Y0-AJI-246

Dearest Richard,

Thanks for all you have done for me. I'll miss you terribly somedays. It will be much harder without you. The only thing that makes it a little easier is I know with out a doubt you are happy with our precious Jesus & the Lord can't wait to be with you. I'm so sorry I couldn't do more for you. I love you Rich. Hope to see you soon.

Love You Always
Sara

YOUR WORD IS A LAMP TO MY FEET AND A LIGHT FOR MY PATH. PS 119:105

Presented
TO

Richard

BY

Sara

ON

1/26/07

YOU KNIT ME TOGETHER IN MY MOTHER'S WOMB. PS 139:13

Births

NAME

BORN TO   DATE

NAME

BORN TO   DATE

NAME

BORN TO   DATE

NAME

BORN TO   DATE

NAME

BORN TO   DATE

NAME

BORN TO   DATE

NAME

BORN TO   DATE

*THE LORD REIGNS,
LET THE EARTH BE GLAD. PS 97:1*

Special Events

EVENT

PLACE   DATE

EVENT

PLACE   DATE

EVENT

PLACE   DATE

EVENT

PLACE   DATE

EVENT

PLACE   DATE

EVENT

PLACE   DATE

A MAN WILL… BE UNITED TO HIS WIFE, AND THEY WILL BECOME ONE FLESH. GE 2:24

This Certifies That

_____

and

_____

were united in

Holy Matrimony

on _____ the _____

day of _____ A.D. _____

at _____

in accordance with the laws of _____

Officiating _____

Witness _____

Witness _____

*LOVE IS PATIENT, LOVE IS KIND…
LOVE NEVER FAILS. 1 CO 13:4,8*

Marriages

HUSBAND

WIFE

PLACE   DATE

HUSBAND

WIFE

PLACE   DATE

HUSBAND

WIFE

PLACE   DATE

HUSBAND

WIFE

PLACE   DATE

HUSBAND

WIFE

PLACE   DATE

HUSBAND

WIFE

PLACE   DATE

*BLESSED IS THE MAN
WHO FEARS THE LORD. PS 112:1*

Husband's Family Tree

NAME

BIRTHPLACE   DATE

BROTHERS AND SISTERS

PARENTS

FATHER
NAME
BIRTHPLACE   DATE

MOTHER
NAME
BIRTHPLACE   DATE

GRANDPARENTS

PATERNAL
GRANDFATHER
BIRTHPLACE   DATE
GRANDMOTHER
BIRTHPLACE   DATE

MATERNAL
GRANDFATHER
BIRTHPLACE   DATE
GRANDMOTHER
BIRTHPLACE   DATE

GREAT-GRANDPARENTS

PATERNAL
GRANDFATHER'S FATHER
BIRTHPLACE   DATE
GRANDFATHER'S MOTHER
BIRTHPLACE   DATE
GRANDMOTHER'S FATHER
BIRTHPLACE   DATE
GRANDMOTHER'S MOTHER
BIRTHPLACE   DATE

MATERNAL
GRANDFATHER'S FATHER
BIRTHPLACE   DATE
GRANDFATHER'S MOTHER
BIRTHPLACE   DATE
GRANDMOTHER'S FATHER
BIRTHPLACE   DATE
GRANDMOTHER'S MOTHER
BIRTHPLACE   DATE

A WOMAN WHO FEARS THE LORD IS TO BE PRAISED. PR 31:30

WIFE'S FAMILY TREE

NAME

BIRTHPLACE _____ DATE

BROTHERS AND SISTERS

PARENTS

FATHER
NAME
BIRTHPLACE _____ DATE

MOTHER
NAME
BIRTHPLACE _____ DATE

GRANDPARENTS

PATERNAL
GRANDFATHER
BIRTHPLACE _____ DATE
GRANDMOTHER
BIRTHPLACE _____ DATE

MATERNAL
GRANDFATHER
BIRTHPLACE _____ DATE
GRANDMOTHER
BIRTHPLACE _____ DATE

GREAT-GRANDPARENTS

PATERNAL
GRANDFATHER'S FATHER
BIRTHPLACE _____ DATE
GRANDFATHER'S MOTHER
BIRTHPLACE _____ DATE
GRANDMOTHER'S FATHER
BIRTHPLACE _____ DATE
GRANDMOTHER'S MOTHER
BIRTHPLACE _____ DATE

MATERNAL
GRANDFATHER'S FATHER
BIRTHPLACE _____ DATE
GRANDFATHER'S MOTHER
BIRTHPLACE _____ DATE
GRANDMOTHER'S FATHER
BIRTHPLACE _____ DATE
GRANDMOTHER'S MOTHER
BIRTHPLACE _____ DATE

FOR TO ME, TO LIVE IS CHRIST AND TO DIE IS GAIN. PHP 1:21

Deaths

NAME

DATE

NAME

DATE

NAME

DATE

NAME

DATE

NAME

DATE

NAME

DATE

NAME

DATE

NIV
PROPHECY
MARKED REFERENCE
STUDY BIBLE

GENERAL EDITOR
GRANT R. JEFFREY

Zondervan Publishing House
Grand Rapids, Michigan 49530, U.S.A.

NIV Prophecy Marked Reference Study Bible
Copyright © 1998 by the Zondervan Corporation
All Rights Reserved

The Holy Bible, New International Version®
Copyright 1973, 1978, 1984 by International Bible Society
All rights reserved

Printed by permission of Zondervan Publishing House

The "NIV" and "New International Version" trademarks are registered in the United States Patent and Trademark Office by International Bible Society. Use of either trademark requires the permission of the International Bible Society.

Artwork:

Solomon's Temple, Zerubbabel's Temple, copyright © 1981 by Hugh Claycombe; Ezekiel's Temple, plan adapted from the design given in the Zondervan Pictorial Bible Dictionary. Copyright © 1975 by the Zondervan Corporation. Used by permission. "Harmony of the Gospels" adapted from "Analytical Outline for the NIV Harmony of the Gospels," pp. 15–23 from *The NIV Harmony of the Gospels*, by Robert L. Thomas and Stanley N. Gundry. Copyright © 1988 by Robert L. Thomas and Stanley N. Gundry. Reprinted by permission of HarperCollins Publishers, Inc..

Notes on the Subjects of Dispensations and Covenants:

Limited quotations and references from C.I. Scofield, taken from the *New Scofield Reference Bible* copyright © 1984 by Oxford University Press, Inc. Used by permission.

The NIV text may be quoted in any form (written, visual, electronic or audio), up to and inclusive of five hundred (500) verses without express written permission of the publisher, providing the verses quoted do not amount to a complete book of the Bible nor do the verses quoted account for 25% or more of the total text of the work in which they are quoted.

Notice of copyright must appear on the title or copyright page of the work as follows:

Scripture taken from the HOLY BIBLE, NEW INTERNATIONAL VERSION. Copyright 1973, 1978, 1984 by International Bible Society. Used by permission of Zondervan Publishing House.
All rights reserved.

The "NIV" and "New International Version" trademarks are registered in the United States Patent and Trademark Office by International Bible Society. Use of either trademark requires the permission of International Bible Society.

When quotations from the NIV text are used in non-salable media such as church bulletins, orders of service, posters, transparencies or similar media, a complete copyright notice is not required, but the initials NIV must appear at the end of each quotation.

Any commentary or other Biblical reference work produced for commercial sale that uses the New International Version must obtain written permission for use of the NIV text.

Permission requests for commercial use within the U.S. and Canada that exceed the above guidelines must be directed to, and approved in writing by, Zondervan Publishing House, 5300 Patterson Avenue, S.E., Grand Rapids, MI 49530.

Permission requests for commercial use within the U.K., EEC, and EFTA countries that exceed the above guidelines must be directed to, and approved in writing by, Hodder & Stoughton Ltd., a member of the Headline Plc. Group, 338 Euston Road, London, NW1 3BH, England.

Permission requests for non-commercial use that exceed the above guidelines must bedirected to, and approved in writing by, International Bible Society, 1820 Jet Stream Drive, Colorado Springs, CO 80921

Library of Congress Catalog Card Number 98-61553
Published by Zondervan Publishing House
Grand Rapids, Michigan 49530, U.S.A.
http://www.zondervan.com

Printed in the United States of America
All rights Reserved

99 00 01 02 7 6 5 4 3 2 1

RRD

You will be pleased to know that a portion of the purchase price of your new NIV Bible has been provided to International Bible Society to help spread the gospel of Jesus Christ around the world!

Table of Contents

Introduction to the *NIV Prophecy Marked Reference Study Bible* iv
Introduction to Prophecy vi
Contents: Articles ix
Contents: Maps, Charts, and Illustrations x
Explanation of Color Markings and Chain of References xi
Prophetic Subjects xii
The Holy Spirit xiii
Salvation xiv
Temporal Blessings xv
A Complete Summary of Chain of References xvi
Preface to the NIV xlix
How To Use the Center Column References lii
Abbreviations to the Books of the Bible liii

The Old Testament

Genesis 1	2 Chronicles 467	Daniel 959
Exodus 69	Ezra 504	Hosea 997
Leviticus 115	Nehemiah 516	Joel 1010
Numbers 151	Esther 532	Amos 1017
Deuteronomy 200	Job 541	Obadiah 1027
Joshua 245	Psalms 579	Jonah 1030
Judges 271	Proverbs 678	Micah 1035
Ruth 296	Ecclesiastes 711	Nahum 1044
1 Samuel 301	Song of Songs 722	Habakkuk 1048
2 Samuel 334	Isaiah 729	Zephaniah 1053
1 Kings 364	Jeremiah 814	Haggai 1058
2 Kings 399	Lamentations 886	Zechariah 1062
1 Chronicles 432	Ezekiel 895	Malachi 1075

The New Testament

Matthew 1083	Ephesians 1354	Hebrews 1405
Mark 1135	Philippians 1361	James 1419
Luke 1161	Colossians 1367	1 Peter 1424
John 1209	1 Thessalonians 1372	2 Peter 1430
Acts 1257	2 Thessalonians 1382	1 John 1435
Romans 1297	1 Timothy 1389	2 John 1441
1 Corinthians 1316	2 Timothy 1395	3 John 1443
2 Corinthians 1336	Titus 1400	Jude 1445
Galatians 1347	Philemon 1403	Revelation 1448

Study Helps

Table of Weights and Measures 1505
Index to Subjects 1506
Index to Articles 1515
Concordance 1516
Index to Color Maps 1572

Introduction
Prophecy Marked Reference Study Bible

ONE OF THE most amazing facts about the Bible is its endurance through the ages. Its persistent popularity into our present day is undiminished in the face of continuous, powerful, and relentless opposition. The Bible is one of the oldest books in the world; sections of it were written more than 25 centuries ago and no part of Scripture is less than 18 centuries old. Very few other ancient works are still circulated and read; those that are circulated and read lie nearly dormant on library shelves, referred to only by a few scholars or by college students as "required reading."

The Bible today is still a best seller, read frequently by millions. Its pages are thumbed and its covers are worn. Passages in the Bible such as the Psalms of David, the prophecies in Isaiah, the Sermon on the Mount in Matthew 5—7, the story of the prodigal son in Luke 15, and well-known chapters such as Romans 8 and John 14 have introduced salvation, encouraged discipleship, and provided hope and security for countless Christians.

It is evident, however, that many people who love to read the Bible have neither the time nor the specialized training for deep systematic study of the Scriptures. To gain a better understanding of the Bible, they must depend upon others who have made special studies of the Word of God. All Christians can be diligent readers of the Bible, but not all can be thorough students of the Scriptures.

The investigations of educated Bible scholars in colleges and seminaries are important, and their conclusions in commentaries, handbooks, and textbooks can be helpful. But for each Christian there is no substitute for reading the Biblical text itself in his or her own personal copy of the Bible. Better than the second-hand study of the Bible is the direct reading of the Word of God.

It is extremely important, however, that the reader learns to read the Bible meaningfully. To assist any follower of Christ who desires to read his own Bible with more purpose and meaning, the original *Marked Reference Bible* was conceived and developed to enable the student to master many of the key ideas and themes of God's Word. J. Gilchrist Lawson devoted many years to the preparation of the original four-theme edition.

The following statistics show the importance of four of the greatest themes of the Bible and over seventy subjects marked in this Bible:

1. On the theme of PROPHETIC SUBJECTS there are nearly 3,900 verses in the Old Testament and nearly 1,500 in the New Testament. One verse in six in the Bible has a more or less important bearing on prophetic subjects.

2. On the theme of THE HOLY SPIRIT there are over 500 verses, or one verse in forty-five, in the Old Testament; and over 660 verses, or one verse in twelve, in the New Testament. The Holy Spirit is mentioned over 400 times in the Bible, under 41 different names and titles. One verse in twenty-six in the Bible concerns the work of the Holy Spirit.

3. Out of a total of over 31,000 verses in the Bible, nearly 7,700 verses, or nearly one verse in four, concern the theme of SALVATION. This includes over 1,900 verses on the necessity of holy living, over 2,500 verses on the temporal punishment of unbelievers, over 400 verses on the future punishment of unbelievers, nearly 600 verses that show God's love for the sinner, and over 180 verses that show that God is no respecter of persons but saves all who are willing to meet the conditions of salvation.

Out of over 23,100 verses in the Old Testament, over 4,700 have some bearing on a person's need of salvation, or on the way of salvation; and nearly 3,000 verses out of a total of nearly 8,000 in the New Testament also concern the salvation of human beings.

4. On the theme of TEMPORAL BLESSINGS there are over 2,400 verses in the Old Testament and 1,091 in the New Testament. This includes nearly 330 verses on promises of examples of food or clothing

provided, and almost 90 verses recording promises and 760 verses recording examples of health and healing for the body, which makes one verse in thirty-six in the Bible on the subject of health or healing for the body. One verse in nine in the Bible concerns temporal blessings.

One-half of the Bible is devoted to these great themes. Thus, wherever there are readers and students of the Bible, there will be those who may receive help from this work. That it will increase interest in the Word of God, strengthen faith, build up true Christian character, and enlarge the kingdom of God is the hope of all who have taken part in its preparation.

Features of the NIV Prophecy Marked Reference Study Bible

Study Notes An outstanding feature of this Bible is the nearly 1200 notes it includes on the same pages as the verses and chapters they explain. Most of these notes illuminate various scriptural passages that have special prophetic significance.

Articles Another important feature of this study Bible is the inclusion of 30 articles on various topics related to Bible prophecy. These articles address significant prophetic topics such as Biblical dispensations, Biblical covenants, the rapture, the tribulation, the resurrection, signs of the Second Coming, the antichrist, Satan, the Millennium, heaven, hell, and many other important topics.

Introductions to Books Each book of the Bible has a unique introduction that includes a short description of the book's author, time of writing, and purpose; an outline of the Biblical book; and a section that gives additional historical, theological, and prophetic information pertaining to the book.

Chain of References The marked reference system color-highlights four key themes in Scripture. The color-highlighted verses along with the color marginal letters, which indicate the subjects, enable the reader to tell in an instant both the theme and the subject of any marked verse or passage. The Scripture references located at the bottom of a column indicate both the previous reference to a subject as well as the next reference to it. The "Complete Summary of Chain of References of Subjects" located on page xvi offers a resource showing a complete listing of all of the marked themes and subjects in the *NIV Prophecy Marked Reference Study Bible*. These references will enable the Bible student to make a careful, complete and objective study of any theme or subject marked in this Bible.

Maps In addition to the beautiful, four-color maps located in the back of this Bible, you will also find six in-text, two-color maps that graphically illustrate various subjects of prophetic significance.

Charts Fifteen in-text charts provide you with a quick pictorial view of various subjects and events, including the Biblical dispensations and covenants, the rapture, the Millennium, and a possible sequence of future events.

Illustrations This Bible also includes four finely detailed illustrations. Three of these depict the temples of Solomon, Ezekiel, and Zerubbabel, while another illustrates the four Gentile world empires described in the book of Daniel.

Concordance A concordance is included in the back of the *NIV Prophecy Marked Reference Study Bible* to help you find Bible verses quickly and easily. Key words in a Bible verse will help you find a verse for which you remember a word or two but not a location.

Subject, Article, and Color Map Indexes The subject index locates other references to persons, places, events and topics mentioned in the Study Bible notes, book introductions, and articles. The map index helps in locating place-names on a variety of full-color maps.

Harmony of the Gospels As an additional study tool for the Gospels and the life of Christ, this Bible contains a harmony of the Gospels.

Introduction to Prophecy

THE STUDY OF prophecy is known as eschatology, that is, "the study of last things." The *NIV Prophecy Marked Reference Study Bible* will focus primarily on the interpretation of the prophetic portions of the Scriptures. However, the role of the prophet and his message is much broader than simply the prediction of spiritually significant future events. In the Hebrew Bible three primary words describe a prophet. Together they reveal the role of the prophet both as seer as well as spokesperson of God's words. The message of the prophet is twofold: God's coming judgment of sin, and his declaration of immediate and ultimate triumph for truth and his sovereign purposes. Both the past and the future unite together in the message of the prophet. Ultimately, God is guiding human history toward the day when the kingdoms of this world will truly become the kingdom of God.

Principles of Prophetic Interpretation

The principles used to interpret Scripture are intimately related to the principles used to interpret the prophetic portions of Scripture. Several basic principles for the interpretation of prophecy include the following:

1. All Scripture should be understood according to its ordinary, usual, and common sense meaning, unless the context clearly indicates that the statement is symbolic.
2. The interpretation of symbolic language is usually clarified by reference to other Biblical passages.
3. God has consistently prophesied and set appointed times for Israel and the nations that have been fulfilled with accuracy and precision. The Lord has always dealt with Israel in terms of specifically appointed time periods and the promised land.
4. Scripture does not pinpoint the specific day or hour for the rapture.
5. The message of the prophet is for his own time and for all generations to follow. Its purpose is not simply to provide information but rather to challenge our behavior and our priorities in life.
6. God has never abandoned his eternal covenant with Israel.
7. Christ will return to usher in the long-awaited Messianic kingdom.

Historically, many in the church have forgotten Israel and the eternal promises that God made to her. They believe that God rejected and abandoned Israel forever because she rejected Jesus Christ, her Messiah. However, the apostle Paul warned the church against this mistake: "I do not want you to be ignorant of this mystery, brothers, so that you may not be conceited: Israel has experienced a hardening in part until the full number of the Gentiles has come in. And so all Israel will be saved, as it is written: 'The deliverer will come from Zion; he will turn godlessness away from Jacob. And this is my covenant with them when I take away their sins'" (Ro 11:25–27). God will still accomplish all of his promises.

The primary focus of this Bible is to present an interpretation of the prophecies concerning Israel, the nations, and the church. The notes and articles will explore the precise fulfillment of past prophecies and examine the prophecies that relate to the second coming of the Messiah. Those prophecies of the Bible, which have already been fulfilled, were fulfilled accurately. Therefore, we can have confidence that the prophecies about the "last days" will also be fulfilled as accurately as the specific predictions in regard to Christ's life, death, and resurrection.

The Bible declares that prophecy is clear evidence that God inspired the Word of God, distinguishing it from all other religious writings. The Lord declares that he is the only one who can prophesy the future and bring it to pass: "Remember the former things, those of long ago; I am God, and there is no other; I am God, and there is none like me. I make known the end from the beginning, from ancient times, what is still to come. I say: My purpose will stand, and I will do all that I please" (Isa 46:9–10).

Since one quarter of the verses in the Bible is prophetic, it is vital for us to properly understand God's revelation to his church. So how can we correctly interpret the prophecies of the Bible? Bible students have used two basic methods of interpretation to understand Biblical prophecy.

Understanding Biblical Prophecy: Two Approaches

The Allegorical Method Some scholars maintain that the prophecies of the Bible should be interpreted allegorically or symbolically rather than literally. This allegorical method of interpretation does not accept that certain prophecies point to second coming of Christ in our generation. For example, they interpret Christ's words in Matthew 24 in an allegorical manner. When they interpret Matthew 24, they understand that all of these prophetic signs were fulfilled when Rome destroyed Jerusalem in A.D. 70. They believe that the prophetic signs of worldwide earthquakes, famines, pestilence, the key prophetic role of Israel, the rebuilt temple, the abomination of desolation, the personal antichrist, and the Battle of Armageddon were totally fulfilled in the burning of the temple and the destruction of Jerusalem nearly 2,000 years ago.

The Literal Method Another method is the literal or common sense method. This approach assumes that the writer wrote his prophecy to be understood as any other type of writing. While the literal method acknowledges that prophecy contains symbols and figures of speech, it interprets these as pointing to a literal reality.

The literal method maintains that all fulfilled prophecies were fulfilled in a literal manner. To illustrate, nearly 50 distinct predictions from the Old Testament pertain to the life, death, and resurrection of Jesus Christ. Yet not one of those predictions was fulfilled in an allegorical or spiritual manner. Thus the conclusion reached by many respected Bible scholars over the centuries is that the Bible's prophecies should be interpreted literally.

This method maintains that the authors of the New Testament interpreted the Old Testament prophecies in a literal manner. For example, the apostle Peter declared, "And we have the word of the prophets made more certain, and you will do well to pay attention to it, as to a light shining in a dark place, until the day dawns and the morning star rises in your hearts. Above all, you must understand that no prophecy of Scripture came about by the prophet's own interpretation. For prophecy never had its origin in the will of man, but men spoke from God as they were carried along by the Holy Spirit" (2Pe 1:19–21). This significant passage explains that prophecy helps Christians in several ways. First, it helps them understand their dark times. Second, it motivates them to holy living. Third, it encourages them to share the Gospel. It also tells us that "prophecy never had its origin in will of man" and that "no prophecy of Scripture came about by the prophet's own interpretation." The message of prophecy is an inspired message from the Holy Spirit to all generations of the church, encouraging the church to live expectantly for Jesus Christ's imminent return.

The Language of Prophecy

Prophecy is often written in a distinct form of religious literature called apocalyptic. While the Bible often uses symbolic language and figures, the Scriptures always interpret their own symbols; we need not guess their meaning. For example, in Revelation 12:7 we read that "Michael and his angels fought against the dragon." Instead of wondering what the dragon symbol represents, Revelation 12:9 reveals its identity: "The great dragon was hurled down—that ancient serpent called the devil, or Satan."

Why Prophecy Is Vital to the Church

There are four major reasons why prophecy is vital to the church.

1. Fulfilled prophecy authenticates the Bible as the inspired Word of God.

2. The message of the prophets calls the church to live in purity and holiness.

3. The prophetic message of the imminent return of Jesus Christ motivates us to witness to those around us.

4. The message of prophecy is a vital evangelistic tool for reaching the lost. God can use prophecy to help convince unbelievers that the Bible is the inspired Word of God, thereby bringing them to a place where they may consider the truth of the Gospel.

Reasons to Study Prophecy

While it is certainly true that many details in the unfolding plan of God will not be known until they come to pass, four factors encourage us to examine those prophecies that point to events leading up to Christ's return:

1. *The importance that God places on prophecy.* Over one quarter of the Bible is prophetic, and the Lord directs us to study prophecy (Rev 1:3).

2. *The literal fulfillment of past prophecies.* This leads us to believe that the prophecies that describe future events will be fulfilled in a similar literal manner. God will continue to fulfill his ancient prophecies as he has in the past, for the Lord himself says, "I the LORD do not change" (Mal 3:6).

3. *Jesus Christ's criticism of the religious leaders of his day.* These leaders failed to pay attention to the prophecies and failed to "interpret the signs of the times" (Mt 16:3).

4. *The apostle Paul's instructions.* Paul specifically reminded Christians that they knew that "the day of the Lord will come like a thief in the night" (1Th 5:2), yet he also reminded them, "But you, brothers, are not in darkness so that this day should surprise you like a thief. You are all sons of the light and sons of the day. We do not belong to the night or to the darkness. So then, let us not be like others, who are asleep, but let us be alert and self-controlled" (5:4–6).

These factors encourage us to carefully and prudently examine those prophecies that clearly relate to our generation. While the textual notes in the *NIV Prophecy Marked Reference Study Bible* will examine numerous prophecies that have already been fulfilled, we will also explore those prophecies that still await fulfillment.

Jesus Christ commanded his disciples to watch for the fulfillment of the prophetic signs that would indicate his coming. And he himself declared, "When these things begin to take place, stand up and lift up your heads, because your redemption is drawing near" (Lk 21:28).

Contents:
Articles

BOOK	TITLE	PAGE
Genesis	The Seven Dispensations	4
	The Biblical Covenants	8
Numbers	The Biblical Anniversaries of Israel	170
Deuteronomy	A Prophet Like Unto Moses	224
Isaiah	The Prophecies of Christ's First Coming	742
Ezekiel	Satan and the Fallen Angels	926
	The Battle of Gog and Magog	942
Daniel	The Four World Empires	964
	The Antichrist	978
	The Vision of the Seventy Weeks	986
	The Tribulation	990
Matthew	Hell	1098
	Signs of the Second Coming	1126
Luke	The Intermediate State	1192
John	The Resurrection of the Body	1218
	The Judgments of God	1234
	Heaven	1238
1 Corinthians	Crowns and Rewards	1326
1 Thessalonians	The Rapture	1376
2 Thessalonians	Reasons for a Pretribulation Rapture	1384
Revelation	The Seven Letters to the Churches	1456
	The Two Witnesses	1468
	The Battle of Armageddon	1474
	The Marriage Supper of the Lamb	1482
	The Millennium	1486
	The Great White Throne Judgment	1490
	A New Heaven and a New Earth	1494
	The New Jerusalem	1498

Contents:
Maps, Charts, Illustrations

Maps

BOOK	TITLE	PAGE
Genesis	Nations Descended from Noah's Sons	19
	Extent of Land Promised to Abraham	22
Ezekiel	The Nations of Ezekiel 38—39	944
	Division of the Land in the Millennium	957
Jonah	The Prophets in Palestine	1032
Revelation	Stages of the Battle of Armageddon	1473

Charts

BOOK	TITLE	PAGE
Genesis	The Seven Dispensations	3
	The Eight Covenants	7
Exodus	Hebrew Calendar and Selected Events	82
Leviticus	Old Testament Sacrifices	121
	Old Testament Feasts and Other Sacred Days	144
Daniel	Daniel's Vision of the Seventy Weeks	984
Matthew	The Four Temples in Israel's History	1115
1 Thessalonians	The Rapture and the Tribulation Period	1380
Revelation	The Millennium	1485

Illustrations

BOOK	TITLE	PAGE
1 Kings	Solomon's Temple	372
Ezekiel	Ezekiel's Temple	946
Daniel	The Four Gentile World Empires	962
Haggai	Zerubbabel's Temple	1060

Explanations:
Color Markings and Chain of References

Color Markings

All verses about **PROPHETIC SUBJECTS** are marked with **BLUE** ink.
All verses about the **HOLY SPIRIT** are marked with **DARK GREEN** ink.
All verses about **SALVATION** are marked with **RED** ink.
All verses about **TEMPORAL BLESSINGS** are marked with **LIGHT GREEN** ink.

Only the verses or words having a *very important* bearing on each subject are marked with colors in this Bible.

A summary of all the Bible verses on each subject marked is given at the front of the Bible (on pages xii–xv). In this summary the marked verses, or very important verses, are printed in colored type. Less important verses are not marked in color but are printed in lightface black type.

The letters on the margin of the verses marked in this Bible indicated the subjects of the verses marked.

The index on the following pages (pages xvi–xlviii) shows the letter that stands for each subject. This index also gives the first verse in the Old Testament and the first verse in the New Testament on each subject. These are given after each subject in the index. Under each subject in the index the most important verses in the Bible on the subject are given.

It will be noted that in the index all subjects are grouped under the four great themes of **PROPHETIC SUBJECTS,** the **HOLY SPIRIT, SALVATION,** and **TEMPORAL BLESSINGS,** and that the letter which stands for each subject is generally the first letter of the most important word in each subject. Thus, under the theme of **SALVATION** the letter **F** stands for FAITH, **H** for HELL, **R** for REPENTANCE, and so on. Under the theme of the **HOLY SPIRIT** the letter **F** stands for FRUITS of the Spirit, the letter **G** for GIFTS of the Spirit, the letter **B** for BAPTISM of the Spirit, and so on.

As *blue* ink is used for marking all verses on subjects under the theme of **PROPHETIC SUBJECTS**, so *blue* letters stand for all subjects under the theme of **PROPHETIC SUBJECTS**. In like manner *green* letters are used for all subjects under the theme of the **HOLY SPIRIT**, *red* letters for all subjects under the theme of **SALVATION,** and *light green* for all subjects under the theme of **TEMPORAL BLESSINGS.**

Chain of Reference System

After each verse or passage marked in this Bible there is a reference to the *next verse* or passage on the subject, thus forming a chain of reference that extends through the whole Bible. The letter in front of each reference corresponds to the same letter in the margin so as to enable the reader to select the proper reference for any subject marked.

The markings in this Bible will enable a person to give a Bible reading at a moment's notice on any subject marked, or a Bible reading may be given from either the Old or New Testament. The first verse on any subject is found by turning to the index on the following pages.

Other subjects may be marked by the Bible student personally, by arranging them under the heading "Miscellaneous Subjects," and using an appropriate letter or sign for each subject of special or personal interest.

Prophetic Subjects

A. Dispensational **Ages** and Covenants — Ge 1:28; Ac 2:1
Ge 2:16; 3:7, 15; 8:15; 9:8–16; 12:1; Ex 19:1; Dt 30:3; 2Sa 7:16; He 8:8–13; Rev 20:4

B. Prophecies About Christ's **Birth** and First Coming — Ge 3:15; Mt 1:21–23
Ge 3:15; Ps. 22:1–18; Isa 9:6–7; 52:13—53:12; Mic 5:1–4; Mt 1:21–23; Lk 1:30–35

C. Prophecies About Christ's Second **Coming** — Ps 97:2–7; Mt 16:27–28
Isa 64:1–2; Da 7:13; Mt 24:26–27, 31, 36–51; 25:1–13; Ac 1:11; 1Th 4:14; 5:4

D. **Descent** of Christ and the Saints — Job 19:25; Mt 25:31
Job 19:25; Ps 96:13; Eze 43:1–2, 4–7; Zec 2:10; 14:4–5; 1Th 3:13; Rev 3:12

E. **Events** that Precede Christ's Second Coming — Da 12:4; Mt 16:3
Da 12:4; Lk 17:26–30; 1Th 5:1–4; 1Ti 4:1–3; 2Ti 3:1–4; 2Pe 3:3–4; Jude 17–18

F. The **First** Resurrection — Job 14:12–15; Mt 22:30–32
Job 19:26; Ps 17:15; Da 12:2; Lk 14:14; 1Co 15:23, 35–55; 1Th 4:16; Rev 20:6

G. Times of the **Gentile's** Ascendancy — Dt 32:21; Mt 21:41
Dt 32:21; Da 2: 28–45; 7; 8; Mt 21:41, 43; Lk 21:24; Ro 11:17–22

H. Marriage Supper and Church in **Heaven** — Ps 45:14–15; Mt 22:2–3
Isa 26:20; Mt 22:1–14; 25:1–13; Eph 1:10; 5:27; Rev. 7:9–17; 14:1–5; 15:2–4; 19:7–9

I. Prophecies About **Israel's** Restoration — Ge 13:15; Mt 2:2
Isa 4; 49:13, 23; 54:1–14; 60; 62; Eze 37; Mt 19:28; Ro 11:25–26; Rev 7:1–8

J. God's Prophetic **Judgments** — Ge 6:2–4; Mt 10:15
Ecc 3:17; 12:14; Mt 10:15; 11:22, 24; 12:36, 42; 25:31–46; 2Co 5:10–11; Rev 20:11–15

K. Triumph of God's **Kingdom** — Ps 10:16; Mt 6:10
Isa 11:9; Hab 2:14; Zec 14:9; Mt 6:10; Ac 3:21; 1Co 15:24–28

M. The **Millennial** Reign of Christ — Nu 14:21; Mt 2:2
Isa 2:1–4; 11:4–10; 35; Jer 23:5–6; Da 2:44; Mic 4:3–4; Zec 9:10; Mt 19:28; Rev 20:1–6

N. The **Never-ending** Life — Dt 4:40; Mt 5:5
Ps 102:25–26; Isa 65:17; Heb 1:10–12; 12:26–28; 2Pe 3:10–14; Rev. 21:1–5; 22:3–5

P. **Period** of Great Tribulation — Nu 24:17–19; Mt 3:12
Ps 10:16; 11:6; 37:34; Pr 2:22; Isa 2:10–21; 13:6–13; Zep 1:14–18; Mal 4:1; Rev 6:12–17

Q. **Question** of Recognizing Friends in Heaven — Ge 15:15; Lk 9:28–33
Ge 15:15; 25:8; 35:29; 49:33; Dt 32:50; Jdg 2:10; Lk 16:23–25; 1Co 13:12

R. **Rejection** and Scattering of Israel — Lev 26:18; Mt 10:6
Dt. 29:22–28; Da 9:26–27; Hos 3:4; Mt 21:41, 43; 22:7; 23:37–39; 24:14–22; Ro 11:17–28

S. **Sorrow** and **Suffering** Cease Forever — Ps 16:11; Rev 7:17
Ps 16:11; Isa 12:3; 25:8; 35:10; 51:11; 61:3; Rev. 7:17; 21:4

T. **Translation** of the Saved — Ps 45:14–15; Mt 3:12
Isa 26:20; Mt 13:30; 24:31; Lk 17:34–36; 1Co 15:50–55; 1Th 4:13–18

U. Hope of **Universal** Peace Realized — Ps 72:7; Mt 5:9
Isa 2:4; Hos 2:18; Mic 4:3–4; Mt 5:9; Lk 2:14; Heb 12:14

V. Christ's Certain **Victory** Over All Enemies — Ps 45:6; Mt 22:44
Isa 45:23; Da 2:44; 7:14; Mt 22:44; Php 2:9–10; Rev 11:15

W. The Resurrection of the **Wicked** — Da 12:2; Jn 5:25–29
Da 12:2; Jn 5:25–29; Ac 24:15; 1Co 15:21–26; 1Ti 6:13; Rev 20:5–6

The Holy Spirit

A.	**ASKING FOR,** or Praying for the Spirit		2Ki 2:9–10
	Isa 44:3; Hos 10:12; Lk 11:9–13; Jn 4:10; Ac 8:14–19; 9:17; 19:1–6		Lk 11:9–13
B.	**BAPTISM** or Filling of the Spirit		Ge 41:38
	Ex 31:2–3; Dt 34:9; Lk 3:16; Jn 14:17; Ac 2:1–18; 8:14–19; 19:1–6; Eph 5:18		Mt 3:11
C.	The Holy Spirit **CONVICTS** of Sin		Ge 6:3
	Ge 6:3; Ps 51:12–13; Mic 3:8; Zec 12:10; Jn 16:8–11; Ac 2:37		Lk 1:17
D.	**DEITY,** or Divinity, of the Holy Spirit		Ps 68:18
	Ps 68:18; Mt 28:19; Ac 5:3–4; 1Co 3:16; 2Co 3:17; 13:14; Eph 2:22; 1Jn 5:7		Mt 12:31–32
E.	**EXAMPLES** of the Holy Spirit's Work		Ge 1:2–3
	Ge 41:38–39; Nu 11:24–29; 1Ki 3:12; Da 1:17–20; Ac 2:1–18; 8:14–19; 19:1–6		Mt 1:18
F.	**FRUITS** of the Holy Spirit		Ps 45:7
	Isa 63:14; Ac 2:46; 9:31; 13:52; Ro 5:5; 8:23; 14:17; 15:13; Gal 5:22–23		Ac 9:31
G.	**GIFTS** of the Holy Spirit		Ge 41:38
	Ps 68:18; Isa 11:2; Joel 2:28; Mk 16:17–18; Ro 12:6–8; 1Co 12:14; Eph 4:7–16		Mt 10:19–20
H.	**HEALING** and Resurrecting Power of the Spirit		Job 33:4
	Eze 37:14; Mt 12:28; Ro 8:11; 1Co 12:9, 28, 30; 15:35–55; 1Pe 3:18; Rev 11:11		Mt 12:28
J.	Comfort or **JOY** of the Holy Spirit		Ps 45:7
	Ps 45:7; Isa 61:3; Jn 14:16, 26; 15:26; 16:7; Ac 2:46; 9:31; 13:52; Ro 14:17		Mt 3:16
L.	**LEADING** or Guiding of the Holy Spirit		Jdg 13:25
	Ex 4:12, 15; Nu 22:38; 1Sa 10:7; 1Ki 22:14; Mt 10:19–20; Jn 16:13; Ac 2:4		Mt 4:1
M.	Great **MIGHT** or Power Given by the Spirit		Ge 1:2–3
	Jdg 14:6; 15:14–15; Mic 3:8; Zec 4:6; Lk 24:49; Ac 1:8; 2Co 10:4; Eph 3:16		Mt 3:11
N.	**NAMES** and Symbols of the Holy Spirit		Ge 1:2
	Job 32:19; Ps 23:5; 39:3; 45:7; Mt 3:16; Lk 3:16; Jn 7:38; Ac 2:2–3		Mt 3:11
P.	The Holy Spirit **PROMISED**		Ps 68:18
	Isa 44:3; Joel 2:28–29; Mal 3:10; Lk 3:16; 11:9–13; Jn 16:7–15; Ac 2:39		Mt 3:11
Q.	**QUENCHING,** Grieving, or Sinning Against the Spirit		Ge 6:3
	Ge 6:3; Isa 63:10; Mt 12:31–32; Eph 4:30; 1Th 5:19; Heb 10:29; 1Jn 5:16		Mt 12:31–32
R.	**REGENERATION** as the Work of the Holy Spirit		1Sa 10:6
	1Sa 10:6; 9:26; Jer 31:33; Jn 3:5–8; Ro 8:15–16; 1Co 6:11; 12:13; Tit 3:5		Lk 1:15–17
S.	**SANCTIFYING** Power of the Holy Spirit		Ex 30:25
	Ex 3:5; Ps 51:10; Eze 36:25–27; Ac 15:8–9; Ro 8:1–14; 15:16; 1Co 3:16–17		Lk 1:17
T.	**TEACHING** or Enlightening of the Spirit		Ge 41:38
	Ge 41:39; 1Ki 3:12; 10:7; Da 1:20; Jn 16:13; Ac 4:13; 1Co 2; 2Co 12:4; 1Jn 2:27		Mt 10:19–20
W.	God **WISHES** Us to be Filled with the Spirit		Nu 11:29
	Nu 11:29; Isa 30:1; Lk 24:49; Jn 16:7; Ac 19:1–2; 1Co 12:1; Eph 5:18; 6:10–18		Lk 24:49

Salvation

A.	**ALL** Unsaved People are Sinners Ps 14:3; Ecc 7:20; Isa 53:6; Ro 3:12, 23; 5:12; Gal 3:22; 1Jn 1:8	1Ki 8:46 Mt 12:30
C.	**CONDITION** of Sinners Described Ps 1:4; 40:2; Isa 1:5–6; 64:6; Jer 17:9; Lk 12:16–21; Rev 3:17	Ge 2:17 Mt 3:7
D.	Christ **DIED** to Save Sinners Isa 53; Zec 13:1; Mt 26:28; Jn 1:29; 3:14–17; 1Pe 2:24; 1Jn 1:7; 2:2	Ge 3:15 Mt 1:21
E.	The Lord Knows **EVERY** Secret Thing Ps 139:1–12; Jer 2:22; Jn 4:29; Heb 4:12–13; 1Jn 3:20	Ge 6:5 Mt 9:4
F.	We are Saved Through **FAITH** 2Ch 20:20; Ps 34:22; Hab 2:4; Jn 3:14–16, 36; Ac 10:43; 16:31; Ro 1:18; 10:8–13	Ge 15:6 Mt. 11:12
G.	**GOOD WORKS** Alone Will Not Save Pr 16:2; Isa 64:6; Jer 17:5; Ro 3:20; 10:3; 1Co 13:3; Gal 2:16; Tit 3:5	Dt 32:31 Mt 5:20
H.	Punishment and **HELL** Await Sinners Da 12:2; Mt 25:46; Lk 16:19–31; Gal 6:7; Heb 6:2; Rev 20:10, 15	Ge 17:14 Mt 3:7
J.	All People will be **JUDGED** by the Lord Ecc 11:9; 12:14; Mt 25:31–46; 2Co 5:10–11; Heb 9:27; Rev 20:11–15	Ge 18:25 Mt 7:1–2
K.	Saving and **KEEPING** Power of God Dt 33:25, 27; Ps 121; Isa 26:4; 40:31; 41:10; 48:18; 59:1; Ro 8:33–39; 2Ti 1:12; Heb 7:25	Ge 15:1 Mt. 1:21
L.	The Lord **LOVES** and Saves Sinners Isa 1:18; 55:7; 65:2; Zec 13:1; Mt 18:11; Lk 15; Jn 6:37; 1Ti 1:15	Ex 20:6 Mt 1:21
M.	We Must be **MEEK** or Humble Before God Ps 34:18; 51:17; 147:3; 149:4; Isa 57:15; 66:2; Mt 18:3; Lk 18:9–14; 1Pe 5:5–6	Ex 32:9–10 Mt 5:3–5
N.	**NEGLECTING** or Rejecting Salvation Pr 1:24–32; 27:1; 29:1; Jer 8:20; Lk 12:16–21; 14:15–24; 2Co 6:2; Heb 2:3; Jas 4:13–14	Ge 6:3 Mt 10:14–15
O.	The Lord is the **ONLY** Way of Salvation Job 8:11–15; Isa 43:11; 45:22; Jer 17:13; Mt 22:37–38; Jn 3:3; 14:6; Ac 4:12; Rev 20:15	Ge 17:4 Mt 7:26–27
P.	The Lord Loves and **PARDONS** Backsliders 2Sa 12:13; 14:14; 2Ch 7:14; 30:9; Jer 3; Hos 14:4; Lk 15; 1Jn 2:1	Lev 26:40–42 Mt 10:6
R.	**REPENTANCE**, Confession, and Restitution Lev 6:1–6; Pr 28:13; Eze 18:27–28; Mt. 4:17; Ac 17:30; 20:21; 26:20; 1Jn 1:9	Ex 22:1–14 Mt 3:2
S.	Holy Living **SHOULD** Follow Conversion Lev 11:44; Ps 24:3–4; Ro 6; 1Th 4:3, 7; Heb 12:14; 1Jn 3:3–10; 5:18	Ge 2:17 Mt 1:21
T.	**TESTIFYING**, or Confessing the Lord Ps 40:10; 107:2; Isa 43:12; Mt 10:32–33; 12:34; Ro 10:8–10; 1Co 14:24–25	Dt 6:7 Mt 10:32–33
W.	"**WHOSOEVER WILL**" May Be Saved Isa 45:22; 55:1; Mt 11:28–30; Jn 3:16; 2Pe 3:9; 1Jn 2:2; Rev 3:20; 22:17	Nu 21:8–9 Mt 7:7–8

Temporal Blessings

A.	**ALL THINGS** Working for Good Ge 21:22; Ps 91:10; 121:7; Pr 12:21; Isa 58:11; Ro 8:28	Ge 21:22 Ro 8:28
B.	The Lord's **BLESSING** on Fields and Flocks Lev 26:3–5; Dt 11:14–15; 28:3–5; Ps 65:9–13; Pr 3:9–10; 2Co 9:10	Ge 24:35 2Co 9:10
C.	**CLOTHING** Provided for God's Children Ge 28:20; Dt 10:8; 29:5; 33:25; Job 27:16–17; Mt 6:25–34	Ge 28:20 Mt 6:25–34
D.	Some Reasons Why **DISEASES** are Allowed Lev 26:16; Dt 7:15; 28:21–22, 27, 35, 59–61; Jn 5:14; 1Co 11:29–32	Ge 12:17 Mt 13:58
E.	**EXAMPLES** of Healing for the Body Nu 21:9; Ps 105:37; Mt 8:16–17; 12:15; Mk 6:13, 54–56; Ac 5:14–16	Ge 17:15–17 Mt 4:23–24
F.	**FOOD** Provided for the Lord's Children Ex 16:35; Dt 10:18; Ps 37:3, 25; Isa 1:19; 33:16; Mt 6:11, 25–34; 2Co 9:10	Ge 21:19 Mt 4:11
H.	**HEALTH** and Healing Promised Ex 15:26; 23:25; Dt 7:15; 33:25; Ps 91:10; 103:3; Isa 40:31; Mt 8:17; Jas 5:14–15	Ge 15:15 Mt 8:17
J.	**JOY** and Trust in Times of Trial Ne 8:10; Job 1:21; 13:15; Ps 23:4; 30:5; Isa 26:3; Hab 3:17–19; Jas 1:2; 1 Jn 4:18	Ne 8:10 Mt 5:11–12
L.	The Lord's **LOVE** and Care for His Children Dt 33:27; Ps 23; 91; Pr 18:24; Jer 31:3; Lk 12:6–7, 22–31; Heb 13:5; 1Jn 3:1	Ge 15:1 Mt 6:8
P.	**PROSPERITY** in Business and Finance Dt 8:18; 15:4–6; 1Sa 2:7–8; Pr 11:24–25; 19:17; Ecc 2:26; 2Co 9:6–11	Ge 15:14 Mt 6:31–33
R.	Blessing on Children, **RELATIVES**, and Friends Ge 26:24; 30:27; Job 42:15; Ps 37:26; 103:17–18; 112:2; 128:3; 144:12; Lk 1:13–15	Ge 26:24 Lk 1:13–15
S.	**SAFETY** From All Harm and Danger Ex 11:7; 1Ch 18:6; Ps 91:10–12; 121:5–8; Na 1:7; Lk 21:18; Ac 18:10	Ex 11:7 Mt 4:6
T.	Why **TEMPTATIONS** and **TRIALS** are Allowed Dt 8:5–6; Job 5:17; Pr 3:11–12; Ro 5:3–4; 2Co 4:17; Heb 5:8; 12:5–13; Jas 1:2–4, 12	Dt 8:2 Ro 5:3–4
U.	The **UPRIGHT** are Blessed and Prospered Dt 28:1–13; 1Sa 2:30; Job 17:9; Ps 37:4–6; 84:11; Pr 4:18; Mk 10:28–30; 1Jn 3:22	Ge 12:1–3 Mt 5:5–12
V.	**VICTORY** Over Enemies and Troubles Jos 23:10; Ps 18:29; 34:17; Pr 16:7; Isa 54:17; Ac 5:39; Ro 8:37; 2Ti 4:18	Ex 23:22 Lk 21:18
W.	**WORRY** and Anxiety Contrary to God's Will Dt 1:21; Jos 1:9; Ps 27:14; 55:22; Mt 6:25–34; Jn 14:1, 27; Php 4:4, 6–7; 1Pe 5:7	Ge 15:1 Mt 6:25–34

Complete Summary
of Chain of References on Subjects Marked in this Bible

The references printed in color type are the important ones, and are the only ones marked in the Bible. Those marked in black type are secondary references.

PROPHETIC SUBJECTS
(BLUE)

A Dispensational **Ages** and Covenants	**B** Prophecies About Christ's **Birth** and First Coming	**C** Prophecies About Christ's Second **Coming**	
Ge 1:28; 2:16–17; 3:7, 15; 8:15; 9:1–3, 7–10, 11–17, 24–27; 12:1–3, 7; 13:14–16; 14:18–20; 15:4–5, 13–16, 18–21; 16:10–12; 17:2–21; 19:22–25; 21:18; 22:15–18; 24:60; 25:23; 26:2–5, 24; 27:28, 39–40; 28:3–4, 13–15; 32:27–28; 35:10–12; 37:6–7, 9; 41:1–7, 25–36, 47–48, 53–54; 46:2–4; 48:3–6, 15–16, 19–22; 49:1–28; 50:24–25 Ex 3:8–12, 17–21; 12:3–9; 23:16, 25–31; 32:13; 34:10–12 Lev 23:33–36; 25:8–17 Nu 23:24 Dt 33:6, 12–29	Ge 3:15–21; 49:10 Nu 19:1–22 Dt 18:15–19 Ps 22:1–18 Isa 7:13–16; 9:6–7; 11:1–5; 50:6–9; 52:13—53:12; 61:1–3 Jer 22:29–30 Da 9:24–26 Mic 5:1–4 Hag 2:9 Zec 9:9; 11:12–13 Mt 1:21–23; 2:14–15, 23; 3:3; 4:13–15; 12:40–41; 27:9–10, 51 Mk 1:7; 8:31; 14:18–21, 27–28, 30, 42 Lk 1:30–35; 2:30–32, 34–35; 3:16; 9:22 Jn 1:29, 33; 2:19; 3:14; 7:42; 19:24, 36–37 Ac 7:37–38; 26:23	2Sa 22:10–13 Ps 77:15–18; 97:2–7; 109:8; 114:7 SS 1:2, 4; 2:7–8, 16, 17; 4:6; 5:6–7, 8; 6:11–12; 7:1–7, 8–9; 8:4, 14 Isa 64:1, 4 Da 7:13 Hag 2:6–7 Mt 16:27–28; 24:3, 4–25, 26–27, 28, 29–33, 34–35, 36–51; 25:1–13, 14–18, 19, 20–30; 26:64 Mk 4:26–28, 29; 8:38; 9:1–13; 13:26, 32–37; 14:62 Lk 9:26; 12:34, 35–47, 48; 17:23–24, 25, 26–30, 31–33, 34–37; 18:8; 19:15, 23; 21:27–31, 32–33, 34–36 Jn 14:2–3; 16:16; 21:22–23 Ac 1:9–10, 11, 20; 4:7, 13 Ro 13:11–12	1Co 1:7–8; 7:29–31; 10:11; 11:26 2Co 1:14 Php 1:6, 10; 2:16; 3:20–21; 4:5 Col 3:4 1Th 1:10; 2:19; 3:13; 4:14—5:4; 5:5–11, 23 2Th 1:7, 10; 2:1–3; 3:5 1Ti 6:14 2Ti 1:12; 4:8 Tit 2:13 Heb 9:26, 28; 10:25, 37 Jas 5:7–9 1Pe 1:5, 7, 13, 20; 4:7, 13 2Pe 1:16–19; 3:3–14 1Jn 2:28; 3:2–3 Rev 1:7, 13–17; 3:11; 22:7, 12, 20 **D** **Descent** of Christ and the Saints Job 19:25 Ps 96:12–13; 98:9; 102:16 SS 8:5 Eze 43:1–2, 4–7; 44:1–2 Zec 2:10; 14:4–7, 14–20

Mt 25:31
Mk 13:26
1Th 3:13
Rev 3:12

E
Events that Precede Christ's Second Coming

SS 5:6–8;
    6:1–2
Da 12:4, 8, 9–10
Mal 4:5
Mt 10:23;
    16:2, 3;
    24:3–6, 7–31, 32–33
Mk 13:5–13, 14–26, 22, 24, 27, 31–32
Lk 12:54–57;
    17:26–30;
    21:25–31
Ac 2:17, 19–20
1Th 5:1–4
2Th 2:1–9, 10–12
1Ti 4:1–3
2Ti 3:1–9;
    4:3–4
Jas 5:1, 3, 4–6, 7
2Pe 3:3–10
1Jn 2:18
Jude 17–18
Rev 1:1, 3, 19;
    4:1, 2;
    5:1—6:11;
    22:6–7, 10

F
The **First** Resurrection

Job 14:12–15;
    19:25–27
Ps 8:3–8;
    16:9, 9–10;
    17:15;
    71:20;
    88:10–12
Isa 25:8;
    26:19
Eze 37:12–14
Da 12:2, 13
Hos 13:14
Mt 22:23–29, 30–32
Mk 12:18–23, 24–25, 26–27
Lk 14:13–14;
    20:27–33, 34–38
Jn 5:21, 25–29;
    6:39–40, 44, 54;
    11:23–25
Ac 17:18;
    23:6, 7, 8, 9;
    24:15, 21;
    26:6–8;

    28:20
Ro 8:11, 17–25, 29
1Co 6:13, 14;
    15:12–19, 20–26, 35–55
2Co 1:9;
    4:14
Php 3:11–15, 21
1Th 4:13–18
1Ti 6:13
2Ti 2:17–18
Heb 6:2;
    11:35
Rev 1:5, 18;
    20:5–6

G
Times of the **Gentile's** Ascendancy

Dt 32:21
2Ch 36:23
Ezr 1:2
Est 1:1
SS 8:8–9
Isa 49:6;
    65:1
Jer 16:19, 20–21
Da 2:1–27, 28–45;
    7:1, 2–28;
    8:1–26, 27;
    9:26–27;
    10:1, 2–13, 14, 15–19, 20—11:5;
    11:6–30, 31, 32–45;
    12:5, 6–7, 11–12
Zec 1:7–15, 18–21
Mal 1:11
Mt 21:41, 43;
    22:9–10
Mk 12:9
Lk 14:21, 22–24;
    20:16;
    21:24
Jn 10:16
Ac 10:1–14, 15, 16–44, 45—11:1;
    11:2–17, 18, 19–21;
    13:44–45, 46–48;
    14:27;
    15:3, 6, 7–9, 10–11, 12, 13–19;
    18:6;
    21:19;
    22:21;
    28:28
Ro 9:30;
    10:19–20;

    11:11–12, 13–14, 15–29;
    15:9–11, 12, 16, 27
Rev 11:2;
    12:3–6;
    13:1–18;
    14:8;
    17:1—18:3

H
Marriage Supper and Church in **Heaven**

Ps 45:14–15
SS 1:4;
    2:4
Isa 26:20–21
Mt 22:1, 2–3, 4–7, 8–10, 11, 13, 14;
    25:1–13
Lk 14:16;
    22:16
Eph 1:10;
    5:25–26, 27
Rev 7:9–17;
    14:1–5;
    15:2–4;
    19:7–9

I
Prophecies About **Israel's** Restoration

Ge 12:7;
    13:15;
    15:18;
    17:7–8, 19;
    48:4
Ex 12:41;
    32:13
Lev 26:40–42, 44–45
Nu 10:29;
    24:7–9, 14–19;
    34:1–12
Dt 1:35–39;
    2:24–25;
    3:2, 21–22;
    4:22, 26–31, 32–38;
    6:3;
    7:4, 6–9, 14–15, 22;
    11:12;
    12:5;
    17:14;
    18:15–19;
    26:19;
    28:1–3;
    30:1–10;
    32:36, 43
Jos 1:2–9;
    3:5, 7;
    6:2–5, 16;

    8:1–2, 7;
    9:27;
    10:8, 12, 19;
    11:6;
    17:18
Jdg 1:2;
    2:1;
    6:16;
    7:13–14;
    13:3, 5;
    20:28
1Sa 7:3;
    9:16;
    12:22;
    14:10;
    17:36–37;
    25:28
2Sa 3:18;
    7:10–12, 23–24
1Ki 2:4;
    5:5;
    9:3;
    18:1, 41
2Ki 7:1–2;
    8:19;
    13:15–19;
    14:27;
    19:30–31
1Ch 14:10, 15;
    16:15–18, 35;
    17:9, 22;
    22:9, 13
2Ch 20:7
Ezr 3:11
Ne 1:9
Ps 14:7;
    28:9;
    29:11;
    33:12;
    47:3–4;
    50:5;
    53:6;
    60:1–12;
    68:13, 22–23;
    69:35–36;
    74:10, 11, 19–20;
    77:7–10, 15;
    79:5, 13;
    80:1–2, 3–7, 14–15, 19;
    85:1–13;
    87:2, 3, 5;
    90:13–17;
    94:14;
    97:8;
    98:3;
    99:4;
    102:13–16, 21–22;
    105:8–11, 12;
    107:3–7;
    111:5–6, 9;
    112:3–9;
    115:12;

Summary of Chain of References

125:1;
126:1–6;
129:1–8;
130:8;
132:13–15;
135:4, 14;
136:21–22;
147:2;
148:14
Isa 1:25–27;
2:1–5;
4:2–6;
9:1–4, 7;
10:20–21;
11:11–15, 14—16;
12:1–6, 4–5, 6;
14:1–3;
18:7;
22:20–24;
25:8–10;
26:1–2, 12, 19;
27:2–6, 7–11, 12–13;
28:5–6;
30:15, 18–26, 29;
31:4–5;
32:15–18;
33:20–22, 24;
37:31–32;
40:1–2, 3–7, 8–11, 27–28, 29–31;
41:2–7, 8–21;
42:16, 17–21;
43:1–4, 5–7, 8–18, 19–21, 22–24, 25, 26;
44:1–8, 21–23, 24–25, 26, 27–28;
45:17–19, 25;
46:3–4, 12–13;
49:5–6, 7, 8–23, 24–26;
50:2;
51:1–2, 3–4, 5–8, 9, 10, 11–12, 13–14, 15–17, 18–21, 22, 23;
52:1–3, 4–5, 6–9, 10;
54:1–14, 15–16, 17;
55:5, 8–11, 12–13;
56:1, 8;
57:16–19;
58:8–12, 14;
59:20, 21;
60:1–22;
61:3—62:12;
65:8–10, 16–25;
66:5–6, 7, 8, 9, 10–14, 15–17, 18–24

Jer 3:14—19;
4:1–2;
10:16;
12:14–17, 14, 16–17;
14:21;
16:14–16;
18:1–8;
23:1–2, 3–8;
25:12;
29:10–14;
30:1–3, 4–6, 7–10, 11–16, 14, 17–22;
23–24;
31:1, 2, 3–14, 15–27, 28–29, 30, 31–34, 35–37, 38–40;
32:36–42, 43, 44;
33:1, 2–3, 4–5, 6–11, 12–14, 15–16, 17–26;
35:18–19;
46:27–28;
50:4–5, 19–20;
51:5, 10, 19–23
La 3:31;
4:22;
5:20–21
Eze 4:4–6;
11:17–20;
16:53, 55, 60–63;
17:17, 22–24;
20:33, 34–38, 39, 40–42, 43–44;
28:25–26;
29:21;
34:11–16, 17–21, 22—31;
36:1–7, 8–12, 13–21;
37:1–28;
38:1–7, 8, 9–10, 11–12, 13, 14, 15, 16, 17–19, 20, 21—39:6;
39:7–10, 11–24, 25–29;
43:4, 5–7, 8, 9, 10–12;
45:1–2, 7, 8;
47:1—48:35
Da 8:19;
12:1
Hos 1:10–11;
2:7, 14–16, 17, 18–23;
3:5;
6:1–3;
11:8–12;
12:9;

13:9–10, 14;
14:4–8
Joel 2:21—3:2;
3:16–18, 19, 20–21
Am 9:11–15
Ob 17; 18–21
Mic 2:12, 13;
4:1–4, 5, 6–8, 9–11, 12–13;
5:1, 2, 3–15;
7:7–9, 10, 11–20
Na 1:12, 13–14, 15
Hab 3:13
Zep 2:6–7;
3:9–20
Hag 2:7
Zec 1:12—2:5;
2:1–5, 6–9, 10–13;
3:1, 2–5, 6–8, 9–10;
8:1–3, 4–6, 7–8, 9–19, 20–23;
9:9–10, 11—10:5;
10:6–8, 9–12;
12:6–7, 8—13:1;
13:2–6, 9;
14:8–11, 12–15, 16–21
Mal 3:2–4, 6–7, 9–12
Mt 2:1, 2, 3–5, 6, 7–20;
19:28;
21:5;
27:11, 28, 29, 30–31, 37, 42
Mk 11:10;
15:2, 9, 12, 16, 17–18, 19–20, 26, 32
Lk 1:32–33, 54–55, 68–79;
2:25–26, 38;
23:2–3, 36, 37–38;
24:13–20, 21
Jn 1:49;
12:12, 13–15, 16;
18:33–37, 38, 39;
19:2–3, 4–5, 12–15, 17–18, 19–22, 37
Ac 1:6–7;
2:29–31
Ro 3:1–2;
9:4, 8–24, 25–28;
10:21—11:5;
11:6–11, 12, 13–14, 15–29

30–31, 32, 33–36;
15:8
2Co 3:16
Heb 8:7, 8–13;
10:16–17
Rev 1:7;
3:7;
7:1–8;
11:1–2;
12:14–17

J
God's Prophetic
JUDGMENTS

Ge 6:2–4, 17;
11:6–8;
40:12–13, 18–19
Ex 14:4, 13;
16:23–30;
17:14, 16
Nu 14:22–30, 43;
24:14–24;
33:55–56
Jos 6:26;
23:13
Jdg 2:3, 21;
9:15, 20
1Sa 2:31;
12:25;
13:14
2Sa 12:14
1Ki 17:1;
21:19, 21–24, 29
2Ki 1:4;
2:3, 5, 9–10;
5:27;
7:19;
8:1, 10–13;
9:8–10, 26;
18:30;
19:7;
20:17–19
1Ch 21:9–13
2Ch 16:9;
21:14–16
Ps 1:5;
7:8;
9:7–8, 19;
69:25;
87:4–6
Ecc 3:17–18;
11:9;
12:14
Isa 10:33–34;
15:1–9;
20:1–6;
21:13–16;
23:1–17;
30:5–7;
48:14–15
Jer 1:13–16, 18–19;
9:26;

Summary of Chain of References

11:20;
27:22;
28:16;
29:21–22, 32;
44:30;
46:26;
47:5
Eze 12:13
21:28–31
24:21, 25–27;
25:15–17;
26:1–5, 12–21;
28:20–24;
29:1–6, 19–20;
35:1–15
Da 4:10–17, 20–26, 31–32;
5:5, 24–28;
7:10–11
Zep 2:4–15
Mt 10:15;
11:22, 24;
12:36, 42;
25:14–18, 19, 20–30, 31–46
Mk 6:11
Lk 10:12, 14;
11:31–32
Jn 12:48
Ac 17:31
Ro 2:5, 16;
14:10–13
1Co 4:5
2Co 5:9–11
2Ti 4:1
Heb 9:27;
10:30
1Pe 4:5
2Pe 2:4, 9;
3:7
1Jn 4:17
Jude 6
Rev 20:11–15

K
Triumph of God's **KINGDOM**

Ps 10:16;
92:9;
145:13
Isa 2:2–4;
11:9;
24:23
Jer 10:10;
31:34
Da 2:33, 35, 44–45;
4:3, 34;
6:26;
7:13–14, 27
Ob 21
Mic 4:7
Hab 2:14
Zec 14:9

Mt 6:10, 13;
13:33;
16:18–20
Mk 4:26–28;
9:1
Lk 11:2
Ac 3:21, 25
1Co 15:24–28
Rev 11:15

2Ki 4:16;
10:30;
20:5–10
2Ch 1:12;
9:8;
20:9;
34:28
Isa 38:18, 21–22;
45:1–5, 13
Jer 39:17–18
Da 2:28–32
Jnh 2:4
Mt 10:17–23;
26:13

M
The **MILLENNIAL** Reign of Christ

Ge 3:15;
49:10
Ex 15:17–18;
19:5
Nu 14:21;
24:17–19
1Sa 2:10
2Sa 7:12, 13–14, 14–15, 16, 17–29;
23:3–5
1Ki 2:45
1Ch 16:30–33, 34;
17:10–13, 13, 14, 15–27, 22;
28:4
2Ch 6:16;
13:5;
21:7
Ps 2:8–9;
9:8;
10:16;
14:7;
22:27–28;
24:1, 2–6, 7–10;
29:10;
45:1–5, 16;
46:4–11;
47:1–9;
48:2, 8;
49:14;
50:1–2, 4–6;
60:6–12;
66:4;
67:4;

68:16;
72:1–19;
76:1–12;
82:8;
85:9–13;
86:9;
89:2, 3–4, 26–32, 30–34, 35–37;
93:1–2;
96:1–3, 7–9, 10–13;
97:1;
98:3–9;
99:1–5, 9;
102:15–16, 22;
108:7–9;
110:1–7;
132:11–18
SS 1:11–17;
2:3–6, 11–13;
4:16—5:1;
7:10–13
Isa 2:1–5;
4:5–6;
9:6–7;
11:4–10, 12;
14:2;
16:5;
19:20–25;
22:20–24;
24:13–15, 23;
25:6–10;
26:1–2, 9;
29:17–24;
32:1–4;
33:6, 20–22;
35:1–10;
40:4–5;
41:18–20;
42:4;
44:3–5;
45:8, 23–24;
49:7–12;
52:13;
55:3, 12–13;
56:1;
57:13;
59:19, 21;
60:1–22;
65:16–25;
66:18–24
Jer 3:17;
23:5–6;
30:9;
33:15
Eze 21:26–27;
34:23–29
34:25–28
37:22–28;
43:5–7;
47:1–21;
48:1–7, 10–35

Da 2:34–35, 44–45;
7:13–14, 18, 22, 27
Hos 2:18, 21–22;
3:5
Joel 3:4, 18–20
Mic 4:3–4;
5:2
Hab 2:14, 20
Hag 2:23
Zec 2:5, 10–13;
6:9–11, 11–15;
8:3–8, 20–23;
9:1, 9–10;
14:9, 16–21
Mal 1:4–5;
3:1, 17–18;
4:2–3
Mt 2:1, 2, 3–5, 6;
5:35;
6:10, 13;
13:31–33, 43;
16:28—17:13;
19:28;
20:20–21, 22–24;
21:1–4, 5, 6–11, 33–37, 38;
22:43, 44;
25:21, 23;
27:11, 28, 29, 30–31, 37, 42
Mk 4:30–32;
10:35–36, 37, 38, 41–45, 39–40;
11:1–9, 10;
12:10–11, 36;
15:2, 9, 12, 16, 17–18, 19–20, 26, 32, 43
Lk 1:32–33;
2:26;
3:4, 5–6;
9:27–36;
11:2;
12:32, 44;
13:18, 19, 20, 21;
17:20–37;
19:11–26, 20–26, 27, 28–40;
20:9–13, 14, 17, 42–43;
22:29–30;
23:2–3, 36, 37–38, 42, 51
Jn 10:16;
12:12, 13–15, 16;
18:33–37, 38, 39, 40—19:5;
19:12–15, 17–18, 19–22
Ac 2:29–31, 34–35;
3:19–21;
17:7

Summary of Chain of References

Ro 4:13;
 8:17–18;
 14:11;
 15:10, 12;
 16:20
1Co 6:2–3;
 10:26, 28;
 15:24–28
Eph 1:10, 22
Php 2:9–11
Col 1:20
1Th 3:13
2Th 1:5
1Ti 6:15
2Ti 2:12;
 4:1, 8, 18
Heb 1:2, 8, 13;
 2:5–8;
 5:6;
 7:1, 2, 3–10, 11,
 12–14, 15–17,
 18, 19, 20–21,
 22–24;
 10:12, 13
1Pe 4:11, 13;
 5:1, 4, 6
2Pe 1:19
Rev 1:5–6;
 2:26–27;
 3:7, 11–12, 21;
 5:10;
 11:15–19;
 12:5;
 19:16;
 20:1–6

N

The Never-Ending Life
Dt 4:40
Job 26:10
Ps 37:9, 11, 22, 29, 34;
 75:3;
 78:69;
 93:1;
 96:10;
 102:25–26;
 104:5;
 119:90
Pr 10:30
Ecc 1:4
Isa 51:16;
 65:16–18
Mt 5:5
Eph 1:10;
 6:3
Heb 1:10–12;
 2:5;
 6:5;
 12:26–28
2Pe 3:13–14
1Jn 2:17

Rev 21:1–5, 6—22:2;
 22:3–5, 14–15

P

Period of Great Tribulation
Nu 24:17–19
Dt 32:22, 41–43
1Sa 2:10
2Sa 22:14–18;
 23:6–7
Job 38:13
Ps 2:1–6, 8–9, 12;
 10:15–16;
 11:6;
 18:7–15;
 37:34;
 45:1–5;
 46:6–9;
 50:3;
 59:5, 8;
 66:3;
 68:1–2;
 72:9;
 75:8, 10;
 76:3–12;
 82:5, 8;
 83:13–17;
 94:1–4;
 98:1–2;
 101:8;
 104:35;
 110:1, 5–6;
 119:119;
 132:18;
 144:5–6
Pr 2:21–22
Isa 1:24, 28, 29, 30–31;
 2:10–21;
 9:18;
 11:4;
 13:1–22;
 24:1, 2, 3, 4–5, 6, 7–12, 17–23;
 25:10–12;
 26:20–21;
 27:1;
 28:17–18, 19–20, 21–22;
 29:20, 21;
 30:27, 28, 30;
 33:3–4, 10–11, 12;
 34:1–4, 5, 5–17;
 40:10, 24;
 42:13–15;
 45:23–24;
 59:17–19;
 61:2;
 63:1–2, 3–6;
 64:2–3;
 66:5–6, 14–17, 24

Jer 9:25–26;
 10:10, 15;
 23:19–20;
 25:29–33;
 30:23–24;
 45:5;
 48:47;
 49:2–6, 23–27, 39
Eze 38:1–23;
 39:1–22
Da 12:1
Joel 1:15;
 2:1–11, 19–32;
 3:1–2, 9–17
Am 1:2–15;
 5:18–20
Ob 1–10; 15–16
Mic 1:3–7, 9;
 5:5, 15
Na 1:1, 2, 3–4, 5–12, 15
Hab 3:3–16
Zep 1:14–18;
 3:8
Hag 2:20–21, 22
Zec 9:2, 5–8, 12–16;
 11:8;
 12:2–6, 9–14;
 13:7–9;
 14:12–21
Mal 3:2–5;
 4:1, 2, 3, 5
Mt 3:12;
 13:24–26, 27–30, 39–42, 47–50;
 22:43–44;
 24:50–51
Mk 13:19–20;
 14:25
Lk 3:17;
 12:45–47;
 17:26–30;
 18:1–6, 7–8;
 19:27;
 20:42–43;
 21:5–7, 9–11, 25–26, 36
Ac 2:19–20
1Co 16:22
1Th 5:3, 4, 9
2Th 1:5–9, 6, 10;
 2:8–9
2Pe 3:10–12
2Jn 7
Jude 14–15
Rev 1:7;
 2:27;
 3:10;
 6:12—9:6;
 9:7–11, 12–15, 16–17, 18, 19, 20, 21—10:4;
 10:5–7, 8—11:13;

 11:14, 15–17, 18–19;
 12:9–17;
 14:6–11, 13, 14—15:1;
 15:2–4, 5—18:13;
 18:14–18, 19—19:3;
 19:4–10, 11—20:3;
 21:9

Q

Question of Recognizing Friends in Heaven
Ge 15:15;
 25:8, 17;
 35:29;
 49:29, 33
Nu 20:24, 26;
 27:13;
 31:2
Dt 32:50
Jdg 2:10
Mt 8:11;
 17:4
Mk 9:4–5
Lk 9:28–33;
 13:28;
 16:23–25
1Co 13:12
Col 1:28
Phm 15
Heb 12:23
Rev 3:5

R

Rejection and Scattering of Israel
Lev 20:22;
 26:5–10, 14–35, 15–17, 18, 19–23, 24, 25–27, 28, 29–30, 31–35, 36–39, 41–43, 43
Dt 4:27, 28, 30;
 28:15–22, 23–25, 26–32, 33, 34–36, 37, 38–44, 45, 46–48, 49, 50–61, 62–65, 66–68;
 29:22–28, 29;
 30:1;
 31:16, 17–18, 29;
 32:9–19, 20, 21–25, 26, 36
Jos 23:15–16;
 24:20

1Ki	9:6–9, 7–8; 11:11, 30–31; 13:2–3, 22, 32; 14:10–16		30:8–12, 13–14, 15–16, 17; 31:2; 32:9, 10, 11–12, 13–14; 38:5; 40:2; 42:22–25; 43:2, 27–28; 44:28; 48:10; 50:1, 2; 51:17, 19, 20; 54:4, 6–8, 11; 59:2, 9–12, 13–15; 60:10, 14–15; 63:17; 64:7, 9–10, 11, 12; 65:6–7		26:2, 3, 4–5, 6, 7–19, 20, 21–24; 29:18; 30:4–6, 7, 17; 31:15–16; 33:5; 34:17, 21, 22; 35:17; 36:1–32; 37:8–9; 38:3, 21–23; 39:1–18; 40:2–3; 42:19—43:7; 44:1, 2, 3–5, 6, 7–10, 11–12, 13–21, 22, 23—45:3; 45:4, 5; 50:6–8, 11, 17; 52:3–30
2Ki	10:32; 13:23; 17:6, 18, 19, 20, 21–22, 23, 24; 18:9–12; 21:7–9, 12–15; 22:15–20; 23:26–27; 24:2–3, 4, 10–13, 14, 15–20; 25:1–6, 7–12, 13–20, 21, 22–26				
1Ch	5:25, 26; 6:15; 9:1				
2Ch	7:20, 20–22; 28:23; 29:8; 30:6–7; 34:24–25; 36:17–21				
Ezr	5:12	Jer	1:3, 11–16; 2:14–17; 3:8, 25; 4:6–19, 20, 21–25, 23, 26–28, 29; 5:2, 3, 4–8, 9–10, 11–18, 19, 20–28, 29, 30; 6:9, 10, 11–12, 13–18, 19, 20–29, 30; 7:12–13, 14–16, 17–19, 20, 21–28, 29, 30–33, 34; 8:4, 5–6, 7–11, 12–14, 15; 9:8, 9–22; 10:17, 18, 19, 20–21, 25; 11:8, 11–17; 12:4, 7–9, 10–13; 13:1–8, 9–11, 12–16, 17–21, 22–23, 24, 25; 14:18, 19, 20; 15:1–4, 5, 6–7, 8–14; 16:1–13, 18; 17:1–3, 4, 27; 18:1–15, 16–17; 19:1–7, 8, 9; 20:6, 22; 21:1–9, 7, 10, 11–14; 22:5, 6–30, 10–12, 18–19; 23:33, 39–40; 24:1–10; 25:8–11, 15–16, 17–18, 34;	La	1:1–2, 3, 4–10, 11, 12, 13–15, 16–17, 18; 2:1–2, 3–5, 6, 7; 3:1–3, 45; 4:22
Ne	1:8			Eze	2:3–10; 4:1—5:2; 5:3–4, 5–13, 14–15, 16— 6:5; 6:6, 7–9, 10, 11—14; 7:1–2, 3–27; 8:17—10:2; 9:4–5; 11:10–12, 13–15, 16; 12:1–14, 15, 16–19, 20, 21–28; 14:21—15:8; 16:35–43; 17:9–10, 21; 19:12—20:32; 20:45; 21:2, 3, 4–25, 18–23, 26–27, 28—22:3; 22:4, 5–14, 15, 16—23:31; 23:32–33, 34— 24:12; 24:13, 14–27; 25:3; 33:23–27, 28–29, 30–33; 34:1–2, 5–10; 35:15; 36:3–7, 16–17, 18–19;
Ps	44:9–14; 60:1–3; 69:21–28; 74:1–2, 3–6, 7–11; 78:67; 79:1, 2–3, 4–7, 8–13; 80:4–6, 7–11, 12–16; 129:1–3; 137:1–3				
SS	1:6				
Isa	1:1–6, 7–9, 21–22; 2:6; 3:1–8, 8, 9–15, 25, 26; 4:1; 5:1–10, 25–30; 6:9–13; 7:3–4, 7–9, 17, 18–25, 23–24; 8:9–10, 17, 18; 9:8–21; 10:3–6, 12, 16–19, 22–27; 14:28–31; 17:4–8, 9–11; 18:2; 22:1–7, 17–19; 26:15–17, 18; 28:13; 29:1–3, 4, 5–12, 13–14, 15–16;				

				39:21–24, 26, 28; 43:8
			Da	1:1–2; 8:11–14, 19, 24; 9:2, 7–8, 11–14, 16–18, 26–27; 11:2, 31, 36; 12:7, 11–12
			Hos	1:1–3, 5, 4, 6, 8–9; 2:1–3, 4–5, 6, 7–10, 11–12, 13; 3:1, 2–4, 4; 4:1–2, 3, 4–5, 6, 7–8, 9, 10— 5:4; 5:5, 6–8, 9, 10–11, 12, 13, 14, 15; 6:11; 8:1–7, 8, 9—9:2; 9:3, 4–5, 6, 7–11, 12, 13–16, 17; 10:6, 7, 8–9, 10; 11:7; 12:2, 14; 13:1–2, 3, 7–9, 13, 15, 16; 14:1
			Joel	1:1–3, 4, 5–6, 7, 8—2:11; 3:2
			Am	2:1–6, 7—5:3; 7:8, 9, 10–15, 16–17; 8:2, 3—9:4; 9:5, 6–7, 8–10
			Mic	1:1–5, 6, 7—2:3; 2:4, 5–11; 3:12; 4:9–10, 11; 6:13, 14–15, 16; 7:1, 13
			Na	2:2
			Hab	1:5–12, 5–11; 2:6–13, 15–19
			Zep	1:1, 2–4, 5–18; 3:1–7
			Zec	1:12–15, 18–21; 2:6–7; 3:3–4; 7:14; 8:1–2; 11:1–8, 9–10, 11–13, 14, 15—12:5; 13:8; 14:1–3
			Mt	10:5, 6; 15:21–22, 23–27, 28;

Summary of Chain of References

21:33–40, 41, 42,
   43, 44–45;
22:3–6, 7–8;
23:34–36, 37–39;
24:1–3, 4–13,
   15–22, 28;
27:25
Mk 12:1–8, 9, 10–12;
   13:1–2, 3–13,
   14–20
Lk 13:1–2, 3, 4, 5,
   6–9, 34–35;
   14:15–23, 24;
   19:41–44;
   20:9–16;
   21:5–19, 20–24;
   23:28, 29–31
Jn 7:35;
   12:37–41
Ro 9:1–24, 25–29,
   30;
   11:1–5, 6, 7–12,
   13–14, 15, 16,
   17–28
2Co 3:14
1Th 2:14–15, 16
Rev 12:1–6, 7–9,
   10–13

S
Sorrow and **Suffering**
Cease Forever
Ps 16:11;
   30:5;
   98:4;
   126:5
Isa 12:3;
   25:8;
   29:19;
   35:2, 10;
   49:13;
   51:11;
   52:9;
   61:3;

   65:14, 18–19
Jer 31:13
Lk 2:10
Jn 15:11;
   16:22;
   17:3
Ac 2:28
Gal 5:22
1Th 5:16
1Pe 1:8–9
1Jn 1:4
Rev 7:17;
   21:4

T
Translation of the Saved
Ps 45:14–15
SS 1:4;
   2:10;
   6:10—12
Isa 26:20
Mt 3:12;
   13:30;
   24:31
Lk 3:17;
   17:34–36
Jn 3:3–7, 8, 9–13;
   14:2–3
Ro 8:17–18, 29
1Co 15:50–55
Php 3:21
1Th 4:15–18

U
Hope of **Universal** Peace Realized
Lev 26:6
Dt 33:28
1Ki 5:4
1Ch 22:9
Job 5:23
Ps 72:7

Isa 2:4;
   9:6;
   11:6–9;
   32:17–18;
   65:25
Jer 23:6;
   31:40
Hos 2:18
Mic 4:3–4
Zec 9:10;
   14:11
Mt 5:9
Lk 1:79;
   2:14
Ro 16:20
Jas 3:18;
   4:1–2

V
Christ's Certain **Victory** Over All Enemies
Ps 2:8–9;
   45:6;
   72:4, 8–9;
   110:1;
   132:11
Isa 9:6–7;
   11:1–9;
   16:5;
   32:1;
   42:1, 4;
   45:23;
   49:6;
   55:4–5;
   60:12
Jer 23:5–6;
   30:9;
   31:34
Eze 21:27;
   34:23–24;
   37:24
Da 2:34–35, 44, 45;
   7:13, 14, 27;
   9:25

Hos 3:5
Zec 9:10
Mt 21:5, 38, 44;
   22:44;
   28:18
Mk 12:36
Lk 1:32, 33;
   2:32;
   19:12, 15;
   20:42–43;
   22:29
Jn 3:35
Ac 2:34–35;
   3:22–23
1Co 15:24–26
Eph 1:21–22
Php 2:9–10
2Th 2:8
1Ti 6:15
Heb 1:2, 8, 13
Rev 2:26–27;
   5:13;
   11:15;
   12:5;
   17:14;
   19:15–16;
   20:7–15

W
The Resurrection of the **Wicked**
Da 12:2
Jn 5:25–29
Ac 24:15
1Co 15:21–26
1Ti 6:13
Rev 20:5–6

THE HOLY SPIRIT
(DARK GREEN)

A
Asking for, or Praying for the Spirit
Ge 32:24–28
1Ki 3:5–12
2Ki 2:9–10
2Ch 1:7–12
Ps 51:10–13
Isa 44:3
Mt 5:6
Lk 11:9–13
Jn 4:10
Ac 1:4, 14;

   4:29–31;
   8:14–17;
   10:31
Eph 1:16–17;
   3:14–19
Col 1:9

B
Baptism or Filling of the Spirit
Ge 41:38
Ex 28:3;
   29:7;
   31:3;

   35:31
Lev 8:12
Nu 27:18
Dt 34:9
2Ki 2:9–10
Job 32:18–19
Ps 45:7;
   51:12–13;
   68:18;
   133:2
Isa 11:2;
   42:1;
   44:3;

   61:1;
   63:11
Eze 11:19;
   36:26–27;
   37:14
Da 4:8–9, 18;
   5:11–12, 14;
   6:3
Joel 2:28–29
Mic 3:8
Mal 3:10
Mt 3:11, 16;
   12:18

Mk	1:8, 10		11:24;	2Sa	7:17;		4:5, 8–9, 13, 18;
Lk	1:15, 41, 67;		22:6–10;		23:1, 2		5:11–12, 14;
	3:16, 21–22;		26:12–14	1Ki	3:5–12;		6:3;
	4:18;	2Co	10:4–5		4:29–34;		7:1–2, 7, 13, 15;
	24:49	Eph	6:17		8:10–11;		8:1–2;
Jn	1:32–33;	Heb	4:12		13:20;		10:1, 7–8
	3:34;	Rev	1:16;		18:12, 46;	Hos	12:10
	4:10, 14;		22:17		22:24	Ob	1
	7:37–39;			2Ki	2:9–10, 15–16;	Mic	3:8
	14:16–17, 26;	**D**			3:11–12, 15;	Na	1:1
	15:26;	**DEITY**, or Divinity, of the			6:8–12, 17	Hab	2:2
	16:7, 13	Holy Spirit		1Ch	12:18;	Hag	2:5
Ac	1:4–5, 8;	Ps	68:18;		17:15;	Zec	4:6;
	2:1–18, 33,		139:7		28:12, 19		6:8;
	38–39;	Isa	40:13	2Ch	1:7–12;		7:12
	4:31;	Mt	12:31–32;		5:13–14;	Mt	1:18, 20;
	5:32;		28:19		7:1–3;		3:16;
	6:3, 5;	Mk	3:28, 29		9:29;		4:1;
	8:14–21;	Ac	5:4		15:1;		12:28;
	9:17;	1Co	3:16–17		20:14;		16:17;
	10:44–47;	2Co	3:17;		24:20;		17:9;
	11:15–17, 24;		6:16;		26:5;		22:43
	13:52;		13:14		32:32	Mk	1:10, 12;
	15:8;	Eph	2:22;	Ne	9:12, 20, 30		12:36
	19:1–7		4:4	Job	4:12–13;	Lk	1:15–17, 22, 41,
Ro	8:23;	Heb	9:14		26:13;		67, 80;
	15:13, 16	1Jn	5:7		32:8, 18–19;		2:25–27, 40;
1Co	6:11;				33:4, 14–15		3:22;
	12:1–11	**E**		Ps	39:3;		4:1, 14;
2Co	1:21–22;	**EXAMPLES** of the Holy			45:7;		24:23, 32
	5:5	Spirit's Work			78:14;	Jn	1:32–33;
Gal	3:5	Ge	1:2–3;		89:10, 20;		3:34;
Eph	1:13–14;		15:1;		104:30;		20:22
	3:16;		32:24–28;		139:7;	Ac	1:2, 16;
	4:8;		41:15, 38;		143:10		2:1–18, 33;
	5:18		46:2	Isa	1:1;		4:8, 13, 31, 33;
Tit	3:5–6	Ex	3:1–6;		6:5–8;		5:3, 9, 32;
Heb	1:9;		13:21–22;		21:2;		6:3, 5, 8–10, 15;
	2:4;		28:3;		22:1;		7:51, 55;
	10:14–15		31:3;		30:1;		8:14–21, 29, 39;
1Pe	1:11;		34:29–35;		34:16;		9:3, 10, 12, 17,
	4:10–11		35:31;		40:7;		31;
1Jn	2:20		40:34–35		48:16;		10:3, 10, 11, 19,
		Nu	9:15–16;		59:21;		38, 44–47;
C			11:17, 25–29;		63:10–11, 14		11:5, 12, 15–17,
The Holy Spirit **CONVICTS**			12:6;	Jer	20:9;		28;
of Sin			14:24;		23:16		12:9;
Ge	6:3		24:2, 4;	La	2:9		13:2, 4, 9, 52;
Ne	9:30		27:18	Eze	1:1, 3, 12, 20;		15:8, 28;
Job	36:8–10	Dt	34:9		2:2–3;		16:6–7, 9–10;
Ps	51:12–13;	Jdg	3:10;		3:12, 14, 22, 24;		18:5, 9;
	139:7		6:34;		7:13;		19:1–7;
Isa	49:2		11:29;		8:1, 3, 4;		20:22–23, 28;
Jer	5:14;		13:25;		10:4;		21:4, 11;
	23:29		14:6, 19;		11:1, 5, 24;		22:6, 17;
Hos	6:5		15:14–15		12:27;		26:19;
Mic	3:8	1Sa	3:1, 15;		13:3;		28:25
Zec	4:6;		10:6–7, 10–12;		33:22;	Ro	1:4, 11;
	12:10		11:6;		37:1;		5:5;
Lk	1:15–17		16:13–14;		40:1–2;		7:6;
Jn	16:7–11		18:12;		43:3–4, 5		8:2, 15, 23,
Ac	2:37;		19:20–23	Da	1:17, 20;		26–27;
	9:3–6;				2:19, 28;		9:1;

Summary of Chain of References

12:6–7;
15:16, 18–19, 30
1Co 2:4–16;
3:1, 16;
6:11, 19;
7:40;
12:1–13, 28–31
2Co 1:21–22;
3:3, 6–18;
12:1–4
Gal 3:2–3, 5;
4:6;
5:5;
6:1
Eph 1:3, 13–14;
2:18, 22;
3:2–5;
4:3, 7–8, 30
Php 3:3
Col 1:8;
2:5
1Th 1:5–6;
4:8
2Th 2:13
1Ti 3:16;
4:1, 14
2Ti 1:6–7, 14
Tit 3:5–6
Heb 1:9;
2:4;
3:7;
9:8, 14;
10:15, 32;
11:11
1Pe 1:2, 11–12, 22;
2:5;
3:18–19;
4:10–11
2Pe 1:21
1Jn 2:20, 27;
3:24;
4:13;
5:6–8
Jude 19–20
Rev 1:4, 10;
2:7, 11, 17, 29;
3:1, 6, 13, 22;
4:2;
5:6;
9:17;
11:11;
14:13;
17:3;
21:10;
22:17

F
FRUITS of the Holy Spirit
Ps 45:7;
51:12
Isa 61:3;
63:14
Mt 3:10;
7:16–20;
12:33;
13:8, 22–23
Mk 4:8, 20
Lk 3:9;
6:43–44;
8:8, 15;
13:9
Jn 4:10–15;
15:1–8
Ac 9:31;
13:52
Ro 5:5;
6:22;
8:6, 23;
14:17;
15:13, 30
2Co 13:14
Gal 5:22–23
Eph 1:3;
4:3;
5:9
Php 1:11;
2:1
Col 1:8
1Th 1:6
2Ti 1:7
Heb 1:9;
12:11
Jas 3:17–18
1Pe 1:22

G
GIFTS of the Holy Spirit
Ge 41:38
Ex 4:10–15;
6:30—7:1;
25:31–40;
28:3;
31:3;
35:31, 34–35;
36:1;
37:17–24
Nu 11:25–29
Dt 34:9
1Sa 10:6–7, 10–12;
18:14–15, 30;
19:20–24
2Sa 14:17, 20;
16:23;
23:2
1Ki 3:5–14, 28;
4:29–34;
5:12;
10:1–9, 23–24;
11:41
2Ki 6:8–12
1Ch 22:12
2Ch 1:7–12;
2:12;
9:1–8, 22–24
Ezr 7:25
Ne 9:20
Job 32:8;
35:10–11;
38:36
Ps 51:6;
68:18
Pr 1:22–23;
2:3–8;
3:13–18
Ecc 2:26
Isa 11:2–3;
28:6, 9, 11;
42:1;
61:1
Jer 1:6–10;
5:14
Da 1:17, 20;
2:20–23;
4:8–9, 18;
5:11–12, 14
Joel 2:28–29
Mic 3:8
Zec 4:1–6
Mt 10:19–20;
12:42
Mk 13:11;
16:17–18
Lk 1:17, 67;
2:40;
11:31;
12:11–12;
21:14–15;
24:49
Jn 3:34;
14:26;
16:13–15
Ac 1:8;
2:3–18;
4:13;
6:3, 8–10;
10:38, 46;
11:27–28;
19:6;
20:28
Ro 1:11;
12:6–8;
15:19
1Co 1:4–7;
2:4–15;
3:1–2;
7:7;
12:1–31;
13:1–2, 8;
14:1–40
Eph 1:16–19;
3:2–5, 7, 14–19;
4:7–8, 11–14
Col 1:9
1Th 5:20
1Ti 4:14
2Ti 1:6–7, 14;
3:16
Heb 2:4
Jas 1:5
1Pe 4:10–11
2Pe 1:19, 21
1Jn 2:20, 27
Rev 1:4;
3:1;
4:5;
5:6;
19:10

H
HEALING and Resurrecting Power of the Spirit
Job 33:4
Eze 37:1–12, 13–14
Mt 12:28
Jn 3:3–8;
6:63
Ro 1:4;
8:2, 11;
15:19
1Co 6:14;
12:9;
15:44–54
2Co 3:6
Eph 1:19–20
Heb 2:4
1Pe 3:18
Rev 11:11

J
Comfort or **JOY** of the Holy Spirit
Ps 45:7;
51:12
Isa 44:3;
61:3;
63:14
Mal 3:10
Mt 3:16;
5:6
Mk 1:10
Lk 3:22
Jn 1:32;
14:16–17, 26;
15:26;
16:7;
20:21–22
Ac 2:46;
9:31;
13:52
Ro 5:5;
8:1, 15;
14:17;
15:13
2Co 3:17
Gal 5:22
1Th 1:6
Heb 1:9

L

LEADING or Guiding of the Holy Spirit
Ge 24:27
Nu 9:21
Jdg 13:25
1Sa 10:6–7
2Sa 5:24;
 23:2
1Ki 18:12;
 22:24
2Ki 2:16
1Ch 14:15
2Ch 18:23
Ne 2:12;
 9:12, 20
Job 32:18–19
Ps 37:23;
 39:3;
 143:10
Pr 3:5–6;
 6:22;
 16:1, 9
Isa 30:21;
 48:16;
 58:1;
 63:14
Jer 10:23;
 20:9
Eze 1:12, 20;
 2:2–3;
 3:14, 22, 24;
 11:1, 5;
 13:3;
 36:27
Mt 4:1;
 10:19–20
Mk 1:12;
 12:36;
 13:11
Lk 2:27;
 4:1, 14;
 12:11–12;
 21:14–15
Jn 4:23–24;
 16:13
Ac 1:2;
 2:4;
 4:8;
 6:10;
 8:29, 39;
 9:31;
 10:19–20;
 11:12;
 13:2, 4, 9;
 15:28;
 16:6–7;
 18:5;
 20:22–23, 28;
 21:4
Ro 7:6;
 8:1–14, 26–27;
 9:1;
 12:6–8
1Co 7:40;
 12:3;
 14:15, 30, 32–33
2Co 12:18
Gal 5:5, 16–18,
 22–25;
 6:8
Eph 4:3–4;
 5:18–19;
 6:18
Php 3:3
1Th 5:19
Heb 9:14
1Pe 1:12, 22;
 2:5;
 3:18–19;
 4:10–11
Jude 19–20
Rev 1:10;
 4:2

M

Great MIGHT or Power Given by the Spirit
Ge 1:2–3;
 41:38
Ex 4:10–12;
 40:34–35
Jdg 3:10;
 6:34;
 11:29;
 14:6, 19;
 15:14–15;
 16:20
1Sa 10:10–12;
 11:6;
 19:20–23
1Ki 3:12;
 4:29–34;
 8:10–11;
 10:1–9
2Ki 2:16
2Ch 5:14;
 7:2
Job 26:13–14;
 32:18–19;
 33:4
Ps 51:12–13;
 104:30;
 139:7
Isa 9:5;
 11:2;
 28:6;
 31:3;
 32:15;
 34:16;
 40:7, 13;
 44:3–4;
 58:11;
 59:19
Jer 1:6–10, 17–19;
 5:14;
 20:9
Eze 2:2–3;
 3:12, 14, 24;
 33:22;
 36:27;
 37:14
Da 4:8–9, 18;
 5:11–12, 14;
 6:3
Joel 2:28
Mic 2:7;
 3:8
Zec 4:6;
 6:8
Mal 3:10;
 4:2–3
Mt 3:11;
 12:28
Mk 13:11
Lk 1:15–17, 80;
 2:40;
 3:16;
 4:14;
 21:14–15;
 24:32, 49
Jn 7:38–39;
 14:26;
 16:7–15
Ac 1:8;
 2:1–18;
 4:13, 29–31, 33;
 6:8–10, 15;
 10:38, 46;
 11:24;
 19:6
Ro 1:4, 11;
 8:2, 26–27;
 15:13, 19
1Co 2:4–10;
 3:1;
 4:20
2Co 3:5–18;
 9:8
Gal 3:5
Eph 1:17–19;
 3:2–5, 14–19;
 6:10
Php 1:19
Col 1:9–11
1Th 1:5
2Ti 1:7
Heb 2:4
2Pe 1:21
1Jn 2:20, 27

N

NAMES and Symbols of the Holy Spirit
Ge 1:2
Ex 3:1–6;
 13:21–22;
 25:31–37;
 29:7;
 30:25;
 34:29–35;
 40:34–35
Lev 1:7;
 6:13
1Ki 8:10–11;
 18:46
2Ki 2:9;
 3:15
2Ch 5:13–14;
 7:1–22
Ne 9:12, 20
Job 26:13;
 32:8, 18–19;
 33:4
Ps 39:3;
 45:2, 7;
 51:12;
 78:14;
 84:11;
 89:20;
 104:30;
 133:2;
 139:7;
 143:10
Ecc 11:5
Isa 4:4, 5;
 6:6;
 9:5;
 11:2;
 12:3;
 30:1;
 40:7;
 44:3–4;
 55:1;
 61:3
Jer 2:13;
 5:14;
 17:13;
 20:9
Eze 1:3–4, 13,
 27–28;
 3:12, 14, 22;
 8:1, 3;
 10:2–4;
 34:26;
 37:1;
 40:1;
 43:4–5
Da 5:12;
 6:3
Hos 10:12
Joel 3:18
Zec 4:1–6;
 6:8;
 12:10
Mal 4:2
Mt 3:11, 16;
 6:22;
 25:4

Summary of Chain of References

Mk 1:10;
  6:13
Lk 3:16, 22;
  11:34–36;
  24:32
Jn 1:32;
  3:5, 8, 34;
  4:10–14;
  7:37–39;
  14:16–17;
  15:26
Ac 2:2–4, 13, 33;
  4:31;
  6:15;
  8:39;
  9:3;
  10:45;
  22:6;
  26:13
Ro 1:4
1Co 2:11;
  12:1–13
2Co 3:17;
  4:6–7;
  11:4
Gal 5:18
Eph 2:18;
  3:16;
  4:4;
  5:18
Heb 9:14;
  10:29
Jas 5:14
1Pe 4:14
1Jn 2:20, 27;
  4:1–2, 6;
  5:6, 7–8
Jude 19
Rev 1:4;
  3:1, 18;
  4:5;
  5:6;
  22:17

P
The Holy Spirit Promised
Nu 11:17;
  12:6
1Sa 10:6
2Ki 2:9–10
Ps 68:18;
  84:11
Pr 1:22–23
Isa 4:4;
  9:5;
  11:2;
  12:3;
  32:15;
  41:17–18;
  42:1;
  44:3–4;
  55:1;

  59:21;
  61:1
Eze 11:19;
  36:26–27;
  37:14;
  39:29
Da 9:24
Hos 6:3;
  10:12
Joel 2:28–29;
  3:18
Zec 12:10
Mal 3:10;
  4:2
Mt 3:11;
  12:18
Mk 1:8
Lk 1:15, 35;
  3:16;
  4:17–18;
  11:9–13;
  24:29
Jn 1:33;
  4:10;
  7:37–39;
  14:16–17, 26;
  15:26;
  16:7–15
Ac 1:4–5, 8;
  2:15–18, 38–39;
  11:16
Ro 15:29
Gal 3:14
2Pe 1:4
Rev 22:17

Q
Quenching, Grieving, or Sinning Against the Spirit
Ge 6:3
Jdg 16:20
1Sa 3:1;
  16:14;
  18:12
1Ki 22:24
2Ch 18:23
Ne 9:30
Ps 51:11
Isa 63:10
La 2:9
Mic 3:6
Zec 6:8
Mt 12:31–32
Mk 3:29
Lk 12:10
Ac 5:3–4, 9;
  7:51
Eph 4:30
1Th 5:19
Heb 6:4–6;
  10:29
1Jn 5:16, 17–18

R
Regeneration as the Work of the Holy Spirit
1Sa 10:6, 9
Ps 51:10, 12–13
Isa 4:4;
  6:5–7;
  61:1–3
Jer 31:33–34;
  32:38–39
Eze 11:19;
  36:25–27
Lk 1:17
Jn 3:3–8;
  6:63
Ro 8:1–16
1Co 6:11;
  12:13
2Co 3:3
Gal 3:2–3;
  4:6, 29
Eph 1:13–14;
  2:18
Tit 3:5
Heb 8:10–12;
  10:16, 22

S
Sanctifying Power of the Holy Spirit
Ex 3:1–6;
  28:41;
  29:21;
  30:25
Lev 8:12;
  21:10–12
Dt 30:6
1Sa 24:6;
  26:9
2Sa 1:14, 21
1Ch 16:22
Ps 51:10
Isa 4:3–4;
  6:5–8;
  9:5
Eze 11:19;
  36:25–27
Mic 2:7
Lk 1:17
Ac 15:8–9
Ro 1:4;
  8:1–16;
  12:1–2;
  15:16
1Co 3:1, 16–17;
  6:11
2Co 3:18
Gal 5:16
Eph 4:22–24;
  5:25–27
1Th 4:7–8;
  5:23

2Th 2:13
Heb 10:14–15, 22, 29
1Pe 1:2, 22
Jude 19–20

T
Teaching or Enlightening of the Spirit
Ge 15:1;
  41:38;
  46:2
Ex 4:15;
  28:3;
  31:3;
  35:31
Nu 11:25–29;
  12:6;
  22:38;
  23:5, 12, 16;
  24:2–3
Dt 34:9
1Sa 3:1;
  10:6–7, 10–12
2Sa 16:23;
  23:1–2
1Ki 3:5–14, 28;
  4:29–34;
  5:12;
  10:1–9, 23–24;
  22:14
2Ki 6:8–12, 17
1Ch 28:12, 19
2Ch 9:1–7, 23;
  18:13;
  20:14–15;
  24:20;
  26:5
Ezr 7:25
Ne 9:20
Job 4:13;
  27:11;
  32:8, 18–19;
  33:14–15;
  35:10–11;
  38:36
Ps 143:10
Pr 1:22–23;
  2:3–9;
  28:5
Ecc 1:16;
  2:26
Isa 11:2–3;
  28:6, 9;
  40:13;
  42:1;
  51:16;
  61:1
Jer 1:6–10, 5–14;
  31:33–34
La 2:9
Eze 1:1;
  7:26;

xxvii Summary of Chain of References

		Ac	1:2, 16;	2Pe	1:21		9:17;
	8:3;		2:1–18;	1Jn	2:20, 27		19:2
	11:24;		4:13;	Rev	1:10;	Ro	1:11;
	13:3;		6:3, 9–10;		2:7, 11, 17, 29;		7:6;
	40:1–2		7:55;		3:6, 13, 18, 22;		8:1–16;
Da	1:17, 20;		10:10–11, 17, 46;		4:2;		12:1–2, 6–8;
	2:19–23, 28;		11:28;		14:13;		14:17
	4:8–9, 18;		16:9;		17:3	1Co	1:4–7;
	5:11–12, 14;		19:6;				2:14;

W
God WISHES Us to be Filled with the Spirit

	7:1;		20:23;				3:1–2;
	8:1–2, 16;		21:4, 11;				12:1–11, 31;
	9:21;		22:17–18;				14:1, 5, 15
	10:1, 8, 16		28:25	Nu	11:29;	2Co	3:6–11, 17–18;
Joel	2:28–29	Ro	12:6–8		14:24;		6:6;
Mic	3:8	1Co	2:4–16;		27:18–20		13:14
Zec	7:12		7:40;	Ps	68:18	Gal	3:3, 14;
Mt	6:22;		12:3, 8, 10;	Pr	1:22–23;		5:16, 25
	10:19–20;		14:30		29:18	Eph	1:16–17;
	12:42;	2Co	12:1–4	Isa	30:1		2:22;
	22:43–44	Gal	1:11–12	Jer	2:13		3:14–19;
Mk	12:36;	Eph	1:17–19;	Hos	10:12		4:3–4, 11–14;
	13:11;		3:2–5, 16–19;	Mic	2:7		5:9, 18
	16:17		6:17	Zec	4:6	Php	3:3
Lk	1:22, 41–42, 67;	1Th	1:5	Lk	24:49	Col	1:9
	2:40, 52;	1Ti	4:1	Jn	4:23–24;	1Th	4:7–8
	4:18;	2Ti	3:16		6:63;	2Th	2:13
	11:31;	Heb	3:7;		14:16–17;	1Ti	4:12
	12:11–12;		6:4;		16:7	1Pe	1:2;
	21:14–15		8:10–11;	Ac	1:4–5;		2:5;
Jn	3:34;		10:16		6:3;		4:10–11
	14:26;	1Pe	1:11, 22;		7:51;	Jude	19–20
	15:26;		4:10–11		8:14–15;	Rev	3:18
	16:7–15						

SALVATION
(RED)

A
ALL Unsaved People are Sinners

Pr	20:9;	Jn	1:12;	2Co	5:14;
	30:12		3:3–7, 18, 19, 36;		13:5
Ecc	7:20		5:38–42;	Gal	1:4;
Isa	53:6		6:53;		2:16, 21;
Mal	1:6;		7:7;		3:10–11, 22
	3:18		8:7–9, 23–24, 33–36, 42–44, 47;	Eph	2:1–3
Mt	4:8–9;			Php	2:21
	6:24;			2Th	1:8
	7:13–14;		10:1, 25–28;	Heb	3:18
	12:30;		12:48;	Jas	2:10;
	13:38;		14:17, 30;		4:4
	18:3;		15:6, 18–19;	1Jn	1:6, 8, 10;
	22:11–14;		16:8–9;		2:15–16, 22;
	25:1–12		17:14, 16, 25		3:1, 9, 10;
Mk	9:40;	Ac	3:22–23		4:3;
	10:15;	Ro	1:20, 21;		5:10, 12, 19
	16:16		3:9–12, 19, 22, 23;	2Jn	9–10
Lk	4:5–6;			Rev	13:8;
	11:23;		5:12, 14–21;		20:15
	12:34;		6:16, 20–21;		
	13:1–5;		7:5, 9, 14;		

Ge	17:10, 14
Ex	12:43–49; 30:15
Dt	1:32; 11:26–28; 18:18–19; 32:20
1Sa	2:12; 8:7
1Ki	8:46
2Ch	6:36; 12:14
Job	9:2–3; 15:12–16; 25:4–6
Ps	14:1–4; 53:1–4; 58:1–2; 78:21–22; 130:3; 143:2

			8:5–9, 13–14;		
			11:32		
		1Co	11:32		
	16:13, 15;				
	18:17				

C
CONDITION of Sinners Described

Ge	2:17; 3:3;

Summary of Chain of References

	6:5, 11, 12;		83:5;	La	3:19–20		3:9–12, 17–20;
	8:21;		94:11;	Eze	2:3, 4, 6;		6:16–17, 20;
	13:13;		95:10;		3:7;		7:5, 9–11, 14–25;
	18:20;		107:10, 17;		12:2;		8:5–8;
	19:4–10		119:53, 158		20:16;		11:8
Ex	9:34;	Pr	1:32;		22:18;	1Co	2:14;
	32:7–9;		2:13–14;		33:30–32		3:19–20;
	33:3, 5		4:16–17, 19;	Da	9:5		6:9–10
Nu	16:38		5:5, 22–23;	Hos	1:9;	2Co	4:3–4;
Dt	9:6, 13, 18;		6:14;		4:2, 17;		5:14;
	13:13;		8:36;		6:4;		10:12
	29:4, 18–19;		10:20, 23;		10:1–2, 13;	Gal	5:19–21
	31:27;		11:18;		13:3	Eph	2:1–3, 12, 19;
	32:5, 20, 28–29		12:5;	Am	5:7;		4:18;
Jdg	2:19;		13:15, 19;		6:12, 13		5:5, 14
	19:22		14:9, 13, 16, 34;	Mic	7:2–4	Php	2:21;
1Sa	2:12, 17, 25;		15:8–9, 26, 29;	Hab	2:4		3:18–19
	8:7;		16:27;	Zep	1:12	Col	1:13, 21;
	24:13;		21:10, 16, 27;	Hag	1:5–7		2:13, 18;
	25:17		30:12–13	Mal	3:13–14		3:5–7
2Sa	23:6–7	Ecc	1:2;	Mt	3:7, 12;	1Th	4:13;
1Ki	21:20, 25–26		5:1;		4:16;		5:6
2Ki	17:14–15, 17;		7:6, 29;		6:23;	2Th	1:8;
	19:22;		8:11;		7:16–20, 26–27;		2:10–12;
	21:22		9:3, 18;		8:22;		3:2
2Ch	12:14;		10:2;		9:10–11, 12;	1Ti	1:9–10;
	24:20;		12:8		10:6;		4:2;
	28:11, 22;	Isa	1:4–6;		12:30, 33;		5:6
	29:6		3:9;		13:14–15, 38;	2Ti	2:26;
Ne	9:16–17		5:18, 20;		15:14, 18–19;		3:1–5, 8, 13;
Job	5:13–14;		6:5, 9–10;		18:11–14;		4:4
	6:18;		9:2;		22:11–14;	Tit	1:15, 16;
	15:16, 20–21,		26:10–11;		23:17, 19, 25–28,		3:3
	23–26, 35;		30:9–10;		33;	Heb	2:15;
	20:4–13, 14–29;		33:11;		25:2–3		3:10
	21:14–15, 17–18;		42:7;	Mk	2:16, 17;	Jas	1:14–15;
	22:10;		43:8;		4:12;		2:14–15;
	24:13, 17;		44:18, 20;		7:15, 20–23		4:5
	27:18		48:4, 22;	Lk	1:79;	1Pe	2:25;
Ps	1:4;		53:6;		3:7;		4:3–5
	5:9;		55:2;		5:30, 31;	2Pe	2:10–15, 17, 22;
	7:14;		57:4, 20–21;		6:39, 43–45, 49;		3:3
	10:4–6, 7–13;		59:2–3, 4–7, 8,		9:60;	1Jn	2:11, 15–17;
	11:2;		12, 13;		11:23, 34–35, 39,		3:8, 14–15;
	12:2;		61:1;		44;		5:12, 19
	14:1–4;		64:6;		12:15, 16–21;	Jude	12; 13; 16
	17:14;		65:2		15:6, 9, 16–17,	Rev	3:17
	28:5;	Jer	2:19, 32;		24, 32;		
	36:1–4;		4:22;		19:10		**D**
	37:12, 14;		5:4, 21–25;	Jn	3:19–20;		Christ D<small>IED</small> to Save
	38:4–5, 7;		6:10, 15, 17, 28,		6:44;		Sinners
	40:2;		30;		8:34, 44;	Ge	3:15;
	49:11–13, 20;		7:24, 25, 26;		11:10;		4:3–5;
	51:5;		8:7, 9;		12:40;		8:20;
	52:1–3, 7;		9:3, 26;		17:25		22:1–6, 7–8,
	53:1–4;		11:8;	Ac	7:51;		9–14;
	58:1–3, 4–5;		13:10, 23;		8:23;		31:54;
	62:9–10;		16:12;		13:10;		46:1
	64:3–6;		17:1, 9, 23;		26:18;	Ex	3:18;
	73:6, 8–9;		23:12;		28:26–27		5:3;
	74:18, 22;		30:12;	Ro	1:20–21, 22–23,		8:8, 25–29;
	78:8, 10, 36–37;		44:10;		24, 25, 26, 27,		
	82:5;		50:6		28–32;		

	12:3–5, 6–12, 13, 14–20, 21–23, 24–28; 20:24; 24:5–8; 28:38; 29:1, 10–13, 14, 15–18, 36–42; 30:10, 15–16; 32:30	Jdg	2:5; 20:26; 21:4	Lk	9:56; 19:10; 22:17–20; 24:25–27, 44–47		7:14; 12:11; 13:8
		1Sa	1:3; 6:15; 7:9; 10:8; 11:15; 13:9–10; 15:15, 21; 20:6	Jn	1:29, 36; 3:14–17; 6:51–56; 10:11, 15; 11:49–52; 12:32, 47; 15:13; 18:14		**E** The Lord Knows **Every** Secret Thing
						Ge	3:8–9; 6:5, 11–12; 13:13; 18:20–21; 19:13; 20:6
Lev	1:1–4, 10; 3:1–2, 6–8, 12–13; 4:1–3, 4–11, 12, 13, 14, 15–19, 20–21, 22, 23, 24–27, 28, 29–31, 32, 33–35; 5:5–6, 7–14, 15, 16–17, 18, 19; 6:6–7, 17, 25; 7:1–2, 7, 37; 8:2, 14, 17–18, 22; 9:2–7, 11, 15–18, 22; 10:16–19; 12:6–8; 14:4–7, 10–14, 19–25, 30–31; 15:14–15, 29–30; 16:3, 5–11, 15, 21, 27; 17:3–10, 11–14; 19:21–22; 22:17–25; 23:4–5, 8, 19, 26–32	2Sa	6:13, 17–18; 24:25	Ac	8:32–35; 20:28; 26:22–23	Ex	32:9
		1Ki	3:4, 15; 8:5, 62–64; 9:25; 18:29, 36	Ro	3:24–25; 5:1–2, 6–21; 8:3, 32, 34; 14:9, 15	Nu	32:23
						Dt	9:13; 31:16, 21
		2Ki	16:13–15; 23:21			Jos	22:22
		1Ch	6:49; 16:1–2, 40; 21:26; 28:21	1Co	5:7; 6:20; 7:23; 8:11; 10:16; 11:23–25; 15:3	1Sa	2:3, 17; 16:7
						1Ki	8:39; 19:18
		2Ch	2:4; 7:4–5; 8:12–13; 13:11; 15:11; 29:21–24, 27, 31–35; 30:1, 5, 15, 22, 24; 31:2–3; 35:1, 7–19			2Ki	19:27
						1Ch	28:9
				2Co	5:14–15, 18–21; 9:15	2Ch	6:30; 16:9
				Gal	1:4; 2:20; 3:13, 16; 4:4–5	Job	4:14; 10:4–7; 13:27; 14:16–17; 20:27; 22:12–17; 23:10; 26:6; 28:24–25; 31:4; 34:21–22, 25; 42:2
		Ezr	3:2–6; 6:17, 19–20; 8:35	Eph	1:4–5, 6–7, 10–11; 2:13–18; 4:32; 5:2, 25		
		Ne	10:33; 12:43	Col	1:14, 20–22		
		Job	1:5; 42:8	1Th	5:9–10	Ps	7:9; 10:11–14; 11:4; 14:2; 17:3; 33:13–15; 44:21; 53:2; 56:8; 59:8–9; 64:5; 66:7; 69:5; 73:11; 87:6; 90:8; 94:7–11; 102:19; 139:1–16
				1Ti	1:15; 2:5–6		
Nu	5:8; 6:12–17; 7:10–88; 8:8, 10–13, 17–18, 21; 9:2–3, 13–14; 15:24–29; 16:46–47; 18:17; 19:1–9, 17; 21:6–9; 23:1–3; 25:13; 28:3–4, 9–10, 15–19, 22–23, 30–31; 29:1–40; 31:50	Ps	22:13–18; 40:6–8; 69:22–21	Tit	2:14		
				Heb	1:3; 2:9, 14–17; 5:1–5; 7:27; 9:7, 11–28; 10:1–11, 12, 13–22; 12:24; 13:11–12, 21		
		Isa	52:14–15; 53:3–12; 56:7				
		Eze	40:39; 42:13; 43:18–27; 44:11, 27, 29; 45:15–25; 46:4–6, 11-12, 13, 14–15, 20				
				1Pe	1:2, 11, 18–19; 2:21, 24; 3:18; 4:1		
		Da	9:24–26	2Pe	2:1		
		Jnh	1:16	1Jn	1:7; 2:2, 12; 3:5, 16; 4:9, 10, 14; 5:8		
		Zec	12:10; 13:1				
Dt	12:5–6, 13–14; 15:21; 16:1–6; 17:1	Mal	1:8, 13–14			Pr	5:21; 15:3, 11; 16:2; 17:3; 21:2; 24:12
		Mt	1:21; 20:28; 26:26–28				
				Rev	1:5; 5:6, 9, 12;		
Jos	5:10; 8:30–31	Mk	10:45; 14:22–24				

Summary of Chain of References

Ecc 12:14
Isa 28:17;
　　29:15;
　　59:12
Jer 2:26;
　　11:20;
　　12:3;
　　13:27;
　　16:17;
　　17:1, 10;
　　18:23;
　　20:12;
　　23:23–24;
　　29:23;
　　32:19;
　　49:10
Eze 8:12;
　　9:9–10;
　　11:5
Da 2:22;
　　5:27
Hos 5:3;
　　7:2
Am 5:12;
　　8:7;
　　9:8
Jnh 1:2;
　　4:4
Zec 4:10
Mt 9:4;
　　10:26, 29–30;
　　12:25, 36
Mk 2:8;
　　4:22;
　　12:15
Lk 5:22;
　　6:8;
　　8:17;
　　9:47;
　　11:17;
　　12:2–3;
　　16:15
Jn 1:47–49;
　　2:24–25;
　　4:17–19, 29, 39;
　　5:42;
　　6:64;
　　10:14;
　　13:11, 21;
　　16:30;
　　21:17
Ac 1:24;
　　15:8, 18;
　　18:10
Ro 2:16;
　　8:27, 29;
　　11:4
1Co 3:13;
　　4:5;
　　8:3
2Co 11:31
1Th 2:4
2Ti 2:19

Heb 4:12–13
Jas 5:4
1Jn 3:20
Rev 2:23;
　　3:1

F
We are Saved Through
FAITH

Ge 15:6
2Sa 22:31
2Ch 20:20
Ps 2:12;
　　18:30;
　　32:10;
　　34:8, 22;
　　37:3, 40;
　　40:4;
　　84:12;
　　116:13;
　　125:1;
　　146:5;
　　147:11
Pr 16:20;
　　29:25
Isa 7:9;
　　26:3–4
Jer 17:7
Hab 2:4
Mt 9:2;
　　11:12;
　　21:31–32
Mk 1:15;
　　2:5;
　　16:16
Lk 5:20;
　　7:50;
　　8:12;
　　16:16;
　　18:42
Jn 1:12;
　　3:14–18, 36;
　　5:24;
　　6:28–29, 35, 40, 47;
　　7:38;
　　8:24;
　　9:35;
　　11:25–26;
　　12:36, 46;
　　14:12;
　　20:29, 31
Ac 8:37;
　　10:43;
　　13:38–39;
　　15:9;
　　16:30–31;
　　19:4;
　　20:21;
　　26:18
Ro 1:16, 17;
　　3:3, 21–30;

4:1–2, 3, 4–15, 16, 17–22, 23–24, 25;
5:1–2;
8:24;
9:30–33;
10:4, 6–11;
11:20, 23;
15:13
1Co 1:21;
　　15:2
Gal 2:16;
　　3:2, 6–9, 11, 14, 22, 24–26;
　　5:5–6
Eph 2:8;
　　3:12
Php 3:9
2Th 2:12–13
1Ti 1:16
2Ti 2:13;
　　3:15
Heb 3:18–19;
　　4:2–3, 6;
　　6:1, 12;
　　10:38–39;
　　11:1, 6, 7, 13
Jas 2:5, 23
1Pe 1:5, 8–9;
　　2:6
1Jn 3:23;
　　4:15;
　　5:1, 4–5, 9–10, 13

G
GOOD WORKS Alone Will Not Save

Ex 20:25
Dt 9:6;
　　10:17;
　　32:31, 37
Jdg 10:13–14
1Sa 2:9;
　　12:21;
　　16:7
1Ki 18:21
2Ch 19:7
Job 8:11–16;
　　9:2–3, 20, 29–31;
　　15:12, 16, 31;
　　27:18;
　　31:24;
　　34:19;
　　36:18–19;
　　40:3–4
Ps 16:4;
　　20:7;
　　33:16-17;
　　44:3, 6;
　　49:6–7;
　　52:7;
　　62:9–11;

75:6–7;
78:36–37;
118:8–9;
127:1;
143:2;
146:3
Pr 3:5–6, 7;
　　11:4, 28;
　　16:2;
　　18:11, 12;
　　19:21;
　　20:9;
　　21:2;
　　26:12;
　　28:26
Ecc 1:14–15;
　　7:13
Isa 1:11–14;
　　28:15–20;
　　29:8, 13–14;
　　30:1;
　　31:1;
　　36:6;
　　41:29;
　　45:20;
　　50:11;
　　52:3;
　　55:1–2;
　　59:6;
　　64:6
Jer 2:13, 22, 28, 35;
　　3:23;
　　4:14, 19–20;
　　8:9, 11;
　　9:23–24;
　　10:15;
　　13:23;
　　16:19;
　　17:5;
　　18:13–15;
　　23:17;
　　30:12;
　　34:17;
　　46:11;
　　48:7
La 3:37
Eze 7:19;
　　13:10–14;
　　29:6–7;
　　33:31
Hos 1:7;
　　5:13;
　　10:13;
　　14:3
Am 2:14–16
Jnh 2:8
Mic 6:7
Hab 2:13
Zep 1:18
Hag 1:5–7
Zec 4:6
Mt 3:9;
　　5:20;

Summary of Chain of References

	7:26–27;		11:7, 8;		35:19, 21		7:10, 13;
	9:13;		12:17;	Dt	1:34–37, 42–44;		12:9, 15, 25;
	15:8–9;		17:14;		2:14–15, 21, 34;		15:1–23, 26, 33;
	18:23–25;		19:11, 13, 24–26;		3:6;		25:29, 38;
	19:16–26;		38:7, 10		4:3, 21, 24, 25,		26:10;
	22:11–14;	Ex	4:24;		27;		28:18–19
	25:1–2, 3, 4–13		7:19–21;		5:9, 11;	2Sa	3:39;
Mk	7:6–7;		8:1–6, 16, 18,		6:15;		6:7;
	10:17–22, 23–27		20–24;		7:1–5, 10,		7:14;
Lk	6:49;		9:1–6, 8–11,		23–24, 26;		12:1–15;
	7:41–42;		13–15, 18–19,		8:19–20;		22:27–28;
	11:39–40;		22–25;		9:3–5, 13–14,		24:10–15
	12:15;		10:4–6, 12–15,		25;	1Ki	2:5–6, 33, 34,
	16:15;		21–23;		10:10;		44;
	18:9–14, 16–22,		11:4–6;		11:4–8, 16–17,		8:32–33, 35, 46;
	23–27		12:13, 15, 29–30;		26–28;		9:6–9;
Jn	1:12–13;		14:23–28, 30;		13:4–11, 15;		13:34;
	3:3, 5;		15:4–5, 10;		17:2–7, 12–13;		14:10–11, 16;
	6:28–29;		19:13;		18:12, 18–19;		16:1–4, 12–13;
	9:39;		20:5, 7;		19:11–13, 21;		17:1;
	10:1;		21:12, 14–17, 20,		20:16–17;		20:42;
	15:4		22–25;		21:21–23;		21:20–24, 29
Ac	15:11		22:9, 20, 24;		24:7;	2Ki	1:10, 12, 14;
Ro	2:11, 28–29;		23:7, 21, 27;		25:1;		2:23–24;
	3:20, 27;		31:14–15;		27:14–26;		9:8–10, 25;
	4:1–4, 13, 14;		32:10, 27–28, 33,		28:15–28, 29,		10:18–25, 32;
	8:9, 14;		34;		30–68		13:3;
	9:11, 15–16,		33:2–3;		29:19–28;		14:5–6;
	31–32;		34:7;		30:1, 15, 17–19;		17:6–7, 18–20,
	10:1–3;		35:2		31:16–17, 29;		22–23, 25;
	11:5–6, 32	Lev	10:1–2, 6–7, 10;		32:22–23, 24–26,		18:11–12;
1Co	1:18–21, 26–31;		18:25, 28;		35, 41, 42, 43,		21:9–15;
	3:11, 19–20;		20:1–6, 9–21, 27;		49–52;		22:13, 16–17;
	13:1–3;		22:9;		34:4–5		23:26–27;
	15:10		23:30;	Jos	5:6;		24:3;
2Co	10:18		25:13–21;		6:17, 21;		25:21
Gal	1:8–9;		26:14–39, 41, 43		7:1–26;	1Ch	2:3;
	2:6, 16, 21;	Nu	1:51;		8:24, 26;		5:25–26;
	3:2, 10–12,		3:4, 10, 38;		9:24;		9:1;
	17–18, 21;		5:27;		10:11, 24–25,		10:13–14;
	4:21–31;		8:17;		28–41;		21:8–14;
	5:4, 6;		9:13;		11:11–12, 14,		27:24;
	6:14–15		11:1, 33–34;		20–22;		28:9
Eph	2:5, 8–9;		14:11–12, 18,		13:22;	2Ch	6:23, 26, 36;
	6:9		22–23, 29–30,		22:17–18, 20;		7:13, 19–22;
Php	3:3–10		32–37, 42–43;		23:12–13, 15–16;		12:1, 2, 5;
1Ti	6:7, 17		15:30–36;		24:18, 19, 20		15:2;
2Ti	1:9		16:29–35, 39–40,	Jdg	1:6–7;		19:2;
Tit	3:5		44–49;		2:14–15, 20–21;		22:7–8;
Heb	11:6		17:12–13;		3:7–8;		24:18, 20, 24;
1Pe	1:18–19, 23–24		18:7, 22;		4:1–2;		25:3–4, 15–16,
Rev	3:17–18		20:12, 24;		5:23, 31;		20, 23;
	H		21:2–3, 6;		6:1;		26:16–21;
	Punishment and **Hell**		22:33;		10:6–9;		28:4–6, 10–11, 13,
	Await Sinners		23:20;		13:1;		19;
Ge	2:17, 18;		24:17, 20, 24;		20:13;		29:7–8;
	3:3, 14–19;		25:3–9, 17;		21:11		30:7;
	4:7, 11–14;		26:10, 61, 64–65;	1Sa	2:9, 10, 24–25,		32:25;
	6:7, 13, 17;		27:13–14;		30–34;		33:10–11;
	7:4, 21–23;		31:16–17;		3:11–12, 13–14;		34:21, 24–25;
	9:6;		32:10–15, 23;		4:7, 8, 10–11;		36:16, 17
			33:4, 52;		5:6–7, 9–12;	Ezr	8:22
					6:4, 19–20;		

Summary of Chain of References

Ne 1:8;
4:5;
9:11, 26–28, 30
Est 7:10
Job 4:8–9;
8:11–15, 20, 22;
9:4;
10:14, 15;
11:20;
15:20–22, 23–26, 30, 31–33, 34;
18:18;
20:5–25, 26–27, 28–29;
21:17–20, 30;
22:15–16;
26:6;
27:7, 8, 19–23;
29:17;
31:3;
34:11–12, 25–26;
36:12–14;
38:15
Ps 1:4–6;
2:4–5, 8–9, 12;
3:7;
5:4–6, 10;
7:11, 12–15, 16;
9:3, 5, 15–16, 17;
10:2, 14–16;
11:6;
12:3;
16:4;
18:13–14, 26;
21:8–9;
25:4–8, 26;
26:9;
27:14–15, 17;
28:1, 3–5;
31:23;
32:10;
34:16, 21;
36:12;
37:1–2, 9–10, 12–13, 20, 22, 28, 33–36, 38;
39:11;
40:14;
50:3, 21–22;
52:5–6;
53:5;
55:9, 15, 23;
57:6;
58:6–10;
59:5, 8, 12–13;
62:3, 12;
63:9–10;
64:7;
68:1–2, 21, 23;
69:22, 23–24, 25, 27–28;
70:2–3;

71:13;
72:9;
73:17–18, 27;
74:1;
75:7–8, 10;
76:7;
78:21–22, 30–34, 43–51, 55–66;
79:5–6;
83:9–11, 13–16, 17;
86:13;
89:10, 23, 32;
91:8;
92:7, 9;
94:1–2, 13, 23;
95:11;
97:3;
101:8;
103:4;
104:35;
105:27–36;
106:11, 14–15, 17–18, 23, 27, 29, 32, 34, 40, 42;
107:17, 33–34;
109:7–16, 17–19;
110:1, 5–6;
112:10;
119:21, 32, 118, 119;
120:3–4;
125:3;
129:4;
135:8–12;
136:10;
139:19;
140:9–11;
141:9–10;
143:7;
144:6;
145:20;
146:9;
147:6;
149:7
Pr 1:24–32;
2:18, 22;
3:25, 33–34;
5:4–5, 22, 23;
6:15, 27–28, 32–33;
7:27;
8:36;
9:18;
10:7, 14, 24–25, 27–31;
11:3, 5–7, 19, 21, 31;
12:2, 13, 21;
13:2–3, 6, 9, 13, 15, 20, 21, 25;

14:11, 12, 13–14, 27, 32;
15:10–11, 24, 25;
16:4–5, 18, 25;
17:19;
18:7, 12;
19:5, 9, 19;
20:17, 20, 26;
21:7, 11–12, 15–16, 28;
22:3, 8;
23:14, 29–32;
24:12, 16, 20;
26:10, 27;
27:12, 20;
29:1;
30:17;
31:6
Ecc 7:6, 17;
8:11–13;
9:12;
10:8, 12
Isa 1:20, 24, 28, 30–31;
2:10–21;
3:8–10, 11, 14–15, 24;
5:5–6, 11–12, 16–18, 23;
8:15;
9:18;
11:4;
13:6–13, 15–22;
14:4–6, 9, 11–12, 15, 19–25;
15:9;
16:6–11;
17:12–14;
23:1–11;
24:1–12, 17–23;
25:5, 10–12;
26:11, 20–21;
28:1–3, 15–18, 22;
29:1–8, 15;
30:1, 12–14, 17, 30, 31, 33;
31:1–2;
33:11–12, 14;
34:1–17;
35:4;
40:2;
42:24–25;
43:17;
50:1;
51:17;
59:18;
60:12;
61:2;
63:3–4, 6, 10;
65:6, 7, 12, 13–14, 15, 20;
66:14–16, 17, 24

Jer 1:16;
2:16–17, 35;
3:3, 8;
4:4, 6–9, 15, 18–20;
5:6, 9, 14–19, 25, 29;
6:11–12, 15, 19, 21, 25–26;
7:12, 19–20, 29, 32–34;
8:12–18, 20;
9:9, 11, 16, 19, 22, 25;
10:10, 15, 18, 25;
11:8, 11, 20, 22;
12:5, 9, 11–13, 17;
13:10, 14, 15–16, 17–23, 24, 25–27;
14:4, 10–12;
15:2–9;
16:4–5, 10–13, 18;
17:4, 5–6, 10, 18;
18:9–11, 16–17, 23;
19:3, 6–15;
20:3–6, 11, 12, 16;
21:4–7, 10, 12, 14;
22:5-13, 24–30;
23:1–2, 12, 15, 17–19, 20, 29, 34, 39, 40;
24:9–10;
25:8–38;
26:3–6;
27:8;
29:17–19, 22, 32;
30:6–7, 15, 20, 23–24;
31:28, 30;
32:18–19, 23–25, 28–29, 36;
33:5;
34:17, 20–22;
35:17;
36:3, 7, 30–31;
42:16–18;
43:11–13;
44:2, 6–7, 11–14, 22–23, 27, 29–30;
46:5–6, 10, 14–16, 19–26;
47:4–7;
48:3–4, 7–10, 15–25, 36–46;
49:2–3, 8–10, 12–18, 20–29, 32–38;
50:3, 12–18, 21–32, 35–46;

Summary of Chain of References

51:3–4, 6, 11, 18, 20–64
La 1:5–8, 12–22; 2:1–12, 20; 3:20, 39, 64–66; 4:5–6, 10–12, 22; 5:1–22
Eze 3:17–20; 5:1; 7:8, 9–16, 17–18, 19; 9:5–7, 10; 11:21; 12:13–15, 25; 13:8–9, 14, 22; 14:8–10, 13–21; 15:7–8; 16:23, 49–50; 17:16, 18–21; 18:4, 13, 20, 23–24, 26, 30; 19:8–9; 20:8, 15, 21, 23; 22:20–22, 31; 23:25–26, 32–34; 24:13–14, 23; 25:7, 13–16, 17; 26:4–8, 14–21; 28:7–10, 18–19; 29:8–10; 30:1–26; 31:11–18; 33:4–5, 8–10, 11, 12, 13, 14–16, 18; 35:3–9, 14; 36:5–7; 38:20–23; 43:8; 44:12
Da 2:44; 5:1–6, 20, 24–28; 6:24; 7:11, 26; 8:25; 9:11–14; 12:1, 2
Hos 1:6; 2:2–3, 13; 4:2–3, 6–9, 14; 5:5, 9–14; 6:4–5; 7:12–13; 8:7, 13–14; 9:9, 12; 10:7–10, 13–15; 12:2; 13:1, 3, 16; 14:1, 9

Joel 1:15; 2:1–2, 3–5, 6, 7–9, 10–11, 31; 3:13–14
Am 1:3; 2:6, 9, 14–16; 3:2, 14; 4:2, 6–11, 12; 5:6, 16–20, 27; 6:1, 11; 8:3, 7, 8–14; 9:1–4, 8, 10
Ob 4, 8–10, 15
Jnh 1:2; 3:4
Mic 1:3–6; 2:1, 3, 10; 5:15; 6:13, 14–15; 7:9–10, 17
Na 1:2–3, 5–6, 8–12; 2:10, 13; 3:1, 10, 13–15
Hab 2:10; 3:12–13
Zep 1:2–3, 6–8, 12, 14–15, 17–18; 2:2–3; 3:8
Hag 2:17
Zec 3:2; 5:1–4; 7:17; 8:14; 9:4–5; 10:3, 5; 11:6; 14:3, 12, 18–19
Mal 1:4; 2:2, 9; 3:2, 5; 4:1, 3
Mt 3:7, 10, 12; 5:13, 22, 29–30; 6:15; 7:13, 19, 23, 26–27; 8:12; 10:14–15, 28, 33; 11:20–24; 12:31–32, 36–37, 41–42; 13:30, 38–42, 46–50; 15:4, 13–14; 16:19, 26–27; 18:3, 6–9, 18, 34–35; 19:24; 21:40–41, 44; 22:1–6, 7, 11–13, 44;

23:14–15, 23, 25, 27, 29, 33, 38; 24:21, 40–41, 50–51; 25:11–12, 30–46; 26:24, 52
Mk 3:28–29; 6:11; 7:10; 8:36–38; 9:42–49; 12:9, 36–40; 13:19; 14:21; 16:16
Lk 1:51; 2:34; 3:7, 9, 17; 6:24, 25, 26, 39, 49; 9:25–26; 10:12–15, 18; 11:31–32, 42–44, 46–47, 50–52; 12:4–5, 9–10, 16–19, 20–21, 46–48; 13:1–4, 5, 6–8, 9, 24–28, 35; 14:16–23, 24; 16:19–31; 17:1–2, 26–30, 32–36; 18:7; 19:27, 41–46; 20:15–16, 18, 42–43, 47; 21:24, 25–26; 22:22; 23:30
Jn 3:3, 5, 16–19, 36; 5:14, 24, 29; 9:39; 12:48; 15:2, 6; 17:12
Ac 1:25; 2:34–35; 3:23; 5:1–11; 12:21–23; 13:6–11, 41; 18:6; 23:3
Ro 1:18, 28–32; 2:2–13; 3:5–6, 8, 16; 5:9, 12; 6:21, 23; 8:6, 13; 9:22;

11:9–10, 14, 20–22, 25; 12:19; 13:2, 4; 14:15
1Co 1:18; 3:17; 6:9–10, 13; 8:11; 9:22; 10:5–12; 11:32; 15:25, 56; 16:22
2Co 2:15–16; 4:3; 5:10–11; 11:15
Gal 1:8–9; 5:19–21; 6:7–8
Eph 5:5–6
Php 1:28; 3:19
Col 3:5–6, 25
1Th 1:10; 2:16; 4:6; 5:3, 9
2Th 1:5–9; 2:8, 11–12
1Ti 4:16; 5:12, 24; 6:9, 10
2Ti 4:14
Heb 1:13; 2:2–3; 3:11, 17–19; 6:2, 7–8; 10:12–13, 26–31, 39; 11:28; 12:20–21, 25, 29; 13:4
Jas 1:15; 2:13; 3:1; 5:1–3
1Pe 3:12; 4:17–18
2Pe 2:1, 3–9, 12–13, 17, 20, 21; 3:6–7, 16
Jude 5–7; 11; 13–15; 23
Rev 1:7; 2:5, 16, 21–23, 27; 3:3, 16; 6:15–17; 8:7–13; 9:1–21; 11:13–14, 18;

Summary of Chain of References

13:10;
14:10–11, 14–20;
15:1, 6–8;
17:8, 11;
18:4–8, 10, 15, 20–21;
19:3, 11–19, 20, 21;
20:2–3, 9–15;
21:8, 27;
22:12, 15

J
All People will be JUDGED by the Lord

Ge 18:25
Jdg 11:27
1Sa 2:10
1Ch 16:33
Ps 1:5;
7:8;
9:7–8;
37:32–3;
50:3–6;
58:11;
67:4;
75:7;
82:8;
94:2;
96:10, 13;
98:9;
109:7;
110:6
Ecc 3:17;
11:9;
12:14
Isa 2:4;
3:13–14;
33:22
Eze 7:27;
18:30;
33:20;
34:17, 20, 22
Da 7:9–10, 26
Joel 3:12
Am 4:12
Mal 3:5
Mt 7:1–2;
10:15;
11:22, 24;
12:36, 41–42;
25:31–46
Mk 6:11
Lk 10:12–14;
11:31–32
Jn 8:50;
12:48;
16:11
Ac 10:42;
17:31;
24:25
Ro 2:2–13, 16;
3:6;

14:10–12
1Co 4:4–5;
5:13
2Co 5:10
1Ti 5:24
2Ti 4:1, 8
Heb 9:27;
10:27, 30;
12:23;
13:4
Jas 2:12–13;
4:12;
5:9
1Pe 4:5
2Pe 2:4, 9;
3:7
1Jn 4:17
Jude 6; 14–15
Rev 11:18;
14:7;
19:11;
20:1–15

K
Saving and KEEPING Power of God

Ge 7:16;
14:19, 22;
15:1;
18:14;
22:18
Ex 12:13, 23;
15:2, 11, 13, 17;
19:5–6;
33:19
Nu 6:24–26;
11:23;
21:8–9;
23:19
Dt 30:6, 20;
32:15, 39;
33:25, 27, 29
Jos 1:5
Jdg 5:31
Ru 2:12
1Sa 2:2, 8–9;
25:29
2Sa 22:31, 36, 47
1Ki 8:57–58
2Ki 6:16–17
1Ch 4:10;
29:11–12
2Ch 2:5–6
Ne 8:10;
9:29
Job 1:10;
5:24;
17:9;
19:25;
36:7;
42:2
Ps 2:12;
3:8;

4:3;
12:7;
16:8;
17:8;
18:2, 16, 35–36, 46;
19:7;
20:5–6;
25:5;
26:1;
27:1;
31:5;
36:9;
37:27–28;
40:2;
51:7;
55:16, 22;
61:2;
62:1–2, 5–10, 11–12;
67:1–2;
68:13, 20;
69:32;
72:17;
73:26;
78:35;
80:3, 7, 19;
84:11;
89:8, 13, 15–16, 26;
91:3, 11;
94:18;
95:1;
103:3–4, 12;
106:8;
107:14;
118:14, 21;
119:130;
121:1–8;
125:1;
128:1–2;
130:7;
135:5–6;
144:15;
145:14;
146:5
Pr 14:17;
16:15;
19:21;
20:22;
23:11
Ecc 7:13
Isa 1:18, 25;
4:4, 6;
12:1–2;
25:4;
26:3–4;
28:16;
32:2;
40:8, 29, 30, 31;
41:10;
43:1–2;
47:4;

48:18;
50:2, 10;
51:6;
52:10;
53:5, 11;
55:7;
57:13;
59:1;
60:19–21;
63:1
Jer 8:22;
17:13–14;
18:14–15;
24:7;
31:33–34;
32:17–18, 27, 38–39;
33:8;
50:20, 34
Eze 11:19–20;
12:25;
20:13, 21;
36:25–26, 29, 33;
37:23
Joel 2:32
Am 5:4, 6, 8
Ob 17
Jnh 2:9
Mic 7:7
Zec 13:1
Mal 3:3
Mt 1:21, 25;
4:4;
6:13;
7:24–25;
9:2–5, 6, 7–8;
11:28–29;
19:26;
24:35;
27:42;
28:18
Mk 2:10;
10:27;
13:31;
14:36;
15:31
Lk 1:31, 37, 69, 77–79;
2:10–11, 21, 32, 38;
3:5–6;
5:24;
6:47–48;
11:4;
18:27;
21:33;
22:31–32;
23:35
Jn 1:4, 12, 29;
3:14–18;
4:10, 13–14, 42;
5:24;

Summary of Chain of References

6:27, 33–35,
 39–40, 50–51,
 54–58, 63, 68;
7:17, **38**;
8:12, 36, 51, **52**;
9:5;
10:7, 9–10,
 28–29;
11:25–26;
12:46, 50;
14:6;
17:3, 11–12;
19:30;
20:23
Ac 2:25–26;
 3:26;
 5:31;
 10:43;
 13:23, 38–39, 47;
 16:31;
 20:32
Ro 1:16;
 3:3–4, 24–25;
 5:1–2, 9–11,
  15–21;
 7:24–25;
 8:1–4, 33–39;
 9:15, 18, 21, 23;
 10:4, 11;
 11:26;
 15:29;
 16:20, 25
1Co 1:9, 18, 23–24,
  25, 30;
 3:7;
 6:9–11;
 15:56–57
2Co 1:20;
 2:14;
 9:8
Eph 1:7;
 2:18;
 3:20;
 5:14
Php 4:13, 19
Col 1:14
1Th 1:10;
 5:9–10
2Th 3:3
1Ti 4:8
2Ti 1:12;
 3:15
Tit 1:2;
 2:11
Heb 2:18;
 5:9;
 6:16–17, 18–19;
 7:25;
 8:10–12;
 9:13–14;
 10:16–17;
 12:24;
 13:6, 8

Jas 1:21;
 4:12
1Pe 1:4–5, 8, 9, 23,
  25;
 2:6, 24
2Pe 2:9
1Jn 1:7;
 2:2;
 3:5, 8;
 4:4, 14;
 5:4–5
Jude 24
Rev 1:18;
 5:9;
 7:9, 14;
 12:11

L

**The Lord Loves and
Saves Sinners**
Ge 15:16;
 17:7;
 18:23–32
Ex 20:6;
 22:27;
 25:17;
 34:6–7
Lev 4:1–19, 20,
  21–25, 26,
  27–30, 31,
  32–34, 35;
 5:5–9, 10, 11–12,
  13, 14–15, 16,
  17, 18, 19;
 6:4–6, 7;
 19:22;
 26:40–42
Nu 14:18–20;
 15:25–28;
 21:7–9;
 30:5, 8, 12
Dt 4:7, 29, 30–31;
 5:10;
 7:7–8, 9;
 11:26–27;
 30:1–3, 11–15, 19
Jdg 3:8–9, 12–15;
 4:1–7;
 6:1–14;
 13:1–5
1Sa 2:8;
 7:9;
 12:10–11, 20
2Sa 12:13;
 22:28
1Ki 8:33–39, 47–50;
 21:25–29
1Ch 16:34, 41;
 28:9
2Ch 5:13;
 6:26–30, 37–39;
 7:3, 6, 14;
 15:2, 3, 4, 15;

 20:21;
 30:9, 18–20;
 33:11–13
Ezr 3:11;
 8:22
Ne 1:9;
 9:16, 17, 18–28,
  31
Job 33:27–28
Ps 9:10;
 22:5, 24, 26;
 25:6–11;
 30:5;
 31:16;
 32:5;
 33:5, 18–19;
 34:8, 18;
 51:1–3, 17;
 65:3;
 68:13;
 69:16, 32;
 77:7–9;
 78:34–37, 38–39;
 79:9;
 85:2–3, 9–10;
 86:5, 13, 15;
 89:34;
 99:8;
 100:5;
 102:19–20;
 103:1–4, 8–14, 17;
 106:7–8, 45;
 107:1, 9, 13, 19;
 108:4;
 109:26;
 111:4;
 112:4;
 113:7;
 116:5, 13;
 118:1–5, 29;
 119:64, 156;
 130:3–4, 7–8;
 136:1–26;
 138:8;
 145:8, 18;
 147:3;
 149:4
Pr 8:17;
 21:21;
 28:13
Isa 1:18–19, 25;
 4:4, 6;
 9:2;
 12:1–3;
 32:2, 3–4;
 33:24;
 38:17;
 40:2;
 42:6–7;
 43:1, 25;
 44:22;
 45:22;
 49:6;

 52:3;
 53:4–6, 11–12;
 55:1–3, 6–7;
 57:15–16, 18–19;
 59:1;
 61:1–3;
 63:7, 9;
 65:1, 2
Jer 3:1, 5, 12, 14, 22;
 5:1;
 9:24;
 14:7;
 18:8, 11–12;
 21:8;
 25:3–5;
 26:3, 13, 19;
 29:12, 13;
 31:3, 20, 34;
 32:18;
 33:8, 11;
 35:15;
 36:3;
 44:4–5;
 50:20
La 3:22, 25, 32–33,
  42
Eze 18:21–23, 27–28,
  32;
 33:11–12, 14–16,
  19;
 34:11–12;
 36:25, 29, 33;
 37:23
Da 9:9, 24
Hos 1:10;
 2:19–20, 23;
 5:15;
 6:1, 3;
 13:9, 14;
 14:4
Joel 2:13
Am 5:4, 6–8;
 7:3, 6
Jnh 3:10;
 4:2, 11
Mic 6:6–8;
 7:18–19
Hab 2:13
Zec 1:3;
 3:1–5, 9;
 13:1
Mal 3:7
Mt 1:21;
 4:16;
 5:5;
 6:14;
 7:7–8;
 9:2, 10–11,
  12–13;
 10:6;
 11:19, 28–29;
 12:20, 31–32;
 15:24;

18:11–14, 21–25, 26–27;
20:1–14;
21:27–30, 31–32;
22:1–8, 9–10;
23:37
Mk 2:5, 15–16, 17;
3:28;
6:34;
11:24–25;
16:9
Lk 1:50, 77–79;
2:10–11, 14, 32;
4:4, 18–19;
5:20, 29–30, 31–32;
6:35–36, 37;
7:34, 36–40, 41–42, 43–46, 47;
9:56;
11:9–10;
12:10;
13:34;
14:12–20, 21–23;
15:1–2, 3–24, 25–31, 32;
16:19–22;
17:3–4;
18:9–14;
19:1–9, 10, 41–42;
23:34, 39–41, 42–43;
24:46–47
Jn 1:7, 9, 12, 29;
3:14–17, 36;
4:6–9, 10, 11–41, 42;
5:24, 34;
6:35, 37, 40, 47;
7:17, 37;
8:3–10, 11–12, 51;
9:35–38, 39;
10:10;
11:25–26;
12:32, 46–47;
15:13;
20:31
Ac 3:14–18, 19, 25, 26;
5:31;
10:43;
11:18;
13:38–39, 47;
14:27;
15:7–10, 11, 14–17;
17:27, 28;
26:17–18, 23;
28:28
Ro 2:4;
3:21–30;
4:6, 12, 16, 22–24;
5:1, 6–21;
8:32;
9:23–26;
10:4–13, 20, 21;
11:23–24, 26–27, 32;
15:8–12, 21
1Co 1:26–31;
6:9–11, 20;
7:23;
15:3
2Co 1:3;
5:18–21;
6:2;
9:15
Gal 1:4;
2:21;
3:8, 22, 26;
4:4–5
Eph 1:6–7;
2:1–9, 11–18;
3:6–8;
4:32;
5:8, 14
Col 1:13–14, 19–22;
2:13;
3:13
1Th 1:10;
2:16;
5:9–10
1Ti 1:13, 15;
2:3–4;
4:10
2Ti 1:9;
2:13
Tit 1:2;
2:11;
3:3–5, 7
Heb 1:3;
2:14–17;
4:15;
5:2, 9;
7:25, 27;
8:12;
9:13–14, 28;
10:17;
13:8
Jas 2:5;
4:10;
5:7, 11
1Pe 1:10, 18–19;
2:6, 9–10, 24–25;
3:18
2Pe 3:9
1Jn 1:7, 9;
2:1–2, 12, 25;
3:5, 16;
4:8–10, 14;
5:1, 9–10, 16
Rev 1:5;
3:20;
21:6;
22:17

M

We Must be MEEK or Humble Before God

Ex 10:3;
32:9–10;
33:3, 5;
34:8, 9
Lev 26:18–19, 40–42
Nu 12:3
Dt 9:13–14;
10:16–17;
31:27
Jos 7:6
Jdg 20:26
1Sa 1:10;
2:3
2Sa 22:28;
24:10
1Ki 8:33–34, 38–39, 47–50;
21:25–29
2Ki 17:14;
20:2–5;
22:19
1Ch 21:8
2Ch 6:24–27, 29–30, 37–39;
7:14;
12:6–7, 12;
30:8;
32:26;
33:12–13;
34:27;
36:12–13
Ezr 9:5–6, 7–15;
10:1, 2–12
Ne 1:4–6;
9:3, 29
Job 5:11;
22:29;
38:15;
40:3–5, 11–12;
41:34
Ps 6:1–4;
9:12;
10:4, 17;
12:3–4;
17:10;
18:27;
22:26;
25:9, 11, 16–18;
27:7–8;
30:5, 11;
31:9–10, 18;
34:18;
37:11, 35–36;
42:1–2;
51:1–17;
59:12;
61:1–2;
63:1–3;
72:12–13;
73:3–18;
76:9;
79:8–9;
84:2;
86:16;
94:2–4;
106:6;
113:7;
116:3–5;
119:21, 81;
123:1–3;
126:5;
138:6;
143:6–7;
145:14;
146:8;
147:3, 6;
149:4
Pr 3:7, 34;
4:24;
6:16–17;
8:13;
11:2;
14:3, 16;
15:25, 33;
16:5, 18;
17:19–20;
18:12;
26:12;
29:1, 20, 23;
30:12–13
Ecc 7:6
Isa 2:10–17;
5:14–16, 21;
10:15, 33;
13:11;
14:12–15;
16:6–11;
23:9;
25:11;
28:1–3;
29:4;
38:2–4;
46:12;
48:4;
57:15;
61:1–3;
66:2
Jer 2:35;
3:3;
4:3–4;
5:3;
6:10, 15;
7:24, 26;
8:12;
9:25–26;
13:9–10, 15–17;
14:7;

17:23;
19:15;
26:18–19;
29:12–13;
48:29–31;
49:16;
50:31–32
La 2:18–19;
3:19–21, 40–42
Eze 2:4;
3:7;
16:50;
31:10–14;
33:13;
34:16;
44:7
Da 4:30–33, 37;
5:20–24;
9:3–5, 6, 19,
20–21
Hos 5:5;
7:10;
10:12;
12:7–8
Joel 1:13;
2:13, 17
Am 7:2–3
Ob 3–4
Jnh 2:1–2;
3:5–10
Hab 2:4
Zep 2:2–3, 10
Mal 3:13;
4:1
Mt 5:3–5;
11:20–23, 25;
18:1–4, 26–27;
19:14, 23–24, 30;
20:16, 27;
23:12
Mk 10:14–15, 23–25,
31
Lk 1:51–52;
6:20–21;
10:13–15;
13:30;
14:11;
18:9–14, 24–25
Jn 7:48;
9:39
Ac 7:51;
8:22;
12:21–23
Ro 1:30;
12:16;
14:11
1Co 1:26–31;
10:12;
14:24–25
Col 2:18
1Ti 6:3–4
2Ti 3:2

Jas 1:10–11;
2:5;
4:6–10
1Pe 5:5–6
1Jn 2:16
Jude 15
Rev 3:17–18;
18:7–8

N

NEGLECTING or Rejecting Salvation

Ge 6:3;
7:16;
19:14, 17
Ex 16:28;
32:9–10;
33:5
Lev 26:14–26, 18, 21,
23–24, 27–28
Nu 14:11, 23, 27
Dt 9:13–14, 23–25;
10:16;
11:26–28;
18:18–19;
28:15;
29:19–20, 21;
30:15, 19;
31:27;
32:35
Jos 24:15
1Sa 12:15
2Sa 14:14
1Ki 18:4, 21;
19:10
2Ki 17:13–15;
18:11–12
1Ch 29:15
2Ch 12:14;
24:20–21;
25:16;
30:8;
33:10–11;
36:12, 13, 16
Ne 9:16, 26, 29–30
Job 4:19–20;
7:1, 6–10;
8:9, 11–15;
9:2–4;
11:20;
14:1–2, 5, 7–12;
15:12–13;
16:22;
20:5, 6–12;
21:13–14;
22:15–17;
24:13;
27:8–9;
34:15;
36:10–12
Ps 2:2–5;
27:8;
39:4–5;

49:10–14;
50:16–17, 21–22;
55:23;
58:4–5;
78:10, 22, 32–33,
39;
81:11–12;
89:48;
90:5–6, 9, 12;
95:8;
103:9, 15–16;
106:24–26;
112:10;
118:22;
144:4;
146:3–4
Pr 1:24–33;
8:17;
11:7;
14:16, 32;
22:3;
27:1, 12;
28:14;
29:1
Ecc 7:6;
8:8, 11–13;
9:4, 10–12;
12:1, 2–7
Isa 26:10–11;
28:12–13;
30:12–13;
40:6;
48:4;
55:6;
60:12;
63:10;
65:12, 13–14;
66:4
Jer 2:27;
3:5;
5:3–4, 12,
21–25;
6:15–17, 19;
7:13–15, 23–29;
8:9, 12, 20;
9:13–15;
11:7–8, 10–11;
13:10, 15–17;
17:23;
18:11–13;
19:15;
22:5;
25:4–5, 7–9;
26:3–6, 22–24;
29:17–19;
32:33;
35:14–15, 17;
37:15;
44:4–6
Eze 3:7;
12:2;
20:15–16;

33:1–3, 4–5, 6–8,
9, 31;
39:6
Da 5:1–6, 20;
8:25
Hos 4:17
Joel 3:14
Am 4:6–11, 12
Zec 1:4–5;
7:11–12
Mal 2:2
Mt 5:12;
10:14–15;
11:15–19, 20–24;
12:41–42;
13:3–9, 13–15,
18–23;
17:17;
21:33–43, 44;
22:1–7;
23:37–38;
24:36–41, 43–44,
50–51;
25:1–9, 10–11;
27:1
Mk 4:3–9, 14–20,
23;
6:11;
12:1–10;
16:15–16
Lk 4:28–29;
7:29–30;
8:4–15;
9:5;
10:10–16;
11:23, 31–32;
12:16–21, 39–40,
46–47;
13:24–25, 34–35;
14:16–24;
16:30–31;
17:26–30;
20:9–17, 18;
21:34–36
Jn 3:18–20, 36;
8:24, 47;
9:39–41;
10:1, 26–27;
12:35–36, 40, 48
Ac 2:23;
3:14–15, 22–23;
4:11–12, 27;
5:30;
7:51–53, 54–60;
12:1–4;
13:41, 46, 50–51;
14:19;
16:22–23;
18:6;
21:27;
24:25;
26:28–29;
28:26–27

Summary of Chain of References

Ro	1:20–22, 28; 2:5, 8; 13:12
1Co	1:18
2Co	2:15–16; 4:3–4; 6:2
1Th	2:15–16; 5:2–3
2Th	1:7–8; 2:10–12
1Ti	4:2
2Ti	3:8; 4:3–4
Heb	2:2–3; 3:7–9, 15, 18—4:2; 4:6–7; 11:36–37; 12:25
Jas	4:13–14
1Pe	1:24; 2:7–8
2Pe	3:10–11
1Jn	5:10, 12
Jude	14; 15
Rev	2:21–22; 3:17–18; 6:15–16; 10:5–6; 13:9; 22:11–12

O
The Lord is the ONLY Way of Salvation

Ge	17:4
Ex	15:11
Dt	3:24; 4:35, 39; 6:4–5; 10:12; 18:15, 18–19; 30:15–16, 20; 32:31–32, 39
Jos	5:2–9
1Sa	2:2, 6–9
2Sa	7:22; 22:32
1Ki	8:60
2Ki	19:15, 19
1Ch	17:20
Job	8:11–15
Ps	3:8; 16:4; 18:31; 36:9; 62:1–2, 5–6, 11–12; 68:20; 73:25–27; 75:6–7; 86:10; 118:22; 127:1
Pr	19:21
Ecc	7:13; 12:13
Isa	37:16; 43:11; 44:6, 8; 45:5–9, 14, 18, 21–22; 46:9; 48:12; 50:10–11
Jer	2:13, 22; 3:23; 9:23–24; 13:23; 17:13–14
La	3:37
Hos	6:1; 13:4; 14:3
Jnh	2:9
Mic	6:7–8
Mt	7:26–27; 10:32–33; 12:21; 15:13; 16:16–18, 19; 18:3, 18; 19:16–22, 25–26; 21:42; 22:11–14, 35–40; 25:1–12
Mk	2:7; 8:38; 10:15, 17, 22, 26–27; 12:10, 28–34; 16:15–16
Lk	5:21; 6:47–49; 10:25–28; 12:8–9; 18:16–17, 18–27; 20:17; 24:46–47
Jn	1:4; 3:3, 5, 18–19, 36; 5:38–42; 6:53; 8:12, 24; 10:1, 7, 9; 12:48; 14:6; 15:1–5, 6; 20:23
Ac	3:22–23; 4:11–12; 13:38–39
Ro	8:9, 14; 9:15–16; 10:3–4; 11:36; 14:17
1Co	1:30–31; 2:2; 3:7, 11; 8:4, 6; 15:17
2Co	10:17–18; 13:5
Gal	1:8–9; 2:16; 3:11; 5:6; 6:14–15
Eph	1:6, 22; 4:15–16
Php	3:8–9
Col	1:16–18
1Ti	2:5
2Ti	2:11–12
Heb	9:22; 11:6
Jas	4:12
1Pe	1:18–19
1Jn	2:22–23; 5:12
Rev	1:8, 18; 3:17–18; 7:9–12, 14; 12:11; 19:1; 21:6; 22:13

P
The Lord Loves and PARDONS Backsliders

Lev	26:40–42
Nu	14:19–20
Dt	4:29–31; 30:2–3
Jdg	10:15–16
1Sa	12:20
2Sa	12:13
1Ki	8:33–36, 38–39, 46–50
2Ch	6:24–27, 29–30, 36–39; 7:14; 15:3–4, 15; 30:9
Ne	1:9; 9:16–17
Ps	32:5; 51:1–10; 78:38; 106:43–45
Isa	49:14–16; 57:15–19
Jer	3:1, 5, 12–14, 20–22; 4:1; 25:3–5; 29:11–13; 30:17; 31:3, 20; 33:6–8; 35:15; 36:3, 7; 44:4, 5
La	3:40–42
Eze	2:3–5; 34:11–12
Da	9:9
Hos	6:1; 14:1–2, 4
Joel	2:12–13
Am	5:4, 6–8
Mic	7:18–19
Zec	1:3
Mal	3:7
Mt	10:6; 18:11–14
Lk	15:3–32
Ro	10:21; 11:23–24
Jas	5:19–20
1Jn	2:1–2; 5:16
Rev	2:5

R
REPENTANCE, Confession, and Restitution

Ge	35:2–3
Ex	22:1–14; 34:13
Lev	5:5, 16; 16:21; 22:14; 26:40–41
Nu	5:6–8; 21:7; 22:34
Dt	4:29–30; 7:5; 12:3; 30:2, 8
Jos	7:19; 24:14, 23
Jdg	10:10, 15–16; 20:26
1Sa	1:14; 7:3–6; 12:3, 10–11; 15:24, 30–31; 26:21
2Sa	12:6, 13; 24:10
1Ki	8:33–36, 47–50; 21:25–29
2Ki	11:17–18; 17:13; 18:4–5; 23:3–8, 14–15

1Ch 21:8
2Ch 6:24–27, 37–39;
    7:14;
    14:3;
    15:4, 8, 12, 15;
    19:3;
    23:16–19;
    29:4–8;
    30:8, 22;
    31:1;
    34:7, 31–33;
    36:13
Ezr 9:5–10;
    10:11, 12
Ne 1:6–7, 9;
    5:11–13;
    9:2–3, 33–35;
    10:29;
    13:3, 30
Job 7:20;
    11:13–14;
    13:23;
    20:18;
    22:23;
    28:28;
    31:33;
    33:27–28;
    34:31–32;
    36:9–11;
    40:3–4;
    42:6
Ps 6:6;
    7:11–12;
    25:11;
    32:5;
    34:14, 18;
    37:27;
    38:1–10, 18;
    39:8;
    40:12–13;
    41:4;
    51:1–3, 17;
    66:16–19;
    78:34;
    80:3, 7, 19;
    106:6;
    126:5;
    147:3
Pr 1:23;
    3:7;
    6:30–31;
    14:16;
    28:13
Ecc 11:10
Isa 1:16–17;
    9:13;
    31:6;
    55:7;
    57:15;
    58:5–10;
    66:2
Jer 3:10, 12–13, 25;
    4:1, 3–4, 14;

    6:15;
    7:3, 5–7;
    8:5–6, 12;
    14:7, 20;
    18:7–8, 11;
    23:22;
    25:4–5;
    26:3, 13;
    29:12–13;
    31:9, 18–19;
    35:15;
    36:3, 7;
    44:5;
    50:4
La 1:16, 18, 20;
    2:11, 18–19;
    3:40–41, 42;
    5:21
Eze 3:19;
    13:22;
    14:6;
    18:21–23, 27–28, 30–32;
    20:43;
    33:9, 11–12, 14–16, 19;
    36:31;
    43:9;
    45:9–12
Da 4:27;
    9:4–5, 15, 20
Hos 2:2, 7;
    5:4, 15;
    7:10;
    10:12;
    12:6;
    14:1–2
Joel 1:13;
    2:12–13
Am 5:14–15
Jnh 3:5–10
Hag 2:17
Zec 1:4–5;
    12:10
Mal 3:7
Mt 3:2, 6, 8, 11;
    4:17;
    6:12, 14–15;
    9:13;
    11:20–22;
    12:41;
    18:35;
    21:28–32;
    26:75
Mk 1:4, 15;
    2:17;
    6:12;
    11:25–26;
    14:72
Lk 3:3, 8;
    5:32;
    6:37;
    10:13–14;

    11:4, 32;
    13:3, 5;
    15:7, 10, 18–22;
    16:30;
    17:3–4;
    18:13–14;
    19:8–9;
    22:62;
    24:47
Ac 2:37–38;
    3:19, 26;
    5:31;
    8:22;
    11:18;
    13:24;
    14:15;
    17:30;
    19:4, 18–20;
    20:21;
    26:18, 20
Ro 2:4
2Co 7:9–10;
    12:21
1Th 1:9
2Ti 2:25
Heb 6:1, 6
Jas 1:21;
    4:8;
    5:16
2Pe 3:9
1Jn 1:9
Rev 2:5, 16, 21–22;
    3:3, 19;
    9:20–21;
    16:9, 11

S
Holy Living Should Follow Conversion

Ge 2:17;
    4:7;
    7:1;
    18:19;
    19:26;
    35:2
Ex 15:26;
    16:28;
    19:5–6;
    20:6;
    22:31;
    23:2, 7, 18, 21;
    32:33, 34;
    34:11
Lev 11:4–8, 44–45;
    18:4–5;
    19:2, 12, 37;
    20:7–8, 22–25, 26;
    22:8, 31–32;
    25:18;
    26:2–4, 14–16, 23–24, 27–28

Nu 14:22–25, 30, 43;
    15:30–31, 37, 40;
    16:7, 23–26;
    32:11, 23
Dt 4:1–2, 9, 40;
    5:29, 32–33;
    6:7, 12–18, 24, 25;
    7:6, 9, 12, 26;
    8:1, 3, 6, 11, 19–20;
    10:12–13;
    11:1, 8, 14, 16–22, 26–27, 32;
    12:19, 25, 28, 32;
    13:4–18;
    14:2;
    15:5;
    16:12, 20;
    17:7, 9–13, 20;
    18:9–12, 13, 18–19;
    19:9, 19–20;
    21:9, 20–21;
    22:21–24;
    23:12–14;
    24:7;
    25:16;
    26:16–19;
    27:1, 9–10;
    28:1–2, 9–10, 13–14, 15, 20, 45, 58–59, 62;
    29:19–20;
    30:2, 6, 8, 10–11, 15–20;
    31:12–13;
    32:5
Jos 1:7, 8;
    5:6;
    6:18;
    7:1–18;
    22:5, 16–20, 29;
    23:6–8, 11, 16;
    24:14, 15–16, 19–24, 27
Jdg 2:2, 11–15, 17, 19–22;
    3:4, 7–8, 12;
    4:1–2;
    6:1, 10;
    8:23;
    10:6–7;
    13:1;
    20:13
1Sa 12:14, 15, 20–23, 24, 25;
    15:1–21, 22–23, 24;
    16:14;
    24:13

Summary of Chain of References   xl

2Sa	12:1–14; 22:21–27; 24:1–15	Ps	1:1–2, 5; 4:2, 3–4; 5:4–6; 6:8; 7:10–11; 11:5; 15:1–2, 5; 18:20, 21–23, 24; 19:12–14; 24:3–5; 26:1, 5–6; 29:2; 34:12–16; 36:4; 37:3, 8–9, 27, 29–31, 34, 37–38; 50:16, 17–22, 23; 62:12; 66:18; 68:21; 69:28; 73:1, 27; 78:7–8, 10, 14, 56–66; 85:8–11; 89:30–32; 93:5; 96:9; 97:10; 101:2–3, 6–8; 105:45; 106:13, 21; 110:3; 119:1–3, 4, 8–9, 11, 15–16, 21, 30–31, 97, 101–106, 112, 115, 119, 126–129, 141, 153, 155, 159, 173; 125:3–4, 5; 128:1–2; 139:23–24; 140:13; 141:4	Ecc	5:6; 8:5; 11:13; 12:13–14	Hos	4:6–7, 16; 6:4; 7:13; 8:1; 10:1, 2, 12–13; 11:7; 12:6; 13:1; 14:1
1Ki	2:3–4; 3:14; 6:12; 8:58, 61; 9:6–9; 11:4–11, 33, 38; 14:8, 16, 22; 15:3, 5, 14, 26, 30, 34; 16:13, 19, 25–26, 30–31, 33; 18:18, 21; 20:36; 22:52–53			SS	6:10	Joel	3:17
				Isa	1:4, 13–17, 19, 20, 27–28; 2:5; 3:10–11; 5:18, 23; 32:17; 33:14–17; 35:8–9; 48:18, 22; 52:1, 11; 57:20–21; 60:21; 62:12; 65:11–12; 66:4	Am	2:4; 3:2, 3; 5:14–15; 6:12; 9:10
2Ki	10:31; 13:2–3, 6, 11; 14:24; 15:9, 18, 28; 17:7–20, 33–41; 18:11–12; 20:3; 21:2, 6, 14–15, 20–22; 22:13, 17; 23:32, 37; 24:9, 19					Ob	17
						Jnh	2:8
						Mic	2:10; 3:4; 6:7–8
1Ch	10:13–14; 16:29; 28:8, 9; 29:19					Na	1:3
				Jer	1:16; 2:13, 17, 19, 20, 29, 32; 3:1, 6, 8; 4:14; 5:7; 6:28–30; 7:3, 5–7, 9–11, 12, 23, 24–29; 8:5; 9:13–15, 25; 11:3–4, 7–8; 12:17; 13:10, 25; 14:10, 11–14; 15:6; 16:10–12; 17:10, 13; 18:9–11; 19:3–4; 22:3, 8–9; 23:16–17, 21–22; 26:4–6, 13; 32:19, 23, 39–40; 40:3; 42:6, 21; 44:4–6, 23	Zep	1:6–7; 2:3; 3:13
2Ch	6:14; 7:14; 8:17, 19–22; 12:1–2, 5; 15:2; 19:7–10; 20:21; 24:18, 20, 24; 27:2; 28:1, 6, 19, 22; 29:4–6; 30:7; 34:2, 21, 24–25, 31–33; 36:12					Zec	7:9–10; 8:16–17; 14:20–21
						Mal	1:6; 2:11, 17; 3:7, 18
						Mt	1:21; 3:10; 5:3–7, 8, 9, 13, 19–20, 29–30, 48; 6:21–24; 7:13–14, 16–24; 10:22, 37–38; 11:29; 12:33–37, 44–45, 50; 13:5–8, 20–22; 16:24, 27; 18:8–9, 15–16, 17, 23–35; 19:16–21; 21:28–31, 33, 34, 35–40, 41; 22:30, 35, 36–40; 23:23, 25–28; 24:13, 42–47, 48–51; 25:14–23, 24–30, 31–33, 34–36, 37–40, 41–43, 44–46; 28:20
Ezr	8:28; 9:1–10, 12						
Ne	1:5, 7–8; 9:16, 28–29; 10:29; 13:26–27			Eze	3:20–21; 5:5–8; 6:9–11; 8:17–18; 9:4–6; 11:19–21; 13:22; 14:6–8, 11; 18:4, 20–27, 30–32; 20:11–13, 19, 21, 27, 39; 33:11–16, 18, 31; 36:25–27, 29; 37:23		
Job	4:8; 8:20; 11:14; 17:9; 22:23; 27:8; 28:7–8; 34:11, 26–27, 32; 36:10–11	Pr	1:10, 15; 3:3, 6–7; 4:14–15, 23, 24–26, 27; 6:22, 27–28; 10:28, 29–30; 11:3–5, 6, 7–8; 14:9, 14, 16; 15:8, 9, 26, 29; 16:6, 7, 17; 17:15; 21:16, 21; 22:8; 24:12, 20, 24; 28:9			Mk	3:35; 4:5–8, 16–20; 8:34; 9:43–50;
				Da	9:4, 11		

Summary of Chain of References

Lk 12:1, 2, 3–9, 28–34;
13:13, 34
1:74–75;
3:8, 9;
6:43–49;
8:6–8, 13–15, 21;
9:23, 62;
10:25–28;
11:28, 34;
12:1, 34–37, 45–47;
13:6–8, 9, 23–28;
14:26–27, 28–31, 33–35;
16:10–12, 13;
17:32;
19:12–27;
20:9, 10, 11–16, 19–21

Jn 4:23–24;
5:14, 29;
8:11–12, 31, 34–35, 44, 51;
9:31;
12:26;
13:35;
14:15, 21;
15:1, 2, 3–5, 6, 7–9, 10, 14, 16;
17:15–20

Ac 1:25;
3:26;
5:1–11, 32;
14:22

Ro 1:18;
2:6–13;
3:31;
6:1–2, 3–5, 6, 7–10, 11–23;
7:4, 5–6;
8:1–14;
11:16–19, 20–22;
12:1–2, 9, 21;
13:8–13, 14;
14:10–12, 15–18

1Co 1:2, 30;
3:8, 12–13, 17;
5:7–8, 11, 13;
6:9–11, 13, 15, 20;
8:11;
9:24–27;
10:5–10, 11–12, 13, 21, 31;
11:27–32;
13:1–7;
15:1, 2, 33–34

2Co 5:10, 15, 17;
6:14;
7:1;

10:2;
12:21;
13:2, 11

Gal 1:10;
2:17–18, 19, 20;
3:1;
5:6, 13, 19–25;
6:7–9, 14–16

Eph 1:4;
2:10;
4:1, 17–19, 20–24, 26–32;
5:1–4, 5–6, 7–12, 25–27

Php 1:27;
2:12, 15;
3:17, 18, 19–20;
4:8–9

Col 1:10, 21–23;
2:6, 11;
3:1–3, 5–10, 12, 17, 23–25;
4:6

1Th 2:11–12;
4:1–2, 3, 4–5, 6–7;
5:22–23

2Th 1:8;
2:13;
3:6, 14

1Ti 1:5, 19;
2:8–10, 15;
4:1–2, 12, 16;
5:8, 12;
6:8–11, 12, 13–14, 18–21

2Ti 2:10–12, 19, 22;
3:1–5;
4:10

Tit 1:16;
2:11–14;
3:1, 8, 14

Heb 2:1–3;
3:6, 10–11, 12–14;
4:1, 11;
5:9;
6:1, 4–7, 8, 11–12;
9:14;
10:26–31, 35–36, 38–39;
12:1, 14, 25;
13:4, 20–21

Jas 1:21–27;
2:8–26;
3:11–13, 14–18;
4:4, 8, 17;
5:9, 19–20

1Pe 1:2, 13–14, 15–17, 22;
2:1, 11–17, 21–22, 24;

3:2–4, 8–9, 10–12, 15;
4:1–7, 15, 17–18;
5:8–9

2Pe 1:4–8, 9–10;
2:9–10, 15, 19–21;
3:7, 11, 13–14

1Jn 1:5–7;
2:1, 3–6, 11, 15, 16–17, 29;
3:3–10, 14, 15, 20–21, 23, 24;
4:8, 20–21;
5:2–3, 4, 16–17, 18

2Jn 8–9
3Jn 11
Jude 5–6; 15, 19–21, 24
Rev 2:4–5, 7, 10, 11, 17, 23, 26;
3:1–5, 14–16, 21;
14:4–5, 13;
20:12–13;
21:7–8, 27;
22:12, 14–15

T

TESTIFYING, or Confessing the Lord

Dt 6:7;
8:10;
26:1–3
Jos 4:1–9, 19–24
1Sa 7:12
2Sa 22:50
1Ch 16:8–10, 23–24, 29, 34–36
Ps 9:11, 14;
20:5;
22:22–23, 25;
29:2, 9;
34:1–3, 4–6;
35:18, 27–28;
40:10, 16;
44:8;
50:23;
51:15;
60:4;
63:3;
66:8, 16–17;
67:3;
68:26;
70:4;
71:8;
77:12;
78:4;
92:1;
96:2–4;
100:4;

105:1–2;
106:1–2;
107:1, 2, 22, 31;
109:30;
111:1;
118:21, 28–29;
119:13, 27, 46, 108, 116–171;
128:2;
132:9;
134:1–3;
135:1–3, 19–20;
140:13;
145:1–7, 10–12, 21;
146:1–2;
147:12;
148:1–14
Isa 12:1–3, 4, 5–6;
38:19;
43:10, 12;
44:8
Jer 1:17
Da 4:37
Joel 2:26
Mal 3:16–17
Mt 10:32–33;
12:34, 37
Mk 5:19;
8:38
Lk 6:45;
9:25–26;
12:8–9
Jn 12:42–43
Ac 1:8
Ro 1:16;
10:8–10, 11
1Co 14:3, 24–25
Php 1:28
2Ti 1:8;
2:12
Phm 6
Heb 2:11–12;
3:13;
13:6, 15–16
1Pe 2:9
1Jn 4:15
Rev 12:11;
19:5

W

"WHOSOEVER WILL" May Be Saved

Ge 12:3;
22:18;
26:4;
28:14
Nu 21:8–9
2Sa 22:31
1Ch 12:22
Ezr 8:22
Ps 2:12;
18:30;
22:27;

Summary of Chain of References

32:10; 34:8, 22; 49:1–2; 50:1; 84:12; 86:5; 145:9, 18 Pr 16:20; 29:25 Isa 1:18; 11:10; 42:3; 45:22; 49:6; 52:10; 53:6; 55:1, 6–7; 57:19; 59:1–2; 63:1 Jer 17:7 Eze 18:23, 32; 33:11 Zec 13:1 Mt 7:7–8, 24; 8:11; 9:12;	10:32; 11:15, 28–29; 12:20, 31–32; 13:9; 20:1–16; 22:1–10; 26:28; 28:19 Mk 3:28; 4:9, 23; 10:45; 14:24; 16:15–16 Lk 1:79; 2:10–11, 30–32; 6:47–48; 11:9–10; 12:8; 13:29; 14:16–23; 15:7; 16:16; 19:10; 24:46–47	Jn 1:7, 9, 12, 29; 3:14–18, 36; 4:10, 42; 5:24; 6:35, 37, 40, 47, 51, 54; 7:17, 37; 9:5; 11:25, 26; 12:32, 46, 47 Ac 2:21; 3:25; 10:34–35, 43; 11:18; 13:26, 38–39, 47; 15:7–11; 17:27; 26:13–18; 28:28 Ro 1:16; 3:21–24, 28–30; 4:6–13, 16; 5:6–17, 18, 19–21;	9:33; 10:4, 6–13; 11:32; 15:10 2Co 5:14–15, 19–21 Gal 3:6–9, 14, 22, 26 Eph 2:17–18; 3:6–8 Col 1:20–21 1Ti 1:15; 2:3–6; 4:10 Tit 2:11 Heb 2:9; 5:9; 7:25; 9:13–14, 22, 28 2Pe 3:9 1Jn 1:7–9; 2:1–2; 4:14–15; 5:1, 9–10, 13 Rev 3:20; 5:9; 7:9; 14:6; 21:6; 22:17

TEMPORAL BLESSINGS
(LIGHT GREEN)

A
ALL THINGS Working for Good
Ge 21:22;
24:1;
45:5–8;
48:16
Dt 14:29;
15:10, 18;
29:9
1Ki 2:3
Ps 91:10;
121:7
Pr 12:21;
19:23
Isa 58:11
Ro 8:28
1Th 5:18

B
The Lord's BLESSING on Fields and Flocks
Ge 15:7;
24:35;
26:12, 14;
27:28, 39;
30:43;
39:5
Ex 9:4–7, 26;
23:26;
33:3

Lev 20:24;
25:19, 20–22, 38;
26:3–5, 19–20
Dt 7:13, 14;
8:7–8, 13;
11:10, 11–12, 13,
14–15;
26:9;
28:3–5, 11–12,
23–24;
30:9
1Ki 8:35
2Ki 2:19–22
Job 42:12
Ps 65:9–13;
67:6;
85:12;
107:38;
144:13
Pr 3:9–10
Isa 4:2;
55:10
Eze 34:26–27;
36:30
Hos 2:8, 21–22
Joel 2:22, 24–26
Am 4:9;
9:13
Hag 1:10;
2:15–19
Zec 8:12

Mal 3:11–12
2Co 9:10

C
CLOTHING Provided for God's Children
Ge 28:20
Dt 2:7;
8:4;
10:18;
29:5;
33:25
Ne 9:21
Job 27:16–17
Eze 16:10
Mt 6:25–34;
10:10
Mk 6:8–9
Lk 9:3;
10:4;
12:22–31;
22:35

D
Some Reasons Why DISEASES are Allowed
Ge 12:17;
19:11;
20:18
Ex 4:6;
5:3;

9:8–10, 11–14,
15;
15:26;
20:12;
23:25;
30:12;
32:35
Lev 14:19, 30–32, 34;
15:13–15;
18:30;
26:14–15, 16,
23–25, 36
Nu 5:20, 21, 27;
8:19;
11:33–34;
12:9–10;
14:12, 37;
16:46, 47–49;
21:6;
25:1–7, 8–9
Dt 7:15;
24:9;
28:21–22, 27, 35,
59–61;
29:22
Jos 22:17
1Sa 1:5–6;
5:6, 9, 11–12;
25:38
2Sa 3:29;
6:23;

	12:15–18;		25:7–8, 21;		7:25–37;		23:25
	24:15		29:31;		8:22–26;	Lev	25:19, 20–22;
1Ki	13:4;		30:17, 22;		9:14–29, 38–39;		26:5
	14:1–11, 12–13;		50:23		10:46–52;	Nu	11:7–9, 18–23,
	17:18	Ex	4:7		16:9		31–32;
2Ki	1:2–4;	Lev	14:3	Lk	1:11–17, 18,		20:7–11;
	5:20–26, 27;	Nu	12:9–15;		19–25, 36–37;		21:16, 17
	6:18;		16:46–50;		4:23–27, 33–41;	Dt	2:7;
	15:5		21:7–9;		5:12–26;		7:13;
1Ch	21:10, 13, 14–15		25:8		6:6–11, 17–19;		8:3, 9–10,
2Ch	7:13;	Dt	8:4;		7:1–22;		15–16;
	13:20;		34:7		8:26–56;		10:18;
	21:14–15, 18–19;	Jos	14:10–11		9:1–2, 6, 11,		11:14–15;
	26:16–18, 19–21	Jdg	13:2–3		37–43, 49–50;		32:13–14
Job	2:3–6, 7, 8;	1Sa	1:5–20;		10:9, 17–20;	Jos	5:12
	30:18–19;		2:5		11:14–26;	Jdg	15:18–19
	33:17–22, 23–28,	2Sa	24:18–24, 25		13:11–17, 32–33;	Ru	1:6
	29–30	1Ki	13:6;		14:1–6;	1Sa	2:5
Ps	78:30–31;		17:17–21, 22–24		17:11–19;	1Ki	17:1–16;
	106:29	2Ki	4:12–31, 32–35,		18:35–43;		19:5–8
Pr	5:8–11		39–41;		22:50–51	2Ki	3:9–20;
Jer	14:12;		5:1–13, 14;	Jn	4:46–54;		4:1–7, 42–44;
	21:6;		6:20;		5:1–16, 17–38;		6:18, 19–20,
	24:10;		8:4–5;		6:2;		24—7:17
	29:17;		13:21;		7:23;	2Ch	20:9
	42:17;		20:1–11		9:1–7, 8–41;	Ne	9:15, 20–21
	44:13	1Ch	21:15–27;		11:1–38, 39–46,	Job	5:20;
Eze	5:12, 17;		29:28		47–54;		15:23
	6:12;	2Ch	32:24		12:9–11, 17–19	Ps	22:26;
	7:15;	Ne	9:21	Ac	2:22;		23:1–2, 5;
	14:19, 21;	Job	42:16–17		3:1–16;		33:18–19;
	28:23;	Ps	30:2–3;		4:8–10, 14–22;		34:9–10;
	33:27;		103:3;		5:14–16;		37:3, 19, 25;
	38:22		105:37;		8:6–7;		78:15–16, 19–29;
Am	4:10		106:30;		9:12, 17, 18,		81:10, 16;
Mt	13:58		107:20		32–35;		103:5;
Mk	6:5–6	Isa	38:1–22		10:38;		104:27;
Lk	1:20;	Da	1:15		14:3, 8–10, 11–18,		105:40–41;
	4:23–27;	Hos	11:3		19–20;		107:9;
	13:16	Mt	4:23–25;		16:16–18, 19–24;		111:5;
Jn	5:14;		7:22;		19:11–12, 13–17;		114:8;
	9:1–3;		8:2–3, 4, 5–17,		20:9–12;		132:15;
	11:4		28–32, 33–34;		22:11–13;		136:25;
Ac	9:8–9;		9:2–8, 18–35;		28:3–9		145:15;
	10:38;		10:1, 7–8;	Ro	15:18–19		146:7;
	13:11		11:4–5;	1Co	12:9, 28, 30		147:9, 14
1Co	7:28;		12:9–13, 15,	2Co	12:12	Pr	10:3;
	10:8;		22–29;	Php	2:25–26, 27		13:25;
	11:29–32		13:58;	Heb	2:4;		30:8
2Co	12:7–10		14:14, 34–36;		11:11–12, 34–35	Ecc	11:1
Php	2:30		15:21–28, 30–31;			Isa	1:19;
Heb	12:5–13		17:14–21;		**F**		33:16;
Rev	16:3		19:1–2;				41:17, 18;
			20:30–34;		**Food** Provided for the		48:21;
	E		21:14		Lord's Children		49:9–10;
		Mk	1:23–34, 39–45;	Ge	6:19–21;		55:10;
	Examples of Healing for		2:3–12;		21:19;		58:11;
	the Body		3:1–5, 7–9,		27:28;		65:13
Ge	5:5, 8, 11, 14, 17,		10–12, 14–15,		28:20;	Hos	2:8;
	20, 23, 27,		22–27;		45:5–7;		11:4;
	31–32;		5:1–20, 22–43;		48:15		13:5–6
	17:15–17;		6:5, 7, 13,	Ex	15:23–25;	Joel	2:19, 24–26
	18:12–14;		54–56;		16:4–36;	Hab	3:17–18
	20:17;				17:5–6;		

Summary of Chain of References

Mt 4:11;
6:11, 25–34;
10:9–10;
14:15–21;
15:32–38;
16:5–10, 11–12
Mk 1:13;
6:8, 33–44;
8:1–9, 14–21
Lk 1:53;
4:25–26;
5:4–9;
9:3, 12–17;
10:4;
11:3;
12:22–31;
22:35
Jn 6:5–14, 31–32;
21:8–13
2Co 9:10
Rev 7:16

H
HEALTH and Healing Promised

Ge 15:15
Ex 9:4–5;
15:26;
20:12;
23:25;
30:12
Dt 4:40;
7:15;
11:21;
25:15;
32:39;
33:25
1Sa 2:6;
6:3
2Sa 12:22
1Ki 3:14;
8:37–39
2Ki 5:7
1Ch 29:12
2Ch 6:28–30;
7:13–14;
16:12;
20:9
Job 5:26;
33:23–30
Ps 34:12–13;
41:3;
67:2;
91:3, 5–7, 10, 16;
103:3, 5;
113:9;
128:6;
146:8
Pr 3:2, 8, 16;
4:10, 22;
9:11;
10:16, 27;
14:30;

17:22;
19:23
Isa 29:18;
32:3–4;
35:3–6;
38:16;
40:29–31;
42:6–7;
53:4
Jer 8:22;
17:14
Eze 34:4, 16;
47:12
Mt 8:17;
10:7–8
Mk 9:23;
16:17–18
Lk 4:18
Eph 6:2–3
Jas 5:13–18
1Pe 3:10
3Jn 2
Rev 22:2

J
JOY and Trust in Times of Trial

Ne 8:10
Job 1:21;
13:15
Ps 3:5–6;
18:29;
23:4;
27:1;
30:5;
31:13, 14;
42:5, 7–8, 11;
43:5;
46:1–3;
56:3–4, 11;
57:1;
61:2–4;
91:5–6;
112:7–8;
118:6;
119:83
Pr 1:33;
14:31
Isa 26:3;
51:12
Hab 3:17–19
Mt 5:11–12
Lk 6:22–23
Jn 16:33
Ac 5:41;
6:15;
16:25
Ro 5:3;
12:12
2Co 1:3–10;
2:14;
4:8–10, 15, 16–18;

7:4;
8:1–2;
11:23–33;
12:10
Eph 5:20
Php 1:28–29;
2:17;
3:8
Col 1:24
Heb 10:34;
13:6
Jas 1:2–4;
5:10, 11
1Pe 2:19–20;
3:14;
4:12–14, 16
1Jn 4:18

L
The Lord's LOVE and Care for His Children

Ge 6:7–8, 17–18;
7:1;
8:1;
12:3;
15:1;
16:13;
19:19–22, 29;
21:17–19, 22;
22:11–12;
24:27, 48;
26:3–4, 24, 28;
27:28–29;
28:15;
31:3, 24, 29;
35:3;
48:16
Ex 2:1–10, 24–25;
3:7–8, 15;
8:22;
9:4, 6, 26;
10:23;
11:7;
13:21–22;
14:19–20, 24–28;
15:13;
18:8–10;
19:4–6;
23:20;
29:45–46;
33:12, 22;
40:36–38
Nu 9:15–23;
14:14;
20:16;
22:12;
23:18–24;
24:9;
31:49
Dt 1:21, 29–33;
2:7;
4:7;
29:5;

31:6, 8, 23;
32:9–14;
33:12, 13–16, 27, 28–29
Jos 1:5, 9, 17;
3:7;
5:13–14;
6:27;
21:45;
23:14;
24:3–13
1Sa 2:9;
12:24;
17:37;
20:13;
25:29
2Sa 4:9;
6:11–12;
7:9–11, 23;
8:6, 14;
22:1, 2–4, 5–51
1Ki 1:29, 37, 47–48;
8:51–53, 56–59, 66;
9:4–5;
17:1–16;
19:5–8
2Ki 4:1–7;
6:16–17
1Ch 13:14;
16:21–22;
17:7–8, 21–22;
18:6;
28:20
2Ch 7:10;
32:22
Ne 9:11, 12, 13–15, 19
Est 4:14;
6:1—7:10;
8:16
Job 5:17–26;
23:6
Ps 3:3;
6:8–9;
13:6;
18:28;
20:1–2;
23:1–6;
27:4–5, 10;
28:7–9;
29:11;
30:5;
31:7, 19–20, 23;
32:8;
33:18, 20;
34:7–10, 15, 19–20, 22;
36:7–8;
37:39–40;
40:17;
41:12;
46:1;

Summary of Chain of References

48:14;
50:15;
54:4;
56:8;
63:3–7;
66:9, 12;
68:5, 19;
71:3, 6;
73:23–24;
78:14–16, 52–53;
81:6–7, 10;
86:7, 17;
90:1;
91:1–16;
94:18, 19, 22;
97:10;
103:13, 17–18;
105:13, 14–15,
   16–45;
106:44;
107:6, 13, 19, 20,
   28, 35–38;
116:15;
118:8, 9;
119:132;
121:1–8;
125:1–2;
138:7–8;
140:7;
142:3, 5, 7;
144:2;
145:18, 20;
146:5
Pr 2:8;
   3:26;
   18:24
SS 1:2, 4, 8–10;
   2:3–4, 6, 8–16;
   4:1, 9–10, 11–15;
   5:1;
   6:1–7
Isa 32:2;
   41:10, 13–14;
   43:2, 5;
   44:2;
   46:3–4;
   48:17;
   49:15–16;
   54:10;
   63:7–8, 9
Jer 1:17–19;
   2:3, 6–7, 20;
   13:11;
   14:8;
   31:3, 32;
   49:11
Eze 16:7–14
Da 2:17–19;
   3:1–24, 25,
   26–30;
   6:4–21, 22;
   9:23;
   10:11

Hos 11:1, 8–9
Joel 2:18, 27–28
Am 2:10;
   7:3, 6
Jnh 1:15;
   2:10
Mic 6:4
Hag 2:4–5
Zec 2:8;
   12:8
Mal 3:16–17
Mt 4:6;
   6:8, 25–34;
   7:7–11;
   8:26;
   10:29–31;
   14:31;
   18:5–6, 10, 19–20;
   21:22;
   28:20
Mk 9:41, 42;
   11:24
Lk 1:30;
   4:10–11;
   11:9–10;
   12:6–7, 22–32;
   17:1, 2;
   18:1–6, 7–8;
   21:18;
   22:31–32, 35
Jn 10:3–4, 5–8, 9–11,
   13, 14–15,
   27–29;
   14:13–14;
   16:22–23, 24,
   26–27;
   17:13
Ac 7:34;
   18:10;
   23:11;
   26:22;
   27:22–44
Ro 8:31–39
1Co 10:13
2Co 1:3–10;
   7:6;
   8:9, 15
Php 4:19
1Ti 6:17
2Ti 3:11;
   4:17–18
Heb 1:14;
   11:32–35;
   13:5–6
Jas 5:10–11
1Pe 3:12;
   5:7
2Pe 2:9
1Jn 3:1;
   5:14–15
Rev 7:16–17;
   12:14

P

PROSPERITY in Business
   and Finance
Ge 13:2;
   15:14;
   24:1, 21, 35, 40,
   56;
   33:11
Ex 12:36
Dt 8:13, 17, 18;
   14:29;
   15:4–6, 7–9, 10,
   18;
   16:15;
   24:19;
   28:8, 11–12;
   30:9
1Sa 2:7–8
1Ki 2:3;
   3:13;
   10:23
1Ch 29:12
2Ch 1:12;
   25:9;
   31:10;
   32:29
Job 1:10;
   22:24–25;
   27:16–17;
   42:10, 12
Ps 37:4;
   105:37;
   112:3;
   128:1–2
Pr 3:9–10, 16;
   8:18;
   10:22;
   11:24–25;
   13:22;
   15:6;
   19:17;
   22:9;
   28:8, 27
Ecc 2:26;
   5:19;
   11:1
Hos 2:8
Mal 3:10–11
Mt 6:31–33;
   10:9;
   17:27
Mk 6:8–9
Lk 5:4–7;
   9:3;
   10:4;
   22:35
Jn 21:3–13
2Co 9:6–11
Php 4:19
1Ti 4:8;
   6:17
Heb 6:10

R

Blessing on Children,
RELATIVES, and Friends
Ge 9:9;
   12:7;
   13:15;
   15:18;
   17:7–8;
   18:17–19;
   19:12, 29;
   21:13;
   22:17–18;
   26:4, 24;
   28:4;
   30:27, 30;
   39:5
Ex 2:24–25
Dt 7:9, 13;
   11:21;
   28:4, 11;
   30:9;
   34:4
2Sa 7:12
1Ki 2:4;
   3:6;
   8:25;
   11:36;
   15:4
2Ki 8:19;
   10:30
2Ch 6:16;
   20:7;
   21:7
Ne 9:8
Job 5:25;
   42:13–14, 15
Ps 18:50;
   25:13;
   37:26;
   89:35–36;
   102:28;
   103:17–18;
   112:1–2;
   115:14;
   128:3;
   132:11–12;
   144:12
Jer 35:19
Lk 1:5–12, 13–15,
   16–17
Ac 3:25
Heb 11:9

S

SAFETY From All Harm
   and Danger
Ge 7:1;
   9:9;
   15:1;
   18:23–32;
   19:16–19, 22, 29;

Summary of Chain of References

	22:12;	Mt	4:6		25:11;	2Ch	1:1, 12;
	26:24	Mk	4:38–39, 40, 41		26:3, 24, 28–29;		6:14;
Ex	8:22;	Lk	8:23–25;		28:3–4, 10–22;		15:2;
	9:4, 6, 26;		21:18		31:3;		16:9;
	11:7;	Ac	18:10;		32:9–12;		19:11;
	12:13, 27;		23:11;		35:9–12;		20:20;
	33:22		27:22, 23–24,		37:5–11;		26:5;
Lev	25:18;		25–44		39:2–3, 6, 21, 23;		27:6;
	26:5, 6	Ro	8:31		41:51–52;		31:5–9, 10, 20, 21;
Nu	14:9;	Heb	11:33–34		48:3–4;		32:26, 30
	31:49	2Pe	2:5, 7		49:22–24, 25–26;	Ezr	8:22
Dt	12:10;				50:24–25	Ne	1:5;
	33:28–29		**T**	Ex	1:21;		13:14, 22
2Sa	8:6, 14;		Why **Temptations** and		3:12, 21;	Job	1:9–10;
	22:3		**Trials** are Allowed		11:3;		4:7;
1Ch	18:6, 13	Dt	8:2, 5–6, 16		15:26;		8:6–7;
Job	5:21;	2Sa	7:14		20:24		11:13–19;
	11:18–19;	Job	5:17;	Lev	26:3–12		17:9;
	34:29		23:10;	Nu	6:23, 24–27;		22:21, 23, 28;
Ps	3:3;		33:17–22;		10:29, 32;		29:1–2, 3, 4–5, 6,
	4:8;		34:31		14:8;		7–25;
	9:9;	Ps	17:3;		23:8–9, 10;		36:7, 11, 16;
	18:2;		39:11;		24:5–9		42:10, 11, 12,
	27:5;		66:10–12;	Dt	4:40;		13–17
	31:20, 23;		89:30–33;		5:10, 29, 33;	Ps	1:1–3;
	32:6–7;		94:12–13;		6:3, 18;		3:8;
	34:9, 12–15;		105:19;		7:12–13, 14–24;		4:7;
	37:4–6;		119:67, 71, 75		11:26–27;		5:11–12;
	46:1;	Pr	3:11–12;		12:28;		7:10;
	59:16;		17:3;		14:29;		11:7;
	71:7;		25:4		15:10, 18;		15:1–2;
	84:11;	Ecc	7:14		22:7;		16:6, 11;
	91:1–16;	Isa	48:10		23:20;		18:19–20, 21, 23,
	97:10;	Jer	24:5;		24:19;		24, 32, 33;
	115:9–11;		31:18–19		26:15, 18–19;		19:11;
	118:6;	Da	9:11–14;		28:1–14;		21:1–7;
	119:117;		11:35;		30:8–9, 15–16;		22:8;
	121:1–8;		12:10		31:23;		24:3–4;
	140:7;	Hag	1:5–11;		33:13, 24, 28–29		25:10, 14, 15;
	142:5;		2:15–19	Jos	1:9		28:25–31;
	144:10	Zec	13:9	Ru	2:12		31:19–20, 23;
Pr	1:33;	Ro	5:3–4	1Sa	2:9, 30, 35;		32:1–2, 10–11;
	3:23–26;	1Co	11:32		3:19;		33:18;
	18:10;	2Co	1:6–9;		16:18;		34:7, 9, 12–15;
	29:25;		4:10–11, 17;		18:12, 14, 28;		36:10;
	30:5		12:7–10		25:28–30		37:4–6, 17–19,
Isa	32:18;	Heb	5:8;	2Sa	7:3, 9;		23–28, 30, 31,
	43:2		12:5–13		22:20–21, 22–28		37;
Jer	16:19;	Jas	1:2–4, 12	1Ki	2:3;		41:1–3;
	23:6;	1Pe	1:6–7;		3:6, 13–14;		45:7;
	32:37;		4:12–13;		5:4;		55:22;
	33:16;		5:10		6:11–13;		64:10;
	42:11–12	Rev	3:10, 19		8:32;		65:4;
Eze	34:25				9:4–5;		68:3;
Da	3:1–16, 17,		**U**		11:38		73:1;
	18–23, 24–25,		The **Upright** are Blessed	2Ki	18:7		81:15–16;
	26, 27, 28–30;		and Prospered	1Ch	4:10;		84:4–5, 7, 10–12;
	6:4–21, 22–23,	Ge	9:1;		11:9;		89:15–16;
	27		12:1–3, 3;		17:2, 7–8;		91:1–16;
Hos	2:18		17:1–8;		22:13;		92:12–14;
Jnh	1:15–16, 17;		21:22;		28:7–8;		97:10–12;
	2:9, 10		22:15–18;		29:25, 28		112:1–10;
Na	1:7		24:1, 35;				115:12–15;

118:15;
119:1–2, 165;
125:4;
128:1–6;
132:9, 16;
140:13;
144:15;
145:18–19;
147:11
Pr 3:1–2, 5–6, 9, 10,
33;
4:18;
10:6, 22, 24;
11:8, 20, 24–25,
28, 31;
12:1–3, 13, 19, 21,
28;
13:21, 22;
14:9, 11, 19, 32;
15:8–9, 29;
16:3, 7, 20;
21:21;
23:17–18;
24:16, 25;
25:21–22;
28:10, 20, 25
Ecc 2:26;
7:18
Isa 1:19;
3:10;
32:17;
33:15–16;
55:2;
56:5, 7;
57:1–2;
58:7, 8, 10, 14;
62:4;
64:4–5;
65:13–14;
66:2
Jer 7:23;
17:7–8;
35:1–18, 19
Eze 34:26–27
Da 1:8–14, 15;
3:1–30;
6:4–23;
9:4;
10:12, 19;
12:3
Hos 13:1
Am 5:14–15
Hag 1:5–11;
2:15–19, 23
Zec 8:12
Mal 2:5;
3:10, 11–12,
16–17
Mt 5:5–12;
6:4, 6, 18, 33;
19:27–28, 29
Mk 10:28–30

Lk 12:31;
18:28, 29–30
Jn 9:31;
12:25–26;
14:21;
15:7, 11
Ac 7:9–10;
10:35
Ro 8:28
1Co 2:9
2Co 5:1, 2–9;
6:17—7:1
Gal 6:16
1Ti 4:8
Jas 5:16
1Pe 3:12
1Jn 1:4;
3:22

V

**VICTORY Over Enemies
and Troubles**
Ge 14:20;
19:10–11;
22:17;
27:29;
31:5–9, 16, 42;
49:8
Ex 1:12;
3:7–10, 16–17,
19–22;
6:1, 6–8;
7:4–5;
11:1, 3;
12:33–36, 42;
13:14–15;
14:13–31;
15:1, 6, 9–10;
18:4, 8–11;
20:2;
23:22, 23, 27, 28;
33:2;
34:11, 24
Lev 26:6–8
Nu 10:9;
14:3, 9;
21:33–35;
22:12;
23:8–12, 19–24;
24:1–9;
33:52–53
Dt 1:29–31;
2:25, 33–36;
3:2–6, 21–24;
4:37–38;
5:6, 15;
6:18–23;
7:1–2, 15–24;
9:1–3;
11:4, 23–24, 25;
12:10;
20:1–3, 4;
23:5, 14;

25:19;
26:8;
28:7;
31:3–8;
32:30
Jos 1:5;
2:8–11, 24;
3:10;
5:1, 13;
6:21;
8:1, 18;
10:8–14, 24–25,
30, 32, 42;
11:1;
12:24;
13:6;
17:18;
21:44;
22:8;
23:3, 5, 9–10;
24:11–13, 17–18
Jdg 1:2–4;
3:10, 28–31;
4:9, 14–16, 23;
5:20;
6:8–9, 16;
7:1–25;
10:11–12;
11:21, 32–33, 36;
15:15;
16:28–30;
18:10
1Sa 2:1;
7:3, 9–13;
10:18–19;
11:13;
12:11;
14:6;
17:36–46, 47,
48–54;
20:15;
23:4–5;
25:29;
30:8
2Sa 3:18;
5:19–25;
7:9–11;
22:1–29, 30,
31–51;
23:10–12
1Ki 8:37–39, 44–45;
20:13, 27–30
2Ki 3:18–19;
6:13–23;
13:17–19;
17:39;
18:13–19, 37;
20:6
1Ch 5:20;
11:14;
14:10–11, 13–17;
17:10;
22:9, 18

2Ch 6:28–30, 34–35;
13:14–16, 18;
14:6, 7, 11, 12–14;
16:8, 9;
18:31;
20:5–14, 15, 16,
17, 27, 29;
32:7–8, 22
Ezr 8:31
Ne 4:4, 14–15, 20;
6:15–16;
9:11, 24–25, 27
Est 4:14;
5:14;
7:10;
8:4–11;
9:16–32
Job 5:15, 20–23, 24
Ps 3:5–6;
6:10;
9:3–4;
17:7;
18:3, 14, 17–18,
29, 34–50;
20:7–8;
22:4–5;
25:2–3;
27:1, 3, 5–6;
31:20;
34:6, 17, 19;
35:1–9, 10;
37:32, 33;
40:14–15;
41:2, 11;
44:1–3, 5–7;
45:5;
47:3;
50:15;
54:7;
55:18;
56:9;
59:1, 10;
60:12;
70:2;
78:42, 55;
81:13–14;
89:22–23;
91:1–16;
97:10;
106:10–11;
107:2;
108:13;
109:29, 31;
110:5;
112:8;
118:6–7, 10–14;
124:1–8;
132:18;
138:7
Pr 12:13;
16:7;
20:22

Summary of Chain of References

Isa	31:4; 36:1; 37:38; 38:6; 41:11–14; 49:25–26; 50:9; 54:15, 17	Ac	5:18, 19, 20–25, 38–39; 7:34; 12:5–6, 7–11, 12–19; 14:19–20; 16:25, 26, 27–28; 18:10; 27:9–44; 28:1–6	Dt	1:21; 20:8; 31:6–8, 23		26:3–4; 32:17
				Jos	1:6–7, 9; 8:1	Jer	10:2
						Mt	6:25–34; 8:26
				Jdg	7:3	Mk	4:40
Jer	1:17–18, 19; 15:20–21; 20:11; 39:17–18; 42:11–12; 51:36			1Ch	22:13; 28:20	Lk	8:24–25; 12:22–32; 18:1
				2Ch	19:11		
				Ne	8:10	Jn	14:1, 27
		Ro	8:31, 35–39	Ps	23:4; 27:1, 14; 31:24; 37:1, 5; 42:5, 11; 43:5; 55:22; 91:5–6; 112:7–8; 119:165	2Co	13:11
		1Co	15:57			Eph	5:20
Da	3:6; 11:32	2Co	2:14			Php	3:1; 4:4, 6–7, 11–13
		2Ti	4:18				
Hos	1:7	Heb	11:32–35			Col	3:15
Joel	2:20	1Jn	5:4–5			1Th	5:16, 18
Zec	4:6; 12:8	**W**				1Ti	6:6, 8
		Worry and Anxiety Contrary to God's Will				Heb	13:5–6
Mt	8:23–27					1Pe	3:14; 5:7
Mk	4:36–39	Ge	15:1; 21:17; 26:24	Pr	1:33		
Lk	8:22–25; 21:18			Isa	12:2–3;	1Jn	4:18

Preface

THE NEW INTERNATIONAL VERSION is a completely new translation of the Holy Bible made by over a hundred scholars working directly from the best available Hebrew, Aramaic and Greek texts. It had its beginning in 1965 when, after several years of exploratory study by committees from the Christian Reformed Church and the National Association of Evangelicals, a group of scholars met at Palos Heights, Illinois, and concurred in the need for a new translation of the Bible in contemporary English. This group, though not made up of official church representatives, was transdenominational. Its conclusion was endorsed by a large number of leaders from many denominations who met in Chicago in 1966.

Responsibility for the new version was delegated by the Palos Heights group to a self-governing body of fifteen, the Committee on Bible Translation, composed for the most part of biblical scholars from colleges, universities and seminaries. In 1967 the New York Bible Society (now the International Bible Society) generously undertook the financial sponsorship of the project—a sponsorship that made it possible to enlist the help of many distinguished scholars. The fact that participants from the United States, Great Britain, Canada, Australia and New Zealand worked together gave the project its international scope. That they were from many denominations—including Anglican, Assemblies of God, Baptist, Brethren, Christian Reformed, Church of Christ, Evangelical Free, Lutheran, Mennonite, Methodist, Nazarene, Presbyterian, Wesleyan and other churches—helped to safeguard the translation from sectarian bias.

How it was made helps to give the New International Version its distinctiveness. The translation of each book was assigned to a team of scholars. Next, one of the Intermediate Editorial Committees revised the initial translation, with constant reference to the Hebrew, Aramaic or Greek. Their work then went to one of the General Editorial Committees, which checked it in detail and made another thorough revision. This revision in turn was carefully reviewed by the Committee on Bible Translation, which made further changes and then released the final version for publication. In this way the entire Bible underwent three revisions, during each of which the translation was examined for its faithfulness to the original languages and for its English style.

All this involved many thousands of hours of research and discussion regarding the meaning of the texts and the precise way of putting them into English. It may well be that no other translation has been made by a more thorough process of review and revision from committee to committee than this one.

From the beginning of the project, the Committee on Bible Translation held to certain goals for the New International Version: that it would be an accurate translation and one that would have clarity and literary quality and so prove suitable for public and private reading, teaching, preaching, memorizing and liturgical use. The Committee also sought to preserve some measure of continuity with the long tradition of translating the Scriptures into English.

In working toward these goals, the translators were united in their commitment to the authority and infallibility of the Bible as God's Word in written form. They believe that it contains the divine answer to the deepest needs of humanity, that it sheds unique light on our path in a dark world, and that it sets forth the way to our eternal well-being.

The first concern of the translators has been the accuracy of the translation and its fidelity to the thought of the biblical writers. They have weighed the significance of the lexical and grammatical details of the Hebrew, Aramaic and Greek texts. At the same time, they have striven for more than a word-for-word translation. Because thought patterns and syntax differ from language to language, faithful communication of the meaning of the writers of the Bible demands frequent modifications in sentence structure and constant regard for the contextual meanings of words.

A sensitive feeling for style does not always accompany scholarship. Accordingly the Committee on Bible Translation submitted the developing version to a number of stylistic consultants. Two of them read every book of both Old and New Testaments twice—once before and once after the last major revision—and made

Preface

invaluable suggestions. Samples of the translation were tested for clarity and ease of reading by various kinds of people—young and old, highly educated and less well educated, ministers and laymen.

Concern for clear and natural English—that the New International Version should be idiomatic but not idiosyncratic, contemporary but not dated—motivated the translators and consultants. At the same time, they tried to reflect the differing styles of the biblical writers. In view of the international use of English, the translators sought to avoid obvious Americanisms on the one hand and obvious Anglicisms on the other. A British edition reflects the comparatively few differences of significant idiom and of spelling.

As for the traditional pronouns "thou," "thee" and "thine" in reference to the Deity, the translators judged that to use these archaisms (along with the old verb forms such as "doest," "wouldest" and "hadst") would violate accuracy in translation. Neither Hebrew, Aramaic nor Greek uses special pronouns for the persons of the Godhead. A present-day translation is not enhanced by forms that in the time of the King James Version were used in everyday speech, whether referring to God or man.

For the Old Testament the standard Hebrew text, the Masoretic Text as published in the latest editions of *Biblia Hebraica*, was used throughout. The Dead Sea Scrolls contain material bearing on an earlier stage of the Hebrew text. They were consulted, as were the Samaritan Pentateuch and the ancient scribal traditions relating to textual changes. Sometimes a variant Hebrew reading in the margin of the Masoretic Text was followed instead of the text itself. Such instances, being variants within the Masoretic tradition, are not specified by footnotes. In rare cases, words in the consonantal text were divided differently from the way they appear in the Masoretic Text. Footnotes indicate this. The translators also consulted the more important early versions—the Septuagint; Aquila, Symmachus and Theodotion; the Vulgate; the Syriac Peshitta; the Targums; and for the Psalms the *Juxta Hebraica* of Jerome. Readings from these versions were occasionally followed where the Masoretic Text seemed doubtful and where accepted principles of textual criticism showed that one or more of these textual witnesses appeared to provide the correct reading. Such instances are footnoted. Sometimes vowel letters and vowel signs did not, in the judgment of the translators, represent the correct vowels for the original consonantal text. Accordingly some words were read with a different set of vowels. These instances are usually not indicated by footnotes.

The Greek text used in translating the New Testament was an eclectic one. No other piece of ancient literature has such an abundance of manuscript witnesses as does the New Testament. Where existing manuscripts differ, the translators made their choice of readings according to accepted principles of New Testament textual criticism. Footnotes call attention to places where there was uncertainty about what the original text was. The best current printed texts of the Greek New Testament were used.

There is a sense in which the work of translation is never wholly finished. This applies to all great literature and uniquely so to the Bible. In 1973 the New Testament in the New International Version was published. Since then, suggestions for corrections and revisions have been received from various sources. The Committee on Bible Translation carefully considered the suggestions and adopted a number of them. These were incorporated in the first printing of the entire Bible in 1978. Additional revisions were made by the Committee on Bible Translation in 1983 and appear in printings after that date.

As in other ancient documents, the precise meaning of the biblical texts is sometimes uncertain. This is more often the case with the Hebrew and Aramaic texts than with the Greek text. Although archaeological and linguistic discoveries in this century aid in understanding difficult passages, some uncertainties remain. The more significant of these have been called to the reader's attention in the footnotes.

In regard to the divine name *YHWH*, commonly referred to as the *Tetragrammaton*, the translators adopted the device used in most English versions of rendering that name as "Lord" in capital letters to distinguish it from *Adonai*, another Hebrew word rendered "Lord," for which small letters are used. Wherever the two names stand together in the Old Testament as a compound name of God, they are rendered "Sovereign Lord."

Because for most readers today the phrases "the Lord of hosts" and "God of hosts" have little meaning, this version renders them "the Lord Almighty" and "God Almighty." These renderings convey the sense of the Hebrew, namely, "he who is sovereign over all the 'hosts' (powers) in heaven and on earth, especially over the 'hosts' (armies) of Israel." For readers unacquainted with Hebrew this does not make clear the distinction between *Sabaoth* ("hosts" or "Almighty") and *Shaddai* (which can also be translated "Almighty"), but the latter occurs infrequently and is always footnoted. When *Adonai* and *YHWH Sabaoth* occur together, they are rendered "the Lord, the Lord Almighty."

As for other proper nouns, the familiar spellings of the King James Version are generally retained. Names traditionally spelled with "ch," except where it is final, are usually spelled in this translation with "k" or "c," since the biblical languages do not have the sound that "ch" frequently indicates in English—for example, in *chant*. For well-known names such as Zechariah, however, the traditional spelling has been retained. Variation in the spelling of names in the original languages has usually not been indicated. Where a person or place has two or more different names in the Hebrew, Aramaic or Greek texts, the more familiar one has generally been used, with footnotes where needed.

To achieve clarity the translators sometimes supplied words not in the original texts but required by the context. If there was uncertainty about such material, it is enclosed in brackets. Also for the sake of clarity or style, nouns, including some proper nouns, are sometimes substituted for pronouns, and vice versa. And though the Hebrew writers often shifted back and forth between first, second and third personal pronouns without change of antecedent, this translation often makes them uniform, in accordance with English style and without the use of footnotes.

Poetical passages are printed as poetry, that is, with indentation of lines and with separate stanzas. These are generally designed to reflect the structure of Hebrew poetry. This poetry is normally characterized by parallelism in balanced lines. Most of the poetry in the Bible is in the Old Testament, and scholars differ regarding the scansion of Hebrew lines. The translators determined the stanza divisions for the most part by analysis of the subject matter. The stanzas therefore serve as poetic paragraphs.

As an aid to the reader, italicized sectional headings are inserted in most of the books. They are not to be regarded as part of the NIV text, are not for oral reading, and are not intended to dictate the interpretation of the sections they head.

The footnotes in this version are of several kinds, most of which need no explanation. Those giving alternative translations begin with "Or" and generally introduce the alternative with the last word preceding it in the text, except when it is a single-word alternative; in poetry quoted in a footnote a slant mark indicates a line division. Footnotes introduced by "Or" do not have uniform significance. In some cases two possible translations were considered to have about equal validity. In other cases, though the translators were convinced that the translation in the text was correct, they judged that another interpretation was possible and of sufficient importance to be represented in a footnote.

In the New Testament, footnotes that refer to uncertainty regarding the original text are introduced by "Some manuscripts" or similar expressions. In the Old Testament, evidence for the reading chosen is given first and evidence for the alternative is added after a semicolon (for example: Septuagint; Hebrew *father*). In such notes the term "Hebrew" refers to the Masoretic Text.

It should be noted that minerals, flora and fauna, architectural details, articles of clothing and jewelry, musical instruments and other articles cannot always be identified with precision. Also measures of capacity in the biblical period are particularly uncertain (see the table of weights and measures following the text).

Like all translations of the Bible, made as they are by imperfect man, this one undoubtedly falls short of its goals. Yet we are grateful to God for the extent to which he has enabled us to realize these goals and for the strength he has given us and our colleagues to complete our task. We offer this version of the Bible to him in whose name and for whose glory it has been made. We pray that it will lead many into a better understanding of the Holy Scriptures and a fuller knowledge of Jesus Christ the incarnate Word, of whom the Scriptures so faithfully testify.

The Committee on Bible Translation
June 1978
(Revised August 1983)

Names of the translators and editors may be secured
from the International Bible Society,
translation sponsors of the New International Version,
1820 Jet Stream Drive, Colorado Springs, Colorado
80921-3696 U.S.A.

How to Use
the Center Column Reference

THE CROSS REFERENCE SYSTEM can be used to explore concepts, as well as specific words. For example, one can either study "angels as protectors" (see Mt 18:10) or focus on the word "angel" (see Jn 20:12).

The NIV cross-reference system resembles a series of interlocking chains with many links. The head, or organizing, link in each concept chain is indicated by the letter "S" (short for "See"). The appearance of a head link in a list of references usually signals another list of references that will cover a slightly different aspect of the concept or word being studied. The various chains in the cross-reference system—which is virtually inexhaustible—continually intersect and diverge.

Cross references are indicated by raised roman letters. When a single word is addressed by both text notes and cross references, the italic NIV text-note letter comes first. The cross references normally appear in the center column and, when necessary, continue at the bottom of the right-hand column preceding the NIV text notes.

The four lists of references are in Biblical order with one exception: If reference is made to a verse within the same chapter, that verse (indicated by "ver") is listed first. If an Old Testament verse is quoted in the New Testament, the New Testament reference is marked with an asterisk (*).

Genesis 1:1 provides a good example of the resources of the cross-reference system.

The four lists of references all relate to creation, but each takes a different perspective. Note a takes up the time of creation: "in the beginning." Note b lists three other occurrences of the word "created" in Genesis 1—2. Note c focuses on "the heavens" as God's creation. Because note d is attached to the end of the verse as well as to the word "earth," it deals with the word "earth," with the phrase "the heavens and the earth" and with creation itself (the whole verse).

Parallel Passages

When two or more passages of Scripture are nearly identical or deal with the same event, this "parallel" is noted at the sectional headings for those passages. Such passages are especially common in Matthew, Mark, Luke and John; and in Samuel, Kings and Chronicles.

Identical or nearly identical passages are noted with *"pp."* Similar passages—those not dealing with the same event—are noted with *"Ref."*

To conserve space and avoid repetition, when a parallel passage is noted at a sectional heading, no further parallels are listed in the cross-reference system. It was compiled and edited by John R. Kohlenberger III and Edward W. Goodrick.

Abbreviations
of the Books of the Bible

Genesis ....Ge	Isaiah ....Isa	Romans........................Ro
Exodus ....Ex	Jeremiah ....Jer	1 Corinthians 1Co
Leviticus ....Lev	Lamentations ....La	2 Corinthians 2Co
Numbers ....Nu	Ezekiel ....Eze	Galatians ....Gal
Deuteronomy ....Dt	Daniel ....Da	Ephesians ....Eph
Joshua ....Jos	Hosea ....Hos	Philippians ....Php
Judges ....Jdg	Joel ....Joel	Colossians ....Col
Ruth ....Ru	Amos ....Am	1 Thessalonians 1Th
1 Samuel 1Sa	Obadiah ....Ob	2 Thessalonians 2Th
2 Samuel 2Sa	Jonah ....Jnh	1 Timothy 1Ti
1 Kings 1Ki	Micah ....Mic	2 Timothy 2Ti
2 Kings 2Ki	Nahum ....Na	Titus ....Tit
1 Chronicles 1Ch	Habakkuk ....Hab	Philemon ....Phm
2 Chronicles 2Ch	Zephaniah ....Zep	Hebrews ....Heb
Ezra ....Ezr	Haggai ....Hag	James ....Jas
Nehemiah ....Ne	Zechariah ....Zec	1 Peter 1Pe
Esther ....Est	Malachi ....Mal	2 Peter 2Pe
Job ....Job	Matthew ....Mt	1 John 1Jn
Psalm ....Ps	Mark ....Mk	2 John 2Jn
Proverbs ....Pr	Luke ....Lk	3 John 3Jn
Ecclesiastes ....Ecc	John ....Jn	Jude ....Jude
Song of Songs ....SS	Acts ....Ac	Revelation ....Rev

OLD TESTAMENT

Genesis

Author: Moses

Theme: The beginning of all things

Date of Writing: C. 1446–1406 B.C.

Outline of Genesis
   I. God's Creation of the Universe (1:1—2:25)
   II. The First Sin and Promise of Redemption (3:1—5:32)
   III. The Flood and the History of Noah (6:1—9:29)
   IV. The Distribution of People (10:1—11:26)
   V. The Life of Abraham (Abram) (11:27—25:18)
   VI. The Life of Isaac (25:19—26:35)
   VII. The Life of Jacob and His Sons (27:1—37:1)
   VIII. The Life of Joseph (37:2—50:26)

GENESIS 1:1 OPENS with the Hebrew word *bereshith*, which means "by way of beginning" or "in [the] beginning." The book of Genesis is truly a book about beginnings, recording God's creation of the heavens, the earth, vegetation, animals and people. Genesis also chronicles the first sin—the disobedience of Adam and Eve to God's commands and their subsequent exile from Eden. The pages of Genesis reveal the breadth of humanity's sinful condition and broken relationship with God. Yet Genesis also introduces the progressive revelation of God's plan to redeem the earth and fallen humanity and defeat Satan through the sacrificial death on the cross of God's Son, Jesus Christ. Thus Genesis records the creation, fall and ultimate redemption of the human race.

The progressive revelation of God's divine nature and his plan of salvation through Jesus Christ are revealed in Scripture through eight major covenants. In each covenant God established specific conditions of relationship between himself and people. Genesis records the four initial covenants—the Edenic (2:15–17), Adamic (3:15–19), Noahic (9:8ff) and Abrahamic (15:4ff; 17:1–22). These four covenants set the stage for the four remaining covenants that are revealed in the balance of Scripture—the Mosaic (Sinaitic), Palestinian,

Davidic and New covenants. Consequently a careful study of Genesis is essential to our understanding of the entire Bible.

The inspiration of Genesis is authenticated by the numerous quotations by the writers of the NT and by the word of Jesus Christ (see Mt 19:4–6; 24:37–39; Lk 17:26–29). Recent scientific discoveries also confirm the incredible accuracy of the scientific and medical statements found in this book. Though critics once doubted the existence of written language during Moses' day, modern-day archeologists have discovered many examples of ancient writing that predate the time of the exodus and further validate the historical reliability of Genesis.

The Beginning

1 In the beginning[a] God created[b] the heavens[c] and the earth.[d] **2** Now the earth was[a] formless[e] and empty,[f] darkness was over the surface of the deep,[g] and the Spirit of God[h] was hovering[i] over the waters.

3 And God said,[j] "Let there be light," and there was light.[k] **4** God saw that the light was good,[l] and he separated the light from the darkness.[m] **5** God called[n] the light "day," and the darkness he called "night."[o] And there was evening, and there was morning[p]—the first day.

6 And God said,[q] "Let there be an expanse[r] between the waters[s] to separate water from water." **7** So God made the expanse and separated the water under the expanse from the water above it.[t] And it was so.[u] **8** God called[v] the expanse "sky."[w] And there was evening, and there was morning[x]—the second day.

9 And God said, "Let the water under the sky be gathered to one place,[y] and let dry ground[z] appear." And it was so.[a] **10** God called[b] the dry ground "land," and the gathered waters[c] he called "seas."[d] And God saw that it was good.[e]

11 Then God said, "Let the land produce vegetation:[f] seed-bearing plants and trees on the land that bear fruit with seed in it, according to their various kinds.[g]" And it was so.[h] **12** The land produced vegetation: plants bearing seed according to their kinds[i] and trees bearing fruit with seed in it according to their kinds. And God saw that it was good.[j] **13** And there was evening, and there was morning[k]—the third day.

14 And God said, "Let there be lights[l] in the expanse of the sky to separate the day from the night,[m] and let them serve as signs[n] to mark seasons[o] and days and years,[p] **15** and let them be lights in the expanse of the sky to give light on the earth." And it was so.[q] **16** God made two great lights—the greater light[r] to govern[s] the day and the lesser light to govern[t] the night.[u] He also made the stars.[v] **17** God set them in the expanse of the sky to give light on the earth, **18** to govern the day and the night,[w] and to separate light from darkness. And God saw that it was good.[x] **19** And there was evening, and there was morning[y]—the fourth day.

20 And God said, "Let the water teem with living creatures,[z] and let birds

---

1:1 a Ps 102:25; Pr 8:23; Isa 40:21; 41:4,26; Jn 1:1-2
b ver 21,27; Ge 2:3
c ver 6; Ne 9:6;
Job 9:8; 37:18;
Ps 96:5; 104:2;
115:15; 121:2;
136:5; Isa 40:22;
42:5; 51:13;
Jer 10:12; 51:15
d Ge 14:19;
2Ki 19:15; Ne 9:6;
Job 38:4; Ps 90:2;
136:6; 146:6;
Isa 37:16; 40:28;
42:5; 44:24; 45:12,
18; Jer 27:5; 32:17;
Ac 14:15; 17:24;
Eph 3:9; Col 1:16;
Heb 3:4; 11:3;
Rev 4:11; 10:6
1:2 e Isa 23:1;
24:10; 27:10;
32:14; 34:11
f Isa 45:18; Jer 4:23
g Ge 8:2; Job 7:12;
26:8; 38:9; Ps 36:6;
42:7; 104:6;
107:24; Pr 30:4
h Ge 2:7; Job 33:4;
Ps 104:30;
Isa 32:15
1:3 i Dt 32:11; Isa 31:5
1:3 j ver 6; Ps 33:6,
9; 148:5; Heb 11:3
k 2Co 4:6*;
1Jn 1:5-7
1:4 l ver 10,12,18,
21,25,31;
Ps 104:31; 119:68;
Jer 31:35 m ver 14;
Ex 10:21-23;
Job 26:10; 38:19;
Ps 18:28; 104:20;
105:28; Isa 42:16;
45:7
1:5 n ver 8,10;
Ge 2:19,23
o Ps 74:16 p ver 8,
13,19,23,31
1:6 q S ver 3
r S ver 1; Isa 44:24;
2Pe 3:5 s ver 9;
Ps 24:2; 136:6
1:7 t Ge 7:11;
Job 26:10; 38:8-11,
16; Ps 68:33;

148:4; Pr 8:28 u ver 9,11,15,24 1:8 v S ver 5 w Job 9:8; 37:18; Ps 19:1; 104:2; Isa 40:22; 44:24; 45:12; Jer 10:12; Zec 12:1 x S ver 5
1:9 v Job 38:8-11; Ps 33:7; 104:6-9; Pr 8:29; Jer 5:22; 2Pe 3:5 z Ps 95:5; Jnh 1:9; Hag 2:6 a S ver 7 1:10 b S ver 5 c Ps 33:7 d Job 38:8; Ps 90:2; 95:5 e S ver 4 1:11 f Ps 65:9-13; 104:14 g ver 12,21,24,25; Ge 2:5; 6:20; 7:14; Lev 11:14,19,22; Dt 14:13,18; 1Co 15:38 h S ver 7 1:12 i S ver 11 j S ver 4 1:13 k S ver 5 1:14 l Ps 74:16; 136:7 m S ver 4 n Jer 10:2 o Ps 104:19 p Ge 8:22; Jer 31:35-36; 33:20,25 1:15 q S ver 7 1:16 r Dt 17:3; Job 31:26; Jer 43:13; Eze 8:16 s Ps 136:8 t Ps 136:9 u Job 38:33; Ps 74:16; 104:19; Jer 31:35; Jas 1:17 v Dt 4:19; Job 9:9; 38:7, 31-32; Ps 8:3; 33:6; Ecc 12:2; Isa 40:26; Jer 8:2; Am 5:8 1:18 w Jer 33:20,25 x S ver 4 1:19 y S ver 5 1:20 z Ps 146:6

E ▶ Ge 41:38   M ▶ Ge 41:38   N ▶ 2Ki 2:9   a 2 Or possibly became

fly above the earth across the expanse of the sky."ᵃ ²¹So God created ᵇ the great creatures of the sea ᶜ and every living and moving thing with which the water teems,ᵈ according to their kinds, and every winged bird according to its kind.ᵉ And God saw that it was good.ᶠ ²²God blessed them and said, "Be fruitful and increase in number and fill the water in the seas, and let the birds increase on the earth."ᵍ ²³And there was evening, and there was morning ʰ—the fifth day.

²⁴And God said, "Let the land produce living creatures ⁱ according to their kinds: ʲ livestock, creatures that move along the ground, and wild animals, each according to its kind." And it was so.ᵏ ²⁵God made the wild animals ˡ according to their kinds, the livestock according to their kinds, and all the creatures that move along the ground according to their kinds.ᵐ And God saw that it was good.ⁿ

²⁶Then God said, "Let usᵒ make manᵖ in our image,ᵠ in our likeness,ʳ and let them rule ˢ over the fish of the sea and the birds of the air,ᵗ over the livestock, over all the earth,ᵇ and over all the creatures that move along the ground."

²⁷So God created ᵘ man ᵛ in his own image,ʷ
in the image of Godˣ he created him;
male and female ʸ he created them.ᶻ

²⁸God blessed them and said to them,ᵃ "Be fruitful and increase in number;ᵇ fill the earth ᶜ and subdue it. Rule overᵈ the fish of the sea and the birds of the air and over every living creature that moves on the ground.ᵉ"

²⁹Then God said, "I give you every seed-bearing plant on the face of the whole earth and every tree that has fruit with seed in it. They will be yours for food.ᶠ ³⁰And to all the beasts of the earth and all the birds of the air and all the creatures that move on the ground—everything that has the breath of lifeᵍ in it—I give every green plant for food.ʰ" And it was so.

³¹God saw all that he had made,ⁱ and it was very good.ʲ And there was

A ▶ *Ge 2:16–17*

1:28 *Dispensation of Innocence.* Throughout Scripture, one can find seven distinct periods of time in which God commands obedience to a specific aspect or revelation of his will. These time periods may be referred to as dispensations. This verse introduces the first of those dispensations—the dispensation of innocence.

Adam and Eve were created as pure and innocent human beings, placed by God in a perfect world. God commanded Adam's adherence to one specific rule—not to eat of the tree of the knowledge of good and evil—and he warned Adam of the consequences of disobedience. But Adam and Eve failed this test of obedience. Eve yielded to Satan's temptation, and Adam chose to follow his wife's sinful rebellion. Their failure to obey God resulted in their eviction from the garden and their ultimate death.

The seven dispensations revealed in Scripture are the dispensations of innocence (Ge 1:28), conscience (3:7), human government (8:15), promise (12:1), law (Ex 19:1), the church (Ac 2:1) and the kingdom (Rev 20:4). For further information on the dispensations, see the article on p. 4.

The Seven Dispensations

Innocence GE 1:28	Conscience GE 3:7	Human Government GE 8:15	Promise GE 12:1	Law EX 19:1		Age of Grace Church Age AC 2:1	Kingdom Age REV 20:4
1	2	3	4	5	✝	6	7
Creation	Fall	Flood	Abraham	Moses	Crucifixion	Battle of Armageddon	Eternity

The Seven Dispensations

A DISPENSATION IS a period of time in God's divine economy during which God gives a special revelation and commands people to obey that specific revelation. Scripture unveils seven distinct dispensations: innocence (Ge 1:28), conscience (3:7), human government (8:15), promise (12:1), law (Ex 19:1), the church (Ac 2:1) and the kingdom (Rev 20:4).

The Dispensation of Innocence (Ge 1:28)
God created Adam and Eve in total innocence and placed them in an environment of perfect harmony. God established one simple test of obedience: Adam and Eve were forbidden to eat from the tree of the knowledge of good and evil. Satan first tempted Eve, and Adam chose to follow his wife's rebellion. They both disobeyed God's test of obedience and instead yielded to sin. The consequence for their failure to obey God was their expulsion from Eden.

The Dispensation of Conscience (Ge 3:7)
As a result of Adam and Eve's sinful rebellion, people now possessed the knowledge of the difference between good and evil. God revealed a new test of obedience. People were to follow the dictates of conscience, rejecting evil and following good. Yet humanity failed this test of obedience too, resulting in worldwide corruption and violence. Consequently God sent a terrible flood to destroy the world, leaving only eight survivors from Noah's family.

The Dispensation of Human Government (Ge 8:15)
Noah's family was given the command to repopulate the world and to organize a society that would follow the principles of God's law. This new dispensation involved the creation of human government, under the command of God, to protect the sanctity of human life and to rule with righteousness on earth. Though God authorized human government, history tragically records humanity's failure to rule in righteousness. Human governments have been marked by cruelty, corruption and injustice. This dispensation of human government will be set aside when Jesus Christ returns at Armageddon to establish his kingdom in Jerusalem and to rule the earth in righteousness forever.

The Dispensation of Promise (Ge 12:1)
This dispensation revealed God's intent to use Abram and his descendants to provide a Savior for all people. Abram and his descendants were to be obedient to God and faithful to him. God unconditionally promised to bless them (see 15:15), make them a great nation (see 12:2) and give them the promised land as their eternal inheritance (see 15:18–21;

17:7–8). In addition, God promised to bless all who would bless Abram and his descendants (see 12:3), while those who cursed Abram and his offspring would reap judgment. The history of the rise and fall of many empires can be understood in light of this promise to bless or curse those who bless or curse Israel.

This dispensation of promise has not been eliminated even though Abram's descendants have not faithfully obeyed God. Though the dispensation of the law given to Moses at Mt. Sinai (see Ex 19:1–3) superseded this dispensation of promise, the Bible contains many promises about Israel's future blessing and restoration to the promised land (see Isa 44; 49: 51:3–9; 66:8–9; Jer 31:3–14).

The Dispensation of the Law (Ex 19:1)

This dispensation covered the time period from the giving of God's Law on Mt. Sinai until the death of Jesus Christ on the cross. Humanity had failed each of the previous tests of obedience, but Israel promised to obey this revelation of God's Law. The law provided Israel with a divinely sanctioned way of life that functioned as a tutor, or disciplinary schoolmaster, to test Israel's obedience to God's will (see Gal 3:24). Though God commanded the sacrifices, personal righteousness, rituals and worship ceremonies, these sacrifices and rituals could not, in themselves, ever eliminate sin. The law merely pointed to the need for a permanent salvation through Jesus Christ, the Lamb of God, slain for the sins of the world. Tragically, history records Israel's continual rebellion and violation of God's Law, proving that Israel failed this test of obedience. Therefore, it was necessary for God to send Jesus Christ to die as the perfect sacrifice for all sin.

The Dispensation of Grace (Ac 2:1)

This dispensation corresponds to the church age, beginning at the cross and continuing until the resurrection of the saints (see 1Th 4:13–17). During this time period, humanity faces the testing of their response to God's offer of salvation based on Jesus' sacrificial death. Many will deny Jesus' claims and introduce false doctrines into the church (see 1Ti 4:1–3). Others will scoff and refuse to accept God's gracious gift. Still others will verbally profess faith in Christ but never truly repent and will join in the apostasy of the false church during the last days. This dispensation of grace will conclude with the rapture of the saints, those who have truly repented and loved Jesus Christ, to their home in heaven.

The Dispensation of the Kingdom (Rev 20:4)

This last dispensation concludes God's plan of redemption for humanity, establishes his eternal kingdom on earth and ultimately fulfills God's unshakable promises to Israel, the Gentile nations, and the church. The Messiah, Jesus Christ, will rule the earth from the throne of David forever. Righteousness and justice will replace oppression and misrule. Israel will be restored and converted. And the final consummation of the dispensation of this coming kingdom will be the deliverance of creation from its bondage since the time of Eden.
For further information about the seven dispensations, see the chart on p. 3 or the study notes at Ge 1:28; 3:7; 8:15; 12:1; Ex 19:1; Ac 2:1 and Rev 20:4.

evening, and there was morning[k]—the sixth day.

2 Thus the heavens and the earth were completed in all their vast array.[l] ²By the seventh day[m] God had finished the work he had been doing; so on the seventh day he rested[c] from all his work.[n] ³And God blessed the seventh day and made it holy,[o] because on it he rested[p] from all the work of creating[q] that he had done.

Adam and Eve

⁴This is the account[r] of the heavens and the earth when they were created.[s]

When the LORD God made the earth and the heavens— ⁵and no shrub of the field had yet appeared on the earth[d] and no plant of the field had yet sprung up,[t] for the LORD God had not sent rain on the earth[d][u] and there was no man to work the ground, ⁶but streams[e] came up from the earth and watered the whole surface of the ground— ⁷the LORD God formed[v] the man,[f][w] from the dust[x] of the ground[y] and breathed into his nostrils the breath[z] of life,[a] and the man became a living being.[b]

⁸Now the LORD God had planted a garden in the east, in Eden;[c] and there he put the man he had formed. ⁹And the LORD God made all kinds of trees grow out of the ground—trees[d] that were pleasing to the eye and good for food. In the middle of the garden were the tree of life[e] and the tree of the knowledge of good and evil.[f]

¹⁰A river[g] watering the garden flowed from Eden;[h] from there it was separated into four headwaters. ¹¹The name of the first is the Pishon; it winds through the entire land of Havilah,[i] where there is gold. ¹²(The gold of that land is good; aromatic resin[g][j] and onyx are also there.) ¹³The name of the second river is the Gihon; it winds through the entire land of Cush.[h] ¹⁴The name of the third river is the Tigris;[k] it runs along the east side of Asshur. And the fourth river is the Euphrates.[l]

¹⁵The LORD God took the man and put him in the Garden of Eden[m] to work it and take care of it. ¹⁶And the LORD God **A** commanded the man, "You are free to eat from any tree in the garden;[n] ¹⁷but you **C** must not eat from the tree of the knowl- **S** edge of good and evil,[o] for when you eat of it you will surely die."[p]

¹⁸The LORD God said, "It is not good for the man to be alone. I will make a helper suitable for him."[q]

A ▶ Ge 1:28 ◀ ▶ Ge 3:7 **C** ▶ Ge 3:3
S ▶ Ge 7:1

2:15–17 *Edenic Covenant.* This passage marks the Edenic covenant—the first of God's eight major covenants with humanity. In this solemn declaration of God's sovereignty the Lord established a relationship between himself and human beings involving the following elements:
1. People were to rule over the whole earth and "over the fish of the sea and the birds of the air and over every living creature that moves on the ground" (1:28).
2. People were to populate and fill the earth.
3. Adam was instructed to be a steward of the garden and allowed to partake of its fruits for food.
4. Adam was not allowed to eat of the fruit of the tree of the knowledge of good and evil on penalty of death.

NOTE: The seven additional covenants include the Adamic (3:15–17), Noahic (9:8ff), Abrahamic (15:4ff; 17:1–22), Mosaic (Ex 19:5), Palestinian (Dt 30:1–10), Davidic (2Sa 7:16) and New (Heb 8:8–12). See chart on p. 7.

2:17 The description of the garden includes the mention of two specific trees. "The tree of the knowledge of good and evil" became the focus of Adam and Eve's temptation to disobey God, transcend themselves and "be like God" (3:5). The other important tree in the middle of the garden was "the tree of life" (2:9). This tree yielded more than mere knowledge; its fruit conveyed immortality (see 3:22). The "tree of life" is referred to again in John's description of the new Jerusalem (see Rev 22:2). The righteous will apparently partake of this "tree of life" because sin's control over them will be destroyed and their eternity with God will be secure.

The Holy Spirit

A. **Asking For, or Praying for the Spirit**
Isa 44:3; Hos 10:12; Lk 11:9-13; Ac 4:10; Jn 4:10, 7:37, 9:17, 19:1-6
2Ki 2:9-10
Lk 11:9-13

B. **Baptism or Filling of the Spirit**
Ex 31:2-3; Dt 34:9; Lk 3:16; Jn 14:17; Ac 2:1-18, 8:14-19, 19:1-6; Eph 5:18
Ge 41:38
Mt 3:11

C. **The Holy Spirit Convicts of Sin**
Ge 6:3; Ps 51:12-13; Mic 3:8; Zec 12:10; Jn 16:8-11; Ac 2:37
Ge 6:3
Lk 1:17

D. **Deity, or Divinity, of the Holy Spirit**
Ps 68:18; Mt 28:19; Ac 5:3-4; 1Co 3:16; 2Co 3:17; 13:14; Eph 2:22; 1Jn 5:7
Ps 68:18
Mt 12:31-32

E. **Examples of the Holy Spirit's Work**
Ge 41:38-39; Nu 11:24-29; 1Ki 3:12; Da 1:17-20; Ac 2:1-18, 8:14-19, 19:1-6
Ge 1:2-3
Mt 1:18

F. **Fruits of the Holy Spirit**
Isa 63:14; Ac 2:46, 9:31; 13:52; Ro 5:5; 8:23; 14:17; 15:13; Gal 5:22-23
Ps 45:7
Ac 9:31

G. **Gifts of the Holy Spirit**
Ps 68:18; Isa 11:2; Joel 2:28; Mk 16:17-18; Ro 12:6-8; 1Co 12:14; Eph 4:7-16
Ge 41:38
Mt 10:19-20

H. **Healing and Resurrecting Power of the Spirit**
Eze 37:14; Mt 12:28; Ro 8:11; 1Co 12:9, 28, 30; 15:35-55; 1Pe 3:18; Rev 11:11
Job 33:4
Mt 12:28

J. **Comfort or Joy of the Holy Spirit**
Ps 45:7; Isa 61:3; Jn 14:16, 26; 15:26; 16:7; Ac 2:46; 9:31; 13:52; Ro 14:17
Ps 45:7
Mt 3:16

L. **Leading or Guiding of the Holy Spirit**
Ex 4:12, 15; Nu 22:38; Isa 10:7; 1Ki 22:14; Mt 10:19-20; Jn 16:13; Ac 2:4
Jdg 13:25
Mt 4:1

M. **Great Might or Power Given by the Spirit**
Jdg 14:6; 15:14-15; Mic 3:8; Zec 4:6; Lk 24:49; Ac 1:8; 2Co 10:4; Eph 3:16
Ge 1:2-3
Mt 3:11

N. **Names and Symbols of the Holy Spirit**
Job 32:19; Ps 23:5; 39:3; 45:7; Mt 3:16; Lk 3:16; Jn 7:38; Ac 2:2-3
Ge 1:2
Mt 3:11

P. **The Holy Spirit Promised**
Isa 44:3; Joel 2:28-29; Mal 3:10; Lk 3:16; Jn 16:7-15; Ac 2:39
Ps 68:18
Mt 3:11

Q. **Quenching, Grieving, or Sinning Against the Spirit**
Ge 6:3; Isa 63:10; Mt 12:31-32; Eph 4:30; 1Th 5:19; Heb 10:29; 1Jn 5:16
Ge 6:3
Mt 12:31-32

R. **Regeneration as the Work of the Holy Spirit**
Isa 10:6; 9:26; Jer 31:33; Jn 3:5-8; Ro 8:15-16; 1Co 6:11; 12:13; Tit 3:5
Isa 10:6
Lk 1:15-17

S. **Sanctifying Power of the Holy Spirit**
Ex 3:5; Ps 51:10; Eze 36:25-27; Ac 15:8-9; Ro 8:1-14; 15:16; 1Co 3:16-17
Ex 30:25
Lk 1:17

T. **Teaching or Enlightening of the Spirit**
Ge 41:39; 1Ki 3:12; Da 1:20; Jn 16:13; Ac 4:13; 1Co 2; 12:4; 1Jn 2:27
Ge 41:38
Mt 10:19-20

W. **God Wishes Us to be Filled with the Spirit**
Nu 11:29; Isa 30:1; Lk 24:49; Ac 19:1-2; 1Co 12:1; Eph 5:18; 6:10-18
Nu 11:29
Lk 24:49

¹⁹Now the LORD God had formed out of the ground all the beasts of the field' and all the birds of the air.ˢ He brought them to the man to see what he would name them; and whatever the man calledᵗ each living creature,ᵘ that was its name. ²⁰So the man gave names to all the livestock, the birds of the air and all the beasts of the field.

But for Adamⁱ no suitable helperᵛ was found. ²¹So the LORD God caused the man to fall into a deep sleep;ʷ and while he was sleeping, he took one of the man's ribs ʲ and closed up the place with flesh. ²²Then the LORD God made a woman from the ribᵏˣ he had taken out of the man, and he brought her to the man.

²³The man said,

"This is now bone of my bones
 and flesh of my flesh;ʸ
she shall be calledᶻ 'woman,'ˡ
 for she was taken out of man.ᵃ"

²⁴For this reason a man will leave his father and mother and be unitedᵇ to his wife, and they will become one flesh.ᶜ

²⁵The man and his wife were both naked,ᵈ and they felt no shame.

The Fall of Man

3 Now the serpentᵉ was more crafty than any of the wild animals the LORD God had made. He said to the woman, "Did God really say, 'You must not eat from any tree in the garden'?ᶠ"

²The woman said to the serpent, "We may eat fruit from the trees in the garden,ᵍ ³but God did say, 'You must not eat C fruit from the tree that is in the middle of the garden, and you must not touch it, or you will die.' "ʰ

⁴"You will not surely die," the serpent said to the woman.ⁱ ⁵"For God knows that when you eat of it your eyes will be opened, and you will be like God,ʲ knowing good and evil."

⁶When the woman saw that the fruit of the tree was good for food and pleasing to the eye, and also desirableᵏ for gaining wisdom, she took some and ate it. She also gave some to her husband,ˡ who was with her, and he ate it.ᵐ ⁷Then the eyes A of both of them were opened, and they realized they were naked;ⁿ so they sewed

C *Ge 2:17* ◀▶ *Ge 6:5*
A *Ge 2:16–17* ◀▶ *Ge 3:15*

ⁱ 20 Or *the man* / *21* Or *took part of the man's side* / *ᵏ 22* Or *part*
ˡ 23 The Hebrew for *woman* sounds like the Hebrew for *man*.

3:7 *Dispensation of Conscience.* Adam and Eve disobeyed God's command and immediately felt a keen sense of guilt as they experienced what had heretofore been theoretical. They now knew the difference between good and evil, but had gained this knowledge by choosing disobedience rather than obedience to God's command. As a result of their sinful rebellion, humanity moved from innocence to a time of moral decision and faced God's test to follow the dictates of conscience, voluntarily choosing righteousness rather than wickedness. Tragically, humanity continued to reject obedience to God's revealed will and failed the test of obedience in this dispensation of conscience (see 6:5).

The seven dispensations revealed in Scripture are the dispensations of innocence (Ge 1:28), conscience (3:7), human government (8:15), promise (12:1), law (Ex 19:1), the church (Ac 2:1) and the kingdom (Rev 20:4). For further information on the dispensations, see the article on p. 4.

The Eight Covenants

| Edenic | Adamic | Noahic | Abrahamic | Mosaic | Palestinian | Davidic | New Covenant |
GE 2:16	GE 3:15	GE 8:15	GE 12:2	EX 19:5	DT 30:3	2 SA 7:16	HEB 8:8
1	**2**	**3**	**4**	**5**	**6**	**7**	**8**
Creation	The fall of Adam	After flood, government begins	Promise of land to Israel	The law given	God gives conditions to enter Promised Land	Promise David's throne forever	God Promised Final Redemption A new heart to be given to Israel

Covenant: A declaration of God in which he establishes man's responsibility to obey a specific revelation from the Lord. Usually, these covenants are unconditional, as God declares "I will . . ." Man's obedience leads to blessing, while disobedience leads to discipline. However, man's sinful disobedience cannot interfere with God's ultimate fulfillment of his covenants.

The Biblical Covenants

A COVENANT IS a formal, binding agreement between two parties to do or not to do something. Biblical covenants reflect God's sovereign declaration to establish a legal agreement between himself and human beings. Many Biblical covenants are unconditional—God commits himself to accomplish something regardless of whether or not humanity executes their part of the agreement. A Biblical covenant, however, usually contains promised blessings for adherence to the terms of the covenant and guarantees punishment for a refusal to comply. Though people may experience punishment in return for disobedience to a Biblical covenant, such disobedience does not negate the ultimate fulfillment of God's covenant promises.

Note that there are eight major covenants found in the Bible. These covenants help us understand God's unfolding plan to redeem humanity from the curse of sin and provide details about the establishment of his Messianic kingdom on earth. For additional details about each of the covenants listed below, refer to the study notes provided at each referenced location and review the chart provided on p. 7.

The Edenic Covenant (Ge 2:15)
The Edenic covenant is the first of God's great covenants with people. This covenant granted several rights and requirements for people: They were to rule the earth and its creatures, populate and fill the earth, take care of Eden and refrain from eating from the tree of the knowledge of good and evil. The blessings of this covenant were a beautiful environment, abundant fruits and food available in the garden and a close, personal relationship with God. The penalty for breaking this covenant was death.

The Adamic Covenant (Ge 3:15)
The Adamic covenant stipulated the conditions under which sinful people must live until the redemption of the earth in the millennial kingdom of Christ. These conditions included a curse upon the snake, a judgment on women because of Eve's fall and temptation of Adam, a curse upon the earth and a certainty of death for all people.

Yet hidden within each of these judgments was a seed of God's mercy. Though used as Satan's tool, the snake was not utterly destroyed but rather was given a lesser place of prominence in the animal kingdom. Though the earth was cursed because of sin, the ground would still yield enough food to allow the continuance of human beings and animals. Though the woman was cursed with sorrow in conception, pain in childbirth and a place of subjection in the marital relationship, God also showed mercy to the woman by granting her joy in the birth of her children (see Jn 16:21) and by establishing guidelines for a husband's leadership in marriage (see Eph 5:22–28).

Even the curse of death carried a promise from God. God had initially created Adam and Eve to live forever if they obeyed his commands. Because of their sin, Adam and Eve forfeited their immortality, received the curse of death and were evicted from the Garden. However, God extended his mercy to humanity in this covenant by promising that a future Redeemer would come through the woman's seed. This Messianic foreshadowing of the virgin birth is the first in a series of prophecies about Christ that occur throughout the Bible. This covenant also foreshadowed the rise of a seed of Satan—the antichrist—and his inevitable defeat. Though Satan would have a temporary victory, Christ would neutralize Satan's power through his triumphant resurrection and victory over death.

The Noahic Covenant (Ge 9:8)

God established the Noahic covenant to reconfirm the conditions of the Adamic covenant and to authorize human government as a control for violence and sin. The articles of this covenant included a confirmation of the seasons, the freedom for people to kill animals for food and a fear of humanity instilled in animals. God also required that people protect human life and control the actions of others through the creation of human government (see 9:5–6; Rom 13:1–7).

Specific instructions in this covenant were given to Noah's sons: Canaan's (Ham's) descendants would be the servants of their brothers; Japheth's line would be enlarged; Shem's descendants would serve the Lord in a unique way. Note that these specific instructions were also prophetic: Many of those gifted in art, science and government in ancient times were descendants of Japheth, while Jesus Christ was a descendant of Shem.

The promise of the Noahic covenant was sealed with a rainbow as God promised to never again destroy every living thing (see 8:21; 9:11–16) or increase the curse placed upon the ground.

The Abrahamic Covenant (Ge 15:4)

The Abrahamic covenant declared God's sovereign choice to bless Israel and the nations through Abraham and his descendant, the Messiah. The major aspects of this covenant included God's eternal promises to Abraham ensuring him innumerable descendants, considerable blessings and a great nation to come from his lineage. In this covenant God's promises of blessing also extended to all of humanity provided people blessed Abraham's descendants. If people chose to denounce Abraham's offspring, however, God would punish them. The reason for the rise and fall of many nations can be found in this solemn promise of God to Abraham and his descendants.

The Mosaic Covenant (Ex 19:5)

The Mosaic covenant did not change the covenant promise made to Abraham but instead expanded it. God promised to make the nation of Israel his chosen people. The people were required to obey God's commandments, judgments and ordinances to gain an understanding of God's righteousness and will for their lives. The law became Israel's schoolteacher, setting the limits for Israel's spiritual life and determining the rules that would govern Israel's daily life. This covenant would remain in effect until the Messiah comes.

The Palestinian Covenant (Dt 30:1–10)
The Palestinian covenant described the divinely appointed conditions that God established for Israel's occupation of the promised land. Blessings and punishments are offset in the terms of this covenant. If Israel rebelled against God, God said they would be removed from their land. Yet God promised that his people would eventually repent and be restored to the land of Canaan. When the Messiah comes Israel will be fully restored to the land, the nation will repent and God will judge Israel's enemies. Then Israel will enjoy eternal prosperity in the promised land.

Israel has never possessed Canaan under the terms of the unconditional Abrahamic covenant. The Palestinian covenant confirms those promises concerning the land and indicates that this covenant will not be totally fulfilled until the Millennium, under the rule of the Messiah.

The Davidic Covenant (2Sa 7:16)
God made additional promises to Israel through the Davidic covenant. This eternal agreement established David's throne and promised that David's descendants would rule his kingdom forever. This covenant was established upon God's promise that the future Messiah would come from David's line and someday rule Israel from David's throne. God guaranteed that despite the sins of David's sons, this covenant with David would be fulfilled eternally.

The New Covenant (Heb 8:8–12)
The New covenant is the last of the eight, major Biblical covenants and is unconditionally based on the promises of God to transform the hearts of his people. The promises of the New covenant affect all believers because this covenant asserts that all sin has been effectively forgiven forever through Christ's atoning work on the cross.

This final covenant also assures Israel that they will remain God's chosen people and that God will transform their sinful hearts so that they will love and obey him forever. God promises through his New covenant to ultimately redeem his chosen people and establish them in a new relationship with him forever in the promised land.

fig leaves together and made coverings for themselves.°
⁸Then the man and his wife heard the sound of the LORD God as he was walking[p] in the garden in the cool of the day, and they hid[q] from the LORD God among the trees of the garden. ⁹But the LORD God called to the man, "Where are you?"[r]
¹⁰He answered, "I heard you in the garden, and I was afraid[s] because I was naked;[t] so I hid."
¹¹And he said, "Who told you that you were naked?[u] Have you eaten from the tree that I commanded you not to eat from?"[v]
¹²The man said, "The woman you put here with me[w]—she gave me some fruit from the tree, and I ate it."

3:7 °ver 21
3:8 pLev 26:12; Dt 23:14
qJob 13:16; 23:7; 31:33; 34:22,23; Ps 5:5; 139:7-12; Isa 29:15; Jer 16:17; 23:24; 49:10; Rev 6:15-16
3:9 rGe 4:9; 16:8; 18:9; 1Ki 19:9,13
3:10 sEx 19:16; 20:18; Dt 5:5; 1Sa 12:18 tGe 2:25
3:11 uGe 2:25 vS Ge 2:17
3:12 wGe 2:22
3:13 xRo 7:11; 2Co 11:3; 1Ti 2:14
3:14 yDt 28:15-20 zPs 72:9; Isa 49:23; 65:25; Mic 7:17

¹³Then the LORD God said to the woman, "What is this you have done?"
The woman said, "The serpent deceived me,[x] and I ate."
¹⁴So the LORD God said to the serpent, "Because you have done this,

"Cursed[y] are you above all the livestock
and all the wild animals!
You will crawl on your belly
and you will eat dust[z]
all the days of your life.
¹⁵And I will put enmity
between you and the woman,

A
B
D

A *Ge 3:7* ◄► *Ge 8:15*   B ► *Ge 49:10*
D ► *Ge 4:3–5*

3:15 This verse has been called the *protevangelium*—the first proclamation of the gospel. It is the first in a chain of Messianic prophecies throughout the Scriptures that prefigure Christ's birth, life, death and resurrection. The first part of the verse infers the spiritual struggle that will arise between the woman's offspring and the offspring of the serpent—the continual battle between the children of the kingdom and the children of Satan. However, this prophecy also reveals that one ultimate victor will win this battle. Though Satan will "strike his heel," inflicting temporary pain and suffering through his many skirmishes (see Rev 12:13–17), Christ will ultimately triumph over death and the grave, crushing the serpent's head and inflicting a mortal wound that will win the war. To the resounding, joyful cries of his children, Christ will one day destroy all of Satan's powers at the final defeat of the antichrist and in the last days deliver a wound to Satan's head that can never be healed.

3:15–17 *Adamic Covenant.* This verse introduces the agreement made between God and Adam and Eve after their sin but before their removal from the garden. This Adamic covenant specifies the elements of life for humanity on this earth until Christ's second coming (see Ro 8:21). The covenant consisted of curses and promises:

1. The curse upon the serpent (see 3:14; Isa 65:25; Ro 16:20; 2Co 11:3; Rev 12:9). Created to be under humanity's dominion and rule but abused as Satan's instrument, the serpent was reduced from a subtle "wild animal" (3:1) to a slithering reptile, cursed more than any other beast and forced to eat dust. Although the words of the curse were directed toward a creature, the underlying thrust of the message was against "that ancient serpent called the devil" (Rev 12:9).

2. The curse upon Satan (3:15; see Eph 2:2; Col 2:13–15; Heb 2:14–15). The time will come when Satan will be completely crushed by the seed of the woman (see note on 3:15 above).

3. The curse upon women (see 3:16). As the one who yielded first to Satan and then tempted another to sin, the woman suffered a special punishment: (a) women would henceforth have multiplied pain, suffering and agony in childbirth as a perpetual reminder of the effects of sin; and (b) women were reduced to a position of subjection to their husbands. Within each of these pronouncements of judgment God also provided a promise. The experience of birth is an agony of the moment, but also a gift of joy: "A woman giving birth to a child has pain because her time has come; but when her baby is born she forgets the anguish because of her joy that a child is born into the world" (Jn 16:21). The authority of a husband in a marriage can also be a blessing. When a husband exercises his leadership in the marriage under God's direction, he will cherish and love his wife "just as Christ loved the church" (Eph 5:25; see Eph 5:23–28).

4. The curse upon the ground (see 3:17). The bountiful abundance of the garden would no longer be available to Adam and Eve. Weeds, thorns and thistles would now cover the ground and make harvesting food a toilsome process.

5. The curse upon humanity (see 3:17–19; Ro 5:12–21). From a life of ease to a life of toilsome labor, God's curse on Adam's sin also included the certainty of death for Adam, Eve and each of their descendants (see 3:19). Yet this judgment also contained a promise of grace—hard work would yield food to sustain life.

6. The promise of a future Redeemer (3:15). "That ancient serpent called the devil, or Satan, who leads the whole world astray"

and between your offspring[m a] and hers;[b]
he will crush[n] your head,[c]
and you will strike his heel."

¹⁶To the woman he said,

"I will greatly increase your pains in childbearing;
with pain you will give birth to children.[d]
Your desire will be for your husband, and he will rule over you.[e]"

¹⁷To Adam he said, "Because you listened to your wife and ate from the tree about which I commanded you, 'You must not eat of it,'[f]

"Cursed[g] is the ground[h] because of you;
through painful toil[i] you will eat of it
all the days of your life.[j]
¹⁸It will produce thorns and thistles[k] for you,
and you will eat the plants of the field.[l]
¹⁹By the sweat of your brow[m]
you will eat your food[n]
until you return to the ground,
since from it you were taken;
for dust you are
and to dust you will return."[o]

²⁰Adam[o] named his wife Eve,[p p] because she would become the mother of all the living.
²¹The LORD God made garments of skin for Adam and his wife and clothed them.[q]
²²And the LORD God said, "The man has now become like one of us,[r] knowing good and evil. He must not be allowed to reach out his hand and take also from the tree of life[s] and eat, and live forever."
²³So the LORD God banished him from the Garden of Eden[t] to work the ground[u]

3:15 ᵃJn 8:44; Ac 13:10; 1Jn 3:8
ᵇGe 6:11; Jdg 13:5; Isa 7:14; 8:3; 9:6; Mt 1:23; Lk 1:31; Gal 4:4; Rev 12:17
ᶜRo 16:20; Heb 2:14
3:16 ᵈPs 48:5-6; Isa 13:8; 21:3; 26:17; Jer 4:31; 6:24; Mic 4:9; 1Ti 2:15
ᵉ1Co 11:3; Eph 5:22
3:17 ᶠS Ge 2:17
ᵍGe 5:29; Nu 35:33; Ps 106:39; Isa 24:5; Jer 3:1; Ro 8:20-22
ʰGe 6:13; 8:21; Isa 54:9 ⁱGe 29:32; 31:42; Ex 3:7; Ps 66:11; 127:2; Ecc 1:13 ʲGe 47:9; Job 5:7; 7:1; 14:1; Ecc 2:23; Jer 20:18
3:18 ᵏJob 31:40; Isa 5:6; Heb 6:8
ˡPs 104:14
3:19 ᵐPs 104:23
ⁿGe 14:18; Dt 8:3, 9; 23:4; Ru 1:6; 2:14; 2Th 3:10
ᵒS Ge 2:7;
S Job 7:21;
S Ps 146:4; 1Co 15:47; Heb 9:27
3:20 ᵖS Ge 2:20; 2Co 11:3; 1Ti 2:13
3:21 ᑫS ver 7
3:22 ʳS Ge 1:26
ˢS Ge 2:9; S Rev 2:7
3:23 ᵗS Ge 2:8
ᵘS Ge 2:7
3:24 ᵛS Ge 2:8
ʷEx 25:18-22; 1Sa 4:4; 2Sa 6:2; 22:11; 1Ki 6:27; 8:6; 2Ki 19:15; 2Ch 5:8; Ps 18:10; 80:1; 99:1; Ps 104:4; Isa 27:1
ˣIsa 37:16; Eze 10:1; 28:16 ʸJob 40:19; Nu 4:3 ᶻGe 2:9
4:1 ᵃver 17,25
ᵃS Ge 2:20
ᵇHeb 11:4; 1Jn 3:12; Jude 1:11
4:2 ᶜMt 23:35;
Lk 11:51; Heb 11:4; 12:24 ᵈS Ge 2:7
4:3 ᵉLev 2:1-2;

---

from which he had been taken. ²⁴After he drove the man out, he placed on the east side[q] of the Garden of Eden[v] cherubim[w] and a flaming sword[x] flashing back and forth to guard the way to the tree of life.[y]

Cain and Abel

4 Adam[o] lay with his wife[z] Eve,[a] and she became pregnant and gave birth to Cain.[rb] She said, "With the help of the LORD I have brought forth[s] a man." ²Later she gave birth to his brother Abel.[c] Now Abel kept flocks, and Cain worked the soil.[d] ³In the course of time Cain brought some of the fruits of the soil as an offering[e] to the LORD.[f] ⁴But Abel brought fat portions[g] from some of the firstborn of his flock.[h] The LORD looked with favor on Abel and his offering,[i] ⁵but on Cain and his offering he did not look with favor. So Cain was very angry, and his face was downcast.

⁶Then the LORD said to Cain, "Why are you angry?[j] Why is your face downcast? ⁷If you do what is right, will you not be accepted? But if you do not do what is right, sin is crouching at your door;[k] it desires to have you, but you must master it.¹"

⁸Now Cain said to his brother Abel, "Let's go out to the field."[t] And while they were in the field, Cain attacked his brother Abel and killed him.[m]

⁹Then the LORD said to Cain, "Where is your brother Abel?"[n]

D *Ge 3:15* ◀▶ *Ge 22:7–8*

Isa 43:23; Jer 41:5 ⁿNu 18:12 **4:4** ᵍLev 3:16; 2Ch 29:35 ʰEx 13:2,12; Dt 15:19 ⁱHeb 11:4 **4:6** ʲJnh 4:4 **4:7** ᵏGe 44:16; Nu 32:23; Isa 59:12
ˡJob 11:15; 22:27; Ps 27:3; 46:2; S Ro 6:14 **4:8** ᵐMt 23:35; Lk 11:51; 1Jn 3:12; Jude 1:11 **4:9** ⁿS Ge 3:9

ᵐ 15 Or *seed* ⁿ 15 Or *strike* ᵒ 20,1 Or *The man* ᵖ 20 *Eve* probably means *living.* ᑫ 24 Or *placed in front* ʳ 1 *Cain* sounds like the Hebrew for *brought forth* or *acquired.* ˢ 1 Or *have acquired* ᵗ 8 Samaritan Pentateuch, Septuagint, Vulgate and Syriac; Masoretic Text does not have "Let's go out to the field."

(Rev 12:9) would be crushed by the seed of the woman, a descendant of Adam. The line of the Redeemer would eventually run from Adam through Seth, Noah, Shem and Abraham and on through the genealogy of the first chapter of Matthew concluding with Jesus (see 6:8–10; 11:10–32; 12:1–5; Mt 1:2–16).

NOTE: The seven additional covenants include the Edenic (Ge 2:15–17), Noahic (9:8ff), Abrahamic (15:4ff; 17:1–22), Mosaic (Ex 19:5), Palestinian (Dt 30:1–10), Davidic (2Sa 7:16) and New (Heb 8:8–12). See the article on p. 8.

3:21 Because of Adam and Eve's awareness of their nakedness, God introduced death into the world by providing the "garments of skin" of animals to clothe them and cover their shame. God's sacrifice of an innocent animal to restore Adam and Eve's fellowship with him prefigures the ultimate sacrifice of Jesus Christ, who died on the cross to cover the shame of our sins and restore us to fellowship with God.

"I don't know," he replied. "Am I my brother's keeper?"

¹⁰The LORD said, "What have you done? Listen! Your brother's blood cries out to me from the ground. ¹¹Now you are under a curse and driven from the ground, which opened its mouth to receive your brother's blood from your hand. ¹²When you work the ground, it will no longer yield its crops for you. You will be a restless wanderer on the earth."

¹³Cain said to the LORD, "My punishment is more than I can bear. ¹⁴Today you are driving me from the land, and I will be hidden from your presence; I will be a restless wanderer on the earth, and whoever finds me will kill me."

¹⁵But the LORD said to him, "Not so; if anyone kills Cain, he will suffer vengeance seven times over." Then the LORD put a mark on Cain so that no one who found him would kill him. ¹⁶So Cain went out from the LORD's presence and lived in the land of Nod, east of Eden.

¹⁷Cain lay with his wife, and she became pregnant and gave birth to Enoch. Cain was then building a city, and he named it after his son Enoch. ¹⁸To Enoch was born Irad, and Irad was the father of Mehujael, and Mehujael was the father of Methushael, and Methushael was the father of Lamech.

¹⁹Lamech married two women, one named Adah and the other Zillah. ²⁰Adah gave birth to Jabal; he was the father of those who live in tents and raise livestock. ²¹His brother's name was Jubal; he was the father of all who play the harp and flute. ²²Zillah also had a son, Tubal-Cain, who forged all kinds of tools out of bronze and iron. Tubal-Cain's sister was Naamah.

²³Lamech said to his wives,

"Adah and Zillah, listen to me;
   wives of Lamech, hear my words.
I have killed a man for wounding
   me,
   a young man for injuring me.
²⁴If Cain is avenged seven times,
   then Lamech seventy-seven times."

²⁵Adam lay with his wife again, and she gave birth to a son and named him Seth, saying, "God has granted me another child in place of Abel, since Cain killed him." ²⁶Seth also had a son, and he named him Enosh.

At that time men began to call on the name of the LORD.

From Adam to Noah

5 This is the written account of Adam's line.

When God created man, he made him in the likeness of God. ²He created them male and female and blessed them. And when they were created, he called them "man."

³When Adam had lived 130 years, he had a son in his own likeness, in his own image; and he named him Seth. ⁴After Seth was born, Adam lived 800 years and had other sons and daughters. ⁵Altogether, Adam lived 930 years, and then he died.

⁶When Seth had lived 105 years, he became the father of Enosh. ⁷And after he became the father of Enosh, Seth lived 807 years and had other sons and daughters. ⁸Altogether, Seth lived 912 years, and then he died.

⁹When Enosh had lived 90 years, he became the father of Kenan. ¹⁰And after he became the father of Kenan, Enosh lived 815 years and had other sons and daughters. ¹¹Altogether, Enosh lived 905 years, and then he died.

¹²When Kenan had lived 70 years, he became the father of Mahalalel. ¹³And after he became the father of Mahalalel, Kenan lived 840 years and had other sons and daughters. ¹⁴Altogether, Kenan lived 910 years, and then he died.

¹⁵When Mahalalel had lived 65 years, he became the father of Jared. ¹⁶And after he became the father of Jared, Mahalalel lived 830 years and had other sons and daughters. ¹⁷Altogether, Mahalalel lived 895 years, and then he died.

¹⁸When Jared had lived 162 years, he became the father of Enoch. ¹⁹And after he became the father of Enoch, Jared lived 800 years and had other sons and daughters. ²⁰Altogether, Jared lived 962 years, and then he died.

²¹When Enoch had lived 65 years, he

became the father of Methuselah.ᵍ ²²And after he became the father of Methuselah, Enoch walked with Godʰ 300 years and had other sons and daughters. ²³Altogether, Enoch lived 365 years. ²⁴Enoch walked with God;ⁱ then he was no more, because God took him away.ʲ

²⁵When Methuselah had lived 187 years, he became the father of Lamech.ᵏ ²⁶And after he became the father of Lamech, Methuselah lived 782 years and had other sons and daughters. ²⁷Altogether, Methuselah lived 969 years, and then he died.

²⁸When Lamech had lived 182 years, he had a son. ²⁹He named him Noahᶜˡ and said, "He will comfort us in the labor and painful toil of our hands caused by the ground the LORD has cursed."ᵐ ³⁰After Noah was born, Lamech lived 595 years and had other sons and daughters. ³¹Altogether, Lamech lived 777 years, and then he died.

³²After Noah was 500 years old,ⁿ he became the father of Shem,ᵒ Ham and Japheth.ᵖ

The Flood

6 When men began to increase in number on the earthᵠ and daughters were born to them, ²the sons of Godʳ saw that the daughters of menˢ were beautiful,ᵗ and they marriedᵘ any of them they chose. ³Then the LORD said, "My Spirit will not contend withᵈ man forever,ʷ for he is mortalᵉ;ˣ his days will be a hundred and twenty years."

⁴The Nephilimʸ were on the earth in those days—and also afterward—when the sons of God went to the daughters of menᶻ and had children by them. They were the heroes of old, men of renown.ᵃ

⁵The LORD saw how great man's wickedness on the earth had become,ᵇ and that every inclination of the thoughts of his heart was only evil all the time.ᶜ ⁶The LORD was grievedᵈ that he had made man on the earth, and his heart was filled with pain. ⁷So the LORD said, "I will wipe mankind, whom I have created, from the face of the earthᵉ—men and animals, and creatures that move along the ground, and birds of the air—for I am grieved that I have made them.'" ⁸But Noahᵍ found favor in the eyes of the LORD.ʰ

⁹This is the accountⁱ of Noah.

Noah was a righteous man, blamelessʲ among the people of his time,ᵏ and he walked with God.ˡ ¹⁰Noah had three sons: Shem,ᵐ Ham and Japheth.ⁿ

¹¹Now the earth was corruptᵒ in God's sight and was full of violence.ᵖ ¹²God saw how corruptᵠ the earth had become, for

J ▶ Ge 6:17   C ▶ Ne 9:30   Q ▶ Jdg 16:20
N ▶ Lev 26:21

C Ge 3:3 ◀▶ Ge 6:12   E ▶ Nu 32:23
C Ge 6:5 ◀▶ Ge 8:21

5:21 ᵍ1Ch 1:3; Lk 3:37
5:22 ʰver 24; Ge 6:9; 17:1; 24:40; 48:15; 2Ki 20:3; Ps 116:9; Mic 6:8; Mal 2:6
5:24 ⁱS ver 22
ʲ2Ki 2:1,11; Ps 49:15; 73:24; 89:48; Heb 11:5
5:25 ᵏ1Ch 1:3; Lk 3:36
5:29 ˡ1Ch 1:3; Lk 3:36
ᵐS Ge 3:17; Ro 8:20
5:32 ⁿGe 7:6,11; 8:13 ᵒLk 3:36
ᵖGe 6:10; 9:18; 10:1; 1Ch 1:4; Isa 65:20
6:1 ᵠS Ge 1:28
6:2 ʳJob 1:6 fn; 2:1 fn ˢver 4
ᵗDt 21:11
ᵘS Ge 4:19
6:3 ᵛJob 34:14; Gal 5:16-17
ʷIsa 57:16; 1Pe 3:20
ˣJob 10:9;
Ps 78:39; 103:14; Isa 40:6
6:4 ʸNu 13:33
ᶻver 2 ᵃGe 11:4
6:5 ᵇGe 38:7; Job 34:26; Jer 1:16; 44:5; Eze 3:19
ᶜGe 8:21; Ps 14:1-3
6:6 ᵈEx 32:14; 1Sa 15:11,35; 2Sa 24:16;
1Ch 21:15; Isa 63:10; Jer 18:7-10; Eph 4:30
6:7 ᵉEze 33:28; Zep 1:2,18 ᶠver 17; Ge 7:4,21;
Dt 28:63; 29:20
6:8 ᵍEx 14:14 ʰGe 19:19; 39:4; Ex 33:12,13,17; 34:9; Nu 11:15; Ru 2:2; Lk 1:30; Ac 7:46

6:9 ⁱS Ge 2:4 ʲGe 17:1; Dt 18:13; 2Sa 22:24; Job 1:1; 4:6; 9:21; 12:4; 31:6; Ps 15:2; 18:23; 19:13; 37:37; Pr 2:7 ᵏGe 7:1; Ps 37:39; Jer 15:1; Eze 14:14,20; Da 10:11; S Lk 1:6; Heb 11:7; 2Pe 2:5 ˡS Ge 5:22
6:10 ᵐLk 3:36 ⁿS Ge 5:32 6:11 ᵒDt 31:29; Jdg 2:19 ᵖPs 7:9; 73:6;
Eze 7:23; 8:17; 28:16; Mal 2:16 6:12 ᵠEx 32:7; Dt 4:16; 9:12,24

ᶜ29 *Noah* sounds like the Hebrew for *comfort.* ᵈ3 Or *My spirit will not remain in* ᵉ3 Or *corrupt*

6:2 The phrase "sons of God" has been interpreted to mean either angels or human beings. Some use references in Job and Jude to apply this phrase to angels, suggesting that angels had sexual relations with human women (see Job 1:6; 2:1; 38:7; Jude 6). While ancient mythologies maintain that intermarriage between angels and human beings took place, Jesus' words refute the idea of angelic marriage (see Mt 22:30; Mk 12:25).

Other scholars believe that these "sons of God" were human beings. They may have been rulers who flaunted their power by having large harems. Others view this phrase figuratively and suggest that these "sons of God" were godly men descended from Seth who married sinful women descended from Cain, thus weakening the influence of the godly and allowing an increase in moral depravity.

6:3 As a result of this intermarriage God pronounced a judgment on humanity. Yet God offered a delay in his judgment for "a hundred and twenty years" giving people time to repent. During this delay, Noah preached repentance to his neighbors (see 1Pe 3:20; 2Pe 2:5), but to no avail.

6:4 The *Nephilim* or "giants" were probably people of great influence. In humanity's eyes they were "heroes of old, men of renown" but in God's eyes they were sinners ripe for judgment. The term *Nephilim* also occurs in Nu 13:33.

6:9 Noah was "a righteous man, blameless among the people of his time." Since no one is sinless, this statement about Noah refers to his lifetime example of love and obedience to God in powerful contrast to the wicked lives of his contemporaries. Apparently Noah's was the last remaining family to follow the path of righteousness.

all the people on earth had corrupted their ways.ᵗ ¹³So God said to Noah, "I am going to put an end to all people, for the earth is filled with violence because of them. I am surely going to destroyˢ both them and the earth.ᵗ ¹⁴So make yourself an ark of cypressᶠ wood;ᵘ make rooms in it and coat it with pitchᵛ inside and out. ¹⁵This is how you are to build it: The ark is to be 450 feet long, 75 feet wide and 45 feet high.ᵍ ¹⁶Make a roof for it and finishʰ the ark to within 18 inchesⁱ of the top. Put a door in the side of the ark and make lower, middle and upper decks. ¹⁷I am going to bring floodwatersʷ on the earth to destroy all life under the heavens, every creature that has the breath of life in it. Everything on earth will perish.ˣ ¹⁸But I will establish my covenant with you,ʸ and you will enter the arkᶻ— you and your sons and your wife and your sons' wives with you. ¹⁹You are to bring into the ark two of all living creatures, male and female, to keep them alive with you.ᵃ ²⁰Twoᵇ of every kind of bird, of every kind of animalᶜ and of every kindᵈ of creature that moves along the ground will come to you to be kept alive.ᵈ ²¹You are to take every kind of food that is to be eaten and store it away as food for you and for them."

²²Noah did everything just as God commanded him.ᵉ

7 The LORD then said to Noah, "Go into the ark, you and your whole family,ᶠ because I have found you righteousᵍ in this generation. ²Take with you sevenʲ of every kind of cleanʰ animal, a male and its mate, and two of every kind of un-

clean animal, a male and its mate, ³and also seven of every kind of bird, male and female, to keep their various kinds aliveⁱ throughout the earth. ⁴Seven days from now I will send rainʲ on the earthᵏ for forty daysˡ and forty nights,ᵐ and I will wipe from the face of the earth every living creature I have made.ⁿ"

⁵And Noah did all that the LORD commanded him.ᵒ

⁶Noah was six hundred years oldᵖ when the floodwaters came on the earth. ⁷And Noah and his sons and his wife and his sons' wives entered the arkᵠ to escape the waters of the flood. ⁸Pairs of clean and uncleanʳ animals, of birds and of all creatures that move along the ground, ⁹male and female, came to Noah and entered the ark, as God had commanded Noah.ˢ ¹⁰And after the seven daysᵗ the floodwaters came on the earth.

¹¹In the six hundredth year of Noah's life,ᵘ on the seventeenth day of the second month—on that day all the springs of the great deepʷ burst forth, and the floodgates of the heavensˣ were opened. ¹²And rain fell on the earth forty days and forty nights.ʸ

¹³On that very day Noah and his sons,ᶻ Shem, Ham and Japheth, together with his wife and the wives of his three sons, entered the ark.ᵃ ¹⁴They had with them every wild animal according to its kind, all livestock according to their kinds, ev-

---

6:12 ʳPs 14:1-3
6:13 ˢDt 28:63; 2Ki 8:19; Ezr 9:14; Jer 44:11 ᵗver 17; Ge 7:4,21-23; Job 34:15; Isa 5:6; 24:1-3; Jer 44:27; Eze 7:2-3
6:14 ᵘHeb 11:7; 1Pe 3:20 ᵛEx 2:3
6:17 ʷPs 29:10 ˣS ver 7,S 13; 2Pe 2:5
6:18 ʸGe 9:9-16; 17:7; 19:12; Ex 6:4; 34:10,27; Dt 29:13, 14-15; Ps 25:10; 74:20; 106:45; Isa 55:3; Jer 32:40; Eze 16:60; Hag 2:5; 1Pe 3:20 ᶻGe 7:1,7, 13
6:19 ᵃGe 7:15
6:20 ᵇGe 7:15 ᶜS Ge 1:11 ᵈGe 7:3
6:22 ᵉGe 7:5,9,16; Ex 7:6; 39:43; 40:16,19,21,23,25, 27,29,32
7:1 ᶠS Ge 6:18; Mt 24:38; Lk 17:26-27; Heb 11:7; 1Pe 3:20; 2Pe 2:5 ᵍGe 6:9; Eze 14:14
7:2 ʰver 8; Ge 8:20; Lev 10:10; 11:1-47; Dt 14:3-20; Eze 44:23; Hag 2:12; Ac 10:14-15
7:3 ⁱGe 6:20
7:4 ʲGe 8:2 ᵏ1Ki 13:34; Jer 28:16 ˡNu 13:25; Dt 9:9; 1Sa 17:16; 1Ki 19:8 ᵐver 12,17; Ex 24:18; 32:1; 34:28; Dt 9:9,11, 18,25; 10:10; Job 37:6,13; Mt 4:2 ⁿS Ge 6:7,13
7:5 ᵒS Ge 6:22
7:6 ᵖS Ge 5:32
7:7 ᵠS Ge 6:18
7:8 ʳS ver 2
7:9 ˢS Ge 6:22
7:10 ᵗS ver 4
7:11 ᵘS Ge 5:32 ᵛGe 8:4,14 ʷS Ge 1:7;

Job 28:11; Ps 36:6; 42:7; Pr 8:24; Isa 51:10; Eze 26:19 ˣGe 8:2; 2Ki 7:2; Ps 78:23; Isa 24:18; Mal 3:10 **7:12** ʸS ver 4; S 1Sa 12:17; S Job 28:26 **7:13** ᶻGe 8:16; 1Pe 3:20; 2Pe 2:5 ᵃS Ge 6:18

ᶠ14 The meaning of the Hebrew for this word is uncertain. ᵍ15 Hebrew *300 cubits long, 50 cubits wide and 30 cubits high* (about 140 meters long, 23 meters wide and 13.5 meters high) ʰ16 Or *Make an opening for light by finishing* ⁱ16 Hebrew *a cubit* (about 0.5 meter) ʲ2 Or *seven pairs*; also in verse 3

J Ge 6:2–4 ◀▶ Ge 11:6–8
S Ge 2:17 ◀▶ Ge 19:26

6:14 God commanded Noah to build a boat that measured 450 feet long, 75 feet wide and 45 feet high. Comparable in size to a modern ocean liner, the ark was 1.5 times the length of a football field with a height equal to a four-story building. Within this ark Noah was to stock sufficient food for a one-year journey for his family and for all of the animals God would send to him. Though most species require less food in a confined area than if they were living in the wild, this was still an enormous amount of cargo. Since there are approximately 18,000 known species of animals on earth today, it is quite possible that Noah and his family might have had to care for 40,000 animals on the ark.

6:17 God prophesied that the coming flood would destroy "all life under the heavens, every creature that has the breath of life in it. Everything on earth." Yet, in the very next verse, God promises a new covenant with Noah and his descendants. Out of universal death God would bring new life and rebuild the earth.

6:19 The Lord commanded that at least one pair of each species be preserved to restock the earth after the waters receded.

7:2 God further commanded Noah to gather seven of each of the ten species of clean animals (seventy clean animals) that were acceptable for sacrifice and for food (see 8:20; 9:3; Dt 14:1–8).

ery creature that moves along the ground according to its kind and every bird according to its kind,[b] everything with wings. [15]Pairs of all creatures that have the breath of life in them came to Noah and entered the ark.[c] [16]The animals going in were male and female of every living thing, as God had commanded Noah.[d] Then the LORD shut him in.

[17]For forty days[e] the flood kept coming on the earth, and as the waters increased they lifted the ark high above the earth. [18]The waters rose and increased greatly on the earth, and the ark floated on the surface of the water. [19]They rose greatly on the earth, and all the high mountains under the entire heavens were covered.[f] [20]The waters rose and covered the mountains to a depth of more than twenty feet.[k,l,g] [21]Every living thing that moved on the earth perished—birds, livestock, wild animals, all the creatures that swarm over the earth, and all mankind.[h] [22]Everything on dry land that had the breath of life[i] in its nostrils died. [23]Every living thing on the face of the earth was wiped out; men and animals and the creatures that move along the ground and the birds of the air were wiped from the earth.[j] Only Noah was left, and those with him in the ark.[k]

[24]The waters flooded the earth for a hundred and fifty days.[l]

8 But God remembered[m] Noah and all the wild animals and the livestock that were with him in the ark, and he sent a wind over the earth,[n] and the waters receded. [2]Now the springs of the deep and the floodgates of the heavens[o] had been closed, and the rain[p] had stopped falling from the sky. [3]The water receded steadily from the earth. At the end of the hundred and fifty days[q] the water had gone down, [4]and on the seventeenth day of the seventh month[r] the ark came to rest on the mountains[s] of Ararat.[t] [5]The waters continued to recede until the tenth month, and on the first day of the tenth month the tops of the mountains became visible.

[6]After forty days[u] Noah opened the window he had made in the ark [7]and sent out a raven,[v] and it kept flying back and forth until the water had dried up from the earth.[w] [8]Then he sent out a dove[x] to see if the water had receded from the surface of the ground. [9]But the dove could find no place to set its feet because there was water over all the surface of the earth; so it returned to Noah in the ark. He reached out his hand and took the dove and brought it back to himself in the ark. [10]He waited seven more days and again sent out the dove from the ark. [11]When the dove returned to him in the evening, there in its beak was a freshly plucked olive leaf! Then Noah knew that the water had receded from the earth.[y] [12]He waited seven more days and sent the dove out again, but this time it did not return to him.

[13]By the first day of the first month of Noah's six hundred and first year,[z] the water had dried up from the earth. Noah then removed the covering from the ark and saw that the surface of the ground was dry. [14]By the twenty-seventh day of the second month[a] the earth was completely dry.

[15]Then God said to Noah, [16]"Come out A

A Ge 3:15 ◀ ▶ Ge 9:1–3

k 20 Hebrew *fifteen cubits* (about 6.9 meters) *l 20* Or *rose more than twenty feet, and the mountains were covered*

7:24 The 150 days mentioned in this verse are, in round numbers, equivalent to five months. This lengthy time period parallels the five months when the locusts will afflict sinners during the future tribulation (see Rev 9:5).

8:4 Due to its considerable size and weight, the ark rested on the mountain almost immediately after the water started to recede. Though the exact location of Ararat is uncertain, the mountain range is most probably in modern Armenia.

8:15 *Dispensation of Human Government.* After the destruction of the earth in the flood it was necessary for God to establish a new dispensation with the eight people who survived on the ark. This third dispensation instituted a new standard of conduct for Noah and his descendants that involved the creation of various laws to govern humanity and organize society. In addition to the internal workings of conscience, God established new external laws of civil government and rule, ways to punish wrongdoers and the means to worship God completely and correctly. By acting in submission to one another and to these laws, people would forge a corporate relationship with each other and live in obedience to God. Though people have failed in obedience to this dispensation, humanity's responsibility to obey government will continue until Christ sets up his heavenly kingdom.

of the ark, you and your wife and your sons and their wives.ᵇ ¹⁷Bring out every kind of living creature that is with you— the birds, the animals, and all the creatures that move along the ground—so they can multiply on the earth and be fruitful and increase in number upon it."ᶜ

¹⁸So Noah came out, together with his sons and his wife and his sons' wives.ᵈ ¹⁹All the animals and all the creatures that move along the ground and all the birds—everything that moves on the earth—came out of the ark, one kind after another.

²⁰Then Noah built an altar to the LORDᵉ and, taking some of all the clean animals and cleanᶠ birds, he sacrificed burnt offeringsᵍ on it. ²¹The LORD smelled the pleasing aromaʰ and said in his heart: "Never again will I curse the groundⁱ because of man, even thoughᵐ every inclination of his heart is evil from childhood.ʲ And never again will I destroyᵏ all living creatures,ˡ as I have done.

²²"As long as the earth endures,
seedtime and harvest,ᵐ
cold and heat,
summer and winter,ⁿ
day and night
will never cease."ᵒ

c Ge 6:12 ◄ ► Dt 9:6

8:16 ᵇ S Ge 7:13
8:17 ᶜ S Ge 1:22
8:18 ᵈ 1Pe 3:20; 2Pe 2:5
8:20 ᵉ Ge 12:7-8; 13:18; 22:9; 26:25; 33:20; 35:7; Ex 17:15; 24:4
ᶠ S Ge 7:8 ᵍ Ge 22:2, 13; Ex 10:25; 20:24; 40:29; Lev 1:3; 4:29; 6:8-13; Nu 6:11; Jdg 6:26; 11:31; 1Sa 20:29; Job 1:5; 42:8
8:21 ʰ Ex 29:18, 25; Lev 1:9,13; 2:9; 4:31; Nu 15:3,7; 2Co 2:15
ⁱ S Ge 3:17 ʲ Ge 6:5; Ps 51:5; Jer 17:9; Mt 15:19; Ro 1:21
ᵏ Jer 44:11
ˡ Ge 9:11,15; Isa 54:9
8:22 ᵐ Jos 3:15; Ps 67:6; Jer 5:24
ⁿ Ps 74:17; Zec 14:8
ᵒ S Ge 1:14
9:1 ᵖ S Ge 1:22
9:2 ᵠ S Ge 1:26
9:3 ʳ S Ge 1:29
ˢ S Ac 10:15; Col 2:16
9:4 ᵗ Lev 3:17; 7:26; 17:10-14; 19:26; Dt 12:16, 23-25; 15:2_3; 1Sa 14:33; Eze 33:25; Ac 15:20,29
9:5 ᵘ Ge 42:22; 50:15; 1Ki 2:32; 2Ch 24:22; Ps 9:12
ᵛ Ex 21:28-32
ʷ Ge 4:10
9:6 ˣ S Ge 4:14; S Jdg 9:24; S Mt 26:52
ʸ S Ge 1:26
9:7 ᶻ S Ge 1:22

God's Covenant With Noah

9 Then God blessed Noah and his sons, saying to them, "Be fruitful and increase in number and fill the earth.ᵖ ²The fear and dread of you will fall upon all the beasts of the earth and all the birds of the air, upon every creature that moves along the ground, and upon all the fish of the sea; they are given into your hands.ᵠ ³Everything that lives and moves will be food for you.ʳ Just as I gave you the green plants, I now give you everything.ˢ

⁴"But you must not eat meat that has its lifeblood still in it.ᵗ ⁵And for your lifeblood I will surely demand an accounting.ᵘ I will demand an accounting from every animal.ᵛ And from each man, too, I will demand an accounting for the life of his fellow man.ʷ

⁶"Whoever sheds the blood of man,
by man shall his blood be shed;ˣ
for in the image of Godʸ
has God made man.

⁷As for you, be fruitful and increase in number; multiply on the earth and increase upon it."ᶻ

⁸Then God said to Noah and to his sons with him: ⁹"I now establish my covenant

A Ge 8:15 ◄ ► Ge 9:7–10
A Ge 9:1–3 ◄ ► Ge 9:11–17

ᵐ 21 Or man, for

The seven dispensations revealed in Scripture are the dispensations of innocence (Ge 1:28), conscience (3:7), human government (8:15), promise (12:1), law (Ex 19:1), the church (Ac 2:1) and the kingdom (Rev 20:4). For further information on the dispensations, see the article on p. 4.

9:8–16 *Noahic Covenant.* This covenant was made between God, Noah, Noah's descendants and all other living creatures on the earth (9:9–10). The Noahic covenant consisted of the following elements:
1. God promised that he would never destroy the earth and "all living creatures" (8:21) with a flood again (9:11–16).
2. God reconfirmed the normal order of the earth and its seasons (see 8:22).
3. God reconfirmed his instructions to humanity to repopulate the earth (see 9:1).
4. God instilled a fear of humans in animals (see 9:2).
5. People were allowed to eat animals for food (see 9:3–4). Apparently humans were vegetarians in the garden and before the flood (see 1:29; 9:3). The only restriction to this allowance was the prohibition against eating "meat that has its lifeblood still in it" (9:4).
6. God instituted basic civil government, including capital punishment for murder and people's accountability to protect human life (see 9:5–6). The NT also confirms God's role in the establishment of government and rulers (see Ro 13:1–5).
7. The covenant was unconditional and perpetual (9:12).
8. The covenant was sealed with the sign of the rainbow (9:13).

NOTE: The seven additional covenants include the Edenic (Ge 2:15–17), Adamic (3:15–19), Abrahamic (15:4ff; 17:1–22), Mosaic (Ex 19:5), Palestinian (Dt 30:1–10), Davidic (2Sa 7:16) and New (Heb 8:8–12). See the article on p. 8.

with you^a and with your descendants after you ¹⁰and with every living creature that was with you—the birds, the livestock and all the wild animals, all those that came out of the ark with you—every living creature on earth. ¹¹I establish my covenant^b with you:^c Never again will all life be cut off by the waters of a flood; never again will there be a flood to destroy the earth.^d"

¹²And God said, "This is the sign of the covenant^e I am making between me and you and every living creature with you, a covenant for all generations to come:^f ¹³I have set my rainbow^g in the clouds, and it will be the sign of the covenant between me and the earth. ¹⁴Whenever I bring clouds over the earth and the rainbow^h appears in the clouds, ¹⁵I will remember my covenantⁱ between me and you and all living creatures of every kind. Never again will the waters become a flood to destroy all life.^j ¹⁶Whenever the rainbow^k appears in the clouds, I will see it and remember the everlasting covenant^l between God and all living creatures of every kind on the earth."

¹⁷So God said to Noah, "This is the sign of the covenant^m I have established between me and all life on the earth."

The Sons of Noah

¹⁸The sons of Noah who came out of the ark were Shem, Ham and Japheth.ⁿ (Ham was the father of Canaan.)^o ¹⁹These were the three sons of Noah,^p and from them came the people who were scattered over the earth.^q

²⁰Noah, a man of the soil, proceededⁿ to plant a vineyard. ²¹When he drank some of its wine,^r he became drunk and lay uncovered inside his tent. ²²Ham, the father of Canaan, saw his father's nakedness^s and told his two brothers outside.

²³But Shem and Japheth took a garment and laid it across their shoulders; then they walked in backward and covered their father's nakedness. Their faces were turned the other way so that they would not see their father's nakedness.

²⁴When Noah awoke from his wine and found out what his youngest son had done to him, ²⁵he said,

"Cursed^t be Canaan!^u
  The lowest of slaves
  will he be to his brothers.^v"

²⁶He also said,

"Blessed be the LORD, the God of
  Shem!^w
May Canaan be the slave^x of Shem.^o
²⁷May God extend the territory of
  Japheth^p;^y
may Japheth live in the tents of
  Shem,^z
and may Canaan be his^q slave."

²⁸After the flood Noah lived 350 years. ²⁹Altogether, Noah lived 950 years, and then he died.^a

The Table of Nations

10 This is the account^b of Shem, Ham and Japheth,^c Noah's sons,^d who themselves had sons after the flood.

The Japhethites

10:2–5pp — 1Ch 1:5–7

²The sons^r of Japheth:
  Gomer,^e Magog,^f Madai, Javan,^g
  Tubal,^h Meshechⁱ and Tiras.
³The sons of Gomer:
  Ashkenaz,^j Riphath and Togarmah.^k
⁴The sons of Javan:

---

n 20 Or soil, was the first o 26 Or be his slave p 27 Japheth sounds like the Hebrew for extend. q 27 Or their r 2 Sons may mean descendants or successors or nations; also in verses 3, 4, 6, 7, 20-23, 29 and 31.

9:25–27 God made some direct promises to Noah's sons. Canaan and his descendants, who were Ham's offspring, would be servants of their brothers because of Ham's disrespectful actions toward his father (9:25–26). Historically, even before the Israelites occupied the promised land, the Canaanites were subject and inferior to the larger powers of Egypt and Assyria thus fulfilling this curse on Ham's (Canaan's) descendants.

On the other hand, Shem and Japheth's respect for their father would be rewarded. Blessings would be accorded to Shem. The Messianic line that began with Seth, Enoch and Noah before the flood would now run from Shem through Abraham and on to Jesus Christ (see 11:10–27; Mt 1:2–16). Japheth would also share in these blessings and would have his territories enlarged (9:27). It is noteworthy that the descendants of Japheth include the Medes and the Greeks, an obvious fulfillment of this prophecy as well.

Elishah, Tarshish, the Kittim and the Rodanim. 5(From these the maritime peoples spread out into their territories by their clans within their nations, each with its own language.)

The Hamites
10:6–20pp — 1Ch 1:8–16

6The sons of Ham:
Cush, Mizraim, Put and Canaan.
7The sons of Cush:
Seba, Havilah, Sabtah, Raamah and Sabteca.
The sons of Raamah:
Sheba and Dedan.

8Cush was the father of Nimrod, who grew to be a mighty warrior on the earth. 9He was a mighty hunter before the LORD; that is why it is said, "Like Nimrod, a mighty hunter before the LORD." 10The first centers of his kingdom were Babylon, Erech, Akkad and Calneh, in Shinar. 11From that land he went to Assyria, where he built Nineveh, Rehoboth Ir, Calah 12and Resen, which is between Nineveh and Calah; that is the great city.

13Mizraim was the father of
the Ludites, Anamites, Lehabites, Naphtuhites, 14Pathrusites, Casluhites (from whom the Philistines came) and Caphtorites.
15Canaan was the father of
Sidon his firstborn, and of the

s 4 Some manuscripts of the Masoretic Text and Samaritan Pentateuch (see also Septuagint and 1 Chron. 1:7); most manuscripts of the Masoretic Text *Dodanim* *t 6* That is, Egypt; also in verse 13 *u 8 Father* may mean *ancestor* or *predecessor* or *founder*; also in verses 13, 15, 24 and 26. *v 10* Or *Erech and Akkad—all of them in* *w 10* That is, Babylonia *x 11* Or *Nineveh with its city squares* *y 15* Or *of the Sidonians, the foremost*

Nations Descended from Noah's Sons
Ge 10:1

Hittites,¹ ¹⁶Jebusites,ᵐ Amorites,ⁿ Girgashites,ᵒ ¹⁷Hivites,ᵖ Arkites, Sinites, ¹⁸Arvadites,ᑫ Zemarites and Hamathites.ʳ

Later the Canaaniteˢ clans scattered ¹⁹and the borders of Canaanᵗ reached from Sidonᵘ toward Gerarᵛ as far as Gaza,ʷ and then toward Sodom, Gomorrah, Admah and Zeboiim,ˣ as far as Lasha.

²⁰These are the sons of Ham by their clans and languages, in their territories and nations.

The Semites

10:21–31pp — Ge 11:10–27; 1Ch 1:17–27

²¹Sons were also born to Shem, whose older brother wasᶻ Japheth; Shem was the ancestor of all the sons of Eber.ʸ

²²The sons of Shem:
Elam,ᶻ Asshur,ᵃ Arphaxad,ᵇ Lud and Aram.ᶜ

²³The sons of Aram:
Uz,ᵈ Hul, Gether and Meshech.ᵃ

²⁴Arphaxad was the father ofᵇ Shelah, and Shelah the father of Eber.ᵉ

²⁵Two sons were born to Eber:
One was named Peleg,ᶜ because in his time the earth was divided; his brother was named Joktan.

²⁶Joktan was the father of
Almodad, Sheleph, Hazarmaveth, Jerah, ²⁷Hadoram, Uzal,ᶠ Diklah, ²⁸Obal, Abimael, Sheba,ᵍ ²⁹Ophir,ʰ Havilah and Jobab. All these were sons of Joktan.

³⁰The region where they lived stretched from Mesha toward Sephar, in the eastern hill country.

³¹These are the sons of Shem by their clans and languages, in their territories and nations.

³²These are the clans of Noah's sons,ⁱ according to their lines of descent, within their nations. From these the nations spread out over the earthʲ after the flood.

The Tower of Babel

11 Now the whole world had one languageᵏ and a common speech. ²As men moved eastward,ᵈ they found a plain in Shinarᵉˡ and settled there.

³They said to each other, "Come, let's make bricksᵐ and bake them thoroughly." They used brick instead of stone,ⁿ and tarᵒ for mortar. ⁴Then they said, "Come, let us build ourselves a city, with a tower that reaches to the heavens,ᵖ so that we may make a nameᑫ for ourselves and not be scatteredʳ over the face of the whole earth."ˢ

⁵But the LORD came downᵗ to see the city and the tower that the men were building. ⁶The LORD said, "If as one people speaking the same languageᵘ they have begun to do this, then nothing they plan to do will be impossible for them. ⁷Come, let usᵛ go downʷ and confuse their language so they will not understand each other."ˣ

⁸So the LORD scattered them from there over all the earth,ʸ and they stopped building the city. ⁹That is why it was called Babelʲᶻ—because there the LORD confused the languageᵃ of the whole world.ᵇ From there the LORD scatteredᶜ them over the face of the whole earth.

From Shem to Abram

11:10–27pp — Ge 10:21–31; 1Ch 1:17–27

¹⁰This is the accountᵈ of Shem.

Two years after the flood, when Shem was 100 years old, he became the fatherᵍ of Arphaxad.ᵉ ¹¹And after he became the father of Arphaxad, Shem lived 500 years and had other sons and daughters.

¹²When Arphaxad had lived 35 years, he became the father of Shelah.ᶠ ¹³And after he became the father of Shelah, Arphaxad lived 403 years and had other sons and daughters.ʰ

¹⁴When Shelah had lived 30 years, he became the father of Eber.ᵍ ¹⁵And after he became the father of Eber, Shelah lived 403 years and had other sons and daughters.

ʲ Ge 6:17 ◀▶ Ge 40:12–13

ᶻ 21 Or Shem, the older brother of ᵃ 23 See Septuagint and 1 Chron. 1:17; Hebrew Mash ᵇ 24 Hebrew; Septuagint father of Cainan, and Cainan was the father of ᶜ 25 Peleg means division. ᵈ 2 Or from the east; or in the east ᵉ 2 That is, Babylonia ᶠ 9 That is, Babylon; Babel sounds like the Hebrew for confused. ᵍ 10 Father may mean ancestor; also in verses 11-25. ʰ 12,13 Hebrew; Septuagint (see also Luke 3:35, 36 and note at Gen. 10:24) 35 years, he became the father of Cainan. ¹³And after he became the father of Cainan, Arphaxad lived 430 years and had other sons and daughters, and then he died. When Cainan had lived 130 years, he became the father of Shelah. And after he became the father of Shelah, Cainan lived 330 years and had other sons and daughters

¹⁶When Eber had lived 34 years, he became the father of Peleg. ¹⁷And after he became the father of Peleg, Eber lived 430 years and had other sons and daughters.

¹⁸When Peleg had lived 30 years, he became the father of Reu. ¹⁹And after he became the father of Reu, Peleg lived 209 years and had other sons and daughters.

²⁰When Reu had lived 32 years, he became the father of Serug. ²¹And after he became the father of Serug, Reu lived 207 years and had other sons and daughters.

²²When Serug had lived 30 years, he became the father of Nahor. ²³And after he became the father of Nahor, Serug lived 200 years and had other sons and daughters.

²⁴When Nahor had lived 29 years, he became the father of Terah. ²⁵And after he became the father of Terah, Nahor lived 119 years and had other sons and daughters.

²⁶After Terah had lived 70 years, he became the father of Abram, Nahor and Haran.

²⁷This is the account of Terah.

Terah became the father of Abram, Nahor and Haran. And Haran became the father of Lot. ²⁸While his father Terah was still alive, Haran died in Ur of the Chaldeans, in the land of his birth. ²⁹Abram and Nahor both married. The name of Abram's wife was Sarai, and the name of Nahor's wife was Milcah; she was the daughter of Haran, the father of both Milcah and Iscah. ³⁰Now Sarai was barren; she had no children.

³¹Terah took his son Abram, his grandson Lot son of Haran, and his daughter-in-law Sarai, the wife of his son Abram, and together they set out from Ur of the Chaldeans to go to Canaan. But when they came to Haran, they settled there.

³²Terah lived 205 years, and he died in Haran.

The Call of Abram

12 The LORD had said to Abram, "Leave your country, your people and your father's household and go to the land I will show you.

² "I will make you into a great nation
 and I will bless you;
I will make your name great,
 and you will be a blessing.
³ I will bless those who bless you,
 and whoever curses you I will curse;
and all peoples on earth
 will be blessed through you."

⁴So Abram left, as the LORD had told him; and Lot went with him. Abram was seventy-five years old when he set out from Haran. ⁵He took his wife Sarai, his nephew Lot, all the possessions they had accumulated and the people they had acquired in Haran, and they set out for the land of Canaan, and they arrived there.

⁶Abram traveled through the land as far as the site of the great tree of Moreh at Shechem. At that time the Canaan-

A Ge 9:24–27 ◀▶ Ge 12:7
U ▶ Ge 22:15–18

12:1 *Dispensation of Promise.* In this time period God designated Abram and his descendants as the people who would be used in the fulfillment of God's plan of salvation. The dispensation of promise tested Abram and his descendants in their faithfulness and obedience to God. God unconditionally promised that individual obedience would be rewarded with individual blessing (see 12:2; 15:15; 22:18; 26:2–5); the promised land would be their eternal inheritance (see 17:7–8); they would be a great nation (see 12:2); and those nations and individuals who blessed Abram and his offspring would receive a blessing in return (see 12:3). This latter promise has seen fulfillment in the rise and fall of many empires. Anti-Semitism has brought many individuals and nations under God's curse.

The seven dispensations revealed in Scripture are the dispensations of innocence (Ge 1:28), conscience (3:7), human government (8:15), promise (12:1), law (Ex 19:1), the church (Ac 2:1) and the kingdom (Rev 20:4). For further information on the dispensations, see the article on p. 4.

ites^v were in the land. ⁷The LORD appeared to Abram^w and said, "To your offspring^i I will give this land."^x"^y So he built an altar there to the LORD,^z who had appeared to him.

⁸From there he went on toward the hills east of Bethel^a and pitched his tent,^b with Bethel on the west and Ai^c on the east. There he built an altar to the LORD and called on the name of the LORD.^d ⁹Then Abram set out and continued toward the Negev.^e

Abram in Egypt
12:10–20Ref — Ge 20:1–18; 26:1–11

¹⁰Now there was a famine in the land,^f and Abram went down to Egypt to live there for a while because the famine was severe.^g ¹¹As he was about to enter Egypt, he said to his wife Sarai,^h "I know what a beautiful woman^i you are. ¹²When the Egyptians see you, they will say, 'This is his wife.' Then they will kill me but will let you live. ¹³Say you are my sister,^j so that I will be treated well for your sake and my life will be spared because of you."

¹⁴When Abram came to Egypt, the Egyptians saw that she was a very beautiful woman.^k ¹⁵And when Pharaoh's officials saw her, they praised her to Pharaoh, and she was taken into his palace. ¹⁶He treated Abram well for her sake, and Abram acquired sheep and cattle, male

A Ge 12:1–3 ◄ ► Ge 13:14–16

12:6 ^v S Ge 10:18
12:7 ^w Ge 17:1; 18:1; 26:2; 35:1; Ex 6:3; Ac 7:2
^x Ex 3:8; Nu 10:29; Dt 30:5; Heb 11:8
^y Ge 13:15,17; 15:18; 17:8; 23:18; 24:7; 26:3-4; 28:13; 35:12; 48:4; 50:24; Ex 6:4,8; 13:5,11; 32:13; 33:1; Nu 11:12; Dt 1:8; 2:31; 9:5; 11:9; 34:4; 2Ki 25:21; 1Ch 16:16; 2Ch 20:7; Ps 105:9-11; Jer 25:5; Eze 47:14; Ac 7:5; Ro 4:13; Gal 3:16*
^z S Ge 8:20; 13:4
12:8 ^a Ge 13:3; 28:11,19; 35:1,8, 15; Jos 7:2; 8:9; 1Sa 7:16; 1Ki 12:29; Hos 12:4; Am 3:14; 4:4 ^b Ge 26:25; 33:19; Heb 11:9
^c Jos 7:2; 12:9; Ezr 2:28; Ne 7:32;

Jer 49:3 ^d S Ge 4:26; S 8:20 12:9 ^e Ge 13:1,3; 20:1; 24:62; Nu 13:17; 33:40; Dt 34:3; Jos 10:40 12:10 ^f Ge 41:27,57; 42:5; 43:1; 47:4,13; Ru 1:1; 2Sa 21:1; 2Ki 8:1; Ps 105:19 ^g Ge 41:30,54,56; 47:20; Ps 105:16
12:11 ^h S Ge 11:29 ^i ver 14; Ge 24:16; 26:7; 29:17; 39:6
12:13 ^j Ge 20:2; 26:7 12:14 ^k S ver 11

^i 7 Or seed

12:7 This verse records a theophany—a visible manifestation of God's presence to someone. Whether in angelic or human form, the Lord frequently appeared to Abram and others, but not in all his glory (see Ex 33:18–20; Jn 1:18). We will not be given that opportunity until Christ's second coming (see 1Jn 3:2).

Extent of Land Promised to Abraham
Ge 13:14–17; 15:18–21

and female donkeys, menservants and maidservants, and camels.¹

D ¹⁷But the LORD inflicted serious diseases on Pharaoh and his household because of Abram's wife Sarai. ¹⁸So Pharaoh summoned Abram. "What have you done to me?" he said. "Why didn't you tell me she was your wife? ¹⁹Why did you say, 'She is my sister,' so that I took her to be my wife? Now then, here is your wife. Take her and go!" ²⁰Then Pharaoh gave orders about Abram to his men, and they sent him on his way, with his wife and everything he had.

Abram and Lot Separate

13 So Abram went up from Egypt to the Negev, with his wife and everything he had, and Lot went with him. ²Abram had become very wealthy in livestock and in silver and gold.

³From the Negev he went from place to place until he came to Bethel, to the place between Bethel and Ai where his tent had been earlier ⁴and where he had first built an altar. There Abram called on the name of the LORD.

⁵Now Lot, who was moving about with Abram, also had flocks and herds and tents. ⁶But the land could not support them while they stayed together, for their possessions were so great that they were not able to stay together. ⁷And quarreling arose between Abram's herdsmen and the herdsmen of Lot. The Canaanites and Perizzites were also living in the land at that time.

⁸So Abram said to Lot, "Let's not have any quarreling between you and me, or between your herdsmen and mine, for we are brothers. ⁹Is not the whole land before you? Let's part company. If you go to the left, I'll go to the right; if you go to the right, I'll go to the left."

¹⁰Lot looked up and saw that the whole plain of the Jordan was well watered, like the garden of the LORD, like the land of Egypt, toward Zoar. (This was before

D ▶ *Ge 19:11*

the LORD destroyed Sodom and Gomorrah.) ¹¹So Lot chose for himself the whole plain of the Jordan and set out toward the east. The two men parted company: ¹²Abram lived in the land of Canaan, while Lot lived among the cities of the plain and pitched his tents near Sodom. ¹³Now the men of Sodom were wicked and were sinning greatly against the LORD.

¹⁴The LORD said to Abram after Lot had **A** parted from him, "Lift up your eyes from where you are and look north and south, east and west. ¹⁵All the land that you see **I** I will give to you and your offspring forever. ¹⁶I will make your offspring like the dust of the earth, so that if anyone could count the dust, then your offspring could be counted. ¹⁷Go, walk through the length and breadth of the land, for I am giving it to you."

¹⁸So Abram moved his tents and went to live near the great trees of Mamre at Hebron, where he built an altar to the LORD.

Abram Rescues Lot

14 At this time Amraphel king of Shinar, Arioch king of Ellasar, Kedorlaomer king of Elam and Tidal king of Goiim ²went to war against Bera king of Sodom, Birsha king of Gomorrah, Shinab king of Admah, Shemeber king of Zeboiim, and the king of Bela (that is, Zoar). ³All these latter kings joined forces in the Valley of Siddim (the Salt Sea). ⁴For twelve years they had been subject to Kedorlaomer, but in the thirteenth year they rebelled.

A *Ge 12:7* ◀ ▶ *Ge 14:18–20*
I ▶ *Ge 17:7–8*

13:14–16 In this passage God promised Abram that his descendants would possess Canaan forever. God's promise cannot be broken. Despite three major dispersions and exiles of the Jews from the promised land, God has always brought his people back to the land—and he always will (see 28:15; Ex 6:8; Jer 24:6; Eze 34:13; Am 9:14–15). In addition, the Lord promised that Abram would have "offspring like the dust of the earth" (13:16) meaning Abram's descendants would be beyond numbering. This prophecy will not be completely fulfilled until the Messianic kingdom of Christ.

⁵In the fourteenth year, Kedorlaomer and the kings allied with him went out and defeated the Rephaites in Ashteroth Karnaim, the Zuzites in Ham, the Emites in Shaveh Kiriathaim ⁶and the Horites in the hill country of Seir, as far as El Paran near the desert. ⁷Then they turned back and went to En Mishpat (that is, Kadesh), and they conquered the whole territory of the Amalekites, as well as the Amorites who were living in Hazazon Tamar.

⁸Then the king of Sodom, the king of Gomorrah, the king of Admah, the king of Zeboiim and the king of Bela (that is, Zoar) marched out and drew up their battle lines in the Valley of Siddim ⁹against Kedorlaomer king of Elam, Tidal king of Goiim, Amraphel king of Shinar and Arioch king of Ellasar—four kings against five. ¹⁰Now the Valley of Siddim was full of tar pits, and when the kings of Sodom and Gomorrah fled, some of the men fell into them and the rest fled to the hills. ¹¹The four kings seized all the goods of Sodom and Gomorrah and all their food; then they went away. ¹²They also carried off Abram's nephew Lot and his possessions, since he was living in Sodom.

¹³One who had escaped came and reported this to Abram the Hebrew. Now Abram was living near the great trees of Mamre the Amorite, a brother of Eshcol and Aner, all of whom were allied with Abram. ¹⁴When Abram heard that his relative had been taken captive, he called out the 318 trained men born in his household and went in pursuit as far as Dan. ¹⁵During the night Abram divided his men to attack them and he routed them, pursuing them as far as Hobah, north of Damascus. ¹⁶He recovered all the goods and brought back his relative Lot and his possessions, together with the women and the other people.

¹⁷After Abram returned from defeating Kedorlaomer and the kings allied with him, the king of Sodom came out to meet him in the Valley of Shaveh (that is, the King's Valley).

¹⁸Then Melchizedek king of Salem brought out bread and wine. He was priest of God Most High, ¹⁹and he blessed Abram, saying,

"Blessed be Abram by God Most High,
    Creator of heaven and earth.
²⁰And blessed be God Most High,
    who delivered your enemies into your hand."

Then Abram gave him a tenth of everything.

²¹The king of Sodom said to Abram, "Give me the people and keep the goods for yourself."

²²But Abram said to the king of Sodom, "I have raised my hand to the LORD, God Most High, Creator of heaven and earth, and have taken an oath ²³that I will accept nothing belonging to you, not even a thread or the thong of a sandal, so that you will never be able to say, 'I made Abram rich.' ²⁴I will accept nothing but what my men have eaten and the share that belongs to the men who went with me—to Aner, Eshcol and Mamre. Let them have their share."

A Ge 13:14–16 ◄► Ge 15:4–5

m 13 Or a relative; or an ally n 18 That is, Jerusalem o 19 Or Possessor; also in verse 22 p 20 Or And praise be to

---

14:18 This verse introduces us to Melchizedek, the king of Salem, a shortened form of "Jerusalem" (see Ps 76:2). Evidently the residents of this city worshiped "God Most High" under the leadership of this king-priest. Because of his double role in leadership, Melchizedek has been described as a type of Christ. (A "type" is an OT event, person, teaching or symbol that foreshadows something to come in the NT.) The psalmist referred to the Messiah as "a priest forever, in the order of Melchizedek" (Ps 110:4) while the writer of the book of Hebrews draws a parallel between Melchizedek's kingly priesthood and Christ's eternal high priesthood (see Heb 5:5–6; 6:20; 7:1ff).

God's Covenant With Abram

15 After this, the word of the LORD came to Abram in a vision:

"Do not be afraid, Abram.
I am your shield,
your very great reward."

²But Abram said, "O Sovereign LORD, what can you give me since I remain childless and the one who will inherit my estate is Eliezer of Damascus?" ³And Abram said, "You have given me no children; so a servant in my household will be my heir."

⁴Then the word of the LORD came to him: "This man will not be your heir, but a son coming from your own body will be your heir." ⁵He took him outside and said, "Look up at the heavens and count the stars—if indeed you can count them." Then he said to him, "So shall your offspring be."

⁶Abram believed the LORD, and he credited it to him as righteousness.

⁷He also said to him, "I am the LORD, who brought you out of Ur of the Chaldeans to give you this land to take possession of it."

⁸But Abram said, "O Sovereign LORD, how can I know that I will gain possession of it?"

⁹So the LORD said to him, "Bring me a heifer, a goat and a ram, each three years old, along with a dove and a young pigeon." ¹⁰Abram brought all these to him, cut them in two and arranged the halves opposite each other; the birds, however, he did not cut in half. ¹¹Then birds of prey came down on the carcasses, but Abram drove them away.

¹²As the sun was setting, Abram fell into a deep sleep, and a thick and dreadful darkness came over him. ¹³Then the LORD said to him, "Know for certain that your descendants will be strangers in a country not their own, and they will be enslaved and mistreated four hundred years. ¹⁴But I will punish the nation they serve as slaves, and afterward they will come out with great possessions. ¹⁵You, however, will go to your fathers in peace and be buried at a good old age. ¹⁶In the fourth generation your descendants will come back here, for the sin of the Amorites has not yet reached its full measure."

15:4 *Abrahamic Covenant.* The Abrahamic covenant is closely allied to the dispensation of promise because of the similarity of their conditions. This covenant revealed God's sovereign plan to bless the world through the seed of Abraham:
1. God promised to make Abram a great nation with innumerable offspring (see 12:2; 13:16; 15:5; 17:6). Ultimately, all who belong to Christ are Abram's offspring too (see Gal 3:29).
2. God promised to personally bless Abram both spiritually and materially (see 15:6, 18; 24:34–35).
3. Abram would receive honor and be a blessing to others (see 12:2; Ro 4:1–22). This promise foreshadows the coming of Christ and the blessing of eternal life made available to all who believe on him.
4. This covenant was unconditional and its ultimate fulfillment rested on God's promise and power rather than on Israel's faithfulness.
5. The sign of this covenant was circumcision (see 17:1–21).

NOTE: The seven additional covenants include the Edenic (Ge 2:15–17), Adamic (3:15–19), Noahic (9:8ff), Mosaic (Ex 19:5), Palestinian (Dt 30:1–10), Davidic (2Sa 7:16) and New (Heb 8:8–12).

15:5 God declared to Abram that his descendants would be as numerous as the stars of the heavens. More than 8,000 stars are visible on a clear night in Israel, and we know that there are literally thousands of galaxies containing millions of stars each. Clearly this promise to Abram will not be completely fulfilled until Christ's kingdom comes, though it was initially fulfilled in Egypt (see Ex 1:7; Dt 1:10; Heb 11:13).

15:13–16 In this prophetic passage, the Lord predicts the slavery of the Israelites in Egypt while at the same time promising their deliverance and return to the promised land.

¹⁷When the sun had set and darkness had fallen, a smoking firepot with a blazing torch appeared and passed between the pieces. ¹⁸On that day the LORD made a covenant with Abram and said, "To your descendants I give this land, from the river of Egypt to the great river, the Euphrates— ¹⁹the land of the Kenites, Kenizzites, Kadmonites, ²⁰Hittites, Perizzites, Rephaites, ²¹Amorites, Canaanites, Girgashites and Jebusites."

Hagar and Ishmael

16 Now Sarai, Abram's wife, had borne him no children. But she had an Egyptian maidservant named Hagar; ²so she said to Abram, "The LORD has kept me from having children. Go, sleep with my maidservant; perhaps I can build a family through her."

Abram agreed to what Sarai said. ³So after Abram had been living in Canaan ten years, Sarai his wife took her Egyptian maidservant Hagar and gave her to her husband to be his wife. ⁴He slept with Hagar, and she conceived.

When she knew she was pregnant, she began to despise her mistress. ⁵Then Sarai said to Abram, "You are responsible for the wrong I am suffering. I put my servant in your arms, and now that she knows she is pregnant, she despises me. May the LORD judge between you and me."

⁶"Your servant is in your hands," Abram said. "Do with her whatever you think best." Then Sarai mistreated Hagar; so she fled from her.

⁷The angel of the LORD found Hagar near a spring in the desert; it was the spring that is beside the road to Shur. ⁸And he said, "Hagar, servant of Sarai, where have you come from, and where are you going?"

"I'm running away from my mistress Sarai," she answered.

⁹Then the angel of the LORD told her, "Go back to your mistress and submit to her." ¹⁰The angel added, "I will so increase your descendants that they will be too numerous to count."

¹¹The angel of the LORD also said to her:

"You are now with child
  and you will have a son.
You shall name him Ishmael,
  for the LORD has heard of your
    misery.
¹²He will be a wild donkey of a man;

15:18–21 Ten Canaanite tribes occupied the land God promised to Abram in this passage. The Israelites only ruled all of this land briefly under the reigns of Solomon and Jeroboam II (see 1Ki 8:65; 2Ki 14:25). Even now, portions of the promised land remain outside Israeli control. Several prophecies in Scripture indicate that Israel will be exiled from the land but will ultimately regain possession of it (see Ge 15:13–16; Dt 28:62–65; 30:1–3). Twice before in history the Israelites have been exiled to foreign lands, but each time they have returned to the promised land as prophesied. The land will be completely theirs again when Christ returns (see Dt 30:3; Jer 23:5–8; Eze 37:21–25; Acts 15:14–17).

16:10 God promised Hagar that he would give her innumerable descendants. This promise was reaffirmed in 17:20, and initially fulfilled in 25:13–16. Today more than 200 million descendants of Ishmael live in the Arab countries surrounding Israel.

16:11 As a result of a lack of faith, Abram entered into a relationship with his wife's servant Hagar, attempting to produce a child to fulfill God's promise. Ishmael was the son born from this relationship. Because of hostility between Abram's wife and Hagar, Ishmael and his mother were forced to leave Abram's camp. Yet God took care of Hagar and Ishmael, as he had promised, and Ishmael fathered twelve sons—the ancestors of modern-day Arabs. The hostility between Ishmael's family and Abram's family continues today in both the political and spiritual arenas. Tragically, many Arabs refuse to follow the teachings of Jesus because he is a descendant of Abraham and choose instead to follow the teachings of Mohammed, a descendant of Ishmael and the founder of Islam.

16:12 The Lord described the future of Ishmael's race as being unceasingly in conflict with others and that Ishmael's enemies would be unable to drive them from the land. The history of Ishmael's descendants, the Arabs, clearly shows the fulfillment of this divine prediction. Even the British historian Edward

his hand will be against everyone and everyone's hand against him, and he will live in hostility toward all his brothers."

¹³She gave this name to the LORD who spoke to her: "You are the God who sees me," for she said, "I have now seen the One who sees me." ¹⁴That is why the well was called Beer Lahai Roi; it is still there, between Kadesh and Bered.

¹⁵So Hagar bore Abram a son, and Abram gave the name Ishmael to the son she had borne. ¹⁶Abram was eighty-six years old when Hagar bore him Ishmael.

The Covenant of Circumcision

17 When Abram was ninety-nine years old, the LORD appeared to him and said, "I am God Almighty; walk before me and be blameless. ²I will confirm my covenant between me and you and will greatly increase your numbers."

³Abram fell facedown, and God said to him, ⁴"As for me, this is my covenant with you: You will be the father of many nations. ⁵No longer will you be called Abram; your name will be Abraham, for I have made you a father of many nations. ⁶I will make you very fruitful; I will make nations of you, and kings will come from you. ⁷I will establish my covenant as an everlasting covenant between me and you and your descendants after you for the generations to come, to be your God and the God of your descendants after you. ⁸The whole land of Canaan, where you are now an alien, I will give as an everlasting possession to you and your descendants after you; and I will be their God."

⁹Then God said to Abraham, "As for you, you must keep my covenant, you and your descendants after you for the generations to come. ¹⁰This is my covenant with you and your descendants after you, the covenant you are to keep: Every male among you shall be circumcised. ¹¹You are to undergo circumcision, and it will be the sign of the covenant between me and you. ¹²For the generations to come every male among you who is eight days old must be circumcised, including those born in your household or bought with money from a foreigner—those who are not your offspring. ¹³Whether born in your household or bought with your money, they must be circumcised. My covenant in your flesh is to be an everlasting covenant. ¹⁴Any uncircumcised male, who has not been circumcised in the flesh, will be cut off from his people; he has broken my covenant."

¹⁵God also said to Abraham, "As for Sarai your wife, you are no longer to call her Sarai; her name will be Sarah. ¹⁶I will bless her and will surely give you a son by her. I will bless her so that she will be the mother of nations; kings of peoples will come from her."

¹⁷Abraham fell facedown; he laughed and said to himself, "Will a son be born to a man a hundred years old? Will Sarah bear a child at the age of ninety?" ¹⁸And Abraham said to God, "If only Ishmael might live under your blessing!"

¹⁹Then God said, "Yes, but your wife

Gibbon declared in *The Decline and Fall of the Roman Empire*: "The arms of Sesostris and Cyrus, of Pompey and Trajan could never achieve the conquest of Arabia."

17:10 The Lord established circumcision as his appointed sign or token of his eternal covenant with Abraham (see 15:4). This act signified Abraham's commitment that the Lord alone would be his God; that he would trust in only God's Word (see Ro 4:11–12); and that he would consecrate himself, his offspring and all he possessed to the Lord's service and mercy. Though other nations practiced circumcision (see Jer 9:25–26; Eze 32:18–19) only Israel observed this practice as a covenantal sign of consecration.

17:19–20 In this passage God reconfirmed his

Sarah will bear you a son,ⁿ and you will call him Isaac.ᵇᵒ I will establish my covenant with himᵖ as an everlasting covenantᑫ for his descendants after him. ²⁰And as for Ishmael, I have heard you: I will surely bless him; I will make him fruitful and will greatly increase his numbers.ʳ He will be the father of twelve rulers,ˢ and I will make him into a great nation.ᵗ ²¹But my covenantᵘ I will establish with Isaac, whom Sarah will bear to youᵛ by this time next year.ʷ ²²When he had finished speaking with Abraham, God went up from him.ˣ

²³On that very day Abraham took his son Ishmael and all those born in his householdʸ or bought with his money, every male in his household, and circumcised them, as God told him.ᶻ ²⁴Abraham was ninety-nine years oldᵃ when he was circumcised,ᵇ ²⁵and his son Ishmaelᶜ was thirteen; ²⁶Abraham and his son Ishmael were both circumcised on that same day. ²⁷And every male in Abraham's householdᵈ, including those born in his household or bought from a foreigner, was circumcised with him.

The Three Visitors

18 The LORD appeared to Abrahamᵉ near the great trees of Mamreᶠ while he was sitting at the entrance to his tentᵍ in the heat of the day. ²Abraham looked upʰ and saw three menⁱ standing nearby. When he saw them, he hurried from the entrance of his tent to meet them and bowed low to the ground.ʲ

³He said, "If I have found favor in your eyes,ᵏ my lord,ᶜ do not pass your servantˡ by. ⁴Let a little water be brought, and then you may all wash your feetᵐ and rest under this tree. ⁵Let me get you something to eat,ⁿ so you can be refreshed and then go on your way—now that you have come to your servant."

"Very well," they answered, "do as you say."

⁶So Abraham hurried into the tent to Sarah. "Quick," he said, "get three seahsᵈ of fine flour and knead it and bake some bread."ᵒ

⁷Then he ran to the herd and selected a choice, tender calfᵖ and gave it to a servant, who hurried to prepare it. ⁸He then brought some curdsᑫ and milkʳ and the calf that had been prepared, and set these before them.ˢ While they ate, he stood near them under a tree.

⁹"Where is your wife Sarah?"ᵗ they asked him.

"There, in the tent,ᵘ" he said.

¹⁰Then the LORDᵉ said, "I will surely return to you about this time next year,ᵛ and Sarah your wife will have a son."ʷ

Now Sarah was listening at the entrance to the tent, which was behind him. ¹¹Abraham and Sarah were already old and well advanced in years,ˣ and Sarah was past the age of childbearing.ʸ ¹²So Sarah laughedᶻ to herself as she thought, "After I am worn out and my masterᶠᵃ is old, will I now have this pleasure?"

¹³Then the LORD said to Abraham, "Why did Sarah laugh and say, 'Will I really have a child, now that I am old?'ᵇ ¹⁴Is anything too hard for the LORD?ᶜ I will return to you at the appointed time next yearᵈ and Sarah will have a son."ᵉ

¹⁵Sarah was afraid, so she lied and said, "I did not laugh."

But he said, "Yes, you did laugh."

Abraham Pleads for Sodom

¹⁶When the menᶠ got up to leave, they looked down toward Sodom, and Abraham walked along with them to see them on their way. ¹⁷Then the LORD said, "Shall I hide from Abrahamᵍ what I am about to do?ʰ ¹⁸Abraham will surely become a great and powerful nation,ⁱ and all nations on earth will be blessed through him. ¹⁹For I have chosen him,ʲ so that he will direct his childrenᵏ and his household after him to keep the way of the LORDˡ by doing what is right and just,ᵐ so that the LORD will bring about for Abraham what he has promised him."ⁿ

E *Ge 17:15–17* ◄► *Ge 20:17*
K *Ge 15:1* ◄► *Ex 12:13*

18:16 ᶠS ver 2 18:17 ᵍAm 3:7 ʰGe 19:24; Job 1:16; Ps 107:34
18:18 ⁱS Ge 12:2; Gal 3:8* 18:19 ʲGe 17:9 ᵏDt 4:9-10; 6:7 ˡJos 24:15; Eph 6:4 ᵐGe 22:12,18; 26:5; 2Sa 8:15; Ps 17:2; 99:4; Jer 23:5 ⁿS Ge 16:11; S Isa 14:1

ᵇ 19 *Isaac* means *he laughs*. ᶜ 3 Or *O Lord* ᵈ 6 That is, probably about 20 quarts (about 22 liters) ᵉ 10 Hebrew *Then he* ᶠ 12 Or *husband*

²⁰Then the LORD said, "The outcry against Sodom and Gomorrah is so great and their sin so grievous ²¹that I will go down and see if what they have done is as bad as the outcry that has reached me. If not, I will know."

²²The men turned away and went toward Sodom, but Abraham remained standing before the LORD. ²³Then Abraham approached him and said: "Will you sweep away the righteous with the wicked? ²⁴What if there are fifty righteous people in the city? Will you really sweep it away and not spare the place for the sake of the fifty righteous people in it? ²⁵Far be it from you to do such a thing—to kill the righteous with the wicked, treating the righteous and the wicked alike. Far be it from you! Will not the Judge of all the earth do right?"

²⁶The LORD said, "If I find fifty righteous people in the city of Sodom, I will spare the whole place for their sake."

²⁷Then Abraham spoke up again: "Now that I have been so bold as to speak to the Lord, though I am nothing but dust and ashes, ²⁸what if the number of the righteous is five less than fifty? Will you destroy the whole city because of five people?"

"If I find forty-five there," he said, "I will not destroy it."

²⁹Once again he spoke to him, "What if only forty are found there?"

He said, "For the sake of forty, I will not do it."

³⁰Then he said, "May the Lord not be angry, but let me speak. What if only thirty can be found there?"

He answered, "I will not do it if I find thirty there."

³¹Abraham said, "Now that I have been so bold as to speak to the Lord, what if only twenty can be found there?"

He said, "For the sake of twenty, I will not destroy it."

³²Then he said, "May the Lord not be angry, but let me speak just once more. What if only ten can be found there?"

He answered, "For the sake of ten, I will not destroy it."

³³When the LORD had finished speaking with Abraham, he left, and Abraham returned home.

Sodom and Gomorrah Destroyed

19 The two angels arrived at Sodom in the evening, and Lot was sitting in the gateway of the city. When he saw them, he got up to meet them and bowed down with his face to the ground. ²"My lords," he said, "please turn aside to your servant's house. You can wash your feet and spend the night and then go on your way early in the morning."

"No," they answered, "we will spend the night in the square."

³But he insisted so strongly that they did go with him and entered his house. He prepared a meal for them, baking bread without yeast, and they ate. ⁴Before they had gone to bed, all the men from every part of the city of Sodom—both young and old—surrounded the house. ⁵They called to Lot, "Where are the men who came to you tonight? Bring them out to us so that we can have sex with them."

⁶Lot went outside to meet them and shut the door behind him ⁷and said, "No, my friends. Don't do this wicked thing. ⁸Look, I have two daughters who have never slept with a man. Let me bring them out to you, and you can do what you like with them. But don't do anything to these men, for they have come under the protection of my roof."

⁹"Get out of our way," they replied. And they said, "This fellow came here as an alien, and now he wants to play the judge! We'll treat you worse than them." They kept bringing pressure on Lot and moved forward to break down the door.

¹⁰But the men inside reached out and pulled Lot back into the house and shut the door. ¹¹Then they struck the men who were at the door of the house, young and old, with blindness so that they could not find the door.

¹²The two men said to Lot, "Do you have anyone else here—sons-in-law, sons or daughters, or anyone else in the city who belongs to you? Get them out of here, ¹³because we are going to destroy this place. The outcry to the LORD

g 22 Masoretic Text; an ancient Hebrew scribal tradition *but the* LORD *remained standing before Abraham* *h 24* Or *forgive;* also in verse 26 *i 25* Or *Ruler*

against its people is so great that he has sent us to destroy it."

¹⁴So Lot went out and spoke to his sons-in-law, who were pledged to marry his daughters. He said, "Hurry and get out of this place, because the LORD is about to destroy the city!" But his sons-in-law thought he was joking.

¹⁵With the coming of dawn, the angels urged Lot, saying, "Hurry! Take your wife and your two daughters who are here, or you will be swept away when the city is punished."

¹⁶When he hesitated, the men grasped his hand and the hands of his wife and of his two daughters and led them safely out of the city, for the LORD was merciful to them. ¹⁷As soon as they had brought them out, one of them said, "Flee for your lives! Don't look back, and don't stop anywhere in the plain! Flee to the mountains or you will be swept away!"

¹⁸But Lot said to them, "No, my lords, please! ¹⁹Your servant has found favor in your eyes, and you have shown great kindness to me in sparing my life. But I can't flee to the mountains; this disaster will overtake me, and I'll die. ²⁰Look, here is a town near enough to run to, and it is small. Let me flee to it—it is very small, isn't it? Then my life will be spared."

²¹He said to him, "Very well, I will grant this request too; I will not overthrow the town you speak of. ²²But flee there quickly, because I cannot do anything until you reach it." (That is why the town was called Zoar.)

²³By the time Lot reached Zoar, the sun had risen over the land. ²⁴Then the LORD rained down burning sulfur on Sodom and Gomorrah—from the LORD out of the heavens. ²⁵Thus he overthrew those cities and the entire plain, including all those living in the cities—and also the vegetation in the land. ²⁶But Lot's wife looked back, and she became a pillar of salt.

²⁷Early the next morning Abraham got up and returned to the place where he had stood before the LORD. ²⁸He looked down toward Sodom and Gomorrah, toward all the land of the plain, and he saw dense smoke rising from the land, like smoke from a furnace.

²⁹So when God destroyed the cities of the plain, he remembered Abraham, and he brought Lot out of the catastrophe that overthrew the cities where Lot had lived.

Lot and His Daughters

³⁰Lot and his two daughters left Zoar and settled in the mountains, for he was afraid to stay in Zoar. He and his two daughters lived in a cave. ³¹One day the older daughter said to the younger, "Our father is old, and there is no man around here to lie with us, as is the custom all over the earth. ³²Let's get our father to drink wine and then lie with him and preserve our family line through our father."

³³That night they got their father to drink wine, and the older daughter went in and lay with him. He was not aware of it when she lay down or when she got up.

³⁴The next day the older daughter said to the younger, "Last night I lay with my father. Let's get him to drink wine again tonight, and you go in and lie with him so we can preserve our family line through our father." ³⁵So they got their father to drink wine that night also, and the younger daughter went and lay with him. Again he was not aware of it when she lay down or when she got up.

³⁶So both of Lot's daughters became pregnant by their father. ³⁷The older

---

19:22–25 The Lord's angels warned Abraham and Lot of the coming judgment on the cities of Sodom and Gomorrah. Lot and his family had to move quickly, choosing whether to obey God's command to flee to safety or disobey, stay and face judgment with the wicked. When Lot chose to obey God, note that God held off his judgment on Sodom and Gomorrah until Lot was safe (19:22). The very presence of godly people within these wicked cities would have prevented God's destruction of them (see 18:23–32). God cares about his people and watches over them to preserve them against indiscriminate judgment (see Eze 9:4; Rev 7:3).

daughter had a son, and she named him Moab[n];[u] he is the father of the Moabites[v] of today. [38]The younger daughter also had a son, and she named him Ben-Ammi[o]; he is the father of the Ammonites[w] of today.

Abraham and Abimelech
20:1–18Ref — Ge 12:10–20; 26:1–11

20 Now Abraham moved on from there[x] into the region of the Negev[y] and lived between Kadesh[z] and Shur.[a] For a while[b] he stayed in Gerar,[c] [2]and there Abraham said of his wife Sarah, "She is my sister.[d]" Then Abimelech[e] king of Gerar sent for Sarah and took her.[f]

[3]But God came to Abimelech[g] in a dream[h] one night and said to him, "You are as good as dead[i] because of the woman you have taken; she is a married woman."[j]

[4]Now Abimelech had not gone near her, so he said, "Lord, will you destroy an innocent nation?[k] [5]Did he not say to me, 'She is my sister,'' and didn't she also say, 'He is my brother'? I have done this with a clear conscience[m] and clean hands."[n]

[6]Then God said to him in the dream, "Yes, I know you did this with a clear conscience, and so I have kept[o] you from sinning against me.[p] That is why I did not let you touch her. [7]Now return the man's wife, for he is a prophet,[q] and he will pray for you[r] and you will live. But if you do not return her, you may be sure that you and all yours will die."[s]

[8]Early the next morning Abimelech summoned all his officials, and when he told them all that had happened, they were very much afraid. [9]Then Abimelech called Abraham in and said, "What have you done to us? How have I wronged you that you have brought such great guilt upon me and my kingdom? You have done things to me that should not be done.[t]" [10]And Abimelech asked Abraham, "What was your reason for doing this?"

[11]Abraham replied, "I said to myself, 'There is surely no fear of God[u] in this place, and they will kill me because of my wife.'[v] [12]Besides, she really is my sister,[w] the daughter of my father though not of my mother; and she became my wife. [13]And when God had me wander[x] from my father's household,[y] I said to her, 'This is how you can show your love to me: Everywhere we go, say of me, "He is my brother." ' "

[14]Then Abimelech[z] brought sheep and cattle and male and female slaves and gave them to Abraham,[a] and he returned Sarah his wife to him. [15]And Abimelech said, "My land is before you; live wherever you like."[b]

[16]To Sarah he said, "I am giving your brother a thousand shekels[p] of silver. This is to cover the offense against you before all who are with you; you are completely vindicated."

[17]Then Abraham prayed to God,[c] and God healed Abimelech, his wife and his slave girls so they could have children again, [18]for the LORD had closed up every womb in Abimelech's household because of Abraham's wife Sarah.[d]

The Birth of Isaac

21 Now the LORD was gracious to Sarah[e] as he had said, and the LORD did for Sarah what he had promised.[f] [2]Sarah became pregnant and bore a son[g] to Abraham in his old age,[h] at the very time God had promised him.[i] [3]Abraham gave the name Isaac[q][j] to the son Sarah bore him. [4]When his son Isaac was eight days old, Abraham circumcised him,[k] as God commanded him. [5]Abraham was a hundred years old[l] when his son Isaac was born to him.

[6]Sarah said, "God has brought me laughter,[m] and everyone who hears about this will laugh with me." [7]And she added, "Who would have said to Abraham that Sarah would nurse children? Yet I have borne him a son in his old age."[n]

Hagar and Ishmael Sent Away

[8]The child grew and was weaned,[o] and on the day Isaac was weaned Abraham held a great feast. [9]But Sarah saw that the son whom Hagar the Egyptian had borne

E Ge 18:12–14 ◀▶ Ge 25:21
D Ge 19:11 ◀▶ Ex 4:6

[n] 37 Moab sounds like the Hebrew for *from father*. [o] 38 Ben-Ammi means *son of my people*. [p] 16 That is, about 25 pounds (about 11.5 kilograms) [q] 3 Isaac means *he laughs*.

to Abraham was mocking, ¹⁰and she said to Abraham, "Get rid of that slave woman and her son, for that slave woman's son will never share in the inheritance with my son Isaac."

¹¹The matter distressed Abraham greatly because it concerned his son. ¹²But God said to him, "Do not be so distressed about the boy and your maidservant. Listen to whatever Sarah tells you, because it is through Isaac that your offspring will be reckoned. ¹³I will make the son of the maidservant into a nation also, because he is your offspring."

¹⁴Early the next morning Abraham took some food and a skin of water and gave them to Hagar. He set them on her shoulders and then sent her off with the boy. She went on her way and wandered in the desert of Beersheba.

¹⁵When the water in the skin was gone, she put the boy under one of the bushes. ¹⁶Then she went off and sat down nearby, about a bowshot away, for she thought, "I cannot watch the boy die." And as she sat there nearby, she began to sob.

¹⁷God heard the boy crying, and the angel of God called to Hagar from heaven and said to her, "What is the matter, Hagar? Do not be afraid; God has heard the boy crying as he lies there. ¹⁸Lift the boy up and take him by the hand, for I will make him into a great nation."

¹⁹Then God opened her eyes and she saw a well of water. So she went and filled the skin with water and gave the boy a drink.

²⁰God was with the boy as he grew up. He lived in the desert and became an archer. ²¹While he was living in the Desert of Paran, his mother got a wife for him from Egypt.

The Treaty at Beersheba

²²At that time Abimelech and Phicol the commander of his forces said to Abraham, "God is with you in everything you do. ²³Now swear to me here before God that you will not deal falsely with me or my children or my descendants. Show to me and the country where you are living as an alien the same kindness I have shown to you."

²⁴Abraham said, "I swear it."

²⁵Then Abraham complained to Abimelech about a well of water that Abimelech's servants had seized. ²⁶But Abimelech said, "I don't know who has done this. You did not tell me, and I heard about it only today."

²⁷So Abraham brought sheep and cattle and gave them to Abimelech, and the two men made a treaty. ²⁸Abraham set apart seven ewe lambs from the flock, ²⁹and Abimelech asked Abraham, "What is the meaning of these seven ewe lambs you have set apart by themselves?"

³⁰He replied, "Accept these seven lambs from my hand as a witness that I dug this well."

³¹So that place was called Beersheba, because the two men swore an oath there.

³²After the treaty had been made at Beersheba, Abimelech and Phicol the commander of his forces returned to the land of the Philistines. ³³Abraham planted a tamarisk tree in Beersheba, and there he called upon the name of the LORD, the Eternal God. ³⁴And Abraham stayed in the land of the Philistines for a long time.

Abraham Tested

22 Some time later God tested Abraham. He said to him, "Abraham!"

"Here I am," he replied.

²Then God said, "Take your son, your only son, Isaac, whom you love, and go to the region of Moriah. Sacrifice him

A Ge 19:22–25 ◀▶ Ge 22:15–18
F ▶ Ge 27:28   A ▶ Ge 24:1

21:18 This prophecy assured Hagar that Ishmael would live and become the great nation that God had promised.

22:2–13 The record of Abraham's obedience to God in offering his son Isaac clearly prefigures the offering of God's own son Jesus to be the ultimate sacrifice for humanity.

there as a burnt offering[h] on one of the mountains I will tell you about.[i]" ³Early the next morning[j] Abraham got up and saddled his donkey. He took with him two of his servants and his son Isaac. When he had cut enough wood for the burnt offering, he set out for the place God had told him about. ⁴On the third day Abraham looked up and saw the place in the distance. ⁵He said to his servants, "Stay here with the donkey while I and the boy go over there. We will worship and then we will come back to you.[k]"

⁶Abraham took the wood for the burnt offering and placed it on his son Isaac,[l] and he himself carried the fire and the knife.[m] As the two of them went on together, ⁷Isaac spoke up and said to his father Abraham, "Father?"

"Yes, my son?" Abraham replied.

"The fire and wood are here," Isaac said, "but where is the lamb[n] for the burnt offering?"

⁸Abraham answered, "God himself will provide[o] the lamb[p] for the burnt offering, my son." And the two of them went on together.

⁹When they reached the place God had told him about,[q] Abraham built an altar[r] there and arranged the wood[s] on it. He bound his son Isaac and laid him on the altar,[t] on top of the wood. ¹⁰Then he reached out his hand and took the knife[u] to slay his son.[v] ¹¹But the angel of the LORD[w] called out to him from heaven,[x] "Abraham! Abraham!"[y]

"Here I am," [z] he replied.

¹²"Do not lay a hand on the boy," he said. "Do not do anything to him. Now I know that you fear God,[a] because you have not withheld from me your son, your only son.[b]"

¹³Abraham looked up and there in a thicket he saw a ram[u] caught by its horns.[c] He went over and took the ram and sacrificed it as a burnt offering instead of his son.[d] ¹⁴So Abraham called[e] that place The LORD[f] Will Provide. And to this day it is said, "On the mountain of the LORD it will be provided.[g]"

¹⁵The angel of the LORD[h] called to Abraham from heaven[i] a second time ¹⁶and said, "I swear by myself,[j] declares the LORD, that because you have done this and have not withheld your son, your only son,[k] ¹⁷I will surely bless you[l] and make your descendants[m] as numerous as the stars in the sky[n] and as the sand on the seashore.[o] Your descendants will take possession of the cities of their enemies,[p] ¹⁸and through your offspring[v] all nations on earth will be blessed,[q] because you have obeyed me."[r]

¹⁹Then Abraham returned to his servants, and they set off together for Beersheba.[s] And Abraham stayed in Beersheba.

Nahor's Sons

²⁰Some time later Abraham was told, "Milcah is also a mother; she has borne sons to your brother Nahor:[t] ²¹Uz[u] the firstborn, Buz[v] his brother, Kemuel (the father of Aram), ²²Kesed, Hazo, Pildash, Jidlaph and Bethuel.[w]" ²³Bethuel became the father of Rebekah.[x] Milcah bore these eight sons to Abraham's brother Nahor.[y] ²⁴His concubine,[z] whose name was Reumah, also had sons: Tebah, Gaham, Tahash and Maacah.

The Death of Sarah

23 Sarah lived to be a hundred and twenty-seven years old. ²She died at Kiriath Arba[a] (that is, Hebron)[b] in the land of Canaan, and Abraham went to mourn for Sarah and to weep over her.[c] ³Then Abraham rose from beside his dead wife and spoke to the Hittites.[w][d] He said, ⁴"I am an alien and a stranger[e] among you. Sell me some property for a burial site here so I can bury my dead.'"

⁵The Hittites replied to Abraham, ⁶"Sir, listen to us. You are a mighty prince^g among us. Bury your dead in the choicest of our tombs. None of us will refuse you his tomb for burying your dead."

⁷Then Abraham rose and bowed down before the people of the land, the Hittites. ⁸He said to them, "If you are willing to let me bury my dead, then listen to me and intercede with Ephron son of Zohar^h on my behalf ⁹so he will sell me the cave of Machpelah,^i which belongs to him and is at the end of his field. Ask him to sell it to me for the full price as a burial site among you."

¹⁰Ephron the Hittite was sitting among his people and he replied to Abraham in the hearing of all the Hittites^j who had come to the gate^k of his city. ¹¹"No, my lord," he said. "Listen to me; I give^l you the field, and I give^x you the cave that is in it. I give^x it to you in the presence of my people. Bury your dead."

¹²Again Abraham bowed down before the people of the land ¹³and he said to Ephron in their hearing, "Listen to me, if you will. I will pay the price of the field. Accept it from me so I can bury my dead there."

¹⁴Ephron answered Abraham, ¹⁵"Listen to me, my lord; the land is worth four hundred shekels^y of silver,^m but what is that between me and you? Bury your dead."

¹⁶Abraham agreed to Ephron's terms and weighed out for him the price he had named in the hearing of the Hittites: four hundred shekels of silver,^n according to the weight current among the merchants.^o

¹⁷So Ephron's field in Machpelah^p near Mamre^q—both the field and the cave in it, and all the trees within the borders of the field—was deeded ¹⁸to Abraham as his property^r in the presence of all the Hittites^s who had come to the gate^t of the city. ¹⁹Afterward Abraham buried his wife Sarah in the cave in the field of Machpelah^u near Mamre (which is at Hebron^v) in the land of Canaan.^w ²⁰So the field and the cave in it were deeded^x to Abraham by the Hittites as a burial site.^y

Isaac and Rebekah

24 Abraham was now old and well advanced in years,^z and the LORD had blessed^a him in every way.^b ²He said to the chief^z servant^c in his household, the one in charge of all that he had,^d "Put your hand under my thigh.^e ³I want you to swear^f by the LORD, the God of heaven^g and the God of earth,^h that you will not get a wife for my son^i from the daughters of the Canaanites,^j among whom I am living,^k ⁴but will go to my country and my own relatives^l and get a wife for my son Isaac.^m"

⁵The servant asked him, "What if the woman is unwilling to come back with me to this land?^n Shall I then take your son back to the country you came from?^o"

⁶"Make sure that you do not take my son back there,"^p Abraham said. ⁷"The LORD, the God of heaven,^q who brought me out of my father's household and my native land^r and who spoke to me and promised me on oath, saying, 'To your offspring^a I will give this land'^t—he will send his angel before you^u so that you can get a wife for my son from there. ⁸If the woman is unwilling to come back with you, then you will be released from this oath^v of mine. Only do not take my son back there."^w ⁹So the servant put his hand under the thigh^x of his master^y Abraham and swore an oath to him concerning this matter.

¹⁰Then the servant took ten of his master's camels^z and left, taking with him all kinds of good things^a from his master. He set out for Aram Naharaim^bb and made his way to the town of Nahor.^c ¹¹He had the camels kneel down near the well^d outside the town; it was toward evening, the time the women go out to draw water.^e

¹²Then he prayed, "O LORD, God of my master Abraham,^f give me success^g today, and show kindness^h to my master Abraham. ¹³See, I am standing beside this spring, and the daughters of the towns-

---

A *Ge 21:22* ◀▶ *Ge 48:16*
P *Ge 15:14* ◀▶ *Ge 24:35*
U *Ge 22:15–18* ◀▶ *Ge 24:35*

h S Ge 19:19; Jos 2:12; Job 10:12

x 11 Or *sell*   y 15 That is, about 10 pounds (about 4.5 kilograms)
z 2 Or *oldest*   a 7 Or *seed*   b 10 That is, Northwest Mesopotamia

people are coming out to draw water.ⁱ ¹⁴May it be that when I say to a girl, 'Please let down your jar that I may have a drink,' and she says, 'Drink,ʲ and I'll water your camels too'ᵏ—let her be the one you have chosen for your servant Isaac.ˡ By this I will knowᵐ that you have shown kindness to my master."

¹⁵Before he had finished praying,ⁿ Rebekahᵒ came out with her jar on her shoulder. She was the daughter of Bethuelᵖ son of Milcah,ᑫ who was the wife of Abraham's brother Nahor.ʳ ¹⁶The girl was very beautiful,ˢ a virgin;ᵗ no man had ever lain with her. She went down to the spring, filled her jar and came up again.

¹⁷The servant hurried to meet her and said, "Please give me a little water from your jar."ᵘ

¹⁸"Drink,ᵛ my lord," she said, and quickly lowered the jar to her hands and gave him a drink.

¹⁹After she had given him a drink, she said, "I'll draw water for your camelsʷ too,ˣ until they have finished drinking." ²⁰So she quickly emptied her jar into the trough, ran back to the well to draw more water, and drew enough for all his camels.ʸ ²¹Without saying a word, the man watched her closely to learn whether or not the LORD had made his journey successful.ᶻ

²²When the camels had finished drinking, the man took out a gold nose ringᵃ weighing a bekaᶜ and two gold braceletsᵇ weighing ten shekels.ᵈ ²³Then he asked, "Whose daughter are you?ᶜ Please tell me, is there room in your father's house for us to spend the night?ᵈ

²⁴She answered him, "I am the daughter of Bethuel, the son that Milcah bore to Nahor.ᵉ" ²⁵And she added, "We have plenty of straw and fodder,ᶠ as well as room for you to spend the night."

²⁶Then the man bowed down and worshiped the LORD,ᵍ ²⁷saying, "Praise be to the LORD,ʰ the God of my master Abraham,ⁱ who has not abandoned his kindness and faithfulnessʲ to my master. As for me, the LORD has led me on the journeyᵏ to the house of my master's relatives."ˡ

²⁸The girl ran and told her mother's household about these things.ᵐ ²⁹Now Rebekah had a brother named Laban,ⁿ and he hurried out to the man at the spring.

³⁰As soon as he had seen the nose ring, and the bracelets on his sister's arms,ᵒ and had heard Rebekah tell what the man said to her, he went out to the man and found him standing by the camels near the spring. ³¹"Come, you who are blessed by the LORD,"ᵖ he said. "Why are you standing out here? I have prepared the house and a place for the camels."

³²So the man went to the house, and the camels were unloaded. Straw and fodderᑫ were brought for the camels, and water for him and his men to wash their feet.ʳ ³³Then food was set before him, but he said, "I will not eat until I have told you what I have to say."

"Then tell us," ⌊Laban⌋ said.

³⁴So he said, "I am Abraham's servant.ˢ ³⁵The LORD has blessedᵗ my master abundantly,ᵘ and he has become wealthy.ᵛ He has given him sheep and cattle, silver and gold, menservants and maidservants, and camels and donkeys.ʷ ³⁶My master's wife Sarah has borne him a son in herᵉ old age,ˣ and he has given him everything he owns.ʸ ³⁷And my master made me swear an oath,ᶻ and said, 'You must not get a wife for my son from the daughters of the Canaanites, in whose land I live,ᵃ ³⁸but go to my father's family and to my own clan, and get a wife for my son.'ᵇ

³⁹Then I asked my master, 'What if the woman will not come back with me?'ᶜ

⁴⁰"He replied, 'The LORD, before whom I have walked,ᵈ will send his angel with youᵉ and make your journey a success,ᶠ so that you can get a wife for my son from my own clan and from my father's family.ᵍ ⁴¹Then, when you go to my clan, you will be released from my oath even if they refuse to give her to you—you will be released from my oath.'ʰ

⁴²"When I came to the spring today, I said, 'O LORD, God of my master Abraham, if you will, please grant successⁱ to the journey on which I have come. ⁴³See, I am standing beside this spring;ʲ if a maidenᵏ comes out to draw water and I say to her, "Please let me drink a little water from your jar,"ˡ ⁴⁴and if she says to

B ▶ *Ge 26:12* P ▶ *Ge 24:1* ◀▶ *Dt 8:13*
U ▶ *Ge 24:1* ◀▶ *Ge 26:3*

ᶜ 22 That is, about 1/5 ounce (about 5.5 grams) ᵈ 22 That is, about 4 ounces (about 110 grams) ᵉ 36 Or *his*

me, "Drink, and I'll draw water for your camels too," let her be the one the LORD has chosen for my master's son.'ᵐ

⁴⁵"Before I finished praying in my heart,ⁿ Rebekah came out, with her jar on her shoulder.ᵒ She went down to the spring and drew water, and I said to her, 'Please give me a drink.'ᵖ

⁴⁶"She quickly lowered her jar from her shoulder and said, 'Drink, and I'll water your camels too.'ᵠ So I drank, and she watered the camels also.ʳ

⁴⁷"I asked her, 'Whose daughter are you?'ˢ

"She said, 'The daughter of Bethuelᵗ son of Nahor, whom Milcah bore to him.'ᵘ

"Then I put the ring in her noseᵛ and the bracelets on her arms,ʷ ⁴⁸and I bowed down and worshiped the LORD.ˣ I praised the LORD, the God of my master Abraham,ʸ who had led me on the right road to get the granddaughter of my master's brother for his son.ᶻ ⁴⁹Now if you will show kindness and faithfulnessᵃ to my master, tell me; and if not, tell me, so I may know which way to turn."

⁵⁰Laban and Bethuelᵇ answered, "This is from the LORD;ᶜ we can say nothing to you one way or the other.ᵈ ⁵¹Here is Rebekah; take her and go, and let her become the wife of your master's son, as the LORD has directed.ᵉ"

⁵²When Abraham's servant heard what they said, he bowed down to the ground before the LORD.ᶠ ⁵³Then the servant brought out gold and silver jewelry and articles of clothingᵍ and gave them to Rebekah; he also gave costly giftsʰ to her brother and to her mother. ⁵⁴Then he and the men who were with him ate and drank and spent the night there.

When they got up the next morning, he said, "Send me on my wayⁱ to my master."

⁵⁵But her brother and her mother replied, "Let the girl remain with us ten days or so;ʲ then youᶠ may go."

⁵⁶But he said to them, "Do not detain me, now that the LORD has granted successᵏ to my journey. Send me on my wayˡ so I may go to my master."

⁵⁷Then they said, "Let's call the girl and ask her about it."ᵐ ⁵⁸So they called Rebekah and asked her, "Will you go with this man?"

"I will go,"ⁿ she said.

⁵⁹So they sent their sister Rebekah on her way,ᵒ along with her nurseᵖ and Abraham's servant and his men. ⁶⁰And they blessedᵠ Rebekah and said to her,

"Our sister, may you increase
  to thousands upon thousands;ʳ
may your offspring possess
  the gates of their enemies."ˢ

⁶¹Then Rebekah and her maidsᵗ got ready and mounted their camels and went back with the man. So the servant took Rebekah and left.

⁶²Now Isaac had come from Beer Lahai Roi,ᵘ for he was living in the Negev.ᵛ ⁶³He went out to the field one evening to meditate,ᵍʷ and as he looked up,ˣ he saw camels approaching. ⁶⁴Rebekah also looked up and saw Isaac. She got down from her camelʸ ⁶⁵and asked the servant, "Who is that man in the field coming to meet us?"

"He is my master," the servant answered. So she took her veilᶻ and covered herself.

⁶⁶Then the servant told Isaac all he had done. ⁶⁷Isaac brought her into the tentᵃ of his mother Sarah,ᵇ and he married Rebekah.ᶜ So she became his wife, and he loved her;ᵈ and Isaac was comforted after his mother's death.ᵉ

The Death of Abraham
25:1–4pp — 1Ch 1:32–33

25 Abraham tookʰ another wife, whose name was Keturah. ²She bore him Zimran,ᶠ Jokshan, Medan, Midian,ᵍ Ishbak and Shuah.ʰ ³Jokshan was the father of Shebaⁱ and Dedan;ʲ the descendants of Dedan were the Asshurites, the Letushites and the Leummites. ⁴The sons of Midian were Ephah,ᵏ Epher, Hanoch, Abida and Eldaah. All these were descendants of Keturah.

⁵Abraham left everything he owned to Isaac.ˡ ⁶But while he was still living, he gave gifts to the sons of his concubinesᵐ and sent them away from his son Isaacⁿ to the land of the east.ᵒ

⁷Altogether, Abraham lived a hundred and seventy-five years.ᵖ ⁸Then Abraham breathed his last and died at a good old

---

A *Ge 22:15–18* ◀ ▶ *Ge 25:23*
Q *Ge 15:15* ◀ ▶ *Ge 35:29*

f 55 Or she *g 63 The meaning of the Hebrew for this word is uncertain.*
h 1 Or had taken

age, an old man and full of years; and he was gathered to his people. ⁹His sons Isaac and Ishmael buried him in the cave of Machpelah near Mamre, in the field of Ephron son of Zohar the Hittite, ¹⁰the field Abraham had bought from the Hittites. There Abraham was buried with his wife Sarah. ¹¹After Abraham's death, God blessed his son Isaac, who then lived near Beer Lahai Roi.

Ishmael's Sons

25:12-16pp — 1Ch 1:29-31

¹²This is the account of Abraham's son Ishmael, whom Sarah's maidservant, Hagar the Egyptian, bore to Abraham.

¹³These are the names of the sons of Ishmael, listed in the order of their birth: Nebaioth the firstborn of Ishmael, Kedar, Adbeel, Mibsam, ¹⁴Mishma, Dumah, Massa, ¹⁵Hadad, Tema, Jetur, Naphish and Kedemah. ¹⁶These were the sons of Ishmael, and these are the names of the twelve tribal rulers according to their settlements and camps. ¹⁷Altogether, Ishmael lived a hundred and thirty-seven years. He breathed his last and died, and he was gathered to his people. ¹⁸His descendants settled in the area from Havilah to Shur, near the border of Egypt, as you go toward Asshur. And they lived in hostility toward all their brothers.

Jacob and Esau

¹⁹This is the account of Abraham's son Isaac.

Abraham became the father of Isaac, ²⁰and Isaac was forty years old when he married Rebekah daughter of Bethuel the Aramean from Paddan Aram and sister of Laban the Aramean. ²¹Isaac prayed to the LORD on behalf of his wife, because she was barren. The LORD answered his prayer, and his wife Rebekah became pregnant. ²²The babies jostled each other within her, and she said, "Why is this happening to me?" So she went to inquire of the LORD.

²³The LORD said to her,

"Two nations are in your womb,
  and two peoples from within you
    will be separated;
one people will be stronger than the other,
  and the older will serve the younger."

²⁴When the time came for her to give birth, there were twin boys in her womb. ²⁵The first to come out was red, and his whole body was like a hairy garment; so they named him Esau. ²⁶After this, his brother came out, with his hand grasping Esau's heel; so he was named Jacob. Isaac was sixty years old when Rebekah gave birth to them.

²⁷The boys grew up, and Esau became a skillful hunter, a man of the open country, while Jacob was a quiet man, staying among the tents. ²⁸Isaac, who had a taste for wild game, loved Esau, but Rebekah loved Jacob.

²⁹Once when Jacob was cooking some stew, Esau came in from the open country, famished. ³⁰He said to Jacob, "Quick, let me have some of that red stew! I'm famished!" (That is why he was also called Edom.)

³¹Jacob replied, "First sell me your birthright."

³²"Look, I am about to die," Esau said. "What good is the birthright to me?"

³³But Jacob said, "Swear to me first." So he swore an oath to him, selling his birthright to Jacob.

³⁴Then Jacob gave Esau some bread and some lentil stew. He ate and drank, and then got up and left.

So Esau despised his birthright.

25:23 God revealed that Rebekah would produce two sons in which "the older will serve the younger" indicating that Esau would be ruled by Jacob, despite Esau's position as the eldest son. God's designation of the younger son illustrates his sovereign right to do "whatever pleases him" (Ps 115:3) in accordance with his perfect will.

Isaac and Abimelech

26:1-11Ref — Ge 12:10-20; 20:1-18

26 Now there was a famine in the land—besides the earlier famine of Abraham's time—and Isaac went to Abimelech king of the Philistines in Gerar. ²The LORD appeared to Isaac and said, "Do not go down to Egypt; live in the land where I tell you to live. ³Stay in this land for a while, and I will be with you and will bless you. For to you and your descendants I will give all these lands and will confirm the oath I swore to your father Abraham. ⁴I will make your descendants as numerous as the stars in the sky and will give them all these lands, and through your offspring all nations on earth will be blessed, ⁵because Abraham obeyed me and kept my requirements, my commands, my decrees and my laws." ⁶So Isaac stayed in Gerar.

⁷When the men of that place asked him about his wife, he said, "She is my sister," because he was afraid to say, "She is my wife." He thought, "The men of this place might kill me on account of Rebekah, because she is beautiful."

⁸When Isaac had been there a long time, Abimelech king of the Philistines looked down from a window and saw Isaac caressing his wife Rebekah. ⁹So Abimelech summoned Isaac and said, "She is really your wife! Why did you say, 'She is my sister'?"

Isaac answered him, "Because I thought I might lose my life on account of her."

¹⁰Then Abimelech said, "What is this you have done to us? One of the men might well have slept with your wife, and you would have brought guilt upon us."

¹¹So Abimelech gave orders to all the people: "Anyone who molests this man or his wife shall surely be put to death."

¹²Isaac planted crops in that land and the same year reaped a hundredfold, because the LORD blessed him. ¹³The man became rich, and his wealth continued to grow until he became very wealthy. ¹⁴He had so many flocks and herds and servants that the Philistines envied him. ¹⁵So all the wells that his father's servants had dug in the time of his father Abraham, the Philistines stopped up, filling them with earth.

¹⁶Then Abimelech said to Isaac, "Move away from us; you have become too powerful for us."

¹⁷So Isaac moved away from there and encamped in the Valley of Gerar and settled there. ¹⁸Isaac reopened the wells that had been dug in the time of his father Abraham, which the Philistines had stopped up after Abraham died, and he gave them the same names his father had given them.

¹⁹Isaac's servants dug in the valley and discovered a well of fresh water there. ²⁰But the herdsmen of Gerar quarreled with Isaac's herdsmen and said, "The water is ours!" So he named the well Esek, because they disputed with him. ²¹Then they dug another well, but they quarreled over that one also; so he named it Sitnah. ²²He moved on from there and dug another well, and no one quarreled over it. He named it Rehoboth, saying, "Now the LORD has given us room and we will flourish in the land."

²³From there he went up to Beersheba. ²⁴That night the LORD appeared to him and said, "I am the God of your father Abraham. Do not be afraid, for I am with you; I will bless you and will increase the number of your descendants for the sake of my servant Abraham."

²⁵Isaac built an altar there and called on the name of the LORD. There he pitched his tent, and there his servants dug a well.

²⁶Meanwhile, Abimelech had come to him from Gerar, with Ahuzzath his per-

A Ge 26:2-5 ◀ ▶ Ge 27:28   R ▶ Ge 30:27

A Ge 25:23 ◀ ▶ Ge 26:24
U Ge 24:35 ◀ ▶ Ge 39:2-3
B Ge 24:35 ◀ ▶ Ge 27:39

o 4 Or seed p 20 Esek means dispute. q 21 Sitnah means opposition.
r 22 Rehoboth means room.

26:3 In this verse the Lord reconfirmed with Isaac the Abrahamic covenant. God's promise to be a sustainer and protector of his people is repeated often throughout Scripture (see 28:13–15; 31:3; 35:11–12; Jos 1:5; Isa 41:10; Jer 1:19; Mt 28:20; Ac 18:10).

sonal adviser and Phicol the commander of his forces.ᵘ ²⁷Isaac asked them, "Why have you come to me, since you were hostile to me and sent me away?"ᵛ

²⁸They answered, "We saw clearly that the LORD was with you;ʷ so we said, 'There ought to be a sworn agreement between us'—between us and you. Let us make a treatyˣ with you ²⁹that you will do us no harm,ʸ just as we did not molest you but always treated you well and sent you away in peace. And now you are blessed by the LORD."ᶻ

³⁰Isaac then made a feastᵃ for them, and they ate and drank. ³¹Early the next morning the men swore an oathᵇ to each other. Then Isaac sent them on their way, and they left him in peace.

³²That day Isaac's servants came and told him about the wellᶜ they had dug. They said, "We've found water!" ³³He called it Shibah,ˢ and to this day the name of the town has been Beersheba.ʳᵈ

³⁴When Esau was forty years old,ᵉ he married Judith daughter of Beeri the Hittite, and also Basemath daughter of Elon the Hittite.ᶠ ³⁵They were a source of grief to Isaac and Rebekah.ᵍ

Jacob Gets Isaac's Blessing

27 When Isaac was old and his eyes were so weak that he could no longer see,ʰ he called for Esau his older sonⁱ and said to him, "My son."

"Here I am," he answered.

²Isaac said, "I am now an old man and don't know the day of my death.ʲ ³Now then, get your weapons—your quiver and bow—and go out to the open countryᵏ to hunt some wild game for me. ⁴Prepare me the kind of tasty food I likeˡ and bring it to me to eat, so that I may give you my blessingᵐ before I die."ⁿ

⁵Now Rebekah was listening as Isaac spoke to his son Esau. When Esau left for the open countryᵒ to hunt game and bring it back, ⁶Rebekah said to her son Jacob,ᵖ "Look, I overheard your father say to your brother Esau, ⁷'Bring me some game and prepare me some tasty food to eat, so that I may give you my blessing in the presence of the LORD before I die.'ᑫ ⁸Now, my son, listen carefully and do what I tell you:ʳ ⁹Go out to the flock and bring me two choice young goats,ˢ so I can prepare some tasty food for your father, just the way he likes it.ᵗ ¹⁰Then take it to your father to eat, so that he may give you his blessingᵘ before he dies."

¹¹Jacob said to Rebekah his mother, "But my brother Esau is a hairy man,ᵛ and I'm a man with smooth skin. ¹²What if my father touches me?ʷ I would appear to be tricking him and would bring down a curseˣ on myself rather than a blessing."

¹³His mother said to him, "My son, let the curse fall on me.ʸ Just do what I say;ᶻ go and get them for me."

¹⁴So he went and got them and brought them to his mother, and she prepared some tasty food, just the way his father liked it.ᵃ ¹⁵Then Rebekah took the best clothesᵇ of Esau her older son,ᶜ which she had in the house, and put them on her younger son Jacob. ¹⁶She also covered his hands and the smooth part of his neck with the goatskins.ᵈ ¹⁷Then she handed to her son Jacob the tasty food and the bread she had made.

¹⁸He went to his father and said, "My father."

"Yes, my son," he answered. "Who is it?"ᵉ

¹⁹Jacob said to his father, "I am Esau your firstborn.ᶠ I have done as you told me. Please sit up and eat some of my gameᵍ so that you may give me your blessing."ʰ

²⁰Isaac asked his son, "How did you find it so quickly, my son?"

"The LORD your God gave me success,ⁱ" he replied.

²¹Then Isaac said to Jacob, "Come near so I can touch you,ʲ my son, to know whether you really are my son Esau or not."

²²Jacob went close to his father Isaac,ᵏ who touchedˡ him and said, "The voice is the voice of Jacob, but the hands are the hands of Esau." ²³He did not recognize him, for his hands were hairy like those of his brother Esau;ᵐ so he blessed him. ²⁴"Are you really my son Esau?" he asked.

"I am," he replied.

²⁵Then he said, "My son, bring me some of your game to eat, so that I may give you my blessing."ⁿ

ˢ 33 *Shibah* can mean *oath* or *seven*.   ᵗ 33 *Beersheba* can mean *well of the oath* or *well of seven*.

Jacob brought it to him and he ate; and he brought some wine and he drank. ²⁶Then his father Isaac said to him, "Come here, my son, and kiss me."

²⁷So he went to him and kissed° him.ᵖ When Isaac caught the smell of his clothes,ᑫ he blessed him and said,

"Ah, the smell of my son
  is like the smell of a field
  that the Lord has blessed.ʳ
²⁸May God give you of heaven's dewˢ
  and of earth's richnessᵗ—
  an abundance of grainᵘ and new
    wine.ᵛ
²⁹May nations serve you
  and peoples bow down to you.ʷ
Be lord over your brothers,
  and may the sons of your mother
    bow down to you.ˣ
May those who curse you be cursed
  and those who bless you be
    blessed."ʸ

³⁰After Isaac finished blessing him and Jacob had scarcely left his father's presence, his brother Esau came in from hunting. ³¹He too prepared some tasty food and brought it to his father. Then he said to him, "My father, sit up and eat some of my game, so that you may give me your blessing."ᶻ

³²His father Isaac asked him, "Who are you?"ᵃ

"I am your son," he answered, "your firstborn, Esau."ᵇ

³³Isaac trembled violently and said, "Who was it, then, that hunted game and brought it to me?ᶜ I ate it just before you came and I blessed him—and indeed he will be blessed!"ᵈ

³⁴When Esau heard his father's words, he burst out with a loud and bitter cryᵉ and said to his father, "Blessᶠ me—me too, my father!"

³⁵But he said, "Your brother came deceitfullyᵍ and took your blessing."ʰ

³⁶Esau said, "Isn't he rightly named Jacobᵘ?ⁱ He has deceivedʲ me these two times: He took my birthright,ᵏ and now he's taken my blessing!"ˡ Then he asked, "Haven't you reserved any blessing for me?"

³⁷Isaac answered Esau, "I have made him lord over you and have made all his relatives his servants, and I have sustained him with grain and new wine.ᵐ So what can I possibly do for you, my son?"

³⁸Esau said to his father, "Do you have only one blessing, my father? Bless me too, my father!" Then Esau wept aloud.ⁿ

³⁹His father Isaac answered him,°

"Your dwelling will be
  away from the earth's richness,
  away from the dewᵖ of heaven
    above.ᑫ
⁴⁰You will live by the sword
  and you will serveʳ your brother.ˢ
But when you grow restless,
  you will throw his yoke
    from off your neck.ᵗ"

Jacob Flees to Laban

⁴¹Esau held a grudgeᵘ against Jacobᵛ because of the blessing his father had given him. He said to himself, "The days of mourningʷ for my father are near; then I will killˣ my brother Jacob."ʸ

⁴²When Rebekah was told what her older son Esauᶻ had said, she sent for her younger son Jacob and said to him, "Your brother Esau is consoling himself with the thought of killing you.ᵃ ⁴³Now then, my son, do what I say:ᵇ Flee at once to my brother Labanᶜ in Haran.ᵈ ⁴⁴Stay with him for a whileᵉ until your brother's fury subsides. ⁴⁵When your brother is no longer angry with you and forgets what you did to him,ᶠ I'll send word for you to come back from there.ᵍ Why should I lose both of you in one day?"

⁴⁶Then Rebekah said to Isaac, "I'm disgusted with living because of these Hittiteʰ women. If Jacob takes a wife from among the women of this land,ⁱ from Hittite women like these, my life will not be worth living."ʲ

28 So Isaac called for Jacob and blessedᵛᵏ him and commanded him: "Do not marry a Canaanite woman.ˡ ²Go at once to Paddan Aram,ʷᵐ to the house of your mother's father Bethuel.ⁿ Take a wife for yourself there, from among the daughters of Laban, your mother's brother.º ³May God Almighty^xp bless^q you and make you fruitful^r and increase your numbers^s until you become a community of peoples. ⁴May he give you and your descendants the blessing given to Abraham,^t so that you may take possession of the land^u where you now live as an alien,^v the land God gave to Abraham." ⁵Then Isaac sent Jacob on his way,^w and he went to Paddan Aram,^x to Laban son of Bethuel the Aramean,^y the brother of Rebekah,^z who was the mother of Jacob and Esau.

⁶Now Esau learned that Isaac had blessed Jacob and had sent him to Paddan Aram to take a wife from there, and that when he blessed him he commanded him, "Do not marry a Canaanite woman,"^a ⁷and that Jacob had obeyed his father and mother and had gone to Paddan Aram. ⁸Esau then realized how displeasing the Canaanite women^b were to his father Isaac;^c ⁹so he went to Ishmael^d and married Mahalath, the sister of Nebaioth^e and daughter of Ishmael son of Abraham, in addition to the wives he already had.^f

Jacob's Dream at Bethel

¹⁰Jacob left Beersheba^g and set out for Haran.^h ¹¹When he reached a certain place,^i he stopped for the night because the sun had set. Taking one of the stones there, he put it under his head^j and lay down to sleep. ¹²He had a dream^k in which he saw a stairway^y resting on the earth, with its top reaching to heaven, and the angels of God were ascending and descending on it.^l ¹³There above it^t stood the LORD,^m and he said: "I am the LORD, the God of your father Abraham and the God of Isaac.^n I will give you and your descendants the land^o on which you are lying.^p ¹⁴Your descendants will be like the dust of the earth, and you^q will spread out to the west and to the east, to the north and to the south.^r All peoples on earth will be blessed through you and your offspring.^s ¹⁵I am with you^t and will watch over you^uv wherever you go,^w and I will bring you back to this land.^x I will not leave you^y until I have done what I have promised you.^z"^a

A Ge 27:39–40 ◀ ▶ Ge 28:13–15
A Ge 28:3–4 ◀ ▶ Ge 32:27–28
L Ge 26:28 ◀ ▶ Ex 11:7

28:2 ºS Ge 21:21; S 24:29
28:3 ᵖS Ge 17:1 ᵠGe 48:16; Nu 6:24; Ru 2:4; Ps 129:8; 134:3; Jer 31:23 ʳS Ge 17:6 ˢS Ge 12:2
28:4 ᵗS Ge 12:2,3 ᵘS Ge 15:7 ᵛS Ge 17:8
28:5 ʷS Ge 11:31 ˣHos 12:12 ʸS Ge 25:20 ᶻS Ge 24:29
28:6 ᵃS ver 1
28:8 ᵇS Ge 10:15-19 ᶜS Ge 26:35
28:9 ᵈS Ge 16:15 ᵉS Ge 25:13 ᶠS Ge 26:34
28:10 ᵍS Ge 21:14 ʰS Ge 11:31
28:11 ⁱS Ge 12:8 ʲver 18
28:12 ᵏS Ge 20:3; 37:19 ˡJn 1:51
28:13 ᵐS Ge 12:7; 35:7,9; 48:3 ⁿS Ge 24:12; 48:16; 49:25; 50:17 ᵒS Ge 12:7 ᵖGe 46:4; 48:21
28:14 ᵠGe 26:4 ʳS Ge 12:2; S 13:14; S 26:24 ˢS Ge 12:3; Ac 3:25; Gal 3:8
28:15 ᵗS Ge 21:20 ᵘPs 121:5,7-8 ᵛver 20 ʷver 22; Ge 35:3 ˣver 21; S Ge 15:16; 30:25; 31:30 ʸDt 31:6,8; Jos 1:5; Ne 4:14; Ps 9:10 ᶻLev 26:42 ᵃPs 105:10
28:16 ᵇ1Ki 3:15; Jer 31:26
28:17 ᶜEx 3:5; 19:21; Jos 5:15; Ps 68:24,35 ᵈver 22; Ge 32:2; 1Ch 22:1; 2Ch 3:1
28:18 ᵉver 11 ᶠver 22; Ge 31:13, 45,51; 35:14; Ex 24:4; Jos 24:26, 27; Isa 19:19 ᵍLev 8:11; Jos 4:9
28:19 ʰS Ge 12:8 ⁱGe 35:6; 48:3; Jos 16:2; 18:13; Jdg 1:23,26
28:20 ʲGe 31:13; Lev 7:16; 22:18; 23:38; 27:2,9; Nu 6:2; 15:3; Dt 12:6; Jdg 11:30; 1Sa 1:21; 2Sa 15:8 ᵏS ver 15 ˡ1Ti 6:8
28:21 ᵐJdg 11:31 ⁿS ver 15 ᵒEx 15:2; Dt 26:17; Jos 24:18; Ps 48:14; 118:28
28:22 ᵖS ver 18; Isa 7:12 ᵠS ver 17 ʳS Ge 14:20; S Nu 18:21; Lk 18:12
29:1 ˢS Ge 25:6
29:2 ᵗS Ge 24:11 ᵘver 3,8,10

¹⁶When Jacob awoke from his sleep,^b he thought, "Surely the LORD is in this place, and I was not aware of it." ¹⁷He was afraid and said, "How awesome is this place!^c This is none other than the house of God;^d this is the gate of heaven."

¹⁸Early the next morning Jacob took the stone he had placed under his head^e and set it up as a pillar^f and poured oil on top of it.^g ¹⁹He called that place Bethel,^ah though the city used to be called Luz.^i

²⁰Then Jacob made a vow,^j saying, "If God will be with me and will watch over me^k on this journey I am taking and will give me food to eat and clothes to wear,^l ²¹so that I return safely^m to my father's house,^n then the LORD^b will be my God^o ²²and^c this stone that I have set up as a pillar^p will be God's house,^q and of all that you give me I will give you a tenth.^r"

Jacob Arrives in Paddan Aram

29 Then Jacob continued on his journey and came to the land of the eastern peoples.^s ²There he saw a well in the field, with three flocks of sheep lying near it because the flocks were watered from that well.^t The stone^u over the mouth of the well was large. ³When all the flocks were gathered there, the shepherds would roll the stone^v away from the well's mouth and water the sheep.^w Then they would return the stone to its place over the mouth of the well.

⁴Jacob asked the shepherds, "My brothers, where are you from?"^x

"We're from Haran,^y" they replied.

⁵He said to them, "Do you know Laban, Nahor's grandson?"^z

"Yes, we know him," they answered.

⁶Then Jacob asked them, "Is he well?"

"Yes, he is," they said, "and here comes his daughter Rachel^a with the sheep.^b"

⁷"Look," he said, "the sun is still high; it is not time for the flocks to be gathered. Water the sheep and take them back to pasture."

⁸"We can't," they replied, "until all the

C ▶ Dt 2:7   F Ge 27:28 ◀ ▶ Ge 48:15

29:3 ᵛS ver 2 ʷver 8 29:4 ˣGe 42:7; Jdg 19:17 ʸS Ge 11:31
29:5 ᶻS Ge 11:29 29:6 ᵃGe 30:22-24; 35:16; 46:19,22 ᵇEx 2:16

ˣ3 Hebrew *El-Shaddai* ʸ12 Or *ladder* ᶻ13 Or *There beside him*
ᵃ19 *Bethel* means *house of God.* ᵇ20,21 Or *Since God . . . father's house, the* LORD ᶜ21,22 Or *house, and the* LORD *will be my God,* ²²*then*

flocks are gathered and the stone[c] has been rolled away from the mouth of the well. Then we will water[d] the sheep."

[9] While he was still talking with them, Rachel came with her father's sheep,[e] for she was a shepherdess. [10] When Jacob saw Rachel[f] daughter of Laban, his mother's brother, and Laban's sheep, he went over and rolled the stone[g] away from the mouth of the well and watered[h] his uncle's sheep.[i] [11] Then Jacob kissed[j] Rachel and began to weep aloud.[k] [12] He had told Rachel that he was a relative[l] of her father and a son of Rebekah.[m] So she ran and told her father.[n]

[13] As soon as Laban[o] heard the news about Jacob, his sister's son, he hurried to meet him. He embraced him[p] and kissed him and brought him to his home, and there Jacob told him all these things. [14] Then Laban said to him, "You are my own flesh and blood."[q]

Jacob Marries Leah and Rachel

After Jacob had stayed with him for a whole month, [15] Laban said to him, "Just because you are a relative[r] of mine, should you work for me for nothing? Tell me what your wages[s] should be."

[16] Now Laban had two daughters; the name of the older was Leah,[t] and the name of the younger was Rachel.[u] [17] Leah had weak[d] eyes, but Rachel[v] was lovely in form, and beautiful.[w] [18] Jacob was in love with Rachel[x] and said, "I'll work for you seven years in return for your younger daughter Rachel."[y]

[19] Laban said, "It's better that I give her to you than to some other man. Stay here with me." [20] So Jacob served seven years to get Rachel,[z] but they seemed like only a few days to him because of his love for her.[a]

[21] Then Jacob said to Laban, "Give me my wife. My time is completed, and I want to lie with her."[b]

[22] So Laban brought together all the people of the place and gave a feast.[c] [23] But when evening came, he took his daughter Leah[d] and gave her to Jacob, and Jacob lay with her. [24] And Laban gave his servant girl Zilpah[e] to his daughter as her maidservant.[f]

[25] When morning came, there was Leah! So Jacob said to Laban, "What is this you have done to me?[g] I served you for Rachel, didn't I? Why have you deceived me?[h]"

[26] Laban replied, "It is not our custom here to give the younger daughter in marriage before the older one.[i] [27] Finish this daughter's bridal week;[j] then we will give you the younger one also, in return for another seven years of work.[k]"

[28] And Jacob did so. He finished the week with Leah, and then Laban gave him his daughter Rachel to be his wife.[l] [29] Laban gave his servant girl Bilhah[m] to his daughter Rachel as her maidservant.[n] [30] Jacob lay with Rachel also, and he loved Rachel more than Leah.[o] And he worked for Laban another seven years.[p]

Jacob's Children

[31] When the LORD saw that Leah was not loved,[q] he opened her womb,[r] but Rachel was barren. [32] Leah became pregnant and gave birth to a son.[s] She named him Reuben,[e][t] for she said, "It is because the LORD has seen my misery.[u] Surely my husband will love me now."

[33] She conceived again, and when she gave birth to a son she said, "Because the LORD heard that I am not loved,[v] he gave me this one too." So she named him Simeon.[f][w]

[34] Again she conceived, and when she gave birth to a son she said, "Now at last my husband will become attached to me,[x] because I have borne him three sons." So he was named Levi.[g][y]

[35] She conceived again, and when she gave birth to a son she said, "This time I will praise the LORD." So she named him Judah.[h][z] Then she stopped having children.[a]

30

When Rachel saw that she was not bearing Jacob any children,[b] she became jealous of her sister.[c] So she said to Jacob, "Give me children, or I'll die!"

[2] Jacob became angry with her and said,

E Ge 25:21 ◀ ▶ Ge 30:22

d 17 Or *delicate* *e 32 Reuben* sounds like the Hebrew for *he has seen my misery*; the name means *see, a son.* *f 33 Simeon* probably means *one who hears.* *g 34 Levi* sounds like and may be derived from the Hebrew for *attached.* *h 35 Judah* sounds like and may be derived from the Hebrew for *praise.*

"Am I in the place of God,ᵈ who has kept you from having children?"ᵉ

³Then she said, "Here is Bilhah,ᶠ my maidservant.ᵍ Sleep with her so that she can bear children for me and that through her I too can build a family."ʰ

⁴So she gave him her servant Bilhah as a wife.ⁱ Jacob slept with her,ʲ ⁵and she became pregnant and bore him a son. ⁶Then Rachel said, "God has vindicated me;ᵏ he has listened to my plea and given me a son."ˡ Because of this she named him Dan.ⁱᵐ

⁷Rachel's servant Bilhahⁿ conceived again and bore Jacob a second son. ⁸Then Rachel said, "I have had a great struggle with my sister, and I have won."ᵒ So she named him Naphtali.ʲᵖ

⁹When Leahᑫ saw that she had stopped having children,ʳ she took her maidservant Zilpahˢ and gave her to Jacob as a wife.ᵗ ¹⁰Leah's servant Zilpahᵘ bore Jacob a son. ¹¹Then Leah said, "What good fortune!"ᵏ So she named him Gad.ˡᵛ

¹²Leah's servant Zilpah bore Jacob a second son. ¹³Then Leah said, "How happy I am! The women will call me happy."ˣ So she named him Asher.ᵐʸ

¹⁴During wheat harvest,ᶻ Reuben went out into the fields and found some mandrake plants,ᵃ which he brought to his mother Leah. Rachel said to Leah, "Please give me some of your son's mandrakes."

¹⁵But she said to her, "Wasn't it enoughᵇ that you took away my husband? Will you take my son's mandrakes too?"

"Very well," Rachel said, "he can sleep with you tonight in return for your son's mandrakes."ᶜ

¹⁶So when Jacob came in from the fields that evening, Leah went out to meet him. "You must sleep with me," she said. "I have hired you with my son's mandrakes."ᵈ So he slept with her that night.

¹⁷God listened to Leah,ᵉ and she became pregnant and bore Jacob a fifth son. ¹⁸Then Leah said, "God has rewarded me for giving my maidservant to my husband."ᶠ So she named him Issachar.ⁿᵍ

¹⁹Leah conceived again and bore Jacob a sixth son. ²⁰Then Leah said, "God has presented me with a precious gift. This time my husband will treat me with honor,ʰ because I have borne him six sons." So she named him Zebulun.ᵒⁱ

²¹Some time later she gave birth to a daughter and named her Dinah.ʲ

²²Then God remembered Rachel;ᵏ he listened to herˡ and opened her womb.ᵐ ²³She became pregnant and gave birth to a sonⁿ and said, "God has taken away my disgrace."ᵒ ²⁴She named him Joseph,ᵖᵖ and said, "May the Lord add to me another son."ᑫ

Jacob's Flocks Increase

²⁵After Rachel gave birth to Joseph, Jacob said to Laban, "Send me on my wayʳ so I can go back to my own homeland.ˢ ²⁶Give me my wives and children, for whom I have served you,ᵗ and I will be on my way. You know how much work I've done for you."

²⁷But Laban said to him, "If I have found favor in your eyes,ᵘ please stay. I have learned by divinationᵛ thatᑫ the Lord has blessed me because of you."ʷ ²⁸He added, "Name your wages,ˣ and I will pay them."

²⁹Jacob said to him, "You know how I have worked for youʸ and how your livestock has fared under my care.ᶻ ³⁰The little you had before I came has increased greatly, and the Lord has blessed you wherever I have been.ᵃ But now, when may I do something for my own household?"ᵇ

³¹"What shall I give you?" he asked.

"Don't give me anything," Jacob replied. "But if you will do this one thing for me, I will go on tending your flocks and watching over them: ³²Let me go through all your flocks today and remove from them every speckled or spotted sheep, every dark-colored lamb and every spotted or speckled goat.ᶜ They will be my wages.ᵈ ³³And my honesty will testify for me in the future, whenever you check on the wages you have paid me. Any goat in my possession that is not speckled or

---

i 6 Dan here means he has vindicated. j 8 Naphtali means my struggle. k 11 Or "A troop is coming!" l 11 Gad can mean good fortune or a troop. m 13 Asher means happy. n 18 Issachar sounds like the Hebrew for reward. o 20 Zebulun probably means honor. p 24 Joseph means may he add. q 27 Or possibly have become rich and

spotted, or any lamb that is not dark-colored,[e] will be considered stolen.[f]"

34"Agreed," said Laban. "Let it be as you have said." 35That same day he removed all the male goats that were streaked or spotted, and all the speckled or spotted female goats (all that had white on them) and all the dark-colored lambs,[g] and he placed them in the care of his sons.[h] 36Then he put a three-day journey[i] between himself and Jacob, while Jacob continued to tend the rest of Laban's flocks.

37Jacob, however, took fresh-cut branches from poplar, almond[j] and plane trees[k] and made white stripes on them by peeling the bark and exposing the white inner wood of the branches.[l] 38Then he placed the peeled branches[m] in all the watering troughs,[n] so that they would be directly in front of the flocks when they came to drink. When the flocks were in heat[o] and came to drink, 39they mated in front of the branches.[p] And they bore young that were streaked or speckled or spotted.[q] 40Jacob set apart the young of the flock by themselves, but made the rest face the streaked and dark-colored animals[r] that belonged to Laban. Thus he made separate flocks for himself and did not put them with Laban's animals. 41Whenever the stronger females were in heat,[s] Jacob would place the branches in the troughs in front of the animals so they would mate near the branches,[t] 42but if the animals were weak, he would not place them there. So the weak animals went to Laban and the strong ones to Jacob.[u] 43In this way the man grew exceedingly prosperous and came to own large flocks, and maidservants and menservants, and camels and donkeys.[v]

Jacob Flees From Laban

31 Jacob heard that Laban's sons[w] were saying, "Jacob has taken everything our father owned and has gained all this wealth from what belonged to our father."[x] 2And Jacob noticed that Laban's attitude toward him was not what it had been.[y]

3Then the LORD said to Jacob, "Go back[z] to the land of your fathers and to your relatives, and I will be with you."[a]

4So Jacob sent word to Rachel and Leah to come out to the fields where his flocks were. 5He said to them, "I see that your father's[b] attitude toward me is not what it was before,[c] but the God of my father has been with me.[d] 6You know that I've worked for your father with all my strength,[e] 7yet your father has cheated[f] me by changing my wages[g] ten times.[h] However, God has not allowed him to harm me.[i] 8If he said, 'The speckled ones will be your wages,' then all the flocks gave birth to speckled young; and if he said, 'The streaked ones will be your wages,'[j] then all the flocks bore streaked young. 9So God has taken away your father's livestock[k] and has given them to me.[l]

10"In breeding season I once had a dream[m] in which I looked up and saw that the male goats mating with the flock were streaked, speckled or spotted. 11The angel of God[n] said to me in the dream,[o] 'Jacob.' I answered, 'Here I am.'[p] 12And he said, 'Look up and see that all the male goats mating with the flock are streaked, speckled or spotted,[q] for I have seen all that Laban has been doing to you.[r] 13I am the God of Bethel,[s] where you anointed a pillar[t] and where you made a vow[u] to me. Now leave this land at once and go back to your native land.[v]' "

14Then Rachel and Leah replied, "Do we still have any share[w] in the inheritance of our father's estate? 15Does he not regard us as foreigners?[x] Not only has he sold us, but he has used up what was paid for us.[y] 16Surely all the wealth that God took away from our father belongs to us and our children.[z] So do whatever God has told you."

17Then Jacob put his children and his wives[a] on camels,[b] 18and he drove all his livestock ahead of him, along with all the goods he had accumulated[c] in Paddan Aram,[rd] to go to his father Isaac[e] in the land of Canaan.[f]

19When Laban had gone to shear his sheep,[g] Rachel stole her father's household gods.[h] 20Moreover, Jacob deceived[i] Laban the Aramean[j] by not telling him he was running away.[k] 21So he fled[l] with all he had, and crossing the River,[sm] he headed for the hill country of Gilead.[n]

---

m S Ge 2:14 n ver 23,25; Ge 37:25; Nu 26:30; 32:1; Dt 3:10; Jos 12:2; Jer 22:6

r 18 That is, Northwest Mesopotamia s 21 That is, the Euphrates

Laban Pursues Jacob

²²On the third day° Laban was told that Jacob had fled.ᵖ ²³Taking his relativesᵠ with him,ʳ he pursued Jacob for seven days and caught up with him in the hill country of Gilead.ˢ ²⁴Then God came to Laban the Arameanᵗ in a dream at night and said to him,ᵘ "Be careful not to say anything to Jacob, either good or bad."ᵛ

²⁵Jacob had pitched his tent in the hill country of Gileadʷ when Laban overtook him, and Laban and his relatives camped there too. ²⁶Then Laban said to Jacob, "What have you done?ˣ You've deceived me,ʸ and you've carried off my daughters like captives in war.ᶻ ²⁷Why did you run off secretly and deceive me? Why didn't you tell me,ᵃ so I could send you away with joy and singing to the music of tambourinesᵇ and harps?ᶜ ²⁸You didn't even let me kiss my grandchildren and my daughters good-by.ᵈ You have done a foolish thing. ²⁹I have the power to harm you;ᵉ but last night the God of your fatherᶠ said to me, 'Be careful not to say anything to Jacob, either good or bad.'ᵍ ³⁰Now you have gone off because you longed to return to your father's house.ʰ But why did you stealⁱ my gods?ʲ"

³¹Jacob answered Laban, "I was afraid, because I thought you would take your daughters away from me by force.ᵏ ³²But if you find anyone who has your gods, he shall not live.ˡ In the presence of our relatives, see for yourself whether there is anything of yours here with me; and if so, take it." Now Jacob did not know that Rachel had stolen the gods.ᵐ

³³So Laban went into Jacob's tent and into Leah's tentⁿ and into the tent of the two maidservants,° but he found nothing.ᵖ After he came out of Leah's tent, he entered Rachel's tent. ³⁴Now Rachel had taken the household godsᵠ and put them inside her camel's saddleʳ and was sitting on them. Laban searchedˢ through everything in the tent but found nothing.

³⁵Rachel said to her father, "Don't be angry, my lord, that I cannot stand up in your presence;ᵗ I'm having my period.ᵘ" So he searched but could not find the household gods.ᵛ

³⁶Jacob was angry and took Laban to task. "What is my crime?" he asked Laban. "What sin have I committedʷ that you hunt me down?ˣ ³⁷Now that you have searched through all my goods, what have you found that belongs to your household?ʸ Put it here in front of your relativesᶻ and mine, and let them judge between the two of us.ᵃ

³⁸"I have been with you for twenty years now.ᵇ Your sheep and goats have not miscarried,ᶜ nor have I eaten rams from your flocks. ³⁹I did not bring you animals torn by wild beasts; I bore the loss myself. And you demanded payment from me for whatever was stolenᵈ by day or night.ᵉ ⁴⁰This was my situation: The heat consumed me in the daytime and the cold at night, and sleep fled from my eyes.ᶠ ⁴¹It was like this for the twenty yearsᵍ I was in your household. I worked for you fourteen years for your two daughtersʰ and six years for your flocks,ⁱ and you changed my wagesʲ ten times.ᵏ ⁴²If the God of my father,ˡ the God of Abrahamᵐ and the Fear of Isaac,ⁿ had not been with me,° you would surely have sent me away empty-handed. But God has seen my hardship and the toil of my hands,ᵖ and last night he rebuked you.ᵠ"

⁴³Laban answered Jacob, "The women are my daughters, the children are my children, and the flocks are my flocks.ʳ All you see is mine. Yet what can I do today about these daughters of mine, or about the children they have borne? ⁴⁴Come now, let's make a covenant,ˢ you and I, and let it serve as a witness between us."ᵗ

⁴⁵So Jacob took a stone and set it up as a pillar.ᵘ ⁴⁶He said to his relatives, "Gather some stones." So they took stones and piled them in a heap,ᵛ and they ate there by the heap. ⁴⁷Laban called it Jegar Sahadutha,ʳ and Jacob called it Galeed.ᵘʷ

⁴⁸Laban said, "This heapˣ is a witness between you and me today."ʸ That is why it was called Galeed. ⁴⁹It was also called Mizpah,ᵛᶻ because he said, "May the LORD keep watch between you and me when we are away from each other. ⁵⁰If you mistreatᵃ my daughters or if you take any wives besides my daughters, even though no one is with us, remem-

---

ʳ 47 The Aramaic *Jegar Sahadutha* means *witness heap*.   ᵘ 47 The Hebrew *Galeed* means *witness heap*.   ᵛ 49 *Mizpah* means *watchtower*.

ber that God is a witness[b] between you and me."[c]

[51]Laban also said to Jacob, "Here is this heap,[d] and here is this pillar[e] I have set up between you and me. [52]This heap is a witness, and this pillar is a witness,[f] that I will not go past this heap to your side to harm you and that you will not go past this heap[g] and pillar to my side to harm me.[h] [53]May the God of Abraham[i] and the God of Nahor,[j] the God of their father, judge between us."[k]

So Jacob took an oath[l] in the name of the Fear of his father Isaac.[m] [54]He offered a sacrifice[n] there in the hill country and invited his relatives to a meal.[o] After they had eaten, they spent the night there.

[55]Early the next morning Laban kissed his grandchildren and his daughters[p] and blessed[q] them. Then he left and returned home.[r]

Jacob Prepares to Meet Esau

32 Jacob also went on his way, and the angels of God[s] met him. [2]When Jacob saw them, he said, "This is the camp of God!"[t] So he named that place Mahanaim.[w][u]

[3]Jacob sent messengers[v] ahead of him to his brother Esau[w] in the land of Seir,[x] the country of Edom.[y] [4]He instructed them: "This is what you are to say to my master[z] Esau: 'Your servant[a] Jacob says, I have been staying with Laban[b] and have remained there till now. [5]I have cattle and donkeys, sheep and goats, menservants and maidservants.[c] Now I am sending this message to my lord,[d] that I may find favor in your eyes.[e]'"

[6]When the messengers returned to Jacob, they said, "We went to your brother Esau, and now he is coming to meet you, and four hundred men are with him."[f]

[7]In great fear[g] and distress[h] Jacob divided the people who were with him into two groups,[x][i] and the flocks and herds and camels as well. [8]He thought, "If Esau comes and attacks one group,[y] the group[y] that is left may escape."

[9]Then Jacob prayed, "O God of my father Abraham,[j] God of my father Isaac,[k] O LORD, who said to me, 'Go back to your country and your relatives, and I will make you prosper,'[l] [10]I am unworthy of all the kindness and faithfulness[m] you have shown your servant. I had only my staff[n] when I crossed this Jordan, but now I have become two groups.[o] [11]Save me, I pray, from the hand of my brother Esau, for I am afraid[p] he will come and attack me,[q] and also the mothers with their children.[r] [12]But you have said, 'I will surely make you prosper and will make your descendants like the sand[s] of the sea, which cannot be counted.'"

[13]He spent the night there, and from what he had with him he selected a gift[u] for his brother Esau: [14]two hundred female goats and twenty male goats, two hundred ewes and twenty rams,[v] [15]thirty female camels with their young, forty cows and ten bulls, and twenty female donkeys and ten male donkeys.[w] [16]He put them in the care of his servants, each herd by itself, and said to his servants, "Go ahead of me, and keep some space between the herds."[x]

[17]He instructed the one in the lead: "When my brother Esau meets you and asks, 'To whom do you belong, and where are you going, and who owns all these animals in front of you?' [18]then you are to say, 'They belong to your servant[y] Jacob. They are a gift[z] sent to my lord Esau, and he is coming behind us.'"

[19]He also instructed the second, the third and all the others who followed the herds: "You are to say the same thing to Esau when you meet him. [20]And be sure to say, 'Your servant[a] Jacob is coming behind us.'" For he thought, "I will pacify him with these gifts[b] I am sending on ahead;[c] later, when I see him, perhaps he will receive me."[d] [21]So Jacob's gifts[e] went on ahead of him, but he himself spent the night in the camp.

Jacob Wrestles With God

[22]That night Jacob got up and took his two wives, his two maidservants and his eleven sons[f] and crossed the ford of the Jabbok.[g] [23]After he had sent them across the stream, he sent over all his possessions.[h] [24]So Jacob was left alone,[i] and a man[j] wrestled with him till daybreak. [25]When the man saw that he could not overpower him, he touched the socket of

Jacob's hip so that his hip was wrenched as he wrestled with the man. ²⁶Then the man said, "Let me go, for it is daybreak."

But Jacob replied, "I will not let you go unless you bless me."

²⁷The man asked him, "What is your name?"

"Jacob," he answered.

²⁸Then the man said, "Your name will no longer be Jacob, but Israel, because you have struggled with God and with men and have overcome."

²⁹Jacob said, "Please tell me your name."

But he replied, "Why do you ask my name?" Then he blessed him there.

³⁰So Jacob called the place Peniel, saying, "It is because I saw God face to face, and yet my life was spared."

³¹The sun rose above him as he passed Peniel, and he was limping because of his hip. ³²Therefore to this day the Israelites do not eat the tendon attached to the socket of the hip, because the socket of Jacob's hip was touched near the tendon.

Jacob Meets Esau

33 Jacob looked up and there was Esau, coming with his four hundred men; so he divided the children among Leah, Rachel and the two maidservants. ²He put the maidservants and their children in front, Leah and her children next, and Rachel and Joseph in the rear. ³He himself went on ahead and bowed down to the ground seven times as he approached his brother.

⁴But Esau ran to meet Jacob and embraced him; he threw his arms around his neck and kissed him. And they wept. ⁵Then Esau looked up and saw the women and children. "Who are these with you?" he asked.

Jacob answered, "They are the children God has graciously given your servant."

⁶Then the maidservants and their children approached and bowed down. ⁷Next, Leah and her children came and bowed down. Last of all came Joseph and Rachel, and they too bowed down.

⁸Esau asked, "What do you mean by all these droves I met?"

"To find favor in your eyes, my lord," he said.

⁹But Esau said, "I already have plenty, my brother. Keep what you have for yourself."

¹⁰"No, please!" said Jacob. "If I have found favor in your eyes, accept this gift from me. For to see your face is like seeing the face of God, now that you have received me favorably. ¹¹Please accept the present that was brought to you, for God has been gracious to me and I have all I need." And because Jacob insisted, Esau accepted it.

¹²Then Esau said, "Let us be on our way; I'll accompany you."

¹³But Jacob said to him, "My lord knows that the children are tender and that I must care for the ewes and cows that are nursing their young. If they are driven hard just one day, all the animals will die. ¹⁴So let my lord go on ahead of his servant, while I move along slowly at the pace of the droves before me and that of the children, until I come to my lord in Seir."

¹⁵Esau said, "Then let me leave some of my men with you."

"But why do that?" Jacob asked. "Just let me find favor in the eyes of my lord."

¹⁶So that day Esau started on his way back to Seir. ¹⁷Jacob, however, went to Succoth, where he built a place for himself and made shelters for his livestock. That is why the place is called Succoth.

¹⁸After Jacob came from Paddan Aram, he arrived safely at the city of Shechem in Canaan and camped within sight of the city. ¹⁹For a hundred pieces of silver, he bought from the sons of Hamor, the father of Shechem, the plot of ground where he pitched his tent. ²⁰There he set up an altar and called it El Elohe Israel.

Dinah and the Shechemites

34 Now Dinah, the daughter Leah had borne to Jacob, went out to visit the women of the land. ²When Shechem son of Hamor the Hivite, the ruler of that area, saw her, he took her and violated her. ³His heart was drawn to Dinah daughter of Jacob, and he loved the girl and spoke tenderly to

---

28 Israel means *he struggles with God.* *30 Peniel* means *face of God.* *31 Hebrew Penuel,* a variant of *Peniel* *17 Succoth* means *shelters.* *18 That is, Northwest Mesopotamia* *18 Or arrived at Shalem, a* *19 Hebrew hundred kesitahs;* a kesitah was a unit of money of unknown weight and value. *20 El Elohe Israel* can mean *God, the God of Israel* or *mighty is the God of Israel.*

Ge 28:13–15 ◀ ▶ Ge 35:10–12

her. ⁴And Shechem said to his father Hamor, "Get me this girl as my wife."ᵗ

⁵When Jacob heard that his daughter Dinah had been defiled,ᵘ his sons were in the fields with his livestock; so he kept quiet about it until they came home.

⁶Then Shechem's father Hamor went out to talk with Jacob.ᵛ ⁷Now Jacob's sons had come in from the fields as soon as they heard what had happened. They were filled with griefʷ and fury,ˣ because Shechem had done a disgraceful thing inʰ Israelʸ by lying with Jacob's daughter—a thing that should not be done.ᶻ

⁸But Hamor said to them, "My son Shechem has his heart set on your daughter. Please give her to him as his wife.ᵃ ⁹Intermarry with us; give us your daughters and take our daughters for yourselves.ᵇ ¹⁰You can settle among us;ᶜ the land is open to you.ᵈ Live in it, tradeⁱ in it,ᵉ and acquire property in it.ᶠ"

¹¹Then Shechem said to Dinah's father and brothers, "Let me find favor in your eyes,ᵍ and I will give you whatever you ask. ¹²Make the price for the brideʰ and the gift I am to bring as great as you like, and I'll pay whatever you ask me. Only give me the girl as my wife."

¹³Because their sister Dinah had been defiled,ⁱ Jacob's sons replied deceitfullyʲ as they spoke to Shechem and his father Hamor. ¹⁴They said to them, "We can't do such a thing; we can't give our sister to a man who is not circumcised.ᵏ That would be a disgrace to us. ¹⁵We will give our consent to you on one condition only: that you become like us by circumcising all your males.ᵐ ¹⁶Then we will give you our daughters and take your daughters for ourselves.ⁿ We'll settle among you and become one people with you.ᵒ ¹⁷But if you will not agree to be circumcised, we'll take our sisterʲ and go."

¹⁸Their proposal seemed good to Hamor and his son Shechem. ¹⁹The young man, who was the most honoredᵖ of all his father's household, lost no time in doing what they said, because he was delighted with Jacob's daughter.ᑫ ²⁰So Hamor and his son Shechem went to the gate of their cityʳ to speak to their fellow townsmen. ²¹"These men are friendly toward us," they said. "Let them live in our land and trade in it;ˢ the land has plenty of room for them. We can marry their daughters and they can marry ours.ᵗ ²²But the men will consent to live with us as one people only on the condition that our males be circumcised,ᵘ as they themselves are. ²³Won't their livestock, their property and all their other animals become ours?ᵛ So let us give our consent to them, and they will settle among us.ʷ"

²⁴All the men who went out of the city gateˣ agreed with Hamor and his son Shechem, and every male in the city was circumcised.

²⁵Three days later, while all of them were still in pain,ʸ two of Jacob's sons, Simeonᶻ and Levi,ᵃ Dinah's brothers, took their swordsᵇ and attacked the unsuspecting city,ᶜ killing every male.ᵈ ²⁶They put Hamor and his son Shechem to the swordᵉ and took Dinahᶠ from Shechem's house and left. ²⁷The sons of Jacob came upon the dead bodies and looted the cityᵍ whereᵏ their sister had been defiled.ʰ ²⁸They seized their flocks and herds and donkeysⁱ and everything else of theirs in the city and out in the fields.ʲ ²⁹They carried off all their wealth and all their women and children,ᵏ taking as plunderˡ everything in the houses.ᵐ

³⁰Then Jacob said to Simeon and Levi, "You have brought troubleⁿ on me by making me a stenchᵒ to the Canaanites and Perizzites, the people living in this land.ᵖ We are few in number,ᑫ and if they join forces against me and attack me, I and my household will be destroyed."

³¹But they replied, "Should he have treated our sister like a prostitute?ʳ"

Jacob Returns to Bethel

35 Then God said to Jacob, "Go up to Bethelˢ and settle there, and build an altarᵗ there to God,ᵘ who appeared to youᵛ when you were fleeing from your brother Esau."ʷ

²So Jacob said to his householdˣ and to all who were with him, "Get rid of the foreign godsʸ you have with you, and purify yourselves and change your clothes.ᶻ ³Then come, let us go up to Bethel, where I will build an altar to God,ᵃ who answered me in the day of my distressᵇ and who has been with me wherever I

ʰ 7 Or *against* ⁱ 10 Or *move about freely*; also in verse 21 ʲ 17 Hebrew *daughter* ᵏ 27 Or *because*

have gone.ᶜ" ⁴So they gave Jacob all the foreign gods they had and the rings in their ears,ᵈ and Jacob buried them under the oakᵉ at Shechem.ᶠ ⁵Then they set out, and the terror of Godᵍ fell upon the towns all around them so that no one pursued them.ʰ

⁶Jacob and all the people with him came to Luzⁱ (that is, Bethel) in the land of Canaan.ʲ ⁷There he built an altar,ᵏ and he called the place El Bethel,ˡ because it was there that God revealed himself to himᵐ when he was fleeing from his brother.ⁿ

⁸Now Deborah, Rebekah's nurse,ᵒ died and was buried under the oakᵖ below Bethel.ᑫ So it was named Allon Bacuth.ᵐ

⁹After Jacob returned from Paddan Aram,ⁿʳ God appeared to him again and blessed him.ˢ ¹⁰God said to him, "Your name is Jacob,ᵒ but you will no longer be called Jacob; your name will be Israel.ᵖ"ᵗ So he named him Israel.

¹¹And God said to him, "I am God Almighty;ᑫᵘ be fruitful and increase in number.ᵛ A nationʷ and a community of nations will come from you, and kings will come from your body.ˣ ¹²The land I gave to Abraham and Isaac I also give to you, and I will give this land to your descendants after you.ʸ"ᶻ ¹³Then God went up from himᵃ at the place where he had talked with him.

¹⁴Jacob set up a stone pillarᵇ at the place where God had talked with him, and he poured out a drink offeringᶜ on it; he also poured oil on it.ᵈ ¹⁵Jacob called the place where God had talked with him Bethel.ʳᵉ

The Deaths of Rachel and Isaac
35:23–26pp — 1Ch 2:1–2

¹⁶Then they moved on from Bethel. While they were still some distance from Ephrath,ᶠ Rachelᵍ began to give birth and had great difficulty. ¹⁷And as she was having great difficulty in childbirth, the midwifeʰ said to her, "Don't be afraid, for

A Ge 32:27–28 ◀ ▶ Ge 37:6–7

35:3 ᶜS Ge 26:3; 35:4 ᵈS Ge 24:22; Ex 32:3; 35:22; Jdg 8:24; Pr 25:12 ᵉver 8 ᶠS Ge 12:6 35:5 ᵍEx 15:16; 23:27; Dt 2:25; Jos 2:9; 1Sa 7:10; 13:7; 14:15; 2Ch 14:14; 17:10; 20:29; Ps 9:20; Isa 19:17; Zec 14:13 ʰPs 105:14 35:6 ⁱS Ge 28:19 ʲS Ge 10:19 35:7 ᵏS Ge 8:20 ˡGe 28:19 ᵐS Ge 28:13 ⁿS ver 1 35:8 ᵒGe 24:59 ᵖver 4 ᑫS Ge 12:8; 1Sa 10:3 35:9 ʳS Ge 25:20 ˢS Ge 28:13; S 32:29 35:10 ᵗS Ge 17:5 35:11 ᵘS Ge 17:1 ᵛS Ge 12:2 ʷS Ge 12:2 ˣS Ge 17:6 35:12 ʸS Ge 28:13 ᶻS Ge 12:7; S 15:7 35:13 ᵃS Ge 17:22 35:14 ᵇS Ge 28:22 ᶜEx 29:40; Lev 23:13; Nu 6:15, 17; 15:5; 28:7,14; 2Sa 23:13; 2Ch 29:35 ᵈS Ge 28:18 35:15 ᵉS Ge 12:8 35:16 ᶠver 19; Ge 48:7; Ru 1:2; 4:11; 1Sa 17:12; Mic 5:2 ᵍS Ge 29:6 35:17 ʰGe 38:28; Ex 1:15 ⁱS Ge 30:24 35:18 ʲ1Sa 4:21; 14:3 ᵏver 24; Ge 42:4; 43:16,29; 45:12,14; 49:27; Nu 1:36; Dt 33:12 35:19 ˡS ver 16 ᵐGe 48:7; Jos 19:15; Jdg 12:8; 17:7; 19:1,18; Ru 1:1,19; 1Sa 17:12; Mic 5:2 35:20 ⁿJos 4:9; 7:26; 8:28; 10:27; 1Sa 6:18 ᵒ1Sa 10:2 35:21 ᵖJos 15:21 35:22 ᑫS Ge 22:24 ʳS Ge 29:29; S 34:5; S Lev 18:8 35:23 ˢS Ge 29:16 ᵗGe 43:33; 46:8 ᵘS Ge 29:35 ᵛS Ge 30:20 35:24 ʷS Ge 30:24 ˣS ver 18 35:25 ʸS Ge 37:2

you have another son."ⁱ ¹⁸As she breathed her last—for she was dying— she named her son Ben-Oni.ˢʲ But his father named him Benjamin.ʳᵏ

¹⁹So Rachel died and was buried on the way to Ephrathˡ (that is, Bethlehemᵐ). ²⁰Over her tomb Jacob set up a pillar, and to this dayⁿ that pillar marks Rachel's tomb.ᵒ

²¹Israel moved on again and pitched his tent beyond Migdal Eder.ᵖ ²²While Israel was living in that region, Reuben went in and slept with his father's concubineᑫ Bilhah,ʳ and Israel heard of it.

Jacob had twelve sons:

²³The sons of Leah:ˢ
Reuben the firstbornᵗ of Jacob,
Simeon, Levi, Judah,ᵘ Issachar
and Zebulun.ᵛ

²⁴The sons of Rachel:
Josephʷ and Benjamin.ˣ

²⁵The sons of Rachel's maidservant Bilhah:ʸ
Dan and Naphtali.ᶻ

²⁶The sons of Leah's maidservant Zilpah:ᵃ
Gadᵇ and Asher.ᶜ

These were the sons of Jacob,ᵈ who were born to him in Paddan Aram.ᵉ

²⁷Jacob came home to his father Isaacᶠ in Mamre,ᵍ near Kiriath Arbaʰ (that is, Hebron),ⁱ where Abraham and Isaac had stayed.ʲ ²⁸Isaac lived a hundred and eighty years.ᵏ ²⁹Then he breathed his last and died and was gathered to his people,ˡ old and full of years.ᵐ And his sons Esau and Jacob buried him.ⁿ

Q Ge 25:8 ◀ ▶ Ge 49:29

ᶻS Ge 30:8 **35:26** ᵃGe 37:2 ᵇS Ge 30:11 ᶜS Ge 30:13 ᵈS Ge 34:30; 46:8; Ex 1:1-4 ᵉS Ge 25:20 **35:27** ᶠGe 31:18 ᵍS Ge 13:18 ʰGe 23:2; Jos 15:54; Jdg 1:10; Ne 11:25 ⁱS Ge 13:18 ʲS Ge 17:8 **35:28** ᵏS Ge 25:7, 20 **35:29** ˡS Ge 25:8 ᵐS Ge 15:15 ⁿS Ge 23:20; S 25:9

r 7 El Bethel means God of Bethel.   m 8 Allon Bacuth means oak of weeping.   n 9 That is, Northwest Mesopotamia; also in verse 26   o 10 Jacob means he grasps the heel (figuratively, he deceives).   p 10 Israel means he struggles with God.   q 11 Hebrew El-Shaddai   r 15 Bethel means house of God.   s 18 Ben-Oni means son of my trouble.   t 18 Benjamin means son of my right hand.

35:29 Isaac lived for 180 years, the longest living of the patriarchs. The phrase "gathered to his people" occurs often in Scripture as part of a promise to a godly individual. It implies the Hebrew view of life after death that involved the reuniting of family members (see 2Sa 12:23). A thousand years later, Jesus referred to the gathered patriarchs (see Mt 22:32), confirming that ancient believers were indeed still alive and awaiting the resurrection from the dead at Christ's second coming.

Esau's Descendants

36:10–14pp — 1Ch 1:35–37
36:20–28pp — 1Ch 1:38–42

36 This is the account° of Esau (that is, Edom).ᵖ

²Esau took his wives from the women of Canaan:ᑫ Adah daughter of Elon the Hittite,ʳ and Oholibamahˢ daughter of Anahᵗ and granddaughter of Zibeon the Hiviteᵘ— ³also Basemathᵛ daughter of Ishmael and sister of Nebaioth.ʷ ⁴Adah bore Eliphaz to Esau, Basemath bore Reuel,ˣ ⁵and Oholibamah bore Jeush, Jalam and Korah.ʸ These were the sons of Esau, who were born to him in Canaan.

⁶Esau took his wives and sons and daughters and all the members of his household, as well as his livestock and all his other animals and all the goods he had acquired in Canaan,ᶻ and moved to a land some distance from his brother Jacob.ᵃ ⁷Their possessions were too great for them to remain together; the land where they were staying could not support them both because of their livestock.ᵇ ⁸So Esauᶜ (that is, Edom)ᵈ settled in the hill country of Seir.ᵉ

⁹This is the accountᶠ of Esau the father of the Edomitesᵍ in the hill country of Seir.

¹⁰These are the names of Esau's sons:
Eliphaz, the son of Esau's wife Adah, and Reuel, the son of Esau's wife Basemath.ʰ
¹¹The sons of Eliphaz:ⁱ
Teman,ʲ Omar, Zepho, Gatam and Kenaz.ᵏ
¹²Esau's son Eliphaz also had a concubineˡ named Timna, who bore him Amalek.ᵐ These were grandsons of Esau's wife Adah.ⁿ
¹³The sons of Reuel:
Nahath, Zerah, Shammah and Mizzah. These were grandsons of Esau's wife Basemath.°
¹⁴The sons of Esau's wife Oholibamahᵖ daughter of Anah and granddaughter of Zibeon, whom she bore to Esau:
Jeush, Jalam and Korah.ᑫ

¹⁵These were the chiefsʳ among Esau's descendants:

The sons of Eliphaz the firstborn of Esau:
Chiefs Teman,ˢ Omar, Zepho, Kenaz,ᵗ ¹⁶Korah,ᵘ Gatam and Amalek. These were the chiefs descended from Eliphazᵘ in Edom;ᵛ they were grandsons of Adah.ʷ
¹⁷The sons of Esau's son Reuel:ˣ
Chiefs Nahath, Zerah, Shammah and Mizzah. These were the chiefs descended from Reuel in Edom; they were grandsons of Esau's wife Basemath.ʸ
¹⁸The sons of Esau's wife Oholibamah:ᶻ
Chiefs Jeush, Jalam and Korah.ᵃ These were the chiefs descended from Esau's wife Oholibamah daughter of Anah.

¹⁹These were the sons of Esauᵇ (that is, Edom),ᶜ and these were their chiefs.ᵈ

²⁰These were the sons of Seir the Horite,ᵉ who were living in the region:
Lotan, Shobal, Zibeon, Anah,ᶠ ²¹Dishon, Ezer and Dishan. These sons of Seir in Edom were Horite chiefs.ᵍ
²²The sons of Lotan:
Hori and Homam.ᵛ Timna was Lotan's sister.
²³The sons of Shobal:
Alvan, Manahath, Ebal, Shepho and Onam.
²⁴The sons of Zibeon:ʰ
Aiah and Anah. This is the Anah who discovered the hot springsʷⁱ in the desert while he was grazing the donkeysʲ of his father Zibeon.
²⁵The children of Anah:ᵏ
Dishon and Oholibamahˡ daughter of Anah.
²⁶The sons of Dishon:ˣ
Hemdan, Eshban, Ithran and Keran.
²⁷The sons of Ezer:
Bilhan, Zaavan and Akan.
²⁸The sons of Dishan:
Uz and Aran.
²⁹These were the Horite chiefs:
Lotan, Shobal, Zibeon, Anah,ᵐ

ᵘ 16 Masoretic Text; Samaritan Pentateuch (see also Gen. 36:11 and 1 Chron. 1:36) does not have *Korah*. ᵛ 22 Hebrew *Hemam*, a variant of *Homam* (see 1 Chron. 1:39) ʷ 24 Vulgate; Syriac *discovered water*; the meaning of the Hebrew for this word is uncertain. ˣ 26 Hebrew *Dishan*, a variant of *Dishon*

[51 GENESIS 37:14]

30Dishon, Ezer and Dishan. These were the Horite chiefs,ⁿ according to their divisions, in the land of Seir.

The Rulers of Edom
36:31–43pp — 1Ch 1:43–54

31These were the kings who reigned in Edom before any Israelite kingᵒ reignedʸ: 32Bela son of Beor became king of Edom. His city was named Dinhabah. 33When Bela died, Jobab son of Zerah from Bozrahᵖ succeeded him as king. 34When Jobab died, Husham from the land of the Temanitesᵠ succeeded him as king. 35When Husham died, Hadad son of Bedad, who defeated Midianʳ in the country of Moab,ˢ succeeded him as king. His city was named Avith. 36When Hadad died, Samlah from Masrekah succeeded him as king. 37When Samlah died, Shaul from Rehobothᵗ on the riverᶻ succeeded him as king. 38When Shaul died, Baal-Hanan son of Acbor succeeded him as king. 39When Baal-Hanan son of Acbor died, Hadadᵃ succeeded him as king. His city was named Pau, and his wife's name was Mehetabel daughter of Matred, the daughter of Me-Zahab.

40These were the chiefsᵘ descended from Esau, by name, according to their clans and regions:

Timna, Alvah, Jetheth, 41Oholibamah, Elah, Pinon, 42Kenaz, Teman, Mibzar, 43Magdiel and Iram. These were the chiefs of Edom, according to their settlements in the land they occupied.

This was Esau the father of the Edomites.ᵛ

Joseph's Dreams

37 Jacob lived in the land where his father had stayed,ʷ the land of Canaan.ˣ

2This is the accountʸ of Jacob.

Joseph,ᶻ a young man of seventeen,ᵃ was tending the flocksᵇ with his brothers,

the sons of Bilhahᶜ and the sons of Zilpah,ᵈ his father's wives, and he brought their father a bad reportᵉ about them.

3Now Israelᶠ loved Joseph more than any of his other sons,ᵍ because he had been born to him in his old age;ʰ and he made a richly ornamentedᵇ robeⁱ for him.ʲ 4When his brothers saw that their father loved him more than any of them, they hated himᵏ and could not speak a kind word to him.

5Joseph had a dream,ˡ and when he told it to his brothers,ᵐ they hated him all the more.ⁿ 6He said to them, "Listen to this dream I had: 7We were binding sheavesᵒ of grain out in the field when suddenly my sheaf rose and stood upright, while your sheaves gathered around mine and bowed down to it."ᵖ

8His brothers said to him, "Do you intend to reign over us? Will you actually rule us?"ᵠ And they hated him all the moreʳ because of his dream and what he had said.

9Then he had another dream,ˢ and he told it to his brothers. "Listen," he said, "I had another dream, and this time the sun and moon and eleven starsᵗ were bowing down to me."ᵘ

10When he told his father as well as his brothers,ᵛ his father rebukedʷ him and said, "What is this dream you had? Will your mother and I and your brothers actually come and bow down to the ground before you?"ˣ 11His brothers were jealous of him,ʸ but his father kept the matter in mind.ᶻ

Joseph Sold by His Brothers

12Now his brothers had gone to graze their father's flocks near Shechem,ᵃ 13and Israelᵇ said to Joseph, "As you know, your brothers are grazing the flocks near Shechem.ᶜ Come, I am going to send you to them."

"Very well," he replied.

14So he said to him, "Go and see if all is well with your brothersᵈ and with the flocks, and bring word back to me." Then

A *Ge 35:10–12* ◀ ▶ *Ge 37:9*
A *Ge 37:6–7* ◀ ▶ *Ge 41:1–7*

ʸ 31 Or *before an Israelite king reigned over them*   ᶻ 37 Possibly the Euphrates   ᵃ 39 Many manuscripts of the Masoretic Text, Samaritan Pentateuch and Syriac (see also 1 Chron. 1:50); most manuscripts of the Masoretic Text *Hadar*   ᵇ 3 The meaning of the Hebrew for *richly ornamented* is uncertain; also in verses 23 and 32.

he sent him off from the Valley of Hebron.ᵉ

When Joseph arrived at Shechem, ¹⁵a man found him wandering around in the fields and asked him, "What are you looking for?"

¹⁶He replied, "I'm looking for my brothers. Can you tell me where they are grazing their flocks?"

¹⁷"They have moved on from here," the man answered. "I heard them say, 'Let's go to Dothan.ᶠ'"

So Joseph went after his brothers and found them near Dothan. ¹⁸But they saw him in the distance, and before he reached them, they plotted to kill him.ᵍ

¹⁹"Here comes that dreamer!ʰ" they said to each other. ²⁰"Come now, let's kill him and throw him into one of these cisternsⁱ and say that a ferocious animalʲ devoured him.ᵏ Then we'll see what comes of his dreams."ˡ

²¹When Reubenᵐ heard this, he tried to rescue him from their hands. "Let's not take his life," he said.ⁿ ²²"Don't shed any blood. Throw him into this cisternᵒ here in the desert, but don't lay a hand on him." Reuben said this to rescue him from them and take him back to his father.ᵖ

²³So when Joseph came to his brothers, they stripped him of his robe—the richly ornamented robeᑫ he was wearing— ²⁴and they took him and threw him into the cistern.ʳ Now the cistern was empty; there was no water in it.

²⁵As they sat down to eat their meal, they looked up and saw a caravan of Ishmaelitesˢ coming from Gilead.ᵗ Their camels were loaded with spices, balmᵘ and myrrh,ᵛ and they were on their way to take them down to Egypt.ʷ

²⁶Judahˣ said to his brothers, "What will we gain if we kill our brother and cover up his blood?ʸ ²⁷Come, let's sell him to the Ishmaelites and not lay our hands on him; after all, he is our brother,ᶻ our own flesh and blood.ᵃ" His brothers agreed.

²⁸So when the Midianiteᵇ merchants came by, his brothers pulled Joseph up out of the cisternᶜ and soldᵈ him for twenty shekelsᶜ of silverᵉ to the Ishmaelites,ᶠ who took him to Egypt.ᵍ

²⁹When Reuben returned to the cistern and saw that Joseph was not there, he tore his clothes.ʰ ³⁰He went back to his brothers and said, "The boy isn't there! Where can I turn now?"ⁱ

³¹Then they got Joseph's robe,ʲ slaughtered a goat and dipped the robe in the blood.ᵏ ³²They took the ornamented robeˡ back to their father and said, "We found this. Examine it to see whether it is your son's robe."

³³He recognized it and said, "It is my son's robe! Some ferocious animalᵐ has devoured him. Joseph has surely been torn to pieces."ⁿ

³⁴Then Jacob tore his clothes,ᵒ put on sackclothᵖ and mourned for his son many days.ᑫ ³⁵All his sons and daughters came to comfort him,ʳ but he refused to be comforted.ˢ "No," he said, "in mourning will I go down to the graveᵈᵗ to my son.ᵘ" So his father wept for him.

³⁶Meanwhile, the Midianitesᵉᵛ sold Josephʷ in Egypt to Potiphar, one of Pharaoh's officials, the captain of the guard.ˣ

Judah and Tamar

38 At that time, Judahʸ left his brothers and went down to stay with a man of Adullamᶻ named Hirah.ᵃ ²There Judah met the daughter of a Canaanite man named Shua.ᵇ He married her and lay with her; ³she became pregnant and gave birth to a son, who was named Er.ᶜ ⁴She conceived again and gave birth to a son and named him Onan.ᵈ ⁵She gave birth to still another son and named him Shelah.ᵉ It was at Kezib that she gave birth to him.

⁶Judah got a wife for Er, his firstborn, and her name was Tamar.ᶠ ⁷But Er, Judah's firstborn, was wicked in the LORD's sight;ᵍ so the LORD put him to death.ʰ

⁸Then Judah said to Onan, "Lie with your brother's wife and fulfill your duty to her as a brother-in-law to produce offspring for your brother."ⁱ ⁹But Onan knew that the offspring would not be his; so whenever he lay with his brother's wife, he spilled his semen on the ground to keep from producing offspring for his brother. ¹⁰What he did was wicked in the

---

c 28 That is, about 8 ounces (about 0.2 kilogram) *d 35* Hebrew *Sheol*
e 36 Samaritan Pentateuch, Septuagint, Vulgate and Syriac (see also verse 28); Masoretic Text *Medanites*

LORD's sight; so he put him to death also.[j] ¹¹Judah then said to his daughter-in-law[k] Tamar,[l] "Live as a widow in your father's house[m] until my son Shelah[n] grows up."[o] For he thought, "He may die too, just like his brothers." So Tamar went to live in her father's house.

¹²After a long time Judah's wife, the daughter of Shua,[p] died. When Judah had recovered from his grief, he went up to Timnah,[q] to the men who were shearing his sheep,[r] and his friend Hirah the Adullamite[s] went with him.

¹³When Tamar[t] was told, "Your father-in-law is on his way to Timnah to shear his sheep," ¹⁴she took off her widow's clothes,[v] covered herself with a veil[w] to disguise herself, and then sat down[x] at the entrance to Enaim, which is on the road to Timnah.[y] For she saw that, though Shelah[z] had now grown up, she had not been given to him as his wife.

¹⁵When Judah saw her, he thought she was a prostitute,[a] for she had covered her face. ¹⁶Not realizing[b] that she was his daughter-in-law,[c] he went over to her by the roadside and said, "Come now, let me sleep with you."[d]

"And what will you give me to sleep with you?"[e] she asked.

¹⁷"I'll send you a young goat[f] from my flock," he said.

"Will you give me something as a pledge[g] until you send it?" she asked.

¹⁸He said, "What pledge should I give you?"

"Your seal[h] and its cord, and the staff in your hand," she answered. So he gave them to her and slept with her, and she became pregnant by him.[j] ¹⁹After she left, she took off her veil and put on her widow's clothes[k] again.

²⁰Meanwhile Judah sent the young goat by his friend the Adullamite[l] in order to get his pledge[m] back from the woman, but he did not find her. ²¹He asked the men who lived there, "Where is the shrine prostitute[n] who was beside the road at Enaim?"

"There hasn't been any shrine prostitute here," they said.

²²So he went back to Judah and said, "I didn't find her. Besides, the men who lived there said, 'There hasn't been any shrine prostitute here.'"

²³Then Judah said, "Let her keep what she has,[o] or we will become a laughingstock.[p] After all, I did send her this young goat, but you didn't find her."

²⁴About three months later Judah was told, "Your daughter-in-law Tamar is guilty of prostitution, and as a result she is now pregnant."

Judah said, "Bring her out and have her burned to death!"[q]

²⁵As she was being brought out, she sent a message to her father-in-law. "I am pregnant by the man who owns these," she said. And she added, "See if you recognize whose seal and cord and staff these are."[r]

²⁶Judah recognized them and said, "She is more righteous than I,[s] since I wouldn't give her to my son Shelah.[t]" And he did not sleep with her again.

²⁷When the time came for her to give birth, there were twin boys in her womb.[u] ²⁸As she was giving birth, one of them put out his hand; so the midwife[v] took a scarlet thread and tied it on his wrist[w] and said, "This one came out first." ²⁹But when he drew back his hand, his brother came out,[x] and she said, "So this is how you have broken out!" And he was named Perez.[f y] ³⁰Then his brother, who had the scarlet thread on his wrist,[z] came out and he was given the name Zerah.[g a]

Joseph and Potiphar's Wife

39 Now Joseph[b] had been taken down to Egypt. Potiphar, an Egyptian who was one of Pharaoh's officials, the captain of the guard,[c] bought him from the Ishmaelites who had taken him there.[d]

²The LORD was with Joseph[e] and he prospered, and he lived in the house of his Egyptian master. ³When his master saw that the LORD was with him[f] and that the LORD gave him success in everything he did,[g] ⁴Joseph found favor in his eyes[h] and became his attendant. Potiphar put him in charge of his household,[i] and he entrusted to his care everything he owned.[j] ⁵From the time he put him in charge of his household and of all that he

U Ge 26:3 ◄► Ge 39:23
B Ge 27:39 ◄► Ex 23:26
R Ge 30:27 ◄► Job 42:15

j ver 8,22; Ge 40:4; 42:37

f 29 Perez means breaking out. g 30 Zerah can mean scarlet or brightness.

owned, the LORD blessed the household of the Egyptian because of Joseph.¹ The blessing of the LORD was on everything Potiphar had, both in the house and in the field.ᵐ ⁶So he left in Joseph's care everything he had;ⁿ with Joseph in charge, he did not concern himself with anything except the food he ate.

Now Joseph was well-built and handsome,° ⁷and after a while his master's wife took notice of Joseph and said, "Come to bed with me!"ᵖ

⁸But he refused.ᑫ "With me in charge," he told her, "my master does not concern himself with anything in the house; everything he owns he has entrusted to my care.ʳ ⁹No one is greater in this house than I am.ˢ My master has withheld nothing from me except you, because you are his wife. How then could I do such a wicked thing and sin against God?"ᵗ ¹⁰And though she spoke to Joseph day after day, he refusedᵘ to go to bed with her or even be with her.

¹¹One day he went into the house to attend to his duties,ᵛ and none of the household servantsʷ was inside. ¹²She caught him by his cloakˣ and said, "Come to bed with me!"ʸ But he left his cloak in her hand and ran out of the house.ᶻ

¹³When she saw that he had left his cloak in her hand and had run out of the house, ¹⁴she called her household servants.ᵃ "Look," she said to them, "this Hebrewᵇ has been brought to us to make sport of us!ᶜ He came in here to sleep with me, but I screamed.ᵈ ¹⁵When he heard me scream for help, he left his cloak beside me and ran out of the house."ᵉ

¹⁶She kept his cloak beside her until his master came home. ¹⁷Then she told him this story:ᶠ "That Hebrewᵍ slaveʰ you brought us came to me to make sport of me. ¹⁸But as soon as I screamed for help, he left his cloak beside me and ran out of the house."

¹⁹When his master heard the story his wife told him, saying, "This is how your slave treated me," he burned with anger.ⁱ ²⁰Joseph's master took him and put him in prison,ʲ the place where the king's prisoners were confined.

But while Joseph was there in the prison, ²¹the LORD was with him;ᵏ he showed him kindnessˡ and granted him favor in the eyes of the prison warden.ᵐ ²²So the warden put Joseph in charge of all those held in the prison, and he was made responsible for all that was done there.ⁿ ²³The warden paid no attention to anything under Joseph's° care, because the LORD was with Joseph and gave him success in whatever he did.ᵖ

The Cupbearer and the Baker

40 Some time later, the cupbearerᑫ and the bakerʳ of the king of Egypt offended their master, the king of Egypt. ²Pharaoh was angryˢ with his two officials,ᵗ the chief cupbearer and the chief baker, ³and put them in custody in the house of the captain of the guard,ᵘ in the same prison where Joseph was confined. ⁴The captain of the guardᵛ assigned them to Joseph,ʷ and he attended them.

After they had been in custodyˣ for some time, ⁵each of the two men—the cupbearer and the baker of the king of Egypt, who were being held in prison— had a dreamʸ the same night, and each dream had a meaning of its own.ᶻ

⁶When Joseph came to them the next morning, he saw that they were dejected. ⁷So he asked Pharaoh's officials who were in custodyᵃ with him in his master's house, "Why are your faces so sad today?"ᵇ

⁸"We both had dreams," they answered, "but there is no one to interpret them."ᶜ

Then Joseph said to them, "Do not interpretations belong to God?ᵈ Tell me your dreams."

⁹So the chief cupbearerᵉ told Joseph his dream. He said to him, "In my dream I saw a vine in front of me, ¹⁰and on the vine were three branches. As soon as it budded, it blossomed,ᶠ and its clusters ripened into grapes. ¹¹Pharaoh's cup was in my hand, and I took the grapes, squeezed them into Pharaoh's cup and put the cup in his hand."

¹²"This is what it means,"ᵍ Joseph said to him. "The three branches are three days.ʰ ¹³Within three daysⁱ Pharaoh will lift up your headʲ and restore you to your position, and you will put Pharaoh's cup in his hand, just as you used to do when you were his cupbearer.ᵏ ¹⁴But when all goes well with you, remember meˡ and

show me kindness; mention me to Pharaoh and get me out of this prison. ¹⁵For I was forcibly carried off from the land of the Hebrews, and even here I have done nothing to deserve being put in a dungeon."

¹⁶When the chief baker saw that Joseph had given a favorable interpretation, he said to Joseph, "I too had a dream: On my head were three baskets of bread. ¹⁷In the top basket were all kinds of baked goods for Pharaoh, but the birds were eating them out of the basket on my head."

¹⁸"This is what it means," Joseph said. "The three baskets are three days. ¹⁹Within three days Pharaoh will lift off your head and hang you on a tree. And the birds will eat away your flesh."

²⁰Now the third day was Pharaoh's birthday, and he gave a feast for all his officials. He lifted up the heads of the chief cupbearer and the chief baker in the presence of his officials: ²¹He restored the chief cupbearer to his position, so that he once again put the cup into Pharaoh's hand, ²²but he hanged the chief baker, just as Joseph had said to them in his interpretation.

²³The chief cupbearer, however, did not remember Joseph; he forgot him.

Pharaoh's Dreams

41 When two full years had passed, Pharaoh had a dream: He was standing by the Nile, ²when out of the river there came up seven cows, sleek and fat, and they grazed among the reeds. ³After them, seven other cows, ugly and gaunt, came up out of the Nile and stood beside those on the riverbank. ⁴And the cows that were ugly and gaunt ate up the seven sleek, fat cows. Then Pharaoh woke up.

⁵He fell asleep again and had a second dream: Seven heads of grain, healthy and good, were growing on a single stalk. ⁶After them, seven other heads of grain sprouted—thin and scorched by the east wind. ⁷The thin heads of grain swallowed up the seven healthy, full heads. Then Pharaoh woke up; it had been a dream.

⁸In the morning his mind was troubled, so he sent for all the magicians and wise men of Egypt. Pharaoh told them his dreams, but no one could interpret them for him.

⁹Then the chief cupbearer said to Pharaoh, "Today I am reminded of my shortcomings. ¹⁰Pharaoh was once angry with his servants, and he imprisoned me and the chief baker in the house of the captain of the guard. ¹¹Each of us had a dream the same night, and each dream had a meaning of its own. ¹²Now a young Hebrew was there with us, a servant of the captain of the guard. We told him our dreams, and he interpreted them for us, giving each man the interpretation of his dream. ¹³And things turned out exactly as he interpreted them to us: I was restored to my position, and the other man was hanged."

¹⁴So Pharaoh sent for Joseph, and he was quickly brought from the dungeon. When he had shaved and changed his clothes, he came before Pharaoh.

¹⁵Pharaoh said to Joseph, "I had a dream, and no one can interpret it. But I have heard it said of you that when you hear a dream you can interpret it."

¹⁶"I cannot do it," Joseph replied to Pharaoh, "but God will give Pharaoh the answer he desires."

¹⁷Then Pharaoh said to Joseph, "In my dream I was standing on the bank of the Nile, ¹⁸when out of the river there came up seven cows, fat and sleek, and they grazed among the reeds. ¹⁹After them, seven other cows came up—scrawny and very ugly and lean. I had never seen such ugly cows in all the land of Egypt. ²⁰The lean, ugly cows ate up the seven fat cows that came up first. ²¹But even after they ate them, no one could tell that they had done so; they looked just as ugly as before. Then I woke up.

²²"In my dreams I also saw seven heads of grain, full and good, growing on a single stalk. ²³After them, seven other heads sprouted—withered and thin and scorched by the east wind. ²⁴The thin heads of grain swallowed up the seven good heads. I told this to the magicians, but none could explain it to me."

²⁵Then Joseph said to Pharaoh, "The

h 16 Or *three wicker baskets* *i 19* Or *and impale you on a pole* *j 22,13* Or *impaled*

dreams of Pharaoh are one and the same.ᵏ God has revealed to Pharaoh what he is about to do.ˡ ²⁶The seven good cowsᵐ are seven years, and the seven good heads of grain are seven years; it is one and the same dream. ²⁷The seven lean, ugly cows that came up afterward are seven years, and so are the seven worthless heads of grain scorched by the east wind: They are seven years of famine.ⁿ

²⁸"It is just as I said to Pharaoh: God has shown Pharaoh what he is about to do.ᵒ ²⁹Seven years of great abundanceᵖ are coming throughout the land of Egypt, ³⁰but seven years of famineᑫ will follow them. Then all the abundance in Egypt will be forgotten, and the famine will ravage the land.ʳ ³¹The abundance in the land will not be remembered, because the famine that follows it will be so severe. ³²The reason the dream was given to Pharaoh in two forms is that the matter has been firmly decidedˢ by God, and God will do it soon.ᵗ

³³"And now let Pharaoh look for a discerning and wise manᵘ and put him in charge of the land of Egypt.ᵛ ³⁴Let Pharaoh appoint commissionersʷ over the land to take a fifthˣ of the harvest of Egypt during the seven years of abundance.ʸ ³⁵They should collect all the food of these good years that are coming and store up the grain under the authority of Pharaoh, to be kept in the cities for food.ᶻ ³⁶This food should be held in reserve for the country, to be used during the seven years of famine that will come upon Egypt,ᵃ so that the country may not be ruined by the famine."

³⁷The plan seemed good to Pharaoh **B** and to all his officials.ᵇ ³⁸So Pharaoh **E** asked them, "Can we find anyone like **G** this man, one in whom is the spirit of **M** God?"ᶜ **T**

³⁹Then Pharaoh said to Joseph, "Since God has made all this known to you,ᵈ there is no one so discerning and wise as you.ᵉ ⁴⁰You shall be in charge of my palace,ᶠ and all my people are to submit to your orders.ᵍ Only with respect to the throne will I be greater than you."ʰ

B ▶ Ex 28:3   **E** Ge 1:2–3 ◀ ▶ Ex 28:3
G ▶ Ex 28:3   **M** Ge 1:2–3 ◀ ▶ Jdg 3:10
T ▶ Ex 28:3

41:25 ᵏS Ge 40:12
ˡS Ge 40:8;
Isa 46:11; Da 2:45
41:26 ᵐS ver 2
41:27 ⁿS Ge 12:10
41:28 ᵒS Ge 40:8
41:29 ᵖver 47
41:30 ᑫver 54;
Ge 45:6,11; 47:13;
Ps 105:16 ʳver 56;
S Ge 12:10
41:32 ˢDa 2:5
ᵗS Ge 40:8
41:33 ᵘver 39
ᵛS Ge 39:9
41:34 ʷEst 2:3
ˣGe 47:24,26;
1Sa 8:15 ʸver 48;
Ge 47:14
41:35 ᶻver 48
41:36 ᵃver 56;
Ge 42:6; 47:14
41:37 ᵇGe 45:16;
Est 2:4; Isa 19:11
41:38 ᶜNu 27:18;
Dt 34:9; Da 2:11;
4:8,8-9,18; 5:11,14
41:39 ᵈDa 2:11;
5:11 ᵉver 33
41:40 ᶠ1Ki 4:6;
2Ki 15:5; Isa 22:15;
36:3 ᵍS Ge 39:9;
Ps 105:21-22;
Ac 7:10 ʰEst 10:3
41:41 ⁱver 43,55;
Ge 42:6; 45:8,13,
26; Est 8:2;
Jer 40:7; Da 6:3
41:42 ʲS Ge 24:22;
Est 3:10; 8:2,8
ᵏ1Sa 17:38; 18:4;
1Ki 19:19; Est 6:8,
11; Da 5:29;
Zec 3:4 ˡEx 25:4;
Est 8:15; Da 5:29
ᵐPs 73:6; SS 4:9;
Isa 3:18; Eze 16:11;
Da 5:7,16,29
41:43 ⁿGe 46:29;
50:9; Isa 2:7; 22:18
ᵒEst 10:3 ᵖEst 6:9
ᑫS ver 41
41:44 ʳS Ge 37:8;
Est 10:2; Ps 105:22
41:45 ˢEst 2:7
ᵗEx 2:16
ᵘEze 30:17
ᵛver 50; Ge 46:20,
27
41:46 ʷS Ge 37:2
ˣ1Sa 8:11; 16:21;
Pr 22:29; Da 1:19
41:47 ʸver 29
41:48 ᶻS ver 34
41:49 ᵃS Ge 12:2
41:50 ᵇS ver 45
41:51 ᶜGe 48:14,
18,20; 49:3
ᵈGe 46:20; 48:1;
50:23; Nu 1:34;
Dt 33:17; Jos 4:12;
17:1; 1Ch 7:14
41:52 ᵉGe 46:20;
48:1,5; 50:23;
Nu 1:32; 26:28;
Dt 33:17; Jos 14:4;
Jdg 5:14; 1Ch 7:20;
2Ch 30:1; Ps 60:7;
Jer 7:15; Ob 1:19
ᶠS Ge 35:17
41:54 ᵍS Ge 12:10
ʰAc 7:11

Joseph in Charge of Egypt

⁴¹So Pharaoh said to Joseph, "I hereby put you in charge of the whole land of Egypt."ⁱ ⁴²Then Pharaoh took his signet ringʲ from his finger and put it on Joseph's finger. He dressed him in robesᵏ of fine linenˡ and put a gold chain around his neck.ᵐ ⁴³He had him ride in a chariotⁿ as his second-in-command,ᵒ and men shouted before him, "Make way!"ᵖ Thus he put him in charge of the whole land of Egypt.ᑫ

⁴⁴Then Pharaoh said to Joseph, "I am Pharaoh, but without your word no one will lift hand or foot in all Egypt."ʳ ⁴⁵Pharaoh gave Josephˢ the name Zaphenath-Paneah and gave him Asenath daughter of Potiphera, priestᵗ of On,ᵘ to be his wife.ᵛ And Joseph went throughout the land of Egypt.

⁴⁶Joseph was thirty years oldʷ when he entered the serviceˣ of Pharaoh king of Egypt. And Joseph went out from Pharaoh's presence and traveled throughout Egypt. ⁴⁷During the seven years of abundanceʸ the land produced plentifully. ⁴⁸Joseph collected all the food produced in those seven years of abundance in Egypt and stored it in the cities.ᶻ In each city he put the food grown in the fields surrounding it. ⁴⁹Joseph stored up huge quantities of grain, like the sand of the sea;ᵃ it was so much that he stopped keeping records because it was beyond measure.

⁵⁰Before the years of famine came, two sons were born to Joseph by Asenath daughter of Potiphera, priest of On.ᵇ ⁵¹Joseph named his firstbornᶜ Manassehᵈ and said, "It is because God has made me forget all my trouble and all my father's household." ⁵²The second son he named Ephraimᵉ and said, "It is because God has made me fruitfulᶠ in the land of my suffering."

⁵³The seven years of abundance in Egypt came to an end, ⁵⁴and the seven years of famineᵍ began,ʰ just as Joseph had said. There was famine in all the other lands, but in the whole land of

A Ge 41:25–36 ◀ ▶ Ge 41:53–54
A Ge 41:47–48 ◀ ▶ Ge 46:2–4

ᵏ 38 Or of the gods   ˡ 43 Or in the chariot of his second-in-command; or in his second chariot   ᵐ 43 Or Bow down   ⁿ 45 That is, Heliopolis; also in verse 50   ᵒ 51 Manasseh sounds like and may be derived from the Hebrew for forget.   ᵖ 52 Ephraim sounds like the Hebrew for twice fruitful.

Egypt there was food. ⁵⁵When all Egypt began to feel the famine, the people cried to Pharaoh for food. Then Pharaoh told all the Egyptians, "Go to Joseph and do what he tells you."

⁵⁶When the famine had spread over the whole country, Joseph opened the storehouses and sold grain to the Egyptians, for the famine was severe throughout Egypt. ⁵⁷And all the countries came to Egypt to buy grain from Joseph, because the famine was severe in all the world.

Joseph's Brothers Go to Egypt

42 When Jacob learned that there was grain in Egypt, he said to his sons, "Why do you just keep looking at each other?" ²He continued, "I have heard that there is grain in Egypt. Go down there and buy some for us, so that we may live and not die."

³Then ten of Joseph's brothers went down to buy grain from Egypt. ⁴But Jacob did not send Benjamin, Joseph's brother, with the others, because he was afraid that harm might come to him. ⁵So Israel's sons were among those who went to buy grain, for the famine was in the land of Canaan also.

⁶Now Joseph was the governor of the land, the one who sold grain to all its people. So when Joseph's brothers arrived, they bowed down to him with their faces to the ground. ⁷As soon as Joseph saw his brothers, he recognized them, but he pretended to be a stranger and spoke harshly to them. "Where do you come from?" he asked.

"From the land of Canaan," they replied, "to buy food."

⁸Although Joseph recognized his brothers, they did not recognize him. ⁹Then he remembered his dreams about them and said to them, "You are spies! You have come to see where our land is unprotected."

¹⁰"No, my lord," they answered. "Your servants have come to buy food. ¹¹We are all the sons of one man. Your servants are honest men, not spies."

¹²"No!" he said to them. "You have come to see where our land is unprotected."

¹³But they replied, "Your servants were twelve brothers, the sons of one man, who lives in the land of Canaan. The youngest is now with our father, and one is no more."

¹⁴Joseph said to them, "It is just as I told you: You are spies! ¹⁵And this is how you will be tested: As surely as Pharaoh lives, you will not leave this place unless your youngest brother comes here. ¹⁶Send one of your number to get your brother; the rest of you will be kept in prison, so that your words may be tested to see if you are telling the truth. If you are not, then as surely as Pharaoh lives, you are spies!" ¹⁷And he put them all in custody for three days.

¹⁸On the third day, Joseph said to them, "Do this and you will live, for I fear God: ¹⁹If you are honest men, let one of your brothers stay here in prison, while the rest of you go and take grain back for your starving households. ²⁰But you must bring your youngest brother to me, so that your words may be verified and that you may not die." This they proceeded to do.

²¹They said to one another, "Surely we are being punished because of our brother. We saw how distressed he was when he pleaded with us for his life, but we would not listen; that's why this distress has come upon us."

²²Reuben replied, "Didn't I tell you not to sin against the boy? But you wouldn't listen! Now we must give an accounting for his blood." ²³They did not realize that Joseph could understand them, since he was using an interpreter.

²⁴He turned away from them and began to weep, but then turned back and spoke to them again. He had Simeon taken from them and bound before their eyes.

²⁵Joseph gave orders to fill their bags with grain, to put each man's silver back in his sack, and to give them provisions for their journey. After this was done for them, ²⁶they loaded their grain on their donkeys and left.

²⁷At the place where they stopped for the night one of them opened his sack to get feed for his donkey, and he saw his silver in the mouth of his sack. ²⁸"My silver has been returned," he said to his brothers. "Here it is in my sack."

Their hearts sank and they turned to

each other trembling and said, "What is this that God has done to us?"

²⁹When they came to their father Jacob in the land of Canaan, they told him all that had happened to them. They said, ³⁰"The man who is lord over the land spoke harshly to us and treated us as though we were spying on the land. ³¹But we said to him, 'We are honest men; we are not spies.' ³²We were twelve brothers, sons of one father. One is no more, and the youngest is now with our father in Canaan.'

³³"Then the man who is lord over the land said to us, 'This is how I will know whether you are honest men: Leave one of your brothers here with me, and take food for your starving households and go. ³⁴But bring your youngest brother to me so I will know that you are not spies but honest men.' Then I will give your brother back to you, and you can trade in the land.' "

³⁵As they were emptying their sacks, there in each man's sack was his pouch of silver! When they and their father saw the money pouches, they were frightened. ³⁶Their father Jacob said to them, "You have deprived me of my children. Joseph is no more and Simeon is no more, and now you want to take Benjamin. Everything is against me!"

³⁷Then Reuben said to his father, "You may put both of my sons to death if I do not bring him back to you. Entrust him to my care, and I will bring him back."

³⁸But Jacob said, "My son will not go down there with you; his brother is dead and he is the only one left. If harm comes to him on the journey you are taking, you will bring my gray head down to the grave in sorrow."

The Second Journey to Egypt

43 Now the famine was still severe in the land. ²So when they had eaten all the grain they had brought from Egypt, their father said to them, "Go back and buy us a little more food." ³But Judah said to him, "The man warned us solemnly, 'You will not see my face again unless your brother is with you.' ⁴If you will send our brother along with us, we will go down and buy food for you. ⁵But if you will not send him, we will not go down, because the man said to us, 'You will not see my face again unless your brother is with you.' "

⁶Israel asked, "Why did you bring this trouble on me by telling the man you had another brother?"

⁷They replied, "The man questioned us closely about ourselves and our family. 'Is your father still living?' he asked us. 'Do you have another brother?' We simply answered his questions. How were we to know he would say, 'Bring your brother down here'?"

⁸Then Judah said to Israel his father, "Send the boy along with me and we will go at once, so that we and you and our children may live and not die. ⁹I myself will guarantee his safety; you can hold me personally responsible for him. If I do not bring him back to you and set him here before you, I will bear the blame before you all my life. ¹⁰As it is, if we had not delayed, we could have gone and returned twice."

¹¹Then their father Israel said to them, "If it must be, then do this: Put some of the best products of the land in your bags and take them down to the man as a gift—a little balm and a little honey, some spices and myrrh, some pistachio nuts and almonds. ¹²Take double the amount of silver with you, for you must return the silver that was put back into the mouths of your sacks. Perhaps it was a mistake. ¹³Take your brother also and go back to the man at once. ¹⁴And may God Almighty grant you mercy before the man so that he will let your other brother and Benjamin come back with you. As for me, if I am bereaved, I am bereaved."

¹⁵So the men took the gifts and double the amount of silver, and Benjamin also. They hurried down to Egypt and presented themselves to Joseph. ¹⁶When Joseph saw Benjamin with them, he said to the steward of his house, "Take these men to my house, slaughter an animal and prepare dinner; they are to eat with me at noon."

¹⁷The man did as Joseph told him and took the men to Joseph's house. ¹⁸Now the men were frightened when they were taken to his house. They thought, "We were brought here because of the silver that was put back into our sacks

q 34 Or move about freely   r 38 Hebrew Sheol   s 14 Hebrew El-Shaddai

the first time. He wants to attack us[h] and overpower us and seize us as slaves[i] and take our donkeys.[j]"

[19] So they went up to Joseph's steward[k] and spoke to him at the entrance to the house. [20] "Please, sir," they said, "we came down here the first time to buy food.[l] [21] But at the place where we stopped for the night we opened our sacks and each of us found his silver—the exact weight—in the mouth of his sack. So we have brought it back with us.[m] [22] We have also brought additional silver with us to buy food. We don't know who put our silver in our sacks."

[23] "It's all right," he said. "Don't be afraid. Your God, the God of your father,[n] has given you treasure in your sacks;[o] I received your silver." Then he brought Simeon out to them.[p]

[24] The steward took the men into Joseph's house,[q] gave them water to wash their feet[r] and provided fodder for their donkeys. [25] They prepared their gifts[s] for Joseph's arrival at noon,[t] because they had heard that they were to eat there.

[26] When Joseph came home,[u] they presented to him the gifts[v] they had brought into the house, and they bowed down before him to the ground.[w] [27] He asked them how they were, and then he said, "How is your aged father[x] you told me about? Is he still living?"[y]

[28] They replied, "Your servant our father[z] is still alive and well." And they bowed low[a] to pay him honor.[b]

[29] As he looked about and saw his brother Benjamin, his own mother's son,[c] he asked, "Is this your youngest brother, the one you told me about?"[d] And he said, "God be gracious to you,[e] my son." [30] Deeply moved[f] at the sight of his brother, Joseph hurried out and looked for a place to weep. He went into his private room and wept[g] there.

[31] After he had washed his face, he came out and, controlling himself,[h] said, "Serve the food."[i]

[32] They served him by himself, the brothers by themselves, and the Egyptians who ate with him by themselves, because Egyptians could not eat with Hebrews,[j] for that is detestable to Egyptians.[k] [33] The men had been seated before him in the order of their ages, from the firstborn[l] to the youngest;[m] and they looked at each other in astonishment.

[34] When portions were served to them from Joseph's table, Benjamin's portion was five times as much as anyone else's.[n] So they feasted[o] and drank freely with him.

A Silver Cup in a Sack

44 Now Joseph gave these instructions to the steward of his house:[p] "Fill the men's sacks with as much food as they can carry, and put each man's silver in the mouth of his sack.[q] [2] Then put my cup,[r] the silver one,[s] in the mouth of the youngest one's sack, along with the silver for his grain." And he did as Joseph said.

[3] As morning dawned, the men were sent on their way with their donkeys.[t] [4] They had not gone far from the city when Joseph said to his steward,[u] "Go after those men at once, and when you catch up with them, say to them, 'Why have you repaid good with evil?[v] [5] Isn't this the cup[w] my master drinks from and also uses for divination?[x] This is a wicked thing you have done.' "

[6] When he caught up with them, he repeated these words to them. [7] But they said to him, "Why does my lord say such things? Far be it from your servants[y] to do anything like that! [8] We even brought back to you from the land of Canaan[a] the silver[b] we found inside the mouths of our sacks.[c] So why would we steal[d] silver or gold from your master's house? [9] If any of your servants[e] is found to have it, he will die;[f] and the rest of us will become my lord's slaves.[g]"

[10] "Very well, then," he said, "let it be as you say. Whoever is found to have it[h] will become my slave;[i] the rest of you will be free from blame."[j]

[11] Each of them quickly lowered his sack to the ground and opened it. [12] Then the steward[k] proceeded to search,[l] beginning with the oldest and ending with the youngest.[m] And the cup was found in Benjamin's sack.[n] [13] At this, they tore their clothes.[o] Then they all loaded their donkeys[p] and returned to the city.

[14] Joseph was still in the house[q] when Judah[r] and his brothers came in, and they threw themselves to the ground before him.[s] [15] Joseph said to them, "What is this you have done?[t] Don't you know that a man like me can find things out by divination?[u]"

¹⁶"What can we say to my lord?" Judah replied. "What can we say? How can we prove our innocence? God has uncovered your servants' guilt. We are now my lord's slaves—we ourselves and the one who was found to have the cup."

¹⁷But Joseph said, "Far be it from me to do such a thing! Only the man who was found to have the cup will become my slave. The rest of you, go back to your father in peace."

¹⁸Then Judah went up to him and said: "Please, my lord, let your servant speak a word to my lord. Do not be angry with your servant, though you are equal to Pharaoh himself. ¹⁹My lord asked his servants, 'Do you have a father or a brother?' ²⁰And we answered, 'We have an aged father, and there is a young son born to him in his old age. His brother is dead, and he is the only one of his mother's sons left, and his father loves him.'

²¹"Then you said to your servants, 'Bring him down to me so I can see him for myself.' ²²And we said to my lord, 'The boy cannot leave his father; if he leaves him, his father will die.' ²³But you told your servants, 'Unless your youngest brother comes down with you, you will not see my face again.' ²⁴When we went back to your servant my father, we told him what my lord had said.

²⁵"Then our father said, 'Go back and buy a little more food.' ²⁶But we said, 'We cannot go down. Only if our youngest brother is with us will we go. We cannot see the man's face unless our youngest brother is with us.'

²⁷"Your servant my father said to us, 'You know that my wife bore me two sons. ²⁸One of them went away from me, and I said, "He has surely been torn to pieces." And I have not seen him since. ²⁹If you take this one from me too and harm comes to him, you will bring my gray head down to the grave in misery.'

³⁰"So now, if the boy is not with us when I go back to your servant my father and if my father, whose life is closely bound up with the boy's life, ³¹sees that the boy isn't there, he will die. Your servants will bring the gray head of our father down to the grave in sorrow. ³²Your servant guaranteed the boy's safety to my father. I said, 'If I do not bring him back to you, I will bear the blame before you, my father, all my life!'

³³"Now then, please let your servant remain here as my lord's slave in place of the boy, and let the boy return with his brothers. ³⁴How can I go back to my father if the boy is not with me? No! Do not let me see the misery that would come upon my father."

Joseph Makes Himself Known

45 Then Joseph could no longer control himself before all his attendants, and he cried out, "Have everyone leave my presence!" So there was no one with Joseph when he made himself known to his brothers. ²And he wept so loudly that the Egyptians heard him, and Pharaoh's household heard about it.

³Joseph said to his brothers, "I am Joseph! Is my father still living?" But his brothers were not able to answer him, because they were terrified at his presence.

⁴Then Joseph said to his brothers, "Come close to me." When they had done so, he said, "I am your brother Joseph, the one you sold into Egypt! ⁵And now, do not be distressed and do not be angry with yourselves for selling me here, because it was to save lives that God sent me ahead of you. ⁶For two years now there has been famine in the land, and for the next five years there will not be plowing and reaping. ⁷But God sent me ahead of you to preserve for you a remnant on earth and to save your lives by a great deliverance."

⁸"So then, it was not you who sent me here, but God. He made me father to Pharaoh, lord of his entire household and ruler of all Egypt. ⁹Now hurry back to my father and say to him, 'This is what your son Joseph says: God has made me lord of all Egypt. Come down to me; don't delay. ¹⁰You shall live in the region of Goshen and be near me—you, your children and grandchildren, your flocks and herds, and all you have. ¹¹I will provide for you there, because five years of famine are still to come. Otherwise you and

10:24; 47:1 ʰGe 46:6-7 **45:11** ⁱGe 47:12; 50:21 ʲS Ge 41:30

t 29 Hebrew *Sheol*; also in verse 31 *u 7* Or *save you as a great band of survivors*

your household and all who belong to you will become destitute.'ᵏ

¹²"You can see for yourselves, and so can my brother Benjamin,ˡ that it is really I who am speaking to you.ᵐ ¹³Tell my father about all the honor accorded me in Egyptⁿ and about everything you have seen. And bring my father down here quickly.ᵒ"

¹⁴Then he threw his arms around his brother Benjamin and wept, and Benjaminᵖ embraced him,ᑫ weeping. ¹⁵And he kissedʳ all his brothers and wept over them.ˢ Afterward his brothers talked with him.ᵗ

¹⁶When the news reached Pharaoh's palace that Joseph's brothers had come,ᵘ Pharaoh and all his officialsᵛ were pleased.ʷ ¹⁷Pharaoh said to Joseph, "Tell your brothers, 'Do this: Load your animalsˣ and return to the land of Canaan,ʸ ¹⁸and bring your father and your families back to me. I will give you the best of the land of Egyptᶻ and you can enjoy the fat of the land.'ᵃ

¹⁹"You are also directed to tell them, 'Do this: Take some cartsᵇ from Egypt for your children and your wives, and get your father and come. ²⁰Never mind about your belongings,ᶜ because the best of all Egyptᵈ will be yours.' "

²¹So the sons of Israel did this. Joseph gave them carts,ᵉ as Pharaoh had commanded, and he also gave them provisions for their journey.ᶠ ²²To each of them he gave new clothing,ᵍ but to Benjamin he gave three hundred shekelsᵛ of silver and five sets of clothes.ʰ ²³And this is what he sent to his father: ten donkeysⁱ loaded with the best thingsʲ of Egypt, and ten female donkeys loaded with grain and bread and other provisions for his journey.ᵏ ²⁴Then he sent his brothers away, and as they were leaving he said to them, "Don't quarrel on the way!"ˡ

²⁵So they went up out of Egyptᵐ and came to their father Jacob in the land of Canaan.ⁿ ²⁶They told him, "Joseph is still alive! In fact, he is ruler of all Egypt."ᵒ Jacob was stunned; he did not believe them.ᵖ ²⁷But when they told him everything Joseph had said to them, and when he saw the cartsᑫ Joseph had sent to carry him back, the spirit of their father Jacob revived. ²⁸And Israel said, "I'm con-vinced!ʳ My son Joseph is still alive. I will go and see him before I die."ˢ

Jacob Goes to Egypt

46 So Israelᵗ set out with all that was his, and when he reached Beersheba,ᵘ he offered sacrificesᵛ to the God of his father Isaac.ʷ

²And God spoke to Israelˣ in a vision at nightʸ and said, "Jacob! Jacob!"

"Here I am,"ᶻ he replied.

³"I am God, the God of your father,"ᵃ he said. "Do not be afraidᵇ to go down to Egypt,ᶜ for I will make you into a great nationᵈ there.ᵉ ⁴I will go down to Egypt with you, and I will surely bring you back again.ᶠ And Joseph's own hand will close your eyes.ᵍ"

⁵Then Jacob left Beersheba,ʰ and Israel'sⁱ sons took their father Jacob and their children and their wives in the cartsʲ that Pharaoh had sent to transport him. ⁶They also took with them their livestock and the possessionsᵏ they had acquiredˡ in Canaan, and Jacob and all his offspring went to Egypt.ᵐ ⁷He took with him to Egyptⁿ his sons and grandsons and his daughters and granddaughters—all his offspring.ᵒ

⁸These are the names of the sons of Israelᵖ (Jacob and his descendants) who went to Egypt:

Reuben the firstbornᑫ of Jacob.
⁹The sons of Reuben:ʳ
  Hanoch, Pallu,ˢ Hezron and Carmi.ᵗ
¹⁰The sons of Simeon:ᵘ
  Jemuel,ᵛ Jamin, Ohad, Jakin, Zoharʷ and Shaul the son of a Canaanite woman.
¹¹The sons of Levi:ˣ
  Gershon,ʸ Kohathᶻ and Merari.ᵃ
¹²The sons of Judah:ᵇ
  Er,ᶜ Onan,ᵈ Shelah, Perezᵉ and Zerahᶠ (but Er and Onan had died in the land of Canaan).ᵍ
  The sons of Perez:ʰ
  Hezron and Hamul.ⁱ
¹³The sons of Issachar:ʲ

GENESIS 46:14

Tola, Puah,[w,k] Jashub[x,l] and Shimron.

[14]The sons of Zebulun:[m]
Sered, Elon and Jahleel.

[15]These were the sons Leah bore to Jacob in Paddan Aram,[n] besides his daughter Dinah.[o] These sons and daughters of his were thirty-three in all.

[16]The sons of Gad:[p]
Zephon,[z,q] Haggi, Shuni, Ezbon, Eri, Arodi and Areli.

[17]The sons of Asher:[r]
Imnah, Ishvah, Ishvi and Beriah. Their sister was Serah.
The sons of Beriah:
Heber and Malkiel.

[18]These were the children born to Jacob by Zilpah,[s] whom Laban had given to his daughter Leah[t]—sixteen in all.

[19]The sons of Jacob's wife Rachel:[u]
Joseph and Benjamin.[v] [20]In Egypt, Manasseh[w] and Ephraim[x] were born to Joseph[y] by Asenath daughter of Potiphera, priest of On.[a,z]

[21]The sons of Benjamin:[a]
Bela, Beker, Ashbel, Gera, Naaman, Ehi, Rosh, Muppim, Huppim and Ard.[b]

[22]These were the sons of Rachel[c] who were born to Jacob—fourteen in all.

[23]The son of Dan:[d]
Hushim.[e]

[24]The sons of Naphtali:[f]
Jahziel, Guni, Jezer and Shillem.

[25]These were the sons born to Jacob by Bilhah,[g] whom Laban had given to his daughter Rachel[h]—seven in all.

[26]All those who went to Egypt with Jacob—those who were his direct descendants, not counting his sons' wives—numbered sixty-six persons.[i] [27]With the two sons[b] who had been born to Joseph in Egypt,[j] the members of Jacob's family, which went to Egypt, were seventy[c] in all.[k]

[28]Now Jacob sent Judah[l] ahead of him to Joseph to get directions to Goshen.[m] When they arrived in the region of Goshen, [29]Joseph had his chariot[n] made ready and went to Goshen to meet his father Israel.[o] As soon as Joseph appeared before him, he threw his arms around his father[d] and wept[p] for a long time.[q]

[30]Israel[r] said to Joseph, "Now I am ready to die, since I have seen for myself that you are still alive."[s]

[31]Then Joseph said to his brothers and to his father's household, "I will go up and speak to Pharaoh and will say to him, 'My brothers and my father's household, who were living in the land of Canaan,[t] have come to me.[u] [32]The men are shepherds;[v] they tend livestock,[w] and they have brought along their flocks and herds and everything they own.'[x] [33]When Pharaoh calls you in and asks, 'What is your occupation?'[y] [34]you should answer, 'Your servants[z] have tended livestock from our boyhood on, just as our fathers did.'[a] Then you will be allowed to settle[b] in the region of Goshen,[c] for all shepherds are detestable to the Egyptians.[d]"

47 Joseph went and told Pharaoh, "My father and brothers, with their flocks and herds and everything they own, have come from the land of Canaan[e] and are now in Goshen."[f] [2]He chose five of his brothers and presented them[g] before Pharaoh.

[3]Pharaoh asked the brothers, "What is your occupation?"[h]

"Your servants[i] are shepherds,[j]" they replied to Pharaoh, "just as our fathers were." [4]They also said to him, "We have come to live here awhile,[k] because the famine is severe in Canaan[l] and your servants' flocks have no pasture.[m] So now, please let your servants settle in Goshen."[n]

[5]Pharaoh said to Joseph, "Your father and your brothers have come to you, [6]and the land of Egypt is before you; settle[o] your father and your brothers in the best part of the land.[p] Let them live in Goshen. And if you know of any among them with special ability,[q] put them in charge of my own livestock.[r]"

[7]Then Joseph brought his father Jacob in and presented him[s] before Pharaoh. After Jacob blessed[e] Pharaoh,[t] [8]Pharaoh asked him, "How old are you?"

[9]And Jacob said to Pharaoh, "The years of my pilgrimage are a hundred and

---

[w 13] Samaritan Pentateuch and Syriac (see also 1 Chron. 7:1); Masoretic Text *Puvah*   [x 13] Samaritan Pentateuch and some Septuagint manuscripts (see also Num. 26:24 and 1 Chron. 7:1); Masoretic Text *Iob*   [y 15] That is, Northwest Mesopotamia   [z 16] Samaritan Pentateuch and Septuagint (see also Num. 26:15); Masoretic Text *Ziphion*   [a 20] That is, Heliopolis   [b 27] Hebrew; Septuagint *the nine children*   [c 27] Hebrew (see also Exodus 1:5 and footnote); Septuagint (see also Acts 7:14) *seventy-five*   [d 29] Hebrew *around him*   [e 7] Or *greeted*

thirty.ᵘ My years have been few and difficult,ᵛ and they do not equal the years of the pilgrimage of my fathers.ʷ" ¹⁰Then Jacob blessedʲ Pharaohˣ and went out from his presence.

¹¹So Joseph settled his father and his brothers in Egypt and gave them property in the best part of the land,ʸ the district of Rameses,ᶻ as Pharaoh directed. ¹²Joseph also provided his father and his brothers and all his father's household with food, according to the number of their children.ᵃ

Joseph and the Famine

¹³There was no food, however, in the whole region because the famine was severe; both Egypt and Canaan wasted away because of the famine.ᵇ ¹⁴Joseph collected all the money that was to be found in Egypt and Canaan in payment for the grain they were buying,ᶜ and he brought it to Pharaoh's palace.ᵈ ¹⁵When the money of the people of Egypt and Canaan was gone,ᵉ all Egypt came to Josephᶠ and said, "Give us food. Why should we die before your eyes?ᵍ Our money is used up."

¹⁶"Then bring your livestock,ʰ" said Joseph. "I will sell you food in exchange for your livestock, since your money is gone.ⁱ" ¹⁷So they brought their livestock to Joseph, and he gave them food in exchange for their horses,ʲ their sheep and goats, their cattle and donkeys.ᵏ And he brought them through that year with food in exchange for all their livestock.

¹⁸When that year was over, they came to him the following year and said, "We cannot hide from our lord the fact that since our money is goneˡ and our livestock belongs to you,ᵐ there is nothing left for our lord except our bodies and our land. ¹⁹Why should we perish before your eyesⁿ—we and our land as well? Buy us and our land in exchange for food,ᵒ and we with our land will be in bondage to Pharaoh.ᵖ Give us seed so that we may live and not die,ᑫ and that the land may not become desolate."

²⁰So Joseph bought all the land in Egypt for Pharaoh. The Egyptians, one and all, sold their fields, because the famine was too severeʳ for them. The land became Pharaoh's, ²¹and Joseph reduced the people to servitude,ᵍˢ from one end of Egypt to the other. ²²However, he did not buy

the land of the priests,ᵗ because they received a regular allotment from Pharaoh and had food enough from the allotmentᵘ Pharaoh gave them. That is why they did not sell their land.

²³Joseph said to the people, "Now that I have bought you and your land today for Pharaoh, here is seedᵛ for you so you can plant the ground.ʷ ²⁴But when the crop comes in, give a fifthˣ of it to Pharaoh. The other four-fifths you may keep as seed for the fields and as food for yourselves and your households and your children."

²⁵"You have saved our lives," they said. "May we find favor in the eyes of our lord;ʸ we will be in bondage to Pharaoh."ᶻ

²⁶So Joseph established it as a law concerning land in Egypt—still in force today—that a fifthᵃ of the produce belongs to Pharaoh. It was only the land of the priests that did not become Pharaoh's.ᵇ

²⁷Now the Israelites settled in Egypt in the region of Goshen.ᶜ They acquired property thereᵈ and were fruitful and increased greatly in number.ᵉ

²⁸Jacob lived in Egyptᶠ seventeen years, and the years of his life were a hundred and forty-seven.ᵍ ²⁹When the time drew near for Israelʰ to die,ⁱ he called for his son Joseph and said to him, "If I have found favor in your eyes,ʲ put your hand under my thighᵏ and promise that you will show me kindnessˡ and faithfulness.ᵐ Do not bury me in Egypt, ³⁰but when I rest with my fathers,ⁿ carry me out of Egypt and bury me where they are buried."ᵒ

"I will do as you say," he said.

³¹"Swear to me,"ᵖ he said. Then Joseph swore to him,ᑫ and Israelʳ worshiped as he leaned on the top of his staff.ʰˢ

Manasseh and Ephraim

48 Some time later Joseph was told, "Your father is ill." So he took his two sons Manasseh and Ephraimᵗ along with him. ²When Jacob was told, "Your son Joseph has come to you," Israelᵘ rallied his strength and sat up on the bed.

³Jacob said to Joseph, "God Almightyⁱᵛ A

A *Ge 46:2–4* ◀▶ *Ge 48:15–16*

ᶠ10 Or *said farewell to* ᵍ21 Samaritan Pentateuch and Septuagint (see also Vulgate); Masoretic Text *and he moved the people into the cities*
ʰ31 Or *Israel bowed down at the head of his bed* ⁱ3 Hebrew *El-Shaddai*

appeared to me at Luz^w in the land of Canaan, and there he blessed me^x ⁴and said to me, 'I am going to make you fruitful and will increase your numbers.^y I will make you a community of peoples, and I will give this land^z as an everlasting possession to your descendants after you.'^a

⁵"Now then, your two sons born to you in Egypt^b before I came to you here will be reckoned as mine; Ephraim and Manasseh will be mine,^c just as Reuben^d and Simeon^e are mine. ⁶Any children born to you after them will be yours; in the territory they inherit they will be reckoned under the names of their brothers. ⁷As I was returning from Paddan,^f to my sorrow^g Rachel died in the land of Canaan while we were still on the way, a little distance from Ephrath. So I buried her there beside the road to Ephrath" (that is, Bethlehem).^h

⁸When Israelⁱ saw the sons of Joseph,^j he asked, "Who are these?"

⁹"They are the sons God has given me here,"^k Joseph said to his father.

Then Israel said, "Bring them to me so I may bless^l them."

¹⁰Now Israel's eyes were failing because of old age, and he could hardly see.^m So Joseph brought his sons close to him, and his father kissed themⁿ and embraced them.^o

¹¹Israel^p said to Joseph, "I never expected to see your face again,^q and now God has allowed me to see your children too."^r

¹²Then Joseph removed them from Israel's knees^s and bowed down with his face to the ground.^t ¹³And Joseph took both of them, Ephraim on his right toward Israel's left hand and Manasseh on his left toward Israel's right hand,^u and brought them close to him. ¹⁴But Israel reached out his right hand and put it on Ephraim's head,^w though he was the younger,^x and crossing his arms, he put his left hand on Manasseh's head, even though Manasseh was the firstborn.^y

I Ge 17:7-8 ◀ ▶ Ex 12:41

¹⁵Then he blessed^z Joseph and said,

"May the God before whom my fathers
  Abraham and Isaac walked,^a
the God who has been my shepherd^b
  all my life to this day,
¹⁶the Angel^c who has delivered me from
  all harm^d
—may he bless^e these boys.^f
May they be called by my name
  and the names of my fathers
    Abraham and Isaac,^g
and may they increase greatly
  upon the earth."^h

¹⁷When Joseph saw his father placing his right handⁱ on Ephraim's head^j he was displeased; so he took hold of his father's hand to move it from Ephraim's head to Manasseh's head. ¹⁸Joseph said to him, "No, my father, this one is the firstborn; put your right hand on his head."^k

¹⁹But his father refused and said, "I know, my son, I know. He too will become a people, and he too will become great.^l Nevertheless, his younger brother will be greater than he,^m and his descendants will become a group of nations."ⁿ ²⁰He blessed^o them that day^p and said,

"In your^k name will Israel^q pronounce
    this blessing:^r
  'May God make you like Ephraim^s
    and Manasseh.'"

So he put Ephraim ahead of Manasseh.

²¹Then Israel said to Joseph, "I am about to die, but God will be with you^u and take you^l back to the land of your^l fathers.^v ²²And to you, as one who is over your brothers,^w I give the ridge of land^{m x} I took from the Amorites with my sword and my bow."

A Ge 48:3-6 ◀ ▶ Ge 48:19-22
F Ge 28:20 ◀ ▶ Ex 15:23-25
A Ge 24:7 ◀ ▶ Dt 14:29
A Ge 48:15-16 ◀ ▶ Ge 49:1-28

¹⁷ That is, Northwest Mesopotamia   ^k20 The Hebrew is singular.   ^l21 The Hebrew is plural.   ^m22 Or *And to you I give one portion more than to your brothers—the portion*

48:4 In this verse Jacob briefly summarizes and reconfirms the divine covenant made with Abraham and his descendants.

Jacob Blesses His Sons

49:1–28Ref — Dt 33:1–29

49 Then Jacob called for his sons and said: "Gather around so I can tell you what will happen to you in days to come.[z]

[2] "Assemble[a] and listen, sons of Jacob;
  listen to your father Israel.[b]

[3] "Reuben, you are my firstborn,[c]
  my might, the first sign of my strength,[d]
  excelling in honor,[e] excelling in power.
[4] Turbulent as the waters,[f] you will no longer excel,
  for you went up onto your father's bed,
  onto my couch and defiled it.[g]

[5] "Simeon[h] and Levi[i] are brothers—
  their swords[n] are weapons of violence.[j]
[6] Let me not enter their council,
  let me not join their assembly,[k]
  for they have killed men in their anger[l]
  and hamstrung[m] oxen as they pleased.
[7] Cursed be their anger, so fierce,
  and their fury,[n] so cruel![o]
  I will scatter them in Jacob
  and disperse them in Israel.[p]

[8] "Judah,[o,q] your brothers will praise you;
  your hand will be on the neck[r] of your enemies;
  your father's sons will bow down to you.[s]
[9] You are a lion's[t] cub,[u] O Judah;[v]
  you return from the prey,[w] my son.
  Like a lion he crouches and lies down,

A Ge 48:19–22 ◀▶ Ge 50:24–25

49:1 ᶻNu 24:14; Dt 31:29; Jer 23:20; Da 2:28,45
49:2 ᵃJos 24:1 ᵇver 16,28; Ps 34:11
49:3 ᶜS Ge 29:32; S 41:51 ᵈDt 21:17; Ps 78:51; 105:36 ᵉS Ge 34:19
49:4 ᶠIsa 57:20; Jer 49:23 ᵍS Ge 29:29; S 34:5
49:5 ʰS Ge 29:33 ⁱGe 29:34 ʲS Ge 34:25; S Pr 4:17
49:6 ᵏPs 1:1; Pr 1:15; Eph 5:11 ˡS Ge 34:26 ᵐJos 11:6,9; 2Sa 8:4; 1Ch 18:4
49:7 ⁿGe 34:7 ᵒJos 34:25 ᵖJos 19:1,9; 21:1-42
49:8 ᑫS Ge 29:35 ʳDt 28:48 ˢS Ge 9:25; 1Ch 5:2
49:9 ᵗNu 24:9; Ps 7:2; 10:9; Eze 19:5; Mic 5:8 ᵘEze 19:2 ᵛRev 5:5 ʷver 27; Nu 23:24; Job 38:39;

Ps 17:12; 22:13; 104:21

n 5 The meaning of the Hebrew for this word is uncertain. *o 8 Judah sounds like and may be derived from the Hebrew for praise.*

49:1 The phrase "days to come" appears in this verse for the first time in the Scripture and is used repeatedly throughout the remainder of the Bible. Referring to a final point in history when God's purposes for a people or an individual will be completed, this expression is primarily used in the OT in conjunction with Israel's rebellion against God and return to him (see Dt 4:30 ["later days"]; 31:29; Hos 3:5 ["last days"]). The NT writers use this phrase in connection with the coming of Christ (see Heb 1:2; 1Pe 1:20); the end of the dispensation of the church (see 2Ti 3:1; 1Pe 1:5; 2Pe 3:3); and the final resurrection (see Jn 6:39–40, 44, 54; 11:24; 12:48).

49:1–27 It was common practice in the Middle East for a dying patriarch to announce his last blessings to his family (see 27:1–4). In this deathbed prophecy, Jacob covers the future destiny of his sons and their tribes from the occupation of the promised land to the return of Christ. Note that the way each son lived his life affected the final blessing they received.

49:3 Reuben, as the oldest son, was entitled to special privileges. Jacob acknowledged Reuben's position in the family line and noted his excellent qualities, but Jacob also prophesied that Reuben would not achieve excellence in leadership because of his unstable character. In addition, due to Reuben's sexual encounter with Jacob's concubine Bilhah (see 35:22), Reuben's birthright, a double portion, would ultimately be divided between Joseph's sons Ephraim and Manasseh (see 48:4–22, 1Ch 5:1). In fulfillment of this prophecy, no leader, judge, prophet or national hero ever came from Reuben's line, and Reuben's tribe was the first tribe of Israel to be carried into captivity by Assyria (see Jdg 5:15–16; 1Ch 5:26).

49:5–7 In addition to their blood relationship as brothers, Simeon and Levi shared the traits of violence, anger and cruelty (see 34:25). When the time came for Jacob to bless these two sons, Jacob prophesied that their descendants would be divided and scattered throughout the promised land. As fulfillment of this prophecy, during Israel's desert wanderings the tribe of Simeon decreased in size. When Israel was ready to conquer the promised land, Simeon was the smallest of the twelve tribes and was therefore only allotted to settle a few cities within the boundaries of Judah (see Jos 19:1). The Levites were not assigned a specific territory in Canaan but were given cities throughout the promised land (see Jos 21:1–3). Because of their opposition to the idolatry of the golden calf God also allowed them to serve as the priestly tribe of Israel (see Ex 32:26).

49:8 Judah was the fourth son born to Jacob (see 29:35). Since Reuben, Simeon and Levi had forfeited their right to leadership, Jacob assigned the leadership position to Judah. Prefiguring the future royalty of Judah's offspring with "your father's sons will bow down to you" and likening Judah's increased military strength to a lion's, Jacob prophesied strength, success, and security for Judah's descendants. In fulfillment of this prophecy, the tribe of Judah grew in power and produced mighty leaders like Caleb, David and Solomon. Significantly, Jesus Christ is a descendant of Judah and called "the Lion of the tribe of Judah, the Root of David" (Rev 5:5).

like a lioness—who dares to rouse him?

10 The scepter will not depart from Judah,
nor the ruler's staff from between his feet,
until he comes to whom it belongs
and the obedience of the nations is his.

11 He will tether his donkey to a vine,
his colt to the choicest branch;
he will wash his garments in wine,
his robes in the blood of grapes.

12 His eyes will be darker than wine,
his teeth whiter than milk.

13 "Zebulun will live by the seashore
and become a haven for ships;
his border will extend toward Sidon.

14 "Issachar is a rawboned donkey
lying down between two saddlebags.

15 When he sees how good is his resting place
and how pleasant is his land,
he will bend his shoulder to the burden
and submit to forced labor.

16 "Dan will provide justice for his people
as one of the tribes of Israel.

17 Dan will be a serpent by the roadside,
a viper along the path,
that bites the horse's heels
so that its rider tumbles backward.

18 "I look for your deliverance, O LORD.

19 "Gad will be attacked by a band of raiders,
but he will attack them at their heels.

20 "Asher's food will be rich;
he will provide delicacies fit for a king.

21 "Naphtali is a doe set free
that bears beautiful fawns.

22 "Joseph is a fruitful vine,

---

p 10 Or until Shiloh comes; or until he comes to whom tribute belongs   q 12 Or will be dull from wine, / his teeth white from milk   r 14 Or strong   s 14 Or campfires   t 16 Dan here means he provides justice.   u 19 Gad can mean attack and band of raiders.   v 21 Or free; / he utters beautiful words

B Ge 3:15-21 ◀▶ Nu 19:1-22

49:10-12 This prophecy was initially fulfilled in Judah's superiority among the twelve tribes and in David's ascendancy to the kingly throne of Israel but will find its final fulfillment in the Messianic reign of Jesus Christ. All the nations will be subject to the Messiah when he returns to establish his eternal and just kingdom.

The phrases "his donkey" and "his colt" (49:11) echo Zechariah's reference to the donkey used as the Messiah's mount (see Zec 9:9) and Christ's fulfillment of this prophecy on his entry into Jerusalem on Palm Sunday (see Lk 19:33-38). The symbolism of washing clothes in wine gives a graphic picture of abundance and fruitfulness (see 27:28) as the Messiah ushers in spiritual blessings and restores what Adam had lost.

49:13 Though landlocked by the tribes of Asher and Manasseh, Zebulun would be within ten miles of the Mediterranean—close enough to "become a haven for ships."

49:14-15 Issachar was prophetically compared to a strong, powerful donkey. In the ancient Middle East this was not a slanderous description but rather an indication that Issachar would be strong but docile, a people able to carry the burden of others but often satisfied with sitting on the sidelines. Issachar's location within the promised land placed it along one of the major trade routes and allowed this tribe to flourish. Yet Issachar was slow to help fight Israel's battles and its name is missing from the description of the conquest of Canaan recorded in Judges (see Jdg 1).

49:16-17 Dan's assigned territory in the promised land was close to the Philistines. Though small in size, the tribe of Dan was warlike and withstood the threats of this powerful neighbor. One of the more famous Danites was a judge named Samson who celebrated several victories over the Philistines (see Jdg 16:30).

49:19 Jacob prophesied that enemies would attack Gad's descendants but the tribe would rally and be successful in driving them out of their territory (see Jdg 10:7ff; 11:1; 1Ch 5:18-22). The judge and deliverer Jephthah was from Gad.

49:20 Asher would be allotted territory in the fertile farmlands near the Mediterranean, ensuring Asher's prosperity and future blessing. Even today this area is one of the more fertile areas of Israel, producing large supplies of olive oil, wine and fragrances.

49:21 Naphtali's territory was a very fertile region in the hill country north of the Sea of Galilee. Somewhat isolated from the other tribes, Naphtali exhibited an independent spirit that manifested itself in swift, skilled warriors who were a strong defense for the nation against its enemies.

49:22 The blessing given to Joseph was eloquent and befitting Jacob's favorite son. Joseph's sons

a fruitful vine near a spring,
   whose branches[b] climb over a wall."[c]
[23]With bitterness archers attacked him;[d]
   they shot at him with hostility.[d]
[24]But his bow remained steady,[e]
   his strong arms[f] stayed[x] limber,
because of the hand of the Mighty One
   of Jacob,[g]
because of the Shepherd,[h] the Rock
   of Israel,[i]
[25]because of your father's God,[j] who
      helps[k] you,
   because of the Almighty,[y][l] who
      blesses you
with blessings of the heavens above,
   blessings of the deep that lies
      below,[m]
   blessings of the breast[n] and womb.[o]
[26]Your father's blessings are greater
   than the blessings of the ancient
      mountains,
   than[z] the bounty of the age-old
      hills.[p]
Let all these rest on the head of
      Joseph,[q]
   on the brow of the prince among[a]
      his brothers.[r]

[27]"Benjamin[s] is a ravenous wolf;[t]
   in the morning he devours the
      prey,[u]
   in the evening he divides the
      plunder."[v]

[28]All these are the twelve tribes of Israel,[w] and this is what their father said to them when he blessed them, giving each the blessing[x] appropriate to him.

The Death of Jacob

[29]Then he gave them these instructions:[y] "I am about to be gathered to my people.[z] Bury me with my fathers[a] in the cave in the field of Ephron the Hittite,[b] [30]the cave in the field of Machpelah,[c] near Mamre[d] in Canaan, which Abraham bought as a burial place[e] from Ephron the Hittite, along with the field.[f] [31]There Abraham[g] and his wife Sarah[h] were buried, there Isaac and his wife Rebekah[i] were buried, and there I buried Leah.[j] [32]The field and the cave in it were bought from the Hittites.[b][k]"

[33]When Jacob had finished giving instructions to his sons, he drew his feet up into the bed, breathed his last and was gathered to his people.[l]

50 Joseph threw himself upon his father and wept over him and kissed him.[m] [2]Then Joseph directed the physicians in his service to embalm his father Israel. So the physicians embalmed him,[n] [3]taking a full forty days, for that was the time required for embalming. And the Egyptians mourned for him seventy days.[o]

[4]When the days of mourning[p] had passed, Joseph said to Pharaoh's court,[q] "If I have found favor in your eyes,[r] speak to Pharaoh for me. Tell him, [5]'My father made me swear an oath[s] and said, "I am about to die;[t] bury me in the tomb I dug for myself[u] in the land of Canaan."[v] Now let me go up and bury my father;[w] then I will return.' "

[6]Pharaoh said, "Go up and bury your father, as he made you swear to do."

[7]So Joseph went up to bury his father. All Pharaoh's officials[x] accompanied him—the dignitaries of his court[y] and all the dignitaries of Egypt— [8]besides all the members of Joseph's household and his

Q Ge 49:29 ◀ ▶ Nu 20:24

Isa 22:16; Mt 27:60 ᵛGe 47:31 ʷMt 8:21 **50:7** ˣGe 45:16 ʸver 4

ʷ 22 Or Joseph is a wild colt, / a wild colt near a spring, / a wild donkey on a terraced hill ˣ 23,24 Or archers will attack . . . will shoot . . . will remain . . . will stay ʸ 25 Hebrew Shaddai ᶻ 26 Or of my progenitors, / as great as ᵃ 26 The one separated from ᵇ 32 Or the sons of Heth

---

Ephraim and Manasseh would carry this blessing into Canaan and were allotted the most favored territories in the promised land, straddling both sides of the Jordan River. Jacob's flowery words also mentioned that Joseph's branches would "climb over a wall," a prediction of the extra land Ephraim would need when settling in Canaan (see Jos 17:14–18).
49:27 Benjamin was known as a warlike tribe, filled with mighty, vigorous warriors who were skilled with the sling and bow (see Jdg 5:14; 1Ch 12:2).

Ehud, Saul and Jonathan were some of Benjamin's more famous warriors who fulfilled this prophecy (see Jdg 3:12–30; 1Sa 11—15).
49:29 Jacob realized that the land of his fathers was his God-appointed homeland, so he requested that he be buried in the cave at Machpelah. Scripture records that Jacob "was gathered to his people" (49:33) supporting Jacob's belief that his faithful ancestors, though dead, still existed and would one day be resurrected (see note at 35:29).

brothers and those belonging to his father's household.ᶻ Only their children and their flocks and herds were left in Goshen.ᵃ ⁹Chariotsᵇ and horsemenᶜ also went up with him. It was a very large company.

¹⁰When they reached the threshing floorᶜ of Atad, near the Jordan, they lamented loudly and bitterly;ᵈ and there Joseph observed a seven-day periodᵉ of mourningᶠ for his father.ᵍ ¹¹When the Canaanitesʰ who lived there saw the mourning at the threshing floor of Atad, they said, "The Egyptians are holding a solemn ceremony of mourning."ⁱ That is why that place near the Jordan is called Abel Mizraim.ᵈ

¹²So Jacob's sons did as he had commanded them:ʲ ¹³They carried him to the land of Canaan and buried him in the cave in the field of Machpelah,ᵏ near Mamre,ˡ which Abraham had bought as a burial place from Ephron the Hittite,ᵐ along with the field.ⁿ ¹⁴After burying his father, Joseph returned to Egypt, together with his brothers and all the others who had gone with him to bury his father.ᵒ

Joseph Reassures His Brothers

¹⁵When Joseph's brothers saw that their father was dead, they said, "What if Joseph holds a grudgeᵖ against us and pays us back for all the wrongs we did to him?"ᑫ ¹⁶So they sent word to Joseph, saying, "Your father left these instructionsʳ before he died: ¹⁷'This is what you are to say to Joseph: I ask you to forgive your brothers the sinsˢ and the wrongs they committed in treating you so badly.'ᵗ Now please forgive the sins of

the servants of the God of your father.'ᵘ" When their message came to him, Joseph wept.ᵛ

¹⁸His brothers then came and threw themselves down before him.ʷ "We are your slaves,"ˣ they said.

¹⁹But Joseph said to them, "Don't be afraid. Am I in the place of God?ʸ ²⁰You intended to harm me,ᶻ but God intendedᵃ it for goodᵇ to accomplish what is now being done, the saving of many lives.ᶜ ²¹So then, don't be afraid. I will provide for you and your children.ᵈ" And he reassured them and spoke kindlyᵉ to them.

The Death of Joseph

²²Joseph stayed in Egypt, along with all his father's family. He lived a hundred and ten years.ᶠ ²³and saw the third generationᵍ of Ephraim'sʰ children.ⁱ Also the children of Makirʲ son of Manassehᵏ were placed at birth on Joseph's knees.ᵉˡ

²⁴Then Joseph said to his brothers, "I am about to die.ᵐ But God will surely come to your aidⁿ and take you up out of this land to the landᵒ he promised on oath to Abraham,ᵖ Isaacᑫ and Jacob."ʳ ²⁵And Joseph made the sons of Israel swear an oathˢ and said, "God will surely come to your aid, and then you must carry my bonesᵗ up from this place."ᵘ ²⁶So Joseph diedᵛ at the age of a hundred and ten.ʷ And after they embalmed him,ˣ he was placed in a coffin in Egypt.

A Ge 49:1–28 ◀ ▶ Ex 3:8–12
U Ge 49:25–26 ◀ ▶ Lev 26:3–12

ᵒ S Ge 15:14 ᵖ S Ge 13:17 ᑫ S Ge 17:19 ʳ S Ge 12:7; S 15:16
50:25 ˢ S Ge 24:37 ᵗ S Ge 49:29 ᵘ S Ge 47:29-30; Heb 11:22
50:26 ᵛ Ge 1:6 ʷ S Ge 25:7 ˣ S ver 2

ᶜ 9 Or charioteers ᵈ 11 *Abel Mizraim* means *mourning of the Egyptians.*
ᵉ 23 That is, were counted as his

50:24–25 God had promised to make Abraham's family into a great nation and bring them into the promised land. Joseph's dying words clearly emphasized his belief that God would do what he had promised (see 15:16; 46:4; 48:21; Heb 11:25). In addition, Joseph expressed his confidence in his descendants' ability to transfer his bones from Egypt to his homeland in Canaan. Though several generations would pass before this prophecy was fulfilled, Moses brought Joseph's bones out of Egypt during the exodus. Joseph's bones were reburied at Shechem (see 33:19; Ex 13:19; Jos 24:32).

Exodus

Author: Moses

Theme: Israel's deliverance from bondage

Date of Writing: c. 1440–1406 B.C.

Outline of Exodus
  I. Israel Under Bondage in Egypt (1:1—12:36)
     A. The slavery of Israel (1:1–22)
     B. The rise of a deliverer (2:1—4:31)
     C. Moses' struggle with Pharaoh (5:1—12:36)
  II. The Exodus From Egypt (12:37—18:27)
     A. Leaving Egypt (12:37—13:16)
     B. Crossing the "Red Sea" (13:17—15:21)
     C. The journey to Sinai (15:22—18:27)
  III. Israel's Experience in the Wilderness (19:1—40:38)
     A. God gives the law on Mt. Sinai (19:1—24:18)
     B. Building the tabernacle (25:1—40:38)

THE BOOK OF Exodus derives its name not from Hebrew but from the Greek word *exodos*, which means "exit" or "departure." The Septuagint, a Greek translation of the OT, uses this term in Ex 19:1 and titles this book *Exodus*—an apt title for a book that chronicles the escape of the Israelites from centuries of bondage as slaves in Egypt.

Exodus records God's deliverance of his chosen people from slavery in Egypt through a series of supernatural interventions. Observing the plagues that Pharaoh's hard heart brought on the land, the Israelites soon realized that their deliverance hinged on faithful obedience to God's revealed law. One such act of obedience was expressed through the sacrifice of an innocent lamb at the institution of the Passover (see Ex 12:1–13). Though the sacrificial system inaugurated in the book of Exodus could not fully eliminate a sinner's guilt, Israel's obedience to God's system of sacrifices foreshadowed the sacrifice of Jesus Christ, who paid the full price for the redemption of sins with his death on the cross.

After the deliverance from Egypt, Exodus documents the elements of a foundational theology in which God reveals his name, his attributes, his redemption, his law and how he is to be worshiped. God gave Moses the Ten Commandments on Mt. Sinai and commanded the Israelites to obey his law. Yet the Israelites' disobedience to God's commandments created the need for a system of priests and blood sacrifices. The book of Exodus details the rules for worship in the tabernacle and for Israel's forgiveness and cleansing from sin and restoration to fellowship, blessing and proper worship.

This second book of the Pentateuch also continues the progressive revelation of God's divine nature and his plan of salvation as revealed in the covenants. Genesis closed with the Abrahamic covenant (see Ge 15:4). The book of Exodus relates how the ancient covenant relationship between God and his people expands under the Mosaic covenant (see Ex 19:5) as God establishes his unbreakable covenant with the nation of Israel.

Note also a multitude of types presented throughout the book of Exodus. Moses, the Passover and the tabernacle all point to the future Messiah, Jesus Christ. See "The Language of Prophecy" section in the article entitled "Introduction to Prophecy," p. vi.

The Israelites Oppressed

1 These are the names of the sons of Israel[a] who went to Egypt with Jacob, each with his family: [2]Reuben, Simeon, Levi and Judah; [3]Issachar, Zebulun and Benjamin; [4]Dan and Naphtali; Gad and Asher.[b] [5]The descendants of Jacob numbered seventy[a] in all;[c] Joseph was already in Egypt.

[6]Now Joseph and all his brothers and all that generation died,[d] [7]but the Israelites were fruitful and multiplied greatly and became exceedingly numerous,[e] so that the land was filled with them.

[8]Then a new king, who did not know about Joseph, came to power in Egypt.[f] [9]"Look," he said to his people, "the Israelites have become much too numerous[g] for us.[h] [10]Come, we must deal shrewdly[i] with them or they will become even more numerous and, if war breaks out, will join our enemies, fight against us and leave the country."[j]

[11]So they put slave masters[k] over them to oppress them with forced labor,[l] and they built Pithom and Rameses[m] as store cities[n] for Pharaoh. [12]But the more they were oppressed, the more they multiplied and spread; so the Egyptians came to dread the Israelites [13]and worked them ruthlessly.[o] [14]They made their lives bitter with hard labor[p] in brick[q] and mortar and with all kinds of work in the fields; in all their hard labor the Egyptians used them ruthlessly.[r]

[15]The king of Egypt said to the Hebrew midwives,[s] whose names were Shiphrah and Puah, [16]"When you help the Hebrew women in childbirth and observe them on the delivery stool, if it is a boy, kill him; but if it is a girl, let her live."[t] [17]The midwives, however, feared[u] God and did not do what the king of Egypt had told them to do;[v] they let the boys live. [18]Then the king of Egypt summoned the midwives and asked them, "Why have you done this? Why have you let the boys live?"

[19]The midwives answered Pharaoh, "Hebrew women are not like Egyptian women; they are vigorous and give birth before the midwives arrive."[w]

[20]So God was kind to the midwives[x]

1:1 a S Ge 46:8
1:4 b Ge 35:22-26; Nu 1:20-43
1:5 c S Ge 46:26
1:6 d Ge 50:26; Ac 7:15
1:7 e ver 9; S Ge 12:2; Dt 7:13; Eze 16:7
1:8 f Jer 43:11; 46:2
1:9 g S ver 7
h S Ge 26:16
1:10 i Ge 15:13; Ex 3:7; 18:11; Ps 64:2; 71:10; 83:3; Isa 53:3
j Ps 105:24-25; Ac 7:17-19
1:11 k Ex 3:7; 5:10,13,14
l S Ge 15:13; Ex 2:11; 5:4; 6:6-7; Jos 9:27; 1Ki 9:21; 1Ch 22:2; Isa 60:10
m S Ge 47:11
n 1Ki 9:19; 2Ch 8:4
1:13 o ver 14; Ge 15:13-14; Ex 5:21; 16:3; Lev 25:43,46,53; Dt 4:20; 26:6; 1Ki 8:51; Ps 129:1; Isa 30:6; 48:10; Jer 11:4
1:14 p Dt 26:6; Ezr 9:9; Isa 14:3
q S Ex 11:3
r Ex 2:23; 3:9; Nu 20:15; 1Sa 10:18; 2Ki 13:4; Ps 66:11; 81:6; Ac 7:19
1:15 s S Ge 35:17
1:16 t ver 22 1:17 u ver 21; Pr 16:6 v 1Sa 22:17; Da 3:16-18; Ac 4:18-20; 5:29 1:19 w Lev 19:11; Jos 2:4-6; 1Sa 19:14; 2Sa 17:20 1:20 x Pr 11:18; 22:8; Ecc 8:12; Isa 3:10; Heb 6:10

[a] 5 Masoretic Text (see also Gen. 46:27); Dead Sea Scrolls and Septuagint (see also Acts 7:14 and note at Gen. 46:27) *seventy-five*

and the people increased and became even more numerous. ²¹And because the midwives feared^y God, he gave them families^z of their own.

²²Then Pharaoh gave this order to all his people: "Every boy that is born^b you must throw into the Nile,^a but let every girl live."^b

The Birth of Moses

2 Now a man of the house of Levi^c married a Levite woman,^d ²and she became pregnant and gave birth to a son. When she saw that he was a fine^e child, she hid him for three months.^f ³But when she could hide him no longer, she got a papyrus^g basket for him and coated it with tar and pitch.^h Then she placed the child in it and put it among the reeds^i along the bank of the Nile. ⁴His sister^j stood at a distance to see what would happen to him.

⁵Then Pharaoh's daughter went down to the Nile to bathe, and her attendants were walking along the river bank.^k She saw the basket among the reeds and sent her slave girl to get it. ⁶She opened it and saw the baby. He was crying, and she felt sorry for him. "This is one of the Hebrew babies," she said.

⁷Then his sister asked Pharaoh's daughter, "Shall I go and get one of the Hebrew women to nurse the baby for you?"

⁸"Yes, go," she answered. And the girl went and got the baby's mother. ⁹Pharaoh's daughter said to her, "Take this baby and nurse him for me, and I will pay you." So the woman took the baby and nursed him. ¹⁰When the child grew older, she took him to Pharaoh's daughter and he became her son. She named^l him Moses,^c saying, "I drew^m him out of the water."

Moses Flees to Midian

¹¹One day, after Moses had grown up, he went out to where his own people^n were and watched them at their hard labor.^o He saw an Egyptian beating a Hebrew, one of his own people. ¹²Glancing this way and that and seeing no one, he killed the Egyptian and hid him in the sand. ¹³The next day he went out and saw two Hebrews fighting. He asked the one in the wrong, "Why are you hitting your fellow Hebrew?"^p

¹⁴The man said, "Who made you ruler and judge over us?^q Are you thinking of killing me as you killed the Egyptian?" Then Moses was afraid and thought, "What I did must have become known."

¹⁵When Pharaoh heard of this, he tried to kill^r Moses, but Moses fled^s from Pharaoh and went to live in Midian,^t where he sat down by a well. ¹⁶Now a priest of Midian^u had seven daughters, and they came to draw water^v and fill the troughs^w to water their father's flock. ¹⁷Some shepherds came along and drove them away, but Moses got up and came to their rescue^x and watered their flock.^y

¹⁸When the girls returned to Reuel^z their father, he asked them, "Why have you returned so early today?"

¹⁹They answered, "An Egyptian rescued us from the shepherds. He even drew water for us and watered the flock."

²⁰"And where is he?" he asked his daughters. "Why did you leave him? Invite him to have something to eat."^a

²¹Moses agreed to stay with the man, who gave his daughter Zipporah^b to Moses in marriage. ²²Zipporah gave birth to a son, and Moses named him Gershom,^d^c saying, "I have become an alien^d in a foreign land."

²³During that long period,^e the king of Egypt died.^f The Israelites groaned in their slavery^g and cried out, and their cry^h for help because of their slavery went up to God. ²⁴God heard their groaning and he remembered^i his covenant^j with Abraham, with Isaac and with Jacob. ²⁵So God looked on the Israelites and was concerned^k about them.

Moses and the Burning Bush

3 Now Moses was tending the flock of Jethro^l his father-in-law, the priest of Midian,^m and he led the flock to the far side of the desert and came to Horeb,^n the mountain^o of God. ²There the angel of the LORD^p appeared to him in flames of fire^q from within a bush.^r Moses saw that though the bush was on fire it did not burn up. ³So Moses thought, "I will go over and see this strange sight—why the bush does not burn up."

⁴When the LORD saw that he had gone

---

^b 22 Masoretic Text; Samaritan Pentateuch, Septuagint and Targums *born to the Hebrews*   ^c 10 *Moses* sounds like the Hebrew for *draw out*.
^d 22 *Gershom* sounds like the Hebrew for *an alien there*.

over to look, God called to him from within the bush, "Moses! Moses!"

And Moses said, "Here I am."

5 "Do not come any closer," God said. "Take off your sandals, for the place where you are standing is holy ground." 6 Then he said, "I am the God of your father, the God of Abraham, the God of Isaac and the God of Jacob." At this, Moses hid his face, because he was afraid to look at God.

7 The LORD said, "I have indeed seen the misery of my people in Egypt. I have heard them crying out because of their slave drivers, and I am concerned about their suffering. 8 So I have come down to rescue them from the hand of the Egyptians and to bring them up out of that land into a good and spacious land, a land flowing with milk and honey— the home of the Canaanites, Hittites, Amorites, Perizzites, Hivites and Jebusites. 9 And now the cry of the Israelites has reached me, and I have seen the way the Egyptians are oppressing them. 10 So now, go. I am sending you to Pharaoh to bring my people the Israelites out of Egypt."

11 But Moses said to God, "Who am I, that I should go to Pharaoh and bring the Israelites out of Egypt?"

12 And God said, "I will be with you. And this will be the sign to you that it is I who have sent you: When you have brought the people out of Egypt, you will worship God on this mountain."

13 Moses said to God, "Suppose I go to the Israelites and say to them, 'The God of your fathers has sent me to you,' and they ask me, 'What is his name?' Then what shall I tell them?"

14 God said to Moses, "I AM WHO I AM. This is what you are to say to the Israelites: 'I AM has sent me to you.'"

15 God also said to Moses, "Say to the Israelites, 'The LORD, the God of your fathers—the God of Abraham, the God of Isaac and the God of Jacob—has sent me to you.' This is my name forever, the name by which I am to be remembered from generation to generation.

16 "Go, assemble the elders of Israel and say to them, 'The LORD, the God of your fathers—the God of Abraham, Isaac and Jacob—appeared to me and said: I have watched over you and have seen what has been done to you in Egypt. 17 And I have promised to bring you up out of your misery in Egypt into the land of the Canaanites, Hittites, Amorites, Perizzites, Hivites and Jebusites—a land flowing with milk and honey.'

18 "The elders of Israel will listen to you. Then you and the elders are to go to the king of Egypt and say to him, 'The LORD, the God of the Hebrews, has met with us. Let us take a three-day journey into the desert to offer sacrifices to the LORD our God.' 19 But I know that the king of Egypt will not let you go unless a mighty hand compels him. 20 So I will stretch out my hand and strike the Egyptians with all the wonders that I will perform among them. After that, he will let you go.

21 "And I will make the Egyptians favorably disposed toward this people, so that when you leave you will not go empty-handed. 22 Every woman is to ask her neighbor and any woman living in her house for articles of silver and gold and for clothing, which you will put on your sons and daughters. And so you will plunder the Egyptians."

Signs for Moses

4 Moses answered, "What if they do not believe me or listen to me and say, 'The LORD did not appear to you'?"

2 Then the LORD said to him, "What is that in your hand?"

"A staff," he replied.

3 The LORD said, "Throw it on the ground."

Moses threw it on the ground and it became a snake, and he ran from it. 4 Then the LORD said to him, "Reach out

e 12 The Hebrew is plural. *f* 14 Or I WILL BE WHAT I WILL BE
g 15 The Hebrew for LORD sounds like and may be derived from the Hebrew for I AM in verse 14.

your hand and take it by the tail." So Moses reached out and took hold of the snake and it turned back into a staff in his hand. ⁵"This," said the LORD, "is so that they may believe[t] that the LORD, the God of their fathers—the God of Abraham, the God of Isaac and the God of Jacob—has appeared to you."

⁶Then the LORD said, "Put your hand inside your cloak." So Moses put his hand into his cloak, and when he took it out, it was leprous,[h] like snow.[u] ⁷"Now put it back into your cloak," he said. So Moses put his hand back into his cloak, and when he took it out, it was restored,[v] like the rest of his flesh.

⁸Then the LORD said, "If they do not believe[w] you or pay attention to the first miraculous sign,[x] they may believe the second. ⁹But if they do not believe these two signs or listen to you, take some water from the Nile and pour it on the dry ground. The water you take from the river will become blood[y] on the ground."

¹⁰Moses said to the LORD, "O Lord, I have never been eloquent, neither in the past nor since you have spoken to your servant. I am slow of speech and tongue."[z]

¹¹The LORD said to him, "Who gave man his mouth? Who makes him deaf or mute?[a] Who gives him sight or makes him blind?[b] Is it not I, the LORD? ¹²Now go;[c] I will help you speak and will teach you what to say."[d]

¹³But Moses said, "O Lord, please send someone else to do it."[e]

¹⁴Then the LORD's anger burned[f] against Moses and he said, "What about your brother, Aaron the Levite? I know he can speak well. He is already on his way to meet[g] you, and his heart will be glad when he sees you. ¹⁵You shall speak to him and put words in his mouth;[h] I will help both of you speak and will teach you what to do. ¹⁶He will speak to the people for you, and it will be as if he were your mouth[i] and as if you were God to him.[j] ¹⁷But take this staff[k] in your hand[l] so you can perform miraculous signs[m] with it."

Moses Returns to Egypt

¹⁸Then Moses went back to Jethro his father-in-law and said to him, "Let me go back to my own people in Egypt to see if any of them are still alive."

Jethro said, "Go, and I wish you well."

¹⁹Now the LORD had said to Moses in Midian, "Go back to Egypt, for all the men who wanted to kill[n] you are dead.[o]" ²⁰So Moses took his wife and sons,[p] put them on a donkey and started back to Egypt. And he took the staff[q] of God in his hand.

²¹The LORD said to Moses, "When you return to Egypt, see that you perform before Pharaoh all the wonders[r] I have given you the power to do. But I will harden his heart[s] so that he will not let the people go.[t] ²²Then say to Pharaoh, 'This is what the LORD says: Israel is my firstborn son,[u] ²³and I told you, "Let my son go,[v] so he may worship[w] me." But you refused to let him go; so I will kill your firstborn son.' "[x]

²⁴At a lodging place on the way, the LORD met ⌊Moses⌋[i] and was about to kill[y] him. ²⁵But Zipporah[z] took a flint knife, cut off her son's foreskin[a] and touched ⌊Moses'⌋ feet with it.[j] "Surely you are a bridegroom of blood to me," she said. ²⁶So the LORD let him alone. (At that time she said "bridegroom of blood," referring to circumcision.)

²⁷The LORD said to Aaron, "Go into the desert to meet Moses." So he met Moses at the mountain[b] of God and kissed[c] him. ²⁸Then Moses told Aaron everything the LORD had sent him to say, and also about all the miraculous signs he had commanded him to perform.

²⁹Moses and Aaron brought together all the elders[d] of the Israelites, ³⁰and Aaron told them everything the LORD had said to Moses. He also performed the signs[e] before the people, ³¹and they believed.[f] And when they heard that the LORD was concerned[g] about them and had seen their misery,[h] they bowed down and worshiped.[i]

D Ge 20:18 ◀ ▶ Ex 9:8–10
E Ge 30:22 ◀ ▶ Nu 12:9–15

h 6 The Hebrew word was used for various diseases affecting the skin—not necessarily leprosy. *i* 24 Or ⌊Moses' son⌋; Hebrew *him* *j* 25 Or *and drew near* ⌊Moses'⌋ *feet*

Bricks Without Straw

5 Afterward Moses and Aaron went to Pharaoh and said, "This is what the LORD, the God of Israel, says: 'Let my people go, so that they may hold a festival to me in the desert.'"

²Pharaoh said, "Who is the LORD, that I should obey him and let Israel go? I do not know the LORD and I will not let Israel go."

³Then they said, "The God of the Hebrews has met with us. Now let us take a three-day journey into the desert to offer sacrifices to the LORD our God, or he may strike us with plagues or with the sword."

⁴But the king of Egypt said, "Moses and Aaron, why are you taking the people away from their labor? Get back to your work!" ⁵Then Pharaoh said, "Look, the people of the land are now numerous, and you are stopping them from working."

⁶That same day Pharaoh gave this order to the slave drivers and foremen in charge of the people: ⁷"You are no longer to supply the people with straw for making bricks; let them go and gather their own straw. ⁸But require them to make the same number of bricks as before; don't reduce the quota. They are lazy; that is why they are crying out, 'Let us go and sacrifice to our God.' ⁹Make the work harder for the men so that they keep working and pay no attention to lies."

¹⁰Then the slave drivers and the foremen went out and said to the people, "This is what Pharaoh says: 'I will not give you any more straw. ¹¹Go and get your own straw wherever you can find it, but your work will not be reduced at all.'" ¹²So the people scattered all over Egypt to gather stubble to use for straw. ¹³The slave drivers kept pressing them, saying, "Complete the work required of you for each day, just as when you had straw." ¹⁴The Israelite foremen appointed by Pharaoh's slave drivers were beaten and were asked, "Why didn't you meet your quota of bricks yesterday or today, as before?"

¹⁵Then the Israelite foremen went and appealed to Pharaoh: "Why have you treated your servants this way? ¹⁶Your servants are given no straw, yet we are told, 'Make bricks!' Your servants are being beaten, but the fault is with your own people."

¹⁷Pharaoh said, "Lazy, that's what you are—lazy! That is why you keep saying, 'Let us go and sacrifice to the LORD.' ¹⁸Now get to work. You will not be given any straw, yet you must produce your full quota of bricks."

¹⁹The Israelite foremen realized they were in trouble when they were told, "You are not to reduce the number of bricks required of you for each day." ²⁰When they left Pharaoh, they found Moses and Aaron waiting to meet them, ²¹and they said, "May the LORD look upon you and judge you! You have made us a stench to Pharaoh and his officials and have put a sword in their hand to kill us."

God Promises Deliverance

²²Moses returned to the LORD and said, "O Lord, why have you brought trouble upon this people? Is this why you sent me? ²³Ever since I went to Pharaoh to speak in your name, he has brought trouble upon this people, and you have not rescued your people at all."

6 Then the LORD said to Moses, "Now you will see what I will do to Pharaoh: Because of my mighty hand he will let them go; because of my mighty hand he will drive them out of his country."

²God also said to Moses, "I am the LORD. ³I appeared to Abraham, to Isaac and to Jacob as God Almighty, but by my name the LORD I did not make myself known to them. ⁴I also established my covenant with them to give them the land of Canaan, where they lived as aliens. ⁵Moreover, I have heard the groaning of the Israelites, whom the Egyptians are enslaving, and I have remembered my covenant.

⁶"Therefore, say to the Israelites: 'I am the LORD, and I will bring you out from under the yoke of the Egyptians. I will free you from being slaves to them, and I will redeem you with an outstretched arm and with mighty acts of judgment. ⁷I will take you as my own people, and I

---

k 3 Hebrew *El-Shaddai* *l 3* See note at Exodus 3:15. *m 3* Or *Almighty, and by my name the LORD did I not let myself be known to them?*

will be your God. Then you will know that I am the LORD your God, who brought you out from under the yoke of the Egyptians. ⁸And I will bring you to the land I swore with uplifted hand to give to Abraham, to Isaac and to Jacob. I will give it to you as a possession. I am the LORD.'"

⁹Moses reported this to the Israelites, but they did not listen to him because of their discouragement and cruel bondage.

¹⁰Then the LORD said to Moses, ¹¹"Go, tell Pharaoh king of Egypt to let the Israelites go out of his country."

¹²But Moses said to the LORD, "If the Israelites will not listen to me, why would Pharaoh listen to me, since I speak with faltering lips[n]?"

Family Record of Moses and Aaron

¹³Now the LORD spoke to Moses and Aaron about the Israelites and Pharaoh king of Egypt, and he commanded them to bring the Israelites out of Egypt.

¹⁴These were the heads of their families[o]:

The sons of Reuben the firstborn son of Israel were Hanoch and Pallu, Hezron and Carmi. These were the clans of Reuben.

¹⁵The sons of Simeon were Jemuel, Jamin, Ohad, Jakin, Zohar and Shaul the son of a Canaanite woman. These were the clans of Simeon.

¹⁶These were the names of the sons of Levi according to their records: Gershon, Kohath and Merari. Levi lived 137 years.

¹⁷The sons of Gershon, by clans, were Libni and Shimei.

¹⁸The sons of Kohath were Amram, Izhar, Hebron and Uzziel. Kohath lived 133 years.

¹⁹The sons of Merari were Mahli and Mushi.

These were the clans of Levi according to their records.

²⁰Amram married his father's sister Jochebed, who bore him Aaron and Moses. Amram lived 137 years.

²¹The sons of Izhar were Korah, Nepheg and Zicri.

²²The sons of Uzziel were Mishael, Elzaphan and Sithri.

²³Aaron married Elisheba, daughter of Amminadab and sister of Nahshon, and she bore him Nadab and Abihu, Eleazar and Ithamar.

²⁴The sons of Korah were Assir, Elkanah and Abiasaph. These were the Korahite clans.

²⁵Eleazar son of Aaron married one of the daughters of Putiel, and she bore him Phinehas.

These were the heads of the Levite families, clan by clan.

²⁶It was this same Aaron and Moses to whom the LORD said, "Bring the Israelites out of Egypt by their divisions." ²⁷They were the ones who spoke to Pharaoh king of Egypt about bringing the Israelites out of Egypt. It was the same Moses and Aaron.

Aaron to Speak for Moses

²⁸Now when the LORD spoke to Moses in Egypt, ²⁹he said to him, "I am the LORD. Tell Pharaoh king of Egypt everything I tell you."

³⁰But Moses said to the LORD, "Since I speak with faltering lips, why would Pharaoh listen to me?"

7 Then the LORD said to Moses, "See, I have made you like God to Pharaoh, and your brother Aaron will be your prophet. ²You are to say everything I command you, and your brother Aaron is to tell Pharaoh to let the Israelites go out of his country. ³But I will harden Pharaoh's heart, and though I multiply my miraculous signs and wonders in Egypt, ⁴he will not listen to you. Then I will lay my hand on Egypt and with mighty acts of judgment I will bring out my divisions, my people the Israelites. ⁵And the Egyptians will know that I am the LORD when I stretch out my hand against Egypt and bring the Israelites out of it."

⁶Moses and Aaron did just as the LORD commanded them. ⁷Moses was eighty years old and Aaron eighty-three when they spoke to Pharaoh.

Aaron's Staff Becomes a Snake

⁸The LORD said to Moses and Aaron, ⁹"When Pharaoh says to you, 'Perform a

---

[n] 12 Hebrew *I am uncircumcised of lips*; also in verse 30
[o] 14 The Hebrew for *families* here and in verse 25 refers to units larger than clans.

miracle,'ʷ' then say to Aaron, 'Take your staff and throw it down before Pharaoh,' and it will become a snake.'"ˣ

¹⁰So Moses and Aaron went to Pharaoh and did just as the LORD commanded. Aaron threw his staff down in front of Pharaoh and his officials, and it became a snake. ¹¹Pharaoh then summoned wise men and sorcerers,ʸ and the Egyptian magiciansᶻ also did the same things by their secret arts:ᵃ ¹²Each one threw down his staff and it became a snake. But Aaron's staff swallowed up their staffs. ¹³Yet Pharaoh's heartᵇ became hard and he would not listenᶜ to them, just as the LORD had said.

The Plague of Blood

¹⁴Then the LORD said to Moses, "Pharaoh's heart is unyielding;ᵈ he refuses to let the people go. ¹⁵Go to Pharaoh in the morning as he goes out to the water.ᵉ Wait on the bank of the Nileᶠ to meet him, and take in your hand the staff that was changed into a snake. ¹⁶Then say to him, 'The LORD, the God of the Hebrews, has sent me to say to you: Let my people go, so that they may worshipᵍ me in the desert. But until now you have not listened.ʰ ¹⁷This is what the LORD says: By this you will know that I am the LORD:ⁱ With the staff that is in my hand I will strike the water of the Nile, and it will be changed into blood.ʲ ¹⁸The fish in the Nile will die, and the river will stink;ᵏ the Egyptians will not be able to drink its water.' "ˡ

¹⁹The LORD said to Moses, "Tell Aaron, 'Take your staffᵐ and stretch out your handⁿ over the waters of Egypt—over the streams and canals, over the ponds and all the reservoirs'—and they will turn to blood. Blood will be everywhere in Egypt, even in the wooden buckets and stone jars."

²⁰Moses and Aaron did just as the LORD had commanded.ᵒ He raised his staff in the presence of Pharaoh and his officials and struck the water of the Nile,ᵖ and all the water was changed into blood.ᵠ ²¹The fish in the Nile died, and the river smelled so bad that the Egyptians could not drink its water. Blood was everywhere in Egypt.

²²But the Egyptian magiciansʳ did the same things by their secret arts,ˢ and Pharaoh's heartᵗ became hard; he would not listen to Moses and Aaron, just as the LORD had said. ²³Instead, he turned and went into his palace, and did not take even this to heart. ²⁴And all the Egyptians dug along the Nile to get drinking waterᵘ, because they could not drink the water of the river.

The Plague of Frogs

²⁵Seven days passed after the LORD struck the Nile. ¹Then the LORD said to Moses, "Go to Pharaoh and say to him, 'This is what the LORD says: Let my people go, so that they may worshipᵛ me. ²If you refuse to let them go, I will plague your whole country with frogs.ʷ ³The Nile will teem with frogs. They will come up into your palace and your bedroom and onto your bed, into the houses of your officials and on your people,ˣ and into your ovens and kneading troughs.ʸ ⁴The frogs will go up on you and your people and all your officials.' "

⁵Then the LORD said to Moses, "Tell Aaron, 'Stretch out your hand with your staffᶻ over the streams and canals and ponds, and make frogsᵃ come up on the land of Egypt.' "

⁶So Aaron stretched out his hand over the waters of Egypt, and the frogsᵇ came up and covered the land. ⁷But the magicians did the same things by their secret arts;ᶜ they also made frogs come up on the land of Egypt.

⁸Pharaoh summoned Moses and Aaron and said, "Prayᵈ to the LORD to take the frogs away from me and my people, and I will let your people go to offer sacrificesᵉ to the LORD."

⁹Moses said to Pharaoh, "I leave to you the honor of setting the timeᶠ for me to pray for you and your officials and your people that you and your houses may be rid of the frogs, except for those that remain in the Nile."

¹⁰"Tomorrow," Pharaoh said.

Moses replied, "It will be as you say, so that you may know there is no one like the LORD our God.ᵍ ¹¹The frogs will leave you and your houses, your officials and your people; they will remain only in the Nile."

¹²After Moses and Aaron left Pharaoh, Moses cried out to the LORD about the frogs he had brought on Pharaoh. ¹³And the LORD did what Moses asked.ʰ The frogs died in the houses, in the court-

yards and in the fields. ¹⁴They were piled into heaps, and the land reeked of them. ¹⁵But when Pharaoh saw that there was relief,ⁱ he hardened his heartʲ and would not listen to Moses and Aaron, just as the LORD had said.

The Plague of Gnats

¹⁶Then the LORD said to Moses, "Tell Aaron, 'Stretch out your staffᵏ and strike the dust of the ground,' and throughout the land of Egypt the dust will become gnats." ¹⁷They did this, and when Aaron stretched out his hand with the staff and struck the dust of the ground, gnatsˡ came upon men and animals. All the dust throughout the land of Egypt became gnats. ¹⁸But when the magiciansᵐ tried to produce gnats by their secret arts,ⁿ they could not. And the gnats were on men and animals.

¹⁹The magicians said to Pharaoh, "This is the fingerᵒ of God." But Pharaoh's heartᵖ was hard and he would not listen,ᵠ just as the LORD had said.

The Plague of Flies

²⁰Then the LORD said to Moses, "Get up early in the morningʳ and confront Pharaoh as he goes to the water and say to him, 'This is what the LORD says: Let my people go, so that they may worshipˢ me. ²¹If you do not let my people go, I will send swarms of flies on you and your officials, on your people and into your houses. The houses of the Egyptians will be full of flies, and even the ground where they are.

²²" 'But on that day I will deal differently with the land of Goshen,ᵗ where my people live;ᵘ no swarms of flies will be there, so that you will knowᵛ that I, the LORD, am in this land. ²³I will make a distinctionᵖ between my people and your people.ʷ This miraculous sign will occur tomorrow.' "

²⁴And the LORD did this. Dense swarms of flies poured into Pharaoh's palace and into the houses of his officials, and throughout Egypt the land was ruined by the flies.ˣ

²⁵Then Pharaoh summonedʸ Moses and Aaron and said, "Go, sacrifice to your God here in the land."

²⁶But Moses said, "That would not be right. The sacrifices we offer the LORD our God would be detestable to the Egyptians.ᶻ And if we offer sacrifices that are detestable in their eyes, will they not stone us? ²⁷We must take a three-day journeyᵃ into the desert to offer sacrificesᵇ to the LORD our God, as he commands us."

²⁸Pharaoh said, "I will let you go to offer sacrifices to the LORD your God in the desert, but you must not go very far. Now prayᶜ for me."

²⁹Moses answered, "As soon as I leave you, I will pray to the LORD, and tomorrow the flies will leave Pharaoh and his officials and his people. Only be sure that Pharaoh does not act deceitfullyᵈ again by not letting the people go to offer sacrifices to the LORD."

³⁰Then Moses left Pharaoh and prayed to the LORD,ᵉ ³¹and the LORD did what Moses asked: The flies left Pharaoh and his officials and his people; not a fly remained. ³²But this time also Pharaoh hardened his heartᶠ and would not let the people go.

The Plague on Livestock

9 Then the LORD said to Moses, "Go to Pharaoh and say to him, 'This is what the LORD, the God of the Hebrews, says: "Let my people go, so that they may worshipᵍ me." ²If you refuse to let them go and continue to hold them back, ³the handʰ of the LORD will bring a terrible plagueⁱ on your livestock in the field—on your horses and donkeys and camels and on your cattle and sheep and goats. ⁴But the LORD will make a distinction between the livestock of Israel and that of Egypt,ʲ so that no animal belonging to the Israelites will die.' "

⁵The LORD set a time and said, "Tomorrow the LORD will do this in the land." ⁶And the next day the LORD did it: All the livestockᵏ of the Egyptians died,ˡ but not one animal belonging to the Israelites died. ⁷Pharaoh sent men to investigate and found that not even one of the animals of the Israelites had died. Yet his heartᵐ was unyielding and he would not let the people go.ⁿ

The Plague of Boils

⁸Then the LORD said to Moses and Aaron, "Take handfuls of soot from a fur-

---

D Ex 4:6 ◀ ▶ Ex 9:15

p 23 Septuagint and Vulgate; Hebrew will put a deliverance nace and have Moses toss it into the air in the presence of Pharaoh. ⁹It will become fine dust over the whole land of Egypt, and festering boils° will break out on men and animals throughout the land."

¹⁰So they took soot from a furnace and stood before Pharaoh. Moses tossed it into the air, and festering boils broke out on men and animals. ¹¹The magicians^p could not stand before Moses because of the boils that were on them and on all the Egyptians. ¹²But the LORD hardened Pharaoh's heart^q and he would not listen^r to Moses and Aaron, just as the LORD had said to Moses.

The Plague of Hail

¹³Then the LORD said to Moses, "Get up early in the morning, confront Pharaoh and say to him, 'This is what the LORD, the God of the Hebrews, says: Let my people go, so that they may worship^s me, ¹⁴or this time I will send the full force of my plagues against you and against your officials and your people, so you may know^t that there is no one like^u me in all the earth. ¹⁵For by now I could have stretched out my hand and struck you and your people^v with a plague that would have wiped you off the earth. ¹⁶But I have raised you up^q for this very purpose,^w that I might show you my power^x and that my name might be proclaimed in all the earth. ¹⁷You still set yourself against my people and will not let them go. ¹⁸Therefore, at this time tomorrow I will send the worst hailstorm^y that has ever fallen on Egypt, from the day it was founded till now.^z ¹⁹Give an order now to bring your livestock and everything you have in the field to a place of shelter, because the hail will fall on every man and animal that has not been brought in and is still out in the field, and they will die.'"

²⁰Those officials of Pharaoh who feared^a the word of the LORD hurried to bring their slaves and their livestock inside. ²¹But those who ignored^b the word of the LORD left their slaves and livestock in the field.

²²Then the LORD said to Moses, "Stretch out your hand toward the sky so that hail will fall all over Egypt—on men and animals and on everything growing in the fields of Egypt." ²³When Moses stretched out his staff toward the sky, the LORD sent thunder^c and hail,^d and lightning flashed down to the ground. So the LORD rained hail on the land of Egypt; ²⁴hail fell and lightning flashed back and forth. It was the worst storm in all the land of Egypt since it had become a nation.^e ²⁵Throughout Egypt hail struck everything in the fields—both men and animals; it beat down everything growing in the fields and stripped every tree.^f ²⁶The only place it did not hail was the land of Goshen,^g where the Israelites were.^h

²⁷Then Pharaoh summoned Moses and Aaron. "This time I have sinned,"^i he said to them. "The LORD is in the right,^j and I and my people are in the wrong. ²⁸Pray^k to the LORD, for we have had enough thunder and hail. I will let you go;^l you don't have to stay any longer."

²⁹Moses replied, "When I have gone out of the city, I will spread out my hands^m in prayer to the LORD. The thunder will stop and there will be no more hail, so you may know that the earth^n is the LORD's. ³⁰But I know that you and your officials still do not fear° the LORD God."

³¹(The flax and barley^p were destroyed, since the barley had headed and the flax was in bloom. ³²The wheat and spelt,^q however, were not destroyed, because they ripen later.)

³³Then Moses left Pharaoh and went out of the city. He spread out his hands toward the LORD; the thunder and hail stopped, and the rain no longer poured down on the land. ³⁴When Pharaoh saw that the rain and hail and thunder had stopped, he sinned again: He and his officials hardened their hearts. ³⁵So Pharaoh's heart^r was hard and he would not let the Israelites go, just as the LORD had said through Moses.

The Plague of Locusts

10 Then the LORD said to Moses, "Go to Pharaoh, for I have hardened his heart^s and the hearts of his officials so that I may perform these miraculous signs^t of mine among them ²that you may tell your children^u and grandchildren how I dealt harshly^v with the Egyptians

q 16 Or have spared you

and how I performed my signs among them, and that you may know that I am the LORD."ʷ

³So Moses and Aaron went to Pharaoh and said to him, "This is what the LORD, the God of the Hebrews, says: 'How long will you refuse to humbleˣ yourself before me? Let my people go, so that they may worship me. ⁴If you refuseʸ to let them go, I will bring locustsᶻ into your country tomorrow. ⁵They will cover the face of the ground so that it cannot be seen. They will devour what little you have leftᵃ after the hail, including every tree that is growing in your fields.ᵇ ⁶They will fill your housesᶜ and those of all your officials and all the Egyptians—something neither your fathers nor your forefathers have ever seen from the day they settled in this land till now.' "ᵈ Then Moses turned and left Pharaoh.

⁷Pharaoh's officials said to him, "How long will this man be a snareᵉ to us? Let the people go, so that they may worship the LORD their God. Do you not yet realize that Egypt is ruined?"ᶠ

⁸Then Moses and Aaron were brought back to Pharaoh. "Go, worshipᵍ the LORD your God," he said. "But just who will be going?"

⁹Moses answered, "We will go with our young and old, with our sons and daughters, and with our flocks and herds, because we are to celebrate a festivalʰ to the LORD."

¹⁰Pharaoh said, "The LORD be with you—if I let you go, along with your women and children! Clearly you are bent on evil.ʳ ¹¹No! Have only the men go; and worship the LORD, since that's what you have been asking for." Then Moses and Aaron were driven out of Pharaoh's presence.

¹²And the LORD said to Moses, "Stretch out your handⁱ over Egypt so that locusts will swarm over the land and devour everything growing in the fields, everything left by the hail."

¹³So Moses stretched out his staffʲ over Egypt, and the LORD made an east wind blow across the land all that day and all that night. By morning the wind had brought the locusts;ᵏ ¹⁴they invaded all Egypt and settled down in every area of the country in great numbers. Never before had there been such a plague of locusts,ˡ nor will there ever be again.

¹⁵They covered all the ground until it was black. They devouredᵐ all that was left after the hail—everything growing in the fields and the fruit on the trees. Nothing green remained on tree or plant in all the land of Egypt.

¹⁶Pharaoh quickly summonedⁿ Moses and Aaron and said, "I have sinnedᵒ against the LORD your God and against you. ¹⁷Now forgiveᵖ my sin once more and prayᵠ to the LORD your God to take this deadly plague away from me."

¹⁸Moses then left Pharaoh and prayed to the LORD.ʳ ¹⁹And the LORD changed the wind to a very strong west wind, which caught up the locusts and carried them into the Red Sea.ˢ Not a locust was left anywhere in Egypt. ²⁰But the LORD hardened Pharaoh's heart,ˢ and he would not let the Israelites go.

The Plague of Darkness

²¹Then the LORD said to Moses, "Stretch out your hand toward the sky so that darknessᵗ will spread over Egypt—darkness that can be felt." ²²So Moses stretched out his hand toward the sky, and total darknessᵘ covered all Egypt for three days. ²³No one could see anyone else or leave his place for three days. Yet all the Israelites had light in the places where they lived.ᵛ

²⁴Then Pharaoh summoned Moses and said, "Go,ʷ worship the LORD. Even your women and childrenˣ may go with you; only leave your flocks and herds behind."ʸ

²⁵But Moses said, "You must allow us to have sacrifices and burnt offeringsᶻ to present to the LORD our God. ²⁶Our livestock too must go with us; not a hoof is to be left behind. We have to use some of them in worshiping the LORD our God, and until we get there we will not know what we are to use to worship the LORD."

²⁷But the LORD hardened Pharaoh's heart,ᵃ and he was not willing to let them go. ²⁸Pharaoh said to Moses, "Get out of my sight! Make sure you do not appear before me again! The day you see my face you will die."

²⁹"Just as you say," Moses replied, "I will never appearᵇ before you again."

ʳ *10* Or *Be careful, trouble is in store for you!* ˢ *19* Hebrew *Yam Suph;* that is, Sea of Reeds

The Plague on the Firstborn

11 Now the LORD had said to Moses, "I will bring one more plague on Pharaoh and on Egypt. After that, he will let you go^c from here, and when he does, he will drive you out completely.^d ²Tell the people that men and women alike are to ask their neighbors for articles of silver and gold."^e ³(The LORD made the Egyptians favorably disposed^f toward the people, and Moses himself was highly regarded^g in Egypt by Pharaoh's officials and by the people.)

⁴So Moses said, "This is what the LORD says: 'About midnight^h I will go throughout Egypt.ⁱ ⁵Every firstborn^j son in Egypt will die, from the firstborn son of Pharaoh, who sits on the throne, to the firstborn son of the slave girl, who is at her hand mill,^k and all the firstborn of the cattle as well. ⁶There will be loud wailing^l throughout Egypt—worse than there has ever been or ever will be again. ⁷But among the Israelites not a dog will bark at any man or animal.' Then you will know that the LORD makes a distinction^m between Egypt and Israel. ⁸All these officials of yours will come to me, bowing down before me and saying, 'Go,ⁿ you and all the people who follow you!' After that I will leave."^o Then Moses, hot with anger, left Pharaoh.

⁹The LORD had said to Moses, "Pharaoh will refuse to listen^p to you—so that my wonders^q may be multiplied in Egypt." ¹⁰Moses and Aaron performed all these wonders before Pharaoh, but the LORD hardened Pharaoh's heart,^r and he would not let the Israelites go out of his country.

L Ge 28:15 ◀▶ Ex 15:13
S ▶ Lev 25:18

The Passover

12:14–20pp — Lev 23:4–8; Nu 28:16–25; Dt 16:1–8

12 The LORD said to Moses and Aaron in Egypt, ²"This month is to be for you the first month,^s the first month of your year. ³Tell the whole community of Israel that on the tenth day of this month each man is to take a lamb^{f t} for his family, one for each household.^u ⁴If any household is too small for a whole lamb, they must share one with their nearest neighbor, having taken into account the number of people there are. You are to determine the amount of lamb needed in accordance with what each person will eat. ⁵The animals you choose must be year-old males without defect,^v and you may take them from the sheep or the goats. ⁶Take care of them until the fourteenth day of the month,^w when all the people of the community of Israel must slaughter them at twilight.^x ⁷Then they are to take some of the blood^y and put it on the sides and tops of the doorframes of the houses where they eat the lambs. ⁸That same night^z they are to eat the meat roasted^a over the fire, along with bitter herbs,^b and bread made without yeast.^c ⁹Do not eat the meat raw or cooked in water, but roast it over the fire—head, legs and inner parts.^d ¹⁰Do not leave any of it till morning;^e if some is left till morning, you must burn it. ¹¹This is how you are to eat it: with your cloak tucked into your belt, your sandals on your feet and your staff in your hand. Eat it in haste;^f it is the LORD's Passover.^g

¹²"On that same night I will pass through^h Egypt and strike downⁱ every firstborn^j—both men and animals—and

A Ex 3:17–21 ◀▶ Ex 23:16
D Ge 22:7–8 ◀▶ Ex 12:13

^f3 The Hebrew word can mean *lamb* or *kid*; also in verse 4.

12:2 This verse marks the beginning of the religious calendar of the Israelites. The designation of this month as the start of Israel's religious year reminded the people of their deliverance and redemption from Egypt. Corresponding to our March-April, the Israelites called this month Abib after the Canaanite name. The name changed to Nisan, its Babylonian form, during the exile. Israel also maintained an agricultural calendar that began in the fall, with both calendars existing side by side until after the exile.

12:3–6 God commanded Israel to celebrate the Passover sacrifice each year on the fourteenth day of the month Nisan. This festival was to be a perpetual reminder of the first Passover in Egypt, signifying that for the people to be spared from death an innocent life had to be sacrificed in their place.

I will bring judgment on all the gods^k of Egypt. I am the LORD.^l ^13The blood will be a sign for you on the houses where you are; and when I see the blood, I will pass over^m you. No destructive plague will touch you when I strike Egypt.^n

^14"This is a day you are to commemorate;^o for the generations to come you shall celebrate it as a festival to the LORD—a lasting ordinance.^p ^15For seven days you are to eat bread made without yeast.^q On the first day remove the yeast from your houses, for whoever eats anything with yeast in it from the first day through the seventh must be cut off^r from Israel. ^16On the first day hold a sacred assembly, and another one on the seventh day. Do no work^s at all on these days, except to prepare food for everyone to eat—that is all you may do.

^17"Celebrate the Feast of Unleavened Bread,^t because it was on this very day that I brought your divisions out of Egypt.^u Celebrate this day as a lasting ordinance for the generations to come.^v ^18In the first month^w you are to eat bread made without yeast, from the evening of the fourteenth day until the evening of the twenty-first day. ^19For seven days no yeast is to be found in your houses. And whoever eats anything with yeast in it must be cut off^x from the community of Israel, whether he is an alien^y or native-born. ^20Eat nothing made with yeast. Wherever you live,^z you must eat unleavened bread."^a

^21Then Moses summoned all the elders of Israel and said to them, "Go at once and select the animals for your families and slaughter the Passover^b lamb. ^22Take a bunch of hyssop,^c dip it into the blood in the basin and put some of the blood^d on the top and on both sides of the doorframe. Not one of you shall go out the door of his house until morning. ^23When the LORD goes through the land to strike^e down the Egyptians, he will see the blood^f on the top and sides of the doorframe and will pass over^g that doorway, and he will not permit the destroyer^h to enter your houses and strike you down.

^24"Obey these instructions as a lasting

D *Ex 12:3–5* ◄► *Ex 12:21–23*
H *Ge 17:14* ◄► *Ex 23:7*
K *Ge 18:14* ◄► *Ex 15:13*
D *Ex 12:13* ◄► *Ex 24:5–8*

12:12 ^k Ex 15:11; 18:11; Nu 33:4; 2Ch 2:5; Ps 95:3; 97:9; 135:5; Isa 19:1; Jer 43:12; 44:8 ^l S Ex 6:2
12:13 ^m S ver 11, 23; Heb 11:28 ^n S Ex 8:23
12:14 ^o Ex 13:9; 23:14; 32:5 ^p ver 17,24; Ex 13:5,10; 27:21; Lev 3:17; 10:9; 16:29; 17:7; 23:14; 24:3; Nu 18:23
12:15 ^q Ex 13:6-7; 23:15; 34:18; Lev 23:6; Nu 28:17; Dt 16:3; 1Co 5:7 ^r S Ge 17:14
12:16 ^s Nu 29:35
12:17 ^t Ex 23:15; 34:18; Dt 16:16; 2Ch 8:13; 30:21; Ezr 6:22; Mt 26:17; Lk 22:1; Ac 12:3 ^u ver 41; S Ex 6:6, 26; 13:3; Lev 19:36 ^v Lev 3:17
12:18 ^w S ver 2
12:19 ^x S Ge 17:14 ^y Nu 9:14; 15:14; 35:15; Dt 1:16; Jos 8:33
12:20 ^z Lev 3:17; Nu 35:29; Eze 6:6 ^a Ex 13:6
12:21 ^b S ver 11; Mk 14:12-16
12:22 ^c Lev 14:4,6; Nu 19:18; Ps 51:7 ^d Heb 11:28
12:23 ^e Isa 19:22 ^f S ver 7; Rev 7:3 ^g S ver 13 ^h S Ge 16:7; Isa 37:36; Jer 6:26; 48:8; 1Co 10:10; Heb 11:28
12:24 ^i S ver 14
12:25 ^j S Ge 15:14; Ex 3:17
12:26 ^k Ex 10:2
12:27 ^l S ver 11 ^m S Ex 8:23 ^n S Ge 24:26
12:28 ^o ver 50
12:29 ^p S Ex 11:4 ^q S Ge 19:13 ^r S Ex 4:23 ^s S Ex 9:6
12:30 ^t S Ex 11:6
12:31 ^u S Ex 8:8
12:32 ^v Ex 10:9,26 ^w Ge 27:34
12:33 ^x S ver 11 ^y S Ex 6:1; 1Sa 6:6 ^z S Ge 20:3; S Ex 8:19
12:34 ^a Ex 8:3
12:35 ^b S Ex 3:22 ^c S Ge 24:53
12:36 ^d S Ge 39:21 ^e S Ex 3:22
12:37 ^f S Ge 47:11 ^g Ex 13:20; Nu 33:3-5 ^h Ge 12:2; Ex 38:26; Nu 1:46; 2:32; 11:13,21; 26:51
12:38 ^i Nu 11:4; Jos 8:35
12:39 ^j Ex 3:20; 11:1

ordinance^i for you and your descendants. ^25When you enter the land^j that the LORD will give you as he promised, observe this ceremony. ^26And when your children^k ask you, 'What does this ceremony mean to you?' ^27then tell them, 'It is the Passover^l sacrifice to the LORD, who passed over the houses of the Israelites in Egypt and spared our homes when he struck down the Egyptians.' "^m Then the people bowed down and worshiped.^n ^28The Israelites did just what the LORD commanded^o Moses and Aaron.

^29At midnight^p the LORD^q struck down all the firstborn^r in Egypt, from the firstborn of Pharaoh, who sat on the throne, to the firstborn of the prisoner, who was in the dungeon, and the firstborn of all the livestock^s as well. ^30Pharaoh and all his officials and all the Egyptians got up during the night, and there was loud wailing^t in Egypt, for there was not a house without someone dead.

The Exodus

^31During the night Pharaoh summoned Moses and Aaron and said, "Up! Leave my people, you and the Israelites! Go, worship^u the LORD as you have requested. ^32Take your flocks and herds,^v as you have said, and go. And also bless^w me."

^33The Egyptians urged the people to hurry^x and leave^y the country. "For otherwise," they said, "we will all die!"^z ^34So the people took their dough before the yeast was added, and carried it on their shoulders in kneading troughs^a wrapped in clothing. ^35The Israelites did as Moses instructed and asked the Egyptians for articles of silver and gold^b and for clothing.^c ^36The LORD had made the Egyptians favorably disposed^d toward the people, and they gave them what they asked for; so they plundered^e the Egyptians.

^37The Israelites journeyed from Rameses^f to Succoth.^g There were about six hundred thousand men^h on foot, besides women and children. ^38Many other people^i went up with them, as well as large droves of livestock, both flocks and herds. ^39With the dough they had brought from Egypt, they baked cakes of unleavened bread. The dough was without yeast because they had been driven out^j of Egypt

Hebrew Calendar and Selected Events

NUMBER of MONTH		HEBREW NAME	MODERN EQUIVALENT	BIBLICAL REFERENCES	AGRICULTURE	FEASTS
1 Sacred sequence begins	7	Abib; Nisan	March–April	Ex 12:2; 13:4; 23:15; 34:18; Dt 16:1; Ne 2:1; Est 3:7	Spring (later) rains; barley and flax harvest begins	Passover; Unleavened Bread; Firstfruits
2	8	Ziv (Iyyar)*	April–May	1Ki 6:1,37	Barley harvest; dry season begins	
3	9	Sivan	May–June	Est 8:9	Wheat harvest	Pentecost (Weeks)
4	10	(Tammuz)*	June–July		Tending vines	
5	11	(Ab)*	July–August		Ripening of grapes, figs and olives	
6	12	Elul	August–September	Ne 6:15	Processing grapes, figs and olives	
7	1 Civil sequence	Ethanim (Tishri)*	September–October	1Ki 8:2	Autumn (early) rains begin; plowing	Trumpets; Atonement; Tabernacles (Booths)
8	2	Bul (Marcheshvan)*	October–November	1Ki 6:38	Sowing of wheat and barley	
9	3	Kislev	November–December	Ne 1:1; Zec 7:1	Winter rains begin (snow in some areas)	Hanukkah ("Dedication")
10	4	Tebeth	December–January	Est 2:16		
11	5	Shebat	January–February	Zec 1:7		
12	6	Adar	February–March	Ezr 6:15; Est 3:7,13; 8:12; 9:1,15,17,19,21	Almond trees bloom; citrus fruit harvest	Purim
		(Adar Sheni)* Second Adar	— This intercalary month was added about every three years so the lunar calendar would correspond to the solar year.			

*Names in parentheses are not in the Bible

and did not have time to prepare food for themselves.

⁴⁰Now the length of time the Israelite people lived in Egypt^u was 430 years.^k ⁴¹At the end of the 430 years, to the very day, all the LORD's divisions^l left Egypt.^m ⁴²Because the LORD kept vigil that night to bring them out of Egypt, on this night all the Israelites are to keep vigil to honor the LORD for the generations to come.ⁿ

Passover Restrictions

⁴³The LORD said to Moses and Aaron, "These are the regulations for the Passover:^o

"No foreigner^p is to eat of it. ⁴⁴Any slave you have bought may eat of it after you have circumcised^q him, ⁴⁵but a temporary resident and a hired worker^r may not eat of it.

⁴⁶"It must be eaten inside one house; take none of the meat outside the house. Do not break any of the bones.^s ⁴⁷The whole community of Israel must celebrate it.

⁴⁸"An alien living among you who wants to celebrate the LORD's Passover must have all the males in his household circumcised; then he may take part like one born in the land.^t No uncircumcised^u male may eat of it. ⁴⁹The same law applies to the native-born and to the alien^v living among you."

⁵⁰All the Israelites did just what the LORD had commanded^w Moses and Aaron. ⁵¹And on that very day the LORD brought the Israelites out of Egypt^x by their divisions.^y

Consecration of the Firstborn

13 The LORD said to Moses, ²"Consecrate to me every firstborn male.^z The first offspring of every womb among the Israelites belongs to me, whether man or animal."

³Then Moses said to the people, "Commemorate this day, the day you came out of Egypt,^a out of the land of slavery, because the LORD brought you out of it with

l Ge 48:4 ◀ ▶ Ex 32:13

a mighty hand.^b Eat nothing containing yeast.^c ⁴Today, in the month of Abib,^d you are leaving. ⁵When the LORD brings you into the land of the Canaanites,^e Hittites, Amorites, Hivites and Jebusites^f— the land he swore to your forefathers to give you, a land flowing with milk and honey^g—you are to observe this ceremony^h in this month: ⁶For seven days eat bread made without yeast and on the seventh day hold a festivalⁱ to the LORD. ⁷Eat unleavened bread during those seven days; nothing with yeast in it is to be seen among you, nor shall any yeast be seen anywhere within your borders. ⁸On that day tell your son,^j 'I do this because of what the LORD did for me when I came out of Egypt.' ⁹This observance will be for you like a sign on your hand^k and a reminder on your forehead^l that the law of the LORD is to be on your lips. For the LORD brought you out of Egypt with his mighty hand.^m ¹⁰You must keep this ordinanceⁿ at the appointed time^o year after year.

¹¹"After the LORD brings you into the land of the Canaanites^p and gives it to you, as he promised on oath^q to you and your forefathers,^r ¹²you are to give over to the LORD the first offspring of every womb. All the firstborn males of your livestock belong to the LORD.^s ¹³Redeem with a lamb every firstborn donkey,^t but if you do not redeem it, break its neck.^u Redeem^v every firstborn among your sons.^w

¹⁴"In days to come, when your son^x asks you, 'What does this mean?' say to him, 'With a mighty hand the LORD brought us out of Egypt, out of the land of slavery.^y ¹⁵When Pharaoh stubbornly refused to let us go, the LORD killed every firstborn in Egypt, both man and animal. This is why I sacrifice to the LORD the first male offspring of every womb and redeem each of my firstborn sons.'^z ¹⁶And it will be like a sign on your hand and a symbol on your forehead^a that the LORD brought us out of Egypt with his mighty hand."

^u 40 Masoretic Text; Samaritan Pentateuch and Septuagint *Egypt and Canaan*

12:41 Moses records that the exodus occurred on the very day that God said it would when God initiated the Abrahamic covenant 430 years earlier (see Ge 15:13–16).

Crossing the Sea

¹⁷When Pharaoh let the people go, God did not lead them on the road through the Philistine country, though that was shorter. For God said, "If they face war, they might change their minds and return to Egypt." ᵇ ¹⁸So God led ᶜ the people around by the desert road toward the Red Sea.ᵛ The Israelites went up out of Egypt armed for battle.ᵈ

¹⁹Moses took the bones of Joseph ᵉ with him because Joseph had made the sons of Israel swear an oath. He had said, "God will surely come to your aid, and then you must carry my bones up with you from this place."ʷᶠ

²⁰After leaving Succoth ᵍ they camped at Etham on the edge of the desert.ʰ ²¹By day the LORD went ahead ⁱ of them in a pillar of cloud ʲ to guide them on their way and by night in a pillar of fire to give them light, so that they could travel by day or night. ²²Neither the pillar of cloud by day nor the pillar of fire by night left ᵏ its place in front of the people.

14

Then the LORD said to Moses, ²"Tell the Israelites to turn back and encamp near Pi Hahiroth, between Migdol ˡ and the sea. They are to encamp by the sea, directly opposite Baal Zephon.ᵐ ³Pharaoh will think, 'The Israelites are wandering around the land in confusion, hemmed in by the desert.' ⁴And I will harden Pharaoh's heart,ⁿ and he will pursue them.ᵒ But I will gain glory ᵖ for myself through Pharaoh and all his army, and the Egyptians will know that I am the LORD."ᑫ So the Israelites did this.

⁵When the king of Egypt was told that the people had fled,ʳ Pharaoh and his officials changed their minds ˢ about them and said, "What have we done? We have let the Israelites go and have lost their services!" ⁶So he had his chariot made ready and took his army with him. ⁷He took six hundred of the best chariots,ᵗ along with all the other chariots of Egypt,

⌐ Ge 40:18–19 ◄► Ex 14:13

with officers over all of them. ⁸The LORD hardened the heart ᵘ of Pharaoh king of Egypt, so that he pursued the Israelites, who were marching out boldly.ᵛ ⁹The Egyptians—all Pharaoh's horses ʷ and chariots, horsemen ˣ and troops ˣ—pursued the Israelites and overtook ʸ them as they camped by the sea near Pi Hahiroth, opposite Baal Zephon.ᶻ

¹⁰As Pharaoh approached, the Israelites looked up, and there were the Egyptians, marching after them. They were terrified and cried ᵃ out to the LORD. ¹¹They said to Moses, "Was it because there were no graves in Egypt that you brought us to the desert to die?ᵇ What have you done to us by bringing us out of Egypt? ¹²Didn't we say to you in Egypt, 'Leave us alone; let us serve the Egyptians'? It would have been better for us to serve the Egyptians than to die in the desert!"ᶜ

¹³Moses answered the people, "Do not be afraid.ᵈ Stand firm and you will see ᵉ the deliverance the LORD will bring you today. The Egyptians you see today you will never see ᶠ again. ¹⁴The LORD will fight ᵍ for you; you need only to be still."ʰ

¹⁵Then the LORD said to Moses, "Why are you crying out to me?ⁱ Tell the Israelites to move on. ¹⁶Raise your staff ʲ and stretch out your hand over the sea to divide the water ᵏ so that the Israelites can go through the sea on dry ground. ¹⁷I will harden the hearts ˡ of the Egyptians so that they will go in after them.ᵐ And I will gain glory through Pharaoh and all his army, through his chariots and his horsemen. ¹⁸The Egyptians will know that I am the LORDⁿ when I gain glory through Pharaoh, his chariots and his horsemen."

¹⁹Then the angel of God,ᵒ who had been traveling in front of Israel's army, withdrew and went behind them. The

⌐ Ex 14:4 ◄► Ex 16:23–30

14:4 God prophesied that even though Pharaoh would again change his mind and pursue the Israelites, God would receive the ultimate honor. This prophecy was fulfilled in a miraculous way (see 14:13, 28).

14:13 Moses told the Israelites at the moment they faced certain destruction that they would "see the deliverance [of] the LORD." That very day God fulfilled this prophecy as he destroyed the Egyptian army in the Red Sea.

pillar of cloud^p also moved from in front and stood behind^q them, ²⁰coming between the armies of Egypt and Israel. Throughout the night the cloud brought darkness^r to the one side and light to the other side; so neither went near the other all night long.

²¹Then Moses stretched out his hand^s over the sea,^t and all that night the LORD drove the sea back with a strong east wind^u and turned it into dry land.^v The waters were divided,^w ²²and the Israelites went through the sea^x on dry ground,^y with a wall^z of water on their right and on their left.

²³The Egyptians pursued them, and all Pharaoh's horses and chariots and horsemen^a followed them into the sea. ²⁴During the last watch of the night the LORD looked down from the pillar of fire and cloud^b at the Egyptian army and threw it into confusion.^c ²⁵He made the wheels of their chariots come off^y so that they had difficulty driving. And the Egyptians said, "Let's get away from the Israelites! The LORD is fighting^d for them against Egypt."^e

²⁶Then the LORD said to Moses, "Stretch out your hand over the sea so that the waters may flow back over the Egyptians and their chariots and horsemen." ²⁷Moses stretched out his hand over the sea, and at daybreak the sea went back to its place.^f The Egyptians were fleeing toward^z it, and the LORD swept them into the sea.^g ²⁸The water flowed back and covered the chariots and horsemen—the entire army of Pharaoh that had followed the Israelites into the sea.^h Not one of them survived.^i

²⁹But the Israelites went through the sea on dry ground,^j with a wall^k of water on their right and on their left. ³⁰That day the LORD saved^l Israel from the hands of the Egyptians, and Israel saw the Egyptians lying dead on the shore. ³¹And when the Israelites saw the great power^m the LORD displayed against the Egyptians, the people feared^n the LORD and put their trust^o in him and in Moses his servant.

The Song of Moses and Miriam

15 Then Moses and the Israelites sang this song^p to the LORD:

"I will sing^q to the LORD,
  for he is highly exalted.
The horse and its rider^r
  he has hurled into the sea.^s
²The LORD is my strength^t and my song;
  he has become my salvation.^u
He is my God,^v and I will praise him,
  my father's God, and I will exalt^w him.
³The LORD is a warrior;^x
  the LORD is his name.^y
⁴Pharaoh's chariots and his army^z
  he has hurled into the sea.
The best of Pharaoh's officers
  are drowned in the Red Sea.^a
⁵The deep waters^a have covered them;
  they sank to the depths like a stone.^b

⁶"Your right hand,^c O LORD,
  was majestic in power.
Your right hand,^d O LORD,
  shattered^e the enemy.
⁷In the greatness of your majesty^f
  you threw down those who opposed you.
You unleashed your burning anger;^g
  it consumed^h them like stubble.
⁸By the blast of your nostrils^i
  the waters piled up.^j
The surging waters stood firm like a wall;^k
  the deep waters congealed in the heart of the sea.^l

⁹"The enemy boasted,
  'I will pursue,^m I will overtake them.
I will divide the spoils;^n
  I will gorge myself on them.
I will draw my sword
  and my hand will destroy them.'
¹⁰But you blew with your breath,^o
  and the sea covered them.
They sank like lead
  in the mighty waters.^p

14:19 p S Ex 13:21; 1Co 10:1 q Isa 26:7; 42:16; 49:10; 52:12; 58:8 **14:20** r Jos 24:7 **14:21** s S Ex 7:19 t S Ex 4:2; Job 26:12; Isa 14:27; 23:11; 51:15; Jer 31:35; Ac 7:36 u S Ge 41:6; Ex 15:8; 2Sa 22:16; 1Ki 19:11; Job 38:1; 40:6; Jer 23:19; Na 1:3 v S ver 22; S Ge 8:1 w 2Ki 2:8; Ps 74:13; 78:13; 114:5; 136:13; Isa 63:12 **14:22** x ver 16; Nu 33:8; Jos 24:6; Isa 43:16; 63:11; 1Co 10:1 y ver 21, 29; S Ex 3:12; 15:19; Dt 31:6-8; Jos 3:16,17; 4:22; Ne 9:11; Ps 66:6; 77:19; 106:9; Isa 11:15; 41:10; 43:5; 44:27; 50:2; 51:10; 63:13; Jer 46:28; Na 1:4; Heb 11:29 z Ex 15:8; Jos 3:13; Ps 78:13 **14:23** a ver 7 **14:24** b S Ex 13:21; 1Co 10:1 c Ex 23:27; Jos 10:10; 1Sa 5:9; 7:10; 14:15; 2Sa 5:24; 2Ki 7:6; 19:7 **14:25** d S ver 14 e S ver 9; Dt 32:31; 1Sa 2:2; 4:8 **14:27** f Jos 4:18 g ver 28; Ex 15:1, 21; Dt 1:40; 2:1; 11:4; Ps 78:53; 106:11; 136:15; Heb 11:29 **14:28** h ver 23; Ex 15:19; Jos 24:7 i S ver 27; Ex 15:5; Jdg 4:16; Ne 9:11 **14:29** j ver; 21, S 22; Jos 24:11; 2Ki 2:8; Ps 74:15 k Ps 78:13 **14:30** l ver 29; Isa 14:23; 1Ch 11:14; Ps 44:7; 106:8,10,21; Isa 43:3; 50:2; 51:9-10; 60:16; 63:8,11 **14:31** m S Ex 9:16; Ps 147:5 n Ex 20:18; Dt 31:13; Jos 4:24; 1Sa 12:18; Ps 76:7; 112:1 o S Ex 4:5; Ps 22:4; 40:3; 106:12; Jn 2:11; 11:45 **15:1** p Nu 21:17; Jdg 5:1; 2Sa 22:1; 1Ch 16:9; Job 36:24; Ps 59:16; 105:2; Rev 15:3 q Jdg 5:3; Ps 13:6; 21:13; 27:6; 61:8; 104:33; 106:12; Isa 12:5,6; 42:10; 44:23 r Dt 11:4; Ps 76:6; Jer 51:21 s S Ex 14:27 **15:2** t Ps 18:1; 59:17 u S Ge 45:7; Ex 14:13; Ps 18:2,46; 25:5; 27:1; 62:2; 118:14; Isa 12:2; 33:2; Jnh 2:9; Hab 3:18 v S Ge 28:21 w Dt 10:21; 2Sa 22:47; Ps 22:3; 30:1; 34:3; 35:27; 99:5; 103:19; 107:32; 108:5; 109:1; 118:28; 145:11; 148:14; Isa 24:15; 25:1; Jer 17:14; Da 4:37 **15:3** x S Ex 14:14; Rev 19:11 y S Ex 3:15 **15:4** z Ex 14:6-7; Jer 51:21 **15:5** a S Ex 14:28 b ver 10; Ne 9:11 **15:6** c Ps 16:11; 17:7; 21:8; 63:8; 74:11; 77:10; 89:13; 98:1; 118:15; 138:7 d S Ex 3:20; S Job 40:14 e Nu 24:8; Isa 2:10; Ps 2:9 **15:7** f Dt 33:26; Ps 150:2 g Ps 2:5; 78:49-50; Jer 12:13; 25:9 h Est 24:17; Dt 4:24; 9:3; Ps 18:8; 59:13; Heb 12:29 **15:8** i S Ex 14:21; Ps 18:15 j Jos 3:13; Ps 78:13; Isa 43:16 k S Ex 14:22 l Ps 46:2 **15:9** m Ex 14:5-9; Dt 28:45; Ps 7:5; La 1:3 n Jdg 5:30; Isa 9:3; 53:12; Lk 11:22 **15:10** o Job 4:9; 15:30; Isa 11:4; 30:33; 40:7 p ver 5; Ne 9:11; Ps 29:3; 32:6; 77:19

^y 25 Or *He jammed the wheels of their chariots* (see Samaritan Pentateuch, Septuagint and Syriac) ^z 27 Or *from* ^a 4 Hebrew *Yam Suph*; that is, Sea of Reeds; also in verse 22

¹¹ "Who among the gods is like you, O LORD?
Who is like you—
majesty in holiness,
awesome in glory,
working wonders?
¹² You stretched out your right hand
and the earth swallowed them.
¹³ "In your unfailing love you will lead
the people you have redeemed.
In your strength you will guide them
to your holy dwelling.
¹⁴ The nations will hear and tremble;
anguish will grip the people of
Philistia.
¹⁵ The chiefs of Edom will be terrified,
the leaders of Moab will be seized
with trembling,
the people of Canaan will melt away;
¹⁶ terror and dread will fall upon
them.
By the power of your arm
they will be as still as a stone—
until your people pass by, O LORD,
until the people you bought pass
by.
¹⁷ You will bring them in and plant
them
on the mountain of your
inheritance—
the place, O LORD, you made for your
dwelling,
the sanctuary, O Lord, your hands
established.
¹⁸ The LORD will reign
for ever and ever."

¹⁹ When Pharaoh's horses, chariots and horsemen went into the sea, the LORD brought the waters of the sea back over them, but the Israelites walked through the sea on dry ground. ²⁰ Then Miriam the prophetess, Aaron's sister, took a tambourine in her hand, and all the women followed her, with tambourines and dancing. ²¹ Miriam sang to them:

"Sing to the LORD,
for he is highly exalted.
The horse and its rider
he has hurled into the sea."

The Waters of Marah and Elim

²² Then Moses led Israel from the Red Sea and they went into the Desert of Shur. For three days they traveled in the desert without finding water. ²³ When they came to Marah, they could not drink its water because it was bitter. (That is why the place is called Marah.) ²⁴ So the people grumbled against Moses, saying, "What are we to drink?" ²⁵ Then Moses cried out to the LORD, and the LORD showed him a piece of wood. He threw it into the water, and the water became sweet.

There the LORD made a decree and a law for them, and there he tested them. ²⁶ He said, "If you listen carefully to the voice of the LORD your God and do what is right in his eyes, if you pay attention to his commands and keep all his decrees, I will not bring on you any of the diseases I brought on the Egyptians, for I am the LORD, who heals you."

²⁷ Then they came to Elim, where there were twelve springs and seventy palm trees, and they camped there near the water.

Manna and Quail

16 The whole Israelite community set out from Elim and came to the Desert of Sin, which is between Elim and Sinai, on the fifteenth day of the second month after they had come out of Egypt. ² In the desert the whole community grumbled against Moses and Aaron. ³ The Israelites said to them, "If only we had died by the LORD's hand in Egypt! There we sat around pots of meat and ate all the food we wanted, but you have brought us out into this desert to starve this entire assembly to death."

⁴ Then the LORD said to Moses, "I will rain down bread from heaven for you. The people are to go out each day and

gather enough for that day. In this way I will test them and see whether they will follow my instructions. ⁵On the sixth day they are to prepare what they bring in, and that is to be twice as much as they gather on the other days."

⁶So Moses and Aaron said to all the Israelites, "In the evening you will know that it was the LORD who brought you out of Egypt, ⁷and in the morning you will see the glory of the LORD, because he has heard your grumbling against him. Who are we, that you should grumble against us?" ⁸Moses also said, "You will know that it was the LORD when he gives you meat to eat in the evening and all the bread you want in the morning, because he has heard your grumbling against him. Who are we? You are not grumbling against us, but against the LORD."

⁹Then Moses told Aaron, "Say to the entire Israelite community, 'Come before the LORD, for he has heard your grumbling.'"

¹⁰While Aaron was speaking to the whole Israelite community, they looked toward the desert, and there was the glory of the LORD appearing in the cloud.

¹¹The LORD said to Moses, ¹²"I have heard the grumbling of the Israelites. Tell them, 'At twilight you will eat meat, and in the morning you will be filled with bread. Then you will know that I am the LORD your God.'"

¹³That evening quail came and covered the camp, and in the morning there was a layer of dew around the camp. ¹⁴When the dew was gone, thin flakes like frost on the ground appeared on the desert floor. ¹⁵When the Israelites saw it, they said to each other, "What is it?" For they did not know what it was.

Moses said to them, "It is the bread the LORD has given you to eat. ¹⁶This is what the LORD has commanded: 'Each one is to gather as much as he needs. Take an omer for each person you have in your tent.'"

¹⁷The Israelites did as they were told; some gathered much, some little. ¹⁸And when they measured it by the omer, he who gathered much did not have too much, and he who gathered little did not have too little. Each one gathered as much as he needed.

¹⁹Then Moses said to them, "No one is to keep any of it until morning."

²⁰However, some of them paid no attention to Moses; they kept part of it until morning, but it was full of maggots and began to smell. So Moses was angry with them.

²¹Each morning everyone gathered as much as he needed, and when the sun grew hot, it melted away. ²²On the sixth day, they gathered twice as much—two omers for each person—and the leaders of the community came and reported this to Moses. ²³He said to them, "This is what the LORD commanded: 'Tomorrow is to be a day of rest, a holy Sabbath to the LORD. So bake what you want to bake and boil what you want to boil. Save whatever is left and keep it until morning.'"

²⁴So they saved it until morning, as Moses commanded, and it did not stink or get maggots in it. ²⁵"Eat it today," Moses said, "because today is a Sabbath to the LORD. You will not find any of it on the ground today. ²⁶Six days you are to gather it, but on the seventh day, the Sabbath, there will not be any."

²⁷Nevertheless, some of the people went out on the seventh day to gather it, but they found none. ²⁸Then the LORD said to Moses, "How long will you refuse to keep my commands and my instructions? ²⁹Bear in mind that the LORD has given you the Sabbath; that is why on the sixth day he gives you bread for two days. Everyone is to stay where he is on the seventh day; no one is to go out." ³⁰So the people rested on the seventh day.

³¹The people of Israel called the bread manna. It was white like coriander seed and tasted like wafers made with honey. ³²Moses said, "This is what the LORD has commanded: 'Take an omer of manna and keep it for the generations to come, so they can see the bread I gave you to eat in the desert when I brought you out of Egypt.'"

³³So Moses said to Aaron, "Take a jar and put an omer of manna in it. Then place it before the LORD to be kept for the generations to come."

³⁴As the LORD commanded Moses,

J Ex 14:13 ◀ ▶ Ex 17:14

f 16 That is, probably about 2 quarts (about 2 liters); also in verses 18, 32, 33 and 36 g 22 That is, probably about 4 quarts (about 4.5 liters) h 28 The Hebrew is plural. i 31 Manna means What is it? (see verse 15).

Aaron put the manna in front of the Testimony,[x] that it might be kept. [35]The Israelites ate manna[y] forty years,[z] until they came to a land that was settled; they ate manna until they reached the border of Canaan.[a]

[36](An omer[b] is one tenth of an ephah.)[c]

Water From the Rock

17 The whole Israelite community set out from the Desert of Sin,[d] traveling from place to place as the LORD commanded. They camped at Rephidim,[e] but there was no water[f] for the people to drink. [2]So they quarreled with Moses and said, "Give us water[g] to drink."[h]

Moses replied, "Why do you quarrel with me? Why do you put the LORD to the test?"[i]

[3]But the people were thirsty[j] for water there, and they grumbled[k] against Moses. They said, "Why did you bring us up out of Egypt to make us and our children and livestock die[l] of thirst?"

[4]Then Moses cried out to the LORD, "What am I to do with these people? They are almost ready to stone[m] me."

[F] [5]The LORD answered Moses, "Walk on ahead of the people. Take with you some of the elders of Israel and take in your hand the staff[n] with which you struck the Nile,[o] and go. [6]I will stand there before you by the rock at Horeb.[p] Strike[q] the rock, and water[r] will come out of it for the people to drink." So Moses did this in the sight of the elders of Israel. [7]And he called the place Massah[/s] and Meribah[k][t] because the Israelites quarreled and because they tested the LORD saying, "Is the LORD among us or not?"

The Amalekites Defeated

[8]The Amalekites[u] came and attacked the Israelites at Rephidim.[v] [9]Moses said to Joshua,[w] "Choose some of our men and go out to fight the Amalekites. Tomorrow

F *Ex 16:4–36* ◄ ► *Ex 23:25*

16:34 [a]Ex 25:16, 21,22; 27:21; 31:18; 40:20; Lev 16:13; Nu 1:50; 7:89; 10:11; 17:4, 10; Dt 10:2;
1Ki 8:9; 2Ch 5:10
16:35 [y]Jn 6:31,49
[z]Nu 14:33; 33:38; Dt 1:3; 2:7; 8:2-4; Jos 5:6; Jdg 3:11;
Ne 9:21; Ps 95:10;
Am 5:25 [a]Jos 5:12
16:36 [b]S ver 16
[c]Lev 5:11; 6:20;
Nu 5:15; 15:4; 28:5
17:1 [d]S Ex 16:1
[e]ver 8; Ex 19:2;
Nu 33:15 [f]Nu 20:5;
21:5; 33:14
17:2 [g]Nu 20:2;
33:14; Ps 107:5
[h]S Ex 14:12
[i]Dt 6:16; Ps 78:18;
41; 106:14; Mt 4:7;
1Co 10:9
17:3 [j]S Ex 15:22
[k]S Ex 15:24
[l]S Ex 14:11
17:4 [m]Nu 14:10;
1Sa 30:6; S Jn 8:59
17:5 [n]S Ex 4:2;
S 10:12-13
[o]Ex 7:20
17:6 [p]S Ex 3:1
[q]Nu 20:8
[r]Nu 20:11;
Dt 8:15; Jdg 15:19;
2Ki 3:20; Ne 9:15;
Ps 74:15; 78:15-16;
105:41; 107:35;
114:8; Isa 30:25;
35:6; 43:19; 48:21;
1Co 10:4
17:7 [s]Dt 6:16;
9:22; 33:8; Ps 95:8
[t]Nu 20:13,24;
27:14; Ps 81:7;
106:32
17:8 [u]S Ge 36:12
[v]S ver 1
17:9 [w]Ex 24:13;
32:17; 33:11;
Nu 11:28; 27:22;
Dt 1:38; Jos 1:1;
Ac 7:45
[x]S Ex 4:17
17:10 [y]ver 10-12;
Ex 24:14; 31:2
17:11 [z]Jas 5:16
17:12 [a]Jos 8:26
17:13 [b]ver 8
17:14 [c]Ex 24:4;
34:27; Nu 33:2;
Dt 31:9; Job 19:23;
Isa 30:8; Jer 36:2;
45:1; 51:60
[d]Ex 32:33;
Dt 29:20;
Job 18:17; Ps 9:5;
34:16; 109:15;

I will stand on top of the hill with the staff[x] of God in my hands."

[10]So Joshua fought the Amalekites as Moses had ordered, and Moses, Aaron and Hur[y] went to the top of the hill. [11]As long as Moses held up his hands, the Israelites were winning,[z] but whenever he lowered his hands, the Amalekites were winning. [12]When Moses' hands grew tired, they took a stone and put it under him and he sat on it. Aaron and Hur held his hands up—one on one side, one on the other—so that his hands remained steady till sunset.[a] [13]So Joshua overcame the Amalekite[b] army with the sword.

[14]Then the LORD said to Moses, "Write[c] [J] this on a scroll as something to be remembered and make sure that Joshua hears it, because I will completely blot out[d] the memory of Amalek[e] from under heaven."

[15]Moses built an altar[f] and called[g] it The LORD is my Banner. [16]He said, "For [J] hands were lifted up to the throne of the LORD. The[I] LORD will be at war against the Amalekites[h] from generation to generation."[i]

Jethro Visits Moses

18 Now Jethro,[j] the priest of Midian[k] and father-in-law of Moses, heard of everything God had done for Moses and for his people Israel, and how the LORD had brought Israel out of Egypt.[l]

[2]After Moses had sent away his wife Zipporah,[m] his father-in-law Jethro received her [3]and her two sons.[n] One son was named Gershom,[m] for Moses said, "I

J *Ex 16:23–30* ◄ ► *Ex 17:16*
J *Ex 17:14* ◄ ► *Nu 14:22–30*

Eze 18:4 [e]ver 13; S Ge 36:12; Nu 24:7; Jdg 3:13; 1Sa 30:17-18; Ps 83:7
17:15 [f]S Ge 8:20 [g]S Ge 22:14 **17:16** [h]Nu 24:7; 1Sa 15:8,32; 1Ch 4:43;
Est 3:1; 8:3; 9:24 [I]Est 9:5 **18:1** [J]S Ex 2:18 [k]S Ex 2:16 [I]S Ex 6:6
18:2 [m]S Ex 2:21 **18:3** [n]S Ex 4:20; Ac 7:29

j 7 Massah means *testing.* *k 7 Meribah* means *quarreling.*
l 16 Or *"Because a hand was against the throne of the LORD, the*
m 3 Gershom sounds like the Hebrew for *an alien there.*

17:14 Though some Biblical scholars challenge the Mosaic authorship of the first five books of the OT, many Jews and Christians alike have historically accepted the testimony of the Scriptures that Moses authored these books (see Dt 31:9, 24). Jesus Christ also affirmed the authorship and inspiration of these five books in numerous passages (see Mt 19:4–8; Mk 12:26; Jn 5:46; 7:19–23). In addition, recent analysis of the Hebrew text of these books by modern-day scholars and scientists strongly indicates the linguistic unity of the five books. Modern archeological discoveries have also confirmed the historicity of the culture and times reflected in the Pentateuch and strongly support Mosaic authorship and authority.

have become an alien in a foreign land"; ⁴and the other was named Eliezer, for he said, "My father's God was my helper; he saved me from the sword of Pharaoh."

⁵Jethro, Moses' father-in-law, together with Moses' sons and wife, came to him in the desert, where he was camped near the mountain of God. ⁶Jethro had sent word to him, "I, your father-in-law Jethro, am coming to you with your wife and her two sons."

⁷So Moses went out to meet his father-in-law and bowed down and kissed him. They greeted each other and then went into the tent. ⁸Moses told his father-in-law about everything the LORD had done to Pharaoh and the Egyptians for Israel's sake and about all the hardships they had met along the way and how the LORD had saved them.

⁹Jethro was delighted to hear about all the good things the LORD had done for Israel in rescuing them from the hand of the Egyptians. ¹⁰He said, "Praise be to the LORD, who rescued you from the hand of the Egyptians and of Pharaoh, and who rescued the people from the hand of the Egyptians. ¹¹Now I know that the LORD is greater than all other gods, for he did this to those who had treated Israel arrogantly." ¹²Then Jethro, Moses' father-in-law, brought a burnt offering and other sacrifices to God, and Aaron came with all the elders of Israel to eat bread with Moses' father-in-law in the presence of God.

¹³The next day Moses took his seat to serve as judge for the people, and they stood around him from morning till evening. ¹⁴When his father-in-law saw all that Moses was doing for the people, he said, "What is this you are doing for the people? Why do you alone sit as judge, while all these people stand around you from morning till evening?"

¹⁵Moses answered him, "Because the people come to me to seek God's will. ¹⁶Whenever they have a dispute, it is brought to me, and I decide between the parties and inform them of God's decrees and laws."

¹⁷Moses' father-in-law replied, "What you are doing is not good. ¹⁸You and these people who come to you will only wear yourselves out. The work is too heavy for you; you cannot handle it alone. ¹⁹Listen now to me and I will give you some advice, and may God be with you. You must be the people's representative before God and bring their disputes to him. ²⁰Teach them the decrees and laws, and show them the way to live and the duties they are to perform. ²¹But select capable men from all the people—men who fear God, trustworthy men who hate dishonest gain—and appoint them as officials over thousands, hundreds, fifties and tens. ²²Have them serve as judges for the people at all times, but have them bring every difficult case to you; the simple cases they can decide themselves. That will make your load lighter, because they will share it with you. ²³If you do this and God so commands, you will be able to stand the strain, and all these people will go home satisfied."

²⁴Moses listened to his father-in-law and did everything he said. ²⁵He chose capable men from all Israel and made them leaders of the people, officials over thousands, hundreds, fifties and tens. ²⁶They served as judges for the people at all times. The difficult cases they brought to Moses, but the simple ones they decided themselves.

²⁷Then Moses sent his father-in-law on his way, and Jethro returned to his own country.

At Mount Sinai

19 In the third month after the Israelites left Egypt—on the very day—they came to the Desert of Sinai. ²After they set out from Rephidim, they entered the Desert of Sinai, and Israel

n 4 Eliezer means my God is helper.

19:1 *Dispensation of the Law.* The dispensation of promise was superseded, but not annulled, by this dispensation of the law given at Sinai. Covering the time period from the exodus to the preaching of John the Baptist (see Mt 11:13; Lk 16:16), this dispensation was given to test the Israelites' obedience to the Law of Moses in every detail. God gave the Law of Moses so that people would recognize their sinfulness in contrast with his righteousness. Though the Israelites witnessed the power of God through miracles in the wilderness, saw a visible manifestation of his presence day and night, received a special

camped there in the desert in front of the mountain.ᵈ

³Then Moses went up to God,ᵉ and the LORD calledᶠ to him from the mountain and said, "This is what you are to say to the house of Jacob and what you are to tell the people of Israel: ⁴'You yourselves have seen what I did to Egypt,ᵍ and how I carried you on eagles' wingsʰ and brought you to myself.ⁱ ⁵Now if you obey me fullyʲ and keep my covenant,ᵏ then out of all nations you will be my treasured possession.ˡ Although the whole earthᵐ is mine, ⁶youᵒ will be for me a kingdom of priestsⁿ and a holy nation.'ᵒ These are the words you are to speak to the Israelites."

⁷So Moses went back and summoned the eldersᵖ of the people and set before them all the words the LORD had commanded him to speak.ᵍ ⁸The people all responded together, "We will do everything the LORD has said."ʳ So Moses brought their answer back to the LORD.

⁹The LORD said to Moses, "I am going to come to you in a dense cloud,ˢ so that the people will hear me speakingᵗ with you and will always put their trustᵘ in you." Then Moses told the LORD what the people had said.

¹⁰And the LORD said to Moses, "Go to the people and consecrateᵛ them today and tomorrow. Have them wash their clothesʷ ¹¹and be ready by the third day,ˣ because on that day the LORD will come downʸ on Mount Sinaiᶻ in the sight of all the people. ¹²Put limitsᵃ for the people around the mountain and tell them, 'Be careful that you do not go up the mountain or touch the foot of it. Whoever touches the mountain shall surely be put to death. ¹³He shall surely be stonedᵇ or shot with arrows; not a hand is to be laid on him. Whether man or animal, he shall not be permitted to live.' Only when the ram's hornᶜ sounds a long blast may they go up to the mountain."ᵈ

¹⁴After Moses had gone down the mountain to the people, he consecrated them, and they washed their clothes.ᵉ ¹⁵Then he said to the people, "Prepare yourselves for the third day. Abstainᶠ from sexual relations."

¹⁶On the morning of the third day there was thunderᵍ and lightning, with a thick cloudʰ over the mountain, and a very loud trumpet blast.ⁱ Everyone in the camp trembled.ʲ ¹⁷Then Moses led the people out of the camp to meet with God, and they stood at the foot of the mountain.ᵏ ¹⁸Mount Sinai was covered with smoke,ˡ because the LORD descended on it in fire.ᵐ The smoke billowed up from it like smoke from a furnace,ⁿ the whole

L Ex 15:13 ◀ ▶ Ex 33:12
S Ge 19:26 ◀ ▶ Ex 20:6

o 5,6 Or *possession, for the whole earth is mine.* *⁶You*

---

revelation from him containing a complete code of civil and religious laws and covenanted with God to be his consecrated people, their failure of the test of this dispensation is documented throughout the entire OT.

The seven dispensations revealed in Scripture are the dispensations of innocence (Ge 1:28), conscience (Ge 3:7), human government (Ge 8:15), promise (Ge 12:1), law (Ex 19:1), the church (Ac 2:1) and the kingdom (Rev 20:4). For further information on the dispensations, see the article on p. 4.

19:5–6 *Mosaic Covenant.* This conditional covenant between God and Israel at Mt. Sinai represented an enlargement of the covenant God made with Abraham 600 years earlier. In addition to God's promise to be Israel's God, protector and provider, God now called Israel his "treasured possession," a nation separated from all other nations, holy and devoted to God alone, whose citizens were all priests with access to God (see Dt 7:6; 14:2; 26:18; Ps 135:4; Mal 3:17). This feature of the Mosaic covenant foreshadows the divine blessing bestowed on Christians (see 1Pe 2:9; Rev 1:6; 5:10).

Chosen to represent God's way of life, teach his Word and serve as his channel of salvation for the world through the prophesied Messiah (see Ge 18:18; Isa 60:3), Israel's covenantal blessing was conditional upon her faith and obedience. At Mt. Sinai the Israelites promised to consecrate themselves to God, to live by his rule and to serve his purposes, yet history records their repeated failures in each of these areas.

NOTE: The seven additional covenants include the Edenic (Ge 2:15–17), Adamic (Ge 3:15–19), Noahic (Ge 9:8ff), Abrahamic (Ge 15:4ff; 17:1–22), Palestinian (Dt 30:1–10), Davidic (2Sa 7:16) and New (Heb 8:8–12). See article on p. 8.

mountain trembled violently, ¹⁹and the sound of the trumpet grew louder and louder. Then Moses spoke and the voice of God answered him.

²⁰The LORD descended to the top of Mount Sinai and called Moses to the top of the mountain. So Moses went up ²¹and the LORD said to him, "Go down and warn the people so they do not force their way through to see the LORD and many of them perish. ²²Even the priests, who approach the LORD, must consecrate themselves, or the LORD will break out against them."

²³Moses said to the LORD, "The people cannot come up Mount Sinai, because you yourself warned us, 'Put limits around the mountain and set it apart as holy.'"

²⁴The LORD replied, "Go down and bring Aaron up with you. But the priests and the people must not force their way through to come up to the LORD, or he will break out against them."

²⁵So Moses went down to the people and told them.

The Ten Commandments

20:1–17pp — Dt 5:6–21

20 And God spoke all these words:

²"I am the LORD your God, who brought you out of Egypt, out of the land of slavery.

³"You shall have no other gods before me.

⁴"You shall not make for yourself an idol in the form of anything in heaven above or on the earth beneath or in the waters below. ⁵You shall not bow down to them or worship them; for I, the LORD your God, am a jealous God, punishing the children for the sin of the fathers to the third and fourth generation of those who hate me, ⁶but showing love to a thousand ⌞generations⌟ of those who love me and keep my commandments.

⁷"You shall not misuse the name of the LORD your God, for the LORD will not hold anyone guiltless who misuses his name.

⁸"Remember the Sabbath day by keeping it holy. ⁹Six days you shall labor and do all your work, ¹⁰but the seventh day is a Sabbath to the LORD your God. On it you shall not do any work, neither you, nor your son or daughter, nor your manservant or maidservant, nor your animals, nor the alien within your gates. ¹¹For in six days the LORD made the heavens and the earth, the sea, and all that is in them, but he rested on the seventh day. Therefore the LORD blessed the Sabbath day and made it holy.

¹²"Honor your father and your mother, so that you may live long in the land the LORD your God is giving you.

¹³"You shall not murder.

¹⁴"You shall not commit adultery.

¹⁵"You shall not steal.

¹⁶"You shall not give false testimony against your neighbor.

¹⁷"You shall not covet your neighbor's house. You shall not covet your neighbor's wife, or his manservant or maidservant, his ox or donkey, or anything that belongs to your neighbor."

¹⁸When the people saw the thunder and lightning and heard the trumpet and saw the mountain in smoke, they trembled with fear. They stayed at a distance ¹⁹and said to Moses, "Speak to us yourself and we will listen. But do not have God speak to us or we will die."

²⁰Moses said to the people, "Do not be afraid. God has come to test you, so

p 18 Most Hebrew manuscripts; a few Hebrew manuscripts and Septuagint all the people   q 19 Or and God answered him with thunder   r 3 Or besides

that the fear[l] of God will be with you to keep you from sinning.'"[m]

²¹The people remained at a distance, while Moses approached the thick darkness[n] where God was.

Idols and Altars

²²Then the LORD said to Moses, "Tell the Israelites this: 'You have seen for yourselves that I have spoken to you from heaven:[o] ²³Do not make any gods to be alongside me;[p] do not make for yourselves gods of silver or gods of gold.[q]

²⁴"'Make an altar[r] of earth for me and sacrifice on it your burnt offerings[s] and fellowship offerings,[s] your sheep and goats and your cattle. Wherever I cause my name[t] to be honored, I will come to you and bless[u] you. ²⁵If you make an altar of stones for me, do not build it with dressed stones, for you will defile it if you use a tool[v] on it. ²⁶And do not go up to my altar on steps, lest your nakedness[w] be exposed on it.'

21 "These are the laws[x] you are to set before them:

Hebrew Servants

21:2–6pp — Dt 15:12–18
21:2–11Ref — Lev 25:39–55

²"If you buy a Hebrew servant,[y] he is to serve you for six years. But in the seventh year, he shall go free,[z] without paying anything. ³If he comes alone, he is to go free alone; but if he has a wife when he comes, she is to go with him. ⁴If his master gives him a wife and she bears him sons or daughters, the woman and her children shall belong to her master, and only the man shall go free.

⁵"But if the servant declares, 'I love my master and my wife and children and do not want to go free,'[a] ⁶then his master must take him before the judges.[b] He shall take him to the door or the doorpost and pierce[c] his ear with an awl. Then he will be his servant for life.[d]

⁷"If a man sells his daughter as a servant, she is not to go free as menservants do. ⁸If she does not please the master who has selected her for himself,[u] he must let her be redeemed. He has no right to sell her to foreigners, because he has broken faith with her. ⁹If he selects her for his son, he must grant her the rights of a daughter. ¹⁰If he marries another woman, he must not deprive the first one of her food, clothing and marital rights.[e] ¹¹If he does not provide her with these three things, she is to go free, without any payment of money.

Personal Injuries

¹²"Anyone who strikes a man and kills him shall surely be put to death.[f] ¹³However, if he does not do it intentionally, but God lets it happen, he is to flee to a place[g] I will designate. ¹⁴But if a man schemes and kills another man deliberately,[h] take him away from my altar and put him to death.[i]

¹⁵"Anyone who attacks[v] his father or his mother must be put to death.

¹⁶"Anyone who kidnaps another and either sells[j] him or still has him when he is caught must be put to death.[k]

¹⁷"Anyone who curses his father or mother must be put to death.[l]

¹⁸"If men quarrel and one hits the other with a stone or with his fist[w] and he does not die but is confined to bed, ¹⁹the one who struck the blow will not be held responsible if the other gets up and walks around outside with his staff; however, he must pay the injured man for the loss of his time and see that he is completely healed.

²⁰"If a man beats his male or female slave with a rod and the slave dies as a direct result, he must be punished, ²¹but he is not to be punished if the slave gets up after a day or two, since the slave is his property.[m]

²²"If men who are fighting hit a pregnant woman and she gives birth prematurely[x] but there is no serious injury, the offender must be fined whatever the woman's husband demands[n] and the court allows. ²³But if there is serious injury, you are to take life for life,[o] ²⁴eye for eye, tooth for tooth,[p] hand for hand, foot for foot, ²⁵burn for burn, wound for wound, bruise for bruise.

²⁶"If a man hits a manservant or maidservant in the eye and destroys it, he must let the servant go free to compensate for the eye. ²⁷And if he knocks out the tooth of a manservant or maidservant, he must let the servant go free to compensate for the tooth.

---

s 24 Traditionally *peace offerings*   *t* 6 Or *before God*   *u* 8 Or *master so that he does not choose her*   *v* 15 Or *kills*   *w* 18 Or *with a tool*   *x* 22 Or *she has a miscarriage*

^{28}"If a bull gores a man or a woman to death, the bull must be stoned to death,^{q} and its meat must not be eaten. But the owner of the bull will not be held responsible. ^{29}If, however, the bull has had the habit of goring and the owner has been warned but has not kept it penned up^r and it kills a man or woman, the bull must be stoned and the owner also must be put to death. ^{30}However, if payment is demanded of him, he may redeem his life by paying whatever is demanded.^{s} ^{31}This law also applies if the bull gores a son or daughter. ^{32}If the bull gores a male or female slave, the owner must pay thirty shekels^y^{t} of silver to the master of the slave, and the bull must be stoned.

^{33}"If a man uncovers a pit^u or digs one and fails to cover it and an ox or a donkey falls into it, ^{34}the owner of the pit must pay for the loss; he must pay its owner, and the dead animal will be his.

^{35}"If a man's bull injures the bull of another and it dies, they are to sell the live one and divide both the money and the dead animal equally. ^{36}However, if it was known that the bull had the habit of goring, yet the owner did not keep it penned up,^{v} the owner must pay, animal for animal, and the dead animal will be his.

Protection of Property

22 "If a man steals an ox or a sheep and slaughters it or sells it, he must pay back^w five head of cattle for the ox and four sheep for the sheep.

^{2}"If a thief is caught breaking in^x and is struck so that he dies, the defender is not guilty of bloodshed;^{y} ^{3}but if it happens^z after sunrise, he is guilty of bloodshed.

"A thief must certainly make restitution,^{z} but if he has nothing, he must be sold^a to pay for his theft.

^{4}"If the stolen animal is found alive in his possession^b—whether ox or donkey or sheep—he must pay back double.^{c}

^{5}"If a man grazes his livestock in a field or vineyard and lets them stray and they graze in another man's field, he must make restitution^d from the best of his own field or vineyard.

^{6}"If a fire breaks out and spreads into thornbushes so that it burns shocks^e of grain or standing grain or the whole field, the one who started the fire must make restitution.^{f}

^{7}"If a man gives his neighbor silver or goods for safekeeping^g and they are stolen from the neighbor's house, the thief, if he is caught, must pay back double.^{h} ^{8}But if the thief is not found, the owner of the house must appear before the judges^a^{i} to determine whether he has laid his hands on the other man's property. ^{9}In all cases of illegal possession of an ox, a donkey, a sheep, a garment, or any other lost property about which somebody says, 'This is mine,' both parties are to bring their cases before the judges.^{j} The one whom the judges declare^b guilty must pay back double to his neighbor.

^{10}"If a man gives a donkey, an ox, a sheep or any other animal to his neighbor for safekeeping^k and it dies or is injured or is taken away while no one is looking, ^{11}the issue between them will be settled by the taking of an oath^l before the LORD that the neighbor did not lay hands on the other person's property. The owner is to accept this, and no restitution is required. ^{12}But if the animal was stolen from the neighbor, he must make restitution^m to the owner. ^{13}If it was torn to pieces by a wild animal, he shall bring in the remains as evidence and he will not be required to pay for the torn animal.^{n}

^{14}"If a man borrows an animal from his neighbor and it is injured or dies while the owner is not present, he must make restitution.^{o} ^{15}But if the owner is with the animal, the borrower will not have to pay. If the animal was hired, the money paid for the hire covers the loss.^{p}

Social Responsibility

^{16}"If a man seduces a virgin^q who is not pledged to be married and sleeps with her, he must pay the bride-price,^{r} and she shall be his wife. ^{17}If her father absolutely refuses to give her to him, he must still pay the bride-price for virgins.

^{18}"Do not allow a sorceress^s to live.

^{19}"Anyone who has sexual relations with an animal^t must be put to death.

^{20}"Whoever sacrifices to any god^u other than the LORD must be destroyed.^{c}^{v}

---

^{y} 32 That is, about 12 ounces (about 0.3 kilogram) ^{z} 3 Or *if he strikes him* ^{a} 8 Or *before God*; also in verse 9 ^{b} 9 Or *whom God declares* ^{c} 20 The Hebrew term refers to the irrevocable giving over of things or persons to the LORD, often by totally destroying them.

R ▶ Lev 5:5

²¹"Do not mistreat an alien^w or oppress him, for you were aliens^x in Egypt.

²²"Do not take advantage of a widow or an orphan.^y ²³If you do and they cry out^z to me, I will certainly hear their cry.^a ²⁴My anger will be aroused, and I will kill you with the sword; your wives will become widows and your children fatherless.^b

²⁵"If you lend money to one of my people among you who is needy, do not be like a moneylender; charge him no interest.^dc ²⁶If you take your neighbor's cloak as a pledge,^d return it to him by sunset, ²⁷because his cloak is the only covering he has for his body. What else will he sleep in?^e When he cries out to me, I will hear, for I am compassionate.^f

²⁸"Do not blaspheme God^eg or curse^h the ruler of your people.^i

²⁹"Do not hold back offerings^j from your granaries or your vats.^f

"You must give me the firstborn of your sons.^k ³⁰Do the same with your cattle and your sheep.^l Let them stay with their mothers for seven days, but give them to me on the eighth day.^m

³¹"You are to be my holy people.^n So do not eat the meat of an animal torn by wild beasts;^o throw it to the dogs.

Laws of Justice and Mercy

23 "Do not spread false reports.^p Do not help a wicked man by being a malicious witness.^q

²"Do not follow the crowd in doing wrong. When you give testimony in a lawsuit, do not pervert justice^r by siding with the crowd,^s ³and do not show favoritism^t to a poor man in his lawsuit.

⁴"If you come across your enemy's^u ox or donkey wandering off, be sure to take it back to him.^v ⁵If you see the donkey^w of someone who hates you fallen down under its load, do not leave it there; be sure you help him with it.

⁶"Do not deny justice^x to your poor people in their lawsuits. ⁷Have nothing to do with a false charge^y and do not put an innocent^z or honest person to death,^a for I will not acquit the guilty.^b

⁸"Do not accept a bribe,^c for a bribe

S Ex 20:6 ◀ ▶ Ex 23:7
H Ex 12:13 ◀ ▶ Ex 32:33
S Ex 22:31 ◀ ▶ Ex 32:33

22:21 ^w Ex 23:9; Lev 19:33; 24:22; Nu 15:14; Dt 1:16; 24:17; Eze 22:29 ^x Dt 10:19; 27:19; Zec 7:10; Mal 3:5
22:22 ^y ver 26; Dt 10:18; 24:6,10, 12,17; Job 22:6,9; 24:3,21; Ps 68:5; 146:9; Pr 23:10; Isa 1:17; Jer 7:5,6; 21:12; 22:3; Eze 18:5-9,12; Zec 7:9-10; Mal 3:5; Jas 1:27
22:23 ^z Lk 18:7 ^a Dt 10:18; 15:9; 24:15; Job 34:28; 35:9; Ps 10:14,17; 12:5; 18:6; 34:15; Jas 5:4
22:24 ^b Ps 69:24; 109:9; La 5:3
22:25 ^c Lev 25:35-37; Dt 15:7-11; 23:20; Ne 5:7,10; Ps 15:5; Eze 18:8
22:26 ^d S ver 22; Pr 20:16; Eze 33:15; Am 2:8
22:27 ^e Dt 24:13, 17; Job 22:6; 24:7; 29:11; 31:19-20; Eze 18:12,16
22:28 ^f Ex 34:6; Dt 4:31; 2Ch 30:9; Ne 9:17; Ps 99:8; 103:8; 116:5; 145:8; Joel 2:13; Jnh 4:2
22:28 ^g S 2Sa 20:7 ^h 2Sa 16:5,9; 19:21; 1Ki 21:10; 2Ki 2:23; Ps 102:8 ^i Ecc 10:20; Ac 23:5*
22:29 ^j Ex 23:15, 16,19; 34:20,26; Lev 19:24; 23:10; Nu 18:13; 28:26; Dt 18:4; 26:2,10; 1Sa 6:3; Ne 10:35; Pr 3:9; Mal 3:10 ^k S Ex 13:2; Nu 8:16-17; Lk 2:23
22:30 ^l Ex 34:19; Dt 15:19 ^m Ge 17:12; Lev 12:3; 22:27
22:31 ^n Ex 19:6; Lev 19:2; 22:31; Ezr 9:2 ^o Lev 7:24; 17:15; 22:8; Dt 14:21; Eze 4:14; 44:31
23:1 ^p S Ge 39:17; Mt 19:18; Lk 3:14 ^q S Ex 20:16; Ps 27:12; 35:11; Pr 19:5; Ac 6:11
23:2 ^r ver 3,6,9; Lev 19:15,33; Dt 1:17; 16:19; 24:17; 27:19; 1Sa 8:3 ^s Job 31:34
23:3 ^t Dt 1:17
23:4 ^u Ro 12:20
23:5 ^w Dt 22:4
23:6 ^x S ver 2;
Dt 22:1-3
23:6 ^x S ver 2; Dt 23:16; Pr 22:22

blinds those who see and twists the words of the righteous.

⁹"Do not oppress an alien;^d you yourselves know how it feels to be aliens, because you were aliens in Egypt.

Sabbath Laws

¹⁰"For six years you are to sow your fields and harvest the crops, ¹¹but during the seventh year let the land lie unplowed and unused.^e Then the poor among your people may get food from it, and the wild animals may eat what they leave. Do the same with your vineyard and your olive grove.

¹²"Six days do your work,^f but on the seventh day do not work, so that your ox and your donkey may rest and the slave born in your household, and the alien as well, may be refreshed.^g

¹³"Be careful^h to do everything I have said to you. Do not invoke the names of other gods;^i do not let them be heard on your lips.^j

The Three Annual Festivals

¹⁴"Three times^k a year you are to celebrate a festival to me.

¹⁵"Celebrate the Feast of Unleavened Bread;^l for seven days eat bread made without yeast, as I commanded you. Do this at the appointed time in the month of Abib,^m for in that month you came out of Egypt.

"No one is to appear before me empty-handed.^n

¹⁶"Celebrate the Feast of Harvest^o with the firstfruits^p of the crops you sow in your field.

"Celebrate the Feast of Ingathering^q at the end of the year, when you gather in your crops from the field.^r

¹⁷"Three times^s a year all the men are to appear before the Sovereign LORD.

A Ex 12:3–9 ◀ ▶ Ex 23:25–31

23:7 ^y S Ex 20:16; S Eph 4:25 ^z Mt 27:4 ^a S Ge 18:23 ^b Ex 34:7; Dt 19:18; 25:1
23:8 ^c S Ex 18:21; Lev 19:15; Dt 10:17; 27:25; Job 15:34; 36:18; Ps 26:10; Pr 6:35; 15:27; 17:8; Isa 1:23; 5:23; Mic 3:11; 7:3
23:9 ^d S ver 2; S Ex 22:21; Lev 19:33-34; Eze 22:7 **23:11** ^e Lev 25:1-7; Ne 10:31 **23:12** ^f S Ex 20:9; Lk 13:14 ^g Ge 2:2-3 **23:13** ^h Dt 4:9,23; 1Ti 4:16 ^i ver 32; Dt 12:3; Jos 23:7; Ps 16:4; Hos 2:17 **23:14** ^k ver 17; S Ex 12:14; 34:23,24; Dt 16:16; 1Ki 9:25; 2Ch 8:13; Eze 46:9 **23:15** ^l S Ex 12:17; Mt 26:17; Lk 22:1; Ac 12:3 ^m S Ex 12:2 ^n S Ex 22:29 **23:16** ^o Lev 23:15-21; Nu 28:26; Dt 16:9; 2Ch 8:13 ^p S Ex 22:29; S 34:22 ^q Ex 34:22; Lev 23:34,42; Dt 16:16; 31:10; Ezr 3:4; Ne 8:14; Zec 14:16 ^r Lev 23:39; Dt 16:13; Jer 40:10 **23:17** ^s S ver 14

^d 25 Or excessive interest ^e 28 Or Do not revile the judges ^f 29 The meaning of the Hebrew for this phrase is uncertain.

¹⁸"Do not offer the blood of a sacrifice to me along with anything containing yeast.ᵗ

"The fat of my festival offerings must not be kept until morning.ᵘ

¹⁹"Bring the best of the firstfruitsᵛ of your soil to the house of the LORD your God.

"Do not cook a young goat in its mother's milk.ʷ

God's Angel to Prepare the Way

²⁰"See, I am sending an angelˣ ahead of you to guard you along the way and to bring you to the place I have prepared.ʸ ²¹Pay attention to him and listenᶻ to what he says. Do not rebel against him; he will not forgiveᵃ your rebellion,ᵇ since my Nameᶜ is in him. ²²If you listen carefully to what he says and doᵈ all that I say, I will be an enemyᵉ to your enemies and will oppose those who oppose you. ²³My angel will go ahead of you and bring you into the land of the Amorites, Hittites, Perizzites, Canaanites, Hivites and Jebusites,ᶠ and I will wipe them out. ²⁴Do not bow down before their gods or worshipᵍ them or follow their practices.ʰ You must demolishⁱ them and break their sacred stonesʲ to pieces. ²⁵Worship the LORD your God,ᵏ and his blessingˡ will be on your food and water. I will take away sicknessᵐ from among you, ²⁶and none will miscarry or be barrenⁿ in your land. I will give you a full life span.ᵒ

²⁷"I will send my terrorᵖ ahead of you and throw into confusionᵠ every nation you encounter. I will make all your enemies turn their backs and run.ʳ ²⁸I will send the hornetsˢ ahead of you to drive the Hivites, Canaanites and Hittitesᵗ out of your way. ²⁹But I will not drive them out in a single year, because the land would become desolate and the wild animalsᵘ too numerous for you. ³⁰Little by little I will drive them out before you, until you have increased enough to take possession of the land.

³¹"I will establish your borders from the Red Seaᵍ to the Sea of the Philistines,ʰ and from the desert to the River.ⁱʷ I will hand over to you the people who live in the land and you will drive them outˣ before you. ³²Do not make a covenantʸ with them or with their gods. ³³Do not let them live in your land, or they will cause you to sin against me, because the worship of their gods will certainly be a snareᶻ to you."

The Covenant Confirmed

24 Then he said to Moses, "Come up to the LORD, you and Aaron,ᵃ Nadab and Abihu,ᵇ and seventy of the eldersᶜ of Israel. You are to worship at a distance, ²but Moses alone is to approachᵈ the LORD; the others must not come near. And the people may not come up with him."

³When Moses went and told the people all the LORD's words and laws,ᵉ they responded with one voice, "Everything the LORD has said we will do."ᶠ ⁴Moses then wroteᵍ down everything the LORD had said.

He got up early the next morning and built an altarʰ at the foot of the mountain and set up twelve stone pillarsⁱ representing the twelve tribes of Israel. ⁵Then he sent young Israelite men, and they offered burnt offeringsʲ and sacrificed young bulls as fellowship offeringsʲ/ᵏ to the LORD. ⁶Mosesˡ took half of the bloodᵐ and put it in bowls, and the other half he sprinkledⁿ on the altar. ⁷Then he took the Book of the Covenantᵒ and read it to the people. They responded, "We will do everything the LORD has said; we will obey."ᵖ

⁸Moses then took the blood, sprinkled it on the peopleᵠ and said, "This is the blood of the covenantʳ that the LORD has made with you in accordance with all these words."

⁹Moses and Aaron, Nadab and Abihu, and the seventy eldersˢ of Israel went up ¹⁰and sawᵗ the God of Israel. Under his feet was something like a pavement made

D Ex 12:21–23 ◄► Ex 28:38

of sapphire,^(k u) clear as the sky^v itself. ^11But God did not raise his hand against these leaders of the Israelites; they saw^w God, and they ate and drank.^x

^12The LORD said to Moses, "Come up to me on the mountain and stay here, and I will give you the tablets of stone,^y with the law and commands I have written for their instruction."

^13Then Moses set out with Joshua^z his aide, and Moses went up on the mountain^a of God. ^14He said to the elders, "Wait here for us until we come back to you. Aaron and Hur^b are with you, and anyone involved in a dispute^c can go to them."

^15When Moses went up on the mountain, the cloud^d covered it, ^16and the glory^e of the LORD settled on Mount Sinai.^f For six days the cloud covered the mountain, and on the seventh day the LORD called to Moses from within the cloud.^g ^17To the Israelites the glory of the LORD looked like a consuming fire^h on top of the mountain. ^18Then Moses entered the cloud as he went on up the mountain. And he stayed on the mountain forty^i days and forty nights.^j

Offerings for the Tabernacle
25:1–7pp — Ex 35:4–9

25 The LORD said to Moses, ^2"Tell the Israelites to bring me an offering. You are to receive the offering for me from each man whose heart prompts^k him to give. ^3These are the offerings you are to receive from them: gold, silver and bronze; ^4blue, purple and scarlet yarn^l and fine linen; goat hair; ^5ram skins dyed red and hides of sea cows^l;^m acacia wood;^n ^6olive oil^o for the light; spices for the anointing oil and for the fragrant incense;^p ^7and onyx stones and other gems to be mounted on the ephod^q and breastpiece.^r

^8"Then have them make a sanctuary^s for me, and I will dwell^t among them. ^9Make this tabernacle and all its furnishings exactly like the pattern^u I will show you.

The Ark
25:10–20pp — Ex 37:1–9

^10"Have them make a chest^v of acacia wood—two and a half cubits long, a cubit and a half wide, and a cubit and a half high.^m ^11Overlay^w it with pure gold, both inside and out, and make a gold molding around it. ^12Cast four gold rings for it and fasten them to its four feet, with two rings^x on one side and two rings on the other. ^13Then make poles of acacia wood and overlay them with gold.^y ^14Insert the poles^z into the rings on the sides of the chest to carry it. ^15The poles are to remain in the rings of this ark; they are not to be removed.^a ^16Then put in the ark the Testimony,^b which I will give you.

^17"Make an atonement cover^n^c of pure gold—two and a half cubits long and a cubit and a half wide.^o ^18And make two cherubim^d out of hammered gold at the ends of the cover. ^19Make one cherub on one end and the second cherub on the other; make the cherubim of one piece with the cover, at the two ends. ^20The cherubim^e are to have their wings spread upward, overshadowing^f the cover with them. The cherubim are to face each other, looking toward the cover. ^21Place the cover on top of the ark^g and put in the ark the Testimony,^h which I will give you. ^22There, above the cover between the two cherubim^i that are over the ark of the Testimony, I will meet^j with you and give you all my commands for the Israelites.^k

L Ex 20:6 ◀ ▶ Ex 34:6–7

25:8 God commanded Moses to have the Israelites make him "a sanctuary" or holy place where he would dwell among them. This sanctuary was to be a sign or token of his presence in their midst. In the wilderness the Israelites lived in tents, so God's sanctuary was also a tent. When the Israelites conquered Canaan and established permanent dwellings, the temple in Jerusalem provided a more permanent place of worship and sacrifice.

The Table

25:23–29pp — Ex 37:10–16

²³"Make a table¹ of acacia wood—two cubits long, a cubit wide and a cubit and a half high.ᵖ ²⁴Overlay it with pure gold and make a gold molding around it. ²⁵Also make around it a rim a handbreadthᑫ wide and put a gold molding on the rim. ²⁶Make four gold rings for the table and fasten them to the four corners, where the four legs are. ²⁷The rings are to be close to the rim to hold the poles used in carrying the table. ²⁸Make the poles of acacia wood, overlay them with goldᵐ and carry the table with them. ²⁹And make its plates and dishes of pure gold, as well as its pitchers and bowls for the pouring out of offerings.ⁿ ³⁰Put the bread of the Presenceᵒ on this table to be before me at all times.

The Lampstand

25:31–39pp — Ex 37:17–24

³¹"Make a lampstandᵖ of pure gold and hammer it out, base and shaft; its flowerlike cups, buds and blossoms shall be of one piece with it. ³²Six branches are to extend from the sides of the lampstand—three on one side and three on the other. ³³Three cups shaped like almond flowers with buds and blossoms are to be on one branch, three on the next branch, and the same for all six branches extending from the lampstand. ³⁴And on the lampstand there are to be four cups shaped like almond flowers with buds and blossoms. ³⁵One bud shall be under the first pair of branches extending from the lampstand, a second bud under the second pair, and a third bud under the third pair—six branches in all. ³⁶The buds and branches shall all be of one piece with the lampstand, hammered out of pure gold.ᑫ

³⁷"Then make its seven lampsʳ and set them up on it so that they light the space in front of it. ³⁸Its wick trimmers and traysˢ are to be of pure gold. ³⁹A talentʳ of pure gold is to be used for the lampstand and all these accessories. ⁴⁰See that you make them according to the patternᵗ shown you on the mountain.

The Tabernacle

26:1–37pp — Ex 36:8–38

26 "Make the tabernacleᵘ with ten curtains of finely twisted linen and blue, purple and scarlet yarn, with cherubimᵛ worked into them by a skilled craftsman. ²All the curtains are to be the same sizeʷ—twenty-eight cubits long and four cubits wide.ˢ ³Join five of the curtains together, and do the same with the other five. ⁴Make loops of blue material along the edge of the end curtain in one set, and do the same with the end curtain in the other set. ⁵Make fifty loops on one curtain and fifty loops on the end curtain of the other set, with the loops opposite each other. ⁶Then make fifty gold clasps and use them to fasten the curtains together so that the tabernacle is a unit.ˣ

⁷"Make curtains of goat hair for the tent over the tabernacle—eleven altogether. ⁸All eleven curtains are to be the same sizeʸ—thirty cubits long and four cubits wide.ʳ ⁹Join five of the curtains together into one set and the other six into another set. Fold the sixth curtain double at the front of the tent. ¹⁰Make fifty loops along the edge of the end curtain in one set and also along the edge of the end curtain in the other set. ¹¹Then make fifty bronze clasps and put them in the loops to fasten the tent together as a unit.ᶻ ¹²As for the additional length of the tent curtains, the half curtain that is left over is to hang down at the rear of the tabernacle. ¹³The tent curtains will be a cubitᵘ longer on both sides; what is left will hang over the sides of the tabernacle so as to cover it. ¹⁴Make for the tent a coveringᵃ of ram skins dyed red, and over that a covering of hides of sea cows.ᵛᵇ

¹⁵"Make upright frames of acacia wood for the tabernacle. ¹⁶Each frame is to be ten cubits long and a cubit and a half wide,ʷ ¹⁷with two projections set parallel to each other. Make all the frames of the tabernacle in this way. ¹⁸Make twenty frames for the south side of the tabernacle ¹⁹and make forty silver basesᶜ to go under them—two bases for each frame,

p 23 That is, about 3 feet (about 0.9 meter) long and 1 1/2 feet (about 0.5 meter) wide and 2 1/4 feet (about 0.7 meter) high q 25 That is, about 3 inches (about 8 centimeters) r 39 That is, about 75 pounds (about 34 kilograms) s 2 That is, about 42 feet (about 12.5 meters) long and 6 feet (about 1.8 meters) wide t 8 That is, about 45 feet (about 13.5 meters) long and 6 feet (about 1.8 meters) wide u 13 That is, about 1 1/2 feet (about 0.5 meter) v 14 That is, dugongs w 16 That is, about 15 feet (about 4.5 meters) long and 2 1/4 feet (about 0.7 meter) wide

one under each projection. ²⁰For the other side, the north side of the tabernacle, make twenty frames ²¹and forty silver bases[d]—two under each frame. ²²Make six frames for the far end, that is, the west end of the tabernacle, ²³and make two frames for the corners at the far end. ²⁴At these two corners they must be double from the bottom all the way to the top, and fitted into a single ring; both shall be like that. ²⁵So there will be eight frames and sixteen silver bases—two under each frame.

²⁶"Also make crossbars of acacia wood: five for the frames on one side of the tabernacle, ²⁷five for those on the other side, and five for the frames on the west, at the far end of the tabernacle. ²⁸The center crossbar is to extend from end to end at the middle of the frames. ²⁹Overlay the frames with gold and make gold rings to hold the crossbars. Also overlay the crossbars with gold.

³⁰"Set up the tabernacle[e] according to the plan[f] shown you on the mountain.

³¹"Make a curtain[g] of blue, purple and scarlet yarn and finely twisted linen, with cherubim[h] worked into it by a skilled craftsman. ³²Hang it with gold hooks on four posts of acacia wood overlaid with gold and standing on four silver bases.[i] ³³Hang the curtain from the clasps and place the ark of the Testimony behind the curtain.[j] The curtain will separate the Holy Place from the Most Holy Place.[k] ³⁴Put the atonement cover[l] on the ark of the Testimony in the Most Holy Place. ³⁵Place the table[m] outside the curtain on the north side of the tabernacle and put the lampstand[n] opposite it on the south side.

³⁶"For the entrance to the tent make a curtain[o] of blue, purple and scarlet yarn and finely twisted linen—the work of an embroiderer.[p] ³⁷Make gold hooks for this curtain and five posts of acacia wood overlaid with gold. And cast five bronze bases for them.

The Altar of Burnt Offering
27:1–8pp — Ex 38:1–7

27 "Build an altar[q] of acacia wood, three cubits[x] high; it is to be square, five cubits long and five cubits wide.[y] ²Make a horn[r] at each of the four corners, so that the horns and the altar are of one piece, and overlay the altar with bronze. ³Make all its utensils of bronze—its pots to remove the ashes, and its shovels, sprinkling bowls,[s] meat forks and firepans.[t] ⁴Make a grating for it, a bronze network, and make a bronze ring at each of the four corners of the network. ⁵Put it under the ledge of the altar so that it is halfway up the altar. ⁶Make poles of acacia wood for the altar and overlay them with bronze.[u] ⁷The poles are to be inserted into the rings so they will be on two sides of the altar when it is carried.[v] ⁸Make the altar hollow, out of boards. It is to be made just as you were shown[w] on the mountain.

The Courtyard
27:9–19pp — Ex 38:9–20

⁹"Make a courtyard[x] for the tabernacle. The south side shall be a hundred cubits[z] long and is to have curtains of finely twisted linen, ¹⁰with twenty posts and twenty bronze bases and with silver hooks and bands on the posts. ¹¹The north side shall also be a hundred cubits long and is to have curtains, with twenty posts and twenty bronze bases and with silver hooks and bands on the posts.

¹²"The west end of the courtyard shall be fifty cubits[a] wide and have curtains, with ten posts and ten bases. ¹³On the east end, toward the sunrise, the courtyard shall also be fifty cubits wide. ¹⁴Curtains fifteen cubits[b] long are to be on one side of the entrance, with three posts and three bases, ¹⁵and curtains fifteen cubits long are to be on the other side, with three posts and three bases.

¹⁶"For the entrance to the courtyard, provide a curtain[y] twenty cubits[c] long, of blue, purple and scarlet yarn and finely twisted linen—the work of an embroiderer[z]—with four posts and four bases. ¹⁷All the posts around the courtyard are to have silver bands and hooks, and bronze bases. ¹⁸The courtyard shall be a hundred cubits long and fifty cubits wide,[d] with curtains of finely twisted linen five cubits[e] high, and with bronze bases. ¹⁹All the other articles used in the service of the tabernacle, whatever their

---

[x] *1* That is, about 4 1/2 feet (about 1.3 meters) [y] *1* That is, about 7 1/2 feet (about 2.3 meters) long and wide [z] *9* That is, about 150 feet (about 46 meters); also in verse 11 [a] *12* That is, about 75 feet (about 23 meters); also in verse 13 [b] *14* That is, about 22 1/2 feet (about 6.9 meters); also in verse 15 [c] *16* That is, about 30 feet (about 9 meters) [d] *18* That is, about 150 feet (about 46 meters) long and 75 feet (about 23 meters) wide [e] *18* That is, about 7 1/2 feet (about 2.3 meters)

function, including all the tent pegs for it and those for the courtyard, are to be of bronze.

Oil for the Lampstand
27:20–21pp — Lev 24:1–3

[20]"Command the Israelites to bring you clear oil[a] of pressed olives for the light so that the lamps may be kept burning. [21]In the Tent of Meeting,[b] outside the curtain that is in front of the Testimony,[c] Aaron and his sons are to keep the lamps[d] burning before the LORD from evening till morning. This is to be a lasting ordinance[e] among the Israelites for the generations to come.

The Priestly Garments

28 "Have Aaron[f] your brother brought to you from among the Israelites, along with his sons Nadab and Abihu,[g] Eleazar and Ithamar,[h] so they may serve me as priests.[i] [2]Make sacred garments[j] for your brother Aaron, to give him dignity and honor.[k] [3]Tell all the skilled men[l] to whom I have given wisdom[m] in such matters that they are to make garments for Aaron, for his consecration, so he may serve me as priest. [4]These are the garments they are to make: a breastpiece,[n] an ephod,[o] a robe,[p] a woven tunic,[q] a turban[r] and a sash. They are to make these sacred garments for your brother Aaron and his sons, so they may serve me as priests. [5]Have them use gold, and blue, purple and scarlet yarn, and fine linen.[s]

The Ephod
28:6–14pp — Ex 39:2–7

[6]"Make the ephod[t] of gold, and of blue, purple and scarlet yarn, and of finely twisted linen—the work of a skilled craftsman. [7]It is to have two shoulder pieces attached to two of its corners, so it can be fastened. [8]Its skillfully woven waistband[u] is to be like it—of one piece with the ephod and made with gold, and with blue, purple and scarlet yarn, and with finely twisted linen.

[9]"Take two onyx stones and engrave[v] on them the names of the sons of Israel [10]in the order of their birth—six names on one stone and the remaining six on the other. [11]Engrave the names of the sons of Israel on the two stones the way a gem cutter engraves a seal. Then mount the stones in gold filigree settings [12]and fasten them on the shoulder pieces of the ephod as memorial stones for the sons of Israel. Aaron is to bear the names on his shoulders[w] as a memorial[x] before the LORD. [13]Make gold filigree settings [14]and two braided chains of pure gold, like a rope, and attach the chains to the settings.

The Breastpiece
28:15–28pp — Ex 39:8–21

[15]"Fashion a breastpiece[y] for making decisions—the work of a skilled craftsman. Make it like the ephod: of gold, and of blue, purple and scarlet yarn, and of finely twisted linen. [16]It is to be square—a span[f] long and a span wide—and folded double. [17]Then mount four rows of precious stones[z] on it. In the first row there shall be a ruby, a topaz and a beryl; [18]in the second row a turquoise, a sapphire[g] and an emerald; [19]in the third row a jacinth, an agate and an amethyst; [20]in the fourth row a chrysolite, an onyx and a jasper.[h] Mount them in gold filigree settings. [21]There are to be twelve stones, one for each of the names of the sons of Israel,[b] each engraved like a seal with the name of one of the twelve tribes.[c]

[22]"For the breastpiece make braided chains of pure gold, like a rope. [23]Make two gold rings for it and fasten them to two corners of the breastpiece. [24]Fasten the two gold chains to the rings at the corners of the breastpiece, [25]and the other ends of the chains to the two settings, attaching them to the shoulder pieces of the ephod at the front. [26]Make two gold rings and attach them to the other two corners of the breastpiece on the inside edge next to the ephod. [27]Make two more gold rings and attach them to the bottom of the shoulder pieces on the front of the ephod, close to the seam just above the waistband of the ephod. [28]The rings of the breastpiece are to be tied to the rings of the ephod with blue cord, connecting it to the waistband,

---

f 16 That is, about 9 inches (about 22 centimeters)   *g 18* Or *lapis lazuli*   *h 20* The precise identification of some of these precious stones is uncertain.

so that the breastpiece will not swing out from the ephod. ²⁹"Whenever Aaron enters the Holy Place,ᵈ he will bear the names of the sons of Israel over his heart on the breastpiece of decision as a continuing memorial before the LORD. ³⁰Also put the Urim and the Thummimᵉ in the breastpiece, so they may be over Aaron's heart whenever he enters the presence of the LORD. Thus Aaron will always bear the means of making decisions for the Israelites over his heart before the LORD.

Other Priestly Garments
28:31-43pp — Ex 39:22-31

³¹"Make the robe of the ephod entirely of blue cloth, ³²with an opening for the head in its center. There shall be a woven edge like a collarⁱ around this opening, so that it will not tear. ³³Make pomegranatesᶠ of blue, purple and scarlet yarn around the hem of the robe, with gold bells between them. ³⁴The gold bells and the pomegranates are to alternate around the hem of the robe. ³⁵Aaron must wear it when he ministers. The sound of the bells will be heard when he enters the Holy Place before the LORD and when he comes out, so that he will not die.

³⁶"Make a plateᵍ of pure gold and engrave on it as on a seal: HOLY TO THE LORD.ʰ ³⁷Fasten a blue cord to it to attach it to the turban; it is to be on the front of the turban. ³⁸It will be on Aaron's forehead, and he will bear the guiltⁱ involved in the sacred gifts the Israelites consecrate, whatever their gifts may be. It will be on Aaron's forehead continually so that they will be acceptableʲ to the LORD.

³⁹"Weave the tunicᵏ of fine linen and make the turbanˡ of fine linen. The sash is to be the work of an embroiderer. ⁴⁰Make tunics, sashes and headbands for Aaron's sons,ᵐ to give them dignity and honor.ⁿ ⁴¹After you put these clothesᵒ on your brother Aaron and his sons, anointᵖ and ordain them. Consecrate them so they may serve me as priests.ᵠ

⁴²"Make linen undergarmentsʳ as a covering for the body, reaching from the waist to the thigh. ⁴³Aaron and his sons must wear them whenever they enter the Tent of Meetingˢ or approach the altar to minister in the Holy Place,ᵗ so that they will not incur guilt and die.ᵘ

"This is to be a lasting ordinanceᵛ for Aaron and his descendants.

Consecration of the Priests
29:1-37pp — Lev 8:1-36

29 "This is what you are to do to consecrateʷ them, so they may serve me as priests: Take a young bull and two rams without defect.ˣ ²And from fine wheat flour, without yeast, make bread, and cakes mixed with oil, and wafers spread with oil.ʸ ³Put them in a basket and present them in it—along with the bull and the two rams.ᶻ ⁴Then bring Aaron and his sons to the entrance to the Tent of Meeting and wash them with water.ᵃ ⁵Take the garmentsᵇ and dress Aaron with the tunic, the robe of the ephod, the ephod itself and the breastpiece. Fasten the ephod on him by its skillfully woven waistband.ᶜ ⁶Put the turbanᵈ on his head and attach the sacred diademᵉ to the turban. ⁷Take the anointing oilᶠ and anoint him by pouring it on his head. ⁸Bring his sons and dress them in tunicsᵍ ⁹and put headbands on them. Then tie sashes on Aaron and his sons.ʲʰ The priesthood is theirs by a lasting ordinance.ⁱ In this way you shall ordain Aaron and his sons.

¹⁰"Bring the bull to the front of the Tent of Meeting, and Aaron and his sons shall lay their hands on its head.ʲ ¹¹Slaughter it in the LORD's presenceᵏ at the entrance to the Tent of Meeting. ¹²Take some of the bull's blood and put it on the hornsˡ of the altar with your finger, and pour out the rest of it at the base of the altar.ᵐ ¹³Then take all the fatⁿ around the inner parts,ᵒ the covering of the liver, and both kidneys with the fat on them, and burn them on the altar. ¹⁴But burn the bull's flesh and its hide and its offalᵖ outside the camp.ᵠ It is a sin offering.

¹⁵"Take one of the rams,ʳ and Aaron and his sons shall lay their hands on its

head.ˢ ¹⁶Slaughter it and take the blood and sprinkle it against the altar on all sides. ¹⁷Cut the ram into pieces and wash ᵗ the inner parts and the legs, putting them with the head and the other pieces. ¹⁸Then burn the entire ram on the altar. It is a burnt offering to the LORD, a pleasing aroma,ᵘ an offering made to the LORD by fire.

¹⁹"Take the other ram,ᵛ and Aaron and his sons shall lay their hands on its head.ʷ ²⁰Slaughter it, take some of its blood and put it on the lobes of the right ears of Aaron and his sons, on the thumbs of their right hands, and on the big toes of their right feet.ˣ Then sprinkle blood against the altar on all sides.ʸ ²¹And take some of the blood ᶻ on the altar and some of the anointing oilᵃ and sprinkle it on Aaron and his garments and on his sons and their garments. Then he and his sons and their garments will be consecrated.ᵇ

²²"Take from this ram the fat,ᶜ the fat tail, the fat around the inner parts, the covering of the liver, both kidneys with the fat on them, and the right thigh. (This is the ram for the ordination.) ²³From the basket of bread made without yeast, which is before the LORD, take a loaf, and a cake made with oil, and a wafer. ²⁴Put all these in the hands of Aaron and his sons and wave them before the LORD as a wave offering.ᵈ ²⁵Then take them from their hands and burn them on the altar along with the burnt offering for a pleasing aroma to the LORD, an offering made to the LORD by fire.ᵉ ²⁶After you take the breast of the ram for Aaron's ordination, wave it before the LORD as a wave offering, and it will be your share.ᶠ

²⁷"Consecrate those parts of the ordination ram that belong to Aaron and his sons:ᵍ the breast that was waved and the thigh that was presented. ²⁸This is always to be the regular share from the Israelites for Aaron and his sons. It is the contribution the Israelites are to make to the LORD from their fellowship offerings.ᵏ ʰ

²⁹"Aaron's sacred garmentsⁱ will belong to his descendants so that they can be anointed and ordained in them.ʲ ³⁰The sonᵏ who succeeds him as priest and comes to the Tent of Meeting to minister in the Holy Place is to wear them seven days.

³¹"Take the ramˡ for the ordination and cook the meat in a sacred place.ᵐ ³²At the entrance to the Tent of Meeting, Aaron and his sons are to eat the meat of the ram and the breadⁿ that is in the basket. ³³They are to eat these offerings by which atonement was made for their ordination and consecration. But no one else may eatᵒ them, because they are sacred. ³⁴And if any of the meat of the ordination ram or any bread is left over till morning,ᵖ burn it up. It must not be eaten, because it is sacred.

³⁵"Do for Aaron and his sons everything I have commanded you, taking seven days to ordain them. ³⁶Sacrifice a bull each dayᑫ as a sin offering to make atonementʳ. Purify the altar by making atonement for it, and anoint it to consecrateˢ it. ³⁷For seven days make atonement for the altar and consecrate it. Then the altar will be most holy, and whatever touches it will be holy.ᵗ

³⁸"This is what you are to offer on the altar regularly each day:ᵘ two lambs a year old. ³⁹Offer one in the morning and the other at twilight.ᵛ ⁴⁰With the first lamb offer a tenth of an ephahˡ of fine flour mixed with a quarter of a hinᵐ of oilʷ from pressed olives, and a quarter of a hin of wine as a drink offering.ˣ ⁴¹Sacrifice the other lamb at twilightʸ with the same grain offeringᶻ and its drink offering as in the morning—a pleasing aroma, an offering made to the LORD by fire.

⁴²"For the generations to comeᵃ this burnt offering is to be made regularlyᵇ at the entrance to the Tent of Meetingᶜ before the LORD. There I will meet you and speak to you;ᵈ ⁴³there also I will meet with the Israelites, and the place will be consecrated by my glory.ᵉ

⁴⁴"So I will consecrate the Tent of Meeting and the altar and will consecrate Aaron and his sons to serve me as priests.ᶠ ⁴⁵Then I will dwellᵍ among the Israelites and be their God.ʰ ⁴⁶They will know that I am the LORD their God, who brought them out of Egyptⁱ so that I might dwell among them. I am the LORD their God.ʲ

D *Ex 29:14* ◀ ▶ *Ex 30:10*

ᵏ 28 Traditionally *peace offerings* ˡ 40 That is, probably about 2 quarts (about 2 liters) ᵐ 40 That is, probably about 1 quart (about 1 liter)

The Altar of Incense

30:1–5pp — Ex 37:25–28

30 "Make an altar of acacia wood for burning incense.¹ ²It is to be square, a cubit long and a cubit wide, and two cubits high—its horns of one piece with it. ³Overlay the top and all the sides and the horns with pure gold, and make a gold molding around it. ⁴Make two gold rings for the altar below the molding—two on opposite sides—to hold the poles used to carry it. ⁵Make the poles of acacia wood and overlay them with gold. ⁶Put the altar in front of the curtain that is before the ark of the Testimony—before the atonement cover that is over the Testimony—where I will meet with you.

⁷"Aaron must burn fragrant incense on the altar every morning when he tends the lamps. ⁸He must burn incense again when he lights the lamps at twilight so incense will burn regularly before the LORD for the generations to come. ⁹Do not offer on this altar any other incense or any burnt offering or grain offering, and do not pour a drink offering on it. ¹⁰Once a year Aaron shall make atonement on its horns. This annual atonement must be made with the blood of the atoning sin offering for the generations to come. It is most holy to the LORD."

Atonement Money

¹¹Then the LORD said to Moses, ¹²"When you take a census of the Israelites to count them, each one must pay the LORD a ransom for his life at the time he is counted. Then no plague will come on them when you number them. ¹³Each one who crosses over to those already counted is to give a half shekel, according to the sanctuary shekel, which weighs twenty gerahs. This half shekel is an offering to the LORD. ¹⁴All who cross over, those twenty years old or more, are to give an offering to the LORD. ¹⁵The rich are not to give more than a half shekel and the poor are not to give less when you make the offering to the LORD

D Ex 29:36–42 ◀ ▶ Lev 1:1–4

to atone for your lives. ¹⁶Receive the atonement money from the Israelites and use it for the service of the Tent of Meeting. It will be a memorial for the Israelites before the LORD, making atonement for your lives."

Basin for Washing

¹⁷Then the LORD said to Moses, ¹⁸"Make a bronze basin, with its bronze stand, for washing. Place it between the Tent of Meeting and the altar, and put water in it. ¹⁹Aaron and his sons are to wash their hands and feet with water from it. ²⁰Whenever they enter the Tent of Meeting, they shall wash with water so that they will not die. Also, when they approach the altar to minister by presenting an offering made to the LORD by fire, ²¹they shall wash their hands and feet so that they will not die. This is to be a lasting ordinance for Aaron and his descendants for the generations to come."

Anointing Oil

²²Then the LORD said to Moses, ²³"Take the following fine spices: 500 shekels of liquid myrrh, half as much (that is, 250 shekels) of fragrant cinnamon, 250 shekels of fragrant cane, ²⁴500 shekels of cassia—all according to the sanctuary shekel—and a hin of olive oil. ²⁵Make these into a sacred anointing oil, a fragrant blend, the work of a perfumer. It will be the sacred anointing oil. ²⁶Then use it to anoint the Tent of Meeting, the ark of the Testimony, ²⁷the table and all its articles, the lampstand and its accessories, the altar of incense, ²⁸the altar of burnt offering and all its utensils, and the basin with its stand. ²⁹You shall consecrate them so they will be most holy, and whatever touches them will be holy.

S ▶ Lev 8:12

n 2 That is, about 1 1/2 feet (about 0.5 meter) long and wide and about 3 feet (about 0.9 meter) high o 13 That is, about 1/5 ounce (about 6 grams); also in verse 15 p 23 That is, about 12 1/2 pounds (about 6 kilograms) q 24 That is, probably about 4 quarts (about 4 liters)

30:25 Moses recorded God's command to create the "sacred anointing oil" to anoint the tabernacle, its furnishings, the ark of the covenant and the priests. Scripture also records that Solomon was anointed with this oil (see 1Ki 1:39). In addition, Daniel prophesied that this oil will be used "to anoint the most holy" (Da 9:24) in the millennial temple at the conclusion of the seventy weeks.

30 "Anoint Aaron and his sons and consecrate them so they may serve me as priests. 31Say to the Israelites, 'This is to be my sacred anointing oil for the generations to come. 32Do not pour it on men's bodies and do not make any oil with the same formula. It is sacred, and you are to consider it sacred. 33Whoever makes perfume like it and whoever puts it on anyone other than a priest must be cut off from his people.'"

Incense

34Then the LORD said to Moses, "Take fragrant spices—gum resin, onycha and galbanum—and pure frankincense, all in equal amounts, 35and make a fragrant blend of incense, the work of a perfumer. It is to be salted and pure and sacred. 36Grind some of it to powder and place it in front of the Testimony in the Tent of Meeting, where I will meet with you. It shall be most holy to you. 37Do not make any incense with this formula for yourselves; consider it holy to the LORD. 38Whoever makes any like it to enjoy its fragrance must be cut off from his people."

Bezalel and Oholiab
31:2–6pp — Ex 35:30–35

31 Then the LORD said to Moses, 2"See, I have chosen Bezalel son of Uri, the son of Hur, of the tribe of Judah, 3and I have filled him with the Spirit of God, with skill, ability and knowledge in all kinds of crafts— 4to make artistic designs for work in gold, silver and bronze, 5to cut and set stones, to work in wood, and to engage in all kinds of craftsmanship. 6Moreover, I have appointed Oholiab son of Ahisamach, of the tribe of Dan, to help him. Also I have given skill to all the craftsmen to make everything I have commanded you: 7the Tent of Meeting, the ark of the Testimony with the atonement cover on it, and all the other furnishings of the tent— 8the table and its articles, the pure gold lampstand and all its accessories, the altar of incense, 9the altar of burnt offering and all its utensils, the basin with its stand— 10and also the woven garments, both the sacred garments for Aaron the priest and the garments for his sons when they serve as priests, 11and the anointing oil and fragrant incense for the Holy Place. They are to make them just as I commanded you."

The Sabbath

12Then the LORD said to Moses, 13"Say to the Israelites, 'You must observe my Sabbaths. This will be a sign between me and you for the generations to come, so you may know that I am the LORD, who makes you holy.

14"'Observe the Sabbath, because it is holy to you. Anyone who desecrates it must be put to death; whoever does any work on that day must be cut off from his people. 15For six days, work is to be done, but the seventh day is a Sabbath of rest, holy to the LORD. Whoever does any work on the Sabbath day must be put to death. 16The Israelites are to observe the Sabbath, celebrating it for the generations to come as a lasting covenant. 17It will be a sign between me and the Israelites forever, for in six days the LORD made the heavens and the earth, and on the seventh day he abstained from work and rested.'"

18When the LORD finished speaking to Moses on Mount Sinai, he gave him the two tablets of the Testimony, the tablets of stone inscribed by the finger of God.

The Golden Calf

32 When the people saw that Moses was so long in coming down from the mountain, they gathered around Aaron and said, "Come, make us gods who will go before us. As for this fellow

r 13 Or who sanctifies you; or who sets you apart as holy   s 1 Or a god; also in verses 23 and 31

31:13 The Lord established the perpetual observance of the Sabbath to signify God's relationship with Israel as his sanctified people. This was time set aside to rest and remember what God had done for them. Some scholars who subscribe to the view that a "day" in Scripture is actually equivalent to 1,000 years (see Ps 90:4; 2Pe 3:8) suggest that the Sabbath day of rest prefigures the final millennial rest mentioned in the NT (see Rev 20:6–7).

Moses who brought us up out of Egypt, we don't know what has happened to him."ᵘ

²Aaron answered them, "Take off the gold earrings ᵛ that your wives, your sons and your daughters are wearing, and bring them to me." ³So all the people took off their earrings and brought them to Aaron. ⁴He took what they handed him and made it into an idol ʷ cast in the shape of a calf,ˣ fashioning it with a tool. Then they said, "These are your gods,ᵗʸ O Israel, who brought you up out of Egypt."ᶻ

⁵When Aaron saw this, he built an altar in front of the calf and announced, "Tomorrow there will be a festivalᵃ to the LORD." ⁶So the next day the people rose early and sacrificed burnt offerings and presented fellowship offerings.ᵘᵇ Afterward they sat down to eat and drinkᶜ and got up to indulge in revelry.ᵈ

⁷Then the LORD said to Moses, "Go down, because your people, whom you brought up out of Egypt,ᵉ have become corrupt.ᶠ ⁸They have been quick to turn awayᵍ from what I commanded them and have made themselves an idolʰ cast in the shape of a calf.ⁱ They have bowed down to it and sacrificedʲ to it and have said, 'These are your gods, O Israel, who brought you up out of Egypt.'ᵏ

⁹"I have seen these people," the LORD said to Moses, "and they are a stiff-neckedˡ people. ¹⁰Now leave me aloneᵐ so that my anger may burn against them and that I may destroyⁿ them. Then I will make you into a great nation."ᵒ

¹¹But Moses sought the favorᵖ of the LORD his God. "O LORD," he said, "why should your anger burn against your people, whom you brought out of Egypt with great power and a mighty hand?ᑫ ¹²Why should the Egyptians say, 'It was with evil intent that he brought them out, to kill them in the mountains and to wipe them off the face of the earth'?ʳ Turn from your fierce anger; relent and do not bring disasterˢ on your people. ¹³Rememberᵗ your servants Abraham, Isaac and Israel, to whom you swore by your own self:ᵘ 'I will make your descendants as numerous as the stars ᵛ in the sky and I will give your descendants all this landʷ I promised them, and it will be their inheritance forever.'" ¹⁴Then the LORD relentedˣ and did not bring on his people the disaster he had threatened.

¹⁵Moses turned and went down the mountain with the two tablets of the Testimonyʸ in his hands.ᶻ They were inscribedᵃ on both sides, front and back. ¹⁶The tablets were the work of God; the writing was the writing of God, engraved on the tablets.ᵇ

¹⁷When Joshuaᶜ heard the noise of the people shouting, he said to Moses, "There is the sound of war in the camp."

¹⁸Moses replied:

"It is not the sound of victory,
 it is not the sound of defeat;
 it is the sound of singing that I hear."

¹⁹When Moses approached the camp and saw the calfᵈ and the dancing,ᵉ his anger burnedᶠ and he threw the tablets out of his hands, breaking them to piecesᵍ at the foot of the mountain. ²⁰And he took the calf they had made and burnedʰ it in the fire; then he ground it to powder,ⁱ scattered it on the waterʲ and made the Israelites drink it.

²¹He said to Aaron, "What did these people do to you, that you led them into such great sin?"

²²"Do not be angry,ᵏ my lord," Aaron answered. "You know how prone these people are to evil.ˡ ²³They said to me, 'Make us gods who will go before us. As for this fellow Moses who brought us up out of Egypt, we don't know what has happened to him.'ᵐ ²⁴So I told them, 'Whoever has any gold jewelry, take it

---

32:13 In this verse Moses appeals to God's mercy reminding him of his promise to the patriarchs that he would increase their offspring "as the stars in the sky" and give them the promised land.

off.' Then they gave me the gold, and I threw it into the fire, and out came this calf!" ⁿ

²⁵Moses saw that the people were running wild and that Aaron had let them get out of control and so become a laughingstock° to their enemies. ²⁶So he stood at the entrance to the camp and said, "Whoever is for the LORD, come to me." And all the Levites rallied to him.

²⁷Then he said to them, "This is what the LORD, the God of Israel, says: 'Each man strap a sword to his side. Go back and forth through the camp from one end to the other, each killing his brother and friend and neighbor.' " ᵖ ²⁸The Levites did as Moses commanded, and that day about three thousand of the people died. ²⁹Then Moses said, "You have been set apart to the LORD today, for you were against your own sons and brothers, and he has blessed you this day."

³⁰The next day Moses said to the people, "You have committed a great sin.ᑫ But now I will go up to the LORD; perhaps I can make atonementʳ for your sin." ³¹So Moses went back to the LORD and said, "Oh, what a great sin these people have committed!ˢ They have made themselves gods of gold.ᵗ ³²But now, please forgive their sinᵘ—but if not, then blot meᵛ out of the bookʷ you have written."

³³The LORD replied to Moses, "Whoever has sinned against me I will blot outˣ of my book. ³⁴Now go, leadʸ the people to the place ᶻ I spoke of, and my angelᵃ will go before you. However, when the time comes for me to punish,ᵇ I will punish them for their sin."

³⁵And the LORD struck the people with a plague because of what they did with the calfᶜ Aaron had made.

33 Then the LORD said to Moses, "Leave this place, you and the people you brought up out of Egypt, and go up to the land I promised on oathᵈ to Abraham, Isaac and Jacob, saying, 'I will give it to your descendants.'ᵉ ²I will send

H Ex 23:7 ◀ ▶ Ex 34:7
S Ex 23:7 ◀ ▶ Lev 11:44–45
D Ex 15:26 ◀ ▶ Lev 26:16

32:24 ⁿ S ver 4
32:25 ° S Ge 38:23
32:27 ᵖ Nu 25:3,5; Dt 33:9; Eze 9:5
32:30 ᑫ 1Sa 12:20; Ps 25:11; 85:2
ʳ Lev 1:4; 4:20,26; 5:6,10,13; 6:7
32:31 ˢ Ex 34:9; Dt 9:18 ᵗ S Ex 20:23
32:32 ᵘ Nu 14:19
ᵛ Ro 9:3 ʷ Ps 69:28; Eze 13:9; Da 7:10; 12:1; Mal 3:16;
ˢ Lk 10:20
32:33
ˣ S Ex 17:14; S Job 21:20; Rev 3:5
32:34 ʸ S Ex 15:17
ᶻ Ex 3:17
ᵃ S Ex 14:19
ᵇ S Ge 50:19; 94:23; 99:8; 109:20; Isa 27:1; Jer 5:9; 11:22; 23:2; 44:13,29; Hos 12:2; Ro 2:5-6
32:35 ᶜ S ver 4
33:1 ᵈ S Ex 13:11;
S Nu 14:23;
Heb 6:13
ᵉ S Ge 12:7
33:2 ᶠ S Ex 14:19
ᵍ S Ex 23:28
33:3 ʰ S Ex 3:8
ⁱ Ex 32:9; Ac 7:51
ʲ S Ex 32:10
33:4 ᵏ Nu 14:39;
Ezr 9:3; Est 4:1;
Ps 119:53
33:5 ˡ S Ex 32:9
ᵐ S Ex 32:10
33:6 ⁿ S Ex 3:1
33:7 ° S Ex 27:21
ᵖ S Ge 25:22;
S 1Ki 22:5
33:8 ᑫ ver 10;
Nu 16:27
33:9 ʳ Ex 13:21;
S 19:9; Dt 31:15;
1Co 10:1
ˢ S Ex 29:42; 31:18;
Ps 99:7
33:10 ᵗ S ver 8
33:11 ᵘ Nu 12:8;
Dt 5:4; 34:10
ᵛ S Ex 17:9
33:12 ʷ Ex 3:10;
S 15:17 ˣ ver 17;
Isa 43:1; 45:3;
49:1; Jn 10:14-15;
2Ti 2:19 ʸ S Ge 6:8
33:13 ᶻ Ps 25:4;
27:11; 51:13;
86:11; 103:7;
143:8 ᵃ Ex 3:7;
Dt 9:26,29;
Ps 77:15

an angelᶠ before you and drive out the Canaanites, Amorites, Hittites, Perizzites, Hivites and Jebusites.ᵍ ³Go up to the land flowing with milk and honey.ʰ But I will not go with you, because you are a stiff-neckedⁱ people and I might destroyʲ you on the way."

⁴When the people heard these distressing words, they began to mournᵏ and no one put on any ornaments. ⁵For the LORD had said to Moses, "Tell the Israelites, 'You are a stiff-necked people.ˡ If I were to go with you even for a moment, I might destroyᵐ you. Now take off your ornaments and I will decide what to do with you.' " ⁶So the Israelites stripped off their ornaments at Mount Horeb.ⁿ

The Tent of Meeting

⁷Now Moses used to take a tent and pitch it outside the camp some distance away, calling it the "tent of meeting."° Anyone inquiringᵖ of the LORD would go to the tent of meeting outside the camp. ⁸And whenever Moses went out to the tent, all the people rose and stood at the entrances to their tents,ᑫ watching Moses until he entered the tent. ⁹As Moses went into the tent, the pillar of cloudʳ would come down and stay at the entrance, while the LORD spokeˢ with Moses. ¹⁰Whenever the people saw the pillar of cloud standing at the entrance to the tent, they all stood and worshiped, each at the entrance to his tent.ᵗ ¹¹The LORD would speak to Moses face to face,ᵘ as a man speaks with his friend. Then Moses would return to the camp, but his young aide Joshuaᵛ son of Nun did not leave the tent.

Moses and the Glory of the LORD

¹²Moses said to the LORD, "You have been telling me, 'Lead these people,'ʷ but you have not let me know whom you will send with me. You have said, 'I know you by nameˣ and you have found favorʸ with me.' ¹³If you are pleased with me, teach me your waysᶻ so I may know you and continue to find favor with you. Remember that this nation is your people."ᵃ

L Ex 19:4–6 ◀ ▶ Ex 40:36–38

33:1–3 This prophecy includes God's promise to remove the original pagan inhabitants of Canaan and give his people a land "flowing with milk and honey," a phrase that indicated the land's abundance and fertility.

¹⁴The LORD replied, "My Presence will go with you, and I will give you rest." ¹⁵Then Moses said to him, "If your Presence does not go with us, do not send us up from here. ¹⁶How will anyone know that you are pleased with me and with your people unless you go with us? What else will distinguish me and your people from all the other people on the face of the earth?"

¹⁷And the LORD said to Moses, "I will do the very thing you have asked, because I am pleased with you and I know you by name."

¹⁸Then Moses said, "Now show me your glory."

¹⁹And the LORD said, "I will cause all my goodness to pass in front of you, and I will proclaim my name, the LORD, in your presence. I will have mercy on whom I will have mercy, and I will have compassion on whom I will have compassion. ²⁰But," he said, "you cannot see my face, for no one may see me and live."

²¹Then the LORD said, "There is a place near me where you may stand on a rock. ²²When my glory passes by, I will put you in a cleft in the rock and cover you with my hand until I have passed by. ²³Then I will remove my hand and you will see my back; but my face must not be seen."

The New Stone Tablets

34 The LORD said to Moses, "Chisel out two stone tablets like the first ones, and I will write on them the words that were on the first tablets, which you broke. ²Be ready in the morning, and then come up on Mount Sinai. Present yourself to me there on top of the mountain. ³No one is to come with you or be seen anywhere on the mountain; not even the flocks and herds may graze in front of the mountain."

⁴So Moses chiseled out two stone tablets like the first ones and went up Mount Sinai early in the morning, as the LORD had commanded him; and he carried the two stone tablets in his hands. ⁵Then the LORD came down in the cloud and stood there with him and proclaimed his name, the LORD. ⁶And he passed in front of Moses, proclaiming, "The LORD, the LORD, the compassionate and gracious God, slow to anger, abounding in love and faithfulness, ⁷maintaining love to thousands, and forgiving wickedness, rebellion and sin. Yet he does not leave the guilty unpunished; he punishes the children and their children for the sin of the fathers to the third and fourth generation."

⁸Moses bowed to the ground at once and worshiped. ⁹"O Lord, if I have found favor in your eyes," he said, "then let the Lord go with us. Although this is a stiff-necked people, forgive our wickedness and our sin, and take us as your inheritance."

¹⁰Then the LORD said: "I am making a covenant with you. Before all your people I will do wonders never before done in any nation in all the world. The people you live among will see how awesome is the work that I, the LORD, will do for you. ¹¹Obey what I command you today. I will drive out before you the Amorites, Canaanites, Hittites, Perizzites, Hivites and Jebusites. ¹²Be careful not to make a treaty with those who live in the land where you are going, or they will be a snare among you. ¹³Break down their altars, smash their sacred stones and cut

---

34:10–12 Though Israel had broken their covenant with God by worshiping the golden calf, God willingly renewed it, promising miracles and a successful conquest of Canaan. Yet God reminded his people that they could not expect the benefit of his blessing unless they were obedient to his commands to abstain from idolatry and worship him alone. In order that the Israelites would not be tempted into idolatry again, God further instructed the people to abstain from friendship or alliances with the idolatrous people of Canaan. Tragically, the Israelites disobeyed God in this matter and suffered greatly because of it.

down their Asherah poles.*v s* ¹⁴Do not worship any other god,ᵗ for the LORD, whose nameᵘ is Jealous, is a jealous God.ᵛ

¹⁵"Be careful not to make a treatyʷ with those who live in the land; for when they prostituteˣ themselves to their gods and sacrifice to them, they will invite you and you will eat their sacrifices.ʸ ¹⁶And when you choose some of their daughters as wivesᶻ for your sons and those daughters prostitute themselves to their gods,ᵃ they will lead your sons to do the same.

¹⁷"Do not make cast idols.ᵇ

¹⁸"Celebrate the Feast of Unleavened Bread.ᶜ For seven days eat bread made without yeast,ᵈ as I commanded you. Do this at the appointed time in the month of Abib,ᵉ for in that month you came out of Egypt.

¹⁹"The first offspringᶠ of every womb belongs to me, including all the firstborn males of your livestock, whether from herd or flock. ²⁰Redeem the firstborn donkey with a lamb, but if you do not redeem it, break its neck.ᵍ Redeem all your firstborn sons.ʰ

"No one is to appear before me empty-handed.ⁱ

²¹"Six days you shall labor, but on the seventh day you shall rest;ʲ even during the plowing season and harvestᵏ you must rest.

²²"Celebrate the Feast of Weeks with the firstfruitsˡ of the wheat harvest, and the Feast of Ingatheringᵐ at the turn of the year.ʷ ²³Three timesⁿ a year all your men are to appear before the Sovereign LORD, the God of Israel. ²⁴I will drive out nationsᵒ before you and enlarge your territory,ᵖ and no one will covet your land when you go up three times each year to appear before the LORD your God.

²⁵"Do not offer the blood of a sacrifice to me along with anything containing yeast,ᵠ and do not let any of the sacrifice from the Passover Feast remain until morning.ʳ

²⁶"Bring the best of the firstfruitsˢ of your soil to the house of the LORD your God.

"Do not cook a young goat in its mother's milk."ᵗ

²⁷Then the LORD said to Moses, "Writeᵘ down these words, for in accordance with these words I have made a covenantᵛ with you and with Israel." ²⁸Moses was there with the LORD forty days and forty nightsʷ without eating bread or drinking water.ˣ And he wrote on the tabletsʸ the words of the covenant—the Ten Commandments.ᶻ

The Radiant Face of Moses

²⁹When Moses came down from Mount Sinaiᵃ with the two tablets of the Testimony in his hands,ᵇ he was not aware that his face was radiantᶜ because he had spoken with the LORD. ³⁰When Aaron and all the Israelites saw Moses, his face was radiant, and they were afraid to come near him. ³¹But Moses called to them; so Aaron and all the leaders of the communityᵈ came back to him, and he spoke to them. ³²Afterward all the Israelites came near him, and he gave them all the commandsᵉ the LORD had given him on Mount Sinai.

³³When Moses finished speaking to them, he put a veilᶠ over his face. ³⁴But whenever he entered the LORD's presence to speak with him, he removed the veil until he came out. And when he came out and told the Israelites what he had been commanded, ³⁵they saw that his face was radiant.ᵍ Then Moses would put the veil back over his face until he went in to speak with the LORD.

Sabbath Regulations

35 Moses assembled the whole Israelite community and said to them, "These are the things the LORD has commandedʰ you to do: ²For six days, work is to be done, but the seventh day shall be your holy day, a Sabbathⁱ of rest to the LORD. Whoever does any work on it must be put to death.ʲ ³Do not light a fire in any of your dwellings on the Sabbath day.ᵏ"

Materials for the Tabernacle

35:4–9pp — Ex 25:1–7
35:10–19pp — Ex 39:32–41

⁴Moses said to the whole Israelite community, "This is what the LORD has commanded: ⁵From what you have, take an offering for the LORD. Everyone who is willing is to bring to the LORD an offering of gold, silver and bronze; ⁶blue, purple and scarlet yarn and fine linen; goat hair; ⁷ram skins dyed red and hides of sea

---

ᵛ 13 That is, symbols of the goddess Asherah   ʷ 22 That is, in the fall

cows;[x] acacia wood; [8]olive oil[l] for the light; spices for the anointing oil and for the fragrant incense; [9]and onyx stones and other gems to be mounted on the ephod and breastpiece.

[10]"All who are skilled among you are to come and make everything the LORD has commanded:[m] [11]the tabernacle[n] with its tent and its covering, clasps, frames, crossbars, posts and bases; [12]the ark[o] with its poles and the atonement cover and the curtain[p] that shields it; [13]the table[q] with its poles and all its articles and the bread of the Presence; [14]the lampstand[r] that is for light with its accessories, lamps and oil for the light; [15]the altar[s] of incense with its poles, the anointing oil[t] and the fragrant incense;[u] the curtain for the doorway at the entrance to the tabernacle;[v] [16]the altar[w] of burnt offering with its bronze grating, its poles and all its utensils; the bronze basin[x] with its stand; [17]the curtains of the courtyard with its posts and bases, and the curtain for the entrance to the courtyard;[y] [18]the tent pegs[z] for the tabernacle and for the courtyard, and their ropes; [19]the woven garments worn for ministering in the sanctuary—both the sacred garments[a] for Aaron the priest and the garments for his sons when they serve as priests."

[20]Then the whole Israelite community withdrew from Moses' presence, [21]and everyone who was willing and whose heart moved him came and brought an offering to the LORD for the work on the Tent of Meeting, for all its service, and for the sacred garments. [22]All who were willing, men and women alike, came and brought gold jewelry of all kinds: brooches, earrings, rings and ornaments. They all presented their gold as a wave offering to the LORD. [23]Everyone who had blue, purple or scarlet yarn[b] or fine linen, or goat hair, ram skins dyed red or hides of sea cows brought them. [24]Those presenting an offering of silver or bronze brought it as an offering to the LORD, and everyone who had acacia wood for any part of the work brought it. [25]Every skilled woman[c] spun with her hands and brought what she had spun—blue, purple or scarlet yarn or fine linen. [26]And all the women who were willing and had the skill spun the goat hair. [27]The leaders[d] brought onyx stones and other gems[e] to be mounted on the ephod and breastpiece. [28]They also brought spices and olive oil for the light and for the anointing oil and for the fragrant incense.[f] [29]All the Israelite men and women who were willing[g] brought to the LORD freewill offerings[h] for all the work the LORD through Moses had commanded them to do.

Bezalel and Oholiab

35:30–35pp — Ex 31:2-6

[30]Then Moses said to the Israelites, "See, the LORD has chosen Bezalel son of Uri, the son of Hur, of the tribe of Judah, [31]and he has filled him with the Spirit of God, with skill, ability and knowledge in all kinds of crafts[i]— [32]to make artistic designs for work in gold, silver and bronze, [33]to cut and set stones, to work in wood and to engage in all kinds of artistic craftsmanship. [34]And he has given both him and Oholiab[j] son of Ahisamach, of the tribe of Dan, the ability to teach[k] others. [35]He has filled them with skill to do all kinds of work[l] as craftsmen, designers, embroiderers in blue, purple and scarlet yarn and fine linen, and weavers—all of them master craftsmen and designers. **36** [1]So Bezalel, Oholiab and every skilled person[m] to whom the LORD has given skill and ability to know how to carry out all the work of constructing the sanctuary[n] are to do the work just as the LORD has commanded."

[2]Then Moses summoned Bezalel[o] and Oholiab[p] and every skilled person to whom the LORD had given ability and who was willing[q] to come and do the work. [3]They received from Moses all the offerings[r] the Israelites had brought to carry out the work of constructing the sanctuary. And the people continued to bring freewill offerings morning after morning. [4]So all the skilled craftsmen who were doing all the work on the sanctuary left their work [5]and said to Moses, "The people are bringing more than enough[s] for doing the work the LORD commanded to be done."

[6]Then Moses gave an order and they

B *Ex 31:3* ◄ ► *Nu 27:18*
E *Ex 31:3* ◄ ► *Nu 11:17*
G *Ex 31:3* ◄ ► *Nu 11:25–29*
T *Ex 31:3* ◄ ► *Nu 11:25–29*

x 7 That is, dugongs; also in verse 23

sent this word throughout the camp: "No man or woman is to make anything else as an offering for the sanctuary." And so the people were restrained from bringing more, ⁷because what they already had was more^t than enough to do all the work.

The Tabernacle
36:8–38pp — Ex 26:1–37

⁸All the skilled men among the workmen made the tabernacle with ten curtains of finely twisted linen and blue, purple and scarlet yarn, with cherubim worked into them by a skilled craftsman. ⁹All the curtains were the same size—twenty-eight cubits long and four cubits wide.^y ¹⁰They joined five of the curtains together and did the same with the other five. ¹¹Then they made loops of blue material along the edge of the end curtain in one set, and the same was done with the end curtain in the other set. ¹²They also made fifty loops on one curtain and fifty loops on the end curtain of the other set, with the loops opposite each other. ¹³Then they made fifty gold clasps and used them to fasten the two sets of curtains together so that the tabernacle was a unit.^u

¹⁴They made curtains of goat hair for the tent over the tabernacle—eleven altogether. ¹⁵All eleven curtains were the same size—thirty cubits long and four cubits wide.^z ¹⁶They joined five of the curtains into one set and the other six into another set. ¹⁷Then they made fifty loops along the edge of the end curtain in one set and also along the edge of the end curtain in the other set. ¹⁸They made fifty bronze clasps to fasten the tent together as a unit.^v ¹⁹Then they made for the tent a covering of ram skins dyed red, and over that a covering of hides of sea cows.^a

²⁰They made upright frames of acacia wood for the tabernacle. ²¹Each frame was ten cubits long and a cubit and a half wide,^b ²²with two projections set parallel to each other. They made all the frames of the tabernacle in this way. ²³They made twenty frames for the south side of the tabernacle ²⁴and made forty silver bases to go under them—two bases for each frame, one under each projection. ²⁵For the other side, the north side of the tabernacle, they made twenty frames ²⁶and forty silver bases—two under each frame. ²⁷They made six frames for the far end, that is, the west end of the tabernacle, ²⁸and two frames were made for the corners of the tabernacle at the far end. ²⁹At these two corners the frames were double from the bottom all the way to the top and fitted into a single ring; both were made alike. ³⁰So there were eight frames and sixteen silver bases—two under each frame.

³¹They also made crossbars of acacia wood: five for the frames on one side of the tabernacle, ³²five for those on the other side, and five for the frames on the west, at the far end of the tabernacle. ³³They made the center crossbar so that it extended from end to end at the middle of the frames. ³⁴They overlaid the frames with gold and made gold rings to hold the crossbars. They also overlaid the crossbars with gold.

³⁵They made the curtain^w of blue, purple and scarlet yarn and finely twisted linen, with cherubim worked into it by a skilled craftsman. ³⁶They made four posts of acacia wood for it and overlaid them with gold. They made gold hooks for them and cast their four silver bases. ³⁷For the entrance to the tent they made a curtain of blue, purple and scarlet yarn and finely twisted linen—the work of an embroiderer;^x ³⁸and they made five posts with hooks for them. They overlaid the tops of the posts and their bands with gold and made their five bases of bronze.

The Ark
37:1–9pp — Ex 25:10–20

37 Bezalel^y made the ark^z of acacia wood—two and a half cubits long, a cubit and a half wide, and a cubit and a half high.^c ²He overlaid it with pure gold,^a both inside and out, and made a gold molding around it. ³He cast four gold rings for it and fastened them to its four feet, with two rings on one side and two rings on the other. ⁴Then he made poles of acacia wood and overlaid them with gold. ⁵And he inserted the poles into the rings on the sides of the ark to carry it.

⁶He made the atonement cover^b of

---

^y 9 That is, about 42 feet (about 12.5 meters) long and 6 feet (about 1.8 meters) wide   ^z 15 That is, about 45 feet (about 13.5 meters) long and 6 feet (about 1.8 meters) wide   ^a 19 That is, dugongs   ^b 21 That is, about 15 feet (about 4.5 meters) long and 2 1/4 feet (about 0.7 meter) wide   ^c 1 That is, about 3 3/4 feet (about 1.1 meters) long and 2 1/4 feet (about 0.7 meter) wide and high

pure gold—two and a half cubits long and a cubit and a half wide.[d] ⁷Then he made two cherubim[c] out of hammered gold at the ends of the cover. ⁸He made one cherub on one end and the second cherub on the other; at the two ends he made them of one piece with the cover. ⁹The cherubim had their wings spread upward, overshadowing[d] the cover with them. The cherubim faced each other, looking toward the cover.[e]

The Table

37:10-16pp — Ex 25:23-29

¹⁰They[e] made the table[f] of acacia wood—two cubits long, a cubit wide, and a cubit and a half high.[f] ¹¹Then they overlaid it with pure gold[g] and made a gold molding around it. ¹²They also made around it a rim a handbreadth[g] wide and put a gold molding on the rim. ¹³They cast four gold rings for the table and fastened them to the four corners, where the four legs were. ¹⁴The rings[h] were put close to the rim to hold the poles used in carrying the table. ¹⁵The poles for carrying the table were made of acacia wood and were overlaid with gold. ¹⁶And they made from pure gold the articles for the table—its plates and dishes and bowls and its pitchers for the pouring out of drink offerings.

The Lampstand

37:17-24pp — Ex 25:31-39

¹⁷They made the lampstand[i] of pure gold and hammered it out, base and shaft; its flowerlike cups, buds and blossoms were of one piece with it. ¹⁸Six branches extended from the sides of the lampstand—three on one side and three on the other. ¹⁹Three cups shaped like almond flowers with buds and blossoms were on one branch, three on the next branch and the same for all six branches extending from the lampstand. ²⁰And on the lampstand were four cups shaped like almond flowers with buds and blossoms. ²¹One bud was under the first pair of branches extending from the lampstand, a second bud under the second pair, and a third bud under the third pair—six branches in all. ²²The buds and the branches were all of one piece with the lampstand, hammered out of pure gold.[j]

²³They made its seven lamps,[k] as well as its wick trimmers and trays, of pure gold. ²⁴They made the lampstand and all its accessories from one talent[h] of pure gold.

The Altar of Incense

37:25-28pp — Ex 30:1-5

²⁵They made the altar of incense[l] out of acacia wood. It was square, a cubit long and a cubit wide, and two cubits high[i]—its horns[m] of one piece with it. ²⁶They overlaid the top and all the sides and the horns with pure gold, and made a gold molding around it. ²⁷They made two gold rings[n] below the molding—two on opposite sides—to hold the poles used to carry it. ²⁸They made the poles of acacia wood and overlaid them with gold.[o]

²⁹They also made the sacred anointing oil[p] and the pure, fragrant incense[q]—the work of a perfumer.

The Altar of Burnt Offering

38:1-7pp — Ex 27:1-8

38 They[j] built the altar of burnt offering of acacia wood, three cubits[k] high; it was square, five cubits long and five cubits wide.[l] ²They made a horn at each of the four corners, so that the horns and the altar were of one piece, and they overlaid the altar with bronze.[r] ³They made all its utensils[s] of bronze—its pots, shovels, sprinkling bowls, meat forks and firepans. ⁴They made a grating for the altar, a bronze network, to be under its ledge, halfway up the altar. ⁵They cast bronze rings to hold the poles for the four corners of the bronze grating. ⁶They made the poles of acacia wood and overlaid them with bronze. ⁷They inserted the poles into the rings so they would be on the sides of the altar for carrying it. They made it hollow, out of boards.

Basin for Washing

⁸They made the bronze basin[t] and its bronze stand from the mirrors of the women[u] who served at the entrance to the Tent of Meeting.

---

[d] *6* That is, about 3 3/4 feet (about 1.1 meters) long and 2 1/4 feet (about 0.7 meter) wide [e] *10* Or *He*; also in verses 11-29 [f] *10* That is, about 3 feet (about 0.9 meter) long, 1 1/2 feet (about 0.5 meter) wide, and 2 1/4 feet (about 0.7 meter) high [g] *12* That is, about 3 inches (about 8 centimeters) [h] *24* That is, about 75 pounds (about 34 kilograms) [i] *25* That is, about 1 1/2 feet (about 0.5 meter) long and wide, and about 3 feet (about 0.9 meter) high [j] *1* Or *He*; also in verses 2-9 [k] *1* That is, about 4 1/2 feet (about 1.3 meters) [l] *1* That is, about 7 1/2 feet (about 2.3 meters) long and wide

The Courtyard

38:9-20pp — Ex 27:9-19

⁹Next they made the courtyard. The south side was a hundred cubits^m long and had curtains of finely twisted linen, ¹⁰with twenty posts and twenty bronze bases, and with silver hooks and bands on the posts. ¹¹The north side was also a hundred cubits long and had twenty posts and twenty bronze bases, with silver hooks and bands on the posts.

¹²The west end was fifty cubits^n wide and had curtains, with ten posts and ten bases, with silver hooks and bands on the posts. ¹³The east end, toward the sunrise, was also fifty cubits wide. ¹⁴Curtains fifteen cubits^o long were on one side of the entrance, with three posts and three bases, ¹⁵and curtains fifteen cubits long were on the other side of the entrance to the courtyard, with three posts and three bases. ¹⁶All the curtains around the courtyard were of finely twisted linen. ¹⁷The bases for the posts were bronze. The hooks and bands on the posts were silver, and their tops were overlaid with silver; so all the posts of the courtyard had silver bands.

¹⁸The curtain for the entrance to the courtyard was of blue, purple and scarlet yarn and finely twisted linen—the work of an embroiderer. It was twenty cubits^p long and, like the curtains of the courtyard, five cubits^q high, ¹⁹with four posts and four bronze bases. Their hooks and bands were silver, and their tops were overlaid with silver. ²⁰All the tent pegs^v of the tabernacle and of the surrounding courtyard were bronze.

The Materials Used

²¹These are the amounts of the materials used for the tabernacle, the tabernacle of the Testimony,^w which were recorded at Moses' command by the Levites under the direction of Ithamar^x son of Aaron, the priest. ²²(Bezalel^y son of Uri, the son of Hur, of the tribe of Judah, made everything the LORD commanded Moses; ²³with him was Oholiab^z son of Ahisamach, of the tribe of Dan—a craftsman and designer, and an embroiderer in blue, purple and scarlet yarn and fine linen.) ²⁴The total amount of the gold from the wave offering used for all the work on the sanctuary^a was 29 talents and 730 shekels,^r according to the sanctuary shekel.^b

²⁵The silver obtained from those of the community who were counted in the census^c was 100 talents and 1,775 shekels,^s according to the sanctuary shekel— ²⁶one beka per person,^d that is, half a shekel,^t according to the sanctuary shekel,^e from everyone who had crossed over to those counted, twenty years old or more,^f a total of 603,550 men.^g ²⁷The 100 talents^u of silver were used to cast the bases^h for the sanctuary and for the curtain—100 bases from the 100 talents, one talent for each base. ²⁸They used the 1,775 shekels^v to make the hooks for the posts, to overlay the tops of the posts, and to make their bands.

²⁹The bronze from the wave offering was 70 talents and 2,400 shekels.^w ³⁰They used it to make the bases for the entrance to the Tent of Meeting, the bronze altar with its bronze grating and all its utensils, ³¹the bases for the surrounding courtyard and those for its entrance and all the tent pegs for the tabernacle and those for the surrounding courtyard.

The Priestly Garments

39 From the blue, purple and scarlet yarn^i they made woven garments for ministering in the sanctuary.^j They also made sacred garments^k for Aaron, as the LORD commanded Moses.

The Ephod

39:2-7pp — Ex 28:6-14

²They^x made the ephod of gold, and of blue, purple and scarlet yarn, and of finely twisted linen. ³They hammered out thin sheets of gold and cut strands to be worked into the blue, purple and scarlet yarn and fine linen—the work of a skilled craftsman. ⁴They made shoulder pieces for the ephod, which were attached to two of its corners, so it could be fastened. ⁵Its skillfully woven waistband was like it—of one piece with the ephod and

---

^m 9 That is, about 150 feet (about 46 meters) ^n 12 That is, about 75 feet (about 23 meters) ^o 14 That is, about 22 1/2 feet (about 6.9 meters) ^p 18 That is, about 30 feet (about 9 meters) ^q 18 That is, about 7 1/2 feet (about 2.3 meters) ^r 24 The weight of the gold was a little over one ton (about 1 metric ton). ^s 25 The weight of the silver was a little over 3 3/4 tons (about 3.4 metric tons). ^t 26 That is, about 1/5 ounce (about 5.5 grams) ^u 27 That is, about 3 3/4 tons (about 3.4 metric tons) ^v 28 That is, about 45 pounds (about 20 kilograms) ^w 29 The weight of the bronze was about 2 1/2 tons (about 2.4 metric tons). ^x 2 Or *He*; also in verses 7, 8 and 22

made with gold, and with blue, purple and scarlet yarn, and with finely twisted linen, as the LORD commanded Moses.

⁶They mounted the onyx stones in gold filigree settings and engraved them like a seal with the names of the sons of Israel. ⁷Then they fastened them on the shoulder pieces of the ephod as memorial¹ stones for the sons of Israel, as the LORD commanded Moses.

The Breastpiece
39:8–21pp — Ex 28:15–28

⁸They fashioned the breastpiece ᵐ—the work of a skilled craftsman. They made it like the ephod: of gold, and of blue, purple and scarlet yarn, and of finely twisted linen. ⁹It was square—a span ʸ long and a span wide—and folded double. ¹⁰Then they mounted four rows of precious stones on it. In the first row there was a ruby, a topaz and a beryl; ¹¹in the second row a turquoise, a sapphire ᶻ and an emerald; ¹²in the third row a jacinth, an agate and an amethyst; ¹³in the fourth row a chrysolite, an onyx and a jasper.ᵃ They were mounted in gold filigree settings. ¹⁴There were twelve stones, one for each of the names of the sons of Israel, each engraved like a seal with the name of one of the twelve tribes.ⁿ

¹⁵For the breastpiece they made braided chains of pure gold, like a rope. ¹⁶They made two gold filigree settings and two gold rings, and fastened the rings to two of the corners of the breastpiece. ¹⁷They fastened the two gold chains to the rings at the corners of the breastpiece, ¹⁸and the other ends of the chains to the two settings, attaching them to the shoulder pieces of the ephod at the front. ¹⁹They made two gold rings and attached them to the other two corners of the breastpiece on the inside edge next to the ephod. ²⁰Then they made two more gold rings and attached them to the bottom of the shoulder pieces on the front of the ephod, close to the seam just above the waistband of the ephod. ²¹They tied the rings of the breastpiece to the rings of the ephod with blue cord, connecting it to the waistband so that the breastpiece would not swing out from the ephod—as the LORD commanded Moses.

Other Priestly Garments
39:22–31pp — Ex 28:31–43

²²They made the robe of the ephod entirely of blue cloth—the work of a weaver— ²³with an opening in the center of the robe like the opening of a collar,ᵇ and a band around this opening, so that it would not tear. ²⁴They made pomegranates of blue, purple and scarlet yarn and finely twisted linen around the hem of the robe. ²⁵And they made bells of pure gold and attached them around the hem between the pomegranates. ²⁶The bells and pomegranates alternated around the hem of the robe to be worn for ministering, as the LORD commanded Moses.

²⁷For Aaron and his sons, they made tunics of fine linen ᵒ—the work of a weaver— ²⁸and the turban ᵖ of fine linen, the linen headbands and the undergarments of finely twisted linen. ²⁹The sash was of finely twisted linen and blue, purple and scarlet yarn—the work of an embroiderer—as the LORD commanded Moses.

³⁰They made the plate, the sacred diadem, out of pure gold and engraved on it, like an inscription on a seal: HOLY TO THE LORD. ᵠ ³¹Then they fastened a blue cord to it to attach it to the turban,ʳ as the LORD commanded Moses.

Moses Inspects the Tabernacle
39:32–41pp — Ex 35:10–19

³²So all the work on the tabernacle, the Tent of Meeting, was completed. The Israelites did everything just as the LORD commanded Moses.ˢ ³³Then they brought the tabernacle ᵗ to Moses: the tent and all its furnishings, its clasps, frames, crossbars, posts and bases; ³⁴the covering of ram skins dyed red, the covering of hides of sea cows ᶜ and the shielding curtain; ³⁵the ark of the Testimony ᵘ with its poles and the atonement cover; ³⁶the table ᵛ with all its articles and the bread of the Presence;ʷ ³⁷the pure gold lampstand ˣ with its row of lamps and all its accessories,ʸ and the oil ᶻ for the light; ³⁸the gold altar,ᵃ the anointing oil,ᵇ the fragrant incense,ᶜ and the curtain ᵈ for the entrance to the tent; ³⁹the bronze altar ᵉ with its bronze grating, its

---

y 9 That is, about 9 inches (about 22 centimeters)   *z 11* Or *lapis lazuli*
a 13 The precise identification of some of these precious stones is uncertain.   *b 23* The meaning of the Hebrew for this word is uncertain.
c 34 That is, dugongs

poles and all its utensils; the basin with its stand; ⁴⁰the curtains of the courtyard with its posts and bases, and the curtain for the entrance to the courtyard; the ropes and tent pegs for the courtyard; all the furnishings for the tabernacle, the Tent of Meeting; ⁴¹and the woven garments worn for ministering in the sanctuary, both the sacred garments for Aaron the priest and the garments for his sons when serving as priests.

⁴²The Israelites had done all the work just as the LORD had commanded Moses. ⁴³Moses inspected the work and saw that they had done it just as the LORD had commanded. So Moses blessed them.

Setting Up the Tabernacle

40 Then the LORD said to Moses: ²"Set up the tabernacle, the Tent of Meeting, on the first day of the first month. ³Place the ark of the Testimony in it and shield the ark with the curtain. ⁴Bring in the table and set out what belongs on it. Then bring in the lampstand and set up its lamps. ⁵Place the gold altar of incense in front of the ark of the Testimony and put the curtain at the entrance to the tabernacle.

⁶"Place the altar of burnt offering in front of the entrance to the tabernacle, the Tent of Meeting; ⁷place the basin between the Tent of Meeting and the altar and put water in it. ⁸Set up the courtyard around it and put the curtain at the entrance to the courtyard.

⁹"Take the anointing oil and anoint the tabernacle and everything in it; consecrate it and all its furnishings, and it will be holy. ¹⁰Then anoint the altar of burnt offering and all its utensils; consecrate the altar, and it will be most holy. ¹¹Anoint the basin and its stand and consecrate them.

¹²"Bring Aaron and his sons to the entrance to the Tent of Meeting and wash them with water. ¹³Then dress Aaron in the sacred garments, anoint him and consecrate him so he may serve me as priest. ¹⁴Bring his sons and dress them in tunics. ¹⁵Anoint them just as you anointed their father, so they may serve me as priests. Their anointing will be to a priesthood that will continue for all generations to come." ¹⁶Moses did everything just as the LORD commanded him.

¹⁷So the tabernacle was set up on the first day of the first month in the second year. ¹⁸When Moses set up the tabernacle, he put the bases in place, erected the frames, inserted the crossbars and set up the posts. ¹⁹Then he spread the tent over the tabernacle and put the covering over the tent, as the LORD commanded him.

²⁰He took the Testimony and placed it in the ark, attached the poles to the ark and put the atonement cover over it. ²¹Then he brought the ark into the tabernacle and hung the shielding curtain and shielded the ark of the Testimony, as the LORD commanded him.

²²Moses placed the table in the Tent of Meeting on the north side of the tabernacle outside the curtain ²³and set out the bread on it before the LORD, as the LORD commanded him.

²⁴He placed the lampstand in the Tent of Meeting opposite the table on the south side of the tabernacle ²⁵and set up the lamps before the LORD, as the LORD commanded him.

²⁶Moses placed the gold altar in the Tent of Meeting in front of the curtain ²⁷and burned fragrant incense on it, as the LORD commanded him. ²⁸Then he put up the curtain at the entrance to the tabernacle.

²⁹He set the altar of burnt offering near the entrance to the tabernacle, the Tent of Meeting, and offered on it burnt offerings and grain offerings, as the LORD commanded him.

³⁰He placed the basin between the Tent of Meeting and the altar and put water in it for washing, ³¹and Moses and Aaron and his sons used it to wash their hands and feet. ³²They washed whenever they entered the Tent of Meeting or approached the altar, as the LORD commanded Moses.

³³Then Moses set up the courtyard around the tabernacle and altar and put up the curtain at the entrance to the courtyard. And so Moses finished the work.

The Glory of the LORD

³⁴Then the cloud covered the Tent of Meeting, and the glory of the LORD filled the tabernacle. ³⁵Moses could not enter the Tent of Meeting because the cloud

had settled upon it, and the glory¹ of the LORD filled the tabernacle.ᵐ ³⁶In all the travels of the Israelites, whenever the cloud lifted from above the tabernacle, they would set out;ⁿ ³⁷but if the cloud did not lift, they did not set out—until the day it lifted. ³⁸So the cloud° of the LORD was over the tabernacle by day, and fire was in the cloud by night, in the sight of all the house of Israel during all their travels.

L Ex 33:12 ◄ ► Nu 9:15–23

40:35 ˡ S Ex 16:10
ᵐ 1Ki 8:11; 2Ch 5:13-14; 7:2
40:36
ⁿ Nu 9:17-23; 10:13
40:38
° S Ex 13:21; 1Co 10:1

Leviticus

Author: Moses

Theme: Laws and regulations about holy living and worship

Date of Writing: c. 1440–1406 B.C.

Outline of Leviticus
- I. Regulations Concerning Sacrifices (1:1—7:38)
- II. The Priesthood (8:1—10:20)
- III. Regulations for Purity (11:1—15:33)
- IV. The Day of Atonement (16:1-34)
- V. Regulations for Holy Living (17:1—22:33)
- VI. The Festivals, Feasts and Seasons of Israel (23:1—25:55)
- VII. Obedience Brings Blessing (26:1—27:34)

LEVITICUS DERIVES ITS name from the word *Levitikon*, the Septuagint's (the Greek translation of the OT) title for the book, which means "relating to the Levites." The Hebrew title *wayyiqra'* is the first word in the Hebrew text of the book and means "and he [i.e., the Lord] called." After the exodus, the Israelites needed instruction in the proper use of tabernacle, the ark of the covenant and the other elements of worship. This third book in the Pentateuch provides a detailed set of regulations regarding Israel's worship, including instructions for ceremonial cleanness, moral laws and holy days.

The key thought of Leviticus is the holiness of God and Israel's duties as a holy nation. The Hebrew word *qodesh*, which translates as "holy" or "holiness," occurs with frequency throughout Leviticus. God commanded the sanctification of the Israelites in all areas of body and spirit, saying, "Be holy, because I am holy" (11:44). Their sanctification also necessitated a clear knowledge of the difference "between the holy and the common, between the unclean and the clean" (10:10) which Leviticus clearly provides.

Leviticus is also replete with the language of sacrifice. In Leviticus, God's system of sacrifice provided the sinful Israelites with a means for their atonement from sin, both individually and nationally. Repeatedly throughout Leviticus the Israelites were reminded that rec-

INTRODUCTION: LEVITICUS

onciliation was available only through their obedience to God's regulations. The addition of the system of festivals, feasts and Sabbaths further confirmed and reminded the Israelites of their covenant relationship with God.

One of the most powerful proofs for the divine inspiration and authority of the Bible is found within the book of Leviticus. Archeological findings have revealed the limited medical knowledge available to the ancient Egyptians at the time of Moses. Yet the book of Leviticus follows modern medical practice in its recognition of the dangers of improper food preparation, cleanliness and care for disease. God had promised the Israelites, "If you listen carefully to the voice of the LORD your God and do what is right in his eyes, if you pay attention to his commands and keep all his decrees, I will not bring on you any of the diseases I brought on the Egyptians, for I am the LORD, who heals you" (Ex 15:26). The advanced medical knowledge that appears in the chapters of Leviticus could come only from God's hand and further underscores the divine inspiration of this book. Several of the textual notes call attention to these medical practices.

The Burnt Offering

1 The LORD called to Moses[a] and spoke to him from the Tent of Meeting.[b] He said, [2]"Speak to the Israelites and say to them: 'When any of you brings an offering to the LORD,[c] bring as your offering an animal from either the herd or the flock.[d]

[3]"'If the offering is a burnt offering[e] from the herd,[f] he is to offer a male without defect.[g] He must present it at the entrance to the Tent[h] of Meeting so that it[a] will be acceptable[i] to the LORD. [4]He is to lay his hand on the head[j] of the burnt offering,[k] and it will be accepted[l] on his behalf to make atonement[m] for him. [5]He is to slaughter[n] the young bull[o] before the LORD, and then Aaron's sons[p] the priests shall bring the blood and sprinkle it against the altar on all sides[q] at the entrance to the Tent of Meeting. [6]He is to skin[r] the burnt offering and cut it into pieces.[s] [7]The sons of Aaron the priest are to put fire on the altar and arrange wood[t] on the fire. [8]Then Aaron's sons the priests shall arrange the pieces, including the head and the fat,[u] on the burning wood[v] that is on the altar. [9]He is to wash the inner parts and the legs with water,[w] and the priest is to burn all of it[x] on the altar.[y] It is a burnt offering,[z] an offering made by fire,[a] an aroma pleasing to the LORD.[b]

[10]"'If the offering is a burnt offering from the flock, from either the sheep[c] or the goats,[d] he is to offer a male without defect. [11]He is to slaughter it at the north side of the altar[e] before the LORD, and Aaron's sons the priests shall sprinkle its blood against the altar on all sides.[f] [12]He is to cut it into pieces, and the priest shall arrange them, including the head and the fat,[g] on the burning wood that is on the altar. [13]He is to wash the inner parts and the legs with water,[h] and the priest is to bring all of it and burn it[i] on the altar.[j] It is a burnt offering,[k] an offering made by fire, an aroma pleasing to the LORD.

[14]"'If the offering to the LORD is a burnt offering of birds, he is to offer a dove or a young pigeon.[l] [15]The priest shall bring it to the altar, wring off the head[m] and burn it on the altar; its blood shall be drained out on the side of the altar.[n] [16]He is to

D Lev 1:1–4 ◀ ▶ Lev 3:1–2

D Ex 30:10 ◀ ▶ Lev 1:10

1:1 a S Ex 3:4; S 25:22
b S Ex 27:21; S 40:2
1:2 c Lev 7:16,38; 22:21; 23:38; 27:9
d Lev 22:18-19; Nu 15:3
1:3 e S Ge 8:20
f ver 10; Lev 22:27; Ezr 8:35; Mal 1:8
g S ver 5; S Lev 12:5; S Lev 22:19,20; Heb 9:14; 1Pe 1:19
h Lev 6:25; 17:9; Nu 6:16; Dt 12:5-6, 11 i Isa 58:5
1:4 j S Ex 29:10,15
k ver 3; Lev 4:29; 6:25; Eze 45:15
l S Ge 32:20
m S Ex 29:36; S 32:30
1:5 n Ex 29:11; Lev 3:2,8 o S ver 3; Ex 29:1; Nu 15:8; Dt 18:3; Ps 50:9; 69:31 p Lev 8:2; 10:6; 21:1
q S Ex 29:20; Heb 12:24; 1Pe 1:2
1:6 r Lev 7:8
s Ex 29:17
1:7 t ver 17; S Ge 22:9; Lev 3:5; 6:12
1:8 u ver 12; S Ex 29:13;
Lev 8:20 v Lev 9:13
1:9 w S Ex 29:17
x Lev 6:22
y ver 13; Ex 29:18; Lev 9:14 z ver 3
a Lev 23:8,25,36; Nu 28:6,19
b ver 13; Ge 8:21; Lev 2:2; 3:5,16; 17:6; Nu 18:17; 28:11-13; Eph 5:2

1:10 c S Ge 22:7 d S ver 3; Ex 12:5; Lev 3:12; 4:23,28; 5:6; Nu 15:11
1:11 e S Ex 29:11 f S Ex 29:20 1:12 g S ver 8 1:13 h S Ex 29:17
i Lev 6:22 j S ver 9 k S ver 9 1:14 l S Ge 15:9; Lk 2:24 1:15 m Lev 5:8
n Lev 5:9

a 3 Or he

remove the crop with its contents[b] and throw it to the east side of the altar, where the ashes[o] are. [17]He shall tear it open by the wings, not severing it completely,[p] and then the priest shall burn it on the wood[q] that is on the fire on the altar. It is a burnt offering, an offering made by fire, an aroma pleasing to the LORD.

The Grain Offering

2 " 'When someone brings a grain offering[r] to the LORD, his offering is to be of fine flour.[s] He is to pour oil[t] on it,[u] put incense on it[v] [2]and take it to Aaron's sons the priests. The priest shall take a handful of the fine flour[w] and oil, together with all the incense,[x] and burn this as a memorial portion[y] on the altar, an offering made by fire,[z] an aroma pleasing to the LORD.[a] [3]The rest of the grain offering belongs to Aaron and his sons;[b] it is a most holy[c] part of the offerings made to the LORD by fire.

[4]" 'If you bring a grain offering baked in an oven,[d] it is to consist of fine flour: cakes made without yeast and mixed with oil, or[c] wafers[e] made without yeast and spread with oil.[f] [5]If your grain offering is prepared on a griddle,[g] it is to be made of fine flour mixed with oil, and without yeast. [6]Crumble it and pour oil on it; it is a grain offering. [7]If your grain offering is cooked in a pan,[h] it is to be made of fine flour and oil. [8]Bring the grain offering made of these things to the LORD; present it to the priest, who shall take it to the altar. [9]He shall take out the memorial portion[i] from the grain offering and burn it on the altar as an offering made by fire, an aroma pleasing to the LORD.[j] [10]The rest of the grain offering belongs to Aaron and his sons;[k] it is a most holy part of the offerings made to the LORD by fire.[l]

[11]" 'Every grain offering you bring to the LORD must be made without yeast,[m] for you are not to burn any yeast or honey in an offering made to the LORD by fire. [12]You may bring them to the LORD as an offering of the firstfruits,[n] but they are not to be offered on the altar as a pleasing aroma. [13]Season all your grain offerings with salt.[o] Do not leave the salt of the covenant[p] of your God out of your grain offerings; add salt to all your offerings.

[14]" 'If you bring a grain offering of firstfruits[q] to the LORD, offer crushed heads of new grain roasted in the fire. [15]Put oil and incense[r] on it; it is a grain offering. [16]The priest shall burn the memorial portion[s] of the crushed grain and the oil, together with all the incense,[t] as an offering made to the LORD by fire.[u]

The Fellowship Offering

3 " 'If someone's offering is a fellowship offering,[d][v] and he offers an animal from the herd, whether male or female, he is to present before the LORD an animal without defect.[w] [2]He is to lay his hand on the head[x] of his offering and slaughter it[y] at the entrance to the Tent of Meeting.[z] Then Aaron's sons the priests shall sprinkle[a] the blood against the altar[b] on all sides.[c] [3]From the fellowship offering he is to bring a sacrifice made to the LORD by fire: all the fat[d] that covers the inner parts[e] or is connected to them, [4]both kidneys[f] with the fat on them near the loins, and the covering of the liver, which he will remove with the kidneys. [5]Then Aaron's sons[g] are to burn it on the altar[h] on top of the burnt offering[i] that is on the burning wood,[j] as an offering made by fire, an aroma pleasing to the LORD.[k]

[6]" 'If he offers an animal from the flock as a fellowship offering[l] to the LORD, he is to offer a male or female without defect. [7]If he offers a lamb,[m] he is to present it before the LORD.[n] [8]He is to lay his hand on the head of his offering and slaughter it[o] in front of the Tent of Meeting. Then Aaron's sons shall sprinkle its blood against the altar on all sides. [9]From the fellowship offering he is to bring a sacrifice[p] made to the LORD by fire: its fat, the entire fat tail cut off close to the backbone, all the fat that covers the inner parts or is connected to them, [10]both kidneys with the fat on them near the loins, and the covering of the liver, which he will remove with the kidneys. [11]The priest shall burn them on the altar[q] as food,[r] an offering made to the LORD by fire.[s]

D Lev 1:10 ◄ ► Lev 3:6–8
D Lev 3:1–2 ◄ ► Lev 4:1–3

[b] 16 Or *crop and the feathers*; the meaning of the Hebrew for this word is uncertain. [c] 4 Or *and* [d] 1 Traditionally *peace offering*; also in verses 3, 6 and 9

¹²"'If his offering is a goat, he is to present it before the LORD. ¹³He is to lay his hand on its head and slaughter it in front of the Tent of Meeting. Then Aaron's sons shall sprinkle its blood against the altar on all sides. ¹⁴From what he offers he is to make this offering to the LORD by fire: all the fat that covers the inner parts or is connected to them, ¹⁵both kidneys with the fat on them near the loins, and the covering of the liver, which he will remove with the kidneys. ¹⁶The priest shall burn them on the altar as food, an offering made by fire, a pleasing aroma. All the fat is the LORD's.

¹⁷"'This is a lasting ordinance for the generations to come, wherever you live: You must not eat any fat or any blood.'"

The Sin Offering

4 The LORD said to Moses, ²"Say to the Israelites: 'When anyone sins unintentionally and does what is forbidden in any of the LORD's commands—

³"'If the anointed priest sins, bringing guilt on the people, he must bring to the LORD a young bull without defect as a sin offering for the sin he has committed. ⁴He is to present the bull at the entrance to the Tent of Meeting before the LORD. He is to lay his hand on its head and slaughter it before the LORD. ⁵Then the anointed priest shall take some of the bull's blood and carry it into the Tent of Meeting. ⁶He is to dip his finger into the blood and sprinkle some of it seven times before the LORD, in front of the curtain of the sanctuary. ⁷The priest shall then put some of the blood on the horns of the altar of fragrant incense that is before the LORD in the Tent of Meeting. The rest of the bull's blood he shall pour out at the base of the altar of burnt offering at the entrance to the Tent of Meeting. ⁸He shall remove all the fat from the bull of the sin offering—the fat that covers the inner parts or is connected to them, ⁹both kidneys with the fat on them near the loins, and the covering of the liver, which he will remove with the kidneys— ¹⁰just as the fat is removed from the ox sacrificed as a fellowship offering. Then the priest shall burn them on the altar of burnt offering. ¹¹But the hide of the bull and all its flesh, as well as the head and legs, the inner parts and offal— ¹²that is, all the rest of the bull— he must take outside the camp to a place ceremonially clean, where the ashes are thrown, and burn it in a wood fire on the ash heap.

¹³"'If the whole Israelite community sins unintentionally and does what is forbidden in any of the LORD's commands, even though the community is unaware of the matter, they are guilty. ¹⁴When they become aware of the sin they committed, the assembly must bring a young bull as a sin offering and present it before the Tent of Meeting. ¹⁵The elders of the community are to lay their hands on the bull's head before the LORD, and the bull shall be slaughtered before the LORD. ¹⁶Then the anointed priest is to take some of the bull's blood into the Tent of Meeting. ¹⁷He shall dip his finger into the blood and sprinkle it before the LORD seven times in front of the curtain. ¹⁸He is to put some of the blood on the horns of the altar that is before the LORD in the Tent of Meeting. The rest of the blood he shall pour out at the base of the altar of burnt offering at the entrance to the Tent of Meeting. ¹⁹He shall remove all the fat from it and burn it on the altar, ²⁰and do with this bull just as he did with the bull for the sin offering. In this way the priest will make atonement for them, and they will be forgiven. ²¹Then he shall take the bull outside the camp and burn it as he burned the first bull. This is the sin offering for the community.

²²"'When a leader sins unintentionally and does what is forbidden in any of the commands of the LORD his God, he is guilty. ²³When he is made aware of the sin he committed, he must bring as his offering a male goat without defect. ²⁴He is to lay his hand on the goat's head and

D Lev 4:1–3 ◀ ▶ Lev 4:14
D Lev 4:12 ◀ ▶ Lev 4:20–21
D Lev 4:14 ◀ ▶ Lev 4:23
L Ex 34:6–7 ◀ ▶ Lev 4:26
D Lev 4:20–21 ◀ ▶ Lev 4:28

*ver 26,31,35; Nu 15:25 4:21 *ver 2 z*Lev 16:5,15; 2Ch 29:21
4:22 *Nu 31:13 *ver 2 4:23 *ver 3; S Lev 1:10
*10 The Hebrew word can include both male and female.
*10 Traditionally *peace offering*; also in verses 26, 31 and 35

D Lev 3:6–8 ◀ ▶ Lev 4:12

slaughter it at the place where the burnt offering is slaughtered before the LORD.ᵈ It is a sin offering.ᵉ ²⁵Then the priest shall take some of the blood of the sin offering with his finger and put it on the horns of the altarᶠ of burnt offering and pour out the rest of the blood at the base of the altar.ᵍ ²⁶He shall burn all the fat on the altar as he burned the fat of the fellowship offering. In this way the priest will make atonementʰ for the man's sin, and he will be forgiven.ⁱ

²⁷"'If a member of the community sins unintentionallyʲ and does what is forbidden in any of the LORD's commands, he is guilty. ²⁸When he is made aware of the sin he committed, he must bring as his offeringᵏ for the sin he committed a female goatˡ without defect. ²⁹He is to lay his hand on the headᵐ of the sin offeringⁿ and slaughter it at the place of the burnt offering.ᵒ ³⁰Then the priest is to take some of the blood with his finger and put it on the horns of the altar of burnt offeringᵖ and pour out the rest of the blood at the base of the altar. ³¹He shall remove all the fat, just as the fat is removed from the fellowship offering, and the priest shall burn it on the altarᵍ as an aroma pleasing to the LORD.ʳ In this way the priest will make atonementˢ for him, and he will be forgiven.ᵗ

³²"'If he brings a lambᵘ as his sin offering, he is to bring a female without defect.ᵛ ³³He is to lay his hand on its head and slaughter itʷ for a sin offeringˣ at the place where the burnt offering is slaughtered.ʸ ³⁴Then the priest shall take some of the blood of the sin offering with his finger and put it on the horns of the altar of burnt offering and pour out the rest of the blood at the base of the altar.ᶻ ³⁵He shall remove all the fat, just as the fat is removed from the lamb of the fellowship offering, and the priest shall burn it on the altarᵃ on top of the offerings made to the LORD by fire. In this way the priest will make atonement for him for the sin he has committed, and he will be forgiven.

L *Lev 4:20* ◀ ▶ *Lev 4:31*
D *Lev 4:23* ◀ ▶ *Lev 4:32*
L *Lev 4:26* ◀ ▶ *Lev 4:35*
D *Lev 4:28* ◀ ▶ *Lev 5:5–6*
L *Lev 4:31* ◀ ▶ *Lev 5:10*

---

5 "'If a person sins because he does not speak up when he hears a public charge to testifyᵇ regarding something he has seen or learned about, he will be held responsible.ᶜ

²"'Or if a person touches anything ceremonially unclean—whether the carcasses of unclean wild animals or of unclean livestock or of unclean creatures that move along the groundᵈ—even though he is unaware of it, he has become uncleanᵉ and is guilty.

³"'Or if he touches human uncleannessᶠ—anything that would make him uncleanᵍ—even though he is unaware of it, when he learns of it he will be guilty.

⁴"'Or if a person thoughtlessly takes an oathʰ to do anything, whether good or evilⁱ—in any matter one might carelessly swear about—even though he is unaware of it, in any case when he learns of it he will be guilty.

⁵"'When anyone is guilty in any of these ways, he must confessʲ in what way he has sinned ⁶and, as a penalty for the sin he has committed, he must bring to the LORD a female lamb or goatᵏ from the flock as a sin offering;ˡ and the priest shall make atonementᵐ for him for his sin.

⁷"'If he cannot affordⁿ a lamb,ᵒ he is to bring two doves or two young pigeonsᵖ to the LORD as a penalty for his sin—one for a sin offering and the other for a burnt offering. ⁸He is to bring them to the priest, who shall first offer the one for the sin offering. He is to wring its head from its neck,ᵍ not severing it completely,ʳ ⁹and is to sprinkleˢ some of the blood of the sin offering against the side of the altar;ᵗ the rest of the blood must be drained out at the base of the altar.ᵘ It is a sin offering. ¹⁰The priest shall then offer the other as a burnt offering in the prescribed wayᵛ and make atonementʷ for him for the sin he has committed, and he will be forgiven.ˣ

¹¹"'If, however, he cannot affordʸ two doves or two young pigeons,ᶻ he is to bring as an offering for his sin a tenth of

---

D *Lev 4:32* ◀ ▶ *Lev 5:15*
R *Ex 22:1–14* ◀ ▶ *Lev 5:16*
L *Lev 4:35* ◀ ▶ *Lev 5:13*

an ephah of fine flour for a sin offering. He must not put oil or incense on it, because it is a sin offering. ¹²He is to bring it to the priest, who shall take a handful of it as a memorial portion and burn it on the altar on top of the offerings made to the LORD by fire. It is a sin offering. ¹³In this way the priest will make atonement for him for any of these sins he has committed, and he will be forgiven. The rest of the offering will belong to the priest, as in the case of the grain offering.'"

The Guilt Offering

¹⁴The LORD said to Moses: ¹⁵"When a person commits a violation and sins unintentionally in regard to any of the LORD's holy things, he is to bring to the LORD as a penalty a ram from the flock, one without defect and of the proper value in silver, according to the sanctuary shekel. It is a guilt offering. ¹⁶He must make restitution for what he has failed to do in regard to the holy things, add a fifth of the value to that and give it all to the priest, who will make atonement for him with the ram as a guilt offering, and he will be forgiven.

¹⁷"If a person sins and does what is forbidden in any of the LORD's commands, even though he does not know it, he is guilty and will be held responsible. ¹⁸He is to bring to the priest as a guilt offering a ram from the flock, one without defect and of the proper value. In this way the priest will make atonement for him for the wrong he has committed unintentionally, and he will be forgiven. ¹⁹It is a guilt offering; he has been guilty of wrongdoing against the LORD."

6 The LORD said to Moses: ²"If anyone sins and is unfaithful to the LORD by deceiving his neighbor about something entrusted to him or left in his care or stolen, or if he cheats him, ³or if he finds lost property and lies about it, or if he swears falsely, or if he commits any such sin that people may do— ⁴when he thus sins and becomes guilty, he must return what he has stolen or taken by extortion, or what was entrusted to him, or the lost property he found, ⁵or whatever it was he swore falsely about. He must make restitution in full, add a fifth of the value to it and give it all to the owner on the day he presents his guilt offering. ⁶And as a penalty he must bring to the priest, that is, to the LORD, his guilt offering, a ram from the flock, one without defect and of the proper value. ⁷In this way the priest will make atonement for him before the LORD, and he will be forgiven for any of these things he did that made him guilty."

The Burnt Offering

⁸The LORD said to Moses: ⁹"Give Aaron and his sons this command: 'These are the regulations for the burnt offering: The burnt offering is to remain on the altar hearth throughout the night, till morning, and the fire must be kept burning on the altar. ¹⁰The priest shall then put on his linen clothes, with linen undergarments next to his body, and shall remove the ashes of the burnt offering that the fire has consumed on the altar and place them beside the altar. ¹¹Then he is to take off these clothes and put on others, and carry the ashes outside the camp to a place that is ceremonially clean. ¹²The fire on the altar must be kept burning; it must not go out. Every morning the priest is to add firewood and arrange the burnt offering on the fire and burn the fat of the fellowship offerings on it. ¹³The fire must be kept burning on the altar continuously; it must not go out.

The Grain Offering

¹⁴" 'These are the regulations for the grain offering: Aaron's sons are to bring it before the LORD, in front of the altar. ¹⁵The priest is to take a handful of fine flour and oil, together with all the incense on the grain offering, and burn the memorial portion on the altar as an aroma pleasing to the LORD. ¹⁶Aaron and his sons shall eat the rest of it, but it is to be eaten without yeast in a holy

g 11 That is, probably about 2 quarts (about 2 liters) *h 15* That is, about 2/5 ounce (about 11.5 grams) *i 19* Or *has made full expiation for his* *j 12* Traditionally *peace offerings*

Old Testament Sacrifices

SACRIFICE	OT REFERENCES	ELEMENTS	PURPOSE
Burnt Offering	Lev 1; 6:8-13; 8:18-21; 16:24	Bull, ram or male bird (dove or young pigeon for the poor); wholly consumed; no defect	Voluntary act of worship; atonement for unintentional sin in general; expression of devotion, commitment and complete surrender to God
Grain Offering	Lev 2; 6:14-23	Grain, fine flour, olive oil, incense, baked bread (cakes or wafers), salt; no yeast or honey; accompanied burnt offering and fellowship offering (along with drink offering)	Voluntary act of worship; recognition of God's goodness and provisions; devotion to God
Fellowship Offering	Lev 3; 7:11-34	Any animal without defect from herd or flock; variety of breads	Voluntary act of worship; thanksgiving and fellowship (it included a communal meal)
Sin Offering	Lev 4:1–5:13; 6:24-30; 8:14-17; 16:3-22	1. Young bull: for high priest and congregation 2. Male goat: for leader 3. Female goat or lamb: for common person 4. Dove or pigeon: for the poor 5. Tenth of an ephah of fine flour: for the very poor	Mandatory atonement for specific unintentional sin; confession of sin; forgiveness of sin; cleansing from defilement
Guilt Offering	Lev. 5:14–6:7; 7:1-6	Ram or lamb	Mandatory atonement for unintentional sin requiring restitution; cleansing from defilement; make restitution; pay 20% fine

When more than one kind of offering was presented (as in Nu 7:16,17), the procedure was usually as follows: (1) sin offering or guilt offering, (2) burnt offering, (3) fellowship offering and grain offering (along with a drink offering). This sequence furnishes part of the spiritual significance of the sacrificial system. First, sin had to be dealt with (sin offering or guilt offering). Second, the worshiper committed himself completely to God (burnt offering and grain offering). Third, fellowship or communion between the Lord, the priest and the worshiper (fellowship offering) was established. To state it another way, there were sacrifices of expiation (sin offerings and guilt offerings), consecration (burnt offerings and grain offerings) and communion (fellowship offerings—these included vow offerings, thank offerings and freewill offerings).

place; they are to eat it in the courtyard of the Tent of Meeting. ¹⁷It must not be baked with yeast; I have given it as their share of the offerings made to me by fire. Like the sin offering and the guilt offering, it is most holy. ¹⁸Any male descendant of Aaron may eat it. It is his regular share of the offerings made to the LORD by fire for the generations to come. Whatever touches them will become holy.'"

¹⁹The LORD also said to Moses, ²⁰"This is the offering Aaron and his sons are to bring to the LORD on the day he is anointed: a tenth of an ephah of fine flour as a regular grain offering, half of it in the morning and half in the evening. ²¹Prepare it with oil on a griddle; bring it well-mixed and present the grain offering broken in pieces as an aroma pleasing to the LORD. ²²The son who is to succeed him as anointed priest shall prepare it. It is the LORD's regular share and is to be burned completely. ²³Every grain offering of a priest shall be burned completely; it must not be eaten."

The Sin Offering

²⁴The LORD said to Moses, ²⁵"Say to Aaron and his sons: 'These are the regulations for the sin offering: The sin offering is to be slaughtered before the LORD in the place the burnt offering is slaughtered; it is most holy. ²⁶The priest who offers it shall eat it; it is to be eaten in a holy place, in the courtyard of the Tent of Meeting. ²⁷Whatever touches any of the flesh will become holy, and if any of the blood is spattered on a garment, you must wash it in a holy place. ²⁸The clay pot the meat is cooked in must be broken; but if it is cooked in a bronze pot, the pot is to be scoured and rinsed with water. ²⁹Any male in a priest's family may eat it; it is most holy. ³⁰But any sin offering whose blood is brought into the Tent of Meeting to make atonement in the Holy Place must not be eaten; it must be burned.

The Guilt Offering

7 " 'These are the regulations for the guilt offering, which is most holy: ²The guilt offering is to be slaughtered in the place where the burnt offering is slaughtered, and its blood is to be sprinkled against the altar on all sides. ³All its fat shall be offered: the fat tail and the fat that covers the inner parts, ⁴both kidneys with the fat on them near the loins, and the covering of the liver, which is to be removed with the kidneys. ⁵The priest shall burn them on the altar as an offering made to the LORD by fire. It is a guilt offering. ⁶Any male in a priest's family may eat it, but it must be eaten in a holy place; it is most holy.

⁷" 'The same law applies to both the sin offering and the guilt offering: They belong to the priest who makes atonement with them. ⁸The priest who offers a burnt offering for anyone may keep its hide for himself. ⁹Every grain offering baked in an oven or cooked in a pan or on a griddle belongs to the priest who offers it, ¹⁰and every grain offering, whether mixed with oil or dry, belongs equally to all the sons of Aaron.

The Fellowship Offering

¹¹" 'These are the regulations for the fellowship offering a person may present to the LORD:

¹²" 'If he offers it as an expression of thankfulness, then along with this thank offering he is to offer cakes of bread made without yeast and mixed with oil, wafers made without yeast and spread

D *Lev 6:6–7* ◄ ► *Lev 7:37*

---

k 18 Or *Whoever touches them must be holy*; similarly in verse 27
l 20 Or *each* m 20 That is, probably about 2 quarts (about 2 liters)
n 21 The meaning of the Hebrew for this word is uncertain.
o 11 Traditionally *peace offering*; also in verses 13-19

6:28 Since clay was a porous material and absorbed some of the juices of the sacrifice during the cooking, the Lord's command to break the clay cooking pot served two purposes. For religious reasons the clay pot was broken to remove the remnants of the sacrifice that the pot absorbed, thereby ensuring that nothing of the offering was withheld from God. The porous clay pots also had to be destroyed for health reasons. Modern science realizes the peril of germ-laden cookware. Yet God's instructions protected his people centuries before the scientific discovery of germs. Since the Levites were required to eat the sacrifices cooked in these pots, destruction of a pot that harbored germs on its porous surface would prevent illness and contamination for the Levites. Bronze pots could be scoured and cleaned and therefore could be used again.

with oil, and cakes of fine flour well-kneaded and mixed with oil. ¹³Along with his fellowship offering of thanksgiving he is to present an offering with cakes of bread made with yeast. ¹⁴He is to bring one of each kind as an offering, a contribution to the LORD; it belongs to the priest who sprinkles the blood of the fellowship offerings. ¹⁵The meat of his fellowship offering of thanksgiving must be eaten on the day it is offered; he must leave none of it till morning.

¹⁶" 'If, however, his offering is the result of a vow or is a freewill offering, the sacrifice shall be eaten on the day he offers it, but anything left over may be eaten on the next day. ¹⁷Any meat of the sacrifice left over till the third day must be burned up. ¹⁸If any meat of the fellowship offering is eaten on the third day, it will not be accepted. It will not be credited to the one who offered it, for it is impure; the person who eats any of it will be held responsible.

¹⁹" 'Meat that touches anything ceremonially unclean must not be eaten; it must be burned up. As for other meat, anyone ceremonially clean may eat it. ²⁰But if anyone who is unclean eats any meat of the fellowship offering belonging to the LORD, that person must be cut off from his people. ²¹If anyone touches something unclean—whether human uncleanness or an unclean animal or any unclean, detestable thing—and then eats any of the meat of the fellowship offering belonging to the LORD, that person must be cut off from his people.' "

Eating Fat and Blood Forbidden

²²The LORD said to Moses, ²³"Say to the Israelites: 'Do not eat any of the fat of cattle, sheep or goats. ²⁴The fat of an animal found dead or torn by wild animals may be used for any other purpose, but you must not eat it. ²⁵Anyone who eats the fat of an animal from which an offering by fire may be made to the LORD must be cut off from his people. ²⁶And wherever you live, you must not eat the blood of any bird or animal. ²⁷If anyone eats blood, that person must be cut off from his people.' "

The Priests' Share

²⁸The LORD said to Moses, ²⁹"Say to the Israelites: 'Anyone who brings a fellowship offering to the LORD is to bring part of it as his sacrifice to the LORD. ³⁰With his own hands he is to bring the offering made to the LORD by fire; he is to bring the fat, together with the breast, and wave the breast before the LORD as a wave offering. ³¹The priest shall burn the fat on the altar, but the breast belongs to Aaron and his sons. ³²You are to give the right thigh of your fellowship offerings to the priest as a contribution. ³³The son of Aaron who offers the blood and the fat of the fellowship offering shall have the right thigh as his share. ³⁴From the fellowship offerings of the Israelites, I have taken the breast that is waved and the thigh that is presented and have given them to Aaron the priest and his sons as their regular share from the Israelites.' "

³⁵This is the portion of the offerings made to the LORD by fire that were allotted to Aaron and his sons on the day they were presented to serve the LORD as priests. ³⁶On the day they were anointed, the LORD commanded that the Israelites give this to them as their regular share for the generations to come.

³⁷These, then, are the regulations for the burnt offering, the grain offering, the sin offering, the guilt offering, the ordination offering and the fellowship offering, ³⁸which the LORD gave Moses on Mount Sinai on the day he commanded the Israelites to bring their offerings to the LORD, in the Desert of Sinai.

The Ordination of Aaron and His Sons
8:1–36pp — Ex 29:1–37

8 The LORD said to Moses, ²"Bring Aaron and his sons, their garments, the anointing oil, the bull for the sin offering, the two rams and the

D *Lev 7:1–2* ◀ ▶ *Lev 8:14*

p 25 Or *fire is*

7:24 God commanded that the people were not allowed to eat the fat of any animal that died naturally or was violently killed by a predator. Doctors now know that such animals quickly produce harmful germs, especially in a warm climate like the Middle East.

basket containing bread made without yeast,[c] ³and gather the entire assembly[d] at the entrance to the Tent of Meeting." ⁴Moses did as the LORD commanded him, and the assembly gathered at the entrance to the Tent of Meeting.

⁵Moses said to the assembly, "This is what the LORD has commanded to be done.[e]" ⁶Then Moses brought Aaron and his sons forward and washed them with water.[f] ⁷He put the tunic on Aaron, tied the sash around him, clothed him with the robe and put the ephod on him. He also tied the ephod to him by its skillfully woven waistband; so it was fastened on him.[g] ⁸He placed the breastpiece[h] on him and put the Urim and Thummim[i] in the breastpiece. ⁹Then he placed the turban[j] on Aaron's head and set the gold plate, the sacred diadem,[k] on the front of it, as the LORD commanded Moses.[l]

¹⁰Then Moses took the anointing oil[m] and anointed[n] the tabernacle[o] and everything in it, and so consecrated them. ¹¹He sprinkled some of the oil on the altar seven times, anointing the altar and all its utensils and the basin with its stand, to consecrate them.[p] ¹²He poured some of the anointing oil on Aaron's head and anointed[q] him to consecrate him.[r] ¹³Then he brought Aaron's sons[s] forward, put tunics[t] on them, tied sashes around them and put headbands on them, as the LORD commanded Moses.[u]

¹⁴He then presented the bull[v] for the sin offering,[w] and Aaron and his sons laid their hands on its head.[x] ¹⁵Moses slaughtered the bull and took some of the blood,[y] and with his finger he put it on all the horns of the altar[z] to purify the altar.[a] He poured out the rest of the blood at the base of the altar. So he consecrated it to make atonement for it.[b] ¹⁶Moses also took all the fat around the inner parts, the covering of the liver, and both kidneys and their fat, and burned it on the altar. ¹⁷But the bull with its hide and its flesh and its offal[c] he burned up outside the camp,[d] as the LORD commanded Moses.

S *Ex 30:25* ◀ ▶ *Ps 51:10*
D *Lev 7:37* ◀ ▶ *Lev 8:17–18*
D *Lev 8:14* ◀ ▶ *Lev 9:2–7*

8:2 c Ex 29:2-3
8:3 d Nu 8:9
8:5 e Ex 29:1
8:6 f Ex 29:4; S 30:19; S Ac 22:16
8:7 g Ex 28:4
8:8 h S Ex 25:7
       i S Ex 28:30
8:9 j S Ex 39:28
       k S Ex 28:36
       l S Ex 28:2;
       Lev 21:10
8:10 m ver 2
         n S Ex 30:26
         o S Ex 26:1
8:11 p S Ex 30:29
8:12 q S Lev 7:36
         r S Ex 30:30
8:13 s S Ex 28:40
         t S Ex 28:4,39;
         39:27 u Lev 21:10
8:14 v S Lev 4:3
         w S Ex 30:10
         x S Lev 4:15
8:15 y S Lev 4:18
         z S Lev 4:7
         a Heb 9:22
         b Eze 43:20
8:17 c S Lev 4:11
         d S Lev 4:12
8:18 e S ver 2
8:20 f S Lev 1:8
8:22 g S ver 2
         h S Lev 4:15
8:23 i Lev 14:14,25
8:24 j Heb 9:18-22
8:25 k Lev 3:3-5
8:26 l S Lev 2:4
8:27 m Nu 5:25
8:29 n Lev 7:31-34
8:30 o S Ex 28:1
         p S Ex 28:2
         q S Lev 7:36

¹⁸He then presented the ram[e] for the burnt offering, and Aaron and his sons laid their hands on its head. ¹⁹Then Moses slaughtered the ram and sprinkled the blood against the altar on all sides. ²⁰He cut the ram into pieces and burned the head, the pieces and the fat.[f] ²¹He washed the inner parts and the legs with water and burned the whole ram on the altar as a burnt offering, a pleasing aroma, an offering made to the LORD by fire, as the LORD commanded Moses.

²²He then presented the other ram, the ram for the ordination,[g] and Aaron and his sons laid their hands on its head.[h] ²³Moses slaughtered the ram and took some of its blood and put it on the lobe of Aaron's right ear, on the thumb of his right hand and on the big toe of his right foot.[i] ²⁴Moses also brought Aaron's sons forward and put some of the blood on the lobes of their right ears, on the thumbs of their right hands and on the big toes of their right feet. Then he sprinkled blood against the altar on all sides.[j] ²⁵He took the fat[k], the fat tail, all the fat around the inner parts, the covering of the liver, both kidneys and their fat and the right thigh. ²⁶Then from the basket of bread made without yeast, which was before the LORD, he took a cake of bread, and one made with oil, and a wafer;[l] he put these on the fat portions and on the right thigh. ²⁷He put all these in the hands of Aaron and his sons and waved them before the LORD[m] as a wave offering. ²⁸Then Moses took them from their hands and burned them on the altar on top of the burnt offering as an ordination offering, a pleasing aroma, an offering made to the LORD by fire. ²⁹He also took the breast—Moses' share of the ordination ram[n]—and waved it before the LORD as a wave offering, as the LORD commanded Moses.

³⁰Then Moses[o] took some of the anointing oil and some of the blood from the altar and sprinkled them on Aaron and his garments[p] and on his sons and their garments. So he consecrated[q] Aaron and his garments and his sons and their garments.

³¹Moses then said to Aaron and his sons, "Cook the meat at the entrance to

---

8:12 This passage mentions the anointing oil applied to the high priest, foreshadowing the anointing of "the most holy" (see Da 9:24).

the Tent of Meeting and eat it there with the bread from the basket of ordination offerings, as I commanded, saying, 'Aaron and his sons are to eat it.' ³²Then burn up the rest of the meat and the bread. ³³Do not leave the entrance to the Tent of Meeting for seven days, until the days of your ordination are completed, for your ordination will last seven days. ³⁴What has been done today was commanded by the LORD to make atonement for you. ³⁵You must stay at the entrance to the Tent of Meeting day and night for seven days and do what the LORD requires, so you will not die; for that is what I have been commanded." ³⁶So Aaron and his sons did everything the LORD commanded through Moses.

The Priests Begin Their Ministry

9 On the eighth day Moses summoned Aaron and his sons and the elders of Israel. ²He said to Aaron, "Take a bull calf for your sin offering and a ram for your burnt offering, both without defect, and present them before the LORD. ³Then say to the Israelites: 'Take a male goat for a sin offering, a calf and a lamb—both a year old and without defect—for a burnt offering, ⁴and an ox and a ram for a fellowship offering to sacrifice before the LORD, together with a grain offering mixed with oil. For today the LORD will appear to you.'"

⁵They took the things Moses commanded to the front of the Tent of Meeting, and the entire assembly came near and stood before the LORD. ⁶Then Moses said, "This is what the LORD has commanded you to do, so that the glory of the LORD may appear to you."

⁷Moses said to Aaron, "Come to the altar and sacrifice your sin offering and your burnt offering and make atonement for yourself and the people; sacrifice the offering that is for the people and make atonement for them, as the LORD has commanded."

⁸So Aaron came to the altar and slaughtered the calf as a sin offering for himself. ⁹His sons brought the blood to him, and he dipped his finger into the blood and put it on the horns of the altar; the rest of the blood he poured out at the base of the altar. ¹⁰On the altar he burned the fat, the kidneys and the covering of the liver from the sin offering, as the LORD commanded Moses; ¹¹the flesh and the hide he burned up outside the camp.

¹²Then he slaughtered the burnt offering. His sons handed him the blood, and he sprinkled it against the altar on all sides. ¹³They handed him the burnt offering piece by piece, including the head, and he burned them on the altar. ¹⁴He washed the inner parts and the legs and burned them on top of the burnt offering on the altar.

¹⁵Aaron then brought the offering that was for the people. He took the goat for the people's sin offering and slaughtered it and offered it for a sin offering as he did with the first one.

¹⁶He brought the burnt offering and offered it in the prescribed way. ¹⁷He also brought the grain offering, took a handful of it and burned it on the altar in addition to the morning's burnt offering.

¹⁸He slaughtered the ox and the ram as the fellowship offering for the people. His sons handed him the blood, and he sprinkled it against the altar on all sides. ¹⁹But the fat portions of the ox and the ram—the fat tail, the layer of fat, the kidneys and the covering of the liver— ²⁰these they laid on the breasts, and then Aaron burned the fat on the altar. ²¹Aaron waved the breasts and the right thigh before the LORD as a wave offering, as Moses commanded.

²²Then Aaron lifted his hands toward the people and blessed them. And having sacrificed the sin offering, the burnt offering and the fellowship offering, he stepped down.

²³Moses and Aaron then went into the Tent of Meeting. When they came out, they blessed the people; and the glory of the LORD appeared to all the people. ²⁴Fire came out from the presence of the LORD and consumed the burnt offering and the fat portions on the altar. And when all the people saw it, they shouted for joy and fell facedown.

q 31 Or *I was commanded*; *r 4* The Hebrew word can include both male and female; also in verses 18 and 19. *s 4* Traditionally *peace offering*; also in verses 18 and 22

The Death of Nadab and Abihu

10 Aaron's sons Nadab and Abihu took their censers, put fire in them and added incense; and they offered unauthorized fire before the LORD, contrary to his command. ²So fire came out from the presence of the LORD and consumed them, and they died before the LORD. ³Moses then said to Aaron, "This is what the LORD spoke of when he said:

> "'Among those who approach me
> I will show myself holy;
> in the sight of all the people
> I will be honored.'"

Aaron remained silent.

⁴Moses summoned Mishael and Elzaphan, sons of Aaron's uncle Uzziel, and said to them, "Come here; carry your cousins outside the camp, away from the front of the sanctuary." ⁵So they came and carried them, still in their tunics, outside the camp, as Moses ordered.

⁶Then Moses said to Aaron and his sons Eleazar and Ithamar, "Do not let your hair become unkempt, and do not tear your clothes, or you will die and the LORD will be angry with the whole community. But your relatives, all the house of Israel, may mourn for those the LORD has destroyed by fire. ⁷Do not leave the entrance to the Tent of Meeting or you will die, because the LORD's anointing oil is on you." So they did as Moses said.

⁸Then the LORD said to Aaron, ⁹"You and your sons are not to drink wine or other fermented drink whenever you go into the Tent of Meeting, or you will die. This is a lasting ordinance for the generations to come. ¹⁰You must distinguish between the holy and the common, between the unclean and the clean, ¹¹and you must teach the Israelites all the decrees the LORD has given them through Moses."

¹²Moses said to Aaron and his remaining sons, Eleazar and Ithamar, "Take the grain offering left over from the offerings made to the LORD by fire and eat it prepared without yeast beside the altar, for it is most holy. ¹³Eat it in a holy place, because it is your share and your sons' share of the offerings made to the LORD by fire; for so I have been commanded. ¹⁴But you and your sons and your daughters may eat the breast that was waved and the thigh that was presented. Eat them in a ceremonially clean place; they have been given to you and your children as your share of the Israelites' fellowship offerings. ¹⁵The thigh that was presented and the breast that was waved must be brought with the fat portions of the offerings made by fire, to be waved before the LORD as a wave offering. This will be the regular share for you and your children, as the LORD has commanded."

¹⁶When Moses inquired about the goat of the sin offering and found that it had been burned up, he was angry with Eleazar and Ithamar, Aaron's remaining sons, and asked, ¹⁷"Why didn't you eat the sin offering in the sanctuary area? It is most holy; it was given to you to take away the guilt of the community by making atonement for them before the LORD. ¹⁸Since its blood was not taken into the Holy Place, you should have eaten the goat in the sanctuary area, as I commanded.'"

¹⁹Aaron replied to Moses, "Today they sacrificed their sin offering and their burnt offering before the LORD, but such things as this have happened to me. Would the LORD have been pleased if I had eaten the sin offering today?" ²⁰When Moses heard this, he was satisfied.

Clean and Unclean Food

11:1–23pp — Dt 14:3–20

11 The LORD said to Moses and Aaron, ²"Say to the Israelites: 'Of all the animals that live on land, these are the ones you may eat: ³You may eat any

---

t 6 Or Do not uncover your heads   u 14 Traditionally peace offerings

---

10:10 God's laws of sanctification clearly defined the difference between the sacred and the profane, the holy and the common, the right and the wrong. This verse marks the focus of the entire book of Leviticus.

11:2–3 The animals acceptable for human consumption were those that chewed the cud and had a split hoof (11:3). The distinction between these "clean" animals and "unclean" ones had been made since God commanded Noah to take additional clean

animal that has a split hoof completely divided and that chews the cud. 4 " 'There are some that only chew the cud or only have a split hoof, but you must not eat them.ᵘ The camel, though it chews the cud, does not have a split hoof; it is ceremonially unclean for you. ⁵The coney,ᵛ though it chews the cud, does not have a split hoof; it is unclean for you. ⁶The rabbit, though it chews the cud, does not have a split hoof; it is unclean for you. ⁷And the pig,ᵛ though it has a split hoof completely divided, does not chew the cud; it is unclean for you. ⁸You must not eat their meat or touch their carcasses; they are unclean for you.ʷ

⁹" 'Of all the creatures living in the water of the seas and the streams, you may eat any that have fins and scales. ¹⁰But all creatures in the seas or streams that do not have fins and scales—whether among all the swarming things or among all the other living creatures in the water—you are to detest.ˣ ¹¹And since you are to detest them, you must not eat their meat and you must detest their carcasses.ʸ ¹²Anything living in the water that does not have fins and scales is to be detestable to you.ᶻ

¹³" 'These are the birds you are to detest and not eat because they are detestable: the eagle, the vulture, the black vulture, ¹⁴the red kite, any kindᵃ of black kite, ¹⁵any kind of raven,ᵇ ¹⁶the horned owl, the screech owl, the gull, any kind of hawk, ¹⁷the little owl, the cormorant, the great owl, ¹⁸the white owl,ᶜ the desert owl, the osprey, ¹⁹the stork,ᵈ any kindᵉ of heron, the hoopoe and the bat.ʷᶠ

²⁰" 'All flying insects that walk on all fours are to be detestable to you.ᵍ ²¹There are, however, some winged creatures that walk on all fours that you may eat: those that have jointed legs for hopping on the ground. ²²Of these you may eat any kind of locust,ʰ katydid, cricket or grasshopper. ²³But all other winged creatures that have four legs you are to detest.

²⁴" 'You will make yourselves unclean by these;ⁱ whoever touches their carcasses will be unclean till evening.ʲ ²⁵Whoever picks up one of their carcasses must wash his clothes,ᵏ and he will be unclean till evening.ˡ

²⁶" 'Every animal that has a split hoof not completely divided or that does not chew the cud is unclean for you; whoever touches ˌthe carcass of₎ any of them will be unclean. ²⁷Of all the animals that walk on all fours, those that walk on their paws are unclean for you; whoever touches their carcasses will be unclean till evening. ²⁸Anyone who picks up their carcasses must wash his clothes, and he will be unclean till evening.ᵐ They are unclean for you.

²⁹" 'Of the animals that move about on the ground, these are unclean for you:ⁿ the weasel, the rat,ᵒ any kind of great lizard, ³⁰the gecko, the monitor lizard, the wall lizard, the skink and the chameleon. ³¹Of all those that move along the ground, these are unclean for you. Whoever touches them when they are dead will be unclean till evening. ³²When one of them dies and falls on something, that article, whatever its use, will be unclean, whether it is made of wood, cloth, hide or sackcloth.ᵖ Put it in water; it will be unclean till evening, and then it will be clean. ³³If one of them falls into a clay pot, everything in it will be unclean, and you must break the pot.ᵠ ³⁴Any food that could be eaten but has water on it from such a pot is unclean, and any liquid that could be drunk from it is unclean. ³⁵Anything that one of their carcasses falls on becomes unclean; an oven or cooking pot must be broken up. They are unclean, and you are to regard them as unclean. ³⁶A spring, however, or a cistern for collecting water remains clean, but anyone who touches one of these carcasses is unclean. ³⁷If a carcass falls on any seeds that are to be planted, they remain clean. ³⁸But if water has been put on the seed and a carcass falls on it, it is unclean for you.

³⁹" 'If an animal that you are allowed to eat dies,ʳ anyone who touches the car-

ᵛ5 That is, the hyrax or rock badger ʷ19 The precise identification of some of the birds, insects and animals in this chapter is uncertain.

---

animals into the ark for use in future sacrifices (see Ge 7:2–3).

11:32–35 God gave his people special instructions regarding the dead carcasses of unclean animals such as rats, weasels and lizards. These dead creatures could easily contaminate food, cooking pots or ovens.

carcass^s will be unclean till evening. ^{40}Anyone who eats some of the carcass^t must wash his clothes, and he will be unclean till evening.^{u} Anyone who picks up the carcass must wash his clothes, and he will be unclean till evening.

^{41}" 'Every creature that moves about on the ground is detestable; it is not to be eaten. ^{42}You are not to eat any creature that moves about on the ground, whether it moves on its belly or walks on all fours or on many feet; it is detestable. ^{43}Do not defile yourselves by any of these creatures.^{v} Do not make yourselves unclean by means of them or be made unclean by them. ^{44}I am the L<small>ORD</small> your God;^{w} consecrate yourselves^x and be holy,^{y} because I am holy.^{z} Do not make yourselves unclean by any creature that moves about on the ground.^{a} ^{45}I am the L<small>ORD</small> who brought you up out of Egypt^b to be your God;^{c} therefore be holy, because I am holy.^{d}

^{46}" 'These are the regulations concerning animals, birds, every living thing that moves in the water and every creature that moves about on the ground. ^{47}You must distinguish between the unclean and the clean, between living creatures that may be eaten and those that may not be eaten.^{e} '"

Purification After Childbirth

12 The L<small>ORD</small> said to Moses, ^{2}"Say to the Israelites: 'A woman who becomes pregnant and gives birth to a son will be ceremonially unclean for seven days, just as she is unclean during her monthly period.^{f} ^{3}On the eighth day^g the boy is to be circumcised.^{h} ^{4}Then the woman must wait thirty-three days to be purified from her bleeding. She must not touch anything sacred or go to the sanctuary until the days of her purification are over. ^{5}If she gives birth to a daughter, for two weeks the woman will be unclean, as during her period. Then she must wait sixty-six days to be purified from her bleeding.

^{6}" 'When the days of her purification for a son or daughter are over,^{i} she is to bring to the priest at the entrance to the Tent of Meeting a year-old lamb^j for a burnt offering and a young pigeon or a dove for a sin offering.^{k} ^{7}He shall offer

them before the L<small>ORD</small> to make atonement for her, and then she will be ceremonially clean from her flow of blood.

" 'These are the regulations for the woman who gives birth to a boy or a girl. ^{8}If she cannot afford a lamb, she is to bring two doves or two young pigeons,^{l} one for a burnt offering and the other for a sin offering.^{m} In this way the priest will make atonement for her, and she will be clean.^{n} '"

Regulations About Infectious Skin Diseases

13 The L<small>ORD</small> said to Moses and Aaron, ^{2}"When anyone has a swelling^o or a rash or a bright spot^p on his skin that may become an infectious skin disease,$^{x\,q}$ he must be brought to Aaron the priest^r or to one of his sons^y who is a priest. ^{3}The priest is to examine the sore on his skin, and if the hair in the sore has turned white and the sore appears to be more than skin deep,^{z} it is an infectious skin disease. When the priest examines him, he shall pronounce him ceremonially unclean.^{s} ^{4}If the spot^t on his skin is white but does not appear to be more than skin deep and the hair in it has not turned white, the priest is to put the infected person in isolation for seven days.^{u} ^{5}On the seventh day^v the priest is to examine him,^{w} and if he sees that the sore is unchanged and has not spread in the skin, he is to keep him in isolation another seven days. ^{6}On the seventh day the priest is to examine him again, and if the sore has faded and has not spread in the skin, the priest shall pronounce him clean;^{x} it is only a rash. The man must wash his clothes,^{y} and he will be clean.^{z} ^{7}But if the rash does spread in his skin after he has shown himself to the priest to be pronounced clean, he must appear before the priest again.^{a} ^{8}The priest is to examine him, and if the rash has spread in the skin, he shall pronounce him unclean; it is an infectious disease.

^{9}"When anyone has an infectious skin disease, he must be brought to the priest. ^{10}The priest is to examine him, and if there is a white swelling in the skin that has turned the hair white and if there is

---

^{x}2 Traditionally *leprosy*; the Hebrew word was used for various diseases affecting the skin—not necessarily leprosy; also elsewhere in this chapter. ^{y}2 Or *descendants* ^{z}3 Or *be lower than the rest of the skin*; also elsewhere in this chapter

raw flesh in the swelling, ¹¹it is a chronic skin disease[b] and the priest shall pronounce him unclean. He is not to put him in isolation, because he is already unclean.

¹²"If the disease breaks out all over his skin and, so far as the priest can see, it covers all the skin of the infected person from head to foot, ¹³the priest is to examine him, and if the disease has covered his whole body, he shall pronounce that person clean. Since it has all turned white, he is clean. ¹⁴But whenever raw flesh appears on him, he will be unclean. ¹⁵When the priest sees the raw flesh, he shall pronounce him unclean. The raw flesh is unclean; he has an infectious disease.[c] ¹⁶Should the raw flesh change and turn white, he must go to the priest. ¹⁷The priest is to examine him, and if the sores have turned white, the priest shall pronounce the infected person clean;[d] then he will be clean.

¹⁸"When someone has a boil[e] on his skin and it heals, ¹⁹and in the place where the boil was, a white swelling or reddish-white[f] spot[g] appears, he must present himself to the priest. ²⁰The priest is to examine it, and if it appears to be more than skin deep and the hair in it has turned white, the priest shall pronounce him unclean. It is an infectious skin disease[h] that has broken out where the boil was. ²¹But if, when the priest examines it, there is no white hair in it and it is not more than skin deep and has faded, then the priest is to put him in isolation for seven days. ²²If it is spreading in the skin, the priest shall pronounce him unclean; it is infectious. ²³But if the spot is unchanged and has not spread, it is only a scar from the boil, and the priest shall pronounce him clean.[i]

²⁴"When someone has a burn on his skin and a reddish-white or white spot appears in the raw flesh of the burn, ²⁵the priest is to examine the spot, and if the hair in it has turned white, and it appears to be more than skin deep, it is an infectious disease that has broken out in the burn. The priest shall pronounce him unclean; it is an infectious skin disease.[j] ²⁶But if the priest examines it and there is no white hair in the spot and if it is not more than skin deep and has faded, then the priest is to put him in isolation for seven days.[k] ²⁷On the seventh day the priest is to examine him,[l] and if it is spreading in the skin, the priest shall pronounce him unclean; it is an infectious skin disease. ²⁸If, however, the spot is unchanged and has not spread in the skin but has faded, it is a swelling from the burn, and the priest shall pronounce him clean; it is only a scar from the burn.[m]

²⁹"If a man or woman has a sore on the head[n] or on the chin, ³⁰the priest is to examine the sore, and if it appears to be more than skin deep and the hair in it is yellow and thin, the priest shall pronounce that person unclean; it is an itch, an infectious disease of the head or chin. ³¹But if, when the priest examines this kind of sore, it does not seem to be more than skin deep and there is no black hair in it, then the priest is to put the infected person in isolation for seven days.[o] ³²On the seventh day the priest is to examine the sore,[p] and if the itch has not spread and there is no yellow hair in it and it does not appear to be more than skin deep, ³³he must be shaved except for the diseased area, and the priest is to keep him in isolation another seven days. ³⁴On the seventh day the priest is to examine the itch,[q] and if it has not spread in the skin and appears to be no more than skin deep, the priest shall pronounce him clean. He must wash his clothes, and he will be clean.[r] ³⁵But if the itch does spread in the skin after he is pronounced clean, ³⁶the priest is to examine him, and if the itch has spread in the skin, the priest does not need to look for yellow hair; the person is unclean.[s] ³⁷If, however, in his judgment it is unchanged and black hair has grown in it, the itch is healed. He is clean, and the priest shall pronounce him clean.

³⁸"When a man or woman has white spots on the skin, ³⁹the priest is to examine them, and if the spots are dull white, it is a harmless rash that has broken out on the skin; that person is clean.

⁴⁰"When a man has lost his hair and is bald,[t] he is clean. ⁴¹If he has lost his hair from the front of his scalp and has a bald forehead, he is clean. ⁴²But if he has a reddish-white sore on his bald head or forehead, it is an infectious disease breaking out on his head or forehead. ⁴³The priest is to examine him, and if the swollen sore on his head or forehead is reddish-white like an infectious skin disease,

---

13:11 [b] S Ex 4:6; S Lev 14:8; S Nu 12:10; Mt 8:2
13:15 [c] S ver 2
13:17 [d] S ver 6
13:18 [e] S Ex 9:9
13:19 [f] ver 24, 42; Lev 14:37 [g] S ver 2
13:20 [h] ver 2
13:23 [i] S ver 6
13:25 [j] ver 11
13:26 [k] S ver 4
13:27 [l] S ver 5
13:28 [m] S ver 2
13:29 [n] ver 43, 44
13:31 [o] ver 4
13:32 [p] S ver 5
13:34 [q] S ver 5; [r] S Lev 11:25
13:36 [s] ver 30
13:40 [t] Lev 21:5; 2Ki 2:23; Isa 3:24; 15:2; 22:12; Eze 27:31; 29:18; Am 8:10; Mic 1:16

⁴⁴the man is diseased and is unclean. The priest shall pronounce him unclean because of the sore on his head.

⁴⁵"The person with such an infectious disease must wear torn clothes,ᵘ let his hair be unkempt,ᵃ cover the lower part of his faceᵛ and cry out, 'Unclean! Unclean!'ʷ ⁴⁶As long as he has the infection he remains unclean. He must live alone; he must live outside the camp.ˣ

Regulations About Mildew

⁴⁷"If any clothing is contaminated with mildew—any woolen or linen clothing, ⁴⁸any woven or knitted material of linen or wool, any leather or anything made of leather— ⁴⁹and if the contamination in the clothing, or leather, or woven or knitted material, or any leather article, is greenish or reddish, it is a spreading mildew and must be shown to the priest.ʸ ⁵⁰The priest is to examine the mildewᶻ and isolate the affected article for seven days. ⁵¹On the seventh day he is to examine it,ᵃ and if the mildew has spread in the clothing, or the woven or knitted material, or the leather, whatever its use, it is a destructive mildew; the article is unclean.ᵇ ⁵²He must burn up the clothing, or the woven or knitted material of wool or linen, or any leather article that has the contamination in it, because the mildew is destructive; the article must be burned up.ᶜ

⁵³"But if, when the priest examines it, the mildew has not spread in the clothing, or the woven or knitted material, or the leather article, ⁵⁴he shall order that the contaminated article be washed. Then he is to isolate it for another seven days. ⁵⁵After the affected article has been washed, the priest is to examine it, and if the mildew has not changed its appearance, even though it has not spread, it is unclean. Burn it with fire, whether the mildew has affected one side or the other. ⁵⁶If, when the priest examines it, the mildew has faded after the article has been washed, he is to tear the contaminated part out of the clothing, or the leather, or the woven or knitted material. ⁵⁷But if it reappears in the clothing, or in the woven or knitted material, or in the leather article, it is spreading, and whatever has the mildew must be burned with fire. ⁵⁸The clothing, or the woven or knitted material, or any leather article that has been washed and is rid of the mildew, must be washed again, and it will be clean."

⁵⁹These are the regulations concerning contamination by mildew in woolen or linen clothing, woven or knitted material, or any leather article, for pronouncing them clean or unclean.

Cleansing From Infectious Skin Diseases

14 The LORD said to Moses, ²"These are the regulations for the diseased person at the time of his ceremonial cleansing, when he is brought to the priest:ᵈ ³The priest is to go outside the camp and examine him.ᵉ If the person has been healed of his infectious skin disease,ᵇᶠ ⁴the priest shall order that two live clean birds and some cedar wood, scarlet yarn and hyssopᵍ be brought for the one to be cleansed.ʰ ⁵Then the priest shall order that one of the birds be killed over fresh water in a clay pot.ⁱ ⁶He is then to take the live bird and dip it, together with the cedar wood, the scarlet yarn and the hyssop, into the blood of the bird that was killed over the fresh water.ʲ ⁷Seven timesᵏ he shall sprinkleˡ the one to be cleansed of the infectious disease and pronounce him clean. Then he is to release the live bird in the open fields.ᵐ

⁸"The person to be cleansed must wash his clothes,ⁿ shave off all his hair and bathe with water;ᵒ then he will be ceremonially clean.ᵖ After this he may come into the camp,ᵠ but he must stay outside his tent for seven days. ⁹On the seventh dayʳ he must shave off all his hair;ˢ he must shave his head, his beard, his eyebrows and the rest of his hair. He must wash his clothes and bathe himself with water, and he will be clean.ᵗ

¹⁰"On the eighth dayᵘ he must bring two male lambs and one ewe lambᵛ a year old, each without defect, along with

---

ᵃ 45 Or *clothes, uncover his head* ᵇ 3 Traditionally *leprosy*; the Hebrew word was used for various diseases affecting the skin—not necessarily leprosy; also elsewhere in this chapter.

13:46 In this passage Moses divinely demonstrates a knowledge of quarantine—a disease control method that was not formally recognized until the 1870s.

three-tenths of an ephah[c][w] of fine flour mixed with oil for a grain offering,[x] and one log[d] of oil.[y] [11]The priest who pronounces him clean shall present[z] both the one to be cleansed and his offerings before the LORD at the entrance to the Tent of Meeting.[a]

[12]"Then the priest is to take one of the male lambs and offer it as a guilt offering,[b] along with the log of oil; he shall wave them before the LORD as a wave offering.[c] [13]He is to slaughter the lamb in the holy place[d] where the sin offering and the burnt offering are slaughtered. Like the sin offering, the guilt offering belongs to the priest;[e] it is most holy. [14]The priest is to take some of the blood of the guilt offering and put it on the lobe of the right ear of the one to be cleansed, on the thumb of his right hand and on the big toe of his right foot.[f] [15]The priest shall then take some of the log of oil, pour it in the palm of his own left hand,[g] [16]dip his right forefinger into the oil in his palm, and with his finger sprinkle some of it before the LORD seven times.[h] [17]The priest is to put some of the oil remaining in his palm on the lobe of the right ear of the one to be cleansed, on the thumb of his right hand and on the big toe of his right foot, on top of the blood of the guilt offering.[i] [18]The rest of the oil in his palm the priest shall put on the head of the one to be cleansed[j] and make atonement for him before the LORD.

[19]"Then the priest is to sacrifice the sin offering and make atonement for the one to be cleansed from his uncleanness.[k] After that, the priest shall slaughter the burnt offering [20]and offer it on the altar, together with the grain offering, and make atonement for him,[l] and he will be clean.[m]

[21]"If, however, he is poor[n] and cannot afford these,[o] he must take one male lamb as a guilt offering to be waved to make atonement for him, together with a tenth of an ephah[e] of fine flour mixed with oil for a grain offering, a log of oil, [22]and two doves or two young pigeons,[p] which he can afford, one for a sin offering and the other for a burnt offering.[q]

[23]"On the eighth day he must bring them for his cleansing to the priest at the entrance to the Tent of Meeting,[r] before the LORD.[s] [24]The priest is to take the lamb for the guilt offering,[t] together with the log of oil,[u] and wave them before the LORD as a wave offering.[v] [25]He shall slaughter the lamb for the guilt offering and take some of its blood and put it on the lobe of the right ear of the one to be cleansed, on the thumb of his right hand and on the big toe of his right foot.[w] [26]The priest is to pour some of the oil into the palm of his own left hand,[x] [27]and with his right forefinger sprinkle some of the oil from his palm seven times before the LORD. [28]Some of the oil in his palm he is to put on the same places he put the blood of the guilt offering—on the lobe of the right ear of the one to be cleansed, on the thumb of his right hand and on the big toe of his right foot. [29]The rest of the oil in his palm the priest shall put on the head of the one to be cleansed, to make atonement for him before the LORD.[y] [30]Then he shall sacrifice the doves or the young pigeons, which the person can afford,[z] [31]one[f] as a sin offering and the other as a burnt offering,[a] together with the grain offering. In this way the priest will make atonement before the LORD on behalf of the one to be cleansed.[b]"

[32]These are the regulations for anyone who has an infectious skin disease[c] and who cannot afford the regular offerings[d] for his cleansing.

Cleansing From Mildew

[33]The LORD said to Moses and Aaron, [34]"When you enter the land of Canaan,[e] which I am giving you as your possession,[f] and I put a spreading mildew in a house in that land, [35]the owner of the house must go and tell the priest, 'I have seen something that looks like mildew in my house.' [36]The priest is to order the house to be emptied before he goes in to examine the mildew, so that nothing in the house will be pronounced unclean. After this the priest is to go in and inspect the house. [37]He is to examine the mildew on the walls, and if it has greenish or reddish[g] depressions that appear to be deeper than the surface of the wall, [38]the priest shall go out the doorway of the house and close it up for seven days.[h] [39]On the seventh day[i] the priest shall return to inspect the house. If the mildew

---

[c] 10 That is, probably about 6 quarts (about 6.5 liters)   [d] 10 That is, probably about 2/3 pint (about 0.3 liter); also in verses 12, 15, 21 and 24   [e] 21 That is, probably about 2 quarts (about 2 liters)   [f] 31 Septuagint and Syriac; Hebrew 31 such as the person can afford, one

has spread on the walls, ⁴⁰he is to order that the contaminated stones be torn out and thrown into an unclean place outside the town.ʲ ⁴¹He must have all the inside walls of the house scraped and the material that is scraped off dumped into an unclean place outside the town. ⁴²Then they are to take other stones to replace these and take new clay and plaster the house.

⁴³"If the mildew reappears in the house after the stones have been torn out and the house scraped and plastered, ⁴⁴the priest is to go and examine it and, if the mildew has spread in the house, it is a destructive mildew; the house is unclean.ᵏ ⁴⁵It must be torn down—its stones, timbers and all the plaster—and taken out of the town to an unclean place.

⁴⁶"Anyone who goes into the house while it is closed up will be unclean till evening.ˡ ⁴⁷Anyone who sleeps or eats in the house must wash his clothes.ᵐ

⁴⁸"But if the priest comes to examine it and the mildew has not spread after the house has been plastered, he shall pronounce the house clean,ⁿ because the mildew is gone. ⁴⁹To purify the house he is to take two birds and some cedar wood, scarlet yarn and hyssop.ᵒ ⁵⁰He shall kill one of the birds over fresh water in a clay pot.ᵖ ⁵¹Then he is to take the cedar wood, the hyssop,ᑫ the scarlet yarn and the live bird, dip them into the blood of the dead bird and the fresh water, and sprinkle the house seven times.ʳ ⁵²He shall purify the house with the bird's blood, the fresh water, the live bird, the cedar wood, the hyssop and the scarlet yarn. ⁵³Then he is to release the live bird in the open fieldsˢ outside the town. In this way he will make atonement for the house, and it will be clean.'"

⁵⁴These are the regulations for any infectious skin disease,ᵘ for an itch, ⁵⁵for mildewᵛ in clothing or in a house, ⁵⁶and for a swelling, a rash or a bright spot,ʷ ⁵⁷to determine when something is clean or unclean.

These are the regulations for infectious skin diseases and mildew.ˣ

14:40 ʲver 45
14:44 ᵏLev 13:51
14:46 ˡS Lev 11:24
14:47 ᵐS Lev 11:25
14:48 ⁿS Lev 13:6
14:49 ᵒver 4; 1Ki 4:33
14:50 ᵖver 5
14:51 ᑫver 6; Ps 51:7 ʳS ver 4,7
14:53 ˢS ver 7 ᵗver 20
14:54 ᵘLev 13:2
14:55 ᵛLev 13:47-52
14:56 ʷLev 13:2
14:57 ˣS Lev 10:10
15:2 ʸver 16,32; Lev 22:4; Nu 5:2; 2Sa 3:29; Mt 9:20
15:5 ᶻS Lev 11:25 ᵃLev 14:8 ᵇS Lev 11:24
15:7 ᶜver 19; Lev 22:5 ᵈver 16; Lev 22:4
15:8 ᵉNu 12:14
15:10 ᶠNu 19:10
15:12 ᵍS Lev 6:28 ʰS Lev 11:32
15:13 ⁱS Lev 8:33 ʲver 5
15:14 ᵏLev 14:22

Discharges Causing Uncleanness

15 The LORD said to Moses and Aaron, ²"Speak to the Israelites and say to them: 'When any man has a bodily discharge,ʸ the discharge is unclean. ³Whether it continues flowing from his body or is blocked, it will make him unclean. This is how his discharge will bring about uncleanness:

⁴"'Any bed the man with a discharge lies on will be unclean, and anything he sits on will be unclean. ⁵Anyone who touches his bed must wash his clothesᶻ and bathe with water,ᵃ and he will be unclean till evening.ᵇ ⁶Whoever sits on anything that the man with a discharge sat on must wash his clothes and bathe with water, and he will be unclean till evening.

⁷"'Whoever touches the manᶜ who has a dischargeᵈ must wash his clothes and bathe with water, and he will be unclean till evening.

⁸"'If the man with the discharge spitsᵉ on someone who is clean, that person must wash his clothes and bathe with water, and he will be unclean till evening.

⁹"'Everything the man sits on when riding will be unclean, ¹⁰and whoever touches any of the things that were under him will be unclean till evening; whoever picks up those thingsᶠ must wash his clothes and bathe with water, and he will be unclean till evening.

¹¹"'Anyone the man with a discharge touches without rinsing his hands with water must wash his clothes and bathe with water, and he will be unclean till evening.

¹²"'A clay potᵍ that the man touches must be broken, and any wooden articleʰ is to be rinsed with water.

¹³"'When a man is cleansed from his discharge, he is to count off seven daysⁱ for his ceremonial cleansing; he must wash his clothes and bathe himself with fresh water, and he will be clean.ʲ ¹⁴On the eighth day he must take two doves or two young pigeonsᵏ and come before the LORD to the entrance to the Tent of Meeting and give them to the priest. ¹⁵The priest is to sacrifice them, the one for a

---

15:13 The command in this verse for the man to "wash his clothes and bathe himself with fresh water" is as modern as today's hospital manuals. Following God's command to wash in running water could have saved untold millions from disease and death throughout history.

sin offering[1] and the other for a burnt offering.[m] In this way he will make atonement before the LORD for the man because of his discharge.[n]

[16] "'When a man has an emission of semen,[o] he must bathe his whole body with water, and he will be unclean till evening.[p] [17]Any clothing or leather that has semen on it must be washed with water, and it will be unclean till evening. [18]When a man lies with a woman and there is an emission of semen,[q] both must bathe with water, and they will be unclean till evening.

[19] "'When a woman has her regular flow of blood, the impurity of her monthly period[r] will last seven days, and anyone who touches her will be unclean till evening.

[20] "'Anything she lies on during her period will be unclean, and anything she sits on will be unclean. [21]Whoever touches her bed must wash his clothes and bathe with water, and he will be unclean till evening.[s] [22]Whoever touches anything she sits on must wash his clothes and bathe with water, and he will be unclean till evening. [23]Whether it is the bed or anything she was sitting on, when anyone touches it, he will be unclean till evening.

[24] "'If a man lies with her and her monthly flow[t] touches him, he will be unclean for seven days; any bed he lies on will be unclean.

[25] "'When a woman has a discharge of blood for many days at a time other than her monthly period[u] or has a discharge that continues beyond her period, she will be unclean as long as she has the discharge, just as in the days of her period. [26]Any bed she lies on while her discharge continues will be unclean, as is her bed during her monthly period, and anything she sits on will be unclean, as during her period. [27]Whoever touches them will be unclean; he must wash his clothes and bathe with water, and he will be unclean till evening.

[28] "'When she is cleansed from her discharge, she must count off seven days, and after that she will be ceremonially clean. [29]On the eighth day she must take two doves or two young pigeons[v] and bring them to the priest at the entrance to the Tent of Meeting. [30]The priest is to sacrifice one for a sin offering and the other for a burnt offering. In this way he will make atonement for her before the LORD for the uncleanness of her discharge.[w]

[31] "'You must keep the Israelites separate from things that make them unclean, so they will not die in their uncleanness for defiling my dwelling place,[g][x] which is among them.'"

[32]These are the regulations for a man with a discharge, for anyone made unclean by an emission of semen,[y] [33]for a woman in her monthly period, for a man or a woman with a discharge, and for a man who lies with a woman who is ceremonially unclean.[z]

The Day of Atonement
16:2–34pp — Lev 23:26–32; Nu 29:7–11

16 The LORD spoke to Moses after the death of the two sons of Aaron who died when they approached the LORD.[a] [2]The LORD said to Moses: "Tell your brother Aaron not to come whenever he chooses[b] into the Most Holy Place[c] behind the curtain[d] in front of the atonement cover[e] on the ark, or else he will die, because I appear[f] in the cloud[g] over the atonement cover.

[3] "This is how Aaron is to enter the sanctuary area:[h] with a young bull[i] for a sin offering and a ram for a burnt offering.[j] [4]He is to put on the sacred linen tunic,[k] with linen undergarments next to his body; he is to tie the linen sash around his waist and put on the linen turban.[l] These are sacred garments;[m] so he must bathe himself with water[n] before he puts them on.[o] [5]From the Israelite community[p] he is to take two male goats[q] for a sin offering and a ram for a burnt offering.

[6]"Aaron is to offer the bull for his own sin offering to make atonement for himself and his household.[r] [7]Then he is to take the two goats and present them before the LORD at the entrance to the Tent of Meeting. [8]He is to cast lots[s] for the two goats—one lot for the LORD and the other for the scapegoat.[h][t] [9]Aaron shall bring the goat whose lot falls to the LORD and sacrifice it for a sin offering. [10]But the goat chosen by lot as the scapegoat shall

D *Lev 9:11* ◄ ► *Lev 16:21*

g 31 Or my tabernacle   h 8 That is, the goat of removal; Hebrew azazel; also in verses 10 and 26

LEVITICUS 16:11

be presented alive before the LORD to be used for making atonement by sending it into the desert as a scapegoat.

¹¹"Aaron shall bring the bull for his own sin offering to make atonement for himself and his household, and he is to slaughter the bull for his own sin offering. ¹²He is to take a censer full of burning coals from the altar before the LORD and two handfuls of finely ground fragrant incense and take them behind the curtain. ¹³He is to put the incense on the fire before the LORD, and the smoke of the incense will conceal the atonement cover above the Testimony, so that he will not die. ¹⁴He is to take some of the bull's blood and with his finger sprinkle it on the front of the atonement cover; then he shall sprinkle some of it with his finger seven times before the atonement cover.

¹⁵"He shall then slaughter the goat for the sin offering for the people and take its blood behind the curtain and do with it as he did with the bull's blood: He shall sprinkle it on the atonement cover and in front of it. ¹⁶In this way he will make atonement for the Most Holy Place because of the uncleanness and rebellion of the Israelites, whatever their sins have been. He is to do the same for the Tent of Meeting, which is among them in the midst of their uncleanness. ¹⁷No one is to be in the Tent of Meeting from the time Aaron goes in to make atonement in the Most Holy Place until he comes out, having made atonement for himself, his household and the whole community of Israel.

¹⁸"Then he shall come out to the altar that is before the LORD and make atonement for it. He shall take some of the bull's blood and some of the goat's blood and put it on all the horns of the altar. ¹⁹He shall sprinkle some of the blood on it with his finger seven times to cleanse it and to consecrate it from the uncleanness of the Israelites.

²⁰"When Aaron has finished making atonement for the Most Holy Place, the Tent of Meeting and the altar, he shall bring forward the live goat. ²¹He is to lay both hands on the head of the live goat and confess over it all the wickedness and rebellion of the Israelites—all their sins—and put them on the goat's head. He shall send the goat away into the desert in the care of a man appointed for the task. ²²The goat will carry on itself all their sins to a solitary place; and the man shall release it in the desert.

²³"Then Aaron is to go into the Tent of Meeting and take off the linen garments he put on before he entered the Most Holy Place, and he is to leave them there. ²⁴He shall bathe himself with water in a holy place and put on his regular garments. Then he shall come out and sacrifice the burnt offering for himself and the burnt offering for the people, to make atonement for himself and for the people. ²⁵He shall also burn the fat of the sin offering on the altar.

²⁶"The man who releases the goat as a scapegoat must wash his clothes and bathe himself with water; afterward he may come into the camp. ²⁷The bull and the goat for the sin offerings, whose blood was brought into the Most Holy Place to make atonement, must be taken outside the camp; their hides, flesh and offal are to be burned up. ²⁸The man who burns them must wash his clothes and bathe himself with water; afterward he may come into the camp.

²⁹"This is to be a lasting ordinance for you: On the tenth day of the seventh month you must deny yourselves and not do any work—whether native-born or an alien living among you— ³⁰because on this day atonement will be made for you, to cleanse you. Then, before the LORD, you will be clean from all your sins. ³¹It is a sabbath of rest, and you must deny yourselves; it is a lasting ordinance. ³²The priest who is anointed and ordained to succeed his father as high priest is to make atonement. He is to put on the sacred linen garments ³³and make atonement for the Most Holy Place, for the Tent of Meeting and the altar, and for the priests and all the people of the community.

³⁴"This is to be a lasting ordinance for you: Atonement is to be made once a year for all the sins of the Israelites."

And it was done, as the LORD commanded Moses.

Eating Blood Forbidden

17 The LORD said to Moses, ² "Speak to Aaron and his sons and to all the Israelites and say to them: 'This is what the LORD has commanded: ³ Any Israelite who sacrifices an ox, a lamb or a goat in the camp or outside of it ⁴ instead of bringing it to the entrance to the Tent of Meeting to present it as an offering to the LORD in front of the tabernacle of the LORD—that man shall be considered guilty of bloodshed; he has shed blood and must be cut off from his people. ⁵ This is so the Israelites will bring to the LORD the sacrifices they are now making in the open fields. They must bring them to the priest, that is, to the LORD, at the entrance to the Tent of Meeting and sacrifice them as fellowship offerings. ⁶ The priest is to sprinkle the blood against the altar of the LORD at the entrance to the Tent of Meeting and burn the fat as an aroma pleasing to the LORD. ⁷ They must no longer offer any of their sacrifices to the goat idols to whom they prostitute themselves. This is to be a lasting ordinance for them and for the generations to come.'

⁸ "Say to them: 'Any Israelite or any alien living among them who offers a burnt offering or sacrifice ⁹ and does not bring it to the entrance to the Tent of Meeting to sacrifice it to the LORD—that man must be cut off from his people.

¹⁰ "'Any Israelite or any alien living among them who eats any blood—I will set my face against that person who eats blood and will cut him off from his people. ¹¹ For the life of a creature is in the blood, and I have given it to you to make atonement for yourselves on the altar; it is the blood that makes atonement for one's life. ¹² Therefore I say to the Israelites, "None of you may eat blood, nor may an alien living among you eat blood."

¹³ "'Any Israelite or any alien living among you who hunts any animal or bird that may be eaten must drain out the blood and cover it with earth, ¹⁴ because the life of every creature is its blood. That is why I have said to the Israelites, "You must not eat the blood of any creature, because the life of every creature is its blood; anyone who eats it must be cut off."

¹⁵ "'Anyone, whether native-born or alien, who eats anything found dead or torn by wild animals must wash his clothes and bathe with water, and he will be ceremonially unclean till evening; then he will be clean. ¹⁶ But if he does not wash his clothes and bathe himself, he will be held responsible.'"

Unlawful Sexual Relations

18 The LORD said to Moses, ² "Speak to the Israelites and say to them: 'I am the LORD your God. ³ You must not do as they do in Egypt, where you used to live, and you must not do as they do in the land of Canaan, where I am bringing you. Do not follow their practices. ⁴ You must obey my laws and be careful to follow my decrees. I am the LORD your God. ⁵ Keep my decrees and laws, for the man who obeys them will live by them. I am the LORD.

⁶ "'No one is to approach any close relative to have sexual relations. I am the LORD.

⁷ "'Do not dishonor your father by having sexual relations with your mother. She is your mother; do not have relations with her.

⁸ "'Do not have sexual relations with your father's wife; that would dishonor your father.

⁹ "'Do not have sexual relations with your sister, either your father's daughter or your mother's daughter, whether she

S Lev 11:44–45 ◀▶ Lev 19:2

j3 The Hebrew word can include both male and female.   k5 Traditionally peace offerings   l7 Or demons

---

17:11 Since life was sacred to God, the blood was also sacred as a symbol of life. The blood of a sacrificial animal took the place of the sinner's blood and symbolically redeemed the sinner. Thus the blood in the OT sacrifice foreshadowed the blood of "the Lamb of God, who takes away the sin of the world" (Jn 1:29).

18:4–5 These two statements reminded the Israelites that the law was the way of life for the redeemed. Their faithful acts of obedience would result in blessing (see Eze 20:11, 13, 21; Ro 10:5).

was born in the same home or elsewhere.ᵇ

10 "'Do not have sexual relations with your son's daughter or your daughter's daughter; that would dishonor you.

11 "'Do not have sexual relations with the daughter of your father's wife, born to your father; she is your sister.

12 "'Do not have sexual relations with your father's sister;ᶜ she is your father's close relative.

13 "'Do not have sexual relations with your mother's sister,ᵈ because she is your mother's close relative.

14 "'Do not dishonor your father's brother by approaching his wife to have sexual relations; she is your aunt.ᵉ

15 "'Do not have sexual relations with your daughter-in-law.ᶠ She is your son's wife; do not have relations with her.ᵍ

16 "'Do not have sexual relations with your brother's wife;ʰ that would dishonor your brother.

17 "'Do not have sexual relations with both a woman and her daughter.ⁱ Do not have sexual relations with either her son's daughter or her daughter's daughter; they are her close relatives. That is wickedness.

18 "'Do not take your wife's sisterʲ as a rival wife and have sexual relations with her while your wife is living.

19 "'Do not approach a woman to have sexual relations during the uncleannessᵏ of her monthly period.ˡ

20 "'Do not have sexual relations with your neighbor's wifeᵐ and defile yourself with her.

21 "'Do not give any of your childrenⁿ to be sacrificedᵐ to Molech,ᵒ for you must not profane the name of your God.ᵖ I am the LORD.ᵠ

22 "'Do not lie with a man as one lies with a woman;ʳ that is detestable.ˢ

23 "'Do not have sexual relations with an animal and defile yourself with it. A woman must not present herself to an animal to have sexual relations with it; that is a perversion.ᵗ

24 "'Do not defile yourselves in any of these ways, because this is how the nations that I am going to drive out before youᵘ became defiled.ᵛ 25 Even the land was defiled;ʷ so I punished it for its sin,ˣ and the land vomited out its inhabitants.ʸ 26 But you must keep my decrees and my laws.ᶻ The native-born and the aliens liv-

ing among you must not do any of these detestable things, 27 for all these things were done by the people who lived in the land before you, and the land became defiled. 28 And if you defile the land,ᵃ it will vomit you outᵇ as it vomited out the nations that were before you.

29 "'Everyone who does any of these detestable things—such persons must be cut off from their people. 30 Keep my requirementsᶜ and do not follow any of the detestable customs that were practiced before you came and do not defile yourselves with them. I am the LORD your God.ᵈ'"

Various Laws

19 The LORD said to Moses, 2 "Speak to the entire assembly of Israelᵉ and say to them: 'Be holy because I, the LORD your God,ᶠ am holy.ᵍ

3 "'Each of you must respect his mother and father,ʰ and you must observe my Sabbaths.ⁱ I am the LORD your God.ʲ

4 "'Do not turn to idols or make gods of cast metal for yourselves.ᵏ I am the LORD your God.ˡ

5 "'When you sacrifice a fellowship offeringⁿ to the LORD, sacrifice it in such a way that it will be accepted on your behalf. 6 It shall be eaten on the day you sacrifice it or on the next day; anything left over until the third day must be burned up.ᵐ 7 If any of it is eaten on the third day, it is impure and will not be accepted.ⁿ 8 Whoever eats it will be held responsibleᵒ because he has desecrated what is holyᵖ to the LORD; that person must be cut off from his people.ᵠ

9 "'When you reap the harvest of your land, do not reap to the very edgesʳ of your field or gather the gleanings of your harvest.ˢ 10 Do not go over your vineyard a second timeᵗ or pick up the grapes that have fallen.ᵘ Leave them for the poor and the alien.ᵛ I am the LORD your God.

11 "'Do not steal.ʷ

"'Do not lie.ˣ

"'Do not deceive one another.ʸ

12 "'Do not swear falselyᶻ by my nameᵃ

and so profane the name of your God. I am the LORD.

13 " 'Do not defraud your neighbor or rob him.

" 'Do not hold back the wages of a hired man overnight.

14 " 'Do not curse the deaf or put a stumbling block in front of the blind, but fear your God. I am the LORD.

15 " 'Do not pervert justice; do not show partiality to the poor or favoritism to the great, but judge your neighbor fairly.

16 " 'Do not go about spreading slander among your people.

" 'Do not do anything that endangers your neighbor's life. I am the LORD.

17 " 'Do not hate your brother in your heart. Rebuke your neighbor frankly so you will not share in his guilt.

18 " 'Do not seek revenge or bear a grudge against one of your people, but love your neighbor as yourself. I am the LORD.

19 " 'Keep my decrees.

" 'Do not mate different kinds of animals.

" 'Do not plant your field with two kinds of seed.

" 'Do not wear clothing woven of two kinds of material.

20 " 'If a man sleeps with a woman who is a slave girl promised to another man but who has not been ransomed or given her freedom, there must be due punishment. Yet they are not to be put to death, because she had not been freed. 21 The man, however, must bring a ram to the entrance to the Tent of Meeting for a guilt offering to the LORD. 22 With the ram of the guilt offering the priest is to make atonement for him before the LORD for the sin he has committed, and his sin will be forgiven.

23 " 'When you enter the land and plant any kind of fruit tree, regard its fruit as forbidden. For three years you are to consider it forbidden; it must not be eaten. 24 In the fourth year all its fruit will be holy, an offering of praise to the LORD. 25 But in the fifth year you may eat its fruit. In this way your harvest will be increased. I am the LORD your God.

26 " 'Do not eat any meat with the blood still in it.

" 'Do not practice divination or sorcery.

27 " 'Do not cut the hair at the sides of your head or clip off the edges of your beard.

28 " 'Do not cut your bodies for the dead or put tattoo marks on yourselves. I am the LORD.

29 " 'Do not degrade your daughter by making her a prostitute, or the land will turn to prostitution and be filled with wickedness.

30 " 'Observe my Sabbaths and have reverence for my sanctuary. I am the LORD.

31 " 'Do not turn to mediums or seek out spiritists, for you will be defiled by them. I am the LORD your God.

32 " 'Rise in the presence of the aged, show respect for the elderly and revere your God. I am the LORD.

33 " 'When an alien lives with you in your land, do not mistreat him. 34 The alien living with you must be treated as one of your native-born. Love him as yourself, for you were aliens in Egypt. I am the LORD your God.

35 " 'Do not use dishonest standards when measuring length, weight or quantity. 36 Use honest scales and honest weights, an honest ephah and an honest hin. I am the LORD your God, who brought you out of Egypt.

37 " 'Keep all my decrees and all my laws and follow them. I am the LORD.' "

Punishments for Sin

20 The LORD said to Moses, 2 "Say to the Israelites: 'Any Israelite or any alien living in Israel who gives any of his children to Molech must be put to death. The people of the community are to stone him. 3 I will set my face against that man and I will cut him off from his people; for by giving his children to Molech, he has defiled my sanctuary and profaned my holy name. 4 If the people of the community close their eyes when that man gives one of his children to Molech and they fail to put him to death, 5 I will set my face against that man and his family and will cut off from their people both him and all who follow him in prostituting themselves to Molech.

⁶ " 'I will set my face against the person who turns to mediums and spiritists to prostitute himself by following them, and I will cut him off from his people.ᵏ

⁷ " 'Consecrate yourselves' and be holy,ᵐ because I am the LORD your God.ⁿ ⁸Keep my decreesᵒ and follow them. I am the LORD, who makes you holy.ˢᵖ

⁹ " 'If anyone curses his fatherᑫ or mother,ʳ he must be put to death.ˢ He has cursed his father or his mother, and his blood will be on his own head.ᵗ

¹⁰ " 'If a man commits adultery with another man's wifeᵘ—with the wife of his neighbor—both the adulterer and the adulteress must be put to death.ᵛ

¹¹ " 'If a man sleeps with his father's wife, he has dishonored his father.ʷ Both the man and the woman must be put to death; their blood will be on their own heads.ˣ

¹² " 'If a man sleeps with his daughter-in-law,ʸ both of them must be put to death. What they have done is a perversion; their blood will be on their own heads.

¹³ " 'If a man lies with a man as one lies with a woman, both of them have done what is detestable.ᶻ They must be put to death; their blood will be on their own heads.

¹⁴ " 'If a man marries both a woman and her mother,ᵃ it is wicked. Both he and they must be burned in the fire,ᵇ so that no wickedness will be among you.ᶜ

¹⁵ " 'If a man has sexual relations with an animal,ᵈ he must be put to death,ᵉ and you must kill the animal.

¹⁶ " 'If a woman approaches an animal to have sexual relations with it, kill both the woman and the animal. They must be put to death; their blood will be on their own heads.

¹⁷ " 'If a man marries his sister,ᶠ the daughter of either his father or his mother, and they have sexual relations, it is a disgrace. They must be cut off before the eyesᵍ of their people. He has dishonored his sister and will be held responsible.ʰ

¹⁸ " 'If a man lies with a woman during her monthly periodⁱ and has sexual relations with her, he has exposed the source of her flow, and she has also uncovered it. Both of them must be cut off from their people.ʲ

¹⁹ " 'Do not have sexual relations with the sister of either your mother or your father,ᵏ for that would dishonor a close relative; both of you would be held responsible.

²⁰ " 'If a man sleeps with his aunt,¹ he has dishonored his uncle. They will be held responsible; they will die childless.ᵐ

²¹ " 'If a man marries his brother's wife,ⁿ it is an act of impurity; he has dishonored his brother. They will be childless.ᵒ

²² " 'Keep all my decrees and lawsᵖ and follow them, so that the landᑫ where I am bringing you to live may not vomit you out. ²³You must not live according to the customs of the nationsʳ I am going to drive out before you.ˢ Because they did all these things, I abhorred them.ᵗ ²⁴But I said to you, "You will possess their land; I will give it to you as an inheritance, a land flowing with milk and honey."ᵘ I am the LORD your God, who has set you apart from the nations.ᵛ

²⁵ " 'You must therefore make a distinction between clean and unclean animals and between unclean and clean birds.ʷ Do not defile yourselves by any animal or bird or anything that moves along the ground—those which I have set apart as unclean for you. ²⁶You are to be holy to meᶠˣ because I, the LORD, am holy,ʸ and I have set you apart from the nationsᶻ to be my own.

²⁷ " 'A man or woman who is a mediumᵃ or spiritist among you must be put to death.ᵇ You are to stone them;ᶜ their blood will be on their own heads.' "

Rules for Priests

21 The LORD said to Moses, "Speak to the priests, the sons of Aaron,ᵈ and say to them: 'A priest must not make himself ceremonially uncleanᵉ for any of his people who die,ᶠ ²except for a close relative, such as his mother or father,ᵍ his son or daughter, his brother, ³or an unmarried sister who is dependent on him since she has no husband—for her he may make himself unclean.[h] ⁴He must not make himself unclean for people related to him by marriage,[u] and so defile himself.

⁵" 'Priests must not shave[i] their heads or shave off the edges of their beards[j] or cut their bodies.[k] ⁶They must be holy to their God[l] and must not profane the name of their God.[m] Because they present the offerings made to the LORD by fire,[n] the food of their God,[o] they are to be holy.[p]

⁷" 'They must not marry women defiled by prostitution or divorced from their husbands,[q] because priests are holy to their God.[r] ⁸Regard them as holy,[s] because they offer up the food of your God.[t] Consider them holy, because I the LORD am holy—I who make you holy.[v][u]

⁹" 'If a priest's daughter defiles herself by becoming a prostitute, she disgraces her father; she must be burned in the fire.[v]

¹⁰" 'The high priest, the one among his brothers who has had the anointing oil poured on his head[w] and who has been ordained to wear the priestly garments,[x] must not let his hair become unkempt[w] or tear his clothes.[y] ¹¹He must not enter a place where there is a dead body.[z] He must not make himself unclean,[a] even for his father or mother,[b] ¹²nor leave the sanctuary[c] of his God or desecrate it, because he has been dedicated by the anointing oil[d] of his God. I am the LORD.

¹³" 'The woman he marries must be a virgin.[e] ¹⁴He must not marry a widow, a divorced woman, or a woman defiled by prostitution, but only a virgin from his own people, ¹⁵so he will not defile his offspring among his people. I am the LORD, who makes him holy.[x] ' "

¹⁶The LORD said to Moses, ¹⁷"Say to Aaron: 'For the generations to come none of your descendants who has a defect[f] may come near to offer the food of his God.[g] ¹⁸No man who has any defect[h] may come near: no man who is blind[i] or lame,[j] disfigured or deformed; ¹⁹no man with a crippled foot or hand, ²⁰or who is hunchbacked or dwarfed, or who has any eye defect, or who has festering or running sores or damaged testicles.[k] ²¹No descendant of Aaron the priest who has any defect[l] is to come near to present the offerings made to the LORD by fire.[m] He has a defect; he must not come near to offer the food of his God.[n] ²²He may eat the most holy food of his God,[o] as well as the holy food; ²³yet because of his defect,[p] he must not go near the curtain or approach the altar, and so desecrate my sanctuary.[q] I am the LORD, who makes them holy.[r] ' "

²⁴So Moses told this to Aaron and his sons and to all the Israelites.

22 The LORD said to Moses, ²"Tell Aaron and his sons to treat with respect the sacred offerings[s] the Israelites consecrate to me, so they will not profane my holy name.[t] I am the LORD.[u]

³"Say to them: 'For the generations to come, if any of your descendants is ceremonially unclean and yet comes near the sacred offerings that the Israelites consecrate to the LORD,[v] that person must be cut off from my presence.[w] I am the LORD.

⁴" 'If a descendant of Aaron has an infectious skin disease[z] or a bodily discharge,[x] he may not eat the sacred offerings until he is cleansed. He will also be unclean if he touches something defiled by a corpse[y] or by anyone who has an emission of semen, ⁵or if he touches any crawling thing[z] that makes him unclean, or any person[a] who makes him unclean, whatever the uncleanness may be. ⁶The one who touches any such thing will be unclean[b] till evening.[c] He must not eat any of the sacred offerings unless he has bathed himself with water.[d] ⁷When the sun goes down, he will be clean, and after that he may eat the sacred offerings, for they are his food.[e] ⁸He must not eat anything found dead[f] or torn by wild animals,[g] and so become unclean[h] through it. I am the LORD.[i]

⁹" 'The priests are to keep my requirements[j] so that they do not become guilty[k] and die[l] for treating them with contempt. I am the LORD, who makes them holy.[a][m]

¹⁰" 'No one outside a priest's family may eat the sacred offering, nor may the guest of a priest or his hired worker eat it.[n] ¹¹But if a priest buys a slave with money, or if a slave is born in his house-

---

[u] 4 Or *unclean as a leader among his people*   [v] 8 Or *who sanctify you*; or *who set you apart as holy*   [w] 10 Or *not uncover his head*   [x] 15 Or *who sanctifies him*; or *who sets him apart as holy*   [y] 23 Or *who sanctifies them*; or *who sets them apart as holy*   [z] 4 Traditionally *leprosy*; the Hebrew word was used for various diseases affecting the skin—not necessarily leprosy.   [a] 9 Or *who sanctifies them*; or *who sets them apart as holy*; also in verse 16

LEVITICUS 22:12

hold, that slave may eat his food.º ¹²If a priest's daughter marries anyone other than a priest, she may not eat any of the sacred contributions. ¹³But if a priest's daughter becomes a widow or is divorced, yet has no children, and she returns to live in her father's house as in her youth, she may eat of her father's food. No unauthorized person, however, may eat any of it.

¹⁴" 'If anyone eats a sacred offering by mistake,ᵖ he must make restitution to the priest for the offering and add a fifth of the valueᵠ to it. ¹⁵The priests must not desecrate the sacred offeringsʳ the Israelites present to the Lordˢ ¹⁶by allowing them to eatᵗ the sacred offerings and so bring upon them guiltᵘ requiring payment.ᵛ I am the Lord, who makes them holy.ʷ' "

Unacceptable Sacrifices

¹⁷The Lord said to Moses, ¹⁸"Speak to Aaron and his sons and to all the Israelites and say to them: 'If any of you—either an Israelite or an alien living in Israelˣ—presents a giftʸ for a burnt offering to the Lord, either to fulfill a vowᶻ or as a freewill offering,ᵃ ¹⁹you must present a male without defectᵇ from the cattle, sheep or goats in order that it may be accepted on your behalf.ᶜ ²⁰Do not bring anything with a defect,ᵈ because it will not be accepted on your behalf.ᵉ ²¹When anyone brings from the herd or flockᶠ a fellowship offeringᵇ ᵍ to the Lord to fulfill a special vow or as a freewill offering,ʰ it must be without defect or blemishⁱ to be acceptable.ʲ ²²Do not offer to the Lord the blind, the injured or the maimed, or anything with warts or festering or running sores. Do not place any of these on the altar as an offering made to the Lord by fire. ²³You may, however, present as a freewill offering an oxᶜ or a sheep that is deformed or stunted, but it will not be accepted in fulfillment of a vow. ²⁴You must not offer to the Lord an animal whose testicles are

D Lev 17:11-14 ◀ ▶ Lev 23:4-5

22:11 ºGe 17:5; Ex 12:44
22:14 ᵖS Lev 4:2; ᵠLev 5:15
22:15 ʳS Lev 19:8; ˢNu 18:32
22:16 ᵗNu 18:11; ᵘS Ex 28:38; ᵛver 9 ʷLev 20:8
22:18 ˣNu 15:16; 19:10; Jos 8:33; ʸS Lev 1:2 ᶻver 21; ᵃS Ge 28:20; Nu 15:8; Ps 22:25; 76:11; 116:18 ᵇS Lev 7:16
22:19 ᵇS Lev 1:3; 21:18-21; Nu 28:11; Dt 15:21 ᶜS Lev 1:2
22:20 ᵈS Lev 1:3; Dt 15:21; 17:1; Eze 43:23; 45:18; 46:6; Mal 1:8; Heb 9:14; 1Pe 1:19 ᵉS Ex 28:38
22:21 ᶠS Lev 1:2 ᵍS Ex 32:6; ʰS Lev 3:6 ʰS Lev 7:16 ⁱS Ex 12:5; Mal 1:14 ʲAm 4:5
22:24 ᵏS Lev 21:20
22:25 ˡS Lev 21:6 ᵐS Lev 1:3; S 3:1; Nu 19:2
22:27 ⁿS Lev 1:3 ºS Ex 22:30 ᵖS Ex 22:30 ᵠS Ex 28:38
22:28 ʳDt 22:6,7
22:29 ˢS Lev 7:12
22:30 ᵗLev 7:15 ᵘLev 11:44
22:31 ᵛDt 4:2,40; Ps 105:45 ʷS Ex 22:31
22:32 ˣLev 18:21 ʸS Lev 10:3 ᶻLev 20:8
22:33 ᵃS Ex 6:6 ᵇS Ge 17:7
23:2 ᶜver 4,37,44; Nu 29:39; Eze 44:24; Col 2:16 ᵈver 21,27
23:3 ᵉEx 20:9 ᶠS Ex 20:10; Heb 4:9,10 ᵍver 7, 21,35; Nu 28:26

bruised, crushed, torn or cut.ᵏ You must not do this in your own land, ²⁵and you must not accept such animals from the hand of a foreigner and offer them as the food of your God.ˡ They will not be accepted on your behalf, because they are deformed and have defects.ᵐ' "

²⁶The Lord said to Moses, ²⁷"When a calf, a lamb or a goatⁿ is born, it is to remain with its mother for seven days.º From the eighth dayᵖ on, it will be acceptableᵠ as an offering made to the Lord by fire. ²⁸Do not slaughter a cow or a sheep and its young on the same day.ʳ ²⁹When you sacrifice a thank offeringˢ to the Lord, sacrifice it in such a way that it will be accepted on your behalf. ³⁰It must be eaten that same day; leave none of it till morning.ᵗ I am the Lord.ᵘ

³¹"Keepᵛ my commands and follow them.ʷ I am the Lord. ³²Do not profane my holy name.ˣ I must be acknowledged as holy by the Israelites.ʸ I am the Lord, who makesᵈ you holyᵉᶻ ³³and who brought you out of Egyptᵃ to be your God.ᵇ I am the Lord."

23

The Lord said to Moses, ²"Speak to the Israelites and say to them: 'These are my appointed feasts,ᶜ the appointed feasts of the Lord, which you are to proclaim as sacred assemblies.ᵈ

The Sabbath

³" 'There are six days when you may work,ᵉ but the seventh day is a Sabbath of rest,ᶠ a day of sacred assembly. You are not to do any work;ᵍ wherever you live, it is a Sabbath to the Lord.

The Passover and Unleavened Bread

23:4-8pp — Ex 12:14-20; Nu 28:16-25; Dt 16:1-8

⁴" 'These are the Lord's appointed feasts, the sacred assemblies you are to

S Lev 20:26 ◀ ▶ Nu 14:22-25
D Lev 22:17-25 ◀ ▶ Lev 23:26-32

ᵇ 21 Traditionally *peace offering* ᶜ 23 The Hebrew word can include both male and female. ᵈ 32 Or *made* ᵉ 32 Or *who sanctifies you*; or *who sets you apart as holy*

23:2-4 "The Lord's appointed feasts" (23:4) consisted of seven religious celebrations that the Israelites were to observe every year. The apostle Paul admonished young believers to beware of legalism when he spoke of these special days as "a shadow of the things that were to come" (Col 2:17). Though these holy days were commanded, they were intended to be celebrations of God's faithfulness in the past and promised blessing in the future.

proclaim at their appointed times:[h] **⁵The LORD's Passover**[i] **begins at twilight on the fourteenth day of the first month.**[j] ⁶On the fifteenth day of that month the LORD's Feast of Unleavened Bread[k] begins; for seven days[l] you must eat bread made without yeast. ⁷On the first day hold a sacred assembly[m] and do no regular work. ⁸For seven days present an offering made to the LORD by fire.[n] And on the seventh day hold a sacred assembly and do no regular work.' "

Firstfruits

⁹The LORD said to Moses, ¹⁰"Speak to the Israelites and say to them: 'When you enter the land I am going to give you[o] and you reap its harvest,[p] bring to the priest a sheaf[q] of the first grain you harvest.[r] ¹¹He is to wave the sheaf before the LORD[s] so it will be accepted[t] on your behalf; the priest is to wave it on the day after the Sabbath. ¹²On the day you wave the sheaf, you must sacrifice as a burnt offering to the LORD a lamb a year old[u] without defect,[v] ¹³together with its grain offering[w] of two-tenths of an ephah[/x] of fine flour mixed with oil—an offering made to the LORD by fire, a pleasing aroma—and its drink offering[y] of a quarter of a hin[g] of wine.[z] ¹⁴You must not eat any bread, or roasted or new grain,[a] until the very day you bring this offering to your God.[b] This is to be a lasting ordinance for the generations to come,[c] wherever you live.[d]

Feast of Weeks

23:15–22pp — Nu 28:26–31; Dt 16:9–12

¹⁵" 'From the day after the Sabbath, the

---

f 13 That is, probably about 4 quarts (about 4.5 liters); also in verse 17
g 13 That is, probably about 1 quart (about 1 liter)

23:5 The Passover was the first of Israel's major feasts. It was celebrated on the fourteenth day of the first month (Nisan/Abib) of Israel's religious year. Significant anniversaries in the spiritual and national life of Israel have occurred on the Passover.
  1. The first Passover supper in Egypt. On this night God sent the tenth plague on Egypt—the death of "all the firstborn in Egypt" (Ex 12:29). Yet God passed over the homes of his people who had placed lamb's blood on the lintels of their doors. The next morning the Israelites were set free from Egypt (see Ex 12:41).
  2. The first Passover in Canaan. None of the male children born during the forty years of the wilderness wandering had been circumcised. Yet God's law prohibited the uncircumcised from celebrating the Passover (see Ex 12:48). Joshua ordered the circumcision of all the males of Israel and then "on the evening of the fourteenth day of the month . . . celebrated the Passover" (Jos 5:10). The very next day the Israelites ate food from the promised land.
  3. The return from captivity. After the Jews returned to Jerusalem under the decree of Cyrus the Great in 538 B.C., they rebuilt the temple, rededicated it, cleansed themselves and celebrated the Passover (see Ezr 6:19–22).
  4. The Last Supper. Jesus and the disciples met in an upper room to celebrate the Passover. While there, Jesus invoked the words of the new covenant, saying, "This is my body given for you; do this in remembrance of me" (Lk 22:19).

For a full examination of the phenomenon of Biblical anniversaries, see the article on the Biblical Anniversaries, see the article "The Biblical Anniversaries of Israel," p. 170.

23:6–8 Although it begins at almost the same time, the Feast of Unleavened Bread is distinct from the Passover. Israel was required to eat bread made without yeast, hold several assemblies and make several designated offerings for this seven-day celebration. Three important anniversaries in the life of Israel have occurred during the Feast of Unleavened Bread:
  1. The exodus from Egypt. The morning after God's destroying angel had passed over the Israelites' homes the Israelites left Egypt. In their haste, "with the dough they had brought from Egypt, they baked cakes of unleavened bread. The dough was without yeast because they had been driven out of Egypt and did not have time to prepare food for themselves" (Ex 12:39).
  2. The crucifixion of Christ. Jesus referred to himself as "the bread of life" (Jn 6:35). He was crucified, died and was buried during the Feast of Unleavened Bread.
  3. The fall of Massada. A nearly impregnable fortress commanded by Jewish resistance fighters was located at Massada. Flavius Josephus, a Jewish historian, records that this fortress finally fell to Roman soldiers "on the fifteenth day of the month Nisan" in A.D. 72—the first day of the Feast of Unleavened Bread.

23:9–11 The Feast of Firstfruits was celebrated on the sixteenth day of the first month (Nisan/Abib). This feast recognized the Lord's bounty in the land with a wave offering, burnt offering and grain offering. Manna also stopped falling on this feast day after the Israelites enjoyed some of the fruit of the promised land (see Jos 5:12). The NT writers also make reference to firstfruits (see Ro 8:23; 1Co 15:20).

23:15–16 The Feast of Weeks was one of the three annual feasts for which all males of Israel were

day you brought the sheaf of the wave offering, count off seven full weeks. ¹⁶Count off fifty days up to the day after the seventh Sabbath,ᵉ and then present an offering of new grain to the LORD. ¹⁷From wherever you live, bring two loavesᶠ made of two-tenths of an ephah of fine flour, baked with yeast, as a wave offering of firstfruitsᵍ to the LORD. ¹⁸Present with this bread seven male lambs, each a year old and without defect, one young bull and two rams. They will be a burnt offering to the LORD, together with their grain offerings and drink offeringsʰ—an offering made by fire, an aroma pleasing to the LORD. ¹⁹Then sacrifice one male goat for a sin offering and two lambs, each a year old, for a fellowship offering.ʰ ²⁰The priest is to wave the two lambs before the LORD as a wave offering,ⁱ together with the bread of the firstfruits. They are a sacred offering to the LORD for the priest. ²¹On that same day you are to proclaim a sacred assemblyʲ and do no regular work.ᵏ This is to be a lasting ordinance for the generations to come, wherever you live.

²²" 'When you reap the harvestˡ of your land, do not reap to the very edges of your field or gather the gleanings of your harvest.ᵐ Leave them for the poor and the alien.ⁿ I am the LORD your God.' "

Feast of Trumpets
23:23–25pp — Nu 29:1–6

²³The LORD said to Moses, ²⁴"Say to the

23:16 ᵉAc 2:1; 20:16
23:17 ᶠS ver 13; ᵍS Ex 34:22
23:18 ʰver 13; Ex 29:41; 30:9; 37:16; Jer 19:13; 44:18
23:20 ⁱS Ex 29:24
23:21 ʲS ver 2; Ex 32:5 ᵏS ver 3
23:22 ˡS Lev 19:9 ᵐS Lev 19:10; Dt 24:19-21; Ru 2:15 ⁿRu 2:2
23:24 ᵒver 27,36; Ezr 3:1 ᵖLev 25:9; Nu 10:9,10; 29:1; 31:6; 2Ki 11:14; 2Ch 13:12; Ps 98:6
23:25 ᑫver 21 ʳS Lev 1:9
23:27 ˢS Lev 16:29 ᵗS Ex 30:10 ᵘS ver 2,S 24
23:28 ᵛver 31
23:29 ʷGe 17:14; Lev 7:20; Nu 5:2
23:30 ˣS Lev 20:3
23:31 ʸLev 3:17
23:32 ᶻS Lev 16:31 ᵃNe 13:19

Israelites: 'On the first day of the seventh month you are to have a day of rest, a sacred assemblyᵒ commemorated with trumpet blasts.ᵖ ²⁵Do no regular work,ᑫ but present an offering made to the LORD by fire.ʳ' "

Day of Atonement
23:26–32pp — Lev 16:2–34; Nu 29:7–11

²⁶The LORD said to Moses, ²⁷"The tenth day of this seventh monthˢ is the Day of Atonement.ᵗ Hold a sacred assemblyᵘ and deny yourselves,ⁱ and present an offering made to the LORD by fire. ²⁸Do no workᵛ on that day, because it is the Day of Atonement, when atonement is made for you before the LORD your God. ²⁹Anyone who does not deny himself on that day must be cut off from his people.ʷ ³⁰I will destroy from among his peopleˣ anyone who does any work on that day. ³¹You shall do no work at all. This is to be a lasting ordinanceʸ for the generations to come, wherever you live. ³²It is a sabbath of restᶻ for you, and you must deny yourselves. From the evening of the ninth day of the month until the following evening you are to observe your sabbath."ᵃ **D**

D Lev 23:4–5 ◄ ► Nu 8:17–18

ʰ19 Traditionally *peace offering* ⁱ27 Or *and fast*; also in verses 29 and 32

---

required to gather together (see Ex 23:14–19). Celebrated fifty days after the Feast of Firstfruits, the Feast of Weeks was a festival of joy and thanksgiving to the Lord for the blessing of the harvest. Included in the celebration were mandatory and voluntary offerings, including the firstfruits of the wheat harvest. This annual feast also served in part as a remembrance of the giving of the law upon Mt. Sinai fifty days after the Israelites left Egypt.

In the NT, the Feast of Weeks corresponds to the day of Pentecost. Fifty days after Christ's death on the cross God poured out his Spirit upon the apostles (see Ac 2:1). On that day all Jewish males were gathered together in Jerusalem to celebrate the Feast of Weeks (see Ac 2:5). The disciples were given extraordinary spiritual power and ability to witness to those assembled in Jerusalem and "about three thousand were added to their number that day" (Ac 2:41).

23:24–25 The Feast of Trumpets was celebrated on the first day of the seventh month (Tishri). Later called Rosh Hashanah, this celebration was Israel's New Year's Day, the first day of the civil year. This day was a time of rest commemorated with trumpet blasts and sacrifices intended to present Israel before the Lord. The Feast of Trumpets also figures in the historical anniversaries of the Jews. When the exiles returned from Babylon to Jerusalem, Ezra read the law to them on Rosh Hashanah, marking a reaffirmation of Israel's covenant with God.

23:27–32 Known also as Yom Kippur, the Day of Atonement was the holiest day of the Israelite year. On this day of rest, fasting and sacrifice the Israelites mourned and made atonement for their sins, cleansing the priests, the people and the tabernacle. The high priest would enter the holy place and sprinkle the blood of the sacrifice before the mercy seat. The blood sprinkled on the Day of Atonement prefigured the ultimate sacrifice of God's only begotten Son who "entered the Most Holy Place once for all by his own blood, having obtained eternal redemption" (Heb 9:12).

Feast of Tabernacles

23:33–43pp — Nu 29:12–39; Dt 16:13–17

³³The LORD said to Moses, ³⁴"Say to the Israelites: 'On the fifteenth day of the seventh month the LORD's Feast of Tabernacles begins, and it lasts for seven days. ³⁵The first day is a sacred assembly; do no regular work. ³⁶For seven days present offerings made to the LORD by fire, and on the eighth day hold a sacred assembly and present an offering made to the LORD by fire. It is the closing assembly; do no regular work.

³⁷("'These are the LORD's appointed feasts, which you are to proclaim as sacred assemblies for bringing offerings made to the LORD by fire—the burnt offerings and grain offerings, sacrifices and drink offerings required for each day. ³⁸These offerings are in addition to those for the LORD's Sabbaths and/ in addition to your gifts and whatever you have vowed and all the freewill offerings you give to the LORD.)

³⁹"'So beginning with the fifteenth day of the seventh month, after you have gathered the crops of the land, celebrate the festival to the LORD for seven days; the first day is a day of rest, and the eighth day also is a day of rest. ⁴⁰On the first day you are to take choice fruit from the trees, and palm fronds, leafy branches and poplars, and rejoice before the LORD your God for seven days. ⁴¹Celebrate this as a festival to the LORD for seven days each year. This is to be a lasting ordinance for the generations to come; celebrate it in the seventh month. ⁴²Live in booths for seven days: All native-born Israelites are to live in booths ⁴³so your descendants will know that I had the Israelites live in booths when I brought them out of Egypt. I am the LORD your God.'"

⁴⁴So Moses announced to the Israelites the appointed feasts of the LORD.

A Ex 34:10–12 ◀ ▶ Lev 25:8–17

Oil and Bread Set Before the LORD

24:1–3pp — Ex 27:20–21

24 The LORD said to Moses, ²"Command the Israelites to bring you clear oil of pressed olives for the light so that the lamps may be kept burning continually. ³Outside the curtain of the Testimony in the Tent of Meeting, Aaron is to tend the lamps before the LORD from evening till morning, continually. This is to be a lasting ordinance for the generations to come. ⁴The lamps on the pure gold lampstand before the LORD must be tended continually.

⁵"Take fine flour and bake twelve loaves of bread, using two-tenths of an ephah for each loaf. ⁶Set them in two rows, six in each row, on the table of pure gold before the LORD. ⁷Along each row put some pure incense as a memorial portion to represent the bread and to be an offering made to the LORD by fire. ⁸This bread is to be set out before the LORD regularly, Sabbath after Sabbath, on behalf of the Israelites, as a lasting covenant. ⁹It belongs to Aaron and his sons, who are to eat it in a holy place, because it is a most holy part of their regular share of the offerings made to the LORD by fire."

A Blasphemer Stoned

¹⁰Now the son of an Israelite mother and an Egyptian father went out among the Israelites, and a fight broke out in the camp between him and an Israelite. ¹¹The son of the Israelite woman blasphemed the Name with a curse; so they brought him to Moses. (His mother's name was Shelomith, the daughter of Dibri the Danite.) ¹²They put him in custody until the will of the LORD should be made clear to them.

¹³Then the LORD said to Moses: ¹⁴"Take the blasphemer outside the camp. All

j 38 Or *These feasts are in addition to the LORD's Sabbaths, and these offerings are*   *k 5* That is, probably about 4 quarts (about 4.5 liters)

23:34, 39 The Feast of Tabernacles was the last of the three annual celebrations. Lasting seven days, this celebration, also called the Feast of Booths, memorialized the journey from Egypt to Canaan and was characterized by offering sacrifices and by the building of small booths or tents made of branches. During this harvest feast people gave thanks for the productivity of Canaan. In postexilic times the Jews who returned from Babylon responded to Ezra's reading about the Feast of Tabernacles by celebrating it with great joy (see Ne 8:14–18). In fact, Scripture records that "from the days of Joshua son of Nun until that day, the Israelites had not celebrated it like this. And their joy was very great" (Ne 8:17).

Old Testament Feasts and Other Sacred Days

NAME	OLD TESTAMENT REFERENCES	TIME	DESCRIPTION	NEW TESTAMENT REFERENCES
Sabbath	Exodus 20:8-11; 31:12-17; Leviticus 23:3; Deuteronomy 5:12-15	7th day	Day of rest; no work	Matthew 12:1-14; Mark 2:23–3:5; Luke 4:16-30; 6:1-10; 13:10-16; 14:1-5; John 5:1-15; 9:1-34; Acts 13:14-48; 17:2; 18:4; Hebrews 4:1-11
Sabbath Year	Exodus 23:10-11; Leviticus 25:1-7	7th year	Year of rest; fallow fields	
Year of Jubilee	Leviticus 25:8-55; 27:17-24; Numbers 36:4	50th year	Canceled debts; liberation of slaves and indentured servants; land returned to original family owners	
Passover	Exodus 12:1-14; Leviticus 23:5; Numbers 9:1-14; 28:16; Deuteronomy 16:1-7	1st month (Abib) 14	Slaying and eating a lamb, together with bitter herbs and bread made without yeast in every household	Matthew 26:1-2,17-29; Mark 14:12-26; Luke 22:7-38; John 2:13-25; 11:55-56; 13:1-30; 1 Corinthians 5:7
Unleavened Bread	Exodus 12:15-20; 13:3-10; 23:15; Leviticus 23:6-8; Numbers 28:17-25; Deuteronomy 16:3-4,8	1st month (Abib) 15-21	Eating bread made without yeast; holding several assemblies; making designated offerings	Matthew 26:17; Mark 14:1,12; Luke 22:1,7; Acts 12:3; 20:6; 1 Corinthians 5:6-8
Firstfruits	Leviticus 23:9-14	1st month (Abib) 16	Presenting a sheaf of the first of the barley harvest as a wave offering; making a burnt offering and a grain offering	Romans 8:23; 1 Corinthians 15:20-23
Weeks (Pentecost) (Harvest)	Exodus 23:16a; 34:22a; Leviticus 23:15-21; Numbers 28:26-31; Deuteronomy 16:9-12	3rd month (Sivan) 6	A festival of joy; mandatory and voluntary offerings, including the firstfruits of the wheat harvest	Acts 2:1-41; 20:16; 1 Corinthians 16:8
Trumpets (Later: Rosh Hashanah— New Year's Day)	Leviticus 23:23-25; Numbers 29:1-6	7th month (Tishri) 1	An assembly on a day of rest commemorated with trumpet blasts and sacrifices	
Day of Atonement (Yom Kippur)	Leviticus 16; 23:26-32; Numbers 29:7-11	7th month (Tishri) 10	A day of rest, fasting and sacrifices of atonement for priests and people and atonement for the tabernacle and altar	Acts 27:9; Romans 3:24-26; Hebrews 9:1-14,23-26; 10:19-22
Tabernacles (Booths) (Ingathering)	Exodus 23:16b; 34:22b; Leviticus 23:33-36,39-43; Numbers 29:12-34; Deuteronomy 16:13-15	7th month (Tishri) 15-21	A week of celebration for the harvest; living in booths and offering sacrifices	John 7:2-37
Sacred Assembly	Leviticus 23:36; Numbers 29:35-38	7th month (Tishri) 22	A day of convocation, rest and offering sacrifices	John 7:37-44
Dedication		9th month	A commemoration of the purification of the temple in the Maccabean era (166-160 b.c.)	John 10:22-39
Purim	Esther 9:18-32	12th month (Adar) 14,15	A day of joy and feasting and giving presents	

those who heard him are to lay their hands on his head, and the entire assembly is to stone him.[j] [15]Say to the Israelites: 'If anyone curses his God,[k] he will be held responsible;[l] [16]anyone who blasphemes[m] the name of the LORD must be put to death.[n] The entire assembly must stone him. Whether an alien or native-born, when he blasphemes the Name, he must be put to death.

[17]" 'If anyone takes the life of a human being, he must be put to death.[o] [18]Anyone who takes the life of someone's animal must make restitution[p]—life for life. [19]If anyone injures his neighbor, whatever he has done must be done to him: [20]fracture for fracture, eye for eye, tooth for tooth.[q] As he has injured the other, so he is to be injured. [21]Whoever kills an animal must make restitution,[r] but whoever kills a man must be put to death.[s] [22]You are to have the same law for the alien[t] and the native-born.[u] I am the LORD your God.' "

[23]Then Moses spoke to the Israelites, and they took the blasphemer outside the camp and stoned him.[v] The Israelites did as the LORD commanded Moses.

The Sabbath Year

25 The LORD said to Moses on Mount Sinai,[w] [2]"Speak to the Israelites and say to them: 'When you enter the land I am going to give you, the land itself must observe a sabbath to the LORD. [3]For six years sow your fields, and for six years prune your vineyards and gather their crops.[x] [4]But in the seventh year the land is to have a sabbath of rest,[y] a sabbath to the LORD. Do not sow your fields or prune your vineyards.[z] [5]Do not reap what grows of itself[a] or harvest the grapes[b] of your untended vines.[c] The land is to have a year of rest. [6]Whatever the land yields during the sabbath year[d] will be food for you—for yourself, your manservant and maidservant, and the hired worker and temporary resident who live among you, [7]as well as for your livestock and the wild animals[e] in your land. Whatever the land produces may be eaten.

The Year of Jubilee

25:8–38Ref — Dt 15:1–11
25:39–55Ref — Ex 21:2–11; Dt 15:12–18

[8]" 'Count off seven sabbaths of years— A

A Lev 23:33–36 ◄ ► Nu 23:24

25:2–6 When Israel conquered the promised land, God commanded them to let the land stay unplowed every seventh year. This Sabbath for the land actually allowed the ground to rest and replenished some of the nutrients taken out of the soil during the planting and harvesting years. Some crops would self-seed and sprout on their own, providing enough food for the people during the Sabbath year (25:6).

25:8–10, 23 Every fifty years God commanded Israel to allow the land to stay unplowed, to return lands to their former owners and to free all Hebrew slaves. This Year of Jubilee was to be observed after seven Sabbath years. As in the regular Sabbath years, the unplowed ground would have a rest. God promised to provide enough extra food in the sixth year to carry people through the Year of Jubilee and through the succeeding years "until the harvest of the ninth year comes in" (25:22).

The return of lands and property was also an important part of the Year of Jubilee. Since God had divided the land among the twelve tribes as their inheritance, God opposed the permanent transfer of land from one person to another. The Year of Jubilee required that all land and property sold to a creditor be transferred back to the original family. By this arrangement, land and property were not sold permanently; the land was merely leased, and all leases expired in the jubilee year. This arrangement reinforced in the Israelites' mind God's control of the land (25:23). He was the owner; they were the tenants.

In addition, if any Israelites had sold themselves to a fellow Israelite because of crushing debt, they were to be treated as hired hands and not as slaves. Only people from pagan nations could be kept as slaves (see 25:44). In the Year of Jubilee any Israelite people sold into servitude were automatically freed and returned to their families (see 25:54).

Moses warned the people to follow these Sabbath laws. Blessing, safety and productivity were promised for obedience. Yet if the people did not obey and give the land its Sabbath, they would be removed from the land and then "all the time that it lies desolate, the land will have the rest it did not have during the sabbaths you lived in it" (26:35). Apparently the Israelites did not follow these Sabbath regulations for the land (see 2Ch 36:21). Jeremiah's words ring with the Lord's anger: "You have not obeyed me; you have not proclaimed freedom for your fellow countrymen. So I now proclaim 'freedom' for you, declares the LORD— 'freedom' to fall by the sword, plague and famine. I will make you abhorrent to all the kingdoms of the earth" (Jer 34:17). In return for their disobedience to the law of the Sabbaths of the land Israel endured seventy years of captivity in Babylon.

seven times seven years—so that the seven sabbaths of years amount to a period of forty-nine years. ⁹Then have the trumpet^f sounded everywhere on the tenth day of the seventh month;^g on the Day of Atonement^h sound the trumpet throughout your land. ¹⁰Consecrate the fiftieth year and proclaim liberty^i throughout the land to all its inhabitants. It shall be a jubilee^j for you; each one of you is to return to his family property^k and each to his own clan. ¹¹The fiftieth year shall be a jubilee^l for you; do not sow and do not reap what grows of itself or harvest the untended vines.^m ¹²For it is a jubilee and is to be holy for you; eat only what is taken directly from the fields.

¹³" 'In this Year of Jubilee^n everyone is to return to his own property.

¹⁴" 'If you sell land to one of your countrymen or buy any from him, do not take advantage of each other.^o ¹⁵You are to buy from your countryman on the basis of the number of years^p since the Jubilee. And he is to sell to you on the basis of the number of years left for harvesting crops. ¹⁶When the years are many, you are to increase the price, and when the years are few, you are to decrease the price,^q because what he is really selling you is the number of crops. ¹⁷Do not take advantage of each other,^r but fear your God.^s I am the LORD your God.^t

¹⁸" 'Follow my decrees and be careful to obey my laws,^u and you will live safely in the land.^v ¹⁹Then the land will yield its fruit,^w and you will eat your fill and live there in safety.^x ²⁰You may ask, "What will we eat in the seventh year^y if we do not plant or harvest our crops?" ²¹I will send you such a blessing^z in the sixth year that the land will yield enough for three years.^a ²²While you plant during the eighth year, you will eat from the old crop and will continue to eat from it until the harvest of the ninth year comes in.^b

²³" 'The land^c must not be sold permanently, because the land is mine^d and you are but aliens^e and my tenants. ²⁴Throughout the country that you hold as a possession, you must provide for the redemption^f of the land.

S *Ex 11:7* ◀ ▶ *Lev 26:6*
B *Ex 23:26* ◀ ▶ *Lev 26:3–5*
F *Ex 23:25* ◀ ▶ *Lev 26:5*

25:9 f Lev 23:24; Nu 10:8; Jos 6:4; Jdg 3:27; 7:16; 1Sa 13:3; Isa 27:13; Zec 9:14
g S Lev 16:29
h S Ex 30:10
25:10 i Isa 61:1; Jer 34:8,15,17; S Lk 4:19 j ver 11, 28,50; Lev 27:17, 21; Nu 36:4; Eze 46:17 k ver 27
25:11 l S ver 10 m S ver 5
25:13 n ver 10
25:14 o S Lev 19:13; 1Sa 12:3,4; 1Co 6:8
25:15 p ver 27; Lev 27:18,23
25:16 q ver 27,51, 52
25:17 r S Lev 19:13; Job 31:16; Pr 22:22; Jer 7:5,6; 21:12; 22:3,15; Zec 7:9-10; 1Th 4:6 s S Lev 19:14 t S Lev 19:32
25:18 u S Ge 26:5 v ver 19; Lev 26:4, 5; Dt 12:10; 33:28; Job 5:22; Ps 4:8; Jer 23:6; 30:10; 32:37; 33:16; Eze 28:26; 34:25; 38:14
25:19 w Lev 26:4; Dt 11:14; 28:12; Isa 55:10 x S ver 18
25:20 y S ver 4
25:21 z Dt 28:8, 12; Ps 133:3; 134:3; 147:13; Hag 2:19; Mal 3:10
a S Ex 16:5
25:22 b Lev 26:10
25:23 c Nu 36:7; 1Ki 21:3; Eze 46:18 d Ex 19:5 e S Ge 23:4; S Heb 11:13
25:24 f ver 29,48; Ru 4:7
25:25 g ver 48; Ru 2:20; Jer 32:7 h Lev 27:13,19,31; Ru 4:4
25:26 i ver 49
25:27 j S ver 15 k ver 10
25:28 l Lev 27:24 m S ver 10
25:32 n Nu 35:1-8; Jos 21:2
25:34 o Nu 35:2-5; Eze 48:14
25:35 p Dt 24:14, 15 q Dt 15:8; Ps 37:21,26; Pr 21:26; Lk 6:35
25:36 r S Ex 22:25; Jer 15:10 s S Lev 19:32
25:37 t S Ex 22:25
25:38 u S Ge 10:19 v S Ge 17:7

²⁵" 'If one of your countrymen becomes poor and sells some of his property, his nearest relative^g is to come and redeem^h what his countryman has sold. ²⁶If, however, a man has no one to redeem it for him but he himself prospers^i and acquires sufficient means to redeem it, ²⁷he is to determine the value for the years^j since he sold it and refund the balance to the man to whom he sold it; he can then go back to his own property.^k ²⁸But if he does not acquire the means to repay him, what he sold will remain in the possession of the buyer until the Year of Jubilee. It will be returned^l in the Jubilee, and he can then go back to his property.^m

²⁹" 'If a man sells a house in a walled city, he retains the right of redemption a full year after its sale. During that time he may redeem it. ³⁰If it is not redeemed before a full year has passed, the house in the walled city shall belong permanently to the buyer and his descendants. It is not to be returned in the Jubilee. ³¹But houses in villages without walls around them are to be considered as open country. They can be redeemed, and they are to be returned in the Jubilee.

³²" 'The Levites always have the right to redeem their houses in the Levitical towns,^n which they possess. ³³So the property of the Levites is redeemable—that is, a house sold in any town they hold—and is to be returned in the Jubilee, because the houses in the towns of the Levites are their property among the Israelites. ³⁴But the pastureland belonging to their towns must not be sold; it is their permanent possession.^o

³⁵" 'If one of your countrymen becomes poor^p and is unable to support himself among you, help him^q as you would an alien or a temporary resident, so he can continue to live among you. ³⁶Do not take interest^r of any kind^l from him, but fear your God,^s so that your countryman may continue to live among you. ³⁷You must not lend him money at interest^t or sell him food at a profit. ³⁸I am the LORD your God, who brought you out of Egypt to give you the land of Canaan^u and to be your God.^v

l 36 Or take excessive interest; similarly in verse 37

³⁹ 'If one of your countrymen becomes poor among you and sells himself to you, do not make him work as a slave.ʷ ⁴⁰He is to be treated as a hired workerˣ or a temporary resident among you; he is to work for you until the Year of Jubilee. ⁴¹Then he and his children are to be released, and he will go back to his own clan and to the propertyʸ of his forefathers.ᶻ ⁴²Because the Israelites are my servants, whom I brought out of Egypt,ᵃ they must not be sold as slaves. ⁴³Do not rule over them ruthlessly,ᵇ but fear your God.ᶜ

⁴⁴ 'Your male and female slaves are to come from the nations around you; from them you may buy slaves. ⁴⁵You may also buy some of the temporary residents living among you and members of their clans born in your country, and they will become your property. ⁴⁶You can will them to your children as inherited property and can make them slaves for life, but you must not rule over your fellow Israelites ruthlessly.

⁴⁷ 'If an alien or a temporary resident among you becomes rich and one of your countrymen becomes poor and sells himselfᵈ to the alien living among you or to a member of the alien's clan, ⁴⁸he retains the right of redemptionᵉ after he has sold himself. One of his relativesᶠ may redeem him: ⁴⁹An uncle or a cousin or any blood relative in his clan may redeem him. Or if he prospers,ᵍ he may redeem himself. ⁵⁰He and his buyer are to count the time from the year he sold himself up to the Year of Jubilee.ʰ The price for his release is to be based on the rate paid to a hired manⁱ for that number of years. ⁵¹If many years remain, he must pay for his redemption a larger share of the price paid for him. ⁵²If only a few years remain until the Year of Jubilee, he is to compute that and pay for his redemption accordingly.ʲ ⁵³He is to be treated as a man hired from year to year; you must see to it that his owner does not rule over him ruthlessly.ᵏ

⁵⁴ 'Even if he is not redeemed in any of these ways, he and his children are to be released in the Year of Jubilee, ⁵⁵for the Israelites belong to me as servants. They are my servants, whom I brought out of Egypt.ˡ I am the LORD your God.ᵐ

Reward for Obedience

26 " 'Do not make idolsⁿ or set up an imageᵒ or a sacred stoneᵖ for yourselves, and do not place a carved stoneᑫ in your land to bow down before it. I am the LORD your God.

² " 'Observe my Sabbathsʳ and have reverence for my sanctuary.ˢ I am the LORD.

³ " 'If you follow my decrees and are careful to obeyᵗ my commands, ⁴I will send you rainᵘ in its season,ᵛ and the ground will yield its crops and the trees of the field their fruit.ʷ ⁵Your threshing will continue until grape harvest and the grape harvest will continue until planting, and you will eat all the food you wantˣ and live in safety in your land.ʸ

⁶ " 'I will grant peace in the land,ᶻ and you will lie downᵃ and no one will make you afraid.ᵇ I will remove savage beastsᶜ from the land, and the sword will not pass through your country. ⁷You will pursue your enemies,ᵈ and they will fall by the sword before you. ⁸Fiveᵉ of you will chase a hundred, and a hundred of you will chase ten thousand, and your enemies will fall by the sword before you.ᶠ

⁹ " 'I will look on you with favor and make you fruitful and increase your numbers,ᵍ and I will keep my covenantʰ with you. ¹⁰You will still be eating last year's harvest when you will have to move it out to make room for the new.ⁱ ¹¹I will put my dwelling placeᵐʲ among you, and I will not abhor you.ᵏ ¹²I will walkˡ among you and be your God,ᵐ and you will be my people.ⁿ ¹³I am the LORD your God,ᵒ who brought you out of Egyptᵖ so that you would no longer be slaves to the Egyptians; I broke the bars of your yokeᑫ and enabled you to walk with heads held high.

Punishment for Disobedience

¹⁴ " 'But if you will not listen to me and

B *Lev 25:19* ◀ ▶ *Dt 7:13*
U *Ge 50:24–25* ◀ ▶ *Nu 6:24–27*
R ▶ *Lev 26:14–35*
F *Lev 25:19* ◀ ▶ *Nu 11:7–9*
S *Lev 25:18* ◀ ▶ *Nu 31:49*
V *Ex 23:27* ◀ ▶ *Nu 10:9*
R *Lev 26:5–10* ◀ ▶ *Lev 26:18*

28:10; 30:8; Eze 30:18; 34:27; Hos 11:4

ᵐ 11 Or *my tabernacle*

LEVITICUS 26:15

carry out all these commands,ʳ ¹⁵and if you reject my decrees and abhor my lawsˢ and fail to carry out all my commands and so violate my covenant,ᵗ ¹⁶then I will do this to you: I will bring upon you sudden terror, wasting diseases and feverᵘ that will destroy your sight and drain away your life.ᵛ You will plant seed in vain, because your enemies will eat it.ʷ ¹⁷I will set my faceˣ against you so that you will be defeatedʸ by your enemies;ᶻ those who hate you will rule over you,ᵃ and you will flee even when no one is pursuing you.ᵇ

¹⁸"'If after all this you will not listen to me,ᶜ I will punishᵈ you for your sins seven times over.ᵉ ¹⁹I will break down your stubborn prideᶠ and make the sky above you like iron and the ground beneath you like bronze.ᵍ ²⁰Your strength will be spent in vain,ʰ because your soil will not yield its crops, nor will the trees of the land yield their fruit.ⁱ

²¹"'If you remain hostileʲ toward me and refuse to listen to me, I will multiply your afflictions seven times over,ᵏ as your sins deserve. ²²I will send wild animalsˡ against you, and they will rob you of your children, destroy your cattle and make you so fewᵐ in number that your roads will be deserted.ⁿ

²³"'If in spite of these things you do not accept my correctionᵒ but continue to

be hostile toward me, ²⁴I myself will be hostileᵖ toward you and will afflict you for your sins seven times over. ²⁵And I will bring the swordᵠ upon you to avengeʳ the breaking of the covenant. When you withdraw into your cities, I will send a plagueˢ among you, and you will be given into enemy hands. ²⁶When I cut off your supply of bread,ᵗ ten women will be able to bake your bread in one oven, and they will dole out the bread by weight. You will eat, but you will not be satisfied.

²⁷"'If in spite of this you still do not listen to meᵘ but continue to be hostile toward me, ²⁸then in my angerᵛ I will be hostileʷ toward you, and I myself will punish you for your sins seven times over.ˣ ²⁹You will eatʸ the flesh of your sons and the flesh of your daughters.ᶻ ³⁰I will destroy your high places,ᵃ cut down your incense altarsᵇ and pile your dead bodies on the lifeless forms of your idols,ᶜ and I will abhorᵈ you. ³¹I will turn your cities into ruinsᵉ and lay wasteᶠ your

D Ex 32:35 ◀▶ Nu 5:21
R Lev 26:14-35 ◀▶ Lev 26:24
N Ge 6:3 ◀▶ Lev 26:23-24
N Lev 26:21 ◀▶ Lev 26:27-28

R Lev 26:18 ◀▶ Lev 26:28
N Lev 26:23-24 ◀▶ Nu 14:11
R Lev 26:24 ◀▶ Lev 26:31-35
R Lev 26:28 ◀▶ Lev 26:41-43

26:18 This verse highlights a critical principle for the people of Israel. The Lord declares four times in this chapter that, if Israel refuses to repent for its sinful rebellion, then God would make their punishment seven times worse.

26:22 Wild animals were a nuisance in underpopulated areas in the promised land (see Dt 7:22). This verse seems to indicate that one of the punishments for disobedience would be an increase in the number of wild animals and their attacks in all areas of the land (see 2Ki 2:24; 17:26). God will also use wild animals to carry out his punishments in the last days. One of the horrors of the tribulation will be the attack on humans by wild beasts (see Rev 6:8).

26:22-26 According to this prophecy, God's wrath against Israel would involve four key elements: wild animals, the sword, a plague and famine. It is significant that these four elements appear together several times in Scripture (see Jer 15:2-3; Eze 5:12, 17; 14:13-20; 33:27). The prophet Ezekiel refers to them most often and calls them the "four dreadful judgments" (Eze 14:21).

These four elements of the wrath of God are also poured out on sinful humanity during the opening days of the tribulation (see Rev 6:4-8). God's wrath will continue until the end of the Battle of Armageddon. Yet the righteous will be spared such wrath (see Ge 18:23-32; Eze 14:13-20). God chastens his children, but he will deliver them from his wrath. The apostle Paul comforted believers to this end when he urged them to "wait for his Son from heaven, whom he raised from the dead—Jesus, who rescues us from the coming wrath" (1Th 1:10). For more information, see the article entitled "The Rapture," p. 1368.

sanctuaries,ᵍ and I will take no delight in the pleasing aroma of your offerings.ʰ ³²I will lay waste the land,ⁱ so that your enemies who live there will be appalled.ʲ ³³I will scatterᵏ you among the nations¹ and will draw out my swordᵐ and pursue you. Your land will be laid waste,ⁿ and your cities will lie in ruins.ᵒ ³⁴Then the land will enjoy its sabbath years all the time that it lies desolateᵖ and you are in the country of your enemies;ᵠ then the land will rest and enjoy its sabbaths. ³⁵All the time that it lies desolate, the land will have the restʳ it did not have during the sabbaths you lived in it.

³⁶ " 'As for those of you who are left, I will make their hearts so fearful in the lands of their enemies that the sound of a windblown leafˢ will put them to flight.ᵗ They will run as though fleeing from the sword, and they will fall, even though no one is pursuing them.ᵘ ³⁷They will stumble over one anotherᵛ as though fleeing from the sword, even though no one is pursuing them. So you will not be able to stand before your enemies.ʷ ³⁸You will perishˣ among the nations; the land of your enemies will devour you.ʸ ³⁹Those of you who are left will waste away in the lands of their enemies because of their sins; also because of their fathers'ᶻ sins they will waste away.ᵃ

⁴⁰ " 'But if they will confessᵇ their sinsᶜ and the sins of their fathersᵈ—their treachery against me and their hostility toward me, ⁴¹which made me hostileᵉ toward them so that I sent them into the land of their enemies—then when their uncircumcised heartsᶠ are humbledᵍ and they payʰ for their sin, ⁴²I will remember my covenant with Jacobⁱ and my covenant with Isaacʲ and my covenant with Abraham,ᵏ and I will remember the land. ⁴³For the land will be desertedˡ by them and will enjoy its sabbaths while it lies desolate without them. They will pay for their sins because they rejectedᵐ my laws and abhorred my decrees.ⁿ ⁴⁴Yet in spite of this, when they are in the land of their enemies,ᵒ I will not reject them or abhorᵖ them so as to destroy them completely,ᵠ breaking my covenantʳ with them. I am the Lord their God. ⁴⁵But for their sake I will rememberˢ the covenant with their ancestors whom I brought out of Egyptᵗ in the sight of the nations to be their God. I am the Lord.' "

⁴⁶These are the decrees, the laws and the regulations that the Lord established on Mount Sinaiᵘ between himself and the Israelites through Moses.ᵛ

Redeeming What Is the Lord's

27 The Lord said to Moses, ²"Speak to the Israelites and say to them: 'If anyone makes a special vowʷ to dedicate persons to the Lord by giving equivalent values, ³set the value of a male between the ages of twenty and sixty at fifty shekelsⁿ of silver, according to the sanctuary shekel;ᵒˣ ⁴and if it is a female, set her value at thirty shekels.ᵖ ⁵If it is a person between the ages of five and twenty, set the value of a male at twenty shekelsᵠʸ and of a female at ten shekels.ʳ ⁶If it is a person between one month and five years, set the value of a male at five shekelsˢᶻ of silver and that of a female at three shekelsᵗ of silver. ⁷If it is a person sixty years old or more, set the value of a male at fifteen shekelsᵘ and of a female at ten shekels. ⁸If anyone making the vow is too poor to payᵃ the specified amount, he is to present the person to the priest, who will set the valueᵇ for him according to what the man making the vow can afford.

⁹" 'If what he vowed is an animal that is acceptable as an offering to the Lord,ᶜ such an animal given to the Lord becomes holy.ᵈ ¹⁰He must not exchange it or substitute a good one for a bad one, or a bad one for a good one;ᵉ if he should substitute one animal for another, both it and the substitute become holy. ¹¹If what he vowed is a ceremonially unclean animalᶠ—one that is not acceptable as an

---

M Ex 32:9–10 ◀ ▶ Dt 9:13–14
P ▶ Nu 14:19–20
R Lev 5:16 ◀ ▶ Nu 5:6–8
R Lev 26:31–35 ◀ ▶ Lev 26:43
R Lev 26:41–43 ◀ ▶ Dt 4:27
I Ex 32:13 ◀ ▶ Nu 10:29

offering to the LORD—the animal must be presented to the priest, [12]who will judge its quality as good or bad. Whatever value the priest then sets, that is what it will be. [13]If the owner wishes to redeem[g] the animal, he must add a fifth to its value.[h]

[14] 'If a man dedicates his house as something holy to the LORD, the priest will judge its quality as good or bad. Whatever value the priest then sets, so it will remain. [15]If the man who dedicates his house redeems it,[i] he must add a fifth to its value, and the house will again become his.

[16] 'If a man dedicates to the LORD part of his family land, its value is to be set according to the amount of seed required for it—fifty shekels of silver to a homer[v] of barley seed. [17]If he dedicates his field during the Year of Jubilee, the value that has been set remains. [18]But if he dedicates his field after the Jubilee,[j] the priest will determine the value according to the number of years that remain[k] until the next Year of Jubilee, and its set value will be reduced. [19]If the man who dedicates the field wishes to redeem it,[l] he must add a fifth to its value, and the field will again become his. [20]If, however, he does not redeem the field, or if he has sold it to someone else, it can never be redeemed. [21]When the field is released in the Jubilee,[m] it will become holy,[n] like a field devoted to the LORD;[o] it will become the property of the priests.[w]

[22] 'If a man dedicates to the LORD a field he has bought, which is not part of his family land, [23]the priest will determine its value up to the Year of Jubilee,[p] and the man must pay its value on that day as something holy to the LORD. [24]In the Year of Jubilee the field will revert to the person from whom he bought it,[q] the one whose land it was. [25]Every value is to be set according to the sanctuary shekel,[r] twenty gerahs[s] to the shekel.

[26] ' 'No one, however, may dedicate the firstborn of an animal, since the firstborn already belongs to the LORD;[t] whether an ox[x] or a sheep, it is the LORD's. [27]If it is one of the unclean animals,[u] he may buy it back at its set value, adding a fifth of the value to it. If he does not redeem it, it is to be sold at its set value.

[28] 'But nothing that a man owns and devotes[y][v] to the LORD—whether man or animal or family land—may be sold or redeemed; everything so devoted is most holy[w] to the LORD.

[29] ' 'No person devoted to destruction[z] may be ransomed; he must be put to death.[x]

[30] 'A tithe[y] of everything from the land, whether grain from the soil or fruit from the trees, belongs to the LORD; it is holy[z] to the LORD. [31]If a man redeems[a] any of his tithe, he must add a fifth of the value[b] to it. [32]The entire tithe of the herd and flock—every tenth animal that passes under the shepherd's rod[c]—will be holy to the LORD. [33]He must not pick out the good from the bad or make any substitution.[d] If he does make a substitution, both the animal and its substitute become holy and cannot be redeemed.[e]' "

[34]These are the commands the LORD gave Moses on Mount Sinai[f] for the Israelites.[g]

27:13 g S Lev 25:25; h S Lev 5:16
27:15 i ver 13,20
27:18 j Lev 25:10; k Lev 25:15
27:19 l S Lev 25:25
27:21 m S Lev 25:10; n S ver 9 o ver 28; Nu 18:14; Eze 44:29
27:23 p S Lev 25:15
27:24 q Lev 25:28
27:25 r S Ex 30:13; s Nu 3:47; Eze 45:12
27:26 t S Ex 13:12
27:27 u S ver 11
27:28 v Nu 18:14; Jos 6:17-19; w S ver 9
27:29 x Dt 7:26
27:30 y Nu 18:26; Dt 12:6,17; 14:22, 28; 2Ch 31:6; Ne 10:37; 12:44; 13:5; Mal 3:8 z Dt 7:6; Ezr 9:2; Isa 6:13
27:31 a S Lev 25:25; b Lev 5:16
27:32 c Ps 89:32; Jer 33:13; Eze 20:37
27:33 d ver 10; e Nu 18:21
27:34 f S Ex 19:11; g S Lev 7:38; Ac 7:38

[v] 16 That is, probably about 6 bushels (about 220 liters) [w] 21 Or priest [x] 26 The Hebrew word can include both male and female. [y] 28 The Hebrew term refers to the irrevocable giving over of things or persons to the LORD. [z] 29 The Hebrew term refers to the irrevocable giving over of things or persons to the LORD, often by totally destroying them.

Numbers

Author: Moses

Theme: Israel's wilderness wanderings in Sinai

Date of Writing: c. 1440–1406 B.C.

Outline of Numbers
I. Preparing to Depart From Mount Sinai (1:1—9:23)
II. From Mount Sinai to Defiance and Judgment (10:1—14:45)
III. Discipline, Duties and Defeat Along the Journey (15:1—21:35)
IV. Balaam's Prophetic Words (22:1—25:18)
V. Practical Preparations for Entering Canaan (26:1—36:13)

THE TITLE OF the book of Numbers comes from Moses' counting (or numbering) of the Israelites (chs. 1; 26). This census taking occurred twice—once as the Israelites left Egypt and again, almost forty years later, as the Israelites prepared to enter the promised land.

Yet the Hebrew title of the book (*bemidbar*, which means "in the wilderness") more accurately describes Numbers' contents. Continuing the account begun in the book of Exodus, Numbers opens with the conclusion of God's instructions to Moses at Mt. Sinai. The opening chapters of the book (chs. 1—14) chronicle the beginning of Israel's wilderness experience. The majority of the book relates the story of Israel's journey from Mt. Sinai to the borders of Canaan on the eastern side of the Jordan River (chs. 15—20). The book closes by recording the events that transpired in the final few months in the wilderness (chs. 21—36).

The book of Numbers also tells of the murmuring and rebellion of God's people. Despite the miraculous deliverance from their enemies, the divine provision of daily food in the form of manna and the continued presence of God in their lives as evidenced by the pillar of cloud and fire, Numbers reveals the deep-seated unbelief of the Israelites. Rather than displaying attitudes of worship and obedience, the people whom God had redeemed from slavery in Egypt responded to his miracles with constant complaining, rebellion and mutiny. Loudly voicing a desire to return to their chains in Egypt and refusing to believe God's promise to help them overcome their enemies in Canaan, the community of the redeemed tragically lost not only their faith but their part in the promised land as well.

NUMBERS 1:1

The Census

1 The LORD spoke to Moses in the Tent of Meeting[a] in the Desert of Sinai[b] on the first day of the second month[c] of the second year after the Israelites came out of Egypt.[d] He said: [2]"Take a census[e] of the whole Israelite community by their clans and families,[f] listing every man by name,[g] one by one. [3]You and Aaron[h] are to number by their divisions all the men in Israel twenty years old or more[i] who are able to serve in the army.[j] [4]One man from each tribe,[k] each the head of his family,[l] is to help you.[m] [5]These are the names[n] of the men who are to assist you:

from Reuben,[o] Elizur son of Shedeur;[p]
[6]from Simeon,[q] Shelumiel son of Zurishaddai;[r]
[7]from Judah,[s] Nahshon son of Amminadab;[t]
[8]from Issachar,[u] Nethanel son of Zuar;[v]
[9]from Zebulun,[w] Eliab son of Helon;[x]
[10]from the sons of Joseph:
from Ephraim,[y] Elishama son of Ammihud;[z]
from Manasseh,[a] Gamaliel son of Pedahzur;[b]
[11]from Benjamin,[c] Abidan son of Gideoni;[d]
[12]from Dan,[e] Ahiezer son of Ammishaddai;[f]
[13]from Asher,[g] Pagiel son of Ocran;[h]
[14]from Gad,[i] Eliasaph son of Deuel;[j]
[15]from Naphtali,[k] Ahira son of Enan.[l]"

[16]These were the men appointed from the community, the leaders[m] of their ancestral tribes.[n] They were the heads of the clans of Israel.[o]

[17]Moses and Aaron took these men whose names had been given, [18]and they called the whole community together on the first day of the second month.[p] The people indicated their ancestry[q] by their clans and families,[r] and the men twenty years old or more[s] were listed by name, one by one, [19]as the LORD commanded Moses. And so he counted[t] them in the Desert of Sinai:

[20]From the descendants of Reuben[u] the firstborn son[v] of Israel:

All the men twenty years old or more who were able to serve in the army were listed by name, one by one, according to the records of their clans and families. [21]The number from the tribe of Reuben[w] was 46,500.

[22]From the descendants of Simeon:[x]

All the men twenty years old or more who were able to serve in the army were counted and listed by name, one by one, according to the records of their clans and families. [23]The number from the tribe of Simeon was 59,300.[y]

[24]From the descendants of Gad:[z]

All the men twenty years old or more who were able to serve in the army were listed by name, according to the records of their clans and families. [25]The number from the tribe of Gad[a] was 45,650.

[26]From the descendants of Judah:[b]

All the men twenty years old or more who were able to serve in the army were listed by name, according to the records of their clans and families. [27]The number from the tribe of Judah[c] was 74,600.

[28]From the descendants of Issachar:[d]

All the men twenty years old or more who were able to serve in the army were listed by name, according to the records of their clans and families. [29]The number from the tribe of Issachar[e] was 54,400.[f]

[30]From the descendants of Zebulun:[g]

All the men twenty years old or more who were able to serve in the army were listed by name, according to the records of their clans and families. [31]The number from the tribe of Zebulun was 57,400.[h]

[32]From the sons of Joseph:[i]

From the descendants of Ephraim:[j]

All the men twenty years old or more who were able to serve in the army were listed by name, according to the records of their clans and families. [33]The number from the tribe of Ephraim was 40,500.

³⁴From the descendants of Manasseh:
All the men twenty years old or more who were able to serve in the army were listed by name, according to the records of their clans and families. ³⁵The number from the tribe of Manasseh was 32,200.

³⁶From the descendants of Benjamin:
All the men twenty years old or more who were able to serve in the army were listed by name, according to the records of their clans and families. ³⁷The number from the tribe of Benjamin was 35,400.

³⁸From the descendants of Dan:
All the men twenty years old or more who were able to serve in the army were listed by name, according to the records of their clans and families. ³⁹The number from the tribe of Dan was 62,700.

⁴⁰From the descendants of Asher:
All the men twenty years old or more who were able to serve in the army were listed by name, according to the records of their clans and families. ⁴¹The number from the tribe of Asher was 41,500.

⁴²From the descendants of Naphtali:
All the men twenty years old or more who were able to serve in the army were listed by name, according to the records of their clans and families. ⁴³The number from the tribe of Naphtali was 53,400.

⁴⁴These were the men counted by Moses and Aaron and the twelve leaders of Israel, each one representing his family. ⁴⁵All the Israelites twenty years old or more who were able to serve in Israel's army were counted according to their families. ⁴⁶The total number was 603,550.

⁴⁷The families of the tribe of Levi, however, were not counted along with the others. ⁴⁸The LORD had said to Moses: ⁴⁹"You must not count the tribe of Levi or include them in the census of the other Israelites. ⁵⁰Instead, appoint the Levites to be in charge of the tabernacle of the Testimony—over all its furnishings and everything belonging to it. They are to carry the tabernacle and all its furnishings; they are to take care of it and encamp around it. ⁵¹Whenever the tabernacle is to move, the Levites are to take it down, and whenever the tabernacle is to be set up, the Levites shall do it. Anyone else who goes near it shall be put to death. ⁵²The Israelites are to set up their tents by divisions, each man in his own camp under his own standard. ⁵³The Levites, however, are to set up their tents around the tabernacle of the Testimony so that wrath will not fall on the Israelite community. The Levites will be responsible for the care of the tabernacle of the Testimony.'"

⁵⁴The Israelites did all this just as the LORD commanded Moses.

The Arrangement of the Tribal Camps

2 The LORD said to Moses and Aaron: ²"The Israelites are to camp around the Tent of Meeting some distance from it, each man under his standard with the banners of his family."

³On the east, toward the sunrise, the divisions of the camp of Judah are to encamp under their standard. The leader of the people of Judah is

---

1:45–46 This passage chronicles the first census of the Israelites, recording 603,550 as the number of those qualified to serve in the army. Except for Joshua and Caleb, all of these died in the desert. This large number of men suggests a population for the entire community of nearly 2.5 million.

Because Exodus records that "many other people went up with them, as well as large droves of livestock, both flocks and herds" (Ex 12:38) some scholars deny that the route of the exodus led through the Sinai desert, claiming the Sinai's inability to sustain a large population and their flocks. However, archeological discoveries indicate that the northern areas of the Sinai that are now desert were once cultivated, treed and well watered, suggesting that available pasture land existed at the time of the exodus. Since God provided manna for human consumption, it is likely that with a slight increase in rainfall the land could have easily supported abundant flocks and herds.

Nahshon son of Amminadab.ⁿ ⁴His division numbers 74,600.

⁵The tribe of Issachar° will camp next to them. The leader of the people of Issachar is Nethanel son of Zuar.ᵖ ⁶His division numbers 54,400. ⁷The tribe of Zebulun will be next. The leader of the people of Zebulun is Eliab son of Helon.ᵠ ⁸His division numbers 57,400.

⁹All the men assigned to the camp of Judah, according to their divisions, number 186,400. They will set out first.ʳ

¹⁰On the southˢ will be the divisions of the camp of Reuben under their standard. The leader of the people of Reuben is Elizur son of Shedeur.ᵗ ¹¹His division numbers 46,500. ¹²The tribe of Simeonᵘ will camp next to them. The leader of the people of Simeon is Shelumiel son of Zurishaddai.ᵛ ¹³His division numbers 59,300. ¹⁴The tribe of Gadʷ will be next. The leader of the people of Gad is Eliasaph son of Deuel.ᵃˣ ¹⁵His division numbers 45,650.

¹⁶All the men assigned to the camp of Reuben,ʸ according to their divisions, number 151,450. They will set out second.

¹⁷Then the Tent of Meeting and the camp of the Levitesᶻ will set out in the middle of the camps. They will set out in the same order as they encamp, each in his own place under his standard.

¹⁸On the westᵃ will be the divisions of the camp of Ephraimᵇ under their standard. The leader of the people of Ephraim is Elishama son of Ammihud.ᶜ ¹⁹His division numbers 40,500. ²⁰The tribe of Manassehᵈ will be next to them. The leader of the people of Manasseh is Gamaliel son of Pedahzur.ᵉ ²¹His division numbers 32,200. ²²The tribe of Benjaminᶠ will be next. The leader of the people of Benjamin is Abidan son of Gideoni.ᵍ ²³His division numbers 35,400.

²⁴All the men assigned to the camp of Ephraim,ʰ according to their divisions, number 108,100. They will set out third.ⁱ

²⁵On the northʲ will be the divisions of the camp of Dan, under their standard.ᵏ The leader of the people of Dan is Ahiezer son of Ammishaddai.ˡ ²⁶His division numbers 62,700. ²⁷The tribe of Asher will camp next to them. The leader of the people of Asher is Pagiel son of Ocran.ᵐ ²⁸His division numbers 41,500. ²⁹The tribe of Naphtaliⁿ will be next. The leader of the people of Naphtali is Ahira son of Enan.° ³⁰His division numbers 53,400.

³¹All the men assigned to the camp of Dan number 157,600. They will set out last,ᵖ under their standards.

³²These are the Israelites, counted according to their families.ᵠ All those in the camps, by their divisions, number 603,550.ʳ ³³The Levites, however, were not countedˢ along with the other Israelites, as the LORD commanded Moses.

³⁴So the Israelites did everything the LORD commanded Moses; that is the way they encamped under their standards, and that is the way they set out, each with his clan and family.

The Levites

3 This is the account of the family of Aaron and Mosesᵗ at the time the LORD talked with Moses on Mount Sinai.ᵘ ²The names of the sons of Aaron were Nadab the firstbornᵛ and Abihu, Eleazar and Ithamar.ʷ ³Those were the names of Aaron's sons, the anointed priests,ˣ who were ordained to serve as priests. ⁴Nadab and Abihu, however, fell dead before the LORDʸ when they made an offering with unauthorized fire before him in the Desert of Sinai.ᶻ They had no sons; so only Eleazar and Ithamarᵃ served as priests during the lifetime of their father Aaron.ᵇ

⁵The LORD said to Moses, ⁶"Bring the

ᵃ 14 Many manuscripts of the Masoretic Text, Samaritan Pentateuch and Vulgate (see also Num. 1:14); most manuscripts of the Masoretic Text *Reuel*

tribe of Levi[c] and present them to Aaron the priest to assist him.[d] [7]They are to perform duties for him and for the whole community[e] at the Tent of Meeting by doing the work[f] of the tabernacle. [8]They are to take care of all the furnishings of the Tent of Meeting, fulfilling the obligations of the Israelites by doing the work of the tabernacle. [9]Give the Levites to Aaron and his sons;[g] they are the Israelites who are to be given wholly to him.[b] [10]Appoint Aaron[h] and his sons to serve as priests;[i] anyone else who approaches the sanctuary must be put to death."[j]

[11]The LORD also said to Moses, [12]"I have taken the Levites[k] from among the Israelites in place of the first male offspring[l] of every Israelite woman. The Levites are mine,[m] [13]for all the firstborn are mine.[n] When I struck down all the firstborn in Egypt, I set apart for myself every firstborn in Israel, whether man or animal. They are to be mine. I am the LORD."[o]

[14]The LORD said to Moses in the Desert of Sinai,[p] [15]"Count[q] the Levites by their families and clans. Count every male a month old or more."[r] [16]So Moses counted them, as he was commanded by the word of the LORD.

[17]These were the names of the sons of Levi:[s]
Gershon,[t] Kohath[u] and Merari.[v]
[18]These were the names of the Gershonite clans:
Libni and Shimei.[w]
[19]The Kohathite clans:
Amram, Izhar, Hebron and Uzziel.[x]
[20]The Merarite clans:[y]
Mahli and Mushi.[z]
These were the Levite clans, according to their families.

[21]To Gershon[a] belonged the clans of the Libnites and Shimeites;[b] these were the Gershonite clans. [22]The number of all the males a month old or more who were counted was 7,500. [23]The Gershonite clans were to camp on the west, behind the tabernacle.[c] [24]The leader of the families of the Gershonites was Eliasaph son of Lael. [25]At the Tent of Meeting the Gershonites were responsible for the care of the tabernacle[d] and tent, its coverings,[e] the curtain at the entrance[f] to the Tent of Meeting,[g] [26]the curtains of the courtyard[h], the curtain at the entrance to the courtyard surrounding the tabernacle and altar,[i] and the ropes[j]—and everything[k] related to their use.

[27]To Kohath[l] belonged the clans of the Amramites, Izharites, Hebronites and Uzzielites;[m] these were the Kohathite[n] clans. [28]The number of all the males a month old or more[o] was 8,600.[c] The Kohathites were responsible[p] for the care of the sanctuary.[q] [29]The Kohathite clans were to camp on the south side[r] of the tabernacle. [30]The leader of the families of the Kohathite clans was Elizaphan[s] son of Uzziel. [31]They were responsible for the care of the ark,[t] the table,[u] the lampstand,[v] the altars,[w] the articles[x] of the sanctuary used in ministering, the curtain,[y] and everything related to their use.[z] [32]The chief leader of the Levites was Eleazar[a] son of Aaron, the priest. He was appointed over those who were responsible[b] for the care of the sanctuary.[c]

[33]To Merari belonged the clans of the Mahlites and the Mushites;[d] these were the Merarite clans.[e] [34]The number of all the males a month old or more[f] who were counted was 6,200. [35]The leader of the families of the Merarite clans was Zuriel son of Abihail; they were to camp on the north side of the tabernacle.[g] [36]The Merarites were appointed[h] to take care of the frames of the tabernacle,[i] its crossbars,[j] posts,[k] bases, all its equipment, and everything related to their use,[l] [37]as well as the posts of the surrounding courtyard[m] with their bases, tent pegs[n] and ropes.

[38]Moses and Aaron and his sons were to camp to the east[o] of the tabernacle, toward the sunrise, in front of the Tent of Meeting.[p] They were responsible for the care of the sanctuary[q] on behalf of the Israelites. Anyone else who approached the sanctuary was to be put to death.[r]

[39]The total number of Levites counted[s] at the LORD's command by Moses and Aaron according to their clans, including

---

[q] ver 7; Nu 18:5 [r] ver 10; Nu 1:51 **3:39** [s] S ver 15

[b] *9* Most manuscripts of the Masoretic Text; some manuscripts of the Masoretic Text, Samaritan Pentateuch and Septuagint (see also Num. 8:16) *to me* [c] *28* Hebrew; some Septuagint manuscripts *8,300*

every male a month old or more, was 22,000.ᵗ

⁴⁰The LORD said to Moses, "Count all the firstborn Israelite males who are a month old or moreᵘ and make a list of their names.ᵛ ⁴¹Take the Levites for me in place of all the firstborn of the Israelites,ʷ and the livestock of the Levites in place of all the firstborn of the livestock of the Israelites. I am the LORD."ˣ

⁴²So Moses counted all the firstborn of the Israelites, as the LORD commanded him. ⁴³The total number of firstborn males a month old or more,ʸ listed by name, was 22,273.ᶻ

⁴⁴The LORD also said to Moses, ⁴⁵"Take the Levites in place of all the firstborn of Israel, and the livestock of the Levites in place of their livestock. The Levites are to be mine.ᵃ I am the LORD.ᵇ ⁴⁶To redeemᶜ the 273 firstborn Israelites who exceed the number of the Levites, ⁴⁷collect five shekelsᵈᵈ for each one, according to the sanctuary shekel,ᵉ which weighs twenty gerahs.ᶠ ⁴⁸Give the money for the redemptionᵍ of the additional Israelites to Aaron and his sons."ʰ

⁴⁹So Moses collected the redemption moneyⁱ from those who exceeded the number redeemed by the Levites. ⁵⁰From the firstborn of the Israelitesʲ he collected silver weighing 1,365 shekels,ᵉᵏ according to the sanctuary shekel. ⁵¹Moses gave the redemption money to Aaron and his sons, as he was commanded by the word of the LORD.

The Kohathites

4 The LORD said to Moses and Aaron: ²"Take a census¹ of the Kohathite branch of the Levites by their clans and families. ³Countᵐ all the men from thirty to fifty years of ageⁿ who come to serve in the work in the Tent of Meeting.

⁴"This is the workᵒ of the Kohathitesᵖ in the Tent of Meeting: the care of the most holy things.ᑫ ⁵When the camp is to move,ʳ Aaron and his sons are to go in and take down the shielding curtainˢ and cover the ark of the Testimony with it.ᵗ ⁶Then they are to cover this with hides of sea cows,ᵘ spread a cloth of solid blue over that and put the polesᵛ in place.

⁷"Over the table of the Presenceʷ they are to spread a blue cloth and put on it the plates, dishes and bowls, and the jars for drink offerings;ˣ the bread that is continually thereʸ is to remain on it. ⁸Over these they are to spread a scarlet cloth, cover that with hides of sea cows and put its polesᶻ in place.

⁹"They are to take a blue cloth and cover the lampstand that is for light, together with its lamps, its wick trimmers and trays,ᵃ and all its jars for the oil used to supply it. ¹⁰Then they are to wrap it and all its accessories in a covering of hides of sea cows and put it on a carrying frame.ᵇ

¹¹"Over the gold altarᶜ they are to spread a blue cloth and cover that with hides of sea cows and put its polesᵈ in place.

¹²"They are to take all the articlesᵉ used for ministering in the sanctuary, wrap them in a blue cloth, cover that with hides of sea cows and put them on a carrying frame.ᶠ

¹³"They are to remove the ashesᵍ from the bronze altarʰ and spread a purple cloth over it. ¹⁴Then they are to place on it all the utensilsⁱ used for ministering at the altar, including the firepans,ʲ meat forks,ᵏ shovelsˡ and sprinkling bowls.ᵐ Over it they are to spread a covering of hides of sea cows and put its polesⁿ in place.

¹⁵"After Aaron and his sons have finished covering the holy furnishings and all the holy articles, and when the camp is ready to move,ᵒ the Kohathitesᵖ are to come to do the carrying.ᑫ But they must not touch the holy thingsʳ or they will die.ˢᵗ The Kohathites are to carry those things that are in the Tent of Meeting.

¹⁶"Eleazarᵘ son of Aaron, the priest, is to have charge of the oil for the light,ᵛ the fragrant incense,ʷ the regular grain offeringˣ and the anointing oil. He is to be in charge of the entire tabernacle and everything in it, including its holy furnishings and articles."

¹⁷The LORD said to Moses and Aaron, ¹⁸"See that the Kohathite tribal clans are not cut off from the Levites. ¹⁹So that they may live and not die when they come near the most holy things,ʸ do this for them: Aaron and his sonsᶻ are to go into the sanctuary and assign to each man his work and what he is to carry.ᵃ ²⁰But the

---

ᵈ 47 That is, about 2 ounces (about 55 grams) ᵉ 50 That is, about 35 pounds (about 15.5 kilograms) ᶠ 6 That is, dugongs; also in verses 8, 10, 11, 12, 14 and 25

Kohathites must not go in to look[b] at the holy things, even for a moment, or they will die."

The Gershonites

[21]The LORD said to Moses, [22]"Take a census also of the Gershonites by their families and clans. [23]Count all the men from thirty to fifty years of age[c] who come to serve in the work at the Tent of Meeting.

[24]"This is the service of the Gershonite clans as they work and carry burdens: [25]They are to carry the curtains of the tabernacle,[d] the Tent of Meeting,[e] its covering[f] and the outer covering of hides of sea cows, the curtains for the entrance to the Tent of Meeting, [26]the curtains of the courtyard surrounding the tabernacle and altar,[g] the curtain for the entrance,[h] the ropes and all the equipment[i] used in its service. The Gershonites are to do all that needs to be done with these things. [27]All their service, whether carrying or doing other work, is to be done under the direction of Aaron and his sons.[j] You shall assign to them as their responsibility[k] all they are to carry. [28]This is the service of the Gershonite clans[l] at the Tent of Meeting. Their duties are to be under the direction of Ithamar[m] son of Aaron, the priest.

The Merarites

[29]"Count[n] the Merarites by their clans and families.[o] [30]Count all the men from thirty to fifty years of age who come to serve in the work at the Tent of Meeting. [31]This is their duty as they perform service at the Tent of Meeting: to carry the frames of the tabernacle, its crossbars, posts and bases,[p] [32]as well as the posts of the surrounding courtyard with their bases, tent pegs, ropes,[q] all their equipment and everything related to their use. Assign to each man the specific things he is to carry. [33]This is the service of the Merarite clans as they work at the Tent of Meeting under the direction of Ithamar[r] son of Aaron, the priest."

The Numbering of the Levite Clans

[34]Moses, Aaron and the leaders of the community counted the Kohathites[s] by their clans and families. [35]All the men from thirty to fifty years of age[t] who came to serve in the work in the Tent of Meeting, [36]counted by clans, were 2,750. [37]This was the total of all those in the Kohathite clans[u] who served in the Tent of Meeting. Moses and Aaron counted them according to the LORD's command through Moses.

[38]The Gershonites[v] were counted by their clans and families. [39]All the men from thirty to fifty years of age who came to serve in the work at the Tent of Meeting, [40]counted by their clans and families, were 2,630. [41]This was the total of those in the Gershonite clans who served at the Tent of Meeting. Moses and Aaron counted them according to the LORD's command.

[42]The Merarites were counted by their clans and families. [43]All the men from thirty to fifty years of age[w] who came to serve in the work at the Tent of Meeting, [44]counted by their clans, were 3,200. [45]This was the total of those in the Merarite clans.[x] Moses and Aaron counted them according to the LORD's command through Moses.

[46]So Moses, Aaron and the leaders of Israel counted[y] all the Levites by their clans and families. [47]All the men from thirty to fifty years of age[z] who came to do the work of serving and carrying the Tent of Meeting [48]numbered 8,580.[a] [49]At the LORD's command through Moses, each was assigned his work and told what to carry.

Thus they were counted,[b] as the LORD commanded Moses.

The Purity of the Camp

5 The LORD said to Moses, [2]"Command the Israelites to send away from the camp anyone who has an infectious skin disease[g][c] or a discharge[d] of any kind, or who is ceremonially unclean[e] because of a dead body.[f] [3]Send away male and female alike; send them outside the camp so they will not defile their camp, where I dwell among them.[g]" [4]The Israelites did this; they sent them outside the camp. They did just as the LORD had instructed Moses.

Restitution for Wrongs

[5]The LORD said to Moses, [6]"Say to the

R *Lev 26:40–41* ◀ ▶ *Dt 4:29–30*

---

[g] 2 Traditionally *leprosy*; the Hebrew word was used for various diseases affecting the skin—not necessarily leprosy.

Israelites: 'When a man or woman wrongs another in any way[h] and so is unfaithful[h] to the LORD, that person is guilty[i] [7]and must confess[j] the sin he has committed. He must make full restitution[k] for his wrong, add one fifth to it and give it all to the person he has wronged. [8]But if that person has no close relative to whom restitution can be made for the wrong, the restitution belongs to the LORD and must be given to the priest, along with the ram[l] with which atonement is made for him.[m] [9]All the sacred contributions the Israelites bring to a priest will belong to him.[n] [10]Each man's sacred gifts are his own, but what he gives to the priest will belong to the priest.[o]' "

The Test for an Unfaithful Wife

[11]Then the LORD said to Moses, [12]"Speak to the Israelites and say to them: 'If a man's wife goes astray[p] and is unfaithful to him [13]by sleeping with another man,[q] and this is hidden from her husband and her impurity is undetected (since there is no witness against her and she has not been caught in the act), [14]and if feelings of jealousy[r] come over her husband and he suspects his wife and she is impure—or if he is jealous and suspects her even though she is not impure— [15]then he is to take his wife to the priest. He must also take an offering of a tenth of an ephah[s] of barley flour[t] on her behalf. He must not pour oil on it or put incense on it, because it is a grain offering for jealousy,[u] a reminder[v] offering to draw attention to guilt.

[16]"'The priest shall bring her and have her stand before the LORD. [17]Then he shall take some holy water in a clay jar and put some dust from the tabernacle floor into the water. [18]After the priest has had the woman stand before the LORD, he shall loosen her hair[w] and place in her hands the reminder offering, the grain offering for jealousy,[x] while he himself holds the bitter water that brings a curse.[y] [19]Then the priest shall put the woman under oath and say to her, "If no other man has slept with you and you have not gone astray[z] and become impure while married to your husband, may this bitter water that brings a curse[a] not harm you. [20]But if you have gone astray[b] while married to your husband and you have defiled yourself by sleeping with a man other than your husband"— [21]here the priest is to put the woman under this curse of the oath[c]—"may the LORD cause your people to curse and denounce you when he causes your thigh to waste away and your abdomen to swell.[j] [22]May this water[d] that brings a curse[e] enter your body so that your abdomen swells and your thigh wastes away.[k]"

" 'Then the woman is to say, "Amen. So be it.!"'

[23]" 'The priest is to write these curses on a scroll[g] and then wash them off into the bitter water. [24]He shall have the woman drink the bitter water that brings a curse, and this water will enter her and cause bitter suffering. [25]The priest is to take from her hands the grain offering for jealousy, wave it before the LORD[h] and bring it to the altar. [26]The priest is then to take a handful of the grain offering as a memorial offering[i] and burn it on the altar; after that, he is to have the woman drink the water. [27]If she has defiled herself and been unfaithful to her husband, then when she is made to drink the water that brings a curse, it will go into her and cause bitter suffering; her abdomen will swell and her thigh waste away,[i] and she will become accursed[j] among her people. [28]If, however, the woman has not defiled herself and is free from impurity, she will be cleared of guilt and will be able to have children.

[29]" 'This, then, is the law of jealousy when a woman goes astray[k] and defiles herself while married to her husband, [30]or when feelings of jealousy[l] come over a man because he suspects his wife. The priest is to have her stand before the LORD and is to apply this entire law to her. [31]The husband will be innocent of any wrongdoing, but the woman will bear the consequences[m] of her sin.' "

D Lev 26:16 ◀▶ Nu 5:27
D Nu 5:21 ◀▶ Nu 11:33–34

[h] 6 Or *woman commits any wrong common to mankind* [i] 15 That is, probably about 2 quarts (about 2 liters) [j] 21 Or *causes you to have a miscarrying womb and barrenness* [k] 22 Or *body and cause you to be barren and have a miscarrying womb* [l] 27 Or *suffering; she will have barrenness and a miscarrying womb*

The Nazirite

6 The LORD said to Moses, [2]"Speak to the Israelites and say to them: 'If a man or woman wants to make a special vow,[n] a vow of separation[o] to the LORD as a Nazirite,[p] [3]he must abstain from wine[q] and other fermented drink and must not drink vinegar[r] made from wine or from other fermented drink. He must not drink grape juice or eat grapes[s] or raisins. [4]As long as he is a Nazirite, he must not eat anything that comes from the grapevine, not even the seeds or skins.

[5]"'During the entire period of his vow of separation no razor[t] may be used on his head.[u] He must be holy until the period of his separation to the LORD is over; he must let the hair of his head grow long. [6]Throughout the period of his separation to the LORD he must not go near a dead body.[v] [7]Even if his own father or mother or brother or sister dies, he must not make himself ceremonially unclean[w] on account of them, because the symbol of his separation to God is on his head. [8]Throughout the period of his separation he is consecrated to the LORD.

[9]"'If someone dies suddenly in his presence, thus defiling the hair he has dedicated,[x] he must shave his head on the day of his cleansing[y]—the seventh day. [10]Then on the eighth day[z] he must bring two doves or two young pigeons[a] to the priest at the entrance to the Tent of Meeting.[b] [11]The priest is to offer one as a sin offering[c] and the other as a burnt offering[d] to make atonement[e] for him because he sinned by being in the presence of the dead body. That same day he is to consecrate his head. [12]He must dedicate himself to the LORD for the period of his separation and must bring a year-old male lamb[f] as a guilt offering.[g] The previous days do not count, because he became defiled during his separation.

[13]"'Now this is the law for the Nazirite when the period of his separation is over.[h] He is to be brought to the entrance to the Tent of Meeting.[i] [14]There he is to present his offerings to the LORD: a year-old male lamb without defect[j] for a burnt offering, a year-old ewe lamb without defect for a sin offering,[k] a ram[l] without defect for a fellowship offering,[m][m] [15]together with their grain offerings[n] and drink offerings,[o] and a basket of bread made without yeast—cakes made of fine flour mixed with oil, and wafers spread with oil.[p]

[16]"'The priest is to present them[q] before the LORD[r] and make the sin offering and the burnt offering.[s] [17]He is to present the basket of unleavened bread and is to sacrifice the ram as a fellowship offering[t] to the LORD, together with its grain offering[u] and drink offering.[v]

[18]"'Then at the entrance to the Tent of Meeting, the Nazirite must shave off the hair that he dedicated.[w] He is to take the hair and put it in the fire that is under the sacrifice of the fellowship offering.

[19]"'After the Nazirite has shaved off the hair of his dedication, the priest is to place in his hands a boiled shoulder of the ram, and a cake and a wafer from the basket, both made without yeast.[x] [20]The priest shall then wave them before the LORD as a wave offering;[y] they are holy[z] and belong to the priest, together with the breast that was waved and the thigh that was presented.[a] After that, the Nazirite may drink wine.[b]

[21]"'This is the law of the Nazirite[c] who vows his offering to the LORD in accordance with his separation, in addition to whatever else he can afford. He must fulfill the vow[d] he has made, according to the law of the Nazirite.'"

The Priestly Blessing

[22]The LORD said to Moses, [23]"Tell Aaron and his sons, 'This is how you are to bless[e] the Israelites. Say to them:

[24]"'"The LORD bless you[f]
and keep you;[g]

K *Ex 33:19* ◄ ► *Nu 11:23*
U *Lev 26:3–12* ◄ ► *Nu 10:29*

[m] 14 Traditionally *peace offering*; also in verses 17 and 18

6:2–21 This section outlines God's laws concerning the vows of a Nazirite—an Israelite who was completely separated to God for a specified period of time or for some holy service. Though there were many restrictions on a Nazirite, this vow was a positive act of total devotion to the Lord. Samson, Samuel, John the Baptist and the apostle Paul were all Nazirites (see Jdg 13; 1Sa 1:9–11; Lk 1:15; Ac 18:18).

²⁵the LORD make his face shine upon
you,
and be gracious to you;
²⁶the LORD turn his face toward you
and give you peace."'

²⁷"So they will put my name on the Israelites, and I will bless them."

Offerings at the Dedication of the Tabernacle

7 When Moses finished setting up the tabernacle, he anointed it and consecrated it and all its furnishings. He also anointed and consecrated the altar and all its utensils. ²Then the leaders of Israel, the heads of families who were the tribal leaders in charge of those who were counted, made offerings. ³They brought as their gifts before the LORD six covered carts and twelve oxen—an ox from each leader and a cart from every two. These they presented before the tabernacle.

⁴The LORD said to Moses, ⁵"Accept these from them, that they may be used in the work at the Tent of Meeting. Give them to the Levites as each man's work requires."

⁶So Moses took the carts and oxen and gave them to the Levites. ⁷He gave two carts and four oxen to the Gershonites, as their work required, ⁸and he gave four carts and eight oxen to the Merarites, as their work required. They were all under the direction of Ithamar son of Aaron, the priest. ⁹But Moses did not give any to the Kohathites, because they were to carry on their shoulders the holy things, for which they were responsible.

¹⁰When the altar was anointed, the leaders brought their offerings for its dedication and presented them before the altar. ¹¹For the LORD had said to Moses, "Each day one leader is to bring his offering for the dedication of the altar."

¹²The one who brought his offering on the first day was Nahshon son of Amminadab of the tribe of Judah.

¹³His offering was one silver plate weighing a hundred and thirty shekels, and one silver sprinkling bowl weighing seventy shekels, both according to the sanctuary shekel, each filled with fine flour mixed with oil as a grain offering; ¹⁴one gold dish weighing ten shekels, filled with incense; ¹⁵one young bull, one ram and one male lamb a year old, for a burnt offering; ¹⁶one male goat for a sin offering; ¹⁷and two oxen, five rams, five male goats and five male lambs a year old, to be sacrificed as a fellowship offering. This was the offering of Nahshon son of Amminadab.

¹⁸On the second day Nethanel son of Zuar, the leader of Issachar, brought his offering.

¹⁹The offering he brought was one silver plate weighing a hundred and thirty shekels, and one silver sprinkling bowl weighing seventy shekels, both according to the sanctuary shekel, each filled with fine flour mixed with oil as a grain offering; ²⁰one gold dish weighing ten shekels, filled with incense; ²¹one young bull, one ram and one male lamb a year old, for a burnt offering; ²²one male goat for a sin offering; ²³and two oxen, five rams, five male goats and five male lambs a year old, to be sacrificed as a fellowship offering. This was the offering of Nethanel son of Zuar.

²⁴On the third day, Eliab son of Helon, the leader of the people of Zebulun, brought his offering.

²⁵His offering was one silver plate weighing a hundred and thirty shekels, and one silver sprinkling bowl weighing seventy shekels, both according to the sanctuary shekel, each filled with fine flour mixed with oil as a grain offering; ²⁶one gold dish weighing ten shekels, filled with incense; ²⁷one young bull, one ram and one male lamb a year old, for a burnt offering; ²⁸one male goat for a sin offering; ²⁹and two oxen, five rams, five male goats and five male lambs a year old, to be sacrificed as a fellowship offering. This was the offering of Eliab son of Helon.

³⁰On the fourth day Elizur son of Shed-

---

n 13 That is, about 3 1/4 pounds (about 1.5 kilograms); also elsewhere in this chapter   *o 13* That is, about 1 3/4 pounds (about 0.8 kilogram); also elsewhere in this chapter   *p 14* That is, about 4 ounces (about 110 grams); also elsewhere in this chapter   *q 17* Traditionally *peace offering*; also elsewhere in this chapter

eur,ᵖ the leader of the people of Reuben, brought his offering.

³¹His offering was one silver plate weighing a hundred and thirty shekels, and one silver sprinkling bowl weighing seventy shekels, both according to the sanctuary shekel, each filled with fine flour mixed with oil as a grain offering; ³²one gold dish weighing ten shekels, filled with incense; ³³one young bull, one ram and one male lamb a year old, for a burnt offering; ³⁴one male goat for a sin offering; ³⁵and two oxen, five rams, five male goats and five male lambs a year old, to be sacrificed as a fellowship offering. This was the offering of Elizur son of Shedeur.

³⁶On the fifth day Shelumiel son of Zurishaddai,ᑫ the leader of the people of Simeon, brought his offering.

³⁷His offering was one silver plate weighing a hundred and thirty shekels, and one silver sprinkling bowl weighing seventy shekels, both according to the sanctuary shekel, each filled with fine flour mixed with oil as a grain offering; ³⁸one gold dish weighing ten shekels, filled with incense; ³⁹one young bull, one ram and one male lamb a year old, for a burnt offering; ⁴⁰one male goat for a sin offering; ⁴¹and two oxen, five rams, five male goats and five male lambs a year old, to be sacrificed as a fellowship offering. This was the offering of Shelumiel son of Zurishaddai.

⁴²On the sixth day Eliasaph son of Deuel,ʳ the leader of the people of Gad, brought his offering.

⁴³His offering was one silver plate weighing a hundred and thirty shekels, and one silver sprinkling bowl weighing seventy shekels, both according to the sanctuary shekel, each filled with fine flour mixed with oil as a grain offering; ⁴⁴one gold dish weighing ten shekels, filled with incense; ⁴⁵one young bull, one ram and one male lamb a year old, for a burnt offering; ⁴⁶one male goat for a sin offering; ⁴⁷and two oxen, five rams, five male goats and five male lambs a year old, to be sacrificed as a fellowship offering. This was the offering of Eliasaph son of Deuel.

⁴⁸On the seventh day Elishama son of Ammihud,ˢ the leader of the people of Ephraim, brought his offering.

⁴⁹His offering was one silver plate weighing a hundred and thirty shekels, and one silver sprinkling bowl weighing seventy shekels, both according to the sanctuary shekel, each filled with fine flour mixed with oil as a grain offering; ⁵⁰one gold dish weighing ten shekels, filled with incense; ⁵¹one young bull, one ram and one male lamb a year old, for a burnt offering; ⁵²one male goat for a sin offering; ⁵³and two oxen, five rams, five male goats and five male lambs a year old, to be sacrificed as a fellowship offering. This was the offering of Elishama son of Ammihud.ᵗ

⁵⁴On the eighth day Gamaliel son of Pedahzur,ᵘ the leader of the people of Manasseh, brought his offering.

⁵⁵His offering was one silver plate weighing a hundred and thirty shekels, and one silver sprinkling bowl weighing seventy shekels, both according to the sanctuary shekel, each filled with fine flour mixed with oil as a grain offering; ⁵⁶one gold dish weighing ten shekels, filled with incense; ⁵⁷one young bull, one ram and one male lamb a year old, for a burnt offering; ⁵⁸one male goat for a sin offering; ⁵⁹and two oxen, five rams, five male goats and five male lambs a year old, to be sacrificed as a fellowship offering. This was the offering of Gamaliel son of Pedahzur.

⁶⁰On the ninth day Abidan son of Gideoni,ᵛ the leader of the people of Benjamin, brought his offering.

⁶¹His offering was one silver plate weighing a hundred and thirty shekels, and one silver sprinkling bowl weighing seventy shekels, both according to the sanctuary shekel, each filled with fine flour mixed with oil as a grain offering; ⁶²one gold dish weighing ten shekels, filled with incense; ⁶³one young bull, one

ram and one male lamb a year old, for a burnt offering; ⁶⁴one male goat for a sin offering; ⁶⁵and two oxen, five rams, five male goats and five male lambs a year old, to be sacrificed as a fellowship offering. This was the offering of Abidan son of Gideoni.

⁶⁶On the tenth day Ahiezer son of Ammishaddai,ʷ the leader of the people of Dan, brought his offering. ⁶⁷His offering was one silver plate weighing a hundred and thirty shekels, and one silver sprinkling bowl weighing seventy shekels, both according to the sanctuary shekel, each filled with fine flour mixed with oil as a grain offering; ⁶⁸one gold dish weighing ten shekels, filled with incense; ⁶⁹one young bull, one ram and one male lamb a year old, for a burnt offering; ⁷⁰one male goat for a sin offering; ⁷¹and two oxen, five rams, five male goats and five male lambs a year old, to be sacrificed as a fellowship offering. This was the offering of Ahiezer son of Ammishaddai.

⁷²On the eleventh day Pagiel son of Ocran,ˣ the leader of the people of Asher, brought his offering. ⁷³His offering was one silver plate weighing a hundred and thirty shekels, and one silver sprinkling bowl weighing seventy shekels, both according to the sanctuary shekel, each filled with fine flour mixed with oil as a grain offering; ⁷⁴one gold dish weighing ten shekels, filled with incense; ⁷⁵one young bull, one ram and one male lamb a year old, for a burnt offering; ⁷⁶one male goat for a sin offering; ⁷⁷and two oxen, five rams, five male goats and five male lambs a year old, to be sacrificed as a fellowship offering. This was the offering of Pagiel son of Ocran.

⁷⁸On the twelfth day Ahira son of Enan,ʸ the leader of the people of Naphtali, brought his offering. ⁷⁹His offering was one silver plate weighing a hundred and thirty shekels, and one silver sprinkling bowl weighing seventy shekels, both according to the sanctuary shekel, each filled with fine flour mixed with oil as a grain offering; ⁸⁰one gold dish weighing ten shekels, filled with incense; ⁸¹one young bull, one ram and one male lamb a year old, for a burnt offering; ⁸²one male goat for a sin offering; ⁸³and two oxen, five rams, five male goats and five male lambs a year old, to be sacrificed as a fellowship offering. This was the offering of Ahira son of Enan.

⁸⁴These were the offerings of the Israelite leaders for the dedication of the altar when it was anointed:ᶻ twelve silver plates, twelve silver sprinkling bowlsᵃ and twelve gold dishes.ᵇ ⁸⁵Each silver plate weighed a hundred and thirty shekels, and each sprinkling bowl seventy shekels. Altogether, the silver dishes weighed two thousand four hundred shekels,ʳ according to the sanctuary shekel.ᶜ ⁸⁶The twelve gold dishes filled with incense weighed ten shekels each, according to the sanctuary shekel.ᵈ Altogether, the gold dishes weighed a hundred and twenty shekels.ˢ ⁸⁷The total number of animals for the burnt offeringᵉ came to twelve young bulls, twelve rams and twelve male lambs a year old, together with their grain offering.ᶠ Twelve male goats were used for the sin offering.ᵍ ⁸⁸The total number of animals for the sacrifice of the fellowship offeringʰ came to twenty-four oxen, sixty rams, sixty male goats and sixty male lambsⁱ a year old. These were the offerings for the dedication of the altar after it was anointed.ʲ

⁸⁹When Moses entered the Tent of Meetingᵏ to speak with the LORD,ˡ he heard the voice speaking to him from between the two cherubim above the atonement coverᵐ on the ark of the Testimony.ⁿ And he spoke with him.

Setting Up the Lamps

8 The LORD said to Moses, ²"Speak to Aaron and say to him, 'When you set up the seven lamps, they are to light the area in front of the lampstand.ᵒ'"

³Aaron did so; he set up the lamps so that they faced forward on the lampstand,

---

ʳ 85 That is, about 60 pounds (about 28 kilograms) ˢ 86 That is, about 3 pounds (about 1.4 kilograms) just as the LORD commanded Moses. ⁴This is how the lampstand was made: It was made of hammered gold ᵖ—from its base to its blossoms. The lampstand was made exactly like the pattern ᵠ the LORD had shown Moses.

The Setting Apart of the Levites

⁵The LORD said to Moses: ⁶"Take the Levites from among the other Israelites and make them ceremonially clean.ʳ ⁷To purify them, do this: Sprinkle the water of cleansingˢ on them; then have them shave their whole bodiesᵗ and wash their clothes,ᵘ and so purify themselves.ᵛ ⁸Have them take a young bull with its grain offering of fine flour mixed with oil;ʷ then you are to take a second young bull for a sin offering.ˣ ⁹Bring the Levites to the front of the Tent of Meetingʸ and assemble the whole Israelite community.ᶻ ¹⁰You are to bring the Levites before the LORD, and the Israelites are to lay their hands on them.ᵃ ¹¹Aaron is to present the Levites before the LORD as a wave offeringᵇ from the Israelites, so that they may be ready to do the work of the LORD.

¹²"After the Levites lay their hands on the heads of the bulls,ᶜ use the one for a sin offeringᵈ to the LORD and the other for a burnt offering,ᵉ to make atonementᶠ for the Levites. ¹³Have the Levites stand in front of Aaron and his sons and then present them as a wave offeringᵍ to the LORD. ¹⁴In this way you are to set the Levites apart from the other Israelites, and the Levites will be mine.ʰ

¹⁵"After you have purified the Levites and presented them as a wave offering,ⁱ they are to come to do their work at the Tent of Meeting.ʲ ¹⁶They are the Israelites who are to be given wholly to me. I have taken them as my own in place of the firstborn,ᵏ the first male offspring ᶫ from every Israelite woman. ¹⁷Every firstborn male in Israel, whether man or animal,ᵐ is mine. When I struck down all the firstborn in Egypt, I set them apart for myself.ⁿᵒ ¹⁸And I have taken the Levites in place of all the firstborn sons in Israel.ᵖ ¹⁹Of all the Israelites, I have given the Levites as gifts to Aaron and his sonsᵠ to do the work at the Tent of Meeting on behalf of the Israelitesʳ and to make atonement for themˢ so that no plague will strike the Israelites when they go near the sanctuary."

²⁰Moses, Aaron and the whole Israelite community did with the Levites just as the LORD commanded Moses. ²¹The Levites purified themselves and washed their clothes.ᵗ Then Aaron presented them as a wave offering before the LORD and made atonementᵘ for them to purify them.ᵛ ²²After that, the Levites came to do their workʷ at the Tent of Meeting under the supervision of Aaron and his sons. They did with the Levites just as the LORD commanded Moses.

²³The LORD said to Moses, ²⁴"This applies to the Levites: Men twenty-five years old or moreˣ shall come to take part in the work at the Tent of Meeting,ʸ ²⁵but at the age of fifty,ᶻ they must retire from their regular service and work no longer. ²⁶They may assist their brothers in performing their duties at the Tent of Meeting, but they themselves must not do the work.ᵃ This, then, is how you are to assign the responsibilities of the Levites."

The Passover

9 The LORD spoke to Moses in the Desert of Sinai in the first monthᵇ of the second year after they came out of Egypt.ᶜ He said, ²"Have the Israelites celebrate the Passoverᵈ at the appointed time.ᵉ ³Celebrate it at the appointed time, at twilight on the fourteenth day of this month,ᶠ in accordance with all its rules and regulations.ᵍ"

⁴So Moses told the Israelites to celebrate the Passover,ʰ ⁵and they did so in the Desert of Sinaiⁱ at twilight on the fourteenth day of the first month.ʲ The Israelites did everything just as the LORD commanded Moses.ᵏ

⁶But some of them could not celebrate the Passover on that day because they were ceremonially uncleanⁱ on account of a dead body.ᵐ So they came to Moses and Aaronⁿ that same day ⁷and said to Moses, "We have become unclean because of a dead body, but why should we be kept from presenting the LORD's offering with the other Israelites at the appointed time?ᵒ"

⁸Moses answered them, "Wait until I

find out what the LORD commands concerning you."ᵖ

⁹Then the LORD said to Moses, ¹⁰"Tell the Israelites: 'When any of you or your descendants are unclean because of a dead bodyᵠ or are away on a journey, they may still celebrateʳ the LORD's Passover. ¹¹They are to celebrate it on the fourteenth day of the second monthˢ at twilight. They are to eat the lamb, together with unleavened bread and bitter herbs.ᵗ ¹²They must not leave any of it till morningᵘ or break any of its bones.ᵛ When they celebrate the Passover, they must follow all the regulations.ʷ ¹³But if a man who is ceremonially clean and not on a journey fails to celebrate the Passover, that person must be cut off from his peopleˣ because he did not present the LORD's offering at the appointed time. That man will bear the consequences of his sin.

¹⁴" 'An alienʸ living among you who wants to celebrate the LORD's Passover must do so in accordance with its rules and regulations. You must have the same regulations for the alien and the native-born.' "

The Cloud Above the Tabernacle

¹⁵On the day the tabernacle, the Tent of the Testimony,ᶻ was set up,ᵃ the cloudᵇ covered it. From evening till morning the cloud above the tabernacle looked like fire.ᶜ ¹⁶That is how it continued to be; the cloud covered it, and at night it looked like fire.ᵈ ¹⁷Whenever the cloud lifted from above the Tent, the Israelites set out;ᵉ wherever the cloud settled, the Israelites encamped.ᶠ ¹⁸At the LORD's command the Israelites set out, and at his command they encamped. As long as the cloud stayed over the tabernacle, they remainedᵍ in camp. ¹⁹When the cloud remained over the tabernacle a long time, the Israelites obeyed the LORD's orderʰ and did not set out.ⁱ ²⁰Sometimes the cloud was over the tabernacle only a few days; at the LORD's command they would encamp, and then at his command they would set out. ²¹Sometimes the cloud stayed only from evening till morning, and when it lifted in the morning, they set out. Whether by day or by night, whenever the cloud lifted, they set out. ²²Whether the cloud stayed over the tabernacle for two days or a month or a year, the Israelites would remain in camp and not set out; but when it lifted, they would set out. ²³At the LORD's command they encamped, and at the LORD's command they set out. They obeyed the LORD's order, in accordance with his command through Moses.

The Silver Trumpets

10 The LORD said to Moses: ²"Make two trumpetsʲ of hammered silver, and use them for calling the communityᵏ together and for having the camps set out.ˡ ³When both are sounded, the whole community is to assemble before you at the entrance to the Tent of Meeting. ⁴If only one is sounded, the leadersᵐ—the heads of the clans of Israel—are to assemble before you. ⁵When a trumpet blast is sounded, the tribes camping on the east are to set out.ⁿ ⁶At the sounding of a second blast, the camps on the south are to set out.ᵒ The blast will be the signal for setting out. ⁷To gather the assembly, blow the trumpets,ᵖ but not with the same signal.ᵠ

⁸"The sons of Aaron, the priests, are to blow the trumpets. This is to be a lasting ordinance for you and the generations to come.ʳ ⁹When you go into battle in your own land against an enemy who is oppressing you,ˢ sound a blast on the trumpets.ᵗ Then you will be rememberedᵘ by the LORD your God and rescued from your

---

10:2–7 Israel was commanded to make two, silver trumpets—long, straight, slender metal tubes with flared ends. These trumpets were blown to call the whole assembly to the tabernacle or to announce Israel's special feasts. In addition, two blasts were blown from these trumpets when the Israelites were to break camp. The first blast alerted the camp to start to pack up their tents and the tabernacle furnishings. When the second blast was blown, the Israelites were to "set out" (Nu 10:6). This response to the trumpet call may be what Paul had in mind when he wrote, "We will not all sleep, but we will all be changed—in a flash, in the twinkling of an eye, at the last trumpet" (1Co 15:51–52). See the study notes accompanying 1Co 15:51.

enemies. ¹⁰Also at your times of rejoicing—your appointed feasts and New Moon festivals—you are to sound the trumpets over your burnt offerings and fellowship offerings, and they will be a memorial for you before your God. I am the LORD your God."

The Israelites Leave Sinai

¹¹On the twentieth day of the second month of the second year, the cloud lifted from above the tabernacle of the Testimony. ¹²Then the Israelites set out from the Desert of Sinai and traveled from place to place until the cloud came to rest in the Desert of Paran. ¹³They set out, this first time, at the LORD's command through Moses.

¹⁴The divisions of the camp of Judah went first, under their standard. Nahshon son of Amminadab was in command. ¹⁵Nethanel son of Zuar was over the division of the tribe of Issachar, ¹⁶and Eliab son of Helon was over the division of the tribe of Zebulun. ¹⁷Then the tabernacle was taken down, and the Gershonites and Merarites, who carried it, set out.

¹⁸The divisions of the camp of Reuben went next, under their standard. Elizur son of Shedeur was in command. ¹⁹Shelumiel son of Zurishaddai was over the division of the tribe of Simeon, ²⁰and Eliasaph son of Deuel was over the division of the tribe of Gad. ²¹Then the Kohathites set out, carrying the holy things. The tabernacle was to be set up before they arrived.

²²The divisions of the camp of Ephraim went next, under their standard. Elishama son of Ammihud was in command. ²³Gamaliel son of Pedahzur was over the division of the tribe of Manasseh, ²⁴and Abidan son of Gideoni was over the division of the tribe of Benjamin.

²⁵Finally, as the rear guard for all the units, the divisions of the camp of Dan set out, under their standard. Ahiezer son of Ammishaddai was in command. ²⁶Pagiel son of Ocran was over the division of the tribe of Asher, ²⁷and Ahira son of Enan was over the division of the tribe of Naphtali. ²⁸This was the order of march for the Israelite divisions as they set out.

²⁹Now Moses said to Hobab son of Reuel the Midianite, Moses' father-in-law, "We are setting out for the place about which the LORD said, 'I will give it to you.' Come with us and we will treat you well, for the LORD has promised good things to Israel."

³⁰He answered, "No, I will not go; I am going back to my own land and my own people."

³¹But Moses said, "Please do not leave us. You know where we should camp in the desert, and you can be our eyes. ³²If you come with us, we will share with you whatever good things the LORD gives us."

³³So they set out from the mountain of the LORD and traveled for three days. The ark of the covenant of the LORD went before them during those three days to find them a place to rest. ³⁴The cloud of the LORD was over them by day when they set out from the camp.

³⁵Whenever the ark set out, Moses said,

"Rise up, O LORD!
    May your enemies be scattered;
    may your foes flee before you."

³⁶Whenever it came to rest, he said,

"Return, O LORD,
    to the countless thousands of Israel."

Fire From the LORD

11 Now the people complained about their hardships in the hearing of the LORD, and when he heard them his anger was aroused. Then fire from the LORD burned among them and consumed some of the outskirts of the camp. ²When the people cried out to Mo-

l Lev 26:44–45 ◀ ▶ Nu 24:7–9
U Nu 6:24–27 ◀ ▶ Nu 23:10

t 10 Traditionally *peace offerings*

10:29 Moses invited his brother-in-law, Hobab the Midianite, to join the Israelites. Hobab's skills in the desert would have undoubtedly been helpful to the Israelites. Moses recognized this and promised Hobab that he would be well treated and experience the blessings God promised to his chosen people.

ses, he prayed to the LORD and the fire died down. ³So that place was called Taberah, because fire from the LORD had burned among them.

Quail From the LORD

⁴The rabble with them began to crave other food, and again the Israelites started wailing and said, "If only we had meat to eat! ⁵We remember the fish we ate in Egypt at no cost—also the cucumbers, melons, leeks, onions and garlic. ⁶But now we have lost our appetite; we never see anything but this manna!"

⁷The manna was like coriander seed and looked like resin. ⁸The people went around gathering it, and then ground it in a handmill or crushed it in a mortar. They cooked it in a pot or made it into cakes. And it tasted like something made with olive oil. ⁹When the dew settled on the camp at night, the manna also came down.

¹⁰Moses heard the people of every family wailing, each at the entrance to his tent. The LORD became exceedingly angry, and Moses was troubled. ¹¹He asked the LORD, "Why have you brought this trouble on your servant? What have I done to displease you that you put the burden of all these people on me? ¹²Did I conceive all these people? Did I give them birth? Why do you tell me to carry them in my arms, as a nurse carries an infant, to the land you promised on oath to their forefathers? ¹³Where can I get meat for all these people? They keep wailing to me, 'Give us meat to eat!' ¹⁴I cannot carry all these people by myself; the burden is too heavy for me. ¹⁵If this is how you are going to treat me, put me to death right now—if I have found favor in your eyes—and do not let me face my own ruin."

¹⁶The LORD said to Moses: "Bring me seventy of Israel's elders who are known to you as leaders and officials among the people. Have them come to the Tent of Meeting, that they may stand there with you. ¹⁷I will come down and speak with you there, and I will take of the Spirit that is on you and put the Spirit on them. They will help you carry the burden of the people so that you will not have to carry it alone.

¹⁸"Tell the people: 'Consecrate yourselves in preparation for tomorrow, when you will eat meat. The LORD heard you when you wailed, "If only we had meat to eat! We were better off in Egypt!" Now the LORD will give you meat, and you will eat it. ¹⁹You will not eat it for just one day, or two days, or five, ten or twenty days, ²⁰but for a whole month—until it comes out of your nostrils and you loathe it—because you have rejected the LORD, who is among you, and have wailed before him, saying, "Why did we ever leave Egypt?" ' "

²¹But Moses said, "Here I am among six hundred thousand men on foot, and you say, 'I will give them meat to eat for a whole month!' ²²Would they have enough if flocks and herds were slaughtered for them? Would they have enough if all the fish in the sea were caught for them?"

²³The LORD answered Moses, "Is the LORD's arm too short? You will now see whether or not what I say will come true for you."

²⁴So Moses went out and told the people what the LORD had said. He brought together seventy of their elders and had them stand around the Tent. ²⁵Then the LORD came down in the cloud and spoke with him, and he took of the Spirit that was on him and put the Spirit on the seventy elders. When the Spirit rested on them, they prophesied, but they did not do so again.

²⁶However, two men, whose names were Eldad and Medad, had remained in the camp. They were listed among the elders, but did not go out to the Tent. Yet the Spirit also rested on them, and they prophesied in the camp. ²⁷A young man ran and told Moses, "Eldad and Medad are prophesying in the camp."

²⁸Joshua son of Nun, who had been Moses' aide since youth, spoke up and said, "Moses, my lord, stop them!"

²⁹But Moses replied, "Are you jealous

for my sake? I wish that all the LORD's people were prophets[x] and that the LORD would put his Spirit[y] on them!"[z] ³⁰Then Moses and the elders of Israel returned to the camp.

³¹Now a wind went out from the LORD and drove quail[a] in from the sea. It brought them[w] down all around the camp to about three feet[x] above the ground, as far as a day's walk in any direction. ³²All that day and night and all the next day the people went out and gathered quail. No one gathered less than ten homers.[y] Then they spread them out all around the camp. ³³But while the meat was still between their teeth[b] and before it could be consumed, the anger[c] of the LORD burned against the people, and he struck them with a severe plague.[d] ³⁴Therefore the place was named Kibroth Hattaavah,[z][e] because there they buried the people who had craved other food.

³⁵From Kibroth Hattaavah the people traveled to Hazeroth[f] and stayed there.

Miriam and Aaron Oppose Moses

12 Miriam[g] and Aaron began to talk against Moses because of his Cushite wife,[h] for he had married a Cushite. ²"Has the LORD spoken only through Moses?" they asked. "Hasn't he also spoken through us?"[i] And the LORD heard this.[j]

³(Now Moses was a very humble man,[k] more humble than anyone else on the face of the earth.)

⁴At once the LORD said to Moses, Aaron and Miriam, "Come out to the Tent of Meeting, all three of you." So the three of them came out. ⁵Then the LORD came down in a pillar of cloud;[l] he stood at the entrance to the Tent and summoned Aaron and Miriam. When both of them stepped forward, ⁶he said, "Listen to my words:

"When a prophet of the LORD is among you,
I reveal[m] myself to him in visions,[n]
I speak to him in dreams.[o]
⁷But this is not true of my servant Moses;[p]
he is faithful in all my house.[q]
⁸With him I speak face to face,
clearly and not in riddles;[r]

he sees the form of the LORD.[s]
Why then were you not afraid
to speak against my servant
Moses?"[t]

⁹The anger of the LORD burned against them,[u] and he left them.[v] ¹⁰When the cloud lifted from above the Tent,[w] there stood Miriam—leprous,[a] like snow.[x] Aaron turned toward her and saw that she had leprosy;[y] ¹¹and he said to Moses, "Please, my lord, do not hold against us the sin we have so foolishly committed.[z] ¹²Do not let her be like a stillborn infant coming from its mother's womb with its flesh half eaten away."

¹³So Moses cried out to the LORD, "O God, please heal her![a]"

¹⁴The LORD replied to Moses, "If her father had spit in her face,[b] would she not have been in disgrace for seven days? Confine her outside the camp[c] for seven days; after that she can be brought back." ¹⁵So Miriam was confined outside the camp[d] for seven days,[e] and the people did not move on till she was brought back.

¹⁶After that, the people left Hazeroth[f] and encamped in the Desert of Paran.[g]

Exploring Canaan

13 The LORD said to Moses, ²"Send some men to explore[h] the land of Canaan,[i] which I am giving to the Israelites.[j] From each ancestral tribe[k] send one of its leaders."

³So at the LORD's command Moses sent them out from the Desert of Paran. All of them were leaders of the Israelites.[l] ⁴These are their names:

from the tribe of Reuben, Shammua
  son of Zaccur;
⁵from the tribe of Simeon, Shaphat
  son of Hori;
⁶from the tribe of Judah, Caleb son of
  Jephunneh;[m]
⁷from the tribe of Issachar, Igal son
  of Joseph;
⁸from the tribe of Ephraim, Hoshea
  son of Nun;[n]

D ▸ Nu 11:33–34 ◂▸ Nu 14:12
E ▸ Ex 4:7 ◂▸ Nu 16:46–50

w 31 Or They flew x 31 Hebrew two cubits (about 1 meter) y 32 That is, probably about 60 bushels (about 2.2 kiloliters) z 34 Kibroth Hattaavah means graves of craving. a 10 The Hebrew word was used for various diseases affecting the skin—not necessarily leprosy.

F ▸ Nu 11:18–23 ◂▸ Nu 20:7–11
D ▸ Nu 5:27 ◂▸ Nu 12:9–10

⁹from the tribe of Benjamin, Palti son of Raphu;
¹⁰from the tribe of Zebulun, Gaddiel son of Sodi;
¹¹from the tribe of Manasseh (a tribe of Joseph), Gaddi son of Susi;
¹²from the tribe of Dan, Ammiel son of Gemalli;
¹³from the tribe of Asher, Sethur son of Michael;
¹⁴from the tribe of Naphtali, Nahbi son of Vophsi;
¹⁵from the tribe of Gad, Geuel son of Maki.

¹⁶These are the names of the men Moses sent to explore° the land. (Moses gave Hoshea son of Nunᵖ the name Joshua.)ᵠ

¹⁷When Moses sent them to explore Canaan,ʳ he said, "Go up through the Negevˢ and on into the hill country.ᵗ ¹⁸See what the land is like and whether the people who live there are strong or weak, few or many. ¹⁹What kind of land do they live in? Is it good or bad? What kind of towns do they live in? Are they unwalled or fortified? ²⁰How is the soil? Is it fertile or poor? Are there trees on it or not? Do your best to bring back some of the fruit of the land.ᵘ" (It was the season for the first ripe grapes.)ᵛ

²¹So they went up and explored the land from the Desert of Zinʷ as far as Rehob,ˣ toward Leboᵇ Hamath.ʸ ²²They went up through the Negev and came to Hebron,ᶻ where Ahiman, Sheshai and Talmai,ᵃ the descendants of Anak,ᵇ lived. (Hebron had been built seven years before Zoan in Egypt.)ᶜ ²³When they reached the Valley of Eshcol,ᶜᵈ they cut off a branch bearing a single cluster of grapes. Two of them carried it on a pole between them, along with some pomegranatesᵉ and figs.ᶠ ²⁴That place was called the Valley of Eshcol because of the cluster of grapes the Israelites cut off there. ²⁵At the end of forty daysᵍ they returned from exploring the land.ʰ

Report on the Exploration

²⁶They came back to Moses and Aaron and the whole Israelite community at Kadeshⁱ in the Desert of Paran.ʲ There they reported to themᵏ and to the whole assembly and showed them the fruit of the land.ˡ ²⁷They gave Moses this account: "We went into the land to which you sent us, and it does flow with milk and honey!ᵐ Here is its fruit.ⁿ ²⁸But the people who live there are powerful, and the cities are fortified and very large.ᵒ We even saw descendants of Anakᵖ there.ᵠ ²⁹The Amalekitesʳ live in the Negev; the Hittites,ˢ Jebusitesᵗ and Amoritesᵘ live in the hill country;ᵛ and the Canaanitesʷ live near the sea and along the Jordan.ˣ"

³⁰Then Calebʸ silenced the people before Moses and said, "We should go up and take possession of the land, for we can certainly do it."

³¹But the men who had gone up with him said, "We can't attack those people; they are stronger than we are."ᶻ ³²And they spread among the Israelites a bad reportᵃ about the land they had explored. They said, "The land we explored devoursᵇ those living in it. All the people we saw there are of great size.ᶜ ³³We saw the Nephilimᵈ there (the descendants of Anakᵉ come from the Nephilim). We seemed like grasshoppersᶠ in our own eyes, and we looked the same to them."

The People Rebel

14 That night all the people of the community raised their voices and wept aloud.ᵍ ²All the Israelites grumbledʰ against Moses and Aaron, and the

---

ᵇ21 Or *toward the entrance to* ᶜ23 *Eshcol* means *cluster*; also in verse 24.

13:27–33 The report of the ten spies acknowledged that the promised land flowed "with milk and honey" (13:27). They also correctly reported that the cities were walled and well defended and that the people of the land were strong and very large. While Joshua and Caleb saw God's overcoming power through their eyes of faith, ten of the spies saw horrible obstacles through their eyes of fear as they told the terrified Israelites, "We seemed like grasshoppers in our own eyes" (Nu 13:33). See note on Ge 6:4.

14:1–2 The frightening words of the fearful spies caused the Israelites to lose faith in God's promises to help them possess the promised land. They preferred instead to return to slavery in Egypt. Focused on their problems instead of their provider, the Israelites had no hope. When Moses, Aaron and Caleb appealed to them to have faith in God's prophecies "all the congregation bade stone them with stones" (Nu 14:10).

whole assembly said to them, "If only we had died in Egypt!ⁱ Or in this desert! ³Why is the LORD bringing us to this land only to let us fall by the sword?ᵏ Our wives and children¹ will be taken as plunder.ᵐ Wouldn't it be better for us to go back to Egypt?ⁿ" ⁴And they said to each other, "We should choose a leader and go back to Egypt.ᵒ"

⁵Then Moses and Aaron fell facedownᵖ in front of the whole Israelite assemblyᵠ gathered there. ⁶Joshua son of Nunʳ and Caleb son of Jephunneh, who were among those who had explored the land, tore their clothesˢ ⁷and said to the entire Israelite assembly, "The land we passed through and explored is exceedingly good.ᵗ ⁸If the LORD is pleased with us,ᵘ he will lead us into that land, a land flowing with milk and honey,ᵛ and will give it to us.ʷ ⁹Only do not rebelˣ against the LORD. And do not be afraidʸ of the people of the land,ᶻ because we will swallow them up. Their protection is gone, but the LORD is withᵃ us.ᵇ Do not be afraid of them."ᶜ

¹⁰But the whole assembly talked about stoningᵈ them. Then the glory of the LORDᵉ appeared at the Tent of Meeting to all the Israelites. ¹¹The LORD said to Moses, "How long will these people treat me with contempt?ᶠ How long will they refuse to believe in me,ᵍ in spite of all the miraculous signsʰ I have performed among them? ¹²I will strike them down with a plagueⁱ and destroy them, but I will make you into a nationʲ greater and stronger than they."ᵏ

¹³Moses said to the LORD, "Then the Egyptians will hear about it! By your power you brought these people up from among them.ˡ ¹⁴And they will tell the inhabitants of this land about it. They have already heardᵐ that you, O LORD, are with these peopleⁿ and that you, O LORD, have been seen face to face,ᵒ that your cloud stays over them,ᵖ and that you go before them in a pillar of cloud by day and a pillar of fire by night.ᵠ ¹⁵If you put these people to death all at one time, the nations who have heard this report about you will say, ¹⁶'The LORD was not able to bring these people into the land he promised them on oath;ʳ so he slaughtered them in the desert.'ˢ

¹⁷"Now may the Lord's strength be displayed, just as you have declared: ¹⁸'The LORD is slow to anger, abounding in love and forgiving sin and rebellion.ᵗ Yet he does not leave the guilty unpunished; he punishes the children for the sin of the fathers to the third and fourth generation.'ᵘ ¹⁹In accordance with your great love, forgiveᵛ the sin of these people,ʷ just as you have pardoned them from the time they left Egypt until now."ˣ

²⁰The LORD replied, "I have forgiven them,ʸ as you asked. ²¹Nevertheless, as surely as I liveᶻ and as surely as the glory of the LORDᵃ fills the whole earth,ᵇ ²²not one of the men who saw my glory and

---

14:11–12 This passage marks the second time since the exodus that God speaks of starting over with Moses to create a nation that would be faithful to God alone (see Ex 32:10). The Israelites were given the privilege to obey God and participate in his blessings, but many times they chose to disobey him. Yet God did not need their faithfulness to fulfill his purposes. He will always accomplish his perfect plan, with or without human obedience. But we will suffer the consequences of our disobedience, just as the Israelites did.

14:21 The phrase "the glory of the LORD fills the whole earth" appears here for the first time. It occurs throughout Scripture in various forms (see Ps 72:19; 86:9; Isa 6:3; Hab 2:14; Mal 1:11). The coming kingdom of the Messiah will usher in the day when this phrase will be a reality (see Rev 4:11; 15:4).

14:22–23 Although God did not annihilate the Israelites because of their rebellion, justice required punishment. All throughout the exodus the Israelites had repeatedly disobeyed the Lord (see Ex 14:10–12; 15:22–24; 16:1–3, 19–20, 27–30; 17:1–4; 32:1–35; Nu 11:1–3, 4–34; 14:3). Consequently, God declared that every adult, above twenty years of age who had "disobeyed me" (14:22) would die in the desert. In this way the

The Biblical Anniversaries of Israel

JUST AS WE attach special significance to certain happenings in our lives like birthdays or anniversaries, some of the significant happenings in the life of Israel occurred on some of the same days that had been important to their ancestors. In effect these days became Biblical anniversaries, visual reminders of God's sovereignty and plan for his people. Some of these visual reminders were tied to Israel's feasts. In giving the laws to his people, God set several appointed feasts for Israel to observe at specific times during the year (see Lev 23). Each feast commemorated a specific event in God's interaction with Israel. Some feasts were celebrated annually, such as Passover. Others were celebrated more often; the Sabbath was observed every week.

The apostle Paul understood that the feasts and celebrations were intended by the Lord as prophetic signs of future events and referred to them as "a shadow of the things that were to come" (Col 2:17). Looking back from the vantage point of modern history we can observe specific prophecies that were fulfilled on or near several of these special celebrations. Just as we anticipate our next birthday, note that some of these "anniversaries" are still to come.

The First Day of Nisan
The first day of the month of Nisan was a time for ritual cleansing and new beginnings for the Jews. Nisan was the first month in the Jewish civil calendar. Three events symbolizing new beginnings have already transpired in Israel's history on this important anniversary. One event still remains to be fulfilled.
1. The dedication of the tabernacle (see Ex 40:17)
2. The cleansing of the temple by King Hezekiah (see 2Ch 29:2–3, 17)
3. Ezra and the exiles return to Jerusalem from Babylon (see Ezr 7:9)
4. The future cleansing of the millennial temple (see Eze 45:18)

The Tenth Day of Nisan
Sanctification is the theme associated with the tenth day of Nisan. It was the day connected with setting apart someone or something for a holy purpose. There are three major events associated with this special day.
1. The lamb is chosen for the Passover (see Ex 12:3–6)
2. Israel crosses the Jordan River and enters Canaan (see Jos 4:19)
3. Ezekiel's vision of the millennial temple (see Eze 40:1–2)

The Passover
"The LORD's Passover begins at twilight on the fourteenth day of the first month" (Lev 23:5). Passover was the first of three annual feasts that required mandatory attendance of all

men at the temple. The Passover holds forth the promise of a final atonement when the Messiah will redeem all those who look to him for salvation. Six times in their history the Passover has marked a milestone in the spiritual and national life of Israel.
1. The Passover supper eaten in Egypt (see Ex 12:41)
2. The Passover supper eaten at Sinai (see Nu 9:5)
3. The first Passover in Canaan (see Jos 5:10)
4. King Josiah celebrates the Passover (see 2Ch 35:1)
5. Ezra and the exiles celebrate the Passover (see Ezr 6:16–19)
6. The Last Supper observed at Passover (see Lk 22:7–11)

The Feast of Pentecost
Celebrated fifty days after the Feast of Firstfruits, the Feast of Pentecost was the second of the three required celebrations at the temple in Jerusalem. Two special events took place on this feast, introducing a special time of spiritual stewardship to a specific new revelation of God.
1. The giving of the Law (see Ex 19:1–11)
2. The giving of the Holy Spirit (see Ac 2:1–4)

The Feast of Trumpets
This feast signaled the beginning of the agricultural calendar, a New Year's celebration marked by the blowing of trumpets, cessation of work and convening together to celebrate. At this time the people would be reminded of the long-awaited day when the Lord would be revealed as King and accepted as the ruler of the whole world. Two spiritually important events have already occurred on the anniversary of this feast.
1. God institutes the Feast of Trumpets (see Lev 23:23–24)
2. The high priest brings the first offering to the rebuilt altar (see Ezr 3:1–6)
3. Ezra reads the Law to the returned exiles (see Ne 8:2–3)

A Shadow of Things to Come
Of the seven appointed feasts mentioned in Leviticus 23, four of them have found prophetic fulfillment in the major events in the life of Jesus Christ. During the Passover Jesus instituted the Last Supper and the new covenant of his blood. The Feast of Unleavened Bread, the day after Passover, coincided with the crucifixion of Christ, the sinless Son of God who was untainted by the leaven of the Pharisees. The Feast of Firstfruits marked the day of resurrection when Christ became "the firstfruits of those who have fallen asleep" (1Co 15:20). And the Feast of Pentecost heralded the giving of the Holy Spirit.

The three other major celebrations—the Feast of Trumpets, the Day of Atonement and the Feast of Tabernacles—are still only shadows of things to come and may be fulfilled at the climactic Battle of Armageddon as Christ ushers in his millennial kingdom. What better event could happen than the deliverance from persecution and the beginning of the prophesied kingdom of God on earth? That would be worth an anniversary forever in Jerusalem (see Zec 14:16).

the miraculous signs[c] I performed in Egypt and in the desert but who disobeyed me and tested me ten times[d]— [23]not one of them will ever see the land I promised on oath[e] to their forefathers. No one who has treated me with contempt[f] will ever see it.[g] [24]But because my servant Caleb[h] has a different spirit and follows me wholeheartedly,[i] I will bring him into the land he went to, and his descendants will inherit it.[j] [25]Since the Amalekites[k] and Canaanites[l] are living in the valleys, turn[m] back tomorrow and set out toward the desert along the route to the Red Sea.[d][n]"

[26]The LORD said to Moses and Aaron: [27]"How long will this wicked community grumble against me? I have heard the complaints of these grumbling Israelites.[o] [28]So tell them, 'As surely as I live,[p] declares the LORD, I will do to you[q] the very things I heard you say: [29]In this desert your bodies will fall[r]—every one of you twenty years old or more[s] who was counted in the census[t] and who has grumbled against me. [30]Not one of you will enter the land[u] I swore with uplifted hand[v] to make your home, except Caleb son of Jephunneh[w] and Joshua son of Nun.[x] [31]As for your children that you said would be taken as plunder, I will bring them in to enjoy the land you have rejected.[y] [32]But you—your bodies will fall[z] in this desert. [33]Your children will be shepherds here for forty years,[a] suffering for your unfaithfulness, until the last of your bodies lies in the desert. [34]For forty years[b]—one year for each of the forty days you explored the land[c]—you will

suffer for your sins and know what it is like to have me against you.' [35]I, the LORD, have spoken, and I will surely do these things[d] to this whole wicked community, which has banded together against me. They will meet their end in this desert; here they will die.[e]"

[36]So the men Moses had sent[f] to explore the land, who returned and made the whole community grumble[g] against him by spreading a bad report[h] about it— [37]these men responsible for spreading the bad report[i] about the land were struck down and died of a plague[j] before the LORD. [38]Of the men who went to explore the land,[k] only Joshua son of Nun and Caleb son of Jephunneh survived.[l]

[39]When Moses reported this[m] to all the Israelites, they mourned[n] bitterly. [40]Early the next morning they went up toward the high hill country.[o] "We have sinned[p]," they said. "We will go up to the place the LORD promised."

[41]But Moses said, "Why are you disobeying the LORD's command? This will not succeed![q] [42]Do not go up, because the LORD is not with you. You will be defeated by your enemies,[r] [43]for the Amalekites[s] and Canaanites[t] will face you there. Because you have turned away from the LORD, he will not be with you[u] and you will fall by the sword."

[44]Nevertheless, in their presumption they went up[v] toward the high hill coun-

---

nation would be purged of rebellion; only the children born on this arduous journey would see the promised land.

14:32–34 The Lord punished the Israelites with one year in the desert for each day that the spies searched out the land—forty years for forty days. During that time the older generation of Israelites would die, leaving only the younger generation to enter the promised land.

14:36–37 The judgment on the ten spies who sinfully rebelled against the Lord's command to conquer Canaan was immediate—each one died of a plague. The two faithful spies, Joshua and Caleb, were the only adult Israelites who lived through the exodus from Egypt and crossed into Canaan forty years later.

14:39 After Moses' prophecy of judgment the Israelites "mourned bitterly," knowing they would all die in the wilderness. Yet Joshua and Caleb were spared this tragedy because of their faith in God. They were God's believing remnant in a nation of unbelievers. Believers, both Jew and Gentile, can faithfully hold on to God's promises and look expectantly to that great day when their Messiah will come to end their suffering. When the Messianic kingdom arrives, the mournful fasting and sorrow of Israel will be transformed and "will become joyful and glad occasions and happy festivals for Judah" (Zec 8:19).

try, though neither Moses nor the ark of the LORD's covenant moved from the camp.[w] [45]Then the Amalekites and Canaanites[x] who lived in that hill country[y] came down and attacked them and beat them down all the way to Hormah.[z]

Supplementary Offerings

15 The LORD said to Moses, [2]"Speak to the Israelites and say to them: 'After you enter the land I am giving you[a] as a home [3]and you present to the LORD offerings made by fire, from the herd or the flock,[b] as an aroma pleasing to the LORD[c]—whether burnt offerings[d] or sacrifices, for special vows or freewill offerings[e] or festival offerings[f]— [4]then the one who brings his offering shall present to the LORD a grain offering[g] of a tenth of an ephah[e] of fine flour[h] mixed with a quarter of a hin[f] of oil. [5]With each lamb[i] for the burnt offering or the sacrifice, prepare a quarter of a hin of wine[j] as a drink offering.[k]

[6]"'With a ram[l] prepare a grain offering[m] of two-tenths of an ephah[g n] of fine flour mixed with a third of a hin[h] of oil,[o] [7]and a third of a hin of wine[p] as a drink offering.[q] Offer it as an aroma pleasing to the LORD.[r]

[8]"'When you prepare a young bull[s] as a burnt offering or sacrifice, for a special vow[t] or a fellowship offering[u] to the LORD, [9]bring with the bull a grain offering[v] of three-tenths of an ephah[w] of fine flour mixed with half a hin[k] of oil. [10]Also bring half a hin of wine[x] as a drink offering.[y] It will be an offering made by fire, an aroma pleasing to the LORD.[z] [11]Each bull or ram, each lamb or young goat, is to be prepared in this manner. [12]Do this for each one, for as many as you prepare.[a]

[13]"'Everyone who is native-born[b] must do these things in this way when he brings an offering made by fire as an aroma pleasing to the LORD.[c] [14]For the generations to come,[d] whenever an alien[e] or anyone else living among you presents an offering[f] made by fire[g] as an aroma pleasing to the LORD, he must do exactly as you do. [15]The community is to have the same rules for you and for the alien living among you; this is a lasting ordinance for the generations to come.[h] You and the alien shall be the same before the LORD: [16]The same laws and regulations will apply both to you and to the alien living among you.'"

[17]The LORD said to Moses, [18]"Speak to the Israelites and say to them: 'When you enter the land to which I am taking you[j] [19]and you eat the food of the land,[k] present a portion as an offering to the LORD.[l] [20]Present a cake from the first of your ground meal[m] and present it as an offering from the threshing floor.[n o] [21]Throughout the generations to come[p] you are to give this offering to the LORD from the first of your ground meal.[q]

Offerings for Unintentional Sins

[22]"'Now if you unintentionally fail to keep any of these commands the LORD gave Moses[r]— [23]any of the LORD's commands to you through him, from the day the LORD gave them and continuing through the generations to come[s]— [24]and if this is done unintentionally[t] without the community being aware of it,[u] then the whole community is to offer a young bull for a burnt offering[v] as an aroma pleasing to the LORD,[w] along with its prescribed grain offering[x] and drink offering,[y] and a male goat for a sin offering.[z] [25]The priest is to make atonement for the whole Israelite community, and they will be forgiven,[a] for it was not intentional[b] and they have brought to the LORD for their wrong an offering made by fire[c] and a sin offering.[d] [26]The whole Israelite community and the aliens living among them will be forgiven, because all the people were involved in the unintentional wrong.[e]

[27]"'But if just one person sins unintentionally,[f] he must bring a year-old female goat for a sin offering.[g] [28]The priest is to make atonement[h] before the LORD for the one who erred by sinning unintentionally, and when atonement has been made for him, he will be forgiven.[i] [29]One and the same law applies to everyone who sins unintentionally, whether he is a native-born Israelite or an alien.[j]

[30]"'But anyone who sins defiantly,[k] whether native-born or alien,[l] blas-

S *Nu 14:22–25* ◄ ► *Nu 32:11*

[e] *4 That is, probably about 2 quarts (about 2 liters)* [f] *4 That is, probably about 1 quart (about 1 liter); also in verse 5* [g] *6 That is, probably about 4 quarts (about 4.5 liters)* [h] *6 That is, probably about 1 1/4 quarts (about 1.2 liters); also in verse 7* [i] *8 Traditionally* peace offering [j] *9 That is, probably about 6 quarts (about 6.5 liters)* [k] *9 That is, probably about 2 quarts (about 2 liters); also in verse 10*

phemes the LORD,^m and that person must be cut off from his people.^n ^31 Because he has despised^o the LORD's word and broken his commands,^p that person must surely be cut off; his guilt remains on him.^q' "

The Sabbath-Breaker Put to Death

^32 While the Israelites were in the desert,^r a man was found gathering wood on the Sabbath day.^s ^33 Those who found him gathering wood brought him to Moses and Aaron and the whole assembly, ^34 and they kept him in custody, because it was not clear what should be done to him.^t ^35 Then the LORD said to Moses, "The man must die.^u The whole assembly must stone him outside the camp.^v" ^36 So the assembly took him outside the camp and stoned him^w to death,^x as the LORD commanded Moses.^y

Tassels on Garments

^37 The LORD said to Moses, ^38 "Speak to the Israelites and say to them: 'Throughout the generations to come^z you are to make tassels on the corners of your garments,^a with a blue cord on each tassel. ^39 You will have these tassels to look at and so you will remember^b all the commands of the LORD, that you may obey them and not prostitute yourselves^c by going after the lusts of your own hearts^d and eyes. ^40 Then you will remember to obey all my commands^e and will be consecrated to your God.^f ^41 I am the LORD your God, who brought you out of Egypt to be your God.^g I am the LORD your God.^h' "

Korah, Dathan and Abiram

16 Korah^i son of Izhar, the son of Kohath, the son of Levi, and certain Reubenites—Dathan and Abiram,^j sons of Eliab,^k and On son of Peleth—became insolent^l ^2 and rose up against Moses.^l With them were 250 Israelite men, well-known community leaders who had been appointed members of the council.^m ^3 They came as a group to oppose Moses and Aaron^n and said to them, "You have gone too far! The whole community is holy,^o every one of them, and the LORD is with them.^p Why then do you set yourselves above the LORD's assembly?"^q

^4 When Moses heard this, he fell facedown.^r ^5 Then he said to Korah and all his followers: "In the morning the LORD will show who belongs to him and who is holy,^s and he will have that person come near him.^t The man he chooses^u he will cause to come near him. ^6 You, Korah, and all your followers^v are to do this: Take censers^w ^7 and tomorrow put fire^x and incense^y in them before the LORD. The man the LORD chooses^z will be the one who is holy.^a You Levites have gone too far!"

^8 Moses also said to Korah, "Now listen, you Levites! ^9 Isn't it enough^b for you that the God of Israel has separated you from the rest of the Israelite community and brought you near himself to do the work at the LORD's tabernacle and to stand before the community and minister to them?^c ^10 He has brought you and all your fellow Levites near himself, but now you are trying to get the priesthood too.^d ^11 It is against the LORD that you and all your followers have banded together. Who is Aaron that you should grumble^e against him?^f"

^12 Then Moses summoned Dathan and Abiram,^g the sons of Eliab. But they said, "We will not come!^h ^13 Isn't it enough that you have brought us up out of a land flowing with milk and honey^i to kill us in the desert?^j And now you also want to lord it over us?^k ^14 Moreover, you haven't brought us into a land flowing with milk and honey^l or given us an inheritance of fields and vineyards.^m Will you gouge out the eyes of^m these men?^n No, we will not come!^o"

^15 Then Moses became very angry^p and said to the LORD, "Do not accept their offering. I have not taken so much as a donkey^q from them, nor have I wronged any of them."

^16 Moses said to Korah, "You and all your followers are to appear before the LORD tomorrow—you and they and Aaron.^r ^17 Each man is to take his censer and put incense in it—250 censers in all—and present it before the LORD. You and Aaron are to present your censers also.^s" ^18 So each man took his censer,^t put fire and incense in it, and stood with Moses and Aaron at the entrance to the Tent of Meeting. ^19 When Korah had gath-

l 11 Or Peleth—took men.   *m* 14 Or you make slaves of; or you deceive

ered all his followers in opposition to them at the entrance to the Tent of Meeting, the glory of the LORD appeared to the entire assembly. ²⁰The LORD said to Moses and Aaron, ²¹"Separate yourselves from this assembly so I can put an end to them at once."

²²But Moses and Aaron fell facedown and cried out, "O God, God of the spirits of all mankind, will you be angry with the entire assembly when only one man sins?"

²³Then the LORD said to Moses, ²⁴"Say to the assembly, 'Move away from the tents of Korah, Dathan and Abiram.'"

²⁵Moses got up and went to Dathan and Abiram, and the elders of Israel followed him. ²⁶He warned the assembly, "Move back from the tents of these wicked men! Do not touch anything belonging to them, or you will be swept away because of all their sins." ²⁷So they moved away from the tents of Korah, Dathan and Abiram. Dathan and Abiram had come out and were standing with their wives, children and little ones at the entrances to their tents.

²⁸Then Moses said, "This is how you will know that the LORD has sent me to do all these things and that it was not my idea: ²⁹If these men die a natural death and experience only what usually happens to men, then the LORD has not sent me. ³⁰But if the LORD brings about something totally new, and the earth opens its mouth and swallows them, with everything that belongs to them, and they go down alive into the grave,ⁿ then you will know that these men have treated the LORD with contempt."

³¹As soon as he finished saying all this, the ground under them split apart ³²and the earth opened its mouth and swallowed them, with their households and all Korah's men and all their possessions. ³³They went down alive into the grave, with everything they owned; the earth closed over them, and they perished and were gone from the community. ³⁴At their cries, all the Israelites around them fled, shouting, "The earth is going to swallow us too!"

³⁵And fire came out from the LORD and consumed the 250 men who were offering the incense.

³⁶The LORD said to Moses, ³⁷"Tell Elea-

zar son of Aaron, the priest, to take the censers out of the smoldering remains and scatter the coals some distance away, for the censers are holy— ³⁸the censers of the men who sinned at the cost of their lives. Hammer the censers into sheets to overlay the altar, for they were presented before the LORD and have become holy. Let them be a sign to the Israelites."

³⁹So Eleazar the priest collected the bronze censers brought by those who had been burned up, and he had them hammered out to overlay the altar, ⁴⁰as the LORD directed him through Moses. This was to remind the Israelites that no one except a descendant of Aaron should come to burn incense before the LORD, or he would become like Korah and his followers.

⁴¹The next day the whole Israelite community grumbled against Moses and Aaron. "You have killed the LORD's people," they said.

⁴²But when the assembly gathered in opposition to Moses and Aaron and turned toward the Tent of Meeting, suddenly the cloud covered it and the glory of the LORD appeared. ⁴³Then Moses and Aaron went to the front of the Tent of Meeting, ⁴⁴and the LORD said to Moses, ⁴⁵"Get away from this assembly so I can put an end to them at once." And they fell facedown.

⁴⁶Then Moses said to Aaron, "Take your censer and put incense in it, along with fire from the altar, and hurry to the assembly to make atonement for them. Wrath has come out from the LORD; the plague has started." ⁴⁷So Aaron did as Moses said, and ran into the midst of the assembly. The plague had already started among the people, but Aaron offered the incense and made atonement for them. ⁴⁸He stood between the living and the dead, and the plague stopped. ⁴⁹But 14,700 people died from the plague, in addition to those who had died because of Korah. ⁵⁰Then Aaron returned to Moses at the entrance to the Tent of Meeting, for the plague had stopped.

D *Nu 9:13–14* ◀ ▶ *Nu 18:17*
D *Nu 14:37* ◀ ▶ *Nu 21:6*
E *Nu 12:9–15* ◀ ▶ *Nu 21:7–9*

ⁿ 30 Hebrew *Sheol*; also in verse 33

The Budding of Aaron's Staff

17 The LORD said to Moses, ²"Speak to the Israelites and get twelve staffs from them, one from the leader of each of their ancestral tribes. Write the name of each man on his staff. ³On the staff of Levi write Aaron's name, for there must be one staff for the head of each ancestral tribe. ⁴Place them in the Tent of Meeting in front of the Testimony, where I meet with you. ⁵The staff belonging to the man I choose will sprout, and I will rid myself of this constant grumbling against you by the Israelites."

⁶So Moses spoke to the Israelites, and their leaders gave him twelve staffs, one for the leader of each of their ancestral tribes, and Aaron's staff was among them. ⁷Moses placed the staffs before the LORD in the Tent of the Testimony.

⁸The next day Moses entered the Tent of the Testimony and saw that Aaron's staff, which represented the house of Levi, had not only sprouted but had budded, blossomed and produced almonds. ⁹Then Moses brought out all the staffs from the LORD's presence to all the Israelites. They looked at them, and each man took his own staff.

¹⁰The LORD said to Moses, "Put back Aaron's staff in front of the Testimony, to be kept as a sign to the rebellious. This will put an end to their grumbling against me, so that they will not die." ¹¹Moses did just as the LORD commanded him.

¹²The Israelites said to Moses, "We will die! We are lost, we are all lost! ¹³Anyone who even comes near the tabernacle of the LORD will die. Are we all going to die?"

Duties of Priests and Levites

18 The LORD said to Aaron, "You, your sons and your father's family are to bear the responsibility for offenses against the sanctuary, and you and your sons alone are to bear the responsibility for offenses against the priesthood. ²Bring your fellow Levites from your ancestral tribe to join you and assist you when you and your sons minister before the Tent of the Testimony. ³They are to be responsible to you and are to perform all the duties of the Tent, but they must not go near the furnishings of the sanctuary or the altar, or both they and you will die. ⁴They are to join you and be responsible for the care of the Tent of Meeting—all the work at the Tent—and no one else may come near where you are.

⁵"You are to be responsible for the care of the sanctuary and the altar, so that wrath will not fall on the Israelites again. ⁶I myself have selected your fellow Levites from among the Israelites as a gift to you, dedicated to the LORD to do the work at the Tent of Meeting. ⁷But only you and your sons may serve as priests in connection with everything at the altar and inside the curtain. I am giving you the service of the priesthood as a gift. Anyone else who comes near the sanctuary must be put to death."

Offerings for Priests and Levites

⁸Then the LORD said to Aaron, "I myself have put you in charge of the offerings presented to me; all the holy offerings the Israelites give me I give to you and your sons as your portion and regular share. ⁹You are to have the part of the most holy offerings that is kept from the fire. From all the gifts they bring me as most holy offerings, whether grain or sin or guilt offerings, that part belongs to you and your sons. ¹⁰Eat it as something most holy; every male shall eat it. You must regard it as holy.

¹¹"This also is yours: whatever is set aside from the gifts of all the wave offerings of the Israelites. I give this to you and your sons and daughters as your regular share. Everyone in your household who is ceremonially clean may eat it.

¹²"I give you all the finest olive oil and all the finest new wine and grain they

---

17:5-10 To prevent any further uprisings by the Israelites, God initiated a test to determine his choice for Israel's high priest. The head of each tribe brought Moses a dead, wooden walking stick. God said he would cause one of the rods to blossom and bring forth buds. The next day Aaron's rod was covered with buds, blossoms and fully developed almonds confirming God's choice and the exclusive legitimacy of Aaron as high priest. Aaron's rod joined the tablets of the law and the jar of manna within or near the ark of the covenant in the tabernacle (see Ex 16:33-34; Dt 10:1-3; Heb 9:4).

give the LORD as the firstfruits of their harvest. ¹³All the land's firstfruits that they bring to the LORD will be yours. Everyone in your household who is ceremonially clean may eat it.

¹⁴"Everything in Israel that is devoted to the LORD is yours. ¹⁵The first offspring of every womb, both man and animal, that is offered to the LORD is yours. But you must redeem every firstborn son and every firstborn male of unclean animals. ¹⁶When they are a month old, you must redeem them at the redemption price set at five shekels of silver, according to the sanctuary shekel, which weighs twenty gerahs.

¹⁷"But you must not redeem the firstborn of an ox, a sheep or a goat; they are holy. Sprinkle their blood on the altar and burn their fat as an offering made by fire, an aroma pleasing to the LORD. ¹⁸Their meat is to be yours, just as the breast of the wave offering and the right thigh are yours. ¹⁹Whatever is set aside from the holy offerings the Israelites present to the LORD I give to you and your sons and daughters as your regular share. It is an everlasting covenant of salt before the LORD for both you and your offspring."

²⁰The LORD said to Aaron, "You will have no inheritance in their land, nor will you have any share among them; I am your share and your inheritance among the Israelites.

²¹"I give to the Levites all the tithes in Israel as their inheritance in return for the work they do while serving at the Tent of Meeting. ²²From now on the Israelites must not go near the Tent of Meeting, or they will bear the consequences of their sin and will die. ²³It is the Levites who are to do the work at the Tent of Meeting and bear the responsibility for offenses against it. This is a lasting ordinance for the generations to come. They will receive no inheritance among the Israelites. ²⁴Instead, I give to the Levites as their inheritance the tithes that the Israelites present as an offering to the LORD. That is why I said concerning them: 'They will have no inheritance among the Israelites.' "

²⁵The LORD said to Moses, ²⁶"Speak to the Levites and say to them: 'When you receive from the Israelites the tithe I give you¹ as your inheritance, you must present a tenth of that tithe as the LORD's offering. ²⁷Your offering will be reckoned to you as grain from the threshing floor or juice from the winepress. ²⁸In this way you also will present an offering to the LORD from all the tithes you receive from the Israelites. From these tithes you must give the LORD's portion to Aaron the priest. ²⁹You must present as the LORD's portion the best and holiest part of everything given to you.'

³⁰"Say to the Levites: 'When you present the best part, it will be reckoned to you as the product of the threshing floor or the winepress. ³¹You and your households may eat the rest of it anywhere, for it is your wages for your work at the Tent of Meeting. ³²By presenting the best part of it you will not be guilty in this matter; then you will not defile the holy offerings of the Israelites, and you will not die.' "

The Water of Cleansing

19 The LORD said to Moses and Aaron: ²"This is a requirement of the law the LORD has commanded: Tell the Israelites to bring you a red

B *Ge 49:10* ◄ ► *Dt 18:15–19*
D *Nu 18:17* ◄ ► *Nu 21:6–9*

o 14 The Hebrew term refers to the irrevocable giving over of things or persons to the LORD. *p 16* That is, about 2 ounces (about 55 grams)

D *Nu 16:46–47* ◄ ► *Nu 19:1–9*

19:2–12 In every respect the killing of the red heifer is distinct. It is a cow, not a bull or an ox, that is to be killed, not sacrificed. The animal was taken outside the camp, and though the priest was present, he did not identify himself with it. Except for a small amount of blood that the priest sprinkled toward the tabernacle seven times, the entire heifer, including its blood and feces, was burned to ash. When the ash was mixed with water, the solution could be used to purify anyone who had touched a dead body.

This unusual ritual is clearly symbolic. The red hide of the animal symbolized blood, God's requirement for cleansing. The use of a young female cow symbolized the giving of life back to one who had come in contact with death.

The killing of the red heifer is also a prophetic type of the ultimate sacrifice of Christ:

1. God instructed that the people bring a cow "without defect or blemish" (19:2). This same

heifer[w] without defect or blemish[x] and that has never been under a yoke.[y] ³Give it to Eleazar[z] the priest; it is to be taken outside the camp[a] and slaughtered in his presence. ⁴Then Eleazar the priest is to take some of its blood on his finger and sprinkle[b] it seven times toward the front of the Tent of Meeting. ⁵While he watches, the heifer is to be burned—its hide, flesh, blood and offal.[c] ⁶The priest is to take some cedar wood, hyssop[d] and scarlet wool[e] and throw them onto the burning heifer. ⁷After that, the priest must wash his clothes and bathe himself with water.[f] He may then come into the camp, but he will be ceremonially unclean till evening. ⁸The man who burns it must also wash his clothes and bathe with water, and he too will be unclean till evening.

⁹"A man who is clean shall gather up the ashes of the heifer[g] and put them in a ceremonially clean place[h] outside the camp. They shall be kept by the Israelite community for use in the water of cleansing;[i] it is for purification from sin.[j] ¹⁰The man who gathers up[k] the ashes of the heifer must also wash his clothes, and he too will be unclean till evening.[l] This will be a lasting ordinance[m] both for the Israelites and for the aliens living among them.[n]

¹¹"Whoever touches the dead body[o] of anyone will be unclean for seven days.[p] ¹²He must purify himself with the water on the third day and on the seventh day;[q] then he will be clean. But if he does not purify himself on the third and seventh days, he will not be clean.[r] ¹³Whoever touches the dead body[s] of anyone and fails to purify himself defiles the LORD's tabernacle.[t] That person must be cut off from Israel.[u] Because the water of cleansing has not been sprinkled on him, he is unclean;[v] his uncleanness remains on him.

¹⁴"This is the law that applies when a person dies in a tent: Anyone who enters the tent and anyone who is in it will be unclean for seven days, ¹⁵and every open container[w] without a lid fastened on it will be unclean.

¹⁶"Anyone out in the open who touches someone who has been killed with a sword or someone who has died a natural death,[x] or anyone who touches a human bone[y] or a grave,[z] will be unclean for seven days.[a]

¹⁷"For the unclean person, put some ashes[b] from the burned purification offering into a jar and pour fresh water[c] over them. ¹⁸Then a man who is ceremonially clean is to take some hyssop,[d] dip it in the water and sprinkle[e] the tent and all the furnishings and the people who were there. He must also sprinkle anyone who has touched a human bone or a grave[f] or someone who has been killed or someone who has died a natural death. ¹⁹The man who is clean is to sprinkle[g] the unclean person on the third and seventh days, and on the seventh day he is to purify him.[h] The person being cleansed must wash his clothes[i] and bathe with water, and that evening he will be clean. ²⁰But if a person who is unclean does not purify himself, he must be cut off from the community, because he has defiled[j] the sanctuary of the LORD.[k] The water of cleansing has not been sprinkled on him, and he is unclean.[l] ²¹This is a lasting ordinance[m] for them.

"The man who sprinkles the water of cleansing must also wash his clothes, and anyone who touches the water of cleansing will be unclean till evening. ²²Anything that an unclean[n] person touches be-

---

description was applied to Christ, "a lamb without blemish or defect" (1Pe 1:19), the only perfect "Lamb that was slain from the creation of the world" (Rev 13:8). Jesus, who was perfectly sinless, became sin for us so that our sins could be judged and paid for by his completed work on the cross (see 2Co 5:21).

2. The red heifer was a female animal. Jesus was betrayed for thirty pieces of silver, the price of a female slave.

3. God commanded that this slaughter take place "outside the camp" (19:3). Jesus also sanctified people with his blood and "suffered outside the city gate" (Heb 13:12).

Moses' words indicate that this ceremony was to be "a lasting ordinance" (Nu 19:21). Though this ritual has not been performed for centuries, it is possible this ceremony will be reinstated in the last days. Ezekiel prophesied that the Lord would "sprinkle clean water on you, and you will be clean" (Eze 36:25). The red cattle being bred in Israel may be used for reinstatement of this ceremony in the last days.

comes unclean, and anyone who touches it becomes unclean till evening."

Water From the Rock

20 In the first month the whole Israelite community arrived at the Desert of Zin, and they stayed at Kadesh. There Miriam died and was buried.

2 Now there was no water for the community, and the people gathered in opposition to Moses and Aaron. 3 They quarreled with Moses and said, "If only we had died when our brothers fell dead before the LORD! 4 Why did you bring the LORD's community into this desert, that we and our livestock should die here? 5 Why did you bring us up out of Egypt to this terrible place? It has no grain or figs, grapevines or pomegranates. And there is no water to drink!"

6 Moses and Aaron went from the assembly to the entrance to the Tent of Meeting and fell facedown, and the glory of the LORD appeared to them. 7 The LORD said to Moses, 8 "Take the staff, and you and your brother Aaron gather the assembly together. Speak to that rock before their eyes and it will pour out its water. You will bring water out of the rock for the community so they and their livestock can drink."

9 So Moses took the staff from the LORD's presence, just as he commanded him. 10 He and Aaron gathered the assembly together in front of the rock and Moses said to them, "Listen, you rebels, must we bring you water out of this rock?" 11 Then Moses raised his arm and struck the rock twice with his staff. Water gushed out, and the community and their livestock drank.

12 But the LORD said to Moses and Aaron, "Because you did not trust in me enough to honor me as holy in the sight of the Israelites, you will not bring this community into the land I give them."

13 These were the waters of Meribah, where the Israelites quarreled with the LORD and where he showed himself holy among them.

Edom Denies Israel Passage

14 Moses sent messengers from Kadesh to the king of Edom, saying:

"This is what your brother Israel says: You know about all the hardships that have come upon us. 15 Our forefathers went down into Egypt, and we lived there many years. The Egyptians mistreated us and our fathers, 16 but when we cried out to the LORD, he heard our cry and sent an angel and brought us out of Egypt.

"Now we are here at Kadesh, a town on the edge of your territory. 17 Please let us pass through your country. We will not go through any field or vineyard, or drink water from any well. We will travel along the king's highway and not turn to the right or to the left until we have passed through your territory."

18 But Edom answered:

"You may not pass through here; if you try, we will march out and attack you with the sword."

19 The Israelites replied:

"We will go along the main road, and if we or our livestock drink any of your water, we will pay for it. We only want to pass through on foot—nothing else."

20 Again they answered:

"You may not pass through."

Then Edom came out against them with a large and powerful army. 21 Since Edom refused to let them go through their territory, Israel turned away from them.

The Death of Aaron

22 The whole Israelite community set out from Kadesh and came to Mount

q 13 Meribah means quarreling.

20:12 Despite almost forty years of faithful leadership, Moses reacted faithlessly to the Israelites' insistent demand for water. Displaying his lack of faith in God's ability to provide water with a mere word, Moses struck the rock. The end result of his failure to honor God was his exclusion from entering the promised land.

Hor.¹ ²³At Mount Hor, near the border of Edom,ᵐ the LORD said to Moses and Aaron, ²⁴"Aaron will be gathered to his people.ⁿ He will not enter the land I give the Israelites, because both of you rebelled against my commandᵒ at the waters of Meribah.ᵖ ²⁵Get Aaron and his son Eleazar and take them up Mount Hor.ᵠ ²⁶Remove Aaron's garmentsʳ and put them on his son Eleazar, for Aaron will be gathered to his people;ˢ he will die there."

²⁷Moses did as the LORD commanded: They went up Mount Horᵗ in the sight of the whole community. ²⁸Moses removed Aaron's garments and put them on his son Eleazar.ᵘ And Aaron died thereᵛ on top of the mountain. Then Moses and Eleazar came down from the mountain, ²⁹and when the whole community learned that Aaron had died,ʷ the entire house of Israel mourned for himˣ thirty days.

Arad Destroyed

21 When the Canaanite king of Arad,ʸ who lived in the Negev,ᶻ heard that Israel was coming along the road to Atharim, he attacked the Israelites and captured some of them. ²Then Israel made this vowᵃ to the LORD: "If you will deliver these people into our hands, we will totally destroyʳᵇ their cities." ³The LORD listened to Israel's plea and gave the Canaanitesᶜ over to them. They completely destroyed themᵈ and their towns; so the place was named Hormah.ˢ ᵉ

The Bronze Snake

⁴They traveled from Mount Horᶠ along the route to the Red Sea,ʳᵍ to go around Edom.ʰ But the people grew impatient on the way;ⁱ ⁵they spoke against God ʲ and against Moses, and said, "Why have you brought us up out of Egyptᵏ to die in the desert?ˡ There is no bread! There is no water!ᵐ And we detest this miserable food!"ⁿ

⁶Then the LORD sent venomous snakesᵒ among them; they bit the people and many Israelites died.ᵖ ⁷The people came to Mosesᵠ and said, "We sinnedʳ when we spoke against the LORD and against you. Pray that the LORDˢ will take the snakes away from us." So Moses prayedᵗ for the people.

⁸The LORD said to Moses, "Make a snake and put it up on a pole;ᵘ anyone who is bitten can look at it and live." ⁹So Moses made a bronze snakeᵛ and put it up on a pole. Then when anyone was bitten by a snake and looked at the bronze snake, he lived.ʷ

The Journey to Moab

¹⁰The Israelites moved on and camped at Oboth.ˣ ¹¹Then they set out from Oboth and camped in Iye Abarim, in the desert that faces Moabʸ toward the sunrise. ¹²From there they moved on and camped in the Zered Valley.ᶻ ¹³They set out from there and camped alongside the Arnonᵃ, which is in the desert extending into Amorite territory. The Arnon is the border of Moab, between Moab and the Amorites.ᵇ ¹⁴That is why the Book of the Warsᶜ of the LORD says:

"... Waheb in Suphaᵘ and the
    ravines,
the Arnon ¹⁵andᵛ the slopes of the
    ravines

D Nu 19:1–9 ◀ ▶ Nu 28:3–4
D Nu 16:46 ◀ ▶ Nu 25:8–9
E Nu 16:46–50 ◀ ▶ Nu 25:8
K Nu 11:23 ◀ ▶ Nu 23:19   W ▶ 2Sa 22:31

ʳ 2 The Hebrew term refers to the irrevocable giving over of things or persons to the LORD, often by totally destroying them; also in verse 3. ˢ 3 *Hormah* means *destruction.* ᵗ 4 Hebrew *Yam Suph*; that is, Sea of Reeds ᵘ 14 The meaning of the Hebrew for this phrase is uncertain. ᵛ 14,15 Or "*I have been given from Suphah and the ravines / of the Arnon* ¹⁵*to*

Q Ge 49:33 ◀ ▶ Nu 20:26
Q Nu 20:24 ◀ ▶ Nu 27:13

20:24–26 The Lord promised Moses that "Aaron will be gathered to his people" (20:24). This phrase occurs often in Scripture as a promise to a godly person, implying the reuniting of family members after death (see 2Sa 12:23). The promise is ours as well. Those who live godly lives can die secure in the knowledge that they will live eternally with God and their righteous ancestors in heaven. See note at Ge 35:29.

21:8 The bronze serpent on a pole points prophetically as a type of Jesus Christ. Just as the Israelites were saved when they faithfully gazed upon the bronze serpent, those who turn from their sins and gaze in faith upon the crucified and risen Christ will have everlasting life (see Jn 3:14–15).

that lead to the site of Ar
and lie along the border of Moab."

¹⁶From there they continued on to Beer, the well where the LORD said to Moses, "Gather the people together and I will give them water."

¹⁷Then Israel sang this song:

"Spring up, O well!
  Sing about it,
¹⁸about the well that the princes dug,
  that the nobles of the people sank—
  the nobles with scepters and staffs."

Then they went from the desert to Mattanah, ¹⁹from Mattanah to Nahaliel, from Nahaliel to Bamoth, ²⁰and from Bamoth to the valley in Moab where the top of Pisgah overlooks the wasteland.

Defeat of Sihon and Og

²¹Israel sent messengers to say to Sihon king of the Amorites:

²²"Let us pass through your country. We will not turn aside into any field or vineyard, or drink water from any well. We will travel along the king's highway until we have passed through your territory."

²³But Sihon would not let Israel pass through his territory. He mustered his entire army and marched out into the desert against Israel. When he reached Jahaz, he fought with Israel. ²⁴Israel, however, put him to the sword and took over his land from the Arnon to the Jabbok, but only as far as the Ammonites, because their border was fortified. ²⁵Israel captured all the cities of the Amorites and occupied them, including Heshbon and all its surrounding settlements. ²⁶Heshbon was the city of Sihon king of the Amorites, who had fought against the former king of Moab and had taken from him all his land as far as the Arnon. ²⁷That is why the poets say:

"Come to Heshbon and let it be
    rebuilt;
  let Sihon's city be restored.

²⁸"Fire went out from Heshbon,
    a blaze from the city of Sihon.
  It consumed Ar of Moab,
    the citizens of Arnon's heights.

²⁹Woe to you, O Moab!
  You are destroyed, O people of
    Chemosh!
He has given up his sons as fugitives
  and his daughters as captives
  to Sihon king of the Amorites.

³⁰"But we have overthrown them;
  Heshbon is destroyed all the way to
    Dibon.
We have demolished them as far as
    Nophah,
  which extends to Medeba.'"

³¹So Israel settled in the land of the Amorites.

³²After Moses had sent spies to Jazer, the Israelites captured its surrounding settlements and drove out the Amorites who were there. ³³Then they turned and went up along the road toward Bashan, and Og king of Bashan and his whole army marched out to meet them in battle at Edrei.

³⁴The LORD said to Moses, "Do not be afraid of him, for I have handed him over to you, with his whole army and his land. Do to him what you did to Sihon king of the Amorites, who reigned in Heshbon."

³⁵So they struck him down, together with his sons and his whole army, leaving them no survivors. And they took possession of his land.

Balak Summons Balaam

22 Then the Israelites traveled to the plains of Moab and camped along the Jordan across from Jericho.[w] ²Now Balak son of Zippor saw all that Israel had done to the Amorites, ³and Moab was terrified because there were so many people. Indeed, Moab was filled with dread because of the Israelites.

⁴The Moabites said to the elders of Midian, "This horde is going to lick up everything around us, as an ox licks up the grass of the field."

So Balak son of Zippor, who was king of Moab at that time, ⁵sent messengers to summon Balaam son of Beor, who was

F *Nu 20:7–11* ◀ ▶ *Dt 2:7*

[w] 1 Hebrew *Jordan of Jericho*; possibly an ancient name for the Jordan River

NUMBERS 22:6

at Pethor, near the River,[xc] in his native land. Balak said:

"A people has come out of Egypt;[d] they cover the face of the land and have settled next to me. [6]Now come and put a curse[e] on these people, because they are too powerful for me. Perhaps then I will be able to defeat them and drive them out of the country.[f] For I know that those you bless are blessed, and those you curse are cursed."

[7]The elders of Moab and Midian left, taking with them the fee for divination.[g] When they came to Balaam, they told him what Balak had said.

[8]"Spend the night here," Balaam said to them, "and I will bring you back the answer the LORD gives me."[h] So the Moabite princes stayed with him.

[9]God came to Balaam[i] and asked,[j] "Who are these men with you?"

[10]Balaam said to God, "Balak son of Zippor, king of Moab, sent me this message: [11]'A people that has come out of Egypt covers the face of the land. Now come and put a curse on them for me. Perhaps then I will be able to fight them and drive them away.'"

[12]But God said to Balaam, "Do not go with them. You must not put a curse on those people, because they are blessed.[k]"

[13]The next morning Balaam got up and said to Balak's princes, "Go back to your own country, for the LORD has refused to let me go with you."

[14]So the Moabite princes returned to Balak and said, "Balaam refused to come with us."

[15]Then Balak sent other princes, more numerous and more distinguished than the first. [16]They came to Balaam and said:

"This is what Balak son of Zippor says: Do not let anything keep you from coming to me, [17]because I will reward you handsomely[l] and do whatever you say. Come and put a curse[m] on these people for me."

[18]But Balaam answered them, "Even if Balak gave me his palace filled with silver and gold, I could not do anything great or small to go beyond the command of the LORD my God.[n] [19]Now stay here tonight as the others did, and I will find out what else the LORD will tell me."[o]

[20]That night God came to Balaam[p] and said, "Since these men have come to summon you, go with them, but do only what I tell you."[q]

Balaam's Donkey

[21]Balaam got up in the morning, saddled his donkey and went with the princes of Moab. [22]But God was very angry[r] when he went, and the angel of the LORD[s] stood in the road to oppose him. Balaam was riding on his donkey, and his two servants were with him. [23]When the donkey saw the angel of the LORD standing in the road with a drawn sword[t] in his hand, she turned off the road into a field. Balaam beat her[u] to get her back on the road.

[24]Then the angel of the LORD stood in a narrow path between two vineyards, with walls on both sides. [25]When the donkey saw the angel of the LORD, she pressed close to the wall, crushing Balaam's foot against it. So he beat her again.

[26]Then the angel of the LORD moved on ahead and stood in a narrow place where there was no room to turn, either to the right or to the left. [27]When the donkey saw the angel of the LORD, she lay down under Balaam, and he was angry[v] and beat her with his staff. [28]Then the LORD opened the donkey's mouth,[w] and she said to Balaam, "What have I done to you to make you beat me these three times?[x]"

[29]Balaam answered the donkey, "You have made a fool of me! If I had a sword in my hand, I would kill you right now.[y]"

[30]The donkey said to Balaam, "Am I not your own donkey, which you have always ridden, to this day? Have I been in the habit of doing this to you?"

"No," he said.

[31]Then the LORD opened Balaam's eyes,[z] and he saw the angel of the LORD standing in the road with his sword drawn. So he bowed low and fell facedown.

[32]The angel of the LORD asked him, "Why have you beaten your donkey these three times? I have come here to oppose you because your path is a reckless one before me.[y] [33]The donkey saw me and

---

x5 That is, the Euphrates   y32 The meaning of the Hebrew for this clause is uncertain.

turned away from me these three times. If she had not turned away, I would certainly have killed you by now,ᵃ but I would have spared her."

³⁴Balaam said to the angel of the LORD, "I have sinned.ᵇ I did not realize you were standing in the road to oppose me. Now if you are displeased, I will go back."

³⁵The angel of the LORD said to Balaam, "Go with the men, but speak only what I tell you." So Balaam went with the princes of Balak.

³⁶When Balakᶜ heard that Balaam was coming, he went out to meet him at the Moabite town on the Arnonᵈ border, at the edge of his territory. ³⁷Balak said to Balaam, "Did I not send you an urgent summons? Why didn't you come to me? Am I really not able to reward you?"

³⁸"Well, I have come to you now," Balaam replied. "But can I say just anything? I must speak only what God puts in my mouth."ᵉ

³⁹Then Balaam went with Balak to Kiriath Huzoth. ⁴⁰Balak sacrificed cattle and sheep,ᶠ and gave some to Balaam and the princes who were with him. ⁴¹The next morning Balak took Balaam up to Bamoth Baal,ᵍ and from there he saw part of the people.ʰ

Balaam's First Oracle

23 Balaam said, "Build me seven altars here, and prepare seven bullsⁱ and seven ramsⁱ for me." ²Balak did as Balaam said, and the two of them offered a bull and a ram on each altar.ʲ

³Then Balaam said to Balak, "Stay here beside your offering while I go aside. Perhaps the LORD will come to meet with me.ᵏ Whatever he reveals to me I will tell you." Then he went off to a barren height.

⁴God met with him,ˡ and Balaam said, "I have prepared seven altars, and on each altar I have offered a bull and a ram."

⁵The LORD put a message in Balaam's mouth,ᵐⁿ and said, "Go back to Balak and give him this message."ᵒ

⁶So he went back to him and found him standing beside his offering, with all the princes of Moab.ᵖ ⁷Then Balaamᑫ uttered his oracle:ʳ

"Balak brought me from Aram,ˢ
  the king of Moab from the eastern
    mountains.ᵗ
'Come,' he said, 'curse Jacob for me;
  come, denounce Israel.'ᵘ
⁸How can I curse
  those whom God has not cursed?ᵛ
How can I denounce
  those whom the LORD has not
    denounced?ʷ
⁹From the rocky peaks I see them,
  from the heights I view them.ˣ
I see a people who live apart
  and do not consider themselves one
    of the nations.ʸ
¹⁰Who can count the dust of Jacobᶻ
  or number the fourth part of Israel?
Let me die the death of the righteous,ᵃ
  and may my end be like theirs!ᵇ"

¹¹Balak said to Balaam, "What have you done to me? I brought you to curse my enemies,ᶜ but you have done nothing but bless them!"ᵈ

¹²He answered, "Must I not speak what the LORD puts in my mouth?"ᵉ

Balaam's Second Oracle

¹³Then Balak said to him, "Come with me to another placeᶠ where you can see them; you will see only a part but not all of them.ᵍ And from there, curse them for me."ʰ ¹⁴So he took him to the field of Zophim on the top of Pisgah,ⁱ and there he built seven altars and offered a bull and a ram on each altar.ʲ

¹⁵Balaam said to Balak, "Stay here beside your offering while I meet with him over there."

¹⁶The LORD met with Balaam and put a message in his mouthᵏ and said, "Go

U Nu 10:29 ◀▶ Dt 5:10

23:8–10 God led Balaam, the hired, pagan prophet, to prophesy and bless Israel despite the commands of the king of the Moabites. Balaam declared that he could not curse what God had blessed but rather prophesied that the Israelites would be innumerable, echoing God's direct prophecy to make Abram's "offspring like the dust of the earth" (Ge 13:16). With Balaam's own words he fulfilled another of God's promises to Abram: "I will bless those who bless you, and whoever curses you I will curse" (Ge 12:3).

back to Balak and give him this message."

¹⁷So he went to him and found him standing beside his offering, with the princes of Moab. Balak asked him, "What did the LORD say?"

¹⁸Then he uttered his oracle:

"Arise, Balak, and listen;
  hear me, son of Zippor.
¹⁹God is not a man, that he should lie,
  nor a son of man, that he should change his mind.
Does he speak and then not act?
Does he promise and not fulfill?
²⁰I have received a command to bless;
  he has blessed, and I cannot change it.

²¹"No misfortune is seen in Jacob,
  no misery observed in Israel.
The LORD their God is with them;
  the shout of the King is among them.
²²God brought them out of Egypt;
  they have the strength of a wild ox.
²³There is no sorcery against Jacob,
  no divination against Israel.
It will now be said of Jacob
  and of Israel, 'See what God has done!'
²⁴The people rise like a lioness;
  they rouse themselves like a lion
that does not rest till he devours his prey
  and drinks the blood of his victims."

²⁵Then Balak said to Balaam, "Neither curse them at all nor bless them at all!"

²⁶Balaam answered, "Did I not tell you I must do whatever the LORD says?"

Balaam's Third Oracle

²⁷Then Balak said to Balaam, "Come, let me take you to another place. Perhaps it will please God to let you curse them for me from there." ²⁸And Balak took Balaam to the top of Peor, overlooking the wasteland.

²⁹Balaam said, "Build me seven altars here, and prepare seven bulls and seven rams for me." ³⁰Balak did as Balaam had said, and offered a bull and a ram on each altar.

24

Now when Balaam saw that it pleased the LORD to bless Israel, he did not resort to sorcery as at other times, but turned his face toward the desert. ²When Balaam looked out and saw Israel encamped tribe by tribe, the Spirit of God came upon him ³and he uttered his oracle:

"The oracle of Balaam son of Beor,
  the oracle of one whose eye sees clearly,
⁴the oracle of one who hears the words of God,
  who sees a vision from the Almighty,
  who falls prostrate, and whose eyes are opened:

⁵"How beautiful are your tents, O Jacob,
  your dwelling places, O Israel!

⁶"Like valleys they spread out,
  like gardens beside a river,
like aloes planted by the LORD,
  like cedars beside the waters.
⁷Water will flow from their buckets;
  their seed will have abundant water.

"Their king will be greater than Agag;
  their kingdom will be exalted.

⁸"God brought them out of Egypt;
  they have the strength of a wild ox.
They devour hostile nations
  and break their bones in pieces;
  with their arrows they pierce them.
⁹Like a lion they crouch and lie down,
  like a lioness—who dares to rouse them?

"May those who bless you be blessed
  and those who curse you be cursed!"

¹⁰Then Balak's anger burned against Balaam. He struck his hands together and said to him, "I summoned you to curse my enemies, but you have blessed them these three times. ¹¹Now leave at

---

K Nu 21:8–9 ◄ ► Dt 30:6
A Lev 25:8–17 ◄ ► Dt 33:6
E Nu 14:24 ◄ ► Nu 27:18
T Nu 11:25–29 ◄ ► Dt 34:9
I Nu 10:29 ◄ ► Nu 24:14–19

g ver 3-9; Nu 23:7-10,18-24

z 21 Or *He has not looked on Jacob's offenses / or on the wrongs found in Israel*. a 4 Hebrew *Shaddai*; also in verse 16

once and go home!ʰ I said I would reward you handsomely,ⁱ but the Lord has kept you from being rewarded."

¹²Balaam answered Balak, "Did I not tell the messengers you sent me,ʲ ¹³'Even if Balak gave me his palace filled with silver and gold, I could not do anything of my own accord, good or bad, to go beyond the command of the Lordᵏ—and I must say only what the Lord says'?¹ ¹⁴Now I am going back to my people, but come, let me warn you of what this people will do to your people in days to come."ᵐ

Balaam's Fourth Oracle

¹⁵Then he uttered his oracle:

"The oracle of Balaam son of Beor,
    the oracle of one whose eye sees clearly,
¹⁶the oracle of one who hears the wordsⁿ of God,
    who has knowledge from the Most High,ᵒ
who sees a vision from the Almighty,
    who falls prostrate, and whose eyes are opened:

¹⁷"I see him, but not now;
    I behold him, but not near.ᵖ
A star will come out of Jacob;ᑫ
    a scepter will rise out of Israel.ʳ
He will crush the foreheads of Moab,ˢ
    the skullsᵇᵗ ofᶜ all the sons of Sheth.ᵈ
¹⁸Edomᵘ will be conquered;
    Seir,ᵛ his enemy, will be conquered,ʷ
    but Israelˣ will grow strong.
¹⁹A ruler will come out of Jacobʸ
    and destroy the survivors of the city."

I Nu 24:7–9 ◀ ▶ Nu 34:1–12
J Nu 14:43 ◀ ▶ Nu 33:55–56
M Nu 14:21 ◀ ▶ 1Sa 2:10   P ◀ ▶ Dt 32:22

Balaam's Final Oracles

²⁰Then Balaam saw Amalekᶻ and uttered his oracle:

"Amalek was first among the nations,
    but he will come to ruin at last."ᵃ

²¹Then he saw the Kenitesᵇ and uttered his oracle:

"Your dwelling place is secure,ᶜ
    your nest is set in a rock;
²²yet you Kenites will be destroyed
    when Asshurᵈ takes you captive."

²³Then he uttered his oracle:

"Ah, who can live when God does this?ᵉ
²⁴   Ships will come from the shores of Kittim;ᵉ
they will subdue Asshurᶠ and Eber,ᵍ
    but they too will come to ruin."ʰ

²⁵Then Balaamⁱ got up and returned home and Balak went his own way.

Moab Seduces Israel

25 While Israel was staying in Shittim,ʲ the men began to indulge in sexual immoralityᵏ with Moabiteˡ women,ᵐ ²who invited them to the sacrificesⁿ to their gods.ᵒ The people ate and bowed down before these gods. ³So Israel joined in worshipingᵖ the Baal of Peor.ᑫ And the Lord's anger burned against them.

⁴The Lord said to Moses, "Take all the leadersʳ of these people, kill them and exposeˢ them in broad daylight before the Lord,ᵗ so that the Lord's fierce angerᵘ may turn away from Israel."

⁵So Moses said to Israel's judges, "Each

ᵇ 17 Samaritan Pentateuch (see also Jer. 48:45); the meaning of the word in the Masoretic Text is uncertain.   ᶜ 17 Or possibly *Moab, / batter*   ᵈ 17 Or *all the noisy boasters*   ᵉ 23 Masoretic Text; with a different word division of the Hebrew *A people will gather from the north.*

24:17 Though this prophecy was initially fulfilled in David's victory over the Moabites and Edomites (see 2Sa 8:2–14), this verse foreshadows the greater victory of Christ's second coming. This oracle describes the Messiah as "a star ... out of Jacob; a scepter ... out of Israel." It is possible that Balaam's words gave direction to the wise men who saw an unusual star over the land of Judah and went to look for the one "born king of the Jews" (Mt 2:2).
24:19 This prophecy of the rise of the Messiah from the tribe of Jacob confirms the earlier prediction that the "scepter will not depart from Judah, nor the ruler's staff from between his feet, until he comes to whom it belongs" (Ge 49:10).

24:20–24 Amalek was the first of the pagan nations to fight and oppose Israel in the wilderness (see Ex 17:8–16). At that time God promised to annihilate the Amalekites. Balaam's prophecy in these verses confirms God's intent toward Amalek.

of you must put to death those of your men who have joined in worshiping the Baal of Peor."

⁶Then an Israelite man brought to his family a Midianite woman right before the eyes of Moses and the whole assembly of Israel while they were weeping at the entrance to the Tent of Meeting. ⁷When Phinehas son of Eleazar, the son of Aaron, the priest, saw this, he left the assembly, took a spear in his hand ⁸and followed the Israelite into the tent. He drove the spear through both of them—through the Israelite and into the woman's body. Then the plague against the Israelites was stopped; ⁹but those who died in the plague numbered 24,000.

¹⁰The LORD said to Moses, ¹¹"Phinehas son of Eleazar, the son of Aaron, the priest, has turned my anger away from the Israelites; for he was as zealous as I am for my honor among them, so that in my zeal I did not put an end to them. ¹²Therefore tell him I am making my covenant of peace with him. ¹³He and his descendants will have a covenant of a lasting priesthood, because he was zealous for the honor of his God and made atonement for the Israelites."

¹⁴The name of the Israelite who was killed with the Midianite woman was Zimri son of Salu, the leader of a Simeonite family. ¹⁵And the name of the Midianite woman who was put to death was Cozbi daughter of Zur, a tribal chief of a Midianite family.

¹⁶The LORD said to Moses, ¹⁷"Treat the Midianites as enemies and kill them, ¹⁸because they treated you as enemies when they deceived you in the affair of Peor and their sister Cozbi, the daughter of a Midianite leader, the woman who was killed when the plague came as a result of Peor."

The Second Census

26 After the plague the LORD said to Moses and Eleazar son of Aaron, the priest, ²"Take a census of the whole Israelite community by families—all those twenty years old or more who are able to serve in the army of Israel." ³So on the plains of Moab by the Jordan across from Jericho, Moses and Eleazar the priest spoke with them and said, ⁴"Take a census of the men twenty years old or more, as the LORD commanded Moses."

These were the Israelites who came out of Egypt:

⁵The descendants of Reuben, the firstborn son of Israel, were:

through Hanoch, the Hanochite clan;

through Pallu, the Palluite clan;

⁶through Hezron, the Hezronite clan;

through Carmi, the Carmite clan.

⁷These were the clans of Reuben; those numbered were 43,730.

⁸The son of Pallu was Eliab, ⁹and the sons of Eliab were Nemuel, Dathan and Abiram. The same Dathan and Abiram were the community officials who rebelled against Moses and Aaron and were among Korah's followers when they rebelled against the LORD. ¹⁰The earth opened its mouth and swallowed them along with Korah, whose followers died when the fire devoured the 250 men. And they served as a warning sign. ¹¹The line of Korah, however, did not die out.

¹²The descendants of Simeon by their clans were:

through Nemuel, the Nemuelite clan;

through Jamin, the Jaminite clan;

through Jakin, the Jakinite clan;

¹³through Zerah, the Zerahite clan;

through Shaul, the Shaulite clan.

¹⁴These were the clans of Simeon; there were 22,200 men.

¹⁵The descendants of Gad by their clans were:

through Zephon, the Zephonite clan;

through Haggi, the Haggite clan;

through Shuni, the Shunite clan;

¹⁶through Ozni, the Oznite clan;

through Eri, the Erite clan;

¹⁷through Arodi, the Arodite clan;

through Areli, the Arelite clan.

¹⁸These were the clans of Gad; those numbered were 40,500.

3 Hebrew Jordan of Jericho; possibly an ancient name for the Jordan River; also in verse 63   17 Samaritan Pentateuch and Syriac (see also Gen. 46:16); Masoretic Text Arod

¹⁹Er[v] and Onan[w] were sons of Judah, but they died[x] in Canaan.
²⁰The descendants of Judah by their clans were:
   through Shelah,[y] the Shelanite clan;
   through Perez,[z] the Perezite clan;
   through Zerah, the Zerahite clan.[a]
²¹The descendants of Perez[b] were:
   through Hezron,[c] the Hezronite clan;
   through Hamul, the Hamulite clan.
²²These were the clans of Judah;[d] those numbered were 76,500.

²³The descendants of Issachar by their clans were:
   through Tola,[e] the Tolaite clan;
   through Puah, the Puite[h] clan;
²⁴through Jashub,[f] the Jashubite clan;
   through Shimron, the Shimronite clan.
²⁵These were the clans of Issachar;[g] those numbered were 64,300.

²⁶The descendants of Zebulun[h] by their clans were:
   through Sered, the Seredite clan;
   through Elon, the Elonite clan;
   through Jahleel, the Jahleelite clan.
²⁷These were the clans of Zebulun;[i] those numbered were 60,500.

²⁸The descendants of Joseph[j] by their clans through Manasseh and Ephraim[k] were:

²⁹The descendants of Manasseh:[l]
   through Makir,[m] the Makirite clan (Makir was the father of Gilead[n]);
   through Gilead, the Gileadite clan.
³⁰These were the descendants of Gilead:[o]
   through Iezer,[p] the Iezerite clan;
   through Helek, the Helekite clan;
³¹through Asriel, the Asrielite clan;
   through Shechem, the Shechemite clan;
³²through Shemida, the Shemidaite clan;
   through Hepher, the Hepherite clan.
³³(Zelophehad[q] son of Hepher had no sons;[r] he had only daughters, whose names were Mahlah, Noah, Hoglah, Milcah and Tirzah.)[s]
³⁴These were the clans of Manasseh; those numbered were 52,700.[t]

³⁵These were the descendants of Ephraim[u] by their clans:
   through Shuthelah, the Shuthelahite clan;
   through Beker, the Bekerite clan;
   through Tahan, the Tahanite clan.
³⁶These were the descendants of Shuthelah:
   through Eran, the Eranite clan.
³⁷These were the clans of Ephraim;[v] those numbered were 32,500.
These were the descendants of Joseph by their clans.

³⁸The descendants of Benjamin[w] by their clans were:
   through Bela, the Belaite clan;
   through Ashbel, the Ashbelite clan;
   through Ahiram, the Ahiramite clan;
³⁹through Shupham,[i] the Shuphamite clan;
   through Hupham, the Huphamite clan.
⁴⁰The descendants of Bela through Ard[x] and Naaman were:
   through Ard,[j] the Ardite clan;
   through Naaman, the Naamite clan.
⁴¹These were the clans of Benjamin;[y] those numbered were 45,600.

⁴²These were the descendants of Dan[z] by their clans:[a]
   through Shuham,[b] the Shuhamite clan.
These were the clans of Dan: ⁴³All of them were Shuhamite clans; and those numbered were 64,400.

⁴⁴The descendants of Asher[c] by their clans were:
   through Imnah, the Imnite clan;
   through Ishvi, the Ishvite clan;
   through Beriah, the Beriite clan;
⁴⁵and through the descendants of Beriah:
   through Heber, the Heberite clan;
   through Malkiel, the Malkielite clan.

---

[h] 23 Samaritan Pentateuch, Septuagint, Vulgate and Syriac (see also 1 Chron. 7:1); Masoretic Text *through Puvah, the Punite* [i] 39 A few manuscripts of the Masoretic Text, Samaritan Pentateuch, Vulgate and Syriac (see also Septuagint); most manuscripts of the Masoretic Text *Shephupham* [j] 40 Samaritan Pentateuch and Vulgate (see also Septuagint); Masoretic Text does not have *through Ard*.

46(Asher had a daughter named Serah.)
47These were the clans of Asher; those numbered were 53,400.

48The descendants of Naphtali by their clans were:
through Jahzeel, the Jahzeelite clan;
through Guni, the Gunite clan;
49through Jezer, the Jezerite clan;
through Shillem, the Shillemite clan.
50These were the clans of Naphtali; those numbered were 45,400.

51The total number of the men of Israel was 601,730.

52The LORD said to Moses, 53"The land is to be allotted to them as an inheritance based on the number of names. 54To a larger group give a larger inheritance, and to a smaller group a smaller one; each is to receive its inheritance according to the number of those listed. 55Be sure that the land is distributed by lot. What each group inherits will be according to the names for its ancestral tribe. 56Each inheritance is to be distributed by lot among the larger and smaller groups."

57These were the Levites who were counted by their clans:
through Gershon, the Gershonite clan;
through Kohath, the Kohathite clan;
through Merari, the Merarite clan.
58These also were Levite clans:
the Libnite clan,
the Hebronite clan,
the Mahlite clan,
the Mushite clan,
the Korahite clan.
(Kohath was the forefather of Amram; 59the name of Amram's wife was Jochebed, a descendant of Levi, who was born to the Levites in Egypt. To Amram she bore Aaron, Moses and their sister Miriam. 60Aaron was the father of Nadab and Abihu, Eleazar and Ithamar. 61But Nadab and Abihu died when they made an offering before the LORD with unauthorized fire.)

62All the male Levites a month old or more numbered 23,000. They were not counted along with the other Israelites because they received no inheritance among them.

63These are the ones counted by Moses and Eleazar the priest when they counted the Israelites on the plains of Moab by the Jordan across from Jericho. 64Not one of them was among those counted by Moses and Aaron the priest when they counted the Israelites in the Desert of Sinai. 65For the LORD had told those Israelites they would surely die in the desert, and not one of them was left except Caleb son of Jephunneh and Joshua son of Nun.

Zelophehad's Daughters

27:1–11pp — Nu 36:1–12

27 The daughters of Zelophehad son of Hepher, the son of Gilead, the son of Makir, the son of Manasseh, belonged to the clans of Manasseh son of Joseph. The names of the daughters were Mahlah, Noah, Hoglah, Milcah and Tirzah. They approached 2the entrance to the Tent of Meeting and stood before Moses, Eleazar the priest, the leaders and the whole assembly, and said, 3"Our father died in the desert. He was not among Korah's followers, who banded together against the LORD, but he died for his own sin and left no sons. 4Why should our father's name disappear from his clan because he had no son? Give us property among our father's relatives."

5So Moses brought their case before the LORD 6and the LORD said to him, 7"What Zelophehad's daughters are saying is right. You must certainly give them property as an inheritance among their

k 59 Or Jochebed, a daughter of Levi, who was born to Levi

26:51–53 The second census of the Israelites yielded an astonishing result. Though the Israelites had spent forty years in the wilderness as a result of their sinful rebellion and an entire generation had died, the new census was nearly the same as the first. Of the 603,550 original adults, all but Joshua and Caleb died in the desert as decreed by the Lord (see 26:64–65). God replaced the rebellious generation of Israelite slaves with a new generation totaling 601,730 born in the freedom of the desert. This new generation eagerly awaited their land allotments following the conquest of the promised land.

father's relatives and turn their father's inheritance over to them.ᵘ

⁸"Say to the Israelites, 'If a man dies and leaves no son, turn his inheritance over to his daughter. ⁹If he has no daughter, give his inheritance to his brothers. ¹⁰If he has no brothers, give his inheritance to his father's brothers. ¹¹If his father had no brothers, give his inheritance to the nearest relative in his clan, that he may possess it. This is to be a legal requirementᵛ for the Israelites, as the LORD commanded Moses.' "

Joshua to Succeed Moses

¹²Then the LORD said to Moses, "Go up this mountainʷ in the Abarim rangeˣ and see the landʸ I have given the Israelites.ᶻ ¹³After you have seen it, you too will be gathered to your people,ᵃ as your brother Aaronᵇ was, ¹⁴for when the community rebelled at the waters in the Desert of Zin,ᶜ both of you disobeyed my command to honor me as holyᵈ before their eyes." (These were the waters of Meribahᵉ Kadesh, in the Desert of Zin.)

¹⁵Moses said to the LORD, ¹⁶"May the LORD, the God of the spirits of all mankind,ᶠ appoint a man over this community ¹⁷to go out and come in before them, one who will lead them out and bring them in, so the LORD's people will not be like sheep without a shepherd."ᵍ

¹⁸So the LORD said to Moses, "Take Joshua son of Nun, a man in whom is the spirit,ʰ and lay your hand on him.ⁱ ¹⁹Have him stand before Eleazar the priest and the entire assembly and commission himʲ in their presence.ᵏ ²⁰Give him some of your authority so the whole Israelite community will obey him.ˡ ²¹He is to stand before Eleazar the priest, who will obtain decisions for him by inquiringᵐ of the Urimⁿ before the LORD. At his command he and the entire community of the Israelites will go out, and at his command they will come in."

²²Moses did as the LORD commanded him. He took Joshua and had him stand before Eleazar the priest and the whole assembly. ²³Then he laid his hands on him and commissioned him,ᵒ as the LORD instructed through Moses.

Daily Offerings

28 The LORD said to Moses, ²"Give this command to the Israelites and say to them: 'See that you present to me at the appointed timeᵖ the foodᵠ for my offerings made by fire, as an aroma pleasing to me.'ʳ ³Say to them: 'This is the offering made by fire that you are to present to the LORD: two lambs a year old without defect,ˢ as a regular burnt offering each day.ᵗ ⁴Prepare one lamb in the morning and the other at twilight,ᵘ ⁵together with a grain offeringᵛ of a tenth of an ephahᵐ of fine flourʷ mixed with a quarter of a hinⁿ of oilˣ from pressed olives. ⁶This is the regular burnt offeringʸ instituted at Mount Sinaiᶻ as a pleasing aroma, an offering made to the LORD by fire.ᵃ ⁷The accompanying drink offeringᵇ is to be a quarter of a hin of fermented drinkᶜ with each lamb. Pour out the drink offering to the LORD at the sanctuary.ᵈ ⁸Prepare the second lamb at twilight,ᵉ along with the same kind of grain offering and drink offering that you prepare in the morning.ᶠ This is an offering made by fire, an aroma pleasing to the LORD.ᵍ

Sabbath Offerings

⁹" 'On the Sabbathʰ day, make an offering of two lambs a year old without defect,ⁱ together with its drink offering and a grain offering of two-tenths of an ephahᵒʲ of fine flour mixed with oil.ᵏ ¹⁰This is the burnt offering for every Sabbath,ˡ in addition to the regular burnt offeringᵐ and its drink offering.

Monthly Offerings

¹¹" 'On the first of every month,ⁿ present to the LORD a burnt offering of

---

D *Nu 21:6–9* ◀ ▶ *Dt 15:21*

l 18 Or *Spirit* *m* 5 That is, probably about 2 quarts (about 2 liters); also in verses 13, 21 and 29 *n* 5 That is, probably about 1 quart (about 1 liter); also in verses 7 and 14 *o* 9 That is, probably about 4 quarts (about 4.5 liters); also in verses 12, 20 and 28

27:13–14 The Lord allowed Moses a glimpse of the promised land from the top of the mountain, but reconfirmed his judgment on Moses' unfaithfulness at Meribah. Moses' sin and failure to believe God and honor him cost Moses the blessing of entering Canaan. See note at 20:12.

two young bulls, one ram and seven male lambs a year old, all without defect. ¹²With each bull there is to be a grain offering of three-tenths of an ephah of fine flour mixed with oil; with the ram, a grain offering of two-tenths of an ephah of fine flour mixed with oil; ¹³and with each lamb, a grain offering of a tenth of an ephah of fine flour mixed with oil. This is for a burnt offering, a pleasing aroma, an offering made to the LORD by fire. ¹⁴With each bull there is to be a drink offering of half a hin of wine; with the ram, a third of a hin; and with each lamb, a quarter of a hin. This is the monthly burnt offering to be made at each new moon during the year. ¹⁵Besides the regular burnt offering with its drink offering, one male goat is to be presented to the LORD as a sin offering.

The Passover
28:16–25pp — Ex 12:14–20; Lev 23:4–8; Dt 16:1–8

¹⁶" 'On the fourteenth day of the first month the LORD's Passover is to be held. ¹⁷On the fifteenth day of this month there is to be a festival; for seven days eat bread made without yeast. ¹⁸On the first day hold a sacred assembly and do no regular work. ¹⁹Present to the LORD an offering made by fire, a burnt offering of two young bulls, one ram and seven male lambs a year old, all without defect. ²⁰With each bull prepare a grain offering of three-tenths of an ephah of fine flour mixed with oil; with the ram, two-tenths; ²¹and with each of the seven lambs, one-tenth. ²²Include one male goat as a sin offering to make atonement for you. ²³Prepare these in addition to the regular morning burnt offering. ²⁴In this way prepare the food for the offering made by fire every day for seven days as an aroma pleasing to the LORD; it is to be prepared in addition to the regular burnt offering and its drink offering. ²⁵On the seventh day hold a sacred assembly and do no regular work.

Feast of Weeks
28:26–31pp — Lev 23:15–22; Dt 16:9–12

²⁶" 'On the day of firstfruits, when you present to the LORD an offering of new grain during the Feast of Weeks, hold a sacred assembly and do no regular work. ²⁷Present a burnt offering of two young bulls, one ram and seven male lambs a year old as an aroma pleasing to the LORD. ²⁸With each bull there is to be a grain offering of three-tenths of an ephah of fine flour mixed with oil; with the ram, two-tenths; ²⁹and with each of the seven lambs, one-tenth. ³⁰Include one male goat to make atonement for you. ³¹Prepare these together with their drink offerings, in addition to the regular burnt offering and its grain offering. Be sure the animals are without defect.

Feast of Trumpets
29:1–6pp — Lev 23:23–25

29 " 'On the first day of the seventh month hold a sacred assembly and do no regular work. It is a day for you to sound the trumpets. ²As an aroma pleasing to the LORD, prepare a burnt offering of one young bull, one ram and seven male lambs a year old, all without defect. ³With the bull prepare a grain offering of three-tenths of an ephah of fine flour mixed with oil; with the ram, two-tenths; ⁴and with each of the seven lambs, one-tenth. ⁵Include one male goat as a sin offering to make atonement for you. ⁶These are in addition to the monthly and daily burnt offerings with their grain offerings and drink offerings as specified. They are offerings made to the LORD by fire—a pleasing aroma.

Day of Atonement
29:7–11pp — Lev 16:2–34; 23:26–32

⁷" 'On the tenth day of this seventh month hold a sacred assembly. You must deny yourselves and do no work. ⁸Present as an aroma pleasing to the LORD a burnt offering of one young bull, one ram and seven male lambs a year old, all without defect. ⁹With the bull prepare a grain offering of three-tenths of an ephah of fine flour mixed with oil; with the ram, two-tenths; ¹⁰and with each of the seven lambs, one-tenth. ¹¹Include one male goat as a sin offering, in addition to the sin offering for atonement and the regular burnt offering with its grain offering, and their drink offerings.

---

p 12 That is, probably about 6 quarts (about 6.5 liters); also in verses 20 and 28   *q 14* That is, probably about 2 quarts (about 2 liters)   *r 14* That is, probably about 1 1/4 quarts (about 1.2 liters)   *s 3* That is, probably about 6 quarts (about 6.5 liters); also in verses 9 and 14   *t 3* That is, probably about 4 quarts (about 4.5 liters); also in verses 9 and 14   *u 4* That is, probably about 2 quarts (about 2 liters); also in verses 10 and 15
v 7 Or *must fast*

Feast of Tabernacles

29:12-39pp — Lev 23:33-43; Dt 16:13-17

[12] "'On the fifteenth day of the seventh month, hold a sacred assembly and do no regular work. Celebrate a festival to the LORD for seven days. [13]Present an offering made by fire as an aroma pleasing to the LORD, a burnt offering of thirteen young bulls, two rams and fourteen male lambs a year old, all without defect. [14]With each of the thirteen bulls prepare a grain offering of three-tenths of an ephah of fine flour mixed with oil; with each of the two rams, two-tenths; [15]and with each of the fourteen lambs, one-tenth. [16]Include one male goat as a sin offering, in addition to the regular burnt offering with its grain offering and drink offering.

[17]"'On the second day prepare twelve young bulls, two rams and fourteen male lambs a year old, all without defect. [18]With the bulls, rams and lambs, prepare their grain offerings and drink offerings according to the number specified. [19]Include one male goat as a sin offering, in addition to the regular burnt offering with its grain offering, and their drink offerings.

[20]"'On the third day prepare eleven bulls, two rams and fourteen male lambs a year old, all without defect. [21]With the bulls, rams and lambs, prepare their grain offerings and drink offerings according to the number specified. [22]Include one male goat as a sin offering, in addition to the regular burnt offering with its grain offering and drink offering.

[23]"'On the fourth day prepare ten bulls, two rams and fourteen male lambs a year old, all without defect. [24]With the bulls, rams and lambs, prepare their grain offerings and drink offerings according to the number specified. [25]Include one male goat as a sin offering, in addition to the regular burnt offering with its grain offering and drink offering.

[26]"'On the fifth day prepare nine bulls, two rams and fourteen male lambs a year old, all without defect. [27]With the bulls, rams and lambs, prepare their grain offerings and drink offerings according to the number specified. [28]Include one male goat as a sin offering, in addition to the regular burnt offering with its grain offering and drink offering.

[29]"'On the sixth day prepare eight bulls, two rams and fourteen male lambs a year old, all without defect. [30]With the bulls, rams and lambs, prepare their grain offerings and drink offerings according to the number specified. [31]Include one male goat as a sin offering, in addition to the regular burnt offering with its grain offering and drink offering.

[32]"'On the seventh day prepare seven bulls, two rams and fourteen male lambs a year old, all without defect. [33]With the bulls, rams and lambs, prepare their grain offerings and drink offerings according to the number specified. [34]Include one male goat as a sin offering, in addition to the regular burnt offering with its grain offering and drink offering.

[35]"'On the eighth day hold an assembly and do no regular work. [36]Present an offering made by fire as an aroma pleasing to the LORD, a burnt offering of one bull, one ram and seven male lambs a year old, all without defect. [37]With the bull, the ram and the lambs, prepare their grain offerings and drink offerings according to the number specified. [38]Include one male goat as a sin offering, in addition to the regular burnt offering with its grain offering and drink offering.

[39]"'In addition to what you vow and your freewill offerings, prepare these for the LORD at your appointed feasts: your burnt offerings, grain offerings, drink offerings and fellowship offerings.*w s*'"

[40]Moses told the Israelites all that the LORD commanded him.

Vows

30 Moses said to the heads of the tribes of Israel: "This is what the LORD commands: [2]When a man makes a vow to the LORD or takes an oath to obligate himself by a pledge, he must not break his word but must do everything he said.

[3]"When a young woman still living in her father's house makes a vow to the LORD or obligates herself by a pledge [4]and her father hears about her vow or pledge but says nothing to her, then all her vows and every pledge by which she obligated herself will stand. [5]But if her father forbids her when he hears about it, none of her vows or the pledges by which she

---

w 39 Traditionally peace offerings

obligated herself will stand; the LORD will release her because her father has forbidden her.

⁶"If she marries after she makes a vow˟ or after her lips utter a rash promise by which she obligates herself ⁷and her husband hears about it but says nothing to her, then her vows or the pledges by which she obligated herself will stand. ⁸But if her husband ʸ forbids her when he hears about it, he nullifies the vow that obligates her or the rash promise by which she obligates herself, and the LORD will release her.ᶻ

⁹"Any vow or obligation taken by a widow or divorced woman will be binding on her.

¹⁰"If a woman living with her husband makes a vow or obligates herself by a pledge under oath ¹¹and her husband hears about it but says nothing to her and does not forbid her, then all her vows or the pledges by which she obligated herself will stand. ¹²But if her husband nullifies them when he hears about them, then none of the vows or pledges that came from her lips will stand.ᵃ Her husband has nullified them, and the LORD will release her. ¹³Her husband may confirm or nullify any vow she makes or any sworn pledge to deny herself. ¹⁴But if her husband says nothing to her about it from day to day, then he confirms all her vows or the pledges binding on her. He confirms them by saying nothing to her when he hears about them. ¹⁵If, however, he nullifies them ᵇ some time after he hears about them, then he is responsible for her guilt."

¹⁶These are the regulations the LORD gave Moses concerning relationships between a man and his wife, and between a father and his young daughter still living in his house.

Vengeance on the Midianites

Q 31 The LORD said to Moses, ²"Take vengeance on the Midianitesᶜ for the Israelites. After that, you will be gathered to your people.ᵈ"

Q Nu 27:13 ◀▶ Dt 32:50

³So Moses said to the people, "Arm some of your men to go to war against the Midianites and to carry out the LORD's vengeanceᵉ on them. ⁴Send into battle a thousand men from each of the tribes of Israel." ⁵So twelve thousand men armed for battle,ᶠ a thousand from each tribe, were supplied from the clans of Israel. ⁶Moses sent them into battle,ᵍ a thousand from each tribe, along with Phinehasʰ son of Eleazar, the priest, who took with him articles from the sanctuaryⁱ and the trumpetsʲ for signaling.

⁷They fought against Midian, as the LORD commanded Moses,ᵏ and killed every man.ˡ ⁸Among their victims were Evi, Rekem, Zur, Hur and Rebaᵐ—the five kings of Midian.ⁿ They also killed Balaam son of Beorᵒ with the sword.ᵖ ⁹The Israelites captured the Midianite womenᵠ and children and took all the Midianite herds, flocks and goods as plunder.ʳ ¹⁰They burnedˢ all the towns where the Midianites had settled, as well as all their camps.ᵗ ¹¹They took all the plunder and spoils, including the people and animals,ᵘ ¹²and brought the captives, spoilsᵛ and plunder to Moses and Eleazar the priest and the Israelite assemblyʷ at their camp on the plains of Moab, by the Jordan across from Jericho.˟˟

¹³Moses, Eleazar the priest and all the leaders of the community went to meet them outside the camp. ¹⁴Moses was angry with the officers of the armyʸ—the commanders of thousands and commanders of hundreds—who returned from the battle.

¹⁵"Have you allowed all the women to live?" he asked them. ¹⁶"They were the ones who followed Balaam's adviceᶻ and were the means of turning the Israelites away from the LORD in what happened at Peor,ᵃ so that a plagueᵇ struck the LORD's people. ¹⁷Now kill all the boys. And kill every woman who has slept with a man,ᶜ ¹⁸but save for yourselves every girl who has never slept with a man.

¹⁹"All of you who have killed anyone or

x 12 Hebrew *Jordan of Jericho*; possibly an ancient name for the Jordan River

---

31:2 God confirmed that Moses death was imminent but promised that Moses would "be gathered to" his people. The repetition of this promise in Scripture reflects the Hebrew belief that godly individuals will be reunited with their godly ancestors in heaven and will one day be resurrected. See note at Ge 35:29.

touched anyone who was killed[d] must stay outside the camp seven days.[e] On the third and seventh days you must purify yourselves[f] and your captives. [20]Purify every garment[g] as well as everything made of leather, goat hair or wood.[h]

[21]Then Eleazar the priest said to the soldiers who had gone into battle,[i] "This is the requirement of the law that the LORD gave Moses: [22]Gold, silver, bronze, iron,[j] tin, lead [23]and anything else that can withstand fire must be put through the fire,[k] and then it will be clean. But it must also be purified with the water of cleansing.[l] And whatever cannot withstand fire must be put through that water. [24]On the seventh day wash your clothes and you will be clean.[m] Then you may come into the camp.[n]

Dividing the Spoils

[25]The LORD said to Moses, [26]"You and Eleazar the priest and the family heads[o] of the community are to count all the people[p] and animals that were captured.[q] [27]Divide[r] the spoils between the soldiers who took part in the battle and the rest of the community. [28]From the soldiers who fought in the battle, set apart as tribute for the LORD[s] one out of every five hundred, whether persons, cattle, donkeys, sheep or goats. [29]Take this tribute from their half share and give it to Eleazar the priest as the LORD's part. [30]From the Israelites' half, select one out of every fifty, whether persons, cattle, donkeys, sheep, goats or other animals. Give them to the Levites, who are responsible for the care of the LORD's tabernacle.[t] [31]So Moses and Eleazar the priest did as the LORD commanded Moses.

[32]The plunder remaining from the spoils[u] that the soldiers took was 675,000 sheep, [33]72,000 cattle, [34]61,000 donkeys [35]and 32,000 women who had never slept with a man.

[36]The half share of those who fought in the battle was:

337,500 sheep, [37]of which the tribute for the LORD[v] was 675;
[38]36,000 cattle, of which the tribute for the LORD was 72;
[39]30,500 donkeys, of which the tribute for the LORD was 61;
[40]16,000 people, of which the tribute for the LORD was 32.

[41]Moses gave the tribute to Eleazar the priest as the LORD's part,[w] as the LORD commanded Moses.[x]

[42]The half belonging to the Israelites, which Moses set apart from that of the fighting men— [43]the community's half— was 337,500 sheep, [44]36,000 cattle, [45]30,500 donkeys [46]and 16,000 people. [47]From the Israelites' half, Moses selected one out of every fifty persons and animals, as the LORD commanded him, and gave them to the Levites, who were responsible for the care of the LORD's tabernacle.

[48]Then the officers[y] who were over the units of the army—the commanders of thousands and commanders of hundreds—went to Moses [49]and said to him, "Your servants have counted[z] the soldiers under our command, and not one is missing.[a] [50]So we have brought as an offering to the LORD the gold articles each of us acquired—armlets, bracelets, signet rings, earrings and necklaces—to make atonement for ourselves[b] before the LORD."

[51]Moses and Eleazar the priest accepted from them the gold—all the crafted articles. [52]All the gold from the commanders of thousands and commanders of hundreds that Moses and Eleazar presented as a gift to the LORD weighed 16,750 shekels.[y] [53]Each soldier had taken plunder[c] for himself. [54]Moses and Eleazar the priest accepted the gold from the commanders of thousands and commanders of hundreds and brought it into the Tent of Meeting[d] as a memorial[e] for the Israelites before the LORD.

The Transjordan Tribes

32 The Reubenites and Gadites, who had very large herds and flocks,[f] saw that the lands of Jazer[g] and Gilead[h] were suitable for livestock.[i] [2]So they came to Moses and Eleazar the priest and to the leaders of the community,[j] and said, [3]"Ataroth,[k] Dibon,[l] Jazer,[m] Nimrah,[n] Heshbon,[o] Elealeh,[p] Sebam,[q] Nebo[r] and Beon[s]— [4]the land the LORD subdued[t] before the people of Israel— are suitable for livestock,[u] and your servants have livestock. [5]If we have found

L *Nu 14:14* ◀ ▶ *Dt 1:29–33*
S *Lev 26:6* ◀ ▶ *2Sa 8:6*

[y] 52 That is, about 420 pounds (about 190 kilograms)

favor in your eyes," they said, "let this land be given to your servants as our possession. Do not make us cross the Jordan."ᵛ

⁶Moses said to the Gadites and Reubenites, "Shall your countrymen go to war while you sit here? ⁷Why do you discourage the Israelites from going over into the land the LORD has given them?ʷ ⁸This is what your fathers did when I sent them from Kadesh Barnea to look over the land.ˣ ⁹After they went up to the Valley of Eshcolʸ and viewed the land, they discouraged the Israelites from entering the land the LORD had given them. ¹⁰The LORD's anger was arousedᶻ that day and he swore this oath:ᵃ ¹¹'Because they have not followed me wholeheartedly, not one of the men twenty years old or moreᶜ who came up out of Egyptᶜ will see the land I promised on oathᵈ to Abraham, Isaac and Jacobᵉ— ¹²not one except Caleb son of Jephunneh the Kenizzite and Joshua son of Nun, for they followed the LORD wholeheartedly.'ᶠ ¹³The LORD's anger burned against Israelᵍ and he made them wander in the desert forty years, until the whole generation of those who had done evil in his sight was gone.ʰ

¹⁴"And here you are, a brood of sinners, standing in the place of your fathers and making the LORD even more angry with Israel.ⁱ ¹⁵If you turn away from following him, he will again leave all this people in the desert, and you will be the cause of their destruction.ʲ"

¹⁶Then they came up to him and said, "We would like to build pensᵏ here for our livestockˡ and cities for our women and children. ¹⁷But we are ready to arm ourselves and go ahead of the Israelitesᵐ until we have brought them to their place.ⁿ Meanwhile our women and children will live in fortified cities, for protection from the inhabitants of the land. ¹⁸We will not return to our homes until every Israelite has received his inheritance.ᵒ ¹⁹We will not receive any inheritance with them on the other side of the Jordan, because our inheritanceᵖ has come to us on the east side of the Jordan."ᵠ

²⁰Then Moses said to them, "If you will do this—if you will arm yourselves before the LORD for battle,ʳ ²¹and if all of you will go armed over the Jordan before the LORD until he has driven his enemies out before himˢ— ²²then when the land is subdued before the LORD, you may returnᵗ and be free from your obligation to the LORD and to Israel. And this land will be your possessionᵘ before the LORD.ᵛ

²³"But if you fail to do this, you will be sinning against the LORD; and you may be sure that your sin will find you out.ʷ ²⁴Build cities for your women and children, and pens for your flocks,ˣ but do what you have promised.ʸ"

²⁵The Gadites and Reubenites said to Moses, "We your servants will do as our lord commands.ᶻ ²⁶Our children and wives, our flocks and herds will remain here in the cities of Gilead.ᵃ ²⁷But your servants, every man armed for battle, will cross over to fightᵇ before the LORD, just as our lord says."

²⁸Then Moses gave orders about themᶜ to Eleazar the priest and Joshua son of Nunᵈ and to the family heads of the Israelite tribes.ᵉ ²⁹He said to them, "If the Gadites and Reubenites, every man armed for battle, cross over the Jordan with you before the LORD, then when the land is subdued before you,ᶠ give them the land of Gilead as their possession.ᵍ ³⁰But if they do not cross overʰ with you armed, they must accept their possession with you in Canaan.ⁱ"

³¹The Gadites and Reubenites answered, "Your servants will do what the LORD has said.ʲ ³²We will cross over before the LORD into Canaan armed,ᵏ but the property we inherit will be on this side of the Jordan.ˡ"

³³Then Moses gave to the Gadites,ᵐ the Reubenites and the half-tribe of Manassehⁿ son of Joseph the kingdom of Sihon king of the Amoritesᵒ and the kingdom

---

32:11 Moses reminded the people that the disobedience and unfaithfulness of the ten spies resulted in judgment. Complete obedience to the Lord's commands was the only way for the Israelites to achieve blessing and military success.

of Og king of Bashan[p]—the whole land with its cities and the territory around them.[q]

³⁴The Gadites built up Dibon, Ataroth, Aroer,[r] ³⁵Atroth Shophan, Jazer,[s] Jogbehah,[t] ³⁶Beth Nimrah[u] and Beth Haran as fortified cities, and built pens for their flocks.[v] ³⁷And the Reubenites rebuilt Heshbon,[w] Elealeh[x] and Kiriathaim,[y] ³⁸as well as Nebo[z] and Baal Meon (these names were changed) and Sibmah.[a] They gave names to the cities they rebuilt.

³⁹The descendants of Makir[b] son of Manasseh went to Gilead,[c] captured it and drove out the Amorites[d] who were there. ⁴⁰So Moses gave Gilead to the Makirites,[e] the descendants of Manasseh, and they settled there. ⁴¹Jair,[f] a descendant of Manasseh, captured their settlements and called them Havvoth Jair.[z][g] ⁴²And Nobah captured Kenath[h] and its surrounding settlements and called it Nobah[i] after himself.[j]

Stages in Israel's Journey

33 Here are the stages in the journey[k] of the Israelites when they came out of Egypt[l] by divisions under the leadership of Moses and Aaron.[m] ²At the LORD's command Moses recorded[n] the stages in their journey[o]. This is their journey by stages:

³The Israelites set out[p] from Rameses[q] on the fifteenth day of the first month, the day after the Passover.[r] They marched out boldly[s] in full view of all the Egyptians, ⁴who were burying all their firstborn,[t] whom the LORD had struck down among them; for the LORD had brought judgment[u] on their gods.[v]

⁵The Israelites left Rameses and camped at Succoth.[w]

⁶They left Succoth and camped at Etham, on the edge of the desert.[x]

⁷They left Etham, turned back to Pi Hahiroth, to the east of Baal Zephon,[y] and camped near Migdol.[z]

⁸They left Pi Hahiroth[aa] and passed through the sea[b] into the desert, and when they had traveled for three days in the Desert of Etham, they camped at Marah.[c]

⁹They left Marah and went to Elim, where there were twelve springs and seventy palm trees, and they camped[d] there.

¹⁰They left Elim[e] and camped by the Red Sea.[b]

¹¹They left the Red Sea and camped in the Desert of Sin.[f]

¹²They left the Desert of Sin and camped at Dophkah.

¹³They left Dophkah and camped at Alush.

¹⁴They left Alush and camped at Rephidim, where there was no water for the people to drink.[g]

¹⁵They left Rephidim[h] and camped in the Desert of Sinai.[i]

¹⁶They left the Desert of Sinai and camped at Kibroth Hattaavah.[j]

¹⁷They left Kibroth Hattaavah and camped at Hazeroth.[k]

¹⁸They left Hazeroth and camped at Rithmah.

¹⁹They left Rithmah and camped at Rimmon Perez.

²⁰They left Rimmon Perez and camped at Libnah.[l]

²¹They left Libnah and camped at Rissah.

²²They left Rissah and camped at Kehelathah.

²³They left Kehelathah and camped at Mount Shepher.

²⁴They left Mount Shepher and camped at Haradah.

²⁵They left Haradah and camped at Makheloth.

²⁶They left Makheloth and camped at Tahath.

²⁷They left Tahath and camped at Terah.

²⁸They left Terah and camped at Mithcah.

²⁹They left Mithcah and camped at Hashmonah.

³⁰They left Hashmonah and camped at Moseroth.[m]

³¹They left Moseroth and camped at Bene Jaakan.[n]

³²They left Bene Jaakan and camped at Hor Haggidgad.

³³They left Hor Haggidgad and camped at Jotbathah.[o]

³⁴They left Jotbathah and camped at Abronah.

---

[z] 41 Or *them the settlements of Jair*   [a] 8 Many manuscripts of the Masoretic Text, Samaritan Pentateuch and Vulgate; most manuscripts of the Masoretic Text *left from before Hahiroth*   [b] 10 Hebrew *Yam Suph*; that is, Sea of Reeds; also in verse 11

³⁵They left Abronah and camped at Ezion Geber.ᵖ

³⁶They left Ezion Geber and camped at Kadesh, in the Desert of Zin.ᵠ

³⁷They left Kadesh and camped at Mount Hor,ʳ on the border of Edom.ˢ ³⁸At the LORD's command Aaron the priest went up Mount Hor, where he diedᵗ on the first day of the fifth month of the fortieth yearᵘ after the Israelites came out of Egypt.ᵛ ³⁹Aaron was a hundred and twenty-three years old when he died on Mount Hor.

⁴⁰The Canaanite kingʷ of Arad,ˣ who lived in the Negevʸ of Canaan, heard that the Israelites were coming.

⁴¹They left Mount Hor and camped at Zalmonah.

⁴²They left Zalmonah and camped at Punon.

⁴³They left Punon and camped at Oboth.ᶻ

⁴⁴They left Oboth and camped at Iye Abarim, on the border of Moab.ᵃ

⁴⁵They left Iyimᶜ and camped at Dibon Gad.

⁴⁶They left Dibon Gad and camped at Almon Diblathaim.

⁴⁷They left Almon Diblathaim and camped in the mountains of Abarim,ᵇ near Nebo.ᶜ

⁴⁸They left the mountains of Abarimᵈ and camped on the plains of Moabᵉ by the Jordanᶠ across from Jericho.ᵈᵍ ⁴⁹There on the plains of Moab they camped along the Jordan from Beth Jeshimothʰ to Abel Shittim.ⁱ

⁵⁰On the plains of Moab by the Jordan across from Jerichoʲ the LORD said to Moses, ⁵¹"Speak to the Israelites and say to them: 'When you cross the Jordan into Canaan,ᵏ ⁵²drive out all the inhabitants of the land before you. Destroy all their carved images and their cast idols, and demolish all their high places.ˡ ⁵³Take possession of the land and settle in it, for I have given you the land to possess.ᵐ

⁵⁴Distribute the land by lot,ⁿ according to your clans.ᵒ To a larger group give a larger inheritance, and to a smaller group a smaller one.ᵖ Whatever falls to them by lot will be theirs. Distribute it according to your ancestral tribes.ᵠ

⁵⁵" 'But if you do not drive out the inhabitants of the land, those you allow to remain will become barbs in your eyes and thornsʳ in your sides. They will give you trouble in the land where you will live. ⁵⁶And then I will do to you what I plan to do to them.ˢ' "

Boundaries of Canaan

34 The LORD said to Moses, ²"Command the Israelites and say to them: 'When you enter Canaan,ᵗ the land that will be allotted to you as an inheritanceᵘ will have these boundaries:ᵛ

³" 'Your southern side will include some of the Desert of Zinʷ along the border of Edom. On the east, your southern boundary will start from the end of the Salt Sea,ᵉˣ ⁴cross south of Scorpionᶠ Pass,ʸ continue on to Zin and go south of Kadesh Barnea.ᶻ Then it will go to Hazar Addar and over to Azmon,ᵃ ⁵where it will turn, join the Wadi of Egyptᵇ and end at the Sea.ᵍ

⁶" 'Your western boundary will be the coast of the Great Sea.ᶜ This will be your boundary on the west.ᵈ

⁷" 'For your northern boundary,ᵉ run a line from the Great Sea to Mount Horᶠ ⁸and from Mount Hor to Leboʰ Hamath.ᵍ Then the boundary will go to Zedad, ⁹continue to Ziphron and end at Hazar Enan. This will be your boundary on the north.

¹⁰" 'For your eastern boundary,ʰ run a line from Hazar Enan to Shepham. ¹¹The boundary will go down from Shepham to Riblahⁱ on the east side of Ainʲ and con-

J Nu 24:14–24 ◄ ► Jos 6:26
I Nu 24:14–19 ◄ ► Dt 1:35–39

ᶜ 45 That is, Iye Abarim ᵈ 48 Hebrew *Jordan of Jericho;* possibly an ancient name for the Jordan River; also in verse 50 ᵉ 3 That is, the Dead Sea; also in verse 12 ᶠ 4 Hebrew *Akrabbim* ᵍ 5 That is, the Mediterranean; also in verses 6 and 7 ʰ 8 Or *to the entrance to*

34:1–15 Moses records God's detailed outline of the future borders of the territory allotments in the promised land. This outline was not only for information, but to convey to the people again the greatness of God's gifts to his people.

tinue along the slopes east of the Sea of Kinnereth.*j k* ¹²Then the boundary will go down along the Jordan and end at the Salt Sea.

" 'This will be your land, with its boundaries on every side.' "

¹³Moses commanded the Israelites: "Assign this land by lot¹ as an inheritance.*m* The LORD has ordered that it be given to the nine and a half tribes, ¹⁴because the families of the tribe of Reuben, the tribe of Gad and the half-tribe of Manasseh have received their inheritance.*n* ¹⁵These two and a half tribes have received their inheritance on the east side of the Jordan of Jericho,*j* toward the sunrise."

¹⁶The LORD said to Moses, ¹⁷"These are the names of the men who are to assign the land for you as an inheritance: Eleazar the priest and Joshua*o* son of Nun. ¹⁸And appoint one leader from each tribe to help*p* assign the land.*q* ¹⁹These are their names:*r*

Caleb*s* son of Jephunneh,
  from the tribe of Judah;*t*
²⁰Shemuel son of Ammihud,
  from the tribe of Simeon;*u*
²¹Elidad son of Kislon,
  from the tribe of Benjamin;*v*
²²Bukki son of Jogli,
  the leader from the tribe of Dan;
²³Hanniel son of Ephod,
  the leader from the tribe of Manasseh*w* son of Joseph;
²⁴Kemuel son of Shiphtan,
  the leader from the tribe of Ephraim*x* son of Joseph;
²⁵Elizaphan son of Parnach,
  the leader from the tribe of Zebulun;*y*
²⁶Paltiel son of Azzan,
  the leader from the tribe of Issachar;
²⁷Ahihud son of Shelomi,
  the leader from the tribe of Asher;*z*
²⁸Pedahel son of Ammihud,
  the leader from the tribe of Naphtali."

²⁹These are the men the LORD commanded to assign the inheritance to the Israelites in the land of Canaan.*a*

34:11 *k* Dt 3:17; Jos 11:2; 13:27
34:13 *l* S Lev 16:8; Jos 18:10; Mic 2:5
  m Jos 13:6; 14:1-5; Isa 49:8; 65:9; Eze 45:1
34:14 *n* Nu 32:19; Dt 33:21; Jos 14:3
34:17 *o* Nu 11:28; Dt 1:38
34:18 *p* S Nu 1:4
  q Jos 14:1
34:19 *r* ver 29
  s S Nu 26:65
  t Ge 29:35; Dt 33:7; Ps 60:7
34:20 *u* S Ge 29:33
34:21 *v* Ge 49:27; Jdg 5:14; Ps 68:27
34:23 *w* Nu 1:34
34:24 *x* Nu 1:32
34:25 *y* S Ge 30:20
34:27 *z* Nu 1:40
34:29 *a* ver 19

35:1 *b* Nu 22:1
35:2 *c* Lev 25:32-34; Jos 14:3,4
  d Jos 21:1-42
35:3 *e* Dt 18:6; Jos 14:4; 21:2
35:5 *f* Jos 3:4
  g Lev 25:34; 2Ch 11:14; 13:9; 23:2; 31:19
35:6 *h* ver 11; Jos 21:13
35:8 *i* Nu 26:54; 33:54
35:10 *j* Nu 33:51; Dt 9:1; Jos 1:2,11
35:11 *k* ver 22-25
  l S Ex 21:13
35:12 *m* ver 19; Dt 19:6; Jos 20:3; 2Sa 14:11 *n* ver 26, 27,28 *o* ver 24,25
35:13 *p* ver 6,14

Towns for the Levites

35 On the plains of Moab by the Jordan across from Jericho,*k b* the LORD said to Moses, ²"Command the Israelites to give the Levites towns to live in*c* from the inheritance the Israelites will possess. And give them pasturelands*d* around the towns. ³Then they will have towns to live in and pasturelands for their cattle, flocks and all their other livestock.*e*

⁴"The pasturelands around the towns that you give the Levites will extend out fifteen hundred feet*l* from the town wall. ⁵Outside the town, measure three thousand feet*m f* on the east side, three thousand on the south side, three thousand on the west and three thousand on the north, with the town in the center. They will have this area as pastureland for the towns.*g*

Cities of Refuge

35:6-34Ref — Dt 4:41-43; 19:1-14; Jos 20:1-9

⁶"Six of the towns you give the Levites will be cities of refuge, to which a person who has killed someone may flee.*h* In addition, give them forty-two other towns. ⁷In all you must give the Levites forty-eight towns, together with their pasturelands. ⁸The towns you give the Levites from the land the Israelites possess are to be given in proportion to the inheritance of each tribe: Take many towns from a tribe that has many, but few from one that has few."*i*

⁹Then the LORD said to Moses: ¹⁰"Speak to the Israelites and say to them: 'When you cross the Jordan into Canaan,*j* ¹¹select some towns to be your cities of refuge, to which a person who has killed someone*k* accidentally*l* may flee. ¹²They will be places of refuge from the avenger,*m* so that a person accused of murder*n* may not die before he stands trial before the assembly.*o* ¹³These six towns you give will be your cities of refuge.*p* ¹⁴Give three on this side of the Jordan and three in Canaan as cities of refuge. ¹⁵These six towns will be a place of refuge for Israelites, aliens and any other people living among them, so that anyone

j 11 That is, Galilee j 15 Jordan of Jericho was possibly an ancient name for the Jordan River. *k 1* Hebrew *Jordan of Jericho;* possibly an ancient name for the Jordan River *l 4* Hebrew *a thousand cubits* (about 450 meters) *m 5* Hebrew *two thousand cubits* (about 900 meters)

who has killed another accidentally can flee there.

¹⁶"'If a man strikes someone with an iron object so that he dies, he is a murderer; the murderer shall be put to death.ᑫ ¹⁷Or if anyone has a stone in his hand that could kill, and he strikes someone so that he dies, he is a murderer; the murderer shall be put to death. ¹⁸Or if anyone has a wooden object in his hand that could kill, and he hits someone so that he dies, he is a murderer; the murderer shall be put to death. ¹⁹The avenger of bloodʳ shall put the murderer to death; when he meets him, he shall put him to death.ˢ ²⁰If anyone with malice aforethought shoves another or throws something at him intentionallyᵗ so that he dies ²¹or if in hostility he hits him with his fist so that he dies, that person shall be put to death;ᵘ he is a murderer. The avenger of bloodᵛ shall put the murderer to death when he meets him.

²²"'But if without hostility someone suddenly shoves another or throws something at him unintentionallyʷ ²³or, without seeing him, drops a stone on him that could kill him, and he dies, then since he was not his enemy and he did not intend to harm him, ²⁴the assemblyˣ must judge between him and the avenger of blood according to these regulations. ²⁵The assembly must protect the one accused of murder from the avenger of blood and send him back to the city of refuge to which he fled. He must stay there until the death of the high priest,ʸ who was anointedᶻ with the holy oil.ᵃ

²⁶"'But if the accused ever goes outside the limits of the city of refuge to which he has fled ²⁷and the avenger of blood finds him outside the city, the avenger of blood may kill the accused without being guilty of murder. ²⁸The accused must stay in his city of refuge until the death of the high priest; only after the death of the high priest may he return to his own property.

²⁹"'These are to be legal requirementsᵇ for you throughout the generations to come,ᶜ wherever you live.ᵈ

³⁰"'Anyone who kills a person is to be put to death as a murderer only on the testimony of witnesses. But no one is to be put to death on the testimony of only one witness.ᵉ

³¹"'Do not accept a ransomᶠ for the life of a murderer, who deserves to die. He must surely be put to death.

³²"'Do not accept a ransom for anyone who has fled to a city of refuge and so allow him to go back and live on his own land before the death of the high priest.

³³"'Do not pollute the land where you are. Bloodshed pollutes the land,ᵍ and atonement cannot be made for the land on which blood has been shed, except by the blood of the one who shed it. ³⁴Do not defile the landʰ where you live and where I dwell,ⁱ for I, the LORD, dwell among the Israelites.'"

Inheritance of Zelophehad's Daughters
36:1–12pp — Nu 27:1–11

36 The family heads of the clan of Gileadʲ son of Makir,ᵏ the son of Manasseh, who were from the clans of the descendants of Joseph,ˡ came and spoke before Moses and the leaders,ᵐ the heads of the Israelite families. ²They said, "When the LORD commanded my lord to give the land as an inheritance to the Israelites by lot,ⁿ he ordered you to give the inheritance of our brother Zelophehadᵒ to his daughters. ³Now suppose they marry men from other Israelite tribes; then their inheritance will be taken from our ancestral inheritance and added to that of the tribe they marry into. And so part of the inheritance allotted to us will be taken away. ⁴When the Year of Jubileeᵖ for the Israelites comes, their inheritance will be added to that of the tribe into which they marry, and their property will be taken from the tribal inheritance of our forefathers."

⁵Then at the LORD's command Moses gave this order to the Israelites: "What the tribe of the descendants of Joseph is saying is right. ⁶This is what the LORD commands for Zelophehad's daughters: They may marry anyone they please as long as they marry within the tribal clan of their father. ⁷No inheritanceᑫ in Israel is to pass from tribe to tribe, for every Israelite shall keep the tribal land inherited from his forefathers. ⁸Every daughter who inherits land in any Israelite tribe must marry someone in her father's tribal clan,ʳ so that every Israelite will possess the inheritance of his fathers. ⁹No inheritance may pass from tribe to tribe, for each Israelite tribe is to keep the land it inherits."

¹⁰So Zelophehad's daughters did as the LORD commanded Moses. ¹¹Zelophehad's daughters—Mahlah, Tirzah, Hoglah, Milcah and Noahˢ—married their cousins on their father's side. ¹²They married within the clans of the descendants of Manasseh son of Joseph, and their inheritance remained in their father's clan and tribe.ᵗ

¹³These are the commands and regulations the LORD gave through Mosesᵘ to the Israelites on the plains of Moab by the Jordan across from Jericho.ⁿᵛ

36:11 ˢ Nu 26:33
36:12 ᵗ 1Ch 7:15
36:13 ᵘ S Lev 7:38; S 27:34 ᵛ Nu 22:1

ⁿ *13* Hebrew *Jordan of Jericho*; possibly an ancient name for the Jordan River

Deuteronomy

Author: Moses

Theme: Restatement of the laws in Exodus, Leviticus and Numbers

Date of Writing: c. 1406–1400 B.C.

Outline of Deuteronomy
 I. A Historical Review of Israel's Wanderings (1:1—4:43)
 II. A Restatement of God's Laws (4:44—11:32)
 III. Practical Lessons in Righteous Living (12:1—26:19)
 IV. Blessings and Curses (27:1—28:68)
 V. The Palestinian Covenant (29:1—30:20)
 VI. Final Words and Moses' Death (31:1—34:12)

DEUTERONOMY IS THE last book of the Pentateuch. Its name comes from a phrase in Dt 17:18 in the Greek Septuagint which means "second law-giving." The Hebrew title for this book, *debarim*, literally means "words" and is taken from the opening phrase in the first verse.

This was time of great anticipation for the Israelites. Encamped along the Jordan River, the countdown had begun. Everyone in the camp knew that the forty-year judgment promised by God was about to be completed. With the exception of Moses, Joshua and Caleb, a whole generation had died during the forty years in the wilderness. Moses' death loomed, but a new generation of Israelites stood poised on the riverbank, ready to conquer Canaan. The dream of the promised land was almost in their grasp.

Commencing with an overview of their experiences during the exodus and wilderness wandering, Moses admonishes Israel in this farewell address to obey the fundamental laws of God that were given at Sinai. This new generation of Israelites needed to understand their covenant relationship with God—his laws and their required obedience. Moses' words came from his heart as he reminded the people to "be silent, O Israel, and listen! You have now become the people of the LORD your God. Obey the LORD your God and follow his commands and decrees that I give you today" (27:9–10). Moses also dictated a series of blessings and curses that were to be announced from Mt. Ebal and Mt. Gerizim after the Israelites had taken possession of the land. The great lawgiver of Israel concludes his remarks in Deuteronomy with a series of prophecies that span Israel's exile from the land and their ultimate return to Palestine. The book of Deuteronomy closes with God's appointment of Joshua as Moses' successor and the death of Moses on Mt. Nebo.

Deuteronomy's spiritual emphasis and its call to total commitment to the Lord in worship and obedience inspired references to its message throughout the rest of Scripture. The NT writers refer to it more than eighty times and Jesus quoted from Deuteronomy more than from any other OT book (see Mt 4:1–11; 22:37).

The Command to Leave Horeb

1 These are the words Moses spoke to all Israel in the desert east of the Jordan[a]—that is, in the Arabah[b]—opposite Suph, between Paran[c] and Tophel, Laban, Hazeroth and Dizahab. ²(It takes eleven days to go from Horeb[d] to Kadesh Barnea[e] by the Mount Seir[f] road.)[g]

³In the fortieth year,[h] on the first day of the eleventh month,[i] Moses proclaimed[j] to the Israelites all that the LORD had commanded him concerning them. ⁴This was after he had defeated Sihon[k] king of the Amorites,[l] who reigned in Heshbon,[m] and at Edrei had defeated Og[n] king of Bashan, who reigned in Ashtaroth.[o]

⁵East of the Jordan in the territory of Moab,[p] Moses began to expound this law, saying:

⁶The LORD our God said to us[q] at Horeb,[r] "You have stayed long enough[s] at this mountain. ⁷Break camp and advance into the hill country of the Amorites;[t] go to all the neighboring peoples in the Arabah,[u] in the mountains, in the western foothills, in the Negev[v] and along the coast, to the land of the Canaanites[w] and to Lebanon,[x] as far as the great river, the Euphrates.[y] ⁸See, I have given you this land[z].[a] Go in and take possession of the land that the LORD swore[b] he would give to your fathers—to Abraham, Isaac and Jacob—and to their descendants after them."

The Appointment of Leaders

⁹At that time I said to you, "You are too heavy a burden[c] for me to carry alone.[d] ¹⁰The LORD your God has increased[e] your numbers[f] so that today you are as many[g] as the stars in the sky.[h] ¹¹May the LORD, the God of your fathers, increase[i] you a thousand times and bless you as he has promised![j] ¹²But how can I bear your problems and your burdens and your disputes all by myself?[k] ¹³Choose some wise, understanding and respected men[l] from each of your tribes, and I will set them over you."

¹⁴You answered me, "What you propose to do is good."

¹⁵So I took[m] the leading men of your tribes,[n] wise and respected men,[o] and appointed them to have authority over you—as commanders[p] of thousands, of hundreds, of fifties and of tens and as tribal officials.[q] ¹⁶And I charged your judges at that time: Hear the disputes between your brothers and judge[r] fairly,[s]

1:1–3 Moses' last great message confirmed Israel's eternal covenant with God. This discourse was delivered on the first day of the last month of the forty years spent in the wilderness. With the exception of Moses, Joshua and Caleb, the entire generation of Israelites who had escaped from Egypt during the exodus had died in the Sinai wilderness. Within the month Moses would die too, and the new generation would begin the conquest of the land.

whether the case is between brother Israelites or between one of them and an alien. ¹⁷Do not show partiality in judging; hear both small and great alike. Do not be afraid of any man, for judgment belongs to God. Bring me any case too hard for you, and I will hear it. ¹⁸And at that time I told you everything you were to do.

Spies Sent Out

¹⁹Then, as the LORD our God commanded us, we set out from Horeb and went toward the hill country of the Amorites through all that vast and dreadful desert that you have seen, and so we reached Kadesh Barnea. ²⁰Then I said to you, "You have reached the hill country of the Amorites, which the LORD our God is giving us. ²¹See, the LORD your God has given you the land. Go up and take possession of it as the LORD, the God of your fathers, told you. Do not be afraid; do not be discouraged."

²²Then all of you came to me and said, "Let us send men ahead to spy out the land for us and bring back a report about the route we are to take and the towns we will come to."

²³The idea seemed good to me; so I selected twelve of you, one man from each tribe. ²⁴They left and went up into the hill country, and came to the Valley of Eshcol and explored it. ²⁵Taking with them some of the fruit of the land, they brought it down to us and reported, "It is a good land that the LORD our God is giving us."

Rebellion Against the LORD

²⁶But you were unwilling to go up; you rebelled against the command of the LORD your God. ²⁷You grumbled in your tents and said, "The LORD hates us; so he brought us out of Egypt to deliver us into the hands of the Amorites to destroy us. ²⁸Where can we go? Our brothers have made us lose heart. They say, 'The people are stronger and taller than we are; the cities are large, with walls up to the sky. We even saw the Anakites there.'"

²⁹Then I said to you, "Do not be terrified; do not be afraid of them. ³⁰The LORD your God, who is going before you, will fight for you, as he did for you in Egypt, before your very eyes, ³¹and in the desert. There you saw how the LORD your God carried you, as a father carries his son, all the way you went until you reached this place."

³²In spite of this, you did not trust in the LORD your God, ³³who went ahead of you on your journey, in fire by night and in a cloud by day, to search out places for you to camp and to show you the way you should go.

³⁴When the LORD heard what you said, he was angry and solemnly swore: ³⁵"Not a man of this evil generation shall see the good land I swore to give your forefathers, ³⁶except Caleb son of Jephunneh. He will see it, and I will give him and his descendants the land he set his feet on, because he followed the LORD wholeheartedly."

³⁷Because of you the LORD became angry with me also and said, "You shall not enter it, either. ³⁸But your assistant, Joshua son of Nun, will enter it. Encourage him, because he will lead Israel to inherit it. ³⁹And the little ones that you said would be taken captive, your children who do not yet know good from bad—they will enter the land. I will give it to them and they will take possession of it. ⁴⁰But as for you, turn around and set out toward the desert along the route to the Red Sea."

⁴¹Then you replied, "We have sinned against the LORD. We will go up and fight, as the LORD our God commanded us." So every one of you put on his weapons, thinking it easy to go up into the hill country.

⁴²But the LORD said to me, "Tell them, 'Do not go up and fight, because I will not be with you. You will be defeated by your enemies.'"

⁴³So I told you, but you would not listen. You rebelled against the LORD's command and in your arrogance you marched up into the hill country. ⁴⁴The Amorites who lived in those hills came out against you; they chased you like a swarm of bees and beat you down from Seir all the way to Hormah. ⁴⁵You came back and wept before the LORD, but he paid

---

W Ge 15:1 ◀▶ Dt 20:8
L Nu 31:49 ◀▶ Dt 2:7

I Nu 34:1–12 ◀▶ Dt 2:24–25

ᵃ 40 Hebrew *Yam Suph*; that is, Sea of Reeds

no attention[t] to your weeping and turned a deaf ear[u] to you. [46]And so you stayed in Kadesh[v] many days—all the time you spent there.

Wanderings in the Desert

2 Then we turned back and set out toward the desert along the route to the Red Sea,[b][w] as the LORD had directed me. For a long time we made our way around the hill country of Seir.[x]

[2]Then the LORD said to me, [3]"You have made your way around this hill country long enough;[y] now turn north. [4]Give the people these orders:[z] 'You are about to pass through the territory of your brothers the descendants of Esau,[a] who live in Seir.[b] They will be afraid[c] of you, but be very careful. [5]Do not provoke them to war, for I will not give you any of their land, not even enough to put your foot on. I have given Esau the hill country of Seir as his own.[d] [6]You are to pay them in silver for the food you eat and the water you drink.' "

[7]The LORD your God has blessed you in all the work of your hands. He has watched[e] over your journey through this vast desert.[f] These forty years[g] the LORD your God has been with you, and you have not lacked anything.[h]

[8]So we went on past our brothers the descendants of Esau, who live in Seir. We turned from[i] the Arabah[j] road, which comes up from Elath and Ezion Geber,[k] and traveled along the desert road of Moab.[l]

[9]Then the LORD said to me, "Do not harass the Moabites or provoke them to war, for I will not give you any part of their land. I have given Ar[m] to the descendants of Lot[n] as a possession."

[10](The Emites[o] used to live there—a people strong and numerous, and as tall as the Anakites.[p] [11]Like the Anakites, they too were considered Rephaites,[q] but the Moabites called them Emites. [12]Horites[r] used to live in Seir, but the descendants of Esau drove them out. They destroyed the Horites from before them and settled in their place, just as Israel did[s] in the land the LORD gave them as their possession.)

[13]And the LORD said, "Now get up and cross the Zered Valley.[t]" So we crossed the valley.

[14]Thirty-eight years[u] passed from the time we left Kadesh Barnea[v] until we crossed the Zered Valley. By then, that entire generation[w] of fighting men had perished from the camp, as the LORD had sworn to them.[x] [15]The LORD's hand was against them until he had completely eliminated[y] them from the camp.

[16]Now when the last of these fighting men among the people had died, [17]the LORD said to me, [18]"Today you are to pass by the region of Moab at Ar.[z] [19]When you come to the Ammonites,[a] do not harass them or provoke them to war,[b] for I will not give you possession of any land belonging to the Ammonites. I have given it as a possession to the descendants of Lot.[c]"

[20](That too was considered a land of the Rephaites,[d] who used to live there; but the Ammonites called them Zamzummites. [21]They were a people strong and numerous, and as tall as the Anakites.[e] The LORD destroyed them from before the Ammonites, who drove them out and settled in their place. [22]The LORD had done the same for the descendants of Esau, who lived in Seir,[f] when he destroyed the Horites from before them. They drove them out and have lived in their place to this day. [23]And as for the Avites[g] who lived in villages as far as Gaza,[h] the Caphtorites[i] coming from

C Ge 28:20 ◄► Dt 8:4
F Nu 21:16 ◄► Dt 8:3
L Dt 1:29–33 ◄► Dt 4:7

1:45 [t]Job 27:9; 35:13; Ps 18:41; 66:18; Pr 1:28; Isa 1:15; Jer 14:12; La 3:8; Mic 3:4; S Jn 9:31 [u]Ps 28:1; 39:12; Pr 28:9
1:46 [v]S Nu 20:1
2:1 [w]S Ex 14:27; S Nu 21:4 [x]S Nu 24:18
2:3 [y]Dt 1:6
2:4 [z]Nu 20:14-21 [a]Ge 36:8 [b]ver 1 [c]Ex 15:16
2:5 [d]Jos 24:4
2:7 [e]Dt 8:2-4 [f]S Ex 13:21; S Dt 1:19 [g]ver 14; S Nu 14:33; 32:13; Jos 5:6 [h]Ne 9:21; Am 2:10
2:8 [i]S Nu 20:21 [j]S Dt 1:1 [k]Nu 33:35; 1Ki 9:26 [l]S Nu 21:4
2:9 [m]S Nu 21:15 [n]Ge 19:38; Ps 83:8
2:10 [o]Ge 14:5 [p]S Nu 13:22,33
2:11 [q]S Ge 14:5
2:12 [r]S Ge 14:6 [s]Nu 21:25,35
2:13 [t]S Nu 21:12
2:14 [u]S ver 7 [v]S Dt 1:2 [w]Nu 14:29-35 [x]Dt 1:34-35; Jos 5:6
2:15 [y]Ps 106:26; Jude 1:5
2:18 [z]S Nu 21:15
2:19 [a]S Ge 19:38 [b]2Ch 20:10 [c]S ver 9
2:20 [d]S Ge 14:5
2:21 [e]ver 10
2:22 [f]S Ge 14:6
2:23 [g]Jos 13:3; 18:23; 2Ki 17:31 [h]S Ge 10:19 [i]S Ge 10:14

[b] 1 Hebrew *Yam Suph*; that is, Sea of Reeds

2:20–21 The giants that inhabited the territories around Canaan were probably descendants of the early inhabitants of Ashteroth Karnaim on the eastern slopes of the Jordan (see Ge 14:5). These Rephaites were probably descended from the same race, but were given different names by the different peoples who came in contact with them. The races identified with the Rephaites include the Zamzummin (2:20), who may be the same as the Zuzim mentioned in Ge 14:5; the Emim (see 2:10–11), a very tall race who lived in Moabite territory in the time of Abraham (see Ge 14:5); and the Anakim (see 1:28; 2:11), who lived in Hebron, the territory promised to Caleb (see Nu 13:22; Jos 15:13–14; 21:11; Jdg 1:20).

Caphtor[cj] destroyed them and settled in their place.)

Defeat of Sihon King of Heshbon

[24] "Set out now and cross the Arnon Gorge.[k] See, I have given into your hand Sihon the Amorite,[l] king of Heshbon, and his country. Begin to take possession of it and engage[m] him in battle. [25] This very day I will begin to put the terror[n] and fear[o] of you on all the nations under heaven. They will hear reports of you and will tremble[p] and be in anguish because of you."

[26] From the desert of Kedemoth[q] I sent messengers to Sihon[r] king of Heshbon offering peace[s] and saying, [27] "Let us pass through your country. We will stay on the main road; we will not turn aside to the right or to the left.[t] [28] Sell us food to eat[u] and water to drink for their price in silver. Only let us pass through on foot[v]— [29] as the descendants of Esau, who live in Seir, and the Moabites, who live in Ar, did for us—until we cross the Jordan into the land the LORD our God is giving us." [30] But Sihon king of Heshbon refused to let us pass through. For the LORD[w] your God had made his spirit stubborn[x] and his heart obstinate[y] in order to give him into your hands,[z] as he has now done.

[31] The LORD said to me, "See, I have begun to deliver Sihon and his country over to you. Now begin to conquer and possess his land."[a]

[32] When Sihon and all his army came out to meet us in battle[b] at Jahaz, [33] the LORD our God delivered[c] him over to us and we struck him down,[d] together with his sons and his whole army. [34] At that time we took all his towns and completely destroyed[de] them—men, women and children. We left no survivors. [35] But the livestock[f] and the plunder[g] from the towns we had captured we carried off for ourselves. [36] From Aroer[h] on the rim of the Arnon Gorge, and from the town in

Dt 1:35–39 ◄ ► Dt 3:2

2:23 [I] Jer 47:4; Am 9:7
2:24 [k] Nu 21:13-14; Jdg 11:13,18
[l] S Dt 1:7 m Dt 3:6
2:25 [n] S Ge 35:5; Dt 11:25 [o] Jos 2:9, 11; 1Ch 14:17; 2Ch 14:14; 17:10; 20:29; Isa 2:19; 13:13; 19:16
[p] Ex 15:14-16
2:26 [q] Jos 13:18; 1Ch 6:79 r Dt 1:4; Jdg 11:21-22
[s] Dt 20:10; Jdg 21:13; 2Sa 20:19
2:27 [t] Nu 21:21-22
2:28 [u] Dt 23:4
[v] S Nu 20:19
2:30 [w] Jdg 14:4; 1Ki 12:15
[x] S Ex 4:21; Ro 9:18 [y] S Ex 14:17
[z] La 3:65
2:31 [a] S Ge 12:7
2:32 [b] S Nu 21:23
2:33 [c] Ex 23:31; Dt 7:2; 31:5
[d] S Nu 21:24
2:34 [e] S Nu 21:2; Dt 3:6; 7:2; Ps 106:34
2:35 [f] Dt 3:7
[g] S Ge 34:29; S 49:27
2:36 [h] S Nu 32:34
[i] S Nu 32:39
[j] Ps 44:3
2:37 [k] ver 18-19
[l] S Nu 21:24
[m] S Ge 32:22
3:1 [n] S Nu 32:19
[o] S Nu 21:33
3:2 [p] Jos 10:8; 2Ki 19:6; Isa 7:4
3:3 [q] S Nu 21:24
[r] Nu 21:35
3:4 [s] S Nu 21:24
[t] ver 13
[u] S Nu 21:33
3:6 [v] Dt 2:24
3:7 [w] Dt 2:35
3:8 [x] Nu 32:33; Jos 13:8-12
[y] Dt 4:48; Jos 11:3, 17; 12:1; 13:5; Jdg 3:3; 1Ch 5:23; Ps 42:6; 89:12; 133:3; SS 4:8
3:9 [z] Ps 29:6
[a] 1Ch 5:23; SS 4:8; Eze 27:5
3:10 [b] Jos 12:5; 1Ch 5:11

the gorge, even as far as Gilead,[i] not one town was too strong for us. The LORD our God gave[j] us all of them. [37] But in accordance with the command of the LORD our God,[k] you did not encroach on any of the land of the Ammonites,[l] neither the land along the course of the Jabbok[m] nor that around the towns in the hills.

Defeat of Og King of Bashan

3 Next we turned and went up along the road toward Bashan, and Og king of Bashan[n] with his whole army marched out to meet us in battle at Edrei.[o] [2] The LORD said to me, "Do not be afraid[p] of him, for I have handed him over to you with his whole army and his land. Do to him what you did to Sihon king of the Amorites, who reigned in Heshbon."

[3] So the LORD our God also gave into our hands Og king of Bashan and all his army. We struck them down,[q] leaving no survivors.[r] [4] At that time we took all his cities.[s] There was not one of the sixty cities that we did not take from them—the whole region of Argob, Og's kingdom[t] in Bashan.[u] [5] All these cities were fortified with high walls and with gates and bars, and there were also a great many unwalled villages. [6] We completely destroyed[d] them, as we had done with Sihon king of Heshbon, destroying[dv] every city—men, women and children. [7] But all the livestock[w] and the plunder from their cities we carried off for ourselves.

[8] So at that time we took from these two kings of the Amorites[x] the territory east of the Jordan, from the Arnon Gorge as far as Mount Hermon.[y] [9] (Hermon is called Sirion[z] by the Sidonians; the Amorites call it Senir.)[a] [10] We took all the towns on the plateau, and all Gilead, and all Bashan as far as Salecah[b] and Edrei, towns of Og's kingdom in Bashan. [11] (Only Og king of Bashan was left of the

Dt 2:24–25 ◄ ► Dt 3:21–22

[c] 23 That is, Crete [d] 34,6 The Hebrew term refers to the irrevocable giving over of things or persons to the LORD, often by totally destroying them.

3:11 Og was the king of Bashan, the last of the giant races of that part of Canaan. The Israelites conquered Og's kingdom immediately after the conquest of Sihon (see Nu 21:32–35; Dt 3:1–12), and Og and his people were "completely destroyed" (3:6). Og's kingdom became part of the inheritance of Gad, Reuben and the half tribe of Manasseh (see Nu 32:33). The bed mentioned in this verse may refer to Og's sarcophagus (stone coffin) made of basalt, a stone as hard as iron. Yet the bed may have been Og's regular bed. In either case the dimensions of this bed—13.5 feet long by 6 feet wide—

remnant of the Rephaites.^c His bed^e was made of iron and was more than thirteen feet long and six feet wide.^f It is still in Rabbah^d of the Ammonites.)

Division of the Land

¹²Of the land that we took over at that time, I gave the Reubenites and the Gadites the territory north of Aroer^e by the Arnon Gorge, including half the hill country of Gilead, together with its towns. ¹³The rest of Gilead and also all of Bashan, the kingdom of Og, I gave to the half tribe of Manasseh.^f (The whole region of Argob in Bashan used to be known as a land of the Rephaites.^g ¹⁴Jair,^h a descendant of Manasseh, took the whole region of Argob as far as the border of the Geshurites and the Maacathites;ⁱ it was named^j after him, so that to this day Bashan is called Havvoth Jair.^g) ¹⁵And I gave Gilead to Makir.^k ¹⁶But to the Reubenites and the Gadites I gave the territory extending from Gilead down to the Arnon Gorge (the middle of the gorge being the border) and out to the Jabbok River,^l which is the border of the Ammonites. ¹⁷Its western border was the Jordan in the Arabah,^m from Kinnerethⁿ to the Sea of the Arabah^o (the Salt Sea^h^p), below the slopes of Pisgah.

¹⁸I commanded you at that time: "The LORD your God has given^q you this land to take possession of it. But all your able-bodied men, armed for battle, must cross over ahead of your brother Israelites.^r ¹⁹However, your wives,^s your children and your livestock^t (I know you have much livestock) may stay in the towns I have given you, ²⁰until the LORD gives rest to your brothers as he has to you, and they too have taken over the land that the LORD your God is giving them, across the Jordan. After that, each of you may go back to the possession I have given you."

Moses Forbidden to Cross the Jordan

²¹At that time I commanded Joshua: "You have seen with your own eyes all that the LORD your God has done to these two kings. The LORD will do the same to all the kingdoms over there where you are going. ²²Do not be afraid^u of them; the LORD your God himself will fight^w for you."

²³At that time I pleaded^x with the LORD: ²⁴"O Sovereign LORD, you have begun to show to your servant your greatness^y and your strong hand. For what god^z is there in heaven or on earth who can do the deeds and mighty works^a you do?^b ²⁵Let me go over and see the good land^c beyond the Jordan—that fine hill country and Lebanon.^d"

²⁶But because of you the LORD was angry^e with me and would not listen to me. "That is enough," the LORD said. "Do not speak to me anymore about this matter. ²⁷Go up to the top of Pisgah^f and look west and north and south and east.^g Look at the land with your own eyes, since you are not going to cross^h this Jordan.ⁱ ²⁸But commission^j Joshua, and encourage^k and strengthen him, for he will lead this people across^l and will cause them to inherit the land that you will see." ²⁹So we stayed in the valley near Beth Peor.^m

Obedience Commanded

4 Hear now, O Israel, the decreesⁿ and laws I am about to teach^o you. Follow them so that you may live^p and may go in and take possession of the land that the LORD, the God of your fathers, is giving you. ²Do not add^q to what I command you and do not subtract^r from it, but keep^s the commands^t of the LORD your God that I give you.

³You saw with your own eyes what the LORD did at Baal Peor.^u The LORD your God destroyed from among you everyone who followed the Baal of Peor, ⁴but all of you who held fast to the LORD your God are still alive today.

⁵See, I have taught^v you decrees and laws^w as the LORD my God commanded^x me, so that you may follow them in the land you are entering^y to take possession of it. ⁶Observe^z them carefully, for this will show your wisdom^a and understanding to the nations, who will hear about all these decrees and say, "Surely this great nation is a wise and understanding peo-

---

^a Dt 30:19-20; 32:46-47; Ps 19:7; 119:98; Pr 1:7; 2Ti 3:15

^e 11 Or sarcophagus ^f 11 Hebrew nine cubits long and four cubits wide (about 4 meters long and 1.8 meters wide) ^g 14 Or called the settlements of Jair ^h 17 That is, the Dead Sea

---

suggest that Og was a huge man and his defeat was a cause for rejoicing (see Ps 135:11; 136:20).

ple."[b] [7]What other nation is so great[c] as to have their gods near[d] them the way the LORD our God is near us whenever we pray to him? [8]And what other nation is so great as to have such righteous decrees and laws[e] as this body of laws I am setting before you today?

[9]Only be careful,[f] and watch yourselves closely so that you do not forget the things your eyes have seen or let them slip from your heart as long as you live. Teach[g] them to your children[h] and to their children after them. [10]Remember the day you stood before the LORD your God at Horeb,[i] when he said to me, "Assemble the people before me to hear my words so that they may learn[j] to revere me as long as they live in the land[l] and may teach[m] them to their children." [11]You came near and stood at the foot of the mountain[n] while it blazed with fire[o] to the very heavens, with black clouds and deep darkness.[p] [12]Then the LORD spoke[q] to you out of the fire. You heard the sound of words but saw no form;[r] there was only a voice.[s] [13]He declared to you his covenant,[t] the Ten Commandments,[u] which he commanded you to follow and then wrote them on two stone tablets. [14]And the LORD directed me at that time to teach you the decrees and laws[v] you are to follow in the land that you are crossing the Jordan to possess.

Idolatry Forbidden

[15]You saw no form[w] of any kind the day the LORD spoke to you at Horeb[x] out of the fire. Therefore watch yourselves very carefully,[y] [16]so that you do not become corrupt[z] and make for yourselves an idol,[a] an image of any shape, whether formed like a man or a woman, [17]or like any animal on earth or any bird that flies in the air,[b] [18]or like any creature that moves along the ground or any fish in the waters below. [19]And when you look up to the sky and see the sun,[c] the moon and the stars[d]—all the heavenly array[e]—do not be enticed[f] into bowing down to them and worshiping[g] things the LORD your God has apportioned to all the nations under heaven. [20]But as for you, the LORD took you and brought you out of the iron-smelting furnace,[h] out of Egypt,[i] to be the people of his inheritance,[j] as you now are.

[21]The LORD was angry with me[k] because of you, and he solemnly swore that I would not cross the Jordan and enter the good land the LORD your God is giving you as your inheritance. [22]I will die in this land;[l] I will not cross the Jordan; but you are about to cross over and take possession of that good land.[m] [23]Be careful not to forget the covenant[n] of the LORD your God that he made with you; do not make for yourselves an idol[o] in the form of anything the LORD your God has forbidden. [24]For the LORD your God is a consuming fire,[p] a jealous God.[q]

[25]After you have had children and grandchildren and have lived in the land a long time—if you then become corrupt[r] and make any kind of idol,[s] doing evil[t] in the eyes of the LORD your God and provoking him to anger, [26]I call heaven and earth as witnesses[u] against you[v] this day that you will quickly perish[w] from the land that you are crossing the Jordan to possess. You will not live there long but will certainly be destroyed. [27]The LORD

L Dt 3:21–22 ◄ ► Dt 4:26–31
H Nu 32:23 ◄ ► Dt 7:10
I Dt 4:22 ◄ ► Dt 6:3
R Lev 26:43 ◄ ► Dt 4:30

L Nu 14:18–20 ◄ ► Dt 4:29
L Dt 2:7 ◄ ► Dt 29:5

4:21–22 Moses was forbidden to enter the promised land because of his unbelief and failure to honor God at Meribah. (See note at Nu 20:12).

4:23 Because of their ancestors' sin with the golden calf in the desert of Sinai this new generation of Israelites was admonished to remember their covenant with God and his prohibition of idolatry (see Ex 20:4–5).

4:25–28 Moses acknowledged that the sin of idolatry could tempt Israel after their settlement in Canaan. He wanted this new generation to know that God would deal severely with this sin, causing them to "perish from the land" (4:26), be carried off to foreign nations and be forced to serve their gods (4:27–28). Tragically, the Israelites forgot Moses' words and worshiped the idols of Canaan. Moses' prophecy was fulfilled when the Israelites were exiled to Babylon and ordered to worship the golden image of Nebuchadnezzar (see Da 3:4–7).

will scatter you among the peoples, and only a few of you will survive among the nations to which the LORD will drive you. ²⁸There you will worship man-made gods of wood and stone, which cannot see or hear or eat or smell. ²⁹But if from there you seek the LORD your God, you will find him if you look for him with all your heart and with all your soul. ³⁰When you are in distress and all these things have happened to you, then in later days you will return to the LORD your God and obey him. ³¹For the LORD your God is a merciful God; he will not abandon or destroy you or forget the covenant with your forefathers, which he confirmed to them by oath.

The LORD Is God

³²Ask now about the former days, long before your time, from the day God created man on the earth; ask from one end of the heavens to the other. Has anything so great as this ever happened, or has anything like it ever been heard of? ³³Has any other people heard the voice of God speaking out of fire, as you have, and lived? ³⁴Has any god ever tried to take for himself one nation out of another nation, by testings, by miraculous signs and wonders, by war, by a mighty hand and an outstretched arm, or by great and awesome deeds, like all the things the LORD your God did for you in Egypt before your very eyes? ³⁵You were shown these things so that you might know that the LORD is God; besides him there is no other. ³⁶From heaven he made you hear his voice to discipline you. On earth he showed you his great fire, and you heard his words

from out of the fire. ³⁷Because he loved your forefathers and chose their descendants after them, he brought you out of Egypt by his Presence and his great strength, ³⁸to drive out before you nations greater and stronger than you and to bring you into their land to give it to you for your inheritance, as it is today. ³⁹Acknowledge and take to heart this day that the LORD is God in heaven above and on the earth below. There is no other. ⁴⁰Keep his decrees and commands, which I am giving you today, so that it may go well with you and your children after you and that you may live long in the land the LORD your God gives you for all time.

Cities of Refuge

4:41–43Ref — Nu 35:6–34; Dt 19:1–14; Jos 20:1–9

⁴¹Then Moses set aside three cities east of the Jordan, ⁴²to which anyone who had killed a person could flee if he had unintentionally killed his neighbor without malice aforethought. He could flee into one of these cities and save his life. ⁴³The cities were these: Bezer in the desert plateau, for the Reubenites; Ramoth in Gilead, for the Gadites; and Golan in Bashan, for the Manassites.

Introduction to the Law

⁴⁴This is the law Moses set before the Israelites. ⁴⁵These are the stipulations, decrees and laws Moses gave them when they came out of Egypt ⁴⁶and were in the valley near Beth Peor east of the Jordan,

---

4:29–31 God's judgment on the Israelites' idolatry was tempered with mercy. God promised that if the Israelites would repent and turn back to him, he would hear their prayers and forgive them. Nearly a thousand years later Nehemiah refers to these prophetic words of Moses when he appeals for God's forgiveness and mercy for the returning exiles (see Ne 1:1–11).

4:40 If the Israelites kept God's commandments, God made two promises to them in this verse: things would go well for them and they would "live long in the land." Moses wanted the Israelites to understand that obedience to God's laws would bring blessings in all areas of their lives. Isaiah echoes this prophecy of long life with his description of the Messianic kingdom (see Isa 65:20). Earlier, God had also promised good health to the Israelites if they followed his statutes (see Ex 15:26).

in the land of Sihon¹ king of the Amorites, who reigned in Heshbon and was defeated by Moses and the Israelites as they came out of Egypt. ⁴⁷They took possession of his land and the land of Og king of Bashan, the two Amorite kings east of the Jordan. ⁴⁸This land extended from Aroer™ on the rim of the Arnon Gorge to Mount Siyon/ⁿ (that is, Hermon°), ⁴⁹and included all the Arabah east of the Jordan, as far as the Sea of the Arabah,ᵏ below the slopes of Pisgah.

The Ten Commandments
5:6–21pp — Ex 20:1–17

5 Moses summoned all Israel and said: Hear, O Israel, the decrees and lawsᵖ I declare in your hearing today. Learn them and be sure to follow them. ²The LORD our God made a covenantᑫ with us at Horeb.ʳ ³It was not with our fathers that the LORD made this covenant, but with us,ˢ with all of us who are alive here today.ᵗ ⁴The LORD spokeᵘ to you face to faceᵛ out of the fireʷ on the mountain. ⁵(At that time I stood betweenˣ the LORD and you to declare to you the word of the LORD, because you were afraidʸ of the fire and did not go up the mountain.) And he said:

> ⁶"I am the LORD your God, who brought you out of Egypt,ᶻ out of the land of slavery.ᵃ
>
> ⁷"You shall have no other gods beforeᶦ me.
>
> ⁸"You shall not make for yourself an idol in the form of anything in heaven above or on the earth beneath or in the waters below.ᵇ ⁹You shall not bow down to them or worship them; for I, the LORD your God, am a jealous God, punishing the children for the sin of the fathersᶜ to the third and fourth generation of those who hate me,ᵈ ¹⁰but showing love to a thousandᵉ ⌞generations⌟ of those who love me and keep my commandments.ᶠ
>
> ¹¹"You shall not misuse the nameᵍ of the LORD your God, for the LORD will not hold anyone guiltless who misuses his name.ʰ

L Dt 4:29 ◀▶ Dt 7:7–8
U Nu 23:10 ◀▶ Dt 5:29

4:46 ˡNu 21:26
4:48 ᵐDt 2:36
ⁿDt 3:9 ᵒDt 3:8
5:1 ᵖS Ex 18:20
5:2 ᑫEx 19:5; Jer 11:2; Heb 9:15; 10:15-17
ʳS Ge 17:9;
S Ex 3:1
5:3 ˢDt 11:2-7
ᵗNu 26:63-65; Heb 8:9
5:4 ᵘS Dt 4:12
ᵛS Nu 14:14
ʷS Ex 19:18
5:5 ˣS Gal 3:19
ʸS Ge 3:10;
Heb 12:18-21
5:6 ᶻS Ex 13:3;
S 29:46 ᵃLev 26:1;
Dt 6:4; Ps 81:10
5:8 ᵇLev 26:1;
Dt 4:15-18;
Ps 78:58; 97:7
5:9 ᶜS Nu 26:11
ᵈEx 34:7;
S Nu 10:35; 14:18
5:10 ᵉS Ex 34:7
ᶠNu 14:18; Dt 7:9;
Ne 1:5; Jer 32:18;
Da 9:4
5:11 ᵍPs 139:20
ʰLev 19:12;
Dt 10:20;
Mt 5:33-37
5:12 ᶦEx 16:23-30; 31:13-17;
Mk 2:27-28
5:14 ʲS Ge 2:2;
Mt 12:2; Mk 2:27;
Heb 4:4
ᵏJob 31:13;
Jer 34:9-11
ˡJer 17:21,24
5:15 ᵐS Ge 15:13
ⁿEx 6:1; Ps 108:6;
Jer 32:21
ᵒS Dt 4:34
5:16 ᵖMal 1:6
ᑫEx 21:17;
Lev 19:3; Eze 22:7;
Mt 15:4*; 19:19*;
Mk 7:10*; 10:19*;
Lk 18:20*;
Eph 6:2-3*
ʳS Dt 4:40; 11:9;
Pr 3:1-2
5:17 ˢGe 9:6;
Lev 24:17; Ecc 3:3;
Jer 40:15; 41:3;
Mt 5:21-22*;
19:19*; Mk 10:19*;
Lk 18:20*;
Ro 13:9*; Jas 2:11*
5:18 ᵗLev 20:10;
Mt 5:27-30;
19:18*; Mk 10:19*;
Lk 18:20*;
Ro 13:9*; Jas 2:11*
5:19 ᵘLev 19:11;
Mt 19:19*;
Mk 10:19*;
Lk 18:20*;
Ro 13:9*
5:20 ᵛS Ex 23:1;
Mt 19:18*;
Mk 10:19*;
Lk 18:20*
5:21 ʷRo 7:7*;
13:9*
5:22 ˣS Ex 20:21
ʸS Ex 24:12
5:23 ᶻS Ex 3:16

¹²"Observe the Sabbath day by keeping it holy,ᶦ as the LORD your God has commanded you. ¹³Six days you shall labor and do all your work, ¹⁴but the seventh dayʲ is a Sabbath to the LORD your God. On it you shall not do any work, neither you, nor your son or daughter, nor your manservant or maidservant,ᵏ nor your ox, your donkey or any of your animals, nor the alien within your gates, so that your manservant and maidservant may rest, as you do.ˡ ¹⁵Remember that you were slavesᵐ in Egypt and that the LORD your God brought you out of there with a mighty handⁿ and an outstretched arm.ᵒ Therefore the LORD your God has commanded you to observe the Sabbath day.

¹⁶"Honor your fatherᵖ and your mother,ᑫ as the LORD your God has commanded you, so that you may live longʳ and that it may go well with you in the land the LORD your God is giving you.

¹⁷"You shall not murder.ˢ

¹⁸"You shall not commit adultery.ᵗ

¹⁹"You shall not steal.ᵘ

²⁰"You shall not give false testimony against your neighbor.ᵛ

²¹"You shall not covet your neighbor's wife. You shall not set your desire on your neighbor's house or land, his manservant or maidservant, his ox or donkey, or anything that belongs to your neighbor."ʷ

²²These are the commandments the LORD proclaimed in a loud voice to your whole assembly there on the mountain from out of the fire, the cloud and the deep darkness;ˣ and he added nothing more. Then he wrote them on two stone tabletsʸ and gave them to me.

²³When you heard the voice out of the darkness, while the mountain was ablaze with fire, all the leading men of your tribes and your eldersᶻ came to me. ²⁴And you said, "The LORD our God has

j 48 Hebrew; Syriac (see also Deut. 3:9) *Sirion* *k 49* That is, the Dead Sea
l 7 Or *besides*

shown us his glory and his majesty, and we have heard his voice from the fire. Today we have seen that a man can live even if God speaks with him. 25But now, why should we die? This great fire will consume us, and we will die if we hear the voice of the LORD our God any longer. 26For what mortal man has ever heard the voice of the living God speaking out of fire, as we have, and survived? 27Go near and listen to all that the LORD our God says. Then tell us whatever the LORD our God tells you. We will listen and obey."

28The LORD heard you when you spoke to me and the LORD said to me, "I have heard what this people said to you. Everything they said was good. 29Oh, that their hearts would be inclined to fear me and keep all my commands always, so that it might go well with them and their children forever!

30"Go, tell them to return to their tents. 31But you stay here with me so that I may give you all the commands, decrees and laws you are to teach them to follow in the land I am giving them to possess."

32So be careful to do what the LORD your God has commanded you; do not turn aside to the right or to the left. 33Walk in all the way that the LORD your God has commanded you, so that you may live and prosper and prolong your days in the land that you will possess.

Love the LORD Your God

6 These are the commands, decrees and laws the LORD your God directed me to teach you to observe in the land that you are crossing the Jordan to possess, 2so that you, your children and their children after them may fear the LORD your God as long as you live by keeping all his decrees and commands that I give you, and so that you may enjoy long life. 3Hear, O Israel, and be careful to obey so that it may go well with you and that you may increase greatly in a land flowing with milk and honey, just as the LORD, the God of your fathers, promised you.

4Hear, O Israel: The LORD our God, the LORD is one. 5Love the LORD your God with all your heart and with all your soul and with all your strength. 6These commandments that I give you today are to be upon your hearts. 7Impress them on your children. Talk about them when you sit at home and when you walk along the road, when you lie down and when you get up. 8Tie them as symbols on your hands and bind them on your foreheads. 9Write them on the doorframes of your houses and on your gates.

10When the LORD your God brings you into the land he swore to your fathers, to Abraham, Isaac and Jacob, to give you—a land with large, flourishing cities you did not build, 11houses filled with all kinds of good things you did not provide, wells you did not dig, and vineyards and olive groves you did not plant—then when you eat and are satisfied, 12be careful that you do not forget the LORD, who brought you out of Egypt, out of the land of slavery.

13Fear the LORD your God, serve him only and take your oaths in his name. 14Do not follow other gods, the gods of the peoples around you; 15for the LORD your God, who is among you, is a jealous God and his anger will burn against you, and he will destroy you from the face of the land. 16Do not test the LORD your God as you did at Massah. 17Be sure to keep the commands of the LORD your God and the stipulations and decrees he has given you. 18Do what is right and good in the LORD's sight, so that it may go well with you and you may go in and take over the good land that the LORD promised on oath to your forefathers,

S Nu 32:23 ◀ ▶ Dt 6:7
U Dt 5:10 ◀ ▶ Dt 7:12–13
I Dt 4:26–31 ◀ ▶ Dt 7:4

S Dt 5:29 ◀ ▶ Dt 6:25   T ▶ Dt 26:1–3

4:8* m 1Sa 20:3 n S Ex 20:7; S Mt 5:33 6:15 o Dt 4:24; 5:9
6:16 p S Ex 17:2; Mt 4:7*; Lk 4:12* 6:17 q S Lev 26:3 r Dt 11:22;
Ps 119:4,56,100,134,168 6:18 s 2Ki 18:6; Isa 36:7; 38:3 t Dt 4:40
m 4 Or The LORD our God is one LORD; or The LORD our God, the LORD
is one; or The LORD our God, the LORD alone

6:4–9 This passage is known as the *Shema*, a Hebrew word for "hear." These words affirm the Jews' loyalty to the one and only God and are recited daily by the pious (see Mt 22:37–38; Mk 12:29–30; Lk 10:27).

¹⁹thrusting out all your enemies before you, as the LORD said.

²⁰In the future, when your son asks you, "What is the meaning of the stipulations, decrees and laws the LORD our God has commanded you?" ²¹tell him: "We were slaves of Pharaoh in Egypt, but the LORD brought us out of Egypt with a mighty hand. ²²Before our eyes the LORD sent miraculous signs and wonders—great and terrible—upon Egypt and Pharaoh and his whole household. ²³But he brought us out from there to bring us in and give us the land that he promised on oath to our forefathers. ²⁴The LORD commanded us to obey all these decrees and to fear the LORD our God, so that we might always prosper and be kept alive, as is the case today. ²⁵And if we are careful to obey all this law before the LORD our God, as he has commanded us, that will be our righteousness."

Driving Out the Nations

7 When the LORD your God brings you into the land you are entering to possess and drives out before you many nations—the Hittites, Girgashites, Amorites, Canaanites, Perizzites, Hivites and Jebusites, seven nations larger and stronger than you— ²and when the LORD your God has delivered them over to you and you have defeated them, then you must destroy them totally. Make no treaty with them, and show them no mercy. ³Do not intermarry with them. Do not give your daughters to their sons or take their daughters for your sons, ⁴for they will turn your sons away from following me to serve other gods, and the LORD's anger will burn against you and will quickly destroy you. ⁵This is what you are to do to them: Break down their altars, smash their sacred stones, cut down their Asherah poles and burn their idols in the fire. ⁶For you are a people holy to the LORD your God. The LORD your God has chosen you out of all the peoples on the face of the earth to be his people, his treasured possession.

⁷The LORD did not set his affection on you and choose you because you were more numerous than other peoples, for you were the fewest of all peoples. ⁸But it was because the LORD loved you and kept the oath he swore to your forefathers that he brought you out with a mighty hand and redeemed you from the land of slavery, from the power of Pharaoh king of Egypt. ⁹Know therefore that the LORD your God is God; he is the faithful God, keeping his covenant of love to a thousand generations of those who love him and keep his commands. ¹⁰But

> those who hate him he will repay to their face by destruction;
> he will not be slow to repay to their face those who hate him.

¹¹Therefore, take care to follow the commands, decrees and laws I give you today.

¹²If you pay attention to these laws and are careful to follow them, then the LORD your God will keep his covenant of love with you, as he swore to your forefathers. ¹³He will love you and bless you and increase your numbers. He will

---

7:6–10 These verses announced God's decision to choose Israel "out of all the peoples on the face of the earth to be his people, his treasured possession" (7:6). This covenantal relationship was first articulated to Abram (see Ge 12:1–3) and reiterated to the Israelites throughout the OT. This covenant was not based on the numerical greatness of Israel or because of any virtue on their part. God chose Israel as his special people because of his love and mercy. Moses also declared that God would eternally keep his "covenant of love to a thousand generations of those who love him and keep his commands" (7:9).

7:12–14 If Israel kept their part of the covenant, God promised to multiply their people, their livestock and their crops so that they would be "blessed more than any other people" (7:14). Obedience to God's commands would ensure fertility rather than sterility.

bless the fruit of your womb,° the crops of your land—your grain, new wine[p] and oil[q]—the calves of your herds and the lambs of your flocks in the land that he swore to your forefathers to give you.[r] [14]You will be blessed more than any other people; none of your men or women will be childless, nor any of your livestock without young.[s] [15]The LORD will keep you free from every disease.[t] He will not inflict on you the horrible diseases you knew in Egypt,[u] but he will inflict them on all who hate you.[v] [16]You must destroy all the peoples the LORD your God gives over to you.[w] Do not look on them with pity[x] and do not serve their gods,[y] for that will be a snare[z] to you.

[17]You may say to yourselves, "These nations are stronger than we are. How can we drive them out?"[a] [18]But do not be afraid[b] of them; remember well what the LORD your God did to Pharaoh and to all Egypt.[c] [19]You saw with your own eyes the great trials, the miraculous signs and wonders, the mighty hand[d] and outstretched arm, with which the LORD your God brought you out. The LORD your God will do the same to all the peoples you now fear.[e] [20]Moreover, the LORD your God will send the hornet[f] among them until even the survivors who hide from you have perished. [21]Do not be terrified by them, for the LORD your God, who is among you,[g] is a great and awesome God.[h] [22]The LORD your God will drive out those nations before you, little by little.[i] You will not be allowed to eliminate them all at once, or the wild animals will multiply around you. [23]But the LORD your God will deliver them over to you, throwing them into great confusion until they are destroyed.[j] [24]He will give their kings[k] into your hand,[l] and you will wipe out their names from under heaven. No one will be able to stand up against you;[m] you will destroy them.[n] [25]The images of their gods you are to burn[o] in the fire. Do not covet[p] the silver and gold on them, and do not take it for yourselves, or you will be ensnared[q] by it, for it is detestable[r] to the LORD your God. [26]Do not bring a detestable thing into your house or you, like it, will be set apart for destruction.[s] Utterly abhor and detest it, for it is set apart for destruction.

Do Not Forget the LORD

8 Be careful to follow every command I am giving you today, so that you may live[t] and increase and may enter and possess the land that the LORD promised on oath to your forefathers.[u] [2]Remember how the LORD your God led[v] you all the way in the desert these forty years, to humble you and to test[w] you in order to know what was in your heart, whether or not you would keep his commands. [3]He humbled[x] you, causing you to hunger and then feeding you with manna,[y] which neither you nor your fathers had known, to teach[z] you that man does not live on bread[a] alone but on every word that comes from the mouth[b] of the LORD.[c]

I ▶ Dt 7:6–9 ◀▶ Dt 7:22
D ▶ Nu 25:8–9 ◀▶ Dt 28:21–22
H ▶ Ex 23:25 ◀▶ Dt 33:25
I ▶ Dt 7:14–15 ◀▶ Dt 12:5

T ▶ Dt 8:5–6   S ▶ Dt 7:9 ◀▶ Dt 11:26–27
F ▶ Dt 2:7 ◀▶ Dt 8:15–16

7:15 Obedience to God's commands would ensure good health for the Israelites (see Ex 15:26; Dt 28:27, 60), but God would bring disease and ill health "on all who hate you."

7:16 Moses reaffirmed God's command to completely conquer all of the people in the land of Canaan and show them no pity.

7:20 This prophecy indicated that God would send hornets to drive out the remnant of Israel's enemies from the promised land (see Ex 23:28). The use of stinging insects was a metaphor used elsewhere in Scripture (see 1:44; Jos 24:12; Isa 7:18; Ps 118:12).

7:22–24 The Israelites' conquering of Canaan would be gradual so that large territories would not be left abandoned. Wild animals could quickly overtake these deserted areas and make reclamation more difficult for the Israelites. (See note on wild animals at Lev 26:22.) Yet eventually all the pagan kings and their armies would fall to the Israelites because God promised to fight for Israel.

8:2–3 These verses indicate an underlying reason for the forty-year wilderness wandering. In addition to the death of the rebellious generation of adults, the desert experience helped the Israelites see what was in their own hearts, whether or not they "would keep his commands" (8:2). Forty years of experiencing God's miraculous daily provision of water and manna taught the Israelites that "man does not live on bread alone but on every word that comes from the mouth of the LORD" (8:3).

⁴Your clothes did not wear out and your feet did not swell during these forty years.ᵈ ⁵Know then in your heart that as a man disciplines his son, so the LORD your God disciplines you.ᵉ

⁶Observe the commands of the LORD your God, walking in his waysᶠ and revering him.ᵍ ⁷For the LORD your God is bringing you into a good landʰ—a land with streams and pools of water, with springs flowing in the valleys and hills;ⁱ ⁸a land with wheat and barley,ʲ vinesᵏ and fig trees,ˡ pomegranates, olive oil and honey;ᵐ ⁹a land where breadⁿ will not be scarce and you will lack nothing;ᵒ a land where the rocks are iron and you can dig copper out of the hills.ᵖ

¹⁰When you have eaten and are satisfied,ᑫ praise the LORD your God for the good land he has given you. ¹¹Be careful that you do not forgetʳ the LORD your God, failing to observe his commands, his laws and his decrees that I am giving you this day. ¹²Otherwise, when you eat and are satisfied, when you build fine houses and settle down,ˢ ¹³and when your herds and flocks grow large and your silver and gold increase and all you have is multiplied, ¹⁴then your heart will become proud and you will forgetᵗ the LORD your God, who brought you out of Egypt, out of the land of slavery. ¹⁵He led you through the vast and dreadful desert,ᵘ that thirsty and waterless land, with its venomous snakesᵛ and scorpions. He brought you water out of hard rock.ʷ ¹⁶He gave you mannaˣ to eat in the desert, something your fathers had never known,ʸ to humble and to testᶻ you so

C Dt 2:7 ◀▶ Dt 10:18
E Nu 25:8 ◀▶ Dt 34:7
T Dt 8:2 ◀▶ Dt 8:16
P Ge 24:35 ◀▶ Dt 8:18
F Dt 8:3 ◀▶ Dt 10:18
T Dt 8:5–6 ◀▶ 2Sa 7:14

8:4 ᵈDt 29:5; Ne 9:21
8:5 ᵉDt 4:36; 2Sa 7:14; Job 5:17; 33:19; Pr 3:11-12; Heb 12:5-11; Rev 3:19
8:6 ᶠS Ex 33:13; 1Ki 3:14; Ps 81:13; 95:10 ᵍDt 5:33
8:7 ʰPs 106:24; Jer 3:19; Eze 20:6
ⁱDt 11:9-12; Jer 2:7
8:8 ʲS Ex 9:31
ᵏS Ge 49:11
ˡS Nu 13:23;
S 1Ki 4:25
ᵐDt 32:13; Ps 81:16
ⁿS ver 3
ᵒJdg 18:10
ᵖJob 28:2
8:10 ᑫDt 6:10-12
8:11 ʳDt 4:9
8:12 ˢPr 30:9; Hos 13:6
8:14 ᵗver 11; Ps 78:7; 106:21
8:15 ᵘS Dt 1:19; S 32:10 ᵛNu 21:6; Isa 14:29; 30:6
ʷEx 17:6; Dt 32:13; Job 28:9; Ps 78:15; 114:8
8:16 ˣS Ex 16:14
ʸEx 16:15
ᶻS Ge 22:1
8:17 ᵃDt 9:4,7,24; 31:27 ᵇJdg 7:2; Ps 44:3; Isa 10:13
8:18 ᶜGe 26:13; Dt 26:10; 28:4; 1Sa 2:7; Ps 25:13; 112:3; Pr 8:18; 10:22; Ecc 9:11; Hos 2:8
8:19 ᵈDt 6:14; Ps 16:4; Jer 7:6; 13:10; 25:6
ᵉDt 4:26; 30:18
8:20 ᶠ2Ki 21:2; Ps 10:16
ᵍEze 6:5
9:1 ʰS Nu 35:10 ⁱDt 4:38
ʲS Nu 13:28
ᵏS Ge 11:4
9:2 ˡNu 13:22; Jos 11:22
9:3 ᵐDt 31:3; Jos 3:11
ⁿS Ex 15:7;
S 19:18; Heb 12:29
ᵒS Ex 23:31
9:4 ᵖS Dt 8:17
ᑫ2Ki 16:3; 17:8; 21:2; Ezr 9:11

that in the end it might go well with you. ¹⁷You may say to yourself,ᵃ "My power and the strength of my handsᵇ have produced this wealth for me." ¹⁸But remember the LORD your God, for it is he who gives you the ability to produce wealth,ᶜ and so confirms his covenant, which he swore to your forefathers, as it is today.

¹⁹If you ever forget the LORD your God and follow other godsᵈ and worship and bow down to them, I testify against you today that you will surely be destroyed.ᵉ ²⁰Like the nationsᶠ the LORD destroyed before you, so you will be destroyed for not obeying the LORD your God.ᵍ

Not Because of Israel's Righteousness

9 Hear, O Israel. You are now about to cross the Jordanʰ to go in and dispossess nations greater and stronger than you,ⁱ with large citiesʲ that have walls up to the sky.ᵏ ²The people are strong and tall—Anakites! You know about them and have heard it said: "Who can stand up against the Anakites?"ˡ ³But be assured today that the LORD your God is the one who goes across ahead of youᵐ like a devouring fire.ⁿ He will destroy them; he will subdue them before you. And you will drive them out and annihilate them quickly,ᵒ as the LORD has promised you.

⁴After the LORD your God has driven them out before you, do not say to yourself,ᵖ "The LORD has brought me here to take possession of this land because of my righteousness." No, it is on account of the wicknessᑫ of these nationsʳ that the LORD is going to drive them out before you. ⁵It is not because of your righteousness or your integrityˢ that you are going in to take possession of their land; but on account of the wickednessᵗ of these na-

P Dt 8:13 ◀▶ Dt 15:4–6

ʳS Ex 23:24; S Lev 18:21,24-30; Dt 18:9-14 9:5 ˢS Eph 2:9 ᵗDt 18:9

8:4 One of the great miracles of the exodus was God's preservation of the Israelites' clothes and shoes throughout forty years of brutal, desert conditions. Resupply of clothing in the desert was virtually impossible for that many people. Only God's divine intervention could have provided so abundantly (see 29:5).

8:11–20 Forgetfulness comes easily to all of us, so the Israelites were urged to remember the desert's bitter lessons of sin and its punishment. Forgetfulness could result in pride and the Israelites might ascribe their wealth to their own efforts. Therefore, when the Israelites became successful in the promised land, Moses instructed them to "remember the LORD your God, for it is he who gives you the ability to produce wealth" (8:18).

9:1 God commanded Israel to "cross the Jordan" this day to conquer nations that were larger and stronger than themselves. It is possible that this day coincided with the Feast of Firstfruits. See the article "The Biblical Anniversaries of Israel," p. 170.

tions, the LORD your God will drive them out before you, to accomplish what he swore to your fathers, to Abraham, Isaac and Jacob. ⁶Understand, then, that it is not because of your righteousness that the LORD your God is giving you this good land to possess, for you are a stiff-necked people.

The Golden Calf

⁷Remember this and never forget how you provoked the LORD your God to anger in the desert. From the day you left Egypt until you arrived here, you have been rebellious against the LORD. ⁸At Horeb you aroused the LORD's wrath so that he was angry enough to destroy you. ⁹When I went up on the mountain to receive the tablets of stone, the tablets of the covenant that the LORD had made with you, I stayed on the mountain forty days and forty nights; I ate no bread and drank no water. ¹⁰The LORD gave me two stone tablets inscribed by the finger of God. On them were all the commandments the LORD proclaimed to you on the mountain out of the fire, on the day of the assembly.

¹¹At the end of the forty days and forty nights, the LORD gave me the two stone tablets, the tablets of the covenant. ¹²Then the LORD told me, "Go down from here at once, because your people whom you brought out of Egypt have become corrupt. They have turned away quickly from what I commanded them and have made a cast idol for themselves."

¹³And the LORD said to me, "I have seen this people, and they are a stiff-necked people indeed! ¹⁴Let me alone, so that I may destroy them and blot out their name from under heaven. And I will make you into a nation stronger and more numerous than they."

¹⁵So I turned and went down from the mountain while it was ablaze with fire. And the two tablets of the covenant were in my hands. ¹⁶When I looked, I saw that you had sinned against the LORD your God; you had made for yourselves an idol cast in the shape of a calf. You had turned aside quickly from the way that the LORD had commanded you. ¹⁷So I took the two tablets and threw them out of my hands, breaking them to pieces before your eyes.

¹⁸Then once again I fell prostrate before the LORD for forty days and forty nights; I ate no bread and drank no water, because of all the sin you had committed, doing what was evil in the LORD's sight and so provoking him to anger. ¹⁹I feared the anger and wrath of the LORD, for he was angry enough with you to destroy you. But again the LORD listened to me. ²⁰And the LORD was angry enough with Aaron to destroy him, but at that time I prayed for Aaron too. ²¹Also I took that sinful thing of yours, the calf you had made, and burned it in the fire. Then I crushed it and ground it to powder as fine as dust and threw the dust into a stream that flowed down the mountain.

²²You also made the LORD angry at Taberah, at Massah and at Kibroth Hattaavah.

²³And when the LORD sent you out from Kadesh Barnea, he said, "Go up and take possession of the land I have given you." But you rebelled against the command of the LORD your God. You did not trust him or obey him. ²⁴You have been rebellious against the LORD ever since I have known you.

²⁵I lay prostrate before the LORD those forty days and forty nights because the LORD had said he would destroy you. ²⁶I prayed to the LORD and said, "O Sovereign LORD, do not destroy your people, your own inheritance that you redeemed by your great power and brought out of Egypt with a mighty hand. ²⁷Remember your servants Abraham, Isaac and Jacob. Overlook the stubbornness of this people, their wickedness and their sin. ²⁸Otherwise, the country from which you brought us will say, 'Because the LORD was not able to take them into the land he had promised them, and because he hated them, he brought them out to put them to death in the desert.' ²⁹But they are your people, your inheritance that you brought out by your great power and your outstretched arm."

C Ge 8:21 ◄► Dt 9:13
C Dt 9:6 ◄► Dt 29:18–19
M Lev 26:40–42 ◄► Dt 10:16–17

p 15 Or *And I had the two tablets of the covenant with me, one in each hand*

Tablets Like the First Ones

10 At that time the LORD said to me, "Chisel out two stone tablets like the first ones and come up to me on the mountain. Also make a wooden chest. ²I will write on the tablets the words that were on the first tablets, which you broke. Then you are to put them in the chest."

³So I made the ark out of acacia wood and chiseled out two stone tablets like the first ones, and I went up on the mountain with the two tablets in my hands. ⁴The LORD wrote on these tablets what he had written before, the Ten Commandments he had proclaimed to you on the mountain, out of the fire, on the day of the assembly. And the LORD gave them to me. ⁵Then I came back down the mountain and put the tablets in the ark I had made, as the LORD commanded me, and they are there now.

⁶(The Israelites traveled from the wells of the Jaakanites to Moserah. There Aaron died and was buried, and Eleazar his son succeeded him as priest. ⁷From there they traveled to Gudgodah and on to Jotbathah, a land with streams of water. ⁸At that time the LORD set apart the tribe of Levi to carry the ark of the covenant of the LORD, to stand before the LORD to minister and to pronounce blessings in his name, as they still do today. ⁹That is why the Levites have no share or inheritance among their brothers; the LORD is their inheritance, as the LORD your God told them.)

¹⁰Now I had stayed on the mountain forty days and nights, as I did the first time, and the LORD listened to me at this time also. It was not his will to destroy you. ¹¹"Go," the LORD said to me, "and lead the people on their way, so that they may enter and possess the land that I swore to their fathers to give them."

Fear the LORD

¹²And now, O Israel, what does the LORD your God ask of you but to fear the LORD your God, to walk in all his ways, to love him, to serve the LORD your God with all your heart and with all your soul, ¹³and to observe the LORD's commands and decrees that I am giving you today for your own good?

¹⁴To the LORD your God belong the heavens, even the highest heavens, the earth and everything in it. ¹⁵Yet the LORD set his affection on your forefathers and loved them, and he chose you, their descendants, above all the nations, as it is today. ¹⁶Circumcise your hearts, therefore, and do not be stiff-necked any longer. ¹⁷For the LORD your God is God of gods and Lord of lords, the great God, mighty and awesome, who shows no partiality and accepts no bribes. ¹⁸He defends the cause of the fatherless and the widow, and loves the alien, giving him food and clothing. ¹⁹And you are to love those who are aliens, for you yourselves were aliens in Egypt. ²⁰Fear the LORD your God and serve him. Hold fast to him and take your oaths in his name. ²¹He is your praise; he is your God, who performed for you those great and awesome wonders you saw with your own eyes. ²²Your forefathers who went down into Egypt were seventy in all, and now the LORD your God has made you as numerous as the stars in the sky.

Love and Obey the LORD

11 Love the LORD your God and keep his requirements, his decrees, his laws and his commands always. ²Remember today that your children were not the ones who saw and experienced the discipline of the LORD your God: his majesty, his mighty hand, his outstretched arm; ³the signs he performed and the things he did in the heart of Egypt, both to Pharaoh king of Egypt and to his whole country; ⁴what he did to the Egyptian army, to its horses and chariots, how he overwhelmed them with the waters of the Red Sea as they were pursuing you, and how the LORD brought lasting ruin on them. ⁵It was not your children who saw what he did for you in the desert until you arrived at this place, ⁶and what he did to Dathan and Abiram, sons of Eliab the Reubenite, when the earth opened its mouth right

M Dt 9:13–14 ◀▶ 1Sa 2:3
C Dt 8:4 ◀▶ Dt 29:5
F Dt 8:15–16 ◀▶ Dt 11:14–15

q 1 That is, an ark r 4 Hebrew Yam Suph; that is, Sea of Reeds

in the middle of all Israel and swallowed them up with their households, their tents and every living thing that belonged to them. ⁷But it was your own eyes that saw all these great things the LORD has done.ʳ

⁸Observe therefore all the commandsˢ I am giving you today, so that you may have the strength to go in and take over the land that you are crossing the Jordan to possess,ᵗ ⁹and so that you may live longᵘ in the land that the LORD sworeᵛ to your forefathers to give to them and their descendants, a land flowing with milk and honey.ʷ ¹⁰The land you are entering to take over is not like the land of Egypt,ˣ from which you have come, where you planted your seed and irrigated it by foot as in a vegetable garden. ¹¹But the land you are crossing the Jordan to take possession of is a land of mountains and valleysʸ that drinks rain from heaven.ᶻ ¹²It is a land the LORD your God cares for; the eyesᵃ of the LORD your God are continually on it from the beginning of the year to its end.

¹³So if you faithfully obeyᵇ the commands I am giving you today—to loveᶜ the LORD your God and to serve him with all your heart and with all your soulᵈ— ¹⁴then I will send rainᵉ on your land in its season, both autumn and spring rains,ᶠ so that you may gather in your grain, new wine and oil. ¹⁵I will provide grassᵍ in the fields for your cattle, and you will eat and be satisfied.ʰ

¹⁶Be careful, or you will be enticed to turn away and worship other gods and bow down to them.ⁱ ¹⁷Then the LORD'S angerʲ will burn against you, and he will shutᵏ the heavens so that it will not rain and the ground will yield no produce,ˡ and you will soon perishᵐ from the good land the LORD is giving you. ¹⁸Fix these words of mine in your hearts and minds; tie them as symbols on your hands and bind them on your foreheads.ⁿ ¹⁹Teach them to your children,ᵒ talking about them when you sit at home and when you walk along the road, when you lie down and when you get up.ᵖ ²⁰Write them on the doorframes of your houses and on your gates,ᑫ ²¹so that your days and the days of your children may be manyʳ in the land that the LORD swore to give your forefathers, as many as the days that the heavens are above the earth.ˢ

²²If you carefully observeᵗ all these commands I am giving you to follow—to loveᵘ the LORD your God, to walk in all his ways and to hold fastᵛ to him— ²³then the LORD will drive outʷ all these nationsˣ before you, and you will dispossess nations larger and stronger than you.ʸ ²⁴Every place where you set your foot will be yours;ᶻ Your territory will extend from the desert to Lebanon, and from the Euphrates Riverᵃ to the western sea.ˢ ²⁵No man will be able to stand against you. The LORD your God, as he promised you, will put the terrorᵇ and fear of you on the whole land, wherever you go.ᶜ

²⁶See, I am setting before you today a blessingᵈ and a curseᵉ— ²⁷the blessingᶠ if you obey the commands of the LORD your God that I am giving you today; ²⁸the curse if you disobeyᵍ the commands of the LORD your God and turn from the way that I command you today by following other gods,ʰ which you have not known. ²⁹When the LORD your God has brought you into the land you are entering to possess, you are to proclaim on

B Dt 7:13 ◀▶ Dt 11:14–15
B Dt 11:11–12 ◀▶ Dt 28:3–5
F Dt 10:18 ◀▶ Dt 32:13–14

V Nu 14:9 ◀▶ Dt 20:4
L Dt 7:7–8 ◀▶ Dt 30:11–15
N Nu 14:11 ◀▶ Dt 18:18–19
S Dt 8:3 ◀▶ Dt 12:28
U Dt 7:12–13 ◀▶ Dt 14:29

ˢ 24 That is, the Mediterranean

11:11–14 If the Israelites served God and rejected idolatry, God promised rain and abundant crops. Obedience would bring his blessing to them and their possessions. God's promises are still true. If we will love and serve him with all our heart and soul, he will provide for us too.

11:22–28 This passage established the covenant rules that would govern God's agreement with Israel. If the Israelites diligently followed his commands, God promised to drive out their enemies regardless of size or strength. He also set the borders for the promised land, and guaranteed to "put the terror and fear of you on the whole land, wherever you go" (11:25). Yet God also gave a spiritual ultimatum to his chosen people: a promise of blessing if they followed his commandments but a guarantee of judgment if they worshiped false gods.

Mount Gerizim the blessings, and on Mount Ebal the curses. ³⁰As you know, these mountains are across the Jordan, west of the road, toward the setting sun, near the great trees of Moreh, in the territory of those Canaanites living in the Arabah in the vicinity of Gilgal. ³¹You are about to cross the Jordan to enter and take possession of the land the LORD your God is giving you. When you have taken it over and are living there, ³²be sure that you obey all the decrees and laws I am setting before you today.

The One Place of Worship

12 These are the decrees and laws you must be careful to follow in the land that the LORD, the God of your fathers, has given you to possess—as long as you live in the land. ²Destroy completely all the places on the high mountains and on the hills and under every spreading tree where the nations you are dispossessing worship their gods. ³Break down their altars, smash their sacred stones and burn their Asherah poles in the fire; cut down the idols of their gods and wipe out their names from those places.

⁴You must not worship the LORD your God in their way. ⁵But you are to seek the place the LORD your God will choose from among all your tribes to put his Name there for his dwelling. To that place you must go; ⁶there bring your burnt offerings and sacrifices, your tithes and special gifts, what you have vowed to give and your freewill offerings, and the firstborn of your herds and flocks. ⁷There, in the presence of the LORD your God, you and your families shall eat and shall rejoice in everything you have put your hand to, because the LORD your God has blessed you.

⁸You are not to do as we do here today, everyone as he sees fit, ⁹since you have not yet reached the resting place and the inheritance the LORD your God is giving you. ¹⁰But you will cross the Jordan and settle in the land the LORD your God is giving you as an inheritance, and he will give you rest from all your enemies around you so that you will live in safety. ¹¹Then to the place the LORD your God will choose as a dwelling for his Name—there you are to bring everything I command you: your burnt offerings and sacrifices, your tithes and special gifts, and all the choice possessions you have vowed to the LORD. ¹²And there rejoice before the LORD your God, you, your sons and daughters, your menservants and maidservants, and the Levites from your towns, who have no allotment or inheritance of their own. ¹³Be careful not to sacrifice your burnt offerings anywhere you please. ¹⁴Offer them only at the place the LORD will choose in one of your tribes, and there observe everything I command you.

¹⁵Nevertheless, you may slaughter your animals in any of your towns and eat as much of the meat as you want, as if it were gazelle or deer, according to the blessing the LORD your God gives you. Both the ceremonially unclean and the clean may eat it. ¹⁶But you must not eat the blood; pour it out on the ground like water. ¹⁷You must not eat in your own towns the tithe of your grain and new wine and oil, or the firstborn of your herds and flocks, or whatever you have vowed to give, or your freewill offerings or special gifts. ¹⁸Instead, you are to eat them in the presence of the LORD your God at the place the LORD your God will choose—you, your sons and daughters, your menservants and maidservants, and the Levites from your towns—and you are to rejoice before the LORD your God in everything you put your hand to. ¹⁹Be careful not to neglect the Levites as long as you live in your land.

²⁰When the LORD your God has enlarged your territory as he promised you, and you crave meat and say, "I

12:5 God ultimately chose Jerusalem as the location for his sanctuary, but during the exodus and the conquest of Canaan the tabernacle was located in different places as God directed (see 12:10–11; 26:2; Jos 9:27).

would like some meat," then you may eat as much of it as you want. ²¹If the place where the LORD your God chooses to put his Name^h is too far away from you, you may slaughter animals from the herds and flocks the LORD has given you, as I have commanded you, and in your own towns you may eat as much of them as you want.^i ²²Eat them as you would gazelle or deer.^j Both the ceremonially unclean and the clean may eat. ²³But be sure you do not eat the blood,^k because the blood is the life, and you must not eat the life with the meat.^l ²⁴You must not eat the blood; pour it out on the ground like water.^m ²⁵Do not eat it, so that it may go well^n with you and your children after you, because you will be doing what is right^o in the eyes of the LORD.

²⁶But take your consecrated things and whatever you have vowed to give,^p and go to the place the LORD will choose. ²⁷Present your burnt offerings^q on the altar of the LORD your God, both the meat and the blood. The blood of your sacrifices must be poured beside the altar of the LORD your God, but you may eat^r the meat. ²⁸Be careful to obey all these regulations I am giving you, so that it may always go well^s with you and your children after you, because you will be doing what is good and right in the eyes of the LORD your God.

²⁹The LORD your God will cut off^t before you the nations you are about to invade and dispossess. But when you have driven them out and settled in their land,^u ³⁰and after they have been destroyed before you, be careful not to be ensnared^v by inquiring about their gods, saying, "How do these nations serve their gods? We will do the same."^w ³¹You must not worship the LORD your God in their way, because in worshiping their gods, they do all kinds of detestable things the LORD hates.^x They even burn their sons^y and daughters in the fire as sacrifices to their gods.^z

³²See that you do all I command you; do not add^a to it or take away from it.

S Dt 11:26–27 ◀ ▶ Dt 12:32
S Dt 12:28 ◀ ▶ Dt 14:2

12:21 ^h Dt 14:24
^i Lev 17:4
12:22 ^j S ver 15
12:23 ^k S Lev 7:26
^l Eze 33:25
12:24 ^m ver 16
12:25 ^n S Dt 4:40
^o ver 28; Ex 15:26; Dt 13:18;
1Ki 11:38; 2Ki 12:2
12:26 ^p S ver 17; Nu 5:9-10
12:27 ^q S Lev 1:13
^r Lev 3:1-17
12:28 ^s Dt 4:40; Ecc 8:12
12:29 ^t Jos 23:4
^u S Dt 6:10
12:30 ^v S Ex 10:7
^w S ver 4
12:31
^x S Lev 18:25
^y S Lev 18:21
^z S 2Ki 3:27
12:32 ^a S Dt 4:2; Rev 22:18-19
13:1 ^b Mt 24:24; Mk 13:22; 2Th 2:9
^c S Ge 20:3;
Jer 23:25; 27:9; 29:8
13:2 ^d Dt 18:22;
1Sa 2:34; 10:9;
2Ki 19:29; 20:9;
Isa 7:11
^e S Dt 11:28
13:3 ^f 2Pe 2:1
^g 1Sa 28:6,15
^h S Ge 22:1;
1Ki 13:18;
22:22-23;
Jer 29:31; 43:2;
Eze 13:9;
1Co 11:19 ^i Dt 6:5
13:4 ^j 2Ki 23:3;
2Ch 34:31; 2Jn 1:6
^k S Dt 6:13; S Ps 5:7
^l S Dt 10:20
13:5 ^m S Ex 21:12;
S 22:20 ^n ver 10;
Dt 4:19 ^o Dt 17:7,
12; 19:19; 24:7;
Jdg 20:13;
S 1Co 5:13
13:6 ^p Dt 17:2-7;
29:18 ^q S Dt 11:28
13:8 ^r Pr 1:10
^s S Dt 7:2
13:9 ^t ver 5
^u S Lev 24:14
13:10 ^v S Ex 20:3
13:11 ^w Dt 17:13;
19:20; 21:21;
1Ti 5:20
13:13 ^x ver 2,6;
Jdg 19:22; 20:13;
1Sa 2:12; 10:27;
11:12; 25:17;
1Ki 21:10
13:14 ^y Jdg 20:12
^z Dt 17:4

Worshiping Other Gods

13 If a prophet,^b or one who foretells by dreams,^c appears among you and announces to you a miraculous sign or wonder, ²and if the sign^d or wonder of which he has spoken takes place, and he says, "Let us follow other gods"^e (gods you have not known) "and let us worship them," ³you must not listen to the words of that prophet^f or dreamer.^g The LORD your God is testing^h you to find out whether you love^i him with all your heart and with all your soul. ⁴It is the LORD your God you must follow,^j and him you must revere.^k Keep his commands and obey him; serve him and hold fast^l to him. ⁵That prophet or dreamer must be put to death,^m because he preached rebellion against the LORD your God, who brought you out of Egypt and redeemed you from the land of slavery; he has tried to turn^n you from the way the LORD your God commanded you to follow. You must purge the evil^o from among you.

⁶If your very own brother, or your son or daughter, or the wife you love, or your closest friend secretly entices^p you, saying, "Let us go and worship other gods"^q (gods that neither you nor your fathers have known, ⁷gods of the peoples around you, whether near or far, from one end of the land to the other), ⁸do not yield^r to him or listen to him. Show him no pity.^s Do not spare him or shield him. ⁹You must certainly put him to death.^t Your hand^u must be the first in putting him to death, and then the hands of all the people. ¹⁰Stone him to death, because he tried to turn you away^v from the LORD your God, who brought you out of Egypt, out of the land of slavery. ¹¹Then all Israel will hear and be afraid,^w and no one among you will do such an evil thing again.

¹²If you hear it said about one of the towns the LORD your God is giving you to live in ¹³that wicked men^x have arisen among you and have led the people of their town astray, saying, "Let us go and worship other gods" (gods you have not known), ¹⁴then you must inquire, probe and investigate it thoroughly.^y And if it is true and it has been proved that this detestable thing has been done among you,^z ¹⁵you must certainly put to the sword all who live in that town. Destroy

it completely," both its people and its livestock. ¹⁶Gather all the plunder of the town into the middle of the public square and completely burn the town and all its plunder as a whole burnt offering to the LORD your God. It is to remain a ruin forever, never to be rebuilt. ¹⁷None of those condemned things shall be found in your hands, so that the LORD will turn from his fierce anger; he will show you mercy, have compassion on you, and increase your numbers, as he promised on oath to your forefathers, ¹⁸because you obey the LORD your God, keeping all his commands that I am giving you today and doing what is right in his eyes.

Clean and Unclean Food
14:3–20pp — Lev 11:1–23

14 You are the children of the LORD your God. Do not cut yourselves or shave the front of your heads for the dead, ²for you are a people holy to the LORD your God. Out of all the peoples on the face of the earth, the LORD has chosen you to be his treasured possession.

³Do not eat any detestable thing. ⁴These are the animals you may eat: the ox, the sheep, the goat, ⁵the deer, the gazelle, the roe deer, the wild goat, the ibex, the antelope and the mountain sheep. ⁶You may eat any animal that has a split hoof divided in two and that chews the cud. ⁷However, of those that chew the cud or that have a split hoof completely divided you may not eat the camel, the rabbit or the coney. Although they chew the cud, they do not have a split hoof; they are ceremonially unclean for you. ⁸The pig is also unclean; although it has a split hoof, it does not chew the cud. You are not to eat their meat or touch their carcasses.

⁹Of all the creatures living in the water, you may eat any that has fins and scales. ¹⁰But anything that does not have fins and scales you may not eat; for you it is unclean.

¹¹You may eat any clean bird. ¹²But these you may not eat: the eagle, the vulture, the black vulture, ¹³the red kite, the black kite, any kind of falcon, ¹⁴any kind of raven, ¹⁵the horned owl, the screech owl, the gull, any kind of hawk, ¹⁶the little owl, the great owl, the white owl, ¹⁷the desert owl, the osprey, the cormorant, ¹⁸the stork, any kind of heron, the hoopoe and the bat.

¹⁹All flying insects that swarm are unclean to you; do not eat them. ²⁰But any winged creature that is clean you may eat.

²¹Do not eat anything you find already dead. You may give it to an alien living in any of your towns, and he may eat it, or you may sell it to a foreigner. But you are a people holy to the LORD your God.

Do not cook a young goat in its mother's milk.

Tithes

²²Be sure to set aside a tenth of all that your fields produce each year. ²³Eat the tithe of your grain, new wine and oil, and the firstborn of your herds and flocks in the presence of the LORD your God at the place he will choose as a dwelling for his Name, so that you may learn to revere the LORD your God always. ²⁴But if that place is too distant and you have been blessed by the LORD your God and cannot carry your tithe (because the place where the LORD will choose to put his Name is so far away), ²⁵then exchange your tithe for silver, and take the silver with you and go to the place the LORD your God will choose. ²⁶Use the silver to buy whatever you like: cattle, sheep, wine or other fermented drink, or anything you wish. Then you and your household shall eat there in the presence of the LORD your God and rejoice. ²⁷And do not neglect the Levites living in your towns, for they have no allotment or inheritance of their own.

²⁸At the end of every three years, bring all the tithes of that year's produce and store it in your towns, ²⁹so that the Levites (who have no allotment or inheritance of their own) and the aliens, the fatherless and the widows who live in your towns may come and eat and be satisfied, and so that the LORD your God may bless you in all the work of your hands.

A Ge 48:16 ◀▶ Dt 15:10
U Dt 11:26–27 ◀▶ Dt 26:18–19

u 15,17 The Hebrew term refers to the irrevocable giving over of things or persons to the LORD, often by totally destroying them. v 5 The precise identification of some of the birds and animals in this chapter is uncertain. w 7 That is, the hyrax or rock badger

The Year for Canceling Debts

15:1–11Ref — Lev 25:8–38

15 At the end of every seven years you must cancel debts.ᵛ ²This is how it is to be done: Every creditor shall cancel the loan he has made to his fellow Israelite. He shall not require payment from his fellow Israelite or brother, because the LORD's time for canceling debts has been proclaimed. ³You may require payment from a foreigner,ʷ but you must cancel any debt your brother owes you. ⁴However, there should be no poor among you, for in the land the LORD your God is giving you to possess as your inheritance, he will richly blessˣ you, ⁵if only you fully obey the LORD your God and are careful to followʸ all these commands I am giving you today. ⁶For the LORD your God will bless you as he has promised, and you will lend to many nations but will borrow from none. You will rule over many nations but none will rule over you.ᶻ

⁷If there is a poor manᵃ among your brothers in any of the towns of the land that the LORD your God is giving you, do not be hardhearted or tightfistedᵇ toward your poor brother. ⁸Rather be openhandedᶜ and freely lend him whatever he needs. ⁹Be careful not to harbor this wicked thought: "The seventh year, the year for canceling debts,ᵈ is near," so that you do not show ill willᵉ toward your needy brother and give him nothing. He may then appeal to the LORD against you, and you will be found guilty of sin.ᶠ ¹⁰Give generously to him and do so without a grudging heart;ᵍ then because of this the LORD your God will blessʰ you in all your work and in everything you put your hand to. ¹¹There will always be poor peopleⁱ in the land. Therefore I command you to be openhanded toward your brothers and toward the poor and needy in your land.ʲ

Freeing Servants

15:12–18pp — Ex 21:2–6
15:12–18Ref — Lev 25:38–55

¹²If a fellow Hebrew, a man or a woman, sells himself to you and serves you six years, in the seventh year you must let him go free.ᵏ ¹³And when you release him, do not send him away empty-handed. ¹⁴Supply him liberally from your flock, your threshing floorˡ and your winepress. Give to him as the LORD your God has blessed you. ¹⁵Remember that you were slavesᵐ in Egypt and the LORD your God redeemed you.ⁿ That is why I give you this command today.

¹⁶But if your servant says to you, "I do not want to leave you," because he loves you and your family and is well off with you, ¹⁷then take an awl and push it through his ear lobe into the door, and he will become your servant for life. Do the same for your maidservant.

¹⁸Do not consider it a hardship to set your servant free, because his service to you these six years has been worth twice as much as that of a hired hand. And the LORD your God will bless you in everything you do.

The Firstborn Animals

¹⁹Set apart for the LORDᵒ your God every firstborn maleᵖ of your herds and flocks.ᑫ Do not put the firstborn of your oxen to work, and do not shear the firstborn of your sheep.ʳ ²⁰Each year you and your family are to eat them in the presence of the LORD your God at the place he will choose.ˢ ²¹If an animal has a defect,ᵗ is lame or blind, or has any serious flaw, you must not sacrifice it to the LORD your God.ᵘ ²²You are to eat it in your own towns. Both the ceremonially unclean and the clean may eat it, as if it were gazelle or deer.ᵛ ²³But you must not eat the blood; pour it out on the ground like water.ʷ

Passover

16:1–8pp — Ex 12:14–20; Lev 23:4–8; Nu 28:16–25

16 Observe the month of Abibˣ and celebrate the Passoverʸ of the LORD your God, because in the month of Abib he brought you out of Egypt by night. ²Sacrifice as the Passover to the LORD your God an animal from your flock or herd at the place the LORD will choose as a dwelling for his Name.ᶻ ³Do not eat it with bread made with yeast, but for seven days eat unleavened bread, the bread of affliction,ᵃ because you left Egypt in haste ᵇ—so that all the days of your life you may remember the time of your departure from Egypt.ᶜ ⁴Let no yeast be found in your possession in all your land for seven days. Do not let any of the meat you sacrifice on the evening ᵈ of the first day remain until morning.ᵉ

⁵You must not sacrifice the Passover in any town the LORD your God gives you ⁶except in the place he will choose as a dwelling for his Name. There you must sacrifice the Passover in the evening, when the sun goes down, on the anniversary ˣᶠ of your departure from Egypt. ⁷Roast ᵍ it and eat it at the place the LORD your God will choose. Then in the morning return to your tents. ⁸For six days eat unleavened bread and on the seventh day hold an assembly ʰ to the LORD your God and do no work.ⁱ

Feast of Weeks
16:9–12pp — Lev 23:15–22; Nu 28:26–31

⁹Count off seven weeksʲ from the time you begin to put the sickle to the standing grain.ᵏ ¹⁰Then celebrate the Feast of Weeks to the LORD your God by giving a freewill offering in proportion to the blessings the LORD your God has given you. ¹¹And rejoice ˡ before the LORD your God at the place he will choose as a dwelling for his Nameᵐ—you, your sons and daughters, your menservants and maidservants, the Levitesⁿ in your towns, and the aliens,ᵒ the fatherless and the widows living among you.ᵖ ¹²Remember that you were slaves in Egypt,ᑫ and follow carefully these decrees.

Feast of Tabernacles
16:13–17pp — Lev 23:33–43; Nu 29:12–39

¹³Celebrate the Feast of Tabernacles for seven days after you have gathered the produce of your threshing floorʳ and your winepress.ˢ ¹⁴Be joyfulᵗ at your Feast—you, your sons and daughters, your menservants and maidservants, and the Levites, the aliens, the fatherless and the widows who live in your towns. ¹⁵For seven days celebrate the Feast to the LORD your God at the place the LORD will choose. For the LORD your God will bless you in all your harvest and in all the work

P *Dt 15:18* ◀▶ *Dt 24:19*

16:3 ᵃ Ex 12:8,39; 34:18; 1Co 5:8
ᵇ S Ex 12:11
ᶜ Dt 4:9

16:4 ᵈ S Ex 12:6
ᵉ S Ex 12:8; Mk 14:12

16:6 ᶠ S Ex 12:42

16:7 ᵍ S Ex 12:8

16:8 ʰ S Lev 23:8
ⁱ Mt 26:17; Lk 2:41; 22:7; Jn 2:13

16:9 ʲ Ac 2:1
ᵏ S Ex 23:16

16:11 ˡ Dt 12:7
ᵐ S Ex 20:24;
S 2Sa 7:13
ⁿ Dt 12:12
ᵒ S Dt 14:29
ᵖ Ne 8:10

16:12 ᑫ S Dt 15:15

16:13 ʳ S Lev 2:14
ˢ S Ge 27:37;
S Ex 23:16

16:14 ᵗ ver 11

16:15 ᵘ Job 38:7;
Ps 4:7; 28:7; 30:11

16:16 ᵛ Dt 31:11;
Ps 84:7
ʷ S Ex 12:17
ˣ S Ex 23:14,16;
Ezr 3:4 ʸ S Ex 34:20

16:18 ᶻ S Ex 18:21,26
ᵃ S Ge 31:37

16:19 ᵇ S Ex 23:2
ᶜ Lev 19:15
ᵈ S Ex 18:21;
S 1Sa 8:3

16:21 ᵉ S Dt 7:5
ᶠ Ex 34:13;
1Ki 14:15;
2Ki 17:16; 21:3;
2Ch 33:3

16:22 ᵍ S Ex 23:24

17:1 ʰ S Ex 12:5;
S Lev 22:20
ⁱ Dt 7:25
ʲ S Dt 15:21

17:2 ᵏ S Dt 13:6-11

17:3 ˡ Jer 7:31
ᵐ Ex 22:20
ⁿ S Ge 1:16
ᵒ S Ge 2:1; S 37:9

17:4 ᵖ Dt 22:20
ᑫ Dt 13:12-14

17:5 ʳ S Lev 24:14

17:6 ˢ Nu 35:30;
Dt 19:15;
S Mt 18:16

of your hands, and your joy ᵘ will be complete.

¹⁶Three times a year all your men must appear ᵛ before the LORD your God at the place he will choose: at the Feast of Unleavened Bread,ʷ the Feast of Weeks and the Feast of Tabernacles.ˣ No man should appear before the LORD empty-handed:ʸ ¹⁷Each of you must bring a gift in proportion to the way the LORD your God has blessed you.

Judges

¹⁸Appoint judgesᶻ and officials for each of your tribes in every town the LORD your God is giving you, and they shall judge the people fairly.ᵃ ¹⁹Do not pervert justiceᵇ or show partiality.ᶜ Do not accept a bribe,ᵈ for a bribe blinds the eyes of the wise and twists the words of the righteous. ²⁰Follow justice and justice alone, so that you may live and possess the land the LORD your God is giving you.

Worshiping Other Gods

²¹Do not set up any wooden Asherah poleʸᵉ beside the altar you build to the LORD your God,ᶠ ²²and do not erect a sacred stone,ᵍ for these the LORD your God hates.

17
Do not sacrifice to the LORD your God an ox or a sheep that has any defectʰ or flaw in it, for that would be detestableⁱ to him.ʲ

²If a man or woman living among you in one of the towns the LORD gives you is found doing evil in the eyes of the LORD your God in violation of his covenant,ᵏ ³and contrary to my commandˡ has worshiped other gods,ᵐ bowing down to them or to the sunⁿ or the moon or the stars of the sky,ᵒ ⁴and this has been brought to your attention, then you must investigate it thoroughly. If it is trueᵖ and it has been proved that this detestable thing has been done in Israel,ᑫ ⁵take the man or woman who has done this evil deed to your city gate and stone that person to death.ʳ ⁶On the testimony of two or three witnesses a man shall be put to death, but no one shall be put to death on the testimony of only one witness.ˢ ⁷The hands of the witnesses must be the first

D *Dt 16:1–6* ◀▶ *2Ki 23:21*

ˣ 6 *Or down, at the time of day* ʸ 21 *Or Do not plant any tree dedicated to Asherah*

in putting him to death, and then the hands of all the people. You must purge the evil from among you.

Law Courts

⁸If cases come before your courts that are too difficult for you to judge—whether bloodshed, lawsuits or assaults—take them to the place the LORD your God will choose. ⁹Go to the priests, who are Levites, and to the judge who is in office at that time. Inquire of them and they will give you the verdict. ¹⁰You must act according to the decisions they give you at the place the LORD will choose. Be careful to do everything they direct you to do. ¹¹Act according to the law they teach you and the decisions they give you. Do not turn aside from what they tell you, to the right or to the left. ¹²The man who shows contempt for the judge or for the priest who stands ministering there to the LORD your God must be put to death. You must purge the evil from Israel. ¹³All the people will hear and be afraid, and will not be contemptuous again.

The King

¹⁴When you enter the land the LORD your God is giving you and have taken possession of it and settled in it, and you say, "Let us set a king over us like all the nations around us," ¹⁵be sure to appoint over you the king the LORD your God chooses. He must be from among your own brothers. Do not place a foreigner over you, one who is not a brother Israelite. ¹⁶The king, moreover, must not acquire great numbers of horses for himself or make the people return to Egypt to get more of them, for the LORD has told you, "You are not to go back that way again." ¹⁷He must not take many wives, or his heart will be led astray. He must not accumulate large amounts of silver and gold.

¹⁸When he takes the throne of his kingdom, he is to write for himself on a scroll a copy of this law, taken from that of the priests, who are Levites. ¹⁹It is to be with him, and he is to read it all the days of his life so that he may learn to revere the LORD his God and follow carefully all the words of this law and these decrees ²⁰and not consider himself better than his brothers and turn from the law to the right or to the left. Then he and his descendants will reign a long time over his kingdom in Israel.

Offerings for Priests and Levites

18 The priests, who are Levites—indeed the whole tribe of Levi—are to have no allotment or inheritance with Israel. They shall live on the offerings made to the LORD by fire, for that is their inheritance. ²They shall have no inheritance among their brothers; the LORD is their inheritance, as he promised them.

³This is the share due the priests from the people who sacrifice a bull or a sheep: the shoulder, the jowls and the inner parts. ⁴You are to give them the firstfruits of your grain, new wine and oil, and the first wool from the shearing of your sheep, ⁵for the LORD your God has chosen them and their descendants out of all your tribes to stand and minister in the LORD's name always.

⁶If a Levite moves from one of your towns anywhere in Israel where he is living, and comes in all earnestness to the place the LORD will choose, ⁷he may minister in the name of the LORD his God like all his fellow Levites who serve there in the presence of the LORD. ⁸He is to share equally in their benefits, even though he has received money from the sale of family possessions.

Detestable Practices

⁹When you enter the land the LORD your God is giving you, do not learn to

---

18:9–12 This passage contains the most complete list of occult and spiritistic rites in the OT. One of the major Canaanite religions involved the worship of the god Molech and required child sacrifice. The Canaanites believed that such sacrifices would ensure material blessings. God referred to these practices as "detestable ways" (18:9). All forms of fortune telling, sorcery, witchcraft and occult practice were also forbidden in this passage. God's prohibition of these practices continues today; anyone involved with these activities needs to repent of their sin and seek God's forgiveness.

imitate the detestable ways of the nations there. ¹⁰Let no one be found among you who sacrifices his son or daughter in the fire, who practices divination or sorcery, interprets omens, engages in witchcraft, ¹¹or casts spells, or who is a medium or spiritist or who consults the dead. ¹²Anyone who does these things is detestable to the LORD, and because of these detestable practices the LORD your God will drive out those nations before you. ¹³You must be blameless before the LORD your God.

The Prophet

¹⁴The nations you will dispossess listen to those who practice sorcery or divination. But as for you, the LORD your God has not permitted you to do so. ¹⁵The LORD your God will raise up for you a prophet like me from among your own brothers. You must listen to him. ¹⁶For this is what you asked of the LORD your God at Horeb on the day of the assembly when you said, "Let us not hear the voice of the LORD our God nor see this great fire anymore, or we will die."

¹⁷The LORD said to me: "What they say is good. ¹⁸I will raise up for them a prophet like you from among their brothers; I will put my words in his mouth, and he will tell them everything I command him. ¹⁹If anyone does not listen to my words that the prophet speaks in my name, I myself will call him to account. ²⁰But a prophet who presumes to speak in my name anything I have not commanded him to say, or a prophet who speaks in the name of other gods, must be put to death."

²¹You may say to yourselves, "How can we know when a message has not been spoken by the LORD?" ²²If what a prophet proclaims in the name of the LORD does not take place or come true, that is a message the LORD has not spoken. That prophet has spoken presumptuously. Do not be afraid of him.

Cities of Refuge

19:1–14 Ref — Nu 35:6–34; Dt 4:41–43; Jos 20:1–9

19 When the LORD your God has destroyed the nations whose land he is giving you, and when you have driven them out and settled in their towns and houses, ²then set aside for yourselves three cities centrally located in the land the LORD your God is giving you to possess. ³Build roads to them and divide into three parts the land the LORD your God is giving you as an inheritance, so that anyone who kills a man may flee there.

⁴This is the rule concerning the man who kills another and flees there to save his life—one who kills his neighbor unintentionally, without malice aforethought. ⁵For instance, a man may go into the forest with his neighbor to cut wood, and as he swings his ax to fell a tree, the head may fly off and hit his neighbor and kill him. That man may flee to one of these cities and save his life. ⁶Otherwise, the avenger of blood might pursue him in a rage, overtake him if the distance is too great, and kill him even though he is not deserving of death, since he did it to his neighbor without malice aforethought. ⁷This is why I command you to set aside for yourselves three cities.

⁸If the LORD your God enlarges your territory, as he promised on oath to your forefathers, and gives you the whole land he promised them, ⁹because you carefully follow all these laws I command you today—to love the LORD your God and to walk always in his ways—then you are

z 10 Or who makes his son or daughter pass through

18:15–19 These verses contain one of the clearest, prophetic descriptions of Israel's Messiah. Moses indicated that God would raise up a prophet "like me" (18:15). Though this is a collective reference to all of the prophets that would follow Moses, it is also a reference to the Messiah and is uniquely fulfilled in Jesus (see Jn 1:21, 25, 45; 5:46; 6:14; 7:40; Ac 3:22–23; 7:37). Moses specifically warned Israel to listen to this prophet for God would hold everyone responsible if they rejected his words. For a more detailed discussion of the prophetic parallels between the life of Moses and the life of Jesus, see the article "A Prophet Like Unto Moses," p. 224.

to set aside three more cities. ¹⁰Do this so that innocent blood will not be shed in your land, which the LORD your God is giving you as your inheritance, and so that you will not be guilty of bloodshed.

¹¹But if a man hates his neighbor and lies in wait for him, assaults and kills him, and then flees to one of these cities, ¹²the elders of his town shall send for him, bring him back from the city, and hand him over to the avenger of blood to die. ¹³Show him no pity. You must purge from Israel the guilt of shedding innocent blood, so that it may go well with you.

¹⁴Do not move your neighbor's boundary stone set up by your predecessors in the inheritance you receive in the land the LORD your God is giving you to possess.

Witnesses

¹⁵One witness is not enough to convict a man accused of any crime or offense he may have committed. A matter must be established by the testimony of two or three witnesses. ¹⁶If a malicious witness takes the stand to accuse a man of a crime, ¹⁷the two men involved in the dispute must stand in the presence of the LORD before the priests and the judges who are in office at the time. ¹⁸The judges must make a thorough investigation, and if the witness proves to be a liar, giving false testimony against his brother, ¹⁹then do to him as he intended to do to his brother. You must purge the evil from among you. ²⁰The rest of the people will hear of this and be afraid, and never again will such an evil thing be done among you. ²¹Show no pity: life for life, eye for eye, tooth for tooth, hand for hand, foot for foot.

Going to War

20 When you go to war against your enemies and see horses and chariots and an army greater than yours, do not be afraid of them, because the LORD your God, who brought you up out of Egypt, will be with you. ²When you are about to go into battle, the priest shall come forward and address the army. ³He shall say: "Hear, O Israel, today you are going into battle against your enemies. Do not be fainthearted or afraid; do not be terrified or give way to panic before them. ⁴For the LORD your God is the one who goes with you to fight for you against your enemies to give you victory."

⁵The officers shall say to the army: "Has anyone built a new house and not dedicated it? Let him go home, or he may die in battle and someone else may dedicate it. ⁶Has anyone planted a vineyard and not begun to enjoy it? Let him go home, or he may die in battle and someone else enjoy it. ⁷Has anyone become pledged to a woman and not married her? Let him go home, or he may die in battle and someone else marry her." ⁸Then the officers shall add, "Is any man afraid or fainthearted? Let him go home so that his brothers will not become disheartened too." ⁹When the officers have finished speaking to the army, they shall appoint commanders over it.

¹⁰When you march up to attack a city, make its people an offer of peace. ¹¹If they accept and open their gates, all the people in it shall be subject to forced labor and shall work for you. ¹²If they refuse to make peace and they engage you in battle, lay siege to that city. ¹³When the LORD your God delivers it into your hand, put to the sword all the men in it. ¹⁴As for the women, the children, the livestock and everything else in the city, you may take these as plunder for yourselves. And you may use the plunder the LORD your God gives you from your enemies. ¹⁵This is how you are to treat all the cities that are at a distance from you and do not belong to the nations nearby.

¹⁶However, in the cities of the nations the LORD your God is giving you as an inheritance, do not leave alive anything that breathes. ¹⁷Completely destroy[a] them—the Hittites, Amorites, Canaanites, Perizzites, Hivites and Jebusites—as the LORD your God has commanded you. ¹⁸Otherwise, they will teach you to follow all the detestable things they do in worshiping their gods, and you will sin against the LORD your God.

¹⁹When you lay siege to a city for a long time, fighting against it to capture it, do not destroy its trees by putting an ax to

V Dt 11:25 ◀▶ Dt 28:7
W Dt 1:21 ◀▶ Dt 31:6–8

---

[a] 17 The Hebrew term refers to the irrevocable giving over of things or persons to the LORD, often by totally destroying them.

A Prophet Like Unto Moses

MOSES GAVE ISRAEL one of the greatest Messianic prophecies. As a unique leader with abilities as prophet, priest, teacher and lawgiver, Moses prophesied that God would raise up the Messiah to be like Moses so that God's people would recognize him (see Dt 18:15–18; 34:10; Ac 3:22–23; 7:37).

This prophecy was fulfilled in many ways through the life, death and resurrection of Jesus (see Jn 1:21, 45; 6:14; Ac 7:37–38). In fact, an analysis of the life of Moses and the life of Jesus of Nazareth reveals at least fifty parallels in their lives. Both were prophets, priests, lawgivers, teachers and leaders of men. Both taught God's truth and confirmed their teaching with miracles. Both spent their early years in Egypt, miraculously protected from those who sought their lives. Moses' family initially did not accept his role of leadership, but later his brother Aaron and sister Miriam became his assistants. Similarly, Jesus' family initially failed to follow him, but later Jesus' brother James became the leader of the believers in Jerusalem.

The similarities are also evident in their leadership and authority. As Moses appointed seventy rulers over Israel, Jesus anointed seventy disciples to teach the nations. Moses stretched his hand over the Red Sea to command it, and Jesus rebuked the Sea of Galilee to quiet the waves. Moses sent twelve spies to explore Canaan; Jesus sent twelve apostles to reach the world. Moses and Jesus both cured lepers and proved their authority through miracles. The people were ungrateful and rebelled against the leadership of both men. The generations that rebelled against Moses died for their lack of faith in the wilderness. Those who rebelled against Jesus died in the Roman siege of Jerusalem in A.D. 70.

The parallelism is noticeable in the experiences of their personal lives too. The Bible never indicates that either one experienced sickness. Though Moses and Jesus both died on a hilltop, neither of their bodies remained in a tomb. Both fasted for forty days and faced spiritual crises on mountaintops. Both of their faces shone with the glory of heaven—Moses on Mt. Sinai, Jesus on the Mount of Transfiguration.

Yet the greatest resemblance between Moses and Jesus occurred in their ministries among people. During the Passover, both Moses and Jesus freed all people who would listen to them and trust God's Word. While Moses rescued Israel from the dead religion of pagan Egypt, Jesus rescued Israel from the dead letter of the law of tradition. As Moses conquered the great enemy of Israel, the Amalekites, with his upraised arms, Jesus conquered the great enemy of sin and death with his upraised arms on a cross. Moses lifted up the brazen serpent in the wilderness to heal his people; Jesus was lifted up on the cross to heal all people from sin. During the Feast of Firstfruits, God used Moses to bring about the resurrection of the children of Israel as they passed through the Red Sea; on the anniversary of that feast Jesus became the firstfruits of resurrection as he rose from the grave. Fifty days after the Red Sea, on Pentecost, God delivered the great gift to Israel of the Law; fifty days after Jesus' resurrection, God gave believers the great gift of the Holy Spirit.

God is a covenant-keeping God, and the promises made about the Messiah have all come true in Jesus Christ. That all of these similarities are beyond the ability of human control, compels one to believe that Jesus is the prophesied Messiah, a prophet like unto Moses.

them, because you can eat their fruit. Do not cut them down. Are the trees of the field people, that you should besiege them?[b] [20]However, you may cut down trees that you know are not fruit trees[k] and use them to build siege works until the city at war with you falls.

Atonement for an Unsolved Murder

21 If a man is found slain, lying in a field in the land the LORD your God is giving you to possess, and it is not known who killed him,[1] [2]your elders and judges shall go out and measure the distance from the body to the neighboring towns. [3]Then the elders of the town nearest the body shall take a heifer that has never been worked and has never worn a yoke[m] [4]and lead her down to a valley that has not been plowed or planted and where there is a flowing stream. There in the valley they are to break the heifer's neck. [5]The priests, the sons of Levi, shall step forward, for the LORD your God has chosen them to minister and to pronounce blessings[n] in the name of the LORD and to decide all cases of dispute and assault.[o] [6]Then all the elders of the town nearest the body shall wash their hands[p] over the heifer whose neck was broken in the valley, [7]and they shall declare: "Our hands did not shed this blood, nor did our eyes see it done. [8]Accept this atonement for your people Israel, whom you have redeemed, O LORD, and do not hold your people guilty of the blood of an innocent man." And the bloodshed will be atoned for.[q] [9]So you will purge[r] from yourselves the guilt of shedding innocent blood, since you have done what is right in the eyes of the LORD.

Marrying a Captive Woman

[10]When you go to war against your enemies and the LORD your God delivers them into your hands[s] and you take captives,[t] [11]if you notice among the captives a beautiful[u] woman and are attracted to her,[v] you may take her as your wife. [12]Bring her into your home and have her shave her head,[w] trim her nails [13]and put aside the clothes she was wearing when captured. After she has lived in your house and mourned her father and mother for a full month,[x] then you may go to her and be her husband and she shall be your wife. [14]If you are not

pleased with her, let her go wherever she wishes. You must not sell her or treat her as a slave, since you have dishonored her.[y]

The Right of the Firstborn

[15]If a man has two wives,[z] and he loves one but not the other, and both bear him sons but the firstborn is the son of the wife he does not love,[a] [16]when he wills his property to his sons, he must not give the rights of the firstborn to the son of the wife he loves in preference to his actual firstborn, the son of the wife he does not love.[b] [17]He must acknowledge the son of his unloved wife as the firstborn by giving him a double[c] share of all he has. That son is the first sign of his father's strength.[d] The right of the firstborn belongs to him.[e]

A Rebellious Son

[18]If a man has a stubborn and rebellious[f] son[g] who does not obey his father and mother[h] and will not listen to them when they discipline him, [19]his father and mother shall take hold of him and bring him to the elders at the gate of his town. [20]They shall say to the elders, "This son of ours is stubborn and rebellious. He will not obey us. He is a profligate and a drunkard." [21]Then all the men of his town shall stone him to death.[i] You must purge the evil[j] from among you. All Israel will hear of it and be afraid.[k]

Various Laws

[22]If a man guilty of a capital offense[l] is put to death and his body is hung on a tree, [23]you must not leave his body on the tree overnight.[m] Be sure to bury[n] him that same day, because anyone who is hung on a tree is under God's curse.[o] You must not desecrate[p] the land the LORD your God is giving you as an inheritance.

22 If you see your brother's ox or sheep straying, do not ignore it but be sure to take it back to him.[q] [2]If the brother does not live near you or if you do not know who he is, take it home with you and keep it until he comes looking for it. Then give it back to him. [3]Do the same if you find your brother's donkey or his cloak or anything he loses. Do not ignore it.

---

[b] 19 Or *down to use in the siege, for the fruit trees are for the benefit of man.*

⁴If you see your brother's donkey or his ox fallen on the road, do not ignore it. Help him get it to its feet.

⁵A woman must not wear men's clothing, nor a man wear women's clothing, for the LORD your God detests anyone who does this.

⁶If you come across a bird's nest beside the road, either in a tree or on the ground, and the mother is sitting on the young or on the eggs, do not take the mother with the young. ⁷You may take the young, but be sure to let the mother go, so that it may go well with you and you may have a long life.

⁸When you build a new house, make a parapet around your roof so that you may not bring the guilt of bloodshed on your house if someone falls from the roof.

⁹Do not plant two kinds of seed in your vineyard; if you do, not only the crops you plant but also the fruit of the vineyard will be defiled.

¹⁰Do not plow with an ox and a donkey yoked together.

¹¹Do not wear clothes of wool and linen woven together.

¹²Make tassels on the four corners of the cloak you wear.

Marriage Violations

¹³If a man takes a wife and, after lying with her, dislikes her ¹⁴and slanders her and gives her a bad name, saying, "I married this woman, but when I approached her, I did not find proof of her virginity," ¹⁵then the girl's father and mother shall bring proof that she was a virgin to the town elders at the gate. ¹⁶The girl's father will say to the elders, "I gave my daughter in marriage to this man, but he dislikes her. ¹⁷Now he has slandered her and said, 'I did not find your daughter to be a virgin.' But here is the proof of my daughter's virginity." Then her parents shall display the cloth before the elders of the town, ¹⁸and the elders shall take the man and punish him. ¹⁹They shall fine him a hundred shekels of silver and give them to the girl's father, because this man has given an Israelite virgin a bad name. She shall continue to be his wife; he must not divorce her as long as he lives.

²⁰If, however, the charge is true and no proof of the girl's virginity can be found, ²¹she shall be brought to the door of her father's house and there the men of her town shall stone her to death. She has done a disgraceful thing in Israel by being promiscuous while still in her father's house. You must purge the evil from among you.

²²If a man is found sleeping with another man's wife, both the man who slept with her and the woman must die. You must purge the evil from Israel.

²³If a man happens to meet in a town a virgin pledged to be married and he sleeps with her, ²⁴you shall take both of them to the gate of that town and stone them to death—the girl because she was in a town and did not scream for help, and the man because he violated another man's wife. You must purge the evil from among you.

²⁵But if out in the country a man happens to meet a girl pledged to be married and rapes her, only the man who has done this shall die. ²⁶Do nothing to the girl; she has committed no sin deserving death. This case is like that of someone who attacks and murders his neighbor, ²⁷for the man found the girl out in the country, and though the betrothed girl screamed, there was no one to rescue her.

²⁸If a man happens to meet a virgin who is not pledged to be married and rapes her and they are discovered, ²⁹he shall pay the girl's father fifty shekels of silver. He must marry the girl, for he has violated her. He can never divorce her as long as he lives.

³⁰A man is not to marry his father's wife; he must not dishonor his father's bed.

Exclusion From the Assembly

23 No one who has been emasculated by crushing or cutting may enter the assembly of the LORD.

²No one born of a forbidden marriage nor any of his descendants may enter the assembly of the LORD, even down to the tenth generation.

³No Ammonite or Moabite or any of his descendants may enter the assembly of the LORD, even down to the tenth generation. ⁴For they did not come to meet you with bread and water on your way

---

c 9 Or be forfeited to the sanctuary d 19 That is, about 2 1/2 pounds (about 1 kilogram) e 29 That is, about 1 1/4 pounds (about 0.6 kilogram) f 2 Or one of illegitimate birth

when you came out of Egypt, and they hired Balaamq son of Beor from Pethor in Aram Naharaimᵍʳ to pronounce a curse on you.ˢ ⁵However, the LORD your God would not listen to Balaam but turned the curseᵗ into a blessing for you, because the LORD your God lovesᵘ you. ⁶Do not seek a treatyᵛ of friendship with them as long as you live.ʷ

⁷Do not abhor an Edomite,ˣ for he is your brother.ʸ Do not abhor an Egyptian, because you lived as an alien in his country.ᶻ ⁸The third generation of children born to them may enter the assembly of the LORD.

Uncleanness in the Camp

⁹When you are encamped against your enemies, keep away from everything impure.ᵃ ¹⁰If one of your men is unclean because of a nocturnal emission, he is to go outside the camp and stay there.ᵇ ¹¹But as evening approaches he is to wash himself, and at sunsetᶜ he may return to the camp.ᵈ

¹²Designate a place outside the camp where you can go to relieve yourself. ¹³As part of your equipment have something to dig with, and when you relieve yourself, dig a hole and cover up your excrement. ¹⁴For the LORD your God movesᵉ about in your camp to protect you and to deliver your enemies to you. Your camp must be holy,ᶠ so that he will not see among you anything indecent and turn away from you.

Miscellaneous Laws

¹⁵If a slave has taken refugeᵍ with you, do not hand him over to his master.ʰ ¹⁶Let him live among you wherever he likes and in whatever town he chooses. Do not oppressⁱ him.

¹⁷No Israelite manʲ or woman is to become a shrine prostitute.ᵏ ¹⁸You must not bring the earnings of a female prostitute or of a male prostituteʰ into the house of the LORD your God to pay any vow, because the LORD your God detests them both.ˡ

¹⁹Do not charge your brother interest, whether on money or food or anything else that may earn interest.ᵐ ²⁰You may charge a foreignerⁿ interest, but not a brother Israelite, so that the LORD your God may blessᵒ you in everything you put your hand to in the land you are entering to possess.

²¹If you make a vow to the LORD your God, do not be slow to pay it,ᵖ for the LORD your God will certainly demand it of you and you will be guilty of sin.ᑫ ²²But if you refrain from making a vow, you will not be guilty.ʳ ²³Whatever your lips utter you must be sure to do, because you made your vow freely to the LORD your God with your own mouth.

²⁴If you enter your neighbor's vineyard, you may eat all the grapes you want, but do not put any in your basket. ²⁵If you enter your neighbor's grainfield, you may pick kernels with your hands, but you must not put a sickle to his standing grain.ˢ

24

If a man marries a woman who becomes displeasing to himᵗ because he finds something indecent about her, and he writes her a certificate of divorce,ᵘ gives it to her and sends her from his house, ²and if after she leaves his house she becomes the wife of another man, ³and her second husband dislikes her and writes her a certificate of divorce, gives it to her and sends her from his house, or if he dies, ⁴then her first husband, who divorced her, is not allowed to marry her again after she has been defiled. That would be detestable in the eyes of the LORD. Do not bring sin upon the land the LORDᵛ your God is giving you as an inheritance.

⁵If a man has recently married, he must not be sent to war or have any other duty laid on him. For one year he is to be free to stay at home and bring happiness to the wife he has married.ʷ

⁶Do not take a pair of millstones—not even the upper one—as security for a debt, because that would be taking a man's livelihood as security.ˣ

⁷If a man is caught kidnapping one of his brother Israelites and treats him as a slave or sells him, the kidnapper must die.ʸ You must purge the evil from among you.ᶻ

⁸In cases of leprousⁱ diseases be very careful to do exactly as the priests, who are Levites,ᵃ instruct you. You must follow carefully what I have commanded them.ᵇ ⁹Remember what the LORD your

---

ᵍ 4 That is, Northwest Mesopotamia ʰ 18 Hebrew *of a dog*
ⁱ 8 The Hebrew word was used for various diseases affecting the skin—not necessarily leprosy.

God did to Miriam along the way after you came out of Egypt.

¹⁰When you make a loan of any kind to your neighbor, do not go into his house to get what he is offering as a pledge. ¹¹Stay outside and let the man to whom you are making the loan bring the pledge out to you. ¹²If the man is poor, do not go to sleep with his pledge in your possession. ¹³Return his cloak to him by sunset so that he may sleep in it. Then he will thank you, and it will be regarded as a righteous act in the sight of the LORD your God.

¹⁴Do not take advantage of a hired man who is poor and needy, whether he is a brother Israelite or an alien living in one of your towns. ¹⁵Pay him his wages each day before sunset, because he is poor and is counting on it. Otherwise he may cry to the LORD against you, and you will be guilty of sin.

¹⁶Fathers shall not be put to death for their children, nor children put to death for their fathers; each is to die for his own sin.

¹⁷Do not deprive the alien or the fatherless of justice, or take the cloak of the widow as a pledge. ¹⁸Remember that you were slaves in Egypt and the LORD your God redeemed you from there. That is why I command you to do this.

¹⁹When you are harvesting in your field and you overlook a sheaf, do not go back to get it. Leave it for the alien, the fatherless and the widow, so that the LORD your God may bless you in all the work of your hands. ²⁰When you beat the olives from your trees, do not go over the branches a second time. Leave what remains for the alien, the fatherless and the widow. ²¹When you harvest the grapes in your vineyard, do not go over the vines again. Leave what remains for the alien, the fatherless and the widow. ²²Remember that you were slaves in Egypt. That is why I command you to do this.

25

When men have a dispute, they are to take it to court and the judges will decide the case, acquitting the innocent and condemning the guilty. ²If the guilty man deserves to be beaten, the judge shall make him lie down and have him flogged in his presence with the number of lashes his crime deserves, ³but he must not give him more than forty lashes. If he is flogged more than that, your brother will be degraded in your eyes.

⁴Do not muzzle an ox while it is treading out the grain.

⁵If brothers are living together and one of them dies without a son, his widow must not marry outside the family. Her husband's brother shall take her and marry her and fulfill the duty of a brother-in-law to her. ⁶The first son she bears shall carry on the name of the dead brother so that his name will not be blotted out from Israel.

⁷However, if a man does not want to marry his brother's wife, she shall go to the elders at the town gate and say, "My husband's brother refuses to carry on his brother's name in Israel. He will not fulfill the duty of a brother-in-law to me." ⁸Then the elders of his town shall summon him and talk to him. If he persists in saying, "I do not want to marry her," ⁹his brother's widow shall go up to him in the presence of the elders, take off one of his sandals, spit in his face and say, "This is what is done to the man who will not build up his brother's family line." ¹⁰That man's line shall be known in Israel as The Family of the Unsandaled.

¹¹If two men are fighting and the wife of one of them comes to rescue her husband from his assailant, and she reaches out and seizes him by his private parts, ¹²you shall cut off her hand. Show her no pity.

¹³Do not have two differing weights in your bag—one heavy, one light. ¹⁴Do not have two differing measures in your house—one large, one small. ¹⁵You must have accurate and honest weights and measures, so that you may live long in the land the LORD your God is giving you. ¹⁶For the LORD your God detests anyone who does these things, anyone who deals dishonestly.

¹⁷Remember what the Amalekites did to you along the way when you came out of Egypt. ¹⁸When you were weary and worn out, they met you on your journey and cut off all who were lagging behind; they had no fear of God. ¹⁹When the LORD your God gives you rest from all the enemies around you in the land he is

Firstfruits and Tithes

26 When you have entered the land the LORD your God is giving you as an inheritance and have taken possession of it and settled in it, ²take some of the firstfruits of all that you produce from the soil of the land the LORD your God is giving you and put them in a basket. Then go to the place the LORD your God will choose as a dwelling for his Name ³and say to the priest in office at the time, "I declare today to the LORD your God that I have come to the land the LORD swore to our forefathers to give us." ⁴The priest shall take the basket from your hands and set it down in front of the altar of the LORD your God. ⁵Then you shall declare before the LORD your God: "My father was a wandering Aramean, and he went down into Egypt with a few people and lived there and became a great nation, powerful and numerous. ⁶But the Egyptians mistreated us and made us suffer, putting us to hard labor. ⁷Then we cried out to the LORD, the God of our fathers, and the LORD heard our voice and saw our misery, toil and oppression. ⁸So the LORD brought us out of Egypt with a mighty hand and an outstretched arm, with great terror and with miraculous signs and wonders. ⁹He brought us to this place and gave us this land, a land flowing with milk and honey; ¹⁰and now I bring the firstfruits of the soil that you, O LORD, have given me." Place the basket before the LORD your God and bow down before him. ¹¹And you and the Levites and the aliens among you shall rejoice in all the good things the LORD your God has given to you and your household.

¹²When you have finished setting aside a tenth of all your produce in the third year, the year of the tithe, you shall give it to the Levite, the alien, the fatherless and the widow, so that they may eat in your towns and be satisfied. ¹³Then say to the LORD your God: "I have removed from my house the sacred portion and have given it to the Levite, the alien, the fatherless and the widow, according to all you commanded. I have not turned aside from your commands nor have I forgotten any of them. ¹⁴I have not eaten any of the sacred portion while I was in mourning, nor have I removed any of it while I was unclean, nor have I offered any of it to the dead. I have obeyed the LORD my God; I have done everything you commanded me. ¹⁵Look down from heaven, your holy dwelling place, and bless your people Israel and the land you have given us as you promised on oath to our forefathers, a land flowing with milk and honey."

Follow the LORD's Commands

¹⁶The LORD your God commands you this day to follow these decrees and laws; carefully observe them with all your heart and with all your soul. ¹⁷You have declared this day that the LORD is your God and that you will walk in his ways, that you will keep his decrees, commands and laws, and that you will obey him. ¹⁸And the LORD has declared this day that you are his people, his treasured possession as he promised, and that you are to keep all his commands. ¹⁹He has declared that he will set you in praise, fame and honor high above all the nations he has made and that you will be a people holy to the LORD your God, as he promised.

The Altar on Mount Ebal

27 Moses and the elders of Israel commanded the people: "Keep all these commands that I give you today. ²When you have crossed the Jordan into the land the LORD your God is giving you, set up some large stones and coat them with plaster. ³Write on them all the words of this law when you have crossed over to enter the land the LORD your God is giving you, a land flowing with milk and honey, just as the LORD, the God of your fathers, promised you.

⁴And when you have crossed the Jordan, set up these stones on Mount Ebal,ᵉ as I command you today, and coat them with plaster. ⁵Build there an altarᶠ to the LORD your God, an altar of stones. Do not use any iron toolᵍ upon them. ⁶Build the altar of the LORD your God with fieldstones and offer burnt offerings on it to the LORD your God. ⁷Sacrifice fellowship offerings/ʰ there, eating them and rejoicingⁱ in the presence of the LORD your God.ʲ ⁸And you shall write very clearly all the words of this law on these stonesᵏ you have set up."¹

Curses From Mount Ebal

⁹Then Moses and the priests, who are Levites,ᵐ said to all Israel, "Be silent, O Israel, and listen! You have now become the people of the LORD your God.ⁿ ¹⁰Obey the LORD your God and follow his commands and decrees that I give you today."

¹¹On the same day Moses commanded the people:

¹²When you have crossed the Jordan, these tribes shall stand on Mount Gerizimᵒ to bless the people: Simeon, Levi, Judah, Issachar,ᵖ Joseph and Benjamin.ᵠ ¹³And these tribes shall stand on Mount Ebalʳ to pronounce curses: Reuben, Gad, Asher, Zebulun, Dan and Naphtali.

¹⁴The Levites shall recite to all the people of Israel in a loud voice:

¹⁵"Cursed is the man who carves an image or casts an idolˢ—a thing detestableᵗ to the LORD, and the work of the craftsman's hands—and sets it up in secret."

Then all the people shall say, "Amen!"ᵘ

¹⁶"Cursed is the man who dishonors his father or his mother."ᵛ

Then all the people shall say, "Amen!"

¹⁷"Cursed is the man who moves his neighbor's boundary stone."ʷ

Then all the people shall say, "Amen!"

¹⁸"Cursed is the man who leads the blind astray on the road."ˣ

Then all the people shall say, "Amen!"

¹⁹"Cursed is the man who withholds justice from the alien,ʸ the fatherless or the widow."ᶻ

Then all the people shall say, "Amen!"

²⁰"Cursed is the man who sleeps with his father's wife, for he dishonors his father's bed."ᵃ

Then all the people shall say, "Amen!"

²¹"Cursed is the man who has sexual relations with any animal."ᵇ

Then all the people shall say, "Amen!"

²²"Cursed is the man who sleeps with his sister, the daughter of his father or the daughter of his mother."ᶜ

Then all the people shall say, "Amen!"

²³"Cursed is the man who sleeps with his mother-in-law."ᵈ

Then all the people shall say, "Amen!"

²⁴"Cursed is the man who killsᵉ his neighbor secretly."ᶠ

Then all the people shall say, "Amen!"

²⁵"Cursed is the man who accepts a bribe to kill an innocent person."ᵍ

Then all the people shall say, "Amen!"

²⁶"Cursed is the man who does

j 7 Traditionally peace offerings

27:4–10 Moses commanded Israel to gather stones, coat them with plaster, inscribe them with the words of the law and build them into a holy altar on the top of Mt. Ebal in the promised land. In this way the words written on them would stand out clearly, and the people would be reminded of their covenant relationship to obey God's laws and statutes every time they offered a sacrifice.

27:12–14 This curious passage recorded Moses' command to the tribes of Israel to separate into two groups after crossing into the promised land. Some of the tribes were to assemble on Mt. Gerizim and shout out the blessings of the law upon the people. The remaining tribes were to assemble on Mt. Ebal to shout out the curses of the law. Following this, the Levites would loudly shout a series of curses upon those who would violate God's laws. Chapters 28 and 29 contain these blessings and curses and form the basis for the Palestinian covenant established in 30:1–9.

not uphold the words of this law by carrying them out."ʰ

Then all the people shall say, "Amen!"ⁱ

Blessings for Obedience

28 If you fully obey the LORD your God and carefully followʲ all his commandsᵏ I give you today, the LORD your God will set you high above all the nations on earth.ˡ ²All these blessings will come upon youᵐ and accompany you if you obey the LORD your God:

³You will be blessedⁿ in the city and blessed in the country.ᵒ

⁴The fruit of your womb will be blessed, and the crops of your land and the young of your livestock— the calves of your herds and the lambs of your flocks.ᵖ

⁵Your basket and your kneading trough will be blessed.

⁶You will be blessed when you come in and blessed when you go out.ᵍ

⁷The LORD will grant that the enemiesʳ who rise up against you will be defeated before you. They will come at you from one direction but flee from you in seven.ˢ

⁸The LORD will send a blessing on your barns and on everything you put your hand to. The LORD your God will blessᵗ you in the land he is giving you.

⁹The LORD will establish you as his holy people,ᵘ as he promised you on oath, if you keep the commandsᵛ of the LORD your God and walk in his ways. ¹⁰Then all the peoples on earth will see that you are called by the nameʷ of the LORD, and they will fear you. ¹¹The LORD will grant you abundant prosperity—in the fruit of your womb, the young of your livestockˣ and the crops of your ground—in the land he swore to your forefathers to give you.ʸ

¹²The LORD will open the heavens, the storehouseᶻ of his bounty,ᵃ to send rainᵇ on your land in season and to blessᶜ all the work of your hands. You will lend to many nations but will borrow from none.ᵈ ¹³The LORD will make you the head, not the tail. If you pay attention to the commands of the LORD your God that I give you this day and carefully followᵉ them, you will always be at the top, never at the bottom.ᶠ ¹⁴Do not turn aside from any of the commands I give you today, to the right or to the left,ᵍ following other gods and serving them.

Curses for Disobedience

¹⁵However, if you do not obeyʰ the LORD your God and do not carefully follow all his commands and decrees I am giving you today,ⁱ all these curses will come upon you and overtake you:ʲ

¹⁶You will be cursed in the city and cursed in the country.ᵏ

¹⁷Your basket and your kneading trough will be cursed.ˡ

¹⁸The fruit of your womb will be cursed, and the crops of your land, and the calves of your herds and lambs of your flocks.ᵐ

¹⁹You will be cursed when you come in and cursed when you go out.ⁿ

²⁰The LORD will send on you curses,ᵒ confusion and rebukeᵖ in everything you put your hand to, until you are destroyed and come to sudden ruinᵍ because of the evilʳ you have done in forsaking him.ᵏ ²¹The LORD will plague you with diseases until he has destroyed you from the land you are entering to possess.ˢ ²²The LORD will strike you with wasting disease,ᵗ with fever and inflammation, with scorching heat and drought,ᵘ with blightᵛ and mildew, which will plagueʷ you until you perish.ˣ ²³The sky over your head will be bronze, the ground beneath you

---

28:23–25 Moses warned that a severe drought would turn the fertile land to dust if the Israelites broke their covenant with God. Furthermore, if the Israelites broke their covenant, their supernatural

iron.ʸ ²⁴The LORD will turn the rain² of your country into dust and powder; it will come down from the skies until you are destroyed.

²⁵The LORD will cause you to be defeated ᵃ before your enemies. You will come at them from one direction but flee from them in seven,ᵇ and you will become a thing of horrorᶜ to all the kingdoms on earth.ᵈ ²⁶Your carcasses will be food for all the birds of the airᵉ and the beasts of the earth, and there will be no one to frighten them away.ᶠ ²⁷The LORD will afflict you with the boils of Egyptᵍ and with tumors, festering sores and the itch, from which you cannot be cured. ²⁸The LORD will afflict you with madness, blindness and confusion of mind. ²⁹At midday you will gropeʰ about like a blind man in the dark. You will be unsuccessful in everything you do; day after day you will be oppressed and robbed, with no one to rescueⁱ you.

³⁰You will be pledged to be married to a woman, but another will take her and ravish her.ʲ You will build a house, but you will not live in it.ᵏ You will plant a vineyard, but you will not even begin to enjoy its fruit.ˡ ³¹Your ox will be slaughtered before your eyes, but you will eat none of it. Your donkey will be forcibly taken from you and will not be returned. Your sheep will be given to your enemies, and no one will rescue them. ³²Your sons and daughters will be given to another nation,ᵐ and you will wear out your eyes watching for them day after day, powerless to lift a hand. ³³A people that you do not know will eat what your land and labor produce, and you will have nothing but cruel oppressionⁿ all your days.ᵒ ³⁴The sights you see will drive you mad.ᵖ ³⁵The LORD will afflict your knees and legs with painful boilsᑫ that cannot be cured, spreading from the soles of your feet to the top of your head.ʳ

³⁶The LORD will drive you and the kingˢ you set over you to a nation unknown to you or your fathers.ᵗ There you will worship other gods, gods of wood and stone.ᵘ ³⁷You will become a thing of horrorᵛ and an object of scornʷ and ridiculeˣ to all the nations where the LORD will drive you.ʸ

³⁸You will sow much seed in the field but you will harvest little,ᶻ because locustsᵃ will devourᵇ it. ³⁹You will plant vineyards and cultivate them but you will not drink the wineᶜ or gather the grapes, because worms will eatᵈ them.ᵉ ⁴⁰You will have olive trees throughout your country but you will not use the oil, because the olives will drop off.ᶠ ⁴¹You will have sons and daughters but you will not keep them, because they will go into captivity.ᵍ ⁴²Swarms of locustsʰ will take over all your trees and the crops of your land.

⁴³The alien who lives among you will rise above you higher and higher, but you will sink lower and lower.ⁱ ⁴⁴He will lend to you, but you will not lend to him.ʲ He will be the head, but you will be the tail.ᵏ

⁴⁵All these curses will come upon you. They will pursue you and overtake youˡ until you are destroyed,ᵐ because you did not obey the LORD your God and observe the commands and decrees he gave you. ⁴⁶They will be a sign and a wonder to you and your descendants forever.ⁿ ⁴⁷Because you did not serveᵒ the LORD your God joyfully and gladlyᵖ in the time of prosperity,

---

28:23 ʸ S Lev 26:19
28:24 ᶻ Lev 26:19; Dt 11:17; 1Ki 8:35; 17:1; Isa 5:6; Jer 14:1; Hag 1:10
28:25 ᵃ 1Sa 4:10; Ps 78:62
ᵇ S Lev 26:17
ᶜ ver 37 ᵈ 2Ch 29:8; 30:7; Jer 15:4; 24:9; 26:6; 29:18; 44:12; Eze 23:46
28:26 ᵉ S Ge 40:19
ᶠ Ps 79:2; Isa 18:6; Jer 7:33; 12:9; 15:2; 16:4; 19:7; 34:20
28:27 ᵍ Dt 7:15
28:29 ʰ Ge 19:11; Ex 10:21; Job 5:14; 12:25; 24:13; 38:15; Isa 59:10
ⁱ Jdg 3:9; 2Ki 13:5;
28:30 ʲ Job 31:10
ᵏ Isa 65:22; Am 5:11 ˡ Jer 12:13
28:32 ᵐ ver 41
28:33 ⁿ Jer 6:6; 22:17 ᵒ Jer 5:15-17; Eze 25:4
28:34 ᵖ ver 67
28:35 ᑫ Dt 7:15; Rev 16:2 ʳ Job 2:7; 7:5; 13:28; 30:17, 30; Isa 1:6
28:36 ˢ 1Sa 12:25 ᵗ Dt 4:27; 2Ki 24:14; 25:7,11; 2Ch 33:11; 36:21; Ezr 5:12; Jer 15:14; 16:13; 27:20; 39:1-9; 52:28; La 1:3 ᵘ S Dt 4:28
28:37 ᵛ ver 25; ʷ Jer 42:18; Eze 5:15 ʷ Ps 22:7; 39:8; 44:13; 64:8; Jer 18:16; 48:27; Mic 6:16
ˣ 2Ch 7:20; Ezr 9:7; Jer 44:8 ʸ 1Ki 9:7; Ps 44:14; Jer 19:8; 24:9; 25:9,18; 29:18; La 2:15
28:38 ᶻ Lev 26:20; Ps 129:7; Isa 5:10; Jer 12:13; Hos 8:7; Mic 6:15; Hag 1:6, 9; 2:16 ᵃ S Ex 10:4
ᵇ S Ex 10:15
28:39 ᶜ Lev 10:9
ᵈ Joel 1:4; 2:25; Mal 3:11 ᵉ Isa 5:10; 17:10-11; Zep 1:13
28:40 ᶠ Jer 11:16; Mic 6:15
28:41 ᵍ ver 32 **28:42** ʰ ver 38; Jdg 6:5; 7:12; Jer 46:23 **28:43** ⁱ ver 13
28:44 ʲ ver 12 ᵏ S Dt 26:19 **28:45** ˡ S Ex 15:9 ᵐ ver 15; Dt 4:25-26
28:46 ⁿ S Nu 16:38; Ps 71:7; Isa 8:18; 20:3; Eze 3:15; Zec 3:8
28:47 ᵒ S Dt 10:12 ᵖ S Lev 23:40; Ne 9:35

D Dt 28:27 ◀▶ Dt 28:59–61
R Dt 28:33 ◀▶ Dt 28:45
R Dt 28:37 ◀▶ Dt 28:49

D Dt 28:21–22 ◀▶ Dt 28:35
H Dt 18:18–19 ◀▶ Dt 30:15
R Dt 28:23–25 ◀▶ Dt 28:37

---

victories would become ruinous defeats and lead to their exile from the promised land.

28:33 More than 700 years before its fulfillment Moses prophesied about Israel's future destruction at the hands of the Babylonians and warned that this nation would someday oppress, crush and devour everything in the land of Israel.

28:37 Moses prophesied that the Israelites reputation would suffer irreparable damage. The nation that had once been a terror and a power among its neighbors would one day become "a thing of horror and an object of scorn and ridicule to all the nations," thus proving the wisdom of Solomon's words that "sin is a disgrace to any people" (Pr 14:34).

28:45 Over the last twenty-six centuries these curses fell upon the Israelites exactly as Moses had warned because the people refused to hear and obey God's commandments.

⁴⁸therefore in hunger and thirst, in nakedness and dire poverty, you will serve the enemies the LORD sends against you. He will put an iron yoke on your neck until he has destroyed you.

⁴⁹The LORD will bring a nation against you from far away, from the ends of the earth, like an eagle swooping down, a nation whose language you will not understand, ⁵⁰a fierce-looking nation without respect for the old or pity for the young. ⁵¹They will devour the young of your livestock and the crops of your land until you are destroyed. They will leave you no grain, new wine or oil, nor any calves of your herds or lambs of your flocks until you are ruined. ⁵²They will lay siege to all the cities throughout your land until the high fortified walls in which you trust fall down. They will besiege all the cities throughout the land the LORD your God is giving you.

⁵³Because of the suffering that your enemy will inflict on you during the siege, you will eat the fruit of the womb, the flesh of the sons and daughters the LORD your God has given you. ⁵⁴Even the most gentle and sensitive man among you will have no compassion on his own brother or the wife he loves or his surviving children, ⁵⁵and he will not give to one of them any of the flesh of his children that he is eating. It will be all he has left because of the suffering your enemy will inflict on you during the siege of all your cities. ⁵⁶The most gentle and sensitive woman among you—so sensitive and gentle that she would not venture to touch the ground with the sole of her foot—will begrudge the husband she loves and her own son or daughter ⁵⁷the afterbirth from her womb and the children she bears. For she intends to eat them secretly during the siege and in the distress that your enemy will inflict on you in your cities.

⁵⁸If you do not carefully follow all the words of this law, which are written in this book, and do not revere this glorious and awesome name—the LORD your God— ⁵⁹the LORD will send fearful plagues on you and your descendants, harsh and prolonged disasters, and severe and lingering illnesses. ⁶⁰He will bring upon you all the diseases of Egypt that you dreaded, and they will cling to you. ⁶¹The LORD will also bring on you every kind of sickness and disaster not recorded in this Book of the Law, until you are destroyed. ⁶²You who were as numerous as the stars in the sky will be left but few in number, because you did not obey the LORD your God. ⁶³Just as it pleased the LORD to make you prosper and increase in number, so it will please him to ruin and destroy you. You will be uprooted from the land you are entering to possess.

⁶⁴Then the LORD will scatter you among all nations, from one end of the earth to the other. There you will worship other gods—gods of wood and stone, which neither you nor your fathers have known. ⁶⁵Among those nations you will find no repose, no resting place for the sole of your foot. There the LORD will give you an anxious mind, eyes weary with longing, and a despairing heart. ⁶⁶You will live in constant suspense, filled with dread both night and day, never sure of your life. ⁶⁷In the morning you will say, "If only it were evening!" and in the evening, "If only it were morning!"— because of the terror that will fill your hearts and the sights that your eyes will

R Dt 28:45 ◀▶ Dt 28:62–65
D Dt 28:35 ◀▶ Dt 29:22
R Dt 28:49 ◀▶ Dt 29:22–28

28:49 God prophesied that an enemy nation "from the ends of the earth" would conquer the Israelites. This enemy would speak a language that the people would not understand. This prophecy was fulfilled when Nebuchadnezzar of Babylon swiftly conquered Judah in 606 B.C.

28:62–65 Moses prophesied that God's judgment on Israel's sins would reduce the population of the Israelites until they were much fewer in number and dispersed throughout the world. Though God's promise to Abram included offspring as numerous as the stars (see Ge 15:5) the actual number of Jews has grown to only 18 million worldwide today. Yet after almost two thousand years of oppression Jews have begun to return to their homeland and fulfill the words of Ezekiel: "This is what the Sovereign LORD says: I will gather you from the nations and bring you back from the countries where you have been scattered, and I will give you back the land of Israel again" (Eze 11:17).

see. ⁶⁸The LORD will send you back in ships to Egypt on a journey I said you should never make again. There you will offer yourselves for sale to your enemies as male and female slaves, but no one will buy you.

Renewal of the Covenant

29 These are the terms of the covenant the LORD commanded Moses to make with the Israelites in Moab, in addition to the covenant he had made with them at Horeb.

²Moses summoned all the Israelites and said to them:

Your eyes have seen all that the LORD did in Egypt to Pharaoh, to all his officials and to all his land. ³With your own eyes you saw those great trials, those miraculous signs and great wonders. ⁴But to this day the LORD has not given you a mind that understands or eyes that see or ears that hear. ⁵During the forty years that I led you through the desert, your clothes did not wear out, nor did the sandals on your feet. ⁶You ate no bread and drank no wine or other fermented drink. I did this so that you might know that I am the LORD your God.

⁷When you reached this place, Sihon king of Heshbon and Og king of Bashan came out to fight against us, but we defeated them. ⁸We took their land and gave it as an inheritance to the Reubenites, the Gadites and the half-tribe of Manasseh.

⁹Carefully follow the terms of this covenant, so that you may prosper in everything you do. ¹⁰All of you are standing today in the presence of the LORD your God—your leaders and chief men, your elders and officials, and all the other men of Israel, ¹¹together with your children and your wives, and the aliens living in your camps who chop your wood and carry your water. ¹²You are standing here in order to enter into a covenant with the LORD your God, a covenant the LORD is making with you this day and sealing with an oath, ¹³to confirm you this day as his people, that he may be your God as he promised you and as he swore to your fathers, Abraham, Isaac and Jacob. ¹⁴I am making this covenant, with its oath, not only with you ¹⁵who are standing here with us today in the presence of the LORD our God but also with those who are not here today.

¹⁶You yourselves know how we lived in Egypt and how we passed through the countries on the way here. ¹⁷You saw among them their detestable images and idols of wood and stone, of silver and gold. ¹⁸Make sure there is no man or woman, clan or tribe among you today whose heart turns away from the LORD our God to go and worship the gods of those nations; make sure there is no root among you that produces such bitter poison.

¹⁹When such a person hears the words of this oath, he invokes a blessing on himself and therefore thinks, "I will be safe, even though I persist in going my own way." This will bring disaster on the watered land as well as the dry. ²⁰The LORD will never be willing to forgive him; his wrath and zeal will burn against that man. All the curses written in this book will fall upon him, and the LORD will blot out his name from under heaven. ²¹The LORD will single him out from all the tribes of Israel for disaster, according to all the curses of the covenant written in this Book of the Law.

²²Your children who follow you in later generations and foreigners who come from distant lands will see the calamities that have fallen on the land and the diseases with which the LORD has afflicted

C Dt 9:13 ◀▶ Dt 32:5
N Dt 18:18–19 ◀▶ Dt 30:15
S Dt 28:15 ◀▶ Dt 30:6
R Dt 28:62–65 ◀▶ Dt 30:1
D Dt 28:59–61 ◀▶ Jos 22:17

C Dt 10:18 ◀▶ Dt 33:25
L Dt 4:7 ◀▶ Dt 31:6

¹ 19 Or way, in order to add drunkenness to thirst."

29:22–28 This passage reveals that because of God's judgments, pagan nations would know that Israel had broken their covenant with him. Moses warned the Israelites that the desolation of the promised land would astonish all those who traveled through its ruins. Recent archeological discoveries have yielded proof that the land of Israel was once a fertile land that could have easily supported a flourishing population. Israel's sin brought judgment on the people and on the land too.

it. ᵏ ²³The whole land will be a burning waste¹ of salt ᵐ and sulfur—nothing planted, nothing sprouting, no vegetation growing on it. It will be like the destruction of Sodom and Gomorrah,ⁿ Admah and Zeboiim, which the LORD overthrew in fierce anger.ᵒ ²⁴All the nations will ask: "Why has the LORD done this to this land?ᵖ Why this fierce, burning anger?"

²⁵And the answer will be: "It is because this people abandoned the covenant of the LORD, the God of their fathers, the covenant he made with them when he brought them out of Egypt.ᵠ ²⁶They went off and worshiped other gods and bowed down to them, gods they did not know, gods he had not given them. ²⁷Therefore the LORD's anger burned against this land, so that he brought on it all the curses written in this book.ʳ ²⁸In furious anger and in great wrath ˢ the LORD uprooted ᵗ them from their land and thrust them into another land, as it is now."

²⁹The secret things belong to the LORD our God,ᵘ but the things revealed belong to us and to our children forever, that we may follow all the words of this law.ᵛ

Prosperity After Turning to the LORD

30 When all these blessings and curses ʷ I have set before you come upon you and you take them to heart wherever the LORD your God disperses you among the nations,ˣ ²and when you and your children return ʸ to the LORD your God and obey him with all your heart ᶻ and with all your soul according to everything I command you today, ³then the LORD your God will restore your fortunes ᵐᵃ and have compassion ᵇ on you and gather ᶜ you again from all the nations where he scattered ᵈ you.ᵉ ⁴Even if you have been banished to the most distant land under the heavens,ᶠ from there the LORD your God will gather ᵍ you and bring you back.ʰ ⁵He will bring ⁱ you to the land that belonged to your fathers, and you will take possession of it. He will make

I Dt 28:1–3 ◄► Dt 32:36
R Dt 29:22–28 ◄► Dt 31:17–18
R Dt 4:29–30 ◄► Dt 30:8

m 3 Or will bring you back from captivity

29:29 The "secret things" in this verse probably refer to Israel's unknown future. Only God knows these secret things. Yet God had revealed some of these secret things through his law, and the Israelites could determine the secret things of their future by their obedience or disobedience to God's revealed law (see Pr 3:32; Am 3:7).

30:1–20 *Palestinian Covenant.* This restatement of the Abrahamic covenant provides clear answers to Israel's' connection to the promised land. Though Israel had failed to keep their covenant with God, his promise still stood—the land was theirs. The Palestinian covenant contained seven elements:

1. Israel would be taken out of the land because of her disobedience to God's laws (30:1–3; see also 28:63–68; 29:22–28).
2. Israel will repent (30:2; see also 28:63–68).
3. Christ the Messiah will gather the exiles and bring them back to the land (30:3–6; Isa 11:11–12; Jer 23:3–8; Eze 37:21–25; Am 9:14).
4. The land will be restored to the Israelites (30:5). Thus far in history Israel has failed to possess the total area of land promised under God's unconditional covenant to Abram (Ge 12:2; 15:18).
5. Israel will be converted as a nation (30:6; see also Dt 28:9; Ro 11:26–27).
6. Those who oppressed Israel will be judged (30:7; Isa 14:1–2; Joel 3:1–8; Mt 25:31–46).
7. Israel will experience future prosperity (30:9; Am 9:11–15).

Other Biblical authors refer to these elements of the Palestinian covenant. Ezekiel uses it as the framework for his prophecy (see Eze 16:1–7, 35–52), Hosea alludes to the national repentance and conversion which is necessary for its fulfillment (see Hos 2:14–23) and Paul speaks about the salvation of Israel (see Ro 11:26–27). Since all of the elements of this covenant have not been fulfilled, the Palestinian covenant will play a major role in modern history until Christ's second coming.

NOTE: The seven additional covenants include the Edenic (Ge 2:15–17), Adamic (Ge 3:15–19), Noahic (Ge 9:8ff), Abrahamic (Ge 15:4ff; 17:1–22), Mosaic (Ex 19:5), Davidic (2Sa 7:16) and New (Heb 8:8–12). See the article on p. 8.

30:5–10 After many prophecies about the judgments on Israel's disobedience, God promised that he would bring the exiles back "to the land that belonged to your fathers" (30:5) if they repented of their sins and followed his commandments. This prophecy was initially fulfilled during the time of Nehemiah as a remnant returned from exile in Babylon. This century has also seen partial fulfillment of this prophecy as those Jews who have been scattered since NT times have begun to return to their homeland. The final fulfillment of this prophecy will not

you more prosperous and numerous[j] than your fathers. [6]The LORD your God will circumcise your hearts and the hearts of your descendants,[k] so that you may love[l] him with all your heart and with all your soul, and live. [7]The LORD your God will put all these curses[m] on your enemies who hate and persecute you.[n] [8]You will again obey the LORD and follow all his commands I am giving you today. [9]Then the LORD your God will make you most prosperous in all the work of your hands and in the fruit of your womb, the young of your livestock and the crops of your land.[o] The LORD will again delight[p] in you and make you prosperous, just as he delighted in your fathers, [10]if you obey the LORD your God and keep his commands and decrees that are written in this Book of the Law[q] and turn to the LORD your God with all your heart and with all your soul.[r]

The Offer of Life or Death

[11]Now what I am commanding you today is not too difficult for you or beyond your reach.[s] [12]It is not up in heaven, so that you have to ask, "Who will ascend into heaven[t] to get it and proclaim it to us so we may obey it?"[u] [13]Nor is it beyond the sea,[v] so that you have to ask, "Who will cross the sea to get it and proclaim it to us so we may obey it?"[w] [14]No, the word is very near you; it is in your mouth and in your heart so you may obey it.[x]

[15]See, I set before you today life[y] and prosperity,[z] death[a] and destruction.[b] [16]For I command you today to love[c] the LORD your God, to walk in his ways, and to keep his commands, decrees and laws; then you will live[d] and increase, and the LORD your God will bless you in the land you are entering to possess.

[17]But if your heart turns away and you are not obedient, and if you are drawn away to bow down to other gods and worship them, [18]I declare to you this day that you will certainly be destroyed.[e] You will not live long in the land you are crossing the Jordan to enter and possess.

[19]This day I call heaven and earth as witnesses against you[f] that I have set before you life and death, blessings and curses.[g] Now choose life, so that you and your children may live [20]and that you may love[h] the LORD your God, listen to his voice, and hold fast to him. For the LORD is your life,[i] and he will give[j] you many years in the land[k] he swore to give to your fathers, Abraham, Isaac and Jacob.

Joshua to Succeed Moses

31 Then Moses went out and spoke these words to all Israel: [2]"I am now a hundred and twenty years old[l] and I am no longer able to lead you.[m] The LORD has said to me, 'You shall not cross the Jordan.'[n] [3]The LORD your God himself will cross[o] over ahead of you.[p] He will destroy these nations[q] before you, and you will take possession of their land. Joshua also will cross[r] over ahead of you, as the LORD said. [4]And the LORD will do to them what he did to Sihon and Og,[s] the kings of the Amorites, whom he destroyed along with their land. [5]The LORD will deliver[t] them to you, and you must do to them all that I have commanded you. [6]Be strong and courageous.[u] Do not be afraid or terrified[v] because of them, for the LORD your God goes with you;[w] he will never leave you[x] nor forsake[y] you."

[7]Then Moses summoned Joshua and said[z] to him in the presence of all Israel, "Be strong and courageous, for you must go with this people into the land that the LORD swore to their forefathers to give them,[a] and you must divide it among them as their inheritance. [8]The LORD himself goes before you and will be with you;[b] he will never leave you nor forsake

---

K Nu 23:19 ◀▶ Dt 30:20
S Dt 29:19–20 ◀▶ Jos 1:8
R Dt 30:2 ◀▶ Jos 7:19
U Dt 28:1–14 ◀▶ 1Sa 2:30
B Dt 28:11–12 ◀▶ Job 42:12
P Dt 28:11–12 ◀▶ 1Sa 2:7–8
L Dt 11:26–27 ◀▶ Dt 30:19
H Dt 28:29 ◀▶ Dt 32:22–23
N Dt 29:19–20 ◀▶ Dt 30:19

30:5 j S Dt 7:13
30:6 k S Dt 6:24; S 10:16 l Dt 6:5
30:7 m S Ge 12:3 n Dt 7:15
30:9 o Jer 1:10; 24:6; 31:28; 32:41; 42:10; 45:4 p S Dt 28:63
30:10 q S Dt 28:61 r S Dt 4:29
30:11 s Ps 19:8; Isa 45:19,23; 63:1
30:12 t Pr 30:4 u Ro 10:6*
30:13 v Job 28:14 w Ro 10:7*
30:14 x S Dt 6:6; Ro 10:8*
30:15 y Pr 10:16; 11:19; 12:28; Jer 21:8 z Dt 28:11; Job 36:11; Ps 25:13; 106:5; Pr 3:1-2 a S Ge 2:17 b S Dt 11:26
30:16 c Dt 6:5 d ver 19; Dt 4:1; 32:47; Ne 9:29
30:18 e S Dt 8:19
30:19 f Dt 4:26 g S Dt 11:26
30:20 h Dt 6:5 i Dt 4:1; S 8:3; 32:47; Ps 27:1; Pr 3:22; S Jn 5:26; Ac 17:28 j Ge 12:7 k Ps 37:3
31:2 l S Ex 7:7 m Nu 27:17; 1Ki 3:7 n S Dt 3:23, 26
31:3 o Nu 27:18 p Dt 9:3 q S Dt 7:1 r S Dt 3:28
31:4 s S Nu 21:33
31:5 t S Dt 2:33
31:6 u ver 7,23; Nu 1:6,9,18; 10:25; 1Ch 22:13; 28:20; 2Ch 32:7 v Jer 1:8, 17; Eze 2:6 w S Ge 28:15; S Dt 1:29; 20:4; S Mt 28:20 x Ps 56:9; 118:6 y S Dt 4:31; 1Sa 12:22; 1Ki 6:13; Ps 94:14; Isa 41:17; Heb 13:5*
31:7 z ver 23; Nu 27:23 a Jos 1:6
31:8 b S Ex 13:21

L Dt 30:11–15 ◀▶ 1Sa 12:20
N Dt 30:15 ◀▶ Dt 32:35
K Dt 30:6 ◀▶ Dt 32:39
L Dt 29:5 ◀▶ Dt 31:8
W Dt 20:8 ◀▶ Jos 1:6–7
L Dt 31:6 ◀▶ Dt 32:9–14

---

occur until the other elements of the Palestinian covenant are accomplished.

you. Do not be afraid; do not be discouraged."

The Reading of the Law

⁹So Moses wrote down this law and gave it to the priests, the sons of Levi, who carried the ark of the covenant of the LORD, and to all the elders of Israel. ¹⁰Then Moses commanded them: "At the end of every seven years, in the year for canceling debts, during the Feast of Tabernacles, ¹¹when all Israel comes to appear before the LORD your God at the place he will choose, you shall read this law before them in their hearing. ¹²Assemble the people—men, women and children, and the aliens living in your towns—so they can listen and learn to fear the LORD your God and follow carefully all the words of this law. ¹³Their children, who do not know this law, must hear it and learn to fear the LORD your God as long as you live in the land you are crossing the Jordan to possess."

Israel's Rebellion Predicted

¹⁴The LORD said to Moses, "Now the day of your death is near. Call Joshua and present yourselves at the Tent of Meeting, where I will commission him." So Moses and Joshua came and presented themselves at the Tent of Meeting.

¹⁵Then the LORD appeared at the Tent in a pillar of cloud, and the cloud stood over the entrance to the Tent. ¹⁶And the LORD said to Moses: "You are going to rest with your fathers, and these people will soon prostitute themselves to the foreign gods of the land they are entering. They will forsake me and break the covenant I made with them. ¹⁷On that day I will become angry with them and forsake them; I will hide my face from them, and they will be destroyed. Many disasters and difficulties will come upon them, and on that day they will ask, 'Have not these disasters come upon us because our God is not with us?' ¹⁸And I will certainly hide my face on that day because of all their wickedness in turning to other gods.

¹⁹"Now write down for yourselves this song and teach it to the Israelites and have them sing it, so that it may be a witness for me against them. ²⁰When I have brought them into the land flowing with milk and honey, the land I promised on oath to their forefathers, and when they eat their fill and thrive, they will turn to other gods and worship them, rejecting me and breaking my covenant. ²¹And when many disasters and difficulties come upon them, this song will testify against them, because it will not be forgotten by their descendants. I know what they are disposed to do, even before I bring them into the land I promised them on oath." ²²So Moses wrote down this song that day and taught it to the Israelites.

²³The LORD gave this command to Joshua son of Nun: "Be strong and courageous, for you will bring the Israelites into the land I promised them on oath, and I myself will be with you."

²⁴After Moses finished writing in a book the words of this law from beginning to end, ²⁵he gave this command to the Levites who carried the ark of the covenant of the LORD: ²⁶"Take this Book of the Law and place it beside the ark of the covenant of the LORD your God. There it will remain as a witness against you. ²⁷For I know how rebellious and stiff-necked you are. If you have been rebellious against the LORD while I am still alive and with you, how much more will you rebel after I die! ²⁸Assemble before me all the elders of your tribes and all your officials, so that I can speak these words in their hearing and call heaven and earth to testify against them. ²⁹For I know that after my death you are sure to become utterly corrupt and to turn from the way I have commanded you. In days to come, disaster will fall upon you be-

R Dt 30:1 ◄► Dt 31:29

R Dt 31:17–18 ◄► Dt 32:20

31:17–19 In ancient cultures, songs were used to teach and share information. To warn Israel away from the dangerous temptations to idolatry, God commanded Moses to teach the Israelites a song to remind them of their holy covenant, their history of deliverance from Egyptian slavery and their marvelous future when the Messiah returns.

31:29 Despite Moses' warnings, he knew that the Israelites would turn to idolatry after his death. Since he would no longer be able to direct their activities, his predictions were all the more grievous.

cause you will do evil in the sight of the LORD and provoke him to anger by what your hands have made."

The Song of Moses

³⁰And Moses recited the words of this song from beginning to end in the hearing of the whole assembly of Israel:

32 ¹Listen,ᵛ O heavens,ʷ and I will speak;
hear, O earth, the words of my mouth.ˣ
²Let my teaching fall like rainʸ
and my words descend like dew,ᶻᵃ
like showersᵇ on new grass,
like abundant rain on tender plants.
³I will proclaimᶜ the name of the LORD.ᵈ
Oh, praise the greatnessᵉ of our God!
⁴He is the Rock,ᶠ his works are perfect,ᵍ
and all his ways are just.
A faithful Godʰ who does no wrong, uprightⁱ and just is he.ʲ

⁵They have acted corruptly toward him;
to their shame they are no longer his children,
but a warped and crooked generation.ⁿᵏ
⁶Is this the way you repayˡ the LORD,
O foolishᵐ and unwise people?ⁿ
Is he not your Father,ᵒ your Creator,ᵒ
who made you and formed you?ᵖ
⁷Remember the days of old;ᵠ
consider the generations long past.ʳ
Ask your father and he will tell you,
your elders, and they will explain to you.ˢ
⁸When the Most Highᵗ gave the nations their inheritance,
when he divided all mankind,ᵘ
he set up boundariesᵛ for the peoples
according to the number of the sons of Israel.ᵖʷ
⁹For the LORD's portionˣ is his people,
Jacob his allotted inheritance.ʸ

C Dt 29:18-19 ◀ ▶ Dt 32:28-29
L Dt 31:8 ◀ ▶ Dt 33:12

32:1 ᵛPs 49:1; Mic 1:2 ʷJer 2:12 ˣS Dt 4:26
32:2 ʸ2Sa 23:4 ᶻPs 107:20; Isa 9:8; 55:11 ᵃMic 5:7 ᵇPs 65:10; 68:9; 72:6; 147:8
32:3 ᶜPs 118:17; 145:6 ᵈEx 33:19; 34:5-6 ᵉS Dt 3:24
32:4 ᶠS Ge 49:24 ᵍ2Sa 22:31; Ps 18:30; 19:7 ʰS Dt 4:35 ⁱPs 92:15 ʲS Ge 18:25
32:5 ᵏver 20; Mt 17:17; Lk 9:41; Ac 2:40
32:6 ˡPs 116:12 ᵐPs 94:8; Jer 5:21 ⁿver 28 ᵒS Ex 4:22; 2Sa 7:24 ᵖver 15
32:7 ᵠPs 44:1; 74:2; 77:5; Isa 51:9; 63:9 ʳDt 4:32; Job 8:8; 20:4; Ps 78:4; Isa 46:9 ˢS Ex 10:2; Job 15:18
32:8 ᵗPs 7:8 ᵘS Ge 11:8; Ac 8:1 ᵛPs 74:17 ʷNu 23:9; Dt 33:12,28; Jer 23:6
32:9 ˣPs 16:5; 73:26; 119:57; 142:5; Jer 10:16 ʸS Dt 9:29; S 1Sa 26:19
32:10 ᶻS Dt 1:19 ᵃDt 8:15; Job 12:24; Ps 107:40
32:11 ᵈS Ex 19:4 ᵉPs 17:8; 18:10-19; 61:4
32:12 ᶠPs 106:9; Isa 63:13; Jer 31:32 ᵍDt 4:35 ʰver 39; Jdg 2:12; Ps 18:31; 81:9; Isa 43:12; 45:5
32:13 ⁱDt 33:29; 2Sa 22:34; Ps 18:33; Isa 33:16; 58:14; Eze 36:2; Hab 3:19 ʲS Dt 8:8 ᵏDt 33:24; Job 29:6
32:14 ˡS Nu 21:33 ᵐPs 65:9; 81:16; 147:14 ⁿS Ge 49:11
32:15 ᵒDt 33:5, 26; Isa 44:2 ᵖDt 31:20; Jer 5:28 ᵠDt 31:16; Isa 1:4, 28; 58:2; 65:11; Jer 15:6; Eze 14:5 ʳS Ge 49:24

¹⁰In a desertᶻ land he found him,
in a barren and howling waste.ᵃ
He shieldedᵇ him and cared for him;
he guarded him as the apple of his eye,ᶜ
¹¹like an eagle that stirs up its nest
and hovers over its young,ᵈ
that spreads its wings to catch them
and carries them on its pinions.ᵉ
¹²The LORD alone ledᶠ him;ᵍ
no foreign god was with him.ʰ
¹³He made him ride on the heightsⁱ of the land
and fed him with the fruit of the fields.
He nourished him with honey from the rock,ʲ
and with oilᵏ from the flinty crag,
¹⁴with curds and milk from herd and flock
and with fattened lambs and goats,
with choice rams of Bashanˡ
and the finest kernels of wheat.ᵐ
You drank the foaming blood of the grape.ⁿ

¹⁵Jeshurunᵒᵖ grew fatᵖ and kicked;
filled with food, he became heavy and sleek.
He abandonedᵠ the God who made him
and rejected the Rockʳ his Savior.
¹⁶They made him jealousˢ with their foreign gods
and angeredᵗ him with their detestable idols.
¹⁷They sacrificedᵘ to demons,ᵛ which are not God—
gods they had not known,ʷ
gods that recently appeared,ˣ
gods your fathers did not fear.
¹⁸You deserted the Rock, who fathered you;

F Dt 11:14-15 ◀ ▶ Jos 5:12

32:16 ˢS Nu 25:11; S 1Co 10:22 ᵗS Dt 31:17; S 1Ki 14:9
32:17 ᵘS Ex 32:8 ᵛS Ex 22:20; 1Co 10:20 ʷS Dt 28:64 ˣJdg 5:8

ⁿ 5 Or Corrupt are they and not his children, / a generation warped and twisted to their shame   ᵒ 6 Or Father, who bought you   ᵖ 8 Masoretic Text; Dead Sea Scrolls (see also Septuagint) sons of God   ᵠ 15 Jeshurun means the upright one, that is, Israel.

32:8–9 The exact translation of these verses is difficult to determine. If the Hebrew is best translated "sons of Israel," then God may have set the boundaries of the nations during the exodus when Israel left Egypt. Yet if the Hebrew translates as "children of God," then the boundaries of the nations may have been set at an earlier time (see Ac 17:26).

you forgot the God who gave you birth.

¹⁹The LORD saw this and rejected them because he was angered by his sons and daughters.

²⁰"I will hide my face from them," he said,
"and see what their end will be;
for they are a perverse generation,
children who are unfaithful.
²¹They made me jealous by what is no god
and angered me with their worthless idols.
I will make them envious by those who are not a people;
I will make them angry by a nation that has no understanding.
²²For a fire has been kindled by my wrath,
one that burns to the realm of death below.
It will devour the earth and its harvests
and set afire the foundations of the mountains.
²³"I will heap calamities upon them
and spend my arrows against them.
²⁴I will send wasting famine against them,
consuming pestilence and deadly plague;
I will send against them the fangs of wild beasts,
the venom of vipers that glide in the dust.
²⁵In the street the sword will make them childless;
in their homes terror will reign.
Young men and young women will perish,
infants and gray-haired men.
²⁶I said I would scatter them
and blot out their memory from mankind,

²⁷but I dreaded the taunt of the enemy,
lest the adversary misunderstand
and say, 'Our hand has triumphed;
the LORD has not done all this.'"

²⁸They are a nation without sense,
there is no discernment in them.
²⁹If only they were wise and would understand this
and discern what their end will be!
³⁰How could one man chase a thousand,
or two put ten thousand to flight,
unless their Rock had sold them,
unless the LORD had given them up?
³¹For their rock is not like our Rock,
as even our enemies concede.
³²Their vine comes from the vine of Sodom
and from the fields of Gomorrah.
Their grapes are filled with poison,
and their clusters with bitterness.
³³Their wine is the venom of serpents,
the deadly poison of cobras.

³⁴"Have I not kept this in reserve
and sealed it in my vaults?
³⁵It is mine to avenge; I will repay.
In due time their foot will slip;
their day of disaster is near
and their doom rushes upon them."

³⁶The LORD will judge his people
and have compassion on his servants
when he sees their strength is gone
and no one is left, slave or free.
³⁷He will say: "Now where are their gods,

32:20–26 In this passage Moses recorded God's rejection of those who turn from the true God to follow "what is no god" (32:21) and prophesied that those who reject God's truth would burn "to the realm of death below" (32:22). Even the memory about those who reject God's mercy and salvation will be lost forever.

32:36 Though the Lord would stand in judgment of his people, Israel had to realize that God was their only source of hope and help.

the rock they took refuge in,^w
^38 the gods who ate the fat of their
 sacrifices
and drank the wine of their drink
 offerings?^x
Let them rise up to help you!
Let them give you shelter!

^39 "See now that I myself am He!^y
 There is no god besides me.^z
 I put to death^a and I bring to life,^b
 I have wounded and I will heal,^c
 and no one can deliver out of my
  hand.^d
^40 I lift my hand^e to heaven and declare:
 As surely as I live forever,^f
^41 when I sharpen my flashing sword^g
 and my hand grasps it in judgment,
 I will take vengeance^h on my
  adversaries
 and repay those who hate me.^i
^42 I will make my arrows drunk with
  blood,^j
 while my sword devours flesh:^k
 the blood of the slain and the captives,
 the heads of the enemy leaders."

^43 Rejoice,^l O nations, with his people,^s,^t
 for he will avenge the blood of his
  servants;^m
 he will take vengeance on his
  enemies^n
 and make atonement for his land
  and people.^o

^44 Moses came with Joshua^u,^p son of Nun and spoke all the words of this song in the hearing of the people. ^45 When Moses finished reciting all these words to all Israel, ^46 he said to them, "Take to heart all the words I have solemnly declared to you this day,^q so that you may command^r your children to obey carefully all the words of this law. ^47 They are not just idle words for you—they are your life.^s By them you will live long^t in the land you are crossing the Jordan to possess."

Moses to Die on Mount Nebo

^48 On that same day the Lord told Moses,^u ^49 "Go up into the Abarim^v Range to Mount Nebo^w in Moab, across from Jericho,^x and view Canaan,^y the land I am giving the Israelites as their own possession. ^50 There on the mountain that you have climbed you will die^z and be gathered to your people, just as your brother Aaron died^a on Mount Hor^b and was gathered to his people. ^51 This is because both of you broke faith with me in the presence of the Israelites at the waters of Meribah Kadesh^c in the Desert of Zin^d and because you did not uphold my holiness among the Israelites.^e ^52 Therefore, you will see the land only from a distance;^f you will not enter^g the land I am giving to the people of Israel."

Moses Blesses the Tribes

33:1–29Ref — Ge 49:1–28

33 This is the blessing^h that Moses the man of God^i pronounced on the Israelites before his death. ^2 He said:

"The Lord came from Sinai^j
 and dawned over them from Seir;^k

K Dt 30:20 ◀ ▶ Dt 33:25
O Dt 18:18–19 ◀ ▶ 1Sa 2:2
P Dt 32:22 ◀ ▶ 1Sa 2:10
H Dt 32:35 ◀ ▶ Dt 32:43
I Dt 32:36 ◀ ▶ Jos 1:2–9
H Dt 32:41 ◀ ▶ Jos 24:19

Q Nu 31:2 ◀ ▶ Jdg 2:10

^s 43 Or *Make his people rejoice, O nations* ^t 43 Masoretic Text; Dead Sea Scrolls (see also Septuagint) *people, / and let all the angels worship him /* ^u 44 Hebrew *Hoshea*, a variant of *Joshua*

32:41–43 In his last words to the people, Moses declared that although God would execute final vengeance on his enemies, God promised to be merciful to the people as long as they repented of their sins. Echoing Moses' words, the prophet Isaiah reminded the people to "turn to the Lord, and he will have mercy . . . , and to our God, for he will freely pardon" (Isa 55:7).

32:48–52 This is one of the most poignant moments in Biblical history. Moses recorded God's announcement of his approaching death and the reason why he was forbidden from entering the promised land (see the note at Nu 20:12). This notation reminds all who read Moses' words that we serve a holy God who demands obedience from his children. Yet God let Moses view Canaan from the top of the mountain, confirming God's abundant grace and mercy to all who love him.

33:2 Moses recounted the highlight of his ministry—his time with God on Mt. Sinai when he received the law—and traced God's movements with his people from Sinai through Seir (Edom) and on to the northern section of the Sinai peninsula (Paran). Moses also indicated that God's angels accompanied

he shone forth¹ from Mount Paran.ᵐ
He came withᵛ myriads of holy onesⁿ
    from the south, from his mountain
    slopes.ʷ
³Surely it is you who loveᵒ the people;
    all the holy ones are in your hand.ᵖ
At your feet they all bow down,ᵠ
    and from you receive instruction,
⁴the law that Moses gave us,ʳ
    the possession of the assembly of
    Jacob.ˢ
⁵He was kingᵗ over Jeshurunˣᵘ
    when the leaders of the people
    assembled,
    along with the tribes of Israel.

⁶"Let Reuben live and not die,
    norʸ his men be few."ᵛ

⁷And this he said about Judah:ʷ

"Hear, O LORD, the cry of Judah;
    bring him to his people.
With his own hands he defends his
    cause.
Oh, be his help against his foes!"

⁸About Leviˣ he said:

"Your Thummim and Urimʸ belong
    to the man you favored.ᶻ
You testedᵃ him at Massah;
    you contended with him at the
    waters of Meribah.ᵇ
⁹He said of his father and mother,ᶜ
    'I have no regard for them.'
He did not recognize his brothers
    or acknowledge his own children,
but he watched over your word
    and guarded your covenant.ᵈ
¹⁰He teachesᵉ your precepts to Jacob
    and your law to Israel.ᶠ
He offers incense before youᵍ
    and whole burnt offerings on your
    altar.ʰ
¹¹Bless all his skills, O LORD,
    and be pleased with the work of his
    hands.ⁱ
Smite the loins of those who rise up
    against him;
    strike his foes till they rise no
    more."

A Nu 23:24 ◀ ▶ Dt 33:12–29

33:2 ˡPs 50:2; 80:1; 94:1
ᵐS Nu 10:12
ⁿPs 89:7; Da 4:13; 7:10; 8:13;
Zec 14:5; Ac 7:53;
Gal 3:19; Heb 2:2;
Rev 5:11

33:3 ᵒS Dt 4:37
ᵖDt 7:6 ᵠLk 10:39;
Rev 4:10

33:4 ʳDt 4:2;
Jn 1:17; 7:19
ˢPs 119:111

33:5 ᵗS Ex 16:8;
1Sa 10:19;
Ps 10:16; 149:2
ᵘS Nu 23:21;
S Dt 32:15

33:6 ᵛS Ge 34:5

33:7 ʷS Ge 49:10

33:8 ˣS Ge 29:34
ʸEx 28:30
ᶻPs 106:16
ᵃS Nu 14:22
ᵇS Ex 17:7

33:9 ᶜEx 32:26-29
ᵈPs 61:5; Mal 2:5

33:10 ᵉEzr 7:10;
Ne 8:18;
Ps 119:151;
Jer 23:22; Mal 2:6
ᶠS Lev 10:11;
Dt 17:8-11; 31:9-13
ᵍS Ex 30:7;
Lev 16:12-13
ʰPs 51:19

33:11 ⁱ2Sa 24:23;
Ps 20:3; 51:19

33:12 ʲS Ge 35:18
ᵏDt 4:37-38; 12:10;
S 32:8 ˡS Ex 19:4
ᵐPs 60:5; 127:2;
Isa 5:1 ⁿS Ex 28:12

33:13 ᵒS Ge 30:24
ᵖGe 27:28;
Ps 148:7

33:15 ᵠHab 3:6

33:16 ʳS Ex 3:2
ˢS Ge 37:8

33:17 ᵗ1Sa 2:10;
2Sa 22:3; Eze 34:21
ᵘS Nu 23:22
ᵛ1Ki 22:11; Ps 44:5
ʷS Ge 41:52
ˣS Ge 41:51

33:18 ʸS Ge 30:20
ᶻS Ge 30:18

33:19 ᵃS Ex 15:17;
Ps 48:1; Isa 2:3;
65:11; 66:20;
Jer 31:6 ᵇPs 4:5;
51:19

¹²About Benjaminʲ he said:

"Let the beloved of the LORD rest
    secure in him,ᵏ
for he shields him all day long,ˡ
    and the one the LORD lovesᵐ rests
    between his shoulders."ⁿ

¹³About Josephᵒ he said:

"May the LORD bless his land
    with the precious dew from heaven
    above
    and with the deep waters that lie
    below;ᵖ
¹⁴with the best the sun brings forth
    and the finest the moon can yield;
¹⁵with the choicest gifts of the ancient
    mountainsᵠ
    and the fruitfulness of the
    everlasting hills;
¹⁶with the best gifts of the earth and its
    fullness
    and the favor of him who dwelt in
    the burning bush.ʳ
Let all these rest on the head of
    Joseph,
    on the brow of the prince amongᶻ
    his brothers.ˢ
¹⁷In majesty he is like a firstborn bull;
    his hornsᵗ are the horns of a wild
    ox.ᵘ
With them he will goreᵛ the nations,
    even those at the ends of the earth.
Such are the ten thousands of
    Ephraim;ʷ
    such are the thousands of
    Manasseh."ˣ

¹⁸About Zebulunʸ he said:

"Rejoice, Zebulun, in your going out,
    and you, Issachar,ᶻ in your tents.
¹⁹They will summon peoples to the
    mountainᵃ
    and there offer sacrifices of
    righteousness;ᵇ

A Dt 33:6 ◀ ▶
L Dt 32:9–14 ◀ ▶ Dt 33:27

ᵛ2 Or *from* ʷ2 The meaning of the Hebrew for this phrase is uncertain.
ˣ5 *Jeshurun* means *the upright one*, that is, Israel; also in verse 26.
ʸ6 Or *but let* ᶻ16 Or *of the one separated from*

him when he gave the law to Moses. Several NT writers support this statement (see Ac 7:53; Gal 3:19; Heb 2:2).

33:5 *Jeshurun* is a Hebrew term of endearment that means "the upright one" (see Isa 44:2) and refers to Israel. This curious verse reinforces that the Lord, not a mere human, is to be the king over Israel (see 1Sa 12:12; Ps 10:16).

they will feast on the abundance of the
    seas,ᶜ
on the treasures hidden in the
    sand."

²⁰About Gadᵈ he said:

"Blessed is he who enlarges Gad's
    domain!ᵉ
Gad lives there like a lion,
    tearing at arm or head.
²¹He chose the best land for himself;ᶠ
    the leader's portion was kept for
        him.ᵍ
When the heads of the people
        assembled,
    he carried out the LORD's righteous
        will,ʰ
    and his judgments concerning
        Israel."

²²About Danⁱ he said:

"Dan is a lion's cub,
    springing out of Bashan."

²³About Naphtaliʲ he said:

"Naphtali is abounding with the favor
        of the LORD
    and is full of his blessing;
    he will inherit southward to the
        lake."

²⁴About Asherᵏ he said:

"Most blessed of sons is Asher;
    let him be favored by his brothers,
    and let him bathe his feet in oil.ˡ
²⁵The bolts of your gates will be iron and
        bronze,ᵐ
    and your strength will equal your
        days.ⁿ

²⁶"There is no one like the God of
        Jeshurun,ᵒ
    who ridesᵖ on the heavens to help
        youᵠ
    and on the cloudsʳ in his majesty.ˢ
²⁷The eternalᵗ God is your refuge,ᵘ
    and underneath are the everlastingᵛ
        arms.
He will drive out your enemy before
        you,ʷ
    saying, 'Destroy him!'ˣ
²⁸So Israel will live in safety alone;ʸ

K Dt 32:39 ◀▶ Dt 33:27
C Dt 29:5 ◀▶ Ne 9:21
H Dt 7:15 ◀▶ 1Ki 3:14
K Dt 33:25 ◀▶ Dt 33:29
L Dt 33:12 ◀▶ Jos 1:5

33:19 ᶜIsa 18:7;
23:18; 45:14; 60:5,
11; 61:6; Hag 2:7;
Zec 14:14
33:20 ᵈGe 30:11
ᵉDt 3:12-17
33:21 ᶠNu 32:1-5,
31-32 ᵍS Nu 34:14
ʰJos 22:1-3
33:22 ⁱGe 49:16;
S Nu 1:38
33:23 ʲS Ge 30:8
33:24 ᵏS Ge 30:13
ˡS Ge 49:20;
S Dt 32:13
33:25 ᵐNe 3:3;
7:3; Ps 147:13
ⁿS Dt 32:47
33:26 ᵒS Dt 32:15
ᵖPs 18:10; 68:33
ᵠS Dt 10:14;
S Ps 104:3
ʳ2Sa 22:10;
Ps 18:9; 68:4;
Da 7:13 ˢS Ex 15:7
33:27 ᵗEx 15:18;
Isa 40:28; 57:15
ᵘNu 9:5; 84:1; 90:1;
91:9 ᵛS Ge 21:33
ʷEx 34:11;
Jos 24:18 ˣS Dt 7:2
33:28
ʸS Ex 33:16;
S Lev 25:18;
S Dt 32:8; Ps 16:9;
Pr 1:33; Isa 14:30
ᶻver 13; Ge 27:28
33:29 ᵃPs 1:1;
32:1:2; 144:15
ᵇ2Sa 22:45;
Ps 18:44; 66:3;
81:15 ᶜDt 4:7
ᵈGe 15:1; Ex 18:4;
Ps 10:14; 18:1;
27:1,9; 30:10;
54:4; 70:5;
115:9-11; 118:7;
Isa 45:24; Hos 13:9;
Hab 3:19
ᵉS Nu 33:52;
S Dt 32:13
34:1 ᶠS Nu 32:3
ᵍS Nu 21:20
ʰDt 32:49
ⁱDt 32:52
ʲS Ge 14:14
34:2 ᵏS Ex 23:31
34:3 ˡS Ge 12:9
ᵐJdg 1:16; 3:13;
2Ch 28:15
ⁿS Ge 13:10
34:4 ᵒGe 28:13
ᵖJos 21:43
ᵠGe 12:7
ʳS Dt 3:23
34:5 ˢS Nu 12:7
ᵗS Ge 25:8
34:6 ᵘS Dt 3:29
ᵛJude 1:9
34:7 ʷS Ex 7:7
ˣS Ge 27:1
ʸS Ge 15:15
34:8 ᶻS Nu 21:11
ᵃS Ge 37:34;
S Dt 1:3
ᵇ2Sa 11:27
34:9 ᶜS Ge 41:38;
S Ex 28:3; Isa 11:2
ᵈS Dt 31:14; Ac 6:6
34:10 ᵉS Ge 20:7
ᶠDt 18:15,18
ᵍS Ex 33:11

Jacob's spring is secure
    in a land of grain and new wine,
    where the heavens drop dew.ᶻ
²⁹Blessed are you, O Israel!ᵃ
Who is like you,ᵇ
    a people saved by the LORD?ᶜ
He is your shield and helperᵈ
    and your glorious sword.
Your enemies will cower before you,
    and you will trample down their
        high places.ᵃᵉ"

The Death of Moses

34 Then Moses climbed Mount Neboᶠ from the plains of Moab to the top of Pisgah,ᵍ across from Jericho.ʰ There the LORD showedⁱ him the whole land—from Gilead to Dan,ʲ ²all of Naphtali, the territory of Ephraim and Manasseh, all the land of Judah as far as the western sea,ᵇᵏ ³the Negevˡ and the whole region from the Valley of Jericho, the City of Palms,ᵐ as far as Zoar.ⁿ ⁴Then the LORD said to him, "This is the land I promised on oathᵒ to Abraham, Isaac and Jacobᵖ when I said, 'I will give itᵠ to your descendants.' I have let you see it with your eyes, but you will not crossʳ over into it."

⁵And Moses the servant of the LORDˢ diedᵗ there in Moab, as the LORD had said. ⁶He buried himᶜ in Moab, in the valley opposite Beth Peor,ᵘ but to this day no one knows where his grave is.ᵛ ⁷Moses was a hundred and twenty years oldʷ when he died, yet his eyes were not weakˣ nor his strength gone.ʸ ⁸The Israelites grieved for Moses in the plains of Moabᶻ thirty days,ᵃ until the time of weeping and mourningᵇ was over.

⁹Now Joshua son of Nun was filled with the spiritᵈ of wisdomᶜ because Moses had laid his hands on him.ᵈ So the Israelites listened to him and did what the LORD had commanded Moses.

¹⁰Since then, no prophetᵉ has risen in Israel like Moses,ᶠ whom the LORD knew face to face,ᵍ ¹¹who did all those miracu-

K Dt 33:27 ◀▶ Jos 1:5
E Dt 8:4 ◀▶ Jos 14:10–11
B Nu 27:18 ◀▶ Ps 45:7
E Nu 27:18 ◀▶ Jdg 3:10
G Nu 11:25–29 ◀▶ 1Sa 10:6–7
T Nu 24:2–3 ◀▶ 1Sa 10:6–7

ᵃ 29 Or *will tread upon their bodies*   ᵇ That is, the Mediterranean
ᶜ 6 Or *He was buried*   ᵈ 9 Or *Spirit*

lous signs and wondersʰ the LORD sent him to do in Egypt—to Pharaoh and to all his officialsⁱ and to his whole land. ¹²For no one hasʲ ever shown the mighty power or performed the awesome deedsᵏ that Moses did in the sight of all Israel.

34:11 ʰ Dt 4:34; ⁱ S Ex 11:3
34:12 ʲ Heb 3:1-6; ᵏ S Dt 4:34

Joshua

Author: Joshua

Theme: The conquest of Canaan

Date of Writing: c. 1390 B.C.

Outline of Joshua
  I. Preparing to Enter Canaan (1:1—5:12)
  II. Conquering the Land (5:13—12:24)
  III. Dividing the Land by Tribes (13:1—21:45)
  IV. Joshua's Farewell and Death (22:1—24:33)

THE BOOK OF Joshua is the first book in Scripture to bear the name of its author. Appointed by God to succeed Moses as Israel's leader, Joshua had been Moses' willing servant and pupil from the time of the giving of the law at Sinai through the forty years in the desert (see Ex 33:11). Joshua was also one of the twelve spies who originally explored the promised land, returning with a positive report (see Nu 14:6–9, 30). Described by Moses as "a man in whom is the spirit" (Nu 27:18), Joshua faithfully "followed the LORD wholeheartedly" (Nu 32:12).

The book of Joshua records the military battles of the Israelites as they conquered the pagan cities of Canaan. As the Israelites entered the land, they confirmed their acceptance of God's covenant by circumcising all of the males that had been born during the forty years in the wilderness (see Jos 5:2–7). Then, following Joshua's bold leadership and trusting God's promises, the Israelites conquered Canaan, a process that took thirty years. The book concludes with God's detailed instructions for the division of the land among the twelve tribes, including the allotments to Reuben, Gad and the half tribe of Manasseh on the east bank of the Jordan.

Though God provided his presence and constant direction to the Israelites through his law and the visible pillar of cloud and fire, the Israelites rebelliously chose to ignore God's directions. The book of Joshua details the sins of Israel that brought about their numerous defeats. The example of the Israelites profoundly illustrates the opposition God's people will face when they attempt to possess the promises of God and underscores the peril of any disobedience (see Eph 1:3; 6:10–18).

The Lord Commands Joshua

1 After the death of Moses the servant of the Lord,[a] the Lord said to Joshua[b] son of Nun, Moses' aide: [2] "Moses my servant is dead. Now then, you and all these people, get ready to cross the Jordan River[c][d] into the land[e] I am about to give to them[f]—to the Israelites. [3] I will give you every place where you set your foot,[g] as I promised Moses.[h] [4] Your territory will extend from the desert to Lebanon,[i] and from the great river, the Euphrates[j]—all the Hittite[k] country—to the Great Sea on the west.[l] [5] No one will be able to stand up against you[m] all the days of your life. As I was with[n] Moses, so I will be with you; I will never leave you nor forsake[o] you.

[6] "Be strong[p] and courageous,[q] because you will lead these people to inherit the land I swore to their forefathers[r] to give them. [7] Be strong and very courageous. Be careful to obey[s] all the law[t] my servant Moses[u] gave you; do not turn from it to the right or to the left,[v] that you may be successful wherever you go.[w] [8] Do not let this Book of the Law depart from your mouth;[y] meditate[z] on it day and night, so that you may be careful to do everything written in it. Then you will be prosperous and successful.[a] [9] Have I not commanded you? Be strong and courageous. Do not be terrified;[b] do not be discouraged,[c] for the Lord your God will be with you wherever you go."[d]

[10] So Joshua ordered the officers of the people:[e] [11] "Go through the camp[f] and tell the people, 'Get your supplies[g] ready. Three days[h] from now you will cross the Jordan[i] here to go in and take possession[j] of the land the Lord your God is giving you for your own.' "

[12] But to the Reubenites, the Gadites and the half-tribe of Manasseh,[k] Joshua said, [13] "Remember the command that Moses the servant of the Lord gave you: 'The Lord your God is giving you rest[l] and has granted you this land.' [14] Your wives,[m] your children and your livestock may stay in the land[n] that Moses gave you east of the Jordan, but all your fighting men, fully armed,[o] must cross over ahead of your brothers.[p] You are to help your brothers [15] until the Lord gives them rest, as he has done for you, and until they too have taken possession of the land that the Lord your God is giving them. After that, you may go back and occupy your own land, which Moses the servant of the Lord gave you east of the Jordan toward the sunrise."[q]

[16] Then they answered Joshua, "Whatever you have commanded us we will do, and wherever you send us we will go.[r] [17] Just as we fully obeyed Moses, so we will obey you.[s] Only may the Lord your God be with you as he was with Moses. [18] Whoever rebels against your word and does not obey[t] your words, whatever you may command them, will be put to death. Only be strong and courageous!"[u]

Rahab and the Spies

2 Then Joshua son of Nun secretly sent two spies[v] from Shittim.[w] "Go, look over[x] the land," he said, "especially Jericho.[y]" So they went and entered the house of a prostitute[b] named Rahab[z] and stayed there.

[2] The king of Jericho was told, "Look! Some of the Israelites have come here tonight to spy out the land." [3] So the king of Jericho sent this message to Rahab:[a] "Bring out the men who came to you and entered your house, because they have come to spy out the whole land."

[4] But the woman had taken the two men[b] and hidden them.[c] She said, "Yes, the men came to me, but I did not know where they had come from. [5] At dusk,

---

| I Dt 32:43 ◀▶ Jos 3:5 |
| K Dt 33:29 ◀▶ Jdg 5:31 |
| L Dt 33:27 ◀▶ Jos 1:9 |
| V Dt 32:30 ◀▶ Jos 21:44 |
| W Dt 31:6-8 ◀▶ Jos 1:9 |
| S Dt 30:6 ◀▶ Jos 5:6 |
| L Jos 1:5 ◀▶ Jos 21:45 |
| W Jos 1:6-7 ◀▶ Jos 8:1 |

1:1 a Ex 14:31; Dt 34:5; Rev 15:3 b S Ex 17:9 1:2 c S Nu 13:29 d S Nu 35:10 e S Ge 15:14 f Ge 12:7; Dt 1:25 1:3 a S Dt 11:24 h Ge 50:24; Nu 13:2; Dt 1:8 1:4 i S Dt 3:25 j S Ge 2:14 k S Ge 10:15; 23:10; Ex 3:8 l Nu 34:2-12; Ezr 4:20 1:5 m S Dt 7:24 n ver 17; S Ge 26:3; S 39:2; Jdg 6:12; 1Sa 10:7; Jer 1:8; 30:11 o S Ge 28:15; S Dt 4:31 1:6 p S 2Sa 2:7; 1Ki 2:2; Isa 41:6; Joel 3:9-10 q S Dt 1:21; S 31:6; S Jdg 5:21 r Jer 3:18; 7:7 1:7 s Dt 29:9; 1Ki 2:3; 3:3 t Ezr 7:26; Ps 78:10; 119:136; Isa 42:24; Jer 26:4-6; 32:23; 44:10 u ver 2,15; S Nu 12:7; Job 1:8; 42:7 v S Dt 5:32; Jos 23:6 w ver 9; S Dt 4:2; 5:33; S 11:8; Jos 6:15 1:8 x S Dt 28:61; S Ps 147:19 y S Ex 4:15; Isa 59:21 z S Ge 24:63 a Dt 29:9; 1Sa 18:14; Ps 1:1-3; Isa 52:13; 53:10; Jer 23:5 1:9 b S Dt 31:6; Jos 10:8; 2Ki 19:6; Isa 35:4; 37:6 c S Dt 1:21; Job 4:5 d S ver 7; Dt 31:7-8; Jer 1:8 1:10 e S Dt 1:15 1:11 f Jos 3:2 g 1Sa 17:22; Isa 10:28 h S Ge 40:13 i S Nu 35:10 j S Nu 33:53 1:12 k Nu 32:33 1:13 l S Ex 33:14; Ps 55:6; Isa 11:10; 28:12; 30:15; 32:18; 40:31; Jer 6:16; 45:3; La 5:5 1:14 m Dt 3:19 n S Nu 32:26 o S Ex 13:18 p Jos 4:12 1:15 q Nu 32:20-22; Jos 22:1-4 1:16 r S Nu 27:20; S 32:25 1:17 s S Nu 27:20

1:18 t S Nu 32:25 u S Dt 1:21; S 31:6 2:1 v S ver 4; S Ge 42:9 w S Nu 25:1; Jos 3:1; Joel 3:18 x S Nu 21:32; Jdg 18:2 y S Nu 33:48 z Jos 6:17,25; S Heb 11:31 2:3 a Jos 6:23 2:4 b ver 1; Jos 6:22 c Jos 6:17

a 4 That is, the Mediterranean b 1 Or possibly an innkeeper

1:5—9 God's promised presence and strength would be Joshua's so that he could lead the Israelites to a successful conquest of the land promised to Abram and his descendants (see Ge 12:6; 13:14–15; 15:18–21).

when it was time to close the city gate, the men left. I don't know which way they went. Go after them quickly. You may catch up with them." ⁶(But she had taken them up to the roof and hidden them under the stalks of flax she had laid out on the roof.) ⁷So the men set out in pursuit of the spies on the road that leads to the fords of the Jordan, and as soon as the pursuers had gone out, the gate was shut.

⁸Before the spies lay down for the night, she went up on the roof ⁹and said to them, "I know that the LORD has given this land to you and that a great fear of you has fallen on us, so that all who live in this country are melting in fear because of you. ¹⁰We have heard how the LORD dried up the water of the Red Sea for you when you came out of Egypt, and what you did to Sihon and Og, the two kings of the Amorites east of the Jordan, whom you completely destroyed. ¹¹When we heard of it, our hearts melted and everyone's courage failed because of you, for the LORD your God is God in heaven above and on the earth below. ¹²Now then, please swear to me by the LORD that you will show kindness to my family, because I have shown kindness to you. Give me a sure sign ¹³that you will spare the lives of my father and mother, my brothers and sisters, and all who belong to them, and that you will save us from death."

¹⁴"Our lives for your lives!" the men assured her. "If you don't tell what we are doing, we will treat you kindly and faithfully when the LORD gives us the land."

¹⁵So she let them down by a rope through the window, for the house she lived in was part of the city wall. ¹⁶Now she had said to them, "Go to the hills so the pursuers will not find you. Hide yourselves there three days until they return, and then go on your way."

¹⁷The men said to her, "This oath you made us swear will not be binding on us ¹⁸unless, when we enter the land, you have tied this scarlet cord in the window through which you let us down, and unless you have brought your father and mother, your brothers and all your family into your house. ¹⁹If anyone goes outside your house into the street, his blood will be on his own head; we will not be responsible. As for anyone who is in the house with you, his blood will be on our head if a hand is laid on him. ²⁰But if you tell what we are doing, we will be released from the oath you made us swear."

²¹"Agreed," she replied. "Let it be as you say." So she sent them away and they departed. And she tied the scarlet cord in the window.

²²When they left, they went into the hills and stayed there three days, until the pursuers had searched all along the road and returned without finding them. ²³Then the two men started back. They went down out of the hills, forded the river and came to Joshua son of Nun and told him everything that had happened to them. ²⁴They said to Joshua, "The LORD has surely given the whole land into our hands; all the people are melting in fear because of us."

Crossing the Jordan

3 Early in the morning Joshua and all the Israelites set out from Shittim and went to the Jordan, where they camped before crossing over. ²After three days the officers went throughout the camp, ³giving orders to the people: "When you see the ark of the covenant of the LORD your God, and the priests, who are Levites, carrying it, you are to move out from your positions and follow it. ⁴Then you will know which way to go, since you have never been this way before. But keep a distance of about a thousand yards between you and the ark; do not go near it."

⁵Joshua told the people, "Consecrate yourselves, for tomorrow the LORD will do amazing things among you."

⁶Joshua said to the priests, "Take up the ark of the covenant and pass on ahead of the people." So they took it up and went ahead of them.

⁷And the LORD said to Joshua, "Today I will begin to exalt you in the eyes of all Israel, so they may know that I am with

❙ *Jos 1:2–9* ◀ ▶ *Jos 3:7*
❙ *Jos 3:5* ◀ ▶ *Jos 6:2–5*

1Ch 16:9,24; Ps 26:7; 75:1 **3:7** gJos 4:14; 1Ch 29:25

c 10 Hebrew *Yam Suph*; that is, Sea of Reeds *d* 10 The Hebrew term refers to the irrevocable giving over of things or persons to the LORD, often by totally destroying them. *e* 4 Hebrew *about two thousand cubits* (about 900 meters)

you as I was with Moses. ⁸Tell the priests who carry the ark of the covenant: 'When you reach the edge of the Jordan's waters, go and stand in the river.'"

⁹Joshua said to the Israelites, "Come here and listen to the words of the LORD your God. ¹⁰This is how you will know that the living God is among you and that he will certainly drive out before you the Canaanites, Hittites, Hivites, Perizzites, Girgashites, Amorites and Jebusites. ¹¹See, the ark of the covenant of the Lord of all the earth will go into the Jordan ahead of you. ¹²Now then, choose twelve men from the tribes of Israel, one from each tribe. ¹³And as soon as the priests who carry the ark of the LORD—the Lord of all the earth—set foot in the Jordan, its waters flowing downstream will be cut off and stand up in a heap."

¹⁴So when the people broke camp to cross the Jordan, the priests carrying the ark of the covenant went ahead of them. ¹⁵Now the Jordan is at flood stage all during harvest. Yet as soon as the priests who carried the ark reached the Jordan and their feet touched the water's edge, ¹⁶the water from upstream stopped flowing. It piled up in a heap a great distance away, at a town called Adam in the vicinity of Zarethan, while the water flowing down to the Sea of the Arabah (the Salt Sea) was completely cut off. So the people crossed over opposite Jericho. ¹⁷The priests who carried the ark of the covenant of the LORD stood firm on dry ground in the middle of the Jordan, while all Israel passed by until the whole nation had completed the crossing on dry ground.

4 When the whole nation had finished crossing the Jordan, the LORD said to Joshua, ²"Choose twelve men from among the people, one from each tribe, ³and tell them to take up twelve stones from the middle of the Jordan from right where the priests stood and to carry them over with you and put them down at the place where you stay tonight."

⁴So Joshua called together the twelve men he had appointed from the Israelites, one from each tribe, ⁵and said to them, "Go over before the ark of the LORD your God into the middle of the Jordan. Each of you is to take up a stone on his shoulder, according to the number of the tribes of the Israelites, ⁶to serve as a sign among you. In the future, when your children ask you, 'What do these stones mean?' ⁷tell them that the flow of the Jordan was cut off before the ark of the covenant of the LORD. When it crossed the Jordan, the waters of the Jordan were cut off. These stones are to be a memorial to the people of Israel forever."

⁸So the Israelites did as Joshua commanded them. They took twelve stones from the middle of the Jordan, according to the number of the tribes of the Israelites, as the LORD had told Joshua; and they carried them over with them to their camp, where they put them down. ⁹Joshua set up the twelve stones that had been in the middle of the Jordan at the spot where the priests who carried the ark of the covenant had stood. And they are there to this day.

¹⁰Now the priests who carried the ark remained standing in the middle of the Jordan until everything the LORD had commanded Joshua was done by the people, just as Moses had directed Joshua. The people hurried over, ¹¹and as soon as all of them had crossed, the ark of the LORD and the priests came to the other side while the people watched. ¹²The men of Reuben, Gad and the half-tribe of Manasseh crossed over, armed, in front of the Israelites, as Moses had directed them. ¹³About forty thousand armed for battle crossed over before the LORD to the plains of Jericho for war.

¹⁴That day the LORD exalted Joshua in the sight of all Israel; and they revered him all the days of his life, just as they had revered Moses.

¹⁵Then the LORD said to Joshua, ¹⁶"Command the priests carrying the ark of the Testimony to come up out of the Jordan."

¹⁷So Joshua commanded the priests, "Come up out of the Jordan."

¹⁸And the priests came up out of the river carrying the ark of the covenant of the LORD. No sooner had they set their feet on the dry ground than the waters of the Jordan returned to their place and ran at flood stage as before.

¹⁹On the tenth day of the first month the people went up from the Jordan and camped at Gilgal on the eastern border

---

f 16 That is, the Dead Sea *g 9* Or *Joshua also set up twelve stones*

of Jericho. ²⁰And Joshua set up at Gilgal the twelve stones° they had taken out of the Jordan. ²¹He said to the Israelites, "In the future when your descendants ask their fathers, 'What do these stones mean?'ᵖ ²²tell them, 'Israel crossed the Jordan on dry ground.'ᑫ ²³For the LORD your God dried up the Jordan before you until you had crossed over. The LORD your God did to the Jordan just what he had done to the Red Seaʰ when he dried it up before us until we had crossed over.ʳ ²⁴He did this so that all the peoples of the earth might knowˢ that the hand of the LORD is powerfulᵗ and so that you might always fear the LORD your God.ᵘ"

Circumcision at Gilgal

5 Now when all the Amorite kings west of the Jordan and all the Canaanite kings along the coastᵛ heard how the LORD had dried up the Jordan before the Israelites until we had crossed over, their hearts meltedʷ and they no longer had the courage to face the Israelites.

²At that time the LORD said to Joshua, "Make flint knivesˣ and circumciseʸ the Israelites again." ³So Joshua made flint knives and circumcised the Israelites at Gibeath Haaraloth.ⁱ

⁴Now this is why he did so: All those who came out of Egypt—all the men of military ageᶻ—died in the desert on the way after leaving Egypt.ᵃ ⁵All the people that came out had been circumcised, but all the people born in the desert during the journey from Egypt had not. ⁶The Israelites had moved about in the desertʰ forty yearsᶜ until all the men who were of military age when they left Egypt had died, since they had not obeyed the LORD. For the LORD had sworn to them that they would not see the land that he had solemnly promised their fathers to give us,ᵈ a land flowing with milk and honey.ᵉ ⁷So he raised up their sons in their place, and these were the ones Joshua circumcised. They were still uncircumcised because they had not been circumcised on the way. ⁸And after the whole nation had

s *Jos 1:8* ◀ ▶ *Jos 24:14*

4:20 °ver 3,8
4:21 ᵖS ver 6
4:22 ᑫS Ex 14:22
4:23 ʳEx 14:19-22
4:24 ˢ1Ki 8:60; 18:36; 2Ki 5:15; Ps 67:2; 83:18; 106:8; Isa 37:20; 52:10 ᵗEx 15:16; 1Ch 29:12; Ps 44:3; 89:13; 98:1; 118:15-16 ᵘS Ex 14:31
5:1 ᵛS Nu 13:29 ʷS Ge 42:28
5:2 ˣS Ex 4:25 ʸS Ge 17:10,12,14
5:4 ᶻS Nu 1:3 ᵃDt 2:14
5:6 ᵇNu 32:13; Jos 14:10; Ps 107:4 ᶜS Ex 16:35 ᵈNu 14:23,29-35; Dt 2:14 ᵉS Ex 3:8
5:8 ᶠGe 34:25
5:9 ᵍS Dt 11:30
5:10 ʰS Ex 12:6 ⁱS Ex 12:11
5:11 ʲS Nu 15:19 ᵏEx 12:15 ˡS Lev 23:14
5:12 ᵐEx 16:35
5:13 ⁿS Ge 18:2 °Nu 22:23
5:14 ᵖS Ge 17:3 ᑫS Ge 19:1
5:15 ʳS Ge 28:17; Ex 3:5; Ac 7:33
6:1 ˢJos 24:11
6:2 ᵗver 16; Dt 7:24; Jos 8:1
6:4 ᵘS Ex 19:13

been circumcised, they remained where they were in camp until they were healed.ᶠ

⁹Then the LORD said to Joshua, "Today I have rolled away the reproach of Egypt from you." So the place has been called Gilgal/ᵍ to this day.

¹⁰On the evening of the fourteenth day of the month,ʰ while camped at Gilgal on the plains of Jericho, the Israelites celebrated the Passover.ⁱ ¹¹The day after the Passover, that very day, they ate some of the produce of the land:ʲ unleavened breadᵏ and roasted grain.ˡ ¹²The manna stopped the dayᵏ after they ate this food from the land; there was no longer any manna for the Israelites, but that year they ate of the produce of Canaan.ᵐ

The Fall of Jericho

¹³Now when Joshua was near Jericho, he looked up and saw a manⁿ standing in front of him with a drawn sword° in his hand. Joshua went up to him and asked, "Are you for us or for our enemies?"

¹⁴"Neither," he replied, "but as commander of the army of the LORD I have now come." Then Joshua fell facedownᵖ to the groundᑫ in reverence, and asked him, "What message does my Lordˡ have for his servant?"

¹⁵The commander of the LORD's army replied, "Take off your sandals, for the place where you are standing is holy."ʳ And Joshua did so.

6 Now Jerichoˢ was tightly shut up because of the Israelites. No one went out and no one came in.

²Then the LORD said to Joshua, "See, I have deliveredᵗ Jericho into your hands, along with its king and its fighting men. ³March around the city once with all the armed men. Do this for six days. ⁴Have seven priests carry trumpets of rams' hornsᵘ in front of the ark. On the seventh day, march around the city seven times,

F *Dt 32:13–14* ◀ ▶ *Jdg 15:18–19*
I *Jos 3:7* ◀ ▶ *Jos 6:16*

ʰ 23 Hebrew *Yam Suph*; that is, Sea of Reeds ⁱ 3 *Gibeath Haaraloth* means *hill of foreskins*. ʲ 9 *Gilgal* sounds like the Hebrew for *roll*. ᵏ 12 Or *the day* ˡ 14 Or *lord*

5:6 This piece of historical trivia records the fulfillment of the prophecy announced forty years earlier when God pronounced judgment on the Israelites for their lack of faith and rebellion against Moses' leadership (see Nu 14:32–34).

with the priests blowing the trumpets. ⁵When you hear them sound a long blast on the trumpets, have all the people give a loud shout; then the wall of the city will collapse and the people will go up, every man straight in."

⁶So Joshua son of Nun called the priests and said to them, "Take up the ark of the covenant of the LORD and have seven priests carry trumpets in front of it." ⁷And he ordered the people, "Advance! March around the city, with the armed guard going ahead of the ark of the LORD."

⁸When Joshua had spoken to the people, the seven priests carrying the seven trumpets before the LORD went forward, blowing their trumpets, and the ark of the LORD's covenant followed them. ⁹The armed guard marched ahead of the priests who blew the trumpets, and the rear guard followed the ark. All this time the trumpets were sounding. ¹⁰But Joshua had commanded the people, "Do not give a war cry, do not raise your voices, do not say a word until the day I tell you to shout. Then shout!" ¹¹So he had the ark of the LORD carried around the city, circling it once. Then the people returned to camp and spent the night there.

¹²Joshua got up early the next morning and the priests took up the ark of the LORD. ¹³The seven priests carrying the seven trumpets went forward, marching before the ark of the LORD and blowing the trumpets. The armed men went ahead of them and the rear guard followed the ark of the LORD, while the trumpets kept sounding. ¹⁴So on the second day they marched around the city once and returned to the camp. They did this for six days.

¹⁵On the seventh day, they got up at daybreak and marched around the city seven times in the same manner, except that on that day they circled the city seven times. ¹⁶The seventh time around, when the priests sounded the trumpet blast, Joshua commanded the people, "Shout! For the LORD has given you the city! ¹⁷The city and all that is in it are to be devoted to the LORD. Only Rahab the prostitute and all who are with her in her house shall be spared, because she hid the spies we sent. ¹⁸But keep away from the devoted things, so that you will not bring about your own destruction by taking any of them. Otherwise you will make the camp of Israel liable to destruction and bring trouble on it. ¹⁹All the silver and gold and the articles of bronze and iron are sacred to the LORD and must go into his treasury."

²⁰When the trumpets sounded, the people shouted, and at the sound of the trumpet, when the people gave a loud shout, the wall collapsed; so every man charged straight in, and they took the city. ²¹They devoted the city to the LORD and destroyed with the sword every living thing in it—men and women, young and old, cattle, sheep and donkeys.

²²Joshua said to the two men who had spied out the land, "Go into the prostitute's house and bring her out and all who belong to her, in accordance with your oath to her." ²³So the young men who had done the spying went in and brought out Rahab, her father and mother and brothers and all who belonged to her. They brought out her entire family and put them in a place outside the camp of Israel.

²⁴Then they burned the whole city and everything in it, but they put the silver and gold and the articles of bronze and iron into the treasury of the LORD's house. ²⁵But Joshua spared Rahab the prostitute, with her family and all who belonged to her, because she hid the men Joshua had sent as spies to Jericho—and she lives among the Israelites to this day.

²⁶At that time Joshua pronounced this solemn oath: "Cursed before the LORD is the man who undertakes to rebuild this city, Jericho:

"At the cost of his firstborn son
 will he lay its foundations;
at the cost of his youngest
 will he set up its gates."

²⁷So the LORD was with Joshua, and his fame spread throughout the land.

▸ Nu 33:55–56 ◂ ▸ Jos 23:13

m 17 The Hebrew term refers to the irrevocable giving over of things or persons to the LORD, often by totally destroying them; also in verses 18 and 21. *n 17* Or possibly *innkeeper*; also in verses 22 and 25

Achan's Sin

7 But the Israelites acted unfaithfully in regard to the devoted things*ᵒ*; Achan*ʰ* son of Carmi, the son of Zimri,*ᵖ* the son of Zerah,*ⁱ* of the tribe of Judah,*ʲ* took some of them. So the LORD's anger burned*ᵏ* against Israel.*ˡ*

²Now Joshua sent men from Jericho to Ai,*ᵐ* which is near Beth Aven*ⁿ* to the east of Bethel,*ᵒ* and told them, "Go up and spy out*ᵖ* the region." So the men went up and spied out Ai.

³When they returned to Joshua, they said, "Not all the people will have to go up against Ai. Send two or three thousand men to take it and do not weary all the people, for only a few men are there." ⁴So about three thousand men went up; but they were routed by the men of Ai,*ᵠ* ⁵who killed about thirty-six*ʳ* of them. They chased the Israelites from the city gate as far as the stone quarries*ᵠ* and struck them down on the slopes. At this the hearts of the people melted*ˢ* and became like water.

⁶Then Joshua tore his clothes*ᵗ* and fell facedown*ᵘ* to the ground before the ark of the LORD, remaining there till evening.*ᵛ* The elders of Israel*ʷ* did the same, and sprinkled dust*ˣ* on their heads. ⁷And Joshua said, "Ah, Sovereign LORD, why*ʸ* did you ever bring this people across the Jordan to deliver us into the hands of the Amorites to destroy us?*ᶻ* If only we had been content to stay on the other side of the Jordan! ⁸O Lord, what can I say, now that Israel has been routed by its enemies? ⁹The Canaanites and the other people of the country will hear about this and they will surround us and wipe out our name from the earth.*ᵃ* What then will you do for your own great name?"*ᵇ*

¹⁰The LORD said to Joshua, "Stand up! What are you doing down on your face? ¹¹Israel has sinned;*ᶜ* they have violated my covenant,*ᵈ* which I commanded them to keep. They have taken some of the devoted things; they have stolen, they have lied,*ᵉ* they have put them with their own possessions.*ᶠ* ¹²That is why the Israelites cannot stand against their enemies;*ᵍ* they turn their backs*ʰ* and run*ⁱ* because they have been made liable to destruction.*ʲ* I will not be with you anymore*ᵏ* unless you destroy whatever among you is devoted to destruction.

¹³"Go, consecrate the people. Tell them, 'Consecrate yourselves¹ in preparation for tomorrow; for this is what the LORD, the God of Israel, says: That which is devoted is among you, O Israel. You cannot stand against your enemies until you remove it.

¹⁴" 'In the morning, present*ᵐ* yourselves tribe by tribe. The tribe that the LORD takes*ⁿ* shall come forward clan by clan; the clan that the LORD takes shall come forward family by family; and the family that the LORD takes shall come forward man by man. ¹⁵He who is caught with the devoted things*ᵒ* shall be destroyed by fire,*ᵖ* along with all that belongs to him.*ᵠ* He has violated the covenant*ʳ* of the LORD and has done a disgraceful thing in Israel!' "*ˢ*

¹⁶Early the next morning Joshua had Israel come forward by tribes, and Judah was taken. ¹⁷The clans of Judah came forward, and he took the Zerahites.*ᵗ* He had the clan of the Zerahites come forward by families, and Zimri was taken. ¹⁸Joshua had his family come forward man by man, and Achan son of Carmi, the son of Zimri, the son of Zerah, of the tribe of Judah,*ᵘ* was taken.*ᵛ*

¹⁹Then Joshua said to Achan, "My son, give glory*ʷ* to the LORD,*ʳ* the God of Israel, and give him the praise.*ˢ* Tell*ˣ* me what you have done; do not hide it from me." **R**

²⁰Achan replied, "It is true! I have sinned against the LORD, the God of Israel. This is what I have done: ²¹When I saw in the plunder*ʸ* a beautiful robe from Babylonia,*ᵗ* two hundred shekels*ᵘ* of silver and a wedge of gold weighing fifty shekels,*ᵛ* I coveted*ᶻ* them and took them. They are hidden in the ground inside my tent, with the silver underneath."

²²So Joshua sent messengers, and they ran to the tent, and there it was, hidden in his tent, with the silver underneath. ²³They took the things from the tent, brought them to Joshua and all the Israelites and spread them out before the LORD. ²⁴Then Joshua, together with all Israel,

R Dt 30:8 ◀ ▶ Jdg 10:15–16

ᵒ 1 The Hebrew term refers to the irrevocable giving over of things or persons to the LORD, often by totally destroying them; also in verses 11, 12, 13 and 15. *ᵖ 1* See Septuagint and 1 Chron. 2:6; Hebrew *Zabdi;* also in verses 17 and 18. *ᵠ 5 Or as far as Shebarim ʳ 19* A solemn charge to tell the truth *ˢ 19* Or *and confess to him ᵗ 21* Hebrew *Shinar ᵘ 21* That is, about 5 pounds (about 2.3 kilograms) *ᵛ 21* That is, about 1 1/4 pounds (about 0.6 kilogram)

took Achan son of Zerah, the silver, the robe, the gold wedge, his sons[a] and daughters, his cattle, donkeys and sheep, his tent and all that he had, to the Valley of Achor.[b] 25Joshua said, "Why have you brought this trouble[c] on us? The LORD will bring trouble on you today."

Then all Israel stoned him,[d] and after they had stoned the rest, they burned them.[e] 26Over Achan they heaped[f] up a large pile of rocks, which remains to this day.[g] Then the LORD turned from his fierce anger.[h] Therefore that place has been called the Valley of Achor[w][i] ever since.

Ai Destroyed

8 Then the LORD said to Joshua, "Do not be afraid;[j] do not be discouraged.[k] Take the whole army[l] with you, and go up and attack Ai.[m] For I have delivered[n] into your hands the king of Ai, his people, his city and his land. 2You shall do to Ai and its king as you did to Jericho and its king, except that you may carry off their plunder[o] and livestock for yourselves.[p] Set an ambush[q] behind the city."

3So Joshua and the whole army moved out to attack Ai. He chose thirty thousand of his best fighting men and sent them out at night 4with these orders: "Listen carefully. You are to set an ambush behind the city. Don't go very far from it. All of you be on the alert. 5I and all those with me will advance on the city, and when the men come out against us, as they did before, we will flee from them. 6They will pursue us until we have lured them away from the city, for they will say, 'They are running away from us as they did before.' So when we flee from them, 7you are to rise up from ambush and take the city. The LORD your God will give it into your hand." 8When you have taken the city, set it on fire.[s] Do what the LORD has commanded.[t] See to it; you have my orders."

9Then Joshua sent them off, and they went to the place of ambush[u] and lay in wait between Bethel and Ai, to the west of Ai—but Joshua spent that night with the people.

l Jos 6:16 ◀ ▶ Jos 8:7
w Jos 1:9 ◀ ▶ 1Ch 22:13
l Jos 8:1–2 ◀ ▶ Jos 9:27

7:24 a S Nu 16:27
b ver 26; Jos 15:7;
Isa 65:10; Hos 2:15

7:25 c S Ge 6:18
d S Lev 20:2;
Dt 17:5; 1Ki 12:18;
2Ch 10:18; 24:21;
Ne 9:26
e S Ge 38:24

7:26 f 2Sa 18:17
g S Ge 35:20
h S Nu 25:4
i S ver 24

8:1 j Ge 26:24;
Dt 31:6
k S Nu 14:9;
S Dt 1:21 l Jos 10:7
m Jos 7:2; 9:3; 10:1;
12:9 n S Jos 6:2

8:2 o S Ge 49:27
p ver 27; Dt 20:14
q ver 4,12; Jdg 9:43;
20:29

8:7 r Jdg 7:7;
1Sa 23:4

8:8 s Jdg 20:29-38
t ver 19

8:9 u 2Ch 13:13

8:10 v Ge 22:3
w S Jos 7:6

8:14 x S Dt 1:1
y Jdg 20:34

8:15 z S Jdg 20:36
a Jos 15:61; 16:1;
18:12

8:16 b Jdg 20:31

8:18 c Job 41:26;
Ps 35:3 d S Ex 4:2;
17:9-12 e ver 26

8:19 f Jdg 20:33
g S ver 8

8:20 h Jdg 20:40

8:21 i Jdg 20:41

8:22 j Dt 7:2;
Jos 10:1

10Early the next morning[v] Joshua mustered his men, and he and the leaders of Israel[w] marched before them to Ai. 11The entire force that was with him marched up and approached the city and arrived in front of it. They set up camp north of Ai, with the valley between them and the city. 12Joshua had taken about five thousand men and set them in ambush between Bethel and Ai, to the west of the city. 13They had the soldiers take up their positions—all those in the camp to the north of the city and the ambush to the west of it. That night Joshua went into the valley.

14When the king of Ai saw this, he and all the men of the city hurried out early in the morning to meet Israel in battle at a certain place overlooking the Arabah.[x] But he did not know[y] that an ambush had been set against him behind the city. 15Joshua and all Israel let themselves be driven back[z] before them, and they fled toward the desert.[a] 16All the men of Ai were called to pursue them, and they pursued Joshua and were lured away[b] from the city. 17Not a man remained in Ai or Bethel who did not go after Israel. They left the city open and went in pursuit of Israel.

18Then the LORD said to Joshua, "Hold out toward Ai the javelin[c] that is in your hand,[d] for into your hand I will deliver the city." So Joshua held out his javelin[e] toward Ai. 19As soon as he did this, the men in the ambush rose quickly[f] from their position and rushed forward. They entered the city and captured it and quickly set it on fire.[g]

20The men of Ai looked back and saw the smoke of the city rising against the sky,[h] but they had no chance to escape in any direction, for the Israelites who had been fleeing toward the desert had turned back against their pursuers. 21For when Joshua and all Israel saw that the ambush had taken the city and that smoke was going up from the city, they turned around[i] and attacked the men of Ai. 22The men of the ambush also came out of the city against them, so that they were caught in the middle, with Israelites on both sides. Israel cut them down, leaving them neither survivors nor fugitives.[j]

w 26 Achor means trouble.

²³But they took the king of Ai alive[k] and brought him to Joshua.

²⁴When Israel had finished killing all the men of Ai in the fields and in the desert where they had chased them, and when every one of them had been put to the sword, all the Israelites returned to Ai and killed those who were in it. ²⁵Twelve thousand men and women fell that day—all the people of Ai.[l] ²⁶For Joshua did not draw back the hand that held out his javelin[m] until he had destroyed[x][n] all who lived in Ai.[o] ²⁷But Israel did carry off for themselves the livestock and plunder of this city, as the LORD had instructed Joshua.[p]

²⁸So Joshua burned[q] Ai[r] and made it a permanent heap of ruins,[s] a desolate place to this day.[t] ²⁹He hung the king of Ai on a tree and left him there until evening. At sunset,[u] Joshua ordered them to take his body from the tree and throw it down at the entrance of the city gate. And they raised a large pile of rocks[v] over it, which remains to this day.

The Covenant Renewed at Mount Ebal

³⁰Then Joshua built on Mount Ebal[w] an altar[x] to the LORD, the God of Israel, ³¹as Moses the servant of the LORD had commanded the Israelites. He built it according to what is written in the Book of the Law of Moses—an altar of uncut stones, on which no iron tool[y] had been used. On it they offered to the LORD burnt offerings and sacrificed fellowship offerings.[y][z] ³²There, in the presence of the Israelites, Joshua copied on stones the law of Moses, which he had written.[a] ³³All Israel, aliens and citizens[b] alike, with their elders, officials and judges, were standing on both sides of the ark of the covenant of the LORD, facing those who carried it—the priests, who were Levites.[c] Half of the people stood in front of Mount Gerizim and half of them in front of Mount Ebal,[d] as Moses the servant of the LORD had formerly commanded when he gave instructions to bless the people of Israel.

³⁴Afterward, Joshua read all the words of the law—the blessings and the curses—just as it is written in the Book of the Law.[e] ³⁵There was not a word of all that Moses had commanded that Joshua did not read to the whole assembly of Israel, including the women and children, and the aliens who lived among them.[f]

The Gibeonite Deception

9 Now when all the kings west of the Jordan heard about these things—those in the hill country,[g] in the western foothills, and along the entire coast of the Great Sea[zh] as far as Lebanon[i] (the kings of the Hittites, Amorites, Canaanites, Perizzites,[j] Hivites[k] and Jebusites)[l]— ²they came together to make war against Joshua and Israel.

³However, when the people of Gibeon[m] heard what Joshua had done to Jericho and Ai,[n] ⁴they resorted to a ruse: They went as a delegation whose donkeys were loaded[a] with worn-out sacks and old wineskins, cracked and mended. ⁵The men put worn and patched sandals on their feet and wore old clothes. All the bread of their food supply was dry and moldy. ⁶Then they went to Joshua in the camp at Gilgal[o] and said to him and the men of Israel, "We have come from a distant country;[p] make a treaty[q] with us."

⁷The men of Israel said to the Hivites,[r] "But perhaps you live near us. How then can we make a treaty[s] with you?"

⁸"We are your servants,[t]" they said to Joshua.

But Joshua asked, "Who are you and where do you come from?"

⁹They answered: "Your servants have come from a very distant country[u] because of the fame of the LORD your God. For we have heard reports[v] of him: all that he did in Egypt,[w] ¹⁰and all that he did to the two kings of the Amorites east of the Jordan—Sihon king of Heshbon,[x] and Og king of Bashan,[y] who reigned in Ashtaroth.[z] ¹¹And our elders and all those living in our country said to us, 'Take provisions for your journey; go and meet them and say to them, "We are your servants; make a treaty with us."' ¹²This bread of ours was warm when we packed it at home on the day we left to come to you. But now see how dry and moldy it is. ¹³And these wineskins that we filled were new, but see how cracked they are. And our clothes and sandals are worn out by the very long journey."

¹⁴The men of Israel sampled their provisions but did not inquire[a] of the LORD.

---

x 26 The Hebrew term refers to the irrevocable giving over of things or persons to the LORD, often by totally destroying them. *y 31* Traditionally *peace offerings* *z 1* That is, the Mediterranean *a 4* Most Hebrew manuscripts; some Hebrew manuscripts, Vulgate and Syriac (see also Septuagint) *They prepared provisions and loaded their donkeys*

¹⁵Then Joshua made a treaty of peace with them to let them live, and the leaders of the assembly ratified it by oath.

¹⁶Three days after they made the treaty with the Gibeonites, the Israelites heard that they were neighbors, living near them. ¹⁷So the Israelites set out and on the third day came to their cities: Gibeon, Kephirah, Beeroth and Kiriath Jearim. ¹⁸But the Israelites did not attack them, because the leaders of the assembly had sworn an oath to them by the LORD, the God of Israel.

The whole assembly grumbled against the leaders, ¹⁹but all the leaders answered, "We have given them our oath by the LORD, the God of Israel, and we cannot touch them now. ²⁰This is what we will do to them: We will let them live, so that wrath will not fall on us for breaking the oath we swore to them." ²¹They continued, "Let them live, but let them be woodcutters and water carriers for the entire community." So the leaders' promise to them was kept.

²²Then Joshua summoned the Gibeonites and said, "Why did you deceive us by saying, 'We live a long way from you,' while actually you live near us? ²³You are now under a curse: You will never cease to serve as woodcutters and water carriers for the house of my God."

²⁴They answered Joshua, "Your servants were clearly told how the LORD your God had commanded his servant Moses to give you the whole land and to wipe out all its inhabitants from before you. So we feared for our lives because of you, and that is why we did this. ²⁵We are now in your hands. Do to us whatever seems good and right to you."

²⁶So Joshua saved them from the Israelites, and they did not kill them. ²⁷That day he made the Gibeonites woodcutters and water carriers for the community and for the altar of the LORD at the place the LORD would choose. And that is what they are to this day.

The Sun Stands Still

10 Now Adoni-Zedek king of Jerusalem heard that Joshua had taken Ai and totally destroyed it, doing to Ai and its king as he had done to Jericho and its king, and that the people of Gibeon had made a treaty of peace with Israel and were living near them. ²He and his people were very much alarmed at this, because Gibeon was an important city, like one of the royal cities; it was larger than Ai, and all its men were good fighters. ³So Adoni-Zedek king of Jerusalem appealed to Hoham king of Hebron, Piram king of Jarmuth, Japhia king of Lachish and Debir king of Eglon. ⁴"Come up and help me attack Gibeon," he said, "because it has made peace with Joshua and the Israelites."

⁵Then the five kings of the Amorites—the kings of Jerusalem, Hebron, Jarmuth, Lachish and Eglon—joined forces. They moved up with all their troops and took up positions against Gibeon and attacked it.

⁶The Gibeonites then sent word to Joshua in the camp at Gilgal: "Do not abandon your servants. Come up to us quickly and save us! Help us, because all the Amorite kings from the hill country have joined forces against us."

⁷So Joshua marched up from Gilgal with his entire army, including all the best fighting men. ⁸The LORD said to Joshua, "Do not be afraid of them; I have given them into your hand. Not one of them will be able to withstand you."

⁹After an all-night march from Gilgal, Joshua took them by surprise. ¹⁰The LORD threw them into confusion before Israel, who defeated them in a great victory at Gibeon. Israel pursued them along the road going up to Beth Horon and cut them down all the way to Azekah and Makkedah. ¹¹As they fled before Israel on the road down from Beth Horon to Azekah, the LORD hurled large hailstones down on them from the sky, and more of them died from the hailstones than were killed by the swords of the Israelites.

b 1 The Hebrew term refers to the irrevocable giving over of things or persons to the LORD, often by totally destroying them; also in verses 28, 35, 37, 39 and 40.

¹²On the day the LORD gave the Amorites over to Israel, Joshua said to the LORD in the presence of Israel:

"O sun, stand still over Gibeon,
O moon, over the Valley of Aijalon."

¹³So the sun stood still, and the moon stopped, till the nation avenged itself on its enemies,

as it is written in the Book of Jashar. The sun stopped in the middle of the sky and delayed going down about a full day. ¹⁴There has never been a day like it before or since, a day when the LORD listened to a man. Surely the LORD was fighting for Israel!

¹⁵Then Joshua returned with all Israel to the camp at Gilgal.

Five Amorite Kings Killed

¹⁶Now the five kings had fled and hidden in the cave at Makkedah. ¹⁷When Joshua was told that the five kings had been found hiding in the cave at Makkedah, ¹⁸he said, "Roll large rocks up to the mouth of the cave, and post some men there to guard it. ¹⁹But don't stop! Pursue your enemies, attack them from the rear and don't let them reach their cities, for the LORD your God has given them into your hand."

²⁰So Joshua and the Israelites destroyed them completely—almost to a man—but the few who were left reached their fortified cities. ²¹The whole army then returned safely to Joshua in the camp at Makkedah, and no one uttered a word against the Israelites.

²²Joshua said, "Open the mouth of the cave and bring those five kings out to me." ²³So they brought the five kings out of the cave—the kings of Jerusalem, Hebron, Jarmuth, Lachish and Eglon. ²⁴When they had brought these kings to Joshua, he summoned all the men of Israel and said to the army commanders who had come with him, "Come here and put your feet on the necks of these kings." So they came forward and placed their feet on their necks.

²⁵Joshua said to them, "Do not be afraid; do not be discouraged. Be strong and courageous. This is what the LORD will do to all the enemies you are going to fight." ²⁶Then Joshua struck and killed the kings and hung them on five trees, and they were left hanging on the trees until evening.

²⁷At sunset Joshua gave the order and they took them down from the trees and threw them into the cave where they had been hiding. At the mouth of the cave they placed large rocks, which are there to this day.

²⁸That day Joshua took Makkedah. He put the city and its king to the sword and totally destroyed everyone in it. He left no survivors. And he did to the king of Makkedah as he had done to the king of Jericho.

Southern Cities Conquered

²⁹Then Joshua and all Israel with him moved on from Makkedah to Libnah and attacked it. ³⁰The LORD also gave that city and its king into Israel's hand. The city and everyone in it Joshua put to the sword. He left no survivors there. And he did to its king as he had done to the king of Jericho.

³¹Then Joshua and all Israel with him moved on from Libnah to Lachish; he took up positions against it and attacked it. ³²The LORD handed Lachish over to Israel, and Joshua took it on the second day. The city and everyone in it he put to the sword, just as he had done to Libnah. ³³Meanwhile, Horam king of Gezer had come up to help Lachish, but Joshua defeated him and his army—until no survivors were left.

c 13 Or nation triumphed over

10:12–14 This passage records a miraculous answer to Joshua's prayer: "The sun stopped in the middle of the sky and delayed going down about a full day" (10:13). Never before or never since has there been a day like that one. Whether God slowed the rotation of the earth on its axis to lengthen the hours of daylight or whether he cooled the sun's rays for an entire day so that the fighting could continue throughout the afternoon, we cannot say. Scripture does not record how God achieved this effect. It is enough to believe the Biblical record that it happened and trust that the God who created the universe could easily have created this phenomenon to save his chosen people.

³⁴Then Joshua and all Israel with him moved on from Lachish to Eglon;ᑫ they took up positions against it and attacked it. ³⁵They captured it that same day and put it to the sword and totally destroyed everyone in it, just as they had done to Lachish.

³⁶Then Joshua and all Israel with him went up from Eglon to Hebronʳ and attacked it. ³⁷They took the city and put it to the sword, together with its king, its villages and everyoneˢ in it. They left no survivors. Just as at Eglon, they totally destroyed it and everyone in it.

³⁸Then Joshua and all Israel with him turned around and attacked Debir.ᵗ ³⁹They took the city, its king and its villages, and put them to the sword. Everyone in it they totally destroyed. They left no survivors. They did to Debir and its king as they had done to Libnah and its king and to Hebron.ᵘ

⁴⁰So Joshua subdued the whole region, including the hill country, the Negev,ᵛ the western foothills and the mountain slopes,ʷ together with all their kings.ˣ He left no survivors. He totally destroyed all who breathed, just as the LORD, the God of Israel, had commanded.ʸ ⁴¹Joshua subdued them from Kadesh Barneaᶻ to Gazaᵃ and from the whole region of Goshenᵇ to Gibeon. ⁴²All these kings and their lands Joshua conquered in one campaign, because the LORD, the God of Israel, foughtᶜ for Israel.

⁴³Then Joshua returned with all Israel to the camp at Gilgal.ᵈ

Northern Kings Defeated

11 When Jabinᵉ king of Hazorᶠ heard of this, he sent word to Jobab king of Madon, to the kings of Shimronᵍ and Acshaph,ʰ ²and to the northern kings who were in the mountains, in the Arabahⁱ south of Kinnereth,ʲ in the western foothills and in Naphoth Dorᵈᵏ on the west; ³to the Canaanites in the east and west; to the Amorites, Hittites, Perizzitesˡ and Jebusites in the hill country;ᵐ and to the Hivitesⁿ below Hermonᵒ in the region of Mizpah.ᵖ ⁴They came out with all their troops and a large number of horses and chariots—a huge army, as numerous as the sand on the seashore.ᑫ ⁵All these kings joined forcesʳ and made camp together at the Waters of Merom,ˢ to fight against Israel.

⁶The LORD said to Joshua, "Do not be afraid of them, because by this time tomorrow I will hand all of them overᵗ to Israel, slain. You are to hamstringᵘ their horses and burn their chariots."ᵛ

⁷So Joshua and his whole army came against them suddenly at the Waters of Merom and attacked them, ⁸and the LORD gave them into the hand of Israel. They defeated them and pursued them all the way to Greater Sidon,ʷ to Misrephoth Maim,ˣ and to the Valley of Mizpah on the east, until no survivors were left. ⁹Joshua did to them as the LORD had directed: He hamstrung their horses and burned their chariots.

¹⁰At that time Joshua turned back and captured Hazor and put its king to the sword.ʸ (Hazor had been the head of all these kingdoms.) ¹¹Everyone in it they put to the sword. They totally destroyedᵉ them,ᶻ not sparing anything that breathed,ᵃ and he burned upᵇ Hazor itself.

¹²Joshua took all these royal cities and their kings and put them to the sword. He totally destroyed them, as Moses the servant of the LORD had commanded.ᶜ ¹³Yet Israel did not burn any of the cities built on their mounds—except Hazor, which Joshua burned. ¹⁴The Israelites carried off for themselves all the plunder and livestock of these cities, but all the people they put to the sword until they completely destroyed them, not sparing anyone that breathed.ᵈ ¹⁵As the LORD commanded his servant Moses, so Moses commanded Joshua, and Joshua did it; he left nothing undone of all that the LORD commanded Moses.ᵉ

¹⁶So Joshua took this entire land: the hill country,ᶠ all the Negev,ᵍ the whole region of Goshen, the western foothills,ʰ the Arabah and the mountains of Israel with their foothills, ¹⁷from Mount Halak, which rises toward Seir,ⁱ to Baal Gadʲ in the Valley of Lebanonᵏ below Mount Hermon.ˡ He captured all their kings and struck them down, putting them to death.ᵐ ¹⁸Joshua waged war against all these kings for a long time. ¹⁹Except for the Hivitesⁿ living in Gibeon,ᵒ not one

Jos 10:19 ◄ ► Jos 17:18

ᵈ 2 Or *in the heights of Dor* ᵉ 11 The Hebrew term refers to the irrevocable giving over of things or persons to the LORD, often by totally destroying them; also in verses 12, 20 and 21.

city made a treaty of peace[p] with the Israelites, who took them all in battle. [20]For it was the LORD himself who hardened their hearts[q] to wage war against Israel, so that he might destroy them totally, exterminating them without mercy, as the LORD had commanded Moses.[r]

[21]At that time Joshua went and destroyed the Anakites[s] from the hill country: from Hebron, Debir[t] and Anab,[u] from all the hill country of Judah, and from all the hill country of Israel. Joshua totally destroyed them and their towns. [22]No Anakites were left in Israelite territory; only in Gaza,[v] Gath[w] and Ashdod[x] did any survive. [23]So Joshua took the entire land,[y] just as the LORD had directed Moses, and he gave it as an inheritance[z] to Israel according to their tribal divisions.[a][b]

Then the land had rest[c] from war.[d]

List of Defeated Kings

12 These are the kings of the land whom the Israelites had defeated and whose territory they took[e] over east of the Jordan,[f] from the Arnon[g] Gorge to Mount Hermon,[h] including all the eastern side of the Arabah:[i]

[2]Sihon king of the Amorites,
who reigned in Heshbon.[j] He ruled from Aroer[k] on the rim of the Arnon Gorge—from the middle of the gorge—to the Jabbok River,[l] which is the border of the Ammonites.[m] This included half of Gilead.[n] [3]He also ruled over the eastern Arabah from the Sea of Kinnereth[o] to the Sea of the Arabah (the Salt Sea[g][p]), to Beth Jeshimoth,[q] and then southward below the slopes of Pisgah.[r]

[4]And the territory of Og king of Bashan,[s] one of the last of the Rephaites,[t] who reigned in Ashtaroth[u] and Edrei. [5]He ruled over Mount Hermon, Salecah,[v] all of Bashan[w] to the border of the people of Geshur[x] and Maacah,[y] and half of Gilead[z] to the border of Sihon king of Heshbon.

[6]Moses, the servant of the LORD, and the Israelites conquered them.[a] And Moses the servant of the LORD gave their land to the Reubenites, the Gadites and the half-tribe of Manasseh to be their possession.[b]

[7]These are the kings of the land that Joshua and the Israelites conquered on the west side of the Jordan, from Baal Gad in the Valley of Lebanon[c] to Mount Halak, which rises toward Seir (their lands Joshua gave as an inheritance to the tribes of Israel according to their tribal divisions— [8]the hill country, the western foothills, the Arabah, the mountain slopes, the desert and the Negev[d]—the lands of the Hittites, Amorites, Canaanites, Perizzites, Hivites and Jebusites):[e]

[9]the king of Jericho[f]	one
the king of Ai[g] (near Bethel[h])	one
[10]the king of Jerusalem[i]	one
the king of Hebron	one
[11]the king of Jarmuth	one
the king of Lachish[j]	one
[12]the king of Eglon[k]	one
the king of Gezer[l]	one
[13]the king of Debir[m]	one
the king of Geder	one
[14]the king of Hormah[n]	one
the king of Arad[o]	one
[15]the king of Libnah[p]	one
the king of Adullam[q]	one
[16]the king of Makkedah[r]	one
the king of Bethel[s]	one
[17]the king of Tappuah[t]	one
the king of Hepher[u]	one
[18]the king of Aphek[v]	one
the king of Lasharon	one
[19]the king of Madon	one
the king of Hazor[w]	one
[20]the king of Shimron Meron	one
the king of Acshaph[x]	one
[21]the king of Taanach[y]	one
the king of Megiddo[z]	one
[22]the king of Kedesh[a]	one
the king of Jokneam[b] in Carmel[c]	one
[23]the king of Dor (in Naphoth Dor[h][d])	one
the king of Goyim in Gilgal	one
[24]the king of Tirzah[e]	one

thirty-one kings in all.[f]

f 3 That is, Galilee   g 3 That is, the Dead Sea   h 23 Or in the heights of Dor

Land Still to Be Taken

13 When Joshua was old and well advanced in years,[g] the LORD said to him, "You are very old, and there are still very large areas of land to be taken over.

²"This is the land that remains: all the regions of the Philistines[h] and Geshurites:[i] ³from the Shihor River[j] on the east of Egypt to the territory of Ekron[k] on the north, all of it counted as Canaanite (the territory of the five Philistine rulers[l] in Gaza, Ashdod,[m] Ashkelon,[n] Gath and Ekron—that of the Avvites);[o] ⁴from the south, all the land of the Canaanites, from Arah of the Sidonians as far as Aphek,[p] the region of the Amorites,[q] ⁵the area of the Gebalites[i];[r] and all Lebanon[s] to the east, from Baal Gad below Mount Hermon[t] to Lebo[j] Hamath.[u]

⁶"As for all the inhabitants of the mountain regions from Lebanon to Misrephoth Maim,[v] that is, all the Sidonians, I myself will drive them out[w] before the Israelites. Be sure to allocate this land to Israel for an inheritance, as I have instructed you,[x] ⁷and divide it as an inheritance[y] among the nine tribes and half of the tribe of Manasseh."

Division of the Land East of the Jordan

⁸The other half of Manasseh,[k] the Reubenites and the Gadites had received the inheritance that Moses had given them east of the Jordan, as he, the servant of the LORD, had assigned[z] it to them.[a]

⁹It extended from Aroer[b] on the rim of the Arnon Gorge, and from the town in the middle of the gorge, and included the whole plateau[c] of Medeba as far as Dibon,[d] ¹⁰and all the towns of Sihon king of the Amorites, who ruled in Heshbon,[e] out to the border of the Ammonites.[f] ¹¹It also included Gilead,[g] the territory of the people of Geshur and Maacah, all of Mount Hermon and all Bashan as far as Salecah[h]— ¹²that is, the whole kingdom of Og in Bashan,[i] who had reigned in Ashtaroth[j] and Edrei[k] and had survived as one of the last of the Rephaites.[l] Moses had defeated them and taken over their land.[m]

¹³But the Israelites did not drive out the people of Geshur[n] and Maacah,[o] so they continue to live among the Israelites to this day.[p]

¹⁴But to the tribe of Levi he gave no inheritance, since the offerings made by fire to the LORD, the God of Israel, are their inheritance, as he promised them.[q]

¹⁵This is what Moses had given to the tribe of Reuben, clan by clan:

¹⁶The territory from Aroer[r] on the rim of the Arnon Gorge, and from the town in the middle of the gorge, and the whole plateau past Medeba[s] ¹⁷to Heshbon and all its towns on the plateau,[t] including Dibon,[u] Bamoth Baal,[v] Beth Baal Meon,[w] ¹⁸Jahaz,[x] Kedemoth,[y] Mephaath,[z] ¹⁹Kiriathaim,[a] Sibmah,[b] Zereth Shahar on the hill in the valley, ²⁰Beth Peor,[c] the slopes of Pisgah, and Beth Jeshimoth ²¹—all the towns on the plateau[d] and the entire realm of Sihon king of the Amorites, who ruled at Heshbon. Moses had defeated him and the Midianite chiefs,[e] Evi, Rekem, Zur, Hur and Reba[f]—princes allied with Sihon—who lived in that country. ²²In addition to those slain in battle, the Israelites had put to the sword Balaam son of Beor,[g] who practiced divination.[h] ²³The boundary of the Reubenites was the bank of the Jordan. These towns and their villages were the inheritance of the Reubenites, clan by clan.[i]

²⁴This is what Moses had given to the tribe of Gad, clan by clan:

²⁵The territory of Jazer,[j] all the towns of Gilead[k] and half the Ammonite country as far as Aroer, near Rabbah;[l] ²⁶and from Heshbon[m] to Ramath Mizpah and Betonim, and from Mahanaim[n] to the territory of Debir;[o] ²⁷and in the valley, Beth Haram, Beth Nimrah,[p] Succoth[q] and Zaphon[r] with the rest of the realm of Sihon king of Heshbon (the east side of the Jordan, the territory up to the

---

i 5 That is, the area of Byblos j 5 Or to the entrance to k 8 Hebrew With it (that is, with the other half of Manasseh)

end of the Sea of Kinnereth. ²⁸These towns and their villages were the inheritance of the Gadites, clan by clan.

²⁹This is what Moses had given to the half-tribe of Manasseh, that is, to half the family of the descendants of Manasseh, clan by clan:

³⁰The territory extending from Mahanaim and including all of Bashan, the entire realm of Og king of Bashan—all the settlements of Jair in Bashan, sixty towns, ³¹half of Gilead, and Ashtaroth and Edrei (the royal cities of Og in Bashan). This was for the descendants of Makir son of Manasseh—for half of the sons of Makir, clan by clan.

³²This is the inheritance Moses had given when he was in the plains of Moab across the Jordan east of Jericho. ³³But to the tribe of Levi, Moses had given no inheritance; the LORD, the God of Israel, is their inheritance, as he promised them.

Division of the Land West of the Jordan

14 Now these are the areas the Israelites received as an inheritance in the land of Canaan, which Eleazar the priest, Joshua son of Nun and the heads of the tribal clans of Israel allotted to them. ²Their inheritances were assigned by lot to the nine-and-a-half tribes, as the LORD had commanded through Moses. ³Moses had granted the two-and-a-half tribes their inheritance east of the Jordan but had not granted the Levites an inheritance among the rest, ⁴for the sons of Joseph had become two tribes—Manasseh and Ephraim. The Levites received no share of the land but only towns to live in, with pasturelands for their flocks and herds. ⁵So the Israelites divided the land, just as the LORD had commanded Moses.

Hebron Given to Caleb

⁶Now the men of Judah approached Joshua at Gilgal, and Caleb son of Jephunneh the Kenizzite said to him, "You know what the LORD said to Moses the man of God at Kadesh Barnea about you and me. ⁷I was forty years old when Moses the servant of the LORD sent me from Kadesh Barnea to explore the land. And I brought him back a report according to my convictions, ⁸but my brothers who went up with me made the hearts of the people melt with fear. I, however, followed the LORD my God wholeheartedly. ⁹So on that day Moses swore to me, 'The land on which your feet have walked will be your inheritance and that of your children forever, because you have followed the LORD my God wholeheartedly.'

¹⁰"Now then, just as the LORD promised, he has kept me alive for forty-five years since the time he said this to Moses, while Israel moved about in the desert. So here I am today, eighty-five years old! ¹¹I am still as strong today as the day Moses sent me out; I'm just as vigorous to go out to battle now as I was then. ¹²Now give me this hill country that the LORD promised me that day. You yourself heard then that the Anakites were there and their cities were large and fortified, but, the LORD helping me, I will drive them out just as he said."

¹³Then Joshua blessed Caleb son of Jephunneh and gave him Hebron as his inheritance. ¹⁴So Hebron has belonged to Caleb son of Jephunneh the Kenizzite ever since, because he followed the LORD, the God of Israel, wholeheartedly. ¹⁵(Hebron used to be called Kiriath Arba after Arba, who was the greatest man among the Anakites.)

Then the land had rest from war.

Allotment for Judah

15:15–19pp — Jdg 1:11–15

15 The allotment for the tribe of Judah, clan by clan, extended down to the territory of Edom, to the Desert of Zin in the extreme south.

²Their southern boundary started from the bay at the southern end of the Salt Sea, ³crossed south of Scorpion Pass, continued on to Zin and went over to the south of Kadesh Barnea. Then it ran past Hezron up to Addar and curved around to Karka. ⁴It then passed along to Azmon and joined the Wadi of Egypt, ending at the sea. This is their southern boundary.

⁵The eastern boundary^c is the Salt Sea^d as far as the mouth of the Jordan.

The northern boundary^e started from the bay of the sea at the mouth of the Jordan, ⁶went up to Beth Hoglah^f and continued north of Beth Arabah^g to the Stone of Bohan^h son of Reuben. ⁷The boundary then went up to Debirⁱ from the Valley of Achor^j and turned north to Gilgal,^k which faces the Pass of Adummim south of the gorge. It continued along to the waters of En Shemesh^l and came out at En Rogel.^m ⁸Then it ran up the Valley of Ben Hinnomⁿ along the southern slope of the Jebusite^o city (that is, Jerusalem^p). From there it climbed to the top of the hill west of the Hinnom Valley^q at the northern end of the Valley of Rephaim.^r ⁹From the hilltop the boundary headed toward the spring of the waters of Nephtoah,^s came out at the towns of Mount Ephron and went down toward Baalah^t (that is, Kiriath Jearim).^u ¹⁰Then it curved westward from Baalah^v to Mount Seir,^w ran along the northern slope of Mount Jearim (that is, Kesalon), continued down to Beth Shemesh^x and crossed to Timnah.^y ¹¹It went to the northern slope of Ekron,^z turned toward Shikkeron, passed along to Mount Baalah^a and reached Jabneel.^b The boundary ended at the sea.

¹²The western boundary is the coastline of the Great Sea.^{qc} These are the boundaries around the people of Judah by their clans.

¹³In accordance with the LORD's command to him, Joshua gave to Caleb^d son of Jephunneh a portion in Judah—Kiriath Arba^e, that is, Hebron.^f (Arba was the forefather of Anak.)^g ¹⁴From Hebron Caleb drove out the three Anakites^h—Sheshai, Ahiman and Talmaiⁱ—descendants of Anak.^j ¹⁵From there he marched against the people living in Debir (formerly called Kiriath Sepher). ¹⁶And Caleb said, "I will give my daughter Acsah^k in marriage to the man who attacks and captures Kiriath Sepher." ¹⁷Othniel^l son of Kenaz, Caleb's brother, took it; so Caleb gave his daughter Acsah to him in marriage.

¹⁸One day when she came to Othniel, she urged him^r to ask her father for a field. When she got off her donkey, Caleb asked her, "What can I do for you?"

¹⁹She replied, "Do me a special favor. Since you have given me land in the Negev,^m give me also springs of water." So Caleb gave her the upper and lower springs.ⁿ

²⁰This is the inheritance of the tribe of Judah, clan by clan:

²¹The southernmost towns of the tribe of Judah in the Negev^o toward the boundary of Edom were:

Kabzeel,^p Eder,^q Jagur, ²²Kinah, Dimonah, Adadah, ²³Kedesh,^r Hazor,^s Ithnan, ²⁴Ziph,^t Telem, Bealoth, ²⁵Hazor Hadattah, Kerioth Hezron (that is, Hazor),^u ²⁶Amam, Shema, Moladah,^v ²⁷Hazar Gaddah, Heshmon, Beth Pelet, ²⁸Hazar Shual,^w Beersheba,^x Biziothiah, ²⁹Baalah,^y Iim, Ezem,^z ³⁰Eltolad,^a Kesil, Hormah,^b ³¹Ziklag,^c Madmannah,^d Sansannah, ³²Lebaoth, Shilhim, Ain^e and Rimmon^f—a total of twenty-nine towns and their villages.

³³In the western foothills:

Eshtaol,^g Zorah,^h Ashnah,ⁱ ³⁴Zanoah,^j En Gannim,^k Tappuah,^l Enam, ³⁵Jarmuth,^m Adullam,ⁿ Socoh,^o Azekah,^p ³⁶Shaaraim,^q Adithaim and Gederah^r (or Gederothaim)^s—fourteen towns and their villages.

³⁷Zenan, Hadashah, Migdal Gad, ³⁸Dilean, Mizpah,^s Joktheel,^t ³⁹Lachish,^u Bozkath,^v Eglon,^w ⁴⁰Cabbon, Lahmas, Kitlish, ⁴¹Gederoth,^x Beth Dagon,^y Naamah and Makkedah^z—sixteen towns and their villages.

⁴²Libnah,^a Ether, Ashan,^b ⁴³Iphtah, Ashnah,^c Nezib, ⁴⁴Keilah,^d Ac-

^q12 That is, the Mediterranean; also in verse 47 ^r18 Hebrew and some Septuagint manuscripts; other Septuagint manuscripts (see also note at Judges 1:14) *Othniel, he urged her* ^s36 Or *Gederah and Gederothaim*

zib[e] and Mareshah[f]—nine towns and their villages.

⁴⁵Ekron,[g] with its surrounding settlements and villages; ⁴⁶west of Ekron, all that were in the vicinity of Ashdod,[h] together with their villages; ⁴⁷Ashdod,[i] its surrounding settlements and villages; and Gaza, its settlements and villages, as far as the Wadi of Egypt[j] and the coastline of the Great Sea.[k]

⁴⁸In the hill country:
Shamir,[l] Jattir,[m] Socoh,[n] ⁴⁹Dannah, Kiriath Sannah (that is, Debir[o]), ⁵⁰Anab,[p] Eshtemoh,[q] Anim, ⁵¹Goshen,[r] Holon[s] and Giloh[t]—eleven towns and their villages.

⁵²Arab, Dumah,[u] Eshan, ⁵³Janim, Beth Tappuah, Aphekah, ⁵⁴Humtah, Kiriath Arba[v] (that is, Hebron) and Zior—nine towns and their villages.

⁵⁵Maon,[w] Carmel,[x] Ziph,[y] Juttah,[z] ⁵⁶Jezreel,[a] Jokdeam, Zanoah,[b] ⁵⁷Kain, Gibeah[c] and Timnah[d]—ten towns and their villages.

⁵⁸Halhul, Beth Zur,[e] Gedor,[f] ⁵⁹Maarath, Beth Anoth and Eltekon—six towns and their villages.

⁶⁰Kiriath Baal[g] (that is, Kiriath Jearim[h]) and Rabbah[i]—two towns and their villages.

⁶¹In the desert:[j]
Beth Arabah,[k] Middin, Secacah, ⁶²Nibshan, the City of Salt and En Gedi[l]—six towns and their villages.

⁶³Judah could not[m] dislodge the Jebusites,[n] who were living in Jerusalem;[o] to this day the Jebusites live there with the people of Judah.[p]

Allotment for Ephraim and Manasseh

16 The allotment for Joseph began at the Jordan of Jericho,[ʳ] east of the waters of Jericho, and went up from there through the desert[q] into the hill country of Bethel.[r] ²It went on from Bethel (that is, Luz[s]),[u] crossed over to the territory of the Arkites[t] in Ataroth,[u] ³descended westward to the territory of the Japhletites as far as the region of Lower Beth Horon[v] and on to Gezer,[w] ending at the sea.

⁴So Manasseh and Ephraim, the descendants of Joseph, received their inheritance.[x]

⁵This was the territory of Ephraim, clan by clan:

The boundary of their inheritance went from Ataroth Addar[y] in the east to Upper Beth Horon[z] ⁶and continued to the sea. From Micmethath[a] on the north it curved eastward to Taanath Shiloh, passing by it to Janoah[b] on the east. ⁷Then it went down from Janoah[c] to Ataroth[d] and Naarah, touched Jericho and came out at the Jordan. ⁸From Tappuah[e] the border went west to the Kanah Ravine[f] and ended at the sea. This was the inheritance of the tribe of the Ephraimites, clan by clan. ⁹It also included all the towns and their villages that were set aside for the Ephraimites within the inheritance of the Manassites.[g]

¹⁰They did not dislodge the Canaanites living in Gezer; to this day the Canaanites live among the people of Ephraim but are required to do forced labor.[h]

17 This was the allotment for the tribe of Manasseh[i] as Joseph's firstborn,[j] that is, for Makir,[k] Manasseh's firstborn. Makir was the ancestor of the Gileadites, who had received Gilead[l] and Bashan[m] because the Makirites were great soldiers. ²So this allotment was for the rest of the people of Manasseh[n]—the clans of Abiezer,[o] Helek, Asriel,[p] Shechem, Hepher[q] and Shemida.[r] These are the other male descendants of Manasseh son of Joseph by their clans.

³Now Zelophehad son of Hepher,[s] the son of Gilead, the son of Makir, the son of Manasseh, had no sons but only daughters,[t] whose names were Mahlah, Noah, Hoglah, Milcah and Tirzah. ⁴They went to Eleazar the priest, Joshua son of Nun, and the leaders and said, "The LORD commanded Moses to give us an inheritance among our brothers." So Joshua gave them an inheritance along with the brothers of their father, according to the LORD's command.[u] ⁵Manasseh's share consisted of ten tracts of land besides Gilead and Bashan east of the Jordan,[v] ⁶because the daughters of the tribe of Manasseh received an inheritance among the

---

p 1Ch 7:14 q S Nu 27:1 r 1Ch 7:19 **17:3** s S Nu 27:1 t S Nu 26:33
17:4 u Nu 27:5-7 **17:5** v Jos 13:30-31

t 1 Jordan of Jericho was possibly an ancient name for the Jordan River.
u 2 Septuagint; Hebrew Bethel to Luz

sons. The land of Gilead belonged to the rest of the descendants of Manasseh.

⁷The territory of Manasseh extended from Asher to Micmethath east of Shechem. The boundary ran southward from there to include the people living at En Tappuah. ⁸(Manasseh had the land of Tappuah, but Tappuah itself, on the boundary of Manasseh, belonged to the Ephraimites.) ⁹Then the boundary continued south to the Kanah Ravine. There were towns belonging to Ephraim lying among the towns of Manasseh, but the boundary of Manasseh was the northern side of the ravine and ended at the sea. ¹⁰On the south the land belonged to Ephraim, on the north to Manasseh. The territory of Manasseh reached the sea and bordered Asher on the north and Issachar on the east.

¹¹Within Issachar and Asher, Manasseh also had Beth Shan, Ibleam and the people of Dor, Endor, Taanach and Megiddo, together with their surrounding settlements (the third in the list is Naphoth).

¹²Yet the Manassites were not able to occupy these towns, for the Canaanites were determined to live in that region. ¹³However, when the Israelites grew stronger, they subjected the Canaanites to forced labor but did not drive them out completely.

¹⁴The people of Joseph said to Joshua, "Why have you given us only one allotment and one portion for an inheritance? We are a numerous people and the LORD has blessed us abundantly."

¹⁵"If you are so numerous," Joshua answered, "and if the hill country of Ephraim is too small for you, go up into the forest and clear land for yourselves there in the land of the Perizzites and Rephaites."

¹⁶The people of Joseph replied, "The hill country is not enough for us, and all the Canaanites who live in the plain have iron chariots, both those in Beth Shan and its settlements and those in the Valley of Jezreel."

¹⁷But Joshua said to the house of Joseph—to Ephraim and Manasseh—"You are numerous and very powerful. You will have not only one allotment ¹⁸but the forested hill country as well. Clear it, and its farthest limits will be yours; though the Canaanites have iron chariots and though they are strong, you can drive them out."

Division of the Rest of the Land

18 The whole assembly of the Israelites gathered at Shiloh and set up the Tent of Meeting there. The country was brought under their control, ²but there were still seven Israelite tribes who had not yet received their inheritance.

³So Joshua said to the Israelites: "How long will you wait before you begin to take possession of the land that the LORD, the God of your fathers, has given you? ⁴Appoint three men from each tribe. I will send them out to make a survey of the land and to write a description of it, according to the inheritance of each. Then they will return to me. ⁵You are to divide the land into seven parts. Judah is to remain in its territory on the south and the house of Joseph in its territory on the north. ⁶After you have written descriptions of the seven parts of the land, bring them here to me and I will cast lots for you in the presence of the LORD our God. ⁷The Levites, however, do not get a portion among you, because the priestly service of the LORD is their inheritance. And Gad, Reuben and the half-tribe of Manasseh have already received their inheritance on the east side of the Jordan. Moses the servant of the LORD gave it to them."

⁸As the men started on their way to map out the land, Joshua instructed them, "Go and make a survey of the land and write a description of it. Then return to me, and I will cast lots for you here at Shiloh in the presence of the LORD." ⁹So the men left and went through the land. They wrote its description on a scroll, town by town, in seven parts, and returned to Joshua in the camp at Shiloh. ¹⁰Joshua then cast lots for them in Shiloh in the presence of the LORD, and there he distributed the land to the Israelites according to their tribal divisions.

◀ *Jos 11:6* ◀ ▶ *Jdg 1:2*

v 11 That is, Naphoth Dor

Allotment for Benjamin

[11] The lot came up for the tribe of Benjamin, clan by clan. Their allotted territory lay between the tribes of Judah and Joseph:

[12] On the north side their boundary began at the Jordan, passed the northern slope of Jericho and headed west into the hill country, coming out at the desert[m] of Beth Aven.[n] [13] From there it crossed to the south slope of Luz[o] (that is, Bethel[p]) and went down to Ataroth Addar[q] on the hill south of Lower Beth Horon.

[14] From the hill facing Beth Horon[r] on the south the boundary turned south along the western side and came out at Kiriath Baal (that is, Kiriath Jearim),[s] a town of the people of Judah. This was the western side.

[15] The southern side began at the outskirts of Kiriath Jearim on the west, and the boundary came out at the spring of the waters of Nephtoah.[t] [16] The boundary went down to the foot of the hill facing the Valley of Ben Hinnom, north of the Valley of Rephaim.[u] It continued down the Hinnom Valley[v] along the southern slope of the Jebusite city and so to En Rogel.[w] [17] It then curved north, went to En Shemesh, continued to Geliloth,[x] which faces the Pass of Adummim,[y] and ran down to the Stone of Bohan[z] son of Reuben. [18] It continued to the northern slope of Beth Arabah[w][a] and on down into the Arabah.[b] [19] It then went to the northern slope of Beth Hoglah[c] and came out at the northern bay of the Salt Sea,[x][d] at the mouth of the Jordan in the south. This was the southern boundary.

[20] The Jordan formed the boundary on the eastern side.

These were the boundaries that marked out the inheritance of the clans of Benjamin on all sides.[e]

[21] The tribe of Benjamin, clan by clan, had the following cities:

Jericho, Beth Hoglah,[f] Emek Keziz, [22] Beth Arabah,[g] Zemaraim,[h] Bethel,[i] [23] Avvim,[j] Parah, Ophrah,[k] [24] Kephar Ammoni, Ophni and Geba[l]—twelve towns and their villages.

[25] Gibeon,[m] Ramah,[n] Beeroth,[o] [26] Mizpah,[p] Kephirah,[q] Mozah, [27] Rekem, Irpeel, Taralah, [28] Zelah,[r] Haeleph, the Jebusite city[s] (that is, Jerusalem[t]), Gibeah[u] and Kiriath—fourteen towns and their villages.[v]

This was the inheritance of Benjamin for its clans.[w]

Allotment for Simeon

19:2-10pp — 1Ch 4:28-33

19 The second lot came out for the tribe of Simeon, clan by clan. Their inheritance lay within the territory of Judah.[x] [2] It included:

Beersheba[y] (or Sheba),[y] Moladah,[z] [3] Hazar Shual,[a] Balah, Ezem,[b] [4] Eltolad,[c] Bethul, Hormah,[d] [5] Ziklag,[e] Beth Marcaboth, Hazar Susah, [6] Beth Lebaoth and Sharuhen—thirteen towns and their villages;

[7] Ain, Rimmon,[f] Ether and Ashan[g]—four towns and their villages— [8] and all the villages around these towns as far as Baalath Beer (Ramah in the Negev).[h]

This was the inheritance of the tribe of the Simeonites, clan by clan. [9] The inheritance of the Simeonites was taken from the share of Judah,[i] because Judah's portion was more than they needed. So the Simeonites received their inheritance within the territory of Judah.[j]

Allotment for Zebulun

[10] The third lot came up for Zebulun,[k] clan by clan:

The boundary of their inheritance went as far as Sarid.[l] [11] Going west it ran to Maralah, touched Dabbesheth, and extended to the ravine near Jokneam.[m] [12] It turned east from Sarid[n] toward the sunrise to the territory of Kisloth Tabor and went on to Daberath[o] and up to Japhia. [13] Then it continued eastward to Gath Hepher[p] and Eth Kazin; it came out at Rimmon[q] and turned toward Neah. [14] There the boundary went around on the north to Hannathon and ended at the Valley of Iphtah El.[r] [15] Included were Kattath, Nahalal,[s] Shimron,[t] Idalah and

---

w 18 Septuagint; Hebrew *slope facing the Arabah* *x 19* That is, the Dead Sea *y 2* Or *Beersheba, Sheba*; 1 Chron. 4:28 does not have *Sheba*.

Bethlehem. There were twelve towns and their villages.

¹⁶These towns and their villages were the inheritance of Zebulun, clan by clan.

Allotment for Issachar

¹⁷The fourth lot came out for Issachar, clan by clan. ¹⁸Their territory included:

Jezreel, Kesulloth, Shunem, ¹⁹Hapharaim, Shion, Anaharath, ²⁰Rabbith, Kishion, Ebez, ²¹Remeth, En Gannim, En Haddah and Beth Pazzez. ²²The boundary touched Tabor, Shahazumah and Beth Shemesh, and ended at the Jordan. There were sixteen towns and their villages.

²³These towns and their villages were the inheritance of the tribe of Issachar, clan by clan.

Allotment for Asher

²⁴The fifth lot came out for the tribe of Asher, clan by clan. ²⁵Their territory included:

Helkath, Hali, Beten, Acshaph, ²⁶Allammelech, Amad and Mishal. On the west the boundary touched Carmel and Shihor Libnath. ²⁷It then turned east toward Beth Dagon, touched Zebulun and the Valley of Iphtah El, and went north to Beth Emek and Neiel, passing Cabul on the left. ²⁸It went to Abdon, Rehob, Hammon and Kanah, as far as Greater Sidon. ²⁹The boundary then turned back toward Ramah and went to the fortified city of Tyre, turned toward Hosah and came out at the sea in the region of Aczib, ³⁰Ummah, Aphek and Rehob. There were twenty-two towns and their villages.

³¹These towns and their villages were the inheritance of the tribe of Asher, clan by clan.

Allotment for Naphtali

³²The sixth lot came out for Naphtali, clan by clan:

³³Their boundary went from Heleph and the large tree in Zaanannim, passing Adami Nekeb and Jabneel to Lakkum and ending at the Jordan. ³⁴The boundary ran west through Aznoth Tabor and came out at Hukkok. It touched Zebulun on the south, Asher on the west and the Jordan on the east. ³⁵The fortified cities were Ziddim, Zer, Hammath, Rakkath, Kinnereth, ³⁶Adamah, Ramah, Hazor, ³⁷Kedesh, Edrei, En Hazor, ³⁸Iron, Migdal El, Horem, Beth Anath and Beth Shemesh. There were nineteen towns and their villages.

³⁹These towns and their villages were the inheritance of the tribe of Naphtali, clan by clan.

Allotment for Dan

⁴⁰The seventh lot came out for the tribe of Dan, clan by clan. ⁴¹The territory of their inheritance included:

Zorah, Eshtaol, Ir Shemesh, ⁴²Shaalabbin, Aijalon, Ithlah, ⁴³Elon, Timnah, Ekron, ⁴⁴Eltekeh, Gibbethon, Baalath, ⁴⁵Jehud, Bene Berak, Gath Rimmon, ⁴⁶Me Jarkon and Rakkon, with the area facing Joppa.

⁴⁷(But the Danites had difficulty taking possession of their territory, so they went up and attacked Leshem, took it, put it to the sword and occupied it. They settled in Leshem and named it Dan after their forefather.)

⁴⁸These towns and their villages were the inheritance of the tribe of Dan, clan by clan.

Allotment for Joshua

⁴⁹When they had finished dividing the land into its allotted portions, the Israelites gave Joshua son of Nun an inheritance among them, ⁵⁰as the LORD had commanded. They gave him the town he asked for—Timnath Serah*ᵇᵃ* in the hill country of Ephraim. And he built up the town and settled there.

⁵¹These are the territories that Eleazar the priest, Joshua son of Nun and the heads of the tribal clans of Israel assigned by lot at Shiloh in the presence of the LORD at the entrance to the Tent of Meeting. And so they finished dividing the land.

ᶻ 28 Some Hebrew manuscripts (see also Joshua 21:30); most Hebrew manuscripts *Ebron* *ᵃ 34* Septuagint; Hebrew *west, and Judah, the Jordan,* *ᵇ 50* Also known as *Timnath Heres* (see Judges 2:9)

Cities of Refuge

20:1–9 Ref — Nu 35:9–34; Dt 4:41–43; 19:1–14

20 Then the LORD said to Joshua: ²"Tell the Israelites to designate the cities of refuge, as I instructed you through Moses, ³so that anyone who kills a person accidentally and unintentionally may flee there and find protection from the avenger of blood.

⁴"When he flees to one of these cities, he is to stand in the entrance of the city gate and state his case before the elders of that city. Then they are to admit him into their city and give him a place to live with them. ⁵If the avenger of blood pursues him, they must not surrender the one accused, because he killed his neighbor unintentionally and without malice aforethought. ⁶He is to stay in that city until he has stood trial before the assembly and until the death of the high priest who is serving at that time. Then he may go back to his own home in the town from which he fled."

⁷So they set apart Kedesh in Galilee in the hill country of Naphtali, Shechem in the hill country of Ephraim, and Kiriath Arba (that is, Hebron) in the hill country of Judah. ⁸On the east side of the Jordan of Jericho*ᶜ* they designated Bezer in the desert on the plateau in the tribe of Reuben, Ramoth in Gilead in the tribe of Gad, and Golan in Bashan in the tribe of Manasseh. ⁹Any of the Israelites or any alien living among them who killed someone accidentally could flee to these designated cities and not be killed by the avenger of blood prior to standing trial before the assembly.

Towns for the Levites

21:4–39 pp — 1Ch 6:54–80

21 Now the family heads of the Levites approached Eleazar the priest, Joshua son of Nun, and the heads of the other tribal families of Israel ²at Shiloh in Canaan and said to them, "The LORD commanded through Moses that you give us towns to live in, with pasturelands for our livestock." ³So, as the LORD had commanded, the Israelites gave the Levites the following towns and pasturelands out of their own inheritance:

⁴The first lot came out for the Kohathites, clan by clan. The Levites who were descendants of Aaron the priest were allotted thirteen towns from the tribes of Judah, Simeon and Benjamin. ⁵The rest of Kohath's descendants were allotted ten towns from the clans of the tribes of Ephraim, Dan and half of Manasseh.

⁶The descendants of Gershon were allotted thirteen towns from the clans of the tribes of Issachar, Asher, Naphtali and the half-tribe of Manasseh in Bashan.

⁷The descendants of Merari, clan by clan, received twelve towns from the tribes of Reuben, Gad and Zebulun.

⁸So the Israelites allotted to the Levites these towns and their pasturelands, as the LORD had commanded through Moses.

⁹From the tribes of Judah and Simeon they allotted the following towns by name ¹⁰(these towns were assigned to the descendants of Aaron who were from the Kohathite clans of the Levites, because the first lot fell to them):

¹¹They gave them Kiriath Arba (that is, Hebron), with its surrounding pastureland, in the hill country of Judah. (Arba was the forefather of Anak.) ¹²But the fields and villages around the city they had given to Caleb son of Jephunneh as his possession.

¹³So to the descendants of Aaron the priest they gave Hebron (a city of refuge for one accused of murder), Libnah, ¹⁴Jattir, Eshtemoa, ¹⁵Holon, Debir, ¹⁶Ain, Juttah and Beth Shemesh, together with their pasturelands—nine towns from these two tribes.

¹⁷And from the tribe of Benjamin they gave them Gibeon, Geba, ¹⁸Anathoth and Almon, together with their pasturelands—four towns.

¹⁹All the towns for the priests, the descendants of Aaron, were thirteen, together with their pasturelands.

²⁰The rest of the Kohathite clans of the Levites were allotted towns from the tribe of Ephraim:

²¹In the hill country of Ephraim they were given Shechem (a city of refuge for one accused of murder) and Gezer, ²²Kibzaim and Beth Horon, together with their pasturelands—four towns.

---

c 8 Jordan of Jericho was possibly an ancient name for the Jordan River.

²³Also from the tribe of Dan they received Eltekeh, Gibbethon,ᵇ ²⁴Aijalonᶜ and Gath Rimmon,ᵈ together with their pasturelands—four towns.

²⁵From half the tribe of Manasseh they received Taanachᵉ and Gath Rimmon, together with their pasturelands—two towns.

²⁶All these ten towns and their pasturelands were given to the rest of the Kohathite clans.ᶠ

²⁷The Levite clans of the Gershonites were given:

from the half-tribe of Manasseh,
Golan in Bashanᵍ (a city of refuge for one accused of murderʰ) and Be Eshtarah, together with their pasturelands—two towns;

²⁸from the tribe of Issachar,ⁱ
Kishion,ʲ Daberath,ᵏ ²⁹Jarmuthˡ and En Gannim,ᵐ together with their pasturelands—four towns;

³⁰from the tribe of Asher,ⁿ
Mishal,ᵒ Abdon,ᵖ ³¹Helkath and Rehob,ᑫ together with their pasturelands—four towns;

³²from the tribe of Naphtali,
Kedeshʳ in Galilee (a city of refuge for one accused of murderˢ), Hammoth Dor and Kartan, together with their pasturelands—three towns.

³³All the towns of the Gershoniteᵗ clans were thirteen, together with their pasturelands.

³⁴The Merarite clans (the rest of the Levites) were given:

from the tribe of Zebulun,ᵘ
Jokneam,ᵛ Kartah, ³⁵Dimnah and Nahalal,ʷ together with their pasturelands—four towns;

³⁶from the tribe of Reuben,
Bezer,ˣ Jahaz,ʸ ³⁷Kedemoth and Mephaath,ᶻ together with their pasturelands—four towns;

³⁸from the tribe of Gad,
Ramothᵃ in Gileadᵇ (a city of refuge for one accused of murder), Mahanaim,ᶜ ³⁹Heshbon and Jazer,ᵈ together with their pasturelands—four towns in all.

⁴⁰All the towns allotted to the Merarite clans, who were the rest of the Levites, were twelve.ᵉ

⁴¹The towns of the Levites in the territory held by the Israelites were forty-eight in all, together with their pasturelands.ᶠ ⁴²Each of these towns had pasturelands surrounding it; this was true for all these towns.

⁴³So the LORD gave Israel all the land he had sworn to give their forefathers,ᵍ and they took possessionʰ of it and settled there.ⁱ ⁴⁴The LORD gave them restʲ on every side, just as he had sworn to their forefathers. Not one of their enemiesᵏ withstood them; the LORD handed all their enemiesˡ over to them.ᵐ ⁴⁵Not one of all the LORD's good promisesⁿ to the house of Israel failed; every one was fulfilled.

Eastern Tribes Return Home

22 Then Joshua summoned the Reubenites, the Gadites and the half-tribe of Manasseh ²and said to them, "You have done all that Moses the servant of the LORD commanded,ᵒ and you have obeyed me in everything I commanded. ³For a long time now—to this very day—you have not deserted your brothers but have carried out the mission the LORD your God gave you. ⁴Now that the LORD your God has given your brothers restᵖ as he promised, return to your homesᑫ in the land that Moses the servant of the LORD gave you on the other side of the Jordan.ʳ ⁵But be very careful to keep the commandmentˢ and the law that Moses the servant of the LORD gave you: to love the LORDᵗ your God, to walk in all his ways, to obey his commands,ᵘ to hold fast to him and to serve him with all your heart and all your soul.ᵛ"

⁶Then Joshua blessedʷ them and sent them away, and they went to their homes. ⁷(To the half-tribe of Manasseh Moses had given land in Bashan,ˣ and to the other half of the tribe Joshua gave land on the west sideʸ of the Jordan with their brothers.) When Joshua sent them home, he blessed them,ᶻ ⁸saying, "Return to your homes with your great wealth—with large herds of livestock,ᵃ with silver, gold, bronze and iron,ᵇ and a great quantity of clothing—and divideᶜ with your brothers the plunderᵈ from your enemies."

⁹So the Reubenites, the Gadites and the half-tribe of Manasseh left the Israelites at Shilohᵉ in Canaan to return to Gil-

ead,ᶠ their own land, which they had acquired in accordance with the command of the LORD through Moses. ¹⁰When they came to Gelilothᵍ near the Jordan in the land of Canaan, the Reubenites, the Gadites and the half-tribe of Manasseh built an imposing altarʰ there by the Jordan. ¹¹And when the Israelites heard that they had built the altar on the border of Canaan at Geliloth near the Jordan on the Israelite side, ¹²the whole assembly of Israel gathered at Shiloh¹ to go to war against them.

¹³So the Israelites sent Phinehasʲ son of Eleazar,ᵏ the priest, to the land of Gilead—to Reuben, Gad and the half-tribe of Manasseh. ¹⁴With him they sent ten of the chief men, one for each of the tribes of Israel, each the head of a family division among the Israelite clans.¹

¹⁵When they went to Gilead—to Reuben, Gad and the half-tribe of Manasseh—they said to them: ¹⁶"The whole assembly of the LORD says: 'How could you break faithᵐ with the God of Israel like this? How could you turn away from the LORD and build yourselves an altar in rebellionⁿ against him now? ¹⁷Was not the sin of Peorᵒ enough for us? Up to this very day we have not cleansed ourselves from that sin, even though a plague fell on the community of the LORD! ¹⁸And are you now turning away from the LORD?

"'If you rebel against the LORD today, tomorrow he will be angry with the whole communityᵖ of Israel. ¹⁹If the land you possess is defiled, come over to the LORD's land, where the LORD's tabernacleᑫ stands, and share the land with us. But do not rebel against the LORD or against us by building an altarʳ for yourselves, other than the altar of the LORD our God. ²⁰When Achan son of Zerah acted unfaithfully regarding the devoted things,ᵈ did not wrathᵗ come upon the whole communityᵘ of Israel? He was not the only one who died for his sin.'"ᵛ

²¹Then Reuben, Gad and the half-tribe of Manasseh replied to the heads of the clans of Israel: ²²"The Mighty One, God, the LORD! The Mighty One, God,ʷ the LORD!ˣ He knows!ʸ And let Israel know! If this has been in rebellion or disobedience to the LORD, do not spare us this day. ²³If we have built our own altar to turn away from the LORD and to offer burnt offerings and grain offerings,ᶻ or to sacrifice fellowship offeringsᵉ on it, may the LORD himself call us to account.ᵃ

²⁴"No! We did it for fear that some day your descendants might say to ours, 'What do you have to do with the LORD, the God of Israel? ²⁵The LORD has made the Jordan a boundary between us and you—you Reubenites and Gadites! You have no share in the LORD.' So your descendants might cause ours to stop fearing the LORD.

²⁶"That is why we said, 'Let us get ready and build an altar—but not for burnt offerings or sacrifices.' ²⁷On the contrary, it is to be a witnessᵇ between us and you and the generations that follow, that we will worship the LORD at his sanctuary with our burnt offerings, sacrifices and fellowship offerings.ᶜ Then in the future your descendants will not be able to say to ours, 'You have no share in the LORD.'

²⁸"And we said, 'If they ever say this to us, or to our descendants, we will answer: Look at the replica of the LORD's altar, which our fathers built, not for burnt offerings and sacrifices, but as a witnessᵈ between us and you.'

²⁹"Far be it from us to rebelᵉ against the LORD and turn away from him today by building an altar for burnt offerings, grain offerings and sacrifices, other than the altar of the LORD our God that stands before his tabernacle.ᶠ'"

³⁰When Phinehas the priest and the leaders of the community—the heads of the clans of the Israelites—heard what Reuben, Gad and Manasseh had to say, they were pleased. ³¹And Phinehas son of Eleazar, the priest, said to Reuben, Gad and Manasseh, "Today we know that the LORD is with us,ᵍ because you have not acted unfaithfully toward the LORD in this matter. Now you have rescued the Israelites from the LORD's hand."

³²Then Phinehas son of Eleazar, the priest, and the leaders returned to Canaan from their meeting with the Reubenites and Gadites in Gilead and reported to the Israelites.ʰ ³³They were glad to hear the report and praised God.ⁱ And they talked no more about going to war

d 20 The Hebrew term refers to the irrevocable giving over of things or persons to the LORD, often by totally destroying them. *e 23* Traditionally *peace offerings*; also in verse 27

against them to devastate the country where the Reubenites and the Gadites lived.

³⁴And the Reubenites and the Gadites gave the altar this name: A Witness[j] Between Us that the LORD is God.

Joshua's Farewell to the Leaders

23 After a long time had passed and the LORD had given Israel rest[k] from all their enemies around them, Joshua, by then old and well advanced in years,[l] ²summoned all Israel—their elders,[m] leaders, judges and officials[n]—and said to them: "I am old and well advanced in years.[o] ³You yourselves have seen everything the LORD your God has done to all these nations for your sake; it was the LORD your God who fought for you.[p] ⁴Remember how I have allotted[q] as an inheritance[r] for your tribes all the land of the nations that remain—the nations I conquered—between the Jordan and the Great Sea[fs] in the west. ⁵The LORD your God himself will drive them out[t] of your way. He will push them out[u] before you, and you will take possession of their land, as the LORD your God promised you.[v]

⁶"Be very strong; be careful to obey all that is written in the Book of the Law[w] of Moses, without turning aside[x] to the right or to the left.[y] ⁷Do not associate with these nations that remain among you; do not invoke the names of their gods or swear[z] by them. You must not serve them or bow down[a] to them. ⁸But you are to hold fast to the LORD[b] your God, as you have until now.

⁹"The LORD has driven out before you great and powerful nations;[c] to this day no one has been able to withstand you.[d] ¹⁰One of you routs a thousand,[e] because the LORD your God fights for you,[f] just as he promised. ¹¹So be very careful[g] to love the LORD[h] your God.

¹²"But if you turn away and ally yourselves with the survivors of these nations that remain among you and if you intermarry with them[i] and associate with them,[j] ¹³then you may be sure that the LORD your God will no longer drive out[k] these nations before you. Instead, they will become snares[l] and traps for you, whips on your backs and thorns in your eyes,[m] until you perish from this good land,[n] which the LORD your God has given you.

¹⁴"Now I am about to go the way of all the earth.[o] You know with all your heart and soul that not one of all the good promises the LORD your God gave you has failed. Every promise[p] has been fulfilled; not one has failed.[q] ¹⁵But just as every good promise[r] of the LORD your God has come true, so the LORD will bring on you all the evil[s] he has threatened, until he has destroyed you[t] from this good land he has given you.[u] ¹⁶If you violate the covenant of the LORD your God, which he commanded you, and go and serve other gods and bow down to them, the LORD's anger will burn against you, and you will quickly perish from the good land he has given you.[v]"

The Covenant Renewed at Shechem

24 Then Joshua assembled[w] all the tribes of Israel at Shechem.[x] He summoned[y] the elders,[z] leaders, judges and officials of Israel,[a] and they presented themselves before God.

²Joshua said to all the people, "This is what the LORD, the God of Israel, says: 'Long ago your forefathers, including Terah the father of Abraham and Nahor,[b] lived beyond the River[g] and worshiped other gods.[c] ³But I took your father Abraham from the land beyond the River and led him throughout Canaan[d] and gave him many descendants.[e] I gave him Isaac,[f] ⁴and to Isaac I gave Jacob and Esau.[g] I assigned the hill country of Seir[h] to Esau, but Jacob and his sons went down to Egypt.[i]

⁵"'Then I sent Moses and Aaron,[j] and I afflicted the Egyptians by what I did there, and I brought you out.[k] ⁶When I

J Jos 6:26 ◀▶ Jdg 2:3
R Dt 32:36 ◀▶ 1Ki 9:6–9

f 4 That is, the Mediterranean *g* 2 That is, the Euphrates; also in verses 3, 14 and 15

V Jos 21:44 ◀▶ 1Sa 14:31

23:15–16 Joshua's last words to the people confirmed God's promise to bless Israel if they would obey his laws or to judge them if they rejected his laws and worshiped idols.

brought your fathers out of Egypt, you came to the sea,¹ and the Egyptians pursued them with chariots and horsemen as far as the Red Sea. ⁷But they cried to the LORD for help, and he put darkness between you and the Egyptians; he brought the sea over them and covered them. You saw with your own eyes what I did to the Egyptians. Then you lived in the desert for a long time.

⁸" 'I brought you to the land of the Amorites who lived east of the Jordan. They fought against you, but I gave them into your hands. I destroyed them from before you, and you took possession of their land. ⁹When Balak son of Zippor, the king of Moab, prepared to fight against Israel, he sent for Balaam son of Beor to put a curse on you. ¹⁰But I would not listen to Balaam, so he blessed you again and again, and I delivered you out of his hand.

¹¹" 'Then you crossed the Jordan and came to Jericho. The citizens of Jericho fought against you, as did also the Amorites, Perizzites, Canaanites, Hittites, Girgashites, Hivites and Jebusites, but I gave them into your hands. ¹²I sent the hornet ahead of you, which drove them out before you—also the two Amorite kings. You did not do it with your own sword and bow. ¹³So I gave you a land on which you did not toil and cities you did not build; and you live in them and eat from vineyards and olive groves that you did not plant.'

¹⁴"Now fear the LORD and serve him with all faithfulness. Throw away the gods your forefathers worshiped beyond the River and in Egypt, and serve the LORD. ¹⁵But if serving the LORD seems undesirable to you, then choose for yourselves this day whom you will serve, whether the gods your forefathers served beyond the River, or the gods of the Amorites, in whose land you are living. But as for me and my household, we will serve the LORD."

¹⁶Then the people answered, "Far be it from us to forsake the LORD to serve other gods! ¹⁷It was the LORD our God himself who brought us and our fathers up out of Egypt, from that land of slavery, and performed those great signs before our eyes. He protected us on our entire journey and among all the nations through which we traveled. ¹⁸And the LORD drove out before us all the nations, including the Amorites, who lived in the land. We too will serve the LORD, because he is our God."

¹⁹Joshua said to the people, "You are not able to serve the LORD. He is a holy God; he is a jealous God. He will not forgive your rebellion and your sins. ²⁰If you forsake the LORD and serve foreign gods, he will turn and bring disaster on you and make an end of you, after he has been good to you."

²¹But the people said to Joshua, "No! We will serve the LORD."

²²Then Joshua said, "You are witnesses against yourselves that you have chosen to serve the LORD."

"Yes, we are witnesses," they replied.

²³"Now then," said Joshua, "throw away the foreign gods that are among you and yield your hearts to the LORD, the God of Israel."

²⁴And the people said to Joshua, "We will serve the LORD our God and obey him."

²⁵On that day Joshua made a covenant for the people, and there at Shechem he drew up for them decrees and laws. ²⁶And Joshua recorded these things in the Book of the Law of God. Then he took a large stone and set it up there under the oak near the holy place of the LORD.

²⁷"See!" he said to all the people. "This stone will be a witness against us. It has heard all the words the LORD has said

---

24:15 The book of Joshua concludes with an ultimatum that required the Israelites to choose either to worship God or to follow pagan idols. The choices that the people made at this time became one of the most significant turning points in Israel's history.

to us. It will be a witness against you if you are untrueu to your God."v

Buried in the Promised Land
24:29–31pp — Jdg 2:6–9

²⁸Then Joshua sent the people away, each to his own inheritance.w

²⁹After these things, Joshua son of Nun, the servant of the LORD, diedx at the age of a hundred and ten.y ³⁰And they buried him in the land of his inheritance, at Timnath Serah,*/z* in the hill country of Ephraim, north of Mount Gaash.a

³¹Israel served the LORD throughout the lifetime of Joshua and of the eldersb who outlived him and who had experienced everything the LORD had done for Israel.

³²And Joseph's bones,c which the Israelites had brought up from Egypt,d were buried at Shechem in the tract of lande that Jacob bought for a hundred pieces of silverk from the sons of Hamor, the father of Shechem. This became the inheritance of Joseph's descendants.

³³And Eleazar son of Aaronf died and was buried at Gibeah,g which had been allotted to his son Phinehash in the hill countryi of Ephraim.

---

l 30 Also known as *Timnath Heres* (see Judges 2:9) *k 32* Hebrew *hundred kesitahs*; a kesitah was a unit of money of unknown weight and value.

Judges

Author: Tradition suggests Samuel; authorship uncertain

Theme: Israel's disobedience, defeat and deliverance

Date of Writing: c. 1050–1000 B.C.

Outline of Judges
  I. Failure to Purge the Land Leads to Apostasy (1:1—3:6)
  II. The Cycle of Oppression and Deliverance (3:7—16:31)
  III. Spiritual and Civil Disorder (17:1—21:25)

THIS BOOK TAKES its title from the leaders who governed Israel from the time of Joshua's death to the beginning of the monarchy. During this time, men and women from various tribes were chosen by God to provide direction and deliverance for the nation of Israel during times of spiritual disintegration and enemy oppression. These judges ruled over different parts of the promised land for several hundred years. While many of the judges ruled only a portion of the land, God granted some of the judges jurisdiction over the entire territory.

If the book of Joshua is a book of victory, then the book of Judges is a book of defeat. Joshua, who was Moses' second-in-command throughout the exodus, led the Israelites into Canaan and followed God's directions over the next thirty years to conquer the promised land. However, in the leadership vacuum that developed after Joshua's death, Israel did not consistently follow Joshua's example of submission to God. A careful analysis of the chronology of this book reveals that various periods of conquest by their pagan enemies interrupted Israel's peaceful years under the rule of a judge. Israel's spiritual history became a spiral of indifference, disobedience, defeat, domination, deliverance and restored divine approval that was tragically repeated for centuries. The book of Judges chronicles these cycles, noting the numerous defeats of the Israelites as well as their victories, highlighting the righteous judges that God raised up to conquer Israel's enemies and the restoring of his people to covenant fellowship with himself.

Israel Fights the Remaining Canaanites

1:11–15pp — Jos 15:15–19

1 After the death[a] of Joshua, the Israelites asked the LORD, "Who will be the first[b] to go up and fight for us against the Canaanites?[c]"

²The LORD answered, "Judah[d] is to go; I have given the land into their hands.[e]"

³Then the men of Judah said to the Simeonites their brothers, "Come up with us into the territory allotted to us, to fight against the Canaanites. We in turn will go with you into yours." So the Simeonites[f] went with them.

⁴When Judah attacked, the LORD gave the Canaanites and Perizzites[g] into their hands and they struck down ten thousand men at Bezek.[h] ⁵It was there that they found Adoni-Bezek[i] and fought against him, putting to rout the Canaanites and Perizzites. ⁶Adoni-Bezek fled, but they chased him and caught him, and cut off his thumbs and big toes.

⁷Then Adoni-Bezek said, "Seventy kings with their thumbs and big toes cut off have picked up scraps under my table. Now God has paid me back[j] for what I did to them." They brought him to Jerusalem,[k] and he died there.

⁸The men of Judah attacked Jerusalem[l] also and took it. They put the city to the sword and set it on fire.

⁹After that, the men of Judah went down to fight against the Canaanites living in the hill country,[m] the Negev[n] and the western foothills. ¹⁰They advanced against the Canaanites living in Hebron[o] (formerly called Kiriath Arba[p]) and defeated Sheshai, Ahiman and Talmai.[q]

¹¹From there they advanced against the people living in Debir[r] (formerly called Kiriath Sepher). ¹²And Caleb said, "I will give my daughter Acsah in marriage to the man who attacks and captures Kiriath Sepher." ¹³Othniel son of Kenaz, Caleb's younger brother, took it; so Caleb gave his daughter Acsah to him in marriage.

¹⁴One day when she came to Othniel, she urged him[a] to ask her father for a field. When she got off her donkey, Caleb asked her, "What can I do for you?"

¹⁵She replied, "Do me a special favor. Since you have given me land in the Negev, give me also springs of water."

Then Caleb gave her the upper and lower springs.[s]

¹⁶The descendants of Moses' father-in-law,[t] the Kenite,[u] went up from the City of Palms[b][v] with the men of Judah to live among the people of the Desert of Judah in the Negev near Arad.[w]

¹⁷Then the men of Judah went with the Simeonites[x] their brothers and attacked the Canaanites living in Zephath, and they totally destroyed[c] the city. Therefore it was called Hormah.[d][y] ¹⁸The men of Judah also took[e] Gaza,[z] Ashkelon[a] and Ekron—each city with its territory.

¹⁹The LORD was with[b] the men of Judah. They took possession of the hill country,[c] but they were unable to drive the people from the plains, because they had iron chariots.[d] ²⁰As Moses had promised, Hebron[e] was given to Caleb, who drove from it the three sons of Anak.[f] ²¹The Benjamites, however, failed[g] to dislodge the Jebusites, who were living in Jerusalem;[h] to this day the Jebusites live there with the Benjamites.

²²Now the house of Joseph[i] attacked Bethel,[j] and the LORD was with them. ²³When they sent men to spy out Bethel (formerly called Luz),[k] ²⁴the spies saw a man coming out of the city and they said to him, "Show us how to get into the city and we will see that you are treated well.[1]" ²⁵So he showed them, and they put the city to the sword but spared[m] the man and his whole family. ²⁶He then went to the land of the Hittites,[n] where he built a city and called it Luz,[o] which is its name to this day.

²⁷But Manasseh did not[p] drive out the people of Beth Shan or Taanach or Dor[q] or Ibleam[r] or Megiddo[s] and their surrounding settlements, for the Canaanites[t] were determined to live in that land. ²⁸When Israel became strong, they pressed the Canaanites into forced labor but never drove them out completely.[u] ²⁹Nor did Ephraim[v] drive out the Canaanites living in Gezer,[w] but the Canaanites continued to live there among them.[x] ³⁰Neither did Zebulun drive out the Canaanites living in Kitron or Nahalol, who remained among them; but they did sub-

---

[a] 14 Hebrew; Septuagint and Vulgate *Othniel, he urged her* [b] 16 That is, Jericho [c] 17 The Hebrew term refers to the irrevocable giving over of things or persons to the LORD, often by totally destroying them. [d] 17 *Hormah* means *destruction*. [e] 18 Hebrew; Septuagint *Judah did not take*

ject them to forced labor. ³¹Nor did Asher drive out those living in Acco or Sidon or Ahlab or Aczib or Helbah or Aphek or Rehob, ³²and because of this the people of Asher lived among the Canaanite inhabitants of the land. ³³Neither did Naphtali drive out those living in Beth Shemesh or Beth Anath; but the Naphtalites too lived among the Canaanite inhabitants of the land, and those living in Beth Shemesh and Beth Anath became forced laborers for them. ³⁴The Amorites confined the Danites to the hill country, not allowing them to come down into the plain. ³⁵And the Amorites were determined also to hold out in Mount Heres, Aijalon and Shaalbim, but when the power of the house of Joseph increased, they too were pressed into forced labor. ³⁶The boundary of the Amorites was from Scorpion Pass to Sela and beyond.

The Angel of the LORD at Bokim

2 The angel of the LORD went up from Gilgal to Bokim and said, "I brought you up out of Egypt and led you into the land that I swore to give to your forefathers. I said, 'I will never break my covenant with you, ²and you shall not make a covenant with the people of this land, but you shall break down their altars.' Yet you have disobeyed me. Why have you done this? ³Now therefore I tell you that I will not drive them out before you; they will be ⌊thorns⌋ in your sides and their gods will be a snare to you."

⁴When the angel of the LORD had spoken these things to all the Israelites, the people wept aloud, ⁵and they called that place Bokim. There they offered sacrifices to the LORD.

l Jdg 1:2 ◄ ► Jdg 6:16
J Jos 23:13 ◄ ► Jdg 2:21

Disobedience and Defeat
2:6–9pp — Jos 24:29–31

⁶After Joshua had dismissed the Israelites, they went to take possession of the land, each to his own inheritance. ⁷The people served the LORD throughout the lifetime of Joshua and of the elders who outlived him and who had seen all the great things the LORD had done for Israel. ⁸Joshua son of Nun, the servant of the LORD, died at the age of a hundred and ten. ⁹And they buried him in the land of his inheritance, at Timnath Heres[e] in the hill country of Ephraim, north of Mount Gaash.

¹⁰After that whole generation had been gathered to their fathers, another generation grew up, who knew neither the LORD nor what he had done for Israel. ¹¹Then the Israelites did evil in the eyes of the LORD and served the Baals. ¹²They forsook the LORD, the God of their fathers, who had brought them out of Egypt. They followed and worshiped various gods of the peoples around them. They provoked the LORD to anger ¹³because they forsook him and served Baal and the Ashtoreths. ¹⁴In his anger against Israel the LORD handed them over to raiders who plundered them. He sold them to their enemies all around, whom they were no longer able to resist. ¹⁵Whenever Israel went out to fight, the hand of the LORD was against them to defeat them, just as he had sworn to them. They were in great distress.

¹⁶Then the LORD raised up judges,[i] who saved them out of the hands of

Q Dt 32:50 ◄ ► Lk 9:28–33

Job 19:21; Ps 32:4 ᵛGe 35:3; 2Sa 22:7; 2Ch 15:4; Job 5:5; 20:22; Ps 4:1; 18:6 **2:16** ʷRu 1:1; Isa 4:18; 7:6,15; 2Sa 7:11; 1Ch 17:10; Ac 13:20 ˣ1Sa 11:3; Ps 106:43

f 36 Hebrew *Akrabbim* ᵍ 5 *Bokim* means weepers. ʰ 9 Also known as Timnath Serah (see Joshua 19:50 and 24:30) *i 16* Or *leaders;* similarly in verses 17-19

2:1 The angel mentioned in this verse is actually the Lord himself. Whenever God appeared to individuals in the OT it was in this physical, angelic form. Such a visible manifestation of God to humanity is called a theophany. Scripture records other theophanies and other titles given to these visitors, including "the angel of God" (Ge 21:17), "the angel of his presence" (Isa 63:9) and "the messenger of the covenant" (Mal 3:1). Sometimes people recognized the angel's divinity (see Ge 16:13; 48:16) while at other times the angel clearly identified himself as God (see Ge 31:11–13; Ex 3:2–6). In each appearance the angel of the Lord carried out divine actions such as revelation, salvation and judgment, thus preparing God's people for the full expression of God in the form of Jesus Christ.

2:10 This verse refers to the Hebrew view of life after death and the resurrection of the Patriarchs to heaven (see note on Ge 35:29).

these raiders. ¹⁷Yet they would not listen to their judges but prostituted themselves to other gods and worshiped them. Unlike their fathers, they quickly turned from the way in which their fathers had walked, the way of obedience to the LORD's commands. ¹⁸Whenever the LORD raised up a judge for them, he was with the judge and saved them out of the hands of their enemies as long as the judge lived; for the LORD had compassion on them as they groaned under those who oppressed and afflicted them. ¹⁹But when the judge died, the people returned to ways even more corrupt than those of their fathers, following other gods and serving and worshiping them. They refused to give up their evil practices and stubborn ways.

²⁰Therefore the LORD was very angry with Israel and said, "Because this nation has violated the covenant that I laid down for their forefathers and has not listened to me, ²¹I will no longer drive out before them any of the nations Joshua left when he died. ²²I will use them to test Israel and see whether they will keep the way of the LORD and walk in it as their forefathers did." ²³The LORD had allowed those nations to remain; he did not drive them out at once by giving them into the hands of Joshua.

3 These are the nations the LORD left to test all those Israelites who had not experienced any of the wars in Canaan ²(he did this only to teach warfare to the descendants of the Israelites who had not had previous battle experience): ³the five rulers of the Philistines, all the Canaanites, the Sidonians, and the Hivites living in the Lebanon mountains from Mount Baal Hermon to Lebo Hamath. ⁴They were left to test the Israelites to see whether they would obey the LORD's commands, which he had given their forefathers through Moses.

⁵The Israelites lived among the Canaanites, Hittites, Amorites, Perizzites, Hivites and Jebusites. ⁶They took their daughters in marriage and gave their own daughters to their sons, and served their gods.

Othniel

⁷The Israelites did evil in the eyes of the LORD; they forgot the LORD their God and served the Baals and the Asherahs. ⁸The anger of the LORD burned against Israel so that he sold them into the hands of Cushan-Rishathaim king of Aram Naharaim, to whom the Israelites were subject for eight years. ⁹But when they cried out to the LORD, he raised up for them a deliverer, Othniel son of Kenaz, Caleb's younger brother, who saved them. ¹⁰The Spirit of the LORD came upon him, so that he became Israel's judge and went to war. The LORD gave Cushan-Rishathaim king of Aram into the hands of Othniel, who overpowered him. ¹¹So the land had peace for forty years, until Othniel son of Kenaz died.

Ehud

¹²Once again the Israelites did evil in the eyes of the LORD, and because they did this evil the LORD gave Eglon king of Moab power over Israel. ¹³Getting the Ammonites and Amalekites to join him, Eglon came and attacked Israel, and they took possession of the City of Palms. ¹⁴The Israelites were subject to Eglon king of Moab for eighteen years.

¹⁵Again the Israelites cried out to the LORD, and he gave them a deliverer—Ehud, a left-handed man, the son of Gera the Benjamite. The Israelites sent him with tribute to Eglon king of Moab. ¹⁶Now Ehud had made a double-edged sword about a foot and a half long, which he strapped to his right thigh under his clothing. ¹⁷He presented the tribute to Eglon king of Moab, who was a very fat man. ¹⁸After Ehud had presented the tribute, he sent on their way the men who had carried it. ¹⁹At the idols near Gilgal he himself turned back and said, "I have a secret message for you, O king."

The king said, "Quiet!" And all his attendants left him.

²⁰Ehud then approached him while he was sitting alone in the upper room of his

---

E *Dt 34:9* ◀ ▶ *Jdg 6:34*
M *Ge 41:38* ◀ ▶ *Jdg 6:34*

1Ki 4:21; 2Ki 17:3; Est 10:1; Ps 68:29; 72:10; 89:22; Ecc 2:8; Isa 60:5; Hos 10:6 **3:16** ᵇS ver 15 **3:17** ᶜS ver 15 ᵈJob 15:27; Ps 73:4

j 3 Or *to the entrance to* *k 8* That is, Northwest Mesopotamia
l 10 Or *leader* *m 13* That is, Jericho *n 16* Hebrew *a cubit* (about 0.5 meter) *o 19* Or *the stone quarries*; also in verse 26

J *Jdg 2:3* ◀ ▶ *Jdg 9:15*

summer palace[p][e] and said, "I have a message from God for you." As the king rose[f] from his seat, ²¹Ehud reached with his left hand, drew the sword[g] from his right thigh and plunged it into the king's belly. ²²Even the handle sank in after the blade, which came out his back. Ehud did not pull the sword out, and the fat closed in over it. ²³Then Ehud went out to the porch[q]; he shut the doors of the upper room behind him and locked them.

²⁴After he had gone, the servants came and found the doors of the upper room locked. They said, "He must be relieving himself[h] in the inner room of the house." ²⁵They waited to the point of embarrassment,[i] but when he did not open the doors of the room, they took a key and unlocked them. There they saw their lord fallen to the floor, dead.

²⁶While they waited, Ehud got away. He passed by the idols and escaped to Seirah. ²⁷When he arrived there, he blew a trumpet[j] in the hill country of Ephraim, and the Israelites went down with him from the hills, with him leading them.

²⁸"Follow me," he ordered, "for the LORD has given Moab,[k] your enemy, into your hands.[l]" So they followed him down and, taking possession of the fords of the Jordan[m] that led to Moab, they allowed no one to cross over. ²⁹At that time they struck down about ten thousand Moabites, all vigorous and strong; not a man escaped. ³⁰That day Moab[n] was made subject to Israel, and the land had peace[o] for eighty years.

Shamgar

³¹After Ehud came Shamgar son of Anath,[p] who struck down six hundred[q] Philistines[r] with an oxgoad. He too saved Israel.

Deborah

4 After Ehud[s] died, the Israelites once again did evil[t] in the eyes of the LORD.[u] ²So the LORD sold them[v] into the hands of Jabin, a king of Canaan, who reigned in Hazor.[w] The commander of his army was Sisera,[x] who lived in Harosheth Haggoyim. ³Because he had nine hundred iron chariots[y] and had cruelly oppressed[z] the Israelites for twenty years, they cried to the LORD for help.

⁴Deborah,[a] a prophetess,[b] the wife of Lappidoth, was leading[r] Israel at that time. ⁵She held court[c] under the Palm of Deborah between Ramah[d] and Bethel[e] in the hill country of Ephraim, and the Israelites came to have their disputes decided. ⁶She sent for Barak son of Abinoam[f] from Kedesh[g] in Naphtali and said to him, "The LORD, the God of Israel, commands you: 'Go, take with you ten thousand men of Naphtali[h] and Zebulun[i] and lead the way to Mount Tabor.[j] ⁷I will lure Sisera, the commander of Jabin's[k] army, with his chariots and his troops to the Kishon River[l] and give him into your hands.[m]'"

⁸Barak said to her, "If you go with me, I will go; but if you don't go with me, I won't go."

⁹"Very well," Deborah said, "I will go with you. But because of the way you are going about this,[s] the honor will not be yours, for the LORD will hand Sisera over to a woman." So Deborah went with Barak to Kedesh,[n] ¹⁰where he summoned[o] Zebulun and Naphtali. Ten thousand men followed him, and Deborah also went with him.

¹¹Now Heber the Kenite had left the other Kenites,[p] the descendants of Hobab,[q] Moses' brother-in-law,[t] and pitched his tent by the great tree[r] in Zaanannim[s] near Kedesh.

¹²When they told Sisera that Barak son of Abinoam had gone up to Mount Tabor,[t] ¹³Sisera gathered together his nine hundred iron chariots[u] and all the men with him, from Harosheth Haggoyim to the Kishon River.[v]

¹⁴Then Deborah said to Barak, "Go! This is the day the LORD has given Sisera into your hands.[w] Has not the LORD gone ahead[x] of you?" So Barak went down Mount Tabor, followed by ten thousand men. ¹⁵At Barak's advance, the LORD routed[y] Sisera and all his chariots and army by the sword, and Sisera abandoned his chariot and fled on foot. ¹⁶But Barak pursued the chariots and army as far as Harosheth Haggoyim. All the troops of Sisera fell by the sword; not a man was left.[z]

¹⁷Sisera, however, fled on foot to the tent of Jael,[a] the wife of Heber the Kenite,[b] because there were friendly rela-

---

[p] 20 The meaning of the Hebrew for this phrase is uncertain. [q] 23 The meaning of the Hebrew for this word is uncertain. [r] 4 Traditionally *judging* [s] 9 Or *But on the expedition you are undertaking* [t] 11 Or *father-in-law*

tions between Jabin king of Hazor^c and the clan of Heber the Kenite.

^18 Jael^d went out to meet Sisera and said to him, "Come, my lord, come right in. Don't be afraid." So he entered her tent, and she put a covering over him.

^19 "I'm thirsty," he said. "Please give me some water." She opened a skin of milk,^e gave him a drink, and covered him up.

^20 "Stand in the doorway of the tent," he told her. "If someone comes by and asks you, 'Is anyone here?' say 'No.' "

^21 But Jael,^f Heber's wife, picked up a tent peg and a hammer and went quietly to him while he lay fast asleep,^g exhausted. She drove the peg through his temple into the ground, and he died.^h

^22 Barak came by in pursuit of Sisera, and Jael^i went out to meet him. "Come," she said, "I will show you the man you're looking for." So he went in with her, and there lay Sisera with the tent peg through his temple—dead.^j

^23 On that day God subdued^k Jabin,^l the Canaanite king, before the Israelites. ^24 And the hand of the Israelites grew stronger and stronger against Jabin, the Canaanite king, until they destroyed him.^m

The Song of Deborah

5 On that day Deborah^n and Barak son of Abinoam^o sang this song:^p

^2 "When the princes in Israel take the lead,
  when the people willingly offer^q themselves—
  praise the LORD!^r

^3 "Hear this, you kings! Listen, you rulers!
  I will sing to^u the LORD, I will sing;^s
  I will make music to^v the LORD, the God of Israel.^t

^4 "O LORD, when you went out^u from Seir,^v
  when you marched from the land of Edom,
  the earth shook,^w the heavens poured,
  the clouds poured down water.^x
^5 The mountains quaked^y before the LORD, the One of Sinai,
  before the LORD, the God of Israel.

^6 "In the days of Shamgar son of Anath,^z in the days of Jael,^a the roads^b were abandoned;
  travelers took to winding paths.^c
^7 Village life^w in Israel ceased,
  ceased until I,^x Deborah,^d arose,
  arose a mother in Israel.
^8 When they chose new gods,^e
  war came to the city gates,^f
  and not a shield or spear^g was seen among forty thousand in Israel.
^9 My heart is with Israel's princes,
  with the willing volunteers^h among the people.
  Praise the LORD!

^10 "You who ride on white donkeys,^i
  sitting on your saddle blankets,
  and you who walk along the road,
  consider ^11 the voice of the singers^y at the watering places.
  They recite the righteous acts^j of the LORD,
  the righteous acts of his warriors^z in Israel.

"Then the people of the LORD went down to the city gates.^k
^12 'Wake up,^l wake up, Deborah!^m
  Wake up, wake up, break out in song!
  Arise, O Barak!^n
  Take captive your captives,^o O son of Abinoam.'

^13 "Then the men who were left came down to the nobles;
  the people of the LORD came to me with the mighty.
^14 Some came from Ephraim,^p whose roots were in Amalek;^q
  Benjamin^r was with the people who followed you.
  From Makir^s captains came down,
  from Zebulun those who bear a commander's staff.
^15 The princes of Issachar^t were with Deborah;^u
  yes, Issachar was with Barak,^v
  rushing after him into the valley.
  In the districts of Reuben there was much searching of heart.
^16 Why did you stay among the campfires^a^w
  to hear the whistling for the flocks?^x
  In the districts of Reuben

---

^u 3 Or of ^v 3 Or / with song I will praise ^w 7 Or Warriors ^x 7 Or you ^y 11 Or archers; the meaning of the Hebrew for this word is uncertain. ^z 11 Or villagers ^a 16 Or saddlebags

there was much searching of heart.
¹⁷Gileadʸ stayed beyond the Jordan.
And Dan, why did he linger by the
ships?
Asherᶻ remained on the coastᵃ
and stayed in his coves.
¹⁸The people of Zebulunᵇ risked their
very lives;
so did Naphtaliᶜ on the heights of
the field.ᵈ
¹⁹"Kings cameᵉ, they fought;
the kings of Canaan fought
at Taanach by the waters of Megiddo,ᶠ
but they carried off no silver, no
plunder.ᵍ
²⁰From the heavensʰ the stars fought,
from their courses they fought
against Sisera.
²¹The river Kishonⁱ swept them away,
the age-old river, the river Kishon.
March on, my soul; be strong!ʲ
²²Then thundered the horses' hoofs—
galloping, galloping go his mighty
steeds.ᵏ
H ²³'Curse Meroz,' said the angel of the
LORD.
'Curse its people bitterly,
because they did not come to help the
LORD,
to help the LORD against the mighty.'
²⁴"Most blessed of womenˡ be Jael,ᵐ
the wife of Heber the Kenite,ⁿ
most blessed of tent-dwelling
women.
²⁵He asked for water, and she gave him
milk;ᵒ
in a bowl fit for nobles she brought
him curdled milk.
²⁶Her hand reached for the tent peg,
her right hand for the workman's
hammer.
She struck Sisera, she crushed his
head,
she shattered and pierced his
temple.ᵖ
²⁷At her feet he sank,
he fell; there he lay.
At her feet he sank, he fell;
where he sank, there he fell—
dead.ᵠ
²⁸"Through the windowʳ peered Sisera's
mother;
behind the lattice she cried out,ˢ

H Jos 24:19 ◀▶ 1Sa 2:9

5:17 ʸ S Jos 12:2
ᶻ S Jos 17:7
ᵃ Jos 19:29
5:18 ᵇ S Ge 30:20
ᶜ S Ge 30:8;
Ps 68:27 ᵈ S Jdg 4:6,
10
5:19 ᵉ Jos 11:5;
S Jdg 4:13;
Rev 16:16
ᶠ S Jos 12:21
ᵍ ver 30
5:20 ʰ S Jos 10:11
5:21 ⁱ S Jdg 4:7
ʲ Jos 1:6
5:22 ᵏ Jer 8:16
5:24 ˡ Lk 1:42
ᵐ S Jdg 4:17
ⁿ S Ge 15:19
5:25 ᵒ S Ge 18:8
5:26 ᵖ Jdg 4:21
5:27 ᵠ Jdg 4:22
5:28 ʳ S 2:15
ˢ Pr 7:6
5:30 ᵗ Ex 15:9;
1Sa 30:24; Ps 68:12
ᵘ Ps 45:14;
Eze 16:10 ᵛ ver 19;
2Sa 1:24
5:31 ʷ S Nu 10:35
ˣ 2Sa 23:4;
Job 37:21; Ps 19:4;
89:36; Isa 18:4
ʸ 2Sa 18:32
ᶻ S Jdg 3:11
6:1 ᵃ S Jdg 2:11
ᵇ S Ge 25:2
6:2 ᶜ 1Sa 13:6;
Isa 5:30; 8:21;
26:16; 37:3
ᵈ Isa 2:19;
Jer 48:28; 49:8,30
ᵉ Job 24:8; Jer 41:9;
Heb 11:38
6:3 ᶠ Nu 13:29
ᵍ S Ge 25:6;
Isa 11:14; Jer 49:28
6:4 ʰ Lev 26:16;
Dt 28:30,51;
Isa 10:6; 39:6;
42:22 ⁱ S Ge 10:19
6:5 ʲ S Dt 28:42
ᵏ Jdg 8:10; Isa 21:7;
60:6; Jer 49:32
6:6 ˡ S Jdg 3:9
6:7 ᵐ S Jdg 3:9
6:8 ⁿ Dt 18:15;
1Ki 20:13,22;
2Ki 17:13,23;
Ne 9:29; Job 36:10;
Jer 25:5;
Eze 18:30-31
ᵒ S Jdg 2:1
ᵖ Jos 24:17
6:9 ᵠ S Nu 10:9;
Ps 136:24 ʳ Ps 44:2
6:10 ˢ S Ex 20:5
ᵗ S Jos 24:15

'Why is his chariot so long in coming?
Why is the clatter of his chariots
delayed?'
²⁹The wisest of her ladies answer her;
indeed, she keeps saying to herself,
³⁰'Are they not finding and dividing the
spoils:ᵗ
a girl or two for each man,
colorful garments as plunder for
Sisera,
colorful garments embroidered,
highly embroidered garmentsᵘ for
my neck—
all this as plunder?ᵛ'

³¹"So may all your enemies perish,ʷ **K**
O LORD!
But may they who love you be like
the sunˣ
when it rises in its strength."ʸ

Then the land had peaceᶻ forty years.

Gideon

6 Again the Israelites did evil in the eyes of the LORD,ᵃ and for seven years he gave them into the hands of the Midianites.ᵇ ²Because the power of Midian was so oppressive,ᶜ the Israelites prepared shelters for themselves in mountain clefts, cavesᵈ and strongholds.ᵉ ³Whenever the Israelites planted their crops, the Midianites, Amalekitesᶠ and other eastern peoplesᵍ invaded the country. ⁴They camped on the land and ruined the cropsʰ all the way to Gazaⁱ and did not spare a living thing for Israel, neither sheep nor cattle nor donkeys. ⁵They came up with their livestock and their tents like swarms of locusts.ʲ It was impossible to count the men and their camels;ᵏ they invaded the land to ravage it. ⁶Midian so impoverished the Israelites that they cried outˡ to the LORD for help.

⁷When the Israelites criedᵐ to the LORD because of Midian, ⁸he sent them a prophet,ⁿ who said, "This is what the LORD, the God of Israel, says: I brought you up out of Egypt,ᵒ out of the land of slavery.ᵖ ⁹I snatched you from the power of Egypt and from the hand of all your oppressors.ᵠ I drove them from before you and gave you their land.ʳ ¹⁰I said to you, 'I am the LORD your God; do not worshipˢ the gods of the Amorites,ᵗ in whose

K Jos 1:5 ◀▶ Ru 2:12

land you live.' But you have not listened to me." ¹¹The angel of the LORD came and sat down under the oak in Ophrah that belonged to Joash the Abiezrite, where his son Gideon was threshing wheat in a winepress to keep it from the Midianites. ¹²When the angel of the LORD appeared to Gideon, he said, "The LORD is with you, mighty warrior."

¹³"But sir," Gideon replied, "if the LORD is with us, why has all this happened to us? Where are all his wonders that our fathers told us about when they said, 'Did not the LORD bring us up out of Egypt?' But now the LORD has abandoned us and put us into the hand of Midian." ¹⁴The LORD turned to him and said, "Go in the strength you have and save Israel out of Midian's hand. Am I not sending you?"

¹⁵"But Lord," Gideon asked, "how can I save Israel? My clan is the weakest in Manasseh, and I am the least in my family."

¹⁶The LORD answered, "I will be with you, and you will strike down all the Midianites together."

¹⁷Gideon replied, "If now I have found favor in your eyes, give me a sign that it is really you talking to me. ¹⁸Please do not go away until I come back and bring my offering and set it before you."

And the LORD said, "I will wait until you return."

¹⁹Gideon went in, prepared a young goat, and from an ephah of flour he made bread without yeast. Putting the meat in a basket and its broth in a pot, he brought them out and offered them to him under the oak.

²⁰The angel of God said to him, "Take the meat and the unleavened bread, place them on this rock, and pour out the broth." And Gideon did so. ²¹With the tip of the staff that was in his hand, the angel of the LORD touched the meat and the unleavened bread. Fire flared from the rock, consuming the meat and the bread. And the angel of the LORD disappeared. ²²When Gideon realized that it was the angel of the LORD, he exclaimed, "Ah, Sovereign LORD! I have seen the angel of the LORD face to face!"

²³But the LORD said to him, "Peace! Do not be afraid. You are not going to die." ²⁴So Gideon built an altar to the LORD there and called it The LORD is Peace. To this day it stands in Ophrah of the Abiezrites.

²⁵That same night the LORD said to him, "Take the second bull from your father's herd, the one seven years old. Tear down your father's altar to Baal and cut down the Asherah pole beside it. ²⁶Then build a proper kind of altar to the LORD your God on the top of this height. Using the wood of the Asherah pole that you cut down, offer the second bull as a burnt offering." ²⁷So Gideon took ten of his servants and did as the LORD told him. But because he was afraid of his family and the men of the town, he did it at night rather than in the daytime.

²⁸In the morning when the men of the town got up, there was Baal's altar, demolished, with the Asherah pole beside it cut down and the second bull sacrificed on the newly built altar!

²⁹They asked each other, "Who did this?"

When they carefully investigated, they were told, "Gideon son of Joash did it."

³⁰The men of the town demanded of Joash, "Bring out your son. He must die, because he has broken down Baal's altar and cut down the Asherah pole beside it."

³¹But Joash replied to the hostile crowd around him, "Are you going to plead Baal's cause? Are you trying to save him? Whoever fights for him shall be put to death by morning! If Baal really is a god, he can defend himself when someone breaks down his altar." ³²So that day they called Gideon "Jerub-Baal," saying, "Let Baal contend with him," because he broke down Baal's altar.

³³Now all the Midianites, Amalekites and other eastern peoples joined forces and crossed over the Jordan and camped in the Valley of Jezreel. ³⁴Then the Spirit of the LORD came upon Gideon, and he blew a trumpet, summoning the Abiez-

rites^k to follow him. ³⁵He sent messengers throughout Manasseh, calling them to arms, and also into Asher,¹ Zebulun and Naphtali,^m so that they too went up to meet them.^n

³⁶Gideon said to God, "If you will save^o Israel by my hand as you have promised— ³⁷look, I will place a wool fleece^p on the threshing floor.^q If there is dew only on the fleece and all the ground is dry, then I will know^r that you will save Israel by my hand, as you said." ³⁸And that is what happened. Gideon rose early the next day; he squeezed the fleece and wrung out the dew—a bowlful of water.

³⁹Then Gideon said to God, "Do not be angry with me. Let me make just one more request.^s Allow me one more test with the fleece. This time make the fleece dry and the ground covered with dew." ⁴⁰That night God did so. Only the fleece was dry; all the ground was covered with dew.^t

Gideon Defeats the Midianites

7 Early in the morning, Jerub-Baal^u (that is, Gideon^v) and all his men camped at the spring of Harod.^w The camp of Midian^x was north of them in the valley near the hill of Moreh.^y ²The LORD said to Gideon, "You have too many men for me to deliver Midian into their hands. In order that Israel may not boast against me that her own strength^z has saved her, ³announce now to the people, 'Anyone who trembles with fear may turn back and leave Mount Gilead.^a' " So twenty-two thousand men left, while ten thousand remained.

⁴But the LORD said to Gideon, "There are still too many^b men. Take them down to the water, and I will sift them for you there. If I say, 'This one shall go with you,' he shall go; but if I say, 'This one shall not go with you,' he shall not go." ⁵So Gideon took the men down to the water. There the LORD told him, "Separate those who lap the water with their tongues like a dog from those who kneel down to drink." ⁶Three hundred men^c lapped with their hands to their mouths. All the rest got down on their knees to drink.

⁷The LORD said to Gideon, "With the three hundred men that lapped I will save you and give the Midianites into your hands.^d Let all the other men go, each to his own place."^e ⁸So Gideon sent the rest of the Israelites to their tents but kept the three hundred, who took over the provisions and trumpets of the others.

Now the camp of Midian lay below him in the valley. ⁹During that night the LORD said to Gideon, "Get up, go down against the camp, because I am going to give it into your hands.^f ¹⁰If you are afraid to attack, go down to the camp with your servant Purah ¹¹and listen to what they are saying. Afterward, you will be encouraged to attack the camp." So he and Purah his servant went down to the outposts of the camp. ¹²The Midianites, the Amalekites^g and all the other eastern peoples had settled in the valley, thick as locusts.^h Their camels^i could no more be counted than the sand on the seashore.^j

¹³Gideon arrived just as a man was telling a friend his dream. "I had a dream," he was saying. "A round loaf of barley bread came tumbling into the Midianite camp. It struck the tent with such force that the tent overturned and collapsed."

¹⁴His friend responded, "This can be nothing other than the sword of Gideon son of Joash,^k the Israelite. God has given the Midianites and the whole camp into his hands."

¹⁵When Gideon heard the dream and its interpretation, he worshiped God.^l He returned to the camp of Israel and called out, "Get up! The LORD has given the Midianite camp into your hands."^m ¹⁶Dividing the three hundred men^n into three companies,^o he placed trumpets^p and empty jars^q in the hands of all of them, with torches^r inside.

¹⁷"Watch me," he told them. "Follow my lead. When I get to the edge of the camp, do exactly as I do. ¹⁸When I and all who are with me blow our trumpets,^s then from all around the camp blow yours and shout, 'For the LORD and for Gideon.' "

¹⁹Gideon and the hundred men with him reached the edge of the camp at the beginning of the middle watch, just after they had changed the guard. They blew their trumpets and broke the jars^t that were in their hands. ²⁰The three companies blew the trumpets and smashed the jars. Grasping the torches^u in their left

hands and holding in their right hands the trumpets they were to blow, they shouted, "A sword[v] for the LORD and for Gideon!" [21]While each man held his position around the camp, all the Midianites ran, crying out as they fled.[w]

[22]When the three hundred trumpets sounded,[x] the LORD caused the men throughout the camp to turn on each other[y] with their swords.[z] The army fled to Beth Shittah toward Zererah as far as the border of Abel Meholah[a] near Tabbath. [23]Israelites from Naphtali, Asher[b] and all Manasseh were called out,[c] and they pursued the Midianites.[d] [24]Gideon sent messengers throughout the hill country of Ephraim, saying, "Come down against the Midianites and seize the waters of the Jordan[e] ahead of them as far as Beth Barah."

So all the men of Ephraim were called out and they took the waters of the Jordan as far as Beth Barah. [25]They also captured two of the Midianite leaders, Oreb and Zeeb[f]. They killed Oreb at the rock of Oreb,[g] and Zeeb at the winepress of Zeeb. They pursued the Midianites[h] and brought the heads of Oreb and Zeeb to Gideon, who was by the Jordan.[i]

Zebah and Zalmunna

8 Now the Ephraimites asked Gideon,[j] "Why have you treated us like this? Why didn't you call us when you went to fight Midian?[k]"[1] And they criticized him sharply.[m]

[2]But he answered them, "What have I accomplished compared to you? Aren't the gleanings of Ephraim's grapes better than the full grape harvest of Abiezer?[n] [3]God gave Oreb and Zeeb,[o] the Midianite leaders, into your hands. What was I able to do compared to you?" At this, their resentment against him subsided.

[4]Gideon and his three hundred men, exhausted yet keeping up the pursuit, came to the Jordan[p] and crossed it. [5]He said to the men of Succoth,[q] "Give my troops some bread; they are worn out,[r] and I am still pursuing Zebah and Zalmunna,[s] the kings of Midian."

[6]But the officials of Succoth[t] said, "Do you already have the hands of Zebah and Zalmunna in your possession? Why should we give bread[u] to your troops?"[v]

[7]Then Gideon replied, "Just for that, when the LORD has given Zebah and Zalmunna[w] into my hand, I will tear your flesh with desert thorns and briers."

[8]From there he went up to Peniel[i][x] and made the same request of them, but they answered as the men of Succoth had. [9]So he said to the men of Peniel, "When I return in triumph, I will tear down this tower."[y]

[10]Now Zebah and Zalmunna were in Karkor with a force of about fifteen thousand men, all that were left of the armies of the eastern peoples; a hundred and twenty thousand swordsmen had fallen.[z] [11]Gideon went up by the route of the nomads east of Nobah[a] and Jogbehah[b] and fell upon the unsuspecting army. [12]Zebah and Zalmunna, the two kings of Midian, fled, but he pursued them and captured them, routing their entire army.

[13]Gideon son of Joash[c] then returned from the battle by the Pass of Heres.[d] [14]He caught a young man of Succoth and questioned him, and the young man wrote down for him the names of the seventy-seven officials of Succoth,[e] the elders[f] of the town. [15]Then Gideon came and said to the men of Succoth, "Here are Zebah and Zalmunna, about whom you taunted me by saying, 'Do you already have the hands of Zebah and Zalmunna in your possession? Why should we give bread to your exhausted men?[g]'" [16]He took the elders of the town and taught the men of Succoth a lesson[h] by punishing them with desert thorns and briers. [17]He also pulled down the tower of Peniel[i] and killed the men of the town.[j]

[18]Then he asked Zebah and Zalmunna, "What kind of men did you kill at Tabor?[k]"

"Men like you," they answered, "each one with the bearing of a prince."

[19]Gideon replied, "Those were my brothers, the sons of my own mother. As surely as the LORD lives,[l] if you had spared their lives, I would not kill you." [20]Turning to Jether, his oldest son, he said, "Kill them!" But Jether did not draw his sword, because he was only a boy and was afraid.

[21]Zebah and Zalmunna said, "Come, do it yourself. 'As is the man, so is his strength.'" So Gideon stepped forward and killed them, and took the ornaments[m] off their camels' necks.

---

i 8 Hebrew Penuel, a variant of Peniel; also in verses 9 and 17

Gideon's Ephod

²²The Israelites said to Gideon, "Rule over us—you, your son and your grandson—because you have saved us out of the hand of Midian."

²³But Gideon told them, "I will not rule over you, nor will my son rule over you. The LORD will rule over you." ²⁴And he said, "I do have one request, that each of you give me an earring from your share of the plunder." (It was the custom of the Ishmaelites to wear gold earrings.)

²⁵They answered, "We'll be glad to give them." So they spread out a garment, and each man threw a ring from his plunder onto it. ²⁶The weight of the gold rings he asked for came to seventeen hundred shekels, not counting the ornaments, the pendants and the purple garments worn by the kings of Midian or the chains that were on their camels' necks. ²⁷Gideon made the gold into an ephod, which he placed in Ophrah, his town. All Israel prostituted themselves by worshiping it there, and it became a snare to Gideon and his family.

Gideon's Death

²⁸Thus Midian was subdued before the Israelites and did not raise its head again. During Gideon's lifetime, the land enjoyed peace forty years.

²⁹Jerub-Baal son of Joash went back home to live. ³⁰He had seventy sons of his own, for he had many wives. ³¹His concubine, who lived in Shechem, also bore him a son, whom he named Abimelech. ³²Gideon son of Joash died at a good old age and was buried in the tomb of his father Joash in Ophrah of the Abiezrites.

³³No sooner had Gideon died than the Israelites again prostituted themselves to the Baals. They set up Baal-Berith as their god and ³⁴did not remember the LORD their God, who had rescued them from the hands of all their enemies on every side. ³⁵They also failed to show kindness to the family of Jerub-Baal (that is, Gideon) for all the good things he had done for them.

Abimelech

9 Abimelech son of Jerub-Baal went to his mother's brothers in Shechem and said to them and to all his mother's clan, ²"Ask all the citizens of Shechem, 'Which is better for you: to have all seventy of Jerub-Baal's sons rule over you, or just one man?' Remember, I am your flesh and blood."

³When the brothers repeated all this to the citizens of Shechem, they were inclined to follow Abimelech, for they said, "He is our brother." ⁴They gave him seventy shekels of silver from the temple of Baal-Berith, and Abimelech used it to hire reckless adventurers, who became his followers. ⁵He went to his father's home in Ophrah and on one stone murdered his seventy brothers, the sons of Jerub-Baal. But Jotham, the youngest son of Jerub-Baal, escaped by hiding. ⁶Then all the citizens of Shechem and Beth Millo gathered beside the great tree at the pillar in Shechem to crown Abimelech king.

⁷When Jotham was told about this, he climbed up on the top of Mount Gerizim and shouted to them, "Listen to me, citizens of Shechem, so that God may listen to you. ⁸One day the trees went out to anoint a king for themselves. They said to the olive tree, 'Be our king.'

⁹"But the olive tree answered, 'Should I give up my oil, by which both gods and men are honored, to hold sway over the trees?'

¹⁰"Next, the trees said to the fig tree, 'Come and be our king.'

¹¹"But the fig tree replied, 'Should I give up my fruit, so good and sweet, to hold sway over the trees?'

¹²"Then the trees said to the vine, 'Come and be our king.'

¹³"But the vine answered, 'Should I give up my wine, which cheers both gods and men, to hold sway over the trees?'

¹⁴"Finally all the trees said to the thornbush, 'Come and be our king.'

¹⁵"The thornbush said to the trees, 'If you really want to anoint me king over you, come and take refuge in my shade; but if not, then let fire come out of the thornbush and consume the cedars of Lebanon!'

¹⁶"Now if you have acted honorably and in good faith when you made Abimelech king, and if you have been fair to

Jdg 2:21 ◀ ▶ *Jdg 9:20*

j 26 That is, about 43 pounds (about 19.5 kilograms) k 4 That is, about 1 3/4 pounds (about 0.8 kilogram)

JUDGES 9:17

Jerub-Baal and his family, and if you have treated him as he deserves— ¹⁷and to think that my father fought for you, risked[a] his life to rescue you from the hand of Midian ¹⁸(but today you have revolted against my father's family, murdered his seventy sons[b] on a single stone, and made Abimelech, the son of his slave girl, king over the citizens of Shechem because he is your brother)— ¹⁹if then you have acted honorably and in good faith toward Jerub-Baal and his family today,[c] may Abimelech be your joy, and may you be his, too! ²⁰But if you have not, let fire come out[d] from Abimelech and consume you, citizens of Shechem[e] and Beth Millo,[f] and let fire come out from you, citizens of Shechem and Beth Millo, and consume Abimelech!"

²¹Then Jotham[g] fled, escaping to Beer,[h] and he lived there because he was afraid of his brother Abimelech.

²²After Abimelech had governed Israel three years, ²³God sent an evil spirit[i] between Abimelech and the citizens of Shechem, who acted treacherously against Abimelech. ²⁴God did this in order that the crime against Jerub-Baal's seventy sons,[j] the shedding[k] of their blood, might be avenged[l] on their brother Abimelech and on the citizens of Shechem, who had helped him[m] murder his brothers. ²⁵In opposition to him these citizens of Shechem set men on the hilltops to ambush and rob everyone who passed by, and this was reported to Abimelech.

²⁶Now Gaal son of Ebed[n] moved with his brothers into Shechem, and its citizens put their confidence in him. ²⁷After they had gone out into the fields and gathered the grapes and trodden[o] them, they held a festival in the temple of their god.[p] While they were eating and drinking, they cursed Abimelech. ²⁸Then Gaal son of Ebed[q] said, "Who[r] is Abimelech, and who is Shechem, that we should be subject to him? Isn't he Jerub-Baal's son, and isn't Zebul his deputy? Serve the men of Hamor,[s] Shechem's father! Why should we serve Abimelech? ²⁹If only this people were under my command![t] Then I would get rid of him. I would say to Abimelech, 'Call out your whole army!' "[/u]

³⁰When Zebul the governor of the city heard what Gaal son of Ebed said, he was very angry. ³¹Under cover he sent messengers to Abimelech, saying, "Gaal son of Ebed and his brothers have come to Shechem and are stirring up the city against you. ³²Now then, during the night you and your men should come and lie in wait[v] in the fields. ³³In the morning at sunrise, advance against the city. When Gaal and his men come out against you, do whatever your hand finds to do."[w]

³⁴So Abimelech and all his troops set out by night and took up concealed positions near Shechem in four companies. ³⁵Now Gaal son of Ebed had gone out and was standing at the entrance to the city gate[x] just as Abimelech and his soldiers came out from their hiding place.[y]

³⁶When Gaal saw them, he said to Zebul, "Look, people are coming down from the tops of the mountains!"

Zebul replied, "You mistake the shadows of the mountains for men."

³⁷But Gaal spoke up again: "Look, people are coming down from the center of the land, and a company is coming from the direction of the soothsayers' tree."

³⁸Then Zebul said to him, "Where is your big talk now, you who said, 'Who is Abimelech that we should be subject to him?' Aren't these the men you ridiculed?[z] Go out and fight them!"

³⁹So Gaal led out[m] the citizens of Shechem and fought Abimelech. ⁴⁰Abimelech chased him, and many fell wounded in the flight—all the way to the entrance to the gate. ⁴¹Abimelech stayed in Arumah, and Zebul drove Gaal and his brothers out of Shechem.

⁴²The next day the people of Shechem went out to the fields, and this was reported to Abimelech. ⁴³So he took his men, divided them into three companies[a] and set an ambush[b] in the fields. When he saw the people coming out of the city, he rose to attack them. ⁴⁴Abimelech and the companies with him rushed forward to a position at the entrance to the city gate. Then two companies rushed upon those in the fields and struck them down. ⁴⁵All that day Abimelech pressed his attack against the city until he had captured it and killed its people. Then he de-

---

l 29 Septuagint; Hebrew him." Then he said to Abimelech, "Call out your whole army!" m 39 Or Gaal went out in the sight of

J Jdg 9:15 ◀ ▶ 1Sa 2:31

stroyed the city^c and scattered salt^d over it. ^{46}On hearing this, the citizens in the tower of Shechem went into the stronghold of the temple^e of El-Berith. ^{47}When Abimelech heard that they had assembled there, ^{48}he and all his men went up Mount Zalmon.^{f} He took an ax and cut off some branches, which he lifted to his shoulders. He ordered the men with him, "Quick! Do what you have seen me do!" ^{49}So all the men cut branches and followed Abimelech. They piled them against the stronghold and set it on fire over the people inside. So all the people in the tower of Shechem, about a thousand men and women, also died.

^{50}Next Abimelech went to Thebez^g and besieged it and captured it. ^{51}Inside the city, however, was a strong tower, to which all the men and women—all the people of the city—fled. They locked themselves in and climbed up on the tower roof. ^{52}Abimelech went to the tower and stormed it. But as he approached the entrance to the tower to set it on fire, ^{53}a woman dropped an upper millstone on his head and cracked his skull.^{h}

^{54}Hurriedly he called to his armor-bearer, "Draw your sword and kill me,^{i} so that they can't say, 'A woman killed him.'" So his servant ran him through, and he died. ^{55}When the Israelites saw that Abimelech was dead, they went home.

^{56}Thus God repaid the wickedness that Abimelech had done to his father by murdering his seventy brothers. ^{57}God also made the men of Shechem pay for all their wickedness.^{j} The curse of Jotham^k son of Jerub-Baal came on them.

Tola

10 After the time of Abimelech^l a man of Issachar,^{m} Tola son of Puah,^{n} the son of Dodo, rose to save^o Israel. He lived in Shamir,^{p} in the hill country of Ephraim. ^{2}He led^n Israel twenty-three years; then he died, and was buried in Shamir.

Jair

^{3}He was followed by Jair^q of Gilead, who led Israel twenty-two years. ^{4}He had thirty sons, who rode thirty donkeys.^{r} They controlled thirty towns in Gilead, which to this day are called Havvoth Jair.$^{o\,s}$ ^{5}When Jair^t died, he was buried in Kamon.

Jephthah

^{6}Again the Israelites did evil in the eyes of the Lord.^{u} They served the Baals and the Ashtoreths,^{v} and the gods of Aram,^{w} the gods of Sidon,^{x} the gods of Moab, the gods of the Ammonites$^{y\,z}$ and the gods of the Philistines.^{a} And because the Israelites forsook the Lord^b and no longer served him, ^{7}he became angry^c with them. He sold them^d into the hands of the Philistines and the Ammonites, ^{8}who that year shattered and crushed them. For eighteen years they oppressed all the Israelites on the east side of the Jordan in Gilead,^{e} the land of the Amorites. ^{9}The Ammonites also crossed the Jordan to fight against Judah,^{f} Benjamin and the house of Ephraim;^{g} and Israel was in great distress. ^{10}Then the Israelites cried^h out to the Lord, "We have sinned^i against you, forsaking our God and serving the Baals."^{j}

^{11}The Lord replied, "When the Egyptians,^{k} the Amorites,^{l} the Ammonites,^{m} ^{12}the Sidonians, the Amalekites^o and the Maonites^{pp} oppressed you^q and you cried to me for help, did I not save you from their hands? ^{13}But you have forsaken^r me and served other gods,^{s} so I will no longer save you. ^{14}Go and cry out to the gods you have chosen. Let them save^t you when you are in trouble!"^{u}

^{15}But the Israelites said to the Lord, "We have sinned. Do with us whatever you think best,^{v} but please rescue us now." ^{16}Then they got rid of the foreign gods among them and served the Lord.^{w} And he could bear Israel's misery^x no longer.^{y}

^{17}When the Ammonites were called to arms and camped in Gilead, the Israelites assembled and camped at Mizpah.^{z} ^{18}The leaders of the people of Gilead said to each other, "Whoever will launch the at-

P *Dt 4:29–31* ◄ ► *2Sa 12:13*
R *Jos 7:19* ◄ ► *1Sa 12:3*

^{n}2 Traditionally *judged*; also in verse 3 ^{o}4 Or *called the settlements of Jair* ^{p}12 Hebrew; some Septuagint manuscripts *Midianites*

tack against the Ammonites will be the head[a] of all those living in Gilead."

11

Jephthah[b] the Gileadite was a mighty warrior.[c] His father was Gilead;[d] his mother was a prostitute.[e] ²Gilead's wife also bore him sons, and when they were grown up, they drove Jephthah away. "You are not going to get any inheritance in our family," they said, "because you are the son of another woman." ³So Jephthah fled from his brothers and settled in the land of Tob,[f] where a group of adventurers[g] gathered around him and followed him.

⁴Some time later, when the Ammonites[h] made war on Israel, ⁵the elders of Gilead went to get Jephthah from the land of Tob. ⁶"Come," they said, "be our commander, so we can fight the Ammonites."

⁷Jephthah said to them, "Didn't you hate me and drive me from my father's house?[i] Why do you come to me now, when you're in trouble?"

⁸The elders of Gilead said to him, "Nevertheless, we are turning to you now; come with us to fight the Ammonites, and you will be our head[j] over all who live in Gilead."

⁹Jephthah answered, "Suppose you take me back to fight the Ammonites and the LORD gives them to me—will I really be your head?"

¹⁰The elders of Gilead replied, "The LORD is our witness;[k] we will certainly do as you say." ¹¹So Jephthah went with the elders[l] of Gilead, and the people made him head and commander over them. And he repeated[m] all his words before the LORD in Mizpah.[n]

¹²Then Jephthah sent messengers to the Ammonite king with the question: "What do you have against us that you have attacked our country?"

¹³The king of the Ammonites answered Jephthah's messengers, "When Israel came up out of Egypt, they took away my land from the Arnon[o] to the Jabbok,[p] all the way to the Jordan. Now give it back peaceably."

¹⁴Jephthah sent back messengers to the Ammonite king, ¹⁵saying:

"This is what Jephthah says: Israel did not take the land of Moab[q] or the land of the Ammonites.[r] ¹⁶But when they came up out of Egypt, Israel went through the desert to the Red Sea[q][s] and on to Kadesh.[t] ¹⁷Then Israel sent messengers[u] to the king of Edom, saying, 'Give us permission to go through your country,'[v] but the king of Edom would not listen. They sent also to the king of Moab,[w] and he refused.[x] So Israel stayed at Kadesh.

¹⁸"Next they traveled through the desert, skirted the lands of Edom[y] and Moab, passed along the eastern side[z] of the country of Moab, and camped on the other side of the Arnon.[a] They did not enter the territory of Moab, for the Arnon was its border.

¹⁹"Then Israel sent messengers[b] to Sihon king of the Amorites, who ruled in Heshbon,[c] and said to him, 'Let us pass through your country to our own place.'[d] ²⁰Sihon, however, did not trust Israel[r] to pass through his territory. He mustered all his men and encamped at Jahaz and fought with Israel.[e]

²¹"Then the LORD, the God of Israel, gave Sihon and all his men into Israel's hands, and they defeated them. Israel took over all the land of the Amorites who lived in that country, ²²capturing all of it from the Arnon to the Jabbok and from the desert to the Jordan.[f]

²³"Now since the LORD, the God of Israel, has driven the Amorites out before his people Israel, what right have you to take it over? ²⁴Will you not take what your god Chemosh[g] gives you? Likewise, whatever the LORD our God has given us,[h] we will possess. ²⁵Are you better than Balak son of Zippor,[i] king of Moab? Did he ever quarrel with Israel or fight with them?[j] ²⁶For three hundred years Israel occupied[k] Heshbon, Aroer,[l] the surrounding settlements and all the towns along the Arnon. Why didn't you retake them during that time? ²⁷I have not wronged you, but you are doing me wrong by waging war against me. Let the LORD, the Judge,[s][m] decide[n] the dispute this day

---

q 16 Hebrew *Yam Suph*; that is, Sea of Reeds   r 20 Or however, would not make an agreement for Israel   s 27 Or Ruler

between the Israelites and the Ammonites."

²⁸The king of Ammon, however, paid no attention to the message Jephthah sent him.

²⁹Then the Spirit of the Lord came upon Jephthah. He crossed Gilead and Manasseh, passed through Mizpah of Gilead, and from there he advanced against the Ammonites. ³⁰And Jephthah made a vow to the Lord: "If you give the Ammonites into my hands, ³¹whatever comes out of the door of my house to meet me when I return in triumph from the Ammonites will be the Lord's, and I will sacrifice it as a burnt offering."

³²Then Jephthah went over to fight the Ammonites, and the Lord gave them into his hands. ³³He devastated twenty towns from Aroer to the vicinity of Minnith, as far as Abel Keramim. Thus Israel subdued Ammon.

³⁴When Jephthah returned to his home in Mizpah, who should come out to meet him but his daughter, dancing to the sound of tambourines! She was an only child. Except for her he had neither son nor daughter. ³⁵When he saw her, he tore his clothes and cried, "Oh! My daughter! You have made me miserable and wretched, because I have made a vow to the Lord that I cannot break."

³⁶"My father," she replied, "you have given your word to the Lord. Do to me just as you promised, now that the Lord has avenged you of your enemies, the Ammonites. ³⁷But grant me this one request," she said. "Give me two months to roam the hills and weep with my friends, because I will never marry."

³⁸"You may go," he said. And he let her go for two months. She and the girls went into the hills and wept because she would never marry. ³⁹After the two months, she returned to her father and he did to her as he had vowed. And she was a virgin.

From this comes the Israelite custom ⁴⁰that each year the young women of Israel go out for four days to commemorate the daughter of Jephthah the Gileadite.

E *Jdg 6:34* ◄ ► *Jdg 13:25*
M *Jdg 6:34* ◄ ► *Jdg 14:6*

Jephthah and Ephraim

12 The men of Ephraim called out their forces, crossed over to Zaphon and said to Jephthah, "Why did you go to fight the Ammonites without calling us to go with you? We're going to burn down your house over your head."

²Jephthah answered, "I and my people were engaged in a great struggle with the Ammonites, and although I called, you didn't save me out of their hands. ³When I saw that you wouldn't help, I took my life in my hands and crossed over to fight the Ammonites, and the Lord gave me the victory over them. Now why have you come up today to fight me?"

⁴Jephthah then called together the men of Gilead and fought against Ephraim. The Gileadites struck them down because the Ephraimites had said, "You Gileadites are renegades from Ephraim and Manasseh." ⁵The Gileadites captured the fords of the Jordan leading to Ephraim, and whenever a survivor of Ephraim said, "Let me cross over," the men of Gilead asked him, "Are you an Ephraimite?" If he replied, "No," ⁶they said, "All right, say 'Shibboleth.' " If he said, "Sibboleth," because he could not pronounce the word correctly, they seized him and killed him at the fords of the Jordan. Forty-two thousand Ephraimites were killed at that time.

⁷Jephthah led* Israel six years. Then Jephthah the Gileadite died, and was buried in a town in Gilead.

Ibzan, Elon and Abdon

⁸After him, Ibzan of Bethlehem led Israel. ⁹He had thirty sons and thirty daughters. He gave his daughters away in marriage to those outside his clan, and for his sons he brought in thirty young women as wives from outside his clan. Ibzan led Israel seven years. ¹⁰Then Ibzan died, and was buried in Bethlehem.

¹¹After him, Elon the Zebulunite led Israel ten years. ¹²Then Elon died, and buried in Aijalon in the land of Zebulun.

¹³After him, Abdon son of Hillel, from Pirathon, led Israel. ¹⁴He had forty sons and thirty grandsons, who rode on seventy donkeys. He led Israel eight years. ¹⁵Then Abdon son of Hillel died, and was

*7 Traditionally *judged*; also in verses 8-14

buried at Pirathon in Ephraim, in the hill country of the Amalekites.r

The Birth of Samson

13 Again the Israelites did evil in the eyes of the LORD, so the LORD delivered them into the hands of the Philistines[s] for forty years.[t] ²A certain man of Zorah,[u] named Manoah,[v] from the clan of the Danites,[w] had a wife who was sterile and remained childless.[x] ³The angel of the LORD[y] appeared to her[z] and said, "You are sterile and childless, but you are going to conceive and have a son.[a] ⁴Now see to it that you drink no wine or other fermented drink[b] and that you do not eat anything unclean,[c] ⁵because you will conceive and give birth to a son.[d] No razor[e] may be used on his head, because the boy is to be a Nazirite,[f] set apart to God from birth, and he will begin[g] the deliverance of Israel from the hands of the Philistines."

⁶Then the woman went to her husband and told him, "A man of God[h] came to me. He looked like an angel of God,[i] very awesome.[j] I didn't ask him where he came from, and he didn't tell me his name. ⁷But he said to me, 'You will conceive and give birth to a son. Now then, drink no wine[k] or other fermented drink[l] and do not eat anything unclean, because the boy will be a Nazirite of God from birth until the day of his death.'"[m]

⁸Then Manoah[n] prayed to the LORD: "O Lord, I beg you, let the man of God[o] you sent to us come again to teach us how to bring up the boy who is to be born."

⁹God heard Manoah, and the angel of God came again to the woman while she was out in the field; but her husband Manoah was not with her. ¹⁰The woman hurried to tell her husband, "He's here! The man who appeared to me[p] the other day!"

¹¹Manoah got up and followed his wife.

E Jos 14:10–11 ◄ ► 1Sa 1:5–20
I Jdg 7:13–14 ◄ ► Jdg 13:5
I Jdg 13:3 ◄ ► Jdg 20:28

12:15 r Jdg 5:14

13:1 s Jdg 3:31
t Jdg 14:4

13:2 u S Jos 15:33
v ver 8; Jdg 16:31
w S Ge 30:6
x S Ge 11:30

13:3 y S Ge 16:7
z ver 10 a Isa 7:14;
Lk 1:13

13:4 b S Lev 10:9
c ver 14; Nu 6:2-4;
S Lk 1:15

13:5 d S Ge 3:15
e Isa 1:11
f S Nu 6:2,13;
Am 2:11,12
g Isa 7:13

13:6 h ver 8;
1Sa 2:27; 9:6;
1Ki 13:1; 17:18
i S Nu 22:22
j Ps 66:5

13:7 k Jer 35:6
l Lev 10:9
m 1Sa 1:11,28

13:8 n S ver 2
o S ver 6

13:10 p ver 3

13:14 q Lev 10:9
r S ver 4

13:15 s Jdg 6:19

13:16 t S Jdg 11:31
u S Jdg 6:22

13:17 v S Ge 32:29

13:18
w S Ge 32:29

13:19 x Jdg 6:20

13:20 y S Lev 9:24
z S Ge 17:3

13:21 a S Jdg 6:22

13:22
b S Nu 17:12;
S Dt 5:26
c S Ge 16:13;
S Ex 3:6; S 24:10;
S Jdg 6:22

13:23 d Ps 25:14

When he came to the man, he said, "Are you the one who talked to my wife?"

"I am," he said.

¹²So Manoah asked him, "When your words are fulfilled, what is to be the rule for the boy's life and work?"

¹³The angel of the LORD answered, "Your wife must do all that I have told her. ¹⁴She must not eat anything that comes from the grapevine, nor drink any wine or other fermented drink[q] nor eat anything unclean.[r] She must do everything I have commanded her."

¹⁵Manoah said to the angel of the LORD, "We would like you to stay until we prepare a young goat[s] for you."

¹⁶The angel of the LORD replied, "Even though you detain me, I will not eat any of your food. But if you prepare a burnt offering,[t] offer it to the LORD." (Manoah did not realize[u] that it was the angel of the LORD.)

¹⁷Then Manoah inquired of the angel of the LORD, "What is your name,[v] so that we may honor you when your word comes true?"

¹⁸He replied, "Why do you ask my name?[w] It is beyond understanding."[u]

¹⁹Then Manoah took a young goat, together with the grain offering, and sacrificed it on a rock[x] to the LORD. And the LORD did an amazing thing while Manoah and his wife watched: ²⁰As the flame[y] blazed up from the altar toward heaven, the angel of the LORD ascended in the flame. Seeing this, Manoah and his wife fell with their faces to the ground.[z] ²¹When the angel of the LORD did not show himself again to Manoah and his wife, Manoah realized[a] that it was the angel of the LORD.

²²"We are doomed[b] to die!" he said to his wife. "We have seen[c] God!"

²³But his wife answered, "If the LORD had meant to kill us, he would not have accepted a burnt offering and grain offering from our hands, nor shown us all these things or now told us this."[d]

²⁴The woman gave birth to a boy and

u 18 Or is wonderful

13:18 This angelic visitor is a theophany of Christ—a visible manifestation of God to humanity. The word translated "beyond understanding" is a Hebrew term for that which is "secret" or "wonderful." In Isa 9:6 a similar word occurs and is applied to the One who would come as the "Mighty God." Since God is beyond our understanding, we will never be able to "name" him in adequate terms.

named him Samson.ᵉ He grewᶠ and the LORD blessed him,ᵍ ²⁵and the Spirit of the LORD began to stir ʰ him while he was in Mahaneh Dan,ⁱ between Zorah and Eshtaol.

Samson's Marriage

14 Samsonʲ went down to Timnahᵏ and saw there a young Philistine woman. ²When he returned, he said to his father and mother, "I have seen a Philistine woman in Timnah; now get her for me as my wife."ˡ

³His father and mother replied, "Isn't there an acceptable woman among your relatives or among all our people?ᵐ Must you go to the uncircumcisedⁿ Philistines to get a wife?ᵒ"

But Samson said to his father, "Get her for me. She's the right one for me." ⁴(His parents did not know that this was from the LORD,ᵖ who was seeking an occasion to confront the Philistines;ᵠ for at that time they were ruling over Israel.)ʳ ⁵Samson went down to Timnah together with his father and mother. As they approached the vineyards of Timnah, suddenly a young lion came roaring toward him. ⁶The Spirit of the LORD came upon him in powerˢ so that he tore the lion apartᵗ with his bare hands as he might have torn a young goat. But he told neither his father nor his mother what he had done. ⁷Then he went down and talked with the woman, and he liked her.

⁸Some time later, when he went back to marry her, he turned aside to look at the lion's carcass. In it was a swarm of bees and some honey, ⁹which he scooped out with his hands and ate as he went along. When he rejoined his parents, he gave them some, and they too ate it. But he did not tell them that he had taken the honey from the lion's carcass.

¹⁰Now his father went down to see the woman. And Samson made a feastᵘ there, as was customary for bridegrooms. ¹¹When he appeared, he was given thirty companions.

¹²"Let me tell you a riddle,ᵛ" Samson said to them. "If you can give me the answer within the seven days of the feast,ʷ I will give you thirty linen garments and thirty sets of clothes.ˣ ¹³If you can't tell me the answer, you must give me thirty linen garments and thirty sets of clothes."

"Tell us your riddle," they said. "Let's hear it."

¹⁴He replied,

"Out of the eater, something to eat;
   out of the strong, something
      sweet."ʸ

For three days they could not give the answer.

¹⁵On the fourthᵛ day, they said to Samson's wife, "Coaxᶻ your husband into explaining the riddle for us, or we will burn you and your father's household to death.ᵃ Did you invite us here to rob us?"

¹⁶Then Samson's wife threw herself on him, sobbing, "You hate me! You don't really love me.ᵇ You've given my people a riddle, but you haven't told me the answer."

"I haven't even explained it to my father or mother," he replied, "so why should I explain it to you?" ¹⁷She cried the whole seven daysᶜ of the feast. So on the seventh day he finally told her, because she continued to press him. She in turn explained the riddle to her people. ¹⁸Before sunset on the seventh day the men of the town said to him,

"What is sweeter than honey?
   What is stronger than a lion?"ᵈ

Samson said to them,

"If you had not plowed with my heifer,
   you would not have solved my
      riddle."

¹⁹Then the Spirit of the LORD came upon him in power.ᵉ He went down to Ashkelon,ᶠ struck down thirty of their men, stripped them of their belongings and gave their clothes to those who had explained the riddle. Burning with anger,ᵍ he went up to his father's house. ²⁰And Samson's wife was given to the friendʰ who had attended him at his wedding.

Samson's Vengeance on the Philistines

15 Later on, at the time of wheat harvest,^{i} Samson^j took a young goat^k and went to visit his wife. He said, "I'm going to my wife's room."^{l} But her father would not let him go in.

^{2}"I was so sure you thoroughly hated her," he said, "that I gave her to your friend.^{m} Isn't her younger sister more attractive? Take her instead."

^{3}Samson said to them, "This time I have a right to get even with the Philistines; I will really harm them." ^{4}So he went out and caught three hundred foxes^n and tied them tail to tail in pairs. He then fastened a torch^o to every pair of tails, ^{5}lit the torches^p and let the foxes loose in the standing grain of the Philistines. He burned up the shocks^q and standing grain, together with the vineyards and olive groves.

^{6}When the Philistines asked, "Who did this?" they were told, "Samson, the Timnite's son-in-law, because his wife was given to his friend.^{r}"

So the Philistines went up and burned her^s and her father to death.^{t} ^{7}Samson said to them, "Since you've acted like this, I won't stop until I get my revenge on you." ^{8}He attacked them viciously and slaughtered many of them. Then he went down and stayed in a cave in the rock^u of Etam.^{v}

^{9}The Philistines went up and camped in Judah, spreading out near Lehi.^{w} ^{10}The men of Judah asked, "Why have you come to fight us?"

"We have come to take Samson prisoner," they answered, "to do to him as he did to us."

^{11}Then three thousand men from Judah went down to the cave in the rock of Etam and said to Samson, "Don't you realize that the Philistines are rulers over us?^{x} What have you done to us?"

He answered, "I merely did to them what they did to me."

^{12}They said to him, "We've come to tie you up and hand you over to the Philistines."

Samson said, "Swear to me^y that you won't kill me yourselves."

^{13}"Agreed," they answered. "We will only tie you up and hand you over to them. We will not kill you." So they bound him with two new ropes^z and led him up from the rock. ^{14}As he approached Lehi,^{a} the Philistines came toward him shouting. The Spirit of the LORD came upon him in power.^{b} The ropes on his arms became like charred flax,^{c} and the bindings dropped from his hands. ^{15}Finding a fresh jawbone of a donkey, he grabbed it and struck down a thousand men.^{d}

^{16}Then Samson said,

"With a donkey's jawbone
I have made donkeys of them.$^{w\,e}$
With a donkey's jawbone
I have killed a thousand men."

^{17}When he finished speaking, he threw away the jawbone; and the place was called Ramath Lehi.$^{x\,f}$

^{18}Because he was very thirsty, he cried out to the LORD,^{g} "You have given your servant this great victory.^{h} Must I now die of thirst and fall into the hands of the uncircumcised?" ^{19}Then God opened up the hollow place in Lehi, and water came out of it. When Samson drank, his strength returned and he revived.^{i} So the spring^j was called En Hakkore,^{y} and it is still there in Lehi.

^{20}Samson led^z Israel for twenty years^k in the days of the Philistines.

Samson and Delilah

16 One day Samson^l went to Gaza,^{m} where he saw a prostitute.^{n} He went in to spend the night with her. ^{2}The people of Gaza were told, "Samson is here!" So they surrounded the place and lay in wait for him all night at the city gate.^{o} They made no move during the night, saying, "At dawn^p we'll kill him."

^{3}But Samson lay there only until the middle of the night. Then he got up and took hold of the doors of the city gate, together with the two posts, and tore them loose, bar and all. He lifted them to his shoulders and carried them to the top of the hill that faces Hebron.^{q}

^{4}Some time later, he fell in love^r with a woman in the Valley of Sorek whose name was Delilah.^{s} ^{5}The rulers of the

---

E *Jdg 14:19* ◀ ▶ *1Sa 10:6–7*
M *Jdg 14:19* ◀ ▶ *1Sa 10:10–12*
F *Jos 5:12* ◀ ▶ *Ru 1:6*

w 16 Or *made a heap or two*; the Hebrew for *donkey* sounds like the Hebrew for *heap*. x 17 *Ramath Lehi* means *jawbone hill*. y 19 *En Hakkore* means *caller's spring*. z 20 Traditionally *judged*

Philistines went to her and said, "See if you can lure him into showing you the secret of his great strength and how we can overpower him so we may tie him up and subdue him. Each one of us will give you eleven hundred shekels of silver."

⁶So Delilah said to Samson, "Tell me the secret of your great strength and how you can be tied up and subdued."

⁷Samson answered her, "If anyone ties me with seven fresh thongs that have not been dried, I'll become as weak as any other man."

⁸Then the rulers of the Philistines brought her seven fresh thongs that had not been dried, and she tied him with them. ⁹With men hidden in the room, she called to him, "Samson, the Philistines are upon you!" But he snapped the thongs as easily as a piece of string snaps when it comes close to a flame. So the secret of his strength was not discovered.

¹⁰Then Delilah said to Samson, "You have made a fool of me; you lied to me. Come now, tell me how you can be tied."

¹¹He said, "If anyone ties me securely with new ropes that have never been used, I'll become as weak as any other man."

¹²So Delilah took new ropes and tied him with them. Then, with men hidden in the room, she called to him, "Samson, the Philistines are upon you!" But he snapped the ropes off his arms as if they were threads.

¹³Delilah then said to Samson, "Until now, you have been making a fool of me and lying to me. Tell me how you can be tied."

He replied, "If you weave the seven braids of my head into the fabric ⌊on the loom⌋ and tighten it with the pin, I'll become as weak as any other man." So while he was sleeping, Delilah took the seven braids of his head, wove them into the fabric ¹⁴and tightened it with the pin.

Again she called to him, "Samson, the Philistines are upon you!" He awoke from his sleep and pulled up the pin and the loom, with the fabric.

¹⁵Then she said to him, "How can you say, 'I love you,' when you won't confide in me? This is the third time you have made a fool of me and haven't told me the secret of your great strength."

¹⁶With such nagging she prodded him day after day until he was tired to death.

¹⁷So he told her everything. "No razor has ever been used on my head," he said, "because I have been a Nazirite set apart to God since birth. If my head were shaved, my strength would leave me, and I would become as weak as any other man."

¹⁸When Delilah saw that he had told her everything, she sent word to the rulers of the Philistines, "Come back once more; he has told me everything." So the rulers of the Philistines returned with the silver in their hands. ¹⁹Having put him to sleep on her lap, she called a man to shave off the seven braids of his hair, and so began to subdue him. And his strength left him.

²⁰Then she called, "Samson, the Philistines are upon you!"

He awoke from his sleep and thought, "I'll go out as before and shake myself free." But he did not know that the LORD had left him.

²¹Then the Philistines seized him, gouged out his eyes and took him down to Gaza. Binding him with bronze shackles, they set him to grinding in the prison. ²²But the hair on his head began to grow again after it had been shaved.

The Death of Samson

²³Now the rulers of the Philistines assembled to offer a great sacrifice to Dagon their god and to celebrate, saying, "Our god has delivered Samson, our enemy, into our hands."

²⁴When the people saw him, they praised their god, saying,

"Our god has delivered our enemy
  into our hands,
the one who laid waste our land
  and multiplied our slain."

²⁵While they were in high spirits, they shouted, "Bring out Samson to entertain us." So they called Samson out of the prison, and he performed for them.

When they stood him among the pillars, ²⁶Samson said to the servant who

Q Ge 6:3 ◀ ▶ 1Sa 16:14

ᵃ 5 That is, about 28 pounds (about 13 kilograms) ᵇ 7 Or bowstrings; also in verses 8 and 9 ᶜ 13,14 Some Septuagint manuscripts; Hebrew "I can, if you weave the seven braids of my head into the fabric ⌊on the loom⌋." ¹⁴So she ᵈ 19 Hebrew; some Septuagint manuscripts and he began to weaken

held his hand, "Put me where I can feel the pillars that support the temple, so that I may lean against them." ²⁷Now the temple was crowded with men and women; all the rulers of the Philistines were there, and on the roofʷ were about three thousand men and women watching Samson perform. ²⁸Then Samson prayed to the LORD,ˣ "O Sovereign LORD, remember me. O God, please strengthen me just once more, and let me with one blow get revengeʸ on the Philistines for my two eyes." ²⁹Then Samson reached toward the two central pillars on which the temple stood. Bracing himself against them, his right hand on the one and his left hand on the other, ³⁰Samson said, "Let me die with the Philistines!" Then he pushed with all his might, and down came the temple on the rulers and all the people in it. Thus he killed many more when he died than while he lived.

³¹Then his brothers and his father's whole family went down to get him. They brought him back and buried him between Zorah and Eshtaol in the tomb of Manoahᶻ his father. He had ledᵉᵃ Israel twenty years.ᵇ

Micah's Idols

17 Now a man named Micahᶜ from the hill country of Ephraim ²said to his mother, "The eleven hundred shekelsᶠ of silver that were taken from you and about which I heard you utter a curse—I have that silver with me; I took it."

Then his mother said, "The LORD bless you,ᵈ my son!"

³When he returned the eleven hundred shekels of silver to his mother, she said, "I solemnly consecrate my silver to the LORD for my son to make a carved image and a cast idol.ᵉ I will give it back to you."

⁴So he returned the silver to his mother, and she took two hundred shekelsᵍ of silver and gave them to a silversmith, who made them into the image and the idol.ᶠ And they were put in Micah's house.

⁵Now this man Micah had a shrine,ᵍ and he made an ephodʰ and some idolsⁱ and installedʲ one of his sons as his priest.ᵏ ⁶In those days Israel had no king;ˡ everyone did as he saw fit.ᵐ

⁷A young Leviteⁿ from Bethlehem in Judah,ᵒ who had been living within the clan of Judah, ⁸left that town in search of some other place to stay. On his wayʰ he came to Micah's house in the hill country of Ephraim.

⁹Micah asked him, "Where are you from?"

"I'm a Levite from Bethlehem in Judah,ᵖ" he said, "and I'm looking for a place to stay."

¹⁰Then Micah said to him, "Live with me and be my fatherᵠ and priest,ʳ and I'll give you ten shekelsⁱ of silver a year, your clothes and your food." ¹¹So the Levite agreed to live with him, and the young man was to him like one of his sons. ¹²Then Micah installedˢ the Levite, and the young man became his priestᵗ and lived in his house. ¹³And Micah said, "Now I know that the LORD will be good to me, since this Levite has become my priest."ᵘ

Danites Settle in Laish

18 In those days Israel had no king.ᵛ And in those days the tribe of the Danites was seeking a place of their own where they might settle, because they had not yet come into an inheritance among the tribes of Israel.ʷ ²So the Danitesˣ sent five warriorsʸ from Zorah and Eshtaol to spy outᶻ the land and explore it. These men represented all their clans. They told them, "Go, explore the land."ᵃ

The men entered the hill country of Ephraim and came to the house of Micah,ᵇ where they spent the night. ³When they were near Micah's house, they recognized the voice of the young Levite;ᶜ so they turned in there and asked him, "Who brought you here? What are you doing in this place? Why are you here?"

⁴He told them what Micah had done for him, and said, "He has hired me and I am his priest.ᵈ"

⁵Then they said to him, "Please inquire of Godᵉ to learn whether our journey will be successful."

⁶The priest answered them, "Go in peace.ᶠ Your journey has the LORD's approval."

⁷So the five menᵍ left and came to Laish,ʰ where they saw that the people

---

e 31 Traditionally *judged*   *f 2* That is, about 28 pounds (about 13 kilograms)   *g 4* That is, about 5 pounds (about 2.3 kilograms)   *h 8* Or *To carry on his profession*   *i 10* That is, about 4 ounces (about 110 grams)

were living in safety, like the Sidonians, unsuspecting and secure.[i] And since their land lacked nothing, they were prosperous.[j] Also, they lived a long way from the Sidonians[j] and had no relationship with anyone else."[k]

[8] When they returned to Zorah and Eshtaol, their brothers asked them, "How did you find things?"

[9] They answered, "Come on, let's attack them! We have seen that the land is very good. Aren't you going to do something? Don't hesitate to go there and take it over.[k] [10] When you get there, you will find an unsuspecting people and a spacious land that God has put into your hands, a land that lacks nothing[l] whatever.[m]"

[11] Then six hundred men[n] from the clan of the Danites,[o] armed for battle, set out from Zorah and Eshtaol. [12] On their way they set up camp near Kiriath Jearim[p] in Judah. This is why the place west of Kiriath Jearim is called Mahaneh Dan[1q] to this day. [13] From there they went on to the hill country of Ephraim and came to Micah's house.[r]

[14] Then the five men who had spied out the land of Laish[s] said to their brothers, "Do you know that one of these houses has an ephod,[t] other household gods, a carved image and a cast idol?[u] Now you know what to do." [15] So they turned in there and went to the house of the young Levite at Micah's place and greeted him. [16] The six hundred Danites,[v] armed for battle, stood at the entrance to the gate. [17] The five men who had spied out the land went inside and took the carved image, the ephod, the other household gods[w] and the cast idol while the priest and the six hundred armed men[x] stood at the entrance to the gate.

[18] When these men went into Micah's house and took[y] the carved image, the ephod, the other household gods[z] and the cast idol, the priest said to them, "What are you doing?"

[19] They answered him, "Be quiet![a] Don't say a word. Come with us, and be our father and priest.[b] Isn't it better that you serve a tribe and clan[c] in Israel as priest rather than just one man's household?" [20] Then the priest was glad. He took the ephod, the other household gods and the carved image and went along with the people. [21] Putting their little children, their livestock and their possessions in front of them, they turned away and left.

[22] When they had gone some distance from Micah's house, the men who lived near Micah were called together and overtook the Danites. [23] As they shouted after them, the Danites turned and said to Micah, "What's the matter with you that you called out your men to fight?"

[24] He replied, "You took[d] the gods I made, and my priest, and went away. What else do I have? How can you ask, 'What's the matter with you?'"

[25] The Danites answered, "Don't argue with us, or some hot-tempered men will attack you, and you and your family will lose your lives." [26] So the Danites went their way, and Micah, seeing that they were too strong for him,[e] turned around and went back home.

[27] Then they took what Micah had made, and his priest, and went on to Laish, against a peaceful and unsuspecting people.[f] They attacked them with the sword and burned[g] down their city.[h] [28] There was no one to rescue them because they lived a long way from Sidon[i] and had no relationship with anyone else. The city was in a valley near Beth Rehob.[j]

The Danites rebuilt the city and settled there. [29] They named it Dan[k] after their forefather Dan, who was born to Israel—though the city used to be called Laish.[l] [30] There the Danites set up for themselves the idols, and Jonathan son of Gershom,[m] the son of Moses,[m] and his sons were priests for the tribe of Dan until the time of the captivity of the land. [31] They continued to use the idols Micah had made,[n] all the time the house of God[o] was in Shiloh.[p]

A Levite and His Concubine

19 In those days Israel had no king. Now a Levite who lived in a remote area in the hill country of Ephraim[q] took a concubine from Bethlehem in Judah.[r] [2] But she was unfaithful to him. She left him and went back to her father's house in Bethlehem, Judah. After she had been there four months, [3] her husband

---

j 7 The meaning of the Hebrew for this clause is uncertain. k 7 Hebrew; some Septuagint manuscripts with the Arameans *l 12* Mahaneh Dan *means Dan's camp. m 30 An ancient Hebrew scribal tradition, some Septuagint manuscripts and Vulgate; Masoretic Text* Manasseh

went to her to persuade her to return. He had with him his servant and two donkeys. She took him into her father's house, and when her father saw him, he gladly welcomed him. ⁴His father-in-law, the girl's father, prevailed upon him to stay; so he remained with him three days, eating and drinking,ˢ and sleeping there.

⁵On the fourth day they got up early and he prepared to leave, but the girl's father said to his son-in-law, "Refresh yourselfᵗ with something to eat; then you can go." ⁶So the two of them sat down to eat and drink together. Afterward the girl's father said, "Please stay tonight and enjoy yourself.ᵘ" ⁷And when the man got up to go, his father-in-law persuaded him, so he stayed there that night. ⁸On the morning of the fifth day, when he rose to go, the girl's father said, "Refresh yourself. Wait till afternoon!" So the two of them ate together.

⁹Then when the man, with his concubine and his servant, got up to leave, his father-in-law, the girl's father, said, "Now look, it's almost evening. Spend the night here; the day is nearly over. Stay and enjoy yourself. Early tomorrow morning you can get up and be on your way home." ¹⁰But, unwilling to stay another night, the man left and went toward Jebusᵛ (that is, Jerusalem), with his two saddled donkeys and his concubine.

¹¹When they were near Jebus and the day was almost gone, the servant said to his master, "Come, let's stop at this city of the Jebusitesʷ and spend the night." ¹²His master replied, "No. We won't go into an alien city, whose people are not Israelites. We will go on to Gibeah." ¹³He added, "Come, let's try to reach Gibeah or Ramahˣ and spend the night in one of those places." ¹⁴So they went on, and the sun set as they neared Gibeah in Benjamin.ʸ ¹⁵There they stopped to spend the night.ᶻ They went and sat in the city square,ᵃ but no one took them into his home for the night.

¹⁶That eveningᵇ an old man from the hill country of Ephraim,ᶜ who was living in Gibeah (the men of the place were Benjamites), came in from his work in the fields. ¹⁷When he looked and saw the traveler in the city square, the old man asked, "Where are you going? Where did you come from?"ᵈ

¹⁸He answered, "We are on our way from Bethlehem in Judah to a remote area in the hill country of Ephraim where I live. I have been to Bethlehem in Judah and now I am going to the house of the Lord.ᵉ No one has taken me into his house. ¹⁹We have both straw and fodderᶠ for our donkeysᵍ and bread and wineʰ for ourselves your servants—me, your maidservant, and the young man with us. We don't need anything."

²⁰"You are welcome at my house," the old man said. "Let me supply whatever you need. Only don't spend the night in the square." ²¹So he took him into his house and fed his donkeys. After they had washed their feet, they had something to eat and drink.ⁱ

²²While they were enjoying themselves,ʲ some of the wicked menᵏ of the city surrounded the house. Pounding on the door, they shouted to the old man who owned the house, "Bring out the man who came to your house so we can have sex with him.ˡ"

²³The owner of the house went outsideᵐ and said to them, "No, my friends, don't be so vile. Since this man is my guest, don't do this disgraceful thing.ⁿ ²⁴Look, here is my virgin daughter,ᵒ and his concubine. I will bring them out to you now, and you can use them and do to them whatever you wish. But to this man, don't do such a disgraceful thing."

²⁵But the men would not listen to him. So the man took his concubine and sent her outside to them, and they raped herᵖ and abused herᵠ throughout the night, and at dawn they let her go. ²⁶At daybreak the woman went back to the house where her master was staying, fell down at the door and lay there until daylight.

²⁷When her master got up in the morning and opened the door of the house and stepped out to continue on his way, there lay his concubine, fallen in the doorway of the house, with her hands on the threshold. ²⁸He said to her, "Get up; let's go." But there was no answer. Then the man put her on his donkey and set out for home.

²⁹When he reached home, he took a knifeʳ and cut up his concubine, limb by limb, into twelve parts and sent them into all the areas of Israel.ˢ ³⁰Everyone who saw it said, "Such a thing has never been seen or done, not since the day the

Israelites came up out of Egypt. Think about it! Consider it! Tell us what to do!"

Israelites Fight the Benjamites

20 Then all the Israelites from Dan to Beersheba and from the land of Gilead came out as one man and assembled before the LORD in Mizpah. ²The leaders of all the people of the tribes of Israel took their places in the assembly of the people of God, four hundred thousand soldiers armed with swords. ³(The Benjamites heard that the Israelites had gone up to Mizpah.) Then the Israelites said, "Tell us how this awful thing happened."

⁴So the Levite, the husband of the murdered woman, said, "I and my concubine came to Gibeah in Benjamin to spend the night. ⁵During the night the men of Gibeah came after me and surrounded the house, intending to kill me. They raped my concubine, and she died. ⁶I took my concubine, cut her into pieces and sent one piece to each region of Israel's inheritance, because they committed this lewd and disgraceful act in Israel. ⁷Now, all you Israelites, speak up and give your verdict."

⁸All the people rose as one man, saying, "None of us will go home. No, not one of us will return to his house. ⁹But now this is what we'll do to Gibeah: We'll go up against it as the lot directs. ¹⁰We'll take ten men out of every hundred from all the tribes of Israel, and a hundred from a thousand, and a thousand from ten thousand, to get provisions for the army. Then, when the army arrives at Gibeah in Benjamin, it can give them what they deserve for all this vileness done in Israel." ¹¹So all the men of Israel got together and united as one man against the city.

¹²The tribes of Israel sent men throughout the tribe of Benjamin, saying, "What about this awful crime that was committed among you? ¹³Now surrender those wicked men of Gibeah so that we may put them to death and purge the evil from Israel."

But the Benjamites would not listen to their fellow Israelites. ¹⁴From their towns they came together at Gibeah to fight against the Israelites. ¹⁵At once the Benjamites mobilized twenty-six thousand swordsmen from their towns, in addition to seven hundred chosen men from those living in Gibeah. ¹⁶Among all these soldiers there were seven hundred chosen men who were left-handed, each of whom could sling a stone at a hair and not miss.

¹⁷Israel, apart from Benjamin, mustered four hundred thousand swordsmen, all of them fighting men.

¹⁸The Israelites went up to Bethel and inquired of God. They said, "Who of us shall go first to fight against the Benjamites?"

The LORD replied, "Judah shall go first."

¹⁹The next morning the Israelites got up and pitched camp near Gibeah. ²⁰The men of Israel went out to fight the Benjamites and took up battle positions against them at Gibeah. ²¹The Benjamites came out of Gibeah and cut down twenty-two thousand Israelites on the battlefield that day. ²²But the men of Israel encouraged one another and again took up their positions where they had stationed themselves the first day. ²³The Israelites went up and wept before the LORD until evening, and they inquired of the LORD. They said, "Shall we go up again to battle against the Benjamites, our brothers?"

The LORD answered, "Go up against them."

²⁴Then the Israelites drew near to Benjamin the second day. ²⁵This time, when the Benjamites came out from Gibeah to oppose them, they cut down another eighteen thousand Israelites, all of them armed with swords.

²⁶Then the Israelites, all the people, went up to Bethel, and there they sat weeping before the LORD. They fasted that day until evening and presented burnt offerings and fellowship offerings to the LORD. ²⁷And the Israelites inquired of the LORD. (In those days the ark of the covenant of God was there, ²⁸with Phinehas son of Eleazar, the son of Aaron, ministering before it.) They asked, "Shall we go up again to battle with Benjamin our brother, or not?"

◀ *Jdg 13:5* ▶ *1Sa 7:3*

n 10 One Hebrew manuscript; most Hebrew manuscripts *Geba*, a variant of *Gibeah* ○ *18* Or *to the house of God*; also in verse 26
p 26 Traditionally *peace offerings*

The LORD responded, "Go, for tomorrow I will give them into your hands."

²⁹Then Israel set an ambush around Gibeah. ³⁰They went up against the Benjamites on the third day and took up positions against Gibeah as they had done before. ³¹The Benjamites came out to meet them and were drawn away from the city. They began to inflict casualties on the Israelites as before, so that about thirty men fell in the open field and on the roads—the one leading to Bethel and the other to Gibeah.

³²While the Benjamites were saying, "We are defeating them as before," the Israelites were saying, "Let's retreat and draw them away from the city to the roads."

³³All the men of Israel moved from their places and took up positions at Baal Tamar, and the Israelite ambush charged out of its place on the west of Gibeah. ³⁴Then ten thousand of Israel's finest men made a frontal attack on Gibeah. The fighting was so heavy that the Benjamites did not realize how near disaster was. ³⁵The LORD defeated Benjamin before Israel, and on that day the Israelites struck down 25,100 Benjamites, all armed with swords. ³⁶Then the Benjamites saw that they were beaten.

Now the men of Israel had given way before Benjamin, because they relied on the ambush they had set near Gibeah. ³⁷The men who had been in ambush made a sudden dash into Gibeah, spread out and put the whole city to the sword. ³⁸The men of Israel had arranged with the ambush that they should send up a great cloud of smoke from the city, ³⁹and then the men of Israel would turn in the battle.

The Benjamites had begun to inflict casualties on the men of Israel (about thirty), and they said, "We are defeating them as in the first battle." ⁴⁰But when the column of smoke began to rise from the city, the Benjamites turned and saw the smoke of the whole city going up into the sky. ⁴¹Then the men of Israel turned on them, and the men of Benjamin were terrified, because they realized that disaster had come upon them. ⁴²So they fled before the Israelites in the direction of the desert, but they could not escape the battle. And the men of Israel who came out of the towns cut them down there. ⁴³They surrounded the Benjamites, chased them and easily overran them in the vicinity of Gibeah on the east. ⁴⁴Eighteen thousand Benjamites fell, all of them valiant fighters. ⁴⁵As they turned and fled toward the desert to the rock of Rimmon, the Israelites cut down five thousand men along the roads. They kept pressing after the Benjamites as far as Gidom and struck down two thousand more.

⁴⁶On that day twenty-five thousand Benjamite swordsmen fell, all of them valiant fighters. ⁴⁷But six hundred men turned and fled into the desert to the rock of Rimmon, where they stayed four months. ⁴⁸The men of Israel went back to Benjamin and put all the towns to the sword, including the animals and everything else they found. All the towns they came across they set on fire.

Wives for the Benjamites

21 The men of Israel had taken an oath at Mizpah: "Not one of us will give his daughter in marriage to a Benjamite."

²The people went to Bethel, where they sat before God until evening, raising their voices and weeping bitterly. ³"O LORD, the God of Israel," they cried, "why has this happened to Israel? Why should one tribe be missing from Israel today?"

⁴Early the next day the people built an altar and presented burnt offerings and fellowship offerings.

⁵Then the Israelites asked, "Who from all the tribes of Israel has failed to assemble before the LORD?" For they had taken a solemn oath that anyone who failed to assemble before the LORD at Mizpah should certainly be put to death.

⁶Now the Israelites grieved for their brothers, the Benjamites. "Today one tribe is cut off from Israel," they said. ⁷"How can we provide wives for those who are left, since we have taken an oath by the LORD not to give them any of our daughters in marriage?" ⁸Then they asked, "Which one of the tribes of Israel failed to assemble before the LORD at Mizpah?" They discovered that no one from

---

q 33 Some Septuagint manuscripts and Vulgate; the meaning of the Hebrew for this word is uncertain. *r 33* Hebrew *Geba*, a variant of *Gibeah*   *s 43* The meaning of the Hebrew for this word is uncertain.   *t 2* Or *to the house of God*   *u 4* Traditionally *peace offerings*

Jabesh Gilead¹ had come to the camp for the assembly. ⁹For when they counted the people, they found that none of the people of Jabesh Gilead were there.

¹⁰So the assembly sent twelve thousand fighting men with instructions to go to Jabesh Gilead and put to the sword those living there, including the women and children. ¹¹"This is what you are to do," they said. "Kill every male ᵐ and every woman who is not a virgin.ⁿ" ¹²They found among the people living in Jabesh Gilead four hundred young women who had never slept with a man, and they took them to the camp at Shilohᵒ in Canaan.

¹³Then the whole assembly sent an offer of peaceᵖ to the Benjamites at the rock of Rimmon.ᵠ ¹⁴So the Benjamites returned at that time and were given the women of Jabesh Gilead who had been spared. But there were not enough for all of them.

¹⁵The people grieved for Benjamin,ʳ because the LORD had made a gap in the tribes of Israel. ¹⁶And the elders of the assembly said, "With the women of Benjamin destroyed, how shall we provide wives for the men who are left? ¹⁷The Benjamite survivors must have heirs," they said, "so that a tribe of Israel will not be wiped out.ˢ ¹⁸We can't give them our daughters as wives, since we Israelites have taken this oath:ᵗ 'Cursed be anyone who givesᵘ a wife to a Benjamite.' ¹⁹But look, there is the annual festival of the LORD in Shiloh,ᵛ to the north of Bethel,ʷ and east of the road that goes from Bethel to Shechem,ˣ and to the south of Lebonah."

²⁰So they instructed the Benjamites, saying, "Go and hide in the vineyards ²¹and watch. When the girls of Shiloh come out to join in the dancing,ʸ then rush from the vineyards and each of you seize a wife from the girls of Shiloh and go to the land of Benjamin. ²²When their fathers or brothers complain to us, we will say to them, 'Do us a kindness by helping them, because we did not get wives for them during the war, and you are innocent, since you did not giveᶻ your daughters to them.' "

²³So that is what the Benjamites did. While the girls were dancing,ᵃ each man caught one and carried her off to be his wife. Then they returned to their inheritanceᵇ and rebuilt the towns and settled in them.ᶜ

²⁴At that time the Israelites left that place and went home to their tribes and clans, each to his own inheritance.

²⁵In those days Israel had no king; everyone did as he saw fit.ᵈ

Ruth

Author: Unknown

Theme: Devotion yields redemption and restoration

Date of Writing: C. 1000 B.C.

Outline of Ruth
  I. Ruth's Selfless Decision (1:1–22)
  II. Ruth's Favorable Reception (2:1—3:18)
  III. Ruth's Compassionate Redemption (4:1–22)

THIS BOOK IS named after a young woman from Moab named Ruth, the great-grandmother of David and ancestress of Jesus (see 4: 22; Mt 1:1, 5). During a famine in Israel, Elimelech, Naomi and their two sons had abandoned their home in Bethlehem to find food in Moab. While they were there, Ruth met and married one of the sons. Years later, Naomi's and Ruth's husbands died, leaving both women widowed and stranded in Moab. Naomi chose to return to Bethlehem, and Ruth went with her. The book recounts this short story with charming simplicity and further chronicles Ruth's life in Bethlehem, her courtship and marriage, and the birth of her son Obed, the grandfather of King David.

Ancient Jewish manuscripts considered the book of Ruth and the book of Judges as one volume because the events in Ruth occurred during the period of the judges. Later Jewish manuscripts separated the two volumes and included Ruth, because of its literary beauty and subject matter, in a five-book grouping called the megilloth. According to Jewish custom certain books were to be read aloud in the synagogues (see Lk 4:16–17). The books of the megilloth were usually read at feast seasons, with the book of Ruth scheduled to be read at the Feast of Weeks (Pentecost).

The exact dating of this book is uncertain, but because the author explained customs that seemed unfamiliar to readers (see 4:6–8) many scholars believe this book was composed during the time of King David. Note also the reference to David's lineage in the last chapter (see 4:17–22)—a commonplace identifier used during the monarchical period.

Naomi and Ruth

1 In the days when the judges ruled,ᵃ there was a famine in the land,ᵇ and a man from Bethlehem in Judah,ᶜ together with his wife and two sons, went to live for a whileᵈ in the country of Moab.ᵉ ²The man's name was Elimelech,ᶠ his wife's name Naomi, and the names of his two sons were Mahlon and Kilion.ᵍ They were Ephrathitesʰ from Bethlehem,ⁱ Judah. And they went to Moab and lived there.

³Now Elimelech, Naomi's husband, died, and she was left with her two sons. ⁴They married Moabite women,ʲ one named Orpah and the other Ruth.ᵏ After they had lived there about ten years, ⁵both Mahlon and Kilionˡ also died,ᵐ and Naomi was left without her two sons and her husband.

⁶When she heard in Moabⁿ that the LORD had come to the aid of his peopleᵒ by providing foodᵖ for them, Naomi and her daughters-in-lawᵠ prepared to return home from there. ⁷With her two daughters-in-law she left the place where she had been living and set out on the road that would take them back to the land of Judah.

⁸Then Naomi said to her two daughters-in-law, "Go back, each of you, to your mother's home.ʳ May the LORD show kindnessˢ to you, as you have shown to your deadᵗ and to me. ⁹May the LORD grant that each of you will find restᵘ in the home of another husband."

Then she kissedᵛ them and they wept aloudʷ ¹⁰and said to her, "We will go back with you to your people."

¹¹But Naomi said, "Return home, my daughters. Why would you come with me? Am I going to have any more sons, who could become your husbands?ˣ ¹²Return home, my daughters; I am too old to have another husband. Even if I thought there was still hope for me—even if I had a husband tonight and then gave birth to sons— ¹³would you wait until they grew up?ʸ Would you remain unmarried for them? No, my daughters. It is more bitterᶻ for me than for you, because the LORD's hand has gone out against me!ᵃ"

¹⁴At this they weptᵇ again. Then Orpah kissed her mother-in-lawᶜ good-by,ᵈ but Ruth clung to her.ᵉ

F *Jdg 15:18–19* ◄ ► *1Ki 17:1–16*

¹⁵"Look," said Naomi, "your sister-in-lawᶠ is going back to her people and her gods.ᵍ Go back with her."

¹⁶But Ruth replied, "Don't urge me to leave youʰ or to turn back from you. Where you go I will go,ⁱ and where you stay I will stay. Your people will be my peopleʲ and your God my God.ᵏ ¹⁷Where you die I will die, and there I will be buried. May the LORD deal with me, be it ever so severely,ˡ if anything but death separates you and me."ᵐ ¹⁸When Naomi realized that Ruth was determined to go with her, she stopped urging her.ⁿ

¹⁹So the two women went on until they came to Bethlehem.ᵒ When they arrived in Bethlehem, the whole town was stirredᵖ because of them, and the women exclaimed, "Can this be Naomi?"

²⁰"Don't call me Naomi,ᵇ" she told them. "Call me Mara,ᶜ because the Almightyᵈᵠ has made my life very bitter.ʳ ²¹I went away full, but the LORD has brought me back empty.ˢ Why call me Naomi? The LORD has afflictedᵉ me;ᵗ the Almighty has brought misfortune upon me."

²²So Naomi returned from Moab accompanied by Ruth the Moabitess,ᵘ her daughter-in-law,ᵛ arriving in Bethlehem as the barley harvestʷ was beginning.ˣ

Ruth Meets Boaz

2 Now Naomi had a relativeʸ on her husband's side, from the clan of Elimelech,ᶻ a man of standing,ᵃ whose name was Boaz.ᵇ

²And Ruth the Moabitessᶜ said to Naomi, "Let me go to the fields and pick up the leftover grainᵈ behind anyone in whose eyes I find favor.ᵉ"

Naomi said to her, "Go ahead, my daughter." ³So she went out and began to glean in the fields behind the harvesters.ᶠ As it turned out, she found herself working in a field belonging to Boaz, who was from the clan of Elimelech.ᵍ

⁴Just then Boaz arrived from Bethlehem and greeted the harvesters, "The LORD be with you!ʰ"

"The LORD bless you!ⁱ" they called back.

a 1 Traditionally *judged* *b 20* Naomi means *pleasant;* also in verse 21. *c 20* Mara means *bitter.* *d 20* Hebrew *Shaddai;* also in verse 21 *e 21* Or *has testified against*

RUTH 2:5

⁵Boaz asked the foreman of his harvesters, "Whose young woman is that?"

⁶The foreman replied, "She is the Moabitess[j] who came back from Moab with Naomi. ⁷She said, 'Please let me glean and gather among the sheaves[k] behind the harvesters.' She went into the field and has worked steadily from morning till now, except for a short rest[l] in the shelter."

⁸So Boaz said to Ruth, "My daughter, listen to me. Don't go and glean in another field and don't go away from here. Stay here with my servant girls. ⁹Watch the field where the men are harvesting, and follow along after the girls. I have told the men not to touch you. And whenever you are thirsty, go and get a drink from the water jars the men have filled."

¹⁰At this, she bowed down with her face to the ground.[m] She exclaimed, "Why have I found such favor in your eyes that you notice me[n]—a foreigner?[o]"

¹¹Boaz replied, "I've been told all about what you have done for your mother-in-law[p] since the death of your husband[q]— how you left your father and mother and your homeland and came to live with a people you did not know[r] before.[s] ¹²May the LORD repay you for what you have done. May you be richly rewarded by the LORD,[t] the God of Israel,[u] under whose wings[v] you have come to take refuge.[w]"

¹³"May I continue to find favor in your eyes,[x] my lord," she said. "You have given me comfort and have spoken kindly to your servant—though I do not have the standing of one of your servant girls."

¹⁴At mealtime Boaz said to her, "Come over here. Have some bread[y] and dip it in the wine vinegar."

When she sat down with the harvesters,[z] he offered her some roasted grain.[a] She ate all she wanted and had some left over.[b] ¹⁵As she got up to glean, Boaz gave orders to his men, "Even if she gathers among the sheaves,[c] don't embarrass her. ¹⁶Rather, pull out some stalks for her from the bundles and leave them for her to pick up, and don't rebuke[d] her."

¹⁷So Ruth gleaned in the field until evening. Then she threshed[e] the barley she had gathered, and it amounted to about an ephah.[f] ¹⁸She carried it back to town,

2:6 |S Ru 1:22
2:7 kS Ge 37:7; S Lev 19:9 ¹²Sa 4:5
2:10 mS Ge 19:1; S 1Sa 20:41 nver 19; Ps 41:1 oS Ge 31:15; S Dt 15:3
2:11 pS Ru 1:14 qS Ru 1:5 rIsa 55:5 sRu 1:16-17
2:12 t1Sa 24:19; 26:23,25; Ps 18:20; Pr 25:22; Jer 31:16 uS Jos 24:15 vPs 17:8; 36:7; 57:1; 61:4; 63:7; 91:4 wPs 71:1
2:13 xS Ge 18:3
2:14 yS Ge 3:19 zS ver 3 aS Lev 23:14 bver 18
2:15 cS Ge 37:7; S Lev 19:9
2:16 dS Ge 37:10
2:17 eS Jdg 6:11 fS Lev 19:36
2:18 gver 14
2:19 hS ver 10
2:20 iS Jdg 17:2; S 1Sa 23:21 jS Ge 11:31 kS Ge 19:19 lS Lev 25:25 mRu 3:9,12; 4:1,14
2:21 nS Ru 1:22
2:23 oS Ex 9:31 pS Ge 30:14; S 1Sa 6:13
3:1 qRu 1:14 rRu 1:9
3:2 sS Ru 2:1 tS Lev 2:14; S Nu 18:27; S Jdg 6:11
3:3 u2Sa 12:20; 2Ki 5:10; Ps 26:6; 51:2; Isa 1:16; Jer 4:14; Eze 16:9 v2Sa 14:2; Isa 61:3 wS Ge 41:14 xS Ex 32:6 yS Ecc 2:3; S Jer 15:17
3:5 yEph 6:1; Col 3:20
3:6 zS Nu 18:27
3:7 aJdg 19:6,9,22; 1Sa 25:36; 2Sa 13:28; 1Ki 21:7; Est 1:10

and her mother-in-law saw how much she had gathered. Ruth also brought out and gave her what she had left over[g] after she had eaten enough.

¹⁹Her mother-in-law asked her, "Where did you glean today? Where did you work? Blessed be the man who took notice of you![h]"

Then Ruth told her mother-in-law about the one at whose place she had been working. "The name of the man I worked with today is Boaz," she said.

²⁰"The LORD bless him![i]" Naomi said to her daughter-in-law.[j] "He has not stopped showing his kindness[k] to the living and the dead." She added, "That man is our close relative;[l] he is one of our kinsman-redeemers.[m]"

²¹Then Ruth the Moabitess[n] said, "He even said to me, 'Stay with my workers until they finish harvesting all my grain.' "

²²Naomi said to Ruth her daughter-in-law, "It will be good for you, my daughter, to go with his girls, because in someone else's field you might be harmed."

²³So Ruth stayed close to the servant girls of Boaz to glean until the barley[o] and wheat harvests[p] were finished. And she lived with her mother-in-law.

Ruth and Boaz at the Threshing Floor

3 One day Naomi her mother-in-law[q] said to her, "My daughter, should I not try to find a home[gr] for you, where you will be well provided for? ²Is not Boaz, with whose servant girls you have been, a kinsman[s] of ours? Tonight he will be winnowing barley on the threshing floor.[t] ³Wash[u] and perfume yourself,[v] and put on your best clothes.[w] Then go down to the threshing floor, but don't let him know you are there until he has finished eating and drinking.[x] ⁴When he lies down, note the place where he is lying. Then go and uncover his feet and lie down. He will tell you what to do."

⁵"I will do whatever you say,"[y] Ruth answered. ⁶So she went down to the threshing floor[z] and did everything her mother-in-law told her to do.

⁷When Boaz had finished eating and drinking and was in good spirits,[a] he went over to lie down at the far end of

f 17 That is, probably about 3/5 bushel (about 22 liters) *g 1* Hebrew *find rest* (see Ruth 1:9)

K *Jdg 5:31* ◀ ▶ *1Sa 2:2*

the grain pile.[b] Ruth approached quietly, uncovered his feet and lay down. [8]In the middle of the night something startled the man, and he turned and discovered a woman lying at his feet.

[9]"Who are you?" he asked.

"I am your servant Ruth," she said. "Spread the corner of your garment[c] over me, since you are a kinsman-redeemer.[d]"

[10]"The LORD bless you,[e] my daughter," he replied. "This kindness is greater than that which you showed earlier:[f] You have not run after the younger men, whether rich or poor. [11]And now, my daughter, don't be afraid. I will do for you all you ask. All my fellow townsmen know that you are a woman of noble character.[g] [12]Although it is true that I am near of kin, there is a kinsman-redeemer[h] nearer than[i] I. [13]Stay here for the night, and in the morning if he wants to redeem,[j] good; let him redeem. But if he is not willing, as surely as the LORD lives[k] I will do it.[l] Lie here until morning."

[14]So she lay at his feet until morning, but got up before anyone could be recognized; and he said, "Don't let it be known that a woman came to the threshing floor."[m][n]

[15]He also said, "Bring me the shawl[o] you are wearing and hold it out." When she did so, he poured into it six measures of barley and put it on her. Then he[h] went back to town.

[16]When Ruth came to her mother-in-law, Naomi asked, "How did it go, my daughter?"

Then she told her everything Boaz had done for her [17]and added, "He gave me these six measures of barley, saying, 'Don't go back to your mother-in-law empty-handed.'"

[18]Then Naomi said, "Wait, my daughter, until you find out what happens. For the man will not rest until the matter is settled today."[p]

Boaz Marries Ruth

4 Meanwhile Boaz went up to the town gate[q] and sat there. When the kinsman-redeemer[r] he had mentioned[s] came along, Boaz said, "Come over here, my friend, and sit down." So he went over and sat down.

[2]Boaz took ten of the elders[t] of the town and said, "Sit here," and they did so.[u] [3]Then he said to the kinsman-redeemer, "Naomi, who has come back from Moab, is selling the piece of land that belonged to our brother Elimelech.[v] [4]I thought I should bring the matter to your attention and suggest that you buy it in the presence of these seated here and in the presence of the elders of my people. If you will redeem it, do so. But if you[i] will not, tell me, so I will know. For no one has the right to do it except you,[w] and I am next in line."

"I will redeem it," he said.

[5]Then Boaz said, "On the day you buy the land from Naomi and from Ruth the Moabitess,[x] you acquire[j] the dead man's widow, in order to maintain the name of the dead with his property."[y]

[6]At this, the kinsman-redeemer said, "Then I cannot redeem[z] it because I might endanger my own estate. You redeem it yourself. I cannot do it."[a]

[7](Now in earlier times in Israel, for the redemption[b] and transfer of property to become final, one party took off his sandal[c] and gave it to the other. This was the method of legalizing transactions[d] in Israel.)[e]

[8]So the kinsman-redeemer said to Boaz, "Buy it yourself." And he removed his sandal.[f]

[9]Then Boaz announced to the elders and all the people, "Today you are witnesses[g] that I have bought from Naomi all the property of Elimelech, Kilion and Mahlon. [10]I have also acquired Ruth the Moabitess,[h] Mahlon's widow, as my wife,[i] in order to maintain the name of the dead with his property, so that his name will not disappear from among his family or from the town records.[j] Today you are witnesses![k]"

[11]Then the elders and all those at the gate[l] said, "We are witnesses.[m] May the LORD make the woman who is coming into your home like Rachel and Leah,[n] who together built up the house of Israel. May you have standing in Ephrathah[o] and be famous in Bethlehem.[p] [12]Through the offspring the LORD gives you by this young woman, may your family be like that of Perez,[q] whom Tamar[r] bore to Judah."

---

[h] 15 Most Hebrew manuscripts; many Hebrew manuscripts, Vulgate and Syriac *she* / [4] Many Hebrew manuscripts, Septuagint, Vulgate and Syriac; most Hebrew manuscripts *he* / [5] Hebrew; Vulgate and Syriac *Naomi, you acquire Ruth the Moabitess,*

The Genealogy of David
4:18–22pp — 1Ch 2:5–15; Mt 1:3–6; Lk 3:31–33

[13] So Boaz took Ruth and she became his wife. Then he went to her, and the LORD enabled her to conceive,[s] and she gave birth to a son.[t] [14] The women[u] said to Naomi: "Praise be to the LORD,[v] who this day has not left you without a kinsman-redeemer.[w] May he become famous throughout Israel! [15] He will renew your life and sustain you in your old age. For your daughter-in-law,[x] who loves you and who is better to you than seven sons,[y] has given him birth."

[16] Then Naomi took the child, laid him in her lap and cared for him. [17] The women living there said, "Naomi has a son." And they named him Obed. He was the father of Jesse,[z] the father of David.[a]

[18] This, then, is the family line of Perez[b]:

Perez was the father of Hezron,[c]
[19] Hezron the father of Ram,
    Ram the father of Amminadab,[d]
[20] Amminadab the father of Nahshon,[e]
    Nahshon the father of Salmon,[k]
[21] Salmon the father of Boaz,[f]
    Boaz the father of Obed,
[22] Obed the father of Jesse,
    and Jesse the father of David.

4:13 s S Ge 8:1; S 29:31
t S Ge 29:32; S 30:6; Lk 1:57
4:14 u Lk 1:58
v S Ge 24:27
w S Ru 2:20
4:15 x S Ge 11:31
y 1Sa 1:8; 2:5; Job 1:2
4:17 z ver 22; 1Sa 16:1,18; 17:12, 17,58; 1Ch 2:12, 13; Ps 72:20
a 1Sa 16:13; 1Ch 2:15
4:18 b S Ge 38:29
c Nu 26:21
4:19 d S Ex 6:23
4:20 e S Nu 7:12
4:21 f S Ru 2:1

[k] 20 A few Hebrew manuscripts, some Septuagint manuscripts and Vulgate (see also verse 21 and Septuagint of 1 Chron. 2:11); most Hebrew manuscripts *Salma*

1 Samuel

Author: Unknown

Theme: The careers of Samuel, Saul and David

Date of Writing: c. 925 B.C.

Outline of 1 Samuel
I.   Samuel's Birth, Call and Training (1:1—4:22)
II. Samuel's Role as Judge and Deliverer (5:1—8:22)
III. A King Is Anointed and Ultimately Rejected (9:1—15:35)
IV. Saul's Descent and David's Rise (16:1—30:31)
V.   Saul's Death (31:1–13)

ORIGINALLY THE BOOKS of 1 and 2 Samuel were contained on one scroll and considered one volume. Translators of the Greek version of the OT (Septuagint) divided this large book into two parts, referring to them as "The First and Second Books of Kingdoms." However, Hebrew tradition and most modern versions refer to these books as 1 and 2 Samuel since Samuel, more than any other individual during that time period, helped Israel maintain their covenantal relationship with God during the transition from the judges to the monarchy.

Together the books of 1 and 2 Samuel chronicle a seamless history of the establishment of the kingdom of Israel and the foundation of the Hebrew monarchy. The books open with the birth of Samuel during the time of Eli, the high priest, judge and governor of Israel at Shiloh. Several chapters record Samuel's influential career as prophet, priest and judge over Israel and detail the emergence of the monarchy as they describe the anointing of first Saul and then David as Israel's kings. The final chapters of 1 Samuel record Saul's disobedience and sins of presumption that bring about God's rejection of him as king and the anointing of God's replacement, David. Well-known stories in this book include the account of Hannah's infertility (ch. 1), David and Goliath (ch. 17), David and Jonathan (ch. 18) and Saul and the séance at Endor (ch. 28).

The Birth of Samuel

1 There was a certain man from Ramathaim,[a] a Zuphite[ab] from the hill country[c] of Ephraim,[d] whose name was Elkanah[e] son of Jeroham, the son of Elihu, the son of Tohu, the son of Zuph, an Ephraimite. ²He had two wives;[f] one was called Hannah and the other Peninnah. Peninnah had children, but Hannah had none.

³Year after year[g] this man went up from his town to worship[h] and sacrifice to the Lord Almighty at Shiloh,[i] where Hophni and Phinehas, the two sons of Eli,[j] were priests of the Lord. ⁴Whenever the day came for Elkanah to sacrifice,[k] he would give portions of the meat to his wife Peninnah and to all her sons and daughters.[l] ⁵But to Hannah he gave a double portion[m] because he loved her, and the Lord had closed her womb.[n] ⁶And because the Lord had closed her womb, her rival kept provoking her in order to irritate her.[o] ⁷This went on year after year. Whenever Hannah went up to the house of the Lord, her rival provoked her till she wept and would not eat.[p] ⁸Elkanah her husband would say to her, "Hannah, why are you weeping? Why don't you eat? Why are you downhearted? Don't I mean more to you than ten sons?"[q]

⁹Once when they had finished eating and drinking in Shiloh, Hannah stood up. Now Eli the priest was sitting on a chair by the doorpost of the Lord's temple.[br] ¹⁰In bitterness of soul[s] Hannah wept much and prayed to the Lord. ¹¹And she made a vow,[t] saying, "O Lord Almighty[u], if you will only look upon your servant's misery and remember[v] me, and not forget your servant but give her a son, then I will give him to the Lord for all the days of his life,[w] and no razor[x] will ever be used on his head."

¹²As she kept on praying to the Lord, Eli observed her mouth. ¹³Hannah was praying in her heart, and her lips were moving but her voice was not heard. Eli thought she was drunk ¹⁴and said to her, "How long will you keep on getting drunk? Get rid of your wine."

¹⁵"Not so, my lord," Hannah replied, "I am a woman who is deeply troubled.[y] I have not been drinking wine or beer; I was pouring[z] out my soul to the Lord. ¹⁶Do not take your servant for a wicked woman; I have been praying here out of my great anguish and grief."[a]

¹⁷Eli answered, "Go in peace,[b] and may the God of Israel grant you what you have asked of him."[c]

¹⁸She said, "May your servant find favor in your eyes.[d]" Then she went her way and ate something, and her face was no longer downcast.[e]

¹⁹Early the next morning they arose and worshiped before the Lord and then went back to their home at Ramah.[f] Elkanah lay with Hannah his wife, and the Lord remembered[g] her. ²⁰So in the course of time Hannah conceived and gave birth to a son.[h] She named[i] him Samuel,[cj] saying, "Because I asked the Lord for him."

Hannah Dedicates Samuel

²¹When the man Elkanah went up with all his family to offer the annual[k] sacrifice to the Lord and to fulfill his vow,[l] ²²Hannah did not go. She said to her husband, "After the boy is weaned, I will take him and present[m] him before the Lord, and he will live there always."

²³"Do what seems best to you," Elkanah her husband told her. "Stay here until you have weaned him; only may the Lord make good[n] his[d] word." So the woman stayed at home and nursed her son until she had weaned[o] him.

²⁴After he was weaned, she took the boy with her, young as he was, along with a three-year-old bull,[ep] an ephah[f] of flour and a skin of wine, and brought him to the house of the Lord at Shiloh. ²⁵When they had slaughtered the bull, they brought the boy to Eli, ²⁶and she said to him, "As surely as you live, my lord, I am the woman who stood here beside you praying to the Lord. ²⁷I prayed[q] for this child, and the Lord has granted me what I asked of him. ²⁸So now I give him to the Lord. For his whole life[r] he will be given over to the Lord." And he worshiped the Lord there.

---

[a] 1 Or *from Ramathaim Zuphim* [b] 9 That is, tabernacle [c] 20 *Samuel* sounds like the Hebrew for *heard of God*. [d] 23 Masoretic Text; Dead Sea Scrolls, Septuagint and Syriac *your* [e] 24 Dead Sea Scrolls, Septuagint and Syriac; Masoretic Text *with three bulls* [f] 24 That is, probably about 3/5 bushel (about 22 liters)

Hannah's Prayer

2 Then Hannah prayed and said:ˢ

"My heart rejoicesᵗ in the Lord;
in the Lord my hornᵍᵘ is lifted high.
My mouth boastsᵛ over my enemies,ʷ
for I delight in your deliverance.

²"There is no one holyʰˣ likeʸ the Lord;
there is no one besides you;
there is no Rockᶻ like our God.

³"Do not keep talking so proudly
or let your mouth speak such arrogance,ᵃ
for the Lord is a God who knows,ᵇ
and by him deedsᶜ are weighed.ᵈ

⁴"The bows of the warriors are broken,ᵉ
but those who stumbled are armed with strength.ᶠ

⁵Those who were full hire themselves out for food,
but those who were hungryᵍ hunger no more.
She who was barrenʰ has borne seven children,
but she who has had many sons pines away.

⁶"The Lord brings death and makes alive;ⁱ
he brings down to the graveⁱ and raises up.ʲ

⁷The Lord sends poverty and wealth;ᵏ
he humbles and he exalts.ˡ

⁸He raisesᵐ the poorⁿ from the dustᵒ
and lifts the needyᵖ from the ash heap;
he seats them with princes
and has them inherit a throne of honor.ᵍ

"For the foundationsʳ of the earth are the Lord's;
upon them he has set the world.

⁹He will guard the feetˢ of his saints,ᵗ
but the wicked will be silenced in darkness.ᵘ

"It is not by strengthᵛ that one prevails;
¹⁰ those who oppose the Lord will be shattered.ʷ
He will thunderˣ against them from heaven;
the Lord will judgeʸ the ends of the earth.

"He will give strengthᶻ to his king
and exalt the hornᵃ of his anointed."

¹¹Then Elkanah went home to Ramah,ᵇ but the boy ministeredᶜ before the Lord under Eli the priest.

Eli's Wicked Sons

¹²Eli's sons were wicked men; they had no regardᵈ for the Lord. ¹³Now it was the practiceᵉ of the priests with the people that whenever anyone offered a sacrifice and while the meatᶠ was being boiled, the servant of the priest would come with a three-pronged fork in his hand. ¹⁴He would plunge it into the pan or kettle or caldron or pot, and the priest would take for himself whatever the fork brought up. This is how they treated all the Israelites who came to Shiloh. ¹⁵But even before the fat was burned, the servant of the priest would come and say to the man who was sacrificing, "Give the priest some meat to roast; he won't accept boiled meat from you, but only raw."

¹⁶If the man said to him, "Let the fatᵍ be burned up first, and then take whatever you want," the servant would then answer, "No, hand it over now; if you don't, I'll take it by force."

¹⁷This sin of the young men was very great in the Lord's sight, for theyʲ were

---

2:10 Samuel's mother, Hannah, spoke one of the first prophecies in Scripture anticipating the establishment of the monarchy in Israel as well as the future Messianic triumph over the enemies of God in the end times (see Lk 1:69) and the exaltation "of his anointed."

treating the LORD's offering with contempt.ʰ

¹⁸But Samuel was ministeringⁱ before the LORD—a boy wearing a linen ephod.ʲ ¹⁹Each year his mother made him a little robe and took it to him when she went up with her husband to offer the annualᵏ sacrifice. ²⁰Eli would bless Elkanah and his wife, saying, "May the LORD give you children by this woman to take the place of the one she prayed¹ for and gave to the LORD." Then they would go home. ²¹And the LORD was gracious to Hannah;ᵐ she conceived and gave birth to three sons and two daughters. Meanwhile, the boy Samuel grewⁿ up in the presence of the LORD.

²²Now Eli, who was very old, heard about everythingᵒ his sons were doing to all Israel and how they slept with the womenᵖ who served at the entrance to the Tent of Meeting. ²³So he said to them, "Why do you do such things? I hear from all the people about these wicked deeds of yours. ²⁴No, my sons; it is not a good report that I hear spreading among the LORD's people. ²⁵If a man sins against another man, Godᵏ may mediate for him; but if a man sins against the LORD, who willᵠ intercedeʳ for him?" His sons, however, did not listen to their father's rebuke, for it was the LORD's will to put them to death.

²⁶And the boy Samuel continued to growˢ in stature and in favor with the LORD and with men.ᵗ

Prophecy Against the House of Eli

²⁷Now a man of Godᵘ came to Eli and said to him, "This is what the LORD says: 'Did I not clearly reveal myself to your father's house when they were in Egypt under Pharaoh? ²⁸I choseᵛ your father out of all the tribes of Israel to be my priest, to go up to my altar, to burn incense,ʷ and to wear an ephodˣ in my presence. I also gave your father's house all the offeringsʸ made with fire by the Israelites. ²⁹Why do youˡ scorn my sacrifice and offeringᶻ that I prescribed for my dwelling?ᵃ Why do you honor your sons more than me by fattening yourselves on the choice parts of every offering made by my people Israel?'

³⁰"Therefore the LORD, the God of Israel, declares: 'I promised that your house and your father's house would minister before me forever.'ᵇ But now the LORD declares: 'Far be it from me! Those who honor me I will honor,ᶜ but those who despiseᵈ me will be disdained.'ᵉ ³¹The time is coming when I will cut your strength and the strength of your father's house, so that there will not be an old man in your family lineᶠ ³²and you will see distressᵍ in my dwelling. Although good will be done to Israel, in your family line there will never be an old man.ʰ ³³Every one of you that I do not cut off from my altar will be spared only to blind your eyes with tears and to grieve your heart, and all your descendantsⁱ will die in the prime of life.

³⁴" 'And what happens to your two sons, Hophni and Phinehas, will be a signʲ to you—they will both dieᵏ on the same day.ˡ ³⁵I will raise up for myself a faithful priest,ᵐ who will do according to what is in my heart and mind. I will firmly establish his house, and he will minister before my anointedⁿ one always. ³⁶Then everyone left in your family line will come and bow down before him for a piece of silver and a crust of bread and plead,ᵒ "Appoint me to some priestly office so I can have food to eat."ᵖ ' "

The LORD Calls Samuel

3 The boy Samuel ministeredᵠ before the LORD under Eli. In those days the word of the LORD was rare;ʳ there were not many visions.ˢ

²One night Eli, whose eyesᵗ were becoming so weak that he could barely see,ᵘ was lying down in his usual place. ³The lampᵛ of God had not yet gone out, and Samuel was lying down in the templeᵐ of the LORD, where the arkˣ of God was. ⁴Then the LORD called Samuel.

Samuel answered, "Here I am."ʸ ⁵And he ran to Eli and said, "Here I am; you called me."

But Eli said, "I did not call; go back and lie down." So he went and lay down.

⁶Again the LORD called, "Samuel!" And

ᵏ 25 Or *the judges* ˡ 29 The Hebrew is plural. ᵐ 3 That is, tabernacle

Samuel got up and went to Eli and said, "Here I am; you called me."

"My son," Eli said, "I did not call; go back and lie down."

⁷Now Samuel did not yet know^z the LORD: The word^a of the LORD had not yet been revealed^b to him.

⁸The LORD called Samuel a third time, and Samuel got up and went to Eli and said, "Here I am; you called me."

Then Eli realized that the LORD was calling the boy. ⁹So Eli told Samuel, "Go and lie down, and if he calls you, say, 'Speak, LORD, for your servant is listening.'" So Samuel went and lay down in his place.

¹⁰The LORD came and stood there, calling as at the other times, "Samuel! Samuel!"^c

Then Samuel said, "Speak, for your servant is listening."

¹¹And the LORD said to Samuel: "See, I am about to do something in Israel that will make the ears of everyone who hears of it tingle.^d ¹²At that time I will carry out against Eli everything^e I spoke against his family—from beginning to end. ¹³For I told him that I would judge his family forever because of the sin he knew about; his sons made themselves contemptible,ⁿ and he failed to restrain^f them. ¹⁴Therefore, I swore to the house of Eli, 'The guilt of Eli's house will never be atoned^g for by sacrifice or offering.'"

¹⁵Samuel lay down until morning and then opened the doors of the house of the LORD. He was afraid to tell Eli the vision, ¹⁶but Eli called him and said, "Samuel, my son."

Samuel answered, "Here I am."

¹⁷"What was it he said to you?" Eli asked. "Do not hide^h it from me. May God deal with you, be it ever so severely,ⁱ if you hide from me anything he told you." ¹⁸So Samuel told him everything, hiding nothing from him. Then Eli said, "He is the LORD; let him do what is good in his eyes."^j

¹⁹The LORD was with^k Samuel as he grew^l up, and he let none^m of his words fall to the ground. ²⁰And all Israel from Dan to Beershebaⁿ recognized that Samuel was attested as a prophet of the LORD.^o ²¹The LORD continued to appear at Shiloh, and there he revealed^p himself to Samuel through his word.

4 And Samuel's word came to all Israel.

The Philistines Capture the Ark

Now the Israelites went out to fight against the Philistines. The Israelites camped at Ebenezer,^q and the Philistines at Aphek.^r ²The Philistines deployed their forces to meet Israel, and as the battle spread, Israel was defeated by the Philistines, who killed about four thousand of them on the battlefield. ³When the soldiers returned to camp, the elders of Israel asked, "Why^s did the LORD bring defeat upon us today before the Philistines? Let us bring the ark^t of the LORD's covenant from Shiloh,^u so that it^o may go with us^v and save us from the hand of our enemies."

⁴So the people sent men to Shiloh, and they brought back the ark of the covenant of the LORD Almighty, who is enthroned between the cherubim.^w And Eli's two sons, Hophni and Phinehas, were there with the ark of the covenant of God.

⁵When the ark of the LORD's covenant came into the camp, all Israel raised such a great shout^x that the ground shook. ⁶Hearing the uproar, the Philistines asked, "What's all this shouting in the Hebrew^y camp?"

When they learned that the ark of the LORD had come into the camp, ⁷the Philistines were afraid.^z "A god has come into the camp," they said. "We're in trouble! Nothing like this has happened before. ⁸Woe to us! Who will deliver us from the hand of these mighty gods? They are the gods who struck^a the Egyptians with all kinds of plagues^b in the desert. ⁹Be strong, Philistines! Be men, or you will be subject to the Hebrews, as they^c have been to you. Be men, and fight!"

¹⁰So the Philistines fought, and the Israelites were defeated^d and every man fled to his tent. The slaughter was very great; Israel lost thirty thousand foot soldiers. ¹¹The ark of God was captured, and Eli's two sons, Hophni and Phinehas, died.^e

---

ⁿ 13 Masoretic Text; an ancient Hebrew scribal tradition and Septuagint sons blasphemed God   ^o 3 Or he

Death of Eli

[12] That same day a Benjamite[f] ran from the battle line and went to Shiloh, his clothes torn and dust[g] on his head. [13] When he arrived, there was Eli[h] sitting on his chair by the side of the road, watching, because his heart feared for the ark of God. When the man entered the town and told what had happened, the whole town sent up a cry.

[14] Eli heard the outcry and asked, "What is the meaning of this uproar?"

The man hurried over to Eli, [15] who was ninety-eight years old and whose eyes[i] were set so that he could not see. [16] He told Eli, "I have just come from the battle line; I fled from it this very day."

Eli asked, "What happened, my son?"

[17] The man who brought the news replied, "Israel fled before the Philistines, and the army has suffered heavy losses. Also your two sons, Hophni and Phinehas, are dead,[j] and the ark of God has been captured."[k]

[18] When he mentioned the ark of God, Eli fell backward off his chair by the side of the gate. His neck was broken and he died, for he was an old man and heavy. He had led[p][l] Israel forty years.[m]

[19] His daughter-in-law, the wife of Phinehas, was pregnant and near the time of delivery. When she heard the news that the ark of God had been captured and that her father-in-law and her husband were dead, she went into labor and gave birth, but was overcome by her labor pains. [20] As she was dying, the women attending her said, "Don't despair; you have given birth to a son." But she did not respond or pay any attention.

[21] She named the boy Ichabod,[q][n] saying, "The glory[o] has departed from Israel"—because of the capture of the ark of God and the deaths of her father-in-law and her husband. [22] She said, "The glory[p] has departed from Israel, for the ark of God has been captured."[q]

The Ark in Ashdod and Ekron

5 After the Philistines had captured the ark of God, they took it from Ebenezer[r] to Ashdod.[s] [2] Then they carried the ark into Dagon's temple and set it beside Dagon.[t] [3] When the people of Ashdod rose early the next day, there was Dagon, fallen[u] on his face on the ground before the ark of the LORD! They took Dagon and put him back in his place. [4] But the following morning when they rose, there was Dagon, fallen on his face on the ground before the ark of the LORD! His head and hands had been broken[v] off and were lying on the threshold; only his body remained. [5] That is why to this day neither the priests of Dagon nor any others who enter Dagon's temple at Ashdod step on the threshold.[w]

[6] The LORD's hand[x] was heavy upon the people of Ashdod and its vicinity; he brought devastation[y] upon them and afflicted them with tumors.[r][z] [7] When the men of Ashdod saw what was happening, they said, "The ark of the god of Israel must not stay here with us, because his hand is heavy upon us and upon Dagon our god." [8] So they called together all the rulers[a] of the Philistines and asked them, "What shall we do with the ark of the god of Israel?"

They answered, "Have the ark of the god of Israel moved to Gath.[b]" So they moved the ark of the God of Israel.

[9] But after they had moved it, the LORD's hand was against that city, throwing it into a great panic.[c] He afflicted the people of the city, both young and old, with an outbreak of tumors.[s] [10] So they sent the ark of God to Ekron.[d]

As the ark of God was entering Ekron, the people of Ekron cried out, "They have brought the ark of the god of Israel

D *Jos 22:17* ◄ ► *1Sa 5:9*
D *1Sa 5:6* ◄ ► *1Sa 5:11–12*

[p] 18 Traditionally *judged* [q] 21 *Ichabod* means *no glory.* [r] 6 Hebrew; Septuagint and Vulgate *tumors. And rats appeared in their land, and death and destruction were throughout the city* [s] 9 Or *with tumors in the groin* (see Septuagint)

5:10–11 Ekron was the most northerly of the five chief cities of the Philistines and was included in the territory of Dan (see Jos 19:43). After David killed Goliath, the Philistines fled to this fortified city (see 1Sa 17:52). In this story, the people of Ekron urged the other Philistines to return the captured ark of the covenant to Israel in order to avert destruction. The prophets called down God's judgment upon Ekron (see Am 1:8) and the city was destroyed. Recent archeological excavation has uncovered what appear to be the ruins of Ekron, including a stone inscription naming the city and five of its kings.

around to us to kill us and our people." ¹¹So they called together all the rulers^e of the Philistines and said, "Send the ark of the god of Israel away; let it go back to its own place, or it^f will kill us and our people." For death had filled the city with panic; God's hand was very heavy upon it. ¹²Those who did not die^f were afflicted with tumors, and the outcry of the city went up to heaven.

The Ark Returned to Israel

6 When the ark of the LORD had been in Philistine territory seven months, ²the Philistines called for the priests and the diviners^g and said, "What shall we do with the ark of the LORD? Tell us how we should send it back to its place."

³They answered, "If you return the ark of the god of Israel, do not send it away empty,^h but by all means send a guilt offering^i to him. Then you will be healed, and you will know why his hand^j has not been lifted from you."

⁴The Philistines asked, "What guilt offering should we send to him?"

They replied, "Five gold tumors and five gold rats, according to the number^k of the Philistine rulers, because the same plague^l has struck both you and your rulers. ⁵Make models of the tumors^m and of the rats that are destroying the country, and pay honor^n to Israel's god. Perhaps he will lift his hand from you and your gods and your land. ⁶Why do you harden^o your hearts as the Egyptians and Pharaoh did? When he^u treated them harshly,^p did they^q not send the Israelites out so they could go on their way?

⁷"Now then, get a new cart^r ready, with two cows that have calved and have never been yoked.^s Hitch the cows to the cart, but take their calves away and pen them up. ⁸Take the ark of the LORD and put it on the cart, and in a chest beside it put the gold objects you are sending back to him as a guilt offering. Send it on its way, ⁹but keep watching it. If it goes up to its own territory, toward Beth Shemesh,^t then the LORD has brought this great disaster on us. But if it does not, then we will know that it was not his hand that struck us and that it happened to us by chance."

¹⁰So they did this. They took two such cows and hitched them to the cart and penned up their calves. ¹¹They placed the ark of the LORD on the cart and along with it the chest containing the gold rats and the models of the tumors. ¹²Then the cows went straight up toward Beth Shemesh, keeping on the road and lowing all the way; they did not turn to the right or to the left. The rulers of the Philistines followed them as far as the border of Beth Shemesh.

¹³Now the people of Beth Shemesh were harvesting their wheat^u in the valley, and when they looked up and saw the ark, they rejoiced at the sight. ¹⁴The cart came to the field of Joshua of Beth Shemesh, and there it stopped beside a large rock. The people chopped up the wood of the cart and sacrificed the cows as a burnt offering^v to the LORD. ¹⁵The Levites^w took down the ark of the LORD, together with the chest containing the gold objects, and placed them on the large rock.^x On that day the people of Beth Shemesh^y offered burnt offerings and made sacrifices to the LORD. ¹⁶The five rulers of the Philistines saw all this and then returned that same day to Ekron.

¹⁷These are the gold tumors the Philistines sent as a guilt offering to the LORD—one each^z for Ashdod, Gaza, Ashkelon, Gath and Ekron. ¹⁸And the number of the gold rats was according to the number of Philistine towns belonging to the five rulers—the fortified towns with their country villages. The large rock, on which^v they set the ark of the LORD, is a witness to this day in the field of Joshua of Beth Shemesh.

¹⁹But God struck down^a some of the men of Beth Shemesh, putting seventy^w of them to death because they had looked^b into the ark of the LORD. The people mourned because of the heavy blow the LORD had dealt them, ²⁰and the men of Beth Shemesh asked, "Who can stand^c in the presence of the LORD, this holy^d God? To whom will the ark go up from here?"

²¹Then they sent messengers to the people of Kiriath Jearim,^e saying, "The Philistines have returned the ark of the

---

^t 11 Or he   ^u 6 That is, God   ^v 18 A few Hebrew manuscripts (see also Septuagint); most Hebrew manuscripts *villages as far as Greater Abel, where*   ^w 19 A few Hebrew manuscripts; most Hebrew manuscripts and Septuagint *50,070*

LORD. Come down and take it up to your place." ¹So the men of Kiriath Jearim came and took up the ark of the LORD. They took it to Abinadab's house on the hill and consecrated Eleazar his son to guard the ark of the LORD.

Samuel Subdues the Philistines at Mizpah

²It was a long time, twenty years in all, that the ark remained at Kiriath Jearim, and all the people of Israel mourned and sought after the LORD. ³And Samuel said to the whole house of Israel, "If you are returning to the LORD with all your hearts, then rid yourselves of the foreign gods and the Ashtoreths and commit yourselves to the LORD and serve him only, and he will deliver you out of the hand of the Philistines." ⁴So the Israelites put away their Baals and Ashtoreths, and served the LORD only.

⁵Then Samuel said, "Assemble all Israel at Mizpah and I will intercede with the LORD for you." ⁶When they had assembled at Mizpah, they drew water and poured it out before the LORD. On that day they fasted and there they confessed, "We have sinned against the LORD." And Samuel was leader of Israel at Mizpah.

⁷When the Philistines heard that Israel had assembled at Mizpah, the rulers of the Philistines came up to attack them. And when the Israelites heard of it, they were afraid because of the Philistines. ⁸They said to Samuel, "Do not stop crying out to the LORD our God for us, that he may rescue us from the hand of the Philistines." ⁹Then Samuel took a suckling lamb and offered it up as a whole burnt offering to the LORD. He cried out to the LORD on Israel's behalf, and the LORD answered him.

¹⁰While Samuel was sacrificing the burnt offering, the Philistines drew near to engage Israel in battle. But that day the LORD thundered with loud thunder against the Philistines and threw them into such a panic that they were routed before the Israelites. ¹¹The men of Israel rushed out of Mizpah and pursued the Philistines, slaughtering them along the way to a point below Beth Car.

¹²Then Samuel took a stone and set it up between Mizpah and Shen. He named it Ebenezer, saying, "Thus far has the LORD helped us." ¹³So the Philistines were subdued and did not invade Israelite territory again.

Throughout Samuel's lifetime, the hand of the LORD was against the Philistines. ¹⁴The towns from Ekron to Gath that the Philistines had captured from Israel were restored to her, and Israel delivered the neighboring territory from the power of the Philistines. And there was peace between Israel and the Amorites.

¹⁵Samuel continued as judge over Israel all the days of his life. ¹⁶From year to year he went on a circuit from Bethel to Gilgal to Mizpah, judging Israel in all those places. ¹⁷But he always went back to Ramah, where his home was, and there he also judged Israel. And he built an altar there to the LORD.

Israel Asks for a King

⁸When Samuel grew old, he appointed his sons as judges for Israel. ²The name of his firstborn was Joel and the name of his second was Abijah, and they served at Beersheba. ³But his sons did not walk in his ways. They turned aside after dishonest gain and accepted bribes and perverted justice.

⁴So all the elders of Israel gathered together and came to Samuel at Ramah. ⁵They said to him, "You are old, and your sons do not walk in your ways; now appoint a king to lead us, such as all the other nations have."

⁶But when they said, "Give us a king to lead us," this displeased Samuel; so he prayed to the LORD. ⁷And the LORD told him: "Listen to all that the people are saying to you; it is not you they have rejected, but they have rejected me as

T Dt 26:1–3 ◀▶ 1Ch 16:8–10
C 1Sa 2:25 ◀▶ 1Sa 24:13

x 6 Traditionally *judge* *y* 12 *Ebenezer* means *stone of help.*
z 5 Traditionally *judge*; also in verses 6 and 20

7:3 Samuel prophesied Israel's divine deliverance from the Philistines if the Israelites would repent of their idolatry.

their king.ᶠ ⁸As they have done from the day I brought them up out of Egypt until this day, forsakingᵍ me and serving other gods, so they are doing to you. ⁹Now listen to them; but warn them solemnly and let them knowʰ what the king who will reign over them will do."

¹⁰Samuel toldⁱ all the words of the LORD to the people who were asking him for a king. ¹¹He said, "This is what the king who will reign over you will do: He will takeʲ your sons and make them serveᵏ with his chariots and horses, and they will run in front of his chariots.ˡ ¹²Some he will assign to be commandersᵐ of thousands and commanders of fifties, and others to plow his ground and reap his harvest, and still others to make weapons of war and equipment for his chariots. ¹³He will take your daughters to be perfumers and cooks and bakers. ¹⁴He will take the best of yourⁿ fields and vineyardsᵒ and olive groves and give them to his attendants.ᵖ ¹⁵He will take a tenthᑫ of your grain and of your vintage and give it to his officials and attendants. ¹⁶Your menservants and maidservants and the best of your cattleᵃ and donkeys he will take for his own use. ¹⁷He will take a tenth of your flocks, and you yourselves will become his slaves. ¹⁸When that day comes, you will cry out for relief from the king you have chosen, and the LORD will not answerʳ you in that day.ˢ"

¹⁹But the people refusedᵗ to listen to Samuel. "No!" they said. "We wantᵘ a kingᵛ over us. ²⁰Then we will be like all the other nations,ʷ with a king to lead us and to go out before us and fight our battles."

²¹When Samuel heard all that the people said, he repeatedˣ it before the LORD. ²²The LORD answered, "Listenʸ to them and give them a king."

Then Samuel said to the men of Israel, "Everyone go back to his town."

Samuel Anoints Saul

9 There was a Benjamite,ᶻ a man of standing,ᵃ whose name was Kishᵇ son of Abiel, the son of Zeror, the son of Becorath, the son of Aphiah of Benjamin. ²He had a son named Saul, an impressiveᶜ young man without equalᵈ among the Israelites—a head tallerᵉ than any of the others.

³Now the donkeysᶠ belonging to Saul's father Kish were lost, and Kish said to his son Saul, "Take one of the servants with you and go and look for the donkeys." ⁴So he passed through the hillᵍ country of Ephraim and through the area around Shalisha,ʰ but they did not find them. They went on into the district of Shaalim, but the donkeysⁱ were not there. Then he passed through the territory of Benjamin, but they did not find them.

⁵When they reached the district of Zuph,ʲ Saul said to the servant who was with him, "Come, let's go back, or my father will stop thinking about the donkeys and start worryingᵏ about us."

⁶But the servant replied, "Look, in this town there is a man of God;ˡ he is highly respected, and everythingᵐ he says comes true. Let's go there now. Perhaps he will tell us what way to take."

⁷Saul said to his servant, "If we go, what can we give the man? The food in our sacks is gone. We have no giftⁿ to take to the man of God. What do we have?"

⁸The servant answered him again. "Look," he said, "I have a quarter of a shekelᵇ of silver. I will give it to the man of God so that he will tell us what way to take." ⁹(Formerly in Israel, if a man went to inquireᵒ of God, he would say, "Come, let us go to the seer," because the prophet of today used to be called a seer.)ᵖ

¹⁰"Good," Saul said to his servant. "Come, let's go." So they set out for the town where the man of God was.

¹¹As they were going up the hill to the town, they met some girls coming out to drawᑫ water, and they asked them, "Is the seer here?"

¹²"He is," they answered. "He's ahead of you. Hurry now; he has just come to our town today, for the people have a sacrificeʳ at the high place.ˢ ¹³As soon as you enter the town, you will find him before he goes up to the high place to eat. The people will not begin eating until he comes, because he must blessᵗ the sacrifice; afterward, those who are invited will eat. Go up now; you should find him about this time."

¹⁴They went up to the town, and as they were entering it, there was Samuel,

---

ᵃ 16 Septuagint; Hebrew *young men*   ᵇ 8 That is, about 1/10 ounce (about 3 grams) coming toward them on his way up to the high place. ¹⁵Now the day before Saul came, the LORD had revealed this to Samuel: ¹⁶"About this time tomorrow I will send you a man from the land of Benjamin. Anoint him leader over my people Israel; he will deliver my people from the hand of the Philistines. I have looked upon my people, for their cry has reached me."

¹⁷When Samuel caught sight of Saul, the LORD said to him, "This is the man I spoke to you about; he will govern my people."

¹⁸Saul approached Samuel in the gateway and asked, "Would you please tell me where the seer's house is?"

¹⁹"I am the seer," Samuel replied. "Go up ahead of me to the high place, for today you are to eat with me, and in the morning I will let you go and will tell you all that is in your heart. ²⁰As for the donkeys you lost three days ago, do not worry about them; they have been found. And to whom is all the desire of Israel turned, if not to you and all your father's family?"

²¹Saul answered, "But am I not a Benjamite, from the smallest tribe of Israel, and is not my clan the least of all the clans of the tribe of Benjamin? Why do you say such a thing to me?"

²²Then Samuel brought Saul and his servant into the hall and seated them at the head of those who were invited—about thirty in number. ²³Samuel said to the cook, "Bring the piece of meat I gave you, the one I told you to lay aside."

²⁴So the cook took up the leg with what was on it and set it in front of Saul. Samuel said, "Here is what has been kept for you. Eat, because it was set aside for you for this occasion, from the time I said, 'I have invited guests.'" And Saul dined with Samuel that day.

²⁵After they came down from the high place to the town, Samuel talked with Saul on the roof of his house. ²⁶They rose about daybreak and Samuel called to Saul on the roof, "Get ready, and I will send you on your way." When Saul got ready, he and Samuel went outside together. ²⁷As they were going down to the edge of the town, Samuel said to Saul,

"Tell the servant to go on ahead of us"—and the servant did so—"but you stay here awhile, so that I may give you a message from God."

10 Then Samuel took a flask of oil and poured it on Saul's head and kissed him, saying, "Has not the LORD anointed you leader over his inheritance? ²When you leave me today, you will meet two men near Rachel's tomb, at Zelzah on the border of Benjamin. They will say to you, 'The donkeys you set out to look for have been found. And now your father has stopped thinking about them and is worried about you. He is asking, "What shall I do about my son?"'

³"Then you will go on from there until you reach the great tree of Tabor. Three men going up to God at Bethel will meet you there. One will be carrying three young goats, another three loaves of bread, and another a skin of wine. ⁴They will greet you and offer you two loaves of bread, which you will accept from them.

⁵"After that you will go to Gibeah of God, where there is a Philistine outpost. As you approach the town, you will meet a procession of prophets coming down from the high place with lyres, tambourines, flutes and harps being played before them, and they will be prophesying. ⁶The Spirit of the LORD will come upon you in power, and you will prophesy with them; and you will be changed into a different person. ⁷Once these signs are fulfilled, do whatever your hand finds to do, for God is with you.

⁸"Go down ahead of me to Gilgal. I will surely come down to you to sacrifice burnt offerings and fellowship offerings, but you must wait seven days until I come to you and tell you what you are to do."

Saul Made King

⁹As Saul turned to leave Samuel, God changed Saul's heart, and all these

E *Jdg 15:14-15* ◀▶ *1Sa 10:10-12*
G *Dt 34:9* ◀▶ *1Sa 10:10-12*
L *Jdg 13:25* ◀▶ *2Sa 23:2*
T *Dt 34:9* ◀▶ *1Sa 10:10-12*

c 1 Hebrew; Septuagint and Vulgate *over his people Israel? You will reign over the LORD's people and save them from the power of their enemies round about. And this will be a sign to you that the LORD has anointed you leader over his inheritance:* ᵈ *8* Traditionally *peace offerings*

signs were fulfilled that day. ¹⁰When they arrived at Gibeah, a procession of prophets met him; the Spirit of God came upon him in power, and he joined in their prophesying. ¹¹When all those who had formerly known him saw him prophesying with the prophets, they asked each other, "What is this that has happened to the son of Kish? Is Saul also among the prophets?"

¹²A man who lived there answered, "And who is their father?" So it became a saying: "Is Saul also among the prophets?" ¹³After Saul stopped prophesying, he went to the high place.

¹⁴Now Saul's uncle asked him and his servant, "Where have you been?"

"Looking for the donkeys," he said. "But when we saw they were not to be found, we went to Samuel."

¹⁵Saul's uncle said, "Tell me what Samuel said to you."

¹⁶Saul replied, "He assured us that the donkeys had been found." But he did not tell his uncle what Samuel had said about the kingship.

¹⁷Samuel summoned the people of Israel to the LORD at Mizpah ¹⁸and said to them, "This is what the LORD, the God of Israel, says: 'I brought Israel up out of Egypt, and I delivered you from the power of Egypt and all the kingdoms that oppressed you.' ¹⁹But you have now rejected your God, who saves you out of all your calamities and distresses. And you have said, 'No, set a king over us.' So now present yourselves before the LORD by your tribes and clans."

²⁰When Samuel brought all the tribes of Israel near, the tribe of Benjamin was chosen. ²¹Then he brought forward the tribe of Benjamin, clan by clan, and Matri's clan was chosen. Finally Saul son of Kish was chosen. But when they looked for him, he was not to be found. ²²So they inquired further of the LORD, "Has the man come here yet?"

And the LORD said, "Yes, he has hidden himself among the baggage."

²³They ran and brought him out, and as he stood among the people he was a head taller than any of the others. ²⁴Samuel said to all the people, "Do you see the man the LORD has chosen? There is no one like him among all the people."

Then the people shouted, "Long live the king!"

²⁵Samuel explained to the people the regulations of the kingship. He wrote them down on a scroll and deposited it before the LORD. Then Samuel dismissed the people, each to his own home.

²⁶Saul also went to his home in Gibeah, accompanied by valiant men whose hearts God had touched. ²⁷But some troublemakers said, "How can this fellow save us?" They despised him and brought him no gifts. But Saul kept silent.

Saul Rescues the City of Jabesh

11 Nahash the Ammonite went up and besieged Jabesh Gilead. And all the men of Jabesh said to him, "Make a treaty with us, and we will be subject to you."

²But Nahash the Ammonite replied, "I will make a treaty with you only on the condition that I gouge out the right eye of every one of you and so bring disgrace on all Israel."

³The elders of Jabesh said to him, "Give us seven days so we can send messengers throughout Israel; if no one comes to rescue us, we will surrender to you."

⁴When the messengers came to Gibeah of Saul and reported these terms to the people, they all wept aloud. ⁵Just then Saul was returning from the fields, behind his oxen, and he asked, "What is wrong with the people? Why are they weeping?" Then they repeated to him what the men of Jabesh had said.

⁶When Saul heard their words, the Spirit of God came upon him in power, and he burned with anger. ⁷He took a pair of oxen, cut them into pieces, and sent the pieces by messengers throughout Israel, proclaiming, "This is what will be done to the oxen of anyone who does not follow Saul and Samuel." Then the terror of the LORD fell on the people, and they turned out as one man. ⁸When Saul mustered them at Bezek, the men of Israel numbered three hundred thou-

1 SAMUEL 11:9

sand and the men of Judah thirty thousand.

⁹They told the messengers who had come, "Say to the men of Jabesh Gilead, 'By the time the sun is hot tomorrow, you will be delivered.'" When the messengers went and reported this to the men of Jabesh, they were elated. ¹⁰They said to the Ammonites, "Tomorrow we will surrender[c] to you, and you can do to us whatever seems good to you."

¹¹The next day Saul separated his men into three divisions;[d] during the last watch of the night they broke into the camp of the Ammonites[e] and slaughtered them until the heat of the day. Those who survived were scattered, so that no two of them were left together.

Saul Confirmed as King

¹²The people then said to Samuel, "Who[f] was it that asked, 'Shall Saul reign over us?' Bring these men to us and we will put them to death."

¹³But Saul said, "No one shall be put to death today,[g] for this day the LORD has rescued[h] Israel."

¹⁴Then Samuel said to the people, "Come, let us go to Gilgal[i] and there reaffirm the kingship.[j]" ¹⁵So all the people went to Gilgal[k] and confirmed Saul as king[l] in the presence of the LORD. There they sacrificed fellowship offerings[e] before the LORD, and Saul and all the Israelites held a great celebration.

Samuel's Farewell Speech

12 Samuel said to all Israel, "I have listened[m] to everything you said to me and have set a king[n] over you. ²Now you have a king as your leader.[o] As for me, I am old and gray, and my sons[p] are here with you. I have been your leader from my youth until this day. ³Here I stand. Testify against me in the presence of the LORD and his anointed.[q] Whose ox have I taken? Whose donkey have I taken? Whom have I cheated? Whom have I oppressed? From whose hand have I accepted a bribe[s] to make me shut my eyes? If I have done[t] any of these, I will make it right."[u]

⁴"You have not cheated or oppressed us," they replied. "You have not taken anything from anyone's hand."

⁵Samuel said to them, "The LORD is witness[v] against you, and also his anointed is witness this day, that you have not found anything[w] in my hand.[x]"

"He is witness," they said.

⁶Then Samuel said to the people, "It is the LORD who appointed Moses and Aaron and brought[y] your forefathers up out of Egypt. ⁷Now then, stand[z] here, because I am going to confront[a] you with evidence before the LORD as to all the righteous acts[b] performed by the LORD for you and your fathers.

⁸"After Jacob[c] entered Egypt, they cried[d] to the LORD for help, and the LORD sent[e] Moses and Aaron, who brought your forefathers out of Egypt and settled them in this place.

⁹"But they forgot[f] the LORD their God; so he sold them[g] into the hand of Sisera,[h] the commander of the army of Hazor,[i] and into the hands of the Philistines[j] and the king of Moab,[k] who fought against them. ¹⁰They cried[l] out to the LORD and said, 'We have sinned; we have forsaken[m] the LORD and served the Baals and the Ashtoreths.[n] But now deliver us from the hands of our enemies, and we will serve you.' ¹¹Then the LORD sent Jerub-Baal,[o] Barak,[g,p] Jephthah[q] and Samuel,[h,r] and he delivered you from the hands of your enemies on every side, so that you lived securely.

¹²"But when you saw that Nahash[s] king[t] of the Ammonites was moving against you, you said to me, 'No, we want a king to rule[u] over us'—even though the LORD your God was your king. ¹³Now here is the king[v] you have chosen, the one you asked[w] for; see, the LORD has set a king over you. ¹⁴If you fear[x] the LORD and serve and obey him and do not rebel[y] against his commands, and if both you and the king who reigns over you follow the LORD your God—good! ¹⁵But if you do not obey the LORD, and if you rebel against[z] his commands, his hand will be against you, as it was against your fathers.

¹⁶"Now then, stand still[a] and see[b] this great thing the LORD is about to do before your eyes! ¹⁷Is it not wheat harvest[c] now? I will call[d] upon the LORD to send thun-

e 15 Traditionally *peace offerings* / *f* 11 Also called *Gideon* *g* 11 Some Septuagint manuscripts and Syriac; Hebrew *Bedan* *h* 11 Hebrew; some Septuagint manuscripts and Syriac *Samson*

der[e] and rain.[f] And you will realize what an evil[g] thing you did in the eyes of the LORD when you asked for a king."

[18] Then Samuel called upon the LORD,[h] and that same day the LORD sent thunder and rain. So all the people stood in awe[i] of the LORD and of Samuel.

[19] The people all said to Samuel, "Pray[j] to the LORD your God for your servants so that we will not die,[k] for we have added to all our other sins the evil of asking for a king."

[20] "Do not be afraid," Samuel replied. "You have done all this evil;[l] yet do not turn away from the LORD, but serve the LORD with all your heart. [21] Do not turn away after useless[m] idols.[n] They can do you no good, nor can they rescue you, because they are useless. [22] For the sake of his great name[p] the LORD will not reject[q] his people, because the LORD was pleased to make[r] you his own. [23] As for me, far be it from me that I should sin against the LORD by failing to pray[s] for you. And I will teach[t] you the way that is good and right. [24] But be sure to fear[u] the LORD and serve him faithfully with all your heart;[v] consider[w] what great[x] things he has done for you. [25] Yet if you persist[y] in doing evil, both you and your king[z] will be swept[a] away."

Samuel Rebukes Saul

13 Saul was ⌊thirty⌋[/] years old when he became king, and he reigned over Israel ⌊forty⌋[/] two years. [2] Saul[k] chose three thousand men from Israel; two thousand[b] were with him at Micmash[c] and in the hill country of Bethel, and a thousand were with Jonathan at Gibeah[d] in Benjamin. The rest of the men he sent back to their homes.

[3] Jonathan attacked the Philistine outpost[e] at Geba,[f] and the Philistines heard about it. Then Saul had the trumpet[g] blown throughout the land and said, "Let the Hebrews hear!" [4] So all Israel heard the news: "Saul has attacked the Philistine outpost, and now Israel has become a stench[h] to the Philistines." And the people were summoned to join Saul at Gilgal.

[5] The Philistines assembled[i] to fight Israel, with three thousand[/] chariots, six thousand charioteers, and soldiers as numerous as the sand[j] on the seashore. They went up and camped at Micmash,[k] east of Beth Aven.[l] [6] When the men of Israel saw that their situation was critical and that their army was hard pressed, they hid[m] in caves and thickets, among the rocks, and in pits and cisterns.[n] [7] Some Hebrews even crossed the Jordan to the land of Gad[o] and Gilead.

Saul remained at Gilgal, and all the troops with him were quaking[p] with fear. [8] He waited seven[q] days, the time set by Samuel; but Samuel did not come to Gilgal, and Saul's men began to scatter. [9] So he said, "Bring me the burnt offering and the fellowship offerings.[m]" And Saul offered[r] up the burnt offering. [10] Just as he finished making the offering, Samuel[s] arrived, and Saul went out to greet[t] him.

[11] "What have you done?" asked Samuel.

Saul replied, "When I saw that the men were scattering, and that you did not come at the set time, and that the Philistines were assembling at Micmash,[u] [12] I thought, 'Now the Philistines will come down against me at Gilgal,[v] and I have not sought the LORD's favor.[w]' So I felt compelled to offer the burnt offering."

[13] "You acted foolishly,[x]" Samuel said. "You have not kept[y] the command the LORD your God gave you; if you had, he would have established your kingdom over Israel for all time.[z] [14] But now your

---

L Dt 30:19 ◀ ▶ 2Sa 12:13
I 1Sa 9:16 ◀ ▶ 1Sa 14:10
S 1Sa 12:15 ◀ ▶ 1Sa 15:22–23
L 1Sa 2:9 ◀ ▶ 1Sa 25:29
J 1Sa 2:31 ◀ ▶ 1Sa 13:24

12:17 e S Ex 9:23; S 1Sa 2:10
g Ge 7:12; Ex 9:18; Job 37:13; Pr 26:1
a S 1Sa 8:6-7
12:18 h Ps 99:6
i S Ge 3:10; S Ex 14:31
12:19 j S Ex 8:8; S 1Sa 7:8;
S Jer 37:3; Jas 5:18; 1Jn 5:16 k S Dt 9:19
12:20 l S Ex 32:30
12:21 m Isa 40:20; 41:24,29; 44:9;
Jer 2:5,11; 14:22; 16:19; Jnh 2:8;
Hab 2:18; Ac 14:15
n Dt 11:16
12:22 p Ps 25:11; 106:8; Isa 48:9,11;
Jer 14:7; Da 9:19
p S Jos 7:9;
2Sa 7:23; Jn 17:12
q S Lev 26:11;
S Dt 31:6 r Dt 7:7;
1Pe 2:9
12:23 s Nu 11:2;
S 1Sa 1:20; S 7:8;
Ro 1:9-10
t 1Ki 8:36; Ps 25:4;
34:11; 86:11;
94:12; Pr 4:11
12:24 u Dt 6:2;
Ecc 12:13 v Dt 6:5;
S Jos 24:14
w Job 34:27;
Isa 5:12; 22:11;
26:10 x S Dt 10:21
12:25 y 1Sa 31:1-5
z Dt 28:36
a S Jos 24:20;
S 1Ki 14:10
13:2 b ver 15
c ver 5,11,23;
Ne 11:31; Lk 10:28
d S Jdg 19:14
13:3 e S 1Sa 10:5
f S Jos 18:24
g S Lev 25:9;
S Jdg 3:27
13:4 h S Ge 34:30
13:5 i 1Sa 17:1
j S Jos 11:4;
Rev 20:8 k S ver 2
l S Jos 7:2
13:6 m 1Sa 14:11,
22 n S Jdg 6:2;
Eze 33:27
13:7 o S Nu 32:33
p S Ge 35:5;
S Ex 19:16
13:8 q 1Sa 10:8
13:9 r Dt 12:5-14;
2Sa 24:25; 1Ki 3:4
13:10 s 1Sa 15:13
t 1Sa 25:14
13:11 u S ver 2
13:12 v S Jos 10:43
w S Dt 4:29;
Ps 119:58;
Jer 26:19
13:13 x 2Ch 16:9
y ver 14;
S Jos 22:16;
1Sa 15:23,24;
2Sa 7:15; 1Ch 10:13 z Ps 72:5

i 1 A few late manuscripts of the Septuagint; Hebrew does not have thirty. *j* 1 See the round number in Acts 13:21; Hebrew does not have forty. *k* 1,2 Or and when he had reigned over Israel two years, *2*he 15 Some Septuagint manuscripts and Syriac; Hebrew thirty thousand *m* 9 Traditionally peace offerings

▶ 1Sa 12:25 ◀ ▶ 2Sa 12:14

12:22 The Lord reconfirmed the unconditional nature of his eternal covenant with Israel and his intent to set them apart as his chosen nation (see Dt 7:6).

13:14 King Saul had overstepped his bounds and offered a sacrifice that should have only been offered by the high priest. By such a sinful presumption, Saul violated the divine position of trust he had

kingdom[a] will not endure; the LORD has sought out a man after his own heart[b] and appointed[c] him leader[d] of his people, because you have not kept[e] the LORD's command."

[15] Then Samuel left Gilgal[n] and went up to Gibeah[f] in Benjamin, and Saul counted the men who were with him. They numbered about six hundred.[g]

Israel Without Weapons

[16] Saul and his son Jonathan and the men with them were staying in Gibeah[oh] in Benjamin, while the Philistines camped at Micmash. [17] Raiding[i] parties went out from the Philistine camp in three detachments. One turned toward Ophrah[j] in the vicinity of Shual, [18] another toward Beth Horon,[k] and the third toward the borderland overlooking the Valley of Zeboim[l] facing the desert.

[19] Not a blacksmith[m] could be found in the whole land of Israel, because the Philistines had said, "Otherwise the Hebrews will make swords or spears!" [20] So all Israel went down to the Philistines to have their plowshares, mattocks, axes and sickles[p] sharpened. [21] The price was two thirds of a shekel[q] for sharpening plowshares and mattocks, and a third of a shekel[r] for sharpening forks and axes and for repointing goads.

[22] So on the day of the battle not a soldier with Saul and Jonathan[o] had a sword or spear[p] in his hand; only Saul and his son Jonathan had them.

Jonathan Attacks the Philistines

[23] Now a detachment of Philistines had gone out to the pass[q] at Micmash.[r]

14 [1] One day Jonathan son of Saul said to the young man bearing his armor, "Come, let's go over to the Philistine outpost on the other side." But he did not tell his father.

[2] Saul was staying[s] on the outskirts of Gibeah[t] under a pomegranate tree[u] in Migron.[v] With him were about six hundred men, [3] among whom was Ahijah, who was wearing an ephod. He was a son of Ichabod's[w] brother Ahitub[x] son of Phinehas, the son of Eli,[y] the LORD's priest in Shiloh.[z] No one was aware that Jonathan had left.

[4] On each side of the pass[a] that Jonathan intended to cross to reach the Philistine outpost was a cliff; one was called Bozez, and the other Seneh. [5] One cliff stood to the north toward Micmash, the other to the south toward Geba.[b]

[6] Jonathan said to his young armor-bearer, "Come, let's go over to the outpost of those uncircumcised[c] fellows. Perhaps the LORD will act in our behalf. Nothing[d] can hinder the LORD from saving, whether by many[e] or by few.[f]"

[7] "Do all that you have in mind," his armor-bearer said. "Go ahead; I am with you heart and soul."

[8] Jonathan said, "Come, then; we will cross over toward the men and let them see us. [9] If they say to us, 'Wait there until we come to you,' we will stay where we are and not go up to them. [10] But if they say, 'Come up to us,' we will climb up, because that will be our sign[g] that the LORD has given them into our hands.[h]"

[11] So both of them showed themselves to the Philistine outpost. "Look!" said the Philistines. "The Hebrews[i] are crawling out of the holes they were hiding in." [12] The men of the outpost shouted to Jonathan and his armor-bearer, "Come up to us and we'll teach you a lesson.[k]"

So Jonathan said to his armor-bearer, "Climb up after me; the LORD has given them into the hand[l] of Israel."

[13] Jonathan climbed up, using his hands and feet, with his armor-bearer right behind him. The Philistines fell before Jonathan, and his armor-bearer followed and killed behind him. [14] In that first attack Jonathan and his armor-bearer killed some twenty men in an area of about half an acre.[s]

V Jos 23:9–10 ◄► 1Sa 17:47
I 1Sa 12:22 ◄► 1Sa 17:36–37

[n] 15 Hebrew; Septuagint *Gilgal and went his way; the rest of the people went after Saul to meet the army, and they went out of Gilgal*
[o] 16 Two Hebrew manuscripts; most Hebrew manuscripts *Geba*, a variant of *Gibeah* [p] 20 Septuagint; Hebrew *plowshares* [q] 21 Hebrew *pim*; that is, about 1/4 ounce (about 8 grams) [r] 21 That is, about 1/8 ounce (about 4 grams) [s] 14 Hebrew *half a yoke*; a "yoke" was the land plowed by a yoke of oxen in one day.

---

been given as Israel's king and incurred God's judgment. Saul would be removed as king; God had already chosen "a man after his own heart" to be the next king of Israel—David.

Israel Routs the Philistines

¹⁵Then panic^m struck the whole army—those in the camp and field, and those in the outposts and raiding^n parties—and the ground shook. It was a panic sent by God.^t

¹⁶Saul's lookouts° at Gibeah in Benjamin saw the army melting away in all directions. ¹⁷Then Saul said to the men who were with him, "Muster the forces and see who has left us." When they did, it was Jonathan and his armor-bearer who were not there.

¹⁸Saul said to Ahijah, "Bring^p the ark^q of God." (At that time it was with the Israelites.)^u ¹⁹While Saul was talking to the priest, the tumult in the Philistine camp increased more and more. So Saul said to the priest,^r "Withdraw your hand."

²⁰Then Saul and all his men assembled and went to the battle. They found the Philistines in total confusion, striking^s each other with their swords. ²¹Those Hebrews who had previously been with the Philistines and had gone up with them to their camp went^t over to the Israelites who were with Saul and Jonathan. ²²When all the Israelites who had hidden^u in the hill country of Ephraim heard that the Philistines were on the run, they joined the battle in hot pursuit. ²³So the LORD rescued^v Israel that day, and the battle moved on beyond Beth Aven.^w

Jonathan Eats Honey

²⁴Now the men of Israel were in distress that day, because Saul had bound the people under an oath,^x saying, "Cursed be any man who eats food before evening comes, before I have avenged myself on my enemies!" So none of the troops tasted food.

²⁵The entire army^v entered the woods, and there was honey on the ground. ²⁶When they went into the woods, they saw the honey oozing out, yet no one put his hand to his mouth, because they feared the oath. ²⁷But Jonathan had not heard that his father had bound the people with the oath, so he reached out the end of the staff that was in his hand and dipped it into the honeycomb.^y He raised his hand to his mouth, and his eyes brightened.^w ²⁸Then one of the soldiers told him, "Your father bound the army under a strict oath, saying, 'Cursed be any man who eats food today!' That is why the men are faint."

²⁹Jonathan said, "My father has made trouble^z for the country. See how my eyes brightened^x when I tasted a little of this honey. ³⁰How much better it would have been if the men had eaten today some of the plunder they took from their enemies. Would not the slaughter of the Philistines have been even greater?"

³¹That day, after the Israelites had struck down the Philistines from Micmash^a to Aijalon,^b they were exhausted. ³²They pounced on the plunder^c and, taking sheep, cattle and calves, they butchered them on the ground and ate them, together with the blood.^d ³³Then someone said to Saul, "Look, the men are sinning against the LORD by eating meat that has blood^e in it."

"You have broken faith," he said. "Roll a large stone over here at once." ³⁴Then he said, "Go out among the men and tell them, 'Each of you bring me your cattle and sheep, and slaughter them here and eat them. Do not sin against the LORD by eating meat with blood still^f in it.' "

So everyone brought his ox that night and slaughtered it there. ³⁵Then Saul built an altar^g to the LORD; it was the first time he had done this.

³⁶Saul said, "Let us go down after the Philistines by night and plunder them till dawn, and let us not leave one of them alive."

"Do whatever seems best to you," they replied.

But the priest said, "Let us inquire^h of God here."

³⁷So Saul asked God, "Shall I go down after the Philistines? Will you give them into Israel's hand?" But God did not answer^i him that day.

³⁸Saul therefore said, "Come here, all you who are leaders of the army, and let us find out what sin has been committed^j today. ³⁹As surely as the LORD who rescues Israel lives,^k even if it lies with my son Jonathan,^l he must die."^m But not one of the men said a word.

^t 15 Or *a terrible panic*   ^u 18 Hebrew; Septuagint "Bring the ephod." (At that time he wore the ephod before the Israelites.)   ^v 25 Or *Now all the people of the land*   ^w 27 Or *his strength was renewed*   ^x 29 Or *my strength was renewed*

⁴⁰Saul then said to all the Israelites, "You stand over there; I and Jonathan my son will stand over here."

"Do what seems best to you," the men replied.

⁴¹Then Saul prayed to the LORD, the God of Israel, "Give" me the right° answer."ʸ And Jonathan and Saul were taken by lot, and the men were cleared. ⁴²Saul said, "Cast the lotᵖ between me and Jonathan my son." And Jonathan was taken.

⁴³Then Saul said to Jonathan, "Tell me what you have done."ᑫ

So Jonathan told him, "I merely tasted a little honeyʳ with the end of my staff. And now must I die?"

⁴⁴Saul said, "May God deal with me, be it ever so severely,ˢ if you do not die, Jonathan.ᵗ"

⁴⁵But the men said to Saul, "Should Jonathan die—he who has brought about this great deliverance in Israel? Never! As surely as the LORD lives, not a hairᵘ of his head will fall to the ground, for he did this today with God's help." So the men rescuedᵛ Jonathan, and he was not put to death.

⁴⁶Then Saul stopped pursuing the Philistines, and they withdrew to their own land.

⁴⁷After Saul had assumed rule over Israel, he fought against their enemies on every side: Moab,ʷ the Ammonites,ˣ Edom,ʸ the kingsᶻ of Zobah,ᶻ and the Philistines. Wherever he turned, he inflicted punishment on them.ᵃ ⁴⁸He fought valiantly and defeated the Amalekites,ᵃ delivering Israel from the hands of those who had plundered them.

Saul's Family

⁴⁹Saul's sons were Jonathan, Ishvi and Malki-Shua.ᵇ The name of his older daughter was Merab, and that of the younger was Michal.ᶜ ⁵⁰His wife's name was Ahinoam daughter of Ahimaaz. The name of the commander of Saul's army was Abnerᵈ son of Ner, and Ner was Saul's uncle.ᵉ ⁵¹Saul's father Kishᶠ and Abner's father Ner were sons of Abiel.

⁵²All the days of Saul there was bitter war with the Philistines, and whenever Saul saw a mighty or brave man, he tookᵍ him into his service.

14:41 ⁿAc 1:24
°Pr 16:33
14:42 ᵖJnh 1:7
14:43 ᑫS Jos 7:19
ʳS ver 27
14:44 ˢS Ru 1:17
ᵗver 39
14:45 ᵘ1Ki 1:52;
S Mt 10:30
ᵛ2Sa 14:11
14:47
ʷS Ge 19:37
ˣS Ge 19:38;
2Sa 12:31
ʸ1Sa 21:7 ᶻ2Sa 8:3;
10:6; 23:36
14:48
ᵃS Ge 36:12;
Nu 13:29; Jdg 3:13;
1Sa 15:2,7; 27:8;
28:18; 30:13;
2Sa 1:13; 1Ch 4:43
14:49 ᵇ1Sa 31:2;
1Ch 8:33
ᶜS Ge 29:26
14:50 ᵈ2Sa 2:8;
3:6; 1Ki 2:5
ᵉ1Sa 10:14
14:51 ᶠ1Sa 9:1
14:52 ᵍ1Sa 8:11
15:1 ʰS 1Sa 9:16
15:2 ⁱS Ge 14:7;
S 1Sa 14:48;
S 2Sa 1:8
15:3 ʲver 9,19;
S Ge 14:23;
Jos 6:17; 1Sa 22:19;
27:9; 28:18;
Est 3:13; 9:5
15:6 ᵏS Ge 15:19;
Nu 24:22; Jdg 1:16;
1Sa 30:29
15:7 ˡS 1Sa 14:48
ᵐS Ge 16:7
15:8 ⁿEx 17:8-16;
S Nu 24:7
°S Jos 8:23
15:9 ᵖS ver 3
15:11 ᑫS Ge 6:6;
S Ex 32:14
ʳS Jos 22:16
ˢJob 21:14; 34:27;
Ps 28:5; Isa 5:12;
53:6; Jer 48:10;
Eze 18:24
ᵗS ver 35; S 1Sa 8:6
15:12 ᵘJos 15:55
ᵛS Nu 32:42

The LORD Rejects Saul as King

15 Samuel said to Saul, "I am the one the LORD sent to anointʰ you king over his people Israel; so listen now to the message from the LORD. ²This is what the LORD Almighty says: 'I will punish the Amalekitesⁱ for what they did to Israel when they waylaid them as they came up from Egypt. ³Now go, attack the Amalekites and totallyʲ destroyᵇ everything that belongs to them. Do not spare them; put to death men and women, children and infants, cattle and sheep, camels and donkeys.' "

⁴So Saul summoned the men and mustered them at Telaim—two hundred thousand foot soldiers and ten thousand men from Judah. ⁵Saul went to the city of Amalek and set an ambush in the ravine. ⁶Then he said to the Kenites,ᵏ "Go away, leave the Amalekites so that I do not destroy you along with them; for you showed kindness to all the Israelites when they came up out of Egypt." So the Kenites moved away from the Amalekites.

⁷Then Saul attacked the Amalekitesˡ all the way from Havilah to Shur,ᵐ to the east of Egypt. ⁸He took Agagⁿ king of the Amalekites alive,° and all his people he totally destroyed with the sword. ⁹But Saul and the army sparedᵖ Agag and the best of the sheep and cattle, the fat calvesᶜ and lambs—everything that was good. These they were unwilling to destroy completely, but everything that was despised and weak they totally destroyed.

¹⁰Then the word of the LORD came to Samuel: ¹¹"I am grievedᑫ that I have made Saul king, because he has turnedʳ away from me and has not carried out my instructions."ˢ Samuel was troubled,ᵗ and he cried out to the LORD all that night.

¹²Early in the morning Samuel got up and went to meet Saul, but he was told, "Saul has gone to Carmel.ᵘ There he has set up a monumentᵛ in his own honor and has turned and gone on down to Gilgal."

¹³When Samuel reached him, Saul said,

ʸ 41 Hebrew; Septuagint *"Why have you not answered your servant today? If the fault is in me or my son Jonathan, respond with Urim, but if the men of Israel are at fault, respond with Thummim."* ᶻ 47 Masoretic Text; Dead Sea Scrolls and Septuagint *king* ᵃ 47 Hebrew; Septuagint *he was victorious* ᵇ 3 The Hebrew term refers to the irrevocable giving over of things or persons to the LORD, often by totally destroying them; also in verses 8, 9, 15, 18, 20 and 21. ᶜ 9 Or *the grown bulls*; the meaning of the Hebrew for this phrase is uncertain.

"The Lord bless you! I have carried out the Lord's instructions."

¹⁴But Samuel said, "What then is this bleating of sheep in my ears? What is this lowing of cattle that I hear?"

¹⁵Saul answered, "The soldiers brought them from the Amalekites; they spared the best of the sheep and cattle to sacrifice to the Lord your God, but we totally destroyed the rest."

¹⁶"Stop!" Samuel said to Saul. "Let me tell you what the Lord said to me last night."

"Tell me," Saul replied.

¹⁷Samuel said, "Although you were once small in your own eyes, did you not become the head of the tribes of Israel? The Lord anointed you king over Israel. ¹⁸And he sent you on a mission, saying, 'Go and completely destroy those wicked people, the Amalekites; make war on them until you have wiped them out.' ¹⁹Why did you not obey the Lord? Why did you pounce on the plunder and do evil in the eyes of the Lord?"

²⁰"But I did obey the Lord," Saul said. "I went on the mission the Lord assigned me. I completely destroyed the Amalekites and brought back Agag their king. ²¹The soldiers took sheep and cattle from the plunder, the best of what was devoted to God, in order to sacrifice them to the Lord your God at Gilgal."

²²But Samuel replied:

"Does the Lord delight in burnt offerings and sacrifices
 as much as in obeying the voice of the Lord?
To obey is better than sacrifice,
 and to heed is better than the fat of rams.
²³For rebellion is like the sin of divination,
 and arrogance like the evil of idolatry.
Because you have rejected the word of the Lord,
 he has rejected you as king."

S 1Sa 12:24 ◄ ► 1Sa 16:14

²⁴Then Saul said to Samuel, "I have sinned. I violated the Lord's command and your instructions. I was afraid of the people and so I gave in to them. ²⁵Now I beg you, forgive my sin and come back with me, so that I may worship the Lord."

²⁶But Samuel said to him, "I will not go back with you. You have rejected the word of the Lord, and the Lord has rejected you as king over Israel!"

²⁷As Samuel turned to leave, Saul caught hold of the hem of his robe, and it tore. ²⁸Samuel said to him, "The Lord has torn the kingdom of Israel from you today and has given it to one of your neighbors—to one better than you. ²⁹He who is the Glory of Israel does not lie or change his mind; for he is not a man, that he should change his mind."

³⁰Saul replied, "I have sinned. But please honor me before the elders of my people and before Israel; come back with me, so that I may worship the Lord your God." ³¹So Samuel went back with Saul, and Saul worshiped the Lord.

³²Then Samuel said, "Bring me Agag king of the Amalekites."

Agag came to him confidently, thinking, "Surely the bitterness of death is past."

³³But Samuel said,

"As your sword has made women childless,
 so will your mother be childless among women."

And Samuel put Agag to death before the Lord at Gilgal.

³⁴Then Samuel left for Ramah, but Saul went up to his home in Gibeah of Saul. ³⁵Until the day Samuel died, he did not go to see Saul again, though Samuel mourned for him. And the Lord was grieved that he had made Saul king over Israel.

d 32 Or him trembling, yet

15:22 Samuel revealed that God desired obedience more than the formal completion of the required sacrifices. Saul's rebellion and disobedience grew from the root of spiritual pride that in God's eyes was as abominable as witchcraft and idolatry (see 15:23).

Samuel Anoints David

16 The LORD said to Samuel, "How long will you mourn^w for Saul, since I have rejected^x him as king over Israel? Fill your horn with oil^y and be on your way; I am sending you to Jesse^z of Bethlehem. I have chosen^a one of his sons to be king."

²But Samuel said, "How can I go? Saul will hear about it and kill me."

The LORD said, "Take a heifer with you and say, 'I have come to sacrifice to the LORD.' ³Invite Jesse to the sacrifice, and I will show^b you what to do. You are to anoint^c for me the one I indicate."

⁴Samuel did what the LORD said. When he arrived at Bethlehem,^d the elders of the town trembled^e when they met him. They asked, "Do you come in peace?^f"

⁵Samuel replied, "Yes, in peace; I have come to sacrifice to the LORD. Consecrate^g yourselves and come to the sacrifice with me." Then he consecrated Jesse and his sons and invited them to the sacrifice.

⁶When they arrived, Samuel saw Eliab^h and thought, "Surely the LORD's anointed stands here before the LORD."

⁷But the LORD said to Samuel, "Do not consider his appearance or his height, for I have rejected him. The LORD does not look at the things man looks at. Man looks at the outward appearance,^i but the LORD looks at the heart."^j

⁸Then Jesse called Abinadab^k and had him pass in front of Samuel. But Samuel said, "The LORD has not chosen this one either." ⁹Jesse then had Shammah^l pass by, but Samuel said, "Nor has the LORD chosen this one." ¹⁰Jesse had seven of his sons pass before Samuel, but Samuel said to him, "The LORD has not chosen these." ¹¹So he asked Jesse, "Are these all^m the sons you have?"

"There is still the youngest," Jesse an-

E 1Sa 2:3 ◀▶ 1Ki 8:39
G Dt 32:31 ◀▶ Job 8:11–16

16:1 ʷS 1Sa 8:6; S 15:35
ˣS 1Sa 13:14
ʸS 1Sa 10:1
ᶻS Ru 4:17
ᵃ2Sa 5:2; 7:8; 1Ki 8:16; 1Ch 12:23; Ps 78:70; Ac 13:22
16:3 ᵇEx 4:15
ᶜS Dt 17:15
16:4 ᵈS Ge 48:7; Lk 2:4; 1Sa 21:1
ᶠ1Ki 2:13; 2Ki 9:17
16:5 ᵍS Ex 19:10, 22
16:6 ʰ1Sa 17:13; 1Ch 2:13
16:7 ⁱPs 147:10
ʲS 1Sa 2:3; 2Sa 7:20; S Ps 44:21; S 139:23; S Rev 2:23
16:8 ᵏ1Sa 17:13
16:9 ˡ1Sa 17:13; 2Sa 13:3; 21:21
16:11 ᵐ1Sa 17:12
ⁿS Ge 37:2; 2Sa 7:8
16:12 ᵒ1Sa 9:17
ᵖS Ge 39:6
16:13 ᵠS 1Sa 2:35; S 2Sa 22:51
ʳ1Sa 18:12
ˢS 1Sa 11:6
16:14 ᵗS Jdg 16:20
ᵘver 23; S Jdg 9:23; 1Sa 18:10
ᵛ2Sa 7:15
16:16 ʷver 23; S 1Sa 10:5,6; 2Ch 29:26-27; Ps 49:4
16:18 ˣS Ru 4:17
ʸ2Sa 17:8
ᶻS Ge 39:2; 1Sa 17:32-37; 20:13; 1Ch 22:11; Mt 1:23
16:19 ᵃ1Sa 17:15
16:20 ᵇS Ge 32:13; S 1Sa 10:4
16:21 ᶜS Ge 41:26

swered, "but he is tending the sheep."^n

Samuel said, "Send for him; we will not sit down^e until he arrives."

¹²So he^o sent and had him brought in. He was ruddy, with a fine appearance and handsome^p features.

Then the LORD said, "Rise and anoint him; he is the one."

¹³So Samuel took the horn of oil and anointed^q him in the presence of his brothers, and from that day on the Spirit of the LORD^r came upon David in power.^s Samuel then went to Ramah.

David in Saul's Service

¹⁴Now the Spirit of the LORD had departed^t from Saul, and an evil^u spirit from the LORD tormented him.^v Q S

¹⁵Saul's attendants said to him, "See, an evil spirit from God is tormenting you. ¹⁶Let our lord command his servants here to search for someone who can play the harp.^w He will play when the evil spirit from God comes upon you, and you will feel better."

¹⁷So Saul said to his attendants, "Find someone who plays well and bring him to me."

¹⁸One of the servants answered, "I have seen a son of Jesse^x of Bethlehem who knows how to play the harp. He is a brave man and a warrior.^y He speaks well and is a fine-looking man. And the LORD is with^z him."

¹⁹Then Saul sent messengers to Jesse and said, "Send me your son David, who is with the sheep.^a" ²⁰So Jesse took a donkey loaded with bread,^b a skin of wine and a young goat and sent them with his son David to Saul.

²¹David came to Saul and entered his service.^c Saul liked him very much, and David became one of his armor-bearers.

Q Jdg 16:20 ◀▶ 1Ki 22:24
S 1Sa 15:22–23 ◀▶ 1Sa 24:13

^e 11 Some Septuagint manuscripts; Hebrew *not gather around*
^f 14 Or *injurious*; also in verses 15, 16 and 23

16:7 God is more concerned with what is inside the heart than what is outwardly visible to others. Note that no one even considered the possibility that Samuel would anoint David (see 16:7–13). He was a young shepherd. He had no military experience or advantages by virtue of birth order. Yet God knew David's heart. Position, birth order, strength or beauty meant nothing. Though David was young and weak, God in his sovereign grace chose the man he wanted to use in his service regardless of natural advantage for God's "power is made perfect in weakness" (2Co 12:9).

16:13 The anointing of David as the king of Israel prefigures the anointing of the true Messiah of Israel at the conclusion of the seventy weeks (see Da 9:24).

22Then Saul sent word to Jesse, saying, "Allow David to remain in my service, for I am pleased with him."

23Whenever the spirit from God came upon Saul, David would take his harp and play. Then relief would come to Saul; he would feel better, and the evil spirit[d] would leave him.

David and Goliath

17 Now the Philistines gathered their forces for war and assembled[e] at Socoh in Judah. They pitched camp at Ephes Dammim, between Socoh[f] and Azekah.[g] 2Saul and the Israelites assembled and camped in the Valley of Elah[h] and drew up their battle line to meet the Philistines. 3The Philistines occupied one hill and the Israelites another, with the valley between them.

4A champion named Goliath,[i] who was from Gath, came out of the Philistine camp. He was over nine feet[g] tall. 5He had a bronze helmet on his head and wore a coat of scale armor of bronze weighing five thousand shekels[h]; 6on his legs he wore bronze greaves, and a bronze javelin[j] was slung on his back. 7His spear shaft was like a weaver's rod,[k] and its iron point weighed six hundred shekels.[l] His shield bearer[l] went ahead of him.

8Goliath stood and shouted to the ranks of Israel, "Why do you come out and line up for battle? Am I not a Philistine, and are you not the servants of Saul? Choose[m] a man and have him come down to me. 9If he is able to fight and kill me, we will become your subjects; but if I overcome him and kill him, you will become our subjects and serve us." 10Then the Philistine said, "This day I defy[n] the ranks of Israel! Give me a man and let us fight each other."[o] 11On hearing the Philistine's words, Saul and all the Israelites were dismayed and terrified.

12Now David was the son of an Ephrathite[p] named Jesse,[q] who was from Bethlehem[r] in Judah. Jesse had eight[s] sons, and in Saul's time he was old and well advanced in years. 13Jesse's three oldest sons had followed Saul to the war: The firstborn was Eliab;[t] the second, Abinadab;[u] and the third, Shammah.[v] 14David was the youngest. The three oldest followed Saul, 15but David went back and forth from Saul to tend[w] his father's sheep[x] at Bethlehem.

16For forty days the Philistine came forward every morning and evening and took his stand.

17Now Jesse said to his son David, "Take this ephah[y] of roasted grain[z] and these ten loaves of bread for your brothers and hurry to their camp. 18Take along these ten cheeses to the commander of their unit.[k] See how your brothers[a] are and bring back some assurance[l] from them. 19They are with Saul and all the men of Israel in the Valley of Elah, fighting against the Philistines."

20Early in the morning David left the flock with a shepherd, loaded up and set out, as Jesse had directed. He reached the camp as the army was going out to its battle positions, shouting the war cry. 21Israel and the Philistines were drawing up their lines facing each other. 22David left his things with the keeper of supplies,[b] ran to the battle lines and greeted his brothers. 23As he was talking with them, Goliath, the Philistine champion from Gath, stepped out from his lines and shouted his usual[c] defiance, and David heard it. 24When the Israelites saw the man, they all ran from him in great fear.

25Now the Israelites had been saying, "Do you see how this man keeps coming out? He comes out to defy Israel. The king will give great wealth to the man who kills him. He will also give him his daughter[d] in marriage and will exempt his father's family from taxes[e] in Israel."

26David asked the men standing near him, "What will be done for the man who kills this Philistine and removes this disgrace[f] from Israel? Who is this uncircumcised[g] Philistine that he should defy[h] the armies of the living[i] God?"

27They repeated to him what they had been saying and told him, "This is what will be done for the man who kills him."

28When Eliab, David's oldest brother, heard him speaking with the men, he burned with anger[j] at him and asked, "Why have you come down here? And with whom did you leave those few sheep in the desert? I know how conceited you are and how wicked your

---

g 4 Hebrew *was six cubits and a span* (about 3 meters) *h 5* That is, about 125 pounds (about 57 kilograms) *i 7* That is, about 15 pounds (about 7 kilograms) *j 17* That is, probably about 3/5 bushel (about 22 liters) *k 18* Hebrew *thousand* *l 18* Or *some token*; or *some pledge of spoils*

heart is; you came down only to watch the battle."

²⁹"Now what have I done?" said David. "Can't I even speak?" ³⁰He then turned away to someone else and brought up the same matter, and the men answered him as before. ³¹What David said was overheard and reported to Saul, and Saul sent for him.

³²David said to Saul, "Let no one lose heart^k on account of this Philistine; your servant will go and fight him." ³³Saul replied,^l "You are not able to go out against this Philistine and fight him; you are only a boy, and he has been a fighting man from his youth."

³⁴But David said to Saul, "Your servant has been keeping his father's sheep. When a lion^m or a bear came and carried off a sheep from the flock, ³⁵I went after it, struck it and rescued the sheep from its mouth. When it turned on me, I seized^n it by its hair, struck it and killed it. ³⁶Your servant has killed both the lion^o and the bear; this uncircumcised Philistine will be like one of them, because he has defied the armies of the living God. ³⁷The LORD who delivered^p me from the paw of the lion^q and the paw of the bear will deliver me from the hand of this Philistine."

Saul said to David, "Go, and the LORD be with^r you."

³⁸Then Saul dressed David in his own^s tunic. He put a coat of armor on him and a bronze helmet on his head. ³⁹David fastened on his sword over the tunic and tried walking around, because he was not used to them.

"I cannot go in these," he said to Saul, "because I am not used to them." So he took them off. ⁴⁰Then he took his staff in his hand, chose five smooth stones from the stream, put them in the pouch of his shepherd's bag and, with his sling in his hand, approached the Philistine.

⁴¹Meanwhile, the Philistine, with his shield bearer^t in front of him, kept coming closer to David. ⁴²He looked

l *1Sa 14:10* ◄ ► *1Sa 25:28*

over and saw that he was only a boy, ruddy and handsome,^u and he despised^v him. ⁴³He said to David, "Am I a dog,^w that you come at me with sticks?" And the Philistine cursed David by his gods. ⁴⁴"Come here," he said, "and I'll give your flesh to the birds of the air^x and the beasts of the field!"^y

⁴⁵David said to the Philistine, "You come against me with sword and spear and javelin,^z but I come against you in the name^a of the LORD Almighty, the God of the armies of Israel, whom you have defied.^b ⁴⁶This day the LORD will hand^c you over to me, and I'll strike you down and cut off your head. Today I will give the carcasses^d of the Philistine army to the birds of the air and the beasts of the earth, and the whole world^e will know that there is a God in Israel.^f ⁴⁷All those gathered here will know that it is not by sword^g or spear that the LORD saves;^h for the battle^i is the LORD's, and he will give all of you into our hands."

⁴⁸As the Philistine moved closer to attack him, David ran quickly toward the battle line to meet him. ⁴⁹Reaching into his bag and taking out a stone, he slung it and struck the Philistine on the forehead. The stone sank into his forehead, and he fell facedown on the ground.

⁵⁰So David triumphed over the Philistine with a sling^j and a stone; without a sword in his hand he struck down the Philistine and killed him.

⁵¹David ran and stood over him. He took hold of the Philistine's sword and drew it from the scabbard. After he killed him, he cut^k off his head with the sword.^l

When the Philistines saw that their hero was dead, they turned and ran. ⁵²Then the men of Israel and Judah surged forward with a shout and pursued the Philistines to the entrance of Gath^m and to the gates of Ekron.^m Their dead were strewn along the Shaaraim^n road to Gath and Ekron. ⁵³When the Israelites re-

v *1Sa 14:6* ◄ ► *1Sa 25:29*

m 52 Some Septuagint manuscripts; Hebrew *a valley*

17:40 Though David gathered five stones, this is not an indication of a lack of faith in God's power to help him defeat Goliath. Realizing that the death of their champion might anger the Philistines, David prudently gathered these extra stones for additional ammunition in case other Philistines decided to join the fight.

turned from chasing the Philistines, they plundered their camp. ⁵⁴David took the Philistine's head and brought it to Jerusalem, and he put the Philistine's weapons in his own tent.

⁵⁵As Saul watched David° going out to meet the Philistine, he said to Abner, commander of the army, "Abner,ᵖ whose son is that young man?"

Abner replied, "As surely as you live, O king, I don't know."

⁵⁶The king said, "Find out whose son this young man is."

⁵⁷As soon as David returned from killing the Philistine, Abner took him and brought him before Saul, with David still holding the Philistine's head.

⁵⁸"Whose son are you, young man?" Saul asked him.

David said, "I am the son of your servant Jesseᵠ of Bethlehem."

Saul's Jealousy of David

18 After David had finished talking with Saul, Jonathanʳ became one in spirit with David, and he lovedˢ him as himself.ᵗ ²From that day Saul kept David with him and did not let him return to his father's house. ³And Jonathan made a covenantᵘ with David because he loved him as himself. ⁴Jonathan took off the robeᵛ he was wearing and gave it to David, along with his tunic, and even his sword, his bow and his belt.ʷ ⁵Whatever Saul sent him to do, David did it so successfullyⁿˣ that Saul gave him a high rank in the army.ʸ This pleased all the people, and Saul's officers as well.

⁶When the men were returning home after David had killed the Philistine, the women came out from all the towns of Israel to meet King Saul with singing and dancing,ᶻ with joyful songs and with tambourinesᵃ and lutes. ⁷As they danced, they sang:ᵇ

"Saul has slain his thousands,
and David his tensᶜ of thousands."

⁸Saul was very angry; this refrain galled him. "They have credited David with tens of thousands," he thought, "but me with only thousands. What more can he get but the kingdom?ᵈ" ⁹And from that time on Saul kept a jealousᵉ eye on David.

¹⁰The next day an evil° spiritᶠ from God came forcefully upon Saul. He was prophesying in his house, while David was playing the harp,ᵍ as he usuallyʰ did. Saul had a spearⁱ in his hand ¹¹and he hurled it, saying to himself,ʲ "I'll pin David to the wall." But David eludedᵏ him twice.¹

¹²Saul was afraidᵐ of David, because the LORDⁿ was with° David but had leftᵖ Saul. ¹³So he sent David away from him and gave him command over a thousand men, and David ledᵠ the troops in their campaigns.ʳ ¹⁴In everything he did he had great success,ᵖˢ because the LORD was withᵗ him. ¹⁵When Saul saw how successfulᵠ he was, he was afraid of him. ¹⁶But all Israel and Judah loved David, because he led them in their campaigns.ᵘ

¹⁷Saul said to David, "Here is my older daughterᵛ Merab. I will give her to you in marriage;ʷ only serve me bravely and fight the battlesˣ of the LORD." For Saul said to himself,ʸ "I will not raise a hand against him. Let the Philistines do that!"

¹⁸But David said to Saul, "Who am I,ᶻ and what is my family or my father's clan in Israel, that I should become the king's son-in-law?ᵃ" ¹⁹Soʳ when the time came for Merab,ᵇ Saul's daughter, to be given to David, she was given in marriage to Adriel of Meholah.ᶜ

²⁰Now Saul's daughter Michalᵈ was in love with David, and when they told Saul about it, he was pleased.ᵉ ²¹"I will give her to him," he thought, "so that she may be a snareᶠ to him and so that the hand of the Philistines may be against him." So Saul said to David, "Now you have a second opportunity to become my son-in-law."

²²Then Saul ordered his attendants: "Speak to David privately and say, 'Look, the king is pleased with you, and his attendants all like you; now become his son-in-law.'"

²³They repeated these words to David. But David said, "Do you think it is a small matter to become the king's son-in-law?ᵍ I'm only a poor man and little known."

²⁴When Saul's servants told him what David had said, ²⁵Saul replied, "Say to David, 'The king wants no other priceʰ for the bride than a hundred Philistine foreskins, to take revengeⁱ on his enemies.'"

ⁿ 5 Or *wisely* ° 10 Or *injurious* ᵖ 14 Or *he was very wise* ᵠ 15 Or *wise* ʳ 19 Or *However,*

Saul's plan was to have David fall by the hands of the Philistines.

²⁶When the attendants told David these things, he was pleased to become the king's son-in-law. So before the allotted time elapsed, ²⁷David and his men went out and killed two hundred Philistines. He brought their foreskins and presented the full number to the king so that he might become the king's son-in-law. Then Saul gave him his daughter Michal in marriage.

²⁸When Saul realized that the LORD was with David and that his daughter Michal loved David, ²⁹Saul became still more afraid of him, and he remained his enemy the rest of his days.

³⁰The Philistine commanders continued to go out to battle, and as often as they did, David met with more success than the rest of Saul's officers, and his name became well known.

Saul Tries to Kill David

19 Saul told his son Jonathan and all the attendants to kill David. But Jonathan was very fond of David ²and warned him, "My father Saul is looking for a chance to kill you. Be on your guard tomorrow morning; go into hiding and stay there. ³I will go out and stand with my father in the field where you are. I'll speak to him about you and will tell you what I find out."

⁴Jonathan spoke well of David to Saul his father and said to him, "Let not the king do wrong to his servant David; he has not wronged you, and what he has done has benefited you greatly. ⁵He took his life in his hands when he killed the Philistine. The LORD won a great victory for all Israel, and you saw it and were glad. Why then would you do wrong to an innocent man like David by killing him for no reason?"

⁶Saul listened to Jonathan and took this oath: "As surely as the LORD lives, David will not be put to death."

⁷So Jonathan called David and told him the whole conversation. He brought him to Saul, and David was with Saul as before.

⁸Once more war broke out, and David went out and fought the Philistines. He struck them with such force that they fled before him.

⁹But an evil spirit from the LORD came upon Saul as he was sitting in his house with his spear in his hand. While David was playing the harp, ¹⁰Saul tried to pin him to the wall with his spear, but David eluded him as Saul drove the spear into the wall. That night David made good his escape.

¹¹Saul sent men to David's house to watch it and to kill him in the morning. But Michal, David's wife, warned him, "If you don't run for your life tonight, tomorrow you'll be killed." ¹²So Michal let David down through a window, and he fled and escaped. ¹³Then Michal took an idol and laid it on the bed, covering it with a garment and putting some goats' hair at the head.

¹⁴When Saul sent the men to capture David, Michal said, "He is ill."

¹⁵Then Saul sent the men back to see David and told them, "Bring him up to me in his bed so that I may kill him." ¹⁶But when the men entered, there was the idol in the bed, and at the head was some goats' hair.

¹⁷Saul said to Michal, "Why did you deceive me like this and send my enemy away so that he escaped?"

Michal told him, "He said to me, 'Let me get away. Why should I kill you?' "

¹⁸When David had fled and made his escape, he went to Samuel at Ramah and told him all that Saul had done to him. Then he and Samuel went to Naioth and stayed there. ¹⁹Word came to Saul: "David is in Naioth at Ramah"; ²⁰so he sent men to capture him. But when they saw a group of prophets prophesying, with Samuel standing there as their leader, the Spirit of God came upon Saul's men and they also prophesied. ²¹Saul was told about it, and he sent more men, and they prophesied too. Saul sent men a third time, and they also prophesied. ²²Finally, he himself left for Ramah and went to the great cistern at Secu. And he asked, "Where are Samuel and David?"

"Over in Naioth at Ramah," they said.

²³So Saul went to Naioth at Ramah. But the Spirit of God came even upon him, and he walked along prophesying until

E *1Sa 10:10–12* ◀▶ *2Sa 23:2*
G *1Sa 10:10–12* ◀▶ *2Sa 23:2*
M *1Sa 11:6* ◀▶ *2Ki 2:16*

s 30 Or *David acted more wisely* *t 9* Or *injurious* *u 13* Hebrew *teraphim*; also in verse 16

he came to Naioth. ²⁴He stripped¹ off his robes and also prophesied in Samuel's ᵐ presence. He lay that way all that day and night. This is why people say, "Is Saul also among the prophets?"ⁿ

David and Jonathan

20 Then David fled from Naioth at Ramah and went to Jonathan and asked, "What have I done? What is my crime? How have I wronged° your father, that he is trying to take my life?"ᵖ

²"Never!" Jonathan replied. "You are not going to die! Look, my father doesn't do anything, great or small, without confiding in me. Why would he hide this from me? It's not so!"

³But David took an oathᑫ and said, "Your father knows very well that I have found favor in your eyes, and he has said to himself, 'Jonathan must not know this or he will be grieved.' Yet as surely as the LORD lives and as you live, there is only a step between me and death."

⁴Jonathan said to David, "Whatever you want me to do, I'll do for you."

⁵So David said, "Look, tomorrow is the New Moon festival,ʳ and I am supposed to dine with the king; but let me go and hideˢ in the field until the evening of the day after tomorrow. ⁶If your father misses me at all, tell him, 'David earnestly asked my permissionᵗ to hurry to Bethlehem,ᵘ his hometown, because an annualᵛ sacrifice is being made there for his whole clan.' ⁷If he says, 'Very well,' then your servant is safe. But if he loses his temper,ʷ you can be sure that he is determinedˣ to harm me. ⁸As for you, show kindness to your servant, for you have brought him into a covenantʸ with you before the LORD. If I am guilty, then killᶻ me yourself! Why hand me over to your father?"

⁹"Never!" Jonathan said. "If I had the least inkling that my father was determined to harm you, wouldn't I tell you?"

¹⁰David asked, "Who will tell me if your father answers you harshly?"

¹¹"Come," Jonathan said, "let's go out into the field." So they went there together.

¹²Then Jonathan said to David: "By the LORD, the God of Israel, I will surely soundᵃ out my father by this time the day after tomorrow! If he is favorably disposed toward you, will I not send you word and let you know? ¹³But if my father is inclined to harm you, may the LORD deal with me, be it ever so severely,ᵇ if I do not let you know and send you away safely. May the LORD be withᶜ you as he has been with my father. ¹⁴But show me unfailing kindnessᵈ like that of the LORD as long as I live, so that I may not be killed, ¹⁵and do not ever cut off your kindness from my familyᵉ—not even when the LORD has cut off every one of David's enemies from the face of the earth."

¹⁶So Jonathanᶠ made a covenantᵍ with the house of David, saying, "May the LORD call David's enemies to account.ʰ" ¹⁷And Jonathan had David reaffirm his oathⁱ out of love for him, because he loved him as he loved himself.

¹⁸Then Jonathan said to David: "Tomorrow is the New Moon festival. You will be missed, because your seat will be empty.ʲ ¹⁹The day after tomorrow, toward evening, go to the place where you hidᵏ when this trouble began, and wait by the stone Ezel. ²⁰I will shoot three arrowsˡ to the side of it, as though I were shooting at a target. ²¹Then I will send a boy and say, 'Go, find the arrows.' If I say to him, 'Look, the arrows are on this side of you; bring them here,' then come, because, as surely as the LORD lives, you are safe; there is no danger. ²²But if I say to the boy, 'Look, the arrows are beyondᵐ you,' then you must go, because the LORD has sent you away. ²³And about the matter you and I discussed—remember, the LORD is witnessⁿ between you and me forever."

²⁴So David hid in the field, and when the New Moon festival° came, the king sat down to eat. ²⁵He sat in his customary place by the wall, opposite Jonathan,ᵛ and Abner sat next to Saul, but David's place was empty.ᵖ ²⁶Saul said nothing that day, for he thought, "Something must have happened to David to make him ceremonially unclean—surely he is unclean.ᑫ" ²⁷But the next day, the second day of the month, David's place was empty again. Then Saul said to his son Jonathan, "Why hasn't the son of Jesse come to the meal, either yesterday or today?"

²⁸Jonathan answered, "David earnestly asked me for permissionʳ to go to Bethle-

---

ᵛ 25 Septuagint; Hebrew *wall. Jonathan arose*

hem. ²⁹He said, 'Let me go, because our family is observing a sacrificeˢ in the town and my brother has ordered me to be there. If I have found favor in your eyes, let me get away to see my brothers.' That is why he has not come to the king's table."

³⁰Saul's anger flared up at Jonathan and he said to him, "You son of a perverse and rebellious woman! Don't I know that you have sided with the son of Jesse to your own shame and to the shame of the mother who bore you? ³¹As long as the son of Jesse lives on this earth, neither you nor your kingdom^t will be established. Now send and bring him to me, for he must die!"

³²"Why^u should he be put to death? What^v has he done?" Jonathan asked his father. ³³But Saul hurled his spear at him to kill him. Then Jonathan knew that his father intended^w to kill David.

³⁴Jonathan got up from the table in fierce anger; on that second day of the month he did not eat, because he was grieved at his father's shameful treatment of David.

³⁵In the morning Jonathan went out to the field for his meeting with David. He had a small boy with him, ³⁶and he said to the boy, "Run and find the arrows I shoot." As the boy ran, he shot an arrow beyond him. ³⁷When the boy came to the place where Jonathan's arrow had fallen, Jonathan called out after him, "Isn't the arrow beyond^x you?" ³⁸Then he shouted, "Hurry! Go quickly! Don't stop!" The boy picked up the arrow and returned to his master. ³⁹(The boy knew nothing of all this; only Jonathan and David knew.) ⁴⁰Then Jonathan gave his weapons to the boy and said, "Go, carry them back to town."

⁴¹After the boy had gone, David got up from the south side ⌊of the stone⌋ and bowed down before Jonathan three times, with his face to the ground.^y Then they kissed each other and wept together—but David wept the most.

⁴²Jonathan said to David, "Go in peace,^z for we have sworn friendship^a with each other in the name of the LORD,^b saying, 'The LORD is witness^c between you and me, and between your descendants and my descendants forever.^d' " Then David left, and Jonathan went back to the town.

David at Nob

21 David went to Nob,^e to Ahimelech the priest. Ahimelech trembled^f when he met him, and asked, "Why are you alone? Why is no one with you?"

²David answered Ahimelech the priest, "The king charged me with a certain matter and said to me, 'No one is to know anything about your mission and your instructions.' As for my men, I have told them to meet me at a certain place. ³Now then, what do you have on hand? Give me five loaves of bread, or whatever you can find."

⁴But the priest answered David, "I don't have any ordinary bread^g on hand; however, there is some consecrated^h bread here—provided the men have kept^i themselves from women."

⁵David replied, "Indeed women have been kept from us, as usual^j whenever^w I set out. The men's things^x are holy^k even on missions that are not holy. How much more so today!" ⁶So the priest gave him the consecrated bread,^l since there was no bread there except the bread of the Presence that had been removed from before the LORD and replaced by hot bread on the day it was taken away.

⁷Now one of Saul's servants was there that day, detained before the LORD; he was Doeg^m the Edomite,^n Saul's head shepherd.

⁸David asked Ahimelech, "Don't you have a spear or a sword here? I haven't brought my sword or any other weapon, because the king's business was urgent."

⁹The priest replied, "The sword^o of Goliath^p the Philistine, whom you killed in the Valley of Elah,^q is here; it is wrapped in a cloth behind the ephod. If you want it, take it; there is no sword here but that one."

David said, "There is none like it; give it to me."

David at Gath

¹⁰That day David fled from Saul and went^r to Achish king of Gath. ¹¹But the servants of Achish said to him, "Isn't this David, the king of the land? Isn't he the one they sing about in their dances:

---

^w 5 Or *from us in the past few days since* ^x 5 Or *bodies*

" 'Saul has slain his thousands,
and David his tens of thousands'?"

¹²David took these words to heart and was very much afraid of Achish king of Gath. ¹³So he pretended to be insane in their presence; and while he was in their hands he acted like a madman, making marks on the doors of the gate and letting saliva run down his beard.

¹⁴Achish said to his servants, "Look at the man! He is insane! Why bring him to me? ¹⁵Am I so short of madmen that you have to bring this fellow here to carry on like this in front of me? Must this man come into my house?"

David at Adullam and Mizpah

22 David left Gath and escaped to the cave of Adullam. When his brothers and his father's household heard about it, they went down to him there. ²All those who were in distress or in debt or discontented gathered around him, and he became their leader. About four hundred men were with him.

³From there David went to Mizpah in Moab and said to the king of Moab, "Would you let my father and mother come and stay with you until I learn what God will do for me?" ⁴So he left them with the king of Moab, and they stayed with him as long as David was in the stronghold.

⁵But the prophet Gad said to David, "Do not stay in the stronghold. Go into the land of Judah." So David left and went to the forest of Hereth.

Saul Kills the Priests of Nob

⁶Now Saul heard that David and his men had been discovered. And Saul, spear in hand, was seated under the tamarisk tree on the hill at Gibeah, with all his officials standing around him. ⁷Saul said to them, "Listen, men of Benjamin! Will the son of Jesse give all of you fields and vineyards? Will he make all of you commanders of thousands and commanders of hundreds? ⁸Is that why you have all conspired against me? No one tells me when my son makes a covenant with the son of Jesse. None of you is concerned about me or tells me that my son has incited my servant to lie in wait for me, as he does today."

⁹But Doeg the Edomite, who was standing with Saul's officials, said, "I saw the son of Jesse come to Ahimelech son of Ahitub at Nob. ¹⁰Ahimelech inquired of the LORD for him; he also gave him provisions and the sword of Goliath the Philistine."

¹¹Then the king sent for the priest Ahimelech son of Ahitub and his father's whole family, who were the priests at Nob, and they all came to the king. ¹²Saul said, "Listen now, son of Ahitub."

"Yes, my lord," he answered.

¹³Saul said to him, "Why have you conspired against me, you and the son of Jesse, giving him bread and a sword and inquiring of God for him, so that he has rebelled against me and lies in wait for me, as he does today?"

¹⁴Ahimelech answered the king, "Who of all your servants is as loyal as David, the king's son-in-law, captain of your bodyguard and highly respected in your household? ¹⁵Was that day the first time I inquired of God for him? Of course not! Let not the king accuse your servant or any of his father's family, for your servant knows nothing at all about this whole affair."

¹⁶But the king said, "You will surely die, Ahimelech, you and your father's whole family."

¹⁷Then the king ordered the guards at his side: "Turn and kill the priests of the LORD, because they too have sided with David. They knew he was fleeing, yet they did not tell me."

But the king's officials were not willing to raise a hand to strike the priests of the LORD.

¹⁸The king then ordered Doeg, "You turn and strike down the priests." So Doeg the Edomite turned and struck them down. That day he killed eighty-five men who wore the linen ephod. ¹⁹He also put to the sword Nob, the town of the priests, with its men and women, its children and infants, and its cattle, donkeys and sheep.

²⁰But Abiathar, a son of Ahimelech son of Ahitub, escaped and fled to join David. ²¹He told David that Saul had killed the priests of the LORD. ²²Then David said to Abiathar: "That day, when Doeg the Edomite was there, I knew he would be sure to tell Saul. I am responsible for the death of your father's whole family. ²³Stay with me; don't be afraid;

the man who is seeking your life[z] is seeking mine also. You will be safe with me."

David Saves Keilah

23 When David was told, "Look, the Philistines are fighting against Keilah[a] and are looting the threshing floors,"[b] [2]he inquired[c] of the LORD, saying, "Shall I go and attack these Philistines?"

The LORD answered him, "Go, attack the Philistines and save Keilah."

[3]But David's men said to him, "Here in Judah we are afraid. How much more, then, if we go to Keilah against the Philistine forces!"

[4]Once again David inquired[d] of the LORD, and the LORD answered him, "Go down to Keilah, for I am going to give the Philistines[e] into your hand.[f]" [5]So David and his men went to Keilah, fought the Philistines and carried off their livestock. He inflicted heavy losses on the Philistines and saved the people of Keilah. [6](Now Abiathar[g] son of Ahimelech had brought the ephod[h] down with him when he fled to David at Keilah.)

Saul Pursues David

[7]Saul was told that David had gone to Keilah, and he said, "God has handed him over[i] to me, for David has imprisoned himself by entering a town with gates and bars."[j] [8]And Saul called up all his forces for battle, to go down to Keilah to besiege David and his men.

[9]When David learned that Saul was plotting against him, he said to Abiathar[k] the priest, "Bring the ephod.[l]" [10]David said, "O LORD, God of Israel, your servant has heard definitely that Saul plans to come to Keilah and destroy the town on account of me. [11]Will the citizens of Keilah surrender me to him? Will Saul come down, as your servant has heard? O LORD, God of Israel, tell your servant."

And the LORD said, "He will."

[12]Again David asked, "Will the citizens of Keilah surrender[m] me and my men to Saul?"

And the LORD said, "They will."

[13]So David and his men,[n] about six hundred in number, left Keilah and kept moving from place to place. When Saul was told that David had escaped from Keilah, he did not go there.

[14]David stayed in the desert[o] strongholds and in the hills of the Desert of Ziph.[p] Day after day Saul searched[q] for him, but God did not[r] give David into his hands.

[15]While David was at Horesh in the Desert of Ziph, he learned that Saul had come out to take his life.[s] [16]And Saul's son Jonathan went to David at Horesh and helped him find strength[t] in God. [17]"Don't be afraid," he said. "My father Saul will not lay a hand on you. You will be king[u] over Israel, and I will be second to you. Even my father Saul knows this." [18]The two of them made a covenant[v] before the LORD. Then Jonathan went home, but David remained at Horesh.

[19]The Ziphites[w] went up to Saul at Gibeah and said, "Is not David hiding among us[x] in the strongholds at Horesh, on the hill of Hakilah,[y] south of Jeshimon? [20]Now, O king, come down whenever it pleases you to do so, and we will be responsible for handing[z] him over to the king."

[21]Saul replied, "The LORD bless[a] you for your concern[b] for me. [22]Go and make further preparation. Find out where David usually goes and who has seen him there. They tell me he is very crafty. [23]Find out about all the hiding places he uses and come back to me with definite information.[y] Then I will go with you; if he is in the area, I will track[c] him down among all the clans of Judah."

[24]So they set out and went to Ziph ahead of Saul. Now David and his men were in the Desert of Maon,[d] in the Arabah south of Jeshimon.[e] [25]Saul and his men began the search, and when David was told about it, he went down to the rock and stayed in the Desert of Maon. When Saul heard this, he went into the Desert of Maon in pursuit of David.

[26]Saul[f] was going along one side of the mountain, and David and his men were on the other side, hurrying to get away from Saul. As Saul and his forces were closing in on David and his men to capture them, [27]a messenger came to Saul, saying, "Come quickly! The Philistines are raiding the land." [28]Then Saul broke off his pursuit of David and went to meet the Philistines. That is why they call this place Sela Hammahlekoth.[z] [29]And David

---

[y] 23 Or *me at Nacon* [z] 28 *Sela Hammahlekoth* means *rock of parting.*

went up from there and lived in the strongholds^g of En Gedi.^h

David Spares Saul's Life

24 After Saul returned from pursuing the Philistines, he was told, "David is in the Desert of En Gedi.^i" ²So Saul took three thousand chosen men from all Israel and set out to look^j for David and his men near the Crags of the Wild Goats.

³He came to the sheep pens along the way; a cave^k was there, and Saul went in to relieve^l himself. David and his men were far back in the cave. ⁴The men said, "This is the day the LORD spoke^m of when he said^a to you, 'I will give your enemy into your hands for you to deal with as you wish.'"^n Then David crept up unnoticed and cut^o off a corner of Saul's robe.

⁵Afterward, David was conscience-stricken^p for having cut off a corner of his robe. ⁶He said to his men, "The LORD forbid that I should do such a thing to my master, the LORD's anointed,^q or lift my hand against him; for he is the anointed of the LORD." ⁷With these words David rebuked his men and did not allow them to attack Saul. And Saul left the cave and went his way.

⁸Then David went out of the cave and called out to Saul, "My lord the king!" When Saul looked behind him, David bowed down and prostrated himself with his face to the ground.^r ⁹He said to Saul, "Why do you listen^s when men say, 'David is bent on harming^t you'? ¹⁰This day you have seen with your own eyes how the LORD delivered you into my hands in the cave. Some urged me to kill you, but I spared^u you; I said, 'I will not lift my hand against my master, because he is the LORD's anointed.' ¹¹See, my father, look at this piece of your robe in my hand! I cut^v off the corner of your robe but did not kill you. Now understand and recognize that I am not guilty^w of wrongdoing^x or rebellion. I have not wronged^y you, but you are hunting^z me down to take my life.^a ¹²May the LORD judge^b between you and me. And may the LORD avenge^c the wrongs you have done to me, but my hand will not touch you. ¹³As the old saying goes, 'From evildoers come evil deeds,^d' so my hand will not touch you.

¹⁴"Against whom has the king of Israel come out? Whom are you pursuing? A dead dog?^e A flea?^f ¹⁵May the LORD be our judge^g and decide^h between us. May he consider my cause and uphold^i it; may he vindicate^j me by delivering^k me from your hand."

¹⁶When David finished saying this, Saul asked, "Is that your voice,^l David my son?" And he wept aloud. ¹⁷"You are more righteous than I,"^m he said. "You have treated me well,^n but I have treated you badly.^o ¹⁸You have just now told me of the good you did to me; the LORD delivered^p me into your hands, but you did not kill me. ¹⁹When a man finds his enemy, does he let him get away unharmed? May the LORD reward^q you well for the way you treated me today. ²⁰I know that you will surely be king^r and that the kingdom^s of Israel will be established in your hands. ²¹Now swear^t to me by the LORD that you will not cut off my descendants or wipe out my name from my father's family.^u"

²²So David gave his oath to Saul. Then Saul returned home, but David and his men went up to the stronghold.^v

David, Nabal and Abigail

25 Now Samuel died,^w and all Israel assembled and mourned^x for him; and they buried him at his home in Ramah.^y

Then David moved down into the Desert of Maon.^b ²A certain man in Maon,^z who had property there at Carmel, was very wealthy.^a He had a thousand goats and three thousand sheep, which he was shearing^b in Carmel. ³His name was Nabal and his wife's name was Abigail.^c She was an intelligent and beautiful woman, but her husband, a Calebite,^d was surly and mean in his dealings.

⁴While David was in the desert, he heard that Nabal was shearing sheep. ⁵So he sent ten young men and said to them, "Go up to Nabal at Carmel and greet him in my name. ⁶Say to him: 'Long life to you! Good health^e to you and your household! And good health to all that is yours!^f

---

c 1Sa 8:7 ◄► 2Sa 23:6–7
s 1Sa 16:14 ◄► 2Sa 22:21–27

23:29 ^g 1Sa 24:22; ^h S Jos 15:62; 2Ch 20:2; SS 1:14
24:1 ^i S Jos 15:62
24:2 ^j 1Sa 26:2
24:3 ^k Ps 57 Title; 142 Title ^l Jdg 3:24
24:4 ^m 1Sa 25:28-30 ^n 2Sa 4:8 ^o ver 10, 11
24:5 ^p 1Sa 26:9; 2Sa 24:10
24:6 ^q S Ge 26:11; S 1Sa 12:3
24:8 ^r S 1Sa 20:41
24:9 ^s 1Sa 26:19 ^t 1Sa 20:1
24:10 ^u S ver 4
24:11 ^v S ver 4 ^w Ps 7:3 ^x 1Sa 25:28 ^y Ps 35:7 ^z S Ge 31:36; 1Sa 26:20 ^a S 1Sa 20:1
24:12 ^b S Ge 16:5; S 1Sa 25:38; S Job 9:15 ^c S Nu 31:3
24:13 ^d Mt 7:20
24:14 ^e 1Sa 17:43 ^f 1Sa 26:20
24:15 ^g ver 12 ^h S Ge 16:5 ^i Ps 35:1,23; Isa 49:25 ^j Ps 26:1; 35:24; 43:1; 50:4; 54:1; 135:14 ^k Ps 119:134,154
24:16 ^l 1Sa 26:17
24:17 ^m Ge 38:26 ^n Mt 5:44 ^o S Ex 9:27
24:18 ^p 1Sa 26:23
24:19 ^q S Ru 2:12; 2Ch 15:7
24:20 ^r S 1Sa 20:31 ^s 1Sa 13:14
24:21 ^t Ge 21:23; S 47:31; S 1Sa 18:3; 2Sa 21:1-9 ^u 1Sa 20:14-15
24:22 ^v 1Sa 23:29
25:1 ^w 1Sa 28:3 ^x Lev 10:6; Dt 34:8 ^y 1Sa 7:17
25:2 ^z S Jos 15:55 ^a 2Sa 19:32 ^b S Ge 31:19
25:3 ^c Pr 31:10 ^d S Jos 14:13; S 15:13
25:6 ^e Ps 122:7; Mt 10:12 ^f 1Ch 12:18

---

^a 4 Or *"Today the LORD is saying*   ^b 1 Some Septuagint manuscripts; Hebrew *Paran*

7 " 'Now I hear that it is sheep-shearing time. When your shepherds were with us, we did not mistreat them, and the whole time they were at Carmel nothing of theirs was missing. 8 Ask your own servants and they will tell you. Therefore be favorable toward my young men, since we come at a festive time. Please give your servants and your son David whatever you can find for them.' "

9 When David's men arrived, they gave Nabal this message in David's name. Then they waited.

10 Nabal answered David's servants, "Who is this David? Who is this son of Jesse? Many servants are breaking away from their masters these days. 11 Why should I take my bread and water, and the meat I have slaughtered for my shearers, and give it to men coming from who knows where?"

12 David's men turned around and went back. When they arrived, they reported every word. 13 David said to his men, "Put on your swords!" So they put on their swords, and David put on his. About four hundred men went up with David, while two hundred stayed with the supplies.

14 One of the servants told Nabal's wife Abigail: "David sent messengers from the desert to give our master his greetings, but he hurled insults at them. 15 Yet these men were very good to us. They did not mistreat us, and the whole time we were out in the fields near them nothing was missing. 16 Night and day they were a wall around us all the time we were herding our sheep near them. 17 Now think it over and see what you can do, because disaster is hanging over our master and his whole household. He is such a wicked man that no one can talk to him."

18 Abigail lost no time. She took two hundred loaves of bread, two skins of wine, five dressed sheep, five seahs of roasted grain, a hundred cakes of raisins and two hundred cakes of pressed figs, and loaded them on donkeys. 19 Then she told her servants, "Go on ahead; I'll follow you." But she did not tell her husband Nabal.

20 As she came riding her donkey into a mountain ravine, there were David and his men descending toward her, and she met them. 21 David had just said, "It's been useless—all my watching over this fellow's property in the desert so that nothing of his was missing. He has paid me back evil for good. 22 May God deal with David, be it ever so severely, if by morning I leave alive one male of all who belong to him!"

23 When Abigail saw David, she quickly got off her donkey and bowed down before David with her face to the ground. 24 She fell at his feet and said: "My lord, let the blame be on me alone. Please let your servant speak to you; hear what your servant has to say. 25 May my lord pay no attention to that wicked man Nabal. He is just like his name—his name is Fool, and folly goes with him. But as for me, your servant, I did not see the men my master sent.

26 "Now since the LORD has kept you, my master, from bloodshed and from avenging yourself with your own hands, as surely as the LORD lives and as you live, may your enemies and all who intend to harm my master be like Nabal. 27 And let this gift, which your servant has brought to my master, be given to the men who follow you. 28 Please forgive your servant's offense, for the LORD will certainly make a lasting dynasty for my master, because he fights the LORD's battles. Let no wrongdoing be found in you as long as you live. 29 Even though someone is pursuing you to take your life, the life of my master will be bound securely in the bundle of the living by the LORD your God. But the lives of your enemies he will hurl away as from the pocket of a sling. 30 When the LORD has done for my master every good thing he promised concerning him and has appointed him leader over Israel, 31 my master will not have on his conscience the staggering burden of needless bloodshed or of having avenged himself. And when the LORD has brought my master success, remember your servant."

32 David said to Abigail, "Praise be to the LORD, the God of Israel, who has sent

I *1Sa 17:36–37* ◀▶ *2Sa 3:18*
H *1Sa 3:13–14* ◀▶ *2Sa 3:39*
K *1Sa 2:8–9* ◀▶ *2Sa 22:31*
L *1Sa 12:24* ◀▶ *2Sa 22:2–4*
V *1Sa 17:47* ◀▶ *2Sa 22:30*

c 18 That is, probably about a bushel (about 37 liters)   *d 22* Some Septuagint manuscripts; Hebrew *with David's enemies*

you today to meet me. ³³May you be blessed for your good judgment and for keeping me from bloodshed^v this day and from avenging myself with my own hands. ³⁴Otherwise, as surely as the LORD, the God of Israel, lives, who has kept me from harming you, if you had not come quickly to meet me, not one male belonging to Nabal^w would have been left alive by daybreak."

³⁵Then David accepted from her hand what she had brought him and said, "Go home in peace. I have heard your words and granted^x your request."

³⁶When Abigail went to Nabal, he was in the house holding a banquet like that of a king. He was in high^y spirits and very drunk.^z So she told^a him nothing until daybreak. ³⁷Then in the morning, when Nabal was sober, his wife told him all these things, and his heart failed him and he became like a stone.^b ³⁸About ten days later, the LORD struck^c Nabal and he died.

³⁹When David heard that Nabal was dead, he said, "Praise be to the LORD, who has upheld my cause against Nabal for treating me with contempt. He has kept his servant from doing wrong and has brought Nabal's wrongdoing down on his own head."

Then David sent word to Abigail, asking her to become his wife. ⁴⁰His servants went to Carmel and said to Abigail, "David has sent us to you to take you to become his wife."

⁴¹She bowed down with her face to the ground and said, "Here is your maidservant, ready to serve you and wash the feet of my master's servants." ⁴²Abigail^d quickly got on a donkey and, attended by her five maids, went with David's messengers and became his wife. ⁴³David had also married Ahinoam^e of Jezreel, and they both were his wives.^f ⁴⁴But Saul had given his daughter Michal, David's wife, to Paltiel^e ^g son of Laish, who was from Gallim.^h

David Again Spares Saul's Life

26 The Ziphites^i went to Saul at Gibeah and said, "Is not David hiding^j on the hill of Hakilah, which faces Jeshimon?"^k

²So Saul went down to the Desert of Ziph, with his three thousand chosen men of Israel, to search^l there for David. ³Saul made his camp beside the road on the hill of Hakilah^m facing Jeshimon, but David stayed in the desert. When he saw that Saul had followed him there, ⁴he sent out scouts and learned that Saul had definitely arrived.^f

⁵Then David set out and went to the place where Saul had camped. He saw where Saul and Abner^n son of Ner, the commander of the army, had lain down. Saul was lying inside the camp, with the army encamped around him.

⁶David then asked Ahimelech the Hittite^o and Abishai^p son of Zeruiah,^q Joab's brother, "Who will go down into the camp with me to Saul?"

"I'll go with you," said Abishai.

⁷So David and Abishai went to the army by night, and there was Saul, lying asleep inside the camp with his spear stuck in the ground near his head. Abner and the soldiers were lying around him.

⁸Abishai said to David, "Today God has delivered your enemy into your hands. Now let me pin him to the ground with one thrust of my spear; I won't strike him twice."

⁹But David said to Abishai, "Don't destroy him! Who can lay a hand on the LORD's anointed^r and be guiltless?^s ¹⁰As surely as the LORD lives," he said, "the LORD himself will strike^t him; either his time^u will come and he will die,^v or he will go into battle and perish. ¹¹But the LORD forbid that I should lay a hand on the LORD's anointed. Now get the spear and water jug that are near his head, and let's go."

¹²So David took the spear and water jug near Saul's head, and they left. No one saw or knew about it, nor did anyone wake up. They were all sleeping, because the LORD had put them into a deep sleep.^w

¹³Then David crossed over to the other side and stood on top of the hill some distance away; there was a wide space between them. ¹⁴He called out to the army and to Abner son of Ner, "Aren't you going to answer me, Abner?"

Abner replied, "Who are you who calls to the king?"

¹⁵David said, "You're a man, aren't you? And who is like you in Israel? Why didn't you guard your lord the king?

Someone came to destroy your lord the king. ¹⁶What you have done is not good. As surely as the LORD lives, you and your men deserve to die, because you did not guard your master, the LORD's anointed. Look around you. Where are the king's spear and water jug that were near his head?"

¹⁷Saul recognized David's voice and said, "Is that your voice,ˣ David my son?"

David replied, "Yes it is, my lord the king." ¹⁸And he added, "Why is my lord pursuing his servant? What have I done, and what wrongʸ am I guilty of? ¹⁹Now let my lord the king listenᶻ to his servant's words. If the LORD has incited you against me, then may he accept an offering.ᵃ If, however, men have done it, may they be cursed before the LORD! They have now driven me from my share in the LORD's inheritanceᵇ and have said, 'Go, serve other gods.'ᶜ ²⁰Now do not let my bloodᵈ fall to the ground far from the presence of the LORD. The king of Israel has come out to look for a fleaᵉ—as one hunts a partridge in the mountains.'"

²¹Then Saul said, "I have sinned.ᵍ Come back, David my son. Because you considered my life preciousʰ today, I will not try to harm you again. Surely I have acted like a fool and have erred greatly."

²²"Here is the king's spear," David answered. "Let one of your young men come over and get it. ²³The LORD rewardsⁱ every man for his righteousnessʲ and faithfulness. The LORD deliveredᵏ you into my hands today, but I would not lay a hand on the LORD's anointed. ²⁴As surely as I valued your life today, so may the LORD value my life and deliverˡ me from all trouble."

²⁵Then Saul said to David, "May you be blessed,ᵐ my son David; you will do great things and surely triumph."

So David went on his way, and Saul returned home.

David Among the Philistines

27 But David thought to himself, "One of these days I will be destroyed by the hand of Saul. The best thing I can do is to escape to the land of the Philistines. Then Saul will give up searching for me anywhere in Israel, and I will slip out of his hand."

²So David and the six hundred menⁿ with him left and wentº over to Achishᵖ

26:17 ˣ 1Sa 24:16
26:18 ʸ Job 13:23; Jer 37:18
26:19 ᶻ 1Sa 24:9
ᵃ 2Sa 16:11
ᵇ Dt 20:16; 32:9; 2Sa 14:16; 20:19; 21:3 ᶜ S Dt 4:28; S 11:28
26:20 ᵈ S 1Sa 24:11
ᵉ 1Sa 24:14
ᶠ Jer 4:29; 16:16; Am 9:3
26:21 ᵍ S Ex 9:27
ʰ Ps 72:14
26:23 ⁱ S Ge 16:5; S Ru 2:12; Ps 62:12 ʲ 2Sa 22:21,25; Ps 7:8; 18:20,24 ᵏ 1Sa 24:18
26:24 ˡ Ps 54:7
26:25 ᵐ S Ru 2:12
27:2 ⁿ 1Sa 30:9; 2Sa 2:3 º S 1Sa 21:10 ᵖ 1Ki 2:39
27:3 ᵠ S 1Sa 25:43
27:6 ʳ Jos 15:31; 19:5; 1Sa 30:1; 1Ch 12:20; Ne 11:28
27:7 ˢ 1Sa 29:3
27:8 ᵗ S Jos 12:5 ᵘ S Ex 17:14; S 1Sa 14:48; 30:1; 2Sa 1:8; 8:12 ᵛ S Ge 16:7
27:9 ʷ S 1Sa 15:3
27:10 ˣ 1Sa 30:29 ʸ Jdg 1:16
27:12 ᶻ S Ge 34:30 ᵃ 1Sa 29:6
28:1 ᵇ 1Sa 29:1
28:2 ᶜ 1Sa 29:2
28:3 ᵈ 1Sa 25:1 ᵉ 1Sa 7:17 ᶠ ver 9 ᵍ S Ex 22:18

son of Maoch king of Gath. ³David and his men settled in Gath with Achish. Each man had his family with him, and David had his two wives:ᵠ Ahinoam of Jezreel and Abigail of Carmel, the widow of Nabal. ⁴When Saul was told that David had fled to Gath, he no longer searched for him.

⁵Then David said to Achish, "If I have found favor in your eyes, let a place be assigned to me in one of the country towns, that I may live there. Why should your servant live in the royal city with you?"

⁶So on that day Achish gave him Ziklag,ʳ and it has belonged to the kings of Judah ever since. ⁷David livedˢ in Philistine territory a year and four months.

⁸Now David and his men went up and raided the Geshurites,ᵗ the Girzites and the Amalekites.ᵘ (From ancient times these peoples had lived in the land extending to Shurᵛ and Egypt.) ⁹Whenever David attacked an area, he did not leave a man or woman alive,ʷ but took sheep and cattle, donkeys and camels, and clothes. Then he returned to Achish.

¹⁰When Achish asked, "Where did you go raiding today?" David would say, "Against the Negev of Judah" or "Against the Negev of Jerahmeelˣ" or "Against the Negev of the Kenites.ʸ" ¹¹He did not leave a man or woman alive to be brought to Gath, for he thought, "They might inform on us and say, 'This is what David did.'" And such was his practice as long as he lived in Philistine territory. ¹²Achish trusted David and said to himself, "He has become so odiousᶻ to his people, the Israelites, that he will be my servant forever.ᵃ"

Saul and the Witch of Endor

28 In those days the Philistines gatheredᵇ their forces to fight against Israel. Achish said to David, "You must understand that you and your men will accompany me in the army."

²David said, "Then you will see for yourself what your servant can do."

Achish replied, "Very well, I will make you my bodyguardᶜ for life."

³Now Samuel was dead,ᵈ and all Israel had mourned for him and buried him in his own town of Ramah.ᵉ Saul had expelledᶠ the mediums and spiritistsᵍ from the land.

⁴The Philistines assembled and came and set up camp at Shunem,ʰ while Saul gathered all the Israelites and set up camp at Gilboa.ⁱ ⁵When Saul saw the Philistine army, he was afraid; terrorʲ filled his heart. ⁶He inquiredᵏ of the LORD, but the LORD did not answer him by dreamsˡ or Urimᵐ or prophets.ⁿ ⁷Saul then said to his attendants, "Find me a woman who is a medium,ᵒ so I may go and inquire of her."

"There is one in Endor,ᵖ" they said.

⁸So Saul disguisedᵠ himself, putting on other clothes, and at night he and two men went to the woman. "Consultʳ a spirit for me," he said, "and bring up for me the one I name."

⁹But the woman said to him, "Surely you know what Saul has done. He has cut offˢ the mediums and spiritists from the land. Why have you set a trapᵗ for my life to bring about my death?"

¹⁰Saul swore to her by the LORD, "As surely as the LORD lives, you will not be punished for this."

¹¹Then the woman asked, "Whom shall I bring up for you?"

"Bring up Samuel," he said.

¹²When the woman saw Samuel, she cried out at the top of her voice and said to Saul, "Why have you deceived me?ᵘ You are Saul!"

¹³The king said to her, "Don't be afraid. What do you see?"

The woman said, "I see a spiritᵛ coming up out of the ground."ᵛ

¹⁴"What does he look like?" he asked.

"An old man wearing a robeʷ is coming up," she said.

Then Saul knew it was Samuel, and he bowed down and prostrated himself with his face to the ground.

¹⁵Samuel said to Saul, "Why have you disturbed me by bringing me up?"

"I am in great distress," Saul said. "The Philistines are fighting against me, and God has turnedˣ away from me. He no longer answersʸ me, either by prophets or by dreams.ᶻ So I have called on you to tell me what to do."

¹⁶Samuel said, "Why do you consult me, now that the LORD has turned away from you and become your enemy? ¹⁷The LORD has done what he predicted through me. The LORD has tornᵃ the kingdom out of your hands and given it to one of your neighbors—to David. ¹⁸Because you did not obeyᵇ the LORD or carry out his fierce wrathᶜ against the Amalekites,ᵈ the LORD has done this to you today. ¹⁹The LORD will hand over both Israel and you to the Philistines, and tomorrow you and your sonsᵉ will be with me. The LORD will also hand over the army of Israel to the Philistines."

²⁰Immediately Saul fell full length on the ground, filled with fear because of Samuel's words. His strength was gone, for he had eaten nothing all that day and night.

²¹When the woman came to Saul and saw that he was greatly shaken, she said, "Look, your maidservant has obeyed you. I took my lifeᶠ in my hands and did what you told me to do. ²²Now please listen to your servant and let me give you some food so you may eat and have the strength to go on your way."

²³He refusedᵍ and said, "I will not eat."

But his men joined the woman in urging him, and he listened to them. He got up from the ground and sat on the couch.

²⁴The woman had a fattened calfʰ at the house, which she butchered at once. She took some flour, kneaded it and baked bread without yeast. ²⁵Then she set it before Saul and his men, and they ate. That same night they got up and left.

Achish Sends David Back to Ziklag

29 The Philistines gatheredⁱ all their forces at Aphek,ʲ and Israel camped by the spring in Jezreel.ᵏ ²As the Philistine rulers marched with their units of hundreds and thousands, David and his men were marching at the rearˡ with Achish. ³The commanders of the Philistines asked, "What about these Hebrews?"

Achish replied, "Is this not David,ᵐ who was an officer of Saul king of Israel? He has already been with me for over a year,ⁿ and from the day he left Saul until now, I have found no fault in him."

⁴But the Philistine commanders were angry with him and said, "Sendᵒ the man back, that he may return to the place you assigned him. He must not go with us into battle, or he will turnᵖ against us during the fighting. How better could he regain his master's favor than by taking

g 13 Or see spirits; or see gods

the heads of our own men? ⁵Isn't this the David they sang about in their dances:

" 'Saul has slain his thousands,
  and David his tens of thousands'?"ᑫ

⁶So Achish called David and said to him, "As surely as the LORD lives, you have been reliable, and I would be pleased to have you serve with me in the army. From the dayʳ you came to me until now, I have found no fault in you, but the rulersˢ don't approve of you. ⁷Turn back and go in peace; do nothing to displease the Philistine rulers."

⁸"But what have I done?" asked David. "What have you found against your servant from the day I came to you until now? Why can't I go and fight against the enemies of my lord the king?"

⁹Achish answered, "I know that you have been as pleasing in my eyes as an angelᵗ of God; nevertheless, the Philistine commandersᵘ have said, 'He must not go up with us into battle.' ¹⁰Now get up early, along with your master's servants who have come with you, and leaveᵛ in the morning as soon as it is light."

¹¹So David and his men got up early in the morning to go back to the land of the Philistines, and the Philistines went up to Jezreel.

David Destroys the Amalekites

30 David and his men reached Ziklagʷ on the third day. Now the Amalekitesˣ had raided the Negev and Ziklag. They had attacked Ziklag and burnedʸ it, ²and had taken captive the women and all who were in it, both young and old. They killed none of them, but carried them off as they went on their way.

³When David and his men came to Ziklag, they found it destroyed by fire and their wives and sons and daughters taken captive.ᶻ ⁴So David and his men weptᵃ aloud until they had no strength left to weep. ⁵David's two wivesᵇ had been captured—Ahinoam of Jezreel and Abigail, the widow of Nabal of Carmel. ⁶David was greatly distressed because the men were talking of stoningᶜ him; each one was bitterᵈ in spirit because of his sons and daughters. But David found strengthᵉ in the LORD his God.

⁷Then David said to Abiatharᶠ the priest, the son of Ahimelech, "Bring me the ephod.ᵍ" Abiathar brought it to him, ⁸and David inquiredʰ of the LORD, "Shall I pursue this raiding party? Will I overtake them?"

"Pursue them," he answered. "You will certainly overtake them and succeedⁱ in the rescue.ʲ"

⁹David and the six hundred menᵏ with him came to the Besor Ravine, where some stayed behind, ¹⁰for two hundred men were too exhaustedˡ to cross the ravine. But David and four hundred men continued the pursuit.

¹¹They found an Egyptian in a field and brought him to David. They gave him water to drink and food to eat— ¹²part of a cake of pressed figs and two cakes of raisins. He ate and was revived,ᵐ for he had not eaten any food or drunk any water for three days and three nights.

¹³David asked him, "To whom do you belong, and where do you come from?"

He said, "I am an Egyptian, the slave of an Amalekite.ⁿ My master abandoned me when I became ill three days ago. ¹⁴We raided the Negev of the Kerethitesᵒ and the territory belonging to Judah and the Negev of Caleb.ᵖ And we burnedᑫ Ziklag."

¹⁵David asked him, "Can you lead me down to this raiding party?"

He answered, "Swear to me before God that you will not kill me or hand me over to my master,ʳ and I will take you down to them."

¹⁶He led David down, and there they were, scattered over the countryside, eating, drinking and revelingˢ because of the great amount of plunderᵗ they had taken from the land of the Philistines and from Judah. ¹⁷David foughtᵘ them from dusk until the evening of the next day, and none of them got away, except four hundred young men who rode off on camels and fled.ᵛ ¹⁸David recoveredʷ everything the Amalekites had taken, including his two wives. ¹⁹Nothing was missing: young or old, boy or girl, plunder or anything else they had taken. David brought everything back. ²⁰He took all the flocks and herds, and his men drove them ahead of the other livestock, saying, "This is David's plunder."

²¹Then David came to the two hundred men who had been too exhaustedˣ to follow him and who were left behind at the

Besor Ravine. They came out to meet David and the people with him. As David and his men approached, he greeted them. ²²But all the evil men and troublemakers among David's followers said, "Because they did not go out with us, we will not share with them the plunder we recovered. However, each man may take his wife and children and go."

²³David replied, "No, my brothers, you must not do that with what the LORD has given us. He has protected us and handed over to us the forces that came against us. ²⁴Who will listen to what you say? The share of the man who stayed with the supplies is to be the same as that of him who went down to the battle. All will share alike." ²⁵David made this a statute and ordinance for Israel from that day to this.

²⁶When David arrived in Ziklag, he sent some of the plunder to the elders of Judah, who were his friends, saying, "Here is a present for you from the plunder of the LORD's enemies."

²⁷He sent it to those who were in Bethel, Ramoth Negev and Jattir; ²⁸to those in Aroer, Siphmoth, Eshtemoa ²⁹and Racal; to those in the towns of the Jerahmeelites and the Kenites; ³⁰to those in Hormah, Bor Ashan, Athach ³¹and Hebron; and to those in all the other places where David and his men had roamed.

Saul Takes His Life
31:1–13pp — 2Sa 1:4–12; 1Ch 10:1–12

31 Now the Philistines fought against Israel; the Israelites fled before them, and many fell slain on Mount Gilboa. ²The Philistines pressed hard after Saul and his sons, and they killed his sons Jonathan, Abinadab and Malki-Shua. ³The fighting grew fierce around Saul, and when the archers overtook him, they wounded him critically.

⁴Saul said to his armor-bearer, "Draw your sword and run me through, or these uncircumcised fellows will come and run me through and abuse me."

But his armor-bearer was terrified and would not do it; so Saul took his own sword and fell on it. ⁵When the armor-bearer saw that Saul was dead, he too fell on his sword and died with him. ⁶So Saul and his three sons and his armor-bearer and all his men died together that same day.

⁷When the Israelites along the valley and those across the Jordan saw that the Israelite army had fled and that Saul and his sons had died, they abandoned their towns and fled. And the Philistines came and occupied them.

⁸The next day, when the Philistines came to strip the dead, they found Saul and his three sons fallen on Mount Gilboa. ⁹They cut off his head and stripped off his armor, and they sent messengers throughout the land of the Philistines to proclaim the news in the temple of their idols and among their people. ¹⁰They put his armor in the temple of the Ashtoreths and fastened his body to the wall of Beth Shan.

¹¹When the people of Jabesh Gilead heard of what the Philistines had done to Saul, ¹²all their valiant men journeyed through the night to Beth Shan. They took down the bodies of Saul and his sons from the wall of Beth Shan and went to Jabesh, where they burned them. ¹³Then they took their bones and buried them under a tamarisk tree at Jabesh, and they fasted seven days.

2 Samuel

Author: Unknown

Theme: The events of King David's reign

Date of writing: c. 925 B.C.

Outline of 2 Samuel
  I. David's Rise to the Throne (1:1—4:12)
 II. David's Accomplishments as King (5:1—9:13)
III. David's Weaknesses and Failures (10:1—20:26)
IV. Final Reflections About David's Reign (21:1—24:25)

IN THE ORIGINAL Hebrew manuscript the two books of 1 and 2 Samuel were combined into one scroll and identified by the title "Samuel." (For further information about the title, authorship and date of these books, see the introduction to 1 Samuel on p. 301.)

The book of 2 Samuel describes the events following the death of King Saul, detailing the establishment of the kingdom of Israel under King David. Spanning a period of forty years, the book of 2 Samuel records David's military victories over his enemies, his moral failure and adultery with Bathsheba, his flight from Absalom's rebellion and his unauthorized census of the people of Israel. This book also records the Davidic covenant (see 7:8–17), centering its focus on the throne of Jerusalem and the Messiah's promised descent from David's line.

David Hears of Saul's Death

1:4-12pp — 1Sa 31:1-13; 1Ch 10:1-12

1 After the death of Saul, David returned from defeating the Amalekites and stayed in Ziklag two days. ²On the third day a man arrived from Saul's camp, with his clothes torn and with dust on his head. When he came to David, he fell to the ground to pay him honor. ³"Where have you come from?" David asked him.

He answered, "I have escaped from the Israelite camp."

⁴"What happened?" David asked. "Tell me."

He said, "The men fled from the battle. Many of them fell and died. And Saul and his son Jonathan are dead."

⁵Then David said to the young man who brought him the report, "How do you know that Saul and his son Jonathan are dead?"

⁶"I happened to be on Mount Gilboa," the young man said, "and there was Saul, leaning on his spear, with the chariots and riders almost upon him. ⁷When he turned around and saw me, he called out to me, and I said, 'What can I do?'

⁸"He asked me, 'Who are you?'

" 'An Amalekite,' I answered.

⁹"Then he said to me, 'Stand over me and kill me! I am in the throes of death, but I'm still alive.'

¹⁰"So I stood over him and killed him, because I knew that after he had fallen he could not survive. And I took the crown that was on his head and the band on his arm and have brought them here to my lord."

¹¹Then David and all the men with him took hold of their clothes and tore them. ¹²They mourned and wept and fasted till evening for Saul and his son Jonathan, and for the army of the LORD and the house of Israel, because they had fallen by the sword.

¹³David said to the young man who brought him the report, "Where are you from?"

"I am the son of an alien, an Amalekite," he answered.

¹⁴David asked him, "Why were you not afraid to lift your hand to destroy the LORD's anointed?"

¹⁵Then David called one of his men and said, "Go, strike him down!" So he struck him down, and he died. ¹⁶For David had said to him, "Your blood be on your own head. Your own mouth testified against you when you said, 'I killed the LORD's anointed.' "

David's Lament for Saul and Jonathan

¹⁷David took up this lament concerning Saul and his son Jonathan, ¹⁸and ordered that the men of Judah be taught this lament of the bow (it is written in the Book of Jashar):

¹⁹"Your glory, O Israel, lies slain on your heights.
How the mighty have fallen!

²⁰"Tell it not in Gath,
    proclaim it not in the streets of Ashkelon,
lest the daughters of the Philistines be glad,
    lest the daughters of the uncircumcised rejoice.

²¹"O mountains of Gilboa,
    may you have neither dew nor rain,
    nor fields that yield offerings ⌊of grain⌋.
For there the shield of the mighty was defiled,
    the shield of Saul—no longer rubbed with oil.

²²From the blood of the slain,
    from the flesh of the mighty,
the bow of Jonathan did not turn back,
    the sword of Saul did not return unsatisfied.

²³"Saul and Jonathan—
    in life they were loved and gracious,
    and in death they were not parted.
They were swifter than eagles,
    they were stronger than lions.

²⁴"O daughters of Israel,
    weep for Saul,
who clothed you in scarlet and finery,
    who adorned your garments with ornaments of gold.

²⁵"How the mighty have fallen in battle!
    Jonathan lies slain on your heights.
²⁶I grieve for you, Jonathan my brother;
    you were very dear to me.
Your love for me was wonderful,

more wonderful than that of women.

²⁷"How the mighty have fallen!
The weapons of war have perished!"°

David Anointed King Over Judah

2 In the course of time, David inquired[p] of the LORD. "Shall I go up to one of the towns of Judah?" he asked.
The LORD said, "Go up."
David asked, "Where shall I go?"
"To Hebron,"[q] the LORD answered.
²So David went up there with his two wives,[r] Ahinoam of Jezreel and Abigail,[s] the widow of Nabal of Carmel. ³David also took the men who were with him,[t] each with his family, and they settled in Hebron[u] and its towns. ⁴Then the men of Judah came to Hebron[v] and there they anointed[w] David king over the house of Judah.

When David was told that it was the men of Jabesh Gilead[x] who had buried Saul, ⁵he sent messengers to them, "The LORD bless[y] you for showing this kindness to Saul your master by burying him. ⁶May the LORD now show you kindness and faithfulness,[z] and I too will show you the same favor because you have done this. ⁷Now then, be strong[a] and brave, for Saul your master is dead, and the house of Judah has anointed me king over them."

War Between the Houses of David and Saul

3:2–5pp — 1Ch 3:1-4

⁸Meanwhile, Abner[b] son of Ner, the commander of Saul's army, had taken Ish-Bosheth[c] son of Saul and brought him over to Mahanaim.[d] ⁹He made him king over Gilead,[e] Ashuri[af] and Jezreel, and also over Ephraim, Benjamin and all Israel.[g]

¹⁰Ish-Bosheth son of Saul was forty years old when he became king over Israel, and he reigned two years. The house of Judah, however, followed David. ¹¹The length of time David was king in Hebron over the house of Judah was seven years and six months.[h]

¹²Abner son of Ner, together with the men of Ish-Bosheth son of Saul, left Mahanaim and went to Gibeon.[i] ¹³Joab[j] son of Zeruiah and David's men went out and met them at the pool of Gibeon. One group sat down on one side of the pool and one group on the other side.

¹⁴Then Abner said to Joab, "Let's have some of the young men get up and fight hand to hand in front of us."
"All right, let them do it," Joab said.

¹⁵So they stood up and were counted off—twelve men for Benjamin and Ish-Bosheth son of Saul, and twelve for David. ¹⁶Then each man grabbed his opponent by the head and thrust his dagger[k] into his opponent's side, and they fell down together. So that place in Gibeon was called Helkath Hazzurim.[b]

¹⁷The battle that day was very fierce, and Abner and the men of Israel were defeated[l] by David's men.[m]

¹⁸The three sons of Zeruiah[n] were there: Joab,[o] Abishai[p] and Asahel.[q] Now Asahel was as fleet-footed as a wild gazelle.[r] ¹⁹He chased Abner, turning neither to the right nor to the left as he pursued him. ²⁰Abner looked behind him and asked, "Is that you, Asahel?"

"It is," he answered.

²¹Then Abner said to him, "Turn aside to the right or to the left; take on one of the young men and strip him of his weapons." But Asahel would not stop chasing him.

²²Again Abner warned Asahel, "Stop chasing me! Why should I strike you down? How could I look your brother Joab in the face?"[s]

²³But Asahel refused to give up the pursuit; so Abner thrust the butt of his spear into Asahel's stomach,[t] and the spear came out through his back. He fell there and died on the spot. And every man stopped when he came to the place where Asahel had fallen and died.[u]

²⁴But Joab and Abishai pursued Abner, and as the sun was setting, they came to the hill of Ammah, near Giah on the way to the wasteland of Gibeon. ²⁵Then the men of Benjamin rallied behind Abner. They formed themselves into a group and took their stand on top of a hill.

²⁶Abner called out to Joab, "Must the sword devour[v] forever? Don't you realize that this will end in bitterness? How long before you order your men to stop pursuing their brothers?"

---

[a] 9 Or Asher [b] 16 Helkath Hazzurim means field of daggers or field of hostilities.

²⁷Joab answered, "As surely as God lives, if you had not spoken, the men would have continued the pursuit of their brothers until morning." ²⁸So Joab blew the trumpet, and all the men came to a halt; they no longer pursued Israel, nor did they fight anymore.

²⁹All that night Abner and his men marched through the Arabah. They crossed the Jordan, continued through the whole Bithron and came to Mahanaim. ³⁰Then Joab returned from pursuing Abner and assembled all his men. Besides Asahel, nineteen of David's men were found missing. ³¹But David's men had killed three hundred and sixty Benjamites who were with Abner. ³²They took Asahel and buried him in his father's tomb at Bethlehem. Then Joab and his men marched all night and arrived at Hebron by daybreak.

3 The war between the house of Saul and the house of David lasted a long time. David grew stronger and stronger, while the house of Saul grew weaker and weaker.

²Sons were born to David in Hebron:
His firstborn was Amnon the son of Ahinoam of Jezreel;
³his second, Kileab the son of Abigail the widow of Nabal of Carmel;
the third, Absalom the son of Maacah daughter of Talmai king of Geshur;
⁴the fourth, Adonijah the son of Haggith;
the fifth, Shephatiah the son of Abital;
⁵and the sixth, Ithream the son of David's wife Eglah.
These were born to David in Hebron.

Abner Goes Over to David

⁶During the war between the house of Saul and the house of David, Abner had been strengthening his own position in the house of Saul. ⁷Now Saul had had a concubine named Rizpah daughter of Aiah. And Ish-Bosheth said to Abner, "Why did you sleep with my father's concubine?"

⁸Abner was very angry because of what Ish-Bosheth said and he answered, "Am I a dog's head—on Judah's side? This very day I am loyal to the house of your father Saul and to his family and friends. I haven't handed you over to David. Yet now you accuse me of an offense involving this woman! ⁹May God deal with Abner, be it ever so severely, if I do not do for David what the LORD promised him on oath ¹⁰and transfer the kingdom from the house of Saul and establish David's throne over Israel and Judah from Dan to Beersheba." ¹¹Ish-Bosheth did not dare to say another word to Abner, because he was afraid of him.

¹²Then Abner sent messengers on his behalf to say to David, "Whose land is it? Make an agreement with me, and I will help you bring all Israel over to you."

¹³"Good," said David. "I will make an agreement with you. But I demand one thing of you: Do not come into my presence unless you bring Michal daughter of Saul when you come to see me." ¹⁴Then David sent messengers to Ish-Bosheth son of Saul, demanding, "Give me my wife Michal, whom I betrothed to myself for the price of a hundred Philistine foreskins."

¹⁵So Ish-Bosheth gave orders and had her taken away from her husband Paltiel son of Laish. ¹⁶Her husband, however, went with her, weeping behind her all the way to Bahurim. Then Abner said to him, "Go back home!" So he went back.

¹⁷Abner conferred with the elders of Israel and said, "For some time you have wanted to make David your king. ¹⁸Now do it! For the LORD promised David, 'By my servant David I will rescue my people Israel from the hand of the Philistines and from the hand of all their enemies.'"

¹⁹Abner also spoke to the Benjamites in person. Then he went to Hebron to tell David everything that Israel and the whole house of Benjamin wanted to do. ²⁰When Abner, who had twenty men with him, came to David at Hebron, David prepared a feast for him and his men. ²¹Then Abner said to David, "Let

▎1Sa 25:28 ◄ ► 2Sa 7:10–12

c 27 Or *spoken this morning, the men would not have taken up the pursuit of their brothers*; or *spoken, the men would have given up the pursuit of their brothers by morning* d 29 Or *morning*; or *ravine*; the meaning of the Hebrew for this word is uncertain.

me go at once and assemble all Israel for my lord the king, so that they may make a compact[a] with you, and that you may rule over all that your heart desires." [b] So David sent Abner away, and he went in peace.

Joab Murders Abner

22 Just then David's men and Joab returned from a raid and brought with them a great deal of plunder. But Abner was no longer with David in Hebron, because David had sent him away, and he had gone in peace. 23 When Joab and all the soldiers with him arrived, he was told that Abner son of Ner had come to the king and that the king had sent him away and that he had gone in peace.

24 So Joab went to the king and said, "What have you done? Look, Abner came to you. Why did you let him go? Now he is gone! 25 You know Abner son of Ner; he came to deceive you and observe your movements and find out everything you are doing."

26 Joab then left David and sent messengers after Abner, and they brought him back from the well of Sirah. But David did not know it. 27 Now when Abner[c] returned to Hebron, Joab took him aside into the gateway, as though to speak with him privately. And there, to avenge the blood of his brother Asahel, Joab stabbed him[d] in the stomach, and he died.[e]

28 Later, when David heard about this, he said, "I and my kingdom are forever innocent[f] before the LORD concerning the blood of Abner son of Ner. 29 May his blood[g] fall upon the head of Joab and upon all his father's house! [h] May Joab's house never be without someone who has a running sore[i] or leprosy[e] or who leans on a crutch or who falls by the sword or who lacks food."

30 (Joab and his brother Abishai murdered Abner because he had killed their brother Asahel in the battle at Gibeon.)

31 Then David said to Joab and all the people with him, "Tear your clothes and put on sackcloth[j] and walk in mourning[k] in front of Abner." King David himself walked behind the bier. 32 They buried Abner in Hebron, and the king wept[l] aloud at Abner's tomb. All the people wept also.

33 The king sang this lament[m] for Abner:

"Should Abner have died as the
lawless die?
34 Your hands were not bound,
your feet were not fettered.[n]
You fell as one falls before wicked
men."

And all the people wept over him again. 35 Then they all came and urged David to eat something while it was still day; but David took an oath, saying, "May God deal with me, be it ever so severely,[o] if I taste bread[p] or anything else before the sun sets!"

36 All the people took note and were pleased; indeed, everything the king did pleased them. 37 So on that day all the people and all Israel knew that the king had no part[q] in the murder of Abner son of Ner.

38 Then the king said to his men, "Do you not realize that a prince and a great man has fallen[r] in Israel this day? 39 And today, though I am the anointed king, I am weak, and these sons of Zeruiah[s] are too strong[t] for me.[u] May the LORD repay[v] the evildoer according to his evil deeds!"

Ish-Bosheth Murdered

4 When Ish-Bosheth son of Saul heard that Abner[w] had died in Hebron, he lost courage, and all Israel became alarmed. 2 Now Saul's son had two men who were leaders of raiding bands. One was named Baanah and the other Recab; they were sons of Rimmon the Beerothite from the tribe of Benjamin—Beeroth[x] is considered part of Benjamin, 3 because the people of Beeroth fled to Gittaim[y] and have lived there as aliens to this day.

4 (Jonathan[z] son of Saul had a son who was lame in both feet. He was five years old when the news[a] about Saul and Jonathan came from Jezreel. His nurse picked him up and fled, but as she hurried to leave, he fell and became crippled.[b] His name was Mephibosheth.)[c]

5 Now Recab and Baanah, the sons of Rimmon the Beerothite, set out for the house of Ish-Bosheth,[d] and they arrived there in the heat of the day while he was taking his noonday rest.[e] 6 They went into

H 1Sa 25:29 ◀▶ 1Ki 2:33

[e] 29 The Hebrew word was used for various diseases affecting the skin—not necessarily leprosy.

the inner part of the house as if to get some wheat, and they stabbed[f] him in the stomach. Then Recab and his brother Baanah slipped away.

[7] They had gone into the house while he was lying on the bed in his bedroom. After they stabbed and killed him, they cut off his head. Taking it with them, they traveled all night by way of the Arabah.[g] [8] They brought the head[h] of Ish-Bosheth to David at Hebron and said to the king, "Here is the head of Ish-Bosheth son of Saul,[i] your enemy, who tried to take your life. This day the LORD has avenged[j] my lord the king against Saul and his offspring."

[9] David answered Recab and his brother Baanah, the sons of Rimmon the Beerothite, "As surely as the LORD lives, who has delivered[k] me out of all trouble, [10] when a man told me, 'Saul is dead,' and thought he was bringing good news, I seized him and put him to death in Ziklag.[l] That was the reward I gave him for his news! [11] How much more—when wicked men have killed an innocent man in his own house and on his own bed—should I not now demand his blood[m] from your hand and rid the earth of you!"

[12] So David gave an order to his men, and they killed them.[n] They cut off their hands and feet and hung the bodies by the pool in Hebron. But they took the head of Ish-Bosheth and buried it in Abner's tomb at Hebron.

David Becomes King Over Israel
5:1–3pp — 1Ch 11:1–3

5 All the tribes of Israel[o] came to David at Hebron and said, "We are your own flesh and blood.[p] [2] In the past, while Saul was king over us, you were the one who led Israel on their military campaigns.[q] And the LORD said[r] to you, 'You will shepherd[s] my people Israel, and you will become their ruler.'"

[3] When all the elders of Israel had come to King David at Hebron, the king made a compact[u] with them at Hebron before the LORD, and they anointed[v] David king over Israel.

[4] David was thirty years old[w] when he became king, and he reigned[x] forty years. [5] In Hebron he reigned over Judah seven years and six months,[z] and in Jerusalem he reigned over all Israel and Judah thirty-three years.

David Conquers Jerusalem
5:6–10pp — 1Ch 11:4–9
5:11–16pp — 1Ch 3:5–9; 14:1–7

[6] The king and his men marched to Jerusalem[a] to attack the Jebusites,[b] who lived there. The Jebusites said to David, "You will not get in here; even the blind and the lame can ward you off." They thought, "David cannot get in here." [7] Nevertheless, David captured the fortress of Zion,[c] the City of David.[d][e] [8] On that day, David said, "Anyone who conquers the Jebusites will have to use the water shaft[f][t] to reach those 'lame and blind'[g] who are David's enemies.[g]" That is why they say, "The 'blind and lame' will not enter the palace."

[9] David then took up residence in the fortress and called it the City of David. He built up the area around it, from the supporting terraces[h][h] inward. [10] And he became more and more powerful,[i] because the LORD God Almighty[j] was with him.[k]

[11] Now Hiram[l] king of Tyre sent messengers to David, along with cedar logs and carpenters and stonemasons, and they built a palace for David. [12] And David knew that the LORD had established him as king over Israel and had exalted his kingdom[m] for the sake of his people Israel.

[13] After he left Hebron, David took more concubines and wives[n] in Jerusalem, and more sons and daughters were born to him. [14] These are the names of the children born to him there:[o] Shammua, Shobab, Nathan,[p] Solomon, [15] Ibhar, Elishua, Nepheg, Japhia, [16] Elishama, Eliada and Eliphelet.

David Defeats the Philistines
5:17–25pp — 1Ch 14:8–17

[17] When the Philistines heard that David had been anointed king over Israel, they went up in full force to search for him, but David heard about it and went down to the stronghold.[q] [18] Now the Philistines had come and spread out in the Valley of Rephaim;[r] [19] so David inquired[s] of the LORD, "Shall I go and attack the Philistines? Will you hand them over to me?"

The LORD answered him, "Go, for I will surely hand the Philistines over to you."

[20] So David went to Baal Perazim, and

f 8 Or use scaling hooks   g 8 Or are hated by David   h 9 Or the Millo

there he defeated them. He said, "As waters break out, the LORD has broken out against my enemies before me." So that place was called Baal Perazim.*[t]* ²¹The Philistines abandoned their idols there, and David and his men carried them off.*[u]*

²²Once more the Philistines came up and spread out in the Valley of Rephaim; ²³so David inquired of the LORD, and he answered, "Do not go straight up, but circle around behind them and attack them in front of the balsam trees. ²⁴As soon as you hear the sound*[v]* of marching in the tops of the balsam trees, move quickly, because that will mean the LORD has gone out in front*[w]* of you to strike the Philistine army." ²⁵So David did as the LORD commanded him, and he struck down the Philistines*[x]* all the way from Gibeon*[y]* to Gezer.*[z]*

The Ark Brought to Jerusalem
6:1–11pp — 1Ch 13:1–14
6:12–19pp — 1Ch 15:25–16:3

6 David again brought together out of Israel chosen men, thirty thousand in all. ²He and all his men set out from Baalah*[a]* of Judah*[k]* to bring up from there the ark*[b]* of God, which is called by the Name,*[c]* the name of the LORD Almighty, who is enthroned*[d]* between the cherubim*[e]* that are on the ark. ³They set the ark of God on a new cart*[f]* and brought it from the house of Abinadab, which was on the hill.*[g]* Uzzah and Ahio, sons of Abinadab, were guiding the new cart ⁴with the ark of God on it,*[m]* and Ahio was walking in front of it. ⁵David and the whole house of Israel were celebrating*[h]* with all their might before the LORD, with songs*[n]* and with harps, lyres, tambourines, sistrums and cymbals.*[l]*

⁶When they came to the threshing floor of Nacon, Uzzah reached out and took hold of*[j]* the ark of God, because the oxen stumbled. ⁷The LORD's anger burned against Uzzah because of his irreverent act;*[k]* therefore God struck him down*[l]* and he died there beside the ark of God.

⁸Then David was angry because the LORD's wrath*[m]* had broken out against Uzzah, and to this day that place is called Perez Uzzah.*[o][n]*

⁹David was afraid of the LORD that day and said, "How*[o]* can the ark of the LORD ever come to me?" ¹⁰He was not willing to take the ark of the LORD to be with him in the City of David. Instead, he took it aside to the house of Obed-Edom*[p]* the Gittite. ¹¹The ark of the LORD remained in the house of Obed-Edom the Gittite for three months, and the LORD blessed him and his entire household.*[q]*

¹²Now King David*[r]* was told, "The LORD has blessed the household of Obed-Edom and everything he has, because of the ark of God." So David went down and brought up the ark of God from the house of Obed-Edom to the City of David with rejoicing. ¹³When those who were carrying the ark of the LORD had taken six steps, he sacrificed*[s]* a bull and a fattened calf. ¹⁴David, wearing a linen ephod,*[t]* danced*[u]* before the LORD with all his might, ¹⁵while he and the entire house of Israel brought up the ark of the LORD with shouts*[v]* and the sound of trumpets.*[w]*

¹⁶As the ark of the LORD was entering the City of David,*[x]* Michal*[y]* daughter of Saul watched from a window. And when she saw King David leaping and dancing before the LORD, she despised him in her heart.

¹⁷They brought the ark of the LORD and set it in its place inside the tent that David had pitched for it,*[z]* and David sacrificed burnt offerings*[a]* and fellowship offerings*[p]* before the LORD. ¹⁸After he had finished sacrificing*[b]* the burnt offerings and fellowship offerings, he blessed*[c]* the people in the name of the LORD Almighty. ¹⁹Then he gave a loaf of bread, a cake of dates and a cake of raisins*[d]* to each person in the whole crowd of Israelites, both men and women.*[e]* And all the people went to their homes.

²⁰When David returned home to bless his household, Michal daughter of Saul came out to meet him and said, "How the king of Israel has distinguished himself today, disrobing*[f]* in the sight of the slave girls of his servants as any vulgar fellow would!"

²¹David said to Michal, "It was before the LORD, who chose me rather than your father or anyone from his house when he

---

l 20 Baal Perazim means the lord who breaks out. J 25 Septuagint (see also 1 Chron. 14:16); Hebrew Geba k 2 That is, Kiriath Jearim; Hebrew Baale Judah, a variant of Baalah of Judah l 2 Hebrew; Septuagint and Vulgate do not have the Name. m 3,4 Dead Sea Scrolls and some Septuagint manuscripts; Masoretic Text cart ⁴and they brought it with the ark of God from the house of Abinadab, which was on the hill n 5 See Dead Sea Scrolls, Septuagint and 1 Chronicles 13:8; Masoretic Text celebrating before the LORD with all kinds of instruments made of pine. o 8 Perez Uzzah means outbreak against Uzzah. p 17 Traditionally peace offerings; also in verse 18

appointed me ruler over the LORD's people Israel—I will celebrate before the LORD. ²²I will become even more undignified than this, and I will be humiliated in my own eyes. But by these slave girls you spoke of, I will be held in honor."

²³And Michal daughter of Saul had no children to the day of her death.

God's Promise to David
7:1–17pp — 1Ch 17:1–15

7 After the king was settled in his palace and the LORD had given him rest from all his enemies around him, ²he said to Nathan the prophet, "Here I am, living in a palace of cedar, while the ark of God remains in a tent."

³Nathan replied to the king, "Whatever you have in mind, go ahead and do it, for the LORD is with you."

⁴That night the word of the LORD came to Nathan, saying:

⁵"Go and tell my servant David, 'This is what the LORD says: Are you the one to build me a house to dwell in? ⁶I have not dwelt in a house from the day I brought the Israelites up out of Egypt to this day. I have been moving from place to place with a tent as my dwelling. ⁷Wherever I have moved with all the Israelites, did I ever say to any of their rulers whom I commanded to shepherd my people Israel, "Why have you not built me a house of cedar?" '

⁸"Now then, tell my servant David, 'This is what the LORD Almighty says: I took you from the pasture and from following the flock to be ruler over my people Israel. ⁹I have been with you wherever you have gone, and I have cut off all your enemies from before you. Now I will make your name great, like the names of the greatest men of the earth. ¹⁰And I will provide a place for my people Israel and will plant them so that they can have a home of their own and no longer be disturbed. Wicked people will not oppress them anymore, as they did at the beginning ¹¹and have done ever since the time I appointed leaders*q* over my people Israel. I will also give you rest from all your enemies.

" 'The LORD declares to you that the LORD himself will establish a house for you: ¹²When your days are over and you rest with your fathers, I will raise up your offspring to succeed you, who will come from your own body, and I will establish his kingdom. ¹³He is the one who will build a house for my Name, and I will establish the throne of his kingdom forever. ¹⁴I will be his father, and he will be my son. When he does wrong, I will punish him with the rod of men, with floggings inflicted by men. ¹⁵But my love will never be taken away from him, as I took it away from Saul, whom I removed from before you. ¹⁶Your

I 2Sa 3:18 ◀ ▶ 2Sa 7:23–24
M 1Sa 2:10 ◀ ▶ 2Sa 7:16
T Dt 8:16 ◀ ▶ Job 5:17
M 2Sa 7:13–14 ◀ ▶ 2Sa 23:3–5

q 11 Traditionally *judges*

7:10 The Lord promised to give Israel a secure place of their own. This prophecy will find complete fulfillment in the last days as Jewish exiles return to the promised land from all over the world.

7:13 God promised that David would have a son who would build a house for God. That son was Solomon (see 2Ch 6:7–10).

7:16 *Davidic Covenant.* The covenant promise made to Abram concerning the promised land was confirmed and expanded in the Palestinian covenant (see Dt 30:1–3). The Davidic covenant also expands the Abrahamic covenant, but concentrates its focus on the promise of offspring. This eternal covenant contains the following elements:

1. David will have a child who will succeed him and further establish the kingdom (see 7:12). This promise was initially fulfilled in the birth of Solomon.
2. This son (Solomon) will build the temple instead of David (see 7:13). This promise was fulfilled (see 2Ch 6:7–12).
3. Solomon's throne would be established forever (see 7:13). The exile to Babylon interrupted the kingdom, but did not set this promise aside.
4. If Solomon sinned he would be chastised but not removed from God's love (see 7:14–15).

house and your kingdom will endure forever before me'; your throne will be established forever.' "

¹⁷Nathan reported to David all the words of this entire revelation.

David's Prayer
7:18–29pp — 1Ch 17:16–27

¹⁸Then King David went in and sat before the LORD, and he said:

"Who am I, O Sovereign LORD, and what is my family, that you have brought me this far? ¹⁹And as if this were not enough in your sight, O Sovereign LORD, you have also spoken about the future of the house of your servant. Is this your usual way of dealing with man, O Sovereign LORD?

²⁰"What more can David say to you? For you know your servant, O Sovereign LORD. ²¹For the sake of your word and according to your will, you have done this great thing and made it known to your servant.

²²"How great you are, O Sovereign LORD! There is no one like you, and there is no God but you, as we have heard with our own ears. ²³And who is like your people Israel—the one nation on earth that God went out to redeem as a people for himself, and to make a name for himself, and to perform great and awesome wonders by driving out nations and their gods from before your people, whom you redeemed from Egypt? ²⁴You have established your people Israel as your very own forever, and you, O LORD, have become their God.

²⁵"And now, LORD God, keep forever the promise you have made concerning your servant and his house. Do as you promised, ²⁶so that your name will be great forever. Then men will say, 'The LORD Almighty is God over Israel!' And the house of your servant David will be established before you.

²⁷"O LORD Almighty, God of Israel, you have revealed this to your servant, saying, 'I will build a house for you.' So your servant has found courage to offer you this prayer. ²⁸O Sovereign LORD, you are God! Your words are trustworthy, and you have promised these good things to your servant. ²⁹Now be pleased to bless the house of your servant, that it may continue forever in your sight; for you, O Sovereign LORD, have spoken, and with your blessing the house of your servant will be blessed forever."

David's Victories
8:1–14pp — 1Ch 18:1–13

8 In the course of time, David defeated the Philistines and subdued them, and he took Metheg Ammah from the control of the Philistines.

²David also defeated the Moabites. He made them lie down on the ground and measured them off with a length of cord. Every two lengths of them were put to death, and the third length was allowed to live. So the Moabites became subject to David and brought tribute.

³Moreover, David fought Hadadezer son of Rehob, king of Zobah, when he went to restore his control along the Euphrates River. ⁴David captured a thousand of his chariots, seven thousand charioteers and twenty thousand foot

---

r 16 Some Hebrew manuscripts and Septuagint; most Hebrew manuscripts *you.* *s 23* See Septuagint and 1 Chron. 17:21; Hebrew *wonders for your land and before your people, whom you redeemed from Egypt, from the nations and their gods.* *t 4* Septuagint (see also Dead Sea Scrolls and 1 Chron. 18:4); Masoretic Text *captured seventeen hundred of his charioteers*

---

5. David's house, kingdom and throne would be established forever (7:16). This promise will be ultimately fulfilled when David's son, the Christ, returns to earth to reign over David's covenanted kingdom. Each of the elements of this promise is eternal, indicating that there must be no end to the Messiah's reign from David's throne.

NOTE: The seven additional covenants include the Edenic (Ge 2:15–17), Adamic (Ge 3:15–19), Noahic (Ge 9:8ff), Abrahamic (Ge 15:4ff; 17:1–22), Mosaic (Ex 19:5), Palestinian (Dt 30:1–10) and New (Heb 8:8–12). See chart on p. 7.

7:23–24 Israel was unique among the nations because God had chosen them to be his special people (see Ex 19:5–6).

soldiers. He hamstrung^d all but a hundred of the chariot horses. ^5When the Arameans of Damascus^e came to help Hadadezer king of Zobah, David struck down twenty-two thousand of them. ^6He put garrisons^f in the Aramean kingdom of Damascus, and the Arameans became subject^g to him and brought tribute. The LORD gave David victory wherever he went.^h

^7David took the gold shields^i that belonged to the officers of Hadadezer and brought them to Jerusalem. ^8From Tebah^u and Berothai,^j towns that belonged to Hadadezer, King David took a great quantity of bronze.

^9When Tou^v king of Hamath^k heard that David had defeated the entire army of Hadadezer,^l ^10he sent his son Joram^w to King David to greet him and congratulate him on his victory in battle over Hadadezer, who had been at war with Tou. Joram brought with him articles of silver and gold and bronze.

^11King David dedicated^m these articles to the LORD, as he had done with the silver and gold from all the nations he had subdued: ^12Edom^x^n and Moab,^o the Ammonites^p and the Philistines,^q and Amalek.^r He also dedicated the plunder taken from Hadadezer son of Rehob, king of Zobah.

^13And David became famous^s after he returned from striking down eighteen thousand Edomites^y in the Valley of Salt.^t

^14He put garrisons throughout Edom, and all the Edomites^u became subject to David.^v The LORD gave David victory^w wherever he went.^x

David's Officials

8:15–18pp — 1Ch 18:14–17

^15David reigned over all Israel, doing what was just and right^y for all his people. ^16Joab^z son of Zeruiah was over the army; Jehoshaphat^a son of Ahilud was recorder;^b ^17Zadok^c son of Ahitub and Ahimelech son of Abiathar^d were priests; Seraiah was secretary;^e ^18Benaiah^f son of Jehoiada was over the Kerethites^g and Pelethites; and David's sons were royal advisers.^z

S Nu 31:49 ◀▶ 2Sa 8:14
S 2Sa 8:6 ◀▶ 1Ch 18:6

8:4 ^d S Ge 49:6; Jos 11:9
8:5 ^e S Ge 14:15; 2Sa 10:6; 1Ki 11:24; 2Ki 8:7; 14:28
8:6 ^f 1Ki 20:34 ^g 2Sa 10:19 ^h 2Sa 3:18
8:7 ^i 1Ki 10:16; 14:26; 2Ki 11:10
8:8 ^j Eze 47:16
8:9 ^k 1Ki 8:65; 2Ki 14:28; 2Ch 8:4 ^l Lk 14:31-32
8:11 ^m ver 12; 1Ki 7:51; 15:15; 1Ch 26:26; 2Ch 5:1
8:12 ^n S Nu 24:18 ^o ver 2 ^p 2Sa 10:14 ^q S 2Sa 5:25 ^r S Nu 24:20; S 1Sa 27:8
8:13 ^s 2Sa 7:9 ^t 2Ki 14:7; 1Ch 18:12; Ps 60 Title
8:14 ^u Nu 24:17-18; Ps 108:9; Isa 34:5; 63:1; Jer 49:7; Eze 25:12 ^v S Ge 27:29,37-40 ^w Ps 144:10 ^x 2Sa 22:44; Ps 18:43
8:15 ^y S Ge 18:19; 1Ki 11:38; 14:8; 15:11; 22:43; 2Ki 12:2; Job 29:14; Ps 5:12; 119:121; Heb 11:33
8:16 ^z S 2Sa 2:13 ^a 2Sa 20:24; 1Ki 4:3 ^b Isa 36:3,22
8:17 ^c S 1Sa 2:35; 2Sa 15:24,29; 20:25; 1Ki 1:8; 4:4; 1Ch 6:8,53; 16:39; 24:3; 27:17; 2Ch 31:10; Eze 40:46; 43:19; 44:15; 48:11 ^d Mk 2:26 ^e 1Ki 4:3; 2Ki 12:10; 19:2; 22:3; Isa 36:3; Jer 36:12
8:18 ^f 2Sa 20:23; 23:20; 1Ki 1:8,38; 2:25,35,46; 4:4 ^g S 1Sa 30:14
9:1 ^h S 1Sa 20:14-17, 42; S 23:18
9:2 ^i 2Sa 16:1-4; 19:17,26,29
9:3 ^j 1Ch 8:34; 1Sa 20:14
9:4 ^l 2Sa 17:27-29
9:6 ^m S Ge 37:7
9:7 ^n S 1Sa 20:14-15 ^o ver 13; 2Sa 19:28; 21:7; Mt 2:7;
2Ki 25:29; Jer 52:33
9:8 ^p S Dus 4:4
^q S 2Sa 3:8
9:10 ^r 2Sa 16:3

David and Mephibosheth

9 David asked, "Is there anyone still left of the house of Saul to whom I can show kindness for Jonathan's sake?"^h

^2Now there was a servant of Saul's household named Ziba.^i They called him to appear before David, and the king said to him, "Are you Ziba?"

"Your servant," he replied.

^3The king asked, "Is there no one still left of the house of Saul to whom I can show God's kindness?"

Ziba answered the king, "There is still a son of Jonathan;^j he is crippled^k in both feet."

^4"Where is he?" the king asked.

Ziba answered, "He is at the house of Makir^l son of Ammiel in Lo Debar."

^5So King David had him brought from Lo Debar, from the house of Makir son of Ammiel.

^6When Mephibosheth son of Jonathan, the son of Saul, came to David, he bowed down to pay him honor.^m

David said, "Mephibosheth!"

"Your servant," he replied.

^7"Don't be afraid," David said to him, "for I will surely show you kindness for the sake of your father Jonathan.^n I will restore to you all the land that belonged to your grandfather Saul, and you will always eat at my table."^o

^8Mephibosheth^p bowed down and said, "What is your servant, that you should notice a dead dog^q like me?"

^9Then the king summoned Ziba, Saul's servant, and said to him, "I have given your master's grandson everything that belonged to Saul and his family. ^10You and your sons and your servants are to farm the land for him and bring in the crops, so that your master's grandson^r may be provided for. And Mephibosheth, grandson of your master, will always eat at my table." (Now Ziba had fifteen sons and twenty servants.)

^11Then Ziba said to the king, "Your servant will do whatever my lord the king commands his servant to do." So Mephib-

^u 8 See some Septuagint manuscripts (see also 1 Chron. 18:8); Hebrew Betah. ^v 9 Hebrew Toi, a variant of Tou; also in verse 10 ^w 10 A variant of Hadoram ^x 12 Some Hebrew manuscripts, Septuagint and Syriac (see also 1 Chron. 18:11); most Hebrew manuscripts Aram ^y 13 A few Hebrew manuscripts, Septuagint and Syriac (see also 1 Chron. 18:12); most Hebrew manuscripts Aram (that is, Arameans) ^z 18 Or were priests

osheth ate at David's[a] table like one of the king's sons.[s]

[12] Mephibosheth had a young son named Mica, and all the members of Ziba's household were servants of Mephibosheth.[t] [13] And Mephibosheth lived in Jerusalem, because he always ate at the king's table, and he was crippled in both feet.

David Defeats the Ammonites
10:1–19pp — 1Ch 19:1–19

10 In the course of time, the king of the Ammonites died, and his son Hanun succeeded him as king. [2] David thought, "I will show kindness to Hanun son of Nahash,[u] just as his father showed kindness to me." So David sent a delegation to express his sympathy to Hanun concerning his father.

When David's men came to the land of the Ammonites, [3] the Ammonite nobles said to Hanun their lord, "Do you think David is honoring your father by sending men to you to express sympathy? Hasn't David sent them to you to explore the city and spy it out[v] and overthrow it?" [4] So Hanun seized David's men, shaved off half of each man's beard,[w] cut off their garments in the middle at the buttocks,[x] and sent them away.

[5] When David was told about this, he sent messengers to meet the men, for they were greatly humiliated. The king said, "Stay at Jericho till your beards have grown, and then come back."

[6] When the Ammonites realized that they had become a stench[y] in David's nostrils, they hired twenty thousand Aramean[z] foot soldiers from Beth Rehob[a] and Zobah,[b] as well as the king of Maacah[c] with a thousand men, and also twelve thousand men from Tob.[d]

[7] On hearing this, David sent Joab[e] out with the entire army of fighting men. [8] The Ammonites came out and drew up in battle formation at the entrance to their city gate, while the Arameans of Zobah and Rehob and the men of Tob and Maacah were by themselves in the open country.

[9] Joab saw that there were battle lines in front of him and behind him; so he selected some of the best troops in Israel and deployed them against the Arameans. [10] He put the rest of the men under the command of Abishai[f] his brother and deployed them against the Ammonites. [11] Joab said, "If the Arameans are too strong for me, then you are to come to my rescue; but if the Ammonites are too strong for you, then I will come to rescue you. [12] Be strong[g] and let us fight bravely for our people and the cities of our God. The LORD will do what is good in his sight."[h]

[13] Then Joab and the troops with him advanced to fight the Arameans, and they fled before him. [14] When the Ammonites[i] saw that the Arameans were fleeing, they fled before Abishai and went inside the city. So Joab returned from fighting the Ammonites and came to Jerusalem.

[15] After the Arameans saw that they had been routed by Israel, they regrouped. [16] Hadadezer had Arameans brought from beyond the River[b], they went to Helam, with Shobach the commander of Hadadezer's army leading them.

[17] When David was told of this, he gathered all Israel, crossed the Jordan and went to Helam. The Arameans formed their battle lines to meet David and fought against him. [18] But they fled before Israel, and David killed seven hundred of their charioteers and forty thousand of their foot soldiers.[c] He also struck down Shobach the commander of their army, and he died there. [19] When all the kings who were vassals of Hadadezer saw that they had been defeated by Israel, they made peace with the Israelites and became subject[j] to them.

So the Arameans[k] were afraid to help the Ammonites anymore.

David and Bathsheba

11 In the spring,[l] at the time when kings go off to war, David sent Joab[m] out with the king's men and the whole Israelite army.[n] They destroyed the Ammonites and besieged Rabbah.[o] But David remained in Jerusalem.

[2] One evening David got up from his bed and walked around on the roof[p] of the palace. From the roof he saw[q] a woman bathing. The woman was very beautiful, [3] and David sent someone to find out about her. The man said, "Isn't this Bathsheba,[r] the daughter of Eliam[s] and the wife of Uriah[t] the Hittite?"

---
[a] *11* Septuagint; Hebrew *my*   [b] *16* That is, the Euphrates   [c] *18* Some Septuagint manuscripts (see also 1 Chron. 19:18); Hebrew *horsemen*

⁴Then David sent messengers to get her.ᵘ She came to him, and he sleptᵛ with her. (She had purified herself from her uncleanness.)ʷ Thenᵈ she went back home. ⁵The woman conceived and sent word to David, saying, "I am pregnant."

⁶So David sent this word to Joab: "Send me Uriahˣ the Hittite." And Joab sent him to David. ⁷When Uriah came to him, David asked him how Joab was, how the soldiers were and how the war was going. ⁸Then David said to Uriah, "Go down to your house and wash your feet."ʸ So Uriah left the palace, and a gift from the king was sent after him. ⁹But Uriah slept at the entrance to the palace with all his master's servants and did not go down to his house.

¹⁰When David was told, "Uriah did not go home," he asked him, "Haven't you just come from a distance? Why didn't you go home?"

¹¹Uriah said to David, "The arkᶻ and Israel and Judah are staying in tents, and my master Joab and my lord's men are camped in the open fields. How could I go to my house to eat and drink and lieᵃ with my wife? As surely as you live, I will not do such a thing!"

¹²Then David said to him, "Stay here one more day, and tomorrow I will send you back." So Uriah remained in Jerusalem that day and the next. ¹³At David's invitation, he ate and drank with him, and David made him drunk. But in the evening Uriah went out to sleep on his mat among his master's servants; he did not go home.

¹⁴In the morning David wrote a letterᵇ to Joab and sent it with Uriah. ¹⁵In it he wrote, "Put Uriah in the front line where the fighting is fiercest. Then withdraw from him so he will be struck downᶜ and die.ᵈ"

¹⁶So while Joab had the city under siege, he put Uriah at a place where he knew the strongest defenders were. ¹⁷When the men of the city came out and fought against Joab, some of the men in David's army fell; moreover, Uriah the Hittite died.

¹⁸Joab sent David a full account of the battle. ¹⁹He instructed the messenger: "When you have finished giving the king this account of the battle, ²⁰the king's anger may flare up, and he may ask you, 'Why did you get so close to the city to fight? Didn't you know they would shoot arrows from the wall? ²¹Who killed Abimelechᵉ son of Jerub-Beshethᵉ? Didn't a woman throw an upper millstone on him from the wall,ᶠ so that he died in Thebez? Why did you get so close to the wall?' If he asks you this, then say to him, 'Also, your servant Uriah the Hittite is dead.' "

²²The messenger set out, and when he arrived he told David everything Joab had sent him to say. ²³The messenger said to David, "The men overpowered us and came out against us in the open, but we drove them back to the entrance to the city gate. ²⁴Then the archers shot arrows at your servants from the wall, and some of the king's men died. Moreover, your servant Uriah the Hittite is dead."

²⁵David told the messenger, "Say this to Joab: 'Don't let this upset you; the sword devours one as well as another. Press the attack against the city and destroy it.' Say this to encourage Joab."

²⁶When Uriah's wife heard that her husband was dead, she mourned for him. ²⁷After the time of mourningᵍ was over, David had her brought to his house, and she became his wife and bore him a son. But the thing David had done displeasedʰ the LORD.

Nathan Rebukes David
11:1; 12:29–31pp — 1Ch 20:1–3

12 The LORD sent Nathanⁱ to David.ʲ When he came to him,ᵏ he said, "There were two men in a certain town, one rich and the other poor. ²The rich man had a very large number of sheep and cattle, ³but the poor man had nothing except one little ewe lamb he had bought. He raised it, and it grew up with him and his children. It shared his food, drank from his cup and even slept in his arms. It was like a daughter to him.

⁴"Now a traveler came to the rich man, but the rich man refrained from taking one of his own sheep or cattle to prepare a meal for the traveler who had come to him. Instead, he took the ewe lamb that belonged to the poor man and prepared it for the one who had come to him."

⁵Davidˡ burned with angerᵐ against the manⁿ and said to Nathan, "As surely as

---
d 4 Or with her. When she purified herself from her uncleanness,
e 21 Also known as Jerub-Baal (that is, Gideon)

the LORD lives,[o] the man who did this deserves to die! 6He must pay for that lamb
four times over,[p] because he did such a
thing and had no pity."
7Then Nathan said to David, "You are
the man![q] This is what the LORD, the God
of Israel, says: 'I anointed[r] you[s] king over
Israel, and I delivered you from the hand
of Saul. 8I gave your master's house to
you,[t] and your master's wives into your
arms. I gave you the house of Israel and
Judah. And if all this had been too little, I
would have given you even more. 9Why
did you despise[u] the word of the LORD by
doing what is evil in his eyes? You struck
down[v] Uriah[w] the Hittite with the sword
and took his wife to be your own. You
killed[x] him with the sword of the Ammonites. 10Now, therefore, the sword[y]
will never depart from your house, because you despised me and took the wife
of Uriah the Hittite to be your own.'
11"This is what the LORD says: 'Out of
your own household[z] I am going to bring
calamity upon you.[a] Before your very
eyes I will take your wives and give them
to one who is close to you, and he will lie
with your wives in broad daylight.[b] 12You
did it in secret,[c] but I will do this thing in
broad daylight[d] before all Israel.' "
L 13Then David said to Nathan, "I have
P sinned[e] against the LORD."
R Nathan replied, "The LORD has taken
away[f] your sin.[g] You are not going to
J die.[h] 14But because by doing this you
have made the enemies of the LORD show
utter contempt,[f][i] the son born to you
will die."
15After Nathan had gone home, the
LORD struck[j] the child that Uriah's wife
had borne to David, and he became ill.
16David pleaded with God for the child.
He fasted and went into his house and
spent the nights lying[k] on the ground.
17The elders of his household stood beside him to get him up from the ground,
but he refused,[l] and he would not eat
any food with them.[m]
18On the seventh day the child died.
David's servants were afraid to tell him
that the child was dead, for they thought,
"While the child was still living, we
spoke to David but he would not listen to
us. How can we tell him the child is
dead? He may do something desperate."
19David noticed that his servants were
whispering among themselves and he realized the child was dead. "Is the child
dead?" he asked.
"Yes," they replied, "he is dead."
20Then David got up from the ground.
After he had washed,[n] put on lotions and
changed his clothes,[o] he went into the
house of the LORD and worshiped. Then
he went to his own house, and at his request they served him food, and he ate.
21His servants asked him, "Why are
you acting this way? While the child was
alive, you fasted and wept,[p] but now that
the child is dead, you get up and eat!"
22He answered, "While the child was
still alive, I fasted and wept. I thought,
'Who knows?[q] The LORD may be gracious
to me and let the child live.'[r] 23But now
that he is dead, why should I fast? Can I
bring him back again? I will go to him,[s]
but he will not return to me."[t]
24Then David comforted his wife Bathsheba,[u] and he went to her and lay with
her. She gave birth to a son, and they
named him Solomon.[v] The LORD loved
him; 25and because the LORD loved him,
he sent word through Nathan the
prophet to name him Jedidiah.[g][w]
26Meanwhile Joab fought against Rabbah[x] of the Ammonites and captured the
royal citadel. 27Joab then sent messengers
to David, saying, "I have fought against
Rabbah and taken its water supply.
28Now muster the rest of the troops and
besiege the city and capture it. Otherwise
I will take the city, and it will be named
after me."
29So David mustered the entire army
and went to Rabbah, and attacked and
captured it. 30He took the crown[y] from
the head of their king[h]—its weight was a
talent[i] of gold, and it was set with precious stones—and it was placed on David's head. He took a great quantity of
plunder from the city 31and brought out
the people who were there, consigning
them to labor with saws and with iron
picks and axes, and he made them work

12:5 [o] S 1Sa 14:39
12:6 [p] Ex 22:1
12:7 [q] 2Sa 14:13; Da 4:22 [r] S 1Sa 2:35 [s] 1Ki 20:42
12:8 [t] S 2Sa 9:7
12:9 [u] S Nu 15:31; S 1Sa 13:14 [v] S 2Sa 11:15 [w] 1Ki 15:5 [x] Ps 26:9; 51:14
12:10 [y] 2Sa 13:28; 18:14-15; 1Ki 2:25
12:11 [z] 2Sa 16:11 [a] Dt 28:30; 2Sa 16:21-22 [b] S Dt 17:17
12:12 [c] 2Sa 11:4-15 [d] 2Sa 16:22
12:13 [e] S Ge 13:13; S 20:6; S Nu 22:34 [f] Ps 32:1-5; 51:1,9; 103:12; Isa 43:25; 44:22; Zec 3:4,9 [g] Pr 28:13; Jer 2:35; Mic 7:18-19 [h] Lev 20:10; 24:17
12:14 [i] Isa 52:5; Ro 2:24
12:15 [j] S 1Sa 25:38
12:16 [k] Ps 5:7; 95:6
12:17 [l] S Ge 37:35; S 1Sa 1:7 [m] S 2Sa 3:35; Da 6:18
12:20 [n] Mt 6:17 [o] S Ge 41:14
12:21 [p] Jdg 20:26
12:22 [q] Jnh 3:9 [r] Isa 38:1-5
12:23 [s] Ge 37:35 [t] S 1Sa 31:13; 2Sa 13:39; Job 7:10; 10:21
12:24 [u] 1Ki 1:11 [v] 1Ki 1:10; 1Ch 22:9; 28:5; Mt 1:6
12:25 [w] Ne 13:26
12:26 [x] S Dt 3:11
12:30 [y] Est 8:15; Ps 21:3; 132:18

L *1Sa 12:20* ◀ ▶ *1Ch 28:9*
P *Jdg 10:15–16* ◀ ▶ *2Ch 7:14*
R *1Sa 12:3* ◀ ▶ *2Sa 24:10*
J *1Sa 13:14* ◀ ▶ *1Ki 17:1*

[f] 14 Masoretic Text; an ancient Hebrew scribal tradition *this you have shown utter contempt for the LORD* [g] 25 *Jedidiah* means *loved by the LORD.* [h] 30 Or *of Milcom* (that is, Molech) [i] 30 That is, about 75 pounds (about 34 kilograms)

at brickmaking.[j] He did this to all the Ammonite[z] towns. Then David and his entire army returned to Jerusalem.

Amnon and Tamar

13 In the course of time, Amnon[a] son of David fell in love with Tamar,[b] the beautiful sister of Absalom[c] son of David.

[2] Amnon became frustrated to the point of illness on account of his sister Tamar, for she was a virgin, and it seemed impossible for him to do anything to her.

[3] Now Amnon had a friend named Jonadab son of Shimeah,[d] David's brother. Jonadab was a very shrewd man. [4] He asked Amnon, "Why do you, the king's son, look so haggard morning after morning? Won't you tell me?"

Amnon said to him, "I'm in love with Tamar, my brother Absalom's sister."

[5] "Go to bed and pretend to be ill," Jonadab said. "When your father comes to see you, say to him, 'I would like my sister Tamar to come and give me something to eat. Let her prepare the food in my sight so I may watch her and then eat it from her hand.' "

[6] So Amnon lay down and pretended to be ill. When the king came to see him, Amnon said to him, "I would like my sister Tamar to come and make some special bread in my sight, so I may eat from her hand."

[7] David sent word to Tamar at the palace: "Go to the house of your brother Amnon and prepare some food for him." [8] So Tamar went to the house of her brother Amnon, who was lying down. She took some dough, kneaded it, made the bread in his sight and baked it. [9] Then she took the pan and served him the bread, but he refused to eat.

"Send everyone out of here,"[e] Amnon said. So everyone left him. [10] Then Amnon said to Tamar, "Bring the food here into my bedroom so I may eat from your hand." And Tamar took the bread she had prepared and brought it to her brother Amnon in his bedroom. [11] But when she took it to him to eat, he grabbed[f] her and said, "Come to bed with me, my sister."[g]

[12] "Don't, my brother!" she said to him. "Don't force me. Such a thing should not be done in Israel![h] Don't do this wicked thing.[i] [13] What about me?[j] Where could I get rid of my disgrace? And what about you? You would be like one of the wicked fools in Israel. Please speak to the king; he will not keep me from being married to you." [14] But he refused to listen to her, and since he was stronger than she, he raped her.[k]

[15] Then Amnon hated her with intense hatred. In fact, he hated her more than he had loved her. Amnon said to her, "Get up and get out!"

[16] "No!" she said to him. "Sending me away would be a greater wrong than what you have already done to me."

But he refused to listen to her. [17] He called his personal servant and said, "Get this woman out of here and bolt the door after her." [18] So his servant put her out and bolted the door after her. She was wearing a richly ornamented[k] robe,[l] for this was the kind of garment the virgin daughters of the king wore. [19] Tamar put ashes[m] on her head and tore the ornamented[l] robe she was wearing. She put her hand on her head and went away, weeping aloud as she went.

[20] Her brother Absalom said to her, "Has that Amnon, your brother, been with you? Be quiet now, my sister; he is your brother. Don't take this thing to heart." And Tamar lived in her brother Absalom's house, a desolate woman.

[21] When King David heard all this, he was furious.[n] [22] Absalom never said a word to Amnon, either good or bad;[o] he hated[p] Amnon because he had disgraced his sister Tamar.

Absalom Kills Amnon

[23] Two years later, when Absalom's sheepshearers[q] were at Baal Hazor near the border of Ephraim, he invited all the king's sons to come there. [24] Absalom went to the king and said, "Your servant has had shearers come. Will the king and his officials please join me?"

[25] "No, my son," the king replied. "All of us should not go; we would only be a burden to you." Although Absalom urged him, he still refused to go, but gave him his blessing.

[26] Then Absalom said, "If not, please let my brother Amnon come with us."

The king asked him, "Why should he

---

[j] 31 The meaning of the Hebrew for this clause is uncertain.
[k] 18 The meaning of the Hebrew for this phrase is uncertain.
[l] 19 The meaning of the Hebrew for this word is uncertain.

go with you?" ²⁷But Absalom urged him, so he sent with him Amnon and the rest of the king's sons.

²⁸Absalom ordered his men, "Listen! When Amnon is in high spirits from drinking wine and I say to you, 'Strike Amnon down,' then kill him. Don't be afraid. Have not I given you this order? Be strong and brave.'" ²⁹So Absalom's men did to Amnon what Absalom had ordered. Then all the king's sons got up, mounted their mules and fled.

³⁰While they were on their way, the report came to David: "Absalom has struck down all the king's sons; not one of them is left." ³¹The king stood up, tore his clothes and lay down on the ground; and all his servants stood by with their clothes torn.

³²But Jonadab son of Shimeah, David's brother, said, "My lord should not think that they killed all the princes; only Amnon is dead. This has been Absalom's expressed intention ever since the day Amnon raped his sister Tamar. ³³My lord the king should not be concerned about the report that all the king's sons are dead. Only Amnon is dead."

³⁴Meanwhile, Absalom had fled.

Now the man standing watch looked up and saw many people on the road west of him, coming down the side of the hill. The watchman went and told the king, "I see men in the direction of Horonaim, on the side of the hill."ᵐ

³⁵Jonadab said to the king, "See, the king's sons are here; it has happened just as your servant said."

³⁶As he finished speaking, the king's sons came in, wailing loudly. The king, too, and all his servants wept very bitterly.

³⁷Absalom fled and went to Talmai son of Ammihud, the king of Geshur. But King David mourned for his son every day.

³⁸After Absalom fled and went to Geshur, he stayed there three years. ³⁹And the spirit of the king longed to go to Absalom, for he was consoled concerning Amnon's death.

Absalom Returns to Jerusalem

14 Joab son of Zeruiah knew that the king's heart longed for Absalom. ²So Joab sent someone to Tekoa and had a wise woman brought from there. He said to her, "Pretend you are in mourning. Dress in mourning clothes, and don't use any cosmetic lotions. Act like a woman who has spent many days grieving for the dead. ³Then go to the king and speak these words to him." And Joab put the words in her mouth.

⁴When the woman from Tekoa went to the king, she fell with her face to the ground to pay him honor, and she said, "Help me, O king!"

⁵The king asked her, "What is troubling you?"

She said, "I am indeed a widow; my husband is dead. ⁶I your servant had two sons. They got into a fight with each other in the field, and no one was there to separate them. One struck the other and killed him. ⁷Now the whole clan has risen up against your servant; they say, 'Hand over the one who struck his brother down, so that we may put him to death for the life of his brother whom he killed; then we will get rid of the heir as well.' They would put out the only burning coal I have left, leaving my husband neither name nor descendant on the face of the earth."

⁸The king said to the woman, "Go home, and I will issue an order in your behalf."

⁹But the woman from Tekoa said to him, "My lord the king, let the blame rest on me and on my father's family, and let the king and his throne be without guilt."

¹⁰The king replied, "If anyone says anything to you, bring him to me, and he will not bother you again."

¹¹She said, "Then let the king invoke the LORD his God to prevent the avenger of blood from adding to the destruction, so that my son will not be destroyed."

"As surely as the LORD lives," he said, "not one hair of your son's head will fall to the ground.ᵐ"

¹²Then the woman said, "Let your servant speak a word to my lord the king."

"Speak," he replied.

¹³The woman said, "Why then have you devised a thing like this against the people of God? When the king says this, does he not convict himself, for the king

---

m 34 Septuagint; Hebrew does not have this sentence. n 39 Dead Sea Scrolls and some Septuagint manuscripts; Masoretic Text But the spirit of, David the king o 4 Many Hebrew manuscripts, Septuagint, Vulgate and Syriac; most Hebrew manuscripts spoke

has not brought back his banished son? ⁰ ¹⁴Like water ᵖ spilled on the ground, which cannot be recovered, so we must die. ᑫ But God does not take away life; instead, he devises ways so that a banished person ʳ may not remain estranged from him.

¹⁵"And now I have come to say this to my lord the king because the people have made me afraid. Your servant thought, 'I will speak to the king; perhaps he will do what his servant asks. ¹⁶Perhaps the king will agree to deliver his servant from the hand of the man who is trying to cut off both me and my son from the inheritance ˢ God gave us.'

¹⁷"And now your servant says, 'May the word of my lord the king bring me rest, ᵗ for my lord the king is like an angel of God in discerning ᵘ good and evil. May the LORD your God be with you.' "

¹⁸Then the king said to the woman, "Do not keep from me the answer to what I am going to ask you."

"Let my lord the king speak," the woman said.

¹⁹The king asked, "Isn't the hand of Joab ᵛ with you in all this?"

The woman answered, "As surely as you live, my lord the king, no one can turn to the right or to the left from anything my lord the king says. Yes, it was your servant Joab who instructed me to do this and who put all these words into the mouth of your servant. ²⁰Your servant Joab did this to change the present situation. My lord has wisdom ʷ like that of an angel of God—he knows everything that happens in the land." ˣ

²¹The king said to Joab, "Very well, I will do it. Go, bring back the young man Absalom."

²²Joab fell with his face to the ground to pay him honor, and he blessed the king. ʸ Joab said, "Today your servant knows that he has found favor in your eyes, my lord the king, because the king has granted his servant's request."

²³Then Joab went to Geshur and brought Absalom back to Jerusalem. ²⁴But the king said, "He must go to his own house; he must not see my face." So Absalom went to his own house and did not see the face of the king.

²⁵In all Israel there was not a man so highly praised for his handsome appearance as Absalom. From the top of his head to the sole of his foot there was no blemish in him. ²⁶Whenever he cut the hair of his head ᶻ—he used to cut his hair from time to time when it became too heavy for him—he would weigh it, and its weight was two hundred shekels ᵖ by the royal standard.

²⁷Three sons ᵃ and a daughter were born to Absalom. The daughter's name was Tamar, ᵇ and she became a beautiful woman.

²⁸Absalom lived two years in Jerusalem without seeing the king's face. ²⁹Then Absalom sent for Joab in order to send him to the king, but Joab refused to come to him. So he sent a second time, but he refused to come. ³⁰Then he said to his servants, "Look, Joab's field is next to mine, and he has barley ᶜ there. Go and set it on fire." So Absalom's servants set the field on fire.

³¹Then Joab did go to Absalom's house and he said to him, "Why have your servants set my field on fire?" ᵈ

³²Absalom said to Joab, "Look, I sent word to you and said, 'Come here so I can send you to the king to ask, "Why have I come from Geshur? ᵉ It would be better for me if I were still there!" ' Now then, I want to see the king's face, and if I am guilty of anything, let him put me to death." ᶠ

³³So Joab went to the king and told him this. Then the king summoned Absalom, and he came in and bowed down with his face to the ground before the king. And the king kissed ᵍ Absalom.

Absalom's Conspiracy

15 In the course of time, ʰ Absalom provided himself with a chariot ⁱ and horses and with fifty men to run ahead of him. ²He would get up early and stand by the side of the road leading to the city gate. ʲ Whenever anyone came with a complaint to be placed before the king for a decision, Absalom would call out to him, "What town are you from?" He would answer, "Your servant is from one of the tribes of Israel." ³Then Absalom would say to him, "Look, your claims are valid and proper, but there is no representative of the king to hear you." ᵏ

N Jos 24:15 ◄ ► 1Ki 18:21

14:13 ᵒ 2Sa 13:38-39
14:14 ᵖ Job 14:11; Ps 58:7; Isa 19:5
ᑫ Job 10:8; 17:13; 30:23; Ps 22:15; Heb 9:27
ʳ Nu 35:15,25-28
14:16 ˢ S Ex 34:9; S 1Sa 26:19
14:17 ᵗ S 1Sa 29:9
ᵘ 1Ki 3:9; Da 2:21
14:19 ᵛ ver 3
14:20 ʷ 1Ki 3:12, 28; 10:23-24; Isa 28:6 ˣ 2Sa 18:13
14:22 ʸ S Ge 47:5
14:26 ᶻ 2Sa 18:9
14:27 ᵃ 2Sa 18:18
ᵇ S 2Sa 13:1
14:30 ᶜ S Ex 9:31
14:31 ᵈ S Jdg 15:5
14:32 ᵉ S 2Sa 3:3
ᶠ 1Sa 20:8
14:33 ᵍ Lk 15:20
15:1 ʰ S 2Sa 12:11
ⁱ 1Sa 8:11
15:2 ʲ S Ge 23:10; 2Sa 19:8
15:3 ᵏ Pr 12:2

ᵖ 26 That is, about 5 pounds (about 2.3 kilograms)

⁴And Absalom would add, "If only I were appointed judge in the land!¹ Then everyone who has a complaint or case could come to me and I would see that he gets justice." ⁵Also, whenever anyone approached him to bow down before him, Absalom would reach out his hand, take hold of him and kiss him. ⁶Absalom behaved in this way toward all the Israelites who came to the king asking for justice, and so he stole the hearts[m] of the men of Israel.

⁷At the end of four[q] years, Absalom said to the king, "Let me go to Hebron and fulfill a vow I made to the LORD. ⁸While your servant was living at Geshur[n] in Aram, I made this vow:[o] 'If the LORD takes me back to Jerusalem, I will worship the LORD in Hebron.[r]'"

⁹The king said to him, "Go in peace." So he went to Hebron.

¹⁰Then Absalom sent secret messengers throughout the tribes of Israel to say, "As soon as you hear the sound of the trumpets,[p] then say, 'Absalom is king in Hebron.'" ¹¹Two hundred men from Jerusalem had accompanied Absalom. They had been invited as guests and went quite innocently, knowing nothing about the matter. ¹²While Absalom was offering sacrifices, he also sent for Ahithophel[q] the Gilonite, David's counselor,[r] to come from Giloh,[s] his hometown. And so the conspiracy gained strength, and Absalom's following kept on increasing.[t]

David Flees

¹³A messenger came and told David, "The hearts of the men of Israel are with Absalom."

¹⁴Then David said to all his officials who were with him in Jerusalem, "Come! We must flee,[u] or none of us will escape from Absalom.[v] We must leave immediately, or he will move quickly to overtake us and bring ruin upon us and put the city to the sword."

¹⁵The king's officials answered him, "Your servants are ready to do whatever our lord the king chooses."

¹⁶The king set out, with his entire household following him; but he left ten concubines[w] to take care of the palace. ¹⁷So the king set out, with all the people following him, and they halted at a place some distance away. ¹⁸All his men marched past him, along with all the Kerethites[x] and Pelethites; and all the six hundred Gittites who had accompanied him from Gath marched before the king.

¹⁹The king said to Ittai[y] the Gittite, "Why should you come along with us? Go back and stay with King Absalom. You are a foreigner,[z] an exile from your homeland. ²⁰You came only yesterday. And today shall I make you wander[a] about with us, when I do not know where I am going? Go back, and take your countrymen. May kindness and faithfulness[b] be with you."

²¹But Ittai replied to the king, "As surely as the LORD lives, and as my lord the king lives, wherever my lord the king may be, whether it means life or death, there will your servant be."[c]

²²David said to Ittai, "Go ahead, march on." So Ittai the Gittite marched on with all his men and the families that were with him.

²³The whole countryside wept aloud[d] as all the people passed by. The king also crossed the Kidron Valley,[e][f] and all the people moved on toward the desert.

²⁴Zadok[g] was there, too, and all the Levites who were with him were carrying the ark[h] of the covenant of God. They set down the ark of God, and Abiathar[i] offered sacrifices[s] until all the people had finished leaving the city.

²⁵Then the king said to Zadok, "Take the ark of God back into the city. If I find favor in the LORD's eyes, he will bring me back and let me see it and his dwelling place[j] again. ²⁶But if he says, 'I am not pleased with you,' then I am ready; let him do to me whatever seems good to him."[k]

²⁷The king also said to Zadok the priest, "Aren't you a seer?[l] Go back to the city in peace, with your son Ahimaaz and Jonathan[m] son of Abiathar. You and Abiathar take your two sons with you. ²⁸I will wait at the fords[n] in the desert until word comes from you to inform me." ²⁹So Zadok and Abiathar took the ark of God back to Jerusalem and stayed there.

³⁰But David continued up the Mount of Olives, weeping[o] as he went; his head[p] was covered and he was barefoot. All the people with him covered their heads too and were weeping as they went up.

---

[q] 7 Some Septuagint manuscripts, Syriac and Josephus; Hebrew *forty*
[r] 8 Some Septuagint manuscripts; Hebrew does not have *in Hebron.*
[s] 24 Or *Abiathar went up*

³¹Now David had been told, "Ahithophel is among the conspirators with Absalom." So David prayed, "O LORD, turn Ahithophel's counsel into foolishness."

³²When David arrived at the summit, where people used to worship God, Hushai the Arkite was there to meet him, his robe torn and dust on his head. ³³David said to him, "If you go with me, you will be a burden to me. ³⁴But if you return to the city and say to Absalom, 'I will be your servant, O king; I was your father's servant in the past, but now I will be your servant,' then you can help me by frustrating Ahithophel's advice. ³⁵Won't the priests Zadok and Abiathar be there with you? Tell them anything you hear in the king's palace. ³⁶Their two sons, Ahimaaz son of Zadok and Jonathan son of Abiathar, are there with them. Send them to me with anything you hear."

³⁷So David's friend Hushai arrived at Jerusalem as Absalom was entering the city.

David and Ziba

16 When David had gone a short distance beyond the summit, there was Ziba, the steward of Mephibosheth, waiting to meet him. He had a string of donkeys saddled and loaded with two hundred loaves of bread, a hundred cakes of raisins, a hundred cakes of figs and a skin of wine. ²The king asked Ziba, "Why have you brought these?"

Ziba answered, "The donkeys are for the king's household to ride on, the bread and fruit are for the men to eat, and the wine is to refresh those who become exhausted in the desert."

³The king then asked, "Where is your master's grandson?"

Ziba said to him, "He is staying in Jerusalem, because he thinks, 'Today the house of Israel will give me back my grandfather's kingdom.' "

⁴Then the king said to Ziba, "All that belonged to Mephibosheth is now yours."

"I humbly bow," Ziba said. "May I find favor in your eyes, my lord the king."

Shimei Curses David

⁵As King David approached Bahurim, a man from the same clan as Saul's family came out from there. His name was Shimei son of Gera, and he cursed as he came out. ⁶He pelted David and all the king's officials with stones, though all the troops and the special guard were on David's right and left. ⁷As he cursed, Shimei said, "Get out, get out, you man of blood, you scoundrel! ⁸The LORD has repaid you for all the blood you shed in the household of Saul, in whose place you have reigned. The LORD has handed the kingdom over to your son Absalom. You have come to ruin because you are a man of blood!"

⁹Then Abishai son of Zeruiah said to the king, "Why should this dead dog curse my lord the king? Let me go over and cut off his head."

¹⁰But the king said, "What do you and I have in common, you sons of Zeruiah? If he is cursing because the LORD said to him, 'Curse David,' who can ask, 'Why do you do this?' "

¹¹David then said to Abishai and all his officials, "My son, who is of my own flesh, is trying to take my life. How much more, then, this Benjamite! Leave him alone; let him curse, for the LORD has told him to. ¹²It may be that the LORD will see my distress and repay me with good for the cursing I am receiving today."

¹³So David and his men continued along the road while Shimei was going along the hillside opposite him, cursing as he went and throwing stones at him and showering him with dirt. ¹⁴The king and all the people with him arrived at their destination exhausted. And there he refreshed himself.

The Advice of Hushai and Ahithophel

¹⁵Meanwhile, Absalom and all the men of Israel came to Jerusalem, and Ahithophel was with him. ¹⁶Then Hushai the Arkite, David's friend, went to Absalom and said to him, "Long live the king! Long live the king!"

¹⁷Absalom asked Hushai, "Is this the love you show your friend? Why didn't you go with your friend?"

¹⁸Hushai said to Absalom, "No, the one chosen by the LORD, by these people, and by all the men of Israel—his I will be, and I will remain with him. ¹⁹Furthermore, whom should I serve? Should I not serve the son? Just as I served your father, so I will serve you."

²⁰Absalom said to Ahithophel, "Give us your advice. What should we do?"

²¹Ahithophel answered, "Lie with your father's concubines whom he left to take care of the palace. Then all Israel will hear that you have made yourself a stench in your father's nostrils, and the hands of everyone with you will be strengthened." ²²So they pitched a tent for Absalom on the roof, and he lay with his father's concubines in the sight of all Israel.ᵈ

²³Now in those days the adviceᵉ Ahithophel gave was like that of one who inquires of God. That was how both Davidᶠ and Absalom regarded all of Ahithophel's advice.

17 Ahithophel said to Absalom, "I wouldʳ choose twelve thousand men and set out tonight in pursuit of David. ²I wouldᵘ attack him while he is weary and weak.ᵍ I wouldᵘ strike him with terror, and then all the people with him will flee. I wouldᵘ strike down only the kingʰ ³and bring all the people back to you. The death of the man you seek will mean the return of all; all the people will be unharmed." ⁴This plan seemed good to Absalom and to all the elders of Israel.

⁵But Absalom said, "Summon also Hushaiⁱ the Arkite, so we can hear what he has to say." ⁶When Hushai came to him, Absalom said, "Ahithophel has given this advice. Should we do what he says? If not, give us your opinion."

⁷Hushai replied to Absalom, "The advice Ahithophel has given is not good this time. ⁸You know your father and his men; they are fighters, and as fierce as a wild bear robbed of her cubs.ʲ Besides, your father is an experienced fighter;ᵏ he will not spend the night with the troops. ⁹Even now, he is hidden in a cave or some other place.ˡ If he should attack your troops first,ᵛ whoever hears about it will say, 'There has been a slaughter among the troops who follow Absalom.' ¹⁰Then even the bravest soldier, whose heart is like the heart of a lion,ᵐ will meltⁿ with fear, for all Israel knows that your father is a fighter and that those with him are brave.ᵒ

¹¹"So I advise you: Let all Israel, from Dan to Beershebaᵖ—as numerous as the sandᵠ on the seashore—be gathered to you, with you yourself leading them into battle. ¹²Then we will attack him wherever he may be found, and we will fall on him as dew settles on the ground. Neither he nor any of his men will be left alive. ¹³If he withdraws into a city, then all Israel will bring ropes to that city, and we will drag it down to the valleyʳ until not even a piece of it can be found."

¹⁴Absalom and all the men of Israel said, "The adviceˢ of Hushai the Arkite is better than that of Ahithophel."ᵗ For the LORD had determined to frustrateᵘ the good advice of Ahithophel in order to bring disasterᵛ on Absalom.ʷ

¹⁵Hushai told Zadok and Abiathar, the priests, "Ahithophel has advised Absalom and the elders of Israel to do such and such, but I have advised them to do so and so. ¹⁶Now send a message immediately and tell David, 'Do not spend the night at the fords in the desert;ˣ cross over without fail, or the king and all the people with him will be swallowed up.'ʸ "

¹⁷Jonathanᶻ and Ahimaaz were staying at En Rogel.ᵃ A servant girl was to go and inform them, and they were to go and tell King David, for they could not risk being seen entering the city. ¹⁸But a young man saw them and told Absalom. So the two of them left quickly and went to the house of a man in Bahurim.ᵇ He had a well in his courtyard, and they climbed down into it. ¹⁹His wife took a covering and spread it out over the opening of the well and scattered grain over it. No one knew anything about it.ᶜ

²⁰When Absalom's men came to the womanᵈ at the house, they asked, "Where are Ahimaaz and Jonathan?"

The woman answered them, "They crossed over the brook."ʷ The men searched but found no one, so they returned to Jerusalem.

²¹After the men had gone, the two climbed out of the well and went to inform King David. They said to him, "Set out and cross the river at once; Ahithophel has advised such and such against you." ²²So David and all the people with him set out and crossed the Jordan. By daybreak, no one was left who had not crossed the Jordan.

²³When Ahithophel saw that his ad-

---

t 1 Or *Let me* *u 2* Or *will* *v 9* Or *When some of the men fall at the first attack* *w 20* Or *"They passed by the sheep pen toward the water."*

vice[e] had not been followed, he saddled his donkey and set out for his house in his hometown. He put his house in order[f] and then hanged himself. So he died and was buried in his father's tomb.

[24]David went to Mahanaim,[g] and Absalom crossed the Jordan with all the men of Israel. [25]Absalom had appointed Amasa[h] over the army in place of Joab. Amasa was the son of a man named Jether,[xi] an Israelite[y] who had married Abigail,[z] the daughter of Nahash and sister of Zeruiah the mother of Joab. [26]The Israelites and Absalom camped in the land of Gilead.

[27]When David came to Mahanaim, Shobi son of Nahash[j] from Rabbah[k] of the Ammonites, and Makir[l] son of Ammiel from Lo Debar, and Barzillai[m] the Gileadite[n] from Rogelim [28]brought bedding and bowls and articles of pottery. They also brought wheat and barley, flour and roasted grain, beans and lentils,[a] [29]honey and curds, sheep, and cheese from cows' milk for David and his people to eat.[o] For they said, "The people have become hungry and tired and thirsty in the desert.[p]"

Absalom's Death

18 David mustered the men who were with him and appointed over them commanders of thousands and commanders of hundreds. [2]David sent the troops out[q]—a third under the command of Joab, a third under Joab's brother Abishai[r] son of Zeruiah, and a third under Ittai[s] the Gittite. The king told the troops, "I myself will surely march out with you."

[3]But the men said, "You must not go out; if we are forced to flee, they won't care about us. Even if half of us die, they won't care; but you are worth ten[t] thousand of us.[b] It would be better now for you to give us support from the city."[u]

[4]The king answered, "I will do whatever seems best to you."

So the king stood beside the gate while all the men marched out in units of hundreds and of thousands. [5]The king commanded Joab, Abishai and Ittai, "Be gentle with the young man Absalom for my sake." And all the troops heard the king giving orders concerning Absalom to each of the commanders.

[6]The army marched into the field to fight Israel, and the battle took place in the forest[v] of Ephraim. [7]There the army of Israel was defeated by David's men, and the casualties that day were great—twenty thousand men. [8]The battle spread out over the whole countryside, and the forest claimed more lives that day than the sword.

[9]Now Absalom happened to meet David's men. He was riding his mule, and as the mule went under the thick branches of a large oak, Absalom's head[w] got caught in the tree. He was left hanging in midair, while the mule he was riding kept on going.

[10]When one of the men saw this, he told Joab, "I just saw Absalom hanging in an oak tree."

[11]Joab said to the man who had told him this, "What! You saw him? Why didn't you strike[x] him to the ground right there? Then I would have had to give you ten shekels[c] of silver and a warrior's belt."[y]

[12]But the man replied, "Even if a thousand shekels[d] were weighed out into my hands, I would not lift my hand against the king's son. In our hearing the king commanded you and Abishai and Ittai, 'Protect the young man Absalom for my sake.'[e] [13]And if I had put my life in jeopardy[f]—and nothing is hidden from the king[z]—you would have kept your distance from me."

[14]Joab[a] said, "I'm not going to wait like this for you." So he took three javelins in his hand and plunged them into Absalom's heart while Absalom was still alive in the oak tree. [15]And ten of Joab's armor-bearers surrounded Absalom, struck him and killed him.[b]

[16]Then Joab[c] sounded the trumpet, and the troops stopped pursuing Israel, for Joab halted them. [17]They took Absalom, threw him into a big pit in the forest and piled up[d] a large heap of rocks[e] over him. Meanwhile, all the Israelites fled to their homes.

---

[x] 25 Hebrew *Ithra*, a variant of *Jether* [y] 25 Hebrew and some Septuagint manuscripts; other Septuagint manuscripts (see also 1 Chron. 2:17) *Ishmaelite* or *Jezreelite* [z] 25 Hebrew *Abigal*, a variant of *Abigail* [a] 28 Most Septuagint manuscripts and Syriac; Hebrew *lentils, and roasted grain* [b] 3 Two Hebrew manuscripts, some Septuagint manuscripts and Vulgate; most Hebrew manuscripts *care; for now there are ten manuscripts like us* [c] 11 That is, about 4 ounces (about 115 grams) [d] 12 That is, about 25 pounds (about 11 kilograms) [e] 12 A few Hebrew manuscripts, Septuagint, Vulgate and Syriac; most Hebrew manuscripts may be translated *Absalom, whoever you may be.* [f] 13 Or *Otherwise, if I had acted treacherously toward him*

¹⁸During his lifetime Absalom had taken a pillar and erected it in the King's Valley[f] as a monument[g] to himself, for he thought, "I have no son[h] to carry on the memory of my name." He named the pillar after himself, and it is called Absalom's Monument to this day.

David Mourns

¹⁹Now Ahimaaz[i] son of Zadok said, "Let me run and take the news to the king that the LORD has delivered him from the hand of his enemies.[j]"

²⁰"You are not the one to take the news today," Joab told him. "You may take the news another time, but you must not do so today, because the king's son is dead."

²¹Then Joab said to a Cushite, "Go, tell the king what you have seen." The Cushite bowed down before Joab and ran off.

²²Ahimaaz son of Zadok again said to Joab, "Come what may, please let me run behind the Cushite."

But Joab replied, "My son, why do you want to go? You don't have any news that will bring you a reward."

²³He said, "Come what may, I want to run."

So Joab said, "Run!" Then Ahimaaz ran by way of the plain[g] and outran the Cushite.

²⁴While David was sitting between the inner and outer gates, the watchman[k] went up to the roof of the gateway by the wall. As he looked out, he saw a man running alone. ²⁵The watchman called out to the king and reported it.

The king said, "If he is alone, he must have good news." And the man came closer and closer.

²⁶Then the watchman saw another man running, and he called down to the gatekeeper, "Look, another man running alone!"

The king said, "He must be bringing good news,[l] too."

²⁷The watchman said, "It seems to me that the first one runs like[m] Ahimaaz son of Zadok."

"He's a good man," the king said. "He comes with good news."

²⁸Then Ahimaaz called out to the king, "All is well!" He bowed down before the king with his face to the ground and said, "Praise be to the LORD your God! He has delivered up the men who lifted their hands against my lord the king."

²⁹The king asked, "Is the young man Absalom safe?"

Ahimaaz answered, "I saw great confusion just as Joab was about to send the king's servant and me, your servant, but I don't know what it was."

³⁰The king said, "Stand aside and wait here." So he stepped aside and stood there.

³¹Then the Cushite arrived and said, "My lord the king, hear the good news! The LORD has delivered you today from all who rose up against you."

³²The king asked the Cushite, "Is the young man Absalom safe?"

The Cushite replied, "May the enemies of my lord the king and all who rise up to harm you be like that young man."[n]

³³The king was shaken. He went up to the room over the gateway and wept. As he went, he said: "O my son Absalom! My son, my son Absalom! If only I had died[o] instead of you—O Absalom, my son, my son!"[p]

19 Joab was told, "The king is weeping and mourning for Absalom." ²And for the whole army the victory that day was turned into mourning, because on that day the troops heard it said, "The king is grieving for his son." ³The men stole into the city that day as men steal in who are ashamed when they flee from battle. ⁴The king covered his face and cried aloud, "O my son Absalom! O Absalom, my son, my son!"

⁵Then Joab went into the house to the king and said, "Today you have humiliated all your men, who have just saved your life and the lives of your sons and daughters and the lives of your wives and concubines. ⁶You love those who hate you and hate those who love you. You have made it clear today that the commanders and their men mean nothing to you. I see that you would be pleased if Absalom were alive today and all of us were dead. ⁷Now go out and encourage your men. I swear by the LORD that if you don't go out, not a man will be left with you by nightfall. This will be worse for you than all the calamities that have come upon you from your youth till now."[q]

---

[g] 23 That is, the plain of the Jordan

⁸So the king got up and took his seat in the gateway. When the men were told, "The king is sitting in the gateway,"ʳ they all came before him.

David Returns to Jerusalem

Meanwhile, the Israelites had fled to their homes. ⁹Throughout the tribes of Israel, the people were all arguing with each other, saying, "The king delivered us from the hand of our enemies; he is the one who rescued us from the hand of the Philistines.ˢ But now he has fled the country because of Absalom;ᵗ ¹⁰and Absalom, whom we anointed to rule over us, has died in battle. So why do you say nothing about bringing the king back?"

¹¹King David sent this message to Zadokᵘ and Abiathar, the priests: "Ask the elders of Judah, 'Why should you be the last to bring the king back to his palace, since what is being said throughout Israel has reached the king at his quarters? ¹²You are my brothers, my own flesh and blood. So why should you be the last to bring the king back?' ¹³And say to Amasa,ᵛ 'Are you not my own flesh and blood?ʷ May God deal with me, be it ever so severely,ˣ if from now on you are not the commander of my army in place of Joab.'ʸ"

¹⁴He won over the hearts of all the men of Judah as though they were one man. They sent word to the king, "Return, you and all your men." ¹⁵Then the king returned and went as far as the Jordan.

Now the men of Judah had come to Gilgalᶻ to go out and meet the king and bring him across the Jordan. ¹⁶Shimeiᵃ son of Gera, the Benjamite from Bahurim, hurried down with the men of Judah to meet King David. ¹⁷With him were a thousand Benjamites, along with Ziba,ᵇ the steward of Saul's household,ᶜ and his fifteen sons and twenty servants. They rushed to the Jordan, where the king was. ¹⁸They crossed at the ford to take the king's household over and to do whatever he wished.

When Shimei son of Gera crossed the Jordan, he fell prostrate before the king ¹⁹and said to him, "May my lord not hold me guilty. Do not remember how your servant did wrong on the day my lord the king left Jerusalem.ᵈ May the king put it out of his mind. ²⁰For I your servant know that I have sinned, but today I have come here as the first of the whole house of Joseph to come down and meet my lord the king."

²¹Then Abishaiᵉ son of Zeruiah said, "Shouldn't Shimei be put to death for this? He cursedᶠ the LORD's anointed."ᵍ

²²David replied, "What do you and I have in common, you sons of Zeruiah?ʰ This day you have become my adversaries! Should anyone be put to death in Israel today?ⁱ Do I not know that today I am king over Israel?" ²³So the king said to Shimei, "You shall not die." And the king promised him on oath.ʲ

²⁴Mephibosheth,ᵏ Saul's grandson, also went down to meet the king. He had not taken care of his feet or trimmed his mustache or washed his clothes from the day the king left until the day he returned safely. ²⁵When he came from Jerusalem to meet the king, the king asked him, "Why didn't you go with me,ˡ Mephibosheth?"

²⁶He said, "My lord the king, since I your servant am lame,ᵐ I said, 'I will have my donkey saddled and will ride on it, so I can go with the king.' But Zibaⁿ my servant betrayed me. ²⁷And he has slandered your servant to my lord the king. My lord the king is like an angelᵒ of God; so do whatever pleases you. ²⁸All my grandfather's descendants deserved nothing but deathᵖ from my lord the king, but you gave your servant a place among those who eat at your table.ᑫ So what right do I have to make any more appeals to the king?"

²⁹The king said to him, "Why say more? I order you and Ziba to divide the fields."

³⁰Mephibosheth said to the king, "Let him take everything, now that my lord the king has arrived home safely."

³¹Barzillaiʳ the Gileadite also came down from Rogelim to cross the Jordan with the king and to send him on his way from there. ³²Now Barzillai was a very old man, eighty years of age. He had provided for the king during his stay in Mahanaim, for he was a very wealthyˢ man. ³³The king said to Barzillai, "Cross over with me and stay with me in Jerusalem, and I will provide for you."

³⁴But Barzillai answered the king, "How many more years will I live, that I should go up to Jerusalem with the king? ³⁵I am now eightyᵗ years old. Can I tell

the difference between what is good and what is not? Can your servant taste what he eats and drinks? Can I still hear the voices of men and women singers?ᵘ Why should your servant be an addedᵛ burden to my lord the king? ³⁶Your servant will cross over the Jordan with the king for a short distance, but why should the king reward me in this way? ³⁷Let your servant return, that I may die in my own town near the tomb of my fatherʷ and mother. But here is your servant Kimham.ˣ Let him cross over with my lord the king. Do for him whatever pleases you."

³⁸The king said, "Kimham shall cross over with me, and I will do for him whatever pleases you. And anything you desire from me I will do for you."

³⁹So all the people crossed the Jordan, and then the king crossed over. The king kissed Barzillai and gave him his blessing,ʸ and Barzillai returned to his home.

⁴⁰When the king crossed over to Gilgal, Kimham crossed with him. All the troops of Judah and half the troops of Israel had taken the king over.

⁴¹Soon all the men of Israel were coming to the king and saying to him, "Why did our brothers, the men of Judah, steal the king away and bring him and his household across the Jordan, together with all his men?"ᶻ

⁴²All the men of Judah answered the men of Israel, "We did this because the king is closely related to us. Why are you angry about it? Have we eaten any of the king's provisions? Have we taken anything for ourselves?"

⁴³Then the men of Israelᵃ answered the men of Judah, "We have ten shares in the king; and besides, we have a greater claim on David than you have. So why do you treat us with contempt? Were we not the first to speak of bringing back our king?"

But the men of Judah responded even more harshly than the men of Israel.

Sheba Rebels Against David

20 Now a troublemaker named Sheba son of Bicri, a Benjamite, happened to be there. He sounded the trumpet and shouted,

"We have no shareᵇ in David,ᶜ
no part in Jesse's son!ᵈ
Every man to his tent, O Israel!"

²So all the men of Israel deserted David to follow Sheba son of Bicri. But the men of Judah stayed by their king all the way from the Jordan to Jerusalem.

³When David returned to his palace in Jerusalem, he took the ten concubinesᵉ he had left to take care of the palace and put them in a house under guard. He provided for them, but did not lie with them. They were kept in confinement till the day of their death, living as widows.

⁴Then the king said to Amasa,ᶠ "Summon the men of Judah to come to me within three days, and be here yourself." ⁵But when Amasa went to summon Judah, he took longer than the time the king had set for him.

⁶David said to Abishai,ᵍ "Now Sheba son of Bicri will do us more harm than Absalom did. Take your master's men and pursue him, or he will find fortified cities and escape from us." ⁷So Joab's men and the Kerethitesʰ and Pelethites and all the mighty warriors went out under the command of Abishai. They marched out from Jerusalem to pursue Sheba son of Bicri.

⁸While they were at the great rock in Gibeon,ⁱ Amasa came to meet them. Joabʲ was wearing his military tunic, and strapped over it at his waist was a belt with a dagger in its sheath. As he stepped forward, it dropped out of its sheath.

⁹Joab said to Amasa, "How are you, my brother?" Then Joab took Amasa by the beard with his right hand to kiss him. ¹⁰Amasa was not on his guard against the daggerᵏ in Joab'sˡ hand, and Joab plunged it into his belly, and his intestines spilled out on the ground. Without being stabbed again, Amasa died. Then Joab and his brother Abishai pursued Sheba son of Bicri.

¹¹One of Joab's men stood beside Amasa and said, "Whoever favors Joab, and whoever is for David, let him follow Joab!" ¹²Amasa lay wallowing in his blood in the middle of the road, and the man saw that all the troops came to a haltᵐ there. When he realized that everyone who came up to Amasa stopped, he dragged him from the road into a field and threw a garment over him. ¹³After Amasa had been removed from the road, all the men went on with Joab to pursue Sheba son of Bicri.

¹⁴Sheba passed through all the tribes of

Israel to Abel Beth Maacah and through the entire region of the Berites, who gathered together and followed him. ¹⁵All the troops with Joab came and besieged Sheba in Abel Beth Maacah. They built a siege ramp up to the city, and it stood against the outer fortifications. While they were battering the wall to bring it down, ¹⁶a wise woman called from the city, "Listen! Listen! Tell Joab to come here so I can speak to him." ¹⁷He went toward her, and she asked, "Are you Joab?"

"I am," he answered.

She said, "Listen to what your servant has to say."

"I'm listening," he said.

¹⁸She continued, "Long ago they used to say, 'Get your answer at Abel,' and that settled it. ¹⁹We are the peaceful and faithful in Israel. You are trying to destroy a city that is a mother in Israel. Why do you want to swallow up the LORD's inheritance?"

²⁰"Far be it from me!" Joab replied, "Far be it from me to swallow up or destroy! ²¹That is not the case. A man named Sheba son of Bicri, from the hill country of Ephraim, has lifted up his hand against the king, against David. Hand over this one man, and I'll withdraw from the city."

The woman said to Joab, "His head will be thrown to you from the wall."

²²Then the woman went to all the people with her wise advice, and they cut off the head of Sheba son of Bicri and threw it to Joab. So he sounded the trumpet, and his men dispersed from the city, each returning to his home. And Joab went back to the king in Jerusalem.

²³Joab was over Israel's entire army; Benaiah son of Jehoiada was over the Kerethites and Pelethites; ²⁴Adoniram was in charge of forced labor; Jehoshaphat son of Ahilud was recorder; ²⁵Sheva was secretary; Zadok and Abiathar were priests; ²⁶and Ira the Jairite was David's priest.

The Gibeonites Avenged

21 During the reign of David, there was a famine for three successive years; so David sought the face of the LORD. The LORD said, "It is on account of Saul and his blood-stained house; it is because he put the Gibeonites to death."

²The king summoned the Gibeonites and spoke to them. (Now the Gibeonites were not a part of Israel but were survivors of the Amorites; the Israelites had sworn to ⌊spare⌋ them, but Saul in his zeal for Israel and Judah had tried to annihilate them.) ³David asked the Gibeonites, "What shall I do for you? How shall I make amends so that you will bless the LORD's inheritance?"

⁴The Gibeonites answered him, "We have no right to demand silver or gold from Saul or his family, nor do we have the right to put anyone in Israel to death."

"What do you want me to do for you?" David asked.

⁵They answered the king, "As for the man who destroyed us and plotted against us so that we have been decimated and have no place anywhere in Israel, ⁶let seven of his male descendants be given to us to be killed and exposed before the LORD at Gibeah of Saul—the LORD's chosen one."

So the king said, "I will give them to you."

⁷The king spared Mephibosheth son of Jonathan, the son of Saul, because of the oath before the LORD between David and Jonathan son of Saul. ⁸But the king took Armoni and Mephibosheth, the two sons of Aiah's daughter Rizpah, whom she had borne to Saul, together with the five sons of Saul's daughter Merab, whom she had borne to Adriel son of Barzillai the Meholathite. ⁹He handed them over to the Gibeonites, who killed and exposed them on a hill before the LORD. All seven of them fell together; they were put to death during the first days of the harvest, just as the barley harvest was beginning.

¹⁰Rizpah daughter of Aiah took sackcloth and spread it out for herself on a rock. From the beginning of the harvest till the rain poured down from the heavens on the bodies, she did not let the birds of the air touch them by day or the wild animals by night. ¹¹When David

---

h 14 Or *Abel, even Beth Maacah*; also in verse 15   *i 24* Some Septuagint manuscripts (see also 1 Kings 4:6 and 5:14); Hebrew *Adoram*   *j 8* Two Hebrew manuscripts, some Septuagint manuscripts and Syriac (see also 1 Samuel 18:19); most Hebrew and Septuagint manuscripts *Michal*

was told what Aiah's daughter Rizpah, Saul's concubine, had done, ¹²he went and took the bones of Saul[n] and his son Jonathan from the citizens of Jabesh Gilead.[o] (They had taken them secretly from the public square at Beth Shan,[p] where the Philistines had hung[q] them after they struck Saul down on Gilboa.)[r] ¹³David brought the bones of Saul and his son Jonathan from there, and the bones of those who had been killed and exposed were gathered up.

¹⁴They buried the bones of Saul and his son Jonathan in the tomb of Saul's father Kish, at Zela[s] in Benjamin, and did everything the king commanded. After that,[t] God answered prayer[u] in behalf of the land.[v]

Wars Against the Philistines
21:15–22pp — 1Ch 20:4–8

¹⁵Once again there was a battle between the Philistines[w] and Israel. David went down with his men to fight against the Philistines, and he became exhausted. ¹⁶And Ishbi-Benob, one of the descendants of Rapha, whose bronze spearhead weighed three hundred shekels[k] and who was armed with a new sword, said he would kill David. ¹⁷But Abishai[x] son of Zeruiah came to David's rescue; he struck the Philistine down and killed him. Then David's men swore to him, saying, "Never again will you go out with us to battle, so that the lamp[y] of Israel will not be extinguished."[z]

¹⁸In the course of time, there was another battle with the Philistines, at Gob. At that time Sibbecai[a] the Hushathite killed Saph, one of the descendants of Rapha.

¹⁹In another battle with the Philistines at Gob, Elhanan son of Jaare-Oregim[l] the Bethlehemite killed Goliath[m] the Gittite,[b] who had a spear with a shaft like a weaver's rod.[c]

²⁰In still another battle, which took place at Gath, there was a huge man with six fingers on each hand and six toes on each foot—twenty-four in all. He also was descended from Rapha. ²¹When he taunted[d] Israel, Jonathan son of Shimeah,[e] David's brother, killed him.

²²These four were descendants of Rapha in Gath, and they fell at the hands of David and his men.

```
21:12
n 1Sa 31:11-13
o S Jdg 21:8;
  S 1Sa 11:1
p S Jos 17:11
q 1Sa 31:10
r S 1Sa 28:4

21:14 s Jos 18:28
t Jos 7:26
u 2Sa 24:25
v 1Ch 8:34

21:15 w S 2Sa 5:25

21:17 x 2Sa 20:6
y 1Ki 11:36; 15:4;
  2Ki 8:19; 2Ch 21:7;
  Ps 132:17
z 2Sa 18:3

21:18 a 1Ch 11:29;
  27:11

21:19 b S 1Sa 17:4
c S 1Sa 17:7

21:21
d S 1Sa 17:10
e S 1Sa 16:9

22:1 f S Ex 15:1

22:2 g S 1Sa 2:2
h Ps 31:3; 91:2
i Ps 144:2

22:3 j S Dt 23:15;
  S 32:37; Ps 14:6;
  31:2; 59:16; 71:7;
  91:2; 94:22;
  Pr 10:29; Isa 25:4;
  Jer 16:19; Joel 3:16
k S Ge 15:1
l S Dt 33:17;
  S Lk 1:69 m Ps 9:9;
  52:7

22:4 n Ps 48:1;
  96:4; 145:3

22:5 o Ps 69:14-15;
  Jnh 2:3

22:6 p Ps 116:3;
  Ac 2:24

22:7 q Ge 35:3;
  S Jdg 2:15;
  2Ch 15:4; Ps 4:1;
  77:2; 120:1;
  Isa 26:16 r Ps 34:6;
  15; 116:4

22:8 s Jdg 5:4;
  Ps 97:4
t S Ex 19:18;
S Jdg 5:4; Ps 68:8;
77:18; Jer 10:10
u Job 9:6; 26:11;
Ps 75:3

22:9 v Ps 50:3;
97:3; Heb 12:29;
S Rev 11:5
w Isa 6:6; Eze 1:13;
10:2

22:10 x S Ex 19:9;
Lev 16:2;
S Dt 33:26;
1Ki 8:12; Job 26:9;
Ps 104:3; Isa 19:1;
Jer 4:13; Na 1:3

22:11 y S Ge 3:24;
S Ex 25:22
z Ps 104:3

22:12 a S Ex 19:9
```

David's Song of Praise
22:1–51pp — Ps 18:1–50

22 David sang[f] to the LORD the words of this song when the LORD delivered him from the hand of all his enemies and from the hand of Saul. ²He said: L

"The LORD is my rock,[g] my fortress[h]
  and my deliverer;[i]
³ my God is my rock, in whom I take
    refuge,[j]
  my shield[k] and the horn[l] of my
    salvation.
  He is my stronghold,[m] my refuge and
    my savior—
  from violent men you save me.
⁴I call to the LORD, who is worthy[n] of
    praise,
  and I am saved from my enemies.

⁵"The waves[o] of death swirled about
    me;
  the torrents of destruction
    overwhelmed me.
⁶The cords of the grave[o,p] coiled around
    me;
  the snares of death confronted me.
⁷In my distress[q] I called[r] to the LORD;
  I called out to my God.
From his temple he heard my voice;
  my cry came to his ears.

⁸"The earth[s] trembled and quaked,[t]
  the foundations[u] of the heavens[p]
    shook;
  they trembled because he was
    angry.
⁹Smoke rose from his nostrils;
  consuming fire[v] came from his
    mouth,
  burning coals[w] blazed out of it.
¹⁰He parted the heavens and came
    down;
  dark clouds[x] were under his feet.
¹¹He mounted the cherubim[y] and flew;
  he soared[q] on the wings of the
    wind.[z]
¹²He made darkness[a] his canopy around
    him—

L *1Sa 25:29* ◀ ▶ *2Ki 6:16–17*

k 16 That is, about 7 1/2 pounds (about 3.5 kilograms) *l 19* Or *son of Jair the weaver* *m 19* Hebrew and Septuagint; 1 Chron. 20:5 *son of Jair killed Lahmi the brother of Goliath* *n 3 Horn* here symbolizes strength. *o 6* Hebrew *Sheol* *p 8* Hebrew; Vulgate and Syriac (see also Psalm 18:7) *mountains* *q 11* Many Hebrew manuscripts (see also Psalm 18:10); most Hebrew manuscripts *appeared*

the dark^r rain clouds of the sky.
¹³Out of the brightness of his presence
bolts of lightning^b blazed forth.
P ¹⁴The LORD thundered^c from heaven;
the voice of the Most High
resounded.
¹⁵He shot arrows^d and scattered ⌊the
enemies⌋,
bolts of lightning and routed them.
¹⁶The valleys of the sea were exposed
and the foundations of the earth laid
bare
at the rebuke^e of the LORD,
at the blast^f of breath from his
nostrils.
¹⁷"He reached down from on high^g and
took hold of me;
he drew^h me out of deep waters.
¹⁸He rescued^i me from my powerful
enemy,
from my foes, who were too strong
for me.
¹⁹They confronted me in the day of my
disaster,
but the LORD was my support.^j
U ²⁰He brought me out into a spacious^k
place;
he rescued^l me because he
delighted^m in me.^n
S ²¹"The LORD has dealt with me according
to my righteousness;^o
according to the cleanness^p of my
hands^q he has rewarded me.
²²For I have kept^r the ways of the LORD;
I have not done evil by turning from
my God.
²³All his laws are before me;^s
I have not turned^t away from his
decrees.
²⁴I have been blameless^u before him
and have kept myself from sin.
²⁵The LORD has rewarded me according
to my righteousness,^v
according to my cleanness^s in his
sight.
²⁶"To the faithful you show yourself
faithful,

P 1Sa 2:10 ◀▶ 2Sa 23:6–7
U 1Sa 2:30 ◀▶ 1Ki 3:6
S 1Sa 24:13 ◀▶ 1Ki 8:61

22:13 ^b Job 37:3; Ps 77:18
22:14 ^c S 1Sa 2:10
22:15 ^d S Dt 32:23
22:16 ^e Ps 6:1; 50:8,21; 106:9; Na 1:4 ^f S Ex 14:21; Isa 30:33; 40:24
22:17 ^g Ps 144:7 ^h Ex 2:10
22:18 ^i Lk 1:71
22:19 ^j Ps 23:4
22:20 ^k Job 36:16; Ps 31:8 Ps 118:5 ^m Ps 22:8; Isa 42:1; Mt 12:18 ^n S 2Sa 15:26
22:21 ^o S 1Sa 26:23 ^p Ps 26:6 ^q Job 17:9; 22:30; 42:7-8; Ps 24:4
22:22 ^r Ge 18:19; Ps 128:1; Pr 8:32
22:23 ^s Dt 6:4-9; Ps 119:30-32 ^t Ps 119:102
22:24 ^u S Ge 6:9; Eph 1:4
22:25 ^v S 1Sa 26:23
22:27 ^w Mt 5:8 ^x Lev 26:23-24
22:28 ^y S Ex 3:8; 1Sa 2:8-9; Ps 72:12-13 ^z Ps 131:1; Pr 30:13; Da 4:31; Zep 3:11 ^a Isa 2:12, 17; 5:15; S Lk 1:51
22:29 ^b Ps 27:1; Isa 2:5; Mic 7:8; Rev 21:23; 22:5
22:31 ^c S Dt 32:4; Mt 5:48 ^d Ps 12:6; 119:140; Pr 30:5-6 ^e S Ge 15:1
22:32 ^f S 1Sa 2:2 ^g 2Sa 7:22
22:34 ^h Isa 35:6; Hab 3:19 ^i S Dt 32:13
22:35 ^j Ps 144:1 ^k Ps 7:12; 11:2; Zec 9:13
22:36 ^l Eph 6:16
22:37 ^m Pr 4:11
22:39 ^n Ps 44:5; 110:6; Mal 4:3

to the blameless you show yourself
blameless,
²⁷to the pure^w you show yourself pure,
but to the crooked you show
yourself shrewd.^x
²⁸You save the humble,^y
but your eyes are on the haughty^z to
bring them low.^a **M**
²⁹You are my lamp,^b O LORD;
the LORD turns my darkness into
light.
³⁰With your help I can advance against a
troop^r; **V**
with my God I can scale a wall.
³¹"As for God, his way is perfect;^c **K**
the word of the LORD is flawless.^d **W**
He is a shield^e
for all who take refuge in him.
³²For who is God besides the LORD? **O**
And who is the Rock^f except our
God?^g
³³It is God who arms me with strength^u
and makes my way perfect.
³⁴He makes my feet like the feet of a
deer;^h
he enables me to stand on the
heights.^i
³⁵He trains my hands^j for battle;
my arms can bend a bow^k of bronze.
³⁶You give me your shield^l of victory; **K**
you stoop down to make me great.
³⁷You broaden the path^m beneath me,
so that my ankles do not turn.
³⁸"I pursued my enemies and crushed
them;
I did not turn back till they were
destroyed.
³⁹I crushed^n them completely, and they
could not rise;
they fell beneath my feet.
⁴⁰You armed me with strength for battle;

M 1Sa 2:3 ◀▶ 2Sa 24:10
V 1Sa 25:29 ◀▶ 2Ch 14:7
K 1Sa 25:29 ◀▶ 2Sa 22:36
W Nu 21:8–9 ◀▶ Ezr 8:22
O 2Sa 7:22 ◀▶ 1Ki 8:60
K 2Sa 22:31 ◀▶ 2Ki 6:16–17

^r 12 Septuagint and Vulgate (see also Psalm 18:11); Hebrew *massed*   ^s 25 Hebrew; Septuagint and Vulgate (see also Psalm 18:24) *to the cleanness of my hands*   ^t 30 *Or can run through a barricade*   ^u 33 Dead Sea Scrolls, some Septuagint manuscripts, Vulgate and Syriac (see also Psalm 18:32); Masoretic Text *who is my strong refuge*

22:14–18 David's song of praise is also given in Ps 18:1–50. In this song David declares his total dependence upon God's direction and his trust in God's ability to deliver Israel from all their enemies.

you made my adversaries bow at my feet.º
⁴¹You made my enemies turn their backsᵖ in flight,
and I destroyed my foes.
⁴²They cried for help,ᑫ but there was no one to save them—ʳ
to the Lord, but he did not answer.ˢ
⁴³I beat them as fine as the dustᵗ of the earth;
I pounded and trampledᵘ them like mudᵛ in the streets.

⁴⁴"You have deliveredʷ me from the attacks of my people;
you have preservedˣ me as the head of nations.
Peopleʸ I did not know are subject to me,
⁴⁵ and foreigners come cringingᶻ to me;
as soon as they hear me, they obey me.ᵃ
⁴⁶They all lose heart;
they come tremblingᵛᵇ from their strongholds.

⁴⁷"The Lord lives! Praise be to my Rock!
Exaltedᶜ be God, the Rock, my Savior!ᵈ
⁴⁸He is the God who avengesᵉ me,ᶠ
who puts the nations under me,
⁴⁹ who sets me free from my enemies.ᵍ
You exalted meʰ above my foes;
from violent men you rescued me.
⁵⁰Therefore I will praise you, O Lord, among the nations;
I will sing praisesⁱ to your name.ʲ
⁵¹He gives his king great victories;ᵏ
he shows unfailing kindness to his anointed,ˡ
to Davidᵐ and his descendants forever."ⁿ

The Last Words of David

T **23** These are the last words of David:

"The oracle of David son of Jesse,
the oracle of the man exaltedº by the Most High,

the man anointedᵖ by the God of Jacob,
Israel's singer of songs ʷ:

²"The Spiritᑫ of the Lord spoke through me;
his word was on my tongue.
³The God of Israel spoke,
the Rockʳ of Israel said to me:
'When one rules over men in righteousness,ˢ
when he rules in the fearᵗ of God,ᵘ
⁴he is like the lightᵛ of morningʷ at sunriseˣ
on a cloudless morning,
like the brightness after rainʸ
that brings the grass from the earth.'

⁵"Is not my house right with God?
Has he not made with me an everlasting covenant,ᶻ
arranged and secured in every part?
Will he not bring to fruition my salvation
and grant me my every desire?
⁶But evil men are all to be cast aside like thorns,ᵃ
which are not gathered with the hand.
⁷Whoever touches thorns
uses a tool of iron or the shaft of a spear;
they are burned up where they lie."

David's Mighty Men

23:8–39pp — 1Ch 11:10–41

⁸These are the names of David's mighty men:ᵇ
Josheb-Basshebeth,ˣᶜ a Tahkemonite,ʸ was chief of the Three; he raised his

---

23:3–5 These verses clearly declared that God alone sets the standards for righteous government. Humanity must rule one another in conformity to God's justice. See the discussion concerning the dispensation of human government at Ge 8:15.

spear against eight hundred men, whom he killed in one encounter.

⁹Next to him was Eleazar son of Dodai the Ahohite. As one of the three mighty men, he was with David when they taunted the Philistines gathered at Pas Dammim, for battle. Then the men of Israel retreated, ¹⁰but he stood his ground and struck down the Philistines till his hand grew tired and froze to the sword. The LORD brought about a great victory that day. The troops returned to Eleazar, but only to strip the dead.

¹¹Next to him was Shammah son of Agee the Hararite. When the Philistines banded together at a place where there was a field full of lentils, Israel's troops fled from them. ¹²But Shammah took his stand in the middle of the field. He defended it and struck the Philistines down, and the LORD brought about a great victory.

¹³During harvest time, three of the thirty chief men came down to David at the cave of Adullam, while a band of Philistines was encamped in the Valley of Rephaim. ¹⁴At that time David was in the stronghold, and the Philistine garrison was at Bethlehem. ¹⁵David longed for water and said, "Oh, that someone would get me a drink of water from the well near the gate of Bethlehem!" ¹⁶So the three mighty men broke through the Philistine lines, drew water from the well near the gate of Bethlehem and carried it back to David. But he refused to drink it; instead, he poured it out before the LORD. ¹⁷"Far be it from me, O LORD, to do this!" he said. "Is it not the blood of men who went at the risk of their lives?" And David would not drink it.

Such were the exploits of the three mighty men.

¹⁸Abishai the brother of Joab son of Zeruiah was chief of the Three. He raised his spear against three hundred men, whom he killed, and so he became as famous as the Three. ¹⁹Was he not held in greater honor than the Three? He became their commander, even though he was not included among them.

²⁰Benaiah son of Jehoiada was a valiant fighter from Kabzeel, who performed great exploits. He struck down two of Moab's best men. He also went down into a pit on a snowy day and killed a lion. ²¹And he struck down a huge Egyptian. Although the Egyptian had a spear in his hand, Benaiah went against him with a club. He snatched the spear from the Egyptian's hand and killed him with his own spear. ²²Such were the exploits of Benaiah son of Jehoiada; he too was as famous as the three mighty men. ²³He was held in greater honor than any of the Thirty, but he was not included among the Three. And David put him in charge of his bodyguard.

²⁴Among the Thirty were:
Asahel the brother of Joab,
Elhanan son of Dodo from Bethlehem,
²⁵Shammah the Harodite,
Elika the Harodite,
²⁶Helez the Paltite,
Ira son of Ikkesh from Tekoa,
²⁷Abiezer from Anathoth,
Mebunnai the Hushathite,
²⁸Zalmon the Ahohite,
Maharai the Netophathite,
²⁹Heled son of Baanah the Netophathite,
Ithai son of Ribai from Gibeah in Benjamin,
³⁰Benaiah the Pirathonite,
Hiddai from the ravines of Gaash,
³¹Abi-Albon the Arbathite,
Azmaveth the Barhumite,
³²Eliahba the Shaalbonite,
the sons of Jashen,
Jonathan ³³son of Shammah the Hararite,
Ahiam son of Sharar the Hararite,
³⁴Eliphelet son of Ahasbai the Maacathite,
Eliam son of Ahithophel the Gilonite,
³⁵Hezro the Carmelite,
Paarai the Arbite,
³⁶Igal son of Nathan from Zobah,
the son of Hagri,
³⁷Zelek the Ammonite,
Naharai the Beerothite, the ar-

---

z 8 Some Septuagint manuscripts (see also 1 Chron. 11:11); Hebrew and other Septuagint manuscripts *Three; it was Adino the Eznite who killed eight hundred men* *a 9* See 1 Chron. 11:13; Hebrew *gathered there.* *b 18* Most Hebrew manuscripts (see also 1 Chron. 11:20); two Hebrew manuscripts and Syriac *Thirty* *c 27* Hebrew; some Septuagint manuscripts (see also 1 Chron. 11:29) *Sibbecai* *d 29* Some Hebrew manuscripts and Vulgate, most Hebrew manuscripts *Heleb* *e 30* Hebrew; some Septuagint manuscripts (see also 1 Chron. 11:32) *Hurai* *f 33* Some Septuagint manuscripts (see also 1 Chron. 11:34); Hebrew does not have *son of.* *g 33* Hebrew; some Septuagint manuscripts (see also 1 Chron. 11:35) *Sacar* *h 36* Hebrew *Haggadi*

mor-bearer of Joab son of Zeruiah,
[38] Ira the Ithrite,[h]
Gareb the Ithrite
[39] and Uriah[i] the Hittite.
There were thirty-seven in all.

David Counts the Fighting Men

24:1–17pp — 1Ch 21:1–17

[24] Again[j] the anger of the LORD burned against Israel,[k] and he incited David against them, saying, "Go and take a census of[l] Israel and Judah."

[2] So the king said to Joab[m] and the army commanders[i] with him, "Go throughout the tribes of Israel from Dan to Beersheba[n] and enroll[o] the fighting men, so that I may know how many there are."

[3] But Joab[p] replied to the king, "May the LORD your God multiply the troops a hundred times over,[q] and may the eyes of my lord the king see it. But why does my lord the king want to do such a thing?"

[4] The king's word, however, overruled Joab and the army commanders; so they left the presence of the king to enroll the fighting men of Israel.

[5] After crossing the Jordan, they camped near Aroer,[r] south of the town in the gorge, and then went through Gad and on to Jazer.[s] [6] They went to Gilead and the region of Tahtim Hodshi, and on to Dan Jaan and around toward Sidon.[t] [7] Then they went toward the fortress of Tyre[u] and all the towns of the Hivites[v] and Canaanites. Finally, they went on to Beersheba[w] in the Negev[x] of Judah.

[8] After they had gone through the entire land, they came back to Jerusalem at the end of nine months and twenty days.

[9] Joab reported the number of the fighting men to the king: In Israel there were eight hundred thousand able-bodied men who could handle a sword, and in Judah five hundred thousand.[y]

M
R [10] David was conscience-stricken[z] after he had counted the fighting men, and he said to the LORD, "I have sinned[a] greatly in what I have done. Now, O LORD, I beg you, take away the guilt of your servant. I have done a very foolish thing."[b]

[11] Before David got up the next morning, the word of the LORD had come to Gad[c] the prophet, David's seer:[d] [12] "Go

---

23:38 [h] 1Ch 2:53
23:39 [i] 2Sa 11:3
24:1 [j] S Jos 9:15
[k] Job 1:6; Zec 3:1
[l] S Ex 30:12; 1Ch 27:23
24:2 [m] S 2Sa 20:23
[n] S 2Sa 3:10
[o] 2Ch 2:17; 17:14; 25:5
24:3 [p] S 2Sa 2:18
[q] S Dt 1:11
24:5 [r] S Jos 13:9
[s] Nu 21:32
24:6 [t] S Ge 10:19; Jdg 1:31
24:7 [u] S Jos 19:29
[v] S Ex 3:8
[w] Ge 21:31
[x] S Dt 1:7
24:9 [y] S Nu 1:44-46
24:10 [z] S 1Sa 24:5
[a] S Nu 22:34
[b] S Nu 12:11
24:11 [c] S 2Sa 22:5
[d] 1Sa 9:9
24:13 [e] Dt 28:38-42,48; S 32:24; Eze 14:21
[f] S Ex 5:3; S 30:12; S Lev 26:25; Dt 28:21-22,27-28, 35
24:14 [g] Ne 9:28; Ps 4:1; 51:1; 86:5; 103:8,13; 119:132; 130:4; Isa 54:7; 55:7; Jer 33:8; 42:12; Da 9:9
24:15 [h] 1Ch 27:24
24:16 [i] S Ge 6:6
[j] S Ge 16:7; S 19:13; S Ex 12:23; Ac 12:23
24:17 [k] Ps 74:1; 100:3; Jer 49:20
[l] S Ge 18:23
[m] Jnh 1:12
24:18 [n] Ge 22:2; 2Ch 3:1
24:21 [o] Nu 16:44-50
24:22 [p] S 1Sa 6:14

---

and tell David, 'This is what the LORD says: I am giving you three options. Choose one of them for me to carry out against you.'"

[13] So Gad went to David and said to him, "Shall there come upon you three[j] years of famine[e] in your land? Or three months of fleeing from your enemies while they pursue you? Or three days of plague[f] in your land? Now then, think it over and decide how I should answer the one who sent me."

[14] David said to Gad, "I am in deep distress. Let us fall into the hands of the LORD, for his mercy[g] is great; but do not let me fall into the hands of men."

[15] So the LORD sent a plague on Israel from that morning until the end of the time designated, and seventy thousand of the people from Dan to Beersheba died.[h] [16] When the angel stretched out his hand to destroy Jerusalem, the LORD was grieved[i] because of the calamity and said to the angel who was afflicting the people, "Enough! Withdraw your hand." The angel of the LORD[j] was then at the threshing floor of Araunah the Jebusite.

[17] When David saw the angel who was striking down the people, he said to the LORD, "I am the one who has sinned and done wrong. These are but sheep.[k] What have they done?[l] Let your hand fall upon me and my family."[m]

David Builds an Altar

24:18–25pp — 1Ch 21:18–26

[18] On that day Gad went to David and said to him, "Go up and build an altar to the LORD on the threshing floor of Araunah[n] the Jebusite." [19] So David went up, as the LORD had commanded through Gad. [20] When Araunah looked and saw the king and his men coming toward him, he went out and bowed down before the king with his face to the ground.

[21] Araunah said, "Why has my lord the king come to his servant?"

"To buy your threshing floor," David answered, "so I can build an altar to the LORD, that the plague on the people may be stopped."[o]

[22] Araunah said to David, "Let my lord the king take whatever pleases him and offer it up. Here are oxen[p] for the burnt

---

M 2Sa 22:28 ◀ ▶ 1Ki 21:25–29
R 2Sa 12:13 ◀ ▶ 2Ki 17:13

[i] 2 Septuagint (see also verse 4 and 1 Chron. 21:2); Hebrew *Joab the army commander.* [j] 13 Septuagint (see also 1 Chron. 21:12); Hebrew *seven*

offering, and here are threshing sledges and ox yokes for the wood. ²³O king, Araunah gives^q all this to the king." Araunah also said to him, "May the LORD your God accept you."

²⁴But the king replied to Araunah, "No, I insist on paying you for it. I will not sacrifice to the LORD my God burnt offerings that cost me nothing."^r

So David bought the threshing floor and the oxen and paid fifty shekels^k^s of silver for them. ²⁵David built an altar^t to the LORD there and sacrificed burnt offerings and fellowship offerings.^l Then the LORD answered prayer^u in behalf of the land, and the plague on Israel was stopped.

E *1Sa 1:5–20* ◀ ▶ *1Ki 13:6*

24:23 ^q Ge 23:11
24:24 ^r Mal 1:13-14 ^s S Ge 23:16
24:25 ^t S 1Sa 7:17 ^u 2Sa 21:14

^k 24 That is, about 1 1/4 pounds (about 0.6 kilogram) ^l 25 Traditionally *peace offerings*

24:24 Though Araunah had freely offered this land to David, David insisted on paying for it. David declared that an offering must cost the giver something. By purchasing this threshing floor, this land became David's property and ultimately the future site of the temple (see 1Ch 22:1; 2Ch 3:1). The principle of sacrificial giving applies to us as well. While God's gift of grace is free, it was bought with the high price of Jesus' death. We should take our worship of God seriously and offer him only our best, regardless of personal cost (see Lk 21:1–4).

1 Kings

Author: Unknown

Theme: The united and divided kingdom of Israel

Date of Writing: c. 560–550 B.C.

Outline of 1 Kings
  I. King David's Reign Ends (1:1—2:11)
 II. The Reign of Solomon (2:12—11:43)
III. The Kingdom Is Divided (12:1—14:31)
 IV. Kings of Judah and Israel (15:1—16:28)
  V. The Reign of Ahab (16:29—22:40)
 VI. Jehoshaphat and Ahaziah (22:41–53)

THE BOOKS OF 1 and 2 Kings (like 1 and 2 Samuel) were originally treated as one book and called simply "Kings" in the ancient Hebrew manuscripts. Translators of the Septuagint (the Greek version of the OT) divided the larger Hebrew manuscript into the two books modern translations refer to as 1 and 2 Kings. The books of 1 and 2 Kings combined with 1 and 2 Samuel cover the history of Israel through the monarchies of the united and divided kingdoms until its ultimate destruction and exile under the Babylonians. Though authorship of 1 and 2 Kings is uncertain, these books were probably written after King Jehoiachin's release from prison (562 B.C.) but before the end of the Babylonian exile (538 B.C.).

The book of 1 Kings begins with the account of King Solomon's reign, describing the building of the temple and recording Solomon's journey from wisdom to folly. Following Solomon's reign, rebellion among the people broke the nation apart. The northern ten tribes re-formed as the kingdom of Israel and the remaining two southern tribes re-formed as the kingdom of Judah. The remainder of 1 Kings traces the reigns of the kings of these new kingdoms, highlighting the success of the kings who followed God's law while pointing out the destruction that followed those who disobeyed. Note that the majority of the northern kings were evil, but many southern kings initiated revivals and returned their people to the worship of God. The book of 1 Kings closes with the reign of King Ahaziah of Israel and King Jehoshaphat of Judah. Some important stories in 1 Kings include Solomon's prayer for wisdom (ch. 3), the Queen of Sheba's visit (ch. 10), Elijah and the prophets of Baal (ch. 18) and Ahab and Jezebel (chs. 21—22).

Adonijah Sets Himself Up as King

1 When King David was old and well advanced in years, he could not keep warm even when they put covers over him. ²So his servants said to him, "Let us look for a young virgin to attend the king and take care of him. She can lie beside him so that our lord the king may keep warm."

³Then they searched throughout Israel for a beautiful girl and found Abishag,[a] a Shunammite,[b] and brought her to the king. ⁴The girl was very beautiful; she took care of the king and waited on him, but the king had no intimate relations with her.

⁵Now Adonijah, whose mother was Haggith, put himself forward and said, "I will be king." So he got chariots and horses[a] ready, with fifty men to run ahead of him. ⁶(His father had never interfered with him by asking, "Why do you behave as you do?" He was also very handsome and was born next after Absalom.)

⁷Adonijah conferred with Joab son of Zeruiah and with Abiathar the priest, and they gave him their support. ⁸But Zadok the priest, Benaiah son of Jehoiada, Nathan the prophet, Shimei and Rei[b] and David's special guard did not join Adonijah.

⁹Adonijah then sacrificed sheep, cattle and fattened calves at the Stone of Zoheleth near En Rogel. He invited all his brothers, the king's sons, and all the men of Judah who were royal officials, ¹⁰but he did not invite Nathan the prophet or Benaiah or the special guard or his brother Solomon.

¹¹Then Nathan asked Bathsheba, Solomon's mother, "Have you not heard that Adonijah, the son of Haggith, has become king without our lord David's knowing it? ¹²Now then, let me advise you how you can save your own life and the life of your son Solomon. ¹³Go in to King David and say to him, 'My lord the king, did you not swear to me your servant: "Surely Solomon your son shall be king after me, and he will sit on my throne"? Why then has Adonijah become king?' ¹⁴While you are still there talking to the king, I will come in and confirm what you have said."

¹⁵So Bathsheba went to see the aged king in his room, where Abishag the Shunammite was attending him. ¹⁶Bathsheba bowed low and knelt before the king.

"What is it you want?" the king asked.

¹⁷She said to him, "My lord, you yourself swore to me your servant by the LORD your God: 'Solomon your son shall be king after me, and he will sit on my throne.' ¹⁸But now Adonijah has become king, and you, my lord the king, do not know about it. ¹⁹He has sacrificed great numbers of cattle, fattened calves, and sheep, and has invited all the king's sons, Abiathar the priest and Joab the commander of the army, but he has not invited Solomon your servant. ²⁰My lord the king, the eyes of all Israel are on you, to learn from you who will sit on the throne of my lord the king after him. ²¹Otherwise, as soon as my lord the king is laid to rest with his fathers, I and my son Solomon will be treated as criminals."

²²While she was still speaking with the king, Nathan the prophet arrived. ²³And they told the king, "Nathan the prophet is here." So he went before the king and bowed with his face to the ground.

²⁴Nathan said, "Have you, my lord the king, declared that Adonijah shall be king after you, and that he will sit on your

---

a 5 Or *charioteers*   *b 8* Or *and his friends*

throne? ²⁵Today he has gone down and sacrificed great numbers of cattle, fattened calves, and sheep. He has invited all the king's sons, the commanders of the army and Abiathar the priest. Right now they are eating and drinking with him and saying, 'Long live King Adonijah!' ²⁶But me your servant, and Zadok the priest, and Benaiah son of Jehoiada, and your servant Solomon he did not invite.ʸ ²⁷Is this something my lord the king has done without letting his servants know who should sit on the throne of my lord the king after him?"

David Makes Solomon King
1:28-53pp — 1Ch 29:21-25

²⁸Then King David said, "Call in Bathsheba." So she came into the king's presence and stood before him.

²⁹The king then took an oath: "As surely as the LORD lives, who has delivered me out of every trouble,ᶻ ³⁰I will surely carry out today what I sworeᵃ to you by the LORD, the God of Israel: Solomon your son shall be king after me, and he will sit on my throne in my place."

³¹Then Bathsheba bowed low with her face to the ground and, kneeling before the king, said, "May my lord King David live forever!"

³²King David said, "Call in Zadokᵇ the priest, Nathan the prophet and Benaiah son of Jehoiada." When they came before the king, ³³he said to them: "Take your lord's servants with you and set Solomon my son on my own muleᶜ and take him down to Gihon.ᵈ ³⁴There have Zadok the priest and Nathan the prophet anointᵉ him king over Israel. Blow the trumpetᶠ and shout, 'Long live King Solomon!' ³⁵Then you are to go up with him, and he is to come and sit on my throne and reign in my place. I have appointed him ruler over Israel and Judah."

³⁶Benaiah son of Jehoiada answered the king, "Amen! May the LORD, the God of my lord the king, so declare it. ³⁷As the LORD was with my lord the king, so may he be withᵍ Solomon to make his throne even greaterʰ than the throne of my lord King David!"

³⁸So Zadokⁱ the priest, Nathan the prophet, Benaiah son of Jehoiada, the Kerethitesʲ and the Pelethites went down and put Solomon on King David's mule and escorted him to Gihon.ᵏ ³⁹Zadok the priest took the horn of oilˡ from the sacred tentᵐ and anointed Solomon. Then they sounded the trumpetⁿ and all the people shouted,ᵒ "Long live King Solomon!" ⁴⁰And all the people went up after him, playing flutesᵖ and rejoicing greatly, so that the ground shook with the sound.

⁴¹Adonijah and all the guests who were with him heard it as they were finishing their feast. On hearing the sound of the trumpet, Joab asked, "What's the meaning of all the noise in the city?"ᑫ

⁴²Even as he was speaking, Jonathanʳ son of Abiathar the priest arrived. Adonijah said, "Come in. A worthy man like you must be bringing good news."ˢ

⁴³"Not at all!" Jonathan answered. "Our lord King David has made Solomon king. ⁴⁴The king has sent with him Zadok the priest, Nathan the prophet, Benaiah son of Jehoiada, the Kerethites and the Pelethites, and they have put him on the king's mule, ⁴⁵and Zadok the priest and Nathan the prophet have anointed him king at Gihon. From there they have gone up cheering, and the city resoundsᵗ with it. That's the noise you hear. ⁴⁶Moreover, Solomon has taken his seatᵘ on the royal throne. ⁴⁷Also, the royal officials have come to congratulate our lord King David, saying, 'May your God make Solomon's name more famous than yours and his throne greaterᵛ than yours!' And the king bowed in worship on his bed ⁴⁸and said, 'Praise be to the LORD, the God of Israel, who has allowed my eyes to see a successorʷ on my throne today.' "

⁴⁹At this, all Adonijah's guests rose in alarm and dispersed. ⁵⁰But Adonijah, in fear of Solomon, went and took hold of the hornsˣ of the altar. ⁵¹Then Solomon was told, "Adonijah is afraid of King Solomon and is clinging to the horns of the altar. He says, 'Let King Solomon swear to me today that he will not put his servant to death with the sword.' "

⁵²Solomon replied, "If he shows himself to be a worthy man, not a hairʸ of his head will fall to the ground; but if evil is found in him, he will die." ⁵³Then King Solomon sent men, and they brought him down from the altar. And Adonijah came and bowed down to King Solomon, and Solomon said, "Go to your home."

David's Charge to Solomon

2:10–12pp — 1Ch 29:26–28

2 When the time drew near for David to die, he gave a charge to Solomon his son.

² "I am about to go the way of all the earth," he said. "So be strong, show yourself a man, ³ and observe what the LORD your God requires: Walk in his ways, and keep his decrees and commands, his laws and requirements, as written in the Law of Moses, so that you may prosper in all you do and wherever you go, ⁴ and that the LORD may keep his promise to me: 'If your descendants watch how they live, and if they walk faithfully before me with all their heart and soul, you will never fail to have a man on the throne of Israel.'

⁵ "Now you yourself know what Joab son of Zeruiah did to me—what he did to the two commanders of Israel's armies, Abner son of Ner and Amasa son of Jether. He killed them, shedding their blood in peacetime as if in battle, and with that blood stained the belt around his waist and the sandals on his feet. ⁶ Deal with him according to your wisdom, but do not let his gray head go down to the grave in peace.

⁷ "But show kindness to the sons of Barzillai of Gilead and let them be among those who eat at your table. They stood by me when I fled from your brother Absalom.

⁸ "And remember, you have with you Shimei son of Gera, the Benjamite from Bahurim, who called down bitter curses on me the day I went to Mahanaim. When he came down to meet me at the Jordan, I swore to him by the LORD: 'I will not put you to death by the sword.' ⁹ But now, do not consider him innocent. You are a man of wisdom; you will know what to do to him. Bring his gray head down to the grave in blood."

¹⁰ Then David rested with his fathers and was buried in the City of David. ¹¹ He had reigned forty years over Israel—seven years in Hebron and thirty-three in Jerusalem. ¹² So Solomon sat on the throne of his father David, and his rule was firmly established.

Solomon's Throne Established

¹³ Now Adonijah, the son of Haggith, went to Bathsheba, Solomon's mother. Bathsheba asked him, "Do you come peacefully?"

He answered, "Yes, peacefully." ¹⁴ Then he added, "I have something to say to you."

"You may say it," she replied.

¹⁵ "As you know," he said, "the kingdom was mine. All Israel looked to me as their king. But things changed, and the kingdom has gone to my brother; for it has come to him from the LORD. ¹⁶ Now I have one request to make of you. Do not refuse me."

"You may make it," she said.

¹⁷ So he continued, "Please ask King Solomon—he will not refuse you—to give me Abishag the Shunammite as my wife."

¹⁸ "Very well," Bathsheba replied, "I will speak to the king for you."

¹⁹ When Bathsheba went to King Solomon to speak to him for Adonijah, the king stood up to meet her, bowed down to her and sat down on his throne. He had a throne brought for the king's mother, and she sat down at his right hand.

²⁰ "I have one small request to make of you," she said. "Do not refuse me."

The king replied, "Make it, my mother; I will not refuse you."

²¹ So she said, "Let Abishag the Shunammite be given in marriage to your brother Adonijah."

²² King Solomon answered his mother, "Why do you request Abishag the Shunammite for Adonijah? You might as well request the kingdom for him—after all, he is my older brother—yes, for him and for Abiathar the priest and Joab son of Zeruiah!"

²³ Then King Solomon swore by the

---

c 6 Hebrew *Sheol*; also in verse 9

2:2–4 As King David lay on his deathbed he prophesied that God would prosper the reign of Solomon if he would "keep his decrees and commands" (2:3). David then prophesied that his descendants would continue to rule Israel forever if they obeyed God.

LORD: "May God deal with me, be it ever so severely,ʳ if Adonijah does not pay with his life for this request! ²⁴And now, as surely as the LORD lives—he who has established me securely on the throne of my father David and has founded a dynasty for me as he promisedᵍ—Adonijah shall be put to death today!" ²⁵So King Solomon gave orders to Benaiahʰ son of Jehoiada, and he struck down Adonijah and he died.ⁱ

²⁶To Abiatharʲ the priest the king said, "Go back to your fields in Anathoth.ᵏ You deserve to die, but I will not put you to death now, because you carried the arkˡ of the Sovereign LORD before my father David and shared all my father's hardships."ᵐ ²⁷So Solomon removed Abiathar from the priesthood of the LORD, fulfillingⁿ the word the LORD had spoken at Shiloh about the house of Eli.

²⁸When the news reached Joab, who had conspired with Adonijah though not with Absalom, he fled to the tent of the LORD and took hold of the hornsᵒ of the altar. ²⁹King Solomon was told that Joab had fled to the tent of the LORD and was beside the altar.ᵖ Then Solomon ordered Benaiahᑫ son of Jehoiada, "Go, strike him down!"

³⁰So Benaiah entered the tentʳ of the LORD and said to Joab, "The king says, 'Come out!ˢ' "

But he answered, "No, I will die here."

Benaiah reported to the king, "This is how Joab answered me."

³¹Then the king commanded Benaiah, "Do as he says. Strike him down and bury him, and so clear me and my father's house of the guilt of the innocent bloodᵗ that Joab shed. ³²The LORD will repayᵘ him for the blood he shed,ᵛ because without the knowledge of my father David he attacked two men and killed them with the sword. Both of them—Abner son of Ner, commander of Israel's army, and Amasaʷ son of Jether, commander of Judah's army—were betterˣ men and more upright than he. ³³May the guilt of their blood rest on the head of Joab and his descendants forever. But on David and his descendants, his house and his throne, may there be the LORD's peace forever."

³⁴So Benaiahʸ son of Jehoiada went up and struck down Joabᶻ and killed him, and he was buried on his own landᵈ in the desert. ³⁵The king put Benaiahᵃ son of Jehoiada over the army in Joab's position and replaced Abiathar with Zadokᵇ the priest.

³⁶Then the king sent for Shimeiᶜ and said to him, "Build yourself a house in Jerusalem and live there, but do not go anywhere else. ³⁷The day you leave and cross the Kidron Valley,ᵈ you can be sure you will die; your blood will be on your own head."ᵉ

³⁸Shimei answered the king, "What you say is good. Your servant will do as my lord the king has said." And Shimei stayed in Jerusalem for a long time.

³⁹But three years later, two of Shimei's slaves ran off to Achishᶠ son of Maacah, king of Gath, and Shimei was told, "Your slaves are in Gath." ⁴⁰At this, he saddled his donkey and went to Achish at Gath in search of his slaves. So Shimei went away and brought the slaves back from Gath.

⁴¹When Solomon was told that Shimei had gone from Jerusalem to Gath and had returned, ⁴²the king summoned Shimei and said to him, "Did I not make you swear by the LORD and warnᵍ you, 'On the day you leave to go anywhere else, you can be sure you will die'? At that time you said to me, 'What you say is good. I will obey.' ⁴³Why then did you not keep your oath to the LORD and obey the command I gave you?"

⁴⁴The king also said to Shimei, "You know in your heart all the wrongʰ you did to my father David. Now the LORD will repay you for your wrongdoing. ⁴⁵But King Solomon will be blessed, and David's throne will remain secureⁱ before the LORD forever."

⁴⁶Then the king gave the order to Benaiahʲ son of Jehoiada, and he went out and struck Shimeiᵏ down and killed him.

The kingdom was now firmly establishedˡ in Solomon's hands.

M 2Sa 23:3–5 ◀▶ 1Ch 16:30–33

2:45 Solomon reiterates the promise that "David's throne" would continue forever.

Solomon Asks for Wisdom

3:4–15pp — 2Ch 1:2–13

3 Solomon made an alliance with Pharaoh king of Egypt and married his daughter. He brought her to the City of David until he finished building his palace and the temple of the LORD, and the wall around Jerusalem. ² The people, however, were still sacrificing at the high places, because a temple had not yet been built for the Name of the LORD. ³ Solomon showed his love for the LORD by walking according to the statutes of his father David, except that he offered sacrifices and burned incense on the high places.

⁴ The king went to Gibeon to offer sacrifices, for that was the most important high place, and Solomon offered a thousand burnt offerings on that altar. ⁵ At Gibeon the LORD appeared to Solomon during the night in a dream, and God said, "Ask for whatever you want me to give you."

⁶ Solomon answered, "You have shown great kindness to your servant, my father David, because he was faithful to you and righteous and upright in heart. You have continued this great kindness to him and have given him a son to sit on his throne this very day.

⁷ "Now, O LORD my God, you have made your servant king in place of my father David. But I am only a little child and do not know how to carry out my duties. ⁸ Your servant is here among the people you have chosen, a great people, too numerous to count or number. ⁹ So give your servant a discerning heart to govern your people and to distinguish between right and wrong. For who is able to govern this great people of yours?"

¹⁰ The Lord was pleased that Solomon had asked for this. ¹¹ So God said to him, "Since you have asked for this and not for long life or wealth for yourself, nor have asked for the death of your enemies but for discernment in administering justice, ¹² I will do what you have asked. I will give you a wise and discerning heart, so that there will never have been anyone like you, nor will there ever be.

¹³ Moreover, I will give you what you have not asked for—both riches and honor—so that in your lifetime you will have no equal among kings. ¹⁴ And if you walk in my ways and obey my statutes and commands as David your father did, I will give you a long life." ¹⁵ Then Solomon awoke—and he realized it had been a dream.

He returned to Jerusalem, stood before the ark of the Lord's covenant and sacrificed burnt offerings and fellowship offerings. Then he gave a feast for all his court.

A Wise Ruling

¹⁶ Now two prostitutes came to the king and stood before him. ¹⁷ One of them said, "My lord, this woman and I live in the same house. I had a baby while she was there with me. ¹⁸ The third day after my child was born, this woman also had a baby. We were alone; there was no one in the house but the two of us.

¹⁹ "During the night this woman's son died because she lay on him. ²⁰ So she got up in the middle of the night and took my son from my side while I your servant was asleep. She put him by her breast and put her dead son by my breast. ²¹ The next morning, I got up to nurse my son—and he was dead! But when I looked at him closely in the morning light, I saw that it wasn't the son I had borne."

²² The other woman said, "No! The living one is my son; the dead one is yours."

But the first one insisted, "No! The dead one is yours; the living one is mine." And so they argued before the king.

²³ The king said, "This one says, 'My son is alive and your son is dead,' while that one says, 'No! Your son is dead and mine is alive.' "

²⁴ Then the king said, "Bring me a sword." So they brought a sword for the king. ²⁵ He then gave an order: "Cut the living child in two and give half to one and half to the other."

²⁶ The woman whose son was alive was filled with compassion for her son and

said to the king, "Please, my lord, give her the living baby! Don't kill him!"

But the other said, "Neither I nor you shall have him. Cut him in two!"

²⁷Then the king gave his ruling: "Give the living baby to the first woman. Do not kill him; she is his mother."

²⁸When all Israel heard the verdict the king had given, they held the king in awe, because they saw that he had wisdom[x] from God to administer justice.

Solomon's Officials and Governors

4 So King Solomon ruled over all Israel. ²And these were his chief officials:[y]

Azariah[z] son of Zadok—the priest;
³Elihoreph and Ahijah, sons of Shisha—secretaries;[a]
Jehoshaphat[b] son of Ahilud—recorder;
⁴Benaiah[c] son of Jehoiada—commander in chief;
Zadok[d] and Abiathar—priests;
⁵Azariah son of Nathan—in charge of the district officers;
Zabud son of Nathan—a priest and personal adviser to the king;
⁶Ahishar—in charge of the palace;[e]
Adoniram[f] son of Abda—in charge of forced labor.[g]

⁷Solomon also had twelve district governors[h] over all Israel, who supplied provisions for the king and the royal household. Each one had to provide supplies for one month in the year. ⁸These are their names:

Ben-Hur—in the hill country[i] of Ephraim;
⁹Ben-Deker—in Makaz, Shaalbim,[j] Beth Shemesh[k] and Elon Bethhanan;
¹⁰Ben-Hesed—in Arubboth (Socoh[l] and all the land of Hepher[m] were his);
¹¹Ben-Abinadab—in Naphoth Dor[f][n] (he was married to Taphath daughter of Solomon);
¹²Baana son of Ahilud—in Taanach and Megiddo, and in all of Beth Shan[o] next to Zarethan[p] below Jezreel, from Beth Shan to Abel Meholah[q] across to Jokmeam;[r]
¹³Ben-Geber—in Ramoth Gilead (the settlements of Jair[s] son of Manasseh in Gilead[t] were his, as well as the district of Argob in Bashan and its sixty large walled cities[u] with bronze gate bars);
¹⁴Ahinadab son of Iddo—in Mahanaim;[v]
¹⁵Ahimaaz[w]—in Naphtali (he had married Basemath daughter of Solomon);
¹⁶Baana son of Hushai[x]—in Asher and in Aloth;
¹⁷Jehoshaphat son of Paruah—in Issachar;
¹⁸Shimei[y] son of Ela—in Benjamin;
¹⁹Geber son of Uri—in Gilead (the country of Sihon[z] king of the Amorites and the country of Og[a] king of Bashan). He was the only governor over the district.

Solomon's Daily Provisions

²⁰The people of Judah and Israel were as numerous as the sand[b] on the seashore; they ate, they drank and they were happy.[c] ²¹And Solomon ruled[d] over all the kingdoms from the River[g][e] to the land of the Philistines, as far as the border of Egypt.[f] These countries brought tribute[g] and were Solomon's subjects all his life.

²²Solomon's daily provisions[h] were thirty cors[h] of fine flour and sixty cors[i] of meal, ²³ten head of stall-fed cattle, twenty of pasture-fed cattle and a hundred sheep and goats, as well as deer, gazelles, roebucks and choice fowl.[i] ²⁴For he ruled over all the kingdoms west of the River, from Tiphsah[j] to Gaza, and had peace[k] on all sides. ²⁵During Solomon's lifetime Judah and Israel, from Dan to Beersheba,[l] lived in safety,[m] each man under his own vine and fig tree.[n]

²⁶Solomon had four[j] thousand stalls for chariot horses,[o] and twelve thousand horses.[k]

²⁷The district officers,[p] each in his month, supplied provisions for King Solomon and all who came to the king's table. They saw to it that nothing was lacking. ²⁸They also brought to the proper place their quotas of barley and straw for the chariot horses and the other horses.

---

f 11 Or in the heights of Dor   g 21 That is, the Euphrates; also in verse 24   h 22 That is, probably about 185 bushels (about 6.6 kiloliters)   i 22 That is, probably about 375 bushels (about 13.2 kiloliters)   j 26 Some Septuagint manuscripts (see also 2 Chron. 9:25); Hebrew forty   k 26 Or charioteers

Solomon's Wisdom

²⁹God gave Solomon wisdom and very great insight, and a breadth of understanding as measureless as the sand on the seashore. ³⁰Solomon's wisdom was greater than the wisdom of all the men of the East, and greater than all the wisdom of Egypt. ³¹He was wiser than any other man, including Ethan the Ezrahite—wiser than Heman, Calcol and Darda, the sons of Mahol. And his fame spread to all the surrounding nations. ³²He spoke three thousand proverbs and his songs numbered a thousand and five. ³³He described plant life, from the cedar of Lebanon to the hyssop that grows out of walls. He also taught about animals and birds, reptiles and fish. ³⁴Men of all nations came to listen to Solomon's wisdom, sent by all the kings of the world, who had heard of his wisdom.

Preparations for Building the Temple
5:1–16pp — 2Ch 2:1–18

5 When Hiram king of Tyre heard that Solomon had been anointed king to succeed his father David, he sent his envoys to Solomon, because he had always been on friendly terms with David. ²Solomon sent back this message to Hiram:

³"You know that because of the wars waged against my father David from all sides, he could not build a temple for the Name of the LORD his God until the LORD put his enemies under his feet. ⁴But now the LORD my God has given me rest on every side, and there is no adversary or disaster. ⁵I intend, therefore, to build a temple for the Name of the LORD my God, as the LORD told my father David, when he said, 'Your son whom I will put on the throne in your place will build the temple for my Name.'

⁶"So give orders that cedars of Lebanon be cut for me. My men will work with yours, and I will pay you for your men whatever wages you set. You know that we have no one so skilled in felling timber as the Sidonians."

⁷When Hiram heard Solomon's message, he was greatly pleased and said, "Praise be to the LORD today, for he has given David a wise son to rule over this great nation."

⁸So Hiram sent word to Solomon:

"I have received the message you sent me and will do all you want in providing the cedar and pine logs. ⁹My men will haul them down from Lebanon to the sea, and I will float them in rafts by sea to the place you specify. There I will separate them and you can take them away. And you are to grant my wish by providing food for my royal household."

¹⁰In this way Hiram kept Solomon supplied with all the cedar and pine logs he wanted, ¹¹and Solomon gave Hiram twenty thousand cors*ˡ* of wheat as food for his household, in addition to twenty thousand baths*ᵐ,ⁿ* of pressed olive oil. Solomon continued to do this for Hiram year after year. ¹²The LORD gave Solomon wisdom, just as he had promised him. There were peaceful relations between Hiram and Solomon, and the two of them made a treaty.

¹³King Solomon conscripted laborers from all Israel—thirty thousand men. ¹⁴He sent them off to Lebanon in shifts of ten thousand a month, so that they spent one month in Lebanon and two months at home. Adoniram was in charge of the forced labor. ¹⁵Solomon had seventy thousand carriers and eighty thousand stonecutters in the hills, ¹⁶as well as thirty-three hundred foremen who supervised the project and directed the workmen. ¹⁷At the king's command they removed from the quarry large blocks of quality stone to provide a foundation of dressed stone for the temple. ¹⁸The craftsmen of Solomon and Hiram and the men

---

ˡ 11 That is, probably about 125,000 bushels (about 4,400 kiloliters) ᵐ 11 Septuagint (see also 2 Chron. 2:10); Hebrew twenty cors ⁿ 11 That is, about 115,000 gallons (about 440 kiloliters) ᵒ 16 Hebrew; some Septuagint manuscripts (see also 2 Chron. 2:2, 18) thirty-six hundred

---

5:5 Solomon confirms the promise God made to David, that his son would build God's temple (see 2Sa 7:13; 1Ch 17:12).

1 KINGS 6:1

of Gebal[p][u] cut and prepared the timber and stone for the building of the temple.

Solomon Builds the Temple
6:1–29pp — 2Ch 3:1–14

6 In the four hundred and eightieth[q] year after the Israelites had come out of Egypt, in the fourth year of Solomon's reign over Israel, in the month of Ziv, the second month,[v] he began to build the temple of the LORD.[w]

²The temple[x] that King Solomon built for the LORD was sixty cubits long, twenty wide and thirty high.[r] ³The portico[y] at the front of the main hall of the temple extended the width of the temple, that is twenty cubits,[s] and projected ten cubits[t] from the front of the temple. ⁴He made narrow clerestory windows[z] in the temple. ⁵Against the walls of the main hall and inner sanctuary he built a structure around the building, in which there were side rooms.[a] ⁶The lowest floor was five cubits[u] wide, the middle floor six cubits[v] and the third floor seven.[w] He made offset ledges around the outside of the temple so that nothing would be inserted into the temple walls.

⁷In building the temple, only blocks dressed[b] at the quarry were used, and no hammer, chisel or any other iron tool[c] was heard at the temple site while it was being built.

⁸The entrance to the lowest[x] floor was

5:18 [u] S Jos 13:5
[w] Ezr 5:11
6:1 [v] Ezr 3:8
6:2 [x] Ex 26:1
6:3 [y] Eze 40:49
6:4 [z] Eze 41:16
6:5 [a] Jer 35:2; Eze 41:5-6
6:7 [b] S Ex 20:25
[c] S Dt 27:5

[p] 18 That is, Byblos [q] 1 Hebrew; Septuagint *four hundred and fortieth*
[r] 2 That is, about 90 feet (about 27 meters) long and 30 feet (about 9 meters) wide and 45 feet (about 13.5 meters) high [s] 3 That is, about 30 feet (about 9 meters) [t] 3 That is, about 15 feet (about 4.5 meters)
[u] 6 That is, about 7 1/2 feet (about 2.3 meters); also in verses 10 and 24
[v] 6 That is, about 9 feet (about 2.7 meters) [w] 6 That is, about 10 1/2 feet (about 3.1 meters) [x] 8 Septuagint; Hebrew *middle*

Solomon's Temple

960–586 B.C.

Temple source materials are subject to academic interpretation, and subsequent art reconstructions vary.

This reconstruction recognizes influence from the desert tabernacle, accepts general Near Eastern cultural diffusion, and rejects overt pagan Canaanite symbols. It uses known archaeological parallels to supplement the text, and assumes interior dimensions from 1Ki 6:17-20.

Labels: Most Holy Place with ark of the covenant; Holy Place (30 cubits high) with golden tables for Bread of the Presence, gold lampstands, and altar of incense; Portico; Side rooms; The ornate cast bronze pillars, "Jakin and Boaz"; Movable stands of bronze; Sea; Altar; 20; 40 cubits; CUBITS 0 5 10 15 20; FEET 0 10 20 30

©1986 Hugh Claycombe

The temple of Solomon, located adjacent to the king's palace, functioned as God's royal palace and Israel's national center of worship. The Lord said to Solomon, "I have hallowed this house... to put my name there for ever; and mine eyes and mine heart shall be there perpetually" (1Ki 9:3). By its cosmological and royal symbolism, the sanctuary taught the absolute sovereignty of the Lord over the whole creation and his special headship over Israel.

The floor plan is a type that has a long history in Semitic religion, particularly among the West Semites. An early example of the tripartite division into *'ulam, hekal,* and *debir* (portico, main hall, and inner sanctuary) has been found at Syrian Ebla (c. 2300 B.C.) and, much later but more contemporaneous with Solomon, at Tell Tainat in the Orontes basin (c. 900 B.C.). Like Solomon's, the later temple has three divisions, contains two columns supporting the entrance, and is located adjacent to the royal palace.

Many archaeological parallels can be drawn to the methods of construction used in the temple, e.g., the "stone and cedar beam" technique described in 1Ki 6:36. Interestingly, evidence for the largest bronze-casting industry ever found in Palestine comes from the same locale and period as that indicated in Scripture: Zarethan in the Jordan Valley c. 1000 B.C.

on the south side of the temple; a stairway led up to the middle level and from there to the third. ⁹So he built the temple and completed it, roofing it with beams and cedar^d planks. ¹⁰And he built the side rooms all along the temple. The height of each was five cubits, and they were attached to the temple by beams of cedar.

¹¹The word of the LORD came^e to Solomon: ¹²"As for this temple you are building, if you follow my decrees, carry out my regulations and keep all my commands^f and obey them, I will fulfill through you the promise^g I gave to David your father. ¹³And I will live among the Israelites and will not abandon^h my people Israel."

¹⁴So Solomon^i built the temple and completed^j it. ¹⁵He lined its interior walls with cedar boards, paneling them from the floor of the temple to the ceiling,^k and covered the floor of the temple with planks of pine.^l ¹⁶He partitioned off twenty cubits^y at the rear of the temple with cedar boards from floor to ceiling to form within the temple an inner sanctuary, the Most Holy Place.^m ¹⁷The main hall in front of this room was forty cubits^z long. ¹⁸The inside of the temple was cedar,^n carved with gourds and open flowers. Everything was cedar; no stone was to be seen.

¹⁹He prepared the inner sanctuary^o within the temple to set the ark of the covenant^p of the LORD there. ²⁰The inner sanctuary^q was twenty cubits long, twenty wide and twenty high.^a He overlaid the inside with pure gold, and he also overlaid the altar of cedar.^r ²¹Solomon covered the inside of the temple with pure gold, and he extended gold chains across the front of the inner sanctuary, which was overlaid with gold. ²²So he overlaid the whole interior with gold. He also overlaid with gold the altar that belonged to the inner sanctuary.

²³In the inner sanctuary he made a pair of cherubim^s of olive wood, each ten cubits^b high. ²⁴One wing of the first cherub was five cubits long, and the other wing five cubits—ten cubits from wing tip to wing tip. ²⁵The second cherub also measured ten cubits, for the two cherubim were identical in size and shape. ²⁶The height of each cherub was ten cubits. ²⁷He placed the cherubim^t inside the innermost room of the temple, with their wings spread out. The wing of one cherub touched one wall, while the wing of the other touched the other wall, and their wings touched each other in the middle of the room. ²⁸He overlaid the cherubim with gold.

²⁹On the walls^u all around the temple, in both the inner and outer rooms, he carved cherubim,^v palm trees and open flowers. ³⁰He also covered the floors of both the inner and outer rooms of the temple with gold.

³¹For the entrance of the inner sanctuary he made doors of olive wood with five-sided jambs. ³²And on the two olive wood doors^w he carved cherubim, palm trees and open flowers, and overlaid the cherubim and palm trees with beaten gold. ³³In the same way he made four-sided jambs of olive wood for the entrance to the main hall. ³⁴He also made two pine doors, each having two leaves that turned in sockets. ³⁵He carved cherubim, palm trees and open flowers on them and overlaid them with gold hammered evenly over the carvings.

³⁶And he built the inner courtyard^x of three courses^y of dressed stone and one course of trimmed cedar beams.

³⁷The foundation of the temple of the LORD was laid in the fourth year, in the month of Ziv. ³⁸In the eleventh year in the month of Bul, the eighth month, the temple was finished in all its details^z according to its specifications.^a He had spent seven years building it.

Solomon Builds His Palace

7 It took Solomon thirteen years, however, to complete the construction of his palace.^b ²He built the Palace^c of the Forest of Lebanon^d a hundred cubits long, fifty wide and thirty high,^c with four rows of cedar columns supporting trimmed cedar beams. ³It was roofed with cedar above the beams that rested on the columns—forty-five beams, fifteen to a row. ⁴Its windows were placed high in sets of three, facing each other. ⁵All the doorways had rectangular frames; they were in the front part in sets of three, facing each other.^d

^y 16 That is, about 30 feet (about 9 meters)   ^z 17 That is, about 60 feet (about 18 meters)   ^a 20 That is, about 30 feet (about 9 meters) long, wide and high   ^b 23 That is, about 15 feet (about 4.5 meters)   ^c 2 That is, about 150 feet (about 46 meters) long, 75 feet (about 23 meters) wide and 45 feet (about 13.5 meters) high   ^d 5 The meaning of the Hebrew for this verse is uncertain.

⁶He made a colonnade fifty cubits long and thirty wide.ᵉ In front of it was a portico, and in front of that were pillars and an overhanging roof.

⁷He built the throne hall, the Hall of Justice, where he was to judge,ᵉ and he covered it with cedar from floor to ceiling.ᶠᵗ ⁸And the palace in which he was to live, set farther back, was similar in design. Solomon also made a palace like this hall for Pharaoh's daughter, whom he had married.ᵍ

⁹All these structures, from the outside to the great courtyard and from foundation to eaves, were made of blocks of high-grade stone cut to size and trimmed with a saw on their inner and outer faces. ¹⁰The foundations were laid with large stones of good quality, some measuring ten cubitsᵍ and some eight.ʰ ¹¹Above were high-grade stones, cut to size, and cedar beams. ¹²The great courtyard was surrounded by a wall of three courses of dressed stone and one course of trimmed cedar beams, as was the inner courtyard of the temple of the LORD with its portico.

The Temple's Furnishings

7:23–26pp — 2Ch 4:2–5
7:38–51pp — 2Ch 4:6,10–5:1

¹³King Solomon sent to Tyre and brought Huram,ⁱⁱ ¹⁴whose mother was a widow from the tribe of Naphtali and whose father was a man of Tyre and a craftsman in bronze. Huram was highly skilledʲ and experienced in all kinds of bronze work. He came to King Solomon and did allᵏ the work assigned to him.

¹⁵He cast two bronze pillars,ˡ each eighteen cubits high and twelve cubits around,ʲ by line. ¹⁶He also made two capitalsᵐ of cast bronze to set on the tops of the pillars; each capital was five cubitsᵏ high. ¹⁷A network of interwoven chains festooned the capitals on top of the pillars, seven for each capital. ¹⁸He made pomegranates in two rowsˡ encircling each network to decorate the capitals on top of the pillars.ᵐ He did the same for each capital. ¹⁹The capitals on top of the pillars in the portico were in the shape of lilies, four cubitsⁿ high. ²⁰On the capitals of both pillars, above the bowl-shaped part next to the network, were the two hundred pomegranatesⁿ in rows all around. ²¹He erected the pillars at the portico of the temple. The pillar to the south he named Jakinᵒ and the one to the north Boaz.ᵖᵒ ²²The capitals on top were in the shape of lilies. And so the work on the pillarsᵖ was completed.

²³He made the Seaᵠ of cast metal, circular in shape, measuring ten cubitsᵍ from rim to rim and five cubits high. It took a lineʳ of thirty cubitsᵠ to measure around it. ²⁴Below the rim, gourds encircled it— ten to a cubit. The gourds were cast in two rows in one piece with the Sea.

²⁵The Sea stood on twelve bulls,ˢ three facing north, three facing west, three facing south and three facing east. The Sea rested on top of them, and their hindquarters were toward the center. ²⁶It was a handbreadthʳ in thickness, and its rim was like the rim of a cup, like a lily blossom. It held two thousand baths.ˢ

²⁷He also made ten movable standsᵗ of bronze; each was four cubits long, four wide and three high.ᵗ ²⁸This is how the stands were made: They had side panels attached to uprights. ²⁹On the panels between the uprights were lions, bulls and cherubim—and on the uprights as well. Above and below the lions and bulls were wreaths of hammered work. ³⁰Each standᵘ had four bronze wheels with bronze axles, and each had a basin resting on four supports, cast with wreaths on each side. ³¹On the inside of the stand there was an opening that had a circular frame one cubitᵘ deep. This opening was round, and with its basework it measured a cubit and a half.ᵛ Around its opening there was engraving. The panels of the stands were square, not round. ³²The four wheels were under the panels, and the axles of the wheels were attached to the stand. The diameter of each wheel was a cubit and a half. ³³The wheels were made like chariot wheels; the axles, rims,

---

ᵉ 6 That is, about 75 feet (about 23 meters) long and 45 feet (about 13.5 meters) wide ᶠ 7 Vulgate and Syriac; Hebrew *floor* ᵍ 10,23 That is, about 15 feet (about 4.5 meters) ʰ 10 That is, about 12 feet (about 3.6 meters) ⁱ 13 Hebrew *Hiram,* a variant of *Huram;* also in verses 40 and 45 ʲ 15 That is, about 27 feet (about 8.1 meters) high and 18 feet (about 5.4 meters) around ᵏ 16 That is, about 7 1/2 feet (about 2.3 meters); also in verse 23 ˡ 18 Two Hebrew manuscripts and Septuagint; most Hebrew manuscripts *made the pillars, and there were two rows* ᵐ 18 Many Hebrew manuscripts and Syriac; most Hebrew manuscripts *pomegranates* ⁿ 19 That is, about 6 feet (about 1.8 meters); also in verse 38 ᵒ 21 *Jakin* probably means *he establishes.* ᵖ 21 *Boaz* probably means *in him is strength.* ᵠ 23 That is, about 45 feet (about 13.5 meters) ʳ 26 That is, about 3 inches (about 8 centimeters) ˢ 26 That is, probably about 11,500 gallons (about 44 kiloliters); the Septuagint does not have this sentence. ᵗ 27 That is, about 6 feet (about 1.8 meters) long and wide and about 4 1/2 feet (about 1.3 meters) high ᵘ 31 That is, about 1 1/2 feet (about 0.5 meter) ᵛ 31 That is, about 2 1/4 feet (about 0.7 meter); also in verse 32

spokes and hubs were all of cast metal. ³⁴Each stand had four handles, one on each corner, projecting from the stand. ³⁵At the top of the stand there was a circular band half a cubit^w deep. The supports and panels were attached to the top of the stand. ³⁶He engraved cherubim, lions and palm trees on the surfaces of the supports and on the panels, in every available space, with wreaths all around. ³⁷This is the way he made the ten stands. They were all cast in the same molds and were identical in size and shape.

³⁸He then made ten bronze basins,^v each holding forty baths^x and measuring four cubits across, one basin to go on each of the ten stands. ³⁹He placed five of the stands on the south side of the temple and five on the north. He placed the Sea on the south side, at the southeast corner of the temple. ⁴⁰He also made the basins and shovels and sprinkling bowls.^w

So Huram finished all the work he had undertaken for King Solomon in the temple of the LORD:

⁴¹the two pillars;
the two bowl-shaped capitals on top of the pillars;
the two sets of network decorating the two bowl-shaped capitals on top of the pillars;
⁴²the four hundred pomegranates for the two sets of network (two rows of pomegranates for each network, decorating the bowl-shaped capitals^x on top of the pillars);
⁴³the ten stands with their ten basins;
⁴⁴the Sea and the twelve bulls under it;
⁴⁵the pots, shovels and sprinkling bowls.^y

All these objects that Huram^z made for King Solomon for the temple of the LORD were of burnished bronze. ⁴⁶The king had them cast in clay molds in the plain^a of the Jordan between Succoth^b and Zarethan.^c ⁴⁷Solomon left all these things unweighed,^d because there were so many;^e the weight of the bronze^f was not determined.

⁴⁸Solomon also made all^g the furnishings that were in the LORD's temple:

the golden altar;
the golden table^h on which was the bread of the Presence;^i
⁴⁹the lampstands^j of pure gold (five on the right and five on the left, in front of the inner sanctuary); the gold floral work and lamps and tongs;
⁵⁰the pure gold basins, wick trimmers, sprinkling bowls, dishes^k and censers;^l
and the gold sockets for the doors of the innermost room, the Most Holy Place, and also for the doors of the main hall of the temple.

⁵¹When all the work King Solomon had done for the temple of the LORD was finished, he brought in the things his father David had dedicated^m—the silver and gold and the furnishings^n—and he placed them in the treasuries of the LORD's temple.

The Ark Brought to the Temple

8:1–21pp — 2Ch 5:2–6:11

8 Then King Solomon summoned into his presence at Jerusalem the elders of Israel, all the heads of the tribes and the chiefs^o of the Israelite families, to bring up the ark^p of the LORD's covenant from Zion, the City of David.^q ²All the men of Israel came together to King Solomon at the time of the festival^r in the month of Ethanim, the seventh month.^s

³When all the elders of Israel had arrived, the priests^t took up the ark, ⁴and they brought up the ark of the LORD and the Tent of Meeting^u and all the sacred furnishings in it. The priests and Levites^v carried them up, ⁵and King Solomon and the entire assembly of Israel that had gathered about him were before the ark, sacrificing^w so many sheep and cattle that they could not be recorded or counted.

⁶The priests then brought the ark of the LORD's covenant^x to its place in the inner sanctuary of the temple, the Most Holy Place,^y and put it beneath the wings of the cherubim.^z ⁷The cherubim spread their wings over the place of the ark and overshadowed^a the ark and its carrying poles. ⁸These poles were so long that their ends could be seen from the Holy Place in front of the inner sanctuary, but not from outside the Holy Place; and they

---

^w 35 That is, about 3/4 foot (about 0.2 meter) ^x 38 That is, about 230 gallons (about 880 liters)

are still there today.ᵇ ⁹There was nothing in the ark except the two stone tabletsᶜ that Moses had placed in it at Horeb, where the LORD made a covenant with the Israelites after they came out of Egypt.

¹⁰When the priests withdrew from the Holy Place, the cloudᵈ filled the temple of the LORD. ¹¹And the priests could not perform their serviceᵉ because of the cloud, for the gloryᶠ of the LORD filled his temple.

¹²Then Solomon said, "The LORD has said that he would dwell in a dark cloud;ᵍ ¹³I have indeed built a magnificent temple for you, a place for you to dwellʰ forever."

¹⁴While the whole assembly of Israel was standing there, the king turned around and blessedⁱ them. ¹⁵Then he said:

"Praise be to the LORD,ʲ the God of Israel, who with his own hand has fulfilled what he promised with his own mouth to my father David. For he said, ¹⁶'Since the day I brought my people Israel out of Egypt,ᵏ I have not chosen a city in any tribe of Israel to have a temple built for my Nameˡ to be there, but I have chosenᵐ Davidⁿ to rule my people Israel.'

¹⁷"My father David had it in his heartᵒ to build a templeᵖ for the Name of the LORD, the God of Israel. ¹⁸But the LORD said to my father David, 'Because it was in your heart to build a temple for my Name, you did well to have this in your heart. ¹⁹Nevertheless, youᵠ are not the one to build the temple, but your son, who is your own flesh and blood— he is the one who will build the temple for my Name.'ʳ

²⁰"The LORD has kept the promise he made: I have succeededˢ David my father and now I sit on the throne of Israel, just as the LORD promised, and I have builtᵗ the temple for the Name of the LORD, the God of Israel. ²¹I have provided a place there for the ark, in which is the covenant of the LORD that he made with our fathers when he brought them out of Egypt."

Solomon's Prayer of Dedication
8:22–53pp — 2Ch 6:12–40

²²Then Solomon stood before the altar of the LORD in front of the whole assembly of Israel, spread out his handsᵘ toward heaven ²³and said:

"O LORD, God of Israel, there is no God likeᵛ you in heaven above or on earth below—you who keep your covenant of loveʷ with your servants who continue wholeheartedly in your way. ²⁴You have kept your promise to your servant David my father; with your mouth you have promised and with your hand you have fulfilled it—as it is today.

²⁵"Now LORD, God of Israel, keep for your servant David my father the promisesˣ you made to him when you said, 'You shall never fail to have a man to sit before me on the throne of Israel, if only your sons are careful in all they do to walk before me as you have done.' ²⁶And now, O God of Israel, let your word that you promisedʸ your servant David my father come true.

²⁷"But will God really dwellᶻ on earth? The heavens, even the highest heaven,ᵃ cannot containᵇ you. How much less this temple I have built! ²⁸Yet give attention to your servant's prayer and his plea for mercy, O LORD my God. Hear the cry and the prayer that your servant is praying in your presence this day. ²⁹May your eyes be openᶜ towardᵈ this temple night and day, this place of which you said, 'My Nameᵉ shall be there,' so that you will hear the prayer your servant prays toward this place. ³⁰Hear the supplication of your servant and of your people Israel when they prayᶠ toward this place. Hearᵍ from heaven, your

---

8:29 Solomon asked God to graciously listen to the prayers of those who prayed to him when they were at the temple. Even today religious Jews worship and pray at the "wailing wall" in Jerusalem—the only surviving remnant of Solomon's temple—and insert written prayers in the cracks of the stones in this sacred, western wall.

dwelling place, and when you hear, forgive.[h]

31 "When a man wrongs his neighbor and is required to take an oath and he comes and swears the oath[i] before your altar in this temple, 32 then hear from heaven and act. Judge between your servants, condemning the guilty and bringing down on his own head what he has done. Declare the innocent not guilty, and so establish his innocence.[j]

33 "When your people Israel have been defeated[k] by an enemy because they have sinned[l] against you, and when they turn back to you and confess your name, praying and making supplication to you in this temple,[m] 34 then hear from heaven and forgive the sin of your people Israel and bring them back to the land you gave to their fathers.

35 "When the heavens are shut up and there is no rain[n] because your people have sinned[o] against you, and when they pray toward this place and confess your name and turn from their sin because you have afflicted them, 36 then hear from heaven and forgive the sin of your servants, your people Israel. Teach[p] them the right way[q] to live, and send rain[r] on the land you gave your people for an inheritance.

37 "When famine[s] or plague[t] comes to the land, or blight[u] or mildew, locusts or grasshoppers,[v] or when an enemy besieges them in any of their cities, whatever disaster or disease may come, 38 and when a prayer or plea is made by any of your people Israel—each one aware of the afflictions of his own heart, and spreading out his hands[w] toward this temple— 39 then hear[x] from heaven, your dwelling place. Forgive[y] and act; deal with each man according to all he does, since you know[z] his heart (for you alone know the hearts of all men), 40 so that they will fear[a] you all the time they live in the land[b] you gave our fathers.

41 "As for the foreigner[c] who does not belong to your people Israel but has come from a distant land because of your name— 42 for men will hear[d] of your great name and your mighty hand[e] and your outstretched arm—when he comes and prays toward this temple, 43 then hear from heaven, your dwelling place, and do whatever the foreigner asks of you, so that all the peoples of the earth may know[f] your name and fear[g] you, as do your own people Israel, and may know that this house I have built bears your Name.[h]

44 "When your people go to war against their enemies, wherever you send them, and when they pray[i] to the LORD toward the city you have chosen and the temple I have built for your Name, 45 then hear from heaven their prayer and their plea, and uphold their cause.[j]

46 "When they sin against you—for there is no one who does not sin[k]—and you become angry with them and give them over to the enemy, who takes them captive[l] to his own land, far away or near; 47 and if they have a change of heart in the land where they are held captive, and repent and plead[m] with you in the land of their conquerors and say, 'We have sinned, we have done wrong, we have acted wickedly';[n] 48 and if they turn back[o] to you with all their heart[p] and soul in the land of their enemies who took them captive, and pray[q] to you toward the land you gave their fathers, toward the city you have chosen and the temple[r] I have built for your Name;[s] 49 then from heaven, your dwelling place, hear their prayer and their plea, and uphold their cause. 50 And forgive your people, who have sinned against you; forgive all the offenses they have committed against you, and cause their conquerors to show them mercy;[t] 51 for they are your people and your inheritance,[u] whom you brought out of Egypt, out of that iron-smelting furnace.[v]

52 "May your eyes be open[w] to your servant's plea and to the plea of your people Israel, and may you listen to

them whenever they cry out to you.ˣ ⁵³For you singled them out from all the nations of the world to be your own inheritance,ʸ just as you declared through your servant Moses when you, O Sovereign LORD, brought our fathers out of Egypt."

⁵⁴When Solomon had finished all these prayers and supplications to the LORD, he rose up from before the altar of the LORD, where he had been kneeling with his hands spread out toward heaven. ⁵⁵He stood and blessedᶻ the whole assembly of Israel in a loud voice, saying:

⁵⁶"Praise be to the LORD, who has given restᵃ to his people Israel just as he promised. Not one word has failed of all the good promisesᵇ he gave through his servant Moses. ⁵⁷May the LORD our God be with us as he was with our fathers; may he never leave us nor forsakeᶜ us. ⁵⁸May he turn our heartsᵈ to him, to walk in all his ways and to keep the commands, decrees and regulations he gave our fathers. ⁵⁹And may these words of mine, which I have prayed before the LORD, be near to the LORD our God day and night, that he may uphold the cause of his servant and the cause of his people Israel according to each day's need, ⁶⁰so that all the peoplesᵉ of the earth may know that the LORD is God and that there is no other.ᶠ ⁶¹But your heartsᵍ must be fully committedʰ to the LORD our God, to live by his decrees and obey his commands, as at this time."

The Dedication of the Temple
8:62–66pp — 2Ch 7:1–10

⁶²Then the king and all Israel with him offered sacrificesⁱ before the LORD. ⁶³Solomon offered a sacrifice of fellowship offeringsʸ to the LORD: twenty-two thousand cattle and a hundred and twenty thousand sheep and goats. So the king and all the Israelites dedicatedʲ the temple of the LORD.

o 2Sa 22:32 ◀ ▶ 1Ch 17:20
s 2Sa 22:21-27 ◀ ▶ 1Ki 18:21

8:52 ˣJob 30:20; Ps 3:4; 22:2; 77:1; 142:1
8:53 ʸEx 19:5; S 34:9
8:55 ᶻS Ex 39:43; Nu 6:23
8:56 ᵃS Ex 33:14; Dt 12:10; Heb 4:8
ᵇS Jos 23:15; S Jer 29:10
8:57 ᶜS Dt 4:31; S 31:6; S Mt 28:20; Heb 13:5
8:58 ᵈS Jos 24:23
8:60 ᵉS Jos 4:24
ᶠS Dt 4:35
8:61 ᵍDt 6:5
ʰ1Ki 9:4; 11:4; 15:3,14; 22:43; 2Ki 20:3; 1Ch 28:9; 29:19; 2Ch 16:9; 17:6; 25:2; Ps 119:80; Isa 38:3
8:62 ⁱS 2Sa 6:13; 1Ch 29:21; Eze 45:17
8:63 ʲEzr 6:16
8:64 ᵏS Ex 29:13
ˡS Ex 27:1; 2Ki 16:14; 2Ch 4:1; 8:12; 15:8; Eze 43:13-17
ᵐS 2Sa 6:17
8:65 ⁿS ver 2
ᵒS Nu 13:21
ᵖS Ge 15:18
8:66 ᵠS Ex 18:9
9:1 ʳS 2Sa 7:2
9:2 ˢS 1Ki 3:5
9:3 ᵗS 1Sa 9:16; 2Ki 19:20; 20:5; Ps 10:17; 34:17
ᵘS Ex 20:24; S Dt 12:5
ᵛS Dt 11:12
9:4 ʷS Ge 17:1
ˣDt 17:20; 1Ki 14:8; 15:5
ʸS 1Ki 3:14; 1Ch 28:9; Pr 4:4
9:5 ᶻ1Ch 22:10
ᵃS 2Sa 7:15
9:6 ᵇDt 28:15; 2Sa 7:14; 2Ki 18:12; Jer 17:27; 26:4; 32:23; 44:23

⁶⁴On that same day the king consecrated the middle part of the courtyard in front of the temple of the LORD, and there he offered burnt offerings, grain offerings and the fatᵏ of the fellowship offerings, because the bronze altarˡ before the LORD was too small to hold the burnt offerings, the grain offerings and the fat of the fellowship offerings.ᵐ

⁶⁵So Solomon observed the festivalⁿ at that time, and all Israel with him—a vast assembly, people from Leboᶻ Hamathᵒ to the Wadi of Egypt.ᵖ They celebrated it before the LORD our God for seven days and seven days more, fourteen days in all. ⁶⁶On the following day he sent the people away. They blessed the king and then went home, joyful and glad in heart for all the goodᵠ things the LORD had done for his servant David and his people Israel.

The LORD Appears to Solomon
9:1–9pp — 2Ch 7:11–22

9 When Solomon had finishedʳ building the temple of the LORD and the royal palace, and had achieved all he had desired to do, ²the LORD appearedˢ to him a second time, as he had appeared to him at Gibeon. ³The LORD said to him:

"I have heardᵗ the prayer and plea you have made before me; I have consecrated this temple, which you have built, by putting my Nameᵘ there forever. My eyesᵛ and my heart will always be there.

⁴"As for you, if you walk before me in integrity of heartʷ and uprightness, as Davidˣ your father did, and do all I command and observe my decrees and laws,ʸ ⁵I will establishᶻ your royal throne over Israel forever, as I promised David your father when I said, 'You shall never failᵃ to have a man on the throne of Israel.'

⁶"But if youᵃ or your sonsᵇ turn away from me and do not observe the commands and decrees I have

l 1Ki 5:5 ◀ ▶ 1Ki 18:1
R Jos 23:15–16 ◀ ▶ 1Ki 9:7–8

ʸ 63 Traditionally *peace offerings*; also in verse 64   ᶻ 65 Or *from the entrance to*   ᵃ 6 The Hebrew is plural.

9:3 God proclaimed his intent toward the temple to "[put] my Name there forever." This is why orthodox Jews believe they must rebuild the temple on the same site as Solomon's temple.

9:6–9 This prophecy of the future desolation of the temple would come to pass if Israel turned from

given you[b] and go off to serve other gods[c] and worship them, [7]then I will cut off Israel from the land[d] I have given them and will reject this temple I have consecrated for my Name.[e] Israel will then become a byword[f] and an object of ridicule[g] among all peoples. [8]And though this temple is now imposing, all who pass by will be appalled[h] and will scoff and say, 'Why has the LORD done such a thing to this land and to this temple?'[i] [9]People will answer,[j] 'Because they have forsaken[k] the LORD their God, who brought their fathers out of Egypt, and have embraced other gods, worshiping and serving them—that is why the LORD brought all this disaster[l] on them.' "

Solomon's Other Activities
9:10–28pp — 2Ch 8:1–18

[10]At the end of twenty years, during which Solomon built these two buildings—the temple of the LORD and the royal palace— [11]King Solomon gave twenty towns in Galilee to Hiram king of Tyre, because Hiram had supplied him with all the cedar and pine and gold[m] he wanted. [12]But when Hiram went from Tyre to see the towns that Solomon had given him, he was not pleased with them. [13]"What kind of towns are these you have given me, my brother?" he asked. And he called them the Land of Cabul,[cn] a name they have to this day. [14]Now Hiram had sent to the king 120 talents[d] of gold.[o]

[15]Here is the account of the forced labor King Solomon conscripted[p] to build the LORD's temple, his own palace, the supporting terraces,[eq] the wall of Jerusalem, and Hazor,[r] Megiddo and Gezer.[s] [16](Pharaoh king of Egypt had attacked and captured Gezer. He had set it on fire. He killed its Canaanite inhabitants and then gave it as a wedding gift to his daughter,[t] Solomon's wife. [17]And Solomon rebuilt Gezer.) He built up Lower Beth Horon,[u] [18]Baalath,[v] and Tadmor[f] in the desert, within his land, [19]as well as all his store cities[w] and the towns for his chariots[x] and for his horses[g]—whatever he desired to build in Jerusalem, in Lebanon and throughout all the territory he ruled.

[20]All the people left from the Amorites, Hittites,[y] Perizzites, Hivites and Jebusites[z] (these peoples were not Israelites), [21]that is, their descendants[a] remaining in the land, whom the Israelites could not exterminate[hb]—these Solomon conscripted for his slave labor force,[c] as it is to this day. [22]But Solomon did not make slaves[d] of any of the Israelites; they were his fighting men, his government officials, his officers, his captains, and the commanders of his chariots and charioteers. [23]They were also the chief officials[e] in charge of Solomon's projects—550 officials supervising the men who did the work.

[24]After Pharaoh's daughter[f] had come up from the City of David to the palace Solomon had built for her, he constructed the supporting terraces.[g]

[25]Three[h] times a year Solomon sacrificed burnt offerings and fellowship offerings[i] on the altar he had built for the LORD, burning incense before the LORD along with them, and so fulfilled the temple obligations.

[26]King Solomon also built ships[i] at Ezion Geber,[j] which is near Elath[k] in Edom, on the shore of the Red Sea.[j] [27]And Hiram sent his men—sailors[l] who knew the sea—to serve in the fleet with Solomon's men. [28]They sailed to Ophir[m] and brought back 420 talents[k] of gold,[n] which they delivered to King Solomon.

The Queen of Sheba Visits Solomon
10:1–13pp — 2Ch 9:1–12

10 When the queen of Sheba[o] heard about the fame[p] of Solomon and his relation to the name of the LORD, she came to test him with hard questions.[q] [2]Arriving at Jerusalem with a very great

---

[b] 6 The Hebrew is plural. [c] 13 Cabul sounds like the Hebrew for good-for-nothing. [d] 14 That is, about 4 1/2 tons (about 4 metric tons) [e] 15 Or the Millo; also in verse 24 [f] 18 The Hebrew may also be read Tamar. [g] 19 Or charioteers [h] 21 The Hebrew term refers to the irrevocable giving over of things or persons to the LORD, often by totally destroying them. [i] 25 Traditionally peace offerings [j] 26 Hebrew Yam Suph; that is, Sea of Reeds [k] 28 That is, about 16 tons (about 14.5 metric tons)

R 1Ki 9:6–9 ◄► 1Ki 11:11

worshiping the true God to "go off to serve other gods" (9:6). Such destruction would stand as a witness to other nations of Israel's rebellion and God's punishment for their sins.

caravan—with camels carrying spices, large quantities of gold, and precious stones—she came to Solomon and talked with him about all that she had on her mind. ³Solomon answered all her questions; nothing was too hard for the king to explain to her. ⁴When the queen of Sheba saw all the wisdom of Solomon and the palace he had built, ⁵the food on his table, the seating of his officials, the attending servants in their robes, his cupbearers, and the burnt offerings he made at the temple of the LORD, she was overwhelmed.

⁶She said to the king, "The report I heard in my own country about your achievements and your wisdom is true. ⁷But I did not believe these things until I came and saw with my own eyes. Indeed, not even half was told me; in wisdom and wealth you have far exceeded the report I heard. ⁸How happy your men must be! How happy your officials, who continually stand before you and hear your wisdom! ⁹Praise be to the LORD your God, who has delighted in you and placed you on the throne of Israel. Because of the LORD's eternal love for Israel, he has made you king, to maintain justice and righteousness."

¹⁰And she gave the king 120 talents of gold, large quantities of spices, and precious stones. Never again were so many spices brought in as those the queen of Sheba gave to King Solomon.

¹¹(Hiram's ships brought gold from Ophir; and from there they brought great cargoes of almugwood and precious stones. ¹²The king used the almugwood to make supports for the temple of the LORD and for the royal palace, and to make harps and lyres for the musicians. So much almugwood has never been imported or seen since that day.)

¹³King Solomon gave the queen of Sheba all she desired and asked for, besides what he had given her out of his royal bounty. Then she left and returned with her retinue to her own country.

Solomon's Splendor
10:14–29pp — 2Ch 1:14–17; 9:13–28

¹⁴The weight of the gold that Solomon received yearly was 666 talents, ¹⁵not including the revenues from merchants and traders and from all the Arabian kings and the governors of the land.

¹⁶King Solomon made two hundred large shields of hammered gold; six hundred bekas of gold went into each shield. ¹⁷He also made three hundred small shields of hammered gold, with three minas of gold in each shield. The king put them in the Palace of the Forest of Lebanon.

¹⁸Then the king made a great throne inlaid with ivory and overlaid with fine gold. ¹⁹The throne had six steps, and its back had a rounded top. On both sides of the seat were armrests, with a lion standing beside each of them. ²⁰Twelve lions stood on the six steps, one at either end of each step. Nothing like it had ever been made for any other kingdom. ²¹All King Solomon's goblets were gold, and all the household articles in the Palace of the Forest of Lebanon were pure gold. Nothing was made of silver, because silver was considered of little value in Solomon's days. ²²The king had a fleet of trading ships at sea along with the ships of Hiram. Once every three years it returned, carrying gold, silver and ivory, and apes and baboons.

²³King Solomon was greater in riches and wisdom than all the other kings of the earth. ²⁴The whole world sought audience with Solomon to hear the wisdom God had put in his heart. ²⁵Year after year, everyone who came brought a gift—articles of silver and gold, robes, weapons and spices, and horses and mules.

²⁶Solomon accumulated chariots and horses; he had fourteen hundred chariots and twelve thousand horses, which he kept in the chariot cities and also with him in Jerusalem. ²⁷The king made silver as common in Jerusalem as stones, and cedar as plentiful as sycamore-fig trees in the foothills. ²⁸Solomon's horses were imported from Egypt and from Kue— the royal merchants purchased them from Kue. ²⁹They imported a chariot from Egypt for six hundred shekels of silver, and a horse for a hundred and fifty. They

also exported them to all the kings of the Hittites[p] and of the Arameans.

Solomon's Wives

11 King Solomon, however, loved many foreign women[q] besides Pharaoh's daughter—Moabites, Ammonites,[r] Edomites, Sidonians and Hittites. [2]They were from nations about which the LORD had told the Israelites, "You must not intermarry[s] with them, because they will surely turn your hearts after their gods." Nevertheless, Solomon held fast to them in love. [3]He had seven hundred wives of royal birth and three hundred concubines,[t] and his wives led him astray.[u] [4]As Solomon grew old, his wives turned his heart after other gods,[v] and his heart was not fully devoted[w] to the LORD his God, as the heart of David his father had been. [5]He followed Ashtoreth[x] the goddess of the Sidonians, and Molech[w][y] the detestable god of the Ammonites. [6]So Solomon did evil[z] in the eyes of the LORD; he did not follow the LORD completely, as David his father had done.

[7]On a hill east[a] of Jerusalem, Solomon built a high place for Chemosh,[b] the detestable god of Moab, and for Molech[c] the detestable god of the Ammonites. [8]He did the same for all his foreign wives, who burned incense and offered sacrifices to their gods.

[9]The LORD became angry with Solomon because his heart had turned away from the LORD, the God of Israel, who had appeared[d] to him twice. [10]Although he had forbidden Solomon to follow other gods,[e] Solomon did not keep the LORD's command.[f] [11]So the LORD said to Solomon, "Since this is your attitude and you have not kept my covenant and my decrees,[g] which I commanded you, I will most certainly tear[h] the kingdom away from you and give it to one of your subordinates. [12]Nevertheless, for the sake of David[i] your father, I will not do it during your lifetime. I will tear it out of the hand of your son. [13]Yet I will not tear the whole kingdom from him, but will give him one tribe[j] for the sake[k] of David my servant and for the sake of Jerusalem, which I have chosen."[l]

Solomon's Adversaries

[14]Then the LORD raised up against Solomon an adversary,[m] Hadad the Edomite, from the royal line of Edom. [15]Earlier when David was fighting with Edom, Joab the commander of the army, who had gone up to bury the dead, had struck down all the men in Edom.[n] [16]Joab and all the Israelites stayed there for six months, until they had destroyed all the men in Edom. [17]But Hadad, still only a boy, fled to Egypt with some Edomite officials who had served his father. [18]They set out from Midian and went to Paran.[o] Then taking men from Paran with them, they went to Egypt, to Pharaoh king of Egypt, who gave Hadad a house and land and provided him with food.

[19]Pharaoh was so pleased with Hadad that he gave him a sister of his own wife, Queen Tahpenes, in marriage. [20]The sister of Tahpenes bore him a son named Genubath, whom Tahpenes brought up in the royal palace. There Genubath lived with Pharaoh's own children.

[21]While he was in Egypt, Hadad heard that David rested with his fathers and that Joab the commander of the army was also dead. Then Hadad said to Pharaoh, "Let me go, that I may return to my own country."

[22]"What have you lacked here that you want to go back to your own country?" Pharaoh asked.

"Nothing," Hadad replied, "but do let me go!"

[23]And God raised up against Solomon another adversary,[p] Rezon son of Eliada, who had fled from his master, Hadadezer[q] king of Zobah. [24]He gathered men around him and became the leader of a band of rebels when David destroyed the forces[x] of Zobah; the rebels went to Damascus,[r] where they settled and took control. [25]Rezon was Israel's adversary as

---

10:29
p S Nu 13:29

11:1 q S ver 3; S Ex 34:16
r 1Ki 14:21,31

11:2 s S Ex 34:16; 1Ki 16:31

11:3 t S Ge 22:24; S Est 2:14 u ver 1; Dt 17:17; Ne 13:26; Pr 31:3

11:4 v S Ex 34:16 w S 1Ki 8:61; S 1Ch 29:19

11:5 x S Jdg 2:13 y ver 7; S Lev 18:21; Isa 57:9; Zep 1:5

11:6 z S Dt 4:25

11:7 a 2Ki 23:13 b S Nu 21:29 c S Lev 18:21; 20:2-5; Ac 7:43

11:9 d S 1Ki 3:5

11:10 e S 1Ki 9:6 f 1Ki 6:12

11:11 g S Lev 18:4 h ver 31; S 1Sa 15:27; 2Ki 17:21; Mt 21:43

11:12 i Ps 89:33

11:13 j 1Ki 12:20 k S 2Sa 7:15 l Dt 12:11

11:14 m S 1Ki 5:4

11:15 n 1Ch 18:12

11:18 o Nu 10:12

11:23 p S 1Ki 5:4 q S 2Sa 8:3

11:24 r S 2Sa 8:5

R 1Ki 9:7-8 ◀▶ 1Ki 11:30-31

w 5 Hebrew *Milcom*; also in verse 33 x 24 Hebrew *destroyed them*

11:11–13 King Solomon's apostasy in the final years of his reign caused God to declare that he would "most certainly tear the kingdom away from you" (11:11). Yet God's profound love for Solomon's father, David, delayed this judgment until after Solomon's death and allowed Solomon's son Rehoboam to retain rule over Jerusalem and the tribes of Judah.

long as Solomon lived, adding to the trouble caused by Hadad. So Rezon ruled in Aram[s] and was hostile toward Israel.

Jeroboam Rebels Against Solomon

[26]Also, Jeroboam son of Nebat rebelled[t] against the king. He was one of Solomon's officials, an Ephraimite from Zeredah, and his mother was a widow named Zeruah.

[27]Here is the account of how he rebelled against the king: Solomon had built the supporting terraces[y,u] and had filled in the gap in the wall of the city of David his father. [28]Now Jeroboam was a man of standing,[v] and when Solomon saw how well[w] the young man did his work, he put him in charge of the whole labor force of the house of Joseph.

[29]About that time Jeroboam was going out of Jerusalem, and Ahijah[x] the prophet of Shiloh met him on the way, wearing a new cloak. The two of them were alone out in the country, [30]and Ahijah took hold of the new cloak he was wearing and tore[y] it into twelve pieces. [31]Then he said to Jeroboam, "Take ten pieces for yourself, for this is what the LORD, the God of Israel, says: 'See, I am going to tear[z] the kingdom out of Solomon's hand and give you ten tribes. [32]But for the sake[a] of my servant David and the city of Jerusalem, which I have chosen out of all the tribes of Israel, he will have one tribe. [33]I will do this because they have[z] forsaken me and worshiped[b] Ashtoreth the goddess of the Sidonians, Chemosh the god of the Moabites, and Molech the god of the Ammonites, and have not walked[c] in my ways, nor done what is right in my eyes, nor kept my statutes[d] and laws as David, Solomon's father, did.

[34]" 'But I will not take the whole kingdom out of Solomon's hand; I have made him ruler all the days of his life for the sake of David my servant, whom I chose and who observed my commands and statutes. [35]I will take the kingdom from his son's hands and give you ten tribes.

R 1Ki 11:11 ◀ ▶ 1Ki 13:2–3

11:25 [s] S Ge 10:22; S 2Sa 10:19
11:26 [t] 2Ch 13:6
11:27 [u] S 1Ki 9:24
11:28 [v] S Ru 2:1 [w] S Ge 39:4; Pr 22:29
11:29 [x] 1Ki 12:15; 14:2; 2Ch 9:29; 10:15
11:30 [y] 1Sa 15:27
11:31 [z] S ver 11; S 1Sa 15:27
11:32 [a] S 2Sa 7:15
11:33 [b] S Jdg 2:13 [c] 2Ki 21:22 [d] 1Ki 3:3
11:36 [e] 1Ki 12:17 [f] S 2Sa 21:17
11:37 [g] S 1Ki 14:7 [h] 2Sa 3:21
11:38 [i] S Dt 12:25; S 2Sa 8:15 [j] S Dt 17:19 [k] S Ex 1:21
11:40 [l] 1Ki 12:2; 2Ch 10:2 [m] 2Ch 12:2
11:43 [n] Mt 1:7
12:1 [o] ver 25; S Ge 12:6; Jos 24:32
12:2 [p] S 1Ki 11:40
12:4 [q] S 1Sa 8:11-18; 1Ki 4:20-28

[36]I will give one tribe[e] to his son so that David my servant may always have a lamp[f] before me in Jerusalem, the city where I chose to put my Name. [37]However, as for you, I will take you, and you will rule[g] over all that your heart desires;[h] you will be king over Israel. [38]If you do whatever I command you and walk in my ways and do what is right[i] in my eyes by keeping my statutes[j] and commands, as David my servant did, I will be with you. I will build you a dynasty[k] as enduring as the one I built for David and will give Israel to you. [39]I will humble David's descendants because of this, but not forever.' "

[40]Solomon tried to kill Jeroboam, but Jeroboam fled[l] to Egypt, to Shishak[m] the king, and stayed there until Solomon's death.

Solomon's Death
11:41–43pp — 2Ch 9:29–31

[41]As for the other events of Solomon's reign—all he did and the wisdom he displayed—are they not written in the book of the annals of Solomon? [42]Solomon reigned in Jerusalem over all Israel forty years. [43]Then he rested with his fathers and was buried in the city of David his father. And Rehoboam[n] his son succeeded him as king.

Israel Rebels Against Rehoboam
12:1–24pp — 2Ch 10:1–11:4

12 Rehoboam went to Shechem,[o] for all the Israelites had gone there to make him king. [2]When Jeroboam son of Nebat heard this (he was still in Egypt, where he had fled[p] from King Solomon), he returned from[a] Egypt. [3]So they sent for Jeroboam, and he and the whole assembly of Israel went to Rehoboam and said to him: [4]"Your father put a heavy yoke[q] on us, but now lighten the harsh labor and the heavy yoke he put on us, and we will serve you."

[y] 27 Or *the Millo*   [z] 33 Hebrew; Septuagint, Vulgate and Syriac *because he has*   [a] 2 Or *he remained in*

11:28–32 God arranged the meeting of the prophet Ahijah and Jeroboam, governor over the territory of the tribe of Joseph. Ahijah acted out a symbolic prophecy by ripping his garment into twelve pieces. After giving Jeroboam ten pieces, the prophet Ahijah prophesied that God would "tear the kingdom out of Solomon's hand"(11:31) and give the leadership of the ten tribes to Jeroboam. Ahijah reaffirmed that two tribes would remain loyal to the house of David.

⁵Rehoboam answered, "Go away for three days and then come back to me." So the people went away.

⁶Then King Rehoboam consulted the eldersʳ who had served his father Solomon during his lifetime. "How would you advise me to answer these people?" he asked.

⁷They replied, "If today you will be a servant to these people and serve them and give them a favorable answer,ˢ they will always be your servants."

⁸But Rehoboam rejectedᵗ the advice the elders gave him and consulted the young men who had grown up with him and were serving him. ⁹He asked them, "What is your advice? How should we answer these people who say to me, 'Lighten the yoke your father put on us'?"

¹⁰The young men who had grown up with him replied, "Tell these people who have said to you, 'Your father put a heavy yoke on us, but make our yoke lighter'—tell them, 'My little finger is thicker than my father's waist. ¹¹My father laid on you a heavy yoke; I will make it even heavier. My father scourged you with whips; I will scourge you with scorpions.' "

¹²Three days later Jeroboam and all the people returned to Rehoboam, as the king had said, "Come back to me in three days." ¹³The king answered the people harshly. Rejecting the advice given him by the elders, ¹⁴he followed the advice of the young men and said, "My father made your yoke heavy; I will make it even heavier. My father scourgedᵘ you with whips; I will scourge you with scorpions." ¹⁵So the king did not listen to the people, for this turn of events was from the LORD,ᵛ to fulfill the word the LORD had spoken to Jeroboam son of Nebat through Ahijahʷ the Shilonite.

¹⁶When all Israel saw that the king refused to listen to them, they answered the king:

"What shareˣ do we have in David,
  what part in Jesse's son?
To your tents, O Israel!ʸ
Look after your own house,
  O David!"

So the Israelites went home.ᶻ ¹⁷But as for the Israelites who were living in the towns of Judah,ᵃ Rehoboam still ruled over them.

¹⁸King Rehoboam sent out Adoniram,ᵇᵇ who was in charge of forced labor, but all Israel stoned him to death.ᶜ King Rehoboam, however, managed to get into his chariot and escape to Jerusalem. ¹⁹So Israel has been in rebellion against the house of Davidᵈ to this day.

²⁰When all the Israelites heard that Jeroboam had returned, they sent and called him to the assembly and made him king over all Israel. Only the tribe of Judah remained loyal to the house of David.ᵉ

²¹When Rehoboam arrived in Jerusalem, he mustered the whole house of Judah and the tribe of Benjamin—a hundred and eighty thousand fighting men—to make warᶠ against the house of Israel and to regain the kingdom for Rehoboam son of Solomon.

²²But this word of God came to Shemaiahᵍ the man of God:ʰ ²³"Say to Rehoboam son of Solomon king of Judah, to the whole house of Judah and Benjamin, and to the rest of the people, ²⁴'This is what the LORD says: Do not go up to fight against your brothers, the Israelites. Go home, every one of you, for this is my doing.' " So they obeyed the word of the LORD and went home again, as the LORD had ordered.

Golden Calves at Bethel and Dan

²⁵Then Jeroboam fortified Shechemⁱ in the hill country of Ephraim and lived there. From there he went out and built up Peniel.ᶜʲ

²⁶Jeroboam thought to himself, "The kingdom will now likely revert to the house of David. ²⁷If these people go up to offer sacrifices at the temple of the LORD in Jerusalem,ᵏ they will again give their allegiance to their lord, Rehoboam king of Judah. They will kill me and return to King Rehoboam."

²⁸After seeking advice, the king made two golden calves.ˡ He said to the people, "It is too much for you to go up to Jerusalem. Here are your gods, O Israel, who brought you up out of Egypt."ᵐ ²⁹One he set up in Bethel,ⁿ and the other in Dan.ᵒ ³⁰And this thing became a sin;ᵖ the people went even as far as Dan to worship the one there.

³¹Jeroboam built shrinesᵠ on high

ᵇ 18 Some Septuagint manuscripts and Syriac (see also 1 Kings 4:6 and 5:14); Hebrew *Adoram* ᶜ 25 Hebrew *Penuel*, a variant of *Peniel*

places and appointed priests from all sorts of people, even though they were not Levites. ³²He instituted a festival on the fifteenth day of the eighth month, like the festival held in Judah, and offered sacrifices on the altar. This he did in Bethel, sacrificing to the calves he had made. And at Bethel he also installed priests at the high places he had made. ³³On the fifteenth day of the eighth month, a month of his own choosing, he offered sacrifices on the altar he had built at Bethel. So he instituted the festival for the Israelites and went up to the altar to make offerings.

The Man of God From Judah

13 By the word of the LORD a man of God came from Judah to Bethel, as Jeroboam was standing by the altar to make an offering. ²He cried out against the altar by the word of the LORD: "O altar, altar! This is what the LORD says: 'A son named Josiah will be born to the house of David. On you he will sacrifice the priests of the high places who now make offerings here, and human bones will be burned on you.'" ³That same day the man of God gave a sign: "This is the sign the LORD has declared: The altar will be split apart and the ashes on it will be poured out."

⁴When King Jeroboam heard what the man of God cried out against the altar at Bethel, he stretched out his hand from the altar and said, "Seize him!" But the hand he stretched out toward the man shriveled up, so that he could not pull it back. ⁵Also, the altar was split apart and its ashes poured out according to the sign given by the man of God by the word of the LORD.

⁶Then the king said to the man of God, "Intercede with the LORD your God and pray for me that my hand may be restored." So the man of God interceded with the LORD, and the king's hand was restored and became as it was before.

⁷The king said to the man of God, "Come home with me and have something to eat, and I will give you a gift."

⁸But the man of God answered the king, "Even if you were to give me half your possessions, I would not go with you, nor would I eat bread or drink water here. ⁹For I was commanded by the word of the LORD: 'You must not eat bread or drink water or return by the way you came.'" ¹⁰So he took another road and did not return by the way he had come to Bethel.

¹¹Now there was a certain old prophet living in Bethel, whose sons came and told him all that the man of God had done there that day. They also told their father what he had said to the king. ¹²Their father asked them, "Which way did he go?" And his sons showed him which road the man of God from Judah had taken. ¹³So he said to his sons, "Saddle the donkey for me." And when they had saddled the donkey for him, he mounted it ¹⁴and rode after the man of God. He found him sitting under an oak tree and asked, "Are you the man of God who came from Judah?"

"I am," he replied.

¹⁵So the prophet said to him, "Come home with me and eat."

¹⁶The man of God said, "I cannot turn back and go with you, nor can I eat bread or drink water with you in this place. ¹⁷I have been told by the word of the LORD: 'You must not eat bread or drink water there or return by the way you came.'"

¹⁸The old prophet answered, "I too am a prophet, as you are. And an angel said to me by the word of the LORD: 'Bring him back with you to your house so that he may eat bread and drink water.'" (But he was lying to him.) ¹⁹So the man of God returned with him and ate and drank in his house.

²⁰While they were sitting at the table, the word of the LORD came to the old

R 1Ki 11:30–31 ◀ ▶ 1Ki 13:22
D 1Sa 25:38 ◀ ▶ 1Ki 14:12–13
E 2Sa 24:25 ◀ ▶ 1Ki 17:22–24

13:1–3 An unnamed prophet of God from Judah came to Bethel to confront King Jeroboam. Jeroboam had sinfully created two golden calves for the Israelites to worship rather than have them travel south to Jerusalem to worship God (see 12:28). The man of God prophesied that a descendant of David named Josiah would destroy this idol worship by sacrificing the bodies of the idolatrous priests on their idolatrous altar. Three centuries later King Josiah fulfilled this prophecy (see 2Ki 23:1–15).

prophet who had brought him back. ²¹He cried out to the man of God who had come from Judah, "This is what the LORD says: 'You have defied the word of the LORD and have not kept the command the LORD your God gave you. ²²You came back and ate bread and drank water in the place where he told you not to eat or drink. Therefore your body will not be buried in the tomb of your fathers.'"

²³When the man of God had finished eating and drinking, the prophet who had brought him back saddled his donkey for him. ²⁴As he went on his way, a lion met him on the road and killed him, and his body was thrown down on the road, with both the donkey and the lion standing beside it. ²⁵Some people who passed by saw the body thrown down there, with the lion standing beside the body, and they went and reported it in the city where the old prophet lived.

²⁶When the prophet who had brought him back from his journey heard of it, he said, "It is the man of God who defied the word of the LORD. The LORD has given him over to the lion, which has mauled him and killed him, as the word of the LORD had warned him."

²⁷The prophet said to his sons, "Saddle the donkey for me," and they did so. ²⁸Then he went out and found the body thrown down on the road, with the donkey and the lion standing beside it. The lion had neither eaten the body nor mauled the donkey. ²⁹So the prophet picked up the body of the man of God, laid it on the donkey, and brought it back to his own city to mourn for him and bury him. ³⁰Then he laid the body in his own tomb, and they mourned over him and said, "Oh, my brother!"

³¹After burying him, he said to his sons, "When I die, bury me in the grave where the man of God is buried; lay my bones beside his bones. ³²For the message he declared by the word of the LORD against the altar in Bethel and against all the shrines on the high places in the towns of Samaria will certainly come true."

³³Even after this, Jeroboam did not change his evil ways, but once more appointed priests for the high places from all sorts of people. Anyone who wanted to become a priest he consecrated for the high places. ³⁴This was the sin of the house of Jeroboam that led to its downfall and to its destruction from the face of the earth.

Ahijah's Prophecy Against Jeroboam

14 At that time Abijah son of Jeroboam became ill, ²and Jeroboam said to his wife, "Go, disguise yourself, so you won't be recognized as the wife of Jeroboam. Then go to Shiloh. Ahijah the prophet is there—the one who told me I would be king over this people. ³Take ten loaves of bread with you, some cakes and a jar of honey, and go to him. He will tell you what will happen to the boy." ⁴So Jeroboam's wife did what he said and went to Ahijah's house in Shiloh.

Now Ahijah could not see; his sight was gone because of his age. ⁵But the LORD had told Ahijah, "Jeroboam's wife is coming to ask you about her son, for he is ill, and you are to give her such and such an answer. When she arrives, she will pretend to be someone else."

⁶So when Ahijah heard the sound of her footsteps at the door, he said, "Come in, wife of Jeroboam. Why this pretense? I have been sent to you with bad news. ⁷Go, tell Jeroboam that this is what the LORD, the God of Israel, says: 'I raised you up from among the people and made you a leader over my people Israel. ⁸I tore the kingdom away from the house of David and gave it to you, but you have not been like my servant David, who kept my commands and followed me with all his heart, doing only what was right in my eyes. ⁹You have done more evil than all who lived before you. You have made for yourself other gods, idols made of metal; you have provoked me to anger and thrust me behind your back.

¹⁰"'Because of this, I am going to bring

14:10–16 The prophet Ahijah, who earlier prophesied to Jeroboam that he would become king of Israel, now came to the king and announced that all his descendants would die without honor because

disasterg on the house of Jeroboam. I will cut off from Jeroboam every last male in Israel—slave or free.h I will burn up the house of Jeroboam as one burns dung, until it is all gone.i ¹¹Dogsj will eat those belonging to Jeroboam who die in the city, and the birds of the airk will feed on those who die in the country. The LORD has spoken!'

¹²"As for you, go back home. When you set foot in your city, the boy will die. ¹³All Israel will mourn for him and bury him. He is the only one belonging to Jeroboam who will be buried, because he is the only one in the house of Jeroboam in whom the LORD, the God of Israel, has found anything good.l

¹⁴"The LORD will raise up for himself a king over Israel who will cut off the family of Jeroboam. This is the day! What? Yes, even now.d ¹⁵And the LORD will strike Israel, so that it will be like a reed swaying in the water. He will uprootm Israel from this good land that he gave to their forefathers and scatter them beyond the River,e because they provokedn the LORD to anger by making Asheraho poles. ¹⁶And he will give Israel up because of the sinsp Jeroboam has committed and has caused Israel to commit."

¹⁷Then Jeroboam's wife got up and left and went to Tirzah.q As soon as she stepped over the threshold of the house, the boy died. ¹⁸They buried him, and all Israel mourned for him, as the LORD had said through his servant the prophet Ahijah.

¹⁹The other events of Jeroboam's reign, his wars and how he ruled, are written in the book of the annals of the kings of Israel. ²⁰He reigned for twenty-two years and then rested with his fathers. And Nadab his son succeeded him as king.

Rehoboam King of Judah
14:21,25–31pp — 2Ch 12:9–16

²¹Rehoboam son of Solomon was king in Judah. He was forty-one years old when he became king, and he reigned seventeen years in Jerusalem, the city the LORD had chosen out of all the tribes of Israel in which to put his Name. His mother's name was Naamah; she was an Ammonite.r

²²Judahs did evil in the eyes of the LORD. By the sins they committed they stirred up his jealous angert more than their fathers had done. ²³They also set up for themselves high places, sacred stonesu and Asherah polesv on every high hill and under every spreading tree.w ²⁴There were even male shrine prostitutesx in the land; the people engaged in all the detestabley practices of the nations the LORD had driven out before the Israelites.

²⁵In the fifth year of King Rehoboam, Shishak king of Egypt attackedz Jerusalem. ²⁶He carried off the treasures of the templea of the LORD and the treasures of the royal palace. He took everything, including all the gold shieldsb Solomon had made. ²⁷So King Rehoboam made bronze shields to replace them and assigned these to the commanders of the guard on duty at the entrance to the royal palace.c ²⁸Whenever the king went to the LORD's temple, the guards bore the shields, and afterward they returned them to the guardroom.

²⁹As for the other events of Rehoboam's reign, and all he did, are they not written in the book of the annals of the kings of Judah? ³⁰There was continual warfared between Rehoboam and Jeroboam. ³¹And Rehoboam rested with his fathers and was buried with them in the City of David. His mother's name was Naamah; she was an Ammonite.e And Abijahg his son succeeded him as king.

---

d 14 The meaning of the Hebrew for this sentence is uncertain. *e 15* That is, the Euphrates *f 15* That is, symbols of the goddess Asherah; here and elsewhere in 1 Kings *g 31* Some Hebrew manuscripts and Septuagint (see also 2 Chron. 12:16); most Hebrew manuscripts *Abijam*

---

of Jeroboam's idolatry. Ahijah further prophesied that God would raise up another king who would kill King Jeroboam's son and end his dynasty (see 15:28). Because of Jeroboam's evil influence God would also "uproot Israel from this good land that he gave to their forefathers and scatter them beyond the River" (14:15), a prophecy of exile that was fulfilled in 722 B.C.

Abijah King of Judah

15:1-2,6-8pp — 2Ch 13:1-2,22-14:1

15 In the eighteenth year of the reign of Jeroboam son of Nebat, Abijah[h] became king of Judah, [2]and he reigned in Jerusalem three years. His mother's name was Maacah[f] daughter of Abishalom.[i]

[3]He committed all the sins his father had done before him; his heart was not fully devoted[g] to the LORD his God, as the heart of David his forefather had been. [4]Nevertheless, for David's sake the LORD his God gave him a lamp[h] in Jerusalem by raising up a son to succeed him and by making Jerusalem strong. [5]For David had done what was right in the eyes of the LORD and had not failed to keep[i] any of the LORD's commands all the days of his life—except in the case of Uriah[j] the Hittite.

[6]There was war[k] between Rehoboam[j] and Jeroboam throughout ⌊Abijah's⌋ lifetime. [7]As for the other events of Abijah's reign, and all he did, are they not written in the book of the annals of the kings of Judah? There was war between Abijah and Jeroboam. [8]And Abijah rested with his fathers and was buried in the City of David. And Asa his son succeeded him as king.

Asa King of Judah

15:9-22pp — 2Ch 14:2-3; 15:16-16:6
15:23-24pp — 2Ch 16:11-17:1

[9]In the twentieth year of Jeroboam king of Israel, Asa became king of Judah, [10]and he reigned in Jerusalem forty-one years. His grandmother's name was Maacah[l] daughter of Abishalom.

[11]Asa did what was right in the eyes of the LORD, as his father David[m] had done. [12]He expelled the male shrine prostitutes[n] from the land and got rid of all the idols[o] his fathers had made. [13]He even deposed his grandmother Maacah[p] from her position as queen mother,[q] because she had made a repulsive Asherah pole. Asa cut the pole down[r] and burned it in the Kidron Valley. [14]Although he did not remove[s] the high places, Asa's heart was fully committed[t] to the LORD all his life. [15]He brought into the temple of the LORD the silver and gold and the articles that he and his father had dedicated.[u]

[16]There was war[v] between Asa and Baasha king of Israel throughout their reigns. [17]Baasha king of Israel went up against Judah and fortified Ramah[w] to prevent anyone from leaving or entering the territory of Asa king of Judah.

[18]Asa then took all the silver and gold that was left in the treasuries of the LORD's temple[x] and of his own palace. He entrusted it to his officials and sent[y] them to Ben-Hadad[z] son of Tabrimmon, the son of Hezion, the king of Aram, who was ruling in Damascus. [19]"Let there be a treaty[a] between me and you," he said, "as there was between my father and your father. See, I am sending you a gift of silver and gold. Now break your treaty with Baasha king of Israel so he will withdraw from me."

[20]Ben-Hadad agreed with King Asa and sent the commanders of his forces against the towns of Israel. He conquered[b] Ijon, Dan, Abel Beth Maacah and all Kinnereth in addition to Naphtali. [21]When Baasha heard this, he stopped building Ramah[c] and withdrew to Tirzah.[d] [22]Then King Asa issued an order to all Judah—no one was exempt—and they carried away from Ramah[e] the stones and timber Baasha had been using there. With these King Asa[f] built up Geba[g] in Benjamin, and also Mizpah.[h]

[23]As for all the other events of Asa's reign, all his achievements, all he did and the cities he built, are they not written in the book of the annals of the kings of Judah? In his old age, however, his feet became diseased. [24]Then Asa rested with his fathers and was buried with them in the city of his father David. And Jehoshaphat[i] his son succeeded him as king.

Nadab King of Israel

[25]Nadab son of Jeroboam became king of Israel in the second year of Asa king of Judah, and he reigned over Israel two years. [26]He did evil[j] in the eyes of the LORD, walking in the ways of his father[k] and in his sin, which he had caused Israel to commit.

[h] *1* Some Hebrew manuscripts and Septuagint (see also 2 Chron. 12:16); most Hebrew manuscripts *Abijam*; also in verses 7 and 8   [i] *2* A variant of *Absalom*; also in verse 10   [j] *6* Most Hebrew manuscripts; some Hebrew manuscripts and Syriac *Abijam* (that is, Abijah)

²⁷Baasha son of Ahijah of the house of Issachar plotted against him, and he struck him down¹ at Gibbethon,ᵐ a Philistine town, while Nadab and all Israel were besieging it. ²⁸Baasha killed Nadab in the third year of Asa king of Judah and succeeded him as king.

²⁹As soon as he began to reign, he killed Jeroboam's whole family.ⁿ He did not leave Jeroboam anyone that breathed, but destroyed them all, according to the word of the LORD given through his servant Ahijah the Shilonite— ³⁰because of the sinsᵒ Jeroboam had committed and had causedᵖ Israel to commit, and because he provoked the LORD, the God of Israel, to anger.

³¹As for the other events of Nadab's reign, and all he did, are they not written in the book of the annalsᑫ of the kings of Israel? ³²There was warʳ between Asa and Baasha king of Israel throughout their reigns.

Baasha King of Israel

³³In the third year of Asa king of Judah, Baasha son of Ahijah became king of all Israel in Tirzah,ˢ and he reigned twenty-four years. ³⁴He did evilᵗ in the eyes of the LORD, walking in the ways of Jeroboam and in his sin, which he had caused Israel to commit.

16 Then the word of the LORD came to Jehuᵘ son of Hananiᵛ against Baasha: ²"I lifted you up from the dust and made you leaderˣ of my people Israel, but you walked in the ways of Jeroboam and causedʸ my people Israel to sin and to provoke me to anger by their sins. ³So I am about to consume Baashaᶻ and his house,ᵃ and I will make your house like that of Jeroboam son of Nebat. ⁴Dogsᵇ will eat those belonging to Baasha who die in the city, and the birds of the airᶜ will feed on those who die in the country."

⁵As for the other events of Baasha's reign, what he did and his achievements, are they not written in the book of the annalsᵈ of the kings of Israel? ⁶Baasha rested with his fathers and was buried in Tirzah.ᵉ And Elah his son succeeded him as king.

⁷Moreover, the word of the LORD cameᶠ through the prophet Jehuᵍ son of Hanani to Baasha and his house, because of all the evil he had done in the eyes of the LORD, provoking him to anger by the things he did, and becoming like the house of Jeroboam—and also because he destroyed it.

Elah King of Israel

⁸In the twenty-sixth year of Asa king of Judah, Elah son of Baasha became king of Israel, and he reigned in Tirzah two years.

⁹Zimri, one of his officials, who had command of half his chariots, plotted against him. Elah was in Tirzah at the time, getting drunkʰ in the home of Arza, the man in chargeⁱ of the palace at Tirzah. ¹⁰Zimri came in, struck him down and killed him in the twenty-seventh year of Asa king of Judah. Then he succeeded him as king.ʲ

¹¹As soon as he began to reign and was seated on the throne, he killed off Baasha's whole family.ᵏ He did not spare a single male, whether relative or friend. ¹²So Zimri destroyed the whole family of Baasha, in accordance with the word of the LORD spoken against Baasha through the prophet Jehu— ¹³because of all the sins Baasha and his son Elah had committed and had caused Israel to commit, so that they provoked the LORD, the God of Israel, to anger by their worthless idols.ˡ

¹⁴As for the other events of Elah's reign, and all he did, are they not written in the book of the annals of the kings of Israel?

Zimri King of Israel

¹⁵In the twenty-seventh year of Asa king of Judah, Zimri reigned in Tirzah seven days. The army was encamped near Gibbethon,ᵐ a Philistine town. ¹⁶When the Israelites in the camp heard that Zimri had plotted against the king and murdered him, they proclaimed Omri, the commander of the army, king over Israel that very day there in the camp. ¹⁷Then Omri and all the Israelites with him withdrew from Gibbethon and laid siege to Tirzah. ¹⁸When Zimri saw

---

15:27–28 Baasha, from the tribe of Issachar, conspired and killed King Nadab, the son of King Jeroboam, as prophesied by Ahijah years earlier (see 14:14).

that the city was taken, he went into the citadel of the royal palace and set the palace on fire around him. So he died, [19]because of the sins he had committed, doing evil in the eyes of the LORD and walking in the ways of Jeroboam and in the sin he had committed and had caused Israel to commit.

[20]As for the other events of Zimri's reign, and the rebellion he carried out, are they not written in the book of the annals of the kings of Israel?

Omri King of Israel

[21]Then the people of Israel were split into two factions; half supported Tibni son of Ginath for king, and the other half supported Omri. [22]But Omri's followers proved stronger than those of Tibni son of Ginath. So Tibni died and Omri became king.

[23]In the thirty-first year of Asa king of Judah, Omri became king of Israel, and he reigned twelve years, six of them in Tirzah. [24]He bought the hill of Samaria from Shemer for two talents of silver and built a city on the hill, calling it Samaria, after Shemer, the name of the former owner of the hill.

[25]But Omri did evil in the eyes of the LORD and sinned more than all those before him. [26]He walked in all the ways of Jeroboam son of Nebat and in his sin, which he had caused Israel to commit, so that they provoked the LORD, the God of Israel, to anger by their worthless idols.

[27]As for the other events of Omri's reign, what he did and the things he achieved, are they not written in the book of the annals of the kings of Israel? [28]Omri rested with his fathers and was buried in Samaria. And Ahab his son succeeded him as king.

Ahab Becomes King of Israel

[29]In the thirty-eighth year of Asa king of Judah, Ahab son of Omri became king of Israel, and he reigned in Samaria over Israel twenty-two years. [30]Ahab son of Omri did more evil in the eyes of the LORD than any of those before him. [31]He not only considered it trivial to commit the sins of Jeroboam son of Nebat, but he also married Jezebel daughter of Ethbaal king of the Sidonians, and began to serve Baal and worship him. [32]He set up an altar for Baal in the temple of Baal that he built in Samaria. [33]Ahab also made an Asherah pole and did more to provoke the LORD, the God of Israel, to anger than did all the kings of Israel before him.

[34]In Ahab's time, Hiel of Bethel rebuilt Jericho. He laid its foundations at the cost of his firstborn son Abiram, and he set up its gates at the cost of his youngest son Segub, in accordance with the word of the LORD spoken by Joshua son of Nun.

Elijah Fed by Ravens

17 Now Elijah the Tishbite, from Tishbe in Gilead, said to Ahab, "As the LORD, the God of Israel, lives, whom I serve, there will be neither dew nor rain in the next few years except at my word."

[2]Then the word of the LORD came to Elijah: [3]"Leave here, turn eastward and hide in the Kerith Ravine, east of the Jordan. [4]You will drink from the brook, and I have ordered the ravens to feed you there."

[5]So he did what the LORD had told him. He went to the Kerith Ravine, east of the Jordan, and stayed there. [6]The ravens brought him bread and meat in the morning and bread and meat in the evening, and he drank from the brook.

The Widow at Zarephath

[7]Some time later the brook dried up because there had been no rain in the

J 2Sa 12:14 ◀▶ 1Ki 21:19
F Ru 1:6 ◀▶ 1Ki 19:5–8

[k] 24 That is, about 150 pounds (about 70 kilograms) [l] 1 Or *Tishbite, of the settlers*

16:34 This verse records the deaths of Abiram and Segub, the youngest and oldest sons of Hiel, the builder who ignored Joshua's curse uttered six centuries earlier: "Cursed before the LORD is the man who undertakes to rebuild this city, Jericho: At the cost of his firstborn son will he lay its foundations; at the cost of his youngest will he set up its gates" (Jos 6:26).

17:1 Elijah prophesied to King Ahab that there would be a drought. In fulfillment of Elijah's words, it did not rain for over three years (see Jas 5:17). This period of judgment corresponds to the same length of time of the ministry of God's two witnesses during the tribulation period (see Rev 11:3).

land. ⁸Then the word of the LORD came to him: ⁹"Go at once to Zarephath of Sidon and stay there. I have commanded a widow in that place to supply you with food." ¹⁰So he went to Zarephath. When he came to the town gate, a widow was there gathering sticks. He called to her and asked, "Would you bring me a little water in a jar so I may have a drink?" ¹¹As she was going to get it, he called, "And bring me, please, a piece of bread."

¹²"As surely as the LORD your God lives," she replied, "I don't have any bread—only a handful of flour in a jar and a little oil in a jug. I am gathering a few sticks to take home and make a meal for myself and my son, that we may eat it—and die."

¹³Elijah said to her, "Don't be afraid. Go home and do as you have said. But first make a small cake of bread for me from what you have and bring it to me, and then make something for yourself and your son. ¹⁴For this is what the LORD, the God of Israel, says: 'The jar of flour will not be used up and the jug of oil will not run dry until the day the LORD gives rain on the land.'"

¹⁵She went away and did as Elijah had told her. So there was food every day for Elijah and for the woman and her family. ¹⁶For the jar of flour was not used up and the jug of oil did not run dry, in keeping with the word of the LORD spoken by Elijah.

¹⁷Some time later the son of the woman who owned the house became ill. He grew worse and worse, and finally stopped breathing. ¹⁸She said to Elijah, "What do you have against me, man of God? Did you come to remind me of my sin and kill my son?"

¹⁹"Give me your son," Elijah replied. He took him from her arms, carried him to the upper room where he was staying, and laid him on his bed. ²⁰Then he cried out to the LORD, "O LORD my God, have you brought tragedy also upon this widow I am staying with, by causing her son to die?" ²¹Then he stretched himself out on the boy three times and cried to the LORD, "O LORD my God, let this boy's life return to him!"

²²The LORD heard Elijah's cry, and the boy's life returned to him, and he lived. ²³Elijah picked up the child and carried him down from the room into the house. He gave him to his mother and said, "Look, your son is alive!"

²⁴Then the woman said to Elijah, "Now I know that you are a man of God and that the word of the LORD from your mouth is the truth."

Elijah and Obadiah

18 After a long time, in the third year, the word of the LORD came to Elijah: "Go and present yourself to Ahab, and I will send rain on the land." ²So Elijah went to present himself to Ahab.

Now the famine was severe in Samaria, ³and Ahab had summoned Obadiah, who was in charge of his palace. (Obadiah was a devout believer in the LORD. ⁴While Jezebel was killing off the LORD's prophets, Obadiah had taken a hundred prophets and hidden them in two caves, fifty in each, and had supplied them with food and water.) ⁵Ahab had said to Obadiah, "Go through the land to all the springs and valleys. Maybe we can find some grass to keep the horses and mules alive so we will not have to kill any of our animals." ⁶So they divided the land they were to cover, Ahab going in one direction and Obadiah in another.

⁷As Obadiah was walking along, Elijah met him. Obadiah recognized him, bowed down to the ground, and said, "Is it really you, my lord Elijah?"

⁸"Yes," he replied. "Go tell your master, 'Elijah is here.'"

⁹"What have I done wrong," asked Obadiah, "that you are handing your servant over to Ahab to be put to death? ¹⁰As surely as the LORD your God lives, there is not a nation or kingdom where my master has not sent someone to look for

---

17:24 This widow declared that the true test of a prophet's message was in its fulfillment. The words of a man of God would come true.

18:3–4 This verse indicates that there were many godly prophets in Israel who banded together for safety. That Obadiah was able to hide one hundred of these godly prophets from the evil Queen Jezebel during a famine is a miracle of God.

you. And whenever a nation or kingdom claimed you were not there, he made them swear they could not find you. ¹¹But now you tell me to go to my master and say, 'Elijah is here.' ¹²I don't know where the Spirit of the Lord may carry you when I leave you. If I go and tell Ahab and he doesn't find you, he will kill me. Yet I your servant have worshiped the Lord since my youth. ¹³Haven't you heard, my lord, what I did while Jezebel was killing the prophets of the Lord? I hid a hundred of the Lord's prophets in two caves, fifty in each, and supplied them with food and water. ¹⁴And now you tell me to go to my master and say, 'Elijah is here.' He will kill me!"

¹⁵Elijah said, "As the Lord Almighty lives, whom I serve, I will surely present myself to Ahab today."

Elijah on Mount Carmel

¹⁶So Obadiah went to meet Ahab and told him, and Ahab went to meet Elijah. ¹⁷When he saw Elijah, he said to him, "Is that you, you troubler of Israel?"

¹⁸"I have not made trouble for Israel," Elijah replied. "But you and your father's family have. You have abandoned the Lord's commands and have followed the Baals. ¹⁹Now summon the people from all over Israel to meet me on Mount Carmel. And bring the four hundred and fifty prophets of Baal and the four hundred prophets of Asherah, who eat at Jezebel's table."

²⁰So Ahab sent word throughout all Israel and assembled the prophets on Mount Carmel. ²¹Elijah went before the people and said, "How long will you waver between two opinions? If the Lord is God, follow him; but if Baal is God, follow him."

But the people said nothing.

²²Then Elijah said to them, "I am the only one of the Lord's prophets left, but Baal has four hundred and fifty prophets. ²³Get two bulls for us. Let them choose one for themselves, and let them cut it into pieces and put it on the wood but not set fire to it. I will prepare the other bull and put it on the wood but not set fire to it. ²⁴Then you call on the name of your god, and I will call on the name of the Lord. The god who answers by fire—he is God."

Then all the people said, "What you say is good."

²⁵Elijah said to the prophets of Baal, "Choose one of the bulls and prepare it first, since there are so many of you. Call on the name of your god, but do not light the fire." ²⁶So they took the bull given them and prepared it.

Then they called on the name of Baal from morning till noon. "O Baal, answer us!" they shouted. But there was no response; no one answered. And they danced around the altar they had made.

²⁷At noon Elijah began to taunt them. "Shout louder!" he said. "Surely he is a god! Perhaps he is deep in thought, or busy, or traveling. Maybe he is sleeping and must be awakened." ²⁸So they shouted louder and slashed themselves with swords and spears, as was their custom, until their blood flowed. ²⁹Midday passed, and they continued their frantic prophesying until the time for the evening sacrifice. But there was no response, no one answered, no one paid attention.

³⁰Then Elijah said to all the people, "Come here to me." They came to him, and he repaired the altar of the Lord, which was in ruins. ³¹Elijah took twelve stones, one for each of the tribes descended from Jacob, to whom the word of the Lord had come, saying, "Your name shall be Israel." ³²With the stones he built an altar in the name of the Lord, and he dug a trench around it large enough to hold two seahs of seed. ³³He arranged the wood, cut the bull into pieces and laid it on the wood. Then he said to them, "Fill four large jars with water and pour it on the offering and on the wood."

³⁴"Do it again," he said, and they did it again.

"Do it a third time," he ordered, and they did it the third time. ³⁵The water ran down around the altar and even filled the trench.

³⁶At the time of sacrifice, the prophet Elijah stepped forward and prayed: "O Lord, God of Abraham, Isaac and Is-

---

E *2Sa 23:2* ◄ ► *1Ki 22:24*
L *2Sa 23:2* ◄ ► *1Ki 22:24*
N *2Sa 14:14* ◄ ► *2Ki 17:13–15*
S *1Ki 8:61* ◄ ► *1Ch 16:29*

m 32 That is, probably about 13 quarts (about 15 liters)

rael, let it be known[j] today that you are God in Israel and that I am your servant and have done all these things at your command.[k] [37]Answer me, O LORD, answer me, so these people will know[l] that you, O LORD, are God, and that you are turning their hearts back again."

[38]Then the fire[m] of the LORD fell and burned up the sacrifice, the wood, the stones and the soil, and also licked up the water in the trench.

[39]When all the people saw this, they fell prostrate[n] and cried, "The LORD—he is God! The LORD—he is God!"[o]

[40]Then Elijah commanded them, "Seize the prophets of Baal. Don't let anyone get away!" They seized them, and Elijah had them brought down to the Kishon Valley[p] and slaughtered[q] there.

[41]And Elijah said to Ahab, "Go, eat and drink, for there is the sound of a heavy rain." [42]So Ahab went off to eat and drink, but Elijah climbed to the top of Carmel, bent down to the ground and put his face between his knees.[r]

[43]"Go and look toward the sea," he told his servant. And he went up and looked. "There is nothing there," he said.

Seven times Elijah said, "Go back."

[44]The seventh time[s] the servant reported, "A cloud[t] as small as a man's hand is rising from the sea."

So Elijah said, "Go and tell Ahab, 'Hitch up your chariot and go down before the rain stops you.'"

[45]Meanwhile, the sky grew black with clouds, the wind rose, a heavy rain[u] came on and Ahab rode off to Jezreel.[v] [46]The power[w] of the LORD came upon Elijah and, tucking his cloak into his belt,[x] he ran ahead of Ahab all the way to Jezreel.

Elijah Flees to Horeb

19 Now Ahab told Jezebel[y] everything Elijah had done and how he had killed[z] all the prophets with the sword. [2]So Jezebel sent a messenger to Elijah to say, "May the gods deal with me, be it ever so severely,[a] if by this time

◀ 1Ki 18:1 ◀ ▶ 2Ki 7:1–2

tomorrow I do not make your life like that of one of them."[b]

[3]Elijah was afraid[n] and ran[c] for his life.[d] When he came to Beersheba[e] in Judah, he left his servant there, [4]while he himself went a day's journey into the desert. He came to a broom tree,[f] sat down under it and prayed that he might die. "I have had enough, LORD," he said. "Take my life;[g] I am no better than my ancestors." [5]Then he lay down under the tree and fell asleep.[h]

All at once an angel[i] touched him and said, "Get up and eat." [6]He looked around, and there by his head was a cake of bread baked over hot coals, and a jar of water. He ate and drank and then lay down again.

[7]The angel of the LORD came back a second time and touched him and said, "Get up and eat, for the journey is too much for you." [8]So he got up and ate and drank. Strengthened by that food, he traveled forty[j] days and forty nights until he reached Horeb,[k] the mountain of God. [9]There he went into a cave[l] and spent the night.

The LORD Appears to Elijah

And the word of the LORD came to him: "What are you doing here, Elijah?"[m]

[10]He replied, "I have been very zealous[n] for the LORD God Almighty. The Israelites have rejected your covenant,[o] broken down your altars,[p] and put your prophets to death with the sword. I am the only one left,[q] and now they are trying to kill me too."

[11]The LORD said, "Go out and stand on the mountain[r] in the presence of the LORD, for the LORD is about to pass by."[s]

Then a great and powerful wind[t] tore the mountains apart and shattered[u] the rocks before the LORD, but the LORD was not in the wind. After the wind there was an earthquake, but the LORD was not in the earthquake. [12]After the earthquake came a fire,[v] but the LORD was not in the fire. And after the fire came a gentle

F ◀ 1Ki 17:1–16 ◀ ▶ 2Ki 3:9–20

[n]3 Or Elijah saw

18:41–46 Elijah bravely approached the king who hated him and announced that the rains would begin again and end God's judgment of drought and famine throughout Israel. The rains began as promised, and Elijah was miraculously empowered to run from Mt. Carmel to Jezreel (about 17 miles).

whisper.w 13When Elijah heard it, he pulled his cloak over his facex and went out and stood at the mouth of the cave. Then a voice said to him, "What are you doing here, Elijah?"

14He replied, "I have been very zealous for the LORD God Almighty. The Israelites have rejected your covenant, broken down your altars, and put your prophets to death with the sword. I am the only one left,y and now they are trying to kill me too."

15The LORD said to him, "Go back the way you came, and go to the Desert of Damascus. When you get there, anoint Hazaelz king over Aram. 16Also, anointa Jehu son of Nimshi king over Israel, and anoint Elishab son of Shaphat from Abel Meholahc to succeed you as prophet. 17Jehu will put to death any who escape the sword of Hazael,d and Elisha will put to death any who escape the sword of Jehu.e 18Yet I reservef seven thousand in Israel—all whose knees have not bowed down to Baal and all whose mouths have not kissedg him."

The Call of Elisha

19So Elijah went from there and found Elisha son of Shaphat. He was plowing with twelve yoke of oxen, and he himself was driving the twelfth pair. Elijah went up to him and threw his cloakh around him. 20Elisha then left his oxen and ran after Elijah. "Let me kiss my father and mother good-by,"i he said, "and then I will come with you."

"Go back," Elijah replied. "What have I done to you?"

21So Elisha left him and went back. He took his yoke of oxenj and slaughtered them. He burned the plowing equipment to cook the meat and gave it to the people, and they ate. Then he set out to follow Elijah and became his attendant.k

Ben-Hadad Attacks Samaria

20 Now Ben-Hadad1 king of Aram mustered his entire army. Accompanied by thirty-two kings with their horses and chariots, he went up and besieged Samariam and attacked it. 2He sent messengers into the city to Ahab king of Israel, saying, "This is what Ben-Hadad says: 3'Your silver and gold are mine, and the best of your wives and children are mine.' "

4The king of Israel answered, "Just as you say, my lord the king. I and all I have are yours."

5The messengers came again and said, "This is what Ben-Hadad says: 'I sent to demand your silver and gold, your wives and your children. 6But about this time tomorrow I am going to send my officials to search your palace and the houses of your officials. They will seize everything you value and carry it away.' "

7The king of Israel summoned all the eldersn of the land and said to them, "See how this man is looking for trouble!o When he sent for my wives and my children, my silver and my gold, I did not refuse him."

8The elders and the people all answered, "Don't listen to him or agree to his demands."

9So he replied to Ben-Hadad's messengers, "Tell my lord the king, 'Your servant will do all you demanded the first time, but this demand I cannot meet.' " They left and took the answer back to Ben-Hadad.

10Then Ben-Hadad sent another message to Ahab: "May the gods deal with me, be it ever so severely, if enough dustp remains in Samaria to give each of my men a handful."

11The king of Israel answered, "Tell him: 'One who puts on his armor should not boastq like one who takes it off.' "

12Ben-Hadad heard this message while

19:15–18 God commanded Elijah to anoint Hazael as king of Syria, Jehu as king of Israel and Elisha as his successor as the chief prophet of Israel. God promised that none of his evil enemies would escape Hazael, Jehu or Elisha. While Elijah complained bitterly that he was the only faithful man of God left in Israel (see 19:10), God responded that he had "seven thousand in Israel—all whose knees have not bowed down to Baal and all whose mouths have not kissed him" (19:18). God's message is the same today. Despite widespread apostasy, God is still in control and has under his care many men and women who truly love him and his Word.

19:19 Elijah obeyed God's command and found his successor plowing a field. By placing his cloak on the shoulders of this younger man of God, Elijah symbolically passed his prophetic office to Elisha.

he and the kings were drinking[r] in their tents,[o] and he ordered his men: "Prepare to attack." So they prepared to attack the city.

Ahab Defeats Ben-Hadad

[13] Meanwhile a prophet[s] came to Ahab king of Israel and announced, "This is what the LORD says: 'Do you see this vast army? I will give it into your hand today, and then you will know[t] that I am the LORD.'"

[14] "But who will do this?" asked Ahab.

The prophet replied, "This is what the LORD says: 'The young officers of the provincial commanders will do it.'"

"And who will start[u] the battle?" he asked.

The prophet answered, "You will."

[15] So Ahab summoned the young officers of the provincial commanders, 232 men. Then he assembled the rest of the Israelites, 7,000 in all. [16] They set out at noon while Ben-Hadad and the 32 kings allied with him were in their tents getting drunk.[v] [17] The young officers of the provincial commanders went out first.

Now Ben-Hadad had dispatched scouts, who reported, "Men are advancing from Samaria."

[18] He said, "If they have come out for peace, take them alive; if they have come out for war, take them alive."

[19] The young officers of the provincial commanders marched out of the city with the army behind them [20] and each one struck down his opponent. At that, the Arameans fled, with the Israelites in pursuit. But Ben-Hadad king of Aram escaped on horseback with some of his horsemen. [21] The king of Israel advanced and overpowered the horses and chariots and inflicted heavy losses on the Arameans.

[22] Afterward, the prophet[w] came to the king of Israel and said, "Strengthen your position and see what must be done, because next spring[x] the king of Aram will attack you again."

[23] Meanwhile, the officials of the king of Aram advised him, "Their gods are gods[y] of the hills. That is why they were too strong for us. But if we fight them on the plains, surely we will be stronger than they. [24] Do this: Remove all the kings from their commands and replace them with other officers. [25] You must also raise an army like the one you lost—horse for horse and chariot for chariot—so we can fight Israel on the plains. Then surely we will be stronger than they." He agreed with them and acted accordingly.

[26] The next spring[z] Ben-Hadad mustered the Arameans and went up to Aphek[a] to fight against Israel. [27] When the Israelites were also mustered and given provisions, they marched out to meet them. The Israelites camped opposite them like two small flocks of goats, while the Arameans covered the countryside.[b]

[28] The man of God came up and told the king of Israel, "This is what the LORD says: 'Because the Arameans think the LORD is a god of the hills and not a god[c] of the valleys, I will deliver this vast army into your hands, and you will know[d] that I am the LORD.'"

[29] For seven days they camped opposite each other, and on the seventh day the battle was joined. The Israelites inflicted a hundred thousand casualties on the Aramean foot soldiers in one day. [30] The rest of them escaped to the city of Aphek,[e] where the wall collapsed[f] on twenty-seven thousand of them. And Ben-Hadad fled to the city and hid[g] in an inner room.

[31] His officials said to him, "Look, we have heard that the kings of the house of Israel are merciful.[h] Let us go to the king of Israel with sackcloth[i] around our waists and ropes around our heads. Perhaps he will spare your life."

[32] Wearing sackcloth around their waists and ropes around their heads, they went to the king of Israel and said, "Your servant Ben-Hadad says: 'Please let me live.'"

The king answered, "Is he still alive? He is my brother."

[33] The men took this as a good sign and were quick to pick up his word. "Yes, your brother Ben-Hadad!" they said.

"Go and get him," the king said. When Ben-Hadad came out, Ahab had him come up into his chariot.

[34] "I will return the cities[j] my father took from your father," Ben-Hadad[k] offered. "You may set up your own market areas[l] in Damascus,[m] as my father did in Samaria."

[Ahab said,] "On the basis of a treaty[n] I

o 12 Or in Succoth; also in verse 16

will set you free." So he made a treaty with him, and let him go.

A Prophet Condemns Ahab

³⁵By the word of the LORD one of the sons of the prophets^o said to his companion, "Strike me with your weapon," but the man refused.^p ³⁶So the prophet said, "Because you have not obeyed the LORD, as soon as you leave me a lion^q will kill you." And after the man went away, a lion found him and killed him. ³⁷The prophet found another man and said, "Strike me, please." So the man struck him and wounded him. ³⁸Then the prophet went and stood by the road waiting for the king. He disguised himself with his headband down over his eyes. ³⁹As the king passed by, the prophet called out to him, "Your servant went into the thick of the battle, and someone came to me with a captive and said, 'Guard this man. If he is missing, it will be your life for his life,^r or you must pay a talent^p of silver.' ⁴⁰While your servant was busy here and there, the man disappeared."

"That is your sentence,"^s the king of Israel said. "You have pronounced it yourself."

⁴¹Then the prophet quickly removed the headband from his eyes, and the king of Israel recognized him as one of the prophets. ⁴²He said to the king, "This is what the LORD says: 'You^t have set free a man I had determined should die.^{q u} Therefore it is your life for his life,^v your people for his people.' " ⁴³Sullen and angry,^w the king of Israel went to his palace in Samaria.

Naboth's Vineyard

21 Some time later there was an incident involving a vineyard belonging to Naboth^x the Jezreelite. The vineyard was in Jezreel,^y close to the palace of Ahab king of Samaria. ²Ahab said to Naboth, "Let me have your vineyard to use for a vegetable garden, since it is close to my palace. In exchange I will give you a better vineyard or, if you prefer, I will pay you whatever it is worth."

³But Naboth replied, "The LORD forbid that I should give you the inheritance^z of my fathers."

⁴So Ahab went home, sullen and angry^a because Naboth the Jezreelite had said, "I will not give you the inheritance of my fathers." He lay on his bed sulking and refused^b to eat.

⁵His wife Jezebel came in and asked him, "Why are you so sullen? Why won't you eat?"

⁶He answered her, "Because I said to Naboth the Jezreelite, 'Sell me your vineyard; or if you prefer, I will give you another vineyard in its place.' But he said, 'I will not give you my vineyard.' "

⁷Jezebel his wife said, "Is this how you act as king over Israel? Get up and eat! Cheer up. I'll get you the vineyard^c of Naboth the Jezreelite."

⁸So she wrote letters^d in Ahab's name, placed his seal^e on them, and sent them to the elders and nobles who lived in Naboth's city with him. ⁹In those letters she wrote:

> "Proclaim a day of fasting and seat Naboth in a prominent place among the people. ¹⁰But seat two scoundrels^f opposite him and have them testify that he has cursed^g both God and the king. Then take him out and stone him to death."

¹¹So the elders and nobles who lived in Naboth's city did as Jezebel directed in the letters she had written to them. ¹²They proclaimed a fast^h and seated Naboth in a prominent place among the people. ¹³Then two scoundrels came and sat opposite him and brought charges against Naboth before the people, saying, "Naboth has cursed both God and the king." So they took him outside the city and stoned him to death.ⁱ ¹⁴Then they sent word to Jezebel: "Naboth has been stoned and is dead."

¹⁵As soon as Jezebel heard that Naboth had been stoned to death, she said to Ahab, "Get up and take possession of the vineyard^j of Naboth the Jezreelite that he refused to sell you. He is no longer alive, but dead." ¹⁶When Ahab heard that Naboth was dead, he got up and went down to take possession of Naboth's vineyard.

¹⁷Then the word of the LORD came to Elijah the Tishbite: ¹⁸"Go down to meet Ahab king of Israel, who rules in Samaria.

---

^{p 39} That is, about 75 pounds (about 34 kilograms) ^{q 42} The Hebrew term refers to the irrevocable giving over of things or persons to the LORD, often by totally destroying them.

He is now in Naboth's vineyard, where he has gone to take possession of it. ¹⁹Say to him, 'This is what the LORD says: Have you not murdered a man and seized his property?'ᵏ Then say to him, 'This is what the LORD says: In the place where dogs licked up Naboth's blood, dogsᵐ will lick up your blood—yes, yours!' "

²⁰Ahab said to Elijah, "So you have found me, my enemy!"ⁿ

"I have found you," he answered, "because you have soldᵒ yourself to do evil in the eyes of the LORD. ²¹I am going to bring disaster on you. I will consume your descendants and cut off from Ahab every last maleᵖ in Israel—slave or free. ²²I will make your houseʳ like that of Jeroboam son of Nebat and that of Baasha son of Ahijah, because you have provoked me to anger and have caused Israel to sin.'ˢ

²³"And also concerning Jezebel the LORD says: 'Dogsᵗ will devour Jezebel by the wall ofʳ Jezreel.'

²⁴"Dogsᵘ will eat those belonging to Ahab who die in the city, and the birds of the airᵛ will feed on those who die in the country."

²⁵(There was neverʷ a man like Ahab, who sold himself to do evil in the eyes of the LORD, urged on by Jezebel his wife. ²⁶He behaved in the vilest manner by going after idols, like the Amoritesˣ the LORD drove out before Israel.)

²⁷When Ahab heard these words, he tore his clothes, put on sackclothʸ and fasted. He lay in sackcloth and went around meekly.ᶻ

²⁸Then the word of the LORD came to Elijah the Tishbite: ²⁹"Have you noticed how Ahab has humbled himself before me? Because he has humbledᵃ himself, I will not bring this disaster in his day,ᵇ but I will bring it on his house in the days of his son."ᶜ

C 2Sa 23:6–7 ◄► 2Ki 17:14–15
J 1Ki 21:19 ◄► 1Ki 21:29
M 2Sa 24:10 ◄► 2Ki 22:19
J 1Ki 21:21–24 ◄► 2Ki 1:4

21:19 ᵏJob 24:6; 31:39 ²Ki 9:26; Ps 9:12; Isa 14:20 ᵐ1Ki 22:38; Ps 68:23; Jer 15:3
21:20 ⁿS 1Ki 18:17 ᵒ2Ki 17:17; Ro 7:14
21:21 ᵖJdg 9:5; 2Ki 10:7 ᵠS Dt 32:36
21:22 ʳ1Ki 16:3 ˢS 1Ki 12:30
21:23 ᵗ2Ki 9:10, 34-36
21:24 ᵘ1Ki 14:11 ᵛS Ge 40:19; S Dt 28:26
21:25 ʷS 1Ki 14:9; S 16:33
21:26 ˣS Ge 15:16
21:27 ʸS Ge 37:34; S Jer 4:8 ᶻIsa 38:15
21:29 ᵃS Ex 10:3 ᵇS Ex 32:14; 2Ki 22:20 ᶜEx 20:5; 2Ki 9:26; 10:6-10
22:3 ᵈS Dt 4:43
22:4 ᵉ2Ki 3:7
22:5 ᶠEx 33:7; 2Ki 3:11; Job 38:2; Ps 32:8; 73:24; 107:11
22:6 ᵍS Jdg 18:6 ʰS 1Ki 13:18
22:7 ⁱDt 18:15; 2Ki 3:11; 5:8 ʲS Nu 27:21; 2Ki 3:11
22:8 ᵏAm 5:10 ˡver 13; Isa 5:20; 30:10; Jer 23:17
22:10 ᵐS Jdg 6:37
22:11 ⁿver 24 ᵒDt 33:17; Jer 27:2; 28:10; Zec 1:18-21

Micaiah Prophesies Against Ahab

22:1–28pp — 2Ch 18:1–27

22 For three years there was no war between Aram and Israel. ²But in the third year Jehoshaphat king of Judah went down to see the king of Israel. ³The king of Israel had said to his officials, "Don't you know that Ramoth Gileadᵈ belongs to us and yet we are doing nothing to retake it from the king of Aram?"

⁴So he asked Jehoshaphat, "Will you go with me to fightᵉ against Ramoth Gilead?"

Jehoshaphat replied to the king of Israel, "I am as you are, my people as your people, my horses as your horses." ⁵But Jehoshaphat also said to the king of Israel, "First seek the counselᶠ of the LORD."

⁶So the king of Israel brought together the prophets—about four hundred men—and asked them, "Shall I go to war against Ramoth Gilead, or shall I refrain?"

"Go,"ᵍ they answered, "for the Lord will give it into the king's hand."ʰ

⁷But Jehoshaphat asked, "Is there not a prophetⁱ of the LORD here whom we can inquireʲ of?"

⁸The king of Israel answered Jehoshaphat, "There is still one man through whom we can inquire of the LORD, but I hateᵏ him because he never prophesies anything goodˡ about me, but always bad. He is Micaiah son of Imlah."

"The king should not say that," Jehoshaphat replied.

⁹So the king of Israel called one of his officials and said, "Bring Micaiah son of Imlah at once."

¹⁰Dressed in their royal robes, the king of Israel and Jehoshaphat king of Judah were sitting on their thrones at the threshing floorᵐ by the entrance of the gate of Samaria, with all the prophets prophesying before them. ¹¹Now Zedekiahⁿ son of Kenaanah had made iron hornsᵒ and he declared, "This is what the LORD says: 'With these you will gore the Arameans until they are destroyed.' "

ʳ 23 Most Hebrew manuscripts; a few Hebrew manuscripts, Vulgate and Syriac (see also 2 Kings 9:26) *the plot of ground at*

21:21–29 Elijah announced God's verdict upon King Ahab's dynasty because of Ahab's idolatry: all of Ahab's descendants would die dishonorably, his dynasty would be destroyed and dogs would eat his wife's dead body. In response to this terrible judgment, Ahab repented, and God graciously delayed this punishment until after Ahab's death, allowing the judgment to fall on Ahab's evil son instead.

[12]All the other prophets were prophesying the same thing. "Attack Ramoth Gilead and be victorious," they said, "for the LORD will give it into the king's hand."

[13]The messenger who had gone to summon Micaiah said to him, "Look, as one man the other prophets are predicting success for the king. Let your word agree with theirs, and speak favorably."[p]

[14]But Micaiah said, "As surely as the LORD lives, I can tell him only what the LORD tells me."[q]

[15]When he arrived, the king asked him, "Micaiah, shall we go to war against Ramoth Gilead, or shall I refrain?"

"Attack and be victorious," he answered, "for the LORD will give it into the king's hand."

[16]The king said to him, "How many times must I make you swear to tell me nothing but the truth in the name of the LORD?"

[17]Then Micaiah answered, "I saw all Israel scattered[r] on the hills like sheep without a shepherd,[s] and the LORD said, 'These people have no master. Let each one go home in peace.'"

[18]The king of Israel said to Jehoshaphat, "Didn't I tell you that he never prophesies anything good about me, but only bad?"

[19]Micaiah continued, "Therefore hear the word of the LORD: I saw the LORD sitting on his throne[t] with all the host[u] of heaven standing around him on his right and on his left. [20]And the LORD said, 'Who will entice Ahab into attacking Ramoth Gilead and going to his death there?'

"One suggested this, and another that. [21]Finally, a spirit came forward, stood before the LORD and said, 'I will entice him.'

[22]"'By what means?' the LORD asked.

"'I will go out and be a lying[v] spirit in the mouths of all his prophets,' he said.

"'You will succeed in enticing him,' said the LORD. 'Go and do it.'

[23]"So now the LORD has put a lying[w] spirit in the mouths of all these prophets[x] of yours. The LORD has decreed disaster[y] for you."

[24]Then Zedekiah[z] son of Kenaanah went up and slapped[a] Micaiah in the face. "Which way did the spirit from[s] the LORD go when he went from me to speak[b] to you?" he asked.

[25]Micaiah replied, "You will find out on the day you go to hide[c] in an inner room."

[26]The king of Israel then ordered, "Take Micaiah and send him back to Amon the ruler of the city and to Joash the king's son [27]and say, 'This is what the king says: Put this fellow in prison[d] and give him nothing but bread and water until I return safely.'"

[28]Micaiah declared, "If you ever return safely, the LORD has not spoken[e] through me." Then he added, "Mark my words, all you people!"

Ahab Killed at Ramoth Gilead
22:29–36pp — 2Ch 18:28–34

[29]So the king of Israel and Jehoshaphat king of Judah went up to Ramoth Gilead. [30]The king of Israel said to Jehoshaphat, "I will enter the battle in disguise,[f] but you wear your royal robes." So the king of Israel disguised himself and went into battle.

[31]Now the king of Aram[g] had ordered his thirty-two chariot commanders, "Do not fight with anyone, small or great, except the king[h] of Israel." [32]When the chariot commanders saw Jehoshaphat, they thought, "Surely this is the king of Israel." So they turned to attack him, but when Jehoshaphat cried out, [33]the chariot commanders saw that he was not the king of Israel and stopped pursuing him.

[34]But someone drew his bow[i] at random and hit the king of Israel between the sections of his armor. The king told his chariot driver, "Wheel around and get me out of the fighting. I've been wounded." [35]All day long the battle raged, and the king was propped up in his chariot facing the Arameans. The blood from his wound ran onto the floor of the chariot, and that evening he died. [36]As the sun was setting, a cry spread through the army: "Every man to his town; everyone to his land!"[j]

[37]So the king died and was brought to Samaria, and they buried him there. [38]They washed the chariot at a pool in Samaria (where the prostitutes bathed),[t]

22:13 [p] S ver 8
22:14 [q] S Nu 22:18; S 1Sa 3:17
22:17 [r] S Ge 11:4; Na 3:18 [s] Nu 27:17; Isa 13:14; S Mt 9:36
22:19 [t] Ps 47:8; Isa 6:1; 63:15; Eze 1:26; Da 7:9 [u] Job 1:6; 15:8; 38:7; Ps 103:20-21; 148:2; Jer 23:18, 22; Lk 2:13
22:22 [v] S Jdg 9:23; 2Th 2:11
22:23 [w] S Dt 13:3 [x] Eze 14:9 [y] S Dt 31:29
22:24 [z] ver 11 [a] Ac 23:2 [b] Job 26:4
22:25 [c] 1Ki 20:30
22:27 [d] 2Ch 16:10; Jer 20:2; 26:21; 37:15; Heb 11:36
22:28 [e] S Dt 18:22
22:30 [f] S 1Sa 28:8
22:31 [g] S Ge 10:22; S 2Sa 10:19 [h] S 2Sa 17:25
22:34 [i] 2Ki 9:24; 2Ch 35:23
22:36 [j] 2Ki 14:12

[s] 24 Or *Spirit of* [t] 38 Or *Samaria and cleaned the weapons*

E 1Ki 18:12 ◀ ▶ 2Ki 2:9–10
L 1Ki 18:12 ◀ ▶ 2Ki 2:16
Q 1Sa 16:14 ◀ ▶ 2Ch 18:23

and the dogs^k licked up his blood, as the word of the LORD had declared.

^39 As for the other events of Ahab's reign, including all he did, the palace he built and inlaid with ivory,^1 and the cities he fortified, are they not written in the book of the annals of the kings of Israel? ^40 Ahab rested with his fathers. And Ahaziah his son succeeded him as king.

Jehoshaphat King of Judah
22:41–50pp — 2Ch 20:31–21:1

^41 Jehoshaphat son of Asa became king of Judah in the fourth year of Ahab king of Israel. ^42 Jehoshaphat was thirty-five years old when he became king, and he reigned in Jerusalem twenty-five years. His mother's name was Azubah daughter of Shilhi. ^43 In everything he walked in the ways of his father Asa^m and did not stray from them; he did what was right in the eyes of the LORD. The high places,^n however, were not removed, and the people continued to offer sacrifices and burn incense there. ^44 Jehoshaphat was also at peace with the king of Israel.

^45 As for the other events of Jehoshaphat's reign, the things he achieved and his military exploits, are they not written in the book of the annals of the kings of Judah? ^46 He rid the land of the rest of the male shrine prostitutes^o who remained there even after the reign of his father Asa. ^47 There was then no king^p in Edom; a deputy ruled.

^48 Now Jehoshaphat built a fleet of trading ships^{u q} to go to Ophir for gold, but they never set sail—they were wrecked at Ezion Geber.^r ^49 At that time Ahaziah son of Ahab said to Jehoshaphat, "Let my men sail with your men," but Jehoshaphat refused.

^50 Then Jehoshaphat rested with his fathers and was buried with them in the city of David his father. And Jehoram his son succeeded him.

Ahaziah King of Israel

^51 Ahaziah son of Ahab became king of Israel in Samaria in the seventeenth year of Jehoshaphat king of Judah, and he reigned over Israel two years. ^52 He did evil^s in the eyes of the LORD, because he walked in the ways of his father and mother and in the ways of Jeroboam son of Nebat, who caused Israel to sin. ^53 He served and worshiped Baal^t and provoked the LORD, the God of Israel, to anger, just as his father^u had done.

^u 48 Hebrew of ships of Tarshish

2 Kings

Author: Unknown

Theme: The history of the divided kingdom

Date of Writing: c. 560–550 B.C.

Outline of 2 Kings
  I. The Ministries of Elijah and Elisha (1:1—8:15)
  II. Israel's Decline and Exile (8:16—17:41)
  III. Judah's Descent Into Sin (18:1—23:30)
  IV. The Babylonian Exile (23:31—25:30)

THE BOOKS OF 1 and 2 Kings were originally part of one large manuscript that the Hebrews simply called "Kings." (For further information about the title, authorship and date of these books, see the introduction to 1 Kings on p. 364.)

The book of 2 Kings begins with the rebellion of Moab following the death of King Ahab. The narrative describes a short-lived alliance between Israel and Judah and then follows the events in Israel's spiritual apostasy and final fall to the Assyrians. The account of 2 Kings then follows the reigns of Judah's kings until that kingdom's final destruction by the armies of Babylon.

Quoting from various historical records and royal accounts that have not survived the centuries, the author of 2 Kings consistently records God's blessing for obedience and promised judgment for idolatry. Also included in this narrative are the miracles of Elisha, including the healing of a Syrian leper named Naaman (ch. 5).

The LORD's Judgment on Ahaziah

1 After Ahab's death, Moab[a] rebelled against Israel. ²Now Ahaziah had fallen through the lattice of his upper room in Samaria and injured himself. So he sent messengers,[b] saying to them, "Go and consult Baal-Zebub,[c] the god of Ekron,[d] to see if I will recover[e] from this injury."

³But the angel[f] of the LORD said to Elijah[g] the Tishbite, "Go up and meet the messengers of the king of Samaria and ask them, 'Is it because there is no God in Israel[h] that you are going off to consult Baal-Zebub, the god of Ekron?' ⁴Therefore this is what the LORD says: 'You will not leave[i] the bed you are lying on. You will certainly die!' " So Elijah went.

⁵When the messengers returned to the king, he asked them, "Why have you come back?"

⁶"A man came to meet us," they replied. "And he said to us, 'Go back to the king who sent you and tell him, "This is what the LORD says: Is it because there is no God in Israel that you are sending men to consult Baal-Zebub, the god of Ekron? Therefore you will not leave[j] the bed you are lying on. You will certainly die!" ' "

⁷The king asked them, "What kind of man was it who came to meet you and told you this?"

⁸They replied, "He was a man with a garment of hair[k] and with a leather belt around his waist."

The king said, "That was Elijah the Tishbite."

⁹Then he sent[l] to Elijah a captain[m] with his company of fifty men. The captain went up to Elijah, who was sitting on the top of a hill, and said to him, "Man of God, the king says, 'Come down!' "

¹⁰Elijah answered the captain, "If I am a man of God, may fire come down from heaven and consume you and your fifty men!" Then fire[n] fell from heaven and consumed the captain and his men.

¹¹At this the king sent to Elijah another captain with his fifty men. The captain said to him, "Man of God, this is what the king says, 'Come down at once!' "

¹²"If I am a man of God," Elijah replied, "may fire come down from heaven and consume you and your fifty men!" Then the fire of God fell from heaven and consumed him and his fifty men.

¹³So the king sent a third captain with his fifty men. This third captain went up and fell on his knees before Elijah. "Man of God," he begged, "please have respect for my life[o] and the lives of these fifty men, your servants! ¹⁴See, fire has fallen from heaven and consumed the first two captains and all their men. But now have respect for my life!"

¹⁵The angel[p] of the LORD said to Elijah, "Go down with him; do not be afraid[q] of him." So Elijah got up and went down with him to the king.

¹⁶He told the king, "This is what the LORD says: Is it because there is no God in Israel for you to consult that you have sent messengers[r] to consult Baal-Zebub, the god of Ekron? Because you have done this, you will never leave[s] the bed you are lying on. You will certainly die!" ¹⁷So he died,[t] according to the word of the LORD that Elijah had spoken.

Because Ahaziah had no son, Joram[a][u] succeeded him as king in the second year of Jehoram son of Jehoshaphat king of Judah. ¹⁸As for all the other events of Ahaziah's reign, and what he did, are they not written in the book of the annals of the kings of Israel?

Elijah Taken Up to Heaven

2 When the LORD was about to take[v] Elijah up to heaven in a whirlwind,[w] Elijah and Elisha[x] were on their way from Gilgal.[y] ²Elijah said to Elisha, "Stay here;[z] the LORD has sent me to Bethel."

But Elisha said, "As surely as the LORD lives and as you live, I will not leave you."[a] So they went down to Bethel.

³The company[b] of the prophets at Bethel came out to Elisha and asked, "Do you know that the LORD is going to take your master from you today?"

"Yes, I know," Elisha replied, "but do not speak of it."

⁴Then Elijah said to him, "Stay here, Elisha; the LORD has sent me to Jericho.[c]"

And he replied, "As surely as the LORD lives and as you live, I will not leave you." So they went to Jericho.

D 1Ki 14:12–13 ◀▶ 2Ki 5:27
J 1Ki 21:29 ◀▶ 2Ki 2:3

1:1 a S Ge 19:37; 2Ki 3:5
1:2 b ver 16; c S Mk 3:22; d 1Sa 6:2; Isa 2:6; 14:29 e S Jdg 18:5
1:3 f ver 15; g 1Ki 17:1; h S 1Sa 28:8
1:4 i ver 6,16; Ps 41:8
1:6 j S ver 4
1:8 k S 1Ki 18:7; Mt 3:4; Mk 1:6
1:9 l 2Ki 6:14; m Ex 18:25; Isa 3:3
1:10 n S 1Ki 18:38; S Rev 11:5; S 13:13
1:13 o Ps 72:14
1:15 p ver 3; q Isa 51:12; 57:11; Jer 1:17; Eze 2:6
1:16 r S ver 2; s ver 4
1:17 t 2Ki 8:15; Jer 20:6; 28:17; u 2Ki 3:1; 8:16
2:1 v S Ge 5:24; w ver 11; 1Ki 19:11; Isa 5:28; 66:15; Jer 4:13; Na 1:3; x S 1Ki 19:16,21; y S Dt 11:30; 2Ki 4:38
2:2 z ver 6; a Ru 1:16
2:3 b 1Sa 10:5
2:4 c Jos 3:16

J 2Ki 1:4 ◀▶ 2Ki 2:5

a 17 Hebrew *Jehoram*, a variant of *Joram*

⁵The company^d of the prophets at Jericho went up to Elisha and asked him, "Do you know that the LORD is going to take your master from you today?"

"Yes, I know," he replied, "but do not speak of it."

⁶Then Elijah said to him, "Stay here;^e the LORD has sent me to the Jordan."^f

And he replied, "As surely as the LORD lives and as you live, I will not leave you."^g So the two of them walked on. ⁷Fifty men of the company of the prophets went and stood at a distance, facing the place where Elijah and Elisha had stopped at the Jordan. ⁸Elijah took his cloak,^h rolled it up and struck^i the water with it. The water divided^j to the right and to the left, and the two of them crossed over on dry^k ground.

⁹When they had crossed, Elijah said to Elisha, "Tell me, what can I do for you before I am taken from you?"

"Let me inherit a double^l portion of your spirit,"^m Elisha replied.

¹⁰"You have asked a difficult thing," Elijah said, "yet if you see me when I am taken from you, it will be yours—otherwise not."

¹¹As they were walking along and talking together, suddenly a chariot of fire^n and horses of fire appeared and separated the two of them, and Elijah went up to heaven^o in a whirlwind.^p ¹²Elisha saw this and cried out, "My father! My father! The chariots^q and horsemen of Israel!" And Elisha saw him no more. Then he took hold of his own clothes and tore^r them apart.

¹³He picked up the cloak that had fallen from Elijah and went back and stood on the bank of the Jordan. ¹⁴Then he took the cloak^s that had fallen from him and struck^t the water with it. "Where now is the LORD, the God of Elijah?" he asked. When he struck the water, it divided to the right and to the left, and he crossed over.

¹⁵The company^u of the prophets from Jericho, who were watching, said, "The spirit^v of Elijah is resting on Elisha." And they went to meet him and bowed to the ground before him. ¹⁶"Look," they said, "we your servants have fifty able men. Let them go and look for your master. Perhaps the Spirit^w of the LORD has picked him up^x and set him down on some mountain or in some valley."

"No," Elisha replied, "do not send them."

¹⁷But they persisted until he was too ashamed^y to refuse. So he said, "Send them." And they sent fifty men, who searched for three days but did not find him. ¹⁸When they returned to Elisha, who was staying in Jericho, he said to them, "Didn't I tell you not to go?"

Healing of the Water

¹⁹The men of the city said to Elisha, "Look, our lord, this town is well situated, as you can see, but the water is bad and the land is unproductive."

²⁰"Bring me a new bowl," he said, "and put salt in it." So they brought it to him.

²¹Then he went out to the spring and threw^z the salt into it, saying, "This is what the LORD says: 'I have healed this water. Never again will it cause death or make the land unproductive.' " ²²And the water has remained wholesome^a to this day, according to the word Elisha had spoken.

Elisha Is Jeered

²³From there Elisha went up to Bethel. As he was walking along the road, some youths came out of the town and jeered^b at him. "Go up, you baldhead!" they said. "Go on up, you baldhead!" ²⁴He turned around, looked at them and called

---

J 2Ki 2:3 ◀▶ 2Ki 2:9–10
J 2Ki 2:5 ◀▶ 2Ki 5:27
E 1Ki 22:24 ◀▶ 2Ki 2:15–16
N Ge 1:2 ◀▶ Ne 9:20

2:5 ^d ver 3
2:6 ^e ver 2 ^f Jos 3:15 ^g Ru 1:16
2:8 ^h S 1Ki 19:19 ^i ver 14 ^j S Ex 14:21 ^k Ex 14:22,29
2:9 ^l S Dt 21:17 ^m S Nu 11:17
2:11 ^n 2Ki 6:17; Ps 68:17; 104:3,4; Isa 66:15; Hab 3:8; Zec 6:1 ^o S Ge 5:24 ^p S ver 1
2:12 ^q 2Ki 6:17; 13:14 ^r S Ge 37:29
2:14 ^s S 1Ki 19:19 ^t ver 8
2:15 ^u S 1Sa 10:5 ^v S Nu 11:17
2:16 ^w S 1Ki 18:12 ^x Ac 8:39
2:17 ^y S Jdg 3:25
2:21 ^z S Ex 15:25; 2Ki 4:41; 6:6
2:22 ^a Ex 15:25
2:23 ^b S Ex 22:28; 2Ch 30:10; 36:16; Job 19:18; Ps 31:18

E 2Ki 2:9–10 ◀▶ 2Ki 3:15
L 1Ki 22:24 ◀▶ 2Ch 18:23
M 1Sa 19:20–23 ◀▶ Job 26:13–14

2:11–12 These verses mention the second time that God supernaturally took someone to heaven without a death experience. The first such rapture happened to Enoch (see Ge 5:24). These OT raptures foreshadow the final rapture of believers (see 1Co 15:51; 1Th 4:16–17) when Jesus Christ comes again to take his church to the marriage supper of the Lamb (see Rev 19:17–19). Notice that Elisha's description of this miraculous event includes chariots and horsemen, symbols that are used throughout Scripture to indicate strength and might (see Ps 104:3).

down a curse on them in the name of the LORD. Then two bears came out of the woods and mauled forty-two of the youths. ²⁵And he went on to Mount Carmel and from there returned to Samaria.

Moab Revolts

3 Joram son of Ahab became king of Israel in Samaria in the eighteenth year of Jehoshaphat king of Judah, and he reigned twelve years. ²He did evil in the eyes of the LORD, but not as his father and mother had done. He got rid of the sacred stone of Baal that his father had made. ³Nevertheless he clung to the sins of Jeroboam son of Nebat, which he had caused Israel to commit; he did not turn away from them.

⁴Now Mesha king of Moab raised sheep, and he had to supply the king of Israel with a hundred thousand lambs and with the wool of a hundred thousand rams. ⁵But after Ahab died, the king of Moab rebelled against the king of Israel. ⁶So at that time King Joram set out from Samaria and mobilized all Israel. ⁷He also sent this message to Jehoshaphat king of Judah: "The king of Moab has rebelled against me. Will you go with me to fight against Moab?"

"I will go with you," he replied. "I am as you are, my people as your people, my horses as your horses."

⁸"By what route shall we attack?" he asked.

"Through the Desert of Edom," he answered.

⁹So the king of Israel set out with the king of Judah and the king of Edom. After a roundabout march of seven days, the army had no more water for themselves or for the animals with them.

¹⁰"What!" exclaimed the king of Israel. "Has the LORD called us three kings together only to hand us over to Moab?"

¹¹But Jehoshaphat asked, "Is there no prophet of the LORD here, that we may inquire of the LORD through him?"

An officer of the king of Israel answered, "Elisha son of Shaphat is here. He used to pour water on the hands of Elijah."

¹²Jehoshaphat said, "The word of the LORD is with him." So the king of Israel and Jehoshaphat and the king of Edom went down to him.

¹³Elisha said to the king of Israel, "What do we have to do with each other? Go to the prophets of your father and the prophets of your mother."

"No," the king of Israel answered, "because it was the LORD who called us three kings together to hand us over to Moab."

¹⁴Elisha said, "As surely as the LORD Almighty lives, whom I serve, if I did not have respect for the presence of Jehoshaphat king of Judah, I would not look at you or even notice you. ¹⁵But now bring me a harpist."

While the harpist was playing, the hand of the LORD came upon Elisha ¹⁶and he said, "This is what the LORD says: Make this valley full of ditches. ¹⁷For this is what the LORD says: You will see neither wind nor rain, yet this valley will be filled with water, and you, your cattle and your other animals will drink. ¹⁸This is an easy thing in the eyes of the LORD; he will also hand Moab over to you. ¹⁹You will overthrow every fortified city and every major town. You will cut down every good tree, stop up all the springs, and ruin every good field with stones."

²⁰The next morning, about the time for offering the sacrifice, there it was—water flowing from the direction of Edom! And the land was filled with water.

²¹Now all the Moabites had heard that the kings had come to fight against them; so every man, young and old, who could bear arms was called up and stationed on the border. ²²When they got up early in the morning, the sun was shining on the water. To the Moabites across the way, the water looked red—like blood. ²³"That's blood!" they said. "Those kings

E 2Ki 2:15–16 ◀▶ 1Ch 12:18

F 1Ki 19:5–8 ◀▶ 2Ki 4:1–7

b 1 Hebrew *Jehoram,* a variant of *Joram;* also in verse 6 *c 11* That is, was Elijah's personal servant.

3:15–20 Elisha prophesied to the three kings of Judah, Israel and Edom that God would supernaturally fill these man-made ditches in the desolate valley with water. In addition, Elisha prophesied that the three kings would defeat the Moabites and conquer their land because of the Moabite's rebellion from Israel's rule after the death of King Ahab.

must have fought and slaughtered each other. Now to the plunder, Moab!"

²⁴But when the Moabites came to the camp of Israel, the Israelites rose up and fought them until they fled. And the Israelites invaded the land and slaughtered the Moabites. ²⁵They destroyed the towns, and each man threw a stone on every good field until it was covered. They stopped up all the springs and cut down every good tree. Only Kir Hareseth^z was left with its stones in place, but men armed with slings surrounded it and attacked it as well.

²⁶When the king of Moab saw that the battle had gone against him, he took with him seven hundred swordsmen to break through to the king of Edom, but they failed. ²⁷Then he took his firstborn^a son, who was to succeed him as king, and offered him as a sacrifice on the city wall. The fury against Israel was great; they withdrew and returned to their own land.

The Widow's Oil

4 The wife of a man from the company^b of the prophets cried out to Elisha, "Your servant my husband is dead, and you know that he revered the LORD. But now his creditor^c is coming to take my two boys as his slaves."

²Elisha replied to her, "How can I help you? Tell me, what do you have in your house?"

"Your servant has nothing there at all," she said, "except a little oil."^d

³Elisha said, "Go around and ask all your neighbors for empty jars. Don't ask for just a few. ⁴Then go inside and shut the door behind you and your sons. Pour oil into all the jars, and as each is filled, put it to one side."

⁵She left him and afterward shut the door behind her and her sons. They brought the jars to her and she kept pouring. ⁶When all the jars were full, she said to her son, "Bring me another one."

But he replied, "There is not a jar left." Then the oil stopped flowing.

⁷She went and told the man of God,^e and he said, "Go, sell the oil and pay your debts. You and your sons can live on what is left."

The Shunammite's Son Restored to Life

⁸One day Elisha went to Shunem.^f And a well-to-do woman was there, who urged him to stay for a meal. So whenever he came by, he stopped there to eat. ⁹She said to her husband, "I know that this man who often comes our way is a holy man of God. ¹⁰Let's make a small room on the roof and put in it a bed and a table, a chair and a lamp for him. Then he can stay^g there whenever he comes to us."

¹¹One day when Elisha came, he went up to his room and lay down there. ¹²He said to his servant Gehazi, "Call the Shunammite."^h So he called her, and she stood before him. ¹³Elisha said to him, "Tell her, 'You have gone to all this trouble for us. Now what can be done for you? Can we speak on your behalf to the king or the commander of the army?'"

She replied, "I have a home among my own people."

¹⁴"What can be done for her?" Elisha asked.

Gehazi said, "Well, she has no son and her husband is old."

¹⁵Then Elisha said, "Call her." So he called her, and she stood in the doorway. ¹⁶"About this time^i next year," Elisha said, "you will hold a son in your arms."

"No, my lord," she objected. "Don't mislead your servant, O man of God!"

¹⁷But the woman became pregnant, and the next year about that same time she gave birth to a son, just as Elisha had told her.

¹⁸The child grew, and one day he went out to his father, who was with the reapers.^j ¹⁹"My head! My head!" he said to his father.

His father told a servant, "Carry him to his mother." ²⁰After the servant had lifted him up and carried him to his mother, the boy sat on her lap until noon, and then he died. ²¹She went up and laid him on the bed^k of the man of God, then shut the door and went out.

²²She called her husband and said, "Please send me one of the servants and a donkey so I can go to the man of God quickly and return."

²³"Why go to him today?" he asked. "It's not the New Moon^l or the Sabbath."

"It's all right," she said.

²⁴She saddled the donkey and said to her servant, "Lead on; don't slow down for me unless I tell you." ²⁵So she set out and came to the man of God at Mount Carmel.

When he saw her in the distance, the man of God said to his servant Gehazi, "Look! There's the Shunammite! ²⁶Run to meet her and ask her, 'Are you all right? Is your husband all right? Is your child all right?' "

"Everything is all right," she said.

²⁷When she reached the man of God at the mountain, she took hold of his feet. Gehazi came over to push her away, but the man of God said, "Leave her alone! She is in bitter distress, but the LORD has hidden it from me and has not told me why."

²⁸"Did I ask you for a son, my lord?" she said. "Didn't I tell you, 'Don't raise my hopes'?"

²⁹Elisha said to Gehazi, "Tuck your cloak into your belt, take my staff in your hand and run. If you meet anyone, do not greet him, and if anyone greets you, do not answer. Lay my staff on the boy's face."

³⁰But the child's mother said, "As surely as the LORD lives and as you live, I will not leave you." So he got up and followed her.

³¹Gehazi went on ahead and laid the staff on the boy's face, but there was no sound or response. So Gehazi went back to meet Elisha and told him, "The boy has not awakened."

³²When Elisha reached the house, there was the boy lying dead on his couch. ³³He went in, shut the door on the two of them and prayed to the LORD. ³⁴Then he got on the bed and lay upon the boy, mouth to mouth, eyes to eyes, hands to hands. As he stretched himself out upon him, the boy's body grew warm. ³⁵Elisha turned away and walked back and forth in the room and then got on the bed and stretched out upon him once more. The boy sneezed seven times and opened his eyes.

³⁶Elisha summoned Gehazi and said, "Call the Shunammite." And he did. When she came, he said, "Take your son." ³⁷She came in, fell at his feet and bowed to the ground. Then she took her son and went out.

Death in the Pot

³⁸Elisha returned to Gilgal and there was a famine in that region. While the company of the prophets was meeting with him, he said to his servant, "Put on the large pot and cook some stew for these men."

³⁹One of them went out into the fields to gather herbs and found a wild vine. He gathered some of its gourds and filled the fold of his cloak. When he returned, he cut them up into the pot of stew, though no one knew what they were. ⁴⁰The stew was poured out for the men, but as they began to eat it, they cried out, "O man of God, there is death in the pot!" And they could not eat it.

⁴¹Elisha said, "Get some flour." He put it into the pot and said, "Serve it to the people to eat." And there was nothing harmful in the pot.

Feeding of a Hundred

⁴²A man came from Baal Shalishah, bringing the man of God twenty loaves of barley bread baked from the first ripe grain, along with some heads of new grain. "Give it to the people to eat," Elisha said.

⁴³"How can I set this before a hundred men?" his servant asked.

But Elisha answered, "Give it to the people to eat. For this is what the LORD says: 'They will eat and have some left over.' " ⁴⁴Then he set it before them, and they ate and had some left over, according to the word of the LORD.

Naaman Healed of Leprosy

5 Now Naaman was commander of the army of the king of Aram. He was a great man in the sight of his master and highly regarded, because through him the LORD had given victory to Aram. He was a valiant soldier, but he had leprosy.

²Now bands from Aram had gone out and had taken captive a young girl from Israel, and she served Naaman's wife.

ᵈ 1 The Hebrew word was used for various diseases affecting the skin—not necessarily leprosy; also in verses 3, 6, 7, 11 and 27.

³She said to her mistress, "If only my master would see the prophet[h] who is in Samaria! He would cure him of his leprosy." ⁴Naaman went to his master and told him what the girl from Israel had said. ⁵"By all means, go," the king of Aram replied. "I will send a letter to the king of Israel." So Naaman left, taking with him ten talents[e] of silver, six thousand shekels[f] of gold and ten sets of clothing.[i] ⁶The letter that he took to the king of Israel read: "With this letter I am sending my servant Naaman to you so that you may cure him of his leprosy."

⁷As soon as the king of Israel read the letter,[j] he tore his robes and said, "Am I God?[k] Can I kill and bring back to life?[l] Why does this fellow send someone to me to be cured of his leprosy? See how he is trying to pick a quarrel[m] with me!"

⁸When Elisha the man of God heard that the king of Israel had torn his robes, he sent him this message: "Why have you torn your robes? Have the man come to me and he will know that there is a prophet[n] in Israel." ⁹So Naaman went with his horses and chariots and stopped at the door of Elisha's house. ¹⁰Elisha sent a messenger to say to him, "Go, wash yourself seven times[p] in the Jordan, and your flesh will be restored and you will be cleansed."

¹¹But Naaman went away angry and said, "I thought that he would surely come out to me and stand and call on the name of the LORD his God, wave his hand[q] over the spot and cure me of my leprosy. ¹²Are not Abana and Pharpar, the rivers of Damascus, better than any of the waters[r] of Israel? Couldn't I wash in them and be cleansed?" So he turned and went off in a rage.[s]

¹³Naaman's servants went to him and said, "My father,[t] if the prophet had told you to do some great thing, would you not have done it? How much more, then, when he tells you, 'Wash and be cleansed'!" ¹⁴So he went down and dipped himself in the Jordan seven times,[u] as the man of God had told him, and his flesh was restored[v] and became clean like that of a young boy.[w]

¹⁵Then Naaman and all his attendants went back to the man of God.[x] He stood before him and said, "Now I know[y] that there is no God in all the world except in Israel. Please accept now a gift[z] from your servant."

¹⁶The prophet answered, "As surely as the LORD lives, whom I serve, I will not accept a thing." And even though Naaman urged him, he refused.[a]

¹⁷"If you will not," said Naaman, "please let me, your servant, be given as much earth[b] as a pair of mules can carry, for your servant will never again make burnt offerings and sacrifices to any other god but the LORD. ¹⁸But may the LORD forgive your servant for this one thing: When my master enters the temple of Rimmon to bow down and he is leaning[c] on my arm and I bow there also—when I bow down in the temple of Rimmon, may the LORD forgive your servant for this."

¹⁹"Go in peace,"[d] Elisha said.

After Naaman had traveled some distance, ²⁰Gehazi, the servant of Elisha the man of God, said to himself, "My master was too easy on Naaman, this Aramean, by not accepting from him what he brought. As surely as the LORD[e] lives, I will run after him and get something from him."

²¹So Gehazi hurried after Naaman. When Naaman saw him running toward him, he got down from the chariot to meet him. "Is everything all right?" he asked.

²²"Everything is all right," Gehazi answered. "My master sent me to say, 'Two young men from the company of the prophets have just come to me from the hill country of Ephraim. Please give them a talent[g] of silver and two sets of clothing.' "[f]

²³"By all means, take two talents," said Naaman. He urged Gehazi to accept them, and then tied up the two talents of silver in two bags, with two sets of clothing. He gave them to two of his servants, and they carried them ahead of Gehazi. ²⁴When Gehazi came to the hill, he took the things from the servants and put them away in the house. He sent the men away and they left. ²⁵Then he went in and stood before his master Elisha.

"Where have you been, Gehazi?" Elisha asked.

e 5 That is, about 750 pounds (about 340 kilograms) f 5 That is, about 150 pounds (about 70 kilograms) g 22 That is, about 75 pounds (about 34 kilograms)

"Your servant didn't go anywhere," Gehazi answered.

²⁶But Elisha said to him, "Was not my spirit with you when the man got down from his chariot to meet you? Is this the time to take money, or to accept clothes, olive groves, vineyards, flocks, herds, or menservants and maidservants? ²⁷Naaman's leprosy will cling to you and to your descendants forever." Then Gehazi went from Elisha's presence and he was leprous, as white as snow.

An Axhead Floats

6 The company of the prophets said to Elisha, "Look, the place where we meet with you is too small for us. ²Let us go to the Jordan, where each of us can get a pole; and let us build a place there for us to live."

And he said, "Go."

³Then one of them said, "Won't you please come with your servants?"

"I will," Elisha replied. ⁴And he went with them.

They went to the Jordan and began to cut down trees. ⁵As one of them was cutting down a tree, the iron axhead fell into the water. "Oh, my lord," he cried out, "it was borrowed!"

⁶The man of God asked, "Where did it fall?" When he showed him the place, Elisha cut a stick and threw it there, and made the iron float. ⁷"Lift it out," he said. Then the man reached out his hand and took it.

Elisha Traps Blinded Arameans

⁸Now the king of Aram was at war with Israel. After conferring with his officers, he said, "I will set up my camp in such and such a place."

⁹The man of God sent word to the king of Israel: "Beware of passing that place, because the Arameans are going down there." ¹⁰So the king of Israel checked on the place indicated by the man of God. Time and again Elisha warned the king, so that he was on his guard in such places.

¹¹This enraged the king of Aram. He summoned his officers and demanded of them, "Will you not tell me which of us is on the side of the king of Israel?"

¹²"None of us, my lord the king," said one of his officers, "but Elisha, the prophet who is in Israel, tells the king of Israel the very words you speak in your bedroom."

¹³"Go, find out where he is," the king ordered, "so I can send men and capture him." The report came back: "He is in Dothan." ¹⁴Then he sent horses and chariots and a strong force there. They went by night and surrounded the city.

¹⁵When the servant of the man of God got up and went out early the next morning, an army with horses and chariots had surrounded the city. "Oh, my lord, what shall we do?" the servant asked.

¹⁶"Don't be afraid," the prophet answered. "Those who are with us are more than those who are with them."

¹⁷And Elisha prayed, "O LORD, open his eyes so he may see." Then the LORD opened the servant's eyes, and he looked and saw the hills full of horses and chariots of fire all around Elisha.

¹⁸As the enemy came down toward him, Elisha prayed to the LORD, "Strike these people with blindness." So he struck them with blindness, as Elisha had asked.

¹⁹Elisha told them, "This is not the road and this is not the city. Follow me, and I will lead you to the man you are looking for." And he led them to Samaria.

²⁰After they entered the city, Elisha said, "LORD, open the eyes of these men so they can see." Then the LORD opened their eyes and they looked, and there they were, inside Samaria.

²¹When the king of Israel saw them, he

J 2Ki 2:9–10 ◀▶ 2Ki 7:19
D 2Ki 1:2–4 ◀▶ 2Ki 6:18
K 2Sa 22:36 ◀▶ 1Ch 4:10
L 2Sa 22:2–4 ◀▶ 1Ch 16:21–22
D 2Ki 5:27 ◀▶ 2Ki 15:5
F 2Ki 4:42–44 ◀▶ 2Ch 20:9
E 2Ki 5:14 ◀▶ 2Ki 8:4–5

6:15–17 These verses reveal the difference between natural vision and spiritual vision. Though natural vision viewed a difficult situation as overwhelming, spiritual vision recognized God's powerful hosts of heaven outnumbering the enemy. As believers, we are surrounded by angels who do God's bidding and help care for us (see Heb 1:14).

asked Elisha, "Shall I kill them, my father?"[w] Shall I kill them?"

²²"Do not kill them," he answered. "Would you kill men you have captured[x] with your own sword or bow? Set food and water before them so that they may eat and drink and then go back to their master." ²³So he prepared a great feast for them, and after they had finished eating and drinking, he sent them away, and they returned to their master. So the bands[y] from Aram stopped raiding Israel's territory.

Famine in Besieged Samaria

²⁴Some time later, Ben-Hadad[z] king of Aram mobilized his entire army and marched up and laid siege[a] to Samaria. ²⁵There was a great famine[b] in the city; the siege lasted so long that a donkey's head sold for eighty shekels[h] of silver, and a quarter of a cab[i] of seed pods[/c] for five shekels.[k]

²⁶As the king of Israel was passing by on the wall, a woman cried to him, "Help me, my lord the king!"

²⁷The king replied, "If the LORD does not help you, where can I get help for you? From the threshing floor? From the winepress?" ²⁸Then he asked her, "What's the matter?"

She answered, "This woman said to me, 'Give up your son so we may eat him today, and tomorrow we'll eat my son.' ²⁹So we cooked my son and ate[d] him. The next day I said to her, 'Give up your son so we may eat him,' but she had hidden him."

³⁰When the king heard the woman's words, he tore[e] his robes. As he went along the wall, the people looked, and there, underneath, he had sackcloth[f] on his body. ³¹He said, "May God deal with me, be it ever so severely, if the head of Elisha son of Shaphat remains on his shoulders today!"

³²Now Elisha was sitting in his house, and the elders[g] were sitting with him. The king sent a messenger ahead, but be-

---

6:21 ʷS 2Ki 5:13

6:22 ˣS Dt 20:11; 2Ch 28:8-15

6:23 ʸS 2Ki 5:2

6:24 ᶻS 1Ki 15:18; 2Ki 8:7 ᵃDt 28:52

6:25 ᵇS Lev 26:26; S Ru 1:1 ᶜIsa 36:12

6:29 ᵈS Lev 26:29; Dt 28:53-55

6:30 ᵉ2Ki 18:37; Isa 22:15 ᶠS Ge 37:34

6:32 ᵍEze 8:1; 14:1; 20:1 ʰ1Ki 18:4 ⁱver 31

6:33 ʲLev 24:11; Job 2:9; 14:14; Isa 40:31

7:1 ᵏver 16

7:2 ˡ2Ki 5:18 ᵐver 19; Ge 7:11; Ps 78:23; Mal 3:10 ⁿver 17

7:3 ᵒLev 13:45-46; Nu 5:1-4

---

fore he arrived, Elisha said to the elders, "Don't you see how this murderer[h] is sending someone to cut off my head?[i] Look, when the messenger comes, shut the door and hold it shut against him. Is not the sound of his master's footsteps behind him?" ³³While he was still talking to them, the messenger came down to him. And ⌊the king⌋ said, "This disaster is from the LORD. Why should I wait[j] for the LORD any longer?"

7 Elisha said, "Hear the word of the LORD. This is what the LORD says: About this time tomorrow, a seah[l] of flour will sell for a shekel[m] and two seahs[n] of barley for a shekel[k] at the gate of Samaria."

²The officer on whose arm the king was leaning[l] said to the man of God, "Look, even if the LORD should open the floodgates[m] of the heavens, could this happen?"

"You will see it with your own eyes," answered Elisha, "but you will not eat[n] any of it!"

The Siege Lifted

³Now there were four men with leprosy[o] at the entrance of the city gate. They said to each other, "Why stay here until we die? ⁴If we say, 'We'll go into the city'—the famine is there, and we will die. And if we stay here, we will die. So let's go over to the camp of the Arameans and surrender. If they spare us, we live; if they kill us, then we die."

⁵At dusk they got up and went to the camp of the Arameans. When they reached the edge of the camp, not a man

1Ki 18:41 ◀ ▶ 2Ki 8:19

ʰ25 That is, about 2 pounds (about 1 kilogram) ⁱ25 That is, probably about 1/2 pint (about 0.3 liter) ʲ25 Or *of dove's dung* ᵏ25 That is, about 2 ounces (about 55 grams) ˡ1 That is, probably about 7 quarts (about 7.3 liters); also in verses 16 and 18 ᵐ1 That is, about 2/5 ounce (about 11 grams); also in verses 16 and 18 ⁿ1 That is, probably about 13 quarts (about 15 liters); also in verses 16 and 18 ᵒ3 The Hebrew word is used for various diseases affecting the skin—not necessarily leprosy; also in verse 8.

7:1–2 Elisha prophesied that the siege of the Syrian army would miraculously end overnight. Furthermore, Elisha said that the ensuing surplus of food would cause food prices to drop overnight too. One of the nobles of Israel mocked this seemingly impossible prophecy. As a result, Elisha predicted that this doubter would live to see the miracle but he would not live to eat the food. In fulfillment of this prophecy, God supernaturally frightened the Syrian army causing them to flee their camp and leave their enormous stores of food behind. Every detail of Elisha's prediction was fulfilled, including the death of the unbelieving noble (see 7:18–20).

was there, ⁶for the Lord had caused the Arameans to hear the sound of chariots and horses and a great army, so that they said to one another, "Look, the king of Israel has hired the Hittite and Egyptian kings to attack us!" ⁷So they got up and fled in the dusk and abandoned their tents and their horses and donkeys. They left the camp as it was and ran for their lives.

⁸The men who had leprosy reached the edge of the camp and entered one of the tents. They ate and drank, and carried away silver, gold and clothes, and went off and hid them. They returned and entered another tent and took some things from it and hid them also.

⁹Then they said to each other, "We're not doing right. This is a day of good news and we are keeping it to ourselves. If we wait until daylight, punishment will overtake us. Let's go at once and report this to the royal palace."

¹⁰So they went and called out to the city gatekeepers and told them, "We went into the Aramean camp and not a man was there—not a sound of anyone—only tethered horses and donkeys, and the tents left just as they were." ¹¹The gatekeepers shouted the news, and it was reported within the palace.

¹²The king got up in the night and said to his officers, "I will tell you what the Arameans have done to us. They know we are starving; so they have left the camp to hide in the countryside, thinking, 'They will surely come out, and then we will take them alive and get into the city.'"

¹³One of his officers answered, "Have some men take five of the horses that are left in the city. Their plight will be like that of all the Israelites left here—yes, they will only be like all these Israelites who are doomed. So let us send them to find out what happened."

¹⁴So they selected two chariots with their horses, and the king sent them after the Aramean army. He commanded the drivers, "Go and find out what has happened." ¹⁵They followed them as far as the Jordan, and they found the whole road strewn with the clothing and equipment the Arameans had thrown away in their headlong flight. So the messengers returned and reported to the king. ¹⁶Then the people went out and plundered the camp of the Arameans. So a seah of flour sold for a shekel, and two seahs of barley sold for a shekel, as the Lord had said.

¹⁷Now the king had put the officer on whose arm he leaned in charge of the gate, and the people trampled him in the gateway, and he died, just as the man of God had foretold when the king came down to his house. ¹⁸It happened as the man of God had said to the king: "About this time tomorrow, a seah of flour will sell for a shekel and two seahs of barley for a shekel at the gate of Samaria."

¹⁹The officer had said to the man of God, "Look, even if the Lord should open the floodgates of the heavens, could this happen?" The man of God had replied, "You will see it with your own eyes, but you will not eat any of it!" ²⁰And that is exactly what happened to him, for the people trampled him in the gateway, and he died.

The Shunammite's Land Restored

8 Now Elisha had said to the woman whose son he had restored to life, "Go away with your family and stay for a while wherever you can, because the Lord has decreed a famine in the land that will last seven years." ²The woman proceeded to do as the man of God said. She and her family went away and stayed in the land of the Philistines seven years.

³At the end of the seven years she came back from the land of the Philistines and went to the king to beg for her house and land. ⁴The king was talking to Gehazi, the servant of the man of God, and had said, "Tell me about all the great things Elisha has done." ⁵Just as Gehazi was telling the king how Elisha had restored the dead to life, the woman whose son Elisha had brought back to life came to beg the king for her house and land.

Gehazi said, "This is the woman, my lord the king, and this is her son whom Elisha restored to life." ⁶The king asked the woman about it, and she told him. Then he assigned an official to her case and said to him, "Give back everything that belonged to her, including all the income from her land from the day she left the country until now."

Hazael Murders Ben-Hadad

[7]Elisha went to Damascus,[e] and Ben-Hadad[f] king of Aram was ill. When the king was told, "The man of God has come all the way up here," [8]he said to Hazael,[g] "Take a gift[h] with you and go to meet the man of God. Consult[i] the LORD through him; ask him, 'Will I recover from this illness?' "

[9]Hazael went to meet Elisha, taking with him as a gift forty camel-loads of all the finest wares of Damascus. He went in and stood before him, and said, "Your son Ben-Hadad king of Aram has sent me to ask, 'Will I recover from this illness?' "

[10]Elisha answered, "Go and say to him, 'You will certainly recover';[j] but[p] the LORD has revealed to me that he will in fact die." [11]He stared at him with a fixed gaze until Hazael felt ashamed.[k] Then the man of God began to weep.[l]

[12]"Why is my lord weeping?" asked Hazael.

"Because I know the harm[m] you will do to the Israelites," he answered. "You will set fire to their fortified places, kill their young men with the sword, dash[n] their little children[o] to the ground, and rip open[p] their pregnant women."

[13]Hazael said, "How could your servant, a mere dog,[q] accomplish such a feat?"

"The LORD has shown me that you will become king[r] of Aram," answered Elisha.

[14]Then Hazael left Elisha and returned to his master. When Ben-Hadad asked, "What did Elisha say to you?" Hazael replied, "He told me that you would certainly recover." [15]But the next day he took a thick cloth, soaked it in water and spread it over the king's face, so that he died.[s] Then Hazael succeeded him as king.

Jehoram King of Judah

8:16-24pp — 2Ch 21:5-10,20

[16]In the fifth year of Joram[t] son of Ahab king of Israel, when Jehoshaphat was king of Judah, Jehoram[u] son of Jehoshaphat began his reign as king of Judah. [17]He was thirty-two years old when he became king, and he reigned in Jerusalem eight years. [18]He walked in the ways of the kings of Israel, as the house of Ahab had done, for he married a daughter[v] of Ahab. He did evil in the eyes of the LORD. [19]Nevertheless, for the sake of his servant David, the LORD was not willing to destroy[w] Judah. He had promised to maintain a lamp[x] for David and his descendants forever.

[20]In the time of Jehoram, Edom rebelled against Judah and set up its own king.[y] [21]So Jehoram[q] went to Zair with all his chariots. The Edomites surrounded him and his chariot commanders, but he rose up and broke through by night; his army, however, fled back home. [22]To this day Edom has been in rebellion[z] against Judah. Libnah[a] revolted at the same time.

[23]As for the other events of Jehoram's reign, and all he did, are they not written in the book of the annals of the kings of Judah? [24]Jehoram rested with his fathers and was buried with them in the City of David. And Ahaziah his son succeeded him as king.

Ahaziah King of Judah

8:25-29pp — 2Ch 22:1-6

[25]In the twelfth[b] year of Joram son of Ahab king of Israel, Ahaziah son of Jehoram king of Judah began to reign. [26]Ahaziah was twenty-two years old when he became king, and he reigned in Jerusalem one year. His mother's name was Athaliah,[c] a granddaughter of Omri[d] king of Israel. [27]He walked in the ways of the house of Ahab[e] and did evil[f] in the eyes of the LORD, as the house of Ahab had done, for he was related by marriage to Ahab's family.

[28]Ahaziah went with Joram son of Ahab to war against Hazael king of Aram at Ramoth Gilead.[g] The Arameans wounded Joram; [29]so King Joram returned to Jezreel[h] to recover from the wounds the Arameans had inflicted on him at Ramoth[r] in his battle with Hazael[i] king of Aram.

Then Ahaziah[j] son of Jehoram king of Judah went down to Jezreel to see Joram son of Ahab, because he had been wounded.

◀ 2Ki 7:1-2 ◀▶ 2Ki 13:15-19

[p] 10 The Hebrew may also be read *Go and say, 'You will certainly not recover,' for.* [q] 21 Hebrew *Joram,* a variant of *Jehoram;* also in verses 23 and 24 [r] 29 Hebrew *Ramah,* a variant of *Ramoth*

Jehu Anointed King of Israel

9 The prophet Elisha summoned a man from the company[k] of the prophets and said to him, "Tuck your cloak into your belt,[1] take this flask of oil[m] with you and go to Ramoth Gilead.[n] ²When you get there, look for Jehu son of Jehoshaphat, the son of Nimshi. Go to him, get him away from his companions and take him into an inner room. ³Then take the flask and pour the oil[o] on his head and declare, 'This is what the LORD says: I anoint you king over Israel.' Then open the door and run; don't delay!"

⁴So the young man, the prophet, went to Ramoth Gilead. ⁵When he arrived, he found the army officers sitting together. "I have a message for you, commander," he said.

"For which of us?" asked Jehu.

"For you, commander," he replied.

⁶Jehu got up and went into the house. Then the prophet poured the oil[p] on Jehu's head and declared, "This is what the LORD, the God of Israel, says: 'I anoint you king over the LORD's people Israel. ⁷You are to destroy the house of Ahab your master, and I will avenge[q] the blood of my servants[r] the prophets and the blood of all the LORD's servants shed by Jezebel.[s] ⁸The whole house[t] of Ahab will perish. I will cut off from Ahab every last male[u] in Israel—slave or free. ⁹I will make the house of Ahab like the house of Jeroboam[v] son of Nebat and like the house of Baasha[w] son of Ahijah. ¹⁰As for Jezebel, dogs[x] will devour her on the plot of ground at Jezreel, and no one will bury her.'" Then he opened the door and ran.

¹¹When Jehu went out to his fellow officers, one of them asked him, "Is everything all right? Why did this madman[y] come to you?"

"You know the man and the sort of things he says," Jehu replied.

¹²"That's not true!" they said. "Tell us."

Jehu said, "Here is what he told me: 'This is what the LORD says: I anoint you king over Israel.'"

¹³They hurried and took their cloaks and spread[z] them under him on the bare steps. Then they blew the trumpet[a] and shouted, "Jehu is king!"

Jehu Kills Joram and Ahaziah
9:21–29pp — 2Ch 22:7–9

¹⁴So Jehu son of Jehoshaphat, the son of Nimshi, conspired against Joram. (Now Joram and all Israel had been defending Ramoth Gilead[b] against Hazael king of Aram, ¹⁵but King Joram[s] had returned to Jezreel to recover[c] from the wounds the Arameans had inflicted on him in the battle with Hazael king of Aram.) Jehu said, "If this is the way you feel, don't let anyone slip out of the city to go and tell the news in Jezreel." ¹⁶Then he got into his chariot and rode to Jezreel, because Joram was resting there and Ahaziah[d] king of Judah had gone down to see him.

¹⁷When the lookout[e] standing on the tower in Jezreel saw Jehu's troops approaching, he called out, "I see some troops coming."

"Get a horseman," Joram ordered. "Send him to meet them and ask, 'Do you come in peace?'"

¹⁸The horseman rode off to meet Jehu and said, "This is what the king says: 'Do you come in peace?'"

"What do you have to do with peace?" Jehu replied. "Fall in behind me."

The lookout reported, "The messenger has reached them, but he isn't coming back."

¹⁹So the king sent out a second horseman. When he came to them he said, "This is what the king says: 'Do you come in peace?'"

Jehu replied, "What do you have to do with peace? Fall in behind me."

²⁰The lookout reported, "He has reached them, but he isn't coming back either. The driving is like[g] that of Jehu son of Nimshi—he drives like a madman."

²¹"Hitch up my chariot," Joram ordered. And when it was hitched up, Joram king of Israel and Ahaziah king of Judah rode out, each in his own chariot, to meet Jehu. They met him at the plot of

s 15 Hebrew Jehoram, a variant of Joram; also in verses 17 and 21-24

9:4 Some scholars suggest that this young prophet, who was "a man from the company of the prophets" (9:1), was the prophet Jonah, son of Amittai, who was later sent by God to Nineveh.

ground that had belonged to Naboth the Jezreelite. ²²When Joram saw Jehu he asked, "Have you come in peace, Jehu?"

"How can there be peace," Jehu replied, "as long as all the idolatry and witchcraft of your mother Jezebel abound?"

²³Joram turned about and fled, calling out to Ahaziah, "Treachery, Ahaziah!"

²⁴Then Jehu drew his bow and shot Joram between the shoulders. The arrow pierced his heart and he slumped down in his chariot. ²⁵Jehu said to Bidkar, his chariot officer, "Pick him up and throw him on the field that belonged to Naboth the Jezreelite. Remember how you and I were riding together in chariots behind Ahab his father when the LORD made this prophecy about him: ²⁶'Yesterday I saw the blood of Naboth and the blood of his sons, declares the LORD, and I will surely make you pay for it on this plot of ground, declares the LORD.' Now then, pick him up and throw him on that plot, in accordance with the word of the LORD."

²⁷When Ahaziah king of Judah saw what had happened, he fled up the road to Beth Haggan. Jehu chased him, shouting, "Kill him too!" They wounded him in his chariot on the way up to Gur near Ibleam, but he escaped to Megiddo and died there. ²⁸His servants took him by chariot to Jerusalem and buried him with his fathers in his tomb in the City of David. ²⁹(In the eleventh year of Joram son of Ahab, Ahaziah had become king of Judah.)

Jezebel Killed

³⁰Then Jehu went to Jezreel. When Jezebel heard about it, she painted her eyes, arranged her hair and looked out of a window. ³¹As Jehu entered the gate, she asked, "Have you come in peace, Zimri, you murderer of your master?"

³²He looked up at the window and called out, "Who is on my side? Who?" Two or three eunuchs looked down at him. ³³"Throw her down!" Jehu said. So they threw her down, and some of her blood spattered the wall and the horses as they trampled her underfoot.

³⁴Jehu went in and ate and drank. "Take care of that cursed woman," he said, "and bury her, for she was a king's daughter." ³⁵But when they went out to bury her, they found nothing except her skull, her feet and her hands. ³⁶They went back and told Jehu, who said, "This is the word of the LORD that he spoke through his servant Elijah the Tishbite: On the plot of ground at Jezreel dogs will devour Jezebel's flesh. ³⁷Jezebel's body will be like refuse on the ground in the plot at Jezreel, so that no one will be able to say, 'This is Jezebel.'"

Ahab's Family Killed

10 Now there were in Samaria seventy sons of the house of Ahab. So Jehu wrote letters and sent them to Samaria: to the officials of Jezreel, to the elders and to the guardians of Ahab's children. He said, ²"As soon as this letter reaches you, since your master's sons are with you and you have chariots and horses, a fortified city and weapons, ³choose the best and most worthy of your master's sons and set him on his father's throne. Then fight for your master's house."

⁴But they were terrified and said, "If two kings could not resist him, how can we?"

⁵So the palace administrator, the city governor, the elders and the guardians sent this message to Jehu: "We are your servants and we will do anything you say. We will not appoint anyone as king; you do whatever you think best."

⁶Then Jehu wrote them a second letter, saying, "If you are on my side and will obey me, take the heads of your master's sons and come to me in Jezreel by this time tomorrow."

Now the royal princes, seventy of them, were with the leading men of the city, who were rearing them. ⁷When the letter arrived, these men took the princes and slaughtered all seventy of them. They put their heads in baskets and sent them to Jehu in Jezreel. ⁸When the messenger arrived, he told Jehu, "They have brought the heads of the princes."

Then Jehu ordered, "Put them in two piles at the entrance of the city gate until morning."

⁹The next morning Jehu went out. He

stood before all the people and said, "You are innocent. It was I who conspired against my master and killed him, but who killed all these? ¹⁰Know then, that not a word the LORD has spoken against the house of Ahab will fail. The LORD has done what he promised^g through his servant Elijah."^h ¹¹So Jehu^i killed everyone in Jezreel who remained of the house of Ahab, as well as all his chief men, his close friends and his priests, leaving him no survivor.^j

¹²Jehu then set out and went toward Samaria. At Beth Eked of the Shepherds, ¹³he met some relatives of Ahaziah king of Judah and asked, "Who are you?"

They said, "We are relatives of Ahaziah,^k and we have come down to greet the families of the king and of the queen mother.'"

¹⁴"Take them alive!" he ordered. So they took them alive and slaughtered them by the well of Beth Eked—forty-two men. He left no survivor.^m

¹⁵After he left there, he came upon Jehonadab^n son of Recab,^o who was on his way to meet him. Jehu greeted him and said, "Are you in accord with me, as I am with you?"

"I am," Jehonadab answered.

"If so," said Jehu, "give me your hand."^p So he did, and Jehu helped him up into the chariot. ¹⁶Jehu said, "Come with me and see my zeal^q for the LORD." Then he had him ride along in his chariot.

¹⁷When Jehu came to Samaria, he killed all who were left there of Ahab's family;^r he destroyed them, according to the word of the LORD spoken to Elijah.

Ministers of Baal Killed

¹⁸Then Jehu brought all the people together and said to them, "Ahab served^s Baal a little; Jehu will serve him much. ¹⁹Now summon^t all the prophets of Baal, all his ministers and all his priests. See that no one is missing, because I am going to hold a great sacrifice for Baal. Anyone who fails to come will no longer live." But Jehu was acting deceptively in order to destroy the ministers of Baal.

²⁰Jehu said, "Call an assembly^u in honor of Baal." So they proclaimed it. ²¹Then he sent word throughout Israel, and all the ministers of Baal came; not one stayed away. They crowded into the temple of Baal until it was full from one end to the other. ²²And Jehu said to the keeper of the wardrobe, "Bring robes for all the ministers of Baal." So he brought out robes for them.

²³Then Jehu and Jehonadab son of Recab went into the temple of Baal. Jehu said to the ministers of Baal, "Look around and see that no servants of the LORD are here with you—only ministers of Baal." ²⁴So they went in to make sacrifices and burnt offerings. Now Jehu had posted eighty men outside with this warning: "If one of you lets any of the men I am placing in your hands escape, it will be your life for his life."^v

²⁵As soon as Jehu had finished making the burnt offering, he ordered the guards and officers: "Go in and kill^w them; let no one escape."^x So they cut them down with the sword. The guards and officers threw the bodies out and then entered the inner shrine of the temple of Baal. ²⁶They brought the sacred stone^y out of the temple of Baal and burned it. ²⁷They demolished the sacred stone of Baal and tore down the temple^z of Baal, and people have used it for a latrine to this day.

²⁸So Jehu^a destroyed Baal worship in Israel. ²⁹However, he did not turn away from the sins^b of Jeroboam son of Nebat, which he had caused Israel to commit—the worship of the golden calves^c at Bethel^d and Dan.

³⁰The LORD said to Jehu, "Because you have done well in accomplishing what is right in my eyes and have done to the house of Ahab all I had in mind to do, your descendants will sit on the throne of Israel to the fourth generation."^e ³¹Yet Jehu was not careful^f to keep the law of the LORD, the God of Israel, with all his heart. He did not turn away from the sins^g of Jeroboam, which he had caused Israel to commit.

³²In those days the LORD began to reduce^h the size of Israel. Hazael^i overpowered the Israelites throughout their territory ³³east of the Jordan in all the land of Gilead (the region of Gad, Reuben and Manasseh), from Aroer^j by the Arnon^k Gorge through Gilead to Bashan.

³⁴As for the other events of Jehu's reign, all he did, and all his achieve-

L 2Ki 4:16 ◄ ► 2Ki 20:5–10

ments, are they not written in the book of the annals of the kings of Israel? ³⁵Jehu rested with his fathers and was buried in Samaria. And Jehoahaz his son succeeded him as king. ³⁶The time that Jehu reigned over Israel in Samaria was twenty-eight years.

Athaliah and Joash
11:1-21pp — 2Ch 22:10-23:21

11 When Athaliah the mother of Ahaziah saw that her son was dead, she proceeded to destroy the whole royal family. ²But Jehosheba, the daughter of King Jehoram^y and sister of Ahaziah, took Joash son of Ahaziah and stole him away from among the royal princes, who were about to be murdered. She put him and his nurse in a bedroom to hide him from Athaliah; so he was not killed. ³He remained hidden with his nurse at the temple of the LORD for six years while Athaliah ruled the land.

⁴In the seventh year Jehoiada sent for the commanders of units of a hundred, the Carites and the guards and had them brought to him at the temple of the LORD. He made a covenant with them and put them under oath at the temple of the LORD. Then he showed them the king's son. ⁵He commanded them, saying, "This is what you are to do: You who are in the three companies that are going on duty on the Sabbath—a third of you guarding the royal palace, ⁶a third at the Sur Gate, and a third at the gate behind the guard, who take turns guarding the temple— ⁷and you who are in the other two companies that normally go off Sabbath duty are all to guard the temple for the king. ⁸Station yourselves around the king, each man with his weapon in his hand. Anyone who approaches your ranks must be put to death. Stay close to the king wherever he goes."

⁹The commanders of units of a hundred did just as Jehoiada the priest ordered. Each one took his men—those who were going on duty on the Sabbath and those who were going off duty—and came to Jehoiada the priest. ¹⁰Then he gave the commanders the spears and shields that had belonged to King David and that were in the temple of the LORD. ¹¹The guards, each with his weapon in his hand, stationed themselves around the king—near the altar and the temple, from the south side to the north side of the temple.

¹²Jehoiada brought out the king's son and put the crown on him; he presented him with a copy of the covenant and proclaimed him king. They anointed him, and the people clapped their hands and shouted, "Long live the king!"

¹³When Athaliah heard the noise made by the guards and the people, she went to the people at the temple of the LORD. ¹⁴She looked and there was the king, standing by the pillar, as the custom was. The officers and the trumpeters were beside the king, and all the people of the land were rejoicing and blowing trumpets. Then Athaliah tore her robes and called out, "Treason! Treason!"

¹⁵Jehoiada the priest ordered the commanders of units of a hundred, who were in charge of the troops: "Bring her out between the ranks and put to the sword anyone who follows her." For the priest had said, "She must not be put to death in the temple of the LORD." ¹⁶So they seized her as she reached the place where the horses enter the palace grounds, and there she was put to death.

¹⁷Jehoiada then made a covenant between the LORD and the king and people that they would be the LORD's people. He also made a covenant between the king and the people. ¹⁸All the people of the land went to the temple of Baal and tore it down. They smashed the altars and idols to pieces and killed Mattan the priest of Baal in front of the altars.

Then Jehoiada the priest posted guards at the temple of the LORD. ¹⁹He took with him the commanders of hundreds, the Carites, the guards and all the people of the land, and together they brought the king down from the temple of the LORD and went into the palace, entering by way of the gate of the guards. The king then took his place on the royal throne, ²⁰and all the people of the land rejoiced. And the city was quiet, because Athaliah had been slain with the sword at the palace.

²¹Joash was seven years old when he began to reign.

---

y 2 Hebrew Joram, a variant of Jehoram z 8 Or approaches the precincts a 15 Or out from the precincts b 21 Hebrew Jehoash, a variant of Joash

Joash Repairs the Temple

12:1-21pp — 2Ch 24:1-14; 24:23-27

12 In the seventh year of Jehu, Joash[c1] became king, and he reigned in Jerusalem forty years. His mother's name was Zibiah; she was from Beersheba. ²Joash did what was right in the eyes of the LORD all the years Jehoiada the priest instructed him. ³The high places, however, were not removed; the people continued to offer sacrifices and burn incense there.

⁴Joash said to the priests, "Collect all the money that is brought as sacred offerings to the temple of the LORD—the money collected in the census, the money received from personal vows and the money brought voluntarily to the temple. ⁵Let every priest receive the money from one of the treasurers, and let it be used to repair whatever damage is found in the temple."

⁶But by the twenty-third year of King Joash the priests still had not repaired the temple. ⁷Therefore King Joash summoned Jehoiada the priest and the other priests and asked them, "Why aren't you repairing the damage done to the temple? Take no more money from your treasurers, but hand it over for repairing the temple." ⁸The priests agreed that they would not collect any more money from the people and that they would not repair the temple themselves.

⁹Jehoiada the priest took a chest and bored a hole in its lid. He placed it beside the altar, on the right side as one enters the temple of the LORD. The priests who guarded the entrance put into the chest all the money that was brought to the temple of the LORD. ¹⁰Whenever they saw that there was a large amount of money in the chest, the royal secretary and the high priest came, counted the money that had been brought into the temple of the LORD and put it into bags. ¹¹When the amount had been determined, they gave the money to the men appointed to supervise the work on the temple. With it they paid those who worked on the temple of the LORD—the carpenters and builders, ¹²the masons and stonecutters. They purchased timber and dressed stone for the repair of the temple of the LORD, and met all the other expenses of restoring the temple.

¹³The money brought into the temple was not spent for making silver basins, wick trimmers, sprinkling bowls, trumpets or any other articles of gold or silver for the temple of the LORD; ¹⁴it was paid to the workmen, who used it to repair the temple. ¹⁵They did not require an accounting from those to whom they gave the money to pay the workers, because they acted with complete honesty. ¹⁶The money from the guilt offerings and sin offerings was not brought into the temple of the LORD; it belonged to the priests.

¹⁷About this time Hazael king of Aram went up and attacked Gath and captured it. Then he turned to attack Jerusalem. ¹⁸But Joash king of Judah took all the sacred objects dedicated by his fathers—Jehoshaphat, Jehoram and Ahaziah, the kings of Judah—and the gifts he himself had dedicated and all the gold found in the treasuries of the temple of the LORD and of the royal palace, and he sent them to Hazael king of Aram, who then withdrew from Jerusalem.

¹⁹As for the other events of the reign of Joash, and all he did, are they not written in the book of the annals of the kings of Judah? ²⁰His officials conspired against him and assassinated him at Beth Millo, on the road down to Silla. ²¹The officials who murdered him were Jozabad son of Shimeath and Jehozabad son of Shomer. He died and was buried with his fathers in the City of David. And Amaziah his son succeeded him as king.

Jehoahaz King of Israel

13 In the twenty-third year of Joash son of Ahaziah king of Judah, Jehoahaz son of Jehu became king of Israel in Samaria, and he reigned seventeen years. ²He did evil in the eyes of the LORD by following the sins of Jeroboam son of Nebat, which he had caused Israel to commit, and he did not turn away from them. ³So the LORD's anger burned against Israel, and for a long time he kept them under the power of Hazael king of Aram and Ben-Hadad his son.

⁴Then Jehoahaz sought the LORD's favor, and the LORD listened to him, for he saw how severely the king of Aram was oppressing Israel. ⁵The LORD provided a

---

c 1 Hebrew *Jehoash*, a variant of *Joash*; also in verses 2, 4, 6, 7 and 18

deliverer[p] for Israel, and they escaped from the power of Aram. So the Israelites lived in their own homes as they had before. ⁶But they did not turn away from the sins[q] of the house of Jeroboam, which he had caused Israel to commit; they continued in them. Also, the Asherah pole[d][r] remained standing in Samaria.

⁷Nothing had been left[s] of the army of Jehoahaz except fifty horsemen, ten chariots and ten thousand foot soldiers, for the king of Aram had destroyed the rest and made them like the dust[t] at threshing time.

⁸As for the other events of the reign of Jehoahaz, all he did and his achievements, are they not written in the book of the annals of the kings of Israel? ⁹Jehoahaz rested with his fathers and was buried in Samaria. And Jehoash[e] his son succeeded him as king.

Jehoash King of Israel

¹⁰In the thirty-seventh year of Joash king of Judah, Jehoash son of Jehoahaz became king of Israel in Samaria, and he reigned sixteen years. ¹¹He did evil in the eyes of the LORD and did not turn away from any of the sins of Jeroboam son of Nebat, which he had caused Israel to commit; he continued in them.

¹²As for the other events of the reign of Jehoash, all he did and his achievements, including his war against Amaziah[u] king of Judah, are they not written in the book of the annals[v] of the kings of Israel? ¹³Jehoash rested with his fathers, and Jeroboam[w] succeeded him on the throne. Jehoash was buried in Samaria with the kings of Israel.

¹⁴Now Elisha was suffering from the illness from which he died. Jehoash king of Israel went down to see him and wept over him. "My father! My father!" he cried. "The chariots[x] and horsemen of Israel!"

¹⁵Elisha said, "Get a bow and some arrows,"[y] and he did so. ¹⁶"Take the bow in your hands," he said to the king of Israel. When he had taken it, Elisha put his hands on the king's hands.

¹⁷"Open the east window," he said, and he opened it. "Shoot!"[z] Elisha said, and he shot. "The LORD's arrow of victory, the arrow of victory over Aram!" Elisha declared. "You will completely destroy the Arameans at Aphek."[a]

¹⁸Then he said, "Take the arrows," and the king took them. Elisha told him, "Strike the ground." He struck it three times and stopped. ¹⁹The man of God was angry with him and said, "You should have struck the ground five or six times; then you would have defeated Aram and completely destroyed it. But now you will defeat it only three times."[b]

²⁰Elisha died and was buried.

Now Moabite raiders[c] used to enter the country every spring. ²¹Once while some Israelites were burying a man, suddenly they saw a band of raiders; so they threw the man's body into Elisha's tomb. When the body touched Elisha's bones, the man came to life[d] and stood up on his feet.

²²Hazael king of Aram oppressed[e] Israel throughout the reign of Jehoahaz. ²³But the LORD was gracious to them and had compassion and showed concern for them because of his covenant[f] with Abraham, Isaac and Jacob. To this day he has been unwilling to destroy[g] them or banish them from his presence.[h]

²⁴Hazael king of Aram died, and Ben-Hadad[i] his son succeeded him as king. ²⁵Then Jehoash son of Jehoahaz recaptured from Ben-Hadad son of Hazael the towns he had taken in battle from his father Jehoahaz. Three times[j] Jehoash defeated him, and so he recovered[k] the Israelite towns.

Amaziah King of Judah

14:1–7pp — 2Ch 25:1–4,11–12
14:8–22pp — 2Ch 25:17–26:2

14 In the second year of Jehoash[f] son of Jehoahaz king of Israel, Amaziah son of Joash king of Judah began to reign. ²He was twenty-five years old when he became king, and he reigned in Jerusalem twenty-nine years. His mother's name was Jehoaddin; she was from Jerusalem. ³He did what was right in the eyes of the LORD, but not as his father David had done. In everything he followed the example of his father Joash.

---

d 6 That is, a symbol of the goddess Asherah; here and elsewhere in 2 Kings *e 9* Hebrew *Joash,* a variant of *Jehoash;* also in verses 12-14 and 25 *f 1* Hebrew *Joash,* a variant of *Jehoash;* also in verses 13, 23 and 27

⁴The high places,¹ however, were not removed; the people continued to offer sacrifices and burn incense there.

⁵After the kingdom was firmly in his grasp, he executed the officials who had murdered his father the king. ⁶Yet he did not put the sons of the assassins to death, in accordance with what is written in the Book of the Law of Moses where the LORD commanded: "Fathers shall not be put to death for their children, nor children put to death for their fathers; each is to die for his own sins."

⁷He was the one who defeated ten thousand Edomites in the Valley of Salt and captured Sela in battle, calling it Joktheel, the name it has to this day.

⁸Then Amaziah sent messengers to Jehoash son of Jehoahaz, the son of Jehu, king of Israel, with the challenge: "Come, meet me face to face."

⁹But Jehoash king of Israel replied to Amaziah king of Judah: "A thistle in Lebanon sent a message to a cedar in Lebanon, 'Give your daughter to my son in marriage.' Then a wild beast in Lebanon came along and trampled the thistle underfoot. ¹⁰You have indeed defeated Edom and now you are arrogant. Glory in your victory, but stay at home! Why ask for trouble and cause your own downfall and that of Judah also?"

¹¹Amaziah, however, would not listen, so Jehoash king of Israel attacked. He and Amaziah king of Judah faced each other at Beth Shemesh in Judah. ¹²Judah was routed by Israel, and every man fled to his home. ¹³Jehoash king of Israel captured Amaziah king of Judah, the son of Joash, the son of Ahaziah, at Beth Shemesh. Then Jehoash went to Jerusalem and broke down the wall of Jerusalem from the Ephraim Gate to the Corner Gate—a section about six hundred feet long. ¹⁴He took all the gold and silver and all the articles found in the temple of the LORD and in the treasuries of the royal palace. He also took hostages and returned to Samaria.

¹⁵As for the other events of the reign of Jehoash, what he did and his achievements, including his war against Amaziah king of Judah, are they not written in the book of the annals of the kings of Israel? ¹⁶Jehoash rested with his fathers and was buried in Samaria with the kings of Israel. And Jeroboam his son succeeded him as king.

¹⁷Amaziah son of Joash king of Judah lived for fifteen years after the death of Jehoash son of Jehoahaz king of Israel. ¹⁸As for the other events of Amaziah's reign, are they not written in the book of the annals of the kings of Judah?

¹⁹They conspired against him in Jerusalem, and he fled to Lachish, but they sent men after him to Lachish and killed him there. ²⁰He was brought back by horse and was buried in Jerusalem with his fathers, in the City of David.

²¹Then all the people of Judah took Azariah, who was sixteen years old, and made him king in place of his father Amaziah. ²²He was the one who rebuilt Elath and restored it to Judah after Amaziah rested with his fathers.

Jeroboam II King of Israel

²³In the fifteenth year of Amaziah son of Joash king of Judah, Jeroboam son of Jehoash king of Israel became king in Samaria, and he reigned forty-one years. ²⁴He did evil in the eyes of the LORD and did not turn away from any of the sins of Jeroboam son of Nebat, which he had caused Israel to commit. ²⁵He was the one who restored the boundaries of Israel from Lebo Hamath to the Sea of the Arabah, in accordance with the word of the LORD, the God of Israel, spoken through his servant Jonah son of Amittai, the prophet from Gath Hepher.

²⁶The LORD had seen how bitterly everyone in Israel, whether slave or free, was suffering; there was no one to help them. ²⁷And since the LORD had not said he would blot out the name of Israel from under heaven, he saved them by the hand of Jeroboam son of Jehoash. ²⁸As for the other events of Jeroboam's reign, all he did, and his military achieve-

◁ 2Ki 13:15–19 ◀ ▶ 2Ki 19:30–31

⁶ Deut. 24:16 ¹³ Hebrew *four hundred cubits* (about 180 meters) ²¹ Also called *Uzziah* ²⁵ Or *from the entrance to* ²⁵ That is, the Dead Sea

14:27 Though God would judge Israel for its idolatry and rebellion, he would never "blot out the name of Israel from under heaven."

ments, including how he recovered for Israel both Damascus[p] and Hamath,[q] which had belonged to Yaudi,[*l*] are they not written in the book of the annals[r] of the kings of Israel? [29]Jeroboam rested with his fathers, the kings of Israel. And Zechariah his son succeeded him as king.

Azariah King of Judah
15:1–7pp — 2Ch 26:3–4,21–23

[15] In the twenty-seventh year of Jeroboam king of Israel, Azariah[s] son of Amaziah king of Judah began to reign. [2]He was sixteen years old when he became king, and he reigned in Jerusalem fifty-two years. His mother's name was Jecoliah; she was from Jerusalem. [3]He did what was right[t] in the eyes of the LORD, just as his father Amaziah had done. [4]The high places, however, were not removed; the people continued to offer sacrifices and burn incense there.

[5]The LORD afflicted[u] the king with leprosy[m] until the day he died, and he lived in a separate house.[n][v] Jotham[w] the king's son had charge of the palace[x] and governed the people of the land.

[6]As for the other events of Azariah's reign, and all he did, are they not written in the book of the annals of the kings of Judah? [7]Azariah rested[y] with his fathers and was buried near them in the City of David. And Jotham[z] his son succeeded him as king.

Zechariah King of Israel

[8]In the thirty-eighth year of Azariah king of Judah, Zechariah son of Jeroboam became king of Israel in Samaria, and he reigned six months. [9]He did evil[a] in the eyes of the LORD, as his fathers had done. He did not turn away from the sins of Jeroboam son of Nebat, which had caused Israel to commit.

[10]Shallum son of Jabesh conspired against Zechariah. He attacked him in front of the people,[o] assassinated[b] him and succeeded him as king. [11]The other events of Zechariah's reign are written in the book of the annals[c] of the kings of Israel. [12]So the word of the LORD spoken to Jehu was fulfilled:[d] "Your descendants will sit on the throne of Israel to the fourth generation."[p]

D 2Ki 6:18 ◄ ► 1Ch 21:14–15

Shallum King of Israel

[13]Shallum son of Jabesh became king in the thirty-ninth year of Uzziah king of Judah, and he reigned in Samaria[e] one month. [14]Then Menahem son of Gadi went from Tirzah[f] up to Samaria. He attacked Shallum son of Jabesh in Samaria, assassinated[g] him and succeeded him as king.

[15]The other events of Shallum's reign, and the conspiracy he led, are written in the book of the annals[h] of the kings of Israel.

[16]At that time Menahem, starting out from Tirzah, attacked Tiphsah[i] and everyone in the city and its vicinity, because they refused to open[j] their gates. He sacked Tiphsah and ripped open all the pregnant women.

Menahem King of Israel

[17]In the thirty-ninth year of Azariah king of Judah, Menahem son of Gadi became king of Israel, and he reigned in Samaria ten years. [18]He did evil[k] in the eyes of the LORD. During his entire reign he did not turn away from the sins of Jeroboam son of Nebat, which he had caused Israel to commit.

[19]Then Pul[q][*l*] king of Assyria invaded the land, and Menahem gave him a thousand talents[r] of silver to gain his support and strengthen his own hold on the kingdom. [20]Menahem exacted this money from Israel. Every wealthy man had to contribute fifty shekels[s] of silver to be given to the king of Assyria. So the king of Assyria withdrew[m] and stayed in the land no longer.

[21]As for the other events of Menahem's reign, and all he did, are they not written in the book of the annals of the kings of Israel? [22]Menahem rested with his fathers. And Pekahiah his son succeeded him as king.

Pekahiah King of Israel

[23]In the fiftieth year of Azariah king of Judah, Pekahiah son of Menahem became king of Israel in Samaria, and he reigned two years. [24]Pekahiah did evil[n] in the eyes of the LORD. He did not turn away

---

l 28 Or *Judah* *m* 5 The Hebrew word was used for various diseases affecting the skin—not necessarily leprosy. *n* 5 Or *in a house where he was relieved of responsibility* *o* 10 Hebrew; some Septuagint manuscripts *in Ibleam* *p* 12 2 Kings 10:30 *q* 19 Also called *Tiglath-Pileser* *r* 19 That is, about 37 tons (about 34 metric tons) *s* 20 That is, about 1 1/4 pounds (about 0.6 kilogram)

from the sins of Jeroboam son of Nebat, which he had caused Israel to commit. ²⁵One of his chief officers, Pekah son of Remaliah, conspired against him. Taking fifty men of Gilead with him, he assassinated Pekahiah, along with Argob and Arieh, in the citadel of the royal palace at Samaria. So Pekah killed Pekahiah and succeeded him as king.

²⁶The other events of Pekahiah's reign, and all he did, are written in the book of the annals of the kings of Israel.

Pekah King of Israel

²⁷In the fifty-second year of Azariah king of Judah, Pekah son of Remaliah became king of Israel in Samaria, and he reigned twenty years. ²⁸He did evil in the eyes of the LORD. He did not turn away from the sins of Jeroboam son of Nebat, which he had caused Israel to commit.

²⁹In the time of Pekah king of Israel, Tiglath-Pileser king of Assyria came and took Ijon, Abel Beth Maacah, Janoah, Kedesh and Hazor. He took Gilead and Galilee, including all the land of Naphtali, and deported the people to Assyria. ³⁰Then Hoshea son of Elah conspired against Pekah son of Remaliah. He attacked and assassinated him, and then succeeded him as king in the twentieth year of Jotham son of Uzziah.

³¹As for the other events of Pekah's reign, and all he did, are they not written in the book of the annals of the kings of Israel?

Jotham King of Judah
15:33–38pp — 2Ch 27:1–4,7–9

³²In the second year of Pekah son of Remaliah king of Israel, Jotham son of Uzziah king of Judah began to reign. ³³He was twenty-five years old when he became king, and he reigned in Jerusalem sixteen years. His mother's name was Jerusha daughter of Zadok. ³⁴He did what was right in the eyes of the LORD, just as his father Uzziah had done. ³⁵The high places, however, were not removed; the people continued to offer sacrifices and burn incense there. Jotham rebuilt the Upper Gate of the temple of the LORD.

³⁶As for the other events of Jotham's reign, and what he did, are they not written in the book of the annals of the kings of Judah? ³⁷(In those days the LORD began to send Rezin king of Aram and Pekah son of Remaliah against Judah.) ³⁸Jotham rested with his fathers and was buried with them in the City of David, the city of his father. And Ahaz his son succeeded him as king.

Ahaz King of Judah
16:1–20pp — 2Ch 28:1–27

16 In the seventeenth year of Pekah son of Remaliah, Ahaz son of Jotham king of Judah began to reign. ²Ahaz was twenty years old when he became king, and he reigned in Jerusalem sixteen years. Unlike David his father, he did not do what was right in the eyes of the LORD his God. ³He walked in the ways of the kings of Israel and even sacrificed his son* in* the fire, following the detestable ways of the nations the LORD had driven out before the Israelites. ⁴He offered sacrifices and burned incense at the high places, on the hilltops and under every spreading tree.

⁵Then Rezin king of Aram and Pekah son of Remaliah king of Israel marched up to fight against Jerusalem and besieged Ahaz, but they could not overpower him. ⁶At that time, Rezin king of Aram recovered Elath for Aram by driving out the men of Judah. Edomites then moved into Elath and have lived there to this day.

⁷Ahaz sent messengers to say to Tiglath-Pileser king of Assyria, "I am your servant and vassal. Come up and save me out of the hand of the king of Aram and of the king of Israel, who are attacking me." ⁸And Ahaz took the silver and gold found in the temple of the LORD and in the treasuries of the royal palace and sent it as a gift to the king of Assyria. ⁹The king of Assyria complied by attacking Damascus and capturing it. He deported its inhabitants to Kir and put Rezin to death.

¹⁰Then King Ahaz went to Damascus to meet Tiglath-Pileser king of Assyria. He saw an altar in Damascus and sent to Uriah the priest a sketch of the altar, with detailed plans for its construction. ¹¹So Uriah the priest built an altar in accordance with all the plans that King Ahaz had sent from Damascus and finished it before King Ahaz returned. ¹²When the king came back from Damascus and saw the altar, he approached it

t 3 Or even made his son pass through

and presented offerings[uu] on it. [13]He offered up his burnt offering[v] and grain offering,[w] poured out his drink offering,[x] and sprinkled the blood of his fellowship offerings[yy] on the altar. [14]The bronze altar[z] that stood before the LORD he brought from the front of the temple—from between the new altar and the temple of the LORD—and put it on the north side of the new altar.

[15]King Ahaz then gave these orders to Uriah the priest: "On the large new altar, offer the morning[a] burnt offering and the evening grain offering, the king's burnt offering and his grain offering, the burnt offering of all the people of the land, and their grain offering and their drink offering. Sprinkle on the altar all the blood of the burnt offerings and sacrifices. But I will use the bronze altar for seeking guidance."[b] [16]And Uriah the priest did just as King Ahaz had ordered.

[17]King Ahaz took away the side panels and removed the basins from the movable stands. He removed the Sea from the bronze bulls that supported it and set it on a stone base.[c] [18]He took away the Sabbath canopy[w] that had been built at the temple and removed the royal entryway outside the temple of the LORD, in deference to the king of Assyria.[d]

[19]As for the other events of the reign of Ahaz, and what he did, are they not written in the book of the annals of the kings of Judah? [20]Ahaz rested[e] with his fathers and was buried with them in the City of David. And Hezekiah his son succeeded him as king.

Hoshea Last King of Israel
17:3–7pp — 2Ki 18:9–12

17 In the twelfth year of Ahaz king of Judah, Hoshea[f] son of Elah became king of Israel in Samaria, and he reigned nine years. [2]He did evil[g] in the eyes of the LORD, but not like the kings of Israel who preceded him.

[3]Shalmaneser[h] king of Assyria came up to attack Hoshea, who had been Shalmaneser's vassal and had paid him tribute.[i] [4]But the king of Assyria discovered that Hoshea was a traitor, for he had sent envoys to So[x] king of Egypt,[j] and he no longer paid tribute to the king of Assyria, as he had done year by year. Therefore Shalmaneser seized him and put him in prison.[k] [5]The king of Assyria invaded the entire land, marched against Samaria and laid siege[1] to it for three years. [6]In the ninth year of Hoshea, the king of Assyria[m] captured Samaria[n] and deported[o] the Israelites to Assyria. He settled them in Halah, in Gozan[p] on the Habor River and in the towns of the Medes.

Israel Exiled Because of Sin

[7]All this took place because the Israelites had sinned[q] against the LORD their God, who had brought them up out of Egypt[r] from under the power of Pharaoh king of Egypt. They worshiped other gods [8]and followed the practices of the nations[s] the LORD had driven out before them, as well as the practices that the kings of Israel had introduced. [9]The Israelites secretly did things against the LORD their God that were not right. From watchtower to fortified city[t] they built themselves high places in all their towns. [10]They set up sacred stones[u] and Asherah poles[v] on every high hill and under every spreading tree.[w] [11]At every high place they burned incense, as the nations whom the LORD had driven out before them had done. They did wicked things that provoked the LORD to anger. [12]They worshiped idols,[x] though the LORD had said, "You shall not do this."[y] [13]The LORD warned[y] Israel and Judah through all his prophets and seers:[z] "Turn from your evil ways.[a] Observe my commands and decrees, in accordance with the entire Law that I commanded your fathers to obey and that I delivered to you through my servants the prophets."[b] [14]But they would not listen and were as stiff-necked[c] as their fathers, who did not

R *2Ki 13:23* ◀▶ *2Ki 17:18*
N *1Ki 18:21* ◀▶ *1Ch 29:15*
R *2Sa 24:10* ◀▶ *1Ch 21:8*
C *1Ki 21:20* ◀▶ *2Ki 19:22*

u 12 Or and went up   v 13 Traditionally peace offerings   w 18 Or the dais of his throne (see Septuagint)   x 4 Or to Sais, to the; So is possibly an abbreviation for Osorkon.   y 12 Exodus 20:4, 5

17:6 The rebellion of Israel had to be punished, so God let the Assyrians conquer Israel and carry into exile the ten tribes of Israel. This was the first example in history of an enemy transporting an entire conquered population to another location in order to prevent rebellion and assure future loyalty.

trust in the LORD their God. ¹⁵They rejected his decrees and the covenant[d] he had made with their fathers and the warnings he had given them. They followed worthless idols[e] and themselves became worthless.[f] They imitated the nations[g] around them although the LORD had ordered them, "Do not do as they do," and they did the things the LORD had forbidden them to do.

¹⁶They forsook all the commands of the LORD their God and made for themselves two idols cast in the shape of calves,[h] and an Asherah[i] pole. They bowed down to all the starry hosts,[j] and they worshiped Baal.[k] ¹⁷They sacrificed[l] their sons and daughters in[z] the fire. They practiced divination and sorcery[m] and sold[n] themselves to do evil in the eyes of the LORD, provoking him to anger.

R ¹⁸So the LORD was very angry with Israel and removed them from his presence.[o] Only the tribe of Judah was left, ¹⁹and even Judah did not keep the commands of the LORD their God. They followed the practices Israel had introduced.[p] R ²⁰Therefore the LORD rejected all the people of Israel; he afflicted them and gave them into the hands of plunderers,[q] until he thrust them from his presence.[r]

²¹When he tore[s] Israel away from the house of David, they made Jeroboam son of Nebat their king.[t] Jeroboam enticed Israel away from following the LORD and caused them to commit a great sin.[u] ²²The Israelites persisted in all the sins of Jeroboam and did not turn away from R them ²³until the LORD removed them from his presence,[v] as he had warned[w] through all his servants the prophets. So the people of Israel were taken from their homeland[x] into exile in Assyria, and they are still there.

Samaria Resettled

²⁴The king of Assyria[y] brought people from Babylon, Cuthah, Avva, Hamath and Sepharvaim[z] and settled them in the towns of Samaria to replace the Israelites. They took over Samaria and lived in its towns. ²⁵When they first lived there, they did not worship the LORD; so he sent lions[a] among them and they killed some of the people. ²⁶It was reported to the king of Assyria: "The people you deported and resettled in the towns of Samaria do not know what the god of that country requires. He has sent lions among them, which are killing them off, because the people do not know what he requires."

²⁷Then the king of Assyria gave this order: "Have one of the priests you took captive from Samaria go back to live there and teach the people what the god of the land requires." ²⁸So one of the priests who had been exiled from Samaria came to live in Bethel and taught them how to worship the LORD.

²⁹Nevertheless, each national group made its own gods in the several towns[b] where they settled, and set them up in the shrines[c] the people of Samaria had made at the high places.[d] ³⁰The men from Babylon made Succoth Benoth, the men from Cuthah made Nergal, and the men from Hamath made Ashima; ³¹the Avvites made Nibhaz and Tartak, and the Sepharvites burned their children in the fire as sacrifices to Adrammelech[e] and Anammelech, the gods of Sepharvaim.[f] ³²They worshiped the LORD, but they also appointed all sorts[g] of their own people to officiate for them as priests in the shrines at the high places. ³³They worshiped the LORD, but they also served their own gods in accordance with the customs of the nations from which they had been brought.

³⁴To this day they persist in their former practices. They neither worship the LORD nor adhere to the decrees and ordinances, the laws and commands that the LORD gave the descendants of Jacob, whom he named Israel.[h] ³⁵When the LORD made a covenant with the Israelites, he commanded them: "Do not worship[i] any other gods or bow down to them, serve them or sacrifice to them.[j] ³⁶But

R 2Ki 17:6 ◀ ▶ 2Ki 17:20
R 2Ki 17:18 ◀ ▶ 2Ki 17:23
R 2Ki 17:20 ◀ ▶ 2Ki 18:9–12

[z] 17 Or *They made their sons and daughters pass through*

17:18–20 God had allowed Israel's defeat and exile due to their idol worship. Only the southern kingdom of Judah (the tribes of Judah and Benjamin) escaped the Assyrian conquest.

17:23 Scripture repeatedly affirms that God will ultimately restore all twelve tribes to the promised land in the last days (see Eze 37:15–28).

the LORD, who brought you up out of Egypt with mighty power and outstretched arm,[k] is the one you must worship. To him you shall bow down and to him offer sacrifices. ³⁷You must always be careful¹ to keep the decrees[m] and ordinances, the laws and commands he wrote for you. Do not worship other gods. ³⁸Do not forget[n] the covenant I have made with you, and do not worship other gods. ³⁹Rather, worship the LORD your God; it is he who will deliver you from the hand of all your enemies."

⁴⁰They would not listen, however, but persisted in their former practices. ⁴¹Even while these people were worshiping the LORD,[o] they were serving their idols. To this day their children and grandchildren continue to do as their fathers did.

Hezekiah King of Judah

18:2–4pp — 2Ch 29:1–2; 31:1
18:5–7pp — 2Ch 31:20–21
18:9–12pp — 2Ki 17:3–7

18 In the third year of Hoshea son of Elah king of Israel, Hezekiah[p] son of Ahaz king of Judah began to reign. ²He was twenty-five years old when he became king, and he reigned in Jerusalem twenty-nine years.[q] His mother's name was Abijah[a] daughter of Zechariah. ³He did what was right[r] in the eyes of the LORD, just as his father David[s] had done. ⁴He removed[t] the high places,[u] smashed the sacred stones[v] and cut down the Asherah poles. He broke into pieces the bronze snake[w] Moses had made, for up to that time the Israelites had been burning incense to it. (It was called[b] Nehushtan.[c])

⁵Hezekiah trusted[x] in the LORD, the God of Israel. There was no one like him among all the kings of Judah, either before him or after him. ⁶He held fast[y] to the LORD and did not cease to follow him; he kept the commands the LORD had given Moses. ⁷And the LORD was with him; he was successful[z] in whatever he undertook. He rebelled[a] against the king of Assyria and did not serve him. ⁸From watchtower to fortified city,[b] he defeated the Philistines, as far as Gaza and its territory.

⁹In King Hezekiah's fourth year,[c] which was the seventh year of Hoshea son of Elah king of Israel, Shalmaneser king of Assyria marched against Samaria and laid siege to it. ¹⁰At the end of three years the Assyrians took it. So Samaria was captured in Hezekiah's sixth year, which was the ninth year of Hoshea king of Israel. ¹¹The king[d] of Assyria deported Israel to Assyria and settled them in Halah, in Gozan on the Habor River and in towns of the Medes.[e] ¹²This happened because they had not obeyed the LORD their God, but had violated his covenant[f]—all that Moses the servant of the LORD commanded.[g] They neither listened to the commands[h] nor carried them out.

¹³In the fourteenth year[i] of King Hezekiah's reign, Sennacherib king of Assyria attacked all the fortified cities of Judah[j] and captured them. ¹⁴So Hezekiah king of Judah sent this message to the king of Assyria at Lachish:[k] "I have done wrong.¹ Withdraw from me, and I will pay whatever you demand of me." The king of Assyria exacted from Hezekiah king of Judah three hundred talents[d] of silver and thirty talents[e] of gold. ¹⁵So Hezekiah gave[m] him all the silver that was found in the temple of the LORD and in the treasuries of the royal palace.

¹⁶At this time Hezekiah king of Judah stripped off the gold with which he had covered the doors[n] and doorposts of the temple of the LORD, and gave it to the king of Assyria.

Sennacherib Threatens Jerusalem

18:13, 17–37pp — Isa 36:1–22
18:17–35pp — 2Ch 32:9–19

¹⁷The king of Assyria sent his supreme commander,[o] his chief officer and his field commander with a large army, from Lachish to King Hezekiah at Jerusalem. They came up to Jerusalem and stopped

R *2Ki 17:23* ◀ ▶ *2Ki 21:7–9*

[a] 2 Hebrew *Abi,* a variant of *Abijah* [b] 4 Or *He called it* [c] 4 *Nehushtan* sounds like the Hebrew for *bronze* and *snake* and *unclean thing.*
[d] 14 That is, about 11 tons (about 10 metric tons) [e] 14 That is, about 1 ton (about 1 metric ton)

18:9–12 This passage confirms the fulfillment of prophecies that warned of Israel's exile from the promised land if the Israelites persisted in their idolatry and "violated his covenant" (18:12; see Dt 28:62–65).

at the aqueduct of the Upper Pool, on the road to the Washerman's Field. ¹⁸They called for the king; and Eliakim son of Hilkiah the palace administrator, Shebna the secretary, and Joah son of Asaph the recorder went out to them.

¹⁹The field commander said to them, "Tell Hezekiah:

"'This is what the great king, the king of Assyria, says: On what are you basing this confidence of yours? ²⁰You say you have strategy and military strength—but you speak only empty words. On whom are you depending, that you rebel against me? ²¹Look now, you are depending on Egypt, that splintered reed of a staff, which pierces a man's hand and wounds him if he leans on it! Such is Pharaoh king of Egypt to all who depend on him. ²²And if you say to me, "We are depending on the LORD our God"—isn't he the one whose high places and altars Hezekiah removed, saying to Judah and Jerusalem, "You must worship before this altar in Jerusalem"?

²³"'Come now, make a bargain with my master, the king of Assyria: I will give you two thousand horses—if you can put riders on them! ²⁴How can you repulse one officer of the least of my master's officials, even though you are depending on Egypt for chariots and horsemen? ²⁵Furthermore, have I come to attack and destroy this place without word from the LORD? The LORD himself told me to march against this country and destroy it.'"

²⁶Then Eliakim son of Hilkiah, and Shebna and Joah said to the field commander, "Please speak to your servants in Aramaic, since we understand it. Don't speak to us in Hebrew in the hearing of the people on the wall."

²⁷But the commander replied, "Was it only to your master and you that my master sent me to say these things, and not to the men sitting on the wall—who, like you, will have to eat their own filth and drink their own urine?"

²⁸Then the commander stood and called out in Hebrew: "Hear the word of the great king, the king of Assyria! ²⁹This is what the king says: Do not let Hezekiah deceive you. He cannot deliver you from my hand. ³⁰Do not let Hezekiah persuade you to trust in the LORD when he says, 'The LORD will surely deliver us; this city will not be given into the hand of the king of Assyria.'

³¹"Do not listen to Hezekiah. This is what the king of Assyria says: Make peace with me and come out to me. Then every one of you will eat from his own vine and fig tree and drink water from his own cistern, ³²until I come and take you to a land like your own, a land of grain and new wine, a land of bread and vineyards, a land of olive trees and honey. Choose life and not death!

"Do not listen to Hezekiah, for he is misleading you when he says, 'The LORD will deliver us.' ³³Has the god of any nation ever delivered his land from the hand of the king of Assyria? ³⁴Where are the gods of Hamath and Arpad? Where are the gods of Sepharvaim, Hena and Ivvah? Have they rescued Samaria from my hand? ³⁵Who of all the gods of these countries has been able to save his land from me? How then can the LORD deliver Jerusalem from my hand?"

³⁶But the people remained silent and said nothing in reply, because the king had commanded, "Do not answer him."

³⁷Then Eliakim son of Hilkiah the palace administrator, Shebna the secretary and Joah son of Asaph the recorder went to Hezekiah, with their clothes torn, and told him what the field commander had said.

Jerusalem's Deliverance Foretold
19:1–13pp — Isa 37:1–13

19 When King Hezekiah heard this, he tore his clothes and put on sackcloth and went into the temple of the LORD. ²He sent Eliakim the palace administrator, Shebna the secretary and the leading priests, all wearing sackcloth, to the prophet Isaiah son of Amoz. ³They told him, "This is what Hezekiah says: This day is a day of distress and rebuke and disgrace, as when children come to the point of birth and there is no strength to deliver them. ⁴It may be that the LORD your God will hear all the

j 2Ki 9:26 ◀ ▶ 2Ki 19:7

f24 Or charioteers

words of the field commander, whom his master, the king of Assyria, has sent to ridicule° the living God, and that he will rebuke[p] him for the words the LORD your God has heard. Therefore pray for the remnant[q] that still survives."

[5]When King Hezekiah's officials came to Isaiah, [6]Isaiah said to them, "Tell your master, 'This is what the LORD says: Do not be afraid[r] of what you have heard—those words with which the underlings of the king of Assyria have blasphemed[s] me. [7]Listen! I am going to put such a spirit in him that when he hears a certain report,[t] he will return to his own country, and there I will have him cut down with the sword.[u]' "

[8]When the field commander heard that the king of Assyria had left Lachish,[v] he withdrew and found the king fighting against Libnah.[w]

[9]Now Sennacherib received a report that Tirhakah, the Cushite[g] king of Egypt, was marching out to fight against him. So he again sent messengers to Hezekiah with this word: [10]"Say to Hezekiah king of Judah: Do not let the god you depend[x] on deceive[y] you when he says, 'Jerusalem will not be handed over to the king of Assyria.' [11]Surely you have heard what the kings of Assyria have done to all the countries, destroying them completely. And will you be delivered? [12]Did the gods of the nations that were destroyed by my forefathers deliver[z] them: the gods of Gozan,[a] Haran,[b] Rezeph and the people of Eden who were in Tel Assar? [13]Where is the king of Hamath, the king of Arpad, the king of the city of Sepharvaim, or of Hena or Ivvah?"[c]

Hezekiah's Prayer
19:14–19pp — Isa 37:14–20

[14]Hezekiah received the letter[d] from the messengers and read it. Then he went up to the temple of the LORD and spread it out before the LORD. [15]And Hezekiah prayed to the LORD: "O LORD, God of Israel, enthroned between the cherubim,[e] you alone[f] are God over all the kingdoms of the earth. You have made heaven and earth. [16]Give ear,[g] O LORD, and hear;[h] open your eyes,[i] O LORD, and see; listen to the words Sennacherib has sent to insult the living God.

J *2Ki 18:30* ◄ ► *2Ki 20:17–19*

19:4 °S 1Sa 17:26
ᵖ 2Sa 16:12
ᵠ S Ge 45:7;
S Jer 37:3
19:6 ʳ S Dt 3:2;
S Jos 1:9
ˢ S 2Ki 18:25
19:7 ᵗ S Ex 14:24;
Jer 51:46 ᵘ ver 37;
2Ch 32:21;
Isa 10:12
19:8 ᵛ 2Ki 18:14
ʷ S Nu 33:20;
S 2Ki 8:22
19:10 ˣ S 2Ki 18:5
ʸ 2Ki 18:29
19:12 ᶻ 2Ki 18:33;
2Ch 32:17
ᵃ 2Ki 17:6
ᵇ S Ge 11:31
19:13
ᶜ Isa 10:9-11;
Jer 49:23
19:14 ᵈ 2Ki 5:7
19:15 ᵉ S Ge 3:24;
S Ex 25:22
ᶠ S Ge 1:1;
S Jos 2:11
19:16 ᵍ Ps 31:2;
71:2; 88:2; 102:2
ʰ S 1Ki 8:29
ⁱ S Ex 3:16
19:18 ʲ Isa 44:9-11;
Jer 10:3-10
ᵏ Dt 4:28; Ps 115:4;
Ac 17:29
19:19 ˡ 1Sa 12:10;
Job 6:23; Ps 3:7;
71:4 ᵐ S 1Ki 8:43;
1Ch 16:8
ⁿ S Jos 4:24;
S 1Sa 17:46
19:20 °S 1Ki 9:3
19:21 ᵖ Isa 10:5;
33:1 ᵠ Isa 47:1;
Jer 14:17; 18:13;
31:4; 46:11;
La 2:13; Am 5:2
ʳ Ps 53:5 ˢ Pr 1:26;
3:34 ᵗ Job 16:4;
Ps 44:14; 64:8;
109:25; Jer 18:16
19:22
ᵘ S 2Ki 18:25
ᵛ Lev 19:2; Isa 2:2;
Job 6:10; Ps 16:10;
22:3; 71:22; 78:41;
89:18; Isa 1:4; 6:3;
57:15; Hos 11:9
19:23 ʷ Isa 10:18;
Jer 21:14;
Eze 20:47 ˣ Ps 20:7;
Jer 50:37
ʸ Isa 10:34; 14:8;
33:9; Eze 31:3
19:25 ᶻ Isa 40:21,
28 ᵃ Isa 22:11
ᵇ Mic 1:6

[17]"It is true, O LORD, that the Assyrian kings have laid waste these nations and their lands. [18]They have thrown their gods into the fire and destroyed them, for they were not gods[j] but only wood and stone, fashioned by men's hands.[k] [19]Now, O LORD our God, deliver[l] us from his hand, so that all kingdoms[m] on earth may know[n] that you alone, O LORD, are God."

Isaiah Prophesies Sennacherib's Fall
19:20–37pp — Isa 37:21–38
19:35–37pp — 2Ch 32:20–21

[20]Then Isaiah son of Amoz sent a message to Hezekiah: "This is what the LORD, the God of Israel, says: I have heard° your prayer concerning Sennacherib king of Assyria. [21]This is the word that the LORD has spoken against[p] him:

" 'The Virgin Daughter[q] of Zion
   despises[r] you and mocks[s] you.
The Daughter of Jerusalem
   tosses her head[t] as you flee.
[22]Who is it you have insulted and
   blasphemed?[u]
Against whom have you raised your
   voice
and lifted your eyes in pride?
   Against the Holy One[v] of Israel!
[23]By your messengers
   you have heaped insults on the
      Lord.
And you have said,[w]
   "With my many chariots[x]
I have ascended the heights of the
   mountains,
   the utmost heights of Lebanon.
I have cut down[y] its tallest cedars,
   the choicest of its pines.
I have reached its remotest parts,
   the finest of its forests.
[24]I have dug wells in foreign lands
   and drunk the water there.
With the soles of my feet
   I have dried up all the streams of
      Egypt."
[25] 'Have you not heard?[z]
   Long ago I ordained it.
In days of old I planned[a] it;
   now I have brought it to pass,
that you have turned fortified cities
   into piles of stone.[b]

C *2Ki 17:14–15* ◄ ► *2Ki 21:22*

ᵍ 9 That is, from the upper Nile region

^{26}Their people, drained of power,^{c}
   are dismayed^d and put to shame.
They are like plants in the field,
   like tender green shoots,^{e}
like grass sprouting on the roof,
   scorched^f before it grows up.

^{27}"'But I know^g where you stay
   and when you come and go
   and how you rage against me.
^{28}Because you rage against me
   and your insolence has reached my ears,
I will put my hook^h in your nose
   and my bit^i in your mouth,
and I will make you return^j
   by the way you came.'

^{29}"This will be the sign^k for you, O Hezekiah:

"This year you will eat what grows by itself,^{l}
   and the second year what springs from that.
But in the third year sow and reap,
   plant vineyards^m and eat their fruit.
^{30}Once more a remnant^n of the house of Judah
   will take root^o below and bear fruit above.
^{31}For out of Jerusalem will come a remnant,^{p}
   and out of Mount Zion a band of survivors.^{q}

The zeal^r of the LORD Almighty will accomplish this.

^{32}"Therefore this is what the LORD says concerning the king of Assyria:

"He will not enter this city
   or shoot an arrow here.
He will not come before it with shield
   or build a siege ramp against it.
^{33}By the way that he came he will return;^{s}
   he will not enter this city,
          declares the LORD.
^{34}I will defend^t this city and save it,
   for my sake and for the sake of David^u my servant."

E *1Ki 8:39* ◀ ▶ *1Ch 28:9*
I *2Ki 14:27* ◀ ▶ *1Ch 14:10*

^{35}That night the angel of the LORD^v went out and put to death a hundred and eighty-five thousand men in the Assyrian camp. When the people got up the next morning—there were all the dead bodies!^{w} ^{36}So Sennacherib king of Assyria broke camp and withdrew.^{x} He returned to Nineveh^y and stayed there.

^{37}One day, while he was worshiping in the temple of his god Nisroch, his sons Adrammelech^z and Sharezer cut him down with the sword,^{a} and they escaped to the land of Ararat.^{b} And Esarhaddon^c his son succeeded him as king.

Hezekiah's Illness
20:1–11pp — 2Ch 32:24–26; Isa 38:1–8

20 In those days Hezekiah became ill and was at the point of death. The prophet Isaiah son of Amoz went to him and said, "This is what the LORD says: Put your house in order, because you are going to die; you will not recover."

^{2}Hezekiah turned his face to the wall and prayed to the LORD, ^{3}"Remember,^{d} O LORD, how I have walked^e before you faithfully^f and with wholehearted devotion and have done what is good in your eyes." And Hezekiah wept bitterly.

^{4}Before Isaiah had left the middle court, the word of the LORD came to him: ^{5}"Go back and tell Hezekiah, the leader of my people, 'This is what the LORD, the God of your father David, says: I have heard^g your prayer and seen your tears;^{h} I will heal you. On the third day from now you will go up to the temple of the LORD. ^{6}I will add fifteen years to your life. And I will deliver you and this city from the hand of the king of Assyria. I will defend^i this city for my sake and for the sake of my servant David.' "

^{7}Then Isaiah said, "Prepare a poultice of figs." They did so and applied it to the boil,^{j} and he recovered.

^{8}Hezekiah had asked Isaiah, "What will be the sign that the LORD will heal me and that I will go up to the temple of the LORD on the third day from now?"

^{9}Isaiah answered, "This is the LORD's

E *2Ki 13:21* ◀ ▶ *2Ch 32:24*
L *2Ki 10:30* ◀ ▶ *2Ch 1:12*

19:30–31 The Lord promised that some from Judah would escape captivity because they had not yet fallen into idolatry and because of Judah's godly King Hezekiah (see 2Ch 32:22).

sign^k to you that the LORD will do what he has promised: Shall the shadow go forward ten steps, or shall it go back ten steps?"

¹⁰"It is a simple^l matter for the shadow to go forward ten steps," said Hezekiah. "Rather, have it go back ten steps."

¹¹Then the prophet Isaiah called upon the LORD, and the LORD made the shadow go back^m the ten steps it had gone down on the stairway of Ahaz.

Envoys From Babylon

20:12–19pp — Isa 39:1–8
20:20–21pp — 2Ch 32:32–33

¹²At that time Merodach-Baladan son of Baladan king of Babylon sent Hezekiah letters and a gift, because he had heard of Hezekiah's illness. ¹³Hezekiah received the messengers and showed them all that was in his storehouses—the silver, the gold, the spices and the fine oil—his armory and everything found among his treasures. There was nothing in his palace or in all his kingdom that Hezekiah did not show them.

¹⁴Then Isaiah the prophet went to King Hezekiah and asked, "What did those men say, and where did they come from?"

"From a distant land," Hezekiah replied. "They came from Babylon."

¹⁵The prophet asked, "What did they see in your palace?"

"They saw everything in my palace," Hezekiah said. "There is nothing among my treasures that I did not show them."

¹⁶Then Isaiah said to Hezekiah, "Hear the word of the LORD: ¹⁷The time will surely come when everything in your palace, and all that your fathers have stored up until this day, will be carried off to Babylon.ⁿ Nothing will be left, says the LORD. ¹⁸And some of your descendants,^o your own flesh and blood, that will be born to you, will be taken away, and they will become eunuchs in the palace of the king of Babylon."^p

¹⁹"The word of the LORD you have spoken is good," Hezekiah replied. For he

J 2Ki 19:7 ◄ ► 1Ch 21:9–13

20:9 ^kS Dt 13:2; Jer 44:29
20:10 ^lS 2Ki 3:18
20:11 ^mJos 10:13; 2Ch 32:31
20:17 ⁿ2Ki 24:13; 2Ch 36:10; Jer 20:5; 27:22; 52:17-23
20:18 ^o2Ki 24:15; Da 1:3 ^pMic 4:10
20:20 ^qS 2Ki 18:17 ^r2Sa 5:8
21:1 ^sIsa 62:4
21:2 ^tver 16; ^uDt 4:25; Jer 15:4 ^vDt 9:4; S 18:9; S 1Ki 14:24; 2Ki 16:3
21:3 ^vS 1Ki 3:3; S 2Ki 18:4 ^wS Jdg 6:28 ^xS Dt 16:21 ^yS Ge 2:1; Dt 17:3; Jer 19:13
21:4 ^zIsa 66:4; Jer 4:1; 7:30; 23:11; 32:34; Eze 23:39 ^aS Ex 20:24; S 2Sa 7:13
21:5 ^b1Ki 7:12; 2Ki 23:12
21:6 ^cS Lev 18:21; S Dt 18:10; S 2Ki 3:27 ^dDt 18:14 ^eS Lev 19:31 ^f2Ki 23:26
21:7 ^gDt 16:21; 2Ki 23:4 ^hS Lev 15:31 ⁱS Ex 20:24; S 2Sa 7:13
21:8 ^jS 2Sa 7:10 ^kS 2Ki 18:12

thought, "Will there not be peace and security in my lifetime?"

²⁰As for the other events of Hezekiah's reign, all his achievements and how he made the pool^q and the tunnel^r by which he brought water into the city, are they not written in the book of the annals of the kings of Judah? ²¹Hezekiah rested with his fathers. And Manasseh his son succeeded him as king.

Manasseh King of Judah

21:1–10pp — 2Ch 33:1–10
21:17–18pp — 2Ch 33:18–20

21 Manasseh was twelve years old when he became king, and he reigned in Jerusalem fifty-five years. His mother's name was Hephzibah.^s ²He did evil^t in the eyes of the LORD, following the detestable practices^u of the nations the LORD had driven out before the Israelites. ³He rebuilt the high places^v his father Hezekiah had destroyed; he also erected altars to Baal^w and made an Asherah pole,^x as Ahab king of Israel had done. He bowed down to all the starry hosts^y and worshiped them. ⁴He built altars^z in the temple of the LORD, of which the LORD had said, "In Jerusalem I will put my Name."^a ⁵In both courts^b of the temple of the LORD, he built altars to all the starry hosts. ⁶He sacrificed his own son^c in^h the fire, practiced sorcery and divination,^d and consulted mediums and spiritists.^e He did much evil in the eyes of the LORD, provoking^f him to anger.

⁷He took the carved Asherah pole^g he had made and put it in the temple,^h of which the LORD had said to David and to his son Solomon, "In this temple and in Jerusalem, which I have chosen out of all the tribes of Israel, I will put my Nameⁱ forever. ⁸I will not again^j make the feet of the Israelites wander from the land I gave their forefathers, if only they will be careful to do everything I commanded them and will keep the whole Law that my servant Moses^k gave them." ⁹But the people did not listen. Manasseh led them

R 2Ki 18:9–12 ◄ ► 2Ki 21:12–15

^h 6 Or He made his own son pass through

21:7–8 Evil King Manasseh of Judah sacrificed his son to pagan god Molech and established widespread idolatry and wickedness during his long reign. God had warned David and Solomon centuries earlier that he would protect Israel from exile only if Israel obeyed their covenant with God.

astray, so that they did more evil¹ than the nations ᵐ the LORD had destroyed before the Israelites.

¹⁰The LORD said through his servants the prophets: ¹¹"Manasseh king of Judah has committed these detestable sins. He has done more evilⁿ than the Amoritesᵒ who preceded him and has led Judah into sin with his idols.ᵖ ¹²Therefore this is what the LORD, the God of Israel, says: I am going to bring such disasterᑫ on Jerusalem and Judah that the ears of everyone who hears of it will tingle.ʳ ¹³I will stretch out over Jerusalem the measuring line used against Samaria and the plumb lineˢ used against the house of Ahab. I will wipeᵗ out Jerusalem as one wipes a dish, wiping it and turning it upside down. ¹⁴I will forsakeᵘ the remnantᵛ of my inheritance and hand them over to their enemies. They will be looted and plundered by all their foes, ¹⁵because they have done evilʷ in my eyes and have provokedˣ me to anger from the day their forefathers came out of Egypt until this day."

¹⁶Moreover, Manasseh also shed so much innocent bloodʸ that he filled Jerusalem from end to end—besides the sin that he had caused Judahᶻ to commit, so that they did evil in the eyes of the LORD.

¹⁷As for the other events of Manasseh's reign, and all he did, including the sin he committed, are they not written in the book of the annals of the kings of Judah? ¹⁸Manasseh rested with his fathers and was buried in his palace garden,ᵃ the garden of Uzza. And Amon his son succeeded him as king.

Amon King of Judah
21:19–24pp — 2Ch 33:21–25

¹⁹Amon was twenty-two years old when he became king, and he reigned in Jerusalem two years. His mother's name was Meshullemeth daughter of Haruz; she was from Jotbah. ²⁰He did evilᵇ in the eyes of the LORD, as his father Manasseh had done. ²¹He walked in all the ways of his father; he worshiped the idols his father had worshiped, and bowed down to them. ²²He forsookᶜ the LORD, the God of his fathers, and did not walkᵈ in the way of the LORD.

²³Amon's officials conspired against him and assassinatedᵉ the king in his palace. ²⁴Then the people of the land killedᶠ all who had plotted against King Amon, and they made Josiahᵍ his son king in his place.

²⁵As for the other events of Amon's reign, and what he did, are they not written in the book of the annals of the kings of Judah? ²⁶He was buried in his grave in the gardenʰ of Uzza. And Josiah his son succeeded him as king.

The Book of the Law Found
22:1–20pp — 2Ch 34:1–2,8–28

22 Josiahⁱ was eight years old when he became king, and he reigned in Jerusalem thirty-one years. His mother's name was Jedidah daughter of Adaiah; she was from Bozkath.ʲ ²He did what was rightᵏ in the eyes of the LORD and walked in all the ways of his father David, not turning aside to the right¹ or to the left.

³In the eighteenth year of his reign, King Josiah sent the secretary, Shaphanᵐ son of Azaliah, the son of Meshullam, to the temple of the LORD. He said: ⁴"Go up to Hilkiahⁿ the high priest and have him get ready the money that has been brought into the temple of the LORD, which the doorkeepers have collectedᵒ from the people. ⁵Have them entrust it to the men appointed to supervise the work on the temple. And have these men pay the workers who repairᵖ the temple of the LORD— ⁶the carpenters, the builders and the masons. Also have them purchase timber and dressed stone to repair the temple.ᑫ ⁷But they need not account for the money entrusted to them, because they are acting faithfully."ʳ

⁸Hilkiah the high priest said to Shaphan the secretary, "I have found the Book of the Lawˢ in the temple of the LORD." He gave it to Shaphan, who read it. ⁹Then Shaphan the secretary went to the king and reported to him: "Your offi-

---

21:12–15 God announced the destruction of Judah and Jerusalem and the exile of the people as punishment for their continuing sins.

cials have paid out the money that was in the temple of the LORD and have entrusted it to the workers and supervisors at the temple." ¹⁰Then Shaphan the secretary informed the king, "Hilkiah the priest has given me a book." And Shaphan read from it in the presence of the king.ᵗ

¹¹When the king heard the words of the Book of the Law,ᵘ he tore his robes. ¹²He gave these orders to Hilkiah the priest, Ahikamᵛ son of Shaphan, Acbor son of Micaiah, Shaphan the secretary and Asaiah the king's attendant:ʷ ¹³"Go and inquireˣ of the LORD for me and for the people and for all Judah about what is written in this book that has been found. Great is the LORD's angerʸ that burns against us because our fathers have not obeyed the words of this book; they have not acted in accordance with all that is written there concerning us."

¹⁴Hilkiah the priest, Ahikam, Acbor, Shaphan and Asaiah went to speak to the prophetessᶻ Huldah, who was the wife of Shallum son of Tikvah, the son of Harhas, keeper of the wardrobe. She lived in Jerusalem, in the Second District.

R ¹⁵She said to them, "This is what the LORD, the God of Israel, says: Tell the man who sent you to me, ¹⁶'This is what the LORD says: I am going to bring disasterᵃ on this place and its people, according to everything written in the bookᵇ the king of Judah has read. ¹⁷Because they have forsakenᶜ me and burned incense to other gods and provoked me to anger by all the idols their hands have made,ⁱ my anger will burn against this place and will not be quenched.' ¹⁸Tell the king of Judah, who sent you to inquireᵈ of the LORD, 'This is what the LORD, the God of Israel, says concerning the words you heard:
M ¹⁹Because your heart was responsive and you humbledᵉ yourself before the LORD when you heard what I have spoken against this place and its people, that they would become accursedᶠ and laid waste,ᵍ and because you tore your robes and wept in my presence, I have heard you, declares the LORD. ²⁰Therefore I will gather you to your fathers, and you will be buried in peace.ʰ Your eyesⁱ will not see all the disaster I am going to bring on this place.' "

So they took her answer back to the king.

Josiah Renews the Covenant

23:1–3pp — 2Ch 34:29–32
23:4–20Ref — 2Ch 34:3–7,33
23:21–23pp — 2Ch 35:1,18–19
23:28–30pp — 2Ch 35:20–36:1

23 Then the king called together all the elders of Judah and Jerusalem. ²He went up to the temple of the LORD with the men of Judah, the people of Jerusalem, the priests and the prophets—all the people from the least to the greatest. He readʲ in their hearing all the words of the Book of the Covenant,ᵏ which had been found in the temple of the LORD. ³The king stood by the pillarˡ and renewed the covenantᵐ in the presence of the LORD—to followⁿ the LORD and keep his commands, regulations and decrees with all his heart and all his soul, thus confirming the words of the covenant written in this book. Then all the people pledged themselves to the covenant.

⁴The king ordered Hilkiah the high priest, the priests next in rank and the doorkeepersᵒ to removeᵖ from the temple of the LORD all the articles made for Baal and Asherah and all the starry hosts. He burned them outside Jerusalem in the fields of the Kidron Valley and took the ashes to Bethel. ⁵He did away with the pagan priests appointed by the kings of Judah to burn incense on the high places of the towns of Judah and on those around Jerusalem—those who burned incenseᑫ to Baal, to the sun and moon, to the constellations and to all the starry hosts.ʳˢ ⁶He took the Asherah pole from

R 2Ki 21:12–15 ◄ ► 2Ki 23:26–27
M 1Ki 21:25–29 ◄ ► 1Ch 21:8

¹⁷ Or by everything they have done

22:15–20 When Josiah became the king of Judah, he ordered repairs be made to the temple. During these repairs someone found the book of the law (Deuteronomy) that had been misplaced during the years of evil rulers and priests. The prophetess Huldah predicted that God would fulfill the prophecies of judgment because of Judah's sin. However, God promised to delay this judgment until after Josiah's death because of Josiah's genuine repentance.

the temple of the LORD to the Kidron Valley,[t] outside Jerusalem and burned it there. He ground it to powder[u] and scattered the dust over the graves[v] of the common people.[w] [7]He also tore down the quarters of the male shrine prostitutes,[x] which were in the temple of the LORD and where women did weaving for Asherah.

[8]Josiah brought all the priests from the towns of Judah and desecrated the high places, from Geba[y] to Beersheba, where the priests had burned incense. He broke down the shrines[j] at the gates—at the entrance to the Gate of Joshua, the city governor, which is on the left of the city gate. [9]Although the priests of the high places did not serve[z] at the altar of the LORD in Jerusalem, they ate unleavened bread with their fellow priests.

[10]He desecrated Topheth,[a] which was in the Valley of Ben Hinnom,[b] so no one could use it to sacrifice his son[c] or daughter in[k] the fire to Molech. [11]He removed from the entrance to the temple of the LORD the horses that the kings of Judah[d] had dedicated to the sun. They were in the court near the room of an official named Nathan-Melech. Josiah then burned the chariots dedicated to the sun.[e]

[12]He pulled down[f] the altars the kings of Judah had erected on the roof[g] near the upper room of Ahaz, and the altars Manasseh had built in the two courts[h] of the temple of the LORD. He removed them from there, smashed them to pieces and threw the rubble into the Kidron Valley.[i] [13]The king also desecrated the high places that were east of Jerusalem on the south of the Hill of Corruption—the ones Solomon[j] king of Israel had built for Ashtoreth the vile goddess of the Sidonians, for Chemosh the vile god of Moab, and for Molech[l] the detestable[k] god of the people of Ammon.[l] [14]Josiah smashed[m] the sacred stones and cut down the Asherah poles and covered the sites with human bones.[n]

[15]Even the altar[o] at Bethel, the high place made by Jeroboam[p] son of Nebat, who had caused Israel to sin—even that altar and high place he demolished. He burned the high place and ground it to powder, and burned the Asherah pole also. [16]Then Josiah[q] looked around, and

```
23:6 tJer 31:40
uS Ex 32:20
vS Nu 19:16
wJer 26:23

23:7 xS Ge 38:21;
1Ki 14:24;
Eze 16:16

23:8 yS Jos 18:24;
S 1Ki 15:22

23:9
zEze 44:10-14

23:10 aIsa 30:33;
Jer 7:31,32; 19:6
bS Jos 15:8
cS Lev 18:21;
S Dt 18:10

23:11 dver 5,19;
Ne 9:34; Jer 44:9
eS Dt 4:19

23:12 f2Ch 33:15
gJer 19:13; Zep 1:5
hS 2Ki 21:5
iS 2Sa 15:23

23:13 j1Ki 11:7
kS Dt 27:15
lJer 11:13

23:14
mS Ez 23:24
nS Nu 19:16;
S Ps 53:5

23:15 oS Jos 7:2;
1Ki 13:1-3
pS 1Ki 12:33

23:16 qS 1Ki 13:2
rS 1Ki 13:32

23:18 sS 1Ki 13:31
tS 1Ki 13:29

23:20
uS Ex 22:20;
S 2Ki 11:18
vS 1Ki 13:2

23:21
wS Ex 12:11;
Dt 16:1-8
xS Ex 24:7

23:23
yS Ex 12:11;
S Nu 28:16

23:24
zS Lev 19:31;
S Dt 18:11
aS Ge 31:19
bDt 7:26; 2Ki 16:3

23:25 cS 1Sa 7:3
dJer 22:15
```

when he saw the tombs that were there on the hillside, he had the bones removed from them and burned on the altar to defile it, in accordance[r] with the word of the LORD proclaimed by the man of God who foretold these things.

[17]The king asked, "What is that tombstone I see?"

The men of the city said, "It marks the tomb of the man of God who came from Judah and pronounced against the altar of Bethel the very things you have done to it."

[18]"Leave it alone," he said. "Don't let anyone disturb his bones[s]." So they spared his bones and those of the prophet[t] who had come from Samaria.

[19]Just as he had done at Bethel, Josiah removed and defiled all the shrines at the high places that the kings of Israel had built in the towns of Samaria that had provoked the LORD to anger. [20]Josiah slaughtered[u] all the priests of those high places on the altars and burned human bones[v] on them. Then he went back to Jerusalem.

[21]The king gave this order to all the people: "Celebrate the Passover[w] to the LORD your God, as it is written in this Book of the Covenant."[x] **D** [22]Not since the days of the judges who led Israel, nor throughout the days of the kings of Israel and the kings of Judah, had any such Passover been observed. [23]But in the eighteenth year of King Josiah, this Passover was celebrated to the LORD in Jerusalem.[y]

[24]Furthermore, Josiah got rid of the mediums and spiritists,[z] the household gods,[a] the idols and all the other detestable[b] things seen in Judah and Jerusalem. This he did to fulfill the requirements of the law written in the book that Hilkiah the priest had discovered in the temple of the LORD. [25]Neither before nor after Josiah was there a king like him who turned[c] to the LORD as he did—with all his heart and with all his soul and with all his strength, in accordance with all the Law of Moses.[d]

D Dt 17:1 ◄ ► 2Ch 30:1

[j] 8 Or high places   [k] 10 Or to make his son or daughter pass through   [l] 13 Hebrew Milcom

²⁶Nevertheless, the LORD did not turn away from the heat of his fierce anger, which burned against Judah because of all that Manasseh had done to provoke him to anger. ²⁷So the LORD said, "I will remove Judah also from my presence, as I removed Israel, and I will reject Jerusalem, the city I chose, and this temple, about which I said, 'There shall my Name be.'"

²⁸As for the other events of Josiah's reign, and all he did, are they not written in the book of the annals of the kings of Judah?

²⁹While Josiah was king, Pharaoh Neco king of Egypt went up to the Euphrates River to help the king of Assyria. King Josiah marched out to meet him in battle, but Neco faced him and killed him at Megiddo. ³⁰Josiah's servants brought his body in a chariot from Megiddo to Jerusalem and buried him in his own tomb. And the people of the land took Jehoahaz son of Josiah and anointed him and made him king in place of his father.

Jehoahaz King of Judah
23:31–34pp — 2Ch 36:2–4

³¹Jehoahaz was twenty-three years old when he became king, and he reigned in Jerusalem three months. His mother's name was Hamutal daughter of Jeremiah; she was from Libnah. ³²He did evil in the eyes of the LORD, just as his fathers had done. ³³Pharaoh Neco put him in chains at Riblah in the land of Hamath so that he might not reign in Jerusalem, and he imposed on Judah a levy of a hundred talents of silver and a talent of gold. ³⁴Pharaoh Neco made Eliakim son of Josiah king in place of his father Josiah and changed Eliakim's name to Jehoiakim. But he took Jehoahaz and carried him off to Egypt, and there he died. ³⁵Jehoiakim paid Pharaoh Neco the silver and gold he demanded. In order to do so, he taxed the land and exacted the silver and gold from the people of the land according to their assessments.

R 2Ki 22:15–20 ◄ ► 2Ki 24:2–3

23:26 ᵉ 2Ki 21:6; Jer 23:20; 30:24
ᶠ S 2Ki 21:12
23:27 ᵍ 2Ki 21:13
ʰ S Ex 33:15; 2Ki 24:3 ⁱ Jer 27:10; 32:31
23:29 ʲ ver 33-35; Jer 46:2 ᵏ 2Ki 9:27
23:30 ˡ S 2Ki 9:28
23:31 ᵐ 1Ch 3:15; Jer 22:11
ⁿ 2Ki 24:18
23:32 ᵒ 1Ki 15:26
23:33
ᵖ S Nu 34:11
ᑫ 1Ki 8:65
23:34 ʳ 2Ki 24:6; 1Ch 3:15; 2Ch 36:5-8; Jer 1:3
ˢ Jer 22:12
23:35 ᵗ Jer 2:16
23:36 ᵘ Jer 26:1
23:37 ᵛ 1Ki 15:26
24:1 ʷ ver 10; 2Ki 25:11; Ezr 5:12; Jer 4:7; 25:1,9; 39:1; 40:1; 50:17; 52:15; Eze 32:2; Da 1:1; 7:4 ˣ Jer 35:11
ʸ S 2Ki 18:7
24:2 ᶻ Jer 5:15; Hab 1:6 ᵃ Jer 35:11
ᵇ S 2Ki 5:2
ᶜ Isa 28:18-19
ᵈ Jer 12:7-9; 25:1; 26:1; 36:1; Eze 23:23; Da 1:2
24:3 ᵉ S 2Ki 18:25
ᶠ 2Ki 13:23
ᵍ S 1Ki 14:9; S 2Ki 21:12; Jer 15:4
24:4 ʰ S 2Ki 21:16; Jer 22:3
ⁱ S Ex 23:21; La 3:42
24:5 ʲ Jer 22:18-19
24:6 ᵏ Jer 22:19; 36:30 ˡ 1Ch 3:16; Jer 22:24,28; Eze 19:1
24:7 ᵐ S Ge 15:18; S 2Ki 18:21; S Jer 46:25
ⁿ Jer 1:14; 25:9; 46:24
24:8 ᵒ 1Ch 3:16; Jer 22:24; 37:1
ᵖ ver 15; Jer 13:18; 22:26; 29:21

Jehoiakim King of Judah
23:36–24:6pp — 2Ch 36:5–8

³⁶Jehoiakim was twenty-five years old when he became king, and he reigned in Jerusalem eleven years. His mother's name was Zebidah daughter of Pedaiah; she was from Rumah. ³⁷And he did evil in the eyes of the LORD, just as his fathers had done.

24 During Jehoiakim's reign, Nebuchadnezzar king of Babylon invaded the land, and Jehoiakim became his vassal for three years. But then he changed his mind and rebelled against Nebuchadnezzar. ²The LORD sent Babylonian, Aramean, Moabite and Ammonite raiders against him. He sent them to destroy Judah, in accordance with the word of the LORD proclaimed by his servants the prophets. ³Surely these things happened to Judah according to the LORD's command, in order to remove them from his presence because of the sins of Manasseh and all he had done, ⁴including the shedding of innocent blood. For he had filled Jerusalem with innocent blood, and the LORD was not willing to forgive.

⁵As for the other events of Jehoiakim's reign, and all he did, are they not written in the book of the annals of the kings of Judah? ⁶Jehoiakim rested with his fathers. And Jehoiachin his son succeeded him as king.

⁷The king of Egypt did not march out from his own country again, because the king of Babylon had taken all his territory, from the Wadi of Egypt to the Euphrates River.

Jehoiachin King of Judah
24:8–17pp — 2Ch 36:9–10

⁸Jehoiachin was eighteen years old when he became king, and he reigned in Jerusalem three months. His mother's name was Nehushta daughter of Elna-

R 2Ki 23:26–27 ◄ ► 2Ki 24:14

ᵐ 27 1 Kings 8:29 ⁿ 33 Hebrew; Septuagint (see also 2 Chron. 36:3) Neco at Riblah in Hamath removed him ᵒ 33 That is, about 3 3/4 tons (about 3.4 metric tons) ᵖ 33 That is, about 75 pounds (about 34 kilograms) ᑫ 2 Or Chaldean

---

23:26–27 Despite King Josiah's righteousness, God declared that the sins of Judah would receive full judgment in the future generation.

24:2–3 In fulfillment of God's words to his prophets, the Lord sent the combined armies of Babylon, Moab, Ammon and Aramea against Judah.

than; she was from Jerusalem. ⁹He did evil^q in the eyes of the LORD, just as his father had done.

¹⁰At that time the officers of Nebuchadnezzar^r king of Babylon advanced on Jerusalem and laid siege to it, ¹¹and Nebuchadnezzar himself came up to the city while his officers were besieging it. ¹²Jehoiachin king of Judah, his mother, his attendants, his nobles and his officials all surrendered^s to him.

In the eighth year of the reign of the king of Babylon, he took Jehoiachin prisoner. ¹³As the LORD had declared,^t Nebuchadnezzar removed all the treasures^u from the temple of the LORD and from the royal palace, and took away all the gold articles^v that Solomon^w king of Israel had made for the temple of the LORD. ¹⁴He carried into exile^x all Jerusalem: all the officers and fighting men,^y and all the craftsmen and artisans—a total of ten thousand. Only the poorest^z people of the land were left.

¹⁵Nebuchadnezzar took Jehoiachin^a captive to Babylon. He also took from Jerusalem to Babylon the king's mother,^b his wives, his officials and the leading men^c of the land. ¹⁶The king of Babylon also deported to Babylon the entire force of seven thousand fighting men, strong and fit for war, and a thousand craftsmen and artisans.^d ¹⁷He made Mattaniah, Jehoiachin's uncle, king in his place and changed his name to Zedekiah.^e

Zedekiah King of Judah

24:18–20pp — 2Ch 36:11–16; Jer 52:1–3

¹⁸Zedekiah^f was twenty-one years old when he became king, and he reigned in Jerusalem eleven years. His mother's name was Hamutal^g daughter of Jeremiah; she was from Libnah. ¹⁹He did evil^h in the eyes of the LORD, just as Jehoiakim had done. ²⁰It was because of the LORD's anger that all this happened to Je-

R *2Ki 24:2–3 ◀ ▶ 2Ki 25:7–12*

24:9 q 1Ki 15:26
24:10 r S ver 1
24:12 s 2Ki 25:27; Jer 13:18; 22:24-30; 24:1; 29:2
24:13 t 2Ki 20:17 u 2Ki 25:15; Isa 39:6; 42:22 v 2Ki 25:14; Ezr 1:7; Isa 39:6; Jer 15:13; 17:3; 20:5; 27:16; 28:3; Eze 7:21; Da 1:2; 5:2,23; Zep 1:13 w S 1Ki 7:51
24:14 x S Dt 28:36; S 2Ch 36:20; S Mt 1:11 y Isa 3:1-3 z Dt 15:11; 2Ki 25:12; Job 5:16; Ps 9:18; Jer 40:7; 52:16
24:15 a S 2Ki 20:18; Eze 19:9 b S ver 8; S 1Ki 2:19 c Est 2:6; Isa 39:7; La 2:9; Eze 1:2; 17:12-14; Da 1:3
24:16 d Ezr 2:1; Jer 24:1
24:17 e 1Ch 3:15; 2Ch 36:11; Jer 1:3; 37:1; 52:1; Eze 17:13
24:18 f 1Ch 3:16; Jer 39:1 g 2Ki 23:31 Jer 37:2
24:19 h 1Ki 15:26; Jer 37:2
24:20 i Dt 4:26; 29:27 j S Ex 33:15; S 2Ki 13:23
25:1 k Jer 32:1 l Jer 21:2; 34:1-7 m Isa 23:13; 29:3; Jer 4:16-17; 32:2; 33:4; Eze 21:22; 24:2
25:3 n S Lev 26:26; Isa 22:2; Jer 14:18; 37:21; La 2:20; 4:9
25:4 o Job 30:14; Ps 144:14; Jer 50:15; 51:44, 58; Eze 33:21 p Jer 4:17; 6:3
25:5 q S Lev 26:36; Eze 12:14; 17:21
25:6 r Isa 22:3; Jer 38:23 s S Nu 34:11
25:7 t S Dt 28:36; Jer 21:7; 32:4-5; 34:3,21; Eze 12:11; 19:9; 40:1
25:9 u Isa 60:7; 63:15,18; 64:11

rusalem and Judah, and in the end he thrust^i them from his presence.^j

The Fall of Jerusalem

25:1–12pp — Jer 39:1–10
25:1–21pp — 2Ch 36:17–20; Jer 52:4–27
25:22–26pp — Jer 40:7–9; 41:1–3, 16–18

Now Zedekiah rebelled against the king of Babylon.

25 So in the ninth^k year of Zedekiah's reign, on the tenth day of the tenth month, Nebuchadnezzar^l king of Babylon marched against Jerusalem with his whole army. He encamped outside the city and built siege works^m all around it. ²The city was kept under siege until the eleventh year of King Zedekiah. ³By the ninth day of the ⸢fourth⸣ month the famine^n in the city had become so severe that there was no food for the people to eat. ⁴Then the city wall was broken through,^o and the whole army fled at night through the gate between the two walls near the king's garden, though the Babylonians^s were surrounding^p the city. They fled toward the Arabah,^r ⁵but the Babylonian^u army pursued the king and overtook him in the plains of Jericho. All his soldiers were separated from him and scattered,^q ⁶and he was captured.^r He was taken to the king of Babylon at Riblah,^s where sentence was pronounced on him. ⁷They killed the sons of Zedekiah before his eyes. Then they put out his eyes, bound him with bronze shackles and took him to Babylon.^t

⁸On the seventh day of the fifth month, in the nineteenth year of Nebuchadnezzar king of Babylon, Nebuzaradan commander of the imperial guard, an official of the king of Babylon, came to Jerusalem. ⁹He set fire^u to the temple of the LORD, the royal palace and all the houses of Jerusalem. Every important building he

R *2Ki 24:14 ◀ ▶ 2Ki 25:21*

^r 3 See Jer. 52:6. ^s 4 Or *Chaldeans*; also in verses 13, 25 and 26
^t 4 Or *the Jordan Valley* ^u 5 Or *Chaldean*; also in verses 10 and 24

24:14 Nebuchadnezzar of Babylon conquered Jerusalem in 586 B.C., plundering the precious treasures of the temple and taking ten thousand skilled craftsmen, nobles (including Daniel) and fighting men back to Babylon.

25:7–12 The Babylonians killed the sons of King Zedekiah before his eyes and then blinded him in fulfillment of Ezekiel's prophecy (see Eze 12:13). Nebuchadnezzar ordered his troops to burn the city of Jerusalem, destroy the temple and carry off most of the remaining population to slavery in Babylon. Only the poorest people of Judah were left to tend the land under the rule of Babylon.

burned down. ¹⁰The whole Babylonian army, under the commander of the imperial guard, broke down the walls around Jerusalem. ¹¹Nebuzaradan the commander of the guard carried into exile the people who remained in the city, along with the rest of the populace and those who had gone over to the king of Babylon. ¹²But the commander left behind some of the poorest people of the land to work the vineyards and fields.

¹³The Babylonians broke up the bronze pillars, the movable stands and the bronze Sea that were at the temple of the LORD and they carried the bronze to Babylon. ¹⁴They also took away the pots, shovels, wick trimmers, dishes and all the bronze articles used in the temple service. ¹⁵The commander of the imperial guard took away the censers and sprinkling bowls—all that were made of pure gold or silver.

¹⁶The bronze from the two pillars, the Sea and the movable stands, which Solomon had made for the temple of the LORD, was more than could be weighed. ¹⁷Each pillar was twenty-seven feet high. The bronze capital on top of one pillar was four and a half feet high and was decorated with a network and pomegranates of bronze all around. The other pillar, with its network, was similar.

¹⁸The commander of the guard took as prisoners Seraiah the chief priest, Zephaniah the priest next in rank and the three doorkeepers. ¹⁹Of those still in the city, he took the officer in charge of the fighting men and five royal advisers. He also took the secretary who was chief officer in charge of conscripting the people of the land and sixty of his men who were found in the city. ²⁰Nebuzaradan the commander took them all and brought them to the king of Babylon at Riblah. ²¹There at Riblah, in the land of Hamath, the king had them executed. So Judah went into captivity, away from her land.

²²Nebuchadnezzar king of Babylon appointed Gedaliah son of Ahikam, the son of Shaphan, to be over the people he had left behind in Judah. ²³When all the army officers and their men heard that the king of Babylon had appointed Gedaliah as governor, they came to Gedaliah at Mizpah—Ishmael son of Nethaniah, Johanan son of Kareah, Seraiah son of Tanhumeth the Netophathite, Jaazaniah the son of the Maacathite, and their men. ²⁴Gedaliah took an oath to reassure them and their men. "Do not be afraid of the Babylonian officials," he said. "Settle down in the land and serve the king of Babylon, and it will go well with you."

²⁵In the seventh month, however, Ishmael son of Nethaniah, the son of Elishama, who was of royal blood, came with ten men and assassinated Gedaliah and also the men of Judah and the Babylonians who were with him at Mizpah. ²⁶At this, all the people from the least to the greatest, together with the army officers, fled to Egypt for fear of the Babylonians.

Jehoiachin Released
25:27–30pp — Jer 52:31–34

²⁷In the thirty-seventh year of the exile of Jehoiachin king of Judah, in the year Evil-Merodach became king of Babylon, he released Jehoiachin from prison on the twenty-seventh day of the twelfth month. ²⁸He spoke kindly to him and gave him a seat of honor higher than those of the other kings who were with him in Babylon. ²⁹So Jehoiachin put aside his prison clothes and for the rest of his life ate regularly at the king's table. ³⁰Day by day the king gave Jehoiachin a regular allowance as long as he lived.

ᵛ17 Hebrew *eighteen cubits* (about 8.1 meters) ʷ17 Hebrew *three cubits* (about 1.3 meters) ˣ27 Also called *Amel-Marduk*

R 2Ki 25:7–12 ◄► 1Ch 5:26

25:21 The king of Babylon killed the leaders of Judah for their continual rebellion against Babylonian rule. Significantly, rebellion was the same reason for God's judgment against the leaders of Judah.

1 Chronicles

Author: Authorship uncertain; possibly Ezra

Theme: The life and lineage of King David

Date of Writing: c. 450–400 B.C.

Outline of 1 Chronicles
  I. Genealogies From Adam to David (1:1—9:44)
  II. The Death of Saul (10:1—10:14)
  III. The Reign of David (11:1—29:21)
  IV. David's Death and Solomon's Accession (29:22–30)

ORIGINAL HEBREW MANUSCRIPTS combined 1 and 2 Chronicles as one book and titled it "the events (or annals) of the days (or years)," deriving this title from the opening words of the narrative. Septuagint (the Greek translation of the OT) translators called the book "the things omitted" since they regarded its information as supplemental to the narratives of Samuel and Kings. The title "Chronicles" found acceptance after a Latin translation was made of the text by a scholar named Jerome.

The first nine chapters of 1 Chronicles trace the genealogy of King David. This unbroken lineage from the time of the patriarchs to the rise of the monarchy established a rich heritage for the Jewish exiles who returned from Babylon to rebuild their temple and nation. The Chronicles' accounts reflect a priestly view of the events in Israel's life by firmly establishing the basis of God's eternal covenant with his chosen people. The central chapters of 1 Chronicles indicate that this covenantal relationship reached its peak under King David and provide additional details about David's reign that are not recorded in 1 and 2 Kings (see 1Ch 22:1–5; 23—29).

Historical Records From Adam to Abraham

To Noah's Sons

1 Adam,[a] Seth, Enosh, [2]Kenan,[b] Mahalalel,[c] Jared,[d] [3]Enoch,[e] Methuselah,[f] Lamech,[g] Noah.[h]

[4]The sons of Noah:[a][i]
Shem, Ham and Japheth.[j]

The Japhethites
1:5–7pp — Ge 10:2–5

[5]The sons[b] of Japheth:
Gomer, Magog, Madai, Javan, Tubal, Meshech and Tiras.
[6]The sons of Gomer:
Ashkenaz, Riphath[c] and Togarmah.
[7]The sons of Javan:
Elishah, Tarshish, the Kittim and the Rodanim.

The Hamites
1:8–16pp — Ge 10:6–20

[8]The sons of Ham:
Cush, Mizraim,[d] Put and Canaan.
[9]The sons of Cush:
Seba, Havilah, Sabta, Raamah and Sabteca.
The sons of Raamah:
Sheba and Dedan.
[10]Cush was the father[e] of
Nimrod, who grew to be a mighty warrior on earth.
[11]Mizraim was the father of
the Ludites, Anamites, Lehabites, Naphtuhites, [12]Pathrusites, Casluhites (from whom the Philistines came) and Caphtorites.
[13]Canaan was the father of
Sidon his firstborn,[f] and of the Hittites, [14]Jebusites, Amorites, Girgashites, [15]Hivites, Arkites, Sinites, [16]Arvadites, Zemarites and Hamathites.

The Semites
1:17–23pp — Ge 10:21–31; 11:10–27

[17]The sons of Shem:
Elam, Asshur, Arphaxad, Lud and Aram.
The sons of Aram[g]:
Uz, Hul, Gether and Meshech.
[18]Arphaxad was the father of Shelah,
and Shelah the father of Eber.
[19]Two sons were born to Eber:
One was named Peleg,[h] because in his time the earth was divided;
his brother was named Joktan.
[20]Joktan was the father of
Almodad, Sheleph, Hazarmaveth, Jerah, [21]Hadoram, Uzal, Diklah, [22]Obal,[i] Abimael, Sheba, [23]Ophir, Havilah and Jobab. All these were sons of Joktan.

[24]Shem,[k] Arphaxad,[j] Shelah,
[25]Eber, Peleg, Reu,
[26]Serug, Nahor, Terah
[27]and Abram (that is, Abraham).

The Family of Abraham

[28]The sons of Abraham:
Isaac and Ishmael.

Descendants of Hagar
1:29–31pp — Ge 25:12–16

[29]These were their descendants:
Nebaioth the firstborn of Ishmael, Kedar, Adbeel, Mibsam, [30]Mishma, Dumah, Massa, Hadad, Tema, [31]Jetur, Naphish and Kedemah. These were the sons of Ishmael.

Descendants of Keturah
1:32–33pp — Ge 25:1–4

[32]The sons born to Keturah, Abraham's concubine:[l]
Zimran, Jokshan, Medan, Midian, Ishbak and Shuah.
The sons of Jokshan:
Sheba and Dedan.[m]
[33]The sons of Midian:
Ephah, Epher, Hanoch, Abida and Eldaah.
All these were descendants of Keturah.

Descendants of Sarah
1:35–37pp — Ge 36:10–14

[34]Abraham[n] was the father of Isaac.[o]
The sons of Isaac:
Esau and Israel.[p]

---

[a] 4 Septuagint; Hebrew does not have *The sons of Noah*: [b] 5 *Sons* may mean *descendants* or *successors* or *nations*; also in verses 6-10, 17 and 20. [c] 6 Many Hebrew manuscripts and Vulgate (see also Septuagint and Gen. 10:3); most Hebrew manuscripts *Diphath* [d] 8 That is, Egypt; also in verse 11 [e] 10 *Father* may mean *ancestor* or *predecessor* or *founder*; also in verses 11, 13, 18 and 20. [f] 13 Or *of the Sidonians, the foremost* [g] 17 One Hebrew manuscript and some Septuagint manuscripts (see also Gen. 10:23); most Hebrew manuscripts do not have this line. [h] 19 *Peleg* means *division*. [i] 22 Some Hebrew manuscripts and Syriac (see also Gen. 10:28); most Hebrew manuscripts *Ebal* [j] 24 Hebrew; some Septuagint manuscripts *Arphaxad, Cainan* (see also note at Gen. 11:10)

Esau's Sons

35 The sons of Esau:q
Eliphaz, Reuel,ʳ Jeush, Jalam and Korah.
36 The sons of Eliphaz:
Teman, Omar, Zepho,ᵏ Gatam and Kenaz;
by Timna: Amalek.ˡˢ
37 The sons of Reuel:ᵗ
Nahath, Zerah, Shammah and Mizzah.

The People of Seir in Edom
1:38–42pp — Ge 36:20–28

38 The sons of Seir:
Lotan, Shobal, Zibeon, Anah, Dishon, Ezer and Dishan.
39 The sons of Lotan:
Hori and Homam. Timna was Lotan's sister.
40 The sons of Shobal:
Alvan,ᵐ Manahath, Ebal, Shepho and Onam.
The sons of Zibeon:
Aiah and Anah.ᵘ
41 The son of Anah:
Dishon.
The sons of Dishon:
Hemdan,ⁿ Eshban, Ithran and Keran.
42 The sons of Ezer:
Bilhan, Zaavan and Akan.ᵒ
The sons of Dishan:ᵖ
Uz and Aran.

The Rulers of Edom
1:43–54pp — Ge 36:31–43

43 These were the kings who reigned in Edom before any Israelite king reigned:ᵍ
Bela son of Beor, whose city was named Dinhabah.
44 When Bela died, Jobab son of Zerah from Bozrah succeeded him as king.
45 When Jobab died, Husham from the land of the Temanitesᵛ succeeded him as king.
46 When Husham died, Hadad son of Bedad, who defeated Midian in the country of Moab, succeeded him as king. His city was named Avith.
47 When Hadad died, Samlah from Masrekah succeeded him as king.
48 When Samlah died, Shaul from Rehoboth on the riverʳ succeeded him as king.
49 When Shaul died, Baal-Hanan son of Acbor succeeded him as king.
50 When Baal-Hanan died, Hadad succeeded him as king. His city was named Pau,ˢ and his wife's name was Mehetabel daughter of Matred, the daughter of Me-Zahab.
51 Hadad also died.

The chiefs of Edom were:
Timna, Alvah, Jetheth, 52 Oholibamah, Elah, Pinon, 53 Kenaz, Teman, Mibzar, 54 Magdiel and Iram. These were the chiefs of Edom.

Israel's Sons
2:1–2pp — Ge 35:23–26

2 These were the sons of Israel: Reuben, Simeon, Levi, Judah, Issachar, Zebulun, ² Dan, Joseph, Benjamin, Naphtali, Gad and Asher.

Judah
2:5–15pp — Ru 4:18–22; Mt 1:3–6

To Hezron's Sons

³ The sons of Judah:ʷ
Er, Onan and Shelah.ˣ These three were born to him by a Canaanite woman, the daughter of Shua.ʸ Er, Judah's firstborn, was wicked in the LORD's sight; so the LORD put him to death.ᶻ ⁴ Tamar,ᵃ Judah's daughter-in-law,ᵇ bore him Perezᶜ and Zerah. Judah had five sons in all.

⁵ The sons of Perez:ᵈ
Hezronᵉ and Hamul.
⁶ The sons of Zerah:
Zimri, Ethan, Heman, Calcol and Dardaᶠ—five in all.
⁷ The son of Carmi:

ᵏ 36 Many Hebrew manuscripts, some Septuagint manuscripts and Syriac (see also Gen. 36:11); most Hebrew manuscripts *Zephi* ˡ 36 Some Septuagint manuscripts (see also Gen. 36:12); Hebrew *Gatam, Kenaz, Timna and Amalek* ᵐ 40 Many Hebrew manuscripts and some Septuagint manuscripts (see also Gen. 36:23); most Hebrew manuscripts *Alian* ⁿ 41 Many Hebrew manuscripts and some Septuagint manuscripts (see also Gen. 36:26); most Hebrew manuscripts *Hamran* ᵒ 42 Many Hebrew and Septuagint manuscripts (see also Gen. 36:27); most Hebrew manuscripts *Zaavan, Jaakan* ᵖ 42 Hebrew *Dishon*, a variant of *Dishan* ᵍ 43 Or *before an Israelite king reigned over them* ʳ 48 Possibly the Euphrates ˢ 50 Many Hebrew manuscripts, some Septuagint manuscripts, Vulgate and Syriac (see also Gen. 36:39); most Hebrew manuscripts *Pai* ᵗ 6 Many Hebrew manuscripts and some Septuagint manuscripts and Syriac (see also 1 Kings 4:31); most Hebrew manuscripts *Dara*

Achar,[u][f] who brought trouble on Israel by violating the ban on taking devoted things.[v][g]
⁸The son of Ethan:
Azariah.
⁹The sons born to Hezron[h] were: Jerahmeel, Ram and Caleb.[w]

From Ram Son of Hezron

¹⁰Ram[i] was the father of Amminadab[j], and Amminadab the father of Nahshon,[k] the leader of the people of Judah. ¹¹Nahshon was the father of Salmon,[x] Salmon the father of Boaz, ¹²Boaz[l] the father of Obed and Obed the father of Jesse.[m]
¹³Jesse[n] was the father of
Eliab[o] his firstborn; the second son was Abinadab, the third Shimea, ¹⁴the fourth Nethanel, the fifth Raddai, ¹⁵the sixth Ozem and the seventh David. ¹⁶Their sisters were Zeruiah[p] and Abigail. Zeruiah's[q] three sons were Abishai, Joab[r] and Asahel. ¹⁷Abigail was the mother of Amasa,[s] whose father was Jether the Ishmaelite.

Caleb Son of Hezron

¹⁸Caleb son of Hezron had children by his wife Azubah (and by Jerioth). These were her sons: Jesher, Shobab and Ardon. ¹⁹When Azubah died, Caleb[t] married Ephrath, who bore him Hur. ²⁰Hur was the father of Uri, and Uri the father of Bezalel.[u]
²¹Later, Hezron lay with the daughter of Makir the father of Gilead[v] (he had married her when he was sixty years old), and she bore him Segub. ²²Segub was the father of Jair, who controlled twenty-three towns in Gilead. ²³(But Geshur and Aram captured Havvoth Jair,[y][w] as well as Kenath[x] with its surrounding settlements—sixty towns.) All these were descendants of Makir the father of Gilead.

²⁴After Hezron died in Caleb Ephrathah, Abijah the wife of Hezron bore him Ashhur[y] the father[z] of Tekoa.

Jerahmeel Son of Hezron

²⁵The sons of Jerahmeel the firstborn of Hezron:
Ram his firstborn, Bunah, Oren, Ozem and[a] Ahijah. ²⁶Jerahmeel had another wife, whose name was Atarah; she was the mother of Onam.
²⁷The sons of Ram the firstborn of Jerahmeel:
Maaz, Jamin and Eker.
²⁸The sons of Onam:
Shammai and Jada.
The sons of Shammai:
Nadab and Abishur.
²⁹Abishur's wife was named Abihail, who bore him Ahban and Molid.
³⁰The sons of Nadab:
Seled and Appaim. Seled died without children.
³¹The son of Appaim:
Ishi, who was the father of Sheshan.
Sheshan was the father of Ahlai.
³²The sons of Jada, Shammai's brother:
Jether and Jonathan. Jether died without children.
³³The sons of Jonathan:
Peleth and Zaza.
These were the descendants of Jerahmeel.
³⁴Sheshan had no sons—only daughters.
He had an Egyptian servant named Jarha. ³⁵Sheshan gave his

---

[u] 7 *Achar* means *trouble; Achar* is called *Achan* in Joshua.
[v] 7 The Hebrew term refers to the irrevocable giving over of things or persons to the LORD, often by totally destroying them. [w] 9 Hebrew *Kelubai*, a variant of *Caleb* [x] 11 Septuagint (see also Ruth 4:21); Hebrew *Salma* [y] 23 Or *captured the settlements of Jair* [z] 24 *Father* may mean *civic leader* or *military leader;* also in verses 42, 45, 49-52 and possibly elsewhere. [a] 25 Or *Oren and Ozem, by*

2:15 David was not Jesse's firstborn son but rather the seventh in line. No one even considered the possibility of David being the son that Samuel would anoint as Israel's future king (see 1Sa 16:7–13). The customs of ancient Israel provided added benefits to the firstborn son in terms of inheritance and birthright blessings. Yet God in his sovereign grace chose to make Jesse's seventh son the forefather of the Messiah, regardless of his position, birth order or natural advantage.

daughter in marriage to his servant Jarha, and she bore him Attai.
^{36}Attai was the father of Nathan,
Nathan the father of Zabad,^{z}
^{37}Zabad the father of Ephlal,
Ephlal the father of Obed,
^{38}Obed the father of Jehu,
Jehu the father of Azariah,
^{39}Azariah the father of Helez,
Helez the father of Eleasah,
^{40}Eleasah the father of Sismai,
Sismai the father of Shallum,
^{41}Shallum the father of Jekamiah, and Jekamiah the father of Elishama.

The Clans of Caleb

^{42}The sons of Caleb^a the brother of Jerahmeel:
Mesha his firstborn, who was the father of Ziph, and his son Mareshah,^{b} who was the father of Hebron.
^{43}The sons of Hebron:
Korah, Tappuah, Rekem and Shema. ^{44}Shema was the father of Raham, and Raham the father of Jorkeam. Rekem was the father of Shammai. ^{45}The son of Shammai was Maon^b, and Maon was the father of Beth Zur.^{c}
^{46}Caleb's concubine Ephah was the mother of Haran, Moza and Gazez. Haran was the father of Gazez.
^{47}The sons of Jahdai:
Regem, Jotham, Geshan, Pelet, Ephah and Shaaph.
^{48}Caleb's concubine Maacah was the mother of Sheber and Tirhanah. ^{49}She also gave birth to Shaaph the father of Madmannah^d and to Sheva the father of Macbenah and Gibea. Caleb's daughter was Acsah.^{e} ^{50}These were the descendants of Caleb.

The sons of Hur^f the firstborn of Ephrathah:
Shobal the father of Kiriath Jearim,^{g} ^{51}Salma the father of Bethlehem, and Hareph the father of Beth Gader.
^{52}The descendants of Shobal the father of Kiriath Jearim were:
Haroeh, half the Manahathites,

2:36 ^{z}1Ch 11:41

2:42 ^{a}S ver 19

2:45 ^{b}S Jos 15:55
^{c}S Jos 15:58

2:49 ^{d}Jos 15:31
^{e}Jos 15:16

2:50 ^{f}1Ch 4:4
^{g}S ver 19

2:53 ^{h}2Sa 23:38

2:54 ^{i}Ezr 2:22;
Ne 7:26; 12:28

2:55 ^{j}S Ge 15:19;
S Jdg 4:11
^{k}Jos 19:35
^{l}2Ki 10:15,23;
Jer 35:2-19

3:1 ^{m}1Ch 14:3;
28:5 ^{n}S 1Sa 25:43
^{o}S Jos 15:56
^{p}S 1Sa 25:42

3:2 ^{q}1Ki 2:22

3:4 ^{r}S 2Sa 5:4;
1Ch 29:27
^{s}S 2Sa 5:5

3:5 ^{t}2Sa 11:3

3:9 ^{u}S 2Sa 13:1
^{v}1Ch 14:4

^{53}and the clans of Kiriath Jearim: the Ithrites,^{h} Puthites, Shumathites and Mishraites. From these descended the Zorathites and Eshtaolites.
^{54}The descendants of Salma:
Bethlehem, the Netophathites,^{i} Atroth Beth Joab, half the Manahathites, the Zorites, ^{55}and the clans of scribes^c who lived at Jabez: the Tirathites, Shimeathites and Sucathites. These are the Kenites^j who came from Hammath,^{k} the father of the house of Recab.$^{d l}$

The Sons of David
3:1-4pp — 2Sa 3:2-5
3:5-8pp — 2Sa 5:14-16; 1Ch 14:4-7

3 These were the sons of David^m born to him in Hebron:
The firstborn was Amnon the son of Ahinoam^n of Jezreel;^{o}
the second, Daniel the son of Abigail^p of Carmel;
^{2}the third, Absalom the son of Maacah daughter of Talmai king of Geshur;
the fourth, Adonijah^q the son of Haggith;
^{3}the fifth, Shephatiah the son of Abital;
and the sixth, Ithream, by his wife Eglah.
^{4}These six were born to David in Hebron,^{r} where he reigned seven years and six months.^{s}
David reigned in Jerusalem thirty-three years, ^{5}and these were the children born to him there:
Shammua,^{e} Shobab, Nathan and Solomon. These four were by Bathsheba^{ft} daughter of Ammiel.
^{6}There were also Ibhar, Elishua,^{g} Eliphelet, ^{7}Nogah, Nepheg, Japhia, ^{8}Elishama, Eliada and Eliphelet—nine in all. ^{9}All these were the sons of David, besides his sons by his concubines. And Tamar^u was their sister.^{v}

^{b} 42 The meaning of the Hebrew for this phrase is uncertain. ^{c} 55 Or *of the Sopherites* ^{d} 55 Or *father of Beth Recab* ^{e} 5 Hebrew *Shimea*, a variant of *Shammua* ^{f} 5 One Hebrew manuscript and Vulgate (see also Septuagint and 2 Samuel 11:3); most Hebrew manuscripts *Bathshua* ^{g} 6 Two Hebrew manuscripts (see also 2 Samuel 5:15 and 1 Chron. 14:5); most Hebrew manuscripts *Elishama*

The Kings of Judah

¹⁰Solomon's son was Rehoboam,ʷ
  Abijahˣ his son,
  Asaʸ his son,
  Jehoshaphatᶻ his son,
¹¹Jehoramʰᵃ his son,
  Ahaziahᵇ his son,
  Joashᶜ his son,
¹²Amaziahᵈ his son,
  Azariahᵉ his son,
  Jothamᶠ his son,
¹³Ahazᵍ his son,
  Hezekiahʰ his son,
  Manassehⁱ his son,
¹⁴Amonʲ his son,
  Josiahᵏ his son.
¹⁵The sons of Josiah:
  Johanan the firstborn,
  Jehoiakimˡ the second son,
  Zedekiahᵐ the third,
  Shallumⁿ the fourth.
¹⁶The successors of Jehoiakim:
  Jehoiachinⁱᵒ his son,
  and Zedekiah.ᵖ

The Royal Line After the Exile

¹⁷The descendants of Jehoiachin the captive:
  Shealtielᵠ his son, ¹⁸Malkiram, Pedaiah, Shenazzar,ʳ Jekamiah, Hoshama and Nedabiah.ˢ
¹⁹The sons of Pedaiah:
  Zerubbabelᵗ and Shimei.
  The sons of Zerubbabel:
  Meshullam and Hananiah.
  Shelomith was their sister.
²⁰There were also five others:
  Hashubah, Ohel, Berekiah, Hasadiah and Jushab-Hesed.
²¹The descendants of Hananiah:
  Pelatiah and Jeshaiah, and the sons of Rephaiah, of Arnan, of Obadiah and of Shecaniah.
²²The descendants of Shecaniah:
  Shemaiah and his sons:
  Hattush,ᵘ Igal, Bariah, Neariah and Shaphat—six in all.
²³The sons of Neariah:
  Elioenai, Hizkiah and Azrikam—three in all.
²⁴The sons of Elioenai:
  Hodaviah, Eliashib, Pelaiah, Akkub, Johanan, Delaiah and Anani—seven in all.

3:10
ʷ 1Ki 14:21-31;
2Ch 12:16
ˣ 1Ki 15:1-8;
2Ch 13:1
ʸ 1Ki 15:9-24
ᶻ 2Ch 17:1-21:3

3:11 ᵃ 2Ki 8:16-24;
2Ch 21:1
ᵇ 2Ki 8:25-10:14;
2Ch 22:1-10
ᶜ 2Ki 11:1-12:21;
2Ch 22:11-24:27

3:12 ᵈ 2Ki 14:1-22;
2Ch 25:1-28
ᵉ 2Ki 15:1-7;
2Ch 26:1-23
ᶠ 2Ki 15:32-38;
2Ch 27:1; Isa 1:1;
Hos 1:1; Mic 1:1

3:13 ᵍ 2Ki 16:1-20;
2Ch 28:1; Isa 7:1
ʰ 2Ki 18:1-20:21;
2Ch 29:1; Isa 1:1;
Jer 26:19; Hos 1:1;
Mic 1:1
ⁱ 2Ki 21:1-18;
2Ch 33:1

3:14
ʲ 2Ki 21:19-26;
2Ch 33:21; Zep 1:1
ᵏ 2Ki 22:1;
2Ch 34:1; Jer 1:2;
3:6; 25:3

3:15 ˡ 2Ki 23:34
ᵐ Jer 37:1
ⁿ S 2Ki 23:31

3:16 ᵒ S 2Ki 24:6,8
ᵖ S 2Ki 24:18

3:17 ᵠ Ezr 3:2

3:18 ʳ Ezr 1:8; 5:14
ˢ Jer 22:30

3:19 ᵗ Ezr 2:2; 3:2;
5:2; Ne 7:7; 12:1;
Hag 1:1; 2:2;
Zec 4:6

3:22 ᵘ Ezr 8:2-3

4:1 ᵛ S Ge 29:35;
S 1Ch 2:3
ʷ Nu 26:21

4:4 ˣ 1Ch 2:50
ʸ Ru 1:19

4:5 ᶻ 1Ch 2:24

4:13 ᵃ S Jos 15:17

Other Clans of Judah

4 The descendants of Judah:ᵛ
  Perez, Hezron,ʷ Carmi, Hur and Shobal.
²Reaiah son of Shobal was the father of Jahath, and Jahath the father of Ahumai and Lahad. These were the clans of the Zorathites.
³These were the sonsʲ of Etam:
  Jezreel, Ishma and Idbash. Their sister was named Hazzelelponi. ⁴Penuel was the father of Gedor, and Ezer the father of Hushah.
  These were the descendants of Hur,ˣ the firstborn of Ephrathah and fatherᵏ of Bethlehem.ʸ
⁵Ashhurᶻ the father of Tekoa had two wives, Helah and Naarah.
⁶Naarah bore him Ahuzzam, Hepher, Temeni and Haahashtari. These were the descendants of Naarah.
⁷The sons of Helah:
  Zereth, Zohar, Ethnan, ⁸and Koz, who was the father of Anub and Hazzobebah and of the clans of Aharhel son of Harum.

⁹Jabez was more honorable than his brothers. His mother had named him Jabez,ˡ saying, "I gave birth to him in pain." ¹⁰Jabez cried out to the God of Israel, "Oh, that you would bless me and enlarge my territory! Let your hand be with me, and keep me from harm so that I will be free from pain." And God granted his request.

¹¹Kelub, Shuhah's brother, was the father of Mehir, who was the father of Eshton. ¹²Eshton was the father of Beth Rapha, Paseah and Tehinnah the father of Ir Nahash.ᵐ These were the men of Recah.

¹³The sons of Kenaz:
  Othnielᵃ and Seraiah.
  The sons of Othniel:

K *2Ki 6:16–17* ◀▶ *1Ch 29:11–12*
U *1Ki 3:13–14* ◀▶ *1Ch 11:9*

ʰ 11 Hebrew *Joram,* a variant of *Jehoram* ⁱ 16 Hebrew *Jeconiah,* a variant of *Jehoiachin;* also in verse 17 ʲ 3 Some Septuagint manuscripts (see also Vulgate); Hebrew *father* ᵏ 4 *Father* may mean *civic leader* or *military leader;* also in verses 12, 14, 17, 18 and possibly elsewhere. ˡ 9 *Jabez* sounds like the Hebrew for *pain.* ᵐ 12 Or *of the city of Nahash*

Hathath and Meonothai.ⁿ ¹⁴Meonothai was the father of Ophrah. Seraiah was the father of Joab, the father of Ge Harashim.ᵒ It was called this because its people were craftsmen. ¹⁵The sons of Caleb son of Jephunneh:

Iru, Elah and Naam.
The son of Elah:
Kenaz.
¹⁶The sons of Jehallelel:
Ziph, Ziphah, Tiria and Asarel.
¹⁷The sons of Ezrah:
Jether, Mered, Epher and Jalon.

One of Mered's wives gave birth to Miriam,ᵇ Shammai and Ishbah the father of Eshtemoa. ¹⁸(His Judean wife gave birth to Jered the father of Gedor, Heber the father of Soco, and Jekuthiel the father of Zanoah.ᶜ) These were the children of Pharaoh's daughter Bithiah, whom Mered had married. ¹⁹The sons of Hodiah's wife, the sister of Naham:

the father of Keilahᵈ the Garmite, and Eshtemoa the Maacathite.ᵉ
²⁰The sons of Shimon:
Amnon, Rinnah, Ben-Hanan and Tilon.
The descendants of Ishi:
Zoheth and Ben-Zoheth.
²¹The sons of Shelahᶠ son of Judah:

Er the father of Lecah, Laadah the father of Mareshah and the clans of the linen workers at Beth Ashbea, ²²Jokim, the men of Cozeba, and Joash and Saraph, who ruled in Moab and Jashubi Lehem. (These records are from ancient times.) ²³They were the potters who lived at Netaim and Gederah; they stayed there and worked for the king.

Simeon

4:28–33pp — Jos 19:2–10

²⁴The descendants of Simeon:ᵍ
Nemuel, Jamin, Jarib,ʰ Zerah and Shaul;
²⁵Shallum was Shaul's son, Mibsam his son and Mishma his son.
²⁶The descendants of Mishma:
Hammuel his son, Zaccur his son and Shimei his son.
²⁷Shimei had sixteen sons and six

daughters, but his brothers did not have many children; so their entire clan did not become as numerous as the people of Judah. ²⁸They lived in Beersheba,ⁱ Moladah,ʲ Hazar Shual, ²⁹Bilhah, Ezem,ᵏ Tolad, ³⁰Bethuel, Hormah,ˡ Ziklag,ᵐ ³¹Beth Marcaboth, Hazar Susim, Beth Biri and Shaaraim.ⁿ These were their towns until the reign of David. ³²Their surrounding villages were Etam, Ain,ᵒ Rimmon, Token and Ashanᵖ—five towns— ³³and all the villages around these towns as far as Baalath.ᵖ These were their settlements. And they kept a genealogical record.

³⁴Meshobab, Jamlech, Joshah son of Amaziah, ³⁵Joel, Jehu son of Joshibiah, the son of Seraiah, the son of Asiel, ³⁶also Elioenai, Jaakobah, Jeshohaiah, Asaiah, Adiel, Jesimiel, Benaiah, ³⁷and Ziza son of Shiphi, the son of Allon, the son of Jedaiah, the son of Shimri, the son of Shemaiah.

³⁸The men listed above by name were leaders of their clans. Their families increased greatly, ³⁹and they went to the outskirts of Gedorᑫ to the east of the valley in search of pasture for their flocks. ⁴⁰They found rich, good pasture, and the land was spacious, peaceful and quiet.ʳ Some Hamites had lived there formerly. ⁴¹The men whose names were listed came in the days of Hezekiah king of Judah. They attacked the Hamites in their dwellings and also the Meunitesˢ who were there and completely destroyedᑫ them, as is evident to this day. Then they settled in their place, because there was pasture for their flocks. ⁴²And five hundred of these Simeonites, led by Pelatiah, Neariah, Rephaiah and Uzziel, the sons of Ishi, invaded the hill country of Seir.ᵗ ⁴³They killed the remaining Amalekitesᵘ who had escaped, and they have lived there to this day.

Reuben

5 The sons of Reubenᵛ the firstborn of Israel (he was the firstborn, but when he defiled his father's marriage bed,ʷ his rights as firstborn were given to the sons of Josephˣ son of Israel;ʸ so he

---

ⁿ *13* Some Septuagint manuscripts and Vulgate; Hebrew does not have *and Meonothai.* ᵒ *14 Ge Harashim* means *valley of craftsmen.* ᵖ *33* Some Septuagint manuscripts (see also Joshua 19:8); Hebrew *Baal* ᑫ *41* The Hebrew term refers to the irrevocable giving over of things or persons to the LORD, often by totally destroying them.

could not be listed in the genealogical record in accordance with his birthright, ²and though Judah was the strongest of his brothers and a ruler came from him, the rights of the firstborn belonged to Joseph)— ³the sons of Reuben the firstborn of Israel:

Hanoch, Pallu, Hezron and Carmi.

⁴The descendants of Joel:
Shemaiah his son, Gog his son, Shimei his son, ⁵Micah his son, Reaiah his son, Baal his son, ⁶and Beerah his son, whom Tiglath-Pileser king of Assyria took into exile. Beerah was a leader of the Reubenites.

⁷Their relatives by clans, listed according to their genealogical records:

Jeiel the chief, Zechariah, ⁸and Bela son of Azaz, the son of Shema, the son of Joel. They settled in the area from Aroer to Nebo and Baal Meon. ⁹To the east they occupied the land up to the edge of the desert that extends to the Euphrates River, because their livestock had increased in Gilead.

¹⁰During Saul's reign they waged war against the Hagrites, who were defeated at their hands; they occupied the dwellings of the Hagrites throughout the entire region east of Gilead.

Gad

¹¹The Gadites lived next to them in Bashan, as far as Salecah:

¹²Joel was the chief, Shapham the second, then Janai and Shaphat, in Bashan.

¹³Their relatives, by families, were: Michael, Meshullam, Sheba, Jorai, Jacan, Zia and Eber—seven in all.

¹⁴These were the sons of Abihail son of Huri, the son of Jaroah, the son of Gilead, the son of Michael, the son of Jeshishai, the son of Jahdo, the son of Buz.

¹⁵Ahi son of Abdiel, the son of Guni, was head of their family.

¹⁶The Gadites lived in Gilead, in Bashan and its outlying villages, and on all the pasturelands of Sharon as far as they extended.

¹⁷All these were entered in the genealogical records during the reigns of Jotham king of Judah and Jeroboam king of Israel.

¹⁸The Reubenites, the Gadites and the half-tribe of Manasseh had 44,760 men ready for military service—able-bodied men who could handle shield and sword, who could use a bow, and who were trained for battle. ¹⁹They waged war against the Hagrites, Jetur, Naphish and Nodab. ²⁰They were helped in fighting them, and God handed the Hagrites and all their allies over to them, because they cried out to him during the battle. He answered their prayers, because they trusted in him. ²¹They seized the livestock of the Hagrites—fifty thousand camels, two hundred fifty thousand sheep and two thousand donkeys. They also took one hundred thousand people captive, ²²and many others fell slain, because the battle was God's. And they occupied the land until the exile.

The Half-Tribe of Manasseh

²³The people of the half-tribe of Manasseh were numerous; they settled in the land from Bashan to Baal Hermon, that is, to Senir (Mount Hermon).

²⁴These were the heads of their families: Epher, Ishi, Eliel, Azriel, Jeremiah, Hodaviah and Jahdiel. They were brave warriors, famous men, and heads of their families. ²⁵But they were unfaithful to the God of their fathers and prostituted themselves to the gods of the peoples of the land, whom God had destroyed before them. ²⁶So the God of Israel stirred up the spirit of Pul king of Assyria (that is, Tiglath-Pileser king of Assyria), who took the Reubenites, the Gadites and the

R 2Ki 25:21 ◀ ▶ 1Ch 6:15

r 6 Hebrew *Tilgath-Pilneser*, a variant of *Tiglath-Pileser*; also in verse 26

5:26 God used the king of Assyria to accomplish his judgment of sinful Israel. The Assyrians captured the tribes that settled on the eastern side of the Jordan River (Reuben, Gad and the half-tribe of Manasseh) and exiled them to Assyria (modern-day Iraq, Iran and Afghanistan).

half-tribe of Manasseh into exile. He took them to Halah, Habor, Hara and the river of Gozan, where they are to this day.

Levi

6 The sons of Levi:
Gershon, Kohath and Merari.

²The sons of Kohath:
Amram, Izhar, Hebron and Uzziel.

³The children of Amram:
Aaron, Moses and Miriam.
The sons of Aaron:
Nadab, Abihu, Eleazar and Ithamar.

⁴Eleazar was the father of Phinehas,
Phinehas the father of Abishua,
⁵Abishua the father of Bukki,
Bukki the father of Uzzi,
⁶Uzzi the father of Zerahiah,
Zerahiah the father of Meraioth,
⁷Meraioth the father of Amariah,
Amariah the father of Ahitub,
⁸Ahitub the father of Zadok,
Zadok the father of Ahimaaz,
⁹Ahimaaz the father of Azariah,
Azariah the father of Johanan,
¹⁰Johanan the father of Azariah (it was he who served as priest in the temple Solomon built in Jerusalem),
¹¹Azariah the father of Amariah,
Amariah the father of Ahitub,
¹²Ahitub the father of Zadok,
Zadok the father of Shallum,
¹³Shallum the father of Hilkiah,
Hilkiah the father of Azariah,
¹⁴Azariah the father of Seraiah,
and Seraiah the father of Jehozadak.

¹⁵Jehozadak was deported when the LORD sent Judah and Jerusalem into exile by the hand of Nebuchadnezzar.

¹⁶The sons of Levi:
Gershon, Kohath and Merari.

¹⁷These are the names of the sons of Gershon:

R 1Ch 5:26 ◀▶ 1Ch 9:1

Libni and Shimei.
¹⁸The sons of Kohath:
Amram, Izhar, Hebron and Uzziel.
¹⁹The sons of Merari:
Mahli and Mushi.
These are the clans of the Levites listed according to their fathers:
²⁰Of Gershon:
Libni his son, Jehath his son, Zimmah his son, ²¹Joah his son, Iddo his son, Zerah his son and Jeatherai his son.

²²The descendants of Kohath:
Amminadab his son, Korah his son,
Assir his son, ²³Elkanah his son, Ebiasaph his son, Assir his son,
²⁴Tahath his son, Uriel his son, Uzziah his son and Shaul his son.
²⁵The descendants of Elkanah:
Amasai, Ahimoth,
²⁶Elkanah his son, Zophai his son, Nahath his son, ²⁷Eliab his son, Jeroham his son, Elkanah his son
and Samuel his son.

²⁸The sons of Samuel:
Joel the firstborn
and Abijah the second son.

²⁹The descendants of Merari:
Mahli, Libni his son,
Shimei his son, Uzzah his son,
³⁰Shimea his son, Haggiah his son and Asaiah his son.

The Temple Musicians
6:54–80pp — Jos 21:4–39

³¹These are the men David put in charge of the music in the house of the LORD after the ark came to rest there. ³²They ministered with music before the tabernacle, the Tent of Meeting, until Solomon built the temple of the LORD in Jerusalem. They performed their duties ac-

_s 16_ Hebrew _Gershom,_ a variant of _Gershon;_ also in verses 17, 20, 43, 62 and 71 _t 26_ Some Hebrew manuscripts, Septuagint and Syriac; most Hebrew manuscripts _Ahimoth_ ²⁶_and Elkanah. The sons of Elkanah:_ _u 27_ Some Septuagint manuscripts (see also 1 Samuel 1:19,20 and 1 Chron. 6:33,34); Hebrew does not have _and Samuel his son._ _v 28_ Some Septuagint manuscripts and Syriac (see also 1 Samuel 8:2 and 1 Chron. 6:33); Hebrew does not have _Joel._

6:15 Jehozadak, son of the high priest of the temple, was taken captive to Babylon. Apparently he is the same man as Josedech (see Hag 1:1). His son Joshua returned with Zerubbabel, governor of Judah, at the end of the Babylonian captivity to rebuild the temple.

cording to the regulations laid down for them.

³³Here are the men who served, together with their sons:
From the Kohathites:
Heman, the musician,
the son of Joel, the son of Samuel,
³⁴the son of Elkanah, the son of Jeroham,
the son of Eliel, the son of Toah,
³⁵the son of Zuph, the son of Elkanah,
the son of Mahath, the son of Amasai,
³⁶the son of Elkanah, the son of Joel,
the son of Azariah, the son of Zephaniah,
³⁷the son of Tahath, the son of Assir,
the son of Ebiasaph, the son of Korah,
³⁸the son of Izhar, the son of Kohath,
the son of Levi, the son of Israel;
³⁹and Heman's associate Asaph, who served at his right hand:
Asaph son of Berekiah, the son of Shimea,
⁴⁰the son of Michael, the son of Baaseiah,
the son of Malkijah, ⁴¹the son of Ethni,
the son of Zerah, the son of Adaiah,
⁴²the son of Ethan, the son of Zimmah,
the son of Shimei, ⁴³the son of Jahath,
the son of Gershon, the son of Levi;
⁴⁴and from their associates, the Merarites, at his left hand:
Ethan son of Kishi, the son of Abdi,
the son of Malluch, ⁴⁵the son of Hashabiah,
the son of Amaziah, the son of Hilkiah,
⁴⁶the son of Amzi, the son of Bani,
the son of Shemer, ⁴⁷the son of Mahli,
the son of Mushi, the son of Merari,
the son of Levi.

⁴⁸Their fellow Levites were assigned to all the other duties of the tabernacle, the house of God. ⁴⁹But Aaron and his descendants were the ones who presented offerings on the altar of burnt offering and on the altar of incense in connection with all that was done in the Most Holy Place, making atonement for Israel, in accordance with all that Moses the servant of God had commanded.

⁵⁰These were the descendants of Aaron:
Eleazar his son, Phinehas his son, Abishua his son, ⁵¹Bukki his son, Uzzi his son, Zerahiah his son, ⁵²Meraioth his son, Amariah his son,
Ahitub his son, ⁵³Zadok his son and Ahimaaz his son.

⁵⁴These were the locations of their settlements allotted as their territory (they were assigned to the descendants of Aaron who were from the Kohathite clan, because the first lot was for them):

⁵⁵They were given Hebron in Judah with its surrounding pasturelands. ⁵⁶But the fields and villages around the city were given to Caleb son of Jephunneh.

⁵⁷So the descendants of Aaron were given Hebron (a city of refuge), and Libnah, Jattir, Eshtemoa, ⁵⁸Hilen, Debir, ⁵⁹Ashan, Juttah and Beth Shemesh, together with their pasturelands. ⁶⁰And from the tribe of Benjamin they were given Gibeon, Geba, Alemeth and Anathoth, together with their pasturelands.

These towns, which were distributed among the Kohathite clans, were thirteen in all.

⁶¹The rest of Kohath's descendants were allotted ten towns from the clans of half the tribe of Manasseh.

⁶²The descendants of Gershon, clan by clan, were allotted thirteen towns from the tribes of Issachar, Asher and Naphtali, and from the part of the tribe of Manasseh that is in Bashan.

⁶³The descendants of Merari, clan by

---

w 40 Most Hebrew manuscripts; some Hebrew manuscripts, one Septuagint manuscript and Syriac *Maaseiah* *× 57* See Joshua 21:13; Hebrew *given the cities of refuge: Hebron, Libnah.* *y 59* Syriac (see also Septuagint and Joshua 21:16); Hebrew does not have *Juttah.* *z 60* See Joshua 21:17; Hebrew does not have *Gibeon.*

clan, were allotted twelve towns from the tribes of Reuben, Gad and Zebulun. ⁶⁴So the Israelites gave the Levites these towns^z and their pasturelands. ⁶⁵From the tribes of Judah, Simeon and Benjamin they allotted the previously named towns.

⁶⁶Some of the Kohathite clans were given as their territory towns from the tribe of Ephraim. ⁶⁷In the hill country of Ephraim they were given Shechem (a city of refuge), and Gezer,^{aa} ⁶⁸Jokmeam,^b Beth Horon,^c ⁶⁹Aijalon^d and Gath Rimmon,^e together with their pasturelands. ⁷⁰And from half the tribe of Manasseh the Israelites gave Aner and Bileam, together with their pasturelands, to the rest of the Kohathite clans.

⁷¹The Gershonites^f received the following:
From the clan of the half-tribe of Manasseh
  they received Golan in Bashan^g and also Ashtaroth, together with their pasturelands;
⁷²from the tribe of Issachar
  they received Kedesh, Daberath,^h ⁷³Ramoth and Anem, together with their pasturelands;
⁷⁴from the tribe of Asher
  they received Mashal, Abdon,ⁱ ⁷⁵Hukok^j and Rehob,^k together with their pasturelands;
⁷⁶and from the tribe of Naphtali
  they received Kedesh in Galilee, Hammon^l and Kiriathaim,^m together with their pasturelands.

⁷⁷The Merarites (the rest of the Levites) received the following:
From the tribe of Zebulun
  they received Jokneam, Kartah,^b Rimmono and Tabor, together with their pasturelands;
⁷⁸from the tribe of Reuben across the Jordan east of Jericho
  they received Bezerⁿ in the desert, Jahzah, ⁷⁹Kedemoth^o and Mephaath, together with their pasturelands;
⁸⁰and from the tribe of Gad
  they received Ramoth in Gilead,^p Mahanaim,^q ⁸¹Heshbon and Ja-

zer,^r together with their pasturelands.^s

Issachar

7 The sons of Issachar:^t
Tola, Puah,^u Jashub and Shimron—four in all.
²The sons of Tola:
Uzzi, Rephaiah, Jeriel, Jahmai, Ibsam and Samuel—heads of their families. During the reign of David, the descendants of Tola listed as fighting men in their genealogy numbered 22,600.
³The son of Uzzi:
Izrahiah.
The sons of Izrahiah:
Michael, Obadiah, Joel and Isshiah. All five of them were chiefs. ⁴According to their family genealogy, they had 36,000 men ready for battle, for they had many wives and children.
⁵The relatives who were fighting men belonging to all the clans of Issachar, as listed in their genealogy, were 87,000 in all.

Benjamin

⁶Three sons of Benjamin:^v
Bela, Beker and Jediael.
⁷The sons of Bela:
Ezbon, Uzzi, Uzziel, Jerimoth and Iri, heads of families—five in all. Their genealogical record listed 22,034 fighting men.
⁸The sons of Beker:
Zemirah, Joash, Eliezer, Elioenai, Omri, Jeremoth, Abijah, Anathoth and Alemeth. All these were the sons of Beker. ⁹Their genealogical record listed the heads of families and 20,200 fighting men.
¹⁰The son of Jediael:
Bilhan.
The sons of Bilhan:
Jeush, Benjamin, Ehud, Kenaanah, Zethan, Tarshish and Ahishahar. ¹¹All these sons of Jediael were heads of families. There were 17,200 fighting men ready to go out to war.
¹²The Shuppites and Huppites were

---

^a 67 See Joshua 21:21; Hebrew *given the cities of refuge: Shechem, Gezer.* ^b 77 See Septuagint and Joshua 21:34; Hebrew does not have *Jokneam, Kartah.*

the descendants of Ir, and the Hushites the descendants of Aher.

Naphtali

[13] The sons of Naphtali:[w]

Jahziel, Guni, Jezer and Shillem[c]—the descendants of Bilhah.

Manasseh

[14] The descendants of Manasseh:[x]

Asriel was his descendant through his Aramean concubine. She gave birth to Makir the father of Gilead.[y] [15] Makir took a wife from among the Huppites and Shuppites. His sister's name was Maacah.

Another descendant was named Zelophehad,[z] who had only daughters.

[16] Makir's wife Maacah gave birth to a son and named him Peresh. His brother was named Sheresh, and his sons were Ulam and Rakem.

[17] The son of Ulam:

Bedan.

These were the sons of Gilead[a] son of Makir, the son of Manasseh. [18] His sister Hammoleketh gave birth to Ishhod, Abiezer[b] and Mahlah.

[19] The sons of Shemida[c] were:

Ahian, Shechem, Likhi and Aniam.

Ephraim

[20] The descendants of Ephraim:[d]

Shuthelah, Bered his son, Tahath his son, Eleadah his son, Tahath his son, [21] Zabad his son and Shuthelah his son.

Ezer and Elead were killed by the native-born men of Gath, when they went down to seize their livestock. [22] Their father Ephraim mourned for them many days, and his relatives came to comfort him. [23] Then he lay with his wife again, and she became pregnant and gave birth to a son. He named him Beriah,[d] because there had been misfortune in his family. [24] His daughter was Sheerah, who built Lower and Upper Beth Horon[e] as well as Uzzen Sheerah.

[25] Rephah was his son, Resheph his son,[e]

Telah his son, Tahan his son,

[26] Ladan his son, Ammihud his son, Elishama his son, [27] Nun his son and Joshua his son.

[28] Their lands and settlements included Bethel and its surrounding villages, Naaran to the east, Gezer[f] and its villages to the west, and Shechem and its villages all the way to Ayyah and its villages. [29] Along the borders of Manasseh were Beth Shan,[g] Taanach, Megiddo and Dor,[h] together with their villages. The descendants of Joseph son of Israel lived in these towns.

Asher

[30] The sons of Asher:[i]

Imnah, Ishvah, Ishvi and Beriah. Their sister was Serah.

[31] The sons of Beriah:

Heber and Malkiel, who was the father of Birzaith.

[32] Heber was the father of Japhlet, Shomer and Hotham and of their sister Shua.

[33] The sons of Japhlet:

Pasach, Bimhal and Ashvath.

These were Japhlet's sons.

[34] The sons of Shomer:

Ahi, Rohgah,[f] Hubbah and Aram.

[35] The sons of his brother Helem:

Zophah, Imna, Shelesh and Amal.

[36] The sons of Zophah:

Suah, Harnepher, Shual, Beri, Imrah, [37] Bezer, Hod, Shamma, Shilshah, Ithran[g] and Beera.

[38] The sons of Jether:

Jephunneh, Pispah and Ara.

[39] The sons of Ulla:

Arah, Hanniel and Rizia.

[40] All these were descendants of Asher—heads of families, choice men, brave warriors and outstanding leaders. The number of men ready for battle, as listed in their genealogy, was 26,000.

The Genealogy of Saul the Benjamite

8:28-38pp — 1Ch 9:34-44

8 Benjamin[j] was the father of Bela his firstborn,

Ashbel the second son, Aharah the third,

---

c 13 Some Hebrew and Septuagint manuscripts (see also Gen. 46:24 and Num. 26:49); most Hebrew manuscripts *Shallum*   *d 23 Beriah* sounds like the Hebrew for *misfortune*.   *e 25* Some Septuagint manuscripts; Hebrew does not have *his son*.   *f 34* Or *of his brother Shomer: Rohgah*   *g 37* Possibly a variant of *Jether*

²Nohah the fourth and Rapha the fifth.

³The sons of Bela were:
Addar,ᵏ Gera, Abihud,ʰ ⁴Abishua, Naaman, Ahoah,ˡ ⁵Gera, Shephuphan and Huram.

⁶These were the descendants of Ehud,ᵐ who were heads of families of those living in Geba and were deported to Manahath: ⁷Naaman, Ahijah, and Gera, who deported them and who was the father of Uzza and Ahihud.

⁸Sons were born to Shaharaim in Moab after he had divorced his wives Hushim and Baara. ⁹By his wife Hodesh he had Jobab, Zibia, Mesha, Malcam, ¹⁰Jeuz, Sakia and Mirmah. These were his sons, heads of families. ¹¹By Hushim he had Abitub and Elpaal.

¹²The sons of Elpaal:
Eber, Misham, Shemed (who built Onoⁿ and Lod with its surrounding villages), ¹³and Beriah and Shema, who were heads of families of those living in Aijalonᵒ and who drove out the inhabitants of Gath.ᵖ

¹⁴Ahio, Shashak, Jeremoth, ¹⁵Zebadiah, Arad, Eder, ¹⁶Michael, Ishpah and Joha were the sons of Beriah.

¹⁷Zebadiah, Meshullam, Hizki, Heber, ¹⁸Ishmerai, Izliah and Jobab were the sons of Elpaal.

¹⁹Jakim, Zicri, Zabdi, ²⁰Elienai, Zillethai, Eliel, ²¹Adaiah, Beraiah and Shimrath were the sons of Shimei.

²²Ishpan, Eber, Eliel, ²³Abdon, Zicri, Hanan, ²⁴Hananiah, Elam, Anthothijah, ²⁵Iphdeiah and Penuel were the sons of Shashak.

²⁶Shamsherai, Shehariah, Athaliah, ²⁷Jaareshiah, Elijah and Zicri were the sons of Jeroham.

²⁸All these were heads of families, chiefs as listed in their genealogy, and they lived in Jerusalem.

²⁹Jeielⁱ the fatherʲ of Gibeon lived in Gibeon.ᑫ

His wife's name was Maacah, ³⁰and his firstborn son was Abdon, followed by Zur, Kish, Baal, Ner,ᵏ Nadab, ³¹Gedor, Ahio, Zeker ³²and Mikloth, who was the father of Shimeah. They too lived near their relatives in Jerusalem.

³³Nerʳ was the father of Kish,ˢ Kish the father of Saul,ᵗ and Saul the father of Jonathan, Malki-Shua, Abinadab and Esh-Baal.ˡᵘ

³⁴The son of Jonathan:ᵛ
Merib-Baal,ᵐʷ who was the father of Micah.

³⁵The sons of Micah:
Pithon, Melech, Tarea and Ahaz.

³⁶Ahaz was the father of Jehoaddah, Jehoaddah was the father of Alemeth, Azmaveth and Zimri, and Zimri was the father of Moza. ³⁷Moza was the father of Binea; Raphah was his son, Eleasah his son and Azel his son.

³⁸Azel had six sons, and these were their names:
Azrikam, Bokeru, Ishmael, Sheariah, Obadiah and Hanan. All these were the sons of Azel.

³⁹The sons of his brother Eshek:
Ulam his firstborn, Jeush the second son and Eliphelet the third. ⁴⁰The sons of Ulam were brave warriors who could handle the bow. They had many sons and grandsons—150 in all.

All these were the descendants of Benjamin.ˣ

9 All Israelʸ was listed in the genealogies recorded in the book of the kings of Israel.

The People in Jerusalem
9:1–17pp — Ne 11:3–19

The people of Judah were taken captive to Babylonᶻ because of their unfaithfulness.ᵃ ²Now the first to resettle on their

R 1Ch 6:15 ◀ ▶ 2Ch 7:20

ʰ 3 Or *Gera the father of Ehud* ⁱ 29 Some Septuagint manuscripts (see also 1 Chron. 9:35); Hebrew does not have *Jeiel*. ʲ 29 *Father* may mean *civic leader* or *military leader*. ᵏ 30 Some Septuagint manuscripts (see also 1 Chron. 9:36); Hebrew does not have *Ner*. ˡ 33 Also known as *Ish-Bosheth* ᵐ 34 Also known as *Mephibosheth*

9:1 This "book of the kings of Israel" was an official court record that has been lost and should not be confused with our books of 1 and 2 Kings.

own property in their own towns[b] were some Israelites, priests, Levites and temple servants.[c]

³Those from Judah, from Benjamin, and from Ephraim and Manasseh who lived in Jerusalem were:

⁴Uthai son of Ammihud, the son of Omri, the son of Imri, the son of Bani, a descendant of Perez son of Judah.[d]

⁵Of the Shilonites:

Asaiah the firstborn and his sons.

⁶Of the Zerahites:

Jeuel.

The people from Judah numbered 690.

⁷Of the Benjamites:

Sallu son of Meshullam, the son of Hodaviah, the son of Hassenuah;

⁸Ibneiah son of Jeroham; Elah son of Uzzi, the son of Micri; and Meshullam son of Shephatiah, the son of Reuel, the son of Ibnijah.

⁹The people from Benjamin, as listed in their genealogy, numbered 956. All these men were heads of their families.

¹⁰Of the priests:

Jedaiah; Jehoiarib; Jakin;

¹¹Azariah son of Hilkiah, the son of Meshullam, the son of Zadok, the son of Meraioth, the son of Ahitub, the official in charge of the house of God;

¹²Adaiah son of Jeroham, the son of Pashhur,[e] the son of Malkijah; and Maasai son of Adiel, the son of Jahzerah, the son of Meshullam, the son of Meshillemith, the son of Immer.

¹³The priests, who were heads of families, numbered 1,760. They were able men, responsible for ministering in the house of God.

¹⁴Of the Levites:

Shemaiah son of Hasshub, the son of Azrikam, the son of Hashabiah, a Merarite; ¹⁵Bakbakkar, Heresh, Galal and Mattaniah[f] son of Mica, the son of Zicri, the son of Asaph; ¹⁶Obadiah son of Shemaiah, the son of Galal, the son of Jeduthun; and Berekiah son of Asa, the son of Elkanah, who lived in the villages of the Netophathites.[g]

¹⁷The gatekeepers:[h]

Shallum, Akkub, Talmon, Ahiman and their brothers, Shallum their chief ¹⁸being stationed at the King's Gate[i] on the east, up to the present time. These were the gatekeepers belonging to the camp of the Levites. ¹⁹Shallum[j] son of Kore, the son of Ebiasaph, the son of Korah, and his fellow gatekeepers from his family (the Korahites) were responsible for guarding the thresholds of the Tent[n] just as their fathers had been responsible for guarding the entrance to the dwelling of the LORD. ²⁰In earlier times Phinehas[k] son of Eleazar was in charge of the gatekeepers, and the LORD was with him. ²¹Zechariah[l] son of Meshelemiah was the gatekeeper at the entrance to the Tent of Meeting.

²²Altogether, those chosen to be gatekeepers[m] at the thresholds numbered 212. They were registered by genealogy in their villages. The gatekeepers had been assigned to their positions of trust by David and Samuel the seer.[n] ²³They and their descendants were in charge of guarding the gates of the house of the LORD—the house called the Tent. ²⁴The gatekeepers were on the four sides: east, west, north and south. ²⁵Their brothers in their villages had to come from time to time and share their duties for seven-day[o] periods. ²⁶But the four principal gatekeepers, who were Levites, were entrusted with the responsibility for the rooms and treasuries[p] in the house of God. ²⁷They would spend the night stationed around the house of God,[q] because they had to guard it; and they had charge of the key[r] for opening it each morning.

²⁸Some of them were in charge of the articles used in the temple service; they counted them when they were brought in and when they were taken out. ²⁹Others were assigned to take care of the furnishings and all the other articles of the sanctuary,[s] as well as the flour and wine, and the oil, incense and spices. ³⁰But some[t] of the priests took care of mixing the spices. ³¹A Levite named Mattithiah,

---

[n 19] That is, the temple; also in verses 21 and 23

the firstborn son of Shallum the Korahite, was entrusted with the responsibility for baking the offering bread. ³²Some of their Kohathite brothers were in charge of preparing for every Sabbath the bread set out on the table.ᵘ

³³Those who were musicians,ᵛ heads of Levite families, stayed in the rooms of the temple and were exempt from other duties because they were responsible for the work day and night.ʷ

³⁴All these were heads of Levite families, chiefs as listed in their genealogy, and they lived in Jerusalem.

The Genealogy of Saul
9:34-44pp — 1Ch 8:28-38

³⁵Jeielˣ the fatherᵒ of Gibeon lived in Gibeon.

His wife's name was Maacah, ³⁶and his firstborn son was Abdon, followed by Zur, Kish, Baal, Ner, Nadab, ³⁷Gedor, Ahio, Zechariah and Miklah. ³⁸Mikloth was the father of Shimeam. They too lived near their relatives in Jerusalem.

³⁹Nerʸ was the father of Kish,ᶻ Kish the father of Saul, and Saul the father of Jonathan,ᵃ Malki-Shua, Abinadab and Esh-Baal.ᵖᵇ

⁴⁰The son of Jonathan:
Merib-Baal,ᵠᶜ who was the father of Micah.

⁴¹The sons of Micah:
Pithon, Melech, Tahrea and Ahaz.ʳ

⁴²Ahaz was the father of Jadah, Jadahˢ was the father of Alemeth, Azmaveth and Zimri, and Zimri was the father of Moza. ⁴³Moza was the father of Binea; Rephaiah was his son, Eleasah his son and Azel his son.

⁴⁴Azel had six sons, and these were their names:
Azrikam, Bokeru, Ishmael, Sheariah, Obadiah and Hanan. These were the sons of Azel.

Saul Takes His Life
10:1-12pp — 1Sa 31:1-13; 2Sa 1:4-12

10 Now the Philistines fought against Israel; the Israelites fled before them, and many fell slain on Mount Gilboa. ²The Philistines pressed hard after Saul and his sons, and they killed his sons Jonathan, Abinadab and Malki-Shua. ³The fighting grew fierce around Saul, and when the archers overtook him, they wounded him.

⁴Saul said to his armor-bearer, "Draw your sword and run me through, or these uncircumcised fellows will come and abuse me."

But his armor-bearer was terrified and would not do it; so Saul took his own sword and fell on it. ⁵When the armor-bearer saw that Saul was dead, he too fell on his sword and died. ⁶So Saul and his three sons died, and all his house died together.

⁷When all the Israelites in the valley saw that the army had fled and that Saul and his sons had died, they abandoned their towns and fled. And the Philistines came and occupied them.

⁸The next day, when the Philistines came to strip the dead, they found Saul and his sons fallen on Mount Gilboa. ⁹They stripped him and took his head and his armor, and sent messengers throughout the land of the Philistines to proclaim the news among their idols and their people. ¹⁰They put his armor in the temple of their gods and hung up his head in the temple of Dagon.ᵈ

¹¹When all the inhabitants of Jabesh Gileadᵉ heard of everything the Philistines had done to Saul, ¹²all their valiant men went and took the bodies of Saul and his sons and brought them to Jabesh. Then they buried their bones under the great tree in Jabesh, and they fasted seven days.

¹³Saul diedᶠ because he was unfaithfulᵍ to the Lord; he did not keepʰ the word of the Lord and even consulted a mediumⁱ for guidance, ¹⁴and did not inquire of the Lord. So the Lord put him to death and turnedʲ the kingdomᵏ over to David son of Jesse.

David Becomes King Over Israel
11:1-3pp — 2Sa 5:1-3

11 All Israelˡ came together to David at Hebronᵐ and said, "We are your own flesh and blood. ²In the past, even while Saul was king, you were the

---
o 35 Father may mean civic leader or military leader. p 39 Also known as Ish-Bosheth q 40 Also known as Mephibosheth r 41 Vulgate and Syriac (see also Septuagint and 1 Chron. 8:35); Hebrew does not have and Ahaz. s 42 Some Hebrew manuscripts and Septuagint (see also 1 Chron. 8:36); most Hebrew manuscripts Jarah, Jarah

one who led Israel on their military campaigns. And the LORD your God said to you, 'You will shepherd my people Israel, and you will become their ruler.'"

³When all the elders of Israel had come to King David at Hebron, he made a compact with them at Hebron before the LORD, and they anointed David king over Israel, as the LORD had promised through Samuel.

David Conquers Jerusalem
11:4–9pp — 2Sa 5:6–10

⁴David and all the Israelites marched to Jerusalem (that is, Jebus). The Jebusites who lived there ⁵said to David, "You will not get in here." Nevertheless, David captured the fortress of Zion, the City of David.

⁶David had said, "Whoever leads the attack on the Jebusites will become commander-in-chief." Joab son of Zeruiah went up first, and so he received the command.

⁷David then took up residence in the fortress, and so it was called the City of David. ⁸He built up the city around it, from the supporting terraces to the surrounding wall, while Joab restored the rest of the city. ⁹And David became more and more powerful, because the LORD Almighty was with him.

David's Mighty Men
11:10–41pp — 2Sa 23:8–39

¹⁰These were the chiefs of David's mighty men—they, together with all Israel, gave his kingship strong support to extend it over the whole land, as the LORD had promised— ¹¹this is the list of David's mighty men:

Jashobeam, a Hacmonite, was chief of the officers; he raised his spear against three hundred men, whom he killed in one encounter.

¹²Next to him was Eleazar son of Dodai the Ahohite, one of the three mighty men. ¹³He was with David at Pas Dammim when the Philistines gathered there for battle. At a place where there was a field full of barley, the troops fled from the Philistines. ¹⁴But they took their stand in the middle of the field. They defended it and struck the Philistines down, and the LORD brought about a great victory.

¹⁵Three of the thirty chiefs came down to David to the rock at the cave of Adullam, while a band of Philistines was encamped in the Valley of Rephaim. ¹⁶At that time David was in the stronghold, and the Philistine garrison was at Bethlehem. ¹⁷David longed for water and said, "Oh, that someone would get me a drink of water from the well near the gate of Bethlehem!" ¹⁸So the Three broke through the Philistine lines, drew water from the well near the gate of Bethlehem and carried it back to David. But he refused to drink it; instead, he poured it out before the LORD. ¹⁹"God forbid that I should do this!" he said. "Should I drink the blood of these men who went at the risk of their lives?" Because they risked their lives to bring it back, David would not drink it.

Such were the exploits of the three mighty men.

²⁰Abishai the brother of Joab was chief of the Three. He raised his spear against three hundred men, whom he killed, and so he became as famous as the Three. ²¹He was doubly honored above the Three and became their commander, even though he was not included among them.

²²Benaiah son of Jehoiada was a valiant fighter from Kabzeel, who performed great exploits. He struck down two of Moab's best men. He also went down into a pit on a snowy day and killed a lion. ²³And he struck down an Egyptian who was seven and a half feet tall. Although the Egyptian had a spear like a weaver's rod in his hand, Benaiah went against him with a club. He snatched the spear from the Egyptian's hand and killed him with his own spear. ²⁴Such were the exploits of Benaiah son of Jehoiada; he too was as famous as the three mighty men. ²⁵He was held in greater honor than any of the Thirty, but he was not in-

---

t 8 Or the Millo   u 11 Possibly a variant of Jashob-Baal   v 11 Or Thirty; some Septuagint manuscripts Three (see also 2 Samuel 23:8)   w 23 Hebrew five cubits (about 2.3 meters)

cluded among the Three. And David put him in charge of his bodyguard.

26 The mighty men were:
Asahel^g the brother of Joab,
Elhanan son of Dodo from Bethlehem,
27 Shammoth^h the Harorite,
Helez the Pelonite,
28 Ira son of Ikkesh from Tekoa,
Abiezerⁱ from Anathoth,
29 Sibbecai^j the Hushathite,
Ilai the Ahohite,
30 Maharai the Netophathite,
Heled son of Baanah the Netophathite,
31 Ithai son of Ribai from Gibeah in Benjamin,
Benaiah^k the Pirathonite,^l
32 Hurai from the ravines of Gaash,
Abiel the Arbathite,
33 Azmaveth the Baharumite,
Eliahba the Shaalbonite,
34 the sons of Hashem the Gizonite,
Jonathan son of Shagee the Hararite,
35 Ahiam son of Sacar the Hararite,
Eliphal son of Ur,
36 Hepher the Mekerathite,
Ahijah the Pelonite,
37 Hezro the Carmelite,
Naarai son of Ezbai,
38 Joel the brother of Nathan,
Mibhar son of Hagri,
39 Zelek the Ammonite,
Naharai the Berothite, the armor-bearer of Joab son of Zeruiah,
40 Ira the Ithrite,
Gareb the Ithrite,
41 Uriah^m the Hittite,
Zabadⁿ son of Ahlai,
42 Adina son of Shiza the Reubenite, who was chief of the Reubenites, and the thirty with him,
43 Hanan son of Maacah,
Joshaphat the Mithnite,
44 Uzzia the Ashterathite,^o
Shama and Jeiel the sons of Hotham the Aroerite,
45 Jediael son of Shimri,
his brother Joha the Tizite,
46 Eliel the Mahavite,
Jeribai and Joshaviah the sons of Elnaam,
Ithmah the Moabite,
47 Eliel, Obed and Jaasiel the Mezobaite.

Warriors Join David

12 These were the men who came to David at Ziklag,^p while he was banished from the presence of Saul son of Kish (they were among the warriors who helped him in battle; ²they were armed with bows and were able to shoot arrows or to sling stones right-handed or left-handed;^q they were kinsmen of Saul^r from the tribe of Benjamin):

³Ahiezer their chief and Joash the sons of Shemaah the Gibeathite; Jeziel and Pelet the sons of Azmaveth; Beracah, Jehu the Anathothite, ⁴and Ishmaiah the Gibeonite, a mighty man among the Thirty, who was a leader of the Thirty; Jeremiah, Jahaziel, Johanan, Jozabad the Gederathite,^s ⁵Eluzai, Jerimoth, Bealiah, Shemariah and Shephatiah the Haruphite; ⁶Elkanah, Isshiah, Azarel, Joezer and Jashobeam the Korahites; ⁷and Joelah and Zebadiah the sons of Jeroham from Gedor.^t

⁸Some Gadites^u defected to David at his stronghold in the desert. They were brave warriors, ready for battle and able to handle the shield and spear. Their faces were the faces of lions,^v and they were as swift as gazelles^w in the mountains.

⁹Ezer was the chief,
Obadiah the second in command,
Eliab the third,
¹⁰Mishmannah the fourth, Jeremiah the fifth,
¹¹Attai the sixth, Eliel the seventh,
¹²Johanan the eighth, Elzabad the ninth,
¹³Jeremiah the tenth and Macbannai the eleventh.

¹⁴These Gadites were army commanders; the least was a match for a hundred,^x and the greatest for a thousand.^y ¹⁵It was they who crossed the Jordan in the first month when it was overflowing all its banks,^z and they put to flight everyone living in the valleys, to the east and to the west.

¹⁶Other Benjamites^a and some men from Judah also came to David in his stronghold. ¹⁷David went out to meet them and said to them, "If you have come to me in peace, to help me, I am ready to have you unite with me. But if you have

come to betray me to my enemies when my hands are free from violence, may the God of our fathers see it and judge you."

¹⁸Then the Spirit came upon Amasai, chief of the Thirty, and he said:

"We are yours, O David!
We are with you, O son of Jesse!
Success, success to you,
and success to those who help you,
for your God will help you."

So David received them and made them leaders of his raiding bands.

¹⁹Some of the men of Manasseh defected to David when he went with the Philistines to fight against Saul. (He and his men did not help the Philistines because, after consultation, their rulers sent him away. They said, "It will cost us our heads if he deserts to his master Saul.") ²⁰When David went to Ziklag, these were the men of Manasseh who defected to him: Adnah, Jozabad, Jediael, Michael, Jozabad, Elihu and Zillethai, leaders of units of a thousand in Manasseh. ²¹They helped David against raiding bands, for all of them were brave warriors, and they were commanders in his army. ²²Day after day men came to help David, until he had a great army, like the army of God.ˣ

Others Join David at Hebron

²³These are the numbers of the men armed for battle who came to David at Hebron to turn Saul's kingdom over to him, as the LORD had said:

²⁴men of Judah, carrying shield and spear—6,800 armed for battle;
²⁵men of Simeon, warriors ready for battle—7,100;
²⁶men of Levi—4,600, ²⁷including Jehoiada, leader of the family of Aaron, with 3,700 men, ²⁸and Zadok, a brave young warrior, with 22 officers from his family;
²⁹men of Benjamin, Saul's kinsmen—3,000, most of whom had remained loyal to Saul's house until then;
³⁰men of Ephraim, brave warriors, famous in their own clans—20,800;
³¹men of half the tribe of Manasseh, designated by name to come and make David king—18,000;
³²men of Issachar, who understood the times and knew what Israel should do—200 chiefs, with all their relatives under their command;
³³men of Zebulun, experienced soldiers prepared for battle with every type of weapon, to help David with undivided loyalty—50,000;
³⁴men of Naphtali—1,000 officers, together with 37,000 men carrying shields and spears;
³⁵men of Dan, ready for battle—28,600;
³⁶men of Asher, experienced soldiers prepared for battle—40,000;
³⁷and from east of the Jordan, men of Reuben, Gad and the half-tribe of Manasseh, armed with every type of weapon—120,000.

³⁸All these were fighting men who volunteered to serve in the ranks. They came to Hebron fully determined to make David king over all Israel. All the rest of the Israelites were also of one mind to make David king. ³⁹The men spent three days there with David, eating and drinking, for their families had supplied provisions for them. ⁴⁰Also, their neighbors from as far away as Issachar, Zebulun and Naphtali came bringing food on donkeys, camels, mules and oxen. There were plentiful supplies of flour, fig cakes, raisin cakes, wine, oil, cattle and sheep, for there was joy in Israel.

Bringing Back the Ark

13:1–14pp — 2Sa 6:1–11

13 David conferred with each of his officers, the commanders of thousands and commanders of hundreds. ²He then said to the whole assembly of Israel, "If it seems good to you and if it is the

ˣ 22 Or a great and mighty army

12:32 The tribe of Issachar was made up of men "who understood the times and knew what Israel should do." A proper understanding of God's plan is a benefit to any generation. We, too, should be aware of God's plan, live holy lives, long for Christ's return and look for the fulfillment of God's prophecies in our time.

will of the LORD our God, let us send word far and wide to the rest of our brothers throughout the territories of Israel, and also to the priests and Levites who are with them in their towns and pasturelands, to come and join us. ³Let us bring the ark of our God back to us,ˢ for we did not inquireᵗ ofʸ itᶻ during the reign of Saul." ⁴The whole assembly agreed to do this, because it seemed right to all the people.

⁵So David assembled all the Israelites,ᵘ from the Shihor Riverᵛ in Egypt to Lebo Hamath,ʷ to bring the ark of God from Kiriath Jearim.ˣ ⁶David and all the Israelites with him went to Baalahʸ of Judah (Kiriath Jearim) to bring up from there the ark of God the LORD, who is enthroned between the cherubimᶻ—the ark that is called by the Name.

⁷They moved the ark of God from Abinadab'sᵃ house on a new cart, with Uzzah and Ahio guiding it. ⁸David and all the Israelites were celebrating with all their might before God, with songs and with harps, lyres, tambourines, cymbals and trumpets.ᵇ

⁹When they came to the threshing floor of Kidon, Uzzah reached out his hand to steady the ark, because the oxen stumbled. ¹⁰The LORD's angerᶜ burned against Uzzah, and he struck him downᵈ because he had put his hand on the ark. So he died there before God.

¹¹Then David was angry because the LORD's wrath had broken out against Uzzah, and to this day that place is called Perez Uzzah.ᵇᵉ

¹²David was afraid of God that day and asked, "How can I ever bring the ark of God to me?" ¹³He did not take the ark to be with him in the City of David. Instead, he took it aside to the house of Obed-Edomᶠ the Gittite. ¹⁴The ark of God remained with the family of Obed-Edom in his house for three months, and the LORD blessed his householdᵍ and everything he had.

David's House and Family
14:1–7pp — 2Sa 5:11–16; 1Ch 3:5–8

14 Now Hiram king of Tyre sent messengers to David, along with cedar logs,ʰ stonemasons and carpenters to build a palace for him. ²And David

13:3 ˢ 1Sa 7:1-2
ᵗ 2Ch 1:5

13:5 ᵘ 1Ch 11:1;
15:3 ᵛ S Jos 13:3
ʷ S Nu 13:21
ˣ S 1Sa 7:2

13:6 ʸ S Jos 15:9
ᶻ S Ex 25:22;
2Ki 19:15

13:7 ᵃ S 1Sa 7:1

13:8 ᵇ 1Ch 15:16, 19,24; 2Ch 5:12; Ps 92:3

13:10 ᶜ 1Ch 15:13,
15 ᵈ S Lev 10:2

13:11 ᵉ 1Ch 15:13;
Ps 7:11

13:13 ᶠ 1Ch 15:18, 24; 16:38; 26:4-5, 15

13:14 ᵍ S 2Sa 6:11

14:1 ʰ S 1Ki 5:6;
1Ch 17:6; 22:4;
2Ch 2:3; Ezr 3:7;
Hag 1:8

14:2 ⁱ S Nu 24:7;
S Dt 26:19

14:3 ʲ S 1Ch 3:1

14:4 ᵏ S 1Ch 3:9

14:8 ˡ 1Ch 11:1

14:9 ᵐ ver 13;
S Jos 15:8;
S 1Ch 11:15

14:11 ⁿ Ps 94:16;
Isa 28:21

14:12 ᵒ S Ex 32:20
ᵖ S Jos 7:15

14:13 ᵠ S ver 9

14:16 ʳ S Jos 9:3
ˢ Jos 10:33

14:17 ᵗ S Jos 6:27
ᵘ Ex 15:14-16;
S Dt 2:25; Ps 2:1-12

knew that the LORD had established him as king over Israel and that his kingdom had been highly exaltedⁱ for the sake of his people Israel.

³In Jerusalem David took more wives and became the father of more sonsʲ and daughters. ⁴These are the names of the children born to him there:ᵏ Shammua, Shobab, Nathan, Solomon, ⁵Ibhar, Elishua, Elpelet, ⁶Nogah, Nepheg, Japhia, ⁷Elishama, Beeliada and Eliphelet.

David Defeats the Philistines
14:8–17pp — 2Sa 5:17–25

⁸When the Philistines heard that David had been anointed king over all Israel,ˡ they went up in full force to search for him, but David heard about it and went out to meet them. ⁹Now the Philistines had come and raided the Valleyᵐ of Rephaim; ¹⁰so David inquired of God: "Shall I go and attack the Philistines? Will you hand them over to me?"

The LORD answered him, "Go, I will hand them over to you."

¹¹So David and his men went up to Baal Perazim,ⁿ and there he defeated them. He said, "As waters break out, God has broken out against my enemies by my hand." So that place was called Baal Perazim.ᵈ ¹²The Philistines had abandoned their gods there, and David gave orders to burnᵒ them in the fire.ᵖ

¹³Once more the Philistines raided the valley;ᵠ ¹⁴so David inquired of God again, and God answered him, "Do not go straight up, but circle around them and attack them in front of the balsam trees. ¹⁵As soon as you hear the sound of marching in the tops of the balsam trees, move out to battle, because that will mean God has gone out in front of you to strike the Philistine army." ¹⁶So David did as God commanded him, and they struck down the Philistine army, all the way from Gibeonʳ to Gezer.ˢ

¹⁷So David's fameᵗ spread throughout every land, and the LORD made all the nations fearᵘ him.

◀ 2Ki 19:30–31 ◀▶ 1Ch 14:15
◀ 1Ch 14:10 ◀▶ 1Ch 16:15–18

ʸ 3 Or we neglected ᶻ 3 Or him ᵃ 5 Or to the entrance to ᵇ 11 Perez Uzzah means outbreak against Uzzah. ᶜ 7 A variant of Eliada ᵈ 11 Baal Perazim means the lord who breaks out.

The Ark Brought to Jerusalem
15:25–16:3pp — 2Sa 6:12–19

15 After David had constructed buildings for himself in the City of David, he prepared a place for the ark of God and pitched a tent for it. ²Then David said, "No one but the Levites may carry the ark of God, because the LORD chose them to carry the ark of the LORD and to minister before him forever."

³David assembled all Israel in Jerusalem to bring up the ark of the LORD to the place he had prepared for it. ⁴He called together the descendants of Aaron and the Levites:

⁵From the descendants of Kohath,
  Uriel the leader and 120 relatives;
⁶from the descendants of Merari,
  Asaiah the leader and 220 relatives;
⁷from the descendants of Gershon,
  Joel the leader and 130 relatives;
⁸from the descendants of Elizaphan,
  Shemaiah the leader and 200 relatives;
⁹from the descendants of Hebron,
  Eliel the leader and 80 relatives;
¹⁰from the descendants of Uzziel,
  Amminadab the leader and 112 relatives.

¹¹Then David summoned Zadok and Abiathar the priests, and Uriel, Asaiah, Joel, Shemaiah, Eliel and Amminadab the Levites. ¹²He said to them, "You are the heads of the Levitical families; you and your fellow Levites are to consecrate yourselves and bring up the ark of the LORD, the God of Israel, to the place I have prepared for it. ¹³It was because you, the Levites, did not bring it up the first time that the LORD our God broke out in anger against us. We did not inquire of him about how to do it in the prescribed way." ¹⁴So the priests and Levites consecrated themselves in order to bring up the ark of the LORD, the God of Israel. ¹⁵And the Levites carried the ark of God with the poles on their shoulders, as Moses had commanded in accordance with the word of the LORD.

¹⁶David told the leaders of the Levites to appoint their brothers as singers to sing joyful songs, accompanied by musical instruments: lyres, harps and cymbals.

¹⁷So the Levites appointed Heman son of Joel; from his brothers, Asaph son of Berekiah; and from their brothers the Merarites, Ethan son of Kushaiah; ¹⁸and with them their brothers next in rank: Zechariah, Jaaziel, Shemiramoth, Jehiel, Unni, Eliab, Benaiah, Maaseiah, Mattithiah, Eliphelehu, Mikneiah, Obed-Edom and Jeiel, the gatekeepers.

¹⁹The musicians Heman, Asaph and Ethan were to sound the bronze cymbals; ²⁰Zechariah, Aziel, Shemiramoth, Jehiel, Unni, Eliab, Maaseiah and Benaiah were to play the lyres according to *alamoth*, ²¹and Mattithiah, Eliphelehu, Mikneiah, Obed-Edom, Jeiel and Azaziah were to play the harps, directing according to *sheminith*. ²²Kenaniah the head Levite was in charge of the singing; that was his responsibility because he was skillful at it.

²³Berekiah and Elkanah were to be doorkeepers for the ark. ²⁴Shebaniah, Joshaphat, Nethanel, Amasai, Zechariah, Benaiah and Eliezer the priests were to blow trumpets before the ark of God. Obed-Edom and Jehiah were also to be doorkeepers for the ark.

²⁵So David and the elders of Israel and the commanders of units of a thousand went to bring up the ark of the covenant of the LORD from the house of Obed-Edom, with rejoicing. ²⁶Because God had helped the Levites who were carrying the ark of the covenant of the LORD, seven bulls and seven rams were sacrificed. ²⁷Now David was clothed in a robe of fine linen, as were all the Levites who were carrying the ark, and as were the singers, and Kenaniah, who was in charge of the singing of the choirs. David also wore a linen ephod. ²⁸So all Israel brought up the ark of the covenant of the LORD with shouts, with the sounding of rams' horns and trumpets, and of cymbals, and the playing of lyres and harps.

²⁹As the ark of the covenant of the LORD was entering the City of David, Michal daughter of Saul watched from a window. And when she saw King David dancing

---

e 7 Hebrew *Gershom*, a variant of *Gershon*   *f 18* Three Hebrew manuscripts and most Septuagint manuscripts (see also verse 20 and 1 Chron. 16:5); most Hebrew manuscripts *Zechariah son and* or *Zechariah, Ben and*   *g 18* Hebrew; Septuagint (see also verse 21) *Jeiel and Azaziah*   *h 20,21* Probably a musical term

16 They brought the ark of God and set it inside the tent that David had pitched[d] for it, and they presented burnt offerings and fellowship offerings[i] before God. [2]After David had finished sacrificing the burnt offerings and fellowship offerings, he blessed[e] the people in the name of the LORD. [3]Then he gave a loaf of bread, a cake of dates and a cake of raisins[f] to each Israelite man and woman.

[4]He appointed some of the Levites to minister[g] before the ark of the LORD, to make petition, to give thanks, and to praise the LORD, the God of Israel: [5]Asaph was the chief, Zechariah second, then Jeiel, Shemiramoth, Jehiel, Mattithiah, Eliab, Benaiah, Obed-Edom and Jeiel. They were to play the lyres and harps, Asaph was to sound the cymbals, [6]and Benaiah and Jahaziel the priests were to blow the trumpets regularly before the ark of the covenant of God.

David's Psalm of Thanks

16:8–22pp — Ps 105:1–15
16:23–33pp — Ps 96:1–13
16:34–36pp — Ps 106:1,47–48

[7]That day David first committed to Asaph and his associates this psalm[h] of thanks to the LORD:

T [8]Give thanks[i] to the LORD, call on his name;
  make known among the nations[j]
  what he has done.
[9]Sing to him, sing praise[k] to him;
  tell of all his wonderful acts.
[10]Glory in his holy name;[l]
  let the hearts of those who seek the
  LORD rejoice.
[11]Look to the LORD and his strength;
  seek[m] his face always.
[12]Remember[n] the wonders[o] he has done,
  his miracles,[p] and the judgments he pronounced,
[13]O descendants of Israel his servant,
  O sons of Jacob, his chosen ones.

[14]He is the LORD our God;
  his judgments[q] are in all the earth.
[15]He remembers[j][r] his covenant forever,
  the word he commanded, for a
  thousand generations,
[16]the covenant[s] he made with Abraham,
  the oath he swore to Isaac.
[17]He confirmed it to Jacob[t] as a decree,
  to Israel as an everlasting covenant:
[18]"To you I will give the land of Canaan[u]
  as the portion you will inherit."

[19]When they were but few in number,[v]
  few indeed, and strangers in it,
[20]they[k] wandered[w] from nation to nation,
  from one kingdom to another.
[21]He allowed no man to oppress them;
  for their sake he rebuked kings:[x]
[22]"Do not touch my anointed ones;
  do my prophets[y] no harm."

[23]Sing to the LORD, all the earth;
  proclaim his salvation day after day.
[24]Declare his glory[z] among the nations,
  his marvelous deeds among all peoples.
[25]For great is the LORD and most worthy of praise;[a]
  he is to be feared[b] above all gods.[c]
[26]For all the gods of the nations are idols,
  but the LORD made the heavens.[d]
[27]Splendor and majesty are before him;
  strength and joy in his dwelling place.
[28]Ascribe to the LORD, O families of nations,
  ascribe to the LORD glory and strength,[e]
[29]ascribe to the LORD the glory due his name.[f]
  Bring an offering and come before him;

I 1Ch 14:15 ◀ ▶ 1Ch 16:35
L 2Ki 6:16–17 ◀ ▶ 1Ch 28:20
S 1Ki 18:21 ◀ ▶ 1Ch 28:9

[i] 1 Traditionally *peace offerings*; also in verse 2 [j] 15 Some Septuagint manuscripts (see also Psalm 105:8); Hebrew *Remember* [k] 18-20 One Hebrew manuscript, Septuagint and Vulgate (see also Psalm 105:12); most Hebrew manuscripts *inherit,* / [19]*though you are but few in number, / few indeed, and strangers in it.*" / [20]*They*

T 1Sa 7:12 ◀ ▶ Ps 22:22–23

16:15 King David reminded Israel of the eternal covenant that God had made with Abraham regarding their possession of the land of Canaan and their position as God's chosen nation (see note on Abrahamic covenant at Ge 15:4).

worship the LORD in the splendor of
   his holiness.
³⁰Tremble before him, all the earth!
   The world is firmly established; it
   cannot be moved.
³¹Let the heavens rejoice, let the earth
   be glad;
   let them say among the nations,
   "The LORD reigns!"
³²Let the sea resound, and all that is in
   it;
   let the fields be jubilant, and
   everything in them!
³³Then the trees of the forest will sing,
   they will sing for joy before the
   LORD,
   for he comes to judge the earth.

³⁴Give thanks to the LORD, for he is good;
   his love endures forever.
³⁵Cry out, "Save us, O God our Savior;
   gather us and deliver us from the
   nations,
   that we may give thanks to your holy
   name,
   that we may glory in your praise."
³⁶Praise be to the LORD, the God of Israel,
   from everlasting to everlasting.

Then all the people said "Amen" and "Praise the LORD."

³⁷David left Asaph and his associates before the ark of the covenant of the LORD to minister there regularly, according to each day's requirements. ³⁸He also left Obed-Edom and his sixty-eight associates to minister with them. Obed-Edom son of Jeduthun, and also Hosah, were gatekeepers.

³⁹David left Zadok the priest and his fellow priests before the tabernacle of the LORD at the high place in Gibeon ⁴⁰to present burnt offerings to the LORD on the altar of burnt offering regularly, morning and evening, in accordance with everything written in the Law of the LORD, which he had given Israel. ⁴¹With them were Heman and Jeduthun and the rest of those chosen and designated by name to give thanks to the LORD, "for his love endures forever." ⁴²Heman and Jeduthun were responsible for the sounding of the trumpets and cymbals and for the playing of the other instruments for sacred song. The sons of Jeduthun were stationed at the gate.

⁴³Then all the people left, each for his own home, and David returned home to bless his family.

God's Promise to David
17:1–15pp — 2Sa 7:1–17

17 After David was settled in his palace, he said to Nathan the prophet, "Here I am, living in a palace of cedar, while the ark of the covenant of the LORD is under a tent."

²Nathan replied to David, "Whatever you have in mind, do it, for God is with you."

³That night the word of God came to Nathan, saying:

⁴"Go and tell my servant David, 'This is what the LORD says: You are not the one to build me a house to dwell in. ⁵I have not dwelt in a house from the day I brought Israel up out of Egypt to this day. I have moved from one tent site to another, from one dwelling place to another. ⁶Wherever I have moved with all the Israelites, did I ever say to any of their leaders whom I commanded to shepherd my people, "Why have you not built me a house of cedar?" '

⁷"Now then, tell my servant David, 'This is what the LORD Almighty says: I took you from the pasture and from following the flock, to be ruler over my people Israel. ⁸I have been with you wherever you have gone, and I have cut off all your enemies from before you. Now I will make your name like the names of the greatest men of the earth. ⁹And I will

¹29 Or LORD with the splendor of ᵐ6 Traditionally judges; also in verse 10

17:9 God promised to settle Israel in the land, and they would never be removed from it. This prophecy will not be completely fulfilled until the return of Christ.

provide a place for my people Israel and will plant them so that they can have a home of their own and no longer be disturbed. Wicked people will not oppress them anymore, as they did at the beginning ¹⁰and have done ever since the time I appointed leaders over my people Israel. I will also subdue all your enemies.

" 'I declare to you that the LORD will build a house for you: ¹¹When your days are over and you go to be with your fathers, I will raise up your offspring to succeed you, one of your own sons, and I will establish his kingdom. ¹²He is the one who will build a house for me, and I will establish his throne forever. ¹³I will be his father, and he will be my son. I will never take my love away from him, as I took it away from your predecessor. ¹⁴I will set him over my house and my kingdom forever; his throne will be established forever.' "

¹⁵Nathan reported to David all the words of this entire revelation.

David's Prayer
17:16–27pp — 2Sa 7:18–29

¹⁶Then King David went in and sat before the LORD, and he said:

"Who am I, O LORD God, and what is my family, that you have brought me this far? ¹⁷And as if this were not enough in your sight, O God, you have spoken about the future of the house of your servant. You have looked on me as though I were the most exalted of men, O LORD God.

¹⁸"What more can David say to you for honoring your servant? For you know your servant, ¹⁹O LORD. For the sake of your servant and according to your will, you have done this great thing and made known all these great promises.

²⁰"There is no one like you, O LORD, and there is no God but you, as we have heard with our own ears. ²¹And who is like your people Israel—the one nation on earth whose God went out to redeem a people for himself, and to make a name for yourself, and to perform great and awesome wonders by driving out nations from before your people, whom you redeemed from Egypt? ²²You made your people Israel your very own forever, and you, O LORD, have become their God.

²³"And now, LORD, let the promise you have made concerning your servant and his house be established forever. Do as you promised, ²⁴so that it will be established and that your name will be great forever. Then men will say, 'The LORD Almighty, the God over Israel, is Israel's God!' And the house of your servant David will be established before you.

²⁵"You, my God, have revealed to your servant that you will build a house for him. So your servant has found courage to pray to you. ²⁶O LORD, you are God! You have promised these good things to your servant. ²⁷Now you have been pleased to bless the house of your servant, that it may continue forever in your sight; for you, O LORD, have blessed it, and it will be blessed forever."

David's Victories
18:1–13pp — 2Sa 8:1–14

18 In the course of time, David defeated the Philistines and subdued them, and he took Gath and its surrounding villages from the control of the Philistines.

²David also defeated the Moabites, and they became subject to him and brought tribute.

³Moreover, David fought Hadadezer king of Zobah, as far as Hamath, when

---

17:14 Though this prophecy was initially fulfilled in David's son Solomon, this prophecy also extends into the future to David's descendant Jesus Christ, God's Messiah, who will rule Israel forever (see note on Davidic covenant at 2Sa 7:16).

he went to establish his control along the Euphrates River. ⁴David captured a thousand of his chariots, seven thousand charioteers and twenty thousand foot soldiers. He hamstrung all but a hundred of the chariot horses.

⁵When the Arameans of Damascus came to help Hadadezer king of Zobah, David struck down twenty-two thousand of them. ⁶He put garrisons in the Aramean kingdom of Damascus, and the Arameans became subject to him and brought tribute. The LORD gave David victory everywhere he went.

⁷David took the gold shields carried by the officers of Hadadezer and brought them to Jerusalem. ⁸From Tebah and Cun, towns that belonged to Hadadezer, David took a great quantity of bronze, which Solomon used to make the bronze Sea, the pillars and various bronze articles.

⁹When Tou king of Hamath heard that David had defeated the entire army of Hadadezer king of Zobah, ¹⁰he sent his son Hadoram to King David to greet him and congratulate him on his victory in battle over Hadadezer, who had been at war with Tou. Hadoram brought all kinds of articles of gold and silver and bronze.

¹¹King David dedicated these articles to the LORD, as he had done with the silver and gold he had taken from all these nations: Edom and Moab, the Ammonites and the Philistines, and Amalek.

¹²Abishai son of Zeruiah struck down eighteen thousand Edomites in the Valley of Salt. ¹³He put garrisons in Edom, and all the Edomites became subject to David. The LORD gave David victory everywhere he went.

David's Officials

18:14–17pp — 2Sa 8:15–18

¹⁴David reigned over all Israel, doing what was just and right for all his people. ¹⁵Joab son of Zeruiah was over the army; Jehoshaphat son of Ahilud was recorder; ¹⁶Zadok son of Ahitub and Ahimelech son of Abiathar were priests; Shavsha was secretary; ¹⁷Benaiah son of Jehoiada was over the Kerethites and Pelethites; and David's sons were chief officials at the king's side.

S 2Sa 8:14 ◄ ► 1Ch 18:13
S 1Ch 18:6 ◄ ► Job 34:29

The Battle Against the Ammonites

19:1–19pp — 2Sa 10:1–19

19 In the course of time, Nahash king of the Ammonites died, and his son succeeded him as king. ²David thought, "I will show kindness to Hanun son of Nahash, because his father showed kindness to me." So David sent a delegation to express his sympathy to Hanun concerning his father.

When David's men came to Hanun in the land of the Ammonites to express sympathy to him, ³the Ammonite nobles said to Hanun, "Do you think David is honoring your father by sending men to you to express sympathy? Haven't his men come to you to explore and spy out the country and overthrow it?" ⁴So Hanun seized David's men, shaved them, cut off their garments in the middle at the buttocks, and sent them away.

⁵When someone came and told David about the men, he sent messengers to meet them, for they were greatly humiliated. The king said, "Stay at Jericho till your beards have grown, and then come back."

⁶When the Ammonites realized that they had become a stench in David's nostrils, Hanun and the Ammonites sent a thousand talents of silver to hire chariots and charioteers from Aram Naharaim, Aram Maacah and Zobah. ⁷They hired thirty-two thousand chariots and charioteers, as well as the king of Maacah with his troops, who came and camped near Medeba, while the Ammonites were mustered from their towns and moved out for battle.

⁸On hearing this, David sent Joab out with the entire army of fighting men. ⁹The Ammonites came out and drew up in battle formation at the entrance to their city, while the kings who had come were by themselves in the open country.

¹⁰Joab saw that there were battle lines in front of him and behind him; so he selected some of the best troops in Israel and deployed them against the Arameans. ¹¹He put the rest of the men under the command of Abishai his brother, and they were deployed against the Am-

---

n 8 Hebrew *Tibhath*, a variant of *Tebah*   *o 16* Some Hebrew manuscripts, Vulgate and Syriac (see also 2 Samuel 8:17); most Hebrew manuscripts *Abimelech*   *p 6* That is, about 37 tons (about 34 metric tons)   *q 6* That is, Northwest Mesopotamia

monites. ¹²Joab said, "If the Arameans are too strong for me, then you are to rescue me; but if the Ammonites are too strong for you, then I will rescue you. ¹³Be strong and let us fight bravely for our people and the cities of our God. The LORD will do what is good in his sight."

¹⁴Then Joab and the troops with him advanced to fight the Arameans, and they fled before him. ¹⁵When the Ammonites saw that the Arameans were fleeing, they too fled before his brother Abishai and went inside the city. So Joab went back to Jerusalem.

¹⁶After the Arameans saw that they had been routed by Israel, they sent messengers and had Arameans brought from beyond the River,ʳ with Shophach the commander of Hadadezer's army leading them. ¹⁷When David was told of this, he gathered all Israelᵠ and crossed the Jordan; he advanced against them and formed battle lines opposite them. David formed his lines to meet the Arameans in battle, and they fought against him. ¹⁸But they fled before Israel, and David killed seven thousand of their charioteers and forty thousand of their foot soldiers. He also killed Shophach the commander of their army.

¹⁹When the vassals of Hadadezer saw that they had been defeated by Israel, they made peace with David and became subject to him.

So the Arameans were not willing to help the Ammonites anymore.

The Capture of Rabbah
20:1–3pp — 2Sa 11:1; 12:29–31

20 In the spring, at the time when kings go off to war, Joab led out the armed forces. He laid waste the land of the Ammonites and went to Rabbahʳ and besieged it, but David remained in Jerusalem. Joab attacked Rabbah and left it in ruins.ˢ ²David took the crown from the head of their kingˢ—its weight was found to be a talentᵗ of gold, and it was set with precious stones—and it was placed on David's head. He took a great quantity of plunder from the city ³and brought out the people who were there, consigning them to labor with saws and with iron picks and axes.ᵗ David did this to all the Ammonite towns.

Then David and his entire army returned to Jerusalem.

War With the Philistines
2:4–8pp — 2Sa 21:15–22

⁴In the course of time, war broke out with the Philistines, at Gezer.ᵘ At that time Sibbecai the Hushathite killed Sippai, one of the descendants of the Rephaites,ᵛ and the Philistines were subjugated.

⁵In another battle with the Philistines, Elhanan son of Jair killed Lahmi the brother of Goliath the Gittite, who had a spear with a shaft like a weaver's rod.ʷ

⁶In still another battle, which took place at Gath, there was a huge man with six fingers on each hand and six toes on each foot—twenty-four in all. He also was descended from Rapha. ⁷When he taunted Israel, Jonathan son of Shimea, David's brother, killed him.

⁸These were descendants of Rapha in Gath, and they fell at the hands of David and his men.

David Numbers the Fighting Men
21:1–26pp — 2Sa 24:1–25

21 Satanˣ rose up against Israel and incited David to take a censusʸ of Israel. ²So David said to Joab and the commanders of the troops, "Go and countᶻ the Israelites from Beersheba to Dan. Then report back to me so that I may know how many there are."

³But Joab replied, "May the LORD multiply his troops a hundred times over.ᵃ My lord the king, are they not all my lord's subjects? Why does my lord want to do this? Why should he bring guilt on Israel?"

⁴The king's word, however, overruled Joab; so Joab left and went throughout Israel and then came back to Jerusalem. ⁵Joab reported the number of the fighting men to David: In all Israelᵇ there were one million one hundred thousand men who could handle a sword, including four hundred and seventy thousand in Judah.

⁶But Joab did not include Levi and Benjamin in the numbering, because the king's command was repulsive to him. ⁷This command was also evil in the sight of God; so he punished Israel.

r 16 That is, the Euphrates s 2 Or of Milcom, that is, Molech t 2 That is, about 75 pounds (about 34 kilograms)

⁸Then David said to God, "I have sinned greatly by doing this. Now, I beg you, take away the guilt of your servant. I have done a very foolish thing."

⁹The LORD said to Gad,ᶜ David's seer,ᵈ ¹⁰"Go and tell David, 'This is what the LORD says: I am giving you three options. Choose one of them for me to carry out against you.'"

¹¹So Gad went to David and said to him, "This is what the LORD says: 'Take your choice: ¹²three years of famine,ᵉ three months of being swept awayᵘ before your enemies, with their swords overtaking you, or three days of the swordᶠ of the LORDᵍ—days of plague in the land, with the angel of the LORD ravaging every part of Israel.' Now then, decide how I should answer the one who sent me."

¹³David said to Gad, "I am in deep distress. Let me fall into the hands of the LORD, for his mercyʰ is very great; but do not let me fall into the hands of men."

¹⁴So the LORD sent a plague on Israel, and seventy thousand men of Israel fell dead.ⁱ ¹⁵And God sent an angelʲ to destroy Jerusalem.ᵏ But as the angel was doing so, the LORD saw it and was grievedˡ because of the calamity and said to the angel who was destroyingᵐ the people, "Enough! Withdraw your hand." The angel of the LORD was then standing at the threshing floor of Araunahᵛ the Jebusite.

¹⁶David looked up and saw the angel of the LORD standing between heaven and earth, with a drawn sword in his hand extended over Jerusalem. Then David and the elders, clothed in sackcloth, fell facedown.ⁿ

¹⁷David said to God, "Was it not I who ordered the fighting men to be counted? I am the one who has sinned and done wrong. These are but sheep.ᵒ What have they done? O LORD my God, let your hand fall upon me and my family,ᵖ but do not let this plague remain on your people."

¹⁸Then the angel of the LORD ordered Gad to tell David to go up and build an altar to the LORD on the threshing floorᵠ of Araunah the Jebusite. ¹⁹So David went up in obedience to the word that Gad had spoken in the name of the LORD.

²⁰While Araunah was threshing wheat,ʳ he turned and saw the angel; his four sons who were with him hid themselves. ²¹Then David approached, and when Araunah looked and saw him, he left the threshing floor and bowed down before David with his face to the ground.

²²David said to him, "Let me have the site of your threshing floor so I can build an altar to the LORD, that the plague on the people may be stopped. Sell it to me at the full price."

²³Araunah said to David, "Take it! Let my lord the king do whatever pleases him. Look, I will give the oxen for the burnt offerings, the threshing sledges for the wood, and the wheat for the grain offering. I will give all this."

²⁴But King David replied to Araunah, "No, I insist on paying the full price. I will not take for the LORD what is yours, or sacrifice a burnt offering that costs me nothing."

²⁵So David paid Araunah six hundred shekelsʷ of gold for the site. ²⁶David built an altar to the LORD there and sacrificed burnt offerings and fellowship offerings.ˣ He called on the LORD, and the LORD answered him with fireˢ from heaven on the altar of burnt offering.

²⁷Then the LORD spoke to the angel, and he put his sword back into its sheath. ²⁸At that time, when David saw that the LORD had answered him on the threshing floor of Araunah the Jebusite, he offered sacrifices there. ²⁹The tabernacle of the LORD, which Moses had made in the desert, and the altar of burnt offering were at that time on the high place at Gibeon.ᵗ ³⁰But David could not go before it to inquire of God, because he was afraid of the sword of the angel of the LORD.

22 Then David said, "The house of the LORD Godᵘ is to be here, and also the altar of burnt offering for Israel."

Preparations for the Temple

²So David gave orders to assemble the aliensᵛ living in Israel, and from among them he appointed stonecuttersʷ to prepare dressed stone for building the house

---

ᵘ 12 Hebrew; Septuagint and Vulgate (see also 2 Samuel 24:13) *of fleeing*   *ᵛ 15* Hebrew *Ornan,* a variant of *Araunah;* also in verses 18-28   *ʷ 25* That is, about 15 pounds (about 7 kilograms)   *ˣ 26* Traditionally *peace offerings*

of God. ³He provided a large amount of iron to make nails for the doors of the gateways and for the fittings, and more bronze than could be weighed.ˣ ⁴He also provided more cedar logsʸ than could be counted, for the Sidonians and Tyrians had brought large numbers of them to David.

⁵David said, "My son Solomon is youngᶻ and inexperienced, and the house to be built for the LORD should be of great magnificence and fame and splendorᵃ in the sight of all the nations. Therefore I will make preparations for it." So David made extensive preparations before his death.

⁶Then he called for his son Solomon and charged him to buildᵇ a house for the LORD, the God of Israel. ⁷David said to Solomon: "My son, I had it in my heartᶜ to buildᵈ a house for the Nameᵉ of the LORD my God. ⁸But this word of the LORD came to me: 'You have shed much blood and have fought many wars.ᶠ You are not to build a house for my Name,ᵍ because you have shed much blood on the earth in my sight. ⁹But you will have a son who will be a man of peaceʰ and rest,ⁱ and I will give him rest from all his enemies on every side. His name will be Solomon,ʸʲ and I will grant Israel peace and quietᵏ during his reign. ¹⁰He is the one who will build a house for my Name.ˡ He will be my son,ᵐ and I will be his father. And I will establishⁿ the throne of his kingdom over Israel forever.'ᵒ

¹¹"Now, my son, the LORD be withᵖ you, and may you have success and build the house of the LORD your God, as he said you would. ¹²May the LORD give you discretion and understandingᑫ when he puts you in command over Israel, so that you may keep the law of the LORD your God. ¹³Then you will have successʳ if you are careful to observe the decrees and lawsˢ that the LORD gave Moses for Israel. Be strong and courageous.ᵗ Do not be afraid or discouraged.

¹⁴"I have taken great pains to provide

| 1Ch 17:22 ◄ ► 1Ch 22:13
| 1Ch 22:9 ◄ ► 2Ch 20:7
W Jos 8:1 ◄ ► 1Ch 28:20

22:3 ˣS 1Ki 7:47; 1Ch 29:2-5
22:4 ʸS 1Ki 5:6
22:5 ᶻS 1Ki 3:7; 1Ch 29:1 ᵃ2Ch 2:5
22:6 ᵇAc 7:47
22:7 ᶜS 1Ch 17:2 ᵈS 1Ki 8:17 ᵉDt 12:5,11
22:8 ᶠS 1Ki 5:3 ᵍ1Ch 28:3
22:9 ʰS Jos 14:15; S 1Ki 5:4 ⁱver 18; 1Ch 23:25; 2Ch 14:6,7; 15:15; 20:30; 36:21 ʲS 2Sa 12:24; S 1Ch 23:1 ᵏ1Ki 4:20
22:10 ˡS 1Ch 17:12 ᵐS 2Sa 7:13 ⁿ1Ki 9:5 ᵒS 2Sa 7:14; S 1Ch 17:4; 2Ch 6:15
22:11 ᵖS 1Sa 16:18; S 18:12
22:12 ᑫ1Ki 3:9-12
22:13 ʳ1Ki 2:3 ˢDt 31:6
22:14 ᵘ1Ch 29:2-5,19
22:15 ᵛEzr 3:7
22:16 ʷ2Ch 2:7
22:17 ˣ1Ch 28:1-6
22:18 ʸS ver 9 ᶻ2Sa 7:1
22:19 ᵃ2Ch 7:14
23:1 ᵇ1Ch 22:9; 28:5; 2Ch 1:8 ᶜS 1Ki 1:30; 1Ch 29:28
23:3 ᵈNu 8:24 ᵉ1Ch 21:7 ᶠNu 4:3-49
23:4 ᵍEzr 3:8 ʰ2Ch 34:13; Ne 4:10 ⁱ1Ch 26:29; 2Ch 19:8; Eze 44:24
23:5 ʲS 1Ch 15:16; Ps 92:3 ᵏNe 12:45
23:6 ˡ2Ch 8:14; 23:18; 29:25 ᵐS Nu 3:17; 1Ch 24:20
23:7 ⁿ1Ch 6:71

for the temple of the LORD a hundred thousand talentsᶻ of gold, a million talentsᵃ of silver, quantities of bronze and iron too great to be weighed, and wood and stone. And you may add to them.ᵘ ¹⁵You have many workmen: stonecutters, masons and carpenters,ᵛ as well as men skilled in every kind of work ¹⁶in gold and silver, bronze and iron—craftsmenʷ beyond number. Now begin the work, and the LORD be with you."

¹⁷Then David orderedˣ all the leaders of Israel to help his son Solomon. ¹⁸He said to them, "Is not the LORD your God with you? And has he not granted you restʸ on every side?ᶻ For he has handed the inhabitants of the land over to me, and the land is subject to the LORD and to his people. ¹⁹Now devote your heart and soul to seeking the LORD your God.ᵃ Begin to build the sanctuary of the LORD God, so that you may bring the ark of the covenant of the LORD and the sacred articles belonging to God into the temple that will be built for the Name of the LORD."

The Levites

23 When David was old and full of years, he made his son Solomonᵇ king over Israel.ᶜ

²He also gathered together all the leaders of Israel, as well as the priests and Levites. ³The Levites thirty years old or moreᵈ were counted,ᵉ and the total number of men was thirty-eight thousand.ᶠ ⁴David said, "Of these, twenty-four thousand are to superviseᵍ the workʰ of the temple of the LORD and six thousand are to be officials and judges.ⁱ ⁵Four thousand are to be gatekeepers and four thousand are to praise the LORD with the musical instrumentsʲ I have provided for that purpose."ᵏ

⁶David dividedˡ the Levites into groups corresponding to the sons of Levi:ᵐ Gershon, Kohath and Merari.

Gershonites

⁷Belonging to the Gershonites:ⁿ Ladan and Shimei.

ʸ 9 *Solomon* sounds like and may be derived from the Hebrew for *peace*. ᶻ 14 That is, about 3,750 tons (about 3,450 metric tons) ᵃ 14 That is, about 37,500 tons (about 34,500 metric tons)

22:8–10 God had refused to allow David to build the temple. Rather, his son Solomon would rule in peace and would build the temple in Jerusalem. God would also establish his throne forever.

⁸The sons of Ladan:
Jehiel the first, Zetham and Joel—three in all.
⁹The sons of Shimei:
Shelomoth, Haziel and Haran—three in all.
These were the heads of the families of Ladan.
¹⁰And the sons of Shimei:
Jahath, Ziza,[b] Jeush and Beriah. These were the sons of Shimei—four in all.
¹¹Jahath was the first and Ziza the second, but Jeush and Beriah did not have many sons; so they were counted as one family with one assignment.

Kohathites

¹²The sons of Kohath:[o]
Amram, Izhar, Hebron and Uzziel—four in all.
¹³The sons of Amram:[p]
Aaron and Moses.
Aaron was set apart,[q] he and his descendants forever, to consecrate the most holy things, to offer sacrifices before the LORD, to minister[r] before him and to pronounce blessings[s] in his name forever. ¹⁴The sons of Moses the man[t] of God were counted as part of the tribe of Levi.
¹⁵The sons of Moses:
Gershom and Eliezer.[u]
¹⁶The descendants of Gershom:[v]
Shubael was the first.
¹⁷The descendants of Eliezer:
Rehabiah[w] was the first.
Eliezer had no other sons, but the sons of Rehabiah were very numerous.
¹⁸The sons of Izhar:
Shelomith[x] was the first.
¹⁹The sons of Hebron:[y]
Jeriah the first, Amariah the second, Jahaziel the third and Jekameam the fourth.
²⁰The sons of Uzziel:
Micah the first and Isshiah the second.

Merarites

²¹The sons of Merari:[z]
Mahli and Mushi.[a]
The sons of Mahli:
Eleazar and Kish.

²²Eleazar died without having sons: he had only daughters. Their cousins, the sons of Kish, married them.[b]
²³The sons of Mushi:
Mahli, Eder and Jerimoth—three in all.

²⁴These were the descendants of Levi by their families—the heads of families as they were registered under their names and counted individually, that is, the workers twenty years old or more[c] who served in the temple of the LORD. ²⁵For David had said, "Since the LORD, the God of Israel, has granted rest[d] to his people and has come to dwell in Jerusalem forever, ²⁶the Levites no longer need to carry the tabernacle or any of the articles used in its service."[e] ²⁷According to the last instructions of David, the Levites were counted from those twenty years old or more.

²⁸The duty of the Levites was to help Aaron's descendants in the service of the temple of the LORD: to be in charge of the courtyards, the side rooms, the purification[f] of all sacred things and the performance of other duties at the house of God. ²⁹They were in charge of the bread set out on the table,[g] the flour for the grain offerings,[h] the unleavened wafers, the baking and the mixing, and all measurements of quantity and size.[i] ³⁰They were also to stand every morning to thank and praise the LORD. They were to do the same in the evening[j] ³¹and whenever burnt offerings were presented to the LORD on Sabbaths and at New Moon[k] festivals and at appointed feasts.[l] They were to serve before the LORD regularly in the proper number and in the way prescribed for them.

³²And so the Levites[m] carried out their responsibilities for the Tent of Meeting,[n] for the Holy Place and, under their brothers the descendants of Aaron, for the service of the temple of the LORD.[o]

The Divisions of Priests

24 These were the divisions[p] of the sons of Aaron:[q]
The sons of Aaron were Nadab, Abihu, Eleazar and Ithamar.[r] ²But Nadab and Abihu died before their father did,[s] and

---

23:12 °S Ge 46:11; S Ex 6:18
23:13 P Ex 6:20 q Ex 30:7-10 r S 1Ch 15:2 s S Nu 6:23
23:14 t Dt 33:1
23:15 u Ex 18:4
23:16 v 1Ch 26:24-28
23:17 w 1Ch 24:21
23:18 x 1Ch 26:25
23:19 y 1Ch 24:23; 26:31
23:21 z S 1Ch 6:19 a S Ex 6:19
23:22 b Nu 36:8
23:24 c S Nu 4:3
23:25 d S 1Ch 22:9
23:26 e Nu 4:5,15; 7:9; Dt 10:8
23:28 f 2Ch 29:15; Ne 13:9; Mal 3:3
23:29 g S Ex 25:30 h Lev 2:4-7; 6:20-23 i Lev 19:35-36; S 1Ch 9:29,32
23:30 j S 1Ch 9:33; Ps 134:1
23:31 k S 2Ki 4:23 l Nu 28:9-29:39; Isa 1:13-14; Col 2:16
23:32 m 1Ch 6:48 n Nu 3:6-8,38 o 2Ch 23:18; 31:2; Eze 44:14
24:1 p 1Ch 23:6; 28:13; 2Ch 5:11; 8:14; 23:8; 31:2; 35:4,5; Ezr 6:18 q Nu 3:2-4 r S Ex 6:23
24:2 s Lev 10:1-2

---

[b] 10 One Hebrew manuscript, Septuagint and Vulgate (see also verse 11); most Hebrew manuscripts *Zina*

they had no sons; so Eleazar and Ithamar served as the priests. ³With the help of Zadok a descendant of Eleazar and Ahimelech a descendant of Ithamar, David separated them into divisions for their appointed order of ministering. ⁴A larger number of leaders were found among Eleazar's descendants than among Ithamar's, and they were divided accordingly: sixteen heads of families from Eleazar's descendants and eight heads of families from Ithamar's descendants. ⁵They divided them impartially by drawing lots, for there were officials of the sanctuary and officials of God among the descendants of both Eleazar and Ithamar.

⁶The scribe Shemaiah son of Nethanel, a Levite, recorded their names in the presence of the king and of the officials: Zadok the priest, Ahimelech son of Abiathar and the heads of families of the priests and of the Levites—one family being taken from Eleazar and then one from Ithamar.

⁷The first lot fell to Jehoiarib,
 the second to Jedaiah,
⁸the third to Harim,
 the fourth to Seorim,
⁹the fifth to Malkijah,
 the sixth to Mijamin,
¹⁰the seventh to Hakkoz,
 the eighth to Abijah,
¹¹the ninth to Jeshua,
 the tenth to Shecaniah,
¹²the eleventh to Eliashib,
 the twelfth to Jakim,
¹³the thirteenth to Huppah,
 the fourteenth to Jeshebeab,
¹⁴the fifteenth to Bilgah,
 the sixteenth to Immer,
¹⁵the seventeenth to Hezir,
 the eighteenth to Happizzez,
¹⁶the nineteenth to Pethahiah,
 the twentieth to Jehezkel,
¹⁷the twenty-first to Jakin,
 the twenty-second to Gamul,
¹⁸the twenty-third to Delaiah
 and the twenty-fourth to Maaziah.

¹⁹This was their appointed order of ministering when they entered the temple of the LORD, according to the regulations prescribed for them by their forefather Aaron, as the LORD, the God of Israel, had commanded him.

The Rest of the Levites

²⁰As for the rest of the descendants of Levi:
 from the sons of Amram: Shubael;
 from the sons of Shubael: Jehdeiah.
²¹As for Rehabiah, from his sons: Isshiah was the first.
²²From the Izharites: Shelomoth;
 from the sons of Shelomoth: Jahath.
²³The sons of Hebron: Jeriah the first, Amariah the second, Jahaziel the third and Jekameam the fourth.
²⁴The son of Uzziel: Micah;
 from the sons of Micah: Shamir.
²⁵The brother of Micah: Isshiah;
 from the sons of Isshiah: Zechariah.
²⁶The sons of Merari: Mahli and Mushi.
 The son of Jaaziah: Beno.
²⁷The sons of Merari:
 from Jaaziah: Beno, Shoham, Zaccur and Ibri.
²⁸From Mahli: Eleazar, who had no sons.
²⁹From Kish: the son of Kish: Jerahmeel.
³⁰And the sons of Mushi: Mahli, Eder and Jerimoth.

These were the Levites, according to their families. ³¹They also cast lots, just as their brothers the descendants of Aaron did, in the presence of King David and of Zadok, Ahimelech, and the heads of families of the priests and of the Levites. The families of the oldest brother were treated the same as those of the youngest.

The Singers

25 David, together with the commanders of the army, set apart some of the sons of Asaph, Heman and Jeduthun for the ministry of prophesying, accompanied by harps, lyres and cymbals. Here is the list of the men who performed this service:

²From the sons of Asaph:
 Zaccur, Joseph, Nethaniah and Asarelah. The sons of Asaph were under

---

c 23 Two Hebrew manuscripts and some Septuagint manuscripts (see also 1 Chron. 23:19); most Hebrew manuscripts *The sons of Jeriah:*

the supervision of Asaph, who prophesied under the king's supervision. ³As for Jeduthun, from his sons:[n] Gedaliah, Zeri, Jeshaiah, Shimei,[d] Hashabiah and Mattithiah, six in all, under the supervision of their father Jeduthun, who prophesied, using the harp[o] in thanking and praising the LORD. ⁴As for Heman, from his sons: Bukkiah, Mattaniah, Uzziel, Shubael and Jerimoth; Hananiah, Hanani, Eliathah, Giddalti and Romamti-Ezer; Joshbekashah, Mallothi, Hothir and Mahazioth. ⁵All these were sons of Heman the king's seer. They were given him through the promises of God to exalt him.[e] God gave Heman fourteen sons and three daughters.

⁶All these men were under the supervision of their fathers[p] for the music of the temple of the LORD, with cymbals, lyres and harps, for the ministry at the house of God. Asaph, Jeduthun and Heman[q] were under the supervision of the king.[r] ⁷Along with their relatives—all of them trained and skilled in music for the LORD—they numbered 288. ⁸Young and old alike, teacher as well as student, cast lots[s] for their duties.

⁹The first lot, which was for
  Asaph,[t] fell to Joseph,
  his sons and relatives,[f]   12[g]
  the second to Gedaliah,
  he and his relatives and sons,   12
¹⁰the third to Zaccur,
  his sons and relatives,   12
¹¹the fourth to Izri,[h]
  his sons and relatives,   12
¹²the fifth to Nethaniah,
  his sons and relatives,   12
¹³the sixth to Bukkiah,
  his sons and relatives,   12
¹⁴the seventh to Jesarelah,[i]
  his sons and relatives,   12
¹⁵the eighth to Jeshaiah,
  his sons and relatives,   12
¹⁶the ninth to Mattaniah,
  his sons and relatives,   12
¹⁷the tenth to Shimei,
  his sons and relatives,   12
¹⁸the eleventh to Azarel,[j]
  his sons and relatives,   12
¹⁹the twelfth to Hashabiah,
  his sons and relatives,   12
²⁰the thirteenth to Shubael,
  his sons and relatives,   12
²¹the fourteenth to Mattithiah,
  his sons and relatives,   12
²²the fifteenth to Jerimoth,
  his sons and relatives,   12
²³the sixteenth to Hananiah,
  his sons and relatives,   12
²⁴the seventeenth to Joshbekashah,
  his sons and relatives,   12
²⁵the eighteenth to Hanani,
  his sons and relatives,   12
²⁶the nineteenth to Mallothi,
  his sons and relatives,   12
²⁷the twentieth to Eliathah,
  his sons and relatives,   12
²⁸the twenty-first to Hothir,
  his sons and relatives,   12
²⁹the twenty-second to Giddalti,
  his sons and relatives,   12
³⁰the twenty-third to Mahazioth,
  his sons and relatives,   12
³¹the twenty-fourth to Romamti-Ezer,
  his sons and relatives,   12[u]

The Gatekeepers

26 The divisions of the gatekeepers:[v]

From the Korahites: Meshelemiah son of Kore, one of the sons of Asaph. ²Meshelemiah had sons:
  Zechariah[w] the firstborn,
  Jediael the second,
  Zebadiah the third,
  Jathniel the fourth,
  ³Elam the fifth,
  Jehohanan the sixth
  and Eliehoenai the seventh.
⁴Obed-Edom also had sons:
  Shemaiah the firstborn,
  Jehozabad the second,
  Joah the third,
  Sacar the fourth,
  Nethanel the fifth,
  ⁵Ammiel the sixth,

Cross references:
25:3 [n] 1Ch 16:41-42 [o] S Ge 4:21; Ps 33:2
25:6 [p] S 1Ch 15:16 [q] S 1Ch 15:19 [r] 2Ch 23:18; 29:25
25:8 [s] 1Ch 26:13
25:9 [t] S 1Ch 6:39
25:31 [u] S 1Ch 9:33
26:1 [v] S 1Ch 9:17
26:2 [w] S 1Ch 9:21

---

[d] 3 One Hebrew manuscript and some Septuagint manuscripts (see also verse 17); most Hebrew manuscripts do not have *Shimei*.   [e] 5 Hebrew *exalt the horn*   [f] 9 See Septuagint; Hebrew does not have *his sons and relatives*.   [g] 9 See the total in verse 7; Hebrew does not have *twelve*.   [h] 11 A variant of *Zeri*   [i] 14 A variant of *Asarelah*   [j] 18 A variant of *Uzziel*

Issachar the seventh and Peullethai the eighth. (For God had blessed Obed-Edom.ˣ)

⁶His son Shemaiah also had sons, who were leaders in their father's family because they were very capable men. ⁷The sons of Shemaiah: Othni, Rephael, Obed and Elzabad; his relatives Elihu and Semakiah were also able men. ⁸All these were descendants of Obed-Edom; they and their sons and their relatives were capable men with the strength to do the work—descendants of Obed-Edom, 62 in all.

⁹Meshelemiah had sons and relatives, who were able men—18 in all.

¹⁰Hosah the Merarite had sons: Shimri the first (although he was not the firstborn, his father had appointed him the first),ʸ ¹¹Hilkiah the second, Tabaliah the third and Zechariah the fourth. The sons and relatives of Hosah were 13 in all.

¹²These divisions of the gatekeepers, through their chief men, had duties for ministeringᶻ in the temple of the LORD, just as their relatives had. ¹³Lotsᵃ were cast for each gate, according to their families, young and old alike.

¹⁴The lot for the East Gateᵇ fell to Shelemiah.ᵏ Then lots were cast for his son Zechariah,ᶜ a wise counselor, and the lot for the North Gate fell to him. ¹⁵The lot for the South Gate fell to Obed-Edom,ᵈ and the lot for the storehouse fell to his sons. ¹⁶The lots for the West Gate and the Shalleketh Gate on the upper road fell to Shuppim and Hosah.

Guard was alongside of guard: ¹⁷There were six Levites a day on the east, four a day on the north, four a day on the south and two at a time at the storehouse. ¹⁸As for the court to the west, there were four at the road and two at the court itself.

¹⁹These were the divisions of the gatekeepers who were descendants of Korah and Merari.ᵉ

The Treasurers and Other Officials

²⁰Their fellow Levitesᶠ wereˡ in charge of the treasuries of the house of God and the treasuries for the dedicated things.ᵍ

²¹The descendants of Ladan, who were Gershonites through Ladan and who were heads of families belonging to Ladan the Gershonite,ʰ were Jehieli, ²²the sons of Jehieli, Zetham and his brother Joel. They were in charge of the treasuriesⁱ of the temple of the LORD.

²³From the Amramites, the Izharites, the Hebronites and the Uzzielites:ʲ

²⁴Shubael,ᵏ a descendant of Gershom son of Moses, was the officer in charge of the treasuries. ²⁵His relatives through Eliezer: Rehabiah his son, Jeshaiah his son, Joram his son, Zicri his son and Shelomithˡ his son. ²⁶Shelomith and his relatives were in charge of all the treasuries for the things dedicatedᵐ by King David, by the heads of families who were the commanders of thousands and commanders of hundreds, and by the other army commanders. ²⁷Some of the plunder taken in battle they dedicated for the repair of the temple of the LORD. ²⁸And everything dedicated by Samuel the seerⁿ and by Saul son of Kish, Abner son of Ner and Joab son of Zeruiah, and all the other dedicated things were in the care of Shelomith and his relatives.

²⁹From the Izharites: Kenaniah and his sons were assigned duties away from the temple, as officials and judgesᵒ over Israel.

³⁰From the Hebronites: Hashabiahᵖ and his relatives—seventeen hundred able men—were responsible in Israel west of the Jordan for all the work of the LORD and for the king's service. ³¹As for the Hebronites,ᵠ Jeriah was their chief according to the genealogical records of their families. In the fortiethʳ year of David's reign a search was made in the records, and capable men among the Hebronites were found at Jazer in Gilead. ³²Jeriah had twenty-seven hundred relatives, who were able men and heads of families, and

---

ᵏ 14 A variant of *Meshelemiah* ˡ 20 Septuagint; Hebrew *As for the Levites, Ahijah was*

King David put them in charge of the Reubenites, the Gadites and the half-tribe of Manasseh for every matter pertaining to God and for the affairs of the king.

Army Divisions

27 This is the list of the Israelites—heads of families, commanders of thousands and commanders of hundreds, and their officers, who served the king in all that concerned the army divisions that were on duty month by month throughout the year. Each division consisted of 24,000 men.

²In charge of the first division, for the first month, was Jashobeam[s] son of Zabdiel. There were 24,000 men in his division. ³He was a descendant of Perez and chief of all the army officers for the first month. ⁴In charge of the division for the second month was Dodai[t] the Ahohite; Mikloth was the leader of his division. There were 24,000 men in his division. ⁵The third army commander, for the third month, was Benaiah[u] son of Jehoiada the priest. He was chief and there were 24,000 men in his division. ⁶This was the Benaiah who was a mighty man among the Thirty and was over the Thirty. His son Ammizabad was in charge of his division. ⁷The fourth, for the fourth month, was Asahel[v] the brother of Joab; his son Zebadiah was his successor. There were 24,000 men in his division. ⁸The fifth, for the fifth month, was the commander Shamhuth[w] the Izrahite. There were 24,000 men in his division. ⁹The sixth, for the sixth month, was Ira[x] the son of Ikkesh the Tekoite. There were 24,000 men in his division. ¹⁰The seventh, for the seventh month, was Helez[y] the Pelonite, an Ephraimite. There were 24,000 men in his division. ¹¹The eighth, for the eighth month, was Sibbecai[z] the Hushathite, a Zerahite. There were 24,000 men in his division. ¹²The ninth, for the ninth month, was Abiezer[a] the Anathothite, a Benjamite. There were 24,000 men in his division. ¹³The tenth, for the tenth month, was Maharai[b] the Netophathite, a Zerahite. There were 24,000 men in his division. ¹⁴The eleventh, for the eleventh month, was Benaiah[c] the Pirathonite, an Ephraimite. There were 24,000 men in his division. ¹⁵The twelfth, for the twelfth month, was Heldai[d] the Netophathite, from the family of Othniel.[e] There were 24,000 men in his division.

Officers of the Tribes

¹⁶The officers over the tribes of Israel:

over the Reubenites: Eliezer son of Zicri;
over the Simeonites: Shephatiah son of Maacah;
¹⁷over Levi: Hashabiah[f] son of Kemuel;
over Aaron: Zadok;[g]
¹⁸over Judah: Elihu, a brother of David;
over Issachar: Omri son of Michael;
¹⁹over Zebulun: Ishmaiah son of Obadiah;
over Naphtali: Jerimoth son of Azriel;
²⁰over the Ephraimites: Hoshea son of Azaziah;
over half the tribe of Manasseh: Joel son of Pedaiah;
²¹over the half-tribe of Manasseh in Gilead: Iddo son of Zechariah;
over Benjamin: Jaasiel son of Abner;
²²over Dan: Azarel son of Jeroham.

These were the officers over the tribes of Israel.

²³David did not take the number of the men twenty years old or less,[h] because the LORD had promised to make Israel as numerous as the stars[i] in the sky. ²⁴Joab son of Zeruiah began to count the men but did not finish. Wrath came on Israel on account of this numbering,[j] and the number was not entered in the book[m] of the annals of King David.

The King's Overseers

²⁵Azmaveth son of Adiel was in charge of the royal storehouses.

[m] 24 Septuagint; Hebrew *number*

Jonathan son of Uzziah was in charge of the storehouses in the outlying districts, in the towns, the villages and the watchtowers.

²⁶Ezri son of Kelub was in charge of the field workers who farmed the land.

²⁷Shimei the Ramathite was in charge of the vineyards.

Zabdi the Shiphmite was in charge of the produce of the vineyards for the wine vats.

²⁸Baal-Hanan the Gederite was in charge of the olive and sycamore-fig trees in the western foothills.

Joash was in charge of the supplies of olive oil.

²⁹Shitrai the Sharonite was in charge of the herds grazing in Sharon.^l

Shaphat son of Adlai was in charge of the herds in the valleys.

³⁰Obil the Ishmaelite was in charge of the camels.

Jehdeiah the Meronothite was in charge of the donkeys.

³¹Jaziz the Hagrite^m was in charge of the flocks.

All these were the officials in charge of King David's property.

³²Jonathan, David's uncle, was a counselor, a man of insight and a scribe. Jehiel son of Hacmoni took care of the king's sons.

³³Ahithophelⁿ was the king's counselor.

Hushai^o the Arkite was the king's friend. ³⁴Ahithophel was succeeded by Jehoiada son of Benaiah and by Abiathar.^p

Joab^q was the commander of the royal army.

David's Plans for the Temple

28 David summoned^r all the officials^s of Israel to assemble at Jerusalem: the officers over the tribes, the commanders of the divisions in the service of the king, the commanders of thousands and commanders of hundreds, and the officials in charge of all the property and livestock belonging to the king and his sons, together with the palace officials, the mighty men and all the brave warriors.

²King David rose to his feet and said: "Listen to me, my brothers and my people. I had it in my heart^t to build a house as a place of rest^u for the ark of the covenant of the LORD, for the footstool^v of our God, and I made plans to build it.^w ³But God said to me,^x 'You are not to build a house for my Name,^y because you are a warrior and have shed blood.'^z

⁴"Yet the LORD, the God of Israel, chose me^a from my whole family^b to be king over Israel forever. He chose Judah^c as leader, and from the house of Judah he chose my family, and from my father's sons he was pleased to make me king over all Israel.^d ⁵Of all my sons—and the LORD has given me many^e—he has chosen my son Solomon^f to sit on the throne^g of the kingdom of the LORD over Israel. ⁶He said to me: 'Solomon your son is the one who will build^h my house and my courts, for I have chosen him to be my son,ⁱ and I will be his father. ⁷I will establish his kingdom forever if he is unswerving in carrying out my commands and laws,^j as is being done at this time.'

⁸"So now I charge you in the sight of all Israel^k and of the assembly of the LORD, and in the hearing of our God: Be careful to follow all the commands^l of the LORD your God, that you may possess this good land and pass it on as an inheritance to your descendants forever.^m

⁹"And you, my son Solomon, acknowledge the God of your father, and serve him with wholehearted devotionⁿ and with a willing mind, for the LORD searches every heart^o and understands every motive behind the thoughts. If you seek him,^p he will be found by you; but if you forsake^q him, he will reject^r you forever. ¹⁰Consider now, for the LORD has chosen you to build a temple as a sanctuary. Be strong and do the work."

¹¹Then David gave his son Solomon the plans^s for the portico of the temple, its

---

28:4 David declared that God had chosen him "to be king over Israel forever" indicating that one of David's descendants would rule forever from David's throne as the Messiah. This prophecy will be fulfilled when Christ assumes the throne in his Messianic kingdom.

buildings, its storerooms, its upper parts, its inner rooms and the place of atonement. ¹²He gave him the plans of all that the Spirit[t] had put in his mind for the courts of the temple of the LORD and all the surrounding rooms, for the treasuries of the temple of God and for the treasuries for the dedicated things.[u] ¹³He gave him instructions for the divisions[v] of the priests and Levites, and for all the work of serving in the temple of the LORD, as well as for all the articles to be used in its service. ¹⁴He designated the weight of gold for all the gold articles to be used in various kinds of service, and the weight of silver for all the silver articles to be used in various kinds of service: ¹⁵the weight of gold for the gold lampstands[w] and their lamps, with the weight for each lampstand and its lamps; and the weight of silver for each silver lampstand and its lamps, according to the use of each lampstand; ¹⁶the weight of gold for each table[x] for consecrated bread; the weight of silver for the silver tables; ¹⁷the weight of pure gold for the forks, sprinkling bowls[y] and pitchers; the weight of gold for each gold dish; the weight of silver for each silver dish; ¹⁸and the weight of the refined gold for the altar of incense.[z] He also gave him the plan for the chariot,[a] that is, the cherubim of gold that spread their wings and shelter[b] the ark of the covenant of the LORD.

¹⁹"All this," David said, "I have in writing from the hand of the LORD upon me, and he gave me understanding in all the details[c] of the plan.[d]"

²⁰David also said to Solomon his son, "Be strong and courageous,[e] and do the work. Do not be afraid or discouraged, for the LORD God, my God, is with you. He will not fail you or forsake[f] you until all the work for the service of the temple of the LORD is finished.[g] ²¹The divisions of the priests and Levites are ready for all the work on the temple of God, and every willing man skilled[h] in any craft will help you in all the work. The officials and all the people will obey your every command."

E *1Ch 12:18* ◀▶ *2Ch 15:1*
T *2Sa 23:1–2* ◀▶ *2Ch 20:14–15*
L *1Ch 16:21–22* ◀▶ *2Ch 32:22*
W *1Ch 22:13* ◀▶ *2Ch 19:11*

28:12 t S 1Ch 12:18; u 1Ch 26:20
28:13 v S 1Ch 24:1
28:15 w Ex 25:31
28:16 x S Ex 25:23
28:17 y S Ex 27:3
28:18 z Ex 30:1-10; a S Ex 25:22; b S Ex 25:20
28:19 c 1Ki 6:38; d S Ex 25:9
28:20 e S Dt 31:6; 1Ch 22:13; 2Ch 19:11; Hag 2:4; f S Dt 4:31; S Jos 24:20; g S 1Ki 6:14; 2Ch 7:11
28:21 h Ex 35:25-36:5
29:1 i 1Ki 3:7; 1Ch 22:5; 2Ch 13:7
29:2 j ver 7,14,16; Ezr 1:4; 6:5; Hag 2:8 k Isa 54:11 l 1Ch 22:2-5
29:3 m 2Ch 24:10; 31:3; 35:8
29:4 n S Ge 10:29; o 1Ch 22:14
29:6 p 1Ch 27:1; S 28:1 q ver 9; Ex 25:1-8; 35:20-29; 36:2; 2Ch 24:10; Ezr 7:15
29:7 r S Ex 25:2; Ne 7:70-71
29:8 s Ex 35:27; t S 1Ch 26:21
29:9 u 1Ki 8:61

Gifts for Building the Temple

29 Then King David said to the whole assembly: "My son Solomon, the one whom God has chosen, is young and inexperienced.[i] The task is great, because this palatial structure is not for man but for the LORD God. ²With all my resources I have provided for the temple of my God—gold[j] for the gold work, silver for the silver, bronze for the bronze, iron for the iron and wood for the wood, as well as onyx for the settings, turquoise,[n][k] stones of various colors, and all kinds of fine stone and marble—all of these in large quantities.[l] ³Besides, in my devotion to the temple of my God I now give my personal treasures of gold and silver for the temple of my God, over and above everything I have provided[m] for this holy temple: ⁴three thousand talents[o] of gold (gold of Ophir)[n] and seven thousand talents[p] of refined silver,[o] for the overlaying of the walls of the buildings, ⁵for the gold work and the silver work, and for all the work to be done by the craftsmen. Now, who is willing to consecrate himself today to the LORD?"

⁶Then the leaders of families, the officers of the tribes of Israel, the commanders of thousands and commanders of hundreds, and the officials[p] in charge of the king's work gave willingly.[q] ⁷They[r] gave toward the work on the temple of God five thousand talents[q] and ten thousand darics[r] of gold, ten thousand talents[s] of silver, eighteen thousand talents[t] of bronze and a hundred thousand talents[u] of iron. ⁸Any who had precious stones[s] gave them to the treasury of the temple of the LORD in the custody of Jehiel the Gershonite.[t] ⁹The people rejoiced at the willing response of their leaders, for they had given freely and wholeheartedly[u] to the LORD. David the king also rejoiced greatly.

David's Prayer

¹⁰David praised the LORD in the presence of the whole assembly, saying,

"Praise be to you, O LORD,
 God of our father Israel,
 from everlasting to everlasting.

[n] 2 The meaning of the Hebrew for this word is uncertain.   [o] 4 That is, about 110 tons (about 100 metric tons)   [p] 4 That is, about 260 tons (about 240 metric tons)   [q] 7 That is, about 190 tons (about 170 metric tons)   [r] 7 That is, about 185 pounds (about 84 kilograms)   [s] 7 That is, about 375 tons (about 345 metric tons)   [t] 7 That is, about 675 tons (about 610 metric tons)   [u] 7 That is, about 3,750 tons (about 3,450 metric tons)

K ¹¹"Yours, O LORD, is the greatness and the power,
and the glory and the majesty and the splendor,
for everything in heaven and earth is yours.
Yours, O LORD, is the kingdom;
you are exalted as head over all.
P ¹²Wealth and honor come from you;
you are the ruler of all things.
In your hands are strength and power
to exalt and give strength to all.
¹³Now, our God, we give you thanks,
and praise your glorious name.

¹⁴"But who am I, and who are my people, that we should be able to give as generously as this? Everything comes from you, and we have given you only what N comes from your hand. ¹⁵We are aliens and strangers in your sight, as were all our forefathers. Our days on earth are like a shadow, without hope. ¹⁶O LORD our God, as for all this abundance that we have provided for building you a temple for your Holy Name, it comes from your hand, and all of it belongs to you. ¹⁷I know, my God, that you test the heart and are pleased with integrity. All these things have I given willingly and with honest intent. And now I have seen with joy how willingly your people who are here have given to you. ¹⁸O LORD, God of our fathers Abraham, Isaac and Israel, keep this desire in the hearts of your people forever, and keep their hearts loyal to you. ¹⁹And give my son Solomon the wholehearted devotion to keep your commands, requirements and decrees and to do everything to build the palatial structure for which I have provided."

²⁰Then David said to the whole assembly, "Praise the LORD your God." So they all praised the LORD, the God of their fathers; they bowed low and fell prostrate before the LORD and the king.

Solomon Acknowledged as King
29:21–25pp — 1Ki 1:28–53

²¹The next day they made sacrifices to the LORD and presented burnt offerings to him: a thousand bulls, a thousand rams and a thousand male lambs, together with their drink offerings, and other sacrifices in abundance for all Israel. ²²They ate and drank with great joy in the presence of the LORD that day.

Then they acknowledged Solomon son of David as king a second time, anointing him before the LORD to be ruler and Zadok to be priest. ²³So Solomon sat on the throne of the LORD as king in place of his father David. He prospered and all Israel obeyed him. ²⁴All the officers and mighty men, as well as all of King David's sons, pledged their submission to King Solomon.

²⁵The LORD highly exalted Solomon in the sight of all Israel and bestowed on him royal splendor such as no king over Israel ever had before.

The Death of David
29:26–28pp — 1Ki 2:10–12

²⁶David son of Jesse was king over all Israel. ²⁷He ruled over Israel forty years—seven in Hebron and thirty-three in Jerusalem. ²⁸He died at a good old age, having enjoyed long life, wealth and honor. His son Solomon succeeded him as king.

²⁹As for the events of King David's reign, from beginning to end, they are written in the records of Samuel the seer, the records of Nathan the prophet and the records of Gad the seer, ³⁰together with the details of his reign and power, and the circumstances that surrounded him and Israel and the kingdoms of all the other lands.

K 1Ch 4:10 ◀ ▶ Job 1:10
P 1Ki 3:13 ◀ ▶ 2Ch 1:12
N 2Ki 17:13–15 ◀ ▶ 2Ch 12:14

2 Chronicles

Author: Authorship uncertain; possibly Ezra

Theme: The kingdom from Solomon to the Babylonian exile

Date of Writing: c. 450–400 B.C.

Outline of 2 Chronicles
  I. Solomon's Reign (1:1—9:31)
  II. The Kings of Judah (10:1—36:14)
  III. Jerusalem's Destruction (36:15–23)

IN THE ORIGINAL Hebrew canon 1 and 2 Chronicles formed one book. (For further information about the title and character of these books, see the introduction to 1 Chronicles on p. 432.) The book of 2 Chronicles continues the history of King David's family covering the same period of time as 1 and 2 Kings but omitting all references to the kings of the northern kingdom since David's line ran through the southern kings of Judah. The first nine chapters deal with King Solomon's reign, the building of the temple and Solomon's fall into idolatry. The bulk of 2 Chronicles covers the steady decline of the land of Judah and its continual struggle with idolatry. Though the book highlights several spiritual reformations, including a detailed account of the revival under King Hezekiah (chs. 29—31), the continued apostasy of Judah ultimately brought about its destruction and exile to Babylon. The writer concludes this book with a decree from King Cyrus of Persia that allowed the exiles to leave Babylon and end their seventy years of captivity.

Solomon Asks for Wisdom

1:2–13pp — 1Ki 3:4–15
1:14–17pp — 1Ki 10:26–29; 2Ch 9:25–28

1 Solomon son of David established[a] himself firmly over his kingdom, for the LORD his God was with[b] him and made him exceedingly great.[c]

²Then Solomon spoke to all Israel[d]—to the commanders of thousands and commanders of hundreds, to the judges and to all the leaders in Israel, the heads of families— ³and Solomon and the whole assembly went to the high place at Gibeon,[e] for God's Tent of Meeting[f] was there, which Moses[g] the LORD's servant had made in the desert. ⁴Now David had brought up the ark[h] of God from Kiriath Jearim to the place he had prepared for it, because he had pitched a tent[i] for it in Jerusalem. ⁵But the bronze altar[j] that Bezalel[k] son of Uri, the son of Hur, had made was in Gibeon in front of the tabernacle of the LORD; so Solomon and the assembly inquired[l] of him there. ⁶Solomon went up to the bronze altar before the LORD in the Tent of Meeting and offered a thousand burnt offerings on it.

⁷That night God appeared[m] to Solomon and said to him, "Ask for whatever you want me to give you."

⁸Solomon answered God, "You have shown great kindness to David my father and have made me[n] king in his place. ⁹Now, LORD God, let your promise[o] to my father David be confirmed, for you have made me king over a people who are as numerous as the dust of the earth.[p] ¹⁰Give me wisdom and knowledge, that I may lead[q] this people, for who is able to govern this great people of yours?"

¹¹God said to Solomon, "Since this is your heart's desire and you have not asked for wealth,[r] riches or honor, nor for the death of your enemies, and since you have not asked for a long life but for wisdom and knowledge to govern my people over whom I have made you king, ¹²therefore wisdom and knowledge will be given you. And I will also give you wealth, riches and honor,[s] such as no king who was before you ever had and none after you will have.'"

¹³Then Solomon went to Jerusalem from the high place at Gibeon, from before the Tent of Meeting. And he reigned over Israel.

¹⁴Solomon accumulated chariots[u] and horses; he had fourteen hundred chariots and twelve thousand horses,[a] which he kept in the chariot cities and also with him in Jerusalem. ¹⁵The king made silver and gold[v] as common in Jerusalem as stones, and cedar as plentiful as sycamore-fig trees in the foothills. ¹⁶Solomon's horses were imported from Egypt[b] and from Kue[c]—the royal merchants purchased them from Kue. ¹⁷They imported a chariot[w] from Egypt for six hundred shekels[d] of silver, and a horse for a hundred and fifty.[e] They also exported them to all the kings of the Hittites and of the Arameans.

Preparations for Building the Temple

2:1–18pp — 1Ki 5:1–16

2 Solomon gave orders to build a temple[x] for the Name of the LORD and a royal palace for himself.[y] ²He conscripted seventy thousand men as carriers and eighty thousand as stonecutters in the hills and thirty-six hundred as foremen over them.[z]

³Solomon sent this message to Hiram[f][a] king of Tyre:

"Send me cedar logs[b] as you did for my father David when you sent him cedar to build a palace to live in. ⁴Now I am about to build a temple[c] for the Name of the LORD my God and to dedicate it to him for burning fragrant incense[d] before him, for setting out the consecrated bread[e] regularly, and for making burnt offerings[f] every morning and evening and on Sabbaths[g] and New Moons[h] and at the appointed feasts of the LORD our God. This is a lasting ordinance for Israel.

⁵"The temple I am going to build will be great,[i] because our God is greater than all other gods.[j] ⁶But who is able to build a temple for him, since the heavens, even the highest heavens, cannot contain him?[k] Who then am I[l] to build a

---

L 2Ki 20:5–10 ◀▶ 2Ch 9:8
P 1Ch 29:12 ◀▶ 2Ch 25:9
U 1Ch 11:9 ◀▶ 2Ch 6:14

a 14 Or *charioteers*   *b* 16 Or possibly *Muzur*, a region in Cilicia; also in verse 17   *c* 16 Probably Cilicia   *d* 17 That is, about 15 pounds (about 7 kilograms)   *e* 17 That is, about 3 3/4 pounds (about 1.7 kilograms)   *f* 3 Hebrew *Huram*, a variant of *Hiram*; also in verses 11 and 12

temple for him, except as a place to burn sacrifices before him?

⁷"Send me, therefore, a man skilled to work in gold and silver, bronze and iron, and in purple, crimson and blue yarn, and experienced in the art of engraving, to work in Judah and Jerusalem with my skilled craftsmen,ᵐ whom my father David provided.

⁸"Send me also cedar, pine and algumᵍ logs from Lebanon, for I know that your men are skilled in cutting timber there. My men will work with yours ⁹to provide me with plenty of lumber, because the temple I build must be large and magnificent. ¹⁰I will give your servants, the woodsmen who cut the timber, twenty thousand corsʰ of ground wheat, twenty thousand cors of barley, twenty thousand bathsⁱ of wine and twenty thousand baths of olive oil.ⁿ"

¹¹Hiram king of Tyre replied by letter to Solomon:

"Because the LORD lovesᵒ his people, he has made you their king."

¹²And Hiram added:

"Praise be to the LORD, the God of Israel, who made heaven and earth!ᵖ He has given King David a wise son, endowed with intelligence and discernment, who will build a temple for the LORD and a palace for himself.

¹³"I am sending you Huram-Abi,ᵠ a man of great skill, ¹⁴whose mother was from Danʳ and whose father was from Tyre. He is trainedˢ to work in gold and silver, bronze and iron, stone and wood, and with purple and blueᵗ and crimson yarn and fine linen. He is experienced in all kinds of engraving and can execute any design given to him. He will work with your craftsmen and with those of my lord, David your father.

¹⁵"Now let my lord send his servants the wheat and barley and the olive oilᵘ and wine he promised, ¹⁶and we will cut all the logs from Lebanon that you need and will float them in rafts by sea down to Joppa.ᵛ You can then take them up to Jerusalem."

2:7	ᵐ S Ex 35:31; 1Ch 22:16
2:10	ⁿ Ezr 3:7
2:11	ᵒ 1Ki 10:9; 2Ch 9:8
2:12	ᵖ Ne 9:6; Ps 8:3; 33:6; 96:5; 102:25; 146:6
2:13	ᵠ S 1Ki 7:13
2:14	ʳ S Ex 31:6 ˢ S Ex 35:31 ᵗ Ex 35:35
2:15	ᵘ Ezr 3:7
2:16	ᵛ S Jos 19:46; Jnh 1:3
2:17	ʷ 1Ch 22:2 ˣ S 2Sa 24:2
2:18	ʸ 1Ch 22:2; 2Ch 8:8
3:1	ᶻ Ac 7:47 ᵃ S Ge 28:17 ᵇ S 2Sa 24:18
3:2	ᶜ Ezr 5:1
3:3	ᵈ Eze 41:2
3:5	ᵉ Eze 40:16
3:7	ᶠ Ge 3:24; Eze 41:18
3:8	ᵍ S Ex 26:33
3:9	ʰ Ex 26:32
3:10	ⁱ Ex 25:18

¹⁷Solomon took a census of all the aliensʷ who were in Israel, after the censusˣ his father David had taken; and they were found to be 153,600. ¹⁸He assignedʸ 70,000 of them to be carriers and 80,000 to be stonecutters in the hills, with 3,600 foremen over them to keep the people working.

Solomon Builds the Temple
3:1–14pp — 1Ki 6:1–29

3 Then Solomon began to buildᶻ the temple of the LORDᵃ in Jerusalem on Mount Moriah, where the LORD had appeared to his father David. It was on the threshing floor of Araunahʲᵇ the Jebusite, the place provided by David. ²He began building on the second day of the second month in the fourth year of his reign.ᶜ

³The foundation Solomon laid for building the temple of God was sixty cubits long and twenty cubits wideᵏᵈ (using the cubit of the old standard). ⁴The portico at the front of the temple was twenty cubitsˡ long across the width of the building and twenty cubitsᵐ high.

He overlaid the inside with pure gold. ⁵He paneled the main hall with pine and covered it with fine gold and decorated it with palm treeᵉ and chain designs. ⁶He adorned the temple with precious stones. And the gold he used was gold of Parvaim. ⁷He overlaid the ceiling beams, doorframes, walls and doors of the temple with gold, and he carved cherubimᶠ on the walls.

⁸He built the Most Holy Place,ᵍ its length corresponding to the width of the temple—twenty cubits long and twenty cubits wide. He overlaid the inside with six hundred talentsⁿ of fine gold. ⁹The gold nailsʰ weighed fifty shekels.ᵒ He also overlaid the upper parts with gold.

¹⁰In the Most Holy Place he made a pairⁱ of sculptured cherubim and overlaid them with gold. ¹¹The total wingspan of the cherubim was twenty cubits. One wing of the first cherub was five cubitsᵖ long and touched the temple wall, while

ᵍ 8 Probably a variant of almug; possibly juniper   ʰ 10 That is, probably about 125,000 bushels (about 4,400 kiloliters)   ⁱ 10 That is, probably about 115,000 gallons (about 440 kiloliters)   ʲ 1 Hebrew Ornan, a variant of Araunah   ᵏ 3 That is, about 90 feet (about 27 meters) long and 30 feet (about 9 meters) wide   ˡ 4 That is, about 30 feet (about 9 meters); also in verses 8, 11 and 13   ᵐ 4 Some Septuagint and Syriac manuscripts; Hebrew and a hundred and twenty   ⁿ 8 That is, about 23 tons (about 21 metric tons)   ᵒ 9 That is, about 1 1/4 pounds (about 0.6 kilogram)   ᵖ 11 That is, about 7 1/2 feet (about 2.3 meters); also in verse 15 its other wing, also five cubits long, touched the wing of the other cherub. ¹²Similarly one wing of the second cherub was five cubits long and touched the other temple wall, and its other wing, also five cubits long, touched the wing of the first cherub. ¹³The wings of these cherubim^j extended twenty cubits. They stood on their feet, facing the main hall.^q

¹⁴He made the curtain^k of blue, purple and crimson yarn and fine linen, with cherubim^l worked into it.

¹⁵In the front of the temple he made two pillars,^m which ⌊together⌋ were thirty-five cubits^r long, each with a capital^n on top measuring five cubits. ¹⁶He made interwoven chains^s^o and put them on top of the pillars. He also made a hundred pomegranates^p and attached them to the chains. ¹⁷He erected the pillars in the front of the temple, one to the south and one to the north. The one to the south he named Jakin^t and the one to the north Boaz.^u

The Temple's Furnishings
4:2–6,10–5:1pp — 1Ki 7:23–26,38–51

4 He made a bronze altar^q twenty cubits long, twenty cubits wide and ten cubits high.^v ²He made the Sea^r of cast metal, circular in shape, measuring ten cubits from rim to rim and five cubits^w high. It took a line of thirty cubits^x to measure around it. ³Below the rim, figures of bulls encircled it—ten to a cubit.^y The bulls were cast in two rows in one piece with the Sea.

⁴The Sea stood on twelve bulls, three facing north, three facing west, three facing south and three facing east.^s The Sea rested on top of them, and their hindquarters were toward the center. ⁵It was a handbreadth^z in thickness, and its rim was like the rim of a cup, like a lily blossom. It held three thousand baths.^a

⁶He then made ten basins^t for washing and placed five on the south side and five on the north. In them the things to be used for the burnt offerings^u were rinsed, but the Sea was to be used by the priests for washing.

⁷He made ten gold lampstands^v according to the specifications^w for them and placed them in the temple, five on the south side and five on the north.

⁸He made ten tables^x and placed them in the temple, five on the south side and

3:13 JS Ex 25:18
3:14 kS Ex 26:31, 33 lGe 3:24
3:15 mS 1Ki 7:15; Rev 3:12 n1Ki 7:22
3:16 o1Ki 7:17 pS 1Ki 7:20
4:1 qS Ex 20:24; S 40:6; S 1Ki 8:64
4:2 rRev 4:6; 15:2
4:4 sNu 2:3-25; Eze 48:30-34; Rev 21:13
4:6 tS Ex 30:18 uNe 13:5,9; Eze 40:38
4:7 vS Ex 25:31 wEx 25:40
4:8 xS Ex 25:23 yS Nu 4:14
4:9 z1Ki 6:36; 2Ch 33:5
4:11 a1Ki 7:14
4:14 b1Ki 7:27-30
4:16 cS 1Ki 7:13
4:17 dS Ge 33:17
4:18 eS 1Ki 7:23
4:19 fS Ex 25:23, 30
4:20 gS Ex 25:31

five on the north. He also made a hundred gold sprinkling bowls.^y

⁹He made the courtyard^z of the priests, and the large court and the doors for the court, and overlaid the doors with bronze. ¹⁰He placed the Sea on the south side, at the southeast corner.

¹¹He also made the pots and shovels and sprinkling bowls.

So Huram finished^a the work he had undertaken for King Solomon in the temple of God:

¹²the two pillars;
  the two bowl-shaped capitals on top of the pillars;
  the two sets of network decorating the two bowl-shaped capitals on top of the pillars;
¹³the four hundred pomegranates for the two sets of network (two rows of pomegranates for each network, decorating the bowl-shaped capitals on top of the pillars);
¹⁴the stands^b with their basins;
¹⁵the Sea and the twelve bulls under it;
¹⁶the pots, shovels, meat forks and all related articles.

All the objects that Huram-Abi^c made for King Solomon for the temple of the LORD were of polished bronze. ¹⁷The king had them cast in clay molds in the plain of the Jordan between Succoth^d and Zarethan.^b ¹⁸All these things that Solomon made amounted to so much that the weight of the bronze^e was not determined.

¹⁹Solomon also made all the furnishings that were in God's temple:

the golden altar;
the tables^f on which was the bread of the Presence;
²⁰the lampstands^g of pure gold with their lamps, to burn in front of the inner sanctuary as prescribed;

^q 13 Or *facing inward* ^r 15 That is, about 52 feet (about 16 meters) ^s 16 Or possibly *made chains in the inner sanctuary*; the meaning of the Hebrew for this phrase is uncertain. ^t 17 *Jakin* probably means *he establishes*. ^u 17 *Boaz* probably means *in him is strength*. ^v 1 That is, about 30 feet (about 9 meters) long and wide, and about 15 feet (about 4.5 meters) high ^w 2 That is, about 7 1/2 feet (about 2.3 meters) ^x 2 That is, about 45 feet (about 13.5 meters) ^y 3 That is, about 1 1/2 feet (about 0.5 meter) ^z 5 That is, about 3 inches (about 8 centimeters) ^a 5 That is, about 17,500 gallons (about 66 kiloliters) ^b 17 Hebrew *Zeredatha*, a variant of *Zarethan*

²¹the gold floral work and lamps and tongs (they were solid gold); ²²the pure gold wick trimmers, sprinkling bowls, dishes[h] and censers;[i] and the gold doors of the temple: the inner doors to the Most Holy Place and the doors of the main hall.

5 When all the work Solomon had done for the temple of the LORD was finished,[j] he brought in the things his father David had dedicated[k]—the silver and gold and all the furnishings—and he placed them in the treasuries of God's temple.

The Ark Brought to the Temple
5:2–6:11pp — 1Ki 8:1–21

²Then Solomon summoned to Jerusalem the elders of Israel, all the heads of the tribes and the chiefs of the Israelite families, to bring up the ark[l] of the LORD's covenant from Zion, the City of David. ³And all the men of Israel[m] came together to the king at the time of the festival in the seventh month.

⁴When all the elders of Israel had arrived, the Levites took up the ark, ⁵and they brought up the ark and the Tent of Meeting and all the sacred furnishings in it. The priests, who were Levites,[n] carried them up; ⁶and King Solomon and the entire assembly of Israel that had gathered about him were before the ark, sacrificing so many sheep and cattle that they could not be recorded or counted. ⁷The priests then brought the ark[o] of the LORD's covenant to its place in the inner sanctuary of the temple, the Most Holy Place, and put it beneath the wings of the cherubim. ⁸The cherubim[p] spread their wings over the place of the ark and covered the ark and its carrying poles. ⁹These poles were so long that their ends, extending from the ark, could be seen from in front of the inner sanctuary, but not from outside the Holy Place; and they are still there today. ¹⁰There was nothing in the ark except[q] the two tablets[r] that Moses had placed in it at Horeb, where the LORD made a covenant with the Israelites after they came out of Egypt.

¹¹The priests then withdrew from the Holy Place. All the priests who were there had consecrated themselves, regardless of their divisions.[s] ¹²All the Levites who were musicians[t]—Asaph, Heman, Jeduthun and their sons and relatives—stood on the east side of the altar, dressed in fine linen and playing cymbals, harps and lyres. They were accompanied by 120 priests sounding trumpets.[u] ¹³The trumpeters and singers joined in unison, as with one voice, to give praise and thanks to the LORD. Accompanied by trumpets, cymbals and other instruments, they raised their voices in praise to the LORD and sang:

"He is good;
    his love endures forever."[v]

Then the temple of the LORD was filled with a cloud,[w] ¹⁴and the priests could not perform[x] their service because of the cloud,[y] for the glory[z] of the LORD filled the temple of God.

6 Then Solomon said, "The LORD has said that he would dwell in a dark cloud;[a] ²I have built a magnificent temple for you, a place for you to dwell forever.[b]"

³While the whole assembly of Israel was standing there, the king turned around and blessed them. ⁴Then he said:

"Praise be to the LORD, the God of Israel, who with his hands has fulfilled what he promised with his mouth to my father David. For he said, ⁵'Since the day I brought my people out of Egypt, I have not chosen a city in any tribe of Israel to have a temple built for my Name to be there, nor have I chosen anyone to be the leader over my people Israel. ⁶But now I have chosen Jerusalem[c] for my Name[d] to be there, and I have chosen David[e] to rule my people Israel.'

⁷"My father David had it in his heart[f] to build a temple for the Name of the LORD, the God of Israel. ⁸But the LORD said to my father David, 'Because it was in your heart to build a temple for my Name, you did well to have this in your heart. ⁹Nevertheless, you are not the one to build the temple, but your son, who is your own flesh and blood—he is the one who will build the temple for my Name.'

¹⁰"The LORD has kept the promise he made. I have succeeded David my

father and now I sit on the throne of Israel, just as the LORD promised, and I have built the temple for the Name of the LORD, the God of Israel. ¹¹There I have placed the ark, in which is the covenant⁹ of the LORD that he made with the people of Israel."

Solomon's Prayer of Dedication
6:12–40pp — 1Ki 8:22–53
6:41–42pp — Ps 132:8–10

¹²Then Solomon stood before the altar of the LORD in front of the whole assembly of Israel and spread out his hands. ¹³Now he had made a bronze platform,ʰ five cubitsᶜ long, five cubits wide and three cubitsᵈ high, and had placed it in the center of the outer court. He stood on the platform and then knelt downⁱ before the whole assembly of Israel and spread out his hands toward heaven. ¹⁴He said:

"O LORD, God of Israel, there is no God like youʲ in heaven or on earth—you who keep your covenant of loveᵏ with your servants who continue wholeheartedly in your way. ¹⁵You have kept your promise to your servant David my father; with your mouth you have promisedˡ and with your hand you have fulfilled it—as it is today.

¹⁶Now LORD, God of Israel, keep for your servant David my father the promises you made to him when you said, 'You shall never failᵐ to have a man to sit before me on the throne of Israel, if only your sons are careful in all they do to walk before me according to my law,ⁿ as you have done.' ¹⁷And now, O LORD, God of Israel, let your word that you promised your servant David come true.

¹⁸"But will God really dwellᵒ on earth with men? The heavens,ᵖ even the highest heavens, cannot contain you. How much less this temple I have built! ¹⁹Yet give attention to your servant's prayer and his plea for mercy, O LORD my God. Hear the cry and the prayer that your servant is praying in your presence. ²⁰May your eyesᵠ be open toward this temple day and night, this place of which you said you would put your Nameʳ there. May you hearˢ the prayer your servant prays toward this place. ²¹Hear the supplications of your servant and of your people Israel when they pray toward this place. Hear from heaven, your dwelling place; and when you hear, forgive.ᵗ

²²"When a man wrongs his neighbor and is required to take an oathᵘ and he comes and swears the oath before your altar in this temple, ²³then hear from heaven and act. Judge between your servants, repayingᵛ the guilty by bringing down on his own head what he has done. Declare the innocent not guilty and so establish his innocence.

²⁴"When your people Israel have been defeatedʷ by an enemy because they have sinned against you and when they turn back and confess your name, praying and making supplication before you in this temple, ²⁵then hear from heaven and forgive the sin of your people Israel and bring them back to the land you gave to them and their fathers.

²⁶"When the heavens are shut up and there is no rainˣ because your people have sinned against you, and when they pray toward this place and confess your name and turn from their sin because you have afflicted them, ²⁷then hear from heaven and forgiveʸ the sin of your servants, your people Israel. Teach them the right way to live, and send rain on the land you gave your people for an inheritance.

²⁸"When famineᶻ or plague comes to the land, or blight or mildew, locusts or grasshoppers, or when enemies besiege them in any of their cities, whatever disaster or disease may come, ²⁹and when a prayer or plea is made by any of your people Israel—each one aware of his afflictions and pains, and spreading out his hands toward this temple— ³⁰then hear from heaven, your dwelling place.

6:11 ᵍS Dt 10:2; Ps 25:10; 50:5

6:13 ʰNe 8:4
ⁱPs 95:6

6:14 ʲS Ex 8:10; 15:11 ᵏS Dt 7:9

6:15 ˡS 1Ch 22:10

6:16 ᵐS 2Sa 7:13, 15; 2Ch 23:3
ⁿPs 132:12

6:18 ᵒS Rev 21:3
ᵖPs 11:4; Isa 40:22; 66:1

6:20 ᵠS Ex 3:16; Ps 34:15
ʳDt 12:11
ˢ2Ch 7:14; 30:20

6:21 ᵗPs 51:1; Isa 33:24; 40:2; 43:25; 44:22; 55:7; Mic 7:18

6:22 ᵘS Ex 22:11

6:23 ᵛIsa 3:11; 65:6; S Mt 16:27

6:24 ʷS Lev 26:17

6:26 ˣLev 26:19; S Dt 11:17; 28:24; S 2Sa 1:21

6:27 ʸver 30,39; 2Ch 7:14

6:28 ᶻ2Ch 20:9

U 2Ch 1:12 ◀▶ 2Ch 15:2
M 1Ch 28:4 ◀▶ 2Ch 13:5
H 1Ki 8:37–39 ◀▶ 2Ch 7:13–14
E 1Ch 28:9 ◀▶ 2Ch 16:9

ᶜ13 That is, about 7 1/2 feet (about 2.3 meters) ᵈ13 That is, about 4 1/2 feet (about 1.3 meters)

Forgive,ᵃ and deal with each man according to all he does, since you know his heart (for you alone know the hearts of men),ᵇ ³¹so that they will fear youᶜ and walk in your ways all the time they live in the land you gave our fathers.

³²"As for the foreigner who does not belong to your people Israel but has comeᵈ from a distant land because of your great name and your mighty handᵉ and your outstretched arm—when he comes and prays toward this temple, ³³then hear from heaven, your dwelling place, and do whatever the foreignerᶠ asks of you, so that all the peoples of the earth may know your name and fear you, as do your own people Israel, and may know that this house I have built bears your Name.

³⁴"When your people go to war against their enemies,ᵍ wherever you send them, and when they prayʰ to you toward this city you have chosen and the temple I have built for your Name, ³⁵then hear from heaven their prayer and their plea, and uphold their cause.

A ³⁶"When they sin against you—for there is no one who does not sinⁱ—and you become angry with them and give them over to the enemy, who takes them captiveʲ to a land far away or near; ³⁷and if they have a change of heartᵏ in the land where they are held captive, and repent and plead with you in the land of their captivity and say, 'We have sinned, we have done wrong and acted wickedly'; ³⁸and if they turn back to you with all their heart and soul in the land of their captivity where they were taken, and pray toward the land you gave their fathers, toward the city you have chosen and toward the temple I have built for your Name; ³⁹then from heaven, your dwelling place, hear their prayer and their pleas, and uphold their cause. And forgiveˡ your people, who have sinned against you.

⁴⁰"Now, my God, may your eyes be open and your ears attentiveᵐ to the prayers offered in this place.

A 1Ki 8:46 ◀ ▶ Ps 14:1–4

6:30 ᵃS ver 27; ᵇS 1Sa 2:3; Ps 7:9; 44:21; Pr 16:2; 17:3
6:31 ᶜS Dt 6:13; Ps 34:7,9; 103:11,13; Pr 8:13
6:32 ᵈ2Ch 9:6; ᵉS Ex 3:19,20
6:33 ᶠS Ex 12:43
6:34 ᵍDt 28:7; ʰS 1Ch 5:20
6:36 ⁱS 1Ki 8:46; Job 11:12; 15:14; Ps 143:2; Ecc 7:20; Jer 9:5; 13:23; 17:9; S Ro 3:9; Eph 2:3; ʲS Lev 26:34
6:37 ᵏS 1Ki 8:48; 2Ch 7:14; 12:6,12; 30:11; 33:12,19,23; 34:27; 36:12; Isa 58:3; Jer 24:7; 29:13
6:39 ˡS ver 27; 2Ch 30:9
6:40 ᵐS 1Ki 8:29, 52; 2Ch 7:15; Ne 1:6,11; Ps 17:1,6; 116:1; 130:2; Isa 37:17
6:41 ⁿPs 3:7; 7:6; 59:4; Isa 33:10; ᵒ1Ch 28:2; ᵖPs 132:16; ᵠPs 13:6; 27:13; 116:12; 142:7
6:42 ʳPs 2:2; ˢPs 89:24,28
7:1 ᵗS Ex 19:18; S Lev 9:24; S 1Ki 18:38; ᵘS Ex 16:10; ᵛPs 26:8
7:2 ʷS 1Ki 8:11; ˣS Ex 29:43; S 40:35
7:3 ʸS 1Ch 16:34; 2Ch 5:13; Ezr 3:11
7:6 ᶻ1Ch 15:16; ᵃS 1Ch 15:24
7:7 ᵇS Ex 29:13
7:8 ᶜ2Ch 30:26; Ne 8:17 ᵈS 1Ch 9:1

⁴¹"Now arise,ⁿ O LORD God, and come to your resting place,ᵒ
you and the ark of your might.
May your priests,ᵖ O LORD God, be clothed with salvation,
may your saints rejoice in your goodness.ᵠ
⁴²O LORD God, do not reject your anointed one.ʳ
Remember the great loveˢ promised to David your servant."

The Dedication of the Temple
7:1–10pp — 1Ki 8:62–66

7 When Solomon finished praying, fireᵗ came down from heaven and consumed the burnt offering and the sacrifices, and the glory of the LORD filledᵘ the temple.ᵛ ²The priests could not enterʷ the temple of the LORD because the gloryˣ of the LORD filled it. ³When all the Israelites saw the fire coming down and the glory of the LORD above the temple, they knelt on the pavement with their faces to the ground, and they worshiped and gave thanks to the LORD, saying,

"He is good;
his love endures forever."ʸ

⁴Then the king and all the people offered sacrifices before the LORD. ⁵And King Solomon offered a sacrifice of twenty-two thousand head of cattle and a hundred and twenty thousand sheep and goats. So the king and all the people dedicated the temple of God. ⁶The priests took their positions, as did the Levitesᶻ with the LORD's musical instruments,ᵃ which King David had made for praising the LORD and which were used when he gave thanks, saying, "His love endures forever." Opposite the Levites, the priests blew their trumpets, and all the Israelites were standing.

⁷Solomon consecrated the middle part of the courtyard in front of the temple of the LORD, and there he offered burnt offerings and the fatᵇ of the fellowship offerings,ᵉ because the bronze altar he had made could not hold the burnt offerings, the grain offerings and the fat portions.

⁸So Solomon observed the festivalᶜ at that time for seven days, and all Israelᵈ

e 7 Traditionally peace offerings

with him—a vast assembly, people from Lebo Hamath to the Wadi of Egypt. ⁹On the eighth day they held an assembly, for they had celebrated the dedication of the altar for seven days and the festival for seven days more. ¹⁰On the twenty-third day of the seventh month he sent the people to their homes, joyful and glad in heart for the good things the LORD had done for David and Solomon and for his people Israel.

The LORD Appears to Solomon
7:11–22pp — 1Ki 9:1–9

¹¹When Solomon had finished the temple of the LORD and the royal palace, and had succeeded in carrying out all he had in mind to do in the temple of the LORD and in his own palace, ¹²the LORD appeared to him at night and said:

"I have heard your prayer and have chosen this place for myself as a temple for sacrifices.

¹³"When I shut up the heavens so that there is no rain, or command locusts to devour the land or send a plague among my people, ¹⁴if my people, who are called by my name, will humble themselves and pray and seek my face and turn from their wicked ways, then will I hear from heaven and will forgive their sin and will heal their land. ¹⁵Now my eyes will be open and my ears attentive to the prayers offered in this place. ¹⁶I have chosen and consecrated this temple so that my Name may be there forever. My eyes and my heart will always be there.

¹⁷"As for you, if you walk before me as David your father did, and do all I command, and observe my decrees and laws, ¹⁸I will establish your royal throne, as I covenanted with David your father when I said,

'You shall never fail to have a man to rule over Israel.'

¹⁹"But if you turn away and forsake the decrees and commands I have given you and go off to serve other gods and worship them, ²⁰then I will uproot Israel from my land, which I have given them, and will reject this temple I have consecrated for my Name. I will make it a byword and an object of ridicule among all peoples. ²¹And though this temple is now so imposing, all who pass by will be appalled and say, 'Why has the LORD done such a thing to this land and to this temple?' ²²People will answer, 'Because they have forsaken the LORD, the God of their fathers, who brought them out of Egypt, and have embraced other gods, worshiping and serving them—that is why he brought all this disaster on them.'"

Solomon's Other Activities
8:1–18pp — 1Ki 9:10–28

8 At the end of twenty years, during which Solomon built the temple of the LORD and his own palace, ²Solomon rebuilt the villages Hiram had given him, and settled Israelites in them. ³Solomon then went to Hamath Zobah and captured it. ⁴He also built up Tadmor in the desert and all the store cities he had built in Hamath. ⁵He rebuilt Upper Beth Horon and Lower Beth Horon as fortified cities, with walls and with gates and bars, ⁶as well as Baalath and all his store cities, and all the cities for his chariots and for his horses—whatever he desired to build in Jerusalem, in Lebanon and throughout all the territory he ruled.

⁷All the people left from the Hittites, Amorites, Perizzites, Hivites and Jebusites (these peoples were not Israelites), ⁸that is, their descendants remaining in the land, whom the Israelites had not destroyed—these Solomon conscripted for

H 2Ch 6:28–30 ◄ ► 2Ch 16:12
L 1Ch 28:9 ◄ ► 2Ch 15:2
M 1Ch 21:8 ◄ ► 2Ch 12:6–7
P 2Sa 12:13 ◄ ► 2Ch 15:3–4
R 1Ch 21:8 ◄ ► 2Ch 15:4
S 1Ch 28:9 ◄ ► 2Ch 15:2

R 1Ch 9:1 ◄ ► 2Ch 7:20–22
R 2Ch 7:20 ◄ ► 2Ch 28:23

f 8 Or from the entrance to   g 19 The Hebrew is plural.   h 2 Hebrew Huram, a variant of Hiram; also in verse 18   i 6 Or chariotiers

---

7:20 God spoke to Solomon and reminded him of his promise to exile Israel and "uproot" them out of the land if they turned away from God's law.

his slave labor force, as it is to this day. ⁹But Solomon did not make slaves of the Israelites for his work; they were his fighting men, commanders of his captains, and commanders of his chariots and charioteers. ¹⁰They were also King Solomon's chief officials—two hundred and fifty officials supervising the men.

¹¹Solomon brought Pharaoh's daughter^p up from the City of David to the palace he had built for her, for he said, "My wife must not live in the palace of David king of Israel, because the places the ark of the LORD has entered are holy."

¹²On the altar^q of the LORD that he had built in front of the portico, Solomon sacrificed burnt offerings to the LORD, ¹³according to the daily requirement^r for offerings commanded by Moses for Sabbaths,^s New Moons^t and the three annual feasts—the Feast of Unleavened Bread,^v the Feast of Weeks^w and the Feast of Tabernacles.^x ¹⁴In keeping with the ordinance of his father David, he appointed the divisions^y of the priests for their duties, and the Levites^z to lead the praise and to assist the priests according to each day's requirement. He also appointed the gatekeepers^a by divisions for the various gates, because this was what David the man of God^b had ordered.^c ¹⁵They did not deviate from the king's commands to the priests or to the Levites in any matter, including that of the treasuries.

¹⁶All Solomon's work was carried out, from the day the foundation of the temple of the LORD was laid until its completion. So the temple of the LORD was finished.

¹⁷Then Solomon went to Ezion Geber and Elath on the coast of Edom. ¹⁸And Hiram sent him ships commanded by his own officers, men who knew the sea. These, with Solomon's men, sailed to Ophir and brought back four hundred and fifty talents^j of gold,^d which they delivered to King Solomon.

The Queen of Sheba Visits Solomon
9:1–12pp — 1Ki 10:1–13

9 When the queen of Sheba^e heard of Solomon's fame, she came to Jerusalem to test him with hard questions. Arriving with a very great caravan—with camels carrying spices, large quantities of gold, and precious stones—she came to Solomon and talked with him about all she had on her mind. ²Solomon answered all her questions; nothing was too hard for him to explain to her. ³When the queen of Sheba saw the wisdom of Solomon,^f as well as the palace he had built, ⁴the food on his table, the seating of his officials, the attending servants in their robes, the cupbearers in their robes and the burnt offerings he made at^k the temple of the LORD, she was overwhelmed.

⁵She said to the king, "The report I heard in my own country about your achievements and your wisdom is true. ⁶But I did not believe what they said until I came^g and saw with my own eyes. Indeed, not even half the greatness of your wisdom was told me; you have far exceeded the report I heard. ⁷How happy your men must be! How happy your officials, who continually stand before you and hear your wisdom! ⁸Praise be to the LORD your God, who has delighted in you and placed you on his throne^h as king to rule for the LORD your God. Because of the love of your God for Israel and his desire to uphold them forever, he has made you king^i over them, to maintain justice and righteousness."

⁹Then she gave the king 120 talents^j of gold,^j large quantities of spices, and precious stones. There had never been such spices as those the queen of Sheba gave to King Solomon.

¹⁰(The men of Hiram and the men of Solomon brought gold from Ophir;^k they also brought algumwood^m and precious stones. ¹¹The king used the algumwood to make steps for the temple of the LORD and for the royal palace, and to make harps and lyres for the musicians. Nothing like them had ever been seen in Judah.)

¹²King Solomon gave the queen of Sheba all she desired and asked for; he gave her more than she had brought to him. Then she left and returned with her retinue to her own country.

Solomon's Splendor
9:13–28pp — 1Ki 10:14–29; 2Ch 1:14–17

¹³The weight of the gold that Solomon received yearly was 666 talents,^n ¹⁴not

L *2Ch 1:12* ◀ ▶ *2Ch 20:9*

^j 18 That is, about 17 tons (about 16 metric tons) ^k 4 Or *the ascent by which he went up to* ^l 9 That is, about 4 1/2 tons (about 4 metric tons) ^m 10 Probably a variant of *almugwood* ^n 13 That is, about 25 tons (about 23 metric tons)

including the revenues brought in by merchants and traders. Also all the kings of Arabia¹ and the governors of the land brought gold and silver to Solomon.

¹⁵King Solomon made two hundred large shields of hammered gold; six hundred bekas° of hammered gold went into each shield. ¹⁶He also made three hundred small shields^m of hammered gold, with three hundred bekas^p of gold in each shield. The king put them in the Palace of the Forest of Lebanon.^n

¹⁷Then the king made a great throne inlaid with ivory° and overlaid with pure gold. ¹⁸The throne had six steps, and a footstool of gold was attached to it. On both sides of the seat were armrests, with a lion standing beside each of them. ¹⁹Twelve lions stood on the six steps, one at either end of each step. Nothing like it had ever been made for any other kingdom. ²⁰All King Solomon's goblets were gold, and all the household articles in the Palace of the Forest of Lebanon were pure gold. Nothing was made of silver, because silver was considered of little value in Solomon's day. ²¹The king had a fleet of trading ships^q manned by Hiram's^r men. Once every three years it returned, carrying gold, silver and ivory, and apes and baboons.

²²King Solomon was greater in riches and wisdom than all the other kings of the earth.^p ²³All the kings^q of the earth sought audience with Solomon to hear the wisdom God had put in his heart. ²⁴Year after year, everyone who came brought a gift^r—articles of silver and gold, and robes, weapons and spices, and horses and mules.

²⁵Solomon had four thousand stalls for horses and chariots,^s and twelve thousand horses,^s which he kept in the chariot cities and also with him in Jerusalem. ²⁶He ruled^t over all the kings from the River^{t,u} to the land of the Philistines, as far as the border of Egypt.^v ²⁷The king made silver as common in Jerusalem as stones, and cedar as plentiful as sycamore-fig trees in the foothills. ²⁸Solomon's horses were imported from Egypt^u and from all other countries.

Solomon's Death
9:29-31pp — 1Ki 11:41-43

²⁹As for the other events of Solomon's reign, from beginning to end, are they not written in the records of Nathan^w the prophet, in the prophecy of Ahijah^x the Shilonite and in the visions of Iddo the seer concerning Jeroboam^y son of Nebat? ³⁰Solomon reigned in Jerusalem over all Israel forty years. ³¹Then he rested with his fathers and was buried in the city of David^z his father. And Rehoboam his son succeeded him as king.

Israel Rebels Against Rehoboam
10:1-11:4pp — 1Ki 12:1-24

10 Rehoboam went to Shechem, for all the Israelites had gone there to make him king. ²When Jeroboam^a son of Nebat heard this (he was in Egypt, where he had fled^b from King Solomon), he returned from Egypt. ³So they sent for Jeroboam, and he and all Israel^c went to Rehoboam and said to him: ⁴"Your father put a heavy yoke on us,^d but now lighten the harsh labor and the heavy yoke he put on us, and we will serve you."

⁵Rehoboam answered, "Come back to me in three days." So the people went away.

⁶Then King Rehoboam consulted the elders^e who had served his father Solomon during his lifetime. "How would you advise me to answer these people?" he asked.

⁷They replied, "If you will be kind to these people and please them and give them a favorable answer,^f they will always be your servants."

⁸But Rehoboam rejected^g the advice the elders^h gave him and consulted the young men who had grown up with him and were serving him. ⁹He asked them, "What is your advice? How should we answer these people who say to me, 'Lighten the yoke your father put on us'?"

¹⁰The young men who had grown up with him replied, "Tell the people who have said to you, 'Your father put a heavy yoke on us, but make our yoke lighter'—tell them, 'My little finger is thicker than my father's waist. ¹¹My father laid on you a heavy yoke; I will make it even heavier. My father scourged you with whips; I will scourge you with scorpions.'"

° 15 That is, about 7 1/2 pounds (about 3.5 kilograms) ᵖ 16 That is, about 3 3/4 pounds (about 1.7 kilograms) ᵠ 21 Hebrew *of ships that could go to Tarshish* ʳ 21 Hebrew *Huram*, a variant of *Hiram* ˢ 25 Or *chariteers* ᵗ 26 That is, the Euphrates ᵘ 28 Or possibly *Muzur*, a region in Cilicia

¹²Three days later Jeroboam and all the people returned to Rehoboam, as the king had said, "Come back to me in three days." ¹³The king answered them harshly. Rejecting the advice of the elders, ¹⁴he followed the advice of the young men and said, "My father made your yoke heavy; I will make it even heavier. My father scourged you with whips; I will scourge you with scorpions." ¹⁵So the king did not listen to the people, for this turn of events was from God,ⁱ to fulfill the word the LORD had spoken to Jeroboam son of Nebat through Ahijah the Shilonite.ʲ

¹⁶When all Israelᵏ saw that the king refused to listen to them, they answered the king:

"What share do we have in David,ˡ
 what part in Jesse's son?
To your tents, O Israel!
 Look after your own house,
 O David!"

So all the Israelites went home. ¹⁷But as for the Israelites who were living in the towns of Judah, Rehoboam still ruled over them.

¹⁸King Rehoboam sent out Adoniram,ᵛᵐ who was in charge of forced labor, but the Israelites stoned him to death. King Rehoboam, however, managed to get into his chariot and escape to Jerusalem. ¹⁹So Israel has been in rebellion against the house of David to this day.

11 When Rehoboam arrived in Jerusalem,ⁿ he mustered the house of Judah and Benjamin—a hundred and eighty thousand fighting men—to make war against Israel and to regain the kingdom for Rehoboam. ²But this word of the LORD came to Shemaiahᵒ the man of God: ³"Say to Rehoboam son of Solomon king of Judah and to all the Israelites in Judah and Benjamin, ⁴'This is what the LORD says: Do not go up to fight against your brothers.ᵖ Go home, every one of you, for this is my doing.'" So they obeyed the words of the LORD and turned back from marching against Jeroboam.

Rehoboam Fortifies Judah

⁵Rehoboam lived in Jerusalem and built up towns for defense in Judah: ⁶Bethlehem, Etam, Tekoa, ⁷Beth Zur, Soco, Adullam, ⁸Gath, Mareshah, Ziph, ⁹Adoraim, Lachish, Azekah, ¹⁰Zorah, Aijalon and Hebron. These were fortified citiesᵩ in Judah and Benjamin. ¹¹He strengthened their defenses and put commanders in them, with supplies of food, olive oil and wine. ¹²He put shields and spears in all the cities, and made them very strong. So Judah and Benjamin were his.

¹³The priests and Levites from all their districts throughout Israel sided with him. ¹⁴The Levitesʳ even abandoned their pasturelands and property,ˢ and came to Judah and Jerusalem because Jeroboam and his sons had rejected them as priests of the LORD. ¹⁵And he appointedᵗ his own priestsᵘ for the high places and for the goatᵛ and calfʷ idols he had made. ¹⁶Those from every tribe of Israelˣ who set their hearts on seeking the LORD, the God of Israel, followed the Levites to Jerusalem to offer sacrifices to the LORD, the God of their fathers. ¹⁷They strengthenedʸ the kingdom of Judah and supported Rehoboam son of Solomon three years, walking in the ways of David and Solomon during this time.

Rehoboam's Family

¹⁸Rehoboam married Mahalath, who was the daughter of David's son Jerimoth and of Abihail, the daughter of Jesse's son Eliab. ¹⁹She bore him sons: Jeush, Shemariah and Zaham. ²⁰Then he married Maacahᶻ daughter of Absalom, who bore him Abijah,ᵃ Attai, Ziza and Shelomith. ²¹Rehoboam loved Maacah daughter of Absalom more than any of his other wives and concubines. In all, he had eighteen wivesᵇ and sixty concubines, twenty-eight sons and sixty daughters.

²²Rehoboam appointed Abijahᶜ son of Maacah to be the chief prince among his brothers, in order to make him king. ²³He acted wisely, dispersing some of his sons throughout the districts of Judah and Benjamin, and to all the fortified cities. He gave them abundant provisionsᵈ and took many wives for them.

Shishak Attacks Jerusalem
12:9–16pp — 1Ki 14:21, 25–31

12 After Rehoboam's position as king was establishedᵉ and he had become strong,ᶠ he and all Israelʷᵍ with him abandonedʰ the law of the LORD. ²Be-

---
ᵛ 18 Hebrew *Hadoram*, a variant of *Adoniram*   ʷ 1 That is, Judah, as frequently in 2 Chronicles

cause they had been unfaithful to the LORD, Shishak king of Egypt attacked Jerusalem in the fifth year of King Rehoboam. ³With twelve hundred chariots and sixty thousand horsemen and the innumerable troops of Libyans, Sukkites and Cushites[x1] that came with him from Egypt, ⁴he captured the fortified cities of Judah and came as far as Jerusalem.

⁵Then the prophet Shemaiah came to Rehoboam and to the leaders of Judah who had assembled in Jerusalem for fear of Shishak, and he said to them, "This is what the LORD says, 'You have abandoned me; therefore, I now abandon you to Shishak.'"

⁶The leaders of Israel and the king humbled themselves and said, "The LORD is just."

⁷When the LORD saw that they humbled themselves, this word of the LORD came to Shemaiah: "Since they have humbled themselves, I will not destroy them but will soon give them deliverance. My wrath will not be poured out on Jerusalem through Shishak. ⁸They will, however, become subject to him, so that they may learn the difference between serving me and serving the kings of other lands."

⁹When Shishak king of Egypt attacked Jerusalem, he carried off the treasures of the temple of the LORD and the treasures of the royal palace. He took everything, including the gold shields Solomon had made. ¹⁰So King Rehoboam made bronze shields to replace them and assigned these to the commanders of the guard on duty at the entrance to the royal palace. ¹¹Whenever the king went to the LORD's temple, the guards went with him, bearing the shields, and afterward they returned them to the guardroom.

¹²Because Rehoboam humbled himself, the LORD's anger turned from him, and he was not totally destroyed. Indeed, there was some good in Judah.

¹³King Rehoboam established himself firmly in Jerusalem and continued as king. He was forty-one years old when he became king, and he reigned seventeen years in Jerusalem, the city the LORD had chosen out of all the tribes of Israel in which to put his Name. His mother's

M 2Ch 7:14 ◀▶ 2Ch 12:12
M 2Ch 12:6–7 ◀▶ 2Ch 30:8

name was Naamah; she was an Ammonite. ¹⁴He did evil because he had not set his heart on seeking the LORD.

¹⁵As for the events of Rehoboam's reign, from beginning to end, are they not written in the records of Shemaiah the prophet and of Iddo the seer that deal with genealogies? There was continual warfare between Rehoboam and Jeroboam. ¹⁶Rehoboam rested with his fathers and was buried in the City of David. And Abijah his son succeeded him as king.

Abijah King of Judah
13:1–2,22–14:1pp — 1Ki 15:1,2,6–8

13 In the eighteenth year of the reign of Jeroboam, Abijah became king of Judah, ²and he reigned in Jerusalem three years. His mother's name was Maacah,[yc] a daughter of Uriel of Gibeah.

There was war between Abijah and Jeroboam. ³Abijah went into battle with a force of four hundred thousand able fighting men, and Jeroboam drew up a battle line against him with eight hundred thousand able troops.

⁴Abijah stood on Mount Zemaraim, in the hill country of Ephraim, and said, "Jeroboam and all Israel, listen to me! ⁵Don't you know that the LORD, the God of Israel, has given the kingship of Israel to David and his descendants forever by a covenant of salt? ⁶Yet Jeroboam son of Nebat, an official of Solomon son of David, rebelled against his master. ⁷Some worthless scoundrels gathered around him and opposed Rehoboam son of Solomon when he was young and indecisive and not strong enough to resist them.

⁸"And now you plan to resist the kingdom of the LORD, which is in the hands of David's descendants. You are indeed a vast army and have with you the golden calves that Jeroboam made to be your gods. ⁹But didn't you drive out the priests of the LORD, the sons of Aaron, and the Levites, and make priests of your own as the peoples of other lands do?

C 2Ki 21:22 ◀▶ 2Ch 24:20
N 1Ch 29:15 ◀▶ 2Ch 36:13
M 2Ch 6:16 ◀▶ 2Ch 21:7

x 3 That is, people from the upper Nile region   y 2 Most Septuagint manuscripts and Syriac (see also 2 Chron. 11:20 and 1 Kings 15:2); Hebrew *Micaiah*   z Or *granddaughter*

Whoever comes to consecrate himself with a young bull[r] and seven rams[s] may become a priest of what are not gods.[t]

[10] "As for us, the LORD is our God, and we have not forsaken him. The priests who serve the LORD are sons of Aaron, and the Levites assist them. [11] Every morning and evening[u] they present burnt offerings and fragrant incense[v] to the LORD. They set out the bread on the ceremonially clean table[w] and light the lamps[x] on the gold lampstand every evening. We are observing the requirements of the LORD our God. But you have forsaken him. [12] God is with us; he is our leader. His priests with their trumpets will sound the battle cry against you.[y] Men of Israel, do not fight against the LORD,[z] the God of your fathers, for you will not succeed."[a]

[13] Now Jeroboam had sent troops around to the rear, so that while he was in front of Judah the ambush[b] was behind them. [14] Judah turned and saw that they were being attacked at both front and rear. Then they cried out[c] to the LORD. The priests blew their trumpets [15] and the men of Judah raised the battle cry. At the sound of their battle cry, God routed Jeroboam and all Israel[d] before Abijah and Judah. [16] The Israelites fled before Judah, and God delivered[e] them into their hands. [17] Abijah and his men inflicted heavy losses on them, so that there were five hundred thousand casualties among Israel's able men. [18] The men of Israel were subdued on that occasion, and the men of Judah were victorious because they relied[f] on the LORD, the God of their fathers.

[19] Abijah pursued Jeroboam and took from him the towns of Bethel, Jeshanah and Ephron, with their surrounding villages. [20] Jeroboam did not regain power during the time of Abijah. And the LORD struck him down and he died.

[21] But Abijah grew in strength. He married fourteen wives and had twenty-two sons and sixteen daughters.

[22] The other events of Abijah's reign, what he did and what he said, are written in the annotations of the prophet Iddo.

14

And Abijah rested with his fathers and was buried in the City of David. Asa his son succeeded him as king, and in his days the country was at peace for ten years.

Asa King of Judah
14:2–3pp — 1Ki 15:11–12

[2] Asa did what was good and right in the eyes of the LORD his God.[g] [3] He removed the foreign altars[h] and the high places, smashed the sacred stones[i] and cut down the Asherah poles.[a][j] [4] He commanded Judah to seek the LORD,[k] the God of their fathers, and to obey his laws and commands. [5] He removed the high places[l] and incense altars[m] in every town in Judah, and the kingdom was at peace under him. [6] He built up the fortified cities of Judah, since the land was at peace. No one was at war with him during those years, for the LORD gave him rest.[n]

[7] "Let us build up these towns," he said ▼ to Judah, "and put walls around them, with towers, gates and bars. The land is still ours, because we have sought the LORD our God; we sought him and he has given us rest[o] on every side." So they built and prospered.

[8] Asa had an army of three hundred thousand[p] men from Judah, equipped with large shields and with spears, and two hundred and eighty thousand from Benjamin, armed with small shields and with bows. All these were brave fighting men.

[9] Zerah the Cushite[q] marched out against them with a vast army[b] and three hundred chariots, and came as far as Mareshah.[r] [10] Asa went out to meet him, and they took up battle positions in the Valley of Zephathah near Mareshah.

[11] Then Asa called[s] to the LORD his God ▼ and said, "LORD, there is no one like you to help the powerless against the mighty. Help us,[t] O LORD our God, for we rely[u] on you, and in your name[v] we have come against this vast army. O LORD, you are our God; do not let man prevail[w] against you."

[12] The LORD struck down[x] the Cushites before Asa and Judah. The Cushites fled, [13] and Asa and his army pursued them as far as Gerar.[y] Such a great number of Cushites fell that they could not recover; they were crushed[z] before the LORD and his forces. The men of Judah carried off a

▼ 2Sa 22:30 ◀ ▶ 2Ch 14:11
▼ 2Ch 14:7 ◀ ▶ 2Ch 16:9

[a] 3 That is, symbols of the goddess Asherah; here and elsewhere in 2 Chronicles [b] 9 Hebrew *with an army of a thousand thousands* or *with an army of thousands upon thousands*

large amount of plunder.ᵃ ¹⁴They destroyed all the villages around Gerar, for the terrorᵇ of the LORD had fallen upon them. They plundered all these villages, since there was much booty there. ¹⁵They also attacked the camps of the herdsmen and carried off droves of sheep and goats and camels. Then they returned to Jerusalem.

Asa's Reform
15:16–19pp — 1Ki 15:13–16

15 The Spirit of God came uponᵉ Azariah son of Oded. ²He went out to meet Asa and said to him, "Listen to me, Asa and all Judah and Benjamin. The LORD is with youᵈ when you are with him.ᵉ If you seekᶠ him, he will be found by you, but if you forsake him, he will forsake you.ᵍ ³For a long time Israel was without the true God, without a priest to teachʰ and without the law.ⁱ ⁴But in their distress they turned to the LORD, the God of Israel, and sought him,ʲ and he was found by them. ⁵In those days it was not safe to travel about,ᵏ for all the inhabitants of the lands were in great turmoil. ⁶One nation was being crushed by another, and one city by another,ˡ because God was troubling them with every kind of distress. ⁷But as for you, be strongᵐ and do not give up, for your work will be rewarded."ⁿ

⁸When Asa heard these words and the prophecy of Azariah son ofᶜ Oded the prophet, he took courage. He removed the detestable idolsᵒ from the whole land of Judah and Benjamin and from the towns he had capturedᵖ in the hills of Ephraim. He repaired the altarᑫ of the LORD that was in front of the portico of the LORD's temple.

⁹Then he assembled all Judah and Benjamin and the people from Ephraim, Manasseh and Simeon who had settled among them, for large numbersʳ had come over to him from Israel when they saw that the LORD his God was with him.

¹⁰They assembled at Jerusalem in the third monthˢ of the fifteenth year of Asa's reign. ¹¹At that time they sacrificed to the LORD seven hundred head of cattle and seven thousand sheep and goats from the plunderᵗ they had brought back. ¹²They entered into a covenantᵘ to seek the LORD,ᵛ the God of their fathers, with all their heart and soul. ¹³All who would not seek the LORD, the God of Israel, were to be put to death,ʷ whether small or great, man or woman. ¹⁴They took an oath to the LORD with loud acclamation, with shouting and with trumpets and horns. ¹⁵All Judah rejoiced about the oath because they had sworn it wholeheartedly. They sought Godˣ eagerly, and he was found by them. So the LORD gave them restʸ on every side.

¹⁶King Asa also deposed his grandmother Maacahᶻ from her position as queen mother,ᵃ because she had made a repulsive Asherah pole.ᵇ Asa cut the pole down, broke it up and burned it in the Kidron Valley.ᶜ ¹⁷Although he did not remove the high places from Israel, Asa's heart was fully committed ⌊to the LORD⌋ all his life. ¹⁸He brought into the temple of God the silver and gold and the articles that he and his father had dedicated.ᵈ

¹⁹There was no more war until the thirty-fifth year of Asa's reign.

Asa's Last Years
16:1–6pp — 1Ki 15:17–22
16:11–17:1pp — 1Ki 15:23–24

16 In the thirty-sixth year of Asa's reign Baashaᵉ king of Israel went up against Judah and fortified Ramah to prevent anyone from leaving or entering the territory of Asa king of Judah.

²Asa then took the silver and gold out of the treasuries of the LORD's temple and of his own palace and sent it to Ben-Hadad king of Aram, who was ruling in Damascus.ᶠ ³"Let there be a treatyᵍ between me and you," he said, "as there was between my father and your father. See, I am sending you silver and gold. Now break your treaty with Baasha king of Israel so he will withdraw from me."

⁴Ben-Hadad agreed with King Asa and sent the commanders of his forces against the towns of Israel. They conquered Ijon, Dan, Abel Maimᵈ and all the store cities

---

E 1Ch 28:12 ◄► 2Ch 20:14
L 2Ch 7:14 ◄► 2Ch 15:4
S 2Ch 7:14 ◄► 2Ch 20:21
U 2Ch 6:14 ◄► 2Ch 16:9
P 2Ch 7:14 ◄► 2Ch 30:9
L 2Ch 15:2 ◄► 2Ch 15:15
R 2Ch 7:14 ◄► Ezr 10:11

L 2Ch 15:4 ◄► 2Ch 30:9

ᶜ 8 Vulgate and Syriac (see also Septuagint and verse 1); Hebrew does not have *Azariah son of*.   ᵈ 4 Also known as *Abel Beth Maacah*

of Naphtali.ʰ ⁵When Baasha heard this, he stopped building Ramah and abandoned his work. ⁶Then King Asa brought all the men of Judah, and they carried away from Ramah the stones and timber Baasha had been using. With them he built up Geba and Mizpah.ⁱ

⁷At that time Hananiʲ the seer came to Asa king of Judah and said to him: "Because you reliedᵏ on the king of Aram and not on the LORD your God, the army of the king of Aram has escaped from your hand. ⁸Were not the Cushitesᵉˡ and Libyans a mighty army with great numbersᵐ of chariots and horsemenⁿ? Yet when you relied on the LORD, he deliveredⁿ them into your hand. ⁹For the eyesᵒ of the LORD range throughout the earth to strengthen those whose hearts are fully committed to him. You have done a foolishᵖ thing, and from now on you will be at war."ᑫ

¹⁰Asa was angry with the seer because of this; he was so enraged that he put him in prison.ʳ At the same time Asa brutally oppressed some of the people.

¹¹The events of Asa's reign, from beginning to end, are written in the book of the kings of Judah and Israel. ¹²In the thirty-ninth year of his reign Asa was afflictedˢ with a disease in his feet. Though his disease was severe, even in his illness he did not seekᵗ help from the LORD,ᵘ but only from the physicians. ¹³Then in the forty-first year of his reign Asa died and rested with his fathers. ¹⁴They buried him in the tomb that he had cut out for himselfᵛ in the City of David. They laid him on a bier covered with spices and various blended perfumes,ʷ and they made a huge fireˣ in his honor.

Jehoshaphat King of Judah

17 Jehoshaphat his son succeeded him as king and strengthenedʸ himself against Israel. ²He stationed troops in all the fortified citiesᶻ of Judah and put garrisons in Judah and in the towns of Ephraim that his father Asa had captured.ᵃ

³The LORD was with Jehoshaphat because in his early years he walked in the ways his father Davidᵇ had followed. He did not consult the Baals ⁴but soughtᶜ the God of his father and followed his commands rather than the practices of Israel. ⁵The LORD established the kingdom under his control; and all Judah brought giftsᵈ to Jehoshaphat, so that he had great wealth and honor.ᵉ ⁶His heart was devotedᶠ to the ways of the LORD; furthermore, he removed the high placesᵍ and the Asherah polesʰ from Judah.ⁱ

⁷In the third year of his reign he sent his officials Ben-Hail, Obadiah, Zechariah, Nethanel and Micaiah to teachʲ in the towns of Judah. ⁸With them were certain Levitesᵏ—Shemaiah, Nethaniah, Zebadiah, Asahel, Shemiramoth, Jehonathan, Adonijah, Tobijah and Tob-Adonijah—and the priests Elishama and Jehoram. ⁹They taught throughout Judah, taking with them the Book of the Lawˡ of the LORD; they went around to all the towns of Judah and taught the people.

¹⁰The fearᵐ of the LORD fell on all the kingdoms of the lands surrounding Judah, so that they did not make war with Jehoshaphat. ¹¹Some Philistines brought Jehoshaphat gifts and silver as tribute, and the Arabsⁿ brought him flocks:ᵒ seven thousand seven hundred rams and seven thousand seven hundred goats.

¹²Jehoshaphat became more and more powerful; he built forts and store cities in Judah ¹³and had large supplies in the towns of Judah. He also kept experienced fighting men in Jerusalem. ¹⁴Their enrollmentᵖ by families was as follows:

From Judah, commanders of units of 1,000:
  Adnah the commander, with 300,000 fighting men;
¹⁵next, Jehohanan the commander, with 280,000;
¹⁶next, Amasiah son of Zicri, who volunteeredᑫ himself for the service of the LORD, with 200,000.

¹⁷From Benjamin:ʳ
  Eliada, a valiant soldier, with 200,000 men armed with bows and shields;
¹⁸next, Jehozabad, with 180,000 men armed for battle.

¹⁹These were the men who served the

ᵉ 8 That is, people from the upper Nile region ᶠ 8 Or charioteers king, besides those he stationed in the fortified cities throughout Judah.

Micaiah Prophesies Against Ahab
18:1–27pp — 1Ki 22:1–28

18 Now Jehoshaphat had great wealth and honor, and he allied himself with Ahab by marriage. ²Some years later he went down to visit Ahab in Samaria. Ahab slaughtered many sheep and cattle for him and the people with him and urged him to attack Ramoth Gilead. ³Ahab king of Israel asked Jehoshaphat king of Judah, "Will you go with me against Ramoth Gilead?"

Jehoshaphat replied, "I am as you are, and my people as your people; we will join you in the war." ⁴But Jehoshaphat also said to the king of Israel, "First seek the counsel of the LORD."

⁵So the king of Israel brought together the prophets—four hundred men—and asked them, "Shall we go to war against Ramoth Gilead, or shall I refrain?"

"Go," they answered, "for God will give it into the king's hand."

⁶But Jehoshaphat asked, "Is there not a prophet of the LORD here whom we can inquire of?"

⁷The king of Israel answered Jehoshaphat, "There is still one man through whom we can inquire of the LORD, but I hate him because he never prophesies anything good about me, but always bad. He is Micaiah son of Imlah."

"The king should not say that," Jehoshaphat replied.

⁸So the king of Israel called one of his officials and said, "Bring Micaiah son of Imlah at once."

⁹Dressed in their royal robes, the king of Israel and Jehoshaphat king of Judah were sitting on their thrones at the threshing floor by the entrance to the gate of Samaria, with all the prophets prophesying before them. ¹⁰Now Zedekiah son of Kenaanah had made iron horns, and he declared, "This is what the LORD says: 'With these you will gore the Arameans until they are destroyed.'"

¹¹All the other prophets were prophesying the same thing. "Attack Ramoth Gilead and be victorious," they said, "for the LORD will give it into the king's hand."

¹²The messenger who had gone to summon Micaiah said to him, "Look, as one man the other prophets are predicting success for the king. Let your word agree with theirs, and speak favorably."

¹³But Micaiah said, "As surely as the LORD lives, I can tell him only what my God says."

¹⁴When he arrived, the king asked him, "Micaiah, shall we go to war against Ramoth Gilead, or shall I refrain?"

"Attack and be victorious," he answered, "for they will be given into your hand."

¹⁵The king said to him, "How many times must I make you swear to tell me nothing but the truth in the name of the LORD?"

¹⁶Then Micaiah answered, "I saw all Israel scattered on the hills like sheep without a shepherd, and the LORD said, 'These people have no master. Let each one go home in peace.'"

¹⁷The king of Israel said to Jehoshaphat, "Didn't I tell you that he never prophesies anything good about me, but only bad?"

¹⁸Micaiah continued, "Therefore hear the word of the LORD: I saw the LORD sitting on his throne with all the host of heaven standing on his right and on his left. ¹⁹And the LORD said, 'Who will entice Ahab king of Israel into attacking Ramoth Gilead and going to his death there?'

"One suggested this, and another that. ²⁰Finally, a spirit came forward, stood before the LORD and said, 'I will entice him.'

"'By what means?' the LORD asked.

²¹"'I will go and be a lying spirit in the mouths of all his prophets,' he said.

"'You will succeed in enticing him,' said the LORD. 'Go and do it.'

²²"So now the LORD has put a lying spirit in the mouths of these prophets of yours. The LORD has decreed disaster for you."

==²³Then Zedekiah son of Kenaanah went up and slapped Micaiah in the face. "Which way did the spirit from the LORD go when he went from me to speak to you?" he asked.==

²⁴Micaiah replied, "You will find out on the day you go to hide in an inner room."

L 2Ki 2:16 ◄ ► Job 32:18–19
Q 1Ki 22:24 ◄ ► Ne 9:30

g 23 Or Spirit of

²⁵The king of Israel then ordered, "Take Micaiah and send him back to Amon the ruler of the city and to Joash the king's son, ²⁶and say, 'This is what the king says: Put this fellow in prison^f and give him nothing but bread and water until I return safely.'"

²⁷Micaiah declared, "If you ever return safely, the LORD has not spoken through me." Then he added, "Mark my words, all you people!"

Ahab Killed at Ramoth Gilead
18:28–34pp — 1Ki 22:29–36

²⁸So the king of Israel and Jehoshaphat king of Judah went up to Ramoth Gilead. ²⁹The king of Israel said to Jehoshaphat, "I will enter the battle in disguise, but you wear your royal robes." So the king of Israel disguised^g himself and went into battle.

³⁰Now the king of Aram had ordered his chariot commanders, "Do not fight with anyone, small or great, except the king of Israel." ³¹When the chariot commanders saw Jehoshaphat, they thought, "This is the king of Israel." So they turned to attack him, but Jehoshaphat cried out,^h and the LORD helped him. God drew them away from him, ³²for when the chariot commanders saw that he was not the king of Israel, they stopped pursuing him.

³³But someone drew his bow at random and hit the king of Israel between the sections of his armor. The king told the chariot driver, "Wheel around and get me out of the fighting. I've been wounded." ³⁴All day long the battle raged, and the king of Israel propped himself up in his chariot facing the Arameans until evening. Then at sunset he died.^i

19 When Jehoshaphat king of Judah returned safely to his palace in Jerusalem, ²Jehu^j the seer, the son of Hanani, went out to meet him and said to the king, "Should you help the wicked^k and love^h those who hate the LORD?^l Because of this, the wrath^m of the LORD is upon you. ³There is, however, some good^n in you, for you have rid the land of the Asherah poles^o and have set your heart on seeking God.^p"

Jehoshaphat Appoints Judges

⁴Jehoshaphat lived in Jerusalem, and he went out again among the people from Beersheba to the hill country of Ephraim and turned them back to the LORD, the God of their fathers. ⁵He appointed judges^q in the land, in each of the fortified cities of Judah. ⁶He told them, "Consider carefully what you do,^r because you are not judging for man^s but for the LORD, who is with you whenever you give a verdict. ⁷Now let the fear of the LORD be upon you. Judge carefully, for with the LORD our God there is no injustice^t or partiality^u or bribery."

⁸In Jerusalem also, Jehoshaphat appointed some of the Levites,^v priests^w and heads of Israelite families to administer^x the law of the LORD and to settle disputes. And they lived in Jerusalem. ⁹He gave them these orders: "You must serve faithfully and wholeheartedly in the fear of the LORD. ¹⁰In every case that comes before you from your fellow countrymen who live in the cities—whether bloodshed or other concerns of the law, commands, decrees or ordinances—you are to warn them not to sin against the LORD;^y otherwise his wrath will come on you and your brothers. Do this, and you will not sin.

¹¹"Amariah the chief priest will be over you in any matter concerning the LORD, and Zebadiah son of Ishmael, the leader of the tribe of Judah, will be over you in any matter concerning the king, and the Levites will serve as officials before you. Act with courage,^z and may the LORD be with those who do well."

Jehoshaphat Defeats Moab and Ammon

20 After this, the Moabites^a and Ammonites with some of the Meunites^i^b came to make war on Jehoshaphat.

²Some men came and told Jehoshaphat, "A vast army^c is coming against you from Edom,^j from the other side of the Sea.^k It is already in Hazazon Tamar^d" (that is, En Gedi).^e ³Alarmed, Jehoshaphat resolved to inquire of the LORD, and he proclaimed a fast^f for all Judah. ⁴The people of Judah^g came together to seek help from the LORD;

U *2Ch 16:9* ◄► *2Ch 20:20*
W *1Ch 28:20* ◄► *Ne 8:10*

^h 2 Or *and make alliances with* / ^i 1 Some Septuagint manuscripts; Hebrew *Ammonites* / 2 One Hebrew manuscript; most Hebrew manuscripts, Septuagint and Vulgate *Aram* ^k 2 That is, the Dead Sea

indeed, they came from every town in Judah to seek him.

⁵Then Jehoshaphat stood up in the assembly of Judah and Jerusalem at the temple of the LORD in the front of the new courtyard ⁶and said:

"O LORD, God of our fathers,ʰ are you not the God who is in heaven?ⁱ You rule over all the kingdomsʲ of the nations. Power and might are in your hand, and no one can withstand you.ᵏ ⁷O our God, did you not drive out the inhabitants of this landˡ before your people Israel and give it forever to the descendants of Abraham your friend?ᵐ ⁸They have lived in it and have built in it a sanctuaryⁿ for your Name, saying, ⁹'If calamity comes upon us, whether the sword of judgment, or plague or famine,ᵒ we will stand in your presence before this temple that bears your Name and will cry out to you in our distress, and you will hear us and save us.'

¹⁰"But now here are men from Ammon, Moab and Mount Seir, whose territory you would not allow Israel to invade when they came from Egypt;ᵖ so they turned away from them and did not destroy them. ¹¹See how they are repaying us by coming to drive us out of the possessionᵠ you gave us as an inheritance. ¹²O our God, will you not judge them?ʳ For we have no power to face this vast army that is attacking us. We do not know what to do, but our eyes are upon you.ˢ"

¹³All the men of Judah, with their wives and children and little ones, stood there before the LORD.

¹⁴Then the Spiritᵗ of the LORD came upon Jahaziel son of Zechariah, the son of Benaiah, the son of Jeiel, the son of Mattaniah,ᵘ a Levite and descendant of Asaph, as he stood in the assembly.

¹⁵He said: "Listen, King Jehoshaphat and all who live in Judah and Jerusalem! This is what the LORD says to you: 'Do not be afraid or discouragedᵛ because of this vast army. For the battleʷ is not yours, but God's. ¹⁶Tomorrow march down against them. They will be climbing up by the Pass of Ziz, and you will find them at the end of the gorge in the Desert of Jeruel. ¹⁷You will not have to fight this battle. Take up your positions; stand firm and seeˣ the deliverance the LORD will give you, O Judah and Jerusalem. Do not be afraid; do not be discouraged. Go out to face them tomorrow, and the LORD will be with you.'"

¹⁸Jehoshaphat bowedʸ with his face to the ground, and all the people of Judah and Jerusalem fell down in worship before the LORD. ¹⁹Then some Levites from the Kohathites and Korahites stood up and praised the LORD, the God of Israel, with very loud voice.

²⁰Early in the morning they left for the Desert of Tekoa. As they set out, Jehoshaphat stood and said, "Listen to me, Judah and people of Jerusalem! Have faithᶻ in the LORD your God and you will be upheld; have faith in his prophets and you will be successful.ᵃ" ²¹After consulting the people, Jehoshaphat appointed men to sing to the LORD and to praise him for the splendor of hisᶠ holinessᵇ as they went out at the head of the army, saying:

"Give thanks to the LORD,
  for his love endures forever."ᶜ

²²As they began to sing and praise, the LORD set ambushesᵈ against the men of Ammon and Moab and Mount Seir who were invading Judah, and they were defeated. ²³The men of Ammonᵉ and Moab rose up against the men from Mount Seirᶠ to destroy and annihilate them. Af-

20:6 ʰ Mt 6:9
  ⁱ Dt 4:39
  ʲ 1Ch 29:11-12
  ᵏ 2Ch 25:8;
  Job 25:2; 41:10;
  42:2; Isa 14:27;
  Jer 32:27; 49:19

20:7 ˡ S Ge 12:7
  ᵐ Isa 41:8; Jas 2:23

20:8 ⁿ 2Ch 6:20

20:9 ᵒ S 2Ch 6:28

20:10
  ᵖ Nu 20:14-21;
  Dt 2:4-6,9,18-19

20:11 ᵠ Ps 83:1-12

20:12 ʳ Jdg 11:27
  ˢ Ps 25:15;
  Isa 30:15; 45:22;
  Mic 7:7

20:14
  ᵗ 1Ch 12:18
  ᵘ S 1Ch 9:15

20:15 ᵛ 2Ch 32:7
  ʷ 1Sa 17:47;
  Ps 91:8

20:17 ˣ S Ex 14:13

20:18
  ʸ S Ge 24:26;
  2Ch 29:29

20:20 ᶻ Isa 7:9
  ᵃ S Ge 39:3; Pr 16:3

20:21
  ᵇ S 1Ch 16:29
  ᶜ S 2Ch 5:13;
  Ps 136:1

20:22
  ᵈ S 2Ch 13:13

20:23 ᵉ S Ge 19:38
  ᶠ 2Ch 21:8

I 1Ch 22:13 ◀ ▶ Ezr 3:11
L 2Ch 9:8 ◀ ▶ 2Ch 34:28
F 2Ki 6:18 ◀ ▶ Ne 9:15
H 2Ch 16:12 ◀ ▶ Job 5:26
E 2Ch 15:1 ◀ ▶ 2Ch 24:20
T 1Ch 28:12 ◀ ▶ 2Ch 24:20

V 2Ch 16:9 ◀ ▶ 2Ch 20:17
V 2Ch 20:15 ◀ ▶ 2Ch 32:7-8
F Ge 15:6 ◀ ▶ Ps 2:12
U 2Ch 19:11 ◀ ▶ 2Ch 26:5
S 2Ch 15:2 ◀ ▶ 2Ch 24:20

ᶠ 21 Or him with the splendor of

20:7 King Jehoshaphat reminded God of his eternal covenant with Abraham to give Israel the land of Canaan (see note on the Abrahamic covenant at Ge 15:4).

ter they finished slaughtering the men from Seir, they helped to destroy one another.ᵍ

²⁴When the men of Judah came to the place that overlooks the desert and looked toward the vast army, they saw only dead bodies lying on the ground; no one had escaped. ²⁵So Jehoshaphat and his men went to carry off their plunder, and they found among them a great amount of equipment and clothingᵐ and also articles of value—more than they could take away. There was so much plunder that it took three days to collect it. ²⁶On the fourth day they assembled in the Valley of Beracah, where they praised the LORD. This is why it is called the Valley of Beracahⁿ to this day.

²⁷Then, led by Jehoshaphat, all the men of Judah and Jerusalem returned joyfully to Jerusalem, for the LORD had given them cause to rejoice over their enemies. ²⁸They entered Jerusalem and went to the temple of the LORD with harps and lutes and trumpets.

²⁹The fearʰ of God came upon all the kingdoms of the countries when they heard how the LORD had foughtⁱ against the enemies of Israel. ³⁰And the kingdom of Jehoshaphat was at peace, for his God had given him restʲ on every side.

The End of Jehoshaphat's Reign
20:31–21:1pp — 1Ki 22:41-50

³¹So Jehoshaphat reigned over Judah. He was thirty-five years old when he became king of Judah, and he reigned in Jerusalem twenty-five years. His mother's name was Azubah daughter of Shilhi. ³²He walked in the ways of his father Asa and did not stray from them; he did what was right in the eyes of the LORD. ³³The high places,ᵏ however, were not removed, and the people still had not set their hearts on the God of their fathers.

³⁴The other events of Jehoshaphat's reign, from beginning to end, are written in the annals of Jehuˡ son of Hanani, which are recorded in the book of the kings of Israel.

³⁵Later, Jehoshaphat king of Judah made an allianceᵐ with Ahaziah king of Israel, who was guilty of wickedness.ⁿ ³⁶He agreed with him to construct a fleet of trading ships.ᵒ After these were built at Ezion Geber, ³⁷Eliezer son of Dodavahu of Mareshah prophesied against Jehoshaphat, saying, "Because you have made an alliance with Ahaziah, the LORD will destroy what you have made." The shipsᵒ were wrecked and were not able to set sail to trade.ᵖ

21 Then Jehoshaphat rested with his fathers and was buried with them in the City of David. And Jehoramᵖ his son succeeded him as king. ²Jehoram's brothers, the sons of Jehoshaphat, were Azariah, Jehiel, Zechariah, Azariahu, Michael and Shephatiah. All these were sons of Jehoshaphat king of Israel.ᵠ ³Their father had given them many giftsᵠ of silver and gold and articles of value, as well as fortified citiesʳ in Judah, but he had given the kingdom to Jehoram because he was his firstborn son.

Jehoram King of Judah
21:5–10,20pp — 2Ki 8:16-24

⁴When Jehoram establishedˢ himself firmly over his father's kingdom, he put all his brothersᵗ to the sword along with some of the princes of Israel. ⁵Jehoram was thirty-two years old when he became king, and he reigned in Jerusalem eight years. ⁶He walked in the ways of the kings of Israel,ᵘ as the house of Ahab had done, for he married a daughter of Ahab.ᵛ He did evil in the eyes of the LORD. ⁷Nevertheless, because of the covenant the LORD had made with David,ʷ the LORD was not willing to destroy the house of David.ˣ He had promised to maintain a lampʸ for him and his descendants forever. ⁸In the time of Jehoram, Edomᶻ rebelled against Judah and set up its own king. ⁹So Jehoram went there with his officers and all his chariots. The Edomites surrounded him and his chariot com-

M 2Ch 13:5 ◀ ▶ Ps 2:8–9

ᵐ 25 Some Hebrew manuscripts and Vulgate; most Hebrew manuscripts corpses   ⁿ 26 *Beracah* means *praise.*   ᵒ 36 Hebrew *of ships that could go to Tarshish*   ᵖ 37 Hebrew *sail for Tarshish*   ᵠ 2 That is, Judah, as frequently in 2 Chronicles

---

21:7 Though King Jehoram was an evil king, God showed mercy to David's descendants in faithfulness to his covenant with David to establish David's house forever (see note on the Davidic covenant at 2Sa 7:16).

manders, but he rose up and broke through by night. ¹⁰To this day Edom has been in rebellion against Judah.

Libnah⁽ᵃ⁾ revolted at the same time, because Jehoram had forsaken the LORD, the God of his fathers. ¹¹He had also built high places on the hills of Judah and had caused the people of Jerusalem to prostitute themselves and had led Judah astray.

¹²Jehoram received a letter from Elijah⁽ᵇ⁾ the prophet, which said:

"This is what the LORD, the God of your father⁽ᶜ⁾ David, says: 'You have not walked in the ways of your father Jehoshaphat or of Asa⁽ᵈ⁾ king of Judah. ¹³But you have walked in the ways of the kings of Israel, and you have led Judah and the people of Jerusalem to prostitute themselves, just as the house of Ahab did.⁽ᵉ⁾ You have also murdered your own brothers, members of your father's house, men who were better⁽ᶠ⁾ than you.

¹⁴So now the LORD is about to strike your people, your sons, your wives and everything that is yours, with a heavy blow. ¹⁵You yourself will be very ill with a lingering disease⁽ᵍ⁾ of the bowels, until the disease causes your bowels to come out.'"

¹⁶The LORD aroused against Jehoram the hostility of the Philistines and of the Arabs⁽ʰ⁾ who lived near the Cushites. ¹⁷They attacked Judah, invaded it and carried off all the goods found in the king's palace, together with his sons and wives. Not a son was left to him except Ahaziah,⁽ʳ⁾ the youngest.⁽ⁱ⁾

¹⁸After all this, the LORD afflicted Jehoram with an incurable disease of the bowels. ¹⁹In the course of time, at the end of the second year, his bowels came out because of the disease, and he died in great pain. His people made no fire in his honor,⁽ʲ⁾ as they had for his fathers.

²⁰Jehoram was thirty-two years old when he became king, and he reigned in Jerusalem eight years. He passed away, to no one's regret, and was buried⁽ᵏ⁾ in the City of David, but not in the tombs of the kings.

J *2Ch 16:9* ◀ ▶ *Ps 1:5*

21:10 ᵃ S Nu 33:20

21:12
ᵇ 2Ki 1:16-17
ᶜ 2Ch 17:3-6
ᵈ 2Ch 14:2

21:13
ᵉ 1Ki 16:29-33
ᶠ 1Ki 2:32

21:15 ᵍ S Nu 12:10

21:16
ʰ 2Ch 17:10-11;
22:1; 26:7

21:17 ¹ 2Ki 12:18;
2Ch 22:1; Joel 3:5

21:19
ʲ S 2Ch 16:14

21:20
ᵏ 2Ch 24:25; 28:27;
33:20

22:1 ¹ 2Ch 33:25;
36:1
ᵐ 2Ch 23:20-21;
26:1
ⁿ S 2Ch 21:16-17

22:3 ᵒ 2Ch 18:1
ᵖ S 2Ch 21:6

22:5 ᵠ 2Ch 18:11,
34

22:6 ʳ 1Ki 19:15;
2Ki 8:13-15

22:7 ˢ 2Ki 9:16

22:8 ᵗ S 2Ki 10:13

22:9 ᵘ S Jdg 9:5
ᵛ 2Ch 17:4

Ahaziah King of Judah

22:1–6pp — 2Ki 8:25–29
22:7–9pp — 2Ki 9:21–29

22 The people¹ of Jerusalem⁽ᵐ⁾ made Ahaziah, Jehoram's youngest son, king in his place, since the raiders,⁽ⁿ⁾ who came with the Arabs into the camp, had killed all the older sons. So Ahaziah son of Jehoram king of Judah began to reign.

²Ahaziah was twenty-two⁽ˢ⁾ years old when he became king, and he reigned in Jerusalem one year. His mother's name was Athaliah, a granddaughter of Omri.

³He too walked⁽ᵒ⁾ in the ways of the house of Ahab,⁽ᵖ⁾ for his mother encouraged him in doing wrong. ⁴He did evil in the eyes of the LORD, as the house of Ahab had done, for after his father's death they became his advisers, to his undoing. ⁵He also followed their counsel when he went with Joram⁽ᵗ⁾ son of Ahab king of Israel to war against Hazael king of Aram at Ramoth Gilead.⁽ᵠ⁾ The Arameans wounded Joram; ⁶so he returned to Jezreel to recover from the wounds they had inflicted on him at Ramoth⁽ᵘ⁾ in his battle with Hazael⁽ʳ⁾ king of Aram.

Then Ahaziah⁽ᵛ⁾ son of Jehoram king of Judah went down to Jezreel to see Joram son of Ahab because he had been wounded.

⁷Through Ahaziah's⁽ˢ⁾ visit to Joram, God brought about Ahaziah's downfall. When Ahaziah arrived, he went out with Joram to meet Jehu son of Nimshi, whom the LORD had anointed to destroy the house of Ahab. ⁸While Jehu was executing judgment on the house of Ahab,⁽ᵗ⁾ he found the princes of Judah and the sons of Ahaziah's relatives, who had been attending Ahaziah, and he killed them. ⁹He then went in search of Ahaziah, and his men captured him while he was hiding⁽ᵘ⁾ in Samaria. He was brought to Jehu and put to death. They buried him, for they said, "He was a son of Jehoshaphat, who sought⁽ᵛ⁾ the LORD with all his heart." So there was no one in the house of Ahaziah powerful enough to retain the kingdom.

---

r 17 Hebrew *Jehoahaz,* a variant of *Ahaziah   s 2* Some Septuagint manuscripts and Syriac (see also 2 Kings 8:26); Hebrew *forty-two*.   *t 5* Hebrew *Jehoram,* a variant of *Joram;* also in verses 6 and 7   *u 6* Hebrew *Ramah,* a variant of *Ramoth   v 6* Some Hebrew manuscripts, Septuagint, Vulgate and Syriac (see also 2 Kings 8:29); most Hebrew manuscripts *Azariah*

Athaliah and Joash

22:10–23:21pp — 2Ki 11:1–21

¹⁰When Athaliah the mother of Ahaziah saw that her son was dead, she proceeded to destroy the whole royal family of the house of Judah. ¹¹But Jehosheba,ʷ the daughter of King Jehoram, took Joash son of Ahaziah and stole him away from among the royal princes who were about to be murdered and put him and his nurse in a bedroom. Because Jehosheba,ʷ the daughter of King Jehoram and wife of the priest Jehoiada, was Ahaziah's sister, she hid the child from Athaliah so she could not kill him. ¹²He remained hidden with them at the temple of God for six years while Athaliah ruled the land.

23 In the seventh year Jehoiada showed his strength. He made a covenant with the commanders of units of a hundred: Azariah son of Jeroham, Ishmael son of Jehohanan, Azariah son of Obed, Maaseiah son of Adaiah, and Elishaphat son of Zicri. ²They went throughout Judah and gathered the Levitesʷ and the heads of Israelite families from all the towns. When they came to Jerusalem, ³the whole assembly made a covenantˣ with the king at the temple of God.

Jehoiada said to them, "The king's son shall reign, as the LORD promised concerning the descendants of David.ʸ ⁴Now this is what you are to do: A third of you priests and Levites who are going on duty on the Sabbath are to keep watch at the doors, ⁵a third of you at the royal palace and a third at the Foundation Gate, and all the other men are to be in the courtyards of the temple of the LORD. ⁶No one is to enter the temple of the LORD except the priests and Levites on duty; they may enter because they are consecrated, but all the other men are to guardᶻ what the LORD has assigned to them.ˣ ⁷The Levites are to station themselves around the king, each man with his weapons in his hand. Anyone who enters the temple must be put to death. Stay close to the king wherever he goes."

⁸The Levites and all the men of Judah did just as Jehoiada the priest ordered.ᵃ Each one took his men—those who were going on duty on the Sabbath and those who were going off duty—for Jehoiada the priest had not released any of the divisions.ᵇ ⁹Then he gave the commanders of units of a hundred the spears and the large and small shields that had belonged to King David and that were in the temple of God. ¹⁰He stationed all the men, each with his weapon in his hand, around the king—near the altar and the temple, from the south side to the north side of the temple.

¹¹Jehoiada and his sons brought out the king's son and put the crown on him; they presented him with a copyᶜ of the covenant and proclaimed him king. They anointed him and shouted, "Long live the king!"

¹²When Athaliah heard the noise of the people running and cheering the king, she went to them at the temple of the LORD. ¹³She looked, and there was the king,ᵈ standing by his pillarᵉ at the entrance. The officers and the trumpeters were beside the king, and all the people of the land were rejoicing and blowing trumpets, and singers with musical instruments were leading the praises. Then Athaliah tore her robes and shouted, "Treason! Treason!"

¹⁴Jehoiada the priest sent out the commanders of units of a hundred, who were in charge of the troops, and said to them: "Bring her out between the ranksʸ and put to the sword anyone who follows her." For the priest had said, "Do not put her to death at the temple of the LORD." ¹⁵So they seized her as she reached the entrance of the Horse Gateᶠ on the palace grounds, and there they put her to death.

¹⁶Jehoiada then made a covenantᵍ that he and the people and the kingᶻ would be the LORD's people. ¹⁷All the people went to the temple of Baal and tore it down. They smashed the altars and idols and killedʰ Mattan the priest of Baal in front of the altars.

¹⁸Then Jehoiada placed the oversight of the temple of the LORD in the hands of the priests, who were Levites,ⁱ to whom David had made assignments in the temple,ʲ to present the burnt offerings of the LORD as written in the Law of Moses, with rejoicing and singing, as David had ordered. ¹⁹He also stationed doorkeepersᵏ at the gates of the LORD's temple so that

---

ʷ 11 Hebrew *Jehoshabeath*, a variant of *Jehosheba*   ˣ 6 Or *to observe the LORD's command*, not *to enter*,   ʸ 14 Or *out from the precincts*   ᶻ 16 Or *covenant between the LORD, and the people and the king that they* (see 2 Kings 11:17)

no one who was in any way unclean might enter. ²⁰He took with him the commanders of hundreds, the nobles, the rulers of the people and all the people of the land and brought the king down from the temple of the LORD. They went into the palace through the Upper Gate¹ and seated the king on the royal throne, ²¹and all the people of the land rejoiced. And the city was quiet, because Athaliah had been slain with the sword.ᵐ

Joash Repairs the Temple
24:1–14pp — 2Ki 12:1–16
24:23–27pp — 2Ki 12:17–21

24 Joash was seven years old when he became king, and he reigned in Jerusalem forty years. His mother's name was Zibiah; she was from Beersheba. ²Joash did what was right in the eyes of the LORDⁿ all the years of Jehoiada the priest. ³Jehoiada chose two wives for him, and he had sons and daughters.

⁴Some time later Joash decided to restore the temple of the LORD. ⁵He called together the priests and Levites and said to them, "Go to the towns of Judah and collect the moneyᵒ due annually from all Israel,ᵖ to repair the temple of your God. Do it now." But the Levitesᑫ did not act at once.

⁶Therefore the king summoned Jehoiada the chief priest and said to him, "Why haven't you required the Levites to bring in from Judah and Jerusalem the tax imposed by Moses the servant of the LORD and by the assembly of Israel for the Tent of the Testimony?"ʳ

⁷Now the sons of that wicked woman Athaliah had broken into the temple of God and had used even its sacred objects for the Baals.

⁸At the king's command, a chest was made and placed outside, at the gate of the temple of the LORD. ⁹A proclamation was then issued in Judah and Jerusalem that they should bring to the LORD the tax that Moses the servant of God had required of Israel in the desert. ¹⁰All the officials and all the people brought their contributions gladly,ˢ dropping them into the chest until it was full. ¹¹Whenever the chest was brought in by the Levites to the king's officials and they saw that there was a large amount of money, the royal secretary and the officer of the chief priest would come and empty the chest and carry it back to its place. They did this regularly and collected a great amount of money. ¹²The king and Jehoiada gave it to the men who carried out the work required for the temple of the LORD. They hiredᵗ masons and carpenters to restore the LORD's temple, and also workers in iron and bronze to repair the temple.

¹³The men in charge of the work were diligent, and the repairs progressed under them. They rebuilt the temple of God according to its original design and reinforced it. ¹⁴When they had finished, they brought the rest of the money to the king and Jehoiada, and with it were made articles for the LORD's temple: articles for the service and for the burnt offerings, and also dishes and other objects of gold and silver. As long as Jehoiada lived, burnt offerings were presented continually in the temple of the LORD.

¹⁵Now Jehoiada was old and full of years, and he died at the age of a hundred and thirty. ¹⁶He was buried with the kings in the City of David, because of the good he had done in Israel for God and his temple.

The Wickedness of Joash

¹⁷After the death of Jehoiada, the officials of Judah came and paid homage to the king, and he listened to them. ¹⁸They abandonedᵘ the temple of the LORD, the God of their fathers, and worshiped Asherah poles and idols.ᵛ Because of their guilt, God's angerʷ came upon Judah and Jerusalem. ¹⁹Although the LORD sent prophets to the people to bring them back to him, and though they testified against them, they would not listen.ˣ

²⁰Then the Spiritʸ of God came upon Zechariahᶻ son of Jehoiada the priest. He stood before the people and said, "This is what God says: 'Why do you disobey the LORD's commands? You will not prosper.ᵃ Because you have forsakenᵇ the LORD, he has forsakenᵇ you.'"

²¹But they plotted against him, and by order of the king they stonedᶜ him to death ᵈ in the courtyard of the LORD's tem-

E 2Ch 20:14 ◀▶ Ne 9:20
T 2Ch 20:14–15 ◀▶ Ne 9:20
C 2Ch 12:14 ◀▶ 2Ch 28:11
S 2Ch 20:21 ◀▶ Ezr 8:28

ple.ᵉ ²²King Joash did not remember the kindness Zechariah's father Jehoiada had shown him but killed his son, who said as he lay dying, "May the LORD see this and call you to account."ᶠ

²³At the turn of the year,ᵃ the army of Aram marched against Joash; it invaded Judah and Jerusalem and killed all the leaders of the people.ᵍ They sent all the plunder to their king in Damascus. ²⁴Although the Aramean army had come with only a few men,ʰ the LORD delivered into their hands a much larger army.ⁱ Because Judah had forsaken the LORD, the God of their fathers, judgment was executed on Joash. ²⁵When the Arameans withdrew, they left Joash severely wounded. His officials conspired against him for murdering the son of Jehoiada the priest, and they killed him in his bed. So he died and was buriedʲ in the City of David, but not in the tombs of the kings.

²⁶Those who conspired against him were Zabad,ᵇ son of Shimeath an Ammonite woman, and Jehozabad, son of Shimrithᶜᵏ a Moabite woman.ˡ ²⁷The account of his sons, the many prophecies about him, and the record of the restoration of the temple of God are written in the annotations on the book of the kings. And Amaziah his son succeeded him as king.

Amaziah King of Judah

25:1–4pp — 2Ki 14:1–6
25:11–12pp — 2Ki 14:7
25:17–28pp — 2Ki 14:8–20

25 Amaziah was twenty-five years old when he became king, and he reigned in Jerusalem twenty-nine years. His mother's name was Jehoaddanᵈ; she was from Jerusalem. ²He did what was right in the eyes of the LORD, but not wholeheartedly.ᵐ ³After the kingdom was firmly in his control, he executed the officials who had murdered his father the king. ⁴Yet he did not put their sons to death, but acted in accordance with what is written in the Law, in the Book of Moses,ⁿ where the LORD commanded: "Fathers shall not be put to death for their children, nor children put to death for their fathers; each is to die for his own sins."ᵉᵒ

⁵Amaziah called the people of Judah together and assigned them according to their families to commanders of thousands and commanders of hundreds for all Judah and Benjamin. He then musteredᵖ those twenty years oldᵍ or more and found that there were three hundred thousand men ready for military service,ʳ able to handle the spear and shield. ⁶He also hired a hundred thousand fighting men from Israel for a hundred talentsᶠ of silver.

⁷But a man of God came to him and said, "O king, these troops from Israelˢ must not march with you, for the LORD is not with Israel—not with any of the people of Ephraim. ⁸Even if you go and fight courageously in battle, God will overthrow you before the enemy, for God has the power to help or to overthrow."ᵗ

⁹Amaziah asked the man of God, "But what about the hundred talents I paid for these Israelite troops?"

The man of God replied, "The LORD can give you much more than that."ᵘ

¹⁰So Amaziah dismissed the troops who had come to him from Ephraim and sent them home. They were furious with Judah and left for home in a great rage.ᵛ

¹¹Amaziah then marshaled his strength and led his army to the Valley of Salt, where he killed ten thousand men of Seir. ¹²The army of Judah also captured ten thousand men alive, took them to the top of a cliff and threw them down so that all were dashed to pieces.ʷ

¹³Meanwhile the troops that Amaziah had sent back and had not allowed to take part in the war raided Judean towns from Samaria to Beth Horon. They killed three thousand people and carried off great quantities of plunder.

¹⁴When Amaziah returned from slaughtering the Edomites, he brought back the gods of the people of Seir. He set them up as his own gods,ˣ bowed down to them and burned sacrifices to them. ¹⁵The anger of the LORD burned against Amaziah, and he sent a prophet to him, who said, "Why do you consult this people's gods, which could not saveʸ their own people from your hand?"

¹⁶While he was still speaking, the king said to him, "Have we appointed you an

P 2Ch 1:12 ◀ ▶ 2Ch 31:10

ᵃ 23 Probably in the spring ᵇ 26 A variant of *Jozabad* ᶜ 26 A variant of *Shomer* ᵈ 1 Hebrew *Jehoaddan*, a variant of *Jehoaddin* ᵉ 4 Deut. 24:16 ᶠ 6 That is, about 3 3/4 tons (about 3.4 metric tons); also in verse 9

adviser to the king? Stop! Why be struck down?"

So the prophet stopped but said, "I know that God has determined to destroy you, because you have done this and have not listened to my counsel."

¹⁷After Amaziah king of Judah consulted his advisers, he sent this challenge to Jehoash⁸ son of Jehoahaz, the son of Jehu, king of Israel: "Come, meet me face to face."

¹⁸But Jehoash king of Israel replied to Amaziah king of Judah: "A thistle² in Lebanon sent a message to a cedar in Lebanon, 'Give your daughter to my son in marriage.' Then a wild beast in Lebanon came along and trampled the thistle underfoot. ¹⁹You say to yourself that you have defeated Edom, and now you are arrogant and proud. But stay at home! Why ask for trouble and cause your own downfall and that of Judah also?"

²⁰Amaziah, however, would not listen, for God so worked that he might hand them over to ⌊Jehoash⌋, because they sought the gods of Edom.ᵃ ²¹So Jehoash king of Israel attacked. He and Amaziah king of Judah faced each other at Beth Shemesh in Judah. ²²Judah was routed by Israel, and every man fled to his home. ²³Jehoash king of Israel captured Amaziah king of Judah, the son of Joash, the son of Ahaziah,ʰ at Beth Shemesh. Then Jehoash brought him to Jerusalem and broke down the wall of Jerusalem from the Ephraim Gateᵇ to the Corner Gateᶜ—a section about six hundred feetⁱ long. ²⁴He took all the gold and silver and all the articles found in the temple of God that had been in the care of Obed-Edom,ᵈ together with the palace treasures and the hostages, and returned to Samaria.

²⁵Amaziah son of Joash king of Judah lived for fifteen years after the death of Jehoash son of Jehoahaz king of Israel. ²⁶As for the other events of Amaziah's reign, from beginning to end, are they not written in the book of the kings of Judah and Israel? ²⁷From the time that Amaziah turned away from following the LORD, they conspired against him in Jerusalem and he fled to Lachish,ᵉ but they sent men after him to Lachish and killed him there. ²⁸He was brought back by horse and was buried with his fathers in the City of Judah.

25:18 ᶻ Jdg 9:8-15
25:20 ᵃ S 2Ch 10:15
25:23 ᵇ 2Ki 14:13; Ne 8:16; 12:39
ᶜ 2Ch 26:9; Jer 31:38
25:24 ᵈ S 1Ch 26:15
25:27 ᵉ S Jos 10:3
26:1 ᶠ S 2Ch 22:1
26:5 ᵍ S 2Ch 24:2
ʰ 2Ch 27:6
26:6 ⁱ Isa 2:6; 11:14; 14:29; Jer 25:20 ʲ Am 1:8; 3:9
26:7 ᵏ S 2Ch 21:16
ˡ 2Ch 20:1
26:8 ᵐ S Ge 19:38
26:9 ⁿ 2Ki 14:13; S 2Ch 25:23
ᵒ Ne 2:13; 3:13

Uzziah King of Judah

26:1-4pp — 2Ki 14:21-22; 15:1-3
26:21-23pp — 2Ki 15:5-7

26 Then all the people of Judahᶠ took Uzziah,ʲ who was sixteen years old, and made him king in place of his father Amaziah. ²He was the one who rebuilt Elath and restored it to Judah after Amaziah rested with his fathers.

³Uzziah was sixteen years old when he became king, and he reigned in Jerusalem fifty-two years. His mother's name was Jecoliah; she was from Jerusalem. ⁴He did what was right in the eyes of the LORD, just as his father Amaziah had done. ⁵He sought God during the days of Zechariah, who instructed him in the fearᵏ of God.ᵍ As long as he sought the LORD, God gave him success.ʰ U ⁶He went to war against the Philistines ⁱ and broke down the walls of Gath, Jabneh and Ashdod.ʲ He then rebuilt towns near Ashdod and elsewhere among the Philistines. ⁷God helped him against the Philistines and against the Arabsᵏ who lived in Gur Baal and against the Meunites.ˡ ⁸The Ammonitesᵐ brought tribute to Uzziah, and his fame spread as far as the border of Egypt, because he had become very powerful.

⁹Uzziah built towers in Jerusalem at the Corner Gate,ⁿ at the Valley Gateᵒ and at the angle of the wall, and he fortified them. ¹⁰He also built towers in the desert and dug many cisterns, because he had much livestock in the foothills and in the plain. He had people working his fields and vineyards in the hills and in the fertile lands, for he loved the soil.

¹¹Uzziah had a well-trained army, ready to go out by divisions according to their numbers as mustered by Jeiel the secretary and Maaseiah the officer under the direction of Hananiah, one of the royal officials. ¹²The total number of family leaders over the fighting men was 2,600. ¹³Under their command was an army of 307,500 men trained for war, a powerful force to support the king against his enemies. ¹⁴Uzziah provided shields, spears, helmets, coats of armor,

U 2Ch 20:20 ◄ ► 2Ch 27:6

ᵍ 17 Hebrew *Joash*, a variant of *Jehoash*; also in verses 18, 21, 23 and 25 ʰ 23 Hebrew *Jehoahaz*, a variant of *Ahaziah* ⁱ 23 Hebrew *four hundred cubits* (about 180 meters) ʲ 1 Also called *Azariah* ᵏ 5 Many Hebrew manuscripts, Septuagint and Syriac; other Hebrew manuscripts *vision*

bows and slingstones for the entire army. ¹⁵In Jerusalem he made machines designed by skillful men for use on the towers and on the corner defenses to shoot arrows and hurl large stones. His fame spread far and wide, for he was greatly helped until he became powerful.

¹⁶But after Uzziah became powerful, his pride led to his downfall. He was unfaithful to the LORD his God, and entered the temple of the LORD to burn incense on the altar of incense. ¹⁷Azariah the priest with eighty other courageous priests of the LORD followed him in. ¹⁸They confronted him and said, "It is not right for you, Uzziah, to burn incense to the LORD. That is for the priests, the descendants of Aaron, who have been consecrated to burn incense. Leave the sanctuary, for you have been unfaithful; and you will not be honored by the LORD God."

¹⁹Uzziah, who had a censer in his hand ready to burn incense, became angry. While he was raging at the priests in their presence before the incense altar in the LORD's temple, leprosy broke out on his forehead. ²⁰When Azariah the chief priest and all the other priests looked at him, they saw that he had leprosy on his forehead, so they hurried him out. Indeed, he himself was eager to leave, because the LORD had afflicted him.

²¹King Uzziah had leprosy until the day he died. He lived in a separate house—leprous, and excluded from the temple of the LORD. Jotham his son had charge of the palace and governed the people of the land.

²²The other events of Uzziah's reign, from beginning to end, are recorded by the prophet Isaiah son of Amoz. ²³Uzziah rested with his fathers and was buried near them in a field for burial that belonged to the kings, for people said, "He had leprosy." And Jotham his son succeeded him as king.

Jotham King of Judah
27:1–4,7–9pp — 2Ki 15:33–38

27 Jotham was twenty-five years old when he became king, and he reigned in Jerusalem sixteen years. His mother's name was Jerusha daughter of Zadok. ²He did what was right in the eyes of the LORD, just as his father Uzziah had done, but unlike him he did not enter the temple of the LORD. The people, however, continued their corrupt practices. ³Jotham rebuilt the Upper Gate of the temple of the LORD and did extensive work on the wall at the hill of Ophel. ⁴He built towns in the Judean hills and forts and towers in the wooded areas.

⁵Jotham made war on the king of the Ammonites and conquered them. That year the Ammonites paid him a hundred talents of silver, ten thousand cors of wheat and ten thousand cors of barley. The Ammonites brought him the same amount also in the second and third years.

⁶Jotham grew powerful because he walked steadfastly before the LORD his God.

⁷The other events in Jotham's reign, including all his wars and the other things he did, are written in the book of the kings of Israel and Judah. ⁸He was twenty-five years old when he became king, and he reigned in Jerusalem sixteen years. ⁹Jotham rested with his fathers and was buried in the City of David. And Ahaz his son succeeded him as king.

Ahaz King of Judah
28:1–27pp — 2Ki 16:1–20

28 Ahaz was twenty years old when he became king, and he reigned in Jerusalem sixteen years. Unlike David his father, he did not do what was right in the eyes of the LORD. ²He walked in the ways of the kings of Israel and also made cast idols for worshiping the Baals. ³He burned sacrifices in the Valley of Ben Hinnom and sacrificed his sons in the fire, following the detestable ways of the nations the LORD had driven out before the Israelites. ⁴He offered sacrifices and burned incense at the high places, on the hilltops and under every spreading tree.

⁵Therefore the LORD his God handed him over to the king of Aram. The Arameans defeated him and took many of his

---

26:14 p Jer 46:9

26:16 q S 2Ki 14:10 r Dt 32:15 s S 1Ch 5:25 t 2Ki 16:12

26:17 u S 1Ki 4:2

26:18 v Nu 16:39 w Nu 18:1-7 x S Ex 30:7 y S 1Ch 6:49

26:19 z S Nu 12:10

26:21 a S Ex 4:6; Lev 13:46; S 14:8; Nu 5:2; S 19:12

26:22 b 2Ki 15:1; Isa 1:1; 6:1

26:23 c Isa 1:1; 6:1 d S 2Ki 14:21; Am 1:1

27:1 e S 2Ki 15:5, 32; S 1Ch 3:12

27:3 f 2Ch 33:14; Ne 3:26

27:5 g S Ge 19:38

27:6 h 2Ch 26:5

28:1 i S 1Ch 3:13; Isa 1:1

28:2 j Ex 34:17

28:3 k S Jos 15:8 l S Lev 18:21; S 2Ki 3:27; Eze 20:26 m S Dt 18:9; 2Ch 33:2

28:5 n Isa 7:1

U *2Ch 26:5* ◄ ► *2Ch 31:10*

l 19 The Hebrew word was used for various diseases affecting the skin—not necessarily leprosy; also in verses 20, 21 and 23. *m 21* Or *in a house where he was relieved of responsibilities* *n 5* That is, about 3 3/4 tons (about 3.4 metric tons) *o 5* That is, probably about 62,000 bushels (about 2,200 kiloliters)

D *1Ch 21:14–15* ◄ ► *Job 2:7*

people as prisoners and brought them to Damascus.

He was also given into the hands of the king of Israel, who inflicted heavy casualties on him. ⁶In one day Pekah° son of Remaliah killed a hundred and twenty thousand soldiers in Judah ᵖ—because Judah had forsaken the LORD, the God of their fathers. ⁷Zicri, an Ephraimite warrior, killed Maaseiah the king's son, Azrikam the officer in charge of the palace, and Elkanah, second to the king. ⁸The Israelites took captive from their kinsmen ᑫ two hundred thousand wives, sons and daughters. They also took a great deal of plunder, which they carried back to Samaria.ʳ

⁹But a prophet of the LORD named Oded was there, and he went out to meet the army when it returned to Samaria. He said to them, "Because the LORD, the God of your fathers, was angry ˢ with Judah, he gave them into your hand. But you have slaughtered them in a rage that reaches to heaven.ᵗ ¹⁰And now you intend to make the men and women of Judah and Jerusalem your slaves.ᵘ But aren't you also guilty of sins against the LORD your God? ¹¹Now listen to me! Send back your fellow countrymen you have taken as prisoners, for the LORD's fierce anger rests on you.'"

¹²Then some of the leaders in Ephraim—Azariah son of Jehohanan, Berekiah son of Meshillemoth, Jehizkiah son of Shallum, and Amasa son of Hadlai—confronted those who were arriving from the war. ¹³"You must not bring those prisoners here," they said, "or we will be guilty before the LORD. Do you intend to add to our sin and guilt? For our guilt is already great, and his fierce anger rests on Israel."

¹⁴So the soldiers gave up the prisoners and plunder in the presence of the officials and all the assembly. ¹⁵The men designated by name took the prisoners, and from the plunder they clothed all who were naked. They provided them with clothes and sandals, food and drink,ʷ and healing balm. All those who were weak they put on donkeys. So they took them back to their fellow countrymen at Jericho, the City of Palms,ˣ and returned to Samaria.ʸ

¹⁶At that time King Ahaz sent to the king ᵖ of Assyria ᶻ for help. ¹⁷The Edomites ᵃ had again come and attacked Judah and carried away prisoners,ᵇ ¹⁸while the Philistines ᶜ had raided towns in the foothills and in the Negev of Judah. They captured and occupied Beth Shemesh, Aijalon ᵈ and Gederoth,ᵉ as well as Soco,ᶠ Timnah ᵍ and Gimzo, with their surrounding villages. ¹⁹The LORD had humbled Judah because of Ahaz king of Israel,ᑫ for he had promoted wickedness in Judah and had been most unfaithful ʰ to the LORD. ²⁰Tiglath-Pileser ⁱ king of Assyria ʲ came to him, but he gave him trouble ᵏ instead of help.ˡ ²¹Ahaz ᵐ took some of the things from the temple of the LORD and from the royal palace and from the princes and presented them to the king of Assyria, but that did not help him.ⁿ

²²In his time of trouble King Ahaz became even more unfaithful ° to the LORD. ²³He offered sacrifices to the gods ᵖ of Damascus, who had defeated him; for he thought, "Since the gods of the kings of Aram have helped them, I will sacrifice to them so they will help me." ᑫ But they were his downfall and the downfall of all Israel.ʳ

²⁴Ahaz gathered together the furnishings ˢ from the temple of God ᵗ and took them away.ˢ He shut the doors ᵘ of the LORD's temple and set up altars ᵛ at every street corner in Jerusalem. ²⁵In every town in Judah he built high places to burn sacrifices to other gods and provoked the LORD, the God of his fathers, to anger.

²⁶The other events of his reign and all his ways, from beginning to end, are written in the book of the kings of Judah and Israel. ²⁷Ahaz rested ʷ with his fathers and was buried ˣ in the city of Jerusalem, but

R 2Ch 7:20–22 ◀ ▶ 2Ch 29:8

ᵖ 16 One Hebrew manuscript, Septuagint and Vulgate (see also 2 Kings 16:7); most Hebrew manuscripts *kings* ᑫ 19 That is, Judah, as frequently in 2 Chronicles ʳ 20 Hebrew *Tilgath-Pilneser*, a variant of *Tiglath-Pileser* ˢ 24 Or *and cut them up*

C 2Ch 24:20 ◀ ▶ Ne 9:16–17

28:23 King Ahaz worshiped the idol Molech, which required child sacrifices to ensure prosperity. Such apostasy led to Ahaz's downfall and Israel's destruction.

he was not placed in the tombs of the kings of Israel. And Hezekiah his son succeeded him as king.

Hezekiah Purifies the Temple
29:1–2pp — 2Ki 18:2–3

29 Hezekiah was twenty-five years old when he became king, and he reigned in Jerusalem twenty-nine years. His mother's name was Abijah daughter of Zechariah. ²He did what was right in the eyes of the LORD, just as his father David had done.

³In the first month of the first year of his reign, he opened the doors of the temple of the LORD and repaired them. ⁴He brought in the priests and the Levites, assembled them in the square on the east side ⁵and said: "Listen to me, Levites! Consecrate yourselves now and consecrate the temple of the LORD, the God of your fathers. Remove all defilement from the sanctuary. ⁶Our fathers were unfaithful; they did evil in the eyes of the LORD our God and forsook him. They turned their faces away from the LORD's dwelling place and turned their backs on him. ⁷They also shut the doors of the portico and put out the lamps. They did not burn incense or present any burnt offerings at the sanctuary to the God of Israel. ⁸Therefore, the anger of the LORD has fallen on Judah and Jerusalem; he has made them an object of dread and horror and scorn, as you can see with your own eyes. ⁹This is why our fathers have fallen by the sword and why our sons and daughters and our wives are in captivity. ¹⁰Now I intend to make a covenant with the LORD, the God of Israel, so that his fierce anger will turn away from us. ¹¹My sons, do not be negligent now, for the LORD has chosen you to stand before him and serve him, to minister before him and to burn incense."

¹²Then these Levites set to work:
from the Kohathites,
Mahath son of Amasai and Joel son of Azariah;
from the Merarites,

R 2Ch 28:23 ◀ ▶ 2Ch 30:6–7

Kish son of Abdi and Azariah son of Jehallelel;
from the Gershonites,
Joah son of Zimmah and Eden son of Joah;
¹³from the descendants of Elizaphan, Shimri and Jeiel;
from the descendants of Asaph, Zechariah and Mattaniah;
¹⁴from the descendants of Heman, Jehiel and Shimei;
from the descendants of Jeduthun, Shemaiah and Uzziel.

¹⁵When they had assembled their brothers and consecrated themselves, they went in to purify the temple of the LORD, as the king had ordered, following the word of the LORD. ¹⁶The priests went into the sanctuary of the LORD to purify it. They brought out to the courtyard of the LORD's temple everything unclean that they found in the temple of the LORD. The Levites took it and carried it out to the Kidron Valley. ¹⁷They began the consecration on the first day of the first month, and by the eighth day of the month they reached the portico of the LORD. For eight more days they consecrated the temple of the LORD itself, finishing on the sixteenth day of the first month.

¹⁸Then they went in to King Hezekiah and reported: "We have purified the entire temple of the LORD, the altar of burnt offering with all its utensils, and the table for setting out the consecrated bread, with all its articles. ¹⁹We have prepared and consecrated all the articles that King Ahaz removed in his unfaithfulness while he was king. They are now in front of the LORD's altar."

²⁰Early the next morning King Hezekiah gathered the city officials together and went up to the temple of the LORD. ²¹They brought seven bulls, seven rams, seven male lambs and seven male goats as a sin offering for the kingdom, for the sanctuary and for Judah. The king commanded the priests, the descendants of Aaron, to offer these on the altar of the LORD. ²²So they slaughtered the bulls, and the priests took the blood and sprinkled it on the altar; next they slaughtered the rams and sprinkled their blood on the al-

---

29:8 King Hezekiah repented of the sins of his fathers, recognizing that because of his forefathers' sins of idolatry Judah and Jerusalem were suffering God's judgment.

tar; then they slaughtered the lambs and sprinkled their blood[v] on the altar. 23The goats[w] for the sin offering were brought before the king and the assembly, and they laid their hands[x] on them. 24The priests then slaughtered the goats and presented their blood on the altar for a sin offering to atone[y] for all Israel, because the king had ordered the burnt offering and the sin offering for all Israel.[z]

25He stationed the Levites in the temple of the LORD with cymbals, harps and lyres in the way prescribed by David[a] and Gad[b] the king's seer and Nathan the prophet; this was commanded by the LORD through his prophets. 26So the Levites stood ready with David's instruments,[c] and the priests with their trumpets.[d]

27Hezekiah gave the order to sacrifice the burnt offering on the altar. As the offering began, singing to the LORD began also, accompanied by trumpets and the instruments[e] of David king of Israel. 28The whole assembly bowed in worship, while the singers sang and the trumpeters played. All this continued until the sacrifice of the burnt offering[f] was completed.

29When the offerings were finished, the king and everyone present with him knelt down and worshiped.[g] 30King Hezekiah and his officials ordered the Levites to praise the LORD with the words of David and of Asaph the seer. So they sang praises with gladness and bowed their heads and worshiped.

31Then Hezekiah said, "You have now dedicated yourselves to the LORD. Come and bring sacrifices[h] and thank offerings to the temple of the LORD." So the assembly brought sacrifices and thank offerings, and all whose hearts were willing[i] brought burnt offerings.

32The number of burnt offerings[j] the assembly brought was seventy bulls, a hundred rams and two hundred male lambs—all of them for burnt offerings to the LORD. 33The animals consecrated as sacrifices amounted to six hundred bulls and three thousand sheep and goats. 34The priests, however, were too few to

skin all the burnt offerings;[k] so their kinsmen the Levites helped them until the task was finished and until other priests had been consecrated,[l] for the Levites had been more conscientious in consecrating themselves than the priests had been. 35There were burnt offerings in abundance, together with the fat[m] of the fellowship offerings[fn] and the drink offerings[o] that accompanied the burnt offerings.

So the service of the temple of the LORD was reestablished. 36Hezekiah and all the people rejoiced at what God had brought about for his people, because it was done so quickly.[p]

Hezekiah Celebrates the Passover

30 Hezekiah sent word to all Israel[q] and Judah and also wrote letters to Ephraim and Manasseh,[r] inviting them to come to the temple of the LORD in Jerusalem and celebrate the Passover[s] to the LORD, the God of Israel. 2The king and his officials and the whole assembly in Jerusalem decided to celebrate[t] the Passover in the second month. 3They had not been able to celebrate it at the regular time because not enough priests had consecrated[u] themselves and the people had not assembled in Jerusalem. 4The plan seemed right both to the king and to the whole assembly. 5They decided to send a proclamation throughout Israel, from Beersheba to Dan,[v] calling the people to come to Jerusalem and celebrate the Passover to the LORD, the God of Israel. It had not been celebrated in large numbers according to what was written.

6At the king's command, couriers went throughout Israel and Judah with letters from the king and from his officials, which read:

"People of Israel, return to the LORD, the God of Abraham, Isaac and Israel, that he may return to you

D 2Ki 23:21 ◀ ▶ 2Ch 30:5
D 2Ch 30:1 ◀ ▶ 2Ch 35:1
R 2Ch 29:8 ◀ ▶ 2Ch 34:24–25

[f] 35 Traditionally *peace offerings*

30:6–7 King Hezekiah wrote letters to all of Israel and Judah encouraging them to return to the true worship of God and reject idol worship so that God might reestablish his blessings and protection for his people.

who are left, who have escaped from the hand of the kings of Assyria. ⁷Do not be like your fathers[w] and brothers, who were unfaithful[x] to the LORD, the God of their fathers, so that he made them an object of horror,[y] as you see. ⁸Do not be stiff-necked,[z] as your fathers were; submit to the LORD. Come to the sanctuary, which he has consecrated forever. Serve the LORD your God, so that his fierce anger[a] will turn away from you. ⁹If you return[b] to the LORD, then your brothers and your children will be shown compassion[c] by their captors and will come back to this land, for the LORD your God is gracious and compassionate.[d] He will not turn his face from you if you return to him."

¹⁰The couriers went from town to town in Ephraim and Manasseh, as far as Zebulun, but the people scorned and ridiculed[e] them. ¹¹Nevertheless, some men of Asher, Manasseh and Zebulun humbled[f] themselves and went to Jerusalem.[g] ¹²Also in Judah the hand of God was on the people to give them unity[h] of mind to carry out what the king and his officials had ordered, following the word of the LORD.

¹³A very large crowd of people assembled in Jerusalem to celebrate the Feast of Unleavened Bread[i] in the second month. ¹⁴They removed the altars[j] in Jerusalem and cleared away the incense altars and threw them into the Kidron Valley.[k]

¹⁵They slaughtered the Passover lamb on the fourteenth day of the second month. The priests and the Levites were ashamed and consecrated[l] themselves and brought burnt offerings to the temple of the LORD. ¹⁶Then they took up their regular positions[m] as prescribed in the Law of Moses the man of God. The priests sprinkled the blood handed to them by the Levites. ¹⁷Since many in the crowd had not consecrated themselves, the Levites had to kill[n] the Passover lambs for all those who were not ceremonially clean and could not consecrate ⌊their lambs⌋ to the LORD. ¹⁸Although most of the many people who came from Ephraim, Manasseh, Issachar and Zebu-

M 2Ch 12:12 ◀ ▶ 2Ch 32:26
L 2Ch 15:15 ◀ ▶ Ezr 8:22
P 2Ch 15:3–4 ◀ ▶ Ps 32:5

30:7 ʷPs 78:8,57; 106:6; Jer 11:10; Eze 20:18
ˣS 1Ch 5:25
ʸS Dt 28:25

30:8 ᶻS Ex 32:9
ᵃS Nu 25:4; S 2Ch 29:10

30:9 ᵇDt 30:2-5; Isa 1:16; 55:7; Jer 25:5; Eze 33:11
ᶜS Ex 3:21; S 1Ki 8:50
ᵈS Ex 22:27; S Dt 4:31; S 2Ch 6:39; Mic 7:18

30:10 ᵉ2Ch 36:16

30:11 ᶠS 2Ch 6:37
ᵍver 25

30:12 ʰJer 32:39; Eze 11:19

30:13 ⁱS Nu 28:16

30:14 ʲ2Ch 28:24
ᵏS 2Sa 15:23

30:15 ˡS 2Ch 29:34

30:16 ᵐ2Ch 35:10

30:17 ⁿ2Ch 35:11; Ezr 6:20

30:18 ᵒEx 12:43-49; Nu 9:6-10

30:20 ᵖS 2Ch 6:20
ᵠS 2Ch 7:14; Mal 4:2 ʳJas 5:16

30:21 ˢEx 12:15, 17; 13:6

30:23 ᵗ2Ch 7:9

30:24 ᵘ1Ki 8:5; 2Ch 35:7; Ezr 6:17; 8:35

30:25 ᵛver 11

30:26 ʷS 2Ch 7:8

30:27 ˣS Ex 39:43

31:1 ʸS 2Ki 18:4; 2Ch 32:12; Isa 36:7

lun had not purified themselves,° yet they ate the Passover, contrary to what was written. But Hezekiah prayed for them, saying, "May the LORD, who is good, pardon everyone ¹⁹who sets his heart on seeking God—the LORD, the God of his fathers—even if he is not clean according to the rules of the sanctuary." ²⁰And the LORD heard[p] Hezekiah and healed[q] the people.[r]

²¹The Israelites who were present in Jerusalem celebrated the Feast of Unleavened Bread[s] for seven days with great rejoicing, while the Levites and priests sang to the LORD every day, accompanied by the LORD's instruments of praise.[u]

²²Hezekiah spoke encouragingly to all the Levites, who showed good understanding of the service of the LORD. For the seven days they ate their assigned portion and offered fellowship offerings[v] and praised the LORD, the God of their fathers.

²³The whole assembly then agreed to celebrate[t] the festival seven more days; so for another seven days they celebrated joyfully. ²⁴Hezekiah king of Judah provided[u] a thousand bulls and seven thousand sheep and goats for the assembly, and the officials provided them with a thousand bulls and ten thousand sheep and goats. A great number of priests consecrated themselves. ²⁵The entire assembly of Judah rejoiced, along with the priests and Levites and all who had assembled from Israel[v], including the aliens who had come from Israel and those who lived in Judah. ²⁶There was great joy in Jerusalem, for since the days of Solomon[w] son of David king of Israel there had been nothing like this in Jerusalem. ²⁷The priests and the Levites stood to bless[x] the people, and God heard them, for their prayer reached heaven, his holy dwelling place.

31

When all this had ended, the Israelites who were there went out to the towns of Judah, smashed the sacred stones and cut down[y] the Asherah poles. They destroyed the high places and the altars throughout Judah and Benjamin and in Ephraim and Manasseh. After they had destroyed all of them, the Israelites

u 21 Or priests praised the LORD every day with resounding instruments belonging to the LORD   v 22 Traditionally peace offerings

returned to their own towns and to their own property.

Contributions for Worship
31:20-21pp — 2Ki 18:5-7

²Hezekiah assigned the priests and Levites to divisions—each of them according to their duties as priests or Levites—to offer burnt offerings and fellowship offerings, to minister, to give thanks and to sing praises at the gates of the LORD's dwelling. ³The king contributed from his own possessions for the morning and evening burnt offerings and for the burnt offerings on the Sabbaths, New Moons and appointed feasts as written in the Law of the LORD. ⁴He ordered the people living in Jerusalem to give the portion due the priests and Levites so they could devote themselves to the Law of the LORD. ⁵As soon as the order went out, the Israelites generously gave the firstfruits of their grain, new wine, oil and honey and all that the fields produced. They brought a great amount, a tithe of everything. ⁶The men of Israel and Judah who lived in the towns of Judah also brought a tithe of their herds and flocks and a tithe of the holy things dedicated to the LORD their God, and they piled them in heaps. ⁷They began doing this in the third month and finished in the seventh month. ⁸When Hezekiah and his officials came and saw the heaps, they praised the LORD and blessed his people Israel.

⁹Hezekiah asked the priests and Levites about the heaps; ¹⁰and Azariah the chief priest, from the family of Zadok, answered, "Since the people began to bring their contributions to the temple of the LORD, we have had enough to eat and plenty to spare, because the LORD has blessed his people, and this great amount is left over."

¹¹Hezekiah gave orders to prepare storerooms in the temple of the LORD, and this was done. ¹²Then they faithfully brought in the contributions, tithes and dedicated gifts. Conaniah, a Levite, was in charge of these things, and his brother Shimei was next in rank. ¹³Jehiel, Azaziah, Nahath, Asahel, Jerimoth, Jozabad, Eliel, Ismakiah, Mahath and Benaiah were supervisors under Conaniah and Shimei his brother, by appointment of King Hezekiah and Azariah the official in charge of the temple of God.

¹⁴Kore son of Imnah the Levite, keeper of the East Gate, was in charge of the freewill offerings given to God, distributing the contributions made to the LORD and also the consecrated gifts. ¹⁵Eden, Miniamin, Jeshua, Shemaiah, Amariah and Shecaniah assisted him faithfully in the towns of the priests, distributing to their fellow priests according to their divisions, old and young alike.

¹⁶In addition, they distributed to the males three years old or more whose names were in the genealogical records—all who would enter the temple of the LORD to perform the daily duties of their various tasks, according to their responsibilities and their divisions. ¹⁷And they distributed to the priests enrolled by their families in the genealogical records and likewise to the Levites twenty years old or more, according to their responsibilities and their divisions. ¹⁸They included all the little ones, the wives, and the sons and daughters of the whole community listed in these genealogical records. For they were faithful in consecrating themselves.

¹⁹As for the priests, the descendants of Aaron, who lived on the farm lands around their towns or in any other towns, men were designated by name to distribute portions to every male among them and to all who were recorded in the genealogies of the Levites.

²⁰This is what Hezekiah did throughout Judah, doing what was good and right and faithful before the LORD his God. ²¹In everything that he undertook in the service of God's temple and in obedience to the law and the commands, he sought his God and worked wholeheartedly. And so he prospered.

Sennacherib Threatens Jerusalem
32:9-19pp — 2Ki 18:17-35; Isa 36:2-20
32:20-21pp — 2Ki 19:35-37; Isa 37:36-38

32 After all that Hezekiah had so faithfully done, Sennacherib

w 2 Traditionally *peace offerings*

king of Assyria came and invaded Judah. He laid siege to the fortified cities, thinking to conquer them for himself. ²When Hezekiah saw that Sennacherib had come and that he intended to make war on Jerusalem,ʸ ³he consulted with his officials and military staff about blocking off the water from the springs outside the city, and they helped him. ⁴A large force of men assembled, and they blocked all the springsᶻ and the stream that flowed through the land. "Why should the kingsˣ of Assyria come and find plenty of water?" they said. ⁵Then he worked hard repairing all the broken sections of the wallᵃ and building towers on it. He built another wall outside that one and reinforced the supporting terracesʸᵇ of the City of David. He also made large numbers of weaponsᶜ and shields.

⁶He appointed military officers over the people and assembled them before him in the square at the city gate and encouraged them with these words: ⁷"Be strong and courageous.ᵈ Do not be afraid or discouragedᵉ because of the king of Assyria and the vast army with him, for there is a greater power with us than with him.ᶠ ⁸With him is only the arm of flesh,ᵍ but with usʰ is the LORD our God to help us and to fight our battles."ⁱ And the people gained confidence from what Hezekiah the king of Judah said.

⁹Later, when Sennacherib king of Assyria and all his forces were laying siege to Lachish,ʲ he sent his officers to Jerusalem with this message for Hezekiah king of Judah and for all the people of Judah who were there:

¹⁰"This is what Sennacherib king of Assyria says: On what are you basing your confidence,ᵏ that you remain in Jerusalem under siege? ¹¹When Hezekiah says, 'The LORD our God will save us from the hand of the king of Assyria,' he is misleadingˡ you, to let you die of hunger and thirst. ¹²Did not Hezekiah himself remove this god's high places and altars, saying to Judah and Jerusalem, 'You must worship before one altarᵐ and burn sacrifices on it'?

¹³"Do you not know what I and my fathers have done to all the peoples of the other lands? Were the gods of those nations ever able to deliver their land from my hand?ⁿ ¹⁴Who of all the gods of these nations that my fathers destroyed has been able to save his people from me? How then can your god deliver you from my hand? ¹⁵Now do not let Hezekiah deceiveᵒ you and mislead you like this. Do not believe him, for no god of any nation or kingdom has been able to deliverᵖ his people from my hand or the hand of my fathers.ᑫ How much less will your god deliver you from my hand!"

¹⁶Sennacherib's officers spoke further against the LORD God and against his servant Hezekiah. ¹⁷The king also wrote lettersʳ insultingˢ the LORD, the God of Israel, and saying this against him: "Just as the godsᵗ of the peoples of the other lands did not rescue their people from my hand, so the god of Hezekiah will not rescue his people from my hand." ¹⁸Then they called out in Hebrew to the people of Jerusalem who were on the wall, to terrify them and make them afraid in order to capture the city. ¹⁹They spoke about the God of Jerusalem as they did about the gods of the other peoples of the world—the work of men's hands.ᵘ

²⁰King Hezekiah and the prophet Isaiah son of Amoz cried out in prayerᵛ to heaven about this. ²¹And the LORD sent an angel,ʷ who annihilated all the fighting men and the leaders and officers in the camp of the Assyrian king. So he withdrew to his own land in disgrace. And when he went into the temple of his god, some of his sons cut him down with the sword.ˣ

²²So the LORD saved Hezekiah and the people of Jerusalem from the hand of Sennacherib king of Assyria and from the hand of all others. He took care of themᶻ on every side. ²³Many brought offerings to Jerusalem for the LORD and valuable

Hezekiah's Pride, Success and Death

32:24–33pp — 2Ki 20:1–21; Isa 37:21–38; 38:1–8

²⁴In those days Hezekiah became ill and was at the point of death. He prayed to the LORD, who answered him and gave him a miraculous sign.ᶻ ²⁵But Hezekiah's heart was proudᵃ and he did not respond to the kindness shown him; therefore the LORD's wrathᵇ was on him and on Judah and Jerusalem. ²⁶Then Hezekiah repentedᶜ of the pride of his heart, as did the people of Jerusalem; therefore the LORD's wrath did not come upon them during the days of Hezekiah.ᵈ

²⁷Hezekiah had very great riches and honor,ᵉ and he made treasuries for his silver and gold and for his precious stones, spices, shields and all kinds of valuables. ²⁸He also made buildings to store the harvest of grain, new wine and oil; and he made stalls for various kinds of cattle, and pens for the flocks. ²⁹He built villages and acquired great numbers of flocks and herds, for God had given him very great riches.ᶠ

³⁰It was Hezekiah who blockedᵍ the upper outlet of the Gihonʰ spring and channeledⁱ the water down to the west side of the City of David. He succeeded in everything he undertook. ³¹But when envoys were sent by the rulers of Babylonʲ to ask him about the miraculous signᵏ that had occurred in the land, God left him to testˡ him and to know everything that was in his heart.

³²The other events of Hezekiah's reign and his acts of devotion are written in the vision of the prophet Isaiah son of Amoz in the book of the kings of Judah and Israel. ³³Hezekiah rested with his fathers and was buried on the hill where the tombs of David's descendants are. All Judah and the people of Jerusalem honored him when he died. And Manasseh his son succeeded him as king.

Manasseh King of Judah

33:1–10pp — 2Ki 21:1–10
33:18–20pp — 2Ki 21:17–18

33 Manassehᵐ was twelve years old when he became king, and he reigned in Jerusalem fifty-five years. ²He did evil in the eyes of the LORD,ⁿ following the detestableᵒ practices of the nations the LORD had driven out before the Israelites. ³He rebuilt the high places his father Hezekiah had demolished; he also erected altars to the Baals and made Asherah poles.ᵖ He bowed downᑫ to all the starry hosts and worshiped them. ⁴He built altars in the temple of the LORD, of which the LORD had said, "My Nameʳ will remain in Jerusalem forever." ⁵In both courts of the temple of the LORD,ˢ he built altars to all the starry hosts. ⁶He sacrificed his sonsᵗ inᵃ the fire in the Valley of Ben Hinnom, practiced sorcery, divination and witchcraft, and consulted mediumsᵘ and spiritists.ᵛ He did much evil in the eyes of the LORD, provoking him to anger.

⁷He took the carved image he had made and put it in God's temple,ʷ of which God had said to David and to his son Solomon, "In this temple and in Jerusalem, which I have chosen out of all the tribes of Israel, I will put my Name forever. ⁸I will not again make the feet of the Israelites leave the landˣ I assigned to your forefathers, if only they will be careful to do everything I commanded them concerning all the laws, decrees and ordinances given through Moses." ⁹But Manasseh led Judah and the people of Jerusalem astray, so that they did more evil than the nations the LORD had destroyed before the Israelites.ʸ

¹⁰The LORD spoke to Manasseh and his people, but they paid no attention. ¹¹So the LORD brought against them the army commanders of the king of Assyria, who took Manasseh prisoner,ᶻ put a hookᵃ in his nose, bound him with bronze shacklesᵇ and took him to Babylon. ¹²In his distress he sought the favor of the LORD his God and humbledᶜ himself greatly before the God of his fathers. ¹³And when he prayed to him, the LORD was moved by his

---

a 6 Or He made his sons pass through

entreaty and listened to his plea; so he brought him back to Jerusalem and to his kingdom. Then Manasseh knew that the LORD is God.

¹⁴Afterward he rebuilt the outer wall of the City of David, west of the Gihon spring in the valley, as far as the entrance of the Fish Gate and encircling the hill of Ophel;ᶠ he also made it much higher. He stationed military commanders in all the fortified cities in Judah.

¹⁵He got rid of the foreign gods and removedᵍ the image from the temple of the LORD, as well as all the altars he had built on the temple hill and in Jerusalem; and he threw them out of the city. ¹⁶Then he restored the altar of the LORD and sacrificed fellowship offeringsᵇ and thank offeringsʰ on it, and told Judah to serve the LORD, the God of Israel. ¹⁷The people, however, continued to sacrifice at the high places, but only to the LORD their God.

¹⁸The other events of Manasseh's reign, including his prayer to his God and the words the seers spoke to him in the name of the LORD, the God of Israel, are written in the annals of the kings of Israel.ᶜ ¹⁹His prayer and how God was moved by his entreaty, as well as all his sins and unfaithfulness, and the sites where he built high places and set up Asherah poles and idols before he humbledⁱ himself—all are written in the records of the seers.ᵈʲ ²⁰Manasseh rested with his fathers and was buriedᵏ in his palace. And Amon his son succeeded him as king.

Amon King of Judah
33:21–25pp — 2Ki 21:19–24

²¹Amonˡ was twenty-two years old when he became king, and he reigned in Jerusalem two years. ²²He did evil in the eyes of the LORD, as his father Manasseh had done. Amon worshiped and offered sacrifices to all the idols Manasseh had made. ²³But unlike his father Manasseh, he did not humbleᵐ himself before the LORD; Amon increased his guilt.

²⁴Amon's officials conspired against him and assassinated him in his palace. ²⁵Then the peopleⁿ of the land killed all who had plotted against King Amon, and they made Josiah his son king in his place.

33:14 ᵈS 1Ki 1:33; ᵉNe 3:3; 12:39; Zep 1:10
33:14 ᶠ2Ch 27:3; Ne 3:26
33:15 ᵍ2Ki 23:12
33:16 ʰLev 7:11-18
33:19 ⁱS 2Ch 6:37
33:19 ʲ2Ki 21:17
33:20 ᵏ2Ki 21:18; S 2Ch 21:20
33:21 ˡS 1Ch 3:14
33:23 ᵐS Ex 10:3; 2Ch 7:14; Ps 18:27; 147:6; Pr 3:34
33:25 ⁿS 2Ch 22:1
34:1 ᵒS 1Ch 3:14
ᵖZep 1:1
34:2 ᵍ2Ch 29:2
34:3 ʳS 1Ch 16:11
34:4 ˢS Ex 34:13
ᵗEx 32:20;
S Lev 26:30;
2Ki 23:11; Mic 1:5
34:5 ᵘS 1Ki 13:2
34:7 ᵛS Ex 32:20
34:9 ʷS 1Ch 6:13
34:11 ˣ2Ch 24:12

Josiah's Reforms
34:1–2pp — 2Ki 22:1–2
34:3–7Ref — 2Ki 23:4–20
34:8–13pp — 2Ki 22:3–7

34 Josiahᵒ was eight years old when he became king,ᵖ and he reigned in Jerusalem thirty-one years. ²He did what was right in the eyes of the LORD and walked in the ways of his father David,ᵍ not turning aside to the right or to the left.

³In the eighth year of his reign, while he was still young, he began to seek the Godʳ of his father David. In his twelfth year he began to purge Judah and Jerusalem of high places, Asherah poles, carved idols and cast images. ⁴Under his direction the altars of the Baals were torn down; he cut to pieces the incense altars that were above them, and smashed the Asherah poles,ˢ the idols and the images. These he broke to pieces and scattered over the graves of those who had sacrificed to them.ᵗ ⁵He burnedᵘ the bones of the priests on their altars, and so he purged Judah and Jerusalem. ⁶In the towns of Manasseh, Ephraim and Simeon, as far as Naphtali, and in the ruins around them, ⁷he tore down the altars and the Asherah poles and crushed the idols to powderᵛ and cut to pieces all the incense altars throughout Israel. Then he went back to Jerusalem.

⁸In the eighteenth year of Josiah's reign, to purify the land and the temple, he sent Shaphan son of Azaliah and Maaseiah the ruler of the city, with Joah son of Joahaz, the recorder, to repair the temple of the LORD his God.

⁹They went to Hilkiahʷ the high priest and gave him the money that had been brought into the temple of God, which the Levites who were the doorkeepers had collected from the people of Manasseh, Ephraim and the entire remnant of Israel and from all the people of Judah and Benjamin and the inhabitants of Jerusalem. ¹⁰Then they entrusted it to the men appointed to supervise the work on the LORD's temple. These men paid the workers who repaired and restored the temple. ¹¹They also gave moneyˣ to the carpenters and builders to purchase dressed stone, and timber for joists and

ᵇ 16 Traditionally *peace offerings* ᶜ 18 That is, Judah, as frequently in 2 Chronicles ᵈ 19 One Hebrew manuscript and Septuagint; most Hebrew manuscripts *of Hozai*

beams for the buildings that the kings of Judah had allowed to fall into ruin.ʸ

¹²The men did the work faithfully.ᶻ Over them to direct them were Jahath and Obadiah, Levites descended from Merari, and Zechariah and Meshullam, descended from Kohath. The Levites—all who were skilled in playing musical instruments—ᵃ ¹³had charge of the laborersᵇ and supervised all the workers from job to job. Some of the Levites were secretaries, scribes and doorkeepers.

The Book of the Law Found
34:14–28pp — 2Ki 22:8–20
34:29–32pp — 2Ki 23:1–3

¹⁴While they were bringing out the money that had been taken into the temple of the LORD, Hilkiah the priest found the Book of the Law of the LORD that had been given through Moses. ¹⁵Hilkiah said to Shaphan the secretary, "I have found the Book of the Lawᶜ in the temple of the LORD." He gave it to Shaphan.

¹⁶Then Shaphan took the book to the king and reported to him: "Your officials are doing everything that has been committed to them. ¹⁷They have paid out the money that was in the temple of the LORD and have entrusted it to the supervisors and workers." ¹⁸Then Shaphan the secretary informed the king, "Hilkiah the priest has given me a book." And Shaphan read from it in the presence of the king.

¹⁹When the king heard the words of the Law,ᵈ he toreᵉ his robes. ²⁰He gave these orders to Hilkiah, Ahikam son of Shaphan,ᶠ Abdon son of Micah,ᵉ Shaphan the secretary and Asaiah the king's attendant: ²¹"Go and inquire of the LORD for me and for the remnant in Israel and Judah about what is written in this book that has been found. Great is the LORD's anger that is poured outᵍ on us because our fathers have not kept the word of the LORD; they have not acted in accordance with all that is written in this book."

²²Hilkiah and those the king had sent with himᶠ went to speak to the prophetessʰ Huldah, who was the wife of Shallum son of Tokhath,ᵍ the son of Hasrah,ʰ keeper of the wardrobe. She lived in Jerusalem, in the Second District.

²³She said to them, "This is what the LORD, the God of Israel, says: Tell the man who sent you to me, ²⁴'This is what the LORD says: I am going to bring disasterⁱ on this place and its peopleʲ—all the cursesᵏ written in the book that has been read in the presence of the king of Judah. ²⁵Because they have forsaken meˡ and burned incense to other gods and provoked me to anger by all that their hands have made,ⁱ my anger will be poured out on this place and will not be quenched.' ²⁶Tell the king of Judah, who sent you to inquire of the LORD, 'This is what the LORD, the God of Israel, says concerning the words you heard: ²⁷Because your heart was responsiveᵐ and you humbledⁿ yourself before God when you heard what he spoke against this place and its people, and because you humbled yourself before me and tore your robes and wept in my presence, I have heard you, declares the LORD. ²⁸Now I will gather you to your fathers,ᵒ and you will be buried in peace. Your eyes will not see all the disaster I am going to bring on this place and on those who live here.'"ᵖ

So they took her answer back to the king.

²⁹Then the king called together all the elders of Judah and Jerusalem. ³⁰He went up to the temple of the LORDq with the men of Judah, the people of Jerusalem, the priests and the Levites—all the people from the least to the greatest. He read in their hearing all the words of the Book of the Covenant, which had been found in the temple of the LORD. ³¹The king stood by his pillarʳ and renewed the covenantˢ in the presence of the LORD—to followᵗ the LORD and keep his commands, regulations and decrees with all his heart

R 2Ch 30:6–7 ◄ ► 2Ch 36:17–21
M 2Ch 33:12–13 ◄ ► Ezr 9:5–6
L 2Ch 20:9 ◄ ► Isa 38:18

ᵉ 20 Also called *Acbor son of Micaiah* ᶠ 22 One Hebrew manuscript, Vulgate and Syriac; most Hebrew manuscripts do not have *had sent with him.* ᵍ 22 Also called *Tikvah* ʰ 22 Also called *Harhas* ⁱ 25 Or *by everything they have done*

34:24–25 After the discovery of the book of the law in the temple, Huldah prophesied that God would still deliver his judgment and punishment upon the people because of their idolatry, but God would delay this judgment until after the death of King Josiah.

and all his soul, and to obey the words of the covenant written in this book.

³²Then he had everyone in Jerusalem and Benjamin pledge themselves to it; the people of Jerusalem did this in accordance with the covenant of God, the God of their fathers.

³³Josiah removed all the detestable idols from all the territory belonging to the Israelites, and he had all who were present in Israel serve the LORD their God. As long as he lived, they did not fail to follow the LORD, the God of their fathers.

Josiah Celebrates the Passover
35:1,18–19pp — 2Ki 23:21–23

35 Josiah celebrated the Passover to the LORD in Jerusalem, and the Passover lamb was slaughtered on the fourteenth day of the first month. ²He appointed the priests to their duties and encouraged them in the service of the LORD's temple. ³He said to the Levites, who instructed all Israel and who had been consecrated to the LORD: "Put the sacred ark in the temple that Solomon son of David king of Israel built. It is not to be carried about on your shoulders. Now serve the LORD your God and his people Israel. ⁴Prepare yourselves by families in your divisions, according to the directions written by David king of Israel and by his son Solomon.

⁵"Stand in the holy place with a group of Levites for each subdivision of the families of your fellow countrymen, the lay people. ⁶Slaughter the Passover lambs, consecrate yourselves and prepare ⌊the lambs⌋ for your fellow countrymen, doing what the LORD commanded through Moses."

⁷Josiah provided for all the lay people who were there a total of thirty thousand sheep and goats for the Passover offerings, and also three thousand cattle—all from the king's own possessions.

⁸His officials also contributed voluntarily to the people and the priests and Levites. Hilkiah, Zechariah and Jehiel, the administrators of God's temple, gave the priests twenty-six hundred Passover offerings and three hundred cattle. ⁹Also Conaniah along with Shemaiah and Nethanel, his brothers, and Hashabiah, Jeiel and Jozabad, the leaders of the Levites, provided five thousand Passover offerings and five hundred head of cattle for the Levites.

¹⁰The service was arranged and the priests stood in their places with the Levites in their divisions as the king had ordered. ¹¹The Passover lambs were slaughtered, and the priests sprinkled the blood handed to them, while the Levites skinned the animals. ¹²They set aside the burnt offerings to give them to the subdivisions of the families of the people to offer to the LORD, as is written in the Book of Moses. They did the same with the cattle. ¹³They roasted the Passover animals over the fire as prescribed, and boiled the holy offerings in pots, caldrons and pans and served them quickly to all the people. ¹⁴After this, they made preparations for themselves and for the priests, because the priests, the descendants of Aaron, were sacrificing the burnt offerings and the fat portions until nightfall. So the Levites made preparations for themselves and for the Aaronic priests.

¹⁵The musicians, the descendants of Asaph, were in the places prescribed by David, Asaph, Heman and Jeduthun the king's seer. The gatekeepers at each gate did not need to leave their posts, because their fellow Levites made the preparations for them.

¹⁶So at that time the entire service of the LORD was carried out for the celebration of the Passover and the offering of burnt offerings on the altar of the LORD, as King Josiah had ordered. ¹⁷The Israelites who were present celebrated the Passover at that time and observed the Feast of Unleavened Bread for seven days. ¹⁸The Passover had not been observed like this in Israel since the days of the prophet Samuel; and none of the kings of Israel had ever celebrated such a Passover as did Josiah, with the priests, the Levites and all Judah and Israel who were there with the people of Jerusalem. ¹⁹This Passover was celebrated in the eighteenth year of Josiah's reign.

The Death of Josiah
35:20–36:1pp — 2Ki 23:28–30

²⁰After all this, when Josiah had set the temple in order, Neco king of Egypt went up to fight at Carchemish on the Euphrates, and Josiah marched out to meet

him in battle. ²¹But Neco sent messengers to him, saying, "What quarrel is there between you and me, O king of Judah? It is not you I am attacking at this time, but the house with which I am at war. God has told me to hurry; so stop opposing God, who is with me, or he will destroy you."

²²Josiah, however, would not turn away from him, but disguised himself to engage him in battle. He would not listen to what Neco had said at God's command but went to fight him on the plain of Megiddo.

²³Archers shot King Josiah, and he told his officers, "Take me away; I am badly wounded." ²⁴So they took him out of his chariot, put him in the other chariot he had and brought him to Jerusalem, where he died. He was buried in the tombs of his fathers, and all Judah and Jerusalem mourned for him.

²⁵Jeremiah composed laments for Josiah, and to this day all the men and women singers commemorate Josiah in the laments. These became a tradition in Israel and are written in the Laments.

²⁶The other events of Josiah's reign and his acts of devotion, according to what is written in the Law of the LORD— ²⁷all the events, from beginning to end, are written in the book of the kings of Israel and Judah. ¹And the people of the land took Jehoahaz son of Josiah and made him king in Jerusalem in place of his father.

36

Jehoahaz King of Judah
36:2–4pp — 2Ki 23:31–34

²Jehoahaz was twenty-three years old when he became king, and he reigned in Jerusalem three months. ³The king of Egypt dethroned him in Jerusalem and imposed on Judah a levy of a hundred talents of silver and a talent of gold. ⁴The king of Egypt made Eliakim, a brother of Jehoahaz, king over Judah and Jerusalem and changed Eliakim's name to Jehoiakim. But Neco took Eliakim's brother Jehoahaz and carried him off to Egypt.

Jehoiakim King of Judah
36:5–8pp — 2Ki 23:36–24:6

⁵Jehoiakim was twenty-five years old when he became king, and he reigned in Jerusalem eleven years. He did evil in the eyes of the LORD his God. ⁶Nebuchadnezzar king of Babylon attacked him and bound him with bronze shackles to take him to Babylon. ⁷Nebuchadnezzar also took to Babylon articles from the temple of the LORD and put them in his temple there.

⁸The other events of Jehoiakim's reign, the detestable things he did and all that was found against him, are written in the book of the kings of Israel and Judah. And Jehoiachin his son succeeded him as king.

Jehoiachin King of Judah
36:9–10pp — 2Ki 24:8–17

⁹Jehoiachin was eighteen years old when he became king, and he reigned in Jerusalem three months and ten days. He did evil in the eyes of the LORD. ¹⁰In the spring, King Nebuchadnezzar sent for him and brought him to Babylon, together with articles of value from the temple of the LORD, and he made Jehoiachin's uncle, Zedekiah, king over Judah and Jerusalem.

Zedekiah King of Judah
36:11–16pp — 2Ki 24:18–20; Jer 52:1–3

¹¹Zedekiah was twenty-one years old when he became king, and he reigned in Jerusalem eleven years. ¹²He did evil in the eyes of the LORD his God and did not humble himself before Jeremiah the prophet, who spoke the word of the LORD. ¹³He also rebelled against King Nebuchadnezzar, who had made him take an oath in God's name. He became stiff-necked and hardened his heart and would not turn to the LORD, the God of Israel. ¹⁴Furthermore, all the leaders of the priests and the people became more and more unfaithful, following all the detestable practices of the nations and defiling the temple of the LORD, which he had consecrated in Jerusalem.

N 2Ch 12:14 ◀ ▶ 2Ch 36:16

j2 Hebrew Joahaz, a variant of Jehoahaz; also in verse 4 k3 That is, about 3 3/4 tons (about 3.4 metric tons) l3 That is, about 75 pounds (about 34 kilograms) m7 Or palace n9 One Hebrew manuscript, some Septuagint manuscripts and Syriac (see also 2 Kings 24:8); most Hebrew manuscripts eight o10 Hebrew brother, that is, relative (see 2 Kings 24:17)

The Fall of Jerusalem

36:17–20pp — 2Ki 25:1–21; Jer 52:4–27
36:22–23pp — Ezr 1:1–3

[15] The LORD, the God of their fathers, sent word to them through his messengers again and again, because he had pity on his people and on his dwelling place. [16] But they mocked God's messengers, despised his words and scoffed at his prophets until the wrath of the LORD was aroused against his people and there was no remedy. [17] He brought up against them the king of the Babylonians, who killed their young men with the sword in the sanctuary, and spared neither young man nor young woman, old man or aged. God handed all of them over to Nebuchadnezzar. [18] He carried to Babylon all the articles from the temple of God, both large and small, and the treasures of the LORD's temple and the treasures of the king and his officials. [19] They set fire to God's temple and broke down the wall of Jerusalem; they burned all the palaces and destroyed everything of value there.

[20] He carried into exile to Babylon the remnant, who escaped from the sword, and they became servants to him and his sons until the kingdom of Persia came to power. [21] The land enjoyed its sabbath rests; all the time of its desolation it rested, until the seventy years were completed in fulfillment of the word of the LORD spoken by Jeremiah.

[22] In the first year of Cyrus king of Persia, in order to fulfill the word of the LORD spoken by Jeremiah, the LORD moved the heart of Cyrus king of Persia to make a proclamation throughout his realm and to put it in writing:

[23] "This is what Cyrus king of Persia says:

" 'The LORD, the God of heaven, has given me all the kingdoms of the earth and he has appointed me to build a temple for him at Jerusalem in Judah. Anyone of his people among you—may the LORD his God be with him, and let him go up.' "

H 1Ch 28:9 ◀▶ Ezr 8:22
N 2Ch 36:13 ◀▶ Ne 9:29–30
R 2Ch 34:24–25 ◀▶ Ne 1:8

p 17 Or Chaldeans

36:17–21 In fulfillment of Jeremiah's prophecy, God allowed the Babylonians to overrun Judah, capture Jerusalem, burn the temple and take the population captive to Babylon. This tragedy occurred in part because Israel had refused to follow God's law of the Sabbath of the land (allowing the land lie unplowed every seven years). Because Israel had willingly refused to obey God's Sabbath laws, God would forcibly give the land its Sabbaths by removing Israel from the land for seventy years.

Ezra

Author: Ezra

Theme: Return of the faithful remnant

Date of Writing: c. 440 B.C.

Outline of Ezra
  I. The First Exiles Return to the Land (1:1—2:70)
  II. The Temple Is Rebuilt (3:1—6:22)
  III. Ezra's Return and Ministry (7:1—10:44)

THIS BOOK IS named after Ezra, a scribe in Israel and main character in this story. Though some ancient texts combined Ezra and Nehemiah into one book, later translators divided them. As a historical narrative, Ezra continues Israel's story following the period of Samuel, Kings and Chronicles.

Using genealogies (2:1–70), official documents (4:7–16) and personal letters (7:27—9:15), Ezra relates the exiles' return to their homeland, commencing with King Cyrus's edict that released the exiles from their seventy-year captivity in Babylon. A remnant of Jews returned to Israel at this time under the supervision of Zerubbabel to begin the reconstruction of the temple. Though enemies opposed this rebuilding project for years, an appeal to Cyrus's successor, Darius, re-authorized the project. Encouraged by Haggai and Zechariah, the people redoubled their efforts and completed the temple in 516 B.C.

In 458 B.C. Ezra led another group of Jews back to Jerusalem. Nehemiah returned with a third group in 445 B.C. to rebuild the city's walls. Though Nehemiah was the civil leader of these exiles, Ezra quickly became their teacher, initiating reforms and guiding the people in rebuilding their spiritual foundations as God's chosen nation. Ezra's concern for the people and his personal devotion to God provided effective leadership and spiritual guidance for the people in a very unsettled time.

Cyrus Helps the Exiles to Return
1:1-3pp — 2Ch 36:22-23

1 In the first year of Cyrus king of Persia, in order to fulfill the word of the LORD spoken by Jeremiah,ᵃ the LORD moved the heartᵇ of Cyrus king of Persia to make a proclamation throughout his realm and to put it in writing:

²"This is what Cyrus king of Persia says:

"'The LORD, the God of heaven, has given me all the kingdoms of the earth and he has appointedᶜ me to buildᵈ a temple for him at Jerusalem in Judah. ³Anyone of his people among you—may his God be with him, and let him go up to Jerusalem in Judah and build the temple of the LORD, the God of Israel, the God who is in Jerusalem. ⁴And the people of any place where survivorsᵉ may now be living are to provide him with silver and gold,ᶠ with goods and livestock, and with freewill offeringsᵍ for the temple of Godʰ in Jerusalem.'"ⁱ

⁵Then the family heads of Judah and Benjamin,ʲ and the priests and Levites—everyone whose heart God had movedᵏ—prepared to go up and build the houseˡ of the LORD in Jerusalem. ⁶All their neighbors assisted them with articles of silver and gold,ᵐ with goods and livestock, and with valuable gifts, in addition to all the freewill offerings. ⁷Moreover, King Cyrus brought out the articles belonging to the temple of the LORD, which Nebuchadnezzar had carried away from Jerusalem and had placed in the temple of his god.ᵃⁿ ⁸Cyrus king of Persia had them brought by Mithredath the treasurer, who counted them out to Sheshbazzarᵒ the prince of Judah.

⁹This was the inventory:

gold dishes	30
silver dishes	1,000
silver pansᵇ	29
¹⁰gold bowls	30
matching silver bowls	410
other articles	1,000

¹¹In all, there were 5,400 articles of gold and of silver. Sheshbazzar brought all these along when the exiles came up from Babylon to Jerusalem.

The List of the Exiles Who Returned
2:1-70pp — Ne 7:6-73

2 Now these are the people of the province who came up from the captivity of the exiles,ᵖ whom Nebuchadnezzar king of Babylonᑫ had taken captive to Babylon (they returned to Jerusalem and Judah, each to his own town,ʳ ²in company with Zerubbabel,ˢ Jeshua,ᵗ Nehemiah, Seraiah,ᵘ Reelaiah, Mordecai, Bilshan, Mispar, Bigvai, Rehum and Baanah):

The list of the men of the people of Israel:

³the descendants of Paroshᵛ	2,172
⁴of Shephatiah	372
⁵of Arah	775
⁶of Pahath-Moab (through the line of Jeshua and Joab)	2,812
⁷of Elam	1,254
⁸of Zattu	945
⁹of Zaccai	760
¹⁰of Bani	642
¹¹of Bebai	623
¹²of Azgad	1,222
¹³of Adonikamʷ	666
¹⁴of Bigvai	2,056
¹⁵of Adin	454
¹⁶of Ater (through Hezekiah)	98
¹⁷of Bezai	323
¹⁸of Jorah	112
¹⁹of Hashum	223
²⁰of Gibbar	95
²¹the men of Bethlehemˣ	123
²²of Netophah	56
²³of Anathoth	128
²⁴of Azmaveth	42
²⁵of Kiriath Jearim,ᶜ Kephirah and Beeroth	743
²⁶of Ramahʸ and Geba	621
²⁷of Micmash	122
²⁸of Bethel and Aiᶻ	223
²⁹of Nebo	52
³⁰of Magbish	156
³¹of the other Elam	1,254
³²of Harim	320
³³of Lod, Hadid and Ono	725
³⁴of Jerichoᵃ	345
³⁵of Senaah	3,630

ᵃ 7 Or gods ᵇ 9 The meaning of the Hebrew for this word is uncertain. ᶜ 25 See Septuagint (see also Neh. 7:29); Hebrew Kiriath Arim.

36The priests:

the descendants of Jedaiah[b] (through the family of Jeshua) 973
37of Immer[c] 1,052
38of Pashhur[d] 1,247
39of Harim[e] 1,017

40The Levites:[f]

the descendants of Jeshua[g] and Kadmiel (through the line of Hodaviah) 74

41The singers:[h]

the descendants of Asaph 128

42The gatekeepers[i] of the temple:

the descendants of Shallum, Ater, Talmon, Akkub, Hatita and Shobai 139

43The temple servants:[j]

the descendants of Ziha, Hasupha, Tabbaoth, 44Keros, Siaha, Padon, 45Lebanah, Hagabah, Akkub, 46Hagab, Shalmai, Hanan, 47Giddel, Gahar, Reaiah, 48Rezin, Nekoda, Gazzam, 49Uzza, Paseah, Besai, 50Asnah, Meunim, Nephussim, 51Bakbuk, Hakupha, Harhur, 52Bazluth, Mehida, Harsha, 53Barkos, Sisera, Temah, 54Neziah and Hatipha

55The descendants of the servants of Solomon:

the descendants of Sotai, Hassophereth, Peruda, 56Jaala, Darkon, Giddel, 57Shephatiah, Hattil, Pokereth-Hazzebaim and Ami

58The temple servants[k] and the descendants of the servants of Solomon 392

59The following came up from the towns of Tel Melah, Tel Harsha, Kerub, Addon and Immer, but they could not show that their families were descended[l] from Israel:

60The descendants of Delaiah, Tobiah and Nekoda 652

61And from among the priests:

The descendants of Hobaiah, Hakkoz and Barzillai (a man who had married a daughter of Barzillai the Gileadite[m] and was called by that name).

62These searched for their family records, but they could not find them and so were excluded from the priesthood[n] as unclean. 63The governor ordered them not to eat any of the most sacred food[o] until there was a priest ministering with the Urim and Thummim.[p]

64The whole company numbered 42,360, 65besides their 7,337 menservants and maidservants; and they also had 200 men and women singers.[q] 66They had 736 horses,[r] 245 mules, 67435 camels and 6,720 donkeys.

68When they arrived at the house of the LORD in Jerusalem, some of the heads of the families[s] gave freewill offerings toward the rebuilding of the house of God on its site. 69According to their ability they gave to the treasury for this work 61,000 drachmas[d] of gold, 5,000 minas[e] of silver and 100 priestly garments.

70The priests, the Levites, the singers, the gatekeepers and the temple servants settled in their own towns, along with some of the other people, and the rest of the Israelites settled in their towns.[t]

Rebuilding the Altar

3 When the seventh month came and the Israelites had settled in their towns,[u] the people assembled[v] as one man in Jerusalem. 2Then Jeshua[w] son of Jozadak[x] and his fellow priests and Zerubbabel son of Shealtiel[y] and his associates began to build the altar of the God of Israel to sacrifice burnt offerings on it, in accordance with what is written in the Law of Moses[z] the man of God. 3Despite their fear[a] of the peoples around them, they built the altar on its foundation and sacrificed burnt offerings on it to the LORD, both the morning and evening sacrifices.[b] 4Then in accordance with what is written, they celebrated the Feast of Tabernacles[c] with the required number

[d] 69 That is, about 1,100 pounds (about 500 kilograms) [e] 69 That is, about 3 tons (about 2.9 metric tons)

of burnt offerings prescribed for each day. ⁵After that, they presented the regular burnt offerings, the New Moon[d] sacrifices and the sacrifices for all the appointed sacred feasts of the LORD,[e] as well as those brought as freewill offerings to the LORD. ⁶On the first day of the seventh month they began to offer burnt offerings to the LORD, though the foundation of the LORD's temple had not yet been laid.

Rebuilding the Temple

⁷Then they gave money to the masons and carpenters,[f] and gave food and drink and oil to the people of Sidon and Tyre, so that they would bring cedar logs[g] by sea from Lebanon[h] to Joppa, as authorized by Cyrus[i] king of Persia.

⁸In the second month[j] of the second year after their arrival at the house of God in Jerusalem, Zerubbabel[k] son of Shealtiel, Jeshua son of Jozadak and the rest of their brothers (the priests and the Levites and all who had returned from the captivity to Jerusalem) began the work, appointing Levites twenty[l] years of age and older to supervise the building of the house of the LORD. ⁹Jeshua[m] and his sons and brothers and Kadmiel and his sons (descendants of Hodaviah[f]) and the sons of Henadad and their sons and brothers—all Levites—joined together in supervising those working on the house of God.

¹⁰When the builders laid[n] the foundation of the temple of the LORD, the priests in their vestments and with trumpets,[o] and the Levites (the sons of Asaph) with cymbals, took their places to praise[p] the LORD, as prescribed by David[q] king of Israel.[r] ¹¹With praise and thanksgiving they sang to the LORD:

"He is good;
  his love to Israel endures forever."[s]

And all the people gave a great shout[t] of praise to the LORD, because the foundation[u] of the house of the LORD was laid. ¹²But many of the older priests and Levites and family heads, who had seen the former temple,[v] wept[w] aloud when they

| 2Ch 20:7 ◀ ▶ Ne 1:9

3:5 ᵈS Nu 28:3,11, 14; Col 2:16
ᵉLev 23:1-44;
S Nu 29:39

3:7 ᶠ1Ch 22:15
ᵍS 1Ch 14:1
ʰIsa 35:2; 60:13
ⁱS Ezr 1:2-4

3:8 ʲ1Ki 6:1
ᵏZec 4:9 ˡS Nu 4:3

3:9 ᵐEzr 2:40

3:10 ⁿEzr 5:16;
6:3; Hag 2:15
ᵒS Nu 10:2;
S 2Sa 6:5;
1Ch 16:6;
2Ch 5:13; Ne 12:35
ᵖS 1Ch 25:1
ᵠS 1Ch 6:31
ʳZec 6:12

3:11 ˢ1Ch 16:34, 41; S 2Ch 7:3;
Ps 30:5; 107:1;
118:1; 138:8
ᵗS Jos 6:5,10
ᵘHag 2:18; Zec 4:9; 8:9

3:12 ᵛHag 2:3,9
ʷJer 31:9; 50:4

3:13 ˣJob 8:21; 33:26; Ps 27:6; 42:4; Isa 16:9; Jer 48:33

4:1 ʸNe 2:20

4:2 ᶻS 2Ki 17:24
ᵃS 2Ki 17:41

4:3 ᵇEzr 1:1-4

4:4 ᶜS Ezr 3:3

4:6 ᵈEst 1:1;
Da 9:1 ᵉEst 3:13; 9:5

4:7 ᶠEzr 7:1;
Ne 2:1 ᵍ2Ki 18:26; Isa 36:11; Da 1:4; 2:4

saw the foundation of this temple being laid, while many others shouted for joy. ¹³No one could distinguish the sound of the shouts of joy[x] from the sound of weeping, because the people made so much noise. And the sound was heard far away.

Opposition to the Rebuilding

4 When the enemies of Judah and Benjamin heard that the exiles were building[y] a temple for the LORD, the God of Israel, ²they came to Zerubbabel and to the heads of the families and said, "Let us help you build because, like you, we seek your God and have been sacrificing to him since the time of Esarhaddon[z] king of Assyria, who brought us here."[a]

³But Zerubbabel, Jeshua and the rest of the heads of the families of Israel answered, "You have no part with us in building a temple to our God. We alone will build it for the LORD, the God of Israel, as King Cyrus, the king of Persia, commanded us."[b]

⁴Then the peoples around them set out to discourage the people of Judah and make them afraid to go on building.[g][c] ⁵They hired counselors to work against them and frustrate their plans during the entire reign of Cyrus king of Persia and down to the reign of Darius king of Persia.

Later Opposition Under Xerxes and Artaxerxes

⁶At the beginning of the reign of Xerxes,[h][d] they lodged an accusation against the people of Judah and Jerusalem.[e]

⁷And in the days of Artaxerxes[f] king of Persia, Bishlam, Mithredath, Tabeel and the rest of his associates wrote a letter to Artaxerxes. The letter was written in Aramaic script and in the Aramaic[g] language.[i][j]

⁸Rehum the commanding officer and Shimshai the secretary wrote a letter against Jerusalem to Artaxerxes the king as follows:

ᶠ9 Hebrew Yehudah, probably a variant of Hodaviah ᵍ4 Or and troubled them as they built ʰ6 Hebrew Ahasuerus, a variant of Xerxes' Persian name ⁱ7 Or written in Aramaic and translated ʲ7 The text of Ezra 4:8—6:18 is in Aramaic.

3:11 During this victory celebration, Ezra recorded that the people's praise and thanks were directed toward the Lord because "he is good; his love to Israel endures forever."

⁹Rehum the commanding officer and Shimshai the secretary, together with the rest of their associates[h]— the judges and officials over the men from Tripolis, Persia,[k] Erech[i] and Babylon, the Elamites of Susa,[j] ¹⁰and the other people whom the great and honorable Ashurbanipal[l][k] deported and settled in the city of Samaria and elsewhere in Trans-Euphrates.[l]

¹¹(This is a copy of the letter they sent him.)

To King Artaxerxes,

From your servants, the men of Trans-Euphrates:

¹²The king should know that the Jews who came up to us from you have gone to Jerusalem and are rebuilding that rebellious and wicked city. They are restoring the walls and repairing the foundations.[m]

¹³Furthermore, the king should know that if this city is built and its walls are restored, no more taxes, tribute or duty[n] will be paid, and the royal revenues will suffer. ¹⁴Now since we are under obligation to the palace and it is not proper for us to see the king dishonored, we are sending this message to inform the king, ¹⁵so that a search may be made in the archives[o] of your predecessors. In these records you will find that this city is a rebellious city, troublesome to kings and provinces, a place of rebellion from ancient times. That is why this city was destroyed.[p] ¹⁶We inform the king that if this city is built and its walls are restored, you will be left with nothing in Trans-Euphrates.

¹⁷The king sent this reply:

To Rehum the commanding officer, Shimshai the secretary and the rest of their associates living in Samaria and elsewhere in Trans-Euphrates:[q]

Greetings.

¹⁸The letter you sent us has been read and translated in my presence. ¹⁹I issued an order and a search was made, and it was found that this city has a long history of revolt[r] against kings and has been a place of rebellion and sedition. ²⁰Jerusalem has had powerful kings ruling over the whole of Trans-Euphrates,[s] and taxes, tribute and duty were paid to them. ²¹Now issue an order to these men to stop work, so that this city will not be rebuilt until I so order. ²²Be careful not to neglect this matter. Why let this threat grow, to the detriment of the royal interests?[t]

²³As soon as the copy of the letter of King Artaxerxes was read to Rehum and Shimshai the secretary and their associates,[u] they went immediately to the Jews in Jerusalem and compelled them by force to stop.

²⁴Thus the work on the house of God in Jerusalem came to a standstill until the second year of the reign of Darius[v] king of Persia.

Tattenai's Letter to Darius

5 Now Haggai[w] the prophet and Zechariah[x] the prophet, a descendant of Iddo, prophesied[y] to the Jews in Judah and Jerusalem in the name of the God of Israel, who was over them. ²Then Zerubbabel[z] son of Shealtiel and Jeshua[a] son of Jozadak set to work[b] to rebuild the house of God in Jerusalem. And the prophets of God were with them, helping them.

³At that time Tattenai,[c] governor of Trans-Euphrates, and Shethar-Bozenai[d] and their associates went to them and asked, "Who authorized you to rebuild this temple and restore this structure?"[e] ⁴They also asked, "What are the names of the men constructing this building?"[m] ⁵But the eye of their God[f] was watching over the elders of the Jews, and they were not stopped until a report could go to Darius and his written reply be received.

⁶This is a copy of the letter that Tattenai, governor of Trans-Euphrates, and Shethar-Bozenai and their associates, the officials of Trans-Euphrates, sent to King Darius. ⁷The report they sent him read as follows:

To King Darius:

---

[k] 9 Or *officials, magistrates and governors over the men from*
[l] 10 Aramaic *Osnappar*, a variant of *Ashurbanipal* [m] 4 See Septuagint; Aramaic *⁴We told them the names of the men constructing this building.*

Cordial greetings.

⁸The king should know that we went to the district of Judah, to the temple of the great God. The people are building it with large stones and placing the timbers in the walls. The work is being carried on with diligence and is making rapid progress under their direction.

⁹We questioned the elders and asked them, "Who authorized you to rebuild this temple and restore this structure?" ¹⁰We also asked them their names, so that we could write down the names of their leaders for your information.

¹¹This is the answer they gave us:

"We are the servants of the God of heaven and earth, and we are rebuilding the temple that was built many years ago, one that a great king of Israel built and finished. ¹²But because our fathers angered the God of heaven, he handed them over to Nebuchadnezzar the Chaldean, king of Babylon, who destroyed this temple and deported the people to Babylon.

¹³"However, in the first year of Cyrus king of Babylon, King Cyrus issued a decree to rebuild this house of God. ¹⁴He even removed from the temple of Babylon the gold and silver articles of the house of God, which Nebuchadnezzar had taken from the temple in Jerusalem and brought to the temple in Babylon.

"Then King Cyrus gave them to a man named Sheshbazzar, whom he had appointed governor, ¹⁵and he told him, 'Take these articles and go and deposit them in the temple in Jerusalem. And rebuild the house of God on its site.' ¹⁶So this Sheshbazzar came and laid the foundations of the house of God in Jerusalem. From that day to the present it has been under construction but is not yet finished."

¹⁷Now if it pleases the king, let a search be made in the royal archives of Babylon to see if King Cyrus did in fact issue a decree to rebuild this house of God in Jerusalem.

Then let the king send us his decision in this matter.

The Decree of Darius

6 King Darius then issued an order, and they searched in the archives stored in the treasury at Babylon. ²A scroll was found in the citadel of Ecbatana in the province of Media, and this was written on it:

Memorandum:

³In the first year of King Cyrus, the king issued a decree concerning the temple of God in Jerusalem:

Let the temple be rebuilt as a place to present sacrifices, and let its foundations be laid. It is to be ninety feet[o] high and ninety feet wide, ⁴with three courses of large stones and one of timbers. The costs are to be paid by the royal treasury. ⁵Also, the gold and silver articles of the house of God, which Nebuchadnezzar took from the temple in Jerusalem and brought to Babylon, are to be returned to their places in the temple in Jerusalem; they are to be deposited in the house of God.

⁶Now then, Tattenai, governor of Trans-Euphrates, and Shethar-Bozenai and you, their fellow officials of that province, stay away from there. ⁷Do not interfere with the work on this temple of God. Let the governor of the Jews and the Jewish elders rebuild this house of God on its site.

⁸Moreover, I hereby decree what you are to do for these elders of the Jews in the construction of this house of God:

The expenses of these men are to be fully paid out of the royal treasury, from the revenues of Trans-Euphrates, so that the work will not stop. ⁹Whatever is needed—young bulls, rams, male lambs for burnt offerings to the God of heaven, and wheat, salt, wine and oil, as requested by the priests in Jerusalem—must be given them daily without fail, ¹⁰so that they may offer sacrifices pleasing to the God of

---

n 14 Or palace   o 3 Aramaic sixty cubits (about 27 meters)

heaven and pray for the well-being of the king and his sons.[b] [11]Furthermore, I decree that if anyone changes this edict, a beam is to be pulled from his house and he is to be lifted up and impaled[c] on it. And for this crime his house is to be made a pile of rubble.[d] [12]May God, who has caused his Name to dwell there,[e] overthrow any king or people who lifts a hand to change this decree or to destroy this temple in Jerusalem.

I, Darius,[f] have decreed it. Let it be carried out with diligence.

Completion and Dedication of the Temple

[13]Then, because of the decree King Darius had sent, Tattenai, governor of Trans-Euphrates, and Shethar-Bozenai and their associates[g] carried it out with diligence. [14]So the elders of the Jews continued to build and prosper under the preaching[h] of Haggai the prophet and Zechariah, a descendant of Iddo. They finished building the temple according to the command of the God of Israel and the decrees of Cyrus,[i] Darius[j] and Artaxerxes,[k] kings of Persia. [15]The temple was completed on the third day of the month Adar, in the sixth year of the reign of King Darius.[l]

[16]Then the people of Israel—the priests, the Levites and the rest of the exiles—celebrated the dedication[m] of the house of God with joy. [17]For the dedication of this house of God they offered[n] a hundred bulls, two hundred rams, four hundred male lambs and, as a sin offering for all Israel, twelve male goats, one for each of the tribes of Israel. [18]And they installed the priests in their divisions[o] and the Levites in their groups[p] for the service of God at Jerusalem, according to what is written in the Book of Moses.[q]

The Passover

D [19]On the fourteenth day of the first month, the exiles celebrated the Passover.[r] [20]The priests and Levites had purified themselves and were all ceremonially clean. The Levites slaughtered[s] the Passover lamb for all the exiles, for their brothers the priests and for themselves.

D 2Ch 35:1 ◀▶ Ps 22:13–18

[21]So the Israelites who had returned from the exile ate it, together with all who had separated themselves[t] from the unclean practices[u] of their Gentile neighbors in order to seek the LORD,[v] the God of Israel. [22]For seven days they celebrated with joy the Feast of Unleavened Bread,[w] because the LORD had filled them with joy by changing the attitude[x] of the king of Assyria, so that he assisted them in the work on the house of God, the God of Israel.

Ezra Comes to Jerusalem

7 After these things, during the reign of Artaxerxes[y] king of Persia, Ezra son of Seraiah,[z] the son of Azariah, the son of Hilkiah,[a] [2]the son of Shallum, the son of Zadok,[b] the son of Ahitub,[c] [3]the son of Amariah, the son of Azariah, the son of Meraioth, [4]the son of Zerahiah, the son of Uzzi, the son of Bukki, [5]the son of Abishua, the son of Phinehas,[d] the son of Eleazar, the son of Aaron the chief priest— [6]this Ezra[e] came up from Babylon. He was a teacher well versed in the Law of Moses, which the LORD, the God of Israel, had given. The king had granted[f] him everything he asked, for the hand of the LORD his God was on him.[g] [7]Some of the Israelites, including priests, Levites, singers, gatekeepers and temple servants, also came up to Jerusalem in the seventh year of King Artaxerxes.[h]

[8]Ezra arrived in Jerusalem in the fifth month of the seventh year of the king. [9]He had begun his journey from Babylon on the first day of the first month, and he arrived in Jerusalem on the first day of the fifth month, for the gracious hand of his God was on him.[i] [10]For Ezra had devoted himself to the study and observance of the Law of the LORD, and to teaching[j] its decrees and laws in Israel.

King Artaxerxes' Letter to Ezra

[11]This is a copy of the letter King Artaxerxes had given to Ezra the priest and teacher, a man learned in matters concerning the commands and decrees of the LORD for Israel:

[12p]Artaxerxes, king of kings,[k]

To Ezra the priest, a teacher of the Law of the God of heaven:

p 12 The text of Ezra 7:12-26 is in Aramaic.

Greetings.

¹³Now I decree that any of the Israelites in my kingdom, including priests and Levites, who wish to go to Jerusalem with you, may go. ¹⁴You are sent by the king and his seven advisers[1] to inquire about Judah and Jerusalem with regard to the Law of your God, which is in your hand. ¹⁵Moreover, you are to take with you the silver and gold that the king and his advisers have freely given[m] to the God of Israel, whose dwelling[n] is in Jerusalem, ¹⁶together with all the silver and gold[o] you may obtain from the province of Babylon, as well as the freewill offerings of the people and priests for the temple of their God in Jerusalem.[p] ¹⁷With this money be sure to buy bulls, rams and male lambs,[q] together with their grain offerings and drink offerings,[r] and sacrifice[s] them on the altar of the temple of your God in Jerusalem.

¹⁸You and your brother Jews may then do whatever seems best with the rest of the silver and gold, in accordance with the will of your God. ¹⁹Deliver[t] to the God of Jerusalem all the articles entrusted to you for worship in the temple of your God. ²⁰And anything else needed for the temple of your God that you may have occasion to supply, you may provide from the royal treasury.[u]

²¹Now I, King Artaxerxes, order all the treasurers of Trans-Euphrates to provide with diligence whatever Ezra the priest, a teacher of the Law of the God of heaven, may ask of you— ²²up to a hundred talents[q] of silver, a hundred cors[r] of wheat, a hundred baths[s] of wine, a hundred baths[s] of olive oil, and salt without limit. ²³Whatever the God of heaven has prescribed, let it be done with diligence for the temple of the God of heaven. Why should there be wrath against the realm of the king and his sons?[v] ²⁴You are also to know that you have no authority to impose taxes, tribute or duty[w] on any of the priests, Levites, singers, gatekeepers, temple servants or other workers at this house of God.[x]

²⁵And you, Ezra, in accordance with the wisdom of your God, which you possess, appoint[y] magistrates and judges to administer justice to all the people of Trans-Euphrates—all who know the laws of your God. And you are to teach[z] any who do not know them. ²⁶Whoever does not obey the law of your God and the law of the king must surely be punished by death, banishment, confiscation of property, or imprisonment.[a]

²⁷Praise be to the LORD, the God of our fathers, who has put it into the king's heart[b] to bring honor[c] to the house of the LORD in Jerusalem in this way ²⁸and who has extended his good favor[d] to me before the king and his advisers and all the king's powerful officials. Because the hand of the LORD my God was on me,[e] I took courage and gathered leading men from Israel to go up with me.

List of the Family Heads Returning With Ezra

8 These are the family heads and those registered with them who came up with me from Babylon during the reign of King Artaxerxes:[f]

²of the descendants of Phinehas, Gershom;
of the descendants of Ithamar, Daniel;
of the descendants of David, Hattush ³of the descendants of Shecaniah;[g]

of the descendants of Parosh,[h] Zechariah, and with him were registered 150 men;
⁴of the descendants of Pahath-Moab,[i] Eliehoenai son of Zerahiah, and with him 200 men;
⁵of the descendants of Zattu,[t] Shecaniah son of Jahaziel, and with him 300 men;
⁶of the descendants of Adin,[j] Ebed son of Jonathan, and with him 50 men;

---

q 22 That is, about 3 3/4 tons (about 3.4 metric tons) *r 22* That is, probably about 600 bushels (about 22 kiloliters) *s 22* That is, probably about 600 gallons (about 2.2 kiloliters) *t 5* Some Septuagint manuscripts (also 1 Esdras 8:32); Hebrew does not have *Zattu*.

EZRA 8:7

⁷of the descendants of Elam, Jeshaiah son of Athaliah, and with him 70 men;
⁸of the descendants of Shephatiah, Zebadiah son of Michael, and with him 80 men;
⁹of the descendants of Joab, Obadiah son of Jehiel, and with him 218 men;
¹⁰of the descendants of Bani,ᵘ Shelomith son of Josiphiah, and with him 160 men;
¹¹of the descendants of Bebai, Zechariah son of Bebai, and with him 28 men;
¹²of the descendants of Azgad, Johanan son of Hakkatan, and with him 110 men;
¹³of the descendants of Adonikam,ᵏ the last ones, whose names were Eliphelet, Jeuel and Shemaiah, and with them 60 men;
¹⁴of the descendants of Bigvai, Uthai and Zaccur, and with them 70 men.

The Return to Jerusalem

¹⁵I assembled them at the canal that flows toward Ahava,¹ and we camped there three days. When I checked among the people and the priests, I found no Levitesᵐ there. ¹⁶So I summoned Eliezer, Ariel, Shemaiah, Elnathan, Jarib, Elnathan, Nathan, Zechariah and Meshullam, who were leaders, and Joiarib and Elnathan, who were men of learning, ¹⁷and I sent them to Iddo, the leader in Casiphia. I told them what to say to Iddo and his kinsmen, the temple servantsⁿ in Casiphia, so that they might bring attendants to us for the house of our God. ¹⁸Because the gracious hand of our God was on us,ᵒ they brought us Sherebiah,ᵖ a capable man, from the descendants of Mahli son of Levi, the son of Israel, and Sherebiah's sons and brothers, 18 men; ¹⁹and Hashabiah, together with Jeshaiah from the descendants of Merari, and his brothers and nephews, 20 men. ²⁰They also brought 220 of the temple servantsᵠ—a body that David and the officials had established to assist the Levites. All were registered by name.

²¹There, by the Ahava Canal,ʳ I proclaimed a fast, so that we might humble ourselves before our God and ask him for a safe journeyˢ for us and our children,

8:13 ᵏ Ezr 2:13
8:15 ˡ ver 21,31
      ᵐ S Ezr 2:40
8:17 ⁿ Ezr 2:43
8:18 ᵒ S Ezr 5:5
      ᵖ ver 24
8:20 ᵠ S 1Ch 9:2
8:21 ʳ S ver 15
      ˢ Ps 5:8; 27:11; 107:7
8:22 ᵗ Ne 2:9; Jer 41:16
      ᵘ S Ezr 5:5
      ᵛ S Dt 31:17
8:23 ʷ S 2Ch 20:3; Ac 14:23
8:24 ˣ ver 18
8:25 ʸ ver 33
8:28 ᶻ S Lev 21:6; 22:2-3
8:31 ᵃ S ver 15
      ᵇ S Ezr 5:5
8:32 ᶜ S Ge 40:13
8:33 ᵈ ver 25
      ᵉ Ne 3:4,21

with all our possessions. ²²I was ashamed to ask the king for soldiersᵗ and horsemen to protect us from enemies on the road, because we had told the king, "The gracious hand of our God is on everyoneᵘ who looks to him, but his great anger is against all who forsake him."ᵛ ²³So we fastedʷ and petitioned our God about this, and he answered our prayer.

²⁴Then I set apart twelve of the leading priests, together with Sherebiah,ˣ Hashabiah and ten of their brothers, ²⁵and I weighed outʸ to them the offering of silver and gold and the articles that the king, his advisers, his officials and all Israel present there had donated for the house of our God. ²⁶I weighed out to them 650 talentsᵛ of silver, silver articles weighing 100 talents,ʷ 100 talentsʷ of gold, ²⁷20 bowls of gold valued at 1,000 darics,ˣ and two fine articles of polished bronze, as precious as gold.

²⁸I said to them, "You as well as these articles are consecrated to the LORD.ᶻ The silver and gold are a freewill offering to the LORD, the God of your fathers. ²⁹Guard them carefully until you weigh them out in the chambers of the house of the LORD in Jerusalem before the leading priests and the Levites and the family heads of Israel." ³⁰Then the priests and Levites received the silver and gold and sacred articles that had been weighed out to be taken to the house of our God in Jerusalem.

³¹On the twelfth day of the first month we set out from the Ahava Canalᵃ to go to Jerusalem. The hand of our God was on us,ᵇ and he protected us from enemies and bandits along the way. ³²So we arrived in Jerusalem, where we rested three days.ᶜ

³³On the fourth day, in the house of our God, we weighed outᵈ the silver and gold and the sacred articles into the hands of Meremothᵉ son of Uriah, the

H 2Ch 36:16 ◀▶ Job 4:8–9
L 2Ch 30:9 ◀▶ Ne 9:17
W 2Sa 22:31 ◀▶ Ps 2:12
U 2Ch 32:30 ◀▶ Ne 1:5
S 2Ch 24:20 ◀▶ Job 4:8

ᵘ 10 Some Septuagint manuscripts (also 1 Esdras 8:36); Hebrew does not have *Bani*. ᵛ 26 That is, about 25 tons (about 22 metric tons) ʷ 26 That is, about 3 3/4 tons (about 3.4 metric tons) ˣ 27 That is, about 19 pounds (about 8.5 kilograms)

priest. Eleazar son of Phinehas was with him, and so were the Levites Jozabadᶠ son of Jeshua and Noadiah son of Binnui.ᵍ ³⁴Everything was accounted for by number and weight, and the entire weight was recorded at that time.

³⁵Then the exiles who had returned from captivity sacrificed burnt offerings to the God of Israel: twelve bullsʰ for all Israel,ⁱ ninety-six rams, seventy-seven male lambs and, as a sin offering, twelve male goats.ʲ All this was a burnt offering to the LORD. ³⁶They also delivered the king's ordersᵏ to the royal satraps and to the governors of Trans-Euphrates,ˡ who then gave assistance to the people and to the house of God.ᵐ

Ezra's Prayer About Intermarriage

9 After these things had been done, the leaders came to me and said, "The people of Israel, including the priests and the Levites, have not kept themselves separateⁿ from the neighboring peoples with their detestable practices, like those of the Canaanites, Hittites, Perizzites, Jebusites,ᵒ Ammonites,ᵖ Moabites,ᑫ Egyptians and Amorites.ʳ ²They have taken some of their daughtersˢ as wives for themselves and their sons, and have mingledᵗ the holy raceᵘ with the peoples around them. And the leaders and officials have led the way in this unfaithfulness."ᵛ

³When I heard this, I toreʷ my tunic and cloak, pulled hair from my head and beard and sat down appalled.ˣ ⁴Then everyone who trembledʸ at the words of the God of Israel gathered around me because of this unfaithfulness of the exiles. And I sat there appalledᶻ until the evening sacrifice.

M ⁵Then, at the evening sacrifice,ᵃ I rose from my self-abasement, with my tunic and cloak torn, and fell on my knees with my handsᵇ spread out to the LORD my God ⁶and prayed:

"O my God, I am too ashamedᶜ and disgraced to lift up my face to you, my God, because our sins are higher than our heads and our guilt has reached to the heavens.ᵈ ⁷From the days of our forefathersᵉ until

M 2Ch 34:27 ◀ ▶ Ezr 10:1

now, our guilt has been great. Because of our sins, we and our kings and our priests have been subjected to the swordᶠ and captivity,ᵍ to pillage and humiliationʰ at the hand of foreign kings, as it is today.

⁸"But now, for a brief moment, the LORD our God has been graciousⁱ in leaving us a remnantʲ and giving us a firm placeᵏ in his sanctuary, and so our God gives light to our eyesˡ and a little relief in our bondage. ⁹Though we are slaves,ᵐ our God has not deserted us in our bondage. He has shown us kindnessⁿ in the sight of the kings of Persia: He has granted us new life to rebuild the house of our God and repair its ruins,ᵒ and he has given us a wall of protection in Judah and Jerusalem.

¹⁰"But now, O our God, what can we say after this? For we have disregarded the commandsᵖ ¹¹you gave through your servants the prophets when you said: 'The land you are enteringᑫ to possess is a land pollutedʳ by the corruption of its peoples. By their detestable practicesˢ they have filled it with their impurity from one end to the other. ¹²Therefore, do not give your daughters in marriage to their sons or take their daughters for your sons. Do not seek a treaty of friendship with themᵗ at any time, that you may be strongᵘ and eat the good thingsᵛ of the land and leave it to your children as an everlasting inheritance.'ʷ

¹³"What has happened to us is a result of our evilˣ deeds and our great guilt, and yet, our God, you have punished us less than our sins have deservedʸ and have given us a remnant like this. ¹⁴Shall we again break your commands and intermarryᶻ with the peoples who commit such detestable practices? Would you not be angry enough with us to destroy us,ᵃ leaving us no remnantᵇ or survivor? ¹⁵O LORD, God of Israel, you are righteous!ᶜ We are left this day as a remnant. Here we are before you in our guilt, though because of it not one of us can standᵈ in your presence.ᵉ"

The People's Confession of Sin

10 While Ezra was praying and confessing, weeping and throwing himself down before the house of God, a large crowd of Israelites—men, women and children—gathered around him. They too wept bitterly. ²Then Shecaniah son of Jehiel, one of the descendants of Elam, said to Ezra, "We have been unfaithful to our God by marrying foreign women from the peoples around us. But in spite of this, there is still hope for Israel. ³Now let us make a covenant before our God to send away all these women and their children, in accordance with the counsel of my lord and of those who fear the commands of our God. Let it be done according to the Law. ⁴Rise up; this matter is in your hands. We will support you, so take courage and do it."

⁵So Ezra rose up and put the leading priests and Levites and all Israel under oath to do what had been suggested. And they took the oath. ⁶Then Ezra withdrew from before the house of God and went to the room of Jehohanan son of Eliashib. While he was there, he ate no food and drank no water, because he continued to mourn over the unfaithfulness of the exiles.

⁷A proclamation was then issued throughout Judah and Jerusalem for all the exiles to assemble in Jerusalem. ⁸Anyone who failed to appear within three days would forfeit all his property, in accordance with the decision of the officials and elders, and would himself be expelled from the assembly of the exiles.

⁹Within the three days, all the men of Judah and Benjamin had gathered in Jerusalem. And on the twentieth day of the ninth month, all the people were sitting in the square before the house of God, greatly distressed by the occasion and because of the rain. ¹⁰Then Ezra the priest stood up and said to them, "You have been unfaithful; you have married foreign women, adding to Israel's guilt. ¹¹Now make confession to the LORD, the God of your fathers, and do his will. Separate yourselves from the peoples around you and from your foreign wives."

¹²The whole assembly responded with a loud voice: "You are right! We must do as you say. ¹³But there are many people here and it is the rainy season; so we cannot stand outside. Besides, this matter cannot be taken care of in a day or two, because we have sinned greatly in this thing. ¹⁴Let our officials act for the whole assembly. Then let everyone in our towns who has married a foreign woman come at a set time, along with the elders and judges of each town, until the fierce anger of our God in this matter is turned away from us." ¹⁵Only Jonathan son of Asahel and Jahzeiah son of Tikvah, supported by Meshullam and Shabbethai the Levite, opposed this.

¹⁶So the exiles did as was proposed. Ezra the priest selected men who were family heads, one from each family division, and all of them designated by name. On the first day of the tenth month they sat down to investigate the cases, ¹⁷and by the first day of the first month they finished dealing with all the men who had married foreign women.

Those Guilty of Intermarriage

¹⁸Among the descendants of the priests, the following had married foreign women:

From the descendants of Jeshua son of Jozadak, and his brothers: Maaseiah, Eliezer, Jarib and Gedaliah. ¹⁹(They all gave their hands in pledge to put away their wives, and for their guilt they each presented a ram from the flock as a guilt offering.)

²⁰From the descendants of Immer: Hanani and Zebadiah.

²¹From the descendants of Harim: Maaseiah, Elijah, Shemaiah, Jehiel and Uzziah.

²²From the descendants of Pashhur: Elioenai, Maaseiah, Ishmael, Nethanel, Jozabad and Elasah.

²³Among the Levites:

Jozabad, Shimei, Kelaiah (that is, Kelita), Pethahiah, Judah and Eliezer.

²⁴From the singers:
Eliashib.
From the gatekeepers:
Shallum, Telem and Uri.

²⁵And among the other Israelites:

From the descendants of Parosh:[f]
Ramiah, Izziah, Malkijah, Mijamin, Eleazar, Malkijah and Benaiah.
²⁶From the descendants of Elam:[g]
Mattaniah, Zechariah, Jehiel, Abdi, Jeremoth and Elijah.
²⁷From the descendants of Zattu:
Elioenai, Eliashib, Mattaniah, Jeremoth, Zabad and Aziza.
²⁸From the descendants of Bebai:
Jehohanan, Hananiah, Zabbai and Athlai.
²⁹From the descendants of Bani:
Meshullam, Malluch, Adaiah, Jashub, Sheal and Jeremoth.
³⁰From the descendants of Pahath-Moab:
Adna, Kelal, Benaiah, Maaseiah, Mattaniah, Bezalel, Binnui and Manasseh.
³¹From the descendants of Harim:
Eliezer, Ishijah, Malkijah, Shemaiah, Shimeon, ³²Benjamin, Malluch and Shemariah.
³³From the descendants of Hashum:
Mattenai, Mattattah, Zabad, Eliphelet, Jeremai, Manasseh and Shimei.
³⁴From the descendants of Bani:
Maadai, Amram, Uel, ³⁵Benaiah, Bedeiah, Keluhi, ³⁶Vaniah, Meremoth, Eliashib, ³⁷Mattaniah, Mattenai and Jaasu.
³⁸From the descendants of Binnui:[y]
Shimei, ³⁹Shelemiah, Nathan, Adaiah, ⁴⁰Macnadebai, Shashai, Sharai, ⁴¹Azarel, Shelemiah, Shemariah, ⁴²Shallum, Amariah and Joseph.
⁴³From the descendants of Nebo:
Jeiel, Mattithiah, Zabad, Zebina, Jaddai, Joel and Benaiah.

⁴⁴All these had married foreign women, and some of them had children by these wives.[z]

---

[y] 37,38 See Septuagint (also 1 Esdras 9:34); Hebrew *Jaasu ³⁸and Bani and Binnui,* [z] 44 Or *and they sent them away with their children*

Nehemiah

Author: Nehemiah

Theme: Rebuilding Jerusalem's walls

Date of Writing: c. 430 B.C.

Outline of Nehemiah
I. Nehemiah Returns to Rebuild the Walls (1:1—2:8)
II. Rebuilding the Walls of Jerusalem (2:9—7:73)
III. The Great Revival Under Ezra (8:1—10:39)
IV. Nehemiah's Policies and Programs (11:1—13:31)

THIS BOOK IS named for Nehemiah, a governor of Judah and one of the main characters in this narrative. Containing vivid details, Nehemiah's book completes the history of the restoration of Jerusalem that was begun under Ezra's leadership.

Formerly a cupbearer to King Artaxerxes, Nehemiah was sent to Jerusalem to act as governor and to help rebuild Jerusalem's city walls. The temple had already been rebuilt, as recorded in Ezra, yet the city walls remained in ruins. With energy, piety and honesty, Nehemiah faced the obstacles that had stalled the project and brought the reconstruction to completion in a record fifty-two days. Nehemiah tackled this project with a deep dependence on God, praying for God's help more than ten times in this short book.

The book of Nehemiah is important prophetically because it marks the beginning of Daniel's prophecy that "from the issuing of the decree to restore and rebuild Jerusalem until the Anointed One, the ruler, comes, there will be seven 'sevens' " (Da 9:25). Though other decrees had been issued to other exiles to rebuild the temple, Artaxerxes' decree recorded for the first time that permission had been granted to rebuild the city of Jerusalem (2:1–8). Thus Nehemiah's book inaugurates the divine time period of Daniel's prophecy.

Nehemiah's Prayer

1 The words of Nehemiah son of Hacaliah:

In the month of Kislev[a] in the twentieth year, while I was in the citadel of Susa,[b] ²Hanani,[c] one of my brothers, came from Judah with some other men, and I questioned them about the Jewish remnant[d] that survived the exile, and also about Jerusalem.

³They said to me, "Those who survived the exile and are back in the province are in great trouble and disgrace. The wall of Jerusalem is broken down, and its gates have been burned with fire.[e]"

⁴When I heard these things, I sat down and wept.[f] For some days I mourned and fasted[g] and prayed before the God of heaven. ⁵Then I said:

"O Lord, God of heaven, the great and awesome God,[h] who keeps his covenant of love[i] with those who love him and obey his commands, ⁶let your ear be attentive and your eyes open to hear[j] the prayer[k] your servant is praying before you day and night for your servants, the people of Israel. I confess[l] the sins we Israelites, including myself and my father's house, have committed against you. ⁷We have acted very wickedly[m] toward you. We have not obeyed the commands, decrees and laws you gave your servant Moses.

⁸"Remember[n] the instruction you gave your servant Moses, saying, 'If you are unfaithful, I will scatter[o] you among the nations, ⁹but if you return to me and obey my commands, then even if your exiled people are at the farthest horizon, I will gather[p] them from there and bring them to the place I have chosen as a dwelling for my Name.'[q]

¹⁰"They are your servants and your people, whom you redeemed by your great strength and your mighty hand.[r] ¹¹O Lord, let your ear be attentive[s] to the prayer of this your servant and to the prayer of your servants who delight in revering your name. Give your servant success today by granting him favor[t] in the presence of this man."

I was cupbearer[u] to the king.

Artaxerxes Sends Nehemiah to Jerusalem

2 In the month of Nisan in the twentieth year of King Artaxerxes,[v] when wine was brought for him, I took the wine and gave it to the king. I had not been sad in his presence before; ²so the king asked me, "Why does your face look so sad when you are not ill? This can be nothing but sadness of heart."

I was very much afraid, ³but I said to the king, "May the king live forever![w] Why should my face not look sad when the city[x] where my fathers are buried lies in ruins, and its gates have been destroyed by fire?[y]"

⁴The king said to me, "What is it you want?"

Then I prayed to the God of heaven, ⁵and I answered the king, "If it pleases the king and if your servant has found favor in his sight, let him send me to the city in Judah where my fathers are buried so that I can rebuild it."

⁶Then the king,[z] with the queen sitting beside him, asked me, "How long will your journey take, and when will you get back?" It pleased the king to send me; so I set a time.

⁷I also said to him, "If it pleases the king, may I have letters to the governors of Trans-Euphrates,[a] so that they will provide me safe-conduct until I arrive in Judah? ⁸And may I have a letter to Asaph, keeper of the king's forest, so he will give me timber to make beams for the gates of the citadel[b] by the temple and for the city wall and for the residence I will occupy?" And because the gracious hand of my God was upon me,[c] the king granted my

---

1:8–9 Once again the promise is given, if Israel sins "I will scatter you among the nations" (1:8), but repentance would result in their return to "the place I have chosen as a dwelling for my Name" (1:9). See note on the Palestinian covenant at Dt 30:1–20.

requests.^d ^9So I went to the governors of Trans-Euphrates and gave them the king's letters. The king had also sent army officers and cavalry^e with me.

^10When Sanballat^f the Horonite and Tobiah^g the Ammonite official heard about this, they were very much disturbed that someone had come to promote the welfare of the Israelites.^h

Nehemiah Inspects Jerusalem's Walls

^11I went to Jerusalem, and after staying there three days^i ^12I set out during the night with a few men. I had not told anyone what my God had put in my heart to do for Jerusalem. There were no mounts with me except the one I was riding on.

^13By night I went out through the Valley Gate^j toward the Jackal^a Well and the Dung Gate,^k examining the walls^l of Jerusalem, which had been broken down, and its gates, which had been destroyed by fire. ^14Then I moved on toward the Fountain Gate^m and the King's Pool,^n but there was not enough room for my mount to get through; ^15so I went up the valley by night, examining the wall. Finally, I turned back and reentered through the Valley Gate. ^16The officials did not know where I had gone or what I was doing, because as yet I had said nothing to the Jews or the priests or nobles or officials or any others who would be doing the work.

^17Then I said to them, "You see the trouble we are in: Jerusalem lies in ruins, and its gates have been burned with fire.^o Come, let us rebuild the wall^p of Jerusalem, and we will no longer be in disgrace.^q" ^18I also told them about the gracious hand of my God upon me^r and what the king had said to me.

They replied, "Let us start rebuilding." So they began this good work.

^19But when Sanballat^s the Horonite, Tobiah the Ammonite official and Geshem^t the Arab heard about it, they mocked and ridiculed us.^u "What is this you are doing?" they asked. "Are you rebelling against the king?"

^20I answered them by saying, "The God of heaven will give us success. We his servants will start rebuilding,^v but as for you, you have no share^w in Jerusalem or any claim or historic right to it."

Builders of the Wall

3 Eliashib^x the high priest and his fellow priests went to work and rebuilt^y the Sheep Gate.^z They dedicated it and set its doors in place, building as far as the Tower of the Hundred, which they dedicated, and as far as the Tower of Hananel.^a ^2The men of Jericho^b built the adjoining section, and Zaccur son of Imri built next to them.

^3The Fish Gate^c was rebuilt by the sons of Hassenaah. They laid its beams and put its doors and bolts and bars in place. ^4Meremoth^d son of Uriah, the son of Hakkoz, repaired the next section. Next to him Meshullam son of Berekiah, the son of Meshezabel, made repairs, and next to him Zadok son of Baana also made repairs. ^5The next section was repaired by the men of Tekoa,^e but their nobles would not put their shoulders to the work under their supervisors.^b

^6The Jeshanah^c Gate^f was repaired by Joiada son of Paseah and Meshullam son of Besodeiah. They laid its beams and put its doors and bolts and bars in place. ^7Next to them, repairs were made by men from Gibeon^g and Mizpah—Melatiah of Gibeon and Jadon of Meronoth—places under the authority of the governor of Trans-Euphrates. ^8Uzziel son of Harhaiah, one of the goldsmiths, repaired the next section; and Hananiah, one of the perfume-makers, made repairs next to that. They restored^d Jerusalem as far as the Broad Wall.^h ^9Rephaiah son of Hur, ruler of a half-district of Jerusalem, repaired the next section. ^10Adjoining this, Jedaiah son of Harumaph made repairs opposite his house, and Hattush son of Hashabneiah made repairs next to him. ^11Malkijah son of Harim and Hasshub son of Pahath-Moab repaired another section and the Tower of the Ovens.^i ^12Shallum son of Hallohesh, ruler of a half-district of Jerusalem, repaired the next section with the help of his daughters.

^13The Valley Gate^j was repaired by Hanun and the residents of Zanoah.^k They rebuilt it and put its doors and bolts and bars in place. They also repaired five hun-

---

^a 13 Or Serpent or Fig ^b 5 Or their Lord or the governor ^c 6 Or Old
^d 8 Or They left out part of

dred yards[e] of the wall as far as the Dung Gate.[l]

¹⁴The Dung Gate was repaired by Malkijah son of Recab, ruler of the district of Beth Hakkerem.[m] He rebuilt it and put its doors and bolts and bars in place.

¹⁵The Fountain Gate was repaired by Shallun son of Col-Hozeh, ruler of the district of Mizpah. He rebuilt it, roofing it over and putting its doors and bolts and bars in place. He also repaired the wall of the Pool of Siloam,[f,n] by the King's Garden, as far as the steps going down from the City of David. ¹⁶Beyond him, Nehemiah son of Azbuk, ruler of a half-district of Beth Zur,[o] made repairs up to a point opposite the tombs[g,p] of David, as far as the artificial pool and the House of the Heroes.

¹⁷Next to him, the repairs were made by the Levites under Rehum son of Bani. Beside him, Hashabiah, ruler of half the district of Keilah,[q] carried out repairs for his district. ¹⁸Next to him, the repairs were made by their countrymen under Binnui[h] son of Henadad, ruler of the other half-district of Keilah. ¹⁹Next to him, Ezer son of Jeshua, ruler of Mizpah, repaired another section, from a point facing the ascent to the armory as far as the angle. ²⁰Next to him, Baruch son of Zabbai zealously repaired another section, from the angle to the entrance of the house of Eliashib the high priest. ²¹Next to him, Meremoth[r] son of Uriah, the son of Hakkoz, repaired another section, from the entrance of Eliashib's house to the end of it.

²²The repairs next to him were made by the priests from the surrounding region. ²³Beyond them, Benjamin and Hasshub made repairs in front of their house; and next to them, Azariah son of Maaseiah, the son of Ananiah, made repairs beside his house. ²⁴Next to him, Binnui[s] son of Henadad repaired another section, from Azariah's house to the angle and the corner, ²⁵and Palal son of Uzai worked opposite the angle and the tower projecting from the upper palace near the court of the guard.[t] Next to him, Pedaiah son of Parosh[u] ²⁶and the temple servants[v] living on the hill of Ophel[w] made repairs up to a point opposite the Water Gate[x] toward the east and the projecting tower. ²⁷Next to them, the men of Tekoa[y] repaired another section, from the great projecting tower[z] to the wall of Ophel.

²⁸Above the Horse Gate,[a] the priests made repairs, each in front of his own house. ²⁹Next to them, Zadok son of Immer made repairs opposite his house. Next to him, Shemaiah son of Shecaniah, the guard at the East Gate, made repairs. ³⁰Next to him, Hananiah son of Shelemiah, and Hanun, the sixth son of Zalaph, repaired another section. Next to them, Meshullam son of Berekiah made repairs opposite his living quarters. ³¹Next to him, Malkijah, one of the goldsmiths, made repairs as far as the house of the temple servants and the merchants, opposite the Inspection Gate, and as far as the room above the corner; ³²and between the room above the corner and the Sheep Gate[b] the goldsmiths and merchants made repairs.

Opposition to the Rebuilding

4 When Sanballat[c] heard that we were rebuilding the wall, he became angry and was greatly incensed. He ridiculed the Jews, ²and in the presence of his associates[d] and the army of Samaria, he said, "What are those feeble Jews doing? Will they restore their wall? Will they offer sacrifices? Will they finish in a day? Can they bring the stones back to life from those heaps of rubble[e]—burned as they are?"

³Tobiah[f] the Ammonite, who was at his side, said, "What they are building—if even a fox climbed up on it, he would break down their wall of stones!"[g]

⁴Hear us, O our God, for we are despised.[h] Turn their insults back on their own heads. Give them over as plunder in a land of captivity. ⁵Do not cover up their guilt[i] or blot out their sins from your sight,[j] for they have thrown insults in the face of[i] the builders.

⁶So we rebuilt the wall till all of it reached half its height, for the people worked with all their heart.

⁷But when Sanballat, Tobiah,[k] the Arabs, the Ammonites and the men of Ashdod heard that the repairs to Jerusa-

---

e 13 Hebrew *a thousand cubits* (about 450 meters) *f 15* Hebrew *Shelah*, a variant of *Shiloah*, that is, Siloam *g 16* Hebrew; Septuagint, some Vulgate manuscripts and Syriac *tomb* *h 18* Two Hebrew manuscripts and Syriac (see also Septuagint and verse 24); most Hebrew manuscripts *Bavvai* *i 5* Or *have provoked you to anger before*

lem's walls had gone ahead and that the gaps were being closed, they were very angry. ⁸They all plotted together¹ to come and fight against Jerusalem and stir up trouble against it. ⁹But we prayed to our God and posted a guard day and night to meet this threat.

¹⁰Meanwhile, the people in Judah said, "The strength of the laborers^m is giving out, and there is so much rubble that we cannot rebuild the wall."

¹¹Also our enemies said, "Before they know it or see us, we will be right there among them and will kill them and put an end to the work."

¹²Then the Jews who lived near them came and told us ten times over, "Wherever you turn, they will attack us."

¹³Therefore I stationed some of the people behind the lowest points of the wall at the exposed places, posting them by families, with their swords, spears and bows. ¹⁴After I looked things over, I stood up and said to the nobles, the officials and the rest of the people, "Don't be afraid^n of them. Remember° the Lord, who is great and awesome,^p and fight^q for your brothers, your sons and your daughters, your wives and your homes."

¹⁵When our enemies heard that we were aware of their plot and that God had frustrated it,^r we all returned to the wall, each to his own work.

¹⁶From that day on, half of my men did the work, while the other half were equipped with spears, shields, bows and armor. The officers posted themselves behind all the people of Judah ¹⁷who were building the wall. Those who carried materials did their work with one hand and held a weapon^s in the other, ¹⁸and each of the builders wore his sword at his side as he worked. But the man who sounded the trumpet^t stayed with me.

¹⁹Then I said to the nobles, the officials and the rest of the people, "The work is extensive and spread out, and we are widely separated from each other along the wall. ²⁰Wherever you hear the sound of the trumpet,^u join us there. Our God will fight^v for us!"

²¹So we continued the work with half the men holding spears, from the first light of dawn till the stars came out. ²²At that time I also said to the people, "Have every man and his helper stay inside Jerusalem at night, so they can serve us as guards by night and workmen by day." ²³Neither I nor my brothers nor my men nor the guards with me took off our clothes; each had his weapon, even when he went for water.^j

Nehemiah Helps the Poor

5 Now the men and their wives raised a great outcry against their Jewish brothers. ²Some were saying, "We and our sons and daughters are numerous; in order for us to eat and stay alive, we must get grain."

³Others were saying, "We are mortgaging our fields,^w our vineyards and our homes to get grain during the famine."^x

⁴Still others were saying, "We have had to borrow money to pay the king's tax^y on our fields and vineyards. ⁵Although we are of the same flesh and blood^z as our countrymen and though our sons are as good as theirs, yet we have to subject our sons and daughters to slavery.^a Some of our daughters have already been enslaved, but we are powerless, because our fields and our vineyards belong to others."^b

⁶When I heard their outcry and these charges, I was very angry. ⁷I pondered them in my mind and then accused the nobles and officials. I told them, "You are exacting usury^c from your own countrymen!" So I called together a large meeting to deal with them ⁸and said: "As far as possible, we have bought^d back our Jewish brothers who were sold to the Gentiles. Now you are selling your brothers, only for them to be sold back to us!" They kept quiet, because they could find nothing to say.^e

⁹So I continued, "What you are doing is not right. Shouldn't you walk in the fear of our God to avoid the reproach^f of our Gentile enemies? ¹⁰I and my brothers and my men are also lending the people money and grain. But let the exacting of usury stop!^g ¹¹Give back to them immediately their fields, vineyards, olive groves and houses, and also the usury^h you are charging them—the hundredth part of the money, grain, new wine and oil."

¹²"We will give it back," they said.

---

j 23 The meaning of the Hebrew for this clause is uncertain.

"And we will not demand anything more from them. We will do as you say."

Then I summoned the priests and made the nobles and officials take an oath[i] to do what they had promised. [13]I also shook[j] out the folds of my robe and said, "In this way may God shake out of his house and possessions every man who does not keep this promise. So may such a man be shaken out and emptied!"

At this the whole assembly said, "Amen,"[k] and praised the LORD. And the people did as they had promised.

[14]Moreover, from the twentieth year of King Artaxerxes,[l] when I was appointed to be their governor[m] in the land of Judah, until his thirty-second year—twelve years—neither I nor my brothers ate the food allotted to the governor. [15]But the earlier governors—those preceding me—placed a heavy burden on the people and took forty shekels[k] of silver from them in addition to food and wine. Their assistants also lorded it over the people. But out of reverence for God[n] I did not act like that. [16]Instead,[o] I devoted myself to the work on this wall. All my men were assembled there for the work; we did not acquire any land.

[17]Furthermore, a hundred and fifty Jews and officials ate at my table, as well as those who came to us from the surrounding nations. [18]Each day one ox, six choice sheep and some poultry[p] were prepared for me, and every ten days an abundant supply of wine of all kinds. In spite of all this, I never demanded the food allotted to the governor, because the demands were heavy on these people.

[19]Remember[q] me with favor, O my God, for all I have done for these people.

Further Opposition to the Rebuilding

6 When word came to Sanballat, Tobiah,[r] Geshem[s] the Arab and the rest of our enemies that I had rebuilt the wall and not a gap was left in it—though up to that time I had not set the doors in the gates— [2]Sanballat and Geshem sent me this message: "Come, let us meet together in one of the villages[m] on the plain of Ono.[t]"

But they were scheming to harm me; [3]so I sent messengers to them with this reply: "I am carrying on a great project and cannot go down. Why should the work stop while I leave it and go down to you?" [4]Four times they sent me the same message, and each time I gave them the same answer.

[5]Then, the fifth time, Sanballat[u] sent his aide to me with the same message, and in his hand was an unsealed letter [6]in which was written:

"It is reported among the nations—and Geshem[nv] says it is true—that you and the Jews are plotting to revolt, and therefore you are building the wall. Moreover, according to these reports you are about to become their king [7]and have even appointed prophets to make this proclamation about you in Jerusalem: 'There is a king in Judah!' Now this report will get back to the king; so come, let us confer together."

[8]I sent him this reply: "Nothing like what you are saying is happening; you are just making it up out of your head."

[9]They were all trying to frighten us, thinking, "Their hands will get too weak for the work, and it will not be completed."

But I prayed, "Now strengthen my hands."

[10]One day I went to the house of Shemaiah son of Delaiah, the son of Mehetabel, who was shut in at his home. He said, "Let us meet in the house of God, inside the temple[w], and let us close the temple doors, because men are coming to kill you—by night they are coming to kill you."

[11]But I said, "Should a man like me run away? Or should one like me go into the temple to save his life? I will not go!" [12]I realized that God had not sent him, but that he had prophesied against me[x] because Tobiah and Sanballat[y] had hired him. [13]He had been hired to intimidate me so that I would commit a sin by doing this, and then they would give me a bad name to discredit me.[z]

[14]Remember[a] Tobiah and Sanballat,[b] O my God, because of what they have done; remember also the prophetess[c] Noadiah and the rest of the prophets[d] who have been trying to intimidate me.

---

[k] 15 That is, about 1 pound (about 0.5 kilogram) [l] 16 Most Hebrew manuscripts; some Hebrew manuscripts, Septuagint, Vulgate and Syriac I [m] 2 Or in Kephirim [n] 6 Hebrew Gashmu, a variant of Geshem

The Completion of the Wall

[15] So the wall was completed on the twenty-fifth of Elul, in fifty-two days. [16] When all our enemies heard about this, all the surrounding nations were afraid and lost their self-confidence, because they realized that this work had been done with the help of our God.

[17] Also, in those days the nobles of Judah were sending many letters to Tobiah, and replies from Tobiah kept coming to them. [18] For many in Judah were under oath to him, since he was son-in-law to Shecaniah son of Arah, and his son Jehohanan had married the daughter of Meshullam son of Berekiah. [19] Moreover, they kept reporting to me his good deeds and then telling him what I said. And Tobiah sent letters to intimidate me.

7 After the wall had been rebuilt and I had set the doors in place, the gatekeepers[e] and the singers[f] and the Levites[g] were appointed. [2] I put in charge of Jerusalem my brother Hanani,[h] along with[o] Hananiah[i] the commander of the citadel,[j] because he was a man of integrity and feared[k] God more than most men do. [3] I said to them, "The gates of Jerusalem are not to be opened until the sun is hot. While the gatekeepers are still on duty, have them shut the doors and bar them. Also appoint residents of Jerusalem as guards, some at their posts and some near their own houses."

The List of the Exiles Who Returned
7:6–73pp — Ezr 2:1–70

[4] Now the city was large and spacious, but there were few people in it,[l] and the houses had not yet been rebuilt. [5] So my God put it into my heart to assemble the nobles, the officials and the common people for registration by families. I found the genealogical record of those who had been the first to return. This is what I found written there:

> [6] These are the people of the province who came up from the captivity of the exiles[m] whom Nebuchadnezzar king of Babylon had taken captive (they returned to Jerusalem and Judah, each to his own town, [7] in company with Zerubbabel,[n] Jeshua, Nehemiah, Azariah, Raamiah, Nahamani, Mordecai, Bilshan, Mispereth, Bigvai, Nehum and Baanah):

The list of the men of Israel:

[8] the descendants of Parosh	2,172
[9] of Shephatiah	372
[10] of Arah	652
[11] of Pahath-Moab (through the line of Jeshua and Joab)	2,818
[12] of Elam	1,254
[13] of Zattu	845
[14] of Zaccai	760
[15] of Binnui	648
[16] of Bebai	628
[17] of Azgad	2,322
[18] of Adonikam	667
[19] of Bigvai	2,067
[20] of Adin[o]	655
[21] of Ater (through Hezekiah)	98
[22] of Hashum	328
[23] of Bezai	324
[24] of Hariph	112
[25] of Gibeon	95
[26] the men of Bethlehem and Netophah[p]	188
[27] of Anathoth[q]	128
[28] of Beth Azmaveth	42
[29] of Kiriath Jearim, Kephirah[r] and Beeroth[s]	743
[30] of Ramah and Geba	621
[31] of Micmash	122
[32] of Bethel and Ai[t]	123
[33] of the other Nebo	52
[34] of the other Elam	1,254
[35] of Harim	320
[36] of Jericho[u]	345
[37] of Lod, Hadid and Ono[v]	721
[38] of Senaah	3,930

[39] The priests:

the descendants of Jedaiah (through the family of Jeshua)	973
[40] of Immer	1,052
[41] of Pashhur	1,247
[42] of Harim	1,017

[43] The Levites:

the descendants of Jeshua (through Kadmiel through the line of Hodaviah)	74

[44] The singers:[w]

the descendants of Asaph	148

o 2 Or Hanani, that is,

⁴⁵The gatekeepers:ˣ

the descendants of
Shallum, Ater, Talmon,
Akkub, Hatita and Shobai   138

⁴⁶The temple servants:ʸ

the descendants of
Ziha, Hasupha, Tabbaoth,
⁴⁷Keros, Sia, Padon,
⁴⁸Lebana, Hagaba, Shalmai,
⁴⁹Hanan, Giddel, Gahar,
⁵⁰Reaiah, Rezin, Nekoda,
⁵¹Gazzam, Uzza, Paseah,
⁵²Besai, Meunim, Nephussim,
⁵³Bakbuk, Hakupha, Harhur,
⁵⁴Bazluth, Mehida, Harsha,
⁵⁵Barkos, Sisera, Temah,
⁵⁶Neziah and Hatipha

⁵⁷The descendants of the servants of Solomon:

the descendants of
Sotai, Sophereth, Perida,
⁵⁸Jaala, Darkon, Giddel,
⁵⁹Shephatiah, Hattil,
Pokereth-Hazzebaim and Amon

⁶⁰The temple servants and the
descendants of the servants
of Solomonᶻ   392

⁶¹The following came up from the towns of Tel Melah, Tel Harsha, Kerub, Addon and Immer, but they could not show that their families were descended from Israel:

⁶²the descendants of
Delaiah, Tobiah and
Nekoda   642

⁶³And from among the priests:

the descendants of
Hobaiah, Hakkoz and Barzillai
(a man who had married a
daughter of Barzillai the
Gileadite and was called by that
name).

⁶⁴These searched for their family records, but they could not find them and so were excluded from the priesthood as unclean. ⁶⁵The governor, therefore, ordered them not to eat any of the most sacred food until there should be a priest ministering with the Urim and Thummim.ᵃ

⁶⁶The whole company numbered 42,360, ⁶⁷besides their 7,337 menservants and maidservants; and they also had 245 men and women singers. ⁶⁸There were 736 horses, 245 mules,ᵖ ⁶⁹435 camels and 6,720 donkeys.

⁷⁰Some of the heads of the families contributed to the work. The governor gave to the treasury 1,000 drachmasᵠ of gold, 50 bowls and 530 garments for priests. ⁷¹Some of the heads of the familiesᵇ gave to the treasury for the work 20,000 drachmasʳ of gold and 2,200 minasˢ of silver. ⁷²The total given by the rest of the people was 20,000 drachmas of gold, 2,000 minasᵗ of silver and 67 garments for priests.ᶜ

⁷³The priests, the Levites, the gatekeepers, the singers and the temple servants,ᵈ along with certain of the people and the rest of the Israelites, settled in their own towns.ᵉ

Ezra Reads the Law

When the seventh month came and the Israelites had settled in their towns,ᶠ **8** ¹all the people assembled as one man in the square before the Water Gate.ᵍ They told Ezra the scribe to bring out the Book of the Law of Moses,ʰ which the LORD had commanded for Israel.

²So on the first day of the seventh monthⁱ Ezra the priest brought the Lawʲ before the assembly, which was made up of men and women and all who were able to understand. ³He read it aloud from daybreak till noon as he faced the square before the Water Gateᵏ in the presence of the men, women and others who could understand. And all the people listened attentively to the Book of the Law.

⁴Ezra the scribe stood on a high wooden platformˡ built for the occasion. Beside him on his right stood Mattithiah, Shema, Anaiah, Uriah, Hilkiah and Maaseiah; and on his left were Pedaiah, Mishael, Malkijah, Hashum, Hashbaddanah, Zechariah and Meshullam.

⁵Ezra opened the book. All the people could see him because he was standingᵐ above them; and as he opened it, the people all stood up. ⁶Ezra praised the LORD,

---

p 68 Some Hebrew manuscripts (see also Ezra 2:66); most Hebrew manuscripts do not have this verse.   *q 70* That is, about 19 pounds (about 8.5 kilograms)   *r 71* That is, about 375 pounds (about 170 kilograms); also in verse 72   *s 71* That is, about 1 1/3 tons (about 1.2 metric tons)   *t 72* That is, about 1 1/4 tons (about 1.1 metric tons)

the great God; and all the people lifted their hands and responded, "Amen! Amen!" Then they bowed down and worshiped the LORD with their faces to the ground.

⁷The Levites—Jeshua, Bani, Sherebiah, Jamin, Akkub, Shabbethai, Hodiah, Maaseiah, Kelita, Azariah, Jozabad, Hanan and Pelaiah—instructed the people in the Law while the people were standing there. ⁸They read from the Book of the Law of God, making it clear and giving the meaning so that the people could understand what was being read.

⁹Then Nehemiah the governor, Ezra the priest and scribe, and the Levites who were instructing the people said to them all, "This day is sacred to the LORD your God. Do not mourn or weep." For all the people had been weeping as they listened to the words of the Law.

¹⁰Nehemiah said, "Go and enjoy choice food and sweet drinks, and send some to those who have nothing prepared. This day is sacred to our Lord. Do not grieve, for the joy of the LORD is your strength."

¹¹The Levites calmed all the people, saying, "Be still, for this is a sacred day. Do not grieve."

¹²Then all the people went away to eat and drink, to send portions of food and to celebrate with great joy, because they now understood the words that had been made known to them.

¹³On the second day of the month, the heads of all the families, along with the priests and the Levites, gathered around Ezra the scribe to give attention to the words of the Law. ¹⁴They found written in the Law, which the LORD had commanded through Moses, that the Israelites were to live in booths during the feast of the seventh month ¹⁵and that they should proclaim this word and spread it throughout their towns and in Jerusalem: "Go out into the hill country and bring back branches from olive and wild olive trees, and from myrtles, palms and shade trees, to make booths"—as it is written.

¹⁶So the people went out and brought back branches and built themselves booths on their own roofs, in their courtyards, in the courts of the house of God and in the square by the Water Gate and the one by the Gate of Ephraim. ¹⁷The whole company that had returned from exile built booths and lived in them. From the days of Joshua son of Nun until that day, the Israelites had not celebrated it like this. And their joy was very great.

¹⁸Day after day, from the first day to the last, Ezra read from the Book of the Law of God. They celebrated the feast for seven days, and on the eighth day, in accordance with the regulation, there was an assembly.

The Israelites Confess Their Sins

9 On the twenty-fourth day of the same month, the Israelites gathered together, fasting and wearing sackcloth and having dust on their heads. ²Those of Israelite descent had separated themselves from all foreigners. They stood in their places and confessed their sins and the wickedness of their fathers. ³They stood where they were and read from the Book of the Law of the LORD their God for a quarter of the day, and spent another quarter in confession and in worshiping the LORD their God. ⁴Standing on the stairs were the Levites—Jeshua, Bani, Kadmiel, Shebaniah, Bunni, Sherebiah, Bani and Kenani—who called with loud voices to the LORD their God. ⁵And the Levites—Jeshua, Kadmiel, Bani, Hashabneiah, Sherebiah, Hodiah, Shebaniah and Pethahiah—said: "Stand up and praise the LORD your God, who is from everlasting to everlasting.

"Blessed be your glorious name, and may it be exalted above all blessing and praise. ⁶You alone are the LORD. You made the heavens, even the highest heavens, and all their starry host, the earth and all that is on it, the seas and all that is in them. You give life to everything, and the multitudes of heaven worship you.

⁷"You are the LORD God, who chose Abram and brought him out of Ur of the Chaldeans and named him Abraham. ⁸You found his heart faithful to you, and you made a cov-

M Ne 1:4–6 ◀ ▶ Job 22:29

ᵘ 8 Or God, translating it ᵛ 15 See Lev. 23:37-40. ʷ 5 Or God for ever and ever

J ▶ Job 1:21   **W** 2Ch 19:11 ◀ ▶ Ps 23:4

enant with him to give to his descendants the land of the Canaanites, Hittites, Amorites, Perizzites, Jebusites and Girgashites.ᵘ You have kept your promiseᵛ because you are righteous.ʷ

⁹"You saw the suffering of our forefathers in Egypt;ˣ you heard their cry at the Red Sea.ˣʸ ¹⁰You sent miraculous signsᶻ and wondersᵃ against Pharaoh, against all his officials and all the people of his land, for you knew how arrogantly the Egyptians treated them. You made a nameᵇ for yourself,ᶜ which remains to this day. ¹¹You divided the sea before them,ᵈ so that they passed through it on dry ground, but you hurled their pursuers into the depths,ᵉ like a stone into mighty waters.ᶠ ¹²By dayᵍ you ledʰ them with a pillar of cloud,ⁱ and by night with a pillar of fire to give them light on the way they were to take.

¹³"You came down on Mount Sinai;ʲ you spokeᵏ to them from heaven.ˡ You gave them regulations and laws that are justᵐ and right, and decrees and commands that are good.ⁿ ¹⁴You made known to them your holy Sabbathᵒ and gave them commands, decrees and laws through your servant Moses. ¹⁵In their hunger you gave them bread from heavenᵖ and in their thirst you brought them water from the rock;ᑫ you told them to go in and take possession of the land you had sworn with uplifted handʳ to give them.ˢ

¹⁶"But they, our forefathers, became arrogant and stiff-necked,ᵗ and did not obey your commands.ᵘ ¹⁷They refused to listen and failed to rememberᵛ the miraclesʷ you performed among them. They became stiff-neckedˣ and in their rebellion appointed a leader in order to return to their slavery.ʸ But you are a forgiving God,ᶻ gracious and compassionate,ᵃ slow to angerᵇ and abounding in love.ᶜ Therefore you did not desert them,ᵈ ¹⁸even when they cast

for themselves an image of a calfᵉ and said, 'This is your god, who brought you up out of Egypt,' or when they committed awful blasphemies.ᶠ

¹⁹"Because of your great compassion you did not abandonᵍ them in the desert. By day the pillar of cloudʰ did not cease to guide them on their path, nor the pillar of fire by night to shine on the way they were to take. ²⁰You gave your good Spiritⁱ to instructʲ them. You did not withhold your mannaᵏ from their mouths, and you gave them waterˡ for their thirst. ²¹For forty yearsᵐ you sustained them in the desert; they lacked nothing,ⁿ their clothes did not wear out nor did their feet become swollen.ᵒ

²²"You gave them kingdoms and nations, allotting to them even the remotest frontiers. They took over the country of Sihonʸᵖ king of Heshbon and the country of Og king of Bashan.ᑫ ²³You made their sons as numerous as the stars in the sky,ʳ and you brought them into the land that you told their fathers to enter and possess. ²⁴Their sons went in and took possession of the land.ˢ You subduedᵗ before them the Canaanites, who lived in the land; you handed the Canaanites over to them, along with their kings and the peoples of the land, to deal with them as they pleased. ²⁵They captured fortified cities and fertile land;ᵘ they took possession of houses filled with all kinds of good things,ᵛ wells already dug, vineyards, olive groves and fruit trees in abundance. They ate to the full and were well-nourished;ʷ they reveled in your great goodness.ˣ

²⁶"But they were disobedient and rebelled against you; they put your law behind their backs.ʸ They

L 2Ch 32:22 ◄ ► Est 8:16
F 2Ch 20:9 ◄ ► Ne 9:20–21
C 2Ch 28:11 ◄ ► Job 5:13–14
L Ezr 8:22 ◄ ► Ne 9:31

9:8
ᵘ S Ge 15:18-21; S Ezr 9:1
ᵛ S Jos 21:45
ʷ Ge 15:6; S Ezr 9:15
9:9 ˣ Ex 2:23-25; ʸ Ex 14:10-30
9:10 ᶻ S Ge 10:1; Ps 74:9 ᵃ S Ex 3:20; S 6:6 ᵇ Jer 32:20; Da 9:15 ᶜ S Nu 6:27
9:11 ᵈ Ps 78:13
ᵉ S Ex 14:28
ᶠ Ex 15:4-5,10; Heb 11:29
9:12 ᵍ S Dt 1:33
ʰ S Ex 15:13
ⁱ S Ex 13:21
9:13 ʲ S Ex 19:11
ᵏ S Ex 19:19
ˡ S Ex 20:22
ᵐ Ps 119:137
ⁿ S Ex 20:1; Dt 4:7-8
9:14 ᵒ S Ge 2:3; Ex 20:8-11
9:15 ᵖ S Ex 16:4; Ps 78:24-25; Jn 6:31 ᑫ Ex 17:6; Nu 20:7-13
ʳ S Ge 14:22
ˢ Dt 1:8,21
9:16 ᵗ S Ex 32:9; Jer 7:26; 17:23; 19:15 ᵘ Dt 1:26-33; 31:29
9:17 ᵛ Jdg 8:34; Ps 78:42
ʷ S 77:11; 78:12; 105:5; 106:7
ˣ Jer 7:26; 19:15
ʸ Nu 14:1-4
ᶻ Ps 130:4; Da 9:9
ᵃ S Dt 4:31
ᵇ S Ex 34:6;
Ps 103:8; Na 1:3
ᶜ S Ex 22:27;
Nu 14:17-19;
ᵈ Ps 86:15 ᵈ Ps 78:11;
Eze 5:6
9:18 ᵉ S Ex 32:4
ᶠ S Ex 20:23
9:19 ᵍ Ex 13:22
ʰ S Ex 13:21
9:20 ⁱ Nu 9:17; 11:17; Isa 63:11, 14; Hag 2:5; Zec 4:6 ʲ Ps 23:3; 143:10 ᵏ S Ex 16:15
ˡ Ex 17:6
9:21 ᵐ S Ex 16:35
ⁿ S Dt 2:7 ᵒ Dt 8:4
9:22 ᵖ S Nu 21:21
ᑫ S Nu 21:33; Dt 2:26-3:11
9:23 ʳ S Ge 12:2;
S Lev 26:9;
S Nu 10:36
9:24 ˢ S Jos 11:23
ᵗ S Jdg 4:23;
S 2Ch 14:13
9:25 ᵘ S Dt 11:11
ᵛ S Ex 18:9
ʷ Dt 6:10-12
ˣ 8:8-11; 32:12-15;
Ps 23:6; 25:7;
69:16
9:26 ʸ S 1Ki 14:9;
Jer 44:10

E 2Ch 24:20 ◄ ► Ne 9:30
G 2Sa 23:2 ◄ ► Job 32:8
N 2Ki 2:9 ◄ ► Job 26:13
T 2Ch 24:20 ◄ ► Job 32:8
F Ne 9:15 ◄ ► Job 5:20
C Dt 33:25 ◄ ► Job 27:16–17
E 2Ch 32:24 ◄ ► Job 42:16–17

ˣ 9 Hebrew *Yam Suph*; that is, Sea of Reeds ʸ 22 One Hebrew manuscript and Septuagint; most Hebrew manuscripts *Sihon, that is, the country of the*

killed your prophets, who had admonished them in order to turn them back to you; they committed awful blasphemies. ²⁷So you handed them over to their enemies, who oppressed them. But when they were oppressed they cried out to you. From heaven you heard them, and in your great compassion you gave them deliverers, who rescued them from the hand of their enemies.

²⁸"But as soon as they were at rest, they again did what was evil in your sight. Then you abandoned them to the hand of their enemies so that they ruled over them. And when they cried out to you again, you heard from heaven, and in your compassion you delivered them time after time.

²⁹"You warned them to return to your law, but they became arrogant and disobeyed your commands. They sinned against your ordinances, by which a man will live if he obeys them. Stubbornly they turned their backs on you, became stiff-necked and refused to listen. ³⁰For many years you were patient with them. By your Spirit you admonished them through your prophets. Yet they paid no attention, so you handed them over to the neighboring peoples. ³¹But in your great mercy you did not put an end to them or abandon them, for you are a gracious and merciful God.

³²"Now therefore, O our God, the great, mighty and awesome God, who keeps his covenant of love, do not let all this hardship seem trifling in your eyes—the hardship that has come upon us, upon our kings and leaders, upon our priests and prophets, upon our fathers and all your people, from the days of the kings of Assyria until today. ³³In all that has happened to us, you have been just; you have acted faithfully, while we did wrong. ³⁴Our kings, our leaders,

---

N 2Ch 36:16 ◄► Job 4:19–20
C Ge 6:3 ◄► Ps 51:12–13
E Ne 9:20 ◄► Job 26:13
Q 2Ch 18:23 ◄► Ps 51:11
L Ne 9:17 ◄► Job 33:27–28

9:26 ᶻS Jos 7:25
ᵃJer 2:30; 26:8; Mt 21:35-36; 23:29-36; Ac 7:52
ᵇS Jdg 2:12-13

9:27 ᶜS Nu 25:17; S Jdg 2:14 ᵈPs 51:1; 103:8; 106:45; 119:156 ᵉS Jdg 3:9

9:28 ᶠS Ex 32:22; S Jdg 2:17
ᵍS 2Sa 24:14
ʰPs 22:4; 106:43; 136:24

9:29 ⁱS Jdg 6:8
ʲver 16-17; Isa 2:11; Jer 43:2
ᵏS Dt 30:16
ˡS 1Sa 8:3
ᵐJer 19:15
ⁿZec 7:11-12

9:30
ᵒ2Ki 17:13-18; S 2Ch 36:16
ᵖJer 16:11; Zec 7:12

9:31 ᵠIsa 48:9; 65:9 ʳS Dt 4:31

9:32 ˢJob 9:19; Ps 24:8; 89:8; 93:4
ᵗS Dt 7:21
ᵘS Dt 7:9; S 1Ki 8:23; Da 9:4
ᵛS Ex 18:8

9:33 ʷS Ge 18:25
ˣJer 44:3; Da 9:7-8, 14

9:34 ʸS 2Ki 23:1 ᶻJer 44:17

9:35 ᵃIsa 63:7 ᵇDt 28:45-48

9:36 ᶜS Ezr 9:9

9:37 ᵈDt 28:33; La 5:5

9:38 ᵉS 2Ch 23:16 ᶠIsa 44:5

10:2 ᵍS Ezr 2:2

10:3 ʰS 1Ch 9:12

10:5 ⁱS 1Ch 24:8

10:8 ʲNe 12:1

10:9 ᵏNe 12:1

10:16 ˡS Ezr 8:6

10:20 ᵐ1Ch 24:15

---

ers, our priests and our fathers did not follow your law; they did not pay attention to your commands or the warnings you gave them. ³⁵Even while they were in their kingdom, enjoying your great goodness to them in the spacious and fertile land you gave them, they did not serve you or turn from their evil ways.

³⁶"But see, we are slaves today, slaves in the land you gave our forefathers so they could eat its fruit and the other good things it produces. ³⁷Because of our sins, its abundant harvest goes to the kings you have placed over us. They rule over our bodies and our cattle as they please. We are in great distress.

The Agreement of the People

³⁸"In view of all this, we are making a binding agreement, putting it in writing, and our leaders, our Levites and our priests are affixing their seals to it."

10 Those who sealed it were:

Nehemiah the governor, the son of Hacaliah.

Zedekiah, ²Seraiah, Azariah, Jeremiah,

³Pashhur, Amariah, Malkijah,
⁴Hattush, Shebaniah, Malluch,
⁵Harim, Meremoth, Obadiah,
⁶Daniel, Ginnethon, Baruch,
⁷Meshullam, Abijah, Mijamin,
⁸Maaziah, Bilgai and Shemaiah.

These were the priests.

⁹The Levites:

Jeshua son of Azaniah, Binnui of the sons of Henadad, Kadmiel,

¹⁰and their associates: Shebaniah, Hodiah, Kelita, Pelaiah, Hanan,
¹¹Mica, Rehob, Hashabiah,
¹²Zaccur, Sherebiah, Shebaniah,
¹³Hodiah, Bani and Beninu.

¹⁴The leaders of the people:

Parosh, Pahath-Moab, Elam, Zattu, Bani,

¹⁵Bunni, Azgad, Bebai,
¹⁶Adonijah, Bigvai, Adin,
¹⁷Ater, Hezekiah, Azzur,
¹⁸Hodiah, Hashum, Bezai,
¹⁹Hariph, Anathoth, Nebai,
²⁰Magpiash, Meshullam, Hezir,

²¹Meshezabel, Zadok, Jaddua, ²²Pelatiah, Hanan, Anaiah, ²³Hoshea, Hananiah,ⁿ Hasshub, ²⁴Hallohesh, Pilha, Shobek, ²⁵Rehum, Hashabnah, Maaseiah, ²⁶Ahiah, Hanan, Anan, ²⁷Malluch, Harim and Baanah.

²⁸"The rest of the people—priests, Levites, gatekeepers, singers, temple servants° and all who separated themselves from the neighboring peoplesᵖ for the sake of the Law of God, together with their wives and all their sons and daughters who are able to understand— ²⁹all these now join their brothers the nobles, and bind themselves with a curse and an oathq to follow the Law of God given through Moses the servant of God and to obey carefully all the commands, regulations and decrees of the LORD our Lord.

³⁰"We promise not to give our daughters in marriage to the peoples around us or take their daughters for our sons.ʳ

³¹"When the neighboring peoples bring merchandise or grain to sell on the Sabbath,ˢ we will not buy from them on the Sabbath or on any holy day. Every seventh year we will forgo working the landᵗ and will cancel all debts.ᵘ

³²"We assume the responsibility for carrying out the commands to give a third of a shekelᶻ each year for the service of the house of our God: ³³for the bread set out on the table;ᵛ for the regular grain offerings and burnt offerings; for the offerings on the Sabbaths, New Moonʷ festivals and appointed feasts; for the holy offerings; for sin offerings to make atonement for Israel; and for all the duties of the house of our God.ˣ

³⁴"We—the priests, the Levites and the people—have cast lotsʸ to determine when each of our families is to bring to the house of our God at set times each year a contribution of woodᶻ to burn on the altar of the LORD our God, as it is written in the Law.

³⁵"We also assume responsibility for bringing to the house of the LORD each year the firstfruitsᵃ of our crops and of every fruit tree.ᵇ

³⁶"As it is also written in the Law, we will bring the firstbornᶜ of our sons and of our cattle, of our herds and of our flocks to the house of our God, to the priests ministering there.ᵈ

³⁷"Moreover, we will bring to the storerooms of the house of our God, to the priests, the first of our ground meal, of our ⌊grain⌋ offerings, of the fruit of all our trees and of our new wine and oil.ᵉ And we will bring a titheᶠ of our crops to the Levites,ᵍ for it is the Levites who collect the tithes in all the towns where we work.ʰ ³⁸A priest descended from Aaron is to accompany the Levites when they receive the tithes, and the Levites are to bring a tenth of the tithesⁱ up to the house of our God, to the storerooms of the treasury. ³⁹The people of Israel, including the Levites, are to bring their contributions of grain, new wine and oil to the storerooms where the articles for the sanctuary are kept and where the ministering priests, the gatekeepers and the singers stay.

"We will not neglect the house of our God."ʲ

The New Residents of Jerusalem
11:3–19pp — 1Ch 9:1–17

11 Now the leaders of the people settled in Jerusalem, and the rest of the people cast lots to bring one out of every ten to live in Jerusalem,ᵏ the holy city,ˡ while the remaining nine were to stay in their own towns.ᵐ ²The people commended all the men who volunteered to live in Jerusalem.

³These are the provincial leaders who settled in Jerusalem (now some Israelites, priests, Levites, temple servants and descendants of Solomon's servants lived in the towns of Judah, each on his own property in the various towns,ⁿ ⁴while other people from both Judah and Benjamin° lived in Jerusalem):ᵖ

From the descendants of Judah:

Athaiah son of Uzziah, the son of Zechariah, the son of Amariah, the

---

z 32 That is, about 1/8 ounce (about 4 grams)

son of Shephatiah, the son of Mahalalel, a descendant of Perez; ⁵and Maaseiah son of Baruch, the son of Col-Hozeh, the son of Hazaiah, the son of Adaiah, the son of Joiarib, the son of Zechariah, a descendant of Shelah. ⁶The descendants of Perez who lived in Jerusalem totaled 468 able men.

⁷From the descendants of Benjamin:

Sallu son of Meshullam, the son of Joed, the son of Pedaiah, the son of Kolaiah, the son of Maaseiah, the son of Ithiel, the son of Jeshaiah, ⁸and his followers, Gabbai and Sallai—928 men. ⁹Joel son of Zicri was their chief officer, and Judah son of Hassenuah was over the Second District of the city.

¹⁰From the priests:

Jedaiah; the son of Joiarib; Jakin; ¹¹Seraiah[q] son of Hilkiah, the son of Meshullam, the son of Zadok, the son of Meraioth, the son of Ahitub,[r] supervisor in the house of God, ¹²and their associates, who carried on work for the temple—822 men; Adaiah son of Jeroham, the son of Pelaliah, the son of Amzi, the son of Zechariah, the son of Pashhur, the son of Malkijah, ¹³and his associates, who were heads of families—242 men; Amashsai son of Azarel, the son of Ahzai, the son of Meshillemoth, the son of Immer, ¹⁴and his[a] associates, who were able men—128. Their chief officer was Zabdiel son of Haggedolim.

¹⁵From the Levites:

Shemaiah son of Hasshub, the son of Azrikam, the son of Hashabiah, the son of Bunni; ¹⁶Shabbethai[s] and Jozabad,[t] two of the heads of the Levites, who had charge of the outside work of the house of God; ¹⁷Mattaniah[u] son of Mica, the son of Zabdi, the son of Asaph,[v] the director who led in thanksgiving and prayer; Bakbukiah, second among his associates; and Abda son of Shammua, the son of Galal, the son of Jeduthun.[w] ¹⁸The Levites in the holy city[x] totaled 284.

¹⁹The gatekeepers:

Akkub, Talmon and their associates, who kept watch at the gates—172 men.

²⁰The rest of the Israelites, with the priests and Levites, were in all the towns of Judah, each on his ancestral property.
²¹The temple servants[y] lived on the hill of Ophel, and Ziha and Gishpa were in charge of them.
²²The chief officer of the Levites in Jerusalem was Uzzi son of Bani, the son of Hashabiah, the son of Mattaniah,[z] the son of Mica. Uzzi was one of Asaph's descendants, who were the singers responsible for the service of the house of God. ²³The singers[a] were under the king's orders, which regulated their daily activity.
²⁴Pethahiah son of Meshezabel, one of the descendants of Zerah[b] son of Judah, was the king's agent in all affairs relating to the people.
²⁵As for the villages with their fields, some of the people of Judah lived in Kiriath Arba[c] and its surrounding settlements, in Dibon[d] and its settlements, in Jekabzeel and its villages, ²⁶in Jeshua, in Moladah,[e] in Beth Pelet,[f] ²⁷in Hazar Shual,[g] in Beersheba[h] and its settlements, ²⁸in Ziklag,[i] in Meconah and its settlements, ²⁹in En Rimmon, in Zorah,[j] in Jarmuth,[k] ³⁰Zanoah,[l] Adullam[m] and their villages, in Lachish[n] and its fields, and in Azekah[o] and its settlements. So they were living all the way from Beersheba[p] to the Valley of Hinnom.
³¹The descendants of the Benjamites from Geba[q] lived in Micmash,[r] Aija, Bethel[s] and its settlements, ³²in Anathoth,[t] Nob[u] and Ananiah, ³³in Hazor,[v] Ramah[w] and Gittaim,[x] ³⁴in Hadid, Zeboim[y] and Neballat, ³⁵in Lod and Ono,[z] and in the Valley of the Craftsmen.
³⁶Some of the divisions of the Levites of Judah settled in Benjamin.

Priests and Levites

12 These were the priests[a] and Levites[b] who returned with Zerubbabel[c] son of Shealtiel[d] and with Jeshua:[e]

Seraiah,[f] Jeremiah, Ezra, ²Amariah, Malluch, Hattush, ³Shecaniah, Rehum, Meremoth,

---

[a] 14 Most Septuagint manuscripts; Hebrew *their*

⁴Iddo, Ginnethon, Abijah, ⁵Mijamin, Moadiah, Bilgah, ⁶Shemaiah, Joiarib, Jedaiah, ⁷Sallu, Amok, Hilkiah and Jedaiah. These were the leaders of the priests and their associates in the days of Jeshua.

⁸The Levites were Jeshua, Binnui, Kadmiel, Sherebiah, Judah, and also Mattaniah, who, together with his associates, was in charge of the songs of thanksgiving. ⁹Bakbukiah and Unni, their associates, stood opposite them in the services.

¹⁰Jeshua was the father of Joiakim, Joiakim the father of Eliashib, Eliashib the father of Joiada, ¹¹Joiada the father of Jonathan, and Jonathan the father of Jaddua.

¹²In the days of Joiakim, these were the heads of the priestly families:
of Seraiah's family, Meraiah;
of Jeremiah's, Hananiah;
¹³of Ezra's, Meshullam;
of Amariah's, Jehohanan;
¹⁴of Malluch's, Jonathan;
of Shecaniah's, Joseph;
¹⁵of Harim's, Adna;
of Meremoth's, Helkai;
¹⁶of Iddo's, Zechariah;
of Ginnethon's, Meshullam;
¹⁷of Abijah's, Zicri;
of Miniamin's and of Moadiah's, Piltai;
¹⁸of Bilgah's, Shammua;
of Shemaiah's, Jehonathan;
¹⁹of Joiarib's, Mattenai;
of Jedaiah's, Uzzi;
²⁰of Sallu's, Kallai;
of Amok's, Eber;
²¹of Hilkiah's, Hashabiah;
of Jedaiah's, Nethanel.

²²The family heads of the Levites in the days of Eliashib, Joiada, Johanan and Jaddua, as well as those of the priests, were recorded in the reign of Darius the Persian. ²³The family heads among the descendants of Levi up to the time of Johanan son of Eliashib were recorded in the book of the annals. ²⁴And the leaders of the Levites were Hashabiah, Sherebiah, Jeshua son of Kadmiel, and their associates, who stood opposite them to give praise and thanksgiving, one section responding to the other, as prescribed by David the man of God.

²⁵Mattaniah, Bakbukiah, Obadiah, Meshullam, Talmon and Akkub were gatekeepers who guarded the storerooms at the gates. ²⁶They served in the days of Joiakim son of Jeshua, the son of Jozadak, and in the days of Nehemiah the governor and of Ezra the priest and scribe.

Dedication of the Wall of Jerusalem

²⁷At the dedication of the wall of Jerusalem, the Levites were sought out from where they lived and were brought to Jerusalem to celebrate joyfully the dedication with songs of thanksgiving and with the music of cymbals, harps and lyres. ²⁸The singers also were brought together from the region around Jerusalem—from the villages of the Netophathites, ²⁹from Beth Gilgal, and from the area of Geba and Azmaveth, for the singers had built villages for themselves around Jerusalem. ³⁰When the priests and Levites had purified themselves ceremonially, they purified the people, the gates and the wall.

³¹I had the leaders of Judah go up on top of the wall. I also assigned two large choirs to give thanks. One was to proceed on top of the wall to the right, toward the Dung Gate. ³²Hoshaiah and half the leaders of Judah followed them, ³³along with Azariah, Ezra, Meshullam, ³⁴Judah, Benjamin, Shemaiah, Jeremiah, ³⁵as well as some priests with trumpets, and also Zechariah son of Jonathan, the son of Shemaiah, the son of Mattaniah, the son of Micaiah, the son of Zaccur, the son of Asaph, ³⁶and his associates—Shemaiah, Azarel, Milalai, Gilalai, Maai, Nethanel, Judah and Hanani—with musical instruments prescribed by David the man of God. Ezra the scribe led the procession. ³⁷At the Fountain Gate they continued directly up the steps of the City of David on the ascent to the wall and passed above the house of David to the Water Gate on the east.

³⁸The second choir proceeded in the opposite direction. I followed them on top of the wall, together with half the people—past the Tower of the Ovens to the Broad Wall, ³⁹over the Gate of Ephraim, the Jeshanah Gate, the Fish Gate, the Tower of Hananel and the Tower of the Hundred, as far as the

---

b 4 Many Hebrew manuscripts and Vulgate (see also Neh. 12:16); most Hebrew manuscripts *Ginnethoi* *c 5* A variant of *Miniamin* *d 14* Very many Hebrew manuscripts, some Septuagint manuscripts and Syriac (see also Neh. 12:3); most Hebrew manuscripts *Shebaniah's* *e 15* Some Septuagint manuscripts (see also Neh. 12:3); Hebrew *Meraioth's* *f 31* Or *go alongside* *g 31* Or *proceed alongside* *h 38* Or *them alongside* *i 39* Or *Old*

Sheep Gate. At the Gate of the Guard they stopped.

⁴⁰The two choirs that gave thanks then took their places in the house of God; so did I, together with half the officials, ⁴¹as well as the priests—Eliakim, Maaseiah, Miniamin, Micaiah, Elioenai, Zechariah and Hananiah with their trumpets— ⁴²and also Maaseiah, Shemaiah, Eleazar, Uzzi, Jehohanan, Malkijah, Elam and Ezer. The choirs sang under the direction of Jezrahiah. ⁴³And on that day they offered great sacrifices, rejoicing because God had given them great joy. The women and children also rejoiced. The sound of rejoicing in Jerusalem could be heard far away.

⁴⁴At that time men were appointed to be in charge of the storerooms for the contributions, firstfruits and tithes. From the fields around the towns they were to bring into the storerooms the portions required by the Law for the priests and the Levites, for Judah was pleased with the ministering priests and Levites. ⁴⁵They performed the service of their God and the service of purification, as did also the singers and gatekeepers, according to the commands of David and his son Solomon. ⁴⁶For long ago, in the days of David and Asaph, there had been directors for the singers and for the songs of praise and thanksgiving to God. ⁴⁷So in the days of Zerubbabel and of Nehemiah, all Israel contributed the daily portions for the singers and gatekeepers. They also set aside the portion for the other Levites, and the Levites set aside the portion for the descendants of Aaron.

Nehemiah's Final Reforms

13 On that day the Book of Moses was read aloud in the hearing of the people and there it was found written that no Ammonite or Moabite should ever be admitted into the assembly of God, ²because they had not met the Israelites with food and water but had hired Balaam to call a curse down on them. (Our God, however, turned the curse into a blessing.) ³When the people heard this law, they excluded from Israel all who were of foreign descent.

⁴Before this, Eliashib the priest had been put in charge of the storerooms of the house of our God. He was closely associated with Tobiah, ⁵and he had provided him with a large room formerly used to store the grain offerings and incense and temple articles, and also the tithes of grain, new wine and oil prescribed for the Levites, singers and gatekeepers, as well as the contributions for the priests.

⁶But while all this was going on, I was not in Jerusalem, for in the thirty-second year of Artaxerxes king of Babylon I had returned to the king. Some time later I asked his permission ⁷and came back to Jerusalem. Here I learned about the evil thing Eliashib had done in providing Tobiah a room in the courts of the house of God. ⁸I was greatly displeased and threw all Tobiah's household goods out of the room. ⁹I gave orders to purify the rooms, and then I put back into them the equipment of the house of God, with the grain offerings and the incense.

¹⁰I also learned that the portions assigned to the Levites had not been given to them, and that all the Levites and singers responsible for the service had gone back to their own fields. ¹¹So I rebuked the officials and asked them, "Why is the house of God neglected?" Then I called them together and stationed them at their posts.

¹²All Judah brought the tithes of grain, new wine and oil into the storerooms. ¹³I put Shelemiah the priest, Zadok the scribe, and a Levite named Pedaiah in charge of the storerooms and made Hanan son of Zaccur, the son of Mattaniah, their assistant, because these men were considered trustworthy. They were made responsible for distributing the supplies to their brothers.

¹⁴Remember me for this, O my God, and do not blot out what I have so faithfully done for the house of my God and its services.

¹⁵In those days I saw men in Judah treading winepresses on the Sabbath and bringing in grain and loading it on donkeys, together with wine, grapes, figs and all other kinds of loads. And they were bringing all this into Jerusalem on the Sabbath. Therefore I warned them against selling food on that day. ¹⁶Men from Tyre who lived in Jerusalem were bringing in fish and all kinds of merchandise and selling them in Jerusalem on the

Sabbath to the people of Judah. ¹⁷I rebuked the nobles of Judah and said to them, "What is this wicked thing you are doing—desecrating the Sabbath day? ¹⁸Didn't your forefathers do the same things, so that our God brought all this calamity upon us and upon this city? Now you are stirring up more wrath against Israel by desecrating the Sabbath."

¹⁹When evening shadows fell on the gates of Jerusalem before the Sabbath, I ordered the doors to be shut and not opened until the Sabbath was over. I stationed some of my own men at the gates so that no load could be brought in on the Sabbath day. ²⁰Once or twice the merchants and sellers of all kinds of goods spent the night outside Jerusalem. ²¹But I warned them and said, "Why do you spend the night by the wall? If you do this again, I will lay hands on you." From that time on they no longer came on the Sabbath. ²²Then I commanded the Levites to purify themselves and go and guard the gates in order to keep the Sabbath day holy.

Remember me for this also, O my God, and show mercy to me according to your great love.

²³Moreover, in those days I saw men of Judah who had married women from Ashdod, Ammon and Moab. ²⁴Half of their children spoke the language of Ashdod or the language of one of the other peoples, and did not know how to speak the language of Judah. ²⁵I rebuked them and called curses down on them. I beat some of the men and pulled out their hair. I made them take an oath in God's name and said: "You are not to give your daughters in marriage to their sons, nor are you to take their daughters in marriage for your sons or for yourselves. ²⁶Was it not because of marriages like these that Solomon king of Israel sinned? Among the many nations there was no king like him. He was loved by his God, and God made him king over all Israel, but even he was led into sin by foreign women. ²⁷Must we hear now that you too are doing all this terrible wickedness and are being unfaithful to our God by marrying foreign women?"

²⁸One of the sons of Joiada son of Eliashib the high priest was son-in-law to Sanballat the Horonite. And I drove him away from me.

²⁹Remember them, O my God, because they defiled the priestly office and the covenant of the priesthood and of the Levites.

³⁰So I purified the priests and the Levites of everything foreign, and assigned them duties, each to his own task. ³¹I also made provision for contributions of wood at designated times, and for the firstfruits.

Remember me with favor, O my God.

Esther

Author: Unknown

Theme: God provides for those who trust him

Date of Writing: c. 460–350 B.C.

Outline of Esther
  I. King Xerxes and His Court (1:1—2:23)
  II. Esther's People Are Threatened (3:1—5:14)
  III. The Jews Triumph Over Haman (6:1—10:3)

THIS BOOK BEARS the name of its leading lady, Esther, whom the Persian king Xerxes (Ahasuerus) chose to be his queen. The book of Esther is one book in a five-book grouping in the Hebrew canon known as the megilloth. According to Jewish custom, certain books were to be read aloud in the synagogues (see Lk 4:16–17). The books of the megilloth were read aloud at feast seasons, with the book of Esther scheduled to be read at the Feast of Purim. The four other books in the megilloth are Ruth, Lamentations, Song of Songs and Ecclesiastes.

The events in Esther took place in the Persian capital of Shushan during the reign of King Xerxes and may correspond to a time just after the dedication of the rebuilt temple but prior to Nehemiah's arrival in Judah. Although the name of God does not appear in the text of this book, Esther's story clearly demonstrates God's control over his covenant people as it portrays the plight of the Jews in Persian exile.

Although the author of Esther is unknown, contemporary customs, the royal palace and Persian history are accurately described. Note also the inauguration of the Feast of Purim. While not one of the feasts given to Moses by God in the desert (see Lev 23:1–39), the Feast of Purim is commemorated annually by the Jews worldwide, confirming the historicity of Esther's account.

Queen Vashti Deposed

1 This is what happened during the time of Xerxes,[a] the Xerxes who ruled over 127 provinces[b] stretching from India to Cush[b]:[c] ²At that time King Xerxes reigned from his royal throne in the citadel of Susa,[d] ³and in the third year of his reign he gave a banquet[e] for all his nobles and officials. The military leaders of Persia and Media, the princes, and the nobles of the provinces were present.

⁴For a full 180 days he displayed the vast wealth of his kingdom and the splendor and glory of his majesty. ⁵When these days were over, the king gave a banquet, lasting seven days,[f] in the enclosed garden[g] of the king's palace, for all the people from the least to the greatest, who were in the citadel of Susa. ⁶The garden had hangings of white and blue linen, fastened with cords of white linen and purple material to silver rings on marble pillars. There were couches[h] of gold and silver on a mosaic pavement of porphyry, marble, mother-of-pearl and other costly stones. ⁷Wine was served in goblets of gold, each one different from the other, and the royal wine was abundant, in keeping with the king's liberality.[i] ⁸By the king's command each guest was allowed to drink in his own way, for the king instructed all the wine stewards to serve each man what he wished.

⁹Queen Vashti also gave a banquet[j] for the women in the royal palace of King Xerxes.

¹⁰On the seventh day, when King Xerxes was in high spirits[k] from wine,[l] he commanded the seven eunuchs who served him—Mehuman, Biztha, Harbona,[m] Bigtha, Abagtha, Zethar and Carcas— ¹¹to bring[n] before him Queen Vashti, wearing her royal crown, in order to display her beauty[o] to the people and nobles, for she was lovely to look at. ¹²But when the attendants delivered the king's command, Queen Vashti refused to come. Then the king became furious and burned with anger.[p]

¹³Since it was customary for the king to consult experts in matters of law and justice, he spoke with the wise men who understood the times[q] ¹⁴and were closest to the king—Carshena, Shethar, Admatha, Tarshish, Meres, Marsena and Memucan, the seven nobles[r] of Persia and Media who had special access to the king and were highest in the kingdom.

¹⁵"According to law, what must be done to Queen Vashti?" he asked. "She has not obeyed the command of King Xerxes that the eunuchs have taken to her."

¹⁶Then Memucan replied in the presence of the king and the nobles, "Queen Vashti has done wrong, not only against the king but also against all the nobles and the peoples of all the provinces of King Xerxes. ¹⁷For the queen's conduct will become known to all the women, and so they will despise their husbands and say, 'King Xerxes commanded Queen Vashti to be brought before him, but she would not come.' ¹⁸This very day the Persian and Median women of the nobility who have heard about the queen's conduct will respond to all the king's nobles in the same way. There will be no end of disrespect and discord.[s]

¹⁹"Therefore, if it pleases the king,[t] let him issue a royal decree and let it be written in the laws of Persia and Media, which cannot be repealed,[u] that Vashti is never again to enter the presence of King Xerxes. Also let the king give her royal position to someone else who is better than she. ²⁰Then when the king's edict is proclaimed throughout all his vast realm, all the women will respect their husbands, from the least to the greatest."

²¹The king and his nobles were pleased with this advice, so the king did as Memucan proposed. ²²He sent dispatches to all parts of the kingdom, to each province in its own script and to each people in its own language,[v] proclaiming in each people's tongue that every man should be ruler over his own household.

Esther Made Queen

2 Later when the anger of King Xerxes had subsided,[w] he remembered Vashti and what she had done and what he had decreed about her. ²Then the

---

a 1 Hebrew *Ahasuerus,* a variant of Xerxes' Persian name; here and throughout Esther *b 1* That is, the upper Nile region

---

1:13 The wise men were probably astrologers that advised the royal court of Persia. They were also conversant with the law of Moses (see Ezr 7:14).

king's personal attendants proposed, "Let a search be made for beautiful young virgins for the king. ³Let the king appoint commissioners in every province of his realm to bring all these beautiful girls into the harem at the citadel of Susa. Let them be placed under the care of Hegai, the king's eunuch, who is in charge of the women; and let beauty treatments be given to them. ⁴Then let the girl who pleases the king be queen instead of Vashti." This advice appealed to the king, and he followed it.

⁵Now there was in the citadel of Susa a Jew of the tribe of Benjamin, named Mordecai son of Jair, the son of Shimei, the son of Kish, ⁶who had been carried into exile from Jerusalem by Nebuchadnezzar king of Babylon, among those taken captive with Jehoiachin[c] king of Judah. ⁷Mordecai had a cousin named Hadassah, whom he had brought up because she had neither father nor mother. This girl, who was also known as Esther,[a] was lovely[b] in form and features, and Mordecai had taken her as his own daughter when her father and mother died.

⁸When the king's order and edict had been proclaimed, many girls were brought to the citadel of Susa[c] and put under the care of Hegai. Esther also was taken to the king's palace and entrusted to Hegai, who had charge of the harem. ⁹The girl pleased him and won his favor.[d] Immediately he provided her with beauty treatments and special food.[e] He assigned to her seven maids selected from the king's palace and moved her and her maids into the best place in the harem.

¹⁰Esther had not revealed her nationality and family background, because Mordecai had forbidden her to do so.[f] ¹¹Every day he walked back and forth near the courtyard of the harem to find out how Esther was and what was happening to her.

¹²Before a girl's turn came to go in to King Xerxes, she had to complete twelve months of beauty treatments prescribed for the women, six months with oil of myrrh and six with perfumes[g] and cosmetics. ¹³And this is how she would go to the king: Anything she wanted was given her to take with her from the harem to the king's palace. ¹⁴In the evening she would go there and in the morning return to another part of the harem to the care of Shaashgaz, the king's eunuch who was in charge of the concubines.[h] She would not return to the king unless he was pleased with her and summoned her by name.[i]

¹⁵When the turn came for Esther (the girl Mordecai had adopted, the daughter of his uncle Abihail[j]) to go to the king,[k] she asked for nothing other than what Hegai, the king's eunuch who was in charge of the harem, suggested. And Esther won the favor[l] of everyone who saw her. ¹⁶She was taken to King Xerxes in the royal residence in the tenth month, the month of Tebeth, in the seventh year of his reign.

¹⁷Now the king was attracted to Esther more than to any of the other women, and she won his favor and approval more than any of the other virgins. So he set a royal crown on her head and made her queen[m] instead of Vashti. ¹⁸And the king gave a great banquet,[n] Esther's banquet, for all his nobles and officials.[o] He proclaimed a holiday throughout the provinces and distributed gifts with royal liberality.[p]

Mordecai Uncovers a Conspiracy

¹⁹When the virgins were assembled a second time, Mordecai was sitting at the king's gate.[q] ²⁰But Esther had kept secret her family background and nationality just as Mordecai had told her to do, for she continued to follow Mordecai's instructions as she had done when he was bringing her up.[r]

²¹During the time Mordecai was sitting at the king's gate, Bigthana[d] and Teresh, two of the king's officers[s] who guarded the doorway, became angry[t] and conspired to assassinate King Xerxes. ²²But Mordecai found out about the plot and told Queen Esther, who in turn reported it to the king, giving credit to Mordecai. ²³And when the report was investigated and found to be true, the two officials were hanged[u] on a gallows.[e] All this was recorded in the book of the annals[v] in the presence of the king.[w]

---

[c] 6 Hebrew *Jeconiah*, a variant of *Jehoiachin* [d] 21 Hebrew *Bigthan*, a variant of *Bigthana* [e] 23 Or *were hung* (or *impaled*) *on poles*; similarly elsewhere in Esther

Haman's Plot to Destroy the Jews

3 After these events, King Xerxes honored Haman son of Hammedatha, the Agagite,ˣ elevating him and giving him a seat of honor higher than that of all the other nobles. ²All the royal officials at the king's gate knelt down and paid honor to Haman, for the king had commanded this concerning him. But Mordecai would not kneel down or pay him honor.

³Then the royal officials at the king's gate asked Mordecai, "Why do you disobey the king's command?"ʸ ⁴Day after day they spoke to him but he refused to comply.ᶻ Therefore they told Haman about it to see whether Mordecai's behavior would be tolerated, for he had told them he was a Jew.

⁵When Haman saw that Mordecai would not kneel down or pay him honor, he was enraged.ᵃ ⁶Yet having learned who Mordecai's people were, he scorned the idea of killing only Mordecai. Instead Haman looked for a wayᵇ to destroyᶜ all Mordecai's people, the Jews,ᵈ throughout the whole kingdom of Xerxes.

⁷In the twelfth year of King Xerxes, in the first month, the month of Nisan, they cast the *pur*ᵉ (that is, the lotᶠ) in the presence of Haman to select a day and month. And the lot fell onᶠ the twelfth month, the month of Adar.ᵍ

⁸Then Haman said to King Xerxes, "There is a certain people dispersed and scattered among the peoples in all the provinces of your kingdom whose customsʰ are different from those of all other people and who do not obeyⁱ the king's laws; it is not in the king's best interest to tolerate them.ʲ ⁹If it pleases the king, let a decree be issued to destroy them, and I will put ten thousand talentsᵍ of silver into the royal treasury for the men who carry out this business."ᵏ

¹⁰So the king took his signet ringˡ from his finger and gave it to Haman son of Hammedatha, the Agagite, the enemy of the Jews. ¹¹"Keep the money," the king said to Haman, "and do with the people as you please."

¹²Then on the thirteenth day of the first month the royal secretaries were summoned. They wrote out in the script of each province and in the languageᵐ of each people all Haman's orders to the king's satraps, the governors of the various provinces and the nobles of the various peoples. These were written in the name of King Xerxes himself and sealedⁿ with his own ring. ¹³Dispatches were sent by couriers to all the king's provinces with the order to destroy, kill and annihilate all the Jewsᵒ—young and old, women and little children—on a single day, the thirteenth day of the twelfth month, the month of Adar,ᵖ and to plunderᵠ their goods. ¹⁴A copy of the text of the edict was to be issued as law in every province and made known to the people of every nationality so they would be ready for that day.ʳ

¹⁵Spurred on by the king's command, the couriers went out, and the edict was issued in the citadel of Susa.ˢ The king and Haman sat down to drink,ᵗ but the city of Susa was bewildered.ᵘ

Mordecai Persuades Esther to Help

4 When Mordecai learned of all that had been done, he tore his clothes,ᵛ put on sackcloth and ashes,ʷ and went out into the city, wailingˣ loudly and bitterly. ²But he went only as far as the king's gate,ʸ because no one clothed in sackcloth was allowed to enter it. ³In every province to which the edict and order of the king came, there was great mourning among the Jews, with fasting, weeping and wailing. Many lay in sackcloth and ashes.

⁴When Esther's maids and eunuchs came and told her about Mordecai, she was in great distress. She sent clothes for him to put on instead of his sackcloth, but he would not accept them. ⁵Then Esther summoned Hathach, one of the king's eunuchs assigned to attend her, and ordered him to find out what was troubling Mordecai and why.

⁶So Hathach went out to Mordecai in the open square of the city in front of the king's gate. ⁷Mordecai told him everything that had happened to him, including the exact amount of money Haman had promised to pay into the royal treasury for the destruction of the Jews.ᶻ ⁸He also gave him a copy of the text of the edict for their annihilation, which had been published in Susa, to show to Esther

---

f 7 Septuagint; Hebrew does not have *And the lot fell on*. *g 9* That is, about 375 tons (about 345 metric tons) and explain it to her, and he told him to urge her to go into the king's presence to beg for mercy and plead with him for her people.

⁹Hathach went back and reported to Esther what Mordecai had said. ¹⁰Then she instructed him to say to Mordecai, ¹¹"All the king's officials and the people of the royal provinces know that for any man or woman who approaches the king in the inner court without being summoned[a] the king has but one law:[b] that he be put to death. The only exception to this is for the king to extend the gold scepter[c] to him and spare his life. But thirty days have passed since I was called to go to the king."

¹²When Esther's words were reported to Mordecai, ¹³he sent back this answer: "Do not think that because you are in the king's house you alone of all the Jews will escape. ¹⁴For if you remain silent[d] at this time, relief[e] and deliverance[f] for the Jews will arise from another place, but you and your father's family will perish. And who knows but that you have come to royal position for such a time as this?" ¹⁵Then Esther sent this reply to Mordecai: ¹⁶"Go, gather together all the Jews who are in Susa, and fast[h] for me. Do not eat or drink for three days, night or day. I and my maids will fast as you do. When this is done, I will go to the king, even though it is against the law. And if I perish, I perish."[i]

¹⁷So Mordecai went away and carried out all of Esther's instructions.

Esther's Request to the King

5 On the third day Esther put on her royal robes[j] and stood in the inner court of the palace, in front of the king's[k] hall. The king was sitting on his royal throne in the hall, facing the entrance. ²When he saw Queen Esther standing in the court, he was pleased with her and held out to her the gold scepter that was in his hand. So Esther approached and touched the tip of the scepter.[l]

³Then the king asked, "What is it, Queen Esther? What is your request? Even up to half the kingdom,[m] it will be given you."

⁴"If it pleases the king," replied Esther, "let the king, together with Haman, come today to a banquet I have prepared for him."

⁵"Bring Haman at once," the king said, "so that we may do what Esther asks."

So the king and Haman went to the banquet Esther had prepared. ⁶As they were drinking wine,[n] the king again asked Esther, "Now what is your petition? It will be given you. And what is your request? Even up to half the kingdom,[o] it will be granted."[p]

⁷Esther replied, "My petition and my request is this: ⁸If the king regards me with favor[q] and if it pleases the king to grant my petition and fulfill my request, let the king and Haman come tomorrow to the banquet[r] I will prepare for them. Then I will answer the king's question."

Haman's Rage Against Mordecai

⁹Haman went out that day happy and in high spirits. But when he saw Mordecai at the king's gate and observed that he neither rose nor showed fear in his presence, he was filled with rage[s] against Mordecai.[t] ¹⁰Nevertheless, Haman restrained himself and went home.

Calling together his friends and Zeresh,[u] his wife, ¹¹Haman boasted[v] to them about his vast wealth, his many sons,[w] and all the ways the king had honored him and how he had elevated him above the other nobles and officials. ¹²"And that's not all," Haman added. "I'm the only person[x] Queen Esther in-

---

4:11 a Est 2:14; b Da 2:9 c Est 5:1,2; 8:4; Ps 125:3

4:14 d Job 34:29; Ps 28:1; 35:22; Ecc 3:7; Isa 42:14; 57:11; 62:1; 64:12; Am 5:13 e Est 9:16, 22 f S Ge 45:7; S Dt 28:29 g S Ge 50:20

4:16 h S 2Ch 20:3; Est 9:31 i S Ge 43:14

5:1 j Eze 16:13 k Pr 21:1

5:2 l S Est 4:11

5:3 m Est 7:2; Da 5:16; Mk 6:23

5:6 n S Est 1:10 o Da 5:16; Mk 6:23 p Est 9:12

5:8 q S Est 2:15 r S 1Ki 3:15

5:9 s S Est 2:21; Pr 14:17 t S Est 3:3, 5

5:10 u Est 6:13

5:11 v Pr 13:16 w Est 9:7-10,13

5:12 x Job 22:29; Pr 16:18; 29:23

4:16 Our method of marking time differs from the ancient Jews' method of calculating time. While we follow a full measure of time to calculate the passage of days and years (one day means 24 hours; one year means 365 days; half a day means 12 hours, etc.), in ancient societies any part of one day counted as a whole day when calculating time. When Esther asked Mordecai to fast for three days, she was not referring to a full measure of seventy-two hours, but rather regarded the three days to have begun on the day she spoke with Mordecai, continuing through the next full day and ending sometime during the day after that—the third day. Note that 5:1 bears out this inclusive mode of time calculation.

Understanding this ancient mode of time calculation is important for us in understanding the precise chronology of some key Biblical events such as Jonah's incarceration in the whale (see Jnh 1:17) and Christ's crucifixion and resurrection (see Mt 12:40).

vited to accompany the king to the banquet she gave. And she has invited me along with the king tomorrow. ¹³But all this gives me no satisfaction as long as I see that Jew Mordecai sitting at the king's gate."

¹⁴His wife Zeresh and all his friends said to him, "Have a gallows built, seventy-five feet[h] high, and ask the king in the morning to have Mordecai hanged on it. Then go with the king to the dinner and be happy." This suggestion delighted Haman, and he had the gallows built.

Mordecai Honored

6 That night the king could not sleep; so he ordered the book of the chronicles, the record of his reign, to be brought in and read to him. ²It was found recorded there that Mordecai had exposed Bigthana and Teresh, two of the king's officers who guarded the doorway, who had conspired to assassinate King Xerxes.

³"What honor and recognition has Mordecai received for this?" the king asked.

"Nothing has been done for him," his attendants answered.

⁴The king said, "Who is in the court?" Now Haman had just entered the outer court of the palace to speak to the king about hanging Mordecai on the gallows he had erected for him.

⁵His attendants answered, "Haman is standing in the court."

"Bring him in," the king ordered.

⁶When Haman entered, the king asked him, "What should be done for the man the king delights to honor?"

Now Haman thought to himself, "Who is there that the king would rather honor than me?" ⁷So he answered the king, "For the man the king delights to honor, ⁸have them bring a royal robe the king has worn and a horse the king has ridden, one with a royal crest placed on its head. ⁹Then let the robe and horse be entrusted to one of the king's most noble princes. Let them robe the man the king delights to honor, and lead him on the horse through the city streets, proclaiming before him, 'This is what is done for the man the king delights to honor!'"

¹⁰"Go at once," the king commanded Haman. "Get the robe and the horse and do just as you have suggested for Mordecai the Jew, who sits at the king's gate. Do not neglect anything you have recommended."

¹¹So Haman got the robe and the horse. He robed Mordecai, and led him on horseback through the city streets, proclaiming before him, "This is what is done for the man the king delights to honor!"

¹²Afterward Mordecai returned to the king's gate. But Haman rushed home, with his head covered in grief, ¹³and told Zeresh his wife and all his friends everything that had happened to him.

His advisers and his wife Zeresh said to him, "Since Mordecai, before whom your downfall has started, is of Jewish origin, you cannot stand against him—you will surely come to ruin!" ¹⁴While they were still talking with him, the king's eunuchs arrived and hurried Haman away to the banquet Esther had prepared.

Haman Hanged

7 So the king and Haman went to dine with Queen Esther, ²and as they were drinking wine on that second day, the king again asked, "Queen Esther, what is your petition? It will be given you. What is your request? Even up to half the kingdom, it will be granted."

³Then Queen Esther answered, "If I have found favor with you, O king, and if it pleases your majesty, grant me my life—this is my petition. And spare my people—this is my request. ⁴For I and my people have been sold for destruction and slaughter and annihilation. If we had merely been sold as male and female slaves, I would have kept quiet, because no such distress would justify disturbing the king."

⁵King Xerxes asked Queen Esther, "Who is he? Where is the man who has dared to do such a thing?"

⁶Esther said, "The adversary and enemy is this vile Haman."

Then Haman was terrified before the king and queen. ⁷The king got up in a rage, left his wine and went out into the palace garden. But Haman, realizing that the king had already decided his fate, stayed behind to beg Queen Esther for his life.

---

h 14 Hebrew *fifty cubits* (about 23 meters) *i 4* Or *quiet, but the compensation our adversary offers cannot be compared with the loss the king would suffer*

ESTHER 7:8

⁸Just as the king returned from the palace garden to the banquet hall, Haman was falling on the couchˣ where Esther was reclining.ʸ

The king exclaimed, "Will he even molest the queen while she is with me in the house?"ᶻ

As soon as the word left the king's mouth, they covered Haman's face.ᵃ ⁹Then Harbona,ᵇ one of the eunuchs attending the king, said, "A gallows seventy-five feetᶠ highᶜ stands by Haman's house. He had it made for Mordecai, who spoke up to help the king."

The king said, "Hang him on it!"ᵈ ¹⁰So they hangedᵉ Hamanᶠ on the gallowsᵍ he had prepared for Mordecai.ʰ Then the king's fury subsided.ⁱ

The King's Edict in Behalf of the Jews

8 That same day King Xerxes gave Queen Esther the estate of Haman,ʲ the enemy of the Jews. And Mordecai came into the presence of the king, for Esther had told how he was related to her. ²The king took off his signet ring,ᵏ which he had reclaimed from Haman, and presented it to Mordecai. And Esther appointed him over Haman's estate.ˡ

³Esther again pleaded with the king, falling at his feet and weeping. She begged him to put an end to the evil plan of Haman the Agagite,ᵐ which he had devised against the Jews. ⁴Then the king extended the gold scepterⁿ to Esther and she arose and stood before him.

⁵"If it pleases the king," she said, "and if he regards me with favorᵒ and thinks it the right thing to do, and if he is pleased with me, let an order be written overruling the dispatches that Haman son of Hammedatha, the Agagite, devised and wrote to destroy the Jews in all the king's provinces. ⁶For how can I bear to see disaster fall on my people? How can I bear to see the destruction of my family?"ᵖ

⁷King Xerxes replied to Queen Esther and to Mordecai the Jew, "Because Haman attacked the Jews, I have given his estate to Esther, and they have hangedᵠ him on the gallows. ⁸Now write another decreeʳ in the king's name in behalf of the Jews as seems best to you, and sealˢ it with the king's signet ringᵗ—for no document written in the king's name and sealed with his ring can be revoked."ᵘ

⁹At once the royal secretaries were summoned—on the twenty-third day of the third month, the month of Sivan. They wrote out all Mordecai's orders to the Jews, and to the satraps, governors and nobles of the 127 provinces stretching from India to Cush.ᵏᵛ These orders were written in the script of each province and the language of each people and also to the Jews in their own script and language.ʷ ¹⁰Mordecai wrote in the name of King Xerxes, sealed the dispatches with the king's signet ring, and sent them by mounted couriers, who rode fast horses especially bred for the king.

¹¹The king's edict granted the Jews in every city the right to assemble and protect themselves; to destroy, kill and annihilate any armed force of any nationality or province that might attack them and their women and children; and to plunderˣ the property of their enemies. ¹²The day appointed for the Jews to do this in all the provinces of King Xerxes was the thirteenth day of the twelfth month, the month of Adar.ʸ ¹³A copy of the text of the edict was to be issued as law in every province and made known to the people of every nationality so that the Jews would be ready on that dayᶻ to avenge themselves on their enemies.

¹⁴The couriers, riding the royal horses, raced out, spurred on by the king's command. And the edict was also issued in the citadel of Susa.ᵃ

¹⁵Mordecaiᵇ left the king's presence wearing royal garments of blue and white, a large crown of goldᶜ and a purple robe of fine linen.ᵈ And the city of Susa held a joyous celebration.ᵉ ¹⁶For the Jews it was a time of happiness and joy,ᶠ gladness and honor.ᵍ ¹⁷In every province and in every city, wherever the edict of the king went, there was joyʰ and gladness among the Jews, with feasting and celebrating. And many people of other nationalities became Jews because fearⁱ of the Jews had seized them.ʲ

Triumph of the Jews

9 On the thirteenth day of the twelfth month, the month of Adar,ᵏ the edict commanded by the king was to be carried out. On this day the enemies of

L Ne 9:12 ◀▶ Job 5:17–26

ʲ 9 Hebrew *fifty cubits* (about 23 meters)   *ᵏ 9* That is, the upper Nile region

the Jews had hoped to overpower them, but now the tables were turned and the Jews got the upper hand over those who hated them. ²The Jews assembled in their cities in all the provinces of King Xerxes to attack those seeking their destruction. No one could stand against them, because the people of all the other nationalities were afraid of them. ³And all the nobles of the provinces, the satraps, the governors and the king's administrators helped the Jews, because fear of Mordecai had seized them. ⁴Mordecai was prominent in the palace; his reputation spread throughout the provinces, and he became more and more powerful.

⁵The Jews struck down all their enemies with the sword, killing and destroying them, and they did what they pleased to those who hated them. ⁶In the citadel of Susa, the Jews killed and destroyed five hundred men. ⁷They also killed Parshandatha, Dalphon, Aspatha, ⁸Poratha, Adalia, Aridatha, ⁹Parmashta, Arisai, Aridai and Vaizatha, ¹⁰the ten sons of Haman son of Hammedatha, the enemy of the Jews. But they did not lay their hands on the plunder.

¹¹The number of those slain in the citadel of Susa was reported to the king that same day. ¹²The king said to Queen Esther, "The Jews have killed and destroyed five hundred men and the ten sons of Haman in the citadel of Susa. What have they done in the rest of the king's provinces? Now what is your petition? It will be given you. What is your request? It will also be granted."

¹³"If it pleases the king," Esther answered, "give the Jews in Susa permission to carry out this day's edict tomorrow also, and let Haman's ten sons be hanged on gallows."

¹⁴So the king commanded that this be done. An edict was issued in Susa, and they hanged the ten sons of Haman. ¹⁵The Jews in Susa came together on the fourteenth day of the month of Adar, and they put to death in Susa three hundred men, but they did not lay their hands on the plunder.

¹⁶Meanwhile, the remainder of the Jews who were in the king's provinces also assembled to protect themselves and get relief from their enemies. They killed seventy-five thousand of them but did not lay their hands on the plunder. ¹⁷This happened on the thirteenth day of the month of Adar, and on the fourteenth they rested and made it a day of feasting and joy.

Purim Celebrated

¹⁸The Jews in Susa, however, had assembled on the thirteenth and fourteenth, and then on the fifteenth they rested and made it a day of feasting and joy.

¹⁹That is why rural Jews—those living in villages—observe the fourteenth of the month of Adar as a day of joy and feasting, a day for giving presents to each other.

²⁰Mordecai recorded these events, and he sent letters to all the Jews throughout the provinces of King Xerxes, near and far, ²¹to have them celebrate annually the fourteenth and fifteenth days of the month of Adar ²²as the time when the Jews got relief from their enemies, and as the month when their sorrow was turned into joy and their mourning into a day of celebration. He wrote them to observe the days as days of feasting and joy and giving presents of food to one another and gifts to the poor.

²³So the Jews agreed to continue the celebration they had begun, doing what Mordecai had written to them. ²⁴For Haman son of Hammedatha, the Agagite, the enemy of all the Jews, had plotted against the Jews to destroy them and had cast the *pur* (that is, the lot) for their ruin and destruction. ²⁵But when the plot came to the king's attention, he issued written orders that the evil scheme Haman had devised against the Jews should come back onto his own head, and that he and his sons should be hanged on the gallows. ²⁶(Therefore these days were called Purim, from the word *pur*.) Because of everything written in this letter and because of what they had seen and what had happened to them, ²⁷the Jews took it upon themselves to establish the custom that they and their descendants and all who join them should without fail observe these two days every year, in the way prescribed and at the time appointed. ²⁸These days should be remembered and observed in

---

25 Or when Esther came before the king

every generation by every family, and in every province and in every city. And these days of Purim should never cease to be celebrated by the Jews, nor should the memory of them die out among their descendants.

²⁹So Queen Esther, daughter of Abihail,ʷ along with Mordecai the Jew, wrote with full authority to confirm this second letter concerning Purim. ³⁰And Mordecai sent letters to all the Jews in the 127 provincesˣ of the kingdom of Xerxes—words of goodwill and assurance— ³¹to establish these days of Purim at their designated times, as Mordecai the Jew and Queen Esther had decreed for them, and as they had established for themselves and their descendants in regard to their times of fastingʸ and lamentation.ᶻ ³²Esther's decree confirmed these regulations about Purim, and it was written down in the records.

The Greatness of Mordecai

10 King Xerxes imposed tribute throughout the empire, to its distant shores.ᵃ ²And all his acts of power and might, together with a full account of the greatness of Mordecaiᵇ to which the king had raised him,ᶜ are they not written in the book of the annalsᵈ of the kings of Media and Persia? ³Mordecai the Jew was secondᵉ in rankᶠ to King Xerxes,ᵍ preeminent among the Jews, and held in high esteem by his many fellow Jews, because he worked for the good of his people and spoke up for the welfare of all the Jews.ʰ

Job

Author: Unknown

Theme: The problem of human suffering

Date of Writing: Unknown

Outline of Job
  I. Behind the Scenes of Job's Life (1:1—2:13)
  II. Job's Dialogue With His Three Friends (3:1—27:23)
  III. What Is Wisdom? (28:1–28)
  IV. Job, Elihu and God Speak (29:1—42:6)
  V. Job's Fortunes Restored (42:7–17)

ALTHOUGH THIS BOOK consists of the words of Job and his friends, Job himself was not the author. Jewish tradition suggests that Job was written before the time of Moses, but it may have been written as late as the time of Esther. Authorship is uncertain, but that the writer was an Israelite sharing the story of a non-Israelite from Uz. Using unusual words and literary styles, this book is difficult to translate, but the overarching message of God's justice despite human suffering is clear.

The dialogue between Job and his three friends forms the major part of the book. Job and his friends did not know about Satan's contest with God to test Job's. Missing this vital piece of the puzzle, Job's friends proceeded to dissect Job's life, attitudes and actions to explain away Job's suffering. Despite his overwhelming losses, calamities and betrayal by his friends and family, Job continued in his complete devotion to God (see 1:6–22; 2:1—3:26). Though Job did eventually succumb to self-pity, he never attacked God or questioned his sovereignty but expressed his confidence in God's redemption (see 19:25).

The book also presents several clear Messianic passages (see 9:33; 16:19; 19:25; 33:23–24; 36:18) pointing the reader to an eternal hope of deliverance. Job acknowledges that though the righteous may suffer, God has a purpose in suffering that may be beyond human comprehension. It is the response of the righteous to merely trust and obey.

Prologue

1 In the land of Uz[a] there lived a man whose name was Job.[b] This man was blameless[c] and upright;[d] he feared God[e] and shunned evil.[f] ²He had seven sons[g] and three daughters,[h] ³and he owned seven thousand sheep, three thousand camels, five hundred yoke of oxen and five hundred donkeys,[i] and had a large number of servants.[j] He was the greatest man[k] among all the people of the East.[l]

⁴His sons used to take turns holding feasts[m] in their homes, and they would invite their three sisters to eat and drink with them. ⁵When a period of feasting had run its course, Job would send and have them purified.[n] Early in the morning he would sacrifice a burnt offering[o] for each of them, thinking, "Perhaps my children have sinned[p] and cursed God[q] in their hearts." This was Job's regular custom.

Job's First Test

⁶One day the angels[a][r] came to present themselves before the LORD, and Satan[b][s] also came with them.[t] ⁷The LORD said to Satan, "Where have you come from?"

Satan answered the LORD, "From roaming through the earth and going back and forth in it."[u]

⁸Then the LORD said to Satan, "Have you considered my servant Job?[v] There is no one on earth like him; he is blameless and upright, a man who fears God[w] and shuns evil."[x]

⁹"Does Job fear God for nothing?"[y] Satan replied. ¹⁰"Have you not put a hedge[z] around him and his household and everything he has?[a] You have blessed the work of his hands, so that his flocks and herds are spread throughout the land.[b] ¹¹But stretch out your hand and strike everything he has,[c] and he will surely curse you to your face."[d]

¹²The LORD said to Satan, "Very well, then, everything he has[e] is in your hands, but on the man himself do not lay a finger."[f]

Then Satan went out from the presence of the LORD.

¹³One day when Job's sons and daughters[g] were feasting[h] and drinking wine at the oldest brother's house, ¹⁴a messenger came to Job and said, "The oxen were plowing and the donkeys were grazing[i] nearby, ¹⁵and the Sabeans[j] attacked and carried them off. They put the servants to the sword, and I am the only one who has escaped to tell you!"

¹⁶While he was still speaking, another messenger came and said, "The fire of God fell from the sky[k] and burned up the sheep and the servants,[l] and I am the only one who has escaped to tell you!"

¹⁷While he was still speaking, another messenger came and said, "The Chaldeans[m] formed three raiding parties and swept down on your camels and carried them off. They put the servants to the sword, and I am the only one who has escaped to tell you!"

¹⁸While he was still speaking, yet another messenger came and said, "Your sons and daughters[n] were feasting[o] and drinking wine at the oldest brother's house, ¹⁹when suddenly a mighty wind[p] swept in from the desert and struck the four corners of the house. It collapsed on them and they are dead,[q] and I am the only one who has escaped to tell you!"[r]

²⁰At this, Job got up and tore his robe[s] and shaved his head.[t] Then he fell to the ground in worship[u] ²¹and said:

> "Naked I came from my mother's womb,
>   and naked I will depart.[c][v]
> The LORD gave and the LORD has taken away;[w]

1:1 ᵃS Ge 10:23; ᵇEze 14:14,20; Jas 5:11 ᶜS Ge 6:9; S Job 23:10 ᵈJob 23:7; Ps 11:7; 107:42; Pr 21:29; Mic 7:2 ᵉS Ge 22:12 ᶠver 8; ᵍS Dt 4:6; Job 2:3; 1Th 5:22 1:2 ᵍS Ru 4:15 ʰver 13,18; Job 42:13; 1:3 ⁱS Ge 13:2 ʲS Ge 12:16 ᵏver 8; Job 29:25 ˡS Ge 25:6; Job 42:10; Ps 103:10 1:4 ᵐver 13,18 1:5 ⁿS Ne 12:30 ᵒS Ge 8:20 ᵖJob 8:4 ᵠ1Ki 21:10,13; Ps 10:3; 74:10 1:6 ʳS 1Ki 22:19; ᵃⁿGe 6:2 ˢS 2Sa 24:1; S 2Ch 18:21; S Ps 109:6; Lk 22:31 ᵗJob 2:1 1:7 ᵘS Ge 3:1; 1Pe 5:8 1:8 ᵛS Jos 1:7 ʷPs 25:12; 112:1; 128:4 ˣS ver 1; S Ex 20:20 1:9 ʸ1Ti 6:5 1:10 ᶻS 1Sa 25:16 ᵃver 12; Job 2:4; Ps 34:7 ᵇver 3; Job 8:7; 29:6; 42:12,17 1:11 ᶜJob 19:21; Lk 22:31 ᵈLev 24:11; Job 2:5; Isa 3:8; 65:3; Rev 12:9-10 1:12 ᵉS ver 10 ᶠJob 2:6; 1Co 10:13 1:13 ᵍS ver 2 ʰS ver 4 1:14 ⁱGe 36:24 1:15 ʲS Ge 10:7; S Job 9:24 1:16 ᵏS 1Ki 18:38; 2Ki 1:12; Job 20:26 ˡS Ge 18:17; S Lev 10:2; S Nu 11:1-3 1:17 ᵐS Ge 11:28, 31; S Job 9:24 1:18 ⁿS ver 2 ᵒS ver 4 1:19 ᵖPs 11:6; Isa 5:28; 21:1; Jer 4:11; 13:24; 18:17; Eze 17:10; Hos 13:15; Mt 7:25 ᵠJob 16:7; 19:13-15 ʳEze 24:26 1:20 ˢS Ge 37:29; S Mk 14:63 ᵗIsa 3:24; 15:2; 22:12; Jer 7:29; 16:6; Eze 27:31; 29:18; Mic 1:16 ᵘ1Pe 5:6 1:21 ᵛEcc 5:15; 1Ti 6:7 ʷRu 1:21; 1Sa 2:7

ᵃ6 Hebrew the sons of God ᵇ6 Satan means accuser. ᶜ21 Or will return empty

U Ne 1:5 ◀ ▶ Job 8:6–7
K 1Ch 29:11–12 ◀ ▶ Job 17:9
P 2Ch 32:29 ◀ ▶ Job 22:24–25

J Ne 8:10 ◀ ▶ Job 13:15

1:6–7 Satan, the chief of the fallen angels, "prowls around like a roaring lion looking for someone to devour" (1Pe 5:8). Satan's freedom will end when Christ casts him into the bottomless pit for a thousand years following the defeat of the antichrist at the end of the Battle of Armageddon (see Rev 20:1–3).

may the name of the Lord be praised."ˣ

²²In all this, Job did not sin by charging God with wrongdoing.ʸ

Job's Second Test

2 On another day the angels*ᵈᶻ* came to present themselves before the Lord, and Satan also came with themᵃ to present himself before him. ²And the Lord said to Satan, "Where have you come from?"

Satan answered the Lord, "From roaming through the earth and going back and forth in it."ᵇ

³Then the Lord said to Satan, "Have you considered my servant Job? There is no one on earth like him; he is blameless and upright, a man who fears God and shuns evil.ᶜ And he still maintains his integrity,ᵈ though you incited me against him to ruin him without any reason."ᵉ

⁴"Skin for skin!" Satan replied. "A man will give all he hasᶠ for his own life. ⁵But stretch out your hand and strike his flesh and bones,ᵍ and he will surely curse you to your face."ʰ

⁶The Lord said to Satan, "Very well, then, he is in your hands;ⁱ but you must spare his life."ʲ

⁷So Satan went out from the presence of the Lord and afflicted Job with painful sores from the soles of his feet to the top of his head.ᵏ ⁸Then Job took a piece of broken pottery and scraped himself with it as he sat among the ashes.ˡ

⁹His wife said to him, "Are you still holding on to your integrity?ᵐ Curse God and die!"ⁿ

¹⁰He replied, "You are talking like a foolishᵉ woman. Shall we accept good from God, and not trouble?"ᵒ

In all this, Job did not sin in what he said.ᵖ

Job's Three Friends

¹¹When Job's three friends, Eliphaz the Temanite,ᑫ Bildad the Shuhiteʳ and Zophar the Naamathite,ˢ heard about all the troubles that had come upon him, they set out from their homes and met together by agreement to go and sympathize with him and comfort him.ᵗ ¹²When they saw him from a distance, they could hardly recognize him;ᵘ they began to weep aloud,ᵛ and they tore their robesʷ and sprinkled dust on their heads.ˣ ¹³Then they sat on the groundʸ with him for seven days and seven nights.ᶻ No one said a word to him,ᵃ because they saw how great his suffering was.

Job Speaks

3 After this, Job opened his mouth and cursed the day of his birth.ᵇ ²He said:

³"May the day of my birth perish,
   and the night it was said, 'A boy is born!'ᶜ
⁴That day—may it turn to darkness;
   may God above not care about it;
   may no light shine upon it.
⁵May darkness and deep shadow*ᶠᵈ*
   claim it once more;
   may a cloud settle over it;
   may blackness overwhelm its light.
⁶That night—may thick darknessᵉ seize it;
   may it not be included among the days of the year
   nor be entered in any of the months.
⁷May that night be barren;
   may no shout of joyᶠ be heard in it.
⁸May those who curse daysᵍ curse that day,ᵍ
   those who are ready to rouse Leviathan.ʰ
⁹May its morning stars become dark;
   may it wait for daylight in vain
   and not see the first rays of dawn,ⁱ
¹⁰for it did not shut the doors of the womb on me
   to hide trouble from my eyes.

¹¹"Why did I not perish at birth,
   and die as I came from the womb?ʲ
¹²Why were there knees to receive meᵏ
   and breasts that I might be nursed?
¹³For now I would be lying downˡ in peace;
   I would be asleep and at restᵐ
¹⁴with kings and counselors of the earth,ⁿ
   who built for themselves places now lying in ruins,ᵒ

d 1 Hebrew *the sons of God* *e 10* The Hebrew word rendered *foolish* denotes moral deficiency. *f 5* Or *and the shadow of death* *g 8* Or *the sea*

¹⁵with rulers who had gold,
    who filled their houses with silver.
¹⁶Or why was I not hidden in the
    ground like a stillborn child,
    like an infant who never saw the
    light of day?
¹⁷There the wicked cease from turmoil,
    and there the weary are at rest.
¹⁸Captives also enjoy their ease;
    they no longer hear the slave
    driver's shout.
¹⁹The small and the great are there,
    and the slave is freed from his
    master.
²⁰"Why is light given to those in misery,
    and life to the bitter of soul,
²¹to those who long for death that does
    not come,
    who search for it more than for
    hidden treasure,
²²who are filled with gladness
    and rejoice when they reach the
    grave?
²³Why is life given to a man
    whose way is hidden,
    whom God has hedged in?
²⁴For sighing comes to me instead of
    food;
    my groans pour out like water.
²⁵What I feared has come upon me;
    what I dreaded has happened to
    me.
²⁶I have no peace, no quietness,
    I have no rest, but only turmoil."

Eliphaz

4 Then Eliphaz the Temanite replied:

²"If someone ventures a word with you,
    will you be impatient?
    But who can keep from speaking?
³Think how you have instructed many,
    how you have strengthened feeble
    hands.
⁴Your words have supported those who
    stumbled;
    you have strengthened faltering
    knees.
⁵But now trouble comes to you, and you
    are discouraged;
    it strikes you, and you are
    dismayed.
⁶Should not your piety be your
    confidence
    and your blameless ways your
    hope?

⁷"Consider now: Who, being innocent,
    has ever perished?
    Where were the upright ever
    destroyed?
⁸As I have observed, those who plow
    evil
    and those who sow trouble reap it.
⁹At the breath of God they are
    destroyed;
    at the blast of his anger they perish.
¹⁰The lions may roar and growl,
    yet the teeth of the great lions are
    broken.
¹¹The lion perishes for lack of prey,
    and the cubs of the lioness are
    scattered.

¹²"A word was secretly brought to me,
    my ears caught a whisper of it.
¹³Amid disquieting dreams in the night,
    when deep sleep falls on men,
¹⁴fear and trembling seized me
    and made all my bones shake.
¹⁵A spirit glided past my face,
    and the hair on my body stood on
    end.
¹⁶It stopped,
    but I could not tell what it was.
    A form stood before my eyes,
    and I heard a hushed voice:
¹⁷'Can a mortal be more righteous than
    God?
    Can a man be more pure than his
    Maker?
¹⁸If God places no trust in his servants,
    if he charges his angels with error,
¹⁹how much more those who live in
    houses of clay,
    whose foundations are in the dust,
    who are crushed more readily than
    a moth!
²⁰Between dawn and dusk they are
    broken to pieces;

H Ezr 8:22 ◄ ► Job 8:22
S Ezr 8:28 ◄ ► Job 8:20
E 2Ch 16:9 ◄ ► Job 14:16–17
N Ne 9:29–30 ◄ ► Job 7:1

unnoticed, they perish forever.ᶜ
²¹Are not the cords of their tent pulled
up,ᵈ
so that they dieᵉ without
wisdom?'ʰᶠ

5 "Call if you will, but who will
answer you?ᵍ
To which of the holy onesʰ will you
turn?
²Resentmentⁱ kills a fool,
and envy slays the simple.ʲ
³I myself have seenᵏ a fool taking root,ˡ
but suddenlyᵐ his house was
cursed.ⁿ
⁴His childrenᵒ are far from safety,ᵖ
crushed in courtᵠ without a
defender.ʳ
⁵The hungry consume his harvest,ˢ
taking it even from among thorns,
and the thirsty pant after his wealth.
⁶For hardship does not spring from the
soil,
nor does trouble sprout from the
ground.ᵗ
⁷Yet man is born to troubleᵘ
as surely as sparks fly upward.
⁸"But if it were I, I would appeal to
God;
I would lay my cause before him.ᵛ
⁹He performs wondersʷ that cannot be
fathomed,ˣ
miracles that cannot be counted.ʸ
¹⁰He bestows rain on the earth;ᶻ
he sends water upon the
countryside.ᵃ
¹¹The lowly he sets on high,ᵇ
and those who mournᶜ are liftedᵈ to
safety.
¹²He thwarts the plansᵉ of the crafty,
so that their hands achieve no
success.ᶠ
¹³He catches the wiseᵍ in their
craftiness,ʰ
and the schemes of the wily are
swept away.ⁱ
¹⁴Darknessʲ comes upon them in the
daytime;
at noon they grope as in the night.ᵏ
¹⁵He saves the needyˡ from the sword in
their mouth;
he saves them from the clutches of
the powerful.ᵐ
¹⁶So the poorⁿ have hope,
and injustice shuts its mouth.ᵒ

¹⁷"Blessed is the man whom God
corrects;ᵖ
so do not despise the disciplineᵠ of
the Almighty.ⁱʳ
¹⁸For he wounds, but he also binds up;ˢ
he injures, but his hands also heal.ᵗ
¹⁹From six calamities he will rescueᵘ
you;
in seven no harm will befall you.ᵛ
²⁰In famineʷ he will ransom you from
death,
and in battle from the stroke of the
sword.ˣ
²¹You will be protected from the lash of
the tongue,ʸ
and need not fearᶻ when destruction
comes.ᵃ
²²You will laughᵇ at destruction and
famine,ᶜ
and need not fear the beasts of the
earth.ᵈ
²³For you will have a covenantᵉ with the
stonesᶠ of the field,
and the wild animals will be at
peace with you.ᵍ
²⁴You will know that your tent is
secure;ʰ
you will take stock of your property
and find nothing missing.ⁱ
²⁵You will know that your children will
be many,ʲ
and your descendants like the grass
of the earth.ᵏ
²⁶You will come to the grave in full
vigor,ˡ
like sheaves gathered in season.ᵐ
²⁷"We have examined this, and it is
true.
So hear itⁿ and apply it to yourself."ᵒ

ʰ 21 Some interpreters end the quotation after verse 17. ⁱ 17 Hebrew *Shaddai*; here and throughout Job

Job

6 Then Job replied:

² "If only my anguish could be weighed
and all my misery be placed on the
scales!ᵖ
³ It would surely outweigh the sandᵠ of
the seas—
no wonder my words have been
impetuous.ʳ
⁴ The arrowsˢ of the Almightyᵗ are in
me,ᵘ
my spirit drinksᵛ in their poison;ʷ
God's terrorsˣ are marshaled against
me.ʸ
⁵ Does a wild donkeyᶻ brayᵃ when it has
grass,
or an ox bellow when it has
fodder?ᵇ
⁶ Is tasteless food eaten without salt,
or is there flavor in the white of an
egg/?ᶜ
⁷ I refuse to touch it;
such food makes me ill.ᵈ

⁸ "Oh, that I might have my request,
that God would grant what I hope
for,ᵉ
⁹ that God would be willing to crushᶠ
me,
to let loose his hand and cut me
off!ᵍ
¹⁰ Then I would still have this
consolationʰ—
my joy in unrelenting painⁱ—
that I had not denied the wordsʲ of
the Holy One.ᵏ

¹¹ "What strength do I have, that I should
still hope?
What prospects, that I should be
patient?ˡ
¹² Do I have the strength of stone?
Is my flesh bronze?ᵐ
¹³ Do I have any power to help myself,ⁿ
now that success has been driven
from me?

¹⁴ "A despairing manᵒ should have the
devotionᵖ of his friends,ᵠ
even though he forsakes the fear of
the Almighty.ʳ
¹⁵ But my brothers are as undependable
as intermittent streams,ˢ
as the streams that overflow
¹⁶ when darkened by thawing ice
and swollen with melting snow,ᵗ
¹⁷ but that cease to flow in the dry
season,
and in the heatᵘ vanish from their
channels.
¹⁸ Caravans turn aside from their
routes;
they go up into the wasteland and
perish.
¹⁹ The caravans of Temaᵛ look for water,
the traveling merchants of Shebaʷ
look in hope.
²⁰ They are distressed, because they had
been confident;
they arrive there, only to be
disappointed.ˣ
²¹ Now you too have proved to be of no
help;
you see something dreadful and are
afraid.ʸ
²² Have I ever said, 'Give something on
my behalf,
pay a ransomᶻ for me from your
wealth,ᵃ
²³ deliver me from the hand of the
enemy,
ransom me from the clutches of the
ruthless'?ᵇ

²⁴ "Teach me, and I will be quiet;ᶜ
show me where I have been
wrong.ᵈ
²⁵ How painful are honest words!ᵉ
But what do your arguments
prove?
²⁶ Do you mean to correct what I say,
and treat the words of a despairing
man as wind?ᶠ
²⁷ You would even cast lotsᵍ for the
fatherlessʰ
and barter away your friend.

²⁸ "But now be so kind as to look at me.
Would I lie to your face?ⁱ
²⁹ Relent, do not be unjust;ʲ
reconsider, for my integrityᵏ is at
stake.ᵏˡ
³⁰ Is there any wickedness on
my lips?ᵐ
Can my mouth not discernⁿ
malice?

c Job 5:13–14 ◀ ▶ Job 15:16

l 6 The meaning of the Hebrew for this phrase is uncertain. *k 29* Or *my righteousness still stands*

7 "Does not man have hard service on earth?
Are not his days like those of a hired man?
²Like a slave longing for the evening shadows,
or a hired man waiting eagerly for his wages,
³so I have been allotted months of futility,
and nights of misery have been assigned to me.
⁴When I lie down I think, 'How long before I get up?'
The night drags on, and I toss till dawn.
⁵My body is clothed with worms and scabs,
my skin is broken and festering.
⁶"My days are swifter than a weaver's shuttle,
and they come to an end without hope.
⁷Remember, O God, that my life is but a breath;
my eyes will never see happiness again.
⁸The eye that now sees me will see me no longer;
you will look for me, but I will be no more.
⁹As a cloud vanishes and is gone,
so he who goes down to the grave does not return.
¹⁰He will never come to his house again;
his place will know him no more.
¹¹"Therefore I will not keep silent;
I will speak out in the anguish of my spirit,
I will complain in the bitterness of my soul.
¹²Am I the sea, or the monster of the deep,
that you put me under guard?
¹³When I think my bed will comfort me
and my couch will ease my complaint,
¹⁴even then you frighten me with dreams
and terrify me with visions,
¹⁵so that I prefer strangling and death,
rather than this body of mine.
¹⁶I despise my life; I would not live forever.
Let me alone; my days have no meaning.
¹⁷"What is man that you make so much of him,
that you give him so much attention,
¹⁸that you examine him every morning
and test him every moment?
¹⁹Will you never look away from me,
or let me alone even for an instant?
²⁰If I have sinned, what have I done to you,
O watcher of men?
Why have you made me your target?
Have I become a burden to you?
²¹Why do you not pardon my offenses
and forgive my sins?
For I will soon lie down in the dust;
you will search for me, but I will be no more."

Bildad

8 Then Bildad the Shuhite replied:

²"How long will you say such things?
Your words are a blustering wind.
³Does God pervert justice?
Does the Almighty pervert what is right?
⁴When your children sinned against him,
he gave them over to the penalty of their sin.
⁵But if you will look to God
and plead with the Almighty,
⁶if you are pure and upright,
even now he will rouse himself on your behalf

19 Hebrew *Sheol* *20* A few manuscripts of the Masoretic Text, an ancient Hebrew scribal tradition and Septuagint; most manuscripts of the Masoretic Text *I have become a burden to myself.*

7:1–3 These verses indicate that God is in charge of the destiny of every one of us (see Ps 31:15; Ac 17:26).

and restore you to your rightful
   place.ᵗ
⁷Your beginnings will seem humble,
   so prosperousᵘ will your future be.ᵛ

⁸"Ask the former generationsʷ
   and find out what their fathers
      learned,
⁹for we were born only yesterday and
      know nothing,ˣ
   and our days on earth are but a
      shadow.ʸ
¹⁰Will they not instructᶻ you and tell
      you?
   Will they not bring forth words from
      their understanding?ᵃ

¹¹Can papyrus grow tall where there is
      no marsh?ᵇ
   Can reedsᶜ thrive without water?
¹²While still growing and uncut,
   they wither more quickly than
      grass.ᵈ
¹³Such is the destinyᵉ of all who forget
      God;ᶠ
   so perishes the hope of the godless.ᵍ
¹⁴What he trusts in is fragileⁿ;
   what he relies on is a spider's
      web.ʰ
¹⁵He leans on his web,ⁱ but it gives
      way;
   he clings to it, but it does not hold.ʲ
¹⁶He is like a well-watered plant in the
      sunshine,
   spreading its shootsᵏ over the
      garden;ˡ
¹⁷it entwines its roots around a pile of
      rocks
   and looks for a place among the
      stones.
¹⁸But when it is torn from its spot,
   that place disownsᵐ it and says, 'I
      never saw you.'ⁿ
¹⁹Surely its life withersᵒ away,
   andᵒ from the soil other plants
      grow.ᵖ

²⁰"Surely God does not reject a
      blamelessᵠ man
   or strengthen the hands of
      evildoers.ʳ
²¹He will yet fill your mouth with
      laughterˢ
   and your lips with shouts of joy.ᵗ

N *Job 7:1* ◀ ▶ *Job 9:2–4*
G *1Sa 16:7* ◀ ▶ *Job 9:20*
O *1Ch 17:20* ◀ ▶ *Ps 3:8*
S *Job 4:8* ◀ ▶ *Job 11:14*

8:6 ᵗS Job 5:24
8:7 ᵘJob 21:13; 22:21; 36:11; Ps 25:13
ᵛS Job 1:10; Jer 29:11; 31:17
8:8 ʷS Dt 32:7; S Ps 71:18
8:9 ˣS Ge 47:9
ʸS 1Ch 29:15; S 2Ch 10:6; S Ps 39:6
8:10 ᶻPr 1:8
ᵃPr 2:1-2; 4:1
8:11 ᵇJob 40:21
ᶜEx 2:3; Isa 19:6; 35:7
8:12 ᵈver 19; S 2Ki 19:26; Job 18:16; 20:5; Ps 90:5-6; 102:11; Isa 34:4; 40:7,24
8:13 ᵉPs 37:38; 73:17 ᶠPs 9:17; 50:22; Isa 51:13; Jer 17:6 ᵍJob 6:9; 11:20; 15:34; 20:5; 27:8; 34:30; Ps 37:1-2; 112:10; Pr 10:28; 11:7; Jer 15:9
8:14 ʰver 15; Job 27:18; Isa 59:5
8:15 ⁱS ver 14
ʲPs 49:11; Mt 7:26-27
8:16 ᵏPs 80:11; Isa 16:8 ˡPs 37:35; Jer 11:16
8:18 ᵐJob 20:9; Ps 103:16
ⁿS Job 7:8; S 14:20
8:19 ᵒS ver 12; S Job 15:30
ᵖJob 119:90; Ecc 1:4
8:20 ᵠJob 1:1
ʳGe 18:25
8:21 ˢS Job 5:22
ᵗS Ezr 3:13; Job 35:10; Ps 47:5; 107:22; 118:15; 126:2; 132:16; Isa 35:6
8:22 ᵘJob 27:7; Ps 6:10; 35:26; 44:7; 53:5; 71:13; 86:17; 109:29; 132:18; Eze 7:27; 26:16 ᵛS Job 4:21 ʷS 1Sa 8:3; Job 18:6,14,21; 21:28; 27:8,18; 34:26; 36:6; 38:13; Ps 52:5; Pr 14:11
9:2 ˣS Job 4:17; Ro 3:20
9:3 ʸver 32; Job 40:5 ᶻver 12, 14,29,32; Job 10:2; 12:14; 13:9,14; 22:4; 23:7,13; 37:19; 40:2; Ps 44:21; Isa 14:24
9:4 ᵃJob 11:6; 28:12,20,23; 38:36; Ps 51:6; Pr 14:28; Ecc 2:26 ᵇver 19; S Job 5:9; 12:13,16; 23:6; 24:22; 26:12; 30:18; Ps 93:4; 95:3; Pr 8:14; Isa 40:26; 63:1; Da 2:20; 4:35
ᶜJer 50:24

²²Your enemies will be clothed in
      shame,ᵘ
   and the tentsᵛ of the wicked will be
      no more."ʷ

Job
9 Then Job replied:

²"Indeed, I know that this is true.
   But how can a mortal be righteous
      before God?ˣ
³Though one wished to dispute with
      him,ʸ
   he could not answer him one time
      out of a thousand.ᶻ
⁴His wisdomᵃ is profound, his power is
      vast.ᵇ
   Who has resistedᶜ him and come
      out unscathed?ᵈ
⁵He moves mountainsᵉ without their
      knowing it
   and overturns them in his anger.ᶠ
⁶He shakes the earthᵍ from its place
   and makes its pillars tremble.ʰ
⁷He speaks to the sun and it does not
      shine;ⁱ
   he seals off the light of the stars.ʲ
⁸He alone stretches out the heavensᵏ
   and treads on the waves of the sea.ˡ
⁹He is the Makerᵐ of the Bear and
      Orion,
   the Pleiades and the constellations
      of the south.ⁿ
¹⁰He performs wondersᵒ that cannot be
      fathomed,
   miracles that cannot be counted.ᵖ
¹¹When he passes me, I cannot see him;
   when he goes by, I cannot perceive
      him.ᵠ
¹²If he snatches away, who can stop
      him?ʳ
   Who can say to him, 'What are you
      doing?'ˢ

H *Job 4:8–9* ◀ ▶ *Job 9:4*
N *Job 8:9* ◀ ▶ *Job 11:20*
H *Job 8:22* ◀ ▶ *Job 10:14*

ᵈ2Ch 13:12; S Job 5:13 9:5 ᵉMt 17:20 ᶠPs 18:7; 46:2-3; Isa 13:13; Mic 1:4 9:6 ᵍS Ex 19:18; Isa 2:21; 13:13; 24:18-20; Am 8:8; Heb 12:26 ʰS 2Sa 22:8; Job 26:14; 36:29; 37:4-5; Ps 75:3; Hab 3:4 9:7 ⁱIsa 34:4; Jer 4:28; Joel 2:2,10,31; 3:15; Zep 1:15; Zec 14:6 ʲIsa 13:10; Jer 4:23; Eze 32:8 9:8 ᵏS Ge 1:1,8; S Isa 48:13 ˡJob 38:16; Ps 77:19; Pr 8:28; Hab 3:15; Mt 14:25; Mk 6:48; Jn 6:19 9:9 ᵐJob 32:22; 40:15,19 ⁿS Ge 1:16 9:10 ᵒDt 6:22; Ps 72:18; 136:4; Jer 32:20 ᵖS Job 5:9 9:11 ᵠJob 23:8-9; 35:14 9:12 ʳNu 23:20; Job 11:10; Isa 14:27; 43:13 ˢS ver 3; S Dt 32:39; Isa 29:16; 45:9; Da 2:21; 4:32; Ro 9:20

ⁿ 14 The meaning of the Hebrew for this word is uncertain.
ᵒ 19 Or *Surely all the joy it has / is that*

¹³God does not restrain his anger;ᵗ
    even the cohorts of Rahabᵘ cowered
        at his feet.

¹⁴"How then can I dispute with him?
    How can I find words to argue with
        him?ᵛ
¹⁵Though I were innocent, I could not
        answer him;ʷ
    I could only pleadˣ with my Judgeʸ
        for mercy.ᶻ
¹⁶Even if I summoned him and he
        responded,
    I do not believe he would give me a
        hearing.ᵃ
¹⁷He would crush meᵇ with a stormᶜ
    and multiplyᵈ my wounds for no
        reason.ᵉ
¹⁸He would not let me regain my breath
    but would overwhelm me with
        misery.ᶠ
¹⁹If it is a matter of strength, he is
        mighty!ᵍ
    And if it is a matter of justice, who
        will summon himᵖ?ʰ

G ²⁰Even if I were innocent, my mouth
        would condemn me;
    if I were blameless, it would
        pronounce me guilty.ⁱ

²¹"Although I am blameless,ʲ
    I have no concern for myself;ᵏ
    I despise my own life.ˡ
²²It is all the same; that is why I say,
    'He destroys both the blameless and
        the wicked.'ᵐ
²³When a scourgeⁿ brings sudden death,
    he mocks the despair of the
        innocent.ᵒ
²⁴When a land falls into the hands of the
        wicked,ᵖ
    he blindfolds its judges.ᵠ
    If it is not he, then who is it?ʳ

²⁵"My days are swifter than a runner;ˢ
    they fly away without a glimpse of
        joy.ᵗ
²⁶They skim pastᵘ like boats of papyrus,ᵛ
    like eagles swooping down on their
        prey.ʷ
²⁷If I say, 'I will forget my complaint,ˣ
    I will change my expression, and
        smile,'
²⁸I still dreadʸ all my sufferings,
    for I know you will not hold me
        innocent.ᶻ

G Job 8:11–16 ◄► Job 9:29–31

9:13 ᵗNu 14:18; Job 10:15; Ps 78:38; Isa 3:11; 6:5; 48:9 ᵘJob 26:12; Ps 87:4; 89:10; Isa 30:7; 51:9
9:14 ᵛS ver 3
9:15 ʷJob 10:15; 13:19; 34:5-6; 40:5; 42:7 ˣJob 8:5 ʸS Ge 18:25; 1Sa 24:12; Ps 50:6; 96:13 ᶻver 20,29; Job 15:6; 23:4; 40:2
9:16 ᵃJob 13:22; Ro 9:20-21
9:17 ᵇJob 16:12; 30:16; Ps 10:10; Isa 38:13 ᶜJob 30:22; Ps 83:15; Jnh 1:4 ᵈJob 16:14 ᵉS Job 2:3
9:18 ᶠS Job 7:19; S 10:1
9:19 ᵍS ver 4; ʰS Ne 9:32 ʰver 33; Jer 49:19
9:20 ⁱS ver 15
9:21 ʲS Ge 6:9; Job 34:6,7 ᵏver 14; S Job 6:29; 10:1; 13:13 ˡS Nu 11:15; S Job 7:16
9:22 ᵐS Job 3:19; 10:8; Ecc 9:2,3; Eze 21:3
9:23 ⁿHeb 11:36 ᵒJob 24:1,12; Ps 64:4; Hab 1:3; 1Pe 1:7
9:24 ᵖJob 1:15,17; 10:3; 16:11; 21:16; 22:18; 27:2; 40:8; Ps 73:3 ᵠS Job 3:14; 12:6; 19:7; 21:7; 24:23; 31:35; 35:15; Ps 73:12; Ecc 8:11; Jer 12:1; La 3:0 ʳJob 12:9; 13:1; 24:12; Isa 41:20
9:25 ˢS Job 7:6 ᵗJob 7:7; 10:20
9:26 ᵘJob 24:18; Ps 46:3 ᵛIsa 18:2 ʷJob 39:29; Hab 1:8
9:27 ˣS Job 7:11
9:28 ʸS Job 3:25 ᶻS Ex 34:7; S Job 7:21
9:29 ᵃS ver 3,S 15; Ps 37:33
9:30 ᵇMal 3:2 ᶜJob 17:9; 31:7; Isa 1:15 ᵈJob 14:4, 17; 33:9; Isa 1:18; Jer 2:22; Hos 13:12
9:31 ᵉPs 35:7; 40:2; 51:9; Jer 2:22; Na 3:6; Mal 2:3 ᶠS Job 7:20; 34:9; 35:3; Ps 73:13
9:32 ᵍS Nu 23:19 ʰS ver 3; Hab 1:3 ⁱPs 143:2; Ecc 6:10
9:33 ʲS 1Sa 2:25 ᵏS ver 19
9:34 ˡJob 21:9; Ps 39:10; 73:5

²⁹Since I am already found guilty, G
    why should I struggle in vain?ᵃ
³⁰Even if I washed myself with soapᵍᵇ
    and my handsᶜ with washing soda,ᵈ
³¹you would plunge me into a slime pitᵉ
    so that even my clothes would
        detest me.ᶠ

³²"He is not a manᵍ like me that I might
        answer him,ʰ
    that we might confront each other
        in court.ⁱ
³³If only there were someone to arbitrate
        between us,ʲ
    to lay his hand upon us both,ᵏ
³⁴someone to remove God's rod from
        me,ˡ
    so that his terror would frighten me
        no more.ᵐ
³⁵Then I would speak up without fear of
        him,ⁿ
    but as it now stands with me, I
        cannot.ᵒ

10 "I loathe my very life;ᵖ
    therefore I will give free rein to
        my complaint
    and speak out in the bitterness of
        my soul.ᵠ
²I will say to God:ʳ Do not condemn
        me,
    but tell me what chargesˢ you have
        against me.ᵗ
³Does it please you to oppress me,ᵘ
    to spurn the work of your hands,ᵛ
    while you smile on the schemes of
        the wicked?ʷ
⁴Do you have eyes of flesh?
    Do you see as a mortal sees?ˣ
⁵Are your days like those of a mortal
    or your years like those of a man,ʸ
⁶that you must search out my faults
    and probe after my sinᶻ—
⁷though you know that I am not guiltyᵃ
    and that no one can rescue me from
        your hand?ᵇ

G Job 9:20 ◄► Job 15:12

9:35 ⁿS Job 7:11 ᵒJob 7:15; 13:21 10:1 ᵖS Nu 11:15; S 1Ki 19:4 ᵠS 1Sa 1:10; S Job 7:11; 9:18,21 10:2 ʳJob 13:3; 40:1 ˢIsa 3:13; Hos 4:1; 5:1; 12:2; Mic 6:2; Ro 8:33 ᵗS Job 9:3 10:3 ᵘS Job 9:22; 16:9,14; 19:6, 21; 22:10; 30:13,21; 31:23; 34:6 ᵛver 8; S Ge 1:26; S Job 4:17; 14:15; 34:19; Ps 8:6; 95:6; 100:3; 138:8; 149:2; Isa 60:21; 64:8 ʷS Job 9:24 10:4 ˣIsa 16:7; Job 1:11; 14:16; 24:23; 28:24; 31:4; 34:21; 41:11; Ps 11:4; 33:15; 119:168; 139:1-3; 5:3; Jer 11:20-23; 16:17 10:5 ʸJob 36:26; Ps 39:5; 90:2,4; 102:24; 2Pe 3:8 10:6 ᶻJob 14:16 10:7 ᵃver 15; S Job 6:29; 11:4; 16:17; 27:5,6; 31:6; 32:1 ᵇS Dt 32:39

ᵖ 19 See Septuagint; Hebrew me. ᵠ 30 Or snow

⁸"Your hands shaped me and made me.
　Will you now turn and destroy me?
⁹Remember that you molded me like clay.
　Will you now turn me to dust again?
¹⁰Did you not pour me out like milk
　and curdle me like cheese,
¹¹clothe me with skin and flesh
　and knit me together with bones and sinews?
¹²You gave me life and showed me kindness,
　and in your providence watched over my spirit.

¹³"But this is what you concealed in your heart,
　and I know that this was in your mind:
¹⁴If I sinned, you would be watching me
　and would not let my offense go unpunished.
¹⁵If I am guilty—woe to me!
　Even if I am innocent, I cannot lift my head,
　for I am full of shame
　and drowned in my affliction.
¹⁶If I hold my head high, you stalk me like a lion
　and again display your awesome power against me.
¹⁷You bring new witnesses against me
　and increase your anger toward me;
　your forces come against me wave upon wave.

¹⁸"Why then did you bring me out of the womb?
　I wish I had died before any eye saw me.
¹⁹If only I had never come into being,
　or had been carried straight from the womb to the grave!
²⁰Are not my few days almost over?
　Turn away from me so I can have a moment's joy
²¹before I go to the place of no return,
　to the land of gloom and deep shadow,
²²to the land of deepest night,
　of deep shadow and disorder,
　where even the light is like darkness."

Zophar

11 Then Zophar the Naamathite replied:

²"Are all these words to go unanswered?
　Is this talker to be vindicated?
³Will your idle talk reduce men to silence?
　Will no one rebuke you when you mock?
⁴You say to God, 'My beliefs are flawless
　and I am pure in your sight.'
⁵Oh, how I wish that God would speak,
　that he would open his lips against you
⁶and disclose to you the secrets of wisdom,
　for true wisdom has two sides.
　Know this: God has even forgotten some of your sin.

⁷"Can you fathom the mysteries of God?
　Can you probe the limits of the Almighty?
⁸They are higher than the heavens—what can you do?
　They are deeper than the depths of the grave—what can you know?
⁹Their measure is longer than the earth
　and wider than the sea.

¹⁰"If he comes along and confines you in prison
　and convenes a court, who can oppose him?
¹¹Surely he recognizes deceitful men;
　and when he sees evil, does he not take note?
¹²But a witless man can no more become wise
　than a wild donkey's colt can be born a man.

R ¹³"Yet if you devote your heart to him
and stretch out your hands to him,
S ¹⁴if you put away the sin that is in your hand
and allow no evil to dwell in your tent,
¹⁵then you will lift up your face without shame;
you will stand firm and without fear.
¹⁶You will surely forget your trouble,
recalling it only as waters gone by.
¹⁷Life will be brighter than noonday,
and darkness will become like morning.
¹⁸You will be secure, because there is hope;
you will look about you and take your rest in safety.
¹⁹You will lie down, with no one to make you afraid,
and many will court your favor.
H ²⁰But the eyes of the wicked will fail,
N and escape will elude them;
their hope will become a dying gasp."

Job

12 Then Job replied:

²"Doubtless you are the people,
and wisdom will die with you!
³But I have a mind as well as you;
I am not inferior to you.
Who does not know all these things?

⁴"I have become a laughingstock to my friends,
though I called upon God and he answered—
a mere laughingstock, though righteous and blameless!
⁵Men at ease have contempt for misfortune
as the fate of those whose feet are slipping.
⁶The tents of marauders are undisturbed,
and those who provoke God are secure—

R Ezr 10:11 ◀▶ Job 31:33
S Job 8:20 ◀▶ Job 17:9
H Job 10:14 ◀▶ Job 15:23–26
N Job 9:2–4 ◀▶ Job 15:12–13

those who carry their god in their hands.

⁷"But ask the animals, and they will teach you,
or the birds of the air, and they will tell you;
⁸or speak to the earth, and it will teach you,
or let the fish of the sea inform you.
⁹Which of all these does not know
that the hand of the LORD has done this?
¹⁰In his hand is the life of every creature
and the breath of all mankind.
¹¹Does not the ear test words
as the tongue tastes food?
¹²Is not wisdom found among the aged?
Does not long life bring understanding?

¹³"To God belong wisdom and power;
counsel and understanding are his.
¹⁴What he tears down cannot be rebuilt;
the man he imprisons cannot be released.
¹⁵If he holds back the waters, there is drought;
if he lets them loose, they devastate the land.
¹⁶To him belong strength and victory;
both deceived and deceiver are his.
¹⁷He leads counselors away stripped
and makes fools of judges.
¹⁸He takes off the shackles put on by kings
and ties a loincloth around their waist.
¹⁹He leads priests away stripped
and overthrows men long established.
²⁰He silences the lips of trusted advisers
and takes away the discernment of elders.
²¹He pours contempt on nobles
and disarms the mighty.

v 6 Or *secure / in what God's hand brings them*   *w 18* Or *shackles of kings / and ties a belt*

²²He reveals the deep things of darkness,
  and brings deep shadows into the light.
²³He makes nations great, and destroys them;
  he enlarges nations, and disperses them.
²⁴He deprives the leaders of the earth of their reason;
  he sends them wandering through a trackless waste.
²⁵They grope in darkness with no light;
  he makes them stagger like drunkards.

13 "My eyes have seen all this,
  my ears have heard and understood it.
²What you know, I also know;
  I am not inferior to you.
³But I desire to speak to the Almighty
  and to argue my case with God.
⁴You, however, smear me with lies;
  you are worthless physicians, all of you!
⁵If only you would be altogether silent!
  For you, that would be wisdom.
⁶Hear now my argument;
  listen to the plea of my lips.
⁷Will you speak wickedly on God's behalf?
  Will you speak deceitfully for him?
⁸Will you show him partiality?
  Will you argue the case for God?
⁹Would it turn out well if he examined you?
  Could you deceive him as you might deceive men?
¹⁰He would surely rebuke you
  if you secretly showed partiality.
¹¹Would not his splendor terrify you?
  Would not the dread of him fall on you?
¹²Your maxims are proverbs of ashes;
  your defenses are defenses of clay.
¹³"Keep silent and let me speak;
  then let come to me what may.
¹⁴Why do I put myself in jeopardy
  and take my life in my hands?

¹⁵Though he slay me, yet will I hope in him;
  I will surely defend my ways to his face.
¹⁶Indeed, this will turn out for my deliverance,
  for no godless man would dare come before him!
¹⁷Listen carefully to my words;
  let your ears take in what I say.
¹⁸Now that I have prepared my case,
  I know I will be vindicated.
¹⁹Can anyone bring charges against me?
  If so, I will be silent and die.
²⁰"Only grant me these two things, O God,
  and then I will not hide from you:
²¹Withdraw your hand far from me,
  and stop frightening me with your terrors.
²²Then summon me and I will answer,
  or let me speak, and you reply.
²³How many wrongs and sins have I committed?
  Show me my offense and my sin.
²⁴Why do you hide your face
  and consider me your enemy?
²⁵Will you torment a windblown leaf?
  Will you chase after dry chaff?
²⁶For you write down bitter things against me
  and make me inherit the sins of my youth.
²⁷You fasten my feet in shackles;
  you keep close watch on all my paths
  by putting marks on the soles of my feet.
²⁸"So man wastes away like something rotten,
  like a garment eaten by moths.

Job 1:21 ◀▶ Ps 3:5–6

x 15 Or *He will surely slay me; I have no hope* — / *yet I will*

13:15 Job expressed his unshakable confidence in God when he surrendered his own life to God's will despite his circumstances. Satan had intimated that Job's obedience hinged only on God's hand of blessing. When God allowed Satan to remove all that Job possessed, it was clear that Job's righteousness was motivated by his love of God, not by his blessings. Job's struggles illustrate that though circumstances change, our relationship with God is eternal.

14 ¹"Man born of woman
is of few days and full of
trouble.

²He springs up like a flower and
withers away;
like a fleeting shadow, he does not
endure.

³Do you fix your eye on such a one?
Will you bring him before you for
judgment?

⁴Who can bring what is pure from the
impure?
No one!

⁵Man's days are determined;
you have decreed the number of his
months
and have set limits he cannot
exceed.

⁶So look away from him and let him
alone,
till he has put in his time like a
hired man.

⁷"At least there is hope for a tree:
If it is cut down, it will sprout again,
and its new shoots will not fail.

⁸Its roots may grow old in the ground
and its stump die in the soil,

⁹yet at the scent of water it will bud
and put forth shoots like a plant.

¹⁰But man dies and is laid low;
he breathes his last and is no more.

¹¹As water disappears from the sea
or a riverbed becomes parched and
dry,

F ¹²so man lies down and does not rise;
till the heavens are no more, men
will not awake
or be roused from their sleep.

¹³"If only you would hide me in the
grave
and conceal me till your anger has
passed!
If only you would set me a time
and then remember me!

¹⁴If a man dies, will he live again?
All the days of my hard service

F ▶ *Job 19:25–27*

I will wait for my renewal to
come.
¹⁵You will call and I will answer you;
you will long for the creature your
hands have made.

¹⁶Surely then you will count my steps
but not keep track of my sin.
¹⁷My offenses will be sealed up in a
bag;
you will cover over my sin.

¹⁸"But as a mountain erodes and
crumbles
and as a rock is moved from its
place,

¹⁹as water wears away stones
and torrents wash away the soil,
so you destroy man's hope.

²⁰You overpower him once for all, and
he is gone;
you change his countenance and
send him away.

²¹If his sons are honored, he does not
know it;
if they are brought low, he does not
see it.

²²He feels but the pain of his own body
and mourns only for himself."

Eliphaz

15 ¹Then Eliphaz the Temanite replied:

²"Would a wise man answer with
empty notions
or fill his belly with the hot east
wind?

³Would he argue with useless words,
with speeches that have no value?

⁴But you even undermine piety
and hinder devotion to God.

⁵Your sin prompts your mouth;

E ◀ *Job 4:14* ◀ ▶ *Job 22:12–17*

14:12 The phrase "till the heavens are no more" foreshadows the new heaven that will be created after the white throne judgment (see Rev 21:1).

14:14 The book of Job asks three questions that have puzzled humanity for centuries: (1) Where can we find God? (2) How can one be righteous before God? and the question posed in this verse (3) "If a man dies, will he live again?" The answer to each of these questions can only be found in Jesus Christ: He is God incarnate; his atoning death purchased our salvation; and we can only find immortality through his resurrection.

you adopt the tongue of the crafty.ᵃ
⁶Your own mouth condemns you, not
    mine;
  your own lips testify against you.ᵇ

⁷"Are you the first man ever born?ᶜ
  Were you brought forth before the
    hills?ᵈ
⁸Do you listen in on God's council?ᵉ
  Do you limit wisdom to yourself?ᶠ
⁹What do you know that we do not
    know?
  What insights do you have that we
    do not have?ᵍ
¹⁰The gray-haired and the agedʰ are on
    our side,
  men even older than your father.ⁱ
¹¹Are God's consolationsʲ not enough
    for you,
  wordsᵏ spoken gently to you?ˡ
¹²Why has your heartᵐ carried you away,
    and why do your eyes flash,
¹³so that you vent your rageⁿ against
    God
  and pour out such wordsᵒ from your
    mouth?ᵖ
¹⁴"What is man, that he could be pure,
  or one born of woman,ᑫ that he
    could be righteous?ʳ
¹⁵If God places no trust in his holy
    ones,ˢ
  if even the heavens are not pure in
    his eyes,ᵗ
¹⁶how much less man, who is vile and
    corrupt,ᵘ
  who drinks up evilᵛ like water!ʷ

¹⁷"Listen to me and I will explain to you;
  let me tell you what I have seen,ˣ
¹⁸what wise men have declared,
  hiding nothing received from their
    fathersʸ
¹⁹(to whom alone the landᶻ was given
  when no alien passed among them):
²⁰All his days the wicked man suffers
    torment,ᵃ
  the ruthless through all the years
    stored up for him.ᵇ
²¹Terrifying sounds fill his ears;ᶜ
  when all seems well, marauders
    attack him.ᵈ

²²He despairs of escaping the darkness;ᵉ
  he is marked for the sword.ᶠ
²³He wanders aboutᵍ—food for
    vulturesᵇ,ʰ;
  he knows the day of darknessⁱ is at
    hand.ʲ
²⁴Distress and anguishᵏ fill him with
    terror,ˡ
  they overwhelm him, like a kingᵐ
    poised to attack,
²⁵because he shakes his fistⁿ at God
  and vaunts himself against the
    Almighty,ᵒ
²⁶defiantly charging against him
  with a thick, strong shield.ᵖ

²⁷"Though his face is covered with fat
  and his waist bulges with flesh,ᑫ
²⁸he will inhabit ruined towns
  and houses where no one lives,ʳ
  houses crumbling to rubble.ˢ
²⁹He will no longer be rich and his
    wealth will not endure,ᵗ
  nor will his possessions spread over
    the land.ᵘ
³⁰He will not escape the darkness;ᵛ
  a flameʷ will wither his shoots,ˣ
  and the breath of God's mouthʸ will
    carry him away.ᶻ
³¹Let him not deceiveᵃ himself by
    trusting what is worthless,ᵇ
  for he will get nothing in return.ᶜ
³²Before his timeᵈ he will be paid in
    full,ᵉ
  and his branches will not flourish.ᶠ
³³He will be like a vine stripped of its
    unripe grapes,ᵍ
  like an olive tree shedding its
    blossoms.ʰ
³⁴For the company of the godlessⁱ will
    be barren,
  and fire will consumeʲ the tents of
    those who love bribes.ᵏ

ᵇ 23 Or about, looking for food

35They conceive trouble¹ and give birth to evil;ᵐ
their womb fashions deceit."

Job

16 Then Job replied:

²"I have heard many things like these;
miserable comfortersⁿ are you all!°
³Will your long-winded speeches never end?ᵖ
What ails you that you keep on arguing?ᑫ
⁴I also could speak like you,
if you were in my place;
I could make fine speeches against you
and shake my headʳ at you.
⁵But my mouth would encourage you;
comfortˢ from my lips would bring you relief.ᵗ

⁶"Yet if I speak, my pain is not relieved;
and if I refrain, it does not go away.ᵘ
⁷Surely, O God, you have worn me out;ᵛ
you have devastated my entire household.ʷ
⁸You have bound me—and it has become a witness;
my gauntnessˣ rises up and testifies against me.ʸ
⁹God assails me and tearsᶻ me in his angerᵃ
and gnashes his teeth at me;ᵇ
my opponent fastens on me his piercing eyes.ᶜ
¹⁰Men open their mouthsᵈ to jeer at me;ᵉ
they strike my cheekᶠ in scorn
and unite together against me.ᵍ
¹¹God has turned me over to evil men
and thrown me into the clutches of the wicked.ʰ
¹²All was well with me, but he shattered me;
he seized me by the neck and crushed me.ⁱ
He has made me his target;ʲ
¹³ his archers surround me.ᵏ
Without pity, he pierces¹ my kidneys
and spills my gall on the ground.
¹⁴Again and againᵐ he bursts upon me;
he rushes at me like a warrior.ⁿ
¹⁵"I have sewed sackcloth° over my skin
and buried my brow in the dust.ᵖ
¹⁶My face is red with weeping,ᑫ

deep shadows ring my eyes;ʳ
¹⁷yet my hands have been free of violenceˢ
and my prayer is pure.ᵗ

¹⁸"O earth, do not cover my blood;ᵘ
may my cryᵛ never be laid to rest!ʷ
¹⁹Even now my witnessˣ is in heaven;ʸ
my advocate is on high.ᶻ
²⁰My intercessorᵃ is my friendᶜᵇ
as my eyes pour outᶜ tearsᵈ to God;
²¹on behalf of a man he pleadsᵉ with God
as a man pleads for his friend.

²²"Only a few years will pass
before I go on the journey of no return.ᶠ   N

17 ¹My spiritᵍ is broken,
my days are cut short,ʰ
the grave awaits me.ⁱ
²Surely mockersʲ surround me;ᵏ
my eyes must dwell on their hostility.

³"Give me, O God, the pledge you demand.¹
Who else will put up securityᵐ for me?ⁿ
⁴You have closed their minds to understanding;°
therefore you will not let them triumph.
⁵If a man denounces his friends for reward,ᵖ
the eyes of his children will fail.ᑫ

⁶"God has made me a bywordʳ to everyone,ˢ
a man in whose face people spit.ᵗ
⁷My eyes have grown dim with grief;ᵘ
my whole frame is but a shadow.ᵛ
⁸Upright men are appalled at this;
the innocent are arousedʷ against the ungodly.
⁹Nevertheless, the righteousˣ will hold to their ways,   K
                                                          S
                                                          U

N *Job 15:12–13* ◄ ► *Job 20:5*
K *Job 1:10* ◄ ► *Job 19:25*
S *Job 11:14* ◄ ► *Job 27:8*
U *Job 8:6–7* ◄ ► *Job 22:21*

and those with clean hands^y will grow stronger.^z

¹⁰"But come on, all of you, try again!
I will not find a wise man among you.^a
¹¹My days have passed,^b my plans are shattered,
and so are the desires of my heart.^c
¹²These men turn night into day;^d
in the face of darkness they say,
'Light is near.'^e
¹³If the only home I hope for is the grave,^{df}
if I spread out my bed^g in darkness,^h
¹⁴if I say to corruption,ⁱ 'You are my father,'
and to the worm,^j 'My mother' or 'My sister,'
¹⁵where then is my hope?^k
Who can see any hope for me?^l
¹⁶Will it go down to the gates of death^d?^m
Will we descend together into the dust?"ⁿ

Bildad

18 Then Bildad the Shuhite^o replied:

²"When will you end these speeches?^p
Be sensible, and then we can talk.
³Why are we regarded as cattle^q
and considered stupid in your sight?^r
⁴You who tear yourself^s to pieces in your anger,^t
is the earth to be abandoned for your sake?
Or must the rocks be moved from their place?^u

⁵"The lamp of the wicked is snuffed out;^v
the flame of his fire stops burning.^w
⁶The light in his tent^x becomes dark;^y
the lamp beside him goes out.^z
⁷The vigor^a of his step is weakened;^b
his own schemes^c throw him down.^d
⁸His feet thrust him into a net^e
and he wanders into its mesh.
⁹A trap seizes him by the heel;
a snare^f holds him fast.^g
¹⁰A noose^h is hidden for him on the ground;
a trapⁱ lies in his path.^j
¹¹Terrors^k startle him on every side^l

and dog^m his every step.
¹²Calamityⁿ is hungry^o for him;
disaster^p is ready for him when he falls.^q
¹³It eats away parts of his skin;^r
death's firstborn devours his limbs.^s
¹⁴He is torn from the security of his tent^t
and marched off to the king^u of terrors.^v
¹⁵Fire resides^e in his tent;^w
burning sulfur^x is scattered over his dwelling.
¹⁶His roots dry up below^y
and his branches wither above.^z
¹⁷The memory of him perishes from the earth;^a
he has no name^b in the land.^c
¹⁸He is driven from light into darkness^d
and is banished^e from the world.^f
¹⁹He has no offspring^g or descendants^h among his people,
no survivorⁱ where once he lived.^j
²⁰Men of the west are appalled^k at his fate;^l
men of the east are seized with horror.
²¹Surely such is the dwelling^m of an evil man;ⁿ
such is the place^o of one who knows not God."^p

Job

19 Then Job replied:

²"How long will you torment^q me
and crush^r me with words?
³Ten times^s now you have reproached^t me;
shamelessly you attack me.
⁴If it is true that I have gone astray,
my error^u remains my concern alone.
⁵If indeed you would exalt yourselves above me^v
and use my humiliation against me,

d 13,16 Hebrew *Sheol* *e 15* Or *Nothing he had remains*

⁶then know that God has wronged me ʷ
and drawn his net ˣ around me.ʸ

⁷"Though I cry, 'I've been wronged!' I get no response; ᶻ
though I call for help,ᵃ there is no justice.ᵇ

⁸He has blocked my way so I cannot pass;ᶜ
he has shrouded my paths in darkness.ᵈ

⁹He has stripped ᵉ me of my honor ᶠ
and removed the crown from my head.ᵍ

¹⁰He tears me down ʰ on every side till I am gone;
he uproots my hope ⁱ like a tree.ʲ

¹¹His anger ᵏ burns against me;
he counts me among his enemies.ˡ

¹²His troops advance in force;ᵐ
they build a siege ramp ⁿ against me
and encamp around my tent.ᵒ

¹³"He has alienated my brothers ᵖ from me;
my acquaintances are completely estranged from me.ᑫ

¹⁴My kinsmen have gone away;
my friends ʳ have forgotten me.

¹⁵My guests ˢ and my maidservants ᵗ
count me a stranger;
they look upon me as an alien.

¹⁶I summon my servant, but he does not answer,
though I beg him with my own mouth.

¹⁷My breath is offensive to my wife,
I am loathsome ᵘ to my own brothers.

¹⁸Even the little boys ᵛ scorn me;
when I appear, they ridicule me.ʷ

¹⁹All my intimate friends ˣ detest me;ʸ
those I love have turned against me.ᶻ

²⁰I am nothing but skin and bones;ᵃ
I have escaped with only the skin of my teeth.ᶠ

²¹"Have pity on me, my friends,ᵇ have pity,
for the hand of God has struck ᶜ me.

²²Why do you pursue ᵈ me as God does?ᵉ

²³"Oh, that my words were recorded,
that they were written on a scroll,ᵍ
²⁴that they were inscribed with an iron tool ʰ on ᵍ lead,
or engraved in rock forever! ⁱ

²⁵I know that my Redeemer ʰʲ lives,ᵏ   D
and that in the end he will stand   F
upon the earth.ˡ   K

²⁶And after my skin has been destroyed,
yet ʲ in ᵏ my flesh I will see God;ˡ
²⁷I myself will see him
with my own eyes ᵐ—I, and not another.
How my heart yearns ⁿ within me!

²⁸"If you say, 'How we will hound ᵒ him,
since the root of the trouble lies in him,'
²⁹you should fear the sword yourselves;
for wrath will bring punishment by the sword,ᵖ
and then you will know that there is judgment.ᵐ"ᑫ

Zophar

20 Then Zophar the Naamathite ʳ replied:

²"My troubled thoughts prompt me to answer
because I am greatly disturbed.ˢ
³I hear a rebuke ᵗ that dishonors me,
and my understanding inspires me to reply.

⁴"Surely you know how it has been from of old,ᵘ   C

D ▶ Ps 96:12–13
F Job 14:12–15 ◀ ▶ Ps 8:3–8
K Job 17:9 ◀ ▶ Job 36:7
C Job 15:23–26 ◀ ▶ Job 21:14–15

19:25–27 Job affirmed his confidence in his redemption and in his physical resurrection noting that "in my flesh I will see God; I myself will see him with my own eyes—I, and not another" (19:26–27). Job's words contradict those who teach that spiritual individuality is lost at the resurrection (see also 14:13–14).

ever since man was placed on the earth,
⁵that the mirth of the wicked is brief,
   the joy of the godless lasts but a moment.
⁶Though his pride reaches to the heavens,
   and his head touches the clouds,
⁷he will perish forever, like his own dung;
   those who have seen him will say, 'Where is he?'
⁸Like a dream he flies away, no more to be found,
   banished like a vision of the night.
⁹The eye that saw him will not see him again;
   his place will look on him no more.
¹⁰His children must make amends to the poor;
   his own hands must give back his wealth.
¹¹The youthful vigor that fills his bones
   will lie with him in the dust.
¹²"Though evil is sweet in his mouth
   and he hides it under his tongue,
¹³though he cannot bear to let it go
   and keeps it in his mouth,
¹⁴yet his food will turn sour in his stomach;
   it will become the venom of serpents within him.
¹⁵He will spit out the riches he swallowed;
   God will make his stomach vomit them up.
¹⁶He will suck the poison of serpents;
   the fangs of an adder will kill him.
¹⁷He will not enjoy the streams,
   the rivers flowing with honey and cream.
¹⁸What he toiled for he must give back uneaten;
   he will not enjoy the profit from his trading.
¹⁹For he has oppressed the poor and left them destitute;
   he has seized houses he did not build.
²⁰"Surely he will have no respite from his craving;
   he cannot save himself by his treasure.
²¹Nothing is left for him to devour;
   his prosperity will not endure.
²²In the midst of his plenty, distress will overtake him;
   the full force of misery will come upon him.
²³When he has filled his belly,
   God will vent his burning anger against him
   and rain down his blows upon him.
²⁴Though he flees from an iron weapon,
   a bronze-tipped arrow pierces him.
²⁵He pulls it out of his back,
   the gleaming point out of his liver.
Terrors will come over him;
²⁶ total darkness lies in wait for his treasures.
   A fire unfanned will consume him
   and devour what is left in his tent.
²⁷The heavens will expose his guilt;
   the earth will rise up against him.
²⁸A flood will carry off his house,
   rushing waters on the day of God's wrath.
²⁹Such is the fate God allots the wicked,
   the heritage appointed for them by God."

Job

21 Then Job replied:

²"Listen carefully to my words;
   let this be the consolation you give me.
³Bear with me while I speak,
   and after I have spoken, mock on.
⁴"Is my complaint directed to man?
   Why should I not be impatient?
⁵Look at me and be astonished;
   clap your hand over your mouth.
⁶When I think about this, I am terrified;
   trembling seizes my body.
⁷Why do the wicked live on,
   growing old and increasing in power?

JOB 21:34

⁸They see their children established around them,
their offspring before their eyes.ʰ
⁹Their homes are safe and free from fear;ⁱ
the rod of God is not upon them.ʲ
¹⁰Their bulls never fail to breed;
their cows calve and do not miscarry.ᵏ
¹¹They send forth their children as a flock;ˡ
their little ones dance about.
¹²They sing to the music of tambourine and harp;ᵐ
they make merry to the sound of the flute.ⁿ
¹³They spend their years in prosperityᵒ
and go down to the graveᵖᵖ in peace.ᵠᵠ
¹⁴Yet they say to God, 'Leave us alone!ʳ
We have no desire to know your ways.ˢ
¹⁵Who is the Almighty, that we should serve him?
What would we gain by praying to him?'ᵗ
¹⁶But their prosperity is not in their own hands,
so I stand aloof from the counsel of the wicked.ᵘ
¹⁷"Yet how often is the lamp of the wicked snuffed out?ᵛ
How often does calamityʷ come upon them,
the fate God allots in his anger?ˣ
¹⁸How often are they like straw before the wind,
like chaffʸ swept awayᶻᵃ by a gale?ᵇ
¹⁹It is said, 'God stores up a man's punishment for his sons.'ᶜ
Let him repay the man himself, so that he will know it!ᵈ
²⁰Let his own eyes see his destruction;ᵉ
let him drinkᶠ of the wrath of the Almighty.ʳᵍ
²¹For what does he care about the family he leaves behindʰ

when his allotted monthsⁱ come to an end?ʲ
²²"Can anyone teach knowledge to God,ᵏ
since he judges even the highest?ˡ
²³One man dies in full vigor,ᵐ
completely secure and at ease,ⁿ
²⁴his bodyˢ well nourished,ᵒ
his bonesᵖ rich with marrow.ᵠ
²⁵Another man dies in bitterness of soul,ʳ
never having enjoyed anything good.
²⁶Side by side they lie in the dust,ˢ
and wormsᵗ cover them both.ᵘ
²⁷"I know full well what you are thinking,
the schemes by which you would wrong me.
²⁸You say, 'Where now is the great man'sᵛ house,
the tents where wicked men lived?'ʷ
²⁹Have you never questioned those who travel?
Have you paid no regard to their accounts—
³⁰that the evil man is spared from the day of calamity,ˣ
that he is delivered fromᵗ the day of wrath?ʸ
³¹Who denounces his conduct to his face?
Who repays him for what he has done?ᶻ
³²He is carried to the grave,
and watch is kept over his tomb.ᵃ
³³The soil in the valley is sweet to him;ᵇ
all men follow after him,
and a countless throng goesᵘ before him.ᶜ
³⁴"So how can you console meᵈ with your nonsense?

H Job 21:17–20 ◀ ▶ Job 27:8

N Job 20:5 ◀ ▶ Job 22:15–17
C Job 20:4–13 ◀ ▶ Job 21:17–18
C Job 21:14–15 ◀ ▶ Job 24:13
H Job 20:26–27 ◀ ▶ Job 21:30

21:8 ʰ Ps 17:14; Mal 3:15
21:9 ⁱ S Job 5:24 ʲ S Job 9:34
21:10 ᵏ Ex 23:26
21:11 ˡ Ps 78:52; 107:41
21:12 ᵐ Ps 33:2 ⁿ S Ge 4:21; S 1Ch 15:16; Ps 71:22; 81:2; 108:2; Isa 5:12; Mt 11:17
21:13 ᵒ S ver 7; S Job 8:7; Ps 10:1-12; 94:3 ᵖ Job 24:19; Ps 49:14; Isa 14:15 ᵠ S Job 3:13
21:14 ʳ S Job 4:17; 22:17; Isa 30:11 ˢ S Dt 32:15; S 1Sa 15:11; Ps 95:10; Pr 1:29; Jer 2:20,31
21:15 ᵗ S Job 5:2; 34:9; 35:3; Ps 73:13; 139:20; Isa 48:5; Jer 9:6; 44:17
21:16 ᵘ Job 22:18; Ps 1:1; 26:5; 36:1
21:17 ᵛ S Job 18:5 ʷ Job 18:12 ˣ S Job 20:22,28
21:18 ʸ S Job 13:25 ᶻ S Ge 19:15 ᵃ S Job 7:10; Pr 10:25 ᵇ S Ge 7:23
21:19 ᶜ Ex 20:5; Jer 31:29; Eze 18:2; Jn 9:2 ᵈ Jer 25:14; 50:29; 51:6,24,56
21:20 ᵉ S Ex 32:33; Nu 16:22; S 2Ki 14:6; Jer 42:16 ᶠ Job 6:4 ᵍ S Job 20:28; Jer 25:15; Rev 14:10
21:21 ʰ Job 14:22 ⁱ S Job 14:5 ʲ S Job 14:21; Ecc 9:5-6
21:22 ᵏ Job 35:11; 36:22; 39:17; Ps 94:12; Isa 40:13-14; Jer 32:33; Ro 11:34 ˡ S Job 4:18; Ps 82:1; 86:8; 135:5
21:23 ᵐ S Ge 15:15; S Job 13:26
21:24 ⁿ Ps 73:4 ᵒ Job 20:11 ᵖ Pr 3:8 ᵠ S Job 10:1
21:26 ʳ S Job 17:16 ˢ Job 7:5 ᵗ Job 24:20; Ecc 9:2-3; Isa 14:11
21:28 ᵛ Job 1:3; 12:21; 29:25;

31:37 ʷ S Job 8:22 21:30 ˣ Job 31:3 ʸ S Job 20:22,28; S Isa 5:30; Ro 2:5; 2Pe 2:9 21:31 ᶻ Job 34:11; Ps 62:12; Pr 24:11-12; Isa 59:18 21:32 ᵃ Isa 14:18 21:33 ᵇ Job 3:22 ᶜ S Job 3:19 21:34 ᵈ ver 2

ᵖ 13 Hebrew *Sheol* ᵠ 13 Or *in an instant* ʳ 17-20 Verses 17 and 18 may be taken as exclamations and 19 and 20 as declarations. ˢ 24 The meaning of the Hebrew for this word is uncertain. ᵗ 30 Or *man is reserved for the day of calamity, / that he is brought forth to* ᵘ 33 Or / *as a countless throng went*

21:30 Job declared that the wicked would be judged and delivered to "the day of wrath" with the same certainty that he affirmed the promise of a heavenly resurrection to those who repented of their sins.

Nothing is left of your answers but falsehood!"ᵉ

Eliphaz

22 Then Eliphaz the Temaniteᶠ replied:

²"Can a man be of benefit to God?ᵍ
  Can even a wise man benefit him?ʰ
³What pleasureⁱ would it give the Almighty if you were righteous?ʲ
  What would he gain if your ways were blameless?ᵏ
⁴"Is it for your piety that he rebukes you
  and brings charges against you?ˡ
⁵Is not your wickedness great?
  Are not your sinsᵐ endless?ⁿ
⁶You demanded securityᵒ from your brothers for no reason;ᵖ
  you stripped men of their clothing, leaving them naked.ᑫ
⁷You gave no waterʳ to the weary
  and you withheld food from the hungry,ˢ
⁸though you were a powerful man, owning landᵗ—
  an honored man,ᵘ living on it.ᵛ
⁹And you sent widowsʷ away empty-handedˣ
  and broke the strength of the fatherless.ʸ
¹⁰That is why snaresᶻ are all around you,ᵃ
  why sudden peril terrifies you,ᵇ
¹¹why it is so darkᶜ you cannot see,
  and why a flood of water covers you.ᵈ

¹²"Is not God in the heights of heaven?ᵉ
  And see how lofty are the highest stars!
¹³Yet you say, 'What does God know?ᶠ
  Does he judge through such darkness?ᵍ
¹⁴Thick cloudsʰ veil him, so he does not see usⁱ
  as he goes about in the vaulted heavens.'ʲ
¹⁵Will you keep to the old path
  that evil menᵏ have trod?ˡ
¹⁶They were carried off before their time,ᵐ

E *Job 14:16–17* ◀▶ *Job 26:6*
N *Job 21:13–14* ◀▶ *Job 27:8–9*

21:34 ᵉS Job 6:15; 8:20
22:1 ᶠS Job 4:1
22:2 ᵍLk 17:10
  ʰS Job 7:17
22:3 ⁱIsa 1:11;
  Hag 1:8 ⁱPs 143:2
  ᵏJob 35:7; Pr 9:12
22:4 ˡS Job 9:3;
  19:29; Ps 143:2;
  Isa 3:14; Eze 20:35
22:5 ᵐS Ezr 9:13;
  S Job 15:5
  ⁿS Job 15:13;
  S 20:29; 29:17
22:6 ᵒS Ex 22:26
  ᵖS 2Ki 4:1
  ᑫS Ex 22:27;
  Dt 24:12-13
22:7 ʳMt 10:42
  ˢver 9; Job 29:12;
  31:17,21,31;
  Isa 58:7,10;
  Eze 18:7; Mt 25:42
22:8 ᵗS Job 15:19
  ᵘIsa 3:3; 5:13; 9:15
  ᵛS Job 12:19
22:9 ʷJob 29:13;
  31:16; Ps 146:9
  ˣJob 24:3,21;
  Isa 10:2; Lk 1:53
  ʸS ver 7;
  S Job 6:27;
  S Isa 1:17
22:10 ᶻS Job 18:9
  ᵃS Job 10:3
  ᵇS Job 15:21
22:11 ᶜS Job 5:14
  ᵈS Ge 7:23;
  Job 36:28; 38:34, 37; Ps 69:1-2; 124:4-5;
  Isa 58:10-11;
  La 3:54
22:12 ᵉS Job 11:8;
  S 16:19
22:13 ᶠver 14;
  Ps 10:11; 59:7;
  64:5; 73:11; 94:7;
  Isa 29:15; Eze 9:9;
  Zep 1:12
  ᵍPs 139:11;
  Eze 8:12; Eph 6:12
22:14 ʰJob 26:9;
  Ps 97:2; 105:39
  ⁱS ver 13;
  S 2Ki 21:16
  ʲJob 37:18;
  Ps 18:11; Pr 8:27;
  Isa 40:22;
  Jer 23:23-24
22:15 ᵏJob 23:10;
  34:36 ˡJob 34:8;
  Ps 1:1; 50:18
22:16 ᵐS Job 15:32
  ⁿS Job 4:19
  ᵒS Ge 7:23;
  Mt 7:26-27

their foundationsⁿ washed away by a flood.ᵒ
¹⁷They said to God, 'Leave us alone!
  What can the Almighty do to us?'ᵖ
¹⁸Yet it was he who filled their houses with good things,ᑫ
  so I stand aloof from the counsel of the wicked.ʳ
¹⁹"The righteous see their ruin and rejoice;ˢ
  the innocent mockᵗ them, saying,
²⁰'Surely our foes are destroyed,ᵘ
  and fireᵛ devours their wealth.'

²¹"Submit to God and be at peaceʷ with him;ˣ
  in this way prosperity will come to you.ʸ
²²Accept instruction from his mouthᶻ
  and lay up his wordsᵃ in your heart.ᵇ
²³If you returnᶜ to the Almighty, you will be restored:ᵈ
  If you remove wickedness far from your tentᵉ
²⁴and assign your nuggetsᶠ to the dust,
  your goldᵍ of Ophirʰ to the rocks in the ravines,ⁱ
²⁵then the Almighty will be your gold,ʲ
  the choicest silver for you.ᵏ
²⁶Surely then you will find delight in the Almightyˡ
  and will lift up your faceᵐ to God.ⁿ
²⁷You will pray to him,ᵒ and he will hear you,ᵖ
  and you will fulfill your vows.ᑫ
²⁸What you decide on will be done,ʳ
  and lightˢ will shine on your ways.ᵗ
²⁹When men are brought lowᵘ and you say, 'Lift them up!'
  then he will save the downcast.ᵛ
³⁰He will deliver even one who is not innocent,ʷ

U *Job 17:9* ◀▶ *Job 22:23*
U *Job 22:21* ◀▶ *Job 22:28*
P *Job 1:10* ◀▶ *Job 27:16–17*
U *Job 22:23* ◀▶ *Job 29:3*
M *Ne 9:3* ◀▶ *Ps 10:4*

22:22 ᶻS Dt 8:3 ᵃS Job 6:10 ᵇS Job 15:11; 28:23; Ps 37:31; 40:8; Pr 2:6; Eze 3:10 22:23 ᶜIsa 31:6; 44:22; 55:7; 59:20; Jer 3:14,22; Eze 18:32; Zec 1:3; Mal 3:7 ᵈS Job 5:24; Isa 19:22; Ac 20:32 ᵉJob 11:14 22:24 ᶠJob 28:6 ᵍPs 19:10 ʰS Job 10:29 ⁱS Job 1:10; 31:25; Isa 2:20; 30:22; 31:7; 40:19-20; Mt 6:19 22:25 ʲJob 31:24; Ps 49:6; 52:7; Pr 11:28 ᵏ2Ki 18:7; Isa 33:6; Mt 6:20-21 22:26 ˡJob 27:10; Ps 2:8; 16:6; Pr 10:28 ᵐJob 11:15 ⁿJob 11:17; 33:26; Ps 27:6; 100:1 22:27 ᵒS Job 5:27 ᵖS Job 5:15; S Ps 86:7; S Isa 30:19 ᑫS Nu 30:2 22:28 ʳPs 103:11; 145:19 ˢJob 33:28; Ps 97:11; Pr 4:18 ᵗS Job 11:17 22:29 ᵘS Est 5:12 ᵛPs 18:27; S Mt 23:12 22:30 ʷIsa 1:18; Ro 4:5

who will be delivered through the
cleanness of your hands." ˣ

Job

23 Then Job replied:

² "Even today my complaint ʸ is bitter; ᶻ
his hand ᵛ is heavy in spite of ʷ my
groaning. ᵃ
³ If only I knew where to find him;
if only I could go to his dwelling! ᵇ
⁴ I would state my case ᶜ before him
and fill my mouth with arguments. ᵈ
⁵ I would find out what he would
answer me, ᵉ
and consider what he would say.
⁶ Would he oppose me with great
power? ᶠ
No, he would not press charges
against me. ᵍ
⁷ There an upright man ʰ could present
his case before him, ⁱ
and I would be delivered forever
from my judge. ʲ

⁸ "But if I go to the east, he is not there;
if I go to the west, I do not find him.
⁹ When he is at work in the north, I do
not see him;
when he turns to the south, I catch
no glimpse of him. ᵏ
¹⁰ But he knows the way that I take; ˡ
when he has tested me, ᵐ I will come
forth as gold. ⁿ
¹¹ My feet have closely followed his
steps; ᵒ
I have kept to his way without
turning aside. ᵖ
¹² I have not departed from the
commands of his lips; ᑫ
I have treasured the words of his
mouth more than my daily
bread. ʳ

¹³ "But he stands alone, and who can
oppose him? ˢ
He does whatever he pleases. ᵗ
¹⁴ He carries out his decree against me,
and many such plans he still has in
store. ᵘ
¹⁵ That is why I am terrified before him; ᵛ
when I think of all this, I fear him. ʷ
¹⁶ God has made my heart faint; ˣ
the Almighty ʸ has terrified me. ᶻ
¹⁷ Yet I am not silenced by the darkness, ᵃ
by the thick darkness that covers my
face.

24 "Why does the Almighty not set
times ᵇ for judgment? ᶜ
Why must those who know him
look in vain for such days? ᵈ
² Men move boundary stones; ᵉ
they pasture flocks they have
stolen. ᶠ
³ They drive away the orphan's donkey
and take the widow's ox in pledge. ᵍ
⁴ They thrust the needy ʰ from the path
and force all the poor ⁱ of the land
into hiding.
⁵ Like wild donkeys ᵏ in the desert,
the poor go about their labor ˡ of
foraging food;
the wasteland ᵐ provides food for
their children.
⁶ They gather fodder ⁿ in the fields
and glean in the vineyards ᵒ of the
wicked. ᵖ
⁷ Lacking clothes, they spend the night
naked;
they have nothing to cover
themselves in the cold. ᑫ
⁸ They are drenched ʳ by mountain rains
and hug ˢ the rocks for lack of
shelter. ᵗ
⁹ The fatherless ᵘ child is snatched ᵛ from
the breast;
the infant of the poor is seized ʷ for
a debt. ˣ
¹⁰ Lacking clothes, they go about naked; ʸ
they carry the sheaves, ᶻ but still go
hungry.

T *Job 5:17* ◀▶ *Job 33:17–22*

23:10 Job declared that God knew in advance what Job's conduct would be when he was subjected to various tests and temptations. These trials were designed to test Job's character and his devotion to God despite his circumstances. Just as an assay test examines the mineral content of an ore sample to determine its purity, Job's tests of character revealed what was in the core of Job's heart—his complete trust in God.

¹¹They crush olives among the terraces^x;
    they tread the winepresses,^a yet
        suffer thirst.^b
¹²The groans of the dying rise from the
        city,
    and the souls of the wounded cry
        out for help.^c
    But God charges no one with
        wrongdoing.^d
¹³"There are those who rebel against the
        light,^e
    who do not know its ways
        or stay in its paths.^f
¹⁴When daylight is gone, the murderer
        rises up
    and kills^g the poor and needy;^h
    in the night he steals forth like a
        thief.^i
¹⁵The eye of the adulterer^j watches for
        dusk;^k
    he thinks, 'No eye will see me,'^l
    and he keeps his face concealed.
¹⁶In the dark, men break into houses,^m
    but by day they shut themselves in;
    they want nothing to do with the
        light.^n
¹⁷For all of them, deep darkness is their
        morning';
    they make friends with the terrors^o
        of darkness.^z^p
¹⁸"Yet they are foam^q on the surface of
        the water;^r
    their portion of the land is cursed,^s
    so that no one goes to the
        vineyards.^t
¹⁹As heat and drought snatch away the
        melted snow,^u
    so the grave^av snatches away those
        who have sinned.
²⁰The womb forgets them,
    the worm^w feasts on them;^x
    evil men are no longer remembered^y
    but are broken like a tree.^z

C Job 21:17–18 ◀ ▶ Job 24:17
C Job 24:13 ◀ ▶ Job 27:18

24:11 ^a Isa 5:2;
16:10; Hag 2:16
^b Mic 6:15
24:12
^c S Job 12:19;
30:28; Ps 5:2;
22:24; 39:12;
119:147; Isa 30:19;
Jer 50:46; 51:52,
54; Eze 26:15;
Rev 6:10
^d S Job 9:23
24:13 ^e ver 16;
Job 38:15;
Jn 3:19-20;
1Th 5:4-5
^f Job 17:12; 38:20;
Ps 18:28; Isa 5:20;
Eph 5:8-14
24:14 ^g Isa 3:15;
Mic 3:3
^h S Job 20:19;
Ps 37:32 ^i Ps 10:9
24:15 ^j Job 31:9,
27; Pr 1:10
^k Pr 7:8-9 ^l Ps 10:11
24:16 ^m S Ex 22:2;
Mt 6:19 ^n S ver 13
24:17
^o S Job 18:11
^p S Job 15:22;
S 18:5
24:18 ^q S Job 9:26;
Jude 1:13
Isa 57:20 ^s S Job 5:3
^t ver 6
24:19 ^u Job 6:17
^v S Job 21:13
24:20 ^w S Job 7:5
^x S Job 21:26
^y S Job 18:17
^z S Job 14:7;
Ps 31:12; Da 4:14
24:21 ^a S Job 22:9
24:22 ^b S Job 9:4
^c S Job 12:19
^d Dt 28:66;
Mt 6:27; Jas 4:14
24:23 ^e S Job 9:24;
Am 6:1 ^f S 2Ch 16:9
^g S Job 10:4
24:24
^h S 2Ki 19:35;
S Job 4:20;
Ps 37:10; 83:13;
Isa 5:24; 17:13;
40:24; 41:2,15
^i S Job 3:19
^j Isa 17:5
24:25 ^k S Job 6:28;
S 16:17
25:1 ^l S Job 8:1
25:2 ^m S Job 9:4;
Ps 47:9; 89:18;
Zec 9:7; Rev 1:6
^n S 2Ch 20:6;
S Job 11:8; S 16:19
25:3 ^o Mt 5:45;
Jas 1:17

²¹They prey on the barren and childless
        woman,
    and to the widow show no
        kindness.^a
²²But God drags away the mighty by his
        power;^b
    though they become established,^c
        they have no assurance of life.^d
²³He may let them rest in a feeling of
        security,^e
    but his eyes^f are on their ways.^g
²⁴For a little while they are exalted, and
        then they are gone;^h
    they are brought low and gathered
        up like all others;^i
    they are cut off like heads of grain.^j
²⁵"If this is not so, who can prove me
        false
    and reduce my words to nothing?"^k

Bildad

25 Then Bildad the Shuhite¹ replied:

²"Dominion and awe belong to God;^m
    he establishes order in the heights
        of heaven.^n
³Can his forces be numbered?
    Upon whom does his light not rise?^o
⁴How then can a man be righteous
        before God?
    How can one born of woman be
        pure?^p
⁵If even the moon^q is not bright
    and the stars are not pure in his
        eyes,^r
⁶how much less man, who is but a
        maggot—
    a son of man,^s who is only a
        worm!"^t

25:4 ^p S Job 4:17 25:5 ^q Job 31:26 ^r S Job 4:18 25:6 ^s Ps 80:17; 144:3;
Eze 2:1 ^t S Job 4:19; S 7:5

^x 11 Or olives between the millstones; the meaning of the Hebrew for this
word is uncertain.   ^y 17 Or them, their morning is like the shadow of
death   ^z 17 Or of the shadow of death   ^a 19 Hebrew Sheol

25:4 Job's question of justification mirrors the discussion Jesus had with Nicodemus (see Jn 3:1–16) and provides the framework for the book of Romans. God is holy and he cannot ignore our sinfulness. However, we are incapable of living a sinless life and are in need of justification to satisfy God's entrance requirements to heaven (see Ro 3:23). The only way we can obtain this justification is through repentance and acceptance of Christ's sacrificial atonement for our sins. When a person repents of their sins, asks God for forgiveness and accepts Christ's death on the cross as payment for their sin, God wipes away the sin in their life and views that repentant sinner through the righteousness of Christ. Christ's perfect obedience and righteousness, applied to the heart of each repentant sinner, qualifies each one for acceptance into the holiness of heaven.

Job

26 Then Job replied:

² "How you have helped the powerless!ᵘ
How you have saved the arm that is feeble!ᵛ
³ What advice you have offered to one without wisdom!
And what great insightʷ you have displayed!
⁴ Who has helped you utter these words?
And whose spirit spoke from your mouth?ˣ

⁵ "The dead are in deep anguish,ʸ
those beneath the waters and all that live in them.
⁶ Deathᵇᶻ is naked before God;
Destructionᶜᵃ lies uncovered.ᵇ
⁷ He spreads out the northern skies⌐ᶜ over empty space;
he suspends the earth over nothing.ᵈ
⁸ He wraps up the watersᵉ in his clouds,ᶠ
yet the clouds do not burst under their weight.
⁹ He covers the face of the full moon, spreading his cloudsᵍ over it.
¹⁰ He marks out the horizon on the face of the waters ʰ
for a boundary between light and darkness.ⁱ
¹¹ The pillars of the heavens quake,ʲ
aghast at his rebuke.
¹² By his power he churned up the sea;ᵏ
by his wisdomˡ he cut Rahabᵐ to pieces.
¹³ By his breath the skiesⁿ became fair;
his hand pierced the gliding serpent.ᵒ

¹⁴ And these are but the outer fringe of his works;
how faint the whisperᵖ we hear of him!ᵠ
Who then can understand the thunder of his power?"ʳ

27 And Job continued his discourse:ˢ

² "As surely as God lives, who has denied me justice,ᵗ
the Almighty,ᵘ who has made me taste bitterness of soul,ᵛ
³ as long as I have life within me,
the breath of Godʷ in my nostrils,
⁴ my lips will not speak wickedness,
and my tongue will utter no deceit.ˣ
⁵ I will never admit you are in the right;
till I die, I will not deny my integrity.ʸ
⁶ I will maintain my righteousnessᶻ and never let go of it;
my conscienceᵃ will not reproach me as long as I live.ᵇ

⁷ "May my enemies be like the wicked,ᶜ
my adversariesᵈ like the unjust!
⁸ For what hope has the godlessᵉ when he is cut off,
when God takes away his life?ᶠ
⁹ Does God listen to his cry when distress comes upon him?ᵍ
¹⁰ Will he find delight in the Almighty?ʰ
Will he call upon God at all times?

¹¹ "I will teach you about the power of God;
the waysⁱ of the Almighty I will not conceal.ʲ
¹² You have all seen this yourselves.
Why then this meaningless talk?

¹³ "Here is the fate God allots to the wicked,

E Job 22:12–17 ◀▶ Job 28:24–25
N Dt 4:40 ◀▶ Ps 37:9
E Ne 9:30 ◀▶ Job 32:8
M 2Ki 2:16 ◀▶ Job 32:18–19
N Ne 9:20 ◀▶ Job 32:8

H Job 21:30 ◀▶ Job 27:19–23
N Job 22:15–17 ◀▶ Ps 27:8
S Job 17:9 ◀▶ Job 28:7–8

ᵇ 6 Hebrew *Sheol* ᶜ 6 Hebrew *Abaddon*

26:7 The Hebrew for this verse indicates that God created a zone of emptiness in space to the north of the earth. To the naked eye, the northern area of the night sky seems just as full of stars as other parts of the heavens. Yet scientists have recently discovered an area just north of the axis of the earth (near the north polar star) that seems to be almost empty of stars for millions of light-years, as if there were a hole in space, confirming the accuracy of Job's words. **26:10** Note the similarity between this verse and 38:8. God is in control of the boundaries of the water and the land as he promised Noah he would be (see Ge 9:15).

the heritage a ruthless man receives
    from the Almighty:^k
^14However many his children,^l their fate
    is the sword;^m
his offspring will never have enough
    to eat.^n
^15The plague will bury those who
    survive him,
and their widows will not weep for
    them.^o
^16Though he heaps up silver like dust^p
    and clothes like piles of clay,^q
^17what he lays up^r the righteous will
    wear,^s
and the innocent will divide his
    silver.^t
^18The house^u he builds is like a moth's
    cocoon,^v
like a hut^w made by a watchman.
^19He lies down wealthy, but will do so
    no more;^x
when he opens his eyes, all is gone.^y
^20Terrors^z overtake him like a flood;^a
    a tempest snatches him away in the
    night.^b
^21The east wind^c carries him off, and he
    is gone;^d
it sweeps him out of his place.^e
^22It hurls itself against him without
    mercy^f
as he flees headlong^g from its
    power.^h
^23It claps its hands^i in derision
    and hisses him out of his place.^j

28 "There is a mine for silver
    and a place where gold is
    refined.^k
^2Iron is taken from the earth,
    and copper is smelted from ore.^l
^3Man puts an end to the darkness;^m
    he searches the farthest recesses
    for ore in the blackest darkness."^n
^4Far from where people dwell he cuts a
    shaft,^o
in places forgotten by the foot of
    man;
far from men he dangles and sways.
^5The earth, from which food comes,^p
    is transformed below as by fire;
^6sapphires^d^q come from its rocks,
    and its dust contains nuggets of
    gold.^r

C Ne 9:21 ◀▶ Eze 16:10
P Job 22:24–25 ◀▶ Job 42:10
C Job 24:17 ◀▶ Ps 1:4
H Job 27:8 ◀▶ Job 31:3

27:13
^k S Job 16:19;
S 20:29
27:14 ^l S Job 5:4
^m S Job 15:22;
S La 2:22
^n S Job 4:11
27:15 ^o Ps 78:64
27:16
^p S 1Ki 10:27
^q Zec 9:3
27:17 ^r Ps 39:6;
49:10; Ecc 2:26
^s S Job 7:8;
Pr 13:22; 28:8;
Ecc 2:26 ^t Ex 3:22;
S Job 3:15
27:18 ^u S Job 8:22
^v S Job 8:14
^w Isa 1:8; 24:20
27:19 ^x S Job 3:13;
S 7:8 ^y S Job 14:20
27:20 ^z S Job 6:4
^a S Job 15:21
^b S Job 20:8
27:21 ^c Job 38:24;
Jer 13:24; 22:22
^d Job 30:22
^e S Job 7:10
27:22 ^f Jer 13:14;
Eze 5:11; 24:14
^g 2Ki 7:15
^h S Job 11:20
27:23
^i S Nu 24:10;
Na 3:19 ^j S Job 7:10
28:1 ^k Ps 12:6;
66:10; Jer 9:7;
Da 11:35; Mal 3:3
28:2 ^l Dt 8:9
28:3 ^m Ecc 1:13;
7:25; 8:17
^n S Job 26:10; 38:19
28:4 ^o ver 10;
2Sa 5:8
28:5 ^p Ge 1:29;
Ps 104:14; 145:15
28:6 ^q ver 16;
SS 5:14; Isa 54:11
^r S Job 22:24
28:7 ^s ver 21
28:8 ^t Job 41:34
^u Isa 35:9
28:9 ^v S Dt 8:15
^w Jnh 2:6
28:10 ^x S ver 4
^y Pr 2:4
28:11 ^z S Ge 7:11
^a Isa 48:6; Jer 33:3
28:12 ^b ver 28;
Pr 1:20; 3:13-20;
8:1; 9:1-3; Ecc 7:24
^c ver 20,23
28:13 ^d Pr 3:15;
Mt 13:44-46
^e Dt 29:29;
Ps 27:13; 52:5;
116:9; 142:5;
Isa 38:11;
Jer 11:19;
Eze 26:20; 32:24
28:14 ^f Ps 42:7;
Ro 10:7 ^g Dt 30:13
28:15 ^h ver 17;
Pr 3:13-14;
8:10-11; 16:16;
Ac 8:20
28:16 ^i S Ge 10:29
^j ver 6; S Ex 24:10
28:17 ^k Ps 119:72;
Pr 8:10 ^l S ver 15
28:18 ^m Eze 27:16
^n Rev 21:11
^o Pr 3:15; 8:11
28:19 ^p Ex 28:17

^7No bird of prey knows that hidden
    path,
no falcon's eye has seen it.^s
^8Proud beasts^t do not set foot on it,
    and no lion prowls there.^u
^9Man's hand assaults the flinty rock^v
    and lays bare the roots of the
    mountains.^w
^10He tunnels through the rock;^x
    his eyes see all its treasures.^y
^11He searches^e the sources of the rivers^z
    and brings hidden things^a to light.
^12"But where can wisdom be found?^b
    Where does understanding dwell?^c
^13Man does not comprehend its worth;^d
    it cannot be found in the land of the
    living.^e
^14The deep^f says, 'It is not in me';
    the sea^g says, 'It is not with me.'
^15It cannot be bought with the finest
    gold,
nor can its price be weighed in
    silver.^h
^16It cannot be bought with the gold of
    Ophir,^i
with precious onyx or sapphires.^j
^17Neither gold nor crystal can compare
    with it,^k
nor can it be had for jewels of gold.^l
^18Coral^m and jasper^n are not worthy of
    mention;
the price of wisdom is beyond
    rubies.^o
^19The topaz^p of Cush^q cannot compare
    with it;
it cannot be bought with pure gold.^r
^20"Where then does wisdom come from?
    Where does understanding dwell?^s
^21It is hidden from the eyes of every
    living thing,
concealed even from the birds of the
    air.^t
^22Destruction^f^u and Death^v say,
    'Only a rumor of it has reached our
    ears.'
^23God understands the way to it
    and he alone^w knows where it
    dwells,^x

S Job 27:8 ◀▶ Job 34:11

^q Isa 11:11 ^r Pr 3:14-15; 8:10-11,19 **28:20** ^s S Job 9:4 **28:21** ^t ver 7
28:22 ^u S Job 20:26; S Rev 9:11 ^v Pr 8:32-36 **28:23** ^w Ecc 3:11; 8:17
^x S Job 9:4; S 22:22; Pr 8:22-31

^d 6 Or *lapis lazuli*; also in verse 16   ^e 11 Septuagint, Aquila and Vulgate;
Hebrew *He dams up*   ^f 22 Hebrew *Abaddon*

²⁴for he views the ends of the earth^y
  and sees everything under the
    heavens.^z
²⁵When he established the force of the
    wind
  and measured out the waters,^a
²⁶when he made a decree for the rain^b
  and a path for the thunderstorm,^c
²⁷then he looked at wisdom and
    appraised it;
  he confirmed it and tested it.^d
²⁸And he said to man,
  'The fear of the Lord—that is
      wisdom,
    and to shun evil^e is
      understanding.'"

29

Job continued his discourse:^g

²"How I long for the months gone by,^h
  for the days when God watched over
    me,^i
³when his lamp shone upon my head
  and by his light I walked through
      darkness!^j
⁴Oh, for the days when I was in my
    prime,
  when God's intimate friendship^k
    blessed my house,^l
⁵when the Almighty was still with me
  and my children^m were around me,^n
⁶when my path was drenched with
    cream^o
  and the rock^p poured out for me
    streams of olive oil.^q
⁷"When I went to the gate^r of the city
  and took my seat in the public
    square,
⁸the young men saw me and stepped
    aside^s
  and the old men rose to their feet;^t
⁹the chief men refrained from
    speaking^u
  and covered their mouths with their
    hands;^v
¹⁰the voices of the nobles were hushed,^w
  and their tongues stuck to the roof
    of their mouths.^x
¹¹Whoever heard me spoke well of me,
  and those who saw me commended
    me,^y
¹²because I rescued the poor^z who cried
    for help,

E Job 26:6 ◀ ▶ Job 31:4
U Job 22:28 ◀ ▶ Job 29:6
U Job 29:3 ◀ ▶ Job 36:7

28:24 ^y Job 36:32;
37:3; 38:18,24,35;
Ps 33:13-14; 66:7;
Isa 11:12
^z S Jos 3:11;
S Job 10:4;
S Heb 4:13
28:25
^a S Job 12:15;
38:8-11
28:26 ^b Job 36:28;
37:6; Jer 51:16
^c Job 36:33; 37:3,8,
11; 38:25,27;
Ps 65:12; 104:14;
147:8; Isa 35:7
28:27 ^d Pr 3:19;
8:22-31
28:28 ^e Ps 11:5;
97:10; Pr 3:7; 8:13
^f Ex 20:20;
S Dt 4:6;
S Job 37:24
29:1 ^g Job 27:1
29:2 ^h S Ge 31:30
^i Jer 1:12; 31:28;
44:27
29:3 ^j S Job 11:17;
S 12:25
29:4 ^k S Job 15:8
^l Ps 25:14; Pr 3:32
29:5 ^m Ps 127:3-5;
128:3 ^n Ru 4:1
29:6 ^o S Job 20:17
^p Ps 81:16
^q Ge 49:20;
S Dt 32:13
29:7 ^r ver 21;
Job 5:4; 31:21;
Jer 20:2; 38:7
29:8 ^s 1Ti 5:1
^t S Lev 19:32
29:9 ^u ver 21;
Job 31:21
29:10 ^w ver 22
29:11 ^y S Job 4:4;
Heb 11:4
29:12 ^z S Job 24:4
^a S Dt 24:17;
Job 31:17,21
^b Ps 72:12; Pr 21:13
29:13 ^c Job 31:20
^d S Dt 10:18;
S Job 22:9
29:14 ^e S 2Sa 8:15;
S Job 27:6;
Eph 4:24; 6:14
^f S Job 19:9
29:15 ^g Nu 10:31
^h S Job 4:4
29:16 ^i S Job 24:4
^j Ex 18:26
^k S Job 4:4;
Pr 22:22-23
29:17 ^l Job 24:9
^m S Job 4:10,11;
S Ps 3:7
29:18 ^n Ps 1:1-3;
15:5; 16:8; 30:6;
62:5; 139:18;
Pr 3:1-2
29:19 ^o S Nu 24:6;
S Job 14:9
^p S Ge 27:8;
S Job 15:30;
S Ps 133:3
29:20 ^q Ps 92:14
^r Job 30:11;
Ps 18:34; Isa 38:12
^s Ge 49:24
29:21 ^t S ver 7, S 9
29:22 ^u ver 10

and the fatherless^a who had none to
    assist him.^b
¹³The man who was dying blessed me;^c
  I made the widow's^d heart sing.
¹⁴I put on righteousness^e as my clothing;
  justice was my robe and my turban.^f
¹⁵I was eyes^g to the blind
  and feet to the lame.^h
¹⁶I was a father to the needy;^i
  I took up the case^j of the stranger.^k
¹⁷I broke the fangs of the wicked
  and snatched the victims^l from their
    teeth.^m
¹⁸"I thought, 'I will die in my own
      house,
  my days as numerous as the grains
    of sand.^n
¹⁹My roots will reach to the water,^o
  and the dew will lie all night on my
    branches.^p
²⁰My glory will remain fresh^q in me,
  the bow^r ever new in my hand.'^s
²¹"Men listened to me expectantly,
  waiting in silence for my counsel.^t
²²After I had spoken, they spoke no
    more;^u
  my words fell gently on their ears.^v
²³They waited for me as for showers
  and drank in my words as the spring
    rain.^w
²⁴When I smiled at them, they scarcely
    believed it;
  the light of my face^x was precious to
    them.^y
²⁵I chose the way for them and sat as
    their chief;^z
  I dwelt as a king^a among his troops;
  I was like one who comforts
    mourners.^b

30

"But now they mock me,^c
  men younger than I,
whose fathers I would have disdained
  to put with my sheep dogs.^d
²Of what use was the strength of their
    hands to me,
  since their vigor had gone from
    them?
³Haggard from want and hunger,
  they roamed^h the parched land^e
  in desolate wastelands^f at night.^g

^v Dt 32:2 29:23 ^w S Job 4:3 29:24 ^x S Nu 6:25 ^y Pr 16:14,15
29:25 ^z S Job 21:28 ^a S Job 1:3 ^b S Job 4:4 30:1 ^c S Job 6:14; S 11:3;
S Ps 119:21 ^d Isa 56:10 30:3 ^e Isa 8:21 ^f Job 24:5 ^g Jer 17:6
^g 24 The meaning of the Hebrew for this clause is uncertain.
^h 3 Or gnawed

⁴"In the brush they gathered salt herbs,ʰ
 and their foodⁱ was the root of the
   broom tree.ʲ
⁵They were banished from their fellow
   men,
 shouted at as if they were thieves.
⁶They were forced to live in the dry
   stream beds,
 among the rocks and in holes in the
   ground.ʲ
⁷They brayedᵏ among the bushesˡ
 and huddled in the undergrowth.
⁸A base and nameless brood,ᵐ
 they were driven out of the land.ⁿ

⁹"And now their sons mock meᵒ in
   song;ᵖ
 I have become a bywordᵠ among
   them.
¹⁰They detest meʳ and keep their
   distance;
 they do not hesitate to spit in my
   face.ˢ
¹¹Now that God has unstrung my bowᵗ
   and afflicted me,ᵘ
 they throw off restraintᵛ in my
   presence.
¹²On my rightʷ the tribeʲ attacks;
 they lay snaresˣ for my feet,ʸ
 they build their siege ramps against
   me.ᶻ
¹³They break up my road;ᵃ
 they succeed in destroying meᵇ—
 without anyone's helping them.ᵏ
¹⁴They advance as through a gaping
   breach;ᶜ
 amid the ruins they come rolling in.
¹⁵Terrorsᵈ overwhelm me;ᵉ
 my dignity is driven away as by the
   wind,
 my safety vanishes like a cloud.ᶠ

¹⁶"And now my life ebbs away;ᵍ
 days of suffering grip me.ʰ
¹⁷Night pierces my bones;
 my gnawing pains never rest.ⁱ
¹⁸In his great powerʲ ⌊God⌋ becomes like
   clothing to me;
 he binds me like the neck of my
   garment.
¹⁹He throws me into the mud,ᵏ
 and I am reduced to dust and
   ashes.ˡ
²⁰"I cry out to you,ᵐ O God, but you do
   not answer;ⁿ
 I stand up, but you merely look at
   me.

²¹You turn on me ruthlessly;ᵒ
 with the might of your handᵖ you
   attack me.ᵠ
²²You snatch me up and drive me before
   the wind;ʳ
 you toss me about in the storm.ˢ
²³I know you will bring me down to
   death,ᵗ
 to the place appointed for all the
   living.ᵘ

²⁴"Surely no one lays a hand on a broken
   manᵛ
 when he cries for help in his
   distress.ʷ
²⁵Have I not wept for those in trouble?ˣ
 Has not my soul grieved for the
   poor?ʸ
²⁶Yet when I hoped for good, evil came;
 when I looked for light, then came
   darkness.ᶻ
²⁷The churning inside me never stops;ᵃ
 days of suffering confront me.ᵇ
²⁸I go about blackened,ᶜ but not by the
   sun;
 I stand up in the assembly and cry
   for help.ᵈ
²⁹I have become a brother of jackals,ᵉ
 a companion of owls.ᶠ
³⁰My skin grows blackᵍ and peels;ʰ
 my body burns with fever.ⁱ
³¹My harp is tuned to mourning,ʲ
 and my fluteᵏ to the sound of
   wailing.

31 "I made a covenant with my
   eyesˡ
 not to look lustfully at a girl.ᵐ
²For what is man's lotⁿ from God
   above,
 his heritage from the Almighty on
   high?ᵒ
³Is it not ruinᵖ for the wicked,
 disasterᵠ for those who do wrong?ʳ
⁴Does he not see my waysˢ
 and count my every step?ᵗ
⁵"If I have walked in falsehood

H Job 27:19–23 ◀▶ Ps 2:8–9
E Job 28:24–25 ◀▶ Job 34:21–22

⁴ Or *fuel* / 12 The meaning of the Hebrew for this word is uncertain. / 13 Or *me.* / 'No one can help him,' *they say.* / 18 Hebrew; Septuagint *God, grasps my clothing*

or my foot has hurried after deceit[u]—
⁶let God weigh me[v] in honest scales[w]
and he will know that I am blameless[x]—
⁷if my steps have turned from the path,[y]
if my heart has been led by my eyes,
or if my hands[z] have been defiled,[a]
⁸then may others eat what I have sown,[b]
and may my crops be uprooted.[c]
⁹"If my heart has been enticed[d] by a woman,[e]
or if I have lurked at my neighbor's door,
¹⁰then may my wife grind[f] another man's grain,
and may other men sleep with her.[g]
¹¹For that would have been shameful,[h] a sin to be judged.[i]
¹²It is a fire[j] that burns to Destruction[m];[k]
it would have uprooted my harvest.[l]
¹³"If I have denied justice to my menservants and maidservants[m]
when they had a grievance against me,[n]
¹⁴what will I do when God confronts me?[o]
What will I answer when called to account?[p]
¹⁵Did not he who made me in the womb make them?[q]
Did not the same one form us both within our mothers?[r]
¹⁶"If I have denied the desires of the poor[s]
or let the eyes of the widow[t] grow weary,[u]
¹⁷if I have kept my bread to myself, not sharing it with the fatherless[v]—
¹⁸but from my youth I reared him as would a father,
and from my birth I guided the widow[w]—
¹⁹if I have seen anyone perishing for lack of clothing,[x]
or a needy[y] man without a garment,
²⁰and his heart did not bless me[z]
for warming him with the fleece[a] from my sheep,
²¹if I have raised my hand against the fatherless,[b]
knowing that I had influence in court,[c]

²²then let my arm fall from the shoulder,
let it be broken off at the joint.[d]
²³For I dreaded destruction from God,[e]
and for fear of his splendor[f] I could not do such things.[g]
²⁴"If I have put my trust in gold[h]
or said to pure gold, 'You are my security,'[i]
²⁵if I have rejoiced over my great wealth,[j]
the fortune my hands had gained,[k]
²⁶if I have regarded the sun[l] in its radiance
or the moon[m] moving in splendor,
²⁷so that my heart was secretly enticed[n]
and my hand offered them a kiss of homage,[o]
²⁸then these also would be sins to be judged,[p]
for I would have been unfaithful to God on high.[q]
²⁹"If I have rejoiced at my enemy's misfortune[r]
or gloated over the trouble that came to him[s]—
³⁰I have not allowed my mouth to sin
by invoking a curse against his life[t]—
³¹if the men of my household have never said,
'Who has not had his fill of Job's meat?'[u]—
³²but no stranger had to spend the night in the street,
for my door was always open to the traveler[v]—
³³if I have concealed[w] my sin as men do,[n]
by hiding[x] my guilt in my heart
³⁴because I so feared the crowd[y]
and so dreaded the contempt of the clans
that I kept silent[z] and would not go outside
³⁵("Oh, that I had someone to hear me![a]
I sign now my defense—let the Almighty answer me;
let my accuser[b] put his indictment in writing.

R Job 11:13–14 ◀ ▶ Job 33:27–28

m 12 Hebrew *Abaddon* *n* 33 Or *as Adam did*

36 Surely I would wear it on my shoulder,c
I would put it on like a crown.d
37 I would give him an account of my every step;e
like a princef I would approach him.)—
38 "if my land cries out against meg
and all its furrows are weth with tears,
39 if I have devoured its yield without paymenti
or broken the spirit of its tenants,j
40 then let briersk come up instead of wheat
and weedsl instead of barley."

The words of Job are ended.m

Elihu

32 So these three men stopped answering Job,n because he was righteous in his own eyes.o 2 But Elihu son of Barakel the Buzite,p of the family of Ram, became very angry with Job for justifying himselfq rather than God.r 3 He was also angry with the three friends,s because they had found no way to refute Job,t and yet had condemned him.o u 4 Now Elihu had waited before speaking to Job because they were older than he.v 5 But when he saw that the three men had nothing more to say, his anger was aroused.

6 So Elihu son of Barakel the Buzite said:

"I am young in years,
and you are old;w
that is why I was fearful,
not daring to tell you what I know.
7 I thought, 'Age should speak;
advanced years should teach wisdom.'x
8 But it is the spiritp y in a man,
the breath of the Almighty,z that gives him understanding.a
9 It is not only the oldq who are wise,b
not only the agedc who understand what is right.d
10 "Therefore I say: Listen to me;e
I too will tell you what I know.f

E *Job 26:13* ◀ ▶ *Job 32:18-19*
G *Ne 9:20* ◀ ▶ *Ps 68:18*
N *Job 26:13* ◀ ▶ *Job 33:4*
T *Ne 9:20* ◀ ▶ *Job 32:18-19*

31:36 cS Ex 28:12
d Job 29:14
31:37 eS ver 14;
S Job 11:11
f S Job 21:28
31:38 gS Ge 4:10
h Ps 65:10
31:39 iS 1Ki 21:19
j S Lev 19:13;
Jas 5:4
31:40 kS Ge 3:18;
Mt 13:7 l Zep 2:9;
Mt 13:26
m Ps 72:20;
Jer 51:64
32:1 n ver 15
o S Job 2:3; S 10:7
32:2 pS Ge 22:21
q ver 1
r S Job 13:19; 27:5;
30:21; 35:2
32:3 sJob 42:7
t ver 12-13
u S Job 15:13
32:4 vS Lev 19:32
32:6 wJob 15:10
32:7
x S 1Ch 29:15;
S 2Ch 10:6
32:8 y ver 18
z S Job 27:3
a S Job 12:13;
S Ps 119:34; Jas 1:5
32:9 b 1Co 1:26
c Ps 119:100
d S Job 12:12,20;
Lk 2:47; 1Ti 4:12
32:10 e Job 33:1,
31,33; 34:2,16;
37:2,14; Ps 34:11
f S Job 5:27
32:12 g ver 3
32:13 hS Job 4:12;
S Ecc 9:11
i S Job 11:5
32:14 j Job 23:4
32:15 k ver 1
32:17 l S Job 5:27;
33:3; 36:4
32:18 m ver 8
n Ac 4:20;
1Co 9:16; 2Co 5:14
32:19 o Jer 20:9;
Am 3:8; Mt 9:17
32:20 pS Job 4:2;
S Jer 6:11
32:21
qS Lev 19:15;
S 2Ch 19:7;
S Job 13:10
r Mt 22:16
s Pr 29:5; 1Th 2:5
32:22 tS Job 4:17;
S 9:4 uS Ps 12:2-4
33:1 v Job 32:10
w S Job 6:28; S 13:6
33:3 x 1Ki 3:6;
Ps 7:10; 11:2;
64:10 yS Job 6:28
33:4 zS Ge 1:2
a Job 10:3

11 I waited while you spoke,
I listened to your reasoning;
while you were searching for words,
12 I gave you my full attention.
But not one of you has proved Job wrong;
none of you has answered his arguments.g
13 Do not say, 'We have found wisdom;h
let God refutei him, not man.'
14 But Job has not marshaled his words against me,j
and I will not answer him with your arguments.
15 "They are dismayed and have no more to say;
words have failed them.k
16 Must I wait, now that they are silent,
now that they stand there with no reply?
17 I too will have my say;
I too will tell what I know.l
18 For I am full of words,
and the spiritm within me compels me;n
19 inside I am like bottled-up wine,
like new wineskins ready to burst.o
20 I must speak and find relief;
I must open my lips and reply.p
21 I will show partialityq to no one,r
nor will I flatter any man;s
22 for if I were skilled in flattery,
my Makert would soon take me away.u

33 "But now, Job, listenv to my words;
pay attention to everything I say.w
2 I am about to open my mouth;
my words are on the tip of my tongue.
3 My words come from an upright heart;x
my lips sincerely speak what I know.y
4 The Spiritz of God has made me;a

E *Job 32:8* ◀ ▶ *Job 33:4*
L *2Ch 18:23* ◀ ▶ *Ps 39:3*
M *Job 26:13-14* ◀ ▶ *Job 33:4*
T *Job 32:8* ◀ ▶ *Ps 143:10*
E *Job 32:18-19* ◀ ▶ *Ps 104:30*
H ▶ *Eze 37:13-14*
M *Job 32:18-19* ◀ ▶ *Ps 51:12-13*
N *Job 32:8* ◀ ▶ *Ps 51:12*

o 3 Masoretic Text; an ancient Hebrew scribal tradition *Job, and so had condemned God* p 8 Or *Spirit*; also in verse 18 q 9 Or *many*; or *great*

the breath of the Almighty[b] gives
  me life.[c]
⁵Answer me[d] then, if you can;
  prepare[e] yourself and confront me.[f]
⁶I am just like you before God;[g]
  I too have been taken from clay.[h]
⁷No fear of me should alarm you,
  nor should my hand be heavy upon
    you.[i]
⁸"But you have said in my hearing—
  I heard the very words—
⁹'I am pure[j] and without sin;[k]
  I am clean and free from guilt.[l]
¹⁰Yet God has found fault with me;
  he considers me his enemy.[m]
¹¹He fastens my feet in shackles;[n]
  he keeps close watch on all my
    paths.'[o]
¹²"But I tell you, in this you are not
    right,
  for God is greater than man.[p]
¹³Why do you complain to him[q]
  that he answers none of man's
    words[r]?[r]
¹⁴For God does speak[s]—now one way,
    now another[t]—
  though man may not perceive it.[u]
¹⁵In a dream,[v] in a vision[w] of the night,[x]
  when deep sleep[y] falls on men
  as they slumber in their beds,
¹⁶he may speak[z] in their ears
  and terrify them[a] with warnings,[b]
¹⁷to turn man from wrongdoing
  and keep him from pride,[c]
¹⁸to preserve his soul from the pit,[s]
  his life from perishing by the
    sword.[r][e]
¹⁹Or a man may be chastened[f] on a bed
    of pain[g]
  with constant distress in his bones,[h]
²⁰so that his very being finds food[i]
    repulsive
  and his soul loathes the choicest
    meal.[j]
²¹His flesh wastes away to nothing,
  and his bones,[k] once hidden, now
    stick out.[l]
²²His soul draws near to the pit,[u][m]
  and his life to the messengers of
    death.[v][n]
²³"Yet if there is an angel on his side

as a mediator,[o] one out of a
    thousand,
  to tell a man what is right for him,[p]
²⁴to be gracious to him and say,
  'Spare him from going down to the
    pit[w];[q]
  I have found a ransom for him'[r]—
²⁵then his flesh is renewed[s] like a
    child's;
  it is restored as in the days of his
    youth.[t]
²⁶He prays to God and finds favor with
    him,[u]
  he sees God's face and shouts for
    joy;[v]
  he is restored by God to his
    righteous state.[w]
²⁷Then he comes to men and says,
  'I sinned,[x] and perverted what was
    right,[y]
  but I did not get what I deserved.[z]
²⁸He redeemed[a] my soul from going
    down to the pit,[x][b]
  and I will live to enjoy the light.'[c]
²⁹"God does all these things to a man[d]—
  twice, even three times[e]—
³⁰to turn back[f] his soul from the pit,[y][g]
  that the light of life[h] may shine on
    him.[i]
³¹"Pay attention, Job, and listen[j] to me;[k]
  be silent,[l] and I will speak.
³²If you have anything to say, answer
    me;[m]
  speak up, for I want you to be
    cleared.[n]
³³But if not, then listen to me;[o]
  be silent,[p] and I will teach you
    wisdom.[q]"

34

Then Elihu said:
²"Hear my words, you wise men;
  listen to me,[r] you men of learning.

³For the ear tests words
    as the tongue tastes food.ˢ
⁴Let us discern for ourselves what is
        right;ᵗ
    let us learn together what is good.ᵘ

⁵"Job says, 'I am innocent,ᵛ
    but God denies me justice.ʷ
⁶Although I am right,
    I am considered a liar;ˣ
although I am guiltless,ʸ
    his arrow inflicts an incurable
        wound.'ᶻ
⁷What man is like Job,
    who drinks scorn like water?ᵃ
⁸He keeps company with evildoers;
    he associates with wicked men.ᵇ
⁹For he says, 'It profits a man nothing
    when he tries to please God.'ᶜ

¹⁰"So listen to me,ᵈ you men of
        understanding.ᵉ
    Far be it from God to do evil,ᶠ
        from the Almighty to do wrong.ᵍ
ˢ¹¹He repays a man for what he has
        done;ʰ
    he brings upon him what his
        conduct deserves.ⁱ
¹²It is unthinkable that God would do
        wrong,ʲ
    that the Almighty would pervert
        justice.ᵏ
¹³Who appointedˡ him over the earth?
    Who put him in charge of the whole
        world?ᵐ
¹⁴If it were his intention
    and he withdrew his spiritⁿ and
        breath,ᵒ
¹⁵all mankind would perishᵖ together
    and man would return to the dust.ᑫ

¹⁶"If you have understanding,ʳ hear this;
    listen to what I say.ˢ
¹⁷Can he who hates justice govern?ᵗ
    Will you condemn the just and
        mighty One?ᵘ
¹⁸Is he not the One who says to kings,
    'You are worthless,'
    and to nobles,ᵛ 'You are wicked,'ʷ
¹⁹who shows no partialityˣ to princes
    and does not favor the rich over the
        poor,ʸ
    for they are all the work of his
        hands?ᶻ
²⁰They die in an instant, in the middle of
        the night;ᵃ

the people are shaken and they pass
        away;
    the mighty are removed without
        human hand.ᵇ

²¹"His eyes are on the ways of men;ᶜ
    he sees their every step.ᵈ
²²There is no dark place,ᵉ no deep
        shadow,ᶠ
    where evildoers can hide.ᵍ
²³God has no need to examine men
        further,ʰ
    that they should come before him
        for judgment.ⁱ
²⁴Without inquiry he shattersʲ the
        mightyᵏ
    and sets up others in their place.ˡ
²⁵Because he takes note of their deeds,ᵐ
    he overthrows them in the nightⁿ
        and they are crushed.ᵒ
²⁶He punishes them for their
        wickednessᵖ
    where everyone can see them,
²⁷because they turned from following
        himᑫ
    and had no regard for any of his
        ways.ʳ
²⁸They caused the cry of the poor to
        come before him,
    so that he heard the cry of the
        needy.ˢ

²⁹But if he remains silent,ᵗ who can
        condemn him?ᵘ
    If he hides his face,ᵛ who can see
        him?
    Yet he is over man and nation alike,ʷ
³⁰ to keep a godlessˣ man from ruling,ʸ
    from laying snares for the people.ᶻ

³¹"Suppose a man says to God,
    'I am guiltyᵃ but will offend no
        more.
³²Teach me what I cannot see;ᵇ
    if I have done wrong, I will not do
        so again.'ᶜ

³³Should God then reward you on your terms,
    when you refuse to repent?ᵈ
You must decide, not I;
    so tell me what you know.
³⁴"Men of understanding declare,
    wise men who hear me say to me,
³⁵'Job speaks without knowledge;ᵉ
    his words lack insight.'ᶠ
³⁶Oh, that Job might be tested to the utmost
    for answering like a wicked man!ᵍ
³⁷To his sin he adds rebellion;
    scornfully he claps his handsʰ among us
    and multiplies his wordsⁱ against God."ʲ

35 Then Elihu said:

²"Do you think this is just?
    You say, 'I will be clearedᵏ by God.'ᵃ
³Yet you ask him, 'What profit is it to me,ᵇ
    and what do I gain by not sinning?'ᵐ
⁴"I would like to reply to you
    and to your friends with you.
⁵Look up at the heavensⁿ and see;
    gaze at the clouds so high above you.ᵒ
⁶If you sin, how does that affect him?
    If your sins are many, what does that do to him?ᵖ
⁷If you are righteous, what do you give to him,ᵠ
    or what does he receiveʳ from your hand?ˢ
⁸Your wickedness affects only a man like yourself,ᵗ
    and your righteousness only the sons of men.ᵘ
⁹"Men cry outᵛ under a load of oppression;ʷ
    they plead for relief from the arm of the powerful.ˣ
¹⁰But no one says, 'Where is God my Maker,ʸ
    who gives songsᶻ in the night,ᵃ
¹¹who teachesᵇ more toᶜ us than toᶜ the beasts of the earth
    and makes us wiserᵈ than the birds of the air?'
¹²He does not answerᵈ when men cry out

because of the arroganceᵉ of the wicked.ᶠ
¹³Indeed, God does not listen to their empty plea;
    the Almighty pays no attention to it.ᵍ
¹⁴How much less, then, will he listen when you say that you do not see him,ʰ
    that your caseⁱ is before him
    and you must wait for him,ʲ
¹⁵and further, that his anger never punishesᵏ
    and he does not take the least notice of wickedness.ᵉˡ
¹⁶So Job opens his mouth with empty talk;ᵐ
    without knowledge he multiplies words."ⁿ

36 Elihu continued:

²"Bear with me a little longer and I will show you
    that there is more to be said in God's behalf.
³I get my knowledge from afar;ᵒ
    I will ascribe justice to my Maker.ᵖ
⁴Be assured that my words are not false;ᵠ
    one perfect in knowledgeʳ is with you.ˢ
⁵"God is mighty,ᵗ but does not despise men;ᵘ
    he is mighty, and firm in his purpose.ᵛ
⁶He does not keep the wicked aliveʷ
    but gives the afflicted their rights.ˣ
⁷He does not take his eyes off the righteous;ʸ
    he enthrones them with kingsᶻ
    and exalts them forever.ᵃ
⁸But if men are bound in chains,ᵇ
    held fast by cords of affliction,ᶜ
⁹he tells them what they have done—
    that they have sinned arrogantly.ᵈ
¹⁰He makes them listenᵉ to correctionᶠ

and commands them to repent of
their evil.ᵍ
U ¹¹If they obey and serve him,ʰ
they will spend the rest of their days
in prosperityⁱ
and their years in contentment.ʲ
¹²But if they do not listen,
they will perish by the sword/ᵏ
and die without knowledge.ˡ
¹³"The godless in heartᵐ harbor
resentment;ⁿ
even when he fetters them, they do
not cry for help.ᵒ
¹⁴They die in their youth,ᵖ
among male prostitutes of the
shrines.ᵠ
¹⁵But those who sufferʳ he delivers in
their suffering;ˢ
he speaksᵗ to them in their
affliction.ᵘ

U ¹⁶"He is wooingᵛ you from the jaws of
distress
to a spacious placeʷ free from
restriction,ˣ
to the comfort of your tableʸ laden
with choice food.ᶻ

¹⁷But now you are laden with the
judgment due the wicked;ᵃ
judgment and justice have taken
hold of you.ᵇ
¹⁸Be careful that no one entices you by
riches;
do not let a large bribeᶜ turn you
aside.ᵈ
¹⁹Would your wealthᵉ
or even all your mighty efforts
sustain you so you would not be in
distress?
²⁰Do not long for the night,ᶠ
to drag people away from their
homes.ᵍ
²¹Beware of turning to evil,ᵍ
which you seem to prefer to
affliction.ʰ
²²"God is exalted in his power.ⁱ
Who is a teacher like him?ʲ
²³Who has prescribed his waysᵏ for
him,ˡ
or said to him, 'You have done
wrong'?ᵐ
²⁴Remember to extol his work,ⁿ
which men have praised in song.ᵒ
²⁵All mankind has seen it;ᵖ

men gaze on it from afar.
²⁶How great is God—beyond our
understanding!ᵠ
The number of his years is past
finding out.ʳ
²⁷"He draws up the drops of water,ˢ
which distill as rain to the
streamsʰ;ᵗ
²⁸the clouds pour down their moisture
and abundant showersᵘ fall on
mankind.ᵛ
²⁹Who can understand how he spreads
out the clouds,
how he thundersʷ from his
pavilion?ˣ
³⁰See how he scatters his lightningʸ
about him,
bathing the depths of the sea.ᶻ
³¹This is the way he governsⁱ the
nationsᵃ
and provides foodᵇ in abundance.ᶜ
³²He fills his hands with lightning
and commands it to strike its mark.ᵈ
³³His thunder announces the coming
storm;ᵉ
even the cattle make known its
approach.ʲᶠ

37 "At this my heart poundsᵍ
and leaps from its place.
²Listen!ʰ Listen to the roar of his
voice,ⁱ
to the rumbling that comes from his
mouth.ʲ
³He unleashes his lightningᵏ beneath
the whole heaven
and sends it to the ends of the
earth.ˡ
⁴After that comes the sound of his roar;
he thundersᵐ with his majestic
voice.ⁿ
When his voice resounds,
he holds nothing back.
⁵God's voice thundersᵒ in marvelous
ways;ᵖ
he does great things beyond our
understanding.ᵠ

U Job 36:7 ◄► Job 36:16
U Job 36:11 ◄► Job 42:10

⁶He says to the snow, 'Fall on the earth,'
and to the rain shower, 'Be a mighty downpour.'ˢ
⁷So that all men he has made may know his work,ᵗ
he stops every man from his labor.ᵏᵘ
⁸The animals take cover;ᵛ
they remain in their dens.ʷ
⁹The tempest comes out from its chamber,ˣ
the cold from the driving winds.ʸ
¹⁰The breath of God produces ice,
and the broad waters become frozen.ᶻ
¹¹He loads the clouds with moisture;ᵃ
he scatters his lightningᵇ through them.ᶜ
¹²At his direction they swirl around
over the face of the whole earth
to do whatever he commands them.ᵈ
¹³He brings the clouds to punish men,ᵉ
or to water his earthᶠ and show his love.ᶠ
¹⁴"Listenᵍ to this, Job;
stop and consider God's wonders.ʰ
¹⁵Do you know how God controls the clouds
and makes his lightningⁱ flash?ʲ
¹⁶Do you know how the clouds hang poised,ᵏ
those wonders of him who is perfect in knowledge?ˡ
¹⁷You who swelter in your clothes
when the land lies hushed under the south wind,ᵐ
¹⁸can you join him in spreading out the skies,ⁿ
hard as a mirror of cast bronze?ᵒ
¹⁹"Tell us what we should say to him;ᵖ
we cannot draw up our caseᑫ
because of our darkness.ʳ
²⁰Should he be told that I want to speak?
Would any man ask to be swallowed up?
²¹Now no one can look at the sun,ˢ
bright as it is in the skies
after the wind has swept them clean.
²²Out of the north he comes in golden splendor;ᵗ
God comes in awesome majesty.ᵘ
²³The Almighty is beyond our reach and exalted in power;ᵛ
in his justiceʷ and great righteousness, he does not oppress.ˣ
²⁴Therefore, men revere him,ʸ
for does he not have regard for all the wiseᶻ in heart?ᵐ"

The LORD Speaks

38 Then the LORD answered Jobᵃ out of the storm.ᵇ He said:

²"Who is this that darkens my counselᶜ
with words without knowledge?ᵈ
³Brace yourself like a man;
I will question you,
and you shall answer me.ᵉ

⁴"Where were you when I laid the earth's foundation?ᶠ
Tell me, if you understand.ᵍ
⁵Who marked off its dimensions?ʰ
Surely you know!
Who stretched a measuring lineⁱ across it?
⁶On what were its footings set,ʲ
or who laid its cornerstoneᵏ—
⁷while the morning starsˡ sang togetherᵐ
and all the angelsⁿⁿ shouted for joy?ᵒ

⁸"Who shut up the sea behind doorsᵖ
when it burst forth from the womb,ᑫ
⁹when I made the clouds its garment
and wrapped it in thick darkness,ʳ
¹⁰when I fixed limits for itˢ
and set its doors and bars in place,ᵗ
¹¹when I said, 'This far you may come and no farther;ᵘ

---

⁶ʳDt 28:12; Job 38:22
ˢS Ge 7:4;
S Job 5:10; S 28:26
37:7 ᵗPs 109:27
ᵘPs 104:19-23; 111:2
37:8 ᵛS Job 28:26
ʷJob 38:40;
Ps 104:22
37:9 ˣPs 50:3
ʸPs 147:17
37:10
ᶻJob 38:29-30; Ps 147:17
37:11 ᵃS Job 26:8
ᵇS Job 36:30
ᶜS Job 28:26
37:12 ᵈS ver 3; Ps 147:16; 148:8
37:13 ᵉS Ge 7:4; Ex 9:22-23;
S 1Sa 12:17
ᶠS 1Ki 18:45;
S Job 5:10; S 36:31; 38:27
37:14 ᵏS Job 32:10
ʰS Job 5:9
37:15 ⁱS Job 36:30
ʲS Job 36:32
37:16
ᵏS Job 36:29
ˡS Job 5:9; S 36:4
37:17 ᵐAc 27:13
37:18 ⁿS Ge 1:1,8;
S Job 22:14
ᵒDt 28:23
37:19 ᵖRo 8:26
ᑫS Job 13:18
ʳS Job 9:3
37:21 ˢS Jdg 5:31;
Ac 22:11; 26:13
37:22 ᵗPs 19:5
ᵘEx 24:17
37:23 ᵛS Job 5:9;
S 36:4; Ro 11:33;
1Ti 6:16 ʷS Job 8:3
ˣS Job 4:17;
Ps 44:1; Isa 63:9;
Jer 25:5; La 3:33;
Eze 18:23,32
37:24
ʸS Ge 22:12;
Job 28:28;
Ecc 12:13; Mic 6:8;
Mt 10:28
ᶻS Job 5:13;
Eph 5:15
38:1 ᵃS Job 11:5
ᵇS Ex 14:21;
S 1Sa 2:10;
Job 40:6; Isa 21:1;
Eze 1:4
38:2 ᶜS 1Ki 22:5;
Isa 40:13
ᵈS Job 34:35;
Mk 10:38; 1Ti 1:7
38:3 ᵉJob 40:7;
42:4; Mk 11:29
38:4 ᶠS ver 5;
S Ge 1:1; S 1Sa 2:8
ᵍver 18;
S Job 34:13; Pr 30:4
38:5 ʰver 4;
Ps 102:25; Pr 8:29;
Isa 40:12; 48:13;
Jer 31:37 ⁱJer 31:39; Zec 1:16; 4:9-10 38:6 ʲPr 8:25 ᵏS Job 26:7
38:7 ˡS Ge 1:16 ᵐPs 19:1-4; 148:2-3 ⁿS 1Ki 22:19 ᵒS Dt 16:15
38:8 ᵖver 11; Ps 33:7; Pr 8:29; Jer 5:22 ᑫS Ge 1:9-10 38:9 ʳS Ge 1:2
38:10 ˢS Job 28:25; Ps 33:7; 104:9; Isa 40:12 ᵗNe 3:3; Job 7:12; 26:10
38:11 ᵘS ver 8
ᵏ7 Or / he fills all men with fear by his power ˡ13 Or to favor them
ᵐ24 Or for he does not have regard for any who think they are wise.
ⁿ7 Hebrew the sons of God

37:16 Elihu mentioned God's marvelously complex influence on the world's climate as "how the clouds hang poised." Scientists now recognize that the amount of water vapor within the clouds influences the amount of rain, evaporation and global weather patterns. Once again, science upholds the Word of God written more than 3,000 years ago.

here is where your proud waves halt'?ᵛ

¹²"Have you ever given orders to the morning,ʷ
or shown the dawn its place,ˣ

¹³that it might take the earth by the edges
and shake the wickedʸ out of it?ᶻ

¹⁴The earth takes shape like clay under a seal;ᵃ
its features stand out like those of a garment.

¹⁵The wicked are denied their light,ᵇ
and their upraised arm is broken.ᶜ

¹⁶"Have you journeyed to the springs of the sea
or walked in the recesses of the deep?ᵈ

¹⁷Have the gates of deathᵉ been shown to you?
Have you seen the gates of the shadow of deathᵒ?ᶠ

¹⁸Have you comprehended the vast expanses of the earth?ᵍ
Tell me, if you know all this.ʰ

¹⁹"What is the way to the abode of light?
And where does darkness reside?ⁱ

²⁰Can you take them to their places?
Do you know the pathsʲ to their dwellings?

²¹Surely you know, for you were already born!ᵏ
You have lived so many years!

²²"Have you entered the storehouses of the snowˡ
or seen the storehousesᵐ of the hail,ⁿ

²³which I reserve for times of trouble,ᵒ
for days of war and battle?ᵖ

²⁴What is the way to the place where the lightning is dispersed,ᵠ
or the place where the east winds are scattered over the earth?ʳ

²⁵Who cuts a channel for the torrents of rain,
and a path for the thunderstorm,ᵗ

²⁶to waterᵘ a land where no man lives,
a desert with no one in it,ᵛ

²⁷to satisfy a desolate wasteland
and make it sprout with grass?ʷ

²⁸Does the rain have a father?ˣ
Who fathers the drops of dew?

²⁹From whose womb comes the ice?
Who gives birth to the frost from the heavensʸ

³⁰when the waters become hard as stone,
when the surface of the deep is frozen?ᶻ

³¹"Can you bind the beautifulᵖ Pleiades?
Can you loose the cords of Orion?ᵃ

³²Can you bring forth the constellationsᵇ in their seasonsᵠ
or lead out the Bearʳ with its cubs?ᶜ

³³Do you know the lawsᵈ of the heavens?ᵉ
Can you set up ⌊God's⌋ dominion over the earth?

³⁴"Can you raise your voice to the clouds
and cover yourself with a flood of water?ᶠ

³⁵Do you send the lightning bolts on their way?ᵍ
Do they report to you, 'Here we are'?

³⁶Who endowed the heartᵗ with wisdomʰ
or gave understandingⁱ to the mindʳ?

³⁷Who has the wisdom to count the clouds?
Who can tip over the water jarsʲ of the heavensᵏ

³⁸when the dust becomes hardˡ
and the clods of earth stick together?ᵐ

³⁹"Do you hunt the prey for the lioness
and satisfy the hunger of the lionsⁿ

⁴⁰when they crouch in their densᵒ

ᵒ 17 Or *gates of deep shadows* ᵖ 31 Or *the twinkling*; or *the chains of the* ᵠ 32 Or *the morning star in its season* ʳ 32 Or *out Leo* ˢ 33 Or *his*; or *their* ᵗ 36 The meaning of the Hebrew for this word is uncertain.

ᴾ 2Sa 23:6–7 ◀▶ Ps 2:1–6

38:13 This verse metaphorically says that dawn will shake the wicked out of the earth. These words may allude prophetically to the final battle of this age (Armageddon) when God will destroy the wicked leaders and armies of this world and "shake [them] out of it."

38:30 Job's words confirm the divine inspiration of this book in this reference to frozen waters that are as hard as stone. Since Job lived in the Middle East it is unlikely that he had ever seen a frozen body of water or a polar ice cap, yet his description of both is profoundly accurate.

or lie in wait in a thicket?
⁴¹Who provides food for the raven
when its young cry out to God
and wander about for lack of food?

39
"Do you know when the mountain goats give birth?
Do you watch when the doe bears her fawn?
²Do you count the months till they bear?
Do you know the time they give birth?
³They crouch down and bring forth their young;
their labor pains are ended.
⁴Their young thrive and grow strong in the wilds;
they leave and do not return.

⁵"Who let the wild donkey go free?
Who untied his ropes?
⁶I gave him the wasteland as his home,
the salt flats as his habitat.
⁷He laughs at the commotion in the town;
he does not hear a driver's shout.
⁸He ranges the hills for his pasture
and searches for any green thing.

⁹"Will the wild ox consent to serve you?
Will he stay by your manger at night?
¹⁰Can you hold him to the furrow with a harness?
Will he till the valleys behind you?
¹¹Will you rely on him for his great strength?
Will you leave your heavy work to him?
¹²Can you trust him to bring in your grain
and gather it to your threshing floor?

¹³"The wings of the ostrich flap joyfully,
but they cannot compare with the pinions and feathers of the stork.
¹⁴She lays her eggs on the ground
and lets them warm in the sand,
¹⁵unmindful that a foot may crush them,
that some wild animal may trample them.
¹⁶She treats her young harshly, as if they were not hers;
she cares not that her labor was in vain,
¹⁷for God did not endow her with wisdom
or give her a share of good sense.
¹⁸Yet when she spreads her feathers to run,
she laughs at horse and rider.

¹⁹"Do you give the horse his strength
or clothe his neck with a flowing mane?
²⁰Do you make him leap like a locust,
striking terror with his proud snorting?
²¹He paws fiercely, rejoicing in his strength,
and charges into the fray.
²²He laughs at fear, afraid of nothing;
he does not shy away from the sword.
²³The quiver rattles against his side,
along with the flashing spear and lance.
²⁴In frenzied excitement he eats up the ground;
he cannot stand still when the trumpet sounds.
²⁵At the blast of the trumpet he snorts, 'Aha!'
He catches the scent of battle from afar,
the shout of commanders and the battle cry.

²⁶"Does the hawk take flight by your wisdom
and spread his wings toward the south?
²⁷Does the eagle soar at your command
and build his nest on high?
²⁸He dwells on a cliff and stays there at night;
a rocky crag is his stronghold.
²⁹From there he seeks out his food;
his eyes detect it from afar.
³⁰His young ones feast on blood,
and where the slain are, there is he."

40
The LORD said to Job:

²"Will the one who contends with the Almighty correct him?
Let him who accuses God answer him!"

³Then Job answered the LORD:

⁴"I am unworthy[i]—how can I reply to you?
I put my hand over my mouth.[j]
⁵I spoke once, but I have no answer[k]—
twice, but I will say no more."[l]

⁶Then the LORD spoke to Job out of the storm:[m]

⁷"Brace yourself like a man;
I will question you,
and you shall answer me.[n]

⁸"Would you discredit my justice?[o]
Would you condemn me to justify yourself?[p]
⁹Do you have an arm like God's,[q]
and can your voice[r] thunder like his?[s]
¹⁰Then adorn yourself with glory and splendor,
and clothe yourself in honor and majesty.[t]
¹¹Unleash the fury of your wrath,[u]
look at every proud man and bring him low,[v]
¹²look at every proud[w] man and humble him,[x]
crush[y] the wicked where they stand.
¹³Bury them all in the dust together;[z]
shroud their faces in the grave.[a]
¹⁴Then I myself will admit to you
that your own right hand can save you.[b]

¹⁵"Look at the behemoth,[u]
which I made[c] along with you
and which feeds on grass like an ox.[d]
¹⁶What strength[e] he has in his loins,
what power in the muscles of his belly![f]
¹⁷His tail[v] sways like a cedar;
the sinews of his thighs are close-knit.[g]
¹⁸His bones are tubes of bronze,
his limbs[h] like rods of iron.[i]
¹⁹He ranks first among the works of God,
yet his Maker[k] can approach him with his sword.[l]
²⁰The hills bring him their produce,[m]
and all the wild animals play[n] nearby.[o]
²¹Under the lotus plants he lies,
hidden among the reeds[p] in the marsh.[q]
²²The lotuses conceal him in their shadow;
the poplars by the stream[r] surround him.
²³When the river rages,[s] he is not alarmed;
he is secure, though the Jordan[t] should surge against his mouth.
²⁴Can anyone capture him by the eyes,[w]
or trap him and pierce his nose?[u]

41

"Can you pull in the leviathan[xv]
with a fishhook[w]
or tie down his tongue with a rope?
²Can you put a cord through his nose[x]
or pierce his jaw with a hook?[y]
³Will he keep begging you for mercy?[z]
Will he speak to you with gentle words?
⁴Will he make an agreement with you
for you to take him as your slave for life?[a]
⁵Can you make a pet of him like a bird
or put him on a leash for your girls?
⁶Will traders barter for him?
Will they divide him up among the merchants?
⁷Can you fill his hide with harpoons
or his head with fishing spears?[b]
⁸If you lay a hand on him,
you will remember the struggle and never do it again![c]
⁹Any hope of subduing him is false;
the mere sight of him is overpowering.[d]
¹⁰No one is fierce enough to rouse him.[e]
Who then is able to stand against me?[f]
¹¹Who has a claim against me that I must pay?[g]
Everything under heaven belongs to me.[h]

¹²"I will not fail to speak of his limbs,[i]
his strength[j] and his graceful form.
¹³Who can strip off his outer coat?
Who would approach him with a bridle?[k]
¹⁴Who dares open the doors of his mouth,[l]
ringed about with his fearsome teeth?
¹⁵His back has[y] rows of shields

40:4 ⁱJob 42:6
ʲS Jdg 18:19; S Job 29:9
40:5 ᵏS Job 9:3
ˡS Job 9:15
40:6 ᵐS Ex 14:21; S Job 38:1
40:7 ⁿS Job 38:3
40:8 ᵒS Job 15:25; S 27:2; Ro 3:3
ᵖS Job 2:3; S 34:17
40:9 ᵠS 2Ch 32:8; S Ps 98:1
ʳIsa 6:8; Eze 10:5
ˢS Ex 20:19; S Job 36:33
40:10 ᵗPs 29:1-2; 45:3; 93:1; 96:6; 104:1; 145:5
40:11
ᵘS Job 20:28; Ps 7:11; Isa 5:25; 9:12,19; 10:5; 13:3,5; 30:27; 42:25; 51:20; Jer 7:20; Na 1:6; Zep 1:18 ᵛPs 18:27; Isa 2:11,12,17; 23:9; 24:10; 25:12; 26:5; 32:19
40:12 ʷPs 10:4; Isa 25:11; Jer 48:29; 49:16; Zep 2:10
ˣS 1Sa 2:7; S Ps 52:5; 1Pe 5:5
ʸPs 60:12; Isa 22:5; 28:3; 63:2-3,6; Da 5:20; Mic 5:8; 7:10; Zec 10:5; Mal 4:3
40:13
ᶻNu 16:31-34
ᵃS Job 4:9
40:14 ᵇEx 15:6, 12; Ps 18:35; 20:6; 48:10; 60:5; 108:6; Isa 41:10; 63:5
40:15 ᶜS Job 9:9
ᵈIsa 11:7; 65:25
40:16
ᵉS Job 39:11
ᶠJob 41:9
40:17 ᵍJob 41:15
40:18 ʰJob 41:12
ⁱIsa 11:4; 49:2
40:19 ʲJob 41:33; Ps 40:5; 139:14; Isa 27:1
ᵏS Job 4:17; S 9:9
ˡS Ge 3:24
40:20 ᵐPs 104:14
ⁿPs 104:26
ᵒS Job 5:23
40:21 ᵖS Ge 41:2; Ps 68:30; Isa 35:7
ᵠJob 8:11
40:22 ʳPs 1:3; Isa 44:4
40:23 ˢIsa 8:7; 11:15 ᵗS Jos 3:1
40:24 ᵘ2Ki 19:28; Job 41:2,7,26; Isa 37:29
41:1 ᵛS Job 3:8
ʷAm 4:2
41:2 ˣS Job 40:24
ʸEze 19:4
41:3 ᶻ1Ki 20:31
41:4 ᵃS Ex 21:6
41:7 ᵇS Job 40:24
41:8 ᶜS Job 3:8
41:9 ᵈJob 40:16
41:10 ᵉS Job 3:8
ᶠS 2Ch 20:6;

S Isa 46:5; Jer 50:44; Rev 6:17 **41:11** ᵍS Job 34:33; Ro 11:35 ʰS Jos 3:11; S Job 10:4; Ac 4:24; 1Co 10:26 **41:12** ⁱJob 40:18 ʲS Job 39:11 **41:13** ᵏS Job 39:10; S 39:10 **41:14** ˡPs 22:13

ᵘ 15 Possibly the hippopotamus or the elephant ᵛ 17 Possibly trunk ʷ 24 Or *by a water hole* ˣ 1 Possibly the crocodile ʸ 15 Or *His pride is his*

tightly sealed together;ᵐ
¹⁶each is so close to the next
  that no air can pass between.
¹⁷They are joined fast to one another;
  they cling together and cannot be
  parted.
¹⁸His snorting throws out flashes of
  light;
  his eyes are like the rays of dawn.ⁿ
¹⁹Firebrandsᵒ stream from his mouth;
  sparks of fire shoot out.
²⁰Smoke pours from his nostrilsᵖ
  as from a boiling pot over a fire of
  reeds.
²¹His breathᵠ sets coals ablaze,
  and flames dart from his mouth.ʳ
²²Strengthˢ resides in his neck;
  dismay goes before him.
²³The folds of his flesh are tightly
  joined;
  they are firm and immovable.
²⁴His chest is hard as rock,
  hard as a lower millstone.ᵗ
²⁵When he rises up, the mighty are
  terrified;ᵘ
  they retreat before his thrashing.ᵛ
²⁶The sword that reaches him has no
  effect,
  nor does the spear or the dart or the
  javelin.ʷˣ
²⁷Iron he treats like strawʸ
  and bronze like rotten wood.
²⁸Arrows do not make him flee;ᶻ
  slingstones are like chaff to him.
²⁹A club seems to him but a piece of
  straw;ᵃ
  he laughsᵇ at the rattling of the
  lance.
³⁰His undersides are jagged potsherds,
  leaving a trail in the mud like a
  threshing sledge.ᶜ
³¹He makes the depths churn like a
  boiling caldronᵈ
  and stirs up the sea like a pot of
  ointment.ᵉ
³²Behind him he leaves a glistening
  wake;
  one would think the deep had white
  hair.
³³Nothing on earth is his equalᶠ—
  a creature without fear.

³⁴He looks down on all that are
  haughty;ᵍ
  he is king over all that are proud."ʰ

Job

42 Then Job replied to the LORD:

²"I know that you can do all things;ⁱ
  no plan of yours can be thwarted.ʲ
³You asked, 'Who is this that obscures
  my counsel without
  knowledge?'ᵏ
  Surely I spoke of things I did not
  understand,
  things too wonderful for me to
  know.ˡ
⁴"You said, 'Listen now, and I will
  speak;
  I will question you,
  and you shall answer me.'ᵐ
⁵My ears had heard of youⁿ
  but now my eyes have seen you.ᵒ
⁶Therefore I despise myselfᵖ
  and repentᵠ in dust and ashes."ʳ

Epilogue

⁷After the LORD had said these things to Job,ˢ he said to Eliphaz the Temanite, "I am angry with you and your two friends,ᵗ because you have not spoken of me what is right, as my servant Job has.ᵘ ⁸So now take seven bulls and seven ramsᵛ and go to my servant Jobʷ and sacrifice a burnt offeringˣ for yourselves. My servant Job will pray for you, and I will accept his prayerʸ and not deal with you according to your folly.ᶻ You have not spoken of me what is right, as my servant Job has."ᵃ ⁹So Eliphaz the Temanite, Bildad the Shuhite and Zophar the Naamathiteᵇ did what the LORD told them; and the LORD accepted Job's prayer.ᶜ

¹⁰After Job had prayed for his friends, the LORD made him prosperous againᵈ and gave him twice as much as he had be-

E *Job 34:21–22* ◀▶ *Ps 7:9*
K *Job 36:7* ◀▶ *Ps 2:12*
R *Job 36:9–11* ◀▶ *Ps 32:5*
P *Job 27:16–17* ◀▶ *Job 42:12*
U *Job 36:16* ◀▶ *Job 42:12*

42:10 God reversed the fortunes of Job and prospered him "after Job had prayed for his friends." When Job looked beyond his own pain and prayed for God to bless his friends despite their accusations and useless advice, the Lord answered his prayer, reconciling him to his friends and restoring to Job more than he had lost to Satan's attacks.

fore.ᵉ ¹¹All his brothers and sisters and everyone who had known him beforeᶠ came and ate with him in his house. They comforted and consoled him over all the trouble the Lord had brought upon him,ᵍ and each one gave him a piece of silverᶻ and a gold ring.

¹²The Lord blessed the latter part of Job's life more than the first. He had fourteen thousand sheep, six thousand camels, a thousand yoke of oxen and a thousand donkeys. ¹³And he also had seven sons and three daughters. ¹⁴The first daughter he named Jemimah, the second Keziah and the third Keren-Happuch. ¹⁵Nowhere in all the land were there found women as beautiful as Job's daughters, and their father granted them an inheritance along with their brothers.

¹⁶After this, Job lived a hundred and forty years; he saw his children and their children to the fourth generation. ¹⁷And so he died, old and full of years.ʰ

42:10 ᵉS Job 1:3; Ps 85:1-3; 126:5-6; Php 2:8-9; Jas 5:11
42:11 ᶠS Job 19:13 ᵍS Ge 37:35
R Ge 39:5 ◀▶ Ps 37:26
E Ne 9:21 ◀▶ Ps 30:2-3

B Dt 30:9 ◀▶ Ps 65:9-13
P Job 42:10 ◀▶ Ps 105:37
U Job 42:10 ◀▶ Ps 1:1-3

ᶻ 11 Hebrew *him a kesitah*; a kesitah was a unit of money of unknown weight and value.
42:17 ʰS Ge 15:15

42:12 Despite Job's terrible trials, God's love for Job remained unchanged and "The Lord blessed the latter part of Job's life more than the first."

Psalms

Author: King David and others

Theme: Prayer and praise

Date of Writing: c. 1400–400 B.C.

Outline of Psalms
Book I.   (1—41)
Book II. (42—72)
Book III. (73—89)
Book IV. (90—106)
Book V.   (107—150)

THE COMBINATION OF poems, songs and laments included in the book of Psalms was originally called in Hebrew *tehillim*, meaning "praises." The name "Psalms" or "Psalter" came from the Septuagint (the Greek translation of the OT) title for this collection of poetry and is the title commonly used today. Characterized throughout by heartfelt praise to God, the 150 poems in the book of Psalms reflect a wide variety of feelings, attitudes and circumstances from its various authors. King David authored the majority of the psalms (73). Other authors include Solomon, Moses, Asaph, the sons of Korah, Heman and Ethan. Still other psalms are anonymous. Superscriptions preceding each psalm indicate its authorship, its use in worship and the circumstance for the writing of the psalm, if known.

Because it contains more verses than any other book of the Bible, the book of Psalms is usually divided into five sections. Each psalm within the section is separate and complete, with the last psalm in the section serving as a doxology. Significantly, the final psalm ends with its own doxology: "Let everything that has breath praise the LORD. Praise the LORD" (Ps 150:6).

The psalms may also be classified into categories. Psalms 104—106 are historical, Psalms 120—130 are liturgical and Psalms 95—100 and 146—150 are psalms of praise. In addition, several of the psalms are Messianic in content (2; 21; 22; 45; 50; 69; 72; 97; 98; 110) with Psalm 110 being the most frequently quoted psalm in the entire NT. Though Psalms is not a prophetical book, the NT quotes these passages as testimonies to Christ, for in him they are truly fulfilled (see Lk 24:44).

BOOK I

Psalms 1–41

Psalm 1

¹Blessed is the man
  who does not walk in the counsel
    of the wicked
  or stand in the way of sinners
  or sit in the seat of mockers.
²But his delight is in the law of the
    LORD,
  and on his law he meditates day
    and night.
³He is like a tree planted by streams
    of water,
  which yields its fruit in season
  and whose leaf does not wither.
  Whatever he does prospers.

⁴Not so the wicked!
  They are like chaff
    that the wind blows away.
⁵Therefore the wicked will not stand
    in the judgment,
  nor sinners in the assembly of the
    righteous.

⁶For the LORD watches over the way of
    the righteous,
  but the way of the wicked will
    perish.

Psalm 2

¹Why do the nations conspire
    and the peoples plot in vain?
²The kings of the earth take their
    stand
  and the rulers gather together
    against the LORD
  and against his Anointed One.
³"Let us break their chains," they say,
  "and throw off their fetters."

⁴The One enthroned in heaven
    laughs;
  the Lord scoffs at them.
⁵Then he rebukes them in his anger
  and terrifies them in his wrath,
    saying,
⁶"I have installed my King
  on Zion, my holy hill."

⁷I will proclaim the decree of the LORD:

He said to me, "You are my Son;
  today I have become your Father.
⁸Ask of me,
  and I will make the nations your
    inheritance,
  the ends of the earth your
    possession.
⁹You will rule them with an iron
    scepter;
  you will dash them to pieces like
    pottery."

¹⁰Therefore, you kings, be wise;
  be warned, you rulers of the earth.
¹¹Serve the LORD with fear
  and rejoice with trembling.
¹²Kiss the Son, lest he be angry
  and you be destroyed in your way,

---

a 1 Hebrew; Septuagint *rage* *b 2* Or *anointed one* *c 6* Or *king*
d 7 Or *son; also in verse 12* *e 7* Or *have begotten you* *f 9* Or *will break them with a rod of iron*

1:5 This verse affirms the principle that the ungodly will be unable to withstand God's wrath in the day of judgment. Furthermore, sinners will not be allowed to assemble in God's sanctuary because God will separate them out to judgment in hell.

2:1–3 This is the first of the major Messianic psalms. It foreshadows Christ's victory in the final battle of Armageddon. David used the phrase "his Anointed One" (2:2) referring to Jesus as the Messiah (see Ac 4:25–28). Other psalms also speak of the role of the Messiah (see 21; 22; 45; 50; 69; 72; 97; 98; 110).

2:8–9 These verses confirm God's plan to make the nations the messiah's eternal possession when he establishes his kingdom. Ultimately the Messiah's rule will encompass all that God himself rules.

2:12 The "Son" clearly refers to the Messiah; and the NT defines the Messiah as Jesus Christ (see Heb 5:5). A kiss was a sign of submission (see 1Sa 10:1; 1Ki 19:18).

for his wrath[x] can flare up in a
    moment.
Blessed[y] are all who take refuge[z] in
    him.

Psalm 3

A psalm of David. When he fled from his
    son Absalom.[a]

[1] O LORD, how many are my foes!
    How many rise up against me!
[2] Many are saying of me,
    "God will not deliver him.[b]" Selah[g]

[3] But you are a shield[c] around me,
    O LORD;
you bestow glory on me and lift[h] up
    my head.[d]
[4] To the LORD I cry aloud,[e]
    and he answers me from his holy
    hill.[f] Selah

[5] I lie down and sleep;[g]
    I wake again,[h] because the LORD
    sustains me.
[6] I will not fear[i] the tens of thousands
    drawn up against me on every side.[j]

[7] Arise,[k] O LORD!
    Deliver me,[l] O my God!
Strike[m] all my enemies on the jaw;
    break the teeth[n] of the wicked.

[8] From the LORD comes deliverance.[o]
    May your blessing[p] be on your
    people. Selah

Psalm 4

For the director of music. With stringed
    instruments. A psalm of David.

[1] Answer me[q] when I call to you,
    O my righteous God.
Give me relief from my distress;[r]
    be merciful[s] to me and hear my
    prayer.[t]

[2] How long, O men, will you turn my
    glory[u] into shame[i]?[v]
How long will you love delusions
    and seek false gods[j]?[w] Selah

[3] Know that the LORD has set apart the
    godly[x] for himself;

J Job 13:15 ◀▶ Ps 18:29
V Job 5:20–23 ◀▶ Ps 9:3–4
K Ps 2:12 ◀▶ Ps 12:7
O Job 8:11–15 ◀▶ Ps 18:31
U Ps 1:1–3 ◀▶ Ps 4:7
S Ps 1:5 ◀▶ Ps 5:4–6

2:12 ˣS Dt 9:8;
Rev 6:16 ʸPs 84:12
ᶻPs 5:11; 34:8;
64:10
3 Title ᵃ2Sa 15:14
3:2 ᵇPs 22:8;
71:11; Isa 36:15;
37:20
3:3 ᶜS Ge 15:1
ᵈPs 27:6
3:4 ᵉS Job 30:20
ᶠPs 2:6
3:5 ᵍS Lev 26:6
ʰPs 17:15; 139:18
3:6 ⁱJob 11:15;
Ps 23:4; 27:3
ʲPs 118:11
3:7 ᵏS 2Ch 6:41
ˡPs 6:4; 7:1; 59:1;
109:21; 119:153;
Isa 25:9; 33:22;
35:4; 36:15; 37:20;
Jer 42:11; Mt 6:13
ᵐJob 16:10
ⁿJob 29:17;
Ps 57:4; Pr 30:14;
La 3:16
3:8 ᵒPs 27:1;
37:39; 62:1;
Isa 43:3,11; 44:6,8;
45:21; Hos 13:4;
Jnh 2:9; Rev 7:10
ᵖNu 6:23;
Ps 29:11; 129:8
4:1 ᵠPs 13:3; 27:7;
69:16; 86:7; 102:2
ʳS Ge 32:7;
S Jdg 2:15
ˢPs 30:10 ᵗPs 17:6;
54:2; 84:8; 88:2
4:2 ᵘEx 16:7;
1Sa 4:21
ᵛ2Ki 19:26;
Job 8:22; Ps 35:26
ʷJdg 2:17; Ps 31:6;
40:4; Jer 13:25;
16:19; Am 2:4
4:3 ˣPs 12:1; 30:4;
31:23; 79:2;
Mic 7:2; 1Ti 4:7;
2Pe 3:11
ʸPs 6:8; Mic 7:7
4:4 ᶻEph 4:26*
ᵃPs 63:6; Da 2:28
4:5 ᵇPs 31:6;
115:9; Pr 3:5;
28:26; Isa 26:4;
Jn 14:1
4:6 ᶜNu 6:25
4:7 ᵈAc 14:17
ᵉIsa 9:3; 35:10;
65:14,18
ᶠS Ge 27:28;
S Dt 28:51
4:8 ᵍS Lev 26:6
ʰS Nu 6:26;
S Job 11:18
ⁱS Dt 33:28;
S Jer 32:37
5:1 ʲS 1Ki 8:29;
Ps 17:1; 40:1;
116:2; Da 9:18
ᵏPs 38:9; Isa 35:10;
51:11
5:2 ˡS Job 19:7;
S 24:12; S 36:5
ᵐPs 44:4; 68:24;
84:3
5:3 ⁿIsa 28:19;
50:4; Jer 21:12;
Eze 46:13; Zep 3:5
ᵒPs 62:1; 119:81;
130:5; Hab 2:1;
Ro 8:19
5:4 ᵖPs 1:5; 11:5;

the LORD will hear[y] when I call to
    him.
[4] In your anger do not sin;[z]
    when you are on your beds,[a]
search your hearts and be silent.
        Selah
[5] Offer right sacrifices
    and trust in the LORD.[b]

[6] Many are asking, "Who can show us
    any good?"
Let the light of your face shine upon
    us,[c] O LORD.
[7] You have filled my heart[d] with greater U
    joy[e]
than when their grain and new
    wine[f] abound.
[8] I will lie down and sleep[g] in peace,[h] S
    for you alone, O LORD,
make me dwell in safety.[i]

Psalm 5

For the director of music. For flutes.
    A psalm of David.

[1] Give ear[j] to my words, O LORD,
    consider my sighing.[k]
[2] Listen to my cry for help,[l]
    my King and my God,[m]
    for to you I pray.
[3] In the morning,[n] O LORD, you hear my
    voice;
in the morning I lay my requests
    before you
    and wait in expectation.[o]

[4] You are not a God who takes pleasure H
    in evil; S
with you the wicked[p] cannot dwell.
[5] The arrogant[q] cannot stand[r] in your
    presence;
    you hate[s] all who do wrong.
[6] You destroy those who tell lies;[t]
bloodthirsty and deceitful men
    the LORD abhors.

[7] But I, by your great mercy,

U Ps 3:8 ◀▶ Ps 5:11–12
S Job 34:29 ◀▶ Ps 27:5
H Ps 2:12 ◀▶ Ps 7:11
S Ps 4:3–4 ◀▶ Ps 7:10–11

104:35; Pr 2:22 5:5 ᵠ2Ki 19:32; Ps 73:3; 75:4; Isa 33:19; 37:33 ʳPs 1:5
ˢPs 45:7; 101:3; 119:104; Pr 8:13 5:6 ᵗPr 19:22; S Jn 8:44; Ac 5:3;
Rev 21:8

ᵍ2 A word of uncertain meaning, occurring frequently in the Psalms;
possibly a musical term ʰ3 Or LORD, / my Glorious One, who lifts
ⁱ2 Or you dishonor my Glorious One ʲ2 Or seek lies

will come into your house;
in reverence[u] will I bow down[v]
  toward your holy temple.[w]
⁸Lead me, O LORD, in your righteousness[x]
  because of my enemies—
  make straight your way[y] before me.

⁹Not a word from their mouth can be trusted;
  their heart is filled with destruction.
Their throat is an open grave;[z]
  with their tongue they speak deceit.[a]
¹⁰Declare them guilty, O God!
  Let their intrigues be their downfall.
Banish them for their many sins,[b]
  for they have rebelled[c] against you.

¹¹But let all who take refuge in you be glad;
  let them ever sing for joy.[d]
Spread your protection over them,
  that those who love your name[e] may rejoice in you.[f]
¹²For surely, O LORD, you bless the righteous;[g]
  you surround them[h] with your favor as with a shield.[i]

Psalm 6

For the director of music. With stringed instruments. According to *sheminith*.[k] A psalm of David.

¹O LORD, do not rebuke me in your anger[j]
  or discipline me in your wrath.
²Be merciful to me,[k] LORD, for I am faint;[l]
  O LORD, heal me,[m] for my bones are in agony.[n]
³My soul is in anguish.[o]
  How long,[p] O LORD, how long?

⁴Turn,[q] O LORD, and deliver me;
  save me because of your unfailing love.[r]
⁵No one remembers you when he is dead.
  Who praises you from the grave[?]?[s]

⁶I am worn out[t] from groaning;[u]

U ◄ Ps 4:7 ► Ps 7:10

5:7 ᵘDt 13:4; Jer 44:10; Da 6:26
   ᵛS 2Sa 12:16; Ps 138:2
   ʷS 1Ki 8:48
5:8 ˣPs 23:3; 31:1; 71:2; 85:13; 89:16; Pr 8:20
   ʸS 1Ki 8:36; Jn 1:23
5:9 ᶻJer 5:16; Lk 11:44 ᵃPs 12:2; 28:3; 36:3; Pr 15:4; Jer 9:8; Ro 3:13ᵃ
5:10 ᵇLa 1:5
   ᶜPs 78:40; 106:7; 107:11; La 3:42
5:11 ᵈPs 33:1; 81:1; 90:14; 92:4; 95:1; 145:7
   ᵉPs 69:36; 119:132
5:12 ᶠPs 112:2
   ʰPs 32:7
   ⁱS Ge 15:1
6:1 ʲS Ps 2:5
6:2 ᵏPs 4:1; 26:11; Jer 3:12; 12:15; 31:20 ⁱPs 61:2; 77:3; 142:3; Isa 40:31; Jer 8:18; Eze 21:7
   ᵐS Nu 12:13
   ⁿPs 22:14; 31:10; 32:3; 38:3; 42:10; 102:3
6:3 ᵒS Job 7:11; Ps 31:7; 38:8; 55:4; S Jn 12:27; Ro 9:2; 2Co 2:4 ᵖ1Sa 1:14; 1Ki 18:21; Ps 4:2; 89:46; Isa 6:11; Jer 4:14; Hab 1:2; Zec 1:12
6:4 ᵠPs 25:16; 31:2; 69:16; 71:2; 86:16; 88:2; 102:2; 119:132 ʳPs 13:5; 31:16; 77:8; 85:7; 119:41; Isa 54:8,10
6:5 ˢPs 30:9; 88:10-12; 115:17; Ecc 9:10; Isa 38:18
6:6 ᵗS Jdg 8:5
   ᵘS Job 3:24; S 23:2; Ps 12:5; 77:3; 102:5; La 1:8,11, 21,22
   ᵛS Job 16:16
   ʷS Job 7:3; Lk 7:38; Ac 20:19
6:7 ˣS Job 16:8; Ps 31:9; 69:3; 119:82; Isa 38:14
6:8 ʸPs 119:115; 139:19 ᶻPs 5:5; S Mt 7:23
6:9 ᵃPs 28:6; 116:1
6:10 ᵇS 2Ki 19:26
   ᶜPs 40:14
7 Title ᵈHab 3:1
7:1 ᵉPs 2:12; 11:1; 31:1 ᶠS Ps 3:7
   ᵍPs 31:15; 119:86; 157,161
7:2 ʰPs Ge 49:9; Rev 4:7 ⁱPs 3:2; 71:11

all night long I flood my bed with weeping[v]
  and drench my couch with tears.[w]
⁷My eyes grow weak[x] with sorrow;
  they fail because of all my foes.

⁸Away from me,[y] all you who do evil,[z]
  for the LORD has heard my weeping.
⁹The LORD has heard my cry for mercy;[a]
  the LORD accepts my prayer.
¹⁰All my enemies will be ashamed and dismayed;[b]
  they will turn back in sudden disgrace.[c]

Psalm 7

A *shiggaion*[m] of David, which he sang to the LORD concerning Cush, a Benjamite.

¹O LORD my God, I take refuge[e] in you;
  save and deliver me[f] from all who pursue me,[g]
²or they will tear me like a lion[h]
  and rip me to pieces with no one to rescue[i] me.

³O LORD my God, if I have done this
  and there is guilt on my hands[j]—
⁴if I have done evil to him who is at peace with me
  or without cause[k] have robbed my foe—
⁵then let my enemy pursue and overtake[l] me;
  let him trample my life to the ground[m]
  and make me sleep in the dust.[n]
    Selah

⁶Arise,[o] O LORD, in your anger;
  rise up against the rage of my enemies.[p]
  Awake,[q] my God; decree justice.
⁷Let the assembled peoples gather around you.
  Rule over them from on high;[r]
⁸ let the LORD judge[s] the peoples.   J
                                        J

J Ps 1:5 ◄ ► Ps 9:7-8
J Ps 1:5 ◄ ► Ps 9:7-8

7:3 ʲIsa 59:3 7:4 ᵏPs 35:7,19; Pr 24:28 7:5 ˡS Ex 15:9 ᵐS 2Sa 22:43; 2Ki 9:33; Isa 10:6; La 3:16 ⁿS Job 7:21 7:6 ᵒS 2Ch 6:41 ᵖPs 138:7 ᵠPs 35:23; 44:23 7:7 ʳPs 68:18 7:8 ˢS 1Ch 16:33

ᵏ Title: Probably a musical term ˡ⁵ Hebrew *Sheol* ᵐ Title: Probably a literary or musical term

---

7:8 The psalmist appeals to God to judge all the people of the earth according to God's standards of righteousness and integrity.

Judge me, O LORD, according to my
  righteousness,[t]
  according to my integrity,[u] O Most
  High.[v]
⁹O righteous God,[w]
  who searches minds and hearts,[x]
  bring to an end the violence of the
    wicked
  and make the righteous secure.[y]
¹⁰My shield[n][z] is God Most High,
  who saves the upright in heart.[a]
¹¹God is a righteous judge,[b]
  a God who expresses his wrath[c]
    every day.
¹²If he does not relent,[d]
  he[o] will sharpen his sword;[e]
  he will bend and string his bow.[f]
¹³He has prepared his deadly weapons;
  he makes ready his flaming arrows.[g]
¹⁴He who is pregnant with evil
  and conceives trouble gives birth[h] to
    disillusionment.
¹⁵He who digs a hole and scoops it out
  falls into the pit[i] he has made.[j]
¹⁶The trouble he causes recoils on
    himself;
  his violence comes down on his own
    head.

¹⁷I will give thanks to the LORD because
    of his righteousness[k]
  and will sing praise[l] to the name of
    the LORD Most High.[m]

Psalm 8

For the director of music. According to
  gittith.[p] A psalm of David.

¹O LORD, our Lord,
  how majestic is your name[n] in all
    the earth!
You have set your glory[o]
  above the heavens.[p]
²From the lips of children and infants
  you have ordained praise[q][q]
  because of your enemies,
  to silence the foe[r] and the avenger.

³When I consider your heavens,[s]
    the work of your fingers,[t]
  the moon and the stars,[u]
  which you have set in place,
⁴what is man that you are mindful of
    him,
  the son of man that you care for
    him?[v]
⁵You made him a little lower than the
    heavenly beings[r][w]
  and crowned him with glory and
    honor.[x]
⁶You made him ruler[y] over the works of
    your hands;[z]
  you put everything under his feet:[a][b]
⁷all flocks and herds,[c]
  and the beasts of the field,[d]
⁸the birds of the air,
  and the fish of the sea,[e]
  all that swim the paths of the seas.

⁹O LORD, our Lord,
  how majestic is your name in all the
    earth![f]

Psalm 9[s]

For the director of music. To ⌊the tune of⌋
  "The Death of the Son." A psalm of David.

¹I will praise you, O LORD, with all my
    heart;[g]
  I will tell of all your wonders.[h]
²I will be glad and rejoice[i] in you;
  I will sing praise[j] to your name,[k]
  O Most High.

F Job 19:25–27 ◀ ▶ Ps 16:9

Zep 3:14; S Mt 5:12; Rev 19:7 S 2Ch 31:2 k Ps 92:1

[n] 10 Or *sovereign*   [o] 12 Or *If a man does not repent, / God*   [p] Title: Probably a musical term   [q] 2 Or *strength*   [r] 5 Or *than God*   [s] Psalms 9 and 10 may have been originally a single acrostic poem, the stanzas of which begin with the successive letters of the Hebrew alphabet. In the Septuagint they constitute one psalm.

8:4 Though this psalm is not eschatological in character, Heb 2:6–9 applies these verses to Jesus. Adam, representing the human race, fell from perfect obedience. Jesus, who is both the perfect man and the one in whom humanity's destiny is fully realized, provided redemption for humanity with his atoning death on the cross.

8:8 The phrase "the paths of the seas" refers to the huge currents of water that flow beneath the ocean's surface, such as the Gulf Stream, the Japan Current and the Humboldt Current.

³My enemies turn back;
    they stumble and perish before you.
⁴For you have upheld my right and my cause;
    you have sat on your throne,
    judging righteously.
⁵You have rebuked the nations and destroyed the wicked;
    you have blotted out their name for ever and ever.
⁶Endless ruin has overtaken the enemy,
    you have uprooted their cities;
    even the memory of them has perished.

⁷The LORD reigns forever;
    he has established his throne for judgment.
⁸He will judge the world in righteousness;
    he will govern the peoples with justice.
⁹The LORD is a refuge for the oppressed,
    a stronghold in times of trouble.
¹⁰Those who know your name will trust in you,
    for you, LORD, have never forsaken those who seek you.

¹¹Sing praises to the LORD, enthroned in Zion;
    proclaim among the nations what he has done.
¹²For he who avenges blood remembers;
    he does not ignore the cry of the afflicted.

¹³O LORD, see how my enemies persecute me!
    Have mercy and lift me up from the gates of death,
¹⁴that I may declare your praises
    in the gates of the Daughter of Zion
    and there rejoice in your salvation.

¹⁵The nations have fallen into the pit they have dug;
    their feet are caught in the net they have hidden.
¹⁶The LORD is known by his justice;
    the wicked are ensnared by the work of their hands.
    Higgaion. Selah

¹⁷The wicked return to the grave,
    all the nations that forget God.
¹⁸But the needy will not always be forgotten,
    nor the hope of the afflicted ever perish.

¹⁹Arise, O LORD, let not man triumph;
    let the nations be judged in your presence.
²⁰Strike them with terror, O LORD;
    let the nations know they are but men.   Selah

Psalm 10

¹Why, O LORD, do you stand far off?
    Why do you hide yourself in times of trouble?

²In his arrogance the wicked man hunts down the weak,
    who are caught in the schemes he devises.
³He boasts of the cravings of his heart;
    he blesses the greedy and reviles the LORD.
⁴In his pride the wicked does not seek him;
    in all his thoughts there is no room for God.
⁵His ways are always prosperous;
    he is haughty and your laws are far from him;
    he sneers at all his enemies.
⁶He says to himself, "Nothing will shake me;

V Ps 3:5–6 ◀▶ Ps 17:7
H Ps 7:16 ◀▶ Ps 9:17
J Ps 7:8 ◀▶ Ps 69:25
J Ps 7:8 ◀▶ Ps 50:3–6
L Job 33:27–28 ◀▶ Ps 22:26

H Ps 9:5 ◀▶ Ps 11:6
C Ps 7:14 ◀▶ Ps 14:1–4
M Job 22:29 ◀▶ Ps 12:3–4

t 16 Or *Meditation*; possibly a musical notation   *u 17* Hebrew *Sheol*
v Psalms 9 and 10 may have been originally a single acrostic poem, the stanzas of which begin with the successive letters of the Hebrew alphabet. In the Septuagint they constitute one psalm.

9:7–8 David confirmed that God will ultimately judge the nations according to God's standards of righteousness.

I'll always be happy[i] and never have trouble."
[7]His mouth is full of curses[j] and lies and threats;[k]
   trouble and evil are under his tongue.[l]
[8]He lies in wait[m] near the villages;
   from ambush he murders the innocent,[n]
   watching in secret for his victims.
[9]He lies in wait like a lion in cover;
   he lies in wait to catch the helpless;[o]
   he catches the helpless and drags them off in his net.[p]
[10]His victims are crushed,[q] they collapse;
   they fall under his strength.
[11]He says to himself, "God has forgotten;[r]
   he covers his face and never sees."[s]
[12]Arise,[t] LORD! Lift up your hand,[u] O God.
   Do not forget the helpless.[v]
[13]Why does the wicked man revile God?[w]
   Why does he say to himself,
   "He won't call me to account"?[x]
[14]But you, O God, do see trouble[y] and grief;
   you consider it to take it in hand.
   The victim commits himself to you;[z]
   you are the helper[a] of the fatherless.
[15]Break the arm of the wicked and evil man;[b]
   call him to account for his wickedness
   that would not be found out.
[16]The LORD is King for ever and ever;[c]
   the nations[d] will perish from his land.
[17]You hear, O LORD, the desire of the afflicted;[e]
   you encourage them, and you listen to their cry,[f]
[18]defending the fatherless[g] and the oppressed,[h]
   in order that man, who is of the earth, may terrify no more.

E *Ps 7:9* ◀ ▶ *Ps 11:4*   P *Ps 2:12* ◀ ▶ *Ps 11:6*
K *Ps 92:9*   M *Ps 2:8–9* ◀ ▶ *Ps 14:7*

10:6 [i] Rev 18:7
10:7 [j] Ro 3:14*
[k] Ps 73:8; 119:134; Ecc 4:1; Isa 30:12
[l] S Job 20:12
10:8 [m] Ps 37:32; 59:3; 71:10; Pr 1:11; Jer 5:26; Mic 7:2 [n] Hos 6:9
10:9 [o] S ver 2
[p] S Job 18:8
10:10 [q] S Job 9:17
10:11 [r] Job 22:13; Ps 42:9; 77:9
[s] S Job 22:14
10:12 [t] Ps 3:7
[u] Ps 17:7; 20:6; 106:26; Isa 26:11; Mic 5:9 [v] Ps 9:12
10:13 [w] ver 3
[x] S Job 31:14
10:14 [y] ver 7; Ps 22:11 [z] Ps 37:5
[a] S Dt 33:29
10:15
[b] S Job 31:22
10:16 [c] S Ex 15:18
[d] S Dt 8:20
10:17 [e] S Ps 9:12
[f] S Ex 22:23
10:18 [g] S Dt 24:17; Ps 146:9 [h] S Ps 9:9
11:1 [i] S Ps 7:1
[j] S Ge 14:10
[k] Ps 50:11
11:2 [l] S 2Sa 22:35
[m] S Ps 7:13; S 58:7
[n] Ps 10:8
[o] S Job 33:3; Ps 7:10
11:3 [p] Ps 18:15; 82:5; Isa 24:18
11:4 [q] S 1Ki 8:48; Ps 18:6; 27:4; Jnh 2:7; Mic 1:2; Hab 2:20
[r] S 2Ch 6:18; S Ps 9:7; Mt 5:34; 23:22; S Rev 4:2
[s] Pr 15:3 [t] Ps 33:18; 66:7
11:5 [u] S Dt 7:13; S Job 23:10
[v] S Job 28:28; Ps 5:5; 45:7; Isa 1:14
11:6 [w] S Ge 19:24; S Rev 9:17
[x] S Ge 41:6; S Job 1:19
11:7 [y] S 2Ch 12:6; S Ezr 9:15; 2Ti 4:8
[z] S Ps 9:8; 33:5; 99:4; Isa 28:17; 30:18; 56:1; 61:8; Jer 9:24 [a] S Job 1:1; Lk 23:50
[b] Ps 17:5; 140:13
12:1 [c] Isa 57:1; Mic 7:2
12:2 [d] Ps 5:6; 34:13; 141:3; Pr 6:19; 12:17; 13:3; Isa 32:7
[e] S Ps 5:9; Ro 10:18
12:3 [f] Pr 26:28; 28:23

Psalm 11

For the director of music. Of David.

[1]In the LORD I take refuge.[i]
   How then can you say to me:
   "Flee[j] like a bird to your mountain.[k]
[2]For look, the wicked bend their bows;[l]
   they set their arrows[m] against the strings
   to shoot from the shadows[n]
   at the upright in heart.[o]
[3]When the foundations[p] are being destroyed,
   what can the righteous do[w]?"

[4]The LORD is in his holy temple;[q]
   the LORD is on his heavenly throne.[r]
   He observes the sons of men;[s]
   his eyes examine[t] them.
[5]The LORD examines the righteous,[u]
   but the wicked[x] and those who love violence
   his soul hates.[v]
[6]On the wicked he will rain fiery coals and burning sulfur;[w]
   a scorching wind[x] will be their lot.
[7]For the LORD is righteous,[y]
   he loves justice;[z]
   upright men[a] will see his face.[b]

Psalm 12

For the director of music. According to sheminith.[y] *A psalm of David.*

[1]Help, LORD, for the godly are no more;[c]
   the faithful have vanished from among men.
[2]Everyone lies[d] to his neighbor;
   their flattering lips speak with deception.[e]
[3]May the LORD cut off all flattering lips[f]

E *Ps 10:11–14* ◀ ▶ *Ps 33:13–15*
S *Ps 7:10–11* ◀ ▶ *Ps 15:1–2*
P *Ps 10:15–16* ◀ ▶ *Ps 18:7–15*
H *Ps 9:17* ◀ ▶ *Ps 21:8–9*
U *Ps 7:10* ◀ ▶ *Ps 15:1–2*
M *Ps 10:4* ◀ ▶ *Ps 25:11*

[w] 3 Or *what is the Righteous One doing* [x] 5 Or *The LORD, the Righteous One, examines the wicked,* / [y] Title: Probably a musical term

---

10:15–16 The wicked will be destroyed by God who is the "King for ever and ever" (10:16).
11:6 This verse may be recalling God's judgment on Sodom and Gomorrah as it predicts the ultimate destruction of the wicked (see Rev. 14:10; 20:10; 21:8).

and every boastful tongue—
⁴that says, "We will triumph with our tongues;
we own our lips—who is our master?"

⁵"Because of the oppression of the weak
and the groaning of the needy,
I will now arise," says the LORD.
"I will protect them from those who malign them."

⁶And the words of the LORD are flawless,
like silver refined in a furnace of clay,
purified seven times.

⁷O LORD, you will keep us safe
and protect us from such people forever.

⁸The wicked freely strut about
when what is vile is honored among men.

Psalm 13

For the director of music. A psalm of David.

¹How long, O LORD? Will you forget me forever?
How long will you hide your face from me?

²How long must I wrestle with my thoughts
and every day have sorrow in my heart?
How long will my enemy triumph over me?

³Look on me and answer, O LORD my God.
Give light to my eyes, or I will sleep in death;

⁴my enemy will say, "I have overcome him,"
and my foes will rejoice when I fall.

⁵But I trust in your unfailing love;
my heart rejoices in your salvation.

⁶I will sing to the LORD,
for he has been good to me.

Psalm 14

14:1–7pp — Ps 53:1–6

For the director of music. Of David.

¹The fool says in his heart,
"There is no God."
They are corrupt, their deeds are vile;
there is no one who does good.

²The LORD looks down from heaven
on the sons of men
to see if there are any who understand,
any who seek God.

³All have turned aside,
they have together become corrupt;
there is no one who does good,
not even one.

⁴Will evildoers never learn—
those who devour my people as men eat bread
and who do not call on the LORD?

⁵There they are, overwhelmed with dread,
for God is present in the company of the righteous.

⁶You evildoers frustrate the plans of the poor,
but the LORD is their refuge.

⁷Oh, that salvation for Israel would come out of Zion!
When the LORD restores the fortunes of his people,
let Jacob rejoice and Israel be glad!

Psalm 15

A psalm of David.

¹LORD, who may dwell in your sanctuary?
Who may live on your holy hill?

²He whose walk is blameless
and who does what is righteous,

14:7 The psalmist looks forward to Israel's ultimate deliverance from her enemies through the victory of the Messiah.

who speaks the truth from his heart
³ and has no slander on his tongue,
who does his neighbor no wrong
   and casts no slur on his fellowman,
⁴who despises a vile man
   but honors those who fear the
     LORD,
who keeps his oath
   even when it hurts,
⁵who lends his money without usury
   and does not accept a bribe against
     the innocent.

He who does these things
   will never be shaken.

Psalm 16

A *miktam* of David.

¹Keep me safe, O God,
   for in you I take refuge.

²I said to the LORD, "You are my Lord;
   apart from you I have no good
     thing."
³As for the saints who are in the land,
   they are the glorious ones in whom
     is all my delight.
⁴The sorrows of those will increase
   who run after other gods.
I will not pour out their libations of
     blood
   or take up their names on my lips.

⁵LORD, you have assigned me my
     portion and my cup;
   you have made my lot secure.
⁶The boundary lines have fallen for me
     in pleasant places;
   surely I have a delightful
     inheritance.

⁷I will praise the LORD, who counsels
     me;
   even at night my heart instructs
     me.
⁸I have set the LORD always before me.
   Because he is at my right hand,
     I will not be shaken.

⁹Therefore my heart is glad and my
     tongue rejoices;
   my body also will rest secure,
¹⁰because you will not abandon me to
     the grave,
   nor will you let your Holy One see
     decay.
¹¹You have made known to me the path
     of life;
   you will fill me with joy in your
     presence,
   with eternal pleasures at your right
     hand.

Psalm 17

A prayer of David.

¹Hear, O LORD, my righteous plea;
   listen to my cry.
Give ear to my prayer—
   it does not rise from deceitful lips.
²May my vindication come from you;
   may your eyes see what is right.

³Though you probe my heart and
     examine me at night,
   though you test me, you will find
     nothing;
   I have resolved that my mouth will
     not sin.
⁴As for the deeds of men—
   by the word of your lips
I have kept myself
   from the ways of the violent.
⁵My steps have held to your paths;
   my feet have not slipped.

⁶I call on you, O God, for you will
     answer me;
   give ear to me and hear my
     prayer.
⁷Show the wonder of your great love,
   you who save by your right hand

16:9–11 Hidden in these words of assurance is David's confidence in a personal resurrection (see 17:15; 73:24). Peter declares that David's words also foretold Christ's resurrection and his victory over death and the grave (see Ac 2:25–31).

those who take refuge[x] in you from
 their foes.
⁸Keep me[y] as the apple of your eye;[z]
 hide me[a] in the shadow of your
 wings[b]
⁹from the wicked who assail me,
 from my mortal enemies who
 surround me.[c]

¹⁰They close up their callous hearts,[d]
 and their mouths speak with
 arrogance.[e]
¹¹They have tracked me down, they now
 surround me,[f]
 with eyes alert, to throw me to the
 ground.
¹²They are like a lion[g] hungry for prey,[h]
 like a great lion crouching in cover.
¹³Rise up,[i] O LORD, confront them, bring
 them down;[j]
 rescue me from the wicked by your
 sword.
¹⁴O LORD, by your hand save me from
 such men,
 from men of this world[k] whose
 reward is in this life.[l]
You still the hunger of those you
 cherish;
 their sons have plenty,
 and they store up wealth[m] for their
 children.
¹⁵And I—in righteousness I will see
 your face;
 when I awake,[n] I will be satisfied
 with seeing your likeness.[o]

Psalm 18

18:Title-50pp — 2Sa 22:1-51

For the director of music. Of David the
servant of the LORD. He sang to the LORD
the words of this song when the LORD
delivered him from the hand of all his
enemies and from the hand of Saul. He said:

¹I love you, O LORD, my strength.[p]
²The LORD is my rock,[q] my fortress[r] and
 my deliverer;[s]

K *Ps 16:8* ◀ ▶ *Ps 18:2*
C *Ps 14:1-4* ◀ ▶ *Ps 36:1-4*
F *Ps 16:9-10* ◀ ▶ *Ps 71:20*
K *Ps 17:8* ◀ ▶ *Ps 18:16*

17:7 ˣPs 2:12
17:8 ʸS Nu 6:24
 ᶻS Dt 32:10; Pr 7:2
 ᵃPs 27:5; 31:20;
 32:7 ᵇRu 2:12;
 Ps 36:7; 63:7;
 Isa 34:15
17:9 ᶜPs 109:3
17:10 ᵈPs 73:7;
 119:70; Isa 6:10
 ᵉS 1Sa 2:3
17:11 ᶠPs 88:17
17:12 ᵍPs 7:2;
 Jer 5:6; 12:8;
 La 3:10 ʰS Ge 49:9
17:13 ⁱS Nu 10:35
 ʲPs 35:8; 55:23;
 73:18
17:14 ᵏLk 16:8
 ˡPs 49:17; Lk 16:25
 ᵐIsa 2:7; 57:17
17:15 ⁿS Ps 3:5
 ᵒS Nu 12:8;
 S Mt 5:8; 1Jn 3:2
18:1 ᵖS Ex 15:2;
 S Dt 33:29;
 S 1Sa 2:10;
 Ps 22:19; 28:7;
 59:9; 81:1;
 Isa 12:2; 49:5;
 Jer 16:19
18:2 ᵠS Ex 33:22
 ʳPs 28:8; 31:2,3;
 Isa 17:10; Jer 16:19
 Ps 40:17
 ᵗPs 2:12; 9:9; 94:22
 ᵘS Ge 15:1;
 Ps 28:7; 84:9;
 119:114; 144:2
 ᵛS 1Sa 2:1;
 S Lk 1:69
18:3
 ʷS 1Ch 16:25
 ˣS Ps 9:13
18:4 ʸPs 116:3
 ᶻPs 93:4; 124:4;
 Isa 5:30; 17:12;
 Jer 6:23; 51:42,55;
 Eze 43:2
18:5 ᵃPr 13:14
18:6 ᵇS Dt 4:30
 ᶜPs 30:2; 99:6;
 102:2; 120:1
 ᵈPs 66:19; 116:1
 ᵉS Job 16:18
18:7 ᶠPs 97:4;
 Isa 5:25; 64:3
 ᵍS Jdg 5:4
 ʰS Jdg 5:5
 ⁱS Job 9:5;
 Jer 10:10
18:8 ʲS Job 41:20
 ᵏS Ex 15:7;
 S 19:18;
 S Job 41:21;
 Ps 50:3; 97:3;
 Da 7:10 ˡPr 25:22;
 Ro 12:20
18:9 ᵐS Ge 11:5;
 S Ps 57:3
 ⁿS Ex 20:21;
 S Dt 33:26;
 Ps 104:3
18:10 ᵒS Ge 3:24;
 Eze 10:18
 ᵖS Dt 33:26
 ᵠPs 104:3
18:11 ʳS Ex 19:9;
 S Dt 4:11

my God is my rock, in whom I take
 refuge.[t]
He is my shield[u] and the horn[g] of
 my salvation,[v] my stronghold.
³I call to the LORD, who is worthy of
 praise,[w]
 and I am saved from my enemies.[x]

⁴The cords of death[y] entangled me;
 the torrents[z] of destruction
 overwhelmed me.
⁵The cords of the grave[h] coiled around
 me;
 the snares of death[a] confronted me.
⁶In my distress[b] I called to the LORD;[c]
 I cried to my God for help.
From his temple he heard my voice;[d]
 my cry came[e] before him, into his
 ears.

⁷The earth trembled[f] and quaked,[g]
 and the foundations of the
 mountains shook;[h]
 they trembled because he was
 angry.[i]
⁸Smoke rose from his nostrils;[j]
 consuming fire[k] came from his
 mouth,
 burning coals[l] blazed out of it.
⁹He parted the heavens and came
 down;[m]
 dark clouds[n] were under his feet.
¹⁰He mounted the cherubim[o] and flew;
 he soared[p] on the wings of the
 wind.[q]
¹¹He made darkness his covering,[r] his
 canopy[s] around him—
 the dark rain clouds of the sky.
¹²Out of the brightness of his presence[t]
 clouds advanced,
 with hailstones[u] and bolts of
 lightning.[v]
¹³The LORD thundered[w] from heaven;
 the voice of the Most High
 resounded.[i]

V *Ps 17:7* ◀ ▶ *Ps 18:29*
P *Ps 11:6* ◀ ▶ *Ps 37:34*

ˢS Job 22:14; Isa 4:5; Jer 43:10 **18:12** ᵗPs 104:2 ᵘS Jos 10:11
ᵛS Job 36:30 **18:13** ʷS Ex 9:23; S 1Sa 2:10

g 2 *Horn* here symbolizes strength. *h* 5 Hebrew *Sheol* *i* 13 Some
Hebrew manuscripts and Septuagint (see also 2 Samuel 22:14); most
Hebrew manuscripts *resounded, / amid hailstones and bolts of lightning*

18:7–15 This psalm is a restatement of 2Sa 22 and celebrates David's deliverance from his mortal
enemies.

¹⁴He shot his arrows* and scattered ⌊the enemies⌋,
 great bolts of lightningʸ and routed them.ᶻ
¹⁵The valleys of the sea were exposed
 and the foundationsᵃ of the earth laid bare
at your rebuke,ᵇ O LORD,
 at the blast of breath from your nostrils.ᶜ
¹⁶He reached down from on high and took hold of me;
 he drew me out of deep waters.ᵈ
¹⁷He rescued me from my powerful enemy,ᵉ
 from my foes, who were too strong for me.ᶠ
¹⁸They confronted me in the day of my disaster,ᵍ
 but the LORD was my support.ʰ
¹⁹He brought me out into a spacious place;ⁱ
 he rescued me because he delighted in me.ʲ
²⁰The LORD has dealt with me according to my righteousness;ᵏ
 according to the cleanness of my handsˡ he has rewarded me.ᵐ
²¹For I have kept the ways of the LORD;ⁿ
 I have not done evil by turningᵒ from my God.
²²All his laws are before me;ᵖ
 I have not turned away from his decrees.
²³I have been blamelessᑫ before him
 and have kept myself from sin.
²⁴The LORD has rewarded me according to my righteousness,ʳ
 according to the cleanness of my hands in his sight.
²⁵To the faithfulˢ you show yourself faithful,ᵗ
 to the blameless you show yourself blameless,
²⁶to the pureᵘ you show yourself pure,
 but to the crooked you show yourself shrewd.ᵛ
²⁷You save the humbleʷ
 but bring low those whose eyes are haughty.ˣ

²⁸You, O LORD, keep my lampʸ burning;
 my God turns my darkness into light.ᶻ
²⁹With your helpᵃ I can advance against a troop;ʲ
 with my God I can scale a wall.
³⁰As for God, his way is perfect;ᵇ
 the word of the LORD is flawless.ᶜ
He is a shieldᵈ
 for all who take refugeᵉ in him.
³¹For who is God besides the LORD?ᶠ
 And who is the Rockᵍ except our God?
³²It is God who arms me with strengthʰ
 and makes my way perfect.ⁱ
³³He makes my feet like the feet of a deer;ʲ
 he enables me to stand on the heights.ᵏ
³⁴He trains my hands for battle;ˡ
 my arms can bend a bow of bronze.
³⁵You give me your shield of victory,
 and your right hand sustainsᵐ me;
 you stoop down to make me great.
³⁶You broaden the pathⁿ beneath me,
 so that my ankles do not turn.ᵒ
³⁷I pursued my enemiesᵖ and overtook them;
 I did not turn back till they were destroyed.
³⁸I crushed themᑫ so that they could not rise;ʳ
 they fell beneath my feet.ˢ
³⁹You armed me with strengthᵗ for battle;
 you made my adversaries bowᵘ at my feet.
⁴⁰You made my enemies turn their backsᵛ in flight,
 and I destroyedʷ my foes.
⁴¹They cried for help, but there was no one to save them*—
 to the LORD, but he did not answer.ʸ

K *Ps 18:2* ◄ ► *Ps 18:35–36*
U *Ps 16:11* ◄ ► *Ps 18:24*
S *Ps 15:5* ◄ ► *Ps 19:12–14*
U *Ps 18:19–20* ◄ ► *Ps 18:32*

L *Ps 13:6* ◄ ► *Ps 23:1–6*
J *Ps 3:5–6* ◄ ► *Ps 23:4*
V *Ps 18:3* ◄ ► *Ps 20:7–8*
W *Ps 2:12* ◄ ► *Ps 34:8*
O *Ps 3:8* ◄ ► *Ps 36:9*
U *Ps 18:24* ◄ ► *Ps 19:11*
K *Ps 18:16* ◄ ► *Ps 19:7*

j29 Or can run through a barricade

⁴²I beat them as fine as dust borne on the wind;
I poured them out like mud in the streets.

⁴³You have delivered me from the attacks of the people;
you have made me the head of nations;
people I did not know are subject to me.
⁴⁴As soon as they hear me, they obey me;
foreigners cringe before me.
⁴⁵They all lose heart;
they come trembling from their strongholds.

⁴⁶The LORD lives! Praise be to my Rock!
Exalted be God my Savior!
⁴⁷He is the God who avenges me,
who subdues nations under me,
⁴⁸ who saves me from my enemies.
You exalted me above my foes;
from violent men you rescued me.
⁴⁹Therefore I will praise you among the nations, O LORD;
I will sing praises to your name.
⁵⁰He gives his king great victories;
he shows unfailing kindness to his anointed,
to David and his descendants forever.

Psalm 19

For the director of music. A psalm of David.

¹The heavens declare the glory of God;
the skies proclaim the work of his hands.
²Day after day they pour forth speech;
night after night they display knowledge.
³There is no speech or language where their voice is not heard.
⁴Their voice goes out into all the earth,
their words to the ends of the world.

In the heavens he has pitched a tent for the sun,
⁵which is like a bridegroom coming forth from his pavilion,
like a champion rejoicing to run his course.
⁶It rises at one end of the heavens
and makes its circuit to the other;
nothing is hidden from its heat.

⁷The law of the LORD is perfect, reviving the soul.
The statutes of the LORD are trustworthy,
making wise the simple.
⁸The precepts of the LORD are right,
giving joy to the heart.
The commands of the LORD are radiant,
giving light to the eyes.
⁹The fear of the LORD is pure,
enduring forever.
The ordinances of the LORD are sure
and altogether righteous.
¹⁰They are more precious than gold,
than much pure gold;
they are sweeter than honey,
than honey from the comb.
¹¹By them is your servant warned;
in keeping them there is great reward.

¹²Who can discern his errors?
Forgive my hidden faults.
¹³Keep your servant also from willful sins;
may they not rule over me.
Then will I be blameless,
innocent of great transgression.

¹⁴May the words of my mouth and the meditation of my heart
be pleasing in your sight,
O LORD, my Rock and my Redeemer.

K Ps 18:35–36 ◄► Ps 20:5–6
U Ps 18:32 ◄► Ps 21:1–7
S Ps 18:21–23 ◄► Ps 24:3–5

k 3 Or They have no speech, there are no words; / no sound is heard from them   14 Septuagint, Jerome and Syriac; Hebrew line

---

19:6 While the sun is easily observed in its path from east to west during daylight hours, recent scientific discoveries have found that the sun also makes a "circuit" or orbit through the galaxy, confirming this divinely inspired record.

Psalm 20

For the director of music. A psalm of David.

¹May the LORD answer you when you are in distress;ᵈ
may the name of the God of Jacobᵉ protect you.ᶠ
²May he send you helpᵍ from the sanctuaryʰ
and grant you supportⁱ from Zion.ʲ
³May he rememberᵏ all your sacrifices
and accept your burnt offerings.ˡ
Selah

⁴May he give you the desire of your heartᵐ
and make all your plans succeed.ⁿ
⁵We will shout for joyᵒ when you are victorious
and will lift up our bannersᵖ in the name of our God.
May the LORD grant all your requests.ᑫ
⁶Now I know that the LORD saves his anointed;ʳ
he answers him from his holy heaven
with the saving power of his right hand.ˢ
⁷Some trust in chariotsᵗ and some in horses,ᵘ
but we trust in the name of the LORD our God.ᵛ
⁸They are brought to their knees and fall,ʷ
but we rise upˣ and stand firm.ʸ
⁹O LORD, save the king!
Answerᵐ usᶻ when we call!

Psalm 21

For the director of music. A psalm of David.

¹O LORD, the king rejoices in your strength.ᵃ
How great is his joy in the victories you give!ᵇ
²You have granted him the desire of his heartᶜ
and have not withheld the request of his lips. *Selah*

³You welcomed him with rich blessings
and placed a crown of pure goldᵈ on his head.ᵉ
⁴He asked you for life, and you gave it to him—
length of days, for ever and ever.ᶠ
⁵Through the victoriesᵍ you gave, his glory is great;
you have bestowed on him splendor and majesty.ʰ
⁶Surely you have granted him eternal blessings
and made him glad with the joyⁱ of your presence.ʲ
⁷For the king trusts in the LORD;ᵏ
through the unfailing loveˡ of the Most Highᵐ
he will not be shaken.ⁿ
⁸Your hand will lay holdᵒ on all your enemies;
your right hand will seize your foes.
⁹At the time of your appearing
you will make them like a fiery furnace.
In his wrath the LORD will swallow them up,
and his fire will consume them.ᵖ
¹⁰You will destroy their descendants from the earth,
their posterity from mankind.ᑫ
¹¹Though they plot evilʳ against you
and devise wicked schemes,ˢ they cannot succeed;
¹²for you will make them turn their backsᵗ
when you aim at them with drawn bow.
¹³Be exalted,ᵘ O LORD, in your strength;ᵛ
we will sing and praise your might.

Psalm 22

For the director of music. To ₗthe tune ofⱼ "The Doe of the Morning." A psalm of David.

¹My God, my God, why have you forsaken me?ʷ
Why are you so farˣ from saving me,

K Ps 19:7 ◀ ▶ Ps 26:1
V Ps 18:29 ◀ ▶ Ps 22:4–5
U Ps 19:11 ◀ ▶ Ps 24:3–4

20:1 ᵈPs 4:1
ᵉEx 3:6; Ps 46:7,11
ᶠPs 59:1; 69:29; 91:14
20:2 ᵍPs 30:10; 33:20; 37:40; 40:1; 54:4; 118:7
ʰS Nu 3:28
ⁱS Ps 18:18 ʲPs 2:6; 128:5; 134:3; 135:21
20:3 ᵏAc 10:4
ˡS Dt 33:11
20:4 ᵐPs 21:2; 37:4; 145:16,19; Isa 26:8; Eze 24:25; Ro 10:1 ⁿPs 140:8; Pr 16:3; Da 11:17
20:5 ᵒS Job 3:7
ᵖS Nu 1:52; Ps 60:4; Isa 5:26; 11:10,12; 13:2; 30:17; 49:22; 62:10; Jer 50:2; 51:12,27 ᑫ1Sa 1:17
20:6 ʳS 2Sa 23:1; Ps 28:8
ˢS Job 40:14; Hab 3:13
20:7 ᵗS 2Ki 19:23
ᵘS Dt 17:16; Ps 33:17; 147:10; Pr 21:31; Isa 31:1; 36:8,9 ᵛS 2Ch 32:8
20:8 ʷPs 27:2; Isa 40:30; Jer 46:6; 50:32 ˣMic 7:8
ʸJob 11:15; Ps 37:23; Pr 10:25; Isa 7:9
20:9 ᶻPs 17:5
21:1 ᵃS 1Sa 2:10
ᵇ2Sa 22:51
21:2 ᶜS Ps 20:4
21:3 ᵈS 2Sa 12:30; Rev 14:14
ᵉZec 6:11
21:4 ᶠPs 10:16; 45:17; 48:14; 133:3
21:5 ᵍver 1; Ps 18:50; 44:5
ʰS Ps 8:5; 45:3; 93:1; 96:6; 104:1
21:6 ⁱPs 43:4; 126:3 ʲS 1Ch 17:22
21:7 ᵏS 2Ki 18:5
ˡPs 6:4 ᵐGe 14:18
ⁿPs 15:5; S 55:22
21:8 ᵒIsa 10:10
21:9 ᵖS Dt 32:22; Ps 50:3; Jer 15:14
21:10 ᑫDt 28:18
21:11 ʳPs 2:1
ˢJob 10:3; Ps 10:2; 26:10; 37:7
21:12 ᵗS Ex 23:27
21:13 ᵘS Ps 18:46
ᵛPs 18:1
22:1 ʷS Job 6:15; S Ps 9:10; Mt 27:46*; Mk 15:34*
ˣPs 10:1

H Ps 11:6 ◀ ▶ Ps 26:9
B Dt 18:15–19 ◀ ▶ Isa 7:13–16

ᵐ 9 Or save! / O King, answer

22:1–2 The prophetic words of the psalmist "My God, my God, why have you forsaken me?" (22:1) were reiterated in Jesus' cry from the cross (see Mt 27:46). When Jesus took the sins of the

so far from the words of my
    groaning?[y]
[2]O my God, I cry out by day, but you do
    not answer,[z]
  by night,[a] and am not silent.

[3]Yet you are enthroned as the Holy
    One;[b]
  you are the praise[c] of Israel.[n]
[V] [4]In you our fathers put their trust;
  they trusted and you delivered
    them.[d]
[5]They cried to you[e] and were saved;
  in you they trusted[f] and were not
    disappointed.[g]

[6]But I am a worm[h] and not a man,
  scorned by men[i] and despised[j] by
    the people.
[7]All who see me mock me;[k]
  they hurl insults,[l] shaking their
    heads:[m]
[8]"He trusts in the LORD;
    let the LORD rescue him.[n]
  Let him deliver him,[o]
    since he delights[p] in him."

[9]Yet you brought me out of the womb;[q]
  you made me trust[r] in you
    even at my mother's breast.
[10]From birth[s] I was cast upon you;
  from my mother's womb you have
    been my God.
[11]Do not be far from me,[t]
  for trouble is near[u]
  and there is no one to help.[v]

[12]Many bulls[w] surround me;[x]
  strong bulls of Bashan[y] encircle me.
[D] [13]Roaring lions[z] tearing their prey[a]

[V] Ps 20:7-8 ◄► Ps 25:2-3
[D] Ezr 6:19-20 ◄► Ps 69:22-21

22:1 [y]S Job 3:24
22:2 [z]S Job 19:7
  [a]Ps 42:3; 88:1
22:3 [b]S 2Ki 19:22;
  Ps 71:22;
  S Mk 1:24
  [c]S Ex 15:2;
  Ps 148:14
22:4 [d]Ps 78:53;
  107:6
22:5 [e]S 1Ch 5:20
  [f]Isa 8:17; 25:9;
  26:3; 30:18
  [g]S 2Ch 13:18;
  Ps 25:3; 31:17;
  71:1; Isa 49:23;
  Ro 9:33
22:6 [h]S Job 4:19
  [i]S 2Sa 12:14;
  Ps 31:11; 64:8;
  69:19; 109:25
  [j]Ps 119:141;
  Isa 49:7; 53:3;
  60:14; Mal 2:9;
  Mt 16:21
22:7 [k]S Job 17:2;
  Ps 35:16; 69:12;
  74:18; Mt 27:41;
  Mk 15:31; Lk 23:36
  [l]Mt 27:39,44;
  Mk 15:32; Lk 23:39
  [m]Mk 15:29
22:8 [n]Ps 91:14
  [o]S Ps 3:2
  [p]S 2Sa 22:20;
  S Mt 3:17; 27:43
22:9 [q]Job 10:18;
  Ps 71:6 [r]Ps 78:7;
  Na 1:7
22:10 [s]Ps 71:6;
  Isa 46:3; 49:1
22:11 [t]ver 19;
  S Ps 10:1
  [u]S Ps 10:14
  [v]S 2Ki 14:26;
  S Isa 41:28
22:12 [w]Ps 68:30
  [x]Ps 17:9; 27:6;
  49:5; 109:3; 140:9
  [y]Dt 32:14; Isa 2:13;
  Eze 27:6; 39:18;
  Am 4:1
22:13 [z]ver 21;
  Eze 22:25; Zep 3:3
  [a]S Ge 49:9
  [b]La 3:46
22:14 [c]S Ps 6:2
  [d]Job 23:16;
  Ps 68:2; 97:5;
  Mic 1:4 [e]Jos 7:5;
  Ps 107:26; Da 5:6
22:15 [f]Isa 45:9

open their mouths wide[b] against
    me.
[14]I am poured out like water,
  and all my bones are out of joint.[c]
  My heart has turned to wax;[d]
    it has melted away[e] within me.
[15]My strength is dried up like a
    potsherd,[f]
  and my tongue sticks to the roof of
    my mouth;[g]
  you lay me[o] in the dust[h] of death.
[16]Dogs[i] have surrounded me;
  a band of evil men has encircled
    me,
  they have pierced[p][j] my hands and
    my feet.
[17]I can count all my bones;
  people stare[k] and gloat over me.[l]
[18]They divide my garments among
    them
  and cast lots[m] for my clothing.[n]

[19]But you, O LORD, be not far off;[o]
  O my Strength,[p] come quickly[q] to
    help me.[r]
[20]Deliver my life from the sword,[s]
  my precious life[t] from the power of
    the dogs.[u]
[21]Rescue me from the mouth of the
    lions;[v]
  save[q] me from the horns of the wild
    oxen.[w]

[g]Ps 137:6; La 4:4; Eze 3:26; Jn 19:28 [h]S Job 7:21; Ps 104:29
22:16 [i]Php 3:2 [j]Isa 51:9; 53:5; Zec 12:10; Jn 20:25 22:17 [k]Lk 23:35
[l]Ps 25:2; 30:1; 35:19; 38:16; La 2:17; Mic 7:8 22:18 [m]S Lev 16:8;
Mt 27:35*; Mk 15:24; Lk 23:34; Jn 19:24* [n]Mk 9:12 22:19 [o]S ver 11
[p]S Ps 18:1 [q]S Ps 38:22; 70:5; 141:1 [r]Ps 40:13 22:20 [s]S Job 5:20;
Ps 37:14 [t]S Ps 35:17 [u]Php 3:2 22:21 [v]S ver 13; S Job 4:10 [w]ver 12;
S Nu 23:22

[n]3 Or *Yet you are holy, / enthroned on the praises of Israel* [o]15 Or / I
am laid [p]16 Some Hebrew manuscripts, Septuagint and Syriac; most
Hebrew manuscripts / like the lion, [q]21 Or / you have heard

---

world upon himself so that those sins could be judged and justified through his sacrifice, God in his holiness had to turn away (see 2Co 5:21).

22:6–8 David's prophecy described the rejection and the mockery that Jesus took upon himself on the cross. Matthew records the fulfillment of this psalm in his record of the crucifixion (see Mt 27:39–43).

22:9–10 In contrast to other OT references that identify a person through their father's lineage, this prophecy of the Messiah mentioned only the mother of the Messiah, foreshadowing the virgin birth.

22:11–18 This psalm predicted the horrible aspects of the crucifixion including thirst (see Jn 19:28) and the mocking of the priests and soldiers (see Jn 19:1–3). The startling prophetic words "they have pierced my hands and my feet" (22:16) describe a method of execution that was not known until the Roman occupation several centuries later. The reference to gambling for the clothes of the victim was also fulfilled as the Roman soldiers gambled for the robe of Jesus (see Jn 19:24). Though some suggest that Jesus' familiarity with the Scriptures allowed him to arrange his life so that he could conveniently fulfill the Messianic prophecies, this argument does not bear itself out in Scripture. Overwhelming historical evidence proves that Jesus of Nazareth is God's Messiah, the one who fulfilled the prophecies recorded in Scripture centuries before he was born.

²²I will declare your name to my brothers;
in the congregation˟ I will praise you.ʸ
²³You who fear the LORD, praise him!
All you descendants of Jacob, honor him!ᵃ
Revere him,ᵇ all you descendants of Israel!
²⁴For he has not despisedᶜ or disdained
the suffering of the afflicted one;ᵈ
he has not hidden his faceᵉ from him
but has listened to his cry for help.ᶠ

²⁵From you comes the theme of my praise in the great assembly;ᵍ
before those who fear youʳ will I fulfill my vows.ʰ
²⁶The poor will eatⁱ and be satisfied;
they who seek the LORD will praise him—ʲ
may your hearts live forever!
²⁷All the ends of the earthᵏ
will remember and turn to the LORD,
and all the families of the nations
will bow down before him,ˡ
²⁸for dominion belongs to the LORDᵐ
and he rules over the nations.

²⁹All the richⁿ of the earth will feast and worship;ᵒ
all who go down to the dustᵖ will kneel before him—
those who cannot keep themselves alive.ᑫ
³⁰Posterityʳ will serve him;
future generationsˢ will be told about the Lord.
³¹They will proclaim his righteousnessᵗ
to a people yet unbornᵘ—
for he has done it.ᵛ

T 1Ch 16:8–10 ◀ ▶ Ps 22:25
T Ps 22:22–23 ◀ ▶ Ps 34:1–3
L Ps 9:10 ◀ ▶ Ps 30:5
F Job 5:20 ◀ ▶ Ps 23:1–2
M Ps 14:7 ◀ ▶ Ps 24:1

22:22 ˣPs 26:12; 40:9,10; 68:26
ʸPs 35:18; Heb 2:12*
22:23 ᶻPs 33:2; 66:8; 86:12; 103:1; 106:1; 113:1; 117:1; 135:19
ᵃPs 50:15; Isa 24:15; 25:3; 49:23; 60:9;
ᵇJer 3:17
ᵇDt 14:23; Ps 33:8
22:24 ᶜPs 102:17
ᵈS Ps 9:12
ᵉPs 13:1; 27:9; 69:17; 102:2; 143:7 ᶠS Job 24:12; S 36:5; Heb 5:7
22:25 ᵍPs 26:12; 35:18; 40:9; 82:1
ʰS Nu 30:2
22:26 ⁱPs 107:9
ʲPs 40:16
22:27 ᵏPs 2:8
ˡPs 86:9; 102:22; Da 7:27; Mic 4:1
22:28 ᵐPs 47:7-8; Zec 14:9
22:29 ⁿPs 45:12
ᵒPs 95:6; 96:9; 99:5; Isa 27:13; 49:7; 66:23; Zec 14:16
ᵖIsa 26:19
ᑫPs 89:48
22:30 ʳIsa 53:10; 54:3; 61:9; 66:22
ˢPs 102:18
22:31 ᵗS Ps 5:8; 40:9 ᵘPs 71:18; 78:6; 102:18
ᵛLk 18:31; 24:44
23:1 ʷS Ge 48:15; S Ps 28:9; S Jn 10:11
ˣPs 34:9,10; 84:11; 107:9; Php 4:19
23:2 ʸPs 36:8; 46:4; Rev 7:17
23:3 ᶻS Ps 19:7
ᵃPs 25:9; 73:24; Isa 42:16 ᵇS Ps 5:8
ᶜPs 25:11; 31:3; 79:9; 106:8; 109:21; 143:11
23:4 ᵈS Job 3:5; Ps 107:14 ᵉPs 3:6; 27:1 ᶠPs 16:8; Isa 43:2
23:5 ᵍS Job 36:16 ʰPs 45:7; 92:10; Lk 7:46 ⁱS Ps 16:5
23:6 ʲS Ne 9:25
24:1 ᵏS Ex 9:29; Job 41:11
ˡ1Co 10:26*

Psalm 23

A psalm of David.

¹The LORD is my shepherd,ʷ I shall not be in want.ˣ
² He makes me lie down in green pastures,
he leads me beside quiet waters,ʸ
³ he restores my soul.ᶻ
He guides meᵃ in paths of righteousnessᵇ
for his name's sake.ᶜ
⁴Even though I walk
through the valley of the shadow of death,ˢ ᵈ
I will fear no evil,ᵉ
for you are with me;ᶠ
your rod and your staff,
they comfort me.
⁵You prepare a tableᵍ before me
in the presence of my enemies.
You anoint my head with oil;ʰ
my cupⁱ overflows.
⁶Surely goodness and loveʲ will follow me
all the days of my life,
and I will dwell in the house of the LORD forever.

Psalm 24

Of David. A psalm.

¹The earth is the LORD's,ᵏ and everything in it,
the world, and all who live in it;ˡ
²for he founded it upon the seas

F Ps 22:26 ◀ ▶ Ps 23:5
L Ps 18:28 ◀ ▶ Ps 27:4–5
J Ps 18:29 ◀ ▶ Ps 27:1
W Ne 8:10 ◀ ▶ Ps 27:1
F Ps 23:1–2 ◀ ▶ Ps 33:18–19
M Ps 22:27–28 ◀ ▶ Ps 24:7–10

ʳ25 Hebrew *him*   ˢ4 Or *through the darkest valley*

22:27–31 David predicted that "all the ends of the earth will remember and turn to the LORD" (22:27). The world already remembers the Lord when they record a date in history using the notation B.C. (Before Christ) or A.D. (*Anno Domini*, meaning "in the year of our Lord"). However, the final fulfillment of this prophecy will occur in the millennial kingdom of Christ. Note that vv. 30 and 31 may refer to those who witness about Christ to the survivors of Armageddon and those that are born during the millenium. These people must decide whether they will repent and follow Jesus or not. Some will still reject faith in Christ and join Satan's final rebellion at the end of the Millennium (see Rev 20:3). See the article on "The Millennium," p. 1486.

24:1, 7–10 This psalm foreshadows the establishment of the Messianic kingdom when the whole world will acknowledge Jesus as the "King of glory" (24:7).

and established it upon the waters.ᵐ

³Who may ascend the hillⁿ of the LORD?
Who may stand in his holy place?ᵒ
⁴He who has clean handsᵖ and a pure heart,ᵠ
who does not lift up his soul to an idolʳ
or swear by what is false.ᵗ
⁵He will receive blessingsˢ from the LORD
and vindicationᵗ from God his Savior.
⁶Such is the generation of those who seek him,
who seek your face,ᵘ O God of Jacob.ᵘ   *Selah*

⁷Lift up your heads, O you gates;ᵛ
be lifted up, you ancient doors,
that the Kingʷ of gloryˣ may come in.ʸ
⁸Who is this King of glory?
The LORD strong and mighty,ᶻ
the LORD mighty in battle.ᵃ
⁹Lift up your heads, O you gates;
lift them up, you ancient doors,
that the King of glory may come in.
¹⁰Who is he, this King of glory?
The LORD Almightyᵇ—
he is the King of glory.   *Selah*

Psalm 25ᵛ

Of David.

¹To you, O LORD, I lift up my soul;ᶜ
² in you I trust,ᵈ O my God.
Do not let me be put to shame,
nor let my enemies triumph over me.
³No one whose hope is in you
will ever be put to shame,ᵉ
but they will be put to shame
who are treacherousᶠ without excuse.

⁴Show me your ways, O LORD,
teach me your paths;ᵍ
⁵guide me in your truthʰ and teach me,
for you are God my Savior,ⁱ
and my hope is in youʲ all day long.
⁶Remember, O LORD, your great mercy and love,ᵏ
for they are from of old.

⁷Remember not the sins of my youthˡ
and my rebellious ways;ᵐ
according to your loveⁿ remember me,
for you are good,ᵒ O LORD.

⁸Good and uprightᵖ is the LORD;
therefore he instructsᵠ sinners in his ways.
⁹He guidesʳ the humble in what is right
and teaches themˢ his way.
¹⁰All the ways of the LORD are loving and faithfulᵗ
for those who keep the demands of his covenant.ᵘ

¹¹For the sake of your name,ᵛ O LORD,
forgiveʷ my iniquity,ˣ though it is great.
¹²Who, then, is the man that fears the LORD?ʸ
He will instruct him in the wayᶻ chosen for him.
¹³He will spend his days in prosperity,ᵃ
and his descendants will inherit the land.ᵇ
¹⁴The LORD confidesᶜ in those who fear him;
he makes his covenant knownᵈ to them.
¹⁵My eyes are ever on the LORD,ᵉ
for only he will release my feet from the snare.ᶠ
¹⁶Turn to meᵍ and be gracious to me,ʰ
for I am lonelyⁱ and afflicted.
¹⁷The troublesʲ of my heart have multiplied;
free me from my anguish.ᵏ
¹⁸Look upon my afflictionˡ and my distressᵐ
and take away all my sins.ⁿ
¹⁹See how my enemiesᵒ have increased
and how fiercely they hate me!ᵖ
²⁰Guard my lifeᵠ and rescue me;ʳ
let me not be put to shame,ˢ
for I take refugeᵗ in you.

t 4 Or *swear falsely* *u 6* Two Hebrew manuscripts and Syriac (see also Septuagint); most Hebrew manuscripts *face, Jacob* *v* This psalm is an acrostic poem, the verses of which begin with the successive letters of the Hebrew alphabet.

²¹May integrity^u and uprightness^v
    protect me,
    because my hope is in you.^w

²²Redeem Israel,^x O God,
    from all their troubles!

Psalm 26

Of David.

¹Vindicate me,^y O LORD,
    for I have led a blameless life;^z
    I have trusted^a in the LORD
        without wavering.^b
²Test me,^c O LORD, and try me,
    examine my heart and my mind;^d
³for your love^e is ever before me,
    and I walk continually^f in your
        truth.^g
⁴I do not sit^h with deceitful men,
    nor do I consort with hypocrites;^i
⁵I abhor^j the assembly of evildoers
    and refuse to sit with the wicked.
⁶I wash my hands in innocence,^k
    and go about your altar, O LORD,
⁷proclaiming aloud your praise^l
    and telling of all your wonderful
        deeds.^m
⁸I love^n the house where you live,
    O LORD,
    the place where your glory dwells.^o

⁹Do not take away my soul along with
        sinners,
    my life with bloodthirsty men,^p
¹⁰in whose hands are wicked schemes,^q
    whose right hands are full of
        bribes.^r
¹¹But I lead a blameless life;
    redeem me^s and be merciful to me.
¹²My feet stand on level ground;^t
    in the great assembly^u I will praise
        the LORD.

Psalm 27

Of David.

¹The LORD is my light^v and my
        salvation^w—

K Ps 20:5–6 ◄ ► Ps 27:1
S Ps 24:3–5 ◄ ► Ps 26:5–6
S Ps 26:1 ◄ ► Ps 29:2
H Ps 21:8–9 ◄ ► Ps 36:12
K Ps 26:1 ◄ ► Ps 36:9
J Ps 23:4 ◄ ► Ps 30:5
W Ps 23:4 ◄ ► Ps 27:14

25:21 ^u Ge 20:5;
  Pr 10:9 ^v 1Ki 9:4;
  Ps 85:10; 111:8;
  Isa 60:17; Mal 2:6
  ^w ver 3
25:22 ^x Ps 130:8;
  Lk 24:21
26:1 ^y S 1Sa 24:15
  ^z Ps 15:2; Pr 20:7
  ^a Ps 22:4; 40:4;
  Isa 12:2; 25:9;
  Jer 17:7; Da 3:28
  ^b 2Ki 20:3;
  Heb 10:23
26:2 ^c Ps 66:10
  ^d Dt 6:6; S Ps 7:9;
  Jer 11:20; 20:12;
  Eze 11:5
26:3 ^e Ps 6:4
  ^f S 1Ki 2:4
  ^g Ps 40:11; 43:3;
  86:11; 119:30
26:4 ^h Ps 1:1
  ^i Ps 28:3; Mt 6:2
26:5 ^j Ps 139:21
26:6 ^k Ps 73:13;
  Mt 27:24
26:7 ^l Isa 42:12;
  60:6 ^m S Jos 3:5;
  Ps 9:1
26:8 ^n Ps 122:6;
  Isa 66:10
  ^o S Ex 29:43;
  2Ch 7:1; Ps 96:6
26:9 ^p Ps 5:6; 28:3;
  55:23; 139:19;
  Pr 29:10
26:10 ^q S Ps 21:11
  ^r S Job 36:18;
  S Isa 1:23;
  S Eze 22:12
26:11 ^s Ps 31:5;
  69:18; 119:134;
  Tit 2:14
26:12 ^t Ps 27:11;
  40:2; 143:10;
  Isa 26:7; 40:3-4;
  45:13; Zec 4:7;
  Lk 6:17
  ^u S Ps 22:25
27:1 ^v S 2Sa 22:29
  ^w S Ex 15:2;
  Ps 3:8
  ^x Ps 9:9
  ^y S Job 13:15;
  Ps 56:4,11; 118:6
27:2 ^z Ps 9:3;
  S 20:8; 37:24;
  Da 11:19; Ro 11:11
27:3 ^a S Ge 4:7;
  S Ps 3:6 ^b Job 4:6
27:4 ^c Lk 10:42
  ^d Ps 23:6; 61:4
27:5 ^e S Job 38:23
  ^f S Ps 12:7
  ^g S Ps 17:8 ^h Ps 40:2
27:6 ^i 2Sa 22:49;
  Ps 3:3; 18:48
  ^j S Ps 22:12
  ^k Ps 50:14; 54:6;
  107:22; 116:17
  ^l S Ezr 3:13;
  S Job 22:26
  ^m S Ex 15:1
  ^n Ps 33:2; 92:1;
  147:7; S Eph 5:19
27:7 ^o Ps 5:3; 18:6;
  55:17; 119:149;
  130:2; Isa 28:23
  ^p S Ps 4:1
27:8 ^q S 1Ch 16:11
27:9 ^r S Dt 31:17;
  S Ps 22:24
  ^s S Ps 2:5
  ^t S Ge 49:25;

whom shall I fear?
The LORD is the stronghold^x of my
        life—
    of whom shall I be afraid?^y
²When evil men advance against me
    to devour my flesh,^w
when my enemies and my foes attack
        me,
    they will stumble and fall.^z
³Though an army besiege me,
    my heart will not fear;^a
though war break out against me,
    even then will I be confident.^b

⁴One thing^c I ask of the LORD,
    this is what I seek:
that I may dwell in the house of the
        LORD
    all the days of my life,^d
to gaze upon the beauty of the LORD
    and to seek him in his temple.
⁵For in the day of trouble^e
    he will keep me safe^f in his
        dwelling;
he will hide me^g in the shelter of his
        tabernacle
    and set me high upon a rock.^h
⁶Then my head will be exalted^i
    above the enemies who surround
        me;^j
at his tabernacle will I sacrifice^k with
        shouts of joy;^l
    I will sing^m and make music^n to the
        LORD.

⁷Hear my voice^o when I call, O LORD;
    be merciful to me and answer me.^p
⁸My heart says of you, "Seek his^x
        face!^q"
    Your face, LORD, I will seek.
⁹Do not hide your face^r from me,
    do not turn your servant away in
        anger;^s
you have been my helper.^t
    Do not reject me or forsake^u me,
    O God my Savior.^v
¹⁰Though my father and mother forsake
        me,
    the LORD will receive me.

V Ps 25:2–3 ◄ ► Ps 34:6
L Ps 23:1–6 ◄ ► Ps 27:10
S Ps 4:8 ◄ ► Ps 31:20
N Job 27:8–9 ◄ ► Ps 49:10–14
L Ps 27:4–5 ◄ ► Ps 31:19–20

S Dt 33:29 ^u Dt 4:31; Ps 37:28; 119:8; Isa 41:17; 62:12; Jer 14:9
^v Ps 18:46

^w 2 Or *to slander me*   ^x 8 Or *To you, O my heart, he has said, "Seek my*

¹¹Teach me your way,ʷ O LORD;
  lead me in a straight pathˣ
  because of my oppressors.ʸ
¹²Do not turn me over to the desire of
    my foes,
  for false witnessesᶻ rise up against
    me,
  breathing out violence.
¹³I am still confident of this:
  I will see the goodness of the LORDᵃ
    in the land of the living.ᵇ
¹⁴Waitᶜ for the LORD;
  be strongᵈ and take heart
  and wait for the LORD.

Psalm 28

Of David.

¹To you I call, O LORD my Rock;
  do not turn a deaf earᵉ to me.
  For if you remain silent,ᶠ
  I will be like those who have gone
    down to the pit.ᵍ
²Hear my cry for mercyʰ
  as I call to you for help,
  as I lift up my handsⁱ
  toward your Most Holy Place.ʲ

³Do not drag me away with the wicked,
  with those who do evil,
  who speak cordially with their
    neighbors
  but harbor malice in their hearts.ᵏ
⁴Repay them for their deeds
  and for their evil work;
  repay them for what their hands have
    doneˡ
  and bring back upon them what
    they deserve.ᵐ
⁵Since they show no regard for the
    works of the LORD
  and what his hands have done,ⁿ
  he will tear them down
  and never build them up again.

⁶Praise be to the LORD,ᵒ
  for he has heard my cry for mercy.ᵖ
⁷The LORD is my strengthᑫ and my
    shield;
  my heart trustsʳ in him, and I am
    helped.

W Ps 27:1 ◀ ▶ Ps 31:24

My heart leaps for joyˢ
  and I will give thanks to him in
    song.ᵗ

⁸The LORD is the strengthᵘ of his people,
  a fortress of salvationᵛ for his
    anointed one.ʷ
⁹Save your peopleˣ and bless your
    inheritance;ʸ
  be their shepherdᶻ and carry themᵃ
    forever.

Psalm 29

A psalm of David.

¹Ascribe to the LORD,ᵇ O mighty ones,ᶜ
  ascribe to the LORD gloryᵈ and
    strength.
²Ascribe to the LORD the glory due his
    name;
  worship the LORD in the splendor of
    hisʸ holiness.ᵉ

³The voiceᶠ of the LORD is over the
    waters;
  the God of gloryᵍ thunders,ʰ
  the LORD thunders over the mighty
    waters.ⁱ
⁴The voice of the LORD is powerful;ʲ
  the voice of the LORD is majestic.
⁵The voice of the LORD breaks the
    cedars;
  the LORD breaks in pieces the cedars
    of Lebanon.ᵏ
⁶He makes Lebanon skipˡ like a calf,
  Sirionᶻᵐ like a young wild ox.ⁿ
⁷The voice of the LORD strikes
  with flashes of lightning.ᵒ
⁸The voice of the LORD shakes the
    desert;
  the LORD shakes the Desert of
    Kadesh.ᵖ
⁹The voice of the LORD twists the oaksᵃᑫ
  and strips the forests bare.
  And in his temple all cry, "Glory!"ʳ

I Ps 14:7 ◀ ▶ Ps 47:3–4
S Ps 26:5–6 ◀ ▶ Ps 34:12–16

29:6 ¹Ps 114:4 ᵐDt 3:9 ⁿS Nu 23:22; Job 39:9; Ps 92:10
29:7 ᵒEze 1:14; Rev 8:5 29:8 ᵖNu 13:26; S 20:1 29:9 ᑫIsa 2:13;
Eze 27:6; Am 2:9 ʳPs 26:8
ʸ2 Or LORD with the splendor of ᶻ6 That is, Mount Hermon
ᵃ9 Or LORD makes the deer give birth

28:9 David appealed to the Lord to save and bless his people. Note the eternal nature of this appeal that forms a restatement of God's covenant with his people to care for them forever.

¹⁰The LORD sits[b] enthroned over the
    flood;[s]
  the LORD is enthroned as King
    forever.[t]
¹¹The LORD gives strength to his people;[u]
  the LORD blesses his people with
    peace.[v]

Psalm 30

A psalm. A song. For the dedication of the
temple.[c] Of David.

¹I will exalt[w] you, O LORD,
  for you lifted me out of the depths[x]
  and did not let my enemies gloat
    over me.[y]
²O LORD my God, I called to you for
    help[z]
  and you healed me.[a]
³O LORD, you brought me up from the
    grave[d],[b]
  you spared me from going down into
    the pit.[c]

⁴Sing[d] to the LORD, you saints[e] of his;
  praise his holy name.[f]
⁵For his anger[g] lasts only a moment,[h]
  but his favor lasts a lifetime;[i]
weeping[j] may remain for a night,
  but rejoicing comes in the morning.[k]

⁶When I felt secure, I said,
  "I will never be shaken."[l]
⁷O LORD, when you favored me,
  you made my mountain[e] stand firm;
but when you hid your face,[m]
  I was dismayed.

⁸To you, O LORD, I called;
  to the Lord I cried for mercy:
⁹"What gain is there in my
    destruction,[f]
  in my going down into the pit?[n]
Will the dust praise you?
  Will it proclaim your faithfulness?[o]
¹⁰Hear,[p] O LORD, and be merciful to me;[q]
  O LORD, be my help.[r]"

¹¹You turned my wailing[s] into dancing;[t]
  you removed my sackcloth[u] and
    clothed me with joy,[v]
¹²that my heart may sing to you and not
    be silent.

E Job 42:16–17 ◀▶ Ps 103:3
L Ps 22:26 ◀▶ Ps 32:5
M Ps 25:11 ◀▶ Ps 34:18
J Ps 27:1 ◀▶ Ps 31:14

O LORD my God, I will give you
    thanks[w] forever.[x]

Psalm 31

31:1–4pp — Ps 71:1–3

For the director of music. A psalm of David.

¹In you, O LORD, I have taken refuge;[y]
  let me never be put to shame;
  deliver me in your righteousness.[z]
²Turn your ear to me,[a]
  come quickly to my rescue;[b]
be my rock of refuge,[c]
  a strong fortress to save me.
³Since you are my rock and my
    fortress,[d]
  for the sake of your name[e] lead and
    guide me.
⁴Free me from the trap[f] that is set for
    me,
  for you are my refuge.[g]
⁵Into your hands I commit my spirit;[h]
  redeem me, O LORD, the God of
    truth.[i]

⁶I hate those who cling to worthless
    idols;[j]
  I trust in the LORD.[k]
⁷I will be glad and rejoice in your love,
  for you saw my affliction[l]
  and knew the anguish[m] of my soul.
⁸You have not handed me over[n] to the
    enemy
  but have set my feet in a spacious
    place.[o]

⁹Be merciful to me, O LORD, for I am in
    distress;[p]
  my eyes grow weak with sorrow,[q]
  my soul and my body[r] with grief.
¹⁰My life is consumed by anguish[s]
  and my years by groaning;[t]
my strength fails[u] because of my
    affliction,[g][v]
  and my bones grow weak.[w]
¹¹Because of all my enemies,[x]
  I am the utter contempt[y] of my
    neighbors;[z]
I am a dread to my friends—
  those who see me on the street flee
    from me.
¹²I am forgotten by them as though I
    were dead;[a]
  I have become like broken pottery.
¹³For I hear the slander[b] of many;

[b] 10 Or sat [c] Title: Or palace [d] 3 Hebrew Sheol [e] 7 Or hill country
[f] 9 Or there if I am silenced [g] 10 Or guilt

PSALM 31:14

there is terror on every side;^c
they conspire against me^d
and plot to take my life.^e

¹⁴But I trust^f in you, O LORD;
I say, "You are my God."
¹⁵My times^g are in your hands;
deliver me from my enemies
and from those who pursue me.
¹⁶Let your face shine^h on your servant;
save me in your unfailing love.ⁱ
¹⁷Let me not be put to shame,^j
O LORD,
for I have cried out to you;
but let the wicked be put to shame
and lie silent^k in the grave.^h
¹⁸Let their lying lips^l be silenced,
for with pride and contempt
they speak arrogantly^m against the righteous.

¹⁹How great is your goodness,ⁿ
which you have stored up for those who fear you,
which you bestow in the sight of men^o
on those who take refuge^p in you.
²⁰In the shelter^q of your presence you hide^r them
from the intrigues of men;^s
in your dwelling you keep them safe
from accusing tongues.

²¹Praise be to the LORD,^t
for he showed his wonderful love^u to me
when I was in a besieged city.^v
²²In my alarm^w I said,
"I am cut off^x from your sight!"
Yet you heard my cry^y for mercy
when I called to you for help.

²³Love the LORD, all his saints!^z
The LORD preserves the faithful,^a
but the proud he pays back^b in full.
²⁴Be strong and take heart,^c
all you who hope in the LORD.

J Ps 30:5 ◄ ► Ps 42:5
L Ps 27:10 ◄ ► Ps 31:23
U Ps 25:14 ◄ ► Ps 31:23
S Ps 27:5 ◄ ► Ps 31:23
L Ps 31:19–20 ◄ ► Ps 32:8
S Ps 31:20 ◄ ► Ps 32:6–7
U Ps 31:19–20 ◄ ► Ps 32:1–2
W Ps 27:14 ◄ ► Ps 37:1

31:13
^c S Job 18:11;
Isa 13:8; Jer 6:25;
20:3,10; 46:5;
49:5; La 2:22
^d Ps 41:7; 56:6;
71:10; 83:3
^e S Ge 37:18;
S Mt 12:14

31:14 ^f Ps 4:5
31:15 ^g S Job 14:5
31:16 ^h S Nu 6:25
ⁱ S Ps 6:4

31:17 ^j S Ps 22:5
^k 1Sa 2:9; Ps 94:17;
115:17

31:18 ^l Ps 120:2;
Pr 10:18; 26:24
^m S 1Sa 2:3;
Jude 1:15

31:19 ⁿ S Ps 27:13;
Ro 11:22 ^o Ps 23:5
^p Ps 2:12

31:20 ^q Ps 55:8
^r S Ps 17:8
^s S Ge 37:18

31:21 ^t Ps 28:6
^u S Ps 17:7
^v 1Sa 23:7

31:22 ^w Ps 116:11
^x Job 6:9; 17:1;
Ps 37:9; 88:5;
Isa 38:12 ^y Ps 6:9;
66:19; 116:1;
145:19

31:23 ^z S Ps 4:3
^a S Ps 18:25;
Rev 2:10
^b Dt 32:41; Ps 94:2

31:24 ^c Ps 27:14

32:1 ^d Ps 85:2; 103:3

32:2 ^e S Ro 4:7-8*
^f Jn 1:47; Rev 14:5

32:3 ^g S Job 31:34
^h Ps 31:10
ⁱ S Job 3:24; Ps 6:6

32:4 ^j 1Sa 5:6;
S Job 9:34; Ps 38:2;
39:10 ^k Ps 22:15

32:5 ^l Job 31:33
^m Pr 28:13
ⁿ Ps 103:12
^o S Lev 26:40;
1Jn 1:9

32:6 ^p Ps 69:13;
Isa 55:6
^q S Ex 15:10
^r Ps 69:1 ^s Isa 43:2

32:7 ^t S Jdg 9:35
^u Ps 9:9 ^v S Jdg 5:1

32:8 ^w S Ps 25:8
^x Ps 34:11
^y Ps 33:18

32:9 ^z S Job 30:11;
S 39:10; Jas 3:3

32:10 ^a Ro 2:9
^b Ps 4:5; Pr 16:20

Psalm 32

Of David. A *maskil*.ⁱ

¹Blessed is he
whose transgressions are forgiven,
whose sins are covered.^d
²Blessed is the man
whose sin the LORD does not count against him^e
and in whose spirit is no deceit.^f

³When I kept silent,^g
my bones wasted away^h
through my groaningⁱ all day long.
⁴For day and night
your hand was heavy^j upon me;
my strength was sapped^k
as in the heat of summer. *Selah*

⁵Then I acknowledged my sin to you
and did not cover up my iniquity.^l
I said, "I will confess^m
my transgressionsⁿ to the LORD"—
and you forgave
the guilt of my sin.^o *Selah*

⁶Therefore let everyone who is godly pray to you
while you may be found;^p
surely when the mighty waters^q rise,^r
they will not reach him.^s
⁷You are my hiding place;^t
you will protect me from trouble^u
and surround me with songs of deliverance.^v *Selah*

⁸I will instruct^w you and teach you^x in the way you should go;
I will counsel you and watch over^y you.
⁹Do not be like the horse or the mule,
which have no understanding
but must be controlled by bit and bridle^z
or they will not come to you.
¹⁰Many are the woes of the wicked,^a
but the LORD's unfailing love
surrounds the man who trusts^b in him.

U Ps 31:23 ◄ ► Ps 32:10–11
L Ps 30:5 ◄ ► Ps 34:8
P 2Ch 30:9 ◄ ► Ps 78:38
R Job 42:6 ◄ ► Ps 34:14
S Ps 31:23 ◄ ► Ps 34:14
L Ps 31:23 ◄ ► Ps 34:7–10
U Ps 32:1–2 ◄ ► Ps 34:9

^h 17 Hebrew *Sheol* ⁱ Title: Probably a literary or musical term

¹¹Rejoice in the LORD^c and be glad, you righteous;
sing, all you who are upright in heart!

Psalm 33

¹Sing joyfully^d to the LORD, you righteous;
it is fitting^e for the upright^f to praise him.
²Praise the LORD with the harp;^g
make music to him on the ten-stringed lyre.^h
³Sing to him a new song;ⁱ
play skillfully, and shout for joy.^j

⁴For the word of the LORD is right^k and true;^l
he is faithful^m in all he does.
⁵The LORD loves righteousness and justice;ⁿ
the earth is full of his unfailing love.^o

⁶By the word^p of the LORD were the heavens made,^q
their starry host^r by the breath of his mouth.
⁷He gathers the waters^s of the sea into jars;^{j,t}
he puts the deep into storehouses.

⁸Let all the earth fear the LORD;^u
let all the people of the world^v revere him.^w
⁹For he spoke, and it came to be;
he commanded,^x and it stood firm.

¹⁰The LORD foils^y the plans^z of the nations;^a
he thwarts the purposes of the peoples.
¹¹But the plans of the LORD stand firm^b forever,
the purposes^c of his heart through all generations.

¹²Blessed is the nation whose God is the LORD,^d
the people he chose^e for his inheritance.^f

¹³From heaven the LORD looks down^g
and sees all mankind;^h
¹⁴from his dwelling placeⁱ he watches all who live on earth—
¹⁵he who forms^j the hearts of all,
who considers everything they do.^k

¹⁶No king is saved by the size of his army;^l
no warrior escapes by his great strength.
¹⁷A horse^m is a vain hope for deliverance;
despite all its great strength it cannot save.

¹⁸But the eyesⁿ of the LORD are on those who fear him,
on those whose hope is in his unfailing love,^o
¹⁹to deliver them from death^p
and keep them alive in famine.^q

²⁰We wait^r in hope for the LORD;
he is our help and our shield.
²¹In him our hearts rejoice,^s
for we trust in his holy name.^t
²²May your unfailing love^u rest upon us, O LORD,
even as we put our hope in you.

Psalm 34^k

Of David. When he pretended to be insane^v before Abimelech, who drove him away, and he left.

¹I will extol the LORD at all times;^w
his praise will always be on my lips.
²My soul will boast^x in the LORD;
let the afflicted hear and rejoice.^y
³Glorify the LORD^z with me;
let us exalt^a his name together.

⁴I sought the LORD,^b and he answered me;
he delivered^c me from all my fears.
⁵Those who look to him are radiant;^d
their faces are never covered with shame.^e
⁶This poor man called, and the LORD heard him;
he saved him out of all his troubles.^f
⁷The angel of the LORD^g encamps around those who fear him,
and he delivers^h them.

F Ps 23:5 ◀ ▶ Ps 34:9–10
T Ps 22:25 ◀ ▶ Ps 35:18
V Ps 27:3 ◀ ▶ Ps 34:17
L Ps 32:8 ◀ ▶ Ps 34:15

^h Ps 22:4; 37:40; 41:1; 97:10; Isa 31:5; Ac 12:11

i 7 Or *sea as into a heap*   ^k This psalm is an acrostic poem, the verses of which begin with the successive letters of the Hebrew alphabet.

E Ps 11:4 ◀ ▶ Ps 44:21

⁸Taste and see that the LORD is good;
 blessed is the man who takes
  refuge in him.
⁹Fear the LORD, you his saints,
 for those who fear him lack
  nothing.
¹⁰The lions may grow weak and hungry,
 but those who seek the LORD lack no
  good thing.
¹¹Come, my children, listen to me;
 I will teach you the fear of the
  LORD.
¹²Whoever of you loves life
 and desires to see many good days,
¹³keep your tongue from evil
 and your lips from speaking lies.
¹⁴Turn from evil and do good;
 seek peace and pursue it.
¹⁵The eyes of the LORD are on the
  righteous
 and his ears are attentive to their
  cry;
¹⁶the face of the LORD is against those
  who do evil,
 to cut off the memory of them from
  the earth.
¹⁷The righteous cry out, and the LORD
  hears them;
 he delivers them from all their
  troubles.
¹⁸The LORD is close to the
  brokenhearted
 and saves those who are crushed in
  spirit.
¹⁹A righteous man may have many
  troubles,
 but the LORD delivers him from them
  all;

²⁰he protects all his bones,
 not one of them will be broken.
²¹Evil will slay the wicked;
 the foes of the righteous will be
  condemned.
²²The LORD redeems his servants;
 no one will be condemned who
  takes refuge in him.

Psalm 35

Of David.

¹Contend, O LORD, with those who
  contend with me;
 fight against those who fight against
  me.
²Take up shield and buckler;
 arise and come to my aid.
³Brandish spear and javelin
 against those who pursue me.
Say to my soul,
 "I am your salvation."
⁴May those who seek my life
 be disgraced and put to shame;
 may those who plot my ruin
 be turned back in dismay.
⁵May they be like chaff before the
  wind,
 with the angel of the LORD driving
  them away;
⁶may their path be dark and slippery,
 with the angel of the LORD pursuing
  them.
⁷Since they hid their net for me
  without cause
 and without cause dug a pit for me,
⁸may ruin overtake them by
  surprise—
 may the net they hid entangle them,
 may they fall into the pit, to their
  ruin.
⁹Then my soul will rejoice in the LORD
 and delight in his salvation.
¹⁰My whole being will exclaim,
 "Who is like you, O LORD?
You rescue the poor from those too
  strong for them,
 the poor and needy from those who
  rob them."

¹³ Or and block the way

¹¹Ruthless witnessesⁱ come forward;
  they question me on things I know
    nothing about.
¹²They repay me evil for goodʲ
  and leave my soul forlorn.
¹³Yet when they were ill, I put on
    sackclothᵏ
  and humbled myself with fasting.ˡ
  When my prayers returned to me
    unanswered,
¹⁴   I went about mourningᵐ
  as though for my friend or brother.
  I bowed my head in grief
  as though weeping for my mother.
¹⁵But when I stumbled, they gathered in
    glee;ⁿ
  attackers gathered against me when
    I was unaware.
  They slanderedᵒ me without
    ceasing.
¹⁶Like the ungodly they maliciously
    mocked;ᵐ'ᵖ
  they gnashed their teethᑫ at me.
¹⁷O Lord, how longʳ will you look on?
  Rescue my life from their ravages,
  my precious lifeˢ from these lions.ᵗ

¹⁸I will give you thanks in the great
    assembly;ᵘ
  among throngsᵛ of people I will
    praise you.ʷ

¹⁹Let not those gloat over me
  who are my enemiesˣ without
    cause;
  let not those who hate me without
    reasonʸ
  maliciously wink the eye.ᶻ
²⁰They do not speak peaceably,
  but devise false accusationsᵃ
  against those who live quietly in the
    land.
²¹They gapeᵇ at me and say, "Aha! Aha!ᶜ
  With our own eyes we have seen
    it."

²²O Lord, you have seenᵈ this; be not
    silent.
  Do not be farᵉ from me, O Lord.
²³Awake,ᶠ and riseᵍ to my defense!
  Contendʰ for me, my God and Lord.
²⁴Vindicate me in your righteousness,
    O Lord my God;
  do not let them gloatⁱ over me.
²⁵Do not let them think, "Aha,ʲ just
    what we wanted!"

or say, "We have swallowed him
    up."ᵏ
²⁶May all who gloatˡ over my distressᵐ
  be put to shameⁿ and confusion;
  may all who exalt themselves
    over meᵒ
  be clothed with shame and
    disgrace.
²⁷May those who delight in my
    vindicationᵖ
  shout for joyᑫ and gladness;
  may they always say, "The Lord be
    exalted,
  who delightsʳ in the well-being of
    his servant."ˢ
²⁸My tongue will speak of your
    righteousnessᵗ
  and of your praises all day long.ᵘ

Psalm 36

*For the director of music. Of David the
servant of the Lord.*

¹An oracle is within my heart
    concerning the sinfulness of the
      wicked:ⁿ'ᵛ
  There is no fearʷ of God
    before his eyes.ˣ
²For in his own eyes he flatters
    himself
  too much to detect or hate his sin.ʸ
³The words of his mouthᶻ are wicked
    and deceitful;ᵃ
  he has ceased to be wiseᵇ and to do
    good.ᶜ
⁴Even on his bed he plots evil;ᵈ
  he commits himself to a sinful
    courseᵉ
  and does not reject what is wrong.ᶠ

⁵Your love, O Lord, reaches to the
    heavens,
  your faithfulnessᵍ to the skies.ʰ
⁶Your righteousnessⁱ is like the mighty
    mountains,ʲ
  your justice like the great deep.ᵏ
  O Lord, you preserve both man and
    beast.ˡ

⁷   How priceless is your unfailing
      love!ᵐ
  Both high and low among men

C Ps 17:14 ◀▶ Ps 38:4–5
L Ps 34:22 ◀▶ Ps 37:39–40

ᵐ 16 Septuagint; Hebrew may mean *ungodly circle of mockers.*
ⁿ 1 Or *heart: / Sin proceeds from the wicked.*

T Ps 34:1–3 ◀▶ Ps 40:10

find° refuge in the shadow of your wings.ⁿ
⁸They feast on the abundance of your house;°
you give them drink from your riverᵖ of delights.ᵩ
⁹For with you is the fountain of life;ʳ
in your lightˢ we see light.
¹⁰Continue your loveᵗ to those who know you,ᵘ
your righteousness to the upright in heart.ᵛ
¹¹May the foot of the proud not come against me,
nor the hand of the wickedʷ drive me away.
¹²See how the evildoers lie fallen—
thrown down, not able to rise!ˣ

Psalm 37ᵖ

Of David.

¹Do not fret because of evil men
or be enviousʸ of those who do wrong;ᶻ
²for like the grass they will soon wither,ᵃ
like green plants they will soon die away.ᵇ
³Trust in the LORD and do good;
dwell in the landᶜ and enjoy safe pasture.ᵈ
⁴Delightᵉ yourself in the LORD
and he will give you the desires of your heart.ᶠ
⁵Commit your way to the LORD;
trust in himᵍ and he will do this:
⁶He will make your righteousnessʰ shine like the dawn,ⁱ

the justice of your cause like the noonday sun.
⁷Be stillʲ before the LORD and wait patientlyᵏ for him;
do not fretˡ when men succeed in their ways,ᵐ
when they carry out their wicked schemes.ⁿ
⁸Refrain from anger° and turn from wrath;
do not fretᵖ—it leads only to evil.
⁹For evil men will be cut off,ᵩ
but those who hopeʳ in the LORD will inherit the land.ˢ
¹⁰A little while, and the wicked will be no more;ᵗ
though you look for them, they will not be found.
¹¹But the meek will inherit the landᵘ
and enjoy great peace.ᵛ
¹²The wicked plotʷ against the righteous
and gnash their teethˣ at them;
¹³but the Lord laughs at the wicked,
for he knows their day is coming.ʸ
¹⁴The wicked draw the swordᶻ
and bend the bowᵃ
to bring down the poor and needy,ᵇ
to slay those whose ways are upright.
¹⁵But their swords will pierce their own hearts,ᶜ
and their bows will be broken.ᵈ
¹⁶Better the little that the righteous have
than the wealthᵉ of many wicked;
¹⁷for the power of the wicked will be broken,ᶠ
but the LORD upholdsᵍ the righteous.

K Ps 27:1 ◀ ▶ Ps 37:27–28
O Ps 18:31 ◀ ▶ Ps 62:11–12
H Ps 26:9 ◀ ▶ Ps 37:12–13
W Ps 31:24 ◀ ▶ Ps 37:5
F Ps 34:22 ◀ ▶ Ps 84:12
S Ps 34:12–16 ◀ ▶ Ps 37:8–9
F Ps 34:9–10 ◀ ▶ Ps 37:19
S Ps 34:12–15 ◀ ▶ Ps 46:1
U Ps 34:12–15 ◀ ▶ Ps 37:17–19
W Ps 37:1 ◀ ▶ Ps 42:5

S Ps 37:3 ◀ ▶ Ps 37:27
N Job 26:10 ◀ ▶ Ps 37:11
N Ps 37:9 ◀ ▶ Ps 37:22
H Ps 36:12 ◀ ▶ Ps 37:20
U Ps 37:4–6 ◀ ▶ Ps 37:23–28

o 7 Or *love, O God! / Men find*; or *love! / Both heavenly beings and men / find* *p* This psalm is an acrostic poem, the stanzas of which begin with the successive letters of the Hebrew alphabet.

37:9–34 Several times throughout this passage the psalmist says that God will ultimately punish and "cut off" those who choose to reject his mercy and forgiveness. However, those "who hope in the LORD" (37:9) will ultimately be blessed forever in Christ's Messianic kingdom when they "inherit the land" (37:22) and witness with their own eyes God's final judgment of the wicked (37:34).

¹⁸The days of the blameless are known
    to the Lord,ʰ
  and their inheritance will endure
    forever.ⁱ
¹⁹In times of disaster they will not
    wither;
  in days of famine they will enjoy
    plenty.
²⁰But the wicked will perish:ʲ
  The Lord's enemies will be like the
    beauty of the fields,
  they will vanish—vanish like
    smoke.ᵏ

²¹The wicked borrow and do not repay,
  but the righteous give generously;ˡ
²²those the Lord blesses will inherit the
    land,
  but those he cursesᵐ will be cut off.ⁿ

²³If the Lord delightsᵒ in a man's way,
  he makes his steps firm;ᵖ
²⁴though he stumble, he will not fall,ᵠ
  for the Lord upholdsʳ him with his
    hand.

²⁵I was young and now I am old,
  yet I have never seen the righteous
    forsakenˢ
  or their children beggingᵗ bread.
²⁶They are always generous and lend
    freely;ᵘ
  their children will be blessed.ᵛ
²⁷Turn from evil and do good;ʷ
  then you will dwell in the land
    forever.ˣ
²⁸For the Lord loves the just
  and will not forsake his faithful
    ones.ʸ

They will be protected forever,
  but the offspring of the wicked will
    be cut off;ᶻ
²⁹the righteous will inherit the landᵃ
  and dwell in it forever.ᵇ

37:18
ʰ S Job 23:10;
Ps 44:21 ⁱ ver 27,29
37:20 ʲ S Ps 34:21
ᵏ Ps 68:2; 102:3;
Isa 51:6
37:21
ˡ Lev 25:35;
Ps 112:5
37:22 ᵐ S Job 5:3
ⁿ ver 9
37:23 ᵒ S Nu 14:8;
Ps 147:11
ᵖ S Job 11:15;
S Ps 7:9; 66:9
37:24 ᵠ S Ps 13:4;
27:2; S 38:17; 55:22;
119:165; Pr 3:23;
10:9 ʳ 2Ch 9:8;
Ps 41:12; 145:14
37:25 ˢ ver 28;
S Ge 15:1;
Heb 13:5
ᵗ Ps 111:5; 145:15;
Mk 10:46
37:26
ᵘ S Lev 25:35
ᵛ Dt 28:4; Ps 112:2
37:27 ʷ Ps 34:14;
3Jn 1:11
ˣ S Nu 24:21
37:28 ʸ Dt 7:6;
S Ps 18:25; S 97:10
ᶻ S Ge 17:14;
S Dt 32:26; Pr 2:22
37:29 ᵃ ver 9;
Pr 2:21 ᵇ Isa 34:17
37:30 ᶜ Ps 49:3;
Pr 10:13
37:31 ᵈ S Dt 6:6;
S Job 22:22
ᵉ S Dt 32:35
37:32 ᶠ S Ps 10:8
ᵍ Ps 11:5
37:33 ʰ Job 32:3;
Ps 34:22; 79:11
ⁱ 2Pe 2:9
37:34 ʲ Ps 27:14
ᵏ S Ps 18:21 ˡ ver 9
ᵐ Ps 52:6
37:35 ⁿ S Job 5:3
37:36 ᵒ ver 10;
Pr 12:7; Isa 41:12;
Da 11:19
37:37 ᵖ ver 18;
S Ge 6:9; Ps 18:25
ᵠ Ps 11:7
ʳ Isa 57:1-2
37:38 ˢ S Ps 1:1
ᵗ S ver 2; Ps 73:19
ᵘ ver 9
37:39 ᵛ S Ps 3:8
ʷ Ps 9:9
37:40
ˣ S 1Ch 5:20;
S Ps 20:2
ʸ S Ps 34:7
ᶻ S Ps 18:48
ᵃ Ps 2:12

---

³⁰The mouth of the righteous man utters
    wisdom,ᶜ
  and his tongue speaks what is just.
³¹The law of his God is in his heart;ᵈ
  his feet do not slip.ᵉ

³²The wicked lie in waitᶠ for the
    righteous,ᵍ
  seeking their very lives;
³³but the Lord will not leave them in
    their power
  or let them be condemnedʰ when
    brought to trial.ⁱ

³⁴Wait for the Lordʲ
  and keep his way.ᵏ
He will exalt you to inherit the
    land;
  when the wicked are cut off,ˡ you
    will seeᵐ it.

³⁵I have seen a wicked and ruthless
    man
  flourishingⁿ like a green tree in its
    native soil,
³⁶but he soon passed away and was no
    more;
  though I looked for him, he could
    not be found.ᵒ

³⁷Consider the blameless,ᵖ observe the
    upright;ᵠ
  there is a futureᵠ for the man of
    peace.ʳ
³⁸But all sinnersˢ will be destroyed;ᵗ
  the futureʳ of the wicked will be cut
    off.ᵘ

³⁹The salvationᵛ of the righteous comes
    from the Lord;
  he is their stronghold in time of
    trouble.ʷ
⁴⁰The Lord helpsˣ them and deliversʸ
    them;
  he delivers them from the wicked
    and savesᶻ them,
  because they take refugeᵃ in him.

F Ps 37:3 ◀ ▶ Ps 37:25
H Ps 37:12–13 ◀ ▶ Ps 37:38
N Ps 37:11 ◀ ▶ Ps 37:29
U Ps 37:17–19 ◀ ▶ Ps 37:31
F Ps 37:19 ◀ ▶ Ps 78:15–16
R Job 42:15 ◀ ▶ Ps 102:28
K Ps 36:9 ◀ ▶ Ps 40:2
R Ps 34:18 ◀ ▶ Ps 38:18
S Ps 37:8–9 ◀ ▶ Ps 37:29–31
N Ps 37:22 ◀ ▶ Ps 37:34
S Ps 37:27 ◀ ▶ Ps 37:34

U Ps 37:23–28 ◀ ▶ Ps 37:37
V Ps 35:10 ◀ ▶ Ps 41:2
N Ps 37:29 ◀ ▶ Ps 75:3
P Ps 18:7–15 ◀ ▶ Ps 45:1–5
S Ps 37:29–31 ◀ ▶ Ps 37:37–38
S Ps 37:34 ◀ ▶ Ps 50:16
U Ps 37:31 ◀ ▶ Ps 41:1–3
H Ps 37:20 ◀ ▶ Ps 50:3
L Ps 36:7–8 ◀ ▶ Ps 46:1

ᵠ 37 Or *there will be posterity* ʳ 38 Or *posterity*

Psalm 38

A psalm of David. A petition.

¹ O LORD, do not rebuke me in your anger
   or discipline me in your wrath.
² For your arrows have pierced me,
   and your hand has come down upon me.
³ Because of your wrath there is no health in my body;
   my bones have no soundness because of my sin.
⁴ My guilt has overwhelmed me
   like a burden too heavy to bear.
⁵ My wounds fester and are loathsome
   because of my sinful folly.
⁶ I am bowed down and brought very low;
   all day long I go about mourning.
⁷ My back is filled with searing pain;
   there is no health in my body.
⁸ I am feeble and utterly crushed;
   I groan in anguish of heart.
⁹ All my longings lie open before you, O Lord;
   my sighing is not hidden from you.
¹⁰ My heart pounds, my strength fails me;
    even the light has gone from my eyes.
¹¹ My friends and companions avoid me because of my wounds;
    my neighbors stay far away.
¹² Those who seek my life set their traps,
    those who would harm me talk of my ruin;
    all day long they plot deception.
¹³ I am like a deaf man, who cannot hear,
    like a mute, who cannot open his mouth;
¹⁴ I have become like a man who does not hear,
    whose mouth can offer no reply.
¹⁵ I wait for you, O LORD;
    you will answer, O Lord my God.
¹⁶ For I said, "Do not let them gloat
    or exalt themselves over me when my foot slips."
¹⁷ For I am about to fall,
    and my pain is ever with me.
¹⁸ I confess my iniquity;
    I am troubled by my sin.
¹⁹ Many are those who are my vigorous enemies;
    those who hate me without reason are numerous.
²⁰ Those who repay my good with evil
    slander me when I pursue what is good.
²¹ O LORD, do not forsake me;
    be not far from me, O my God.
²² Come quickly to help me,
    O Lord my Savior.

Psalm 39

For the director of music. For Jeduthun. A psalm of David.

¹ I said, "I will watch my ways
   and keep my tongue from sin;
   I will put a muzzle on my mouth
   as long as the wicked are in my presence."
² But when I was silent and still,
   not even saying anything good,
   my anguish increased.
³ My heart grew hot within me,
   and as I meditated, the fire burned;
   then I spoke with my tongue:
⁴ "Show me, O LORD, my life's end
   and the number of my days;
   let me know how fleeting is my life.
⁵ You have made my days a mere handbreadth;
   the span of my years is as nothing before you.
   Each man's life is but a breath.
       Selah
⁶ Man is a mere phantom as he goes to and fro;
   He bustles about, but only in vain;
   he heaps up wealth, not knowing who will get it.
⁷ "But now, Lord, what do I look for?
   My hope is in you.
⁸ Save me from all my transgressions;
   do not make me the scorn of fools.

⁹I was silent;° I would not open my mouth,ᵖ
for you are the one who has done this.ᵍ
¹⁰Remove your scourge from me;
I am overcome by the blowʳ of your hand.ˢ
¹¹You rebukeᵗ and disciplineᵘ men for their sin;
you consumeᵛ their wealth like a mothʷ—
each man is but a breath.ˣ   *Selah*

¹²"Hear my prayer, O Lᴏʀᴅ,
listen to my cry for help;ʸ
be not deafᶻ to my weeping.ᵃ
For I dwell with you as an alien,ᵇ
a stranger,ᶜ as all my fathers were.ᵈ
¹³Look away from me, that I may rejoice again
before I depart and am no more."ᵉ

Psalm 40

40:13–17pp — Ps 70:1–5

For the director of music. Of David. A psalm.

¹I waited patientlyᶠ for the Lᴏʀᴅ;
he turned to me and heard my cry.ᵍ
²He lifted me out of the slimy pit,ʰ
out of the mudⁱ and mire;ʲ
he set my feetᵏ on a rockˡ
and gave me a firm place to stand.
³He put a new songᵐ in my mouth,
a hymn of praise to our God.
Many will see and fearⁿ
and put their trust° in the Lᴏʀᴅ.
⁴Blessed is the manᵖ
who makes the Lᴏʀᴅ his trust,ᵍ
who does not look to the proud,ʳ
to those who turn aside to false gods.ˢ*
⁵Many, O Lᴏʀᴅ my God,
are the wondersᵗ you have done.
The things you planned for us
no one can recountᵘ to you;
were I to speak and tell of them,
they would be too manyᵛ to declare.

⁶Sacrifice and offering you did not desire,ʷ
but my ears you have pierced,ᵗ,ᵘ,ˣ
burnt offeringsʸ and sin offerings
you did not require.
⁷Then I said, "Here I am, I have come—
it is written about me in the scroll.ᵛ,ᶻ
⁸I desire to do your will,ᵃ O my God;ᵇ
your law is within my heart."ᶜ
⁹I proclaim righteousnessᵈ in the great assembly;ᵉ
I do not seal my lips,
as you know,ᶠ O Lᴏʀᴅ.
¹⁰I do not hide your righteousness in my heart;
I speak of your faithfulnessᵍ and salvation.
I do not conceal your love and your truth
from the great assembly.ʰ

¹¹Do not withhold your mercyⁱ from me, O Lᴏʀᴅ;
may your loveʲ and your truthᵏ
always protectˡ me.
¹²For troublesᵐ without number surround me;
my sins have overtaken me, and I cannot see.ⁿ
They are more than the hairs of my head,°
and my heart failsᵖ within me.

¹³Be pleased, O Lᴏʀᴅ, to save me;
O Lᴏʀᴅ, come quickly to help me.ᵍ
¹⁴May all who seek to take my lifeʳ
be put to shame and confusion;ˢ
may all who desire my ruinᵗ
be turned back in disgrace.
¹⁵May those who say to me, "Aha! Aha!"ᵘ
be appalled at their own shame.
¹⁶But may all who seek youᵛ
rejoice and be gladʷ in you;
may those who love your salvation
always say,
"The Lᴏʀᴅ be exalted!"ˣ

¹⁷Yet I am poor and needy;ʸ
may the Lord thinkᶻ of me.
You are my helpᵃ and my deliverer;ᵇ
O my God, do not delay.ᶜ

s 4 Or *to falsehood* *t 6* Hebrew; Septuagint *but a body you have prepared for me* (see also Symmachus and Theodotion) *u 6* Or *opened* *v 7* Or *come* / *with the scroll written for me*

Psalm 41

For the director of music. A psalm of David.

¹Blessed is he who has regard for the weak;
the LORD delivers him in times of trouble.
²The LORD will protect him and preserve his life;
he will bless him in the land
and not surrender him to the desire of his foes.
³The LORD will sustain him on his sickbed
and restore him from his bed of illness.

⁴I said, "O LORD, have mercy on me;
heal me, for I have sinned against you."
⁵My enemies say of me in malice,
"When will he die and his name perish?"
⁶Whenever one comes to see me,
he speaks falsely, while his heart gathers slander;
then he goes out and spreads it abroad.

⁷All my enemies whisper together against me;
they imagine the worst for me, saying,
⁸"A vile disease has beset him;
he will never get up from the place where he lies."
⁹Even my close friend, whom I trusted,
he who shared my bread,
has lifted up his heel against me.

¹⁰But you, O LORD, have mercy on me;
raise me up, that I may repay them.
¹¹I know that you are pleased with me,
for my enemy does not triumph over me.
¹²In my integrity you uphold me
and set me in your presence forever.

¹³Praise be to the LORD, the God of Israel,
from everlasting to everlasting.
Amen and Amen.

BOOK II

Psalms 42–72

Psalm 42ʷ

For the director of music. A *maskil* of the Sons of Korah.

¹As the deer pants for streams of water,
so my soul pants for you, O God.
²My soul thirsts for God, for the living God.
When can I go and meet with God?
³My tears have been my food day and night,
while men say to me all day long,
"Where is your God?"
⁴These things I remember as I pour out my soul:
how I used to go with the multitude,
leading the procession to the house of God,
with shouts of joy and thanksgiving among the festive throng.

⁵Why are you downcast, O my soul?
Why so disturbed within me?
Put your hope in God,
for I will yet praise him,
my Savior and ⁶my God.

My soul is downcast within me;
therefore I will remember you
from the land of the Jordan,

ʷ In many Hebrew manuscripts Psalms 42 and 43 constitute one psalm.
ˣ Title: Probably a literary or musical term ʸ 5,6 A few Hebrew manuscripts, Septuagint and Syriac; most Hebrew manuscripts *praise him for his saving help.* / ⁶O my God, my

---

41:9 David's prophecy of betrayal by a close friend prefigures two future events: the betrayal of King David and the betrayal of Jesus. David's trusted counselor Ahithophel betrayed him by joining Absalom's rebellion and advising David's son how to defeat his father and steal his throne. The words of this psalm also portend the betrayal of Jesus Christ by Judas Iscariot for thirty pieces of silver (see Jn 13:18–19).

the heights of Hermon[d]—from
  Mount Mizar.
⁷Deep calls to deep[e]
  in the roar of your waterfalls;
all your waves and breakers
  have swept over me.[f]

⁸By day the LORD directs his love,[g]
  at night[h] his song[i] is with me—
  a prayer to the God of my life.[j]

⁹I say to God my Rock,[k]
  "Why have you forgotten[l] me?
Why must I go about mourning,[m]
  oppressed[n] by the enemy?"[o]
¹⁰My bones suffer mortal agony[p]
  as my foes taunt[q] me,
saying to me all day long,
  "Where is your God?"[r]

¹¹Why are you downcast, O my soul?
  Why so disturbed within me?
Put your hope in God,
  for I will yet praise him,
  my Savior and my God.[s]

Psalm 43[z]

¹Vindicate me, O God,
  and plead my cause[t] against an
    ungodly nation;
rescue me[u] from deceitful and
  wicked men.[v]
²You are God my stronghold.
  Why have you rejected[w] me?
Why must I go about mourning,[x]
  oppressed by the enemy?[y]
³Send forth your light[z] and your truth,[a]
  let them guide me;[b]
let them bring me to your holy
  mountain,[c]
to the place where you dwell.[d]
⁴Then will I go[e] to the altar[f] of God,
  to God, my joy[g] and my delight.[h]
I will praise you with the harp,[i]
  O God, my God.

⁵Why are you downcast, O my soul?
  Why so disturbed within me?
Put your hope in God,
  for I will yet praise him,
  my Savior and my God.[j]

J Ps 42:5 ◀▶ Ps 42:11
J Ps 42:7–8 ◀▶ Ps 43:5
W Ps 42:5 ◀▶ Ps 43:5
J Ps 42:11 ◀▶ Ps 46:1–3
W Ps 42:11 ◀▶ Ps 55:22

42:6 ᵈ S Dt 3:8; S 4:48
42:7 ᵉ S Ge 1:2; S 7:11 ᶠ Ps 69:2; Jnh 2:3
42:8 ᵍ Ps 57:3 ʰ S Ps 16:7 ⁱ Ps 77:6 ʲ Ps 133:3; Ecc 5:18; 8:15
42:9 ᵏ Ps 18:31 ˡ S Ps 10:11 ᵐ S Ps 35:14 ⁿ Job 20:19; Ps 43:2; 106:42 ᵒ Ps 9:13; 43:2
42:10 ᵖ S Ps 6:2 ᑫ Dt 32:27; Ps 44:16; 89:51; 102:8; 119:42 ʳ S ver 3
42:11 ˢ ver 5; Ps 43:5
43:1 ᵗ S Jdg 6:31 ᵘ Ps 25:20 ᵛ Ps 36:3; 109:2
43:2 ʷ Ps 44:9; 74:1; 88:14; 89:38 ˣ S Ps 35:14 ʸ Ps 42:9
43:3 ᶻ Ps 27:1 ᵃ S Ps 26:3 ᵇ S Ps 25:5 ᶜ Ps 2:6 ᵈ S 2Sa 15:25
43:4 ᵉ S Ps 42:2 ᶠ Ps 26:6; 84:3 ᵍ S Ps 21:6 ʰ Ps 16:3 ⁱ S Ge 4:21
43:5 ʲ S Ps 42:6
44:1 ᵏ 2Sa 7:22; 1Ch 17:20; Jer 26:11
ˡ S Jdg 6:13 ᵐ S Dt 32:7; S Job 37:23
44:2 ⁿ S Jos 3:10; Ac 7:45 ᵒ S Ex 15:17; S Isa 60:21 ᵖ S Jdg 4:23; S 2Ch 14:13
ᑫ Ps 80:9; Jer 32:23
44:3 ʳ Jos 24:12 ˢ Ps 78:54 ᵗ Ex 15:16; Ps 77:15; 79:11; 89:10; 98:1; Isa 40:10; 52:10; 63:5 ᵘ Ps 89:15 ᵛ S Dt 4:37
44:4 ʷ S Ps 24:7 ˣ Ps 5:2 ʸ S Ps 21:5
44:5 ᶻ S Jos 23:5 ᵃ Ps 60:12; 108:13
44:6 ᵇ Ge 48:22; Hos 1:7
44:7 ᶜ S Dt 20:4 ᵈ S Job 8:22
44:8 ᵉ S Ps 34:2; 1Co 1:31; 2Co 10:17 ᶠ Ps 52:1 ᵍ S Ps 30:12
44:9 ʰ S Ps 43:2 ⁱ S Dt 8:3; S 31:17; Ps 107:39; Isa 5:15 ʲ S Jos 7:12; Ps 108:11
44:10 ᵏ Lev 26:17 ˡ S Jdg 2:14
44:11 ᵐ ver 22; Jer 12:3 ⁿ S Lev 26:33; S Ps 9:11; Eze 6:8; Zec 2:6

Psalm 44

For the director of music. Of the Sons of Korah. A *maskil*.[a]

¹We have heard with our ears,[k] O God;
  our fathers have told us[l]
what you did in their days,
  in days long ago.[m]
²With your hand you drove out[n] the
    nations
  and planted[o] our fathers;
you crushed[p] the peoples
  and made our fathers flourish.[q]
³It was not by their sword[r] that they
    won the land,
  nor did their arm bring them
    victory;
it was your right hand,[s] your arm,[t]
  and the light[u] of your face, for you
    loved[v] them.

⁴You are my King[w] and my God,[x]
  who decrees[b] victories[y] for Jacob.
⁵Through you we push back[z] our
    enemies;
  through your name we trample[a] our
    foes.
⁶I do not trust in my bow,[b]
  my sword does not bring me victory;
⁷but you give us victory[c] over our
    enemies,
  you put our adversaries to shame.[d]
⁸In God we make our boast[e] all day
    long,[f]
  and we will praise your name
    forever.[g]   *Selah*

⁹But now you have rejected[h] and
    humbled us;[i]
  you no longer go out with our
    armies.[j]
¹⁰You made us retreat[k] before the
    enemy,
  and our adversaries have plundered[l]
    us.
¹¹You gave us up to be devoured like
    sheep[m]
  and have scattered us among the
    nations.[n]
¹²You sold your people for a pittance,[o]
  gaining nothing from their sale.

V Ps 41:11 ◀▶ Ps 50:15

44:12 ᵒ S Dt 32:30; Isa 52:3; Jer 15:13; 50:1; 52:3; Jer 15:13

ᶻ In many Hebrew manuscripts Psalms 42 and 43 constitute one psalm.
ᵃ Title: Probably a literary or musical term ᵇ 4 Septuagint, Aquila and Syriac; Hebrew *King, O God; / command*

¹³You have made us a reproach to our neighbors,
  the scorn and derision of those around us.
¹⁴You have made us a byword among the nations;
  the peoples shake their heads at us.
¹⁵My disgrace is before me all day long,
  and my face is covered with shame
¹⁶at the taunts of those who reproach and revile me,
  because of the enemy, who is bent on revenge.

¹⁷All this happened to us,
  though we had not forgotten you
  or been false to your covenant.
¹⁸Our hearts had not turned back;
  our feet had not strayed from your path.
¹⁹But you crushed us and made us a haunt for jackals
  and covered us over with deep darkness.

²⁰If we had forgotten the name of our God
  or spread out our hands to a foreign god,
²¹would not God have discovered it,
  since he knows the secrets of the heart?
²²Yet for your sake we face death all day long;
  we are considered as sheep to be slaughtered.

²³Awake, O Lord! Why do you sleep?
  Rouse yourself! Do not reject us forever.
²⁴Why do you hide your face
  and forget our misery and oppression?
²⁵We are brought down to the dust;
  our bodies cling to the ground.
²⁶Rise up and help us;
  redeem us because of your unfailing love.

Psalm 45

For the director of music. To the tune of "Lilies." Of the Sons of Korah. A *maskil*. A wedding song.

¹My heart is stirred by a noble theme
  as I recite my verses for the king;
  my tongue is the pen of a skillful writer.

²You are the most excellent of men
  and your lips have been anointed with grace,
  since God has blessed you forever.
³Gird your sword upon your side, O mighty one;
  clothe yourself with splendor and majesty.
⁴In your majesty ride forth victoriously
  in behalf of truth, humility and righteousness;
  let your right hand display awesome deeds.
⁵Let your sharp arrows pierce the hearts of the king's enemies;
  let the nations fall beneath your feet.
⁶Your throne, O God, will last for ever and ever;
  a scepter of justice will be the scepter of your kingdom.
⁷You love righteousness and hate wickedness;
  therefore God, your God, has set you above your companions
  by anointing you with the oil of joy.
⁸All your robes are fragrant with myrrh and aloes and cassia;
  from palaces adorned with ivory
  the music of the strings makes you glad.
⁹Daughters of kings are among your honored women;
  at your right hand is the royal bride in gold of Ophir.

Title: Probably a literary or musical term

45:1–6 This psalm describes the certainty of Messiah's victory over his enemies at the end of the tribulation period and the establishment of his eternal throne and sceptre (see Ge 49:10).

¹⁰Listen, O daughter, consider and
    give ear:
  Forget your people and your
    father's house.
¹¹The king is enthralled by your beauty;
  honor him, for he is your lord.
¹²The Daughter of Tyre will come with
    a gift,
  men of wealth will seek your favor.
¹³All glorious is the princess within
    ⸤her chamber⸥;
  her gown is interwoven with gold.
¹⁴In embroidered garments she is led to
    the king;
  her virgin companions follow her
    and are brought to you.
¹⁵They are led in with joy and gladness;
    they enter the palace of the king.
¹⁶Your sons will take the place of your
    fathers;
  you will make them princes
    throughout the land.
¹⁷I will perpetuate your memory through
    all generations;
  therefore the nations will praise
    you for ever and ever.

Psalm 46

For the director of music. Of the Sons of Korah. According to alamoth. *A song.*

¹God is our refuge and strength,
    an ever-present help in trouble.
²Therefore we will not fear, though
    the earth give way
  and the mountains fall into the
    heart of the sea,
³though its waters roar and foam
  and the mountains quake with
    their surging. *Selah*

H ▶ SS 1:4   T ▶ SS 1:4
M Ps 24:7–10 ◀▶ Ps 46:4–11
J Ps 43:5 ◀▶ Ps 56:3–4
L Ps 37:39–40 ◀▶ Ps 48:14
S Ps 37:4–6 ◀▶ Ps 91:1–16

45:10 ˣRu 1:11
  ʸJer 5:1 ᶻRu 1:16
45:11 ᵃS Est 1:11;
  S La 2:15
  ᵇEph 5:33 ᶜ1Pe 3:6
45:12 ᵈS Jos 19:29
  ᵉS 1Ki 9:16;
  S 2Ch 9:24
45:13 ᶠIsa 61:10
  ᵍEx 39:3
45:14 ʰS Jdg 5:30
  ⁱEst 2:15 ʲSS 1:3
45:15 ᵏS Est 8:17
45:16 ˡIsa 2:8;
  Ps 68:27; 113:8
45:17 ᵐS Ex 3:15;
  Ps 33:11; 119:90;
  135:13 ᵐPs 138:4
  ᵒS Ps 21:4;
  Rev 22:5
46:1 ᵖPs 9:9;
  37:39; 61:3; 73:26;
  91:2,9; 142:5;
  Isa 33:16;
  Jer 16:19; 17:17;
  Joel 3:16; Na 1:7
  ᵠPs 18:1 ʳPs 34:18;
  La 3:57 ˢPs 18:6;
  Lk 1:54 ᵗS Dt 4:30;
  Ps 25:17
46:2 ᵘS Ge 4:7;
  Ps 3:6 ᵛPs 82:5;
  Isa 13:13; 24:1,19,
  Da 11:19; Am 8:14;
  S Rev 6:14 ʷver 6;
  Ps 18:7; 97:5;
  Isa 54:10; Am 9:5;
  Mic 1:4; Na 1:5;
  Hab 3:6 ˣEx 15:8
46:3 ʸPs 93:3;
  Rev 22:1 ᶻS Job 9:26
  ᵃS Jdg 5:5
46:4 ᵇS Ge 2:10;
  ᶜPs 48:1,8; 87:3;
  101:8; Rev 3:12
  ᵉGe 14:18
  ᶠS 2Sa 15:25
46:5 ᵈDt 23:14;
  S Ps 26:8; Isa 12:6;
  Zec 2:5 ʰPs 125:1
  ⁱS 1Ch 5:20
46:6 ʲS Job 12:23
  ᵏPs 74:23; Isa 5:30;
  17:12 ˡPs 68:32;
  102:22; Isa 13:4,
  13; 23:11;
  Eze 26:18; Mt 4:8
  ᵐS Ps 29:3;
  Isa 33:3 ⁿS ver 2
46:7 ᵒS 1Sa 1:11
  ᵖS Ge 21:22
  ᵠS Ps 20:1 ʳver 11;
  Ps 18:2
46:8 ˢPs 66:5
  ᵗIsa 17:9; 64:10;
  Da 9:26; Lk 21:20

---

⁴There is a river whose streams make
    glad the city of God,
  the holy place where the Most
    High dwells.
⁵God is within her, she will not fall;
    God will help her at break of day.
⁶Nations are in uproar, kingdoms
    fall;
  he lifts his voice, the earth melts.
⁷The LORD Almighty is with us;
    the God of Jacob is our fortress.
              Selah
⁸Come and see the works of the LORD,
    the desolations he has brought on
    the earth.
⁹He makes wars cease to the ends of
    the earth;
  he breaks the bow and shatters the
    spear,
  he burns the shields with fire.
¹⁰"Be still, and know that I am God;
    I will be exalted among the nations,
    I will be exalted in the earth."
¹¹The LORD Almighty is with us;
    the God of Jacob is our fortress.
              Selah

Psalm 47

For the director of music. Of the Sons of Korah. A psalm.

¹Clap your hands, all you nations;
    shout to God with cries of joy.
²How awesome is the LORD Most
    High,

M Ps 45:16 ◀▶ Ps 47:1–9
P Ps 45:1–5 ◀▶ Ps 50:3
M Ps 46:4–11 ◀▶ Ps 48:2

46:9 ᵘIsa 2:4 ᵛS Ps 37:15; S Isa 22:6 ʷIsa 9:5; Eze 39:9; Hos 2:18
46:10 ˣDt 4:35; 1Ki 18:36,39; Ps 100:3; Isa 37:16,20; 43:11; 45:21;
  Eze 36:23 ʸPs 18:46; Isa 2:11 46:11 ᶻS Ps 20:1 ᵃS ver 7
47:1 ᵇS 2Ki 11:12 ᶜS Ps 33:3 47:2 ᵈS Dt 7:21 ᵉGe 14:18

ᵈ 12 Or *A Tyrian robe is among the gifts* ᵉ Title: Probably a musical term
ᶠ 9 Or *chariots*

45:14–16 David prophetically described the resurrected saints and the glorious marriage supper of the Lamb (see Mt 22:2–14; 25:10–13; Rev 19:7–9).

46:4–5 David foresaw the joy and peace that would accompany Christ's presence in Jerusalem during the millennial kingdom of God on earth.

46:6–11 This psalm celebrates the security of Jerusalem as God's great city as it declares the effects of God's triumph over the nations. These words also prophetically envision God's climactic salvation in the birth, life, death, resurrection and second coming of Christ. Only when the Messiah rules in his kingdom will Israel experience this glorious peace.

47:1–9 This psalm exalts the glorious and powerful victory of God over the heathen enemies of Israel and foreshadows God's rule through Jesus Christ in the millennial kingdom. God will vindicate those who

the great King[f] over all the earth!
³He subdued[g] nations under us,
  peoples under our feet.
⁴He chose our inheritance[h] for us,
  the pride of Jacob,[i] whom he loved.
      Selah

⁵God has ascended[j] amid shouts of
    joy,[k]
  the LORD amid the sounding of
    trumpets.[l]
⁶Sing praises[m] to God, sing praises;
  sing praises to our King, sing
    praises.
⁷For God is the King of all the earth;[n]
  sing to him a psalm[g][o] of praise.
⁸God reigns[p] over the nations;
  God is seated on his holy throne.[q]
⁹The nobles of the nations assemble
    as the people of the God of
    Abraham,
  for the kings[h] of the earth belong to
    God;[r]
  he is greatly exalted.[s]

Psalm 48

A song. A psalm of the Sons of Korah.

¹Great is the LORD,[t] and most worthy of
    praise,[u]
  in the city of our God,[v] his holy
    mountain.[w]
²It is beautiful[x] in its loftiness,
  the joy of the whole earth.
Like the utmost heights of Zaphon[j][y] is
    Mount Zion,[z]
  the[j] city of the Great King.[a]
³God is in her citadels;[b]
  he has shown himself to be her
    fortress.[c]
⁴When the kings joined forces,
  when they advanced together,[d]
⁵they saw ⌊her⌋ and were astounded;
  they fled in terror.[e]

I *Ps 28:9 ◄ ► Ps 50:5*
M *Ps 47:1-9 ◄ ► Ps 48:8*

47:2 [f]Ps 2:6; 48:2; 95:3; Mt 5:35
47:3 [g]Ps 18:39,47; Isa 14:6
47:4 [h]Ps 2:8; 16:6; 78:55; 1Pe 1:4
  [i]Am 6:8; 8:7
47:5 [j]Ps 68:18; Eph 4:8
  [k]S Job 8:21; S Ps 106:5
  [l]S Nu 10:2; S 2Sa 6:15
47:6 [m]S 2Sa 22:50
47:7 [n]Zec 14:9
  [o]1Ch 16:7; Col 3:16
47:8 [p]S 1Ch 16:31
  [q]S 1Ki 22:19; S Ps 9:4; Rev 4:9
47:9 [r]S Job 25:2
  [s]Ps 46:10; 97:9
48:1 [t]Ps 86:10; 96:4; 99:2; 135:5; 147:5; Jer 10:6
  [u]S 2Sa 22:4; S 1Ch 16:25; Ps 18:3 vS Ps 46:4
  [w]S Dt 33:19; Ps 2:6; 87:1; Isa 11:9; 32:16; Jer 31:23; Da 9:16; Mic 4:1; Zec 8:3
48:2 [x]Ps 50:2; La 2:15; Eze 16:14
  [y]S Jos 13:27
  [z]S Ps 2:6 [a]Mt 5:35
48:3 [b]ver 13; Ps 122:7 [c]Ps 18:2
48:4 [d]2Sa 10:1-19
48:5 [e]Ex 15:16; Isa 13:8; Jer 46:5; Da 5:9
48:6 [f]S Job 4:14
  [g]S Ge 3:16
48:7 [h]S Ge 10:4; S 1Ki 10:22; 22:48
  [i]S Ge 41:6
48:8 [j]Jer 23:6; Zec 8:13; 14:11
48:9 [k]S Ps 39:3
  [l]Ps 6:4
48:10 [m]S Ex 6:3; S Jos 7:9 [n]1Sa 2:10; Ps 22:27; 65:5; 98:3; 100:1; Isa 11:12; 24:16; 42:10; 49:6
48:11 [o]Ps 97:8
48:12 [p]S Ne 3:1
48:13 [q]2Sa 20:15; Isa 26:1; La 2:8; Hab 2:1 [r]S ver 3
  [s]Ps 71:18; 78:6; 109:13
48:14 [t]Ps 25:5; 73:24; Pr 6:22; Isa 49:10; 57:11; 58:11
49:1 [u]Isa 1:2
  [v]Ps 78:1

⁶Trembling seized[f] them there,
  pain like that of a woman in labor.[g]
⁷You destroyed them like ships of
    Tarshish[h]
  shattered by an east wind.[i]

⁸As we have heard,
  so have we seen
in the city of the LORD Almighty,
  in the city of our God:
God makes her secure forever.[j]
      Selah

⁹Within your temple, O God,
  we meditate[k] on your unfailing
    love.[l]
¹⁰Like your name,[m] O God,
  your praise reaches to the ends of
    the earth;[n]
  your right hand is filled with
    righteousness.
¹¹Mount Zion rejoices,
  the villages of Judah are glad
  because of your judgments.[o]
¹²Walk about Zion, go around her,
  count her towers,[p]
¹³consider well her ramparts,[q]
  view her citadels,[r]
that you may tell of them to the next
    generation.[s]
¹⁴For this God is our God for ever and
    ever;
  he will be our guide[t] even to the
    end.

Psalm 49

For the director of music. Of the Sons of Korah. A psalm.

¹Hear[u] this, all you peoples;[v]
  listen, all who live in this world,[w]

M *Ps 48:2 ◄ ► Ps 50:1-2*
L *Ps 46:1 ◄ ► Ps 50:15*

[w] *Ps 33:8*

[g] 7 Or a *maskil* (probably a literary or musical term) [h] 9 Or *shields*
[i] 2 *Zaphon* can refer to a sacred mountain or the direction north.
[j] 2 Or *earth, / Mount Zion, on the northern side / of the*

---

have faith in him and will defeat the armies of the ungodly nations.

48:2 David likened Jerusalem to Mt. Zaphon, the residence of the Phoenicians' chief god El, thus signifying that Mt. Zion is "the joy of the whole earth" and abode of the only true God.

48:12-13 This curious command to walk around the city and take note of its construction would ultimately serve two purposes. Not only would it give the current residents of Jerusalem a sense of God's blessing in providing such a beautiful city for his habitation, but by remembering the city and sharing its wonders with future generations, those who ultimately returned from Babylonian exile would have verbal reminders to help them rebuild the city and its temple.

²both low and high,ˣ
    rich and poor alike:
³My mouth will speak words of
    wisdom;ʸ
    the utterance from my heart will
    give understanding.ᶻ
⁴I will turn my ear to a proverb;ᵃ
    with the harpᵇ I will expound my
    riddle:ᶜ
⁵Why should I fearᵈ when evil days
    come,
    when wicked deceivers surround
    me—
⁶those who trust in their wealthᵉ
    and boastᶠ of their great riches?ᵍ
⁷No man can redeem the life of another
    or give to God a ransom for him—
⁸the ransomʰ for a life is costly,
    no payment is ever enough—ⁱ
⁹that he should live onʲ forever
    and not see decay.ᵏ
¹⁰For all can see that wise men die;ˡ
    the foolish and the senselessᵐ alike
    perish
    and leave their wealthⁿ to others.ᵒ
¹¹Their tombsᵖ will remain their houses
    forever,
    their dwellings for endless
    generations,ᵠ
    though theyⁱ namedʳ lands after
    themselves.
¹²But man, despite his riches, does not
    endure;ˢ
    he isᵐ like the beasts that perish.ᵗ
¹³This is the fate of those who trust in
    themselves,ᵘ
    and of their followers, who approve
    their sayings.   *Selah*
¹⁴Like sheep they are destinedᵛ for the
    grave,ⁿʷ
    and death will feed on them.
    The upright will ruleˣ over them in the
    morning;
    their forms will decay in the grave,ⁿ
    far from their princely mansions.
¹⁵But God will redeem my lifeᵒ from the
    grave;ʸ
    he will surely take me to himself.ᶻ
                                    Selah

N Ps 27:8 ◀ ▶ Ps 78:39

49:2 ˣ Ps 62:9
49:3 ʸ S Ps 37:30
  ᶻ Ps 119:130
49:4 ᵃ Ps 78:2;
  Pr 1:6; Eze 12:22;
  16:44; 18:2,3;
  Lk 4:23
  ᵇ S 1Sa 16:16;
  Ps 33:2 ᶜ S Nu 12:8
49:5 ᵈ Ps 23:4;
  27:1
49:6 ᵉ S Job 22:25;
  Ps 73:12; Jer 48:7
  ᶠ S Ps 10:3
  ᵍ S Job 36:19
49:8 ʰ S Nu 35:31
  ⁱ Mt 16:26
49:9 ʲ Ps 22:29;
  89:48 ᵏ Ps 16:10
49:10 ˡ Ecc 2:16
  ᵐ Ps 92:6; 94:8
  ⁿ S Job 27:17
  ᵒ Ecc 2:18,21;
  Lk 12:20
49:11 ᵖ Mk 5:3;
  Lk 8:27 ᵠ Ps 106:31
  ʳ S Dt 3:14
49:12 ˢ S Job 14:2
  ᵗ ver 20; 2Pe 2:12
49:13 ᵘ Lk 12:20
49:14 ʲ Jer 43:11;
  Eze 31:14
  ʷ Nu 16:30;
  S Job 21:13;
  Ps 9:17; 55:15
  ˣ Isa 14:2; Da 7:18;
  1Co 6:2
49:15 ʸ Ps 56:13;
  Hos 13:14
  ᶻ S Ge 5:24
49:17 ᵃ 1Ti 6:7
  ᵇ S Ps 17:14
49:18 ᶜ Ps 10:6;
  Lk 12:19
49:19 ᵈ S Ge 15:15
  ᵉ Job 33:30
49:20 ᶠ Pr 16:16
  ᵍ S ver 12
50:1 ʰ Jos 22:22
  ⁱ Ps 113:3
50:2 ʲ Ps 2:6
  ᵏ S Ps 48:2;
  S La 2:15
  ˡ S Dt 33:2
50:3 ᵐ Ps 96:13
  ⁿ ver 21; Isa 42:14;
  64:12; 65:6
  ᵒ S Lev 10:2
  ᵖ S Ps 18:8
  ᵠ Job 37:9;
  Ps 83:15; 107:25;
  147:18; Isa 29:6;
  30:28; Jnh 1:4;
  Na 1:3
50:4 ʳ Dt 4:26;
  31:28; Isa 1:2
  ˢ Heb 10:30
50:5 ᵗ S Dt 7:6;
  S Ps 18:25
  ᵘ Ex 24:7;
  S 2Ch 6:11
50:6 ᵛ S Ps 19:1
  ʷ S Ge 16:5;
  S Job 9:15

¹⁶Do not be overawed when a man
    grows rich,
    when the splendor of his house
    increases;
¹⁷for he will take nothingᵃ with him
    when he dies,
    his splendor will not descend with
    him.ᵇ
¹⁸Though while he lived he counted
    himself blessed—ᶜ
    and men praise you when you
    prosper—
¹⁹he will join the generation of his
    fathers,ᵈ
    who will never see the lightᵉ ⌊of life⌋.
²⁰A man who has riches without
    understandingᶠ
    is like the beasts that perish.ᵍ

Psalm 50

A psalm of Asaph.

¹The Mighty One, God, the LORD,ʰ
    speaks and summons the earth
    from the rising of the sun to the
    place where it sets.ⁱ
²From Zion,ʲ perfect in beauty,ᵏ
    God shines forth.ˡ
³Our God comesᵐ and will not be
    silent;ⁿ
    a fire devoursᵒ before him,ᵖ
    and around him a tempestᵠ rages.
⁴He summons the heavens above,
    and the earth,ʳ that he may judge
    his people:ˢ
⁵"Gather to me my consecrated ones,ᵗ
    who made a covenantᵘ with me by
    sacrifice."
⁶And the heavens proclaimᵛ his
    righteousness,
    for God himself is judge.ʷ   *Selah*

M Ps 48:8 ◀ ▶ Ps 50:4–6
W Ps 34:22 ◀ ▶ Ps 86:5
P Ps 46:6–9 ◀ ▶ Ps 59:5
H Ps 37:38 ◀ ▶ Ps 55:23
J Ps 9:7–8 ◀ ▶ Ps 67:4
M Ps 50:1–2 ◀ ▶ Ps 66:4
I Ps 47:3–4 ◀ ▶ Ps 53:6

ᵏ 11 Septuagint and Syriac; Hebrew *In their thoughts their houses will remain*   ˡ 11 Or */ for they have*   ᵐ 12 Hebrew; Septuagint and Syriac read verse 12 the same as verse 20.   ⁿ 14 Hebrew *Sheol*; also in verse 15   ᵒ 15 Or *soul*

50:1–6 This psalm of Asaph warns the Israelites that the God of Zion is the God of the covenant (see Ex 19:16–20), and he is coming to correct and rebuke his people for their sins.

⁷"Hear, O my people, and I will speak,
  O Israel, and I will testify against
    you:
  I am God, your God.
⁸I do not rebuke you for your sacrifices
  or your burnt offerings, which are
    ever before me.
⁹I have no need of a bull from your
    stall
  or of goats from your pens,
¹⁰for every animal of the forest is mine,
  and the cattle on a thousand hills.
¹¹I know every bird in the mountains,
  and the creatures of the field are
    mine.
¹²If I were hungry I would not tell you,
  for the world is mine, and all that is
    in it.
¹³Do I eat the flesh of bulls
  or drink the blood of goats?
¹⁴Sacrifice thank offerings to God,
  fulfill your vows to the Most High,
¹⁵and call upon me in the day of
    trouble;
  I will deliver you, and you will
    honor me."

¹⁶But to the wicked, God says:

"What right have you to recite my
    laws
  or take my covenant on your lips?
¹⁷You hate my instruction
  and cast my words behind you.
¹⁸When you see a thief, you join with
    him;
  you throw in your lot with
    adulterers.
¹⁹You use your mouth for evil
  and harness your tongue to deceit.
²⁰You speak continually against your
    brother
  and slander your own mother's son.
²¹These things you have done and I kept
    silent;
  you thought I was altogether like
    you.
  But I will rebuke you
  and accuse you to your face.

²²"Consider this, you who forget God,
  or I will tear you to pieces, with
    none to rescue:

²³He who sacrifices thank offerings
    honors me,
  and he prepares the way
  so that I may show him the
    salvation of God.'"

Psalm 51

For the director of music. A psalm of David. When the prophet Nathan came to him after David had committed adultery with Bathsheba.

¹Have mercy on me, O God,
  according to your unfailing love;
  according to your great compassion
  blot out my transgressions.
²Wash away all my iniquity
  and cleanse me from my sin.

³For I know my transgressions,
  and my sin is always before me.
⁴Against you, you only, have I sinned
  and done what is evil in your sight,
  so that you are proved right when you
    speak
  and justified when you judge.
⁵Surely I was sinful at birth,
  sinful from the time my mother
    conceived me.
⁶Surely you desire truth in the inner
    parts;
  you teach me wisdom in the
    inmost place.

⁷Cleanse me with hyssop, and I will
    be clean;
  wash me, and I will be whiter than
    snow.
⁸Let me hear joy and gladness;
  let the bones you have crushed
    rejoice.
⁹Hide your face from my sins
  and blot out all my iniquity.

¹⁰Create in me a pure heart, O God,

and renew a steadfast spirit within
    me.ᵉ
¹¹Do not castᶠ me from your presenceᵍ
    or take your Holy Spiritʰ from me.
¹²Restore to me the joy of your
        salvationⁱ
    and grant me a willing spirit,ʲ to
        sustain me.ᵏ
¹³Then I will teach transgressors your
        ways,ˡ
    and sinnersᵐ will turn back to you.ⁿ
¹⁴Save meᵒ from bloodguilt,ᵖ O God,
    the God who saves me,ᑫ
    and my tongue will sing of your
        righteousness.ʳ
¹⁵O Lord, open my lips,ˢ
    and my mouth will declare your
        praise.
¹⁶You do not delight in sacrifice,ᵗ or I
        would bring it;
    you do not take pleasure in burnt
        offerings.
¹⁷The sacrificesᵘ of God areᵗ a broken
        spirit;
    a broken and contrite heart,ᵛ
    O God, you will not despise.

¹⁸In your good pleasure make Zionʷ
        prosper;
    build up the walls of Jerusalem.ˣ
¹⁹Then there will be righteous
        sacrifices,ʸ
    whole burnt offeringsᶻ to delight
        you;
    then bullsᵃ will be offered on your
        altar.

Psalm 52

For the director of music. A *maskil*ᵘ
of David. When Doeg the Edomiteᵇ had
gone to Saul and told him: "David has gone
to the house of Ahimelech."

¹Why do you boast of evil, you mighty
        man?
    Why do you boastᶜ all day long,ᵈ

Q *Ne 9:30* ◀ ▶ *Isa 63:10*
B *Ps 45:7* ◀ ▶ *Isa 11:2*
C *Ne 9:30* ◀ ▶ *Ps 139:7*
F *Ps 45:7* ◀ ▶ *Isa 63:14*
J *Ps 45:7* ◀ ▶ *Isa 44:3*
M *Job 33:4* ◀ ▶ *Ps 104:30*
N *Job 33:4* ◀ ▶ *Ps 104:30*
R *Ps 51:10* ◀ ▶ *Isa 4:4*
L *Ps 51:1–3* ◀ ▶ *Ps 65:3*
R *Ps 51:1–3* ◀ ▶ *Ps 126:5*

51:10 ᵉEze 18:31; 36:26
51:11 ᶠPs 27:9; 71:9; 138:8
ᵍS Ge 4:14; S Ex 33:15
ʰPs 106:33; Isa 63:10; Eph 4:30
51:12 ⁱS Job 33:26
ʲPs 110:3
ᵏS Ps 18:35
51:13 ˡS Ex 33:13; Ac 9:21-22
ᵐS Ps 1:1
ⁿS Job 33:27
51:14 ᵒS Ps 39:8
ᵖ2Sa 12:9
ᑫPs 25:5; 68:20; 88:1 ʳS Ps 5:8; 35:28; 71:15
51:15 ˢS Ex 4:15
51:16
ᵗS 1Sa 15:22
51:17 ᵘPr 15:8; Hag 2:14
ᵛMt 11:29
51:18 ʷPs 102:16; 147:2; Isa 14:32; 51:3; Zec 1:16-17
ˣPs 69:35; Isa 44:26
51:19 ʸDt 33:19
ᶻPs 66:13; 96:8; Jer 17:26 ᵃPs 66:15

52 Title ᵇ1Sa 21:7; 22:9
52:1 ᶜPs 10:3; 94:4 ᵈPs 44:8
52:2 ᵉPs 5:9
ᶠNu 6:5
ᵍS Ps 50:19
52:3 ʰEx 10:10; 1Sa 12:25; Am 5:14-15; Jn 3:20 ⁱPs 58:3; Jer 9:5; Rev 21:8
52:4 ʲPs 5:9; 10:7; 109:2; 120:2,3; Pr 10:31; 12:19
52:5 ᵏS Dt 29:28; S Job 40:12; Isa 22:19; Eze 17:24
ˡS Dt 28:63
ᵐS Job 28:13
52:6 ⁿS Job 22:19
52:7 ᵒS 2Sa 22:3
ᵖPs 49:6; S Pr 11:28; Mk 10:23
52:8 ᑫPs 1:3; S Rev 11:4 ʳPs 6:4; 13:5
52:9 ˢS Ps 30:12
ᵗS Job 7:6; Ps 25:3
ᵘPs 54:6 ᵛS Dt 7:6; Ps 16:3
53:1 ʷPs 74:22; 107:17; Pr 10:23
ˣPs 10:4
53:2 ʸS Ps 33:13
ᶻPs 82:5; Jer 4:22; 8:8

you who are a disgrace in the eyes
    of God?
²Your tongue plots destruction;ᵉ
    it is like a sharpened razor,ᶠ
    you who practice deceit.ᵍ
³You love evilʰ rather than good,
    falsehoodⁱ rather than speaking the
        truth.   *Selah*
⁴You love every harmful word,
    O you deceitful tongue!ʲ
⁵Surely God will bring you down to
        everlasting ruin:
    He will snatch you up and tearᵏ you
        from your tent;
    he will uprootˡ you from the land of
        the living.ᵐ   *Selah*
⁶The righteous will see and fear;
    they will laughⁿ at him, saying,
⁷"Here now is the man
    who did not make God his
        strongholdᵒ
    but trusted in his great wealthᵖ
    and grew strong by destroying
        others!"
⁸But I am like an olive treeᑫ
    flourishing in the house of God;
    I trustʳ in God's unfailing love
        for ever and ever.
⁹I will praise you foreverˢ for what you
        have done;
    in your name I will hope,ᵗ for your
        name is good.ᵘ
    I will praise you in the presence of
        your saints.ᵛ

Psalm 53

53:1–6pp — Ps 14:1–7

For the director of music. According to
*mahalath.*ᵛ A *maskil*ᵘ of David.

¹The foolʷ says in his heart,
    "There is no God."ˣ
They are corrupt, and their ways are
        vile;
    there is no one who does good.

²God looks down from heavenʸ
        on the sons of men
    to see if there are any who
        understand,ᶻ

G *Job 15:31* ◀ ▶ *Ps 62:9–11*
A *Ps 14:1–4* ◀ ▶ *Ps 130:3*
C *Ps 51:5* ◀ ▶ *Ps 58:1–3*

ᵗ17 Or *My sacrifice, O God, is*   ᵘTitle: Probably a literary or musical term
ᵛTitle: Probably a musical term

any who seek God.ᵃ
³Everyone has turned away,
 they have together become corrupt;
there is no one who does good,
 not even one.ᵇ
⁴Will the evildoers never learn—
 those who devour my people as men eat bread
 and who do not call on God?
⁵There they were, overwhelmed with dread,
 where there was nothing to dread.ᶜ
God scattered the bonesᵈ of those who attacked you;ᵉ
 you put them to shame,ᶠ for God despised them.ᵍ

⁶Oh, that salvation for Israel would come out of Zion!
 When God restores the fortunes of his people,
 let Jacob rejoice and Israel be glad!

Psalm 54

For the director of music. With stringed instruments. A *maskil*ʷ of David. When the Ziphitesʰ had gone to Saul and said, "Is not David hiding among us?"

¹Save me,ⁱ O God, by your name;ʲ
 vindicate me by your might.ᵏ
²Hear my prayer, O God;ˡ
 listen to the words of my mouth.

³Strangers are attacking me;ᵐ
 ruthless menⁿ seek my life°—
 men without regard for God.ᵖ *Selah*

⁴Surely God is my help;ᑫ
 the Lord is the one who sustains me.ʳ

⁵Let evil recoilˢ on those who slander me;
 in your faithfulnessᵗ destroy them.

⁶I will sacrifice a freewill offeringᵘ to you;
 I will praiseᵛ your name, O Lᴏʀᴅ,
 for it is good.ʷ

I Ps 50:5 ◀ ▶ Ps 68:13
L Ps 50:15 ◀ ▶ Ps 56:8

53:2 ᵃ 2Ch 15:2
53:3 ᵇ Ro 3:10-12*
53:5 ᶜ S Lev 26:17
 ᵈ 2Ki 23:14;
 Ps 141:7; Jer 8:1;
 Eze 6:5 ᵉ 2Ki 17:20
 ᶠ S Job 8:22
 ᵍ Jer 6:30; 14:19;
 La 5:22
54 Title
 ʰ 1Sa 23:19; 26:1
54:1 ⁱ 1Sa 24:15
 ʲ Ps 20:1 ᵏ 2Ch 20:6
54:2 ˡ S Ps 4:1; 5:1;
 55:1
54:3 ᵐ Ps 86:14
 ⁿ Ps 18:48; 140:1,4,
 11 ° S 1Sa 20:1
 ᵖ Ps 36:1
54:4 ᑫ S 1Ch 5:20;
 S Ps 20:2
 ʳ S Ps 18:35
54:5 ˢ S Dt 32:35;
 Ps 94:23; Pr 24:12
 ᵗ Ps 89:49; Isa 42:3
54:6 ᵘ S Lev 7:12,
 16; S Ezr 1:4;
 S Ps 27:6 ᵛ Ps 44:8;
 69:30; 138:2;
 142:7; 145:1
 ʷ Ps 52:9

54:7 ˣ Ps 34:6
 ʸ Ps 59:10; 92:11;
 112:8; 118:7

55:1 ᶻ Ps 27:9;
 La 3:56
55:2 ᵃ Ps 4:1
 ᵇ 1Sa 1:15-16;
 Ps 77:3; 86:6-7;
 142:2
55:3
 ᶜ S 2Sa 16:0-8;
 Ps 17:9; 143:3
 ᵈ S Ps 44:16
 ᵉ Ps 71:11
55:4 ᶠ S Ps 6:3
 ᵍ S Job 18:11
55:5 ʰ S Job 4:14;
 S 2Co 7:15
 ⁱ Dt 28:67; Isa 21:4;
 Jer 46:5; 49:5;
 Eze 7:18
55:7 ʲ 1Sa 23:14
55:8 ᵏ Ps 31:20
 ˡ Ps 77:18; Isa 4:6;
 25:4; 28:2; 29:6;
 32:2
55:9 ᵐ Ge 11:9;
 Ac 2:4 ⁿ Ps 11:5;
 Isa 59:6; Jer 6:7;
 Eze 7:11; Hab 1:3
 ° Ge 4:17
55:10 ᵖ 1Pe 5:8
55:11 ᑫ Ps 5:9
 ʳ Ps 10:7

⁷For he has delivered meˣ from all my troubles,
 and my eyes have looked in triumph on my foes.ʸ

Psalm 55

For the director of music. With stringed instruments. A *maskil*ʷ of David.

¹Listen to my prayer, O God,
 do not ignore my plea;ᶻ
² hear me and answer me.ᵃ
My thoughts trouble me and I am distraughtᵇ
³ at the voice of the enemy,
 at the stares of the wicked;
for they bring down suffering upon meᶜ
 and revileᵈ me in their anger.ᵉ

⁴My heart is in anguishᶠ within me;
 the terrorsᵍ of death assail me.
⁵Fear and tremblingʰ have beset me;
 horrorⁱ has overwhelmed me.
⁶I said, "Oh, that I had the wings of a dove!
 I would fly away and be at rest—
⁷I would flee far away
 and stay in the desert;ʲ *Selah*
⁸I would hurry to my place of shelter,ᵏ
 far from the tempest and storm.ˡ"

⁹Confuse the wicked, O Lord, confound their speech,ᵐ
 for I see violence and strifeⁿ in the city.°
¹⁰Day and night they prowlᵖ about on its walls;
 malice and abuse are within it.
¹¹Destructive forcesᑫ are at work in the city;
 threats and liesʳ never leave its streets.

¹²If an enemy were insulting me,
 I could endure it;
if a foe were raising himself against me,
 I could hide from him.
¹³But it is you, a man like myself,

V Ps 50:15 ◀ ▶ Ps 56:9

ʷ Title: Probably a literary or musical term

53:6 This psalm contains material similar to Ps 14. David longed for the ultimate deliverance of his people from their enemies and that God's kingdom on earth would be established. Then his people could rejoice and be glad.

my companion, my close friend,^s
¹⁴with whom I once enjoyed sweet
   fellowship^t
as we walked with the throng at the
   house of God.^u

¹⁵Let death take my enemies by
   surprise;^v
let them go down alive to the
   grave,^{xw}
for evil finds lodging among them.

¹⁶But I call to God,
   and the LORD saves me.
¹⁷Evening,^x morning^y and noon^z
   I cry out in distress,
   and he hears my voice.
¹⁸He ransoms me unharmed
   from the battle waged against me,
   even though many oppose me.
¹⁹God, who is enthroned forever,^a
   will hear^b them and afflict them—
                                       Selah
men who never change their ways
   and have no fear of God.^c

²⁰My companion attacks his friends;^d
   he violates his covenant.^e
²¹His speech is smooth as butter,^f
   yet war is in his heart;
his words are more soothing than oil,^g
   yet they are drawn swords.^h

²²Cast your cares on the LORD
   and he will sustain you;ⁱ
   he will never let the righteous fall.^j
²³But you, O God, will bring down the
   wicked
   into the pit^k of corruption;
bloodthirsty and deceitful men^l
   will not live out half their days.^m

But as for me, I trust in you.ⁿ

Psalm 56

For the director of music. To the tune of "A
Dove on Distant Oaks." Of David. A
miktam.^y When the Philistines had seized
him in Gath.

¹Be merciful to me,^o O God, for men
   hotly pursue me;^p
   all day long they press their attack.^q
²My slanderers pursue me all day long;^r

K *Ps 51:7* ◀ ▶ *Ps 62:1–2*
K *Ps 51:7* ◀ ▶ *Ps 55:16*
U *Ps 45:7* ◀ ▶ *Ps 64:10*
W *Ps 43:5* ◀ ▶ *Ps 91:5–6*
H *Ps 50:3* ◀ ▶ *Ps 68:1–2*

55:13
^s S 2Sa 15:12
55:14 ^t Ac 1:16-17
^u Ps 42:4
55:15 ^v Ps 64:7;
Pr 6:15; Isa 29:5;
47:9,11; 1Th 5:3
^w S Ps 49:14
55:17 ^x Ps 141:2;
Ac 3:1; 10:3,30
^y Ps 5:3; 88:13;
92:2 ^z Ac 10:9
55:19
^a S Ex 15:18;
Dt 33:27; Ps 29:10
^b Ps 78:59 ^c Ps 36:1;
64:4
55:20 ^d Ps 7:4
^e S Ps 41:9
55:21 ^f Ps 12:2
^g Pr 5:3; 6:24
^h Ps 57:4; 59:7;
64:3; Pr 12:18;
Rev 1:16
55:22 ⁱ S Ps 18:35;
Mt 6:25-34; 1Pe 5:7
^j Ps 15:5; 21:7;
37:24; 112:6
55:23 ^k Ps 9:15;
S 30:3; 73:18;
94:13; Isa 14:15;
Eze 28:8; S Lk 8:31
^l Ps 5:6
^m S Job 15:32
ⁿ Ps 11:1; 25:2;
56:3
56:1 ^o Ps 6:2
^p Ps 57:1-3
^q Ps 17:9
56:2 ^r Ps 35:25;
124:3
^s Ps 35:1
56:3 ^t Ps 55:4-5
^u S Ps 55:23
56:4 ^v ver 10
^w S Ps 27:1
^x Ps 118:6;
Mt 10:28; Heb 13:6
56:5 ^y Ps 41:7;
2Pe 3:16
56:6 ^z Ps 59:3;
94:21; Mk 3:6
^a Ps 17:11
^b Ps 71:10
56:7 ^c Pr 19:5;
Eze 17:15; Ro 2:3;
Heb 12:25
^d Ps 36:12; 55:23
56:8 ^e S 2Ki 20:5
^f Isa 4:3; Da 7:10;
12:1; Mal 3:16
56:9 ^g Ps 9:3
^h Ps 102:2
ⁱ S Nu 14:8;
S Dt 31:6; Ro 8:31
56:12 ^j Ps 50:14
56:13 ^k Ps 30:3;
33:19; 49:15;
86:13; 107:20;
116:8 ^l S Job 33:30
57 Title ^m 1Sa 22:1;
24:3; Ps 142 Title
57:1 ⁿ Ps 2:12; 9:9;
34:22

---

many are attacking me in their
   pride.^s

³When I am afraid,^t
   I will trust in you.^u
⁴In God, whose word I praise,^v
   in God I trust; I will not be afraid.^w
   What can mortal man do to me?^x

⁵All day long they twist my words;^y
   they are always plotting to harm me.
⁶They conspire,^z they lurk,
   they watch my steps,^a
   eager to take my life.^b

⁷On no account let them escape;^c
   in your anger, O God, bring down
     the nations.^d

⁸Record my lament;
   list my tears on your scroll^{ze}—
   are they not in your record?^f

⁹Then my enemies will turn back^g
   when I call for help.^h
By this I will know that God is for
   me.ⁱ

¹⁰In God, whose word I praise,
   in the LORD, whose word I praise—
¹¹in God I trust; I will not be afraid.
   What can man do to me?

¹²I am under vows^j to you, O God;
   I will present my thank offerings to
     you.
¹³For you have delivered me^a from
   death^k
   and my feet from stumbling,
that I may walk before God
   in the light of life.^{bl}

Psalm 57

57:7–11pp — Ps 108:1–5

For the director of music. To the tune of
"Do Not Destroy." Of David. A *miktam*.^y
When he had fled from Saul into the cave.^m

¹Have mercy on me, O God, have
   mercy on me,
   for in you my soul takes refuge.ⁿ

J *Ps 46:1–3* ◀ ▶ *Ps 56:11*
E *Ps 44:21* ◀ ▶ *Ps 66:7*
L *Ps 54:4* ◀ ▶ *Ps 63:3–7*
V *Ps 54:7* ◀ ▶ *Ps 60:12*
J *Ps 56:3–4* ◀ ▶ *Ps 57:1*
J *Ps 56:11* ◀ ▶ *Ps 61:2–4*

^x 15 Hebrew *Sheol*   ^y Title: Probably a literary or musical term   ^z 8 Or / *put my tears in your wineskin*   ^a 13 Or *my soul*   ^b 13 Or *the land of the living*

I will take refuge in the shadow of
   your wings°
   until the disaster has passed.ᵖ
²I cry out to God Most High,
   to God, who fulfills ⌊his purpose⌋ for
      me.q
³He sends from heaven and saves me,ʳ
   rebuking those who hotly pursue
      me;ˢ   Selah
   God sends his love and his
      faithfulness.ᵗ
⁴I am in the midst of lions;ᵘ
   I lie among ravenous beasts—
   men whose teeth are spears and
      arrows,
   whose tongues are sharp swords.ᵛ
⁵Be exalted, O God, above the heavens;
   let your glory be over all the earth.ʷ
⁶They spread a net for my feetˣ—
   I was bowed downʸ in distress.
   They dug a pitᶻ in my path—
   but they have fallen into it
      themselves.ᵃ   Selah
⁷My heart is steadfast, O God,
   my heart is steadfast;ᵇ
   I will sing and make music.
⁸Awake, my soul!
   Awake, harp and lyre!ᶜ
   I will awaken the dawn.
⁹I will praise you, O Lord, among the
      nations;
   I will sing of you among the peoples.
¹⁰For great is your love, reaching to the
      heavens;
   your faithfulness reaches to the
      skies.ᵈ
¹¹Be exalted, O God, above the
      heavens;ᵉ
   let your glory be over all the earth.ᶠ

Psalm 58

For the director of music. ⌊To the tune of⌋
"Do Not Destroy." Of David. A *miktam*.ᶜ

c ¹Do you rulers indeed speak justly?ᵍ
   Do you judge uprightly among men?
²No, in your heart you devise injustice,ʰ
   and your hands mete out violence
      on the earth.ⁱ
³Even from birth the wicked go astray;

c Ps 53:1–4 ◄► Ps 74:18

57:1 °S Ru 2:12;
S Mt 23:37
ᵖ Isa 26:20
57:2 ᵠ Ps 138:8
57:3 ʳ Ps 18:9,16;
69:14; 142:6;
144:5,7 ˢ Ps 56:1
ᵗ Ps 25:10; 40:11;
115:1
57:4 ᵘ S Ps 35:17
ᵛ S Ps 55:21;
Pr 30:14
57:5 ʷ ver 11;
Ps 108:5
57:6 ˣ Ps 10:9;
31:4; 140:5
ʸ S Ps 38:6; 145:14
ᶻ S Ps 9:15
ᵃ S Est 6:13;
Ps 7:15; Pr 28:10;
Ecc 10:8
57:7 ᵇ Ps 112:7
57:8 ᶜ Ps 33:2;
149:3; 150:3
57:10 ᵈ S Ps 36:5
57:11 ᵉ S Ps 8:1;
113:4 ᶠ S ver 5
58:1 ᵍ Ps 82:2
58:2 ʰ Mt 15:19
ⁱ Ps 94:20; Isa 10:1;
Lk 6:38
58:4 ʲ S Nu 21:6
58:5 ᵏ Ps 81:11
ˡ Ecc 10:11; Jer 8:17
58:6 ᵐ Ps 3:7
ⁿ Job 4:10
58:7 ° S Lev 26:36;
S Job 11:16
ᵖ Ps 11:2; 57:4;
64:3
58:8 ᵠ Isa 13:7
ʳ Job 3:16
58:9 ˢ Ps 118:12;
Ecc 7:6 ᵗ S Job 7:10;
S 21:18
58:10
ᵘ S Job 22:19
ᵛ Dt 32:35; Ps 7:9;
91:8; Jer 11:20;
Ro 12:17-21
ʷ Ps 68:23
58:11 ˣ S Ge 15:1;
S Ps 128:2; Lk 6:23
ʸ S Ge 18:25
59 Title ᶻ 1Sa 19:11
59:1 ᵃ Ps 143:9
ᵇ S Ps 20:1
59:2 ᶜ Ps 14:4;
36:12; 53:4; 92:7;
94:16 ᵈ S Ps 26:9;
139:19; Pr 29:10
59:3 ᵉ S Ps 56:0

from the womb they are wayward
   and speak lies.
⁴Their venom is like the venom of a
      snake,ʲ
   like that of a cobra that has stopped
      its ears,
⁵that will not heedᵏ the tune of the
      charmer,ˡ
   however skillful the enchanter may
      be.
⁶Break the teeth in their mouths,
      O God;ᵐ
   tear out, O Lᴏʀᴅ, the fangs of the
      lions!ⁿ
⁷Let them vanish like water that flows
      away;°
   when they draw the bow, let their
      arrows be blunted.ᵖ
⁸Like a slug melting away as it moves
      along,ᵠ
   like a stillborn child,ʳ may they not
      see the sun.
⁹Before your pots can feel ⌊the heat of⌋
      the thornsˢ—
   whether they be green or dry—the
      wicked will be swept away.ᵈᵗ
¹⁰The righteous will be gladᵘ when they
      are avenged,ᵛ
   when they bathe their feet in the
      blood of the wicked.ʷ
¹¹Then men will say,
   "Surely the righteous still are
      rewarded;ˣ
   surely there is a God who judges the
      earth."ʸ

Psalm 59

For the director of music. ⌊To the tune of⌋
"Do Not Destroy." Of David. A *miktam*.ᶜ
When Saul had sent men to watch David's
houseᶻ in order to kill him.

¹Deliver me from my enemies, O God;ᵃ
   protect me from those who rise up
      against me.ᵇ
²Deliver me from evildoersᶜ
   and save me from bloodthirsty
      men.ᵈ
³See how they lie in wait for me!
   Fierce men conspireᵉ against me
   for no offense or sin of mine,
      O Lᴏʀᴅ.

ᶜ Title: Probably a literary or musical term   ᵈ 9 The meaning of the
Hebrew for this verse is uncertain.

⁴I have done no wrong, yet they are ready to attack me.
Arise to help me; look on my plight!

P ⁵O LORD God Almighty, the God of Israel,
rouse yourself to punish all the nations;
show no mercy to wicked traitors.
Selah

⁶They return at evening,
snarling like dogs,
and prowl about the city.
⁷See what they spew from their mouths—
they spew out swords from their lips,
and they say, "Who can hear us?"

P ⁸But you, O LORD, laugh at them;
you scoff at all those nations.

⁹O my Strength, I watch for you;
you, O God, are my fortress, ¹⁰my loving God.

God will go before me
and will let me gloat over those who slander me.
¹¹But do not kill them, O Lord our shield,
or my people will forget.
In your might make them wander about,
and bring them down.
¹²For the sins of their mouths,
for the words of their lips,
let them be caught in their pride.
For the curses and lies they utter,
¹³ consume them in wrath,
consume them till they are no more.
Then it will be known to the ends of the earth
that God rules over Jacob. *Selah*

¹⁴They return at evening,
snarling like dogs,
and prowl about the city.
¹⁵They wander about for food
and howl if not satisfied.

P Ps 50:3 ◀ ▶ Ps 59:8
P Ps 59:5 ◀ ▶ Ps 66:3

59:4 ᶠPs 119:3
ᵍMt 5:11
ʰS Ps 13:3
59:5 ⁱPs 69:6; 80:4; 84:8
ʲS Ps 44:23
ᵏS Ps 9:5;
S Isa 10:3
ˡJer 18:23
59:6 ᵐver 14;
Ps 22:16
59:7 ⁿPs 94:4; Pr 10:32; 12:23; 15:2,28
ᵒS Ps 55:21
ᵖS Job 22:13
59:8 ᵠPs 37:13; Pr 1:26 ʳPs 2:4
59:9 ˢS Ps 18:1
ᵗPs 9:9; 18:2; 62:2; 71:3
59:11 ᵘPs 3:3; 84:9 ᵛDt 4:9; 6:12
ʷPs 89:10; 106:27; 144:6; Isa 33:3
59:12 ˣPs 10:7
ʸPs 64:8; Pr 10:14; 12:13 ᶻIsa 2:12; 5:15; Zep 3:11
59:13 ᵃPs 104:35
ᵇPs 83:18
59:15 ᶜJob 15:23
59:16 ᵈPs 108:1
ᵉS 1Sa 2:10
ᶠPs 5:3; 88:13
ᵍPs 101:1
ʰS 2Sa 22:3
ⁱS Dt 4:30
59:17 ʲver 10
60 Title ᵏ2Sa 8:13
60:1 ˡ2Sa 5:20;
Ps 44:9 ᵐPs 79:5
ⁿPs 80:3
60:2 ᵒPs 18:7
ᵖS 2Ch 7:14
60:3 ᵠPs 71:20
ʳPs 75:8; Isa 29:9; 51:17; 63:6;
Jer 25:16; Zec 12:2; Rev 14:10
60:4 ˢIsa 5:26; 11:10,12; 18:3
60:5 ᵗS Job 40:14
ᵘDt 33:12
60:6 ᵛS Ge 12:6
ʷS Ge 33:17
60:7 ˣJos 13:31
ʸS Ge 41:52
ᶻS Nu 34:19
ᵃS Ge 49:10

¹⁶But I will sing of your strength,
in the morning I will sing of your love;
for you are my fortress,
my refuge in times of trouble.

¹⁷O my Strength, I sing praise to you;
you, O God, are my fortress, my loving God.

Psalm 60

60:5-12pp — Ps 108:6-13

For the director of music. To the tune of "The Lily of the Covenant." A miktam of David. For teaching. When he fought Aram Naharaim and Aram Zobah, and when Joab returned and struck down twelve thousand Edomites in the Valley of Salt.

¹You have rejected us, O God, and burst forth upon us;
you have been angry—now restore us!
²You have shaken the land and torn it open;
mend its fractures, for it is quaking.
³You have shown your people desperate times;
you have given us wine that makes us stagger.
⁴But for those who fear you, you have raised a banner **T**
to be unfurled against the bow. *Selah*

⁵Save us and help us with your right hand,
that those you love may be delivered.
⁶God has spoken from his sanctuary:
"In triumph I will parcel out Shechem
and measure off the Valley of Succoth.
⁷Gilead is mine, and Manasseh is mine;
Ephraim is my helmet,
Judah my scepter.

T Ps 50:23 ◀ ▶ Ps 66:8

ᵉ 11 Or *sovereign* ᶠ Title: Probably a literary or musical term ᵍ Title: That is, Arameans of Northwest Mesopotamia ʰ Title: That is, Arameans of central Syria

---

59:5, 8 The psalmist asked God not to show mercy to the heathen in the day of judgment because they were "wicked traitors" (59:5). Rather God should openly show contempt for those who have derided him and his people.

⁸Moab is my washbasin,
 upon Edom I toss my sandal;
 over Philistia I shout in triumph.ᵇ"
⁹Who will bring me to the fortified city?
 Who will lead me to Edom?
¹⁰Is it not you, O God, you who have rejected us
 and no longer go out with our armies?ᶜ
¹¹Give us aid against the enemy,
 for the help of man is worthless.ᵈ
¹²With God we will gain the victory,
 and he will trample down our enemies.ᵉ

Psalm 61

For the director of music. With stringed instruments. Of David.

¹Hear my cry, O God;ᶠ
 listen to my prayer.ᵍ
²From the ends of the earth I call to you,
 I call as my heart grows faint;ʰ
 lead me to the rockⁱ that is higher than I.
³For you have been my refuge,ʲ
 a strong tower against the foe.ᵏ
⁴I long to dwellˡ in your tent forever
 and take refuge in the shelter of your wings.ᵐ   Selah
⁵For you have heard my vows,ⁿ O God;
 you have given me the heritage of those who fear your name.ᵒ
⁶Increase the days of the king's life,ᵖ
 his years for many generations.ᵠ
⁷May he be enthroned in God's presence forever;ʳ
 appoint your love and faithfulness to protect him.ˢ
⁸Then will I ever sing praise to your nameᵗ
 and fulfill my vows day after day.ᵘ

Psalm 62

For the director of music. For Jeduthun. A psalm of David.

¹My soul finds restᵛ in God alone;ʷ
 my salvation comes from him.
²He alone is my rockˣ and my salvation;ʸ
 he is my fortress,ᶻ I will never be shaken.ᵃ
³How long will you assault a man?
 Would all of you throw him down—
 this leaning wall,ᵇ this tottering fence?
⁴They fully intend to topple him from his lofty place;
 they take delight in lies.
 With their mouths they bless,
 but in their hearts they curse.ᶜ Selah
⁵Find rest, O my soul, in God alone;ᵈ
 my hope comes from him.
⁶He alone is my rock and my salvation;
 he is my fortress, I will not be shaken.
⁷My salvation and my honor depend on God[7];
 he is my mighty rock, my refuge.ᵉ
⁸Trust in him at all times, O people;ᶠ
 pour out your hearts to him,ᵍ
 for God is our refuge.   Selah
⁹Lowborn menʰ are but a breath,ⁱ
 the highborn are but a lie;
 if weighed on a balance,ʲ they are nothing;
 together they are only a breath.
¹⁰Do not trust in extortionᵏ
 or take pride in stolen goods;ˡ
 though your riches increase,
 do not set your heart on them.ᵐ
¹¹One thing God has spoken,
 two things have I heard:
 that you, O God, are strong,ⁿ
¹² and that you, O Lord, are loving.ᵒ
 Surely you will reward each person according to what he has done.ᵖ

Psalm 63

A psalm of David. When he was in the Desert of Judah.

¹O God, you are my God,
 earnestly I seek you;
 my soul thirsts for you,ᵠ
 my body longs for you,

[7] Or / God Most High is my salvation and my honor

in a dry and weary land
  where there is no water.ʳ

²I have seen you in the sanctuaryˢ
  and beheld your power and your
    glory.ᵗ
³Because your love is better than life,ᵘ
  my lips will glorify you.
⁴I will praise you as long as I live,ᵛ
  and in your name I will lift up my
    hands.ʷ
⁵My soul will be satisfied as with the
    richest of foods;ˣ
  with singing lips my mouth will
    praise you.

⁶On my bed I remember you;
  I think of you through the watches
    of the night.ʸ
⁷Because you are my help,ᶻ
  I sing in the shadow of your wings.ᵃ
⁸My soul clings to you;ᵇ
  your right hand upholds me.ᶜ

⁹They who seek my life will be
    destroyed;ᵈ
  they will go down to the depths of
    the earth.ᵉ
¹⁰They will be given over to the swordᶠ
  and become food for jackals.ᵍ
¹¹But the king will rejoice in God;
  all who swear by God's name will
    praise him,ʰ
  while the mouths of liars will be
    silenced.ⁱ

Psalm 64

For the director of music. A psalm of David.

¹Hear me, O God, as I voice my
    complaint;ʲ
  protect my life from the threat of the
    enemy.ᵏ
²Hide me from the conspiracy¹ of the
    wicked,ᵐ
  from that noisy crowd of evildoers.
³They sharpen their tongues like
    swordsⁿ
  and aim their words like deadly
    arrows.ᵒ
⁴They shoot from ambush at the
    innocent man;ᵖ
  they shoot at him suddenly, without
    fear.ᵠ

L Ps 56:8 ◀ ▶ Ps 68:5

63:1 ʳPs 143:6
63:2 ˢS Ps 15:1; 27:4; 68:24
    ᵗS Ex 16:7
63:3 ᵘPs 36:7; 69:16; 106:45; 109:21
63:4 ᵛPs 104:33; 146:2; Isa 38:20
    ʷS Ps 28:2; 1Ti 2:8
63:5 ˣS Ps 36:8; Mt 5:6
63:6 ʸDt 6:4-9; Ps 16:7; 119:148; Mt 14:25
63:7 ᶻPs 27:9; 118:7 ᵃS Ru 2:12
63:8 ᵇS Nu 32:12; Hos 6:3 ᶜS Ps 41:12
63:9 ᵈPs 40:14 ᵉPs 55:15; 71:20; 95:4; 139:15
63:10 ᶠJer 18:21; Eze 35:5; Am 1:11
    ᵍLa 5:18
63:11 ʰIsa 19:18; 45:23; 65:16
    ⁱS Job 5:16; Ro 3:19
64:1 ʲPs 142:2
    ᵏPs 140:1
64:2 ˡS Ex 1:10
    ᵐPs 56:6; 59:2
64:3 ⁿS Ps 55:21; Isa 49:2 ᵒS Ps 7:13;
    S 58:7
64:4 ᵖS Job 9:23; Ps 10:8; 11:2
    ᵠS Ps 55:19
64:5 ʳPs 91:3; 119:110; 140:5; 141:9 ˢS Job 22:13
64:8 ᵗS Ps 59:12; Pr 18:7
    ᵘS 2Ki 19:21; Ps 109:25
    ᵛS Dt 28:37
64:9 ʷS Ps 40:3
    ˣJer 51:10
64:10 ʸS Job 22:19
    ᶻPs 11:1; 25:20; 31:2 ᵃPs 32:11
65:1 ᵇPs 2:6
    ᶜS Dt 23:21; Ps 116:18
65:2 ᵈPs 80:9; Isa 66:23
65:3 ᵉS Ps 40:12
    ᶠPs 79:9; Ro 3:25; Heb 9:14
65:4 ᵍS Ps 33:12
    ʰS Nu 16:5
    ⁱS Ps 36:8
65:5 ʲS Dt 4:34; S Ps 45:4; 106:22; Isa 64:3 ᵏS Ps 18:46; 68:19; 85:4
    ˡS Ps 48:10
    ᵐPs 107:23
65:6 ⁿAm 4:13
    ᵒS Ps 18:1; 93:1; Isa 51:9
65:7 ᵖPs 89:9; 93:3-4; 107:29;
    S Mt 8:26

⁵They encourage each other in evil
    plans,
  they talk about hiding their snares;ʳ
  they say, "Who will see them¹?"ˢ
⁶They plot injustice and say,
  "We have devised a perfect plan!"
  Surely the mind and heart of man
    are cunning.

⁷But God will shoot them with arrows;
  suddenly they will be struck down.
⁸He will turn their own tongues against
    themᵗ
  and bring them to ruin;
  all who see them will shake their
    headsᵘ in scorn.ᵛ
⁹All mankind will fear;ʷ
  they will proclaim the works of God
  and ponder what he has done.ˣ
¹⁰Let the righteous rejoice in the Lordʸ
  and take refuge in him;ᶻ
  let all the upright in heart praise
    him!ᵃ

Psalm 65

For the director of music. A psalm of David.
A song.

¹Praise awaitsᵏ you, O God, in Zion;ᵇ
  to you our vows will be fulfilled.ᶜ
²O you who hear prayer,
  to you all men will come.ᵈ
³When we were overwhelmed by sins,ᵉ
  you forgave¹ our transgressions.ᶠ
⁴Blessed are those you chooseᵍ
  and bring nearʰ to live in your
    courts!
  We are filled with the good things of
    your house,ⁱ
  of your holy temple.

⁵You answer us with awesome deeds of
    righteousness,ʲ
  O God our Savior,ᵏ
  the hope of all the ends of the earthˡ
  and of the farthest seas,ᵐ
⁶who formed the mountainsⁿ by your
    power,
  having armed yourself with
    strength,ᵒ
⁷who stilled the roaring of the seas,ᵖ

U Ps 55:22 ◀ ▶ Ps 65:4
L Ps 51:17 ◀ ▶ Ps 68:13
U Ps 64:10 ◀ ▶ Ps 68:3

¹⁵ Or us ᵏ¹ Or befits; the meaning of the Hebrew for this word is uncertain. ¹³ Or made atonement for

the roaring of their waves,
and the turmoil of the nations.q
⁸Those living far away fear your wonders;
where morning dawns and evening fades
you call forth songs of joy.r

⁹You care for the land and water it;s
you enrich it abundantly.t
The streams of God are filled with water
to provide the people with grain,u
for so you have ordained it.m
¹⁰You drench its furrows
and level its ridges;
you soften it with showersv
and bless its crops.
¹¹You crown the year with your bounty,w
and your carts overflow with abundance.x
¹²The grasslands of the desert overflow;y
the hills are clothed with gladness.z
¹³The meadows are covered with flocksa
and the valleys are mantled with grain;b
they shout for joy and sing.c

Psalm 66

For the director of music. A song. A psalm.

¹Shout with joy to God, all the earth!d
² Sing the glory of his name;e
make his praise glorious!f
³Say to God, "How awesome are your deeds!g
So great is your power
that your enemies cringeh before you.
⁴All the earth bows downi to you;
they sing praisej to you,
they sing praise to your name."
Selah

⁵Come and see what God has done,
how awesome his worksk in man's behalf!
⁶He turned the sea into dry land,l

B Job 42:12 ◄► Ps 67:6
P Ps 59:8 ◄► Ps 68:1–2
M Ps 50:4–6 ◄► Ps 67:4

65:7 qDt 32:41; Ps 2:1; 74:23; 139:20; Isa 17:12-13
65:8 rPs 100:2; 107:22; 126:2; Isa 24:16; 52:9
65:9 sS Lev 26:4 tPs 104:24 uS Ge 27:28; S Dt 32:14; Ps 104:14
65:10 vS Dt 32:2; S 2Sa 1:21; S Job 36:28; Ac 14:17
65:11 wS Dt 28:12; Ps 104:28; Jn 10:10 xJob 36:28; Ps 147:14; Lk 6:38
65:12 yS Job 28:26; Joel 2:22 zPs 98:8
65:13 aPs 144:13; Isa 30:23; Zec 8:12 bPs 72:16 cPs 98:8; Isa 14:8; 44:23; 49:13; 55:12
66:1 dPs 81:1; 84:8; 95:1; 98:4; 100:1
66:2 ePs 79:9; 86:9 fIsa 42:8,12; 43:21
66:3 gS Dt 7:21; S 10:21; Ps 65:5; 106:22; 111:6; 145:6 hS 2Sa 22:45
66:4 iPs 22:27 jPs 7:17; 67:3
66:5 kver 3; Ps 106:22
66:6 lS Ge 8:1; S Ex 14:22 mICo 10:1 nS Lev 23:40
66:7 oS Ex 15:18; Ps 145:13 pS Ex 3:16; S Ps 11:4 qS Nu 17:10; Ps 112:10; 140:8
66:8 rS Ps 22:23
66:9 sPs 30:3 tS Dt 32:35; S Job 12:5
66:10 uS Ex 15:25 vS Job 6:29; S 28:1; S Ps 12:6
66:11 wPs 142:7; 146:7; Isa 42:7,22; 61:1 xS Ge 3:17; S Ex 1:14; Ps 38:4; Isa 10:27
66:12 yIsa 51:23 zPs 18:19
66:13 aS Ps 51:19 bPs 22:25; 50:14; 116:14; Ecc 5:4; Jnh 2:9
66:15 cS Lev 16:5; Ps 51:19
66:16 dPs 34:11 ePs 71:15,24
66:18 fS Dt 1:45; S 1Sa 8:18; Jas 4:3
66:19 gS Ps 18:6
66:20 hPs 22:24

they passed throughm the waters on foot—
come, let us rejoicen in him.
⁷He rules forevero by his power,
his eyes watchp the nations—
let not the rebelliousq rise up against him.
Selah

⁸Praiser our God, O peoples,
let the sound of his praise be heard;
⁹he has preserved our livess
and kept our feet from slipping.t
¹⁰For you, O God, testedu us;
you refined us like silver.v
¹¹You brought us into prisonw
and laid burdensx on our backs.
¹²You let men ride over our heads;y
we went through fire and water,
but you brought us to a place of abundance.z

¹³I will come to your temple with burnt offeringsa
and fulfill my vowsb to you—
¹⁴vows my lips promised and my mouth spoke
when I was in trouble.
¹⁵I will sacrifice fat animals to you
and an offering of rams;
I will offer bulls and goats.c
Selah

¹⁶Come and listen,d all you who fear God;
let me telle you what he has done for me.
¹⁷I cried out to him with my mouth;
his praise was on my tongue.
¹⁸If I had cherished sin in my heart,
the Lord would not have listened;f
¹⁹but God has surely listened
and heard my voiceg in prayer.
²⁰Praise be to God,
who has not rejectedh my prayer
or withheld his love from me!

E Ps 56:8 ◄► Ps 69:5
T Ps 60:4 ◄► Ps 66:16–17
T Ps 39:11 ◄► Ps 89:30–33
T Ps 66:8 ◄► Ps 78:4

m 9 Or for that is how you prepare the land

66:3–4 The psalmist indicates that in the millennial kingdom God's enemies will "cringe before you" (66:3) and that all nations and peoples throughout the earth will join in glorious worship of God forever.

Psalm 67

For the director of music. With stringed instruments. A psalm. A song.

1 May God be gracious to us and bless us
and make his face shine upon us,[i]
Selah

2 that your ways may be known on earth,
your salvation[j] among all nations.[k]

3 May the peoples praise you, O God;
may all the peoples praise you.[l]

4 May the nations be glad and sing for joy,[m]
for you rule the peoples justly[n]
and guide the nations of the earth.[o]
Selah

5 May the peoples praise you, O God;
may all the peoples praise you.

6 Then the land will yield its harvest,[p]
and God, our God, will bless us.[q]

7 God will bless us,
and all the ends of the earth[r] will fear him.[s]

Psalm 68

For the director of music. Of David. A psalm. A song.

1 May God arise,[t] may his enemies be scattered;[u]
may his foes flee[v] before him.

2 As smoke[w] is blown away by the wind,
may you blow them away;
as wax melts[x] before the fire,
may the wicked perish[y] before God.

3 But may the righteous be glad
and rejoice[z] before God;
may they be happy and joyful.

K Ps 62:11–12 ◄ ► Ps 68:13
H Ps 41:3 ◄ ► Ps 91:3
M Ps 66:4 ◄ ► Ps 68:16
J Ps 50:3–6 ◄ ► Ps 96:10
B Ps 65:9–13 ◄ ► Ps 85:12
P Ps 66:3 ◄ ► Ps 72:9
H Ps 55:23 ◄ ► Ps 68:21
U Ps 65:4 ◄ ► Ps 73:1

67:1 i Nu 6:24-26
67:2 j Isa 40:5; 52:10; 62:1
k Ps 98:2; Isa 62:2; Ac 10:35; Tit 2:11
67:3 l ver 5
67:4 m Ps 100:1-2
n S Ps 9:4; 96:10-13
o Ps 68:32
67:6 p S Ge 8:22; S Lev 26:4; Ps 85:12; Isa 55:10; Eze 34:27; Zec 8:12
q S Ge 12:2
67:7 r S Ps 2:8
s Ps 33:8
68:1 t Ps 12:5; 132:8 u Ps 18:14; 89:10; 92:9; 144:6
v Nu 10:35; Isa 17:13; 21:15; 33:3
68:2 w S Ps 37:20
x S Ps 22:14
y S Nu 10:35; Ps 9:3; 80:16
68:3 z Ps 64:10; 97:12
68:4 a S 2Sa 22:50; Ps 7:17; S 30:4; 66:2; 96:2; 100:4; 135:3 b ver 33;
S Ex 20:21;
S Dt 33:26
c S Ex 6:3; Ps 83:18
68:5 d Ps 10:14
e S Ex 22:22;
S Dt 10:18
f S Dt 26:15;
Jer 25:30
68:6 g Ps 25:16
h Ps 113:9
i Ps 79:11; 102:20; 146:7; Isa 61:1; Lk 4:18 j Isa 35:7; 49:10; 58:11
68:7 k S Ex 13:21
l Ps 78:40; 106:14
68:8 m S 2Sa 22:8
n S Jdg 5:4;
2Sa 21:10; Ecc 11:3
o S Dt 33:2
p S Jdg 5:5
68:9 q S Dt 32:2;
S Job 36:28;
S Eze 34:26
68:10 r S Dt 28:12
s Ps 65:9
68:11 t Lk 2:13
68:12 u Jos 10:16
v S Jdg 5:30
68:13
w S Ge 49:14
68:14 x 2Sa 22:15

---

4 Sing to God, sing praise to his name,[a]
extol him who rides on the clouds[n][b]—
his name is the LORD[c]—
and rejoice before him.

5 A father to the fatherless,[d] a defender of widows,[e]
is God in his holy dwelling.[f]

6 God sets the lonely[g] in families,[o][h]
he leads forth the prisoners[i] with singing;
but the rebellious live in a sun-scorched land.[j]

7 When you went out[k] before your people, O God,
when you marched through the wasteland,[l]
Selah

8 the earth shook,[m]
the heavens poured down rain,[n]
before God, the One of Sinai,[o]
before God, the God of Israel.[p]

9 You gave abundant showers,[q] O God;
you refreshed your weary inheritance.

10 Your people settled in it,
and from your bounty,[r] O God, you provided[s] for the poor.

11 The Lord announced the word,
and great was the company[t] of those who proclaimed it:

12 "Kings and armies flee[u] in haste;
in the camps men divide the plunder.[v]

13 Even while you sleep among the campfires,[p][w]
the wings of ⌊my⌋ dove are sheathed with silver,
its feathers with shining gold."

14 When the Almighty[q] scattered[x] the kings in the land,

L Ps 63:3–7 ◄ ► Ps 68:19
I Ps 53:6 ◄ ► Ps 68:22–23
K Ps 67:1–2 ◄ ► Ps 68:20
L Ps 65:3 ◄ ► Ps 69:32

---

n 4 Or | prepare the way for him who rides through the deserts
o 6 Or the desolate in a homeland   p 13 Or saddlebags   q 14 Hebrew Shaddai

---

67:4 One of the great blessings of the Millennium will be that Jesus Christ will "rule the peoples justly and guide the nations." The oppressed of our world cry out for justice, but only Christ's millennial kingdom will bring true justice and peace.

68:1–2 David exults in the certain knowledge that God's enemies will "be scattered" (68:1) and that the wicked will "perish before God" (68:2) during the coming tribulation period.

68:13 Despite the apparent difficulties facing Israel, David prophesied that God would restore the nation. He likened Israel unto a dove that is covered with silver and gold—symbols of glory and victory.

it was like snow fallen on Zalmon.ʸ

¹⁵The mountains of Bashanᶻ are majestic mountains;ᵃ
rugged are the mountains of Bashan.

M ¹⁶Why gaze in envy, O rugged mountains,
at the mountain where God choosesᵇ to reign,
where the LORD himself will dwell forever?ᶜ

¹⁷The chariotsᵈ of God are tens of thousands
and thousands of thousands;ᵉ
the Lord ⌊has come⌋ from Sinai into his sanctuary.

D ¹⁸When you ascendedᶠ on high,ᵍ
G   you led captivesʰ in your train;
P   you received gifts from men,ⁱ
W   even fromʳ the rebellious;ʲ—
       that you,ˢ O LORD God, might dwell there.

L ¹⁹Praise be to the Lord, to God our Savior,ᵏ
who daily bears our burdens.ˡ   *Selah*

K ²⁰Our God is a God who saves;ᵐ
O   from the Sovereign LORD comes escape from death.ⁿ

H ²¹Surely God will crush the headsᵒ of his enemies,
S   the hairy crowns of those who go on in their sins.

I ²²The Lord says, "I will bring them from Bashan;
I will bring them from the depths of the sea,ᵖ
²³that you may plunge your feet in the blood of your foes,ᑫ
while the tongues of your dogsʳ have their share."

²⁴Your procession has come into view, O God,
the procession of my God and King into the sanctuary.ˢ
²⁵In front are the singers,ᵗ after them the musicians;ᵘ
with them are the maidens playing tambourines.ᵛ
²⁶Praise God in the great congregation;ʷ
praise the LORD in the assembly of Israel.ˣ
²⁷There is the little tribeʸ of Benjamin,ᶻ leading them,
there the great throng of Judah's princes,
and there the princes of Zebulun and of Naphtali.ᵃ

²⁸Summon your power,ᵇ O God‡;
show us your strength,ᶜ O God, as you have doneᵈ before.
²⁹Because of your temple at Jerusalem
kings will bring you gifts.ᵉ
³⁰Rebuke the beastᶠ among the reeds,ᵍ
the herd of bullsʰ among the calves of the nations.
Humbled, may it bring bars of silver.
Scatter the nationsⁱ who delight in war.ʲ
³¹Envoys will come from Egypt;ᵏ
Cushᵘˡ will submit herself to God.

³²Sing to God, O kingdoms of the earth,ᵐ
sing praiseⁿ to the Lord,   *Selah*
³³to him who ridesᵒ the ancient skies above,
who thundersᵖ with mighty voice.ᑫ
³⁴Proclaim the powerʳ of God,
whose majestyˢ is over Israel,
whose power is in the skies.

ʳ 18 Or *gifts for men,* / *even*   ˢ 18 Or *they*   ᵗ 28 Many Hebrew manuscripts, Septuagint and Syriac; most Hebrew manuscripts *Your God has summoned power for you*   ᵘ 31 That is, the upper Nile region

M ▶ Ps 67:4 ◀▶ Ps 72:1–19   D ▶ Ps 139:7
G ▶ Job 32:8 ◀▶ Pr 1:22–23
P ▶ Pr 1:22–23
W ▶ Nu 11:29 ◀▶ Pr 1:22–23
L Ps 68:5 ◀▶ Ps 71:3
K Ps 68:13 ◀▶ Ps 69:32
O Ps 62:11–12 ◀▶ Ps 73:25–27
H Ps 68:1–2 ◀▶ Ps 69:23–24
S Ps 62:12 ◀▶ Ps 69:28
I Ps 68:13 ◀▶ Ps 69:35–36

68:16 Though the mountains of Bashan, including Mt. Hermon, were taller than Mt. Zion (also called Mt. Moriah), God had chosen it as the place for his eternal temple (see 2Ch 3:1). Note that this hill is probably the same location where God commanded Abraham to sacrifice a ram as a divinely-provided substitute for his son, Isaac (see Ge 22:2). This hill was also the site of Araunah's threshing floor and the place where David offered a sacrifice to halt the plague of the avenging angel (see note at 2Sa 24:24).

68:22–23 David foresaw the restoration of Israel from the highest plateaus of Bashan to the deepest depths of the sea. This return of God's people to the promised land is still under way and will find its ultimate fulfillment when Christ returns.

35 You are awesome, O God, in your
    sanctuary;
  the God of Israel gives power and
    strength to his people.

Praise be to God!

Psalm 69

For the director of music. To the tune of
"Lilies." Of David.

1 Save me, O God,
    for the waters have come up to my
      neck.
2 I sink in the miry depths,
    where there is no foothold.
  I have come into the deep waters;
    the floods engulf me.
3 I am worn out calling for help;
    my throat is parched.
  My eyes fail,
    looking for my God.
4 Those who hate me without reason
    outnumber the hairs of my head;
  many are my enemies without cause,
    those who seek to destroy me.
  I am forced to restore
    what I did not steal.

5 You know my folly, O God;
    my guilt is not hidden from you.

6 May those who hope in you
    not be disgraced because of me,
    O Lord, the LORD Almighty;
  may those who seek you
    not be put to shame because of me,
    O God of Israel.
7 For I endure scorn for your sake,
    and shame covers my face.
8 I am a stranger to my brothers,
    an alien to my own mother's sons;
9 for zeal for your house consumes me,
    and the insults of those who insult
      you fall on me.
10 When I weep and fast,
    I must endure scorn;
11 when I put on sackcloth,
    people make sport of me.
12 Those who sit at the gate mock me,
    and I am the song of the drunkards.

E Ps 66:7 ◀▶ Ps 87:6

13 But I pray to you, O LORD,
    in the time of your favor;
  in your great love, O God,
    answer me with your sure salvation.
14 Rescue me from the mire,
    do not let me sink;
  deliver me from those who hate me,
    from the deep waters.
15 Do not let the floodwaters engulf me
    or the depths swallow me up
    or the pit close its mouth over me.
16 Answer me, O LORD, out of the
    goodness of your love;
  in your great mercy turn to me.
17 Do not hide your face from your
    servant;
  answer me quickly, for I am in
    trouble.
18 Come near and rescue me;
    redeem me because of my foes.

19 You know how I am scorned,
    disgraced and shamed;
    all my enemies are before you.
20 Scorn has broken my heart
    and has left me helpless;
  I looked for sympathy, but there was
    none,
  for comforters, but I found none.
21 They put gall in my food
    and gave me vinegar for my thirst.

22 May the table set before them become
    a snare;
  may it become retribution and a
    trap.
23 May their eyes be darkened so they
    cannot see,
    and their backs be bent forever.
24 Pour out your wrath on them;
    let your fierce anger overtake them.
25 May their place be deserted;
    let there be no one to dwell in their
      tents.
26 For they persecute those you wound
    and talk about the pain of those you
      hurt.

D Ps 22:13–18 ◀▶ Isa 52:14–15
H Ps 68:21 ◀▶ Ps 69:27–28
J Ps 9:7–8 ◀▶ Ps 87:4–6

v 22 Or snare / and their fellowship become

69:25 The apostle Peter applied this verse to Judas after his betrayal of Jesus and subsequent suicide. Since Judas sought to remove Jesus from his place as Messiah, Peter said that Judas was removed from his place among the twelve disciples and another leader had to be found to take his place (see Acts 1:20).

PSALM 69:27

H ²⁷Charge them with crime upon crime;ᵖ
  do not let them share in your
    salvation.ᵠ
S ²⁸May they be blotted out of the book of
    lifeʳ
  and not be listed with the
    righteous.ˢ

²⁹I am in pain and distress;
  may your salvation, O God, protect
    me.ᵗ
³⁰I will praise God's name in songᵘ
  and glorify himᵛ with thanksgiving.
³¹This will please the LORD more than an
    ox,
  more than a bull with its horns and
    hoofs.ʷ
K ³²The poor will see and be gladˣ—
L   you who seek God, may your hearts
    live!ʸ
³³The LORD hears the needyᶻ
  and does not despise his captive
    people.
³⁴Let heaven and earth praise him,
  the seas and all that move in them,ᵃ
I ³⁵for God will save Zionᵇ
  and rebuild the cities of Judah.ᶜ
  Then people will settle there and
    possess it;
³⁶ the children of his servants will
    inherit it,ᵈ
  and those who love his name will
    dwell there.ᵉ

Psalm 70

70:1–5pp — Ps 40:13–17

For the director of music. Of David.
A petition.

¹Hasten, O God, to save me;
  O LORD, come quickly to help me.ᶠ
²May those who seek my lifeᵍ
  be put to shame and confusion;
  may all who desire my ruin
    be turned back in disgrace.ʰ

H *Ps 69:23–24* ◀▶ *Ps 73:17–18*
S *Ps 68:21* ◀▶ *Ps 73:27*
K *Ps 68:20* ◀▶ *Ps 73:26*
L *Ps 68:13* ◀▶ *Ps 77:7–9*
I *Ps 68:22–23* ◀▶ *Ps 74:10*

69:27 ᵖNe 4:5
  ᵠPs 109:14
69:28
  ʳEx 32:32-33;
  S Lk 10:20
  ˢEze 13:9
69:29 ᵗS Ps 20:1
69:30 ᵘPs 28:7
  ᵛPs 34:3
69:31
  ʷPs 50:9-13; 51:16
69:32 ˣS Ps 34:2
  ʸPs 22:26
69:33 ᶻPs 12:5
69:34 ᵃPs 96:11;
  98:7; Isa 44:23
69:35 ᵇOb 1:17
  ᶜS Ezr 9:9;
  S Ps 51:18
69:36 ᵈPs 25:13
  ᵉS Ps 37:29
70:1 ᶠPs 22:19;
  71:12
70:2 ᵍPs 35:4
  ʰPs 6:10; 35:26;
  71:13; 109:29;
  129:5
70:3 ⁱS Ps 35:21
70:4 ʲPs 9:10
  ᵏPs 31:6-7; 32:11;
  118:24 ˡPs 35:27
70:5 ᵐPs 86:1;
  109:22 ⁿPs 141:1
  ᵒPs 30:10; 33:20
  ᵖPs 18:2
  ᵠPs 119:60
71:1 ʳS Dt 23:15;
  Ru 2:12 ˢPs 22:5
71:2 ˢ2Ki 19:16
71:3 ᵘPs 18:2
71:4 ᵛS 2Ki 19:19
  ʷPs 140:4
  ˣS Ge 48:16
71:5 ʸS Ps 9:18;
  S 25:5 ᶻS Job 4:6;
  Jer 17:7
71:6 ᵃS Ps 22:10
  ᵇS Job 3:16;
  S Ps 22:9 ᶜPs 9:1;
  34:1; 52:9;
  119:164; 145:2
71:7 ᵈS Dt 28:46;
  Isa 8:18; 1Co 4:9
  ᵉS 2Sa 22:3;
  Ps 61:3
71:8 ᶠver 15;
  Ps 51:15; 63:5
  ᵍPs 96:6; 104:1
71:9 ʰS Ps 51:11
  ⁱPs 92:14; Isa 46:4
  ʲS Dt 4:31; S 31:6
71:10 ᵏPs 3:7

---

³May those who say to me, "Aha!
    Aha!"ⁱ
  turn back because of their shame.
⁴But may all who seek youʲ
  rejoice and be gladᵏ in you;
  may those who love your salvation
    always say,
    "Let God be exalted!"ˡ

⁵Yet I am poor and needy;ᵐ
  come quickly to me,ⁿ O God.
  You are my helpᵒ and my deliverer;ᵖ
  O LORD, do not delay.ᵠ

Psalm 71

71:1–3pp — Ps 31:1–4

¹In you, O LORD, I have taken refuge;ʳ
  let me never be put to shame.ˢ
²Rescue me and deliver me in your
    righteousness;
  turn your earᵗ to me and save me.
L ³Be my rock of refuge,
  to which I can always go;
  give the command to save me,
  for you are my rock and my
    fortress.ᵘ
⁴Deliverᵛ me, O my God, from the hand
    of the wicked,ʷ
  from the grasp of evil and cruel
    men.ˣ

⁵For you have been my hope,ʸ
  O Sovereign LORD,
  my confidenceᶻ since my youth.
L ⁶From birthᵃ I have relied on you;
  you brought me forth from my
    mother's womb.ᵇ
  I will ever praiseᶜ you.

⁷I have become like a portentᵈ to many,
  but you are my strong refuge.ᵉ
⁸My mouthᶠ is filled with your praise,
  declaring your splendorᵍ all day
    long.

⁹Do not castʰ me away when I am old;ⁱ
  do not forsakeʲ me when my
    strength is gone.
¹⁰For my enemiesᵏ speak against me;

L *Ps 68:19* ◀▶ *Ps 71:6*
L *Ps 71:3* ◀▶ *Ps 73:23–24*

69:35–36 These predictive verses were initially fulfilled when the exiles returned from their Babylonian captivity. The ultimate fulfillment will occur in the coming Millennium when Jesus Christ, God's Messiah, will obtain victory over his enemies. Then Jerusalem will be rebuilt and "those who love his name will dwell there" (69:36).

those who wait to kill me conspire
together.
¹¹They say, "God has forsaken him;
pursue him and seize him,
for no one will rescue him."
¹²Be not far from me, O God;
come quickly, O my God, to help
me.
¹³May my accusers perish in shame;
may those who want to harm me
be covered with scorn and
disgrace.
¹⁴But as for me, I will always have
hope;
I will praise you more and more.
¹⁵My mouth will tell of your
righteousness,
of your salvation all day long,
though I know not its measure.
¹⁶I will come and proclaim your mighty
acts, O Sovereign LORD;
I will proclaim your righteousness,
yours alone.
¹⁷Since my youth, O God, you have
taught me,
and to this day I declare your
marvelous deeds.
¹⁸Even when I am old and gray,
do not forsake me, O God,
till I declare your power to the next
generation,
your might to all who are to come.
¹⁹Your righteousness reaches to the
skies, O God,
you who have done great things.
Who, O God, is like you?
F ²⁰Though you have made me see
troubles, many and bitter,
you will restore my life again;
from the depths of the earth
you will again bring me up.
²¹You will increase my honor
and comfort me once again.
²²I will praise you with the harp

F *Ps 17:15 ◄ ▶ Ps 88:10–12*

71:10 ˡS Ps 10:8; 59:3; Pr 1:18
ᵐS Ex 1:10; S Ps 31:13; S Mt 12:14
71:11 ⁿS Ps 9:10; Isa 40:27; 54:7; La 5:20; Mt 27:46
ᵒS Ps 7:2
71:12 ᵖS Ps 38:21
ᑫPs 22:19; 38:22
71:13 ʳJer 18:19
ˢS Job 8:22; Ps 25:3
ᵗS Ps 70:2
71:14 ᵘPs 25:3; 42:5; 130:7; 131:3
71:15 ᵛS ver 8; S Ps 66:16
ʷS Ps 51:14
71:16 ˣPs 9:1; 77:12; 106:2; 118:15; 145:4
71:17 ʸS Dt 4:5; S Jer 7:13
ᶻS Job 5:9; Ps 26:7; 86:10; 96:3
71:18 ᵃIsa 46:4
ᵇS Ex 9:16
ᶜJob 8:8; Ps 22:30, 31; 78:4; 145:4; Joel 1:3
71:19 ᵈS Ps 36:5
ᵉPs 126:2; Lk 1:49
ᶠPs 35:10; 77:13; 89:8
71:20 ᵍPs 25:17
ʰPs 80:3,19; 85:4; Hos 6:2 ⁱS Ps 63:9
71:21 ʲPs 18:35
ᵏPs 23:4; 86:17; Isa 12:1; 40:1-2; 49:13; 54:10
71:22 ˡPs 33:2
ᵐS Job 21:12; Ps 92:3; 144:9
ⁿS 2Ki 19:22
71:23 ᵒPs 20:5
ᵖS Ex 15:13
71:24 ᑫS Ps 35:28
ʳver 13 ˢS Est 9:2
72:1 ᵗS Dt 1:16; S Ps 9:8
72:2 ᵘIsa 9:7; 11:4-5; 16:5; 32:1; 59:17; 63:1; Jer 23:5; 33:15
72:4 ᵛS Ps 9:12; 76:9; Isa 49:13
ʷver 13; Isa 11:4; 29:19; 32:7
ˣS Ps 27:11
72:5 ʸIsa 13:13
ᶻPs 33:11
72:6 ᵃS Dt 32:2
72:7 ᵇPs 92:12; Pr 14:11

for your faithfulness, O my God;
I will sing praise to you with the lyre,
O Holy One of Israel.
²³My lips will shout for joy
when I sing praise to you—
I, whom you have redeemed.
²⁴My tongue will tell of your righteous
acts
all day long,
for those who wanted to harm me
have been put to shame and
confusion.

Psalm 72

Of Solomon.

¹Endow the king with your justice, **M**
O God,
the royal son with your
righteousness.
²He will judge your people in
righteousness,
your afflicted ones with justice.
³The mountains will bring prosperity to
the people,
the hills the fruit of righteousness.
⁴He will defend the afflicted among
the people
and save the children of the needy;
he will crush the oppressor.

⁵He will endure as long as the sun,
as long as the moon, through all
generations.
⁶He will be like rain falling on a mown
field,
like showers watering the earth.
⁷In his days the righteous will flourish; **U**
prosperity will abound till the moon
is no more.

⁸He will rule from sea to sea **V**

M *Ps 68:16 ◄ ▶ Ps 82:8*   **U** *▶ Isa 2:4*
V *Ps 45:6 ◄ ▶ Ps 110:1*

w 2 Or May he; similarly in verses 3-11 and 17 *ˣ 5 Septuagint; Hebrew You will be feared*

71:20 This is a clear OT prophecy of physical resurrection from "the depths of the earth" for God's righteous saints.

72:1–19 This prophetic psalm is a prayer for the king, a son of David, expressing the desire that the king's reign will be a just and righteous reign. Note that this description for the king can also apply to the Messiah, who will rule righteously in glory and power in his eternal kingdom on earth.

72:5–7 This psalm of Solomon prophesied the eternal reverence and fear of God that the nations will express during the coming Millennium.

72:8 This prophecy looks forward to the ultimate dominion of Jesus Christ as the Messiah who will rule the earth forever because of his righteousness.

and from the River[yc] to the ends of
the earth.[zd]

⁹The desert tribes will bow before him
and his enemies will lick the dust.
¹⁰The kings of Tarshish[e] and of distant
shores[f]
will bring tribute to him;
the kings of Sheba[g] and Seba
will present him gifts.[h]
¹¹All kings will bow down[i] to him
and all nations will serve[j] him.

¹²For he will deliver the needy who cry
out,
the afflicted who have no one to
help.
¹³He will take pity[k] on the weak and the
needy
and save the needy from death.
¹⁴He will rescue[l] them from oppression
and violence,
for precious[m] is their blood in his
sight.

¹⁵Long may he live!
May gold from Sheba[n] be given him.
May people ever pray for him
and bless him all day long.[o]
¹⁶Let grain[p] abound throughout the land;
on the tops of the hills may it sway.
Let its fruit[q] flourish like Lebanon;[r]
let it thrive like the grass of the
field.[s]
¹⁷May his name endure forever;[t]
may it continue as long as the sun.[u]

All nations will be blessed through
him,
and they will call him blessed.[v]

¹⁸Praise be to the LORD God, the God of
Israel,[w]
who alone does marvelous deeds.[x]
¹⁹Praise be to his glorious name[y]
forever;
may the whole earth be filled with
his glory.[z]
Amen and Amen.[a]

²⁰This concludes the prayers of David
son of Jesse.[b]

P Ps 68:1-2 ◀ ▶ Ps 75:8

BOOK III

Psalms 73–89

Psalm 73

A psalm of Asaph.

¹Surely God is good to Israel,
to those who are pure in heart.[c]

²But as for me, my feet had almost
slipped;[d]
I had nearly lost my foothold.[e]
³For I envied[f] the arrogant
when I saw the prosperity of the
wicked.[g]

⁴They have no struggles;
their bodies are healthy and strong.[a]
⁵They are free[h] from the burdens
common to man;
they are not plagued by human ills.
⁶Therefore pride[i] is their necklace;[j]
they clothe themselves with
violence.[k]
⁷From their callous hearts[l] comes
iniquity[b];
the evil conceits of their minds
know no limits.
⁸They scoff, and speak with malice;[m]
in their arrogance[n] they threaten
oppression.[o]
⁹Their mouths lay claim to heaven,
and their tongues take possession of
the earth.
¹⁰Therefore their people turn to them
and drink up waters in abundance.[c]
¹¹They say, "How can God know?
Does the Most High have
knowledge?"

¹²This is what the wicked are like—
always carefree,[p] they increase in
wealth.[q]
¹³Surely in vain[r] have I kept my heart
pure;

U Ps 68:3 ◀ ▶ Ps 81:15-16

---

[y] 8 That is, the Euphrates [z] 8 Or the end of the land [a] 4 With a different word division of the Hebrew; Masoretic Text *struggles at their death;* / *their bodies are healthy* [b] 7 Syriac (see also Septuagint); Hebrew *Their eyes bulge with fat* [c] 10 The meaning of the Hebrew for this verse is uncertain.

72:17 Solomon's words conclude with a benediction that the Messiah's eternal and prosperous reign will bless the entire world.

in vain have I washed my hands in innocence.ˢ
¹⁴All day long I have been plagued;ᵗ
I have been punished every morning.

¹⁵If I had said, "I will speak thus,"
I would have betrayed your children.
¹⁶When I tried to understandᵘ all this,
it was oppressive to me
¹⁷till I entered the sanctuaryᵛ of God;
then I understood their final destiny.ʷ

¹⁸Surely you place them on slippery ground;ˣ
you cast them down to ruin.ʸ
¹⁹How suddenlyᶻ are they destroyed,
completely swept awayᵃ by terrors!
²⁰As a dreamᵇ when one awakes,ᶜ
so when you arise, O Lord,
you will despise them as fantasies.ᵈ

²¹When my heart was grieved
and my spirit embittered,
²²I was senselessᵉ and ignorant;
I was a brute beastᶠ before you.

²³Yet I am always with you;
you hold me by my right hand.ᵍ
²⁴You guideʰ me with your counsel,ⁱ
and afterward you will take me into glory.

²⁵Whom have I in heaven but you?ʲ
And earth has nothing I desire besides you.ᵏ
²⁶My flesh and my heartˡ may fail,ᵐ
but God is the strengthⁿ of my heart
and my portionᵒ forever.

²⁷Those who are far from you will perish;ᵖ
you destroy all who are unfaithfulᵠ to you.
²⁸But as for me, it is good to be near God.ʳ

H Ps 69:27–28 ◀▶ Ps 75:7–8
L Ps 71:6 ◀▶ Ps 78:52–53
O Ps 68:20 ◀▶ Ps 75:6–7
K Ps 69:32 ◀▶ Ps 80:3
S Ps 69:28 ◀▶ Ps 93:5

73:13 ˢ S Ge 44:16
73:14 ᵗ ver 5
73:16 ᵘ Ecc 8:17
73:17 ᵛ Ex 15:17; Ps 15:1
ʷ S Job 8:13; Php 3:19
73:18 ˣ S Dt 32:35; Ps 35:6 ʸ Ps 17:13
73:19 ᶻ Dt 28:20; Pr 24:22; Isa 47:11
ᵃ S Ge 19:15
73:20 ᵇ S Job 20:8
ᶜ Ps 78:65; Isa 29:8
ᵈ Pr 12:11; 28:19
73:22 ᵉ Ps 49:10; 92:6; 94:8
ᶠ Ps 49:12,20; Ecc 3:18; 9:12
73:23 ᵍ S Ge 48:13
73:24 ʰ S Ps 48:14
ⁱ S 1Ki 22:5
73:25 ʲ Ps 16:2
ᵏ Php 3:8
73:26 ˡ Ps 84:2
ᵐ S Ps 31:10; 40:12
ⁿ Ps 18:1
ᵒ S Dt 32:9
73:27 ᵖ S Ps 34:21
ᵠ S Lev 6:2; Jer 5:11; Hos 4:12; 9:1
73:28 ʳ Zep 3:2; Heb 10:22; Jas 4:8
ˢ Ps 9:9 ᵗ Ps 26:7; 40:5
74:1 ᵘ S Ps 43:2
ᵛ S Ps 44:23
ʷ Ps 79:13; 95:7; 100:3
74:2 ˣ S Ex 15:16; S 1Co 6:20
ʸ S Dt 32:7
ᶻ S Ex 34:9
ᵃ S Ex 15:13; S Isa 48:20 ᵇ Ps 2:6
ᶜ Ps 43:3; 68:16; Isa 46:13; Joel 3:17, 21; Ob 1:17
74:3 ᵈ Isa 44:26; 52:9
74:4 ᵉ La 2:7
ᶠ S Nu 2:2; S Jer 4:6
74:5 ᵍ Jer 46:22
74:6 ʰ S 1Ki 6:18
74:7 ⁱ S Lev 20:3; Ac 21:28
ʲ S Lev 15:31
ᵏ Ps 75:1
74:8 ˡ Ps 94:5
ᵐ 2Ki 25:9; 2Ch 36:19; Jer 21:10; 34:22; 52:13
74:9 ⁿ S Ex 4:17; S 10:1 ᵒ S Isa 3:1
74:10 ᵖ Ps 6:3; 79:5; 80:4 ᵠ ver 22
ʳ S Ps 44:16

I have made the Sovereign LORD my refuge;ˢ
I will tell of all your deeds.ᵗ

Psalm 74

A *maskil*ᵈ of Asaph.

¹Why have you rejectedᵘ us forever,ᵛ O God?
Why does your anger smolder against the sheep of your pasture?ʷ
²Remember the people you purchasedˣ of old,ʸ
the tribe of your inheritance,ᶻ
whom you redeemedᵃ—
Mount Zion,ᵇ where you dwelt.ᶜ
³Turn your steps toward these everlasting ruins,ᵈ
all this destruction the enemy has brought on the sanctuary.

⁴Your foes roaredᵉ in the place where you met with us;
they set up their standardsᶠ as signs.
⁵They behaved like men wielding axes
to cut through a thicket of trees.ᵍ
⁶They smashed all the carvedʰ paneling
with their axes and hatchets.
⁷They burned your sanctuary to the ground;
they defiledⁱ the dwelling placeʲ of your Name.ᵏ
⁸They said in their hearts, "We will crushˡ them completely!"
They burnedᵐ every place where God was worshiped in the land.
⁹We are given no miraculous signs;ⁿ
no prophetsᵒ are left,
and none of us knows how long this will be.
¹⁰How longᵖ will the enemy mockᵠ you, O God?
Will the foe revileʳ your name forever?ˢ

R Ne 1:8 ◀▶ Ps 74:7–11
R Ps 74:1–2 ◀▶ Ps 78:67
I Ps 69:35–36 ◀▶ Ps 79:5

ᵈ Title: Probably a literary or musical term

74:1–2 Asaph prophesied the rejection and scattering of Israel. This prophecy was fulfilled when the Assyrians and Babylonians carried Israel and Judah into exile.

74:7–11 Asaph declared that God's people would cry in despair that "no prophets are left" (74:9). Both of the prophets Ezekiel and Jeremiah had been carried into exile, leaving no one behind to tell the people how long their suffering would last.

¹¹Why do you hold back your hand, your right hand?ˢ
Take it from the folds of your garmentᵗ and destroy them!

¹²But you, O God, are my kingᵘ from of old;
you bring salvationᵛ upon the earth.
¹³It was you who split open the seaʷ by your power;
you broke the heads of the monsterˣ in the waters.
¹⁴It was you who crushed the heads of Leviathanʸ
and gave him as food to the creatures of the desert.ᶻ
¹⁵It was you who opened up springsᵃ and streams;
you driedᵇ up the ever flowing rivers.
¹⁶The day is yours, and yours also the night;
you established the sun and moon.ᶜ
¹⁷It was you who set all the boundariesᵈ of the earth;
you made both summer and winter.ᵉ

¹⁸Remember how the enemy has mocked you, O Lᴏʀᴅ,
how foolish peopleᶠ have reviled your name.
¹⁹Do not hand over the life of your doveᵍ to wild beasts;
do not forget the lives of your afflictedʰ people forever.
²⁰Have regard for your covenant,ⁱ
because haunts of violence fill the dark placesʲ of the land.
²¹Do not let the oppressedᵏ retreat in disgrace;
may the poor and needyˡ praise your name.

²²Rise up,ᵐ O God, and defend your cause;
remember how foolsⁿ mock you all day long.
²³Do not ignore the clamorᵒ of your adversaries,ᵖ

C Ps 58:1–3 ◄ ► Ps 74:22
C Ps 74:18 ◄ ► Ps 94:11

74:11 ˢS Ex 15:6
ᵗNe 5:13; Eze 5:3
74:12 ᵘPs 2:6;
S 24:7; 68:24
ᵛPs 27:1
74:13
ʷS Ex 14:21
ˣIsa 27:1; 51:9;
Eze 29:3; 32:2
74:14 ʸS Job 3:8
ᶻIsa 13:21; 23:13;
34:14; Jer 50:39
74:15 ᵃS Ex 17:6;
S Nu 20:11
ᵇS Ex 14:29;
S Jos 2:10
74:16 ᶜS Ge 1:16;
Ps 136:7-9
74:17 ᵈDt 32:8;
Ac 17:26
ᵉS Ge 8:22
74:18 ᶠDt 32:6
74:19 ᵍS Ge 8:8;
S Isa 59:11
ʰS Ps 9:18
74:20 ⁱS Ge 6:18
ʲJob 34:22
74:21 ᵏPs 9:9;
10:18; 103:6;
Isa 58:10
ˡS Ps 35:10
74:22 ᵐPs 17:13
ⁿS Ps 53:1
74:23 ᵒIsa 31:4
ᵖPs 65:7
ᵠS Ps 46:6
ʳS Nu 25:17

75:1 ˢPs 145:18
ᵗS Jos 3:5; Ps 44:1;
S 71:16; 77:12;
105:2; 107:8,15;
145:5,12
75:2 ᵘS Ex 13:10
ᵛPs 7:11
75:3 ʷIsa 24:19
ˣ1Sa 2:8;
S 2Sa 22:8
75:4 ʸS Ps 5:5
ᶻ1Sa 2:3
ᵃZec 1:21
75:5 ᵇS Job 15:25
75:7 ᶜS Ge 16:5;
Ps 50:6; 58:11;
Rev 18:8 ᵈ1Sa 2:7;
S Job 5:11;
Ps 147:6;
Eze 21:26; Da 2:21
75:8 ᵉPr 23:30
ᶠIsa 51:17;
Jer 25:15; Zec 12:2
75:9 ᵍPs 40:10
ʰPs 108:1
ⁱS Ge 24:12;
Ps 76:5

the uproarᵠ of your enemies,ʳ which rises continually.

Psalm 75

For the director of music. ⌞To the tune of⌟ "Do Not Destroy." A psalm of Asaph. A song.

¹We give thanks to you, O God,
we give thanks, for your Name is near;ˢ
men tell of your wonderful deeds.ᵗ

²You say, "I choose the appointed time;ᵘ
it is I who judge uprightly.ᵛ
³When the earth and all its people quake,ʷ
it is I who hold its pillarsˣ firm.
Selah

⁴To the arrogantʸ I say, 'Boast no more,'ᶻ
and to the wicked, 'Do not lift up your horns.ᵃ
⁵Do not lift your horns against heaven;
do not speak with outstretched neck.ᵇ'"

⁶No one from the east or the west
or from the desert can exalt a man.
⁷But it is God who judges:ᶜ
He brings one down, he exalts another.ᵈ

⁸In the hand of the Lᴏʀᴅ is a cup
full of foaming wine mixedᵉ with spices;
he pours it out, and all the wicked of the earth
drink it down to its very dregs.ᶠ

⁹As for me, I will declareᵍ this forever;
I will singʰ praise to the God of Jacob.ⁱ
¹⁰I will cut off the horns of all the wicked,

N Ps 37:34 ◄ ► Ps 78:69
G Ps 62:9–11 ◄ ► Ps 143:2
O Ps 73:25–27 ◄ ► Ps 127:1
H Ps 73:17–18 ◄ ► Ps 75:10
P Ps 72:9 ◄ ► Ps 75:10
P Ps 75:8 ◄ ► Ps 83:13–17
H Ps 75:7–8 ◄ ► Ps 76:7

75:3 This prophecy anticipates the ultimate redemption of the earth when the Messiah returns. Though the whole moral order of the world seems to have crumbled, God is still in control and will uphold "its pillars."

75:8–10 This prophecy looks forward to the final victory of Jesus Christ over the wicked during the terrors of the great tribulation when God will defeat the wicked, "but the horns of the righteous will be lifted up" (75:10).

but the horns of the righteous will
        be lifted up.ʲ

Psalm 76

For the director of music. With stringed instruments. A psalm of Asaph. A song.

¹In Judah God is known;
        his name is greatᵏ in Israel.
²His tent is in Salem,ˡ
        his dwelling place in Zion.ᵐ
³There he broke the flashing arrows,ⁿ
        the shields and the swords, the
                weapons of war.ᵒ   *Selah*

⁴You are resplendent with light,ᵖ
        more majestic than mountains rich
                with game.
⁵Valiant menᑫ lie plundered,
        they sleep their last sleep;ʳ
        not one of the warriors
                can lift his hands.
⁶At your rebuke,ˢ O God of Jacob,
        both horse and chariotᵗ lie still.

⁷You alone are to be feared.ᵘ
        Who can standᵛ before you when
                you are angry?ʷ
⁸From heaven you pronounced
                judgment,
        and the land fearedˣ and was
                quiet—
⁹when you, O God, rose up to judge,ʸ
        to save all the afflictedᶻ of the land.
                                              Selah
¹⁰Surely your wrath against men brings
                you praise,ᵃ
        and the survivors of your wrath are
                restrained.ᵉ

¹¹Make vows to the Lᴏʀᴅ your God and
                fulfill them;ᵇ
        let all the neighboring lands
                bring giftsᶜ to the One to be feared.
¹²He breaks the spirit of rulers;
        he is feared by the kings of the
                earth.

Psalm 77

For the director of music. For Jeduthun. Of Asaph. A psalm.

¹I cried out to Godᵈ for help;
        I cried out to God to hear me.
²When I was in distress,ᵉ I sought the
                Lord;

75:10 ʲ Ps 89:17; 92:10; 112:9; 148:14
76:1 ᵏ Ps 99:3
76:2 ˡ S Ge 14:18; Heb 7:1
ᵐ S 2Sa 5:7; Ps 2:6
76:3 ⁿ Eze 39:9
ᵒ Ps 46:9
76:4 ᵖ S Ps 36:9
76:5 ᑫ S Jdg 20:44
ʳ S Ps 13:3;
S Mt 9:24
76:6 ˢ S Ps 50:21
ᵗ S Ex 15:1
76:7 ᵘ S 1Ch 16:25
ᵛ S Ezr 9:15;
Rev 6:17 ʷ Ps 2:5;
Na 1:6
76:8
ˣ S 1Ch 16:30;
Eze 38:20
76:9 ʸ S Ps 9:8; 58:11; 74:22; 82:8; 96:13 ᶻ S Ps 72:4
76:10 ᵃ Ex 9:16; Ro 9:17
76:11
ᵇ S Lev 22:18;
S Ps 50:14;
Ecc 5:4-5
ᶜ S 2Ch 32:23
77:1 ᵈ S 1Ki 8:52
77:2 ᵉ S Ge 32:7;
S 2Sa 22:7;
S Ps 118:5
ᶠ Ps 6:6; 22:2; 88:1;
ᵍ S Ex 9:29;
S Job 11:13
ʰ S Ge 37:35;
Mt 2:18
77:3 ⁱ Ps 78:35
ʲ Ex 2:23; S Ps 6:6;
Jer 45:3 ᵏ S Ps 6:2
77:4 ˡ S Ps 39:2
77:5 ᵐ Dt 32:7;
S Ps 44:1; 143:5;
Ecc 7:10
77:7 ⁿ S 1Ch 28:9
ᵒ Ps 85:1; 102:13;
106:4
77:8 ᵖ S Ps 6:4; 90:14 ᑫ 2Pe 3:9
77:9 ʳ Ps 25:6; 40:11; 51:1
ˢ Isa 49:15
77:10 ᵗ S Ex 15:6
77:11 ᵘ S Ne 9:17
77:12 ᵛ S Ge 24:63
ʷ Ps 143:5
77:13
ˣ S Ex 15:11;
S Ps 71:19; 86:8
77:14 ʸ S Ex 3:20; S 34:10
77:15 ᶻ S Ex 6:6
77:16 ᵃ Ex 14:21, 28; Isa 50:2;
Hab 3:8 ᵇ Ps 114:3;
Hab 3:10
77:17 ᶜ S Jdg 5:4
ᵈ S Ex 9:23;
S Ps 29:3
ᵉ S Dt 32:23
77:18 ᶠ S Ps 55:8
ᵍ S 2Sa 22:13

at night ᶠ I stretched out untiring
                handsᵍ
        and my soul refused to be
                comforted.ʰ
³I rememberedⁱ you, O God, and I
                groaned;ʲ
        I mused, and my spirit grew faint.ᵏ
                                              Selah
⁴You kept my eyes from closing;
        I was too troubled to speak.ˡ
⁵I thought about the former days,ᵐ
        the years of long ago;
⁶I remembered my songs in the night.
        My heart mused and my spirit
                inquired:

⁷"Will the Lord reject forever?ⁿ
        Will he never show his favorᵒ again?
⁸Has his unfailing loveᵖ vanished
                forever?
        Has his promiseᑫ failed for all time?
⁹Has God forgotten to be merciful?ʳ
        Has he in anger withheld his
                compassion?ˢ"   *Selah*

¹⁰Then I thought, "To this I will appeal:
        the years of the right handᵗ of the
                Most High."
¹¹I will remember the deeds of the Lᴏʀᴅ;
        yes, I will remember your miraclesᵘ
                of long ago.
¹²I will meditateᵛ on all your works
        and consider all your mighty deeds.ʷ
¹³Your ways, O God, are holy.
        What god is so great as our God?ˣ
¹⁴You are the God who performs
                miracles;ʸ
        you display your power among the
                peoples.
¹⁵With your mighty arm you redeemed
                your people,ᶻ
        the descendants of Jacob and Joseph.
                                              Selah
¹⁶The watersᵃ saw you, O God,
        the waters saw you and writhed;ᵇ
        the very depths were convulsed.
¹⁷The clouds poured down water,ᶜ
        the skies resounded with thunder;ᵈ
        your arrowsᵉ flashed back and forth.
¹⁸Your thunder was heard in the
                whirlwind,ᶠ
        your lightningᵍ lit up the world;

L Ps 69:32 ◄ ► Ps 78:38–39

ᵉ 10 Or Surely the wrath of men brings you praise, / and with the remainder of wrath you arm yourself

H Ps 75:10 ◄ ► Ps 83:17

the earth trembled and quaked.ʰ
¹⁹Your pathⁱ led through the sea,ʲ
your way through the mighty
waters,
though your footprints were not
seen.
²⁰You led your peopleᵏ like a flockˡ
by the hand of Moses and Aaron.ᵐ

Psalm 78

A *maskil*ʲ of Asaph.

¹O my people, hear my teaching;ⁿ
listen to the words of my mouth.
²I will open my mouth in parables,ᵒ
I will utter hidden things, things
from of old—
³what we have heard and known,
what our fathers have told us.ᵖ
⁴We will not hide them from their
children;ᵠ
we will tell the next generationʳ
the praiseworthy deedsˢ of the LORD,
his power, and the wondersᵗ he has
done.
⁵He decreed statutesᵘ for Jacobᵛ
and established the law in Israel,
which he commanded our forefathers
to teach their children,
⁶so the next generation would know
them,
even the children yet to be born,ʷ
and they in turn would tell their
children.
⁷Then they would put their trust in God
and would not forgetˣ his deeds
but would keep his commands.ʸ
⁸They would not be like their
forefathersᶻ—
a stubbornᵃ and rebelliousᵇ
generation,
whose hearts were not loyal to God,
whose spirits were not faithful to
him.
⁹The men of Ephraim, though armed
with bows,ᶜ
turned back on the day of battle;ᵈ
¹⁰they did not keep God's covenantᵉ
and refused to live by his law.ᶠ

T Ps 66:16–17 ◀ ▶ Ps 105:1–2

77:18 ʰS Jdg 5:4
77:19 ⁱS Ex 14:22
ʲS Job 9:8
77:20 ᵏS Ex 13:21
ˡPs 78:52; Isa 63:11
ᵐS Ex 4:16;
S Nu 33:1
78:1 ⁿIsa 51:4;
55:3
78:2 ᵒS Ps 49:4;
S Mt 13:35*
78:3 ᵖS Jdg 6:13
78:4 ᵠS Dt 11:19
ʳDt 32:7;
S Ps 71:18
ˢPs 26:7; 71:17
ᵗS Job 5:9
78:5 ᵘPs 19:7;
81:5 ᵛPs 147:19
78:6 ʷS Ps 22:31
78:7 ˣS Dt 6:12
ʸS Dt 5:29
78:8 ᶻS 2Ch 30:7
ᵃS Ex 32:9
ᵇS Ex 23:21;
S Dt 21:18;
Isa 30:9; 65:2
78:9 ᶜver 57;
1Ch 12:2; Hos 7:16
ᵈS Jdg 20:39
78:10 ᵉS Jos 7:11;
S 2Ki 17:15
ᶠS Ex 16:28;
S Jer 11:8
78:11 ᵍS Ps 106:13
78:12 ʰS Ne 9:17;
Ps 106:22 ⁱEx 11:9
ʲS Nu 13:22
78:13
ᵏS Ex 14:21;
Ps 66:6; 136:13
ˡS Ex 14:22; S 15:8
78:14 ᵐS Ex 13:21;
Ps 105:39
78:15
ⁿS Nu 20:11;
1Co 10:4
78:17 ᵒver 32,40;
Dt 9:22; Isa 30:1;
63:10; Heb 3:16
78:18 ᵖS Ex 17:2;
1Co 10:9
ᵠS Ex 15:24;
Nu 11:4
78:19 ʳNu 21:5
78:20
ˢS Nu 20:11;
S Isa 35:6
ᵗNu 11:18
78:21 ᵘS Nu 11:1
78:22 ᵛS Dt 1:32;
Heb 3:19
78:23 ʷGe 7:11;
S 2Ki 7:2
78:24 ˣEx 6:4;
Jn 6:31*

¹¹They forgot what he had done,ᵍ
the wonders he had shown them.
¹²He did miraclesʰ in the sight of their
fathers
in the land of Egypt,ⁱ in the region
of Zoan.ʲ
¹³He divided the seaᵏ and led them
through;
he made the water stand firm like a
wall.ˡ
¹⁴He guided them with the cloud by day
and with light from the fire all
night.ᵐ
¹⁵He split the rocksⁿ in the desert
and gave them water as abundant as
the seas;
¹⁶he brought streams out of a rocky crag
and made water flow down like
rivers.
¹⁷But they continued to sinᵒ against him,
rebelling in the desert against the
Most High.
¹⁸They willfully put God to the testᵖ
by demanding the food they craved.ᵠ
¹⁹They spoke against God,ʳ saying,
"Can God spread a table in the
desert?
²⁰When he struck the rock, water
gushed out,ˢ
and streams flowed abundantly.
But can he also give us food?
Can he supply meatᵗ for his
people?"
²¹When the LORD heard them, he was
very angry;
his fire broke outᵘ against Jacob,
and his wrath rose against Israel,
²²for they did not believe in God
or trustᵛ in his deliverance.
²³Yet he gave a command to the skies
above
and opened the doors of the
heavens;ʷ
²⁴he rained down mannaˣ for the people
to eat,
he gave them the grain of heaven.
²⁵Men ate the bread of angels;

F Ps 37:25 ◀ ▶ Ps 78:19–29
F Ps 78:15–16 ◀ ▶ Ps 81:10

ʲTitle: Probably a literary or musical term

78:24–25 The psalmist calls this heavenly manna "the bread of angels" (78:25), indicating that the angels have the capacity to eat (see Ge 18:1–8). The NT also suggests that resurrected bodies will still eat (see Lk 24:36–43; Rev 19:7–9).

he sent them all the food they could eat.
²⁶He let loose the east wind^y from the heavens
and led forth the south wind by his power.
²⁷He rained meat down on them like dust,
flying birds^z like sand on the seashore.
²⁸He made them come down inside their camp,
all around their tents.
²⁹They ate till they had more than enough,^a
for he had given them what they craved.
³⁰But before they turned from the food they craved,
even while it was still in their mouths,^b
³¹God's anger rose against them;
he put to death the sturdiest^c among them,
cutting down the young men of Israel.
³²In spite of all this, they kept on sinning;^d
in spite of his wonders,^e they did not believe.^f
³³So he ended their days in futility^g
and their years in terror.
³⁴Whenever God slew them, they would seek^h him;
they eagerly turned to him again.
³⁵They remembered that God was their Rock,^i
that God Most High was their Redeemer.^j
³⁶But then they would flatter him with their mouths,^k
lying to him with their tongues;
³⁷their hearts were not loyal^l to him,
they were not faithful to his covenant.

L
P
³⁸Yet he was merciful;^m
he forgave^n their iniquities^o
and did not destroy them.
Time after time he restrained his anger^p
and did not stir up his full wrath.

N
³⁹He remembered that they were but flesh,^q

L Ps 77:7–9 ◀ ▶ Ps 85:2–3
P Ps 32:5 ◀ ▶ Isa 57:15–19
N Ps 49:10–14 ◀ ▶ Ps 89:48

78:26 ^y S Nu 11:31
78:27 ^z S Ex 16:13; Nu 11:31
78:29 ^a S Nu 11:20
78:30 ^b S Nu 11:33
78:31 ^c Isa 10:16
78:32 ^d S ver 17 ^e ver 11 ^f ver 22
78:33 ^g Nu 14:29, 35
78:34 ^h S Dt 4:29; Hos 5:15
78:35 ^i S Ge 49:24 ^j S Dt 9:26
78:36 ^k Eze 33:31
78:37 ^l ver 8; Ac 8:21
78:38 ^m S Ex 34:6 ^n Isa 1:25; 27:9; 48:10; Da 11:35 ^o Ps 25:11; 85:2 ^p S Job 9:13; S Isa 30:18
78:39 ^q S Ge 6:3; S Isa 29:5 ^r S Job 7:7; Jas 4:14
78:40 ^s S Ex 23:21 ^t Ps 95:8; 106:14 ^u Eph 4:30
78:41 ^v S Ex 17:2 ^w S 2Ki 19:22; Ps 71:22; 89:18
78:42 ^x S Jdg 3:7; S Ne 9:17 ^y S Ps 27:11
78:43 ^z Ex 10:1 ^a S Ex 3:20
78:44 ^b Ex 7:20-21; Ps 105:29
78:45 ^c S Ex 8:24; Ps 105:31 ^d S Ex 8:2,6
78:46 ^e Na 3:15 ^f S Ex 10:13
78:47 ^g Ex 9:23; Ps 105:32; 147:17
78:48 ^h Ex 9:25
78:49 ^i Ex 15:7 ^j S Ge 19:13; 1Co 10:10
78:51 ^k S Ex 12:12; Ps 135:8 ^l Ps 105:23; 106:22
78:52 ^m S Job 21:11; S Ps 28:9; 77:20
78:53 ^n S Ex 14:28 ^o Ex 15:7; Ps 106:10
78:54 ^p Ps 44:3
78:55 ^q Ps 44:2 ^r Dt 1:38; S Jos 13:7; Ac 13:19

a passing breeze^r that does not return.
⁴⁰How often they rebelled^s against him in the desert^t
and grieved him^u in the wasteland!
⁴¹Again and again they put God to the test;^v
they vexed the Holy One of Israel.^w
⁴²They did not remember^x his power—
the day he redeemed them from the oppressor,^y
⁴³the day he displayed his miraculous signs^z in Egypt,
his wonders^a in the region of Zoan.
⁴⁴He turned their rivers to blood;^b
they could not drink from their streams.
⁴⁵He sent swarms of flies^c that devoured them,
and frogs^d that devastated them.
⁴⁶He gave their crops to the grasshopper,^e
their produce to the locust.^f
⁴⁷He destroyed their vines with hail^g
and their sycamore-figs with sleet.
⁴⁸He gave over their cattle to the hail,
their livestock^h to bolts of lightning.
⁴⁹He unleashed against them his hot anger,^i
his wrath, indignation and hostility—
a band of destroying angels.^j
⁵⁰He prepared a path for his anger;
he did not spare them from death
but gave them over to the plague.
⁵¹He struck down all the firstborn of Egypt,^k
the firstfruits of manhood in the tents of Ham.^l
⁵²But he brought his people out like a flock;^m
he led them like sheep through the desert.
⁵³He guided them safely, so they were unafraid;
but the sea engulfed^n their enemies.^o
⁵⁴Thus he brought them to the border of his holy land,
to the hill country his right hand^p had taken.
⁵⁵He drove out nations^q before them
and allotted their lands to them as an inheritance;^r

L

L Ps 73:23–24 ◀ ▶ Ps 81:10

he settled the tribes of Israel in their homes.
⁵⁶But they put God to the test
and rebelled against the Most High;
they did not keep his statutes.
⁵⁷Like their fathers they were disloyal and faithless,
as unreliable as a faulty bow.
⁵⁸They angered him with their high places;
they aroused his jealousy with their idols.
⁵⁹When God heard them, he was very angry;
he rejected Israel completely.
⁶⁰He abandoned the tabernacle of Shiloh,
the tent he had set up among men.
⁶¹He sent ⌊the ark of⌋ his might into captivity,
his splendor into the hands of the enemy.
⁶²He gave his people over to the sword;
he was very angry with his inheritance.
⁶³Fire consumed their young men,
and their maidens had no wedding songs;
⁶⁴their priests were put to the sword,
and their widows could not weep.
⁶⁵Then the Lord awoke as from sleep,
as a man wakes from the stupor of wine.
⁶⁶He beat back his enemies;
he put them to everlasting shame.
⁶⁷Then he rejected the tents of Joseph,
he did not choose the tribe of Ephraim;
⁶⁸but he chose the tribe of Judah,
Mount Zion, which he loved.
⁶⁹He built his sanctuary like the heights,

like the earth that he established forever.
⁷⁰He chose David his servant
and took him from the sheep pens;
⁷¹from tending the sheep he brought him
to be the shepherd of his people Jacob,
of Israel his inheritance.
⁷²And David shepherded them with integrity of heart;
with skillful hands he led them.

Psalm 79

A psalm of Asaph.

¹O God, the nations have invaded your inheritance;
they have defiled your holy temple,
they have reduced Jerusalem to rubble.
²They have given the dead bodies of your servants
as food to the birds of the air,
the flesh of your saints to the beasts of the earth.
³They have poured out blood like water all around Jerusalem,
and there is no one to bury the dead.
⁴We are objects of reproach to our neighbors,
of scorn and derision to those around us.
⁵How long, O LORD? Will you be angry forever?
How long will your jealousy burn like fire?
⁶Pour out your wrath on the nations that do not acknowledge you,
on the kingdoms

R Ps 74:7–11 ◀▶ Ps 79:1
N Ps 75:3 ◀▶ Ps 93:1

R Ps 78:67 ◀▶ Ps 79:4–7
R Ps 79:1 ◀▶ Ps 80:4–6
l Ps 74:10 ◀▶ Ps 79:13

78:67–70 God had chosen Mt. Zion, in the territory allocated to the tribe of Judah, as the location for his temple. This sanctuary was as secure and enduring as the earth. A new earth will be revealed at the end of the Millennium (see Rev 21:1) and will be the home of the people who survive the Millennium. The new Jerusalem will descend to this perfected earth, and the resurrected believers will continue to rule there forever. For further information, see the article entitled "A New Heaven and a New Earth," p. 1494.

79:1 In this psalm Asaph complained to God that the enemies of Israel had defiled God's temple and destroyed Jerusalem, referring to the conquest of Jerusalem by the Babylonian army of Nebuchadnezzar in 586 B.C.

79:4–7 Note the similarity between vv. 6–7 and Jer 10:25. Perhaps Asaph is quoting the prophet here in his prayer for justice.

that do not call on your name;ʰ
⁷for they have devouredⁱ Jacob
and destroyed his homeland.

⁸Do not hold against us the sins of the
fathers;ʲ
may your mercy come quickly to
meet us,
for we are in desperate need.ᵏ

⁹Help us,ˡ O God our Savior,
for the glory of your name;
deliver us and forgive our sins
for your name's sake.ᵐ

¹⁰Why should the nations say,
"Where is their God?"ⁿ
Before our eyes, make known among
the nations
that you avengeᵒ the outpoured
bloodᵖ of your servants.

¹¹May the groans of the prisoners come
before you;
by the strength of your arm
preserve those condemned to die.

¹²Pay back into the lapsᵠ of our
neighbors seven timesʳ
the reproach they have hurled at
you, O Lord.

¹³Then we your people, the sheep of
your pasture,ˢ
will praise you forever;ᵗ
from generation to generation
we will recount your praise.

Psalm 80

For the director of music. To the tune of
"The Lilies of the Covenant." Of Asaph.
A psalm.

¹Hear us, O Shepherd of Israel,
you who lead Joseph like a flock;ᵘ
you who sit enthroned between the
cherubim,ᵛ shine forth
² before Ephraim, Benjamin and
Manasseh.ʷ
Awakenˣ your might;
come and save us.ʸ

³Restoreᶻ us,ᵃ O God;

I Ps 79:5 ◀ ▶ Ps 80:3–7
I Ps 79:13 ◀ ▶ Ps 80:14–15
K Ps 73:26 ◀ ▶ Ps 80:7

79:6 ʰ Ps 14:4
79:7 ⁱ Isa 9:12;
Jer 10:25

79:8 ʲ S Ge 9:25;
Jer 44:21
ᵏ Ps 116:6; 142:6
79:9 ˡ 2Ch 14:11
ᵐ Ps 25:11; 31:3;
Jer 14:7

79:10 ⁿ S Ps 42:3
ᵒ Ps 94:1;
S Rev 6:10 ᵖ ver 3

79:12 ᵠ Isa 65:6;
Jer 32:18
ʳ S Ge 4:15

79:13 ˢ S Ps 74:1
ᵗ Ps 44:8

80:1 ᵘ S Ps 77:20
ᵛ S Ex 25:22

80:2 ʷ Nu 2:18-24
ˣ S Ps 35:23
ʸ Ps 54:1; 69:1;
71:2; 109:26;
116:4; 119:94

80:3 ᶻ S Ps 71:20;
85:4; Jer 31:18;
La 5:21 ᵃ S Nu 6:25
ᵇ ver 7,19

80:4 ᶜ S Ps 74:10
ᵈ S Dt 29:20

80:5 ᵉ S Job 3:24
ᶠ Isa 30:20

80:6 ᵍ S Ps 79:4

80:7 ʰ ver 3

80:8 ⁱ Isa 5:1-2;
Jer 2:21;
Mt 21:33-41
ʲ Ex 23:28-30;
S Jos 13:6; Ac 7:45
ᵏ S Ex 15:17

80:11 ˡ Ps 72:8

80:12 ᵐ Ps 89:40;
Isa 5:5; 30:13;
Jer 39:8

80:13 ⁿ Jer 5:6

80:14 ᵒ S Dt 26:15

80:16 ᵖ Ps 79:1
ᵠ S Dt 28:20

make your face shine upon us,
that we may be saved.ᵇ

⁴O LORD God Almighty,
how longᶜ will your anger smolderᵈ
against the prayers of your people?
⁵You have fed them with the bread of
tears;ᵉ
you have made them drink tears by
the bowlful.ᶠ
⁶You have made us a source of
contention to our neighbors,
and our enemies mock us.ᵍ

⁷Restore us, O God Almighty;
make your face shine upon us,
that we may be saved.ʰ

⁸You brought a vineⁱ out of Egypt;
you drove outʲ the nations and
plantedᵏ it.
⁹You cleared the ground for it,
and it took root and filled the land.
¹⁰The mountains were covered with its
shade,
the mighty cedars with its branches.
¹¹It sent out its boughs to the Sea,ᵍ
its shoots as far as the River.ʰ

¹²Why have you broken down its walls,ᵐ
so that all who pass by pick its
grapes?
¹³Boars from the forest ravageⁿ it
and the creatures of the field feed on
it.
¹⁴Return to us, O God Almighty!
Look down from heaven and see!ᵒ
Watch over this vine,
¹⁵ the root your right hand has planted,
the sonⁱ you have raised up for
yourself.

¹⁶Your vine is cut down, it is burned
with fire;ᵖ
at your rebukeᵠ your people perish.

¹⁷Let your hand rest on the man at your
right hand,

R Ps 79:4–7 ◀ ▶ Ps 80:12–16
K Ps 80:3 ◀ ▶ Ps 80:19
R Ps 80:4–6 ◀ ▶ Isa 1:7–9
I Ps 80:3–7 ◀ ▶ Ps 80:19

ᵍ 11 Probably the Mediterranean ʰ 11 That is, the Euphrates
ⁱ 15 Or branch

79:13 The psalmist rejoiced in his prophetic vision of the final victory over the heathen.
80:3 The psalmist calls upon God for restoration and revival with words that echo the priestly benediction of Nu 6:25.
80:3–16, 19 Asaph expressed his confidence in God's ultimate sovereignty and deliverance despite a time of great destruction.

the son of man' you have raised up
    for yourself.
¹⁸Then we will not turn away from you;
    revive us, and we will call on your
        name.

¹⁹Restore us, O LORD God Almighty;
    make your face shine upon us,
    that we may be saved.

Psalm 81

For the director of music. According to
    gittith.ʲ Of Asaph.

¹Sing for joy to God our strength;
    shout aloud to the God of Jacob!ᵗ
²Begin the music, strike the
        tambourine,ᵘ
    play the melodious harpᵛ and lyre.ʷ
³Sound the ram's hornˣ at the New
        Moon,ʸ
    and when the moon is full, on the
        day of our Feast;
⁴this is a decree for Israel,
    an ordinance of the God of Jacob.ᶻ
⁵He established it as a statute for Joseph
    when he went out against Egypt,ᵃ
    where we heard a language we did
        not understand.ᵏᵇ
⁶He says, "I removed the burdenᶜ from
        their shoulders;ᵈ
    their hands were set free from the
        basket.
⁷In your distress you calledᵉ and I
        rescued you,
    I answeredᶠ you out of a
        thundercloud;
    I tested you at the waters of
        Meribah.ᵍ   Selah
⁸"Hear, O my people,ʰ and I will warn
        you—
    if you would but listen to me,
        O Israel!
⁹You shall have no foreign godⁱ among
        you;
    you shall not bow down to an alien
        god.
¹⁰I am the LORD your God,
    who brought you up out of Egypt.ʲ
    Openᵏ wide your mouth and I will
        fillˡ it.

I Ps 80:14-15 ◀ ▶ Ps 85:1-13
K Ps 80:7 ◀ ▶ Ps 84:11
F Ps 78:19-29 ◀ ▶ Ps 81:16
L Ps 78:52-53 ◀ ▶ Ps 86:7

80:17 ʳS Job 25:6
80:18 ˢPs 85:6;
    Isa 57:15; Hos 6:2
81:1 ᵗS Ps 66:1
81:2 ᵘS Ex 15:20
    ᵛPs 92:3
    ʷS Job 21:12
81:3 ˣS Ex 19:13
    ʸS Ne 10:33
81:4 ᶻver 1
81:5 ᵃS Ex 11:4
    ᵇPs 114:1
81:6 ᶜS Ex 1:14
    ᵈIsa 9:4; 52:2
81:7 ᵉS Ex 2:23
    ᶠEx 19:19
    ᵍS Ex 17:7;
    S Dt 33:8
81:8 ʰPs 50:7;
    78:1
81:9 ⁱS Ex 20:3
81:10 ʲS Ex 6:6;
    S 13:3; S 29:46
    ᵏEze 2:8 ˡPs 107:9
81:11 ᵐEx 32:1-6
81:12 ⁿEze 20:25;
    Ac 7:42; Ro 1:24
81:13 ᵒS Dt 5:29
81:14 ᵖPs 47:3
    ᵠAm 1:8
81:15
    ʳS 2Sa 22:45
81:16 ˢS Dt 32:14

82:1 ᵗPs 7:8;
    58:11; Isa 3:13;
    66:16; Joel 3:12
    ᵘS Job 21:22
82:2 ᵛDt 1:17
    ʷPs 58:1-2; Pr 18:5
82:3 ˣS Dt 24:17
    ʸPs 140:12;
    Jer 5:28; 22:16
82:5 ᶻS Ps 14:4;
    S 53:2 ᵃJob 30:26;
    Isa 5:30; 8:21-22;
    9:2; 59:9; 60:2;
    Jer 13:16; 23:12;
    La 3:2 ᵇS Jdg 5:4;
    S Ps 11:3
82:6 ᶜJn 10:34*
82:7 ᵈPs 49:12;
    Eze 31:14

¹¹"But my people would not listen to
        me;
    Israel would not submit to me.ᵐ
¹²So I gave them overⁿ to their stubborn
        hearts
    to follow their own devices.

¹³"If my people would but listen to me,ᵒ
    if Israel would follow my ways,
¹⁴how quickly would I subdueᵖ their
        enemies
    and turn my hand againstᵠ their
        foes!
¹⁵Those who hate the LORD would
        cringeʳ before him,
    and their punishment would last
        forever.
¹⁶But you would be fed with the finest of
        wheat;ˢ
    with honey from the rock I would
        satisfy you."

Psalm 82

A psalm of Asaph.

¹God presides in the great assembly;
    he gives judgmentᵗ among the
        "gods":ᵘ

²"How long will youᵛ defend the unjust
    and show partialityᵛ to the wicked?ʷ
                            Selah
³Defend the cause of the weak and
        fatherless;ˣ
    maintain the rights of the poorʸ and
        oppressed.
⁴Rescue the weak and needy;
    deliver them from the hand of the
        wicked.

⁵"They know nothing, they understand
        nothing.ᶻ
    They walk about in darkness;ᵃ
    all the foundationsᵇ of the earth are
        shaken.

⁶"I said, 'You are "gods";ᶜ
    you are all sons of the Most High.'
⁷But you will dieᵈ like mere men;
    you will fall like every other ruler."

V Ps 60:12 ◀ ▶ Ps 89:22-23
U Ps 73:1 ◀ ▶ Ps 84:4-5
F Ps 81:10 ◀ ▶ Ps 103:5

ʲTitle: Probably a musical term ᵏ5 Or / and we heard a voice we had not
known ˡ2 The Hebrew is plural.

⁸Rise up, O God, judge the earth,
   for all the nations are your
      inheritance.

Psalm 83

A song. A psalm of Asaph.

¹O God, do not keep silent;
   be not quiet, O God, be not still.
²See how your enemies are astir,
   how your foes rear their heads.
³With cunning they conspire against
      your people;
   they plot against those you cherish.
⁴"Come," they say, "let us destroy
      them as a nation,
   that the name of Israel be
      remembered no more."

⁵With one mind they plot together;
   they form an alliance against you—
⁶the tents of Edom and the
      Ishmaelites,
   of Moab and the Hagrites,
⁷Gebal, Ammon and Amalek,
   Philistia, with the people of Tyre.
⁸Even Assyria has joined them
   to lend strength to the descendants
      of Lot.   *Selah*

⁹Do to them as you did to Midian,
   as you did to Sisera and Jabin at
      the river Kishon,
¹⁰who perished at Endor
   and became like refuse on the
      ground.
¹¹Make their nobles like Oreb and
      Zeeb,
   all their princes like Zebah and
      Zalmunna,
¹²who said, "Let us take possession
      of the pasturelands of God."

¹³Make them like tumbleweed, O my
      God,
   like chaff before the wind.
¹⁴As fire consumes the forest
   or a flame sets the mountains
      ablaze,
¹⁵so pursue them with your tempest
   and terrify them with your storm.
¹⁶Cover their faces with shame
   so that men will seek your name,
      O LORD.

¹⁷May they ever be ashamed and
      dismayed;
   may they perish in disgrace.
¹⁸Let them know that you, whose name
      is the LORD—
   that you alone are the Most High
      over all the earth.

Psalm 84

For the director of music. According to *gittith*. Of the Sons of Korah. A psalm.

¹How lovely is your dwelling place,
   O LORD Almighty!
²My soul yearns, even faints,
   for the courts of the LORD;
my heart and my flesh cry out
   for the living God.

³Even the sparrow has found a home,
   and the swallow a nest for herself,
   where she may have her young—
a place near your altar,
   O LORD Almighty, my King and my
      God.

⁴Blessed are those who dwell in your
      house;
   they are ever praising you. *Selah*
⁵Blessed are those whose strength is in
      you,
   who have set their hearts on
      pilgrimage.
⁶As they pass through the Valley of
      Baca,
   they make it a place of springs;
   the autumn rains also cover it with
      pools.
⁷They go from strength to strength,

82:8 Asaph confirmed the great truth that God will ultimately judge all of his inheritance.
83:13–17 These verses plead for God to destroy his enemies so that God's kingdom of righteousness and peace will come. Though this was the plea of most of the kings of Israel and Judah, these words also foreshadow the time when Jesus Christ will defeat his enemies during the seven years of the great tribulation.

till each appears[f] before God in Zion.[g]

⁸Hear my prayer,[h] O LORD God Almighty;
    listen to me, O God of Jacob.   Selah
⁹Look upon our shield,[p,i] O God;
    look with favor on your anointed one.[j]

¹⁰Better is one day in your courts
    than a thousand elsewhere;
I would rather be a doorkeeper[k] in the house of my God
    than dwell in the tents of the wicked.
¹¹For the LORD God is a sun[l] and shield;[m]
    the LORD bestows favor and honor;
no good thing does he withhold[n]
    from those whose walk is blameless.

¹²O LORD Almighty,
    blessed[o] is the man who trusts in you.

Psalm 85

For the director of music. Of the Sons of Korah. A psalm.

¹You showed favor to your land, O LORD;
    you restored the fortunes[p] of Jacob.
²You forgave[q] the iniquity[r] of your people
    and covered all their sins.   Selah
³You set aside all your wrath[s]
    and turned from your fierce anger.[t]

⁴Restore[u] us again, O God our Savior,[v]
    and put away your displeasure toward us.
⁵Will you be angry with us forever?[w]
    Will you prolong your anger through all generations?
⁶Will you not revive[x] us again,
    that your people may rejoice[y] in you?

U Ps 84:7 ◄ ► Ps 89:15–16
K Ps 80:19 ◄ ► Ps 89:15–16
F Ps 37:3 ◄ ► Ps 125:1
I Ps 80:19 ◄ ► Ps 87:3
L Ps 78:38–39 ◄ ► Ps 85:9–10

84:7 ᶠS Dt 16:16; ᵍ1Ki 8:1
84:8 ʰPs 4:1
84:9 ⁱS Ps 59:11; ʲ1Sa 16:6; Ps 2:2; 18:50; 132:17
84:10 ᵏ1Ch 23:5
84:11 ˡIsa 60:19; Jer 43:13; Rev 21:23; ᵐS Ge 15:1; ⁿPs 34:10
84:12 ᵒPs 2:12
85:1 ᵖS Dt 30:3; Ps 14:7
85:2 ᵠS Nu 14:19; ʳS Ex 32:30; S Ps 78:38
85:3 ˢPs 106:23; Da 9:16 ᵗEx 32:12; Dt 13:17; Ps 78:38; Jnh 3:9
85:4 ᵘS Ps 71:20; ᵛS Ps 65:5
85:5 ʷS Ps 50:21
85:6 ˣS Ps 80:18; ʸPhp 3:1
85:7 ᶻS Ps 6:4; ᵃPs 27:1
85:8 ᵇS Lev 26:6; S Isa 60:17; S Jn 14:27; 2Th 3:16; ᶜPr 26:11; 27:22
85:9 ᵈPs 27:1; Isa 43:3; 45:8; 46:13; 51:5; 56:1; 62:11 ᵉS Ex 29:43; Isa 60:19; Hag 2:9; Zec 2:5
85:10 ᶠPs 89:14; 115:1; Pr 3:3 ᵍPs 72:2-3; Isa 32:17
85:11 ʰIsa 45:8
85:12 ⁱPs 84:11; Jas 1:17; Lev 26:4; S Ps 67:6; Zec 8:12
86:1 ᵏPs 17:6
86:2 ˡPs 25:2; 31:14
86:3 ᵐPs 4:1; S 9:13; 57:1; ⁿPs 88:9
86:4 ᵒPs 46:5; 143:5
86:5 ᵖEx 34:6; Ne 9:17; Ps 103:8; 145:8; Joel 2:13; Jnh 4:2
86:6 ᵠPs 5:2; 17:1

⁷Show us your unfailing love,[z] O LORD,
    and grant us your salvation.[a]

⁸I will listen to what God the LORD will say;
    he promises peace[b] to his people, his saints—
    but let them not return to folly.[c]
⁹Surely his salvation[d] is near those who fear him,
    that his glory[e] may dwell in our land.

¹⁰Love and faithfulness[f] meet together;
    righteousness[g] and peace kiss each other.
¹¹Faithfulness springs forth from the earth,
    and righteousness[h] looks down from heaven.
¹²The LORD will indeed give what is good,[i]
    and our land will yield[j] its harvest.
¹³Righteousness goes before him
    and prepares the way for his steps.

Psalm 86

A prayer of David.

¹Hear, O LORD, and answer[k] me,
    for I am poor and needy.
²Guard my life, for I am devoted to you.
    You are my God; save your servant who trusts in you.[l]
³Have mercy[m] on me, O Lord,
    for I call[n] to you all day long.
⁴Bring joy to your servant,
    for to you, O Lord,
    I lift[o] up my soul.
⁵You are forgiving and good, O Lord,
    abounding in love[p] to all who call to you.
⁶Hear my prayer, O LORD;
    listen to my cry[q] for mercy.

M Ps 82:8 ◄ ► Ps 86:9
L Ps 85:2–3 ◄ ► Ps 86:5
B Ps 67:6 ◄ ► Ps 107:38
L Ps 85:9–10 ◄ ► Ps 86:15
W Ps 50:1 ◄ ► Ps 145:9

p 9 Or sovereign

85:1–13 This psalm recalls God's powerful deeds and his past faithfulness to help bring hope in a difficult time. In the Millennium, people will enjoy the blessings of God's victory again as the Messiah overcomes the nations that have resisted God's commands. This victory will allow for the proclamation of his righteousness among the captive nations.

⁷In the day of my trouble^r I will call^s to you,
for you will answer^t me.

⁸Among the gods^u there is none like you,^v O Lord;
no deeds can compare with yours.
⁹All the nations you have made
will come^w and worship^x before you, O Lord;
they will bring glory^y to your name.
¹⁰For you are great^z and do marvelous deeds;^a
you alone^b are God.

¹¹Teach me your way,^c O LORD,
and I will walk in your truth;^d
give me an undivided^e heart,
that I may fear^f your name.
¹²I will praise you, O Lord my God, with all my heart;^g
I will glorify your name forever.
¹³For great is your love toward me;
you have delivered me^h from the depths of the grave.^{q i}

¹⁴The arrogant are attacking me, O God;
a band of ruthless men seeks my life—
men without regard for you.^j
¹⁵But you, O Lord, are a compassionate and gracious^k God,
slow to anger,^l abounding^m in love and faithfulness.ⁿ
¹⁶Turn to me^o and have mercy^p on me;
grant your strength^q to your servant
and save the son of your maidservant.^{rr}
¹⁷Give me a sign^s of your goodness,
that my enemies may see it and be put to shame,
for you, O LORD, have helped me and comforted me.

L Ps 81:10 ◀▶ Ps 90:1
M Ps 85:9–13 ◀▶ Ps 89:3–4
H Ps 83:17 ◀▶ Ps 92:7
L Ps 86:5 ◀▶ Ps 99:8

Psalm 87

Of the Sons of Korah. A psalm. A song.

¹He has set his foundation on the holy mountain;^t
² the LORD loves the gates of Zion^u
more than all the dwellings of Jacob.

³Glorious things are said of you,
O city of God:^v   *Selah*
⁴"I will record Rahab^{s w} and Babylon
among those who acknowledge me—
Philistia^x too, and Tyre^y, along with Cush^t—
and will say, 'This^u one was born in Zion.^z'"
⁵Indeed, of Zion it will be said,
"This one and that one were born in her,
and the Most High himself will establish her."
⁶The LORD will write in the register^a of the peoples:
"This one was born in Zion." *Selah*
⁷As they make music^b they will sing,
"All my fountains^c are in you."

Psalm 88

A song. A psalm of the Sons of Korah. For the director of music. According to mahalath leannoth.^v *A* maskil^w *of Heman the Ezrahite.*

¹O LORD, the God who saves me,^d
day and night I cry out^e before you.
²May my prayer come before you;
turn your ear to my cry.

³For my soul is full of trouble^f
and my life draws near the grave.^{q g}
⁴I am counted among those who go down to the pit;^h

I Ps 85:1–13 ◀▶ Ps 87:5
J Ps 69:25 ◀▶ Ecc 3:17–18
I Ps 87:3 ◀▶ Ps 94:14
E Ps 69:5 ◀▶ Ps 90:8

^q 13,3 Hebrew *Sheol*   ^r 16 Or *save your faithful son*   ^s 4 A poetic name for Egypt   ^t 4 That is, the upper Nile region   ^u 4 Or *"O Rahab and Babylon, / Philistia, Tyre and Cush, / I will record concerning those who acknowledge me: / 'This'*   ^v Title: Possibly a tune, "The Suffering of Affliction"   ^w Title: Probably a literary or musical term

---

86:9 David prophetically announced that humanity would finally repent of its sin and glorify God. This prophecy will not be fulfilled until the Millennium.

87:3–5 One day, in the Millennium, humanity will speak glorious things of Jerusalem. Note that at that time native-born citizens will have special honor and privileges.

I am like a man without strength.
⁵I am set apart with the dead,
  like the slain who lie in the grave,
  whom you remember no more,
  who are cut off from your care.
⁶You have put me in the lowest pit,
  in the darkest depths.
⁷Your wrath lies heavily upon me;
  you have overwhelmed me with all
    your waves. *Selah*
⁸You have taken from me my closest
    friends
  and have made me repulsive to
    them.
  I am confined and cannot escape;
⁹ my eyes are dim with grief.

  I call to you, O LORD, every day;
  I spread out my hands to you.
¹⁰Do you show your wonders to the
    dead?
  Do those who are dead rise up and
    praise you? *Selah*
¹¹Is your love declared in the grave,
  your faithfulness in Destruction?
¹²Are your wonders known in the place
    of darkness,
  or your righteous deeds in the land
    of oblivion?

¹³But I cry to you for help, O LORD;
  in the morning my prayer comes
    before you.
¹⁴Why, O LORD, do you reject me
  and hide your face from me?
¹⁵From my youth I have been afflicted
    and close to death;
  I have suffered your terrors and am
    in despair.
¹⁶Your wrath has swept over me;
  your terrors have destroyed me.
¹⁷All day long they surround me like a
    flood;
  they have completely engulfed me.

F Ps 71:20 ◀ ▶ Isa 25:8

¹⁸You have taken my companions and
    loved ones from me;
  the darkness is my closest friend.

Psalm 89

A *maskil* of Ethan the Ezrahite.

¹I will sing of the LORD's great love
    forever;
  with my mouth I will make your
    faithfulness known through all
    generations.
²I will declare that your love stands firm
    forever,
  that you established your
    faithfulness in heaven itself.

³You said, "I have made a covenant
    with my chosen one,
  I have sworn to David my servant,
⁴'I will establish your line forever
  and make your throne firm through
    all generations.'" *Selah*

⁵The heavens praise your wonders,
    O LORD,
  your faithfulness too, in the
    assembly of the holy ones.
⁶For who in the skies above can
    compare with the LORD?
  Who is like the LORD among the
    heavenly beings?
⁷In the council of the holy ones God
    is greatly feared;
  he is more awesome than all who
    surround him.
⁸O LORD God Almighty, who is like
    you?
  You are mighty, O LORD, and your
    faithfulness surrounds you.
⁹You rule over the surging sea;

M Ps 86:9 ◀ ▶ Ps 89:26–32

x 11 Hebrew *Abaddon* y Title: Probably a literary or musical term

---

88:10–12 This psalm expressed a cry of abandonment from one who felt the heavy hand of God's judgment on Israel. The Scriptures often record the deep emotions of the godly as they face struggles. Yet other passages provide God's answer to those questions of the heart: In everything God reigns supreme, "for the LORD Almighty has purposed, and who can thwart him?" (Isa 14:27).

89:3–4 Though it appeared that God had violated his covenant with David in allowing his downfall, the Lord reconfirmed the unbreakable covenant that he had made centuries earlier with David (see note at 2Sa 7:16). In the NT, the apostle Peter reminded his listeners that God had promised by an oath to King David that "he would place one of his descendants on his throne" (Ac 2:30). The genealogical records trace Jesus' line back to the throne of David (see Mt 1:1–16; Lk 3:23–38) giving him the legal status as David's descendant to rule from David's throne as the Messiah.

when its waves mount up, you still them.ᵘ
¹⁰You crushed Rahabᵛ like one of the slain;
with your strong arm you scatteredʷ your enemies.
¹¹The heavens are yours,ˣ and yours also the earth;ʸ
you founded the world and all that is in it.ᶻ
¹²You created the north and the south;
Taborᵃ and Hermonᵇ sing for joyᶜ at your name.
¹³Your arm is endued with power;
your hand is strong, your right hand exalted.ᵈ
¹⁴Righteousness and justice are the foundation of your throne;ᵉ
love and faithfulness go before you.ᶠ
K ¹⁵Blessed are those who have learned to acclaim you,
U who walkᵍ in the lightʰ of your presence, O LORD.
¹⁶They rejoice in your nameⁱ all day long;
they exult in your righteousness.
¹⁷For you are their glory and strength,ʲ
and by your favor you exalt our horn.ᶻᵏ
¹⁸Indeed, our shieldᵃ¹ belongs to the LORD,
our kingᵐ to the Holy One of Israel.
¹⁹Once you spoke in a vision,
to your faithful people you said:
"I have bestowed strength on a warrior;
I have exalted a young man from among the people.
²⁰I have found Davidⁿ my servant;ᵒ
with my sacred oilᵖ I have anointedᑫ him.
²¹My hand will sustain him;
surely my arm will strengthen him.ʳ
V ²²No enemy will subject him to tribute;ˢ

K Ps 84:11 ◀ ▶ Ps 91:3
U Ps 84:10–12 ◀ ▶ Ps 91:1–16
V Ps 81:13–14 ◀ ▶ Ps 91:1–16

89:9 ᵘS Ps 65:7
89:10 ᵛS Job 9:13
ʷS Ps 59:11; S 68:1; 92:9
89:11 ˣS Dt 10:14; Ps 115:16
ʸ1Ch 29:11; S Ps 24:1 ᶻS Ge 1:1
89:12 ᵃS Jos 19:22
ᵇS Dt 3:8; S 4:48
ᶜPs 98:8
89:13 ᵈS Jos 4:24
89:14 ᵉPs 97:2
ᶠPs 85:10-11
89:15 ᵍPs 1:1
ʰPs 44:3
89:16 ⁱPs 30:4; 105:3
89:17 ʲPs 18:1
ᵏver 24; Ps 75:10; 92:10; 112:9; 148:14
89:18 ᵃ¹Ps 18:2
ᵐPs 47:9; Isa 16:5; 33:17,22
89:20 ⁿAc 13:22
ᵒPs 78:70
ᵖEx 29:7; S 1Ki 1:39
ᑫS 1Sa 2:35; S 2Sa 22:51
89:21 ʳver 13; Ps 18:35
89:22 ˢS Jdg 3:15
ᵗ2Sa 7:10
89:23 ᵘPs 18:40
ᵛ2Sa 7:9
89:24 ʷS 2Sa 7:15
89:25 ˣPs 72:8
89:26 ʸS 2Sa 7:14; S Jer 3:4; Heb 1:5
ᶻS Ps 62:2
ᵃ2Sa 22:47
89:27 ᵇS Col 1:18
ᶜS Nu 24:7 ᵈPs 2:6; Rev 1:5; 19:16
89:28 ᵉver 33-34; Isa 55:3
89:29 ᶠver 4,36
89:32 ᵍ2Sa 7:14
89:33 ʰ2Sa 7:15
89:34 ⁱS Nu 23:19
89:36 ʲver 4
89:37 ᵏJer 33:20-21

no wicked man will oppressᵗ him.
²³I will crush his foes before himᵘ
and strike down his adversaries.ᵛ
²⁴My faithful love will be with him,ʷ
and through my name his hornᵇ will be exalted.
²⁵I will set his hand over the sea,
his right hand over the rivers.ˣ
²⁶He will call out to me, 'You are my Father,ʸ
my God, the Rockᶻ my Savior.'ᵃ
²⁷I will also appoint him my firstborn,ᵇ
the most exaltedᶜ of the kingsᵈ of the earth.
²⁸I will maintain my love to him forever,
and my covenant with him will never fail.ᵉ
²⁹I will establish his line forever,
his throne as long as the heavens endure.ᶠ
³⁰"If his sons forsake my law
and do not follow my statutes,
³¹if they violate my decrees
and fail to keep my commands,
³²I will punish their sin with the rod,
their iniquity with flogging;ᵍ
³³but I will not take my love from him,ʰ
nor will I ever betray my faithfulness.
³⁴I will not violate my covenant
or alter what my lips have uttered.ⁱ
³⁵Once for all, I have sworn by my holiness—
and I will not lie to David—
³⁶that his line will continue forever
and his throne endure before me like the sun;ʲ
³⁷it will be established forever like the moon,
the faithful witness in the sky."ᵏ
Selah

M Ps 89:3–4 ◀ ▶ Ps 89:35–37
T Ps 66:10–12 ◀ ▶ Ps 94:12–13
M Ps 89:26–32 ◀ ▶ Ps 93:1–2

ᶻ 17 *Horn* here symbolizes strong one. ᵃ 18 Or *sovereign* ᵇ 24 *Horn* here symbolizes strength.

89:27–29 Note the similarity between this prophecy about the Messiah as God's "firstborn, the most exalted of the kings of the earth" (89:27) and the description of Jesus Christ as "the image of the invisible God, the firstborn over all creation" (Col 1:15) and "his one and only Son" (Jn 3:16).
89:34–37 The Lord reconfirmed his unbreakable covenant with David and his descendants. However, he warned David's descendants that disobedience to God's laws would be punished severely. The downward spiral of Israel's refusal to repent and return to worship God resulted in the division of David's kingdom (see 1Ki 11:26–40) and the Assyrian and Babylonian captivities.

⁳⁸But you have rejected,¹ you have spurned,
 you have been very angry with your anointed one.
³⁹You have renounced the covenant with your servant
 and have defiled his crown in the dust.ᵐ
⁴⁰You have broken through all his wallsⁿ
 and reduced his strongholdsᵒ to ruins.
⁴¹All who pass by have plunderedᵖ him;
 he has become the scorn of his neighbors.ᵠ
⁴²You have exalted the right hand of his foes;
 you have made all his enemies rejoice.ʳ
⁴³You have turned back the edge of his sword
 and have not supported him in battle.ˢ
⁴⁴You have put an end to his splendor
 and cast his throne to the ground.
⁴⁵You have cut shortᵗ the days of his youth;
 you have covered him with a mantle of shame.ᵘ Selah
⁴⁶How long, O Lord? Will you hide yourself forever?
 How long will your wrath burn like fire?ᵛ
⁴⁷Remember how fleeting is my life.ʷ
 For what futility you have created all men!
⁴⁸What man can live and not see death,
 or save himself from the power of the grave?ᶜˣ Selah
⁴⁹O Lord, where is your former great love,

N Ps 78:39 ◀ ▶ Ps 90:5–6

89:38 ¹1Ch 28:9; Ps 44:9; 78:59
89:39 ᵐLa 5:16
89:40 ⁿS Ps 80:12
 ᵒIsa 22:5; La 2:2
89:41 ᵖS Jdg 2:14
 ᵠS Ps 44:13
89:42 ʳPs 13:2; 80:6
89:43 ˢPs 44:10
89:45 ᵗS Ps 39:5
 ᵘPs 44:15; 109:29
89:46 ᵛPs 79:5
89:47 ʷS Ge 47:9; S Job 7:7; Ps 39:5; 1Pe 1:24
89:48 ˣS Ge 5:24; Ps 22:29
89:50 ʸPs 69:19
89:51 ᶻPs 74:10
89:52 ᵃS Ps 41:13; S 72:19
90:1 ᵇS Dt 33:27; Eph 2:22; Rev 21:3
90:2 ᶜS Job 15:7
 ᵈIsa 9:6; 57:15
 ᵉS Ge 21:33;
 S Job 10:5;
 Ps 102:24-27;
 Pr 8:23-26
90:3 ᶠS Ge 2:7;
 S Job 7:21; 34:15;
 1Co 15:47
90:4 ᵍS Job 10:5;
 2Pe 3:8
90:5 ʰS Ge 19:15

which in your faithfulness you swore to David?
⁵⁰Remember, Lord, how your servant hasᵈ been mocked,ʸ
 how I bear in my heart the taunts of all the nations,
⁵¹the taunts with which your enemies have mocked, O Lord,
 with which they have mocked every step of your anointed one.ᶻ
⁵²Praise be to the Lord forever!
 Amen and Amen.ᵃ

BOOK IV

Psalms 90–106

Psalm 90

A prayer of Moses the man of God.

¹Lord, you have been our dwelling placeᵇ
 throughout all generations.
²Before the mountains were bornᶜ
 or you brought forth the earth and the world,
 from everlasting to everlastingᵈ you are God.ᵉ
³You turn men back to dust,
 saying, "Return to dust, O sons of men."ᶠ
⁴For a thousand years in your sight
 are like a day that has just gone by,
 or like a watch in the night.ᵍ
⁵You sweep men awayʰ in the sleep of death;

L Ps 86:7 ◀ ▶ Ps 91:1–16
N Ps 89:48 ◀ ▶ Ps 90:9

ᶜ48 Hebrew *Sheol* ᵈ50 Or *your servants have*

90:4 The eternal God is not bound by our sense of time; one thousand years to him is but one day. In the NT the apostle Peter also reminded believers of this view of time (see 2Pe 3:8). These verses have prompted various interpretations. Some early church scholars taught that the relationship of one day to a thousand years could be used to determine a Biblical timeline. They believed that the six days of creation symbolized six thousand years of humanity's dominion on earth and concluded that the Sabbath day of rest was a symbol for the peaceful Millennium.

While this theory was widely taught in the early church, Scripture warns against any dogmatic declarations of when certain Biblical events will occur because "no one knows about that day or hour, not even the angels in heaven, nor the Son, but only the Father" (Mk 13:32). Instead, we should be watchful and aware of the prophecies in Scripture, looking for their fulfillment, so that "when these things begin to take place" we can then "stand up and lift up your heads, because your redemption is drawing near" (Lk 21:28). Until our Lord returns and the trumpet calls us to meet him in the air, we should be actively going about his business so that he will number us among his faithful servants (see Mt 25:21; Col 3:17; 2Ti 4:8).

they are like the new grass of the
    morning—
⁶though in the morning it springs up
    new,
  by evening it is dry and withered.ⁱ

⁷We are consumed by your anger
  and terrified by your indignation.
⁸You have set our iniquities before
    you,
  our secret sinsʲ in the light of your
    presence.ᵏ
⁹All our days pass away under your
    wrath;
  we finish our years with a moan.ˡ
¹⁰The length of our days is seventy
    yearsᵐ—
  or eighty,ⁿ if we have the strength;
  yet their spanᵉ is but trouble and
    sorrow,ᵒ
  for they quickly pass, and we fly
    away.ᵖ
¹¹Who knows the power of your
    anger?
  For your wrathq is as great as the
    fear that is due you.ʳ
¹²Teach us to number our daysˢ aright,
  that we may gain a heart of
    wisdom.ᵗ

¹³Relent, O LORD! How longᵘ will
    it be?
  Have compassion on your
    servants.ᵛ
¹⁴Satisfyʷ us in the morning with your
    unfailing love,ˣ
  that we may sing for joyʸ and be
    glad all our days.ᶻ
¹⁵Make us glad for as many days as you
    have afflicted us,
  for as many years as we have seen
    trouble.
¹⁶May your deeds be shown to your
    servants,
  your splendor to their children.ᵃ

¹⁷May the favorᶠ of the Lord our God
    rest upon us;
  establish the work of our hands for
    us—
  yes, establish the work of our
    hands.ᵇ

E Ps 87:6 ◄► Ps 94:7–11
N Ps 90:5–6 ◄► Ps 90:12
N Ps 90:9 ◄► Ps 95:8

90:6 ⁱ Isa 40:6-8; Mt 6:30; Jas 1:10
90:8 ʲ S Ps 19:12; 2Co 4:2; Eph 5:12
  ᵏ S Heb 4:13
90:9 ˡ Ps 78:33
90:10 ᵐ Isa 23:15, 17; Jer 25:11
  ⁿ 2Sa 19:35
  ᵒ S Job 5:7
  ᵖ S Job 20:8; S 34:15
90:11 q Ps 7:11
  ʳ Ps 76:7
90:12 ˢ Ps 39:4; 139:16; Pr 16:9; 20:24 ᵗ Dt 32:29
90:13 ᵘ Ps 6:3
  ᵛ S Dt 32:36
90:14 ʷ Ps 103:5; 107:9; 145:16,19
  ˣ S Ps 77:8; 143:8
  ʸ S Ps 5:11 ᶻ Ps 31:7
90:16 ᵃ Ps 44:1; Hab 3:2
90:17 ᵇ Isa 26:12

91:1 ᶜ S Ex 33:22
  ᵈ Ps 63:7; Isa 49:2; La 4:20
91:2 ᵉ ver 9; S 2Sa 22:3; Ps 9:9
  ᶠ S 2Sa 22:2
91:3 ᵍ Ps 124:7; Pr 6:5 ʰ 1Ki 8:37
91:4 ⁱ S Ru 2:12; Ps 17:8
  ʲ S Dt 32:10; Ps 35:2; Isa 27:3; 31:5; Zec 12:8
91:5 ᵏ S Job 5:21
91:8 ˡ Ps 37:34; S 58:10
91:10 ᵐ Pr 12:21
91:11 ⁿ S Ge 32:1; Heb 1:14 ᵒ Ps 34:7
91:12 ᵖ Mt 4:6*; Lk 4:10-11*

Psalm 91

¹He who dwells in the shelterᶜ of the
    Most High
  will rest in the shadowᵈ of the
    Almighty.ᵍ
²I will sayʰ of the LORD, "He is my
    refugeᵉ and my fortress,ᶠ
  my God, in whom I trust."

³Surely he will save you from the
    fowler's snareᵍ
  and from the deadly pestilence.ʰ
⁴He will cover you with his feathers,
  and under his wings you will find
    refuge;ⁱ
  his faithfulness will be your shieldʲ
    and rampart.
⁵You will not fearᵏ the terror of night,
  nor the arrow that flies by day,
⁶nor the pestilence that stalks in the
    darkness,
  nor the plague that destroys at
    midday.
⁷A thousand may fall at your side,
  ten thousand at your right hand,
  but it will not come near you.
⁸You will only observe with your eyes
  and see the punishment of the
    wicked.ˡ

⁹If you make the Most High your
    dwelling—
  even the LORD, who is my refuge—
¹⁰then no harmᵐ will befall you,
  no disaster will come near your tent.
¹¹For he will command his angelsⁿ
    concerning you
  to guard you in all your ways;ᵒ
¹²they will lift you up in their hands,
  so that you will not strike your foot
    against a stone.ᵖ
¹³You will tread upon the lion and the
    cobra;

L Ps 90:1 ◄► Ps 94:18
S Ps 46:1 ◄► Ps 118:6
U Ps 89:15–16 ◄► Ps 97:10–12
V Ps 89:22–23 ◄► Ps 97:10
K Ps 89:15–16 ◄► Ps 91:11
H Ps 67:2 ◄► Ps 91:5–7
H Ps 91:3 ◄► Ps 91:10
J Ps 61:2–4 ◄► Ps 112:7–8
W Ps 55:22 ◄► Ps 112:7–8
A 1Ki 2:3 ◄► Ps 121:7
H Ps 91:5–7 ◄► Ps 91:16
K Ps 91:3 ◄► Ps 94:18

ᵉ 10 Or yet the best of them   ᶠ 17 Or beauty   ᵍ 1 Hebrew Shaddai   ʰ 2 Or He says

you will trample the great lion and
the serpent.^q

¹⁴"Because he loves me," says the LORD,
"I will rescue him;
I will protect him, for he
acknowledges my name.
¹⁵He will call upon me, and I will
answer him;
I will be with him in trouble,
I will deliver him and honor him.^r
¹⁶With long life^s will I satisfy him
and show him my salvation.^t"

Psalm 92

A psalm. A song. For the Sabbath day.

¹It is good to praise the LORD
and make music^u to your name,^v
O Most High,^w
²to proclaim your love in the morning^x
and your faithfulness at night,
³to the music of the ten-stringed lyre^y
and the melody of the harp.^z

⁴For you make me glad by your deeds,
O LORD;
I sing for joy^a at the works of your
hands.^b
⁵How great are your works,^c O LORD,
how profound your thoughts!^d
⁶The senseless man^e does not know,
fools do not understand,
⁷that though the wicked spring up like
grass
and all evildoers flourish,
they will be forever destroyed.^f

⁸But you, O LORD, are exalted forever.

⁹For surely your enemies^g, O LORD,
surely your enemies will perish;
all evildoers will be scattered.^h
¹⁰You have exalted my horn^{/i} like that
of a wild ox;^j
fine oils^k have been poured upon
me.

H *Ps 91:10* ◀▶ *Ps. 103:3*
H *Ps 86:13* ◀▶ *Ps 109:17–19*
K *Ps 10:16* ◀▶ *Ps 145:13*

91:13 ^qDa 6:22;
Lk 10:19
91:15 ^rS 1Sa 2:30;
Jn 12:26
91:16 ^sDt 6:2;
S Ps 21:4
^tS Ps 50:23

92:1 ^uS Ps 27:6
^vS Ps 9:2; 147:1
^wPs 135:3
92:2 ^xS Ps 55:17
92:3 ^yS Ps 71:22
^zS 1Sa 10:5;
S Ne 12:27;
S Ps 33:2; 81:2
92:4 ^aS Ps 5:11;
27:6 ^bS Ps 8:6;
111:7; 143:5
92:5 ^cS Job 36:24;
Rev 15:3 ^dPs 40:5;
139:17; Isa 28:29;
31:2; Ro 11:33
92:6 ^eS Ps 73:22
92:7 ^fS Ps 37:2
92:9 ^gS Ps 45:5
^hS Ps 68:1; S 89:10
92:10 ⁱS Ps 89:17
^jS Ps 29:6
^kS Ps 23:5
92:11 ^lS Ps 54:7;
91:8
92:12 ^mS Ps 72:7
ⁿS Ps 1:3; 52:8;
Jer 17:8; Hos 14:6
92:13 ^oPs 135:2
92:14 ^pS Ps 1:3;
S Jn 15:2
92:15
^qS Job 34:10
93:1
^rS 1Ch 16:31;
S Ps 97:1
^sS Job 40:10;
S Ps 21:5 ^tS Ps 65:6
^uPs 24:2; 78:69;
119:90
^v1Ch 16:30;
Ps 96:10
93:2 ^wS 2Sa 7:16
^xS Ge 21:33
93:3 ^yPs 96:11;
98:7; Isa 5:30;
17:12-13; Jer 6:23
^zS Ps 46:3 ^aJob 9:8;
Ps 107:25,29;
Isa 51:15;
Jer 31:35; Hab 3:10
93:4 ^bPs 65:7;
Jer 6:23 ^cS Ps 18:4;
Jnh 1:15
^dS Ne 9:32;
S Job 9:41
93:5 ^ePs 29:2;
96:9 ^fPs 5:7; 23:6
94:1 ^gS Ge 4:24;
Ro 12:19
^hS Dt 33:2; Ps 80:1

¹¹My eyes have seen the defeat of my
adversaries;
my ears have heard the rout of my
wicked foes.^l

¹²The righteous will flourish^m like a palm
tree,
they will grow like a cedar of
Lebanon;ⁿ
¹³planted in the house of the LORD,
they will flourish in the courts of our
God.^o
¹⁴They will still bear fruit^p in old age,
they will stay fresh and green,
¹⁵proclaiming, "The LORD is upright;
he is my Rock, and there is no
wickedness in him.^q"

Psalm 93

¹The LORD reigns,^r he is robed in
majesty;^s
the LORD is robed in majesty
and is armed with strength.^t
The world is firmly established;^u
it cannot be moved.^v
²Your throne was established^w long ago;
you are from all eternity.^x

³The seas^y have lifted up, O LORD,
the seas have lifted up their voice;^z
the seas have lifted up their
pounding waves.^a
⁴Mightier than the thunder^b of the
great waters,
mightier than the breakers^c of the
sea—
the LORD on high is mighty.^d

⁵Your statutes stand firm;
holiness^e adorns your house^f
for endless days, O LORD.

Psalm 94

¹O LORD, the God who avenges,^g
O God who avenges, shine forth.^h

M *Ps 89:35–37* ◀▶ *Ps 96:10–13*
N *Ps 78:69* ◀▶ *Ps 96:10*
S *Ps 73:27* ◀▶ *Ps 96:9*
P *Ps 83:13–17* ◀▶ *Ps 98:1–2*

ⁱ *10 Horn here symbolizes strength.*

92:9 This psalm was a song for the Sabbath that prophetically declared the certainty of God's judgment on "all evildoers ."

93:1–2 This hymn of prophecy anticipated the glorious appearance of Jesus Christ as the reigning Messiah in the coming millennial kingdom.

94:1–4 This lament voiced the complaint of the writer as he witnessed the apparent victory of the wicked and prophetically called upon God to fulfill his promise of judgment.

²Rise up, O Judge of the earth;
    pay back to the proud what they
        deserve.
³How long will the wicked, O LORD,
    how long will the wicked be
        jubilant?

⁴They pour out arrogant words;
    all the evildoers are full of boasting.
⁵They crush your people, O LORD;
    they oppress your inheritance.
⁶They slay the widow and the alien;
    they murder the fatherless.
⁷They say, "The LORD does not see;
    the God of Jacob pays no heed."

⁸Take heed, you senseless ones among
        the people;
    you fools, when will you become
        wise?
⁹Does he who implanted the ear not
        hear?
    Does he who formed the eye not
        see?
¹⁰Does he who disciplines nations not
        punish?
    Does he who teaches man lack
        knowledge?
¹¹The LORD knows the thoughts of man;
    he knows that they are futile.

¹²Blessed is the man you discipline,
        O LORD,
    the man you teach from your law;
¹³you grant him relief from days of
        trouble,
    till a pit is dug for the wicked.
¹⁴For the LORD will not reject his
        people;
    he will never forsake his
        inheritance.
¹⁵Judgment will again be founded on
        righteousness,
    and all the upright in heart will
        follow it.

¹⁶Who will rise up for me against the
        wicked?
    Who will take a stand for me against
        evildoers?

E Ps 90:8 ◀ ▶ Ps 102:19
C Ps 74:22 ◀ ▶ Ps 95:10
T Ps 89:30–33 ◀ ▶ Ps 105:19
I Ps 87:5 ◀ ▶ Ps 97:8

¹⁷Unless the LORD had given me help,
    I would soon have dwelt in the
        silence of death.
¹⁸When I said, "My foot is slipping,"
    your love, O LORD, supported me.
¹⁹When anxiety was great within me,
    your consolation brought joy to my
        soul.

²⁰Can a corrupt throne be allied with
        you—
    one that brings on misery by its
        decrees?
²¹They band together against the
        righteous
    and condemn the innocent to
        death.
²²But the LORD has become my fortress,
    and my God the rock in whom I
        take refuge.
²³He will repay them for their sins
    and destroy them for their
        wickedness;
    the LORD our God will destroy them.

Psalm 95

¹Come, let us sing for joy to the LORD;
    let us shout aloud to the Rock of
        our salvation.
²Let us come before him with
        thanksgiving
    and extol him with music and song.

³For the LORD is the great God,
    the great King above all gods.
⁴In his hand are the depths of the
        earth,
    and the mountain peaks belong to
        him.
⁵The sea is his, for he made it,
    and his hands formed the dry land.

⁶Come, let us bow down in worship,
    let us kneel before the LORD our
        Maker;
⁷for he is our God
    and we are the people of his
        pasture,
    the flock under his care.

K Ps 91:11 ◀ ▶ Ps 103:3–4
L Ps 91:1–16 ◀ ▶ Ps 97:10

94:14 The psalmist reconfirmed God's faithfulness to Israel and his guarantee that he will never forget his inheritance.

Today, if you hear his voice,
8 do not harden your hearts° as you
   did at Meribah,ᴶᵖ
   as you did that day at Massahᵏ in the
   desert,ᵠ
9 where your fathers testedʳ and tried
   me,
   though they had seen what I did.
10 For forty yearsˢ I was angry with that
    generation;
    I said, "They are a people whose
    hearts go astray,ᵗ
    and they have not known my
    ways."ᵘ
11 So I declared on oathᵛ in my anger,
   "They shall never enter my rest."ʷ

Psalm 96

96:1–13pp — 1Ch 16:23–33

1 Sing to the LORDˣ a new song;ʸ
   sing to the LORD, all the earth.
2 Sing to the LORD, praise his name;ᶻ
   proclaim his salvationᵃ day after
   day.
3 Declare his gloryᵇ among the nations,
   his marvelous deedsᶜ among all
   peoples.

4 For great is the LORD and most worthy
   of praise;ᵈ
   he is to be fearedᵉ above all gods.ᶠ
5 For all the gods of the nations are
   idols,ᵍ
   but the LORD made the heavens.ʰ
6 Splendor and majestyⁱ are before
   him;
   strength and gloryʲ are in his
   sanctuary.

7 Ascribe to the LORD,ᵏ O families of
   nations,ˡ
   ascribe to the LORD glory and
   strength.
8 Ascribe to the LORD the glory due his
   name;
   bring an offeringᵐ and come into his
   courts.ⁿ

N Ps 90:12 ◀ ▶ Ps 103:15–16
C Ps 94:11 ◀ ▶ Ps 107:10

95:8 ᵒMk 10:5;
Heb 3:8
ᵖS Ex 17:7;
S Dt 33:8;
Heb 3:15*; 4:7
ᵠS Ps 78:40
95:9 ʳS Nu 14:22;
1Co 10:9
95:10 ˢS Ex 16:35;
S Nu 14:34;
Ac 7:36; Heb 3:17
ᵗPs 58:3; 119:67,
176; Pr 12:26;
16:29; Isa 53:6;
Jer 31:19; 50:6;
Eze 34:6 ᵘS Dt 8:6
95:11 ᵛS Nu 14:23
ʷDt 1:35;
Heb 3:7-11*; 4:3*
96:1 ˣPs 30:4
ʸDt 1:35; S 40:3;
98:1; 144:9; 149:1;
Isa 42:10; S Rev 5:9
96:2 ᶻS Ps 68:4
ᵃPs 27:1; 71:15
96:3 ᵇPs 8:1
ᶜS Ps 71:17;
Rev 15:3
96:4 ᵈS Ps 48:1
ᵉS Dt 28:58;
S 1Ch 16:25;
Ps 89:7 ᶠS Ps 95:3
96:5 ᵍS Lev 19:4
ʰS Ge 1:1;
S 2Ch 2:12
96:6 ⁱS Ps 21:5
ʲPs 29:1; 89:17
96:7 ᵏPs 29:1
ˡPs 22:27
96:8 ᵐPs 45:12;
S 51:19; 72:10
ⁿPs 65:4; 84:10;
92:13; 100:4
96:9 ᵒEx 23:25;
Jnh 1:9 ᵖS Ps 93:5
ᵠS Ex 15:14;
Ps 114:7 ʳPs 33:8
96:10 ˢPs 97:1
ᵗPs 24:2; 78:69;
119:90 ᵘS Ps 93:1
ᵛPs 58:11
ʷPs 67:4; 98:9
96:11
ˣS Rev 12:12
ʸPs 97:1; Isa 49:13
96:12 ᶻIsa 44:23;
55:12; Eze 17:24
ᵃPs 65:13
96:13 ᵇRev 19:11
ᶜS Ps 7:11;
Ac 17:31 ᵈPs 86:11
97:1 ᵉEx 15:18;
Ps 93:1; 96:10;
99:1; Isa 24:23;
52:7 ᶠS Ps 96:11
ᵍS Est 10:1
97:2 ʰS Job 22:14
ⁱS Ex 19:9
ʲPs 89:14
97:3 ᵏIsa 9:19;
Da 7:10; Joel 1:19;
2:3 ˡHab 3:5
ᵐS 2Sa 22:9
97:4 ⁿS Job 36:30
ᵒS 2Sa 22:8

9 Worship the LORD° in the splendor of
   hisʲ holiness;ᵖ
   trembleᵠ before him, all the earth.ʳ

10 Say among the nations, "The LORD
    reigns.ˢ"
    The world is firmly established,ᵗ it
    cannot be moved;ᵘ
    he will judgeᵛ the peoples with
    equity.ʷ
11 Let the heavens rejoice,ˣ let the earth
    be glad;ʸ
    let the sea resound, and all that is
    in it;
12 let the fields be jubilant, and
    everything in them.
    Then all the trees of the forestᶻ will
    sing for joy;ᵃ
13 they will sing before the LORD, for he
    comes,
    he comes to judgeᵇ the earth.
    He will judge the world in
    righteousnessᶜ
    and the peoples in his truth.ᵈ

Psalm 97

1 The LORD reigns,ᵉ let the earth be
   glad;ᶠ
   let the distant shoresᵍ rejoice.
2 Cloudsʰ and thick darknessⁱ surround
   him;
   righteousness and justice are the
   foundation of his throne.ʲ
3 Fireᵏ goes beforeˡ him
   and consumesᵐ his foes on every
   side.
4 His lightningⁿ lights up the world;
   the earthᵒ sees and trembles.ᵖ

S Ps 93:5 ◀ ▶ Ps 97:10
M Ps 93:1–2 ◀ ▶ Ps 97:1
N Ps 93:1 ◀ ▶ Ps 102:25–26
J Ps 67:4 ◀ ▶ Ps 96:13
D Job 19:25 ◀ ▶ Ps 98:9
J Ps 96:10 ◀ ▶ Ps 98:9
M Ps 96:10–13 ◀ ▶ Ps 98:3–9
C ▶ Ps 109:8

ᵖPs 18:7; 104:32; S Rev 6:12

J 8 Meribah means quarreling. *k 8 Massah* means testing. *l 9* Or LORD *with the splendor of*

96:10–13 This psalm reflects the universal joy that all nations will express when the Messiah "will judge the peoples with equity" (96:10) and rule the earth from the throne of David with truth and justice.

97:1–8 This prophetic psalm describes the victory of the Messiah and prophesies about the battles that will defeat the armies of the antichrist, ushering in the millennial reign of Christ.

⁵The mountains melt^q like wax^r before the LORD,
before the Lord of all the earth.^s
⁶The heavens proclaim his righteousness,^t
and all the peoples see his glory.^u
⁷All who worship images^v are put to shame,^w
those who boast in idols^x—
worship him,^y all you gods!^z
⁸Zion hears and rejoices
and the villages of Judah are glad^a
because of your judgments,^b O LORD.
⁹For you, O LORD, are the Most High^c
over all the earth;^d
you are exalted^e far above all gods.
¹⁰Let those who love the LORD hate evil,^f
for he guards^g the lives of his faithful ones^h
and deliversⁱ them from the hand of the wicked.^j
¹¹Light is shed^k upon the righteous^l
and joy on the upright in heart.^m
¹²Rejoice in the LORD,ⁿ you who are righteous,
and praise his holy name.^o

Psalm 98

A psalm.

¹Sing to the LORD^p a new song,^q
for he has done marvelous things;^r
his right hand^s and his holy arm^t
have worked salvation^u for him.
²The LORD has made his salvation known^v
and revealed his righteousness^w to the nations.^x
³He has remembered^y his love
and his faithfulness to the house of Israel;
all the ends of the earth^z have seen the salvation of our God.^a

⁴Shout for joy^b to the LORD, all the earth,
burst into jubilant song with music;
⁵make music to the LORD with the harp,^c
with the harp and the sound of singing,^d
⁶with trumpets^e and the blast of the ram's horn^f—
shout for joy^g before the LORD, the King.^h

⁷Let the seaⁱ resound, and everything in it,
the world, and all who live in it.^j
⁸Let the rivers clap their hands,^k
let the mountains^l sing together for joy;
⁹let them sing before the LORD,
for he comes to judge the earth.
He will judge the world in righteousness
and the peoples with equity.^m

Psalm 99

¹The LORD reigns,ⁿ
let the nations tremble;^o
he sits enthroned^p between the cherubim,^q
let the earth shake.
²Great is the LORD^r in Zion;^s
he is exalted^t over all the nations.
³Let them praise^u your great and awesome name^v—
he is holy.^w

⁴The King^x is mighty, he loves justice^y—
you have established equity;^z
in Jacob you have done
what is just and right.^a
⁵Exalt^b the LORD our God
and worship at his footstool;
he is holy.

⁶Moses^c and Aaron^d were among his priests,

98:1—9 The beginning and ending of this psalm echoes Ps 96 in its description of humanity's joy at the establishment of Christ's righteous government in the millennial kingdom.

Samuel was among those who
  called on his name;
they called on the LORD
  and he answered them.
⁷He spoke to them from the pillar of
  cloud;
they kept his statutes and the
  decrees he gave them.

⁸O LORD our God,
  you answered them;
you were to Israel a forgiving God,
  though you punished their
  misdeeds.

⁹Exalt the LORD our God
  and worship at his holy mountain,
for the LORD our God is holy.

Psalm 100

A psalm. For giving thanks.

¹Shout for joy to the LORD, all the
  earth.
² Worship the LORD with gladness;
  come before him with joyful songs.
³Know that the LORD is God.
  It is he who made us, and we are
  his;
  we are his people, the sheep of his
  pasture.

⁴Enter his gates with thanksgiving
  and his courts with praise;
  give thanks to him and praise his
  name.
⁵For the LORD is good and his love
  endures forever;
  his faithfulness continues through
  all generations.

Psalm 101

Of David. A psalm.

¹I will sing of your love and justice;
  to you, O LORD, I will sing praise.
²I will be careful to lead a blameless
  life —
  when will you come to me?

I will walk in my house
  with blameless heart.
³I will set before my eyes
  no vile thing.

The deeds of faithless men I hate;
  they will not cling to me.

L Ps 86:15 ◀ Ps 102:19–20

99:6 e 1Sa 7:5
fPs 4:3; 91:15
99:7 gS Ex 13:21;
S 19:9; S Nu 11:25
99:8 hS Ex 22:27;
S Nu 14:20
iS Lev 26:18
100:1 jS Ps 98:6
100:2 kS Dt 10:12
lS Ps 95:2
100:3
mS 1Ki 18:21;
S Ps 46:10
nS Job 10:3
oPs 79:13;
Isa 19:25; 63:8,
17-19; 64:9
pS 2Sa 24:17;
S Ps 74:1
100:4 qS Ps 42:4
rS Ps 96:8
sPs 116:17
100:5
tS 1Ch 16:34
uS Ezr 3:11;
Ps 106:1 vPs 108:4;
119:90
101:1 wPs 33:1;
51:14; 89:1; 145:7
101:2 xS Ge 17:1;
Php 1:10
yS 1Ki 3:14
101:3 zJer 16:18;
Eze 11:21;
Hos 9:10 aS Ps 55:5
101:4 bPr 3:32;
6:16-19; 11:20
101:5
cS Ex 20:16;
S Lev 19:16
dS Ps 10:5
101:6 ever 2;
Ps 119:1
101:8 fPs 5:3;
Jer 21:12 gPs 75:10
hS 2Sa 3:39;
Ps 118:10-12
iS Ps 46:4
102:1 jPs 4:1
kS Ex 2:23
102:2 lS Ps 22:24
mS 2Ki 19:16;
Ps 31:2; 88:2
102:3 nS Ps 37:20;
S Jas 4:14 oLa 1:13
102:4 pS Ps 37:2;
90:5-6 qS 1Sa 1:7;
S Ezr 10:6;
S Job 33:20
102:5 rS Ps 6:6
102:6
sS Dt 14:15-17;
Job 30:29;
Isa 34:11; Zep 2:14
102:7 tPs 77:4
uPs 38:11
102:8 vS Ps 31:11
wS Ps 42:10;
Lk 22:63-65;
23:35-37
xS Ex 22:28;
Isa 65:15; Jer 24:9;
25:18; 42:18;
44:12; Eze 14:8;
Zec 8:13
102:9 yIsa 44:20

⁴Men of perverse heart shall be far
  from me;
  I will have nothing to do with evil.

⁵Whoever slanders his neighbor in
  secret,
  him will I put to silence;
whoever has haughty eyes and a
  proud heart,
  him will I not endure.

⁶My eyes will be on the faithful in the
  land,
  that they may dwell with me;
he whose walk is blameless
  will minister to me.

⁷No one who practices deceit
  will dwell in my house;
no one who speaks falsely
  will stand in my presence.

⁸Every morning I will put to silence
  all the wicked in the land;
I will cut off every evildoer
  from the city of the LORD.

Psalm 102

A prayer of an afflicted man. When he is
faint and pours out his lament
before the LORD.

¹Hear my prayer, O LORD;
  let my cry for help come to you.
²Do not hide your face from me
  when I am in distress.
Turn your ear to me;
  when I call, answer me quickly.

³For my days vanish like smoke;
  my bones burn like glowing
  embers.
⁴My heart is blighted and withered like
  grass;
  I forget to eat my food.
⁵Because of my loud groaning
  I am reduced to skin and bones.
⁶I am like a desert owl,
  like an owl among the ruins.
⁷I lie awake; I have become
  like a bird alone on a roof.
⁸All day long my enemies taunt me;
  those who rail against me use my
  name as a curse.
⁹For I eat ashes as my food

S Ps 97:10 ◀ Ps 119:1–3

m 8 Hebrew them n 8 Or / an avenger of the wrongs done to them
o 3 Or and not we ourselves

and mingle my drink with tears[z]
[10]because of your great wrath,[a]
for you have taken me up and
thrown me aside.
[11]My days are like the evening shadow;[b]
I wither[c] away like grass.

[12]But you, O LORD, sit enthroned
forever;[d]
your renown endures[e] through all
generations.[f]

[13]You will arise[g] and have compassion[h]
on Zion,
for it is time[i] to show favor[j] to her;
the appointed time[k] has come.
[14]For her stones are dear to your
servants;
her very dust moves them to pity.
[15]The nations will fear[l] the name of the
LORD,
all the kings[m] of the earth will revere
your glory.
[16]For the LORD will rebuild Zion[n]
and appear in his glory.[o]
[17]He will respond to the prayer[p] of the
destitute;
he will not despise their plea.

[18]Let this be written[q] for a future
generation,
that a people not yet created[r] may
praise the LORD:
[19]"The LORD looked down[s] from his
sanctuary on high,
from heaven he viewed the earth,
[20]to hear the groans of the prisoners[t]
and release those condemned to
death."

[21]So the name of the LORD will be
declared[u] in Zion
and his praise[v] in Jerusalem
[22]when the peoples and the kingdoms
assemble to worship[w] the LORD.

[23]In the course of my life[p] he broke my
strength;
he cut short my days.[x]
[24]So I said:
"Do not take me away, O my God,
in the midst of my days;
your years go on[y] through all
generations.
[25]In the beginning[z] you laid the
foundations of the earth,
and the heavens[a] are the work of
your hands.[b]
[26]They will perish,[c] but you remain;
they will all wear out like a
garment.
Like clothing you will change them
and they will be discarded.
[27]But you remain the same,[d]
and your years will never end.[e]
[28]The children of your servants[f] will live
in your presence;
their descendants[g] will be
established before you."

102:9 [z] Ps 6:6; 42:3; 80:5
102:10 [a] Ps 7:11; 38:3
102:11 [b] S 1Ch 29:15; S Job 14:2; S Ps 39:6 [c] S Job 8:12; Jas 1:10
102:12 [d] S Ex 15:18 [e] Ps 135:13; Isa 55:13; 63:12 [f] S Ex 3:15
102:13 [g] S Ps 44:26 [h] S Dt 32:36; S 1Ki 3:26; Isa 54:8; 60:10; Zec 10:6 [i] Ps 119:126 [j] S Ps 77:7 [k] S Ex 13:10; Da 8:19; Ac 1:7
102:15 [l] 1Ki 8:43; Ps 67:7; Isa 2:2 [m] Ps 76:12; 138:4; 148:11
102:16 [n] S Ps 51:18 [o] Ps 8:1; Isa 60:1-2
102:17 [p] 1Ki 8:29; Ps 4:1; 6:9
102:18 [q] S Ro 4:24 [r] S Ps 22:31
102:19 [s] Ps 53:2
102:20 [t] S Ps 68:6; S Lk 4:19
102:21 [u] Ps 22:22 [v] Ps 9:14
102:22 [w] S Ps 22:27; Isa 49:22-23; Zec 8:20-23
102:23 [x] S Ps 39:5
102:24 [y] S Ge 21:33; Job 36:26; Ps 90:2
102:25 [z] S Ge 1:1; Heb 1:10-12* [a] S 2Ch 2:12 [b] S Ps 8:3
102:26 [c] Isa 13:10, 13; 34:4; 51:6; Eze 32:8; Joel 2:10; Mt 24:35; 2Pe 3:7-10; Rev 20:11
102:27 [d] S Nu 23:19; Heb 13:8; Jas 1:17 [e] Ps 9:7 102:28 [f] Ps 69:36 [g] Ps 25:13; 89:4

[p] 23 Or *By his power*

I Ps 102:13–16 ◀▶ Ps 105:8–11
M Ps 102:15–16 ◀▶ Ps 110:1–7
N Ps 96:10 ◀▶ Ps 104:5
R Ps 37:26 ◀▶ Ps 103:17–18

I Ps 98:3 ◀▶ Ps 102:21–22
M Ps 98:3–9 ◀▶ Ps 102:22
E Ps 94:7–11 ◀▶ Ps 139:1–16
L Ps 99:8 ◀▶ Ps 103:1–4

102:13–18 Several different interpretations have been given for this passage. Some scholars suggest that these verses pertain to our time. They suggest that Christ will return in our generation, basing their belief on the phrase "the appointed time has come" (102:13) and citing the increase of modern-day Israel's interest in archeology as a prophetic fulfillment of "her stones are dear to your servants; her very dust moves them to pity" (102:14). Other scholars view these verses as prophecies from the time of the exile, noting that after seventy years of Babylonian captivity God's "appointed time" had transpired and the exiles could now return to the city that meant so much to them.

Still others view this psalm as a prophecy about the millennial kingdom and the eternal King who will hear the prayer of the destitute and restore Zion. These scholars note that though the promised land has experienced an influx of returning Jews in our century and that Jerusalem is being restored to her former strength and beauty, these verses will find their full expression in the new Jerusalem of Christ's millennial kingdom (see Rev 21).

102:21–22 The psalmist announced in this millennial prophecy that the name of the LORD will be declared in Zion and Jerusalem "when the peoples and the kingdoms assemble to worship the LORD" (102:22). This prophecy will be fulfilled after the victory at Armageddon.

102:25–26 This prophecy deals with "a new heaven and a new earth" (Rev 21:1).

Psalm 103

Of David.

¹Praise the LORD, O my soul;
  all my inmost being, praise his holy
    name.
²Praise the LORD, O my soul,
  and forget not all his benefits—
³who forgives all your sins
  and heals all your diseases,
⁴who redeems your life from the pit
  and crowns you with love and
    compassion,
⁵who satisfies your desires with good
    things
  so that your youth is renewed like
    the eagle's.

⁶The LORD works righteousness
  and justice for all the oppressed.

⁷He made known his ways to Moses,
  his deeds to the people of Israel:
⁸The LORD is compassionate and
    gracious,
  slow to anger, abounding in love.
⁹He will not always accuse,
  nor will he harbor his anger
    forever;
¹⁰he does not treat us as our sins
    deserve
  or repay us according to our
    iniquities.
¹¹For as high as the heavens are above
    the earth,
  so great is his love for those who
    fear him;
¹²as far as the east is from the west,
  so far has he removed our
    transgressions from us.
¹³As a father has compassion on his
    children,
  so the LORD has compassion on those
    who fear him;
¹⁴for he knows how we are formed,
  he remembers that we are dust.
¹⁵As for man, his days are like grass,
  he flourishes like a flower of the
    field;
¹⁶the wind blows over it and it is gone,
  and its place remembers it no
    more.
¹⁷But from everlasting to everlasting
  the LORD's love is with those who
    fear him,
  and his righteousness with their
    children's children—
¹⁸with those who keep his covenant
  and remember to obey his
    precepts.

¹⁹The LORD has established his throne
    in heaven,
  and his kingdom rules over all.

²⁰Praise the LORD, you his angels,
  you mighty ones who do his
    bidding,
  who obey his word.
²¹Praise the LORD, all his heavenly
    hosts,
  you his servants who do
    his will.
²²Praise the LORD, all his works
  everywhere in his dominion.

Praise the LORD, O my soul.

Psalm 104

¹Praise the LORD, O my soul.

O LORD my God, you are very great;
  you are clothed with splendor and
    majesty.
²He wraps himself in light as with a
    garment;
  he stretches out the heavens like a
    tent
³ and lays the beams of his upper
    chambers on their waters.
He makes the clouds his chariot
  and rides on the wings of the
    wind.
⁴He makes winds his messengers,
  flames of fire his servants.

Old Testament Prophecies Fulfilled in Christ

OT TEXT	NT TEXT	SUBJECT
Ge 3:15	Lk 22:53	Satan against Jesus
Ge 3:15	Heb 2:14; 1Jn 3:8	Jesus' victory over Satan
Ge 12:3	Ac 3:25; Gal 3:8	Gentiles blessed through Christ as the seed of Abraham
Ge 13:15	Gal 3:15–16, 19	Messiah as the seed of Abraham
Ge 14:18–20	Heb 7	Jesus' priesthood according to the likeness of Melchizedek
Ge 18:18	Ac 3:25; Gal 3:8	Gentiles blessed through Christ as the seed of Abraham
Ge 22:18	Ac 3:25; Gal 3:8	Gentiles blessed through Christ as the seed of Abraham
Ge 26:4	Ac 3:25; Gal 3:8	Gentiles blessed through Christ as the seed of Abraham
Ge 49:10	Lk 1:32–33	Coming ruler from Judah
Ex 12:1—14:46	Jn 19:31–36; 1Co 5:7; 1Pe 1:19	The Messiah as the Passover Lamb
Ex 16:4	Jn 6:31–33	Messiah to give true bread from heaven
Ex 24:8	Heb 9:11–28	The Messiah's blood to be shed as sacrifice
Lev 16:15–17	Ro 3:25; Heb 9:1–14, 24; 1Jn 2:2	Atoning sacrifice of blood
Nu 21:8–9	Jn 3:14–15	Life through looking at one on a cross
Nu 24:17	Lk 1:32–33	Coming ruler from Jacob
Nu 24:17	Rev 22:16	Coming Star out of Jacob
Dt 18:17	Jn 6:14; 12:49–50; Ac 3:22–23	Coming prophet sent from God
Dt 21:23	Gal 3:13	Messiah cursed for hanging on a tree
Dt 30:12–14	Ro 10:6–8	Jesus is God's word near to us
2Sa 7:14	Heb 1:5	Messiah to be God's Son
2Sa 7:16	Lk 1:32–33; Rev 19:11–16	David's Son as eternal king
1Ch 17:13	Heb 1:5	Messiah to be God's Son
1Ch 17:14	Lk 1:32–33; Rev 19:11–16	David's Son as eternal king
Ps 2:7	Mt 3:17; 17:5; Mk 1:11; 9:7; Lk 3:22; 9:35; Ac 13:33; Heb 1:5	God's address to his Son
Ps 2:9	Rev 2:27	Messiah to rule the nations with power
Ps 8:2	Mt 21:16	Children to praise God's Son

Old Testament Prophecies Fulfilled in Christ

OT TEXT	NT TEXT	SUBJECT
Ps 8:4–5	Heb 2:6–9	Jesus lower than the angels
Ps 8:6	1Co 15:27–28; Eph 1:22	Everything subject to God's Son
Ps 16:8–11	Ac 2:25–32; 13:35–37	David's Son to be raised from the dead
Ps 22:1	Mt 27:46; Mk 15:34	God-forsaken cry by the Messiah
Ps 22:7–8	Mt 27:29, 41–44; Mk 15:18, 29–32; Lk 23:35–39	Messiah mocked by a crowd
Ps 22:18	Mt 27:35; Mk 15:24; Lk 23:34; Jn 19:24	Casting lots for Jesus' clothes
Ps 22:22	Heb 2:12	Jesus to declare his name in the church
Ps 31:5	Lk 23:46	Messiah to commit his spirit to God
Ps 34:20	Jn 19:31–36	Messiah to have no broken bones
Ps 35:19	Jn 15:25	Messiah experiencing hatred for no reason
Ps 40:6–8	Jn 6:48; Heb 10:5–9	Messiah to do God's perfect will
Ps 41:9	Jn 13:18	The Messiah's betrayal by a friend
Ps 45:6–7	Heb 1:8–9	Characteristics of the coming King
Ps 68:18	Eph 4:7–11	Ascension and giving gifts to humans
Ps 69:4	Jn 15:25	Messiah experiencing hatred for no reason
Ps 69:9	Jn 2:14–22	The Messiah's zeal for God's house
Ps 69:21	Jn 19:29	The thirst of the suffering Messiah
Ps 69:25	Ac 1:20	Judgment on the Messiah's persecutor
Ps 78:2	Mt 13:34–35	Messiah to speak in parables
Ps 102:25–27	Heb 1:10–12	Characteristics of the coming King
Ps 110:1	Ac 2:34–35; 1Co 15:25; Eph 1:20–22; Heb 1:13; 10:12–13	Jesus exalted in power at God's right hand
Ps 110:1	Mt 22:41–45; Mk 12:35–37; Lk 20:41–44	Jesus as Son and Lord of David
Ps 110:4	Heb 5:6; 7:11–22	Jesus' priesthood after Melchizedek
Ps 118:22–23	Mt 21:42–44; Mk 12:10–12; Lk 20:17–19; Ac 4:10–11; 1Pe 2:7–8	Rejected stone to become capstone
Ps 118:26	Mt 21:9; Mk 11:9; Lk 19:38; Jn 12:13	Messiah to come in the name of the Lord
Isa 6:9–10	Mt 13:14–15; Mk 4:12; Lk 8:10; Jn 12:37–41	Hearts to be closed to the gospel
Isa 7:14	Mt 1:18–23; Lk 1:26–35	Virgin birth of the Messiah
Isa 8:14	Ro 9:32–33; 1Pe 2:7–8	A stone on which people stumble
Isa 9:1–2	Mt 4:13–16; Mk 1:14–15; Lk 4:14–15	Ministry to begin in Galilee

Old Testament Prophecies Fulfilled in Christ

OT TEXT	NT TEXT	SUBJECT
Isa 9:6–7	Lk 1:32–33	David's Son as eternal king
Isa 9:7	Jn 1:1, 18	The Messiah to be God
Isa 9:7	Eph 2:14–17	The Messiah to be a man of peace
Isa 11:1–2	Mt 3:16; Mk 1:16; Lk 3:21–22	Rod of Jesse (David) to receive the Spirit
Isa 11:10	Lk 1:32–33	Rod of Jesse (David) as coming ruler
Isa 11:10	Ro 15:12	Salvation to be available for Gentiles
Isa 22:22	Rev 3:7	Jesus to receive the key of David
Isa 25:8	1Co 15:54	Death to be swallowed up in victory
Isa 28:16	Ro 9:32–33; 1Pe 2:6	Messiah to be the chief cornerstone
Isa 35:5–6	Mt 11:4–6; Lk 7:22	Messiah to be a mighty worker of miracles
Isa 40:3–5	Mt 3:3; Mk 1:3; Lk 3:4–6; Jn 1:23	Jesus' forerunner, a voice in the wilderness
Isa 42:1–4	Mt 12:15–21	Messiah as the chosen servant of the Lord
Isa 45:23	Ro 14:11; Php 2:10	Every knee to bow before the Messiah
Isa 49:6	Ac 13:46–47	Messiah as a light to the Gentiles
Isa 50:6	Mt 27:26–30; Mk 14:65; 15:15, 19; Lk 22:63; Jn 19:1, 3	Beating God's servant
Isa 50:6	Mt 26:67; Mk 14:65	Spitting on God's servant
Isa 53:1	Jn 12:38; Ro 10:16	Israel not to believe in the Messiah
Isa 53:3	Jn 1:11	Messiah to be rejected by his own people
Isa 53:4–5	Mt 8:16–17; Mk 1:32–34; Lk. 4:40–41; 1Pe 2:24	Healing ministry of God's servant
Isa 53:7–8	Jn 1:29, 36; Ac 8:30–35; 1Pe 1:19; Rev 5:6, 12	Suffering Lamb of God
Isa 53:9	Heb 4:15; 1Pe 2:22	The sinless servant of God
Isa 53:9	Mt 27:57–60	Messiah to be buried in a rich man's grave
Isa 53:12	Mt 27:38; Mk 15:27–28; Lk 22:37; 23:33; Jn 19:18	God's servant numbered with transgressors
Isa 55:3	Lk 22:20; 1Co 11:25	Everlasting covenant through the Messiah
Isa 55:3	Ac 13:33	Blessings of David given to the Messiah
Isa 59:20–21	Ro 11:26–27	Israel's Deliverer to come from Zion
Isa 60:1–3	Mt 2:11; Ro 15:8–12	Gentiles coming to worship the Messiah
Isa 61:1–2	Mt 3:16; Mk 1:10; Lk 4:18–21	The Messiah anointed by the Holy Spirit
Isa 65:1	Ro 10:20	Gentiles would believe in the Messiah
Isa 65:2	Ro 10:21	Israel would reject the Messiah
Jer 23:5	Lk 1:32–33	David's Son to be a great King
Jer 23:6	Mt 1:21	David's Son to be Savior

Old Testament Prophecies Fulfilled in Christ

OT TEXT	NT TEXT	SUBJECT
Jer 23:6	1Co 1:30	Messiah to be named "Our Righteousness"
Jer 31:5	Mt 2:16–18	Rachel weeping when God's Son is born
Jer 31:31–34	Lk 22:20; 1Co 11:25; Heb 8:8–12; 10:15–18	Jesus and the new covenant
Jer 32:40	Lk 22:20; 1Co 11:25	Everlasting covenant through the Messiah
Jer 33:15	Lk 1:32–33	David's Son to be a great King
Jer 33:16	Mt 1:21	David's Son to be Savior
Jer 33:16	1Co 1:30	Messiah to be named "Our Righteousness"
Eze 21:26–27	Lk 1:32–33	A rightful crown for the Messiah
Eze 34:23–24	Jn 10:11, 14, 16; Heb 13:20; 1Pe 5:4	The coming good shepherd
Eze 37:24–25	Lk 1:32–33	Messiah to be David's Son and a king
Eze 37:24–25	Jn 10:11, 14, 16; Heb 13:20; 1Pe 5:4	The coming good shepherd
Eze 37:26	Lk 22:20; 1Co 11:25	Messiah's everlasting covenant of peace
Da 7:13–14	Mt 24:30; 26:64; Mk 13:26; 14:62; Lk 21:27; Rev 1:13; 14:14	The coming of the Son of Man
Da 7:27	Rev 11:15	The coming everlasting kingdom of the Messiah
Da 9:24–26	Gal 4:4	Timetable for the Messiah's coming
Hos 11:1	Mt 2:14–15	Jesus to return from Egypt
Joel 2:28–32	Ac 2:14–21	God's Spirit to be poured out
Am 9:11–12	Ac 15:13–18	Gentiles would believe in the Messiah
Jnh 1:17	Mt 12:39–40	Messiah to be three days and nights in grave
Mic 5:2	Mt 2:1–6	The Messiah to be born in Bethlehem
Mic 5:2	Lk 1:32–33	The Messiah as an eternal king
Mic 5:4	Jn 10:11, 14	The coming shepherd of God's flock
Mic 5:5	Eph 2:14–17	The Messiah to be a man of peace
Zec 9:9	Mt 21:1–9; Mk 11:1–10; Lk 19:28–38; Jn 12:12–16	The coming ruler on a donkey
Zec 11:12–13	Mt 27:1–10	Thirty pieces of silver for a potter's field
Zec 12:10	Jn 19:37; Rev 1:7	Looking on the pierced Messiah
Zec 13:7	Mt 26:31; 26:55–56; Mk 14:27; 14:48–50	Striking the coming shepherd; the sheep flee
Mal 3:1	Mt 11:7–10; Mk 1:2–4; Lk 7:24–27	The forerunner to the Messiah
Mal 4:5–6	Mt 11:14; 17:11–13; Mk 9:11–13; Lk 1:16–17	The forerunner as Elijah returned

⁵He set the earth on its foundations;
   it can never be moved.
⁶You covered it with the deep as with a garment;
   the waters stood above the mountains.
⁷But at your rebuke the waters fled,
   at the sound of your thunder they took to flight;
⁸they flowed over the mountains,
   they went down into the valleys,
   to the place you assigned for them.
⁹You set a boundary they cannot cross;
   never again will they cover the earth.
¹⁰He makes springs pour water into the ravines;
   it flows between the mountains.
¹¹They give water to all the beasts of the field;
   the wild donkeys quench their thirst.
¹²The birds of the air nest by the waters;
   they sing among the branches.
¹³He waters the mountains from his upper chambers;
   the earth is satisfied by the fruit of his work.
¹⁴He makes grass grow for the cattle,
   and plants for man to cultivate—
   bringing forth food from the earth:
¹⁵wine that gladdens the heart of man,
   oil to make his face shine,
   and bread that sustains his heart.
¹⁶The trees of the LORD are well watered,
   the cedars of Lebanon that he planted.
¹⁷There the birds make their nests;
   the stork has its home in the pine trees.
¹⁸The high mountains belong to the wild goats;
   the crags are a refuge for the coneys.
¹⁹The moon marks off the seasons,
   and the sun knows when to go down.

²⁰You bring darkness, it becomes night,
   and all the beasts of the forest prowl.
²¹The lions roar for their prey
   and seek their food from God.
²²The sun rises, and they steal away;
   they return and lie down in their dens.
²³Then man goes out to his work,
   to his labor until evening.
²⁴How many are your works, O LORD!
   In wisdom you made them all;
   the earth is full of your creatures.
²⁵There is the sea, vast and spacious,
   teeming with creatures beyond number—
   living things both large and small.
²⁶There the ships go to and fro,
   and the leviathan, which you formed to frolic there.
²⁷These all look to you
   to give them their food at the proper time.
²⁸When you give it to them,
   they gather it up;
   when you open your hand,
   they are satisfied with good things.
²⁹When you hide your face,
   they are terrified;
   when you take away their breath,
   they die and return to the dust.
³⁰When you send your Spirit,
   they are created,
   and you renew the face of the earth.
³¹May the glory of the LORD endure forever;
   may the LORD rejoice in his works—
³²he who looks at the earth, and it trembles,
   who touches the mountains, and they smoke.

104:5 In this hymn to the Creator the psalmist echoes God's question to Job: "Where were you when I laid the earth's foundation?" (Job 38:4). The NT clearly answers the question of Creator's identity—he is Jesus Christ (see Jn 1:3; Eph 3:9).

⁳³I will singʳ to the Lord all my life;
   I will sing praise to my God as long
      as I live.
³⁴May my meditation be pleasing to him,
   as I rejoiceˢ in the Lord.
³⁵But may sinners vanishᵗ from the
      earth
   and the wicked be no more.ᵘ

Praise the Lord, O my soul.
Praise the Lord.ˢᵛ

Psalm 105

105:1–15pp — 1Ch 16:8–22

¹Give thanks to the Lord,ʷ call on his
      name;ˣ
   make known among the nations
      what he has done.
²Sing to him,ʸ sing praiseᶻ to him;
   tell of all his wonderful acts.ᵃ
³Glory in his holy name;ᵇ
   let the hearts of those who seek the
      Lord rejoice.
⁴Look to the Lord and his strength;
   seek his faceᶜ always.
⁵Remember the wondersᵈ he has done,
   his miracles, and the judgments he
      pronounced,ᵉ
⁶O descendants of Abraham his
      servant,ᶠ
   O sons of Jacob, his chosenᵍ ones.
⁷He is the Lord our God;
   his judgments are in all the earth.
⁸He remembers his covenantʰ forever,
   the word he commanded, for a
      thousand generations,
⁹the covenant he made with Abraham,ⁱ
   the oath he swore to Isaac.
¹⁰He confirmed itʲ to Jacob as a decree,
   to Israel as an everlasting covenant:ᵏ
¹¹"To you I will give the land of Canaanˡ
      as the portion you will inherit."ᵐ
¹²When they were but few in number,ⁿ
   few indeed, and strangers in it,ᵒ
¹³they wandered from nation to nation,ᵖ
   from one kingdom to another.
¹⁴He allowed no one to oppressᵠ them;
   for their sake he rebuked kings:ʳ
¹⁵"Do not touchˢ my anointed ones;
   do my prophetsᵗ no harm."
¹⁶He called down famineᵘ on the land
   and destroyed all their supplies of
      food;
¹⁷and he sent a man before them—
   Joseph, sold as a slave.ᵛ
¹⁸They bruised his feet with shackles,ʷ
   his neck was put in irons,
¹⁹till what he foretoldˣ came to pass,
   till the wordʸ of the Lord proved
      him true.
²⁰The king sent and released him,
   the ruler of peoples set him free.ᶻ
²¹He made him master of his household,
   ruler over all he possessed,
²²to instruct his princesᵃ as he pleased
   and teach his elders wisdom.ᵇ
²³Then Israel entered Egypt;ᶜ
   Jacobᵈ lived as an alien in the land
      of Ham.ᵉ
²⁴The Lord made his people very fruitful;
   he made them too numerousᶠ for
      their foes,
²⁵whose hearts he turnedᵍ to hate his
      people,
   to conspireʰ against his servants.
²⁶He sent Mosesⁱ his servant,
   and Aaron,ʲ whom he had chosen.ᵏ

P Ps 98:1–2 ◄► Ps 110:1
T Ps 78:4 ◄► Ps 107:2
I Ps 102:21–22 ◄► Ps 111:5–6

L Ps 103:17–18 ◄► Ps 107:6
T Ps 94:12–13 ◄► Ps 119:67

ᵇ S Ge 41:40 105:23 ᶜ Ge 46:6; Ac 7:15; 13:17 ᵈ Ge 47:28 ᵉ S Ps 78:51 105:24 ᶠ Ex 1:7,9; Ac 7:17 105:25 ᵍ S Ex 4:21 ʰ Ex 1:6-10; Ac 7:19 105:26 ⁱ S Ex 3:10 ʲ S Ex 4:16; S Nu 33:1 ᵏ Nu 16:5; 17:5-8

ˢ 35 Hebrew *Hallelu Yah*; in the Septuagint this line stands at the beginning of Psalm 105.

104:35 The psalmist calls for God's judgment on the wicked. This judgment will occur during the seven-year tribulation period when the wicked will be overthrown and refused entrance into God's kingdom (see Rev 21:27). The Scriptures are very clear that the wicked who reject God's forgiveness will continue in hell forever (see Mt 18:8; Mk 3:29; 2Th 1:9).

105:8–11 The psalmist reconfirmed the Abrahamic covenant and the disposition of the land of Canaan (see note at Ge 15:4). Some have attempted to use this passage to determine the exact time of the Lord's second coming, basing their calculations on the length of "a thousand generations" (105:8). However, relating the Lord's second coming to this phrase is inaccurate because the phrase refers specifically to God's "word he commanded" (105:8)—his eternal promise to Abraham and his descendants.

²⁷They performed¹ his miraculous signs^m
    among them,
    his wondersⁿ in the land of Ham.
²⁸He sent darkness° and made the land dark—
    for had they not rebelled against^p his words?
²⁹He turned their waters into blood,^q
    causing their fish to die.^r
³⁰Their land teemed with frogs,^s
    which went up into the bedrooms of their rulers.
³¹He spoke,^t and there came swarms of flies,^u
    and gnats^v throughout their country.
³²He turned their rain into hail,^w
    with lightning throughout their land;
³³he struck down their vines^x and fig trees^y
    and shattered the trees of their country.
³⁴He spoke,^z and the locusts came,^a
    grasshoppers^b without number;^c
³⁵they ate up every green thing in their land,
    ate up the produce of their soil.
³⁶Then he struck down all the firstborn^d in their land,
    the firstfruits of all their manhood.
³⁷He brought out Israel, laden with silver and gold,^e
    and from among their tribes no one faltered.
³⁸Egypt was glad when they left,
    because dread of Israel^f had fallen on them.
³⁹He spread out a cloud^g as a covering,
    and a fire to give light at night.^h
⁴⁰They asked,ⁱ and he brought them quail^j
    and satisfied them with the bread of heaven.^k
⁴¹He opened the rock,^l and water gushed out;
    like a river it flowed in the desert.
⁴²For he remembered his holy promise^m
    given to his servant Abraham.
⁴³He brought out his people with rejoicing,ⁿ
    his chosen ones with shouts of joy;
⁴⁴he gave them the lands of the nations,°

and they fell heir to what others had toiled^p for—
⁴⁵that they might keep his precepts
    and observe his laws.^q

Praise the LORD.^{fr}

Psalm 106

106:1,47–48pp — 1Ch 16:34–36

¹Praise the LORD.^{us}

Give thanks to the LORD, for he is good;^t
    his love endures forever.^u
²Who can proclaim the mighty acts^v of the LORD
    or fully declare his praise?
³Blessed are they who maintain justice,^w
    who constantly do what is right.^x
⁴Remember me,^y O LORD, when you show favor^z to your people,
    come to my aid^a when you save them,
⁵that I may enjoy the prosperity^b of your chosen ones,^c
    that I may share in the joy^d of your nation
    and join your inheritance^e in giving praise.

⁶We have sinned,^f even as our fathers^g did;
    we have done wrong and acted wickedly.^h
⁷When our fathers were in Egypt,
    they gave no thoughtⁱ to your miracles;
    they did not remember^j your many kindnesses,
    and they rebelled by the sea,^k the Red Sea.^v
⁸Yet he saved them¹ for his name's sake,^m
    to make his mighty powerⁿ known.
⁹He rebuked° the Red Sea, and it dried up;^p
    he led them through^q the depths as through a desert.
¹⁰He saved them^r from the hand of the foe;^s

---

^t45 Hebrew *Hallelu Yah* ^u1 Hebrew *Hallelu Yah*; also in verse 48
^v7 Hebrew *Yam Suph*; that is, Sea of Reeds; also in verses 9 and 22

from the hand of the enemy he
    redeemed them.ᵗ
¹¹The waters coveredᵘ their adversaries;
    not one of them survived.
¹²Then they believed his promises
    and sang his praise.ᵛ

¹³But they soon forgotʷ what he had
        done
    and did not wait for his counsel.ˣ
¹⁴In the desertʸ they gave in to their
        craving;
    in the wastelandᶻ they put God to
        the test.ᵃ
¹⁵So he gave themᵇ what they asked for,
    but sent a wasting diseaseᶜ upon
        them.

¹⁶In the camp they grew enviousᵈ of
        Moses
    and of Aaron, who was consecrated
        to the LORD.
¹⁷The earth openedᵉ up and swallowed
        Dathan;ᶠ
    it buried the company of Abiram.ᵍ
¹⁸Fire blazedʰ among their followers;
    a flame consumed the wicked.

¹⁹At Horeb they made a calfⁱ
    and worshiped an idol cast from
        metal.
²⁰They exchanged their Gloryʲ
    for an image of a bull, which eats
        grass.
²¹They forgot the Godᵏ who saved them,
    who had done great thingsˡ in
        Egypt,
²²miracles in the land of Hamᵐ
    and awesome deedsⁿ by the Red
        Sea.
²³So he said he would destroyᵒ them—
    had not Moses, his chosen one,
    stood in the breachᵖ before him
    to keep his wrath from destroying
        them.

²⁴Then they despisedᵠ the pleasant
        land;ʳ
    they did not believeˢ his promise.
²⁵They grumbledᵗ in their tents
    and did not obey the LORD.
²⁶So he swOreᵘ to them with uplifted
        hand
    that he would make them fall in the
        desert,ᵛ
²⁷make their descendants fall among the
        nations
    and scatterʷ them throughout the
        lands.

²⁸They yoked themselves to the Baal of
        Peorˣ
    and ate sacrifices offered to lifeless
        gods;
²⁹they provoked the LORD to angerʸ by
        their wicked deeds,ᶻ
    and a plagueᵃ broke out among
        them.
³⁰But Phinehasᵇ stood up and
        intervened,
    and the plague was checked.ᶜ
³¹This was credited to himᵈ as
        righteousness
    for endless generationsᵉ to come.

³²By the waters of Meribahᶠ they
        angered the LORD,
    and trouble came to Moses because
        of them;
³³for they rebelledᵍ against the Spiritʰ of
        God,
    and rash words came from Moses'
        lips.ʷⁱ

³⁴They did not destroyʲ the peoples
    as the LORD had commandedᵏ them,
³⁵but they mingledˡ with the nations
    and adopted their customs.
³⁶They worshiped their idols,ᵐ
    which became a snareⁿ to them.
³⁷They sacrificed their sonsᵒ
    and their daughters to demons.ᵖ
³⁸They shed innocent blood,
    the blood of their sonsᵠ and
        daughters,
    whom they sacrificed to the idols of
        Canaan,
    and the land was desecrated by their
        blood.
³⁹They defiled themselvesʳ by what they
        did;
    by their deeds they prostitutedˢ
        themselves.

⁴⁰Therefore the LORD was angryᵗ with
        his people
    and abhorred his inheritance.ᵘ
⁴¹He handed them overᵛ to the nations,
    and their foes ruled over them.
⁴²Their enemies oppressedʷ them
    and subjected them to their power.

D *Job 33:29–30* ◀ ▶ *Jer 21:6*

ʷ33 Or *against his spirit, / and rash words came from his lips*

⁴³Many times he delivered them,ˣ
but they were bent on rebellionʸ
and they wasted away in their sin.

⁴⁴But he took note of their distress
when he heard their cry;ᶻ
⁴⁵for their sake he remembered his
covenantᵃ
and out of his great loveᵇ he
relented.ᶜ
⁴⁶He caused them to be pitiedᵈ
by all who held them captive.

⁴⁷Save us,ᵉ O LORD our God,
and gather usᶠ from the nations,
that we may give thanksᵍ to your holy
nameʰ
and glory in your praise.

⁴⁸Praise be to the LORD, the God of
Israel,
from everlasting to everlasting.
Let all the people say, "Amen!"ⁱ

Praise the LORD.

BOOK V

Psalms 107–150

Psalm 107

¹Give thanks to the LORD,ʲ for he is
good;ᵏ
his love endures forever.

²Let the redeemedˡ of the LORD say
this—
those he redeemed from the hand of
the foe,
³those he gatheredᵐ from the lands,
from east and west, from north and
south.ˣ

⁴Some wandered in desertⁿ wastelands,
finding no way to a cityᵒ where they
could settle.
⁵They were hungryᵖ and thirsty,ᑫ
and their lives ebbed away.
⁶Then they cried outʳ to the LORD in
their trouble,
and he delivered them from their
distress.
⁷He led them by a straight wayˢ
to a cityᵗ where they could settle.
⁸Let them give thanksᵘ to the LORD for
his unfailing loveᵛ
and his wonderful deedsʷ for men,

⁹for he satisfiesˣ the thirsty
and fills the hungry with good
things.ʸ
¹⁰Some sat in darknessᶻ and the deepest
gloom,
prisoners sufferingᵃ in iron chains,ᵇ
¹¹for they had rebelledᶜ against the
words of God
and despisedᵈ the counselᵉ of the
Most High.
¹²So he subjected them to bitter labor;
they stumbled, and there was no
one to help.ᶠ
¹³Then they cried to the LORD in their
trouble,
and he saved themᵍ from their
distress.
¹⁴He brought them out of darknessʰ and
the deepest gloomⁱ
and broke away their chains.ʲ

¹⁵Let them give thanksᵏ to the LORD for
his unfailing loveˡ
and his wonderful deedsᵐ for men,
¹⁶for he breaks down gates of bronze
and cuts through bars of iron.
¹⁷Some became foolsⁿ through their
rebellious waysᵒ
and suffered afflictionᵖ because of
their iniquities.
¹⁸They loathed all foodᑫ
and drew near the gates of death.ʳ
¹⁹Then they criedˢ to the LORD in their
trouble,
and he saved themᵗ from their
distress.
²⁰He sent forth his wordᵘ and healed
them;ᵛ
he rescuedʷ them from the grave.ˣ
²¹Let them give thanksʸ to the LORD for
his unfailing loveᶻ
and his wonderful deedsᵃ for men.
²²Let them sacrifice thank offeringsᵇ
and tell of his worksᶜ with songs of
joy.ᵈ

²³Others went out on the sea^e in ships;^f
they were merchants on the mighty
waters.
²⁴They saw the works of the LORD,^g
his wonderful deeds in the deep.
²⁵For he spoke^h and stirred up a
tempest^i
that lifted high the waves.^j
²⁶They mounted up to the heavens and
went down to the depths;
in their peril^k their courage melted^l
away.
²⁷They reeled^m and staggered like
drunken men;
they were at their wits' end.
²⁸Then they cried^n out to the LORD in
their trouble,
and he brought them out of their
distress.^o
²⁹He stilled the storm^p to a whisper;
the waves^q of the sea were hushed.^r
³⁰They were glad when it grew calm,
and he guided them^s to their
desired haven.
³¹Let them give thanks^t to the LORD for
his unfailing love^u
and his wonderful deeds^v for men.
³²Let them exalt^w him in the assembly^x
of the people
and praise him in the council of the
elders.
³³He turned rivers into a desert,^y
flowing springs^z into thirsty ground,
³⁴and fruitful land into a salt waste,^a
because of the wickedness of those
who lived there.
³⁵He turned the desert into pools of
water^b
and the parched ground into flowing
springs;^c
³⁶there he brought the hungry to live,
and they founded a city where they
could settle.
³⁷They sowed fields and planted
vineyards^d
that yielded a fruitful harvest;
³⁸he blessed them, and their numbers
greatly increased,^e
and he did not let their herds
diminish.^f
³⁹Then their numbers decreased,^g and
they were humbled^h
by oppression, calamity and sorrow;

⁴⁰he who pours contempt on nobles^i
made them wander in a trackless
waste.^j
⁴¹But he lifted the needy^k out of their
affliction
and increased their families like
flocks.^l
⁴²The upright see and rejoice,^m
but all the wicked shut their
mouths.^n
⁴³Whoever is wise,^o let him heed these
things
and consider the great love^p of the
LORD.

Psalm 108

108:1–5pp — Ps 57:7–11
108:6–13pp — Ps 60:5–12

A song. A psalm of David.

¹My heart is steadfast,^q O God;
I will sing^r and make music with all
my soul.
²Awake, harp and lyre!^s
I will awaken the dawn.
³I will praise you, O LORD, among the
nations;
I will sing of you among the peoples.
⁴For great is your love,^t higher than the
heavens;
your faithfulness^u reaches to the
skies.^v
⁵Be exalted, O God, above the
heavens,^w
and let your glory be over all the
earth.^x
⁶Save us and help us with your right
hand,^y
that those you love may be
delivered.
⁷God has spoken^z from his sanctuary:^a
"In triumph I will parcel out
Shechem^b
and measure off the Valley of
Succoth.^c
⁸Gilead is mine, Manasseh is mine;
Ephraim is my helmet,
Judah^d my scepter.
⁹Moab^e is my washbasin,
upon Edom^f I toss my sandal;
over Philistia^g I shout in triumph."
¹⁰Who will bring me to the fortified city?
Who will lead me to Edom?

¹¹Is it not you, O God, you who have
rejected us
and no longer go out with our
armies?ʰ
¹²Give us aid against the enemy,
for the help of man is worthless.ⁱ
V ¹³With God we will gain the victory,
and he will trample downʲ our
enemies.

Psalm 109

For the director of music. Of David.
A psalm.

¹O God, whom I praise,ᵏ
do not remain silent,ˡ
²for wicked and deceitful menᵐ
have opened their mouths against
me;
they have spoken against me with
lying tongues.ⁿ
³With words of hatredᵒ they surround
me;
they attack me without cause.ᵖ
⁴In return for my friendship they accuse
me,
but I am a man of prayer.ᵠ
⁵They repay me evil for good,ʳ
and hatred for my friendship.
⁶Appointʸ an evil manᶻ to oppose him;
let an accuserᵃˢ stand at his right
hand.
⁷When he is tried, let him be found
guilty,ᵗ
and may his prayers condemnᵘ him.
C ⁸May his days be few;ᵛ
may another take his placeʷ of
leadership.
⁹May his children be fatherless
and his wife a widow.ˣ
¹⁰May his children be wandering
beggars;ʸ
may they be drivenᵇ from their
ruined homes.
¹¹May a creditorᶻ seize all he has;
may strangers plunderᵃ the fruits of
his labor.ᵇ

V Ps 97:10 ◀ ▶ Ps 112:8
C Ps 97:2-7 ◀ ▶ SS 2:7-8

108:11 ʰ S Ps 44:9
108:12 ⁱ Ps 118:8;
146:3; Isa 10:3;
30:5; 31:3;
Jer 2:36; 17:5
108:13 ʲ Ps 44:5;
Isa 22:5; 63:3,6
109:1 ᵏ S Ex 15:2;
Jer 17:14
ˡ S Job 34:29
109:2 ᵐ S Ps 43:1
ⁿ S Ps 52:4
109:3 ᵒ Ps 69:4
ᵖ Ps 35:7; Jn 15:25
109:4 ᵠ Ps 69:13;
141:5
109:5 ʳ S Ge 44:4
109:6 ˢ 1Ch 21:1;
Job 1:6; Zec 3:1
109:7 ᵗ Ps 1:5
ᵘ Pr 28:9; Isa 41:24
109:8 ᵛ S Job 15:32
ʷ Ac 1:20*
109:9 ˣ Ex 22:24;
Jer 18:21
109:10 ʸ S Ge 4:12
109:11 ᶻ Ne 5:3
ᵃ S Nu 14:3; Isa 1:7;
6:11; 36:1; La 5:2
ᵇ Job 20:18
109:12 ᶜ S Job 5:4
109:13
ᵈ Job 18:19;
Ps 21:10
ᵉ S Nu 14:12;
Ps 9:5; Pr 10:7
109:14 ᶠ Ex 20:5;
Nu 14:18;
Isa 65:6-7;
Jer 32:18
109:15 ᵍ Ps 90:8
ʰ S Ex 17:14;
S Dt 32:26
109:16
ⁱ S Job 20:19;
S Ps 35:10
ʲ S Ps 34:18
109:17 ᵏ Pr 28:27;
S Mt 7:2
109:18 ˡ Ps 10:7
ᵐ Nu 5:22
109:19 ⁿ ver 29;
Ps 73:6; Eze 7:27
109:20
ᵒ S Ex 32:34;
Ps 54:5; 94:23;
Isa 3:11; 2Ti 4:14
ᵖ Ps 71:10
109:21
ᵠ S Ex 9:16;
S Ps 23:3 Ps 69:16
ˢ S Ps 3:7
109:23 ᵗ S Job 14:2
109:24
ᵘ Heb 12:12
ᵛ S Ps 35:13
ʷ S Job 16:8

¹²May no one extend kindness to him
or take pityᶜ on his fatherless
children.
¹³May his descendants be cut off,ᵈ
their names blotted outᵉ from the
next generation.
¹⁴May the iniquity of his fathersᶠ be
remembered before the Lord;
may the sin of his mother never be
blotted out.
¹⁵May their sins always remain beforeᵍ
the Lord,
that he may cut off the memoryʰ of
them from the earth.
¹⁶For he never thought of doing a
kindness,
but hounded to death the poor
and the needyⁱ and the
brokenhearted.ʲ
¹⁷He loved to pronounce a curse—
may itᶜ come on him;ᵏ
he found no pleasure in blessing—
may it beᵈ far from him.
¹⁸He wore cursingˡ as his garment;
it entered into his body like water,ᵐ
into his bones like oil.
¹⁹May it be like a cloak wrappedⁿ about
him,
like a belt tied forever around him. **H**
²⁰May this be the Lord's paymentᵒ to my
accusers,
to those who speak evilᵖ of me.
²¹But you, O Sovereign Lord,
deal well with me for your name's
sake;ᵠ
out of the goodness of your love,ʳ
deliver me.ˢ
²²For I am poor and needy,
and my heart is wounded within
me.
²³I fade away like an evening shadow;ᵗ
I am shaken off like a locust.
²⁴My knees giveᵘ way from fasting;ᵛ
my body is thin and gaunt.ʷ

H Ps 92:7 ◀ ▶ Ps 110:1

ʸ 6 Or *They say:* "Appoint (with quotation marks at the end of verse 19)
ᶻ 6 Or *the Evil One* ᵃ 6 Or *let Satan* ᵇ 10 Septuagint; Hebrew *sought*
ᶜ 17 Or *curse, / and it has* ᵈ 17 Or *blessing, / and it is*

109:8 The apostle Peter combined this verse with Ps 69:25 in reference to Judas after his betrayal of Jesus (see Ac 1:20). Judas's suicide removed him from his place among the twelve disciples and another leader had to be found to take his place. The early church chose Matthias, one who had been with Jesus and could testify to his words and deeds based on eyewitness accounts of his ministry, as Judas's successor (see Ac 1:12-26).

25 I am an object of scorn[x] to my accusers;
when they see me, they shake their heads.[y]

26 Help me,[z] O LORD my God;
save me in accordance with your love.
27 Let them know[a] that it is your hand,
that you, O LORD, have done it.
28 They may curse,[b] but you will bless;
when they attack they will be put to shame,
but your servant will rejoice.[c]
29 My accusers will be clothed with disgrace
and wrapped in shame[d] as in a cloak.

30 With my mouth I will greatly extol the LORD;
in the great throng[e] I will praise him.
31 For he stands at the right hand[f] of the needy one,
to save his life from those who condemn him.

Psalm 110

Of David. A psalm.

1 The LORD says[g] to my Lord:
"Sit at my right hand[h]
until I make your enemies
a footstool for your feet."[i]

2 The LORD will extend your mighty scepter[j] from Zion;[k]
you will rule[l] in the midst of your enemies.
3 Your troops will be willing
on your day of battle.
Arrayed in holy majesty,[m]
from the womb of the dawn
you will receive the dew of your youth.[e][n]

4 The LORD has sworn
and will not change his mind:[o]
"You are a priest forever,[p]
in the order of Melchizedek."[q]

5 The Lord is at your right hand;[r]
he will crush kings[s] on the day of his wrath.[t]
6 He will judge the nations,[u] heaping up the dead[v]
and crushing the rulers[w] of the whole earth.
7 He will drink from a brook beside the way;[f]
therefore he will lift up his head.[x]

Psalm 111[g]

1 Praise the LORD.[h]

I will extol the LORD[y] with all my heart[z]
in the council[a] of the upright and in the assembly.[b]

2 Great are the works[c] of the LORD;
they are pondered by all[d] who delight in them.
3 Glorious and majestic are his deeds,
and his righteousness endures[e] forever.
4 He has caused his wonders to be remembered;
the LORD is gracious and compassionate.[f]
5 He provides food[g] for those who fear him;[h]
he remembers his covenant[i] forever.

109:25 x S Ps 22:6
y S Job 16:4; S Mt 27:39; Mk 15:29
109:26 z S Ps 12:1; 119:86
109:27 a S Job 37:7
109:28 b S 2Sa 10:12
c Ps 66:4; Isa 35:10; 51:11; 54:1; 65:14
109:29 d S Ps 35:26
109:30 e S Ps 35:18
109:31 f Ps 16:8; 108:6
110:1 g Mt 22:44*; Mk 12:36*; Lk 20:42*; Ac 2:34*
h S Mk 16:19; Heb 1:13*; 12:2
i S Jos 10:24; S 1Ki 5:3; 1Co 15:25
110:2 j S Ge 49:10; Ps 45:6; Isa 14:5; Jer 48:17 k S Ps 2:6
l Ps 72:8
110:3 m S Ex 15:11
n Mic 5:7
110:4 o S Nu 23:19
p Zec 6:13; Heb 5:6*; 7:21*
q S Ge 14:18; Heb 5:10; 7:15-17*
110:5 r Ps 16:8
s S Dt 7:24; Ps 2:12; 68:21; 76:12; Isa 60:12; Da 2:44
t S Ps 2:5; Ro 2:5; Rev 6:17; 11:18
110:6 u S Ps 9:19
v Isa 5:25; 34:3; 66:24 w S Ps 18:38
110:7 x Ps 3:3; 27:5
111:1 y Ps 34:1; 109:30; 115:18; 145:10 z S Ps 9:1
a Ps 89:7 b S Ps 1:5
111:2 c S Job 36:24; Ps 143:5; Rev 15:3
d Ps 64:9
111:3 e Ps 112:3,9; 119:142
111:4 f S Dt 4:31; S Ps 86:15
111:5 g S Ge 1:30; S Ps 37:25; Mt 6:26,31-33
h Ps 103:11
i S 1Ch 16:15; S Ps 105:8

M Ps 102:22 ◀ ▶ Ps 132:11-18
P Ps 104:35 ◀ ▶ Ps 110:4-8
V Ps 72:8-9 ◀ ▶ Isa 9:6-7
H Ps 109:17-19 ◀ ▶ Ps 119:32

P Ps 110:1 ◀ ▶ Ps 144:5-6
L Ps 108:4 ◀ ▶ Ps 112:4
I Ps 105:8-11 ◀ ▶ Ps 111:9
F Ps 105:40-41 ◀ ▶ Ps 114:8

e 3 Or / *your young men will come to you like the dew* *f* 7 Or / *The One who grants succession will set him in authority* *g* This psalm is an acrostic poem, the lines of which begin with the successive letters of the Hebrew alphabet. *h* 1 Hebrew *Hallelu Yah*

110:1–7 This psalm is frequently referred to in the NT because of its vivid description of the Messiah. Beginning with the coronation of the King, David affirms the kingly and priestly roles of the Messiah (see Ge 14:18; Jn 14:6; 1Ti 2:5–6; Heb 5:6; 7:1–28; Rev 3:21). David also alludes to the conversion of Israel (see Dt 30:1–9; Joel 2:27; Zec 13:9) and the tribulation period when Jesus, as God's "mighty scepter from Zion" (110:2), will defeat the antichrist and "judge the nations" (110:6).

111:5–9 The psalmist praised God for fulfilling his covenant with Israel by delivering them from the heathen and sending them redemption.

⁶He has shown his people the power of his works,ʲ
giving them the lands of other nations.ᵏ
⁷The works of his hands¹ are faithful and just;
all his precepts are trustworthy.ᵐ
⁸They are steadfast for everⁿ and ever,
done in faithfulness and uprightness.
⁹He provided redemption° for his people;
he ordained his covenant forever—
holy and awesomeᵖ is his name.

¹⁰The fear of the LORDᑫ is the beginning of wisdom;ʳ
all who follow his precepts have good understanding.ˢ
To him belongs eternal praise.ᵗ

Psalm 112ⁱ

¹Praise the LORD.ʲᵘ

Blessed is the manᵛ who fears the LORD,ʷ
who finds great delightˣ in his commands.

²His childrenʸ will be mighty in the land;
the generation of the upright will be blessed.
³Wealth and richesᶻ are in his house,
and his righteousness enduresᵃ forever.
⁴Even in darkness light dawnsᵇ for the upright,
for the gracious and compassionate and righteousᶜ man.ᵏ
⁵Good will come to him who is generous and lends freely,ᵈ
who conducts his affairs with justice.
⁶Surely he will never be shaken;ᵉ
a righteous man will be rememberedᶠ forever.
⁷He will have no fear of bad news;
his heart is steadfast,ᵍ trusting in the LORD.ʰ

⁸His heart is secure, he will have no fear;ⁱ
in the end he will look in triumph on his foes.ʲ
⁹He has scattered abroad his gifts to the poor,ᵏ
his righteousness endures¹ forever;
his hornⁱ will be liftedᵐ high in honor.

¹⁰The wicked man will seeⁿ and be vexed,
he will gnash his teeth° and waste away;ᵖ
the longings of the wicked will come to nothing.ᑫ

Psalm 113

¹Praise the LORD.ᵐʳ

Praise, O servants of the LORD,ˢ
praise the name of the LORD.
²Let the name of the LORD be praised,ᵗ
both now and forevermore.ᵘ
³From the rising of the sunᵛ to the place where it sets,
the name of the LORD is to be praised.

⁴The LORD is exaltedʷ over all the nations,
his glory above the heavens.ˣ
⁵Who is like the LORD our God,ʸ
the One who sits enthronedᶻ on high,ᵃ
⁶who stoops down to lookᵇ
on the heavens and the earth?

⁷He raises the poorᶜ from the dust
and lifts the needyᵈ from the ash heap;
⁸he seats themᵉ with princes,
with the princes of their people.
⁹He settles the barrenᶠ woman in her home
as a happy mother of children.

Praise the LORD.

I Ps 111:5–6 ◀ ▶ Ps 126:1–6
R Ps 103:17–18 ◀ ▶ Ps 128:3
U Ps 97:10–12 ◀ ▶ Ps 115:12–15
P Ps 105:37 ◀ ▶ Pr 3:9–10
L Ps 111:4 ◀ ▶ Ps 116:5
J Ps 91:5–6 ◀ ▶ Ps 118:6
W Ps 91:5–6 ◀ ▶ Ps 119:165

V Ps 108:13 ◀ ▶ Ps 138:7
H Ps 103:5 ◀ ▶ Ps 128:6

i This psalm is an acrostic poem, the lines of which begin with the successive letters of the Hebrew alphabet. / *j* Hebrew *Hallelu Yah* / *k4* Or / *for* the LORD, *is gracious and compassionate and righteous* / *l9* *Horn* here symbolizes dignity. / *m1* Hebrew *Hallelu Yah;* also in verse 9

Psalm 114

¹ When Israel came out of Egypt,
   the house of Jacob from a people of foreign tongue,
² Judah became God's sanctuary,
   Israel his dominion.

³ The sea looked and fled,
   the Jordan turned back;
⁴ the mountains skipped like rams,
   the hills like lambs.

⁵ Why was it, O sea, that you fled,
   O Jordan, that you turned back,
⁶ you mountains, that you skipped like rams,
   you hills, like lambs?

⁷ Tremble, O earth, at the presence of the Lord,
   at the presence of the God of Jacob,
⁸ who turned the rock into a pool,
   the hard rock into springs of water.

Psalm 115

115:4–11pp — Ps 135:15–20

¹ Not to us, O LORD, not to us
   but to your name be the glory,
   because of your love and faithfulness.

² Why do the nations say,
   "Where is their God?"
³ Our God is in heaven;
   he does whatever pleases him.
⁴ But their idols are silver and gold,
   made by the hands of men.
⁵ They have mouths, but cannot speak,
   eyes, but they cannot see;
⁶ they have ears, but cannot hear,
   noses, but they cannot smell;
⁷ they have hands, but cannot feel,
   feet, but they cannot walk;
   nor can they utter a sound with their throats.
⁸ Those who make them will be like them,
   and so will all who trust in them.

⁹ O house of Israel, trust in the LORD—
   he is their help and shield.
¹⁰ O house of Aaron, trust in the LORD—
   he is their help and shield.
¹¹ You who fear him, trust in the LORD—
   he is their help and shield.

¹² The LORD remembers us and will bless us:
He will bless the house of Israel,
   he will bless the house of Aaron,
¹³ he will bless those who fear the LORD—
   small and great alike.

¹⁴ May the LORD make you increase,
   both you and your children.
¹⁵ May you be blessed by the LORD,
   the Maker of heaven and earth.

¹⁶ The highest heavens belong to the LORD,
   but the earth he has given to man.
¹⁷ It is not the dead who praise the LORD,
   those who go down to silence;
¹⁸ it is we who extol the LORD,
   both now and forevermore.

Praise the LORD.

Psalm 116

¹ I love the LORD, for he heard my voice;
   he heard my cry for mercy.
² Because he turned his ear to me,
   I will call on him as long as I live.

³ The cords of death entangled me,
   the anguish of the grave came upon me;
   I was overcome by trouble and sorrow.
⁴ Then I called on the name of the LORD:
   "O LORD, save me!"

⁵ The LORD is gracious and righteous;
   our God is full of compassion.
⁶ The LORD protects the simplehearted;
   when I was in great need, he saved me.

⁷ Be at rest once more, O my soul,
   for the LORD has been good to you.

⁸ For you, O LORD, have delivered my soul from death,
   my eyes from tears,
   my feet from stumbling,
⁹ that I may walk before the LORD
   in the land of the living.

n 18 Hebrew Hallelu Yah   o 3 Hebrew Sheol

¹⁰I believed;ᵇ thereforeᵖ I said,
  "I am greatly afflicted."ᶜ
¹¹And in my dismay I said,
  "All men are liars."ᵈ

¹²How can I repay the LORD
  for all his goodnessᵉ to me?
¹³I will lift up the cup of salvation
  and call on the nameᶠ of the LORD.
¹⁴I will fulfill my vowsᵍ to the LORD
  in the presence of all his people.

¹⁵Precious in the sightʰ of the LORD
  is the death of his saints.ⁱ
¹⁶O LORD, truly I am your servant;ʲ
  I am your servant, the son of your
    maidservantᵠ;ᵏ
  you have freed me from my chains.ˡ
¹⁷I will sacrifice a thank offeringᵐ to you
  and call on the name of the LORD.
¹⁸I will fulfill my vowsⁿ to the LORD
  in the presence of all his people,
¹⁹in the courtsᵒ of the house of the
    LORD—
  in your midst, O Jerusalem.ᵖ

Praise the LORD.ʳ

Psalm 117

¹Praise the LORD,ᵠ all you nations;ʳ
  extol him, all you peoples.
²For great is his loveˢ toward us,
  and the faithfulness of the LORDᵗ
    endures forever.

Praise the LORD.ʳ

Psalm 118

¹Give thanks to the LORD,ᵘ for he is
    good;ᵛ
  his love endures forever.ʷ

²Let Israel say:ˣ
  "His love endures forever."ʸ
³Let the house of Aaron say:ᶻ
  "His love endures forever."
⁴Let those who fear the LORDᵃ say:
  "His love endures forever."

⁵In my anguishᵇ I cried to the LORD,
  and he answeredᶜ by setting me
    free.
⁶The LORD is with me;ᵈ I will not be
    afraid.
  What can man do to me?ᵉ

L Ps 107:28 ◀▶ Ps 118:8
J Ps 112:7-8 ◀▶ Pr 1:33
S Ps 91:1-16 ◀▶ Ps 119:117

116:10 ᵇ2Co 4:13*
ᶜPs 9:18; 72:2;
S 107:17; 119:67,
71, 75
116:11 ᵈJer 9:3-5;
Hos 7:13; Mic 6:12;
Ro 3:4
116:12 ᵉPs 103:2;
106:1
116:13 ᶠS Ps 105:1
116:14 ᵍS Nu 30:2;
S Ps 66:13
116:15 ʰPs 72:14
ⁱS Nu 23:10
116:16 ʲPs 119:125;
143:12 ᵏS Ps 86:16
ˡS Job 12:18
116:17 ᵐS Lev 7:12;
S Ezr 2:1
116:18 ⁿver 14;
S Lev 22:18
116:19 ᵒPs 92:13;
96:8; 100:4; 135:2
ᵖPs 102:21
117:1 ᵠS Ps 22:23;
S 103:2 ʳRo 15:11*
117:2 ˢS Ps 17:7;
S 103:11
ᵗPs 119:90; 146:6
118:1 ᵘS 1Ch 16:8
ᵛS 2Ch 5:13; S 7:3
ʷS Ezr 3:11
118:2 ˣPs 115:9
ʸPs 106:1;
136:1-26
118:3 ᶻEx 30:30;
Ps 115:10
118:4
ᵃS Ps 115:11
118:5 ᵇPs 18:6;
31:7; 77:2; 120:1
ᶜver 21; Ps 34:4;
86:7; 116:1; 138:3
118:6 ᵈS Dt 31:6;
Heb 13:6*
ᵉS Ps 56:4
118:7 ᶠS Dt 33:29
ᵍS Ps 54:7
118:8 ʰPs 2:12;
5:11; 9:9; 37:3;
40:4; Isa 25:4;
57:13 ⁱ2Ch 32:7-8;
Ps 108:12;
S Isa 2:22
118:9 ʲPs 146:3
118:10 ᵏS Ps 37:9
118:11 ˡPs 88:17
ᵐPs 3:6
118:12 ⁿDt 1:44
ᵒS Ps 58:9 ᵖPs 37:9
118:13 ᵠver 7;
2Ch 18:31;
Ps 86:17
118:14 ʳS Ex 15:2
ˢS Ps 62:2
118:15
ᵗS Job 8:21;
S Ps 106:5
ᵘS Ex 15:6;
Ps 89:13; 108:6
ᵛLk 1:51
118:17 ʷHab 1:12
ˣS Dt 32:3; Ps 64:9;
71:16; 73:28
118:18
ʸJer 31:18;
1Co 11:32;
Heb 12:5 ᶻPs 86:13
118:19 ᵃS Ps 24:7
ᵇPs 100:4

⁷The LORD is with me; he is my helper.ᶠ
  I will look in triumph on my
    enemies.ᵍ

⁸It is better to take refuge in the LORDʰ
  than to trust in man.ⁱ
⁹It is better to take refuge in the LORD
  than to trust in princes.ʲ

¹⁰All the nations surrounded me,
  but in the name of the LORD I cut
    them off.ᵏ
¹¹They surrounded meˡ on every side,ᵐ
  but in the name of the LORD I cut
    them off.
¹²They swarmed around me like bees,ⁿ
  but they died out as quickly as
    burning thorns;ᵒ
  in the name of the LORD I cut them
    off.ᵖ
¹³I was pushed back and about to fall,
  but the LORD helped me.ᵠ
¹⁴The LORD is my strengthʳ and my song;
  he has become my salvation.ˢ

¹⁵Shouts of joyᵗ and victory
  resound in the tents of the
    righteous:
  "The LORD's right handᵘ has done
    mighty things!ᵛ
¹⁶ The LORD's right hand is lifted high;
  the LORD's right hand has done
    mighty things!"

¹⁷I will not dieʷ but live,
  and will proclaimˣ what the LORD
    has done.
¹⁸The LORD has chastenedʸ me severely,
  but he has not given me over to
    death.ᶻ

¹⁹Open for me the gatesᵃ of
    righteousness;
  I will enterᵇ and give thanks to the
    LORD.
²⁰This is the gate of the LORDᶜ
  through which the righteous may
    enter.ᵈ
²¹I will give you thanks, for you
    answered me;ᵉ
  you have become my salvation.ᶠ

L Ps 116:15 ◀▶ Ps 121:1-8
U Ps 115:12-15 ◀▶ Ps 119:1-2

118:20 ᶜPs 122:1-2 ᵈPs 15:1-2; 24:3-4; Rev 22:14 118:21 ᵉS ver 5
ᶠPs 27:1

ᵖ 10 Or believed even when   ᵠ 16 Or servant, your faithful son
ʳ 19,2 Hebrew Hallelu Yah

²²The stoneᵍ the builders rejected
 has become the capstone;ʰ
²³the LORD has done this,
 and it is marvelousⁱ in our eyes.
²⁴This is the day the LORD has made;
 let us rejoice and be gladʲ in it.
²⁵O LORD, save us;ᵏ
 O LORD, grant us success.
²⁶Blessed is he who comesˡ in the name of the LORD.
 From the house of the LORD we bless you.ˢᵐ
²⁷The LORD is God,ⁿ
 and he has made his light shineᵒ upon us.
 With boughs in hand,ᵖ join in the festal procession
 upʳ to the horns of the altar.ᵠ
²⁸You are my God, and I will give you thanks;
 you are my God,ʳ and I will exaltˢ you.
²⁹Give thanks to the LORD, for he is good;
 his love endures forever.

Psalm 119ᵘ

א Aleph

¹Blessed are they whose ways are blameless,ᵗ
 who walkᵘ according to the law of the LORD.ᵛ
²Blessedʷ are they who keep his statutesˣ
 and seek himʸ with all their heart.ᶻ
³They do nothing wrong;ᵃ
 they walk in his ways.ᵇ
⁴You have laid down preceptsᶜ
 that are to be fully obeyed.ᵈ
⁵Oh, that my ways were steadfast
 in obeying your decrees!ᵉ
⁶Then I would not be put to shameᶠ
 when I consider all your commands.ᵍ
⁷I will praise you with an upright heart
 as I learn your righteous laws.ʰ
⁸I will obey your decrees;
 do not utterly forsake me.ⁱ

ב Beth

⁹How can a young man keep his way pure?ʲ
 By living according to your word.ᵏ

118:22 ᵍ Isa 8:14
ʰ Isa 17:10; 19:13; 28:16; Zec 4:7; 10:4; Mt 21:42; Mk 12:10; Lk 20:17*; S Ac 4:11*; 1Pe 2:7*
118:23
ⁱ Mt 21:42*; Mk 12:11*
118:24 ʲ S Ps 70:4
118:25
ᵏ S Ps 28:9; 116:4
118:26
ˡ S Mt 11:3; 21:9*; 23:39*; Mk 11:9*; Lk 13:35*; 19:38*; Jn 12:13*
ᵐ Ps 129:8
118:27
ⁿ S 1Ki 18:21
ᵒ Ps 27:1; Isa 58:10; 60:1,19,20; Mal 4:2; 1Pe 2:9
ᵖ S Lev 23:40
ᵠ Ex 27:2
118:28
ʳ S Ge 28:21; S Ps 16:2; 63:1; Isa 25:1 ˢ S Ex 15:2
119:1 ᵗ S Ge 17:1; S Dt 18:13; Pr 11:20 ᵘ S Ps 128:1
ᵛ S Ps 1:2
119:2 ʷ Ps 112:1; Isa 56:2 ˣ ver 146; Ps 99:7
ʸ S 1Ch 16:11; S Ps 40:16
ᶻ S Dt 10:12
119:3 ᵃ S Ps 59:4; 1Jn 3:9; 5:18
ᵇ Ps 128:1; Jer 6:16; 7:23
119:4 ᶜ Ps 103:18
ᵈ S ver 56; S Dt 6:17
119:5
ᵉ S Lev 19:37
119:6 ᶠ ver 46,80
ᵍ ver 117
119:7 ʰ S Dt 4:8
119:8 ⁱ S Ps 38:21
119:9 ʲ S Ps 39:1
ᵏ ver 65,169
119:10 ˡ S Ps 9:1
ᵐ ver 21,118
119:11 ⁿ S Dt 6:6;
S Job 22:22
ᵒ ver 133,165;
Ps 18:22-23; 19:13; Pr 3:23; Isa 63:13
119:12 ᵖ Ps 28:6
ᵠ Ps 143:8,10
ʳ S Ex 18:20
119:13 ˢ ver 72
119:14 ᵗ ver 111
119:15 ᵘ ver 97, 148; Ps 1:2
119:16
ᵛ S Ps 112:1
119:17 ʷ Ps 13:6; 116:7 ˣ ver 67;
Ps 103:20
119:19
ʸ S Ge 23:4; Heb 11:13
119:20 ᶻ Ps 42:2; 84:2 ᵃ ver 131;
S Ps 63:1; Isa 26:9
119:21 ᵇ ver 51; Job 30:1; Ps 5:5;
Jer 20:7; 50:32; Da 4:37; Mal 3:15

---

¹⁰I seek you with all my heart;ˡ
 do not let me stray from your commands.ᵐ
¹¹I have hidden your word in my heartⁿ
 that I might not sinᵒ against you.
¹²Praise beᵖ to you, O LORD;
 teach meᵠ your decrees.ʳ
¹³With my lips I recount
 all the laws that come from your mouth.ˢ
¹⁴I rejoice in following your statutesᵗ
 as one rejoices in great riches.
¹⁵I meditate on your preceptsᵘ
 and consider your ways.
¹⁶I delightᵛ in your decrees;
 I will not neglect your word.

ג Gimel

¹⁷Do good to your servant,ʷ and I will live;
 I will obey your word.ˣ
¹⁸Open my eyes that I may see
 wonderful things in your law.
¹⁹I am a stranger on earth;ʸ
 do not hide your commands from me.
²⁰My soul is consumedᶻ with longing
 for your lawsᵃ at all times.
²¹You rebuke the arrogant,ᵇ who are cursedᶜ
 and who strayᵈ from your commands.
²²Remove from me scornᵉ and contempt,
 for I keep your statutes.ᶠ
²³Though rulers sit together and slander me,
 your servant will meditate on your decrees.
²⁴Your statutes are my delight;
 they are my counselors.

ד Daleth

²⁵I am laid low in the dust;ᵍ
 preserve my lifeʰ according to your word.ⁱ
²⁶I recounted my ways and you answered me;
 teach me your decrees.ʲ
²⁷Let me understand the teaching of your precepts;

ᶜ Dt 27:26 ᵈ S ver 10 119:22 ᵉ Ps 39:8 ᶠ ver 2 119:25 ᵍ Ps 44:25
ʰ ver 50,107; Ps 143:11 ⁱ ver 9 119:26 ʲ Ps 25:4; 27:11; 86:11

ˢ 26 The Hebrew is plural. ᵗ 27 Or Bind the festal sacrifice with ropes / and take it ᵘ This psalm is an acrostic poem; the verses of each stanza begin with the same letter of the Hebrew alphabet.

S Ps 101:6-8 ◀▶ Ps 119:119
U Ps 118:15 ◀▶ Ps 119:165

then I will meditate on your wonders.ᵏ
²⁸My soul is weary with sorrow;ˡ
strengthen meᵐ according to your word.ⁿ
²⁹Keep me from deceitful ways;ᵒ
be gracious to meᵖ through your law.
³⁰I have chosenᵠ the way of truth;ʳ
I have set my heartˢ on your laws.
³¹I hold fastᵗ to your statutes, O LORD;
do not let me be put to shame.
³²I run in the path of your commands,
for you have set my heart free.

ה He

³³Teach me,ᵘ O LORD, to follow your decrees;
then I will keep them to the end.
³⁴Give me understanding,ᵛ and I will keep your lawʷ
and obey it with all my heart.ˣ
³⁵Direct meʸ in the path of your commands,ᶻ
for there I find delight.ᵃ
³⁶Turn my heartᵇ toward your statutes
and not toward selfish gain.ᶜ
³⁷Turn my eyes away from worthless things;
preserve my lifeᵈ according to your word.ᵛᵉ
³⁸Fulfill your promiseᶠ to your servant,
so that you may be feared.
³⁹Take away the disgraceᵍ I dread,
for your laws are good.
⁴⁰How I longʰ for your precepts!
Preserve my lifeⁱ in your righteousness.

ו Waw

⁴¹May your unfailing loveʲ come to me, O LORD,
your salvation according to your promise;ᵏ
⁴²then I will answerˡ the one who taunts me,ᵐ
for I trust in your word.
⁴³Do not snatch the word of truth from my mouth,ⁿ
for I have put my hopeᵒ in your laws.
⁴⁴I will always obey your law,ᵖ
for ever and ever.
⁴⁵I will walk about in freedom,
for I have sought out your precepts.ᵠ

H Ps 110:1 ◀ ▶ Ps 119:119

119:27 ᵏ Ps 105:2; 145:5
119:28 ˡ Ps 6:7; 116:3; Isa 51:11; Jer 45:3 ᵐ Ps 18:1; Isa 40:29; 41:10 ⁿ ver 9
119:29 ᵒ Ps 26:4 ᵖ S Nu 6:25
119:30 ᵠ S Jos 24:22 ʳ S Ps 26:3 ˢ S Ps 108:1
119:31 ᵗ S Dt 10:20
119:33 ᵘ ver 12
119:34 ᵛ ver 27, 73,144,169; S Job 32:8; Pr 2:6; Da 2:21; Jas 1:5 ʷ S Dt 6:25 ˣ ver 69
119:35 ʸ Ps 25:4-5 ᶻ ver 32 ᵃ S Ps 1:2
119:36 ᵇ S Jos 24:23 ᶜ Eze 33:31
119:37 ᵈ ver 25; Ps 71:20 ᵉ ver 9
119:38 ᶠ S Nu 23:19
119:39 ᵍ ver 22; Ps 69:9; 89:51; Isa 25:8; 51:7; 54:4
119:40 ʰ ver 20 ⁱ ver 25,149,154
119:41 ʲ S Ps 6:4 ᵏ ver 76,116,154, 170
119:42 ˡ Pr 27:11 ᵐ S Ps 42:10
119:43 ⁿ S 1Ki 17:24 ᵒ ver 74,81,114, 147
119:44 ᵖ ver 33, 34,55; S Dt 6:25
119:45 ᵠ ver 94, 155
119:46 ʳ Mt 10:18; Ac 26:1-2 ˢ S ver 6
119:47 ᵗ ver 77, 143; S Ps 112:1 ᵘ ver 97,127,159, 163,165
119:48 ᵛ S Ge 24:63
119:49 ʷ ver 9 ˣ ver 43
119:50 ʸ S ver 25
119:51 ᶻ S ver 21; S Job 16:10; S 17:2 ᵃ S Job 23:11
119:52 ᵇ Ps 103:18
119:53 ᶜ S Ex 32:19; S 33:4 ᵈ Ps 89:30
119:54 ᵉ ver 172; Ps 101:1; 138:5
119:55 ᶠ ver 62, 72; Ps 1:2; 42:8; S 63:6; 77:2; Isa 26:9; Ac 16:25 ᵍ S ver 44
119:56 ʰ ver 4, 100,134,168; S Nu 15:40
119:57 ⁱ S Dt 32:9; Jer 51:19; La 3:24 ʲ ver 17,67,101
119:58 ᵏ S Dt 4:29; S 1Ch 16:11; Ps 34:4 ˡ S Ge 43:29;

119:27 ᵏ Ps 105:2;

⁴⁶I will speak of your statutes before kings,ʳ
and will not be put to shame,ˢ
⁴⁷for I delightᵗ in your commands
because I love them.ᵘ
⁴⁸I lift up my hands toʷ your commands, which I love,
and I meditateᵛ on your decrees.

ז Zayin

⁴⁹Remember your wordʷ to your servant,
for you have given me hope.ˣ
⁵⁰My comfort in my suffering is this:
Your promise preserves my life.ʸ
⁵¹The arrogant mock meᶻ without restraint,
but I do not turnᵃ from your law.
⁵²I rememberᵇ your ancient laws, O LORD,
and I find comfort in them.
⁵³Indignation grips meᶜ because of the wicked,
who have forsaken your law.ᵈ
⁵⁴Your decrees are the theme of my songᵉ
wherever I lodge.
⁵⁵In the night I rememberᶠ your name, O LORD,
and I will keep your law.ᵍ
⁵⁶This has been my practice:
I obey your precepts.ʰ

ח Heth

⁵⁷You are my portion,ⁱ O LORD;
I have promised to obey your words.ʲ
⁵⁸I have soughtᵏ your face with all my heart;
be gracious to meˡ according to your promise.ᵐ
⁵⁹I have considered my waysⁿ
and have turned my steps to your statutes.
⁶⁰I will hasten and not delay
to obey your commands.ᵒ
⁶¹Though the wicked bind me with ropes,
I will not forgetᵖ your law.
⁶²At midnightᵠ I rise to give you thanks
for your righteous laws.ʳ

T Ps 107:2 ◀ ▶ Ps 119:108

S Ezr 9:8 ᵐ ver 41 119:59 ⁿ Jos 24:14-15; S Ps 39:1 119:60 ᵒ ver 115 119:61 ᵖ ver 83,109,153,176 119:62 ᵠ S ver 55; Ac 16:25 ʳ ver 7

ᵛ 37 Two manuscripts of the Masoretic Text and Dead Sea Scrolls; most manuscripts of the Masoretic Text *life in your way* ʷ 48 Or *for*

⁶³I am a friend to all who fear you,
  to all who follow your precepts.
⁶⁴The earth is filled with your love,
    O LORD;
  teach me your decrees.

ט Teth

⁶⁵Do good to your servant
  according to your word, O LORD.
⁶⁶Teach me knowledge and good
    judgment,
  for I believe in your commands.
⁶⁷Before I was afflicted I went astray,
  but now I obey your word.
⁶⁸You are good, and what you do is
    good;
  teach me your decrees.
⁶⁹Though the arrogant have smeared me
    with lies,
  I keep your precepts with all my
    heart.
⁷⁰Their hearts are callous and
    unfeeling,
  but I delight in your law.
⁷¹It was good for me to be afflicted
  so that I might learn your decrees.
⁷²The law from your mouth is more
    precious to me
  than thousands of pieces of silver
    and gold.

י Yodh

⁷³Your hands made me and formed me;
  give me understanding to learn your
    commands.
⁷⁴May those who fear you rejoice when
    they see me,
  for I have put my hope in your
    word.
⁷⁵I know, O LORD, that your laws are
    righteous,
  and in faithfulness you have
    afflicted me.
⁷⁶May your unfailing love be my
    comfort,
  according to your promise to your
    servant.
⁷⁷Let your compassion come to me that
    I may live,
  for your law is my delight.
⁷⁸May the arrogant be put to shame for
    wronging me without cause;
  but I will meditate on your precepts.

⁷⁹May those who fear you turn to me,
  those who understand your
    statutes.
⁸⁰May my heart be blameless toward
    your decrees,
  that I may not be put to shame.

כ Kaph

⁸¹My soul faints with longing for your
    salvation,
  but I have put my hope in your
    word.
⁸²My eyes fail, looking for your
    promise;
  I say, "When will you comfort me?"
⁸³Though I am like a wineskin in the
    smoke,
  I do not forget your decrees.
⁸⁴How long must your servant wait?
  When will you punish my
    persecutors?
⁸⁵The arrogant dig pitfalls for me,
  contrary to your law.
⁸⁶All your commands are trustworthy;
  help me, for men persecute me
    without cause.
⁸⁷They almost wiped me from the earth,
  but I have not forsaken your
    precepts.
⁸⁸Preserve my life according to your
    love,
  and I will obey the statutes of your
    mouth.

ל Lamedh

⁸⁹Your word, O LORD, is eternal;
  it stands firm in the heavens.
⁹⁰Your faithfulness continues through
    all generations;
  you established the earth, and it
    endures.
⁹¹Your laws endure to this day,
  for all things serve you.
⁹²If your law had not been my delight,
  I would have perished in my
    affliction.
⁹³I will never forget your precepts,
  for by them you have preserved my
    life.
⁹⁴Save me, for I am yours;
  I have sought out your precepts.
⁹⁵The wicked are waiting to destroy
    me,
  but I will ponder your statutes.

⁹⁶To all perfection I see a limit;
  but your commands are boundless.ᵈ

מ Mem

⁹⁷Oh, how I love your law!ᵉ
  I meditateᶠ on it all day long.
⁹⁸Your commands make me wiserᵍ than my enemies,
  for they are ever with me.
⁹⁹I have more insight than all my teachers,
  for I meditate on your statutes.ʰ
¹⁰⁰I have more understanding than the elders,
  for I obey your precepts.ⁱ
¹⁰¹I have kept my feetʲ from every evil path
  so that I might obey your word.ᵏ
¹⁰²I have not departed from your laws,ˡ
  for you yourself have taughtᵐ me.
¹⁰³How sweet are your words to my taste,
  sweeter than honeyⁿ to my mouth!ᵒ
¹⁰⁴I gain understandingᵖ from your precepts;
  therefore I hate every wrong path.ᵠ

נ Nun

¹⁰⁵Your word is a lampʳ to my feet
  and a lightˢ for my path.
¹⁰⁶I have taken an oathᵗ and confirmed it,
  that I will follow your righteous laws.ᵘ
¹⁰⁷I have suffered much;
  preserve my life,ᵛ O LORD, according to your word.

**T ¹⁰⁸Accept, O LORD, the willing praise of my mouth,ʷ
  and teach me your laws.ˣ**

¹⁰⁹Though I constantly take my life in my hands,ʸ
  I will not forgetᶻ your law.
¹¹⁰The wicked have set a snareᵃ for me,
  but I have not strayedᵇ from your precepts.
¹¹¹Your statutes are my heritage forever;
  they are the joy of my heart.ᶜ
¹¹²My heart is setᵈ on keeping your decrees
  to the very end.ᵉ

ס Samekh

¹¹³I hate double-minded men,ᶠ
  but I love your law.ᵍ

¹¹⁴You are my refuge and my shield;ʰ
  I have put my hopeⁱ in your word.
¹¹⁵Away from me,ʲ you evildoers,
  that I may keep the commands of my God!
¹¹⁶Sustain meᵏ according to your promise,ˡ and I will live;
  do not let my hopes be dashed.ᵐ

**¹¹⁷Uphold me,ⁿ and I will be delivered;ᵒ
  I will always have regard for your decrees.ᵖ**

¹¹⁸You reject all who strayᵠ from your decrees,
  for their deceitfulness is in vain.

**¹¹⁹All the wicked of the earth you discard like dross;ʳ
  therefore I love your statutes.ˢ**

¹²⁰My flesh tremblesᵗ in fear of you;ᵘ
  I stand in aweᵛ of your laws.

ע Ayin

¹²¹I have done what is righteous and just;ʷ
  do not leave me to my oppressors.
¹²²Ensure your servant's well-being;ˣ
  let not the arrogant oppress me.ʸ
¹²³My eyes fail,ᶻ looking for your salvation,ᵃ
  looking for your righteous promise.ᵇ
¹²⁴Deal with your servant according to your loveᶜ
  and teach me your decrees.ᵈ
¹²⁵I am your servant;ᵉ give me discernment
  that I may understand your statutes.ᶠ
¹²⁶It is time for you to act, O LORD;
  your law is being broken.ᵍ
¹²⁷Because I love your commandsʰ
  more than gold,ⁱ more than pure gold,ʲ
¹²⁸and because I consider all your precepts right,ᵏ
  I hate every wrong path.ˡ

פ Pe

¹²⁹Your statutes are wonderful;ᵐ
  therefore I obey them.ⁿ
¹³⁰The unfolding of your words gives light;ᵒ

PSALM 119:131

it gives understanding to the
      simple.ᵖ
¹³¹I open my mouth and pant,ᑫ
      longing for your commands.ʳ
¹³²Turn to meˢ and have mercyᵗ on me,
      as you always do to those who love
         your name.ᵘ
¹³³Direct my footsteps according to your
      word;ᵛ
      let no sinʷ rule over me.
¹³⁴Redeem me from the oppression of
      men,ˣ
      that I may obey your precepts.ʸ
¹³⁵Make your face shineᶻ upon your
      servant
      and teach me your decrees.ᵃ
¹³⁶Streams of tearsᵇ flow from my eyes,
      for your law is not obeyed.ᶜ

צ Tsadhe

¹³⁷Righteous are you,ᵈ O LORD,
      and your laws are right.ᵉ
¹³⁸The statutes you have laid down are
      righteous;ᶠ
      they are fully trustworthy.ᵍ
¹³⁹My zeal wears me out,ʰ
      for my enemies ignore your words.
¹⁴⁰Your promisesⁱ have been thoroughly
      tested,ʲ
      and your servant loves them.ᵏ
¹⁴¹Though I am lowly and despised,ˡ
      I do not forget your precepts.ᵐ
¹⁴²Your righteousness is everlasting
      and your law is true.ⁿ
¹⁴³Trouble and distress have come
      upon me,
      but your commands are my delight.ᵒ
¹⁴⁴Your statutes are forever right;
      give me understandingᵖ that I may
         live.

ק Qoph

¹⁴⁵I call with all my heart;ᑫ answer me,
      O LORD,
      and I will obey your decrees.ʳ
¹⁴⁶I call out to you; save meˢ
      and I will keep your statutes.
¹⁴⁷I rise before dawnᵗ and cry for help;
      I have put my hope in your word.
¹⁴⁸My eyes stay open through the
      watches of the night,ᵘ
      that I may meditate on your
         promises.
¹⁴⁹Hear my voiceᵛ in accordance with
      your love;ʷ
      preserve my life,ˣ O LORD, according
         to your laws.

¹⁵⁰Those who devise wicked schemesʸ
      are near,
      but they are far from your law.
¹⁵¹Yet you are near,ᶻ O LORD,
      and all your commands are true.ᵃ
¹⁵²Long ago I learned from your
      statutesᵇ
      that you established them to last
         forever.ᶜ

ר Resh

¹⁵³Look upon my sufferingᵈ and
      deliver me,ᵉ
      for I have not forgottenᶠ your law.
¹⁵⁴Defend my causeᵍ and redeem me;ʰ
      preserve my lifeⁱ according to your
         promise.ʲ
¹⁵⁵**Salvation is far from the wicked,**
      for they do not seek outᵏ your
         decrees.
¹⁵⁶Your compassion is great,ˡ O LORD;
      preserve my lifeᵐ according to your
         laws.ⁿ
¹⁵⁷Many are the foes who
      persecute me,ᵒ
      but I have not turnedᵖ from your
         statutes.
¹⁵⁸I look on the faithless with loathing,ᑫ
      for they do not obey your word.ʳ
¹⁵⁹See how I love your precepts;
      preserve my life,ˢ O LORD, according
         to your love.
¹⁶⁰All your words are true;
      all your righteous laws are eternal.ᵗ

ש Sin and Shin

¹⁶¹Rulers persecute meᵘ without cause,
      but my heart tremblesᵛ at your
         word.
¹⁶²I rejoiceʷ in your promise
      like one who finds great spoil.ˣ
¹⁶³I hate and abhorʸ falsehood
      but I love your law.ᶻ
¹⁶⁴Seven times a day I praise you
      for your righteous laws.ᵃ
¹⁶⁵**Great peaceᵇ have they who love your**
      law,
      and nothing can make them
         stumble.ᶜ

S Ps 119:119 ◀▶ Ps 125:5
U Ps 119:1–2 ◀▶ Ps 128:1–6
W Ps 112:7–8 ◀▶ Pr 1:33

¹⁶⁶I wait for your salvation,ᵈ O LORD,
and I follow your commands.
¹⁶⁷I obey your statutes,
for I love themᵉ greatly.
¹⁶⁸I obey your preceptsᶠ and your
statutes,ᵍ
for all my ways are knownʰ to you.

ת Taw

¹⁶⁹May my cry comeⁱ before you,
O LORD;
give me understandingʲ according to
your word.ᵏ
¹⁷⁰May my supplication comeˡ before
you;
deliver meᵐ according to your
promise.ⁿ
¹⁷¹May my lips overflow with praise,ᵒ
for you teach meᵖ your decrees.
¹⁷²May my tongue singᑫ of your word,
for all your commands are
righteous.ʳ
¹⁷³May my hand be ready to helpˢ me,
for I have chosenᵗ your precepts.
¹⁷⁴I long for your salvation,ᵘ O LORD,
and your law is my delight.ᵛ
¹⁷⁵Let me liveʷ that I may praise you,
and may your laws sustain me.
¹⁷⁶I have strayed like a lost sheep.ˣ
Seek your servant,
for I have not forgottenʸ your
commands.

Psalm 120

A song of ascents.

¹I call on the LORDᶻ in my distress,ᵃ
and he answers me.
²Save me, O LORD, from lying lipsᵇ
and from deceitful tongues.ᶜ

³What will he do to you,
and what more besides, O deceitful
tongue?
⁴He will punish you with a warrior's
sharp arrows,ᵈ
with burning coals of the broom
tree.

⁵Woe to me that I dwell in Meshech,
that I live among the tents of
Kedar!ᵉ
⁶Too long have I lived
among those who hate peace.
⁷I am a man of peace;
but when I speak, they are for war.

119:166 ᵈver 81
119:167 ᵉver 47
119:168
 ᶠS ver 56,S 88
 ᵍver 2,22
 ʰS Job 10:4;
 S 23:10; Ps 139:3;
 Pr 5:21
119:169
 ⁱS Job 16:18
 ʲS ver 34 ᵏS ver 9
119:170
 ˡ1Ki 8:30;
 2Ch 6:24; Ps 28:2;
 140:6; 143:1
 ᵐPs 3:7; 22:20;
 59:1 ⁿS ver 41
119:171
 ᵒPs 51:15; 63:3
 ᵖPs 94:12; Isa 2:3;
 Mic 4:2
119:172
 ᑫPs 51:14 ʳver 7,
 S 75
119:173
 ˢPs 37:24; 73:23;
 Isa 41:10
 ᵗS Jos 24:22
119:174 ᵘver 166
 ᵛver 16,24
119:175
 ʷver 116,159;
 Isa 55:3
119:176 ˣver 10;
 S Ps 95:10;
 Jer 50:17;
 Eze 34:11;
 S Lk 15:4
 ʸS Ps 44:17
120:1 ᶻS Ps 18:6
 ᵃS 2Sa 22:7;
 S Ps 118:5
120:2 ᵇS Ps 31:18
 ᶜS Ps 52:4
120:4 ᵈS Dt 32:23
120:5
 ᵉS Ge 25:13;
 Jer 2:10
121:2 ᶠS Ge 1:1
 ᵍS Ps 104:5;
 Ps 115:15
121:4 ʰS Ps 127:1
121:5 ⁱS Ps 1:6
121:6 ʲIsa 49:10
121:7 ᵏS Ps 9:9
121:8 ˡDt 28:6
122:6 ᵐS Ps 26:8
122:7 ⁿS 1Sa 25:6
 ᵒS Ps 48:3

Psalm 121

A song of ascents.

¹I lift up my eyes to the hills—
where does my help come from?
²My help comes from the LORD,
the Maker of heavenᶠ and earth.ᵍ

³He will not let your foot slip—
he who watches over you will not
slumber;
⁴indeed, he who watchesʰ over Israel
will neither slumber nor sleep.

⁵The LORD watches overⁱ you—
the LORD is your shade at your right
hand;
⁶the sunʲ will not harm you by day,
nor the moon by night.

⁷The LORD will keep you from all
harmᵏ—
he will watch over your life;
⁸the LORD will watch over your coming
and going
both now and forevermore.ˡ

Psalm 122

A song of ascents. Of David.

¹I rejoiced with those who said to me,
"Let us go to the house of the LORD."
²Our feet are standing
in your gates, O Jerusalem.

³Jerusalem is built like a city
that is closely compacted together.
⁴That is where the tribes go up,
the tribes of the LORD,
to praise the name of the LORD
according to the statute given to
Israel.
⁵There the thrones for judgment stand,
the thrones of the house of David.

⁶Pray for the peace of Jerusalem:
"May those who loveᵐ you be
secure.
⁷May there be peaceⁿ within your walls
and security within your citadels.ᵒ"
⁸For the sake of my brothers and
friends,
I will say, "Peace be within you."

K *Ps 107:14* ◀▶ *Ps 125:1*
L *Ps 118:8* ◀▶ *Ps 125:1–2*
S *Ps 119:117* ◀▶ *Ps 140:7*
A *Ps 91:10* ◀▶ *Pr 12:21*

⁹For the sake of the house of the LORD our God,
 I will seek your prosperity.ᵖ

Psalm 123

A song of ascents.

¹I lift up my eyes to you,
 to you whose throneᵍ is in heaven.
²As the eyes of slaves look to the hand of their master,
 as the eyes of a maid look to the hand of her mistress,
so our eyes look to the LORDʳ our God,
 till he shows us his mercy.

³Have mercy on us, O LORD, have mercy on us,
 for we have endured much contempt.
⁴We have endured much ridicule from the proud,
 much contempt from the arrogant.

Psalm 124

A song of ascents. Of David.

¹If the LORD had not been on our side—
 let Israel sayˢ—
²if the LORD had not been on our side
 when men attacked us,
³when their anger flared against us,
 they would have swallowed us alive;
⁴the floodᵗ would have engulfed us,
 the torrentᵘ would have swept over us,
⁵the raging waters
 would have swept us away.

⁶Praise be to the LORD,
 who has not let us be torn by their teeth.
⁷We have escaped like a bird
 out of the fowler's snare;ᵛ
the snare has been broken,ʷ
 and we have escaped.
⁸Our help is in the nameˣ of the LORD,
 the Maker of heavenʸ and earth.

122:9 ᵖ Ps 128:5
123:1 ᵍ S Ps 68:5; Isa 6:1; 63:15
123:2 ʳ S Ps 25:15
124:1 ˢ Ps 129:1
124:4 ᵗ Ps 88:17
 ᵘ S Ps 18:4
124:7 ᵛ S Ps 91:3
 ʷ Ps 25:15
124:8 ˣ S 1Sa 17:45
 ʸ Ge 1:1; Ps 115:15; 121:2; 134:3
125:1 ᶻ Ps 48:12; Isa 33:20 ᵃ Ps 46:5; 48:2-5
125:2 ᵇ 1Ch 21:15
 ᶜ Ps 32:10; Zec 2:4-5
125:3 ᵈ S Est 4:11
 ᵉ Ps 89:22; Pr 22:8; Isa 13:11; 14:5
 ᶠ Isa 24:10
125:4 ᵍ S Ps 119:65
 ʰ S Ps 36:10
125:5 ⁱ S Job 23:11
 ʲ Pr 2:15; Isa 59:8
 ᵏ Ps 92:7 ˡ Ps 128:6; Gal 6:16
126:1 ᵐ Ezr 1:1-3; Ps 85:1; Hos 6:11
126:2 ⁿ S Ge 21:6
 ᵒ S Job 8:21; S Ps 65:8
 ᵖ S Dt 10:21; Ps 71:19; Lk 1:49
126:3 ᵍ Ps 106:21; Joel 2:21,26
 ʳ S Ps 9:2; 16:11
126:4 ˢ S Dt 30:3
 ᵗ S Ps 107:35; Isa 43:19; 51:3

Psalm 125

A song of ascents.

¹Those who trust in the LORD are like Mount Zion,ᶻ
 which cannot be shakenᵃ but endures forever.
²As the mountains surround Jerusalem,ᵇ
 so the LORD surroundsᶜ his people both now and forevermore.

³The scepterᵈ of the wicked will not remainᵉ
 over the land allotted to the righteous,
for then the righteous might use their hands to do evil.ᶠ

⁴Do good, O LORD,ᵍ to those who are good,
 to those who are upright in heart.ʰ
⁵But those who turnⁱ to crooked waysʲ
 the LORD will banishᵏ with the evildoers.

Peace be upon Israel.ˡ

Psalm 126

A song of ascents.

¹When the LORD brought backᵐ the captives toˣ Zion,
 we were like men who dreamed.ʸ
²Our mouths were filled with laughter,ⁿ
 our tongues with songs of joy.ᵒ
Then it was said among the nations,
 "The LORD has done great thingsᵖ for them."
³The LORD has done great thingsᵍ for us,
 and we are filled with joy.ʳ

⁴Restore our fortunes,ᶻˢ O LORD,
 like streams in the Negev.ᵗ

F Ps 84:12 ◀ ▶ Pr 29:25
K Ps 121:1-8 ◀ ▶ Ps 128:1-2
L Ps 121:1-8 ◀ ▶ Ps 142:3
S Ps 119:155 ◀ ▶ Ps 139:23-24
I Ps 111:9 ◀ ▶ Ps 130:8

ˣ 1 Or LORD restored the fortunes of ʸ 1 Or men restored to health ᶻ 4 Or Bring back our captives

---

126:1–6 This psalm of praise rejoices in the exiles' restoration to Zion and prefigures the rejoicing that will accompany the Messiah's victory in the millennial kingdom. The psalmist also reminds his readers that we must remain faithful despite adversity for "those who sow in tears will reap with songs of joy" (126:5).

⁵Those who sow in tears
 will reap with songs of joy.
⁶He who goes out weeping,
 carrying seed to sow,
will return with songs of joy,
 carrying sheaves with him.

Psalm 127

A song of ascents. Of Solomon.

¹Unless the LORD builds the house,
 its builders labor in vain.
Unless the LORD watches over the
 city,
 the watchmen stand guard in vain.
²In vain you rise early
 and stay up late,
 toiling for food to eat—
 for he grants sleep to those he
 loves.
³Sons are a heritage from the LORD,
 children a reward from him.
⁴Like arrows in the hands of a warrior
 are sons born in one's youth.
⁵Blessed is the man
 whose quiver is full of them.
They will not be put to shame
 when they contend with their
 enemies in the gate.

Psalm 128

A song of ascents.

¹Blessed are all who fear the LORD,
 who walk in his ways.
²You will eat the fruit of your labor;
 blessings and prosperity will be
 yours.
³Your wife will be like a fruitful vine
 within your house;
 your sons will be like olive shoots
 around your table.
⁴Thus is the man blessed
 who fears the LORD.

⁵May the LORD bless you from Zion
 all the days of your life;
may you see the prosperity of
 Jerusalem,
⁶and may you live to see your
 children's children.

Peace be upon Israel.

Psalm 129

A song of ascents.

¹They have greatly oppressed me from
 my youth—
 let Israel say—
²they have greatly oppressed me from
 my youth,
 but they have not gained the
 victory over me.
³Plowmen have plowed my back
 and made their furrows long.
⁴But the LORD is righteous;
 he has cut me free from the cords
 of the wicked.
⁵May all who hate Zion
 be turned back in shame.
⁶May they be like grass on the roof,
 which withers before it can grow;
⁷with it the reaper cannot fill his
 hands,
 nor the one who gathers fill his
 arms.
⁸May those who pass by not say,
 "The blessing of the LORD be upon
 you;
we bless you in the name of the
 LORD."

Psalm 130

A song of ascents.

¹Out of the depths I cry to you,
 O LORD;
² O Lord, hear my voice.
Let your ears be attentive
 to my cry for mercy.
³If you, O LORD, kept a record of sins,
 O Lord, who could stand?
⁴But with you there is forgiveness;
 therefore you are feared.
⁵I wait for the LORD, my soul waits,
 and in his word I put my hope.
⁶My soul waits for the Lord

a 2 Or eat— / for while they sleep he provides for

more than watchmen wait for the
  morning,
more than watchmen wait for the
  morning.

⁷O Israel, put your hope in the LORD,
  for with the LORD is unfailing love
  and with him is full redemption.
⁸He himself will redeem Israel
  from all their sins.

Psalm 131

A song of ascents. Of David.

¹My heart is not proud, O LORD,
  my eyes are not haughty;
I do not concern myself with great
    matters
  or things too wonderful for me.
²But I have stilled and quieted my
    soul;
like a weaned child with its mother,
  like a weaned child is my soul
    within me.

³O Israel, put your hope in the LORD
  both now and forevermore.

Psalm 132

132:8–10pp — 2Ch 6:41-42

A song of ascents.

¹O LORD, remember David
  and all the hardships he endured.
²He swore an oath to the LORD
  and made a vow to the Mighty One
    of Jacob:
³"I will not enter my house
  or go to my bed—
⁴I will allow no sleep to my eyes,
  no slumber to my eyelids,
⁵till I find a place for the LORD,
  a dwelling for the Mighty One of
    Jacob."

⁶We heard it in Ephrathah,

K Ps 128:1-2 ◄► Pr 23:11
L Ps 130:3-4 ◄► Ps 145:8
I Ps 126:1-6 ◄► Ps 132:13-15

130:6 ᵗPs 63:6
  ᵘS 2Sa 23:4
130:7 ᵛS Ps 25:5;
  S 71:14
  ʷS 1Ch 21:13
  ˣS Ps 111:9;
  S Ro 3:24
130:8 ʸLk 1:68
  ᶻS Ex 34:7;
  S Mt 1:21
131:1 ᵃPs 101:5;
  Isa 2:12; Ro 12:16
  ᵇS 2Sa 22:28;
  S Job 41:34
  ᶜJer 45:5
  ᵈJob 5:9;
  Ps 139:6
131:2 ᵉS Ps 116:7
  ᶠMt 18:3;
  1Co 13:11; 14:20
131:3 ᵍS Ps 25:5;
  119:43; 130:7
  ʰS Ps 113:2
132:1 ⁱ1Sa 18:11;
  S 2Sa 15:14
132:2 ʲS Ge 49:24;
  Isa 49:26; 60:16
132:3 ᵏS Ps 7:2, 27
132:5 ˡS 1Ki 8:17;
  Ac 7:46
132:6
  ᵐS 1Sa 17:12
  ⁿS Jos 9:17;
  S 1Sa 7:2
132:7
  ᵒS 2Sa 15:25;
  Ps 5:7; 122:1
  ᵖS 1Ch 28:2
132:8
  ᑫS Nu 10:35
132:9 ʳS Job 27:6;
  Isa 61:3,10;
  Zec 3:4; Mal 3:3;
  Eph 6:14 ˢS 16:3;
  30:4; 149:5
132:11
  ᵗS Ps 89:3-4,35
  ᵘS 1Ch 17:11-14;
  S Mt 1:1; Lk 3:31
132:12
  ᵛ2Ch 6:16;
  S Ps 25:10
  ʷLk 1:32; Ac 2:30
132:13
  ˣS Ex 15:17;
  Ps 48:1-2; S 68:16
  ʸS 1Ki 8:13
132:14 ᶻver 8;
  Ps 68:16
  ᵃS 2Sa 6:2; Ps 80:1
132:15 ᵇPs 107:9;
  147:14
132:16
  ᶜS 2Ch 6:41
  ᵈJob 8:21;
  Ps 149:5
132:17
  ᵉS 1Sa 2:10;
  Ps 92:10;
  Eze 29:21;
  ᶠS Lk 1:69
  ᵍ1Ki 11:36;
  2Ki 8:19; 2Ch 21:7;

---

we came upon it in the fields of
    Jaar:
⁷"Let us go to his dwelling place;
  let us worship at his footstool—
⁸arise, O LORD, and come to your
    resting place,
  you and the ark of your might.
⁹May your priests be clothed with
    righteousness;
  may your saints sing for joy."
¹⁰For the sake of David your servant,
  do not reject your anointed one.

¹¹The LORD swore an oath to David,
  a sure oath that he will not revoke:
"One of your own descendants
  I will place on your throne—
¹²if your sons keep my covenant
    and the statutes I teach them,
  then their sons will sit
    on your throne for ever and ever."

¹³For the LORD has chosen Zion,
  he has desired it for his dwelling:
¹⁴"This is my resting place for ever and
    ever;
  here I will sit enthroned, for I have
    desired it—
¹⁵I will bless her with abundant
    provisions;
  her poor will I satisfy with food.
¹⁶I will clothe her priests with
    salvation,
  and her saints will ever sing for joy.

¹⁷"Here I will make a horn grow for
    David
  and set up a lamp for my anointed
    one.
¹⁸I will clothe his enemies with shame,

T Ps 119:108 ◄► Ps 134:1-3
U Ps 128:1-6 ◄► Ps 132:16
M Ps 110:1-7 ◄► SS 2:3-6
I Ps 130:8 ◄► Ps 135:14
F Ps 114:8 ◄► Ps 146:7
U Ps 132:9 ◄► Ps 140:13

Ps 18:28 ᵍS Ps 84:7 132:18 ʰS Job 8:22

ᵇ 6 That is, Kiriath Jearim   ᶜ 6 Or heard of it in Ephrathah, / we found it in the fields of Jaar. (And no quotes around verses 7-9)   ᵈ 17 Horn here symbolizes strong one, that is, king.

130:8 This prophecy confirmed God's promise to redeem Israel from their sins if they would turn from iniquity and repent of their sins.

132:11–18 This psalm prophetically confirmed God's unbreakable promise to David to establish David's seed upon the throne of Israel forever. The final fulfillment of this prophecy will be realized during the millennial kingdom. When the Messiah returns, the temple will be reestablished, sacred worship reinstated and righteous priests will worship God in true holiness.

but the crown on his head[i] will be resplendent."

Psalm 133

A song of ascents. Of David.

[1] How good and pleasant it is
  when brothers live together[j] in unity![k]
[2] It is like precious oil poured on the head,[l]
  running down on the beard,
  running down on Aaron's beard,
  down upon the collar of his robes.
[3] It is as if the dew[m] of Hermon[n]
  were falling on Mount Zion.[o]
For there the LORD bestows his blessing,[p]
  even life forevermore.[q]

Psalm 134

A song of ascents.

T [1] Praise the LORD, all you servants[r] of the LORD
  who minister[s] by night[t] in the house of the LORD.
[2] Lift up your hands[u] in the sanctuary[v]
  and praise the LORD.[w]

[3] May the LORD, the Maker of heaven[x] and earth,
  bless you from Zion.[y]

Psalm 135

135:15–20pp — Ps 115:4–11

[1] Praise the LORD.[e]

Praise the name of the LORD;
  praise him, you servants[z] of the LORD,
[2] you who minister in the house[a] of the LORD,
  in the courts[b] of the house of our God.

[3] Praise the LORD, for the LORD is good;[c]
  sing praise to his name,[d] for that is pleasant.[e]
[4] For the LORD has chosen Jacob[f] to be his own,
  Israel to be his treasured possession.[g]

[5] I know that the LORD is great,[h]

T *Ps 132:9* ◄ ► *Ps 145:1–7*

132:18 [i] S 2Sa 12:30
133:1 [j] S Ge 13:8; S Ro 12:10
[k] Jn 17:11
133:2 [l] S Ex 29:7
133:3 [m] Job 29:19; Pr 19:12; Isa 18:4; 26:19; 45:8; Hos 14:5; Mic 5:7
[n] S Dt 3:8; S 4:48
[o] S Ex 15:17; S Ps 2:6; 74:2
[p] S Lev 25:21
[q] S Ps 21:4
134:1 [r] S Ps 113:1; 135:1-2; Rev 19:5
[s] Nu 16:9; S 1Ch 15:2
[t] S 1Ch 23:30
134:2 [u] S Ps 28:2; 1Ti 2:8 v Ps 15:1
[w] Ps 33:2; 103:1
134:3 [x] S Ps 124:8
[y] S Lev 25:21; S Ps 20:2
135:1 [z] Ne 7:73
135:2 [a] S 1Ch 15:2; Lk 2:37
[b] S Ps 116:19
135:3 [c] S 1Ch 16:34; S Ps 119:68
[d] S Ps 68:4
[e] S Ps 92:1; 147:1
135:4 [f] S Dt 10:15
[g] Ex 19:5; Dt 7:6; Mal 3:17; S Tit 2:14
135:5 [h] S Ps 48:1; 145:3
[i] S Ex 12:12; S 1Ch 16:25; S Job 21:22
135:6 [j] Ps 115:3; Da 4:35 [k] Mt 6:10
135:7 [l] S Job 5:10; Ps 68:9; Isa 30:23; Jer 10:13; 51:16; Joel 2:23; Zec 10:1
[m] Am 4:13
135:8 [n] S Dt 28:12
[o] S Ex 4:23; S 12:12
135:9 [p] S Ex 7:9
[q] Ps 136:10-15
135:10 [r] Nu 21:21-25; Jos 24:8-11; Ps 44:2; 78:55; 136:17-21
135:11 [s] S Nu 21:21
[t] S Nu 21:26
[u] S Nu 21:33
[v] S Jos 12:7-24; 24:12
135:12 [w] S Dt 29:8
135:13 [x] S Ex 3:15
[y] S Ps 102:12
135:14 [z] S 1Sa 24:15; Heb 10:30*
[a] S Dt 32:36
135:15 [b] Ps 96:5; Rev 9:20 [c] Isa 2:8; 31:7; 37:19; 40:19; Jer 1:16; 10:5
135:16 [d] S 1Ki 18:26
135:17 [e] Jer 10:14; Hab 2:19
135:19

that our Lord is greater than all gods.[i]
[6] The LORD does whatever pleases him,[j]
  in the heavens and on the earth,[k]
  in the seas and all their depths.
[7] He makes clouds rise from the ends of the earth;
  he sends lightning with the rain[l]
  and brings out the wind[m] from his storehouses.[n]

[8] He struck down the firstborn[o] of Egypt,
  the firstborn of men and animals.
[9] He sent his signs[p] and wonders into your midst, O Egypt,
  against Pharaoh and all his servants.[q]
[10] He struck down many[r] nations
  and killed mighty kings—
[11] Sihon[s] king of the Amorites,[t]
  Og king of Bashan[u]
  and all the kings of Canaan[v]—
[12] and he gave their land as an inheritance,[w]
  an inheritance to his people Israel.

[13] Your name, O LORD, endures forever,[x]
  your renown,[y] O LORD, through all generations.
[14] For the LORD will vindicate his people[z]
  and have compassion on his servants.[a]

[15] The idols of the nations[b] are silver and gold,
  made by the hands of men.[c]
[16] They have mouths, but cannot speak,[d]
  eyes, but they cannot see;
[17] they have ears, but cannot hear,
  nor is there breath[e] in their mouths.
[18] Those who make them will be like them,
  and so will all who trust in them.

[19] O house of Israel, praise the LORD;[f]
  O house of Aaron, praise the LORD;
[20] O house of Levi, praise the LORD;
  you who fear him, praise the LORD.
[21] Praise be to the LORD from Zion,[g]
  to him who dwells in Jerusalem.[h]

Praise the LORD.

I *Ps 132:13–15* ◄ ► *Ps 147:2*

[f] S Ps 22:23 **135:21** [g] Ps 128:5; 134:3 [h] S 1Ki 8:13; S 2Ch 6:2

[e] *1* Hebrew *Hallelu Yah*; also in verses 3 and 21

Psalm 136

¹Give thanks to the LORD, for he is good.
His love endures forever.
²Give thanks to the God of gods.
His love endures forever.
³Give thanks to the Lord of lords:
His love endures forever.
⁴to him who alone does great wonders,
His love endures forever.
⁵who by his understanding made the heavens,
His love endures forever.
⁶who spread out the earth upon the waters,
His love endures forever.
⁷who made the great lights—
His love endures forever.
⁸the sun to govern the day,
His love endures forever.
⁹the moon and stars to govern the night;
His love endures forever.
¹⁰to him who struck down the firstborn of Egypt
His love endures forever.
¹¹and brought Israel out from among them
His love endures forever.
¹²with a mighty hand and outstretched arm;
His love endures forever.
¹³to him who divided the Red Sea/ᵃ asunder
His love endures forever.
¹⁴and brought Israel through the midst of it,
His love endures forever.
¹⁵but swept Pharaoh and his army into the Red Sea;
His love endures forever.
¹⁶to him who led his people through the desert,
His love endures forever.
¹⁷who struck down great kings,
His love endures forever.
¹⁸and killed mighty kings—
His love endures forever.
¹⁹Sihon king of the Amorites
His love endures forever.
²⁰and Og king of Bashan—
His love endures forever.
²¹and gave their land as an inheritance,
His love endures forever.
²²an inheritance to his servant Israel;
His love endures forever.
²³to the One who remembered us in our low estate
His love endures forever.
²⁴and freed us from our enemies,
His love endures forever.
²⁵and who gives food to every creature.
His love endures forever.
²⁶Give thanks to the God of heaven.
His love endures forever.

Psalm 137

¹By the rivers of Babylon we sat and wept
when we remembered Zion.
²There on the poplars
we hung our harps,
³for there our captors asked us for songs,
our tormentors demanded songs of joy;
they said, "Sing us one of the songs of Zion!"
⁴How can we sing the songs of the LORD
while in a foreign land?
⁵If I forget you, O Jerusalem,
may my right hand forget ⌊its skill⌋.
⁶May my tongue cling to the roof of my mouth
if I do not remember you,
if I do not consider Jerusalem my highest joy.
⁷Remember, O LORD, what the Edomites did
on the day Jerusalem fell.
"Tear it down," they cried,
"tear it down to its foundations!"
⁸O Daughter of Babylon, doomed to destruction,
happy is he who repays you
for what you have done to us—
⁹he who seizes your infants
and dashes them against the rocks.

ƒ13 Hebrew *Yam Suph*; that is, Sea of Reeds; also in verse 15

Psalm 138

Of David.

¹I will praise you, O LORD, with all my heart;
  before the "gods"¹ I will sing your praise.
²I will bow down toward your holy temple
  and will praise your name
  for your love and your faithfulness,
for you have exalted above all things
  your name and your word.
³When I called, you answered me;
  you made me bold and stouthearted.
⁴May all the kings of the earth praise you, O LORD,
  when they hear the words of your mouth.
⁵May they sing of the ways of the LORD,
  for the glory of the LORD is great.
⁶Though the LORD is on high, he looks upon the lowly,
  but the proud he knows from afar.
⁷Though I walk in the midst of trouble, you preserve my life;
  you stretch out your hand against the anger of my foes,
  with your right hand you save me.
⁸The LORD will fulfill [his purpose] for me;
  your love, O LORD, endures forever—
  do not abandon the works of your hands.

Psalm 139

For the director of music. Of David. A psalm.

¹O LORD, you have searched me
  and you know me.
²You know when I sit and when I rise;
  you perceive my thoughts from afar.
³You discern my going out and my lying down;
  you are familiar with all my ways.
⁴Before a word is on my tongue
  you know it completely, O LORD.
⁵You hem me in—behind and before;
  you have laid your hand upon me.
⁶Such knowledge is too wonderful for me,
  too lofty for me to attain.
⁷Where can I go from your Spirit?
  Where can I flee from your presence?
⁸If I go up to the heavens, you are there;
  if I make my bed in the depths,⁸ you are there.
⁹If I rise on the wings of the dawn,
  if I settle on the far side of the sea,
¹⁰even there your hand will guide me,
  your right hand will hold me fast.
¹¹If I say, "Surely the darkness will hide me
  and the light become night around me,"
¹²even the darkness will not be dark to you;
  the night will shine like the day,
  for darkness is as light to you.
¹³For you created my inmost being;
  you knit me together in my mother's womb.
¹⁴I praise you because I am fearfully and wonderfully made;
  your works are wonderful,
  I know that full well.
¹⁵My frame was not hidden from you
  when I was made in the secret place.
When I was woven together in the depths of the earth,
¹⁶ your eyes saw my unformed body.
All the days ordained for me
  were written in your book
  before one of them came to be.
¹⁷How precious to me are your thoughts, O God!
  How vast is the sum of them!
¹⁸Were I to count them,
  they would outnumber the grains of sand.
When I awake,
  I am still with you.

---

g 8 Hebrew *Sheol*   *h 17* Or *concerning*

¹⁹If only you would slay the wicked,° O God!
Away from me,ᵖ you bloodthirsty men!ᑫ
²⁰They speak of you with evil intent;
your adversariesʳ misuse your name.ˢ
²¹Do I not hate thoseᵗ who hate you, O LORD,
and abhorᵘ those who rise up against you?
²²I have nothing but hatred for them;
I count them my enemies.ᵛ
²³Search me,ʷ O God, and know my heart;ˣ
test me and know my anxious thoughts.
²⁴See if there is any offensive wayʸ in me,
and lead meᶻ in the way everlasting.

Psalm 140

For the director of music. A psalm of David.

¹Rescue me,ᵃ O LORD, from evil men;
protect me from men of violence,ᵇ
²who devise evil plansᶜ in their hearts
and stir up warᵈ every day.
³They make their tongues as sharp asᵉ a serpent's;
the poison of vipersᶠ is on their lips. *Selah*

⁴Keep me,ᵍ O LORD, from the hands of the wicked;ʰ
protect me from men of violence
who plan to trip my feet.
⁵Proud men have hidden a snareⁱ for me;
they have spread out the cords of their netʲ
and have set trapsᵏ for me along my path. *Selah*

⁶O LORD, I say to you, "You are my God."ˡ
Hear, O LORD, my cry for mercy.ᵐ
⁷O Sovereign LORD,ⁿ my strong deliverer,
who shields my head in the day of battle—
⁸do not grant the wicked° their desires, O LORD;

do not let their plans succeed,
or they will become proud. *Selah*

⁹Let the heads of those who surround me
be covered with the trouble their lips have caused.ᵖ
¹⁰Let burning coals fall upon them;
may they be thrown into the fire,ᑫ
into miry pits, never to rise.
¹¹Let slanderers not be established in the land;
may disaster hunt down men of violence.ʳ

¹²I know that the LORD secures justice for the poorˢ
and upholds the causeᵗ of the needy.ᵘ

¹³Surely the righteous will praise your nameᵛ
and the upright will liveʷ before you.ˣ

Psalm 141

A psalm of David.

¹O LORD, I call to you; come quicklyʸ to me.
Hear my voiceᶻ when I call to you.
²May my prayer be set before you like incense;ᵃ
may the lifting up of my handsᵇ be like the evening sacrifice.ᶜ

³Set a guard over my mouth,ᵈ O LORD;
keep watch over the door of my lips.ᵉ
⁴Let not my heartᶠ be drawn to what is evil,
to take part in wicked deedsᵍ
with men who are evildoers;
let me not eat of their delicacies.ʰ

⁵Let a righteous manⁱ strike me—it is a kindness;
let him rebuke meⁱ—it is oil on my head.ʲ
My head will not refuse it.
Yet my prayer is ever against the deeds of evildoers;
⁶ their rulers will be thrown down from the cliffs,ᵏ

ⁱ⁵ Or *Let the Righteous One*

and the wicked will learn that my
    words were well spoken.
⁷They will say, "As one plows¹ and
    breaks up the earth,ᵐ
so our bones have been scattered at
    the mouthⁿ of the grave."

⁸But my eyes are fixedᵒ on you,
    O Sovereign LORD;
in you I take refugeᵖ—do not give
    me over to death.
⁹Keep meᵠ from the snares they have
    laidʳ for me,
from the traps setˢ by evildoers.
¹⁰Let the wicked fallᵗ into their own
    nets,
while I pass by in safety.ᵘ

Psalm 142

A *maskil*ᵏ of David. When he was in the cave.ᵛ A prayer.

¹I cry aloudʷ to the LORD;
    I lift up my voice to the LORD for
    mercy.ˣ
²I pour out my complaintʸ before
    him;
before him I tell my trouble.ᶻ

³When my spirit grows faintᵃ within
    me,
    it is you who know my way.
In the path where I walk
    men have hidden a snare for me.
⁴Look to my right and see;
    no one is concerned for me.
I have no refuge;ᵇ
    no one caresᶜ for my life.

⁵I cry to you, O LORD;
    I say, "You are my refuge,ᵈ
my portionᵉ in the land of the
    living."ᶠ
⁶Listen to my cry,ᵍ
    for I am in desperate need;ʰ
rescue meⁱ from those who pursue
    me,
    for they are too strongʲ for me.
⁷Set me free from my prison,ᵏ
    that I may praise your name.ˡ

Then the righteous will gather about
    me
because of your goodness to me.ᵐ

L *Ps 125:1–2* ◀ ▶ *Ps 144:2*

141:7 ¹Ps 129:3
ᵐNu 16:32-33
ⁿS Nu 16:30

141:8 ᵒPs 123:2
ᵖPs 2:12; 11:1

141:9 ᵠPs 140:4
ʳS Ps 64:5
ˢS Ps 38:12

141:10 ᵗPs 7:15; 35:8; 57:6
ᵘPs 124:7

142 Title
ᵛ1Sa 22:1; 24:3; Ps 57 Title

142:1
ʷS 1Ki 8:52; Ps 3:4
ˣPs 30:8

142:2 ʸPs 64:1
ᶻS Ps 50:15

142:3 ᵃPs 6:2; 77:3; 84:2; 88:4; 143:4,7; Jer 8:18; La 1:22

142:4 ᵇJer 25:35
ᶜJer 30:17

142:5 ᵈS Ps 46:1
ᵉDt 32:9; Ps 16:5
ᶠS Job 28:13; Ps 27:13

142:6 ᵍS Ps 17:1
ʰS Ps 79:8
ⁱS Ps 25:20
ʲJer 31:11

142:7 ᵏS Ps 66:11
ˡPs 7:17; 9:2
ᵐS 2Ch 6:41

143:1 ⁿS Ps 141:1
ᵒS Ps 28:2; 130:2
ᵖS Ex 34:6; Ps 89:1-2 ᵠS Ps 71:2

143:2 ʳS Ps 14:3;
Ro 3:10

143:3
ˢS Ps 107:10
ᵗLa 3:6

143:4 ᵘPs 30:7

143:5 ᵛPs 77:6
ʷS Ge 24:63

143:6 ˣS Ex 9:29;
S Job 11:13

143:7 ʸS Ps 69:17
ᶻS Ps 142:3
ᵃS Ps 22:24; 27:9; 30:7

143:8 ᵇPs 6:4; 90:14 ᶜS Ex 33:13; S Job 34:32;
Ps 27:11; 32:8
ᵈPs 25:1-2; S 86:4

143:9 ᵉS Ps 140:1
ᶠS Ps 18:17; 31:15

143:10
ᵍS Ps 119:12
ʰPs 31:14
ⁱS Ne 9:20;
Ps 25:4-5 ʲPs 26:12

143:11 ᵏS Ps 25:11
ˡS Ps 41:2
ᵐS Ps 31:1; 71:2

Psalm 143

A psalm of David.

¹O LORD, hear my prayer,ⁿ
    listen to my cry for mercy;ᵒ
in your faithfulnessᵖ and
    righteousnessᵠ
come to my relief.

²Do not bring your servant into
    judgment,
    for no one living is righteousʳ before
    you.

³The enemy pursues me,
    he crushes me to the ground;
he makes me dwell in darknessˢ
    like those long dead.ᵗ
⁴So my spirit grows faint within me;
    my heart within me is dismayed.ᵘ
⁵I rememberᵛ the days of long ago;
    I meditateʷ on all your works
    and consider what your hands have
    done.
⁶I spread out my handsˣ to you;
    my soul thirsts for you like a
    parched land.   *Selah*

⁷Answer me quickly,ʸ O LORD;
    my spirit fails.ᶻ
Do not hide your faceᵃ from me
    or I will be like those who go down
    to the pit.
⁸Let the morning bring me word of
    your unfailing love,ᵇ
    for I have put my trust in you.
Show me the wayᶜ I should go,
    for to you I lift up my soul.ᵈ
⁹Rescue meᵉ from my enemies,ᶠ
    O LORD,
    for I hide myself in you.
¹⁰Teach meᵍ to do your will,
    for you are my God;ʰ
may your good Spirit
    leadⁱ me on level ground.ʲ

¹¹For your name's sake,ᵏ O LORD,
    preserve my life;ˡ
in your righteousness,ᵐ bring me out
    of trouble.

A *Ps 130:3* ◀ ▶ *Pr 20:9*
G *Ps 75:6–7* ◀ ▶ *Pr 3:5–6*
E *Ps 139:7* ◀ ▶ *Isa 30:1*
L *Ps 39:3* ◀ ▶ *Isa 48:16*
N *Ps 139:7* ◀ ▶ *Isa 4:4*
T *Job 32:18–19* ◀ ▶ *Pr 1:22–23*

j7 Hebrew *Sheol*   ᵏTitle: Probably a literary or musical term

12In your unfailing love, silence my
enemies;[n]
destroy all my foes,[o]
for I am your servant.[p]

Psalm 144

Of David.

1Praise be to the LORD my Rock,[q]
who trains my hands for war,
my fingers for battle.
L 2He is my loving God and my fortress,[r]
my stronghold[s] and my deliverer,
my shield,[t] in whom I take refuge,
who subdues peoples[l][u] under me.
3O LORD, what is man[v] that you care for
him,
the son of man that you think of
him?
N 4Man is like a breath;[w]
his days are like a fleeting shadow.[x]
P 5Part your heavens,[y] O LORD, and come
down;[z]
touch the mountains, so that they
smoke.[a]
6Send forth lightning[b] and scatter[c] ⌞the
enemies⌟;
shoot your arrows[d] and rout them.
7Reach down your hand from on high;[e]
deliver me and rescue me[f]
from the mighty waters,[g]
from the hands of foreigners[h]
8whose mouths are full of lies,[i]
whose right hands[j] are deceitful.[k]

9I will sing a new song[l] to you, O God;
on the ten-stringed lyre[m] I will make
music to you,
10to the One who gives victory to kings,[n]
who delivers his servant David[o]
from the deadly sword.[p]

11Deliver me and rescue me[q]
from the hands of foreigners[r]
whose mouths are full of lies,[s]
whose right hands are deceitful.[t]

R 12Then our sons in their youth
will be like well-nurtured plants,[u]
and our daughters will be like pillars[v]
carved to adorn a palace.
13Our barns will be filled[w]
with every kind of provision.
Our sheep will increase by thousands,
by tens of thousands in our fields;
14 our oxen[x] will draw heavy loads.[m]
There will be no breaching of walls,[y]
no going into captivity,
no cry of distress in our streets.[z]
15Blessed are the people[a] of whom this
is true; U
blessed are the people whose God is
the LORD.

Psalm 145[n]

A psalm of praise. Of David.

1I will exalt you,[b] my God the King;[c] T
I will praise your name[d] for ever and
ever.
2Every day I will praise[e] you
and extol your name[f] for ever and
ever.

3Great is the LORD[g] and most worthy of
praise;[h]
his greatness no one can fathom.[i]
4One generation[j] will commend your
works to another;
they will tell[k] of your mighty acts.[l]
5They will speak of the glorious
splendor[m] of your majesty,
and I will meditate on your
wonderful works.[o][n]
6They will tell[o] of the power of your
awesome works,[p]
and I will proclaim[q] your great
deeds.[r]
7They will celebrate your abundant
goodness[s]
and joyfully sing[t] of your
righteousness.[u]

L Ps 142:3 ◀ ▶ Ps 145:18
N Ps 103:15–16 ◀ ▶ Pr 1:24–33
P Ps 110:4–8 ◀ ▶ Pr 2:21–22
R Ps 128:3 ◀ ▶ Lk 1:13–15
U Ps 140:13 ◀ ▶ Ps 147:11
T Ps 134:1–3 ◀ ▶ Ps 145:10–12

143:12 [n]Ps 8:2 [o]Ps 54:5 [p]S Ps 116:16 **144:1** [q]S Ge 49:24 **144:2** [r]Ps 59:9; 91:2 [s]Ps 27:1; 37:39; 43:2 [t]S Ge 15:1; S Ps 18:2 [u]S Jdg 4:23; S Ps 18:39 **144:3** [v]Heb 2:6 **144:4** [w]S Job 7:7; 27:3; Isa 2:22 [x]S 1Ch 29:15; S Job 14:2; S Jas 4:14 **144:5** [y]Ps 18:9; Isa 64:1 [z]S Ge 11:5; S Ps 57:3 [a]Ps 104:32 **144:6** [b]Hab 3:11; Zec 9:14 [c]S Ps 59:11; S 68:1 [d]Ps 7:12-13; 18:14 **144:7** [e]S 2Sa 22:17 [f]Ps 3:7; S 57:3 [g]Ps 69:2 [h]S Ps 18:44 **144:8** [i]Ps 12:2; 41:6 [j]Ge 14:22; Dt 32:40 [k]S Ps 36:3 **144:9** [l]S Ps 28:7; S 96:1 [m]Ps 33:2-3; S 71:22 **144:10** [n]S 2Sa 8:14 [o]Ps 18:50 [p]S Job 5:20 **144:11** [q]Ps 3:7; S 25:20 [r]S Ps 18:44 [s]Ps 41:6-7 [t]Ps 12:2; S 36:3; 106:26; Isa 44:20 **144:12** [u]Ps 92:12-14; S 128:3 [v]SS 4:4; 7:4 **144:13** [w]Pr 3:10 **144:14** [x]Pr 14:4 [y]2Ki 25:11 [z]Isa 24:11; Jer 14:2-3 **144:15** [a]Dt 28:3 **145:1** [b]Ps 30:1; 34:1 [c]Ps 2:6; 5:2 [d]S Ps 54:6 **145:2** [e]S Ps 71:6 [f]Ps 34:1; Isa 25:1; 26:8 **145:3** [g]S Ps 95:3 [h]S 2Sa 22:4; Ps 96:4 [i]S Job 5:9 **145:4** [j]Ps 22:30 [k]S Dt 11:19 [l]S Ps 71:16 **145:5** [m]Ps 96:6; 148:13 [n]S Ps 75:1 **145:6** [o]Ps 78:4 [p]S Ps 66:3 [q]S Dt 32:3 [r]Ps 75:1; 106:22 **145:7** [s]S Ex 18:9; S Ps 27:13 [t]S Ps 5:11; S 101:1 [u]S Ps 138:5

[l]*2* Many manuscripts of the Masoretic Text, Dead Sea Scrolls, Aquila, Jerome and Syriac; most manuscripts of the Masoretic Text *subdues my people* [m]*14* Or *our chieftains will be firmly established* [n]This psalm is an acrostic poem, the verses of which (including verse 13b) begin with the successive letters of the Hebrew alphabet. [o]*5* Dead Sea Scrolls and Syriac (see also Septuagint); Masoretic Text *On the glorious splendor of your majesty / and on your wonderful works I will meditate*

144:5–6 This prayer for deliverance over treacherous enemies bears some resemblance to Ps 18:9, 14.

⁸The LORD is gracious and
    compassionate,ᵛ
  slow to anger and rich in love.ʷ
⁹The LORD is goodˣ to all;
  he has compassionʸ on all he has
    made.
¹⁰All you have made will praise you,ᶻ
    O LORD;
  your saints will extolᵃ you.ᵇ
¹¹They will tell of the glory of your
    kingdomᶜ
  and speak of your might,ᵈ
¹²so that all men may know of your
    mighty actsᵉ
  and the glorious splendor of your
    kingdom.ᶠ
¹³Your kingdom is an everlasting
    kingdom,ᵍ
  and your dominion endures through
    all generations.

The LORD is faithfulʰ to all his
    promisesⁱ
  and loving toward all he has made.ᵖ
¹⁴The LORD upholdsʲ all those who fall
  and lifts up allᵏ who are bowed
    down.ˡ
¹⁵The eyes of all look to you,
  and you give them their foodᵐ at the
    proper time.
¹⁶You open your hand
  and satisfy the desiresⁿ of every
    living thing.
¹⁷The LORD is righteousᵒ in all his ways
  and loving toward all he has made.ᵖ
¹⁸The LORD is nearᵠ to all who call on
    him,ʳ
  to all who call on him in truth.
¹⁹He fulfills the desiresˢ of those who
    fear him;ᵗ
  he hears their cryᵘ and saves them.ᵛ
²⁰The LORD watches overʷ all who love
    him,ˣ
  but all the wicked he will destroy.ʸ

L Ps 130:7–8 ◀▶ Ps 145:18
W Ps 86:5 ◀▶ Ps 145:18
T Ps 145:1–7 ◀▶ Isa 12:4
K Ps 92:9 ◀▶ Isa 11:9
L Ps 145:8 ◀▶ Ps 147:3
W Ps 145:9 ◀▶ Pr 29:25
L Ps 144:2 ◀▶ Ps 145:20
L Ps 145:18 ◀▶ Ps 146:5

145:8 ᵛS Ps 86:15;
103:8 ʷS Ps 86:5
145:9
ˣS 1Ch 16:34;
S Ps 136:1;
Mt 19:17;
Mk 10:18
ʸPs 103:13-14
145:10 ᶻS Ps 8:6;
S 103:22; S 139:14
ᵃPs 30:4; 148:14;
149:9
ᵇPs 115:17-18
145:11
ᶜver 12-13;
S Ex 15:2; Mt 6:33
ᵈPs 21:13
145:12
ᵉS Ps 75:1; 105:1
ᶠver 11; Ps 103:19;
Isa 2:10,19,21
145:13
ᵍS Ex 15:18;
1Ti 1:17; 2Pe 1:11;
Rev 11:15
ʰS Dt 7:9;
S 1Co 1:9
ⁱS Jos 23:14
145:14
ʲS Ps 37:17
ᵏS 1Sa 2:8;
Ps 146:8 ˡS Ps 38:6
145:15
ᵐS Ge 1:30;
S Job 28:5;
S Ps 37:25;
S Mt 6:26
145:16
ⁿS Ps 90:14;
S 104:28
145:17
ᵒS Ex 9:27;
S Ezr 9:15 ᵖver 13
145:18
ᵠS Nu 23:21;
S Ps 40:1; Php 4:5
ʳPs 18:6; 80:18
145:19 ˢS Ps 20:4
ᵗS Job 22:28
ᵘS Ps 31:22; S 40:1
ᵛS Ps 10:19;
Ps 7:10; 34:18
145:20 ʷS Ps 1:6
ˣPs 31:23; 91:14;
97:10 ʸS Ps 94:23
145:21 ᶻPs 71:8
ᵃPs 65:2; 150:6
ᵇS Ex 3:15;
S Ps 30:4; S 99:3
146:1 ᶜPs 103:1;
104:1
146:2 ᵈPs 104:33
ᵉS Ps 105:2
ᶠS Ps 63:4
146:3 ᵍPs 118:9
ʰPs 60:11;
S 108:12; Isa 2:22
146:4 ⁱS Ge 3:19;
S Job 7:21;
Ps 103:14; Ecc 12:7
ʲPs 33:10; 1Co 2:6
146:5 ᵏPs 33:18;
37:9; 119:43;
144:15; Jer 17:7
ˡPs 70:5; 71:5;
121:2
146:6
ᵐS 2Ch 2:12;
Ps 115:15;

²¹My mouth will speakᶻ in praise of the
    LORD.
  Let every creatureᵃ praise his holy
    nameᵇ
  for ever and ever.

Psalm 146

¹Praise the LORD.ᵠ

Praise the LORD,ᶜ O my soul.
² I will praise the LORD all my life;ᵈ
  I will sing praiseᵉ to my God as long
    as I live.ᶠ

³Do not put your trust in princes,ᵍ
  in mortal men,ʰ who cannot save.
⁴When their spirit departs, they return
    to the ground;ⁱ
  on that very day their plans come to
    nothing.ʲ

⁵Blessed is heᵏ whose helpˡ is the God
    of Jacob,
  whose hope is in the LORD his God,
⁶the Maker of heavenᵐ and earth,
  the sea, and everything in them—
  the LORD, who remains faithfulⁿ
    forever.
⁷He upholdsᵒ the cause of the
    oppressedᵖ
  and gives food to the hungry.ᵠ
  The LORD sets prisoners free,ʳ
⁸ the LORD gives sightˢ to the blind,ᵗ
  the LORD lifts up those who are bowed
    down,ᵘ
  the LORD loves the righteous.ᵛ
⁹The LORD watches over the alienʷ
  and sustains the fatherlessˣ and the
    widow,ʸ
  but he frustrates the ways of the
    wicked.

¹⁰The LORD reignsᶻ forever,

L Ps 145:20 ◀▶ Pr 2:8
F Ps 132:15 ◀▶ Ps 147:9
H Ps 128:6 ◀▶ Pr 3:2

Ac 14:15; S Rev 10:6 ⁿS Dt 7:9; S Ps 18:25; 108:4; 117:2
146:7 ᵒS Ps 37:17 ᵖPs 103:6 ᵠPs 107:9; 145:15 ʳS Ps 66:11; S 68:6
146:8 ᵖPr 20:12; Isa 29:18; 32:3; 35:5; 42:7,18-19; 43:8; Mt 11:5
ᵗS Ex 4:11 ᵘS Ps 38:6 ᵛS Job 23:10 146:9 ʷS Lev 19:34
ˣPs 10:18 ʸS Ex 22:22; Jas 1:27 146:10 ᶻS Ge 21:33; S 1Ch 16:31;
Ps 93:1; 99:1; Rev 11:15

ᵖ 13 One manuscript of the Masoretic Text, Dead Sea Scrolls and Syriac
(see also Septuagint); most manuscripts of the Masoretic Text do not have
the last two lines of verse 13.   ᵠ 1 Hebrew *Hallelu Yah*; also in verse 10

145:13 Unlike earthly kingdoms that flourish for a few centuries and then fade away, the kingdom of the Messiah "is an everlasting kingdom."

your God, O Zion, for all
generations.
Praise the LORD.

Psalm 147

¹Praise the LORD.ʳ

How good it is to sing praises to our God,
how pleasantᵃ and fitting to praise him!ᵇ
²The LORD builds up Jerusalem;ᶜ
he gathers the exilesᵈ of Israel.
³He heals the brokenheartedᵉ
and binds up their wounds.ᶠ
⁴He determines the number of the starsᵍ
and calls them each by name.
⁵Great is our Lordʰ and mighty in power;ⁱ
his understanding has no limit.ʲ
⁶The LORD sustains the humbleᵏ
but casts the wickedˡ to the ground.
⁷Sing to the LORDᵐ with thanksgiving;ⁿ
make musicᵒ to our God on the harp.ᵖ
⁸He covers the sky with clouds;ᵠ
he supplies the earth with rainʳ
and makes grass growˢ on the hills.
⁹He provides foodᵗ for the cattle
and for the young ravensᵘ when they call.
¹⁰His pleasure is not in the strengthᵛ of the horse,ʷ
nor his delight in the legs of a man;
¹¹the LORD delightsˣ in those who fear him,ʸ
who put their hopeᶻ in his unfailing love.ᵃ
¹²Extol the LORD, O Jerusalem;ᵇ
praise your God, O Zion,
¹³for he strengthens the bars of your gatesᶜ
and blesses your peopleᵈ within you.

I Ps 135:14 ◀▶ Isa 1:25–27
L Ps 145:18 ◀▶ Ps 149:4
R Ps 126:5 ◀▶ Pr 3:7
F Ps 146:7 ◀▶ Ps 147:14
U Ps 144:15 ◀▶ Pr 3:5–6

147:1 ᵃS Ps 135:3
ᵇ Ps 33:1
147:2 ᶜS Ps 51:18
ᵈS Ps 106:47
147:3 ᵉS Ps 34:18
ᶠS Nu 12:13;
S Job 5:18; Isa 1:6;
Eze 34:16
147:4 ᵍS Ge 15:5
147:5 ʰS Ps 48:1
ⁱS Ex 14:31
ʲ Ps 145:3; Isa 40:28
147:6
ᵏ S 2Ch 33:23;
Ps 146:8-9
ˡ Ps 37:9-10; 145:20
147:7 ᵐ Ps 30:4;
33:3 ⁿS Ps 42:4
ᵒS Ps 27:6
ᵖ S Ps 98:5
147:8 ᵠS Job 26:8
ʳS Dt 11:14; S 32:2;
S 2Sa 1:21;
ˢ Job 5:10
ᵗ S Job 28:26;
S Ps 104:14
147:9 ᵘS Ge 1:30;
Ps 104:27-28;
S Mt 6:26
ᵘS Ge 8:7
147:10
ᵛS 1Sa 16:7
ʷS Job 39:11;
Ps 33:16-17
147:11
ˣS Ps 35:27
ʸPs 33:18; 103:11
ᶻPs 119:43 ᵃPs 6:4
147:12 ᵇPs 48:1
147:13
ᶜS Dt 33:25
ᵈS Lev 25:21;
Ps 128:5; 134:3
147:14
ᵉS Lev 26:6;
S 2Sa 7:10;
S Isa 48:18
ᶠS Ps 132:15
ᵍS Dt 32:14
147:15
ʰJob 37:12;
Ps 33:9; 148:5
ⁱIsa 55:11
147:16 ʲPs 148:8
ᵏS Job 37:12; 38:29
147:17
ˡEx 9:22-23;
S Job 38:22;
S Ps 78:47
147:18 ᵐver 15;
Ps 33:9; 107:20
ⁿS Ps 50:3
147:19
ᵒS Ex 20:1; Ro 3:2
ᵖ Ps 78:5
ᵠS Dt 33:4; Jos 1:8;
2Ki 22:8; Mal 4:4;
Ro 9:4
147:20 ʳDt 4:7-8,
32-34 ˢS Ps 79:6
ᵗPs 33:2; 103:1
148:1 ᵘPs 33:2;
103:1 ᵛPs 19:1;
69:34; 150:1
148:2 ʷPs 103:20
ˣS 1Ki 22:19
148:3 ʸPs 19:1
148:4 ᶻS Dt 10:14
ᵃS Ge 1:7

¹⁴He grants peaceᵉ to your borders
and satisfies youᶠ with the finest of wheat.ᵍ
¹⁵He sends his commandʰ to the earth;
his word runsⁱ swiftly.
¹⁶He spreads the snowʲ like wool
and scatters the frostᵏ like ashes.
¹⁷He hurls down his hailˡ like pebbles.
Who can withstand his icy blast?
¹⁸He sends his wordᵐ and melts them;
he stirs up his breezes,ⁿ and the waters flow.
¹⁹He has revealed his wordᵒ to Jacob,ᵖ
his laws and decreesᵠ to Israel.
²⁰He has done this for no other nation;ʳ
they do not knowˢ his laws.

Praise the LORD.ᵗ

Psalm 148

¹Praise the LORD.ˢ ᵘ

Praise the LORD from the heavens,ᵛ
praise him in the heights above.
²Praise him, all his angels,ʷ
praise him, all his heavenly hosts.ˣ
³Praise him, sunʸ and moon,
praise him, all you shining stars.
⁴Praise him, you highest heavensᶻ
and you waters above the skies.ᵃ
⁵Let them praise the nameᵇ of the LORD,
for he commandedᶜ and they were created.
⁶He set them in place for ever and ever;
he gave a decreeᵈ that will never pass away.

⁷Praise the LORDᵉ from the earth,
you great sea creaturesᶠ and all ocean depths,ᵍ
⁸lightning and hail,ʰ snow and clouds,
stormy winds that do his bidding,ⁱ
⁹you mountains and all hills,ʲ
fruit trees and all cedars,
¹⁰wild animalsᵏ and all cattle,

F Ps 147:9 ◀▶ Pr 10:3

148:5 ᵇPs 145:21 ᶜS Ps 147:15 148:6 ᵈJer 31:35-36; 33:25
148:7 ᵉPs 33:2 ᶠS Ge 1:21; Ps 74:13-14 ᵍS Dt 33:13 148:8 ʰS Ex 9:18;
S Jos 10:11 ⁱJob 37:11-12; S Ps 103:20; 147:15-18 148:9 ʲIsa 44:23;
49:13; 55:12 148:10 ᵏIsa 43:20; Hos 2:18

ʳ Hebrew *Hallelu Yah*; also in verse 20   ˢ Hebrew *Hallelu Yah*; also in verse 14

147:2 This verse refers to the postexilic return of the Jews to Palestine that began in Nehemiah's day and has gained momentum in this generation, initially fulfilling this ancient prophecy.

small creatures and flying birds,
¹¹kings¹ of the earth and all nations,
you princes and all rulers on earth,
¹²young men and maidens,
old men and children.

¹³Let them praise the name of the LORD,ᵐ
for his name alone is exalted;
his splendorⁿ is above the earth and
the heavens.ᵒ
¹⁴He has raised up for his people a
horn,ᵗᵖ
the praiseᵍ of all his saints,ʳ
of Israel, the people close to his
heart.ˢ

Praise the LORD.

Psalm 149

¹Praise the LORD.ᵘᵗ

Sing to the LORD a new song,ᵘ
his praise in the assemblyᵛ of the
saints.
²Let Israel rejoiceʷ in their Maker;ˣ
let the people of Zion be glad in
their King.ʸ
³Let them praise his name with
dancingᶻ
and make music to him with
tambourine and harp.ᵃ
**⁴For the LORD takes delightᵇ in his
people;
he crowns the humble with
salvation.ᶜ**
⁵Let the saints rejoiceᵈ in this honor
and sing for joy on their beds.ᵉ

L *Ps 147:3* ◀ ▶ *Pr 8:17*
M *Ps 138:6* ◀ ▶ *Pr 3:7*

148:11
ˡS Ps 102:15
148:13
ᵐS Ps 113:2; 138:4
ⁿS Ps 145:5
ᵒS Ps 8:1
148:14 ᵖS 1Sa 2:1
ᵠS Ex 15:2; 2Sa 22:3
ʳS Ps 145:10
ˢS Dt 26:19
149:1 ᵗPs 33:2;
103:1 ᵘS Ps 28:7;
S 96:1; Rev 5:9
ᵛS Ps 1:5
149:2 ʷS Isa 13:3;
Jer 51:48
ˣS Job 10:3;
Ps 95:6; Isa 44:2;
45:11; 54:5
ʸPs 10:16; 47:6;
Isa 32:1; Zec 9:9
149:3 ᶻS Ex 15:20
ᵃS Ps 57:8
149:4 ᵇPs 35:27;
147:11 ᶜPs 132:11
149:5
ᵈS Ps 132:16
ᵉJob 35:10; Ps 42:8
149:6 ᶠPs 66:17
ᵍHeb 4:12;
Rev 1:16 ʰNe 4:17
149:7 ⁱS Nu 31:3;
S Dt 32:41
ʲPs 81:15
149:8 ᵏS 2Sa 3:34;
S Isa 14:1-2
ˡ2Ch 33:11
149:9 ᵐDt 7:1;
Eze 28:26
ⁿS Ps 145:10
150:1 ᵒS Ps 112:1
ᵖPs 68:24-26;
73:17; 102:19
ᵠS Ps 148:1
150:2 ʳS Dt 3:24
ˢS Ex 15:7
150:3 ᵗS Nu 10:2
ᵘS Ps 57:8
150:4 ᵛS Ex 15:20
ʷS Ps 45:8
ˣS Ge 4:21
150:5 ʸS 2Sa 6:5
150:6
ᶻS Ps 103:22

⁶May the praise of God be in their
mouthsᶠ
and a double-edgedᵍ sword in their
hands,ʰ
⁷to inflict vengeanceⁱ on the nations
and punishmentʲ on the peoples,
⁸to bind their kings with fetters,ᵏ
their nobles with shackles of iron,ˡ
⁹to carry out the sentence written
against them.ᵐ
This is the glory of all his saints.ⁿ

Praise the LORD.

Psalm 150

¹Praise the LORD.ᵛᵒ

Praise God in his sanctuary;ᵖ
praise him in his mighty heavens.ᵠ
²Praise him for his acts of power;ʳ
praise him for his surpassing
greatness.ˢ
³Praise him with the sounding of the
trumpet,ᵗ
praise him with the harp and lyre,ᵘ
⁴praise him with tambourine and
dancing,ᵛ
praise him with the stringsʷ and
flute,ˣ
⁵praise him with the clash of cymbals,ʸ
praise him with resounding cymbals.

⁶Let everythingᶻ that has breath praise
the LORD.

Praise the LORD.

ᵗ *14 Horn here symbolizes strong one, that is, king.* ᵘ *1 Hebrew Hallelu Yah; also in verse 9* ᵛ *1 Hebrew Hallelu Yah; also in verse 6*

150:6 This psalm follows the pattern of the rest of the book by ending this section of Psalms with a doxology. In fact, this particular psalm may have been composed specifically to close this book with a final call to "praise the LORD."

Proverbs

Author: King Solomon and others

Theme: God's wisdom gives guidance for right living

Date of Writing: c. 970–700 B.C.

Outline of Proverbs
   I. Purpose and Theme Are Introduced (1:1–7)
   II. Following the Way of Wisdom (1:8—9:18)
   III. Proverbs of Solomon (10:1—22:16)
   IV. Words From the Wise (22:17—24:34)
   V. More Proverbs of Solomon (25:1—29:27)
   VI. Proverbs of Agur and Lemuel (30:1—31:9)
   VII. An Excellent Wife (31:10–31)

COMPLETED ABOUT 700 B.C., the book of Proverbs consists of wise sayings, comparisons and moral assertions that illustrate truths about human behavior. The use of proverbs as a teaching tool was widely accepted in ancient societies. Since a proverb usually describes a self-evident or axiomatic truth, the 900 maxims in this book helped provide practical knowledge in discerning between good and evil, truth and error, uprightness and foolishness.

The proverbs used in this book came from a variety of sources. Many of the maxims in the opening chapters of this book probably came from Solomon's personal experience. In fact, Proverbs credits these wise sayings to King Solomon (see 1:1; 10:1). Additional proverbs may have been well known in the literature of that period and recorded by other authors. Later, King Solomon's reputation for wisdom prompted scholars in Hezekiah's day to copy down more of Solomon's proverbs (see 25:1; 1 Ki 4:29–32), adding chapters 25—29 to the original collection. Additional entries by Agur and Lemuel complete the book as it appears today.

Prologue: Purpose and Theme

1 The proverbs[a] of Solomon[b] son of David, king of Israel:[c]

[2] for attaining wisdom and discipline;
for understanding words of insight;
[3] for acquiring a disciplined and prudent life,
doing what is right and just and fair;
[4] for giving prudence to the simple,[d]
knowledge and discretion[e] to the young—
[5] let the wise listen and add to their learning,[f]
and let the discerning get guidance—
[6] for understanding proverbs and parables,[g]
the sayings and riddles[h] of the wise.[i]
[7] The fear of the LORD[j] is the beginning of knowledge,
but fools[a] despise wisdom[k] and discipline.[l]

Exhortations to Embrace Wisdom

Warning Against Enticement

[8] Listen, my son,[m] to your father's[n] instruction
and do not forsake your mother's teaching.[o]
[9] They will be a garland to grace your head
and a chain to adorn your neck.[p]

[10] My son, if sinners entice[q] you,
do not give in[r] to them.[s]
[11] If they say, "Come along with us;
let's lie in wait[t] for someone's blood,
let's waylay some harmless soul;
[12] let's swallow[u] them alive, like the grave,[v]
and whole, like those who go down to the pit;[v]
[13] we will get all sorts of valuable things
and fill our houses with plunder;
[14] throw in your lot with us,
and we will share a common purse[w]"—
[15] my son, do not go along with them,
do not set foot[x] on their paths;[y]
[16] for their feet rush into sin,[z]
they are swift to shed blood.[a]
[17] How useless to spread a net
in full view of all the birds!
[18] These men lie in wait[b] for their own blood;
they waylay only themselves![c]
[19] Such is the end of all who go after ill-gotten gain;
it takes away the lives of those who get it.[d]

Warning Against Rejecting Wisdom

[20] Wisdom calls aloud[e] in the street,
she raises her voice in the public squares;
[21] at the head of the noisy streets[c] she cries out,
in the gateways of the city she makes her speech:

[22] "How long will you simple ones[d f] love your simple ways?
How long will mockers delight in mockery
and fools hate[g] knowledge?
[23] If you had responded to my rebuke,
I would have poured out my heart to you
and made my thoughts known to you.
[24] But since you rejected[h] me when I called[i]
and no one gave heed[j] when I stretched out my hand,
[25] since you ignored all my advice
and would not accept my rebuke,
[26] I in turn will laugh[k] at your disaster;[l]
I will mock[m] when calamity overtakes you[n]—
[27] when calamity overtakes you like a storm,
when disaster[o] sweeps over you like a whirlwind,
when distress and trouble overwhelm you.

[28] "Then they will call to me but I will not answer;[p]
they will look for me but will not find me.[q]

1:1 [a] Mt 13:3 [b] 1Ki 4:29-34 [c] Pr 10:1; 25:1; Ecc 1:1
1:4 [d] Pr 8:5 [e] Pr 8:12
1:5 [f] Pr 9:9
1:6 [g] S Ps 49:4; Mt 13:10-17 [h] S Nu 12:8; S Jdg 14:12 [i] Pr 22:17; 24:23
1:7 [j] S Ex 20:20; S Job 23:15; Ps 34:4-22; S 112:1; Pr 9:10; 15:33; Isa 33:6; 50:10; 59:19 [k] S Dt 4:6; Jer 8:9 [l] Pr 8:33-36; 9:7-9; 12:1; 13:18; 15:32
1:8 [m] ver 8-9; Pr 2:1; 3:1; 4:1; 5:1; 6:1; 7:1; 19:27; 22:17; 23:26-28 [n] Jer 35:8 [o] S Dt 21:18; Pr 6:20
1:9 [p] Pr 3:21-22; 4:1-9
1:10 [q] S Job 24:15 [r] Dt 13:8 [s] ver 15; Ps 1:1; Pr 16:29
1:11 [t] S Ps 10:8
1:12 [u] Ps 35:25 [v] ver 16-18; S Job 33:18; S Ps 30:3
1:14 [w] ver 19
1:15 [x] S Ps 119:101 [y] S Ge 49:6; Pr 4:14
1:16 [z] S Job 15:31 [a] Pr 6:18; Isa 59:7
1:18 [b] S Ps 71:10 [c] S ver 11-12
1:19 [d] S ver 13-14; Pr 4:14-17; 11:19
1:20 [e] S Job 28:12; Pr 7:10-13; 9:1-3, 13-15
1:22 [f] Pr 6:32; 7:7; 8:5; 9:4,16 [g] Ps 50:17
1:24 [h] Jer 26:5; 35:17; 36:31 [i] Isa 65:12; 66:4; Jer 7:13 [j] S Isa 8:19
1:26 [k] S Ps 2:4 [l] ver 33; S Ps 59:8 [m] S 2Ki 19:21 [n] S Dt 28:63
1:27 [o] S Ps 18:18; Pr 5:12-14
1:28 [p] S Dt 1:45; S 1Sa 8:18; S Jer 1:11 [q] S Job 27:9; Pr 8:17; Eze 8:18; Hos 5:6; Zec 7:13

G Ps 68:18 ◀ ▶ Isa 11:2-3
P Ps 68:18 ◀ ▶ Isa 4:4
T Ps 143:10 ◀ ▶ Isa 11:2-3
W Ps 68:18 ◀ ▶ Isa 30:1
H Ps 119:119 ◀ ▶ Pr 5:4-5
N Ps 144:4 ◀ ▶ Pr 8:17

[a] 7 The Hebrew words rendered *fool* in Proverbs, and often elsewhere in the Old Testament, denote one who is morally deficient. [b] 12 Hebrew *Sheol* [c] 21 Hebrew; Septuagint / *on the tops of the walls* [d] 22 The Hebrew word rendered *simple* in Proverbs generally denotes one without moral direction and inclined to evil.

²⁹Since they hated knowledge
    and did not choose to fear the LORD,ʳ
³⁰since they would not accept my advice
    and spurned my rebuke,ˢ
³¹they will eat the fruit of their ways
    and be filled with the fruit of their
        schemes.ᵗ
³²For the waywardness of the simple will
        kill them,
    and the complacency of fools will
        destroy them;ᵘ
³³but whoever listens to me will live in
        safetyᵛ
    and be at ease, without fear of
        harm."ʷ

Moral Benefits of Wisdom

2 My son,ˣ if you accept my words
    and store up my commands within
        you,
²turning your ear to wisdom
    and applying your heart to
        understanding,ʸ
³and if you call out for insightᶻ
    and cry aloud for understanding,
⁴and if you look for it as for silver
    and search for it as for hidden
        treasure,ᵃ
⁵then you will understand the fear of
        the LORD
    and find the knowledge of God.ᵇ
⁶For the LORD gives wisdom,ᶜ
    and from his mouth come
        knowledge and understanding.ᵈ
⁷He holds victory in store for the
        upright,
    he is a shieldᵉ to those whose walk
        is blameless,ᶠ
⁸for he guards the course of the just
    and protects the way of his faithful
        ones.ᵍ
⁹Then you will understandʰ what is
        right and just
    and fair—every good path.
¹⁰For wisdom will enter your heart,ⁱ
    and knowledge will be pleasant to
        your soul.

J Ps 118:6 ◄► Isa 26:3
S Ps 140:7 ◄► Pr 3:23–26
W Ps 119:165 ◄► Isa 12:2–3
L Ps 146:5 ◄► Pr 18:24

1:29 ʳS Job 21:14
1:30 ˢver 25
1:31 ᵗS 2Ch 36:16;
    Pr 14:14; Jer 6:19;
    14:16; 21:14;
    30:15
1:32 ᵘPr 5:22;
    15:10; Isa 66:4
1:33 ᵛS Nu 24:21;
    S Dt 33:28; S Pr 3:23
    ʷS ver 21-26;
    S Ps 112:8
2:1 ˣS Pr 1:8
2:2 ʸPr 22:17;
    23:12
2:3 ᶻJas 1:5
2:4 ᵃS Job 3:21;
    Mt 13:44
2:5 ᵇS Dt 4:6
2:6 ᶜS Job 12:13;
    S Ps 119:34
    ᵈS Job 9:4; S 22:22
2:7 ᵉS Ge 15:1;
    Pr 30:5-6 ᶠS Ge 6:9;
    Ps 84:11
2:8 ᵍ1Sa 2:9;
    S Ps 18:25; S 97:10
2:9 ʰS Dt 1:16
2:10 ⁱPr 14:33
2:11 ʲPr 4:6
2:12 ᵏver 16;
    Pr 3:13-18; 4:5
2:13 ˡPr 4:19
2:14 ᵐPr 10:23;
    15:21
2:15 ⁿS Ps 125:5
    ᵒPr 21:8
2:16 ᵖPr 5:1-6;
    6:20-29; 7:5-27
2:17 ᵠMal 2:14
2:18 ʳPr 5:5; 7:27;
    9:18
2:19 ˢPr 3:16-18;
    5:8; Ecc 7:26
2:21 ᵗS Ps 37:29
2:22 ᵘS Ps 5:4
    ᵛS Job 18:17
    ʷDt 28:63;
    S 29:28; Ps 37:9,
    28-29; Pr 10:30
3:1 ˣS Pr 1:8
    ʸS Ps 44:17
3:2 ᶻS Dt 11:21
    ᵃS Dt 5:16;
    S 30:15,16;
    S 1Ki 3:13,14;
    Pr 9:6,10-11
3:3 ᵇS Ps 85:10

¹¹Discretion will protect you,
    and understanding will guard you.ʲ
¹²Wisdom will saveᵏ you from the ways
        of wicked men,
    from men whose words are
        perverse,
¹³who leave the straight paths
    to walk in dark ways,ˡ
¹⁴who delight in doing wrong
    and rejoice in the perverseness of
        evil,ᵐ
¹⁵whose paths are crookedⁿ
    and who are devious in their ways.ᵒ
¹⁶It will save you also from the
        adulteress,ᵖ
    from the wayward wife with her
        seductive words,
¹⁷who has left the partner of her youth
    and ignored the covenant she made
        before God.ᵉᵠ
¹⁸For her house leads down to death
    and her paths to the spirits of the
        dead.ʳ
¹⁹None who go to her return
    or attain the paths of life.ˢ
²⁰Thus you will walk in the ways of good
        men
    and keep to the paths of the
        righteous.
²¹For the upright will live in the land,ᵗ
    and the blameless will remain in it;
²²but the wickedᵘ will be cut off from
        the land,ᵛ
    and the unfaithful will be torn from
        it.ʷ

Further Benefits of Wisdom

3 My son,ˣ do not forget my
        teaching,ʸ
    but keep my commands in your
        heart,
²for they will prolong your life many
        yearsᶻ
    and bring you prosperity.ᵃ
³Let love and faithfulnessᵇ never leave
        you;

P Ps 144:5–6 ◄► Isa 1:24
H Ps 146:8 ◄► Pr 3:8

ᵉ17 Or covenant of her God

2:21–22 Solomon announced prophetically the final victory of the righteous and the defeat of the wicked who will be "cut off from the land" (2:22). This prophecy will be fulfilled at the Battle of Armageddon and will usher in the Millennium.

bind them around your neck,
write them on the tablet of your heart.c
⁴Then you will win favor and a good name
in the sight of God and man.d
⁵Trust in the LORDe with all your heart
and lean not on your own understanding;
⁶in all your ways acknowledge him,
and he will make your pathsf straight.fg
⁷Do not be wise in your own eyes;h
fear the LORDi and shun evil.j
⁸This will bring health to your bodyk
and nourishment to your bones.l
⁹Honor the LORD with your wealth,
with the firstfruitsm of all your crops;
¹⁰then your barns will be filledn to overflowing,
and your vats will brim over with new wine.o
¹¹My son,p do not despise the LORD's disciplineq
and do not resent his rebuke,
¹²because the LORD disciplines those he loves,r
as a fatherg the son he delights in.s
¹³Blessed is the man who finds wisdom,
the man who gains understanding,
¹⁴for she is more profitable than silver
and yields better returns than gold.t
¹⁵She is more precious than rubies;u
nothing you desire can compare with her.v
¹⁶Long life is in her right hand;w
in her left hand are riches and honor.x
¹⁷Her ways are pleasant ways,
and all her paths are peace.y
¹⁸She is a tree of lifez to those who embrace her;

G Ps 143:2 ◀ ▶ Pr 16:2
U Ps 147:11 ◀ ▶ Pr 3:9
S Ps 139:23–24 ◀ ▶ Pr 4:23
M Ps 149:4 ◀ ▶ Pr 3:34
R Ps 147:3 ◀ ▶ Pr 14:16
H Pr 3:2 ◀ ▶ Pr 3:16
B Ps 107:38 ◀ ▶ Eze 34:26–27
P Ps 112:3 ◀ ▶ Pr 3:16
U Pr 3:5–6 ◀ ▶ Pr 3:33
T Ps 119:75 ◀ ▶ Pr 17:3
H Pr 3:8 ◀ ▶ Pr 4:10
P Pr 3:9–10 ◀ ▶ Pr 8:18

3:3 c S Ex 13:9; S Dt 6:6; Pr 6:21; 7:3; S 2Co 3:3
3:4 d S 1Sa 2:26; Lk 2:52
3:5 e S Ps 4:5
3:6 f S Job 33:11; S Isa 30:11 gPs 5:8; Pr 16:3; Isa 40:3; Jer 42:3
3:7 h Pr 26:5,12; Isa 5:21 i Ps 111:10 j S Ex 20:20; S Dt 4:6; S Job 1:1
3:8 k S Ps 38:3; Pr 4:22 l Job 21:24
3:9 m S Ex 22:29; Dt 26:1-15
3:10 n Ps 144:13 o S Job 22:21; Joel 2:24; Mal 3:10-12
3:11 p Pr 1:8-9 q S Job 5:17
3:12 r Pr 13:24; Rev 3:19 s S Dt 8:5; S Job 5:17; Heb 12:5-6*
3:14 t S Job 28:15; Pr 8:19; 16:16
3:15 u S Job 28:18 v S Job 28:17-19
3:16 w S Ge 15:15 x S 1Ki 3:13,14
3:17 y Mt 11:28-30
3:18 z S Ge 2:9; S Pr 10:11; S Rev 2:7 a S Pr 2:12; 4:3-9,8; 8:17-21
3:19 b S Ge 1:31; Ps 136:5-9 c S Job 28:25-27 d Pr 8:27-29
3:21 e Pr 1:8-9; 6:20 f Pr 4:20-22
3:22 g S Dt 30:20; Pr 4:13 h S Pr 1:8-9
3:23 i S Pr 1:33 j S Ps 37:24; S 119:11; Pr 4:12
3:24 k S Lev 26:6 l Ps 91:5; 112:8 m S Job 11:18; Jer 31:26
3:26 n S 2Ki 18:5; S Job 4:6 o S 1Sa 2:9 p S Job 5:19
3:28 q Lev 19:13; Dt 24:15; Lk 10:25-37
3:29 r Zec 8:17
3:31 s S Ps 37:1; Pr 24:1-2
3:32 t S Ps 101:4 u S Job 29:4
3:33 v S Job 5:3 w Zec 5:4
x Ps 37:22; Pr 14:11

those who lay hold of her will be blessed.a
¹⁹By wisdomb the LORD laid the earth's foundations,c
by understanding he set the heavensd in place;
²⁰by his knowledge the deeps were divided,
and the clouds let drop the dew.
²¹My son,e preserve sound judgment and discernment,
do not let them out of your sight;f
²²they will be life for you,g
an ornament to grace your neck.h
²³Then you will go on your way in safety,i
and your foot will not stumble;j
²⁴when you lie down,k you will not be afraid;l
when you lie down, your sleepm will be sweet.
²⁵Have no fear of sudden disaster
or of the ruin that overtakes the wicked,
²⁶for the LORD will be your confidencen
and will keep your footo from being snared.p
²⁷Do not withhold good from those who deserve it,
when it is in your power to act.
²⁸Do not say to your neighbor,
"Come back later; I'll give it tomorrow"—
when you now have it with you.q
²⁹Do not plot harm against your neighbor,
who lives trustfully near you.r
³⁰Do not accuse a man for no reason—
when he has done you no harm.
³¹Do not envys a violent man
or choose any of his ways,
³²for the LORD detests a perverse mant
but takes the upright into his confidence.u
³³The LORD's cursev is on the house of the wicked,w
but he blesses the home of the righteous.x

S Pr 1:33 ◀ ▶ Pr 18:10
U Pr 3:9 ◀ ▶ Pr 4:18

f 6 Or will direct your paths   g 12 Hebrew; Septuagint / and he punishes

PROVERBS 3:34

M ³⁴He mocks^y proud mockers^z
but gives grace to the humble.^a
³⁵The wise inherit honor,
but fools he holds up to shame.

Wisdom Is Supreme

4 Listen, my sons,^b to a father's
instruction;^c
pay attention and gain
understanding.^d
² I give you sound learning,
so do not forsake my teaching.
³ When I was a boy in my father's
house,
still tender, and an only child of my
mother,
⁴ he taught me and said,
"Lay hold^e of my words with all
your heart;
keep my commands and you will
live.^f
⁵ Get wisdom,^g get understanding;
do not forget my words or swerve
from them.
⁶ Do not forsake wisdom, and she will
protect you;^h
love her, and she will watch over
you.^i
⁷ Wisdom is supreme; therefore get
wisdom.
Though it cost all^j you have,^h get
understanding.^k
⁸ Esteem her, and she will exalt you;
embrace her, and she will honor
you.^l
⁹ She will set a garland of grace on your
head
and present you with a crown of
splendor.^m"

H ¹⁰ Listen, my son,^n accept what I say,
and the years of your life will be
many.^o

¹¹ I guide^p you in the way of wisdom
and lead you along straight paths.^q
¹² When you walk, your steps will not be
hampered;
when you run, you will not
stumble.^r
¹³ Hold on to instruction, do not let it go;
guard it well, for it is your life.^s
¹⁴ Do not set foot on the path of the
wicked
or walk in the way of evil men.^t
¹⁵ Avoid it, do not travel on it;

M Pr 3:7 ◀▶ Pr 6:16–17
H Pr 3:16 ◀▶ Pr 4:22

3:34 ^y S 2Ki 19:21
^z S Ps 40:4
^a S Ps 18:25-27;
S Mt 23:12;
Jas 4:6*; 1Pe 5:5*
4:1 ^b S Pr 1:8
^c Pr 19:20
^d S Job 8:10
4:4 ^e S 1Ki 9:4
^f Pr 7:2
4:5 ^g S Pr 2:12;
3:13-18
4:6 ^h 2Th 2:10
^i S Pr 2:11
4:7 ^j Mt 13:44-46
^k Pr 23:23
4:8 ^l S Pr 3:18
4:9 ^m S Pr 1:8-9
4:10 ^n Ps 34:11-16;
Pr 1:8-9
^o S Dt 11:21
4:11 ^p S 1Sa 12:23
^q 2Sa 22:37; Ps 5:8
4:12 ^r S Job 18:7;
Pr 3:23
4:13 ^s S Pr 3:22
4:14 ^t Ps 1:1;
S Pr 1:15
4:16 ^u Ps 36:4;
Mic 7:3
4:17 ^v Ge 49:5;
Ps 73:6; Pr 1:10-19;
14:22; Isa 59:6;
Jer 22:3; Hab 1:2;
Mal 2:16
4:18 ^w Job 17:9
^x S Job 22:28
^y S 2Sa 23:4;
Da 12:3; Mt 5:14;
Jn 8:12; Php 2:15
4:19 ^z S Pr 2:13
^a Dt 32:35;
S Job 3:23; Pr 13:9;
S Isa 8:15
4:20 ^b Ps 34:11-16;
Pr 1:8-9 ^c Pr 5:1
4:21 ^d Pr 3:21
4:22 ^e S Pr 3:8
4:23 ^f S 2Ki 10:31
^g Pr 10:11; Lk 6:45
4:25 ^h S Job 31:1
4:26 ^i Heb 12:13*
4:27 ^j S Lev 10:11;
S Dt 5:32
5:1 ^k S Pr 1:8
^l Pr 4:20
5:3 ^m S Ps 55:21;
Pr 7:5
5:4 ^n Ecc 7:26
5:5 ^o Ps 9:17;
S Pr 2:18; 7:26-27

turn from it and go on your way.
¹⁶ For they cannot sleep till they do evil;^u
they are robbed of slumber till they
make someone fall.
¹⁷ They eat the bread of wickedness
and drink the wine of violence.^v

¹⁸ The path of the righteous^w is like the **U**
first gleam of dawn,^x
shining ever brighter till the full
light of day.^y
¹⁹ But the way of the wicked is like deep **C**
darkness;^z
they do not know what makes them
stumble.^a

²⁰ My son,^b pay attention to what I say;
listen closely to my words.^c
²¹ Do not let them out of your sight,^d
keep them within your heart;
²² for they are life to those who find **H**
them
and health to a man's whole body.^e
²³ Above all else, guard^f your heart, **S**
for it is the wellspring of life.^g
²⁴ Put away perversity from your mouth;
keep corrupt talk far from your lips.
²⁵ Let your eyes^h look straight ahead,
fix your gaze directly before you.
²⁶ Make level^i paths for your feet^i
and take only ways that are firm.
²⁷ Do not swerve to the right or the left;^j **S**
keep your foot from evil.

Warning Against Adultery

5 My son,^k pay attention to my
wisdom,
listen well to my words^l of insight,
² that you may maintain discretion
and your lips may preserve
knowledge.
³ For the lips of an adulteress drip
honey,
and her speech is smoother than
oil;^m
⁴ but in the end she is bitter as gall,^n **H**
sharp as a double-edged sword.
⁵ Her feet go down to death;
her steps lead straight to the
grave.^o

U Pr 3:33 ◀▶ Pr 10:6
C Ps 107:10 ◀▶ Pr 5:22–23
H Pr 4:10 ◀▶ Pr 9:11
S Pr 3:6–7 ◀▶ Pr 4:27
S Pr 4:23 ◀▶ Pr 10:29–30
H Pr 1:24–32 ◀▶ Pr 5:22

^h 7 Or *Whatever else you get*   ^i 26 Or *Consider the*   ^j 5 Hebrew *Sheol*

⁶She gives no thought to the way of life;
  her paths are crooked, but she
    knows it not.ᵖ

⁷Now then, my sons, listenᑫ to me;
  do not turn aside from what I say.
⁸Keep to a path far from her,ʳ
  do not go near the door of her
    house,
⁹lest you give your best strength to
    others
  and your years to one who is cruel,
¹⁰lest strangers feast on your wealth
  and your toil enrich another man's
    house.ˢ
¹¹At the end of your life you will groan,
  when your flesh and body are spent.
¹²You will say, "How I hated discipline!
  How my heart spurned correction!ᵗ
¹³I would not obey my teachers
  or listen to my instructors.
¹⁴I have come to the brink of utter ruinᵘ
  in the midst of the whole
    assembly."ᵛ

¹⁵Drink water from your own cistern,
  running water from your own well.
¹⁶Should your springs overflow in the
    streets,
  your streams of water in the public
    squares?
¹⁷Let them be yours alone,
  never to be shared with strangers.
¹⁸May your fountainʷ be blessed,
  and may you rejoice in the wife of
    your youth.ˣ
¹⁹A loving doe, a graceful deerʸ—
  may her breasts satisfy you always,
  may you ever be captivated by her
    love.
²⁰Why be captivated, my son, by an
    adulteress?
  Why embrace the bosom of another
    man's wife?

E ²¹For a man's ways are in full viewᶻ of
    the Lord,
  and he examinesᵃ all his paths.ᵇ
C ²²The evil deeds of a wicked man
H   ensnare him;ᶜ
  the cords of his sin hold him fast.ᵈ
²³He will die for lack of discipline,ᵉ
  led astray by his own great folly.ᶠ

E Ps 139:1–16 ◀▶ Pr 15:3
C Pr 4:19 ◀▶ Pr 8:36
H Pr 5:4–5 ◀▶ Pr 6:15

5:6 ᵖPr 9:13; 30:20
5:7 ᑫPr 1:8–9
5:8 ʳS Pr 2:16-19; 6:20-29; 7:1-27
5:10 ˢPr 29:3
5:12 ᵗPr 12:1
5:14 ᵘPr 1:24-27; 6:33 ᵛPr 31:3
5:18 ʷSS 4:12-15 ˣS Dt 20:7; Pr 2:17; Ecc 9:9; Mal 2:14
5:19 ʸSS 4:5; 8:14
5:21 ᶻS Ps 119:168 ᵃJer 29:23 ᵇS Job 10:4; S 14:16; Pr 15:3; Jer 32:19; S Heb 4:13
5:22 ᶜPs 9:16 ᵈNu 32:23; S Job 18:9; Ps 7:15-16; S Pr 1:31-32
5:23 ᵉS Job 4:21; Pr 10:21 ᶠJob 34:21-25; Pr 11:5
6:1 ᵍS Pr 1:8 ʰJob 17:3 ⁱPr 17:18 ʲPr 11:15; 22:26-27
6:4 ᵏPs 132:4
6:5 ˡS 2Sa 2:18 ᵐIsa 13:14 ⁿS Ps 91:3
6:6 ᵒver 6-11; Pr 20:4
6:8 ᵖPr 30:24-25 ᑫPr 10:4
6:9 ʳPr 24:30-34; 26:13-16
6:10 ˢPr 24:33; Ecc 4:5
6:11 ᵗver 10-11; Pr 20:13; 24:30-34
6:13 ᵘPs 35:19; Pr 16:30 ᵛIsa 58:9
6:14 ʷS Ps 140:2 ˣver 16-19
6:15 ʸS Ps 55:15 ᶻJob 5:3 ᵃPr 14:32; 29:1
6:16 ᵇver 16-19; Pr 3:32; 8:13; 15:8, 9,26; 16:5

Warnings Against Folly

6 My son,ᵍ if you have put up
    securityʰ for your neighbor,ⁱ
  if you have struck hands in pledgeʲ
    for another,
²if you have been trapped by what you
    said,
  ensnared by the words of your
    mouth,
³then do this, my son, to free yourself,
  since you have fallen into your
    neighbor's hands:
  Go and humble yourself;
  press your plea with your neighbor!
⁴Allow no sleep to your eyes,
  no slumber to your eyelids.ᵏ
⁵Free yourself, like a gazelle¹ from the
    hand of the hunter,ᵐ
  like a bird from the snare of the
    fowler.ⁿ

⁶Go to the ant, you sluggard;ᵒ
  consider its ways and be wise!
⁷It has no commander,
  no overseer or ruler,
⁸yet it stores its provisions in summerᵖ
  and gathers its food at harvest.ᑫ
⁹How long will you lie there, you
    sluggard?ʳ
  When will you get up from your
    sleep?
¹⁰A little sleep, a little slumber,
  a little folding of the hands to
    restˢ—
¹¹and povertyᵗ will come on you like a
    bandit
  and scarcity like an armed man.ᵏ

¹²A scoundrel and villain,
  who goes about with a corrupt
    mouth,
¹³ who winks with his eye,ᵘ
  signals with his feet
  and motions with his fingers,ᵛ
¹⁴ who plots evilʷ with deceit in his
    heart—
  he always stirs up dissension.ˣ
H ¹⁵Therefore disaster will overtake him in
    an instant;ʸ
  he will suddenlyᶻ be destroyed—
    without remedy.ᵃ
M ¹⁶There are six things the Lord hates,ᵇ

H Pr 5:22 ◀▶ Pr 9:18
M Pr 3:34 ◀▶ Pr 14:16

ᵏ 11 Or like a vagrant / and scarcity like a beggar

seven that are detestable to him:
17 haughty eyes,ᶜ
a lying tongue,ᵈ
hands that shed innocent blood,ᵉ
18 a heart that devises wicked schemes,
feet that are quick to rush into evil,ᶠ
19 a false witnessᵍ who pours out lies,ʰ
and a man who stirs up dissension among brothers.ⁱ

Warning Against Adultery

²⁰My son,ʲ keep your father's commands
and do not forsake your mother's teaching.ᵏ
²¹Bind them upon your heart forever;
fasten them around your neck.ˡ
²²When you walk, they will guide you;
when you sleep, they will watch over you;
when you awake, they will speak to you.
²³For these commands are a lamp,
this teaching is a light,ᵐ
and the corrections of discipline are the way to life,ⁿ
²⁴keeping you from the immoral woman,
from the smooth tongue of the wayward wife.ᵒ
²⁵Do not lust in your heart after her beauty
or let her captivate you with her eyes,
²⁶for the prostitute reduces you to a loaf of bread,
and the adulteress preys upon your very life.ᵖ
²⁷Can a man scoop fire into his lap
without his clothes being burned?
²⁸Can a man walk on hot coals
without his feet being scorched?
²⁹So is he who sleepsᑫ with another man's wife;ʳ
no one who touches her will go unpunished.
³⁰Men do not despise a thief if he steals
to satisfy his hunger when he is starving.
³¹Yet if he is caught, he must pay sevenfold,ˢ
though it costs him all the wealth of his house.
³²But a man who commits adulteryᵗ
lacks judgment;ᵘ

whoever does so destroys himself.
³³Blows and disgrace are his lot,
and his shame will neverᵛ be wiped away;
³⁴for jealousyʷ arouses a husband's fury,ˣ
and he will show no mercy when he takes revenge.
³⁵He will not accept any compensation;
he will refuse the bribe, however great it is.ʸ

Warning Against the Adulteress

7 My son,ᶻ keep my words
and store up my commands within you.
²Keep my commands and you will live;ᵃ
guard my teachings as the apple of your eye.
³Bind them on your fingers;
write them on the tablet of your heart.ᵇ
⁴Say to wisdom, "You are my sister,"
and call understanding your kinsman;
⁵they will keep you from the adulteress,
from the wayward wife with her seductive words.ᶜ
⁶At the window of my house
I looked out through the lattice.
⁷I saw among the simple,
I noticed among the young men,
a youth who lacked judgment.ᵈ
⁸He was going down the street near her corner,
walking along in the direction of her house
⁹at twilight,ᵉ as the day was fading,
as the dark of night set in.
¹⁰Then out came a woman to meet him,
dressed like a prostitute and with crafty intent.
¹¹(She is loudᶠ and defiant,
her feet never stay at home;
¹²now in the street, now in the squares,
at every corner she lurks.)ᵍ
¹³She took hold of himʰ and kissed him
and with a brazen face she said:ⁱ
¹⁴"I have fellowship offeringsʲ¹⁴ at home;
today I fulfilled my vows.
¹⁵So I came out to meet you;
I looked for you and have found you!
¹⁶I have covered my bed
with colored linens from Egypt.
¹⁷I have perfumed my bedᵏ

ˡ14 Traditionally peace offerings

with myrrh,¹ aloes and cinnamon.
¹⁸Come, let's drink deep of love till morning;
let's enjoy ourselves with love!ᵐ
¹⁹My husband is not at home;
he has gone on a long journey.
²⁰He took his purse filled with money
and will not be home till full moon."
²¹With persuasive words she led him astray;
she seduced him with her smooth talk.ⁿ
²²All at once he followed her
like an ox going to the slaughter,
like a deerᵐ stepping into a nooseⁿᵒ
²³ till an arrow piercesᵖ his liver,
like a bird darting into a snare,
little knowing it will cost him his life.ᵠ
²⁴Now then, my sons, listenʳ to me;
pay attention to what I say.
²⁵Do not let your heart turn to her ways
or stray into her paths.ˢ
²⁶Many are the victims she has brought down;
her slain are a mighty throng.
²⁷Her house is a highway to the grave,ᵒ
leading down to the chambers of death.ᵗ

Wisdom's Call

8 Does not wisdom call out?ᵘ
Does not understanding raise her voice?
²On the heights along the way,
where the paths meet, she takes her stand;
³beside the gates leading into the city,
at the entrances, she cries aloud:ᵛ
⁴"To you, O men, I call out;ʷ
I raise my voice to all mankind.
⁵You who are simple,ˣ gain prudence;ʸ
you who are foolish, gain understanding.
⁶Listen, for I have worthy things to say;
I open my lips to speak what is right.
⁷My mouth speaks what is true,ᶻ
for my lips detest wickedness.
⁸All the words of my mouth are just;
none of them is crooked or perverse.
⁹To the discerning all of them are right;
they are faultless to those who have knowledge.
¹⁰Choose my instruction instead of silver,

knowledge rather than choice gold,ᵃ
¹¹for wisdom is more preciousᵇ than rubies,
and nothing you desire can compare with her.ᶜ

¹²"I, wisdom, dwell together with prudence;
I possess knowledge and discretion.ᵈ
¹³To fear the LORDᵉ is to hate evil;ᶠ
I hateᵍ pride and arrogance,
evil behavior and perverse speech.
¹⁴Counsel and sound judgment are mine;
I have understanding and power.ʰ
¹⁵By me kings reign
and rulersⁱ make laws that are just;
¹⁶by me princes govern,ʲ
and all nobles who rule on earth.ᵖ
¹⁷I love those who love me,ᵏ
and those who seek me find me.ˡ
¹⁸With me are riches and honor,ᵐ
enduring wealth and prosperity.ⁿ
¹⁹My fruit is better than fine gold;ᵒ
what I yield surpasses choice silver.ᵖ
²⁰I walk in the way of righteousness,ᵠ
along the paths of justice,
²¹bestowing wealth on those who love me
and making their treasuries full.ʳ

²²"The LORD brought me forth as the first of his works,ᵠ,ʳ
before his deeds of old;
²³I was appointedˢ from eternity,
from the beginning, before the world began.
²⁴When there were no oceans, I was given birth,
when there were no springs abounding with water;ˢ
²⁵before the mountains were settled in place,ᵗ
before the hills, I was given birth,ᵘ
²⁶before he made the earth or its fields
or any of the dust of the world.ᵛ
²⁷I was there when he set the heavens in place,ʷ

L Ps 149:4 ◄► Pr 28:13
N Pr 1:24–33 ◄► Pr 14:16
P Pr 3:16 ◄► Pr 10:22

m 22 Syriac (see also Septuagint); Hebrew *fool* *n 22* The meaning of the Hebrew for this line is uncertain. *o 27* Hebrew *Sheol* *p 16* Many Hebrew manuscripts and Septuagint; most Hebrew manuscripts *and nobles—all righteous rulers* *q 22* Or *way*; or *dominion* *r 22* Or *The LORD possessed me at the beginning of his work*; or *The LORD brought me forth at the beginning of his work* *s 23* Or *fashioned*

when he marked out the horizon*
on the face of the deep,
²⁸when he established the clouds above
and fixed securely the fountains of
the deep,
²⁹when he gave the sea its boundary
so the waters would not overstep his
command,
and when he marked out the
foundations of the earth.
³⁰ Then I was the craftsman at his
side.
I was filled with delight day after day,
rejoicing always in his presence,
³¹rejoicing in his whole world
and delighting in mankind.
³²"Now then, my sons, listen to me;
blessed are those who keep my
ways.
³³Listen to my instruction and be wise;
do not ignore it.
³⁴Blessed is the man who listens to me,
watching daily at my doors,
waiting at my doorway.
³⁵For whoever finds me finds life
and receives favor from the LORD.
³⁶But whoever fails to find me harms
himself;
all who hate me love death."

Invitations of Wisdom and of Folly

9 Wisdom has built her house;
she has hewn out its seven pillars.
²She has prepared her meat and mixed
her wine;
she has also set her table.
³She has sent out her maids, and she
calls
from the highest point of the city.
⁴"Let all who are simple come in
here!"
she says to those who lack
judgment.
⁵"Come, eat my food
and drink the wine I have mixed.
⁶Leave your simple ways and you will
live;
walk in the way of understanding.
⁷"Whoever corrects a mocker invites
insult;
whoever rebukes a wicked man
incurs abuse.
⁸Do not rebuke a mocker or he will
hate you;

rebuke a wise man and he will love
you.
⁹Instruct a wise man and he will be
wiser still;
teach a righteous man and he will
add to his learning.
¹⁰"The fear of the LORD is the beginning
of wisdom,
and knowledge of the Holy One is
understanding.
¹¹For through me your days will be
many,
and years will be added to your life.
¹²If you are wise, your wisdom will
reward you;
if you are a mocker, you alone will
suffer."
¹³The woman Folly is loud;
she is undisciplined and without
knowledge.
¹⁴She sits at the door of her house,
on a seat at the highest point of the
city,
¹⁵calling out to those who pass by,
who go straight on their way.
¹⁶"Let all who are simple come in here!"
she says to those who lack
judgment.
¹⁷"Stolen water is sweet;
food eaten in secret is delicious!"
¹⁸But little do they know that the dead
are there,
that her guests are in the depths of
the grave.

Proverbs of Solomon

10 The proverbs of Solomon:

A wise son brings joy to his father,
but a foolish son grief to his mother.

²Ill-gotten treasures are of no value,
but righteousness delivers from
death.

³The LORD does not let the righteous go
hungry
but he thwarts the craving of the
wicked.

H Pr 4:22 ◀▶ Pr 10:16
H Pr 6:15 ◀▶ Pr 11:21
F Ps 147:14 ◀▶ Pr 13:25

ᵗ 18 Hebrew *Sheol*

C Pr 5:22–23 ◀▶ Pr 11:18

⁴Lazy hands make a man poor,
  but diligent hands bring wealth.

⁵He who gathers crops in summer is a wise son,
  but he who sleeps during harvest is a disgraceful son.

⁶Blessings crown the head of the righteous,
  but violence overwhelms the mouth of the wicked.ᵘ

⁷The memory of the righteous will be a blessing,
  but the name of the wicked will rot.

⁸The wise in heart accept commands,
  but a chattering fool comes to ruin.

⁹The man of integrity walks securely,
  but he who takes crooked paths will be found out.

¹⁰He who winks maliciously causes grief,
  and a chattering fool comes to ruin.

¹¹The mouth of the righteous is a fountain of life,
  but violence overwhelms the mouth of the wicked.

¹²Hatred stirs up dissension,
  but love covers over all wrongs.

¹³Wisdom is found on the lips of the discerning,
  but a rod is for the back of him who lacks judgment.

¹⁴Wise men store up knowledge,
  but the mouth of a fool invites ruin.

¹⁵The wealth of the rich is their fortified city,
  but poverty is the ruin of the poor.

¹⁶The wages of the righteous bring them life,
  but the income of the wicked brings them punishment.

¹⁷He who heeds discipline shows the way to life,
  but whoever ignores correction leads others astray.

¹⁸He who conceals his hatred has lying lips,
  and whoever spreads slander is a fool.

¹⁹When words are many, sin is not absent,
  but he who holds his tongue is wise.

²⁰The tongue of the righteous is choice silver,
  but the heart of the wicked is of little value.

²¹The lips of the righteous nourish many,
  but fools die for lack of judgment.

²²The blessing of the LORD brings wealth,
  and he adds no trouble to it.

²³A fool finds pleasure in evil conduct,
  but a man of understanding delights in wisdom.

²⁴What the wicked dreads will overtake him;
  what the righteous desire will be granted.

²⁵When the storm has swept by, the wicked are gone,
  but the righteous stand firm forever.

²⁶As vinegar to the teeth and smoke to the eyes,
  so is a sluggard to those who send him.

²⁷The fear of the LORD adds length to life,
  but the years of the wicked are cut short.

²⁸The prospect of the righteous is joy,
  but the hopes of the wicked come to nothing.

²⁹The way of the LORD is a refuge for the righteous,
  but it is the ruin of those who do evil.

ᵘ 6 Or but the mouth of the wicked conceals violence; also in verse 11

N ³⁰The righteous will never be uprooted, but the wicked will not remain in the land.¹

³¹The mouth of the righteous brings forth wisdom,ᵐ
but a perverse tongueⁿ will be cut out.

³²The lips of the righteous know what is fitting,°
but the mouth of the wicked only what is perverse.ᵖ

11
The LORD abhors dishonest scales,ᑫ
but accurate weights are his delight.ʳ

²When pride comes, then comes disgrace,ˢ
but with humility comes wisdom.ᵗ

³The integrity of the upright guides them,
but the unfaithful are destroyed by their duplicity.ᵘ

⁴Wealthᵛ is worthless in the day of wrath,ʷ
but righteousness delivers from death.ˣ

⁵The righteousness of the blameless makes a straight wayʸ for them,
but the wicked are brought down by their own wickedness.ᶻ

S ⁶The righteousness of the upright delivers them,
but the unfaithful are trapped by evil desires.ᵃ

⁷When a wicked man dies, his hope perishes;ᵇ
all he expected from his power comes to nothing.ᶜ

U ⁸The righteous man is rescued from trouble,
and it comes on the wicked instead.ᵈ

⁹With his mouth the godless destroys his neighbor,

N Ps 104:5 ◀ ▶ Ecc 1:4
S Pr 10:29–30 ◀ ▶ Pr 14:9
U Pr 10:24 ◀ ▶ Pr 11:20

10:30 ¹Ps 37:9, 28-29; S Pr 2:20-22
10:31 ᵐS ver 13; S Pr 15:2; 31:26 ⁿS Ps 52:4
10:32 ᵒEcc 10:12 ᵖS Ps 59:7
11:1 ᑫS Lev 19:36; Dt 25:13-16; S Job 6:2; Pr 20:10, 23 ʳPr 16:11; Eze 45:10
11:2 ˢPr 16:18 ᵗPr 18:12; 29:23
11:3 ᵘver 5; Pr 13:6
11:4 ᵛEze 27:27 ʷS Job 20:20; S Eze 7:19 ˣS Pr 10:2
11:5 ʸS 1Ki 8:36 ᶻS ver 3; Pr 5:21-23; 13:6; 21:7
11:6 ᵃS Est 7:9
11:7 ᵇS Job 8:13 ᶜS Pr 10:28
11:8 ᵈPr 21:18
11:9 ᵉPr 12:6; Jer 45:5
11:10 ᶠS 2Ki 11:20 ᵍS Est 8:17
11:11 ʰPr 14:34 ⁱPr 29:8
11:12 ʲPr 14:21 ᵏS Job 6:24
11:13 ˡPr 20:19 ᵐS Pr 10:14
11:14 ⁿPr 20:18 ᵒS 2Sa 15:34; Pr 15:22; 24:6
11:15 ᵖS Pr 6:1 ᑫPr 17:18; 22:26-27
11:16 ʳPr 31:31
11:18 ˢS Ex 1:20; S Job 4:8; Hos 10:12-13
11:19 ᵗS Dt 30:15; S Pr 10:2 ᵘ1Sa 2:6; Ps 89:48; Pr 1:18-19; Ecc 7:2; Jer 43:11
11:20 ᵛPr 3:32 ʷS Nu 14:8 ˣ1Ch 29:17; S Ps 15:2; 101:1-4; S 119:1; Pr 12:2, 22; 15:9

but through knowledge the righteous escape.ᵉ

¹⁰When the righteous prosper, the city rejoices;ᶠ
when the wicked perish, there are shouts of joy.ᵍ

¹¹Through the blessing of the upright a city is exalted,ʰ
but by the mouth of the wicked it is destroyed.ⁱ

¹²A man who lacks judgment derides his neighbor,ʲ
but a man of understanding holds his tongue.ᵏ

¹³A gossip betrays a confidence,ˡ
but a trustworthy man keeps a secret.ᵐ

¹⁴For lack of guidance a nation falls,ⁿ
but many advisers make victory sure.ᵒ

¹⁵He who puts up securityᵖ for another will surely suffer,
but whoever refuses to strike hands in pledge is safe.ᑫ

¹⁶A kindhearted woman gains respect,ʳ
but ruthless men gain only wealth.

¹⁷A kind man benefits himself,
but a cruel man brings trouble on himself.

C ¹⁸The wicked man earns deceptive wages,
but he who sows righteousness reaps a sure reward.ˢ

¹⁹The truly righteous man attains life,ᵗ
but he who pursues evil goes to his death.ᵘ

U ²⁰The LORD detests men of perverse heartᵛ
but he delightsʷ in those whose ways are blameless.ˣ

H ²¹Be sure of this: The wicked will not go unpunished,

C Pr 8:36 ◀ ▶ Pr 12:5
U Pr 11:8 ◀ ▶ Pr 11:24–25
H Pr 9:18 ◀ ▶ Pr 13:6

10:30 Solomon declared that the wicked will be destroyed and have no place in the coming millennial kingdom of Christ.

but those who are righteous will go free.^y

²²Like a gold ring in a pig's snout
is a beautiful woman who shows no discretion.

²³The desire of the righteous ends only in good,
but the hope of the wicked only in wrath.

²⁴One man gives freely, yet gains even more;
another withholds unduly, but comes to poverty.

²⁵A generous^z man will prosper;
he who refreshes others will himself be refreshed.^a

²⁶People curse the man who hoards grain,
but blessing crowns him who is willing to sell.

²⁷He who seeks good finds goodwill,
but evil comes to him who searches for it.^b

²⁸Whoever trusts in his riches will fall,^c
but the righteous will thrive like a green leaf.^d

²⁹He who brings trouble on his family will inherit only wind,
and the fool will be servant to the wise.^e

³⁰The fruit of the righteous is a tree of life,^f
and he who wins souls is wise.

³¹If the righteous receive their due^g on earth,
how much more the ungodly and the sinner!

12

Whoever loves discipline loves knowledge,
but he who hates correction is stupid.^h

²A good man obtains favor from the LORD,ⁱ
but the LORD condemns a crafty man.^j

³A man cannot be established through wickedness,
but the righteous cannot be uprooted.^k

⁴A wife of noble character^l is her husband's crown,
but a disgraceful wife is like decay in his bones.^m

⁵The plans of the righteous are just,
but the advice of the wicked is deceitful.

⁶The words of the wicked lie in wait for blood,
but the speech of the upright rescues them.ⁿ

⁷Wicked men are overthrown and are no more,^o
but the house of the righteous stands firm.^p

⁸A man is praised according to his wisdom,
but men with warped^q minds are despised.

⁹Better to be a nobody and yet have a servant
than pretend to be somebody and have no food.

¹⁰A righteous man cares for the needs of his animal,^r
but the kindest acts of the wicked are cruel.

¹¹He who works his land will have abundant food,
but he who chases fantasies lacks judgment.^s

¹²The wicked desire the plunder of evil men,
but the root of the righteous flourishes.

¹³An evil man is trapped by his sinful talk,^t
but a righteous man escapes trouble.^u

¹⁴From the fruit of his lips a man is filled with good things^v
as surely as the work of his hands rewards him.^w

¹⁵The way of a fool seems right to him,ˣ
but a wise man listens to advice.ʸ

¹⁶A fool ᶻ shows his annoyance at once,ᵃ
but a prudent man overlooks an insult.ᵇ

¹⁷A truthful witness gives honest testimony,
but a false witness tells lies.ᶜ

¹⁸Reckless words pierce like a sword,ᵈ
but the tongue of the wise brings healing.ᵉ

¹⁹Truthful lips endure forever,
but a lying tongue lasts only a moment.

²⁰There is deceit in the hearts of those who plot evil,
but joy for those who promote peace.ᶠ

²¹No harm befalls the righteous,ᵍ
but the wicked have their fill of trouble.

²²The LORD detests lying lips,ʰ
but he delightsⁱ in men who are truthful.ʲ

²³A prudent man keeps his knowledge to himself,ᵏ
but the heart of fools blurts out folly.ˡ

²⁴Diligent hands will rule,
but laziness ends in slave labor.ᵐ

²⁵An anxious heart weighs a man down,ⁿ
but a kind word cheers him up.

²⁶A righteous man is cautious in friendship,ᵛ
but the way of the wicked leads them astray.ᵒ

²⁷The lazy man does not roastʷ his game,
but the diligent man prizes his possessions.

²⁸In the way of righteousness there is life;ᵖ
along that path is immortality.

13 A wise son heeds his father's instruction,
but a mocker does not listen to rebuke.ᑫ

²From the fruit of his lips a man enjoys good things,ʳ
but the unfaithful have a craving for violence.

³He who guards his lips ˢ guards his life,ᵗ
but he who speaks rashly will come to ruin.ᵘ

⁴The sluggard craves and gets nothing,ᵛ
but the desires of the diligent are fully satisfied.

⁵The righteous hate what is false,ʷ
but the wicked bring shame and disgrace.

⁶Righteousness guards the man of integrity,
but wickedness overthrows the sinner.ˣ

⁷One man pretends to be rich, yet has nothing;ʸ
another pretends to be poor, yet has great wealth.ᶻ

⁸A man's riches may ransom his life,
but a poor man hears no threat.ᵃ

⁹The light of the righteous shines brightly,
but the lamp of the wicked is snuffed out.ᵇ

¹⁰Pride only breeds quarrels,
but wisdom is found in those who take advice.ᶜ

¹¹Dishonest money dwindles away,ᵈ
but he who gathers money little by little makes it grow.

¹²Hope deferred makes the heart sick,
but a longing fulfilled is a tree of life.ᵉ

¹³He who scorns instruction will pay for it,ᶠ
but he who respectsᵍ a command is rewarded.ʰ

¹⁴The teaching of the wise is a fountain of life,ⁱ
turning a man from the snares of death.ʲ

H Pr 11:21 ◄ ► Pr 13:9
H Pr 13:6 ◄ ► Pr 13:15

ᵛ 26 Or *man is a guide to his neighbor*   ʷ 27 The meaning of the Hebrew for this word is uncertain.

C
H ¹⁵Good understanding wins favor,
   but the way of the unfaithful is hard.ˣ

¹⁶Every prudent man acts out of knowledge,
   but a fool exposesᵏ his folly.ˡ

¹⁷A wicked messenger falls into trouble,ᵐ
   but a trustworthy envoy brings healing.ⁿ

¹⁸He who ignores discipline comes to poverty and shame,ᵒ
   but whoever heeds correction is honored.ᵖ

C ¹⁹A longing fulfilled is sweet to the soul,ᑫ
   but fools detest turning from evil.

²⁰He who walks with the wise grows wise,
   but a companion of fools suffers harm.ʳ

H ²¹Misfortune pursues the sinner,ˢ
U   but prosperityᵗ is the reward of the righteous.ᵘ

P ²²A good man leaves an inheritance for his children's children,
   but a sinner's wealth is stored up for the righteous.ᵛ

²³A poor man's field may produce abundant food,
   but injustice sweeps it away.

²⁴He who spares the rodʷ hates his son,
   but he who loves him is careful to disciplineˣ him.ʸ

F ²⁵The righteous eat to their hearts' content,
   but the stomach of the wicked goes hungry.ᶻ

14 The wise woman builds her house,ᵃ
   but with her own hands the foolish one tears hers down.

²He whose walk is upright fears the LORD,

C Pr 12:5 ◄ ► Pr 13:19
H Pr 13:9 ◄ ► Pr 13:21
C Pr 13:15 ◄ ► Pr 14:9
H Pr 13:15 ◄ ► Pr 14:12
U Pr 12:28 ◄ ► Pr 14:9
P Pr 11:24–25 ◄ ► Pr 15:6
F Pr 10:3 ◄ ► Isa 1:19

13:16 ᵏEcc 10:3
    ˡEst 5:11; S Ps 38:5
13:17 ᵐS Pr 10:26
    ⁿPr 25:13
13:18 ᵒS Pr 1:7;
    S 12:1 ᵖPs 141:5;
    Pr 25:12; Ecc 7:5
13:19 ᑫS Pr 10:11
13:20 ʳ2Ch 10:8
13:21 ˢ2Sa 3:39;
    Jer 40:3; 50:7;
    Eze 14:13; 18:4
    ᵗPs 25:13
    ᵘPs 32:10
13:22 ᵛS Est 8:2;
    S Job 27:17;
    Ecc 2:26
13:24 ʷS 2Sa 7:14
    ˣS Pr 3:12
    ʸPr 19:18; 22:15;
    23:13-14; 29:15,17;
    Eph 6:4; Heb 12:7
13:25 ᶻPr 10:3
14:1 ᵃS Ru 3:11;
    Pr 24:3
14:3 ᵇS Pr 10:14;
    Ecc 10:12
    ᶜS Pr 10:13; S 12:6
14:4 ᵈPs 144:14
14:5 ᵉS Ps 12:2;
    S Pr 12:17
14:6 ᶠS Pr 9:9
14:8 ᵍver 15;
    Pr 15:28; 21:29
    ʰver 24
14:11 ⁱS Job 8:22;
    Pr 21:12 ʲS Ps 72:7;
    S Pr 3:33; S 12:7
14:12 ᵏS Pr 12:15
    ˡPr 16:25
14:13 ᵐEcc 2:2;
    7:3,6
14:14 ⁿS Pr 1:31
    ᵒS 2Ch 15:7;
    Pr 12:14
14:15 ᵖS ver 8

but he whose ways are devious despises him.

³A fool's talk brings a rod to his back,ᵇ
   but the lips of the wise protect them.ᶜ

⁴Where there are no oxen, the manger is empty,
   but from the strength of an oxᵈ comes an abundant harvest.

⁵A truthful witness does not deceive,
   but a false witness pours out lies.ᵉ

⁶The mocker seeks wisdom and finds none,
   but knowledge comes easily to the discerning.ᶠ

⁷Stay away from a foolish man,
   for you will not find knowledge on his lips.

⁸The wisdom of the prudent is to give thought to their ways,ᵍ
   but the folly of fools is deception.ʰ

⁹Fools mock at making amends for sin,   C
   but goodwill is found among the   S
   upright.   U

¹⁰Each heart knows its own bitterness,
   and no one else can share its joy.

¹¹The house of the wicked will be destroyed,ⁱ   U
   but the tent of the upright will flourish.ʲ

¹²There is a way that seems right to a man,ᵏ   H
   but in the end it leads to death.ˡ

¹³Even in laughterᵐ the heart may ache,   C
   and joy may end in grief.

¹⁴The faithless will be fully repaid for their ways,ⁿ   S
   and the good man rewarded for his.ᵒ

¹⁵A simple man believes anything,
   but a prudent man gives thought to his steps.ᵖ

C Pr 13:19 ◄ ► Pr 14:13
S Pr 11:6 ◄ ► Pr 14:14
U Pr 13:21 ◄ ► Pr 14:11
U Pr 14:9 ◄ ► Pr 14:32
H Pr 13:21 ◄ ► Pr 15:24
C Pr 14:9 ◄ ► Pr 14:16
S Pr 14:9 ◄ ► Pr 15:9

ˣ15 Or *unfaithful does not endure*

PROVERBS 14:16

¹⁶A wise man fears the LORD and shuns evil,ᵍ
but a foolʳ is hotheaded and reckless.

¹⁷A quick-temperedˢ man does foolish things,ᵗ
and a crafty man is hated.ᵘ

¹⁸The simple inherit folly,
but the prudent are crowned with knowledge.

¹⁹Evil men will bow down in the presence of the good,
and the wicked at the gates of the righteous.ᵛ

²⁰The poor are shunned even by their neighbors,
but the rich have many friends.ʷ

²¹He who despises his neighbor sins,ˣ
but blessed is he who is kind to the needy.ʸ

²²Do not those who plot evil go astray?ᶻ
But those who plan what is good findʸ love and faithfulness.

²³All hard work brings a profit,
but mere talk leads only to poverty.

²⁴The wealth of the wise is their crown,
but the folly of fools yields folly.ᵃ

²⁵A truthful witness saves lives,
but a false witness is deceitful.ᵇ

²⁶He who fears the LORD has a secure fortress,ᶜ
and for his children it will be a refuge.ᵈ

²⁷The fear of the LORD is a fountain of life,ᵉ
turning a man from the snares of death.ᶠ

²⁸A large population is a king's glory,
but without subjects a prince is ruined.ᵍ

²⁹A patient man has great understanding,ʰ
but a quick-tempered man displays folly.ⁱ

³⁰A heart at peace gives life to the body,
but envy rots the bones.ʲ

³¹He who oppresses the poor shows contempt for their Maker,ᵏ
but whoever is kind to the needy honors God.ˡ

³²When calamity comes, the wicked are brought down,ᵐ
but even in death the righteous have a refuge.ⁿ

³³Wisdom reposes in the heart of the discerningᵒ
and even among fools she lets herself be known.ᶻ

³⁴Righteousness exalts a nation,ᵖ
but sin is a disgrace to any people.

³⁵A king delights in a wise servant,
but a shameful servant incurs his wrath.ᵍ

15

¹A gentle answerʳ turns away wrath,ˢ
but a harsh word stirs up anger.

²The tongue of the wise commends knowledge,ᵗ
but the mouth of the fool gushes folly.ᵘ

³The eyesᵛ of the LORD are everywhere,ʷ
keeping watch on the wicked and the good.ˣ

⁴The tongueʸ that brings healing is a tree of life,ᶻ
but a deceitful tongue crushes the spirit.ᵃ

⁵A fool spurns his father's discipline,
but whoever heeds correction shows prudence.ᵇ

⁶The house of the righteous contains great treasure,ᶜ
but the income of the wicked brings them trouble.ᵈ

H *Pr 10:27* ◀ ▶ *Pr 17:22*
N *Pr 14:16* ◀ ▶ *Pr 27:1*
U *Pr 14:11* ◀ ▶ *Pr 15:8–9*
C *Pr 14:16* ◀ ▶ *Pr 15:8–9*
E *Pr 5:21* ◀ ▶ *Pr 15:11*
P *Pr 13:22* ◀ ▶ *Pr 19:17*

ʸ 22 Or *show*   ᶻ 33 Hebrew; Septuagint and Syriac / *but in the heart of fools she is not known*

C *Pr 14:13* ◀ ▶ *Pr 14:34*
M *Pr 6:16–17* ◀ ▶ *Pr 15:33*
N *Pr 8:17* ◀ ▶ *Pr 14:32*
R *Pr 3:7* ◀ ▶ *Pr 28:13*

⁷The lips of the wise spread knowledge;ᵉ
  not so the hearts of fools.

⁸The LORD detests the sacrificeᶠ of the wicked,ᵍ
  but the prayer of the upright pleases him.ʰ

⁹The LORD detests the way of the wickedⁱ
  but he loves those who pursue righteousness.ʲ

¹⁰Stern discipline awaits him who leaves the path;
  he who hates correction will die.ᵏ

¹¹Death and Destructionᵃ lie open before the LORDˡ—
  how much more the hearts of men!ᵐ

¹²A mocker resents correction;ⁿ
  he will not consult the wise.

¹³A happy heart makes the face cheerful,ᵒ
  but heartache crushes the spirit.ᵖ

¹⁴The discerning heart seeks knowledge,ᑫ
  but the mouth of a fool feeds on folly.

¹⁵All the days of the oppressed are wretched,
  but the cheerful heart has a continual feast.ʳ

¹⁶Better a little with the fear of the LORD
  than great wealth with turmoil.ˢ

¹⁷Better a meal of vegetables where there is love
  than a fattened calf with hatred.ᵗ

¹⁸A hot-tempered man stirs up dissension,ᵘ
  but a patient man calms a quarrel.ᵛ

¹⁹The way of the sluggard is blocked with thorns,ʷ
  but the path of the upright is a highway.

²⁰A wise son brings joy to his father,ˣ
  but a foolish man despises his mother.

C Pr 14:34 ◄► Pr 15:26
U Pr 14:32 ◄► Pr 15:29
S Pr 14:14 ◄► Pr 15:29
E Pr 15:3 ◄► Pr 16:2

15:7 ᵉS ver 2; S Pr 10:13
15:8 ᶠS Ps 51:17; S Isa 1:13 ᵍS Pr 6:16; 21:27 ʰver 29; Job 35:13; Pr 28:9; S Jn 9:31
15:9 ⁱS Pr 6:16 ʲS Dt 7:13; S Pr 11:20
15:10 ᵏS Pr 1:31-32; S 12:1
15:11 ˡS Job 26:6 ᵐS 1Sa 2:3; S 2Ch 6:30; S Ps 44:21; S Rev 2:23
15:12 ⁿS Pr 9:8; S 12:1
15:13 ᵒver 15 ᵖS Pr 12:25; 17:22; 18:14
15:14 ᑫPr 18:15
15:15 ʳver 13
15:16 ˢver 17; Ps 37:16-17; Pr 13:8; 16:8; 17:1
15:17 ᵗS ver 16; Pr 17:1; Ecc 4:6
15:18 ᵘS Pr 6:1-19; S 14:17 ᵛS Ge 13:8
15:19 ʷPr 22:5
15:20 ˣS Pr 10:1
15:21 ʸS Pr 2:14
15:22 ᶻS Ps 16:7 ᵃ1Ki 1:12; Pr 24:6 ᵇS Pr 11:14
15:23 ᶜS Pr 12:14 ᵈPr 25:11
15:25 ᵉS Pr 12:7 ᶠS Dt 19:14; Pr 23:10-11
15:26 ᵍS Ps 94:11 ʰS Pr 6:16 ⁱS Ps 18:26
15:27 ʲS Ex 23:8; S Ps 15:5; Isa 1:23; 33:15
15:28 ᵏS Pr 14:8 ˡS Ps 59:7
15:29 ᵐS ver 8; S Job 15:31; Ps 145:18-19; Isa 59:2; S Jn 9:31
15:30 ⁿPr 25:25
15:31 ᵒS Pr 9:7-9; S 12:1
15:32 ᵖS Pr 1:7; S 12:1 ᑫS Pr 9:7-9; S 12:1; Ecc 7:5

²¹Folly delights a man who lacks judgment,ʸ
  but a man of understanding keeps a straight course.

²²Plans fail for lack of counsel,ᶻ
  but with many advisersᵃ they succeed.ᵇ

²³A man finds joy in giving an apt replyᶜ—
  and how good is a timely word!ᵈ

²⁴The path of life leads upward for the wise
  to keep him from going down to the grave.ᵇ

²⁵The LORD tears down the proud man's houseᵉ
  but he keeps the widow's boundaries intact.ᶠ

²⁶The LORD detests the thoughtsᵍ of the wicked,ʰ
  but those of the pureⁱ are pleasing to him.

²⁷A greedy man brings trouble to his family,
  but he who hates bribes will live.ʲ

²⁸The heart of the righteous weighs its answers,ᵏ
  but the mouth of the wicked gushes evil.ˡ

²⁹The LORD is far from the wicked
  but he hears the prayer of the righteous.ᵐ

³⁰A cheerful look brings joy to the heart,
  and good news gives health to the bones.ⁿ

³¹He who listens to a life-giving rebuke
  will be at home among the wise.ᵒ

³²He who ignores discipline despises himself,ᵖ
  but whoever heeds correction gains understanding.ᑫ

H Pr 14:12 ◄► Pr 16:4-5
C Pr 15:8-9 ◄► Pr 15:29
C Pr 15:26 ◄► Pr 21:16
S Pr 15:9 ◄► Pr 16:6
U Pr 15:8-9 ◄► Pr 16:7

ᵃ 11 Hebrew *Sheol* and *Abaddon* ᵇ 24 Hebrew *Sheol*

M ³³The fear of the Lord^r teaches a man wisdom,^c
and humility comes before honor.^s

16 To man belong the plans of the heart,
but from the Lord comes the reply of the tongue.^t

E ²All a man's ways seem innocent to him,^u
G but motives are weighed^v by the Lord.^w

³Commit to the Lord whatever you do,
and your plans will succeed.^x

H ⁴The Lord works out everything for his own ends^y—
even the wicked for a day of disaster.^z

M ⁵The Lord detests all the proud of heart.^a
Be sure of this: They will not go unpunished.^b

S ⁶Through love and faithfulness sin is atoned for;
through the fear of the Lord^c a man avoids evil.^d

U ⁷When a man's ways are pleasing to the Lord,
V he makes even his enemies live at peace^e with him.^f

⁸Better a little with righteousness
than much gain^g with injustice.^h

⁹In his heart a man plans his course,
but the Lord determines his steps.ⁱ

¹⁰The lips of a king speak as an oracle,
and his mouth should not betray justice.^j

¹¹Honest scales and balances are from the Lord;

M Pr 14:16 ◀▶ Pr 16:5
E Pr 15:11 ◀▶ Pr 17:3
G Pr 3:5–6 ◀▶ Pr 19:21
H Pr 15:24 ◀▶ Pr 16:18
M Pr 15:33 ◀▶ Pr 16:18
S Pr 15:29 ◀▶ Pr 16:17
U Pr 15:29 ◀▶ Pr 21:21
V Pr 12:13 ◀▶ Pr 20:22

15:33 ʳS Pr 1:7
ˢPr 16:18; 18:12; 22:4; 29:23;
Isa 66:2
16:1 ᵗver 9;
Pr 19:21
16:2 ᵘS Pr 12:15; 30:12 ᵛS 1Sa 2:3
ʷS 2Ch 6:30;
Pr 20:27; 21:2;
Lk 16:15
16:3
ˣS 2Ch 20:20;
S Ps 20:4; 37:5-6;
S Pr 3:5-6
16:4 ʸEx 9:16
ᶻS 2Ch 34:24;
S Ps 18:18; Ro 9:22
16:5 ᵃS Ps 40:4;
S Pr 6:16
ᵇPr 11:20-21
16:6 ᶜS Ge 20:11;
S Ex 1:17
ᵈS Ex 20:20
16:7 ᵉS Ge 39:21
ᶠPs 105:15;
Jer 39:12; 40:1;
42:12; Da 1:9
16:8 ᵍS Ps 37:16
ʰS Pr 15:16; 17:1;
Ecc 4:6
16:9 ⁱS ver 1;
S Job 33:29;
S Ps 90:12
16:10 ʲPr 17:7
16:11 ᵏS Pr 11:1;
Eze 45:10
16:12 ˡPr 26:28;
25:5; 29:14; 31:5
16:13 ᵐPr 22:11
16:14 ⁿS Ge 40:2;
S Job 29:24; Pr 20:2
ᵒPr 25:15; 29:8;
Ecc 10:4
16:15 ᵖS Ge 40:2;
S Job 29:24
ᵠPr 19:12; 25:2-7
16:16 ʳPs 49:20
ˢS Job 28:15;
S Pr 3:13-14
16:17 ᵗPr 19:16
16:18
ᵘS 1Sa 17:42
ᵛPs 18:27;
Isa 13:11; Jer 48:29
ʷS Est 5:12;
Pr 11:2; S 15:33;
18:12; 29:23
16:20 ˣPr 13:13
ʸS Ps 32:10; 40:4;
Pr 19:8; 29:25;
Jer 17:7
16:21 ᶻver 23
16:22 ᵃS Pr 10:11

all the weights in the bag are of his making.^k

¹²Kings detest wrongdoing,
for a throne is established through righteousness.^l

¹³Kings take pleasure in honest lips;
they value a man who speaks the truth.^m

¹⁴A king's wrath is a messenger of death,ⁿ
but a wise man will appease it.^o

¹⁵When a king's face brightens, it means life;^p
his favor is like a rain cloud in spring.^q

¹⁶How much better to get wisdom than gold,
to choose understanding^r rather than silver!^s

¹⁷The highway of the upright avoids evil; S
he who guards his way guards his life.^t

¹⁸Pride^u goes before destruction, H
a haughty spirit^v before a fall.^w M

¹⁹Better to be lowly in spirit and among the oppressed
than to share plunder with the proud.

²⁰Whoever gives heed to instruction prospers,^x
and blessed is he who trusts in the Lord.^y

²¹The wise in heart are called discerning,
and pleasant words promote instruction.^{d z}

²²Understanding is a fountain of life to those who have it,^a
but folly brings punishment to fools.

S Pr 16:6 ◀▶ Pr 17:15
H Pr 16:4–5 ◀▶ Pr 16:25
M Pr 16:5 ◀▶ Pr 18:12

^c 33 Or *Wisdom teaches the fear of the Lord*   ^d 21 Or *words make a man persuasive*

16:6 When people repent of their sin in the fear of God and live their lives according to his law, God will forgive them. God, in his love and mercy, has provided a way to remove our iniquity and that is through the shed blood of Jesus Christ on the cross.

²³A wise man's heart guides his mouth,
and his lips promote instruction.

²⁴Pleasant words are a honeycomb,
sweet to the soul and healing to the bones.

²⁵There is a way that seems right to a man,
but in the end it leads to death.

²⁶The laborer's appetite works for him;
his hunger drives him on.

²⁷A scoundrel plots evil,
and his speech is like a scorching fire.

²⁸A perverse man stirs up dissension,
and a gossip separates close friends.

²⁹A violent man entices his neighbor
and leads him down a path that is not good.

³⁰He who winks with his eye is plotting perversity;
he who purses his lips is bent on evil.

³¹Gray hair is a crown of splendor;
it is attained by a righteous life.

³²Better a patient man than a warrior,
a man who controls his temper than one who takes a city.

³³The lot is cast into the lap,
but its every decision is from the LORD.

17

Better a dry crust with peace and quiet
than a house full of feasting, with strife.

²A wise servant will rule over a disgraceful son,
and will share the inheritance as one of the brothers.

³The crucible for silver and the furnace for gold,
but the LORD tests the heart.

⁴A wicked man listens to evil lips;
a liar pays attention to a malicious tongue.

⁵He who mocks the poor shows contempt for their Maker;
whoever gloats over disaster will not go unpunished.

⁶Children's children are a crown to the aged,
and parents are the pride of their children.

⁷Arrogant lips are unsuited to a fool—
how much worse lying lips to a ruler!

⁸A bribe is a charm to the one who gives it;
wherever he turns, he succeeds.

⁹He who covers over an offense promotes love,
but whoever repeats the matter separates close friends.

¹⁰A rebuke impresses a man of discernment
more than a hundred lashes a fool.

¹¹An evil man is bent only on rebellion;
a merciless official will be sent against him.

¹²Better to meet a bear robbed of her cubs
than a fool in his folly.

¹³If a man pays back evil for good,
evil will never leave his house.

¹⁴Starting a quarrel is like breaching a dam;
so drop the matter before a dispute breaks out.

¹⁵Acquitting the guilty and condemning the innocent—
the LORD detests them both.

¹⁶Of what use is money in the hand of a fool,
since he has no desire to get wisdom?

¹⁷A friend loves at all times,
and a brother is born for adversity.

¹⁸A man lacking in judgment strikes hands in pledge
and puts up security for his neighbor.

¹⁹He who loves a quarrel loves sin;

H *Pr 16:18* ◀▶ *Pr 18:12*
E *Pr 16:2* ◀▶ *Pr 21:2*
T *Pr 3:11–12* ◀▶ *Pr 25:4*

S *Pr 16:17* ◀▶ *Pr 21:16*

e 23 Or mouth / and makes his lips persuasive   f 1 Hebrew sacrifices   g 7 Or Eloquent he who builds a high gate invites destruction.

²⁰A man of perverse heart does not prosper;
  he whose tongue is deceitful falls into trouble.

²¹To have a fool for a son brings grief;
  there is no joy for the father of a fool.ᵐ

**²²A cheerful heart is good medicine,
  but a crushedⁿ spirit dries up the bones.ᵒ**

²³A wicked man accepts a bribeᵖ in secret
  to pervert the course of justice.ᵠ

²⁴A discerning man keeps wisdom in view,
  but a fool's eyesʳ wander to the ends of the earth.

²⁵A foolish son brings grief to his father
  and bitterness to the one who bore him.ˢ

²⁶It is not good to punish an innocent man,ᵗ
  or to flog officials for their integrity.

²⁷A man of knowledge uses words with restraint,ᵘ
  and a man of understanding is even-tempered.ᵛ

²⁸Even a fool is thought wise if he keeps silent,
  and discerning if he holds his tongue.ʷ

18 An unfriendly man pursues selfish ends;
  he defies all sound judgment.

²A fool finds no pleasure in understanding
  but delights in airing his own opinions.ˣ

³When wickedness comes, so does contempt,
  and with shame comes disgrace.

⁴The words of a man's mouth are deep waters,ʸ
  but the fountain of wisdom is a bubbling brook.

H Pr 14:30 ◄ ► Pr 19:23

17:21 ᵐ S Pr 10:1
17:22 ⁿ S Ps 38:8
  ᵒ S Ex 12:46;
  Pr 14:30; S 15:13;
  18:14
17:23 ᵖ S Ex 18:21;
  S 23:8; S 1Sa 8:3
  ᵠ S Job 34:33
17:24 ʳ S Job 31:1
17:25 ˢ S Pr 10:1
17:26 ᵗ S Ps 94:21
17:27 ᵘ S Job 6:24
  ᵛ S Pr 14:29
17:28 ʷ S Job 2:13;
  13:5; S Pr 10:19
18:2 ˣ S Pr 12:23
18:4 ʸ S Ps 18:16
18:5 ᶻ Pr 24:23-25;
  28:21 ᵃ S Ps 82:2;
  S Pr 17:15
18:6 ᵇ S Pr 10:14
18:7 ᶜ Ps 140:9
  ᵈ S Ps 64:8;
  S Pr 10:14; S 12:13;
  S 13:3; Ecc 10:12
18:8 ᵉ Pr 26:22
18:9 ᶠ Pr 28:24
18:10 ᵍ S Ps 61:3
  ʰ S Ps 20:1;
  Pr 14:26
18:11 ⁱ Pr 10:15
18:12 ʲ S Pr 11:2;
  15:33; S 16:18
18:13 ᵏ Pr 20:25
18:14 ˡ S Pr 15:13;
  S 17:22
18:15 ᵐ S Pr 15:14
18:16 ⁿ S Ge 32:13;
  S 1Sa 10:4; Pr 19:6
18:18 ᵒ S Pr 16:33
18:19 ᵖ S 1Sa 17:28

---

⁵It is not good to be partial to the wicked ᶻ
  or to deprive the innocent of justice.ᵃ

⁶A fool's lips bring him strife,
  and his mouth invites a beating.ᵇ

⁷A fool's mouth is his undoing,
  and his lips are a snareᶜ to his soul.ᵈ

⁸The words of a gossip are like choice morsels;
  they go down to a man's inmost parts.ᵉ

⁹One who is slack in his work
  is brother to one who destroys.ᶠ

**¹⁰The name of the LORD is a strong tower;ᵍ
  the righteous run to it and are safe.ʰ**

¹¹The wealth of the rich is their fortified city;ⁱ
  they imagine it an unscalable wall.

**¹²Before his downfall a man's heart is proud,
  but humility comes before honor.ʲ**

¹³He who answers before listening—
  that is his folly and his shame.ᵏ

¹⁴A man's spirit sustains him in sickness,
  but a crushed spirit who can bear?ˡ

¹⁵The heart of the discerning acquires knowledge;ᵐ
  the ears of the wise seek it out.

¹⁶A giftⁿ opens the way for the giver
  and ushers him into the presence of the great.

¹⁷The first to present his case seems right,
  till another comes forward and questions him.

¹⁸Casting the lot settles disputesᵒ
  and keeps strong opponents apart.

¹⁹An offendedᵖ brother is more unyielding than a fortified city,
  and disputes are like the barred gates of a citadel.

²⁰From the fruit of his mouth a man's stomach is filled;

S Pr 3:23–26 ◄ ► Pr 29:25
H Pr 16:25 ◄ ► Pr 22:3
M Pr 16:18 ◄ ► Pr 26:12

with the harvest from his lips he is
   satisfied.q
21The tongue has the power of life and
   death,r
and those who love it will eat its
   fruit.s
22He who finds a wife finds what is
   goodt
and receives favor from the LORD.u
23A poor man pleads for mercy,
but a rich man answers harshly.
24A man of many companions may come
   to ruin,
but there is a friend who sticks
   closer than a brother.v

19

Better a poor man whose walk is
   blameless
than a fool whose lips are perverse.w
2It is not good to have zeal without
   knowledge,
nor to be hasty and miss the way.x
3A man's own follyy ruins his life,
yet his heart rages against the LORD.z
4Wealth brings many friends,
but a poor man's friend deserts
   him.a
5A false witnessb will not go
   unpunished,c
and he who pours out lies will not
   go free.d
6Many curry favor with a ruler,e
and everyone is the friend of a man
   who gives gifts.f
7A poor man is shunned by all his
   relatives—
how much more do his friends avoid
   him!g
Though he pursues them with
   pleading,
they are nowhere to be found.h h
8He who gets wisdom loves his own
   soul;
he who cherishes understanding
   prospers.i
9A false witness will not go
   unpunished,
and he who pours out lies will
   perish.j

10It is not fitting for a foolk to live in
   luxury—
how much worse for a slave to rule
   over princes!l
11A man's wisdom gives him patience;m
it is to his glory to overlook an
   offense.
12A king's rage is like the roar of a lion,n
but his favor is like dewo on the
   grass.p
13A foolish son is his father's ruin,q
and a quarrelsome wife is like a
   constant dripping.r
14Houses and wealth are inherited from
   parents,s
but a prudent wife is from the LORD.t
15Laziness brings on deep sleep,
and the shiftless man goes hungry.u
16He who obeys instructions guards his
   life,
but he who is contemptuous of his
   ways will die.v
17He who is kind to the poor lends to
   the LORD,w
and he will reward him for what he
   has done.x
18Discipline your son, for in that there is
   hope;
do not be a willing party to his
   death.y
19A hot-tempered man must pay the
   penalty;
if you rescue him, you will have to
   do it again.
20Listen to advice and accept
   instruction,z
and in the end you will be wise.a
21Many are the plans in a man's heart,
but it is the LORD's purpose that
   prevails.b
22What a man desires is unfailing lovei;
better to be poor than a liar.

h 7 The meaning of the Hebrew for this sentence is uncertain.   i 22 Or A man's greed is his shame

²³The fear of the LORD leads to life:
Then one rests content, untouched by trouble.^c

²⁴The sluggard buries his hand in the dish;
he will not even bring it back to his mouth!^d

²⁵Flog a mocker, and the simple will learn prudence;
rebuke a discerning man,^e and he will gain knowledge.^f

²⁶He who robs his father and drives out his mother^g
is a son who brings shame and disgrace.

²⁷Stop listening to instruction, my son,^h
and you will stray from the words of knowledge.

²⁸A corrupt witness mocks at justice,
and the mouth of the wicked gulps down evil.ⁱ

²⁹Penalties are prepared for mockers,
and beatings for the backs of fools.^j

20

Wine^k is a mocker^l and beer a brawler;
whoever is led astray^m by them is not wise.ⁿ

²A king's wrath is like the roar of a lion;^o
he who angers him forfeits his life.^p

³It is to a man's honor to avoid strife,
but every fool^q is quick to quarrel.^r

⁴A sluggard^s does not plow in season;
so at harvest time he looks but finds nothing.^t

⁵The purposes of a man's heart are deep waters,^u
but a man of understanding draws them out.

⁶Many a man claims to have unfailing love,
but a faithful man who can find?^v

⁷The righteous man leads a blameless life;^w
blessed are his children after him.^x

⁸When a king sits on his throne to judge,^y
he winnows out all evil with his eyes.^z

⁹Who can say, "I have kept my heart pure;^a
I am clean and without sin"?^b

¹⁰Differing weights and differing measures—
the LORD detests them both.^c

¹¹Even a child is known by his actions,
by whether his conduct is pure^d and right.

¹²Ears that hear and eyes that see—
the LORD has made them both.^e

¹³Do not love sleep or you will grow poor;^f
stay awake and you will have food to spare.

¹⁴"It's no good, it's no good!" says the buyer;
then off he goes and boasts about his purchase.

¹⁵Gold there is, and rubies in abundance,
but lips that speak knowledge are a rare jewel.

¹⁶Take the garment of one who puts up security for a stranger;
hold it in pledge^g if he does it for a wayward woman.^h

¹⁷Food gained by fraud tastes sweet to a man,ⁱ
but he ends up with a mouth full of gravel.^j

¹⁸Make plans by seeking advice;
if you wage war, obtain guidance.^k

¹⁹A gossip betrays a confidence;^l
so avoid a man who talks too much.

²⁰If a man curses his father or mother,^m
his lamp will be snuffed out in pitch darkness.ⁿ

²¹An inheritance quickly gained at the beginning
will not be blessed at the end.

²²Do not say, "I'll pay you back for this wrong!"^o

> Wait for the LORD, and he will
> deliver you.ᵖ

²³The LORD detests differing weights,
and dishonest scales do not please
him.ᑫ

²⁴A man's steps are directedʳ by the
LORD.ˢ
How then can anyone understand
his own way?ᵗ

²⁵It is a trap for a man to dedicate
something rashly
and only later to consider his vows.ᵘ

²⁶A wise king winnows out the wicked;
he drives the threshing wheel over
them.ᵛ

²⁷The lamp of the LORDʷ searches the
spirit of a man;ʲ
it searches out his inmost being.ˣ

²⁸Love and faithfulness keep a king safe;
through loveʸ his throne is made
secure.ᶻ

²⁹The glory of young men is their
strength,
gray hair the splendor of the old.ᵃ

³⁰Blows and wounds cleanseᵇ away evil,
and beatingsᶜ purge the inmost
being.

21

The king's heart is in the hand of
the LORD;
he directs it like a watercourse
wherever he pleases.ᵈ

E
G ²All a man's ways seem right to him,
but the LORD weighs the heart.ᵉ

³To do what is right and just
is more acceptable to the LORD than
sacrifice.ᶠ

⁴Haughty eyesᵍ and a proud heart,
the lamp of the wicked, are sin!

⁵The plans of the diligent lead to profitʰ
as surely as haste leads to poverty.

⁶A fortune made by a lying tongue
is a fleeting vapor and a deadly
snare.ᵏⁱ

⁷The violence of the wicked will drag
them away,ʲ
for they refuse to do what is right.

20:22 ᵖ Isa 37:20; Jer 1:19; 42:11; Ro 12:19
20:23 ᑫ S ver 10; S Dt 25:13
20:24 ʳ S Ps 90:12
ˢ S Job 33:29
ᵗ S Pr 19:21; Jer 10:23
20:25 ᵘ S Pr 10:19; 18:13; Ecc 5:2,4-5; Jer 44:25
20:26 ᵛ S ver 8
20:27 ʷ S Ps 119:105
ˣ S Pr 16:2
20:28 ʸ Ps 40:11
ᶻ S Pr 16:12; Isa 16:5
20:29 ᵃ Pr 16:31
20:30 ᵇ S Ps 51:2; Pr 22:15 ᶜ Isa 1:5
21:1 ᵈ Est 5:1; Jer 39:11-12
21:2 ᵉ S Pr 16:2
21:3 ᶠ S 1Sa 15:22; Isa 1:11; Mic 6:6-8
21:4 ᵍ S Job 41:34
21:5 ʰ S Pr 10:4
21:6 ⁱ S Pr 10:2
21:7 ʲ S Pr 11:5
21:8 ᵏ S Pr 2:15
21:9 ˡ ver 19; Pr 19:13; 25:24
21:11 ᵐ S Pr 19:25
21:12 ⁿ S Pr 14:11
21:13 ᵒ S Ex 11:6
ᵖ S Job 29:12
21:14 ᑫ S Ge 32:20
21:15 ʳ S Pr 10:29
21:16 ˢ Eze 18:24
21:17 ᵗ Pr 23:20-21,29-35
21:18 ᵘ Pr 11:8; Isa 43:3
21:19 ᵛ S ver 9

⁸The way of the guilty is devious,ᵏ
but the conduct of the innocent is
upright.

⁹Better to live on a corner of the roof
than share a house with a
quarrelsome wife.ˡ

¹⁰The wicked man craves evil;
his neighbor gets no mercy from
him.

¹¹When a mocker is punished, the
simple gain wisdom;
when a wise man is instructed, he
gets knowledge.ᵐ

¹²The Righteous Oneˡ takes note of the
house of the wicked
and brings the wicked to ruin.ⁿ

¹³If a man shuts his ears to the cry of the
poor,
he too will cry outᵒ and not be
answered.ᵖ

¹⁴A gift given in secret soothes anger,
and a bribe concealed in the cloak
pacifies great wrath.ᑫ

¹⁵When justice is done, it brings joy to
the righteous
but terror to evildoers.ʳ

> ¹⁶A man who strays from the path of
> understanding   C
> comes to rest in the company of the   S
> dead.ˢ

¹⁷He who loves pleasure will become
poor;
whoever loves wine and oil will
never be rich.ᵗ

¹⁸The wicked become a ransomᵘ for the
righteous,
and the unfaithful for the upright.

¹⁹Better to live in a desert
than with a quarrelsome and
ill-tempered wife.ᵛ

²⁰In the house of the wise are stores of
choice food and oil,
but a foolish man devours all he has.

C Pr 15:29 ◀▶ Pr 21:27
S Pr 17:15 ◀▶ Pr 22:8

l 27 Or The spirit of man is the LORD's lamp k 6 Some Hebrew manuscripts, Septuagint and Vulgate; most Hebrew manuscripts *vapor for those who seek death l 12* Or *The righteous man*

E Pr 17:3 ◀▶ Pr 24:12
G Pr 20:9 ◀▶ Pr 26:12

PROVERBS 21:21

²¹He who pursues righteousness and love
  finds life, prosperity^m^w and honor.^x
²²A wise man attacks the city of the mighty^y
  and pulls down the stronghold in which they trust.
²³He who guards his mouth^z and his tongue
  keeps himself from calamity.^a
²⁴The proud and arrogant^b man—
  "Mocker" is his name;
  he behaves with overweening pride.
²⁵The sluggard's craving will be the death of him,^c
  because his hands refuse to work.
²⁶All day long he craves for more,
  but the righteous^d give without sparing.^e
²⁷The sacrifice of the wicked is detestable^f—
  how much more so when brought with evil intent!^g
²⁸A false witness^h will perish,^i
  and whoever listens to him will be destroyed forever.^n
²⁹A wicked man puts up a bold front,
  but an upright man gives thought to his ways.^j
³⁰There is no wisdom,^k no insight, no plan
  that can succeed against the LORD.^l
³¹The horse is made ready for the day of battle,
  but victory rests with the LORD.^m

22 A good name is more desirable than great riches;
  to be esteemed is better than silver or gold.^n
²Rich and poor have this in common:
  The LORD is the Maker of them all.^o
³A prudent man sees danger and takes refuge,^p
  but the simple keep going and suffer for it.^q
⁴Humility and the fear of the LORD
  bring wealth and honor^r and life.^s

⁵In the paths of the wicked lie thorns and snares,^t
  but he who guards his soul stays far from them.
⁶Train^o^u a child in the way he should go,^v
  and when he is old he will not turn from it.^w
⁷The rich rule over the poor,
  and the borrower is servant to the lender.
⁸He who sows wickedness reaps trouble,^x
  and the rod of his fury will be destroyed.^y
⁹A generous man will himself be blessed,^z
  for he shares his food with the poor.^a
¹⁰Drive out the mocker, and out goes strife;
  quarrels and insults are ended.^b
¹¹He who loves a pure heart and whose speech is gracious
  will have the king for his friend.^c
¹²The eyes of the LORD keep watch over knowledge,
  but he frustrates the words of the unfaithful.
¹³The sluggard says, "There is a lion outside!"^d
  or, "I will be murdered in the streets!"
¹⁴The mouth of an adulteress is a deep pit;^e
  he who is under the LORD's wrath will fall into it.^f
¹⁵Folly is bound up in the heart of a child,
  but the rod of discipline will drive it far from him.^g
¹⁶He who oppresses the poor to increase his wealth
  and he who gives gifts to the rich—
  both come to poverty.

21:21 ^w Ps 25:13 ^x Mt 5:6
21:22 ^y S Pr 8:14
21:23 ^z S Ps 34:13 ^a S Pr 10:19; 12:13; S 13:3
21:24 ^b Jer 43:2
21:25 ^c Pr 13:4
21:26 ^d S 2Sa 17:27 ^e S Lev 25:35
21:27 ^f S 1Ki 14:24 ^g S Pr 15:8
21:28 ^h Isa 29:21 ^i S Pr 19:5
21:29 ^j S Pr 14:8
21:30 ^k S Job 12:13; S 15:25 ^l 2Ch 13:12; S Job 5:13; Isa 8:10
21:31 ^m Ps 33:12-19; Isa 31:1
22:1 ^n Ecc 7:1
22:2 ^o S Job 31:15; Pr 29:13; Mt 5:45
22:3 ^p S Pr 14:16 ^q Pr 27:12
22:4 ^r S Pr 15:33 ^s S Pr 10:27; Da 4:36
22:5 ^t Pr 15:19
22:6 ^u S Ge 14:14 ^v Eph 6:4 ^w S Dt 6:7
22:8 ^x S Ex 1:20; S Job 4:8; Gal 6:7-8 ^y Hos 8:7
22:9 ^z S Dt 14:29 ^a S Pr 11:25; S 19:17; 28:27
22:10 ^b Pr 26:20
22:11 ^c Pr 16:13; Mt 5:8
22:13 ^d Pr 26:13
22:14 ^e S Pr 5:3-5; 23:27 ^f Ecc 7:26
22:15 ^g S Pr 13:24; S 20:30

S *Pr 21:16* ◀ ▶ *Pr 24:12*
P *Pr 19:17* ◀ ▶ *Pr 28:8*
^m 21 Or *righteousness* ^n 28 Or / *but the words of an obedient man will live on* ^o 6 Or *Start*

U *Pr 16:7* ◀ ▶ *Pr 24:16*
C *Pr 21:16* ◀ ▶ *Pr 30:12–13*
H *Pr 18:12* ◀ ▶ *Pr 23:14*

Sayings of the Wise

¹⁷Pay attention and listen to the sayings of the wise;
  apply your heart to what I teach,
¹⁸for it is pleasing when you keep them in your heart
  and have all of them ready on your lips.
¹⁹So that your trust may be in the LORD,
  I teach you today, even you.
²⁰Have I not written thirty sayings for you,
  sayings of counsel and knowledge,
²¹teaching you true and reliable words,
  so that you can give sound answers to him who sent you?

²²Do not exploit the poor because they are poor
  and do not crush the needy in court,
²³for the LORD will take up their case
  and will plunder those who plunder them.

²⁴Do not make friends with a hot-tempered man,
  do not associate with one easily angered,
²⁵or you may learn his ways
  and get yourself ensnared.

²⁶Do not be a man who strikes hands in pledge
  or puts up security for debts;
²⁷if you lack the means to pay,
  your very bed will be snatched from under you.

²⁸Do not move an ancient boundary stone
  set up by your forefathers.

²⁹Do you see a man skilled in his work?
  He will serve before kings;
  he will not serve before obscure men.

23

When you sit to dine with a ruler,
  note well what is before you,
²and put a knife to your throat
  if you are given to gluttony.
³Do not crave his delicacies,
  for that food is deceptive.

⁴Do not wear yourself out to get rich;
  have the wisdom to show restraint.
⁵Cast but a glance at riches, and they are gone,
  for they will surely sprout wings
  and fly off to the sky like an eagle.

⁶Do not eat the food of a stingy man,
  do not crave his delicacies;
⁷for he is the kind of man
  who is always thinking about the cost.
"Eat and drink," he says to you,
  but his heart is not with you.
⁸You will vomit up the little you have eaten
  and will have wasted your compliments.

⁹Do not speak to a fool,
  for he will scorn the wisdom of your words.

¹⁰Do not move an ancient boundary stone
  or encroach on the fields of the fatherless,
¹¹for their Defender is strong;
  he will take up their case against you.

¹²Apply your heart to instruction
  and your ears to words of knowledge.

¹³Do not withhold discipline from a child;
  if you punish him with the rod, he will not die.
¹⁴Punish him with the rod
  and save his soul from death.

¹⁵My son, if your heart is wise,
  then my heart will be glad;
¹⁶my inmost being will rejoice
  when your lips speak what is right.

¹⁷Do not let your heart envy sinners,
  but always be zealous for the fear of the LORD.
¹⁸There is surely a future hope for you,
  and your hope will not be cut off.

¹⁹Listen, my son, and be wise,
  and keep your heart on the right path.

K Ps 130:7 ◄ ► Isa 1:18
H Pr 22:3 ◄ ► Pr 24:20

p 20 Or not formerly written; or not written excellent   q 1 Or who   r 7 Or for as he thinks within himself, / so he is; or as he puts on a feast, / so he is   s 14 Hebrew Sheol

PROVERBS 23:20

²⁰Do not join those who drink too much
    wine,
  or gorge themselves on meat,
²¹for drunkards and gluttons become
    poor,
  and drowsiness clothes them
    in rags.
²²Listen to your father, who gave you
    life,
  and do not despise your mother
    when she is old.
²³Buy the truth and do not sell it;
  get wisdom, discipline and
    understanding.
²⁴The father of a righteous man has great
    joy;
  he who has a wise son delights in
    him.
²⁵May your father and mother be glad;
  may she who gave you birth
    rejoice!
²⁶My son, give me your heart
  and let your eyes keep to my
    ways,
²⁷for a prostitute is a deep pit
  and a wayward wife is a narrow
    well.
²⁸Like a bandit she lies in wait,
  and multiplies the unfaithful among
    men.
²⁹Who has woe? Who has sorrow?
  Who has strife? Who has
    complaints?
  Who has needless bruises? Who has
    bloodshot eyes?
³⁰Those who linger over wine,
  who go to sample bowls of mixed
    wine.
³¹Do not gaze at wine when it
    is red,
  when it sparkles in the cup,
  when it goes down smoothly!
³²In the end it bites like a snake
  and poisons like a viper.
³³Your eyes will see strange sights
  and your mind imagine confusing
    things.
³⁴You will be like one sleeping on the
    high seas,
  lying on top of the rigging.
³⁵"They hit me," you will say, "but I'm
    not hurt!
  They beat me, but I don't feel it!
  When will I wake up
    so I can find another drink?"

24

Do not envy wicked men,
  do not desire their company;
²for their hearts plot violence,
  and their lips talk about making
    trouble.
³By wisdom a house is built,
  and through understanding it is
    established;
⁴through knowledge its rooms are filled
  with rare and beautiful treasures.
⁵A wise man has great power,
  and a man of knowledge increases
    strength;
⁶for waging war you need guidance,
  and for victory many advisers.
⁷Wisdom is too high for a fool;
  in the assembly at the gate he has
    nothing to say.
⁸He who plots evil
  will be known as a schemer.
⁹The schemes of folly are sin,
  and men detest a mocker.
¹⁰If you falter in times of trouble,
  how small is your strength!
¹¹Rescue those being led away to death;
  hold back those staggering toward
    slaughter.
¹²If you say, "But we knew nothing
    about this,"
  does not he who weighs the heart
    perceive it?
  Does not he who guards your life
    know it?
  Will he not repay each person
    according to what he has
    done?
¹³Eat honey, my son, for it is good;
  honey from the comb is sweet to
    your taste.
¹⁴Know also that wisdom is sweet to
    your soul;
  if you find it, there is a future hope
    for you,
  and your hope will not be cut off.
¹⁵Do not lie in wait like an outlaw
    against a righteous man's
    house,
  do not raid his dwelling place;

E Pr 21:2 ◀ ▶ Isa 29:15
S Pr 22:8 ◀ ▶ Pr 24:20

¹⁶for though a righteous man falls seven times, he rises again,
but the wicked are brought down by calamity.¹

¹⁷Do not gloat^m when your enemy falls;
when he stumbles, do not let your heart rejoice,^n
¹⁸or the LORD will see and disapprove
and turn his wrath away from him.^o

¹⁹Do not fret^p because of evil men
or be envious of the wicked,
²⁰for the evil man has no future hope,
and the lamp of the wicked will be snuffed out.^q

²¹Fear the LORD and the king,^r my son,
and do not join with the rebellious,
²²for those two will send sudden destruction^s upon them,
and who knows what calamities they can bring?

Further Sayings of the Wise

²³These also are sayings of the wise:^t

To show partiality^u in judging is not good:^v
²⁴Whoever says to the guilty, "You are innocent"^w —
peoples will curse him and nations denounce him.
²⁵But it will go well with those who convict the guilty,
and rich blessing will come upon them.

²⁶An honest answer
is like a kiss on the lips.

²⁷Finish your outdoor work
and get your fields ready;
after that, build your house.

²⁸Do not testify against your neighbor without cause,^x
or use your lips to deceive.
²⁹Do not say, "I'll do to him as he has done to me;
I'll pay that man back for what he did."^y

³⁰I went past the field of the sluggard,^z
past the vineyard of the man who lacks judgment;

U Pr 21:21 ◀ ▶ Pr 25:21–22
H Pr 23:14 ◀ ▶ Pr 26:10
S Pr 24:12 ◀ ▶ Pr 24:24
S Pr 24:20 ◀ ▶ Ecc 12:13–14

24:16 ˡS Job 5:19; S Ps 34:21
24:17 ᵐOb 1:12 ⁿS 2Sa 3:32; Mic 7:8
24:18 ᵒS Job 31:29
24:19 ᵖPs 37:1
24:20 ᵠS Job 18:5; S Pr 23:17-18
24:21 ʳRo 13:1-5
24:22 ˢS Ps 73:19
24:23 ᵗS Pr 1:6 ᵘS Ex 18:16; S Lev 19:15 ᵛPs 72:2; Pr 28:21; 31:8-9; Jer 22:16
24:24 ʷS Pr 17:15
24:28 ˣS Ps 7:4
24:29 ʸPr 20:22; Mt 5:38-41
24:30 ᶻPr 6:6-11; 26:13-16
24:33 ᵃS Pr 6:10
24:34 ᵇS Pr 10:4; Ecc 10:18
25:1 ᶜS 1Ki 4:32 ᵈS Pr 1:1
25:2 ᵉPr 16:10-15
25:5 ᶠS Pr 20:8 ᵍS 2Sa 7:13 ʰS Pr 16:12; 29:14
25:7 ⁱLk 14:7-10
25:8 ʲMt 5:25-26

³¹thorns had come up everywhere,
the ground was covered with weeds,
and the stone wall was in ruins.
³²I applied my heart to what I observed
and learned a lesson from what I saw:
³³A little sleep, a little slumber,
a little folding of the hands to rest^a —
³⁴and poverty will come on you like a bandit
and scarcity like an armed man.^rb

More Proverbs of Solomon

25 These are more proverbs^c of Solomon, copied by the men of Hezekiah king of Judah:^d

²It is the glory of God to conceal a matter;
to search out a matter is the glory of kings.^e

³As the heavens are high and the earth is deep,
so the hearts of kings are unsearchable.

⁴Remove the dross from the silver,
and out comes material for^u the silversmith;
⁵remove the wicked from the king's presence,^f
and his throne will be established^g through righteousness.^h

⁶Do not exalt yourself in the king's presence,
and do not claim a place among great men;
⁷it is better for him to say to you, "Come up here,"^i
than for him to humiliate you before a nobleman.

What you have seen with your eyes
⁸ do not bring^v hastily to court,
for what will you do in the end
if your neighbor puts you to shame?^j

⁹If you argue your case with a neighbor,
do not betray another man's confidence,
¹⁰or he who hears it may shame you

T Pr 17:3 ◀ ▶ Ecc 7:14

^r 34 Or like a vagrant / and scarcity like a beggar   ^u 4 Or comes a vessel from   ^v 7,8 Or nobleman / on whom you had set your eyes.   ^8 Do not go

and you will never lose your bad
      reputation.
¹¹A word aptly spoken
    is like apples of gold in settings of
      silver.ᵏ
¹²Like an earring of gold or an ornament
      of fine gold
    is a wise man's rebuke to a listening
      ear.ˡ
¹³Like the coolness of snow at harvest
      time
    is a trustworthy messenger to those
      who send him;
    he refreshes the spirit of his
      masters.ᵐ
¹⁴Like clouds and wind without rain
    is a man who boasts of gifts he does
      not give.
¹⁵Through patience a ruler can be
      persuaded,ⁿ
    and a gentle tongue can break a
      bone.ᵒ
¹⁶If you find honey, eat just enough—
    too much of it, and you will vomit.ᵖ
¹⁷Seldom set foot in your neighbor's
      house—
    too much of you, and he will hate
      you.
¹⁸Like a club or a sword or a sharp arrow
    is the man who gives false testimony
      against his neighbor.ᑫ
¹⁹Like a bad tooth or a lame foot
    is reliance on the unfaithful in times
      of trouble.
²⁰Like one who takes away a garment on
      a cold day,
    or like vinegar poured on soda,
    is one who sings songs to a heavy
      heart.
U ²¹If your enemy is hungry, give him food
      to eat;
    if he is thirsty, give him water to
      drink.
²²In doing this, you will heap burning
      coalsʳ on his head,
    and the Lord will reward you.ˢ
²³As a north wind brings rain,
    so a sly tongue brings angry looks.
²⁴Better to live on a corner of the roof

than share a house with a
      quarrelsome wife.ᵗ
²⁵Like cold water to a weary soul
    is good news from a distant land.ᵘ
²⁶Like a muddied spring or a polluted
      well
    is a righteous man who gives way to
      the wicked.
²⁷It is not good to eat too much honey,ᵛ
    nor is it honorable to seek one's
      own honor.ʷ
²⁸Like a city whose walls are broken
      down
    is a man who lacks self-control.

26

Like snow in summer or rainˣ in
      harvest,
    honor is not fitting for a fool.ʸ
²Like a fluttering sparrow or a darting
      swallow,
    an undeserved curse does not come
      to rest.ᶻ
³A whip for the horse, a halter for the
      donkey,ᵃ
    and a rod for the backs of fools!ᵇ
⁴Do not answer a fool according to his
      folly,
    or you will be like him yourself.ᶜ
⁵Answer a fool according to his folly,
    or he will be wise in his own eyes.ᵈ
⁶Like cutting off one's feet or drinking
      violence
    is the sending of a message by the
      hand of a fool.ᵉ
⁷Like a lame man's legs that hang limp
    is a proverb in the mouth of a fool.ᶠ
⁸Like tying a stone in a sling
    is the giving of honor to a fool.ᵍ
⁹Like a thornbush in a drunkard's hand
    is a proverb in the mouth of a fool.ʰ
¹⁰Like an archer who wounds at random **H**
    is he who hires a fool or any
      passer-by.
¹¹As a dog returns to its vomit,ⁱ
    so a fool repeats his folly.ʲ

¹²Do you see a man wise in his own
    eyes?ᵏ
There is more hope for a fool than
    for him.ˡ

¹³The sluggard says,ᵐ "There is a lion in
    the road,
a fierce lion roaming the streets!"ⁿ

¹⁴As a door turns on its hinges,
so a sluggard turns on his bed.ᵒ

¹⁵The sluggard buries his hand in the
    dish;
he is too lazy to bring it back to his
    mouth.ᵖ

¹⁶The sluggard is wiser in his own eyes
than seven men who answer
    discreetly.

¹⁷Like one who seizes a dog by the ears
is a passer-by who meddles in a
    quarrel not his own.

¹⁸Like a madman shooting
    firebrands or deadly arrows
¹⁹is a man who deceives his neighbor
and says, "I was only joking!"

²⁰Without wood a fire goes out;
without gossip a quarrel dies down.ᵠ

²¹As charcoal to embers and as wood to
    fire,
so is a quarrelsome man for kindling
    strife.ʳ

²²The words of a gossip are like choice
    morsels;
they go down to a man's inmost
    parts.ˢ

²³Like a coating of glazeʷ over
    earthenware
are fervent lips with an evil heart.

²⁴A malicious man disguises himself
    with his lips,ᵗ
but in his heart he harbors deceit.ᵘ

²⁵Though his speech is charming,ᵛ do
    not believe him,
for seven abominations fill his
    heart.ʷ

²⁶His malice may be concealed by
    deception,
but his wickedness will be exposed
    in the assembly.

²⁷If a man digs a pit,ˣ he will fall into it;

G Pr 21:2 ◀▶ Pr 28:26
M Pr 18:12 ◀▶ Pr 29:1

26:12 ᵏ S Pr 3:7
  l Pr 29:20
26:13 ᵐ Pr 6:6-11;
  24:30-34 ⁿ Pr 22:13
26:14 ᵒ S Pr 6:9
26:15 ᵖ Pr 19:24
26:20 ᵠ Pr 22:10
26:21 ʳ S Pr 14:17
26:22 ˢ Pr 18:8
26:24 ᵗ S Ps 31:18
  ᵘ Ps 41:6
26:25 ᵛ Ps 28:3
  ʷ Jer 9:4-8
26:27 ˣ S Ps 7:15
  ʸ S Est 6:13
  ᶻ S Est 2:23; S 7:9;
  Ps 35:8; 141:10;
  Pr 28:10; 29:6;
  Isa 50:11
26:28 ᵃ S Ps 12:3;
  Pr 29:5
27:1 ᵇ S 1Ki 20:11
  ᶜ Mt 6:34;
  Jas 4:13-16
27:2 ᵈ S Pr 25:27
27:3 ᵉ S Job 6:3
27:4 ᶠ S Nu 5:14
27:6 ᵍ Ps 141:5;
  Pr 28:23
27:8 ʰ Isa 16:2
27:9 ⁱ S Est 2:12;
  S Ps 45:8
27:10 ʲ S Pr 17:17
27:11 ᵏ S Pr 10:1;
  S 23:15-16
  ˡ S Ge 24:60
27:12 ᵐ Pr 22:3

if a man rolls a stone, it will roll
    back on him.ᶻ

²⁸A lying tongue hates those it hurts,
and a flattering mouthᵃ works ruin.

27 Do not boastᵇ about tomorrow,
    for you do not know what a day
    may bring forth.ᶜ

²Let another praise you, and not your
    own mouth;
someone else, and not your own
    lips.ᵈ

³Stone is heavy and sandᵉ a burden,
but provocation by a fool is heavier
    than both.

⁴Anger is cruel and fury overwhelming,
but who can stand before jealousy?ᶠ

⁵Better is open rebuke
than hidden love.

⁶Wounds from a friend can be trusted,
but an enemy multiplies kisses.ᵍ

⁷He who is full loathes honey,
but to the hungry even what is
    bitter tastes sweet.

⁸Like a bird that strays from its nestʰ
is a man who strays from his home.

⁹Perfumeⁱ and incense bring joy to the
    heart,
and the pleasantness of one's friend
    springs from his earnest
    counsel.

¹⁰Do not forsake your friend and the
    friend of your father,
and do not go to your brother's
    house when disasterʲ strikes
    you—
better a neighbor nearby than a
    brother far away.

¹¹Be wise, my son, and bring joy to my
    heart;ᵏ
then I can answer anyone who
    treats me with contempt.ˡ

¹²The prudent see danger and take
    refuge,
but the simple keep going and suffer
    for it.ᵐ

N Pr 14:32 ◀▶ Pr 29:1
H Pr 26:10 ◀▶ Pr 29:1

ʷ 23 With a different word division of the Hebrew; Masoretic Text *of silver dross*

¹³Take the garment of one who puts up
       security for a stranger;
   hold it in pledge if he does it for a
       wayward woman.ⁿ

¹⁴If a man loudly blesses his neighbor
       early in the morning,
   it will be taken as a curse.

¹⁵A quarrelsome wife is like
   a constant dripping° on a rainy day;
¹⁶restraining her is like restraining the
       wind
   or grasping oil with the hand.

¹⁷As iron sharpens iron,
   so one man sharpens another.

¹⁸He who tends a fig tree will eat its
       fruit,ᵖ
   and he who looks after his master
       will be honored.ᑫ

¹⁹As water reflects a face,
   so a man's heart reflects the man.

²⁰Death and Destructionˣ are never
       satisfied,ʳ
   and neither are the eyes of man.ˢ

²¹The crucible for silver and the furnace
       for gold,ᵗ
   but man is tested by the praise he
       receives.

²²Though you grind a fool in a mortar,
       grinding him like grain with a
       pestle,
   you will not remove his folly from
       him.

²³Be sure you know the condition of
       your flocks,ᵘ
   give careful attention to your herds;
²⁴for riches do not endure forever,ᵛ
   and a crown is not secure for all
       generations.

²⁵When the hay is removed and new
       growth appears
   and the grass from the hills is
       gathered in,
²⁶the lambs will provide you with
       clothing,
   and the goats with the price of a
       field.

²⁷You will have plenty of goats' milk
   to feed you and your family
   and to nourish your servant girls.

27:13 ⁿ Pr 20:16
27:15 ° S Est 1:18
27:18 ᵖ 1Co 9:7
       ᑫ Lk 19:12-27
27:20 ʳ Pr 30:15-16;
       Hab 2:5 ˢ Ecc 1:8;
       6:7
27:21 ᵗ S Pr 17:3
27:23 ᵘ Pr 12:10
27:24 ᵛ Pr 23:5
28:1 ʷ S 2Ki 7:7
     ˣ S Lev 26:17
     ʸ S Ps 138:3
28:6 ᶻ Pr 19:1
28:7 ᵃ Pr 23:19-21
28:8 ᵇ S Ex 18:21;
     Eze 18:8
     ᶜ S Job 27:17
     ᵈ S Job 3:15;
     Ps 112:9;
     Lk 14:12-14
28:9 ᵉ S Ps 109:7;
     S Pr 15:8; S Isa 1:13
28:10 ᶠ S Ps 57:6;
      S Pr 26:27
28:12
     ᵍ S 2Ki 11:20
     ʰ ver 28; Job 24:4;
     Pr 29:2

28

The wicked man fleesʷ though
       no one pursues,ˣ
   but the righteous are as bold as a
       lion.ʸ

²When a country is rebellious, it has
       many rulers,
   but a man of understanding and
       knowledge maintains order.

³A rulerʸ who oppresses the poor
   is like a driving rain that leaves no
       crops.

⁴Those who forsake the law praise the
       wicked,
   but those who keep the law resist
       them.

⁵Evil men do not understand justice,
   but those who seek the LORD
       understand it fully.

⁶Better a poor man whose walk is
       blameless
   than a rich man whose ways are
       perverse.ᶻ

⁷He who keeps the law is a discerning
       son,
   but a companion of gluttons
       disgraces his father.ᵃ

⁸He who increases his wealth by   ᵖ
       exorbitant interestᵇ
   amasses it for another,ᶜ who will be
       kind to the poor.ᵈ

⁹If anyone turns a deaf ear to the law,
   even his prayers are detestable.ᵉ

¹⁰He who leads the upright along an evil   ᵘ
       path
   will fall into his own trap,ᶠ
   but the blameless will receive a good
       inheritance.

¹¹A rich man may be wise in his own
       eyes,
   but a poor man who has
       discernment sees through him.

¹²When the righteous triumph, there is
       great elation;ᵍ
   but when the wicked rise to power,
       men go into hiding.ʰ

ᵖ Pr 22:9 ◄ ► Pr 28:27
ᵘ Pr 25:21-22 ◄ ► Pr 28:20

ˣ20 Hebrew *Sheol and Abaddon* ʸ3 Or *A poor man*

¹³He who conceals his sins does not prosper,
but whoever confesses and renounces them finds mercy.

¹⁴Blessed is the man who always fears the LORD,
but he who hardens his heart falls into trouble.

¹⁵Like a roaring lion or a charging bear
is a wicked man ruling over a helpless people.

¹⁶A tyrannical ruler lacks judgment,
but he who hates ill-gotten gain will enjoy a long life.

¹⁷A man tormented by the guilt of murder
will be a fugitive till death;
let no one support him.

¹⁸He whose walk is blameless is kept safe,
but he whose ways are perverse will suddenly fall.

¹⁹He who works his land will have abundant food,
but the one who chases fantasies will have his fill of poverty.

²⁰A faithful man will be richly blessed,
but one eager to get rich will not go unpunished.

²¹To show partiality is not good—
yet a man will do wrong for a piece of bread.

²²A stingy man is eager to get rich
and is unaware that poverty awaits him.

²³He who rebukes a man will in the end gain more favor
than he who has a flattering tongue.

²⁴He who robs his father or mother
and says, "It's not wrong"—
he is partner to him who destroys.

²⁵A greedy man stirs up dissension,
but he who trusts in the LORD will prosper.

²⁶He who trusts in himself is a fool,
but he who walks in wisdom is kept safe.

²⁷He who gives to the poor will lack nothing,
but he who closes his eyes to them receives many curses.

²⁸When the wicked rise to power, people go into hiding;
but when the wicked perish, the righteous thrive.

29 A man who remains stiff-necked after many rebukes
will suddenly be destroyed—without remedy.

²When the righteous thrive, the people rejoice;
when the wicked rule, the people groan.

³A man who loves wisdom brings joy to his father,
but a companion of prostitutes squanders his wealth.

⁴By justice a king gives a country stability,
but one who is greedy for bribes tears it down.

⁵Whoever flatters his neighbor
is spreading a net for his feet.

⁶An evil man is snared by his own sin,
but a righteous one can sing and be glad.

⁷The righteous care about justice for the poor,
but the wicked have no such concern.

⁸Mockers stir up a city,
but wise men turn away anger.

⁹If a wise man goes to court with a fool,
the fool rages and scoffs, and there is no peace.

¹⁰Bloodthirsty men hate a man of integrity
and seek to kill the upright.

¹¹A fool gives full vent to his anger,ˢ
but a wise man keeps himself under control.ᵗ

¹²If a rulerᵘ listens to lies,
all his officials become wicked.ᵛ

¹³The poor man and the oppressor have this in common:
The LORD gives sight to the eyes of both.ʷ

¹⁴If a king judges the poor with fairness,
his throne will always be secure.ˣ

¹⁵The rod of correction imparts wisdom,
but a child left to himself disgraces his mother.ʸ

¹⁶When the wicked thrive, so does sin,
but the righteous will see their downfall.ᶻ

¹⁷Discipline your son, and he will give you peace;
he will bring delight to your soul.ᵃ

¹⁸Where there is no revelation, the people cast off restraint;
but blessed is he who keeps the law.ᵇ

¹⁹A servant cannot be corrected by mere words;
though he understands, he will not respond.

²⁰Do you see a man who speaks in haste?
There is more hope for a fool than for him.ᶜ

²¹If a man pampers his servant from youth,
he will bring griefᶻ in the end.

²²An angry man stirs up dissension,
and a hot-tempered one commits many sins.ᵈ

²³A man's pride brings him low,ᵉ
but a man of lowly spirit gains honor.ᶠ

²⁴The accomplice of a thief is his own enemy;
he is put under oath and dare not testify.ᵍ

²⁵Fearʰ of man will prove to be a snare,
but whoever trusts in the LORDⁱ is kept safe.ʲ

²⁶Many seek an audience with a ruler,ᵏ
but it is from the LORD that man gets justice.ˡ

²⁷The righteous detest the dishonest;
the wicked detest the upright.ᵐ

Sayings of Agur

30 The sayingsⁿ of Agur son of Jakeh—an oracleᵃ:

This man declared to Ithiel,
to Ithiel and to Ucal:ᵇ

²"I am the most ignorant of men;
I do not have a man's understanding.

³I have not learned wisdom,
nor have I knowledge of the Holy One.ᵒ

⁴Who has gone upᵖ to heaven and come down?
Who has gathered up the wind in the hollowᵠ of his hands?
Who has wrapped up the watersʳ in his cloak?ˢ
Who has established all the ends of the earth?
What is his name,ᵗ and the name of his son?
Tell me if you know!

⁵"Every word of God is flawless;ᵘ
he is a shieldᵛ to those who take refuge in him.

⁶Do not addʷ to his words,
or he will rebuke you and prove you a liar.

⁷"Two things I ask of you, O LORD;
do not refuse me before I die:

⁸Keep falsehood and lies far from me;
give me neither poverty nor riches,
but give me only my daily bread.ˣ

⁹Otherwise, I may have too much and disownʸ you
and say, 'Who is the LORD?'ᶻ
Or I may become poor and steal,
and so dishonor the name of my God.ᵃ

29:11 ˢ S Job 15:13; ᵗ Pr 12:16
29:12 ᵘ 2Ki 21:9; ᵛ S Job 34:30
29:13 ʷ S Pr 22:2; Mt 5:45
29:14 ˣ S ver 4; Ps 72:1-5; S Pr 16:12
29:15 ʸ ver 17; S Pr 13:24
29:16 ᶻ S Ps 91:8; S 92:11
29:17 ᵃ S ver 15
29:18 ᵇ Ps 1:1-2; 19:11; 119:1-2
29:20 ᶜ Pr 19:2; 26:12
29:22 ᵈ S Pr 14:17
29:23 ᵉ Est 5:12; ᶠ S Pr 11:2; S 15:33; S 16:18
29:24 ᵍ S Lev 5:1
29:25 ʰ S Isa 15:24; ⁱ Pr 28:25; ʲ S Pr 16:20
29:26 ᵏ Pr 19:6; ˡ Pr 16:33
29:27 ᵐ S ver 10
30:1 ⁿ S Pr 22:17
30:3 ᵒ Pr 9:10
30:4 ᵖ Dt 30:12; Ps 24:1-2; S Pr 8:22-31; Jn 3:13; Eph 4:7-10; ᵠ Isa 40:12; ʳ Job 26:8 ˢ S Ge 1:2; ᵗ Rev 19:12
30:5 ᵘ S Ps 12:6; S 18:30 ᵛ S Ge 15:1
30:6 ʷ S Dt 4:2
30:8 ˣ Mt 6:11
30:9 ʸ Jos 24:27; Isa 1:4; 59:13; ᶻ Dt 6:12; 8:10-14; Hos 13:6; ᵃ S Dt 8:12

S Pr 29:25 ◀ ▶ Isa 32:18

F Ps 125:1 ◀ ▶ Isa 7:9
W Ps 145:18 ◀ ▶ Isa 1:18
S Pr 18:10 ◀ ▶ Pr 30:5

ᶻ 21 The meaning of the Hebrew for this word is uncertain. ᵃ 1 Or *Jakeh of Massa* ᵇ 1 Masoretic Text; with a different word division of the Hebrew declared, "I am weary, O God; / I am weary, O God, and faint.

¹⁰"Do not slander a servant to his master,
or he will curse you, and you will pay for it.

¹¹"There are those who curse their fathers
and do not bless their mothers;ᵇ
¹²those who are pure in their own eyesᶜ
and yet are not cleansed of their filth;ᵈ
¹³those whose eyes are ever so haughty,ᵉ
whose glances are so disdainful;
¹⁴those whose teethᶠ are swords
and whose jaws are set with knivesᵍ
to devourʰ the poorⁱ from the earth,
the needy from among mankind.ʲ

¹⁵"The leech has two daughters.
'Give! Give!' they cry.

"There are three things that are never satisfied,ᵏ
four that never say, 'Enough!':
¹⁶the grave,ᶜ¹ the barren womb,
land, which is never satisfied with water,
and fire, which never says, 'Enough!'

¹⁷"The eye that mocksᵐ a father,
that scorns obedience to a mother,
will be pecked out by the ravens of the valley,
will be eaten by the vultures.ⁿ

¹⁸"There are three things that are too amazing for me,
four that I do not understand:
¹⁹the way of an eagle in the sky,
the way of a snake on a rock,
the way of a ship on the high seas,
and the way of a man with a maiden.

²⁰"This is the way of an adulteress:
She eats and wipes her mouth
and says, 'I've done nothing wrong.'ᵒ

²¹"Under three things the earth trembles,
under four it cannot bear up:
²²a servant who becomes king,ᵖ
a fool who is full of food,
²³an unloved woman who is married,

and a maidservant who displaces her mistress.

²⁴"Four things on earth are small,
yet they are extremely wise:
²⁵Ants are creatures of little strength,
yet they store up their food in the summer;ᑫ
²⁶coneysᵈʳ are creatures of little power,
yet they make their home in the crags;
²⁷locustsˢ have no king,
yet they advance together in ranks;
²⁸a lizard can be caught with the hand,
yet it is found in kings' palaces.

²⁹"There are three things that are stately in their stride,
four that move with stately bearing:
³⁰a lion, mighty among beasts,
who retreats before nothing;
³¹a strutting rooster, a he-goat,
and a king with his army around him.ᵉ

³²"If you have played the fool and exalted yourself,
or if you have planned evil,
clap your hand over your mouth!ᵗ
³³For as churning the milk produces butter,
and as twisting the nose produces blood,
so stirring up anger produces strife."

Sayings of King Lemuel

31 The sayingsᵘ of King Lemuel—an oracleᶠ his mother taught him:

²"O my son, O son of my womb,
O son of my vows,ᵍᵛ
³do not spend your strength on women,
your vigor on those who ruin kings.ʷ

⁴"It is not for kings, O Lemuel—
not for kings to drink wine,ˣ
not for rulers to crave beer,
⁵lest they drinkʸ and forget what the law decrees,ᶻ
and deprive all the oppressed of their rights.
⁶Give beer to those who are perishing,
wineᵃ to those who are in anguish;
⁷let them drinkᵇ and forget their poverty

---

c 16 Hebrew *Sheol*   *d 26* That is, the hyrax or rock badger   *e 31* Or *king secure against revolt*   *f 1* Or *of Lemuel king of Massa, which*   *g 2* Or *I the answer to my prayers*

and remember their misery no
   more.
⁸"Speakᶜ up for those who cannot speak
   for themselves,
   for the rights of all who are
      destitute.
⁹Speak up and judge fairly;
   defend the rights of the poor and
      needy."ᵈ

Epilogue: The Wife of Noble Character

¹⁰ʰA wife of noble characterᵉ who can
      find?ᶠ
   She is worth far more than rubies.
¹¹Her husbandᵍ has full confidence in
      her
   and lacks nothing of value.ʰ
¹²She brings him good, not harm,
   all the days of her life.
¹³She selects wool and flax
   and works with eager hands.ⁱ
¹⁴She is like the merchant ships,
   bringing her food from afar.
¹⁵She gets up while it is still dark;
   she provides food for her family
   and portions for her servant girls.
¹⁶She considers a field and buys it;
   out of her earnings she plants a
      vineyard.
¹⁷She sets about her work vigorously;
   her arms are strong for her tasks.
¹⁸She sees that her trading is profitable,
   and her lamp does not go out at
      night.
¹⁹In her hand she holds the distaff
   and grasps the spindle with her
      fingers.
²⁰She opens her arms to the poor
   and extends her hands to the
      needy.ʲ
²¹When it snows, she has no fear for her
      household;
   for all of them are clothed in scarlet.
²²She makes coverings for her bed;
   she is clothed in fine linen and
      purple.
²³Her husband is respected at the city
      gate,
   where he takes his seat among the
      eldersᵏ of the land.
²⁴She makes linen garments and sells
      them,
   and supplies the merchants with
      sashes.
²⁵She is clothed with strength and
      dignity;
   she can laugh at the days to come.
²⁶She speaks with wisdom,
   and faithful instruction is on her
      tongue.ˡ
²⁷She watches over the affairs of her
      household
   and does not eat the bread of
      idleness.
²⁸Her children arise and call her blessed;
   her husband also, and he praises
      her:
²⁹"Many women do noble things,
   but you surpass them all."
³⁰Charm is deceptive, and beauty is
      fleeting;
   but a woman who fears the LORD is
      to be praised.
³¹Give her the reward she has earned,
   and let her works bring her praiseᵐ
      at the city gate.

31:8 ᶜS 1Sa 19:4
31:9 ᵈS Pr 24:23; 29:7
31:10 ᵉS Ru 3:11; S Pr 18:22 ᶠPr 8:35
31:11 ᵍS Ge 2:18 ʰS Pr 12:4
31:13 ⁱ1Ti 2:9-10
31:20 ʲDt 15:11
31:23 ᵏS Ex 3:16
31:26 ˡS Pr 10:31
31:31 ᵐPr 11:16

ʰ 10 Verses 10-31 are an acrostic, each verse beginning with a successive letter of the Hebrew alphabet.

Ecclesiastes

Author: King Solomon

Theme: Only a life centered on God has meaning

Date of Writing: c. 950 B.C.

Outline of Ecclesiastes
　I. Working for Gain Is Profitless (1:1–11)
　II. Enjoy God's Gift of Life (1:12—11:6)
　III. Enjoy Life While Young for God Will Judge (11:7—12:7)
　IV. Reverently Trust and Obey God (12:8–14)

THE BOOK OF Ecclesiastes identifies its author as "the Teacher," a title derived from the Hebrew word *qoheleth*. When scholars of the Septuagint (the Greek translation of the OT) translated this book, they titled it *ecclesiastes*, which is the Greek word meaning "teacher." Most English translations use the Septuagint title. Because several passages strongly suggest that King Solomon was "the Teacher," Jewish and Christian scholars traditionally ascribe authorship to him (see 1:1; 2:4–9; 7:26–29). Several references to Aramaic and Phoenician customs also help place this book in Solomon's time.

Included in the Jewish megilloth (a five-book grouping read aloud in the Jewish synagogues) and annually read during the Feast of the Tabernacles, Ecclesiastes measures life as a whole to determine its worth and significance. Examining the "vanity" and futility of wisdom, education, knowledge, pleasure, happiness, power, influence and religion, the author concludes that life is meaningless unless it is centered on a proper respect and reverence for God. The mood of the book is sad, mournful and depressed, intimating that these are the philosophical and theological reflections of an older person whose life "under the sun" (1:3) was meaningless because he had not relied on God. While unequaled wisdom, vast wealth, pleasure in abundance and ideal working conditions all have temporary value, the Teacher declares that these blessings have lasting value only when life is lived in obedience to God.

ECCLESIASTES 1:1

Everything Is Meaningless

1 The words of the Teacher,[a] son of David, king in Jerusalem:[b]

²"Meaningless! Meaningless!"
 says the Teacher.
"Utterly meaningless!
 Everything is meaningless."[c]

³What does man gain from all his labor
 at which he toils under the sun?[d]
⁴Generations come and generations go,
 but the earth remains forever.[e]
⁵The sun rises and the sun sets,
 and hurries back to where it rises.[f]
⁶The wind blows to the south
 and turns to the north;
round and round it goes,
 ever returning on its course.
⁷All streams flow into the sea,
 yet the sea is never full.
To the place the streams come from,
 there they return again.[g]
⁸All things are wearisome,
 more than one can say.
The eye never has enough of seeing,[h]
 nor the ear its fill of hearing.
⁹What has been will be again,
 what has been done will be done again;[i]
there is nothing new under the sun.
¹⁰Is there anything of which one can say,
 "Look! This is something new"?
It was here already, long ago;
 it was here before our time.
¹¹There is no remembrance of men of old,[j]
 and even those who are yet to come
will not be remembered
 by those who follow.[k]

Wisdom Is Meaningless

¹²I, the Teacher,[1] was king over Israel in Jerusalem.[m] ¹³I devoted myself to study and to explore by wisdom all that is done under heaven.[n] What a heavy burden God has laid on men![o] ¹⁴I have seen all the things that are done under the sun; all of them are meaningless, a chasing after the wind.[p]

¹⁵What is twisted cannot be
 straightened;[q]
what is lacking cannot be counted.

¹⁶I thought to myself, "Look, I have grown and increased in wisdom more than anyone who has ruled over Jerusalem before me;[r] I have experienced much of wisdom and knowledge." ¹⁷Then I applied myself to the understanding of wisdom,[s] and also of madness and folly,[t] but I learned that this, too, is a chasing after the wind.

¹⁸For with much wisdom comes much
 sorrow;[u]
the more knowledge, the more
 grief.[v]

Pleasures Are Meaningless

2 I thought in my heart, "Come now, I will test you with pleasure[w] to find out what is good." But that also proved to be meaningless. ²"Laughter,"[x] I said, "is foolish. And what does pleasure accomplish?" ³I tried cheering myself with wine,[y] and embracing folly[z]—my mind still guiding me with wisdom. I wanted to see what was worthwhile for men to do under heaven during the few days of their lives.

⁴I undertook great projects: I built houses for myself[a] and planted vineyards.[b] ⁵I made gardens and parks and planted all kinds of fruit trees in them. ⁶I made reservoirs to water groves of flourishing trees. ⁷I bought male and female slaves and had other slaves[c] who were born in my house. I also owned more herds and flocks than anyone in Jerusalem before me. ⁸I amassed silver and gold[d] for myself, and the treasure of kings and provinces.[e] I acquired men and

[a] 1 Or *leader of the assembly*; also in verses 2 and 12

1:1 ᵃver 12; Ecc 7:27; 12:10
ᵇS Pr 1:1
1:2 ᶜPs 39:5-6; 62:9; Ecc 12:8; Ro 8:20-21
1:3 ᵈEcc 2:11,22; 3:9; 5:15-16
1:4 ᵉS Job 8:19
1:5 ᶠPs 19:5-6
1:7 ᵍJob 36:28
1:8 ʰPr 27:20
1:9 ⁱEcc 2:12; 3:15
1:11 ʲGe 40:23; Ecc 9:15 ᵏPs 88:12; Ecc 2:16; 8:10; 9:5
1:12 ˡS ver 1 ᵐEcc 2:9
1:13 ⁿS Job 28:3 ᵒS Ge 3:17; Ecc 3:10
1:14 ᵖEcc 2:11,17; 4:4; 6:9
1:15 ᵠEcc 7:13
1:16 ʳS 1Ki 3:12
1:17 ˢEcc 7:23; 8:16 ᵗEcc 2:3,12; 7:25
1:18 ᵘJer 45:3 ᵛEcc 2:23; 12:12
2:1 ʷver 24; Ecc 7:4; 8:15
2:2 ˣS Pr 14:13
2:3 ʸver 24-25; S Jdg 9:13; Ru 3:3; Ecc 3:12-13; 5:18; 8:15 ᶻS Ecc 1:17
2:4 ᵃ2Ch 2:1; 8:1-6 ᵇSS 8:11
2:7 ᶜ2Ch 8:7-8
2:8 ᵈ1Ki 9:28 ᵉS Jdg 3:15

N Pr 10:30 ◀ ▶ Isa 65:16–18
G Pr 28:26 ◀ ▶ Isa 28:15–20

1:4 Solomon declared that "the earth remains forever," indicating that by contrast, humanity's lifespan is fleeting.

1:6 When Solomon described these circular wind patterns he was accurately describing the major patterns of global weather that scientists have only recently been able to verify with satellite photos—another marvelous confirmation of the divine inspiration of Scripture.

1:7 This verse describes the hydrological cycle that governs evaporation, cloud formation and precipitation. Even Job was familiar with this water cycle (see Job 26:27–33).

women singers,ʳ and a harem*ᵇ* as well—
the delights of the heart of man. ⁹I became greater by far than anyone in Jerusalem*ᵍ* before me.ʰ In all this my wisdom
stayed with me.

¹⁰I denied myself nothing my eyes
  desired;
  I refused my heart no pleasure.
  My heart took delight in all my work,
  and this was the reward for all my
  labor.
¹¹Yet when I surveyed all that my hands
  had done
  and what I had toiled to achieve,
  everything was meaningless, a chasing
  after the wind;ⁱ
  nothing was gained under the sun.ʲ

Wisdom and Folly Are Meaningless

¹²Then I turned my thoughts to consider
  wisdom,
  and also madness and folly.ᵏ
What more can the king's successor do
  than what has already been done?ˡ
¹³I saw that wisdomᵐ is better than
  folly,ⁿ
  just as light is better than darkness.
¹⁴The wise man has eyes in his head,
  while the fool walks in the darkness;
  but I came to realize
  that the same fate overtakes them
  both.ᵒ

¹⁵Then I thought in my heart,
"The fate of the fool will overtake me
  also.
  What then do I gain by being
  wise?"ᵖ
I said in my heart,
"This too is meaningless."
¹⁶For the wise man, like the fool, will
  not be long remembered;ᑫ
  in days to come both will be
  forgotten.ʳ
Like the fool, the wise man too must
  die!ˢ

Toil Is Meaningless

¹⁷So I hated life, because the work that
is done under the sun was grievous to
me. All of it is meaningless, a chasing after the wind.ᵗ ¹⁸I hated all the things I
had toiled for under the sun, because I
must leave them to the one who comes
after me.ᵘ ¹⁹And who knows whether he
will be a wise man or a fool?ᵛ Yet he will
have control over all the work into which

2:8 ʳS 2Sa 19:35
2:9 ᵍEcc 1:12
 ʰ1Ch 29:25
2:11 ⁱS Ecc 1:14
 ʲS Ecc 1:3
2:12 ᵏS Ecc 1:17
 ˡS Ecc 1:9
2:13 ᵐEcc 7:19;
9:18 ⁿEcc 7:11-12
2:14 ᵒPs 49:10;
Ecc 3:19; 6:6; 7:2;
9:3,11-12
2:15 ᵖver 19;
Ecc 6:8
2:16 ᑫS Ps 112:6
 ʳS Ecc 1:11
 ˢPs 49:10
2:17 ᵗS Ecc 1:14
2:18 ᵘPs 39:6;
49:10
2:19 ᵛS ver 15
2:22 ʷS Ecc 1:3
2:23 ˣS Ecc 1:18
 ʸGe 3:17;
S Job 7:2
2:24 ᶻver 3;
1Co 15:32 ᵃS ver 1;
Ecc 3:22
 ᵇS Job 2:10;
Ecc 3:12-13;
5:17-19; 7:14;
9:7-10; 11:7-10
2:25 ᶜS Ps 127:2
2:26 ᵈS Job 9:4
 ᵉS Job 27:17
 ᶠS Pr 13:22
3:1 ᵍver 11,17;
Ecc 8:6
3:2 ʰIsa 28:24
3:3 ⁱS Dt 5:17
3:7 ʲS Est 4:14

I have poured my effort and skill under
the sun. This too is meaningless. ²⁰So my
heart began to despair over all my toilsome labor under the sun. ²¹For a man
may do his work with wisdom, knowledge and skill, and then he must leave all
he owns to someone who has not worked
for it. This too is meaningless and a great
misfortune. ²²What does a man get for all
the toil and anxious striving with which
he labors under the sun?ʷ ²³All his days
his work is pain and grief;ˣ even at night
his mind does not rest.ʸ This too is meaningless.

²⁴A man can do nothing better than to
eat and drinkᶻ and find satisfaction in his
work.ᵃ This too, I see, is from the hand
of God,ᵇ ²⁵for without him, who can eat
or find enjoyment?ᶜ ²⁶To the man who
pleases him, God gives wisdom,ᵈ knowledge and happiness, but to the sinner he
gives the task of gathering and storing up
wealthᵉ to hand it over to the one who
pleases God.ᶠ This too is meaningless, a
chasing after the wind.

A Time for Everything

3 There is a timeᵍ for everything,
  and a season for every activity under
  heaven:

² a time to be born and a time to die,
  a time to plant and a time to
    uproot,ʰ
³ a time to killⁱ and a time to heal,
  a time to tear down and a time to
    build,
⁴ a time to weep and a time to laugh,
  a time to mourn and a time to
    dance,
⁵ a time to scatter stones and a time to
    gather them,
  a time to embrace and a time to
    refrain,
⁶ a time to search and a time to give
    up,
  a time to keep and a time to throw
    away,
⁷ a time to tear and a time to mend,
  a time to be silentʲ and a time to
    speak,
⁸ a time to love and a time to hate,
  a time for war and a time for peace.

P *Pr 28:27* ◀ ▶ *Ecc 5:19*
U *Pr 28:25* ◀ ▶ *Ecc 7:18*

ᵇ 8 The meaning of the Hebrew for this phrase is uncertain.

⁹What does the worker gain from his toil?ᵏ ¹⁰I have seen the burden God has laid on men.ˡ ¹¹He has made everything beautiful in its time.ᵐ He has also set eternity in the hearts of men; yet they cannot fathomⁿ what God has done from beginning to end.ᵒ ¹²I know that there is nothing better for men than to be happy and do good while they live. ¹³That everyone may eat and drink,ᵖ and find satisfactionᑫ in all his toil—this is the gift of God.ʳ ¹⁴I know that everything God does will endure forever; nothing can be added to it and nothing taken from it. God does it so that men will revere him.ˢ

¹⁵Whatever is has already been,ᵗ
and what will be has been before;ᵘ
and God will call the past to account.ᶜ

¹⁶And I saw something else under the sun:

In the place of judgment—wickedness was there,
in the place of justice—wickedness was there.

¹⁷I thought in my heart,

"God will bring to judgmentᵛ
both the righteous and the wicked,
for there will be a time for every activity,
a time for every deed."ʷ

¹⁸I also thought, "As for men, God tests them so that they may see that they are like the animals.ˣ ¹⁹Man's fateʸ is like that of the animals; the same fate awaits them both: As one dies, so dies the other. All have the same breathᵈ; man has no advantage over the animal. Everything is meaningless. ²⁰All go to the same place; all come from dust, and to dust all return.ᶻ ²¹Who knows if the spirit of man rises upwardᵃ and if the spirit of the animalᵉ goes down into the earth?"

²²So I saw that there is nothing better for a man than to enjoy his work,ᵇ because that is his lot.ᶜ For who can bring him to see what will happen after him?

J Ps 87:4–6 ◀▶ Ecc 11:9
J Ps 98:9 ◀▶ Ecc 11:9

3:9 ᵏ S Ecc 1:3
3:10 ˡ S Ecc 1:13
3:11 ᵐ S ver 1; ⁿ S Job 11:7; ᵒ S Job 28:23; Ro 11:33
3:13 ᵖ Ecc 2:3; ᑫ Ps 34:12; ʳ S Dt 12:7,18; S Ecc 2:24
3:14 ˢ S Job 23:15; Ecc 5:7; 7:18; 8:12-13
3:15 ᵗ Ecc 6:10; ᵘ S Ecc 1:9
3:17 ᵛ S Job 19:29; Ecc 11:9; 12:14; ʷ ver 1
3:18 ˣ S Ps 73:22
3:19 ʸ S Ecc 2:14
3:20 ᶻ S Ge 2:7; S Job 34:15
3:21 ᵃ Ecc 12:7
3:22 ᵇ S Ecc 2:24; ᶜ S Job 31:2
4:1 ᵈ S Ps 12:5; ᵉ La 1:16
4:2 ᶠ Jer 20:17-18; 22:10 ᵍ S Job 3:17; S 10:18
4:3 ʰ S Job 3:16; ⁱ S Job 3:22
4:4 ʲ S Ecc 1:14
4:5 ᵏ S Pr 6:10
4:6 ˡ Pr 15:16-17; S 16:8
4:8 ᵐ Pr 27:20

Oppression, Toil, Friendlessness

4 Again I looked and saw all the oppressionᵈ that was taking place under the sun:

I saw the tears of the oppressed—
and they have no comforter;
power was on the side of their oppressors—
and they have no comforter.ᵉ
²And I declared that the dead,ᶠ
who had already died,
are happier than the living,
who are still alive.ᵍ
³But better than both
is he who has not yet been,ʰ
who has not seen the evil
that is done under the sun.ⁱ

⁴And I saw that all labor and all achievement spring from man's envy of his neighbor. This too is meaningless, a chasing after the wind.ʲ

⁵The fool folds his handsᵏ
and ruins himself.
⁶Better one handful with tranquillity
than two handfuls with toilˡ
and chasing after the wind.

⁷Again I saw something meaningless under the sun:

⁸There was a man all alone;
he had neither son nor brother.
There was no end to his toil,
yet his eyes were not contentᵐ with his wealth.
"For whom am I toiling," he asked,
"and why am I depriving myself of enjoyment?"
This too is meaningless—
a miserable business!

⁹Two are better than one,
because they have a good return for their work:
¹⁰If one falls down,
his friend can help him up.
But pity the man who falls
and has no one to help him up!
¹¹Also, if two lie down together, they will keep warm.
But how can one keep warm alone?
¹²Though one may be overpowered,
two can defend themselves.

ᶜ 15 Or *God calls back the past*   ᵈ 19 Or *spirit*   ᵉ 21 Or *Who knows the spirit of man, which rises upward, or the spirit of the animal, which*

A cord of three strands is not quickly broken.

Advancement Is Meaningless

¹³Better a poor but wise youth than an old but foolish king who no longer knows how to take warning. ¹⁴The youth may have come from prison to the kingship, or he may have been born in poverty within his kingdom. ¹⁵I saw that all who lived and walked under the sun followed the youth, the king's successor. ¹⁶There was no end to all the people who were before them. But those who came later were not pleased with the successor. This too is meaningless, a chasing after the wind.

Stand in Awe of God

5 Guard your steps when you go to the house of God. Go near to listen rather than to offer the sacrifice of fools, who do not know that they do wrong.

²Do not be quick with your mouth,
  do not be hasty in your heart
  to utter anything before God.ⁿ
God is in heaven
  and you are on earth,
  so let your words be few.°
³As a dreamᵖ comes when there are many cares,
  so the speech of a fool when there are many words.ᑫ

⁴When you make a vow to God, do not delay in fulfilling it.ʳ He has no pleasure in fools; fulfill your vow.ˢ ⁵It is better not to vow than to make a vow and not fulfill it.ᵗ ⁶Do not let your mouth lead you into sin. And do not protest to the ⌊temple⌋ messenger, "My vow was a mistake." Why should God be angry at what you say and destroy the work of your hands? ⁷Much dreaming and many words are meaningless. Therefore stand in awe of God.ᵘ

Riches Are Meaningless

⁸If you see the poor oppressedᵛ in a district, and justice and rights denied, do not be surprised at such things; for one official is eyed by a higher one, and over them both are others higher still. ⁹The increase from the land is taken by all; the king himself profits from the fields.

¹⁰Whoever loves money never has money enough;
  whoever loves wealth is never satisfied with his income.
  This too is meaningless.

¹¹As goods increase,
  so do those who consume them.
And what benefit are they to the owner
  except to feast his eyes on them?

¹²The sleep of a laborer is sweet,
  whether he eats little or much,
but the abundance of a rich man
  permits him no sleep.ʷ

¹³I have seen a grievous evil under the sun:ˣ

wealth hoarded to the harm of its owner,
¹⁴ or wealth lost through some misfortune,
so that when he has a son
  there is nothing left for him.
¹⁵Naked a man comes from his mother's womb,
  and as he comes, so he departs.ʸ
He takes nothing from his laborᶻ
  that he can carry in his hand.ᵃ

¹⁶This too is a grievous evil:

As a man comes, so he departs,
  and what does he gain,
  since he toils for the wind?ᵇ
¹⁷All his days he eats in darkness,
  with great frustration, affliction and anger.

¹⁸Then I realized that it is good and proper for a man to eat and drink,ᶜ and to find satisfaction in his toilsome laborᵈ under the sun during the few days of life God has given him—for this is his lot. ¹⁹Moreover, when God gives any man ᴾ wealth and possessions,ᵉ and enables him to enjoy them,ᶠ to accept his lotᵍ and be happy in his work—this is a gift of God.ʰ ²⁰He seldom reflects on the days of his life, because God keeps him occupied with gladness of heart.ⁱ

6 I have seen another evil under the sun, and it weighs heavily on men: ²God gives a man wealth, possessions and honor, so that he lacks nothing his heart desires, but God does not enable him to enjoy them,ʲ and a stranger enjoys them

ᴾ *Ecc 2:26* ◄ ► *Ecc 11:1*

ECCLESIASTES 6:3

instead. This is meaningless, a grievous evil.ᵏ

³A man may have a hundred children and live many years; yet no matter how long he lives, if he cannot enjoy his prosperity and does not receive proper burial, I say that a stillborn¹ child is better off than he.ᵐ ⁴It comes without meaning, it departs in darkness, and in darkness its name is shrouded. ⁵Though it never saw the sun or knew anything, it has more rest than does that man— ⁶even if he lives a thousand years twice over but fails to enjoy his prosperity. Do not all go to the same place?ⁿ

⁷All man's efforts are for his mouth,
  yet his appetite is never satisfied.ᵒ
⁸What advantage has a wise man
    over a fool?ᵖ
  What does a poor man gain
    by knowing how to conduct himself
      before others?
⁹Better what the eye sees
    than the roving of the appetite.
  This too is meaningless,
    a chasing after the wind.ᵠ

¹⁰Whatever exists has already been named,ʳ
  and what man is has been known;
  no man can contend
    with one who is stronger than he.
¹¹The more the words,
    the less the meaning,
    and how does that profit anyone?

¹²For who knows what is good for a man in life, during the few and meaningless daysˢ he passes through like a shadow?ᵗ Who can tell him what will happen under the sun after he is gone?

Wisdom

7 A good name is better than fine perfume,ᵘ
    and the day of death better than the day of birth.ᵛ
² It is better to go to a house of mourning
    than to go to a house of feasting,
    for deathʷ is the destinyˣ of every man;
    the living should take this to heart.
³ Sorrow is better than laughter,ʸ
    because a sad face is good for the heart.

6:2 ᵏEcc 5:13
6:3 ˡS Job 3:16
    ᵐS Job 3:3
6:6 ⁿEcc 2:14
6:7 ᵒS Pr 27:20
6:8 ᵖS Ecc 2:15
6:9 ᵠS Ecc 1:14
6:10 ʳEcc 3:15
6:12 ˢS Job 10:20;
     S 20:8
     ᵗS 1Ch 29:15;
     S Job 14:2;
     S Ps 39:6
7:1 ᵘPr 22:1;
    SS 1:3 ᵛS Job 10:18
7:2 ʷS Pr 11:19
    ˣS Ecc 2:14
7:3 ʸS Pr 14:13
7:4 ᶻS Ecc 2:1;
    Jer 16:8
7:5 ᵃS Pr 13:18;
    15:31-32
7:6 ᵇS Ps 58:9
    ᶜS Pr 14:13
7:7 ᵈS Ex 18:21;
    S 23:8
7:8 ᵉPr 14:29
7:9 ᶠS Mt 5:22
    ᵍS Pr 14:29
7:10 ʰS Ps 77:5
7:11 ⁱEcc 2:13
     ʲEcc 11:5
7:13 ᵏEcc 2:24
     ˡEcc 1:15
7:14 ᵐS Job 1:21;
     S Ecc 2:24
7:15 ⁿS Job 7:7
     ᵒS Job 21:7;
     Ecc 8:12-14;
     Jer 12:1

⁴The heart of the wise is in the house of mourning,
  but the heart of fools is in the house of pleasure.ᶻ
⁵It is better to heed a wise man's rebukeᵃ
  than to listen to the song of fools.
⁶Like the crackling of thornsᵇ under the pot,
  so is the laughterᶜ of fools.
  This too is meaningless.

⁷Extortion turns a wise man into a fool,
    and a bribeᵈ corrupts the heart.
⁸The end of a matter is better than its beginning,
    and patienceᵉ is better than pride.
⁹Do not be quickly provokedᶠ in your spirit,
    for anger resides in the lap of fools.ᵍ
¹⁰Do not say, "Why were the old daysʰ better than these?"
    For it is not wise to ask such questions.

¹¹Wisdom, like an inheritance, is a good thingⁱ
    and benefits those who see the sun.ʲ
¹²Wisdom is a shelter
    as money is a shelter,
  but the advantage of knowledge is this:
    that wisdom preserves the life of its possessor.

¹³Consider what God has done:ᵏ ᵒ

Who can straighten
    what he has made crooked?ˡ

¹⁴When times are good, be happy; ᵀ
    but when times are bad, consider:
  God has made the one
    as well as the other.ᵐ
  Therefore, a man cannot discover
    anything about his future.

¹⁵In this meaningless lifeⁿ of mine I have seen both of these:
  a righteous man perishing in his righteousness,
  and a wicked man living long in his wickedness.ᵒ
¹⁶Do not be overrighteous,
    neither be overwise—
    why destroy yourself?
¹⁷Do not be overwicked,

ᵒ Pr 19:21 ◄► Isa 43:11
ᵀ Pr 25:4 ◄► Isa 48:10

and do not be a fool—
    why die before your time?^p
¹⁸It is good to grasp the one
    and not let go of the other.
    The man who fears God^q will avoid
        all ⌊extremes⌋.^f

¹⁹Wisdom^r makes one wise man more
        powerful^s
    than ten rulers in a city.

²⁰There is not a righteous man^t on earth
    who does what is right and never
        sins.^u

²¹Do not pay attention to every word
        people say,
    or you^v may hear your servant
        cursing you—
²²for you know in your heart
    that many times you yourself have
        cursed others.

²³All this I tested by wisdom and I said,

"I am determined to be wise"^w—
    but this was beyond me.
²⁴Whatever wisdom may be,
    it is far off and most profound—
    who can discover it?^x
²⁵So I turned my mind to understand,
    to investigate and to search out
        wisdom and the scheme of
        things^y
    and to understand the stupidity of
        wickedness
    and the madness of folly.^z

²⁶I find more bitter than death
    the woman who is a snare,^a
    whose heart is a trap
        and whose hands are chains.
    The man who pleases God will escape
        her,
    but the sinner she will ensnare.^b

²⁷"Look," says the Teacher,^{gc} "this is what I have discovered:

"Adding one thing to another to
        discover the scheme of
        things—
²⁸ while I was still searching
    but not finding—
    I found one ⌊upright⌋ man among a
        thousand,
    but not one ⌊upright⌋ woman^d among
        them all.

²⁹This only have I found:
    God made mankind upright,
    but men have gone in search of
        many schemes."

8 Who is like the wise man?
    Who knows the explanation of
        things?
Wisdom brightens a man's face
    and changes its hard appearance.

Obey the King

²Obey the king's command, I say, because you took an oath before God. ³Do not be in a hurry to leave the king's presence.^e Do not stand up for a bad cause, for he will do whatever he pleases. ⁴Since a king's word is supreme, who can say to him, "What are you doing?^f"

⁵Whoever obeys his command will
        come to no harm,
    and the wise heart will know the
        proper time and procedure.
⁶For there is a proper time and
        procedure for every matter,^g
    though a man's misery weighs
        heavily upon him.

⁷Since no man knows the future,
    who can tell him what is to come?
⁸No man has power over the wind to
        contain it^h;
    so no one has power over the day of
        his death.
As no one is discharged in time of war,
    so wickedness will not release those
        who practice it.

⁹All this I saw, as I applied my mind to everything done under the sun. There is a time when a man lords it over others to his ownⁱ hurt. ¹⁰Then too, I saw the wicked buried^h—those who used to come and go from the holy place and receive praise^j in the city where they did this. This too is meaningless.

¹¹When the sentence for a crime is not quickly carried out, the hearts of the people are filled with schemes to do wrong.

---

^f 18 Or *will follow them both* ^g 27 Or *leader of the assembly* ^h 8 Or *over his spirit to retain it* ⁱ 9 Or *to their* ^j 10 Some Hebrew manuscripts and Septuagint (Aquila); most Hebrew manuscripts *and are forgotten*

¹²Although a wicked man commits a hundred crimes and still lives a long time, I know that it will go better with God-fearing men, who are reverent before God. ¹³Yet because the wicked do not fear God, it will not go well with them, and their days will not lengthen like a shadow.

¹⁴There is something else meaningless that occurs on earth: righteous men who get what the wicked deserve, and wicked men who get what the righteous deserve. This too, I say, is meaningless. ¹⁵So I commend the enjoyment of life, because nothing is better for a man under the sun than to eat and drink and be glad. Then joy will accompany him in his work all the days of the life God has given him under the sun.

¹⁶When I applied my mind to know wisdom and to observe man's labor on earth—his eyes not seeing sleep day or night— ¹⁷then I saw all that God has done. No one can comprehend what goes on under the sun. Despite all his efforts to search it out, man cannot discover its meaning. Even if a wise man claims he knows, he cannot really comprehend it.

A Common Destiny for All

9 So I reflected on all this and concluded that the righteous and the wise and what they do are in God's hands, but no man knows whether love or hate awaits him. ²All share a common destiny—the righteous and the wicked, the good and the bad, the clean and the unclean, those who offer sacrifices and those who do not.

As it is with the good man,
  so with the sinner;
as it is with those who take oaths,
  so with those who are afraid to take them.

³This is the evil in everything that happens under the sun: The same destiny overtakes all. The hearts of men, moreover, are full of evil and there is madness in their hearts while they live, and afterward they join the dead. ⁴Anyone who is among the living has hope—even a live dog is better off than a dead lion!

⁵For the living know that they will die,

but the dead know nothing;
they have no further reward,
  and even the memory of them is forgotten.
⁶Their love, their hate
  and their jealousy have long since vanished;
never again will they have a part
  in anything that happens under the sun.

⁷Go, eat your food with gladness, and drink your wine with a joyful heart, for it is now that God favors what you do. ⁸Always be clothed in white, and always anoint your head with oil. ⁹Enjoy life with your wife, whom you love, all the days of this meaningless life that God has given you under the sun—all your meaningless days. For this is your lot in life and in your toilsome labor under the sun. ¹⁰Whatever your hand finds to do, do it with all your might, for in the grave, where you are going, there is neither working nor planning nor knowledge nor wisdom.

¹¹I have seen something else under the sun:

The race is not to the swift
  or the battle to the strong,
nor does food come to the wise
  or wealth to the brilliant
  or favor to the learned;
but time and chance happen to them all.

¹²Moreover, no man knows when his hour will come:

As fish are caught in a cruel net,
  or birds are taken in a snare,
so men are trapped by evil times
  that fall unexpectedly upon them.

Wisdom Better Than Folly

¹³I also saw under the sun this example of wisdom that greatly impressed me: ¹⁴There was once a small city with only a few people in it. And a powerful king came against it, surrounded it and built huge siegeworks against it. ¹⁵Now there lived in that city a man poor but wise,

k 2 Septuagint (Aquila), Vulgate and Syriac; Hebrew does not have and the bad. 14 Or What then is to be chosen? With all who live, there is hope m 10 Hebrew Sheol

and he saved the city by his wisdom. But nobody remembered that poor man.ᵛ ¹⁶So I said, "Wisdom is better than strength." But the poor man's wisdom is despised, and his words are no longer heeded.ʷ

¹⁷The quiet words of the wise are more to be heeded
than the shouts of a ruler of fools.
¹⁸Wisdomˣ is better than weapons of war,
but one sinner destroys much good.

10 As dead flies give perfume a bad smell,
so a little follyʸ outweighs wisdom and honor.
²The heart of the wise inclines to the right,
but the heart of the fool to the left.
³Even as he walks along the road,
the fool lacks sense
and shows everyoneᶻ how stupid he is.
⁴If a ruler's anger rises against you,
do not leave your post;ᵃ
calmness can lay great errors to rest.ᵇ

⁵There is an evil I have seen under the sun,
the sort of error that arises from a ruler:
⁶Fools are put in many high positions,ᶜ
while the rich occupy the low ones.
⁷I have seen slaves on horseback,
while princes go on foot like slaves.ᵈ

⁸Whoever digs a pit may fall into it;ᵉ
whoever breaks through a wall may be bitten by a snake.ᶠ
⁹Whoever quarries stones may be injured by them;
whoever splits logs may be endangered by them.ᵍ

¹⁰If the ax is dull
and its edge unsharpened,
more strength is needed
but skill will bring success.
¹¹If a snake bites before it is charmed,
there is no profit for the charmer.ʰ

¹²Words from a wise man's mouth are gracious,ⁱ

c *Ecc 9:3* ◀ ▶ *Isa 1:4–6*

9:15 ᵛS Ge 40:14; S Ecc 1:11
9:16 ʷEst 6:3
9:18 ˣS Ecc 2:13
10:1 ʸPr 13:16; 18:2
10:3 ᶻPr 13:16
10:4 ᵃEcc 8:3
ᵇS Pr 16:14
10:6 ᶜS Pr 29:2
10:7 ᵈPr 19:10
10:8 ᵉS Ps 57:6
ᶠS Est 2:23; Ps 9:16; Am 5:19
10:9 ᵍS Pr 26:27
10:11 ʰS Ps 58:5; S Isa 3:3
10:12 ⁱPr 10:32
ʲS Pr 10:6; S 14:3; S 15:2; S 18:7
10:14 ᵏEcc 5:3
ˡEcc 9:1
10:16 ᵐIsa 3:4-5, 12
10:17 ⁿS Dt 14:26; S 1Sa 25:36; S Pr 31:4
10:18 ᵒPr 20:4; S 24:30-34
10:19 ᵖS Ge 14:18; S Jdg 9:13
10:20 ᵠS Ex 22:28
11:1 ʳver 6; Isa 32:20; Hos 10:12
ˢS Dt 24:19

but a fool is consumed by his own lips.ʲ
¹³At the beginning his words are folly;
at the end they are wicked madness—
¹⁴ and the fool multiplies words.ᵏ

No one knows what is coming—
who can tell him what will happen after him?ˡ

¹⁵A fool's work wearies him;
he does not know the way to town.

¹⁶Woe to you, O land whose king was a servant ⁿᵐ
and whose princes feast in the morning.
¹⁷Blessed are you, O land whose king is of noble birth
and whose princes eat at a proper time—
for strength and not for drunkenness.ⁿ

¹⁸If a man is lazy, the rafters sag;
if his hands are idle, the house leaks.ᵒ

¹⁹A feast is made for laughter,
and wineᵖ makes life merry,
but money is the answer for everything.

²⁰Do not revile the kingᵠ even in your thoughts,
or curse the rich in your bedroom,
because a bird of the air may carry your words,
and a bird on the wing may report what you say.

Bread Upon the Waters

11 Castʳ your bread upon the waters,
for after many days you will find it again.ˢ
²Give portions to seven, yes to eight,
for you do not know what disaster may come upon the land.

³If clouds are full of water,
they pour rain upon the earth.
Whether a tree falls to the south or to the north,
in the place where it falls, there will it lie.

P *Ecc 5:19* ◀ ▶ *Hos 2:8*

n 16 Or *king is a child*

⁴Whoever watches the wind will not plant;
  whoever looks at the clouds will not reap.

⁵As you do not know the path of the wind,ᵗ
  or how the body is formedᵒ in a mother's womb,ᵘ
so you cannot understand the work of God,
  the Maker of all things.

⁶Sow your seed in the morning,
  and at evening let not your hands be idle,ᵛ
for you do not know which will succeed,
  whether this or that,
  or whether both will do equally well.

Remember Your Creator While Young

⁷Light is sweet,
  and it pleases the eyes to see the sun.ʷ
⁸However many years a man may live,
  let him enjoy them all.
But let him rememberˣ the days of darkness,
  for they will be many.
  Everything to come is meaningless.

J ⁹Be happy, young man, while you are young,
J   and let your heart give you joy in the days of your youth.
Follow the ways of your heart
  and whatever your eyes see,
but know that for all these things God will bring you to judgment.ʸ

¹⁰So then, banish anxietyᶻ from your heart
  and cast off the troubles of your body,
for youth and vigor are meaningless.ᵃ

N **12** Rememberᵇ your Creator
  in the days of your youth,
before the days of troubleᶜ come
  and the years approach when you will say,
  "I find no pleasure in them"—
²before the sun and the light

and the moon and the stars grow dark,
  and the clouds return after the rain;
³when the keepers of the house tremble,
  and the strong men stoop,
when the grinders cease because they are few,
  and those looking through the windows grow dim;
⁴when the doors to the street are closed
  and the sound of grinding fades;
when men rise up at the sound of birds,
  but all their songs grow faint;ᵈ
⁵when men are afraid of heights
  and of dangers in the streets;
when the almond tree blossoms
  and the grasshopper drags himself along
  and desire no longer is stirred.
Then man goes to his eternal homeᵉ
  and mournersᶠ go about the streets.

⁶Remember him—before the silver cord is severed,
  or the golden bowl is broken;
before the pitcher is shattered at the spring,
  or the wheel broken at the well,
⁷and the dust returnsᵍ to the ground it came from,
  and the spirit returns to Godʰ who gave it.ⁱ

⁸"Meaningless! Meaningless!" says the Teacher.ᵖʲ
  "Everything is meaningless!"ᵏ

The Conclusion of the Matter

⁹Not only was the Teacher wise, but also he imparted knowledge to the people. He pondered and searched out and set in order many proverbs.ˡ ¹⁰The Teacherᵐ searched to find just the right words, and what he wrote was upright and true.ⁿ ¹¹The words of the wise are like goads, their collected sayings like firmly embedded nailsᵒ—given by one Shepherd. ¹²Be warned, my son, of anything in addition to them.
  Of making many books there is no end, and much study wearies the body.ᵖ

J Ecc 3:17–18 ◀ ▶ Ecc 12:14
J Ecc 3:17 ◀ ▶ Ecc 12:14
N Ecc 9:10–12 ◀ ▶ Isa 26:10–11

ᵒ 5 Or *know how life* (or *the spirit*) / *enters the body being formed*
ᵖ 8 Or *the leader of the assembly*; also in verses 9 and 10

¹³Now all has been heard;
here is the conclusion of the matter:
Fear God^q and keep his
commandments,^r
for this is the whole ⌊duty⌋ of man.^s

¹⁴For God will bring every deed into
judgment,^t
including every hidden thing,^u
whether it is good or evil.

12:13
qS Ex 20:20; S 1Sa 12:24; S Job 23:15; S Ps 19:9 rS Dt 4:2
sS Dt 4:6; S Job 37:24

12:14
tS Job 19:29; S Ecc 3:17

S Pr 24:24 ◀▶ Isa 1:13–17

J Ecc 11:9 ◀▶ Isa 10:33–34
J Ecc 11:9 ◀▶ Da 7:9–10
uS Job 34:21; S Ps 19:12; Jer 16:17; 23:24

12:14 God will ultimately judge every act according to his righteousness.

Song of Songs

Author: Uncertain; possibly Solomon

Theme: Marital love mirrors God's love for his people

Date of Writing: c. 965 B.C.

Outline of Song of Songs
  I. Courtship (1:1—3:5)
  II. The Wedding Procession (3:6–11)
  III. Declarations of Love (4:1—5:1)
  IV. Conflict and Resolution (5:2—6:13)
  V. More Loving Words (7:1—8:4)
  VI. Conclusion (8:5–14)

THE TITLE IN Hebrew for this delightful love song is "Solomon's Song of Songs," meaning a great song by, for or about Solomon. After the opening verse, Solomon is mentioned five more times in the text (see 1:5; 3:9, 11; 8:11–12), adding credence to the early church recognition of Solomon's authorship of this short book. In addition, the numerous references to customs, local geography and nature fit the context of Solomon's day.

While there are no specific prophecies in Song of Songs, the book is nonetheless difficult to interpret. Some people view it literally, as a secular love song between Solomon and his bride, reflecting Solomon's actual experiences and expressing warm emotions of human love. This interpretation attaches little spiritual significance to the words or situations. Others understand the book to be a collection of love songs without a specific story to tell.

A third way to approach this love song is to view it allegorically, applying OT and NT types to each of the participants. In this way Solomon, the one who loves his chosen bride, is an OT type of God and a NT type of Christ, while the Shulamite bride, the one who resists her lover's advances, is an OT type of Israel and a NT type of the church. The whole love story becomes an allegory that depicts both God's love for Israel and Christ's love for the church. Scripture does treat Solomon as a type of Christ (see Ps 72; Mt 12:42) lending credence to this last interpretation. Yet whether interpreted by any of these means, the intent of Song of Songs is clear: Love is a precious gift that cannot be bought. "If one were to give all the wealth of his house for love, it would be utterly scorned" (8:7).

1

Solomon's Song of Songs.[a]

Beloved[a]

²Let him kiss me with the kisses of his mouth—
for your love[b] is more delightful than wine.[c]
³Pleasing is the fragrance of your perfumes;[d]
your name[e] is like perfume poured out.
No wonder the maidens[f] love you!
⁴Take me away with you—let us hurry!
Let the king bring me into his chambers.[g]

Friends

We rejoice and delight[h] in you[b];
we will praise your love[i] more than wine.

Beloved

How right they are to adore you!
⁵Dark am I, yet lovely,[j]
O daughters of Jerusalem,[k]
dark like the tents of Kedar,[l]
like the tent curtains of Solomon.[c]
⁶Do not stare at me because I am dark,
because I am darkened by the sun.
My mother's sons were angry with me
and made me take care of the vineyards;[m]
my own vineyard I have neglected.
⁷Tell me, you whom I love, where you graze your flock
and where you rest your sheep[n] at midday.
Why should I be like a veiled[o] woman
beside the flocks of your friends?

Friends

⁸If you do not know, most beautiful of women,[p]
follow the tracks of the sheep
and graze your young goats
by the tents of the shepherds.

Lover

⁹I liken you, my darling, to a mare
harnessed to one of the chariots[q] of Pharaoh.
¹⁰Your cheeks[r] are beautiful with earrings,
your neck with strings of jewels.[s]

¹¹We will make you earrings of gold,
studded with silver.

Beloved

¹²While the king was at his table,
my perfume spread its fragrance.[t]
¹³My lover is to me a sachet of myrrh[u]
resting between my breasts.
¹⁴My lover[v] is to me a cluster of henna[w] blossoms
from the vineyards of En Gedi.[x]

Lover

¹⁵How beautiful[y] you are, my darling!
Oh, how beautiful!
Your eyes are doves.[z]

Beloved

¹⁶How handsome you are, my lover![a]
Oh, how charming!
And our bed is verdant.

Lover

¹⁷The beams of our house are cedars;[b]
our rafters are firs.

Beloved[d]

2

I am a rose[e,c] of Sharon,[d]
a lily[e] of the valleys.

Lover

²Like a lily among thorns
is my darling among the maidens.

Beloved

³Like an apple tree among the trees of the forest
is my lover[f] among the young men.
I delight[g] to sit in his shade,
and his fruit is sweet to my taste.[h]
⁴He has taken me to the banquet hall,[i]
and his banner[j] over me is love.
⁵Strengthen me with raisins,
refresh me with apples,[k]
for I am faint with love.[l]
⁶His left arm is under my head,
and his right arm embraces me.[m]
⁷Daughters of Jerusalem, I charge you[n]

M Ps 132:11–18 ◀ ▶ SS 2:11–13
L Pr 18:24 ◀ ▶ SS 2:6
H SS 1:4 ◀ ▶ Isa 26:20–21
L SS 2:3–4 ◀ ▶ SS 4:9–10
C Ps 109:8 ◀ ▶ SS 2:17

H Ps 45:14–15 ◀ ▶ SS 2:4
T Ps 45:14–15 ◀ ▶ SS 2:10

---

[a] Primarily on the basis of the gender of the Hebrew pronouns used, male and female speakers are indicated in the margins by the captions *Lover* and *Beloved* respectively. The words of others are marked *Friends*. In some instances the divisions and their captions are debatable. [b] 4 The Hebrew is masculine singular. [c] 5 Or *Salma* [d] 1 Or *Lover* [e] 1 Possibly a member of the crocus family

by the gazelles and by the does of
    the field:
Do not arouse or awaken love
    until it so desires.°

⁸Listen! My lover!
    Look! Here he comes,
leaping across the mountains,
    bounding over the hills.ᵖ
⁹My lover is like a gazelleᵠ or a young
    stag.ʳ
Look! There he stands behind our
    wall,
gazing through the windows,
    peering through the lattice.

T ¹⁰My lover spoke and said to me,
"Arise, my darling,
    my beautiful one, and come with
        me.
M ¹¹See! The winter is past;
    the rains are over and gone.
¹²Flowers appear on the earth;
    the season of singing has come,
the cooing of doves
    is heard in our land.
¹³The fig tree forms its early fruit;ˢ
    the blossomingᵗ vines spread their
        fragrance.
Arise, come, my darling;
    my beautiful one, come with me."

Lover

¹⁴My doveᵘ in the clefts of the rock,
    in the hiding places on the
        mountainside,
show me your face,
    let me hear your voice;
for your voice is sweet,
    and your face is lovely.ᵛ
¹⁵Catch for us the foxes,ʷ
    the little foxes
that ruin the vineyards,ˣ
    our vineyards that are in bloom.ʸ

Beloved

¹⁶My lover is mine and I am his;ᶻ
    he browses among the lilies.ᵃ
C ¹⁷Until the day breaks
    and the shadows flee,ᵇ
turn, my lover,ᶜ
    and be like a gazelle
or like a young stagᵈ
    on the rugged hills.ᶠᵉ

T SS 1:4 ◀▶ SS 6:10
M SS 2:3–6 ◀▶ SS 4:16
C SS 2:7–8 ◀▶ SS 4:6

2:7 °SS 3:5; 8:4

2:8 ᵖver 17;
SS 8:14

2:9 ᵠS 2Sa 2:18
ʳver 17; SS 8:14

2:13 ˢIsa 28:4;
Jer 24:2; Hos 9:10;
Mic 7:1; Na 3:12
ᵗSS 7:12

2:14 ᵘS Ge 8:8;
S SS 1:15 ᵛS SS 1:5

2:15 ʷJdg 15:4
ˣS SS 1:6 ʸSS 7:12

2:16 ᶻSS 7:10
ᵃSS 4:5; 6:3

2:17 ᵇSS 4:6
ᶜS SS 1:14 ᵈS ver 9
ᵉS ver 8

3:1 ᶠSS 5:6

3:3 ᵍSS 5:7

3:4 ʰSS 8:2
ⁱSS 6:9; 8:5

3:5 ʲS SS 2:7
ᵏSS 8:4

3:6 ˡSS 8:5
ᵐSS 4:6,14
ⁿEx 30:34

3:7 °S 1Sa 8:11

3:8 ᵖS Job 15:22;
Ps 91:5

3:11 ᵠIsa 3:16;
4:4; 32:9-13

3 All night long on my bed
I lookedᶠ for the one my heart loves;
    I looked for him but did not find
        him.
²I will get up now and go about the
    city,
through its streets and squares;
I will search for the one my heart
    loves.
So I looked for him but did not find
    him.
³The watchmen found me
    as they made their rounds in the
        city.ᵍ
"Have you seen the one my heart
    loves?"
⁴Scarcely had I passed them
    when I found the one my heart
        loves.
I held him and would not let him go
    till I had brought him to my
        mother's house,ʰ
    to the room of the one who
        conceived me.ⁱ
⁵Daughters of Jerusalem, I charge youʲ
    by the gazelles and by the does of
        the field:
Do not arouse or awaken love
    until it so desires.ᵏ

⁶Who is this coming up from the
    desertˡ
like a column of smoke,
perfumed with myrrhᵐ and incense
    made from all the spicesⁿ of the
        merchant?
⁷Look! It is Solomon's carriage,
    escorted by sixty warriors,°
    the noblest of Israel,
⁸all of them wearing the sword,
    all experienced in battle,
each with his sword at his side,
    prepared for the terrors of the
        night.ᵖ
⁹King Solomon made for himself the
    carriage;
he made it of wood from Lebanon.
¹⁰Its posts he made of silver,
    its base of gold.
Its seat was upholstered with purple,
    its interior lovingly inlaid
byᵍ the daughters of Jerusalem.
¹¹Come out, you daughters of Zion,ᵠ
    and look at King Solomon wearing
        the crown,

ᶠ17 Or the hills of Bether ᵍ10 Or its inlaid interior a gift of love / from

the crown with which his mother
        crowned him
on the day of his wedding,
    the day his heart rejoiced.

Lover

4 How beautiful you are, my darling!
    Oh, how beautiful!
    Your eyes behind your veil are
        doves.
Your hair is like a flock of goats
    descending from Mount Gilead.
²Your teeth are like a flock of sheep just
        shorn,
    coming up from the washing.
Each has its twin;
    not one of them is alone.
³Your lips are like a scarlet ribbon;
    your mouth is lovely.
Your temples behind your veil
    are like the halves of a
        pomegranate.
⁴Your neck is like the tower of David,
    built with elegance;
on it hang a thousand shields,
    all of them shields of warriors.
⁵Your two breasts are like two fawns,
    like twin fawns of a gazelle
    that browse among the lilies.
⁶Until the day breaks
    and the shadows flee,
I will go to the mountain of myrrh
    and to the hill of incense.
⁷All beautiful you are, my darling;
    there is no flaw in you.

⁸Come with me from Lebanon, my
        bride,
    come with me from Lebanon.
Descend from the crest of Amana,
    from the top of Senir, the summit
        of Hermon,
from the lions' dens
    and the mountain haunts of the
        leopards.

⁹You have stolen my heart, my sister,
        my bride;
    you have stolen my heart
with one glance of your eyes,
    with one jewel of your necklace.
¹⁰How delightful is your love, my
        sister, my bride!
    How much more pleasing is your
        love than wine,
    and the fragrance of your perfume
        than any spice!

¹¹Your lips drop sweetness as the
        honeycomb, my bride;
    milk and honey are under your
        tongue.
The fragrance of your garments is
    like that of Lebanon.
¹²You are a garden locked up, my sister,
        my bride;
    you are a spring enclosed, a sealed
        fountain.
¹³Your plants are an orchard of
        pomegranates
    with choice fruits,
    with henna and nard,
¹⁴   nard and saffron,
    calamus and cinnamon,
    with every kind of incense tree,
    with myrrh and aloes
    and all the finest spices.
¹⁵You are a garden fountain,
    a well of flowing water
    streaming down from Lebanon.

Beloved

¹⁶Awake, north wind,
    and come, south wind!
Blow on my garden,
    that its fragrance may spread
        abroad.
Let my lover come into his garden
    and taste its choice fruits.

Lover

5 I have come into my garden, my
        sister, my bride;
    I have gathered my myrrh with my
        spice.
I have eaten my honeycomb and my
        honey;
    I have drunk my wine and my milk.

Friends

Eat, O friends, and drink;
    drink your fill, O lovers.

Beloved

²I slept but my heart was awake.
    Listen! My lover is knocking:
"Open to me, my sister, my darling,
    my dove, my flawless one.
My head is drenched with dew,
    my hair with the dampness of the
        night."

h 4 The meaning of the Hebrew for this word is uncertain. *i* 15 Or *I am* (spoken by the *Beloved*)

SONG OF SONGS 5:3

³I have taken off my robe—
　　must I put it on again?
I have washed my feet—
　　must I soil them again?
⁴My lover thrust his hand through the
　　　latch-opening;
　　my heart began to pound for him.
⁵I arose to open for my lover,
　　and my hands dripped with myrrh,°
my fingers with flowing myrrh,
　　on the handles of the lock.
⁶I opened for my lover,ᵖ
　　but my lover had left; he was gone.ᵠ
My heart sank at his departure.ʲ
I looked ʳ for him but did not find him.
　　I called him but he did not answer.
⁷The watchmen found me
　　as they made their rounds in the
　　　city.ˢ
They beat me, they bruised me;
　　they took away my cloak,
　　those watchmen of the walls!

⁸O daughters of Jerusalem, I charge
　　you ᵗ—
if you find my lover,ᵘ
what will you tell him?
Tell him I am faint with love.ᵛ

Friends

⁹How is your beloved better than
　　others,
　　most beautiful of women?ʷ
How is your beloved better than
　　others,
　　that you charge us so?

Beloved

¹⁰My lover is radiant and ruddy,
　　outstanding among ten thousand.ˣ
¹¹His head is purest gold;
　　his hair is wavy
　　and black as a raven.
¹²His eyes are like doves ʸ
　　by the water streams,
washed in milk,ᶻ
　　mounted like jewels.
¹³His cheeks ᵃ are like beds of spice ᵇ
　　yielding perfume.
His lips are like lilies ᶜ
　　dripping with myrrh.ᵈ
¹⁴His arms are rods of gold
　　set with chrysolite.
His body is like polished ivory
　　decorated with sapphires.ᵏ ᵉ
¹⁵His legs are pillars of marble

set on bases of pure gold.
His appearance is like Lebanon,ᶠ
　　choice as its cedars.
¹⁶His mouth ᵍ is sweetness itself;
　　he is altogether lovely.
This is my lover,ʰ this my friend,
O daughters of Jerusalem.ⁱ

Friends

6 Where has your lover ʲ gone,
　　most beautiful of women?ᵏ
Which way did your lover turn,
　　that we may look for him with you?

Beloved

²My lover has gone ˡ down to his
　　　garden,ᵐ
to the beds of spices,ⁿ
to browse in the gardens
　　and to gather lilies.
³I am my lover's and my lover is mine;°
　　he browses among the lilies.ᵖ

Lover

⁴You are beautiful, my darling, as
　　　Tirzah,ᵠ
lovely as Jerusalem,ʳ
majestic as troops with banners.ˢ
⁵Turn your eyes from me;
　　they overwhelm me.
Your hair is like a flock of goats
　　descending from Gilead.ᵗ
⁶Your teeth are like a flock of sheep
　　coming up from the washing.
Each has its twin,
　　not one of them is alone.ᵘ
⁷Your temples behind your veil ᵛ
　　are like the halves of a
　　　pomegranate.ʷ
⁸Sixty queens ˣ there may be,
　　and eighty concubines,ʸ
　　and virgins beyond number;
⁹but my dove,ᶻ my perfect one,ᵃ is
　　　unique,
the only daughter of her mother,
the favorite of the one who bore
　　her.ᵇ
The maidens saw her and called her
　　blessed;
the queens and concubines praised
　　her.

Friends

¹⁰Who is this that appears like the dawn, ᵀ

ᵀ SS 2:10 ◀ ▶ Isa 26:20

j 6 Or heart had gone out to him when he spoke　　*k 14 Or lapis lazuli*

fair as the moon, bright as the sun,
    majestic as the stars in procession?"

Lover

¹¹I went down to the grove of nut trees
    to look at the new growth in the
        valley,
    to see if the vines had budded
    or the pomegranates were in
        bloom.^c
¹²Before I realized it,
    my desire set me among the royal
        chariots of my people.^l

Friends

¹³Come back, come back,
    O Shulammite;
come back, come back, that we may
    gaze on you!

Lover

Why would you gaze on the
    Shulammite
    as on the dance^d of Mahanaim?

7 How beautiful your sandaled feet,
    O prince's^e daughter!
Your graceful legs are like jewels,
    the work of a craftsman's hands.
²Your navel is a rounded goblet
    that never lacks blended wine.
Your waist is a mound of wheat
    encircled by lilies.
³Your breasts^f are like two fawns,
    twins of a gazelle.
⁴Your neck is like an ivory tower.^g
Your eyes are the pools of Heshbon^h
    by the gate of Bath Rabbim.
Your nose is like the tower of
    Lebanonⁱ
    looking toward Damascus.
⁵Your head crowns you like Mount
    Carmel.^j
Your hair is like royal tapestry;
    the king is held captive by its
        tresses.
⁶How beautiful^k you are and how
    pleasing,
    O love, with your delights!^l
⁷Your stature is like that of the palm,
    and your breasts^m like clusters of
        fruit.
⁸I said, "I will climb the palm tree;
    I will take hold of its fruit."

C *SS 5:8* ◀▶ *SS 7:8–9*
C *SS 6:11–12* ◀▶ *SS 8:4*

6:11 ^c SS 7:12
6:13 ^d S Ex 15:20
7:1 ^e Ps 45:13
7:3 ^f SS 4:5
7:4 ^g S Ps 144:12
^h Nu 21:26
ⁱ S SS 5:15
7:5 ^j Isa 35:2
7:6 ^k S SS 1:15
^l SS 4:10
7:7 ^m SS 4:5
7:8 ⁿ SS 2:5
7:9 ^o S S 5:16
7:10 ^p Ps 45:11
^q SS 2:16; 6:3
7:12 ^r S SS 1:6
^s SS 2:15 ^t SS 2:13
^u S SS 4:13 ^v S SS 6:11
7:13 ^w S Ge 30:14
^x SS 4:16
8:2 ^y SS 3:4
8:3 ^z SS 2:6
8:4 ^a SS 2:7; S 3:5
8:5 ^b SS 3:6

May your breasts be like the clusters of
    the vine,
    the fragrance of your breath like
        apples,ⁿ
⁹ and your mouth like the best wine.

Beloved

May the wine go straight to my lover,^o
    flowing gently over lips and teeth.^m
¹⁰I belong to my lover,
    and his desire^p is for me.^q
¹¹Come, my lover, let us go to the
        countryside,
    let us spend the night in the
        villages.ⁿ
¹²Let us go early to the vineyards^r
    to see if the vines have budded,^s
    if their blossoms^t have opened,
    and if the pomegranates^u are in
        bloom^v—
    there I will give you my love.
¹³The mandrakes^w send out their
        fragrance,
    and at our door is every delicacy,
        both new and old,
    that I have stored up for you, my
        lover.^x

8 If only you were to me like a
    brother,
    who was nursed at my mother's
        breasts!
Then, if I found you outside,
    I would kiss you,
    and no one would despise me.
²I would lead you
    and bring you to my mother's
        house^y—
    she who has taught me.
I would give you spiced wine to drink,
    the nectar of my pomegranates.
³His left arm is under my head
    and his right arm embraces me.^z
⁴Daughters of Jerusalem, I charge you:
    Do not arouse or awaken love
    until it so desires.^a

Friends

⁵Who is this coming up from the
        desert^b
    leaning on her lover?

C *SS 7:8–9* ◀▶ *SS 8:14*
D *Ps 98:9* ◀▶ *Eze 43:1–2*

^l 12 Or *among the chariots of Amminadab;* or *among the chariots of the people of the prince* ^m 9 Septuagint, Aquila, Vulgate and Syriac; Hebrew *lips of sleepers* ⁿ 11 Or *henna bushes*

Beloved

Under the apple tree I roused you;
   there your mother conceived[c] you,
   there she who was in labor gave you
      birth.
⁶Place me like a seal over your heart,
   like a seal on your arm;
for love[d] is as strong as death,
   its jealousy[o][e] unyielding as the
      grave.[p]
It burns like blazing fire,
   like a mighty flame.[q]
⁷Many waters cannot quench love;
   rivers cannot wash it away.
If one were to give
   all the wealth of his house for love,
   it[r] would be utterly scorned.[f]

Friends

⁸We have a young sister,
   and her breasts are not yet grown.
What shall we do for our sister
   for the day she is spoken for?
⁹If she is a wall,
   we will build towers of silver on
      her.
If she is a door,
   we will enclose her with panels of
      cedar.

Beloved

¹⁰I am a wall,
   and my breasts are like towers.
Thus I have become in his eyes
   like one bringing contentment.
¹¹Solomon had a vineyard[g] in Baal
      Hamon;
he let out his vineyard to tenants.
Each was to bring for its fruit
   a thousand shekels[s][h] of silver.
¹²But my own vineyard[i] is mine to give;
   the thousand shekels are for you,
      O Solomon,
   and two hundred[t] are for those who
      tend its fruit.

Lover

¹³You who dwell in the gardens
   with friends in attendance,
   let me hear your voice!

Beloved

¹⁴Come away, my lover,
   and be like a gazelle[j]
   or like a young stag[k]
   on the spice-laden mountains.[l]

8:5 [c]S SS 3:4
8:6 [d]S SS 1:2 [e]S Nu 5:14
8:7 [f]S Pr 6:35
8:11 [g]Ecc 2:4 [h]Isa 7:23
8:12 [i]S SS 1:6
8:14 [j]S Pr 5:19 [k]S SS 2:9 [l]S SS 2:8, 17

[c] SS 8:4 ◀ ▶ Isa 64:1

[o] 6 Or *ardor* [p] 6 Hebrew *Sheol* [q] 6 Or / *like the very flame of the* LORD [r] 7 Or *he* [s] 11 That is, about 25 pounds (about 11.5 kilograms); also in verse 12 [t] 12 That is, about 5 pounds (about 2.3 kilograms)

[G] Dt 32:21 ◀ ▶ Isa 65:1

Isaiah

Author: Isaiah

Theme: God, the sovereign Lord, judge and redeemer

Date of Writing: c. 700–680 B.C.

Outline of Isaiah
  I. God's Judgment and Promise (1:1—6:13)
  II. Immanuel's Kingdom (7:1—12:6)
  III. Judgment Against the Nations (13:1—23:18)
  IV. Judgment of Israel and a Promise (24:1—27:13)
  V. Warnings to Israel and Assyria (28:1—33:24)
  VI. Judgment and Promise (34:1—35:10)
  VII. The Assyrian Threat and Babylonian Exile (36:1—39:8)
  VIII. Israel's Deliverance and Restoration (40:1—48:22)
  IX. The Servant's Ministry (49:1—57:21)
  X. Judgment and Everlasting Deliverance (58:1—66:24)

ISAIAH, THE SON of Amoz, was a prophet in the southern kingdom of Judah. Respected in royal circles despite his repeated warnings of the approaching judgment of God, Isaiah prophesied during a troublesome time in the life of Israel and Judah. Israel faced the threat of domination by the Assyrians. Isaiah warned that Judah too would face capture and captivity because of their sins unless they placed their total reliance on God, not on political alliances, religious ritual or material possessions. A contemporary of Amos, Hosea and Micah, Isaiah echoed their warnings of judgment. Yet his literary style, beautiful images and insights into God's character make Isaiah the greatest of the writing prophets and the most quoted OT prophet in the entire NT.

Isaiah began this book during King Uzziah's reign and continued his prophetic ministry for more than sixty years through the reigns of Jotham, Ahaz and Hezekiah. More than half of his written record concerns prophetic events. The time period covered in chapters 1—39 took place during Isaiah's ministry, including the prediction and fulfillment of the destruc-

INTRODUCTION: ISAIAH

tion of Jerusalem. Note that Jerusalem appears numerous times with different prophetic names in Isaiah's prophecies.

The remainder of the book focuses on events that were to happen centuries after Isaiah's time. Covering the deliverance of his people from the Babylonians and prefiguring the coming of the Messiah, these chapters may have been completed during Isaiah's later years. The predictions in these later chapters also describe the destiny of virtually every nation on earth. In addition, many of these prophecies directly relate to the Messiah's birth, lineage, ministry, death on a cross and plan of redemption as well as the establishment of the Messianic kingdom during the end times.

1 The vision[a] concerning Judah and Jerusalem[b] that Isaiah son of Amoz saw[c] during the reigns of Uzziah,[d] Jotham,[e] Ahaz[f] and Hezekiah,[g] kings of Judah.

A Rebellious Nation

[2] Hear, O heavens! Listen, O earth![h]
 For the LORD has spoken:[i]
"I reared children[j] and brought them up,
 but they have rebelled[k] against me.
[3] The ox knows[l] his master,
 the donkey his owner's manger,[m]
but Israel does not know,[n]
 my people do not understand."[o]

C [4] Ah, sinful nation,
 a people loaded with guilt,[p]
a brood of evildoers,[q]
 children given to corruption![r]
They have forsaken[s] the LORD;
 they have spurned the Holy One[t] of Israel
 and turned their backs[u] on him.

[5] Why should you be beaten[v] anymore?
 Why do you persist[w] in rebellion?[x]
Your whole head is injured,
 your whole heart[y] afflicted.[z]
[6] From the sole of your foot to the top of your head[a]

there is no soundness[b]—
 only wounds and welts[c]
 and open sores,
not cleansed or bandaged[d]
 or soothed with oil.[e]

[7] Your country is desolate,[f]
 your cities burned with fire;[g]
your fields are being stripped by foreigners[h]
 right before you,
 laid waste as when overthrown by strangers.[i]
[8] The Daughter of Zion[j] is left[k]
 like a shelter in a vineyard,
 like a hut[l] in a field of melons,
 like a city under siege.
[9] Unless the LORD Almighty
 had left us some survivors,[m]
we would have become like Sodom,
 we would have been like Gomorrah.[n]

[10] Hear the word of the LORD,[o]
 you rulers of Sodom;[p]
listen to the law[q] of our God,

R

R Ps 80:12-16 ◀▶ Isa 1:21-22

C Ecc 9:18 ◀▶ Isa 3:9

1:1 [a] Isa 3:1; Isa 22:1,5; Ob 1:1; [b] Na 1:1 [b] Isa 40:9; 44:26 [c] Isa 2:1; 13:1 [d] S 2Ki 14:21; S 2Ch 26:22 [e] S 1Ch 3:12 [f] S 2Ki 16:1 [g] S 1Ch 3:13 1:2 [h] S Dt 4:26 [i] Jdg 11:10; Jer 42:5; Mic 1:2 [j] Isa 23:4; 63:16 [k] ver 4,23; Isa 24:5, 20; 30:1,9; 46:8; 48:8; 57:4; 65:2; 66:24; Eze 24:3; Hag 1:12; Mal 1:6; 3:5 1:3 [l] Job 12:9 [m] S Ge 42:27 [n] Jer 4:22; 5:4; 9:3, 6; Hos 2:8; 4:1 [o] S Dt 32:28; Isa 42:25; 48:8; Hos 4:6; 7:9 1:4 [p] Isa 5:18 [q] S ver 2; Isa 9:17; 14:20; 31:2; Jer 23:14 [r] Ps 14:3 [s] S Dt 32:15; S Ps 119:87 [t] S 2Ki 19:22; Isa 5:19,24; 31:1; 37:23; 41:14; 43:14; 45:11; 47:4; Eze 39:7 [u] S Pr 30:9; Isa 59:13 1:5 [v] Pr 20:30 [w] Jer 2:30; 5:3; 8:5 [x] S ver 2; Isa 31:6; Jer 44:16-17; Heb 3:16 [y] La 2:11; 5:17 [z] Isa 30:26; 33:6,24; 58:8; Jer 30:17 1:6 [a] S Dt 28:35 [b] Ps 38:3 [c] Isa 53:5

[d] S Ps 147:3; Isa 30:26; Jer 8:22; 14:19; 30:17; La 2:13; Eze 34:4 [e] 2Sa 14:2; Ps 23:5; 45:7; 104:15; Isa 61:3; Lk 10:34 1:7 [f] S Lev 26:31; S Dt 29:23 [h] Lev 26:16; Jdg 6:3-6; Isa 62:8; Jer 5:17 [i] S 2Ki 18:13; S Ps 109:11 1:8 [j] S Ps 9:14; Isa 10:32 [k] S Mt 30:17; 49:21 [l] Job 27:18 1:9 [m] S Ge 45:7; S 2Ki 21:14; Isa 4:2; 6:13; 27:12; 28:5; 37:4,31-32; 45:25; 56:8; Jer 23:3; Joel 2:32 [n] S Ge 19:24; Ro 9:29 1:10 [o] Isa 28:14 [p] S Ge 13:13; S 18:20; Eze 16:49; Ro 9:29; Rev 11:8 [q] Isa 5:24; 8:20; 30:9

1:7–9 Isaiah prophesied about God's rejection of Judah and Jerusalem due to their continued wickedness, describing their future destruction in the past tense to emphasize its certainty and noting that unless God showed mercy to a small remnant, the kingdom of Judah would be annihilated like Sodom and Gomorrah.

you people of Gomorrah!

¹¹"The multitude of your sacrifices—
what are they to me?" says the LORD.
"I have more than enough of burnt offerings,
of rams and the fat of fattened animals;
I have no pleasure
in the blood of bulls and lambs and goats.

¹²When you come to appear before me,
who has asked this of you,
this trampling of my courts?

¹³Stop bringing meaningless offerings!
Your incense is detestable to me.
New Moons, Sabbaths and convocations—
I cannot bear your evil assemblies.

¹⁴Your New Moon festivals and your appointed feasts
my soul hates.
They have become a burden to me;
I am weary of bearing them.

¹⁵When you spread out your hands in prayer,
I will hide my eyes from you;
even if you offer many prayers,
I will not listen.
Your hands are full of blood;

¹⁶ wash and make yourselves clean.
Take your evil deeds
out of my sight!
Stop doing wrong,

¹⁷ learn to do right!
Seek justice,
encourage the oppressed.ᵃ
Defend the cause of the fatherless,
plead the case of the widow.

¹⁸"Come now, let us reason together,"
says the LORD.
"Though your sins are like scarlet,
they shall be as white as snow;
though they are red as crimson,
they shall be like wool.

¹⁹If you are willing and obedient,
you will eat the best from the land;

²⁰but if you resist and rebel,
you will be devoured by the sword."
For the mouth of the LORD has spoken.

²¹See how the faithful city has become a harlot!
She once was full of justice;
righteousness used to dwell in her—
but now murderers!

²²Your silver has become dross,
your choice wine is diluted with water.

²³Your rulers are rebels,
companions of thieves;
they all love bribes
and chase after gifts.
They do not defend the cause of the fatherless;
the widow's case does not come before them.

²⁴Therefore the Lord, the LORD Almighty, the Mighty One of Israel, declares:
"Ah, I will get relief from my foes
and avenge myself on my enemies.

²⁵I will turn my hand against you;

ᵃ 17 Or / rebuke the oppressor

1:21–22 Using the imagery of an unfaithful harlot, God condemns Judah's compromise with evil and corruption.

1:24 God promised Judah that he would take vengeance against those nations that had helped turn Judah away from him.

1:25–28 God promises to cleanse his people of their sin and redeem them "with justice" (1:27). This prophecy was initially fulfilled when Jerusalem fell in 586 B.C. to the Babylonians, but will find its fullest fulfillment during the great tribulation and the final judgment of God's people. At that time God will "restore your judges as in days of old" (1:26) under the Messiah, and Jerusalem will become "the Faithful

I will thoroughly purge° away your
    dross,ᵖ
and remove all your impurities.ᵠ
²⁶I will restore your judges as in days of
    old,ʳ
your counselors as at the beginning.
Afterward you will be calledˢ
the City of Righteousness,ᵗ
the Faithful City."ᵘ

²⁷Zion will be redeemed with justice,
her penitentᵛ ones with
    righteousness.ʷ
²⁸But rebels and sinnersˣ will both be
    broken,
and those who forsakeʸ the LORD will
    perish.ᶻ

²⁹"You will be ashamedᵃ because of the
    sacred oaksᵇ
in which you have delighted;
you will be disgraced because of the
    gardensᶜ
that you have chosen.
³⁰You will be like an oak with fading
    leaves,ᵈ
like a garden without water.
³¹The mighty man will become tinder
and his work a spark;
both will burn together,
with no one to quench the fire."ᵉ

The Mountain of the LORD

2:1–4pp — Mic 4:1–3

2 This is what Isaiah son of Amoz saw
concerning Judah and Jerusalem:ᶠ

²In the last daysᵍ

the mountainʰ of the LORD's temple
    will be established
as chief among the mountains;ⁱ

it will be raisedʲ above the hills,
and all nations will stream to it.ᵏ

³Many peoplesˡ will come and say,

"Come, let us goᵐ up to the mountainⁿ
    of the LORD,
to the house of the God of Jacob.
He will teach us his ways,
so that we may walk in his paths."
The lawº will go out from Zion,
the word of the LORD from
    Jerusalem.ᵖ
⁴He will judgeᵠ between the nations
and will settle disputesʳ for many
    peoples.
They will beat their swords into
    plowshares
and their spears into pruning
    hooks.ˢ
Nation will not take up sword against
    nation,ᵗ
nor will they train for war anymore.

⁵Come, O house of Jacob,ᵘ
let us walk in the lightᵛ of the LORD.

The Day of the LORD

⁶You have abandonedʷ your people,
the house of Jacob.ˣ
They are full of superstitions from the
    East;
they practice divinationʸ like the
    Philistinesᶻ
and clasp handsᵃ with pagans.ᵇ
⁷Their land is full of silver and gold;ᶜ
there is no end to their treasures.ᵈ
Their land is full of horses;ᵉ
there is no end to their chariots.ᶠ
⁸Their land is full of idols;ᵍ

S *Isa 1:19* ◀ ▶ *Isa 5:18*
P *Isa 1:24* ◀ ▶ *Isa 1:30–31*
H *Isa 1:24* ◀ ▶ *Isa 1:30–31*
P *Isa 1:28* ◀ ▶ *Isa 2:10–21*
H *Isa 1:28* ◀ ▶ *Isa 2:10–21*
I *Isa 1:25–27* ◀ ▶ *Isa 4:2–6*
M *SS 4:16* ◀ ▶ *Isa 4:5–6*

U *Ps 72:7* ◀ ▶ *Isa 9:6*
R *Isa 1:21–22* ◀ ▶ *Isa 3:1–8*

City" (1:26).
1:30–31 These verses likely refer to the destruction of the oak groves and gardens that were used in pagan idolatrous rituals.
2:1–6 Despite the certainty of God's approaching judgment, Isaiah also prophesied the final redemption of Israel and Judah in the millennial kingdom when the Lord will bring about the restoration of the nation and the rebuilding of the temple. Isaiah also prophesied that all the nations would come to Jerusalem to worship God during the Messiah's reign. Christ will then "teach us his ways" (2:3) as he proclaims God's laws throughout the earth from his throne in Jerusalem. Isaiah therefore urged Judah to repent and "walk in the light of the LORD" (2:5).

they bow down ʰ to the work of their hands, ⁱ
to what their fingers ʲ have made.
⁹So man will be brought low ᵏ
and mankind humbled ˡ—
do not forgive them. ᵇ ᵐ

P ¹⁰Go into the rocks,
H   hide ⁿ in the ground
M   from dread of the LORD
     and the splendor of his majesty! ᵒ
¹¹The eyes of the arrogant ᵖ man will be humbled ᵠ
and the pride ʳ of men brought low; ˢ
the LORD alone will be exalted ᵗ in that day. ᵘ
¹²The LORD Almighty has a day ᵛ in store
for all the proud ʷ and lofty, ˣ
for all that is exalted ʸ
(and they will be humbled), ᶻ
¹³for all the cedars of Lebanon, ᵃ tall and lofty, ᵇ
and all the oaks of Bashan, ᶜ
¹⁴for all the towering mountains
and all the high hills, ᵈ
¹⁵for every lofty tower ᵉ
and every fortified wall, ᶠ
¹⁶for every trading ship ᶜ ᵍ
and every stately vessel.
¹⁷The arrogance of man will be brought low ʰ
and the pride of men humbled; ⁱ
the LORD alone will be exalted in that day, ʲ
¹⁸ and the idols ᵏ will totally disappear. ˡ

¹⁹Men will flee to caves ᵐ in the rocks
and to holes in the ground ⁿ
from dread ᵒ of the LORD
and the splendor of his majesty, ᵖ
when he rises to shake the earth. ᵠ
²⁰In that day ʳ men will throw away
to the rodents and bats ˢ
their idols of silver and idols of gold, ᵗ
which they made to worship. ᵘ
²¹They will flee to caverns in the rocks ᵛ
and to the overhanging crags
from dread of the LORD
and the splendor of his majesty, ʷ
when he rises ˣ to shake the earth. ʸ

P *Isa 1:30–31* ◄► *Isa 11:4*
H *Isa 1:30–31* ◄► *Isa 3:11*
M *Pr 30:12–13* ◄► *Isa 5:14–16*

2:8 ʰ Isa 44:17
ⁱ S 2Ch 32:19;
S Ps 135:15;
Mic 5:13 ʲ Isa 17:8
2:9 ᵏ Ps 62:9
ˡ ver 11,17;
Isa 5:15; 13:11
ᵐ S Ne 4:5
2:10 ⁿ ver 19;
Na 3:11
ᵒ S Ps 145:12;
2Th 1:9;
Rev 6:15-16
2:11 ᵖ S Ne 9:29;
Hab 2:5 ᵠ S ver 9
ʳ Isa 5:15; 10:12;
37:23; Eze 31:10
ˢ S Job 40:11
ᵗ S Ps 46:10
ᵘ ver 17,20; Isa 3:7,
18; 4:1,2; 5:30;
7:18; 17:4,7;
24:21; 25:9; 26:1;
27:1
2:12 ᵛ Isa 13:6,9;
22:5,8,12; 34:8;
61:2; Jer 30:7;
La 1:12; Eze 7:7;
30:3; Joel 1:15;
2:11; Am 5:18;
Zep 1:14
ʷ S Ps 59:12
ˣ S 2Sa 22:28
ʸ Ps 76:12; Isa 24:4,
21; 60:11; Mal 4:1
ᶻ S Job 40:11
2:13 ᵃ S Jdg 9:15;
Isa 10:34; 29:17;
Eze 27:5 ᵇ Isa 10:33
ᶜ S Ps 22:12;
Zec 11:2
2:14 ᵈ Isa 30:25;
40:4
2:15 ᵉ Isa 30:25;
32:14; 33:18
ᶠ Isa 25:2,12;
Zep 1:16
2:16
ᵍ ᶠⁿ S Ge 10:4;
S 1Ki 9:26
2:17 ʰ S Job 40:11 ⁱ S ver 9
ʲ S ver 11
2:18 ᵏ S Isa 5:2;
Eze 36:25
ˡ S Dt 9:21;
Isa 21:9; Jer 10:11;
Mic 5:13
2:19 ᵐ S Jdg 6:2;
Isa 7:19 ⁿ S Jdg 6:2;
S Job 30:6;
Lk 23:30; Rev 6:15
ᵒ S Dt 2:25
ᵖ S Ps 145:12
ᵠ ver 21; S Job 9:6;
S Isa 14:16;
Heb 12:26
2:20 ʳ S ver 11
ˢ Lev 11:19
ᵗ S Job 22:24;
Eze 36:25; Rev 9:20
ᵘ Eze 7:19-20; 14:6
2:21 ᵛ S Ex 33:22
ʷ S Ps 145:12
ˣ Isa 33:10
ʸ S ver 19
2:22 ᶻ Ps 118:6,8;
146:3; Isa 51:12;
Jer 17:5 ᵃ S Ge 2:7;

²²Stop trusting in man, ᶻ
who has but a breath ᵃ in his nostrils.
Of what account is he? ᵇ

Judgment on Jerusalem and Judah

3 See now, the Lord,
the LORD Almighty,
is about to take from Jerusalem and Judah
both supply and support: ᶜ
all supplies of food ᵈ and all supplies of water, ᵉ
² the hero and warrior, ᶠ
the judge and prophet,
the soothsayer ᵍ and elder, ʰ
³the captain of fifty ⁱ and man of rank, ʲ
the counselor, skilled craftsman ᵏ
and clever enchanter. ˡ
⁴I will make boys their officials;
mere children will govern them. ᵐ
⁵People will oppress each other—
man against man, neighbor against neighbor. ⁿ
The young will rise up against the old,
the base against the honorable.
⁶A man will seize one of his brothers
at his father's home, and say,
"You have a cloak, you be our leader;
take charge of this heap of ruins!"
⁷But in that day ᵒ he will cry out,
"I have no remedy. ᵖ
I have no food ᵠ or clothing in my house;
do not make me the leader of the people." ʳ

⁸Jerusalem staggers,
Judah is falling; ˢ
their words ᵗ and deeds ᵘ are against the LORD,
defying ᵛ his glorious presence.

R *Isa 2:6* ◄► *Isa 3:8*
R *Isa 3:1–8* ◄► *Isa 3:26*

S Ps 144:4 ᵇ S Job 12:19; Ps 8:4; 18:42; 144:3; Isa 17:13; 29:5; 40:15;
S Jas 4:14 **3:1** ᶜ S Ps 18:18 ᵈ S Lev 26:26; Am 4:6 ᵉ Isa 5:13; 65:13;
Eze 4:16 **3:2** ᶠ Eze 17:13 ᵍ Dt 18:10 ʰ Jos 9:14-15 **3:3** ⁱ S 2Ki 1:9
ʲ S Job 22:8 ᵏ 2Ki 24:14 ˡ S Ecc 10:11; Jer 8:17 **3:4** ᵐ ver 12; Ecc 10:16 ᶠⁿ
3:5 ⁿ Ps 28:3; Isa 9:19; Jer 9:8; Mic 7:2,6 **3:7** ᵒ S Isa 2:11 ᵖ Jer 30:12;
Eze 34:4; Hos 5:13 ᵠ Joel 1:16 ʳ Isa 42:22; ˢ Isa 9:15,17; 28:15;
30:9; 59:3,13 ᵘ 2Ch 33:6 ᵛ S Job 1:11; Ps 73:9,11; Isa 65:7

ᵇ 9 Or *not raise them up* ᶜ 16 Hebrew *every ship of Tarshish*

2:10–21 Isaiah describes the desperate actions and fear that will afflict the world during the tribulation under the cruel rule of the antichrist before the Messiah's return.

⁹The look on their faces testifies against them;
 they parade their sin like Sodom;
 they do not hide it.
Woe to them!
 They have brought disaster upon themselves.

¹⁰Tell the righteous it will be well with them,
 for they will enjoy the fruit of their deeds.

¹¹Woe to the wicked! Disaster is upon them!
 They will be paid back for what their hands have done.

¹²Youths oppress my people,
 women rule over them.
O my people, your guides lead you astray;
 they turn you from the path.

¹³The LORD takes his place in court;
 he rises to judge the people.
¹⁴The LORD enters into judgment
 against the elders and leaders of his people:
"It is you who have ruined my vineyard;
 the plunder from the poor is in your houses.
¹⁵What do you mean by crushing my people
 and grinding the faces of the poor?"
declares the Lord,
 the LORD Almighty.

¹⁶The LORD says,
"The women of Zion are haughty,
 walking along with outstretched necks,
flirting with their eyes,
tripping along with mincing steps,
 with ornaments jingling on their ankles.

C *Isa 1:4–6* ◀ ▶ *Isa 5:18*
U *Isa 1:19* ◀ ▶ *Isa 32:17*
H *Isa 2:10–21* ◀ ▶ *Isa 3:14–15*
H *Isa 3:11* ◀ ▶ *Isa 3:24*

¹⁷Therefore the Lord will bring sores on the heads of the women of Zion;
 the LORD will make their scalps bald."

¹⁸In that day the Lord will snatch away their finery: the bangles and headbands and crescent necklaces, ¹⁹the earrings and bracelets and veils, ²⁰the headdresses and ankle chains and sashes, the perfume bottles and charms, ²¹the signet rings and nose rings, ²²the fine robes and the capes and cloaks, the purses ²³and mirrors, and the linen garments and tiaras and shawls.

²⁴Instead of fragrance there will be a stench;
 instead of a sash, a rope;
 instead of well-dressed hair, baldness;
 instead of fine clothing, sackcloth;
 instead of beauty, branding.
²⁵Your men will fall by the sword,
 your warriors in battle.
²⁶The gates of Zion will lament and mourn;
 destitute, she will sit on the ground.

4 In that day seven women will take hold of one man and say, "We will eat our own food and provide our own clothes; only let us be called by your name. Take away our disgrace!"

The Branch of the LORD

²In that day the Branch of the LORD will be beautiful and glorious, and the fruit of the land will be the pride and glory of the survivors in Israel. ³Those who are left in Zion, who remain in Jerusalem, will be called holy, all who

H *Isa 3:14–15* ◀ ▶ *Isa 8:15*
R *Isa 3:8* ◀ ▶ *Isa 5:1–10*
I *Isa 2:1–5* ◀ ▶ *Isa 9:1–4*
S *Ps 51:10* ◀ ▶ *Eze 11:19*

4:1–6 This unusual prophecy reveals that the unprecedented slaughter of humanity during the wars of the tribulation period will severely reduce the number of marriageable men. Yet when the Messiah returns, God's glory will provide a defense for the people, worship in the temple will resume and the temple will become a place of refuge for God's people.

are recorded among the living in Jerusalem. ⁴The Lord will wash away the filth of the women of Zion; he will cleanse the bloodstains from Jerusalem by a spirit of judgment and a spirit of fire. ⁵Then the Lord will create over all of Mount Zion and over those who assemble there a cloud of smoke by day and a glow of flaming fire by night; over all the glory will be a canopy. ⁶It will be a shelter and shade from the heat of the day, and a refuge and hiding place from the storm and rain.

The Song of the Vineyard

5 I will sing for the one I love
    a song about his vineyard:
My loved one had a vineyard
    on a fertile hillside.
²He dug it up and cleared it of stones
    and planted it with the choicest vines.
He built a watchtower in it
    and cut out a winepress as well.
Then he looked for a crop of good grapes,
    but it yielded only bad fruit.

³"Now you dwellers in Jerusalem and men of Judah,
    judge between me and my vineyard.
⁴What more could have been done for my vineyard
    than I have done for it?
When I looked for good grapes,
    why did it yield only bad?
⁵Now I will tell you
    what I am going to do to my vineyard:
I will take away its hedge,
    and it will be destroyed;
I will break down its wall,
    and it will be trampled.
⁶I will make it a wasteland,
    neither pruned nor cultivated,

N *Ps 143:10* ◀▶ *Isa 11:2*
P *Pr 1:22–23* ◀▶ *Isa 32:15*
R *Ps 51:12–13* ◀▶ *Isa 61:1–3*
M *Isa 2:1–5* ◀▶ *Isa 9:6–7*
K *Isa 1:25* ◀▶ *Isa 25:4*
L *Isa 1:25* ◀▶ *Isa 9:2*
R *Isa 3:26* ◀▶ *Isa 5:25–30*

4:3 ᶜS Ps 56:8; S 87:6; S Lk 10:20
4:4 ᵈIsa 3:24
ᵉS SS 3:11
ᶠS Ps 51:2
ᵍS Isa 1:15
ʰIsa 28:6
ⁱS Isa 1:31; S 30:30; S Zec 13:9; Mt 3:11; Lk 3:17
4:5 ʲIsa 41:20; 65:18 ᵏRev 14:1
ˡS Ex 13:21
ᵐIsa 35:2; 58:8; 60:1 ⁿS Ps 18:11; Rev 7:15
4:6 ᵒLev 23:34-43; Ps 27:5; Isa 8:14; 25:4; Eze 11:16
ᵖIsa 14:32; 25:4; 30:2; 57:13
ᵠS Ps 55:8
5:1 ʳPs 80:8-9; Isa 27:2; Jn 15:1
5:2 ˢS Ex 15:17; Isa 16:8 ᵗIsa 2:9; Isa 27:3; 31:5; 49:8; Mt 21:33
ᵘS Job 24:11
ᵛMt 21:19; Mk 11:13; Lk 13:6
5:3 ʷMt 21:40
5:4 ˣS 2Ch 36:15; Jer 2:5-7; Mic 6:3:4; Mt 23:37 ʸJer 2:21; 24:2; 29:17
5:5 ᶻ2Ch 36:21; Isa 6:12; 27:10
ᵃPs 80:12; S Isa 22:5
ᵇIsa 10:6; 26:6; 28:3,18; 41:25; 63:3; Jer 12:10; 34:22; La 1:15; Hos 2:12; Mic 7:10; Mal 4:3; S Lk 21:24
5:6 ᶜS Ge 6:13; S Lev 26:32; Isa 6:13; 49:17,19; 51:3; Joel 1:10
ᵈver 10,17; S 2Sa 23:6; Isa 7:23,24; 32:13; 34:13; 55:13; Eze 28:24; Hos 2:12; Heb 6:8
ᵉS Dt 28:24; S 2Sa 1:21; Am 4:7
5:7 ᶠPs 80:8; Isa 17:10; 18:5; 37:30 ᵍIsa 10:2; 29:21; 32:7; 59:15; 61:8; Eze 9:9; 22:29 ʰS Isa 1:21
ⁱS Ps 12:5
5:8 ʲver 11,18,20; 24:16; Jer 22:13
ᵏJob 20:19; Mic 2:2; Hab 2:9-12
5:9 ˡJer 44:11
ᵐIsa 22:14
ⁿIsa 6:11-12; Mt 23:38
5:10 ᵒS ver 6; Lev 26:26; S Dt 28:38; Zec 8:10

and briers and thorns will grow there.
I will command the clouds
    not to rain on it."

⁷The vineyard of the Lord Almighty
    is the house of Israel,
and the men of Judah
    are the garden of his delight.
And he looked for justice, but saw bloodshed;
for righteousness, but heard cries of distress.

Woes and Judgments

⁸Woe to you who add house to house
    and join field to field
till no space is left
    and you live alone in the land.

⁹The Lord Almighty has declared in my hearing:

"Surely the great houses will become desolate,
    the fine mansions left without occupants.
¹⁰A ten-acre vineyard will produce only a bath of wine,
    a homer of seed only an ephah of grain."

¹¹Woe to those who rise early in the morning
    to run after their drinks,
who stay up late at night
    till they are inflamed with wine.
¹²They have harps and lyres at their banquets,
    tambourines and flutes and wine,
but they have no regard for the deeds of the Lord,
    no respect for the work of his hands.

¹³Therefore my people will go into exile
    for lack of understanding;

5:11 ᵖver 8 ᵠS Isa 25:36; S Pr 23:29-30 5:12 ʳPs 68:25; Isa 24:8
ˢS Job 21:12 ᵗS Isa 12:24 ᵘPs 28:5; Eze 26:13 5:13 ᵛIsa 49:21
ʷS Pr 10:21; S Isa 1:3; Hos 4:6

ᵈ4 *Or the Spirit*   ᵉ10 Hebrew *ten-yoke,* that is, the land plowed by 10 yoke of oxen in one day   ᶠ10 That is, probably about 6 gallons (about 22 liters)   ᵍ10 That is, probably about 6 bushels (about 220 liters)   ʰ10 That is, probably about 3/5 bushel (about 22 liters)

5:1–10 This passage reveals the judgment of God upon the nation as a result of their continued sin. Elsewhere in Scripture the nation is also pictured as a vineyard that yields evil fruit (see Ps 80:8–9; Jer 12:10; Mt 21:33–44; Mk 12:1–11; Lk 20:9–18).

their men of rank˟ will die of hunger
 and their masses will be parched
  with thirst.ʸ

M ¹⁴Therefore the graveⁱᶻ enlarges its
  appetite
 and opens its mouthᵃ without limit;
 into it will descend their nobles and
  masses
 with all their brawlers and revelers.ᵇ
¹⁵So man will be brought lowᶜ
 and mankind humbled,ᵈ
 the eyes of the arroganteᵉ humbled.
¹⁶But the LORD Almighty will be exaltedᶠ
  by his justice,ᵍ
 and the holy God will show himself
  holyʰ by his righteousness.
¹⁷Then sheep will graze as in their own
  pasture;ⁱ
 lambs will feedʲ among the ruins of
  the rich.

C ¹⁸Woeʲ to those who draw sin along
S with cordsᵏ of deceit,
 and wickednessˡ as with cart ropes,
¹⁹to those who say, "Let God hurry,
 let him hastenᵐ his work
 so we may see it.
 Let it approach,
 let the plan of the Holy Oneⁿ of
  Israel come,
 so we may know it."ᵒ

C ²⁰Woeᵖ to those who call evil goodᑫ
 and good evil,ʳ
 who put darkness for light
  and light for darkness,ˢ
 who put bitter for sweet
  and sweet for bitter.ᵗ

M ²¹Woe to those who are wise in their
  own eyesᵘ
 and clever in their own sight.

²²Woe to those who are heroes at
  drinking wineᵛ
 and champions at mixing drinks,ʷ
²³who acquit the guilty for a bribe,ˣ
 but deny justiceʸ to the innocent.ᶻ

M Isa 2:10–17 ◀▶ Isa 5:21
C Isa 3:9 ◀▶ Isa 5:20
S Isa 1:27–28 ◀▶ Isa 32:17
C Isa 5:18 ◀▶ Isa 6:5
M Isa 5:14–16 ◀▶ Isa 10:15

5:13 ˣS Job 22:8
ʸS Isa 3:1
5:14 ᶻS Pr 30:16
ᵃS Nu 16:30
ᵇIsa 22:2,13; 23:7; 24:8
5:15 ᶜIsa 10:33
ᵈS Isa 2:9
ᵉS Isa 2:11
5:16 ᶠPs 97:9; Isa 33:10
ᵍIsa 28:17; 30:18; 33:5; 61:8
ʰS Lev 10:3; Isa 29:23; Eze 36:23
5:17 ⁱIsa 7:25; 17:2; 32:14; Zep 2:6,14
5:18 ʲS ver 8
ᵏHos 11:4
ˡIsa 59:4-8; Jer 23:14
5:19 ᵐIsa 60:22
ⁿS Isa 1:4; 29:23; 30:11,12
ᵒJer 17:15; Eze 12:25; 2Pe 3:4
5:20 ᵖS ver 8
ᑫS Ge 18:25; S 1Ki 22:8
ʳS Ps 94:21
ˢS Job 24:13; Mt 6:22-23; Lk 11:34-35
ᵗAm 5:7
5:21 ᵘS Pr 3:7; Isa 47:10; Ro 12:16; 1Co 3:18-20
5:22 ᵛS Isa 25:36; S Pr 23:20; S Isa 22:13
ʷS Pr 31:4; Isa 65:11; Jer 7:18
5:23 ˣS Ex 23:8; S Eze 22:12 ʸver 7; S Isa 1:17; 10:2; 29:21; 59:4,13-15
ᶻS Ps 94:21; Am 5:12; Jas 5:6
5:24 ᵃS Isa 1:31
ᵇIsa 47:14; Na 1:10
ᶜS 2Ki 19:30; S Job 18:16
ᵈS Job 24:24; Isa 40:8
ᵉPs 107:11; Isa 8:6; 30:9,12 ᶠJob 6:10; Isa 1:4; 10:20; 12:6
5:25 ᵍS 2Ki 22:13; S Job 40:11; Isa 10:17; 26:11; 31:9; 66:15; S Jer 6:12
ʰS Ex 19:18
ⁱS Ps 110:6
ʲS 2Ki 9:37
ᵏS 2Sa 22:43
ˡJer 4:8; Da 9:16
ᵐIsa 9:12,17,21; 10:4
5:26 ⁿS Ps 20:5
ᵒIsa 7:18; Zec 10:8
ᵖDt 28:49;
Isa 13:5; 18:3
5:27 ᑫIsa 14:31; 40:29-31

²⁴Therefore, as tongues of fireᵃ lick up
  strawᵇ
 and as dry grass sinks down in the
  flames,
 so their roots will decayᶜ
 and their flowers blow away like
  dust;ᵈ
 for they have rejected the law of the
  LORD Almighty
 and spurned the wordᵉ of the Holy
  Oneᶠ of Israel.

R ²⁵Therefore the LORD's angerᵍ burns
  against his people;
 his hand is raised and he strikes
  them down.
 The mountains shake,ʰ
 and the dead bodiesⁱ are like refuseʲ
  in the streets.ᵏ
 Yet for all this, his anger is not turned
  away,ˡ
 his hand is still upraised.ᵐ

²⁶He lifts up a bannerⁿ for the distant
  nations,
 he whistlesᵒ for those at the ends of
  the earth.ᵖ
 Here they come,
  swiftly and speedily!
²⁷Not one of them grows tiredᑫ or
  stumbles,
 not one slumbers or sleeps;
 not a beltʳ is loosened at the waist,ˢ
 not a sandal thong is broken.ᵗ
²⁸Their arrows are sharp,ᵘ
 all their bowsᵛ are strung;
 their horses' hoofsʷ seem like flint,
 their chariot wheels like a
  whirlwind.ˣ
²⁹Their roar is like that of the lion,ʸ
 they roar like young lions;
 they growl as they seizeᶻ their prey
 and carry it off with no one to
  rescue.ᵃ
³⁰In that dayᵇ they will roar over it
 like the roaring of the sea.ᶜ

R Isa 5:1–10 ◀▶ Isa 6:9–13

ʳIsa 22:21; Eze 23:15 ˢS Job 12:18 ᵗJoel 2:7-8 **5:28** ᵘS Job 39:23; Ps 45:5 ᵛS Ps 7:12 ʷEze 26:11 ˣS 2Ki 2:1; S Job 1:19 **5:29** ʸS 2Ki 17:25; Jer 51:38; Zep 3:3; Zec 11:3 ᶻIsa 10:6; 49:24-25 ᵃIsa 42:22; Mic 5:8 **5:30** ᵇS Isa 2:11 ᶜS Ps 93:3; Jer 50:42; Lk 21:25

ⁱ 14 Hebrew *Sheol* ʲ 17 Septuagint; Hebrew / *strangers will eat*

5:25 Isaiah declares God's determination to punish his people as a result of their continued rebellion.

5:30 God affirms his coming judgment at the hands of a destroying enemy due to the nation's rebellion.

And if one looks at the land,
    he will see darkness and distress;
    even the light will be darkened by
        the clouds.

Isaiah's Commission

6 In the year that King Uzziah died, I saw the Lord seated on a throne, high and exalted, and the train of his robe filled the temple. ² Above him were seraphs, each with six wings: With two wings they covered their faces, with two they covered their feet, and with two they were flying. ³ And they were calling to one another:

"Holy, holy, holy is the LORD Almighty;
    the whole earth is full of his
        glory."

⁴ At the sound of their voices the doorposts and thresholds shook and the temple was filled with smoke.

⁵ "Woe to me!" I cried. "I am ruined! For I am a man of unclean lips, and I live among a people of unclean lips, and my eyes have seen the King, the LORD Almighty."

⁶ Then one of the seraphs flew to me with a live coal in his hand, which he had taken with tongs from the altar. ⁷ With it he touched my mouth and said, "See, this has touched your lips; your guilt is taken away and your sin atoned for."

⁸ Then I heard the voice of the Lord saying, "Whom shall I send? And who will go for us?"

And I said, "Here am I. Send me!"

⁹ He said, "Go and tell this people:

" 'Be ever hearing, but never
    understanding;
be ever seeing, but never
    perceiving.'

C Isa 5:20 ◄► Isa 6:9–10
R Isa 5:25–30 ◄► Isa 7:3–4
C Isa 6:5 ◄► Isa 9:2

¹⁰ Make the heart of this people calloused;
    make their ears dull
    and close their eyes.
Otherwise they might see with their
    eyes,
    hear with their ears,
    understand with their hearts,
and turn and be healed."

¹¹ Then I said, "For how long, O Lord?"

And he answered:

"Until the cities lie ruined
    and without inhabitant,
until the houses are left deserted
    and the fields ruined and ravaged,
¹² until the LORD has sent everyone far
    away
    and the land is utterly forsaken.
¹³ And though a tenth remains in the
    land,
    it will again be laid waste.
But as the terebinth and oak
    leave stumps when they are cut
        down,
so the holy seed will be the stump
    in the land."

The Sign of Immanuel

7 When Ahaz son of Jotham, the son of Uzziah, was king of Judah, King Rezin of Aram and Pekah son of Remaliah king of Israel marched up to fight against Jerusalem, but they could not overpower it.

² Now the house of David was told, "Aram has allied itself with Ephraim"; so the hearts of Ahaz and his people were

9,10 Hebrew; Septuagint 'You will be ever hearing, but never understanding; / you will be ever seeing, but never perceiving.' / ¹⁰ This people's heart has become calloused; / they hardly hear with their ears, / and they have closed their eyes ¹² Or has set up camp in

---

6:1–8 This remarkable passage tells of a vision that Isaiah received when he went to the temple to pray. Isaiah saw God in all his majesty and glory, "high and exalted" (6:1). In response to this vision Isaiah declared his sinfulness and the sinfulness of the nation too, so God sent an angel to cleanse Isaiah from his sin. Note that only after acknowledging his sin and receiving cleansing can Isaiah answer God's question "Whom shall I send?" with a firm "Here am I. Send me!" (6:8).

6:9–13 God declared that those who received Isaiah's prophecy would fail to hear or understand his inspired words. Until the threatened destruction was fulfilled, the people would not understand God's warning.

ISAIAH 7:3

shaken,[g] as the trees of the forest are shaken by the wind."

[R] ³Then the LORD said to Isaiah, "Go out, you and your son Shear-Jashub,[m,h] to meet Ahaz at the end of the aqueduct of the Upper Pool, on the road to the Washerman's Field.[i] ⁴Say to him, 'Be careful, keep calm[j] and don't be afraid.[k] Do not lose heart[l] because of these two smoldering stubs[m] of firewood—because of the fierce anger[n] of Rezin and Aram and of the son of Remaliah.[o] ⁵Aram, Ephraim and Remaliah's[p] son have plotted[q] your ruin, saying, ⁶"Let us invade Judah; let us tear it apart and divide it among ourselves, and make the son of Tabeel king [R] over it." ⁷Yet this is what the Sovereign LORD says:[r]

" 'It will not take place,
   it will not happen,[s]
⁸for the head of Aram is Damascus,[t]
   and the head of Damascus is only
      Rezin.[u]
Within sixty-five years
   Ephraim will be too shattered[v] to be
      a people.
[F] ⁹The head of Ephraim is Samaria,[w]
   and the head of Samaria is only
      Remaliah's son.
If you do not stand[x] firm in your faith,[y]
   you will not stand at all.' "[z]

¹⁰Again the LORD spoke to Ahaz, ¹¹"Ask the LORD your God for a sign,[a] whether in the deepest depths or in the highest heights.[b]"

¹²But Ahaz said, "I will not ask; I will not put the LORD to the test.[c]"

[B] ¹³Then Isaiah said, "Hear now, you

[R] Isa 6:9–13 ◄ ► Isa 7:7–9
[R] Isa 7:3–4 ◄ ► Isa 7:17
[F] Pr 29:25 ◄ ► Isa 26:3–4
[B] Ps 22:1–18 ◄ ► Isa 9:6–7

7:2 [g] Isa 6:4; Da 5:6
7:3 [h] Isa 10:21-22
   [i] 2Ki 18:17; Isa 36:2
7:4 [j] Isa 30:15; La 3:26 [k] S Ge 15:1; S Dt 3:2; Isa 8:12; 12:2; 35:4; 37:6; Mt 24:6 [l] S Dt 20:3; S Isa 21:4
   [m] Am 4:11; Zec 3:2
   [n] Isa 10:24; 51:13; 54:14 [o] S 2Ki 15:27
7:5 [p] S ver 1 [q] ver 2
7:7 [r] Isa 24:3; 25:8; 28:16 [s] Ps 2:1; Isa 8:10; 14:24; 28:18; 40:8; 46:10; Ac 4:25
7:8 [t] S Ge 14:15
   [u] ver 1; Isa 9:11
   [v] 2Ki 17:24; Isa 8:4; 17:1-3
   [w] S 2Ki 15:29; Isa 9:9; 28:1,3
   [x] S Ps 20:8; Isa 8:10; 40:8
   [y] 2Ch 20:20
   [z] Isa 8:6-8; 30:12-14
7:11 [a] S Ex 7:9; S Dt 13:2
   [b] Ps 139:8
7:12 [c] Dt 4:34
7:13 [d] S ver 1
   [e] S Ge 30:15
   [f] S Isa 1:14
   [g] Ps 63:1; 118:28; Isa 25:1; 49:4; 61:10
7:14 [h] S Ex 3:12;
   S Lk 2:12
   [i] S Ge 24:43
   [j] S Ge 3:15; Lk 1:31
   [k] S Ge 21:22;
   Isa 8:8,10;
   Mt 1:23*
7:15 [l] S Ge 18:8
   [m] ver 22
7:16 [n] Isa 8:4
   [o] Dt 1:39
   [p] S Dt 13:16; Isa 17:3; Jer 7:15; Hos 5:9,13; Am 1:3-5
7:17 [q] 1Ki 12:16
   [r] S ver 20; S 2Ch 28:20
7:18 [s] ver 20,21; S Isa 2:11
   [t] S Isa 5:26
   [u] Isa 13:5
7:19 [v] S Isa 2:19
   [w] ver 25; Isa 17:9; 34:13; 55:13
7:20 [x] S ver 18

house of David![d] Is it not enough[e] to try the patience of men? Will you try the patience[f] of my God[g] also? ¹⁴Therefore the Lord himself will give you[n] a sign:[h] The virgin[i] will be with child and will give birth to a son,[j] and[o] will call him Immanuel.[p,k] ¹⁵He will eat curds[l] and honey[m] when he knows enough to reject the wrong and choose the right. ¹⁶But before the boy knows[n] enough to reject the wrong and choose the right,[o] the land of the two kings you dread will be laid waste.[p] ¹⁷The LORD will bring on you and [R] on your people and on the house of your father a time unlike any since Ephraim broke away[q] from Judah—he will bring the king of Assyria.'"

¹⁸In that day[s] the LORD will whistle[r] for [R] flies from the distant streams of Egypt and for bees from the land of Assyria.[u] ¹⁹They will all come and settle in the steep ravines and in the crevices[v] in the rocks, on all the thornbushes[w] and at all the water holes. ²⁰In that day[x] the Lord will use[y] a razor hired from beyond the River[a,z]—the king of Assyria[a]—to shave your head and the hair of your legs, and to take off your beards[b] also.[c] ²¹In that day,[d] a man will keep alive a young cow and two goats.[e] ²²And because of the abundance of the milk they give, he will have curds to eat. All who remain in the land will eat curds[f] and honey.[g] ²³In that [R] day,[h] in every place where there were a

[R] Isa 7:7–9 ◄ ► Isa 7:18–25
[R] Isa 7:17 ◄ ► Isa 7:23–24
[R] Isa 7:18–25 ◄ ► Isa 8:9–10

[y] Isa 10:15; 29:16 [z] Isa 11:15; Jer 2:18 [a] ver 17; 2Ki 18:16; Isa 8:7; 10:5
[b] S 2Sa 10:4 [c] S Dt 28:49 7:21 [d] ver 23; Isa 2:17 [e] Jer 39:10
7:22 [f] S Ge 18:8 [g] ver 15; Isa 14:30 7:23 [h] ver 21

[m] 3 *Shear-Jashub* means *a remnant will return.* [n] 14 The Hebrew is plural. [o] 14 Masoretic Text; Dead Sea Scrolls *and he* or *and they* [p] 14 *Immanuel* means *God with us.* [q] 20 That is, the Euphrates

---

7:3 Isaiah calls his son "Shear-Jashub" (7:3), which prophetically means "a remnant will return."

7:8–9 This fascinating prophecy was fulfilled 65 years later in 670 B.C. when the conquering Assyrian king settled Assyrian colonists in Israel. The intermarriage of theses colonists with the remaining Israelites who had not been exiled resulted in the people group called the Samaritans (see 2Ki 17:24–34) and marked the end of the tribe of Ephraim.

7:14 This prophecy is the clearest prediction of the virgin birth of the Messiah in the OT. It expands the earlier prophecy found in Genesis that the seed of the woman would defeat the seed of Satan (see Ge 3:15). By using the Hebrew word *almah* (translated "virgin") to denote an unmarried young woman as the mother of this child, Isaiah's prophecy declared that this miraculous conception and birth would be "a sign" from God, and that her miraculous son would be named Immanuel, which means "God with us" (Mt 1:23). Centuries later, the virgin Mary gave birth to the Christ-child Jesus in fulfillment of this extraordinary prophecy (see Lk 1:26–37).

thousand vines worth a thousand silver shekels,[ri] there will be only briers and thorns.[j] [24]Men will go there with bow and arrow, for the land will be covered with briers[k] and thorns. [25]As for all the hills[l] once cultivated by the hoe, you will no longer go there for fear of the briers and thorns;[m] they will become places where cattle are turned loose and where sheep run.[n]

Assyria, the LORD's Instrument

8 The LORD said to me, "Take a large scroll[o] and write on it with an ordinary pen: Maher-Shalal-Hash-Baz.[sp] [2]And I will call in Uriah[q] the priest and Zechariah son of Jeberekiah as reliable witnesses[r] for me."

[3]Then I went to the prophetess,[s] and she conceived and gave birth to a son.[t] And the LORD said to me, "Name him Maher-Shalal-Hash-Baz.[u] [4]Before the boy knows[v] how to say 'My father' or 'My mother,' the wealth of Damascus[w] and the plunder of Samaria will be carried off by the king of Assyria.[x]"

[5]The LORD spoke to me again:

[6]"Because this people has rejected[y]
the gently flowing waters of Shiloah[z]
and rejoices over Rezin
and the son of Remaliah,[a]
[7]therefore the Lord is about to bring against them
the mighty floodwaters[b] of the River[r]—
the king of Assyria[c] with all his pomp.[d]
It will overflow all its channels,
run over all its banks[e]
[8]and sweep on into Judah, swirling over it,[f]
passing through it and reaching up to the neck.
Its outspread wings[g] will cover the breadth of your land,
O Immanuel[u]!"[h]

[9]Raise the war cry,[vi] you nations, and be shattered![j]
Listen, all you distant lands.
Prepare[k] for battle, and be shattered!
Prepare for battle, and be shattered!

[10]Devise your strategy, but it will be thwarted;[l]
propose your plan, but it will not stand,[m]
for God is with us.[wn]

Fear God

[11]The LORD spoke to me with his strong hand upon me,[o] warning me not to follow[p] the way of this people. He said:

[12]"Do not call conspiracy[q]
everything that these people call conspiracy[x];
do not fear what they fear,[r]
and do not dread it.[s]
[13]The LORD Almighty is the one you are to regard as holy,[t]
he is the one you are to fear,[u]
he is the one you are to dread,[v]
[14]and he will be a sanctuary;[w]
but for both houses of Israel he will be
a stone[x] that causes men to stumble[y]
and a rock that makes them fall.[z]
And for the people of Jerusalem he will be
a trap and a snare.[a]
[15]Many of them will stumble;[b]
they will fall and be broken,
they will be snared and captured."

[16]Bind up the testimony[c]
and seal[d] up the law among my disciples.
[17]I will wait[e] for the LORD,
who is hiding[f] his face from the house of Jacob.
I will put my trust in him.[g]

[18]Here am I, and the children the LORD has given me.[h] We are signs[i] and symbols[j] in Israel from the LORD Almighty, who dwells on Mount Zion.[k]

[19]When men tell you to consult[l] mediums and spiritists,[m] who whisper and

---

H *Isa 3:24* ◀ ▶ *Isa 9:18*
R *Isa 8:9–10* ◀ ▶ *Isa 10:12*

[i]S Ex 3:12; Eze 4:3; 12:6; 24:24; Lk 2:34 [j]S Dt 28:46; S Eze 12:11 [k]S Ps 9:11
8:19 [l]S Isa 28:8 [m]S Lev 19:31

[r]*23 That is, about 25 pounds (about 11.5 kilograms)*
[s]*1 Maher-Shalal-Hash-Baz means quick to the plunder, swift to the spoil; also in verse 3.* [t]*7 That is, the Euphrates* [u]*8 Immanuel means God with us.* [v]*9 Or Do your worst* [w]*10 Hebrew Immanuel* [x]*12 Or Do not call for a treaty / every time these people call for a treaty*

R *Isa 7:23–24* ◀ ▶ *Isa 8:17*

7:23–24 Isaiah predicted that the fertility of the land of Palestine would turn to barrenness as a result of the nation's continued rebellion against God.

mutter,ⁿ should not a people inquire° of their God? Why consult the dead on behalf of the living? ²⁰To the lawᵖ and to the testimony!ᑫ If they do not speak according to this word, they have no light ʳ of dawn. ²¹Distressed and hungry,ˢ they will roam through the land;ᵗ when they are famished, they will become enraged and, looking upward, will curseᵘ their king and their God. ²²Then they will look toward the earth and see only distress and darkness and fearful gloom,ᵛ and they will be thrust into utter darkness.ʷ

To Us a Child Is Born

9 Nevertheless, there will be no more gloomˣ for those who were in distress. In the past he humbled the land of Zebulun and the land of Naphtali,ʸ but in the future he will honor Galilee of the Gentiles, by the way of the sea, along the Jordan—

²The people walking in darkness ᶻ
  have seen a great light;ᵃ
on those living in the land of the
    shadow of death,ʸᵇ
  a light has dawned.ᶜ
³You have enlarged the nationᵈ
  and increased their joy;ᵉ
they rejoice before you
  as people rejoice at the harvest,
as men rejoice
  when dividing the plunder.ᶠ
⁴For as in the day of Midian's defeat,ᵍ
  you have shattered ʰ
the yokeⁱ that burdens them,
  the bar across their shoulders,ʲ
  the rod of their oppressor.ᵏ
⁵Every warrior's boot used in battle
  and every garment rolled in blood

I Isa 4:2–6 ◀▶ Isa 9:7
C Isa 6:9–10 ◀▶ Isa 26:10–11
L Isa 4:6 ◀▶ Isa 12:1–3

will be destined for burning,ˡ
  will be fuel for the fire.
⁶For to us a child is born,ᵐ
  to us a son is given,ⁿ
  and the government° will be on his
    shoulders.ᵖ
And he will be called
  Wonderful Counselor,ᶻᑫ Mighty
    God,ʳ
  Everlastingˢ Father,ᵗ Prince of
    Peace.ᵘ
⁷Of the increase of his governmentᵛ
    and peaceʷ
  there will be no end.ˣ
He will reignʸ on David's throne
  and over his kingdom,
establishing and upholding it
  with justice ᶻ and righteousnessᵃ
  from that time on and forever.ᵇ
The zealᶜ of the Lᴏʀᴅ Almighty
  will accomplish this.

The Lᴏʀᴅ's Anger Against Israel

⁸The Lord has sent a messageᵈ against
    Jacob;
  it will fall on Israel.
⁹All the people will know it—
  Ephraimᵉ and the inhabitants of
    Samariaᶠ—
who say with pride
  and arroganceᵍ of heart,
¹⁰"The bricks have fallen down,

B Isa 7:13–16 ◀▶ Isa 11:1–5
M Isa 4:5–6 ◀▶ Isa 11:4–10
U Isa 2:4 ◀▶ Isa 11:6–9
V Ps 110:1 ◀▶ Isa 11:1–9
I Isa 9:1–4 ◀▶ Isa 11:11–15

ʸ2 Or *land of darkness* ᶻ6 Or *Wonderful, Counselor*

9:1–2 This prophecy notes that though Zebulun and Naphtali were humbled by the Assyrians (see 2Ki 15:29), Galilee would be the center of the Messiah's ministry, bringing glory back to these humbled tribes. Many of the people of Galilee responded favorably to the message of Christ during his ministry there (see Mk 4:13–16), leaving their darkness for his "great light" (9:2).

9:6–7 Isaiah's famous prophecy of the Messiah points to Christ's ultimate establishment of his millennial kingdom. Christ will rule in those days as the Prince of Peace from David's throne in Zion. Isaiah predicts that this kingdom will increase forever. Some scholars believe that Christ will only rule during the Millennium for a period of a thousand years (see Rev 20:6). Other scholars suggest that this millennial rule is only one piece of God's plan following the Battle of Armageddon. These scholars contend that after Satan's final rebellion at the end of the Millennium, God's kingdom will continue forever on the new earth as Christians rule over the earth under the leadership of Christ the Messiah (see 2Ti 2:12; Rev 3:21; 22:5).

ISAIAH 10:6

but we will rebuild with dressed
   stone;[h]
the fig trees have been felled,
but we will replace them with
   cedars.'"
[11]But the LORD has strengthened Rezin's[k]
   foes against them
and has spurred their enemies on.
[12]Arameans[l] from the east and
   Philistines[m] from the west
have devoured[n] Israel with open
   mouth.

Yet for all this, his anger[o] is not turned
   away,
   his hand is still upraised.[p]

[13]But the people have not returned[q] to
   him who struck[r] them,
   nor have they sought[s] the LORD
      Almighty.
[14]So the LORD will cut off from Israel
   both head and tail,
both palm branch and reed[t] in a
   single day;[u]
[15]the elders[v] and prominent men[w] are
   the head,
the prophets[x] who teach lies[y] are
   the tail.
[16]Those who guide[z] this people mislead
   them,
and those who are guided are led
   astray.[a]
[17]Therefore the Lord will take no
   pleasure in the young men,[b]
nor will he pity[c] the fatherless and
   widows,
for everyone is ungodly[d] and wicked,[e]
every mouth speaks vileness.[f]

Yet for all this, his anger is not turned
   away,
   his hand is still upraised.[g]

H [18]Surely wickedness burns like a fire;[h]
   it consumes briers and thorns,[i]
   it sets the forest thickets ablaze,[j]
   so that it rolls upward in a column of
      smoke.
[19]By the wrath[k] of the LORD Almighty
   the land will be scorched[l]

H *Isa 8:15* ◀ ▶ *Isa 11:4*

and the people will be fuel for the
   fire;[m]
no one will spare his brother.[n]
[20]On the right they will devour,
   but still be hungry;[o]
on the left they will eat,[p]
   but not be satisfied.
Each will feed on the flesh of his own
   offspring[a]:
[21] Manasseh will feed on Ephraim, and
   Ephraim on Manasseh;[q]
together they will turn against
   Judah.[r]

Yet for all this, his anger is not turned
   away,
   his hand is still upraised.[s]

10
Woe[t] to those who make unjust
   laws,
to those who issue oppressive
   decrees,[u]
[2]to deprive[v] the poor of their rights
   and withhold justice from the
      oppressed of my people,[w]
making widows their prey
   and robbing the fatherless.[x]
[3]What will you do on the day of
   reckoning,[y]
when disaster[z] comes from afar?
To whom will you run for help?[a]
Where will you leave your riches?
[4]Nothing will remain but to cringe
   among the captives[b]
or fall among the slain.[c]

Yet for all this, his anger is not turned
   away,[d]
   his hand is still upraised.

God's Judgment on Assyria

[5]"Woe[e] to the Assyrian,[f] the rod[g] of my
   anger,
in whose hand is the club[h] of my
   wrath![i]
[6]I send him against a godless[j] nation,

[a] 20 Or *arm*

10:5–6 This prediction referred initially to the Assyrian king whom God sent to judge his people. The prophetic title of "the Assyrian" (10:5) also refers to the antichrist, who will come against the nation of Israel in the last days during the tribulation.

The Prophecies of Christ's First Coming

THOUGH THE WRITINGS of other religious beliefs do not contain detailed, specific prophecies, one of the strongest evidences of the divine inspiration of Scripture can be attributed to the hundreds of verifiable, detailed prophecies spanning thousands of years and concerning various nations, events and individuals. When we examine the prophecies in the Bible, we find predictions of events which historians and archeologists verify have been fulfilled. God declared that these prophecies and their fulfillments are verification that the Bible is truly the inspired Word of God (see Isa 46:9–10).

Out of hundreds of Biblical prophecies concerning the promised Messiah's birth, life, death and resurrection, some are quite specific, including the eleven listed below. Note that the chart below suggests an estimate of the probability of each prophecy's fulfillment, with more commonplace customs showing a higher probability of occurrence and the more restrictive prophecies reflecting a lesser probability of occurrence. Though the odds assigned in this chart are arbitrary, they are presented to give the reader an indication of the preponderance of evidence for the divine inspiration of Scripture.

Note also that statistical theory holds that if the probability of one event occurring is one in five, and the probability of another event occurring is one in ten, then the probability of both events being fulfilled in sequence is one in fifty. The following eleven Messianic predictions were made more than four hundred years before they were fulfilled. If these arbitrarily assigned odds were statistically calculated, there is only one chance in 10^{19} that the prophets could have accurately predicted these eleven specific prophecies. Searching the Scriptures for the other specific prophecies regarding Christ's first coming and factoring in their mathematical probabilities reveal the virtual impossibility that these prophecies could be fulfilled by chance alone. God made these promises, and God kept his promises.

Eleven Predictions About the Promised Messiah

PREDICTION & PROBABILITY	OT PREDICTION	NT FULFILLMENT
1. Be born in Bethlehem 1 in 200	But you, Bethlehem Ephrathah, though you are small among the clans of Judah, out of you will come for me one who will be ruler over Israel (Mic 5:2).	Jesus was born in Bethlehem in Judea, during the time of King Herod (Mt 2:1).
2. Be preceded by a messenger 1 in 20	A voice of one calling: "In the desert prepare the way for the LORD; make straight in the wilderness a highway for our God" (Isa 40:3).	In those days John the Baptist came, preaching in the Desert of Judea and saying, "Repent, for the kingdom of heaven is near" (Mt 3:1–2).

PREDICTION & PROBABILITY	OT PREDICTION	NT FULFILLMENT
3. Enter Jerusalem on a colt *1 in 50*	Rejoice greatly, O Daughter of Zion! Shout, Daughter of Jerusalem! See, your king comes to you, righteous and having salvation, gentle and riding on a donkey, on a colt, the foal of a donkey (Zec 9:9).	They brought it to Jesus, threw their cloaks on the colt and put Jesus on it. As he went along, people spread their cloaks on the road. When he came near the place where the road goes down the Mount of Olives, the whole crowd of disciples began joyfully to praise God in loud voices for all the miracles they had seen (Lk 19:35–37).
4. Be betrayed by a friend *1 in 10*	Even my close friend, whom I trusted, he who shared my bread, has lifted up his heel against me (Ps 41:9).	While he was still speaking, Judas, one of the Twelve, arrived. With him was a large crowd armed with swords and clubs, sent from the chief priests and the elders of the people. Now the betrayer had arranged a signal with them: "The one I kiss is the man; arrest him".... Jesus replied, "Friend, do what you came for" (Mt 26:47-50).
5. Have his hands and feet pierced *1 in 100*	A band of evil men has encircled me, they have pierced my hands and my feet (Ps 22:16).	When they came to the place called the Skull, there they crucified him, along with the criminals—one on his right, the other on his left (Lk 23:33).
6. Be wounded and whipped by his enemies *1 in 25*	But he was pierced for our transgressions, he was crushed for our iniquities; the punishment that brought us peace was upon him, and by his wounds we are healed (Isa 53:5).	Then he released Barabbas to them. But he had Jesus flogged, and handed him over to be crucified (Mt 27:26).
7. Be sold for thirty pieces of silver *1 in 100*	I told them, "If you think it best, give me my pay; but if not, keep it." So they paid me thirty pieces of silver (Zec 11:12).	"What are you willing to give me if I hand him over to you?" So they counted out for him thirty silver coins (Mt 26:15).
8. Be spit upon and beaten *1 in 10*	I offered my back to those who beat me, my cheeks to those who pulled out my beard; I did not hide my face from mocking and spitting (Isa 50:6).	Then they spit in his face and struck him with their fists (Mt 26:67).
9. Have his betrayal money thrown in the temple and given for a potter's field *1 in 200*	And the LORD said to me, "Throw it to the potter"—the handsome price at which they priced me! So I took the thirty pieces of silver and threw them into the house of the LORD to the potter (Zec 11:13).	So Judas threw the money into the temple and left. Then he went away and hanged himself. The chief priests picked up the coins and said, "It is against the law to put this into the treasury, since it is blood money." So they decided to use the money to buy the potter's field as a burial place for foreigners (Mt 27:5–7).
10. Be silent before his accusers *1 in 100*	He was oppressed and afflicted, yet he did not open his mouth; he was led like a lamb to the slaughter, and as a sheep before her shearers is silent, so he did not open his mouth (Isa 53:7).	When he was accused by the chief priests and the elders, he gave no answer. Then Pilate asked him, "Don't you hear the testimony they are bringing against you?" But Jesus made no reply, not even to a single charge to the great amazement of the governor (Mt 27:12–14).
11. Be crucified with thieves *1 in 100*	He poured out his life unto death, and was numbered with the transgressors. For he bore the sin of many, and made intercession for the transgressors (Isa 53:12).	Two robbers were crucified with him, one on his right and one on his left (Mt 27:38).

I dispatch^k him against a people who anger me,^l
to seize loot and snatch plunder,^m
and to trample^n them down like mud in the streets.
⁷But this is not what he intends,^o
this is not what he has in mind;
his purpose is to destroy,
to put an end to many nations.
⁸'Are not my commanders^p all kings?' he says.
⁹ 'Has not Calno^q fared like Carchemish?^r
Is not Hamath^s like Arpad,^t
and Samaria^u like Damascus?^v
¹⁰As my hand seized the kingdoms of the idols,^w
kingdoms whose images excelled those of Jerusalem and Samaria—
¹¹shall I not deal with Jerusalem and her images
as I dealt with Samaria and her idols?^x '"

R ¹²When the Lord has finished all his work^y against Mount Zion^z and Jerusalem, he will say, "I will punish the king of Assyria^a for the willful pride^b of his heart and the haughty look^c in his eyes. ¹³For he says:

" 'By the strength of my hand^d I have done this,^e
and by my wisdom, because I have understanding.
I removed the boundaries of nations,
I plundered their treasures;^f
like a mighty one I subdued^b their kings.^g
¹⁴As one reaches into a nest,^h
so my hand reached for the wealth^i of the nations;
as men gather abandoned eggs,
so I gathered all the countries;^j
not one flapped a wing,
or opened its mouth to chirp.^k ' "

R *Isa 8:17* ◀▶ *Isa 10:16–19*

10:6 ^k Hab 1:12
^l S 2Ch 28:9;
Isa 9:19 ^m S Jdg 6:4;
S Isa 5:29; 8:1
^n S 2Sa 22:43;
S Ps 7:5; S Isa 5:5;
37:26-27
10:7 ^o S Ge 50:20;
Ac 4:23-28
10:8 ^p 2Ki 18:24
10:9 ^q S Ge 10:10
^r S 2Ch 35:20
^s Nu 34:8; 2Ch 8:4;
Isa 11:11
^t 2Ki 18:34
^u 2Ki 17:6
^v S Ge 14:15;
2Ki 16:9; Jer 49:24
10:10 ^w 2Ki 19:18
10:11
^x S 2Ki 19:13;
S Isa 2:8; 36:18-20;
37:10-13
10:12
^y Isa 28:21-22;
65:7; 66:4; Jer 5:29
^z 2Ki 19:31
^a ver 5;
S 2Ki 19:7;
Isa 30:31-33;
37:36-38; Jer 50:18
^b S Isa 2:11;
S Eze 28:17
^c Ps 18:27
10:13 ^d S Dt 8:17
^e Dt 32:26-27;
Isa 47:7; Da 4:30
^f Eze 28:4
^g Isa 14:13-14
10:14 ^h Jer 49:16;
Ob 1:4; Hab 2:6-11
^i S Job 31:25
^j Isa 14:6
^k 2Ki 19:22-24;
Isa 37:24-25
10:15 ^l S Isa 7:20;
45:9; Ro 9:20-21
^m S ver 5
10:16 ^n ver 18;
S Nu 11:33;
Isa 17:4 ^o Ps 78:31
^p S Isa 8:7
^q Jer 21:14
10:17
^r S Job 41:21;
S Isa 1:31; 31:9;
Zec 2:5 ^s Isa 37:23
^t S Nu 11:1-3;
S 2Sa 23:6
^u S Isa 9:18
10:18
^v S 2Ki 19:23
^w S ver 5
10:19 ^x ver 33-34;
Isa 32:19 ^y Isa 17:6;
21:17; 27:13;
Jer 44:28
10:20 ^z ver 27;
Isa 11:10,11; 12:1,
4; 19:18,19; 24:21;
28:5; 52:6;
Zec 9:16 ^a S Isa 1:9;
Eze 7:16
^b S 2Ki 16:7

¹⁵Does the ax raise itself above him who M swings it,
or the saw boast against him who uses it?^l
As if a rod were to wield him who lifts it up,
or a club^m brandish him who is not wood!

¹⁶Therefore, the Lord, the LORD Almighty, R
will send a wasting disease^n upon his sturdy warriors;^o
under his pomp^p a fire^q will be kindled like a blazing flame.
¹⁷The Light of Israel will become a fire,^r
their Holy One^s a flame;
in a single day it will burn and consume
his thorns^t and his briers.^u
¹⁸The splendor of his forests^v and fertile fields
it will completely destroy,^w
as when a sick man wastes away.
¹⁹And the remaining trees of his forests^x
will be so few^y
that a child could write them down.

The Remnant of Israel

²⁰In that day^z the remnant of Israel,
the survivors^a of the house of Jacob,
will no longer rely^b on him
who struck them down^c
but will truly rely^d on the LORD,
the Holy One of Israel.^e
²¹A remnant^f will return,^c,g a remnant of Jacob
will return to the Mighty God.^h
²²Though your people, O Israel, be like R
the sand^i by the sea,
only a remnant will return.^j

M *Isa 5:21* ◀▶ *Isa 13:11*
R *Isa 10:12* ◀▶ *Isa 10:22–27*
R *Isa 10:16–19* ◀▶ *Isa 14:28–31*

^c 2Ch 28:20 ^d 2Ch 14:11; Isa 17:7; 48:2; 50:10; Jer 21:2; Hos 3:5; 6:1;
Mic 3:11; 7:7 ^e Isa 5:24 10:21 ^f S Ge 45:7; Isa 6:13; Zep 3:13 ^g Isa 7:3
^h Isa 9:6 10:22 ^i S Ge 12:2; Isa 48:19; Jer 33:22 ^j Ezr 1:4; Isa 11:11;
46:3

^b 13 Or / I subdued the mighty, ^c 21 Hebrew *shear-jashub*; also in verse 22

10:12 This verse found its initial fulfillment in God's punishment of the nation of Assyria. Though God used this wicked nation to carry out his judgment on his people, Assyria was still punished for its misdeeds. The final punishment of the antichrist, "the king of Assyria" (10:12), will come at the end times.

10:21–23 Isaiah prophesied that although the nation of Israel would be dispersed throughout the nations, a remnant would return to establish their nation in the last days.

Destruction has been decreed,ᵏ
overwhelming and righteous.
²³The Lord, the LORD Almighty, will carry out
the destruction decreedˡ upon the whole land.ᵐ

²⁴Therefore, this is what the Lord, the LORD Almighty, says:

"O my people who live in Zion,ⁿ
do not be afraidᵒ of the Assyrians,
who beatᵖ you with a rodᵠ
and lift up a club against you, as Egypt did.
²⁵Very soonʳ my anger against you will end
and my wrathˢ will be directed to their destruction.ᵗ"

²⁶The LORD Almighty will lashᵘ them with a whip,
as when he struck down Midianᵛ at the rock of Oreb;
and he will raise his staffʷ over the waters,ˣ
as he did in Egypt.
²⁷In that dayʸ their burdenᶻ will be lifted from your shoulders,
their yokeᵃ from your neck;ᵇ
the yokeᶜ will be broken
because you have grown so fat.ᵈ

²⁸They enter Aiath;
they pass through Migron;ᵈ
they store suppliesᵉ at Micmash.ᶠ
²⁹They go over the pass, and say,
"We will camp overnight at Geba."ᵍ
Ramahʰ trembles;
Gibeahⁱ of Saul flees.ʲ
³⁰Cry out, O Daughter of Gallim!ᵏ
Listen, O Laishah!
Poor Anathoth!ˡ
³¹Madmenah is in flight;
the people of Gebim take cover.
³²This day they will halt at Nob;ᵐ
they will shake their fistⁿ
at the mount of the Daughter of Zion,ᵒ
at the hill of Jerusalem.

³³See, the Lord, the LORD Almighty,
will lop offᵖ the boughs with great power.
The lofty trees will be felled,ᵠ
the tallʳ ones will be brought low.ˢ
³⁴He will cut downᵗ the forest thickets with an ax;
Lebanonᵘ will fall before the Mighty One.ᵛ

The Branch From Jesse

11 A shootʷ will come up from the stumpˣ of Jesse;ʸ
from his roots a Branchᶻ will bear fruit.ᵃ
²The Spiritᵇ of the LORD will rest on him—
the Spirit of wisdomᶜ and of understanding,
the Spirit of counsel and of power,ᵈ
the Spirit of knowledge and of the fear of the LORD—
³and he will delight in the fearᵉ of the LORD.

10:24–27 The prophet assured the people that God's judgment on Israel would come to an end and that God would punish the Assyrians for their part in Israel's judgment. Note also that this prophecy may be applied to the end times when the antichrist, prophetically called "the Assyrian" (see 10:5), will finally be destroyed by God.

11:1 This powerful prophecy described the coming Messiah as David's descendant, "a Branch," that would come from David's roots (see 4:2). This messianic title, "the Branch," is also mentioned by other OT prophets: "I will raise up to David a righteous Branch" (Jer 23:5) and "Here is the man whose name is the Branch" (Zec 6:12). Note that the Hebrew word for branch, *neser*, is also the root word for the city of Nazareth. Since Jesus came from that city, he is truly that Branch (see Mt 2:23).

11:2 Compare this prophecy with Zec 4:10. Note that Isaiah's prophecy described the anointing of the Messiah with seven characteristics of God: "the Spirit of the LORD," the Spirit of wisdom, understanding, counsel, might, knowledge and the Spirit of the fear of the Lord.

11:3–5 Though the rulers of Isaiah's day lacked all of these qualities, the Messiah will possess God's understanding, allowing him to rule with perfect justice. His government will be characterized by righteousness for the poor and judgment for the wicked.

He will not judge by what he sees with his eyes,ᶠ
or decide by what he hears with his ears;ᵍ
⁴but with righteousnessʰ he will judge the needy,ⁱ
with justiceʲ he will give decisions for the poorᵏ of the earth.
He will strikeˡ the earth with the rod of his mouth;ᵐ
with the breathⁿ of his lips he will slay the wicked.ᵒ
⁵Righteousness will be his beltᵖ
and faithfulnessᑫ the sash around his waist.ʳ

⁶The wolf will live with the lamb,ˢ
the leopard will lie down with the goat,
the calf and the lion and the yearlingᵉ together;
and a little child will lead them.
⁷The cow will feed with the bear,
their young will lie down together,
and the lion will eat straw like the ox.ᵗ
⁸The infantᵘ will play near the hole of the cobra,
and the young child put his hand into the viper'sᵛ nest.
⁹They will neither harm nor destroyʷ on all my holy mountain,ˣ
for the earthʸ will be full of the knowledgeᶻ of the Lord
as the waters cover the sea.
¹⁰In that dayᵃ the Root of Jesseᵇ will stand as a bannerᶜ for the peoples; the

M Isa 9:6–7 ◀ ▶ Isa 14:2
P Isa 2:10–21 ◀ ▶ Isa 13:1–22
H Isa 9:18 ◀ ▶ Isa 13:6–13
U Isa 9:6 ◀ ▶ Isa 32:17–18
K Ps 145:13 ◀ ▶ Jer 31:34

11:3 ᶠJn 7:24
ᵍJn 2:25
11:4 ʰS Ps 72:2
ⁱS Ps 72:4;
S Isa 14:30
ʲS Isa 9:7;
Rev 19:11
ᵏS Job 5:16;
S Isa 3:14 ˡIsa 27:7;
30:31; Zec 14:12;
Mal 4:6
ᵐS Job 40:18;
Ps 2:9; Rev 19:15
ⁿS Job 4:9; Ps 18:8;
Isa 30:28,33;
40:24; 59:19;
Eze 21:31; 2Th 2:8
ᵒS Ps 139:19
11:5 ᵖEx 12:11;
1Ki 18:46 ᑫIsa 25:1
ʳEph 6:14
11:6 ˢIsa 65:25
11:7 ᵗS Job 40:15
11:8 ᵘIsa 65:20
ᵛIsa 14:29; 30:6;
59:5
11:9 ʷS Nu 25:12;
S Isa 2:4; S 9:7
ˣS Ps 48:1;
S Isa 2:2
ʸIsa 17:46;
Ps 98:2-3;
Isa 45:22; 48:20;
52:10 ᶻEx 7:5;
Isa 19:21; 45:6,14;
49:26; Jer 24:7;
31:34; Hab 2:14
11:10 ᵃS Isa 10:20
ᵇver 1 ᶜS Ps 20:5;
Isa 18:3; Jer 4:6;
Jn 12:32
ᵈIsa 2:4; 14:1;
49:23; 56:3,6;
60:5,10; Lk 2:32;
Ac 11:18
ᵉRo 15:12*
ᶠS Ps 116:7;
Isa 14:3; 28:12;
32:17-18; 40:2;
Jer 6:16; 30:10;
46:27 ᵍHag 2:9;
Zec 2:5
11:11 ʰS Isa 10:20
ⁱS Dt 30:4; S Isa 1:9
ʲIsa 19:24;
Hos 11:11
Mic 7:12;
Zec 10:10
ᵏJer 44:1,15;
Eze 29:14; 30:14
ˡS Ge 10:6; Ac 8:27
ᵐS Ge 10:22
ⁿS Isa 10:9

nationsᵈ will rally to him,ᵉ and his place of restᶠ will be glorious.ᵍ ¹¹In that dayʰ the Lord will reach out his hand a second time to reclaim the remnantⁱ that is left of his people from Assyria,ʲ from Lower Egypt, from Upper Egypt,ᶠᵏ from Cush,ᵍˡ from Elam,ᵐ from Babylonia,ʰ from Hamathⁿ and from the islandsᵒ of the sea.ᵖ

¹²He will raise a bannerᑫ for the nations
and gatherʳ the exiles of Israel;ˢ
he will assemble the scattered peopleᵗ of Judah
from the four quarters of the earth.ᵘ
¹³Ephraim's jealousy will vanish,
and Judah's enemiesⁱ will be cut off;
Ephraim will not be jealous of Judah,
nor Judah hostile toward Ephraim.ᵛ
¹⁴They will swoop down on the slopes of Philistiaʷ to the west;
together they will plunder the people to the east.ˣ
They will lay hands on Edomʸ and Moab,ᶻ
and the Ammonitesᵃ will be subject to them.ᵇ
¹⁵The Lord will dry upᶜ
the gulf of the Egyptian sea;
with a scorching windᵈ he will sweep his handᵉ

ˡ Isa 9:7 ◀ ▶ Isa 12:1–6

ᵒIsa 24:15; 41:1,5; 42:4,10,12; 49:1; 51:5; 59:18; 60:9; 66:19
ᵖIsa 49:12; Jer 16:15; 46:27; Eze 38:8; Zec 8:7 11:12 ᑫS Ps 20:5
ʳIsa 14:2; 43:5; 49:22; 54:7; Jer 16:15; 31:10; 32:37 ˢS Ne 1:9;
S Ps 106:47; Isa 14:1; 41:14; 49:5 ᵗEze 28:25; Zep 3:10 ᵘS Ps 48:10;
67:7; Isa 41:5; Rev 7:1 11:13 ᵛ2Ch 28:6; Jer 3:18; Eze 37:16-17,22;
Hos 1:11 11:14 ʷ2Ch 26:6; S 28:18 ˣS Jdg 6:3 ʸS Nu 24:18;
S Ps 137:7; Isa 34:5-6; 63:1; Jer 49:22; Eze 25:12; Da 11:41; Joel 3:19;
Ob 1:1; Mal 1:4 ᶻIsa 15:1; 16:14; 25:10; Jer 48:40; Zep 2:8-11
ᵃJdg 11:4-18 ᵇIsa 25:3; 60:12 11:15 ᶜS Ex 14:22; S Dt 11:10;
Isa 37:25; 42:15; Jer 50:38; 51:36 ᵈS Ge 41:6 ᵉIsa 19:16; 30:32

ᵉ 6 Hebrew; Septuagint *lion will feed* ᶠ 11 Hebrew *from Pathros*
ᵍ 11 That is, the upper Nile region ʰ 11 Hebrew *Shinar* ⁱ 13 Or *hostility*

11:6–9 Isaiah described the future millennial reign of Christ as a time in which the curse of sin and violence will be lifted from the earth. Carnivorous animals will no longer kill to eat. Violence will be eliminated. This prediction is paralleled by other OT prophecies that confirm the peace and safety of the Messiah's rule (see Eze 34:25–28; Hos 2:18).

11:10 This prediction indicates the full acceptance of the Messiah by all nations.

11:11–12 At the second coming, Christ will bring about the return of all of the Jews to the promised land. Eight specific areas of the world are named in this passage. Note that this promised return "from the four quarters of the earth" (11:12) does not mean that Isaiah taught that the earth was flat. Isaiah also refers to the earth as a sphere in other prophecies (see 40:22). Rather, this metaphor indicates that God will bring his people back from all over the world to resettle the promised land.

11:13–16 The division between the two kingdoms of Israel and Judah will be healed by the return of the Messiah. Aided by God's miraculous intervention, the armies of the reunited kingdom of Israel will march across former rivers to attack their surrounding enemies (see Rev 16:12). Isaiah also foresaw the peaceful millennial kingdom of the Messiah, and described a highway for the Jewish refugees who would return to the promised land.

over the Euphrates River.*j f*
He will break it up into seven streams
so that men can cross over in
sandals.*g*

¹⁶There will be a highway*h* for the
remnant*i* of his people
that is left from Assyria,*j*
as there was for Israel
when they came up from Egypt.*k*

Songs of Praise

12 In that day*l* you will say:

"I will praise*m* you, O LORD.
Although you were angry with me,
your anger has turned away*n*
and you have comforted*o* me.

²Surely God is my salvation;*p*
I will trust*q* and not be afraid.
The LORD, the LORD,*r* is my strength*s*
and my song;
he has become my salvation."*t*

³With joy you will draw water*u*
from the wells*v* of salvation.

⁴In that day*w* you will say:

"Give thanks to the LORD, call on his
name;*x*
make known among the nations*y*
what he has done,
and proclaim that his name is
exalted.*z*

⁵Sing*a* to the LORD, for he has done
glorious things;*b*
let this be known to all the world.

l Isa 11:11–15 ◀ ▶ Isa 12:6
L Isa 9:2 ◀ ▶ Isa 32:2
W Pr 1:33 ◀ ▶ Isa 26:3–4
S Ps 16:11 ◀ ▶ Isa 25:8
T Ps 145:10–12 ◀ ▶ Isa 43:10

11:15 *f* S Isa 7:20
g S Ex 14:29
11:16 *h* Isa 19:23; 35:8; 40:3; 49:11; 51:10; 57:14; 62:10; Jer 50:5
i S Ge 45:7
j S ver 11
k Ex 14:26-31
12:1 *l* S Isa 10:20
m Ps 9:1; Isa 25:1
n S Job 13:16
o S Ps 71:21
12:2 *p* Isa 17:10; 25:9; 33:6; 45:17; 51:5,6; 54:8; 59:16; 61:10; 62:11 *q* S Job 13:15; S Ps 26:1; S 112:7; Isa 26:3; Da 6:23
r Isa 26:4; 38:11
s S Ps 18:1
t S Ex 15:2
12:3 *u* S 2Ki 3:17; Ps 36:9; Jer 2:13; 17:13; Jn 4:10,14
v Ex 15:25
12:4 *w* S Isa 10:20
x Ex 3:15; Ps 80:18; 105:1; Isa 24:15; 25:1; 26:8,13; Hos 12:5 *y* Isa 54:5; 60:3; Jer 10:7; Zep 2:11; Mal 1:11
z S Ps 113:2
12:5 *a* S Ex 15:1
b S Ps 98:1
12:6 *c* S Ge 21:6; S Ps 98:4; Isa 24:14; 48:20; 52:8; Jer 20:13; 31:7; Zec 2:10
d Ps 48:1
e S Ps 78:41; 99:2; Isa 1:24; 10:20; 17:7; 29:19; 37:23; 43:3,14; 45:11; 49:26; 55:5; Eze 39:7 *f* S Ps 46:5; Zep 3:14-17
13:1 *g* Isa 14:28; 15:1; 21:1; Na 1:1; Hab 1:1; Zec 9:1; 12:1; Mal 1:1
h ver 19; S Ge 10:10; Isa 14:4; 21:9; 46:1-2; 48:14; Jer 24:1; 25:12; Rev 14:8 *i* Isa 20:2; 37:2 *j* S Isa 1:1
13:2 *k* S Ps 20:5; Jer 50:2; 51:27

⁶Shout aloud and sing for joy,*c* people of
Zion,
for great*d* is the Holy One of Israel*e*
among you."*f*

A Prophecy Against Babylon

13 An oracle*g* concerning Babylon*h*
that Isaiah son of Amoz*i* saw:*j*

²Raise a banner*k* on a bare hilltop,
shout to them;
beckon to them
to enter the gates*l* of the nobles.

³I have commanded my holy ones;
I have summoned my warriors*m* to
carry out my wrath*n*—
those who rejoice*o* in my triumph.

⁴Listen, a noise on the mountains,
like that of a great multitude!*p*
Listen, an uproar*q* among the
kingdoms,
like nations massing together!
The LORD Almighty*r* is mustering*s*
an army for war.

⁵They come from faraway lands,
from the ends of the heavens*t*—
the LORD and the weapons*u* of his
wrath*v*—
to destroy*w* the whole country.

⁶Wail,*x* for the day of the LORD is near;
it will come like destruction*z* from
the Almighty.*k a*

l Isa 12:1–6 ◀ ▶ Isa 18:7
P Isa 11:4 ◀ ▶ Isa 24:1
H Isa 11:4 ◀ ▶ Isa 24:17–23

l Isa 24:12; 45:2; Jer 51:58 **13:3** *m* ver 17; Isa 21:2; Jer 51:11; Da 5:28, 31; Joel 3:11 *n* S Job 40:11; S Isa 10:5 *o* S Ps 149:2 **13:4** *p* Joel 3:14
q S Ps 46:6 *r* Isa 47:4; 51:15 *s* Isa 42:13; Jer 50:41 **13:5** *t* S Isa 5:26
u Isa 45:1; Jer 50:25 *v* S Isa 10:25 *w* S Jos 6:17; Isa 24:1; 30:25; 34:2 **13:6** *x* Isa 14:31; 15:2; 16:7; 23:1; Eze 30:2; Jas 5:1 *y* S Isa 2:12
z S Isa 10:3; S 14:15 *a* S Ge 17:1

j 15 Hebrew *the River* *k* 6 Hebrew *Shaddai*

12:1–6 This prophecy confidently foreshadowed Israel's final deliverance and reconciliation with God. Note also the final fulfillment of the role that God originally intended for his chosen people—to "make known among the nations what he has done" (12:4).

13:1–22 In this passage, Isaiah prophesied God's final judgment and destruction on Babylon that would occur during "the day of the LORD" (13:6). Though Babylon was initially destroyed by Cyrus the Persian in 539 B.C., its final destruction is announced here and in Rev 14:8; 16:19; 17—18. Paralleling Babylon's devastation with the destruction of Sodom and Gomorrah, Isaiah's words of doom signal the total victory of the Messiah over the satanic forces of the antichrist, prophetically called "the king of Babylon" (14:4).

Though for centuries Arab shepherds have used the region that formerly was the Babylonian empire as a grazing land, the ruins of the city of Babylon lay buried under desert sand and have only recently been discovered by archaeologists. Some Arab nations have begun to rebuild the city, however, in an attempt to restore Babylon to its glory. Isaiah's prediction that no Arab will pitch a tent in that region (13:20) has not been fulfilled yet in history and therefore must refer to Babylon's final destruction when Christ returns to defeat the forces of Satan at Armageddon.

ISAIAH 13:7

⁷Because of this, all hands will go
   limp,ᵇ
   every man's heart will melt.ᶜ
⁸Terrorᵈ will seize them,
   pain and anguish will gripᵉ them;
   they will writhe like a woman in
      labor.ᶠ
They will look aghast at each other,
   their faces aflame.ᵍ

⁹See, the dayʰ of the LORD is coming
   —a cruelⁱ day, with wrathʲ and
      fierce angerᵏ—
to make the land desolate
   and destroy the sinners within it.
¹⁰The stars of heaven and their
      constellations
   will not show their light.ˡ
The rising sunᵐ will be darkenedⁿ
   and the moon will not give its light.ᵒ
M ¹¹I will punishᵖ the world for its evil,
   the wickedᵠ for their sins.
I will put an end to the arrogance of
      the haughty,ʳ
   and will humbleˢ the pride of the
      ruthless.ᵗ
¹²I will make manᵘ scarcer than pure
      gold,
   more rare than the gold of Ophir.ᵛ
¹³Therefore I will make the heavens
      tremble;ʷ
   and the earth will shakeˣ from its
      place
at the wrathʸ of the LORD Almighty,
   in the day of his burning anger.ᶻ

¹⁴Like a huntedᵃ gazelle,
   like sheep without a shepherd,ᵇ
each will return to his own people,
   each will fleeᶜ to his native land.ᵈ
¹⁵Whoever is captured will be thrust
      through;
   all who are caught will fallᵉ by the
      sword.ᶠ
¹⁶Their infantsᵍ will be dashed to pieces
   before their eyes;

M Isa 10:15 ◀ ▶ Isa 46:12

13:7 ᵇS 2Ki 19:26; S Job 4:3; S Jer 47:3
ᶜS Jos 2:11; Eze 21:7
13:8 ᵈS Ps 31:13; S 48:5; S Isa 21:4
ᵉEx 15:14
ᶠS Ge 3:16; S Jn 16:21
ᵍJoel 2:6; Na 2:10
13:9 ʰS Isa 2:12; Jer 51:2 ⁱJer 6:23 ʲS Isa 9:19
ᵏIsa 26:21; 66:16; Jer 25:31; Joel 3:2
13:10 ˡS Job 9:7
ᵐIsa 24:23; Zec 14:7
ⁿS Ex 10:22; S Isa 5:30; Rev 8:12
ᵒEze 32:7; Am 5:20; 8:9; S Mt 24:29*; Mk 13:24*
13:11 ᵖS Pr 3:11; 11:4; 26:21; 65:6-7; 66:16 ᵠS Ps 125:3
ʳS Ps 10:5; S Pr 16:18; Da 5:23
ˢS Isa 2:9; 23:9; Eze 28:2; Da 4:37
ᵗS Isa 25:3,5; 29:5, 20; 49:25,26
13:12 ᵘS Isa 4:1 ᵛS Ge 10:29
13:13 ʷS Ps 102:26; Isa 34:4; 51:6
ˣS Job 9:6; S Isa 14:16; Mt 24:7; Mk 13:8
ʸS Isa 9:19
ᶻS Job 9:5
13:14 ᵃPr 6:5
ᵇS 1Ki 22:17; S Mt 9:36; S Jn 10:11
ᶜS Ge 11:9; Isa 17:13; 21:15; 22:3; 33:3; Jer 4:9
ᵈJer 46:16; 50:16; 51:9; Na 3:7
13:15 ᵉJer 51:4
ᶠIsa 14:19; Jer 50:25
13:16 ᵍver 18; S Nu 16:27; S 2Ki 8:12
ʰS Ge 34:29; S Hos 13:16
13:17 ⁱJer 50:9, 41; 51:1 ʲS ver 3
ᵏ2Ki 18:14-16; Pr 6:34-35
13:18 ˡS Ps 7:12; Isa 41:2; Jer 50:9, 14,29 ᵐS Dt 32:25; Jer 49:26; 50:30; 51:4 ⁿIsa 47:6; Jer 6:23; 50:42
ᵒS ver 16;

their houses will be looted and their
   wives ravished.ʰ

¹⁷See, I will stir upⁱ against them the
      Medes,ʲ
   who do not care for silver
   and have no delight in gold.ᵏ
¹⁸Their bowsˡ will strike down the
      young men;ᵐ
   they will have no mercyⁿ on infants
   nor will they look with compassion
      on children.ᵒ
¹⁹Babylon,ᵖ the jewel of kingdoms,ᵠ
   the gloryʳ of the Babylonians'ⁱ
      pride,
will be overthrownˢ by God
   like Sodom and Gomorrah.ᵗ
²⁰She will never be inhabitedᵘ
   or lived in through all generations;
no Arabᵛ will pitch his tent there,
   no shepherd will rest his flocks
      there.
²¹But desert creaturesʷ will lie there,
   jackalsˣ will fill her houses;
there the owlsʸ will dwell,
   and there the wild goatsᶻ will leap
      about.
²²Hyenasᵃ will howl in her strongholds,ᵇ
   jackalsᶜ in her luxurious palaces.
Her time is at hand,ᵈ
   and her days will not be prolonged.ᵉ

14 The LORD will have compassionᶠ
   on Jacob;
once again he will chooseᵍ Israel
   and will settle them in their own
      land.ʰ
Aliensⁱ will join them
   and unite with the house of Jacob.

Isa 14:22; 47:9 13:19 ᵖS ver 1 ᵠIsa 47:5; Da 2:37-38 ʳDa 4:30
ˢS Ps 137:8; S Rev 14:8 ᵗS Ge 19:25; Isa 1:9-10; Ro 9:29
13:20 ᵘIsa 14:23; 34:10-15; Jer 51:29,37-43,62 ᵛ2Ch 17:11
13:21 ʷS Ps 74:14; Rev 18:2 ˣJer 14:6 ʸS Lev 11:16-18; S Dt 14:15-17
ᶻLev 17:7; 2Ch 11:15 13:22 ᵃIsa 34:14 ᵇIsa 25:2; 32:14 ᶜIsa 34:13; 35:7; 43:20; Jer 9:11; 49:33; 51:37; Mal 1:3 ᵈDt 32:35; Jer 48:16; 51:33
ᵉJer 50:39 14:1 ᶠPs 102:13; Isa 49:10,13; 54:7-8,10; Jer 33:26; Zec 10:6
ᵍEze 18:19; 2Ch 6:6; Isa 4:3; 42:1; 44:1; 45:4; 49:7; 65:9,22; Zec 1:17; 2:12; 3:2 ʰJer 3:18; 16:15; 23:8 ⁱS Ex 12:43; S Isa 11:10; Eze 47:22; Zec 8:22-23; Eph 2:12-19
ⁱ19 Or *Chaldeans'*

14:1–27 God promised that Babylon's fall would be linked to the nation's restoration. Despite their coming judgment and exile, God would ultimately "have compassion on Jacob" (14:1). In this taunt, Isaiah prophesied that the grave would welcome the wicked king of Babylon (14:9) as he is brought down at the hand of God. Isaiah also refers to this wicked ruler as "the Assyrian" (14:25), a title used earlier to refer to the antichrist (see 10:5).
Note also that the list of the sins of the king of Babylon can be directly attributed to Satan (14:13–14). Addressed as the "son of the dawn" (14:12), Satan, the antichrist, desired to become like God and set his throne up "above the stars of God" (14:13). Satan's sinful pride is the essence of all sin—the desire to become like God (see Ge 3:5).

²Nations will take them
 and bring them to their own place.
And the house of Israel will possess
 the nations
 as menservants and maidservants in
 the LORD's land.
They will make captives of their
 captors
 and rule over their oppressors.

³On the day the LORD gives you relief from suffering and turmoil and cruel bondage, ⁴you will take up this taunt against the king of Babylon:

How the oppressor has come to an
 end!
How his fury has ended!
⁵The LORD has broken the rod of the
 wicked,
 the scepter of the rulers,
⁶which in anger struck down peoples
 with unceasing blows,
 and in fury subdued nations
 with relentless aggression.
⁷All the lands are at rest and at peace;
 they break into singing.
⁸Even the pine trees and the cedars of
 Lebanon
 exult over you and say,
"Now that you have been laid low,
 no woodsman comes to cut us
 down."
⁹The grave below is all astir
 to meet you at your coming;
 it rouses the spirits of the departed to
 greet you—
 all those who were leaders in the
 world;
 it makes them rise from their
 thrones—
 all those who were kings over the
 nations.
¹⁰They will all respond,
 they will say to you,
"You also have become weak, as we
 are;
 you have become like us."
¹¹All your pomp has been brought down
 to the grave,
 along with the noise of your harps;
 maggots are spread out beneath you
 and worms cover you.

¹²How you have fallen from heaven,
 O morning star, son of the dawn!

You have been cast down to the earth,
 you who once laid low the nations!
¹³You said in your heart,
"I will ascend to heaven;
 I will raise my throne
 above the stars of God;
 I will sit enthroned on the mount of
 assembly,
 on the utmost heights of the sacred
 mountain.
¹⁴I will ascend above the tops of the
 clouds;
 I will make myself like the Most
 High."
¹⁵But you are brought down to the
 grave,
 to the depths of the pit.

¹⁶Those who see you stare at you,
 they ponder your fate:
"Is this the man who shook the earth
 and made kingdoms tremble,
¹⁷the man who made the world a
 desert,
 who overthrew its cities
 and would not let his captives go
 home?"

¹⁸All the kings of the nations lie in state,
 each in his own tomb.
¹⁹But you are cast out of your tomb
 like a rejected branch;
 you are covered with the slain,
 with those pierced by the sword,
 those who descend to the stones of
 the pit.
Like a corpse trampled underfoot,
20 you will not join them in burial,
 for you have destroyed your land
 and killed your people.

The offspring of the wicked
 will never be mentioned again.
²¹Prepare a place to slaughter his sons
 for the sins of their forefathers;
 they are not to rise to inherit the land
 and cover the earth with their cities.

²²"I will rise up against them,"
 declares the LORD Almighty.
"I will cut off from Babylon her name
 and survivors,

M Isa 11:4–10 ◀▶ Isa 16:5

m 4 Dead Sea Scrolls, Septuagint and Syriac; the meaning of the word in the Masoretic Text is uncertain. n 9 Hebrew *Sheol*; also in verses 11 and 15. o 13 Or *the north*; Hebrew *Zaphon*

her offspring and descendants,ʳ"
                        declares the LORD.
²³"I will turn her into a place for owlsˢ
     and into swampland;
  I will sweep her with the broom of
     destruction,'"
     declares the LORD Almighty.ᵘ

A Prophecy Against Assyria

²⁴The LORD Almighty has sworn,ᵛ

  "Surely, as I have planned,ʷ so it will
     be,
   and as I have purposed, so it will
     stand.ˣ
²⁵I will crush the Assyrianʸ in my land;
     on my mountains I will trample him
     down.
  His yokeᶻ will be taken from my
     people,
   and his burden removed from their
     shoulders.ᵃ"
²⁶This is the planᵇ determined for the
     whole world;
  this is the handᶜ stretched out over
     all nations.
²⁷For the LORD Almighty has purposed,ᵈ
     and who can thwart him?
  His handᵉ is stretched out, and who
     can turn it back?ᶠ

A Prophecy Against the Philistines

²⁸This oracleᵍ came in the yearʰ King
     Ahaziⁱ died:

²⁹Do not rejoice, all you Philistines,ʲ
     that the rod that struck you is
     broken;
  from the root of that snake will spring
     up a viper,ᵏ
   its fruit will be a darting, venomous
     serpent.ˡ
³⁰The poorest of the poor will find
     pasture,
   and the needyᵐ will lie down in
     safety.ⁿ
  But your root I will destroy by famine;ᵒ
     it will slayᵖ your survivors.ᵠ

³¹Wail,ʳ O gate!ˢ Howl, O city!
     Melt away, all you Philistines!ᵗ

R Isa 10:22–27 ◀ ▶ Isa 17:9–11

14:22 ʳ 2Sa 18:15; 1Ki 14:10; Job 18:19; S Ps 9:6; S Isa 13:18
14:23 ˢ S Lev 11:16-18; Isa 34:11-15; Zep 2:14
ᵗ S Isa 10:3; Jer 25:12 ᵘ Jer 50:3; 51:62
14:24 ᵛ Isa 45:23; 49:18; 54:9; 62:8
ʷ Isa 19:12,17; 23:8-9; 25:1; Da 4:35 ˣ S Job 9:3; S Isa 7:7; 46:10-11; Eze 12:25; Ac 4:28
14:25 ʸ S Isa 10:5, 12; 37:36-38
ᶻ S Isa 9:4
ᵃ S Isa 10:27
14:26 ᵇ Isa 23:9
ᶜ Ex 15:12; S Job 30:21
14:27 ᵈ Jer 49:20
ᵉ S Ex 14:21
ᶠ S 2Ch 20:6; Isa 43:13; Da 4:35
14:28 ᵍ S Isa 13:1
ʰ S 2Ki 15:7
ⁱ S 2Ki 16:1
14:29 ʲ S Jos 13:3; S 2Ki 1:2; S 2Ch 26:6
ᵏ S Isa 11:8
ˡ S Dt 8:15
14:30 ᵐ Isa 3:15; 25:4 ⁿ S Isa 7:21-22
ᵒ Isa 8:21; 9:20; 51:19 ᵖ Jer 25:16; Zec 9:5-6
ᵠ Eze 25:15-17; Zep 2:5
14:31 ʳ S Isa 13:6
ˢ S Isa 3:26
ᵗ S Ge 10:14
ᵘ Isa 41:25; Jer 1:14; 4:6; 6:1, 22; 10:22; 13:20; 25:9; 46:20,24; 47:2; 50:41; Eze 32:30
ᵛ S Isa 5:27
14:32 ʷ Isa 37:9
ˣ S Ps 51:18; 87:2, 5; Isa 2:2; 26:1; 28:16; 31:5; 33:5, 20; 44:28; 51:21; 54:11 ʸ S Isa 4:6; Jas 2:5
15:1 ᶻ S Isa 13:1
ᵃ Nu 22:3-6; S Dt 23:6; S Isa 11:14
ᵇ S Nu 21:15
ᶜ S Nu 17:12; Isa 25:12; 26:5; Jer 48:24,41; 51:58
ᵈ S 2Ki 3:25
15:2 ᵉ S Nu 21:30
ᶠ 1Ki 11:7; Isa 16:12; Jer 48:35
ᵍ S Isa 13:6; 65:14
ʰ S Nu 32:38
ⁱ S Lev 13:40;

A cloud of smoke comes from the
     north,ᵘ
     and there is not a straggler in its
     ranks.ᵛ
³²What answer shall be given
     to the envoysʷ of that nation?
  "The LORD has established Zion,ˣ
     and in her his afflicted people will
     find refuge.ʸ"

A Prophecy Against Moab

16:6–12pp — Jer 48:29–36

15

An oracleᶻ concerning Moab:ᵃ

Arᵇ in Moab is ruined,ᶜ
     destroyed in a night!
  Kirᵈ in Moab is ruined,
     destroyed in a night!
²Dibonᵉ goes up to its temple,
     to its high placesᶠ to weep;
  Moab wailsᵍ over Neboʰ and
     Medeba.
  Every head is shavedⁱ
     and every beard cut off.ʲ
³In the streets they wear sackcloth;ᵏ
     on the roofsˡ and in the public
     squaresᵐ
  they all wail,ⁿ
     prostrate with weeping.ᵒ
⁴Heshbonᵖ and Elealehᵠ cry out,
     their voices are heard all the way to
     Jahaz.ʳ
  Therefore the armed men of Moab cry
     out,
     and their hearts are faint.

⁵My heart cries outˢ over Moab;ᵗ
     her fugitivesᵘ flee as far as Zoar,ᵛ
     as far as Eglath Shelishiyah.
  They go up the way to Luhith,
     weeping as they go;
  on the road to Horonaimʷ
     they lament their destruction.ˣ
⁶The waters of Nimrim are dried upʸ

J Isa 10:33–34 ◀ ▶ Isa 20:1–6

S Job 1:20 ʲ S 2Sa 10:4 **15:3** ᵏ S Isa 3:24 ˡ S Jos 2:8 ᵐ Jer 48:38
ⁿ Isa 14:31; Jer 47:2 ᵒ ver 5; Isa 16:9; 22:4; La 2:11; Eze 7:18; Mic 1:8
15:4 ᵖ S Nu 21:25; S Jos 13:26 ᵠ S Nu 32:3 ʳ S Nu 21:23 **15:5** ˢ S ver 3
ᵗ Isa 16:11; Jer 48:31 ᵘ S Nu 21:29 ᵛ S Ge 13:10 ʷ Jer 48:3,34 ˣ Jer 4:20;
48:5 **15:6** ʸ Isa 19:5-7; Jer 48:34

14:29–31 Isaiah also predicted the coming judgment of God upon the wicked inhabitants of Palestine, involving famine and war with their northern enemies. This prophecy was fulfilled in a succession of Assyrian invasions of Israel under the Assyrian King Shalmaneser and his successor King Sargon (727–705 B.C.).

and the grass is withered;^{z}
the vegetation is gone^a
and nothing green is left.^{b}
^{7}So the wealth they have acquired^c and stored up
they carry away over the Ravine of the Poplars.
^{8}Their outcry echoes along the border of Moab;
their wailing reaches as far as Eglaim,
their lamentation as far as Beer^d Elim.
^{9}Dimon's^p waters are full of blood,
but I will bring still more upon Dimon^p—
a lion^e upon the fugitives of Moab^f
and upon those who remain in the land.

16 Send lambs^g as tribute^h
to the ruler of the land,
from Sela,^{i} across the desert,
to the mount of the Daughter of Zion.^{j}
^{2}Like fluttering birds
pushed from the nest,^{k}
so are the women of Moab^l
at the fords^m of the Arnon.^{n}

^{3}"Give us counsel,
render a decision.
Make your shadow like night—
at high noon.
Hide the fugitives,^{o}
do not betray the refugees.
^{4}Let the Moabite fugitives stay with you;
be their shelter^p from the destroyer."

The oppressor^q will come to an end,
and destruction will cease;^{r}
the aggressor will vanish from the land.
^{5}In love a throne^s will be established;^{t}
in faithfulness a man will sit on it—
one from the house^q of David^u—
one who in judging seeks justice^v

M *Isa 14:2* ◀ ▶ *Isa 24:13–15*

and speeds the cause of righteousness.

^{6}We have heard of Moab's^w pride^x—
her overweening pride and conceit,
her pride and her insolence—
but her boasts are empty.
^{7}Therefore the Moabites wail,^{y}
they wail together for Moab.
Lament and grieve
for the men^{rz} of Kir Hareseth.^{a}
^{8}The fields of Heshbon^b wither,^{c}
the vines of Sibmah^d also.
The rulers of the nations
have trampled down the choicest vines,^{e}
which once reached Jazer^f
and spread toward the desert.
Their shoots spread out^g
and went as far as the sea.^{h}
^{9}So I weep,^{i} as Jazer weeps,
for the vines of Sibmah.
O Heshbon, O Elealeh,^{j}
I drench you with tears!^{k}
The shouts of joy^l over your ripened fruit
and over your harvests^m have been stilled.
^{10}Joy and gladness are taken away from the orchards;^{n}
no one sings or shouts^o in the vineyards;
no one treads^p out wine at the presses,^{q}
for I have put an end to the shouting.
^{11}My heart laments for Moab^r like a harp,^{s}
my inmost being^t for Kir Hareseth.
^{12}When Moab appears at her high place,^{u}
she only wears herself out;
when she goes to her shrine^v to pray,
it is to no avail.^{w}

^{13}This is the word the LORD has already spoken concerning Moab. ^{14}But now the LORD says: "Within three years,^{x} as a ser-

15:6 ^{z} Ps 37:2; Isa 16:8; 24:4,7,11; 33:9; 34:4; 37:27; 40:7; 51:6,12; Hos 4:3; Joel 1:12 ^{a} S Isa 14:17 ^{b} Jer 14:5
15:7 ^{c} Isa 30:6; Jer 48:36
15:8 ^{d} S Nu 21:16
15:9 ^{e} S 2Ki 17:25 ^{f} Eze 25:8-11
16:1 ^{g} S 2Ki 3:4 ^{h} S 2Ch 32:23 ^{i} S Jdg 1:36; Ob 3 *fn* ^{j} S Isa 10:32
16:2 ^{k} Pr 27:8 ^{l} Nu 21:29 ^{m} Jdg 12:5 ^{n} Nu 21:13-14; Jer 48:20
16:3 ^{o} S 1Ki 18:4
16:4 ^{p} Isa 58:7 ^{q} S Isa 9:4 ^{r} Isa 2:2-4
16:5 ^{s} S Isa 13:14; Da 7:14; Mic 4:7 ^{t} S Pr 20:28 ^{u} S Isa 7:2; Lk 1:32 ^{v} S Isa 9:7
16:6 ^{w} Jer 25:21; Eze 25:8; Am 2:1; Zep 2:8 ^{x} S Lev 26:19; S Job 20:6; Jer 49:16; Ob 1:3; Zep 2:10
16:7 ^{y} S Isa 13:6; Jer 48:20; 49:3 ^{z} S 1Ch 16:3 ^{a} S 2Ki 3:25
16:8 ^{b} S Nu 21:25 ^{c} S Isa 15:6 ^{d} S Nu 32:3 ^{e} S Isa 5:2 ^{f} S Nu 21:32 ^{g} S Job 8:16 ^{h} Ps 80:11
16:9 ^{i} S Isa 15:3; Eze 27:31 ^{j} S Nu 32:3 ^{k} S Job 7:3 ^{l} S Ezr 3:13 ^{m} Jer 40:12
16:10 ^{n} Isa 24:7-8 ^{o} Jer 25:30 ^{p} S Jdg 9:27 ^{q} S Job 24:11; S Isa 5:2
16:11 ^{r} S Isa 15:5 ^{s} S Job 30:31 ^{t} Isa 63:15; Hos 11:8; Php 2:1
16:12 ^{u} 1Ki 11:7 ^{v} S Isa 15:2 ^{w} S 1Ki 18:29; Ps 115:4-7; Isa 44:17-18; 1Co 8:4
16:14 ^{x} Isa 20:3; 37:30

^{p} 9 Masoretic Text; Dead Sea Scrolls, some Septuagint manuscripts and Vulgate *Dibon* ^{q} 5 Hebrew *tent* ^{r} 7 Or *"raisin cakes,"* a wordplay

---

16:1–5 The immediate explanation of these verses concerned the nation of Moab. Sela was the fortified capital of Edom, situated on a cliff overlooking nearby Petra (see 42:11). Moabite refugees had settled in Sela and had requested asylum in Israel. The interpretation of this passage with a view to the future suggests that refugees will once again seek asylum in Israel and that Gentile nations will participate in the Millennium.

vant bound by contractʸ would count them,ᶻ Moab's splendor and all her many people will be despised,ᵃ and her survivors will be very few and feeble."ᵇ

An Oracle Against Damascus

17 An oracleᶜ concerning Damascus:ᵈ

"See, Damascus will no longer be a city
but will become a heap of ruins.ᵉ
²The cities of Aroerᶠ will be deserted
and left to flocks,ᵍ which will lie down,ʰ
with no one to make them afraid.ⁱ
³The fortifiedʲ city will disappear from Ephraim,
and royal power from Damascus;
the remnant of Aram will be
like the gloryᵏ of the Israelites,"ˡ
declares the LORD Almighty.

⁴"In that dayᵐ the gloryⁿ of Jacob will fade;
the fat of his body will wasteᵒ away.
⁵It will be as when a reaper gathers the standing grain
and harvestsᵖ the grain with his arm—
as when a man gleans heads of grainᵠ
in the Valley of Rephaim.ʳ
⁶Yet some gleanings will remain,ˢ
as when an olive tree is beaten,ᵗ
leaving two or three olives on the topmost branches,
four or five on the fruitful boughs,"
declares the LORD,
the God of Israel.

⁷In that dayᵘ men will lookᵛ to their Makerʷ
and turn their eyes to the Holy Oneˣ of Israel.
⁸They will not look to the altars,ʸ
the work of their hands,ᶻ
and they will have no regard for the Asherah polesˢᵃ
and the incense altars their fingersᵇ have made.

⁹In that day their strong cities, which they left because of the Israelites, will be like places abandoned to thickets and undergrowth.ᶜ And all will be desolation.

¹⁰You have forgottenᵈ God your Savior;ᵉ
you have not remembered the Rock,ᶠ your fortress.ᵍ
Therefore, though you set out the finest plants
and plant imported vines,ʰ
¹¹though on the day you set them out, you make them grow,
and on the morningⁱ when you plant them, you bring them to bud,
yet the harvestʲ will be as nothingᵏ
in the day of disease and incurableˡ pain.ᵐ

¹²Oh, the ragingⁿ of many nations—
they rage like the raging sea!ᵒ
Oh, the uproarᵖ of the peoples—
they roar like the roaring of great waters!ᵠ
¹³Although the peoples roarʳ like the roar of surging waters,
when he rebukesˢ them they fleeᵗ far away,
driven before the wind like chaffᵘ on the hills,
like tumbleweed before a gale.ᵛ
¹⁴In the evening, suddenʷ terror!ˣ
Before the morning, they are gone!ʸ
This is the portion of those who loot us,
the lot of those who plunder us.

A Prophecy Against Cush

18 Woeᶻ to the land of whirring wingsᵃ
along the rivers of Cush,ᵘᵃ
²which sends envoysᵇ by sea
in papyrusᶜ boats over the water.

R Isa 14:28–31 ◀ ▶ Isa 18:2
R Isa 17:9–11 ◀ ▶ Isa 22:17–19

ᵛJob 21:18; S Ps 65:7 ¹⁷:¹⁴ ʷIsa 29:5; 30:13; 47:11; 48:3 ˣIsa 33:18; 54:14 ʸS 2Ki 19:35 ¹⁸:¹ ᶻIsa 5:8 ᵃS Ge 10:6; S Ps 68:31; S Eze 29:10 ¹⁸:² ᵇOb 1:1 ᶜEx 2:3; Job 9:26

ˢ 8 That is, symbols of the goddess Asherah ᵗ 1 Or of locusts ᵘ 1 That is, the upper Nile region

---

17:1 Isaiah directed his prophecy to Damascus, the capital city of Syria, declaring that it "will become a heap of ruins" (17:1). Compare this prophecy against the nation's enemy with Jer 49:27.

17:9–11 God declared that he would reject his people because of their sins.

18:2–4 The Cushites were an ancient Ethiopian dynasty established in Egypt c. 714 B.C. (This nation is not to be confused with modern-day Ethiopia that is further to the southeast than ancient Cush.) Some

Go, swift messengers,
to a people tall and smooth-skinned,
to a people feared far and wide,
an aggressive nation of strange
    speech,
whose land is divided by rivers.

³All you people of the world,
you who live on the earth,
when a banner is raised on the
    mountains,
you will see it,
and when a trumpet sounds,
you will hear it.
⁴This is what the LORD says to me:
"I will remain quiet and will look
    on from my dwelling place,
like shimmering heat in the sunshine,
like a cloud of dew in the heat of
    harvest."
⁵For, before the harvest, when the
    blossom is gone
and the flower becomes a ripening
    grape,
he will cut off the shoots with
    pruning knives,
and cut down and take away the
    spreading branches.
⁶They will all be left to the mountain
    birds of prey
and to the wild animals;
the birds will feed on them all
    summer,
the wild animals all winter.

⁷At that time gifts will be brought to
the LORD Almighty

from a people tall and
    smooth-skinned,
from a people feared far and wide,
an aggressive nation of strange speech,
whose land is divided by rivers—
the gifts will be brought to Mount Zion,
the place of the Name of the LORD Almighty.

A Prophecy About Egypt

19 An oracle concerning Egypt:

See, the LORD rides on a swift cloud
and is coming to Egypt.

◀ Isa 12:6 ◀▶ Isa 25:8–10

The idols of Egypt tremble before him,
and the hearts of the Egyptians
    melt within them.

²"I will stir up Egyptian against
    Egyptian—
brother will fight against brother,
neighbor against neighbor,
city against city,
kingdom against kingdom.
³The Egyptians will lose heart,
and I will bring their plans to
    nothing;
they will consult the idols and the
    spirits of the dead,
the mediums and the spiritists.
⁴I will hand the Egyptians over
to the power of a cruel master,
and a fierce king will rule over
    them,"
declares the Lord, the LORD
    Almighty.

⁵The waters of the river will dry up,
and the riverbed will be parched
    and dry.
⁶The canals will stink;
the streams of Egypt will dwindle
    and dry up.
The reeds and rushes will wither,
⁷ also the plants along the Nile,
at the mouth of the river.
Every sown field along the Nile
will become parched, will blow
    away and be no more.
⁸The fishermen will groan and lament,
all who cast hooks into the Nile;
those who throw nets on the water
will pine away.
⁹Those who work with combed flax
    will despair,
the weavers of fine linen will lose
    hope.
¹⁰The workers in cloth will be dejected,
and all the wage earners will be sick
    at heart.

¹¹The officials of Zoan are nothing but
    fools;
the wise counselors of Pharaoh give
    senseless advice.
How can you say to Pharaoh,
"I am one of the wise men,
a disciple of the ancient kings"?

---

believe that the ark of the covenant survived Nebuchadnezzar's destruction of the temple and accompanied the remnant of Jews who fled to Egypt (Cush).

ISAIAH 19:12

¹²Where are your wise men now?
  Let them show you and make
    known
  what the Lord Almighty
    has planned against Egypt.
¹³The officials of Zoan have become
    fools,
  the leaders of Memphis are
    deceived;
  the cornerstones of her peoples
    have led Egypt astray.
¹⁴The Lord has poured into them
  a spirit of dizziness;
  they make Egypt stagger in all that she
    does,
  as a drunkard staggers around in
    his vomit.
¹⁵There is nothing Egypt can do—
  head or tail, palm branch or
    reed.

¹⁶In that day the Egyptians will be like women. They will shudder with fear at the uplifted hand that the Lord Almighty raises against them. ¹⁷And the land of Judah will bring terror to the Egyptians; everyone to whom Judah is mentioned will be terrified, because of what the Lord Almighty is planning against them.

¹⁸In that day five cities in Egypt will speak the language of Canaan and swear allegiance to the Lord Almighty. One of them will be called the City of Destruction.

¹⁹In that day there will be an altar to the Lord in the heart of Egypt, and a monument to the Lord at its border. ²⁰It will be a sign and witness to the Lord Almighty in the land of Egypt. When they cry out to the Lord because of their oppressors, he will send them a savior and defender, and he will rescue them. ²¹So the Lord will make himself known to the Egyptians, and in that day they will acknowledge the Lord. They will worship with sacrifices and grain offerings; they will make vows to the Lord and keep them. ²²The Lord will strike Egypt with a plague; he will strike them and heal them. They will turn to the Lord, and he will respond to their pleas and heal them.

²³In that day there will be a highway from Egypt to Assyria. The Assyrians will go to Egypt and the Egyptians to Assyria. The Egyptians and Assyrians will worship together. ²⁴In that day Israel will be the third, along with Egypt and Assyria, a blessing on the earth. ²⁵The Lord Almighty will bless them, saying, "Blessed be Egypt my people, Assyria my handiwork, and Israel my inheritance."

A Prophecy Against Egypt and Cush

20 In the year that the supreme commander, sent by Sargon king of Assyria, came to Ashdod and attacked and captured it— ²at that time the Lord spoke through Isaiah son of Amoz. He said to him, "Take off the sackcloth from your body and the sandals from your feet." And he did so, going around stripped and barefoot.

³Then the Lord said, "Just as my servant Isaiah has gone stripped and barefoot for three years, as a sign and portent against Egypt and Cush, ⁴so the king of Assyria will lead away stripped and barefoot the Egyptian captives and Cushite exiles, young and old, with buttocks bared—to Egypt's shame. ⁵Those who trusted in Cush and boasted in Egypt will be afraid and put to shame. ⁶In that day the people who live on this coast will say, 'See what has happened to those we relied on, those we fled to for help and deliverance from the king of Assyria! How then can we escape?'"

Isa 15:1–9 ◀ ▶ *Isa 21:13–16*

19:18 This prophecy suggested that the entire land of Egypt would one day worship the true God. The "City of Destruction" was probably a reference to Heliopolis, the center of worship for the Egyptian sun god that was destroyed by Nebuchadnezzar (see Jer 43:12–13).

A Prophecy Against Babylon

21 An oracle concerning the Desert by the Sea:

Like whirlwinds sweeping through the southland,
an invader comes from the desert,
from a land of terror.

²A dire vision has been shown to me:
The traitor betrays, the looter takes loot.
Elam, attack! Media, lay siege!
I will bring to an end all the groaning she caused.

³At this my body is racked with pain,
pangs seize me, like those of a woman in labor;
I am staggered by what I hear,
I am bewildered by what I see.
⁴My heart falters,
fear makes me tremble;
the twilight I longed for
has become a horror to me.

⁵They set the tables,
they spread the rugs,
they eat, they drink!
Get up, you officers,
oil the shields!

⁶This is what the Lord says to me:

"Go, post a lookout
and have him report what he sees.
⁷When he sees chariots
with teams of horses,
riders on donkeys
or riders on camels,
let him be alert,
fully alert."

⁸And the lookout shouted,

"Day after day, my lord, I stand on the watchtower;
every night I stay at my post.
⁹Look, here comes a man in a chariot
with a team of horses.
And he gives back the answer:
'Babylon has fallen, has fallen!
All the images of its gods
lie shattered on the ground!' "

¹⁰O my people, crushed on the threshing floor,
I tell you what I have heard
from the LORD Almighty,
from the God of Israel.

A Prophecy Against Edom

¹¹An oracle concerning Dumah:

Someone calls to me from Seir,
"Watchman, what is left of the night?
Watchman, what is left of the night?"
¹²The watchman replies,
"Morning is coming, but also the night.
If you would ask, then ask;
and come back yet again."

A Prophecy Against Arabia

¹³An oracle concerning Arabia:

You caravans of Dedanites,
who camp in the thickets of Arabia,
¹⁴ bring water for the thirsty;
you who live in Tema,
bring food for the fugitives.
¹⁵They flee from the sword,
from the drawn sword,
from the bent bow
and from the heat of battle.

¹⁶This is what the Lord says to me: "Within one year, as a servant bound by contract would count it, all the pomp of Kedar will come to an end. ¹⁷The survivors of the bowmen, the warriors of Kedar, will be few." The LORD, the God of Israel, has spoken.

A Prophecy About Jerusalem

22 An oracle concerning the Valley of Vision:

What troubles you now,
that you have all gone up on the roofs,
²O town full of commotion,
O city of tumult and revelry?
Your slain were not killed by the sword,
nor did they die in battle.
³All your leaders have fled together;
they have been captured without using the bow.
All you who were caught were taken prisoner together,
having fled while the enemy was still far away.
⁴Therefore I said, "Turn away from me;

y 8 Dead Sea Scrolls and Syriac; Masoretic Text A lion z 11 Dumah means silence or stillness, a wordplay on Edom.

let me weep[p] bitterly.
Do not try to console me
 over the destruction of my people."[q]

[5]The Lord, the LORD Almighty, has a day[r]
 of tumult and trampling[s] and terror[t]
 in the Valley of Vision,[u]
a day of battering down walls[v]
 and of crying out to the mountains.
[6]Elam[w] takes up the quiver,[x]
 with her charioteers and horses;
Kir[y] uncovers the shield.
[7]Your choicest valleys[z] are full of chariots,
 and horsemen are posted at the city gates;[a]
[8] the defenses of Judah are stripped away.

And you looked in that day[b]
 to the weapons[c] in the Palace of the Forest;[d]
[9]you saw that the City of David
 had many breaches[e] in its defenses;
you stored up water
 in the Lower Pool.[f]
[10]You counted the buildings in Jerusalem
 and tore down houses[g] to strengthen the wall.[h]
[11]You built a reservoir between the two walls[i]
 for the water of the Old Pool,[j]
but you did not look to the One who made it,
 or have regard[k] for the One who planned[l] it long ago.

[12]The Lord, the LORD Almighty,
 called you on that day[m]
to weep[n] and to wail,
 to tear out your hair[o] and put on sackcloth.[p]
[13]But see, there is joy and revelry,[q]
 slaughtering of cattle and killing of sheep,
 eating of meat and drinking of wine![r]
"Let us eat and drink," you say,
 "for tomorrow we die!"[s]

[14]The LORD Almighty has revealed this in my hearing:[t] "Till your dying day this sin will not be atoned[u] for," says the Lord, the LORD Almighty.

[15]This is what the Lord, the LORD Almighty, says:

"Go, say to this steward,
 to Shebna,[v] who is in charge[w] of the palace:[x]
[16]What are you doing here and who gave you permission
 to cut out a grave[y] for yourself[z] here,
hewing your grave on the height
 and chiseling your resting place in the rock?

[17]"Beware, the LORD is about to take firm hold of you R
 and hurl[a] you away, O you mighty man.
[18]He will roll you up tightly like a ball
 and throw[b] you into a large country.
There you will die
 and there your splendid chariots[c] will remain—
 you disgrace to your master's house!
[19]I will depose you from your office,
 and you will be ousted[d] from your position.[e]

[20]"In that day[f] I will summon my servant,[g] Eliakim[h] son of Hilkiah. [21]I will clothe him with your robe and fasten your sash[i] around him and hand your authority[j] over to him. He will be a father to those who live in Jerusalem and to the house of Judah. [22]I will place on his shoulder[k] the key[l] to the house of David;[m] what he opens no one can shut, and what he shuts no one can open.[n] [23]I will drive him like a peg[o] into a firm place;[p] he will be a seat[a] of honor[q] for the house of his father. [24]All the glory of his family will hang on him: its offspring and offshoots—all its lesser vessels, from the bowls to all the jars.

[25]"In that day,[r]" declares the LORD Almighty, "the peg[s] driven into the firm place will give way; it will be sheared off and will fall, and the load hanging on it will be cut down." The LORD has spoken.[t]

R *Isa 18:2* ◀ ▶ *Isa 26:15–17*

[S] Job 36:7 **22:25** [r] ver 20 [s] ver 23 [t] Isa 46:11; Mic 4:1
[a] 23 Or *throne*

22:17–19 This prophecy was spoken to one of the officials in Hezekiah's court who coveted a tomb worthy of a king (22:16; see 2Ch 16:14).

A Prophecy About Tyre

23 An oracle concerning Tyre:

Wail, O ships of Tarshish!
  For Tyre is destroyed
  and left without house or harbor.
From the land of Cyprus
  word has come to them.

² Be silent, you people of the island
  and you merchants of Sidon,
  whom the seafarers have enriched.
³ On the great waters
  came the grain of the Shihor;
the harvest of the Nile was the
  revenue of Tyre,
and she became the marketplace of
  the nations.

⁴ Be ashamed, O Sidon, and you,
  O fortress of the sea,
  for the sea has spoken:
"I have neither been in labor nor given
  birth;
I have neither reared sons nor
  brought up daughters."
⁵ When word comes to Egypt,
  they will be in anguish at the
  report from Tyre.

⁶ Cross over to Tarshish;
  wail, you people of the island.
⁷ Is this your city of revelry,
  the old, old city,
whose feet have taken her
  to settle in far-off lands?
⁸ Who planned this against Tyre,
  the bestower of crowns,
whose merchants are princes,
  whose traders are renowned in the
  earth?
⁹ The LORD Almighty planned it,
  to bring low the pride of all glory
  and to humble all who are
  renowned on the earth.

¹⁰ Till your land as along the Nile,
  O Daughter of Tarshish,
  for you no longer have a harbor.
¹¹ The LORD has stretched out his hand
  over the sea
  and made its kingdoms tremble.

He has given an order concerning
  Phoenicia
  that her fortresses be destroyed.
¹² He said, "No more of your reveling,
  O Virgin Daughter of Sidon, now
  crushed!

"Up, cross over to Cyprus;
  even there you will find no rest."
¹³ Look at the land of the Babylonians,
  this people that is now of no
  account!
The Assyrians have made it
  a place for desert creatures;
they raised up their siege towers,
  they stripped its fortresses bare
  and turned it into a ruin.

¹⁴ Wail, you ships of Tarshish;
  your fortress is destroyed!

¹⁵ At that time Tyre will be forgotten for seventy years, the span of a king's life. But at the end of these seventy years, it will happen to Tyre as in the song of the prostitute:

¹⁶ "Take up a harp, walk through the
  city,
  O prostitute forgotten;
play the harp well, sing many a song,
  so that you will be remembered."

¹⁷ At the end of seventy years, the LORD will deal with Tyre. She will return to her hire as a prostitute and will ply her trade with all the kingdoms on the face of the earth. ¹⁸ Yet her profit and her earnings will be set apart for the LORD; they will not be stored up or hoarded. Her profits will go to those who live before the LORD, for abundant food and fine clothes.

The LORD's Devastation of the Earth

24 See, the LORD is going to lay
  waste the earth
  and devastate it;
he will ruin its face

---

b 1,12 Hebrew *Kittim* *c 2,3* Masoretic Text; one Dead Sea Scroll *Sidon, / who cross over the sea; / your envoys* ³*are on the great waters. / The grain of the Shihor, / the harvest of the Nile,* *d 10* Dead Sea Scrolls and some Septuagint manuscripts; Masoretic Text *Go through* *e 11* Hebrew *Canaan* *f 13* Or *Chaldeans*

24:1, 3, 6 This prophecy foretells the great destruction of the earth's population during the tribulation period.

and scatter^q its inhabitants—
²it will be the same
  for priest as for people,^r
  for master as for servant,
  for mistress as for maid,
  for seller as for buyer,^s
  for borrower as for lender,
  for debtor as for creditor.^t

P ³The earth will be completely laid waste^u
  and totally plundered.^v
      The LORD has spoken^w
          this word.

⁴The earth dries up^x and withers,^y
  the world languishes and withers,
  the exalted^z of the earth languish.^a
⁵The earth is defiled^b by its people;
  they have disobeyed^c the laws,
  violated the statutes
  and broken the everlasting covenant.^d

P ⁶Therefore a curse^e consumes the earth;
  its people must bear their guilt.
Therefore earth's inhabitants are burned up,^f
  and very few are left.
⁷The new wine dries up^g and the vine withers;^h
  all the merrymakers groan.^i
⁸The gaiety of the tambourines^j is stilled,
  the noise^k of the revelers^l has stopped,
  the joyful harp^m is silent.^n
⁹No longer do they drink wine^o with a song;
  the beer is bitter^p to its drinkers.
¹⁰The ruined city^q lies desolate;^r
  the entrance to every house is barred.
¹¹In the streets they cry out^s for wine;^t
  all joy turns to gloom,^u
  all gaiety is banished from the earth.
¹²The city is left in ruins,^v
  its gate^w is battered to pieces.

M ¹³So will it be on the earth
  and among the nations,
as when an olive tree is beaten,^x
  or as when gleanings are left after the grape harvest.^y

¹⁴They raise their voices, they shout for joy;^z
  from the west^a they acclaim the LORD's majesty.
¹⁵Therefore in the east^b give glory^c to the LORD;
  exalt^d the name^e of the LORD, the God of Israel,
  in the islands^f of the sea.
¹⁶From the ends of the earth^g we hear singing:^h
  "Glory^i to the Righteous One."^j

But I said, "I waste away, I waste away!^k
Woe^l to me!
The treacherous^m betray!
  With treachery the treacherous betray!"^n

P H ¹⁷Terror^o and pit and snare^p await you,
  O people of the earth.^q
¹⁸Whoever flees^r at the sound of terror
  will fall into a pit;^s
whoever climbs out of the pit
  will be caught in a snare.^t

The floodgates of the heavens^u are opened,
  the foundations of the earth shake.^v
¹⁹The earth is broken up,^w
  the earth is split asunder,^x
  the earth is thoroughly shaken.
²⁰The earth reels like a drunkard,^y
  it sways like a hut^z in the wind;
so heavy upon it is the guilt of its rebellion^a
  that it falls^b—never to rise again.^c

²¹In that day^d the LORD will punish^e
  the powers^f in the heavens above
  and the kings^g on the earth below.

P *Isa 24:1* ◀ ▶ *Isa 24:6*
P *Isa 24:3* ◀ ▶ *Isa 24:17–23*
M *Isa 16:5* ◀ ▶ *Isa 24:23*

P *Isa 24:6* ◀ ▶ *Isa 26:20–21*
H *Isa 13:6–13* ◀ ▶ *Isa 26:20–21*

24:13–15 Isaiah foresaw the peace of the millennial kingdom.
24:17–23 Isaiah reveals the coming punishment of God upon his enemies during the tribulation period, ending in the complete destruction of the antichrist in the final conflict and the establishment of the glorious reign of the Messiah.

²²They will be herded together
    like prisoners bound in a dungeon;
they will be shut up in prison
    and be punished after many days.
²³The moon will be abashed, the sun ashamed;
    for the LORD Almighty will reign
on Mount Zion and in Jerusalem,
    and before its elders, gloriously.

Praise to the LORD

25 O LORD, you are my God;
    I will exalt you and praise your name,
for in perfect faithfulness
    you have done marvelous things,
    things planned long ago.
²You have made the city a heap of rubble,
    the fortified town a ruin,
    the foreigners' stronghold a city no more;
    it will never be rebuilt.
³Therefore strong peoples will honor you;
    cities of ruthless nations will revere you.
⁴You have been a refuge for the poor,
    a refuge for the needy in his distress,
a shelter from the storm
    and a shade from the heat.
For the breath of the ruthless
    is like a storm driving against a wall
⁵   and like the heat of the desert.

You silence the uproar of foreigners;
    as heat is reduced by the shadow of a cloud,
so the song of the ruthless is stilled.

⁶On this mountain the LORD Almighty will prepare
    a feast of rich food for all peoples,
    a banquet of aged wine—
    the best of meats and the finest of wines.
⁷On this mountain he will destroy
the shroud that enfolds all peoples,
    the sheet that covers all nations;
⁸   he will swallow up death forever.
The Sovereign LORD will wipe away the tears
    from all faces;
he will remove the disgrace of his people
    from all the earth.
        The LORD has spoken.

⁹In that day they will say,

"Surely this is our God;
    we trusted in him, and he saved us.
This is the LORD, we trusted in him;
    let us rejoice and be glad in his salvation."

¹⁰The hand of the LORD will rest on this mountain;
    but Moab will be trampled under him
    as straw is trampled down in the manure.
¹¹They will spread out their hands in it,
    as a swimmer spreads out his hands to swim.
God will bring down their pride
    despite the cleverness of their hands.
¹²He will bring down your high fortified walls
    and lay them low;
he will bring them down to the ground,
    to the very dust.

M Isa 24:13–15 ◀ ▶ Isa 25:6–10
K Isa 4:6 ◀ ▶ Isa 26:3–4
M Isa 24:23 ◀ ▶ Isa 26:1–2

F Ps 88:10–12 ◀ ▶ Isa 26:19
I Isa 18:7 ◀ ▶ Isa 26:1–2
S Isa 12:3 ◀ ▶ Isa 35:10

25:6 This prophecy will be ultimately fulfilled during the marriage supper of the Lamb (see Rev 19:9).
25:7–10 Isaiah prophesied the Lord's ultimate victory over death (compare with 1Co 15:54; Rev 21:4). This victory will be total and absolute, a complete fulfillment of the ancient prophecies.

A Song of Praise

26 In that day this song will be sung in the land of Judah:

We have a strong city;
  God makes salvation
    its walls and ramparts.
²Open the gates
  that the righteous nation may
    enter,
  the nation that keeps faith.
³You will keep in perfect peace
  him whose mind is steadfast,
  because he trusts in you.
⁴Trust in the LORD forever,
  for the LORD, the LORD, is the Rock
    eternal.
⁵He humbles those who dwell on high,
  he lays the lofty city low;
  he levels it to the ground
  and casts it down to the dust.
⁶Feet trample it down—
  the feet of the oppressed,
  the footsteps of the poor.
⁷The path of the righteous is level;
  O upright One, you make the way
    of the righteous smooth.
⁸Yes, LORD, walking in the way of your
    laws,
  we wait for you;
  your name and renown
    are the desire of our hearts.
⁹My soul yearns for you in the night;
  in the morning my spirit longs for
    you.
  When your judgments come upon the
    earth,
  the people of the world learn
    righteousness.
¹⁰Though grace is shown to the wicked,
  they do not learn righteousness;
  even in a land of uprightness they go
    on doing evil

I Isa 25:8–10 ◀▶ Isa 26:12
M Isa 25:6–10 ◀▶ Isa 29:17–24
F Isa 7:9 ◀▶ Jer 17:7
K Isa 25:4 ◀▶ Isa 28:16
J Pr 1:33 ◀▶ Isa 51:2
W Isa 12:2–3 ◀▶ Isa 32:17
C Isa 9:2 ◀▶ Isa 30:9–10
N Ecc 12:1 ◀▶ Isa 28:12–13

and regard not the majesty of the
    LORD.
¹¹O LORD, your hand is lifted high,
  but they do not see it.
  Let them see your zeal for your
    people and be put to shame;
  let the fire reserved for your
    enemies consume them.
¹²LORD, you establish peace for us;
  all that we have accomplished you
    have done for us.
¹³O LORD, our God, other lords besides
    you have ruled over us,
  but your name alone do we
    honor.
¹⁴They are now dead, they live no
    more;
  those departed spirits do not rise.
  You punished them and brought them
    to ruin;
  you wiped out all memory of them.
¹⁵You have enlarged the nation, O LORD;
  you have enlarged the nation.
  You have gained glory for yourself;
  you have extended all the borders
    of the land.
¹⁶LORD, they came to you in their
    distress;
  when you disciplined them,
  they could barely whisper a
    prayer.
¹⁷As a woman with child and about to
    give birth
  writhes and cries out in her pain,
  so were we in your presence,
    O LORD.
¹⁸We were with child, we writhed in
    pain,
  but we gave birth to wind.
  We have not brought salvation to the
    earth;
  we have not given birth to people of
    the world.

I Isa 26:1–2 ◀▶ Isa 26:19
R Isa 22:17–19 ◀▶ Isa 28:13

Ps 17:14 d Isa 42:6; 49:6; 51:4; Jer 12:16
ı8 Or judgments ı16 The meaning of the Hebrew for this clause is uncertain.

26:1–2 This prophecy anticipates the victory of the Messiah as he ushers in the millennial kingdom and reconciles the nation to God.
26:12 The final reward of true peace will be won by Israel's Messiah.
26:15–17 Isaiah likened the approaching crisis in the last days to a pregnant woman in labor, awaiting the delivery of her child.

ISAIAH 27:11

19 But your dead will live;
 their bodies will rise.
You who dwell in the dust,
 wake up and shout for joy.
Your dew is like the dew of the morning;
 the earth will give birth to her dead.

20 Go, my people, enter your rooms
 and shut the doors behind you;
hide yourselves for a little while
 until his wrath has passed by.
21 See, the LORD is coming out of his dwelling
 to punish the people of the earth for their sins.
The earth will disclose the blood shed upon her;
 she will conceal her slain no longer.

Deliverance of Israel

27 In that day,

the LORD will punish with his sword,
 his fierce, great and powerful sword,
Leviathan the gliding serpent,
 Leviathan the coiling serpent;
he will slay the monster of the sea.

2 In that day—

"Sing about a fruitful vineyard:
3 I, the LORD, watch over it;
 I water it continually.
I guard it day and night
 so that no one may harm it.
4 I am not angry.
If only there were briers and thorns confronting me!
 I would march against them in battle;
 I would set them all on fire.
5 Or else let them come to me for refuge;
 let them make peace with me,
 yes, let them make peace with me."

6 In days to come Jacob will take root,
 Israel will bud and blossom
 and fill all the world with fruit.

7 Has the LORD struck her
 as he struck down those who struck her?
Has she been killed
 as those were killed who killed her?
8 By warfare and exile you contend with her—
 with his fierce blast he drives her out,
 as on a day the east wind blows.
9 By this, then, will Jacob's guilt be atoned for,
 and this will be the full fruitage of the removal of his sin:
When he makes all the altar stones
 to be like chalk stones crushed to pieces,
no Asherah poles or incense altars
 will be left standing.
10 The fortified city stands desolate,
 an abandoned settlement, forsaken like the desert;
there the calves graze,
 there they lie down;
 they strip its branches bare.
11 When its twigs are dry, they are broken off
 and women come and make fires with them.
For this is a people without understanding;
 so their Maker has no compassion on them,

26:19–21 Isaiah prophesied a word of reassurance to God's people by promising the future resurrection of the righteous (see Job 19:26; Da 12:2). Their oppression would end and God would avenge their deaths (see Ge 4:10; Rev 20:13).

27:2–6 Isaiah spoke another vineyard song (see 5:1–7) picturing the nation's lukewarm attitude toward God as not "briers and thorns" (27:4) but neither a relationship of complete trust. Yet when the Messiah comes "Israel will bud and blossom and fill all the world with fruit" (27:6). This prophecy is being fulfilled in our generation as the returning Jews transform the landscape of Palestine. Where once there was desert, there are now farms. Where once there was desolation, there are now vineyards and orchards.

and their Creator^w shows them no favor.^x

¹²In that day the LORD will thresh^y from the flowing Euphrates^m to the Wadi of Egypt,^z and you, O Israelites, will be gathered^a up one by one. ¹³And in that day^b a great trumpet^c will sound. Those who were perishing in Assyria and those who were exiled^d in Egypt^e will come and worship^f the LORD on the holy mountain^g in Jerusalem.

Woe to Ephraim

28 Woe^h to that wreath, the pride
of Ephraim'sⁱ drunkards,
to the fading flower, his glorious
beauty,
set on the head of a fertile valley^j—
to that city, the pride of those laid
low by wine!^k
²See, the Lord has one who is
powerful^l and strong.
Like a hailstorm^m and a destructive
wind,ⁿ
like a driving rain and a flooding^o
downpour,
he will throw it forcefully to the
ground.
³That wreath, the pride of Ephraim's^p
drunkards,
will be trampled^q underfoot.
⁴That fading flower, his glorious beauty,
set on the head of a fertile valley,^r
will be like a fig^s ripe before harvest—
as soon as someone sees it and takes
it in his hand,
he swallows it.

⁵In that day^t the LORD Almighty
will be a glorious^u crown,^v
a beautiful wreath
for the remnant^w of his people.
⁶He will be a spirit of justice^x
to him who sits in judgment,^y

a source of strength
to those who turn back the battle^z at the gate.

⁷And these also stagger^a from wine^b
and reel^c from beer:
Priests^d and prophets^e stagger from beer
and are befuddled with wine;
they reel from beer,
they stagger when seeing visions,^f
they stumble when rendering decisions.
⁸All the tables are covered with vomit^g
and there is not a spot without filth.
⁹"Who is it he is trying to teach?^h
To whom is he explaining his message?ⁱ
To children weaned^j from their milk,^k
to those just taken from the breast?
¹⁰For it is:
Do and do, do and do,
rule on rule, rule on ruleⁿ;
a little here, a little there.¹"

¹¹Very well then, with foreign lips and
strange tongues^m
God will speak to this people,ⁿ
¹²to whom he said,
"This is the resting place, let the
weary rest";^o
and, "This is the place of repose"—
but they would not listen.
¹³So then, the word of the LORD to them
will become:
Do and do, do and do,
rule on rule, rule on rule;
a little here, a little there^p—
so that they will go and fall backward,
be injured^q and snared and
captured.^r

N Isa 26:10–11 ◀▶ Isa 40:6
R Isa 26:15–17 ◀▶ Isa 29:4

I Isa 27:2–6 ◀▶ Isa 28:5–6
I Isa 27:12–13 ◀▶ Isa 30:15
G Isa 11:2–3 ◀▶ Isa 42:1
M Isa 11:2 ◀▶ Isa 31:3
T Isa 11:2–3 ◀▶ Isa 40:13

27:12–13 This passage reconfirmed the return of the Jews to their homeland. Isaiah specifically refers to the blowing of a "trumpet" (27:13) in connection with this return of God's people from their captivity "in Assyria" (27:13). The trumpet mentioned here is the shophar, a ram's horn used to call the troops together (see 1Sa 13:3).

28:5–6 Isaiah foresaw the future millennial rule of the coming Messiah who will be "a glorious crown" (28:5) for the nation. He will usher in a reign of righteousness and justice that the nation has anticipated for centuries.

¹⁴Therefore hear the word of the LORD,
    you scoffers
    who rule this people in Jerusalem.
¹⁵You boast, "We have entered into a
    covenant with death,
    with the grave° we have made an
    agreement.
    When an overwhelming scourge
    sweeps by,
    it cannot touch us,
    for we have made a lie our refuge
    and falsehood our hiding place."
¹⁶So this is what the Sovereign LORD
    says:

"See, I lay a stone in Zion,
    a tested stone,
    a precious cornerstone for a sure
    foundation;
    the one who trusts will never be
    dismayed.
¹⁷I will make justice the measuring line
    and righteousness the plumb line;
    hail will sweep away your refuge, the
    lie,
    and water will overflow your hiding
    place.
¹⁸Your covenant with death will be
    annulled;
    your agreement with the grave will
    not stand.
    When the overwhelming scourge
    sweeps by,
    you will be beaten down by it.
¹⁹As often as it comes it will carry you
    away;
    morning after morning, by day and
    by night,
    it will sweep through."

The understanding of this message
    will bring sheer terror.
²⁰The bed is too short to stretch out on,
    the blanket too narrow to wrap
    around you.
²¹The LORD will rise up as he did at
    Mount Perazim,
    he will rouse himself as in the Valley
    of Gibeon—
    to do his work, his strange work,
    and perform his task, his alien task.
²²Now stop your mocking,
    or your chains will become heavier;
    the Lord, the LORD Almighty, has told
    me
    of the destruction decreed against
    the whole land.

²³Listen and hear my voice;
    pay attention and hear what I say.
²⁴When a farmer plows for planting,
    does he plow continually?
    Does he keep on breaking up and
    harrowing the soil?
²⁵When he has leveled the surface,
    does he not sow caraway and scatter
    cummin?
    Does he not plant wheat in its place,
    barley in its plot,
    and spelt in its field?
²⁶His God instructs him
    and teaches him the right way.

²⁷Caraway is not threshed with a
    sledge,
    nor is a cartwheel rolled over
    cummin;
    caraway is beaten out with a rod,
    and cummin with a stick.
²⁸Grain must be ground to make bread;
    so one does not go on threshing it
    forever.
    Though he drives the wheels of his
    threshing cart over it,
    his horses do not grind it.
²⁹All this also comes from the LORD
    Almighty,

G Ecc 1:14–15 ◀▶ Isa 29:8
H Isa 26:20–21 ◀▶ Isa 28:22
K Isa 26:3–4 ◀▶ Isa 32:2
P Isa 26:20–21 ◀▶ Isa 28:21–22

P Isa 28:17–18 ◀▶ Isa 29:20
H Isa 28:15–18 ◀▶ Isa 30:30

° 15 Hebrew *Sheol*; also in verse 18   P 15 Or *false gods*
q 25 The meaning of the Hebrew for this word is uncertain.

28:14–22 This prophecy reviled the unrighteous leaders of the nation who preferred to trust in their alliances "with death, with the grave" (28:15), the nation's deadly enemies, rather than obey God. Isaiah predicted the staggering consequences that such alliances would bring about in the final conflict.

However, Isaiah also predicted that God would intervene to save the nation from total destruction, referring to Israel's deliverance from her enemies at the Battle of Armageddon (see Rev 19:21). Isaiah's words in 28:22 tie this prediction to Daniel's prophecy of the destruction of the antichrist and his armies in Da 9:24–27.

wonderful in counsel[d] and
    magnificent in wisdom.[e]

Woe to David's City

29 Woe[f] to you, Ariel, Ariel,[g]
    the city[h] where David settled!
Add year to year
    and let your cycle of festivals[i] go on.
[2] Yet I will besiege Ariel;[j]
    she will mourn and lament,[k]
    she will be to me like an altar
        hearth.[r][l]
[3] I will encamp against you all around;
    I will encircle[m] you with towers
    and set up my siege works[n] against
        you.
[4] Brought low, you will speak from the
        ground;
    your speech will mumble[o] out of the
        dust.[p]
Your voice will come ghostlike[q] from
        the earth;
    out of the dust your speech will
        whisper.[r]

[5] But your many enemies will become
        like fine dust,[s]
    the ruthless[t] hordes like blown
        chaff.[u]
Suddenly,[v] in an instant,
[6] the LORD Almighty will come[w]
with thunder[x] and earthquake[y] and
        great noise,
    with windstorm and tempest[z] and
        flames of a devouring fire.[a]
[7] Then the hordes of all the nations[b]
    that fight against Ariel,[c]
    that attack her and her fortress and
        besiege her,
will be as it is with a dream,[d]
    with a vision in the night—
[8] as when a hungry man dreams that he
        is eating,
    but he awakens,[e] and his hunger
        remains;
as when a thirsty man dreams that he
        is drinking,
    but he awakens faint, with his thirst
        unquenched.[f]
So will it be with the hordes of all the
        nations
    that fight against Mount Zion.[g]

[9] Be stunned and amazed,[h]
    blind yourselves and be sightless;[i]
be drunk,[j] but not from wine,[k]
    stagger,[l] but not from beer.
[10] The LORD has brought over you a deep
        sleep:[m]
He has sealed your eyes[n] (the
        prophets);[o]
he has covered your heads (the
        seers).[p]

[11] For you this whole vision[q] is nothing but words sealed[r] in a scroll. And if you give the scroll to someone who can read, and say to him, "Read this, please," he will answer, "I can't; it is sealed." [12] Or if you give the scroll to someone who cannot read, and say, "Read this, please," he will answer, "I don't know how to read."

[13] The Lord says:

"These people[s] come near to me with
        their mouth
    and honor me with their lips,[t]
    but their hearts are far from me.[u]
Their worship of me
    is made up only of rules taught by
        men.[s][v]
[14] Therefore once more I will astound
        these people
    with wonder upon wonder;[w]
the wisdom of the wise[x] will perish,
    the intelligence of the intelligent
        will vanish.[y]"

[15] Woe to those who go to great depths
        to hide[z] their plans from the LORD,

R Isa 29:4 ◀▶ Isa 30:13–14
G Isa 29:8 ◀▶ Isa 30:1
E Pr 24:12 ◀▶ Jer 11:20

49:4 y Isa 6:9–10; 1Co 1:19* 29:15 z Ge 3:8; S Isa 28:15
r 2 The Hebrew for *altar hearth* sounds like the Hebrew for *Ariel.*
s 13 Hebrew; Septuagint *They worship me in vain, / their teachings are but rules taught by men*

R Isa 28:13 ◀▶ Isa 29:13–14
G Isa 28:15–20 ◀▶ Isa 29:13–14

29:4 Isaiah indicated that Judah's alliance with death (see 28:15–18) would only bring about the nation's death.

29:13–14 In their insincere worship of God, the people rejected God's Word and followed the "rules taught by men" (29:13) instead. Note that Jesus quoted from this prophecy to illustrate the hypocrisy of the Pharisees (see Mt 15:8–9).

who do their work in darkness and
    think,
  "Who sees us?ᵃ Who will know?"ᵇ
¹⁶You turn things upside down,
  as if the potter were thought to be
    like the clay!ᶜ
  Shall what is formed say to him who
    formedᵈ it,
  "He did not make me"?
  Can the pot say of the potter,ᵉ
  "He knows nothing"?ᶠ

M ¹⁷In a very short time,ᵍ will not
    Lebanonʰ be turned into a
    fertile fieldⁱ
  and the fertile field seem like a
    forest?ʲ
¹⁸In that dayᵏ the deafˡ will hear the
    words of the scroll,
  and out of gloom and darknessᵐ
  the eyes of the blind will see.ⁿ
¹⁹Once more the humbleᵒ will rejoice in
    the LORD;
  the needyᵖ will rejoice in the Holy
    Oneᑫ of Israel.
P ²⁰The ruthlessʳ will vanish,ˢ
  the mockersᵗ will disappear,
  and all who have an eye for evilᵘ
    will be cut down—
²¹those who with a word make a man
    out to be guilty,
  who ensnare the defender in courtᵛ
  and with false testimonyʷ deprive
    the innocent of justice.ˣ

²²Therefore this is what the LORD, who
redeemedʸ Abraham,ᶻ says to the house
of Jacob:

  "No longer will Jacob be ashamed;ᵃ
  no longer will their faces grow
    pale.ᵇ
²³When they see among them their
    children,ᶜ
  the work of my hands,ᵈ
  they will keep my name holy;ᵉ
  they will acknowledge the holiness
    of the Holy Oneᶠ of Jacob,
  and will stand in awe of the God of
    Israel.
²⁴Those who are waywardᵍ in spirit will
    gain understanding;ʰ

M Isa 26:1–2 ◀ ▶ Isa 32:1–4
P Isa 28:21–22 ◀ ▶ Isa 30:27

29:15 ᵃS Job 8:3;
Ps 10:11-13; 94:7;
Isa 47:10; 57:12;
Eze 8:12; 9:9
ᵇS 2Ki 21:16;
S Job 22:13
29:16 ᶜS Job 10:9;
S Isa 10:15
ᵈS Ge 2:7
ᵉIsa 45:9; 64:8;
Jer 18:6;
Ro 9:20-21*
ᶠS Job 9:12
29:17 ᵍS Isa 10:25
ʰS Isa 2:13
ⁱPs 84:6; 107:33
ʲIsa 32:15
29:18 ᵏS Isa 28:5
ˡMk 7:37
ᵐS Ps 107:14
ⁿS Ps 146:8;
S Isa 32:3; Mt 11:5;
Lk 7:22
29:19 ᵒPs 25:9;
37:11; Isa 61:1;
Mt 5:5; 11:29
ᵖPs 72:4;
S Isa 3:15; S 14:30;
Mt 11:5; Lk 7:22;
Jas 1:9; 2:5
ᑫver 23; Isa 1:4;
S 5:19; S 12:6;
30:11
29:20 ʳS Isa 9:4;
S 13:11 ˢIsa 34:12
ᵗS 2Ch 36:16;
Isa 28:22
ᵘS Job 15:35;
Ps 7:14; Isa 32:7;
33:11; 59:4;
Eze 11:2; Mic 2:1;
Na 1:11
29:21 ᵛAm 5:10,
15 ʷPr 21:28
ˣS Isa 2:7; Hab 1:4
29:22 ʸS Ex 6:6
ᶻGe 17:16;
Isa 41:8; 51:2;
63:16 ᵃPs 22:5;
25:3; S Isa 28:16;
49:23; 61:7;
Joel 2:26; Zep 3:11
ᵇJer 30:6,10;
Joel 2:6,21; Na 2:10
29:23
ᶜIsa 49:20-26;
53:10; 54:1-3
ᵈS Ps 8:6;
S Isa 19:25 ᵉMt 6:9
ᶠS ver 19; S Isa 5:19
29:24 ᵍPs 95:10;
S Pr 12:8; Isa 28:7;
Heb 5:2 ʰIsa 1:3;
32:4; 41:20; 60:16
ⁱIsa 30:21; 42:16
30:1 ʲS Isa 28:1
ᵏS Dt 21:18;
S Isa 1:2
ˡS 2Ki 17:4;
S Isa 8:12
30:2 ᵐ2Ki 25:26;
Isa 31:1; 36:6;
Jer 2:18,36; 42:14;
Eze 17:15; 29:16
ⁿS Ge 25:22;
S Nu 27:21
ᵒIsa 36:9 ᵖS Isa 4:6
30:3 ᑫJdg 9:8-15
ʳver 5; S Ps 44:15;

those who complain will accept
    instruction."ⁱ

Woe to the Obstinate Nation

30 "Woeʲ to the obstinate
    children,"ᵏ
  declares the LORD,
  "to those who carry out plans that are
    not mine,
  forming an alliance,ˡ but not by my
    Spirit,
  heaping sin upon sin;
²who go down to Egyptᵐ
  without consultingⁿ me;
  who look for help to Pharaoh's
    protection,ᵒ
  to Egypt's shade for refuge.ᵖ
³But Pharaoh's protection will be to
    your shame,
  Egypt's shadeᑫ will bring you
    disgrace.ʳ
⁴Though they have officials in Zoanˢ
  and their envoys have arrived in
    Hanes,
⁵everyone will be put to shame
  because of a peopleᵗ uselessᵘ to
    them,
  who bring neither helpᵛ nor
    advantage,
  but only shame and disgrace.ʷ"

⁶An oracleˣ concerning the animals of
the Negev:ʸ

  Through a land of hardship and
    distress,ᶻ
  of lionsᵃ and lionesses,
  of adders and darting snakes,ᵇ
  the envoys carry their riches on
    donkeys'ᶜ backs,
  their treasuresᵈ on the humps of
    camels,
  to that unprofitable nation,

E Ps 143:10 ◀ ▶ Isa 34:16
N Isa 11:2 ◀ ▶ Isa 40:7
W Pr 1:22–23 ◀ ▶ Mic 2:7
G Isa 29:13–14 ◀ ▶ Isa 50:11
J Isa 23:1–17 ◀ ▶ Isa 48:14–15

Isa 20:4-5; 36:6 30:4 ˢNu 13:22 30:5 ᵗver 7; Isa 20:5; 31:1; 36:6
ᵘ2Ki 18:21 ᵛS Ps 108:12; Jer 37:3-5 ʷS ver 3; S 2Ki 18:21; Eze 17:15
30:6 ˣIsa 13:1 ʸJdg 1:9 ᶻS Ex 1:13; 5:10,21; S Isa 5:30; 8:22; Jer 11:4
ᵃS Isa 5:29; 35:9 ᵇS Dt 8:15 ᶜS Ge 42:26; S 1Sa 25:18 ᵈS Isa 15:7

29:17–20 These wondrous prophecies saw an initial fulfillment when Jesus healed the deaf and the blind and will be completely fulfilled during the Millennium.

⁷ to Egypt, whose help is utterly
useless.ᵉ
Therefore I call her
Rahabᶠ the Do-Nothing.

⁸Go now, write it on a tabletᵍ for them,
inscribe it on a scroll,ʰ
that for the days to come
it may be an everlasting witness.ⁱ

⁹These are rebelliousʲ people,
deceitfulᵏ children,
children unwilling to listen to the
LORD's instruction.ˡ
¹⁰They say to the seers,ᵐ
"See no more visionsⁿ!"
and to the prophets,
"Give us no more visions of what is
right!
Tell us pleasant things,ᵒ
prophesy illusions.ᵖ
¹¹Leave this way,ᵠ
get off this path,
and stop confrontingʳ us
with the Holy Oneˢ of Israel!"

¹²Therefore, this is what the Holy Oneᵗ
of Israel says:

"Because you have rejected this
message,ᵘ
relied on oppressionᵛ
and depended on deceit,
¹³this sin will become for you
like a high wall,ʷ cracked and
bulging,
that collapsesˣ suddenly,ʸ in an
instant.
¹⁴It will break in pieces like pottery,ᶻ
shattered so mercilessly
that among its pieces not a fragment
will be found
for taking coals from a hearth
or scooping water out of a cistern."

¹⁵This is what the Sovereignᵃ LORD, the
Holy Oneᵇ of Israel, says:

"In repentance and restᶜ is your
salvation,
in quietness and trustᵈ is your
strength,
but you would have none of it.ᵉ

¹⁶You said, 'No, we will fleeᶠ on
horses.'ᵍ
Therefore you will flee!
You said, 'We will ride off on swift
horses.'
Therefore your pursuers will be
swift!
¹⁷A thousand will flee
at the threat of one;
at the threat of fiveʰ
you will all fleeⁱ away,
till you are leftʲ
like a flagstaff on a mountaintop,
like a bannerᵏ on a hill."

¹⁸Yet the LORD longsˡ to be gracious to
you;
he rises to show you compassion.ᵐ
For the LORD is a God of justice.ⁿ
Blessed are all who wait for him!ᵒ

¹⁹O people of Zion, who live in Jerusalem, you will weep no more.ᵖ How gracious he will be when you cry for help!ᵠ As soon as he hears, he will answerʳ you. ²⁰Although the Lord gives you the breadˢ of adversity and the water of affliction, your teachersᵗ will be hiddenᵘ no more; with your own eyes you will see them. ²¹Whether you turn to the right or to the left, your ears will hear a voiceᵛ behind you, saying, "This is the way;ʷ walk in it." ²²Then you will defile your idolsˣ overlaid with silver and your images covered with gold;ʸ you will throw them away like a menstrualᶻ cloth and say to them, "Away with you!ᵃ"

²³He will also send you rainᵇ for the

30:13–15 Though the people had allowed oppression and deceit to become their wall of security, Isaiah said it would be shattered. The only way to true security was through repentance.

30:17–27 Isaiah began this passage by foretelling the fear and terror that would afflict the Jews when their enemies would attack in the last days. Note his mention of the Battle of Armageddon (30:25) and the description of the intense burning of the sun and the moon (30:17, 26) indicating the supernatural judgments of God which will be displayed during the closing moments of the tribulation.

seed you sow in the ground, and the food that comes from the land will be rich[c] and plentiful.[d] In that day[e] your cattle will graze in broad meadows.[f] ²⁴The oxen[g] and donkeys that work the soil will eat fodder[h] and mash, spread out with fork[i] and shovel. ²⁵In the day of great slaughter,[j] when the towers[k] fall, streams of water will flow[l] on every high mountain and every lofty hill. ²⁶The moon will shine like the sun,[m] and the sunlight will be seven times brighter, like the light of seven full days, when the LORD binds up the bruises of his people and heals[n] the wounds he inflicted.

²⁷See, the Name[o] of the LORD comes from afar,
with burning anger[p] and dense clouds of smoke;
his lips are full of wrath,[q]
and his tongue is a consuming fire.[r]
²⁸His breath[s] is like a rushing torrent,[t] rising up to the neck.[u]
He shakes the nations in the sieve[v] of destruction;
he places in the jaws of the peoples
a bit[w] that leads them astray.

²⁹And you will sing
as on the night you celebrate a holy festival;[x]
your hearts will rejoice[y]
as when people go up with flutes[z]
to the mountain[a] of the LORD,
to the Rock[b] of Israel.
³⁰The LORD will cause men to hear his majestic voice[c]
and will make them see his arm[d] coming down
with raging anger[e] and consuming fire,[f]
with cloudburst, thunderstorm[g] and hail.[h]

P *Isa 29:20* ◄ ► *Isa 30:30*
I *Isa 30:18–26* ◄ ► *Isa 32:15–18*
P *Isa 30:27* ◄ ► *Isa 33:12*
H *Isa 28:22* ◄ ► *Isa 30:33*

30:23 ᶜIsa 25:6; 55:2; Jer 31:14
ᵈS Job 36:31; Isa 62:8 ᵉS Isa 28:5
ᶠS Ps 65:13
30:24 ᵍIsa 32:14, 20 ʰS Job 6:5
ⁱMt 3:12; Lk 3:17
30:25 ʲS Isa 13:5; 34:6; 65:12;
Jer 25:32; 50:27
ᵏS Isa 2:15
ˡS Ex 17:6;
Isa 32:2; 41:18;
Joel 3:18; Zec 14:8
30:26 ᵐIsa 24:23; 60:19-20; Zec 14:7;
Rev 21:23; 22:5
ⁿS Dt 32:39;
S 2Ch 7:14;
Ps 107:20;
S Isa 1:5; Jer 3:22;
17:14; Hos 14:4
30:27 ᵒ1Ki 18:24;
Ps 20:1; Isa 59:19;
64:2 ᵖIsa 26:20;
66:14; Eze 22:31
ᵠIsa 10:5; 13:5
ʳS ver 30;
S Job 41:21
30:28 ˢS Isa 11:4
ᵗS Ps 50:3;
S Isa 28:15
ᵘS Isa 8:8 ᵛAm 9:9
ʷ2Ki 19:28
30:29 ˣIsa 25:6
ʸIsa 12:1
ᶻS 1Sa 10:5
ᵃS Ps 42:4;
Mt 26:30
ᵇS Ge 49:24
30:30 ᶜS Ps 68:33
ᵈIsa 9:12; 40:10;
51:9; 52:10; 53:1;
59:16; 62:8; 63:12
ᵉS ver 27;
S Isa 10:25
ᶠS Isa 4:4; 47:14
ᵍEx 20:18; Ps 29:3
ʰS Ex 9:18
30:31 ⁱS Isa 10:5, 12
ʲS Isa 11:4
30:32 ᵏIsa 10:26
ˡS Ex 15:20
ᵐS Isa 11:15;
Eze 32:10
30:33 ⁿS 2Ki 23:10
ᵒS Ex 15:10;
S 2Sa 22:16
ᵖS Ge 19:24;
S Rev 9:17
ᵠS Isa 1:31
31:1 ʳS Isa 28:1
ˢS Dt 17:16;
Isa 30:2,5;
S Jer 37:5
ᵗS Isa 30:16
ᵘS Isa 2:7
ᵛJob 6:10; S Isa 1:4;
S 30:12
ʷS Dt 20:1;
S Pr 21:31;
S Isa 9:13; Jer 46:9;

³¹The voice of the LORD will shatter Assyria;[i]
with his scepter he will strike[j] them down.
³²Every stroke the LORD lays on them
with his punishing rod[k]
will be to the music of tambourines[l] and harps,
as he fights them in battle with the blows of his arm.[m]
³³Topheth[n] has long been prepared; H
it has been made ready for the king.
Its fire pit has been made deep and wide,
with an abundance of fire and wood;
the breath[o] of the LORD,
like a stream of burning sulfur,[p]
sets it ablaze.[q]

Woe to Those Who Rely on Egypt

31 Woe[r] to those who go down to Egypt[s] for help,
who rely on horses,[t]
who trust in the multitude of their chariots[u]
and in the great strength of their horsemen,
but do not look to the Holy One[v] of Israel,
or seek help from the LORD.[w]
²Yet he too is wise[x] and can bring disaster;[y]
he does not take back his words.[z]
He will rise up against the house of the wicked,[a]
against those who help evildoers.
³But the Egyptians[b] are men and not God;[c] M

H *Isa 30:30* ◄ ► *Isa 33:11–12*
M *Isa 28:6* ◄ ► *Isa 32:15*

Eze 29:16 **31:2** ˣS Ps 92:5; Ro 16:27 ʸIsa 45:7; 47:11; Am 3:6
ᶻNu 23:19; S Pr 19:21 ᵃS Isa 1:4; 29:15; 32:6 **31:3** ᵇIsa 20:5; 36:9
ᶜS Ps 9:20; Eze 28:9; 2Th 2:4

30:30–33 This passage carries a double meaning: the wrath of God on the Assyrian army as well as God's judgment on the future antichrist, referred to in 10:5 as "the Assyrian" (see 14:25). Isaiah further declared that Tophet, which is a name for "hell," is prepared and ready for its king. Despite his satanic power, the antichrist will be utterly destroyed by Jesus Christ and cast into hell forever (see Rev 19:19–20).

their horses^d are flesh and not
    spirit.
When the LORD stretches out his
    hand,^{e}
he who helps will stumble,
he who is helped^f will fall;
both will perish together.^{g}

⁴This is what the LORD says to me:

"As a lion^h growls,
    a great lion over his prey—
and though a whole band of
    shepherds^i
is called together against him,
he is not frightened by their shouts
    or disturbed by their clamor^j—
so the LORD Almighty will come
    down^k
to do battle on Mount Zion and on
    its heights.
⁵Like birds hovering^l overhead,
    the LORD Almighty will shield^m
        Jerusalem;
he will shield it and deliver^n it,
he will 'pass over'^{o} it and will
    rescue it."

⁶Return^p to him you have so greatly revolted^q against, O Israelites. ⁷For in that day^r every one of you will reject the idols of silver and gold^s your sinful hands have made.^{t}

⁸"Assyria^u will fall by a sword that is
    not of man;
a sword, not of mortals, will devour^v
    them.
They will flee before the sword
    and their young men will be put to
        forced labor.^{w}
⁹Their stronghold^x will fall because of
    terror;
at sight of the battle standard^y their
    commanders will panic,"^{z}
declares the LORD,
    whose fire^a is in Zion,
    whose furnace^b is in Jerusalem.

^{d} S Isa 30:16
^{e} Ne 1:10;
  S Job 30:21;
  Isa 9:17,21;
  Jer 51:25;
  Eze 20:34
^{f} Isa 10:3
^{g} S Isa 20:6;
  Jer 17:5
31:4 ^{h} Nu 24:9;
  S 1Sa 17:34;
  Hos 11:10; Am 3:8
^{i} Jer 3:15; Eze 34:23;
  Na 3:18 ^{j} Ps 74:23
^{k} Isa 42:13
31:5 ^{l} S Ge 1:2;
  S Mt 23:37
^{m} S Ps 91:4;
  S Isa 5:2; S Zec 9:15
^{n} S Ps 34:7;
^{o} S Ex 12:23
31:6 ^{p} S Job 22:23
^{q} S Isa 1:5
31:7 ^{r} Isa 29:18
^{s} S Isa 30:22
^{t} S Ps 135:15
31:8 ^{u} S Isa 10:12
^{v} S Ex 12:12;
  Isa 10:12; S 27:1;
  Jer 25:12; Hab 2:8
^{w} S Ge 49:15;
  S Dt 20:11
31:9 ^{x} Dt 32:31,37
^{y} S Isa 18:3;
^{z} S Jer 4:6 ^{z} Jer 51:9;
  Na 3:7 ^{a} S Isa 10:17
^{b} Ps 21:9; Mal 4:1
32:1 ^{c} S Ps 149:2;
  S Isa 0:5; Eze 37:24
^{d} Ps 72:1-4;
  S Isa 9:7; S 28:6
32:2 ^{e} S 1Ki 18:4
^{f} S Ps 55:8
^{g} S Isa 25:3;
  S Isa 30:25; Jer 31:9
^{h} S Ps 107:35
32:3 ^{i} S Isa 29:18
^{j} S Dt 29:4
32:4 ^{k} Isa 6:10;
  S 29:24 ^{l} Isa 35:6
32:5 ^{m} S 1Sa 25:25
32:6 ^{n} S Pr 19:3
^{o} S Pr 24:2
^{p} S Isa 9:17
^{q} Isa 3:12; 9:16
^{r} S Isa 3:15
32:7 ^{s} Jer 5:26-28;
  Da 12:10
^{t} S Isa 29:20;
  Mic 7:3 ^{u} S Ps 72:4;
  Isa 29:19; 61:1
^{v} S Isa 29:21
32:8 ^{w} 1Ch 29:9;
  S Pr 11:25
^{x} Isa 14:24
32:9 ^{y} S Isa 4:1
^{z} Isa 28:23 ^{a} ver 11;
  Isa 47:8; Da 4:4;
  Am 6:1; Zep 2:15

The Kingdom of Righteousness

32 See, a king^c will reign in
    righteousness
    and rulers will rule with justice.^{d}
²Each man will be like a shelter^e from
        the wind
    and a refuge from the storm,^{f}
like streams of water^g in the desert^h
    and the shadow of a great rock in a
        thirsty land.
³Then the eyes of those who see will no
        longer be closed,^{i}
    and the ears^j of those who hear will
        listen.
⁴The mind of the rash will know and
        understand,^{k}
    and the stammering tongue^l will be
        fluent and clear.

⁵No longer will the fool^m be called noble
    nor the scoundrel be highly
        respected.
⁶For the fool speaks folly,^{n}
    his mind is busy with evil:^{o}
He practices ungodliness^p
    and spreads error^q concerning the
        LORD;
the hungry he leaves empty^r
    and from the thirsty he withholds
        water.
⁷The scoundrel's methods are wicked,^{s}
    he makes up evil schemes^t
to destroy the poor with lies,
    even when the plea of the needy^u is
        just.^{v}
⁸But the noble man makes noble plans,
    and by noble deeds^w he stands.^{x}

The Women of Jerusalem

⁹You women^y who are so complacent,
    rise up and listen^z to me;
you daughters who feel secure,^{a}
    hear what I have to say!

M Isa 29:17–24 ◀ ▶ Isa 33:20–22
K Isa 28:16 ◀ ▶ Isa 40:8
L Isa 12:1–3 ◀ ▶ Isa 38:17
L SS 4:9–10 ◀ ▶ Isa 41:10

31:5 This prophecy likened God's protection of Jerusalem to a bird that hovers over its nest protecting its young from marauders. Note that the phrase "pass over" is the same word used of the destroying angel in Egypt at the first Passover (see Ex 12:12–13).

31:8–9 This passage may also carry a double meaning. The Assyrians that amassed against Hezekiah were defeated by a supernatural intervention of God (see 37:36) as an initial fulfillment of this prophecy. The final fulfillment may be realized at the final destruction of the antichrist, "the Assyrian" (see 10:5) who will "fall by a sword" (31:8) of the Lord in the end times (see Rev 19:11–21).

32:1–4 The Messiah is again in view in this prophecy as Isaiah describes the rule and government that will be established in the Millennium when "a king will reign in righteousness" (32:1).

¹⁰In little more than a year,
  you who feel secure will tremble;
the grape harvest will fail,
  and the harvest of fruit will not come.
¹¹Tremble, you complacent women;
  shudder, you daughters who feel secure!
Strip off your clothes,
  put sackcloth around your waists.
¹²Beat your breasts for the pleasant fields,
  for the fruitful vines
¹³and for the land of my people,
  a land overgrown with thorns and briers—
yes, mourn for all houses of merriment
  and for this city of revelry.
¹⁴The fortress will be abandoned,
  the noisy city deserted;
citadel and watchtower will become a wasteland forever,
  the delight of donkeys, a pasture for flocks,
¹⁵till the Spirit is poured upon us from on high,
  and the desert becomes a fertile field,
  and the fertile field seems like a forest.
¹⁶Justice will dwell in the desert
  and righteousness live in the fertile field.
¹⁷The fruit of righteousness will be peace;
  the effect of righteousness will be quietness and confidence forever.
¹⁸My people will live in peaceful dwelling places,
  in secure homes,
  in undisturbed places of rest.
¹⁹Though hail flattens the forest
  and the city is leveled completely,
²⁰how blessed you will be,
  sowing your seed by every stream,
  and letting your cattle and donkeys range free.

Distress and Help

33 Woe to you, O destroyer,
  you who have not been destroyed!
Woe to you, O traitor,
  you who have not been betrayed!
When you stop destroying,
  you will be destroyed;
when you stop betraying,
  you will be betrayed.

²O LORD, be gracious to us;
  we long for you.
Be our strength every morning,
  our salvation in time of distress.
³At the thunder of your voice, the peoples flee;
  when you rise up, the nations scatter.
⁴Your plunder, O nations, is harvested as by young locusts;
  like a swarm of locusts men pounce on it.

⁵The LORD is exalted, for he dwells on high;
  he will fill Zion with justice and righteousness.
⁶He will be the sure foundation for your times,
  a rich store of salvation and wisdom and knowledge;
  the fear of the LORD is the key to this treasure.
⁷Look, their brave men cry aloud in the streets;
  the envoys of peace weep bitterly.
⁸The highways are deserted,
  no travelers are on the roads.
The treaty is broken,

32:13–18 This passage envisioned both the rejection of the nation by God (as judgment for their rebellion) as well as their future millennial blessing when they shall be restored to God's blessing under their Messiah.

its witnesses^u are despised,
no one is respected.
⁹The land mourns^v[1] and wastes away,
Lebanon^j is ashamed and withers;^k
Sharon^l is like the Arabah,
and Bashan^m and Carmelⁿ drop their leaves.

¹⁰"Now will I arise,^o" says the LORD.
"Now will I be exalted;^p
now will I be lifted up.
¹¹You conceive^q chaff,
you give birth^r to straw;
your breath is a fire^s that consumes you.
¹²The peoples will be burned as if to lime;^t
like cut thornbushes^u they will be set ablaze."^v

¹³You who are far away,^w hear^x what I have done;
you who are near, acknowledge my power!
¹⁴The sinners^y in Zion are terrified;
trembling^z grips the godless:
"Who of us can dwell with the consuming fire?^a
Who of us can dwell with everlasting burning?"

¹⁵He who walks righteously^b
and speaks what is right,^c
who rejects gain from extortion^d
and keeps his hand from accepting bribes,^e
who stops his ears against plots of murder
and shuts his eyes^f against contemplating evil—
¹⁶this is the man who will dwell on the heights,^g
whose refuge^h will be the mountain fortress.ⁱ

His bread will be supplied,
and water will not fail^j him.

¹⁷Your eyes will see the king^k in his beauty^l
and view a land that stretches afar.^m
¹⁸In your thoughts you will ponder the former terror:ⁿ
"Where is that chief officer?
Where is the one who took the revenue?
Where is the officer in charge of the towers?^o"
¹⁹You will see those arrogant people^p no more,
those people of an obscure speech,
with their strange, incomprehensible tongue.^q

²⁰Look upon Zion,^r the city of our festivals;
your eyes will see Jerusalem,
a peaceful abode,^s a tent^t that will not be moved;^u
its stakes will never be pulled up,
nor any of its ropes broken.
²¹There the LORD will be our Mighty^v One.
It will be like a place of broad rivers and streams.^w
No galley with oars will ride them,
no mighty ship^x will sail them.
²²For the LORD is our judge,^y
the LORD is our lawgiver,^z
the LORD is our king;^a
it is he who will save^b us.

²³Your rigging hangs loose:
The mast is not held secure,
the sail is not spread.
Then an abundance of spoils will be divided
and even the lame^c will carry off plunder.^d
²⁴No one living in Zion will say, "I am ill";^e
and the sins of those who dwell there will be forgiven.^f

H Isa 30:33 ◄ ► Isa 33:14
P Isa 30:30 ◄ ► Isa 34:1–4
H Isa 33:11–12 ◄ ► Isa 35:4
S Isa 32:15 ◄ ► Isa 35:8–9
U Isa 32:17 ◄ ► Isa 55:2
F Isa 1:19 ◄ ► Isa 41:17

I Isa 32:15–18 ◄ ► Isa 37:31–32
M Isa 32:1–4 ◄ ► Isa 35:1–10

^u 8 Dead Sea Scrolls; Masoretic Text / *the cities* ^v 9 Or *dries up*

33:20–22 The prophet foresaw the Millennium when the nation would be restored to God's blessing and the Messiah would rule, ushering in peace and security.

Judgment Against the Nations

34 Come near, you nations, and listen;
pay attention, you peoples!
Let the earth hear, and all that is in it,
the world, and all that comes out of it!
² The LORD is angry with all nations;
his wrath is upon all their armies.
He will totally destroy them,
he will give them over to slaughter.
³ Their slain will be thrown out,
their dead bodies will send up a stench;
the mountains will be soaked with their blood.
⁴ All the stars of the heavens will be dissolved
and the sky rolled up like a scroll;
all the starry host will fall
like withered leaves from the vine,
like shriveled figs from the fig tree.

⁵ My sword has drunk its fill in the heavens;
see, it descends in judgment on Edom,
the people I have totally destroyed.
⁶ The sword of the LORD is bathed in blood,
it is covered with fat—
the blood of lambs and goats,
fat from the kidneys of rams.
For the LORD has a sacrifice in Bozrah
and a great slaughter in Edom.
⁷ And the wild oxen will fall with them,
the bull calves and the great bulls.
Their land will be drenched with blood,
and the dust will be soaked with fat.

⁸ For the LORD has a day of vengeance,
a year of retribution, to uphold Zion's cause.
⁹ Edom's streams will be turned into pitch,
her dust into burning sulfur;
her land will become blazing pitch!
¹⁰ It will not be quenched night and day;
its smoke will rise forever.
From generation to generation it will lie desolate;
no one will ever pass through it again.

¹¹ The desert owl and screech owl will possess it;
the great owl and the raven will nest there.
God will stretch out over Edom
the measuring line of chaos
and the plumb line of desolation.
¹² Her nobles will have nothing there to be called a kingdom,
all her princes will vanish away.
¹³ Thorns will overrun her citadels,
nettles and brambles her strongholds.
She will become a haunt for jackals,
a home for owls.
¹⁴ Desert creatures will meet with hyenas,
and wild goats will bleat to each other;
there the night creatures will also repose
and find for themselves places of rest.
¹⁵ The owl will nest there and lay eggs,
she will hatch them, and care for her young under the shadow of her wings;
there also the falcons will gather, each with its mate.

¹⁶ Look in the scroll of the LORD and read:
None of these will be missing,
not one will lack her mate.
For it is his mouth that has given the order,
and his Spirit will gather them together.
¹⁷ He allots their portions;

P *Isa 33:12* ◀ ▶ *Isa 34:5–17*
P *Isa 34:1–4* ◀ ▶ *Isa 40:24*

E *Isa 30:1* ◀ ▶ *Isa 40:7*
M *Isa 32:15* ◀ ▶ *Isa 40:7*

w 2 The Hebrew term refers to the irrevocable giving over of things or persons to the LORD, often by totally destroying them; also in verse 5.
x 11 The precise identification of these birds is uncertain.

34:1–4 This prophecy described the concluding judgments of God to be poured out upon the unrepentant nations during the final years of the tribulation period. See the judgments described in Rev 6.

Joy of the Redeemed

his hand distributes them by measure.
They will possess it forever
 and dwell there from generation to generation.

35 The desert and the parched land will be glad;
 the wilderness will rejoice and blossom.
Like the crocus, ²it will burst into bloom;
 it will rejoice greatly and shout for joy.
The glory of Lebanon will be given to it,
 the splendor of Carmel and Sharon;
they will see the glory of the LORD,
 the splendor of our God.

³Strengthen the feeble hands,
 steady the knees that give way;
⁴say to those with fearful hearts,
 "Be strong, do not fear;
your God will come,
 he will come with vengeance;
with divine retribution
 he will come to save you."

⁵Then will the eyes of the blind be opened
 and the ears of the deaf unstopped.
⁶Then will the lame leap like a deer,
 and the mute tongue shout for joy.
Water will gush forth in the wilderness
 and streams in the desert.
⁷The burning sand will become a pool,
 the thirsty ground bubbling springs.
In the haunts where jackals once lay,
 grass and reeds and papyrus will grow.

⁸And a highway will be there;
 it will be called the Way of Holiness.
The unclean will not journey on it;
 it will be for those who walk in that Way;
 wicked fools will not go about on it.
⁹No lion will be there,
 nor will any ferocious beast get up on it;
 they will not be found there.
But only the redeemed will walk there,
¹⁰ and the ransomed of the LORD will return.
They will enter Zion with singing;
 everlasting joy will crown their heads.
Gladness and joy will overtake them,
 and sorrow and sighing will flee away.

Sennacherib Threatens Jerusalem
36:1–22pp — 2Ki 18:13,17–37; 2Ch 32:9–19

36 In the fourteenth year of King Hezekiah's reign, Sennacherib king of Assyria attacked all the fortified cities of Judah and captured them. ²Then the king of Assyria sent his field commander with a large army from Lachish to King Hezekiah at Jerusalem. When the commander stopped at the aqueduct of the Upper Pool, on the road to the Washerman's Field, ³Eliakim son of Hilkiah the palace administrator, Shebna the secretary, and Joah son of Asaph the recorder went out to him.

⁴The field commander said to them, "Tell Hezekiah,

" 'This is what the great king, the king of Assyria, says: On what are you basing this confidence of yours? ⁵You say you have strategy and military strength—but you speak only empty words. On whom are you depending, that you rebel against me? ⁶Look now, you are depending on Egypt, that splintered reed of a

---

35:1–10 Isaiah prophesied the blessings of the millennial kingdom when the Messiah's rule is established. Notice the confirmations of the different parts of this prophecy throughout the book of Isaiah: the fertility of the land (see 41:18); peace within the animal kingdom (see 11:6–9); the return of the exiles from all over the world (see 11:11–16).

staff, which pierces a man's hand and wounds him if he leans on it! Such is Pharaoh king of Egypt to all who depend on him. ⁷And if you say to me, "We are depending¹ on the LORD our God"—isn't he the one whose high places and altars Hezekiah removed,ᵐ saying to Judah and Jerusalem, "You must worship before this altar"?ⁿ

⁸" 'Come now, make a bargain with my master, the king of Assyria: I will give you two thousand horsesᵒ—if you can put riders on them! ⁹How then can you repulse one officer of the least of my master's officials, even though you are depending on Egyptᵖ for chariotsᑫ and horsemen?ʳ ¹⁰Furthermore, have I come to attack and destroy this land without the LORD? The LORD himself toldˢ me to march against this country and destroy it.' "

¹¹Then Eliakim, Shebna and Joahᵗ said to the field commander, "Please speak to your servants in Aramaic,ᵘ since we understand it. Don't speak to us in Hebrew in the hearing of the people on the wall."

¹²But the commander replied, "Was it only to your master and you that my master sent me to say these things, and not to the men sitting on the wall—who, like you, will have to eat their own filth and drink their own urine?ᵛ"

¹³Then the commander stood and called out in Hebrew,ʷ "Hear the words of the great king, the king of Assyria!ˣ ¹⁴This is what the king says: Do not let Hezekiah deceiveʸ you. He cannot deliver you! ¹⁵Do not let Hezekiah persuade you to trust in the LORD when he says, 'The LORD will surely deliverᶻ us; this city will not be given into the hand of the king of Assyria.'ᵃ

¹⁶"Do not listen to Hezekiah. This is what the king of Assyria says: Make peace with me and come out to me. Then every one of you will eat from his own vine and fig treeᵇ and drink water from his own cistern,ᶜ ¹⁷until I come and take you to a land like your ownᵈ—a land of grain and new wine,ᵉ a land of bread and vineyards.

¹⁸"Do not let Hezekiah mislead you when he says, 'The LORD will deliver us.' Has the god of any nation ever delivered his land from the hand of the king of Assyria? ¹⁹Where are the gods of Hamath and Arpad?ᶠ Where are the gods of Sepharvaim?ᵍ Have they rescued Samariaʰ from my hand? ²⁰Who of all the godsⁱ of these countries has been able to save his land from me? How then can the LORD deliver Jerusalem from my hand?"ʲ

²¹But the people remained silent and said nothing in reply, because the king had commanded, "Do not answer him."ᵏ

²²Then Eliakimˡ son of Hilkiah the palace administrator, Shebna the secretary, and Joah son of Asaph the recorderᵐ went to Hezekiah, with their clothes torn,ⁿ and told him what the field commander had said.

Jerusalem's Deliverance Foretold
37:1–13pp — 2Ki 19:1–13

37 When King Hezekiah heard this, he tore his clothesᵒ and put on sackclothᵖ and went into the templeᑫ of the LORD. ²He sent Eliakimʳ the palace administrator, Shebnaˢ the secretary, and the leading priests, all wearing sackcloth, to the prophet Isaiah son of Amoz.ᵗ ³They told him, "This is what Hezekiah says: This day is a day of distressᵘ and rebuke and disgrace, as when children come to the point of birthᵛ and there is no strength to deliver them. ⁴It may be that the LORD your God will hear the words of the field commander, whom his master, the king of Assyria, has sent to ridiculeʷ the living God,ˣ and that he will rebuke him for the words the LORD your God has heard.ʸ Therefore prayᶻ for the remnantᵃ that still survives."

⁵When King Hezekiah's officials came to Isaiah, ⁶Isaiah said to them, "Tell your master, 'This is what the LORD says: Do not be afraidᵇ of what you have heard—those words with which the underlings of the king of Assyria have blasphemedᶜ me. ⁷Listen! I am going to put a spiritᵈ in him so that when he hears a certain report,ᵉ he will return to his own country, and there I will have him cut downᶠ with the sword.' "

⁸When the field commander heard that the king of Assyria had left Lachish,ᵍ he withdrew and found the king fighting against Libnah.ʰ

⁹Now Sennacheribⁱ received a reportʲ

that Tirhakah, the Cushite king of Egypt, was marching out to fight against him. When he heard it, he sent messengers to Hezekiah with this word: [10]"Say to Hezekiah king of Judah: Do not let the god you depend on deceive you when he says, 'Jerusalem will not be handed over to the king of Assyria.' [11]Surely you have heard what the kings of Assyria have done to all the countries, destroying them completely. And will you be delivered? [12]Did the gods of the nations that were destroyed by my forefathers deliver them—the gods of Gozan, Haran, Rezeph and the people of Eden who were in Tel Assar? [13]Where is the king of Hamath, the king of Arpad, the king of the city of Sepharvaim, or of Hena or Ivvah?"

Hezekiah's Prayer
37:14–20pp — 2Ki 19:14–19

[14]Hezekiah received the letter from the messengers and read it. Then he went up to the temple of the LORD and spread it out before the LORD. [15]And Hezekiah prayed to the LORD: [16]"O LORD Almighty, God of Israel, enthroned between the cherubim, you alone are God over all the kingdoms of the earth. You have made heaven and earth. [17]Give ear, O LORD, and hear; open your eyes, O LORD, and see; listen to all the words Sennacherib has sent to insult the living God. [18]"It is true, O LORD, that the Assyrian kings have laid waste all these peoples and their lands. [19]They have thrown their gods into the fire and destroyed them, for they were not gods but only wood and stone, fashioned by human hands. [20]Now, O LORD our God, deliver us from his hand, so that all kingdoms on earth may know that you alone, O LORD, are God."

Sennacherib's Fall
37:21–38pp — 2Ki 19:20–37; 2Ch 32:20–21

[21]Then Isaiah son of Amoz sent a message to Hezekiah: "This is what the LORD, the God of Israel, says: Because you have prayed to me concerning Sennacherib king of Assyria, [22]this is the word the LORD has spoken against him:

"The Virgin Daughter of Zion
  despises and mocks you.
The Daughter of Jerusalem
  tosses her head as you flee.
[23]Who is it you have insulted and
  blasphemed?
Against whom have you raised your
  voice
and lifted your eyes in pride?
Against the Holy One of Israel!
[24]By your messengers
  you have heaped insults on the
    Lord.
And you have said,
  'With my many chariots
I have ascended the heights of the
  mountains,
  the utmost heights of Lebanon.
I have cut down its tallest cedars,
  the choicest of its pines.
I have reached its remotest
  heights,
  the finest of its forests.
[25]I have dug wells in foreign lands
  and drunk the water there.
With the soles of my feet
  I have dried up all the streams of
    Egypt.'

[26]"Have you not heard?
  Long ago I ordained it.
In days of old I planned it;
  now I have brought it to pass,
that you have turned fortified
  cities
  into piles of stone.
[27]Their people, drained of power,
  are dismayed and put to shame.
They are like plants in the field,
  like tender green shoots,
like grass sprouting on the roof,
  scorched before it grows up.

[28]"But I know where you stay
  and when you come and go
  and how you rage against me.
[29]Because you rage against me
  and because your insolence has
    reached my ears,
I will put my hook in your nose
  and my bit in your mouth,
and I will make you return
  by the way you came.

---

[z] 9 That is, from the upper Nile region   [a] 20 Dead Sea Scrolls (see also 2 Kings 19:19); Masoretic Text *alone are the LORD*   [b] 25 Dead Sea Scrolls (see also 2 Kings 19:24); Masoretic Text does not have *in foreign lands.*   [c] 27 Some manuscripts of the Masoretic Text, Dead Sea Scrolls and some Septuagint manuscripts (see also 2 Kings 19:26); most manuscripts of the Masoretic Text *roof / and terraced fields*

30"This will be the sign for you, O Hezekiah:

"This year you will eat what grows by itself,
 and the second year what springs from that.
But in the third year sow and reap,
 plant vineyards and eat their fruit.
31Once more a remnant of the house of Judah
 will take root below and bear fruit above.
32For out of Jerusalem will come a remnant,
 and out of Mount Zion a band of survivors.
The zeal of the LORD Almighty will accomplish this.

33"Therefore this is what the LORD says concerning the king of Assyria:

"He will not enter this city
 or shoot an arrow here.
He will not come before it with shield
 or build a siege ramp against it.
34By the way that he came he will return;
 he will not enter this city,"
           declares the LORD.
35"I will defend this city and save it,
 for my sake and for the sake of David my servant!"

36Then the angel of the LORD went out and put to death a hundred and eighty-five thousand men in the Assyrian camp. When the people got up the next morning—there were all the dead bodies! 37So Sennacherib king of Assyria broke camp and withdrew. He returned to Nineveh and stayed there. 38One day, while he was worshiping in the temple of his god Nisroch, his sons Adrammelech and Sharezer cut him down with the sword, and they escaped to the land of Ararat. And Esarhaddon his son succeeded him as king.

Isa 33:20–22 ◀ ▶ Isa 40:1–2

Hezekiah's Illness

38:1–8pp — 2Ki 20:1–11; 2Ch 32:24–26

38 In those days Hezekiah became ill and was at the point of death. The prophet Isaiah son of Amoz went to him and said, "This is what the LORD says: Put your house in order, because you are going to die; you will not recover." 2Hezekiah turned his face to the wall and prayed to the LORD, 3"Remember, O LORD, how I have walked before you faithfully and with wholehearted devotion and have done what is good in your eyes." And Hezekiah wept bitterly.

4Then the word of the LORD came to Isaiah: 5"Go and tell Hezekiah, 'This is what the LORD, the God of your father David, says: I have heard your prayer and seen your tears; I will add fifteen years to your life. 6And I will deliver you and this city from the hand of the king of Assyria. I will defend this city.

7" 'This is the LORD's sign to you that the LORD will do what he has promised: 8I will make the shadow cast by the sun go back the ten steps it has gone down on the stairway of Ahaz.'" So the sunlight went back the ten steps it had gone down.

9A writing of Hezekiah king of Judah after his illness and recovery:

10I said, "In the prime of my life
 must I go through the gates of death
 and be robbed of the rest of my years?"
11I said, "I will not again see the LORD,
 the LORD, in the land of the living;
no longer will I look on mankind,
 or be with those who now dwell in this world.
12Like a shepherd's tent my house has been pulled down and taken from me.
Like a weaver I have rolled up my life,

E Ps 107:20 ◀ ▶ Da 1:15
R Isa 32:13–14 ◀ ▶ Isa 40:2

d 10 Hebrew Sheol e 11 A few Hebrew manuscripts; most Hebrew manuscripts in the place of cessation

---

37:31–32, 36 Isaiah prophesied to King Hezekiah that, despite the seemingly overwhelming military force of Assyria, God would save Judah from destruction. Isaiah's words record an astonishing miracle when God defeated the Assyrian army by destroying 185,000 Assyrian soldiers in one night.

and he has cut me off from the
    loom;
day and night you made an end of
    me.
¹³I waited patiently till dawn,
    but like a lion he broke all my
        bones;
day and night you made an end of
    me.
¹⁴I cried like a swift or thrush,
    I moaned like a mourning dove.
My eyes grew weak as I looked to the
    heavens.
    I am troubled; O Lord, come to my
        aid!"

¹⁵But what can I say?
    He has spoken to me, and he
        himself has done this.
    I will walk humbly all my years
        because of this anguish of my
            soul.
¹⁶Lord, by such things men live;
    and my spirit finds life in
        them too.
    You restored me to health
        and let me live.
¹⁷Surely it was for my benefit
    that I suffered such anguish.
    In your love you kept me
        from the pit of destruction;
    you have put all my sins
        behind your back.
¹⁸For the grave cannot praise you,
    death cannot sing your praise;
    those who go down to the pit
        cannot hope for your faithfulness.
¹⁹The living, the living—they praise
    you,
    as I am doing today;
    fathers tell their children
        about your faithfulness.

²⁰The Lord will save me,
    and we will sing with stringed
        instruments
    all the days of our lives
        in the temple of the Lord.

²¹Isaiah had said, "Prepare a poultice of figs and apply it to the boil, and he will recover."

²²Hezekiah had asked, "What will be the sign that I will go up to the temple of the Lord?"

Envoys From Babylon
39:1–8pp — 2Ki 20:12–19

39 At that time Merodach-Baladan son of Baladan king of Babylon sent Hezekiah letters and a gift, because he had heard of his illness and recovery. ²Hezekiah received the envoys gladly and showed them what was in his storehouses—the silver, the gold, the spices, the fine oil, his entire armory and everything found among his treasures. There was nothing in his palace or in all his kingdom that Hezekiah did not show them.

³Then Isaiah the prophet went to King Hezekiah and asked, "What did those men say, and where did they come from?"

"From a distant land," Hezekiah replied. "They came to me from Babylon."

⁴The prophet asked, "What did they see in your palace?"

"They saw everything in my palace," Hezekiah said. "There is nothing among my treasures that I did not show them."

⁵Then Isaiah said to Hezekiah, "Hear the word of the Lord Almighty: ⁶The time will surely come when everything in your palace, and all that your fathers have stored up until this day, will be carried off to Babylon. Nothing will be left, says the Lord. ⁷And some of your descendants, your own flesh and blood who will be born to you, will be taken away, and they will become eunuchs in the palace of the king of Babylon."

⁸"The word of the Lord you have spoken is good," Hezekiah replied. For he thought, "There will be peace and security in my lifetime."

f 18 Hebrew Sheol

39:5–7 Isaiah's tragic prophecy foretold the final destruction of Hezekiah's reign by the pagan Babylonians. Hezekiah's proud revelation of the treasures in his palace to the representatives of Babylon would ultimately cause Babylon to plunder all of Hezekiah's riches; "nothing will be left" (39:6). Isaiah also prophesied the future castration of Hezekiah's sons—a procedure that would ensure no royal heir to usurp Babylonian authority.

ISAIAH 40:15

Comfort for God's People

40 Comfort, comfort[w] my people,
    says your God.
² Speak tenderly[x] to Jerusalem,
    and proclaim to her
that her hard service[y] has been completed,[z]
    that her sin has been paid for,[a]
that she has received from the LORD's hand
    double[b] for all her sins.

³ A voice of one calling:
"In the desert prepare
    the way[c] for the LORD;[g]
make straight[d] in the wilderness
    a highway for our God.[h][e]
⁴ Every valley shall be raised up,[f]
    every mountain and hill[g] made low;
the rough ground shall become level,[h]
    the rugged places a plain.
⁵ And the glory[i] of the LORD will be revealed,
    and all mankind together will see it.[j]
        For the mouth of the LORD has spoken."[k]

⁶ A voice says, "Cry out."
    And I said, "What shall I cry?"

"All men are like grass,[l]
    and all their glory is like the flowers of the field.
⁷ The grass withers[m] and the flowers fall,
    because the breath[n] of the LORD blows[o] on them.
    Surely the people are grass.
⁸ The grass withers and the flowers[p] fall,
    but the word[q] of our God stands[r] forever."[s]

⁹ You who bring good tidings[t] to Zion,
    go up on a high mountain.
You who bring good tidings to Jerusalem,[u]
    lift up your voice with a shout,
lift it up, do not be afraid;
    say to the towns of Judah,
    "Here is your God!"[v]
¹⁰ See, the Sovereign LORD comes[w] with power,[x]
    and his arm[y] rules[z] for him.
See, his reward[a] is with him,
    and his recompense accompanies him.
¹¹ He tends his flock like a shepherd:[b]
    He gathers the lambs in his arms[c]
and carries them close to his heart;[d]
    he gently leads[e] those that have young.[f]

¹² Who has measured the waters[g] in the hollow of his hand,[h]
    or with the breadth of his hand marked off the heavens?[i]
Who has held the dust of the earth in a basket,
    or weighed the mountains on the scales
    and the hills in a balance?[j]
¹³ Who has understood the mind[j][k] of the LORD,
    or instructed him as his counselor?[l]
¹⁴ Whom did the LORD consult to enlighten him,
    and who taught him the right way?
Who was it that taught him knowledge[m]
    or showed him the path of understanding?[n]
¹⁵ Surely the nations are like a drop in a bucket;
    they are regarded as dust on the scales;[o]

I Isa 37:31–32 ◀ ▶ Isa 40:8–11
R Isa 38:5 ◀ ▶ Isa 42:22–25
M Isa 35:1–10 ◀ ▶ Isa 41:18–20
N Isa 28:12–13 ◀ ▶ Isa 48:4
E Isa 34:16 ◀ ▶ Isa 48:16
M Isa 34:16 ◀ ▶ Isa 40:13
N Isa 30:1 ◀ ▶ Isa 44:3–4
I Isa 40:1–2 ◀ ▶ Isa 40:27–28
K Isa 32:2 ◀ ▶ Isa 40:29

40:1 w Isa 12:1; 49:13; 51:3,12; 52:9; 57:18; 61:2; 66:13; Jer 31:13; Zep 3:14-17; Zec 1:17; 2Co 1:3
40:2 x S Ge 34:3; S Isa 35:4
    y S Job 7:1
    z Isa 41:11-13; 49:25 a S Lev 26:41
    b Isa 51:19; 61:7; Jer 16:18; 17:18; Zec 9:12; Rev 18:6
40:3 c S Isa 11:16; 43:19; Mal 3:1
    d S Pr 3:5-6
    e Mt 3:3*; Mk 1:3*; Jn 1:23*
40:4 f Isa 49:11
    g S Isa 2:14
    h S Isa 26:7; 45:2,13; Jer 31:9
40:5 i S Ex 16:7; S Nu 14:21; Isa 59:19
    j Isa 52:10; 62:2; Lk 2:30; 3:4-6*
    k S Isa 1:20; 58:14
40:6 l S Ge 6:3; S Isa 29:5
40:7 m S Job 8:12; S Isa 15:6
    n S Ex 15:10; S Job 41:21
    o S Ps 103:16; S Eze 22:21
40:8 p S Isa 5:24; Jas 1:10 q Isa 55:11; 59:21 r S Pr 19:21; S Isa 7:7,9; S Jer 39:16
    s S Ps 119:89; S Mt 5:18; 1Pe 1:24-25*
40:9 t Isa 41:27; 44:28; 52:7-10; 61:1; Na 1:15; S Ac 13:32; Ro 10:15; 1Co 15:1-4
    u S Isa 1:1 v Isa 25:9
40:10 w Isa 35:4; 59:20; Mt 21:5; Rev 22:7 x Isa 28:2
    y S Ps 44:3; S Isa 30:30; S 33:2
    z Isa 9:6-7
    a S Isa 35:4; Rev 22:12
40:11 b S Ge 48:15; S Ps 28:9; S Mic 5:4; S Jn 10:11
    c S Nu 11:12
    d S Dt 26:19
    e Isa 49:10
    f S Ge 33:13; S Dt 30:4
40:12 g S Job 12:15; S 38:10 h Pr 30:4
    i S Job 38:5; Heb 1:10-12

D Ps 139:7 ◀ ▶ Mt 12:31–32
M Isa 40:7 ◀ ▶ Isa 44:3–4
T Isa 28:6 ◀ ▶ Isa 42:1

j S Job 38:18; Pr 16:11 40:13 k Isa 11:2; 42:1 l S Job 15:8; Ro 11:34*; 1Co 2:16* 40:14 m Job 21:22; Col 2:3 n S Job 12:13; S 34:13; Isa 55:9 40:15 o S Ps 62:9

g 3 Or *A voice of one calling in the desert: / "Prepare the way for the LORD*
h 3 Hebrew; Septuagint *make straight the paths of our God*
i 9 Or *O Zion, bringer of good tidings, / go up on a high mountain. / O Jerusalem, bringer of good tidings* 13 Or *Spirit; or spirit*

40:1–11 This prophecy foreshadowed three events: the return from the exile (see 52:7–9); the first coming of Christ (see Mt 21:5); and the glorious blessing of the millennial kingdom when the Messiah will rule on earth (see 62:11; Rev 22:12). Note that the NT links the voice of John the Baptist with 40:3 (see Mt 3:3; Mk 1:3; Lk 3:4; Jn 1:23).

he weighs the islands as though they
    were fine dust.ᵖ
¹⁶Lebanonq is not sufficient for altar
    fires,
  nor its animalsʳ enough for burnt
    offerings.
¹⁷Before him all the nationsˢ are as
    nothing;ᵗ
  they are regarded by him as
    worthless
  and less than nothing.ᵘ

¹⁸To whom, then, will you compare
    God?ᵛ
  What imageʷ will you compare him
    to?
¹⁹As for an idol,ˣ a craftsman casts it,
  and a goldsmithʸ overlays it with
    goldᶻ
  and fashions silver chains for it.
²⁰A man too poor to present such an
    offering
  selects woodᵃ that will not rot.
  He looks for a skilled craftsman
  to set up an idolᵇ that will not
    topple.ᶜ

²¹Do you not know?
  Have you not heard?ᵈ
  Has it not been toldᵉ you from the
    beginning?ᶠ
  Have you not understoodᵍ since the
    earth was founded?ʰ
²²He sits enthronedⁱ above the circle of
    the earth,
  and its people are like
    grasshoppers.ʲ
  He stretches out the heavensᵏ like a
    canopy,ˡ
  and spreads them out like a tentᵐ to
    live in.ⁿ
²³He brings princesᵒ to naught
  and reduces the rulers of this world
    to nothing.ᵖ
²⁴No sooner are they planted,
    no sooner are they sown,
    no sooner do they take rootq in the
      ground,
  than he blowsʳ on them and they
    witherˢ
  and a whirlwind sweeps them away
    like chaff.ᵗ

²⁵"To whom will you compare me?ᵘ
  Or who is my equal?" says the Holy
    One.ᵛ
²⁶Lift your eyes and look to the
    heavens:ʷ
  Who createdˣ all these?
  He who brings out the starry hostʸ one
    by one,
  and calls them each by name.
  Because of his great power and mighty
    strength,ᶻ
  not one of them is missing.ᵃ

²⁷Why do you say, O Jacob,
    and complain, O Israel,
  "My way is hidden from the Lᴏʀᴅ;
    my cause is disregarded by my
      God"?ᵇ
²⁸Do you not know?
    Have you not heard?ᶜ
  The Lᴏʀᴅ is the everlastingᵈ God,
    the Creatorᵉ of the ends of the
      earth.ᶠ
  He will not grow tired or weary,ᵍ
    and his understanding no one can
      fathom.ʰ
²⁹He gives strengthⁱ to the wearyʲ
    and increases the power of the
      weak.
³⁰Even youths grow tired and weary,
    and young menᵏ stumble and fall;ˡ
³¹but those who hopeᵐ in the Lᴏʀᴅ
    will renew their strength.ⁿ
  They will soar on wings like eagles;ᵒ
    they will run and not grow weary,
    they will walk and not be faint.ᵖ

The Helper of Israel

41 "Be silentq before me, you
        islands!ʳ
    Let the nations renew their
      strength!ˢ
    Let them come forwardᵗ and speak;
      let us meet togetherᵘ at the place of
        judgment.

l Isa 40:8-11 ◀ ▶ Isa 41:8-21
K Isa 40:8 ◀ ▶ Isa 40:31
H Isa 38:16 ◀ ▶ Isa 53:4
K Isa 40:29 ◀ ▶ Isa 41:10

P Isa 34:5-17 ◀ ▶ Isa 42:13-15

40:15 ᵖ Dt 9:21; Isa 2:22
40:16 q Isa 33:9; 37:24 ʳ Ps 50:9-11; Mic 6:7; Heb 10:5-9
40:17 ˢ Isa 30:28 ᵗ S Job 12:19; Isa 29:7 ᵘ S Isa 37:19;
40:18 ᵛ S Ex 8:10; S 1Sa 2:2 ʷ S Dt 4:15; Ac 17:29
40:19 ˣ S Ex 20:4; Ps 115:4; S Isa 37:19; 42:17; Jer 2:8,28; 10:8; 16:19; Hab 2:18; Zec 10:2 ʸ Isa 41:7; 46:6; Jer 10:3 ᶻ Isa 2:20; 31:7
40:20 ᵃ Isa 44:19 ᵇ S Isa 12:21 ᶜ S Isa 5:3
40:21 ᵈ ver 28; 2Ki 19:25; Isa 41:22; 42:9; 44:8; 48:3,5 ᵉ Ps 19:1; 50:6; Ac 14:17 ᶠ S Ge 1:1 ᵍ Ro 1:19 ʰ Isa 48:13; 51:13
40:22 ⁱ 2Ch 6:18; S Ps 2:4 ʲ S Nu 13:33 ᵏ S Ge 1:1; S Isa 48:13 ˡ S Ge 1:8; S Job 22:14 ᵐ S Job 36:29 ⁿ S Job 26:7
40:23 ᵒ S Job 12:18; S Isa 34:12 ᵖ S Job 12:19; Am 2:3
40:24 q S Isa 5:3 ʳ S 2Sa 22:16; S Isa 11:4; 41:16 ˢ S Job 8:12; S 18:16 ᵗ S Job 24:24; S Isa 41:2
40:25 ᵘ S 1Sa 2:2; S 1Ch 16:25 ᵛ Isa 1:4; 37:23
40:26 ʷ Isa 51:6 ˣ ver 28; Ps 89:11-13; Isa 42:5; 66:2 ʸ S 2Ki 17:16; S Ne 9:6; S Job 38:32 ᶻ S Job 9:4; S Isa 45:24; Eph 1:19 ᵃ S Isa 34:16
40:27 ᵇ S Job 6:29; S 27:2; Lk 18:7-8
40:28 ᶜ S ver 21 ᵈ S Dt 33:27; S Ps 90:2 ᵉ S ver 26 ᶠ S Isa 37:16 ᵍ Isa 44:12 ʰ S Ps 147:5; Ro 11:33
40:29 ⁱ S Ge 18:14; S 1Sa 2:4 ʲ Isa 48:16; 57:3
S Ps 68:35; S 119:28 ʲ Isa 50:4; 57:19; Jer 31:25 40:30 ᵏ Isa 9:17; Jer 6:11; 9:21 ˡ Ps 20:8; Isa 5:27 40:31 ᵐ Isa 37:9; 40:1; S Isa 30:18; Lk 18:1 ⁿ S 1Sa 2:4; S 2Ki 6:33; S 2Co 4:16 ᵒ S Ex 19:4 ᵖ 2Co 4:1; Heb 12:1-3 41:1 q Ps 37:7; Hab 2:20; Zep 1:7; Zec 2:13 ʳ S Isa 11:11 ˢ S 1Sa 2:4 ᵗ Isa 48:16; 57:3 ᵘ S Lk 1:18; 34:1; 50:8

40:27—28 The prophet confirms that God's understanding and purposes are beyond the understanding of those who do not listen to God's Spirit.

²"Who has stirred up one from the east,
 calling him in righteousness to his service?
He hands nations over to him
 and subdues kings before him.
He turns them to dust with his sword,
 to windblown chaff with his bow.
³He pursues them and moves on unscathed,
 by a path his feet have not traveled before.
⁴Who has done this and carried it through,
 calling forth the generations from the beginning?
I, the LORD—with the first of them
 and with the last—I am he.

⁵The islands have seen it and fear;
 the ends of the earth tremble.
They approach and come forward;
⁶ each helps the other
 and says to his brother, "Be strong!"
⁷The craftsman encourages the goldsmith,
 and he who smooths with the hammer
 spurs on him who strikes the anvil.
He says of the welding, "It is good."
 He nails down the idol so it will not topple.

⁸"But you, O Israel, my servant,
 Jacob, whom I have chosen,
 you descendants of Abraham my friend,
⁹I took you from the ends of the earth,
 from its farthest corners I called you.
I said, 'You are my servant';
 I have chosen you and have not rejected you.
¹⁰So do not fear, for I am with you;
 do not be dismayed, for I am your God.
I will strengthen you and help you;
 I will uphold you with my righteous right hand.

¹¹"All who rage against you
 will surely be ashamed and disgraced;
those who oppose you
 will be as nothing and perish.
¹²Though you search for your enemies,
 you will not find them.
Those who wage war against you
 will be as nothing at all.
¹³For I am the LORD, your God,
 who takes hold of your right hand
and says to you, Do not fear;
 I will help you.
¹⁴Do not be afraid, O worm Jacob,
 O little Israel,
for I myself will help you," declares the LORD,
 your Redeemer, the Holy One of Israel.

¹⁵"See, I will make you into a threshing sledge,
 new and sharp, with many teeth.
You will thresh the mountains and crush them,
 and reduce the hills to chaff.
¹⁶You will winnow them, the wind will pick them up,
 and a gale will blow them away.
But you will rejoice in the LORD
 and glory in the Holy One of Israel.

¹⁷"The poor and needy search for water,
 but there is none;
 their tongues are parched with thirst.
But I the LORD will answer them;
 I, the God of Israel, will not forsake them.

41:8–20 God declares that he has chosen Israel as his servant and that he would not cast his people away. He promised, "Do not fear; I will help you" (41:13).

ISAIAH 41:18

¹⁸I will make rivers flow^b on barren heights,
  and springs within the valleys.
I will turn the desert^c into pools of water,^d
  and the parched ground into springs.^e
¹⁹I will put in the desert^f
  the cedar and the acacia,^g the myrtle and the olive.
I will set pines^h in the wasteland,
  the fir and the cypress^i together,^j
²⁰so that people may see and know,^k
  may consider and understand,^l
that the hand^m of the LORD has done this,
  that the Holy One^n of Israel has created^o it.

²¹"Present your case,^p says the LORD.
  "Set forth your arguments," says Jacob's King.^q
²²"Bring in ⌊your idols⌋ to tell us what is going to happen.^r
Tell us what the former things^s were,
  so that we may consider them
  and know their final outcome.
Or declare to us the things to come,^t
²³ tell us what the future holds,
  so we may know^u that you are gods.
Do something, whether good or bad,^v
  so that we will be dismayed^w and filled with fear.
²⁴But you are less than nothing^x
  and your works are utterly worthless;^y
  he who chooses you is detestable.^z

²⁵"I have stirred^a up one from the north,^b and he comes—
  one from the rising sun who calls on my name.
He treads^c on rulers as if they were mortar,
  as if he were a potter treading the clay.
²⁶Who told of this from the beginning,^d
  so we could know,

M Isa 40:4-5 ◀▶ Isa 42:4

or beforehand, so we could say, 'He was right'?
No one told of this,
  no one foretold^e it,
  no one heard any words^f from you.
²⁷I was the first to tell^g Zion, 'Look, here they are!'
  I gave to Jerusalem a messenger of good tidings.^h
²⁸I look but there is no one^i—
  no one among them to give counsel,^j
  no one to give answer^k when I ask them.
²⁹See, they are all false!
  Their deeds amount to nothing;^l
  their images^m are but wind^n and confusion.

The Servant of the LORD

42 "Here is my servant,^o whom I uphold,
  my chosen one^p in whom I delight;^q
I will put my Spirit^r on him
  and he will bring justice^s to the nations.^t
²He will not shout or cry out,^u
  or raise his voice in the streets.
³A bruised reed^v he will not break,^w
  and a smoldering wick he will not snuff out.^x
In faithfulness he will bring forth justice;^y
⁴he will not falter or be discouraged
  till he establishes justice^z on earth.
  In his law^a the islands^b will put their hope."^c

⁵This is what God the LORD says—
he who created the heavens^d and stretched them out,
who spread out the earth^e and all that comes out of it,^f

B Isa 11:2 ◀▶ Isa 44:3
G Isa 28:6 ◀▶ Isa 61:1
T Isa 40:13 ◀▶ Isa 61:1
W Isa 1:18 ◀▶ Isa 45:22
M Isa 41:18-20 ◀▶ Isa 44:3-5

41:21-24 God's prophet challenged the pagan idols to bring forth their predictions of future events to prove that they were truly powerful. Since the idols could neither predict nor perform powerful deeds, God declared that the idols were nothing and that the people who worshiped them were "detestable" (41:24).

42:4 The prophet predicted a day when Jesus Christ, the Messiah, would return to establish his righteous judgment and law on earth.

who gives breath to its people,
   and life to those who walk on it:
⁶"I, the LORD, have called you in
   righteousness;
I will take hold of your hand.
I will keep you and will make you
   to be a covenant for the people
   and a light for the Gentiles,
⁷to open eyes that are blind,
   to free captives from prison
   and to release from the dungeon
   those who sit in darkness.

⁸"I am the LORD; that is my name!
I will not give my glory to another
   or my praise to idols.
⁹See, the former things have taken
   place,
   and new things I declare;
before they spring into being
   I announce them to you."

Song of Praise to the LORD

¹⁰Sing to the LORD a new song,
   his praise from the ends of the
      earth,
you who go down to the sea, and all
   that is in it,
you islands, and all who live in
   them.
¹¹Let the desert and its towns raise
   their voices;
let the settlements where Kedar
   lives rejoice.
Let the people of Sela sing for joy;
   let them shout from the
      mountaintops.
¹²Let them give glory to the LORD
   and proclaim his praise in the
      islands.

¹³The LORD will march out like a mighty
   man,
like a warrior he will stir up his
   zeal;
with a shout he will raise the battle
   cry
and will triumph over his enemies.
¹⁴"For a long time I have kept silent,

L Isa 38:17 ◀ ▶ Isa 43:25
P Isa 40:24 ◀ ▶ Isa 45:23–24

I have been quiet and held myself
   back.
But now, like a woman in childbirth,
   I cry out, I gasp and pant.
¹⁵I will lay waste the mountains and
   hills
   and dry up all their vegetation;
I will turn rivers into islands
   and dry up the pools.
¹⁶I will lead the blind by ways they
   have not known,
along unfamiliar paths I will guide
   them;
I will turn the darkness into light
   before them
   and make the rough places smooth.
These are the things I will do;
   I will not forsake them.
¹⁷But those who trust in idols,
   who say to images, 'You are our
      gods,'
will be turned back in utter shame.

Israel Blind and Deaf

¹⁸"Hear, you deaf;
   look, you blind, and see!
¹⁹Who is blind but my servant,
   and deaf like the messenger I send?
Who is blind like the one committed
   to me,
blind like the servant of the LORD?
²⁰You have seen many things, but have
   paid no attention;
your ears are open, but you hear
   nothing."
²¹It pleased the LORD
   for the sake of his righteousness
   to make his law great and glorious.
²²But this is a people plundered and
   looted,
all of them trapped in pits
   or hidden away in prisons.
They have become plunder,

I Isa 41:8–21 ◀ ▶ Isa 43:5–7
R Isa 40:2 ◀ ▶ Isa 43:27–28

42:13–16 Isaiah prophesied that when the Messiah returns he would display his supernatural power, defeat his enemies and establish his victorious millennial kingdom.

42:22–25 Israel was punished by God not because Babylon was stronger than the Lord, but because Israel had sinned. This punishment would give Israel a foretaste of the final day of the Lord.

with no one to rescue them;^o
they have been made loot,
   with no one to say, "Send them
     back."

²³Which of you will listen to this
  or pay close attention^p in time to
    come?
²⁴Who handed Jacob over to become
    loot,
  and Israel to the plunderers?^q
Was it not the Lord,^r
  against whom we have sinned?
For they would not follow^s his ways;
  they did not obey his law.^t
²⁵So he poured out on them his burning
    anger,^u
  the violence of war.
It enveloped them in flames,^v yet they
    did not understand;^w
  it consumed them, but they did not
    take it to heart.^x

Israel's Only Savior

43 But now, this is what the Lord
    says—
  he who created^y you, O Jacob,
  he who formed^z you, O Israel:^a
"Fear not, for I have redeemed^b you;
  I have summoned you by name;^c
    you are mine.^d
²When you pass through the waters,^e
  I will be with you;^f
and when you pass through the rivers,
  they will not sweep over you.
When you walk through the fire,^g
  you will not be burned;
  the flames will not set you ablaze.^h
³For I am the Lord, your God,ⁱ
  the Holy One^j of Israel, your
    Savior;^k
I give Egypt^l for your ransom,
  Cush^m and Sebaⁿ in your stead.^o
⁴Since you are precious and honored^p
    in my sight,
  and because I love^q you,
I will give men in exchange for you,
  and people in exchange for your life.
⁵Do not be afraid,^r for I am with you;^s
  I will bring your children^t from the
    east
  and gather^u you from the west.^v
⁶I will say to the north, 'Give them up!'
  and to the south,^w 'Do not hold
    them back.'
Bring my sons from afar
  and my daughters^x from the ends of
    the earth^y—
⁷everyone who is called by my name,^z
  whom I created^a for my glory,^b
  whom I formed and made.^c"

⁸Lead out those who have eyes but are
    blind,^d
  who have ears but are deaf.^e
⁹All the nations gather together^f
  and the peoples assemble.
Which of them foretold^g this
  and proclaimed to us the former
    things?
Let them bring in their witnesses to
    prove they were right,
  so that others may hear and say, "It
    is true."

¹⁰"You are my witnesses,^h" declares the
    Lord,
"and my servantⁱ whom I have
    chosen,
so that you may know^j and believe
    me
  and understand that I am he.
Before me no god^k was formed,
  nor will there be one after me.^l
¹¹I, even I, am the Lord,^m
  and apart from me there is no
    savior.ⁿ
¹²I have revealed and saved and
    proclaimed—

l Isa 42:16 ◀ ▶ Isa 43:19–21
c Isa 30:9–10 ◀ ▶ Isa 44:18
t Isa 12:4 ◀ ▶ Isa 43:12
o Ecc 7:13 ◀ ▶ Isa 44:6
t Isa 43:10 ◀ ▶ Isa 44:8

l Isa 41:13–14 ◀ ▶ Isa 46:3–4
s Isa 32:18 ◀ ▶ Da 3:17

1 That is, the upper Nile region

43:5–7 This prophecy found its initial fulfillment in the return of Israel from exile in Babylon. In modern times, Jews from all over the world have been resettling in the promised land. At Christ's second coming this prophecy will be ultimately fulfilled when the Jews will return to Palestine from all parts of the earth.

I, and not some foreign god among you.
You are my witnesses," declares the LORD, "that I am God.

13 Yes, and from ancient days I am he.
No one can deliver out of my hand.
When I act, who can reverse it?"

God's Mercy and Israel's Unfaithfulness

14 This is what the LORD says—
your Redeemer, the Holy One of Israel:
"For your sake I will send to Babylon
and bring down as fugitives all the Babylonians,
in the ships in which they took pride.

15 I am the LORD, your Holy One,
Israel's Creator, your King."

16 This is what the LORD says—
he who made a way through the sea,
a path through the mighty waters,

17 who drew out the chariots and horses,
the army and reinforcements together,
and they lay there, never to rise again,
extinguished, snuffed out like a wick:

18 "Forget the former things;
do not dwell on the past.

19 See, I am doing a new thing!
Now it springs up; do you not perceive it?
I am making a way in the desert
and streams in the wasteland.

20 The wild animals honor me,
the jackals and the owls,
because I provide water in the desert
and streams in the wasteland,

to give drink to my people, my chosen,

21 the people I formed for myself
that they may proclaim my praise.

22 "Yet you have not called upon me, O Jacob,
you have not wearied yourselves for me, O Israel.

23 You have not brought me sheep for burnt offerings,
nor honored me with your sacrifices.
I have not burdened you with grain offerings
nor wearied you with demands for incense.

24 You have not bought any fragrant calamus for me,
or lavished on me the fat of your sacrifices.
But you have burdened me with your sins
and wearied me with your offenses.

25 "I, even I, am he who blots out your transgressions, for my own sake,
and remembers your sins no more.

26 Review the past for me,
let us argue the matter together;
state the case for your innocence.

27 Your first father sinned;
your spokesmen rebelled against me.

28 So I will disgrace the dignitaries of your temple,
and I will consign Jacob to destruction
and Israel to scorn.

I Isa 43:5–7 ◀ ▶ Isa 43:25
I Isa 43:19–21 ◀ ▶ Isa 44:1–8
L Isa 42:6–7 ◀ ▶ Isa 44:22
R Isa 42:22–25 ◀ ▶ Isa 44:28

43:19–21 Isaiah prophesied that the astonishing rebirth of the nation of Israel would be so wonderful as to make the other miracles of Israel's history seem as nothing.

43:25 In spite of the punishment God's people would suffer, Isaiah declared God's commitment to forgive their sins.

43:27–28 God declared that Abraham had sinned (see Ge 12:18; 20:9) and so had the priests and leaders, so destruction would come.

Israel the Chosen

44 "But now listen, O Jacob, my servant,[n]
Israel, whom I have chosen.[o]
[2] This is what the LORD says—
he who made[p] you, who formed you in the womb,[q]
and who will help[r] you:
Do not be afraid,[s] O Jacob, my servant,[t]
Jeshurun,[u] whom I have chosen.
[3] For I will pour water[v] on the thirsty land,
and streams on the dry ground;[w]
I will pour out my Spirit[x] on your offspring,
and my blessing[y] on your descendants.[z]
[4] They will spring up like grass[a] in a meadow,
like poplar trees[b] by flowing streams.[c]
[5] One will say, 'I belong[d] to the LORD';
another will call himself by the name of Jacob;
still another will write on his hand,[e] 'The LORD's,'[f]
and will take the name Israel.

The LORD, Not Idols

[6] "This is what the LORD says—
Israel's King[g] and Redeemer,[h] the LORD Almighty:
I am the first and I am the last;[i]
apart from me there is no God.[j]
[7] Who then is like me?[k] Let him proclaim it.
Let him declare and lay out before me
what has happened since I established my ancient people,
and what is yet to come—
yes, let him foretell[l] what will come.
[8] Do not tremble, do not be afraid.
Did I not proclaim[m] this and foretell it long ago?
You are my witnesses. Is there any God[n] besides me?
No, there is no other Rock;[o] I know not one."

[9] All who make idols[p] are nothing,
and the things they treasure are worthless.[q]
Those who would speak up for them are blind;[r]
they are ignorant, to their own shame.[s]
[10] Who shapes a god and casts an idol,[t]
which can profit him nothing?[u]
[11] He and his kind will be put to shame;[v]
craftsmen are nothing but men.
Let them all come together and take their stand;
they will be brought down to terror and infamy.[w]
[12] The blacksmith[x] takes a tool
and works with it in the coals;
he shapes an idol with hammers,
he forges it with the might of his arm.[y]
He gets hungry and loses his strength;
he drinks no water and grows faint.[z]
[13] The carpenter[a] measures with a line
and makes an outline with a marker;
he roughs it out with chisels
and marks it with compasses.
He shapes it in the form of man,[b]
of man in all his glory,
that it may dwell in a shrine.[c]
[14] He cut down cedars,
or perhaps took a cypress or oak.
He let it grow among the trees of the forest,
or planted a pine,[d] and the rain made it grow.
[15] It is man's fuel[e] for burning;
some of it he takes and warms himself,
he kindles a fire and bakes bread.
But he also fashions a god and worships[f] it;
he makes an idol and bows[g] down to it.

I Isa 43:25 ◀ ▶ Isa 44:21–23
M Isa 42:4 ◀ ▶ Isa 45:8
B Isa 42:1 ◀ ▶ Isa 61:1
J Ps 51:12 ◀ ▶ Isa 63:14
M Isa 40:13 ◀ ▶ Isa 59:19
N Isa 40:7 ◀ ▶ Eze 3:12
P Isa 32:15 ◀ ▶ Eze 11:19
O Isa 43:11 ◀ ▶ Isa 44:8
O Isa 44:6 ◀ ▶ Isa 45:5–9
T Isa 43:12 ◀ ▶ Jer 1:17

44:1 [n] ver 21; [o] S Ge 16:11; S Isa 14:1
44:2 [p] ver 21; S Ps 149:2; [q] S Ge 2:7; S Ps 139:13; [r] S Isa 27:11; [s] S Isa 41:10; [t] S Isa 43:5; [t] Jer 30:10; 46:27; [u] S Nu 23:21; S Dt 32:15
44:3 [v] Joel 3:18; Jn 4:10 [w] S Pr 9:5; S Isa 32:2; S 35:7; [x] S Isa 11:2; Eze 36:27; S Mk 1:8; S Ac 2:17 [y] Mal 3:10 [z] Isa 61:9; 65:23
44:4 [a] S Job 5:25; S Ps 72:16 [b] S Lev 23:40 [c] S Job 40:22
44:5 [d] S Ps 116:5; Isa 19:21; Jer 50:5 [e] Ex 13:9 [f] Isa 60:3; 66:23; Zec 8:20-22; 13:9; 14:16
44:6 [g] S Isa 41:21 [h] S Job 19:25; Isa 43:1 S Isa 41:4; Rev 1:8,17 [j] S Dt 6:4; S 1Ch 17:20; S Ps 18:31; S Isa 43:10
44:7 [k] S Dt 32:39 [l] S Isa 41:22,26
44:8 [m] S Isa 40:21; S 42:9 [n] S Isa 43:10 [o] S Ge 49:24
44:9 [p] S Ex 20:4; S Lev 19:4; Isa 40:19 [q] S Isa 41:24 [r] S Isa 26:11 [s] S Isa 1:29; 65:13; 66:5; Jer 22:22
44:10 [t] S Isa 40:19 [u] Isa 41:29; Jer 10:5; Ac 19:26
44:11 [v] S ver 9; S Isa 1:29; [w] S 2Ki 19:18; S Isa 37:19
44:12 [x] S Isa 40:19; 41:6-7; 54:16 [y] Ac 17:29 [z] Isa 40:28
44:13 [a] S Isa 41:7 [b] Ps 115:4-7 [c] S Jdg 17:4-5
44:14 [d] S Isa 41:19
44:15 [e] ver 19; [f] S Ex 20:5; Rev 9:20 [g] S 2Ch 25:14

44:1–8 Isaiah proclaimed that God alone knows the future and that he alone is God.

¹⁶Half of the wood he burns in the fire;
over it he prepares his meal,
he roasts his meat and eats his fill.
He also warms himself and says,
"Ah! I am warm; I see the fire."
¹⁷From the rest he makes a god, his idol;
he bows down to it and worships.
He prays to it and says,
"Save me; you are my god."
¹⁸They know nothing, they understand nothing;
their eyes are plastered over so they cannot see,
and their minds closed so they cannot understand.
¹⁹No one stops to think,
no one has the knowledge or understanding to say,
"Half of it I used for fuel;
I even baked bread over its coals,
I roasted meat and I ate.
Shall I make a detestable thing from what is left?
Shall I bow down to a block of wood?"
²⁰He feeds on ashes, a deluded heart misleads him;
he cannot save himself, or say,
"Is not this thing in my right hand a lie?"
²¹"Remember these things, O Jacob,
for you are my servant, O Israel.
I have made you, you are my servant;
O Israel, I will not forget you.
²²I have swept away your offenses like a cloud,
your sins like the morning mist.
Return to me,
for I have redeemed you."
²³Sing for joy, O heavens, for the LORD has done this;
shout aloud, O earth beneath.
Burst into song, you mountains,
you forests and all your trees,

C *Isa 43:8* ◀ ▶ *Isa 44:20*
C *Isa 44:18* ◀ ▶ *Isa 48:4*
I *Isa 44:1–8* ◀ ▶ *Isa 44:26*
L *Isa 43:25* ◀ ▶ *Isa 45:22*

44:16 ʰ Isa 47:14
44:17 ⁱ S Ex 20:5; Isa 2:8; Jer 1:16
ʲ S 1Ki 18:26
ᵏ S Jdg 10:14; Isa 45:20; 46:7; 47:15
44:18 ˡ Isa 1:3; S 16:12; Jer 4:22; 10:8,14,14-15
ᵐ S Isa 6:9-10; S 29:10
44:19 ⁿ ver 18-19; Isa 5:13; 27:11; 45:20 ᵒ ver 15
ᵖ S Dt 27:15
ᵠ Isa 40:20
44:20 ʳ Ps 102:9
ˢ S Job 15:31; Ro 1:21-23,28; 2Ti 2:11; 2Ti 3:13
ᵗ S Dt 4:28; Hos 10:5; 13:2
ᵘ Isa 59:3,4,13; Jer 9:3; 10:14; 51:17; Ro 1:25
44:21 ᵛ Isa 46:8; Zec 10:9
ʷ S Isa 43:1
ˣ S Ps 136:22; S Isa 27:11
ʸ Ps 27:10; Isa 49:15; Jer 31:20
44:22 ᶻ 2Sa 12:13; S 2Ch 6:21; Ac 3:19
ᵃ S Job 22:23; Isa 45:22; 55:7; Jer 36:3; Mal 3:7
ᵇ S Isa 33:24; S Mt 20:28; 1Co 6:20
44:23 ᶜ S Ps 98:4; S Isa 12:6
ᵈ S 1Ch 16:31; Ps 148:7 ᵉ S Ps 98:8
ᶠ S Ps 65:13
ᵍ S Ex 6:6; Isa 51:11; 62:12
ʰ S Ex 16:7; S Lev 10:3; S Isa 4:2; 43:7; 46:13; 49:3; 52:1; 55:5; 60:9,21; 61:3; Jer 30:19
44:24 ⁱ S Job 19:25; Isa 43:14
ʲ S Isa 27:11
ᵏ S Ps 139:13
ˡ S Ge 2:1; S Isa 42:5
ᵐ S Ge 1:1
44:25 ⁿ Ps 33:10
ᵒ Lev 19:26; 1Sa 6:2; Isa 2:6; 8:19; 47:13; Jer 27:9; Da 2:2,10; 4:7; Mic 3:7; Zec 10:2
ᵖ S Job 5:13; 1Co 1:27
ᵠ 2Sa 15:31; 1Co 1:19-20

for the LORD has redeemed Jacob,
he displays his glory in Israel.

Jerusalem to Be Inhabited

²⁴"This is what the LORD says—
your Redeemer, who formed you in the womb:

I am the LORD,
who has made all things,
who alone stretched out the heavens,
who spread out the earth by myself,
²⁵who foils the signs of false prophets
and makes fools of diviners,
who overthrows the learning of the wise
and turns it into nonsense,
²⁶who carries out the words of his servants
and fulfills the predictions of his messengers,
who says of Jerusalem, 'It shall be inhabited,'
of the towns of Judah, 'They shall be built,'
and of their ruins, 'I will restore them,'
²⁷who says to the watery deep, 'Be dry,
and I will dry up your streams,'
²⁸who says of Cyrus, 'He is my shepherd
and will accomplish all that I please;
he will say of Jerusalem, "Let it be rebuilt,"
and of the temple, "Let its foundations be laid."'

45 "This is what the LORD says to his anointed,
to Cyrus, whose right hand I take hold of

I *Isa 44:21–23* ◀ ▶ *Isa 45:17–19*
R *Isa 43:27–28* ◀ ▶ *Isa 50:1*
L *Isa 38:21–22* ◀ ▶ *Isa 45:13*

44:26 ʳ Isa 59:21; Zec 1:6 ˢ Isa 46:10; 55:11; Jer 23:20; 39:16; La 2:17; Da 9:12; S Mt 5:18 ᵗ S Isa 1:1 ᵘ S Ps 74:3; S Isa 51:3 ᵛ S Ezr 9:9; S Ps 51:18; Isa 49:8-21; S 61:4 44:27 ʷ S Isa 11:15; S 19:5; Rev 16:12 44:28 ˣ S 2Ch 36:22; S Isa 41:2 ʸ S Isa 14:32 ᶻ Ezr 1:2-4 ᵃ S Isa 28:16; 58:12 45:1 ᵇ S Ps 45:7 ᶜ S 2Ch 36:22; S Isa 41:2 ᵈ S Ps 73:23; S Isa 41:13; 42:6

44:21–23 Israel's suffering has paved the way for God's forgiveness and the final restoration of his people in the millennial kingdom.

44:26–28 Isaiah predicted the return of the exiles under King Cyrus of Persia more than a hundred years before it happened. His words also foreshadow the final restoration of Jerusalem and the kingdom of Judah in the coming millennial kingdom, when the Messiah will reign from the throne of David.

ISAIAH 45:2

to subdue nations^e before him
and to strip kings of their armor,
to open doors before him
so that gates will not be shut:
²I will go before you^f
and will level^g the mountains^o;
I will break down gates^h of bronze
and cut through bars of iron.^i
³I will give you the treasures^j of darkness,
riches stored in secret places,^k
so that you may know^l that I am the LORD,
the God of Israel, who summons you by name.^m
⁴For the sake of Jacob my servant,^n
of Israel my chosen,
I summon you by name
and bestow on you a title of honor,
though you do not acknowledge^o me.
⁵I am the LORD, and there is no other;^p
apart from me there is no God.^q
I will strengthen you,^r
though you have not acknowledged me,
⁶so that from the rising of the sun
to the place of its setting^s
men may know^t there is none besides me.^u
I am the LORD, and there is no other.
⁷I form the light and create darkness,^v
I bring prosperity and create disaster;^w
I, the LORD, do all these things.

⁸"You heavens above, rain^x down righteousness;^y
let the clouds shower it down.
Let the earth open wide,
let salvation^z spring up,
let righteousness grow with it;
I, the LORD, have created it.

⁹"Woe to him who quarrels^a with his Maker,^b
to him who is but a potsherd^c
among the potsherds on the ground.
Does the clay say to the potter,^d
'What are you making?'^e

O Isa 44:8 ◀ ▶ Isa 45:18
M Isa 44:3–5 ◀ ▶ Isa 45:23–24

45:1 ^e Isa 48:14; Jer 50:35; 51:20, 24; Mic 4:13
45:2 ^f Ex 23:20 ^g S Isa 40:4 ^h S Isa 13:2 ^i Ps 107:16; 147:13; Jer 51:30; La 2:9; Na 3:13
45:3 ^j S 2Ki 24:13; Jer 50:37; 51:13 ^k Jer 41:8 ^l Isa 41:23 ^m S Ex 33:12; S Isa 43:1
45:4 ^n S Isa 14:1; 41:8-9 ^o Ac 17:23
45:5 ^p S Isa 44:8 ^q S Dt 32:12; S Ps 18:31; S Isa 43:10 ^r S Ps 18:39; Eze 30:24-25
45:6 ^s S Ps 113:3; Isa 43:5 ^t S Isa 11:9 ^u ver 5,18; Isa 14:13-14; 47:8, 10; Zep 2:15
45:7 ^v S Ge 1:4; S Ex 10:22 ^w S Isa 14:15; S 31:2; La 3:38
45:8 ^x Ps 72:6; S 133:3; Joel 3:18 ^y ver 24; Ps 85:11; S Isa 41:2; 46:13; 48:18; 60:21; 61:10,11; 62:1; Hos 10:12; Joel 2:23; Am 5:24; Mal 4:2 ^z S Ps 85:9; Isa 12:3
45:9 ^a S Job 12:13; S 15:25; S 27:2; 1Co 10:22 ^b S Job 33:13 ^c Ps 22:15 ^d S Isa 29:16; Ro 9:20-21 ^e Job 9:12; Da 4:35
45:11 ^g S Isa 1:4 ^h Ps 149:2; S Isa 51:13 ^i Ps 8:6; S Isa 19:25
45:12 ^j S Ge 1:1 ^k S Ge 2:1; S Isa 48:13 ^l S Ne 9:6; S Job 38:32
45:13 ^m S 2Ch 36:22; S Isa 41:2 ^n S 1Ki 8:36; S Ps 26:12; S Isa 40:4 ^o S Ezr 1:2 ^p Isa 52:3
45:14 ^q 2Sa 8:2; Isa 18:7; 60:5 ^r Isa 2:3; 60:11; 62:2; Zec 8:20-22 ^s S Isa 2:3 ^t S Ge 27:29 ^u 2Sa 3:34; S Isa 14:1-2 ^v Jer 16:19;

Does your work say,
'He has no hands'?^f
¹⁰Woe to him who says to his father,
'What have you begotten?'
or to his mother,
'What have you brought to birth?'

¹¹"This is what the LORD says—
the Holy One^g of Israel, and its Maker:^h
Concerning things to come,
do you question me about my children,
or give me orders about the work of my hands?^i
¹²It is I who made the earth^j
and created mankind upon it.
My own hands stretched out the heavens;^k
I marshaled their starry hosts.^l
¹³I will raise up Cyrus^p^m in my righteousness:
I will make all his ways straight.^n
He will rebuild my city^o
and set my exiles free,
but not for a price or reward,^p
says the LORD Almighty."

¹⁴This is what the LORD says:

"The products^q of Egypt and the merchandise of Cush,^q
and those tall Sabeans^r—
they will come over to you^s
and will be yours;
they will trudge behind you,^t
coming over to you in chains.^u
They will bow down before you
and plead^v with you, saying,
'Surely God is with you,^w and there is no other;
there is no other god.^x' "

¹⁵Truly you are a God who hides^y himself,
O God and Savior^z of Israel.

L Isa 45:1–5 ◀ ▶ Jer 39:17–18

Zec 8:20-23 ^w 1Co 14:25 ^x S Ps 18:31; S Isa 11:9; S 43:10
45:15 ^y S Dt 31:17; Ps 44:24; S Isa 1:15 ^z S Isa 25:9

^o 2 Dead Sea Scrolls and Septuagint; the meaning of the word in the Masoretic Text is uncertain. ^p 13 Hebrew him ^q 14 That is, the upper Nile region

45:8 This prophecy foreshadowed the abundance, deliverance, peace and justice under the millennial reign of Christ.

¹⁶All the makers of idols will be put to shame and disgraced;ᵃ
they will go off into disgrace together.
¹⁷But Israel will be saved ᵇ by the LORD
with an everlasting salvation;ᶜ
you will never be put to shame or disgraced,ᵈ
to ages everlasting.
¹⁸For this is what the LORD says—
he who created the heavens,
he is God;
he who fashioned and made the earth,ᵉ
he founded it;
he did not create it to be empty,ᶠ
but formed it to be inhabited ᵍ—
he says:
"I am the LORD,
and there is no other.ʰ
¹⁹I have not spoken in secret,ⁱ
from somewhere in a land of darkness;ʲ
I have not said to Jacob's descendants,ᵏ
'Seekˡ me in vain.'
I, the LORD, speak the truth;
I declare what is right.ᵐ

²⁰"Gather togetherⁿ and come;
assemble, you fugitives from the nations.
Ignorantᵒ are those who carry ᵖ about idols of wood,
who pray to gods that cannot save.ᵠ
²¹Declare what is to be, present it—
let them take counsel together.
Who foretold ʳ this long ago,
who declared it from the distant past?ˢ
Was it not I, the LORD?
And there is no God apart from me,ᵗ
a righteous Godᵘ and a Savior;ᵛ
there is none but me.

l Isa 44:26 ◀▶ Isa 45:25
o Isa 45:5–9 ◀▶ Isa 45:21–22
o Isa 45:18 ◀▶ Isa 46:9

45:16 ᵃ S Ps 35:4; S Isa 1:29
45:17 ᵇ Jer 23:6; 33:16; Ro 11:26
ᶜ S Isa 12:2
ᵈ S Ge 30:23; S Isa 29:22; S 41:11
45:18 ᵉ S Ge 1:1
ᶠ S Ge 1:2
ᵍ Ge 1:26 ʰ ver 5; Dt 4:35
45:19 ⁱ Isa 48:16; 65:4 ʲ Jer 2:31
ᵏ ver 25; Isa 41:8; 65:9; Jer 31:36
ˡ S Dt 4:29; S 2Ch 15:2
ᵐ S Dt 30:11
45:20 ⁿ S Isa 43:9
ᵒ S Isa 44:19
ᵖ Ps 115:7; Isa 46:1; Jer 10:5 ᵠ Dt 32:37; S Isa 44:17; Jer 1:16; 2:28
45:21 ʳ S Isa 41:22
ˢ Isa 46:10 ᵗ ver 5; S Ps 46:10; Isa 46:9; Mk 12:32
ᵘ Ps 11:7 ᵛ S Ps 3:8; Isa 25:9
45:22 ʷ S Isa 44:22; Zec 12:10
ˣ Nu 21:8-9; S 2Ch 20:12
ʸ S Ge 49:10; S Isa 11:9,12; 49:6, 12 ᶻ Hos 13:4
45:23 ᵃ S Ge 22:16; S Isa 14:24
ᵇ S Dt 30:11; Heb 6:13
ᶜ Isa 55:11
ᵈ S ver 14
ᵉ S Ps 63:11; S Isa 19:18; Ro 14:11*; Php 2:10-11
45:24 ᶠ S ver 8; Jer 33:16
ᵍ S Dt 33:29; S Ps 18:39; S Isa 40:26; 63:1
ʰ S Isa 41:11
45:25 ⁱ S ver 19
ʲ S Isa 4:3; S 49:4
ᵏ S Isa 24:23; S 41:16
46:1 ˡ S Isa 21:9; Jer 50:2; 51:44
ᵐ S 1Sa 5:2 ⁿ ver 7; S Isa 45:20
46:2 ᵒ S Jdg 18:17-18; S 2Sa 5:21; Jer 51:47
46:3 ᵖ ver 12; Isa 48:12; 51:1
ᵠ S Isa 1:9
ʳ S Ps 139:13; Isa 44:2 ˢ S Dt 1:31;

²²"Turnʷ to me and be saved,ˣ
all you ends of the earth;ʸ
for I am God, and there is no other.ᶻ
²³By myself I have sworn,ᵃ
my mouth has uttered in all integrityᵇ
a word that will not be revoked:ᶜ
Before me every knee will bow;ᵈ
by me every tongue will swear.ᵉ
²⁴They will say of me, 'In the LORD alone are righteousnessᶠ and strength.ᵍ'"
All who have raged against him
will come to him and be put to shame.ʰ
²⁵But in the LORD all the descendantsⁱ of Israel
will be found righteousʲ and will exult.ᵏ

Gods of Babylon

46 Belˡ bows down, Nebo stoops low;
their idolsᵐ are borne by beasts of burden.ʳ
The images that are carriedⁿ about are burdensome,
a burden for the weary.
²They stoop and bow down together;
unable to rescue the burden,
they themselves go off into captivity.ᵒ

³"Listenᵖ to me, O house of Jacob,
all you who remainᵠ of the house of Israel,
you whom I have upheld since you were conceived,ʳ
and have carriedˢ since your birth.ᵗ

L Isa 44:22 ◀▶ Isa 49:6
W Isa 42:3 ◀▶ Isa 49:6
M Isa 45:8 ◀▶ Isa 49:7–12
P Isa 42:13–15 ◀▶ Isa 61:2
V Isa 11:1–9 ◀▶ Jer 23:5–6
I Isa 45:17–19 ◀▶ Isa 46:3–4
I Isa 45:25 ◀▶ Isa 46:12–13
L Isa 43:2 ◀▶ Isa 48:17

S Ps 28:9 ᵗ S Ps 22:10

r Or *are but beasts and cattle*

45:17–19 God has repeatedly proclaimed that "Israel will be saved by the LORD with an everlasting salvation" (45:17).

45:23–25 The apostle Paul quoted this prophecy to confirm Christ's exalted position (see Ro 14:11; Php 2:10–11). Note too that while those who love Jesus willingly bow to him as their Savior, even those who are unrepentant will be forced to bow their knee to him when he is revealed in all of his glory as the King of Kings.

46:3–4 Isaiah declared God's deliverance and power to carry Israel, echoing Moses' words in the desert: "The LORD your God carried you, as a father carries his son, all the way you went" (Dt 1:31).

⁴Even to your old age and gray hairs ᵘ
I am he,ᵛ I am he who will sustain
  you.
I have made you and I will carry you;
I will sustainʷ you and I will rescue
  you.

⁵"To whom will you compare me or
    count me equal?
To whom will you liken me that we
    may be compared?ˣ
⁶Some pour out gold from their bags
  and weigh out silver on the scales;
they hire a goldsmithʸ to make it into
    a god,
and they bow down and worship it.ᶻ
⁷They lift it to their shoulders and
    carryᵃ it;
they set it up in its place, and there
    it stands.
From that spot it cannot move.ᵇ
Though one cries out to it, it does not
    answer;ᶜ
it cannot saveᵈ him from his
    troubles.

⁸"Rememberᵉ this, fix it in mind,
    take it to heart, you rebels.ᶠ
O ⁹Remember the former things,ᵍ those of
    long ago;ʰ
I am God, and there is no other;
I am God, and there is none like
    me.ⁱ
¹⁰I make known the end from the
    beginning,ʲ
from ancient times,ᵏ what is still to
    come.ˡ
I say: My purpose will stand,ᵐ
  and I will do all that I please.
¹¹From the east I summonⁿ a bird of
    prey;ᵒ
from a far-off land, a man to fulfill
    my purpose.
What I have said, that will I bring
    about;
what I have planned,ᵖ that will I
    do.ᵠ
I ¹²Listenʳ to me, you stubborn-hearted,ˢ
M

O Isa 45:21–22 ◀▶ Isa 50:10–11
I Isa 46:3–4 ◀▶ Isa 49:5–6
M Isa 13:11 ◀▶ Isa 48:4

46:4 ᵘPs 71:18
ᵛDt 32:39;
S Isa 43:13
ʷS Ps 18:35;
S 119:117
46:5 ˣS Ex 15:11;
Job 41:10;
Isa 40:18,25;
Jer 49:19
46:6 ʸS Isa 40:19
ᶻS Ex 20:5;
Isa 44:17; Hos 13:2
46:7 ᵃS ver 1
ᵇS 1Sa 5:3;
S Isa 41:7
ᶜS 1Ki 18:26
ᵈS Isa 44:17;
S 47:13
46:8 ᵉS Isa 44:21
ᶠS Isa 1:2
46:9 ᵍS Isa 41:22
ʰS Dt 32:7
ⁱS Ex 8:10;
S Isa 45:5,21;
Mk 12:32
46:10 ʲS Isa 41:4
ᵏS Isa 45:21
ˡS Isa 41:22
ᵐS Pr 19:21;
S Isa 7:7,9; S 44:26;
Ac 5:39; Eph 1:11
46:11 ⁿS Jdg 4:10;
S Ezr 1:2 ᵒS Isa 8:8
ᵖS Isa 25:1
ᵠS Ge 41:25;
Jer 44:28
46:12 ʳS ver 3
ˢS Ex 32:9;
S Isa 9:9
ᵗPs 119:150;
Isa 48:1; Jer 2:5
46:13 ᵘS Isa 1:26;
S 45:8; Ro 3:21
ᵛS Ps 85:9
ʷS Ps 74:2;
Joel 2:32
ˣS Isa 44:23
47:1 ʸS Job 2:13;
S Isa 29:4
ᶻS Isa 21:9; S 23:12
ᵃPs 137:8;
Jer 50:42; 51:33;
Zec 2:7 ᵇDt 28:56
47:2 ᶜEx 11:5;
Mt 24:41
ᵈS Jdg 16:21
ᵉS Ge 24:65
ᶠS Isa 32:11
47:3 ᵍS Ge 2:25;
Eze 16:37; Na 3:5
ʰS Isa 20:4
ⁱS Isa 1:24; S 34:8
ʲIsa 13:18-19
47:4 ᵏS Job 19:25
ˡS Isa 13:4
ᵐIsa 48:2;
Jer 50:34; Am 4:13
ⁿIsa 1:4; 48:17
47:5 ᵒS Job 2:13
ᵖIsa 9:2; 13:10
ᵠS Isa 21:9 ʳver 7;
La 1:1; Rev 18:7
ˢIsa 13:19;
Rev 17:18
47:6 ᵗS 2Ch 28:9
ᵘDt 13:15;
S Isa 42:24; Jer 2:7;
50:11 ᵛIsa 10:3

you who are far from
    righteousness.ᵗ
¹³I am bringing my righteousnessᵘ near,
  it is not far away;
and my salvationᵛ will not be
    delayed.
I will grant salvation to Zion,ʷ
  my splendorˣ to Israel.

The Fall of Babylon

47 "Go down, sit in the dust,ʸ
    Virgin Daughterᶻ of Babylon;
sit on the ground without a throne,
    Daughter of the Babylonians.ˢᵃ
No more will you be called
    tender or delicate.ᵇ
²Take millstonesᶜ and grindᵈ flour;
  take off your veil.ᵉ
Lift up your skirts,ᶠ bare your legs,
  and wade through the streams.
³Your nakednessᵍ will be exposed
  and your shameʰ uncovered.
I will take vengeance;ⁱ
  I will spare no one.ʲ"

⁴Our Redeemerᵏ—the LORD Almightyˡ
    is his nameᵐ—
is the Holy Oneⁿ of Israel.

⁵"Sit in silence,ᵒ go into darkness,ᵖ
    Daughter of the Babylonians;ᵠ
no more will you be called
    queenʳ of kingdoms.ˢ
⁶I was angryᵗ with my people
  and desecrated my inheritance;ᵘ
I gave them into your hand,ᵛ
  and you showed them no mercy.ʷ
Even on the aged
  you laid a very heavy yoke.
⁷You said, 'I will continue foreverˣ—
    the eternal queen!'ʸ
But you did not consider these things
  or reflectᶻ on what might happen.ᵃ

⁸"Now then, listen, you wanton
    creature,
lounging in your securityᵇ
and saying to yourself,
  'I am, and there is none besides
    me.ᶜ

ʷIsa 14:6 47:7 ˣS Isa 10:13; Da 4:30 ʸS ver 5; Rev 18:7 ᶻS Isa 42:23, 25 ᵃS Dt 32:29 47:8 ᵇS Isa 32:9 ᶜS Isa 45:6

ˢ1 Or *Chaldeans*; also in verse 5

46:9–10 Only God alone knows the details of future events before they occur, and only he can accurately predict the final end of events before they begin.

46:12–13 Isaiah declared that God would ultimately deliver his people Israel in the last days.

I will never be a widow[d]
    or suffer the loss of children.'
[9]Both of these will overtake you
    in a moment,[e] on a single day:
  loss of children[f] and widowhood.[g]
They will come upon you in full
    measure,
  in spite of your many sorceries[h]
  and all your potent spells.[i]
[10]You have trusted[j] in your wickedness
  and have said, 'No one sees me.'[k]
Your wisdom[l] and knowledge
    mislead[m] you
  when you say to yourself,
  'I am, and there is none besides
    me.'
[11]Disaster[n] will come upon you,
  and you will not know how to
    conjure it away.
A calamity will fall upon you
  that you cannot ward off with a
    ransom;
a catastrophe you cannot foresee
  will suddenly[o] come upon you.

[12]"Keep on, then, with your magic spells
    and with your many sorceries,[p]
  which you have labored at since
    childhood.
Perhaps you will succeed,
  perhaps you will cause terror.
[13]All the counsel you have received has
    only worn you out![q]
  Let your astrologers[r] come forward,
those stargazers who make predictions
    month by month,
  let them save[s] you from what is
    coming upon you.
[14]Surely they are like stubble;[t]
  the fire[u] will burn them up.
They cannot even save themselves
  from the power of the flame.[v]
Here are no coals to warm anyone;
  here is no fire to sit by.
[15]That is all they can do for you—
  these you have labored with
  and trafficked[w] with since
    childhood.
Each of them goes on in his error;
  there is not one that can save[x] you.

Stubborn Israel

48

"Listen to this, O house of Jacob,
  you who are called by the name
    of Israel[y]
  and come from the line of Judah,[z]

47:8 [d]Isa 49:21; 54:4; La 1:1; Rev 18:7
47:9 [e]S Ps 55:15; 73:19; 1Th 5:3; Rev 18:8-10
[f]S Isa 13:18
[g]S Isa 4:1; Jer 15:8; 18:21 [h]ver 12; Na 3:4; Mal 3:5
[i]Dt 18:10-11; Rev 9:21; 18:23
47:10
[j]S Job 15:31; Ps 52:7; 62:10
[k]S 2Ki 21:16; S Isa 29:15
[l]S Isa 5:21
[m]Isa 44:20
47:11 [n]S Isa 10:3; S 14:15; S 21:9; S 31:2; Lk 17:27
[o]S Ps 55:15; S Isa 17:14; 1Th 5:3
47:12 [p]S ver 9; S Ex 7:11
47:13 [q]Isa 57:10; Jer 51:58; Hab 2:13
[r]S Isa 19:3; S 44:25
[s]ver 15; S Isa 5:29; 43:13; 46:7
47:14 [t]S Isa 5:24
[u]S Isa 30:30
[v]Isa 10:17; Jer 51:30,32,58
47:15 [w]Rev 18:11
[x]S ver 13; S Isa 44:17
48:1 [y]S Ge 17:5
[z]S Ge 29:35
[a]S Isa 19:18
[b]S Isa 20:42;
S Isa 43:7
[c]Ex 23:13; 2Sa 14:11; Ps 50:16; Isa 58:2; Jer 7:9-10; 44:26
[d]Isa 59:14; Jer 4:2; 5:2; Da 8:12; Zec 8:3
48:2 [e]S Ne 11:1; S Isa 1:26; S Mt 4:5
[f]S Isa 10:20; Ro 2:17 [g]S Isa 47:4
48:3 [h]S Isa 41:22
[i]S Isa 40:21; 45:21
[j]S Isa 17:14; 30:13
48:4 [k]S Isa 9:9
[l]S Ex 32:9; S Dt 9:27; Ac 7:51
[m]Eze 3:9
48:5 [n]S Isa 40:21; S 42:9
[o]Jer 44:15-18
48:6 [p]S Isa 41:22; S Ro 16:25
48:7 [q]Isa 65:18
[r]Isa 45:21
[s]S Ex 6:7
48:8 [t]S Isa 1:3
[u]S Dt 29:4
[v]Isa 41:24; Mal 2:11,14
[w]Dt 9:7,24; Ps 58:3; Isa 1:2; 43:27; 58:1
48:9 [x]S Isa 12:22; S Isa 37:35
[y]S Job 9:13; S Ne 9:31
48:10 [a]S Isa 1:25; Zec 13:9; Mal 3:3; 1Pe 1:7

you who take oaths[a] in the name of
    the LORD[b]
  and invoke[c] the God of Israel—
    but not in truth[d] or righteousness—
[2]you who call yourselves citizens of the
    holy city[e]
  and rely[f] on the God of Israel—
    the LORD Almighty is his name:[g]
[3]I foretold the former things[h] long ago,
  my mouth announced[i] them and I
    made them known;
  then suddenly[j] I acted, and they
    came to pass.
[4]For I knew how stubborn[k] you were;   C
  the sinews of your neck[l] were iron, M
  your forehead[m] was bronze.   N
[5]Therefore I told you these things long
    ago;
  before they happened I announced[n]
    them to you
so that you could not say,
  'My idols did them;[o]
  my wooden image and metal god
    ordained them.'
[6]You have heard these things; look at
    them all.
  Will you not admit them?

"From now on I will tell you of new
    things,[p]
  of hidden things unknown to you.
[7]They are created[q] now, and not long
    ago;[r]
  you have not heard of them before
    today.
So you cannot say,
  'Yes, I knew[s] of them.'
[8]You have neither heard nor
    understood;[t]
  from of old your ear[u] has not been
    open.
Well do I know how treacherous[v] you
    are;
  you were called a rebel[w] from
    birth.
[9]For my own name's sake[x] I delay my
    wrath;[y]
  for the sake of my praise I hold it
    back from you,
  so as not to cut you off.[z]
[10]See, I have refined[a] you, though not as   T
    silver;

C *Isa 44:20* ◀ ▶ *Isa 48:22*
M *Isa 46:12* ◀ ▶ *Isa 57:15*
N *Isa 40:6* ◀ ▶ *Isa 55:6*
T *Ecc 7:14* ◀ ▶ *Da 12:10*

I have tested[b] you in the furnace[c] of
    affliction.
[11] For my own sake,[d] for my own sake, I
    do this.
How can I let myself be defamed?[e]
I will not yield my glory to another.[f]

Israel Freed

[12] "Listen[g] to me, O Jacob,
    Israel, whom I have called:[h]
I am he;[i]
I am the first and I am the last.[j]
[13] My own hand laid the foundations of
    the earth,[k]
and my right hand spread out the
    heavens;[l]
when I summon them,
    they all stand up together.[m]

[14] "Come together,[n] all of you, and listen:
Which of ⸤the idols⸥ has foretold[o]
    these things?
The LORD's chosen ally[p]
    will carry out his purpose[q] against
        Babylon;[r]
    his arm will be against the
        Babylonians.[r]
[15] I, even I, have spoken;
    yes, I have called[s] him.
I will bring him,
    and he will succeed[t] in his mission.

[16] "Come near[u] me and listen[v] to this:

"From the first announcement I have
    not spoken in secret;[w]
    at the time it happens, I am there."

And now the Sovereign LORD[x] has
    sent[y] me,
    with his Spirit.[z]

[17] This is what the LORD says—
    your Redeemer,[a] the Holy One[b] of
        Israel:
"I am the LORD your God,
    who teaches[c] you what is best for
        you,
    who directs[d] you in the way[e] you
        should go.
[18] If only you had paid attention[f] to my
    commands,
    your peace[g] would have been like a
        river,[h]

J Isa 30:5–7 ◀▶ Jer 1:13–16
E Isa 40:7 ◀▶ Isa 59:21
L Ps 143:10 ◀▶ Isa 63:14
L Isa 46:3–4 ◀▶ Isa 49:15–16
K Isa 41:10 ◀▶ Isa 50:2

48:10 [b]S Ex 15:25
[c]S Ex 1:13;
S 1Ki 8:51
48:11
[d]S Isa 12:22;
S Isa 37:35
[e]S Lev 18:21;
Dt 32:27; Jer 14:7,
21; Eze 20:9,14,22,
44 [f]Isa 42:8
48:12 [g]S Isa 46:3
[h]Isa 41:8; 42:6;
43:1 [i]S Isa 43:13
[j]S Isa 41:4;
S Rev 1:17
48:13
[k]Heb 1:10-12
[l]S Ge 2:1;
Ex 20:11; Job 9:8;
Isa 40:22; S 42:5;
45:18; 51:16;
65:17 [m]S Isa 34:16
48:14 [n]S Isa 43:9
[o]S Isa 41:22
[p]S Isa 41:2
[q]Isa 46:10-11
[r]S Isa 21:9; S 45:1;
Jer 50:45
48:15 [s]S Jdg 4:10;
Isa 45:1
[t]Isa 44:28-45:4
48:16 [u]S Isa 41:1
[v]S Isa 33:13
[w]S Isa 45:19
[x]S Isa 50:5,7,9
[y]Zec 2:9,11
[z]S Isa 11:2
48:17
[a]S Job 19:25;
Isa 49:7; 54:8
[b]S Isa 47:4
[c]S Isa 28:9;
S Jer 7:13
[d]Isa 49:10; 57:18;
58:11 [e]S Isa 30:11
48:18 [f]S Isa 42:23
[g]Ps 147:14;
S Isa 9:7; 54:13;
66:12 [h]S Isa 33:21
48:19 [i]S Isa 1:26; S 45:8
[j]Isa 43:5;
44:3; 61:9
[k]S Ge 12:2
[l]S Job 5:25
[m]Isa 56:5; 65:23;
66:22; Jer 35:19
48:20 [n]Isa 52:11;
Jer 48:6; 50:8;
51:6,45; Zec 2:6-7;
Rev 18:4
[o]S Isa 12:6; 49:13;
51:11 [p]S Ge 49:10;
S Dt 30:4;
S Jer 25:22
[q]S Ex 6:6;
S Isa 33:24; 52:9;
63:9; Mic 4:10
48:21 [r]S Isa 33:16
[s]S Isa 30:25
[t]S Nu 20:11;
S Isa 35:6
48:22 [u]S Job 3:26
[v]S Isa 3:11; 57:21
49:1 [w]S Isa 33:13
[x]S Isa 11:11
[y]Isa 44:24; 46:3;
Mt 1:20 [z]Isa 7:14;
9:6; 44:2; Jer 1:5;
Gal 1:15
[a]S Ex 33:12;
S Isa 43:1
49:2 [b]S Job 40:18
[c]Ps 64:3;
Eph 6:17;
S Rev 1:16

---

your righteousness[i] like the waves
    of the sea.
[19] Your descendants[j] would have been
    like the sand,[k]
    your children like its numberless
        grains;[l]
their name would never be cut off[m]
    nor destroyed from before me."

[20] Leave Babylon,
    flee[n] from the Babylonians!
Announce this with shouts of joy[o]
    and proclaim it.
Send it out to the ends of the earth;[p]
    say, "The LORD has redeemed[q] his
        servant Jacob."
[21] They did not thirst[r] when he led them
    through the deserts;
he made water flow[s] for them from
    the rock;
he split the rock
    and water gushed out.[t]

[22] "There is no peace,"[u] says the LORD,
    "for the wicked."[v]

The Servant of the LORD

49 Listen[w] to me, you islands;[x]
    hear this, you distant nations:
Before I was born[y] the LORD called[z]
    me;
    from my birth he has made mention
        of my name.[a]
[2] He made my mouth[b] like a sharpened
    sword,[c]
in the shadow of his hand[d] he hid
    me;
he made me into a polished arrow[e]
    and concealed me in his quiver.
[3] He said to me, "You are my servant,[f]
    Israel, in whom I will display my
        splendor.[g]
[4] But I said, "I have labored to no
    purpose;
I have spent my strength in vain[h]
    and for nothing.
Yet what is due me is in the LORD's
    hand,[i]
    and my reward[j] is with my God."[k]

F Isa 41:17 ◀▶ Isa 49:9–10
C Isa 48:4 ◀▶ Isa 53:6
S Isa 35:8–9 ◀▶ Isa 60:21

[d]S Ex 33:22; S Ps 91:1 [e]S Dt 32:23; Zec 9:13 **49:3** [f]S Isa 20:3; Zec 3:8
[g]S Lev 10:3; S Isa 44:23 **49:4** [h]S Lev 26:20; Isa 55:2; 65:23 [i]S Isa 45:25;
50:8; 53:10; 54:17 [j]S Isa 35:4 [k]S Job 27:2

[t] 14 Or *Chaldeans*; also in verse 20

⁵And now the LORD says—
  he who formed me in the womb¹ to be his servant
to bring Jacob back to him
  and gather Israel to himself,
for I am honored in the eyes of the LORD
  and my God has been my strength—
⁶he says:
"It is too small a thing for you to be my servant
  to restore the tribes of Jacob
  and bring back those of Israel I have kept.
I will also make you a light for the Gentiles,
  that you may bring my salvation to the ends of the earth."

⁷This is what the LORD says—
  the Redeemer and Holy One of Israel—
to him who was despised and abhorred by the nation,
  to the servant of rulers:
"Kings will see you and rise up,
  princes will see and bow down,
because of the LORD, who is faithful,
  the Holy One of Israel, who has chosen you."

Restoration of Israel

⁸This is what the LORD says:

"In the time of my favor I will answer you,
  and in the day of salvation I will help you;
I will keep you and will make you
  to be a covenant for the people,
to restore the land
  and to reassign its desolate inheritances,

⁹to say to the captives, 'Come out,'
  and to those in darkness, 'Be free!'

"They will feed beside the roads
  and find pasture on every barren hill.
¹⁰They will neither hunger nor thirst,
  nor will the desert heat or the sun beat upon them.
He who has compassion on them will guide them
  and lead them beside springs of water.
¹¹I will turn all my mountains into roads,
  and my highways will be raised up.
¹²See, they will come from afar—
  some from the north, some from the west,
  some from the region of Aswan."

¹³Shout for joy, O heavens;
  rejoice, O earth;
  burst into song, O mountains!
For the LORD comforts his people
  and will have compassion on his afflicted ones.

¹⁴But Zion said, "The LORD has forsaken me,
  the Lord has forgotten me."

¹⁵"Can a mother forget the baby at her breast
  and have no compassion on the child she has borne?
Though she may forget,
  I will not forget you!
¹⁶See, I have engraved you on the palms of my hands;
  your walls are ever before me.
¹⁷Your sons hasten back,
  and those who laid you waste depart from you.
¹⁸Lift up your eyes and look around;

u 12 Dead Sea Scrolls; Masoretic Text Sinim

49:5–6 God has promised that he will "bring back those of Israel I have kept" to "make you a light for the Gentiles" (49:6) indicating that the Messiah would be the light of the world during the last days. See also Ac 13:46–48; 26:23.

49:8–23 Compare 49:8 with 2Co 6:2. Isaiah prophesied that the return from exile would bring the same restoration of land for the people as the Year of Jubilee did (see Lev 25:10). Note that under Joshua the land had been divided among the tribes. When Israel is completely restored in the Millennium, the Messiah will justly reassign the promised land. Compare also the description of heaven with Rev 7:16–17.

all your sons gather' and come to you.
As surely as I live,ᵍ" declares the LORD,
"you will wearʰ them all as ornaments;
you will put them on, like a bride.

¹⁹"Though you were ruined and made desolate,ⁱ
and your land laid waste,ʲ
now you will be too small for your people,ᵏ
and those who devoured¹ you will be far away.

²⁰The children born during your bereavement
will yet say in your hearing,
'This place is too small for us;
give us more space to live in.'ᵐ

²¹Then you will say in your heart,
'Who bore me these?ⁿ
I was bereavedᵒ and barren;
I was exiled and rejected.ᵖ
Who brought theseᵠ up?
I was leftʳ all alone,ˢ
but these—where have they come from?' "

²²This is what the Sovereign LORDᵗ says:

"See, I will beckon to the Gentiles,
I will lift up my bannerᵘ to the peoples;
they will bringᵛ your sons in their arms
and carry your daughters on their shoulders.ʷ

²³Kingsˣ will be your foster fathers,
and their queens your nursing mothers.ʸ
They will bow downᶻ before you with their faces to the ground;
they will lick the dustᵃ at your feet.
Then you will know that I am the LORD;ᵇ
those who hopeᶜ in me will not be disappointed."ᵈ

²⁴Can plunder be taken from warriors,ᵉ
or captives rescued from the fierceᵛ?

²⁵But this is what the LORD says:

"Yes, captivesᶠ will be taken from warriors,ᵍ
and plunder retrieved from the fierce;ʰ
I will contend with those who contend with you,ⁱʲ
and your children I will save.ᵏ

²⁶I will make your oppressors¹ eatᵐ their own flesh;
they will be drunk on their own blood,ⁿ as with wine.
Then all mankind will knowᵒ
that I, the LORD, am your Savior,ᵖ
your Redeemer,ᵠ the Mighty One of Jacob."ʳ

Israel's Sin and the Servant's Obedience

50 This is what the LORD says: R

"Where is your mother's certificate of divorceˢ
with which I sent her away?
Or to which of my creditors
did I sellᵗ you?
Because of your sinsᵘ you were sold;ᵛ
because of your transgressions your mother was sent away.

²When I came, why was there no one? I
When I called, why was there no one to answer?ʷ K
Was my arm too shortˣ to ransom you?
Do I lack the strengthʸ to rescue you?
By a mere rebukeᶻ I dry up the sea,ᵃ
I turn rivers into a desert;ᵇ
their fish rot for lack of water
and die of thirst.

³I clothe the sky with darknessᶜ
and make sackclothᵈ its covering."

⁴The Sovereign LORDᵉ has given me an instructed tongue,ᶠ
to know the word that sustains the weary.ᵍ

R *Isa 44:28* ◄► *Isa 51:17*
I *Isa 49:8–23* ◄► *Isa 51:3–4*
K *Isa 48:18* ◄► *Isa 50:10*

ᵍ S Isa 40:29; Mt 11:28

ᵛ 24 Dead Sea Scrolls, Vulgate and Syriac (see also Septuagint and verse 25); Masoretic Text *righteous*

50:1 Isaiah's words reminded the people that their own disobedience led to their judgment before God.

He wakens me morning by morning,[h]
 wakens my ear to listen like one
  being taught.[i]
⁵The Sovereign LORD[j] has opened my
  ears,[k]
 and I have not been rebellious;[l]
 I have not drawn back.
⁶I offered my back to those who beat[m]
  me,
 my cheeks to those who pulled out
  my beard;[n]
 I did not hide my face
  from mocking and spitting.[o]
⁷Because the Sovereign LORD[p] helps[q]
  me,
 I will not be disgraced.
 Therefore have I set my face like
  flint,[r]
 and I know I will not be put to
  shame.[s]
⁸He who vindicates[t] me is near.[u]
 Who then will bring charges against
  me?[v]
 Let us face each other![w]
 Who is my accuser?
 Let him confront me!
⁹It is the Sovereign LORD[x] who helps[y]
  me.
 Who is he that will condemn[z]
  me?
 They will all wear out like a garment;
  the moths[a] will eat them up.

¹⁰Who among you fears[b] the LORD
  and obeys[c] the word of his
   servant?[d]
 Let him who walks in the dark,
  who has no light,[e]
 trust[f] in the name of the LORD
  and rely on his God.
¹¹But now, all you who light fires
  and provide yourselves with flaming
   torches,[g]
 go, walk in the light of your fires[h]
  and of the torches you have set
   ablaze.
 This is what you shall receive from my
  hand:[i]
 You will lie down in torment.[j]

B Isa 11:1–5 ◀ ▶ Isa 52:13
V Isa 41:11–14 ◀ ▶ Isa 54:15
K Isa 50:2 ◀ ▶ Isa 51:6
O Isa 46:9 ◀ ▶ Jer 2:13
G Isa 30:1 ◀ ▶ Isa 64:6

50:4 [h]Ps 5:3
 [i]S Isa 28:9
50:5 [j]S Isa 48:16
 [k]Isa 35:5 [l]Eze 2:8;
 24:3; S Mt 26:39;
 Jn 8:29; Ac 26:19;
 Heb 5:8
50:6 [m]Isa 53:5;
 Mt 27:30;
 Mk 14:65; 15:19;
 Lk 22:63; Jn 19:1
 [n]S 2Sa 10:4
 [o]S Nu 12:14;
 La 3:30; Mt 26:67;
 Mk 10:34
50:7 [p]S Isa 48:16
 [q]S Isa 41:10; 42:1
 [r]Jer 1:18; 15:20;
 Eze 3:8-9
 [s]S Isa 28:16;
 S 29:22
50:8 [t]S Isa 26:2;
 S 49:4 [u]S Ps 34:18
 [v]S Job 13:19;
 S Isa 43:26;
 Ro 8:32-34
 [w]S Isa 41:1
50:9 [x]S Isa 48:16
 [y]S Isa 41:10
 [z]Ro 8:1,34
 [a]S Job 13:28;
 S Isa 51:8
50:10 [b]S Pr 1:7
 [c]Isa 1:19; Hag 1:12
 [d]S Isa 49:3
 [e]S Ps 107:14;
 Ac 26:18
 [f]S Isa 10:20; S 26:4
50:11 [g]Pr 26:18
 [h]Isa 1:31; Jas 3:6
 [i]S Dt 21:22-23;
 S Pr 26:27
 [j]S Job 15:20;
 Isa 65:13-15
51:1 [k]S Isa 46:3
 [l]ver 7; S Dt 7:13;
 16:20; Ps 94:15;
 Isa 63:8; Ro 9:30-31
 [m]Isa 55:6; 65:10
 [n]Isa 17:10
51:2 [o]S Ge 17:6;
 S Isa 29:22;
 Ro 4:16; Heb 11:11
 [p]S Ge 12:2
51:3 [q]S Isa 40:1
 [r]S Ps 51:18;
 S Isa 61:4
 [s]Isa 44:26; 52:9;
 61:4 [t]S Ge 2:8
 [u]S Isa 5:6; S 41:19
 [v]S Isa 25:9; 35:10;
 65:18; 66:10;
 Jer 16:9
 [w]Jer 17:26; 30:19;
 33:11
51:4 [x]Ex 6:7;
 Ps 50:7; Isa 3:15;
 63:8; 64:9
 [y]S Ps 78:1
 [z]S Dt 18:18
 [a]S Isa 2:4
 [b]S Isa 26:18; S 49:6
51:5 [c]S Ps 85:9;
 S Isa 12:2
 [d]S Isa 35:4
 [e]Ps 98:1; Isa 40:10;
 63:1,5 [f]S Isa 11:1
 [g]S Ge 49:10;
 S Ps 37:9
51:6 [h]S Ps 37:20;
 S 102:26;

Everlasting Salvation for Zion

51 "Listen[k] to me, you who pursue
  righteousness[l]
 and who seek[m] the LORD:
 Look to the rock[n] from which you
  were cut
 and to the quarry from which you
  were hewn;
²look to Abraham,[o] your father,
 and to Sarah, who gave you birth.
 When I called him he was but one,
  and I blessed him and made him
   many.[p]
³The LORD will surely comfort[q] Zion[r]
 and will look with compassion on all
  her ruins;[s]
 he will make her deserts like Eden,[t]
  her wastelands[u] like the garden of
   the LORD.
 Joy and gladness[v] will be found in her,
  thanksgiving[w] and the sound of
   singing.

⁴"Listen to me, my people;[x]
 hear me,[y] my nation:
 The law[z] will go out from me;
  my justice[a] will become a light to
   the nations.[b]
⁵My righteousness draws near speedily,
  my salvation[c] is on the way,[d]
 and my arm[e] will bring justice to the
  nations.
 The islands[f] will look to me
  and wait in hope[g] for my arm.

⁶Lift up your eyes to the heavens,
 look at the earth beneath;
 the heavens will vanish like smoke,[h]
 the earth will wear out like a
  garment[i]
 and its inhabitants die like flies.
 But my salvation[j] will last forever,[k]
 my righteousness will never fail.[l]

⁷"Hear me, you who know what is
  right,[m]
 you people who have my law in your
  hearts:[n]
 Do not fear the reproach of men
  or be terrified by their insults.[o]

I Isa 50:2 ◀ ▶ Isa 51:9
K Isa 50:10 ◀ ▶ Isa 53:5

Mt 24:35; Lk 21:33; 2Pe 3:10 [i]Ps 102:25-26; Heb 1:10-12 [j]S Isa 12:2
[k]ver 8; S Ps 119:89 [l]Ps 89:33; Isa 54:10 **51:7** [m]S ver 1 [n]S Dt 6:6;
Ps 119:11 [o]S Ps 119:39; Isa 50:7; 54:5; Mt 5:11; Lk 6:22; Ac 5:41

51:3–9 Israel prophesied Israel's ultimate restoration in these verses.

ISAIAH 51:8

⁸For the moth will eat them up like a
    garment;ᵖ
  the wormᵠ will devour them like
    wool.
But my righteousness will last
    forever,ʳ
  my salvation through all
    generations."

⁹Awake, awake!ˢ Clothe yourself with
    strength,ᵗ
  O armᵘ of the Lord;
awake, as in days gone by,
  as in generations of old.ᵛ
Was it not you who cut Rahabʷ to
    pieces,
  who pierced that monsterˣ through?
¹⁰Was it not you who dried up the sea,ʸ
  the waters of the great deep,ᶻ
who made a road in the depths of the
    seaᵃ
  so that the redeemedᵇ might cross
    over?
¹¹The ransomedᶜ of the Lord will return.
  They will enter Zion with singing;ᵈ
  everlasting joy will crown their
    heads.
Gladness and joyᵉ will overtake them,
  and sorrow and sighing will flee
    away.ᶠ

¹²"I, even I, am he who comfortsᵍ you.
  Who are you that you fearʰ mortal
    men,ⁱ
  the sons of men, who are but grass,ʲ
¹³that you forgetᵏ the Lord your Maker,ˡ
  who stretched out the heavensᵐ
  and laid the foundations of the
    earth,
that you live in constant terrorⁿ every
    day
  because of the wrath of the
    oppressor,
  who is bent on destruction?
For where is the wrath of the
    oppressor?ᵒ

◀ *Isa 51:3–4* ◀ ▶ *Isa 51:11–12*
◀ *Isa 51:9* ◀ ▶ *Isa 51:15–17*
S *Isa 35:10* ◀ ▶ *Isa 61:3*
J *Isa 26:13* ◀ ▶ *Hab 3:11*

51:8 ᵖS Job 13:28;
Jas 5:2 ᵠS Isa 14:11
ʳS ver 6
51:9 ˢS Jdg 5:12
ᵗS Ge 18:14;
S Ps 65:6;
Isa 40:31; 52:1
ᵘS Ps 98:1;
S Isa 30:30; S 33:2
ᵛEx 6:6; Dt 4:34;
S 32:7 ʷS Job 9:13
ˣS Ps 68:30;
S 74:13
51:10
ʸS Ex 14:22;
Zec 10:11;
Rev 16:12
ᶻEx 15:5,8
ᵃS Job 36:30
ᵇS Ex 15:13
51:11 ᶜS Isa 35:9;
S 44:23
ᵈS Ps 109:28;
Isa 65:14;
Jer 30:19; Zep 3:14
ᵉS Isa 48:20;
Jer 33:11
ᶠS Isa 30:19;
Jer 31:13;
S Rev 7:17
51:12 ᵍS Isa 40:1;
S 2Co 1:4
ʰS 2Ki 1:15
ⁱS Isa 2:22
ʲS Isa 15:6; 40:6-7;
1Pe 1:24
51:13 ᵏS Job 8:13;
S Isa 17:10
ˡS Job 4:17;
Isa 17:7; 45:11;
54:5 ᵐS Ge 1:1;
S Isa 48:13
ⁿS Isa 7:4
ᵒS Isa 9:4
51:14 ᵖS Isa 42:7
ᵠS Isa 49:10
51:15 ʳS Ex 14:21
ˢS Ps 93:3
ᵗS Isa 13:4
51:16 ᵘS Ex 4:12,
15 ᵛS Ex 33:22
ʷS Isa 48:13
ˣJer 7:23; 11:4;
24:7; Eze 14:11;
Zec 8:8
51:17 ʸS Jdg 5:12;
Isa 52:1 ᶻS ver 22;
S Ps 16:5;
S Mt 20:22 ᵃver 20;
Job 21:20;
Isa 42:25; 66:15;
Rev 14:10; 16:19
ᵇS Ps 75:8
ᶜver 23; S Ps 60:3
51:18 ᵈS Ps 88:18
ᵉS Job 31:18;
S Isa 49:21
ᶠS Isa 41:13
51:19 ᵍS Isa 40:2;
47:9 ʰIsa 49:13;
54:11; Jer 15:5;
Na 3:7 ⁱIsa 60:18;
62:4; Jer 48:3;
La 3:47 ʲS Isa 14:30
ᵏJer 14:12; 24:11
51:20 ˡIsa 5:25; Jer 14:16; La 2:19 ᵐS Job 18:10 ⁿS ver 17; S Job 40:11;
Jer 44:6 ᵒS Dt 28:20

¹⁴The cowering prisoners will soon be
    set free;ᵖ
  they will not die in their dungeon,
  nor will they lack bread.ᵠ
¹⁵For I am the Lord your God,
  who churns up the seaʳ so that its
    waves roarˢ—
  the Lord Almightyᵗ is his name.
¹⁶I have put my words in your mouthᵘ
  and covered you with the shadow of
    my handᵛ—
I who set the heavens in place,
  who laid the foundations of the
    earth,ʷ
  and who say to Zion, 'You are my
    people.'ˣ "

The Cup of the Lord's Wrath

¹⁷Awake, awake!ʸ
  Rise up, O Jerusalem,
you who have drunk from the hand of
    the Lord
  the cupᶻ of his wrath,ᵃ
you who have drained to its dregsᵇ
  the goblet that makes men stagger.ᶜ
¹⁸Of all the sonsᵈ she bore
  there was none to guide her;ᵉ
of all the sons she reared
  there was none to take her by the
    hand.ᶠ
¹⁹These double calamitiesᵍ have come
    upon you—
  who can comfort you?ʰ—
ruin and destruction,ⁱ famineʲ and
    swordᵏ—
  who canʷ console you?
²⁰Your sons have fainted;
  they lie at the head of every street,ˡ
  like antelope caught in a net.ᵐ
They are filled with the wrathⁿ of the
    Lord
  and the rebukeᵒ of your God.

◀ *Isa 51:11–12* ◀ ▶ *Isa 51:22*
R *Isa 50:1* ◀ ▶ *Isa 51:19*
R *Isa 51:17* ◀ ▶ *Isa 54:3*

ʷ 19 Dead Sea Scrolls, Septuagint, Vulgate and Syriac; Masoretic Text /
how can I

51:11 Note that this verse is the same as 35:10 and reconfirmed the same promise of comfort and blessing.

51:15–16 The prophet reaffirmed God's declaration of love and care for his people "covered . . . with the shadow" (51:16) of his almighty hand.

51:19–23 God promised that even though his people would suffer, that "cup that made you stagger" (51:22) would be removed and given instead to their enemies.

²¹Therefore hear this, you afflicted one,
   made drunk, but not with wine.
²²This is what your Sovereign LORD says,
   your God, who defends his people:
"See, I have taken out of your hand
   the cup that made you stagger;
from that cup, the goblet of my wrath,
   you will never drink again.
²³I will put it into the hands of your
   tormentors,
who said to you,
   'Fall prostrate that we may walk
      over you.'
And you made your back like the
   ground,
like a street to be walked over."

52

Awake, awake, O Zion,
   clothe yourself with strength.
Put on your garments of splendor,
O Jerusalem, the holy city.
The uncircumcised and defiled
   will not enter you again.
²Shake off your dust;
   rise up, sit enthroned, O Jerusalem.
Free yourself from the chains on your
   neck,
O captive Daughter of Zion.

³For this is what the LORD says:

"You were sold for nothing,
   and without money you will be
   redeemed."

⁴For this is what the Sovereign LORD
says:

"At first my people went down to
   Egypt to live;
lately, Assyria has oppressed them.

⁵"And now what do I have here?" declares the LORD.

"For my people have been taken away
   for nothing,
   and those who rule them mock,"
      declares the LORD.

◀ Isa 51:15–17 ◀▶ Isa 52:1–3
◀ Isa 51:22 ◀▶ Isa 52:6–9
L Isa 49:6 ◀▶ Isa 53:4–6

"And all day long
   my name is constantly
      blasphemed.
⁶Therefore my people will know my
   name;
therefore in that day they will
   know
that it is I who foretold it.
Yes, it is I."

⁷How beautiful on the mountains
   are the feet of those who bring good
      news,
who proclaim peace,
   who bring good tidings,
   who proclaim salvation,
who say to Zion,
   "Your God reigns!"
⁸Listen! Your watchmen lift up their
      voices;
   together they shout for joy.
When the LORD returns to Zion,
   they will see it with their own
      eyes.
⁹Burst into songs of joy together,
   you ruins of Jerusalem,
for the LORD has comforted his
   people,
he has redeemed Jerusalem.
¹⁰The LORD will lay bare his holy arm
   in the sight of all the nations,
and all the ends of the earth will see
   the salvation of our God.

¹¹Depart, depart, go out from there!
   Touch no unclean thing!
Come out from it and be pure,
   you who carry the vessels of the
      LORD.
¹²But you will not leave in haste
   or go in flight;
for the LORD will go before you,
   the God of Israel will be your rear
      guard.

◀ Isa 52:1–3 ◀▶ Isa 54:1–14

*5 Dead Sea Scrolls and Vulgate; Masoretic Text *wail*

52:1–3 Isaiah prophesied that Israel would be delivered from the control of the "uncircumcised and defiled" (52:1) Babylonians without having to pay any ransom.

52:6–9 Though the prophet declared these words as a promise that God's people would one day be returned to Jerusalem, the apostle Paul used this prophecy to describe the ministry of missionaries of the Gospel (see Ro 10:15).

ISAIAH 52:13

The Suffering and Glory of the Servant

13 See, my servant will act wisely;
he will be raised and lifted up and
highly exalted.

14 Just as there were many who were
appalled at him—
his appearance was so disfigured
beyond that of any man
and his form marred beyond human
likeness—

15 so will he sprinkle many nations,
and kings will shut their mouths
because of him.
For what they were not told, they will
see,
and what they have not heard, they
will understand.

53

Who has believed our message
and to whom has the arm of the
LORD been revealed?

2 He grew up before him like a tender
shoot,
and like a root out of dry ground.
He had no beauty or majesty to attract
us to him,
nothing in his appearance that we
should desire him.

3 He was despised and rejected by men,
a man of sorrows, and familiar with
suffering.
Like one from whom men hide their
faces
he was despised, and we esteemed
him not.

4 Surely he took up our infirmities
and carried our sorrows,
yet we considered him stricken by
God,
smitten by him, and afflicted.

5 But he was pierced for our
transgressions,
he was crushed for our iniquities;
the punishment that brought us
peace was upon him,
and by his wounds we are healed.

6 We all, like sheep, have gone astray,
each of us has turned to his own
way;
and the LORD has laid on him
the iniquity of us all.

7 He was oppressed and afflicted,
yet he did not open his mouth;
he was led like a lamb to the
slaughter,
and as a sheep before her shearers is
silent,
so he did not open his mouth.

8 By oppression and judgment he was
taken away.
And who can speak of his
descendants?

53:1–12 In this detailed prophecy, Isaiah describes God's suffering servant, Jesus Christ, including the revelation that God's own people would reject these words. Isaiah's prophecy details events in the life of Jesus seven centuries before his birth.

1. Isaiah prophesied that he would be "despised and rejected by men" (53:3). Jesus was rejected by his own people during his life and at his death.
2. Isaiah said that the servant would bear our griefs but we would consider him worthy of God's punishment (53:4). The majority of the Jews and Roman authorities rejected Jesus, desiring only his execution.
3. Isaiah portrayed the wounds that were laid on the servant (53:5), indicating the death Jesus would die on the cross for our sins.
4. Isaiah prophesied that the servant would be silent before his oppressors as "a sheep before her shearers is silent" (53:7). Scripture records that when Jesus stood before his accusers "he gave no answer" (Mt 27:12).
5. Isaiah accurately predicted that Jesus would be "taken away" (53:8) and killed.
6. Isaiah declared that "he was assigned a grave with the wicked, and with the rich in his death" (53:9), foreshadowing Jesus' burial in a rich man's tomb (Joseph of Arimathea).
7. Isaiah's prediction stated that God's servant would be "numbered with the transgressors" (53:12), a startling prophecy that affirmed Jesus' execution with sinners. At the crucifixion Jesus was executed with two criminals, exactly as prophesied in the book of Isaiah.

For he was cut off from the land of the living;[b]
for the transgression[c] of my people he was stricken.[c]

⁹He was assigned a grave with the wicked,[d]
and with the rich[e] in his death,
though he had done no violence,[f]
nor was any deceit in his mouth.[g]

¹⁰Yet it was the LORD's will[h] to crush[i] him and cause him to suffer,[j]
and though the LORD makes[d] his life a guilt offering,[k]
he will see his offspring[l] and prolong his days,
and the will of the LORD will prosper[m] in his hand.

¹¹After the suffering[n] of his soul,
he will see the light[o] ⌊of life⌉[e] and be satisfied[f];
by his knowledge[g] my righteous servant[p] will justify[q] many,
and he will bear their iniquities.[r]

¹²Therefore I will give him a portion among the great,[h,s]
and he will divide the spoils[t] with the strong,[i]
because he poured out his life unto death,[u]
and was numbered with the transgressors.[v]
For he bore[w] the sin of many,[x]
and made intercession[y] for the transgressors.

The Future Glory of Zion

54 "Sing, O barren woman,[z]
you who never bore a child;
burst into song, shout for joy,[a]
you who were never in labor;[b]
because more are the children[c] of the desolate[d] woman
than of her who has a husband,[e]" says the LORD.

²"Enlarge the place of your tent,[f]
stretch your tent curtains wide,
do not hold back;
lengthen your cords,
strengthen your stakes.[g]

³For you will spread out to the right and to the left;
your descendants[h] will dispossess nations[i]
and settle in their desolate[j] cities.

⁴"Do not be afraid;[k] you will not suffer shame.[l]
Do not fear disgrace;[m] you will not be humiliated.
You will forget the shame of your youth[n]
and remember no more the reproach[o] of your widowhood.[p]

⁵For your Maker[q] is your husband[r]—
the LORD Almighty is his name—
the Holy One[s] of Israel is your Redeemer;[t]
he is called the God of all the earth.[u]

⁶The LORD will call you back[v]
as if you were a wife deserted[w] and distressed in spirit—
a wife who married young,[x]
only to be rejected," says your God.

⁷"For a brief moment[y] I abandoned[z] you,
but with deep compassion[a] I will bring you back.[b]

⁸In a surge of anger[c]
I hid[d] my face from you for a moment,
but with everlasting kindness[e]
I will have compassion[f] on you,"
says the LORD your Redeemer.[g]

⁹"To me this is like the days of Noah,
when I swore that the waters of Noah would never again cover the earth.[h]

R *Isa 51:19* ◀ ▶ *Isa 54:6–8*
R *Isa 54:4* ◀ ▶ *Isa 54:11*

53:8 ᵇ Ps 88:5; Da 9:26; Ac 8:32-33*
ᶜ ver 12; S Ps 39:8
53:9 ᵈ Mt 27:38; Mk 15:27; Lk 23:32; Jn 19:18
ᵉ Mt 27:57-60; Mk 15:43-46; Lk 23:50-53; Jn 19:38-41
ᶠ Isa 42:1-3
ᵍ S Job 16:17; 1Pe 2:22*; 1Jn 3:5; Rev 14:5
53:10 ʰ Isa 46:10; 55:11; Ac 2:23
ⁱ ver 5 ʲ S ver 3;
ʲ S Ge 12:17
ᵏ S Lev 5:15;
Jn 3:17 ˡ S Ps 22:30
ᵐ S Jos 1:8;
S Isa 49:4
53:11
ⁿ Jn 10:14-18
ᵒ S Job 33:30
ᵖ S Isa 20:3;
Ac 7:52 ᵍ S Isa 6:7;
Jn 1:29; Ac 10:43;
S Ro 4:25
ʳ S Ex 28:38
53:12 ˢ S Isa 6:1;
S Php 2:9
ᵗ S Ex 15:9;
S Ps 119:162;
Lk 11:22
ᵘ Mt 26:28,38,39, 42 ᵛ Mt 27:38;
Mk 15:27*;
Lk 22:37*; 23:32
ʷ S ver 6; 1Pe 2:24
ˣ Heb 9:28
ʸ Isa 59:16;
S Ro 8:34
54:1 ᶻ S Ge 30:1
ᵃ S Ge 21:6;
S Ps 98:4 ᵇ Isa 66:7
ᶜ Isa 49:20
ᵈ S Isa 49:19
ᵉ S Isa 2:5;
Gal 4:27*
54:2 ᶠ S Ge 26:22;
Isa 26:15; 49:19-20
ᵍ Ex 35:18; 39:40
54:3 ʰ S Ge 13:14;
S Isa 48:19
ⁱ S Job 12:23;
S Isa 14:2; 60:4-11
ʲ S Isa 49:19
54:4 ᵏ Jer 30:10;
Joel 2:21
ˡ S Isa 28:16;
S 29:22
ᵐ S Ge 30:23;
S Ps 119:39;
S Isa 41:11
ⁿ S Ps 25:7;
S Jer 2:2; S 22:21
ᵒ S Isa 51:7
ᵖ S Isa 47:8
54:5 ᑫ S Ps 95:6;
S 149:2; S Isa 51:13
ʳ SS 3:1,1;
Jer 3:14; 31:32;
Hos 2:7,16
ˢ S Isa 1:4; 49:7;
55:5; 60:9
ᵗ S Isa 48:17

ᵘ S Isa 6:3; S 12:4 **54:6** ᵛ Isa 49:14-21 ʷ ver 6-7; Isa 1:4; 50:1-2; 60:15; 62:4,12; Jer 44:2; Hos 1:10 ˣ S Ex 20:14; Mal 2:15 **54:7** ʸ S Job 14:13; Isa 26:20 ᶻ S Ps 71:11; S Isa 27:8 ᵃ S Ps 51:1 ᵇ Isa 49:18 **54:8** ᶜ Isa 9:12; 26:20; 60:10 ᵈ S Isa 1:15 ᵉ ver 10; S Ps 25:6; 92:2; Isa 55:3; 63:7 ᶠ S Ps 102:13; S Isa 14:1; Hos 2:19 ᵍ S Isa 48:17 **54:9** ʰ S Ge 8:21

ᶜ 8 *Or away.* / *Yet who of his generation considered* / *that he was cut off from the land of the living* / *for the transgression of my people,* / *to whom the blow was due?* ᵈ 10 *Hebrew though you make* ᵉ 11 *Dead Sea Scrolls (see also Septuagint); Masoretic Text does not have* the light ⌊of life⌉. ᶠ 11 *Or (with Masoretic Text)* ¹¹He will see the result of the suffering of his soul / and be satisfied ᵍ 11 *Or by knowledge of him* ʰ 12 *Or many* ⁱ 12 *Or numerous*

K *Isa 53:5* ◀ ▶ *Isa 55:7*
L *Isa 53:4–6* ◀ ▶ *Isa 55:1–3*
I *Isa 52:6–9* ◀ ▶ *Isa 54:17*

54:1–14, 17 This series of prophetic verses confirmed God's promise to make Israel a great nation (see note at Ge 15:4). Israel's descendants would finally "dispossess nations" (54:3) and inherit their lands in the coming millennial kingdom.

So now I have sworn to not be angry with you,
never to rebuke you again.
¹⁰Though the mountains be shaken
and the hills be removed,
yet my unfailing love for you will not be shaken
nor my covenant of peace be removed,"
says the LORD, who has compassion on you.

¹¹"O afflicted city, lashed by storms
and not comforted,
I will build you with stones of turquoise,
your foundations with sapphires.
¹²I will make your battlements of rubies,
your gates of sparkling jewels,
and all your walls of precious stones.
¹³All your sons will be taught by the LORD,
and great will be your children's peace.
¹⁴In righteousness you will be established:
Tyranny will be far from you;
you will have nothing to fear.
Terror will be far removed;
it will not come near you.
¹⁵If anyone does attack you, it will not be my doing;
whoever attacks you will surrender to you.

¹⁶"See, it is I who created the blacksmith
who fans the coals into flame
and forges a weapon fit for its work.
And it is I who have created the destroyer to work havoc;
¹⁷no weapon forged against you will prevail,
and you will refute every tongue that accuses you.
This is the heritage of the servants of the LORD,

and this is their vindication from me,"
declares the LORD.

Invitation to the Thirsty

55 "Come, all you who are thirsty,
come to the waters;
and you who have no money,
come, buy and eat!
Come, buy wine and milk
without money and without cost.
²Why spend money on what is not bread,
and your labor on what does not satisfy?
Listen, listen to me, and eat what is good,
and your soul will delight in the richest of fare.
³Give ear and come to me;
hear me, that your soul may live.
I will make an everlasting covenant with you,
my faithful love promised to David.
⁴See, I have made him a witness to the peoples,
a leader and commander of the peoples.
⁵Surely you will summon nations you know not,
and nations that do not know you will hasten to you,
because of the LORD your God,
the Holy One of Israel,
for he has endowed you with splendor."

⁶Seek the LORD while he may be found;

55:5 Isaiah prophesied that nations would be attracted to Zion and the God of Israel in the last days because they would be restored both physically and spiritually.

call[j] on him while he is near.
⁷Let the wicked forsake[k] his way
and the evil man his thoughts.[l]
Let him turn[m] to the LORD, and he will
have mercy[n] on him,
and to our God, for he will freely
pardon.[o]

⁸"For my thoughts[p] are not your
thoughts,
neither are your ways my ways,"[q]
declares the LORD.
⁹"As the heavens are higher than the
earth,[r]
so are my ways higher than your
ways
and my thoughts than your
thoughts.[s]
¹⁰As the rain[t] and the snow
come down from heaven,
and do not return to it
without watering the earth
and making it bud and flourish,[u]
so that it yields seed[v] for the
sower and bread for the
eater,[w]
¹¹so is my word[x] that goes out from my
mouth:
It will not return to me
empty,[y]
but will accomplish what I
desire
and achieve the purpose[z] for which
I sent it.

¹²You will go out in joy[a]
and be led forth in peace;[b]
the mountains and hills
will burst into song[c] before you,
and all the trees[d] of the field
will clap their hands.[e]
¹³Instead of the thornbush will grow the
pine tree,
and instead of briers[f] the myrtle[g]
will grow.
This will be for the LORD's
renown,[h]
for an everlasting sign,
which will not be destroyed."

K Isa 53:11 ◄► Isa 57:13
R Isa 1:16–17 ◄► Isa 57:15
I Isa 55:5 ◄► Isa 56:8
M Isa 55:3 ◄► Isa 59:19

55:6 jS Ps 50:15; Isa 65:24; Jer 29:12; 33:3
55:7 kS 2Ch 7:14; S 30:9; Eze 18:27-28
l Isa 32:7; 59:7
m S Isa 44:22; S Jer 26:3; S Eze 18:32
n S Isa 54:10
o S 2Ch 6:21; Isa 1:18; 40:2
55:8 p Php 2:5; 4:8
q Isa 53:6; Mic 4:12
55:9 r S Job 11:8; Ps 103:11
s S Nu 23:19; S Isa 40:13-14
55:10 t Isa 30:23
u S Lev 25:19; S Job 14:9; S Ps 67:6
v S Ge 47:23
w 2Co 9:10
55:11 x S Dt 32:2; Jn 1:1; y Isa 40:8; 45:23; S Mt 5:18; Heb 4:12
z S Pr 19:21; S Isa 44:26; Eze 12:25
55:12 a S Ps 98:4; S Isa 35:2
b Isa 54:10,13
c S Ps 65:12-13; S 96:12-13
d S 1Ch 16:33
e Ps 98:8
55:13 f S Nu 33:55; S Isa 5:6 g Isa 41:19
h S Ps 102:12; Isa 63:12; Jer 32:20; 33:9
56:1 i S Ps 11:7; S Isa 1:17; S Jer 22:3
j S Isa 26:8
k Ps 85:9
l Jer 23:6; Da 9:24
56:2 m S Ps 119:2
n S Ex 20:8,10
56:3 o S Ex 12:43; S 1Ki 8:41; S Isa 11:10; Zec 8:20-23
p Dt 23:3
q S Lev 21:20; Jer 38:7 fn; Ac 8:27
56:4 r Jer 38:7 fn
s S Ex 31:13
56:5 t Isa 26:1; 60:18 u S Nu 32:42; 1Sa 15:12
v S Isa 43:7
w S Isa 48:19; 55:13
56:6 x S Ex 12:43; S 1Ki 8:41
y S 1Ch 22:2; Isa 60:7,10; 61:5
z Mal 1:11 a ver 2,4
56:7 b S Isa 2:2; Eze 20:40
c S Isa 19:21; Ro 12:1; Php 4:18; Heb 13:15
d Mt 21:13*; Lk 19:46*
e Mk 11:17*

Salvation for Others

56 This is what the LORD says:

"Maintain justice[i]
and do what is right,[j]
for my salvation[k] is close at hand
and my righteousness[l] will soon be
revealed.
²Blessed[m] is the man who does this,
the man who holds it fast,
who keeps the Sabbath[n] without
desecrating it,
and keeps his hand from doing any
evil."

³Let no foreigner[o] who has bound
himself to the LORD say,
"The LORD will surely exclude me
from his people."[p]
And let not any eunuch[q] complain,
"I am only a dry tree."

⁴For this is what the LORD says:

"To the eunuchs[r] who keep my
Sabbaths,
who choose what pleases me
and hold fast to my covenant[s]—
⁵to them I will give within my temple
and its walls[t]
a memorial[u] and a name
better than sons and daughters;
I will give them an everlasting name[v]
that will not be cut off.[w]
⁶And foreigners[x] who bind themselves
to the LORD
to serve[y] him,
to love the name[z] of the LORD,
and to worship him,
all who keep the Sabbath[a] without
desecrating it
and who hold fast to my covenant—
⁷these I will bring to my holy
mountain[b]
and give them joy in my house of
prayer.
Their burnt offerings and sacrifices[c]
will be accepted on my altar;
for my house will be called
a house of prayer for all nations.[d]"[e]

55:12–13 The prophet gave the people a glimpse of life in the millennial kingdom when Jesus Christ will rule with power and peace, allowing the increased fertility of the land of Israel.

ISAIAH 56:8

⁸The Sovereign LORD declares—
   he who gathers the exiles of Israel:
"I will gather' still others to them
   besides those already gathered."

God's Accusation Against the Wicked

⁹Come, all you beasts of the field,ᵍ
   come and devour, all you beasts of
      the forest!
¹⁰Israel's watchmenʰ are blind,
   they all lack knowledge;ⁱ
they are all mute dogs,
   they cannot bark;
they lie around and dream,
   they love to sleep.ʲ
¹¹They are dogs with mighty appetites;
   they never have enough.
They are shepherdsᵏ who lack
   understanding;ˡ
they all turn to their own way,ᵐ
   each seeks his own gain.ⁿ
¹²"Come," each one cries, "let me get
      wine!ᵒ
   Let us drink our fill of beer!
And tomorrow will be like today,
   or even far better."ᵖ

57 The righteous perish,ᑫ
   and no one ponders it in his
      heart;ʳ
devout men are taken away,
   and no one understands
that the righteous are taken away
   to be spared from evil.ˢ
²Those who walk uprightlyᵗ
   enter into peace;
they find restᵘ as they lie in death.

³"But you—come here, you sons of a
      sorceress,ᵛ
   you offspring of adulterersʷ and
      prostitutes!ˣ
⁴Whom are you mocking?
   At whom do you sneer
      and stick out your tongue?
Are you not a brood of rebels,ʸ
   the offspring of liars?
⁵You burn with lust among the oaksᶻ
   and under every spreading tree;ᵃ

you sacrifice your childrenᵇ in the
   ravines
and under the overhanging crags.
⁶The idols⸝ᶜ among the smooth stones
   of the ravines are your portion;
they, they are your lot.
Yes, to them you have poured out
   drink offeringsᵈ
and offered grain offerings.
In the light of these things, should I
   relent?ᵉ
⁷You have made your bed on a high and
   lofty hill;ᶠ
there you went up to offer your
   sacrifices.ᵍ
⁸Behind your doors and your doorposts
   you have put your pagan symbols.
Forsaking me, you uncovered your
   bed,
you climbed into it and opened it
   wide;
you made a pact with those whose
   beds you love,ʰ
and you looked on their nakedness.ⁱ
⁹You went to Molechʲ⁾ with olive oil
   and increased your perfumes.ᵏ
You sent your ambassadorsᵐ⁾ far away;
   you descended to the graveⁿ⁾ itself!
¹⁰You were weariedⁿ by all your ways,
   but you would not say, 'It is
      hopeless.'ᵒ
You found renewal of your strength,ᵖ
   and so you did not faint.

¹¹"Whom have you so dreaded and
      fearedᑫ
that you have been false to me,
   and have neither rememberedʳ me
      nor ponderedˢ this in your hearts?
Is it not because I have long been
      silentᵗ
that you do not fear me?
¹²I will expose your righteousness and
      your works,ᵘ
   and they will not benefit you.
¹³When you cry outᵛ for help,
   let your collection ⸝of idols⸝ saveʷ
      you!

56:8 Isaiah described the return of the Jewish exiles to Israel, as well as the Gentiles who will attach themselves to the Jewish people in recognition of their favored position with God in the millennial kingdom.

The wind will carry all of them off,
  a mere breath will blow them
    away.
But the man who makes me his
  refuge
  will inherit the land
  and possess my holy mountain."

Comfort for the Contrite

¹⁴And it will be said:

"Build up, build up, prepare the road!
  Remove the obstacles out of the way
    of my people."

¹⁵For this is what the high and lofty
    One says—
  he who lives forever, whose name
    is holy:
"I live in a high and holy place,
  but also with him who is contrite
    and lowly in spirit,
  to revive the spirit of the lowly
  and to revive the heart of the
    contrite.
¹⁶I will not accuse forever,
  nor will I always be angry,
for then the spirit of man would grow
    faint before me—
  the breath of man that I have
    created.
¹⁷I was enraged by his sinful greed;
  I punished him, and hid my face in
    anger,
  yet he kept on in his willful ways.
¹⁸I have seen his ways, but I will heal
    him;
  I will guide him and restore
    comfort to him,
¹⁹ creating praise on the lips of the
    mourners in Israel.
Peace, peace, to those far and near,"
  says the LORD. "And I will heal
    them."

²⁰But the wicked are like the tossing
    sea,

which cannot rest,
  whose waves cast up mire and
    mud.
²¹"There is no peace," says my God,
  "for the wicked."

True Fasting

58 "Shout it aloud, do not hold
    back.
  Raise your voice like a trumpet.
Declare to my people their rebellion
  and to the house of Jacob their sins.
²For day after day they seek me out;
  they seem eager to know my ways,
  as if they were a nation that does what
    is right
  and has not forsaken the
    commands of its God.
They ask me for just decisions
  and seem eager for God to come
    near them.
³'Why have we fasted,' they say,
  'and you have not seen it?
Why have we humbled ourselves,
  and you have not noticed?'

"Yet on the day of your fasting, you do
    as you please
  and exploit all your workers.
⁴Your fasting ends in quarreling and
    strife,
  and in striking each other with
    wicked fists.
You cannot fast as you do today
  and expect your voice to be heard
    on high.
⁵Is this the kind of fast I have chosen,
  only a day for a man to humble
    himself?
Is it only for bowing one's head like a
    reed
  and for lying on sackcloth and
    ashes?
Is that what you call a fast,
  a day acceptable to the LORD?

⁶"Is not this the kind of fasting I have
    chosen:
to loose the chains of injustice
  and untie the cords of the yoke,

57:16–19 The prophet declared that God would not punish his people forever for their rebellion but would finally heal them and restore them. This ultimate restoration and healing of Israel's sins is one of the unshakable covenant promises God made to Abraham and his descendants (see note at Ge 15:4).

to set the oppressed free
 and break every yoke?
⁷Is it not to share your food with the hungry
 and to provide the poor wanderer with shelter—
 when you see the naked, to clothe him,
 and not to turn away from your own flesh and blood?

⁸Then your light will break forth like the dawn,
 and your healing will quickly appear;
 then your righteousness will go before you,
 and the glory of the LORD will be your rear guard.
⁹Then you will call, and the LORD will answer;
 you will cry for help, and he will say: Here am I.

"If you do away with the yoke of oppression,
 with the pointing finger and malicious talk,
¹⁰and if you spend yourselves in behalf of the hungry
 and satisfy the needs of the oppressed,
 then your light will rise in the darkness,
 and your night will become like the noonday.
¹¹The LORD will guide you always;
 he will satisfy your needs in a sun-scorched land
 and will strengthen your frame.
You will be like a well-watered garden,
 like a spring whose waters never fail.
¹²Your people will rebuild the ancient ruins

 and will raise up the age-old foundations;
 you will be called Repairer of Broken Walls,
 Restorer of Streets with Dwellings.

¹³"If you keep your feet from breaking the Sabbath
 and from doing as you please on my holy day,
 if you call the Sabbath a delight
 and the LORD's holy day honorable,
 and if you honor it by not going your own way
 and not doing as you please or speaking idle words,
¹⁴then you will find your joy in the LORD,
 and I will cause you to ride on the heights of the land
 and to feast on the inheritance of your father Jacob."
 The mouth of the LORD has spoken.

Sin, Confession and Redemption

59 Surely the arm of the LORD is not too short to save,
 nor his ear too dull to hear.
²But your iniquities have separated you from your God;
 your sins have hidden his face from you,
 so that he will not hear.
³For your hands are stained with blood,
 your fingers with guilt.
Your lips have spoken lies,
 and your tongue mutters wicked things.
⁴No one calls for justice;
 no one pleads his case with integrity.

o 8 Or *your righteous One*

58:8–12 This passage contained God's promises for his covenant people if they would follow his law, show justice to the oppressed, share with the poor and turn away from vain practices and sinful idolatry.

58:13–14 Isaiah reminded the people to keep God's Sabbath and thereby show their love for him and his law. Such obedience would bring blessings.

59:2 Israel's sins were the reason for their alienation from God and his refusal to hear their cries.

They rely[j] on empty arguments and
  speak lies;[k]
  they conceive trouble and give birth
    to evil.[l]
[5]They hatch the eggs of vipers[m]
  and spin a spider's web.[n]
Whoever eats their eggs will die,
  and when one is broken, an adder is
    hatched.
[6]Their cobwebs are useless for clothing;
  they cannot cover themselves with
    what they make.[o]
Their deeds are evil deeds,
  and acts of violence[p] are in their
    hands.
[7]Their feet rush into sin;
  they are swift to shed innocent
    blood.[q]
Their thoughts are evil thoughts;[r]
  ruin and destruction mark their
    ways.[s]
[8]The way of peace they do not know;[t]
  there is no justice in their paths.
They have turned them into crooked
    roads;[u]
  no one who walks in them will
    know peace.[v]

[9]So justice is far from us,
  and righteousness does not reach us.
We look for light, but all is darkness;[w]
  for brightness, but we walk in deep
    shadows.
[10]Like the blind[x] we grope along the
    wall,
  feeling our way like men without
    eyes.
At midday we stumble[y] as if it were
    twilight;
  among the strong, we are like the
    dead.[z]
[11]We all growl like bears;
  we moan mournfully like doves.[a]
We look for justice, but find none;
  for deliverance, but it is far away.

C *Isa 59:2–3* ◀ ▶ *Isa 59:12*
R *Isa 59:2* ◀ ▶ *Isa 60:10*

59:4 [j]S Job 15:31
  [k]S Isa 44:20
  [l]S Job 4:8;
  S Isa 29:20; Jas 1:15
59:5 [m]S Isa 11:8;
  Mt 3:7 [n]S Job 8:14
59:6 [o]Isa 28:20
  [p]Ps 55:9;
  S Pr 4:17; S Isa 58:4
59:7 [q]S 2Ki 21:16;
  S Pr 6:17;
  S Mic 3:10
  [r]S Pr 24:2;
  S Isa 26:10;
  Mk 7:21-22
  [s]Ro 3:15-17*
59:8 [t]Ro 3:15-17*
  [u]S Jdg 5:6
  [v]S Isa 57:21;
  Lk 1:79
59:9 [w]S Job 19:8;
  S Ps 107:14;
  S Isa 5:30; S 8:20;
  S Lk 1:79
59:10 [x]Dt 28:29;
  S Isa 6:9-10; 56:10;
  La 4:14; Zep 1:17
  [y]S Job 3:23;
  S Isa 8:15;
  Jn 11:9-10 [z]La 3:6
59:11 [a]S Ge 8:8;
  Ps 74:19; Isa 38:14;
  Jer 48:28; Eze 7:16;
  Na 2:7
59:12 [b]S Ezr 9:6;
  S Isa 57:12
  [c]S Ge 4:7; S Isa 3:9;
  S Jer 2:19 [d]S Ps 51:3
59:13 [e]Isa 46:8;
  48:8 [f]S Nu 11:20;
  S Pr 30:9;
  Mt 10:33; Tit 1:16
  [g]S Ps 12:5;
  S Isa 5:7 [h]S Isa 3:8;
  S 44:20;
  Mk 7:21-22
59:14 [i]S Isa 29:21
  [j]S Isa 1:21
  [k]S Isa 48:1;
  S Jer 33:16
59:15 [l]Jer 7:28;
  9:5; Da 8:12
  [m]S Isa 5:7
59:16 [n]S Isa 41:28
  [o]S Isa 53:12
  [p]S Isa 51:5
  [q]Isa 45:8,13; 46:13
59:17 [r]Eph 6:14;
  1Th 5:8 [s]Eph 6:17;
  1Th 5:8
  [t]S Job 27:6;
  Isa 63:3 [u]S Isa 1:24
  [v]S Isa 9:7; Eze 5:13
59:18
  [w]S Lev 26:28;
  S Nu 10:35;
  S Isa 34:8;
  S Mt 16:27
  [x]Isa 11:11; 41:5
59:19
  [y]S Isa 49:12;
  S Mt 8:11

[12]For our offenses[b] are many in your
    sight,
  and our sins testify[c] against us.
Our offenses are ever with us,
  and we acknowledge our iniquities:[d]
[13]rebellion[e] and treachery against the
    LORD,
  turning our backs[f] on our God,
  fomenting oppression[g] and revolt,
  uttering lies[h] our hearts have
    conceived.
[14]So justice[i] is driven back,
  and righteousness[j] stands at a
    distance;
  truth[k] has stumbled in the streets,
  honesty cannot enter.
[15]Truth[l] is nowhere to be found,
  and whoever shuns evil becomes a
    prey.

The LORD looked and was displeased
  that there was no justice.[m]
[16]He saw that there was no one,[n]
  he was appalled that there was no
    one to intervene;[o]
so his own arm worked salvation[p] for
    him,
  and his own righteousness[q]
    sustained him.
[17]He put on righteousness as his
    breastplate,[r]
  and the helmet[s] of salvation on his
    head;
he put on the garments[t] of vengeance[u]
  and wrapped himself in zeal[v] as in a
    cloak.
[18]According to what they have done,
  so will he repay[w]
  wrath to his enemies
    and retribution to his foes;
  he will repay the islands[x] their due.
[19]From the west,[y] men will fear the
    name of the LORD,

C *Isa 59:8* ◀ ▶ *Isa 61:1*
H *Isa 35:4* ◀ ▶ *Isa 61:2*
M *Isa 55:12–13* ◀ ▶ *Isa 59:21*
M *Isa 44:3–4* ◀ ▶ *Eze 2:2–3*

59:9–12 Isaiah declared that the people could not find justice or light because their transgressions against God cut them off from his justice and blessings.

59:17–21 Despite Israel's past rebellion, God promised to send the Messiah as their deliverer who would bring "wrath to his enemies and retribution to his foes" (59:18). This passage parallels other prophecies that confirm the powerful deliverance that Messiah will bring to his chosen people at Armageddon (see Jude 14–15; Rev 19:11–21). God has not rejected Israel forever, but rather has promised to save all "in Jacob who repent of their sins" (59:20).

and from the rising of the sun,[z] they
    will revere his glory.[a]
For he will come like a pent-up flood
    that the breath[b] of the LORD drives
    along.[p]

[20] "The Redeemer[c] will come to Zion,[d]
    to those in Jacob who repent of their
    sins,"[e]
                    declares the LORD.

[21] "As for me, this is my covenant[f] with
them," says the LORD. "My Spirit,[g] who is
on you, and my words that I have put in
your mouth[h] will not depart from your
mouth,[i] or from the mouths of your children, or from the mouths of their descendants from this time on and forever," says
the LORD.

The Glory of Zion

60 "Arise,[j] shine, for your light[k]
    has come,
    and the glory[l] of the LORD rises upon
    you.
[2] See, darkness[m] covers the earth
    and thick darkness[n] is over the
    peoples,
but the LORD rises upon you
    and his glory appears over you.
[3] Nations[o] will come to your light,[p]
    and kings[q] to the brightness of your
    dawn.
[4] "Lift up your eyes and look about you:
    All assemble[r] and come to you;
    your sons come from afar,[s]
    and your daughters[t] are carried on
    the arm.[u]
[5] Then you will look and be radiant,[v]
    your heart will throb and swell with
    joy;[w]

the wealth[x] on the seas will be
    brought to you,
to you the riches of the nations will
    come.
[6] Herds of camels[y] will cover your land,
    young camels of Midian[z] and
    Ephah.[a]
And all from Sheba[b] will come,
    bearing gold and incense[c]
    and proclaiming the praise[d] of the
    LORD.
[7] All Kedar's[e] flocks will be gathered to
    you,
    the rams of Nebaioth will serve you;
they will be accepted as offerings[f] on
    my altar,[g]
    and I will adorn my glorious
    temple.[h]

[8] "Who are these[i] that fly along like
    clouds,[j]
    like doves to their nests?
[9] Surely the islands[k] look to me;
    in the lead are the ships of
    Tarshish,[q]
bringing[m] your sons from afar,
    with their silver and gold,[n]
to the honor[o] of the LORD your God,
    the Holy One[p] of Israel,
for he has endowed you with
    splendor.[q]

[10] "Foreigners[r] will rebuild your walls,
    and their kings[s] will serve you.
Though in anger I struck you,
    in favor[t] I will show you
    compassion.[u]
[11] Your gates[v] will always stand open,

60:1–18 Though this prophecy of restored blessing and God's favor was initially fulfilled when the
exiles returned from Babylon, final fulfillment of
these marvelous words will not be realized until the
Messiah returns to defeat the enemies of his people
and establish his millennial kingdom. At that time Israel will be acknowledged for its supremacy among
the millennial nations and will receive both gifts and
assistance from Gentile nations for rebuilding their
land. In addition, Isaiah prophesied that God would
severely punish any Gentile nation that failed to
serve Israel (60:12).
  Note too that the blessings on Israel and Jerusalem will not be limited by time but rather will
be "the joy of all generations" (60:15), indicating
God's eternal blessing for his chosen people. The
peace of the millennial kingdom of the Messiah is
assured with God's words, "No longer will violence
be heard in your land" (60:18).

they will never be shut, day or
night,
so that men may bring you the wealth
of the nations—
their kings led in triumphal
procession.
¹²For the nation or kingdom that will not
serve you will perish;
it will be utterly ruined.
¹³"The glory of Lebanon will come to
you,
the pine, the fir and the cypress
together,
to adorn the place of my sanctuary;
and I will glorify the place of my
feet.
¹⁴The sons of your oppressors will come
bowing before you;
all who despise you will bow down
at your feet
and will call you the City of the LORD,
Zion of the Holy One of Israel.
¹⁵"Although you have been forsaken
and hated,
with no one traveling through,
I will make you the everlasting pride
and the joy of all generations.
¹⁶You will drink the milk of nations
and be nursed at royal breasts.
Then you will know that I, the LORD,
am your Savior,
your Redeemer, the Mighty One of
Jacob.
¹⁷Instead of bronze I will bring you
gold,
and silver in place of iron.
Instead of wood I will bring you
bronze,
and iron in place of stones.
I will make peace your governor
and righteousness your ruler.
¹⁸No longer will violence be heard in
your land,

nor ruin or destruction within your
borders,
but you will call your walls Salvation
and your gates Praise.
¹⁹The sun will no more be your light by
day,
nor will the brightness of the moon
shine on you,
for the LORD will be your everlasting
light,
and your God will be your glory.
²⁰Your sun will never set again,
and your moon will wane no more;
the LORD will be your everlasting light,
and your days of sorrow will end.
²¹Then will all your people be righteous
and they will possess the land
forever.
They are the shoot I have planted,
the work of my hands,
for the display of my splendor.
²²The least of you will become a
thousand,
the smallest a mighty nation.
I am the LORD;
in its time I will do this swiftly."

The Year of the LORD's Favor

61 The Spirit of the Sovereign
LORD is on me,
because the LORD has anointed me
to preach good news to the poor.
He has sent me to bind up the
brokenhearted,

60:19–22 Isaiah's prophecy looked forward to the blessings of the new Jerusalem. There would be no need for the sun or moon since the Lamb will be the source of light (see Rev 21:23). There would be no more sorrow or nighttime (see Rev 21:4; 22:5) but only the light of joy and salvation. Only the redeemed would enter into those full blessings (see Rev 21:27).

61:1–3 The background for this prophecy is probably the Year of Jubilee (see Lev 25:10) because the restoration of Israel prophesied here is as significant as the restoration for the land during that year of liberty. Jesus began his public ministry in Nazareth by reading the first part of this prophecy in Isaiah and declaring that, "today this scripture is fulfilled in your hearing" (Lk 4:21). With this declaration Jesus claimed that he was the Messiah Isaiah had prophesied about centuries before. Some scholars believe that by dividing 61:2 in half with this reading in the synagogue, Jesus read only what applied to his min-

to proclaim freedom for the
    captives
and release from darkness for the
    prisoners,
²to proclaim the year of the LORD's
    favor
and the day of vengeance of our
    God,
to comfort all who mourn,
³ and provide for those who grieve in
    Zion—
to bestow on them a crown of beauty
    instead of ashes,
the oil of gladness
    instead of mourning,
and a garment of praise
    instead of a spirit of despair.
They will be called oaks of
    righteousness,
a planting of the LORD
    for the display of his splendor.

⁴They will rebuild the ancient ruins
    and restore the places long
    devastated;
they will renew the ruined cities
    that have been devastated for
    generations.
⁵Aliens will shepherd your flocks;
    foreigners will work your fields and
    vineyards.
⁶And you will be called priests of the
    LORD,
you will be named ministers of our
    God.
You will feed on the wealth of
    nations,
and in their riches you will boast.
⁷Instead of their shame
    my people will receive a double
    portion,
and instead of disgrace

P Isa 45:23–24 ◄ ► Isa 63:3–6
H Isa 59:18 ◄ ► Isa 63:3–4
I Isa 60:1–22 ◄ ► Isa 65:8–10
S Isa 51:11 ◄ ► Rev 7:17

61:1 q S Lev 25:10
r S Ps 68:6;
S Isa 49:9
61:2 s S Isa 49:8;
S Lk 4:18-19*
t S Isa 1:24
u S Isa 40:1; Mt 5:4
v S Job 5:11;
Lk 6:21
61:3 w S Isa 3:23
x S Job 2:8
y S Ru 3:3; S Isa 1:6;
Heb 1:9 z Jer 31:13;
Mt 5:4 a Ps 1:3;
92:12-13;
Mt 15:13; 1Co 3:9
b S Isa 44:23
61:4 c S Isa 44:26;
51:3; 65:21;
Eze 36:33;
Am 9:14;
Zec 1:16-17
61:5 d S Isa 14:1-2;
S 56:6
61:6 e S Ex 19:6;
1Pe 2:5 f Dt 33:19;
S Isa 60:11
61:7 g S Isa 29:22;
S 41:11
h S Dt 21:17;
S Isa 40:2
i S Isa 60:21
j S Ps 126:5;
S Isa 25:9
61:8 k S Ps 11:7;
S Isa 1:17; S 5:16
l S Ge 9:16;
S Isa 42:6;
S Heb 13:20
61:9 m S Isa 43:5;
S 48:19
n S Ge 12:2;
S Dt 28:3-12
61:10 o S Ps 2:11;
S Isa 7:13; S 25:9;
Hab 3:18; S Lk 1:47
p S Job 27:6;
S Ps 132:9;
S Isa 52:1; Rev 19:8
q S Ex 39:28
r S Isa 49:18;
Rev 21:2
61:11
s S Ge 47:23;
Isa 58:11
t S Isa 45:8
62:1 u S Est 4:14;
S Ps 50:21; S 83:1
v S Isa 1:26; S 45:8
w S Job 11:17
x S Ps 67:2
62:2 y S Ps 67:2;
S Isa 40:5; S 45:14;
52:10

they will rejoice in their inheritance;
and so they will inherit a double
    portion in their land,
and everlasting joy will be theirs.

⁸"For I, the LORD, love justice;
I hate robbery and iniquity.
In my faithfulness I will reward them
    and make an everlasting covenant
    with them.
⁹Their descendants will be known
    among the nations
and their offspring among the
    peoples.
All who see them will acknowledge
    that they are a people the LORD has
    blessed."

¹⁰I delight greatly in the LORD;
    my soul rejoices in my God.
For he has clothed me with garments
    of salvation
and arrayed me in a robe of
    righteousness,
as a bridegroom adorns his head like
    a priest,
and as a bride adorns herself with
    her jewels.
¹¹For as the soil makes the sprout come
    up
and a garden causes seeds to grow,
so the Sovereign LORD will make
    righteousness and praise
spring up before all nations.

Zion's New Name

62 For Zion's sake I will not keep
    silent,
for Jerusalem's sake I will not
    remain quiet,
till her righteousness shines out like
    the dawn,
her salvation like a blazing torch.
²The nations will see your
    righteousness,
and all kings your glory;

r 1 Hebrew; Septuagint *the blind*

istry on earth at his first coming. These scholars contend that the remainder of this passage will find its fulfillment in Christ's second coming.

61:4–11 Isaiah continued with his description of the millennial kingdom's reign of the Messiah. Israel will be rebuilt with the assistance of the Gentiles and the Lord will rule with justice. Those living on the earth will prosper, have children and live in an atmosphere of righteousness and praise for God.

Note that Isaiah also declares that nations will still exist in the Millennium (61:11). Compare this verse with John's prophecy in Rev 21:24–26.

62:1–12 God declares his commitment to defend his people and bring them salvation in the last days. He even promises to give Israel a new name. This prophecy of restoration affirmed that Israel's desolate condition would become a time of blessing and forgiveness both physically and spiritually.

you will be called by a new name
that the mouth of the LORD will
bestow.
³You will be a crown of splendor in
the LORD's hand,
a royal diadem in the hand of your
God.
⁴No longer will they call you Deserted,
or name your land Desolate.
But you will be called Hephzibah,
and your land Beulah;
for the LORD will take delight in you,
and your land will be married.
⁵As a young man marries a maiden,
so will your sons marry you;
as a bridegroom rejoices over his
bride,
so will your God rejoice over you.
⁶I have posted watchmen on your
walls, O Jerusalem;
they will never be silent day or
night.
You who call on the LORD,
give yourselves no rest,
⁷and give him no rest till he
establishes Jerusalem
and makes her the praise of the
earth.
⁸The LORD has sworn by his right hand
and by his mighty arm:
"Never again will I give your grain
as food for your enemies,
and never again will foreigners drink
the new wine
for which you have toiled;
⁹but those who harvest it will eat it
and praise the LORD,
and those who gather the grapes will
drink it
in the courts of my sanctuary."
¹⁰Pass through, pass through the gates!
Prepare the way for the people.
Build up, build up the highway!
Remove the stones.
Raise a banner for the nations.

U Isa 58:14 ◀ ▶ Isa 64:4–5

¹¹The LORD has made proclamation
to the ends of the earth:
"Say to the Daughter of Zion,
'See, your Savior comes!
See, his reward is with him,
and his recompense accompanies
him.'"
¹²They will be called the Holy People,
the Redeemed of the LORD;
and you will be called Sought After,
the City No Longer Deserted.

God's Day of Vengeance and Redemption

63 Who is this coming from Edom,
from Bozrah, with his garments
stained crimson?
Who is this, robed in splendor,
striding forward in the greatness of
his strength?

"It is I, speaking in righteousness,
mighty to save."

²Why are your garments red,
like those of one treading the
winepress?

³"I have trodden the winepress alone;
from the nations no one was with
me.
I trampled them in my anger
and trod them down in my wrath;
their blood spattered my garments,
and I stained all my clothing.
⁴For the day of vengeance was in my
heart,
and the year of my redemption has
come.
⁵I looked, but there was no one to
help,
I was appalled that no one gave
support;

K Isa 60:19–21 ◀ ▶ Jer 8:22
P Isa 61:2 ◀ ▶ Isa 64:2–3
H Isa 61:2 ◀ ▶ Isa 65:6

s 4 Hephzibah means *my delight is in her*. t 4 Beulah means *married*.
u 5 Or *Builder*

63:1–3 Isaiah prophesied that the Messiah would come "from Edom" (63:1) with his garments covered with blood. Edom symbolized the world that hated God's people. Isaiah's imagery pictured Christ coming again in judgment (see Rev 14:17–20; 19:15) at the end of the great tribulation. Christ will return to save Israel from annihilation (see Mt 24:30; Jude 14–15; Rev 19:11–21).

63:4–6 Isaiah continued his prophecy with the words that Israel would find themselves in danger of total destruction with no allies to come to their aid. Christ would then return in wrath to judge Israel's unrighteous enemies. Compare these words with Isaiah's prophecy in 61:1–3.

so my own arm worked salvation for me,
and my own wrath sustained me.
⁶I trampled the nations in my anger;
in my wrath I made them drunk
and poured their blood on the ground."

Praise and Prayer

⁷I will tell of the kindnesses of the LORD,
the deeds for which he is to be praised,
according to all the LORD has done for us—
yes, the many good things he has done
for the house of Israel,
according to his compassion and many kindnesses.
⁸He said, "Surely they are my people,
sons who will not be false to me";
and so he became their Savior.
⁹In all their distress he too was distressed,
and the angel of his presence saved them.
In his love and mercy he redeemed them;
he lifted them up and carried them
all the days of old.
¹⁰Yet they rebelled
and grieved his Holy Spirit.
So he turned and became their enemy
and he himself fought against them.
¹¹Then his people recalled the days of old,
the days of Moses and his people—
where is he who brought them through the sea,
with the shepherd of his flock?
Where is he who set his Holy Spirit among them,
¹²who sent his glorious arm of power
to be at Moses' right hand,

L *Isa 61:1–3* ◀ ▶ *Isa 65:2*
L *Isa 54:10* ◀ ▶ *Jer 31:3*
E *Isa 59:21* ◀ ▶ *Isa 63:14*
Q *Ps 51:11* ◀ ▶ *La 2:9*
N *Isa 55:6* ◀ ▶ *Isa 65:12*
B *Isa 61:1* ◀ ▶ *Eze 11:19*

63:5 p S Ps 44:3; S 98:1; S Isa 33:2
q Isa 59:16
63:6 r S Job 40:12; S Ps 108:13
s S Isa 29:9; La 4:21
t S Isa 34:3
63:7 u S Isa 54:8
v S Ex 18:9
w S Ps 51:1; Eph 2:4
63:8 x S Ps 100:3; S Isa 51:4
y S Ex 14:30; S Isa 25:9
63:9 z S Isa 14:19
a S Ex 33:14
b Dt 7:7-8; S Ezr 9:9; S Isa 48:20
c S Dt 1:31; S Ps 28:9
d S Dt 32:7; S Job 37:23
63:10 e S Ps 78:17; Eze 20:8; Ac 7:39-42
f S Ps 51:11; Ac 7:51; Eph 4:30
g Ps 106:40; S Isa 10:4
h S Jos 10:14
63:11 i S Ex 14:22, 30; S Ps 77:20
k S Nu 11:17
63:12 l S Ge 49:24; S Ex 3:20
m Ex 14:21-22; Isa 11:15
n S Ps 102:12; S Isa 55:13; S Jer 13:11
63:13 o S Dt 32:12
p S Ex 14:22
q S Ps 119:11; Jer 31:9
63:14 r S Ex 33:14; S Dt 12:9
63:15 s S Dt 26:15; La 3:50
t S 1Ki 22:19; S Ps 123:1
u S Isa 9:7; S 26:11
v S 1Ki 3:26; S Ps 25:6
w S Ge 43:31; Isa 64:12
63:16 x S Ex 4:22; S Jer 3:4; Jn 8:41
y S Job 14:21
z Isa 41:14; 44:6; S 59:20
63:17 a S Ge 20:13; La 3:9
b S Ex 4:21
c Isa 29:13
d S Nu 10:36
e S Ex 34:9
63:18 f Dt 4:26; 11:17 g S Isa 28:18; Da 8:13; S Lk 21:24
h S Lev 26:31; S 2Ki 25:9
63:19 i S Isa 43:7; S Jer 14:9

who divided the waters before them,
to gain for himself everlasting renown,
¹³who led them through the depths?
Like a horse in open country,
they did not stumble;
¹⁴like cattle that go down to the plain,
they were given rest by the Spirit of the LORD.
This is how you guided your people
to make for yourself a glorious name.

¹⁵Look down from heaven and see
from your lofty throne, holy and glorious.
Where are your zeal and your might?
Your tenderness and compassion are withheld from us.
¹⁶But you are our Father,
though Abraham does not know us
or Israel acknowledge us;
you, O LORD, are our Father,
our Redeemer from of old is your name.
¹⁷Why, O LORD, do you make us wander
from your ways
and harden our hearts so we do not revere you?
Return for the sake of your servants,
the tribes that are your inheritance.
¹⁸For a little while your people possessed your holy place,
but now our enemies have trampled down your sanctuary.
¹⁹We are yours from of old;
but you have not ruled over them,
they have not been called by your name.

¹¹ Or But may he recall ʷ 19 Or We are like those you have never ruled, / like those never called by your name

E *Isa 63:10–11* ◀ ▶ *Eze 1:12*
F *Ps 51:12* ◀ ▶ *Ac 9:31*
J *Isa 44:3* ◀ ▶ *Mt 3:16*
L *Isa 48:16* ◀ ▶ *Eze 1:12*
R *Isa 60:14–15* ◀ ▶ *Isa 64:7*

63:16–19 Isaiah's words reaffirmed God's concern for his people when he stated that though human fathers might abandon Israel, God would not abandon them. Though all twelve tribes of Israel and Judah strayed from God's plan, God let them wander and then punished them with exile because of the hardness of their hearts; but he never stopped loving his chosen people.

64

¹Oh, that you would rend the heavens and come down,
that the mountains would tremble before you!
²As when fire sets twigs ablaze and causes water to boil,
come down to make your name known to your enemies
and cause the nations to quake before you!
³For when you did awesome things that we did not expect,
you came down, and the mountains trembled before you.
⁴Since ancient times no one has heard, no ear has perceived,
no eye has seen any God besides you, who acts on behalf of those who wait for him.
⁵You come to the help of those who gladly do right,
who remember your ways.
But when we continued to sin against them,
you were angry.
How then can we be saved?
⁶All of us have become like one who is unclean,
and all our righteous acts are like filthy rags;
we all shrivel up like a leaf,
and like the wind our sins sweep us away.
⁷No one calls on your name or strives to lay hold of you;
for you have hidden your face from us
and made us waste away because of our sins.
⁸Yet, O LORD, you are our Father.

We are the clay, you are the potter;
we are all the work of your hand.
⁹Do not be angry beyond measure, O LORD;
do not remember our sins forever.
Oh, look upon us, we pray, for we are all your people.
¹⁰Your sacred cities have become a desert;
even Zion is a desert, Jerusalem a desolation.
¹¹Our holy and glorious temple, where our fathers praised you,
has been burned with fire,
and all that we treasured lies in ruins.
¹²After all this, O LORD, will you hold yourself back?
Will you keep silent and punish us beyond measure?

Judgment and Salvation

65

"I revealed myself to those who did not ask for me;
I was found by those who did not seek me.
To a nation that did not call on my name,
I said, 'Here am I, here am I.'
²All day long I have held out my hands to an obstinate people,
who walk in ways not good, pursuing their own imaginations—
³a people who continually provoke me to my very face,
offering sacrifices in gardens and burning incense on altars of brick;
⁴who sit among the graves and spend their nights keeping secret vigil;
who eat the flesh of pigs,

64:1–4 In this passage Isaiah prayed for God's intervention on behalf of Israel with the kind of prayer that Israel might pray during the tribulation period. Note the similarity of 64:4 with Paul's words in 1Co 2:9.

64:7–12 This prophecy revealed the "desolation" (64:10) that fell on Israel because of her sinfulness. Yet Isaiah reminds us that we are only clay and God is the potter (64:8); our lives and future are in God's hands.

65:1 Isaiah prophesied that the Gentile nations would find God because God would reveal himself to them. This prophecy found its fulfillment in the missionary effort of the early Christians in the first century (see Ac 10:19–45) and is still being fulfilled today.

and whose pots hold broth of
  unclean meat;
⁵who say, 'Keep away; don't come near
    me,
  for I am too sacredʸ for you!'
Such people are smokeᶻ in my nostrils,
  a fire that keeps burning all day.

⁶"See, it stands written before me:
  I will not keep silentᵃ but will pay
    backᵇ in full;
  I will pay it back into their lapsᶜ—
⁷both your sinsᵈ and the sins of your
    fathers,"ᵉ
  says the LORD.
"Because they burned sacrifices on the
    mountains
  and defied me on the hills,ᶠ
I will measure into their laps
  the full paymentᵍ for their former
    deeds."

⁸This is what the LORD says:

"As when juice is still found in a
    cluster of grapesʰ
  and men say, 'Don't destroy it,
    there is yet some good in it,'
so will I do in behalf of my servants;ⁱ
  I will not destroy them all.
⁹I will bring forth descendantsʲ from
    Jacob,
  and from Judah those who will
    possessᵏ my mountains;
my chosenˡ people will inherit them,
  and there will my servants live.ᵐ
¹⁰Sharonⁿ will become a pasture for
    flocks,ᵒ
  and the Valley of Achorᵖ a resting
    place for herds,
  for my people who seekᑫ me.

¹¹"But as for you who forsakeʳ the LORD
  and forget my holy mountain,ˢ
  who spread a table for Fortune

H *Isa 63:3–4* ◀ ▶ *Isa 65:13–14*
I *Isa 61:3* ◀ ▶ *Isa 65:16–25*

65:5 ʸS Ps 40:4;
Mt 9:11; Lk 7:39;
18:9-12 ᶻPr 10:26
65:6 ᵃS Ps 50:3
ᵇS 2Ch 6:23;
Isa 59:18; Jer 16:18
ᶜS Ps 79:12;
Eze 9:10; Lk 6:38
65:7 ᵈS Isa 22:14
ᵉEx 20:5; Jer 32:18
ᶠS Isa 57:7
ᵍS Pr 10:24;
S Isa 10:12
65:8 ʰS Isa 5:2
ⁱS Isa 54:17
65:9 ʲS Isa 45:19
ᵏS Nu 34:13;
S Isa 60:21;
Jer 50:19;
Am 9:11-15
ˡS Isa 14:1
ᵐIsa 32:18
65:10 ⁿS 1Ch 27:29;
S Isa 35:2; Ac 9:35
ᵒJer 31:12; 33:12;
Eze 34:13-14
ᵖS Jos 7:26
ᑫS Isa 51:1
65:11 ʳDt 28:20;
29:24-25; S 32:15;
Isa 1:28; Jer 2:13;
19:4 ˢS Dt 33:19;
S Ps 137:5
ᵗS Isa 5:22
65:12 ᵘS Isa 1:20;
S 27:1 ᵛS Isa 30:25
ʷS Pr 1:24-25;
S Isa 41:28; 66:4;
Jer 7:27
ˣ2Ch 36:15-16;
Jer 7:13; 13:11;
25:3; 26:5
ʸPs 149:7; Isa 1:24;
66:4; Mic 5:15
65:13 ᶻS Isa 1:19
ᵃJob 18:12;
Lk 6:25
ᵇS Isa 33:16
ᶜS Isa 3:1; 41:17
ᵈS Isa 60:5; 61:7
ᵉS Isa 44:9
65:14
ᶠS Ps 109:28;
Zep 3:14-20;
Jas 5:13
ᵍS Isa 15:2;
Mt 8:12; Lk 13:28
65:15 ʰS Nu 5:27;
S Ps 102:8
ⁱS Ge 32:28;
Rev 2:17
65:16 ʲS Dt 29:19
ᵏPs 31:5; Rev 3:14
ˡS Ps 63:11;
S Isa 19:18
ᵐS Job 11:16

and fill bowls of mixed wineᵗ for
  Destiny,
¹²I will destine you for the sword,ᵘ
  and you will all bend down for the
    slaughter;ᵛ
for I called but you did not answer,ʷ
  I spoke but you did not listen.ˣ
You did evil in my sight
  and chose what displeases me."ʸ

¹³Therefore this is what the Sovereign
  LORD says:

"My servants will eat,ᶻ
  but you will go hungry;ᵃ
my servants will drink,ᵇ
  but you will go thirsty;ᶜ
my servants will rejoice,ᵈ
  but you will be put to shame.ᵉ
¹⁴My servants will singᶠ
  out of the joy of their hearts,
but you will cry outᵍ
  from anguish of heart
  and wail in brokenness of spirit.
¹⁵You will leave your name
  to my chosen ones as a curse;ʰ
the Sovereign LORD will put you to
    death,
  but to his servants he will give
    another name.ⁱ
¹⁶Whoever invokes a blessingʲ in the
    land
  will do so by the God of truth;ᵏ
he who takes an oath in the land
  will swearˡ by the God of truth.
For the past troublesᵐ will be forgotten
  and hidden from my eyes.

New Heavens and a New Earth

¹⁷"Behold, I will create

N *Isa 63:10* ◀ ▶ *Isa 65:13–14*
H *Isa 65:6* ◀ ▶ *Isa 66:14–16*
N *Isa 65:12* ◀ ▶ *Isa 66:4*
F *Isa 58:11* ◀ ▶ *Hos 2:8*
U *Isa 64:4–5* ◀ ▶ *Jer 7:23*
I *Isa 65:8–10* ◀ ▶ *Isa 66:5–6*
M *Isa 60:1–22* ◀ ▶ *Isa 66:18–24*
N *Ecc 1:4* ◀ ▶ *Mt 5:5*

65:8–10 Despite the prophesied judgments against Israel, God promised to leave a remnant who would one day repossess the promised land under their Messiah.

65:16 Isaiah proclaimed that God's people needed nothing more than God; he is enough. Those who are concerned with worldly things bless themselves with the abundance of worldly things (see Ps 49:18; Lk 12:19). We who are God's children should bless ourselves in him for he alone is our strength (see 12:2). We should only swear by him and not false gods of power or materialism. We should honor him as the God of truth and covenant with him who is "the Amen, the faithful and true witness" (Rev 3:14).

65:17–19 The climax of Isaiah's prophecies was this promise that one day God would create "new heavens and a new earth" (65:17) where things that

new heavens and a new earth.ⁿ
The former things will not be
    remembered,ᵒ
nor will they come to mind.
¹⁸But be glad and rejoiceᵖ forever
    in what I will create,
for I will create Jerusalemᑫ to be a
    delight
    and its people a joy.
¹⁹I will rejoiceʳ over Jerusalem
    and take delightˢ in my people;
the sound of weeping and of cryingᵗ
    will be heard in it no more.
²⁰"Never again will there be in it
    an infantᵘ who lives but a few days,
    or an old man who does not live out
    his years;ᵛ
he who dies at a hundred
    will be thought a mere youth;
he who fails to reachˣ a hundred
    will be considered accursed.
²¹They will build housesʷ and dwell in
    them;
they will plant vineyards and eat
    their fruit.ˣ
²²No longer will they build houses and
    others live in them,ʸ
    or plant and others eat.
For as the days of a tree,ᶻ
    so will be the daysᵃ of my people;
my chosenᵇ ones will long enjoy
    the works of their hands.
²³They will not toil in vainᶜ
    or bear children doomed to
    misfortune;ᵈ
for they will be a people blessedᵉ by
    the LORD,
they and their descendantsᶠ with
    them.
²⁴Before they callᵍ I will answer;ʰ
    while they are still speakingⁱ I will
    hear.

²⁵The wolf and the lambʲ will feed
    together,
and the lion will eat straw like the
    ox,ᵏ
but dust will be the serpent's¹ food.
They will neither harm nor destroy
    on all my holy mountain,"ᵐ
        says the LORD.

Judgment and Hope

66 This is what the LORD says:

"Heaven is my throne,ⁿ
    and the earth is my footstool.ᵒ
Where is the houseᵖ you will build for
    me?
Where will my resting place be?
²Has not my hand made all these
    things,ᑫ
    and so they came into being?"
        declares the LORD.

"This is the one I esteem:
he who is humble and contrite in
    spirit,ʳ
and trembles at my word.ˢ

³But whoever sacrifices a bullᵗ
    is like one who kills a man,
and whoever offers a lamb,
    like one who breaks a dog's neck;
whoever makes a grain offering
    is like one who presents pig'sᵘ
    blood,
and whoever burns memorial
    incense,ᵛ
    like one who worships an idol.
They have chosen their own ways,ʷ

U *Isa 32:17–18* ◀▶ *Hos 2:18*
M *Isa 57:15* ◀▶ *Jer 2:35*
R *Isa 58:5–10* ◀▶ *Jer 3:12–13*

---

happened in the past will no longer be remembered. The inhabitants of this future world will not be robbed of the joy of heaven by the memories of past events. Notice also that the portrait of the new Jerusalem is painted in terms of rejoicing: "the sound of weeping and of crying will be heard in it no more" (65:19).

65:20–24 Isaiah's prophecy includes a description of the Millennium that will precede these "new" things. While there will be no death or sin forever in the new heavens and new earth, there will be some degree of sin and punishment for sin during the Millennium (65:20). Infant mortality will no longer exist and people will live longer lives than we commonly experience today. The inhabitants of the Millennium will live in peace and security, able to "enjoy the works of their hands" (65:22) with no fear of war or being cast out of their homes. Above all, the relationship between humanity and God will be so close that "before they call I will answer" (65:24).

65:25 Isaiah included a final word about the remarkable transformation of the animal kingdom that will occur when Christ renews the earth from its curse of sin and death. When Christ returns, even the most ferocious beast will become a harmless vegetarian.

and their souls delight in their abominations;

⁴so I also will choose harsh treatment for them
and will bring upon them what they dread.
For when I called, no one answered,
when I spoke, no one listened.
They did evil in my sight
and chose what displeases me."

⁵Hear the word of the LORD,
you who tremble at his word:
"Your brothers who hate you,
and exclude you because of my name, have said,
'Let the LORD be glorified,
that we may see your joy!'
Yet they will be put to shame.
⁶Hear that uproar from the city,
hear that noise from the temple!
It is the sound of the LORD
repaying his enemies all they deserve.

⁷"Before she goes into labor,
she gives birth;
before the pains come upon her,
she delivers a son.
⁸Who has ever heard of such a thing?
Who has ever seen such things?
Can a country be born in a day
or a nation be brought forth in a moment?
Yet no sooner is Zion in labor
than she gives birth to her children.
⁹Do I bring to the moment of birth
and not give delivery?" says the LORD.
"Do I close up the womb
when I bring to delivery?" says your God.

¹⁰"Rejoice with Jerusalem and be glad for her,
all you who love her;
rejoice greatly with her,
all you who mourn over her.
¹¹For you will nurse and be satisfied
at her comforting breasts;
you will drink deeply
and delight in her overflowing abundance."

¹²For this is what the LORD says:

"I will extend peace to her like a river,
and the wealth of nations like a flooding stream;
you will nurse and be carried on her arm
and dandled on her knees.
¹³As a mother comforts her child,
so will I comfort you;
and you will be comforted over Jerusalem."

¹⁴When you see this, your heart will rejoice
and you will flourish like grass;
the hand of the LORD will be made known to his servants,
but his fury will be shown to his foes.
¹⁵See, the LORD is coming with fire,
and his chariots are like a whirlwind;
he will bring down his anger with fury,
and his rebuke with flames of fire.
¹⁶For with fire and with his sword
the LORD will execute judgment upon all men,
and many will be those slain by the LORD.

N Isa 65:13-14 ◀▶ Jer 2:27
I Isa 65:16-25 ◀▶ Isa 66:8
P Isa 64:2-3 ◀▶ Isa 66:14-17
I Isa 66:5-6 ◀▶ Isa 66:10-14

I Isa 66:8 ◀▶ Isa 66:18-24
P Isa 66:5-6 ◀▶ Isa 66:24
H Isa 65:13-14 ◀▶ Isa 66:24

66:5-6 This prophecy declared that when the Messiah comes Israel's enemies would be repaid for their sarcasm and derision.
66:8-9 Isaiah predicted that the final restoration of Israel will be astonishing and complete and that the nation will "be brought forth in a moment" (66:8) during a period of great travail. This prophecy found its partial fulfillment when Israel declared its independence on May 15, 1948, and will find its final fulfillment when Christ returns.
66:10-14 This prophecy confirmed Israel's blessings in the Millennium. She will finally experience the peace that has eluded her throughout history.
66:15-17 Isaiah declared that the Messiah would judge all sinners "with fire and with his sword" (66:16; see Rev 19:11-21). Whether their sins were public or committed in secret, God promised to punish "all men" (66:16).

ISAIAH 66:24

¹⁷"Those who consecrate and purify themselves to go into the gardens,ᵐ following the one in the midst ofʸ those who eat the flesh of pigsⁿ and ratsᵒ and other abominable things—they will meet their endᵖ together," declares the LORD.

¹⁸"And I, because of their actions and their imaginations,ᑫ am about to comeᶻ and gather all nationsʳ and tongues, and they will come and see my glory.ˢ ¹⁹I will set a signᵗ among them, and I will send some of those who surviveᵘ to the nations—to Tarshish,ᵛ to the Libyansᵃ and Lydiansʷ (famous as archers), to Tubalˣ and Greece,ʸ and to the distant islandsᶻ that have not heard of my fame or seen my glory.ᵃ They will proclaim my glory among the nations. ²⁰And they will bringᵇ all your brothers, from all the nations, to my holy mountainᶜ in Jerusalem as an offering to the LORD—on horses, in chariots and wagons, and on mules and camels,"ᵈ says the LORD. "They will bring them, as the Israelites bring their grain offerings, to the temple of the LORD in ceremonially clean vessels.ᵉ ²¹And I will select some of them also to be priestsᶠ and Levites," says the LORD.

²²"As the new heavens and the new earthᵍ that I make will endure before me," declares the LORD, "so will your name and descendants endure.ʰ ²³From one New Moon to another and from one Sabbathⁱ to another, all mankind will come and bow downʲ before me," says the LORD. ²⁴"And they will go out and look upon the dead bodiesᵏ of those who rebelledˡ against me; their wormᵐ will not die, nor will their fire be quenched,ⁿ and they will be loathsome to all mankind."

P *Isa 66:14–17* ◀ ▶ *Jer 10:10*
H *Isa 66:14–16* ◀ ▶ *Jer 4:4*

66:17 ᵐ S Isa 1:29
ⁿ S Lev 11:7
ᵒ Lev 11:29
ᵖ Ps 37:20; Isa 1:28
66:18 ᑫ S Pr 24:2;
S Isa 65:2
ʳ S Isa 2:3;
S Zec 12:3
ˢ S Ex 16:7;
S Isa 59:19
66:19 ᵗ Isa 11:10;
49:22; Mt 24:30
ᵘ S 2Ki 19:31
ᵛ S Isa 2:16
ʷ Jer 46:9;
ˣ S Ge 10:2
ʸ Jer 31:10;
Da 11:18
ᶻ Isa 11:11
ᵃ S 1Ch 16:24;
S Isa 24:15
66:20
ᵇ S Isa 11:12;
S Jer 25:22;
Eze 34:13
ᶜ S Dt 33:19;
S Isa 2:2; Jer 31:23
ᵈ S Ezr 2:66
ᵉ Isa 52:11
66:21 ᶠ S Ex 19:6;
1Pe 2:5,9
66:22
ᵍ S Isa 65:17;
Heb 12:26-27;
S 2Pe 3:13
ʰ S Isa 48:19;
Jn 10:27-29;
1Pe 1:4-5
66:23 ⁱ Eze 46:1-3 ʲ S Ps 22:29; S Isa 19:21; S 44:5; Rev 15:4
66:24 ᵏ S Ps 110:6 ˡ S Isa 1:2 ᵐ S Isa 14:11 ⁿ S Isa 1:31; S Mt 25:41; Mk 9:48*

ʸ 17 Or *gardens behind one of your temples, and* ᶻ 18 The meaning of the Hebrew for this clause is uncertain. ᵃ 19 Some Septuagint manuscripts *Put* (Libyans); Hebrew *Pul*

I *Isa 66:10–14* ◀ ▶ *Jer 3:14–19*
M *Isa 65:16–25* ◀ ▶ *Jer 3:17*

66:18–21 Isaiah revealed that even the Gentiles would recognize God's glory and acknowledge his kingdom in the last days. God also promised to reestablish the priesthood and the Levites for leading worship in the rebuilt temple (see 2:1–3; Rev 11:1–2).

66:22–24 Isaiah concluded his prophecy with God's declaration that Israel would endure forever (66:22). Note the reference also to the continuation of a way to mark time (66:23). For further information about the passage of time in heaven, see the article on "Heaven," p. 1238.

Jeremiah

Author: Jeremiah

Theme: God's warning and subsequent judgment for Judah's sins

Date of Writing: c. 585–580 B.C.

Outline of Jeremiah
 I. Jeremiah's Call (1:1–19)
 II. Judah's Sinful Condition (2:1—12:17)
 III. The Certainty of Captivity (13:1—29:32)
 IV. The Promise of Restoration (30:1—33:26)
 V. Disintegration Before Jerusalem Falls (34:1—35:19)
 VI. Jeremiah Suffers (36:1—38:28)
 VII. The Fall of Jerusalem (39:1—45:5)
 VIII. Foreign Nations Judged (46:1—51:64)
 IX. Historical Appendix (52:1–34)

JEREMIAH WAS A priest from the city of Anathoth. The book that bears his name is replete with personal details about Jeremiah's life, including his confessions of self-criticism and bold statements about his feelings toward God. His words of doom and woe earned Jeremiah a nickname as the "weeping prophet." Jeremiah's faithful secretary, Baruch, helped him compile the prophecies in this book. Since the messages in Jeremiah are not arranged chronologically, it is vital to read the books of Kings and Chronicles to bring Jeremiah's prophecies into historical perspective.

Jeremiah chronicles life in Judah from the time of King Josiah until Jerusalem's overthrow by Babylon in 586 B.C. Jeremiah repeatedly warned his listeners of impending destruction because of the people's continued wickedness. Though King Josiah instituted a religious reformation during his reign, Jeremiah's words failed to inspire lasting repentance. The people based their security on their possession of the law, God's covenant and the temple. Jeremiah warned that possessions, regardless of their religious significance, were not enough. God required obedience, or judgment would come.

Under King Josiah's rule Judah experienced religious revival. But following Josiah's death in 609 B.C., political and religious leaders returned to their wicked ways. Jeremiah faced constant opposition because of his continued warnings of God's impending judgment. He went into hiding, using Baruch to deliver his messages of doom. Yet the leaders refused to repent, and the kingdom continued to disintegrate. Finally in 586 B.C. the Babylonians under Nebuchadnezzar destroyed the city of Jerusalem and the temple. The remaining citizens of Judah fled to Egypt for safety, and Jeremiah went with them.

The book of Jeremiah offers profound prophetic insight into the conditions of the kingdom of Judah during its final forty years of existence. More than half of the book is concerned with prophetic messages, some of which were fulfilled in Jeremiah's lifetime. Other messages deal with prophecies about Judah's future, including the duration of the Babylonian captivity and its relation to Judah's failure to observe the Sabbath of the land (see 25:11; 2Ch 36:21).

1 The words of Jeremiah son of Hilkiah,ª one of the priests at Anathothª in the territory of Benjamin. ²The word of the LORD came ᵇ to him in the thirteenth year of the reign of Josiah ᶜ son of Amon king of Judah, ³and through the reign of Jehoiakim ᵈ son of Josiah king of Judah, down to the fifth month of the eleventh year of Zedekiah ᵉ son of Josiah king of Judah, when the people of Jerusalem went into exile.ᶠ

The Call of Jeremiah

⁴The word of the LORD came to me, saying,

⁵"Before I formed you in the womb ᵍ I
    knew ᵃʰ you,
before you were born ⁱ I set you
    apart;ʲ
I appointed you as a prophet to the
    nations." ᵏ

⁶"Ah, Sovereign LORD," I said, "I do not know how to speak;ˡ I am only a child." ᵐ ⁷But the LORD said to me, "Do not say, 'I am only a child.' You must go to everyone I send you to and say whatever I command you. ⁸Do not be afraid ⁿ of them, for I am with you ᵒ and will rescue ᵖ you," declares the LORD. ᑫ

⁹Then the LORD reached out his hand and touched ʳ my mouth and said to me, "Now, I have put my words in your mouth.ˢ ¹⁰See, today I appoint you over nations ᵗ and kingdoms to uproot ᵘ and tear down, to destroy and overthrow, to build and to plant." ᵛ

¹¹The word of the LORD came to me: "What do you see, Jeremiah?" ʷ

"I see the branch of an almond tree," I replied.

¹²The LORD said to me, "You have seen correctly, for I am watching ᵇˣ to see that my word is fulfilled."

¹³The word of the LORD came to me again: "What do you see?" ʸ

"I see a boiling pot, tilting away from the north," I answered.

¹⁴The LORD said to me, "From the north ᶻ disaster will be poured out on all who live in the land. ¹⁵I am about to summon all the peoples of the northern kingdoms," declares the LORD.

"Their kings will come and set up
    their thrones
in the entrance of the gates of
    Jerusalem;
they will come against all her
    surrounding walls
and against all the towns of Judah.ª
¹⁶I will pronounce my judgments ᵇ on my
    people

1:1 ª S Jos 21:18
1:2 ᵇ Eze 1:3;
    Hos 1:1; Joel 1:1
    ᶜ S 2Ki 22:1
1:3 ᵈ S 2Ki 23:34
    ᵉ S 2Ki 24:17
    ᶠ Ezr 5:12; Jer 52:15
1:5 ᵍ Ps 139:13
    ʰ Ps 139:16
    ⁱ Isa 49:1
    ʲ Jn 10:36 ᵏ ver 10;
    Jer 25:15-26
1:6 ˡ S Ex 3:11;
    S 6:12 ᵐ 1Ki 3:7
1:8 ⁿ S Ge 15:1;
    S Jos 8:1
    ᵒ S Ge 26:3;
    S Jos 1:5; Jer 15:20
    ᵖ ver 19; Jer 15:21;
    26:24; 36:26;
    42:11 ᑫ Jer 20:11
1:9 ʳ S Isa 6:7
    ˢ S Ex 4:12
1:10 ᵗ Jer 25:17;
    46:1 ᵘ Jer 12:17
    ᵛ Jer 18:7-10; 24:6;
    31:4,28
1:11 ʷ Jer 24:3;
    Am 7:8
1:12 ˣ S Job 29:2;
    Jer 44:27
1:13 ʸ Jer 24:3;
    Zec 4:2; 5:2
1:14 ᶻ S Isa 14:31
1:15 ª Jer 4:16;
    9:11; 10:22
1:16 ᵇ Jer 4:12

ʲ Isa 48:14–15 ◀ ▶ Jer 1:18–19

ª 5 Or *chose* ᵇ 12 The Hebrew for *watching* sounds like the Hebrew for *almond tree*.

JEREMIAH 1:17

because of their wickedness in
forsaking me,
in burning incense to other gods
and in worshiping what their hands
have made.

T ¹⁷"Get yourself ready! Stand up and say to them whatever I command you. Do not be terrified by them, or I will

J terrify you before them. ¹⁸Today I have made you a fortified city, an iron pillar and a bronze wall to stand against the whole land—against the kings of Judah, its officials, its priests and the people of

V the land. ¹⁹They will fight against you but will not overcome you, for I am with you and will rescue you," declares the LORD.

Israel Forsakes God

2 The word of the LORD came to me: ²"Go and proclaim in the hearing of Jerusalem:

" 'I remember the devotion of your youth,
how as a bride you loved me
and followed me through the desert,
through a land not sown.
³Israel was holy to the LORD,
the firstfruits of his harvest;
all who devoured her were held guilty,
and disaster overtook them,' "
declares the LORD.

⁴Hear the word of the LORD, O house of Jacob,
all you clans of the house of Israel.

⁵This is what the LORD says:

"What fault did your fathers find in me,
that they strayed so far from me?
They followed worthless idols
and became worthless themselves.
⁶They did not ask, 'Where is the LORD,
who brought us up out of Egypt
and led us through the barren wilderness,
through a land of deserts and rifts,

1:16 ᶜS Ge 6:5; Jer 44:5 ᵈJer 2:13; 17:13 ᵉS Ex 20:3; Jer 7:9; 19:4; 44:3 ᶠS Nu 25:3 ᵍPs 115:4-8; S 135:15
1:17 ʰver 7; Jer 7:27; 26:2,15; 42:4 ⁱS Dt 31:6; S 2Ki 1:15
1:18 ʲS Isa 50:7
1:19 ᵏS Ps 129:2 ˡS Ge 26:3; Isa 43:2; Jer 20:11 ᵐS ver 8; S Pr 20:22; Ac 26:17
2:1 ⁿIsa 38:4; Eze 1:3; Mic 1:1
2:2 ᵒPs 71:17; Isa 54:4; Jer 3:4; Eze 16:8-14,60; Hos 2:15; 11:1; Rev 2:4
ᵖS Ex 13:21; S Dt 1:19
2:3 ᑫS Dt 7:6 ʳS Ex 19:6; S Dt 7:6 ˢLev 23:9-14; Jas 1:18; Rev 14:4 ᵗIsa 41:11; Jer 10:25; 30:16 ᵘJer 50:7
2:5 ᵛS Dt 32:21; S 1Sa 12:21; Ps 31:6 ʷ2Ki 17:15
2:6 ˣS Ex 6:6; Hos 13:4 ʸS Dt 1:19 ᶻS Dt 32:10 ᵃJer 51:43
2:7 ᵇS Nu 13:27; Dt 8:7-9; 11:10-12 ᶜPs 106:34-39; Jer 3:9; 7:30; 16:18; Eze 11:21; 36:17
2:8 ᵈS Isa 2:12; Jer 4:22 ᵉJer 3:15; 23:1; 25:34; 50:6 ᶠS 1Ki 18:22 ᵍver 25; S Isa 40:19; S 56:10; Jer 5:19; 9:14; 16:19; 22:9
2:9 ʰJer 25:31; Hos 4:1; Mic 6:2
2:10 ⁱS Ge 10:4 ʲS Ge 25:13
2:11 ᵏS Isa 37:19; Jer 16:20; Gal 4:8 ˡS Isa 4:21; Ro 1:23
2:13 ᵐS Dt 31:16; S Isa 65:11 ⁿS Isa 12:3; Jn 4:14
2:14 ᵒEx 4:22; Jer 31:9
2:15 ᵖJer 4:7; 50:17 ᑫS Isa 1:7 ʳS 2Ki 25:9 ˢS Lev 26:43

a land of drought and darkness,
a land where no one travels and no one lives?'
⁷I brought you into a fertile land
to eat its fruit and rich produce.
But you came and defiled my land
and made my inheritance detestable.
⁸The priests did not ask,
'Where is the LORD?'
Those who deal with the law did not know me;
the leaders rebelled against me.
The prophets prophesied by Baal,
following worthless idols.

⁹"Therefore I bring charges against you again,"
declares the LORD.
"And I will bring charges against your children's children.
¹⁰Cross over to the coasts of Kittim and look,
send to Kedar and observe closely;
see if there has ever been anything like this:
¹¹Has a nation ever changed its gods?
(Yet they are not gods at all.)
But my people have exchanged their Glory
for worthless idols.
¹²Be appalled at this, O heavens,
and shudder with great horror,"
declares the LORD.

¹³"My people have committed two sins: **G**
They have forsaken me, **O**
the spring of living water,
and have dug their own cisterns,
broken cisterns that cannot hold water.

¹⁴Is Israel a servant, a slave by birth? **R**
Why then has he become plunder?
¹⁵Lions have roared;
they have growled at him.
They have laid waste his land;
his towns are burned and deserted.

G Isa 64:6 ◀▶ Jer 2:22
O Isa 50:10-11 ◀▶ Jer 2:22
R Isa 64:12 ◀▶ Jer 3:8

ᶜ6 Or *and the shadow of death* ᵈ10 That is, Cyprus and western coastlands ᵉ10 The home of Bedouin tribes in the Syro-Arabian desert ᶠ11 Masoretic Text; an ancient Hebrew scribal tradition *my*

T Isa 44:8 ◀▶ Joel 2:26
J Jer 1:13-16 ◀▶ Jer 9:26
V Isa 54:17 ◀▶ Jer 15:20-21

2:14–17 Jeremiah prophesied that Judah's approaching judgment was the direct result of their apostasy; they had earned it by "forsaking the LORD" (2:17).

¹⁶Also, the men of Memphis⁸ᵗ and
    Tahpanhes ͧ
  have shaved the crown of your
    head.ʰ
¹⁷Have you not brought this on
    yourselvesᵛ
  by forsakingʷ the LORD your God
    when he led you in the way?
¹⁸Now why go to Egyptˣ
  to drink water from the Shihorⁱ?ʸ
And why go to Assyriaᶻ
  to drink water from the River?ᵃ

¹⁹Your wickedness will punish you;
  your backslidingᵇ will rebukeᶜ you.
Consider then and realize
  how evil and bitterᵈ it is for you
when you forsakeᵉ the LORD your God
  and have no aweᶠ of me,"
                    declares the Lord,
                    the LORD Almighty.

²⁰"Long ago you broke off your yoke⁸
    and tore off your bonds;ʰ
  you said, 'I will not serve you!'ⁱ
Indeed, on every high hillʲ
    and under every spreading treeᵏ
  you lay down as a prostitute.ˡ
²¹I had plantedᵐ you like a choice vineⁿ
    of sound and reliable stock.
  How then did you turn against me
    into a corrupt,ᵒ wild vine?
²²Although you washᵖ yourself with
    soda⁹
  and use an abundance of soap,
  the stain of your guilt is still before
    me,"
        declares the Sovereign LORD.ʳ
²³"How can you say, 'I am not defiled;ˢ
    I have not run after the Baals'?ᵗ
  See how you behaved in the valley;ᵘ
    consider what you have done.
  You are a swift she-camel
    runningᵛ here and there,
²⁴a wild donkeyʷ accustomed to the
    desert,ˣ
  sniffing the wind in her craving—
    in her heat who can restrain her?
  Any males that pursue her need not
    tire themselves;
  at mating time they will find her.
²⁵Do not run until your feet are bare
    and your throat is dry.
  But you said, 'It's no use!'ʸ

C Isa 65:2 ◀ ▶ Jer 2:32
S Isa 60:21 ◀ ▶ Jer 3:8
G Jer 2:13 ◀ ▶ Jer 2:28
O Jer 2:13 ◀ ▶ Jer 13:23

2:16 ᵗS Isa 19:13
  ᵘJer 43:7-9
2:17 ᵛJer 4:18
  ʷS Isa 1:28;
  Jer 17:13; 19:4
2:18 ˣS Isa 30:2
  ʸS Jos 13:3
  ᶻS 2Ki 16:7;
  Hos 5:13; 7:11; 8:9
  ᵃS Isa 7:20
2:19 ᵇJer 3:11,22;
  7:24; 11:10; 14:7;
  Hos 14:4 ᶜIsa 3:9;
  59:12; Hos 5:5
  ᵈS Job 20:14;
  Am 8:10 ᵉJer 19:4
  ᶠS Ps 36:1
2:20 ⁸S Lev 26:13
  ʰS Ps 2:3; Jer 5:5
  ⁱS Job 21:14
  ʲS Isa 57:7; Jer 3:23;
  17:2 ᵏS Dt 12:2
  ˡS Isa 1:21;
  Eze 16:15
2:21 ᵐS Ex 15:17
  ⁿS Ps 80:8
  ᵒS Isa 5:4
2:22 ᵖS Ps 51:2;
  La 1:8,17
  ⁹S Job 9:30
  ʳJer 17:1
2:23 ˢS Pr 30:12
  ᵗver 25; Jer 9:14;
  23:27
  ᵘS 2Ki 23:10;
  Jer 7:31; 19:2;
  31:40 ᵛver 33;
  Jer 31:22
2:24 ʷS Ge 16:12;
  Jer 14:6 ˣS Job 39:6
2:25 ʸS Isa 57:10
  ᶻDt 32:16; Jer 3:13;
  14:10 ᵃS ver 8, S 23
2:26 ᵇJer 48:27;
  La 1:7; Eze 16:54;
  36:4 ᶜEze 22:26
  ᵈJer 32:32; 44:17,
  21
2:27 ᵉJer 10:8
  ᶠJer 3:9
  ⁸S 1Ki 14:9;
  S 2Ch 29:6;
  Ps 14:3; Eze 8:16
  ʰJer 18:17; 32:33;
  Eze 7:22
  ⁱJdg 10:10;
  Isa 26:16
  ʲIsa 37:20;
  Hos 5:15
2:28 ᵏS Isa 45:20
  ˡS Dt 32:37;
  S Isa 40:19
  ᵐS 2Ki 17:29
2:29 ⁿJer 5:1;
  6:13; Da 9:11;
  Mic 3:11; 7:2
2:30 ᵒS Lev 26:23
  ᵖS Ne 9:26;
  S Jer 11:21;
  Ac 7:52; 1Th 2:15
2:31 ⁹Isa 45:19
  ʳS Job 21:14
2:32 ˢS Dt 32:18;
  S Isa 57:11
2:33 ᵗS ver 23
2:34 ᵘS 2Ki 21:16;
  S Pr 6:17
  ᵛS Ex 22:2

  I love foreign gods,ᶻ
    and I must go after them.'ᵃ
²⁶"As a thief is disgracedᵇ when he is
    caught,
  so the house of Israel is disgraced—
  they, their kings and their officials,
    their priestsᶜ and their prophets.ᵈ
²⁷They say to wood,ᵉ 'You are my
    father,'
  and to stone,ᶠ 'You gave me birth.'
They have turned their backs⁸ to me
    and not their faces;ʰ
  yet when they are in trouble,ⁱ they
    say,
  'Come and saveʲ us!'
²⁸Where then are the godsᵏ you made
    for yourselves?
Let them come if they can save you
    when you are in trouble!ˡ
For you have as many gods
    as you have towns,ᵐ O Judah.

²⁹"Why do you bring charges against
    me?
  You have allⁿ rebelled against me,"
                  declares the LORD.
³⁰"In vain I punished your people;
    they did not respond to correction.ᵒ
  Your sword has devoured your
    prophetsᵖ
    like a ravening lion.

³¹"You of this generation, consider the
word of the LORD:

"Have I been a desert to Israel
    or a land of great darkness?⁹
Why do my people say, 'We are free to
    roam;
  we will come to you no more'?ʳ
³²Does a maiden forget her jewelry,
    a bride her wedding ornaments?
Yet my people have forgottenˢ me,
    days without number.
³³How skilled you are at pursuingᵗ love!
  Even the worst of women can learn
    from your ways.
³⁴On your clothes men find
  the lifebloodᵘ of the innocent poor,
    though you did not catch them
      breaking in.ᵛ
  Yet in spite of all this

N Isa 66:4 ◀ ▶ Jer 3:5
G Jer 2:22 ◀ ▶ Jer 2:35
C Jer 2:19 ◀ ▶ Jer 4:22

⁸16 Hebrew Noph   ʰ16 Or have cracked your skull   ⁱ18 That is, a
branch of the Nile   ʲ18 That is, the Euphrates

JEREMIAH 2:35

35 you say, 'I am innocent;
   he is not angry with me.'
But I will pass judgment on you
   because you say, 'I have not
      sinned.'
36 Why do you go about so much,
      changing your ways?
   You will be disappointed by Egypt
      as you were by Assyria.
37 You will also leave that place
      with your hands on your head,
   for the LORD has rejected those you
      trust;
   you will not be helped by them.

3 "If a man divorces his wife
   and she leaves him and marries
      another man,
   should he return to her again?
   Would not the land be completely
      defiled?
   But you have lived as a prostitute with
      many lovers—
   would you now return to me?"
                        declares the LORD.

2 "Look up to the barren heights and
      see.
   Is there any place where you have
      not been ravished?
   By the roadside you sat waiting for
      lovers,
   sat like a nomad in the desert.
   You have defiled the land
      with your prostitution and
         wickedness.
3 Therefore the showers have been
      withheld,
   and no spring rains have fallen.
   Yet you have the brazen look of a
      prostitute;
   you refuse to blush with shame.
4 Have you not just called to me:
   'My Father, my friend from my
      youth,
5 will you always be angry?
   Will your wrath continue forever?'

This is how you talk,
   but you do all the evil you can."

Unfaithful Israel

6 During the reign of King Josiah, the LORD said to me, "Have you seen what faithless Israel has done? She has gone up on every high hill and under every spreading tree and has committed adultery there. 7 I thought that after she had done all this she would return to me but she did not, and her unfaithful sister Judah saw it. 8 I gave faithless Israel her certificate of divorce and sent her away because of all her adulteries. Yet I saw that her unfaithful sister Judah had no fear; she also went out and committed adultery. 9 Because Israel's immorality mattered so little to her, she defiled the land and committed adultery with stone and wood. 10 In spite of all this, her unfaithful sister Judah did not return to me with all her heart, but only in pretense," declares the LORD.

11 The LORD said to me, "Faithless Israel is more righteous than unfaithful Judah. 12 Go, proclaim this message toward the north:

" 'Return, faithless Israel,' declares
      the LORD,
   'I will frown on you no longer,
   for I am merciful,' declares the LORD,
   'I will not be angry forever.
13 Only acknowledge your guilt—
   you have rebelled against the LORD
      your God,
   you have scattered your favors to
      foreign gods
   under every spreading tree,
   and have not obeyed me,' "
                        declares the LORD.

14 "Return, faithless people," declares

3:8 God condemned Judah's apostasy and spiritual adultery just as he condemned Israel's apostasy when he sent her into captivity to Assyria.
3:14–15 Jeremiah predicted that God would re-

the LORD, "for I am your husband. I will choose you—one from a town and two from a clan—and bring you to Zion. ¹⁵Then I will give you shepherds after my own heart, who will lead you with knowledge and understanding. ¹⁶In those days, when your numbers have increased greatly in the land," declares the LORD, "men will no longer say, 'The ark of the covenant of the LORD.' It will never enter their minds or be remembered; it will not be missed, nor will another one be made. ¹⁷At that time they will call Jerusalem The Throne of the LORD, and all nations will gather in Jerusalem to honor the name of the LORD. No longer will they follow the stubbornness of their evil hearts. ¹⁸In those days the house of Judah will join the house of Israel, and together they will come from a northern land to the land I gave your forefathers as an inheritance.

¹⁹"I myself said,

" 'How gladly would I treat you like sons
and give you a desirable land,
the most beautiful inheritance of any nation.'
I thought you would call me 'Father'
and not turn away from following me.

²⁰But like a woman unfaithful to her husband,
so you have been unfaithful to me, O house of Israel,"
declares the LORD.

²¹A cry is heard on the barren heights,

the weeping and pleading of the people of Israel,
because they have perverted their ways
and have forgotten the LORD their God.

²²"Return, faithless people;
I will cure you of backsliding."

"Yes, we will come to you,
for you are the LORD our God.

²³Surely the idolatrous commotion on the hills
and mountains is a deception;
surely in the LORD our God
is the salvation of Israel.

²⁴From our youth shameful gods have consumed
the fruits of our fathers' labor—
their flocks and herds,
their sons and daughters.

²⁵Let us lie down in our shame,
and let our disgrace cover us.
We have sinned against the LORD our God,
both we and our fathers;
from our youth till this day
we have not obeyed the LORD our God."

4 "If you will return, O Israel,
return to me,"
declares the LORD.
"If you put your detestable idols out of my sight
and no longer go astray,

3:14–17 store a remnant of his people and provide "shepherds after my own heart" (3:15). This prophecy was initially fulfilled when the exiles returned to their land to rebuild the temple under the godly leadership of Nehemiah and Ezra. In the last days, when the Messiah rules in the millennial kingdom, this prophecy will find its lasting fulfillment (see Rev 7; 14).

3:16–17 In this millennial prophecy God declared that after the return of all the Jews to the promised land people would no longer talk about, think about, remember or visit the ark of the covenant. Because the ark symbolized God's presence with his people, when the Messiah comes and rules on his throne this symbolic token will no longer be needed. Jeremiah also said that Jerusalem would be known as "the throne of the LORD; and all the nations shall be gathered unto it" (3:17). This places the fulfillment of this prophecy during the Millennium (see Zec 14:16–21).

Jeremiah's reference to the ark of the covenant in this passage raises some questions since the ark has been missing from the temple in Jerusalem since the reign of King Solomon. For Jeremiah to write these words about the ark may suggest that the ark may be found in the last days and play a role in the events of the end times.

3:18–19 Jeremiah confirmed the prophecies given by Isaiah and Ezekiel that the exiles from Israel will be joined to the exiles of Judah and returned to the promised land (see Isa 11:11–12; Eze 37:15–24).

²and if in a truthful, just and righteous way
   you swear,ᶜ 'As surely as the LORD lives,'ᵈ
then the nations will be blessedᵉ by him
   and in him they will glory.ᶠ"

³This is what the LORD says to the men of Judah and to Jerusalem:

"Break up your unplowed groundᵍ
   and do not sow among thorns.ʰ
⁴Circumcise yourselves to the LORD,
   circumcise your hearts,ⁱ
you men of Judah and people of Jerusalem,
or my wrathʲ will break out and burn like fireᵏ
because of the evilˡ you have done—
burn with no one to quenchᵐ it.

Disaster From the North

⁵"Announce in Judah and proclaimⁿ in Jerusalem and say:
   'Sound the trumpetᵒ throughout the land!'
Cry aloud and say:
   'Gather together!
Let us flee to the fortified cities!'ᵖ
⁶Raise the signalᵠ to go to Zion!
   Flee for safety without delay!
For I am bringing disasterʳ from the north,ˢ
   even terrible destruction."

⁷A lionᵗ has come out of his lair;ᵘ
   a destroyerᵛ of nations has set out.
He has left his place
   to lay wasteʷ your land.
Your towns will lie in ruinsˣ
   without inhabitant.
⁸So put on sackcloth,ʸ
   lamentᶻ and wail,
for the fierce angerᵃ of the LORD
   has not turned away from us.

⁹"In that day," declares the LORD,
"the king and the officials will lose heart,ᵇ
   the priests will be horrified,
   and the prophets will be appalled."ᶜ

¹⁰Then I said, "Ah, Sovereign LORD, how completely you have deceivedᵈ this

people and Jerusalem by saying, 'You will have peace,'ᵉ when the sword is at our throats."

¹¹At that time this people and Jerusalem will be told, "A scorching windᶠ from the barren heights in the desert blows toward my people, but not to winnow or cleanse; ¹²a windᵍ too strong for that comes from me.ʰ Now I pronounce my judgmentsʰ against them."

¹³Look! He advances like the clouds,ⁱ
   his chariotsʲ come like a whirlwind,ᵏ
his horsesˡ are swifter than eagles.ᵐ
Woe to us! We are ruined!ⁿ

¹⁴O Jerusalem, washᵒ the evil from your heart and be saved.ᵖ
   How longᵠ will you harbor wicked thoughts?

¹⁵A voice is announcing from Dan,ʳ
   proclaiming disaster from the hills of Ephraim.ˢ
¹⁶"Tell this to the nations,
   proclaim it to Jerusalem:
'A besieging army is coming from a distant land,ᵗ
   raising a war cryᵘ against the cities of Judah.ᵛ
¹⁷They surroundʷ her like men guarding a field,
   because she has rebelledˣ against me,' "
         declares the LORD.

¹⁸"Your own conduct and actionsʸ
   have brought this upon you.ᶻ
This is your punishment.
How bitterᵃ it is!
How it pierces to the heart!"

¹⁹Oh, my anguish, my anguish!ᵇ
   I writhe in pain.ᶜ
Oh, the agony of my heart!
   My heart poundsᵈ within me,
   I cannot keep silent.ᵉ
For I have heard the sound of the trumpet;ᶠ
   I have heard the battle cry.ᵍ

R Jer 4:1 ◄► Jer 7:3
S Jer 3:8 ◄► Jer 7:9-11

M Jer 3:3 ◄► Jer 5:3
H Isa 66:24 ◄► Jer 5:9

²⁰Disaster follows disaster;
 the whole land lies in ruins.
In an instant my tents are destroyed,
 my shelter in a moment.
²¹How long must I see the battle
  standard
 and hear the sound of the trumpet?

²²"My people are fools;
 they do not know me.
They are senseless children;
 they have no understanding.
They are skilled in doing evil;
 they know not how to do good."

²³I looked at the earth,
 and it was formless and empty;
and at the heavens,
 and their light was gone.
²⁴I looked at the mountains,
 and they were quaking;
all the hills were swaying.
²⁵I looked, and there were no people;
 every bird in the sky had flown
 away.
²⁶I looked, and the fruitful land was a
  desert;
 all its towns lay in ruins
 before the LORD, before his fierce
 anger.

²⁷This is what the LORD says:

"The whole land will be ruined,
 though I will not destroy it
 completely.
²⁸Therefore the earth will mourn
 and the heavens above grow dark,
because I have spoken and will not
 relent,
I have decided and will not turn
 back."

²⁹At the sound of horsemen and archers
 every town takes to flight.
Some go into the thickets;
 some climb up among the rocks.
All the towns are deserted;
 no one lives in them.

R Jer 3:8 ◀ ▶ Jer 4:23
C Jer 2:32 ◀ ▶ Jer 5:4
R Jer 4:20 ◀ ▶ Jer 4:26–28
R Jer 4:23 ◀ ▶ Jer 5:3

³⁰What are you doing, O devastated
  one?
Why dress yourself in scarlet
 and put on jewels of gold?
Why shade your eyes with paint?
 You adorn yourself in vain.
Your lovers despise you;
 they seek your life.

³¹I hear a cry as of a woman in labor,
 a groan as of one bearing her first
 child—
 the cry of the Daughter of Zion
 gasping for breath,
 stretching out her hands and
 saying,
"Alas! I am fainting;
 my life is given over to murderers."

Not One Is Upright

5 "Go up and down the streets of
 Jerusalem,
 look around and consider,
 search through her squares.
If you can find but one person
 who deals honestly and seeks the
 truth,
 I will forgive this city.
²Although they say, 'As surely as the
 LORD lives,'
 still they are swearing falsely."

³O LORD, do not your eyes look for
  truth?
You struck them, but they felt no
 pain;
 you crushed them, but they refused
 correction.
They made their faces harder than
 stone
 and refused to repent.
⁴I thought, "These are only the poor;
 they are foolish,
for they do not know the way of the
 LORD,
 the requirements of their God.

R Jer 4:26–28 ◀ ▶ Jer 5:9–10
M Jer 4:3–4 ◀ ▶ Jer 6:15
C Jer 4:22 ◀ ▶ Jer 5:21–25

4:20 Jeremiah predicted the certainty of Judah's destruction.
4:26–28 God declared his resolve to punish his people for their sinful rebellion. Though he would make the land desolate, his punishment would not totally destroy the land.
5:3 Jeremiah noted the lack of repentance among the people in their refusal of God's "correction."

JEREMIAH 5:5

⁵So I will go to the leaders
    and speak to them;
surely they know the way of the LORD,
    the requirements of their God."
But with one accord they too had
    broken off the yoke
    and torn off the bonds.
⁶Therefore a lion from the forest will
    attack them,
    a wolf from the desert will ravage
    them,
a leopard will lie in wait near their
    towns
to tear to pieces any who venture
    out,
for their rebellion is great
    and their backslidings many.

⁷"Why should I forgive you?
    Your children have forsaken me
    and sworn by gods that are not
    gods.
I supplied all their needs,
    yet they committed adultery
    and thronged to the houses of
    prostitutes.
⁸They are well-fed, lusty stallions,
    each neighing for another man's
    wife.
⁹Should I not punish them for this?"
    declares the LORD.
"Should I not avenge myself
    on such a nation as this?

¹⁰"Go through her vineyards and ravage
    them,
    but do not destroy them
    completely.
Strip off her branches,
    for these people do not belong to the
    LORD.
¹¹The house of Israel and the house of
    Judah
have been utterly unfaithful to
    me,"
               declares the LORD.

¹²They have lied about the LORD;
    they said, "He will do nothing!
No harm will come to us;

R *Jer 5:3* ◀ ▶ *Jer 5:19*
H *Jer 4:4* ◀ ▶ *Jer 5:29*

5:5 ᵍ Mic 3:1,9
ʰ S Jer 2:20
5:6 ⁱ S Ps 17:12
ʲ S Lev 26:22
ᵏ Hos 13:7
ˡ Jer 14:7; 30:14
5:7 ᵐ S Jos 23:7
ⁿ Dt 32:21;
Jer 2:11; 16:20;
Gal 4:8 ᵒ S Nu 25:1
ᵖ Jer 13:27
5:8 ᵠ Jer 29:23;
Eze 22:11; 33:26
5:9 ʳ ver 29; Jer 9:9
ˢ S Isa 57:6
5:10 ᵗ S Jer 4:27;
Am 9:8
5:11 ᵘ S 1Ki 19:10;
S Ps 73:27;
S Isa 24:16
5:12 ᵛ Isa 28:15
ʷ Jer 23:17
ˣ Jer 14:13; 27:8
5:13 ʸ Jer 14:15
ᶻ S 2Ch 36:16;
S Job 6:26
5:14 ᵃ Hos 6:5
ᵇ S Ps 39:3;
Jer 23:29
ᶜ S Isa 1:31
5:15 ᵈ S Dt 28:49;
S 2Ki 24:2
ᵉ S Ge 11:7;
S Isa 28:11
5:16 ᶠ S Job 39:23
5:17 ᵍ S Isa 1:7;
Jer 8:16; 30:16
ʰ Lev 26:16
ⁱ Jer 50:7,17
ʲ Dt 28:32
ᵏ Dt 28:31
ˡ S Nu 16:14;
Jer 8:13; Hos 2:12
ᵐ S Lev 26:25
ⁿ S Jos 10:20
ᵒ Dt 28:33
5:18 ᵖ S Jer 4:27
5:19 ᵠ S Dt 4:28;
S 1Ki 9:9 ʳ Jer 2:8;
15:14; 16:13; 17:4
ˢ Dt 28:48
5:20 ᵗ S Jer 4:5
5:21 ᵘ ver 4;
S Dt 32:6;
S Jer 4:22; Hab 2:18
ᵛ Isa 6:10; Eze 12:2
ʷ S Dt 29:4;
S Isa 42:20;
S Mt 13:15;
Mk 8:18

we will never see sword or famine.
¹³The prophets are but wind
    and the word is not in them;
so let what they say be done to
    them."

¹⁴Therefore this is what the LORD God Almighty says:

"Because the people have spoken
    these words,
I will make my words in your
    mouth a fire
and these people the wood it
    consumes.
¹⁵O house of Israel," declares the LORD,
"I am bringing a distant nation
    against you—
an ancient and enduring nation,
    a people whose language you do
    not know,
    whose speech you do not
    understand.
¹⁶Their quivers are like an open grave;
    all of them are mighty warriors.
¹⁷They will devour your harvests and
    food,
    devour your sons and daughters;
they will devour your flocks and
    herds,
    devour your vines and fig trees.
With the sword they will destroy
    the fortified cities in which you
    trust.

¹⁸"Yet even in those days," declares the LORD, "I will not destroy you completely. ¹⁹And when the people ask, 'Why has the LORD our God done all this to us?' you will tell them, 'As you have forsaken me and served foreign gods in your own land, so now you will serve foreigners in a land not your own.'

²⁰"Announce this to the house of Jacob
    and proclaim it in Judah:
²¹Hear this, you foolish and senseless
    people,
who have eyes but do not see,
who have ears but do not hear:

R *Jer 5:9–10* ◀ ▶ *Jer 5:29*
C *Jer 5:4* ◀ ▶ *Jer 6:10*
N *Jer 3:5* ◀ ▶ *Jer 6:15–17*

5:9–10 Once again God declared his intention to deliver his vengeance upon unrepentant Judah.
5:19 As the judgments fall on the nation, people will ask Jeremiah for the reason for the punishments. God provided Jeremiah with a clear answer: because the people have rejected God and "served foreign gods" God would exile them as slaves to a land of strangers.

²²Should you not fear me?" declares the LORD.
  "Should you not tremble in my presence?
  I made the sand a boundary for the sea,
    an everlasting barrier it cannot cross.
  The waves may roll, but they cannot prevail;
    they may roar, but they cannot cross it.
²³But these people have stubborn and rebellious hearts;
  they have turned aside and gone away.
²⁴They do not say to themselves,
  'Let us fear the LORD our God,
  who gives autumn and spring rains in season,
  who assures us of the regular weeks of harvest.'
²⁵Your wrongdoings have kept these away;
  your sins have deprived you of good.

²⁶"Among my people are wicked men
  who lie in wait like men who snare birds
  and like those who set traps to catch men.
²⁷Like cages full of birds,
  their houses are full of deceit;
  they have become rich and powerful
²⁸ and have grown fat and sleek.
  Their evil deeds have no limit;
  they do not plead the case of the fatherless to win it,
  they do not defend the rights of the poor.
²⁹Should I not punish them for this?" declares the LORD.
  "Should I not avenge myself
  on such a nation as this?

³⁰"A horrible and shocking thing has happened in the land:
³¹The prophets prophesy lies,
  the priests rule by their own authority,

R *Jer 5:19* ◀ ▶ *Jer 6:9*
H *Jer 5:9* ◀ ▶ *Jer 6:19*

and my people love it this way.
  But what will you do in the end?

Jerusalem Under Siege

6 "Flee for safety, people of Benjamin!
  Flee from Jerusalem!
  Sound the trumpet in Tekoa!
  Raise the signal over Beth Hakkerem!
  For disaster looms out of the north,
    even terrible destruction.
²I will destroy the Daughter of Zion,
  so beautiful and delicate.
³Shepherds with their flocks will come against her;
  they will pitch their tents around her,
  each tending his own portion."

⁴"Prepare for battle against her!
  Arise, let us attack at noon!
  But, alas, the daylight is fading,
    and the shadows of evening grow long.
⁵So arise, let us attack at night
  and destroy her fortresses!"

⁶This is what the LORD Almighty says:

"Cut down the trees
  and build siege ramps against Jerusalem.
This city must be punished;
  it is filled with oppression.
⁷As a well pours out its water,
  so she pours out her wickedness.
Violence and destruction resound in her;
  her sickness and wounds are ever before me.
⁸Take warning, O Jerusalem,
  or I will turn away from you
  and make your land desolate
  so no one can live in it."

⁹This is what the LORD Almighty says:

"Let them glean the remnant of Israel
  as thoroughly as a vine;
pass your hand over the branches again,
  like one gathering grapes."

R *Jer 5:29* ◀ ▶ *Jer 6:11–12*

5:29 God notes the justice of his decision to judge this rebellious nation.

¹⁰To whom can I speak and give
    warning?
  Who will listen to me?
  Their ears are closed
    so they cannot hear.
  The word of the LORD is offensive to
    them;
  they find no pleasure in it.
¹¹But I am full of the wrath of the LORD,
  and I cannot hold it in.

  "Pour it out on the children in the
    street
  and on the young men gathered
    together;
  both husband and wife will be caught
    in it,
  and the old, those weighed down
    with years.
¹²Their houses will be turned over to
    others,
  together with their fields and their
    wives,
  when I stretch out my hand
    against those who live in the land,"
                    declares the LORD.
¹³"From the least to the greatest,
    all are greedy for gain;
  prophets and priests alike,
    all practice deceit.
¹⁴They dress the wound of my people
    as though it were not serious.
  'Peace, peace,' they say,
    when there is no peace.
¹⁵Are they ashamed of their loathsome
    conduct?
  No, they have no shame at all;
    they do not even know how to
    blush.
  So they will fall among the fallen;
    they will be brought down when I
    punish them,"
                    says the LORD.
¹⁶This is what the LORD says:

  "Stand at the crossroads and look;
    ask for the ancient paths,
  ask where the good way is, and walk
    in it,
  and you will find rest for your
    souls.
  But you said, 'We will not walk in
    it.'
¹⁷I appointed watchmen over you and
    said,
  'Listen to the sound of the
    trumpet!'
  But you said, 'We will not listen.'
¹⁸Therefore hear, O nations;
  observe, O witnesses,
  what will happen to them.
¹⁹Hear, O earth:
  I am bringing disaster on this people,
    the fruit of their schemes,
  because they have not listened to my
    words
  and have rejected my law.
²⁰What do I care about incense from
    Sheba
  or sweet calamus from a distant
    land?
  Your burnt offerings are not
    acceptable;
  your sacrifices do not please me."

²¹Therefore this is what the LORD says:

  "I will put obstacles before this people.
  Fathers and sons alike will stumble
    over them;
  neighbors and friends will perish."

²²This is what the LORD says:

  "Look, an army is coming
    from the land of the north;
  a great nation is being stirred up
    from the ends of the earth.
²³They are armed with bow and spear;
  they are cruel and show no mercy.
  They sound like the roaring sea
    as they ride on their horses;
  they come like men in battle formation
    to attack you, O Daughter of Zion."

²⁴We have heard reports about them,

C *Jer 5:21–25* ◀ ▶ *Jer 6:15*
R *Jer 6:9* ◀ ▶ *Jer 6:19*
C *Jer 6:10* ◀ ▶ *Jer 6:17*
M *Jer 5:3* ◀ ▶ *Jer 8:12*
N *Jer 5:21–25* ◀ ▶ *Jer 6:19*

C *Jer 6:15* ◀ ▶ *Jer 6:28*
R *Jer 6:11–12* ◀ ▶ *Jer 6:30*
H *Jer 5:29* ◀ ▶ *Jer 8:20*
N *Jer 6:15–17* ◀ ▶ *Jer 8:9*

m 10 Hebrew *uncircumcised*

6:11–12, 19 Jeremiah warns of God's coming judgment and explains that the reason for this judgment was Judah's refusal to obey God's Word.

and our hands hang limp.^{y}
Anguish^z has gripped us,
    pain like that of a woman in labor.^{a}
^{25}Do not go out to the fields
    or walk on the roads,
for the enemy has a sword,
    and there is terror on every side.^{b}
^{26}O my people, put on sackcloth^c
    and roll in ashes;^{d}
mourn with bitter wailing^e
    as for an only son,^{f}
for suddenly the destroyer^g
    will come upon us.

^{27}"I have made you a tester^h of metals
    and my people the ore,
that you may observe
    and test their ways.
^{28}They are all hardened rebels,^{i}
    going about to slander.^{j}
They are bronze and iron;^{k}
    they all act corruptly.

^{29}The bellows blow fiercely
    to burn away the lead with fire,
but the refining^l goes on in vain;
    the wicked are not purged out.
^{30}They are called rejected silver,^{m}
    because the LORD has rejected them."^{n}

False Religion Worthless

7 This is the word that came to Jeremiah from the LORD: ^{2}"Stand^o at the gate of the LORD's house and there proclaim this message:

" 'Hear the word of the LORD, all you people of Judah who come through these gates to worship the LORD. ^{3}This is what the LORD Almighty, the God of Israel, says: Reform your ways^p and your actions, and I will let you live^q in this place. ^{4}Do not trust^r in deceptive^s words and say, "This is the temple of the LORD, the temple of the LORD, the temple of the LORD!" ^{5}If you really change^t your ways and your actions and deal with each other

C Jer 6:17 ◀▶ Jer 6:30
R Jer 6:19 ◀▶ Jer 7:14–16
C Jer 6:28 ◀▶ Jer 7:24
R Jer 4:14 ◀▶ Jer 7:5–7
R Jer 7:3 ◀▶ Jer 18:11

6:24 ^{y} Isa 13:7
^{z} S Jer 4:19
^{a} S Jer 4:31; 50:41-43
6:25 ^{b} S Job 15:21; S Ps 31:13; Jer 49:29
6:26 ^{c} S Jer 4:8
^{d} S Job 2:8; Jer 25:34; Eze 27:30; Jnh 3:6
^{e} Jer 9:1; 18:22; 20:16; 25:36
^{f} S Ge 21:16
^{g} S Ex 12:23; S Jer 4:7
6:27 ^{h} Jer 9:7; Zec 13:9
6:28 ^{i} Jer 5:23
^{j} S Lev 19:16
^{k} Eze 22:18
6:29 ^{l} Mal 3:3
6:30 ^{m} Pr 17:3; Eze 22:18
^{n} Ps 53:5; 119:119; Jer 7:29; La 5:22; Hos 9:17
7:2 ^{o} Jer 17:19
7:3 ^{p} Jer 18:11; 26:13; 35:15
^{q} ver 7
7:4 ^{r} S Job 15:31
^{s} ver 8; Jer 28:15; Mic 3:11
7:5 ^{t} ver 3; Jer 18:11; 26:13; 35:15
^{u} S Ex 22:22; S Lev 25:17;
^{S} Isa 1:17
7:6 ^{v} S Jer 5:28; Eze 22:7
^{w} S 2Ki 21:16; Jer 2:34; 19:4; 22:3
^{x} S Ex 20:3; S Dt 8:19
7:7 ^{y} S Dt 4:40
^{z} S Jos 1:6
7:8 ^{a} S Job 15:31
^{b} S ver 4
7:9 ^{c} Ex 20:15
^{d} Ex 20:13
^{e} Ex 20:14;
^{S} Nu 25:1
^{f} Ex 20:16;
S Lev 19:12;
Zec 8:17; Mal 3:5
^{g} S Isa 1:13
^{h} Jer 11:13,17; 32:29 ¦ S Ex 20:3; Hos 2:13
7:10 ^{i} S Isa 48:1
2Ki 21:4-5;
Jer 23:11; 32:34; Eze 23:38-39
^{j} Eze 33:25
7:11 ^{m} Isa 56:7
^{n} Mt 21:13*;
Mk 11:17*;
Lk 19:46*
^{o} Ge 31:50;
Jdg 11:10;
Jer 29:23; 42:5
7:12 ^{p} S Jos 18:1;
S Isa 2:32

justly,^{u} ^{6}if you do not oppress^v the alien, the fatherless or the widow and do not shed innocent blood^w in this place, and if you do not follow other gods^x to your own harm, ^{7}then I will let you live in this place, in the land^y I gave your forefathers^z for ever and ever. ^{8}But look, you are trusting^a in deceptive^b words that are worthless.

^{9} "Will you steal^c and murder,^{d} commit adultery^e and perjury,$^{n f}$ burn incense to Baal$^{g h}$ and follow other gods^i you have not known, ^{10}and then come and stand^j before me in this house,^{k} which bears my Name, and say, "We are safe"—safe to do all these detestable things?^{l} ^{11}Has this house,^{m} which bears my Name, become a den of robbers^n to you? But I have been watching!^{o} declares the LORD.

^{12}" 'Go now to the place in Shiloh^p where I first made a dwelling^q for my Name,^{r} and see what I did^s to it because of the wickedness of my people Israel. ^{13}While you were doing all these things, declares the LORD, I spoke^t to you again and again,^{u} but you did not listen;^{v} I called^w you, but you did not answer.^{x} ^{14}Therefore, what I did to Shiloh^y I will now do to the house that bears my Name,^{z} the temple^a you trust in, the place I gave to you and your fathers. ^{15}I will thrust you from my presence,^{b} just as I did all your brothers, the people of Ephraim.'^{c}

^{16}"So do not pray for this people nor offer any plea^d or petition for them; do not plead with me, for I will not listen^e to you. ^{17}Do you not see what they are doing in the towns of Judah and in the streets of Jerusalem? ^{18}The children gather wood, the fathers light the fire, and the women knead the dough and make cakes of bread for the Queen of

S Jer 4:14 ◀▶ Jer 7:23
R Jer 6:30 ◀▶ Jer 7:20

^{q} S Ex 40:2; S Jos 18:10 ¦ Da 9:18 ¦ S 1Sa 4:10-11,22; Ps 78:60-64
7:13 ^{t} Ps 71:17; Isa 48:17; Jer 32:33 ¦ 2Ch 36:15 ¦ ver 26; S Isa 65:12
^{w} S Pr 1:24 ¦ Jer 35:17 7:14 ^{y} S Jdg 18:31; S 1Sa 2:32 ¦ S 1Ki 9:7 ¦ ver 4;
Eze 24:21 7:15 ^{b} S Ge 4:14; S Ex 33:15; S 2Ki 17:20; Jer 23:39
^{c} Ps 78:67 7:16 ^{d} S Ex 32:10; Dt 9:14; Jer 15:1 ^{e} S Nu 23:19

^{n} 9 Or and swear by false gods

6:30 God rejected his wicked people as a refiner rejects impure silver.
7:14–16 The people had placed their trust in God's temple while openly rebelling against God's law. God said he would destroy the temple, the source of their confidence, and would cast them out of the land just as he had expelled the kingdom of Israel.

Heaven.[f] They pour out drink offerings[g] to other gods to provoke[h] me to anger. [19]But am I the one they are provoking?[i] declares the LORD. Are they not rather harming themselves, to their own shame?[j]

[20]"'Therefore this is what the Sovereign[k] LORD says: My anger[l] and my wrath will be poured[m] out on this place, on man and beast, on the trees of the field and on the fruit of the ground, and it will burn and not be quenched.[n]

[21]"'This is what the LORD Almighty, the God of Israel, says: Go ahead, add your burnt offerings to your other sacrifices[o] and eat[p] the meat yourselves! [22]For when I brought your forefathers out of Egypt and spoke to them, I did not just give them commands[q] about burnt offerings and sacrifices,[r] [23]but I gave them this command:[s] Obey[t] me, and I will be your God and you will be my people.[u] Walk in all the ways[v] I command you, that it may go well[w] with you. [24]But they did not listen[x] or pay attention;[y] instead, they followed the stubborn inclinations of their evil hearts.[z] They went backward[a] and not forward. [25]From the time your forefathers left Egypt until now, day after day, again and again[b] I sent you my servants[c] the prophets.[d] [26]But they did not listen to me or pay attention.[e] They were stiff-necked[f] and did more evil than their forefathers.'[g]

[27]"When you tell[h] them all this, they will not listen[i] to you; when you call to them, they will not answer.[j] [28]Therefore say to them, 'This is the nation that has not obeyed the LORD its God or responded to correction.[k] Truth[l] has perished; it has vanished from their lips. [29]Cut off[m] your hair and throw it away; take up a lament[n] on the barren heights, for the LORD has rejected and abandoned[o] this generation that is under his wrath.

R Jer 7:14–16 ◀ ▶ Jer 7:29
S Jer 7:9–11 ◀ ▶ Jer 14:10
U Isa 65:13–14 ◀ ▶ Jer 17:7–8
C Jer 6:30 ◀ ▶ Jer 7:26
C Jer 7:24 ◀ ▶ Jer 8:9
R Jer 7:20 ◀ ▶ Jer 7:34

7:18 [f]Jer 44:17-19; [g]S Isa 57:6
[h]S Dt 31:17; S 1Ki 14:9
7:19 [i]Dt 32:21; Jer 44:3
[j]S Job 7:20; Jer 9:19; 20:11; 22:22
7:20 [k]S Isa 30:15
[l]S Job 40:11; Jer 42:18; La 2:3-5
[m]Jer 6:11-12; La 4:11 [n]S Isa 1:31; Jer 11:16; 13:14; 15:6,14; 17:4,27; Eze 20:47-48
7:21 [o]S Jer 6:20; Am 5:21-22
[p]S 1Sa 2:12-17; Hos 8:13
7:22 [q]Isa 43:23
[r]S Isa 15:22
7:23 [s]1Jn 3:23
[t]S Ex 19:5
[u]S Lev 26:12; S Isa 51:16
S 1Ki 8:36; S Ps 119:3
[v]S Dt 5:33
7:24 [x]S Jer 6:10
[y]Jer 11:8; 17:23; 34:14 [z]S Jer 3:17
[a]S Jer 2:19; Eze 37:23
7:25 [b]S 2Ch 36:15
[c]S Isa 20:3
[d]S Nu 11:29; Jer 25:4; 35:15
7:26 [e]ver 13,24; S 2Ch 36:16; Ps 81:11; Jer 13:11; 22:21; 25:3; 35:15; Eze 20:8,21
[f]S Ex 32:9; Ac 7:51
[g]Jer 16:12; Mal 3:7; Lk 11:47
7:27 [h]Eze 2:7
[i]ver 13; Eze 3:7; Zec 7:13
[j]S Isa 65:12
7:28 [k]S Isa 26:23; Zep 3:7 [l]S Ps 15:2; S Isa 59:15
7:29 [m]S Lev 21:5; S Job 1:20
[n]S Jer 4:8; S Eze 19:1
[o]S Jer 6:30; 12:7; Hos 11:8; Mic 5:3
7:30 [p]S ver 10; S Lev 18:21
[q]S Jer 2:7; S 4:1; Eze 7:20-22
[r]S Lev 20:3; Jer 32:34
7:31 [s]S 2Ki 23:10
[t]S Jos 15:8; 2Ch 33:6
[u]S Lev 18:21; Eze 16:20
[v]Jer 19:5; 32:35; Eze 20:31; Mic 6:7
7:32 [w]Jer 19:6
[x]Jer 19:11
7:33 [y]S Ge 15:11

The Valley of Slaughter

[30]"'The people of Judah have done evil[p] in my eyes, declares the LORD. They have set up their detestable idols[q] in the house that bears my Name and have defiled[r] it. [31]They have built the high places of Topheth[s] in the Valley of Ben Hinnom[t] to burn their sons and daughters[u] in the fire—something I did not command, nor did it enter my mind.[v] [32]So beware, the days are coming, declares the LORD, when people will no longer call it Topheth or the Valley of Ben Hinnom, but the Valley of Slaughter,[w] for they will bury[x] the dead in Topheth until there is no more room. [33]Then the carcasses[y] of this people will become food[z] for the birds of the air and the beasts of the earth, and there will be no one to frighten them away.[a] [34]I will bring an end to the sounds[b] of joy and gladness and to the voices of bride and bridegroom[c] in the towns of Judah and the streets of Jerusalem,[d] for the land will become desolate.[e]

8 "'At that time, declares the LORD, the bones of the kings and officials of Judah, the bones of the priests and prophets, and the bones[f] of the people of Jerusalem will be removed[g] from their graves. [2]They will be exposed to the sun and the moon and all the stars of the heavens, which they have loved and served[h] and which they have followed and consulted and worshiped.[i] They will not be gathered up or buried,[j] but will be like refuse lying on the ground.[k] [3]Wherever I banish them,[l] all the survivors of this evil nation will prefer death to life,[m] declares the LORD Almighty.'

Sin and Punishment

[4]"Say to them, 'This is what the LORD says:

R Jer 7:29 ◀ ▶ Jer 8:5–6

[z]S Dt 28:26; Eze 29:5 [a]er 6:11; 14:16 7:34 [b]S Isa 24:8 [c]Rev 18:23
[d]Isa 24:7-12; Jer 33:10 [e]S Lev 26:34; Zec 7:14; Mt 23:38 8:1 [f]S Ps 53:5
Jer 14:19 8:2 [h]S 2Ki 23:5; Jer 19:13; Zep 1:5; Mic 6:7 [i]S Job 31:26
[j]er 14:16; Eze 29:5; 37:1 [k]S 2Ki 5:17; Jer 31:40; 36:30 8:3 [l]Dt 29:28
[m]S Job 3:22; Rev 9:6

7:20 God's coming judgment would not be limited to the city, but would be poured upon everything in the whole land of Judah.

7:29 Jeremiah advised his listeners to cut their hair as a sign of mourning because of the coming judgment of God upon the rebellious nation.

7:34 The happy sounds of life would be silenced in the coming desolation of the land.

" 'When men fall down, do they not get up?ⁿ
When a man turns away,º does he not return?
⁵Why then have these people turned away?
Why does Jerusalem always turn away?
They cling to deceit;ᵖ
they refuse to return.ᑫ
⁶I have listenedʳ attentively,
but they do not say what is right.
No one repentsˢ of his wickedness,
saying, "What have I done?"
Each pursues his own courseᵗ
like a horse charging into battle.
⁷Even the stork in the sky
knows her appointed seasons,
and the dove, the swift and the thrush
observe the time of their migration.
But my people do not knowᵘ
the requirements of the LORD.
⁸ " 'How can you say, "We are wise,
for we have the lawᵛ of the LORD,"
when actually the lying pen of the scribes
has handled it falsely?
⁹The wiseʷ will be put to shame;
they will be dismayedˣ and trapped.ʸ
Since they have rejected the wordᶻ of the LORD,
what kind of wisdomᵃ do they have?
¹⁰Therefore I will give their wives to other men
and their fields to new owners.ᵇ
From the least to the greatest,
all are greedy for gain;ᶜ
prophetsᵈ and priests alike,
all practice deceit.ᵉ
¹¹They dress the wound of my people
as though it were not serious.
"Peace, peace," they say,
when there is no peace.ᶠ

R Jer 7:34 ◄ ► Jer 8:12–14
C Jer 7:26 ◄ ► Jer 9:3
N Jer 6:19 ◄ ► Jer 8:20

8:4 ⁿ Pr 24:16; Mic 7:8
º Ps 119:67; Jer 31:19
8:5 ᵖ S Jer 5:27
ᑫ Zec 7:11
8:6 ʳ Mal 3:16
ˢ Rev 9:20
ᵗ Ps 14:1-3
8:7 ᵘ S Dt 32:28;
S Jer 4:22
8:8 ᵛ Ro 2:17
8:9 ʷ S Isa 29:14
ˣ S 2Ki 19:26
ʸ S Job 5:13
ᶻ S Jer 6:19 ᵃ Pr 1:7; 1Co 1:20
8:10 ᵇ S Jer 6:12
ᶜ S Isa 56:11
ᵈ Jer 14:14; La 2:14
ᵉ S Jer 23:11,15
8:11 ᶠ ver 15; S Jer 4:10; Eze 7:25
8:12 ᵍ S Jer 3:3
ʰ Ps 52:5-7; Isa 3:9
ⁱ S Jer 6:15
8:13 ʲ Hos 2:12; Joel 1:7 ᵏ Lk 13:6
ˡ Mt 21:19
ᵐ S Jer 5:17
8:14 ⁿ S Jos 10:20; Jer 35:11
º S Dt 29:18; Jer 9:15; 23:15
ᵖ Jer 14:7,20; Da 9:5
8:15 ᑫ S ver 11
ʳ S Job 19:8; Jer 14:19
8:16 ˢ S Jer 4:29
ᵗ S Ge 30:6
ᵘ Jer 51:29
ᵛ S Jer 5:17
8:17 ʷ Nu 21:6; S Dt 32:24
ˣ S Ps 58:5;
S Isa 3:3

¹²Are they ashamed of their loathsome conduct?
No, they have no shameᵍ at all;
they do not even know how to blush.
So they will fall among the fallen;
they will be brought down when they are punished,ʰ
says the LORD.ⁱ
¹³ " 'I will take away their harvest,
declares the LORD.
There will be no grapes on the vine.ʲ
There will be no figsᵏ on the tree,
and their leaves will wither.ˡ
What I have given them
will be takenᵐ from them.º' "
¹⁴"Why are we sitting here?
Gather together!
Let us flee to the fortified citiesⁿ
and perish there!
For the LORD our God has doomed us to perish
and given us poisoned waterº to drink,
because we have sinnedᵖ against him.
¹⁵We hoped for peaceᑫ
but no good has come,
for a time of healing
but there was only terror.ʳ
¹⁶The snorting of the enemy's horsesˢ
is heard from Dan;ᵗ
at the neighing of their stallions
the whole land trembles.ᵘ
They have come to devourᵛ
the land and everything in it,
the city and all who live there."
¹⁷"See, I will send venomous snakesʷ among you,
vipers that cannot be charmed,ˣ
and they will bite you,"
declares the LORD.
¹⁸O my Comforterᵖ in sorrow,

R Jer 8:5–6 ◄ ► Jer 9:9–22
M Jer 6:15 ◄ ► Jer 13:15–17

º 13 The meaning of the Hebrew for this sentence is uncertain.
ᵖ 18 The meaning of the Hebrew for this word is uncertain.

8:5–6 Because of the people's tendency to "always turn away" (8:5) they refused to abandon their course and rushed headlong to utter destruction "like a horse charging into battle" (8:6).

8:12–14 Again God confirmed his determination to "take away their harvest" (8:13) because of Judah's refusal to repent of their sin.

my heart is faint[y] within me.
[19] Listen to the cry of my people
    from a land far away:[z]
"Is the LORD not in Zion?
    Is her King[a] no longer there?"

"Why have they provoked[b] me to
        anger with their images,
    with their worthless[c] foreign
        idols?"[d]

[20] "The harvest is past,
    the summer has ended,
    and we are not saved."

[21] Since my people are crushed,[e] I am
        crushed;
    I mourn,[f] and horror grips me.
[22] Is there no balm in Gilead?[g]
    Is there no physician[h] there?
    Why then is there no healing[i]
    for the wound of my people?

9

[1] Oh, that my head were a spring of
        water
    and my eyes a fountain of tears![j]
    I would weep[k] day and night
    for the slain of my people.[l]
[2] Oh, that I had in the desert[m]
    a lodging place for travelers,
    so that I might leave my people
    and go away from them;
    for they are all adulterers,[n]
    a crowd of unfaithful[o] people.

[3] "They make ready their tongue
    like a bow, to shoot lies;[p]
    it is not by truth
    that they triumph[q] in the land.
    They go from one sin to another;
    they do not acknowledge[q] me,"
        declares the LORD.

[4] "Beware of your friends;[r]
    do not trust your brothers.[s]
    For every brother is a deceiver,[t]
    and every friend a slanderer.[u]
[5] Friend deceives friend,[v]
    and no one speaks the truth.[w]
    They have taught their tongues to lie;[x]
    they weary themselves with sinning.

H *Jer 6:19* ◄ ► *Jer 9:9*
N *Jer 8:9* ◄ ► *Jer 13:15–17*
K *Isa 63:1* ◄ ► *Jer 17:13–14*
H *Isa 53:4* ◄ ► *Jer 17:14*
C *Jer 8:9* ◄ ► *Jer 11:8*

8:18 y La 5:17
8:19 z Dt 28:64;
Jer 9:16 a Mic 4:9
b Jer 44:3
c S Isa 41:24
d S Dt 32:21

8:21 e Ps 94:5
f Ps 78:40;
Isa 43:24; Jer 4:19;
10:19; 14:17;
30:14; La 2:13;
Eze 6:9

8:22 g S Ge 37:25
h Job 13:4
i S Isa 1:6; Jer 30:12

9:1 j S Ps 119:136
k Jer 13:17; 14:17;
La 2:11,18; 3:48
l Isa 22:4

9:2 m Ps 55:7
n S Nu 25:1;
Jer 23:10; Hos 4:2;
7:4 o S 1Ki 19:10;
S Isa 24:16

9:3 p ver 8;
S Ex 20:16; Ps 64:3;
S Isa 44:20;
Jer 18:18; Mic 6:12
q S Isa 1:3

9:4 r S 2Sa 15:12
s Mic 7:5-6
t S Ge 27:35
u S Ex 20:16;
S Lev 19:16

9:5 v S Lev 6:2
w S Ps 15:2;
S Isa 59:15
x S Ps 52:3

9:6 y S Jer 5:27

9:7 z S Job 28:1;
S Isa 1:25
a S Jer 6:27

9:8 b S ver 3;
S Ps 35:20
c S Isa 3:5
d S Jer 5:26 e ver 4

9:9 f S Dt 32:43;
S Isa 10:3

9:10 g Jer 23:10;
Joel 1:19
h S Jer 4:25; 12:4;
Hos 4:3; Joel 1:18

9:11 i Jer 26:18
j S Job 30:29;
S Isa 34:13
k S Jer 1:15
l S Lev 26:31;
Isa 25:2; S Jer 4:13;
26:9; 33:10; 50:3,
13; 51:62; La 1:4

9:12 m S Ps 107:43

9:13 n S 2Ch 7:19;
S Ps 89:30-32

9:14 o S Jer 2:8,23;
Am 2:4 p S Jer 3:17;
S 7:24

[6] You[s] live in the midst of deception;[y]
    in their deceit they refuse to
        acknowledge me,"
            declares the LORD.

[7] Therefore this is what the LORD Almighty says:

"See, I will refine[z] and test[a] them,
    for what else can I do
    because of the sin of my people?
[8] Their tongue[b] is a deadly arrow;
    it speaks with deceit.
With his mouth each speaks cordially
        to his neighbor,[c]
    but in his heart he sets a trap[d] for
        him.[e]
[9] Should I not punish them for this?"
        declares the LORD.
    "Should I not avenge[f] myself
    on such a nation as this?"

[10] I will weep and wail for the mountains
    and take up a lament concerning the
        desert pastures.[g]
    They are desolate and untraveled,
    and the lowing of cattle is not heard.
    The birds of the air[h] have fled
    and the animals are gone.

[11] "I will make Jerusalem a heap[i] of
        ruins,
    a haunt of jackals;[j]
    and I will lay waste the towns of
        Judah[k]
    so no one can live there."[l]

[12] What man is wise[m] enough to understand this? Who has been instructed by the LORD and can explain it? Why has the land been ruined and laid waste like a desert that no one can cross?

[13] The LORD said, "It is because they have forsaken my law, which I set before them; they have not obeyed me or followed my law.[n] [14] Instead, they have followed[o] the stubbornness of their hearts;[p] they have followed the Baals, as their fathers taught them." [15] Therefore, this is

R *Jer 8:12–14* ◄ ► *Jer 10:18*
H *Jer 8:20* ◄ ► *Jer 10:10*

q 3 Or *lies; / they are not valiant for truth*   r 4 Or *a deceiving Jacob*
s 6 That is, Jeremiah (the Hebrew is singular)

9:9–22 Jeremiah announced God's declaration to utterly destroy Jerusalem "because they have forsaken my law, which I set before them" (9:13) and warned that he would "scatter them among nations" (9:16).

what the Lord Almighty, the God of Israel, says: "See, I will make this people eat bitter food^q and drink poisoned water.^r ¹⁶I will scatter them among nations^s that neither they nor their fathers have known,^t and I will pursue them with the sword^u until I have destroyed them."^v

¹⁷This is what the Lord Almighty says:

"Consider now! Call for the wailing women^w to come;
    send for the most skillful of them.
¹⁸Let them come quickly
    and wail over us
till our eyes overflow with tears
    and water streams from our eyelids.^x
¹⁹The sound of wailing is heard from Zion:
    'How ruined^y we are!
    How great is our shame!
We must leave our land
    because our houses are in ruins.' "
²⁰Now, O women, hear the word of the Lord;
    open your ears to the words of his mouth.^z
Teach your daughters how to wail;
    teach one another a lament.^a
²¹Death has climbed in through our windows^b
    and has entered our fortresses;
it has cut off the children from the streets
    and the young men^c from the public squares.

²²Say, "This is what the Lord declares:

" 'The dead bodies of men will lie
    like refuse^d on the open field,
like cut grain behind the reaper,
    with no one to gather them.' "

²³This is what the Lord says:

"Let not the wise man boast of his wisdom^e
    or the strong man boast of his strength^f
    or the rich man boast of his riches,^g
²⁴but let him who boasts boast^h about this:
    that he understands and knowsⁱ me,
that I am the Lord,^j who exercises kindness,^k
    justice and righteousness^l on earth,

for in these I delight,"
            declares the Lord.

²⁵"The days are coming," declares the Lord, "when I will punish all who are circumcised only in the flesh^m— ²⁶Egypt, Judah, Edom, Ammon, Moab and all who live in the desert in distant places.^{†n} For all these nations are really uncircumcised,^o and even the whole house of Israel is uncircumcised in heart.^p"

God and Idols

10:12–16pp — Jer 51:15–19

10 Hear what the Lord says to you, O house of Israel. ²This is what the Lord says:

"Do not learn the ways of the nations^q
    or be terrified by signs^r in the sky,
    though the nations are terrified by them.
³For the customs of the peoples are worthless;
    they cut a tree out of the forest,
    and a craftsman^s shapes it with his chisel.^t
⁴They adorn it with silver^u and gold;
    they fasten it with hammer and nails
    so it will not totter.^v
⁵Like a scarecrow in a melon patch,
    their idols cannot speak;^w
they must be carried
    because they cannot walk.^x
Do not fear them;
    they can do no harm^y
    nor can they do any good."^z

⁶No one is like you,^a O Lord;
    you are great,^b
    and your name is mighty in power.
⁷Who should not revere^c you,
    O King of the nations?^d
    This is your due.
Among all the wise men of the nations
    and in all their kingdoms,
    there is no one like you.
⁸They are all senseless^e and foolish;^f
    they are taught by worthless wooden idols.^g
⁹Hammered silver is brought from Tarshish^h
    and gold from Uphaz.

---

^{†26} Or *desert and who clip the hair by their foreheads*

What the craftsman and goldsmith
    have made[i]
is then dressed in blue and
    purple—
all made by skilled workers.

P [10]But the LORD is the true God;
H   he is the living God,[j] the eternal
        King.[k]
   When he is angry,[l] the earth
        trembles;[m]
   the nations cannot endure his
        wrath.[n]

[11]"Tell them this: 'These gods, who did not make the heavens and the earth, will perish[o] from the earth and from under the heavens.' "[u]

[12]But God made[p] the earth[q] by his
        power;
he founded the world by his
        wisdom[r]
and stretched out the heavens[s] by
        his understanding.
[13]When he thunders,[t] the waters in the
        heavens roar;
he makes clouds rise from the ends
        of the earth.
He sends lightning[u] with the rain[v]
and brings out the wind from his
        storehouses.[w]

[14]Everyone is senseless and without
        knowledge;
every goldsmith is shamed[x] by his
        idols.
His images are a fraud;[y]
    they have no breath in them.
[15]They are worthless,[z] the objects of
        mockery;
when their judgment comes, they
        will perish.
[16]He who is the Portion[a] of Jacob is not
        like these,
for he is the Maker of all things,[b]
    including Israel, the tribe of his
        inheritance[c]—
the LORD Almighty is his name.[d]

P Isa 66:24 ◀ ▶ Jer 23:19-20
H Jer 9:9 ◀ ▶ Jer 12:5

10:9 [i]Ps 115:4; S Isa 40:19
10:10 [j]S Jos 3:10; S Mt 16:16 [k]S Ge 21:33; Da 6:26 [l]S Ps 18:7 [m]S Jdg 5:4; S Job 9:6; Ps 29:8 [n]Ps 76:7; Jer 21:12; Na 1:6
10:11 [o]S Isa 2:18
10:12 [p]S 1Sa 2:8 [q]S ver 16 [r]S Ge 1:31 [s]S Ge 1:1,8
10:13 [t]S Job 36:29 [u]S Job 36:30 [v]S Ps 104:13; S 135:7 [w]S Dt 28:12
10:14 [x]S Ps 97:7; S Isa 1:29 [y]S Isa 44:20
10:15 [z]S Isa 41:24; S Jer 14:22
10:16 [a]S Dt 32:9; S Ps 119:57 [b]ver 12; Jer 32:17; 33:2 [c]S Ex 34:9; Ps 74:2 [d]Jer 31:35; 32:18
10:17 [e]Eze 12:3-12
10:18 [f]S 1Sa 25:29; S Isa 22:17 [g]S Dt 28:52
10:19 [h]Job 34:6; Jer 14:17; 15:18; 30:12,15; La 2:13; Mic 1:9; Na 3:19
[i]Mic 7:9
10:20 [j]S Jer 4:20 [k]Jer 31:15; La 1:5
10:21 [l]Jer 22:22; 23:1; 25:34; 50:6 [m]ver 8 [n]S Isa 56:10 [o]Jer 22:30 [p]Jer 23:2; Eze 34:6
10:22 [q]Jer 6:22; 27:6; 49:28,30 [r]Eze 12:19 [s]S Isa 34:13
10:23 [t]S Job 33:29; S Pr 3:5-6; 20:24
10:24 [u]Ps 6:1; 38:1; S Jer 7:20; 18:23 [v]Jer 46:28 [w]Jer 30:11
10:25 [x]S Ps 69:24; Zep 2:2; 3:8 [y]S Ps 14:4 [z]S Ps 79:7; S Jer 2:3

Coming Destruction

[17]Gather up your belongings[e] to leave
        the land,
you who live under siege.
[18]For this is what the LORD says: R
    "At this time I will hurl[f] out
        those who live in this land;
    I will bring distress[g] on them
        so that they may be captured."

[19]Woe to me because of my injury!
    My wound[h] is incurable!
Yet I said to myself,
    "This is my sickness, and I must
        endure[i] it."

[20]My tent[j] is destroyed;   R
    all its ropes are snapped.
My sons are gone from me and are no
        more;[k]
no one is left now to pitch my tent
    or to set up my shelter.
[21]The shepherds[l] are senseless[m]
    and do not inquire of the LORD;[n]
so they do not prosper[o]
    and all their flock is scattered.[p]
[22]Listen! The report is coming—
    a great commotion from the land of
        the north![q]
It will make the towns of Judah
        desolate,[r]
    a haunt of jackals.[s]

Jeremiah's Prayer

[23]I know, O LORD, that a man's life is not
        his own;
    it is not for man to direct his steps.[t]
[24]Correct me, LORD, but only with
        justice—
    not in your anger,[u]
    lest you reduce me to nothing.[v][w]
[25]Pour out your wrath on the nations[x]   R
        that do not acknowledge you,
    on the peoples who do not call on
        your name.[y]
For they have devoured[z] Jacob;

R Jer 9:9-22 ◀ ▶ Jer 10:20-21
R Jer 10:18 ◀ ▶ Jer 10:25
R Jer 10:20-21 ◀ ▶ Jer 13:9-11

[u] 11 The text of this verse is in Aramaic.

10:10 Jeremiah declared that only God is the true and living God in contrast to the multitude of pagan idols worshiped by Judah's neighbors.

10:18-25 Jeremiah spoke with despair of the unrighteous disobedience of Judah, the spoiling of the temple and her exile as consequences of her continued rebellion against God.

they have devoured him completely
and destroyed his homeland.ᵃ

The Covenant Is Broken

11 This is the word that came to Jeremiah from the LORD: ²"Listen to the terms of this covenantᵇ and tell them to the people of Judah and to those who live in Jerusalem. ³Tell them that this is what the LORD, the God of Israel, says: 'Cursedᶜ is the man who does not obey the terms of this covenant— ⁴the terms I commanded your forefathers when I brought them out of Egypt,ᵈ out of the iron-smelting furnace.ᵉ' I said, 'Obeyᶠ me and do everything I command you, and you will be my people,ᵍ and I will be your God. ⁵Then I will fulfill the oath I sworeʰ to your forefathers, to give them a land flowing with milk and honey'ⁱ—the land you possess today."

I answered, "Amen,ʲ LORD."

⁶The LORD said to me, "Proclaimᵏ all these words in the towns of Judah and in the streets of Jerusalem: 'Listen to the terms of this covenant and followˡ them. ⁷From the time I brought your forefathers up from Egypt until today, I warned them again and again,ᵐ saying, "Obey me." ⁸But they did not listen or pay attention;ⁿ instead, they followed the stubbornness of their evil hearts.ᵒ So I brought on them all the cursesᵖ of the covenant I had commanded them to follow but that they did not keep.'ᑫ"

⁹Then the LORD said to me, "There is a conspiracyʳ among the people of Judah and those who live in Jerusalem. ¹⁰They have returned to the sins of their forefathers,ˢ who refused to listen to my words.ᵗ They have followed other godsᵘ to serve them.ᵛ Both the house of Israel and the house of Judah have broken the covenantʷ I made with their forefathers. ¹¹Therefore this is what the LORD says: 'I will bring on them a disasterˣ they cannot escape.ʸ Although they cryᶻ out to me, I will not listenᵃ to them. ¹²The towns of Judah and the people of Jerusalem will go and cry out to the gods to whom they burn incense,ᵇ but they will not help them at all when disasterᶜ strikes. ¹³You have as many godsᵈ as you have towns,ᵉ O Judah; and the altars you have set up to burn incenseᶠ to that

shamefulᵍ god Baal are as many as the streets of Jerusalem.'

¹⁴"Do not prayʰ for this people nor offer any plea or petition for them, because I will not listenⁱ when they call to me in the time of their distress.

¹⁵"What is my beloved doing in my
  temple
as she works out her evil schemes
  with many?
Can consecrated meatʲ avert ᴸ your
  punishment,ʲ?ᵏ
When you engage in your wickedness,
  then you rejoice.ᵛ"

¹⁶The LORD called you a thriving olive
  treeˡ
with fruit beautiful in form.
But with the roar of a mighty storm
  he will set it on fire,ᵐ
  and its branches will be broken.ⁿ

¹⁷The LORD Almighty, who plantedᵒ you, has decreed disasterᵖ for you, because the house of Israel and the house of Judah have done evil and provokedᑫ me to anger by burning incense to Baal.ʳ

Plot Against Jeremiah

¹⁸Because the LORD revealed their plot to me, I knew it, for at that time he showed me what they were doing. ¹⁹I had been like a gentle lamb led to the slaughter;ˢ I did not realize that they had plottedᵗ against me, saying,

"Let us destroy the tree and its fruit;
  let us cut him off from the land of
    the living,ᵘ
  that his name be rememberedᵛ no
    more."

²⁰But, O LORD Almighty, you who judge
    righteouslyʷ
  and test the heartˣ and mind,ʸ
let me see your vengeanceᶻ upon
    them,
  for to you I have committed my
    cause.

²¹"Therefore this is what the LORD says about the men of Anathothᵃ who are seeking your lifeᵇ and saying, 'Do not

---

C *Jer 9:3* ◀ ▶ *Jer 13:23*

J *Jer 9:26* ◀ ▶ *Jer 27:22*
E *Isa 29:15* ◀ ▶ *Jer 16:17*

11:21 ᵃS Jos 21:18 ᵇS ver 19; Jer 12:6; 21:7; 34:20

ᵛ 15 Or *Could consecrated meat avert your punishment? / Then you would rejoice*

prophesy^c in the name of the LORD or you will die^d by our hands'—^22 therefore this is what the LORD Almighty says: 'I will punish them. Their young men^e will die by the sword, their sons and daughters by famine. ^23 Not even a remnant^f will be left to them, because I will bring disaster on the men of Anathoth in the year of their punishment.^g '"

Jeremiah's Complaint

12 You are always righteous,^h O LORD,
  when I bring a case^i before you.
Yet I would speak with you about your justice:^j
  Why does the way of the wicked prosper?^k
  Why do all the faithless live at ease?
^2 You have planted^l them, and they have taken root;
  they grow and bear fruit.^m
You are always on their lips
  but far from their hearts.^n
^3 Yet you know me, O LORD;
  you see me and test^o my thoughts about you.
Drag them off like sheep^p to be butchered!
Set them apart for the day of slaughter!^q
^4 How long will the land lie parched^w^r
  and the grass in every field be withered?^s
Because those who live in it are wicked,
  the animals and birds have perished.^t
Moreover, the people are saying,
  "He will not see what happens to us."

God's Answer

H ^5 "If you have raced with men on foot
    and they have worn you out,
  how can you compete with horses?
If you stumble in safe country,^x
  how will you manage in the thickets^u by^y the Jordan?
^6 Your brothers, your own family—
  even they have betrayed you;

H *Jer 10:10* ◀▶ *Jer 13:15–16*

they have raised a loud cry against you.^v
Do not trust them,
  though they speak well of you.^w
^7 "I will forsake^x my house,
  abandon^y my inheritance;
I will give the one I love^z
  into the hands of her enemies.^a
^8 My inheritance has become to me
  like a lion^b in the forest.
She roars at me;
  therefore I hate her.^c
^9 Has not my inheritance become to me
  like a speckled bird of prey
  that other birds of prey surround and attack?
Go and gather all the wild beasts;
  bring them to devour.^d
^10 Many shepherds^e will ruin my vineyard
  and trample down my field;
they will turn my pleasant field
  into a desolate wasteland.^f
^11 It will be made a wasteland,^g
  parched and desolate before me;^h
  the whole land will be laid waste
  because there is no one who cares.
^12 Over all the barren heights in the desert
  destroyers will swarm,
for the sword^i of the LORD^j will devour^k
  from one end of the land to the other;^l
  no one will be safe.^m
^13 They will sow wheat but reap thorns;
  they will wear themselves out but gain nothing.^n
So bear the shame of your harvest
  because of the LORD's fierce anger."^o

I ^14 This is what the LORD says: "As for all my wicked neighbors who seize the inheritance^p I gave my people Israel, I will uproot^q them from their lands and I will uproot^r the house of Judah from among them. ^15 But after I uproot them, I will again have compassion^s and will bring^t each of them back to his own inheritance

I *Jer 3:14–19* ◀▶ *Jer 16:14–16*

^w 4 Or *land mourn* ^x 5 Or *If you put your trust in a land of safety* ^y 5 Or *the flooding of*

12:15 Despite the terrible punishment and exile from the promised land, God promises that he will return his people to their land and "have compassion" on them.

and his own country. ¹⁶And if they learn well the ways of my people and swear by my name, saying, 'As surely as the LORD lives'—even as they once taught my people to swear by Baal—then they will be established among my people. ¹⁷But if any nation does not listen, I will completely uproot and destroy it," declares the LORD.

A Linen Belt

13 This is what the LORD said to me: "Go and buy a linen belt and put it around your waist, but do not let it touch water." ²So I bought a belt, as the LORD directed, and put it around my waist.

³Then the word of the LORD came to me a second time: ⁴"Take the belt you bought and are wearing around your waist, and go now to Perath and hide it there in a crevice in the rocks." ⁵So I went and hid it at Perath, as the LORD told me.

⁶Many days later the LORD said to me, "Go now to Perath and get the belt I told you to hide there." ⁷So I went to Perath and dug up the belt and took it from the place where I had hidden it, but now it was ruined and completely useless.

⁸Then the word of the LORD came to me: ⁹"This is what the LORD says: 'In the same way I will ruin the pride of Judah and the great pride of Jerusalem. ¹⁰These wicked people, who refuse to listen to my words, who follow the stubbornness of their hearts and go after other gods to serve and worship them, will be like this belt—completely useless! ¹¹For as a belt is bound around a man's waist, so I bound the whole house of Israel and the whole house of Judah to me,' declares the LORD, 'to be my people for my renown and praise and honor. But they have not listened.'

Wineskins

¹²"Say to them: 'This is what the LORD, the God of Israel, says: Every wineskin should be filled with wine.' And if they say to you, 'Don't we know that every wineskin should be filled with wine?' ¹³then tell them, 'This is what the LORD says: I am going to fill with drunkenness all who live in this land, including the kings who sit on David's throne, the priests, the prophets and all those living in Jerusalem. ¹⁴I will smash them one against the other, fathers and sons alike, declares the LORD. I will allow no pity or mercy or compassion to keep me from destroying them.' "

Threat of Captivity

¹⁵Hear and pay attention,
  do not be arrogant,
  for the LORD has spoken.
¹⁶Give glory to the LORD your God
  before he brings the darkness,
before your feet stumble
  on the darkening hills.
You hope for light,
  but he will turn it to thick darkness
  and change it to deep gloom.
¹⁷But if you do not listen,
  I will weep in secret
  because of your pride;
my eyes will weep bitterly,
  overflowing with tears,
because the LORD's flock will be
  taken captive.

¹⁸Say to the king and to the queen
    mother,
  "Come down from your thrones,
  for your glorious crowns
    will fall from your heads."
¹⁹The cities in the Negev will be shut
    up,
  and there will be no one to open
    them.
All Judah will be carried into exile,
  carried completely away.

H *Jer 12:5* ◀ ▶ *Jer 13:24*
M *Jer 8:12* ◀ ▶ *Jer 29:12–13*
N *Jer 8:20* ◀ ▶ *Jer 32:33*
R *Jer 13:9–11* ◀ ▶ *Jer 13:24*

z 4 Or possibly the Euphrates; also in verses 5-7

R *Jer 10:25* ◀ ▶ *Jer 13:17–21*

13:9–11 God had commanded Jeremiah to take a linen belt and bury it in a hole in a rock. When Jeremiah retrieved it some time later it was mildewed and rotten, symbolizing the useless, ruined nation of Judah that would soon be destroyed.

13:17–21, 24 God told Jeremiah to warn the king and queen of Judah of the coming exile of their people and destruction of their cities because of their unconfessed sins.

²⁰Lift up your eyes and see
   those who are coming from the
      north.ᵇ
   Where is the flockᶜ that was entrusted
      to you,
   the sheep of which you boasted?
²¹What will you say when ˻the LORD˼ sets
      over you
   those you cultivated as your special
      allies?ᵈ
   Will not pain grip you
   like that of a woman in labor?ᵉ
²²And if you ask yourself,
   "Why has this happened to me?"ᶠ—
   it is because of your many sinsᵍ
   that your skirts have been torn offʰ
   and your body mistreated.ⁱ
C ²³Can the Ethiopianᵃ change his skin
G   or the leopard its spots?
O Neither can you do good
   who are accustomed to doing evil.ʲ
R ²⁴"I will scatter you like chaffᵏ
H   driven by the desert wind.ˡ
²⁵This is your lot,
   the portionᵐ I have decreed for
      you,"
                  declares the LORD,
   "because you have forgottenⁿ me
   and trusted in false gods.ᵒ
²⁶I will pull up your skirts over your face
   that your shame may be seenᵖ—
²⁷your adulteries and lustful neighings,
   your shameless prostitution!ᵠ
   I have seen your detestable acts
      on the hills and in the fields.ʳ
   Woe to you, O Jerusalem!
   How long will you be unclean?"ˢ

Drought, Famine, Sword

14 This is the word of the LORD
      to Jeremiah concerning the
drought:ᵗ

²"Judah mourns,ᵘ
   her cities languish;
   they wail for the land,
   and a cry goes up from Jerusalem.
³The nobles send their servants for
      water;
   they go to the cisterns
   but find no water.ᵛ
   They return with their jars unfilled;

C Jer 11:8 ◀▶ Jer 17:1
G Jer 9:23–24 ◀▶ Jer 17:5
O Jer 2:22 ◀▶ Jer 17:13–14
R Jer 13:17–21 ◀▶ Jer 14:19
H Jer 13:15–16 ◀▶ Jer 17:4

13:20 ᵇJer 6:22; Hab 1:6 ᶜJer 23:2
13:21 ᵈS Ps 41:9; Jer 4:30; 20:10; 38:22; Ob 1:7 ᵉS Jer 4:31
13:22 ᶠS 1Ki 9:9 ᵍJer 9:2-6; 16:10-12 ʰS Isa 20:4 ⁱLa 1:8; Eze 16:37; 23:26; Na 3:5-6
13:23 ʲS 2Ch 6:36
13:24 ᵏS Ps 1:4 ˡS Lev 26:33; S Job 1:19; S 27:21
13:25 ᵐS Job 20:29; Mt 24:51 ⁿS Isa 17:10 ᵒS Dt 31:20; S Ps 4:2; 106:19-21
13:26 ᵖLa 1:8; Eze 16:37; Na 3:5
13:27 ᵠEze 23:29 ʳS Isa 57:7; Eze 6:13 ˢHos 8:5
14:1 ᵗS Dt 28:22; S Isa 5:6
14:2 ᵘS Isa 3:26
14:3 ᵛS Dt 28:48; S 2Ki 18:31; Job 6:19-20 ʷS Est 6:12
14:4 ˣS Jer 3:3; S 12:11; Am 4:8; Zec 14:17
14:5 ʸIsa 15:6
14:6 ᶻS Job 39:5-6; S Ps 104:11; S Jer 2:24
14:7 ᵃS Ge 47:4 ᵇS Isa 3:9; Hos 5:5 ᶜS 1Sa 12:22; S Ps 79:9
14:8 ᵈS Jer 2:19; 5:6 ᵉS Jer 8:14 ᶠS Ps 9:18; Jer 17:13; 50:7 ᵍPs 18:46; S Isa 25:9 ʰS Ps 46:1
14:9 ⁱS Isa 50:2 ʲS Ge 18:19; Jer 8:19 ᵏIsa 63:19; Jer 15:16 ˡS Ps 27:9
14:10 ᵐPs 119:101; Jer 2:25 ⁿJer 6:20; Am 5:22 ᵒHos 7:2; 9:9; Am 8:7 ᵖJer 44:21-23; Hos 8:13; Am 3:2
14:11 ᵠS Ex 32:10; S 1Sa 2:25
14:12 ʳS Dt 1:45; S 1Sa 8:18; S Jer 11:11 ˢLev 1:1-17; Jer 7:21 ᵗLev 2:1-16 ᵘAm 5:22 ᵛS Isa 51:19; S Jer 9:16 ʷJer 15:2; 16:4 ˣJer 21:6; 27:8,13; 32:24; 34:17; Eze 14:21
14:13 ʸDt 18:22; Jer 27:14; 37:19 ᶻS Jer 5:12 ᵃS Isa 30:5; S Jer 4:10

S Jer 7:23 ◀▶ Jer 15:6

   dismayed and despairing,
   they cover their heads.ʷ
⁴The ground is cracked
   because there is no rain in the
      land;ˣ
   the farmers are dismayed
   and cover their heads.
⁵Even the doe in the field
   deserts her newborn fawn
   because there is no grass.ʸ
⁶Wild donkeys stand on the barren
      heightsᶻ
   and pant like jackals;
   their eyesight fails
   for lack of pasture."ᵃ

⁷Although our sins testifyᵇ against us,
   O LORD, do something for the sake
      of your name.ᶜ
   For our backslidingᵈ is great;
   we have sinnedᵉ against you.
⁸O Hopeᶠ of Israel,
   its Saviorᵍ in times of distress,ʰ
   why are you like a stranger in the land,
   like a traveler who stays only a
      night?
⁹Why are you like a man taken by
      surprise,
   like a warrior powerless to save?ⁱ
   You are amongʲ us, O LORD,
   and we bear your name;ᵏ
   do not forsakeˡ us!

¹⁰This is what the LORD says about this **S**
people:

"They greatly love to wander;
   they do not restrain their feet.ᵐ
So the LORD does not acceptⁿ them;
   he will now rememberᵒ their
      wickedness
   and punish them for their sins."ᵖ

¹¹Then the LORD said to me, "Do not
prayᵠ for the well-being of this people.
¹²Although they fast, I will not listen to
their cry;ʳ though they offer burnt offerings ˢ and grain offerings,ᵗ I will not accept ᵘ them. Instead, I will destroy them
with the sword,ᵛ famineʷ and plague."ˣ
¹³But I said, "Ah, Sovereign LORD, the
prophetsʸ keep telling them, 'You will
not see the sword or suffer famine.ᶻ Indeed, I will give you lasting peaceᵃ in this
place.' "

ᵃ 23 Hebrew *Cushite* (probably a person from the upper Nile region)

¹⁴Then the LORD said to me, "The prophets are prophesying lies^b in my name. I have not sent^c them or appointed them or spoken to them. They are prophesying to you false visions,^d divinations,^e idolatries^b and the delusions of their own minds. ¹⁵Therefore, this is what the LORD says about the prophets who are prophesying in my name: I did not send them, yet they are saying, 'No sword or famine will touch this land.' Those same prophets will perish^f by sword and famine.^g ¹⁶And the people they are prophesying to will be thrown out into the streets of Jerusalem because of the famine and sword. There will be no one to bury^h them or their wives, their sons or their daughters.^i I will pour out on them the calamity they deserve.^j

¹⁷"Speak this word to them:

" 'Let my eyes overflow with tears^k
    night and day without ceasing;
for my virgin^l daughter—my people—
    has suffered a grievous wound,
    a crushing blow.^m
¹⁸If I go into the country,
    I see those slain by the sword;
if I go into the city,
    I see the ravages of famine.^n
Both prophet and priest
    have gone to a land they know not.' "

R ¹⁹Have you rejected Judah completely?^p
    Do you despise Zion?
Why have you afflicted us
    so that we cannot be healed?^q
We hoped for peace
    but no good has come,
for a time of healing
    but there is only terror.^r
²⁰O LORD, we acknowledge^s our wickedness
    and the guilt of our fathers;^t
    we have indeed sinned^u against you.
²¹For the sake of your name^v do not despise us;

R *Jer 13:24* ◀ ▶ *Jer 15:1–4*

14:14 ᵇ S Jer 5:1; 23:25; 27:14; Eze 13:2
ᶜ Jer 23:21,32; 29:31; Eze 13:6
ᵈ Jer 23:16; La 2:9
ᵉ Eze 12:24
14:15 ᶠ Jer 20:6; Eze 14:9
ᵍ Jer 5:12-13; 16:4; La 1:19
14:16 ʰ Ps 79:3
ⁱ Jer 7:33
ʲ Pr 1:31; S Jer 17:10
14:17 ᵏ S Ps 119:136
ˡ S 2Ki 19:21; S Isa 23:12
ᵐ S Jer 8:21
14:18 ⁿ Eze 7:15
ᵒ 2Ch 36:10; S Jer 13:17
14:19 ᵖ Jer 7:29
ᵠ S Isa 1:6; Jer 30:12-13
ʳ S Job 19:8; S Jer 8:15
14:20 ˢ S Jer 3:13
ᵗ S Lev 26:40; S 1Ki 8:47; S Ezr 9:6
ᵘ S Jdg 10:10; Da 9:7-8
14:21 ᵛ ver 7; S Jos 7:9
ʷ Isa 62:7; Jer 3:17
ˣ S Ex 2:24
14:22 ʸ S Isa 41:24; S 44:10; Jer 10:15; 16:19; Hab 2:18
ᶻ S 1Ki 8:36; S Ps 135:7
ᵃ S Isa 43:10
15:1 ᵇ S Ex 32:11; Nu 14:13-20
ᶜ S Isa 1:20; S 7:8
ᵈ S Isa 2:25; S Jer 7:16
ᵉ S 2Ki 17:20; Jer 16:13
15:2 ᶠ Jer 42:22; 43:11; 44:13
ᵍ S Dt 28:26; S Jer 14:12; La 4:9
ʰ Eze 12:11; Rev 13:10
15:3 ⁱ S Nu 33:4
ʲ S Lev 26:25
ᵏ S 1Ki 21:19; S 2Ki 9:36
ˡ S Dt 28:26
ᵐ S Lev 26:22; Eze 14:21; 33:27
15:4 ⁿ Jer 24:9; 29:18; 34:17
ᵒ S Dt 28:25; S Job 17:5; S 2Ki 21:2; 23:26-27
15:5 ᵠ Isa 27:11; 51:19; S Jer 13:14; 16:13; 21:7; Na 3:7
15:6 ʳ S Dt 32:15;

do not dishonor your glorious throne.^w
Remember your covenant^x with us
    and do not break it.

²²Do any of the worthless idols^y of the nations bring rain?^z
Do the skies themselves send down showers?
No, it is you, O LORD our God.
Therefore our hope is in you,
    for you are the one who does all this.^a

15 Then the LORD said to me: "Even R if Moses^b and Samuel^c were to stand before me, my heart would not go out to this people.^d Send them away from my presence!^e Let them go! ²And if they ask you, 'Where shall we go?' tell them, 'This is what the LORD says:

" 'Those destined for death, to death;
    those for the sword, to the sword;^f
    those for starvation, to starvation;^g
    those for captivity, to captivity.'^h

³"I will send four kinds of destroyers^i against them," declares the LORD, "the sword^j to kill and the dogs^k to drag away and the birds^l of the air and the beasts of the earth to devour and destroy.^m ⁴I will make them abhorrent^n to all the kingdoms of the earth^o because of what Manasseh^p son of Hezekiah king of Judah did in Jerusalem.

⁵"Who will have pity^q on you,
    O Jerusalem?
Who will mourn for you?
Who will stop to ask how you are?

⁶You have rejected^r me," declares the R
    LORD.   S
"You keep on backsliding.
So I will lay hands^s on you and destroy you;
    I can no longer show compassion.^t

R *Jer 14:19* ◀ ▶ *Jer 15:6–7*
R *Jer 15:1–4* ◀ ▶ *Jer 16:18*
S *Jer 14:10* ◀ ▶ *Jer 17:10*

Jer 6:19 S Isa 31:3; Zep 1:4 S Jer 7:20; Am 7:8
ᵇ 14 Or *visions, worthless divinations*

14:19 Jeremiah prophesied that when the judgment and wrath of God fell upon Judah the people would finally awaken to their terrible fate.

15:1–7 Jeremiah said that even though Moses and Samuel had successfully interceded in the past to prevent God from destroying his people, the apostasy of Judah was so terrible that nothing would prevent the coming wrath of God. Jeremiah's prophecy declared four distinct judgments on Judah in addition to exile: death by sword, dogs, birds and beasts.

JEREMIAH 15:7

⁷"I will winnow*ᵘ them with a
        winnowing fork
    at the city gates of the land.
I will bring bereavementᵛ and
        destruction on my people,ʷ
    for they have not changed their
        ways.ˣ
⁸I will make their widowsʸ more
        numerous
    than the sand of the sea.
At midday I will bring a destroyerᶻ
    against the mothers of their young
        men;
suddenly I will bring down on them
    anguish and terror.ᵃ
⁹The mother of seven will grow faintᵇ
    and breathe her last.ᶜ
Her sun will set while it is still day;
    she will be disgracedᵈ and
        humiliated.
I will put the survivors to the swordᵉ
    before their enemies,"ᶠ
            declares the LORD.

¹⁰Alas, my mother, that you gave me
        birth,ᵍ
    a man with whom the whole land
        strives and contends!ʰ
I have neither lentⁱ nor borrowed,
    yet everyone cursesʲ me.

¹¹The LORD said,

"Surely I will deliver youᵏ for a good
        purpose;
    surely I will make your enemies
        pleadˡ with you
    in times of disaster and times of
        distress.

¹²"Can a man break iron—
    iron from the northᵐ—or bronze?
¹³Your wealthⁿ and your treasures
    I will give as plunder,ᵒ without
        charge,ᵖ
because of all your sins
    throughout your country.ᵠ
¹⁴I will enslave you to your enemies
    inᶜ a land you do not know,ʳ
for my anger will kindle a fireˢ
    that will burn against you."

¹⁵You understand, O LORD;
    remember me and care for me.
Avenge me on my persecutors.ᵗ
You are long-sufferingᵘ—do not take
        me away;
    think of how I suffer reproach for
        your sake.ᵛ

15:7 ᵘ S Isa 41:16
ᵛ Isa 3:26
ʷ Jer 18:21
ˣ S 2Ch 28:22
15:8 ʸ S Isa 47:9
ᶻ S Jer 4:7; S 6:4
ᵃ S Job 18:11
15:9 ᵇ 1Sa 2:5
ᶜ S Job 8:13
ᵈ Jer 7:19 ᵉ Jer 21:7;
25:31 ᶠ 2Ki 25:7;
Jer 19:7
15:10 ᵍ S Job 3:1;
S 10:18-19
ʰ Jer 1:19
ⁱ S Lev 25:36;
Ne 5:1-12
ʲ S Jer 6:10
15:11 ᵏ ver 21;
Jer 40:4 ˡ Jer 21:1-2;
37:3; 42:1-3
15:12
ᵐ S Dt 28:48;
Jer 28:14; La 1:14;
Hos 10:11
15:13
ⁿ S 2Ki 25:15
ᵒ S 2Ki 24:13;
Eze 38:12-13
ᵖ S Ps 44:12
ᵠ Jer 17:3
15:14 ʳ S Dt 28:36;
S Jer 5:19
ˢ S Ps 21:9
15:15 ᵗ Jdg 16:28;
S Ps 119:84
ᵘ Ex 34:6
ᵛ Ps 44:22; 69:7-9;
S Jer 6:10
15:16 ʷ Eze 2:8;
3:3; Rev 10:10
ˣ S Job 15:11;
Ps 119:72,103
ʸ S Isa 43:7;
S Jer 14:9
15:17 ᶻ Ru 3:3;
Ps 1:1; 26:4-5;
Jer 16:8
ᵃ S 2Ki 3:15
15:18 ᵇ S Job 6:4;
S Jer 10:19; 30:12;
Mic 1:9
ᶜ S Job 6:15;
S Ps 9:10
15:19 ᵈ Zec 3:7
ᵉ S Ex 4:16
15:20 ᶠ S Isa 50:7
ᵍ S Ps 129:2
ʰ S Jer 1:8; 20:11;
42:11; Eze 3:8
15:21 ⁱ S Jer 1:8
ʲ S Ps 97:10
ᵏ Jer 50:34
ˡ S Ge 48:16
16:2 ᵐ Mt 19:12;
1Co 7:26-27
16:3 ⁿ Jer 6:21
16:4 ᵒ ver 6;
Jer 25:33
ᵖ S Jer 9:22
ᵠ S Jer 14:15

¹⁶When your words came, I ateʷ them;
    they were my joy and my heart's
        delight,ˣ
for I bear your name,ʸ
    O LORD God Almighty.
¹⁷I never satᶻ in the company of
        revelers,
    never made merry with them;
I sat alone because your handᵃ was on
        me
    and you had filled me with
        indignation.
¹⁸Why is my pain unending
    and my wound grievous and
        incurable?ᵇ
Will you be to me like a deceptive
        brook,
    like a spring that fails?ᶜ

¹⁹Therefore this is what the LORD says:

"If you repent, I will restore you
    that you may serveᵈ me;
if you utter worthy, not worthless,
        words,
    you will be my spokesman.ᵉ
Let this people turn to you,
    but you must not turn to them.
²⁰I will make you a wallᶠ to this people,   ▾
    a fortified wall of bronze;
they will fight against you
    but will not overcomeᵍ you,
for I am with you
    to rescue and save you,"ʰ
            declares the LORD.
²¹"I will saveⁱ you from the hands of the
        wickedʲ
    and redeemᵏ you from the grasp of
        the cruel."ˡ

Day of Disaster

16 Then the word of the LORD came
to me: ²"You must not marryᵐ
and have sons or daughters in this place."
³For this is what the LORD says about the
sons and daughters born in this land and
about the women who are their mothers
and the men who are their fathers:ⁿ
⁴"They will die of deadly diseases. They
will not be mourned or buriedᵒ but will
be like refuse lying on the ground.ᵖ They
will perish by sword and famine,ᵠ and
their dead bodies will become food for

▾ *Jer 1:19* ◂ ▸ *Jer 20:11*

ᶜ 14 Some Hebrew manuscripts, Septuagint and Syriac (see also Jer. 17:4);
most Hebrew manuscripts *I will cause your enemies to bring you / into*

the birds of the air and the beasts of the earth."ʳ

⁵For this is what the LORD says: "Do not enter a house where there is a funeral meal; do not go to mourn or show sympathy, because I have withdrawn my blessing, my love and my pityˢ from this people," declares the LORD. ⁶"Both high and low will die in this land.ᵗ They will not be buried or mourned,ᵘ and no one will cutᵛ himself or shaveʷ his head for them. ⁷No one will offer foodˣ to comfort those who mournʸ for the dead—not even for a father or a mother—nor will anyone give them a drink to consoleᶻ them.

⁸"And do not enter a house where there is feasting and sit down to eat and drink.ᵃ ⁹For this is what the LORD Almighty, the God of Israel, says: Before your eyes and in your days I will bring an end to the soundsᵇ of joy and gladness and to the voices of brideᶜ and bridegroom in this place.ᵈ

¹⁰"When you tell these people all this and they ask you, 'Why has the LORD decreed such a great disaster against us? What wrong have we done? What sin have we committed against the LORD our God?'ᵉ ¹¹then say to them, 'It is because your fathers forsook me,' declares the LORD, 'and followed other gods and served and worshipedᶠ them. They forsook me and did not keep my law.ᵍ ¹²But you have behaved more wickedly than your fathers.ʰ See how each of you is following the stubbornness of his evil heartⁱ instead of obeying me. ¹³So I will throw you out of this landʲ into a land neither you nor your fathers have known,ᵏ and there you will serve other godsˡ day and night, for I will show you no favor.'ᵐ

¹⁴"However, the days are coming,"ⁿ declares the LORD, "when men will no longer say, 'As surely as the LORD lives, who brought the Israelites up out of Egypt,'ᵒ ¹⁵but they will say, 'As surely as the LORD lives, who brought the Israelites

I *Jer 12:14–17* ◄ ► *Jer 23:3–8*

16:4 ʳS Dt 28:26; Ps 79:1-3;
S Jer 14:12; 19:7
16:5 ˢS Jer 15:5
16:6 ᵗJer 9:21;
Eze 9:5-6 ᵘS ver 4
ᵛS Lev 19:28
ʷS Lev 21:5;
S Job 1:20
16:7 ˣS 2Sa 3:35
ʸJer 22:10;
Eze 24:17; Hos 9:4
ᶻLa 1:9,16
16:8 ᵃS Ex 32:6;
S Ecc 7:2,4;
S Jer 15:17
16:9 ᵇS Isa 24:8;
S 51:3; Eze 26:13;
Am 6:4-7
ᶜS Ps 78:63
ᵈS Isa 22:12-14;
Rev 18:23
16:10
ᵉS Dt 29:24;
Jer 5:19
16:11 ᶠS Job 31:21
ᵍDt 29:25-26;
S 1Ki 9:9;
Ps 106:35-43
16:12 ʰS Ex 32:8;
S Jer 7:26;
Eze 20:30; Am 2:4
ⁱS Ecc 9:3;
S Jer 3:17
16:13 ʲS 2Ch 7:20
ᵏS Dt 28:36;
S Jer 5:19
ˡS Dt 4:28;
S 1Ki 9:9
ᵐS Jer 15:5
16:14 ⁿJer 29:10;
30:3; 31:27,38
ᵒS Dt 15:15
16:15 ᵖS Jer 3:18
ᵠS Isa 11:11;
Jer 23:8 ʳPs 53:6;
S Isa 11:12;
Jer 30:3; 32:44;
Eze 38:14; Joel 3:1
ˢS Dt 30:3;
S Isa 14:1
16:16 ᵗAm 4:2;
Hab 1:14-15
ᵘAm 9:3; Mic 7:2
ᵛS 1Sa 26:20
16:17 ʷS Ge 3:8;
S Ecc 12:14;
S Mk 4:22; 1Co 4:5;
S Heb 4:13
ˣS Ps 51:9; Pr 15:3;
Zep 1:12
16:18 ʸS Isa 65:6
ᶻS Isa 40:2;
S Jer 12:3; Rev 18:6
ᵃNu 35:34; Jer 2:7
ᵇS Ps 101:3
ᶜS 1Ki 14:24
ᵈS Jer 2:7; S 4:1;
Eze 5:11; 8:10
16:19 ᵉS 2Sa 22:3;
S Ps 46:1 ᶠS Isa 2:2;
Jer 3:17 ᵍS Ps 4:2

up out of the land of the northᵖ and out of all the countries where he had banished them.'ᵠ For I will restoreʳ them to the land I gave their forefathers.ˢ

¹⁶"But now I will send for many fishermen," declares the LORD, "and they will catch them.ᵗ After that I will send for many hunters, and they will huntᵘ them down on every mountain and hill and from the crevices of the rocks.ᵛ ¹⁷My eyes are on all their ways; they are not hiddenʷ from me, nor is their sin concealed from my eyes.ˣ ¹⁸I will repayʸ them doubleᶻ for their wickedness and their sin, because they have defiled my landᵃ with the lifeless forms of their vile imagesᵇ and have filled my inheritance with their detestable idols.ᶜ"ᵈ

¹⁹O LORD, my strength and my fortress,
  my refugeᵉ in time of distress,
to you the nations will comeᶠ
  from the ends of the earth and say,
"Our fathers possessed nothing but
  false gods,ᵍ
worthless idolsʰ that did them no
  good.ⁱ
²⁰Do men make their own gods?
  Yes, but they are not gods!"ʲ

²¹"Therefore I will teach them—
  this time I will teach them
  my power and might.
Then they will know
  that my nameᵏ is the LORD.

17

"Judah's sin is engraved with an iron tool,ˡ
  inscribed with a flint point,
on the tablets of their heartsᵐ
  and on the horns ⁿ of their altars.

E *Jer 11:20* ◄ ► *Jer 17:1*
R *Jer 15:6–7* ◄ ► *Jer 17:4*
G *Isa 65:1* ◄ ► *Da 2:28–45*
C *Jer 13:23* ◄ ► *Jer 17:9*
E *Jer 16:17* ◄ ► *Jer 17:10*

ʰDt 32:21; S 1Sa 12:21 ⁱS Isa 40:19; S Jer 14:22 **16:20** ʲPs 115:4-7; S 2Co 3:3 ⁿS Ex 27:2 **17:1** ˡJob 19:24 ᵐS Dt 6:6;

16:14–19 This prophecy recounted Israel's history from the exodus (c. 1446 B.C.) to the exile (586 B.C.) and to the promised return to their land (536 B.C.) while also foreshadowing the ultimate fulfillment of this prophecy in the last days. Note Jeremiah's use of the phrase "the land of the north" (16:15) to refer to Judah's destroyers (see 50:3; Zec 2:6–7). Jeremiah also declared that the people would honor God for delivering them from exile just as their ancestors had honored him for delivering them from Egypt. Note that 23:7–8 is almost quoted verbatim from 16:14–15, highlighting the importance of this event.

² Even their children remember
  their altars and Asherah poles
  beside the spreading trees
  and on the high hills.
³ My mountain in the land
  and your wealth and all your
    treasures
  I will give away as plunder,
  together with your high places,
  because of sin throughout your
    country.
⁴ Through your own fault you will lose
    the inheritance I gave you.
  I will enslave you to your enemies
    in a land you do not know,
  for you have kindled my anger,
    and it will burn forever."

⁵ This is what the LORD says:

"Cursed is the one who trusts in
    man,
  who depends on flesh for his
    strength
  and whose heart turns away from
    the LORD.
⁶ He will be like a bush in the
    wastelands;
  he will not see prosperity when it
    comes.
  He will dwell in the parched places of
    the desert,
  in a salt land where no one lives.

⁷ "But blessed is the man who trusts
    in the LORD,
  whose confidence is in him.
⁸ He will be like a tree planted by the
    water
  that sends out its roots by the
    stream.
  It does not fear when heat comes;
    its leaves are always green.
  It has no worries in a year of drought
    and never fails to bear fruit."

⁹ The heart is deceitful above all things
    and beyond cure.
  Who can understand it?

¹⁰ "I the LORD search the heart
    and examine the mind,
  to reward a man according to his
    conduct,
  according to what his deeds
    deserve."

¹¹ Like a partridge that hatches eggs it
    did not lay
  is the man who gains riches by
    unjust means.
  When his life is half gone, they will
    desert him,
  and in the end he will prove to be a
    fool.

¹² A glorious throne, exalted from the
    beginning,
  is the place of our sanctuary.

¹³ O LORD, the hope of Israel,
  all who forsake you will be put to
    shame.
  Those who turn away from you will be
    written in the dust
  because they have forsaken the
    LORD,
  the spring of living water.

¹⁴ Heal me, O LORD, and I will be healed;
  save me and I will be saved,
  for you are the one I praise.
¹⁵ They keep saying to me,
  "Where is the word of the LORD?
  Let it now be fulfilled!"
¹⁶ I have not run away from being your
    shepherd;
  you know I have not desired the day
    of despair.
  What passes my lips is open before
    you.
¹⁷ Do not be a terror to me;
  you are my refuge in the day of
    disaster.
¹⁸ Let my persecutors be put to shame,
  but keep me from shame;

17:4 God declared that unrepentant Judah would serve their enemies in an unknown land as punishment for their sins.

let them be terrified,
    but keep me from terror.
Bring on them the day of disaster;
    destroy them with double destruction.ᶻ

Keeping the Sabbath Holy

¹⁹This is what the LORD said to me: "Go and stand at the gate of the people, through which the kings of Judah go in and out; stand also at all the other gates of Jerusalem.ᵃ ²⁰Say to them, 'Hear the word of the LORD, O kings of Judah and all people of Judah and everyone living in Jerusalemᵇ who come through these gates.ᶜ ²¹This is what the LORD says: Be careful not to carry a load on the Sabbathᵈ day or bring it through the gates of Jerusalem. ²²Do not bring a load out of your houses or do any work on the Sabbath, but keep the Sabbath day holy, as I commanded your forefathers.ᵉ ²³Yet they did not listen or pay attention;ᶠ they were stiff-neckedᵍ and would not listen or respond to discipline.ʰ ²⁴But if you are careful to obey me, declares the LORD, and bring no load through the gates of this city on the Sabbath, but keep the Sabbath day holyⁱ by not doing any work on it, ²⁵then kings who sit on David's throneʲ will come through the gates of this city with their officials. They and their officials will come riding in chariots and on horses, accompanied by the men of Judah and those living in Jerusalem, and this city will be inhabited forever.ᵏ ²⁶People will come from the towns of Judah and the villages around Jerusalem, from the territory of Benjamin and the western foothills, from the hill country and the Negev,ˡ bringing burnt offerings and sacrifices, grain offerings, incense and thank offerings to the house of the LORD. ²⁷But if you do not obeyᵐ me to keep the Sabbathⁿ day holy by not carrying any load as you come through the gates of Jerusalem on the Sabbath day, then I will kindle an unquenchable fireᵒ in the gates of Jerusalem that will consume her fortresses.' "ᵖ

At the Potter's House

18 This is the word that came to Jeremiah from the LORD: ²"Go down to the potter's house, and there I will give you my message." ³So I went down to the potter's house, and I saw him working at the wheel. ⁴But the pot he was shaping from the clay was marred in his hands; so the potter formed it into another pot, shaping it as seemed best to him.

⁵Then the word of the LORD came to me: ⁶"O house of Israel, can I not do with you as this potter does?" declares the LORD. "Like clayq in the hand of the potter, so are you in my hand,ʳ O house of Israel. ⁷If at any time I announce that a nation or kingdom is to be uprooted,ˢ torn down and destroyed, ⁸and if that nation I warned repents of its evil, then I will relentᵗ and not inflict on it the disasterᵘ I had planned. ⁹And if at another time I announce that a nation or kingdom is to be builtᵛ up and planted, ¹⁰and if it does evilʷ in my sight and does not obey me, then I will reconsiderˣ the good I had intended to do for it.ʸ

¹¹"Now therefore say to the people of Judah and those living in Jerusalem, 'This is what the LORD says: Look! I am preparing a disasterᶻ for you and devising a planᵃ against you. So turnᵇ from your evil ways,ᶜ each one of you, and reform your ways and your actions.'ᵈ ¹²But they will reply, 'It's no use.ᵉ We will continue with our own plans; each of us will follow the stubbornness of his evil heart.'ᶠ "

¹³Therefore this is what the LORD says:

"Inquire among the nations:
    Who has ever heard anything like this?ᵍ
A most horribleʰ thing has been done
    by Virginⁱ Israel.
¹⁴Does the snow of Lebanon
    ever vanish from its rocky slopes?
Do its cool waters from distant sources
    ever cease to flow?ᶠ
¹⁵Yet my people have forgottenʲ me;
    they burn incenseᵏ to worthless idols,ˡ
which made them stumbleᵐ in their ways
    and in the ancient paths.ⁿ
They made them walk in bypaths
    and on roads not built up.ᵒ

L Jer 3:22 ◀▶ Jer 21:8
R Jer 7:5–7 ◀▶ Jer 25:4–5
G Jer 17:5 ◀▶ Jer 30:12

f 14 The meaning of the Hebrew for this sentence is uncertain.

JEREMIAH 18:16 840

¹⁶Their land will be laid waste,^p
    an object of lasting scorn;^q
all who pass by will be appalled^r
    and will shake their heads.^s
¹⁷Like a wind^t from the east,
    I will scatter them before their
        enemies;
I will show them my back and not my
        face^u
    in the day of their disaster."

¹⁸They said, "Come, let's make plans^v against Jeremiah; for the teaching of the law by the priest^w will not be lost, nor will counsel from the wise,^x nor the word from the prophets.^y So come, let's attack him with our tongues^z and pay no attention to anything he says."

¹⁹Listen to me, O LORD;
    hear what my accusers^a are saying!
²⁰Should good be repaid with evil?^b
    Yet they have dug a pit^c for me.
Remember that I stood^d before you
    and spoke in their behalf^e
to turn your wrath away from
    them.
²¹So give their children over to famine;^f
    hand them over to the power of the
        sword.^g
Let their wives be made childless and
        widows;^h
    let their men be put to death,
their young menⁱ slain by the sword
    in battle.
²²Let a cry^j be heard from their houses
    when you suddenly bring invaders
        against them,
for they have dug a pit^k to capture me
    and have hidden snares^l for my
        feet.
²³But you know, O LORD,
    all their plots to kill^m me.
Do not forgiveⁿ their crimes
    or blot out their sins from your
        sight.
Let them be overthrown before you;
    deal with them in the time of your
        anger.^o

R *Jer 17:4* ◀ ▶ *Jer 19:8*

18:16
p S Dt 28:37;
Jer 25:9;
Eze 33:28-29
q Jer 19:8; 42:18
r S Lev 26:32
s S 2Ki 19:21;
S Job 16:4; Ps 22:7;
La 1:12
18:17 t S Job 7:10;
Jer 13:24
u S 2Ch 29:6;
S Jer 2:27
18:18 v ver 11;
Jer 11:19 w Jer 2:8;
Hag 2:11; Mal 2:7
x S Job 5:13;
Eze 7:26 y Jer 5:13
z Ps 52:2; 64:2-8;
S Jer 9:3
18:19 a Ps 71:13
18:20 b S Ge 44:4
c Ps 35:7; 57:6;
S 119:85 d Jer 15:1
e S Ge 20:7;
S Dt 9:19;
Ps 106:23;
Jer 14:7-9
18:21 f Jer 11:22;
14:16 g S Ps 63:10
h S 1Sa 15:33;
Ps 109:9;
S Isa 47:9; La 5:3
i Isa 9:17
18:22 j S Jer 6:26
k S Ps 119:85
l Ps 35:15; 140:5;
Jer 5:26; 20:10
18:23
m S Jer 11:21;
37:15 n S Ne 4:5
o Ps 59:5;
S Jer 10:24
19:1 p Jer 18:2
q S Nu 11:17;
1Ki 8:1
19:2 r S Jos 15:8
19:3 s Jer 17:20
t S Jer 6:19
u S 1Sa 3:11
19:4 v S Dt 31:16;
Dt 28:20;
S Isa 65:11
w S Ex 20:3;
S Jer 1:16
x S Lev 18:21
y S 2Ki 21:6
19:5 z S Lev 18:21;
S 2Ki 3:27;
Ps 106:37-38
a S Jer 7:31;
Eze 16:36
19:6 b S 2Ki 23:10
c S Jos 15:8
d Jer 7:32
19:7 e Ps 33:10-11
f S ver 9;
S Lev 26:17;
S Dt 28:25
g S Jer 16:4; 34:20
h S Dt 28:26
19:8 i S Dt 28:37;
S Jer 18:16; 25:9
j S Lev 26:32;
La 2:15-16

19 This is what the LORD says: "Go and buy a clay jar from a potter.^p Take along some of the elders^q of the people and of the priests ²and go out to the Valley of Ben Hinnom,^r near the entrance of the Potsherd Gate. There proclaim the words I tell you, ³and say, 'Hear the word of the LORD, O kings^s of Judah and people of Jerusalem. This is what the LORD Almighty, the God of Israel, says: Listen! I am going to bring a disaster^t on this place that will make the ears of everyone who hears of it tingle.^u ⁴For they have forsaken^v me and made this a place of foreign gods^w; they have burned sacrifices^x in it to gods that neither they nor their fathers nor the kings of Judah ever knew, and they have filled this place with the blood of the innocent.^y ⁵They have built the high places of Baal to burn their sons^z in the fire as offerings to Baal— something I did not command or mention, nor did it enter my mind.^a ⁶So beware, the days are coming, declares the LORD, when people will no longer call this place Topheth^b or the Valley of Ben Hinnom,^c but the Valley of Slaughter.^d

⁷"'In this place I will ruin^g the plans^e of Judah and Jerusalem. I will make them fall by the sword before their enemies,^f at the hands of those who seek their lives, and I will give their carcasses^g as food^h to the birds of the air and the beasts of the earth. ⁸I will devastate this city and make it an object of scorn;ⁱ all who pass by will be appalled^j and will scoff because of all its wounds.^k ⁹I will make them eat^l the flesh of their sons and daughters, and they will eat one another's flesh during the stress of the siege imposed on them by the enemies^m who seek their lives.'

¹⁰"Then break the jarⁿ while those

R *Jer 18:16–17* ◀ ▶ *Jer 20:6*

k S Dt 29:22 19:9 l S Lev 26:29; Dt 28:49-57; La 4:10 m S ver 7; Jer 21:7; 34:20 19:10 n ver 1; S Ps 2:9; Jer 13:14

g 7 The Hebrew for *ruin* sounds like the Hebrew for *jar* (see verses 1 and 10).

18:16–17 Jeremiah prophesied that because Judah had turned her back on God by indulging in idolatry, God would show Judah his back instead of his face. To Judah, God's face symbolized blessing, but God's back stood for desolation and calamity.

19:8 God again declared that the city would be devastated and become an object of ridicule for everyone who passed by due because of the idolatry within Jerusalem's walls.

who go with you are watching, ¹¹and say to them, 'This is what the LORD Almighty says: I will smash° this nation and this city just as this potter's jar is smashed and cannot be repaired. They will bury^p the dead in Topheth until there is no more room. ¹²This is what I will do to this place and to those who live here, declares the LORD. I will make this city like Topheth. ¹³The houses^q in Jerusalem and those of the kings of Judah will be defiled^r like this place, Topheth—all the houses where they burned incense on the roofs^s to all the starry hosts^t and poured out drink offerings^u to other gods.' "

¹⁴Jeremiah then returned from Topheth, where the LORD had sent him to prophesy, and stood in the court^v of the LORD's temple and said to all the people, ¹⁵"This is what the LORD Almighty, the God of Israel, says: 'Listen! I am going to bring on this city and the villages around it every disaster^w I pronounced against them, because they were stiff-necked^x and would not listen^y to my words.' "

Jeremiah and Pashhur

20 When the priest Pashhur son of Immer,^z the chief officer^a in the temple of the LORD, heard Jeremiah prophesying these things, ²he had Jeremiah the prophet beaten^b and put in the stocks^c at the Upper Gate of Benjamin^d at the LORD's temple. ³The next day, when Pashhur released him from the stocks, Jeremiah said to him, "The LORD's name^e for you is not Pashhur, but Magor-Missabib.^h^f ⁴For this is what the LORD says: 'I will make you a terror to yourself and to all your friends; with your own eyes^g you will see them fall by the sword of their enemies. I will hand^h all Judah over to the king of Babylon, who will carry^i them away to Babylon or put them to the sword. ⁵I will hand over to their enemies all the wealth^j of this city—all its products, all its valuables and all the treasures of the kings of Judah. They will take it away^k as plunder and carry it off to Babylon. ⁶And you, Pashhur, and all who live in your house will go into exile to Babylon. There you will die and be buried, you and all your friends to whom you have prophesied^l lies.' "

R *Jer 19:8* ◀▶ *Jer 21:7*

19:11 °Ps 2:9; Isa 30:14 ᵖJer 7:32
19:13 ᑫJer 32:29; 52:13; Eze 16:41
ʳPs 74:7
ˢS 2Ki 23:12
ᵗDt 4:19;
S 2Ki 17:16;
S Job 38:32; Jer 8:2;
Ac 7:42
ᵘS Isa 57:6;
Eze 20:28
19:14 ᵛ2Ch 20:5;
S Jer 7:2; 26:2
19:15 ʷver 3;
Jer 11:11
ˣS Ne 9:16;
Ac 7:51 ʸJer 22:21
20:1 ᶻS 1Ch 24:14
ᵃ2Ki 25:18;
Lk 22:52
20:2 ᵇDt 25:2-3;
S Jer 1:19; 15:15;
37:15; 2Co 11:24
ᶜS Job 13:27;
Jer 29:26;
Ac 16:24;
Heb 11:36
ᵈS Job 29:7;
Jer 37:13; 38:7;
Zec 14:10
20:3 ᵉHos 1:4
ᶠS ver 10;
S Ps 31:13
20:4 ᵍJer 29:21
ʰJer 21:10; 25:9
ⁱJer 13:19; 39:9;
52:27
20:5 ʲS 2Ki 25:15;
Jer 17:3
ᵏS 2Ki 20:17
20:6 ˡS Jer 14:15;
La 2:14
20:7 ᵐS Ex 5:23;
22:16 ⁿIsa 8:11;
Am 3:8; 1Co 9:16
°Job 12:4
ᵖS Job 17:2;
S Ps 119:21
20:8 ᑫJer 6:7; 28:8
ʳS 2Ch 36:16;
S Jer 6:10
20:9 ˢJer 44:16
ᵗS Ps 39:3;
S Jer 4:19
ᵘS Job 4:2;
S Jer 6:11; Am 3:8;
Ac 4:20
20:10 ᵛJer 6:25
ʷNe 6:6-13;
Isa 29:21
ˣS Job 19:14;
S Jer 13:21
ʸS Ps 57:4;
S Jer 18:22;
Lk 11:53-54
ᶻS 1Ki 19:2
ᵃS 1Sa 18:25;
S Jer 11:19
20:11 ᵇJer 1:8;
Ro 8:31 ᶜJer 15:15;
17:18 ᵈS Ps 129:2
ᵉS Jer 7:19; 23:40
20:12 ᶠS Ps 7:9;
S Jer 17:10
ᵍDt 32:35;
S Ro 12:19
ʰPs 62:8; Jer 11:20
20:13 ⁱS Isa 12:6
ʲPs 34:6; 35:10
ᵏS Ps 97:10
20:14 ˡS Job 3:8, 16; Jer 15:10

Jeremiah's Complaint

⁷O LORD, you deceived^i^m me, and I was deceived^i;
 you overpowered^n me and prevailed.
I am ridiculed° all day long;
 everyone mocks^p me.
⁸Whenever I speak, I cry out
 proclaiming violence and destruction. ᑫ
So the word of the LORD has brought me
 insult and reproach^r all day long.
⁹But if I say, "I will not mention him
 or speak any more in his name,"^s
his word is in my heart like a fire,^t
 a fire shut up in my bones.
I am weary of holding it in;^u
 indeed, I cannot.
¹⁰I hear many whispering,
 "Terror^v on every side!
 Report^w him! Let's report him!"
All my friends^x
 are waiting for me to slip,^y saying,
 "Perhaps he will be deceived;
 then we will prevail^z over him
 and take our revenge^a on him."

¹¹But the LORD^b is with me like a mighty warrior;
 so my persecutors^c will stumble and not prevail.^d
They will fail and be thoroughly disgraced;^e
 their dishonor will never be forgotten.
¹²O LORD Almighty, you who examine the righteous
 and probe the heart and mind,^f
let me see your vengeance^g upon them,
 for to you I have committed^h my cause.

¹³Sing^i to the LORD!
 Give praise to the LORD!
He rescues^j the life of the needy
 from the hands of the wicked.^k

¹⁴Cursed be the day I was born!^l
 May the day my mother bore me not be blessed!
¹⁵Cursed be the man who brought my father the news,

H *Jer 17:4* ◀▶ *Jer 23:12*
V *Jer 15:20–21* ◀▶ *Jer 39:17–18*
E *Jer 17:10* ◀▶ *Jer 23:23–24*

^h 3 *Magor-Missabib* means *terror on every side*. ^i 7 Or *persuaded*

who made him very glad, saying,
"A child is born to you—a son!"
[16] May that man be like the towns[m]
   the LORD overthrew without pity.
May he hear wailing[n] in the morning,
   a battle cry at noon.
[17] For he did not kill me in the womb,[o]
   with my mother as my grave,
   her womb enlarged forever.
[18] Why did I ever come out of the womb[p]
   to see trouble[q] and sorrow
   and to end my days in shame?[r]

God Rejects Zedekiah's Request

21 The word came to Jeremiah from the LORD when King Zedekiah[s] sent to him Pashhur[t] son of Malkijah and the priest Zephaniah[u] son of Maaseiah. They said: [2] "Inquire[v] now of the LORD for us because Nebuchadnezzar[w] king of Babylon[x] is attacking us. Perhaps the LORD will perform wonders[y] for us as in times past so that he will withdraw from us."

[3] But Jeremiah answered them, "Tell Zedekiah, [4] 'This is what the LORD, the God of Israel, says: I am about to turn[z] against you the weapons of war that are in your hands, which you are using to fight the king of Babylon and the Babylonians[k] who are outside the wall besieging[a] you. And I will gather them inside this city. [5] I myself will fight[b] against you with an outstretched hand[c] and a mighty arm[d] in anger and fury and great wrath. [6] I will strike[e] down those who live in this city—both men and animals—and they will die of a terrible plague.[f] [7] After that, declares the LORD, I will hand over Zedekiah[g] king of Judah, his officials and the people in this city who survive the plague,[h] sword and famine, to Nebuchadnezzar king of Babylon[i] and to their enemies[j] who seek their lives.[k] He will put them to the sword;[l] he will show them no mercy or pity or compassion.'[m]

[8] "Furthermore, tell the people, 'This is what the LORD says: See, I am setting before you the way of life[n] and the way of death. [9] Whoever stays in this city will die by the sword, famine or plague.[o] But whoever goes out and surrenders[p] to the Babylonians who are besieging you will live; he will escape with his life.[q] [10] I have determined to do this city harm[r] and not good, declares the LORD. It will be given into the hands[s] of the king of Babylon, and he will destroy it with fire.'[t]

[11] "Moreover, say to the royal house[u] of Judah, 'Hear the word of the LORD; [12] O house of David, this is what the LORD says:

" 'Administer justice[v] every morning;
   rescue from the hand of his
      oppressor[w]
   the one who has been robbed,
or my wrath will break out and burn
      like fire[x]
because of the evil[y] you have
      done—
burn with no one to quench[z] it.
[13] I am against[a] you, ⌊Jerusalem,⌋
   you who live above this valley[b]
   on the rocky plateau,
               declares the LORD—
you who say, "Who can come against
      us?
Who can enter our refuge?"[c]
[14] I will punish you as your deeds[d]
      deserve,
               declares the LORD.
I will kindle a fire[e] in your forests[f]
that will consume everything around
      you.' "

Judgment Against Evil Kings

22 This is what the LORD says: "Go down to the palace of the king[g] of Judah and proclaim this message there: [2] 'Hear[h] the word of the LORD, O king of Judah, you who sit on David's throne[i]— you, your officials and your people who come through these gates.[j] [3] This is what

---

20:16 [m] S Ge 19:25 [n] S Jer 6:26
20:17 [o] S Job 3:16; S 10:18-19
20:18 [p] S Job 3:10-11; S Ecc 4:2 [q] S Ge 3:17; [r] S 1Ki 19:4; Ps 90:9; 102:3
21:1 [s] 2Ki 24:18; Jer 52:1 [t] S 1Ch 9:12 [u] S 2Ki 25:18
21:2 [v] S Ge 25:22; S 2Ki 22:18 [w] S 2Ki 25:1 [x] S Ge 10:10 [y] Ps 44:1-4; Jer 32:17
21:4 [z] Jer 32:5 [a] Jer 37:8-10
21:5 [b] S Jos 10:14; Eze 5:8 [c] S 2Ki 22:13; S Jer 6:12 [d] S Ex 3:20
21:6 [e] S Jer 7:20 [f] S Jer 14:12
21:7 [g] S 2Ki 25:7; Jer 52:9; Eze 12:14 [h] Jer 14:12; 27:8 [i] S 2Ch 36:10; Jer 27:6; 32:4; 34:3; 37:17; 38:18; 39:5; Eze 29:19 [j] S Lev 26:17; S Jer 19:9 [k] S Jer 11:21 [l] S Jer 15:9 [m] S 2Ch 36:17; S Jer 15:5; Eze 7:9; Hab 1:6
21:8 [n] S Dt 30:15
21:9 [o] Jer 14:12; Eze 5:12 [p] Jer 27:11; 40:9 [q] Jer 27:12; 38:2, 17; 39:18; 45:5
21:10 [r] Jer 44:11, 27; Am 9:4 [s] S Jer 20:4; 32:28; 38:2-3 [t] S 2Ki 25:9; S 2Ch 36:19
21:11 [u] S Jer 13:18
21:12 [v] S Ex 22:22; S Lev 25:17 [w] S Ps 27:11 [x] S Isa 42:25; S Jer 10:10 [y] Jer 23:2 [z] S Isa 1:31
21:13 [a] Jer 23:30; 50:31; 51:25; Eze 5:8; 13:8; 21:3; 29:10; 34:10; Na 2:13; 3:5 [b] Ps 125:2
[c] 2Sa 5:6-7; Jer 49:4; La 4:12; Ob 1:3-4
21:14 [d] S Pr 1:31; S Isa 3:10-11; [e] S 2Ch 36:19; La 2:3 [f] S 2Ki 19:23; Eze 20:47
22:1 [g] S Jer 13:18; 34:2 22:2 [h] Am 7:16 [i] S Jer 17:25; Lk 1:32 [j] Jer 17:20
[j2] Hebrew *Nebuchadrezzar*, of which *Nebuchadnezzar* is a variant; here and often in Jeremiah and Ezekiel [k4] Or *Chaldeans*; also in verse 9

D Ps 106:29 ◀ ▶ Jer 44:13
R Jer 20:6 ◀ ▶ Jer 21:10
L Jer 18:8 ◀ ▶ Jer 26:13

R Jer 21:7 ◀ ▶ Jer 22:5

21:10 Jeremiah pronounced God's terrible verdict against the wickedness and evil of Jerusalem. The cruel, pagan king of Babylon would destroy the city and carry the people away as slaves.

22:3–5 God commanded the kings of Judah to carry out justice to all otherwise "this palace will become a ruin" (22:5).

the LORD says: Do what is just[k] and right. Rescue from the hand of his oppressor[l] the one who has been robbed. Do no wrong or violence to the alien, the fatherless or the widow,[m] and do not shed innocent blood[n] in this place. [4]For if you are careful to carry out these commands, then kings[o] who sit on David's throne will come through the gates of this palace, riding in chariots and on horses, accompanied by their officials and their people. [5]But if you do not obey[p] these commands, declares the LORD, I swear[q] by myself that this palace will become a ruin.'"

[6]For this is what the LORD says about the palace of the king of Judah:

"Though you are like Gilead[r] to me,
    like the summit of Lebanon,[s]
I will surely make you like a desert,[t]
    like towns not inhabited.
[7]I will send destroyers[u] against you,
    each man with his weapons,
and they will cut[v] up your fine cedar beams
    and throw them into the fire.[w]

[8]"People from many nations will pass by this city and will ask one another, 'Why has the LORD done such a thing to this great city?'[x] [9]And the answer will be: 'Because they have forsaken the covenant of the LORD their God and have worshiped and served other gods.[y] '"

[10]Do not weep for the dead[z] king, or mourn[a] his loss;
rather, weep bitterly for him who is exiled,
because he will never return[b]
    nor see his native land again.

[11]For this is what the LORD says about Shallum[c] son of Josiah, who succeeded his father as king of Judah but has gone from this place: "He will never return. [12]He will die[d] in the place where they have led him captive; he will not see this land again."

[13]"Woe[e] to him who builds[f] his palace by unrighteousness,
    his upper rooms by injustice,
making his countrymen work for nothing,
    not paying[g] them for their labor.

R *Jer 21:10* ◄ ► *Jer 22:10–12*
R *Jer 22:5* ◄ ► *Jer 22:18–19*

22:3 k S Lev 25:17; Isa 56:1; Jer 5:1; Eze 33:14; 45:9; Hos 12:6; Am 5:24; Mic 6:8; Zec 7:9
l Ps 72:4; Jer 21:12
m S Ex 22:22;
n S Jer 7:6
22:4 o S Jer 17:25
22:5 p S Jer 17:27
q S Ge 22:16; Heb 6:13
22:6 r S Ge 31:21; S SS 4:1 s S 1Ki 7:2; S Isa 33:9
t Mic 3:12
22:7 u S Jer 4:7; S 6:4 v Ps 74:5; Isa 10:34
w S 2Ch 36:19; Zec 11:1
22:8 x Dt 29:25-26; 1Ki 9:8-9; Jer 16:10-11
22:9 y S 1Ki 9:9; Jer 16:11; Eze 39:23
22:10 z S Ecc 4:2
a ver 18; Eze 24:16
b ver 27; Jer 24:9; 29:18; 42:18
22:11 c S 2Ki 23:31
22:12 d 2Ki 23:34
22:13 e S Isa 5:8
f Mic 3:10; Hab 2:9
g S Lev 19:13; Jas 5:4
22:14 h Isa 5:8-9
i S 2Sa 7:2
j Eze 23:14
22:15 k 2Ki 23:25
l Ps 128:2; S Isa 3:10
22:16 m Ps 72:1-4, 12-13; S 82:3; S Pr 24:23
n S Ps 36:10
22:17 o S Isa 56:11
p S 2Ki 24:4
q S Dt 28:33; Eze 18:12; Mic 2:2
22:18 r S 2Sa 1:26
22:19 s 2Ki 24:6
t Jer 8:2; 36:30
22:20 u S Isa 57:13
v S Ps 68:15
w S Nu 27:12
x ver 22; Jer 30:14; La 1:19;
Eze 16:33-34; Hos 8:9
22:21 y Zec 7:7
z Dt 9:7; Ps 25:7;
Isa 54:4; Jer 3:25; 31:19; 32:30
a S Jer 3:13;
7:23-28; Zep 3:2
22:22 b S Dt 28:64;
S Job 27:21
c S Jer 10:21
d S ver 20
e S Jer 7:19
22:23 f S 1Ki 7:2; Eze 17:3

[14]He says, 'I will build myself a great palace[h]
    with spacious upper rooms.'
So he makes large windows in it,
    panels it with cedar[i]
    and decorates it in red.[j]

[15]"Does it make you a king
    to have more and more cedar?
Did not your father have food and drink?
    He did what was right and just,[k]
    so all went well[l] with him.
[16]He defended the cause of the poor and needy,[m]
    and so all went well.
Is that not what it means to know[n] me?"
declares the LORD.
[17]"But your eyes and your heart
    are set only on dishonest gain,[o]
on shedding innocent blood[p]
    and on oppression and extortion."[q]

[18]Therefore this is what the LORD says R about Jehoiakim son of Josiah king of Judah:

"They will not mourn[r] for him:
    'Alas, my brother! Alas, my sister!'
They will not mourn for him:
    'Alas, my master! Alas, his splendor!'
[19]He will have the burial[s] of a donkey—
    dragged away and thrown[t]
    outside the gates of Jerusalem."

[20]"Go up to Lebanon and cry out,[u]
    let your voice be heard in Bashan,[v]
cry out from Abarim,[w]
    for all your allies[x] are crushed.
[21]I warned you when you felt secure,[y]
    but you said, 'I will not listen!'
This has been your way from your youth;[z]
    you have not obeyed[a] me.
[22]The wind[b] will drive all your shepherds[c] away,
    and your allies[d] will go into exile.
Then you will be ashamed and disgraced[e]
    because of all your wickedness.
[23]You who live in 'Lebanon,'[m][f]
    who are nestled in cedar buildings,

R *Jer 22:10–12* ◄ ► *Jer 23:39–40*

[l]*11* Also called *Jehoahaz* [m]*23* That is, the palace in Jerusalem (see 1 Kings 7:2)

how you will groan when pangs come
    upon you,
  pain[g] like that of a woman in labor!"

[24] "As surely as I live," declares the
LORD, "even if you, Jehoiachin[n][h] son of
Jehoiakim king of Judah, were a signet
ring[i] on my right hand, I would still pull
you off. [25] I will hand you over[j] to those
who seek your life, those you fear—to
Nebuchadnezzar king of Babylon and to
the Babylonians.[o] [26] I will hurl[k] you and
the mother[l] who gave you birth into another country, where neither of you was
born, and there you both will die. [27] You
will never come back to the land you long
to return[m] to."

[28] Is this man Jehoiachin[n] a despised,
    broken pot,[o]
  an object no one wants?
Why will he and his children be
    hurled[p] out,
  cast into a land[q] they do not know?

[29] O land,[r] land, land,
  hear the word of the LORD!
[30] This is what the LORD says:
  "Record this man as if childless,[s]
  a man who will not prosper[t] in his
    lifetime,
for none of his offspring[u] will prosper,
  none will sit on the throne[v] of David
  or rule anymore in Judah."

The Righteous Branch

23 "Woe to the shepherds[w] who are destroying and scattering[x] the sheep of my pasture!"[y] declares the LORD. [2] Therefore this is what the LORD, the God of Israel, says to the shepherds[z] who tend my people: "Because you have scattered my flock[a] and driven them away and have not bestowed care on them, I will bestow punishment on you for the evil[b] you have done," declares the LORD. [3] "I myself will gather the remnant[c] of my flock out of all the countries where I have driven them and will bring them back to their pasture,[d] where they will be fruitful and increase in number. [4] I will place shepherds[e] over them who will tend them, and they will no longer be afraid[f] or terrified, nor will any be missing,[g]" declares the LORD.

[5] "The days are coming," declares the
    LORD,
  "when I will raise up to David[p] a
    righteous Branch,[h]
  a King[i] who will reign[j] wisely
  and do what is just and right[k] in the
    land.
[6] In his days Judah will be saved
  and Israel will live in safety.[l]
This is the name[m] by which he will be
    called:
  The LORD Our Righteousness.[n]

[7] "So then, the days are coming,"[o] declares the LORD, "when people will no longer say, 'As surely as the LORD lives, who brought the Israelites up out of Egypt,'[p] [8] but they will say, 'As surely as the LORD lives, who brought the descendants of Israel up out of the land of the north and out of all the countries where

l Jer 16:14–16 ◀ ▶ Jer 25:12
M Jer 3:17 ◀ ▶ Jer 30:9
V Isa 45:23 ◀ ▶ Jer 31:34

p S Dt 15:15

n 24 Hebrew *Coniah*, a variant of *Jehoiachin*; also in verse 28
o 25 Or *Chaldeans* p 5 Or *up from David's line*

B Isa 61:1–3 ◀ ▶ Da 9:24–26

22:28–30 The name Coniah is a shortened form of Jeconiah (see Mt 1:11–12) and was an informal name for King Jehoiachin (see 22:24; 1Ch 3:15–17). Because none of Jehoiachin's children ever ruled in Jerusalem, Jeremiah's prophecy appears at first glance to contradict the Davidic covenant that guaranteed the throne to David's seed forever. However, this prophecy will be fulfilled, and the covenant with David upheld, when Jesus the Messiah rules from Jerusalem during the Millennium. When Jesus was born, the genealogical records preserved in the temple at that time would have proved his double right to rule from the throne of David—a legal descent through King Jehoiachin (see Mt 1:1–17) as well as his maternal descent from King David (see Lk 3:23–38).

23:3–8 God stated his ultimate intent to judge the wicked of Judah yet also bring his people back to the promised land from their exile among the nations. Jeremiah foretold the great promise of the Messiah who will "do what is just and right in the land" (23:5). Under the rule of the Messiah, Israel will finally espouse righteousness and experience safety. Jeremiah also declared that the people would honor God for delivering them from exile just as their ancestors had honored him for delivering them from Egypt. Note also that 23:7–8 is quoted almost verbatim from 16:14–15, indicating the significance of this event.

he had banished them.' Then they will live in their own land."ᑫ

Lying Prophets

⁹Concerning the prophets:

My heartʳ is broken within me;
  all my bones tremble.ˢ
I am like a drunken man,
  like a man overcome by wine,
because of the LORD
  and his holy words.ᵗ
¹⁰The land is full of adulterers;ᵘ
  because of the curseᑫᵛ the land lies parchedʳ
  and the pasturesʷ in the desert are withered.ˣ
The ˪prophets˩ follow an evil course
  and use their power unjustly.
¹¹"Both prophet and priest are godless;ʸ
  even in my templeᶻ I find their wickedness,"
          declares the LORD.

¹²"Therefore their path will become slippery;ᵃ
  they will be banished to darkness
  and there they will fall.
I will bring disaster on them
  in the year they are punished,"ᵇ
          declares the LORD.

¹³"Among the prophets of Samaria
  I saw this repulsive thing:
They prophesied by Baalᶜ
  and led my people Israel astray.ᵈ
¹⁴And among the prophets of Jerusalem
  I have seen something horrible:ᵉ
They commit adultery and live a lie.ᶠ
They strengthen the hands of evildoers,ᵍ
  so that no one turns from his wickedness.ʰ
They are all like Sodomⁱ to me;
  the people of Jerusalem are like Gomorrah."ʲ

¹⁵Therefore, this is what the LORD Almighty says concerning the prophets:

"I will make them eat bitter food
  and drink poisoned water,ᵏ

C *Jer 17:9* ◀ ▶ *Jer 44:10*
H *Jer 20:11* ◀ ▶ *Jer 23:17–19*

23:8 ᑫS Isa 14:1; S 43:5-6; Jer 30:10; Eze 20:42; 34:13; Am 9:14-15

23:9 ʳS Jer 4:19; ˢS Job 4:14; ᵗJer 20:8-9

23:10 ᵘS Jer 9:2; ᵛDt 28:23-24; ʷPs 107:34; S Jer 9:10; ˣS Jer 4:26; S 12:11

23:11 ʸJer 6:13; S 8:10; Zep 3:4; ᶻS 2Ki 21:4; S Jer 7:10

23:12 ᵃS Dt 32:35; S Job 3:23; Jer 13:16; ᵇJer 11:23

23:13 ᶜS 1Ki 18:22; ᵈver 32; S Isa 3:12; Eze 13:10

23:14 ᵉS Jer 5:30; Hos 6:10 ᶠJer 29:23 ᵍver 22 ʰS Isa 5:18 ⁱS Ge 18:20; Mt 11:24 ʲJer 20:16; Am 4:11

23:15 ᵏS Jer 8:14; 9:15 ˡS Jer 8:10

23:16 ᵐJer 27:9-10,14; S Mt 7:15 ⁿS Jer 14:14; Eze 13:3 ᵒJer 9:20

23:17 ᵖver 31 ᑫS 1Ki 22:8; S Jer 4:10 ʳS Jer 13:10 ˢJer 5:12; Am 9:10; Mic 3:11

23:18 ᵗS 1Ki 22:19; S Ro 11:34

23:19 ᵘS Isa 30:30; Jer 25:32; 30:23 ᵛZec 7:14

23:20 ʷS 2Ki 23:26 ˣS Jer 4:28

23:21 ʸS Jer 14:14; 27:15

23:22 ᶻS 1Ki 22:19 ᵃS Dt 33:10 ᵇS 2Ki 17:13; Jer 25:5; Zec 1:4 ᶜver 14; Am 3:7

because from the prophets of Jerusalem
  ungodliness¹ has spread throughout the land."

¹⁶This is what the LORD Almighty says:

"Do not listenᵐ to what the prophets
  are prophesying to you;
  they fill you with false hopes.
They speak visionsⁿ from their own minds,
  not from the mouthᵒ of the LORD.
¹⁷They keep sayingᵖ to those who despise me,
  'The LORD says: You will have peace.'ᑫ
And to all who follow the stubbornnessʳ of their hearts
  they say, 'No harmˢ will come to you.'
¹⁸But which of them has stood in the councilᵗ of the LORD
  to see or to hear his word?
Who has listened and heard his word?
¹⁹See, the stormᵘ of the LORD
  will burst out in wrath,
a whirlwindᵛ swirling down
  on the heads of the wicked.
²⁰The angerʷ of the LORD will not turn backˣ
  until he fully accomplishes
  the purposes of his heart.
In days to come
  you will understand it clearly.
²¹I did not sendʸ these prophets,
  yet they have run with their message;
I did not speak to them,
  yet they have prophesied.
²²But if they had stood in my council,ᶻ
  they would have proclaimedᵃ my words to my people
and would have turnedᵇ them from their evil ways
  and from their evil deeds.ᶜ

H *Jer 23:12* ◀ ▶ *Jer 23:40*
P *Jer 10:10* ◀ ▶ *Jer 25:29–33*
S *Jer 17:13* ◀ ▶ *Jer 32:19*

ᑫ 10 Or *because of these things* ʳ 10 Or *land mourns*

23:19–20 Jeremiah's words portray a vivid picture of God's wrath in the last days during the tribulation period.

²³"Am I only a God nearby,
declares the LORD,
"and not a God far away?
²⁴Can anyone hide in secret places
so that I cannot see him?"
declares the LORD.
"Do not I fill heaven and earth?"
declares the LORD.

²⁵"I have heard what the prophets say who prophesy lies in my name. They say, 'I had a dream! I had a dream!' ²⁶How long will this continue in the hearts of these lying prophets, who prophesy the delusions of their own minds? ²⁷They think the dreams they tell one another will make my people forget my name, just as their fathers forgot my name through Baal worship. ²⁸Let the prophet who has a dream tell his dream, but let the one who has my word speak it faithfully. For what has straw to do with grain?" declares the LORD. ²⁹"Is not my word like fire," declares the LORD, "and like a hammer that breaks a rock in pieces?

³⁰"Therefore," declares the LORD, "I am against the prophets who steal from one another words supposedly from me. ³¹Yes," declares the LORD, "I am against the prophets who wag their own tongues and yet declare, 'The LORD declares.' ³²Indeed, I am against those who prophesy false dreams," declares the LORD. "They tell them and lead my people astray with their reckless lies, yet I did not send or appoint them. They do not benefit these people in the least," declares the LORD.

False Oracles and False Prophets

³³"When these people, or a prophet or a priest, ask you, 'What is the oracle of the LORD?' say to them, 'What oracle? I will forsake you, declares the LORD.' ³⁴If a prophet or a priest or anyone else claims, 'This is the oracle of the LORD,' I will punish that man and his household.

E *Jer 20:12* ◄ ► *Jer 32:19*

23:23
ᵈ Ps 139:1-10
23:24 ᵉ S Ge 3:8;
S Job 11:20;
22:12-14;
S Ecc 12:14;
S Isa 28:15;
1Co 4:5 ᶠS 1Ki 8:27
23:25 ᵍver 16;
Jer 14:14; 27:10
ʰ ver 28,32;
S Dt 13:1; Jer 27:9;
29:8
23:26 ⁱS Isa 30:10;
1Ti 4:1-2
ʲJer 14:14; Eze 13:2
23:27 ᵏDt 13:1-3;
Jer 29:8 ˡS Jdg 3:7;
S 8:33-34
ᵐS Jer 2:23
23:28 ⁿS ver 25
ᵒS Isa 3:17
23:29 ᵖS Ps 39:3;
Jer 5:14;
S 1Co 3:13
ᑫHeb 4:12
23:30 ʳS Ps 34:16
ˢver 2; Dt 18:20;
Jer 14:15; S 21:13
23:31 ᵗver 17
23:32 ᵘS ver 25
ᵛS ver 13;
ʷS Jer 50:6
ˣS Job 13:4;
Eze 13:3; 22:28
ˣS Jer 14:14
ʸJer 7:8; La 2:14
23:33 ᶻMal 1:1
ᵃ S 2Ki 21:14
23:34 ᵇLa 2:14
ᶜZec 13:3
23:35 ᵈJer 33:3;
42:4
23:36 ᵉGal 1:7-8;
2Pe 3:16
ᶠS Jos 3:10
23:39 ᵍS Jer 7:15
23:40
ʰS Jer 20:11;
Eze 5:14-15
24:1 ⁱS 2Ki 24:16;
S 2Ch 36:9
ʲEx 23:19; Dt 26:2;
Am 8:1-2
24:2 ᵏS SS 2:13
ˡS Isa 5:4
24:3 ᵐJer 1:11;
Am 8:2

³⁵This is what each of you keeps on saying to his friend or relative: 'What is the LORD's answer?' or 'What has the LORD spoken?' ³⁶But you must not mention 'the oracle of the LORD' again, because every man's own word becomes his oracle and so you distort the words of the living God, the LORD Almighty, our God. ³⁷This is what you keep saying to a prophet: 'What is the LORD's answer to you?' or 'What has the LORD spoken?' ³⁸Although you claim, 'This is the oracle of the LORD,' this is what the LORD says: You used the words, 'This is the oracle of the LORD,' even though I told you that you must not claim, 'This is the oracle of the LORD.' ³⁹Therefore, I will surely forget you and cast you out of my presence along with the city I gave to you and your fathers. ⁴⁰I will bring upon you everlasting disgrace—everlasting shame that will not be forgotten."

Two Baskets of Figs

24 After Jehoiachin son of Jehoiakim king of Judah and the officials, the craftsmen and the artisans of Judah were carried into exile from Jerusalem to Babylon by Nebuchadnezzar king of Babylon, the LORD showed me two baskets of figs placed in front of the temple of the LORD. ²One basket had very good figs, like those that ripen early; the other basket had very poor figs, so bad they could not be eaten.

³Then the LORD asked me, "What do you see, Jeremiah?"

"Figs," I answered. "The good ones are very good, but the poor ones are so bad they cannot be eaten."

⁴Then the word of the LORD came to me: ⁵"This is what the LORD, the God of Israel, says: 'Like these good figs, I regard as good the exiles from Judah, whom I

R *Jer 22:18–19* ◄ ► *Jer 25:17–18*
H *Jer 23:17–19* ◄ ► *Jer 30:23–24*

ˢ 33 Or *burden* (see Septuagint and Vulgate)   ᵗ 33 Hebrew; Septuagint and Vulgate *You are the burden.* (The Hebrew for *oracle* and *burden* is the same.)   ᵘ 1 Hebrew *Jeconiah,* a variant of *Jehoiachin*

23:39–40 God again proclaimed his determination to punish Judah because of her continued rebellion against him.

24:1–10 Jeremiah likened Judah to a basket of figs, a symbolic usage that occurs several times in Scripture (see 8:13; Mic 7:1; Na 3:12). The "good figs" symbolized people of Judah who repented of their sins while in captivity and who would be returned to their land. The "bad figs" symbolized the people who would not repent of their sins and who would be "destroyed from the land" (24:10).

sent[n] away from this place to the land of the Babylonians.[v] ⁶My eyes will watch over them for their good, and I will bring them back[o] to this land. I will build[p] them up and not tear them down; I will plant[q] them and not uproot them. ⁷I will give them a heart to know[r] me, that I am the LORD. They will be my people,[s] and I will be their God, for they will return[t] to me with all their heart.[u]

⁸"'But like the poor[v] figs, which are so bad they cannot be eaten,' says the LORD, 'so will I deal with Zedekiah[w] king of Judah, his officials[x] and the survivors[y] from Jerusalem, whether they remain in this land or live in Egypt.[z] ⁹I will make them abhorrent[a] and an offense to all the kingdoms of the earth, a reproach and a byword,[b] an object of ridicule and cursing,[c] wherever I banish[d] them. ¹⁰I will send the sword,[e] famine[f] and plague[g] against them until they are destroyed from the land I gave to them and their fathers.[h]'"

Seventy Years of Captivity

25 The word came to Jeremiah concerning all the people of Judah in the fourth year of Jehoiakim[i] son of Josiah king of Judah, which was the first year of Nebuchadnezzar[j] king of Babylon. ²So Jeremiah the prophet said to all the people of Judah[k] and to all those living in Jerusalem: ³For twenty-three years—from the thirteenth year of Josiah[l] son of Amon king of Judah until this very day—the word of the LORD has come to me and I have spoken to you again and again,[m] but you have not listened.[n]

⁴And though the LORD has sent all his servants the prophets[o] to you again and again, you have not listened or paid any attention.[p] ⁵They said, "Turn[q] now, each of you, from your evil ways and your evil practices, and you can stay in the land[r] the LORD gave to you and your fathers for

ever and ever. ⁶Do not follow other gods[s] to serve and worship them; do not provoke me to anger with what your hands have made. Then I will not harm you."

⁷"But you did not listen to me," declares the LORD, "and you have provoked[t] me with what your hands have made,[u] and you have brought harm[v] to yourselves."

⁸Therefore the LORD Almighty says this: "Because you have not listened to my words, ⁹I will summon[w] all the peoples of the north[x] and my servant[y] Nebuchadnezzar[z] king of Babylon," declares the LORD, "and I will bring them against this land and its inhabitants and against all the surrounding nations. I will completely destroy[w,a] them and make them an object of horror and scorn,[b] and an everlasting ruin.[c] ¹⁰I will banish from them the sounds[d] of joy and gladness, the voices of bride and bridegroom,[e] the sound of millstones[f] and the light of the lamp.[g] ¹¹This whole country will become a desolate wasteland,[h] and these nations will serve[i] the king of Babylon seventy years.[j]

¹²"But when the seventy years[k] are fulfilled, I will punish the king of Babylon[l] and his nation, the land of the Babylonians,[v] for their guilt," declares the LORD, "and will make it desolate[m] forever. ¹³I will bring upon that land all the things I have spoken against it, all that are written[n] in this book and prophesied by Jeremiah against all the nations. ¹⁴They themselves will be enslaved[o] by many nations[p] and great kings; I will repay[q] them ac-

I *Jer 23:3–8* ◀ ▶ *Jer 30:1–3*

K *Jer 17:13–14* ◀ ▶ *Jer 31:33–34*
R *Jer 18:11* ◀ ▶ *Jer 26:13*

v 5, 12 Or *Chaldeans*   w 9 The Hebrew term refers to the irrevocable giving over of things or persons to the LORD, often by totally destroying them.

25:11–13 Jeremiah delivered one of the most significant prophecies of the OT in this passage, clearly stating who would conquer Judah and how long Judah would be in exile. Since the nation had not followed God's command to let the land lie unplowed every seven years, the seventy-year captivity in Babylon would give the land its Sabbaths (see 2Ch 36:21). God also declared that following this seventy-year captivity he would punish the Babylonians for their pagan idolatry and savage treatment of his people. These prophecies were fulfilled when Nebuchadnezzar conquered Judah in 606 B.C. and when seventy years later Cyrus, the king of Persia, issued his proclamation allowing the exiles to return to the promised land (see Ezr 1:1–4; Da 9:2).

The Cup of God's Wrath

15 This is what the LORD, the God of Israel, said to me: "Take from my hand this cup[r] filled with the wine of my wrath and make all the nations to whom I send[s] you drink it. 16 When they drink[t] it, they will stagger[u] and go mad[v] because of the sword[w] I will send among them."

17 So I took the cup from the LORD's hand and made all the nations to whom he sent[x] me drink it: 18 Jerusalem[y] and the towns of Judah, its kings and officials, to make them a ruin[z] and an object of horror and scorn[a] and cursing,[b] as they are today;[c] 19 Pharaoh king[d] of Egypt, [e] his attendants, his officials and all his people, 20 and all the foreign people there; all the kings of Uz;[f] all the kings of the Philistines[g] (those of Ashkelon,[h] Gaza,[i] Ekron, and the people left at Ashdod); 21 Edom,[j] Moab[k] and Ammon;[l] 22 all the kings of Tyre[m] and Sidon;[n] the kings of the coastlands[o] across the sea; 23 Dedan,[p] Tema,[q] Buz[r] and all who are in distant places[x,s]; 24 all the kings of Arabia[t] and all the kings of the foreign people[u] who live in the desert; 25 all the kings of Zimri,[v] Elam[w] and Media;[x] 26 and all the kings of the north,[y] near and far, one after the other—all the kingdoms[z] on the face of the earth. And after all of them, the king of Sheshach[y,a] will drink it too.

27 "Then tell them, 'This is what the LORD Almighty, the God of Israel, says: Drink, get drunk[b] and vomit, and fall to rise no more because of the sword[c] I will send among you.' 28 But if they refuse to take the cup from your hand and drink[d], tell them, 'This is what the LORD Almighty says: You must drink it! 29 See, I am beginning to bring disaster[e] on the city that bears my Name,[f] and will you indeed go unpunished?[g] You will not go unpunished, for I am calling down a sword[h]

R *Jer 23:39–40* ◀ ▶ *Jer 26:3*
P *Jer 23:19–20* ◀ ▶ *Jer 30:23–24*

upon all[i] who live on the earth,[j] declares the LORD Almighty.'

30 "Now prophesy all these words against them and say to them:

" 'The LORD will roar[k] from on high;
  he will thunder[l] from his holy dwelling[m]
and roar mightily against his land.
He will shout like those who tread[n] the grapes,
  shout against all who live on the earth.
31 The tumult[o] will resound to the ends of the earth,
  for the LORD will bring charges[p] against the nations;
he will bring judgment[q] on all[r] mankind
  and put the wicked to the sword,[s] ' "
    declares the LORD.

32 This is what the LORD Almighty says:

"Look! Disaster[t] is spreading
  from nation to nation;[u]
a mighty storm[v] is rising
  from the ends of the earth."[w]

33 At that time those slain[x] by the LORD will be everywhere—from one end of the earth to the other. They will not be mourned or gathered[y] up or buried,[z] but will be like refuse lying on the ground.

34 Weep and wail, you shepherds;[a]
  roll[b] in the dust, you leaders of the flock.
For your time to be slaughtered[c] has come;
  you will fall and be shattered like fine pottery.[d]
35 The shepherds will have nowhere to flee,

x23 Or *who clip the hair by their foreheads* y26 *Sheshach* is a cryptogram for Babylon.

25:17–18 Jeremiah refers to "the cup" of punishment that God required him to offer to the kings, princes, the cities and Jerusalem itself.

25:29–33 The prophet looks forward to the end of this age when God will unleash his wrath from heaven "against all who live on the earth" (25:30). Note the parallel between this prophecy and Isa 63:1–4. The slaughter during this tribulation will be horrific. Jeremiah states that the dead will cover the earth from one end to the other, indicating that there will be too many bodies to be buried in a timely manner (see Isa 66:16; Rev 19:14–21).

the leaders of the flock no place to
    escape.ᵉ
³⁶Hear the cryᶠ of the shepherds,ᵍ
    the wailing of the leaders of the
      flock,
for the LORD is destroying their
    pasture.
³⁷The peaceful meadows will be laid
    waste
because of the fierce anger of the
    LORD.
³⁸Like a lionʰ he will leave his lair,
    and their land will become desolateⁱ
because of the swordᶻ of the
    oppressorʲ
and because of the LORD's fierce
    anger.ᵏ

Jeremiah Threatened With Death

26 Early in the reign of Jehoiakim¹ son of Josiah king of Judah, this word came from the LORD: ²"This is what the LORD says: Stand in the courtyardᵐ of the LORD's house and speak to all the people of the towns of Judah who come to worship in the house of the LORD.ⁿ Tell them everything I command you; do not omitᵖ a word. ³Perhaps they will listen and each will turnᵠ from his evil way. Then I will relentʳ and not bring on them the disaster I was planning because of the evil they have done. ⁴Say to them, 'This is what the LORD says: If you do not listenˢ to me and follow my law,ᵗ which I have set before you, ⁵and if you do not listen to the words of my servants the prophets, whom I have sent to you again and again (though you have not listenedᵘ), ⁶then I will make this house like Shilohᵛ and this city an object of cursingʷ among all the nations of the earth.' "

⁷The priests, the prophets and all the people heard Jeremiah speak these words in the house of the LORD. ⁸But as soon as Jeremiah finished telling all the people

R *Jer 25:17–18* ◀ ▶ *Jer 26:6*
R *Jer 26:3* ◀ ▶ *Jer 26:20*

25:35
 ᵉ S Job 11:20
25:36 ʳ S Jer 6:26
 ᵍ S Jer 23:1;
   Zec 11:3
25:38
 ʰ S Job 10:16;
   S Jer 4:7 ⁱ Jer 44:22
 ʲ Jer 46:16; 50:16
 ᵏ S Ex 15:7;
   S Jer 4:26
26:1 ¹ 2Ki 23:36
26:2 ᵐ Jer 19:14
 ⁿ S Jer 17:19
 ᵒ ver 12;
   S Jer 1:17;
   Mt 28:20; Ac 20:27
 ᵖ Dt 4:2
26:3 ᵠ Dt 30:2;
   2Ch 33:12-13;
   Isa 55:7; Jer 35:15;
   36:7 ʳ S Jer 18:8
26:4 ˢ Lev 26:14;
   Jer 25:3
 ᵗ Ex 20:1-23:33;
   S 1Ki 9:6; S Jer 11:8
26:5 ᵘ S Pr 1:24;
   S Isa 65:12;
   Jer 25:4; 44:5
26:6 ᵛ S Jos 18:1;
   S Jdg 18:31
 ʷ S Dt 28:25;
   S 2Ki 22:19
26:8 ˣ Jer 43:1
 ʸ Ac 6:12; 21:27
 ᶻ Lev 24:15-16;
   S Ne 9:26;
   S Jer 11:21
26:9 ᵃ S Jer 26:32;
   S Jer 9:11
 ᵇ Ac 21:32
26:10 ᶜ ver 16;
   Jer 34:19;
   Eze 22:27
 ᵈ S Ge 23:10
26:11 ᵉ Dt 18:20;
   S Jer 11:21; 18:23;
   Mt 26:66; Ac 6:11
 ᶠ S Ps 44:1
26:12 ᵍ Jer 1:18
 ʰ S Isa 6:8;
   Am 7:15;
   Ac 4:18-20; 5:29
 ⁱ S ver 2,15
26:13 ʲ S Jer 7:5;
   Joel 2:12-14
 ᵏ Jer 11:4
 ˡ S Jer 18:8
26:14 ᵐ Jos 9:25;
   Jer 38:5
26:15 ⁿ S Dt 19:10
 ᵒ S ver 12;
   S Jer 1:17
26:16 ᵖ S ver 10;
   S Ac 23:9
 ᵠ Ac 23:29
26:18 ʳ Mic 1:1

---

everything the LORD had commandedˣ him to say, the priests, the prophets and all the people seizedʸ him and said, "You must die!ᶻ ⁹Why do you prophesy in the LORD's name that this house will be like Shiloh and this city will be desolate and deserted?"ᵃ And all the people crowdedᵇ around Jeremiah in the house of the LORD.

¹⁰When the officialsᶜ of Judah heard about these things, they went up from the royal palace to the house of the LORD and took their places at the entrance of the New Gateᵈ of the LORD's house. ¹¹Then the priests and the prophets said to the officials and all the people, "This man should be sentenced to deathᵉ because he has prophesied against this city. You have heard it with your own ears!"ᶠ

¹²Then Jeremiah said to all the officialsᵍ and all the people: "The LORD sent me to prophesyʰ against this house and this city all the things you have heard.ⁱ ¹³Now reformʲ your ways and your actions and obeyᵏ the LORD your God. Then the LORD will relentˡ and not bring the disaster he has pronounced against you. ¹⁴As for me, I am in your hands;ᵐ do with me whatever you think is good and right. ¹⁵Be assured, however, that if you put me to death, you will bring the guilt of innocent bloodⁿ on yourselves and on this city and on those who live in it, for in truth the LORD has sent me to you to speak all these wordsᵒ in your hearing."

¹⁶Then the officialsᵖ and all the people said to the priests and the prophets, "This man should not be sentenced to death!ᵠ He has spoken to us in the name of the LORD our God."

¹⁷Some of the elders of the land stepped forward and said to the entire assembly of people, ¹⁸"Micahʳ of Moresh-

L *Jer 21:8* ◀ ▶ *Jer 29:13*
R *Jer 25:4–5* ◀ ▶ *Jer 29:12–13*

ᶻ 38 Some Hebrew manuscripts and Septuagint (see also Jer. 46:16 and 50:16); most Hebrew manuscripts *anger*.

26:6 Shiloh, the former site of the tabernacle and once the home to the ark of the covenant, was only a ruin in Jeremiah's day because Israel's refusal to repent had brought about its destruction.

26:18–24 Some of the princes wanted to kill Jeremiah because of his predictions of coming judgment. Yet the more righteous leaders of the court reminded the people that Micah had prophesied in a similar manner during the reign of King Hezekiah. King Hezekiah and his people responded in repentance and God delayed their punishment. These leaders also pointed out that the prophet Urijah had also prophesied judgment on Judah, but King Jehoiakim had killed him. A righteous man named Ahikam, a friend of King Josiah, came to Jeremiah's defense and persuaded the princes to let Jeremiah live. Note

eth prophesied in the days of Hezekiah king of Judah. He told all the people of Judah, 'This is what the LORD Almighty says:

" 'Zion[s] will be plowed like a field,
Jerusalem will become a heap of rubble,[t]
the temple hill[u] a mound overgrown with thickets.' "[av]

[19]"Did Hezekiah king of Judah or anyone else in Judah put him to death? Did not Hezekiah[w] fear the LORD and seek[x] his favor? And did not the LORD relent,[y] so that he did not bring the disaster[z] he pronounced against them? We are about to bring a terrible disaster[a] on ourselves!" [20](Now Uriah son of Shemaiah from Kiriath Jearim[b] was another man who prophesied in the name of the LORD; he prophesied the same things against this city and this land as Jeremiah did. [21]When King Jehoiakim[c] and all his officers and officials[d] heard his words, the king sought to put him to death.[e] But Uriah heard of it and fled[f] in fear to Egypt. [22]King Jehoiakim, however, sent Elnathan[g] son of Acbor to Egypt, along with some other men. [23]They brought Uriah out of Egypt and took him to King Jehoiakim, who had him struck down with a sword[h] and his body thrown into the burial place of the common people.)[i]

[24]Furthermore, Ahikam[j] son of Shaphan supported Jeremiah, and so he was not handed over to the people to be put to death.

Judah to Serve Nebuchadnezzar

27 Early in the reign of Zedekiah[bk] son of Josiah king of Judah, this word came to Jeremiah from the LORD: [2]This is what the LORD said to me: "Make a yoke[l] out of straps and crossbars and put it on your neck. [3]Then send[m] word to the kings of Edom, Moab, Ammon,[n] Tyre and Sidon[o] through the envoys who have come to Jerusalem to Zedekiah king of Judah. [4]Give them a message for their masters and say, 'This is what the LORD Almighty, the God of Israel, says: "Tell this to your masters: [5]With my great power and outstretched arm[p] I made[q] the earth and its people and the animals[r] that are on it, and I give[s] it to anyone I please. [6]Now I will hand all your countries over to my servant[t] Nebuchadnezzar[u] king of Babylon; I will make even the wild animals subject to him.[v] [7]All nations will serve[w] him and his son and his grandson until the time[x] for his land comes; then many nations and great kings will subjugate[y] him.

[8]" 'If, however, any nation or kingdom will not serve Nebuchadnezzar king of Babylon or bow its neck under his yoke, I will punish[z] that nation with the sword,[a] famine[b] and plague,[c] declares the LORD, until I destroy it by his hand. [9]So do not listen to your prophets,[d] your diviners,[e] your interpreters of dreams,[f] your mediums[g] or your sorcerers[h] who tell you, 'You will not serve[i] the king of Babylon.' [10]They prophesy lies[j] to you that will only serve to remove[k] you far from your lands; I will banish you and you will perish. [11]But if any nation will bow its neck under the yoke[l] of the king of Babylon and serve him, I will let that nation remain in its own land to till it and to live[m] there, declares the LORD.' " '

[12]I gave the same message to Zedekiah king of Judah. I said, "Bow your neck under the yoke[n] of the king of Babylon; serve him and his people, and you will live.[o] [13]Why will you and your people die[p] by the sword, famine and plague[q] with which the LORD has threatened any nation that will not serve the king of Babylon? [14]Do not listen[r] to the words of the prophets[s] who say to you, 'You will not serve the king of Babylon,' for they are prophesying lies[t] to you. [15]'I have not sent[u] them,' declares the LORD. 'They are prophesying lies in my name.[v] Therefore, I will banish you and you will perish,[w] both you and the prophets who prophesy to you.' "

[16]Then I said to the priests and all these people, "This is what the LORD says: Do not listen to the prophets who say, 'Very soon now the articles[x] from the LORD's house will be brought back from

---

[a] 18 Micah 3:12 [b] 1 A few Hebrew manuscripts and Syriac (see also Jer. 27:3, 12 and 28:1); most Hebrew manuscripts *Jehoiakim* (Most Septuagint manuscripts do not have this verse.)

---

that Ahikam's son later became Nebuchadnezzar's governor of Judah (see 40:5; 2Ki 22:12).

Babylon.' They are prophesying lies to you. ¹⁷Do not listen to them. Serve the king of Babylon, and you will live. Why should this city become a ruin? ¹⁸If they are prophets and have the word of the LORD, let them plead with the LORD Almighty that the furnishings remaining in the house of the LORD and in the palace of the king of Judah and in Jerusalem not be taken to Babylon. ¹⁹For this is what the LORD Almighty says about the pillars, the Sea, the movable stands and the other furnishings that are left in this city, ²⁰which Nebuchadnezzar king of Babylon did not take away when he carried Jehoiachin son of Jehoiakim king of Judah into exile from Jerusalem to Babylon, along with all the nobles of Judah and Jerusalem— ²¹yes, this is what the LORD Almighty, the God of Israel, says about the things that are left in the house of the LORD and in the palace of the king of Judah and in Jerusalem: ²²'They will be taken to Babylon and there they will remain until the day I come for them,' declares the LORD. 'Then I will bring them back and restore them to this place.' "

The False Prophet Hananiah

28 In the fifth month of that same year, the fourth year, early in the reign of Zedekiah king of Judah, the prophet Hananiah son of Azzur, who was from Gibeon, said to me in the house of the LORD in the presence of the priests and all the people: ²"This is what the LORD Almighty, the God of Israel, says: 'I will break the yoke of the king of Babylon. ³Within two years I will bring back to this place all the articles of the LORD's house that Nebuchadnezzar king of Babylon removed from here and took to Babylon. ⁴I will also bring back to this place Jehoiachin son of Jehoiakim king of Judah and all the other exiles from Judah who went to Babylon,' declares the LORD, 'for I will break the yoke of the king of Babylon.' "

⁵Then the prophet Jeremiah replied to the prophet Hananiah before the priests and all the people who were standing in the house of the LORD. ⁶He said, "Amen! May the LORD do so! May the LORD fulfill the words you have prophesied by bringing the articles of the LORD's house and all the exiles back to this place from Babylon. ⁷Nevertheless, listen to what I have to say in your hearing and in the hearing of all the people: ⁸From early times the prophets who preceded you and me have prophesied war, disaster and plague against many countries and great kingdoms. ⁹But the prophet who prophesies peace will be recognized as one truly sent by the LORD only if his prediction comes true.' "

¹⁰Then the prophet Hananiah took the yoke off the neck of the prophet Jeremiah and broke it, ¹¹and he said before all the people, "This is what the LORD says: 'In the same way will I break the yoke of Nebuchadnezzar king of Babylon off the neck of all the nations within two years.' " At this, the prophet Jeremiah went on his way.

¹²Shortly after the prophet Hananiah had broken the yoke off the neck of the prophet Jeremiah, the word of the LORD came to Jeremiah: ¹³"Go and tell Hananiah, 'This is what the LORD says: You have broken a wooden yoke, but in its place you will get a yoke of iron. ¹⁴This is what the LORD Almighty, the God of Israel, says: I will put an iron yoke on the necks of all these nations to make them serve Nebuchadnezzar king of Babylon, and they will serve him. I will even give him control over the wild animals.' "

¹⁵Then the prophet Jeremiah said to Hananiah the prophet, "Listen, Hananiah! The LORD has not sent you, yet you have persuaded this nation to trust in lies. ¹⁶Therefore, this is what the LORD says: 'I am about to remove you from the face of the earth. This very year you are going to die, because you have preached rebellion against the LORD.' "

¹⁷In the seventh month of that same year, Hananiah the prophet died.

A Letter to the Exiles

29 This is the text of the letter that the prophet Jeremiah sent from Jerusalem to the surviving elders among the exiles and to the priests, the prophets and all the other people Nebuchadnezzar had carried into exile from Jerusalem to Babylon. ²(This was after King Jehoia-

---

c 20,4 Hebrew Jeconiah, a variant of Jehoiachin

chin^(df) and the queen mother,^g the court officials and the leaders of Judah and Jerusalem, the craftsmen and the artisans had gone into exile from Jerusalem.) ³He entrusted the letter to Elasah son of Shaphan and to Gemariah son of Hilkiah, whom Zedekiah king of Judah sent to King Nebuchadnezzar in Babylon. It said:

⁴This is what the LORD Almighty, the God of Israel, says to all those I carried^h into exile from Jerusalem to Babylon: ⁵"Build^i houses and settle down; plant gardens and eat what they produce. ⁶Marry and have sons and daughters; find wives for your sons and give your daughters in marriage, so that they too may have sons and daughters. Increase in number there; do not decrease.^j ⁷Also, seek^k the peace and prosperity of the city to which I have carried you into exile. Pray^l to the LORD for it, because if it prospers, you too will prosper." ⁸Yes, this is what the LORD Almighty, the God of Israel, says: "Do not let the prophets^m and diviners among you deceive^n you. Do not listen to the dreams^o you encourage them to have.^p ⁹They are prophesying lies^q to you in my name. I have not sent^r them," declares the LORD.

¹⁰This is what the LORD says: "When seventy years^s are completed for Babylon, I will come to you^t and fulfill my gracious promise^u to bring you back^v to this place. **¹¹For I know the plans^w I have for you," declares the LORD, "plans to prosper^x you and not to harm you, plans to give you hope and a future.^y ¹²Then you will call^z upon me and come and pray^a to me, and I will listen^b to you. ¹³You will seek^c me and find me when you seek me with all your heart.^d** ¹⁴I will be found by you," declares the LORD, "and will bring you back^e from captivity.^e I will gather you from all the nations and places where I have banished you," declares the LORD, "and will bring you back to the place from which I carried you into exile."^f

P *Jer 4:1* ◀ ▶ *Jer 31:3*
M *Jer 13:15–17* ◀ ▶ *Jer 49:16*
R *Jer 26:13* ◀ ▶ *Jer 36:3*
L *Jer 26:13* ◀ ▶ *Jer 31:3*

29:2 ^r S 2Ki 24:12; ^g S 2Ki 24:8
29:4 ^h S Jer 24:5
29:5 ^i ver 28
29:6 ^j Jer 30:19
29:7 ^k S Est 3:8; ^l 1Ti 2:1-2
29:8 ^m 1Jn 4:1; ^n Jer 7:9; ^o Dt 13:1; S Jer 23:25; P S Jer 23:27
29:9 ^q S Jer 27:15; La 2:14; Eze 13:6; ^r Jer 23:21
29:10 ^s 2Ch 36:21; S Da 9:2 S Ru 1:6; ^u 1Ki 8:56; Jer 32:42; 33:14; ^v S Jer 16:14; S 24:6
29:11 ^w Ps 40:5; ^x Isa 55:12; ^y S Job 8:7; Zec 8:15
29:12 ^z Hos 2:23; Zep 3:12; Zec 13:9; ^a S 1Ki 8:30; ^b Ps 145:19; S Isa 55:6
29:13 ^c Mt 7:7; ^d Dt 4:29; S 2Ch 6:37
29:14 ^e S Dt 30:3; Jer 30:3; Eze 39:25; Am 9:14; Zep 3:20; ^f Jer 23:3.4; 30:10; 46:27; Eze 37:21
29:17 ^g Jer 27:8; ^h Isa 5:4
29:18 ^i S Jer 15:4; J S Nu 5:27; S Jer 18:16; S 22:10; 44:12; ^k S Dt 28:25; ^l S Dt 28:37; S Isa 28:22; S Mic 2:6
29:19 ^m Jer 6:19; ^n Jer 7:25; ^o S Jer 25:4
29:20 ^p S Jer 24:5
29:21 ^q ver 9; Jer 14:14
29:22 ^r Da 3:6
29:23 ^s S Jer 23:14; ^t S Heb 4:13; ^u S Ge 31:48; S Jer 7:11

¹⁵You may say, "The LORD has raised up prophets for us in Babylon," ¹⁶but this is what the LORD says about the king who sits on David's throne and all the people who remain in this city, your countrymen who did not go with you into exile— ¹⁷yes, this is what the LORD Almighty says: "I will send the sword, famine and plague^g against them and I will make them like poor figs^h that are so bad they cannot be eaten. ¹⁸I will pursue them with the sword, famine and plague and will make them abhorrent^i to all the kingdoms of the earth and an object of cursing^j and horror,^k of scorn^l and reproach, among all the nations where I drive them. ¹⁹For they have not listened to my words,"^m declares the LORD, "words that I sent to them again and again^n by my servants the prophets.^o And you exiles have not listened either," declares the LORD.

²⁰Therefore, hear the word of the LORD, all you exiles whom I have sent^p away from Jerusalem to Babylon. **²¹This is what the LORD Almighty, the God of Israel, says about Ahab son of Kolaiah and Zedekiah son of Maaseiah, who are prophesying lies^q to you in my name: "I will hand them over to Nebuchadnezzar king of Babylon, and he will put them to death before your very eyes. ²²Because of them, all the exiles from Judah who are in Babylon will use this curse: 'The LORD treat you like Zedekiah and Ahab, whom the king of Babylon burned^r in the fire.'** ²³For they have done outrageous things in Israel; they have committed adultery^s with their neighbors' wives and in my name have spoken lies, which I did not tell them to do. I know^t it and am a witness^u to it," declares the LORD.

Message to Shemaiah

²⁴Tell Shemaiah the Nehelamite, ²⁵"This is what the LORD Almighty, the God of Israel, says: You sent letters in your own name to all the people in Jeru-

J *Jer 28:16* ◀ ▶ *Jer 29:32*

^d 2 Hebrew *Jeconiah*, a variant of *Jehoiachin* ^e 14 Or *will restore your fortunes*

salem, to Zephaniah son of Maaseiah the priest, and to all the other priests. You said to Zephaniah, ²⁶"The LORD has appointed you priest in place of Jehoiada to be in charge of the house of the LORD; you should put any madman who acts like a prophet into the stocks and neck-irons. ²⁷So why have you not reprimanded Jeremiah from Anathoth, who poses as a prophet among you? ²⁸He has sent this message to us in Babylon: It will be a long time. Therefore build houses and settle down; plant gardens and eat what they produce.' "

²⁹Zephaniah the priest, however, read the letter to Jeremiah the prophet. ³⁰Then the word of the LORD came to Jeremiah: ³¹"Send this message to all the exiles: 'This is what the LORD says about Shemaiah the Nehelamite: Because Shemaiah has prophesied to you, even though I did not send him, and has led you to believe a lie, ³²this is what the LORD says: I will surely punish Shemaiah the Nehelamite and his descendants. He will have no one left among this people, nor will he see the good things I will do for my people, declares the LORD, because he has preached rebellion against me.' "

Restoration of Israel

30 This is the word that came to Jeremiah from the LORD: ²"This is what the LORD, the God of Israel, says: 'Write in a book all the words I have spoken to you. ³The days are coming,' declares the LORD, 'when I will bring my people Israel and Judah back from captivity and restore them to the land I gave their forefathers to possess,' says the LORD."

⁴These are the words the LORD spoke concerning Israel and Judah: ⁵"This is what the LORD says:

" 'Cries of fear are heard—
terror, not peace.
⁶Ask and see:
Can a man bear children?
Then why do I see every strong man
with his hands on his stomach like a woman in labor,
every face turned deathly pale?
⁷How awful that day will be!
None will be like it.
It will be a time of trouble for Jacob,
but he will be saved out of it.

⁸" 'In that day,' declares the LORD Almighty,
'I will break the yoke off their necks
and will tear off their bonds;
no longer will foreigners enslave them.
⁹Instead, they will serve the LORD their God
and David their king,
whom I will raise up for them.

¹⁰" 'So do not fear, O Jacob my servant;
do not be dismayed, O Israel,'
declares the LORD.
'I will surely save you out of a distant place,
your descendants from the land of their exile.
Jacob will again have peace and security,
and no one will make him afraid.
¹¹I am with you and will save you,'
declares the LORD.
'Though I completely destroy all the nations
among which I scatter you,
I will not completely destroy you.
I will discipline you but only with justice;

f 3 Or will restore the fortunes of my people Israel and Judah

---

30:1–3 Jeremiah recorded God's solemn promise to end the captivity of his people and bring them back to the land. Note God's promise that they would "possess" the land, reaffirming God's covenant with Abraham (see note at Ge 15:4).

30:7–11 In this prophetic passage, Jeremiah declared God's plan to redeem Israel in the last days. Despite "a time of trouble for Jacob" (30:7) and punishment for Israel's sins, Jeremiah prophesied that God would deliver his people and "not completely destroy you" (30:11). God will remove the "yoke" of Israel's enemies and give Israel rest and safety under the rule of the Messiah.

I will not let you go entirely
    unpunished.'ᵉ

¹²"This is what the LORD says:

" 'Your woundᶠ is incurable,
    your injury beyond healing.ᵍ
¹³There is no one to plead your cause,ʰ
    no remedy for your sore,
    no healingⁱ for you.
¹⁴All your alliesʲ have forgotten you;
    they care nothing for you.
I have struck you as an enemyᵏ would
    and punished you as would the
        cruel,ˡ
because your guilt is so great
    and your sinsᵐ so many.
¹⁵Why do you cry out over your wound,
    your pain that has no cure?ⁿ
Because of your great guilt and many
    sins
I have done these things to you.ᵒ

¹⁶" 'But all who devourᵖ you will be
        devoured;
    all your enemies will go into exile.ᵠ
Those who plunderʳ you will be
        plundered;
    all who make spoil of you I will
        despoil.
¹⁷But I will restore you to health
    and healˢ your wounds,'
            declares the LORD,
'because you are called an outcast,ᵗ
    Zion for whom no one cares.'ᵘ

¹⁸"This is what the LORD says:

" 'I will restore the fortunesᵛ of Jacob's
        tentsʷ
    and have compassionˣ on his
        dwellings;
the city will be rebuiltʸ on her ruins,
    and the palace will stand in its
        proper place.
¹⁹From them will come songsᶻ of
        thanksgivingᵃ
    and the sound of rejoicing.ᵇ
I will add to their numbers,ᶜ

G Jer 18:13–15 ◀ ▶ Jer 46:11
I Jer 30:7–10 ◀ ▶ Jer 30:17–22
I Jer 30:14 ◀ ▶ Jer 31:1
R Jer 30:7 ◀ ▶ Jer 34:22

30:11 ᵉHos 11:9;
    Am 9:8
30:12 ᶠS Job 6:4;
    S Jer 10:19
    ᵍS Jer 8:22
30:13 ʰS Jdg 6:31
    ⁱS Jer 8:22; 14:19;
    46:11; Na 3:19
30:14 ʲS Jer 22:20;
    La 1:2 ᵏS Job 13:24
    ˡS Job 30:21
    ᵐS Jer 25:7
30:15 ⁿS Jer 10:19
    ᵒS Pr 1:31; La 1:5
30:16 ᵖS Isa 29:8;
    S 33:1; S Jer 2:3
    ᵠS Isa 14:2;
    Joel 3:4-8 ʳJer 49:2;
    50:10
30:17 ˢS Isa 1:5;
    Hos 6:1 ᵗS Isa 6:12;
    Jer 33:24 ᵘS Ps 142:4
30:18 ᵛver 3;
    S Dt 30:3;
    Jer 31:23; 32:44
    ʷS Nu 24:5
    ˣPs 102:13;
    Jer 33:26;
    Eze 39:25
    ʸJer 31:4,24,38;
    33:7; Eze 36:10,33;
    Am 9:14
30:19 ᶻS Ps 9:2;
    Isa 35:10; S 51:11
    ᵃS Isa 51:3
    ᵇPs 126:1-2;
    Jer 31:4
    ᶜS Ge 15:5; 22:17;
    Jer 33:22;
    Eze 37:26; Zec 2:4
    ᵈS Isa 44:23; S 60:9
30:20 ᵉIsa 54:13;
    Jer 31:17; Zec 8:5
    ᶠIsa 54:14
    ᵍS Ex 23:22
30:21 ʰS ver 9;
    Jer 23:5-6
    ⁱDt 17:15 ʲNu 16:5
30:22
    ᵏS Isa 19:25;
    Hos 2:23
    ˡS Lev 26:12
30:23
    ᵐS Jer 23:19
30:24 ⁿJer 4:8;
    La 1:12 ᵒS Jer 4:28
    ᵖJer 23:19-20
31:1 ᵠS Lev 26:12
31:2 ʳNu 14:20
    ˢS Ex 33:14;
    S Dt 12:9

    and they will not be decreased;
I will bring them honor,ᵈ
    and they will not be disdained.
²⁰Their childrenᵉ will be as in days of
        old,
    and their community will be
        establishedᶠ before me;
I will punishᵍ all who oppress them.
²¹Their leaderʰ will be one of their own;
    their ruler will arise from among
        them.ⁱ
I will bring him nearʲ and he will
        come close to me,
for who is he who will devote
        himself
    to be close to me?'
            declares the LORD.
²²" 'So you will be my people,ᵏ
    and I will be your God.'ˡ "

²³See, the stormᵐ of the LORD
    will burst out in wrath,
a driving wind swirling down
    on the heads of the wicked.
²⁴The fierce angerⁿ of the LORD will not
        turn backᵒ
    until he fully accomplishes
        the purposes of his heart.
In days to come
    you will understandᵖ this.

31 "At that time," declares the LORD,
    "I will be the Godᵠ of all the
clans of Israel, and they will be my
people."

²This is what the LORD says:

"The people who survive the sword
    will find favorʳ in the desert;
I will come to give restˢ to Israel."

³The LORD appeared to us in the past,ᵍ
    saying:

P Jer 25:29–33 ◀ ▶ Jer 45:5
H Jer 23:40 ◀ ▶ Jer 36:7
I Jer 30:17–22 ◀ ▶ Jer 31:3–14
I Jer 31:1 ◀ ▶ Jer 31:28–29
L Jer 29:13 ◀ ▶ Jer 31:20
P Jer 29:11–13 ◀ ▶ Jer 31:20
L Isa 63:9 ◀ ▶ Da 3:25

ᵍ 3 Or LORD has appeared to us from afar

30:17–24 Jeremiah prophesied that despite God's judgment on the sins of Judah, God would ultimately restore Jerusalem.

31:1 God promised that he would "be the God of all the clans of Israel" when their chastening is finished and they are restored in the last days.

31:3–14 In this wonderful prophecy of restoration, God promises to gather his people from all

"I have loved you with an everlasting
    love;
I have drawn you with
    loving-kindness.
⁴I will build you up again
    and you will be rebuilt, O Virgin
    Israel.
Again you will take up your
    tambourines
and go out to dance with the
    joyful.
⁵Again you will plant vineyards
    on the hills of Samaria;
the farmers will plant them
    and enjoy their fruit.
⁶There will be a day when watchmen
    cry out
on the hills of Ephraim,
'Come, let us go up to Zion,
    to the LORD our God.'"

⁷This is what the LORD says:

"Sing with joy for Jacob;
    shout for the foremost of the
    nations.
Make your praises heard, and say,
    'O LORD, save your people,
    the remnant of Israel.'
⁸See, I will bring them from the land of
    the north
and gather them from the ends of
    the earth.
Among them will be the blind and
    the lame,
expectant mothers and women in
    labor;
a great throng will return.
⁹They will come with weeping;
    they will pray as I bring them back.
I will lead them beside streams of
    water
on a level path where they will not
    stumble,
because I am Israel's father,
    and Ephraim is my firstborn son.

¹⁰"Hear the word of the LORD, O nations;
    proclaim it in distant coastlands:
'He who scattered Israel will gather
    them
and will watch over his flock like a
    shepherd.'
¹¹For the LORD will ransom Jacob
    and redeem them from the hand of
    those stronger than they.
¹²They will come and shout for joy on
    the heights of Zion;
they will rejoice in the bounty of
    the LORD—
the grain, the new wine and the oil,
    the young of the flocks and herds.
They will be like a well-watered
    garden,
and they will sorrow no more.
¹³Then maidens will dance and be glad,
    young men and old as well.
I will turn their mourning into
    gladness;
I will give them comfort and joy
    instead of sorrow.
¹⁴I will satisfy the priests with
    abundance,
and my people will be filled with my
    bounty,"
    declares the LORD.

¹⁵This is what the LORD says:

"A voice is heard in Ramah,
    mourning and great weeping,
Rachel weeping for her children
    and refusing to be comforted,
because her children are no more."

¹⁶This is what the LORD says:

"Restrain your voice from weeping
    and your eyes from tears,
for your work will be rewarded,"
    declares the LORD.

31:3 tS Dt 4:37; uHos 11:4; Jn 6:44
31:4 vS Jer 1:10; S 30:18; wS 2Ki 19:21; xS Ge 31:27; yS Ex 15:20; zS Jer 30:19
31:5 aS Dt 20:6; bJer 33:13; 50:19; Ob 1:19; cS Isa 37:30; Am 9:14
31:6 dS Isa 52:8; S 56:10 v ever 12; S Dt 33:19; Jer 50:4-5; Mic 4:2
31:7 fS Isa 12:6; gDt 28:13; Isa 61:9; hPs 14:7; 28:9; iS Isa 37:31
31:8 jS Jer 3:18; kS Ge 33:13; S Dt 30:4; S Ps 106:47; Eze 34:12-14; lIsa 42:16; mEze 34:16; Mic 4:6
31:9 nS Ezr 3:12; Ps 126:5; oIsa 63:13; pS Nu 20:8; S Ps 1:3; S Isa 32:2; qS Isa 40:4; S 49:11; rS Ex 4:22; S Jer 3:4
31:10 sIsa 49:1; S 66:19; S Jer 25:22; tS Lev 26:33; uS Dt 30:4; S Isa 11:12; Jer 50:19; vIsa 40:11; Eze 34:12
31:11 wS Ex 6:6; Zec 9:16 xPs 142:6
31:12 yS Ps 126:5; zEze 17:23; 20:40; 40:2; Mic 4:1; aS Ps 36:8; Joel 3:18; bS Nu 18:12; Hos 2:21-22; Joel 2:19 cver 24; dS SS 4:15; eS Isa 30:19; S 62:5; Jn 16:22; S Rev 7:17
31:13 fS Isa 61:3; gS Isa 40:1; hPs 30:11; S Isa 51:11
31:14 iver 25; jLev 7:35-36; kS Ps 36:8; S Isa 30:23
31:15 lS Jos 18:25; mS Ge 37:35; nS Jer 10:20; Mt 2:17-18*
31:16 oS Ps 30:5; S Isa 25:8; 30:19 pS Ru 2:12; S 2Ch 15:7

---

parts of the world and bring them back to the promised land to fulfill his ancient covenants (see notes at Ge 15:4; Dt 30:1; 2Sa 7:16). God's promise is slowly being fulfilled in our century. Following World War I, Israel was given some territory along the Mediterranean Sea for use as their homeland. Many Jews from every continent have begun to return to this small territory even though some Arab nations continue to dispute the Jews' claim to this land.

31:15–17 This unusual prophecy was partially fulfilled when evil King Herod sent his soldiers to kill all of the male children below the age of two in a vain attempt to kill the young King sought for by the wise men (see Mt 2:17–18). However, this prophecy will be finally fulfilled in the last days. Rachel prophetically symbolizes the mother of the entire nation of Israel. As many as two thirds of both Jews and Gentiles will die during the tribulation. Yet despite these horrible predictions, God still offers hope and promises that the Jews will return in peace to the promised land.

"They will return[q] from the land of
    the enemy."
[17]So there is hope[r] for your future,"
            declares the LORD.
"Your children[s] will return to their
    own land.

[18]"I have surely heard Ephraim's
    moaning:
'You disciplined[t] me like an unruly
    calf,[u]
    and I have been disciplined.
Restore[v] me, and I will return,
    because you are the LORD my God.
[19]After I strayed,[w]
    I repented;
after I came to understand,
    I beat[x] my breast.
I was ashamed[y] and humiliated
    because I bore the disgrace of my
        youth.'[z]

[20]Is not Ephraim my dear son,
    the child[a] in whom I delight?
Though I often speak against him,
    I still remember[b] him.
Therefore my heart yearns for him;
    I have great compassion[c] for him,"
            declares the LORD.

[21]"Set up road signs;
    put up guideposts.[d]
Take note of the highway,[e]
    the road that you take.
Return,[f] O Virgin[g] Israel,
    return to your towns.
[22]How long will you wander,[h]
    O unfaithful[i] daughter?
The LORD will create a new thing[j] on
    earth—
    a woman will surround[hk] a man."

[23]This is what the LORD Almighty, the God of Israel, says: "When I bring them back from captivity,[l] the people in the land of Judah and in its towns will once again use these words: 'The LORD bless[m] you, O righteous dwelling,[n] O sacred mountain.'[o] [24]People will live[p] together in Judah and all its towns—farmers and those who move about with their flocks.[q] [25]I will refresh the weary[r] and satisfy the faint."[s]

[26]At this I awoke[t] and looked around. My sleep had been pleasant to me.

[27]"The days are coming," declares the LORD, "when I will plant[v] the house of Israel and the house of Judah with the offspring of men and of animals. [28]Just as I watched[w] over them to uproot[x] and tear down, and to overthrow, destroy and bring disaster,[y] so I will watch over them to build and to plant,"[z] declares the LORD. [29]"In those days people will no longer say,

'The fathers[a] have eaten sour grapes,
    and the children's teeth are set on
        edge.'[b]

[30]Instead, everyone will die for his own sin;[c] whoever eats sour grapes—his own teeth will be set on edge.

[31]"The time is coming," declares the
        LORD,
    "when I will make a new covenant[d]
with the house of Israel
    and with the house of Judah.
[32]It will not be like the covenant[e]
    I made with their forefathers[f]
when I took them by the hand
    to lead them out of Egypt,[g]
because they broke my covenant,
    though I was a husband[h] to[j]
        them,[k]"
            declares the LORD.

31:16 qJer 30:3; Eze 11:19
31:17 rS Job 8:7; La 3:29 sJer 30:20
31:18 tS Job 5:17 uJer 50:11; Hos 4:16; 10:11 vS Ps 80:3
31:19 wS Ps 95:10; S Jer 8:4; Eze 36:31 xEze 21:12; Lk 18:13 yEzr 9:6 zS Ps 25:7; S Jer 22:21
31:20 aLa 3:33 bS Isa 44:21 cS 1Ki 3:26; S Ps 6:2; Isa 55:7; Mic 7:18
31:21 dEze 21:19 eIsa 35:8; Jer 50:5 fIsa 52:11; S Jer 3:12 gver 4
31:22 hS Jer 2:23 iS Jer 3:6 jIsa 43:19 kS Dt 32:10
31:23 lS Jer 30:18 mS Ge 28:3; S Nu 6:24 nS Isa 1:26 oS Ps 48:1; S Isa 2:2
31:24 pS Jer 30:18; Zec 8:4-8 qS ver 12
31:25 rS Isa 40:29 sJn 4:14
31:26 tZec 4:1
31:27 uS Jer 16:14 vHos 2:23
31:28 wS Job 29:2 xS Dt 29:28 yS Jer 18:8 zS Dt 28:63; S 30:9; S Jer 1:10; Eze 36:10-11; Am 9:14
31:29 aS Ge 9:25; Dt 24:16; La 5:7 bEze 18:2
31:30 cS 2Ki 14:6; S Isa 3:11; Gal 6:7
31:31 dS Dt 29:14; S Isa 42:6; S 54:10; S Lk 22:20; Heb 8:8-12*; 10:16-17
31:32 eS Ex 24:8 fDt 5:3 gJer 11:4 hS Isa 54:5

| Jer 31:3-14 ◄► Jer 31:31-34
| Jer 31:28-29 ◄► Jer 31:38-40

[h]22 Or will go about ,seeking,; or will protect [i]23 Or I restore their fortunes [j]32 Hebrew; Septuagint and Syriac / and I turned away from [k]32 Or was their master

L Jer 31:3 ◄► Jer 31:34
P Jer 31:3 ◄► Jer 33:6-8

31:27–29 Jeremiah predicted that Israel would finally be restored, physically and spiritually, in the last days.

31:31–36 This astonishing prophecy revealed God's commitment to establish a new covenant relationship with his people based on his promise to place his law "in their minds and write it on their hearts" (31:33). This covenant is not merely a restatement of older covenants, but a new covenant through Jesus Christ (see Heb 8:6–13). This new covenant will be an everlasting covenant with the nation of Israel. God's commitment to Israel is unshakable and his plans for her extend into the events of the last days. The prophet Isaiah prophetically revealed Israel's role reminding them that God would "keep you and will make you to be a covenant for the people and a light for the Gentiles" (Isa 42:6) so that "you may bring my salvation to the ends of the earth" (Isa 49:6).

K ³³"This is the covenant I will make with
  the house of Israel
after that time," declares the LORD.
"I will put my law in their minds¹
  and write it on their hearts.ʲ
I will be their God,
  and they will be my people.ᵏ
K ³⁴No longer will a man teachˡ his
V   neighbor,
L or a man his brother, saying, 'Know
    the LORD,'
because they will all knowᵐ me,
  from the least of them to the
    greatest,"
            declares the LORD.
"For I will forgiveⁿ their wickedness
  and will remember their sinsᵒ no
    more."

³⁵This is what the LORD says,

he who appointsᵖ the sun
  to shine by day,
who decrees the moon and stars
  to shine by night,ᵠ
who stirs up the seaʳ
  so that its waves roarˢ—
  the LORD Almighty is his name:ᵗ
³⁶"Only if these decreesᵘ vanish from
    my sight,"
  declares the LORD,
"will the descendantsᵛ of Israel ever
    cease
  to be a nation before me."

³⁷This is what the LORD says:

"Only if the heavens above can be
    measuredʷ
  and the foundations of the earth
    below be searched out
will I rejectˣ all the descendants of
    Israel
  because of all they have done,"
            declares the LORD.

I ³⁸"The days are coming," declares the

K *Jer 24:7* ◄ ► *Jer 32:27*
K *Isa 11:9* ◄ ► *Da 7:13–14*
V *Jer 23:5–6* ◄ ► *Da 2:44*
L *Jer 31:20* ◄ ► *Jer 33:8*
I *Jer 31:31–34* ◄ ► *Jer 32:36–42*

31:33 ¹S Ex 4:15
ʲS Dt 6:6; S 2Co 3:3
ᵏS Jer 11:4;
Heb 10:16

31:34 ˡ1Jn 2:27
ᵐS Isa 11:9;
S Jn 6:45 ⁿS 85:2;
130:4; Jer 33:8;
50:20 ᵒS Job 7:21;
S Isa 38:17;
Mic 7:19;
Heb 10:17*

31:35 ᵖPs 136:7-9
ᵠS Ge 1:16
ʳS Ex 14:21
ˢS Ps 93:3
ᵗS Jer 10:16

31:36
ᵘS Job 38:33;
Jer 33:20-26
ᵛPs 89:36-37

31:37 ʷS Job 38:5;
Jer 33:22
ˣJer 33:24-26;
Ro 11:1-5

31:38 ʸS Jer 30:18
ᶻS Ne 3:1
ᵃS 2Ki 14:13;
S 2Ch 25:23

31:39 ᵇS 1Ki 7:23

31:40 ᶜS Jer 2:23;
7:31-32 ᵈS Jer 8:2
ᵉS 2Sa 15:23;
Jn 18:1
ᶠS 2Ki 11:16
ᵍS Isa 4:3;
Joel 3:17; Zec 14:21

32:1 ʰ2Ki 25:1
ⁱJer 25:1

32:2 ʲS 2Ki 25:1
ᵏS Ps 88:8
ˡS Ne 3:25

32:3 ᵐJer 26:8-9
ⁿver 28; Jer 21:4;
34:2-3

32:4 ᵒJer 34:21;
44:30 ᵖS Jer 21:7;
38:18,23; 39:5-7;
52:9 ᵠver 24

32:5 ʳJer 39:7;
Eze 12:13
ˢS 2Ki 25:7
ᵗJer 21:4; La 1:14

32:7 ᵘS Jos 21:18
ᵛLev 25:24-25;
S Ru 4:3-4;
Mt 27:10*

32:8 ʷver 25

LORD, "when this city will be rebuiltʸ for
me from the Tower of Hananelᶻ to the
Corner Gate.ᵃ ³⁹The measuring lineᵇ will
stretch from there straight to the hill of
Gareb and then turn to Goah. ⁴⁰The
whole valleyᶜ where dead bodiesᵈ and
ashes are thrown, and all the terraces out
to the Kidron Valleyᵉ on the east as far as
the corner of the Horse Gate,ᶠ will be
holyᵍ to the LORD. The city will never
again be uprooted or demolished."

Jeremiah Buys a Field

32 This is the word that came to Jeremiah from the LORD in the tenthʰ year of Zedekiah king of Judah, which was the eighteenthⁱ year of Nebuchadnezzar. ²The army of the king of Babylon was then besiegingʲ Jerusalem, and Jeremiah the prophet was confinedᵏ in the courtyard of the guardˡ in the royal palace of Judah.

³Now Zedekiah king of Judah had imprisoned him there, saying, "Why do you prophesyᵐ as you do? You say, 'This is what the LORD says: I am about to hand this city over to the king of Babylon, and he will captureⁿ it. ⁴Zedekiahᵒ king of Judah will not escapeᵖ out of the hands of the Babylonians,¹ᵠ but will certainly be handed over to the king of Babylon, and will speak with him face to face and see him with his own eyes. ⁵He will takeʳ Zedekiah to Babylon, where he will remain until I deal with him,ˢ declares the LORD. If you fight against the Babylonians, you will not succeed.' "ᵗ

⁶Jeremiah said, "The word of the LORD came to me: ⁷Hanamel son of Shallum your uncle is going to come to you and say, 'Buy my field at Anathoth,ᵘ because as nearest relative it is your right and dutyᵛ to buy it.'

⁸"Then, just as the LORD had said, my cousin Hanamel came to me in the courtyard of the guard and said, 'Buy my fieldʷ at Anathoth in the territory of Benjamin. Since it is your right to redeem it and possess it, buy it for yourself.'

¹⁴ Or *Chaldeans*; also in verses 5, 24, 25, 28, 29 and 43

31:38–40 The rebuilding of the city of Jerusalem will be the first sign of the fulfillment of the new covenant in the last days. Jeremiah described specific details about the rebuilding project, indicating that the city will be restored in its entirety, beginning at the eastern and western ends of the northern wall. Following this prophecy in sequence and direction, history confirms the fulfillment of Jeremiah's words as the various neighborhoods of Jerusalem have been rebuilt in this exact order.

"I knew that this was the word of the LORD; ⁹so I bought the field ˣ at Anathoth from my cousin Hanamel and weighed out for him seventeen shekels ᵐ of silver.ʸ ¹⁰I signed and sealed the deed,ᶻ had it witnessed,ᵃ and weighed out the silver on the scales. ¹¹I took the deed of purchase—the sealed copy containing the terms and conditions, as well as the unsealed copy— ¹²and I gave this deed to Baruch ᵇ son of Neriah,ᶜ the son of Mahseiah, in the presence of my cousin Hanamel and of the witnesses who had signed the deed and of all the Jews sitting in the courtyard of the guard.

¹³"In their presence I gave Baruch these instructions: ¹⁴'This is what the LORD Almighty, the God of Israel, says: Take these documents, both the sealed ᵈ and unsealed copies of the deed of purchase, and put them in a clay jar so they will last a long time. ¹⁵For this is what the LORD Almighty, the God of Israel, says: Houses, fields and vineyards will again be bought in this land.'ᵉ

¹⁶"After I had given the deed of purchase to Baruch ᶠ son of Neriah, I prayed to the LORD:

¹⁷"Ah, Sovereign LORD,ᵍ you have made the heavens and the earth ʰ by your great power and outstretched arm.ⁱ Nothing is too hard ʲ for you. ¹⁸You show love ᵏ to thousands but bring the punishment for the fathers' sins into the laps ˡ of their children ᵐ after them. O great and powerful God,ⁿ whose name is the LORD Almighty,ᵒ ¹⁹great are your purposes and mighty are your deeds.ᵖ Your eyes are open to all the ways of men;ᵠ you reward everyone according to his conduct and as his deeds deserve.ʳ ²⁰You performed miraculous signs and wonders ˢ in Egypt ᵗ and have continued them to this day, both in Israel and among all mankind, and have gained the renown ᵘ that is still yours. ²¹You brought your people Israel out of Egypt with signs and wonders, by a mighty hand ᵛ and an outstretched arm ʷ and with great terror.ˣ ²²You gave them this land you had sworn to give their forefathers, a land flow-

ing with milk and honey.ʸ ²³They came in and took possession ᶻ of it, but they did not obey you or follow your law;ᵃ they did not do what you commanded them to do. So you brought all this disaster ᵇ upon them.

²⁴"See how the siege ramps ᶜ are built up to take the city. Because of the sword, famine and plague,ᵈ the city will be handed over to the Babylonians who are attacking it. What you said ᵉ has happened,ᶠ as you now see. ²⁵And though the city will be handed over to the Babylonians, you, O Sovereign LORD, say to me, 'Buy the field ᵍ with silver and have the transaction witnessed.ʰ' "

²⁶Then the word of the LORD came to Jeremiah: ²⁷**"I am the LORD, the God of all mankind.ⁱ Is anything too hard for me?ʲ** ²⁸Therefore, this is what the LORD says: I am about to hand this city over to the Babylonians and to Nebuchadnezzar ᵏ king of Babylon, who will capture it.ˡ ²⁹The Babylonians who are attacking this city will come in and set it on fire; they will burn it down,ᵐ along with the houses ⁿ where the people provoked me to anger by burning incense on the roofs to Baal and by pouring out drink offerings ᵒ to other gods.ᵖ

³⁰"The people of Israel and Judah have done nothing but evil in my sight from their youth;ᵠ indeed, the people of Israel have done nothing but provoke ʳ me with what their hands have made,ˢ declares the LORD. ³¹From the day it was built until now, this city ᵗ has so aroused my anger and wrath that I must remove ᵘ it from my sight. ³²The people of Israel and Judah have provoked ᵛ me by all the evil ʷ they have done—they, their kings and officials,ˣ their priests and prophets, the men of Judah and the people of Jerusalem. ³³**They turned their backs ʸ to me and not their faces; though I taught ᶻ them again and again, they would not listen or respond to discipline.**ᵃ ³⁴They set up their abominable idols ᵇ in the house that bears my Name ᶜ and defiled ᵈ it.

35They built high places for Baal in the Valley of Ben Hinnom[e] to sacrifice their sons and daughters[n] to Molech,[f] though I never commanded, nor did it enter my mind,[g] that they should do such a detestable[h] thing and so make Judah sin.[i]

36"You are saying about this city, 'By the sword, famine and plague[j] it will be handed over to the king of Babylon'; but this is what the LORD, the God of Israel, says: 37I will surely gather[k] them from all the lands where I banish them in my furious anger[l] and great wrath; I will bring them back to this place and let them live in safety.[m] 38They will be my people,[n] and I will be their God. 39I will give them singleness[o] of heart and action, so that they will always fear[p] me for their own good and the good of their children after them. 40I will make an everlasting covenant[q] with them: I will never stop doing good to them, and I will inspire[r] them to fear me, so that they will never turn away from me.[s] 41I will rejoice[t] in doing them good[u] and will assuredly plant them in this land with all my heart and soul.[w]

42"This is what the LORD says: As I have brought all this great calamity[x] on this people, so I will give them all the prosperity I have promised[y] them. 43Once more fields will be bought[z] in this land of which you say, 'It is a desolate[a] waste, without men or animals, for it has been handed over to the Babylonians.' 44Fields will be bought for silver, and deeds[b] will be signed, sealed and witnessed[c] in the territory of Benjamin, in the villages around Jerusalem, in the towns of Judah and in the towns of the hill country, of the western foothills and of the Negev,[d] because I will restore[e] their fortunes,[o] declares the LORD."

l *Jer 31:38–40* ◀ ▶ *Jer 32:44*
K *Jer 32:27* ◀ ▶ *Jer 33:8*
l *Jer 32:36–42* ◀ ▶ *Jer 33:2–3*

32:35 e Jer 19:2
f S Lev 18:21
g S Jer 19:5
h S 1Ki 14:24
i S Jer 25:7
32:36 j ver 24
32:37 k S Isa 11:12
l Jer 21:5
m S Lev 25:18; Eze 34:28; 39:26
32:38 n Jer 24:7; 2Co 6:16*
32:39
o S 2Ch 30:12; S Ps 86:11; Jn 17:21; Ac 4:32
32:40 q S Ge 9:16; S Isa 42:6
r S Dt 4:10
s S Jer 24:7
32:41 t S Dt 28:63; S Isa 62:4
u S Dt 28:3-12
v Jer 24:6; 31:28
w Mic 7:18
32:42 x La 3:38
y S Jer 29:10
32:43 z ver 15
a Jer 33:12
32:44 b ver 10
c S Ru 4:9; S Isa 8:2
d S Jer 17:26
e S Ezr 9:9; Ps 14:7
33:1 f S Ps 88:8
g Jer 37:21; 38:28
h Jer 13:3
33:2 i S Ps 136:6;
S Jer 10:16
j S Ex 3:15
33:3 k S Isa 55:6
l S Job 28:11
33:4 m S 2Ki 25:1;
Eze 4:2 n Jer 32:24;
Eze 26:8; Hab 1:10
33:5 o Jer 21:4-7
p S Dt 31:17;
S Isa 8:17
33:6 q S Dt 32:39;
S Isa 30:26
r S Isa 9:6
33:7 s Jer 32:44
t Jer 30:3;
Eze 39:25; Am 9:14
u S Jer 24:6
v S Isa 1:26
33:8
w S Lev 16:30;
Heb 9:13-14
x S 2Sa 24:14;
S Jer 31:34
33:9 y S Isa 55:13
z S Isa 60:18
a S Jer 3:17
b S Isa 64:2
33:10 c Jer 32:43

Promise of Restoration

33 While Jeremiah was still confined[f] in the courtyard[g] of the guard, the word of the LORD came to him a second time:[h] 2"This is what the LORD says, he who made the earth,[i] the LORD who formed it and established it—the LORD is his name:[j] 3'Call[k] to me and I will answer you and tell you great and unsearchable[l] things you do not know.' 4For this is what the LORD, the God of Israel, says about the houses in this city and the royal palaces of Judah that have been torn down to be used against the siege[m] ramps[n] and the sword 5in the fight with the Babylonians[o]: 'They will be filled with the dead bodies of the men I will slay in my anger and wrath.[o] I will hide my face[p] from this city because of all its wickedness.

6"'Nevertheless, I will bring health and healing to it; I will heal[q] my people and will let them enjoy abundant peace[r] and security. 7I will bring Judah[s] and Israel back from captivity[qt] and will rebuild[u] them as they were before.[v] 8I will cleanse[w] them from all the sin they have committed against me and will forgive[x] all their sins of rebellion against me. 9Then this city will bring me renown,[y] joy, praise[z] and honor[a] before all nations on earth that hear of all the good things I do for it; and they will be in awe and will tremble[b] at the abundant prosperity and peace I provide for it.'

10"This is what the LORD says: 'You say about this place, "It is a desolate waste, without men or animals."[c] Yet in the towns of Judah and the streets of Jerusa-

l *Jer 32:44* ◀ ▶ *Jer 33:6–11*
l *Jer 33:2–3* ◀ ▶ *Jer 33:15–16*
P *Jer 31:20* ◀ ▶ *Jer 36:3*
K *Jer 32:38–39* ◀ ▶ *Jer 50:20*
L *Jer 31:34* ◀ ▶ *Jer 36:3*

n 35 Or *to make their sons and daughters pass through* ⌊*the fire*⌋
o 44 Or *will bring them back from captivity* p 5 Or *Chaldeans*
q 7 Or *will restore the fortunes of Judah and Israel*

32:36–44 While Jeremiah confirmed the coming destruction of Jerusalem by Babylon, he also delivered God's promise to bring the exiles back to Israel from the nations where their enemies would drive them. The prophet then described legal land transactions as proof that the Babylonian captivity would not be permanent.

33:2–3 God reassured Jeremiah that he was with him, even in prison, and would show Jeremiah incredible things.

33:6–11 Just as God had promised the removal of the sounds of happiness in Judah (see 7:34), this prophecy stated that God's blessings and the sounds of happiness would be once again be restored to Judah.

lem that are deserted,[d] inhabited by neither men nor animals, there will be heard once more ¹¹the sounds of joy and gladness,[e] the voices of bride and bridegroom, and the voices of those who bring thank offerings[f] to the house of the LORD, saying,

"Give thanks to the LORD Almighty,
 for the LORD is good;[g]
 his love endures forever."[h]

For I will restore the fortunes[i] of the land as they were before,[j]' says the LORD.

¹²"This is what the LORD Almighty says: 'In this place, desolate[k] and without men or animals[l]—in all its towns there will again be pastures for shepherds to rest their flocks.[m] ¹³In the towns of the hill country, of the western foothills and of the Negev,[o] in the territory of Benjamin, in the villages around Jerusalem and in the towns of Judah, flocks will again pass under the hand[p] of the one who counts them,' says the LORD.

¹⁴"'The days are coming,' declares the LORD, 'when I will fulfill the gracious promise[q] I made to the house of Israel and the house of Judah.

¹⁵"'In those days and at that time
 I will make a righteous[r] Branch[s]
  sprout from David's line;[t]
 he will do what is just and right in the land.
¹⁶In those days Judah will be saved[u]
 and Jerusalem will live in safety.[v]
This is the name by which it[r] will be called:[w]
 The LORD Our Righteousness.'[x]

¹⁷For this is what the LORD says: 'David will never fail[y] to have a man to sit on the throne of the house of Israel, ¹⁸nor will the priests,[z] who are Levites,[a] ever fail to have a man to stand before me continually to offer burnt offerings, to burn grain offerings and to present sacrifices.[b]'"

¹⁹The word of the LORD came to Jeremiah: ²⁰"This is what the LORD says: 'If you can break my covenant with the day[c] and my covenant with the night, so that day and night no longer come at their appointed time,[d] ²¹then my covenant[e] with David my servant—and my covenant with the Levites[f] who are priests ministering before me—can be broken and David will no longer have a descendant to reign on his throne.[g] ²²I will make the descendants of David my servant and the Levites who minister before me as countless[h] as the stars of the sky and as measureless as the sand on the seashore.'"

²³The word of the LORD came to Jeremiah: ²⁴"Have you not noticed that these people are saying, 'The LORD has rejected the two kingdoms[s] he chose'? So they despise[j] my people and no longer regard them as a nation.[k] ²⁵This is what the LORD says: 'If I have not established my covenant with day and night[l] and the fixed laws[m] of heaven and earth,[n] ²⁶then I will reject[o] the descendants of Jacob[p] and David my servant and will not choose one of his sons to rule over the descendants of Abraham, Isaac and Jacob. For I will restore their fortunes[q] and have compassion[r] on them.'"

Warning to Zedekiah

34 While Nebuchadnezzar king of Babylon and all his army and all the kingdoms and peoples[s] in the empire he ruled were fighting against Jerusalem[t] and all its surrounding towns, this word came to Jeremiah from the LORD: ²"This is what the LORD, the God of Israel, says: Go to Zedekiah[u] king of Judah and tell him, 'This is what the LORD says: I am about to hand this city over to the king of Babylon, and he will burn it down.[v] ³You will not escape from his grasp but will surely be captured and handed over[w] to him. You will see the king of Babylon with your own eyes, and he will speak with you face to face. And you will go to Babylon.

⁴"'Yet hear the promise of the LORD, O Zedekiah king of Judah. This is what

[r] 16 Or he   [s] 24 Or families   [t] 26 Or will bring them back from captivity

---

33:15–16 Jeremiah prophesied the coming blessing in the millennial kingdom of the Messiah when Judah and Jerusalem would live in safety.

33:22 These words echo God's promises to Abraham (see note at Ge 15:4). These numerous descendants will be counted among the great throng who will reign with Christ and those who have been consecrated to be priests with him (see Ro 5:17; 1Co 6:3; 2Ti 2:12; 1Pe 2:5; Rev 1:6; 5:10; 22:5).

the LORD says concerning you: You will not die by the sword; 5you will die peacefully. As people made a funeral fire in honor of your fathers, the former kings who preceded you, so they will make a fire in your honor and lament, "Alas, O master!" I myself make this promise, declares the LORD.' "

6Then Jeremiah the prophet told all this to Zedekiah king of Judah, in Jerusalem, 7while the army of the king of Babylon was fighting against Jerusalem and the other cities of Judah that were still holding out—Lachish and Azekah. These were the only fortified cities left in Judah.

Freedom for Slaves

8The word came to Jeremiah from the LORD after King Zedekiah had made a covenant with all the people in Jerusalem to proclaim freedom for the slaves. 9Everyone was to free his Hebrew slaves, both male and female; no one was to hold a fellow Jew in bondage. 10So all the officials and people who entered into this covenant agreed that they would free their male and female slaves and no longer hold them in bondage. They agreed, and set them free. 11But afterward they changed their minds and took back the slaves they had freed and enslaved them again.

12Then the word of the LORD came to Jeremiah: 13"This is what the LORD, the God of Israel, says: I made a covenant with your forefathers when I brought them out of Egypt, out of the land of slavery. I said, 14'Every seventh year each of you must free any fellow Hebrew who has sold himself to you. After he has served you six years, you must let him go free.' Your fathers, however, did not listen to me or pay attention to me. 15Recently you repented and did what is right in my sight: Each of you proclaimed freedom to his countrymen. You even made a covenant before me in the house that bears my Name. 16But now you have turned around and profaned my name; each of you has taken back the male and female slaves you had set free to go where they wished. You have forced them to become your slaves again.

17"Therefore, this is what the LORD says: You have not obeyed me; you have not proclaimed freedom for your fellow countrymen. So I now proclaim 'freedom' for you, declares the LORD—'freedom' to fall by the sword, plague and famine. I will make you abhorrent to all the kingdoms of the earth. 18The men who have violated my covenant and have not fulfilled the terms of the covenant they made before me, I will treat like the calf they cut in two and then walked between its pieces. 19The leaders of Judah and Jerusalem, the court officials, the priests and all the people of the land who walked between the pieces of the calf, 20I will hand over to their enemies who seek their lives. Their dead bodies will become food for the birds of the air and the beasts of the earth.

21"I will hand Zedekiah king of Judah and his officials over to their enemies who seek their lives, to the army of the king of Babylon, which has withdrawn from you. 22I am going to give the order, declares the LORD, and I will bring them back to this city. They will fight against it, take it and burn it down. And I will lay waste the towns of Judah so no one can live there."

The Recabites

35 This is the word that came to Jeremiah from the LORD during the reign of Jehoiakim son of Josiah king of Judah: 2"Go to the Recabite family and invite them to come to one of the side rooms of the house of the LORD and give them wine to drink."

3So I went to get Jaazaniah son of Jeremiah, the son of Habazziniah, and his brothers and all his sons—the whole family of the Recabites. 4I brought them into the house of the LORD, into the room of the sons of Hanan son of Igdaliah the man of God. It was next to the room of the officials, which was over that of Maaseiah son of Shallum the doorkeeper.

R *Jer 30:17* ◀ ▶ *Jer 38:21–23*

34:22 God declared that the Babylonians would utterly destroy Jerusalem with fire and that the other cities of Judah would meet a similar fate.

⁵Then I set bowls full of wine and some cups before the men of the Recabite family and said to them, "Drink some wine."

⁶But they replied, "We do not drink wine, because our forefather Jonadab^m son of Recab gave us this command: 'Neither you nor your descendants must ever drink wine.^n ⁷Also you must never build houses, sow seed or plant vineyards; you must never have any of these things, but must always live in tents.^o Then you will live a long time in the land^p where you are nomads.' ⁸We have obeyed everything our forefather^q Jonadab son of Recab commanded us. Neither we nor our wives nor our sons and daughters have ever drunk wine ⁹or built houses to live in or had vineyards, fields or crops.^r ¹⁰We have lived in tents and have fully obeyed everything our forefather Jonadab commanded us. ¹¹But when Nebuchadnezzar king of Babylon invaded^s this land, we said, 'Come, we must go to Jerusalem^t to escape the Babylonian^v and Aramean armies.' So we have remained in Jerusalem."

¹²Then the word of the LORD came to Jeremiah, saying, ¹³"This is what the LORD Almighty, the God of Israel, says: Go and tell^u the men of Judah and the people of Jerusalem, 'Will you not learn a lesson^v and obey my words?' declares the LORD. ¹⁴Jonadab son of Recab ordered his sons not to drink wine and this command has been kept. To this day they do not drink wine, because they obey their forefather's command.^w But I have spoken to you again and again,^x yet you have not obeyed^y me. ¹⁵Again and again I sent all my servants the prophets^z to you. They said, "Each of you must turn^a from your wicked ways and reform^b your actions; do not follow other gods^c to serve them. Then you will live in the land^d I have given to you and your fathers." But you have not paid attention or listened^e to me. ¹⁶The descendants of Jonadab son of Recab have carried out the command

their forefather^f gave them, but these people have not obeyed me.'

¹⁷"Therefore, this is what the LORD God Almighty, the God of Israel, says: 'Listen! I am going to bring on Judah and on everyone living in Jerusalem every disaster^g I pronounced against them. I spoke to them, but they did not listen;^h I called to them, but they did not answer.' "^i

¹⁸Then Jeremiah said to the family of the Recabites, "This is what the LORD Almighty, the God of Israel, says: 'You have obeyed the command of your forefather^j Jonadab and have followed all his instructions and have done everything he ordered.' ¹⁹Therefore, this is what the LORD Almighty, the God of Israel, says: 'Jonadab son of Recab will never fail^k to have a man to serve^l me.' "

Jehoiakim Burns Jeremiah's Scroll

36 In the fourth year of Jehoiakim^m son of Josiah king of Judah, this word came to Jeremiah from the LORD: ²"Take a scroll^n and write on it all the words^o I have spoken to you concerning Israel, Judah and all the other nations from the time I began speaking to you in the reign of Josiah^p till now. ³Perhaps^q when the people of Judah hear^r about every disaster I plan to inflict on them, each of them will turn^s from his wicked way; then I will forgive^t their wickedness and their sin."

⁴So Jeremiah called Baruch^u son of Neriah,^v and while Jeremiah dictated^w all the words the LORD had spoken to him, Baruch wrote them on the scroll.^x ⁵Then Jeremiah told Baruch, "I am restricted; I cannot go to the LORD's temple. ⁶So you go to the house of the LORD on a day of fasting^y and read to the people from the

---

I Jer 33:15–16 ◀▶ Jer 46:27–28
U Jer 17:7–8 ◀▶ Eze 34:26–27
L Jer 33:8 ◀▶ Jer 50:20
P Jer 33:6–8 ◀▶ Eze 34:11–12
R Jer 29:12–13 ◀▶ La 3:40–41

^v 11 Or Chaldean

35:18–19 Jeremiah had set wine in front of the Rechabites, a tribe of Kenites (see 2Ki 10:15–16; 1Ch 2:55). Because of a vow their fathers had made to refrain from drinking wine, these Rechabites refused Jeremiah's offer. Jeremiah recorded this incident as an example to Judah of the choices that the people should make to follow the laws of God rather than succumb to temptation.

36:4 Baruch, the son of Neriah, was Jeremiah's personal secretary. We are not told why Baruch recorded these messages, but it is evident that Jeremiah trusted him with both his words and possessions (see 32:12).

scroll the words of the LORD that you wrote as I dictated.ᶻ Read them to all the people of Judahᵃ who come in from their towns. ⁷Perhaps they will bring their petitionᵇ before the LORD, and each will turnᶜ from his wicked ways, for the angerᵈ and wrath pronounced against this people by the LORD are great."

⁸Baruch son of Neriah did everything Jeremiah the prophet told him to do; at the LORD's temple he read the words of the LORD from the scroll. ⁹In the ninth monthᵉ of the fifth year of Jehoiakim son of Josiah king of Judah, a time of fastingᶠ before the LORD was proclaimed for all the people in Jerusalem and those who had come from the towns of Judah. ¹⁰From the room of Gemariahᵍ son of Shaphanʰ the secretary,ⁱ which was in the upper courtyard at the entrance of the New Gateʲ of the temple, Baruch read to all the people at the LORD's temple the words of Jeremiah from the scroll.

¹¹When Micaiah son of Gemariah, the son of Shaphan, heard all the words of the LORD from the scroll, ¹²he went down to the secretary'sᵏ room in the royal palace, where all the officials were sitting: Elishama the secretary, Delaiah son of Shemaiah, Elnathanˡ son of Acbor, Gemariah son of Shaphan, Zedekiah son of Hananiah, and all the other officials.ᵐ ¹³After Micaiah told them everything he had heard Baruch read to the people from the scroll, ¹⁴all the officials sent Jehudiⁿ son of Nethaniah, the son of Shelemiah, the son of Cushi, to say to Baruch, "Bring the scrollᵒ from which you have read to the people and come." So Baruch son of Neriah went to them with the scroll in his hand. ¹⁵They said to him, "Sit down, please, and read it to us."

So Baruch read it to them. ¹⁶When they heard all these words, they looked at each other in fearᵖ and said to Baruch, "We must report all these words to the king." ¹⁷Then they asked Baruch, "Tell us, how did you come to writeᑫ all this? Did Jeremiah dictate it?"

¹⁸"Yes," Baruch replied, "he dictatedʳ all these words to me, and I wrote them in ink on the scroll."

¹⁹Then the officialsˢ said to Baruch, "You and Jeremiah, go and hide.ᵗ Don't let anyone know where you are."

H Jer 30:23–24 ◀ ▶ La 3:39

36:6 ᶻ Ex 4:16
ᵃ 2Ch 20:4
36:7 ᵇ Jer 37:20;
42:2 ᶜ S Jer 26:3
ᵈ S Dt 31:17
36:9 ᵉ ver 22
ᶠ S 2Ch 20:3
36:10 ᵍ ver 12,25;
Jer 29:3 ʰ Jer 26:24
ⁱ Jer 52:25
ʲ S Ge 23:10
36:12 ᵏ S 2Sa 8:17
ˡ S Jer 26:22
ᵐ Jer 38:4
36:14 ⁿ ver 21
ᵒ ver 4
36:16 ᵖ S Ps 36:1
36:17 ᑫ ver 30:2
36:18 ʳ ver 4
36:19 ˢ Jer 26:16
ᵗ S 1Ki 17:3
36:21 ᵘ ver 14
ᵛ 2Ki 22:10
36:22 ʷ Am 3:15
36:23 ˣ ver 2
ʸ 1Ki 22:8
36:24 ᶻ S Ps 36:1
ᵃ S Ge 37:29;
S Nu 14:6
36:25 ᵇ ver 12
ᶜ S ver 10
36:26 ᵈ Mt 23:34
ᵉ S 1Ki 17:3;
Ps 11:1; S Jer 1:8;
15:21
36:27 ᶠ ver 4
36:28 ᵍ ver 2
36:29 ʰ Jer 33:12
ⁱ S Isa 30:10
36:30 ʲ Jer 52:2
ᵏ Isa 14:19
ˡ S 2Ki 24:6
ᵐ S Jer 8:2
36:31 ⁿ Ex 20:5
ᵒ S Pr 29:1
ᵖ S Pr 1:24
36:32 ᑫ ver 4
ʳ Ex 34:1; Jer 30:2
ˢ ver 23

²⁰After they put the scroll in the room of Elishama the secretary, they went to the king in the courtyard and reported everything to him. ²¹The king sent Jehudiᵘ to get the scroll, and Jehudi brought it from the room of Elishama the secretary and read it to the kingᵛ and all the officials standing beside him. ²²It was the ninth month and the king was sitting in the winter apartment,ʷ with a fire burning in the firepot in front of him. ²³Whenever Jehudi had read three or four columns of the scroll,ˣ the king cut them off with a scribe's knife and threw them into the firepot, until the entire scroll was burned in the fire.ʸ ²⁴The king and all his attendants who heard all these words showed no fear,ᶻ nor did they tear their clothes.ᵃ ²⁵Even though Elnathan, Delaiahᵇ and Gemariahᶜ urged the king not to burn the scroll, he would not listen to them. ²⁶Instead, the king commanded Jerahmeel, a son of the king, Seraiah son of Azriel and Shelemiah son of Abdeel to arrestᵈ Baruch the scribe and Jeremiah the prophet. But the LORD had hiddenᵉ them.

²⁷After the king burned the scroll containing the words that Baruch had written at Jeremiah's dictation,ᶠ the word of the LORD came to Jeremiah: ²⁸"Take another scrollᵍ and write on it all the words that were on the first scroll, which Jehoiakim king of Judah burned up. ²⁹Also tell Jehoiakim king of Judah, 'This is what the LORD says: You burned that scroll and said, "Why did you write on it that the king of Babylon would certainly come and destroy this land and cut off both men and animalsʰ from it?"ⁱ ³⁰Therefore, this is what the LORD says about Jehoiakimʲ king of Judah: He will have no one to sit on the throne of David; his body will be thrown outᵏ and exposedˡ to the heat by day and the frost by night.ᵐ ³¹I will punish him and his childrenⁿ and his attendants for their wickedness; I will bring on them and those living in Jerusalem and the people of Judah every disasterᵒ I pronounced against them, because they have not listened.ᵖ'"

³²So Jeremiah took another scroll and gave it to the scribe Baruch son of Neriah, and as Jeremiah dictated,ᑫ Baruch wroteʳ on it all the words of the scroll that Jehoiakim king of Judah had burnedˢ

Jeremiah in Prison

37 Zedekiah[t] son of Josiah was made king[u] of Judah by Nebuchadnezzar king of Babylon; he reigned in place of Jehoiachin[w,v] son of Jehoiakim. ²Neither he nor his attendants nor the people of the land paid any attention[w] to the words the LORD had spoken through Jeremiah the prophet.

³King Zedekiah, however, sent[x] Jehucal[y] son of Shelemiah with the priest Zephaniah[z] son of Maaseiah to Jeremiah the prophet with this message: "Please pray[a] to the LORD our God for us."

⁴Now Jeremiah was free to come and go among the people, for he had not yet been put in prison.[b] ⁵Pharaoh's army had marched out of Egypt,[c] and when the Babylonians[x] who were besieging Jerusalem heard the report about them, they withdrew[d] from Jerusalem.[e]

⁶Then the word of the LORD came to Jeremiah the prophet: ⁷"This is what the LORD, the God of Israel, says: Tell the king of Judah, who sent you to inquire[f] of me, 'Pharaoh's army, which has marched[g] out to support you, will go back to its own land, to Egypt.[h] ⁸Then the Babylonians will return and attack this city; they will capture[i] it and burn[j] it down.'

⁹"This is what the LORD says: Do not deceive[k] yourselves, thinking, 'The Babylonians will surely leave us.' They will not! ¹⁰Even if you were to defeat the entire Babylonian[y] army that is attacking you and only wounded men were left in their tents, they would come out and burn[l] this city down."

¹¹After the Babylonian army had withdrawn[m] from Jerusalem because of Pharaoh's army, ¹²Jeremiah started to leave the city to go to the territory of Benjamin to get his share of the property[n] among the people there. ¹³But when he reached the Benjamin Gate,[o] the captain of the guard, whose name was Irijah son of Shelemiah, the son of Hananiah, arrested him and said, "You are deserting to the Babylonians!"[p]

¹⁴"That's not true!" Jeremiah said. "I am not deserting to the Babylonians." But Irijah would not listen to him; instead, he arrested[q] Jeremiah and brought him to the officials. ¹⁵They were angry with Jeremiah and had him beaten[r] and imprisoned[s] in the house[t] of Jonathan the secretary, which they had made into a prison.

¹⁶Jeremiah was put into a vaulted cell in a dungeon, where he remained a long time. ¹⁷Then King Zedekiah sent[u] for him and had him brought to the palace, where he asked[v] him privately,[w] "Is there any word from the LORD?"

"Yes," Jeremiah replied, "you will be handed over[x] to the king of Babylon."

¹⁸Then Jeremiah said to King Zedekiah, "What crime[y] have I committed against you or your officials or this people, that you have put me in prison? ¹⁹Where are your prophets[z] who prophesied to you, 'The king of Babylon will not attack you or this land'? ²⁰But now, my lord the king, please listen. Let me bring my petition before you: Do not send me back to the house of Jonathan the secretary, or I will die there."[a]

²¹King Zedekiah then gave orders for Jeremiah to be placed in the courtyard of the guard and given bread from the street of the bakers each day until all the bread[b] in the city was gone.[c] So Jeremiah remained in the courtyard of the guard.[d]

Jeremiah Thrown Into a Cistern

38 Shephatiah son of Mattan, Gedaliah son of Pashhur,[e] Jehucal[z,f] son of Shelemiah, and Pashhur son of Malkijah heard what Jeremiah was telling all the people when he said, ²"This is what the LORD says: 'Whoever stays in this city will die by the sword, famine or plague,[g] but whoever goes over to the Babylonians[a] will live. He will escape with his life; he will live.'[h] ³And this is what the LORD says: 'This city will certainly be handed over to the army of the king of Babylon, who will capture it.'"[i]

⁴Then the officials[j] said to the king, "This man should be put to death.[k] He is discouraging[l] the soldiers who are left in this city, as well as all the people, by the things he is saying to them. This man is not seeking the good of these people but their ruin."

⁵"He is in your hands,"[m] King Zedekiah answered. "The king can do nothing[n] to oppose you."

---

w 1 Hebrew Coniah, a variant of Jehoiachin   x 5 Or Chaldeans; also in verses 8, 9, 13 and 14   y 10 Or Chaldean; also in verse 11   z 1 Hebrew Jucal, a variant of Jehucal   a 2 Or Chaldeans; also in verses 18, 19 and 23

⁶So they took Jeremiah and put him into the cistern of Malkijah, the king's son, which was in the courtyard of the guard.ᵒ They lowered Jeremiah by ropesᵖ into the cistern; it had no water in it,ᑫ only mud, and Jeremiah sank down into the mud.ʳ

⁷But Ebed-Melech,ˢ a Cushite,ᵇ an officialᶜᵗ in the royal palace, heard that they had put Jeremiah into the cistern. While the king was sitting in the Benjamin Gate,ᵘ ⁸Ebed-Melech went out of the palace and said to him, ⁹"My lord the king, these men have acted wickedly in all they have done to Jeremiah the prophet. They have thrown him into a cistern,ᵛ where he will starve to death when there is no longer any breadʷ in the city."

¹⁰Then the king commanded Ebed-Melech the Cushite, "Take thirty men from here with you and lift Jeremiah the prophet out of the cistern before he dies."

¹¹So Ebed-Melech took the men with him and went to a room under the treasury in the palace. He took some old rags and worn-out clothes from there and let them down with ropesˣ to Jeremiah in the cistern. ¹²Ebed-Melech the Cushite said to Jeremiah, "Put these old rags and worn-out clothes under your arms to pad the ropes." Jeremiah did so, ¹³and they pulled him up with the ropes and lifted him out of the cistern. And Jeremiah remained in the courtyard of the guard.ʸ

Zedekiah Questions Jeremiah Again

¹⁴Then King Zedekiah sentᶻ for Jeremiah the prophet and had him brought to the third entrance to the temple of the LORD. "I am going to ask you something," the king said to Jeremiah. "Do not hideᵃ anything from me."

¹⁵Jeremiah said to Zedekiah, "If I give you an answer, will you not kill me? Even if I did give you counsel, you would not listen to me."

¹⁶But King Zedekiah swore this oath secretlyᵇ to Jeremiah: "As surely as the LORD lives, who has given us breath,ᶜ I will neither kill you nor hand you over to those who are seeking your life."ᵈ

¹⁷Then Jeremiah said to Zedekiah, "This is what the LORD God Almighty, the God of Israel, says: 'If you surrenderᵉ to the officers of the king of Babylon, your life will be spared and this city will not be burned down; you and your family will live.ᶠ ¹⁸But if you will not surrender to the officers of the king of Babylon, this city will be handed overᵍ to the Babylonians and they will burnʰ it down; you yourself will not escapeⁱ from their hands.'"

¹⁹King Zedekiah said to Jeremiah, "I am afraidʲ of the Jews who have gone overᵏ to the Babylonians, for the Babylonians may hand me over to them and they will mistreat me."

²⁰"They will not hand you over," Jeremiah replied. "Obeyˡ the LORD by doing what I tell you. Then it will go wellᵐ with you, and your lifeⁿ will be spared. ²¹But if you refuse to surrender, this is what the LORD has revealed to me: ²²All the womenᵒ left in the palace of the king of Judah will be brought out to the officials of the king of Babylon. Those women will say to you:

"'They misled you and overcame you—
those trusted friendsᵖ of yours.
Your feet are sunk in the mud;ᑫ
your friends have deserted you.'

²³"All your wives and childrenʳ will be brought out to the Babylonians. You yourself will not escapeˢ from their hands but will be capturedᵗ by the king of Babylon; and this city willᵈ be burned down.'"ᵘ

²⁴Then Zedekiah said to Jeremiah, "Do not let anyone knowᵛ about this conversation, or you may die. ²⁵If the officials hear that I talked with you, and they come to you and say, 'Tell us what you said to the king and what the king said to you; do not hide it from us or we will kill you,' ²⁶then tellʷ them, 'I was pleading with the king not to send me back to Jonathan's houseˣ to die there.'"

²⁷All the officials did come to Jeremiah and question him, and he told them everything the king had ordered him to say. So they said no more to him, for no one had heard his conversation with the king.

²⁸And Jeremiah remained in the courtyard of the guardʸ until the day Jerusalem was captured.

R *Jer 34:22* ◀ ▶ *Jer 44:2*

ᵇ 7 Probably from the upper Nile region   ᶜ 7 Or *a eunuch*   ᵈ 23 Or *and you will cause this city to*

The Fall of Jerusalem

39:1–10pp — 2Ki 25:1–12; Jer 52:4–16

39 This is how Jerusalem[z] was taken: [1]In the ninth year of Zedekiah[a] king of Judah, in the tenth month, Nebuchadnezzar[b] king of Babylon marched against Jerusalem with his whole army and laid siege[c] to it. [2]And on the ninth day of the fourth[d] month of Zedekiah's eleventh year, the city wall[e] was broken through.[f] [3]Then all the officials[g] of the king of Babylon came and took seats in the Middle Gate: Nergal-Sharezer of Samgar, Nebo-Sarsekim[e] a chief officer, Nergal-Sharezer a high official and all the other officials of the king of Babylon. [4]When Zedekiah king of Judah and all the soldiers saw them, they fled; they left the city at night by way of the king's garden, through the gate between the two walls,[h] and headed toward the Arabah.[f]

[5]But the Babylonian[g] army pursued them and overtook Zedekiah[j] in the plains of Jericho. They captured[k] him and took him to Nebuchadnezzar king of Babylon at Riblah[l] in the land of Hamath, where he pronounced sentence on him. [6]There at Riblah the king of Babylon slaughtered the sons of Zedekiah before his eyes and also killed all the nobles[m] of Judah. [7]Then he put out Zedekiah's eyes[n] and bound him with bronze shackles to take him to Babylon.[o]

[8]The Babylonians[h] set fire[p] to the royal palace and the houses of the people and broke down the walls[q] of Jerusalem. [9]Nebuzaradan commander of the imperial guard carried into exile to Babylon the people who remained in the city, along with those who had gone over to him,[r] and the rest of the people.[s] [10]But Nebuzaradan the commander of the guard left behind in the land of Judah some of the poor people, who owned nothing; and at that time he gave them vineyards and fields.

[11]Now Nebuchadnezzar king of Babylon had given these orders about Jeremiah through Nebuzaradan commander of the imperial guard: [12]"Take him and look after him; don't harm[t] him but do for him whatever he asks." [13]So Nebuzaradan the commander of the guard, Nebushazban a chief officer, Nergal-Sharezer a high official and all the other officers[u] of the king of Babylon [14]sent and had Jeremiah taken out of the courtyard of the guard.[v] They turned him over to Gedaliah[w] son of Ahikam,[x] the son of Shaphan,[y] to take him back to his home. So he remained among his own people.[z]

[15]While Jeremiah had been confined in the courtyard of the guard, the word of the LORD came to him: [16]"Go and tell Ebed-Melech[a] the Cushite, 'This is what the LORD Almighty, the God of Israel, says: I am about to fulfill my words[b] against this city through disaster,[c] not prosperity. At that time they will be fulfilled before your eyes. [17]But I will rescue[d] you on that day, declares the LORD; you will not be handed over to those you fear. [18]I will save[e] you; you will not fall by the sword[f] but will escape with your life,[g] because you trust[h] in me, declares the LORD.'"

Jeremiah Freed

40 The word came to Jeremiah from the LORD after Nebuzaradan commander of the imperial guard had released him at Ramah.[i] He had found Jeremiah bound in chains among all the captives[j] from Jerusalem and Judah who were being carried into exile to Babylon. [2]When the commander[k] of the guard found Jeremiah, he said to him, "The LORD your God decreed[l] this disaster[m] for this place.[n] [3]And now the LORD has brought it about; he has done just as he said he would. All this happened because you people sinned[o] against the LORD and did not obey[p] him. [4]But today I am freeing[q] you from the chains[r] on your wrists. Come with me to Babylon, if you like, and I will look after you; but if you do not want to, then don't come. Look, the whole country lies before you; go wher-

L *Isa 45:13* ◄► *Da 2:28–32*
V *Jer 20:11* ◄► *Jer 51:36*

[e]3 Or *Nergal-Sharezer, Samgar-Nebo, Sarsekim* [f]4 Or *the Jordan Valley* [g]5 Or *Chaldean* [h]8 Or *Chaldeans*

39:6–7 Jeremiah recorded that Nebuchadnezzar killed Zedekiah's sons right in front of him and then blinded him before taking him to Babylon in chains. The last thing Zedekiah saw, the last image indelibly imprinted on his mind, was the murder of his own children brought on by his own rebellion.

ever you please."s 5However, before Jeremiah turned to go,' Nebuzaradan added, "Go back to Gedaliaht son of Ahikam,u the son of Shaphan, whom the king of Babylon has appointedv over the townsw of Judah, and live with him among the people, or go anywhere else you please."x

Then the commander gave him provisions and a presenty and let him go. 6So Jeremiah went to Gedaliah son of Ahikam at Mizpahz and stayed with him among the people who were left behind in the land.

Gedaliah Assassinated
40:7–9; 41:1–3pp — 2Ki 25:22–26

7When all the army officers and their men who were still in the open country heard that the king of Babylon had appointed Gedaliah son of Ahikam as governora over the land and had put him in charge of the men, women and children who were the poorestb in the land and who had not been carried into exile to Babylon, 8they came to Gedaliah at Mizpahc—Ishmaeld son of Nethaniah, Johanane and Jonathan the sons of Kareah, Seraiah son of Tanhumeth, the sons of Ephai the Netophathite,f and Jaazaniah/ the son of the Maacathite,g and their men. 9Gedaliah son of Ahikam, the son of Shaphan, took an oath to reassure them and their men. "Do not be afraid to serveh the Babylonians,ki" he said. "Settle down in the land and serve the king of Babylon, and it will go well with you.j 10I myself will stay at Mizpahk to represent you before the Babylonians who come to us, but you are to harvest the wine,l summer fruit and oil, and put them in your storage jars,m and live in the towns you have taken over."n

11When all the Jews in Moab,o Ammon, Edomp and all the other countriesq heard that the king of Babylon had left a remnant in Judah and had appointed Gedaliah son of Ahikam, the son of Shaphan, as governor over them, 12they all came back to the land of Judah, to Gedaliah at Mizpah, from all the countries where they had been scattered.r And they harvested an abundance of wine and summer fruit.

13Johanans son of Kareah and all the army officers still in the open country came to Gedaliah at Mizpaht 14and said to him, "Don't you know that Baalis king of the Ammonitesu has sent Ishmaelv son of Nethaniah to take your life?" But Gedaliah son of Ahikam did not believe them.

15Then Johananw son of Kareah said privately to Gedaliah in Mizpah, "Let me go and killx Ishmael son of Nethaniah, and no one will know it. Why should he take your life and cause all the Jews who are gathered around you to be scatteredy and the remnantz of Judah to perish?"

16But Gedaliah son of Ahikam said to Johanana son of Kareah, "Don't do such a thing! What you are saying about Ishmael is not true."

41 In the seventh month Ishmaelb son of Nethaniah, the son of Elishama, who was of royal blood and had been one of the king's officers, came with ten men to Gedaliah son of Ahikam at Mizpah. While they were eating together there, 2Ishmaelc son of Nethaniah and the ten men who were with him got up and struck down Gedaliah son of Ahikam, the son of Shaphan, with the sword,d killing the one whom the king of Babylon had appointede as governor over the land.f 3Ishmael also killed all the Jews who were with Gedaliah at Mizpah, as well as the Babylonian/ soldiers who were there.

4The day after Gedaliah's assassination, before anyone knew about it, 5eighty men who had shaved off their beards,g torn their clothesh and cuti themselves came from Shechem,j Shilohk and Samaria,l bringing grain offerings and incense m with them to the house of the LORD.n 6Ishmael son of Nethaniah went out from Mizpah to meet them, weepingo as he went. When he met them, he said, "Come to Gedaliah son of Ahikam."p 7When they went into the city, Ishmael son of Nethaniah and the men who were with him slaughtered them and threw them into a cistern.q 8But ten of them said to Ishmael, "Don't kill us! We have wheat and barley, oil and honey, hidden in a field."r So he let them alone and did not kill them with the others. 9Now the cistern where he threw all the bodies of the men he had killed along with Gedaliah was the one King Asas had made as part of his defenset against Baashau king

---

i 5 Or Jeremiah answered / 8 Hebrew Jezaniah, a variant of Jaazaniah   k 9 Or Chaldeans; also in verse 10   l 3 Or Chaldean

of Israel. Ishmael son of Nethaniah filled it with the dead.

¹⁰Ishmael made captives of all the rest of the people who were in Mizpah—the king's daughters along with all the others who were left there, over whom Nebuzaradan commander of the imperial guard had appointed Gedaliah son of Ahikam. Ishmael son of Nethaniah took them captive and set out to cross over to the Ammonites.

¹¹When Johanan son of Kareah and all the army officers who were with him heard about all the crimes Ishmael son of Nethaniah had committed, ¹²they took all their men and went to fight Ishmael son of Nethaniah. They caught up with him near the great pool in Gibeon. ¹³When all the people Ishmael had with him saw Johanan son of Kareah and the army officers who were with him, they were glad. ¹⁴All the people Ishmael had taken captive at Mizpah turned and went over to Johanan son of Kareah. ¹⁵But Ishmael son of Nethaniah and eight of his men escaped from Johanan and fled to the Ammonites.

Flight to Egypt

¹⁶Then Johanan son of Kareah and all the army officers who were with him led away all the survivors from Mizpah whom he had recovered from Ishmael son of Nethaniah after he had assassinated Gedaliah son of Ahikam: the soldiers, women, children and court officials he had brought from Gibeon. ¹⁷And they went on, stopping at Geruth Kimham near Bethlehem on their way to Egypt ¹⁸to escape the Babylonians. They were afraid of them because Ishmael son of Nethaniah had killed Gedaliah son of Ahikam, whom the king of Babylon had appointed as governor over the land.

42 Then all the army officers, including Johanan son of Kareah and Jezaniah son of Hoshaiah, and all the people from the least to the greatest approached ²Jeremiah the prophet and said to him, "Please hear our petition and pray to the LORD your God for this entire remnant. For as you now see, though we were once many, now only a few are left. ³Pray that the LORD your God will tell us where we should go and what we should do."

⁴"I have heard you," replied Jeremiah the prophet. "I will certainly pray to the LORD your God as you have requested; I will tell you everything the LORD says and will keep nothing back from you."

⁵Then they said to Jeremiah, "May the LORD be a true and faithful witness against us if we do not act in accordance with everything the LORD your God sends you to tell us. ⁶Whether it is favorable or unfavorable, we will obey the LORD our God, to whom we are sending you, so that it will go well with us, for we will obey the LORD our God."

⁷Ten days later the word of the LORD came to Jeremiah. ⁸So he called together Johanan son of Kareah and all the army officers who were with him and all the people from the least to the greatest. ⁹He said to them, "This is what the LORD, the God of Israel, to whom you sent me to present your petition, says: ¹⁰'If you stay in this land, I will build you up and not tear you down; I will plant you and not uproot you, for I am grieved over the disaster I have inflicted on you. ¹¹Do not be afraid of the king of Babylon, whom you now fear. Do not be afraid of him, declares the LORD, for I am with you and will save you and deliver you from his hands. ¹²I will show you compassion so that he will have compassion on you and restore you to your land.'

¹³"However, if you say, 'We will not stay in this land,' and so disobey the LORD your God, ¹⁴and if you say, 'No, we will go and live in Egypt, where we will not see war or hear the trumpet or be hungry for bread,' ¹⁵then hear the word of the LORD, O remnant of Judah. This is what the LORD Almighty, the God of Israel, says: 'If you are determined to go to Egypt and you do go to settle there, ¹⁶then the sword you fear will overtake you there, and the famine you dread will follow you into Egypt, and there you will die. ¹⁷Indeed, all who are determined to go to Egypt to settle there will die by the sword, famine and plague; not one of them will survive or escape the disaster I will bring on them.' ¹⁸This is what the LORD Almighty, the God of Israel, says:

---

m 18 Or *Chaldeans*   *n 1* Hebrew; Septuagint (see also 43:2) *Azariah*

'As my anger and wrath have been poured out on those who lived in Jerusalem, so will my wrath be poured out on you when you go to Egypt. You will be an object of cursing and horror, of condemnation and reproach; you will never see this place again.'

19"O remnant of Judah, the LORD has told you, 'Do not go to Egypt.' Be sure of this: I warn you today 20that you made a fatal mistake when you sent me to the LORD your God and said, 'Pray to the LORD our God for us; tell us everything he says and we will do it.' 21I have told you today, but you still have not obeyed the LORD your God in all he sent me to tell you. 22So now, be sure of this: You will die by the sword, famine and plague in the place where you want to go to settle."

43 When Jeremiah finished telling the people all the words of the LORD their God—everything the LORD had sent him to tell them— 2Azariah son of Hoshaiah and Johanan son of Kareah and all the arrogant men said to Jeremiah, "You are lying! The LORD our God has not sent you to say, 'You must not go to Egypt to settle there.' 3But Baruch son of Neriah is inciting you against us to hand us over to the Babylonians, so they may kill us or carry us into exile to Babylon."

4So Johanan son of Kareah and all the army officers and all the people disobeyed the LORD's command to stay in the land of Judah. 5Instead, Johanan son of Kareah and all the army officers led away all the remnant of Judah who had come back to live in the land of Judah from all the nations where they had been scattered. 6They also led away all the men, women and children and the king's daughters whom Nebuzaradan commander of the imperial guard had left with Gedaliah son of Ahikam, the son of Shaphan, and Jeremiah the prophet and Baruch son of Neriah. 7So they entered Egypt in disobedience to the LORD and went as far as Tahpanhes.

8In Tahpanhes the word of the LORD came to Jeremiah: 9"While the Jews are watching, take some large stones with you and bury them in clay in the brick pavement at the entrance to Pharaoh's palace in Tahpanhes. 10Then say to them, 'This is what the LORD Almighty, the God of Israel, says: I will send for my servant Nebuchadnezzar king of Babylon, and I will set his throne over these stones I have buried here; he will spread his royal canopy above them. 11He will come and attack Egypt, bringing death to those destined for death, captivity to those destined for captivity, and the sword to those destined for the sword. 12He will set fire to the temples of the gods of Egypt; he will burn their temples and take their gods captive. As a shepherd wraps his garment around him, so will he wrap Egypt around himself and depart from there unscathed. 13There in the temple of the sun in Egypt he will demolish the sacred pillars and will burn down the temples of the gods of Egypt.' "

Disaster Because of Idolatry

44 This word came to Jeremiah concerning all the Jews living in Lower Egypt—in Migdol, Tahpanhes and Memphis—and in Upper Egypt: 2"This is what the LORD Almighty, the God of Israel, says: You saw the great disaster I brought on Jerusalem and on all the towns of Judah. Today they lie deserted and in ruins 3because of the evil they have done. They provoked me to anger by burning incense and by worshiping other gods that neither they nor you nor your fathers ever knew. 4Again and again I sent my servants the prophets, who said, 'Do not do this detestable thing that I hate!' 5But they did not listen or pay attention; they did not turn from their wickedness or stop burning in-

R Jer 38:21–23 ◄ ► Jer 44:6

44:2–6 God announced that his punishment upon Jerusalem was delivered and that Judah's cities and towns were no longer inhabited. There was no turning back from his judgment.

cense[p] to other gods.[q] [6]Therefore, my fierce anger was poured out;[r] it raged against the towns of Judah and the streets of Jerusalem and made them the desolate ruins[s] they are today.

[7]"Now this is what the LORD God Almighty, the God of Israel, says: Why bring such great disaster[t] on yourselves by cutting off from Judah the men and women,[u] the children and infants, and so leave yourselves without a remnant? [8]Why provoke me to anger with what your hands have made,[w] burning incense[x] to other gods in Egypt,[y] where you have come to live?[z] You will destroy yourselves and make yourselves an object of cursing and reproach[a] among all the nations on earth. [9]Have you forgotten the wickedness committed by your fathers[b] and by the kings[c] and queens[d] of Judah and the wickedness committed by you and your wives[e] in the land of Judah and the streets of Jerusalem?[f] [10]To this day they have not humbled[g] themselves or shown reverence,[h] nor have they followed my law[i] and the decrees[j] I set before you and your fathers.[k]

[11]"Therefore, this is what the LORD Almighty,[l] the God of Israel, says: I am determined to bring disaster[m] on you and to destroy all Judah. [12]I will take away the remnant[n] of Judah who were determined to go to Egypt to settle there. They will all perish in Egypt; they will fall by the sword or die from famine. From the least to the greatest,[o] they will die by sword or famine.[p] They will become an object of cursing and horror, of condemnation and reproach.[q] [13]I will punish[r] those who live in Egypt with the sword,[s] famine and plague,[t] as I punished Jerusalem. [14]None of the remnant of Judah who have gone to live in Egypt will escape or survive to return to the land of Judah, to which they long to return and live; none will return except a few fugitives."[u]

[15]Then all the men who knew that their wives[v] were burning incense[w] to other gods, along with all the women[x] who were present—a large assembly— and all the people living in Lower and Upper Egypt,[u][y] said to Jeremiah, [16]"We will not listen[z] to the message you have spoken to us in the name of the LORD![a] [17]We will certainly do everything we said we would:[b] We will burn incense[c] to the Queen of Heaven[d] and will pour out drink offerings to her just as we and our fathers, our kings and our officials[e] did in the towns of Judah and in the streets of Jerusalem.[f] At that time we had plenty of food[g] and were well off and suffered no harm.[h] [18]But ever since we stopped burning incense to the Queen of Heaven and pouring out drink offerings[i] to her, we have had nothing and have been perishing by sword and famine.[j][k]"

[19]The women added, "When we burned incense[l] to the Queen of Heaven[m] and poured out drink offerings to her, did not our husbands[n] know that we were making cakes[o] like her image[p] and pouring out drink offerings to her?"

[20]Then Jeremiah said to all the people, both men and women, who were answering him, [21]"Did not the LORD remember[q] and think about the incense[r] burned in the towns of Judah and the streets of Jerusalem[s] by you and your fathers,[t] your kings and your officials and the people of the land?[u] [22]When the LORD could no longer endure[v] your wicked actions and the detestable things you did, your land became an object of cursing[w] and a desolate waste[x] without inhabitants, as it is today.[y] [23]Because you have burned incense and have sinned against the LORD and have not obeyed him or followed[z] his law or his decrees[a] or his stipulations,

R Jer 44:11–12 ◀ ▶ Jer 45:4

R Jer 44:2 ◀ ▶ Jer 44:11–12
C Jer 23:12 ◀ ▶ La 3:19–20
R Jer 44:6 ◀ ▶ Jer 44:22
D Jer 21:6 ◀ ▶ Eze 5:12

44:11–12 Many of the remnant of Judah that had escaped the first wave of exiles to Babylon now planned to escape to Egypt. But Jeremiah warned that God would destroy all those who tried to flee south to escape punishment.

44:22 Jeremiah declared that Judah's desolation was the result of their apostasy.

this disaster has come upon you, as you now see.' "

²⁴Then Jeremiah said to all the people, including the women, "Hear the word of the LORD, all you people of Judah in Egypt. ²⁵This is what the LORD Almighty, the God of Israel, says: You and your wives have shown by your actions what you promised when you said, 'We will certainly carry out the vows we made to burn incense and pour out drink offerings to the Queen of Heaven.'

"Go ahead then, do what you promised! Keep your vows! ²⁶But hear the word of the LORD, all Jews living in Egypt: 'I swear by my great name,' says the LORD, 'that no one from Judah living anywhere in Egypt will ever again invoke my name or swear, "As surely as the Sovereign LORD lives."' ²⁷For I am watching over them for harm, not for good; the Jews in Egypt will perish by sword and famine until they are all destroyed. ²⁸Those who escape the sword and return to the land of Judah from Egypt will be very few. Then the whole remnant of Judah who came to live in Egypt will know whose word will stand—mine or theirs.

²⁹" 'This will be the sign to you that I will punish you in this place,' declares the LORD, 'so that you will know that my threats of harm against you will surely stand.' ³⁰This is what the LORD says: 'I am going to hand Pharaoh Hophra king of Egypt over to his enemies who seek his life, just as I handed Zedekiah king of Judah over to Nebuchadnezzar king of Babylon, the enemy who was seeking his life.' "

A Message to Baruch

45 This is what Jeremiah the prophet told Baruch son of Neriah in the fourth year of Jehoiakim son of Josiah king of Judah, after Baruch had written on a scroll the words Jeremiah was then dictating: ²"This is what the LORD, the God of Israel, says to you, Baruch: ³You said, 'Woe to me! The LORD has added sorrow to my pain; I am worn out with groaning and find no rest.' "

⁴The LORD said, "Say this to him: 'This is what the LORD says: I will overthrow what I have built and uproot what I have planted, throughout the land. ⁵Should you then seek great things for yourself? Seek them not. For I will bring disaster on all people,' declares the LORD, 'but wherever you go I will let you escape with your life.' "

A Message About Egypt

46 This is the word of the LORD that came to Jeremiah the prophet concerning the nations:

²Concerning Egypt:

This is the message against the army of Pharaoh Neco king of Egypt, which was defeated at Carchemish on the Euphrates River by Nebuchadnezzar king of Babylon in the fourth year of Jehoiakim son of Josiah king of Judah:

³"Prepare your shields, both large and small,
 and march out for battle!
⁴Harness the horses,
 mount the steeds!
Take your positions
 with helmets on!
Polish your spears,
 put on your armor!
⁵What do I see?
 They are terrified,
they are retreating,
 their warriors are defeated.
They flee in haste
 without looking back,
 and there is terror on every side,"
  declares the LORD.
⁶"The swift cannot flee
 nor the strong escape.

45:4–5 Though God had built up the land of Judah, he promised to tear it down because of its sins. Yet God is merciful. He promised to preserve Baruch "wherever you go" (45:5). Jewish tradition suggests that Baruch joined his people in exile and died in Babylon.

JEREMIAH 46:7

In the north by the River Euphrates[g]
  they stumble and fall.[h]
7 "Who is this that rises like the Nile,
  like rivers of surging waters?[i]
8 Egypt rises like the Nile,[j]
  like rivers of surging waters.
  She says, 'I will rise and cover the
    earth;
  I will destroy cities and their
    people.'[k]
9 Charge, O horses!
  Drive furiously, O charioteers!
  March on, O warriors—
    men of Cush[m] and Put who carry
      shields,
    men of Lydia[n] who draw the bow.
10 But that day[o] belongs to the Lord, the
    LORD Almighty—
    a day of vengeance,[p] for vengeance
      on his foes.
  The sword will devour[q] till it is
    satisfied,
  till it has quenched its thirst with
    blood.[r]
  For the Lord, the LORD Almighty, will
    offer sacrifices[s]
  in the land of the north by the River
    Euphrates.[t]

G 11 "Go up to Gilead and get balm,[u]
    O Virgin[v] Daughter of Egypt.
  But you multiply remedies in vain;
    there is no healing[w] for you.
12 The nations will hear of your shame;
    your cries will fill the earth.
  One warrior will stumble over
    another;
  both will fall[x] down together."

13 This is the message the LORD spoke to
Jeremiah the prophet about the coming of
Nebuchadnezzar king of Babylon[y] to at-
tack Egypt:[z]

14 "Announce this in Egypt, and proclaim
    it in Migdol;
  proclaim it also in Memphis[w a] and
    Tahpanhes:[b]
  'Take your positions and get ready,
    for the sword devours[c] those around
      you.'
15 Why will your warriors be laid low?
    They cannot stand, for the LORD will
      push them down.[d]
16 They will stumble[e] repeatedly;
    they will fall[f] over each other.

46:6 [g] Ge 2:14; 15:18 [h] ver 12,16; S Ps 20:8
46:7 [i] Jer 47:2
46:8 [j] Eze 29:3,9; 30:12; Am 8:8 [k] Da 11:10
46:9 [l] Jer 47:3; Eze 26:10; Na 3:2 [m] S Ge 10:6 [n] S Isa 66:19
46:10 [o] Eze 32:10; Joel 1:15; Ob 1:15 [p] S Nu 31:3; S Dt 32:41; 2Ki 23:29-30 [q] S Dt 32:42; [s] S 2Sa 2:26; Zep 2:12 [r] S Dt 32:42 [s] S Lev 3:9; Zep 1:7 [t] Ge 2:14; 15:18
46:11 [u] S Ge 37:25 [v] S 2Ki 19:21 [w] S Jer 30:13; S Mic 1:9
46:12 [x] S ver 6; Isa 19:4; Na 3:8-10
46:13 [y] ver 26; Eze 32:11 [z] Isa 19:1; Jer 27:7
46:14 [a] S Isa 19:13 [b] S Jer 43:8 [c] S Dt 32:42; S 2Sa 2:26; S Jer 24:8
46:15 [d] S Jos 23:5; Isa 66:15-16
46:16 [e] S Lev 26:37 [f] S ver 6 [g] S Isa 13:14 [h] S Jer 25:38
46:17 [i] 1Ki 20:10-11 [j] Isa 19:11-16
46:18 [k] Jer 48:15 [l] S Isa 19:22 [m] 1Ki 18:42
46:19 [n] S Isa 20:4 [o] S Isa 19:13 [p] Eze 29:10,12; 35:7
46:20 [q] ver 24; S Isa 14:31; Jer 47:2
46:21 [r] S 2Ki 7:6 [s] Lk 15:27 [t] S ver 5; S Job 20:24 [u] Ps 18:18; 37:13; Jer 18:17 [v] S Job 18:20
46:22 [w] Ps 74:5
46:23 [x] S Dt 28:42; S Jdg 7:12
46:24 [y] S 2Ki 24:7
46:25 [z] Eze 30:14; Na 3:8 [a] 2Ki 24:7; Eze 30:22 [b] S Jer 43:12 [c] Isa 20:6
46:26 [d] S Jer 44:30 [e] S ver 13; [f] S Isa 19:4

They will say, 'Get up, let us go back
  to our own people[g] and our native
    lands,
  away from the sword of the
    oppressor.'[h]
17 There they will exclaim,
  'Pharaoh king of Egypt is only a loud
    noise;[i]
  he has missed his opportunity.'[j]
18 "As surely as I live," declares the
    King,[k]
  whose name is the LORD Almighty,
  "one will come who is like Tabor[l]
    among the mountains,
  like Carmel[m] by the sea.
19 Pack your belongings for exile,[n]
  you who live in Egypt,
  for Memphis[o] will be laid waste[p]
  and lie in ruins without inhabitant.
20 "Egypt is a beautiful heifer,
  but a gadfly is coming
    against her from the north.[q]
21 The mercenaries[r] in her ranks
  are like fattened calves.[s]
  They too will turn and flee[t] together,
    they will not stand their ground,
  for the day[u] of disaster is coming upon
    them,
  the time[v] for them to be punished.
22 Egypt will hiss like a fleeing serpent
  as the enemy advances in force;
  they will come against her with axes,
    like men who cut down trees.[w]
23 They will chop down her forest,"
              declares the LORD,
  "dense though it be.
  They are more numerous than
    locusts,[x]
  they cannot be counted.
24 The Daughter of Egypt will be put to
    shame,
  handed over to the people of the
    north.[y]

25 The LORD Almighty, the God of Israel,
says: "I am about to bring punishment on
Amon god of Thebes,[x z] on Pharaoh,[a] on
Egypt and her gods[b] and her kings, and
on those who rely[c] on Pharaoh. 26 I will J
hand them over[d] to those who seek their
lives, to Nebuchadnezzar king[e] of Babylon and his officers. Later, however,

J Jer 44:30 ◀ ▶ Jer 47:5

[v] 9 That is, the upper Nile region [w] 14 Hebrew Noph; also in verse 19
[x] 25 Hebrew No

G Jer 30:12 ◀ ▶ Eze 13:10–14

Egypt will be inhabited as in times past," declares the LORD.

27"Do not fear, O Jacob my servant;
 do not be dismayed, O Israel.
I will surely save you out of a distant place,
 your descendants from the land of their exile.
Jacob will again have peace and security,
 and no one will make him afraid.
28Do not fear, O Jacob my servant,
 for I am with you," declares the LORD.
"Though I completely destroy all the nations
 among which I scatter you,
I will not completely destroy you.
I will discipline you but only with justice;
 I will not let you go entirely unpunished."

A Message About the Philistines

47 This is the word of the LORD that came to Jeremiah the prophet concerning the Philistines before Pharaoh attacked Gaza:

²This is what the LORD says:

"See how the waters are rising in the north;
 they will become an overflowing torrent.
They will overflow the land and everything in it,
 the towns and those who live in them.
The people will cry out;
 all who dwell in the land will wail
³at the sound of the hoofs of galloping steeds,
 at the noise of enemy chariots
 and the rumble of their wheels.
Fathers will not turn to help their children;
 their hands will hang limp.
⁴For the day has come

Jer 35:18-19 ◀▶ Jer 50:19-20

to destroy all the Philistines
 and to cut off all survivors
 who could help Tyre and Sidon.
The LORD is about to destroy the Philistines,
 the remnant from the coasts of Caphtor.
⁵Gaza will shave her head in mourning;
 Ashkelon will be silenced.
O remnant on the plain,
 how long will you cut yourselves?

⁶" 'Ah, sword of the LORD,' you cry,
 'how long till you rest?
Return to your scabbard;
 cease and be still.'
⁷But how can it rest
 when the LORD has commanded it,
 when he has ordered it
 to attack Ashkelon and the coast?"

A Message About Moab

48:29-36pp — Isa 16:6-12

48 Concerning Moab:

This is what the LORD Almighty, the God of Israel, says:

"Woe to Nebo, for it will be ruined.
 Kiriathaim will be disgraced and captured;
 the stronghold will be disgraced and shattered.
²Moab will be praised no more;
 in Heshbon men will plot her downfall:
 'Come, let us put an end to that nation.'
You too, O Madmen, will be silenced;
 the sword will pursue you.
³Listen to the cries from Horonaim,
 cries of great havoc and destruction.
⁴Moab will be broken;
 her little ones will cry out.
⁵They go up the way to Luhith,

Jer 46:26 ◀▶ Eze 12:13

y 4 That is, Crete z 1 Or /Misgab z 2 The Hebrew for Heshbon sounds like the Hebrew for plot. b 2 The name of the Moabite town Madmen sounds like the Hebrew for be silenced. c 4 Hebrew; Septuagint / proclaim it to Zoar

---

46:27-28 Notice the similarity between this passage and 30:10-11. Jeremiah declared that despite the terrible punishment of captivity and exile, God would ultimately restore his people to the promised land. God would also destroy those nations that gloried in their victory over God's people. In fulfillment of this prophecy both the great empires of Assyria and Babylon were so totally destroyed that archeologists have only recently discovered the ruins of their vast cities.

weeping bitterly as they go;
  on the road down to Horonaim^k
  anguished cries over the destruction
    are heard.
⁶Flee!^l Run for your lives;
  become like a bush^d in the desert.^m
⁷Since you trust in your deeds and
    riches,^n
  you too will be taken captive,
  and Chemosh^o will go into exile,^p
    together with his priests and
      officials.^q
⁸The destroyer^r will come against every
    town,
  and not a town will escape.
The valley will be ruined
  and the plateau^s destroyed,
  because the LORD has spoken.
⁹Put salt^t on Moab,
  for she will be laid waste^e;^u
  her towns will become desolate,
    with no one to live in them.

¹⁰"A curse on him who is lax in doing
    the LORD's work!
  A curse on him who keeps his
    sword^v from bloodshed!^w

¹¹"Moab has been at rest^x from youth,
  like wine left on its dregs,^y
  not poured from one jar to another—
    she has not gone into exile.
So she tastes as she did,
  and her aroma is unchanged.

¹²But days are coming,"
    declares the LORD,
  "when I will send men who pour from
    jars,
  and they will pour her out;
  they will empty her jars
    and smash her jugs.
¹³Then Moab will be ashamed^z of
    Chemosh,^a
  as the house of Israel was ashamed
    when they trusted in Bethel.^b

¹⁴"How can you say, 'We are warriors,^c
    men valiant in battle'?
¹⁵Moab will be destroyed and her towns
    invaded;
  her finest young men^d will go down
    in the slaughter,^e"
    declares the King,^f whose name is
      the LORD Almighty.^g
¹⁶"The fall of Moab is at hand;^h
  her calamity will come quickly.
¹⁷Mourn for her, all who live around
    her,

48:5 ^k ver 3
48:6 ^l S Ge 19:17
  ^m Jer 17:6
48:7 ^n S Ps 49:6;
  S Pr 11:28
  ^o S Nu 21:29
  ^p Isa 46:1-2;
  Jer 49:3 ^q Am 2:3
48:8 ^r S Ex 12:23;
  S Jer 4:7 ^s S Jos 13:9
48:9 ^t Jdg 9:45
  ^u Jer 51:29
48:10 ^v S Jer 47:6
  ^w S Isa 15:11;
  1Ki 20:42;
  2Ki 13:15-19
48:11 ^x Zec 1:15
  ^y Zep 1:12
48:13 ^z Hos 10:6
  ^a ver 7 ^b S Jos 7:2
48:14 ^c Ps 33:16
48:15 ^d S Isa 9:17
  ^e Jer 51:40
  ^f S Jer 46:18
  ^g Jer 51:57
48:16 ^h Isa 13:22
48:17 ^i 2Ki 3:4-5
  ^j S Ps 110:2
48:18 ^k Isa 47:1
  ^l S Nu 21:30;
  S Jos 13:9 ^m ver 8
48:19 ^n S Nu 32:34
48:20 ^o S Isa 16:7
  ^p S Nu 21:13
48:21 ^q S Jos 13:9,
  21 ^r S Jos 15:51
  ^s S Nu 21:23;
  S Isa 15:4
  ^t S Jos 13:18
48:22
  ^u S Nu 21:30;
  S Jos 13:9,17
  ^v S Nu 32:38
48:23
  ^w S Nu 32:37;
  S Jos 13:19
  ^x S Jos 13:17
48:24 ^y Am 2:2
  ^z Jer 49:13
  ^a S Isa 15:1
48:25 ^b Ps 75:10
  ^c Ps 10:15; 37:17;
  Eze 30:21
48:26 ^d Jer 25:16,
  27; 51:39 ^e ver 42;
  1Sa 17:26
  ^f S Isa 28:8 ^g ver 39
48:27 ^h S Jer 2:26
  ^i 2Ki 17:3-6
  ^j S Job 16:4;
  Ps 44:14; Jer 18:16
  ^k S Dt 28:37;
  Mic 7:8-10;
  Zep 2:8,10
48:28 ^l S Ge 8:8;
  S SS 1:15
  ^m S Jdg 6:2
48:29
  ^n S Lev 26:19;
  S Job 40:12
  ^o S Ps 10:5;
  S Pr 16:18

all who know her fame;^i
  say, 'How broken is the mighty
    scepter,^j
  how broken the glorious staff!'

¹⁸"Come down from your glory
  and sit on the parched ground,^k
  O inhabitants of the Daughter of
    Dibon,^l
for he who destroys Moab
  will come up against you
  and ruin your fortified cities.^m
¹⁹Stand by the road and watch,
  you who live in Aroer.^n
Ask the man fleeing and the woman
    escaping,
  ask them, 'What has happened?'
²⁰Moab is disgraced, for she is shattered.
  Wail^o and cry out!
Announce by the Arnon^p
  that Moab is destroyed.
²¹Judgment has come to the plateau^q—
  to Holon,^r Jahzah^s and Mephaath,^t
²² to Dibon,^u Nebo^v and Beth
    Diblathaim,
²³ to Kiriathaim,^w Beth Gamul and
    Beth Meon,^x
²⁴ to Kerioth^y and Bozrah^z—
  to all the towns^a of Moab, far and
    near.
²⁵Moab's horn^{/b} is cut off;
  her arm^c is broken,"
            declares the LORD.

²⁶"Make her drunk,^d
  for she has defied^e the LORD.
Let Moab wallow in her vomit;^f
  let her be an object of ridicule.^g
²⁷Was not Israel the object of your
    ridicule?^h
  Was she caught among thieves,^i
  that you shake your head^j in scorn^k
    whenever you speak of her?
²⁸Abandon your towns and dwell among
    the rocks,
  you who live in Moab.
Be like a dove^l that makes its nest
  at the mouth of a cave.^m

²⁹"We have heard of Moab's pride^n—
  her overweening pride and conceit,
  her pride and arrogance
  and the haughtiness^o of her heart.
³⁰I know her insolence but it is futile,"
            declares the LORD,

^d 6 Or like Aroer ^e 9 Or Give wings to Moab, / for she will fly away
^f 25 Horn here symbolizes strength.

"and her boasts accomplish
　　nothing.
³¹Therefore I wail over Moab,
　　for all Moab I cry out,
　I moan for the men of Kir Hareseth.
³²I weep for you, as Jazer weeps,
　　O vines of Sibmah.
　Your branches spread as far as the sea;
　　they reached as far as the sea of
　　　Jazer.
　The destroyer has fallen
　　on your ripened fruit and grapes.
³³Joy and gladness are gone
　　from the orchards and fields of
　　　Moab.
　I have stopped the flow of wine from
　　the presses;
　no one treads them with shouts of
　　joy.
　Although there are shouts,
　　they are not shouts of joy.

³⁴"The sound of their cry rises
　　from Heshbon to Elealeh and
　　　Jahaz,
　from Zoar as far as Horonaim and
　　Eglath Shelishiyah,
　for even the waters of Nimrim are
　　dried up.
³⁵In Moab I will put an end
　　to those who make offerings on the
　　　high places
　and burn incense to their gods,"
　　　　　declares the LORD.
³⁶"So my heart laments for Moab like a
　　flute;
　it laments like a flute for the men of
　　Kir Hareseth.
　The wealth they acquired is gone.
³⁷Every head is shaved
　　and every beard cut off;
　every hand is slashed
　　and every waist is covered with
　　　sackcloth.
³⁸On all the roofs in Moab
　　and in the public squares
　there is nothing but mourning,
　　for I have broken Moab
　like a jar that no one wants,"
　　　　　declares the LORD.
³⁹"How shattered she is! How they
　　wail!
　How Moab turns her back in shame!

Moab has become an object of
　　ridicule,
　an object of horror to all those
　　around her."

⁴⁰This is what the LORD says:

"Look! An eagle is swooping down,
　　spreading its wings over Moab.
⁴¹Kerioth will be captured
　　and the strongholds taken.
　In that day the hearts of Moab's
　　warriors
　will be like the heart of a woman in
　　labor.
⁴²Moab will be destroyed as a nation
　　because she defied the LORD.
⁴³Terror and pit and snare await you,
　　O people of Moab,"
　　　　　declares the LORD.
⁴⁴"Whoever flees from the terror
　　will fall into a pit,
　whoever climbs out of the pit
　　will be caught in a snare;
　for I will bring upon Moab
　　the year of her punishment,"
　　　　　declares the LORD.

⁴⁵"In the shadow of Heshbon
　　the fugitives stand helpless,
　for a fire has gone out from Heshbon,
　　a blaze from the midst of Sihon;
　it burns the foreheads of Moab,
　　the skulls of the noisy boasters.
⁴⁶Woe to you, O Moab!
　The people of Chemosh are
　　destroyed;
　your sons are taken into exile
　　and your daughters into captivity.

⁴⁷"Yet I will restore the fortunes of
　　Moab
　in days to come,"
　　　　　declares the LORD.

Here ends the judgment on Moab.

A Message About Ammon

49
Concerning the Ammonites:

This is what the LORD says:

"Has Israel no sons?

▶ *Jer 45:5* ◀ ▶ *Jer 49:2–6*

ᵍ 41 Or *The cities*

49:1–2, 6 This prophecy told of the destruction of the Ammonites (see Eze 25:1–7; Am 1:13–15; Zep 2:8–11). Ammon was located on the east side of the Jordan and north of Moab. Ammon joined

Has she no heirs?
Why then has Molech[hf] taken
  possession of Gad?[g]
Why do his people live in its towns?

²"But the days are coming,"
  declares the LORD,
"when I will sound the battle cry[h]
  against Rabbah[i] of the Ammonites;
it will become a mound of ruins,[j]
  and its surrounding villages will be
  set on fire.
Then Israel will drive out
  those who drove her out,[k]"
                    says the LORD.

³"Wail, O Heshbon,[l] for Ai[m] is
  destroyed!
Cry out, O inhabitants of Rabbah!
Put on sackcloth[n] and mourn;
  rush here and there inside the walls,
for Molech[o] will go into exile,[p]
  together with his priests and
  officials.
⁴Why do you boast of your valleys,
  boast of your valleys so fruitful?
O unfaithful daughter,[q]
  you trust in your riches[r] and say,
  'Who will attack me?'[s]
⁵I will bring terror on you
  from all those around you,"
              declares the Lord,
            the LORD Almighty.
"Every one of you will be driven away,
  and no one will gather the
  fugitives.[t]

⁶"Yet afterward, I will restore[u] the
  fortunes of the Ammonites,"
              declares the LORD.

A Message About Edom
49:9–10pp — Ob 5–6
49:14–16pp — Ob 1–4

⁷Concerning Edom:[v]

This is what the LORD Almighty says:

"Is there no longer wisdom in
  Teman?[w]
Has counsel perished from the
  prudent?
Has their wisdom decayed?

P Jer 48:47 ◄ ► Jer 49:23–27

49:1 ʳS Lev 18:21
     ᵍGe 30:11
49:2 ʰS Jer 4:19
     ⁱS Dt 3:11
     ʲS Dt 13:16
     ᵏS Isa 14:2;
     S Jer 30:16;
     Eze 21:28-32;
     25:2-11
49:3 ˡS Jos 13:26
     ᵐS Ge 12:8;
     S Jos 8:28
     ⁿS Ge 37:34
     ᵒZep 1:5
     ᵖS Jer 48:7
49:4 ᑫS Jer 3:6
     ʳS Jer 9:23;
     1Ti 6:17
     ˢS Jer 21:13
49:5 ᵗS Jer 44:14
49:6
     ᵘJer 12:14-17;
     S 48:47
49:7 ᵛS Ge 25:30;
     S Ps 83:6
     ʷS Ge 36:11,15,34
49:8 ˣS Jdg 6:2
     ʸGe 10:7; S 25:3
49:10 ᶻS Ge 3:8
     ᵃIsa 34:10-12;
     S Jer 11:23;
     Eze 35:4; Ob 1:18;
     Mal 1:2-5
49:11 ᵇHos 14:3
     ᶜS Dt 10:18;
     Jas 1:27
49:12
     ᵈS Isa 51:23;
     S Jer 25:15;
     Mt 20:22
     ᵉS Pr 11:31
49:13 ᶠS Ge 22:16
     ᵍS Ge 36:33
     ʰver 17 ⁱJer 42:18
     ʲS Jer 19:8;
     Eze 35:9
49:16 ᵏEze 35:13;
     Ob 1:12
     ˡS Job 39:28
     ᵐS Job 39:27

⁸Turn and flee, hide in deep caves,[x]
  you who live in Dedan,[y]
for I will bring disaster on Esau
  at the time I punish him.
⁹If grape pickers came to you,
  would they not leave a few grapes?
If thieves came during the night,
  would they not steal only as much as
  they wanted?
¹⁰But I will strip Esau bare;
  I will uncover his hiding places,[z]
  so that he cannot conceal himself.
His children, relatives and neighbors
  will perish,
  and he will be no more.[a]
¹¹Leave your orphans;[b] I will protect
  their lives.
  Your widows[c] too can trust in me."

¹²This is what the LORD says: "If those who do not deserve to drink the cup[d] must drink it, why should you go unpunished?[e] You will not go unpunished, but must drink it. ¹³I swear[f] by myself," declares the LORD, "that Bozrah[g] will become a ruin and an object of horror,[h] of reproach[i] and of cursing; and all its towns will be in ruins forever."[j]

¹⁴I have heard a message from the LORD:
  An envoy was sent to the nations to
  say,
"Assemble yourselves to attack it!
  Rise up for battle!"

¹⁵"Now I will make you small among the
  nations,
  despised among men.
¹⁶The terror you inspire
  and the pride[k] of your heart have
  deceived you,
you who live in the clefts of the
  rocks,[l]
  who occupy the heights of the hill.
Though you build your nest[m] as high as
  the eagle's,
from there I will bring you down,"
              declares the LORD.

M Jer 29:12–13 ◄ ► La 3:19–21

ʰ 1 Or *their king*; Hebrew *malcam*; also in verse 3

---

forces with Moab and supplied troops to Nebuchadnezzar during the attack on Judah (see 2Ki 24:2). Yet Ammon apparently rebelled against Nebuchadnezzar's governor Gedaliah (see 40:13—41:3). Such treachery would have been punished by Babylon and probably led to an attack that virtually wiped out Ammon. Though Ammon was sentenced to destruction, note that God promised to restore them (49:6).

¹⁷"Edom will become an object of horror;ⁿ
all who pass by will be appalled and will scoff
because of all its wounds.°
¹⁸As Sodomᵖ and Gomorrahq were overthrown,
along with their neighboring towns,"
says the LORD,
"so no one will live there;
no man will dwellʳ in it.

¹⁹"Like a lionˢ coming up from Jordan's thicketsᵗ
to a rich pastureland,
I will chase Edom from its land in an instant.
Who is the chosen one I will appoint for this?
Who is likeᵘ me and who can challenge me?ᵛ
And what shepherdʷ can stand against me?"
²⁰Therefore, hear what the LORD has planned against Edom,ˣ
what he has purposedʸ against those who live in Teman:ᶻ
The young of the flockᵃ will be dragged away;
he will completely destroyᵇ their pasture because of them.ᶜ
²¹At the sound of their fall the earth will tremble;ᵈ
their cryᵉ will resound to the Red Sea.ⁱ
²²Look! An eagle will soar and swoopᶠ down,
spreading its wings over Bozrah.ᵍ
In that day the hearts of Edom's warriorsʰ
will be like the heart of a woman in labor.ⁱ

A Message About Damascus

P ²³Concerning Damascus:ʲ

"Hamathᵏ and Arpadˡ are dismayed,
for they have heard bad news.
They are disheartened,
troubled likeʲ the restless sea.ᵐ

P Jer 49:2–6 ◄ ► Jer 49:39

49:17 ⁿ ver 13
° S Dt 29:22; Eze 35:7
49:18 ᵖ Jer 23:14
ᵠ S Ge 19:24
ʳ ver 33; S Isa 34:10
49:19
ˢ S 1Sa 17:34
ᵗ S Jer 12:5
ᵘ S Ex 8:10; S 2Ch 20:6; S Isa 46:5
ᵛ S Job 9:19; Jer 50:44
ʷ 1Sa 17:35
49:20 ˣ Isa 34:5
ʸ Isa 14:27 ᶻ ver 7; S Ge 36:11
ᵃ Jer 50:45 ᵇ ver 10; Ob 1:10; Mal 1:3-4
ᶜ Jer 50:45
49:21 ᵈ Ps 114:7; Eze 26:15; 27:28; 31:16 ᵉ Jer 50:46; 51:29; Eze 26:18
49:22 ᶠ S Dt 28:49; Hos 8:1; Hab 1:8
ᵍ S Ge 36:33
ʰ Jer 50:36; Na 3:13
ⁱ Isa 13:8
49:23 ʲ S Ge 14:15; 2Ki 14:28; 2Ch 16:2; Ac 9:2
ᵏ 1Ki 8:65; Isa 10:9; Eze 47:16; Am 6:2; Zec 9:2
ˡ S 2Ki 18:34; S 19:13 ᵐ S Ge 49:4
49:24 ⁿ Jer 13:21
49:26 ° S Isa 9:17; S 13:18
ᵖ Isa 17:12-14
49:27 ᵠ Jer 21:14; 43:12; 50:32; Eze 30:8; 39:6; Am 1:4
ʳ S Ge 14:15
ˢ Isa 17:1
ᵗ S 1Ki 15:18
49:28 ᵘ S Ge 25:13
ᵛ S Jos 11:1
ʷ S Jer 10:22
ˣ S Jdg 6:5
49:29 ʸ ver 32
ᶻ S Jer 6:25
49:30 ᵃ S Jdg 6:2
ᵇ Jos 11:1
ᶜ S Jer 10:22
49:31 ᵈ Eze 38:11
49:32 ᵉ S Jdg 6:5
ᶠ ver 29

²⁴Damascus has become feeble,
she has turned to flee
and panic has gripped her;
anguish and pain have seized her,
pain like that of a woman in labor.ⁿ
²⁵Why has the city of renown not been abandoned,
the town in which I delight?
²⁶Surely, her young men° will fall in the streets;
all her soldiers will be silencedᵖ in that day,"
declares the LORD Almighty.
²⁷"I will set fireᵠ to the walls of Damascus;ʳ
it will consumeˢ the fortresses of Ben-Hadad.ᵗ"

A Message About Kedar and Hazor

²⁸Concerning Kedarᵘ and the kingdoms of Hazor,ᵛ which Nebuchadnezzarʷ king of Babylon attacked:

This is what the LORD says:

"Arise, and attack Kedar
and destroy the people of the East.ˣ
²⁹Their tents and their flocksʸ will be taken;
their shelters will be carried off with all their goods and camels.
Men will shout to them,
'Terrorᶻ on every side!'

³⁰"Flee quickly away!
Stay in deep caves,ᵃ you who live in Hazor,ᵇ"
declares the LORD.
"Nebuchadnezzarᶜ king of Babylon has plotted against you;
he has devised a plan against you.

³¹"Arise and attack a nation at ease,
which lives in confidence,"
declares the LORD,
"a nation that has neither gates nor bars;ᵈ
its people live alone.
³²Their camelsᵉ will become plunder,
and their large herdsᶠ will be booty.

i 21 Hebrew *Yam Suph;* that is, Sea of Reeds   *i 23* Hebrew *on* or *by*

49:23–27 Damascus was the capital of Syria, a frequent enemy of Israel. Note that this prophecy about a fire in the wall of Damascus parallels the prophecy found in Isa 17:1. These words may refer to Nebuchadnezzar's overthrow of Syria or may refer to Damascus' destruction in the end times.

I will scatter to the winds those who
    are in distant places,
and will bring disaster on them from
    every side,"
            declares the LORD.
³³"Hazor will become a haunt of
    jackals,
a desolate place forever.
No one will live there;
    no man will dwell in it."

A Message About Elam

³⁴This is the word of the LORD that came to Jeremiah the prophet concerning Elam, early in the reign of Zedekiah king of Judah:

³⁵This is what the LORD Almighty says:

"See, I will break the bow of Elam,
    the mainstay of their might.
³⁶I will bring against Elam the four
    winds
from the four quarters of the
    heavens;
I will scatter them to the four winds,
    and there will not be a nation
where Elam's exiles do not go.
³⁷I will shatter Elam before their foes,
    before those who seek their lives;
I will bring disaster upon them,
    even my fierce anger,"
            declares the LORD.
"I will pursue them with the sword
    until I have made an end of them.
³⁸I will set my throne in Elam
    and destroy her king and officials,"
            declares the LORD.

³⁹"Yet I will restore the fortunes of
    Elam
in days to come,"
            declares the LORD.

A Message About Babylon

51:15–19pp — Jer 10:12–16

50 This is the word the LORD spoke through Jeremiah the prophet concerning Babylon and the land of the Babylonians:

²"Announce and proclaim among the
    nations,
lift up a banner and proclaim it;

P *Jer 49:23–27* ◀ ▶ *Eze 38:1–23*

keep nothing back, but say,
'Babylon will be captured;
Bel will be put to shame,
Marduk filled with terror.
Her images will be put to shame
    and her idols filled with terror.'
³A nation from the north will attack
    her
and lay waste her land.
No one will live in it;
    both men and animals will flee
        away.

⁴"In those days, at that time,"
            declares the LORD,
"the people of Israel and the people of
    Judah together
will go in tears to seek the LORD
    their God.
⁵They will ask the way to Zion
    and turn their faces toward it.
They will come and bind themselves
    to the LORD
in an everlasting covenant
    that will not be forgotten.

⁶"My people have been lost sheep;
    their shepherds have led them
        astray
and caused them to roam on the
    mountains.
They wandered over mountain and
    hill
and forgot their own resting place.
⁷Whoever found them devoured them;
    their enemies said, 'We are not
        guilty,
for they sinned against the LORD, their
    true pasture,
the LORD, the hope of their fathers.'

⁸"Flee out of Babylon;
    leave the land of the Babylonians,
and be like the goats that lead the
    flock.
⁹For I will stir up and bring against
    Babylon
an alliance of great nations from
    the land of the north.
They will take up their positions
    against her,

k 32 Or who clip the hair by their foreheads *l 1 Or* Chaldeans; *also in verses 8, 25, 35 and 45*

50:1, 9–10 Jeremiah ultimately delivered this prophecy to Babylon itself (see 51:59–61), naming the nations who would come against this great empire and ultimately destroy it (see 51:27–28).

and from the north she will be captured.ʸ
Their arrowsᶻ will be like skilled warriors
who do not return empty-handed.
¹⁰So Babyloniaᵐ will be plundered;ᵃ
all who plunder her will have their fill,"
declares the Lord.

¹¹"Because you rejoice and are glad,
you who pillage my inheritance,ᵇ
because you frolic like a heiferᶜ threshing grain
and neigh like stallions,
¹²your mother will be greatly ashamed;
she who gave you birth will be disgraced.ᵈ
She will be the least of the nations—
a wilderness, a dry land, a desert.ᵉ
¹³Because of the Lord's anger she will not be inhabited
but will be completely desolate.ᶠ
All who pass Babylon will be horrifiedᵍ and scoffʰ
because of all her wounds.ⁱ

¹⁴"Take up your positions around Babylon,
all you who draw the bow.ʲ
Shoot at her! Spare no arrows,ᵏ
for she has sinned against the Lord.
¹⁵Shoutˡ against her on every side!
She surrenders, her towers fall,
her wallsᵐ are torn down.
Since this is the vengeanceⁿ of the Lord,
take vengeance on her;
do to herᵒ as she has done to others.ᵖ
¹⁶Cut off from Babylon the sower,
and the reaper with his sickle at harvest.
Because of the swordᑫ of the oppressor
let everyone return to his own people,ʳ
let everyone flee to his own land.ˢ

¹⁷"Israel is a scattered flockᵗ
that lionsᵘ have chased away.
The first to devourᵛ him
was the kingʷ of Assyria;
the last to crush his bonesˣ

50:9 ᵛS ver 2
ᶻS Isa 13:18
50:10 ᵃIsa 47:11; S Jer 30:16
50:11 ᵇS Isa 47:6
ᶜS Jer 31:18
50:12 ᵈJer 51:47
ᵉver 13; S Isa 21:1; Jer 25:12; 51:26
50:13 ᶠver 3, S 12; S Jer 9:11; 48:9; 51:62 ᵍJer 51:41
ʰS Jer 18:16; 51:37; Eze 27:36; Hab 2:6 ⁱS Dt 29:22
50:14 ʲver 29,42
ᵏS Isa 13:18
50:15 ˡJer 51:14
S Jer 51:44,58
ⁿver 28; S Isa 10:3; 63:4; Jer 51:6
ᵒver 29; Ps 137:8; Rev 18:6
ᵖJer 51:24; Hab 2:7-8
50:16 ᑫS Jer 25:38
ʳS Isa 13:14
ˢJer 51:9
50:17 ᵗS Lev 26:33; S Ps 119:176
ᵘS 2Ki 24:1; S Jer 2:15
ᵛS Jer 5:17
ʷS Dt 4:27; S 2Ki 15:29
ˣS Nu 24:8; La 3:4
ʸJer 51:34
ᶻS 2Ki 24:17; S 25:7
50:18 ᵃS Isa 10:12
ᵇEze 31:3; Zep 2:13
50:19 ᶜS Jer 31:10; Eze 34:13
ᵈJer 31:14
ᵉS Jer 31:5
ᶠMic 7:14; Zec 10:10
50:20 ᵍS Ps 17:3
ʰPs 103:12; S Isa 38:17; Eze 33:16; Mic 7:18,19; Zec 3:4,9
ⁱS Isa 33:24
ʲS Ge 45:7; Isa 1:9; 10:20-22; S Ro 9:27
50:21 ᵏEze 23:23
50:22 ˡJer 4:19-21; 51:54
50:23 ᵐS Isa 10:5
ⁿJer 51:25
ᵒS Isa 14:16
50:24 ᵖJer 51:12
ᑫJer 51:31 ʳJob 9:4
50:25 ˢS Isa 13:5

was Nebuchadnezzarʸ kingᶻ of Babylon."

¹⁸Therefore this is what the Lord Almighty, the God of Israel, says:

"I will punish the king of Babylon and his land
as I punished the kingᵃ of Assyria.ᵇ
¹⁹But I will bringᶜ Israel back to his own pasture
and he will graze on Carmel and Bashan;
his appetite will be satisfiedᵈ
on the hillsᵉ of Ephraim and Gilead.ᶠ
²⁰In those days, at that time,"
declares the Lord,
"search will be made for Israel's guilt,
but there will be none,ᵍ
and for the sinsʰ of Judah,
but none will be found,
for I will forgiveⁱ the remnantʲ I spare.

²¹"Attack the land of Merathaim
and those who live in Pekod.ᵏ
Pursue, kill and completely destroyⁿ them,"
declares the Lord.
"Do everything I have commanded you.
²²The noiseˡ of battle is in the land,
the noise of great destruction!
²³How broken and shattered
is the hammerᵐ of the whole earth!ⁿ
How desolateᵒ is Babylon
among the nations!
²⁴I set a trapᵖ for you, O Babylon,
and you were caught before you knew it;
you were found and capturedᑫ
because you opposedʳ the Lord.
²⁵The Lord has opened his arsenal
and brought out the weaponsˢ of his wrath,
for the Sovereign Lord Almighty has work to do

I *Jer 46:27-28* ◀ ▶ *Jer 51:5*
K *Jer 33:8* ◀ ▶ *Eze 11:19-20*
L *Jer 36:3* ◀ ▶ *La 3:25*

ᵐ 10 Or *Chaldea* ⁿ 21 The Hebrew term refers to the irrevocable giving over of things or persons to the Lord, often by totally destroying them; also in verse 26.

50:19-20 In the last days, when the Messiah returns and declares "I will forgive the remnant I spare" (50:20), the Jews will return to the promised land.

in the land of the Babylonians.ᵗ
²⁶Come against her from afar.ᵘ
  Break open her granaries;
    pile her up like heaps of grain.ᵛ
  Completely destroyʷ her
    and leave her no remnant.
²⁷Kill all her young bulls;ˣ
  let them go down to the slaughter!ʸ
  Woe to them! For their dayᶻ has come,
    the timeᵃ for them to be punished.
²⁸Listen to the fugitivesᵇ and refugees
    from Babylon
  declaring in Zionᶜ
  how the Lord our God has taken
    vengeance,ᵈ
    vengeance for his temple.ᵉ

²⁹"Summon archers against Babylon,
    all those who draw the bow.ᶠ
  Encamp all around her;
    let no one escape.ᵍ
  Repayʰ her for her deeds;ⁱ
    do to her as she has done.
  For she has defiedʲ the Lord,
    the Holy Oneᵏ of Israel.
³⁰Therefore, her young menˡ will fall in
    the streets;
  all her soldiers will be silenced in
    that day,"
            declares the Lord.

³¹"See, I am againstᵐ you, O arrogant
    one,"
  declares the Lord, the Lord
    Almighty,
  "for your dayⁿ has come,
    the time for you to be punished.
³²The arrogantᵒ one will stumble and
    fall;ᵖ
  and no one will help her up;ᑫ
  I will kindle a fireʳ in her towns
    that will consume all who are
    around her."

³³This is what the Lord Almighty says:

"The people of Israel are oppressed,ˢ
    and the people of Judah as well.
  All their captors hold them fast,
    refusing to let them go.ᵗ
³⁴Yet their Redeemerᵘ is strong;
    the Lord Almightyᵛ is his name.
  He will vigorously defend their causeʷ
    so that he may bring restˣ to their
    land,
  but unrest to those who live in
    Babylon.

³⁵"A swordʸ against the Babylonians!"ᶻ
    declares the Lord—

"against those who live in Babylon
  and against her officials and wiseᵃ
  men!
³⁶A sword against her false prophets!
  They will become fools.
  A sword against her warriors!ᵇ
  They will be filled with terror.ᶜ
³⁷A sword against her horses and
    chariotsᵈ
  and all the foreigners in her ranks!
  They will become women.ᵉ
  A sword against her treasures!ᶠ
  They will be plundered.
³⁸A drought onᵒ her waters!ᵍ
  They will dryʰ up.
  For it is a land of idols,ⁱ
    idols that will go mad with terror.

³⁹"So desert creaturesʲ and hyenas will
    live there,
  and there the owl will dwell.
  It will never again be inhabited
    or lived in from generation to
    generation.ᵏ
⁴⁰As God overthrew Sodom and
    Gomorrahˡ
  along with their neighboring
    towns,"
            declares the Lord,
  "so no one will live there;
  no man will dwell in it.ᵐ

⁴¹"Look! An army is coming from the
    north;ⁿ
  a great nation and many kings
    are being stirredᵒ up from the ends
    of the earth.ᵖ
⁴²They are armed with bowsᑫ and
    spears;
  they are cruelʳ and without mercy.ˢ
  They sound like the roaring seaᵗ
    as they ride on their horses;
  they come like men in battle formation
    to attack you, O Daughter of
    Babylon.ᵘ
⁴³The king of Babylon has heard reports
    about them,
  and his hands hang limp.ᵛ
  Anguish has gripped him,
    pain like that of a woman in labor.ʷ
⁴⁴Like a lion coming up from Jordan's
    thicketsˣ
  to a rich pastureland,
  I will chase Babylon from its land in an
    instant.

ᵒ 38 Or *A sword against*

Who is the chosen^y one I will
appoint for this?
Who is like me and who can challenge
me?^z
And what shepherd can stand
against me?"
⁴⁵Therefore, hear what the LORD has
planned against Babylon,
what he has purposed^a against the
land of the Babylonians:^b
The young of the flock will be dragged
away;
he will completely destroy their
pasture because of them.
⁴⁶At the sound of Babylon's capture the
earth will tremble;^c
its cry^d will resound among the
nations.

51

This is what the LORD says:

"See, I will stir^e up the spirit of a
destroyer
against Babylon^f and the people of
Leb Kamai.^p
²I will send foreigners^g to Babylon
to winnow^h her and to devastate her
land;
they will oppose her on every side
in the dayⁱ of her disaster.
³Let not the archer string his bow,^j
nor let him put on his armor.^k
Do not spare her young men;
completely destroy^q her army.
⁴They will fall^l down slain in Babylon,^r
fatally wounded in her streets.^m
⁵For Israel and Judah have not been
forsakenⁿ
by their God, the LORD Almighty,
though their land^s is full of guilt^o
before the Holy One of Israel.
⁶"Flee^p from Babylon!
Run for your lives!
Do not be destroyed because of her
sins.^q
It is time^r for the LORD's vengeance;^s
he will pay^t her what she deserves.
⁷Babylon was a gold cup^u in the LORD's
hand;
she made the whole earth drunk.
The nations drank her wine;

therefore they have now gone mad.
⁸Babylon will suddenly fall^v and be
broken.
Wail over her!
Get balm^w for her pain;
perhaps she can be healed.
⁹"'We would have healed Babylon,
but she cannot be healed;
let us leave^x her and each go to his
own land,
for her judgment^y reaches to the
skies,
it rises as high as the clouds.'
¹⁰"'The LORD has vindicated^z us;
come, let us tell in Zion
what the LORD our God has done.'^a
¹¹"Sharpen the arrows,^b
take up the shields!^c
The LORD has stirred up the kings^d of
the Medes,^e
because his purpose^f is to destroy
Babylon.
The LORD will take vengeance,^g
vengeance for his temple.^h
¹²Lift up a bannerⁱ against the walls of
Babylon!
Reinforce the guard,
station the watchmen,^j
prepare an ambush!^k
The LORD will carry out his purpose,^l
his decree against the people of
Babylon.
¹³You who live by many waters^m
and are rich in treasures,ⁿ
your end has come,
the time for you to be cut off.^o
¹⁴The LORD Almighty has sworn by
himself:^p
I will surely fill you with men, as
with a swarm of locusts,^q
and they will shout^r in triumph over
you.

¹⁵"He made the earth by his power;
he founded the world by his
wisdom^s
and stretched^t out the heavens by
his understanding.^u

---

^p 1 *Leb Kamai* is a cryptogram for Chaldea, that is, Babylonia. ^q 3 The Hebrew term refers to the irrevocable giving over of things or persons to the LORD, often by totally destroying them. ^r 4 Or *Chaldea* ^s 5 Or *I and the land of the Babylonians*

Jer 50:19–20 ◀ ▶ *La 3:31*

51:5 God declared that his people have not been utterly forsaken.

¹⁶When he thunders,ᵛ the waters in the heavens roar;
he makes clouds rise from the ends of the earth.
He sends lightning with the rainʷ
and brings out the wind from his storehouses.ˣ

¹⁷"Every man is senseless and without knowledge;
every goldsmith is shamed by his idols.
His images are a fraud;ʸ
they have no breath in them.
¹⁸They are worthless,ᶻ the objects of mockery;
when their judgment comes, they will perish.
¹⁹He who is the Portionᵃ of Jacob is not like these,
for he is the Maker of all things, including the tribe of his inheritanceᵇ—
the LORD Almighty is his name.

²⁰"You are my war club,ᶜ
my weapon for battle—
with you I shatterᵈ nations,ᵉ
with you I destroy kingdoms,
²¹with you I shatter horse and rider,ᶠ
with you I shatter chariotᵍ and driver,
²²with you I shatter man and woman,
with you I shatter old man and youth,
with you I shatter young man and maiden,ʰ
²³with you I shatter shepherd and flock,
with you I shatter farmer and oxen,
with you I shatter governors and officials.ⁱ

²⁴"Before your eyes I will repayʲ Babylonᵏ and all who live in Babyloniaᵗ for all the wrong they have done in Zion," declares the LORD.

²⁵"I am againstˡ you, O destroying mountain,
you who destroy the whole earth,"ᵐ declares the LORD.
"I will stretch out my handⁿ against you,
roll you off the cliffs,
and make you a burned-out mountain.°
²⁶No rock will be taken from you for a cornerstone,
nor any stone for a foundation,
for you will be desolateᵖ forever," declares the LORD.

²⁷"Lift up a bannerq in the land!
Blow the trumpet among the nations!
Prepare the nations for battle against her;
summon against her these kingdoms:ʳ
Ararat,ˢ Minni and Ashkenaz.ᵗ
Appoint a commander against her;
send up horses like a swarm of locusts.ᵘ
²⁸Prepare the nations for battle against her—
the kings of the Medes,ᵛ
their governors and all their officials,
and all the countries they rule.ʷ
²⁹The land tremblesˣ and writhes,
for the LORD's purposesʸ against Babylon stand—
to lay wasteᶻ the land of Babylon
so that no one will live there.ᵃ
³⁰Babylon's warriorsᵇ have stopped fighting;
they remain in their strongholds.
Their strength is exhausted;
they have become like women.ᶜ
Her dwellings are set on fire;ᵈ
the barsᵉ of her gates are broken.
³¹One courierᶠ follows another
and messenger follows messenger
to announce to the king of Babylon
that his entire city is captured,ᵍ
³²the river crossings seized,
the marshes set on fire,ʰ
and the soldiers terrified.ⁱ"

³³This is what the LORD Almighty, the God of Israel, says:

"The Daughter of Babylonʲ is like a threshing floorᵏ
at the time it is trampled;
the time to harvestˡ her will soon come."ᵐ

³⁴"Nebuchadnezzarⁿ king of Babylon has devoured° us,ᵖ
he has thrown us into confusion,
he has made us an empty jar.
Like a serpent he has swallowed us
and filled his stomach with our delicacies,
and then has spewedq us out.

ᵗ 24 Or Chaldea; also in verse 35

³⁵"May the violence' done to our flesh"
       be upon Babylon,"
   say the inhabitants of Zion.
"May our blood be on those who live
       in Babylonia,"
   says Jerusalem.ˢ

³⁶Therefore, this is what the LORD says:

"See, I will defend your causeᵗ
   and avengeᵘ you;
I will dry upᵛ her sea
   and make her springs dry.
³⁷Babylon will be a heap of ruins,
   a hauntʷ of jackals,
an object of horror and scorn,ˣ
   a place where no one lives.ʸ
³⁸Her people all roar like young lions,ᶻ
   they growl like lion cubs.
³⁹But while they are aroused,
   I will set out a feast for them
   and make them drunk,ᵃ
so that they shout with laughter—
   then sleep foreverᵇ and not awake,"
       declares the LORD.ᶜ
⁴⁰"I will bring them down
   like lambs to the slaughter,
   like rams and goats.ᵈ

⁴¹"How Sheshachᵛᵉ will be captured,ᶠ
   the boast of the whole earth seized!
What a horrorᵍ Babylon will be
   among the nations!
⁴²The sea will rise over Babylon;
   its roaring wavesʰ will cover her.
⁴³Her towns will be desolate,
   a dry and desertⁱ land,
a land where no one lives,
   through which no man travels.ʲ
⁴⁴I will punish Belᵏ in Babylon
   and make him spew outˡ what he
       has swallowed.
The nations will no longer stream to
       him.
And the wallᵐ of Babylon will fall.

⁴⁵"Come outⁿ of her, my people!
   Runᵒ for your lives!
   Run from the fierce angerᵖ of the
       LORD.
⁴⁶Do not lose heartᵠ or be afraidʳ
   when rumorsˢ are heard in the land;

V Jer 39:17-18 ◄ ► Da 11:32

51:35 ʳJoel 3:19; Hab 2:17 ˢver 24; Ps 137:8
51:36 ᵗPs 140:12; Jer 50:34; La 3:58 ᵘver 6; Jer 20:12; ˢRo 12:19 ᵛˢIsa 11:15; ˢ19:5; Hos 13:15
51:37 ʷˢIsa 13:22; Rev 18:2 ˣNa 3:6; Mal 2:9 ʸˢJer 50:13,39
51:38 ᶻˢIsa 5:29
51:39 ᵃˢIsa 21:5 ᵇˢPs 13:3 ᶜver 57; ˢJer 50:24
51:40 ᵈEze 39:18
51:41 ᵉˢJer 25:26 ᶠIsa 13:19 ᵍJer 50:13
51:42 ʰˢPs 18:4; Isa 8:7
51:43 ⁱˢIsa 21:1 ʲˢver 29,62; ˢIsa 13:20; Jer 2:6
51:44 ᵏˢIsa 21:9; ˢ46:1 ˡˢver 34 ᵐver 58; ˢ2Ki 25:4; Isa 25:12; Jer 50:15
51:45 ⁿver 50 ᵒˢIsa 48:20 ᵖPs 76:10; 79:6
51:46 ᵠPs 18:45 ʳˢJer 46:27 ˢˢ2Ki 19:7
51:47 ᵗˢIsa 46:1-2; ˢJer 50:2 ᵘJer 50:12 ᵛˢJer 27:7
51:48 ʷˢJob 3:7; ˢPs 149:2; Rev 18:20 ˣver 11; ˢIsa 41:25; ˢJer 25:26 ʸver 53, 56
51:49 ᶻPs 137:8; ˢJer 50:29
51:50 ᵃver 45 ᵇˢPs 137:6 ᶜJer 23:23
51:51 ᵈPs 44:13-16; 79:4 ᵉLa 1:10
51:52 ᶠver 47 ᵍˢJob 24:12
51:53 ʰˢGe 11:4; ˢIsa 14:13-14 ⁱˢver 48; ˢJob 15:21
51:54 ʲˢJob 24:12 ᵏˢJer 50:22
51:55 ˡIsa 25:5

one rumor comes this year, another
       the next,
   rumors of violence in the land
   and of ruler against ruler.
⁴⁷For the time will surely come
   when I will punish the idolsᵗ of
       Babylon;
her whole land will be disgracedᵘ
   and her slain will all lie fallen within
       her.ᵛ
⁴⁸Then heaven and earth and all that is
       in them
   will shoutʷ for joy over Babylon,
for out of the northˣ
   destroyersʸ will attack her,"
       declares the LORD.

⁴⁹"Babylon must fall because of Israel's
       slain,
just as the slain in all the earth
   have fallen because of Babylon.ᶻ
⁵⁰You who have escaped the sword,
   leaveᵃ and do not linger!
Rememberᵇ the LORD in a distant
       land,ᶜ
   and think on Jerusalem."

⁵¹"We are disgraced,ᵈ
   for we have been insulted
and shame covers our faces,
   because foreigners have entered
   the holy places of the LORD's
       house."ᵉ

⁵²"But days are coming," declares the
       LORD,
   "when I will punish her idols,ᶠ
and throughout her land
   the wounded will groan.ᵍ
⁵³Even if Babylon reaches the skyʰ
   and fortifies her lofty stronghold,
I will send destroyersⁱ against her,"
       declares the LORD.

⁵⁴"The sound of a cryʲ comes from
       Babylon,
   the sound of great destructionᵏ
   from the land of the Babylonians.ʷ
⁵⁵The LORD will destroy Babylon;
   he will silenceˡ her noisy din.

ᵘ 35 Or done to us and to our children ᵛ 41 Sheshach is a cryptogram for Babylon. ʷ 54 Or Chaldeans

51:37 Jeremiah prophesied that Babylon would meet her own fate and be totally destroyed. This prophecy was amply fulfilled when the Medes and Persians destroyed Babylon in 538 B.C. The city became a ruin that was ultimately covered by desert sand for almost two thousand years.

Waves[m] ⌊of enemies⌋ will rage like great waters;
the roar of their voices will resound.
⁵⁶A destroyer[n] will come against Babylon;
her warriors will be captured,
and their bows will be broken.[o]
For the LORD is a God of retribution;
he will repay[p] in full.
⁵⁷I will make her officials[q] and wise[r] men drunk,[s]
her governors, officers and warriors as well;
they will sleep[t] forever and not awake,"
declares the King,[u] whose name is the LORD Almighty.

⁵⁸This is what the LORD Almighty says:

"Babylon's thick wall[v] will be leveled
and her high gates[w] set on fire;
the peoples[x] exhaust[y] themselves for nothing,
the nations' labor is only fuel for the flames."[z]

⁵⁹This is the message Jeremiah gave to the staff officer Seraiah son of Neriah,[a] the son of Mahseiah, when he went to Babylon with Zedekiah[b] king of Judah in the fourth[c] year of his reign. ⁶⁰Jeremiah had written on a scroll[d] about all the disasters that would come upon Babylon—all that had been recorded concerning Babylon. ⁶¹He said to Seraiah, "When you get to Babylon, see that you read all these words aloud. ⁶²Then say, 'O LORD, you have said you will destroy this place, so that neither man nor animal will live in it; it will be desolate[e] forever.' ⁶³When you finish reading this scroll, tie a stone to it and throw it into the Euphrates.[f] ⁶⁴Then say, 'So will Babylon sink to rise no more[g] because of the disaster I will bring upon her. And her people[h] will fall.' "[i]

The words of Jeremiah end[j] here.

The Fall of Jerusalem

52:1–3pp — 2Ki 24:18–20; 2Ch 36:11–16
52:4–16pp — Jer 39:1–10
52:4–21pp — 2Ki 25:1–21; 2Ch 36:17–20

52 Zedekiah[k] was twenty-one years old when he became king, and he reigned in Jerusalem eleven years. His mother's name was Hamutal daughter of Jeremiah; she was from Libnah.[l] ²He did evil in the eyes of the LORD, just as Jehoiakim[m] had done. ³It was because of the LORD's anger that all this happened to Jerusalem and Judah,[n] and in the end he thrust them from his presence.[o]

Now Zedekiah rebelled[p] against the king of Babylon.

⁴So in the ninth year of Zedekiah's reign, on the tenth[q] day of the tenth month, Nebuchadnezzar king of Babylon marched against Jerusalem[r] with his whole army. They camped outside the city and built siege works[s] all around it.[t] ⁵The city was kept under siege until the eleventh year of King Zedekiah.

⁶By the ninth day of the fourth month the famine in the city had become so severe that there was no food for the people to eat.[u] ⁷Then the city wall was broken through, and the whole army fled.[v] They left the city at night through the gate between the two walls near the king's garden, though the Babylonians[x] were surrounding the city. They fled toward the Arabah,[y] ⁸but the Babylonian[z] army pursued King Zedekiah and overtook him in the plains of Jericho. All his soldiers were separated from him and scattered, ⁹and he was captured.[w]

He was taken to the king of Babylon at Riblah[x] in the land of Hamath,[y] where he pronounced sentence on him. ¹⁰There at Riblah the king of Babylon slaughtered the sons[z] of Zedekiah before his eyes; he also killed all the officials of Judah. ¹¹Then he put out Zedekiah's eyes, bound him with bronze shackles and took him to Babylon, where he put him in prison till the day of his death.[a]

¹²On the tenth day of the fifth[b] month, in the nineteenth year of Nebuchadnezzar king of Babylon, Nebuzaradan[c] commander of the imperial guard, who served the king of Babylon, came to Jerusalem. ¹³He set fire[d] to the temple[e] of the LORD, the royal palace and all the houses[f] of Jerusalem. Every important building he burned down. ¹⁴The whole Babylonian army under the commander of the imperial guard broke down all the walls[g] around Jerusalem. ¹⁵Nebuzaradan the commander of the guard carried into exile[h] some of the poorest people and those who remained in the city, along with the

---

[x] 7 Or *Chaldeans*; also in verse 17   [y] 7 Or *the Jordan Valley*
[z] 8 Or *Chaldean*; also in verse 14

rest of the craftsmen[a] and those who had gone over to the king of Babylon. ¹⁶But Nebuzaradan left behind the rest of the poorest people of the land to work the vineyards and fields.

¹⁷The Babylonians broke up the bronze pillars, the movable stands and the bronze Sea that were at the temple of the LORD and they carried all the bronze to Babylon. ¹⁸They also took away the pots, shovels, wick trimmers, sprinkling bowls, dishes and all the bronze articles used in the temple service. ¹⁹The commander of the imperial guard took away the basins, censers, sprinkling bowls, pots, lampstands, dishes and bowls used for drink offerings—all that were made of pure gold or silver.

²⁰The bronze from the two pillars, the Sea and the twelve bronze bulls under it, and the movable stands, which King Solomon had made for the temple of the LORD, was more than could be weighed. ²¹Each of the pillars was eighteen cubits high and twelve cubits in circumference[b]; each was four fingers thick, and hollow. ²²The bronze capital on top of the one pillar was five cubits[c] high and was decorated with a network and pomegranates of bronze all around. The other pillar, with its pomegranates, was similar. ²³There were ninety-six pomegranates on the sides; the total number of pomegranates above the surrounding network was a hundred.

²⁴The commander of the guard took as prisoners Seraiah the chief priest, Zephaniah the priest next in rank and the three doorkeepers. ²⁵Of those still in the city, he took the officer in charge of the fighting men, and seven royal advisers. He also took the secretary who was chief officer in charge of conscripting the people of the land and sixty of his men who were found in the city. ²⁶Nebuzaradan the commander took them all and brought them to the king of Babylon at Riblah. ²⁷There at Riblah, in the land of Hamath, the king had them executed.

So Judah went into captivity, away from her land. ²⁸This is the number of the people Nebuchadnezzar carried into exile:

in the seventh year, 3,023 Jews;
²⁹in Nebuchadnezzar's eighteenth year,
832 people from Jerusalem;
³⁰in his twenty-third year,
745 Jews taken into exile by Nebuzaradan the commander of the imperial guard.

There were 4,600 people in all.

Jehoiachin Released
52:31–34pp — 2Ki 25:27–30

³¹In the thirty-seventh year of the exile of Jehoiachin king of Judah, in the year Evil-Merodach[d] became king of Babylon, he released Jehoiachin king of Judah and freed him from prison on the twenty-fifth day of the twelfth month. ³²He spoke kindly to him and gave him a seat of honor higher than those of the other kings who were with him in Babylon. ³³So Jehoiachin put aside his prison clothes and for the rest of his life ate regularly at the king's table. ³⁴Day by day the king of Babylon gave Jehoiachin a regular allowance as long as he lived, till the day of his death.

---
[a] 15 Or *populace* [b] 21 That is, about 27 feet (about 8.1 meters) high and 18 feet (about 5.4 meters) in circumference [c] 22 That is, about 7 1/2 feet (about 2.3 meters) [d] 31 Also called *Amel-Marduk*

Lamentations

Author: Probably Jeremiah

Theme: Sadness over the fall of Jerusalem

Date of Writing: 586 B.C.

Outline of Lamentations
  I. Jerusalem's Desolation (1:1–22)
  II. God's Wrath Against the People (2:1–22)
  III. The Reason for Comfort (3:1–66)
  IV. Jerusalem's Past Glory and Present Misery (4:1–22)
  V. A Prayer for God's Mercy (5:1–22)

The book of Lamentations does not name its author but has traditionally been ascribed to the prophet Jeremiah. Since Jeremiah lived in Jerusalem, warned the people about the city's coming destruction and then witnessed this terrible judgment, is it assumed that Jeremiah authored this book. In addition, the similarity of vocabulary and style between the books of Lamentations and Jeremiah suggests one author for both books. The book's English title is derived from the Septuagint (the Greek translation of the OT) title that means "to cry aloud." Written as a reminder of the fall of Jerusalem and the destruction of the temple, Lamentations mournfully cries its sense of loss and anguish in its five funeral poems, or laments.

In the Hebrew text the first four chapters are acrostically arranged. Each of the twenty-two verses in chapters 1, 2 and 4 begin with a successive letter of the Hebrew alphabet. The third chapter divides its sixty-six verses into twenty-two groups and follows the same acrostic poem arrangement. The last chapter of the book is not alphabetic but still mirrors the somber mood of the previous four. This stylistic form reflects the meter used in funeral dirges and indicates that despite the passionate tone of these poems, they were composed with expert precision.

While other books in the OT contain community laments, this composition focuses on the terrible calamity that has befallen Jerusalem. The author recognizes that its destruction is the judgment of a righteous God and appeals to God for mercy. Note the similarity between the author's concern for Jerusalem and Jesus' words about the city (see Mt 23:37–38).

R ¹ᵃHow deserted ᵃ lies the city,
  once so full of people!ᵇ
How like a widowᶜ is she,
  who once was greatᵈ among the nations!
She who was queen among the provinces
  has now become a slave.ᵉ

²Bitterly she weepsᶠ at night,
  tears are upon her cheeks.
Among all her loversᵍ
  there is none to comfort her.
All her friends have betrayedʰ her;
  they have become her enemies.ⁱ

³After affliction and harsh labor,
  Judah has gone into exile.ʲ
She dwells among the nations;
  she finds no resting place.ᵏ
All who pursue her have overtaken herˡ
  in the midst of her distress.

R ⁴The roads to Zion mourn,ᵐ
  for no one comes to her appointed feasts.
All her gateways are desolate,ⁿ
  her priests groan,
  her maidens grieve,
  and she is in bitter anguish.ᵒ

⁵Her foes have become her masters;
  her enemies are at ease.
The LORD has brought her griefᵖ
  because of her many sins.ᵠ
Her children have gone into exile,ʳ
  captive before the foe.ˢ

⁶All the splendor has departed
  from the Daughter of Zion.ᵗ

R *Jer 45:4* ◀ ▶ *La 1:4–10*
R *La 1:1–2* ◀ ▶ *La 1:12*

1:1 ᵃS Lev 26:43
ᵇS Jer 42:2
ᶜS Isa 47:8
ᵈS 1Ki 4:21
ᵉIsa 3:26;
S Jer 40:9; Eze 5:5

1:2 ᶠPs 6:6
ᵍS Jer 3:1
ʰS Jer 4:30;
Mic 7:5 ⁱver 16;
S Jer 30:14

1:3 ʲS Jer 13:19
ᵏDt 28:65
ˡS Ex 15:9

1:4 ᵐS Ps 137:1
ⁿS Isa 27:10;
S Jer 9:11 ᵒver 21;
Joel 1:8-13

1:5 ᵖS Jer 22:5;
S Jer 30:15
ᵠS Ps 5:10
ʳS Jer 10:20;
S 39:9; 52:28-30
ˢS Ps 137:3;
La 2:17

1:6 ᵗS Ps 9:14;
Jer 13:18
ᵘS Lev 26:36

1:7 ᵛS 2Ki 14:26;
S Jer 37:7; La 4:17
ʷS Jer 2:26

1:8 ˣver 20;
Isa 59:2-13
ʸS Jer 2:22
ᶻS Jer 13:22,26
ᵃver 21,22;
S Ps 6:6; S 38:8

1:9 ᵇDt 32:28-29;
Eze 24:13
ᶜJer 13:18
ᵈS Ecc 4:1;
S Jer 16:7
ᵉPs 25:18

1:10 ᶠS Isa 64:11
ᵍPs 74:7-8; 79:1;
Jer 51:51 ʰS Dt 23:3

1:11 ⁱS Ps 6:6;
S 38:8 ʲS Jer 37:21;
S 52:6

Her princes are like deer
  that find no pasture;
in weakness they have fledᵘ
  before the pursuer.

⁷In the days of her affliction and wandering
Jerusalem remembers all the treasures
  that were hers in days of old.
When her people fell into enemy hands,
  there was no one to help her.ᵛ
Her enemies looked at her
  and laughedʷ at her destruction.

⁸Jerusalem has sinnedˣ greatly
  and so has become unclean.ʸ
All who honored her despise her,
  for they have seen her nakedness;ᶻ
she herself groansᵃ
  and turns away.

⁹Her filthiness clung to her skirts;
  she did not consider her future.ᵇ
Her fallᶜ was astounding;
  there was none to comfortᵈ her.
"Look, O LORD, on my affliction,ᵉ
  for the enemy has triumphed."

¹⁰The enemy laid hands
  on all her treasures;ᶠ
she saw pagan nations
  enter her sanctuaryᵍ—
those you had forbiddenʰ
  to enter your assembly.

¹¹All her people groanⁱ
  as they search for bread;ʲ
they barter their treasures for food

ᵃ This chapter is an acrostic poem, the verses of which begin with the successive letters of the Hebrew alphabet.

1:1 The prophet lamented over the destruction of Jerusalem which was once "great among the nations" but now is left desolate because of her destruction at the hands of Babylon.

1:4–12 Jeremiah lamented the utter destruction of his beloved city while recognizing that this is God's judgment for "her many sins" (1:5).

to keep themselves alive.
"Look, O LORD, and consider,
for I am despised."

¹²"Is it nothing to you, all you who pass by?ᵏ
Look around and see.
Is any suffering like my sufferingˡ
that was inflicted on me,
that the LORD brought on me
in the day of his fierce anger?ᵐ

¹³"From on high he sent fire,
sent it down into my bones.ⁿ
He spread a netᵒ for my feet
and turned me back.
He made me desolate,ᵖ
faintᵠ all the day long.

¹⁴"My sins have been bound into a yokeᵇ;ʳ
by his hands they were woven together.
They have come upon my neck
and the Lord has sapped my strength.
He has handed me overˢ
to those I cannot withstand.

¹⁵"The Lord has rejected
all the warriors in my midst;ᵗ
he has summoned an armyᵘ against me
toᶜ crush my young men.ᵛ
In his winepressʷ the Lord has trampledˣ
the Virgin Daughterʸ of Judah.

¹⁶"This is why I weep
and my eyes overflow with tears.ᶻ
No one is near to comfortᵃ me,
no one to restore my spirit.
My children are destitute
because the enemy has prevailed."ᵇ

¹⁷Zion stretches out her hands,ᶜ
but there is no one to comfort her.
The LORD has decreed for Jacob
that his neighbors become his foes;ᵈ
Jerusalem has become
an uncleanᵉ thingᶠ among them.

¹⁸"The LORD is righteous,ᵍ
yet I rebelledʰ against his command.

R La 1:4–10 ◀ ▶ La 1:16–17
R La 1:12 ◀ ▶ La 2:1–2

1:12 ᵏ S Jer 18:16
ˡ ver 18
ᵐ S Isa 10:4; 13:13;
S Jer 30:24

1:13 ⁿ S Job 30:30;
Ps 102:3
ᵒ S Job 18:8
ᵖ S Jer 44:6
ᵠ Hab 3:16

1:14 ʳ S Dt 28:48;
S Isa 47:6;
S Jer 15:12
ˢ S Jer 32:5

1:15 ᵗ Jer 37:10
ᵘ Isa 41:2
ᵛ Isa 28:18;
S Jer 18:21
ʷ S Jdg 6:11
ˣ S Isa 5:5
ʸ Jer 14:17

1:16 ᶻ S Job 7:3;
S Ps 119:136;
S Isa 22:4; La 2:11,
18; 3:48-49
ᵃ S Ps 69:20;
Ecc 4:1; S Jer 16:7
ᵇ S ver 2; Jer 13:17;
14:17

1:17 ᶜ S Jer 4:31
ᵈ Ex 23:21
ᵉ Jer 2:22
ᶠ S Lev 18:25-28

1:18 ᵍ S Ex 9:27;
S Ezr 9:15
ʰ S 1Sa 12:14
ⁱ ver 12 ʲ Dt 28:32, 41

1:19 ᵏ S Jer 22:20
ˡ S Jer 14:15;
La 2:20

1:20 ᵐ S Jer 4:19
ⁿ La 2:11
ᵒ S Job 20:2
ᵖ S ver 8
ᵠ S Dt 32:25;
Eze 7:15

1:21 ʳ S ver 8;
S Ps 6:6; S 38:8
ˢ ver 4 ᵗ La 2:15
ᵘ Isa 47:11;
Jer 30:16

1:22 ᵛ Ne 4:5
ʷ S ver 8; S Ps 6:6

2:1 ˣ La 3:44
ʸ Ps 99:5; 132:7
ᶻ S Jer 12:7

2:2 ᵃ ver 17;
La 3:43 ᵇ Ps 21:9

Listen, all you peoples;
look upon my suffering.ⁱ
My young men and maidens
have gone into exile.ʲ

¹⁹"I called to my alliesᵏ
but they betrayed me.
My priests and my elders
perishedˡ in the city
while they searched for food
to keep themselves alive.

²⁰"See, O LORD, how distressedᵐ I am!
I am in tormentⁿ within,
and in my heart I am disturbed,ᵒ
for I have been most rebellious.ᵖ
Outside, the sword bereaves;
inside, there is only death.ᵠ

²¹"People have heard my groaning,ʳ
but there is no one to comfort me.ˢ
All my enemies have heard of my distress;
they rejoiceᵗ at what you have done.
May you bring the dayᵘ you have announced
so they may become like me.

²²"Let all their wickedness come before you;
deal with them
as you have dealt with me
because of all my sins.ᵛ
My groansʷ are many
and my heart is faint."

2 ᵈHow the Lord has covered the
Daughter of Zion
with the cloud of his angerᵉ!ˣ
He has hurled down the splendor of Israel
from heaven to earth;
he has not remembered his footstoolʸ
in the day of his anger.ᶻ

²Without pityᵃ the Lord has swallowedᵇ up
all the dwellings of Jacob;

R La 1:16–17 ◀ ▶ La 2:6

ᵇ 14 Most Hebrew manuscripts; Septuagint *He kept watch over my sins*
ᶜ 15 Or *has set a time for me / when he will* ᵈ This chapter is an acrostic poem, the verses of which begin with the successive letters of the Hebrew alphabet. ᵉ 1 Or *How the Lord in his anger / has treated the Daughter of Zion with contempt*

1:16–17 Jeremiah lamented that at the time of Jerusalem's desolation there was no one to help because God had sent enemies to surround the city.

2:1–2 The image here is of a falling star (see Isa 14:12) being hurled from God's presence.

in his wrath he has torn down
    the strongholds[c] of the Daughter of
        Judah.
He has brought her kingdom and its
        princes
    down to the ground[d] in dishonor.

³In fierce anger he has cut off
    every horn[f][e] of Israel.
He has withdrawn his right hand[f]
    at the approach of the enemy.
He has burned in Jacob like a flaming
        fire
    that consumes everything around
        it.[g]

⁴Like an enemy he has strung his bow;[h]
    his right hand is ready.
Like a foe he has slain
    all who were pleasing to the eye;[i]
he has poured out his wrath[j] like fire[k]
    on the tent[l] of the Daughter of Zion.

⁵The Lord is like an enemy;[m]
    he has swallowed up Israel.
He has swallowed up all her palaces
    and destroyed her strongholds.[n]
He has multiplied mourning and
        lamentation[o]
    for the Daughter of Judah.[p]

R ⁶He has laid waste his dwelling like a
        garden;
    he has destroyed[q] his place of
        meeting.[r]
The LORD has made Zion forget
    her appointed feasts and her
        Sabbaths;[s]
in his fierce anger he has spurned
    both king and priest.[t]

⁷The Lord has rejected his altar
    and abandoned his sanctuary.[u]
He has handed over to the enemy
    the walls of her palaces;[v]
they have raised a shout in the house
        of the LORD
    as on the day of an appointed feast.[w]

⁸The LORD determined to tear down
    the wall around the Daughter of
        Zion.[x]
He stretched out a measuring line[y]

R *La 2:1–2* ◀ ▶ *La 3:1–3*

2:2 [c] Ps 89:39-40; Mic 5:11
[d] S Isa 25:12
2:3 [e] Ps 75:5,10 [f] Ps 74:11 [g] S Isa 42:25; Jer 21:4-5,14
2:4 [h] S Job 3:23; 16:13; La 3:12-13 [i] S Ps 48:2; Eze 24:16,23 [j] S 2Ch 34:21; Eze 20:34 [k] Isa 42:25; S Jer 7:20 [l] S Jer 4:20
2:5 [m] S Job 13:24 [n] ver 2 [o] S Isa 29:2 [p] S Jer 7:20; 9:17-20
2:6 [q] 2Ch 36:19 [r] S Jer 52:13 [s] Zep 3:18 [t] Isa 43:28; S Jer 7:14; La 4:16; 5:12
2:7 [u] S Lev 26:31; S Eze 7:24 [v] Ps 74:7-8; S Isa 64:11; Jer 33:4-5; Eze 7:21-22 [w] Jer 21:4; 52:13
2:8 [x] ver 18 [y] S 2Ki 21:13 [z] S Ps 48:13 [a] Isa 3:26; S Jer 39:8; S 52:14
2:9 [b] S Ne 1:3 [c] S Isa 45:2; Hos 11:6 [d] Dt 28:36; S 2Ki 24:15; Jer 16:13; Hos 3:4 [e] S 2Ch 15:3 [f] S 1Sa 3:1 [g] S Jer 14:14
2:10 [h] La 3:28 [i] Jos 7:6 [j] Job 2:12 [k] S Isa 3:24 [l] S Job 2:13; S Isa 3:26; Eze 27:30-31
2:11 [m] S Ps 119:82; S Isa 15:3; S La 1:16; 3:48-51 [n] S Job 30:27; La 1:20 [o] S Isa 1:5 [p] ver 19; Ps 22:14 [q] S Jer 9:1 [r] La 4:4
2:12 [s] Isa 24:11 [t] S Job 3:24 [u] La 4:4
2:13 [v] S Isa 1:6 [w] S 2Ki 19:21 [x] Isa 37:22 [y] Jer 14:17; 30:12-15; La 1:12
2:14 [z] S Jer 28:15 [a] Jer 8:11

and did not withhold his hand from
        destroying.
He made ramparts[z] and walls lament;
    together they wasted away.[a]

⁹Her gates[b] have sunk into the ground; Q
    their bars[c] he has broken and
        destroyed.
Her king and her princes are exiled[d]
    among the nations,
    the law[e] is no more,
and her prophets[f] no longer find
    visions[g] from the LORD.

¹⁰The elders of the Daughter of Zion
    sit on the ground in silence;[h]
they have sprinkled dust[i] on their
        heads[j]
    and put on sackcloth.[k]
The young women of Jerusalem
    have bowed their heads to the
        ground.[l]

¹¹My eyes fail from weeping,[m]
    I am in torment within,[n]
my heart[o] is poured out[p] on the
        ground
because my people are destroyed,[q]
because children and infants faint[r]
    in the streets of the city.

¹²They say to their mothers,
    "Where is bread and wine?"[s]
as they faint like wounded men
    in the streets of the city,
as their lives ebb away[t]
    in their mothers' arms.[u]

¹³What can I say for you?[v]
    With what can I compare you,
    O Daughter[w] of Jerusalem?
To what can I liken you,
    that I may comfort you,
    O Virgin Daughter of Zion?[x]
Your wound is as deep as the sea.[y]
    Who can heal you?

¹⁴The visions of your prophets
    were false[z] and worthless;
they did not expose your sin
    to ward off your captivity.[a]

Q *Isa 63:10* ◀ ▶ *Mic 3:6*

[f] *3 Or / all the strength; or every king; horn here symbolizes strength.*

2:6 Destruction fell on the temple, the place where God met with his people, destroying the feasts and Sabbath remembrances, the kings and the priests.

The oracles they gave you
  were false and misleading.[b]

[15] All who pass your way
  clap their hands at you;[c]
they scoff[d] and shake their heads[e]
  at the Daughter of Jerusalem:[f]
"Is this the city that was called
  the perfection of beauty,[g]
  the joy of the whole earth?"[h]

[16] All your enemies open their mouths
  wide against you;[i]
they scoff and gnash their teeth[j]
  and say, "We have swallowed her
    up.[k]
This is the day we have waited for;
  we have lived to see it."[l]

[17] The LORD has done what he planned;
  he has fulfilled[m] his word,
  which he decreed long ago.[n]
He has overthrown you without pity,[o]
  he has let the enemy gloat over
    you,[p]
  he has exalted the horn[g] of your
    foes.[q]

[18] The hearts of the people
  cry out to the Lord.[r]
O wall of the Daughter of Zion,[s]
  let your tears[t] flow like a river
  day and night;[u]
give yourself no relief,
  your eyes no rest.[v]

[19] Arise, cry out in the night,
  as the watches of the night begin;
pour out your heart[w] like water
  in the presence of the Lord.[x]
Lift up your hands[y] to him
  for the lives of your children,
who faint[z] from hunger
  at the head of every street.

[20] "Look, O LORD, and consider:
  Whom have you ever treated like
    this?
Should women eat their offspring,[a]
  the children they have cared for?[b]
Should priest and prophet be killed[c]
  in the sanctuary of the Lord?[d]

[21] "Young and old lie together
  in the dust of the streets;
my young men and maidens
have fallen by the sword.[e]
You have slain them in the day of your
    anger;
  you have slaughtered them without
    pity.[f]

[22] "As you summon to a feast day,
  so you summoned against me
    terrors[g] on every side.
In the day of the LORD's anger
  no one escaped[h] or survived;
  those I cared for and reared,[i]
    my enemy has destroyed."

3

[h] I am the man who has seen
  affliction[i]
  by the rod of his wrath.[k]
[2] He has driven me away and made me
    walk
  in darkness[l] rather than light;
[3] indeed, he has turned his hand against
    me[m]
  again and again, all day long.

[4] He has made my skin and my flesh
    grow old[n]
  and has broken my bones.[o]
[5] He has besieged me and surrounded
    me
  with bitterness[p] and hardship.[q]
[6] He has made me dwell in darkness
  like those long dead.[r]
[7] He has walled me in so I cannot
    escape;[s]
  he has weighed me down with
    chains.[t]
[8] Even when I call out or cry for help,[u]
  he shuts out my prayer.[v]
[9] He has barred[w] my way with blocks of
    stone;
  he has made my paths crooked.[x]
[10] Like a bear lying in wait,
  like a lion[y] in hiding,[z]
[11] he dragged me from the path and
    mangled[a] me
  and left me without help.
[12] He drew his bow[b]

R *La 2:6* ◀ ▶ *La 3:45*

g 17 Horn here symbolizes strength. *h* This chapter is an acrostic poem; the verses of each stanza begin with the successive letters of the Hebrew alphabet, and the verses within each stanza begin with the same letter.

3:1–3 God had allowed his servant, the prophet, to witness this destruction of Jerusalem at the hands of Babylon.

and made me the targetc for his
arrows.d

¹³He pierced my heart
with arrows from his quiver.

¹⁴I became the laughingstock of all my
people;
they mock me in song all day long.

¹⁵He has filled me with bitter herbs
and sated me with gall.

¹⁶He has broken my teeth with gravel;
he has trampled me in the dust.

¹⁷I have been deprived of peace;
I have forgotten what prosperity is.

¹⁸So I say, "My splendor is gone
and all that I had hoped from the
LORD."

¹⁹I remember my affliction and my
wandering,
the bitterness and the gall.

²⁰I well remember them,
and my soul is downcast within
me.

²¹Yet this I call to mind
and therefore I have hope:

²²Because of the LORD's great love we
are not consumed,
for his compassions never fail.

²³They are new every morning;
great is your faithfulness.

²⁴I say to myself, "The LORD is my
portion;
therefore I will wait for him."

²⁵The LORD is good to those whose hope
is in him,
to the one who seeks him;

²⁶it is good to wait quietly
for the salvation of the LORD.

²⁷It is good for a man to bear the yoke
while he is young.

²⁸Let him sit alone in silence,
for the LORD has laid it on him.

²⁹Let him bury his face in the dust—
there may yet be hope.

³⁰Let him offer his cheek to one who
would strike him,
and let him be filled with disgrace.

³¹For men are not cast off
by the Lord forever.

³²Though he brings grief, he will show
compassion,
so great is his unfailing love.

³³For he does not willingly bring
affliction
or grief to the children of men.

³⁴To crush underfoot
all prisoners in the land,

³⁵to deny a man his rights
before the Most High,

³⁶to deprive a man of justice—
would not the Lord see such
things?

³⁷Who can speak and have it happen
if the Lord has not decreed it?

³⁸Is it not from the mouth of the Most
High
that both calamities and good things
come?

³⁹Why should any living man complain
when punished for his sins?

⁴⁰Let us examine our ways and test
them,
and let us return to the LORD.

⁴¹Let us lift up our hearts and our hands
to God in heaven, and say:

⁴²"We have sinned and rebelled
and you have not forgiven.

⁴³"You have covered yourself with anger
and pursued us;
you have slain without pity.

⁴⁴You have covered yourself with a
cloud
so that no prayer can get through.

⁴⁵You have made us scum and refuse
among the nations.

C Jer 44:10 ◄► Eze 2:4
M Jer 49:16 ◄► Eze 3:7
L Jer 50:20 ◄► La 3:32–33
I Jer 51:5 ◄► Eze 4:4–6
L La 3:25 ◄► Eze 18:21–23
O Jer 17:13–14 ◄► Hos 13:4
H Jer 36:7 ◄► Eze 7:8
R Jer 36:3 ◄► Eze 14:6
R La 3:1–3 ◄► La 4:22

3:31 Despite God's judgment, the people would not be cast away from God forever because of God's promise to Abraham (see note at Ge 15:4).
3:45 Jeremiah described the city as refuse because of God's terrible judgment fulfilled at the hands of the Babylonians. Moses had warned the people of such judgments for disobedience (see Dt 28:13; 28:37).

⁴⁶"All our enemies have opened their
    mouths
    wide˟ against us.ʸ
⁴⁷We have suffered terror and pitfalls,ᶻ
    ruin and destruction.ᵃ"
⁴⁸Streams of tearsᵇ flow from my eyesᶜ
    because my people are destroyed.ᵈ

⁴⁹My eyes will flow unceasingly,
    without relief,ᵉ
⁵⁰until the LORD looks down
    from heaven and sees.ᶠ
⁵¹What I see brings grief to my soul
    because of all the women of my city.

⁵²Those who were my enemies without
    cause
    hunted me like a bird.ᵍ
⁵³They tried to end my life in a pitʰ
    and threw stones at me;
⁵⁴the waters closed over my head,ⁱ
    and I thought I was about to be cut
    off.ʲ

⁵⁵I called on your name, O LORD,
    from the depthsᵏ of the pit.ˡ
⁵⁶You heard my plea:ᵐ "Do not close
    your ears
    to my cry for relief."
⁵⁷You came nearⁿ when I called you,
    and you said, "Do not fear."ᵒ

⁵⁸O Lord, you took up my case;ᵖ
    you redeemed my life.ᑫ
⁵⁹You have seen, O LORD, the wrong
    done to me.ʳ
    Uphold my cause!ˢ
⁶⁰You have seen the depth of their
    vengeance,
    all their plots against me.ᵗ

⁶¹O LORD, you have heard their
    insults,ᵘ
    all their plots against me—
⁶²what my enemies whisper and mutter
    against me all day long.ᵛ
⁶³Look at them! Sitting or standing,
    they mock me in their songs.ʷ

⁶⁴Pay them back what they deserve,
    O LORD,
    for what their hands have done.ˣ
⁶⁵Put a veil over their hearts,ʸ
    and may your curse be on them!
⁶⁶Pursueᶻ them in anger and destroy
    them
    from under the heavens of the
    LORD.

3:46 ˣPs 22:13
ʸLa 2:16
3:47 ᶻJer 48:43
ᵃS Isa 24:17-18;
S 51:19
3:48
ᵇS Ps 119:136
ᶜS Jer 9:1,18;
La 1:16 ᵈLa 2:11
3:49 ᵉJer 14:17;
S La 2:18
3:50 ᶠS Ps 14:2;
80:14; S Isa 63:15
3:52 ᵍPs 35:7
3:53 ʰJer 37:16;
S 38:6
3:54 ⁱPs 69:2;
Jnh 2:3-5 ʲver 18;
Ps 88:5; Eze 37:11
3:55 ᵏS Ps 88:6
ˡPs 130:1; Jnh 2:2
3:56 ᵐS Ps 55:1;
116:1-2
3:57 ⁿS Ps 46:1
ᵒIsa 41:10
3:58 ᵖS Jer 51:36
ᑫPs 34:22;
S Jer 50:34
3:59 ʳJer 18:19-20
ˢPs 35:23; 43:1
3:60 ᵗS Jer 11:20;
18:18
3:61 ᵘPs 89:50;
Zep 2:8
3:62 ᵛEze 36:3
3:63 ʷS Job 30:9
3:64 ˣS Ps 28:4;
S Jer 51:6
3:65 ʸEx 14:8;
Dt 2:30; Isa 6:10
3:66 ᶻS ver 43
4:1 ᵃEze 7:19
4:2 ᵇIsa 51:18
4:3 ᶜS Job 39:16
4:4 ᵈS Dt 28:48;
S 2Ki 18:31
ᵉS Ps 22:15
ᶠLa 2:11,12
4:5 ᵍJer 6:2
ʰS Isa 3:26;
Am 6:3-7
4:6 ⁱS Ge 19:25
4:8 ʲS Job 30:28
ᵏPs 102:3-5;
S La 3:4
4:9 ˡS 2Ki 25:3
ᵐS Jer 15:2; S 16:4;
La 5:10
4:10 ⁿS Lev 26:29;
Dt 28:53-57;
Jer 19:9; La 2:20;
Eze 5:10
4:11 ᵒS Job 20:23
ᵖS 2Ch 34:21
ᑫNa 1:6; Zep 2:2;
3:8 ʳJer 17:27
ˢS Dt 32:22;
S Jer 7:20;
Eze 22:31

4

ᵗ'How the gold has lost its luster,
   the fine gold become dull!
The sacred gems are scattered
   at the head of every street.ᵃ

²How the precious sons of Zion,ᵇ
   once worth their weight in gold,
are now considered as pots of clay,
   the work of a potter's hands!

³Even jackals offer their breasts
   to nurse their young,
but my people have become heartless
   like ostriches in the desert.ᶜ

⁴Because of thirstᵈ the infant's tongue
   sticks to the roof of its mouth;ᵉ
the children beg for bread,
   but no one gives it to them.ᶠ

⁵Those who once ate delicacies
   are destitute in the streets.
Those nurtured in purpleᵍ
   now lie on ash heaps.ʰ

⁶The punishment of my people
   is greater than that of Sodom,ⁱ
which was overthrown in a moment
   without a hand turned to help her.

⁷Their princes were brighter than snow
   and whiter than milk,
their bodies more ruddy than rubies,
   their appearance like sapphires.ʲ

⁸But now they are blackerʲ than soot;
   they are not recognized in the
   streets.
Their skin has shriveled on their
   bones;ᵏ
   it has become as dry as a stick.

⁹Those killed by the sword are better
   off
than those who die of famine;ˡ
racked with hunger, they waste away
   for lack of food from the field.ᵐ

¹⁰With their own hands compassionate
   women
have cooked their own children,ⁿ
   who became their food
when my people were destroyed.

¹¹The LORD has given full vent to his
   wrath;ᵒ
   he has poured outᵖ his fierce anger.ᑫ
He kindled a fireʳ in Zion
   that consumed her foundations.ˢ

ᵗ This chapter is an acrostic poem, the verses of which begin with the successive letters of the Hebrew alphabet. *7* Or *lapis lazuli*

¹²The kings of the earth did not believe,
    nor did any of the world's people,
    that enemies and foes could enter
    the gates of Jerusalem.ᵗ
¹³But it happened because of the sins of
    her prophets
    and the iniquities of her priests,ᵘ
    who shed within her
    the bloodᵛ of the righteous.
¹⁴Now they grope through the streets
    like men who are blind.ʷ
    They are so defiled with bloodˣ
    that no one dares to touch their
    garments.
¹⁵"Go away! You are unclean!" men cry
    to them.
    "Away! Away! Don't touch us!"
    When they flee and wanderʸ about,
    people among the nations say,
    "They can stay here no longer."ᶻ
¹⁶The LORD himself has scattered them;
    he no longer watches over them.ᵃ
    The priests are shown no honor,
    the eldersᵇ no favor.ᶜ
¹⁷Moreover, our eyes failed,
    looking in vainᵈ for help;ᵉ
    from our towers we watched
    for a nationᶠ that could not save us.
¹⁸Men stalked us at every step,
    so we could not walk in our streets.
    Our end was near, our days were
    numbered,
    for our end had come.ᵍ
¹⁹Our pursuers were swifter
    than eaglesʰ in the sky;
    they chased usⁱ over the mountains
    and lay in wait for us in the desert.ʲ
²⁰The LORD's anointed,ᵏ our very life
    breath,
    was caught in their traps.ˡ
    We thought that under his shadowᵐ
    we would live among the nations.
²¹Rejoice and be glad, O Daughter of
    Edom,
    you who live in the land of Uz.ⁿ
    But to you also the cupᵒ will be
    passed;
    you will be drunk and stripped
    naked.ᵖ
²²O Daughter of Zion, your punishment
    will end;ᑫ
    he will not prolong your exile.
    But, O Daughter of Edom, he will
    punish your sin
    and expose your wickedness.ʳ

5 Remember, O LORD, what has
    happened to us;
    look, and see our disgrace.ˢ
²Our inheritanceᵗ has been turned over
    to aliens,ᵘ
    our homesᵛ to foreigners.ʷ
³We have become orphans and
    fatherless,
    our mothers like widows.ˣ
⁴We must buy the water we drink;ʸ
    our wood can be had only at a
    price.ᶻ
⁵Those who pursue us are at our heels;
    we are wearyᵃ and find no rest.ᵇ
⁶We submitted to Egypt and Assyriaᶜ
    to get enough bread.
⁷Our fathersᵈ sinned and are no more,
    and we bear their punishment.ᵉ
⁸Slavesᶠ rule over us,
    and there is none to free us from
    their hands.ᵍ
⁹We get our bread at the risk of our
    lives
    because of the sword in the desert.
¹⁰Our skin is hot as an oven,
    feverish from hunger.ʰ
¹¹Women have been ravishedⁱ in Zion,
    and virgins in the towns of Judah.
¹²Princes have been hung up by their
    hands;
    eldersʲ are shown no respect.ᵏ
¹³Young men toil at the millstones;
    boys stagger under loads of wood.
¹⁴The elders are gone from the city gate;
    the young men have stopped their
    music.ˡ
¹⁵Joy is gone from our hearts;
    our dancing has turned to
    mourning.ᵐ
¹⁶The crownⁿ has fallen from our head.ᵒ
    Woe to us, for we have sinned!ᵖ
¹⁷Because of this our heartsᑫ are faint,ʳ

R *La 3:45* ◀ ▶ *Eze 5:3-4*

4:22 The prophet declares that the savage defilement of Jerusalem and God's punishment of Judah will end. Once Israel is reestablished in the promised land they will never again be carried into captivity.

because of these things our eyes[s]
    grow dim[t]
[18]for Mount Zion,[u] which lies desolate,[v]
    with jackals prowling over it.

[19]You, O LORD, reign forever;[w]
    your throne endures[x] from
        generation to generation.
[20]Why do you always forget us?[y]
    Why do you forsake[z] us so long?
[21]Restore[a] us to yourself, O LORD, that
        we may return;
    renew our days as of old
[22]unless you have utterly rejected us[b]
    and are angry with us beyond
        measure.[c]

5:17 [s] Ps 6:7 [t] S Job 16:8
5:18 [u] Ps 74:2-3 [v] S Isa 27:10; Mic 3:12
5:19 [w] S 1Ch 16:31 [x] S Ps 45:6; 102:12, 24-27
5:20 [y] S Ps 13:1; 44:24 [z] S Ps 71:11
5:21 [a] S Ps 80:3; Isa 60:20-22 5:22 [b] S Ps 53:5; 60:1-2; S Jer 6:30 [c] S Isa 64:9

Ezekiel

Author: Ezekiel

Theme: God is active in the events of human history

Date of Writing: c. 571 B.C.

Outline of Ezekiel
  I. Ezekiel's Call and Divine Commission (1:1—3:27)
  II. Sinful Conditions and Promised Doom (4:1—19:14)
  III. The Last Full Measure of Judgment (20:1—24:27)
  IV. Judgment Against Foreign Nations (25:1—32:32)
  V. Hope for Restoration (33:1—39:29)
  VI. Restoration and Renewal (40:1—48:35)

THIS BOOK IS named after the prophet Ezekiel, whose name means "God is strong." Born into a priestly family who served in the temple, Ezekiel witnessed the wickedness of his people and was among the captives taken by Nebuchadnezzar into Babylonian exile in 597 B.C. While in Babylon, Ezekiel received God's call to the prophetic ministry (see 1:1) and shared God's messages concerning the destiny of Israel with his fellow exiles. Ezekiel's book contains more dates than any other Biblical record, indicating that his messages were given between 593–571 B.C. Jewish tradition suggests that Ezekiel, God's watchman of judgment, died during the Babylonian captivity.

Over half of this major prophetic book contains promises about Israel's future. During his early ministry, Ezekiel proclaimed the same message as Jeremiah—that the sinfulness and idolatry that prevailed in Jerusalem, even after Babylon's initial conquest, would finally result in God's abandonment and the city's destruction. The first twenty-four chapters of Ezekiel reflect this theme.

After the news reached Babylon that Jerusalem had actually been destroyed, Ezekiel's message became a message of hope and restoration. Ezekiel prophesied that God, the great Shepherd, would gather the exiles from the ends of the earth and establish them in their own land forever. Gentile nations who dared to challenge Israel's return to the promised land would face defeat and God's judgment. In addition, Ezekiel was given a vision of the millennial temple to be established by the Messiah for use in Israel's future worship.

The Living Creatures and the Glory of the LORD

1 In the[a] thirtieth year, in the fourth month on the fifth day, while I was among the exiles[a] by the Kebar River,[b] the heavens were opened[c] and I saw visions[d] of God.

² On the fifth of the month—it was the fifth year of the exile of King Jehoiachin[e]— ³ the word of the LORD came to Ezekiel[f] the priest, the son of Buzi,[b] by the Kebar River in the land of the Babylonians.[c] There the hand of the LORD was upon him.[g]

⁴ I looked, and I saw a windstorm[h] coming out of the north[i]—an immense cloud with flashing lightning and surrounded by brilliant light. The center of the fire looked like glowing metal,[j] ⁵ and in the fire was what looked like four living creatures.[k] In appearance their form was that of a man,[l] ⁶ but each of them had four faces[m] and four wings. ⁷ Their legs were straight; their feet were like those of a calf and gleamed like burnished bronze.[n] ⁸ Under their wings on their four sides they had the hands of a man.[o] All four of them had faces and wings, ⁹ and their wings touched one another. Each one went straight ahead; they did not turn as they moved.[p]

¹⁰ Their faces looked like this: Each of the four had the face of a man, and on the right side each had the face of a lion, and on the left the face of an ox; each also had the face of an eagle.[q] ¹¹ Such were their faces. Their wings[r] were spread out upward; each had two wings, one touching the wing of another creature on either side, and two wings covering its body. ¹² Each one went straight ahead. Wherever the spirit would go, they would go, without turning as they went.[s] ¹³ The appearance of the living creatures was like burning coals[t] of fire or like torches. Fire moved back and forth among the creatures; it was bright, and lightning[u] flashed out of it. ¹⁴ The creatures sped back and forth like flashes of lightning.[v]

¹⁵ As I looked at the living creatures,[w] I saw a wheel[x] on the ground beside each creature with its four faces. ¹⁶ This was the appearance and structure of the wheels: They sparkled like chrysolite,[y] and all four looked alike. Each appeared to be made like a wheel intersecting a wheel. ¹⁷ As they moved, they would go in any one of the four directions the creatures faced; the wheels did not turn[z] about[d] as the creatures went. ¹⁸ Their rims were high and awesome, and all four rims were full of eyes[a] all around. ¹⁹ When the living creatures moved, the wheels beside them moved; and when the living creatures rose from the ground, the wheels also rose. ²⁰ Wherever the spirit would go, they would go,[b] and

---

1:1 [a] S Dt 21:10; Eze 11:24-25 [b] S Ps 137:1 [c] S Mt 3:16 [d] S Ex 24:10
1:2 [e] S 2Ki 24:15
1:3 [f] Eze 24:24 [g] S 2Ki 3:15; Isa 8:11; Eze 3:14, 22; 8:1; 33:22; 37:1; 40:1
1:4 [h] S Job 38:1 [i] Jer 1:14 [j] Eze 8:2
1:5 [k] S Isa 6:2; Rev 4:6 [l] ver 26; Da 7:13
1:6 [m] Eze 10:14
1:7 [n] Eze 40:3; Da 10:6; S Rev 1:15
1:8 [o] Eze 10:8
1:9 [p] Eze 10:22
1:10 [q] Eze 10:14; Rev 4:7
1:11 [r] Isa 6:2
1:12 [s] Eze 10:16-19
1:13 [t] S 2Sa 22:9 [u] Rev 4:5
1:14 [v] S Ps 29:7
1:15 [w] Eze 3:13 [x] Eze 10:2; Da 7:9
1:16 [y] S Ex 28:20
1:17 [z] ver 9
1:18 [a] Rev 4:6
1:20 [b] ver 12

E Isa 63:14 ◀ ▶ Eze 1:20
L Isa 63:14 ◀ ▶ Eze 1:20
E Eze 1:12 ◀ ▶ Eze 2:2-3
L Eze 1:12 ◀ ▶ Eze 2:2-3

[a] 1 Or *my*, [b] 3 Or *Ezekiel son of Buzi the priest* [c] 3 Or *Chaldeans* [d] 17 Or *aside*

1:1 This verse indicates that Ezekiel began to write his prophecy when he was approximately thirty years old, the age that a person entered the Levitical priesthood (see Nu 4:3). Ezekiel was from a priestly family but could not commence his service in the temple because he had been exiled to Babylon. God gave Ezekiel another commission—that of a prophet.
1:4–6, 10 Ezekiel's commission as God's prophet began with this vision of "four living creatures" (1:5). The four creatures represented all the facets of God's creation: "man" (1:5), God's ruler of creation; "lion" (1:10), the strongest of the wild animals; "ox" (1:10), the strongest domesticated animal; and "eagle" (1:10), the greatest bird. Compare this vision with Rev 4:7.

the wheels would rise along with them, because the spirit of the living creatures was in the wheels. ²¹When the creatures moved, they also moved; when the creatures stood still, they also stood still; and when the creatures rose from the ground, the wheels rose along with them, because the spirit of the living creatures was in the wheels.^c

²²Spread out above the heads of the living creatures was what looked like an expanse,^d sparkling like ice, and awesome. ²³Under the expanse their wings were stretched out one toward the other, and each had two wings covering its body. ²⁴When the creatures moved, I heard the sound of their wings, like the roar of rushing^e waters, like the voice^f of the Almighty,^e like the tumult of an army.^g When they stood still, they lowered their wings.

²⁵Then there came a voice from above the expanse over their heads as they stood with lowered wings. ²⁶Above the expanse over their heads was what looked like a throne^h of sapphire,^{f,i} and high above on the throne was a figure like that of a man.^j ²⁷I saw that from what appeared to be his waist up he looked like glowing metal, as if full of fire, and that from there down he looked like fire; and brilliant light surrounded him.^k ²⁸Like the appearance of a rainbow^l in the clouds on a rainy day, so was the radiance around him.^m

This was the appearance of the likeness of the gloryⁿ of the LORD. When I saw it, I fell facedown,^o and I heard the voice of one speaking.

Ezekiel's Call

2 He said to me, "Son of man,^p stand^q up on your feet and I will speak to
E you."^r ²As he spoke, the Spirit came into
L me and raised me^s to my feet, and I
M heard him speaking to me.

³He said: "Son of man, I am sending you to the Israelites, to a rebellious nation that has rebelled against me; they and their fathers have been in revolt
C against me to this very day.^t ⁴The people to whom I am sending you are obstinate

E *Eze 1:20* ◀ ▶ *Eze 3:12*
L *Eze 1:20* ◀ ▶ *Eze 3:14*
M *Isa 59:19* ◀ ▶ *Eze 3:12*
C *La 3:19–20* ◀ ▶ *Eze 2:6*

1:21 ^c Eze 10:9-12
1:22 ^d Eze 10:1
1:24 ^e S Ps 46:3; Eze 3:13 ^f Eze 10:5; 43:2; Da 10:6; Rev 1:15; 14:2; 19:6 ^g S 2Ki 7:6
1:26 ^h S 1Ki 22:19; Isa 6:1; S Jer 3:17 ⁱ S Ex 24:10 ^j S ver 5; S Eze 2:1; S Rev 1:13
1:27 ^k Eze 8:2
1:28 ^l S Ge 9:13; Rev 10:1
^m S Rev 4:2
S 24:16; Lk 2:9
^o S Ge 17:3;
S Nu 14:5
2:1 ^p S Job 25:6; Ps 8:4; S Eze 1:26; Da 7:13; 8:15
^q Da 10:11;
Ac 14:10; 26:16
^r Ac 9:6
2:2 ^s Eze 3:24; Da 8:18
2:3 ^t S Jer 3:25; Eze 5:6; 20:8-24; 24:3
2:4 ^u S Ex 32:9; S Isa 9:9; Eze 3:7
^v Am 7:15
2:5 ^w Eze 3:11
^x Eze 3:27
^y S Jer 5:3;
Eze 33:33; Jn 15:22
2:6 ^z S Dt 31:6; S 2Ki 1:15
^a S Nu 33:55; Isa 9:18; Mic 7:4
^b S Isa 1:2; 30:9; Eze 24:3; 44:6
2:7 ^c Jer 7:27
^d Jer 1:7; S 42:21; Eze 3:10-11
2:8 ^e Nu 20:10-13
^f Isa 8:11
^g S Isa 50:5
^h Ps 81:10;
S Jer 15:16;
Rev 10:9
2:9 ⁱ Eze 8:3
^j S Ps 40:7;
S Jer 36:4;
Rev 5:1-5; 10:8-10
2:10 ^k Isa 3:11; Rev 8:13
3:3 ^l S Jer 15:16
^m S Ps 19:10; Rev 10:9-10
3:4 ⁿ Eze 11:4,25
3:5 ^o S Isa 28:11; Jnh 1:2
3:6 ^p Jnh 3:5-10; Mt 11:21-23; Ac 13:46-48
3:7 ^q S Jer 7:27
^r Isa 48:4; Jer 3:3; S Eze 2:4; Jn 15:20-23
3:8 ^s Jer 1:18; S 15:20
3:9 ^t S Isa 48:4
^u S Jer 5:3
^v Isa 50:7; Eze 2:6; 44:6; Mic 3:8

and stubborn.^u Say to them, 'This is what the Sovereign LORD says.'^v ⁵And whether they listen or fail to listen^w—for they are a rebellious house^x—they will know that a prophet has been among them.^y ⁶And C you, son of man, do not be afraid^z of them or their words. Do not be afraid, though briers and thorns^a are all around you and you live among scorpions. Do not be afraid of what they say or terrified by them, though they are a rebellious house.^b ⁷You must speak^c my words to them, whether they listen or fail to listen, for they are rebellious.^d ⁸But you, son of man, listen to what I say to you. Do not rebel^{e,f} like that rebellious house;^g open your mouth and eat^h what I give you."

⁹Then I looked, and I saw a handⁱ stretched out to me. In it was a scroll,^j ¹⁰which he unrolled before me. On both sides of it were written words of lament and mourning and woe.^k

3 And he said to me, "Son of man, eat what is before you, eat this scroll; then go and speak to the house of Israel." ²So I opened my mouth, and he gave me the scroll to eat.

³Then he said to me, "Son of man, eat this scroll I am giving you and fill your stomach with it." So I ate¹ it, and it tasted as sweet as honey^m in my mouth.

⁴He then said to me: "Son of man, go now to the house of Israel and speak my words to them.ⁿ ⁵You are not being sent to a people of obscure speech and difficult language,^o but to the house of Israel— ⁶not to many peoples of obscure speech and difficult language, whose words you cannot understand. Surely if I had sent you to them, they would have listened to you.^p ⁷But the house of Israel C is not willing to listen^q to you because C they are not willing to listen to me, for M the whole house of Israel is hardened and N obstinate.^r ⁸But I will make you as unyielding and hardened as they are.^s ⁹I will make your forehead^t like the hardest stone, harder than flint.^u Do not be afraid of them or terrified by them, though they are a rebellious house.^v"

¹⁰And he said to me, "Son of man, lis-

C *Eze 2:4* ◀ ▶ *Eze 3:7*
C *Eze 2:6* ◀ ▶ *Eze 12:2*
M *La 3:19–21* ◀ ▶ *Da 9:3–5*
N *Jer 32:33* ◀ ▶ *Eze 33:4–5*

^e 24 Hebrew *Shaddai* ^f 26 Or *lapis lazuli*

EZEKIEL 3:11

ten carefully and take to heart[w] all the words I speak to you. ¹¹Go[x] now to your countrymen in exile and speak to them. Say to them, 'This is what the Sovereign LORD says,'[y] whether they listen or fail to listen.[z]"

E
M
N
¹²Then the Spirit lifted me up,[a] and I heard behind me a loud rumbling sound—May the glory of the LORD be praised in his dwelling place!— ¹³the sound of the wings of the living creatures[b] brushing against each other and the sound of the wheels beside them, a

E
L
M
N
loud rumbling sound.[c] ¹⁴The Spirit[d] then lifted me up[e] and took me away, and I went in bitterness and in the anger of my spirit, with the strong hand of the LORD[f] upon me. ¹⁵I came to the exiles who lived at Tel Abib near the Kebar River.[g] And there, where they were living, I sat among them for seven days[h]—overwhelmed.

Warning to Israel

¹⁶At the end of seven days the word of the LORD came to me:[i] ¹⁷"Son of man, I have made you a watchman[j] for the house of Israel; so hear the word I speak and give them warning from me.[k] ¹⁸When I say to a wicked man, 'You will surely die,'¹ and you do not warn him or speak out to dissuade him from his evil ways in order to save his life, that wicked man will die for[g] his sin, and I will hold you accountable for his blood.[m] ¹⁹But if you do warn the wicked man and he does not turn[n] from his wickedness[o] or from his evil ways, he will die[p] for his sin; but you will have saved yourself.[q]

S ²⁰"Again, when a righteous man turns[r]

E *Eze 2:2–3* ◀ ▶ *Eze 3:14*
M *Eze 2:2–3* ◀ ▶ *Eze 3:14*
N *Isa 44:3–4* ◀ ▶ *Eze 3:14*
E *Eze 3:12* ◀ ▶ *Eze 3:24*
L *Eze 2:2–3* ◀ ▶ *Eze 3:24*
M *Eze 3:12* ◀ ▶ *Eze 3:24*
N *Eze 3:12* ◀ ▶ *Eze 8:3*
S *Jer 32:19* ◀ ▶ *Eze 9:4–6*

3:10 w S Job 22:22
3:11 x S Isa 6:9
y ver 27 w Eze 2:4-5, 7; 11:24-25
3:12 a ver 14; Eze 8:3; 43:5
3:13 b Eze 1:15
c Eze 1:24; 10:5, 16-17
3:14 d S 1Ki 18:12
e ver 12 f ver 22;
S Isa 8:11; Eze 37:1
3:15 g S Ps 137:1
h S Ge 50:10
3:16 i Jer 42:7
3:17 j S Isa 52:8
k S Isa 58:1;
Jer 1:17; Eze 11:4;
Hab 2:1
3:18 l S Ge 2:17;
Jn 8:21,24 m ver 20
3:19 n S Ps 7:12
o S Ge 6:5
p S Jer 42:16
q S 2Ki 17:13;
Eze 14:14,20;
Ac 18:6; 20:26;
1Ti 4:14-16
3:20 r S Jer 34:16
s S Lev 26:37;
S Isa 8:14;
S Eze 7:19 t ver 18;
Ps 125:5;
Eze 18:24; 33:12, 18
3:21 u Ac 20:31
3:22 v S ver 14;
S Eze 1:3 w Ac 9:6
x Eze 8:4
3:23 y Eze 1:1
z S Ge 17:3
3:24 a S Eze 2:2
b Jer 15:17
3:25 c Eze 4:8
3:26 d S Ps 22:15
e Eze 2:5; 24:27;
33:22; Hos 4:4
3:27 f ver 11
g Eze 2:5; 12:3;
24:27; 29:21;
33:22; Rev 22:11
4:2 h S Jer 6:6;
Eze 17:17;
Da 11:15
i S Jer 33:4;
Eze 21:22
4:3 j S Lev 2:5

from his righteousness and does evil, and I put a stumbling block[s] before him, he will die. Since you did not warn him, he will die for his sin. The righteous things he did will not be remembered, and I will hold you accountable for his blood.[t] ²¹But if you do warn the righteous man not to sin and he does not sin, he will surely live because he took warning, and you will have saved yourself.[u]"

²²The hand of the LORD[v] was upon me there, and he said to me, "Get up and go[w] out to the plain,[x] and there I will speak to you." ²³So I got up and went out to the plain. And the glory of the LORD was standing there, like the glory I had seen by the Kebar River,[y] and I fell facedown.[z]

E
L
M
²⁴Then the Spirit came into me and raised me[a] to my feet. He spoke to me and said: "Go, shut yourself inside your house.[b] ²⁵And you, son of man, they will tie with ropes; you will be bound so that you cannot go out among the people.[c] ²⁶I will make your tongue stick to the roof[d] of your mouth so that you will be silent and unable to rebuke them, though they are a rebellious house.[e] ²⁷But when I speak to you, I will open your mouth and you shall say to them, 'This is what the Sovereign LORD says.'[f] Whoever will listen let him listen, and whoever will refuse let him refuse; for they are a rebellious house.[g]

Siege of Jerusalem Symbolized

4 "Now, son of man, take a clay tablet, put it in front of you and draw the city of Jerusalem on it. ²Then lay siege to it: Erect siege works against it, build a ramp[h] up to it, set up camps against it and put battering rams around it.[i] ³Then take an iron pan,[j] place it as an iron wall

E *Eze 3:14* ◀ ▶ *Eze 8:3*
L *Eze 3:14* ◀ ▶ *Eze 11:1*
M *Eze 3:14* ◀ ▶ *Eze 36:27*

g 18 Or in; *also in verses 19 and 20*

4:3–6 Jeremiah had prophesied that Judah would serve seventy years of captivity in Babylon. Ezekiel was serving that sentence when God gave him these additional time markers to symbolize Israel and Judah's sins and set a time for their punishment.

Lying on his left side while he prophesied for 390 days, Ezekiel faced north, symbolizing the northern kingdom of Israel. Lying on his right side for 40 days and facing south, Ezekiel symbolized the southern kingdom of Judah. Scripture records that each day represented one year (4:6).

Determining the actual events of these time periods has been difficult. The 40-year period may correspond to the long reign of wicked King Manasseh before he repented. Or it may refer to the time between the fall of Jerusalem and the defeat of

between you and the city and turn your face toward it. It will be under siege, and you shall besiege it. This will be a sign to the house of Israel.

⁴"Then lie on your left side and put the sin of the house of Israel upon yourself. You are to bear their sin for the number of days you lie on your side. ⁵I have assigned you the same number of days as the years of their sin. So for 390 days you will bear the sin of the house of Israel. ⁶"After you have finished this, lie down again, this time on your right side, and bear the sin of the house of Judah. I have assigned you 40 days, a day for each year. ⁷Turn your face toward the siege of Jerusalem and with bared arm prophesy against her. ⁸I will tie you up with ropes so that you cannot turn from one side to the other until you have finished the days of your siege.

⁹"Take wheat and barley, beans and lentils, millet and spelt; put them in a storage jar and use them to make bread for yourself. You are to eat it during the 390 days you lie on your side. ¹⁰Weigh out twenty shekels of food to eat each day and eat it at set times. ¹¹Also measure out a sixth of a hin of water and drink it at set times. ¹²Eat the food as you would a barley cake; bake it in the sight of the people, using human excrement for fuel." ¹³The LORD said, "In this way the people of Israel will eat defiled food among the nations where I will drive them."

¹⁴Then I said, "Not so, Sovereign LORD! I have never defiled myself. From my youth until now I have never eaten anything found dead or torn by wild animals. No unclean meat has ever entered my mouth."

¹⁵"Very well," he said, "I will let you bake your bread over cow manure instead of human excrement."

¹⁶He then said to me: "Son of man, I will cut off the supply of food in Jerusa-

lem. The people will eat rationed food in anxiety and drink rationed water in despair, ¹⁷for food and water will be scarce. They will be appalled at the sight of each other and will waste away because of their sin.

5 "Now, son of man, take a sharp sword and use it as a barber's razor to shave your head and your beard. Then take a set of scales and divide up the hair. ²When the days of your siege come to an end, burn a third of the hair with fire inside the city. Take a third and strike it with the sword all around the city. And scatter a third to the wind. For I will pursue them with drawn sword. ³But take a few strands of hair and tuck them away in the folds of your garment. ⁴Again, take a few of these and throw them into the fire and burn them up. A fire will spread from there to the whole house of Israel.

⁵"This is what the Sovereign LORD says: This is Jerusalem, which I have set in the center of the nations, with countries all around her. ⁶Yet in her wickedness she has rebelled against my laws and decrees more than the nations and countries around her. She has rejected my laws and has not followed my decrees.

⁷"Therefore this is what the Sovereign LORD says: You have been more unruly than the nations around you and have not followed my decrees or kept my laws. You have not even conformed to the standards of the nations around you.

⁸"Therefore this is what the Sovereign LORD says: I myself am against you, Jerusalem, and I will inflict punishment on you in the sight of the nations. ⁹Because of all your detestable idols, I will do to you what I have never done before and will never do again. ¹⁰Therefore in your midst fathers will eat their children, and

---

5:1–4, 12 Ezekiel again acted out a specific prophecy of God. The hair from Ezekiel's head demonstrated the tragic fate of his people: one third destroyed in the city by famine and plague; one third consumed by battle; one third scattered into exile (5:12). Only a small remnant (5:3) would be spared.

Babylon by Persia. Some scholars believe that the 390 years refer to the time between Solomon's kingdom and the fall of Jerusalem. Others believe that this time period covers the years from the division of the kingdom until the emancipation from Babylon. Still others suggest that the 390 years calculate the rebirth of modern Israel as a nation.

children will eat their fathers. I will inflict punishment on you and will scatter all your survivors to the winds. ¹¹Therefore as surely as I live, declares the Sovereign LORD, because you have defiled my sanctuary with all your vile images and detestable practices, I myself will withdraw my favor; I will not look on you with pity or spare you. ¹²A third of your people will die of the plague or perish by famine inside you; a third will fall by the sword outside your walls; and a third I will scatter to the winds and pursue with drawn sword.

¹³"Then my anger will cease and my wrath against them will subside, and I will be avenged. And when I have spent my wrath upon them, they will know that I the LORD have spoken in my zeal.

¹⁴"I will make you a ruin and a reproach among the nations around you, in the sight of all who pass by. ¹⁵You will be a reproach and a taunt, a warning and an object of horror to the nations around you when I inflict punishment on you in anger and in wrath and with stinging rebuke. I the LORD have spoken. ¹⁶When I shoot at you with my deadly and destructive arrows of famine, I will shoot to destroy you. I will bring more and more famine upon you and cut off your supply of food. ¹⁷I will send famine and wild beasts against you, and they will leave you childless. Plague and bloodshed will sweep through you, and I will bring the sword against you. I the LORD have spoken."

A Prophecy Against the Mountains of Israel

6 The word of the LORD came to me: ²"Son of man, set your face against the mountains of Israel; prophesy against them ³and say: 'O mountains of Israel, hear the word of the Sovereign LORD. This is what the Sovereign LORD says to the mountains and hills, to the ravines and valleys: I am about to bring a sword against you, and I will destroy your high places. ⁴Your altars will be demolished and your incense altars will be smashed; and I will slay your people in front of your idols. ⁵I will lay the dead bodies of the Israelites in front of their idols, and I will scatter your bones around your altars. ⁶Wherever you live, the towns will be laid waste and the high places demolished, so that your altars will be laid waste and devastated, your idols smashed and ruined, your incense altars broken down, and what you have made wiped out. ⁷Your people will fall slain among you, and you will know that I am the LORD.

⁸"'But I will spare some, for some of you will escape the sword when you are scattered among the lands and nations. ⁹Then in the nations where they have been carried captive, those who escape will remember me—how I have been grieved by their adulterous hearts, which have turned away from me, and by their eyes, which have lusted after their idols. They will loathe themselves for the evil they have done and for all their detestable practices. ¹⁰And they will know that I am the LORD; I did not threaten in vain to bring this calamity on them.

¹¹"'This is what the Sovereign LORD says: Strike your hands together and stamp your feet and cry out "Alas!" because of all the wicked and detestable practices of the house of Israel, for they will fall by the sword, famine and

---

5:15 God said that this destruction of Jerusalem would become a proverb among the nations as they recognized God's hand of judgment against his disobedient servants.

5:17 God declared that four specific judgments—famine, evil beasts, pestilence, the sword—represented his wrath against the sinful nation. Compare this prophecy with the four seals of Rev 6, noting that God's wrath will be poured out against unrepentant sinners during the tribulation.

6:6 Ezekiel confirmed that God would destroy their cities, homes and places of idol worship.

6:10 The fulfillment of God's prophecies would prove his prophets' divine inspiration and God's determination to bring judgment on his people.

plague.ᵐ ¹²He that is far away will die of the plague, and he that is near will fall by the sword, and he that survives and is spared will die of famine. So will I spend my wrathⁿ upon them.ᵒ ¹³And they will know that I am the Lord, when their people lie slain among their idolsᵖ around their altars, on every high hill and on all the mountaintops, under every spreading tree and every leafy oakᑫ—places where they offered fragrant incense to all their idols.ʳ ¹⁴And I will stretch out my handˢ against them and make the land a desolate waste from the desert to Diblahᵐ— wherever they live. Then they will know that I am the Lord.ᵗ' "

The End Has Come

R **7** The word of the Lord came to me: ²"Son of man, this is what the Sovereign Lord says to the land of Israel: The end!ᵘ The end has come upon the four cornersᵛ of the land. ³The end is now upon you and I will unleash my anger against you. I will judge you according to your conductʷ and repay you for all your detestable practices.ˣ ⁴I will not look on you with pityʸ or spare you; I will surely repay you for your conduct and the detestable practices among you. Then you will know that I am the Lord.ᶻ

⁵"This is what the Sovereign Lord says: Disaster!ᵃ An unheard-ofⁿ disaster is coming. ⁶The endᵇ has come! The end has come! It has roused itself against you. It has come! ⁷Doom has come upon you—you who dwell in the land. The time has come, the dayᶜ is near;ᵈ there is H panic, not joy, upon the mountains. ⁸I am about to pour out my wrathᵉ on you and spend my anger against you; I will judge you according to your conduct and repay you for all your detestable practices.ᶠ ⁹I will not look on you with pity or spare you;ᵍ I will repay you in accordance with your conduct and the detestable practices among you.ʰ Then you will know that it is I the Lord who strikes the blow.ⁱ

¹⁰"The day is here! It has come! Doom has burst forth, the rodʲ has budded, arrogance has blossomed! ¹¹Violenceᵏ has

grown intoᵒ a rod to punish wickedness; none of the people will be left, none of that crowd—no wealth, nothing of value.ˡ ¹²The time has come, the day has arrived. Let not the buyerᵐ rejoice nor the seller grieve, for wrath is upon the whole crowd.ⁿ ¹³The seller will not recover the land he has sold as long as both of them live, for the vision concerning the whole crowd will not be reversed. Because of their sins, not one of them will preserve his life.ᵒ ¹⁴Though they blow the trumpetᵖ and get everything ready, no one will go into battle, for my wrathᑫ is upon the whole crowd.

¹⁵"Outside is the sword, inside are D plague and famine; those in the country will die by the sword, and those in the city will be devoured by famine and plague.ʳ ¹⁶All who surviveˢ and escape will be in the mountains, moaning like dovesᵗ of the valleys, each because of his sins.ᵘ ¹⁷Every hand will go limp,ᵛ and ev- H ery knee will become as weak as water.ʷ ¹⁸They will put on sackclothˣ and be clothed with terror.ʸ Their faces will be covered with shame and their heads will be shaved.ᶻ ¹⁹They will throw their silver into the streets,ᵃ and their gold will be an unclean thing. Their silver and gold will not be able to save them in the day of the Lord's wrath.ᵇ They will not satisfyᶜ their hunger or fill their stomachs with it, for it has made them stumbleᵈ into sin.ᵉ ²⁰They were proud of their beautiful jewelry and used it to makeᶠ their detestable idols and vile images.ᵍ Therefore I will turn these into an unclean thing for them.ʰ ²¹I will hand it all over as plunderⁱ to foreigners and as loot to the wicked of the earth, and they will defile it.ʲ ²²I will turn my faceᵏ away from them, and they will desecrate my treasured place; robbers will enter it and desecrate it.ˡ

D Eze 5:12 ◀ ▶ Eze 14:19
H Eze 7:8 ◀ ▶ Eze 9:10

ᵍ S Eze 5:11 ʰ S Isa 2:20; 30:22; Eze 16:17 ⁱ 7:21 ʲ S Nu 14:3 ʲ S 2Ki 24:13
7:22 ᵏ S Jer 2:27; Eze 39:23-24 ˡ Ps 74:7-8; Jer 19:13; S La 2:7

ᵐ 14 Most Hebrew manuscripts; a few Hebrew manuscripts Riblah
ⁿ 5 Most Hebrew manuscripts; some Hebrew manuscripts and Syriac Disaster after ᵒ 11 Or The violent one has become

R Eze 6:10 ◀ ▶ Eze 9:4–5
H La 3:39 ◀ ▶ Eze 7:17–18

7:1–2 After centuries of warning, the time of judgment finally arrived.

23 "Prepare chains, because the land is full of bloodshed and the city is full of violence. 24 I will bring the most wicked of the nations to take possession of their houses; I will put an end to the pride of the mighty, and their sanctuaries will be desecrated. 25 When terror comes, they will seek peace, but there will be none. 26 Calamity upon calamity will come, and rumor upon rumor. They will try to get a vision from the prophet; the teaching of the law by the priest will be lost, as will the counsel of the elders. 27 The king will mourn, the prince will be clothed with despair, and the hands of the people of the land will tremble. I will deal with them according to their conduct, and by their own standards I will judge them. Then they will know that I am the LORD."

Idolatry in the Temple

8 In the sixth year, in the sixth month on the fifth day, while I was sitting in my house and the elders of Judah were sitting before me, the hand of the Sovereign LORD came upon me there. 2 I looked, and I saw a figure like that of a man. From what appeared to be his waist down he was like fire, and from there up his appearance was as bright as glowing metal. 3 He stretched out what looked like a hand and took me by the hair of my head. The Spirit lifted me up between earth and heaven and in visions of God he took me to Jerusalem, to the entrance to the north gate of the inner court, where the idol that provokes to jealousy stood. 4 And there before me was the glory of the God of Israel, as in the vision I had seen in the plain.

5 Then he said to me, "Son of man, look toward the north." So I looked, and in the entrance north of the gate of the altar I saw this idol of jealousy.

6 And he said to me, "Son of man, do you see what they are doing—the utterly detestable things the house of Israel is doing here, things that will drive me far from my sanctuary? But you will see things that are even more detestable."

7 Then he brought me to the entrance to the court. I looked, and I saw a hole in the wall. 8 He said to me, "Son of man, now dig into the wall." So I dug into the wall and saw a doorway there.

9 And he said to me, "Go in and see the wicked and detestable things they are doing here." 10 So I went in and looked, and I saw portrayed all over the walls all kinds of crawling things and detestable animals and all the idols of the house of Israel. 11 In front of them stood seventy elders of the house of Israel, and Jaazaniah son of Shaphan was standing among them. Each had a censer in his hand, and a fragrant cloud of incense was rising.

12 He said to me, "Son of man, have you seen what the elders of the house of Israel are doing in the darkness, each at the shrine of his own idol? They say, 'The LORD does not see us; the LORD has forsaken the land.'" 13 Again, he said, "You will see them doing things that are even more detestable."

14 Then he brought me to the entrance to the north gate of the house of the LORD, and I saw women sitting there, mourning for Tammuz. 15 He said to me, "Do you see this, son of man? You will see things that are even more detestable than this."

16 He then brought me into the inner court of the house of the LORD, and there at the entrance to the temple, between the portico and the altar, were about twenty-five men. With their backs toward the temple of the LORD and their faces toward the east, they were bowing down to the sun in the east.

17 He said to me, "Have you seen this, son of man? Is it a trivial matter for the house of Judah to do the detestable things they are doing here? Must they also fill the land with violence and continually provoke me to anger? Look at them putting the branch to their nose! 18 Therefore I will deal with them in anger; I will not look on them with pity or spare them. Although they shout in my ears, I will not listen to them."

Idolaters Killed

9 Then I heard him call out in a loud voice, "Bring the guards of the city here, each with a weapon in his hand." ²And I saw six men coming from the direction of the upper gate, which faces north, each with a deadly weapon in his hand. With them was a man clothed in linen^f who had a writing kit at his side. They came in and stood beside the bronze altar.

³Now the glory^g of the God of Israel went up from above the cherubim,^h where it had been, and moved to the threshold of the temple. Then the LORD called to the man clothed in linen who had the writing kit at his side. ⁴and said to him, "Go throughout the city of Jerusalem^i and put a mark^j on the foreheads of those who grieve and lament^k over all the detestable things that are done in it.^l"

⁵As I listened, he said to the others, "Follow him through the city and kill, without showing pity^m or compassion.^n ⁶Slaughter^o old men, young men and maidens, women and children,^p but do not touch anyone who has the mark.^q Begin at my sanctuary." So they began with the elders^r who were in front of the temple.^s

⁷Then he said to them, "Defile the temple and fill the courts with the slain.^t Go!" So they went out and began killing throughout the city. ⁸While they were killing and I was left alone, I fell facedown,^u crying out, "Ah, Sovereign LORD! Are you going to destroy the entire remnant of Israel in this outpouring of your wrath^w on Jerusalem?^x"

⁹He answered me, "The sin of the house of Israel and Judah is exceedingly great; the land is full of bloodshed and the city is full of injustice.^y They say, 'The LORD has forsaken the land; the LORD does not see.'^z ¹⁰So I will not look on them with pity^a or spare them, but I will bring down on their own heads what they have done.^b"

¹¹Then the man in linen with the writing kit at his side brought back word, saying, "I have done as you commanded."

R *Eze 7:1–2* ◀▶ *Eze 11:10–12*
S *Eze 3:20–21* ◀▶ *Eze 11:19–21*
E *Eze 8:12* ◀▶ *Eze 11:5*
H *Eze 7:17–18* ◀▶ *Eze 11:21*

9:2 ʳS Lev 16:4; Eze 10:2; Da 10:5; 12:6; Rev 15:6
9:3 ᵍS 1Sa 4:21; Eze 10:4
ʰ Eze 11:22
9:4 ⁱJer 25:29
ʲS Ge 4:15; Ex 12:7; 2Co 1:22;
S Rev 7:3
ᵏS Ps 119:136;
Jer 7:29; 13:17;
Eze 21:6; Am 6:6
ˡPs 119:53
9:5 ᵐS Jer 13:14;
S Eze 5:11
ⁿS Ex 32:27;
Isa 13:18
9:6 ᵒJer 7:32
ᵖS Jer 16:6
qS Ge 4:15;
S Ex 12:7
ʳEze 8:11-13,16
ˢS 2Ch 36:17;
Jer 25:29;
S Eze 6:4; 1Pe 4:17
9:7 ᵗEze 6:7
9:8 ᵘS Jos 7:6
ᵛS Eze 4:14
ʷS Eze 7:8
ˣEze 11:13;
Am 7:1-6
9:9 ʸS Ps 58:2;
Jer 12:1; Eze 22:29;
Hab 1:4
ᶻS Job 22:13;
S Eze 8:12; 14:23
9:10 ᵃS Jer 13:14;
S Eze 8:18
ᵇS Isa 22:5; S 65:6;
Eze 11:21; 23:49
10:1 ᶜS Rev 4:2
ᵈS Ex 24:10
ᵉ Eze 1:22
ᶠS Ge 3:24
10:2 ᵍS Eze 9:2
ʰS Eze 1:15
ⁱRev 8:5
ʲS 2Sa 22:9
10:4 ᵏS Ex 24:16; Eze 9:3; 44:4
10:5 ˡS Job 40:9
ᵐS Eze 3:13
10:6 ⁿDa 7:9
10:7 ᵒS Eze 5:4
10:8 ᵖEze 1:8
10:9 qS Eze 28:20;
Rev 21:20
10:12 ʳRev 4:6-8
ˢEze 1:15-21
10:14 ᵗ1Ki 7:36
ᵘGe 1:6 v 1Ki 7:29
ʷEze 1:10; 41:19;
Rev 4:7

The Glory Departs From the Temple

10 I looked, and I saw the likeness of a throne^c of sapphire^qd above the expanse^e that was over the heads of the cherubim.^f ²The LORD said to the man clothed in linen,^g "Go in among the wheels^h beneath the cherubim. Fill^i your hands with burning coals^j from among the cherubim and scatter them over the city." And as I watched, he went in.

³Now the cherubim were standing on the south side of the temple when the man went in, and a cloud filled the inner court. ⁴Then the glory of the LORD^k rose from above the cherubim and moved to the threshold of the temple. The cloud filled the temple, and the court was full of the radiance of the glory of the LORD. ⁵The sound of the wings of the cherubim could be heard as far away as the outer court, like the voice^l of God Almighty^r when he speaks.^m

⁶When the LORD commanded the man in linen, "Take fire from among the wheels,^n from among the cherubim," the man went in and stood beside a wheel. ⁷Then one of the cherubim reached out his hand to the fire^o that was among them. He took up some of it and put it into the hands of the man in linen, who took it and went out. ⁸(Under the wings of the cherubim could be seen what looked like the hands of a man.)^p

⁹I looked, and I saw beside the cherubim four wheels, one beside each of the cherubim; the wheels sparkled like chrysolite.^q ¹⁰As for their appearance, the four of them looked alike; each was like a wheel intersecting a wheel. ¹¹As they moved, they would go in any one of the four directions the cherubim faced; the wheels did not turn about^s as the cherubim went. The cherubim went in whatever direction the head faced, without turning as they went. ¹²Their entire bodies, including their backs, their hands and their wings, were completely full of eyes,^r as were their four wheels.^s ¹³I heard the wheels being called "the whirling wheels." ¹⁴Each of the cherubim^t had four faces:^u One face was that of a cherub, the second the face of a man, the third the face of a lion,^v and the fourth the face of an eagle.^w

¹⁵Then the cherubim rose upward.

---

^q 1 Or *lapis lazuli*   ^r 5 Hebrew *El-Shaddai*   ^s 11 Or *aside*

These were the living creatures I had seen by the Kebar River. ⁱ⁶When the cherubim moved, the wheels beside them moved; and when the cherubim spread their wings to rise from the ground, the wheels did not leave their side. ¹⁷When the cherubim stood still, they also stood still; and when the cherubim rose, they rose with them, because the spirit of the living creatures was in them.

¹⁸Then the glory of the LORD departed from over the threshold of the temple and stopped above the cherubim. ¹⁹While I watched, the cherubim spread their wings and rose from the ground, and as they went, the wheels went with them. They stopped at the entrance to the east gate of the LORD's house, and the glory of the God of Israel was above them.

²⁰These were the living creatures I had seen beneath the God of Israel by the Kebar River, and I realized that they were cherubim. ²¹Each had four faces and four wings, and under their wings was what looked like the hands of a man. ²²Their faces had the same appearance as those I had seen by the Kebar River. Each one went straight ahead.

Judgment on Israel's Leaders

11 Then the Spirit lifted me up and brought me to the gate of the house of the LORD that faces east. There at the entrance to the gate were twenty-five men, and I saw among them Jaazaniah son of Azzur and Pelatiah son of Benaiah, leaders of the people. ²The LORD said to me, "Son of man, these are the men who are plotting evil and giving wicked advice in this city. ³They say, 'Will it not soon be time to build houses?' This city is a cooking pot, and we are the meat.' ⁴Therefore prophesy against them; prophesy, son of man."

⁵Then the Spirit of the LORD came upon me, and he told me to say: "This is what the LORD says: That is what you are saying, O house of Israel, but I know what is going through your mind. ⁶You have killed many people in this city and filled its streets with the dead.

⁷"Therefore this is what the Sovereign LORD says: The bodies you have thrown there are the meat and this city is the pot, but I will drive you out of it. ⁸You fear the sword, and the sword is what I will bring against you, declares the Sovereign LORD. ⁹I will drive you out of the city and hand you over to foreigners and inflict punishment on you. ¹⁰You will fall by the sword, and I will execute judgment on you at the borders of Israel. Then you will know that I am the LORD. ¹¹This city will not be a pot for you, nor will you be the meat in it; I will execute judgment on you at the borders of Israel. ¹²And you will know that I am the LORD, for you have not followed my decrees or kept my laws but have conformed to the standards of the nations around you.'"

¹³Now as I was prophesying, Pelatiah son of Benaiah died. Then I fell facedown and cried out in a loud voice, "Ah, Sovereign LORD! Will you completely destroy the remnant of Israel?"

¹⁴The word of the LORD came to me: ¹⁵"Son of man, your brothers—your brothers who are your blood relatives and the whole house of Israel—are those of whom the people of Jerusalem have said, 'They are far away from the LORD; this land was given to us as our possession.'

E *Eze 8:3* ◀ ▶ *Eze 11:5*
L *Eze 3:24* ◀ ▶ *Eze 11:5*

E *Eze 11:1* ◀ ▶ *Eze 11:24*
L *Eze 11:1* ◀ ▶ *Eze 13:3*
E *Eze 9:9–10* ◀ ▶ *Da 2:22*
R *Eze 9:4–5* ◀ ▶ *Eze 11:16*

t 3 Or *This is not the time to build houses.* u 15 Or *are in exile with you* (see Septuagint and Syriac) v 15 Or *those to whom the people of Jerusalem have said, 'Stay*

10:18–19 The glory of the Lord departed to the threshold of the temple (see 9:3) and then moved out of the temple to the east gate of the outer court (10:19). Some scholars believe that this was the gate Jesus used to enter the temple on Palm Sunday. Others state that this is the same site as the modern "Golden Gate" of Jerusalem that was sealed off centuries ago. Ezekiel later prophesies that the glory of the Lord will reenter the temple "through the gate facing east" (43:4). The rebuilt temple will be cleansed (see Da 8:14) and the millennial kingdom of the Messiah will be ushered in.

Promised Return of Israel

¹⁶"Therefore say: 'This is what the Sovereign LORD says: Although I sent them far away among the nations and scattered them among the countries, yet for a little while I have been a sanctuary^g for them in the countries where they have gone.'

¹⁷"Therefore say: 'This is what the Sovereign LORD says: I will gather you from the nations and bring you back from the countries where you have been scattered, and I will give you back the land of Israel again.'^h

¹⁸"They will return to it and remove all its vile images^i and detestable idols.^j ¹⁹I will give them an undivided heart^k and put a new spirit in them; I will remove from them their heart of stone^l and give them a heart of flesh.^m ²⁰Then they will follow my decrees and be careful to keep my laws.^n They will be my people,^o and I will be their God.^p ²¹But as for those whose hearts are devoted to their vile images and detestable idols,^q I will bring down on their own heads what they have done, declares the Sovereign LORD.^r"

²²Then the cherubim, with the wheels beside them, spread their wings, and the glory^s of the God of Israel was above them.^t ²³The glory^u of the LORD went up from within the city and stopped above the mountain^v east of it. ²⁴The Spirit^w lifted me up and brought me to the exiles in Babylonia^w in the vision^x given by the Spirit of God.

Then the vision I had seen went up from me, ²⁵and I told the exiles everything the LORD had shown me.^y

R Eze 11:10–12 ◀ ▶ Eze 12:15
I Eze 4:4–6 ◀ ▶ Eze 16:53
B Isa 63:11 ◀ ▶ Eze 36:26–27
P Isa 44:3–4 ◀ ▶ Eze 36:26–27
R Isa 61:1–3 ◀ ▶ Eze 36:25–27
S Isa 4:3–4 ◀ ▶ Eze 36:25–27
K Jer 50:20 ◀ ▶ Eze 12:25
S Eze 9:4–6 ◀ ▶ Eze 13:22
H Eze 9:10 ◀ ▶ Eze 13:14
E Eze 11:5 ◀ ▶ Eze 13:3
T Eze 8:3 ◀ ▶ Eze 13:3

11:16 ^g Ps 31:20; 90:1; 91:9; S Isa 4:6
11:17 ^h S Ne 1:9; S Jer 3:18; 24:5-6; S 31:16; Eze 20:41; 28:25; 34:13; 36:28
11:18 ^i S Eze 5:11 ^j Eze 37:23
11:19 ^k 2Ch 30:12; S Ps 86:11 ^l Zec 7:12; Ro 2:5 ^m Eze 18:31; S 2Co 3:3
11:20 ^n S Ps 1:2 ^o S Jer 11:4; 32:38 ^p S Ex 6:7; Eze 14:11; 34:30; 36:26-28; Hos 1:9; Zec 8:8; Heb 8:10
11:21 ^q Jer 16:18 ^r Jer 16:11; S Eze 9:10; 16:43
11:22 ^s S Ex 24:16 ^t Eze 9:3; S 10:19
11:23 ^u Eze 1:28; S 10:4 ^v Zec 14:4
11:24 ^w Eze 37:1; 43:5 ^x 2Co 12:2-4
11:25 ^y S Eze 3:4, 11
12:2 ^z Ps 78:40; S Jer 42:21 ^a S Isa 6:10; S Mt 13:15; Mk 4:12; 8:18
12:3 ^b S Jer 36:3 ^c Jer 26:3 ^d ver 11; S Eze 3:27; 2Ti 2:25-26
12:4 ^e ver 12; 2Ki 25:4; S Jer 39:4
12:5 ^f Jer 52:7; Am 4:3
12:6 ^g ver 12; S Isa 8:18; S 20:3
12:7 ^h Eze 24:18; 37:10
12:9 ^i Eze 17:12; 20:49; 24:19
12:11 ^j Isa 8:18; Zec 3:8 ^k S 2Ki 25:7; S Jer 15:2; 52:15
12:12 ^l S Jer 39:4 ^m Jer 52:7

The Exile Symbolized

12 The word of the LORD came to me: ²"Son of man, you are living among a rebellious people.^z They have eyes to see but do not see and ears to hear but do not hear, for they are a rebellious people.^a

³"Therefore, son of man, pack your belongings for exile and in the daytime, as they watch, set out and go from where you are to another place. Perhaps^b they will understand,^c though they are a rebellious house.^d ⁴During the daytime, while they watch, bring out your belongings packed for exile. Then in the evening, while they are watching, go out like those who go into exile.^e ⁵While they watch, dig through the wall^f and take your belongings out through it. ⁶Put them on your shoulder as they are watching and carry them out at dusk. Cover your face so that you cannot see the land, for I have made you a sign^g to the house of Israel."

⁷So I did as I was commanded.^h During the day I brought out my things packed for exile. Then in the evening I dug through the wall with my hands. I took my belongings out at dusk, carrying them on my shoulders while they watched.

⁸In the morning the word of the LORD came to me: ⁹"Son of man, did not that rebellious house of Israel ask you, 'What are you doing?'^i

¹⁰"Say to them, 'This is what the Sovereign LORD says: This oracle concerns the prince in Jerusalem and the whole house of Israel who are there.' ¹¹Say to them, 'I am a sign^j to you.'

"As I have done, so it will be done to them. They will go into exile as captives.^k

¹²"The prince among them will put his things on his shoulder at dusk^l and leave, and a hole will be dug in the wall for him to go through. He will cover his face so that he cannot see the land.^m ¹³I will

C Eze 3:7 ◀ ▶ Eze 22:18
J Jer 47:5 ◀ ▶ Exe 21:28–31

^w 24 Or *Chaldea*

11:17–20 Ezekiel prophesied that God would bring all of the exiles back to the promised land. God will also transform the hearts of his chosen people so that they will willingly follow him and keep his laws.

spread my net[n] for him, and he will be caught in my snare;[o] I will bring him to Babylonia, the land of the Chaldeans,[p] but he will not see[q] it, and there he will die.[r] [14]I will scatter to the winds all those around him—his staff and all his troops—and I will pursue them with drawn sword.[s]

[15]"They will know that I am the LORD, when I disperse them among the nations[t] and scatter them through the countries. [16]But I will spare a few of them from the sword, famine and plague, so that in the nations where they go they may acknowledge all their detestable practices. Then they will know that I am the LORD."[u]

[17]The word of the LORD came to me: [18]"Son of man, tremble as you eat your food,[v] and shudder in fear as you drink your water. [19]Say to the people of the land: 'This is what the Sovereign LORD says about those living in Jerusalem and in the land of Israel: They will eat their food in anxiety and drink their water in despair, for their land will be stripped of everything[w] in it because of the violence of all who live there.[x] [20]The inhabited towns will be laid waste and the land will be desolate. Then you will know that I am the LORD.'"[y]

[21]The word of the LORD came to me: [22]"Son of man, what is this proverb[z] you have in the land of Israel: 'The days go by and every vision comes to nothing'?[a] [23]Say to them, 'This is what the Sovereign LORD says: I am going to put an end to this proverb, and they will no longer quote it in Israel.' Say to them, 'The days are near[b] when every vision will be fulfilled.[c] [24]For there will be no more false visions or flattering divinations[d] among the people of Israel. [25]But I the LORD will speak what I will, and it shall be fulfilled without delay.[e] For in your days, you rebellious house, I will fulfill[f] whatever I say, declares the Sovereign LORD.[g]'"

[26]The word of the LORD came to me: [27]"Son of man, the house of Israel is say-

ing, 'The vision he sees is for many years from now, and he prophesies about the distant future.'[h] [28]"Therefore say to them, 'This is what the Sovereign LORD says: None of my words will be delayed any longer; whatever I say will be fulfilled, declares the Sovereign LORD.'"

False Prophets Condemned

13 The word of the LORD came to me: [2]"Son of man, prophesy against the prophets[i] of Israel who are now prophesying. Say to those who prophesy out of their own imagination:[j] 'Hear the word of the LORD![k] [3]This is what the Sovereign LORD says: Woe to the foolish[x] prophets[l] who follow their own spirit and have seen nothing![m] [4]Your prophets, O Israel, are like jackals among ruins. [5]You have not gone up to the breaks in the wall to repair[n] it for the house of Israel so that it will stand firm in the battle on the day of the LORD.[o] [6]Their visions are false[p] and their divinations a lie. They say, "The LORD declares," when the LORD has not sent[q] them; yet they expect their words to be fulfilled.[r] [7]Have you not seen false visions[s] and uttered lying divinations when you say, "The LORD declares," though I have not spoken?

[8]"'Therefore this is what the Sovereign LORD says: Because of your false words and lying visions, I am against you,[t] declares the Sovereign LORD. [9]My hand will be against the prophets who see false visions and utter lying[u] divinations. They will not belong to the council of my people or be listed in the records[v] of the house of Israel, nor will they enter the land of Israel. Then you will know that I am the Sovereign LORD.[w]

[10]"'Because they lead my people astray,[x] saying, "Peace,"[y] when there is no peace, and because, when a flimsy wall is built, they cover it with white-

R Eze 11:16 ◀ ▶ Eze 12:20
R Eze 12:15 ◀ ▶ Eze 17:9–10
K Eze 11:19–20 ◀ ▶ Eze 36:25–26

E Eze 11:24 ◀ ▶ Eze 37:1
L Eze 11:5 ◀ ▶ Eze 36:27
T Eze 11:24 ◀ ▶ Eze 40:1–2
G Jer 46:11 ◀ ▶ Eze 33:31

[x3] Or *wicked*

12:15, 20 The phrase "they will know that I am the LORD" occurs more than 20 times in Ezekiel to emphasize the fact that God is in control of everything, whether judgment or restoration.

wash,ᶻ ¹¹therefore tell those who cover it with whitewash that it is going to fall. Rain will come in torrents, and I will send hailstonesᵃ hurtling down,ᵇ and violent winds will burst forth.ᶜ ¹²When the wall collapses, will people not ask you, "Where is the whitewash you covered it with?"

¹³ "Therefore this is what the Sovereign LORD says: In my wrath I will unleash a violent wind, and in my anger hailstonesᵈ and torrents of rainᵉ will fall with destructive fury.ᶠ ¹⁴I will tear down the wallᵍ you have covered with whitewash and will level it to the ground so that its foundationʰ will be laid bare. When it' falls,ⁱ you will be destroyed in it; and you will know that I am the LORD. ¹⁵So I will spend my wrath against the wall and against those who covered it with whitewash. I will say to you, "The wall is gone and so are those who whitewashed it, ¹⁶those prophets of Israel who prophesied to Jerusalem and saw visions of peace for her when there was no peace, declares the Sovereign LORD.ʲ ' "

¹⁷"Now, son of man, set your faceᵏ against the daughtersˡ of your people who prophesy out of their own imagination. Prophesy against themᵐ ¹⁸and say, 'This is what the Sovereign LORD says: Woe to the women who sew magic charms on all their wrists and make veils of various lengths for their heads in order to ensnare people. Will you ensnare the lives of my people but preserve your own? ¹⁹You have profanedⁿ me among my people for a few handfuls of barley and scraps of bread.ᵒ By lying to my people, who listen to lies, you have killed those who should not have died and have spared those who should not live.ᵖ

²⁰ "Therefore this is what the Sovereign LORD says: I am against your magic charms with which you ensnare people like birds and I will tear them from your arms; I will set free the people that you ensnare like birds.ᵠ ²¹I will tear off your veils and save my people from your hands, and they will no longer fall prey to your power. Then you will know that I am the LORD.ʳ ²²Because you disheartened the righteous with your lies,ˢ when I had brought them no grief, and because you encouraged the wicked not to turn from their evil ways and so save their lives,ᵗ ²³therefore you will no longer see false visionsᵘ or practice divination.ᵛ I will saveʷ my people from your hands. And then you will know that I am the LORD.ˣ ' "

Idolaters Condemned

14 Some of the elders of Israel came to me and sat down in front of me.ʸ ²Then the word of the LORD came to me: ³"Son of man, these men have set up idols in their heartsᶻ and put wicked stumbling blocksᵃ before their faces. Should I let them inquire of me at all?ᵇ ⁴Therefore speak to them and tell them, 'This is what the Sovereign LORD says: When any Israelite sets up idols in his heart and puts a wicked stumbling block before his face and then goes to a prophet, I the LORD will answer him myself in keeping with his great idolatry. ⁵I will do this to recapture the hearts of the people of Israel, who have all desertedᶜ me for their idols.'ᵈ

⁶"Therefore say to the house of Israel, 'This is what the Sovereign LORD says: Repent!ᵉ Turn from your idols and renounce all your detestable practices!ᶠ

⁷" 'When any Israelite or any alienᵍ living in Israel separates himself from me and sets up idols in his heart and puts a wicked stumbling blockʰ before his face and then goes to a prophet to inquireⁱ of me, I the LORD will answer him myself. ⁸I will set my face againstʲ that man and make him an exampleᵏ and a byword.ˡ I will cut him off from my people. Then you will know that I am the LORD.ᵐ

⁹" 'And if the prophetⁿ is enticedᵒ to utter a prophecy, I the LORD have enticed that prophet, and I will stretch out my hand against him and destroy him from among my people Israel.ᵖ ¹⁰They will bear their guilt—the prophet will be as guilty as the one who consults him. ¹¹Then the people of Israel will no longer strayᵠ from me, nor will they defile themselves anymore with all their sins. They will be my people,ʳ and I will be their God, declares the Sovereign LORD.ˢ ' "

Judgment Inescapable

[12] The word of the LORD came to me: [13] "Son of man, if a country sins[t] against me by being unfaithful and I stretch out my hand against it to cut off its food supply[u] and send famine upon it and kill its men and their animals,[v] [14] even if these three men—Noah,[w] Daniel[z x] and Job[y]—were in it, they could save only themselves by their righteousness,[z] declares the Sovereign LORD.

[15] "Or if I send wild beasts[a] through that country and they leave it childless and it becomes desolate so that no one can pass through it because of the beasts,[b] [16] as surely as I live, declares the Sovereign LORD, even if these three men were in it, they could not save their own sons or daughters. They alone would be saved, but the land would be desolate.[c]

[17] "Or if I bring a sword[d] against that country and say, 'Let the sword pass throughout the land,' and I kill its men and their animals,[e] [18] as surely as I live, declares the Sovereign LORD, even if these three men were in it, they could not save their own sons or daughters. They alone would be saved.

D [19] "Or if I send a plague into that land and pour out my wrath[f] upon it through bloodshed,[g] killing its men and their animals,[h] [20] as surely as I live, declares the Sovereign LORD, even if Noah, Daniel and Job were in it, they could save neither son nor daughter. They would save only themselves by their righteousness.[i]

D [21] "For this is what the Sovereign LORD says: How much worse will it be when I send against Jerusalem my four dreadful judgments[j]—sword[k] and famine[l] and wild beasts and plague[m]—to kill its men and their animals![n] [22] Yet there will be some survivors[o]—sons and daughters who will be brought out of it.[p] They will come to you, and when you see their conduct[q] and their actions, you will be consoled[r] regarding the disaster I have brought upon Jerusalem—every disaster I have brought upon it. [23] You will be con-

D *Eze 7:15* ◀▶ *Eze 14:21*
D *Eze 14:19* ◀▶ *Eze 28:23*

14:13 [t] S Pr 13:21
[u] S Lev 26:26
[v] S Eze 5:16; 6:14; 15:8
14:14 [w] Ge 6:8
[x] ver 20; Eze 28:3;
Da 1:6; 6:13
[y] S Job 1:1
[z] S Ge 6:9;
S Job 42:9; Jer 15:1;
S Eze 3:19; 18:20
14:15 [a] Eze 5:17
[b] S Lev 26:22
14:16
[c] S Ge 19:29;
Eze 18:20
14:17
[d] S Lev 26:25;
S Jer 25:27; S 42:16
[e] Eze 25:13;
Zep 1:3
14:19 [f] S Eze 7:8
[g] S Isa 34:3
[h] Jer 14:12;
Eze 38:22
14:20 [i] S ver 14
14:21 [j] S Nu 33:4
[k] Isa 31:8; 34:6;
66:16; Eze 21:3,19
[l] S 2Sa 24:13
[m] S Jer 14:12; 27:8
[n] S Jer 15:3;
S Eze 5:17; 33:27;
Am 4:6-10; Rev 6:8
14:22 [o] S Jer 41:16
[p] S Eze 12:16
[q] Eze 20:43
[r] Eze 31:16; 32:31
14:23
[s] S Jer 22:8-9;
Eze 8:6-18; S 9:9
15:2 [t] Ps 80:8-16;
Isa 5:1-7; 27:2-6;
Jer 2:21; Hos 10:1;
S Jn 15:2
15:3 [u] Jer 13:10
[v] S Isa 22:23
15:4
[w] Eze 17:3-10;
19:14; Jn 15:6
15:7 [x] S Lev 26:17;
Ps 34:16; Eze 14:8
[y] S Eze 5:2
[z] S Eze 5:4
[a] Isa 24:18;
Am 9:1-4
15:8 [b] S Eze 14:13
[c] Eze 17:20; 18:24
16:2 [d] S Isa 57:12;
Eze 23:36
[e] Eze 8:17; 20:4; 22:2
16:3 [f] Ge 11:25-29;
Eze 21:30
[g] S Ge 12:18
[h] S Ge 15:16
[i] ver 45;
S Ge 10:15;
S Dt 7:1;
Jos 24:14-15
16:4 [j] Hos 2:3

---

soled when you see their conduct and their actions, for you will know that I have done nothing in it without cause, declares the Sovereign LORD.[s]"

Jerusalem, A Useless Vine

15 The word of the LORD came to me: [2] "Son of man, how is the wood of a vine[t] better than that of a branch on any of the trees in the forest? [3] Is wood ever taken from it to make anything useful?[u] Do they make pegs[v] from it to hang things on? [4] And after it is thrown on the fire as fuel and the fire burns both ends and chars the middle, is it then useful for anything?[w] [5] If it was not useful for anything when it was whole, how much less can it be made into something useful when the fire has burned it and it is charred?

[6] "Therefore this is what the Sovereign LORD says: As I have given the wood of the vine among the trees of the forest as fuel for the fire, so will I treat the people living in Jerusalem. [7] I will set my face against[x] them. Although they have come out of the fire[y z], the fire will yet consume them. And when I set my face against them, you will know that I am the LORD.[a] [8] I will make the land desolate[b] because they have been unfaithful,[c] declares the Sovereign LORD."

An Allegory of Unfaithful Jerusalem

16 The word of the LORD came to me: [2] "Son of man, confront[d] Jerusalem with her detestable practices[e] [3] and say, 'This is what the Sovereign LORD says to Jerusalem: Your ancestry[f] and birth were in the land of the Canaanites; your father[g] was an Amorite[h] and your mother a Hittite.[i] [4] On the day you were born[j] your cord was not cut, nor were you washed with water to make you clean, nor were you rubbed with salt or wrapped in cloths. [5] No one looked on you with pity or had compassion enough to do any of these things for you. Rather, you were thrown out into the open field,

[z] 14 Or *Danel*; the Hebrew spelling may suggest a person other than the prophet Daniel; also in verse 20.

14:21 Ezekiel described the wrath of God in terms of four severe judgments: sword, famine, wild beasts and plague. Compare these judgments with those listed in 5:17 and the judgments of the tribulation (see Rev 6:1–8).

for on the day you were born you were despised.

⁶ "'Then I passed by and saw you kicking about in your blood, and as you lay there in your blood I said to you, "Live!"ᵃᵏ ⁷I made you grow¹ like a plant of the field. You grew up and developed and became the most beautiful of jewels.ᵇ Your breasts were formed and your hair grew, you who were naked and bare.ᵐ

⁸ "'Later I passed by, and when I looked at you and saw that you were old enough for love, I spread the corner of my garmentⁿ over you and covered your nakedness. I gave you my solemn oath and entered into a covenantᵒ with you, declares the Sovereign LORD, and you became mine.ᵖ

⁹ "'I bathedᶜ you with water and washedᑫ the blood from you and put ointments on you. ¹⁰I clothed you with an embroideredʳ dress and put leather sandals on you. I dressed you in fine linenˢ and covered you with costly garments.ᵗ ¹¹I adorned you with jewelry:ᵘ I put braceletsᵛ on your arms and a necklaceʷ around your neck, ¹²and I put a ring on your nose,ˣ earringsʸ on your ears and a beautiful crownᶻ on your head.ᵃ ¹³So you were adorned with gold and silver; your clothesᵇ were of fine linen and costly fabric and embroidered cloth. Your food was fine flour, honey and olive oil.ᶜ You became very beautiful and rose to be a queen.ᵈ ¹⁴And your fameᵉ spread among the nations on account of your beauty,ᶠ because the splendor I had given you made your beauty perfect, declares the Sovereign LORD.ᵍ

¹⁵ "'But you trusted in your beauty and used your fame to become a prostitute. You lavished your favors on anyone who passed byʰ and your beauty became his.ᵈⁱ ¹⁶You took some of your garments to make gaudy high places,ʲ where you carried on your prostitution.ᵏ Such things should not happen, nor should they ever occur. ¹⁷You also took the fine jewelry I gave you, the jewelry made of my gold and silver, and you made for yourself male idols and engaged in prostitution with them.ˡ ¹⁸And you took your embroidered clothes to put on them, and you offered my oil and incenseᵐ before them. ¹⁹Also the food I provided for you—the fine flour, olive oil and honey I gave you to eat—you offered as fragrant incense before them. That is what happened, declares the Sovereign LORD.ⁿ

²⁰ "'And you took your sons and daughtersᵒ whom you bore to meᵖ and sacrificed them as food to the idols. Was your prostitution not enough?ᑫ ²¹You slaughtered my children and sacrificed themᵉ to the idols.ʳ ²²In all your detestable practices and your prostitution you did not remember the days of your youth,ˢ when you were naked and bare,ᵗ kicking about in your blood.ᵘ

²³ "'Woe!ᵛ Woe to you, declares the Sovereign LORD. In addition to all your other wickedness, ²⁴you built a mound for yourself and made a lofty shrineʷ in every public square.ˣ ²⁵At the head of every streetʸ you built your lofty shrines and degraded your beauty, offering your body with increasing promiscuity to anyone who passed by.ᶻ ²⁶You engaged in prostitutionᵃ with the Egyptians,ᵇ your lustful neighbors, and provokedᶜ me to anger with your increasing promiscuity.ᵈ ²⁷So I stretched out my handᵉ against you and reduced my territory; I gave you overᶠ to the greed of your enemies, the daughters of the Philistines,ᵍ who were shocked by your lewd conduct. ²⁸You engaged in prostitution with the Assyriansʰ too, because you were insatiable; and even after that, you still were not satisfied.ⁱ ²⁹Then you increased your promiscuity to include Babylonia,ᶠʲ a land of merchants, but even with this you were not satisfied.ᵏ

³⁰ "'How weak-willed you are, declares the Sovereign LORD, when you do all these things, acting like a brazen prostitute!ˡ ³¹When you built your mounds at the head of every street and made your lofty shrinesᵐ in every public square, you were unlike a prostitute, because you scorned payment.

³² "'You adulterous wife! You prefer strangers to your own husband! ³³Every prostitute receives a fee,ⁿ but you give giftsᵒ to all your lovers, bribing them to

H *Eze 13:14* ◀ ▶ *Eze 18:4*

ᵃ 6 A few Hebrew manuscripts, Septuagint and Syriac; most Hebrew manuscripts *"Live!" And as you lay there in your blood I said to you, "Live!"* ᵇ 7 Or *became mature* ᶜ 9 Or *I had bathed* ᵈ 15 Most Hebrew manuscripts; one Hebrew manuscript (see some Septuagint manuscripts) *by. Such a thing should not happen* ᵉ 21 Or *and made them pass through the fire* ᶠ 29 Or *Chaldea*

come to you from everywhere for your illicit favors. ³⁴So in your prostitution you are the opposite of others; no one runs after you for your favors. You are the very opposite, for you give payment and none is given to you.

³⁵"'Therefore, you prostitute, hear the word of the Lord! ³⁶This is what the Sovereign Lord says: Because you poured out your wealth and exposed your nakedness in your promiscuity with your lovers, and because of all your detestable idols, and because you gave them your children's blood, ³⁷therefore I am going to gather all your lovers, with whom you found pleasure, those you loved as well as those you hated. I will gather them against you from all around and will strip you in front of them, and they will see all your nakedness. ³⁸I will sentence you to the punishment of women who commit adultery and who shed blood; I will bring upon you the blood vengeance of my wrath and jealous anger. ³⁹Then I will hand you over to your lovers, and they will tear down your mounds and destroy your lofty shrines. They will strip you of your clothes and take your fine jewelry and leave you naked and bare. ⁴⁰They will bring a mob against you, who will stone you and hack you to pieces with their swords. ⁴¹They will burn down your houses and inflict punishment on you in the sight of many women. I will put a stop to your prostitution, and you will no longer pay your lovers. ⁴²Then my wrath against you will subside and my jealous anger will turn away from you; I will be calm and no longer angry.

⁴³"'Because you did not remember the days of your youth but enraged me with all these things, I will surely bring down on your head what you have done, declares the Sovereign Lord. Did you not add lewdness to all your other detestable practices?

⁴⁴"'Everyone who quotes proverbs will quote this proverb about you: "Like mother, like daughter." ⁴⁵You are a true daughter of your mother, who despised her husband and her children; and you are a true sister of your sisters, who despised their husbands and their children. Your mother was a Hittite and your father an Amorite. ⁴⁶Your older sister was Samaria, who lived to the north of you with her daughters; and your younger sister, who lived to the south of you with her daughters, was Sodom. ⁴⁷You not only walked in their ways and copied their detestable practices, but in all your ways you soon became more depraved than they. ⁴⁸As surely as I live, declares the Sovereign Lord, your sister Sodom and her daughters never did what you and your daughters have done.

⁴⁹"'Now this was the sin of your sister Sodom: She and her daughters were arrogant, overfed and unconcerned; they did not help the poor and needy. ⁵⁰They were haughty and did detestable things before me. Therefore I did away with them as you have seen. ⁵¹Samaria did not commit half the sins you did. You have done more detestable things than they, and have made your sisters seem righteous by all these things you have done. ⁵²Bear your disgrace, for you have furnished some justification for your sisters. Because your sins were more vile than theirs, they appear more righteous than you. So then, be ashamed and bear your disgrace, for you have made your sisters appear righteous.

⁵³"'However, I will restore the fortunes of Sodom and her daughters and of Samaria and her daughters, and your fortunes along with them, ⁵⁴so that you may bear your disgrace and be ashamed of all you have done in giving them comfort. ⁵⁵And your sisters, Sodom with her daughters and Samaria with her daughters, will return to what they were before; and you and your daughters will return to what you were before. ⁵⁶You would not even mention your sister Sodom in the day of your pride, ⁵⁷before your wickedness was uncovered. Even so, you are now scorned by the daugh-

---

16:53–63 The prophet declared that even though God would punish his people for their sin, God would restore the exiles to their promised land and fulfill his everlasting covenant with the descendants of Abraham.

ters of Edom[hd] and all her neighbors and the daughters of the Philistines—all those around you who despise you. [58]You will bear the consequences of your lewdness and your detestable practices, declares the Lord.[e]

[59]"'This is what the Sovereign Lord says: I will deal with you as you deserve, because you have despised my oath by breaking the covenant.[f] [60]Yet I will remember the covenant[g] I made with you in the days of your youth,[h] and I will establish an everlasting covenant[i] with you. [61]Then you will remember your ways and be ashamed[j] when you receive your sisters, both those who are older than you and those who are younger. I will give them to you as daughters,[k] but not on the basis of my covenant with you. [62]So I will establish my covenant[l] with you, and you will know that I am the Lord.[m] [63]Then, when I make atonement[n] for you for all you have done, you will remember and be ashamed[o] and never again open your mouth[p] because of your humiliation, declares the Sovereign Lord.[q]'"

Two Eagles and a Vine

17 The word of the Lord came to me: [2]"Son of man, set forth an allegory and tell the house of Israel a parable.[r] [3]Say to them, 'This is what the Sovereign Lord says: A great eagle[s] with powerful wings, long feathers and full plumage of varied colors came to Lebanon.[t] Taking hold of the top of a cedar, [4]he broke off[u] its topmost shoot and carried it away to a land of merchants, where he planted it in a city of traders.

[5]"'He took some of the seed of your land and put it in fertile soil. He planted it like a willow by abundant water,[v] [6]and it sprouted and became a low, spreading vine. Its branches[w] turned toward him, but its roots remained under it. So it became a vine and produced branches and put out leafy boughs.[x]

[7]"'But there was another great eagle with powerful wings and full plumage. The vine now sent out its roots toward

l *Eze 16:55* ◀ ▶ *Eze 17:17*

him from the plot where it was planted and stretched out its branches to him for water.[y] [8]It had been planted in good soil by abundant water so that it would produce branches,[z] bear fruit and become a splendid vine.'

[9]"Say to them, 'This is what the Sovereign Lord says: Will it thrive? Will it not be uprooted and stripped of its fruit so that it withers? All its new growth will wither. It will not take a strong arm or many people to pull it up by the roots.[a] [10]Even if it[b] is transplanted, will it thrive? Will it not wither completely when the east wind strikes it—wither away in the plot where it grew?[c]'"   R

[11]Then the word of the Lord came to me: [12]"Say to this rebellious house, 'Do you not know what these things mean?[d] Say to them: 'The king of Babylon went to Jerusalem and carried off her king and her nobles,[e] bringing them back with him to Babylon.[f] [13]Then he took a member of the royal family and made a treaty[g] with him, putting him under oath.[h] He also carried away the leading men[i] of the land, [14]so that the kingdom would be brought low,[j] unable to rise again, surviving only by keeping his treaty. [15]But the king rebelled[k] against him by sending his envoys to Egypt[l] to get horses and a large army.[m] Will he succeed? Will he who does such things escape? Will he break the treaty and yet escape?[n]

[16]"'As surely as I live, declares the Sovereign Lord, he shall die[o] in Babylon, in the land of the king who put him on the throne, whose oath he despised and whose treaty he broke.[p] [17]Pharaoh[q] with   I his mighty army and great horde will be of no help to him in war, when ramps[r] are built and siege works erected to destroy many lives.[s] [18]He despised the oath by breaking the covenant. Because he had given his hand in pledge[t] and yet did all these things, he shall not escape.

[19]"'Therefore this is what the Sovereign Lord says: As surely as I live, I will

R *Eze 12:20* ◀ ▶ *Eze 21:3*
I *Eze 16:60–63* ◀ ▶ *Eze 17:22–24*

[h 57] Many Hebrew manuscripts and Syriac; most Hebrew manuscripts, Septuagint and Vulgate *Aram*

17:10 In this verse, Ezekiel likened Nebuchadnezzar and his Babylonian army to the hot, dry winds from the east that withered all vegetation.

bring down on his head my oath that he despised and my covenant that he broke.ᵘ ²⁰I will spread my netᵛ for him, and he will be caught in my snare. I will bring him to Babylon and execute judgment ʷ upon him there because he was unfaithfulˣ to me. ²¹All his fleeing troops will fall by the sword,ʸ and the survivorsᶻ will be scattered to the winds.ᵃ Then you will know that I the LORD have spoken.ᵇ

²²"'This is what the Sovereign LORD says: I myself will take a shootᶜ from the very top of a cedar and plant it; I will break off a tender sprig from its topmost shoots and plant it on a high and lofty mountain.ᵈ ²³On the mountain heightsᵉ of Israel I will plant it; it will produce branches and bear fruitᶠ and become a splendid cedar. Birds of every kind will nest in it; they will find shelter in the shade of its branches.ᵍ ²⁴All the trees of the fieldʰ will know that I the LORD bring downⁱ the tall tree and make the low tree grow tall. I dry up the green tree and make the dry tree flourish.ʲ

"'I the LORD have spoken, and I will do it.'ᵏ"

The Soul Who Sins Will Die

18 The word of the LORD came to me: ²"What do you people mean by quoting this proverb about the land of Israel:

" 'The fathers eat sour grapes,
and the children's teeth are set on edge'?¹

³"As surely as I live, declares the Sovereign LORD, you will no longer quote this proverbᵐ in Israel. ⁴For every living soul belongs to me, the father as well as the son—both alike belong to me. The soul who sinsⁿ is the one who will die.º

⁵"Suppose there is a righteous man who does what is just and right. ⁶He does not eat at the mountainᵖ shrines

l Eze 17:17 ◀ ▶ Eze 20:34–38
H Eze 16:23 ◀ ▶ Eze 18:20
S Eze 14:6–8 ◀ ▶ Eze 18:20–27

17:19 ᵘJer 7:9; S Eze 16:59; 21:23; Hos 10:4
17:20 ᵛS Eze 12:13; 32:3 ʷS Jer 2:35 ˣS Eze 15:8
17:21 ʸS Eze 12:14 ᶻ2Ki 25:11 ᵃS Lev 26:33; S 2Ki 25:5; Zec 2:6 ᵇS Jer 27:8
17:22 ᶜS 2Ki 19:30; S Isa 4:2 ᵈver 23; Isa 2:2; S Jer 23:5; Eze 20:40; 36:1,36; 37:22; 40:2; 43:12
17:23 ᵉS ver 22; ᶠS Jer 31:12 ᶠS Isa 27:6 ᵍPs 92:12; S Isa 2:2; Eze 31:6; Da 4:12; Hos 14:5-7; S Mt 13:32
17:24 ʰS Ps 96:12; Isa 2:13 ⁱS Ps 52:5 ʲS Nu 17:8; Da 5:21 ᵏS 1Sa 2:7-8; Eze 19:12; 21:26; 22:14; 37:13; Am 9:11
18:2 ˡS Job 21:19; Isa 3:15; Jer 31:29
18:3 ᵐS Ps 49:4
18:4 ⁿS 2Ki 14:6; S Pr 13:21 º ver 20; S Ge 18:23; S Ex 17:14; S Job 21:20; Isa 42:5; Eze 33:8; S Ro 6:23
18:6 ᵖS Eze 6:2 ᵠDt 4:19; S Eze 6:13; 20:24; Am 5:26 ʳS Lev 12:2; S 15:24
18:7 ˢS Ex 22:21; Mal 3:5; Jas 5:4 ᵗS Ex 22:26 ᵘS Ex 20:15 ᵛS Job 22:7 ʷDt 15:11; S Eze 16:49; S Mt 25:36; Lk 3:11
18:8 ˣS Ex 18:21; 22:25; S Lev 25:35-37; Dt 23:19-20 ʸS Jer 22:3; Zec 8:16
18:9 ᶻS Lev 19:37 ᵃHab 2:4 ᵇS Lev 18:5; S Eze 11:12; 20:11; Am 5:4
18:10 ᶜEx 21:12; Eze 22:6
18:11 ᵈEze 22:9
18:12 ᵉS Ex 22:22; S Job 24:9; Am 4:1 ᶠS Ex 22:27 ᵍ2Ki 21:11; Isa 59:6-7;

or look to the idolsᵠ of the house of Israel.
He does not defile his neighbor's wife
or lie with a woman during her period.ʳ
⁷He does not oppressˢ anyone,
but returns what he took in pledgeᵗ
for a loan.
He does not commit robberyᵘ
but gives his food to the hungryᵛ
and provides clothing for the
naked.ʷ
⁸He does not lend at usury
or take excessive interest.ⁱˣ
He withholds his hand from doing
wrong
and judges fairlyʸ between man and
man.
⁹He follows my decreesᶻ
and faithfully keeps my laws.
That man is righteous;ᵃ
he will surely live,ᵇ
declares the Sovereign LORD.

¹⁰"Suppose he has a violent son, who sheds bloodᶜ or does any of these other things/ ¹¹(though the father has done none of them):

"He eats at the mountain shrines.ᵈ
He defiles his neighbor's wife.
¹²He oppresses the poorᵉ and needy.
He commits robbery.
He does not return what he took in pledge.ᶠ
He looks to the idols.
He does detestable things.ᵍ
¹³He lends at usury and takes excessive interest.ʰ

Will such a man live? He will not! Because he has done all these detestable things, he will surely be put to death and his blood will be on his own head.ⁱ

¹⁴"But suppose this son has a son who sees all the sins his father commits, and though he sees them, he does not do such things:ʲ

S Jer 22:17; S Eze 16:49; Hab 2:6 **18:13** ʰEx 22:25 ⁱS Lev 20:9; Eze 33:4-5; Hos 12:14 **18:14** ʲ2Ch 34:21; S Pr 23:24

/⁸ Or *take interest*; similarly in verses 13 and 17 /¹⁰ Or *things to a brother*

17:22–24 Though this Messianic promise used the same imagery of a branch, this prophecy used it in an unexpected way to describe the Messiah's rule in Jerusalem. Compare this prophecy with Isa 11:1; Jer 23:5; Zec 3:8; 6:12.

15"He does not eat at the mountain shrines
or look to the idols of the house of Israel.
He does not defile his neighbor's wife.
16He does not oppress anyone
or require a pledge for a loan.
He does not commit robbery
but gives his food to the hungry
and provides clothing for the naked.
17He withholds his hand from sin
and takes no usury or excessive interest.
He keeps my laws and follows my decrees.

He will not die for his father's sin; he will surely live. 18But his father will die for his own sin, because he practiced extortion, robbed his brother and did what was wrong among his people.

19"Yet you ask, 'Why does the son not share the guilt of his father?' Since the son has done what is just and right and has been careful to keep all my decrees, he will surely live. 20The soul who sins is the one who will die. The son will not share the guilt of the father, nor will the father share the guilt of the son. The righteousness of the righteous man will be credited to him, and the wickedness of the wicked will be charged against him.

21"But if a wicked man turns away from all the sins he has committed and keeps all my decrees and does what is just and right, he will surely live; he will not die. 22None of the offenses he has committed will be remembered against him. Because of the righteous things he has done, he will live. 23Do I take any pleasure in the death of the wicked? declares the Sovereign LORD. Rather, am I not pleased when they turn from their ways and live?

24"But if a righteous man turns from his righteousness and commits sin and does the same detestable things the wicked man does, will he live? None of the righteous things he has done will be remembered. Because of the unfaithfulness he is guilty of and because of the sins he has committed, he will die.

25"Yet you say, 'The way of the Lord is not just.' Hear, O house of Israel: Is my way unjust? Is it not your ways that are unjust? 26If a righteous man turns from his righteousness and commits sin, he will die for it; because of the sin he has committed he will die. 27But if a wicked man turns away from the wickedness he has committed and does what is just and right, he will save his life. 28Because he considers all the offenses he has committed and turns away from them, he will surely live; he will not die. 29Yet the house of Israel says, 'The way of the Lord is not just.' Are my ways unjust, O house of Israel? Is it not your ways that are unjust?

30"Therefore, O house of Israel, I will judge you, each one according to his ways, declares the Sovereign LORD. Repent! Turn away from all your offenses; then sin will not be your downfall. 31Rid yourselves of all the offenses you have committed, and get a new heart and a new spirit. Why will you die, O house of Israel? 32For I take no pleasure in the death of anyone, declares the Sovereign LORD. Repent and live!

A Lament for Israel's Princes

19 "Take up a lament concerning the princes of Israel 2and say:

" 'What a lioness was your mother among the lions!
She lay down among the young lions and reared her cubs.
3She brought up one of her cubs,
and he became a strong lion.
He learned to tear the prey
and he devoured men.
4The nations heard about him,
and he was trapped in their pit.
They led him with hooks
to the land of Egypt.

5" 'When she saw her hope unfulfilled,

her expectation gone,
she took another of her cubs[t]
and made him a strong lion.[u]
⁶He prowled among the lions,
for he was now a strong lion.
He learned to tear the prey
and he devoured men.[v]
⁷He broke down[f] their strongholds
and devastated[w] their towns.
The land and all who were in it
were terrified by his roaring.
⁸Then the nations[x] came against him,
those from regions round about.
They spread their net[y] for him,
and he was trapped in their pit.[z]
⁹With hooks[a] they pulled him into a cage
and brought him to the king of Babylon.[b]
They put him in prison,
so his roar[c] was heard no longer
on the mountains of Israel.[d]

¹⁰" 'Your mother was like a vine in your vineyard[me]
planted by the water;[f]
it was fruitful and full of branches
because of abundant water.[g]
¹¹Its branches were strong,
fit for a ruler's scepter.
It towered high
above the thick foliage,
conspicuous for its height
and for its many branches.[h]
¹²But it was uprooted[i] in fury
and thrown to the ground.
The east wind[j] made it shrivel,
it was stripped of its fruit;
its strong branches withered
and fire consumed them.[k]
¹³Now it is planted in the desert,[l]
in a dry and thirsty land.[m]
¹⁴Fire spread from one of its main[n] branches
and consumed[n] its fruit.
No strong branch is left on it
fit for a ruler's scepter.' "[o]

This is a lament[p] and is to be used as a lament."

Rebellious Israel

20 In the seventh year, in the fifth month on the tenth day, some of the elders of Israel came to inquire[q] of the LORD, and they sat down in front of me.[r]

²Then the word of the LORD came to me: ³"Son of man, speak to the elders[s] of Israel and say to them, 'This is what the Sovereign LORD says: Have you come to inquire[t] of me? As surely as I live, I will not let you inquire of me, declares the Sovereign LORD.'[u]

⁴"Will you judge them? Will you judge them, son of man? Then confront them with the detestable practices of their fathers[v] ⁵and say to them: 'This is what the Sovereign LORD says: On the day I chose[w] Israel, I swore with uplifted hand[x] to the descendants of the house of Jacob and revealed myself to them in Egypt. With uplifted hand I said to them, "I am the LORD your God.[y]" ⁶On that day I swore[z] to them that I would bring them out of Egypt into a land I had searched out for them, a land flowing with milk and honey,[a] the most beautiful of all lands.[b] ⁷And I said to them, "Each of you, get rid of the vile images[c] you have set your eyes on, and do not defile yourselves with the idols[d] of Egypt. I am the LORD your God."[e]

⁸" 'But they rebelled against me and would not listen to me;[f] they did not get rid of the vile images they had set their eyes on, nor did they forsake the idols of Egypt.[g] So I said I would pour out my wrath on them and spend my anger against them in Egypt.[h] ⁹But for the sake of my name I did what would keep it from being profaned[i] in the eyes of the nations they lived among and in whose sight I had revealed myself to the Israelites by bringing them out of Egypt.[j] ¹⁰Therefore I led them out of Egypt and brought them into the desert.[k] ¹¹I gave them my decrees and made known to them my laws, for the man who obeys them will live by them.[l] ¹²Also I gave them my Sabbaths[m] as a sign[n] between us,[o] so they would know that I the LORD made them holy.[p]

¹³" 'Yet the people of Israel rebelled[q] against me in the desert. They did not follow my decrees but rejected my laws[r]—although the man who obeys them will live by them—and they utterly desecrated my Sabbaths.[s] So I said I would pour out my wrath[t] on them and destroy[u] them in the desert.[v] ¹⁴But for the sake of my name I did what would keep it from being profaned[w] in the eyes

l 7 Targum (see Septuagint); Hebrew He knew m 10 Two Hebrew manuscripts; most Hebrew manuscripts your blood n 14 Or from under its

of the nations in whose sight I had brought them out.ˣ ¹⁵Also with uplifted hand I sworeʸ to them in the desert that I would not bring them into the land I had given them—a land flowing with milk and honey, most beautiful of all lands— ¹⁶because they rejected my lawsᵃ and did not follow my decrees and desecrated my Sabbaths. For their heartsᵇ were devoted to their idols.ᶜ ¹⁷Yet I looked on them with pityᵈ and did not destroy them or put an end to them in the desert. ¹⁸I said to their children in the desert, "Do not follow the statutesᵉ of your fathersᵉ or keep their laws or defile yourselvesᶠ with their idols. ¹⁹I am the LORD your God;ᵍ follow my decrees and be careful to keep my laws.ʰ ²⁰Keep my Sabbathsⁱ holy, that they may be a signʲ between us. Then you will know that I am the LORD your God."ᵏ

²¹ "'But the children rebelled against me: They did not follow my decrees, they were not careful to keep my lawsˡ—although the man who obeys them will live by them—and they desecrated my Sabbaths. So I said I would pour out my wrath on them and spend my angerᵐ against them in the desert.ⁿ ²²But I withheldᵒ my hand, and for the sake of my nameᵖ I did what would keep it from being profaned in the eyes of the nations in whose sight I had brought them out. ²³Also with uplifted hand I swore to them in the desert that I would disperse them among the nations and scatterᵠ them through the countries, ²⁴because they had not obeyed my laws but had rejected my decreesʳ and desecrated my Sabbaths,ˢ and their eyes lusted after their fathers' idols.ᵘ ²⁵I also gave them overᵛ to statutes that were not good and laws they could not live by;ʷ ²⁶I let them become defiled through their gifts—the sacrificeˣ of every firstborn⁰—that I might fill them with horror so they would know that I am the LORD.ʸ

²⁷"Therefore, son of man, speak to the people of Israel and say to them, 'This is what the Sovereign LORD says: In this also your fathersᶻ blasphemedᵃ me by forsaking me:ᵇ ²⁸When I brought them into the landᶜ I had sworn to give them and they saw any high hill or any leafy tree, there they offered their sacrifices, made offerings that provoked me to anger, presented their fragrant incense and poured out their drink offerings.ᵈ ²⁹Then I said to them: What is this high placeᵉ you go to?'" (It is called Bamahᵖ to this day.)

Judgment and Restoration

³⁰"Therefore say to the house of Israel: 'This is what the Sovereign LORD says: Will you defile yourselvesᶠ the way your fathers did and lust after their vile images?ᵍ ³¹When you offer your gifts—the sacrifice of your sonsʰ inᵠ the fire—you continue to defile yourselves with all your idols to this day. Am I to let you inquire of me, O house of Israel? As surely as I live, declares the Sovereign LORD, I will not let you inquire of me.ⁱ

³²'You say, "We want to be like the nations, like the peoples of the world, who serve wood and stone." But what you have in mind will never happen. ³³As surely as I live, declares the Sovereign LORD, I will rule over you with a mighty hand and an outstretched armʲ and with outpoured wrath.ᵏ ³⁴I will bring you from the nationsˡ and gatherᵐ you from the countries where you have been scattered—with a mighty handⁿ and an outstretched arm and with outpoured wrath.ᵒ ³⁵I will bring you into the desertᵖ of the nations and there, face to face, I will execute judgmentᵠ upon you. ³⁶As I judged your fathers in the desert of the land of Egypt, so I will judge you, declares the Sovereign LORD.ʳ ³⁷I will take note of you as you pass under my rod,ˢ and I will bring you into the bond of the covenant.ᵗ ³⁸I will purgeᵘ you of those who revolt

▎ *Eze 17:22–24* ◀ ▶ *Eze 20:40–42*

20:34–38 The prophet announced that the exile would seem to the Israelites like a return to their ancestors' time in the desert (see Hos 2:14). Yet God promised to restore his people to their promised land after the completion of their exile. Note also that this passage foreshadows the coming judgment of the Jews in the tribulation period. Only those who follow the Messiah willingly will be allowed to live in his millennial kingdom.

and rebel against me. Although I will bring them out of the land where they are living, yet they will not enter the land of Israel. Then you will know that I am the LORD.'

39 " 'As for you, O house of Israel, this is what the Sovereign LORD says: Go and serve your idols,^w every one of you! But afterward you will surely listen to me and no longer profane my holy name^x with your gifts and idols.^y 40 For on my holy mountain, the high mountain of Israel,^z declares the Sovereign LORD, there in the land the entire house of Israel will serve me, and there I will accept them. There I will require your offerings^a and your choice gifts,^r along with all your holy sacrifices.^b 41 I will accept you as fragrant incense^c when I bring you out from the nations and gather^d you from the countries where you have been scattered, and I will show myself holy^e among you in the sight of the nations.^f 42 Then you will know that I am the LORD,^g when I bring you into the land of Israel,^h the land I had sworn with uplifted hand to give to your fathers.^i 43 There you will remember your conduct^j and all the actions by which you have defiled yourselves, and you will loathe yourselves^k for all the evil you have done.^l 44 You will know that I am the LORD, when I deal with you for my name's sake^m and not according to your evil ways and your corrupt practices, O house of Israel, declares the Sovereign LORD.^n ' "

Prophecy Against the South

45 The word of the LORD came to me: 46 "Son of man, set your face toward^o the south; preach against the south and prophesy against^p the forest of the southland.^q 47 Say to the southern forest:^r 'Hear the word of the LORD. This is what the Sovereign LORD says: I am about to set fire to you, and it will consume^s all your trees, both green and dry. The blazing flame will not be quenched, and every face from south to north^t will be scorched by it.^u 48 Everyone will see that I

| Eze 20:34–38 ◀ ▶ Eze 28:25–26

20:38 ^v Ps 95:11; Jer 44:14; S Eze 13:9; 23:49; Hos 2:14; Zec 13:8-9; Mal 3:3; 4:1-3; Heb 4:3
20:39 ^w S Jer 44:25 ^x S Ex 20:7; S Eze 13:19 ^y Eze 43:7; Am 4:4
20:40 ^z S Eze 17:22; 34:14 ^a S Isa 60:7 ^b S Isa 56:7; Mal 3:4
20:41 ^c S 2Co 2:14 ^d S Dt 30:4 ^e Eze 28:25; 36:23 ^f S Isa 5:16; S Eze 11:17; 2Co 6:17
20:42 ^g Eze 38:23 ^h S Jer 23:8; Eze 34:13; 36:24 ^i Jer 30:3; Eze 34:27; 37:21
20:43 ^j Eze 14:22 ^k Lev 26:41 ^l S Eze 6:9; S 16:61; Hos 5:15
20:44 ^m Ps 109:21; Isa 43:25; Eze 36:22 ^n S Eze 16:62; 36:32
20:46 ^o S Eze 4:3; S 13:17 ^p Eze 21:2; Am 7:16 ^q Isa 30:6; Jer 13:19
20:47 ^r S 2Ki 19:23 ^s Eze 19:14 ^t Eze 21:4 ^u Isa 9:18-19; S 13:8
20:48 ^v S Jer 7:20; Eze 21:5,32; 23:25
20:49 ^w S Eze 4:14 ^x S Jdg 14:12; S Ps 78:2; S Eze 12:9; Mt 13:13; S Jn 16:25
21:1 ^y S Eze 20:1
21:2 ^z S Eze 13:17 ^a Eze 9:6 ^b Jer 26:11-12; S Eze 20:46
21:3 ^c S Jer 21:13 ^d S Isa 27:1; S Eze 14:21 ^e ver 9-11; S Job 9:22; S Isa 57:1; Jer 47:6-7
21:4 ^f S Lev 26:25; S Jer 25:27 ^g Eze 20:47
21:5 ^h S Isa 34:5 ^i ver 30 ^j S Eze 20:47-48; Na 1:9
21:6 ^k ver 12; S Isa 22:4; Jer 30:6; S Eze 9:4
21:7 ^l S Job 23:2

the LORD have kindled it; it will not be quenched.^v ' "

49 Then I said, "Ah, Sovereign LORD!^w They are saying of me, 'Isn't he just telling parables?^x ' "

Babylon, God's Sword of Judgment

21 The word of the LORD came to me:^y 2 "Son of man, set your face against^z Jerusalem and preach against the sanctuary.^a Prophesy against^b the land of Israel 3 and say to her: 'This is what the LORD says: I am against you.^c I will draw my sword^d from its scabbard and cut off from you both the righteous and the wicked.^e 4 Because I am going to cut off the righteous and the wicked, my sword^f will be unsheathed against everyone from south to north.^g 5 Then all people will know that I the LORD have drawn my sword^h from its scabbard; it will not return^i again.'^j

6 "Therefore groan, son of man! Groan before them with broken heart and bitter grief.^k 7 And when they ask you, 'Why are you groaning?^l' you shall say, 'Because of the news that is coming. Every heart will melt^m and every hand go limp;^n every spirit will become faint^o and every knee become as weak as water.'^p It is coming! It will surely take place, declares the Sovereign LORD."

8 The word of the LORD came to me: 9 "Son of man, prophesy and say, 'This is what the Lord says:

" 'A sword, a sword,
   sharpened and polished—
10 sharpened for the slaughter,^q
   polished to flash like lightning!

" 'Shall we rejoice in the scepter of my son ⌊Judah⌋? The sword despises every such stick.^r

11 " 'The sword is appointed to be
   polished,^s

R Eze 17:9–10 ◀ ▶ Eze 21:18–23

^m Jos 7:5 ^n S Jer 47:3; Eze 22:14 ^o S Ps 6:2 ^p S Lev 26:36; S Job 11:16
21:10 ^q Ps 110:5-6; Isa 34:5-6 ^r Dt 32:41 21:11 ^s Jer 46:4

^40 Or *and the gifts of your firstfruits*

20:40–42 Ezekiel prophesied that in the Millennium the returned Jews would willingly serve God and enjoy God's blessings in the promised land.
21:3 This is the first of five oracles that involved the sword of the Lord's judgment (see 21:8–17, 18–24, 25–27, 28–32). God's judgment would come and no one, not even the righteous, would be able to escape.

to be grasped with the hand;
it is sharpened and polished,
made ready for the hand of the slayer.
¹²Cry out and wail, son of man,
for it is against my people;
it is against all the princes of Israel.
They are thrown to the sword
along with my people.
Therefore beat your breast.ᵗ

¹³" 'Testing will surely come. And what if the scepter ⌊of Judah⌋, which the sword despises, does not continue? declares the Sovereign LORD.'

¹⁴"So then, son of man, prophesy
and strike your handsᵘ together.
Let the sword strike twice,
even three times.
It is a sword for slaughter—
a sword for great slaughter,
closing in on them from every side.ᵛ
¹⁵So that hearts may meltʷ
and the fallen be many,
I have stationed the sword for slaughterˢ
at all their gates.
Oh! It is made to flash like lightning,
it is grasped for slaughter.ˣ
¹⁶O sword, slash to the right,
then to the left,
wherever your blade is turned.
¹⁷I too will strike my handsʸ together,
and my wrathᶻ will subside.
I the LORD have spoken.ᵃ"

R ¹⁸The word of the LORD came to me: ¹⁹"Son of man, mark out two roads for the swordᵇ of the king of Babylon to take, both starting from the same country. Make a signpostᶜ where the road branches off to the city. ²⁰Mark out one road for the sword to come against Rabbah of the Ammonitesᵈ and another against Judah and fortified Jerusalem. ²¹For the king of Babylon will stop at the fork in the road, at the junction of the two roads, to seek an omen: He will cast lotsᵉ with arrows, he will consult his idols,ᶠ he will examine the liver.ᵍ ²²Into

R Eze 21:3 ◀ ▶ Eze 21:26–27

21:12 ᵗJer 31:19
21:14 ᵘver 17; S Nu 24:10 ᵛS Eze 6:11; 30:24
21:15 ʷS 2Sa 17:10 ˣPs 22:14
21:17 ʸver 14; Eze 22:13 ᶻS Eze 5:13 ᵃS Eze 6:11; S 16:42
21:19 ᵇS Eze 14:21; 32:11 ᶜJer 31:21
21:20 ᵈS Dt 3:11
21:21 ᵉS Pr 16:33 ᶠZec 10:2 ᵍNu 22:7; S 23:23
21:22 ʰS Jer 4:16 ⁱJer 32:24 ʲS 2Ki 25:1; S Eze 4:2; 26:9
21:23 ᵏS Nu 5:15 ˡS Eze 17:19
21:25 ᵐEze 22:4 ⁿEze 35:5
21:26 ᵒS Isa 28:5; S Jer 13:18 ᵖS Ps 75:7; Isa 40:4; S Eze 17:24; S Mt 23:12
21:27 ᵠGe 49:10 ʳPs 2:6; Jer 23:5-6; Eze 37:24; Hag 2:21-22
21:28 ˢS Ge 19:38; Zep 2:8 ᵗS Jer 12:12
21:29 ᵘJer 27:9 ᵛver 25; Eze 22:28; 35:5
21:30 ʷver 5; Jer 47:6 ˣS Eze 16:3

his right hand will come the lot for Jerusalem, where he is to set up battering rams, to give the command to slaughter, to sound the battle cry,ʰ to set battering rams against the gates, to build a rampⁱ and to erect siege works.ʲ ²³It will seem like a false omen to those who have sworn allegiance to him, but he will remindᵏ them of their guiltˡ and take them captive.

²⁴"Therefore this is what the Sovereign LORD says: 'Because you people have brought to mind your guilt by your open rebellion, revealing your sins in all that you do—because you have done this, you will be taken captive.

²⁵" 'O profane and wicked prince of Israel, whose day has come,ᵐ whose time of punishment has reached its climax,ⁿ ²⁶this is what the Sovereign LORD says: **M** Take off the turban, remove the crown.ᵒ **R** It will not be as it was: The lowly will be exalted and the exalted will be brought low.ᵖ ²⁷A ruin! A ruin! I will make it a ruin! It will not be restored until he comes to whom it rightfully belongs;ᵠ to him I will give it.'ʳ

²⁸"And you, son of man, prophesy and **J** say, 'This is what the Sovereign LORD says about the Ammonitesˢ and their insults:

" 'A sword,ᵗ a sword,
drawn for the slaughter,
polished to consume
and to flash like lightning!
²⁹Despite false visions concerning you
and lying divinationsᵘ about you,
it will be laid on the necks
of the wicked who are to be slain,
whose day has come,
whose time of punishment has reached its climax.ᵛ
³⁰Return the sword to its scabbard.ʷ
In the place where you were created,
in the land of your ancestry,ˣ

M Jer 33:15 ◀ ▶ Eze 34:23–29
R Eze 21:18–23 ◀ ▶ Eze 22:4
J Eze 12:13 ◀ ▶ Eze 24:21

ˢ 15 Septuagint; the meaning of the Hebrew for this word is uncertain.

21:26–27 Ezekiel declared that because of Israel's continued wickedness, no Israelite king would rule until the coming of the rightful king, the Messiah, in the last days. As a sidelight, the coronation of former British monarchs has limited the length of the monarch's reign with Ezekiel's words: "until he come whose right it is" (21:27 KJV).

I will judge you.
³¹I will pour out my wrath upon you
and breathe out my fiery anger
against you;
I will hand you over to brutal men,
men skilled in destruction.
³²You will be fuel for the fire,
your blood will be shed in your land,
you will be remembered no more;
for I the LORD have spoken.' "

Jerusalem's Sins

22 The word of the LORD came to me: ²"Son of man, will you judge her? Will you judge this city of bloodshed? Then confront her with all her detestable practices ³and say: 'This is what the Sovereign LORD says: O city that brings on herself doom by shedding blood in her midst and defiles herself by making idols, ⁴you have become guilty because of the blood you have shed and have become defiled by the idols you have made. You have brought your days to a close, and the end of your years has come. Therefore I will make you an object of scorn to the nations and a laughingstock to all the countries. ⁵Those who are near and those who are far away will mock you, O infamous city, full of turmoil.

⁶" 'See how each of the princes of Israel who are in you uses his power to shed blood. ⁷In you they have treated father and mother with contempt; in you they have oppressed the alien and mistreated the fatherless and the widow. ⁸You have despised my holy things and desecrated my Sabbaths. ⁹In you are slanderous men bent on shedding blood; in you are those who eat at the mountain shrines and commit lewd acts. ¹⁰In you are those who dishonor their fathers' bed; in you are those who violate women during their period, when they are ceremonially unclean. ¹¹In you one man commits a detestable offense with his neighbor's wife, an-

R Eze 21:26–27 ◀ ▶ Eze 22:15

other shamefully defiles his daughter-in-law, and another violates his sister, his own father's daughter. ¹²In you men accept bribes to shed blood; you take usury and excessive interest and make unjust gain from your neighbors by extortion. And you have forgotten me, declares the Sovereign LORD.

¹³" 'I will surely strike my hands together at the unjust gain you have made and at the blood you have shed in your midst. ¹⁴Will your courage endure or your hands be strong in the day I deal with you? I the LORD have spoken, and I will do it. ¹⁵I will disperse you among the nations and scatter you through the countries; and I will put an end to your uncleanness. ¹⁶When you have been defiled in the eyes of the nations, you will know that I am the LORD.' "

¹⁷Then the word of the LORD came to me: ¹⁸"Son of man, the house of Israel has become dross to me; all of them are the copper, tin, iron and lead left inside a furnace. They are but the dross of silver. ¹⁹Therefore this is what the Sovereign LORD says: 'Because you have all become dross, I will gather you into Jerusalem. ²⁰As men gather silver, copper, iron, lead and tin into a furnace to melt it with a fiery blast, so will I gather you in my anger and my wrath and put you inside the city and melt you. ²¹I will gather you and I will blow on you with my fiery wrath, and you will be melted inside her. ²²As silver is melted in a furnace, so you will be melted inside her, and you will know that I the LORD have poured out my wrath upon you.' "

²³Again the word of the LORD came to me: ²⁴"Son of man, say to the land, 'You

R Eze 22:4 ◀ ▶ Eze 23:32–33
C Eze 12:2 ◀ ▶ Da 9:5
H Eze 18:30 ◀ ▶ Eze 25:17

22:4 God detailed the grave sins that forced him to judge his people.
22:15 God's divine purpose for the exile of his people was to purge them from their idolatry and pagan religious practices. Though the Jews may have resisted the worship of stone statues and pagan rituals since their return from exile, they still face the temptations of idolatry manifested in materialism, power, status and position—the same idols that threaten to topple the faith of NT believers (see Mt 6:24 ; Col 3:1–2).

are a land that has had no rain or showers in the day of wrath.' 25There is a conspiracy of her princes within her like a roaring lion tearing its prey; they devour people, take treasures and precious things and make many widows within her. 26Her priests do violence to my law and profane my holy things; they do not distinguish between the holy and the common; they teach that there is no difference between the unclean and the clean; and they shut their eyes to the keeping of my Sabbaths, so that I am profaned among them. 27Her officials within her are like wolves tearing their prey; they shed blood and kill people to make unjust gain. 28Her prophets whitewash these deeds for them by false visions and lying divinations. They say, 'This is what the Sovereign LORD says'— when the LORD has not spoken. 29The people of the land practice extortion and commit robbery; they oppress the poor and needy and mistreat the alien, denying them justice.

30"I looked for a man among them who would build up the wall and stand before me in the gap on behalf of the land so I would not have to destroy it, but I found none. 31So I will pour out my wrath on them and consume them with my fiery anger, bringing down on their own heads all they have done, declares the Sovereign LORD."

Two Adulterous Sisters

23 The word of the LORD came to me: 2"Son of man, there were two women, daughters of the same mother. 3They became prostitutes in Egypt, engaging in prostitution from their youth. In that land their breasts were fondled and their virgin bosoms caressed. 4The older was named Oholah, and her sister was Oholibah. They were mine and gave birth to sons and daughters. Oholah is Samaria, and Oholibah is Jerusalem.

5"Oholah engaged in prostitution while she was still mine; and she lusted after her lovers, the Assyrians—warriors 6clothed in blue, governors and commanders, all of them handsome young men, and mounted horsemen. 7She gave herself as a prostitute to all the elite of the Assyrians and defiled herself with all the idols of everyone she lusted after.

8She did not give up the prostitution she began in Egypt, when during her youth men slept with her, caressed her virgin bosom and poured out their lust upon her.

9"Therefore I handed her over to her lovers, the Assyrians, for whom she lusted. 10They stripped her naked, took away her sons and daughters and killed her with the sword. She became a byword among women, and punishment was inflicted on her.

11"Her sister Oholibah saw this, yet in her lust and prostitution she was more depraved than her sister. 12She too lusted after the Assyrians—governors and commanders, warriors in full dress, mounted horsemen, all handsome young men. 13I saw that she too defiled herself; both of them went the same way.

14"But she carried her prostitution still further. She saw men portrayed on a wall, figures of Chaldeans portrayed in red, 15with belts around their waists and flowing turbans on their heads; all of them looked like Babylonian chariot officers, natives of Chaldea. 16As soon as she saw them, she lusted after them and sent messengers to them in Chaldea. 17Then the Babylonians came to her, to the bed of love, and in their lust they defiled her. After she had been defiled by them, she turned away from them in disgust. 18When she carried on her prostitution openly and exposed her nakedness, I turned away from her in disgust, just as I had turned away from her sister. 19Yet she became more and more promiscuous as she recalled the days of her youth, when she was a prostitute in Egypt. 20There she lusted after her lovers, whose genitals were like those of donkeys and whose emission was like that of horses. 21So you longed for the lewdness of your youth, when in Egypt your bosom was caressed and your young breasts fondled.

22"Therefore, Oholibah, this is what the Sovereign LORD says: I will stir up your lovers against you, those you turned away from in disgust, and I will bring them against you from every

---

v 24 Septuagint; Hebrew has not been cleansed or rained on
w 25 Septuagint; Hebrew prophets   x 14 Or Babylonians
y 15 Or Babylonia; also in verse 16   z 21 Syriac (see also verse 3); Hebrew caressed because of your young breasts

side— ²³the Babylonians and all the Chaldeans, the men of Pekod and Shoa and Koa, and all the Assyrians with them, handsome young men, all of them governors and commanders, chariot officers and men of high rank, all mounted on horses. ²⁴They will come against you with weapons, chariots and wagons and with a throng of people; they will take up positions against you on every side with large and small shields and with helmets. I will turn you over to them for punishment, and they will punish you according to their standards. ²⁵I will direct my jealous anger against you, and they will deal with you in fury. They will cut off your noses and your ears, and those of you who are left will fall by the sword. They will take away your sons and daughters, and those of you who are left will be consumed by fire. ²⁶They will also strip you of your clothes and take your fine jewelry. ²⁷So I will put a stop to the lewdness and prostitution you began in Egypt. You will not look on these things with longing or remember Egypt anymore.

²⁸"For this is what the Sovereign LORD says: I am about to hand you over to those you hate, to those you turned away from in disgust. ²⁹They will deal with you in hatred and take away everything you have worked for. They will leave you naked and bare, and the shame of your prostitution will be exposed. Your lewdness and promiscuity ³⁰have brought this upon you, because you lusted after the nations and defiled yourself with their idols. ³¹You have gone the way of your sister; so I will put her cup into your hand.

³²"This is what the Sovereign LORD says:

"You will drink your sister's cup,
    a cup large and deep;
it will bring scorn and derision,
    for it holds so much.
³³You will be filled with drunkenness
        and sorrow,
    the cup of ruin and desolation,
    the cup of your sister Samaria.

R Eze 22:15 ◀ ▶ Eze 24:13

³⁴You will drink it and drain it dry;
    you will dash it to pieces
    and tear your breasts.

I have spoken, declares the Sovereign LORD.

³⁵"Therefore this is what the Sovereign LORD says: Since you have forgotten me and thrust me behind your back, you must bear the consequences of your lewdness and prostitution."

³⁶The LORD said to me: "Son of man, will you judge Oholah and Oholibah? Then confront them with their detestable practices, ³⁷for they have committed adultery and blood is on their hands. They committed adultery with their idols; they even sacrificed their children, whom they bore to me, as food for them. ³⁸They have also done this to me: At that same time they defiled my sanctuary and desecrated my Sabbaths. ³⁹On the very day they sacrificed their children to their idols, they entered my sanctuary and desecrated it. That is what they did in my house.

⁴⁰"They even sent messengers for men who came from far away, and when they arrived you bathed yourself for them, painted your eyes and put on your jewelry. ⁴¹You sat on an elegant couch, with a table spread before it on which you had placed the incense and oil that belonged to me.

⁴²"The noise of a carefree crowd was around her; Sabeans were brought from the desert along with men from the rabble, and they put bracelets on the arms of the woman and her sister and beautiful crowns on their heads. ⁴³Then I said about the one worn out by adultery, 'Now let them use her as a prostitute, for that is all she is.' ⁴⁴And they slept with her. As men sleep with a prostitute, so they slept with those lewd women, Oholah and Oholibah. ⁴⁵But righteous men will sentence them to the punishment of women who commit adultery

a 24 The meaning of the Hebrew for this word is uncertain. *b* 37 Or even made the children they bore to me pass through the fire. *c* 42 Or drunkards

---

23:32—33 Ezekiel warned Judah that because of her continued failure to repent of her rebellion, Judah would experience the same fate of Israel—exile to a pagan nation.

and shed blood,ᵉ because they are adulterous and blood is on their hands.ᶠ

⁴⁶"This is what the Sovereign LORD says: Bring a mobᵍ against them and give them over to terror and plunder.ʰ ⁴⁷The mob will stone them and cut them down with their swords; they will kill their sons and daughtersⁱ and burnʲ down their houses.ᵏ

⁴⁸"So I will put an endˡ to lewdness in the land, that all women may take warning and not imitate you.ᵐ ⁴⁹You will suffer the penalty for your lewdness and bear the consequences of your sins of idolatry.ⁿ Then you will know that I am the Sovereign LORD.°"

The Cooking Pot

24 In the ninth year, in the tenth month on the tenth day, the word of the LORD came to me:ᵖ ²"Son of man, recordq this date, this very date, because the king of Babylon has laid siege to Jerusalem this very day.ʳ ³Tell this rebellious houseˢ a parableᵗ and say to them: 'This is what the Sovereign LORD says:

" 'Put on the cooking pot;ᵘ put it on
 and pour water into it.
⁴Put into it the pieces of meat,
 all the choice pieces—the leg and the shoulder.
Fill it with the best of these bones;ᵛ
⁵ take the pick of the flock.ʷ
Pile wood beneath it for the bones;
 bring it to a boil
 and cook the bones in it.ˣ

⁶" 'For this is what the Sovereign LORD says:

" 'Woeʸ to the city of bloodshed,ᶻ
 to the pot now encrusted,
 whose deposit will not go away!
Empty it piece by piece
 without casting lotsᵃ for them.ᵇ

⁷" 'For the blood she shed is in her midst:
 She poured it on the bare rock;
 she did not pour it on the ground,
 where the dust would cover it.ᶜ
⁸To stir up wrath and take revenge
 I put her blood on the bare rock,
 so that it would not be covered.

⁹" 'Therefore this is what the Sovereign LORD says:

" 'Woe to the city of bloodshed!
 I, too, will pile the wood high.
¹⁰So heap on the wood
 and kindle the fire.
Cook the meat well,
 mixing in the spices;
 and let the bones be charred.
¹¹Then set the empty pot on the coals
 till it becomes hot and its copper glows
so its impurities may be melted
 and its deposit burned away.ᵈ
¹²It has frustrated all efforts;
 its heavy deposit has not been removed,
 not even by fire.

¹³" 'Now your impurity is lewdness. ᴿ Because I tried to cleanse you but you would not be cleansedᵉ from your impurity, you will not be clean again until my wrath against you has subsided.ᶠ

¹⁴" 'I the LORD have spoken.ᵍ The time has come for me to act.ʰ I will not hold back; I will not have pity,ⁱ nor will I relent.ʲ You will be judged according to your conduct and your actions,ᵏ declares the Sovereign LORD.' "

Ezekiel's Wife Dies

¹⁵The word of the LORD came to me: ¹⁶"Son of man, with one blowᵐ I am about to take away from you the delight of your eyes.ⁿ Yet do not lament or weep or shed any tears.° ¹⁷Groan quietly;ᵖ do not mourn for the dead. Keep your turbanq fastened and your sandals on your feet; do not cover the lower part of your faceˢ or eat the customary food ˻of mourners˼.ᵗ"

¹⁸So I spoke to the people in the morning, and in the evening my wife died. The next morning I did as I had been commanded.ᵘ

¹⁹Then the people asked me, "Won't you tell us what these things have to do with us?ᵛ"

²⁰So I said to them, "The word of the

R *Eze 23:32–33* ◀ ▶ *Eze 33:28–29*

24:13 Despite earlier judgments, Judah had refused to repent of her widespread idolatry, so God would purge her sin by exiling Judah to Babylon.

LORD came to me: ²¹Say to the house of Israel, 'This is what the Sovereign LORD says: I am about to desecrate my sanctuary—the stronghold in which you take pride, the delight of your eyes, the object of your affection. The sons and daughters you left behind will fall by the sword. ²²And you will do as I have done. You will not cover the lower part of your face or eat the customary food of mourners. ²³You will keep your turbans on your heads and your sandals on your feet. You will not mourn or weep but will waste away because of your sins and groan among yourselves. ²⁴Ezekiel will be a sign to you; you will do just as he has done. When this happens, you will know that I am the Sovereign LORD.'

²⁵"And you, son of man, on the day I take away their stronghold, their joy and glory, the delight of their eyes, their heart's desire, and their sons and daughters as well— ²⁶on that day a fugitive will come to tell you the news. ²⁷At that time your mouth will be opened; you will speak with him and will no longer be silent. So you will be a sign to them, and they will know that I am the LORD.'

A Prophecy Against Ammon

25 The word of the LORD came to me: ²"Son of man, set your face against the Ammonites and prophesy against them. ³Say to them, 'Hear the word of the Sovereign LORD. This is what the Sovereign LORD says: Because you said "Aha!" over my sanctuary when it was desecrated and over the land of Israel when it was laid waste and over the people of Judah when they went into exile, ⁴therefore I am going to give you to the people of the East as a possession. They will set up their camps and pitch their tents among you; they will eat your fruit and drink your milk. ⁵I will turn Rabbah into a pasture for camels and Ammon into a resting place for sheep. Then you will know that I am the LORD. ⁶For this is what the Sovereign LORD says: Because you have clapped your hands and stamped your feet, rejoicing with all the malice of your heart against the land of Israel, ⁷therefore I will stretch out my hand against you and give you as plunder to the nations. I will cut you off from the nations and exterminate you from the countries. I will destroy you, and you will know that I am the LORD.'"

A Prophecy Against Moab

⁸"This is what the Sovereign LORD says: 'Because Moab and Seir said, "Look, the house of Judah has become like all the other nations," ⁹therefore I will expose the flank of Moab, beginning at its frontier towns—Beth Jeshimoth, Baal Meon and Kiriathaim—the glory of that land. ¹⁰I will give Moab along with the Ammonites to the people of the East as a possession, so that the Ammonites will not be remembered among the nations; ¹¹and I will inflict punishment on Moab. Then they will know that I am the LORD.'"

A Prophecy Against Edom

¹²"This is what the Sovereign LORD says: 'Because Edom took revenge on the house of Judah and became very guilty by doing so, ¹³therefore this is what the Sovereign LORD says: I will stretch out my hand against Edom and kill its men and their animals. I will lay it waste, and from Teman to Dedan they will fall by the sword. ¹⁴I will take vengeance on Edom by the hand of my people Israel, and they will deal with Edom in accordance with my anger and my wrath; they will know my vengeance, declares the Sovereign LORD.'"

A Prophecy Against Philistia

¹⁵"This is what the Sovereign LORD says: 'Because the Philistines acted in vengeance and took revenge with malice in their hearts, and with ancient hostility sought to destroy Judah, ¹⁶therefore this is what the Sovereign LORD says: I am about to stretch out my hand against the Philistines, and I will cut off the Kerethites and destroy those remaining along the coast. ¹⁷I will carry out great vengeance on them and punish them in my wrath. Then they will know that I am

the LORD,[d] when I take vengeance on them.'[e][f]" "

A Prophecy Against Tyre

26 In the eleventh year, on the first day of the month, the word of the LORD came to me:[g] 2"Son of man, because Tyre[h] has said of Jerusalem, 'Aha! The gate to the nations is broken, and its doors have swung open to me; now that she lies in ruins I will prosper,' 3therefore this is what the Sovereign LORD says: I am against you, O Tyre, and I will bring many nations against you, like the sea casting up its waves. 4They will destroy the walls of Tyre[i] and pull down her towers; I will scrape away her rubble and make her a bare rock. 5Out in the sea[m] she will become a place to spread fishnets,[n] for I have spoken, declares the Sovereign LORD. She will become plunder[o] for the nations,[p] 6and her settlements on the mainland will be ravaged by the sword. Then they will know that I am the LORD.

7"For this is what the Sovereign LORD says: From the north I am going to bring against Tyre Nebuchadnezzar[e][q] king of Babylon, king of kings,[r] with horses and chariots,[s] with horsemen and a great army. 8He will ravage your settlements on the mainland with the sword; he will set up siege works[t] against you, build a ramp[u] up to your walls and raise his shields against you. 9He will direct the blows of his battering rams against your walls and demolish your towers with his weapons.[v] 10His horses will be so many that they will cover you with dust. Your walls will tremble at the noise of the war horses, wagons and chariots[w] when he enters your gates as men enter a city whose walls have been broken through. 11The hoofs[x] of his horses will trample all your streets; he will kill your people with the sword, and your strong pillars[y] will fall to the ground.[z] 12They will plunder your wealth and loot your merchandise; they will break down your walls and demolish your fine houses and throw your stones, timber and rubble into the sea.[a] 13I will put an end[b] to your noisy songs,[c] and the music of your harps[d] will be heard no more.[e] 14I will make you a bare rock, and you will become a place to spread fishnets. You will never be rebuilt,[f] for I the LORD have spoken, declares the Sovereign LORD.

15"This is what the Sovereign LORD says to Tyre: Will not the coastlands[g] tremble[h] at the sound of your fall, when the wounded groan[i] and the slaughter takes place in you? 16Then all the princes of the coast will step down from their thrones and lay aside their robes and take off their embroidered[j] garments. Clothed[k] with terror, they will sit on the ground,[l] trembling[m] every moment, appalled[n] at you. 17Then they will take up a lament[o] concerning you and say to you:

" 'How you are destroyed, O city of renown,
  peopled by men of the sea!
You were a power on the seas,
  you and your citizens;
you put your terror
  on all who lived there.[p]
18Now the coastlands tremble[q]
  on the day of your fall;
the islands in the sea
  are terrified at your collapse.'[r]

19"This is what the Sovereign LORD says: When I make you a desolate city, like cities no longer inhabited, and when I bring the ocean depths[s] over you and its vast waters cover you,[t] 20then I will bring you down with those who go down to the pit,[u] to the people of long ago. I will make you dwell in the earth below, as in ancient ruins, with those who go down to the pit, and you will not return or take your place[f] in the land of the living.[v] 21I will bring you to a horrible end and you will be no more.[w] You will be sought, but you will never again be found, declares the Sovereign LORD."[x]

A Lament for Tyre

27 The word of the LORD came to me: 2"Son of man, take up a lament[y] concerning Tyre. 3Say to Tyre,[z] situated at the gateway to the sea,[a] merchant of peoples on many coasts, 'This is what the Sovereign LORD says:

" 'You say, O Tyre,
  "I am perfect in beauty.[b]

---

[e] 7 Hebrew *Nebuchadrezzar*, of which *Nebuchadnezzar* is a variant; here and often in Ezekiel and Jeremiah [f] 20 Septuagint; Hebrew *return, and I will give glory*

⁴Your domain was on the high seas;
  your builders brought your beauty to
    perfection.
⁵They made all your timbers
  of pine trees from Senir;
  they took a cedar from Lebanon
    to make a mast for you.
⁶Of oaks from Bashan
    they made your oars;
  of cypress wood from the coasts of
      Cyprus
    they made your deck, inlaid with
      ivory.
⁷Fine embroidered linen from Egypt
    was your sail
    and served as your banner;
  your awnings were of blue and purple
    from the coasts of Elishah.
⁸Men of Sidon and Arvad were your
    oarsmen;
  your skilled men, O Tyre, were
    aboard as your seamen.
⁹Veteran craftsmen of Gebal were on
    board
    as shipwrights to caulk your seams.
  All the ships of the sea and their
    sailors
    came alongside to trade for your
      wares.

¹⁰"'Men of Persia, Lydia and Put
    served as soldiers in your army.
  They hung their shields and helmets
    on your walls,
    bringing you splendor.
¹¹Men of Arvad and Helech
    manned your walls on every side;
  men of Gammad
    were in your towers.
  They hung their shields around your
    walls;
    they brought your beauty to
      perfection.

¹²"'Tarshish did business with you because of your great wealth of goods; they exchanged silver, iron, tin and lead for your merchandise.
¹³"'Greece, Tubal and Meshech traded with you; they exchanged slaves and articles of bronze for your wares.
¹⁴"'Men of Beth Togarmah exchanged work horses, war horses and mules for your merchandise.
¹⁵"'The men of Rhodes traded with you, and many coastlands were your customers; they paid you with ivory tusks and ebony.

¹⁶"'Aram did business with you because of your many products; they exchanged turquoise, purple fabric, embroidered work, fine linen, coral and rubies for your merchandise.
¹⁷"'Judah and Israel traded with you; they exchanged wheat from Minnith and confections, honey, oil and balm for your wares.
¹⁸"'Damascus, because of your many products and great wealth of goods, did business with you in wine from Helbon and wool from Zahar.
¹⁹"'Danites and Greeks from Uzal bought your merchandise; they exchanged wrought iron, cassia and calamus for your wares.
²⁰"'Dedan traded in saddle blankets with you.
²¹"'Arabia and all the princes of Kedar were your customers; they did business with you in lambs, rams and goats.
²²"'The merchants of Sheba and Raamah traded with you; for your merchandise they exchanged the finest of all kinds of spices and precious stones, and gold.
²³"'Haran, Canneh and Eden and merchants of Sheba, Asshur and Kilmad traded with you. ²⁴In your marketplace they traded with you beautiful garments, blue fabric, embroidered work and multicolored rugs with cords twisted and tightly knotted.

²⁵"'The ships of Tarshish serve
    as carriers for your wares.
  You are filled with heavy cargo
    in the heart of the sea.
²⁶Your oarsmen take you
    out to the high seas.
  But the east wind will break you to
      pieces
    in the heart of the sea.
²⁷Your wealth, merchandise and wares,
    your mariners, seamen and
      shipwrights,
  your merchants and all your soldiers,
    and everyone else on board
  will sink into the heart of the sea
    on the day of your shipwreck.
²⁸The shorelands will quake
    when your seamen cry out.
²⁹All who handle the oars

---

g 5 That is, Hermon   h 6 Targum; the Masoretic Text has a different division of the consonants.   i 6 Hebrew Kittim   j 9 That is, Byblos   k 15 Septuagint; Hebrew Dedan   l 16 Most Hebrew manuscripts; some Hebrew manuscripts and Syriac Edom   m 17 The meaning of the Hebrew for this word is uncertain.

will abandon their ships;
the mariners and all the seamen
will stand on the shore.
³⁰They will raise their voice
and cry bitterly over you;
they will sprinkle dust[e] on their heads
and roll[f] in ashes.[g]
³¹They will shave their heads[h] because of you
and will put on sackcloth.
They will weep[i] over you with anguish of soul
and with bitter mourning.[j]
³²As they wail and mourn over you,
they will take up a lament[k] concerning you:
"Who was ever silenced like Tyre,
surrounded by the sea?"
³³When your merchandise went out on the seas,[m]
you satisfied many nations;
with your great wealth[n] and your wares
you enriched the kings of the earth.
³⁴Now you are shattered by the sea
in the depths of the waters;
your wares and all your company
have gone down with you.[o]
³⁵All who live in the coastlands[p]
are appalled[q] at you;
their kings shudder with horror
and their faces are distorted with fear.[r]
³⁶The merchants among the nations hiss at you;[s]
you have come to a horrible end
and will be no more.'[t]'"

A Prophecy Against the King of Tyre

28 The word of the LORD came to me: ²"Son of man[u], say to the ruler of Tyre, 'This is what the Sovereign LORD says:

"'In the pride of your heart
you say, "I am a god;
I sit on the throne[v] of a god
in the heart of the seas."[w]
But you are a man and not a god,
though you think you are as wise as a god.[x]
³Are you wiser than Daniel[n]?[y]
Is no secret hidden from you?
⁴By your wisdom and understanding
you have gained wealth for yourself
and amassed gold and silver
in your treasuries.[z]
⁵By your great skill in trading[a]
you have increased your wealth,[b]
and because of your wealth
your heart has grown proud.[c]

⁶"'Therefore this is what the Sovereign LORD says:

"'Because you think you are wise,
as wise as a god,
⁷I am going to bring foreigners against you,
the most ruthless of nations;[d]
they will draw their swords against
your beauty and wisdom[e]
and pierce your shining splendor.[f]
⁸They will bring you down to the pit,[g]
and you will die a violent death[h]
in the heart of the seas.[i]
⁹Will you then say, "I am a god,"
in the presence of those who kill you?
You will be but a man, not a god,[j]
in the hands of those who slay you.[k]
¹⁰You will die the death of the uncircumcised[l]
at the hands of foreigners.

[n] 3 Or *Danel*; the Hebrew spelling may suggest a person other than the prophet Daniel.

28:1–19 This prophecy, like many in Ezekiel, contains a double meaning. Note that the prophecy is delivered against Tyre, and that the first part of the prophecy is directed at the "ruler" of Tyre (28:2), while the latter part of the prophecy is directed against the "king" of Tyre (28:12). While some scholars view this entire prophecy in light of the end times and liken the ruler of Tyre to the antichrist, other scholars suggest that the ruler was probably the king of Tyre in Ezekiel's day—Ittobaal. Though this ruler was so proud of his accomplishments that he viewed himself as a god, his wickedness was merely an instrument of the "king"—Satan. Ezekiel reminded this ruler that he was merely a man and would "die the death of the uncircumcised at the hands of foreigners" (28:10).

Ezekiel then turned his attention to the "king" of Tyre, describing his unique privileges in the garden of Eden as a created being (28:15) and recounting his sin and methods of violence that culminated in his removal from the "mount of God" (28:16). Ezekiel's prophecy closed with a vivid description of Satan's judgment, indicating that these verses will not be completely fulfilled until Satan is forever cast into the lake of fire (see Rev 20:10).

Satan and the Fallen Angels

ANGELS ARE CREATED, immortal beings who play significant roles in God's plan for humanity (see Ps 148:2, 5; Lk 20:36; Eph 3:10; Col 1:16). Present at pivotal points in the spiritual history of the world, God's angels are spiritual messengers, sent to minister to believers (see Heb 1:14). Because angels are spiritual beings, they may be visible to animals but are usually invisible to humans (see Nu 22:22–27). When angels do appear to people they take on human form and may encourage some type of action (see Ge 21:18; Jdg 6:14; Mt 2:13; Ac 8:26; 12:7). At other times God sends his angels to protect his people (see Ps 34:7; Da 3:21; 6:22). Angels are also sent to comfort or share a special message from God (see Mt 1:20; Lk 2:10–11; Ac 27:24). God's angels will return with Jesus Christ at the second coming to establish the Messianic kingdom (see Mt 16:27).

Yet some of these created spiritual beings chose to join Satan and rebel against God. These fallen angels display the same hate, anger, lust and pride that motivated Satan to exalt himself above God (see Isa 14:13–14). Referred to in Isaiah as "Lucifer, son of the morning" (Isa 14:12), Satan left heaven to wander "back and forth in [the earth]" (Job 2:2) with those angels who joined his rebellion. Many scholars also believe that Ezekiel's title "king of Tyre" (Eze 28:12) refers to Satan when Ezekiel described this ruler as "anointed as a guardian cherub . . . blameless in your ways from the day you were created till wickedness was found in you" (Eze 28:14–15).

Scripture sheds abundant light on the role of Satan and his minions. The book of Job describes the scene of Satan appearing before the throne of God to accuse Job of a self-centered worship of God (see Job 1:6). Zechariah prophesied about Satan's resistance against the high priest Joshua and the angel of the Lord (see Zec 3:1). Paul warns that Satan often appears as "an angel of light" (2Co 11:14) to deceive believers. Jesus himself was tempted by Satan but did not sin (see Mt 4:1–10) and was likened by the Jewish leaders to one of Satan's servants (see Mt 12:24–28). Satan can even use well-meaning people to work his plans (see Mt 16:22–23; Rev 2:9, 13; 3:9).

The book of Revelation gives additional information about Satan's involvement in the last days. At that time Satan's angels will tempt the nations to resist God (see Rev 16:14). Because of this increased rebellion, Satan and his angels will be denied access to heaven by the archangel Michael and the angels of the Lord (see Rev 12:7–9). In retaliation, Satan will attempt to destroy the righteous during the perilous last half of the great tribulation. God will supernaturally intervene to protect his people, and Satan will be defeated by Jesus Christ at the Battle of Armageddon and be cast into the bottomless pit (see Rev 20:2).

Yet this imprisonment is not final. When Satan is released from his thousand-year imprisonment, he will be allowed to tempt humanity one last time. Those who choose to join Satan and his angels in a last attempt to overthrow Christ's rule will find themselves destroyed. They will face a final judgment for their rebellion (see Jude 6) and be cast into "into the eternal fire prepared for the devil and his angels" (Mt 25:41; see Rev 20:10–15). Jesus Christ will destroy Satan because of his age-long opposition to God's kingdom. From that moment on there will be no possibility of sin or temptation in the universe. The holiness and justice of our Lord Jesus Christ will cover the earth as the waters cover the sea.

I have spoken, declares the Sovereign
  LORD.' "

¹¹The word of the LORD came to me: ¹²"Son of man, take up a lament^m concerning the king of Tyre and say to him: 'This is what the Sovereign LORD says:

" 'You were the model of perfection,
    full of wisdom and perfect in
      beauty.^n
¹³You were in Eden,^o
    the garden of God;^p
  every precious stone^q adorned you:
    ruby, topaz and emerald,
    chrysolite, onyx and jasper,
    sapphire,^o turquoise^r and beryl.^p
  Your settings and mountings^q were
      made of gold;
    on the day you were created they
      were prepared.^s
¹⁴You were anointed^t as a guardian
      cherub,^u
    for so I ordained you.
  You were on the holy mount of God;
    you walked among the fiery stones.
¹⁵You were blameless in your ways
    from the day you were created
    till wickedness was found in you.
¹⁶Through your widespread trade
    you were filled with violence,^v
      and you sinned.
  So I drove you in disgrace from the
      mount of God,
    and I expelled you, O guardian
      cherub,^w
    from among the fiery stones.
¹⁷Your heart became proud^x
    on account of your beauty,
  and you corrupted your wisdom
    because of your splendor.
  So I threw you to the earth;
    I made a spectacle of you before
      kings.^y
¹⁸By your many sins and dishonest trade
    you have desecrated your
      sanctuaries.
  So I made a fire^z come out from you,
    and it consumed you,
  and I reduced you to ashes^a on the
      ground
    in the sight of all who were
      watching.^b
¹⁹All the nations who knew you

are appalled^c at you;
  you have come to a horrible end
    and will be no more.^d ' "

A Prophecy Against Sidon

²⁰The word of the LORD came to me: ²¹"Son of man, set your face against^e Sidon;^f prophesy against her ²²and say: 'This is what the Sovereign LORD says:

" 'I am against you, O Sidon,
    and I will gain glory^g within you.
  They will know that I am the LORD,
    when I inflict punishment^h on her
    and show myself holy^i within her.
²³I will send a plague upon her
    and make blood flow in her streets.
  The slain will fall within her,
    with the sword against her on every
      side.
  Then they will know that I am the
      LORD.^j

²⁴" 'No longer will the people of Israel have malicious neighbors who are painful briers and sharp thorns.^k Then they will know that I am the Sovereign LORD.

²⁵"This is what the Sovereign LORD says: When I gather^l the people of Israel from the nations where they have been scattered,^m I will show myself holy^n among them in the sight of the nations. Then they will live in their own land, which I gave to my servant Jacob.^o ²⁶They will live there in safety^p and will build houses and plant^q vineyards; they will live in safety when I inflict punishment^r on all their neighbors who maligned them. Then they will know that I am the LORD their God.^s ' "

A Prophecy Against Egypt

29 In the tenth year, in the tenth month on the twelfth day, the word of the LORD came to me:^t ²"Son of man, set your face against^u Pharaoh king of Egypt^v and prophesy against him and

J Eze 26:12–21 ◄► Eze 29:1–6
D Eze 14:21 ◄► Eze 33:27
I Eze 20:40–42 ◄► Eze 34:11–16
J Eze 28:20–24 ◄► Eze 29:19–20

^o 13 Or *lapis lazuli*   ^p 13 The precise identification of some of these precious stones is uncertain.   ^q 13 The meaning of the Hebrew for this phrase is uncertain.

28:25–26 This passage confirmed the final restoration of God's people to safety and security in the promised land. This prophecy will be fulfilled in the Millennium after the return of the Messiah.

against all Egypt.ʷ ³Speak to him and say: 'This is what the Sovereign LORD says:

" 'I am against you, Pharaohˣ king of Egypt,
you great monsterʸ lying among your streams.
You say, "The Nileᶻ is mine;
I made it for myself."
⁴But I will put hooksᵃ in your jaws
and make the fish of your streams stick to your scales.
I will pull you out from among your streams,
with all the fish sticking to your scales.ᵇ
⁵I will leave you in the desert,
you and all the fish of your streams.
You will fall on the open field
and not be gatheredᶜ or picked up.
I will give you as food
to the beasts of the earth and the birds of the air.ᵈ

⁶Then all who live in Egypt will know that I am the LORD.

" 'You have been a staff of reedᵉ for the house of Israel. ⁷When they grasped you with their hands, you splinteredᶠ and you tore open their shoulders; when they leaned on you, you broke and their backs were wrenched.ʳᵍ

⁸" 'Therefore this is what the Sovereign LORD says: I will bring a sword against you and kill your men and their animals.ʰ ⁹Egypt will become a desolate wasteland. Then they will know that I am the LORD.

" 'Because you said, "The Nileⁱ is mine; I made it,"ʲ ¹⁰therefore I am against youᵏ and against your streams, and I will make the land of Egyptˡ a ruin and a desolate wasteᵐ from Migdol to Aswan,ᵒ as far as the border of Cush.ˢᵖ ¹¹No foot of man or animal will pass through it; no one will live there for forty years.ᵠ ¹²I will make the land of Egypt desolateʳ among devastated lands, and her cities will lie desolate forty years among ruined cities. And I will disperse the Egyptians among the nations and scatter them through the countries.ˢ

¹³" 'Yet this is what the Sovereign LORD says: At the end of forty years I will gather the Egyptians from the nations where they were scattered. ¹⁴I will bring them back from captivity and return them to Upper Egypt,ʳᵗ the land of their ancestry. There they will be a lowlyᵘ kingdom.ᵛ ¹⁵It will be the lowliest of kingdoms and will never again exalt itself above the other nations.ʷ I will make it so weak that it will never again rule over the nations. ¹⁶Egypt will no longer be a source of confidenceˣ for the people of Israel but will be a reminderʸ of their sin in turning to her for help.ᶻ Then they will know that I am the Sovereign LORD.ᵃ' "

¹⁷In the twenty-seventh year, in the first month on the first day, the word of the LORD came to me:ᵇ ¹⁸"Son of man, Nebuchadnezzarᶜ king of Babylon drove his army in a hard campaign against Tyre; every head was rubbed bareᵈ and every shoulder made raw.ᵉ Yet he and his army got no reward from the campaign he led against Tyre. ¹⁹Therefore this is what the Sovereign LORD says: I am going to give Egypt to Nebuchadnezzar kingᶠ of Babylon, and he will carry off its wealth. He will loot and plunderᵍ the land as pay for his army.ʰ ²⁰I have given him Egyptⁱ as a reward for his efforts because he and his army did it for me, declares the Sovereign LORD.ʲ

²¹On that day I will make a hornᵘᵏ grow for the house of Israel, and I will open your mouthˡ among them. Then they will know that I am the LORD.ᵐ"

ʲ Eze 29:1–6 ◀ ▶ Eze 35:1–15

ʳ 7 Syriac (see also Septuagint and Vulgate); Hebrew *and you caused their backs to stand* ˢ 10 That is, the upper Nile region ᵗ 14 Hebrew *to Pathros* ᵘ 21 *Horn* here symbolizes strength.

29:10–15 In this oracle against Egypt, Ezekiel declared God's intent to punish the nation of Egypt and make its land desolate and its cities ruined. Ezekiel also named Nebuchadnezzar as God's means to deliver this judgment (see 29:19). According to history, Nebuchadnezzar suffered such great losses in his attack on Tyre (585–572 B.C.) that he sent his troops to plunder Egypt and carry off thousands of Egyptians as slaves.

A Lament for Egypt

30 The word of the LORD came to me: ² "Son of man, prophesy and say: 'This is what the Sovereign LORD says:

" 'Wail and say,
  "Alas for that day!"
³For the day is near,
  the day of the LORD is near—
a day of clouds,
  a time of doom for the nations.
⁴A sword will come against Egypt,
  and anguish will come upon Cush.
When the slain fall in Egypt,
  her wealth will be carried away
  and her foundations torn down.

⁵Cush and Put, Lydia and all Arabia, Libya and the people of the covenant land will fall by the sword along with Egypt.

⁶" 'This is what the LORD says:

" 'The allies of Egypt will fall
  and her proud strength will fail.
From Migdol to Aswan
  they will fall by the sword within her,
    declares the Sovereign LORD.
⁷" 'They will be desolate
  among desolate lands,
and their cities will lie
  among ruined cities.
⁸Then they will know that I am the LORD,
  when I set fire to Egypt
  and all her helpers are crushed.

⁹" 'On that day messengers will go out from me in ships to frighten Cush out of her complacency. Anguish will take hold of them on the day of Egypt's doom, for it is sure to come.

¹⁰" 'This is what the Sovereign LORD says:

" 'I will put an end to the hordes of Egypt
  by the hand of Nebuchadnezzar king of Babylon.
¹¹He and his army—the most ruthless of nations—
  will be brought in to destroy the land.
They will draw their swords against Egypt
  and fill the land with the slain.
¹²I will dry up the streams of the Nile
  and sell the land to evil men;
by the hand of foreigners
  I will lay waste the land and everything in it.
I the LORD have spoken.

¹³" 'This is what the Sovereign LORD says:

" 'I will destroy the idols
  and put an end to the images in Memphis.
No longer will there be a prince in Egypt,
  and I will spread fear throughout the land.
¹⁴I will lay waste Upper Egypt,
  set fire to Zoan
  and inflict punishment on Thebes.
¹⁵I will pour out my wrath on Pelusium,
  the stronghold of Egypt,
  and cut off the hordes of Thebes.
¹⁶I will set fire to Egypt;
  Pelusium will writhe in agony.
Thebes will be taken by storm;
  Memphis will be in constant distress.
¹⁷The young men of Heliopolis and Bubastis
  will fall by the sword,
  and the cities themselves will go into captivity.
¹⁸Dark will be the day at Tahpanhes
  when I break the yoke of Egypt;
there her proud strength will come to an end.
She will be covered with clouds,
  and her villages will go into captivity.
¹⁹So I will inflict punishment on Egypt,
  and they will know that I am the LORD.' "

²⁰In the eleventh year, in the first month on the seventh day, the word of the LORD came to me: ²¹"Son of man, I have broken the arm of Pharaoh king of Egypt. It has not been bound up for healing or put in a splint so as to become strong enough to hold a sword. ²²Therefore this is what the Sovereign LORD says: I am against Pharaoh king of Egypt. I will

---

v 4 That is, the upper Nile region; also in verses 5 and 9 w 5 Hebrew Cub x 13 Hebrew Noph; also in verse 16 y 14 Hebrew waste Pathros z 14 Hebrew No; also in verses 15 and 16 a 15 Hebrew Sin; also in verse 16 b 17 Hebrew Awen (or On) c 17 Hebrew Pi Beseth

break both his arms, the good arm as well as the broken one, and make the sword fall from his hand.ᵈ ²³I will disperse the Egyptians among the nations and scatter them through the countries.ᵉ ²⁴I will strengthenᶠ the arms of the king of Babylon and put my swordᵍ in his hand, but I will break the arms of Pharaoh, and he will groanʰ before him like a mortally wounded man. ²⁵I will strengthen the arms of the king of Babylon, but the arms of Pharaoh will fall limp. Then they will know that I am the LORD, when I put my swordⁱ into the hand of the king of Babylon and he brandishes it against Egypt.ʲ ²⁶I will disperse the Egyptians among the nations and scatter them through the countries. Then they will know that I am the LORD.ᵏ"

A Cedar in Lebanon

31 In the eleventh year,¹ in the third month on the first day, the word of the LORD came to me:ᵐ ²"Son of man, say to Pharaoh king of Egypt and to his hordes:

" 'Who can be compared with you in majesty?
³Consider Assyria,ⁿ once a cedar in Lebanon,ᵒ
with beautiful branches
overshadowing the forest;
it towered on high,
its top above the thick foliage.ᵖ
⁴The watersᵠ nourished it,
deep springs made it grow tall;
their streams flowed
all around its base
and sent their channels
to all the trees of the field.ʳ
⁵So it towered higherˢ
than all the trees of the field;
its boughs increased
and its branches grew long,
spreading because of abundant
waters.ᵗ
⁶All the birds of the air
nested in its boughs,
all the beasts of the field
gave birthᵘ under its branches;
all the great nations
lived in its shade.ᵛ
⁷It was majestic in beauty,
with its spreading boughs,
for its roots went down
to abundant waters.ʷ

⁸The cedarsˣ in the garden of God
could not rival it,
nor could the pine trees
equal its boughs,
nor could the plane treesʸ
compare with its branches—
no tree in the garden of God
could match its beauty.ᶻ
⁹I made it beautiful
with abundant branches,
the envy of all the trees of Edenᵃ
in the garden of God.ᵇ

¹⁰" 'Therefore this is what the Sovereign LORD says: Because it towered on high, lifting its top above the thick foliage, and because it was proudᶜ of its height, ¹¹I handed it over to the ruler of the nations, for him to deal with according to its wickedness. I cast it aside,ᵈ ¹²and the most ruthless of foreign nationsᵉ cut it down and left it. Its boughs fell on the mountains and in all the valleys;ᶠ its branches lay broken in all the ravines of the land. All the nations of the earth came out from under its shade and left it.ᵍ ¹³All the birds of the air settled on the fallen tree, and all the beasts of the field were among its branches.ʰ ¹⁴Therefore no other trees by the waters are ever to tower proudly on high, lifting their tops above the thick foliage. No other trees so well-watered are ever to reach such a height; they are all destinedⁱ for death,ʲ for the earth below, among mortal men, with those who go down to the pit.ᵏ

¹⁵" 'This is what the Sovereign LORD says: On the day it was brought down to the graveᵈ I covered the deep springs with mourning for it; I held back its streams, and its abundant waters were restrained. Because of it I clothed Lebanon with gloom, and all the trees of the field withered away.ˡ ¹⁶I made the nations trembleᵐ at the sound of its fall when I brought it down to the grave with those who go down to the pit. Then all the treesⁿ of Eden,ᵒ the choicest and best of Lebanon, all the trees that were well-watered, were consoledᵖ in the earth below.ᵠ ¹⁷Those who lived in its shade, its allies among the nations, had also gone down to the grave with it, joining those killed by the sword.ʳ

ᵈ 15 Hebrew *Sheol*; also in verses 16 and 17

18 "'Which of the trees of Eden can be compared with you in splendor and majesty? Yet you, too, will be brought down with the trees of Eden to the earth below; you will lie among the uncircumcised,ˢ with those killed by the sword.

"'This is Pharaoh and all his hordes, declares the Sovereign LORD.'"

A Lament for Pharaoh

32 In the twelfth year, in the twelfth month on the first day, the word of the LORD came to me:ᵗ ²"Son of man, take up a lamentᵘ concerning Pharaoh king of Egypt and say to him:

"'You are like a lionᵛ among the nations;
you are like a monsterʷ in the seasˣ
thrashing about in your streams,
churning the water with your feet
and muddying the streams.ʸ

³"'This is what the Sovereign LORD says:

"'With a great throng of people
I will cast my net over you,
and they will haul you up in my net.ᶻ
⁴I will throw you on the land
and hurl you on the open field.
I will let all the birds of the air settle on you
and all the beasts of the earth gorge themselves on you.ᵃ
⁵I will spread your flesh on the mountains
and fill the valleysᵇ with your remains.
⁶I will drench the land with your flowing bloodᶜ
all the way to the mountains,
and the ravines will be filled with your flesh.ᵈ
⁷When I snuff you out, I will cover the heavens
and darken their stars;
I will cover the sun with a cloud,
and the moon will not give its light.ᵉ
⁸All the shining lights in the heavens
I will darkenᶠ over you;
I will bring darkness over your land,ᵍ
declares the Sovereign LORD.
⁹I will trouble the hearts of many peoples

when I bring about your destruction among the nations,
amongᵉ lands you have not known.
¹⁰I will cause many peoples to be appalled at you,
and their kings will shudder with horror because of you
when I brandish my swordʰ before them.
On the dayⁱ of your downfall
each of them will tremble
every moment for his life.ʲ

¹¹"'For this is what the Sovereign LORD says:

"'The swordᵏ of the king of Babylonˡ
will come against you.ᵐ
¹²I will cause your hordes to fall
by the swords of mighty men—
the most ruthless of all nations.ⁿ
They will shatter the pride of Egypt,
and all her hordes will be overthrown.ᵒ
¹³I will destroy all her cattle
from beside abundant waters
no longer to be stirred by the foot of man
or muddied by the hoofs of cattle.ᵖ
¹⁴Then I will let her waters settle
and make her streams flow like oil,
declares the Sovereign LORD.
¹⁵When I make Egypt desolate
and strip the land of everything in it,
when I strike down all who live there,
then they will know that I am the LORD.ᑫ

¹⁶"This is the lamentʳ they will chant for her. The daughters of the nations will chant it; for Egypt and all her hordes they will chant it, declares the Sovereign LORD."

¹⁷In the twelfth year, on the fifteenth day of the month, the word of the LORD came to me:ˢ ¹⁸"Son of man, wail for the hordes of Egypt and consignᵗ to the earth below both her and the daughters of mighty nations, with those who go down to the pit.ᵘ ¹⁹Say to them, 'Are you more favored than others? Go down and be laid among the uncircumcised.'ᵛ ²⁰They will fall among those killed by the sword. The sword is drawn; let her be draggedʷ off with all her hordes.ˣ ²¹From within the

ᵉ 9 Hebrew; Septuagint *bring you into captivity among the nations,* / to

grave,[y] the mighty leaders will say of Egypt and her allies, 'They have come down and they lie with the uncircumcised,[z] with those killed by the sword.'

[22] "Assyria is there with her whole army; she is surrounded by the graves of all her slain, all who have fallen by the sword. [23] Their graves are in the depths of the pit[a] and her army lies around her grave.[b] All who had spread terror in the land of the living are slain, fallen by the sword.

[24] "Elam[c] is there, with all her hordes around her grave. All of them are slain, fallen by the sword.[d] All who had spread terror in the land of the living[e] went down uncircumcised to the earth below. They bear their shame with those who go down to the pit.[f] [25] A bed is made for him among the slain, with all his hordes around her grave. All of them are uncircumcised,[g] killed by the sword. Because their terror had spread in the land of the living, they bear their shame with those who go down to the pit; they are laid among the slain.

[26] "Meshech and Tubal[h] are there, with all their hordes around their graves. All of them are uncircumcised, killed by the sword because they spread their terror in the land of the living. [27] Do they not lie with the other uncircumcised[i] warriors who have fallen, who went down to the grave with their weapons of war, whose swords were placed under their heads? The punishment for their sins rested on their bones, though the terror of these warriors had stalked through the land of the living.

[28] "You too, O Pharaoh, will be broken and will lie among the uncircumcised, with those killed by the sword.

[29] "Edom[j] is there, her kings and all her princes; despite their power, they are laid with those killed by the sword. They lie with the uncircumcised, with those who go down to the pit.[k]

[30] "All the princes of the north[l] and all the Sidonians[m] are there; they went down with the slain in disgrace despite the terror caused by their power. They lie uncircumcised[n] with those killed by the sword and bear their shame with those who go down to the pit.[o]

[31] "Pharaoh—he and all his army—will see them and he will be consoled[p] for all his hordes that were killed by the sword, declares the Sovereign LORD. [32] Although I had him spread terror in the land of the living, Pharaoh[q] and all his hordes will be laid among the uncircumcised, with those killed by the sword, declares the Sovereign LORD."[r]

Ezekiel a Watchman

33 The word of the LORD came to me: [2] "Son of man, speak to your countrymen and say to them: 'When I bring the sword[s] against a land, and the people of the land choose one of their men and make him their watchman,[t] [3] and he sees the sword coming against the land and blows the trumpet[u] to warn the people, [4] then if anyone hears the trumpet but does not take warning[v] and the sword comes and takes his life, his blood will be on his own head.[w] [5] Since he heard the sound of the trumpet but did not take warning, his blood will be on his own head.[x] If he had taken warning, he would have saved himself.[y] [6] But if the watchman sees the sword coming and does not blow the trumpet to warn the people and the sword comes and takes the life of one of them, that man will be taken away because of his sin, but I will hold the watchman accountable for his blood.'[z]

[7] "Son of man, I have made you a watchman[a] for the house of Israel; so hear the word I speak and give them warning from me.[b] [8] When I say to the wicked, 'O wicked man, you will surely die,'[c] and you do not speak out to dissuade him from his ways, that wicked man will die for[g] his sin, and I will hold you accountable for his blood.[d] [9] But if you do warn the wicked man to turn from his ways and he does not do so,[e] he will die for his sin, but you will have saved yourself.[f]

[10] "Son of man, say to the house of Israel, 'This is what you are saying: "Our offenses and sins weigh us down, and we are wasting away[g] because of[h] them.

N *Eze 3:7* ◀ ▶ *Eze 33:9*
N *Eze 33:4–5* ◀ ▶ *Eze 33:31*
R *Eze 18:30–32* ◀ ▶ *Eze 33:11–12*

f 21 Hebrew *Sheol*; also in verse 27 *g 8* Or *in*; also in verse 9 *h 10* Or *away in*

How then can we live?"ʰ" ¹¹Say to them, 'As surely as I live, declares the Sovereign LORD, I take no pleasure in the death of the wicked, but rather that they turn from their ways and live.ⁱ Turn!ʲ Turn from your evil ways! Why will you die, O house of Israel?'ᵏ

¹²"Therefore, son of man, say to your countrymen,ˡ 'The righteousness of the righteous man will not save him when he disobeys, and the wickedness of the wicked man will not cause him to fall when he turns from it. The righteous man, if he sins, will not be allowed to live because of his former righteousness.'ᵐ ¹³If I tell the righteous man that he will surely live, but then he trusts in his righteousness and does evil, none of the righteous things he has done will be remembered; he will die for the evil he has done.ⁿ ¹⁴And if I say to the wicked man, 'You will surely die,' but he then turns away from his sin and does what is justᵒ and right— ¹⁵if he gives back what he took in pledgeᵖ for a loan, returns what he has stolen,ᵠ follows the decrees that give life, and does no evil, he will surely live; he will not die. ¹⁶None of the sinsʳ he has committed will be remembered against him. He has done what is just and right; he will surely live.ᵗ

¹⁷"Yet your countrymen say, 'The way of the Lord is not just.' But it is their way that is not just. ¹⁸If a righteous man turns from his righteousness and does evil,ᵘ he will die for it.ᵛ ¹⁹And if a wicked man turns away from his wickedness and does what is just and right, he will live by doing so.ʷ ²⁰Yet, O house of Israel, you say, 'The way of the Lord is not just.' But I will judge each of you according to his own ways."ˣ

H Eze 25:17 ◀ ▶ Eze 33:13
L Eze 18:32 ◀ ▶ Eze 33:14–16
R Eze 33:9 ◀ ▶ Eze 33:14–16
S Eze 18:30–32 ◀ ▶ Eze 33:18
W Eze 18:32 ◀ ▶ Mt 7:7–8
H Eze 33:11 ◀ ▶ Eze 35:14
L Eze 33:11–12 ◀ ▶ Eze 33:19
R Eze 33:11–12 ◀ ▶ Eze 33:19
S Eze 33:11–16 ◀ ▶ Eze 33:31
L Eze 33:14–16 ◀ ▶ Eze 34:11–12
R Eze 33:14–16 ◀ ▶ Da 4:27

33:10 ʰS Lev 26:39; S Eze 4:17
33:11 ⁱS La 3:33; ʲS 2Ch 30:9; S Isa 19:22; S Jer 3:12; ᵏJer 44:7-8; S Eze 18:23; Hos 11:8; Joel 2:12; S 1Ti 2:4
33:12 ˡver 2; ᵐ2Ch 7:14; S Eze 3:20; S 18:21
33:13 ⁿHeb 10:38; 2Pe 2:20-21
33:14 ᵒS Jer 22:3
33:15 ᵖS Ex 22:26; ᵠEx 22:1-4; S Lev 6:2-5; ʳIsa 55:7; Jer 18:7-8; S Lk 19:8
33:16 ˢS Jer 50:20; ᵗS Isa 43:25
33:18 ᵘJer 18:10; ᵛS Eze 3:20
33:19 ʷS ver 14-15
33:20 ˣS Job 34:11
33:21 ʸEze 24:26; ᶻS 2Ki 25:4,10; Jer 39:1-2; 52:4-7; S Eze 32:1
33:22 ᵃS Eze 1:3; ᵇEze 29:21; Lk 1:64; ᶜEze 3:26-27; S 24:27
33:24 ᵈEze 36:4; ᵉS Dt 1:10; ᶠIsa 51:2; Jer 40:7; Eze 11:15; Lk 3:8; Ac 7:5
33:25 ᵍJer 7:21; ʰS Ge 9:4; ⁱJer 7:9-10; S Eze 22:6,27
33:26 ʲJer 41:7; ᵏEze 22:11
33:27 ˡS Isa 13:6; Isa 2:19; S Jer 42:22; S Eze 7:15; S 14:21; 39:4
33:28 ᵐS Isa 41:15; ⁿS Ge 6:7; Jer 9:10
33:29 ᵒS Lev 26:34; ᵖS Jer 18:16; S 44:22; Eze 36:4; Mic 7:13
33:31 ᵠS Eze 8:1

Jerusalem's Fall Explained

²¹In the twelfth year of our exile, in the tenth month on the fifth day, a man who had escapedʸ from Jerusalem came to me and said, "The city has fallen!"ᶻ ²²Now the evening before the man arrived, the hand of the LORD was upon me,ᵃ and he opened my mouthᵇ before the man came to me in the morning. So my mouth was opened and I was no longer silent.ᶜ

²³Then the word of the LORD came to me: ²⁴"Son of man, the people living in those ruinsᵈ in the land of Israel are saying, 'Abraham was only one man, yet he possessed the land. But we are many;ᵉ surely the land has been given to us as our possession.'ᶠ ²⁵Therefore say to them, 'This is what the Sovereign LORD says: Since you eatᵍ meat with the bloodʰ still in it and look to your idols and shed blood, should you then possess the land?ⁱ ²⁶You rely on your sword, you do detestable things,ʲ and each of you defiles his neighbor's wife.ᵏ Should you then possess the land?'

²⁷"Say this to them: 'This is what the Sovereign LORD says: As surely as I live, those who are left in the ruins will fall by the sword, those out in the country I will give to the wild animals to be devoured, and those in strongholds and caves will die of a plague.ˡ ²⁸I will make the land a desolate waste, and her proud strength will come to an end, and the mountainsᵐ of Israel will become desolate so that no one will cross them.ⁿ ²⁹Then they will know that I am the LORD, when I have made the land a desolateᵒ waste because of all the detestable things they have done.'ᵖ

³⁰"As for you, son of man, your countrymen are talking together about you by the walls and at the doors of the houses, saying to each other, 'Come and hear the message that has come from the LORD.' ³¹My people come to you, as they usually do, and sit beforeᵠ you to listen to your

D Eze 28:23 ◀ ▶ Eze 38:22
R Eze 24:13 ◀ ▶ Eze 34:1–2
G Eze 13:10–14 ◀ ▶ Zep 1:18
N Eze 33:9 ◀ ▶ Da 5:1–6
S Eze 33:18 ◀ ▶ Eze 36:25–27

33:28–29 God declared that all nations would recognize that the desolation of Israel was due to their continued rebellion and apostasy against God.

words, but they do not put them into practice. With their mouths they express devotion, but their hearts are greedy˻ for unjust gain.ˢ ³²Indeed, to them you are nothing more than one who sings love songsᵗ with a beautiful voice and plays an instrument well, for they hear your words but do not put them into practice.ᵘ

³³"When all this comes true—and it surely will—then they will know that a prophet has been among them.ᵛ

Shepherds and Sheep

R **34** The word of the LORD came to me: ²"Son of man, prophesy against the shepherds of Israel; prophesy and say to them: 'This is what the Sovereign LORD says: Woe to the shepherds of Israel who only take care of themselves! Should not shepherds take care of the flock?ʷ ³You eat the curds, clothe yourselves with the wool and slaughter the choice animals, but you do not take care of the flock.ˣ ⁴You have not strengthened the weak or healedʸ the sick or bound upᶻ the injured. You have not brought back the strays or searched for the lost. You have ruled them harshly and bru-

R tally.ᵃ ⁵So they were scattered because there was no shepherd,ᵇ and when they were scattered they became food for all the wild animals.ᶜ ⁶My sheep wandered over all the mountains and on every high hill.ᵈ They were scatteredᵉ over the whole earth, and no one searched or looked for them.ᶠ

⁷"'Therefore, you shepherds, hear the word of the LORD: ⁸As surely as I live, declares the Sovereign LORD, because my flock lacks a shepherd and so has been plunderedᵍ and has become food for all the wild animals,ʰ and because my shepherds did not search for my flock but cared for themselves rather than for my flock,ⁱ ⁹therefore, O shepherds, hear the word of the LORD: ¹⁰This is what the Sovereign LORD says: I am againstʲ the shep-

R Eze 33:28–29 ◀▶ Eze 34:5–10
R Eze 34:1–2 ◀▶ Eze 36:3–7

herds and will hold them accountable for my flock. I will remove them from tending the flock so that the shepherds can no longer feed themselves. I will rescueᵏ my flock from their mouths, and it will no longer be food for them.ˡ

¹¹"'For this is what the Sovereign LORD **I** says: I myself will search for my sheepᵐ **L** and look after them. ¹²As a shepherdⁿ **P** looks after his scattered flock when he is with them, so will I look after my sheep. I will rescue them from all the places where they were scattered on a day of clouds and darkness.ᵒ ¹³I will bring them out from the nations and gatherᵖ them from the countries, and I will bring them into their own land.ᵠʳˢᵗ I will pasture them on the mountains of Israel, in the ravines and in all the settlements in the land.ᵘᵛʷ ¹⁴I will tend them in a good pasture, and the mountain heights of Israelˣ will be their grazing land. There they will lie down in good grazing land, and there they will feed in a rich pastureʸ on the mountains of Israel.ᶻ ¹⁵I myself will tend my sheep and have them lie down,ᵃ declares the Sovereign LORD.ᵇ ¹⁶I **H** will search for the lost and bring back the strays. I will bind upᶜ the injured and strengthen the weak,ᵈ but the sleek and the strong I will destroy.ᵉ I will shepherd the flock with justice.ᶠ

¹⁷"'As for you, my flock, this is what the Sovereign LORD says: I will judge between one sheep and another, and between rams and goats.ᵍ ¹⁸Is it not enoughʰ for you to feed on the good pasture? Must you also trample the rest of your pasture with your feet?ⁱ Is it not enough for you to drink clear water? Must you also muddy the rest with your feet? ¹⁹Must my flock feed on what you have trampled and drink what you have muddied with your feet?

I Eze 28:25–26 ◀▶ Eze 34:22
L Eze 33:19 ◀▶ Eze 36:25
P Jer 36:3 ◀▶ Da 9:9
H Jer 17:14 ◀▶ Eze 47:12

34:5–6 This image of Israel without a shepherd is used often in the Bible (see Mk 6:34).
34:11–16 Using the imagery of a shepherd and his flock, God declared his intent to care for his people when their punishment was finished. He would bring his people back to their land and restore their possessions. Compare this imagery with Isa 40:11 and Jn 10:11.

20 " 'Therefore this is what the Sovereign LORD says to them: See, I myself will judge between the fat sheep and the lean sheep.^j 21Because you shove with flank and shoulder, butting all the weak sheep with your horns^k until you have driven them away, 22I will save my flock, and they will no longer be plundered. I will judge between one sheep and another.^l 23I will place over them one shepherd, my servant David, and he will tend^m them; he will tend them and be their shepherd.^n 24I the LORD will be their God,^o and my servant David^p will be prince among them.^q I the LORD have spoken.^r

25 " 'I will make a covenant^s of peace^t with them and rid the land of wild beasts^u so that they may live in the desert and sleep in the forests in safety.^v 26I will bless^w them and the places surrounding my hill.^i I will send down showers in season;^x there will be showers of blessing.^y 27The trees of the field will yield their fruit^z and the ground will yield its crops; the people will be secure^b in their land. They will know that I am the LORD, when I break the bars of their yoke^c and rescue them from the hands of those who enslaved them.^d 28They will no longer be plundered by the nations, nor will wild animals devour them. They will live in safety,^e and no one will make them afraid.^f 29I will provide for them a land renowned^g for its crops, and they will no longer be victims of famine^h in the land or bear the scorn^i of the nations.^j 30Then they will know that I, the LORD their God, am with them and that they, the house of Israel, are my people, declares the Sovereign LORD.^k 31You my sheep,^l the sheep of my pasture,^m are people, and I am your God, declares the Sovereign LORD.' "

l Eze 34:11–16 ◀▶ Eze 36:8–12
M Eze 21:26–27 ◀▶ Eze 34:25–28
M Eze 34:23–29 ◀▶ Eze 37:22–28
B Pr 3:9–10 ◀▶ Eze 36:30
U Jer 35:19 ◀▶ Da 1:15

34:20 j Mt 25:32
34:21 k S Dt 33:17
34:22
l Ps 72:12-14;
Jer 23:2-3;
Eze 20:37-38
34:23 m Isa 40:11
n S Isa 31:4;
Mic 5:4
34:24 o Eze 36:28
p Ps 89:49
q S Isa 53:4;
Zec 13:7
r Jer 23:4-5; S 30:9;
S 33:14; Jn 10:16;
Rev 7:17
34:25
s S Eze 16:62
t S Nu 25:12
u Lev 26:6
v S Lev 25:18;
Isa 11:6-9; Hos 2:18
34:26 w S Ge 12:2
x Ps 68:9; Joel 2:23
y Dt 11:13-15;
S 28:12; Isa 44:3
34:27 z S Ps 72:16
a S Job 14:9;
S Ps 67:6
b S Nu 24:21
c S Lev 26:13
d S Jer 30:8;
S Eze 20:42;
S 28:25
34:28 e S Jer 32:37
f S Jer 30:10;
S Eze 28:26; 39:26;
Hos 11:11;
Am 9:15; Zep 3:13;
Zec 14:11
34:29 g S Isa 4:2
h Eze 36:29
i S Ps 137:3;
Eze 36:6; Joel 2:19
j Eze 36:15
34:30
k S Eze 14:11;
37:27
34:31 l S Ps 28:9
m S Jer 23:1
35:2 n S Ge 14:6
35:3 o S Jer 6:12
p S Isa 34:10;
Eze 25:12-14
35:4 q Jer 44:2
r ver 9; S Jer 49:10
35:5 s S Ps 63:10
t Ob 1:13
u Ps 137:7;
S Eze 21:29
35:6 v S Isa 34:3
w Isa 63:2-6
35:7 x S Jer 46:19
y S Jer 49:17
35:8 z S Eze 31:12
35:9 a Ob 1:10
b S Isa 34:5-6;
S Jer 49:13
35:10 c S Ps 83:12;
Eze 36:2,5
35:11 d S Eze 25:14
e S Ps 9:16;
Ob 1:15; S Mt 7:2
35:12 f S Jer 50:7
35:13 g S Jer 49:16

A Prophecy Against Edom

35 The word of the LORD came to me: 2"Son of man, set your face against Mount Seir;^n prophesy against it 3and say: 'This is what the Sovereign LORD says: I am against you, Mount Seir, and I will stretch out my hand^o against you and make you a desolate waste.^p 4I will turn your towns into ruins^q and you will be desolate. Then you will know that I am the LORD.^r

5 " 'Because you harbored an ancient hostility and delivered the Israelites over to the sword^s at the time of their calamity,^t the time their punishment reached its climax,^u 6therefore as surely as I live, declares the Sovereign LORD, I will give you over to bloodshed^v and it will pursue you.^w Since you did not hate bloodshed, bloodshed will pursue you. 7I will make Mount Seir a desolate waste^x and cut off from it all who come and go.^y 8I will fill your mountains with the slain; those killed by the sword will fall on your hills and in your valleys and in all your ravines.^z 9I will make you desolate forever;^a your towns will not be inhabited. Then you will know that I am the LORD.^b

10 " 'Because you have said, "These two nations and countries will be ours and we will take possession^c of them," even though I the LORD was there, 11therefore as surely as I live, declares the Sovereign LORD, I will treat you in accordance with the anger^d and jealousy you showed in your hatred of them and I will make myself known among them when I judge you.^e 12Then you will know that I the LORD have heard all the contemptible things you have said against the mountains of Israel. You said, "They have been laid waste and have been given over to us to devour.^f " 13You boasted^g against me and spoke against me without restraint,

J Eze 29:19–20 ◀▶ Da 4:10–17

i 26 Or I will make them and the places surrounding my hill a blessing

---

34:22–31 God promised to "place over them one shepherd" (34:23), indicating that the Messiah, the Son of David, would finally rule over God's people in his peaceful millennial kingdom. Note that this prophecy involved a removal of the wild beasts (34:25, 28) that could kill the sheep. This imagery confirms that Israel will find peace, security and an absence of hostility when the Messiah rules in power and glory.

and I heard it. ¹⁴This is what the Sovereign LORD says: While the whole earth rejoices, I will make you desolate. ¹⁵Because you rejoiced when the inheritance of the house of Israel became desolate, that is how I will treat you. You will be desolate, O Mount Seir, you and all of Edom. Then they will know that I am the LORD.' "

A Prophecy to the Mountains of Israel

36 "Son of man, prophesy to the mountains of Israel and say, 'O mountains of Israel, hear the word of the LORD. ²This is what the Sovereign LORD says: The enemy said of you, "Aha! The ancient heights have become our possession."' ³Therefore prophesy and say, 'This is what the Sovereign LORD says: Because they ravaged and hounded you from every side so that you became the possession of the rest of the nations and the object of people's malicious talk and slander, ⁴therefore, O mountains of Israel, hear the word of the Sovereign LORD: This is what the Sovereign LORD says to the mountains and hills, to the ravines and valleys, to the desolate ruins and the deserted towns that have been plundered and ridiculed by the rest of the nations around you— ⁵this is what the Sovereign LORD says: In my burning zeal I have spoken against the rest of the nations, and against all Edom, for with glee and with malice in their hearts they made my land their own possession so that they might plunder its pastureland.' ⁶Therefore prophesy concerning the land of Israel and say to the mountains and hills, to the ravines and valleys: 'This is what the Sovereign LORD says: I speak in my jealous wrath because you have suffered the scorn of the nations. ⁷Therefore this is what the Sovereign LORD says: I swear with uplifted hand that the nations around you will also suffer scorn.

⁸" 'But you, O mountains of Israel, will produce branches and fruit for my people Israel, for they will soon come home. ⁹I am concerned for you and will look on you with favor; you will be plowed and sown, ¹⁰and I will multiply the number of people upon you, even the whole house of Israel. The towns will be inhabited and the ruins rebuilt. ¹¹I will increase the number of men and animals upon you, and they will be fruitful and become numerous. I will settle people on you as in the past and will make you prosper more than before. Then you will know that I am the LORD. ¹²I will cause people, my people Israel, to walk upon you. They will possess you, and you will be their inheritance; you will never again deprive them of their children.

¹³" 'This is what the Sovereign LORD says: Because people say to you, "You devour men and deprive your nation of its children," ¹⁴therefore you will no longer devour men or make your nation childless, declares the Sovereign LORD. ¹⁵No longer will I make you hear the taunts of the nations, and no longer will you suffer the scorn of the peoples or cause your nation to fall, declares the Sovereign LORD.' "

¹⁶Again the word of the LORD came to me: ¹⁷"Son of man, when the people of Israel were living in their own land, they defiled it by their conduct and their actions. Their conduct was like a woman's monthly uncleanness in my sight. ¹⁸So I poured out my wrath on them because they had shed blood in the land and because they had defiled it with their idols. ¹⁹I dispersed them among the nations, and they were scattered through the countries; I judged them according to their conduct and their actions. ²⁰And wherever they went among the nations they profaned my holy name, for it was said of them, 'These are the LORD's people, and yet they had to leave his land.' ²¹I had concern for my holy name, which the house of Israel profaned among the nations where they had gone.

36:8–12 Despite God's imminent judgment, God promised restoration for his people, their cities and their land. In fact, their blessings in the last days will exceed their former blessings. Compare this promise with Job's account (see Job 42:10).

36:18–19 God declared that the Jews' exile was a direct result of their wickedness.

²²"Therefore say to the house of Israel, 'This is what the Sovereign LORD says: It is not for your sake, O house of Israel, that I am going to do these things, but for the sake of my holy name,ʷ which you have profaned ˣ among the nations where you have gone.ʸ ²³I will show the holiness of my great name,ᶻ which has been profaned ᵃ among the nations, the name you have profaned among them. Then the nations will know that I am the LORD,ᵇ declares the Sovereign LORD, when I show myself holy ᶜ through you before their eyes.ᵈ

²⁴" 'For I will take you out of the nations; I will gather you from all the countries and bring you back into your own land.ᵉ ²⁵I will sprinkle ᶠ clean water on you, and you will be clean; I will cleanse ᵍ you from all your impurities ʰ and from all your idols.ⁱ ²⁶I will give you a new heart ʲ and put a new spirit in you; I will remove from you your heart of stone ᵏ and give you a heart of flesh.ˡ ²⁷And I will put my Spirit ᵐ in you and move you to follow my decrees ⁿ and be careful to keep my laws.ᵒ ²⁸You will live in the land I gave your forefathers; you will be my people,ᵖ and I will be your God.ᵠ ²⁹I will save you from all your uncleanness. I will call for the grain and make it plentiful and will not bring famine ʳ upon you. ³⁰I will increase the fruit of the trees and the crops of the field, so that you will no longer suffer dis-

R *Eze 11:19* ◀▶ *Lk 1:17*
S *Eze 11:19* ◀▶ *Mic 2:7*
K *Eze 12:25* ◀▶ *Eze 36:29*
L *Eze 34:11–12* ◀▶ *Eze 36:29*
S *Eze 33:31* ◀▶ *Eze 36:29*
B *Eze 11:19* ◀▶ *Eze 37:14*
P *Eze 11:19* ◀▶ *Joel 2:28–29*
L *Eze 13:3* ◀▶ *Mt 4:1*
M *Eze 3:24* ◀▶ *Eze 37:14*
K *Eze 36:25–26* ◀▶ *Eze 36:33*
L *Eze 36:25* ◀▶ *Da 9:9*
S *Eze 36:25–27* ◀▶ *Hos 10:2*
B *Eze 34:26–27* ◀▶ *Hos 2:21–22*

36:22
ʷ S Isa 37:35;
S Eze 20:44
ˣ Ro 2:24*
ʸ Dt 9:5-6;
Ps 106:8;
S Eze 20:9
36:23 ᶻ S Nu 6:27
ᵃ S Isa 37:23
ᵇ S Ps 46:10
ᶜ S Eze 20:41
ᵈ Ps 126:2;
S Isa 5:16;
Eze 20:14; 38:23;
39:7,27-28
36:24
ᵉ S Isa 43:5-6;
S Eze 34:13; 37:21
36:25 ᶠ S Lev 14:7;
S 16:14-15;
Heb 9:13
ᵍ S Ps 51:2,7
ʰ S Ezr 6:21
ⁱ Isa 2:18; Joel 3:21;
Zec 3:4; 13:2;
S Ac 22:16
36:26 ʲ Jer 24:7
ᵏ S Jer 5:3
ˡ S Ps 51:10;
S Eze 18:31;
S 2Co 3:3
36:27 ᵐ S Isa 44:3;
Joel 2:29; Jn 3:5
ⁿ S Jer 50:20; 1Th 4:8
36:28 ᵖ S Jer 30:22;
31:33
ᵠ S Eze 11:17;
S 14:11; 34:24;
S 37:14,27; Zec 8:8
36:29 ʳ Eze 34:29
36:30 ˢ S Lev 26:4-5;
S Eze 34:13-14;
Hos 2:21-22
36:31 ᵗ Eze 6:5;
S Jer 31:19;
S Eze 6:9
36:32 ᵘ Eze 16:63
ᵛ Dt 9:5
36:33
ʷ S Lev 16:30
ˣ S Lev 26:31
ʸ S Isa 49:8
36:35 ᶻ S Ge 2:8
ᵃ Am 9:14
36:36
ᵇ S Jer 42:10;
S Eze 17:22; 37:14;
39:27-28
36:37 ᶜ Zec 10:6;
13:9 ᵈ Ps 102:17;
Jer 29:12-14
36:38 ᵉ 1Ki 8:63;
2Ch 35:7-9
ᶠ S Ex 6:2
37:1 ᵍ S Eze 1:3
ʰ S Eze 11:24;
Lk 4:1; Ac 8:39
ⁱ Jer 7:32 ʲ S Jer 8:2;
Eze 40:1

grace among the nations because of famine.ˢ ³¹Then you will remember your evil ways and wicked deeds, and you will loathe yourselves for your sins and detestable practices.ᵗ ³²I want you to know that I am not doing this for your sake, declares the Sovereign LORD. Be ashamed ᵘ and disgraced for your conduct, O house of Israel!ᵛ

³³" 'This is what the Sovereign LORD says: On the day I cleanse ʷ you from all your sins, I will resettle your towns, and the ruins ˣ will be rebuilt.ʸ ³⁴The desolate land will be cultivated instead of lying desolate in the sight of all who pass through it. ³⁵They will say, "This land that was laid waste has become like the garden of Eden;ᶻ the cities that were lying in ruins, desolate and destroyed, are now fortified and inhabited.ᵃ" ³⁶Then the nations around you that remain will know that I the LORD have rebuilt what was destroyed and have replanted what was desolate. I the LORD have spoken, and I will do it.'ᵇ

³⁷"This is what the Sovereign LORD says: Once again I will yield to the plea ᶜ of the house of Israel and do this for them: I will make their people as numerous as sheep,ᵈ ³⁸as numerous as the flocks for offerings ᵉ at Jerusalem during her appointed feasts. So will the ruined cities be filled with flocks of people. Then they will know that I am the LORD.'ᶠ

The Valley of Dry Bones

37 The hand of the LORD was upon me,ᵍ and he brought me out by the Spirit ʰ of the LORD and set me in the middle of a valley;ⁱ it was full of bones.ʲ ²He led me back and forth among them, and I saw a great many bones on the floor

K *Eze 36:29* ◀▶ *Eze 37:23*
I *Eze 36:8–12* ◀▶ *Eze 38:8*
E *Eze 13:3* ◀▶ *Eze 43:5*
N *Eze 8:3* ◀▶ *Eze 43:4–5*

36:22–24 God's determination to restore his chosen people to their land was not because of anything they had done, but rather to show his holiness and faithfulness to them. When the nations witnessed this restoration then they would also "know that I am the LORD" (36:23).

36:25–38 The ritual of sprinkling water upon someone removed their religious depravity (see Ex 30:17–21; Lev 14:52; Nu 19:17–19). The outpouring of the Holy Spirit is also a sign of the Messiah's kingdom. In this prophecy God promised to cleanse his people, give them a new heart and fill them with his Spirit. Other millennial blessings include repossession of the land, renewed relationship with God, increased fertility in the land and the end of Israel's continued rebellion against God.

37:1–14 Though this is one of Ezekiel's major visions, no date is given in this passage. Israel was a

of the valley, bones that were very dry. ³He asked me, "Son of man, can these bones live?"

I said, "O Sovereign LORD, you alone know."ᵏ

⁴Then he said to me, "Prophesy to these bones and say to them, 'Dry bones, hear the word of the LORD!¹ ⁵This is what the Sovereign LORD says to these bones: I will make breathʲ enter you, and you will come to life.ᵐ ⁶I will attach tendons to you and make flesh come upon you and cover you with skin; I will put breath in you, and you will come to life. Then you will know that I am the LORD.ⁿ'"

⁷So I prophesied as I was commanded. And as I was prophesying, there was a noise, a rattling sound, and the bones came together, bone to bone. ⁸I looked, and tendons and flesh appeared on them and skin covered them, but there was no breath in them.

⁹Then he said to me, "Prophesy to the breath;ᵒ prophesy, son of man, and say to it, 'This is what the Sovereign LORD says: Come from the four winds,ᵖ O breath, and breathe into these slain, that they may live.'" ¹⁰So I prophesied as he commandedᑫ me, and breath entered them; they came to life and stood up on their feet—a vast army.ʳ

¹¹Then he said to me: "Son of man, these bones are the whole house of Israel. They say, 'Our bones are dried up and our hope is gone; we are cut off.'ˢ ¹²Therefore prophesy and say to them: 'This is what the Sovereign LORD says: O my people, I am going to open your graves and bring you up from them; I will bring you back to the land of Israel.ᵗ ¹³Then you, my people, will know that I am the LORD,ᵘ when I open your graves and bring you up from them.ᵛ ¹⁴I will put my Spiritʷ in you and you will live, and I will settleˣ you in your own land. Then you will know that I the LORD have spoken, and I have done it, declares the LORD.ʸ'"

One Nation Under One King

¹⁵The word of the LORD came to me: ¹⁶"Son of man, take a stick of wood and write on it, 'Belonging to Judah and the Israelitesᶻ associated with him.ᵃ' Then take another stick of wood, and write on it, 'Ephraim's stick, belonging to Joseph and all the house of Israel associated with him.' ¹⁷Join them together into one stick so that they will become one in your hand.ᵇ

¹⁸"When your countrymen ask you, 'Won't you tell us what you mean by this?'ᶜ ¹⁹say to them, 'This is what the Sovereign LORD says: I am going to take the stick of Joseph—which is in Ephraim's hand—and of the Israelite tribes associated with him, and join it to Judah's stick, making them a single stick of wood, and they will become one in my hand.'ᵈ ²⁰Hold before their eyes the sticks you have written on ²¹and say to them, 'This is what the Sovereign LORD says: I will take the Israelites out of the nations where they have gone. I will gather them from all around and bring them back into their own land.ᵉ ²²I will make them one nation in the land, on the mountains of Israel.ᶠ There will be one king over all of them and they will never again be two

---

37:3 ᵏ Dt 32:39; S 1Sa 2:6; Isa 26:19; 1Co 15:35
37:4 ʲ Jer 22:29
37:5 ᵐ S Ge 2:7; Ps 104:29-30; Rev 11:11
37:6 ⁿ S Ex 6:2; Eze 38:23
37:9 ᵒ ver 14; Ps 104:30; Isa 32:15; Eze 39:29; Zec 12:10 ᵖ Jer 49:36; Da 7:2; 8:8; 11:4; Zec 2:6; 6:5; Rev 7:1
37:10 ᑫ S Eze 12:7 ʳ Rev 11:11
37:11 ˢ Job 17:15; S La 3:54
37:12 ᵗ ver 21; Dt 32:39; 1Sa 2:6; Isa 26:19; Jer 29:14; Hos 13:14; Am 9:14-15; Zep 3:20; Zec 8:8
37:13 ᵘ S Ex 6:2 ᵛ S Eze 17:24; Hos 13:14
37:14 ʷ S ver 9; S Isa 11:2; Joel 2:28-29 ˣ S Jer 43:2 ʸ Eze 36:27-28,36; Rev 11:11
37:16 ᶻ S 1Ki 12:20; 2Ch 10:17-19 ᵃ Nu 17:2-3; 2Ch 15:9
37:17 ᵇ ver 24; Isa 11:13; S Jer 50:4; Hos 1:11
37:18 ᶜ S Eze 24:19
37:19 ᵈ Zec 10:6
37:21 ᵉ S ver 12; S Isa 43:5-6; S Eze 20:42; 39:27; Mic 4:6
37:22 ᶠ S Eze 17:22; S 34:13-14

F *Isa 26:19* ◄ ► *Da 12:2*
H *Job 33:4* ◄ ► *Mt 12:28*

B *Eze 36:26–27* ◄ ► *Da 4:8–9*
M *Eze 36:27* ◄ ► *Da 4:8–9*
M *Exe 34:25–28* ◄ ► *Eze 43:5–7*

j 5 The Hebrew for this word can also mean *wind* or *spirit* (see verses 6-14).

---

hopeless nation, languishing like dry bones in a land of exile. Ezekiel's words gave immediate hope to the exiles that they would be restored to their land (37:14). Yet Ezekiel's words also foreshadowed the spiritual restoration of Israel at Christ's second coming. Israel's restoration would be God's proof of his power and rule.

37:15–28 The prophet indicated that in the last days God would finally restore the northern kingdom of Israel that was exiled in 721 B.C. and join them with the exiled kingdom of Judah so that they would never again "be divided into two kingdoms" (37:22). James echoed this prophecy in his salutation to "the twelve tribes scattered among the nations" (Jas 1:1). Though Jews of each tribe have begun to return to Palestine, a careful examination of Ezekiel's prophecy reveals that these words will not be completely fulfilled until the second coming of Christ.

Note also that this passage called the Messiah "David" because he would be a descendant of David and bring to Israel all the good aspects of David's rule—and much more (37:24).

nations or be divided into two kingdoms.^g ²³They will no longer defile^h themselves with their idols and vile images or with any of their offenses, for I will save them from all their sinful backsliding,^{ki} and I will cleanse them. They will be my people, and I will be their God.^j

²⁴"'My servant David^k will be king^l over them, and they will all have one shepherd.^m They will follow my laws and be careful to keep my decrees.ⁿ ²⁵They will live in the land I gave to my servant Jacob, the land where your fathers lived.^o They and their children and their children's children will live there forever,^p and David my servant will be their prince forever.^q ²⁶I will make a covenant of peace^r with them; it will be an everlasting covenant.^s I will establish them and increase their numbers,^t and I will put my sanctuary among them^u forever.^v ²⁷My dwelling place^w will be with them; I will be their God, and they will be my people.^x ²⁸Then the nations will know that I the LORD make Israel holy,^y when my sanctuary is among them forever.^{z a'}

A Prophecy Against Gog

38 The word of the LORD came to me: ²"Son of man, set your face against Gog,^b of the land of Magog,^c the chief prince of^l Meshech and Tubal;^d prophesy against him ³and say: 'This is what the Sovereign LORD says: I am against you, O Gog, chief prince of^m Meshech and Tubal.^e ⁴I will turn you around, put hooks^f in your jaws and bring you out with your whole army—your horses, your horsemen fully armed, and a great horde with large and small shields, all of them brandishing their swords.^g ⁵Persia, Cush^{nh} and Putⁱ will be with them, all with shields and helmets, ⁶also Gomer^j with all its troops, and Beth Togarmah^k from the far north^l with all its troops—the many nations with you.

⁷"'Get ready; be prepared,^m you and all the hordes gathered about you, and take command of them. ⁸After many daysⁿ you will be called to arms. In future years you will invade a land that has recovered from war, whose people were gathered from many nations^o to the mountains of Israel, which had long been desolate. They had been brought out from the nations, and now all of them live in safety.^p ⁹You and all your troops and the many nations with you will go up, advancing like a storm;^q you will be like a cloud^r covering the land.^s

¹⁰"'This is what the Sovereign LORD says: On that day thoughts will come into your mind^t and you will devise an evil

◀ Eze 37:1–28 ◀▶ Eze 38:11–12

^p ver 14; Jer 23:6; S Eze 28:26; Joel 3:1 ^{38:9} ^q Isa 25:4; 28:2 ^r ver 16; Jer 4:13; Joel 2:2 ^s Rev 20:8 ^{38:10} ^t S Jer 17:10

^k 23 Many Hebrew manuscripts (see also Septuagint); most Hebrew manuscripts *all their dwelling places where they sinned* ^l 2 Or *the prince of Rosh*, ^m 3 Or *Gog, prince of Rosh*, ⁿ 5 That is, the upper Nile region

---

38:1–7 Ezekiel prophesied that in the last days, after the return of the Jews to the promised land, a confederacy of nations would join together militarily to invade and destroy Palestine. Ezekiel called the leader of this alliance "Gog," who was "the chief prince of Meshech and Tubal" (38:2).

Ezekiel declared God's determination to stand against Gog and destroy the armies and leaders that attempt to destroy God's people. Though the alliance is strong, God is the one who will control the outcome of the battle and will lead Gog around like a beast with a bit in its mouth. For more information about Gog and Magog, see the article "The Battle of Gog and Magog," p. 942.

38:8–16 The phrase "in future years" (38:8) designates the time when Gog will invade Israel. At this time in the future, the people of Israel are living in their own land (38:8) in relative safety (38:11). Their army has been strengthened, convincing the people of their ability to defeat all of their enemies. However, the size of the armies of the coalition and their sophisticated weapons will be overwhelming. This enemy alliance will attack Israel and "invade a land of unwalled villages" (38:11) and swarm over them like "a cloud that covers the land" (38:16) and plunder Israel's wealth. Ezekiel's vision could well relate to our century or beyond because modern warfare with tanks, cruise missiles, bombers and paratroopers would find city walls and gates no hindrance to an invasion force.

Ezekiel's words about Sheba, Dedan and Tarshish, seem to reflect only a diplomatic complaint from these nations about this invasion, without any military response or aid being offered to Israel by these nations. Yet when God destroys Israel's enemies, he will forever demonstrate that he is the God of Israel. For more information about Gog and Magog, see the article "The Battle of Gog and Magog," p. 942.

scheme. ᵘ ¹¹You will say, "I will invade a land of unwalled villages; I will attack a peaceful and unsuspecting people ᵛ—all of them living without walls and without gates and bars. ʷ ¹²I will plunder and loot and turn my hand against the resettled ruins and the people gathered from the nations, rich in livestock and goods, living at the center of the land." ¹³Sheba ˣ and Dedan ʸ and the merchants of Tarshish ᶻ and all her villages ᵒ will say to you, "Have you come to plunder? Have you gathered your hordes to loot, to carry off silver and gold, to take away livestock and goods and to seize much plunder?"ᵃ'

¹⁴"Therefore, son of man, prophesy and say to Gog: 'This is what the Sovereign LORD says: In that day, when my people Israel are living in safety,ᵇ will you not take notice of it? ¹⁵You will come from your place in the far north,ᶜ you and many nations with you, all of them riding on horses, a great horde, a mighty army.ᵈ ¹⁶You will advance against my people Israel like a cloudᵉ that covers the land.ᶠ In days to come, O Gog, I will bring you against my land, so that the nations may know me when I show myself holyᵍ through you before their eyes.ʰ

¹⁷"'This is what the Sovereign LORD says: Are you not the one I spoke of in former days by my servants the prophets of Israel? At that time they prophesied for years that I would bring you against them. ¹⁸This is what will happen in that day: When Gog attacks the land of Israel, my hot anger will be aroused, declares the Sovereign LORD. ¹⁹In my zeal and fiery wrath I declare that at that time there shall be a great earthquakeⁱ in the land of Israel.ʲ ²⁰The fish of the sea, the birds of the air, the beasts of the field, every creature that moves along the ground, and all the people on the face of the earth will

▎ Eze 38:8 ◀ ▶ Eze 38:14
▎ Eze 38:11–12 ◀ ▶ Eze 38:16
▎ Eze 38:14 ◀ ▶ Eze 38:20
▎ Eze 38:16 ◀ ▶ Eze 39:7–10

tremble ᵏ at my presence. The mountains will be overturned,ˡ the cliffs will crumbleᵐ and every wall will fall to the ground.ⁿ ²¹I will summon a swordᵒ against Gog on all my mountains, declares the Sovereign LORD. Every man's sword will be against his brother.ᵖ ²²I will execute judgmentᵠ upon him with plague and bloodshed;ʳ I will pour down torrents of rain, hailstonesˢ and burning sulfurᵗ on him and on his troops and on the many nations with him.ᵘ ²³And so I will show my greatness and my holiness, and I will make myself known in the sight of many nations. Then they will know that I am the LORD.ᵛ'

39 "Son of man, prophesy against Gogʷ and say: 'This is what the Sovereign LORD says: I am against you, O Gog, chief prince ofᵖ Meshechˣ and Tubal.ʸ ²I will turn you around and drag you along. I will bring you from the far northᶻ and send you against the mountains of Israel.ᵃ ³Then I will strike your bowᵇ from your left hand and make your arrowsᶜ drop from your right hand. ⁴On the mountains of Israel you will fall, you and all your troops and the nations with you. I will give you as food to all kinds of carrion birdsᵈ and to the wild animals.ᵉ ⁵You will fall in the open field, for I have spoken, declares the Sovereign LORD.ᶠ ⁶I will send fireᵍ on Magogʰ and on those who live in safety in the coastlands,ⁱ and they will knowʲ that I am the LORD.

⁷"'I will make known my holy name among my people Israel. I will no longer let my holy name be profaned,ᵏ and the nations will knowˡ that I the LORD am the Holy One in Israel.ᵐ ⁸It is coming! It will surely take place, declares the Sovereign LORD. This is the dayⁿ I have spoken of.

⁹"'Then those who live in the towns of

▎ D Eze 33:27 ◀ ▶ Mt 13:58
▎ P Eze 38:1–23 ◀ ▶ Da 12:1
▎ I Eze 38:20 ◀ ▶ Eze 39:25–29

ᵒ 13 Or *her strong lions* ᵖ 1 Or *Gog, prince of Rosh,*

38:17–23 Ezekiel prophesied that the destruction of Israel's enemies would come through divine intervention. When the coalition comes against Israel, God will send a great earthquake, plagues, rain, hail and "burning sulfur" (38:22) to destroy Israel's enemies and demonstrate his power and might.

39:1–10 God declared that the destruction of Gog and his forces would be horrific, not only involving two-thirds of their armies but their homelands too. The amount of weapons gathered by Israel from this battle would also be so large that Israel would be able to use these weapons as fuel for their fires for seven years.

The Battle of Gog and Magog

WHILE SOME SCHOLARS contend that Ezekiel's prophecy in chs. 38—39 is merely a symbol of the apocalyptic war between good and evil, specific details in Ezekiel's prophecy point to this event as a literal battle that will be waged sometime in the future. This war is referred to as the Battle of Gog and Magog.

The Identification of Gog and Magog

Ezekiel 38:3 describes Gog as the leader of a confederacy of northern nations. Described as a very strong leader, he will have the power to commit his allies to war. God will control Gog's mind and direct him to attack Israel (see 38:11). Gog will come from the land of Magog, a nation composed of three parts: Rosh, Meshech and Tubal. Therefore the identification of the land of Magog is of great interest to prophecy scholars.

Studying Genesis 10, scholars note that after the flood, Noah's descendants dispersed to various parts of Asia. Among them was Magog, a son of Japheth (see Ge 10:1–2). History indicates that Magog settled in what is now called the Caucasus region between the Black and Caspian Seas. The Greeks called Magog's descendants "Scythians." While some of these Scythians moved farther north into Europe, others remained in Asia and emigrated as far as the Urals, becoming the ancestors of the Tartars, Cossacks, Mongols and others. Thus identifying Magog with this area of southwest Russia seems feasible.

The Motive for the Battle

Ezekiel's prophecy indicates that Magog will attempt to destroy Israel and capture her land as a geographically strategic prize. This narrow strip of land has historically been fought over by any empire that wanted to dominate the world. Today, whoever controls this small strip of land along the Mediterranean controls the Middle East as well as the vital oil supplies that flow through it. Because of worldwide dependence on Middle East oil, this outcome of this strategic battle will affect the economies of all industrialized nations.

According to Ezekiel, Magog (Russia) will need help in acquiring the land of Israel and will form a confederation of nations to attack the promised land (see 38:1–6). Historians and Biblical scholars have identified these nations as modern-day Iran, some of the Arab states adjacent to Iran, Germany, Turkey and the central Asiatic peoples allied with Russia.

The Attack of the Confederation

The Bible describes several battles that will occur in the last days. The Battle of Gog and Magog will be the first major struggle against the land of Israel.

Biblical scholars generally agree that the battle described in Ezekiel will take place following an alliance between Magog (Russia) and its allies (38:2, 5–6). Though some nations will protest the invasion, it will proceed unhindered as Gog's armies marshal themselves in an open field (38:13; 39:5).

The Lord will unleash the greatest earthquake in history in response to the attack of Magog and the confederation. Other natural disasters will require seven months for Israel to bury the dead and seven years to burn up the confederation's weapons (39:4–12). God's intervention will cause many to repent (39:21–22). Even the Gentile nations will acknowledge God's power. Russia and her allies' military devastation will set the stage for the rebuilding of the temple in Jerusalem and the rise of antichrist.

The Time of the Battle

A final question in the minds of Bible scholars concerns the timing of this future battle. Scholars generally agree that this battle has not yet occurred because no invasion in Israel's history sufficiently fulfills the details of this prophecy. Though scholars agree that the conflict will occur at some point in the near future, before Armageddon, they differ on the exact timing of this battle. In fact, six different theories exist about its timing.

Some scholars believe this battle will occur either before, in the middle of, or after the tribulation. Others suggest that the battle will occur either at the beginning of or the end of the Millennium. Still others believe this conflict will occur prior to the rapture of the church. Because Scripture gives varying support to each of these theories, we cannot be dogmatic about the details.

However, this author subscribes to the belief that the battle will occur prior to the tribulation for several reasons. Note that Ezekiel's prophecy does not mention the antichrist, the seven-year treaty or Israel's expectation that anyone would protect them from an invading army. It seems inconsistent with the prophet to omit these details from his precise prediction if this invasion will occur during the seven-year period of peace between Israel and the antichrist. Note also that 38:11–12 indicates that Israel appears to be at peace. Ezekiel's vision does not suggest that Israel is living in total peace with her neighbors prior to the attack, but rather that Israel is secure in her position and not expecting an attack.

The results of this battle also help to place the event prior to the tribulation. Ezekiel prophesied that when the battle ends, only one-sixth of Magog's armies will remain (39:2). This massive destruction will profoundly alter the political and military balance of power, effectively removing Russia and her allies from a major role in future conflicts, and clearing the way for the antichrist's kingdom and final struggle at Armageddon.

Israel will go out and use the weapons for fuel and burn them up—the small and large shields, the bows and arrows,ᵒ the war clubs and spears. For seven years they will use them for fuel.ᵖ ¹⁰They will not need to gather wood from the fields or cut it from the forests, because they will use the weapons for fuel. And they will plunderᑫ those who plundered them and loot those who looted them, declares the Sovereign LORD.ʳ

¹¹ "On that day I will give Gog a burial place in Israel, in the valley of those who travel east towardᑫ the Sea.ʳ It will block the way of travelers, because Gog and all his hordes will be buriedˢ there. So it will be called the Valley of Hamon Gog.ˢᵗ

¹² "For seven months the house of Israel will be burying them in order to cleanse the land.ᵘ ¹³All the people of the land will bury them, and the day I am glorifiedᵛ will be a memorable day for them, declares the Sovereign LORD.

¹⁴ "Men will be regularly employed to cleanse the land. Some will go throughout the land and, in addition to them, others will bury those that remain on the ground. At the end of the seven months they will begin their search. ¹⁵As they go through the land and one of them sees a human bone, he will set up a marker be-

39:9 ᵒ Ps 76:3
ᵖ S Ps 46:9
39:10 ᑫ S Ex 3:22
ʳ S Isa 14:2; S 33:1; Hab 2:8
39:11 ˢ S Isa 34:3
ᵗ S Eze 38:2
39:12 ᵘ Dt 21:23
39:13 ᵛ Eze 28:22

ᑫ 11 Or *of*   ʳ 11 That is, the Dead Sea   ˢ 11 *Hamon Gog* means *hordes of Gog.*

39:11—20 God declared he would provide a cemetery for the slain of Gog's armies. The number of dead bodies would be so extensive it would take seven months to bury them all. The slaughter would be so terrible that predatory animals and birds would gorge on the bodies of Gog's soldiers killed in this battle.

The Nations of Ezekiel 38—39

The War of Gog and Magog

side it until the gravediggers have buried it in the Valley of Hamon Gog. ¹⁶(Also a town called Hamonah' will be there.) And so they will cleanse the land.'

¹⁷"Son of man, this is what the Sovereign LORD says: Call out to every kind of bird^w and all the wild animals: 'Assemble and come together from all around to the sacrifice I am preparing for you, the great sacrifice on the mountains of Israel. There you will eat flesh and drink blood.^x ¹⁸You will eat the flesh of mighty men and drink the blood of the princes of the earth as if they were rams and lambs, goats and bulls—all of them fattened animals from Bashan.^y ¹⁹At the sacrifice^z I am preparing for you, you will eat fat till you are glutted and drink blood till you are drunk. ²⁰At my table you will eat your fill of horses and riders, mighty men and soldiers of every kind,' declares the Sovereign LORD.^a

²¹"I will display my glory among the nations, and all the nations will see the punishment I inflict and the hand I lay upon them.^b ²²From that day forward the house of Israel will know that I am the LORD their God. ²³And the nations will know that the people of Israel went into exile for their sin, because they were unfaithful to me. So I hid my face from them and handed them over to their enemies, and they all fell by the sword.^c ²⁴I dealt with them according to their uncleanness and their offenses, and I hid my face from them.^d

²⁵"Therefore this is what the Sovereign LORD says: I will now bring Jacob back from captivity^u ^e and will have compassion^f on all the people of Israel, and I will be zealous for my holy name.^g ²⁶They will forget their shame and all the unfaithfulness they showed toward me when they lived in safety^h in their land with no one to make them afraid.^i ²⁷When I have brought them back from the nations and

R Eze 36:18–19 ◀ ▶ Eze 39:26
I Eze 39:7–10 ◀ ▶ Eze 43:5–7
R Eze 39:21–24 ◀ ▶ Eze 39:28

have gathered them from the countries of their enemies, I will show myself holy through them in the sight of many nations.^j ²⁸Then they will know that I am the LORD their God, for though I sent them into exile among the nations, I will gather them^k to their own land, not leaving any behind.^l ²⁹I will no longer hide my face^m from them, for I will pour out my Spirit^n on the house of Israel, declares the Sovereign LORD.^o

The New Temple Area

40 In the twenty-fifth year of our exile, at the beginning of the year, on the tenth of the month, in the fourteenth year after the fall of the city^p—on that very day the hand of the LORD was upon me^q and he took me there. ²In visions^r of God he took me to the land of Israel and set me on a very high mountain,^s on whose south side were some buildings that looked like a city. ³He took me there, and I saw a man whose appearance was like bronze;^t he was standing in the gateway with a linen cord and a measuring rod^u in his hand. ⁴The man said to me, "Son of man, look with your eyes and hear with your ears and pay attention to everything I am going to show you,^v for that is why you have been brought here. Tell^w the house of Israel everything you see.^x"

The East Gate to the Outer Court

⁵I saw a wall completely surrounding the temple area. The length of the measuring rod in the man's hand was six long cubits, each of which was a cubit^v and a handbreadth.^w He measured^y the wall; it was one measuring rod thick and one rod high.

⁶Then he went to the gate facing east.^z He climbed its steps and measured the

R Eze 39:26 ◀ ▶ Da 8:11–14
T Eze 13:3 ◀ ▶ Da 4:8–9

^t 16 *Hamonah* means horde. ^u 25 Or *now restore the fortunes of Jacob* ^v 5 The common cubit was about 1 1/2 feet (about 0.5 meter). ^w 5 That is, about 3 inches (about 8 centimeters)

39:21–29 As a postscript to the horror of the battle, God declared his intent to graciously restore Israel in the last days so that the nations would acknowledge God's glory. God's visible presence and intervention in history would be a glorious display of his power to the heathen nations.

40:1—42:20 In these chapters Ezekiel describes a vision of the rebuilding of the temple when Israel is reestablished in their land in the Millennium. This temple will be larger and different in construction than Solomon's temple, but it is difficult to comment with precision about its details.

Ezekiel's Temple

- A. Wall (40:5,16-20)
- B. East gate (40:6-14,16)
- C. Portico (40:8)
- D. Outer court (40:17)
- E. Pavement (40:17)
- F. Inner court (40:19)
- G. North gate (40:20-22)
- H. Inner court (40:23)
- I. South gate (40:24-26)
- J. South inner court (40:27)
- K. Gateway (40:28-31)
- L. Gateway (40:32-34)
- M. Gateway (40:35-38)
- N. Priests' rooms (40:44-45)
- O. Court (40:47)
- P. Temple portico (40:48-49)
- Q. Outer sanctuary (41:1-2)
- R. Most Holy Place (41:3-4)
- S. Temple walls (41:5-7,9,11)
- T. Base (41:8)
- U. Open area (41:10)
- V. West building (41:12)
- W. Priests' rooms (42:1-10)
- X. Altar (43:13-17)
- AA. Rooms for preparing sacrifices (40:39-43)
- BB. Ovens (46:19-20)
- CC. Kitchens (46:21-24)

Ezekiel uses a long or "royal" cubit, 20.4 inches or 51.81 cm ("cubit and a handbreadth," Eze 40:5) as opposed to the standard Hebrew cubit of 17.6 inches or 44.7 cm.

Scripture describes a floor plan, but provides few height dimensions. This artwork shows an upward projection of the temple over the floor plan. This temple existed only in a vision of Ezekiel (Eze 40:2), and has never actually been built as were the temples of Solomon, Zerubbabel and Herod.

Height of this wall has been exaggerated slightly to avoid optical illusion

Kitchens were in all four corners

Plan adapted from the design given in *The Zondervan Pictorial Bible Dictionary*. Copyright © 1975 by The Zondervan Corporation. Used by permission.

threshold of the gate; it was one rod deep.ˣ ⁷The alcovesᵃ for the guards were one rod long and one rod wide, and the projecting walls between the alcoves were five cubits thick. And the threshold of the gate next to the portico facing the temple was one rod deep.

⁸Then he measured the portico of the gateway; ⁹itʸ was eight cubits deep and its jambs were two cubits thick. The portico of the gateway faced the temple.

¹⁰Inside the east gate were three alcoves on each side; the three had the same measurements, and the faces of the projecting walls on each side had the same measurements. ¹¹Then he measured the width of the entrance to the gateway; it was ten cubits and its length was thirteen cubits. ¹²In front of each alcove was a wall one cubit high, and the alcoves were six cubits square. ¹³Then he measured the gateway from the top of the rear wall of one alcove to the top of the opposite one; the distance was twenty-five cubits from one parapet opening to the opposite one. ¹⁴He measured along the faces of the projecting walls all around the inside of the gateway—sixty cubits. The measurement was up to the porticoᶻ facing the courtyard.ᵃᵇ ¹⁵The distance from the entrance of the gateway to the far end of its portico was fifty cubits. ¹⁶The alcoves and the projecting walls inside the gateway were surmounted by narrow parapet openings all around, as was the portico; the openings all around faced inward. The faces of the projecting walls were decorated with palm trees.ᶜ

The Outer Court

¹⁷Then he brought me into the outer court.ᵈ There I saw some rooms and a pavement that had been constructed all around the court; there were thirty roomsᵉ along the pavement.ᶠ ¹⁸It abutted the sides of the gateways and was as wide as they were long; this was the lower pavement. ¹⁹Then he measured the distance from the inside of the lower gateway to the outside of the inner court;ᵍ it was a hundred cubitsʰ on the east side as well as on the north.

The North Gate

²⁰Then he measured the length and width of the gate facing north, leading into the outer court. ²¹Its alcovesⁱ— three on each side—its projecting walls and its porticoʲ had the same measurements as those of the first gateway. It was fifty cubits long and twenty-five cubits wide. ²²Its openings, its porticoᵏ and its palm tree decorations had the same measurements as those of the gate facing east. Seven steps led up to it, with its portico opposite them.ˡ ²³There was a gate to the inner court facing the north gate, just as there was on the east. He measured from one gate to the opposite one; it was a hundred cubits.ᵐ

The South Gate

²⁴Then he led me to the south side and I saw a gate facing south. He measured its jambs and its portico, and they had the same measurementsⁿ as the others. ²⁵The gateway and its portico had narrow openings all around, like the openings of the others. It was fifty cubits long and twenty-five cubits wide.ᵒ ²⁶Seven steps led up to it, with its portico opposite them; it had palm tree decorations on the faces of the projecting walls on each side.ᵖ ²⁷The inner courtᑫ also had a gate facing south, and he measured from this gate to the outer gate on the south side; it was a hundred cubits.ʳ

Gates to the Inner Court

²⁸Then he brought me into the inner court through the south gate, and he measured the south gate; it had the same measurementsˢ as the others. ²⁹Its alcoves,ᵗ its projecting walls and its portico had the same measurements as the others. The gateway and its portico had openings all around. It was fifty cubits long and twenty-five cubits wide.ᵘ ³⁰(The porticoesᵛ of the gateways around the inner court were twenty-five cubits wide and five cubits deep.) ³¹Its porticoʷ faced the outer court; palm trees decorated its jambs, and eight steps led up to it.ˣ

³²Then he brought me to the inner court on the east side, and he measured the gateway; it had the same measurementsʸ as the others. ³³Its alcoves,ᶻ its projecting walls and its portico had the same measurements as the others. The

---

ˣ 6 Septuagint; Hebrew deep, the first threshold, one rod deep
ʸ 8,9 Many Hebrew manuscripts, Septuagint, Vulgate and Syriac; most Hebrew manuscripts gateway facing the temple; it was one rod deep.
ᵃ Then he measured the portico of the gateway; it ᶻ 14 Septuagint; Hebrew projecting wall ᵃ 14 The meaning of the Hebrew for this verse is uncertain.

gateway and its portico had openings all around. It was fifty cubits long and twenty-five cubits wide. ³⁴Its portico[a] faced the outer court; palm trees decorated the jambs on either side, and eight steps led up to it.

³⁵Then he brought me to the north gate[b] and measured it. It had the same measurements[c] as the others, ³⁶as did its alcoves,[d] its projecting walls and its portico, and it had openings all around. It was fifty cubits long and twenty-five cubits wide. ³⁷Its portico[b][e] faced the outer court; palm trees decorated the jambs on either side, and eight steps led up to it.[f]

The Rooms for Preparing Sacrifices

³⁸A room with a doorway was by the portico in each of the inner gateways, where the burnt offerings[g] were washed. ³⁹In the portico of the gateway were two tables on each side, on which the burnt offerings,[h] sin offerings[i] and guilt offerings[j] were slaughtered.[k] ⁴⁰By the outside wall of the portico of the gateway, near the steps at the entrance to the north gateway were two tables, and on the other side of the steps were two tables. ⁴¹So there were four tables on one side of the gateway and four on the other—eight tables in all—on which the sacrifices were slaughtered. ⁴²There were also four tables of dressed stone[l] for the burnt offerings, each a cubit and a half long, a cubit and a half wide and a cubit high. On them were placed the utensils for slaughtering the burnt offerings and the other sacrifices.[m] ⁴³And double-pronged hooks, each a handbreadth long, were attached to the wall all around. The tables were for the flesh of the offerings.

Rooms for the Priests

⁴⁴Outside the inner gate, within the inner court, were two rooms, one[c] at the side of the north gate and facing south, and another at the side of the south[d] gate and facing north. ⁴⁵He said to me, "The room facing south is for the priests who have charge of the temple,[n] ⁴⁶and the room facing north[o] is for the priests who have charge of the altar.[p] These are the sons of Zadok,[q] who are the only Levites who may draw near to the Lord to minister before him.[r]"

⁴⁷Then he measured the court: It was square—a hundred cubits long and a hundred cubits wide. And the altar was in front of the temple.[s]

The Temple

⁴⁸He brought me to the portico of the temple[t] and measured the jambs of the portico; they were five cubits wide on either side. The width of the entrance was fourteen cubits and its projecting walls were[e] three cubits wide on either side. ⁴⁹The portico[u] was twenty cubits wide, and twelve[f] cubits from front to back. It was reached by a flight of stairs,[g] and there were pillars[v] on each side of the jambs.

41 Then the man brought me to the outer sanctuary[w] and measured the jambs; the width of the jambs was six cubits[h] on each side.[i] ²The entrance was ten cubits wide, and the projecting walls on each side of it were five cubits wide. He also measured the outer sanctuary; it was forty cubits long and twenty cubits wide.[x]

³Then he went into the inner sanctuary and measured the jambs of the entrance; each was two cubits wide. The entrance was six cubits wide, and the projecting walls on each side of it were seven cubits wide. ⁴And he measured the length of the inner sanctuary; it was twenty cubits, and its width was twenty cubits across the end of the outer sanctuary.[y] He said to me, "This is the Most Holy Place.[z]"

⁵Then he measured the wall of the temple; it was six cubits thick, and each side room around the temple was four cubits wide. ⁶The side rooms were on three levels, one above another, thirty[a] on each level. There were ledges all around the wall of the temple to serve as supports for the side rooms, so that the supports were not inserted into the wall of the temple.[b] ⁷The side rooms all around the temple were wider at each successive level. The structure surrounding the temple was built in ascending stages, so that the rooms widened as one went upward. A stairway[c] went up from the lowest floor to the top floor through the middle floor.

⁸I saw that the temple had a raised base

---

b 37 Septuagint (see also verses 31 and 34); Hebrew *jambs*
c 44 Septuagint; Hebrew *were rooms for singers, which were*
d 44 Septuagint; Hebrew *east*   *e 48* Septuagint; Hebrew *entrance was*
f 49 Septuagint; Hebrew *eleven*   *g 49* Hebrew; Septuagint *Ten steps led up to it*   *h 1* The common cubit was about 1 1/2 feet (about 0.5 meter).
i 1 One Hebrew manuscript and Septuagint; most Hebrew manuscripts *side, the width of the tent*

all around it, forming the foundation of the side rooms. It was the length of the rod, six long cubits. ⁹The outer wall of the side rooms was five cubits thick. The open area between the side rooms of the temple ¹⁰and the ⌞priests'⌟ rooms was twenty cubits wide all around the temple. ¹¹There were entrances to the side rooms from the open area, one on the north and another on the south; and the base adjoining the open area was five cubits wide all around.

¹²The building facing the temple courtyard on the west side was seventy cubits wide. The wall of the building was five cubits thick all around, and its length was ninety cubits.

¹³Then he measured the temple; it was a hundred cubits long, and the temple courtyard and the building with its walls were also a hundred cubits long. ¹⁴The width of the temple courtyard on the east, including the front of the temple, was a hundred cubits.ᵈ

¹⁵Then he measured the length of the building facing the courtyard at the rear of the temple, including its galleriesᵉ on each side; it was a hundred cubits.

The outer sanctuary, the inner sanctuary and the portico facing the court, ¹⁶as well as the thresholds and the narrow windowsᶠ and galleries around the three of them—everything beyond and including the threshold was covered with wood. The floor, the wall up to the windows, and the windows were covered.ᵍ ¹⁷In the space above the outside of the entrance to the inner sanctuary and on the walls at regular intervals all around the inner and outer sanctuary ¹⁸were carvedʰ cherubimⁱ and palm trees.ʲ Palm trees alternated with cherubim. Each cherub had two faces:ᵏ ¹⁹the face of a man toward the palm tree on one side and the face of a lion toward the palm tree on the other. They were carved all around the whole temple.ˡ ²⁰From the floor to the area above the entrance, cherubim and palm trees were carved on the wall of the outer sanctuary.

²¹The outer sanctuaryᵐ had a rectangular doorframe, and the one at the front of the Most Holy Place was similar. ²²There was a wooden altarⁿ three cubits high and two cubits square;ʲ its corners, its baseᵏ and its sides were of wood. The man said to me, "This is the tableᵒ that is before the LORD." ²³Both the outer sanctuaryᵖ and the Most Holy Place had double doors.ᑫ ²⁴Each door had two leaves—two hinged leavesʳ for each door. ²⁵And on the doors of the outer sanctuary were carved cherubim and palm trees like those carved on the walls, and there was a wooden overhang on the front of the portico. ²⁶On the sidewalls of the portico were narrow windows with palm trees carved on each side. The side rooms of the temple also had overhangs.ˢ

Rooms for the Priests

42 Then the man led me northward into the outer court and brought me to the roomsᵗ opposite the temple courtyardᵘ and opposite the outer wall on the north side.ᵛ ²The building whose door faced north was a hundred cubitsⁱ long and fifty cubits wide. ³Both in the section twenty cubits from the inner court and in the section opposite the pavement of the outer court, galleryʷ faced gallery at the three levels.ˣ ⁴In front of the rooms was an inner passageway ten cubits wide and a hundred cubitsᵐ long. Their doors were on the north.ʸ ⁵Now the upper rooms were narrower, for the galleries took more space from them than from the rooms on the lower and middle floors of the building. ⁶The rooms on the third floor had no pillars, as the courts had; so they were smaller in floor space than those on the lower and middle floors. ⁷There was an outer wall parallel to the rooms and the outer court; it extended in front of the rooms for fifty cubits. ⁸While the row of rooms on the side next to the outer court was fifty cubits long, the row on the side nearest the sanctuary was a hundred cubits long. ⁹The lower rooms had an entranceᶻ on the east side as one enters them from the outer court.

¹⁰On the south sideⁿ along the length of the wall of the outer court, adjoining the temple courtyardᵃ and opposite the outer wall, were roomsᵇ ¹¹with a passageway in front of them. These were like the rooms on the north; they had the same length and width, with similar exits and dimensions. Similar to the doorways on

---

41:14 ᵈEze 40:47
41:15 ᵉEze 42:3
41:16 ᶠ1Ki 6:4
  ᵍver 25-26;
  1Ki 6:15; Eze 42:3
41:18 ʰS 1Ki 6:18
  ⁱEx 37:7; S 2Ch 3:7
  ʲS 1Ki 6:29; 7:36
  ᵏEze 10:21
41:19 ˡS Eze 10:14
41:21 ᵐver 1
41:22 ⁿS Ex 30:1
  ᵒS Ex 25:23;
  S Eze 23:41
41:23 ᵖver 1
  ᑫ1Ki 6:32
41:24 ʳ1Ki 6:34
41:26 ˢver 15-16;
  Eze 40:16
42:1 ᵗver 13
  ᵘS Ex 27:9;
  Eze 41:12-14
  ᵛEze 40:17
42:3 ʷEze 41:15
  ˣEze 41:16
42:4 ʸEze 46:19
42:9 ᶻEze 44:5;
  46:19
42:10
  ᵃEze 41:12-14
  ᵇver 1

ʲ 22 Septuagint; Hebrew *long*   ᵏ 22 Septuagint; Hebrew *length*
ˡ 2 The common cubit was about 1 1/2 feet (about 0.5 meter).
ᵐ 4 Septuagint and Syriac; Hebrew *and one cubit*   ⁿ 10 Septuagint; Hebrew *Eastward*

the north ¹²were the doorways of the rooms on the south. There was a doorway at the beginning of the passageway that was parallel to the corresponding wall extending eastward, by which one enters the rooms.

¹³Then he said to me, "The north[c] and south rooms[d] facing the temple courtyard[e] are the priests' rooms, where the priests who approach the LORD will eat the most holy offerings. There they will put the most holy offerings—the grain offerings,[f] the sin offerings[g] and the guilt offerings[h]—for the place is holy.[i] ¹⁴Once the priests enter the holy precincts, they are not to go into the outer court until they leave behind the garments[j] in which they minister, for these are holy. They are to put on other clothes before they go near the places that are for the people.[k]"

¹⁵When he had finished measuring what was inside the temple area, he led me out by the east gate[l] and measured the area all around: ¹⁶He measured the east side with the measuring rod; it was five hundred cubits.[o] ¹⁷He measured the north side; it was five hundred cubits[p] by the measuring rod. ¹⁸He measured the south side; it was five hundred cubits by the measuring rod. ¹⁹Then he turned to the west side and measured; it was five hundred cubits by the measuring rod. ²⁰So he measured[m] the area[n] on all four sides. It had a wall around it,[o] five hundred cubits long and five hundred cubits wide,[p] to separate the holy from the common.[q]

The Glory Returns to the Temple

D 43 Then the man brought me to the gate facing east,[r] ²and I saw the glory of the God of Israel coming from the east. His voice was like the roar of rushing waters,[s] and the land was radiant with his glory.[t] ³The vision I saw was like the vision I had seen when he[q] came to destroy the city and like the visions I had seen by the Kebar River, and I fell facedown. ⁴The glory[u] of the LORD entered the temple through the gate facing east.[v] ⁵Then the Spirit[w] lifted me up[x] and brought me into the inner court, and the glory[y] of the LORD filled the temple.[z]

⁶While the man was standing beside me, I heard someone speaking to me from inside the temple. ⁷He said: "Son of man, this is the place of my throne[a] and the place for the soles of my feet. This is where I will live among the Israelites forever. The house of Israel will never again defile[b] my holy name—neither they nor their kings—by their prostitution[r] and the lifeless idols[s] of their kings at their high places.[c] ⁸When they placed their threshold next to my threshold and their doorposts beside my doorposts, with only a wall between me and them, they defiled my holy name by their detestable practices. So I destroyed them in my anger. ⁹Now let them put away from me their prostitution and the lifeless idols of their kings, and I will live among them forever.[d]

¹⁰"Son of man, describe the temple to the people of Israel, that they may be ashamed[e] of their sins. Let them consider the plan, ¹¹and if they are ashamed of all they have done, make known to them the design of the temple—its arrangement, its exits and entrances—its whole design and all its regulations[f] and laws. Write these down before them so that they may be faithful to its design and follow all its regulations.[f]

¹²"This is the law of the temple: All the surrounding area[g] on top of the mountain

42:13 c Eze 40:46; d ver 1; e Eze 41:12-14; f Jer 41:5; g S Lev 10:17; h Lev 14:13; i S Ex 29:31; S Lev 6:29; 7:6; 10:12-13; Nu 18:9-10
42:14 j Lev 16:23; Eze 44:19; k Ex 29:9; S Lev 8:7-9
42:15 l Eze 43:1
42:20 m Eze 40:5; n Eze 43:12; o Zec 2:5; p Eze 45:2; Rev 21:16; q S Eze 22:26
43:1 r S 1Ch 9:18; S Eze 8:16; 42:15; 44:1
43:2 s S Ps 18:4; S Rev 1:15 • Isa 6:3; Rev 18:1; 21:11
43:4 u Eze 1:28; v Eze 10:19; 44:2
43:5 w S Eze 11:24; x S Eze 3:12; y S Ex 16:7; z S Isa 6:4
43:7 a S Jer 3:17; b S Eze 37:23; c S Lev 26:30; S Eze 20:29,39
43:9
43:10 e S Eze 16:61
43:11 f Eze 44:5
43:12 g Eze 42:20

D Eze 43:1–2 ◀▶ Eze 44:1–2
N Eze 37:1 ◀▶ Da 5:12
I Eze 39:25–29 ◀▶ Eze 43:9
M Eze 37:22–28 ◀▶ Eze 47:1–21
E Eze 37:1 ◀▶ Da 4:8–9
I Eze 43:5–7 ◀▶ Eze 45:1–2

[o] 16 See Septuagint of verse 17; Hebrew *rods*; also in verses 18 and 19.
[p] Septuagint; Hebrew *rods*   [q] 3 Some Hebrew manuscripts and Vulgate; most Hebrew manuscripts *I*   [r] 7 Or *their spiritual adultery*; also in verse 9   [s] 7 Or *the corpses*; also in verse 9   [t] 11 Some Hebrew manuscripts and Septuagint; most Hebrew manuscripts *regulations and its whole design*.

D SS 8:5 ◀▶ Eze 43:4–7

43:1–9 Ezekiel saw in his vision the return of the Lord to the temple via the east gate, which was the gate through which he had earlier departed (see 10:18–19). God then declared his intent to "live among the Israelites forever" (43:7) and that his people would renounce their sins and receive transformed hearts.

will be most holy.[h] Such is the law of the temple.

The Altar

[13] "These are the measurements of the altar[i] in long cubits, that cubit being a cubit[u] and a handbreadth[v]: Its gutter is a cubit deep and a cubit wide, with a rim of one span[w] around the edge. And this is the height of the altar: [14] From the gutter on the ground up to the lower ledge it is two cubits high and a cubit wide, and from the smaller ledge up to the larger ledge it is four cubits high and a cubit wide. [15] The altar hearth[j] is four cubits high, and four horns[k] project upward from the hearth. [16] The altar hearth is square, twelve cubits long and twelve cubits wide.[l] [17] The upper ledge[m] also is square, fourteen cubits long and fourteen cubits wide, with a rim of half a cubit and a gutter of a cubit all around. The steps[n] of the altar face east.[o]"

[18] Then he said to me, "Son of man, this is what the Sovereign LORD says: These will be the regulations for sacrificing burnt offerings[p] and sprinkling blood[q] upon the altar when it is built: [19] You are to give a young bull[r] as a sin offering to the priests, who are Levites, of the family of Zadok,[s] who come near[t] to minister before me, declares the Sovereign LORD. [20] You are to take some of its blood and put it on the four horns of the altar[u] and on the four corners of the upper ledge[v] and all around the rim, and so purify the altar[w] and make atonement for it. [21] You are to take the bull for the sin offering and burn it in the designated part of the temple area outside the sanctuary.[x]

[22] "On the second day you are to offer a male goat without defect for a sin offering, and the altar is to be purified as it was purified with the bull. [23] When you have finished purifying it, you are to offer a young bull and a ram from the flock, both without defect.[y] [24] You are to offer them before the LORD, and the priests are to sprinkle salt[z] on them and sacrifice them as a burnt offering to the LORD.

[25] "For seven days[a] you are to provide a male goat daily for a sin offering; you are also to provide a young bull and a ram from the flock, both without defect.[b] [26] For seven days they are to make atonement for the altar and cleanse it; thus they will dedicate it. [27] At the end of these days, from the eighth day[c] on, the priests are to present your burnt offerings[d] and fellowship offerings[xe] on the altar. Then I will accept you, declares the Sovereign LORD."

The Prince, the Levites, the Priests

44 Then the man brought me back D to the outer gate of the sanctuary, the one facing east,[f] and it was shut. [2] The LORD said to me, "This gate is to remain shut. It must not be opened; no one may enter through it.[g] It is to remain shut because the LORD, the God of Israel, has entered through it. [3] The prince himself is the only one who may sit inside the gateway to eat in the presence[h] of the LORD. He is to enter by way of the portico of the gateway and go out the same way.[i]"

[4] Then the man brought me by way of the north gate[j] to the front of the temple. I looked and saw the glory of the LORD filling the temple[k] of the LORD, and I fell facedown.[l]

[5] The LORD said to me, "Son of man, look carefully, listen closely and give attention to everything I tell you concerning all the regulations regarding the temple of the LORD. Give attention to the entrance[m] of the temple and all the exits

D Eze 43:4-7 ◄ ► Zec 2:10

[u] 13 The common cubit was about 1 1/2 feet (about 0.5 meter). [v] 13 That is, about 3 inches (about 8 centimeters) [w] 13 That is, about 9 inches (about 22 centimeters) [x] 27 Traditionally *peace offerings*

44:1–2 Ezekiel's vision revealed that the Eastern Gate of the temple would be shut because the Lord entered through it. That the gate remained shut may reaffirm God's promise in 43:7 to dwell with his children forever, or it may merely signify its holy status since the Lord crossed its threshold. Note that Jerusalem has many city gates. The Eastern (Golden) Gate in the old walled city which surrounds the Moslem area of Jerusalem has been walled shut since the sixteenth century, possibly as a result of a related Moslem tradition. Other city gates have suffered similar fates in order to control public access to Moslem mosques in that area.

of the sanctuary.ⁿ ⁶Say to the rebellious house° of Israel, 'This is what the Sovereign LORD says: Enough of your detestable practices, O house of Israel! ⁷In addition to all your other detestable practices, you brought foreigners uncircumcised in heartᵖ and flesh into my sanctuary, desecrating my temple while you offered me food, fat and blood, and you broke my covenant.ᵍ ⁸Instead of carrying out your duty in regard to my holy things, you put others in charge of my sanctuary.ʳ ⁹This is what the Sovereign LORD says: No foreigner uncircumcised in heart and flesh is to enter my sanctuary, not even the foreigners who live among the Israelites.ˢ

¹⁰" 'The Levites who went far from me when Israel went astrayᵗ and who wandered from me after their idols must bear the consequences of their sin.ᵘ ¹¹They may serve in my sanctuary, having charge of the gates of the temple and serving in it; they may slaughter the burnt offeringsᵛ and sacrifices for the people and stand before the people and serve them.ʷ ¹²But because they served them in the presence of their idols and made the house of Israel fallˣ into sin, therefore I have sworn with uplifted handʸ that they must bear the consequences of their sin, declares the Sovereign LORD.ᶻ ¹³They are not to come near to serve me as priests or come near any of my holy things or my most holy offerings; they must bear the shameᵃ of their detestable practices.ᵇ ¹⁴Yet I will put them in charge of the duties of the temple and all the work that is to be done in it.ᶜ

¹⁵" 'But the priests, who are Levites and descendants of Zadokᵈ and who faithfully carried out the duties of my sanctuary when the Israelites went astray from me, are to come near to minister before me; they are to stand before me to offer sacrifices of fatᵉ and blood, declares the Sovereign LORD.ᶠ ¹⁶They alone are to enter my sanctuary; they alone are to come near my tableᵍ to minister before me and perform my service.ʰ

¹⁷" 'When they enter the gates of the inner court, they are to wear linen clothes;ⁱ they must not wear any woolen garment while ministering at the gates of the inner court or inside the temple. ¹⁸They are to wear linen turbansʲ on their heads and linen undergarmentsᵏ around their waists. They must not wear anything that makes them perspire.ˡ ¹⁹When they go out into the outer court where the people are, they are to take off the clothes they have been ministering in and are to leave them in the sacred rooms, and put on other clothes, so that they do not consecrateᵐ the people by means of their garments.ⁿ

²⁰" 'They must not shave° their heads or let their hair grow long, but they are to keep the hair of their heads trimmed.ᵖ ²¹No priest is to drink wine when he enters the inner court.ᵍ ²²They must not marry widows or divorced women; they may marry only virgins of Israelite descent or widows of priests.ʳ ²³They are to teach my people the difference between the holy and the commonˢ and show them how to distinguish between the unclean and the clean.ᵗ

²⁴" 'In any dispute, the priests are to serve as judgesᵘ and decide it according to my ordinances. They are to keep my laws and my decrees for all my appointed feasts,ᵛ and they are to keep my Sabbaths holy.ʷ

²⁵" 'A priest must not defile himself by going near a dead person; however, if the dead person was his father or mother, son or daughter, brother or unmarried sister, then he may defile himself.ˣ ²⁶After he is cleansed, he must wait seven days.ʸ ²⁷On the day he goes into the inner court of the sanctuaryᶻ to minister in the sanctuary, he is to offer a sin offeringᵃ for himself, declares the Sovereign LORD.

²⁸" 'I am to be the only inheritanceᵇ the priests have. You are to give them no possession in Israel; I will be their possession. ²⁹They will eatᶜ the grain offerings, the sin offerings and the guilt offerings; and everything in Israel devotedʸ to the LORDᵈ will belong to them.ᵉ ³⁰The best of all the firstfruitsᶠ and of all your special gifts will belong to the priests. You are to give them the first portion of your ground mealᵍ so that a blessingʰ may rest on your household.ⁱ ³¹The priests must not eat anything, bird or animal, found deadʲ or torn by wild animals.ᵏ

ʸ29 The Hebrew term refers to the irrevocable giving over of things or persons to the LORD.

Division of the Land

45 " 'When you allot the land as an inheritance,¹ you are to present to the LORD a portion of the land as a sacred district, 25,000 cubits long and 20,000 cubits wide; the entire area will be holy. ²Of this, a section 500 cubits square is to be for the sanctuary, with 50 cubits around it for open land. ³In the sacred district, measure off a section 25,000 cubits long and 10,000 cubits wide. In it will be the sanctuary, the Most Holy Place. ⁴It will be the sacred portion of the land for the priests, who minister in the sanctuary and who draw near to minister before the LORD. It will be a place for their houses as well as a holy place for the sanctuary. ⁵An area 25,000 cubits long and 10,000 cubits wide will belong to the Levites, who serve in the temple, as their possession for towns to live in.

⁶" 'You are to give the city as its property an area 5,000 cubits wide and 25,000 cubits long, adjoining the sacred portion; it will belong to the whole house of Israel.

⁷" 'The prince will have the land bordering each side of the area formed by the sacred district and the property of the city. It will extend westward from the west side and eastward from the east side, running lengthwise from the western to the eastern border parallel to one of the tribal portions. ⁸This land will be his possession in Israel. And my princes will no longer oppress my people but will allow the house of Israel to possess the land according to their tribes.

⁹" 'This is what the Sovereign LORD says: You have gone far enough, O princes of Israel! Give up your violence and oppression and do what is just and right. Stop dispossessing my people, declares the Sovereign LORD. ¹⁰You are to use accurate scales, an accurate ephah and an accurate bath. ¹¹The ephah and the bath are to be the same size, the bath containing a tenth of a homer and the ephah a tenth of a homer; the homer is to be the standard measure for both. ¹²The shekel is to consist of twenty gerahs. Twenty shekels plus twenty-five shekels plus fifteen shekels equal one mina.

Offerings and Holy Days

¹³" 'This is the special gift you are to offer: a sixth of an ephah from each homer of wheat and a sixth of an ephah from each homer of barley. ¹⁴The prescribed portion of oil, measured by the bath, is a tenth of a bath from each cor (which consists of ten baths or one homer, for ten baths are equivalent to a homer). ¹⁵Also one sheep is to be taken from every flock of two hundred from the well-watered pastures of Israel. These will be used for the grain offerings, burnt offerings and fellowship offerings to make atonement for the people, declares the Sovereign LORD. ¹⁶All the people of the land will participate in this special gift for the use of the prince in Israel. ¹⁷It will be the duty of the prince to provide the burnt offerings, grain offerings and drink offerings at the festivals, the New Moons and the Sabbaths—at all the appointed feasts of the house of Israel. He will provide the sin offerings, grain offerings, burnt offerings and fellowship offerings to make atonement for the house of Israel.

¹⁸" 'This is what the Sovereign LORD says: In the first month on the first day you are to take a young bull without defect and purify the sanctuary. ¹⁹The priest is to take some of the blood of the sin offering and put it on the doorposts of the temple, on the four corners of the upper ledge of the altar and on the gateposts of the inner court. ²⁰You are to do the same on the seventh day of the month for anyone who sins unintention-

45:1–2 The prophet declared that in the Millennium the land of Israel would be divided by lot for purposes of inheritance and that a portion of the land would be set aside for the temple.

45:8 Ezekiel declared that the oppression of God's people by their own rulers would cease forever in the millennial kingdom.

ally or through ignorance; so you are to make atonement for the temple.

²¹ "'In the first month on the fourteenth day you are to observe the Passover, a feast lasting seven days, during which you shall eat bread made without yeast. ²²On that day the prince is to provide a bull as a sin offering for himself and for all the people of the land. ²³Every day during the seven days of the Feast he is to provide seven bulls and seven rams without defect as a burnt offering to the LORD, and a male goat for a sin offering. ²⁴He is to provide as a grain offering an ephah for each bull and an ephah for each ram, along with a hin of oil for each ephah.

²⁵ "'During the seven days of the Feast, which begins in the seventh month on the fifteenth day, he is to make the same provision for sin offerings, burnt offerings, grain offerings and oil.

46 "'This is what the Sovereign LORD says: The gate of the inner court facing east is to be shut on the six working days, but on the Sabbath day and on the day of the New Moon it is to be opened. ²The prince is to enter from the outside through the portico of the gateway and stand by the gatepost. The priests are to sacrifice his burnt offering and his fellowship offerings. He is to worship at the threshold of the gateway and then go out, but the gate will not be shut until evening. ³On the Sabbaths and New Moons the people of the land are to worship in the presence of the LORD at the entrance to that gateway. ⁴The burnt offering the prince brings to the LORD on the Sabbath day is to be six male lambs and a ram, all without defect. ⁵The grain offering given with the ram is to be an ephah, and the grain offering with the lambs is to be as much as he pleases, along with a hin of oil for each ephah. ⁶On the day of the New Moon he is to offer a young bull, six lambs and a ram, all without defect. ⁷He is to provide as a grain offering one ephah with the bull, one ephah with the ram, and with the lambs as much as he wants to give, along with a hin of oil with each ephah. ⁸When the prince enters, he is to go in through the portico of the gateway, and he is to come out the same way.

⁹ "'When the people of the land come before the LORD at the appointed feasts, whoever enters by the north gate to worship is to go out the south gate; and whoever enters by the south gate is to go out the north gate. No one is to return through the gate by which he entered, but each is to go out the opposite gate. ¹⁰The prince is to be among them, going in when they go in and going out when they go out.

¹¹ "'At the festivals and the appointed feasts, the grain offering is to be an ephah with a bull, an ephah with a ram, and with the lambs as much as one pleases, along with a hin of oil for each ephah. ¹²When the prince provides a freewill offering to the LORD—whether a burnt offering or fellowship offerings—the gate facing east is to be opened for him. He shall offer his burnt offering or his fellowship offerings as he does on the Sabbath day. Then he shall go out, and after he has gone out, the gate will be shut.

¹³ "'Every day you are to provide a year-old lamb without defect for a burnt offering to the LORD; morning by morning you shall provide it. ¹⁴You are also to provide with it morning by morning a grain offering, consisting of a sixth of an ephah with a third of a hin of oil to moisten the flour. The presenting of this grain offering to the LORD is a lasting ordinance. ¹⁵So the lamb and the grain offering and the oil shall be provided morning by morning for a regular burnt offering.

¹⁶ "'This is what the Sovereign LORD says: If the prince makes a gift from his inheritance to one of his sons, it will also belong to his descendants; it is to be their property by inheritance. ¹⁷If, however, he makes a gift from his inheritance to one of his servants, the servant may keep it until the year of freedom; then it will revert to the prince. His inheritance belongs to his sons only; it is theirs. ¹⁸The prince must not take any of the inheritance of the people, driving them off their property. He is to give his sons their inheritance out of his own property, so that none of my people will be separated from his property.'"

¹⁹Then the man brought me through the entrance at the side of the gate to

D Isa 53:3–12 ◄ ► Da 9:24–26

j 24,5 That is, probably about 4 quarts (about 4 liters) *k* 2 Traditionally *peace offerings*; also in verse 12 *l* 5 That is, probably about 3/5 bushel (about 22 liters)

the sacred rooms facing north,y which belonged to the priests, and showed me a place at the western end. ²⁰He said to me, "This is the place where the priests will cook the guilt offering and the sin offering and bake the grain offering, to avoid bringing them into the outer court and consecrating² the people."ᵃ

²¹He then brought me to the outer court and led me around to its four corners, and I saw in each corner another court. ²²In the four corners of the outer court were enclosedᵐ courts, forty cubits long and thirty cubits wide; each of the courts in the four corners was the same size. ²³Around the inside of each of the four courts was a ledge of stone, with places for fire built all around under the ledge. ²⁴He said to me, "These are the kitchens where those who minister at the temple will cook the sacrifices of the people."

The River From the Temple

47 The man brought me back to the entrance of the temple, and I saw waterᵇ coming out from under the threshold of the temple toward the east (for the temple faced east). The water was coming down from under the south side of the temple, south of the altar.ᶜ ²He then brought me out through the north gateᵈ and led me around the outside to the outer gate facing east, and the water was flowing from the south side.

³As the man went eastward with a measuring lineᵉ in his hand, he measured off a thousand cubitsⁿ and then led me through water that was ankle-deep. ⁴He measured off another thousand cubits and led me through water that was knee-deep. He measured off another thousand and led me through water that was up to the waist. ⁵He measured off another thousand, but now it was a riverᶠ that I could not cross, because the water had risen and was deep enough to swim in—a river that no one could cross.ᵍ ⁶He asked me, "Son of man, do you see this?"

Then he led me back to the bank of the river. ⁷When I arrived there, I saw a great number of trees on each side of the river.ʰ ⁸He said to me, "This water flows toward the eastern region and goes down into the Arabah,ᵒⁱ where it enters the Sea.ᵖ When it empties into the Sea,ᵖ the water there becomes fresh.ʲ ⁹Swarms of living creatures will live wherever the river flows. There will be large numbers of fish, because this water flows there and makes the salt water fresh; so where the river flows everything will live.ᵏ ¹⁰Fishermenˡ will stand along the shore; from En Gediᵐ to En Eglaim there will be places for spreading nets.ⁿ The fish will be of many kindsᵒ—like the fish of the Great Sea.ᵠᵖ ¹¹But the swamps and marshes will not become fresh; they will be left for salt.ᵠ ¹²Fruit trees of all kinds will grow on both banks of the river.ʳ Their leaves will not wither, nor will their fruitˢ fail. Every month they will bear, because the water from the sanctuaryᵗ flows to them. Their fruit will serve for food and their leaves for healing.ᵘ"

The Boundaries of the Land

¹³This is what the Sovereign LORD says: "These are the boundariesᵛ by which you are to divide the land for an inheritance among the twelve tribes of Israel, with two portions for Joseph.ʷ ¹⁴You are to divide it equally among them. Because I swore with uplifted hand to give it to your forefathers, this land will become your inheritance.ˣ

¹⁵"This is to be the boundary of the land:ʸ

"On the north side it will run from the Great Seaᶻ by the Hethlon roadᵃ past

---

Ref	Cross-reference
46:19	ʸ Eze 42:4
46:20	ᶻ S Lev 6:27
	ᵃ ver 24; Zec 14:20
47:1	ᵇ S Isa 55:1
	ᶜ Ps 46:4; Joel 3:18; Rev 22:1
47:2	ᵈ S Eze 40:35
47:3	ᵉ S Eze 40:3
47:5	ᶠ S Ge 2:10
	ᵍ Isa 11:9; Hab 2:14
47:7	ʰ ver 12; Rev 22:2
47:8	ⁱ S Dt 1:1; S 3:17 ʲ Isa 41:18
47:9	ᵏ Isa 12:3; 55:1; Jn 4:14; 7:37-38
47:10	ˡ S Isa 19:8; Mt 4:19
	ᵐ S Jos 15:62
	ⁿ Eze 26:5
	ᵒ S Ps 104:25; Mt 13:47
	ᵖ S Nu 34:6
47:11	ᵠ S Dt 29:23
47:12	ʳ ver 7; Rev 22:2 ˢ S Ps 1:3
	ᵗ S Isa 55:1
	ᵘ S Ge 2:9; S Jer 17:8; Eze 36:8
47:13	ᵛ Nu 34:2-12 ʷ S Ge 48:16; S 49:26
47:14	ˣ S Ge 12:7; S Dt 1:8; S Eze 36:12
47:15	ʸ Nu 34:2 ᶻ ver 19; S Nu 34:6 ᵃ Eze 48:1

I Eze 45:8 ◀ ▶ Da 8:19
M Eze 43:5-7 ◀ ▶ Eze 48:1-7

H Eze 34:16 ◀ ▶ Mt 8:17

ᵐ 22 The meaning of the Hebrew for this word is uncertain. ⁿ 3 That is, about 1,500 feet (about 450 meters) ᵒ 8 Or *the Jordan Valley* ᵖ 8 That is, the Dead Sea ᵠ 10 That is, the Mediterranean; also in verses 15, 19 and 20

47:1–23 Ezekiel's vision of the new temple concluded with a view of water flowing out from under the temple. This water would transform the barren landscape into fertile fields and refresh the Dead Sea so that it could support fish again. Note also that Ezekiel outlined the boundaries of Israel's kingdom during the Millennium (47:15–21), a reaffirmation of God's promise to restore all of the promised land to Israel's possession when the Messiah returns.

Lebo' Hamath to Zedad, ¹⁶Berothah^sb and Sibraim (which lies on the border between Damascus and Hamath),^c as far as Hazer Hatticon, which is on the border of Hauran. ¹⁷The boundary will extend from the sea to Hazar Enan,^r along the northern border of Damascus, with the border of Hamath to the north. This will be the north boundary.^d

¹⁸"On the east side the boundary will run between Hauran and Damascus, along the Jordan between Gilead and the land of Israel, to the eastern sea and as far as Tamar.^u This will be the east boundary.^e

¹⁹"On the south side it will run from Tamar as far as the waters of Meribah Kadesh,^f then along the Wadi of Egypt,^g to the Great Sea.^h This will be the south boundary.

²⁰"On the west side, the Great Sea will be the boundary to a point opposite Lebo^v Hamath.^i This will be the west boundary.^j

²¹"You are to distribute this land among yourselves according to the tribes of Israel. ²²You are to allot it as an inheritance^k for yourselves and for the aliens^l who have settled among you and who have children. You are to consider them as native-born Israelites; along with you they are to be allotted an inheritance among the tribes of Israel.^m ²³In whatever tribe the alien settles, there you are to give him his inheritance," declares the Sovereign LORD.^n

The Division of the Land

48 "These are the tribes, listed by name: At the northern frontier, Dan^o will have one portion; it will follow the Hethlon road^p to Lebo^w Hamath;^q Hazar Enan and the northern border of Damascus next to Hamath will be part of its border from the east side to the west side.

²"Asher^r will have one portion; it will border the territory of Dan from east to west.

³"Naphtali^s will have one portion; it will border the territory of Asher from east to west.

⁴"Manasseh^t will have one portion; it will border the territory of Naphtali from east to west.

⁵"Ephraim^u will have one portion; it will border the territory of Manasseh^v from east to west.^w

⁶"Reuben^x will have one portion; it

M Eze 47:1–21 ◀ ▶ Eze 48:10–35

r 15 Or *past the entrance to* *s 15,16* See Septuagint and Ezekiel 48:1; Hebrew *road to go into Zedad,* *16 Hamath, Berothah* *t 17* Hebrew *Enon,* a variant of *Enan* *u 18* Septuagint and Syriac; Hebrew *Israel. You will measure to the eastern sea* *v 20* Or *opposite the entrance to* *w 1* Or *to the entrance to*

48:1–29 Ezekiel then shared his vision of the disposition of the land during the Millennium for each of the tribes of Israel. Notice that these allotments differ slightly from Joshua's original apportionments as the tribes entered Canaan because Ezekiel's allotments run all the way from the eastern to the western borders of the land. See the map of Israel during the Millennium on p. 957.

The northernmost allotment went to the tribe of Dan, descendants of Rachel's maidservant Bilhah (see Ge 35:25). The other northern allotments went to Asher and Naphtali, sons of Leah's and Rachel's maidservants (see Ge 35:25–26), because the tribes descended from maidservants were placed farthest from the sanctuary. The furthest allotment to the south was given to the tribe of Gad, descendants of Zilpah, Leah's maidservant (see Ge 35:25) for the same reason.

Next in line from the north were Manasseh and Ephraim, Joseph's two sons who were adopted by Jacob (see Ge 48:17–20). Since the tribe of Levi received no land (see 44:28) Manasseh and Ephraim received the allotments for Joseph and Levi (48:4–5).

Reuben's allotment came next, and Judah occupied the most prestigious northern allotment alongside the holy portion that was set aside for the temple. Note that in Joshua's allotment of the land of Canaan the tribe of Judah settled in the south. Yet prophecy said that out of the tribe of Judah would come the Messiah (see Ge 49:8–12). Possibly settling the tribe of Judah with the northern tribes in the reunited Israel would signify that these northern tribes would finally have a "share in David" (2Sa 20:1; see 1Ki 12:16; 2Ch 10:16).

The central portion of the promised land included the area of Jerusalem and the area set aside as a sacred district to house the temple, the priests and Levites, and the prince.

Directly to the south of the sacred land was the allotment for the tribe of Benjamin, followed by the allotments for the tribes of Simeon, Issachar and Zebulun. Note that this arrangement is different from the allotments given in Joshua's day (see Jos 13—17).

will border the territory of Ephraim from east to west.

⁷"Judah^y will have one portion; it will border the territory of Reuben from east to west.

⁸"Bordering the territory of Judah from east to west will be the portion you are to present as a special gift. It will be 25,000 cubits^x wide, and its length from east to west will equal one of the tribal portions; the sanctuary will be in the center of it.^z

⁹"The special portion you are to offer to the LORD will be 25,000 cubits long and 10,000 cubits^y wide.^a ¹⁰This will be the sacred portion for the priests. It will be 25,000 cubits long on the north side, 10,000 cubits wide on the west side, 10,000 cubits wide on the east side and 25,000 cubits long on the south side. In the center of it will be the sanctuary of the LORD.^b ¹¹This will be for the consecrated priests, the Zadokites,^c who were faithful in serving me^d and did not go astray as the Levites did when the Israelites went astray.^e ¹²It will be a special gift to them from the sacred portion of the land, a most holy portion, bordering the territory of the Levites.

¹³"Alongside the territory of the priests, the Levites will have an allotment 25,000 cubits long and 10,000 cubits wide. Its total length will be 25,000 cubits and its width 10,000 cubits.^f ¹⁴They must not sell or exchange any of it. This is the best of the land and must not pass into other hands, because it is holy to the LORD.^g

¹⁵"The remaining area, 5,000 cubits wide and 25,000 cubits long, will be for the common use of the city, for houses and for pastureland. The city will be in the center of it ¹⁶and will have these measurements: the north side 4,500 cubits, the south side 4,500 cubits, the east side 4,500 cubits, and the west side 4,500 cubits.^h ¹⁷The pastureland for the city will

M Eze 48:1-7 ◀ ▶ Da 2:34-35

48:7 ʸ Jos 15:1-63
48:8 ᶻ ver 21
48:9 ᵃ S Eze 45:1
48:10 ᵇ ver 21; S Eze 45:3-4
48:11 ᶜ S 2Sa 8:17 ᵈ S Lev 8:35 ᵉ Eze 14:11; S 44:15
48:13 ᶠ Eze 45:5
48:14 ᵍ S Lev 25:34; 27:10,28
48:16 ʰ Rev 21:16

^x8 That is, about 7 miles (about 12 kilometers) ^y9 That is, about 3 miles (about 5 kilometers)

Division of the Land in the Millennium

Eze 47—48

be 250 cubits on the north, 250 cubits on the south, 250 cubits on the east, and 250 cubits on the west. ¹⁸What remains of the area, bordering on the sacred portion and running the length of it, will be 10,000 cubits on the east side and 10,000 cubits on the west side. Its produce will supply food for the workers of the city.ⁱ ¹⁹The workers from the city who farm it will come from all the tribes of Israel. ²⁰The entire portion will be a square, 25,000 cubits on each side. As a special gift you will set aside the sacred portion, along with the property of the city.

²¹"What remains on both sides of the area formed by the sacred portion and the city property will belong to the prince. It will extend eastward from the 25,000 cubits of the sacred portion to the eastern border, and westward from the 25,000 cubits to the western border. Both these areas running the length of the tribal portions will belong to the prince, and the sacred portion with the temple sanctuary will be in the center of them.ʲ ²²So the property of the Levites and the property of the city will lie in the center of the area that belongs to the prince. The area belonging to the prince will lie between the border of Judah and the border of Benjamin.

²³"As for the rest of the tribes: Benjaminᵏ will have one portion; it will extend from the east side to the west side.

²⁴"Simeonˡ will have one portion; it will border the territory of Benjamin from east to west.

²⁵"Issacharᵐ will have one portion; it will border the territory of Simeon from east to west.

²⁶"Zebulunⁿ will have one portion; it will border the territory of Issachar from east to west.

²⁷"Gadᵒ will have one portion; it will border the territory of Zebulun from east to west.

²⁸"The southern boundary of Gad will run south from Tamarᵖ to the waters of Meribah Kadesh, then along the Wadi ⌊of Egypt⌋ to the Great Sea.ᶻᑫ

²⁹"This is the land you are to allot as an inheritance to the tribes of Israel, and these will be their portions," declares the Sovereign Lord.ʳ

The Gates of the City

³⁰"These will be the exits of the city: Beginning on the north side, which is 4,500 cubits long, ³¹the gates of the city will be named after the tribes of Israel. The three gates on the north side will be the gate of Reuben, the gate of Judah and the gate of Levi.

³²"On the east side, which is 4,500 cubits long, will be three gates: the gate of Joseph, the gate of Benjamin and the gate of Dan.

³³"On the south side, which measures 4,500 cubits, will be three gates: the gate of Simeon, the gate of Issachar and the gate of Zebulun.

³⁴"On the west side, which is 4,500 cubits long, will be three gates: the gate of Gad, the gate of Asher and the gate of Naphtali.ˢ

³⁵"The distance all around will be 18,000 cubits.

"And the name of the city from that time on will be:

THE LORD IS THERE.ᵗ"

ᶻ 28 That is, the Mediterranean

Daniel

Author: Daniel

Theme: God is sovereign over human governments

Date of Writing: c. 536–530 B.C.

Outline of Daniel
  I. Background Information About Daniel (1:1–21)
  II. The Nations Are in God's Hands (2:1—7:28)
   A. Nebuchadnezzar's Dreams, Idols and Madness (2:1—4:37)
   B. Belshazzar's Feast and Babylon's Fall (5:1–31)
   C. King Cyrus and the Lion's Den (6:1–28)
   D. Four World Empires (7:1–28)
  III. Israel Is in God's Hands (8:1—12:13)
   A. The Vision of the Ram and Goat (8:1–27)
   B. Daniel's Messianic Vision of the Seventy "Sevens" (9:1–27)
   C. A Vision of Israel's Future and Final Victory (10:1—12:13)

THE BOOK OF Daniel takes its name from its author, a man of God who was granted a divine ability to see through time and describe the future. Taken captive to Babylon by Nebuchadnezzar after the destruction of Jerusalem in 605 B.C., Daniel rose from his position as the king's servant to a position as royal advisor for several Babylonian and Persian kings. As God's prophet, Daniel, whose name means "God is my judge," faithfully and wisely served the kings who had conquered his people. Through his book and ministry, Daniel demonstrates God's sovereign control over the destiny of all nations and brings a clearer understanding of God's plan to redeem the earth from sin's curse.

Scholars consider Daniel's prophecies fundamental to understanding the main themes of the end times. Apocalyptic in style, Daniel's predictions refer to future events using many figures of speech and symbols to convey God's message, sometimes even fixing the time when these events would occur. Because of this, ancient Jewish historians held Daniel's prophecies in highest honor in their theology of the Messiah. In addition, Daniel's predictions harmonize the prophetic details found in Mt 24, 2 Thessalonians, and Revelation. The most notable prophecies in Daniel concern the rise and fall of the four Gentile empires and the establishment of the millennial kingdom of the Messiah.

The book of Daniel also reaffirms the need for consistent holiness and bears out God's triumph over evil. Daniel's record of the persecution of his three companions and himself (chs. 3; 6) by their pagan conquerors foreshadows the persecution of the saints by the antichrist during the tribulation period. Also, King Nebuchadnezzar's statue and King Darius's prohibition of the worship of God warn of the attacks on the true worship of God during the conflict between the antichrist and God's children.

Despite attacks denying Daniel's divine inspiration concerning future events, Jesus confirmed Daniel's accuracy and inspiration by basing some of his prophetic words on Daniel's prophecies (see Mt 24:15). Recent archeological and scientific discoveries also confirm Daniel's divine visions.

Daniel's Training in Babylon

1 In the third year of the reign of Jehoiakim[a] king of Judah, Nebuchadnezzar[b] king of Babylon[c] came to Jerusalem and besieged it.[d] 2 And the Lord delivered Jehoiakim king of Judah into his hand, along with some of the articles from the temple of God. These he carried[e] off to the temple of his god in Babylonia[a] and put in the treasure house of his god.[f]

3 Then the king ordered Ashpenaz, chief of his court officials, to bring in some of the Israelites from the royal family and the nobility[g]— 4 young men without any physical defect, handsome,[h] showing aptitude for every kind of learning,[i] well informed, quick to understand, and qualified to serve in the king's palace. He was to teach them the language[j] and literature of the Babylonians.[b] 5 The king assigned them a daily amount of food and wine[k] from the king's table.[l] They were to be trained for three years,[m] and after that they were to enter the king's service.[n]

6 Among these were some from Judah: Daniel,[o] Hananiah, Mishael and Azariah.[p] 7 The chief official gave them new names: to Daniel, the name Belteshaz-

[a] 2 Hebrew *Shinar* [b] 4 Or *Chaldeans*

1:1–2 The deportation referred to in this passage was the first in a series of deportations of Jewish exiles to Babylon located some 600 miles across the desert in what is now southwestern Iraq (see Jer 25:11). The prophet Ezekiel was taken captive in the second deportation in 598 B.C.

The Babylonian army under King Nebuchadnezzar also captured some of the temple vessels in fulfillment of Isaiah's prophecy to King Hezekiah (see Isa 39:1–6). Daniel recorded that Nebuchadnezzar placed them in "the treasure house of his god" (1:2) which was probably the temple of Marduk (Bel), the chief god of Babylon. However, some of the temple vessels in Jerusalem escaped this first desecration (see Jer 27:19–22).

1:3–4 The nobles and talented artisans of the exiles were taken to the capital of Babylon to be trained for service (see 2Ki 24:14). These captives were selected from the royal dynasty of the kingdom of Judah because they were still of a teachable age, possessed good health and were intelligent and wise. Babylonian history records that young teenage boys were often chosen for an intensive training period to ready them to serve the court as royal advisors.

1:6 Because of their royal standing, skills and abilities, Daniel and his three companions were chosen to join the king's staff.

1:7 It was customary in ancient pagan courts to rename foreign captives to further emphasize their subjection to the conquering king. The original Hebrew names of these Jewish captives honored the

zar;^q to Hananiah, Shadrach; to Mishael, Meshach; and to Azariah, Abednego.^r

⁸But Daniel resolved not to defile^s himself with the royal food and wine, and he asked the chief official for permission not to defile himself this way. ⁹Now God had caused the official to show favor^t and sympathy^u to Daniel, ¹⁰but the official told Daniel, "I am afraid of my lord the king, who has assigned your^c food and drink.^v Why should he see you looking worse than the other young men your age? The king would then have my head because of you."

¹¹Daniel then said to the guard whom the chief official had appointed over Daniel, Hananiah, Mishael and Azariah, ¹²"Please test^w your servants for ten days: Give us nothing but vegetables to eat and water to drink. ¹³Then compare our appearance with that of the young men who eat the royal food, and treat your servants in accordance with what you see."^x ¹⁴So he agreed to this and tested^y them for ten days. ¹⁵At the end of the ten days they looked healthier and better nourished than any of the young men who ate the royal food.^z ¹⁶So the guard took away their choice food and the wine they were to drink and gave them vegetables instead.^a

E Isa 38:1–22 ◀ ▶ Hos 11:3
U Eze 34:26–27 ◀ ▶ Da 10:12

1:7 ^q Da 2:26; 4:8; 5:12; 10:1
^r S Isa 39:7; Da 2:49; 3:12
1:8 ^s Eze 4:13-14
1:9 ^t S Ge 39:21; S Pr 16:7
^u S 1Ki 8:50
1:10 ^v ver 5
1:12 ^w Rev 2:10
1:13 ^x ver 16
1:14 ^y Rev 2:10
1:15 ^z Ex 23:25
1:16 ^a ver 12-13
1:17 ^b S Job 12:13
^c Da 2:23; Col 1:9; Jas 1:5 ^d Da 2:19, 30; 5:11; 7:1; 8:1
1:18 ^e ver 5
1:19 ^f S Ge 41:46
1:20 ^g S Ge 41:8
^h S 1Ki 4:30; Est 2:15; S Eze 28:3; Da 2:13,28; 4:18; 6:3
1:21 ^i S 2Ch 36:22; Da 6:28; 10:1
2:1 ^j ver 3; S Ge 20:3; S Job 33:15,18; Da 4:5 ^k Ge 41:8 ^l S Est 6:1
2:2 ^m S Ge 41:8
^n Ex 7:11; Jer 27:9
^o S ver 10; S Isa 19:3; S 44:25 ^p Da 4:6
2:3 ^q Da 4:5
2:4 ^r S Ezr 4:7 ^s S Ne 2:3

¹⁷To these four young men God gave knowledge and understanding^b of all kinds of literature and learning.^c And Daniel could understand visions and dreams of all kinds.^d

¹⁸At the end of the time^e set by the king to bring them in, the chief official presented them to Nebuchadnezzar. ¹⁹The king talked with them, and he found none equal to Daniel, Hananiah, Mishael and Azariah; so they entered the king's service.^f ²⁰In every matter of wisdom and understanding about which the king questioned them, he found them ten times better than all the magicians^g and enchanters in his whole kingdom.^h

²¹And Daniel remained there until the first year of King Cyrus.^i

Nebuchadnezzar's Dream

2 In the second year of his reign, Nebuchadnezzar had dreams;^j his mind was troubled^k and he could not sleep.^l ²So the king summoned the magicians,^m enchanters, sorcerers^n and astrologers^d ^o to tell him what he had dreamed.^p When they came in and stood before the king, ³he said to them, "I have had a dream that troubles^q me and I want to know what it means.^e "

⁴Then the astrologers answered the king in Aramaic,^f ^r "O king, live forever!^s

^c 10 The Hebrew for *your* and *you* in this verse is plural.
^d 2 Or *Chaldeans*; also in verses 4, 5 and 10   ^e 3 Or *was*   ^f 4 The text from here through chapter 7 is in Aramaic.

---

name of God in their construction and meaning. Their Babylonian names reflected Nebuchadnezzar's desire to honor his pagan god Bel (see note at 1:1–2).

Daniel's Hebrew name means "God is (my) Judge." His name was changed to *Belteshazzar*, which probably meant in Babylonian "Bel protect his life!" *Hananiah* was the Hebrew for "The LORD shows grace"; his changed name *Shadrach* probably meant "at the command of Aku." (Aku was a Sumerian moon-god.) *Mishael*, meaning "Who is what God is?" found his name changed to *Meshach*, which probably meant "Who is what Aku is?" And *Azariah*, meaning "The LORD helps," was renamed after another Babylonian god when he was given the name *Abednego*, which probably meant "servant of Nego."

1:8 Daniel and his friends respectfully rejected the king's food because of their determination to follow God's dietary commands in the Law of Moses (see Lev 11:1–31). Note that Daniel's submissive attitude earned him favor in the eyes of his masters.

1:19–20 At the end of the training period, the king interviewed all of the young men. Daniel, Hananiah, Mishael and Azariah stood out from all the rest, exhibiting the wisdom of God (see Jas 1:5).

1:21 Daniel's remarkable career spanned the reign of several kings and different empires (605–539 B.C.) because of his resolve to obey God and honestly serve his masters.

2:1 The date of this verse could apply to the second year that Nebuchadnezzar ruled over Israel—604 B.C.—or it could refer to the Babylonian system of dating the years of a king's reign. The Babylonians did not count the year of a king's accession to the throne as a numbered year of that king's reign. Thus calculating the second year of Nebuchadnezzar's reign in the Babylonian way would mean that this dream coincided with Daniel's last year of training.

2:4 Since the king's advisors came from different racial backgrounds, they spoke to the king in Aramaic (Syriac), a language that was familiar to everyone. This language was the accepted language for commerce and politics in the Babylonian and Persian

Tell your servants the dream, and we will interpret it." ⁵The king replied to the astrologers, "This is what I have firmly decided:ᵗ If you do not tell me what my dream was and interpret it, I will have you cut into pieces" and your houses turned into piles of rubble.ᵛ ⁶But if you tell me the dream and explain it, you will receive from me gifts and rewards and great honor.ʷ So tell me the dream and interpret it for me."

⁷Once more they replied, "Let the king tell his servants the dream, and we will interpret it."

⁸Then the king answered, "I am certain that you are trying to gain time, because you realize that this is what I have firmly decided: ⁹If you do not tell me the dream, there is just one penaltyˣ for you. You have conspired to tell me misleading and wicked things, hoping the situation will change. So then, tell me the dream, and I will know that you can interpret it for me."ʸ

¹⁰The astrologersᶻ answered the king, "There is not a man on earth who can do what the king asks! No king, however great and mighty, has ever asked such a thing of any magician or enchanter or astrologer.ᵃ ¹¹What the king asks is too difficult. No one can reveal it to the king

2:5 ᵗGe 41:32
ᵘver 12 ᵛEzr 6:11;
Da 3:29

2:6 ʷver 48;
Da 5:7,16

2:9 ˣEst 4:11
ʸIsa 41:22-24

2:10 ᶻver 2;
ᵃver 27; Da 5:8

empires. Note that in the original manuscript chapters 2—7 of Daniel were written in Aramaic since the information included in these chapters was important for the Gentile nations of the Near East to understand too. The latter chapters of Daniel revert to Hebrew text since that material is primarily directed to God's chosen people.

2:5–11 The king demanded something extraordinary: that the wise men describe his forgotten dream and then interpret it for him. The wise men declared correctly that no one could fulfill the king's command "except the gods" (2:11).

The Four Gentile World Empires

Identification of the Four Kingdoms

Vision in Daniel 2	Vision in Daniel 7	Vision in Daniel 8	Identification	Chronology of Major Empires in Daniel
				626 B.C.
HEAD OF GOLD	LION		BABYLON DANIEL 2:37	BABYLON
				539 B.C.
CHEST AND ARMS OF SILVER	BEAR	RAM	MEDO-PERSIA DANIEL 8:20	MEDO-PERSIA
				330 B.C.
BELLY AND THIGHS OF BRONZE	LEOPARD	GOAT	GREECE DANIEL 8:21	GREECE (Including Ptolemies and Seleucids) (167 B.C. Maccabees and Hasmoneans)
				63 B.C.
LEGS OF IRON	DREADFUL AND TERRIBLE BEAST		ROME	ROME
FEET OF CLAY & IRON MIXED				A.D. 70 Fall of Jerusalem

except the gods,[b] and they do not live among men."

[12]This made the king so angry and furious[c] that he ordered the execution[d] of all the wise men of Babylon. [13]So the decree was issued to put the wise men to death, and men were sent to look for Daniel and his friends to put them to death.[e]

[14]When Arioch, the commander of the king's guard, had gone out to put to death the wise men of Babylon, Daniel spoke to him with wisdom and tact. [15]He asked the king's officer, "Why did the king issue such a harsh decree?" Arioch then explained the matter to Daniel. [16]At this, Daniel went in to the king and asked for time, so that he might interpret the dream for him.

[17]Then Daniel returned to his house and explained the matter to his friends Hananiah, Mishael and Azariah.[f] [18]He urged them to plead for mercy[g] from the God of heaven[h] concerning this mystery,[i] so that he and his friends might not be executed with the rest of the wise men of Babylon. [19]During the night the mystery[j] was revealed to Daniel in a vision.[k] Then Daniel praised the God of heaven[l] [20]and said:

"Praise be to the name of God for ever and ever;[m]
wisdom and power[n] are his.
[21]He changes times and seasons;[o]
he sets up kings[p] and deposes[q] them.
He gives wisdom[r] to the wise
and knowledge to the discerning.[s]
E [22]He reveals deep and hidden things;[t]
he knows what lies in darkness,[u]
and light[v] dwells with him.
[23]I thank and praise you, O God of my fathers:[w]
You have given me wisdom[x] and power,

E *Eze 11:5* ◀ ▶ *Da 5:27*

2:11 [b] S Ge 41:38
2:12 [c] Da 3:13,19
[d] ver 5
2:13 [e] S Da 1:20; 5:19
2:17 [f] S Da 1:6
2:18 [g] S Isa 37:4
[h] Ezr 1:2; Ne 1:4; Jnh 1:9; Rev 11:13
[i] ver 23; Jer 33:3
2:19 [j] ver 28
[k] S Da 3:15; S Da 1:17
[l] S Jos 22:33
2:20 [m] S Ps 113:2; 145:1-2 [n] S Job 9:4; S Jer 32:19
2:21 [o] Da 7:25
[p] Da 4:17
[q] S Job 12:19; Ps 75:6-7; Ro 13:1
[r] Ps 139:11-12; Jas 1:5
[s] S 2Sa 14:15
2:22 [t] S Ge 40:8; S Job 12:22; Da 5:11; 1Co 2:10
[u] Job 12:22; Ps 139:11-12; Jer 23:24; S Heb 4:13
[v] Isa 45:7; Jas 1:17
2:23 [w] S Ge 31:5; S Ex 3:15
[x] S Da 1:17
[y] S Eze 28:3
2:24 [z] ver 14
2:25 [a] S Dt 21:10
[b] S Da 1:6; 5:13; 6:13
2:26 [c] S Da 1:7
2:27 [d] S ver 10; S Ge 41:8
2:28 [e] S Ge 40:8; Jer 10:7; Mt 4:13
[f] S Ge 49:1; Da 10:14; Mt 24:6; Rev 1:1; 22:6
[g] Da 4:5 [h] S Ps 4:4
[i] S Eze 28:3; S Da 1:20
2:29 [j] S Ge 41:25
2:30 [k] Isa 45:3; S Da 1:17; Am 4:13
2:31 [l] Hab 1:7
[m] Isa 25:3-5

you have made known to me what we asked of you,
you have made known to us the dream of the king."[y]

Daniel Interprets the Dream

[24]Then Daniel went to Arioch,[z] whom the king had appointed to execute the wise men of Babylon, and said to him, "Do not execute the wise men of Babylon. Take me to the king, and I will interpret his dream for him."

[25]Arioch took Daniel to the king at once and said, "I have found a man among the exiles[a] from Judah[b] who can tell the king what his dream means."

[26]The king asked Daniel (also called Belteshazzar),[c] "Are you able to tell me what I saw in my dream and interpret it?"

[27]Daniel replied, "No wise man, enchanter, magician or diviner can explain to the king the mystery he has asked about,[d] [28]but there is a God in heaven **G** who reveals mysteries.[e] He has shown **L** King Nebuchadnezzar what will happen in days to come.[f] Your dream and the visions that passed through your mind[g] as you lay on your bed[h] are these:[i]

[29]"As you were lying there, O king, your mind turned to things to come, and the revealer of mysteries showed you what is going to happen.[j] [30]As for me, this mystery has been revealed[k] to me, not because I have greater wisdom than other living men, but so that you, O king, may know the interpretation and that you may understand what went through your mind.

[31]"You looked, O king, and there before you stood a large statue—an enormous, dazzling statue,[l] awesome[m] in appearance. [32]The head of the statue was made of pure gold, its chest and arms of

G *Jer 16:19* ◀ ▶ *Da 7:2–28*
L *Jer 39:17–18* ◀ ▶ *Jnh 2:4*

2:17–27 Rather than take personal credit for this revelation, Daniel repeatedly affirmed that only God "reveals deep and hidden things" (2:22).
2:28 Daniel affirmed that God alone knew the future and could reveal the secrets of the future through his prophets (see Ge 40:8; 41:16; Isa 46:9–10).
2:31 Daniel interpreted the king's dream, describing a great, metallic image that represented the future course of Gentile world rule through four successive world empires. King Nebuchadnezzar's curiosity about the future of his empire and those that would follow was answered with this divinely inspired prophetic dream that outlined the course of world history. Note that both the beginning and end of these Gentile world empires are marked by the setting up of a pagan image (see Da 2:31; 3:1; Rev 13:14–15).

The Four World Empires

KING NEBUCHADNEZZAR OF Babylon meditated on what course history would follow after his death and received a vision from God of a great metallic image. God gave the young prophet Daniel the interpretation to this vision. Daniel told the king that the dream symbolized the great world kingdoms that would follow after Nebuchadnezzar's death. Daniel described the great metallic image as a man's body with a head of gold, a chest of silver, an abdomen of bronze, legs of iron and feet and toes made of a mixture of iron and clay. In Nebuchadnezzar's vision, a stone "cut out, but not by human hands" (2:34) suddenly destroyed this magnificent statue, pulverizing the iron and clay feet and grinding the rest of the metals in the image into dust. The stone grew to become a great mountain and filled the entire earth.

Daniel interpreted this curious dream as a clear prophecy of the four future world empires that would rule the earth from Nebuchadnezzar's death until the Messiah sets up his kingdom. True to Daniel's prophecy, the four empires appeared in the exact order that Daniel said they would. And despite repeated efforts, no single nation has succeeded in establishing a fifth world empire to replace ancient Rome. The final world empire will be the kingdom of the Messiah. Nebuchadnezzar's vision is described in the table below.

The Great Image of Daniel 2

THE SYMBOL	THE EMPIRE	THE PROPHECY
Head of gold	Babylon	"You are that head of gold" (2:38).
Chest of silver	Medo-Persia	"After you, another kingdom will rise, inferior to yours" (2:39).
Belly of brass	Greece	"Next, a third kingdom, one of bronze, will rule over the whole earth" (2:39).
Legs of iron	Rome	"Finally, there will be a fourth kingdom, strong as iron . . . iron breaks and smashes everything" (2:40).
Toes of iron and clay	Ten Nations	"this will be a divided kingdom . . . partly strong and partly brittle" (2:41–42).
Stone cut without hands	Messianic Kingdom	"In the time of those kings, the God of heaven will set up a kingdom that will never be destroyed" (2:44).

In 608 B.C. the Babylonian empire under King Nebuchadnezzar was strong, powerful and wealthy, aptly fulfilling the position as the image's head of god. Yet, as predicted by Jeremiah (see Jer 25:12), Babylon was destroyed within seventy years by the rise of Medo-Persia under the rule of King Cyrus. In one night the Medes and Persians conquered the kingdom of Babylon while Babylon's king Belshazzar feasted in his palace. Using the vessels from the temple in Jerusalem for profane purposes, Belshazzar was shaken from his revelry when the finger of God wrote a verdict of judgment on the wall of the palace. Daniel, now an old man and probably forgotten by the new rulers after Nebuchadnezzar's death, was called upon by the queen mother to interpret the writing. Daniel declared to Belshazzar God's judgment: God had decided to finish Belshazzar's reign; Belshazzar had been judged and "found wanting" (5:27) and Belshazzar's kingdom would be "divided and given to the Medes and Persians" (5:28).

The Euphrates River cut through the mighty city of Babylon. Waterways were guarded with gates of strong brass. While Belshazzar feasted, the rebel Medo-Persian army under the leadership of Darius diverted the Euphrates River so that when the riverbed emptied, the Medo-Persian soldiers could slip right under the river gates into the heart of the city. Though Daniel was promoted to the third most powerful position in the kingdom of Babylon, he held that position for only a few hours before the city fell to Darius the Mede (see 5:30).

Nebuchadnezzar's image symbolized the second empire as a chest of silver. This indicated that the next empire would be stronger since silver is a stronger metal than gold but of inferior value. True to Nebuchadnezzar's vision, the Medo-Persians raised enormous armies and were powerful in battle, yet they lacked the nobility and wealth of Babylon. The Medo-Persian empire lasted only 207 years until it was destroyed by the swiftly moving armies of Alexander the Great in a climactic battle in 331 B.C.

The third world empire was symbolized by brass, a stronger metal than silver but a metal of less value. The Greek empire, based on the democratic governments of the Greek city-states, broke its world empire into four divisions led by Alexander's four generals. In a supplementary vision of a rapidly moving male goat that is recorded in ch. 8, Daniel predicted that the Greek empire would destroy Medo-Persia (represented by a ram). History records that the aggressive Alexander the Great exacted his revenge on the Persians for the Persian king Xerxes' earlier attack on Greece. The young Alexander conquered the known world from the Mediterranean to India with only 32,000 men in less than ten years.

Alexander's rule in Greece was short but full of conquests. After conquering the ancient seaport of Tyre in 332 B.C. he moved on, intending to destroy the city of Jerusalem because the Jews had resisted his demands. As Alexander approached the city, he was met by the high priest of the temple and informed that God had revealed to the prophet Daniel more than 300 years earlier that a great king would arise from Greece and subdue the entire world. When the priest showed Alexander the exact prophecies in the ancient Scriptures, Alexander was so moved that he worshiped in the temple and gave orders not to destroy Jerusalem or the land of Israel.

Yet Daniel had also prophesied that at the peak of Alexander's power the male goat's great horn would be broken and instead up would come "four prominent horns . . . toward the four winds of heaven" (8:8). When Alexander died suddenly at a young age, he left no heir as successor. The huge empire was divided among his top four generals, just as Daniel had predicted 300 years earlier.

In this fourfold state, Greece continued to rule from the borders of India to Europe from 331 B.C. until the year 63 B.C. when the Roman army under General Pompey successfully attacked the independent kingdom of Israel and captured the temple. Pompey entered the Holy of Holies and installed his Roman garrisons throughout Palestine, occupying the fortress north of the temple that was later named the Tower of Antonia after Mark Antony.

Pompey's occupation of Palestine marked the end of the Greek empire. The fourth world empire of Nebuchadnezzar's vision was represented as two strong legs of iron that broke in pieces all which stood before it. This fourth world empire was Rome. One of the characteristics of the Roman empire was its incredible military might, and Rome transformed the various parts of its empire into an enormous military machine. Combining strength with an efficient police and judicial system, Rome completely supplanted the three preceding kingdoms. Rome's influence was so pervasive that even today, after two thousand years, many of our governmental institutions, bureaucracy, judicial codes and languages are based on the systems used in the Roman empire.

The fourth world empire of Nebuchadnezzar's vision ruled the known world longer than any of the other three. Exactly as foretold, the Roman empire split into two portions after the rule of Emperor Constantine. The western arm of the empire was based in Rome, and the eastern arm of the empire ruled from Constantinople (today's Istanbul, Turkey). Barbarians destroyed Rome's influence in the west in A.D. 476, while the eastern arm of the Roman empire became known as the Byzantine empire and continued its rule until its defeat by the Turks in A.D. 1453.

The last part of Nebuchadnezzar's dream concerned the final stage of the world's empires represented by the ten toes of iron and clay. God clearly predicted that in the days immediately before the establishment of the Messianic kingdom of the stone "cut out of a mountain, but not by human hands" (2:45), there would be a final revival of the Roman empire consisting of ten nations united together in a confederacy. Since Israel's rebirth as a nation in 1948 Europe has begun to come together more and more as a united federation for economic, trade and security reasons.

In 1948 the North Atlantic Treaty Organization (NATO) was formed to defend Europe against the threat of the massed armies of Communist Russia. In 1957 many European nations banded together in a confederation of economic and trade relationships. In 1992 European nations gathered to discuss future moves toward full integration of member economies, utilizing one economic system, a common monetary system as well as a common defense capability and foreign policy. Today, fifteen member states belong to the European Union, creating one of the largest economic, political and military powers in the western world. Daniel prophesied about a united federation under the revived Roman empire. For the first time in two thousand years, a united Europe would be able to fulfill this specific prophecy.

silver, its belly and thighs of bronze, ³³its legs of iron, its feet partly of iron and partly of baked clay. ³⁴While you were watching, a rock was cut out, but not by human hands.ⁿ It struck the statue on its feet of iron and clay and smashed° them.ᵖ ³⁵Then the iron, the clay, the bronze, the silver and the gold were broken to pieces at the same time and became like chaff on a threshing floor in the summer. The wind swept them awayᑫ without leaving a trace. But the rock that struck the statue became a huge mountainʳ and filled the whole earth.ˢ

³⁶"This was the dream, and now we will interpret it to the king.ᵗ ³⁷You, O king, are the king of kings.ᵘ The God of heaven has given you dominionᵛ and power and might and glory; ³⁸in your hands he has placed mankind and the beasts of the field and the birds of the air. Wherever they live, he has made you ruler over them all.ʷ You are that head of gold.

³⁹"After you, another kingdom will rise, inferior to yours. Next, a third kingdom, one of bronze, will rule over the whole earth.ˣ ⁴⁰Finally, there will be a fourth kingdom, strong as iron—for iron breaks and smashes everything—and as iron breaks things to pieces, so it will crush and break all the others.ʸ ⁴¹Just as you saw that the feet and toes were partly of baked clay and partly of iron, so this will be a divided kingdom; yet it will have some of the strength of iron in it, even as you saw iron mixed with clay. ⁴²As the toes were partly iron and partly clay, so this kingdom will be partly strong and partly brittle. ⁴³And just as you saw the iron mixed with baked clay, so the people will be a mixture and will not remain united, any more than iron mixes with clay.

⁴⁴"In the time of those kings, the God of heaven will set up a kingdom that will never be destroyed, nor will it be left to another people. It will crushᶻ all those kingdomsᵃ and bring them to an end, but it will itself endure forever.ᵇ ⁴⁵This is the meaning of the vision of the rockᶜ cut out of a mountain, but not by human handsᵈ—a rock that broke the iron, the bronze, the clay, the silver and the gold to pieces.

"The great God has shown the king

M Eze 48:10-35 ◄ ► Da 2:44-45
M Da 2:34-35 ◄ ► Da 7:13-14
V Jer 31:34 ◄ ► Da 7:14

2:34–35 The stone "cut out, but not by human hands" (2:34) represented Jesus Christ who would utterly destroy the Gentile world empires with a sudden blow at the Battle of Armageddon. This vivid imagery does not evoke a gradual conquest but rather suggests full-scale destruction of the fourth world kingdom (see Rev 16:13–16; 19:17). This destruction is immediately followed by the establishment of the kingdom of the "stone"—the kingdom of Christ.

This vision clearly foreshadowed Christ's ultimate victory with the defeat of the antichrist during the last days. Note also that the stone (rock) is used elsewhere in Scripture as a symbol for the Messiah (see Ge 49:24; Isa 8:14; 28:16; Zec 3:9).

2:37–40 The four metals of the great statue symbolized four Gentile world empires (Babylon, Medo-Persia, Greece and Rome) that would dominate the world from the time of Daniel (606 B.C.) until the end of this age. Note that the diminishing value of the metals from gold to silver to bronze to iron represented the decreasing grandeur and individual power of the successive kings and their empires. Yet each successive metal was stronger than the previous, indicating that each succeeding empire would last longer than the previous one.

Note that of all the empires the fourth and final world power (Rome) would be divided. The two legs of the image would ultimately become the divided Roman empire with its eastern (Byzantine) territory and its western (Roman) region. The ten toes of the image were also forged of iron and also represented the Roman influence. At the end of this age this last portion of Nebuchadnezzar's image will rise as a new Roman confederacy of ten nations. See the article on "The Four World Empires," p. 964.

2:38 The golden head of the image represented the kingdom of Babylon. God had given Nebuchadnezzar the authority to rule over all the nations of the known world at that time.

2:41 The feet and toes of the image were a composite blend of iron and clay symbolizing both strong and weak people. The ten toes symbolized ten confederate nations that will rule the earth during the last years of this age.

2:44 The ten kings of the confederated kingdoms (symbolized by the ten toes of Nebuchadnezzar's image) will be in existence when Christ comes again. These ten kings did not exist during the time of Christ's first coming, nor at any other time since Christ's ascension into heaven, but will be in power when Christ returns to deliver his people and establish his millennial kingdom (see Ps 2:1–9; Zec 14:1–9).

what will take place in the future.ᵉ The dream is trueᶠ and the interpretation is trustworthy."

⁴⁶Then King Nebuchadnezzar fell prostrateᵍ before Daniel and paid him honor and ordered that an offeringʰ and incense be presented to him. ⁴⁷The king said to Daniel, "Surely your God is the God of godsⁱ and the Lord of kingsʲ and a revealer of mysteries,ᵏ for you were able to reveal this mystery.ˡ"

⁴⁸Then the king placed Daniel in a highᵐ position and lavished many gifts on him. He made him ruler over the entire province of Babylon and placed him in charge of all its wise men.ⁿ ⁴⁹Moreover, at Daniel's request the king appointed Shadrach, Meshach and Abednego administrators over the province of Babylon,ᵒ while Daniel himself remained at the royal court.ᵖ

The Image of Gold and the Fiery Furnace

3 King Nebuchadnezzar made an imageᵠ of gold, ninety feet high and nine feetᵍ wide, and set it up on the plain of Dura in the province of Babylon. ²He then summoned the satraps,ʳ prefects, governors, advisers, treasurers, judges, magistrates and all the other provincial officialsˢ to come to the dedication of the image he had set up. ³So the satraps, prefects, governors, advisers, treasurers, judges, magistrates and all the other provincial officials assembled for the dedication of the image that King Nebuchadnezzar had set up, and they stood before it.

⁴Then the herald loudly proclaimed, "This is what you are commanded to do, O peoples, nations and men of every language:ᵗ ⁵As soon as you hear the sound of the horn, flute, zither, lyre, harp,ᵘ pipes and all kinds of music, you must fall down and worship the imageᵛ of gold that King Nebuchadnezzar has set up.ʷ ⁶Whoever does not fall down and worship will immediately be thrown into a blazing furnace."ˣ

⁷Therefore, as soon as they heard the sound of the horn, flute, zither, lyre, harp and all kinds of music, all the peoples, nations and men of every language fell down and worshiped the image of gold that King Nebuchadnezzar had set up.ʸ

⁸At this time some astrologersʰ ᶻ came forward and denounced the Jews. ⁹They said to King Nebuchadnezzar, "O king, live forever!ᵃ ¹⁰You have issued a decree,ᵇ O king, that everyone who hears the sound of the horn, flute, zither, lyre, harp, pipes and all kinds of music must fall down and worship the image of gold,ᶜ ¹¹and that whoever does not fall down and worship will be thrown into a blazing furnace. ¹²But there are some Jews whom you have set over the affairs of the province of Babylon—Shadrach, Meshach and Abednegoᵈ—who pay no attentionᵉ to you, O king. They neither serve your gods nor worship the image of gold you have set up."ᶠ

¹³Furiousᵍ with rage, Nebuchadnezzar summoned Shadrach, Meshach and Abednego. So these men were brought before the king, ¹⁴and Nebuchadnezzar said to them, "Is it true, Shadrach, Meshach and Abednego, that you do not serve my godsʰ or worship the imageⁱ of gold I have set up? ¹⁵Now when you hear the sound of the horn, flute, zither, lyre, harp, pipes and all kinds of music, if you are ready to fall down and worship the image I made, very good. But if you do not worship it, you will be thrown immediately into a blazing furnace. Then what godʲ will be able to rescueᵏ you from my hand?"

¹⁶Shadrach, Meshach and Abednegoˡ replied to the king, "O Nebuchadnezzar, we do not need to defend ourselves before you in this matter. ¹⁷If we are thrown into the blazing furnace, the God

s Isa 43:2 ◀▶ Da 3:24–25

g 1 Aramaic *sixty cubits high and six cubits wide* (about 27 meters high and 2.7 meters wide)   *h 8* Or *Chaldeans*

3:1 The inauguration of the first Gentile empire of Nebuchadnezzar's vision was marked by the enforced public worship of a golden image created by King Nebuchadnezzar. This golden image may have been human in form, though probably not a likeness of the king himself. Its measurements (90' x 9') probably included a lofty pedestal. Notice that the last empire in Nebuchadnezzar's vision will also enforce the worship of an idolatrous image during the great tribulation (see Rev 13:14–15).

3:6 This command to worship required the recognition of Nebuchadnezzar's gods (see 3:12).

3:17 The faithfulness of Daniel's three companions is an inspiration to all believers to stand fast in

we serve is able to save us from it, and he will rescue us from your hand, O king. ¹⁸But even if he does not, we want you to know, O king, that we will not serve your gods or worship the image of gold you have set up."

¹⁹Then Nebuchadnezzar was furious with Shadrach, Meshach and Abednego, and his attitude toward them changed. He ordered the furnace heated seven times hotter than usual ²⁰and commanded some of the strongest soldiers in his army to tie up Shadrach, Meshach and Abednego and throw them into the blazing furnace. ²¹So these men, wearing their robes, trousers, turbans and other clothes, were bound and thrown into the blazing furnace. ²²The king's command was so urgent and the furnace so hot that the flames of the fire killed the soldiers who took up Shadrach, Meshach and Abednego, ²³and these three men, firmly tied, fell into the blazing furnace.

²⁴Then King Nebuchadnezzar leaped to his feet in amazement and asked his advisers, "Weren't there three men that we tied up and threw into the fire?"

They replied, "Certainly, O king."

²⁵He said, "Look! I see four men walking around in the fire, unbound and unharmed, and the fourth looks like a son of the gods."

²⁶Nebuchadnezzar then approached the opening of the blazing furnace and shouted, "Shadrach, Meshach and Abednego, servants of the Most High God, come out! Come here!"

So Shadrach, Meshach and Abednego came out of the fire, ²⁷and the satraps, prefects, governors and royal advisers crowded around them. They saw that the fire had not harmed their bodies, nor was a hair of their heads singed; their robes were not scorched, and there was no smell of fire on them.

²⁸Then Nebuchadnezzar said, "Praise be to the God of Shadrach, Meshach and Abednego, who has sent his angel and rescued his servants! They trusted in him and defied the king's command and were willing to give up their lives rather than serve or worship any god except their own God. ²⁹Therefore I decree that the people of any nation or language who say anything against the God of Shadrach, Meshach and Abednego be cut into pieces and their houses be turned into piles of rubble, for no other god can save in this way."

³⁰Then the king promoted Shadrach, Meshach and Abednego in the province of Babylon.

Nebuchadnezzar's Dream of a Tree

4 King Nebuchadnezzar,

To the peoples, nations and men of every language, who live in all the world:

May you prosper greatly!

²It is my pleasure to tell you about the miraculous signs and wonders that the Most High God has performed for me.

³How great are his signs,
 how mighty his wonders!
His kingdom is an eternal kingdom;
 his dominion endures from generation to generation.

⁴I, Nebuchadnezzar, was at home in my palace, contented and pros-

---

the day of trial. Whether they received deliverance or martyrdom, Daniel's friends left their lives in God's hands. In the coming tribulation, millions will be martyred for their faith (see Rev 7:14–17).

3:25 There are different interpretations regarding the identity of the fourth person visible in the furnace. Some suggest it was an angel, for angels are referred to in Scripture as God's messengers and ministers (see Heb 1:14), and God used an angel to deliver Daniel (see 6:22). Others think that this person was Jesus, the eternal Son of God, and not a created angel. Nebuchadnezzar, with his limited, pagan polytheism was unsure of this person's identity too, referring to him as "a son of the gods" (3:25) and as God's "angel" (3:28). The important thing is that the king recognized that this being was mightier than any of the Babylonian gods because he was able to rescue the three men from the fire.

4:1 This chapter is a public decree written by King Nebuchadnezzar that acknowledged God's greatness over the king and all humanity. The seven years of madness likely occurred during the last ten years of Nebuchadnezzar's reign.

perous. ⁵I had a dream¹ that made me afraid. As I was lying in my bed,ᵐ the images and visions that passed through my mindⁿ terrified me.ᵒ ⁶So I commanded that all the wise men of Babylon be brought before me to interpretᵖ the dream for me. ⁷When the magicians,ᵠ enchanters, astrologers,ʳ and diviners r came, I told them the dream, but they could not interpret it for me.ˢ ⁸Finally, Daniel came into my presence and I told him the dream. (He is called Belteshazzar,ᵗ after the name of my god, and the spirit of the holy godsᵘ is in him.) ⁹I said, "Belteshazzar, chiefᵛ of the magicians, I know that the spirit of the holy godsʷ is in you, and no mystery is too difficult for you. Here is my dream; interpret it for me. ¹⁰These are the visions I saw while lying in my bed:ˣ I looked, and there before me stood a tree in the middle of the land. Its height was enormous.ʸ ¹¹The tree grew large and strong and its top touched the sky; it was visible to the ends of the earth.ᶻ ¹²Its leaves were beautiful, its fruit abundant, and on it was food for all. Under it the beasts of the field found shelter, and the birds of the air lived in its branches;ᵃ from it every creature was fed.

¹³"In the visions I saw while lying in my bed,ᵇ I looked, and there before me was a messenger,ʲ a holy one,ᶜ coming down from heaven. ¹⁴He called in a loud voice: 'Cut down the treeᵈ and trim off its branches; strip off its leaves and scatter its fruit. Let the animals flee from under it and the birds from its branches.ᵉ ¹⁵But let the stump and its roots, bound with iron and bronze, remain in the ground, in the grass of the field.

" 'Let him be drenched with the dew of heaven, and let him live with the animals among the plants of the earth. ¹⁶Let his mind be changed from that of a man and let him be given the mind of an animal, till seven timesᵏ pass by for him.ˡ

¹⁷ 'The decision is announced by messengers, the holy ones declare the verdict, so that the living may know that the Most Highᵍ is sovereignʰ over the kingdoms of men and gives them to anyone he wishes and sets over them the lowliestⁱ of men.'

¹⁸"This is the dream that I, King Nebuchadnezzar, had. Now, Belteshazzar, tell me what it means, for none of the wise men in my kingdom can interpret it for me.ʲ But you can,ᵏ because the spirit of the holy godsˡ is in you."ᵐ

Daniel Interprets the Dream

¹⁹Then Daniel (also called Belteshazzar) was greatly perplexed for a time, and his thoughts terrifiedⁿ him. So the king said, "Belteshazzar, do not let the dream or its meaning alarm you."ᵒ

Belteshazzar answered, "My lord,

4:5 ˡS Da 2:1; ᵐPs 4:4 ⁿDa 2:28 ᵒver 19; S Ge 41:8; S Job 3:26; Da 2:3; 5:6
4:6 ᵖDa 2:2
4:7 ᵠS Ge 41:8 ʳS Isa 44:25; S Da 2:2 ˢS Da 2:10
4:8 ᵗS Da 1:7 ᵘS Ge 41:38
4:9 ᵛDa 2:48 ʷDa 5:11-12
4:10 ˣS ver 5; Ps 4:4 ʸEze 31:3-4
4:11 ᶻS Eze 19:11; 31:5
4:12 ᵃS Eze 17:23; S Mt 13:32
4:13 ᵇver 10; Da 7:1 ᶜS ver 23; S Dt 33:2
4:14 ᵈS Job 24:20 ᵉS Eze 31:12; S Mt 3:10
4:16 ᶠver 23,32
4:17 ᵍver 2,25; Ps 83:18 ʰS Ps 103:19; Jer 27:5-7; Da 2:21; 5:18-21; Ro 13:1 ⁱDa 11:21; Mt 23:12
4:18 ʲS Ge 41:8; Da 5:8,15 ᵏS Ge 41:15 ˡS Ge 41:38 ᵐver 7-9; S Da 1:20
4:19 ⁿS ver 5; S Ge 41:8; Da 7:15, 28; 8:27; 10:16-17 ᵒS Ge 40:12

B Eze 37:14 ◀▶ Da 4:18
E Eze 43:5 ◀▶ Da 4:18
G Isa 61:1 ◀▶ Da 4:18
M Eze 37:14 ◀▶ Da 4:18
T Eze 40:1-2 ◀▶ Da 4:18
J Eze 35:1-15 ◀▶ Da 4:20-26

B Da 4:8-9 ◀▶ Da 5:11-12
E Da 4:8-9 ◀▶ Da 5:11-12
G Da 4:8-9 ◀▶ Da 5:11-12
M Da 4:8-9 ◀▶ Da 5:11-12
T Da 4:8-9 ◀▶ Da 5:11-12

ⁱ 7 Or *Chaldeans* ʲ 13 Or *watchman*; also in verses 17 and 23
ᵏ 16 Or *years*; also in verses 23, 25 and 32

4:13 This mysterious messenger may refer to one of the special angels charged with oversight over the affairs of a particular nation (see 10:13, 20–21; 12:1). This idea of angels overseeing the affairs of the nations finds its roots in ancient Persian angelology and would have been taught to Daniel during his training. The concept does not contradict any Scriptural teaching, however, and might have comforted the exiled Jews.

4:16 God condemned Nebuchadnezzar to seven years of madness because of Nebuchadnezzar's sinful boasting of his accomplishments without acknowledging God's blessings. Note that Nebuchadnezzar, the defiler of the temple in Jerusalem, was struck with madness for same period of time it took King Solomon to build the temple—seven years.

4:17 God ultimately chooses who will rule the kingdoms of this earth, and he will one day deliver the direct rule of all the nations of this world to the Messiah, Jesus Christ (see Rev 11:15–17).

if only the dream applied to your enemies and its meaning to your adversaries! ²⁰The tree you saw, which grew large and strong, with its top touching the sky, visible to the whole earth, ²¹with beautiful leaves and abundant fruit, providing food for all, giving shelter to the beasts of the field, and having nesting places in its branches for the birds of the air—²²you, O king, are that tree! You have become great and strong; your greatness has grown until it reaches the sky, and your dominion extends to distant parts of the earth.

²³"You, O king, saw a messenger, a holy one, coming down from heaven and saying, 'Cut down the tree and destroy it, but leave the stump, bound with iron and bronze, in the grass of the field, while its roots remain in the ground. Let him be drenched with the dew of heaven; let him live like the wild animals, until seven times pass by for him.'

²⁴"This is the interpretation, O king, and this is the decree the Most High has issued against my lord the king: ²⁵You will be driven away from people and will live with the wild animals; you will eat grass like cattle and be drenched with the dew of heaven. Seven times will pass by for you until you acknowledge that the Most High is sovereign over the kingdoms of men and gives them to anyone he wishes. ²⁶The command to leave the stump of the tree with its roots means that your kingdom will be restored to you when you acknowledge that Heaven rules. ²⁷Therefore, O king, be pleased to accept my advice: Renounce your sins by doing what is right, and your wickedness by being kind to the oppressed. It may be that then your prosperity will continue."

The Dream Is Fulfilled

²⁸All this happened to King Nebuchadnezzar. ²⁹Twelve months later, as the king was walking on the roof of the royal palace of Babylon, ³⁰he said, "Is not this the great Babylon I have built as the royal residence, by my mighty power and for the glory of my majesty?"

³¹The words were still on his lips when a voice came from heaven, "This is what is decreed for you, King Nebuchadnezzar: Your royal authority has been taken from you. ³²You will be driven away from people and will live with the wild animals; you will eat grass like cattle. Seven times will pass by for you until you acknowledge that the Most High is sovereign over the kingdoms of men and gives them to anyone he wishes."

³³Immediately what had been said about Nebuchadnezzar was fulfilled. He was driven away from people and ate grass like cattle. His body was drenched with the dew of heaven until his hair grew like the feathers of an eagle and his nails like the claws of a bird.

³⁴At the end of that time, I, Nebuchadnezzar, raised my eyes toward heaven, and my sanity was restored. Then I praised the Most High; I honored and glorified him who lives forever.

His dominion is an eternal dominion;
 his kingdom endures from
   generation to generation.
³⁵All the peoples of the earth
 are regarded as nothing.
He does as he pleases
 with the powers of heaven
 and the peoples of the earth.
No one can hold back his hand

4:29 Despite God's clear warning issued one year earlier, Nebuchadnezzar proudly boasted about his own accomplishments, and God instantly inflicted the prophesied judgment of seven years of insanity. **4:34** Following his horrible experience of seven years of insanity, King Nebuchadnezzar recovered his right mind and acknowledged that God's kingdom was far superior in power and duration to any human kingdom.

or say to him: "What have you done?"ᵗ

³⁶At the same time that my sanity was restored, my honor and splendor were returned to me for the glory of my kingdom.ᵘ My advisers and nobles sought me out, and I was restored to my throne and became even greater than before. ³⁷Now I, Nebuchadnezzar, praise and exaltᵛ and glorifyʷ the King of heaven, because everything he does is right and all his ways are just.ˣ And those who walk in prideʸ he is able to humble.ᶻ

The Writing on the Wall

5 King Belshazzarᵃ gave a great banquetᵇ for a thousand of his noblesᶜ and drank wine with them. ²While Belshazzar was drinkingᵈ his wine, he gave orders to bring in the gold and silver gobletsᵉ that Nebuchadnezzar his father had taken from the temple in Jerusalem, so that the king and his nobles, his wives and his concubinesᶠ might drink from them.ᵍ ³So they brought in the gold goblets that had been taken from the temple of God in Jerusalem, and the king and his nobles, his wives and his concubines drank from them. ⁴As they drank the wine, they praised the godsʰ of gold and silver, of bronze, iron, wood and stone.ⁱ

⁵Suddenly the fingers of a human hand appeared and wrote on the plaster of the wall, near the lampstand in the royal palace. The king watched the hand as it wrote. ⁶His face turned paleʲ and he was so frightenedᵏ that his knees knockedˡ together and his legs gave way.ᵐ

⁷The king called out for the enchanters,ⁿ astrologersᵐᵒ and divinersᵖ to be brought and said to these wiseᵍ men of Babylon, "Whoever reads this writing and tells me what it means will be clothed in purple and have a gold chain placed around his neck,ʳ and he will be made the thirdˢ highest ruler in the kingdom."ᵗ

⁸Then all the king's wise menᵘ came in, but they could not read the writing or tell the king what it meant.ᵛ ⁹So King Belshazzar became even more terrifiedʷ and his face grew more pale. His nobles were baffled.

¹⁰The queen,ⁿ hearing the voices of the king and his nobles, came into the banquet hall. "O king, live forever!"ˣ she said. "Don't be alarmed! Don't look so pale! ¹¹There is a man in your kingdom who has the spirit of the holy godsʸ in him. In the time of your father he was found to have insight and intelligence and wisdomᶻ like that of the gods.ᵃ King Nebuchadnezzar your father—your father the king, I say—appointed him chief of the magicians, enchanters, astrologers and diviners.ᵇ ¹²This man Daniel, whom the king called Belteshazzar,ᶜ was found to have a keen mind and knowledge and understanding, and also the ability to interpret dreams, explain riddlesᵈ and solve difficult problems.ᵉ Call for Daniel, and he will tell you what the writing means.ᶠ"

¹³So Daniel was brought before the king, and the king said to him, "Are you Daniel, one of the exiles my father the king brought from Judah?ᵍ ¹⁴I have heard

---

4:35 ᵗS Job 9:4; S Isa 14:24; S 45:9; Da 5:21; Ro 9:20
4:36 ᵘS Pr 22:4; Da 5:18
4:37 ᵛS Ex 15:2; ʷS Ps 34:3; ˣDt 32:4; Ps 33:4-5; ʸPs 18:27; S 119:21; ᶻS Job 31:4; 40:11-12; S Isa 13:11; Da 5:20,23; Mt 23:12

5:1 ᵃver 30; Da 7:1; 8:1; ᵇS 1Ki 3:15; ᶜJer 50:35
5:2 ᵈS Isa 21:5; ᵉS 2Ki 24:13; S 2Ch 36:10; S Jer 52:19; ᶠS Est 2:14; S Est 1:7; Da 1:2
5:4 ⁱJdg 16:24; S Est 1:10; Ps 135:15-18; Hab 2:19; Rev 9:20
5:6 ʲS Job 4:15; ᵏS Da 4:5 ˡS Isa 7:2; ᵐS Ps 22:14; Eze 7:17
5:7 ⁿS Ge 41:8; ᵒS Isa 19:3; ᵖIsa 44:25; ᵍJer 50:35; ʳDa 4:6-7; ˢGe 41:42; ᵗEst 10:3; ᵘDa 2:5-6,48
5:8 ᵛS Ex 8:18; ʷS Da 2:10,27; S 4:18
5:9 ʷS Ps 48:5; S Isa 21:4
5:10 ˣS Ne 2:3; S Da 3:9
5:11 ʸS Ge 41:38; ᶻver 14; S Da 1:17; ᵃS Da 2:22; ᵇDa 2:47-48
5:12 ᶜS Da 1:7; ᵈS Nu 12:8; ᵉver 14-16; Da 6:3; ᶠS Eze 28:3
5:13 ᵍS Est 2:5-6; Da 6:13

B Da 4:18 ◀ ▶ Da 5:14
E Da 4:18 ◀ ▶ Da 5:14
G Da 4:18 ◀ ▶ Da 5:14
M Da 4:18 ◀ ▶ Da 5:14
T Da 4:18 ◀ ▶ Da 5:14
N Eze 43:4–5 ◀ ▶ Da 6:3
B Da 5:11–12 ◀ ▶ Da 6:3
E Da 5:11–12 ◀ ▶ Da 6:3
G Da 5:11–12 ◀ ▶ Joel 2:28–29
M Da 5:11–12 ◀ ▶ Da 6:3
T Da 5:11–12 ◀ ▶ Joel 2:28–29

¹² Or *ancestor*, or *predecessor*; also in verses 11, 13 and 18
ᵐ⁷ Or *Chaldeans*; also in verse 11   ⁿ¹⁰ Or *queen mother*

H Eze 35:14 ◀ ▶ Da 12:1
N Eze 33:31 ◀ ▶ Hos 4:17
J Da 4:31–32 ◀ ▶ Da 5:24–28

5:2 The Aramaic word for "father" in this verse indicates a direct ancestor such as a grandson, descendant or successor, but not necessarily an immediate father. In a similar manner, the NT refers to Jesus as David's son (see Mt 1:1; Lk 1:32).

5:3 The king's wives did not usually attend public festivals with the king (see Est 1:9). Belshazzar's decision to include women in his feast while defiling the holy temple vessels was another indication of his contempt for the God of Israel.

5:5 God instantly responded to Belshazzar's blasphemy with a message of judgment supernaturally written on the wall of Belshazzar's palace.

5:12 Daniel's official Babylonian name "Belteshazzar" replaced his Jewish name whenever he appeared at court or served in an advisor's position.

that the spirit of the gods[h] is in you and that you have insight, intelligence and outstanding wisdom.[i] [15]The wise men and enchanters were brought before me to read this writing and tell me what it means, but they could not explain it.[j] [16]Now I have heard that you are able to give interpretations and to solve difficult problems.[k] If you can read this writing and tell me what it means, you will be clothed in purple and have a gold chain placed around your neck,[l] and you will be made the third highest ruler in the kingdom."[m]

[17]Then Daniel answered the king, "You may keep your gifts for yourself and give your rewards to someone else.[n] Nevertheless, I will read the writing for the king and tell him what it means.

[18]"O king, the Most High God gave your father Nebuchadnezzar[o] sovereignty and greatness and glory and splendor.[p] [19]Because of the high position he gave him, all the peoples and nations and men of every language dreaded and feared him. Those the king wanted to put to death, he put to death;[q] those he wanted to spare, he spared; those he wanted to promote, he promoted; and those he wanted to humble, he humbled.[r] [20]But when his heart became arrogant and hardened with pride,[s] he was deposed from his royal throne[t] and stripped[u] of his glory.[v] [21]He was driven away from people and given the mind of an animal; he lived with the wild donkeys and ate grass like cattle; and his body was drenched with the dew of heaven, until he acknowledged that the Most High God is sovereign[w] over the kingdoms of men and sets over them anyone he wishes.[x]

[22]"But you his son,[o] O Belshazzar, have not humbled[y] yourself, though you knew all this. [23]Instead, you have set yourself up against[z] the Lord of heaven. You had the goblets from his temple brought to you, and you and your nobles, your wives[a] and your concubines drank wine from them. You praised the gods of silver and gold, of bronze, iron, wood and stone, which cannot see or hear or understand.[b] But you did not honor the God who holds in his hand your life[c] and all your ways.[d] [24]Therefore he sent the hand that wrote the inscription.

[25]"This is the inscription that was written:

MENE, MENE, TEKEL, PARSIN[p]

[26]"This is what these words mean:

Mene[q]: God has numbered the days[e] of your reign and brought it to an end.[f]
[27]*Tekel*[r]: You have been weighed on the scales[g] and found wanting.[h]
[28]*Peres*[s]: Your kingdom is divided and given to the Medes[i] and Persians."[j]

[29]Then at Belshazzar's command, Daniel was clothed in purple, a gold chain was placed around his neck,[k] and he was

5:14 [h]S Ge 41:38; [i]S Da 2:22
5:15 [j]S Da 4:18
5:16 [k]S Ge 41:15; [l]S Ge 41:42; [m]S Est 5:3; S Da 2:6
5:17 [n]S 2Ki 5:16
5:18 [o]S Jer 28:14; [p]S Jer 27:7; S Da 2:37-38; S 4:36
5:19 [q]Da 2:12-13; S 3:6 [r]S Da 4:22
5:20 [s]Da 4:30 [t]Jer 43:10 [u]Jer 13:18; S Da 4:31 [v]S Job 40:12; Isa 14:13-15; Eze 31:10-11; Da 8:8
5:21 [w]S Eze 17:24 [x]Da 4:16-17,35
5:22 [y]S Ex 10:3
5:23 [z]S Isa 14:13; S Jer 50:29 [a]Jer 44:9 [b]Ps 115:4-8; Hab 2:19; Rev 9:20 [c]Job 12:10; Ac 17:28 [d]S Job 31:4; S Isa 13:11; Jer 10:23; S 48:26
5:26 [e]Jer 27:7 [f]Isa 13:6
5:27 [g]S Job 6:2 [h]Ps 62:9
5:28 [i]Isa 13:17; [j]S Jer 27:7; 50:41-43; Da 6:28
5:29 [k]S Ge 41:42

J Da 5:5 ◀ ▶ Da 7:10–11
E Da 2:22 ◀ ▶ Hos 7:2

[o] 22 Or *descendant*; or *successor* [p] 25 Aramaic UPARSIN (that is, AND PARSIN) [q] 26 *Mene* can mean *numbered* or *mina* (a unit of money). [r] 27 *Tekel* can mean *weighed* or *shekel*. [s] 28 *Peres* (the singular of *Parsin*) can mean *divided* or *Persia* or *a half mina* or *a half shekel*.

5:16 The third in command of the Babylonian kingdom would be like a prime minister. Nabonidus was the king ex officio, Belshazzar occupied the throne and Daniel would be elevated to the chief advisor to the king or prime minister's position.

5:18 Many kings ruled Babylon during Daniel's life. Recent archeological discoveries have confirmed the chronology of the last rulers of Babylon: Nebuchadnezzar died in 562 B.C. and was succeeded on the throne by his son Evil-Merodach (see Jer 52:31). Evil-Merodach was soon murdered and succeeded by Nergal-Sharezer in 560 B.C. (see Jer 39:3, 13). Though his son Labash-Merodach succeeded him in 556 B.C., rebels immediately assassinated this son and crowned Nabonidus as king from 556–539 B.C. When King Nabonidus retired to Tema in the province of Arabia, he left his son Belshazzar in charge of Babylon. In that very year Babylon fell to the Medo-Persians.

5:25 The finger wrote upon the wall of the Babylonian palace these fateful Aramaic words: MENE, MENE, TEKEL, UPHARSIN. Because Aramaic was a common language among the Babylonians (see note at 2:4) Belshazzar should have been able to interpret it. Possibly this message was written as an acrostic. Or, since written Aramaic follows the written Hebrew style of omitting vowels, this message may have seemed to be disconnected letters without a clear meaning. Daniel's divine interpretation of God's judgment upon this Gentile empire reverberates down through the ages upon all kingdoms that reject the laws of God.

proclaimed the third highest ruler in the kingdom.¹

³⁰That very night Belshazzar,ᵐ kingⁿ of the Babylonians,ʳ was slain,ᵒ ³¹and Dariusᵖ the Medeᑫ took over the kingdom, at the age of sixty-two.

Daniel in the Den of Lions

6 It pleased Dariusʳ to appoint 120 satrapsˢ to rule throughout the kingdom, ²with three administrators over them, one of whom was Daniel.ᵗ The satraps were made accountableᵘ to them so that the king might not suffer loss. ³Now Daniel so distinguished himself among the administrators and the satraps by his exceptional qualities that the king planned to set him over the whole kingdom.ᵛ ⁴At this, the administrators and the satraps tried to find grounds for chargesʷ against Daniel in his conduct of government affairs, but they were unable to do so. They could find no corruption in him, because he was trustworthy and neither corrupt nor negligent. ⁵Finally these men said, "We will never find any basis for charges against this man Daniel unless it has something to do with the law of his God."ˣ

⁶So the administrators and the satraps went as a group to the king and said: "O King Darius, live forever!ʸ ⁷The royal administrators, prefects, satraps, advisers and governorsᶻ have all agreed that the king should issue an edict and enforce the decree that anyone who prays to any god or man during the next thirty days, except to you, O king, shall be thrown into the lions' den.ᵃ ⁸Now, O king, issue

B Da 5:14 ◄ ► Joel 2:28–29
E Da 5:14 ◄ ► Mic 3:8
M Da 5:14 ◄ ► Joel 2:28
N Da 5:12 ◄ ► Zec 6:8

5:29 ¹S Da 2:6

5:30 ᵐS ver 1
ⁿJer 50:35
ᵒS Isa 21:9;
S Jer 51:31

5:31 ᵖJer 50:41;
Da 6:1; 9:1; 11:1
ᑫS Isa 13:3

6:1 ʳS Da 5:31
ˢS Est 1:1

6:2 ᵗDa 2:48-49
ᵘEzr 4:22

6:3 ᵛS Ge 41:41;
S Est 10:3;
S Da 1:20; 5:12-14

6:4 ʷJer 20:10

6:5 ˣAc 24:13-16

6:6 ʸS Ne 2:3

6:7 ᶻS Da 3:2
ᵃPs 59:3; 64:2-6;
S Da 3:6

6:8 ᵇS Est 1:19

6:10 ᶜS 1Ki 8:29
ᵈPs 95:6 ᵉMt 6:6;
Ac 5:29

6:11 ᶠ1Ki 8:48-50;
Ps 55:17;
1Th 5:17-18

6:12 ᵍS Est 1:19;
Da 3:8-12

6:13 ʰS Eze 14:14;
Da 2:25 ⁱS ver 3:8

6:14 ʲMk 6:26

6:15 ᵏS Est 8:8

6:16 ˡS ver 7

the decree and put it in writing so that it cannot be altered—in accordance with the laws of the Medes and Persians, which cannot be repealed."ᵇ ⁹So King Darius put the decree in writing.

¹⁰Now when Daniel learned that the decree had been published, he went home to his upstairs room where the windows opened towardᶜ Jerusalem. Three times a day he got down on his kneesᵈ and prayed, giving thanks to his God, just as he had done before.ᵉ ¹¹Then these men went as a group and found Daniel praying and asking God for help.ᶠ ¹²So they went to the king and spoke to him about his royal decree: "Did you not publish a decree that during the next thirty days anyone who prays to any god or man except to you, O king, would be thrown into the lions' den?"

The king answered, "The decree stands—in accordance with the laws of the Medes and Persians, which cannot be repealed."ᵍ

¹³Then they said to the king, "Daniel, who is one of the exiles from Judah,ʰ pays no attentionⁱ to you, O king, or to the decree you put in writing. He still prays three times a day." ¹⁴When the king heard this, he was greatly distressed;ʲ he was determined to rescue Daniel and made every effort until sundown to save him.

¹⁵Then the men went as a group to the king and said to him, "Remember, O king, that according to the law of the Medes and Persians no decree or edict that the king issues can be changed."ᵏ

¹⁶So the king gave the order, and they brought Daniel and threw him into the lions' den.ˡ The king said to Daniel,

ᵗ 30 Or Chaldeans

5:30 God's judgment announced by the writing on the wall was immediately fulfilled. The decadent King Belshazzar was killed that night and the kingdom of Babylon was given to Darius the Mede exactly as God foretold (see Jer 25:12).

5:31 Darius the Mede might be another name for Gubaru, referred to in some Babylonian inscriptions as the governor assigned by Cyrus to rule newly conquered Babylon. Or, Darius the Mede may be the official court name for Cyrus who ruled Babylon from 539–530 B.C. This interchange of names was common in the ancient political world to reflect the different languages of the conquered nations

(see 1Ch 5:26). Note that Darius the Mede is not the same individual as King Darius who ruled Persia from 521–486 B.C. (see Ezr 4:5).

6:10 Scripture indicates that "three times a day [Daniel] got down on his knees and prayed." Both King Solomon and Ezra used this same posture in their prayers (see 1Ki 8:54; Ezr 9:5). While kneeling in prayer has fallen out of favor among many modern-day Jews and Christians, this humble posture is a symbol of reverence and submission to God and an indication of our reliance on him for our very lives.

"May your God, whom you serve continually, rescue™ you!"

¹⁷A stone was brought and placed over the mouth of the den, and the king sealed" it with his own signet ring and with the rings of his nobles, so that Daniel's situation might not be changed. ¹⁸Then the king returned to his palace and spent the night without eating° and without any entertainment being brought to him. And he could not sleep.ᵖ

¹⁹At the first light of dawn, the king got up and hurried to the lions' den. ²⁰When he came near the den, he called to Daniel in an anguished voice, "Daniel, servant of the living God, has your God, whom you serve continually, been able to rescue you from the lions?"ᵠ

²¹Daniel answered, "O king, live forever!ʳ ²²My God sent his angel,ˢ and he shut the mouths of the lions.ᵗ They have not hurt me, because I was found innocent in his sight.ᵘ Nor have I ever done any wrong before you, O king."

²³The king was overjoyed and gave orders to lift Daniel out of the den. And when Daniel was lifted from the den, no woundᵛ was found on him, because he had trustedʷ in his God.

²⁴At the king's command, the men who had falsely accused Daniel were brought in and thrown into the lions' den,ˣ along with their wives and children.ʸ And before they reached the floor of the den, the lions overpowered them and crushed all their bones.ᶻ

²⁵Then King Darius wrote to all the peoples, nations and men of every languageᵃ throughout the land:

L Da 3:25 ◀ ▶ Da 9:23
S Da 3:27 ◀ ▶ Jnh 1:17

"May you prosper greatly!ᵇ

²⁶"I issue a decree that in every part of my kingdom people must fear and reverenceᶜ the God of Daniel.ᵈ

"For he is the living Godᵉ
  and he endures forever;ᶠ
his kingdom will not be destroyed,
  his dominion will never end.ᵍ
²⁷He rescues and he saves;ʰ
he performs signs and wondersⁱ
  in the heavens and on the earth.
He has rescued Daniel
  from the power of the lions."ʲ

²⁸So Daniel prospered during the reign of Darius and the reign of Cyrusᵘᵏ the Persian.ˡ

Daniel's Dream of Four Beasts

7 In the first year of Belshazzarᵐ king of Babylon, Daniel had a dream, and visionsⁿ passed through his mind° as he was lying on his bed.ᵖ He wroteᵠ down the substance of his dream.

²Daniel said: "In my vision at night I **G** looked, and there before me were the four winds of heavenʳ churning up the great sea. ³Four great beasts,ˢ each different from the others, came up out of the sea.

⁴"The first was like a lion,ᵗ and it had the wings of an eagle.ᵘ I watched until its wings were torn off and it was lifted from the ground so that it stood on two feet like a man, and the heart of a man was given to it.

⁵"And there before me was a second beast, which looked like a bear. It was

G Da 2:28–45 ◀ ▶ Da 8:1–26

ᵘ 28 Or Darius, that is, the reign of Cyrus

6:28 The overthrow of the Babylonian empire by the Medo-Persians fulfilled the second stage of Nebuchadnezzar's vision of the metallic image (see Da 2:31–40). King Cyrus, monarch of Medo-Persia, ruled in Babylon from 538–530 B.C. Note that more than one hundred years earlier this Persian king was mentioned by Isaiah as the king who would release the Jewish exiles (see Isa 44:28; 45:13; see also Ezr 1:1–4).

7:1 Since the events of ch. 7 precede the events described in ch. 5, Daniel's vision of the four beasts probably occurred in 553 B.C.

7:2 The large sea was used to indicate the multitudes, the great political world (see Isa 60:5;

Rev 13:1).

7:3 Daniel's vision of the four beasts paralleled Nebuchadnezzar's vision of the metallic image recorded in Da 2 as they both foreshadowed the future course of the Gentile world empires that would precede the kingdom of the Messiah. However, while King Nebuchadnezzar noted the glory and power of these empires, Daniel's vision concentrated on the true spiritual character of the four empires that would rule the known world until the end of this age. Note that each of the four beasts were predatory and violent, indicating that these empires would rule by force, greed and war.

7:5 The three ribs in the bear's mouth may refer

raised up on one of its sides, and it had three ribs in its mouth between its teeth. It was told, 'Get up and eat your fill of flesh!'ᵛ

⁶"After that, I looked, and there before me was another beast, one that looked like a leopard.ʷ And on its back it had four wings like those of a bird. This beast had four heads, and it was given authority to rule.

⁷"After that, in my vision˟ at night I looked, and there before me was a fourth beast—terrifying and frightening and very powerful. It had large ironʸ teeth; it crushed and devoured its victims and trampledᶻ underfoot whatever was left.ᵃ It was different from all the former beasts, and it had ten horns.ᵇ

⁸"While I was thinking about the horns, there before me was another horn, a littleᶜ one, which came up among them; and three of the first horns were uprooted before it. This horn had eyes like the eyes of a manᵈ and a mouth that spoke boastfully.ᵉ

⁹"As I looked,

"thrones were set in place,
    and the Ancient of Daysᶠ took his seat.ᵍ
His clothing was as white as snow;ʰ
    the hair of his head was white like wool.ⁱ
His throne was flaming with fire,
    and its wheelsʲ were all ablaze.

J Ecc 12:14 ◀ ▶ Am 4:12

7:5 ᵛ Da 2:39
7:6 ʷ Rev 13:2
7:7 ˣ S Eze 40:2
  ʸ S Da 2:40
  ᶻ Da 8:10 ᵃ Da 8:7
  ᵇ S Rev 12:3
7:8 ᶜ Da 8:9
  ᵈ Rev 9:7
  ᵉ S Ps 12:3;
  Rev 13:5-6
7:9 ᶠ ver 22
  ᵍ S 1Ki 22:19;
  2Ch 18:18;
  Mt 19:28; Rev 4:2;
  20:4 ʰ S Mt 28:3
  ⁱ Rev 1:14
  ʲ S Eze 1:15; 10:6
7:10 ᵏ Ps 50:3;
  97:3; Isa 30:27
  ˡ Dt 33:2;
  Ps 68:17; Jude 1:14;
  Rev 5:11
  ᵐ S Ex 32:32;
  S Ps 56:8;
  Rev 20:11-15
7:11 ⁿ Rev 13:5-6
  ᵒ Rev 19:20
7:13 ᵖ Eze 1:5;
  S 2:1; Mt 8:20*;
  Rev 1:13*; 14:14*
  ᑫ Isa 13:6; Zep 1:14;
  Mal 3:2; 4:1
  ʳ S Dt 33:26;
  S Rev 1:7
7:14 ˢ S Mt 28:18
  ᵗ Ps 72:11; 102:22
  ᵘ S Isa 16:5
  ᵛ S Da 2:44;
  Heb 12:28;
  Rev 11:15
7:15 ʷ S Job 4:15;
  S Da 4:19

¹⁰A river of fireᵏ was flowing,
    coming out from before him.ˡ
Thousands upon thousands attended him;
    ten thousand times ten thousand stood before him.
The court was seated,
    and the booksᵐ were opened.

¹¹"Then I continued to watch because of the boastful words the horn was speaking.ⁿ I kept looking until the beast was slain and its body destroyed and thrown into the blazing fire.ᵒ ¹²(The other beasts had been stripped of their authority, but were allowed to live for a period of time.)

¹³"In my vision at night I looked, and there before me was one like a son of man,ᵖ comingᑫ with the clouds of heaven.ʳ He approached the Ancient of Days and was led into his presence. ¹⁴He was given authority,ˢ glory and sovereign power; all peoples, nations and men of every language worshiped him.ᵗ His dominion is an everlasting dominion that will not pass away, and his kingdomᵘ is one that will never be destroyed.ᵛ

The Interpretation of the Dream

¹⁵"I, Daniel, was troubled in spirit, and the visions that passed through my mind disturbed me.ʷ ¹⁶I approached one of

J Da 5:24-28 ◀ ▶ Zep 2:4-15
C Isa 64:4 ◀ ▶ Hag 2:6-7
K Jer 31:34 ◀ ▶ Hab 2:14
M Da 2:44-45 ◀ ▶ Da 7:18
V Da 2:44 ◀ ▶ Zec 9:10

---

to the three provincial territories that were conquered by the Medo-Persians: Lydia (546 B.C.), Babylon (539 B.C.) and Egypt (525 B.C.). The Medo-Persian empire ultimately encompassed twenty-seven provinces from northern Africa to India—every nation in the known world at that time.

7:6 The leopard with four wings referred to the empire of Alexander the Great from Greece. The greatest general of the ancient world, Alexander conquered the nations from India to Africa in less than ten years.

7:7–8 The fourth creature in Daniel's vision represented the Roman empire. The ten little horns corresponded to the metallic image's ten toes (see 2:40–42) and indicated the totality of the beast's sphere of authority. Some interpret these ten horns as ten kingdoms, a revived Roman empire, that will arise in the last days (see 7:24–25; Rev 17:12). The smaller horn that appeared in the middle of the other horns is believed to represent the antichrist (see 7:25; 11:36; 12:11; 2Th 2:3, 4, 8; Rev 13:5–6). Daniel describes the antichrist's evil rule in Da 8:23–26 and 11:36–45.

7:9 This title "the Ancient of Days" refers to Jesus Christ who is God eternal and the righteous judge of the world (see Isa 57:15).

7:11 Compare this verse with Rev 19:20. Daniel witnessed the ultimate defeat of Satan's antichrist, destroyed by Jesus Christ when he returns from heaven to establish his kingdom. Though the antichrist's body will die, his spirit will be consigned to the lake of fire (hell) for eternity.

7:13–14 This passage is the first reference to the Messiah as the "son of man" (7:13), a title that Jesus often used for himself (see Mt 8:20; 9:6; 10:23; 12:40; Mk 14:41; Lk 6:5). This prophecy clearly foretells the Messiah's coronation and rule over all nations forever in justice and peace. See also note at 7:9.

those standing there and asked him the true meaning of all this.

"So he told me and gave me the interpretation of these things: ¹⁷'The four great beasts are four kingdoms that will rise from the earth. ¹⁸But the saints of the Most High will receive the kingdom and will possess it forever—yes, for ever and ever.'

¹⁹"Then I wanted to know the true meaning of the fourth beast, which was different from all the others and most terrifying, with its iron teeth and bronze claws—the beast that crushed and devoured its victims and trampled underfoot whatever was left. ²⁰I also wanted to know about the ten horns on its head and about the other horn that came up, before which three of them fell—the horn that looked more imposing than the others and that had eyes and a mouth that spoke boastfully. ²¹As I watched, this horn was waging war against the saints and defeating them, ²²until the Ancient of Days came and pronounced judgment in favor of the saints of the Most High, and the time came when they possessed the kingdom.

²³"He gave me this explanation: 'The fourth beast is a fourth kingdom that will appear on earth. It will be different from all the other kingdoms and will devour the whole earth, trampling it down and crushing it. ²⁴The ten horns are ten kings who will come from this kingdom. After them another king will arise, different from the earlier ones; he will subdue three kings. ²⁵He will speak against the Most High and oppress his saints and try to change the set times and the laws. The saints will be handed over to him for a time, times and half a time.ᵛ

²⁶"'But the court will sit, and his power will be taken away and completely destroyed forever. ²⁷Then the sovereignty, power and greatness of the kingdoms under the whole heaven will be handed over to the saints, the people of the Most High. His kingdom will be an everlasting kingdom, and all rulers will worship and obey him.'

²⁸"This is the end of the matter. I, Daniel, was deeply troubled by my thoughts, and my face turned pale, but I kept the matter to myself."

Daniel's Vision of a Ram and a Goat

8 In the third year of King Belshazzar's reign, I, Daniel, had a vision, after the one that had already appeared to

ᵛ 25 Or for a year, two years and half a year

7:17 The four great beasts represented the kings of the four empires that would rule the world until the return of Jesus the Messiah.

7:18 The "saints" of God are Christ's followers who will enjoy exalted privileges during the Messianic kingdom (see Mt 19:28–29; Lk 22:29–30). John records God's promise to the saints who participate in the first resurrection that they will "reign with him for a thousand years" (Rev 20:6). Other NT passages confirm that Christ's followers will rule over the Gentiles and Jews living on the new earth following the Millennium (see Ro 8:17; 2Ti 2:10–12; Rev 3:21; 5:10).

7:24 The other horn referred to here is the antichrist, the "little horn" of 7:7–8. For additional information about the antichrist, see the notes on Rev 13:1–18.

7:25 The antichrist will "speak against the Most High and oppress his saints" indicating the severe persecution of the Jewish and Gentile tribulation saints. The antichrist will also "try to change the set times and the laws," which may mean that he may introduce new laws restricting the worship of God while promoting his own glorification. The antichrist may also create a new calendar that will no longer acknowledge the role of Jesus Christ in history. Even now such discussions are under way in an attempt to circumvent the technological difficulties raised by the current calendar system.

Note the expression "time, times and half a time." Found in Daniel and Revelation (see 12:7; Rev 12:14), this expression referred to a three-and-a-half-year period that will occur during the last seven-year tribulation period (Daniel's seventieth week). Jesus referred to this time as the great tribulation (see Mt 24:21).

7:26 This verse foretells the final defeat of the antichrist and the ten-nation confederacy of the fourth beast (v. 7). This will occur at the Battle of Armageddon (see Rev 16:16–19; 19:14–21).

8:1–7 Daniel received this vision of the ram (8:3) two years after the vision in chapter 7 and just prior to the destruction of Babylon. Daniel described the Medes and Persians as a ram with two horns (see 8:20). The first horn represented the Medes who dominated the empire during the first few

The Antichrist

THOUGH WE ARE often unaware of the spiritual warfare going on around us, from the time of Satan's rebellion against God this spiritual battle has affected every life on earth. Satan's emissary, the antichrist, will ultimately do battle with Jesus Christ in the last days to put an end to the war against good and evil. This antichrist will be a liar and a deceiver because he is Satan's tool (see 1Jn 2:22). Some suggest that he may be a Jew who is either a eunuch or a homosexual since Daniel warned that he would have no regard "for the gods of his fathers or for the one desired by women" (11:37). Both the OT and NT use various names and titles to describe this satanic deceiver's career, nature and ultimate defeat by the Messiah.

The Antichrist in the Old Testament

Satan's Seed The Bible's first prophecy describes the antichrist as Satan's seed because he will attempt to do the will of his father, Satan, the father of all lies (see Ge 3:15; Jn 8:44).

The King of Babylon He is called the "king of Babylon" (Isa 14:4) because he will make the rebuilt city of Babylon one of his capitals during his brief reign.

Ruler of Tyrus Ezekiel called the antichrist the "ruler of Tyrus" (Eze 28:2) declaring that though he would be possessed by Satan, he was still a man and not a god. The antichrist will exalt himself to be worshiped, exactly as Satan wanted the worship of the fallen angels.

The Little Horn Daniel calls him "another horn, a little one" (7:8) in contrast to the ten horns that represent ten nations arising out of the revived Roman empire. Endowed with satanic powers, he will be a powerful speaker, able to impress people with his brilliant speech.

A Stern-faced King The antichrist will be "a stern-faced king" (8:23), a leader with a striking appearance and great charisma.

The Prince That Shall Come Daniel 9:26 says that a people would come to destroy Jerusalem and the temple. The Romans fulfilled this prophecy in A.D. 70. Therefore the "ruler who will come" (9:26) will come from the revived Roman empire.

The Willful King Jesus came to do his Father's will (see Lk 2:49). In total contrast, the antichrist will "do as he pleases" (Da 11:36).

The Assyrian Prior to 608 B.C. ancient Assyria occupied the same geographic area as Babylon. Isaiah's words may identify the antichrist as coming from "the Assyrians" (Isa 10:24) because of his future role in Babylon.

The Worthless Shepherd The antichrist is called the "worthless shepherd" (Zec 11:17) because his purpose is to use, abandon and destroy God's flock for Satan's benefit. This title may also be applied to the antichrist because he will make an image of himself in the rebuilt temple and require people to worship it (see Rev 13:14–15).

The Destroyer and the Oppressor Isaiah describes the antichrist as "the destroyer" and "the oppressor" (Isa 16:4) because he will attempt to destroy all who resist his claims to be a god while using coercion to gain great riches.

The Lawless One The apostle Paul describes the antichrist as "the lawless one" (2Th 2:8) because he will give himself entirely to Satan's evil designs to destroy God's people and purposes.

The Antichrist in the New Testament

The Man of Lawlessness Paul tells us that the antichrist will not appear until there has been a falling away first. Then "the man of lawlessness" (2Th 2:3) will be revealed after God has removed his restraining Spirit (see 2Th 2:6–7).

The Man Doomed to Destruction Paul calls the antichrist "the man doomed to destruction" (2Th 2:3) because the antichrist is destined to destroy and be destroyed by God. Judas Iscariot was also referred to by this name (see Jn 17:12).

Antichrist The title "antichrist" (1Jn 2:18) is the most common one used to describe this last enemy of humanity. The antichrist will appear to emulate Jesus but will be a counterfeit.

The First Beast The antichrist is identified as "the beast" (Rev 11:7) that comes up "out of the sea" (Rev 13:1). The sea usually depicts Gentile nations so this title indicates the antichrist's power within the ten-nation kingdom.

The One Who Comes in His Own Name Though people rejected Jesus' claim to be the Messiah who came in the name of his Father, the Jews will one day accept the antichrist who "comes in his own name" (Jn 5:43).

The Defilement of the Temple

Daniel and Paul both mention the defilement of the rebuilt temple when the antichrist will enter the Holy of Holies (see 9:27; 2Th 2:4). What he will do there is uncertain, but this act will surely qualify as "the abomination that causes desolation" (Mt 24:15) that Jesus warned his disciples to flee (see Mt 24:15–17). God's wrath will be instantly poured out when the antichrist defiles the temple half way through the seven-year treaty period. This will usher in the final great tribulation.

Many Jews will recognize that the antichrist is the false Messiah when he defiles the temple. As these Jews rebel, Satan will empower the antichrist to supernaturally fight the righteous and attack Israel as she flees into the wilderness seeking God's power and protection (see Rev 12:17).

The Worship of the Antichrist

The antichrist will suffer a deadly wound but will be miraculously healed and restored (see Rev 13:12–13). After this miracle, the false prophet will convince the world that the antichrist is the long-awaited Messiah. The false prophet will force everyone under the jurisdiction of his world government to worship the antichrist. From that point on it will be spiritual and physical warfare for three and a half years for those who choose to serve God.

The Destruction of the Antichrist

In the final years of the tribulation the kings of the east will mobilize a vast army to rebel against the tyranny of the antichrist (see Rev 9:16). They will march across Asia killing one third of humanity as they move towards Armageddon (see Rev 9:18). When they approach the Euphrates River it will dry up to allow their army to march across its dry riverbed to the final Battle of Armageddon (see Rev 9:14–15; 16:12).

When the enormous armies of the kings of the east, north, south and the ten-nation federation of the antichrist join battle, Jesus Christ will descend with his heavenly army of saints to defeat the antichrist and his allies (see Rev 19:19–21). The antichrist and the false prophet will be thrown into the lake of fire, while the sword of the Lord will kill their allies. A remnant of the antichrist's armies will escape and invade Jerusalem a few days later, taking the population captive. Jesus will descend to Jerusalem to destroy the last of the wicked armies and save all of the Jews who repent (see Zec 12:8-11; 14:1-5). Christ will then enter the rebuilt temple through the newly opened eastern gate and usher in the millennial kingdom (see Eze 43:1-5).

DANIEL 8:14

me. ²In my vision I saw myself in the citadel of Susa,ʷ in the province of Elam;ˣ in the vision I was beside the Ulai Canal. ³I looked up,ʸ and there before me was a ramᶻ with two horns, standing beside the canal, and the horns were long. One of the horns was longer than the other but grew up later. ⁴I watched the ram as he charged toward the west and the north and the south. No animal could stand against him, and none could rescue from his power.ᵃ He did as he pleasedᵇ and became great.

⁵As I was thinking about this, suddenly a goat with a prominent horn between his eyes came from the west, crossing the whole earth without touching the ground. ⁶He came toward the two-horned ram I had seen standing beside the canal and charged at him in great rage. ⁷I saw him attack the ram furiously, striking the ram and shattering his two horns. The ram was powerless to stand against him; the goat knocked him to the ground and trampled on him,ᶜ and none could rescue the ram from his power.ᵈ ⁸The goat became very great, but at the height of his power his large horn was broken off, and in its place four prominent horns grew up toward the four winds of heaven.ᶠ

⁹Out of one of them came another horn, which started smallᵍ but grew in power to the south and to the east and toward the Beautiful Land.ʰ ¹⁰It grew until it reachedⁱ the host of the heavens, and it threw some of the starry host down to the earthʲ and trampledᵏ on them. ¹¹It set itself up to be as great as the Princeˡ of the host;ᵐ it took away the daily sacrificeⁿ from him, and the place of his sanctuary was brought low.ᵒ ¹²Because of rebellion, the host ˌof the saints,ʷ and the daily sacrifice were given over to it. It prospered in everything it did, and truth was thrown to the ground.ᵖ

¹³Then I heard a holy oneᑫ speaking, and another holy one said to him, "How long will it take for the vision to be fulfilledʳ—the vision concerning the daily sacrifice, the rebellion that causes desolation, and the surrender of the sanctuary and of the host that will be trampledˢ underfoot?"

¹⁴He said to me, "It will take 2,300

R Eze 39:28 ◀ ▶ Da 8:19

8:2 ʷ S Ezr 4:9; S Est 2:8
ˣ S Ge 10:22
8:3 ʸ Da 10:5
ᶻ Rev 13:11
8:4 ᵃ Isa 41:3
ᵇ Da 11:3,16
8:7 ᶜ S Da 7:7
ᵈ Da 11:11,16
8:8 ᵉ 2Ch 26:16-21; S Da 5:20
ᶠ S Da 7:2; Rev 7:1
8:9 ᵍ Da 7:8
ʰ S Eze 20:6; Da 11:16
8:10 ⁱ S Isa 14:13
ʲ Rev 8:10; 12:4
ᵏ S Da 7:7
8:11 ˡ ver 25
ᵐ Da 11:36-37
ⁿ Eze 46:13-14
ᵒ Da 11:31; 12:11
8:12 ᵖ S Isa 48:1
8:13 ᑫ S Dt 33:2; S Da 4:23 ʳ Da 12:6
ˢ S Isa 28:18;
S Lk 21:24;
Rev 11:2

ʷ 12 Or *rebellion, the armies*

---

years, but the second horn, the highest, reflected the predominant position and superior strength of Persia. Daniel also saw a male goat that came from the west. It too had a horn on its head. This goat charged at the ram with great speed and power, breaking the ram's horns. The goat symbolized the Greek empire under the rule of Alexander the Great. True to Daniel's vision, Alexander's armies, utilizing brilliant military strategy and awesome courage, swiftly invaded Persia and destroyed it.

8:8 Daniel's vision prophesied the early death of Alexander the Great (the image of the broken goat horn) and prophetically described the breakup of Alexander's empire into four kingdoms. True to this prophecy, Alexander died at the age of 32, and the empire was divided among his four generals—Cassander, Lysimachus, Seleucus and Ptolemy. See notes at 8:22 and 11:4.

8:9 Daniel's prophecy envisioned a "little horn" growing up from the territory of one of the four horns. Note that this "little horn" arises from the remnants of the third world empire and is a different person than the "little horn" of 7:8 who will arise from the fourth world empire. Though both of these small horns hate the Jews and would profane the temple at Jerusalem, they are different individuals.

The small horn in this passage found fulfillment in Antiochus Epiphanes. During the last years of his reign in 171–165 B.C., Antiochus Epiphanes attempted to eradicate the Jewish faith by persecuting the Palestinian Jews and defiling the temple. He even set himself up to be the equal of God (see 8:11) and ordered an end to daily sacrifices in the temple. Antiochus Epiphanes was finally overthrown when Judas Maccabeus recaptured Jerusalem and rededicated the temple in 165 B.C.

8:13 Daniel used the word "desolation" many times in this book. The first desolation (8:13) predicted the defilement of the sanctuary by Antiochus Epiphanes. The second desolation (see 9:17) occurred when Nebuchadnezzar destroyed Solomon's temple. The word was used again to describe the condition of Palestine during its occupation by its enemies (see 9:18). The fourth desolation occurred when the Messiah was cut off and Jerusalem and the temple were destroyed by Rome in A.D. 70 (see 9:26). Daniel also used the word "desolation" three more times to describe the future defilement of the temple by the "beast," the future antichrist.

8:14 This prediction of the 2300 days was fulfilled during the bitter persecution under Antiochus Epiphanes, beginning when peaceful relations ended between the Jews and this Syrian king in 171 B.C. and ending with the cleansing of the temple in Jerusalem by Judas Maccabeus in 165 B.C. Yet this prophecy also foreshadows the future tribulation of

evenings and mornings; then the sanctuary will be reconsecrated."ᵗ

The Interpretation of the Vision

¹⁵While I, Daniel, was watching the visionᵘ and trying to understand it, there before me stood one who looked like a man.ᵛ ¹⁶And I heard a man's voice from the Ulaiʷ calling, "Gabriel,ˣ tell this man the meaning of the vision."ʸ

¹⁷As he came near the place where I was standing, I was terrified and fell prostrate.ᶻ "Son of man," he said to me, "understand that the vision concerns the time of the end."ᵃ

¹⁸While he was speaking to me, I was in a deep sleep, with my face to the ground.ᵇ Then he touched me and raised me to my feet.ᶜ

¹⁹He said: "I am going to tell you what will happen later in the time of wrath,ᵈ because the vision concerns the appointed timeᵉ of the end.ˣᶠ ²⁰The two-horned ram that you saw represents the kings of Media and Persia.ᵍ ²¹The shaggy goat is the king of Greece,ʰ and the large horn between his eyes is the first king.ⁱ ²²The four horns that replaced the one that was broken off represent four kingdoms that will emerge from his nation but will not have the same power.

²³"In the latter part of their reign, when rebels have become completely wicked, a stern-faced king, a master of intrigue, will arise. ²⁴He will become very strong, but not by his own power. He will cause astounding devastation and will succeed in whatever he does. He will destroy the mighty men and the holy people.ʲ ²⁵He will cause deceitᵏ to prosper, and he will consider himself superior. When they feel secure, he will destroy many and take his stand against the Prince of princes.ˡ Yet he will be destroyed, but not by human power.ᵐ

²⁶"The vision of the evenings and mornings that has been given you is true,ⁿ but sealᵒ up the vision, for it concerns the distant future."ᵖ

²⁷I, Daniel, was exhausted and lay illᑫ for several days. Then I got up and went about the king's business.ʳ I was ap-

---

l Eze 47:1 ◄ ► Da 12:1
R Da 8:11–14 ◄ ► Da 8:24

8:14 ᵗ Da 12:11-12
8:15 ᵘ ver 1
  ᵛ S Eze 2:1;
  Da 10:16-18
8:16 ʷ ver 2
  ˣ Da 9:21; S Lk 1:19
  ʸ S Da 7:16
8:17 ᶻ Eze 1:28;
  44:4; S Da 2:46;
  Rev 1:17 ᵃ ver 19;
  Hab 2:3
8:18 ᵇ Da 10:9
  ᶜ S Eze 2:2;
  Da 10:16-18;
  Zec 4:1
8:19 ᵈ S Isa 10:25
  ᵉ S Ps 102:13
  ᶠ Hab 2:3
8:20 ᵍ S Eze 27:10
8:21 ʰ Da 10:20
  ⁱ Da 11:3
8:24 ʲ S Da 7:25;
  11:36
8:25 ᵏ Da 11:23
  ˡ Da 11:36
  ᵐ S Da 2:34; 11:21
8:26 ⁿ Da 10:1
  ᵒ S Isa 8:16;
  S 29:11; Rev 10:4;
  22:10 ᵖ Da 10:14
8:27 ᑫ Da 10:8
  ʳ S Da 2:48

R Da 8:19 ◄ ► Da 9:2

ˣ19 Or *because the end will be at the appointed time*

---

the last days. When Christ returns the sanctuary will be cleansed and the antichrist destroyed.

8:17–26 This prophecy concerning "the time of the end" (see also 12:4) seems to be one of double fulfillment. Initially fulfilled when Medo-Persia was destroyed by Alexander the Great and by the cruel reign of Antiochus Epiphanes, the second and final fulfillment of this prophecy will occur when the Gentile kingdoms will be replaced by the Messianic kingdom of Christ (see Lk 21:24–25; Rev 16:19).

8:22 The four separate subkingdoms of the Greek empire—Macedonia, Syria, Egypt, Asia Minor—were ruled by four generals following the death of Alexander the Great in 323 B.C.

8:23 This verse viewed Antiochus Epiphanes as a symbol of the satanic power of the future antichrist that will arise in the end times. Evil will abound in the last days "when rebels have become completely wicked," and the antichrist will be fearsome in appearance and deeply involved in satanic practices and occult rituals.

8:24 Though the details of this verse can be applied directly to Antiochus Epiphanes, the final fulfillment of this prophecy will come in the end times when the antichrist will be strong in battle (see Rev 13:4) and find success in his endeavors (see Rev 13:16–18). His power will come from Satan (see Rev 13:2), and he will also oppress "the holy people" during the final great tribulation as is suggested in 12:1 and Rev 12:6–17.

8:25 This verse found initial fulfillment in the reign of Antiochus Epiphanes. Through deceit, intrigue and treachery, Antiochus brought great wealth to his kingdom. But he also oppressed God's people and was ultimately destroyed by an unexplained illness in 164 B.C. The final fulfillment of Daniel's words revolves around the rule of the antichrist. Daniel stated that this antichrist would experience an economic success that would solidify his popularity (see 11:39). The antichrist would boastfully "consider himself superior" and deceitfully offer a false peace to destroy his enemies. Daniel also prophesied that the antichrist would oppose Jesus Christ, "the Prince of princes. Yet he will be destroyed, but not by human power" at the Battle of Armageddon (see Rev 16:16).

8:26 The angel Gabriel confirmed that this prophecy would be completely fulfilled at the final end of this age.

8:27 Daniel admitted that he was astonished at the vision, but unable to understand it. We, too, can only understand the prophetic outline of God's plan for history when we harmonize the predictions of Daniel with the prophecies of Mt 24, 2 Thessalonians and Revelation.

palled by the vision; it was beyond understanding.

Daniel's Prayer

9 In the first year of Darius son of Xerxes (a Mede by descent), who was made ruler over the Babylonian kingdom— ²in the first year of his reign, I, Daniel, understood from the Scriptures, according to the word of the LORD given to Jeremiah the prophet, that the desolation of Jerusalem would last seventy years. ³So I turned to the Lord God and pleaded with him in prayer and petition, in fasting, and in sackcloth and ashes.

⁴I prayed to the LORD my God and confessed:

"O Lord, the great and awesome God, who keeps his covenant of love with all who love him and obey his commands, ⁵we have sinned and done wrong. We have been wicked and have rebelled; we have turned away from your commands and laws. ⁶We have not listened to your servants the prophets, who spoke in your name to our kings, our princes and our fathers, and to all the people of the land.

⁷"Lord, you are righteous, but this day we are covered with shame—the men of Judah and people of Jerusalem and all Israel, both near and far, in all the countries where you have scattered us because of our unfaithfulness to you. ⁸O LORD, we and our kings, our princes and our fathers are covered with shame because we have sinned against you. ⁹The Lord our God is merciful and forgiving, even though we have rebelled against him; ¹⁰we have not obeyed the LORD our God or kept the laws he gave us through his servants the prophets. ¹¹All Israel has transgressed your laws and turned away, refusing to obey you.

"Therefore the curses and sworn judgments written in the Law of Moses, the servant of God, have been poured out on us, because we have sinned against you. ¹²You have fulfilled the words spoken against us and against our rulers by bringing upon us great disaster. Under the whole heaven nothing has ever been done like what has been done to Jerusalem. ¹³Just as it is written in the Law of Moses, all this disaster has come upon us, yet we have not sought the favor of the LORD our God by turning from our sins and giving attention to your truth. ¹⁴The LORD did not hesitate to bring the disaster upon us, for the LORD our God is righteous in everything he does; yet we have not obeyed him.

¹⁵"Now, O Lord our God, who brought your people out of Egypt with a mighty hand and who made for yourself a name that endures to this day, we have sinned, we have done wrong. ¹⁶O Lord, in keeping with all your righteous acts, turn away your anger and your wrath from Jerusalem, your city, your holy hill. Our sins and the iniquities of our fathers have made Jerusalem and your people an object of scorn to all those around us.

¹⁷"Now, our God, hear the prayers and petitions of your servant. For your sake, O Lord, look with favor on your desolate sanctuary. ¹⁸Give ear, O God, and hear; open your

R *Da 8:24* ◀ ▶ *Da 9:16–18*
M *Eze 3:7* ◀ ▶ *Da 9:20–21*
C *Eze 22:18* ◀ ▶ *Hos 1:9*
L *Eze 36:29* ◀ ▶ *Hos 6:3*
P *Eze 34:11–12* ◀ ▶ *Hos 6:1*

R *Da 9:2* ◀ ▶ *Da 9:26–27*

y 1 Hebrew *Ahasuerus* z 1 Or *Chaldean*

9:1–19 In his prayer, Daniel repented for the nation of Israel for the sins that led to the destruction of Jerusalem. Daniel understood that Israel's punishment was the fulfillment of Solomon's prayer (see 1Ki 8:33–36). Daniel's prayer expressed his deep adoration of God (9:4), his confession of Israel's sins (9:5–15) and his heartfelt petition that God would forgive and limit Israel's desolation to seventy years (9:16–19; see also Jer 25:11–12). Daniel's life reminds us that our study of the deep truths of prophecy should lead us to a deeper spiritual life.

9:2 Daniel declared that the time had come for the ending of the Jews' seventy-year captivity in Babylon as prophesied by Jeremiah (see Jer 25:11–12).

eyes and seeq the desolation of the city that bears your Name.r We do not make requests of you because we are righteous, but because of your great mercy.s ¹⁹O Lord, listen! O Lord, forgive!t O Lord, hear and act! For your sake,u O my God, do not delay, because your city and your people bear your Name."

The Seventy "Sevens"

²⁰While I was speaking and praying, confessingv my sin and the sin of my people Israel and making my request to the LORD my God for his holy hillw — ²¹while I was still in prayer, Gabriel,x the man I had seen in the earlier vision, came to me in swift flight about the time of the evening sacrifice.y ²²He instructed me and said to me, "Daniel, I have now come to give you insight and understanding.z ²³As soon as you began to pray,a an answer was given, which I have come to tell you, for you are highly esteemed.b Therefore, consider the message and understand the vision:c

²⁴"Seventy 'sevens'a are decreed for your people and your holy cityd to finishb transgression, to put an end to sin, to atonee for wickedness, to bring in everlasting righteousness,f to seal up vision and prophecy and to anoint the most holy.c

---

9:18 qPs 80:14
rS Dt 28:10;
S Isa 37:17;
Jer 7:10-12; 25:29
sLk 18:13
9:19 tPs 44:23
uS 1Sa 12:22
9:20 vS Ezr 10:1
wS ver 3;
Ps 145:18;
S Isa 58:5
9:21 xS Da 8:16;
S Lk 1:19
yS Ex 29:39
9:22 aS Da 7:16;
10:14; Am 3:7
9:23 aS Isa 65:24
bDa 10:19; Lk 1:28
cDa 10:11-12;
Mt 24:15
9:24 dS Isa 1:26
eS Isa 53:10
fS Isa 56:1;
Heb 9:12

L Da 6:22 ◄ ► Joel 2:27–28
B Jer 22:29–30 ◄ ► Mic 5:1–4
D Eze 46:13 ◄ ► Zec 12:10

M Da 9:3–5 ◄ ► Hos 10:12

a 24 Or 'weeks'; also in verses 25 and 26 b 24 Or restrain c 24 Or Most Holy Place; or most holy One

---

9:24–27 Careful study of Daniel's prophecy of the "seventy 'sevens' " is essential to a proper understanding of the unfolding of end time events. This prophecy of the seventy sevens, or "weeks" (KJV), provides an outline of history from the time between the command to rebuild the walls of Jerusalem to the coming of the Messiah and the final establishment of his kingdom. Though the interpretation of these verses varies among scholars, most agree that each "week" symbolizes the passage of seven years. (For the Biblical usage of a "week" referring to a period of seven years, see Ge 29:26–28.) Daniel's seventy weeks of years are then subdivided into three distinct units: 49 years (corresponding to the "seven 'sevens' " of 9:25), 434 years (corresponding to the "sixty-two 'sevens' " of 9:26) and 7 more years (corresponding to "the 'seven' " of 9:27).

Note that the focus of this prophecy is on the Jews and Jerusalem. Daniel fixed the date of the beginning of his vision from the time of the decree to rebuild Jerusalem (9:25). Though various edicts were issued to rebuild the temple, history records only one decree issued in 445 B.C. that authorized the rebuilding of the city (see Ne 2:1–8).

Daniel also noted that the Messiah would come "seven 'sevens,' and sixty-two 'sevens' " (9:25) after this historic decree. Yet Daniel indicated that the Messiah would "be cut off" (9:26). This portion of Daniel's prophecy was fulfilled precisely 483 years later when Jesus entered Jerusalem on a donkey on Palm Sunday, was rejected by the Jews, and crucified by the Romans. Note too that Daniel recorded the future destruction of Jerusalem by "the ruler who will come" (9:26), referring to "another horn, a little one" of 7:8. Many scholars agree that this prophecy was fulfilled when Rome destroyed Jerusalem in A.D. 70.

There appears to be a period of time between the conclusion of the sixty-ninth week and the beginning of the seventieth week in Daniel's prophecy. This time period will encompass certain "desolations" (9:26) that are not described here.

Daniel's Vision of the Seventy Weeks

69 WEEKS OF YEARS			70TH WEEK	
7 WKS ⟶ plus ⟶ 62 WKS = 69 WKS 69 WKS X 7 YRS = 483 BIBLICAL YRS OF 360 DAYS = 173,880 DAYS			7 YRS	
7 WKS (OF YEARS) X 7 YRS = 49 YRS	62 WKS (OF YEARS) X 7 YRS = 434 YRS		3.5 YRS	3.5 YRS
Command to Rebuild Walls of Jerusalem March 14, 445 B.C.		**Cutting Off of the Messiah** April 6, A.D. 32	**The Church Age**	**Antichrist in the Temple** 7 Year Treaty

²⁵"Know and understand this: From the issuing of the decree^d to restore and rebuild^g Jerusalem until the Anointed One,^e^h the ruler,^i comes, there will be seven 'sevens,' and sixty-two 'sevens.' It will be rebuilt with streets and a trench, but in times of trouble.^j ²⁶After the sixty-two 'sevens,' the Anointed One will be cut off^k and will have nothing.^l The people of the ruler who will come will destroy the city and the sanctuary. The end will come like a flood:^l War will continue until the end, and desolations^m have been decreed.^n ²⁷He will confirm a covenant with many for one 'seven.'^g In the middle of the 'seven'^g he will put an end to sacrifice and offering. And on a wing ₒf the temple₎ he will set up an abomination that causes desolation, until the end that is decreed° is poured out on him.^h"^i

Daniel's Vision of a Man

10 In the third year of Cyrus^p king of Persia, a revelation was given to Daniel (who was called Belteshazzar).^q Its message was true^r and it concerned a great war.^j The understanding of the message came to him in a vision.

²At that time I, Daniel, mourned^s for three weeks. ³I ate no choice food; no meat or wine touched my lips;^t and I used no lotions at all until the three weeks were over.

⁴On the twenty-fourth day of the first month, as I was standing on the bank^u of the great river, the Tigris,^v ⁵I looked up^w and there before me was a man dressed in linen,^x with a belt of the finest gold^y around his waist. ⁶His body was like chrysolite,^z his face like lightning,^a his eyes like flaming torches,^b his arms and legs like the gleam of burnished bronze,^c and his voice^d like the sound of a multitude.

⁷I, Daniel, was the only one who saw the vision; the men with me did not see it,^e but such terror overwhelmed them that they fled and hid themselves. ⁸So I was left alone,^f gazing at this great vision; I had no strength left,^g my face turned deathly pale^h and I was helpless.^i ⁹Then I heard him speaking, and as I listened to him, I fell into a deep sleep, my face to the ground.^j

¹⁰A hand touched me^k and set me trembling on my hands and knees.^l ¹¹He said, "Daniel, you who are highly esteemed,^m consider carefully the words I

G *Da 8:1–26* ◀ ▶ *Da 10:1*
R *Da 9:16–18* ◀ ▶ *Da 11:2*
G *Da 9:26–27* ◀ ▶ *Da 10:14*

9:25 gS Ezr 4:24; S 6:15 hS Mt 1:17; Jn 4:25 iS Isa 13:14 jS Ezr 3:3
9:26 kS Isa 53:8; Mt 16:21 iIsa 28:2; Da 11:10; Na 1:8 mS Ps 46:8 nIsa 61:1; S Eze 4:5-6; Hag 2:23; Zec 4:14
9:27 oS Isa 10:22
10:1 pS Da 1:21 qS Da 1:7 rDa 8:26
10:2 sS Ezr 9:4
10:3 tS Da 6:18
10:4 uDa 12:5 vS Ge 2:14
10:5 wDa 8:3 xS Eze 9:2; Rev 15:6 yJer 10:9
10:6 zS Ex 28:20 aMt 17:2; S 28:3 bJob 41:19; Rev 19:12 cS Eze 1:7; S Rev 1:15 dS Eze 1:24
10:7 eS 2Ki 6:17-20; Ac 9:7
10:8 fGe 32:24 gS Job 4:14; Da 8:27 hS Job 4:15 iHab 3:16
10:9 jDa 8:18; Mt 17:6
10:10 kJer 1:9 lRev 1:17
10:11 mS Da 6:9; Da 9:23

---

^d 25 Or *word*   ^e 25 Or *an anointed one*; also in verse 26   ^f 26 Or *off and will have no one*; or *off, but not for himself*   ^g 27 Or *'week'*   ^h 27 Or *it*   ^i 27 Or *And one who causes desolation will come upon the pinnacle of the abominable ₎temple₎, until the end that is decreed is poured out on the desolated ₍city₎*   ^j 1 Or *true and burdensome*

9:27 Though some scholars feel that this verse found its fulfillment during the reign of Antiochus Epiphanes and his oppression of the Jews, other scholars suggest that this last "week" of Daniel's prophecy refers to the end times. This futurist view suggests that the last "week" covers the seven-year tribulation period that will occur in the end times, with the second half of those seven years referred to as "a time, times and half a time" (Da 7:25; Rev 12:14). According to futurist scholars, during this "week" the antichrist ("another horn, a little one" in 7:8) will make a covenant between himself and the Jews. At the midpoint of this "week," after only 3 1/2 years, the antichrist will break this covenant, interrupt Jewish worship in the temple, defile the sanctuary and begin to persecute the Jews. For further information on the futurist interpretation of prophecy, refer to the article entitled "Introduction to Prophecy," p. vi.

Jesus' words seem to confirm that this final "week" is still in the future and that these events will transpire just prior to his second coming (see Mt 24:6–15) thus placing several centuries between the sixty-ninth week and the seventieth week of Daniel's prophecy. When Christ returns, he will destroy the antichrist at the end of the seventieth week and introduce a time of "everlasting righteousness" (9:24). Note Daniel's reference to the anointing of the Messiah when he comes again to rule. (Compare this verse with 1Sa 16:13.) The oil used for anointing a king was made from special ingredients (see Ex 30:25–26). A sample of this oil was discovered in recent archeological digs near the Dead Sea.

10:2–3 Daniel mourned for 21 days, "three weeks" (10:2). This reference to "weeks" is clearly differentiated from the "sevens" of 9:24–27. Daniel was probably mourning the destruction of Jerusalem and the exile of his people to Babylon.

10:10–17 While Daniel prayed, an angel came to strengthen him and give him additional prophetic information. Note that the angel's reason for delay was because of demonic interference (10:13). This seems to indicate that demonic spirits or fallen angels have been given authority under the direction of Satan to disturb the affairs of the nations (see 10:20).

The Vision of the Seventy Weeks

DANIEL'S VISION OF the seventy weeks contains a brief outline of the future history of the world (see 9:24-27). The prophet Jeremiah had declared that Israel's captivity in Babylon would last seventy years (see Jer 25:11). Daniel was aware of Jeremiah's prediction and realized in 538 B.C. that the seventy years of Israel's Babylonian captivity were about to end. Daniel asked God to show him what would happen to the Jews after their captivity. God responded by giving Daniel this astonishing vision that foretold Israel's rejection of their promised Messiah and the rise of an evil ruler who would ally himself with Israel in the last days.

The Length of a Year

An important but often ignored factor in determining the chronology of prophecy is determining the length of a year. Our solar year of 365.25 days was unknown to ancient civilizations. The ancient Jews followed the Chaldean lunar-solar year. This method of marking time recognized four distinct seasons and determined the length of months by the course of the moon. Four full seasons and twelve lunar months of 30 days each totaled 360 days or one year in ancient Jewish records.

Abraham followed this method of marking years when he migrated to Canaan from Ur. The Bible also confirms the use of the 30-day month in the record of the flood. Noah and his family were shut up in the ark on the seventeenth day of the second month and did not land on the mountain until five months later on the seventeenth day of the seventh month. Scripture says that the elapsed time was a total of 150 days, indicating that each month contained 30 days each (see Ge 7:11; 7:24; 8:3–4). In the book of Revelation, John indicated that the last half of the great tribulation would last 1260 days (see Rev 12:6). This period also corresponds to the "time, times and half a time" (Rev 12:14) and the "forty-two months" (Rev 13:5)—all references to three and a half Biblical years of 360 days each.

The Years of Daniel's Prophecy

To better understand the time involved in the fulfillment of Daniel's prophecy, we need to remember to use the 360-day Biblical year. Note that Daniel's prophecy began with the words "from the issuing of the decree to restore and rebuild Jerusalem" (9:25). The command to restore Jerusalem was issued by King Artaxerxes of Persia in the twentieth year of his reign, during the month of Nisan (see Ne 2:1). Thus the starting date for Daniel's prophecy corresponds to 444 B.C.

Most scholars agree that Daniel's vision of weeks describes the passage of years; seven weeks are equivalent to seven years. Thus seven Biblical years are equivalent to 2520 days. Understanding these basics makes calculating the remainder of Daniel's prophecy fairly simple, since Daniel divides his prophecy into different sections.

The time period from the decree of Artaxerxes "to rebuild Jerusalem until the Anointed One, the ruler, comes, there will be seven 'sevens,' and sixty-two 'sevens.'" (9:25)—a total of 483 Biblical years. A careful calculation reveals that exactly 483 Biblical years from the beginning of Daniel's prophecy in 444 B.C., Jesus Christ entered Jerusalem through the Eastern Gate on Palm Sunday and presented himself to Israel as their promised Messiah. Yet according to Daniel's prophecy, at the end of the sixty-nine weeks (483 years) the Messiah would be cut off (9:26). The first sixty-nine weeks of Daniel's vision of the seventy weeks were precisely fulfilled because, just a few days later, Jesus Christ the Messiah was cut off and crucified on the cross, rose from the grave and ascended to heaven.

The Seventieth Week

The seventieth "week" of Daniel's prophecy has yet to be fulfilled. When Israel rejected Jesus Christ as their promised Messiah at the conclusion of Daniel's sixty-ninth week, God's prophetic clock for Israel stopped ticking. As a consequence of Israel's rejection of the Messiah, God postponed Israel's prophesied kingdom for almost two thousand years. During the interval between Daniel's sixty-ninth and seventieth weeks, God has instituted a church of believers from all nations to witness to the world of his offer of salvation.

Daniel prophesied that the full seventy weeks were decreed for the Jews (9:24). In fact, the central focus of this final week will be God's dealing with his chosen people. This final week of years will culminate with the tyranny of the antichrist, the terror of the tribulation and the mark of the beast. Until then, wars and desolations will continue until the end of the age.

The seventieth will begin when the antichrist signs a seven-year treaty, or covenant, with Israel (9:27). The preceding verse helps identify this antichrist as "the ruler who will come" from the people who will "destroy the city and the sanctuary" (9:26). History reveals that the Romans destroyed Jerusalem and the temple in A.D. 70. Therefore, the antichrist, "the prince," must rise out of the territories and nations of the Roman empire. In the last days this antichrist will lead his armies in a relentless campaign to conquer the nations of the whole earth.

After three and a half years, the antichrist will break his treaty with Israel, halt the daily sacrifices in the rebuilt temple and defile the Holy of Holies, claiming his own divinity. This defilement of the temple is referred to as "the abomination that causes desolation" (Mk 13:14).

The Abomination of Desolation

The strange phrase "the abomination that causes desolation" is mentioned by Jesus in Mt 24:15 as part of Daniel's prophecy of the seventy weeks. Jesus warned his disciples to watch for the events that will transpire during the countdown to the Battle of Armageddon and to "flee to the mountains" (Mt 24:16) if they saw these things occur. Jesus confirmed Daniel's prediction that the antichrist would defile the temple and commit an act of supreme spiritual defiance against heaven by entering the Holy of Holies. Paul called this antichrist a "man of lawlessness" and a "man doomed to destruction" (2Th 2:3) who would exalt himself above God and sit in the temple accepting worship like a god. But the antichrist will not go unchallenged. The seventieth week will end when Jesus Christ descends from heaven to defeat the antichrist's armies at the Battle of Armageddon.

am about to speak to you, and stand up, for I have now been sent to you." And when he said this to me, I stood up trembling.

¹²Then he continued, "Do not be afraid, Daniel. Since the first day that you set your mind to gain understanding and to humble yourself before your God, your words were heard, and I have come in response to them. ¹³But the prince of the Persian kingdom resisted me twenty-one days. Then Michael, one of the chief princes, came to help me, because I was detained there with the king of Persia. ¹⁴Now I have come to explain to you what will happen to your people in the future, for the vision concerns a time yet to come."

¹⁵While he was saying this to me, I bowed with my face toward the ground and was speechless. ¹⁶Then one who looked like a man touched my lips, and I opened my mouth and began to speak. I said to the one standing before me, "I am overcome with anguish because of the vision, my lord, and I am helpless. ¹⁷How can I, your servant, talk with you, my lord? My strength is gone and I can hardly breathe."

¹⁸Again the one who looked like a man touched me and gave me strength. ¹⁹"Do not be afraid, O man highly esteemed," he said. "Peace! Be strong now; be strong."

U *Da 1:15* ◄ ► *Da 10:19*
G *Da 10:1* ◄ ► *Da 10:20*
U *Da 10:12* ◄ ► *Da 12:3*

10:11 ⁿS Eze 2:1
10:12 ᵒS Mt 14:27
ᵖS Lev 16:31;
S Da 9:3
qS Isa 65:24
ʳDa 9:20
10:13 ˢIsa 24:21
ᵗver 21; Da 12:1;
S Jude 1:9
10:14 ᵘS Da 9:22
ᵛS Eze 12:27
ʷS Da 2:28; 8:26;
Hab 2:3
10:15 ˣS Eze 24:27;
Lk 1:20
10:16 ʸS Isa 6:7;
Jer 1:9; Da 8:15-18
ᶻS Isa 21:3
10:17 ᵃS Da 4:19
10:18 ᵇver 16
ᶜS Da 8:18
10:19 ᵈS Da 9:23
ᵉJdg 6:23;
S Isa 35:4 ᶠJos 1:9
ᵍIsa 6:1-8
10:20 ʰDa 8:21;
11:2
10:21 ⁱDa 11:2
ʲS ver 13;
S Jude 1:9
11:1 ᵏS Da 5:31
11:2 ˡDa 10:21
ᵐS Da 10:20
11:3 ⁿS Da 8:4,21
11:4 ᵒS Da 7:2;
8:22 ᵖS Jer 42:10

When he spoke to me, I was strengthened and said, "Speak, my lord, since you have given me strength."

²⁰So he said, "Do you know why I have come to you? Soon I will return to fight against the prince of Persia, and when I go, the prince of Greece will come; ²¹but first I will tell you what is written in the Book of Truth. (No one supports me against them except Michael, your prince. ¹And in the first year of Darius the Mede, I took my stand to support and protect him.)

The Kings of the South and the North

²"Now then, I tell you the truth: Three more kings will appear in Persia, and then a fourth, who will be far richer than all the others. When he has gained power by his wealth, he will stir up everyone against the kingdom of Greece. ³Then a mighty king will appear, who will rule with great power and do as he pleases. ⁴After he has appeared, his empire will be broken up and parceled out toward the four winds of heaven. It will not go to his descendants, nor will it have the power he exercised, because his empire will be uprooted and given to others.

⁵"The king of the South will become strong, but one of his commanders will

G *Da 10:14* ◄ ► *Da 11:31*
R *Da 9:26–27* ◄ ► *Da 11:31*

ᵏ 16 Most manuscripts of the Masoretic Text; one manuscript of the Masoretic Text, Dead Sea Scrolls and Septuagint *Then something that looked like a man's hand*

11:1 The series of predictions found in this chapter refer to the complex events that transpired following the death of Alexander the Great. The details concerning personal, political and military events of the reign of Antiochus Epiphanes are remarkable for their accuracy, correctly predicting the wars between the Seleucids of Syria and the Ptolemies of Egypt and their struggle to rule the Holy Land between 323–165 B.C. Only a divinely inspired prophecy could be this accurate.

11:2–35 The prophecies in the first part of this chapter concern the future of the Medo-Persian and Greek empires. Daniel's vision revealed that four kings would rule Medo-Persia in quick succession. These kings were probably Cambyses (530–522 B.C.), Pseudo-Smerdis (522–521 B.C.), Darius I Hystaspes (521–486 B.C.; see Ezr 5—6) and Xerxes I, also known as Ahasuerus (486–465 B.C.; see Ezr 4:6). Despite these rulers, Persia would fall to Greece, and this Greek empire would quickly be divided into four parts (see 8:22). The complicated history of the battles between the Syrian and Egyptian kingdoms is outlined with precision between 11:5–20.

11:3 The "mighty king" referred to in this verse is Alexander the Great, who ruled Greece from 330–323 B.C. See also 7:6; 8:5–8, 21–22.

11:4 After the untimely death of Alexander the Great in 323 B.C., the Greek empire was quickly divided into four kingdoms ruled by Alexander's four generals. Cassander became king of Macedonia, the original kingdom in Alexander's empire. Lysimachus ruled Asia Minor and Thrace. Ptolemy and his successors ruled the kingdom of Egypt and her territories for three centuries. Seleucus and his descendants ruled Syria and the surrounding territories of the Middle East until the Roman conquest in 65 B.C.

11:5 This "king of the South" is Ptolemy I Soter of

The Tribulation

JESUS REFERRED SEVERAL times to the terrible persecution that would occur before his return, intimating that it would be worse than anything that has happened since the beginning of the world (see Mt 24:21). This time of persecution is called the tribulation, derived from a root word that means "squeeze" or "press." Prophecy about the tribulation begins in the OT and runs through the entire NT, providing substantial information about this important eschatological doctrine.

The exact timing of this period of suffering is uncertain. Those who teach the preterist view of prophecy suggest that the predictions concerning the tribulation were fulfilled during the destruction of Jerusalem in A.D. 70. However, the futurist view contends that the tribulation period will occur just prior to Christ's second coming and will coincide with what Scripture calls the great day of the Lord. Though the tribulation will last only seven years, the great day of the Lord will continue until the end of the Millennium (see 2Pe 3:10).

The involvement that believers will play in the tribulation is also a matter of some debate. Some scholars feel that believers will be translated to heaven before the beginning of the tribulation. Using a literal method of the interpretation of the Bible, these pretribulation scholars believe that the passages of Scripture that deal with the tribulation relate only to God's interaction with Israel; therefore the church will not be a participant in it. Others suggest that believers will be raptured to heaven during the tribulation. These midtribulation scholars believe the church will endure the first half of this period of suffering but will be raptured to heaven before the full outpouring of God's wrath. Still other scholars subscribe to a posttribulation view of the rapture, basing their belief on the Scriptures that state the church will have to go through a period of testing and tribulation. Because of the varied opinions about the church's role in the tribulation it is vital to understand the events that will transpire. (For additional information about the translation of believers to heaven, see the article entitled "The Rapture" on p. 1376.)

Commencing when the antichrist signs a seven-year treaty with Israel (9:27), the tribulation will continue until the return of Jesus Christ to defeat the antichrist at Armageddon. The seven years of tribulation will be a time of unparalleled evil, war, persecution and martyrdom (see Rev 12:12). The Bible indicates that as many as four billion people will die as the wrath of God is poured out during the judgments of the great tribulation. Unrepentant sinners in that day will still defy God, and the consequences will be catastrophic (see Rev 9:20–21).

God's wrath will be poured out during the tribulation in a sevenfold series of judgments from heaven that begin with the seven seals (see Rev 6:1–17). The first four seals are opened by the Lord and handed over for implementation to the four horsemen of the apocalypse: The white horseman represents false peace; the red horseman symbolizes war; the black horseman stands for famine; the pale horseman represents death. The remaining seals are opened and symbolize the martyrdom of the tribulation saints and the convulsions of the whole earth and the heavens. When the seventh seal is opened, silence falls in heaven for half an hour (see Rev 8:1) as the world waits for the beginning of the seven trumpet judgments.

The seven trumpet judgments begin in the middle of the tribulation and continue to its end, unleashing the wrath of God upon the earth, sea, waters and heavens (see Rev 8:7–13). As these judgments continue, demonic spirits released from the bottomless pit will torment humanity for five months, four angels from the Euphrates River will marshal the armies of the East to attack and the final crisis will lead to Christ's return (see Rev 9:1–19; 11:15). There are also seven vial judgments described in Revelation that will occur just before Armageddon (see Rev 16:1–21). Though similar to the trumpet judgments, these judgments occur at the end of the tribulation and are primarily directed against unbelievers.

At the beginning of the tribulation, the treaty between the antichrist and Israel will be in effect. Though initially allied with only ten nations, the antichrist will bring more nations under his power until the whole world allies with his kingdom. At the midpoint of the seven-year treaty, Satan will be expelled from heaven, and the antichrist will suffer a mortal wound that will be miraculously healed (see Rev 13:3). This miracle will convince many that he is the Messiah. The antichrist will capitalize on this miracle and consciously try to fulfill the ancient prophetic expectations of the Jews. The false prophet will introduce the system of the mark of the beast that will continue until the Battle of Armageddon and will also force people to worship a statue of the antichrist or face death (see Rev 13:14).

Though many Jews will be constrained to accept the antichrist as their Messiah, when the antichrist violates the Holy of Holies, many righteous Jews in Israel will realize that he is not their true Messiah. They will attempt to break with the antichrist for the remainder of the tribulation and will also reject the false prophet's words (see Rev 12:6). Other nations will follow Israel and attempt to rebel against the antichrist. As nation after nation tries to throw off the yoke of the antichrist, the entire tribulation will be filled with war and famine.

The antichrist will establish a military base in Israel. The kings of the northern alliance and the king of the south will attack the antichrist's forces in Palestine, but he will defeat their armies (see Da 11:40). As the antichrist reinforces his military position near Jerusalem, the nations of the east will realize that they must act immediately if they wish to throw off the chains of the world dictator. The final focus of their rebellion will result in the Battle of Armageddon and will involve all the armies of the world (see 11:44; see Rev 16:16).

The armies will fight all across Asia, killing one third of humanity, but the final war will center on the Valley of Jezreel in a place called Armageddon. Whether through the miraculous intervention of God or through a complete closure of the spillways of the

Ataturk Dam in Turkey, the Euphrates River will dry up, allowing the army of the east to cross into northern Israel (see Rev 16:12).

Despite the antichrist's huge military and satanic forces, he will be defeated (see Da 11:45). Jesus Christ, with his army of saints from heaven, will return to defeat the antichrist and his powerful armies, throwing this prince of darkness into the lake of fire (see 8:25; Rev 19:11–14; 19–20). The tribulation will conclude and Jesus Christ will establish his millennial kingdom.

become even stronger than he and will rule his own kingdom with great power. ⁶After some years, they will become allies. The daughter of the king of the South will go to the king of the North to make an alliance, but she will not retain her power, and he and his power' will not last. In those days she will be handed over, together with her royal escort and her father^m and the one who supported her.

⁷"One from her family line will arise to take her place. He will attack the forces of the king of the North^q and enter his fortress; he will fight against them and be victorious. ⁸He will also seize their gods,^r their metal images and their valuable articles of silver and gold and carry them off to Egypt.^s For some years he will leave the king of the North alone. ⁹Then the king of the North will invade the realm of the king of the South but will retreat to his own country. ¹⁰His sons will prepare for war and assemble a great army, which will sweep on like an irresistible flood^t and carry the battle as far as his fortress.

¹¹"Then the king of the South will march out in a rage and fight against the king of the North, who will raise a large army, but it will be defeated.^u ¹²When the army is carried off, the king of the South will be filled with pride and will slaughter many thousands, yet he will not remain triumphant. ¹³For the king of the North will muster another army, larger than the first; and after several years, he will advance with a huge army fully equipped.

¹⁴"In those times many will rise against the king of the South. The violent men among your own people will rebel in fulfillment of the vision, but without success. ¹⁵Then the king of the North will come and build up siege ramps^v and will capture a fortified city. The forces of the South will be powerless to resist; even their best troops will not have the strength to stand. ¹⁶The invader will do as he pleases;^w no one will be able to stand against him.^x He will establish himself in the Beautiful Land and will have the power to destroy it.^y ¹⁷He will determine to come with the might of his entire kingdom and will make an alliance with the king of the South. And he will give him a daughter in marriage in order to overthrow the kingdom, but his plans^n will not succeed^z or help him. ¹⁸Then he will turn his attention to the coastlands^a and will take many of them, but a commander will put an end to his insolence and will turn his insolence back upon him.^b ¹⁹After this, he will turn back toward the fortresses of his own country but will stumble and fall,^c to be seen no more.^d

²⁰"His successor will send out a tax collector to maintain the royal splendor.^e In a few years, however, he will be destroyed, yet not in anger or in battle.

²¹"He will be succeeded by a contemptible^f person who has not been given the honor of royalty.^g He will invade the kingdom when its people feel secure, and he will seize it through intrigue. ²²Then an overwhelming army will be swept away^h before him; both it and a prince of the covenant will be destroyed.^i ²³After coming to an agreement with him, he will act deceitfully,^j and with only a few people he will rise to power. ²⁴When the richest provinces feel secure, he will invade them and will achieve what neither his fathers nor his forefathers did. He will distribute plunder, loot and wealth among his followers.^k He will plot the

l 6 Or offspring m 6 Or child (see Vulgate and Syriac) n 17 Or but she

---

Egypt (323–285 B.C.).
11:6 This "king of the South" is probably Ptolemy II Philadelphus who ruled Egypt from 285–246 B.C. His daughter was named Berenice.
11:7–9 Berenice's brother, Ptolemy III Euergetes (246–221 B.C.) engineered the death of Laodice, Antiochus II Theos' wife who had attempted to murder Berenice.
11:10 The sons mentioned in this verse refer to two of the Seleucids: Seleucus III Ceraunus (226–223 B.C.) and Antiochus III the Great (223–187 B.C.).

11:11 This "king of the South" was Ptolemy IV Philopator (221–203 B.C.) of Egypt.
11:14 This "king of the South" was Ptolemy V Epiphanes (203–181 B.C.) of Egypt.
11:15 This "king of the North" was Seleucus IV Philopator (187–175 B.C.) of Syria.
11:21 The northern king described here is clearly Antiochus IV Epiphanes who ruled in Syria from 175–164 B.C. Antiochus Epiphanes (the "another horn, which started small" of 8:9) oppressed the Jews, defiled the temple and typifies the future antichrist who will rule the earth at the end of the age.

DANIEL 11:25

overthrow of fortresses—but only for a time.

25 "With a large army he will stir up his strength and courage against the king of the South. The king of the South will wage war with a large and very powerful army, but he will not be able to stand because of the plots devised against him. 26 Those who eat from the king's provisions will try to destroy him; his army will be swept away, and many will fall in battle. 27 The two kings, with their hearts bent on evil,¹ will sit at the same table and lie to each other, but to no avail, because an end will still come at the appointed time. 28 The king of the North will return to his own country with great wealth, but his heart will be set against the holy covenant. He will take action against it and then return to his own country.

29 "At the appointed time he will invade the South again, but this time the outcome will be different from what it was before. 30 Ships of the western coastlands°° will oppose him, and he will lose heart. Then he will turn back and vent his fury against the holy covenant. He will return and show favor to those who forsake the holy covenant.

31 "His armed forces will rise up to desecrate the temple fortress and will abolish the daily sacrifice. Then they will set up the abomination that causes desolation. 32 With flattery he will corrupt those who have violated the covenant, but the people who know their God will firmly resist him.

G *Da 10:20* ◄ ► *Da 12:6–7*
R *Da 11:2* ◄ ► *Da 11:36*
V *Jer 51:36* ◄ ► *Zec 4:6*

11:27 ¹Ps 64:6
m Ps 12:2; Jer 9:5
n Hab 2:3

11:30 °°S Ge 10:4
p S 1Sa 17:32
q S Job 15:13

11:31 r Hos 3:4
s S Jer 19:4;
Da 8:11-13; S 9:27;
Mt 24:15*;
Mk 13:14*

11:32 t Mic 5:7-9

11:33 u Da 12:3;
Mal 2:7 v Mt 24:9;
Jn 16:2;
Heb 11:32-38

11:34 w Mt 7:15;
Ro 16:18

11:35 x S Job 28:1;
S Ps 78:38;
S Isa 48:10;
Da 12:10; Zec 13:9;
Jn 15:2

11:36 y Jude 1:16
z Rev 13:5-6
a S Dt 10:17;
S Isa 14:13-14;
S Da 7:25; 8:11-12,
25; 2Th 2:4
b S Isa 10:25; 26:20
c Eze 35:13;
S Da 8:24

11:40 d S Isa 21:1
e Isa 5:28 f S Isa 8:7;
S Eze 38:4

33 "Those who are wise will instruct many, though for a time they will fall by the sword or be burned or captured or plundered. 34 When they fall, they will receive a little help, and many who are not sincere will join them. 35 Some of the wise will stumble, so that they may be refined, purified and made spotless until the time of the end, for it will still come at the appointed time.

The King Who Exalts Himself

36 "The king will do as he pleases. He will exalt and magnify himself above every god and will say unheard-of things against the God of gods. He will be successful until the time of wrath is completed, for what has been determined must take place. 37 He will show no regard for the gods of his fathers or for the one desired by women, nor will he regard any god, but will exalt himself above them all. 38 Instead of them, he will honor a god of fortresses; a god unknown to his fathers he will honor with gold and silver, with precious stones and costly gifts. 39 He will attack the mightiest fortresses with the help of a foreign god and will greatly honor those who acknowledge him. He will make them rulers over many people and will distribute the land at a price.

40 "At the time of the end the king of the South will engage him in battle, and the king of the North will storm out against him with chariots and cavalry and a great fleet of ships. He will invade many countries and sweep through them like a flood. 41 He will also invade the Beautiful

R *Da 11:31* ◄ ► *Da 12:7*

o 30 Hebrew *of Kittim* p 39 Or *land for a reward*

11:25–28 This passage prophesied a series of military expeditions by Antiochus Epiphanes against the kingdom of Egypt.
11:30 Roman ships under the command of Gaius Popilius Laenas challenged Antiochus Epiphanes to cease his attacks toward Egypt.
11:31–35 This passage prophesied the defilement of the temple in Jerusalem by the Antiochus Epiphanes (the "another horn, which started small" of ch. 8). In 168 B.C. Antiochus Epiphanes erected a statue of Zeus in the Holy Place of the temple. This defilement of the temple prefigured the abomination that Jesus predicted would occur in the end times (see Mt 24:15; Lk 21:20).

11:36–45 Some scholars suggest that the willful king in this passage is Antiochus Epiphanes, the same individual described in ch. 8 as "another horn, which started small." The reign of Antiochus Epiphanes was marked by satanic ritual and cruel attacks on God's chosen people. However, other scholars suggest that the prophetic details revealed about this willful king (11:36–45) describe the antichrist, the future head of the revived Roman empire.

11:37 This willful king will have no respect for religion or religious practices and will utterly disregard Israel's God. In addition, this willful king will only worship himself.

Land. Many countries will fall, but Edom, Moab and the leaders of Ammon will be delivered from his hand. ⁴²He will extend his power over many countries; Egypt will not escape. ⁴³He will gain control of the treasures of gold and silver and all the riches of Egypt, with the Libyans and Nubians in submission. ⁴⁴But reports from the east and the north will alarm him, and he will set out in a great rage to destroy and annihilate many. ⁴⁵He will pitch his royal tents between the seas at the beautiful holy mountain. Yet he will come to his end, and no one will help him.

The End Times

12 "At that time Michael, the great prince who protects your people, will arise. There will be a time of distress such as has not happened from the beginning of nations until then. But at that time your people—everyone whose name is found written in the book—will be delivered. ²Multitudes who sleep in the dust of the earth will awake: some to everlasting life, others to shame and everlasting contempt. ³Those who are wise will shine like the brightness of the heavens, and those who lead many to righteousness, like the stars for ever and ever. ⁴But you, Daniel, close up and seal the words of the scroll until the time of the end. Many will go here and there to increase knowledge."

⁵Then I, Daniel, looked, and there before me stood two others, one on this bank of the river and one on the opposite bank. ⁶One of them said to the man clothed in linen, who was above the waters of the river, "How long will it be before these astonishing things are fulfilled?"

⁷The man clothed in linen, who was above the waters of the river, lifted his right hand and his left hand toward heaven, and I heard him swear by him who lives forever, saying, "It will be for a time, times and half a time. When the power of the holy people has been finally broken, all these things will be completed."

⁸I heard, but I did not understand. So I asked, "My lord, what will the outcome of all this be?"

⁹He replied, "Go your way, Daniel, because the words are closed up and sealed until the time of the end. ¹⁰Many will be purified, made spotless and refined, but the wicked will continue to be wicked. None of the wicked will understand, but those who are wise will understand.

¹¹"From the time that the daily sacri-

q 45 Or the sea and r 3 Or who impart wisdom s 7 Or a year, two years and half a year

---

11:45 Despite his powerful armies and success in battle, the antichrist will be defeated at the second coming of Christ and the Battle of Armageddon (see Rev 13:11–18).

12:2 This verse is the clearest confirmation in the OT of God's promise of the physical resurrection of his saints "to everlasting life" and the resurrection of unrepentant sinners "to shame and everlasting contempt." This final resurrection will occur at the end of the seven-year tribulation period. The participants in this resurrection will be those who accept Christ during the tribulation. The resurrection of the saints of the church, known as the rapture, will occur before the signing of the seven-year covenant with the antichrist. For further information on the resurrection of the body and the rapture of the saints, see the articles on pp. 1218 and 1376.

12:4 Note the similarity between this verse and 8:17–19; 9:26; 11:35, 40, 45; 12:4, 6, 9. Daniel was to seal the scroll, indicating that the words of the prophecy were complete as given and should be kept unaltered until the predictions were fulfilled.

12:7 The angel declared that until all these things would be finished would be a period of 3 1/2 years (see 7:25; 12:7; Rev.13:5). This same period of time was referred to by Jesus as the "great distress, unequaled from the beginning of the world until now" (Mt 24:21).

12:11–12 These verses represent further calculations for the end times. Beginning at the time of the desecration of the temple, the midpoint of Daniel's seventieth week (see 9:27; Mt 24:14–15; 2Th 2:4),

fice is abolished and the abomination that causes desolation is set up, there will be 1,290 days. ¹²Blessed is the one who waits for and reaches the end of the 1,335 days.

¹³"As for you, go your way till the end. You will rest, and then at the end of the days you will rise to receive your allotted inheritance."

there will be 1,290 days until the end of the tribulation and the judgments after Christ's second coming. This 3-1/2 year period marks the great tribulation. The 1,335 days corresponds to an additional 45 days beyond the Battle of Armageddon and must mark the final state of millennial blessing. The additional 75 extra days may be needed to prepare the earth for the blessings that will be revealed when Jesus Christ rules the earth.

12:13 The angel's promise to Daniel suggested that Daniel would be resurrected in the last days to witness the final victory of Jesus Christ over the kingdoms of this world.

Hosea

Author: Hosea

Theme: God's undying love for his people

Date of Writing: c. 715 B.C.

Outline of Hosea
  I. Hosea's Life and God's Relationship With Israel (1:1—3:5)
 II. Israel's Wickedness (4:1—6:3)
III. Israel's Punishment (6:4—10:15)
IV. God's Unchanging Love (11:1—13:8)
 V. Israel's Final Restoration (13:9—14:9)

THIS BOOK TAKES its name from the prophet whose message it records. Hosea, meaning "salvation," prophesied during the final days of the kingdom of Israel, beginning with the reign of King Jeroboam II and continuing until the Assyrian destruction of Israel. Hosea's ministry coincided with that of the prophet Amos, also a prophet to Israel, and with Isaiah and Micah, who prophesied to Judah. Scripture records that Hosea was the "son of Beeri" (1:1). Some Jewish scholars believe this was the same man referred to in 1 Chronicles 5:6 who was a "leader of the Reubenites" carried into captivity by Tiglath-Pileser of Assyria. Such a heritage would have made this book's message of God's unchanging love for Israel especially meaningful to Hosea and to the NT writers who borrow from his writings (see Mt 2:15; 9:13; 12:7; Ro 9:25–26; 1Pe 2:10).

Hosea's prophecies warn of God's imminent judgment due to Israel's evil lifestyle of open idolatry. Hosea's wife's infidelity serves as a vivid symbol of Israel's spiritual unfaithfulness in her covenant relationship with God. Instead of responding in gratitude and love to God's grace, the Israelites offered worship to pagan idols.

Hosea's three children also bear names that symbolize the breakdown of Israel's relationship with God. Hosea's oldest son was named Jezreel, meaning "God sows," as a forewarning of the great slaughter to befall Israel's evil king, a descendant of Jehu (see 2Ki 10:1–14). Hosea's daughter was named Lo-Ruhamah, meaning "not pitied, not

INTRODUCTION: HOSEA

favored." Such a name indicated that God would no longer show mercy to Israel as he had in the past. Hosea's third child, a son, was named Lo-Ammi. His name meant "not my people" and symbolized God's rejection of his people because of their wickedness. Despite the sins of the people and the certainty of judgment, Hosea ends his message with the reassurance of God's undying love and Israel's future restoration.

1 The word of the LORD that came[a] to Hosea son of Beeri during the reigns of Uzziah,[b] Jotham,[c] Ahaz[d] and Hezekiah,[e] kings of Judah,[f] and during the reign of Jeroboam[g] son of Jehoash[a] king of Israel:[h]

Hosea's Wife and Children

[2] When the LORD began to speak through Hosea, the LORD said to him, "Go, take to yourself an adulterous[i] wife and children of unfaithfulness, because the land is guilty of the vilest adultery[j] in departing from the LORD." [3] So he married Gomer[k] daughter of Diblaim, and she conceived and bore him a son.

[4] Then the LORD said to Hosea, "Call him Jezreel,[l] because I will soon punish the house of Jehu for the massacre at Jezreel, and I will put an end to the kingdom of Israel. [5] In that day I will break Israel's bow in the Valley of Jezreel."[m]

[6] Gomer[n] conceived again and gave birth to a daughter. Then the LORD said to Hosea, "Call her Lo-Ruhamah,[b][o] for I will no longer show love to the house of Israel,[p] that I should at all forgive them. [7] Yet I will show love to the house of Judah; and I will save them—not by bow,[q] sword or battle, or by horses or horsemen, but by the LORD their God."[r]

[8] After she had weaned Lo-Ruhamah,[s] Gomer had another son. [9] Then the LORD said, "Call him Lo-Ammi,[c] for you are not my people, and I am not your God.[t]

[10] "Yet the Israelites will be like the sand on the seashore, which cannot be measured or counted.[u] In the place where it was said to them, 'You are not my people,' they will be called 'sons of the living God.'[v][w] [11] The people of Judah and the people of Israel will be reunited,[x] and they will appoint one leader[y] and will come up out of the land,[z] for great will be the day of Jezreel.[a]

1:1 [a] S Jer 1:2; [b] 2Ki 14:21; [c] S 1Ch 3:12; [d] S 1Ch 3:13; [e] S 1Ch 3:13; [f] Isa 1:1; Mic 1:1; [g] S 2Ki 13:13; [h] Am 1:1
1:2 [i] S Jer 3:1; Hos 2:2,5; 3:1; [j] Dt 31:16; Jer 3:14; Eze 23:3-21; Hos 5:3
1:3 [k] ver 6
1:4 [l] ver 11; S 1Sa 29:1; 1Ki 18:45; 2Ki 10:1-14; Hos 2:22
1:5 [m] S Jos 15:56; S 1Sa 29:1; 2Ki 15:29
1:6 [n] ver 3 [o] ver 8; Hos 2:23 [p] Hos 2:4
1:7 [q] S Ps 44:6 [r] Zec 4:6
1:8 [s] S ver 6
1:9 [t] ver 10; S Eze 11:19-20; 1Pe 2:10
1:10 [u] S Ge 22:17; S Jer 33:22 [v] S ver 9; Hos 2:23; Ro 9:26* [w] S Jos 3:10
1:11 [x] S Isa 11:12, 13 [y] Jer 23:5-8; 30:9 [z] S Eze 37:15-28 [a] S ver 4

[a] 1 Hebrew *Joash*, a variant of *Jehoash*   [b] 6 *Lo-Ruhamah* means *not loved*.   [c] 9 *Lo-Ammi* means *not my people*.

R Da 12:11-12 ◀▶ Hos 1:6
R Hos 1:4 ◀▶ Hos 1:8-9

R Hos 1:6 ◀▶ Hos 2:1-3
C Da 9:5 ◀▶ Hos 6:4
I Da 12:1 ◀▶ Hos 2:7

1:4 God commanded Hosea to name his son *Jezreel* meaning "God scatters." This conveyed God's warning that Israel's period of grace was almost expired. Note that the valley named Jezreel has witnessed more significant battles than any other place in the Middle East and is named as the site of the Battle of Armageddon (see Zec 12:11; Rev 16:16).
1:6 Israel's coming judgment was indicated by naming Hosea's daughter *Lo-Ruhamah*, which means, "not loved." This name symbolized God's withdrawal of his mercy from Israel.
1:8–11 Hosea's third child, a son, was named *Lo-Ammi* which meant "not my people." This name indicated a break in the covenant relationship between the Lord and Israel. God would reject Israel as his people for a time because of their continual idolatry. However, the prophet recorded God's promise that judgment would be tempered with mercy. The covenant would be restored and the people would be reconciled to God. The future population of Israel would be "like the sand on the seashore" (1:10). Furthermore, the Lord promised that the restoration of his people would include the reconciliation and reunion of the ten tribes of Israel and the two tribes of Judah into one united nation under "one leader," the Messiah (1:11).

2

R "Say of your brothers, 'My people,'
and of your sisters, 'My loved one.'[b]

Israel Punished and Restored

[2] "Rebuke your mother,[c] rebuke her,
 for she is not my wife,
 and I am not her husband.
Let her remove the adulterous[d] look
 from her face
and the unfaithfulness from between
 her breasts.
[3] Otherwise I will strip[e] her naked
 and make her as bare as on the day
  she was born;[f]
I will make her like a desert,[g]
 turn her into a parched land,
 and slay her with thirst.
[4] I will not show my love to her
 children,[h]
 because they are the children of
  adultery.[i]
[5] Their mother has been unfaithful
 and has conceived them in disgrace.
She said, 'I will go after my lovers,[j]
 who give me my food and my water,
 my wool and my linen, my oil and
  my drink.'[k]

R [6] Therefore I will block her path with
 thornbushes;
I I will wall her in so that she cannot
 find her way.[l]
[7] She will chase after her lovers but not
 catch them;
she will look for them but not find
 them.[m]
Then she will say,
 'I will go back to my husband[n] as at
  first,[o]
 for then I was better off[p] than now.'
F [8] She has not acknowledged[q] that I was
P the one
 who gave her the grain, the new
  wine and oil,[r]

R Hos 1:8–9 ◀ ▶ Hos 2:6
R Hos 2:1–3 ◀ ▶ Hos 2:11–12
I Hos 1:10–11 ◀ ▶ Hos 2:14–16
F Isa 65:13 ◀ ▶ Hos 11:4
P Ecc 11:1 ◀ ▶ Mal 3:10–11

2:1 [b]ver 23; 1Pe 2:10
2:2 [c]ver 5; S Isa 50:1; S Hos 1:2; 4:5 [d]S Isa 1:21; S Eze 23:45
2:3 [e]S Eze 16:37 [f]Eze 16:4,22 [g]Isa 32:13-14
2:4 [h]S Eze 8:18; Hos 1:6 [i]Hos 5:7
2:5 [j]S Jer 3:6; S Hos 1:2 [k]Jer 44:17-18
2:6 [l]S Job 3:23; S 19:8; S La 3:9
2:7 [m]Hos 5:13 [n]S Isa 54:5 [o]Jer 2:2; S 3:1 [p]S Eze 16:8
2:8 [q]S Isa 1:3 [r]S Nu 18:12 [s]S Dt 8:18 [t]ver 13; Eze 16:15-19; Hos 8:4
2:9 [u]Hos 8:7 [v]Hos 9:2
2:10 [w]Eze 23:10 [x]Jer 13:26 [y]S Eze 16:37
2:11 [z]Jer 7:34 [a]S Isa 24:8 [b]S Isa 1:14; Jer 16:9; Hos 3:4; 9:5; Am 5:21; 8:10
2:12 [c]S Isa 7:23; S Jer 8:13 [d]S Jer 5:17 [e]S Jer 3:1 [f]S Isa 5:6 [g]Hos 5:7; 13:8
2:13 [h]Isa 65:7 [i]ver 8; S Jer 7:9; Hos 11:2 [j]S Eze 16:17; S 23:40 [k]Hos 4:13 [l]Hos 4:6; 8:14; 13:6 [m]S Jer 44:17; Hos 13:1
2:14 [n]S Eze 19:15
2:15 [o]S Jos 7:24, 26 [p]Eze 15:1-18 [q]S Jer 2:2; S Eze 16:22 [r]S Eze 28:26; Hos 12:9
2:16 [s]S Isa 54:5

who lavished on her the silver and
  gold[s]—
which they used for Baal.[t]

[9] "Therefore I will take away my grain[u]
 when it ripens,
 and my new wine[v] when it is ready.
I will take back my wool and my linen,
 intended to cover her nakedness.
[10] So now I will expose[w] her lewdness
 before the eyes of her lovers;[x]
 no one will take her out of my
  hands.[y]

R [11] I will stop[z] all her celebrations:[a]
 her yearly festivals, her New Moons,
 her Sabbath days—all her appointed
  feasts.[b]
[12] I will ruin her vines[c] and her fig
 trees,[d]
which she said were her pay from
 her lovers;[e]
I will make them a thicket,[f]
 and wild animals will devour them.[g]
[13] I will punish her for the days
 she burned incense[h] to the Baals;[i]
she decked herself with rings and
 jewelry,[j]
and went after her lovers,[k]
 but me she forgot,[l]"
  declares the LORD.[m]

I [14] "Therefore I am now going to allure
 her;
I will lead her into the desert[n]
 and speak tenderly to her.
[15] There I will give her back her
 vineyards,
 and will make the Valley of Achor[d][o]
  a door of hope.
There she will sing[e][p] as in the days of
 her youth,[q]
 as in the day she came up out of
  Egypt.[r]

[16] "In that day," declares the LORD,
 "you will call me 'my husband';[s]

R Hos 2:6 ◀ ▶ Hos 3:2–4
I Hos 2:7 ◀ ▶ Hos 2:18–23

[d] 15 Achor means trouble. [e] 15 Or respond

2:1–6 Hosea urged Israel to reject her sinful ways as he plead with his unfaithful wife to turn from her infidelities.
2:7 Hosea prophesied that Israel would eventually desire to return to God once she recognized the hopelessness of her relationship with pagan gods.
2:11–12 God promised Israel that judgment would fall on her for her idolatry.
2:14–16 This passage prophesied Israel's final reconciliation to the Lord. Note the symbolism as Israel calls God "my husband" (2:16) instead of addressing him as "my master" (2:16).

you will no longer call me 'my
  master.'
17I will remove the names of the Baals
  from her lips;
no longer will their names be
  invoked.
18In that day I will make a covenant for
  them
with the beasts of the field and the
  birds of the air
and the creatures that move along
  the ground.
Bow and sword and battle
I will abolish from the land,
so that all may lie down in safety.
19I will betroth you to me forever;
I will betroth you in righteousness
  and justice,
in love and compassion.
20I will betroth you in faithfulness,
and you will acknowledge the
  LORD.
21"In that day I will respond,"
  declares the LORD—
"I will respond to the skies,
  and they will respond to the earth;
22and the earth will respond to the
  grain,
the new wine and oil,
and they will respond to Jezreel.
23I will plant her for myself in the land;
I will show my love to the one I
  called 'Not my loved one.'
I will say to those called 'Not my
  people,' 'You are my people';

and they will say, 'You are my
  God.'"

Hosea's Reconciliation With His Wife

3 The LORD said to me, "Go, show your love to your wife again, though she is loved by another and is an adulteress. Love her as the LORD loves the Israelites, though they turn to other gods and love the sacred raisin cakes."

2So I bought her for fifteen shekels of silver and about a homer and a lethek of barley. 3Then I told her, "You are to live with me many days; you must not be a prostitute or be intimate with any man, and I will live with you."

4For the Israelites will live many days without king or prince, without sacrifice or sacred stones, without ephod or idol. 5Afterward the Israelites will return and seek the LORD their God and David their king. They will come trembling to the LORD and to his blessings in the last days.

The Charge Against Israel

4 Hear the word of the LORD, you Israelites,
because the LORD has a charge to bring
against you who live in the land:
"There is no faithfulness, no love,

f 16 Hebrew *baal*   *g 19* Or *with*; also in verse 20   *h 19* Or *with*   *i 22 Jezreel* means *God plants.*   *j 23* Hebrew *Lo-Ruhamah*   *k 23* Hebrew *Lo-Ammi*   *l 2* That is, about 6 ounces (about 170 grams)   *m 2* That is, probably about 10 bushels (about 330 liters)   *n 3* Or *wait for*

2:18–23 This curious prophecy revealed that God would make a covenant with the beasts, birds and creeping things on the earth. Where before they had been instruments of destruction (see 2:12), all the animals, birds and insects would no longer threaten life. Every created thing would live in peace. This peaceful creation is confirmed in Isa 11:6–9; 65:25. Contrast this peaceful scene, however, with the tribulation judgment of the fourth horseman of the apocalypse (see Rev 6:8). Wild animals with no fear of people will become instruments of judgment and death on one fourth of the earth.

Note also that the Lord promised to restore his eternal covenant with his people: "I will betroth you to me forever" (2:19). God's unshakable promise of ultimate reconciliation with the children of Abraham is expressed in his prophetic declaration: "I will say . . . , 'You are my people'; and they will say, 'You are my God' " (2:23).

3:4–5 Hosea's prophecy was precisely fulfilled. While these verses picture the exile and Israel's return to their homeland, this passage also foreshadows the centuries following the Jews' rejection of Jesus as Messiah. Even today the Jews remain scattered among the Gentile nations, without their beloved temple or a king. However, Hosea prophesied the final restoration of Israel "in the last days" (3:5) when the Jews would return to the promised land, seeking the Lord and David's descendant.

no acknowledgment[y] of God in the land.[z]
²There is only cursing,[o] lying[a] and murder,[b]
stealing[c] and adultery;[d]
they break all bounds,
and bloodshed follows bloodshed.[e]

R ³Because of this the land mourns,[p f]
and all who live in it waste away;[g]
the beasts of the field and the birds of the air
and the fish of the sea are dying.[h]

⁴"But let no man bring a charge,
let no man accuse another,
for your people are like those
who bring charges against a priest.[i]
⁵You stumble[j] day and night,
and the prophets stumble with you.
So I will destroy your mother[k]—
R ⁶ my people are destroyed from lack of knowledge.[l]

"Because you have rejected knowledge,
I also reject you as my priests;
because you have ignored the law[m] of your God,
I also will ignore your children.

⁷The more the priests increased,
the more they sinned against me;
they exchanged[q] their[r] Glory[n] for something disgraceful.[o]
⁸They feed on the sins of my people
and relish their wickedness.[p]

R ⁹And it will be: Like people, like priests.[q]
I will punish both of them for their ways
and repay them for their deeds.[r]

¹⁰"They will eat but not have enough;[s]
they will engage in prostitution[t] but not increase,
because they have deserted[u] the Lord
to give themselves ¹¹to prostitution,[v]
to old wine[w] and new,

R Hos 3:4 ◄ ► Hos 4:6
R Hos 4:3 ◄ ► Hos 4:9
R Hos 4:6 ◄ ► Hos 5:5

which take away the understanding[x]
¹²of my people.
They consult a wooden idol[y]
and are answered by a stick of wood.[z]
A spirit of prostitution[a] leads them astray;[b]
they are unfaithful[c] to their God.
¹³They sacrifice on the mountaintops
and burn offerings on the hills,
under oak,[d] poplar and terebinth,
where the shade is pleasant.[e]
Therefore your daughters turn to prostitution[f]
and your daughters-in-law to adultery.[g]

¹⁴"I will not punish your daughters
when they turn to prostitution,
nor your daughters-in-law
when they commit adultery,
because the men themselves consort with harlots[h]
and sacrifice with shrine prostitutes[i]—
a people without understanding[j]
will come to ruin![k]

¹⁵"Though you commit adultery,
O Israel,
let not Judah become guilty.

"Do not go to Gilgal;[l]
do not go up to Beth Aven.[s m]
And do not swear, 'As surely as the Lord lives!'[n]

¹⁶The Israelites are stubborn,[o]
like a stubborn heifer.[p]
How then can the Lord pasture them
like lambs[q] in a meadow?
¹⁷Ephraim is joined to idols;
leave him alone! **N**
¹⁸Even when their drinks are gone,
they continue their prostitution;

N Da 5:1–6 ◄ ► Joel 3:14

[o] 2 That is, to pronounce a curse upon [p] 3 Or dries up [q] 7 Syriac and an ancient Hebrew scribal tradition; Masoretic Text *I will exchange* [r] 7 Masoretic Text; an ancient Hebrew scribal tradition *my* [s] 15 Beth Aven means *house of wickedness* (a name for Bethel, which means *house of God*).

4:3–9 This passage sternly warned the priests against passing blame for Israel's judgment on the people. Hosea proceeded to charge the priests with their guilt for not instructing the people in the correct way to worship. Israel's judgment was directly related to her "lack of knowledge" (4:6) and obedience to God's law. Hosea's indictment, "like people, like priests" (4:9), conveyed God's judgment on Israel's people and her leaders. The land, too, would suffer and be left desolate during the time of judgment.

their rulers dearly love shameful
    ways.
¹⁹A whirlwind' will sweep them away,
    and their sacrifices will bring them
    shame.ˢ

Judgment Against Israel

5 "Hear this, you priests!
    Pay attention, you Israelites!
Listen, O royal house!
    This judgmentᵗ is against you:
You have been a snareᵘ at Mizpah,
    a netᵛ spread out on Tabor.
²The rebels are deep in slaughter.ʷ
    I will discipline all of them.ˣ
³I know all about Ephraim;
    Israel is not hiddenʸ from me.
Ephraim, you have now turned to
    prostitution;
    Israel is corrupt.ᶻ

⁴"Their deeds do not permit them
    to returnᵃ to their God.
A spirit of prostitutionᵇ is in their
    heart;
    they do not acknowledgeᶜ the LORD.
⁵Israel's arrogance testifiesᵈ against
    them;
    the Israelites, even Ephraim,
    stumbleᵉ in their sin;
    Judah also stumbles with them.ᶠ
⁶When they go with their flocks and
    herds
    to seek the LORD,ᵍ
they will not find him;
    he has withdrawnʰ himself from
    them.
⁷They are unfaithfulⁱ to the LORD;
    they give birth to illegitimateʲ
    children.
Now their New Moon festivalsᵏ
    will devourˡ them and their fields.

⁸"Sound the trumpetᵐ in Gibeah,ⁿ
    the horn in Ramah.ᵒ
Raise the battle cry in Beth Aven';ᵖ
    lead on, O Benjamin.

R *Hos 4:9* ◀ ▶ *Hos 5:9*

4:19 ʳHos 12:1;
13:15 ᵛver 13-14;
Isa 1:29
5:1 ᵗS Job 10:2
ᵘHos 6:9; 9:8
ᵛS Jer 5:26
5:2 ʷS Hos 4:2
ˣHos 9:15
5:3 ʸAm 5:12
ᶻS Eze 23:7;
S Hos 1:2; 6:10
5:4 ᵃHos 7:10
ᵇS Hos 4:11
ᶜS Jer 4:22; S
Hos 4:6
5:5 ᵈS Isa 3:9;
S Jer 2:19; Hos 7:10
ᵉS Eze 14:7
ᶠHos 14:1
5:6 ᵍMic 6:6-7
ʰS Pr 1:28;
Isa 1:15; Eze 8:6;
Mal 1:10
5:7 ⁱS Isa 24:16;
Hos 6:7 ʲHos 2:4
ᵏIsa 1:14
ˡS Hos 2:11-12
5:8 ᵐS Nu 10:2;
S Jer 4:21;
S Eze 33:3
ⁿJdg 19:12;
Hos 9:9; 10:9
ᵒS Isa 10:29
ᵖS Jos 7:2;
Hos 4:15; 10:5
5:9 ᵠS Isa 7:16
ʳIsa 37:3;
Hos 9:11-17
ˢIsa 46:10; Zec 1:6
5:10 ᵗS Dt 19:14
ᵘS Eze 7:8
5:11 ᵛHos 9:16;
Mic 6:16
5:12 ʷS Job 13:28;
S Isa 51:8
ˣS Job 18:16
5:13 ʸS Isa 7:16
ᶻS Eze 23:5;
Hos 7:11; 8:9; 12:1
ᵃLa 5:6; Hos 7:8;
10:6 ᵇS Isa 3:7;
Hos 14:3 ᶜHos 2:7
5:14 ᵈS Job 10:16;
S Jer 4:7; Am 3:4
ᵉHos 6:1
ᶠS Dt 32:39;
Mic 5:8
5:15 ᵍS Isa 18:4
ʰS Lev 26:40
ⁱS Nu 21:7;
S Ps 24:6; S Hos 3:5
ʲPs 50:15;
S Jer 2:27
ᵏIsa 64:9;
S Eze 20:43
6:1 ˡS Hos 10:20;
S 19:22
ᵐS Job 16:9;
La 3:11; Hos 5:14
ⁿS Nu 12:13;
S Jer 3:22

⁹Ephraim will be laid wasteᵠ
    on the day of reckoning.ʳ
Among the tribes of Israel
    I proclaim what is certain.ˢ
¹⁰Judah's leaders are like those
    who move boundary stones.ᵗ
I will pour out my wrathᵘ on them
    like a flood of water.
¹¹Ephraim is oppressed,
    trampled in judgment,
    intent on pursuing idols.ᵘᵛ
¹²I am like a mothʷ to Ephraim,
    like rotˣ to the people of Judah.

¹³"When Ephraimʸ saw his sickness,
    and Judah his sores,
then Ephraim turned to Assyria,ᶻ
    and sent to the great king for help.ᵃ
But he is not able to cureᵇ you,
    not able to heal your sores.ᶜ
¹⁴For I will be like a lionᵈ to Ephraim,
    like a great lion to Judah.
I will tear them to piecesᵉ and go
    away;
I will carry them off, with no one to
    rescue them.ᶠ
¹⁵Then I will go back to my placeᵍ
    until they admit their guilt.ʰ
And they will seek my face;ⁱ
    in their miseryʲ they will earnestly
    seek me.ᵏ"

Israel Unrepentant

6 "Come, let us returnˡ to the LORD.
    He has torn us to piecesᵐ
    but he will heal us;ⁿ
    he has injured us

R *Hos 5:5* ◀ ▶ *Hos 5:12*
R *Hos 5:9* ◀ ▶ *Hos 5:14*
R *Hos 5:12* ◀ ▶ *Hos 6:11*
R *Da 4:27* ◀ ▶ *Hos 10:12*
I *Hos 3:5* ◀ ▶ *Hos 12:9*
P *Da 9:9* ◀ ▶ *Hos 14:1–2*

ᵗ 8 *Beth Aven* means *house of wickedness* (a name for Bethel, which means *house of God*). ᵘ 11 The meaning of the Hebrew for this word is uncertain.

5:5–14 Hosea predicted that God would judge both Israel and Judah for their proud rebellion. Ephraim (Israel) would be desolate and Judah would be rotten, and no one would be able to rescue them from the certainty of God's impending judgment.
6:1–3 This passage contains one of the greatest OT prophecies of the Messiah. God urged Israel to repent and return to him knowing that he would heal their wounds. God's wrath would only be temporary, lasting only a figurative two or three days (see Lk 13:32–33). Israel would be restored when Christ returns (see Ro 11:26). As surely as the seasonal rains fell and revived the earth, God's favor would return and restore Israel (see Joel 2:23; Zec 10:1).

but he will bind up our wounds.º
²After two days he will revive us;ᵖ
  on the third dayᑫ he will restoreʳ us,
  that we may live in his presence.
³Let us acknowledge the Lᴏʀᴅ;
  let us press on to acknowledge him.
As surely as the sun rises,
  he will appear;
he will come to us like the winter
  rains,ˢ
like the spring rains that water the
  earth.ᵗ"

⁴"What can I do with you, Ephraim?ᵘ
  What can I do with you, Judah?
Your love is like the morning mist,
  like the early dew that disappears.ᵛ
⁵Therefore I cut you in pieces with my
  prophets,
  I killed you with the words of my
  mouth;ʷ
  my judgments flashed like lightning
  upon you.ˣ
⁶For I desire mercy, not sacrifice,ʸ
  and acknowledgmentᶻ of God rather
  than burnt offerings.ᵃ
⁷Like Adam,ᵛ they have broken the
  covenantᵇ—
  they were unfaithfulᶜ to me there.
⁸Gilead is a city of wicked men,ᵈ
  stained with footprints of blood.
⁹As marauders lie in ambush for a
  man,ᵉ
so do bands of priests;
  they murderᶠ on the road to Shechem,
  committing shameful crimes.ᵍ
¹⁰I have seen a horribleʰ thing
  in the house of Israel.
There Ephraim is given to prostitution
  and Israel is defiled.ⁱ

¹¹"Also for you, Judah,
  a harvestʲ is appointed.

"Whenever I would restore the
  fortunesᵏ of my people,
7 ¹whenever I would heal Israel,
  the sins of Ephraim are exposed
  and the crimes of Samaria revealed.ˡ
They practice deceit,ᵐ
  thieves break into houses,ⁿ
  bandits rob in the streets;ᵒ
²but they do not realize

L Da 9:9 ◀▶ Hos 13:9
C Hos 1:9 ◀▶ Hos 10:1–2
R Hos 5:14 ◀▶ Hos 8:8
E Da 5:27 ◀▶ Am 8:7

6:1 ᵒS Dt 32:39;
S Job 5:18;
S Jer 30:17;
Hos 14:4
6:2 ᵖS Ps 30:5;
S 80:18
ᑫS Mt 16:21
ʳS Ps 71:20
6:3 ˢS Job 4:3;
Joel 2:23 ᵗS Ps 72:6;
Hos 11:10; 12:6
6:4 ᵘHos 11:8
ᵛHos 7:1; 13:3
6:5 ʷJer 1:9-10;
5:14; 23:29
ˣHeb 4:12
6:6 ʸS 1Sa 15:22;
S Isa 1:11;
Mt 9:13*; 12:7*;
Mk 12:33
ᶻS Jer 4:22;
S Hos 2:20
ᵃS Ps 40:6; Mic 6:8
6:7 ᵇS Ge 9:11;
S Jer 11:10; Hos 8:1
ᶜS Hos 5:7
6:8 ᵈHos 12:11
6:9 ᵉPs 10:8
ᶠS Hos 4:2
ᵍJer 5:30-31;
7:9-10; S Eze 22:9;
S Hos 5:1; 7:1
6:10 ʰS Jer 5:30
ⁱS Jer 23:14;
S Eze 23:7;
S Hos 5:3
6:11 ʲJer 51:33;
Joel 3:13
ᵏS Ps 126:1;
Zep 2:7
7:1 ˡS Eze 24:13;
S Hos 6:4 ᵐver 13
ⁿS Ex 22:2; Hos 4:2
ᵒS Hos 6:9; 12:1
7:2 ᵖS Jer 14:10;
S 44:21; S Hos 8:13
ᑫS Job 35:15;
Hos 9:15 ʳJer 2:19;
4:18
7:3 ˢS Jer 28:1-4;
S Hos 4:2; 10:13;
Mic 7:3
7:4 ᵗS Jer 9:2
7:5 ᵘS Isa 28:1,7
ᵛS Ps 1:1
7:6 ʷS Ps 21:9
7:7 ˣHos 13:10
ʸver 16; S Ps 14:4;
S Isa 9:13; Zep 1:6
7:8 ᶻver 11;
Ps 106:35;
S Hos 5:13
7:9 ᵃIsa 1:7;
Hos 8:7
7:10 ᵇHos 5:5
ᶜHos 5:4 ᵈver 14;
S Isa 9:13
7:11 ᵉS Ge 8:8
ᶠver 16; Hos 9:6
ᵍS ver 8; S Jer 2:18;
S La 5:6; Hos 9:3;
12:1
7:12 ʰS Eze 12:13;
S 32:3
7:13 ⁱHos 9:12
ʲJer 14:10;
S Eze 34:4-6;
Hos 9:17

that I rememberᵖ all their evil
  deeds.ᑫ
Their sins engulf them;ʳ
  they are always before me.

³"They delight the king with their
  wickedness,
  the princes with their lies.ˢ
⁴They are all adulterers,ᵗ
  burning like an oven
whose fire the baker need not stir
  from the kneading of the dough till
  it rises.
⁵On the day of the festival of our king
  the princes become inflamed with
  wine,ᵘ
and he joins hands with the
  mockers.ᵛ
⁶Their hearts are like an oven;ʷ
  they approach him with intrigue.
Their passion smolders all night;
  in the morning it blazes like a
  flaming fire.
⁷All of them are hot as an oven;
  they devour their rulers.
All their kings fall,ˣ
  and none of them callsʸ on me.

⁸"Ephraim mixesᶻ with the nations;
  Ephraim is a flat cake not turned
  over.
⁹Foreigners sap his strength,ᵃ
  but he does not realize it.
His hair is sprinkled with gray,
  but he does not notice.
¹⁰Israel's arrogance testifies against
  him,ᵇ
  but despite all this
he does not returnᶜ to the Lᴏʀᴅ his
  God
  or searchᵈ for him.

¹¹"Ephraim is like a dove,ᵉ
  easily deceived and senseless—
  now calling to Egypt,ᶠ
  now turning to Assyria.ᵍ
¹²When they go, I will throw my netʰ
  over them;
I will pull them down like birds of
  the air.
When I hear them flocking together,
  I will catch them.
¹³Woeⁱ to them,
  because they have strayedʲ from me!
Destruction to them,

ᵛ 7 Or *As at Adam*; or *Like men*

because they have rebelled against
    me!
I long to redeem them
    but they speak lies^k against me.^l
^14 They do not cry out to me from their
        hearts^m
    but wail upon their beds.
They gather together^w for grain and
        new wine^n
    but turn away from me.^o
^15 I trained^p them and strengthened
        them,
    but they plot evil^q against me.
^16 They do not turn to the Most High;^r
    they are like a faulty bow.^s
Their leaders will fall by the
        sword
    because of their insolent^t words.
For this they will be ridiculed^u
    in the land of Egypt.^v

Israel to Reap the Whirlwind

8 "Put the trumpet^w to your lips!
    An eagle^x is over the house of the
        LORD
because the people have broken my
        covenant^y
    and rebelled against my law.^z
^2 Israel cries out to me,
    'O our God, we acknowledge you!'
^3 But Israel has rejected what is good;
    an enemy will pursue him.^a
^4 They set up kings without my
        consent;
    they choose princes without my
        approval.^b
With their silver and gold
    they make idols^c for themselves
    to their own destruction.
^5 Throw out your calf-idol, O Samaria!^d
    My anger burns against them.
    How long will they be incapable of
        purity?^e
^6   They are from Israel!
    This calf—a craftsman has made it;
        it is not God.^f
    It will be broken in pieces,
        that calf^g of Samaria.^h

^7 "They sow the wind
    and reap the whirlwind.^i
The stalk has no head;
    it will produce no flour.^j
Were it to yield grain,
    foreigners would swallow it up.^k

H Da 12:1 ◀▶ Hos 13:3

7:13 ^k S Ps 116:11
^l ver 1; Jer 51:9;
Mt 23:37
7:14 ^m Jer 3:10
^n Am 2:8 ^o S ver 10;
S Hos 4:10; 9:1;
13:16
7:15 ^p Hos 11:3
^q Ps 2:1; S 140:2;
Na 1:9,11
7:16 ^r S ver 7
^s S Ps 78:9,57
^t Mal 3:14
^u S Eze 23:32
^v S ver 11; Hos 9:3;
11:5
8:1 ^w S Nu 10:2;
S Eze 33:3
^x S Dt 28:49;
Jer 4:13
^y S Jer 11:10
^z S Hos 4:6; S 6:7
8:3 ^a S Mt 7:23;
Tit 1:16
8:4 ^b Hos 13:10
^c S Hos 2:8; 13:1-2
8:5 ^d ver 6;
Hos 10:5
^e Jer 13:27
8:6 ^f S Jer 16:20;
Hos 14:3
^g S Ex 32:4 ^h S ver 5
8:7 ^i S Job 4:8;
Pr 22:8; Isa 66:15;
Hos 10:12-13;
Na 1:3; Gal 6:8
^j S Dt 28:38;
S Isa 17:11;
Hos 9:16
^k Hos 2:9; S 7:9
8:8 ^l Jer 51:34
^m Jer 22:28
8:9 ^n S Jer 2:18
^o S Ge 16:12
^p S Jer 22:20;
Eze 23:5;
S Hos 5:13
8:10 ^q S Eze 16:37;
S 22:20 ^r Jer 42:2
8:11 ^s Hos 10:1;
12:11
8:12 ^t S ver 1
8:13 ^u S Jer 7:21
^v S Jer 6:20; Hos 9:4
^w Hos 7:2; 9:9;
Am 8:7 ^x S Hos 4:9
^y Hos 9:3,6
8:14 ^z S Dt 32:18;
S Isa 17:10;
S Hos 2:13
^a Ps 95:6
^b Jer 5:17; S 17:27;
Am 2:5
9:1 ^c Isa 22:12-13
^d Ps 73:27;
S Isa 24:16;
S Hos 7:14; 10:5
^e S Ge 30:15
9:2 ^f Isa 24:7;
Hos 2:9; Joel 1:10
9:3 ^g Lev 25:23
^h S Hos 7:16; S 8:13

^8 Israel is swallowed up;^l
    now she is among the nations
    like a worthless^m thing.
^9 For they have gone up to Assyria^n
    like a wild donkey^o wandering
        alone.
Ephraim has sold herself to lovers.^p
^10 Although they have sold themselves
        among the nations,
    I will now gather them together.^q
They will begin to waste away^r
    under the oppression of the mighty
        king.

^11 "Though Ephraim built many altars for
        sin offerings,
    these have become altars for
        sinning.^s
^12 I wrote for them the many things of
        my law,
    but they regarded them as
        something alien.^t
^13 They offer sacrifices given to me
    and they eat^u the meat,
    but the LORD is not pleased with
        them.^v
Now he will remember^w their
        wickedness
    and punish their sins:^x
They will return to Egypt.^y
^14 Israel has forgotten^z his Maker^a
    and built palaces;
Judah has fortified many towns.
But I will send fire upon their
        cities
    that will consume their
        fortresses."^b

Punishment for Israel

9 Do not rejoice, O Israel;
    do not be jubilant^c like the other
        nations.
For you have been unfaithful^d to your
        God;
    you love the wages of a prostitute^e
    at every threshing floor.
^2 Threshing floors and winepresses will
        not feed the people;
    the new wine^f will fail them.
^3 They will not remain^g in the LORD's
        land;
Ephraim will return to Egypt^h

R Hos 6:11 ◀▶ Hos 9:3
R Hos 8:8 ◀▶ Hos 9:6

^w 14 Most Hebrew manuscripts; some Hebrew manuscripts and
Septuagint *They slash themselves*

and eat unclean[x] food in Assyria.[i]

⁴They will not pour out wine offerings[j] to the LORD,
nor will their sacrifices please[k] him.
Such sacrifices will be to them like the bread of mourners;[1]
all who eat them will be unclean.[m]
This food will be for themselves;
it will not come into the temple of the LORD.[n]

⁵What will you do[o] on the day of your appointed feasts,[p]
on the festival days of the LORD?

⁶Even if they escape from destruction,
Egypt will gather them,[q]
and Memphis[r] will bury them.[s]
Their treasures of silver[t] will be taken over by briers,
and thorns[u] will overrun their tents.

⁷The days of punishment[v] are coming,
the days of reckoning[w] are at hand.
Let Israel know this.
Because your sins[x] are so many
and your hostility so great,
the prophet is considered a fool,[y]
the inspired man a maniac.[z]

⁸The prophet, along with my God,
is the watchman over Ephraim,[y]
yet snares[a] await him on all his paths,
and hostility in the house of his God.[b]

⁹They have sunk deep into corruption,[c]
as in the days of Gibeah.[d]
God will remember[e] their wickedness
and punish them for their sins.[f]

¹⁰"When I found Israel,
it was like finding grapes in the desert;
when I saw your fathers,
it was like seeing the early fruit[g] on the fig[h] tree.
But when they came to Baal Peor,[i]
they consecrated themselves to that shameful idol[j]
and became as vile as the thing they loved.

R *Hos 9:3* ◀ ▶ *Hos 9:12*

¹¹Ephraim's glory[k] will fly away like a bird[l]—
no birth, no pregnancy, no conception.[m]

¹²Even if they rear children,
I will bereave[n] them of every one.
Woe[o] to them
when I turn away from them![p]

¹³I have seen Ephraim,[q] like Tyre,
planted in a pleasant place.[r]
But Ephraim will bring out
their children to the slayer."[s]

¹⁴Give them, O LORD—
what will you give them?
Give them wombs that miscarry
and breasts that are dry.[t]

¹⁵"Because of all their wickedness in Gilgal,[u]
I hated them there.
Because of their sinful deeds,[v]
I will drive them out of my house.
I will no longer love them;[w]
all their leaders are rebellious.[x]

¹⁶Ephraim[y] is blighted,
their root is withered,
they yield no fruit.[z]
Even if they bear children,
I will slay[a] their cherished offspring."

¹⁷My God will reject[b] them
because they have not obeyed[c] him;
they will be wanderers among the nations.[d]

10 Israel was a spreading vine;[e]
he brought forth fruit for himself.
As his fruit increased,
he built more altars;[f]
as his land prospered,[g]
he adorned his sacred stones.[h]

R *Hos 9:6* ◀ ▶ *Hos 9:17*
R *Hos 9:12* ◀ ▶ *Hos 10:7*
C *Hos 6:4* ◀ ▶ *Hos 10:13*

x 3 That is, ceremonially unclean   y 8 Or *The prophet is the watchman over Ephraim, / the people of my God*

8:8 The prophet confirmed the exile of Israel as God's judgment upon his people for their apostasy.
9:3–17 This woeful passage promised punishment for Israel that would include exile from their beloved land into Egypt and Assyria. In fulfillment of this prophecy, Assyria conquered Israel in 721 B.C. and carried her people away captive. God further warned that Israel would be "wanderers among the nations" (9:17). This prophecy too has been tragically fulfilled as millions of Jews have searched for a peaceful life over the centuries in nation after nation without finding refuge.

² Their heart is deceitful,ⁱ
 and now they must bear their guilt.ʲ
 The LORD will demolish their altarsᵏ
 and destroy their sacred stones.ˡ

³ Then they will say, "We have no king
 because we did not revere the LORD.
 But even if we had a king,
 what could he do for us?"
⁴ They make many promises,
 take false oathsᵐ
 and make agreements;ⁿ
 therefore lawsuits spring up
 like poisonous weedsᵒ in a plowed field.
⁵ The people who live in Samaria fear
 for the calf-idolᵖ of Beth Aven.ᵍ
 Its people will mourn over it,
 and so will its idolatrous priests,ʳ
 those who had rejoiced over its splendor,
 because it is taken from them into exile.ˢ
⁶ It will be carried to Assyriaᵗ
 as tributeᵘ for the great king.ᵛ
 Ephraim will be disgraced;ʷ
 Israel will be ashamedˣ of its wooden idols.ᵃ

⁷ Samaria and its king will float awayʸ
 like a twig on the surface of the waters.
⁸ The high placesᶻ of wickednessᵇᵃ will be destroyed—
 it is the sin of Israel.
 Thornsᵇ and thistles will grow up
 and cover their altars.ᶜ
 Then they will say to the mountains, "Cover us!"ᵈ
 and to the hills, "Fall on us!"ᵉ

⁹ "Since the days of Gibeah,ᶠ you have sinned,ᵍ O Israel,
 and there you have remained.ᶜ
 Did not war overtake
 the evildoers in Gibeah?

¹⁰ When I please, I will punishʰ them;
 nations will be gathered against them
 to put them in bonds for their double sin.

¹¹ Ephraim is a trained heifer
 that loves to thresh;
 so I will put a yokeⁱ
 on her fair neck.
 I will drive Ephraim,
 Judah must plow,
 and Jacob must break up the ground.

¹² Sowʲ for yourselves righteousness,ᵏ
 reap the fruit of unfailing love,
 and break up your unplowed ground;ˡ
 for it is time to seekᵐ the LORD,
 until he comes
 and showers righteousnessⁿ on you.
¹³ But you have planted wickedness,
 you have reaped evil,ᵒ
 you have eaten the fruit of deception.ᵖ
 Because you have depended on your own strength
 and on your many warriors,ᵍ
¹⁴ the roar of battle will rise against your people,
 so that all your fortresses will be devastated—
 as Shalmanˢ devastated Beth Arbel on the day of battle,
 when mothers were dashed to the ground with their children.ᵗ
¹⁵ Thus will it happen to you, O Bethel,
 because your wickedness is great.
 When that day dawns,
 the king of Israel will be completely destroyed.ᵘ

God's Love for Israel

11 "When Israel was a child,ᵛ I lovedʷ him,
 and out of Egypt I called my son.ˣ
² But the more Iᵈ called Israel,
 the further they went from me.ᵉʸ
 They sacrificed to the Baalsᶻ
 and they burned incense to images.ᵃ
³ It was I who taught Ephraim to walk,
 taking them by the arms;ᵇ

10:2 ⁱ 1Ki 18:21; ʲ Hos 13:16 ᵏ ver 8 ˡ Mic 5:13
10:4 ᵐ S Hos 4:2 ⁿ S Eze 17:19; Am 5:7 ᵒ Am 6:12
10:5 ᵖ S Ex 32:4; S Isa 44:17-20 ᵍ ver 8; S Hos 5:8 ʳ S 2Ki 23:5; Zep 1:4 ˢ S Jdg 18:17-18; S Hos 8:5; S 9:1,3, 11
10:6 ᵗ S 2Ki 16:7; Hos 11:5 ᵘ S Jdg 3:15 ᵛ S Hos 5:13 ʷ Isa 30:3; S Hos 4:7 ˣ Jer 48:13
10:7 ʸ ver 15; Hos 13:11
10:8 ᶻ S Eze 6:6 ᵃ ver 5; 1Ki 12:28-30; S Hos 4:13 ᵇ S Hos 9:6 ᶜ ver 2; S Isa 32:13 ᵈ S Job 30:6; Am 3:14-15 ᵉ Am 7:9; Lk 23:30*; Rev 6:16
10:9 ᶠ S Hos 5:8 ᵍ S Jos 7:11
10:10 ʰ S Eze 5:13; S Hos 4:9
10:11 ⁱ S Jer 15:12; S 31:18
10:12 ʲ S Ecc 11:1 ᵏ S Pr 11:18; Jas 3:18 ˡ Jer 4:3 ᵐ S Isa 19:22; Hos 12:6 ⁿ S Isa 45:8
10:13 ᵒ S Job 4:8; S Hos 7:3; 11:12; Gal 6:7-8 ᵖ S Pr 11:18; S Hos 8:7 ᵍ Ps 33:16
10:14 ʳ S Isa 17:3; Mic 5:11 ˢ 2Ki 17:3 ᵗ S Isa 13:16; Hos 13:16
10:15 ᵘ S ver 7
11:1 ᵛ S Jer 2:2; S Eze 16:22 ʷ S Dt 4:37 ˣ S Ex 4:22; Hos 12:9,13; 13:4; Mt 2:15*
11:2 ʸ ver 7 ᶻ S Hos 2:13 ᵃ S 2Ki 17:15; Isa 65:7; S Jer 18:15; Hos 4:13; 13:1
11:3 ᵇ S Dt 1:31; S 32:11; Hos 7:15

M Da 9:20–21 ◄ Joel 2:13
R Hos 5:15 ◄ Joel 2:12–13
C Hos 10:1–2 ◄ Hos 13:3
E Da 1:15 ◄ Mt 4:23–25

ᶻ 5 Beth Aven means *house of wickedness* (a name for Bethel, which means *house of God*). ᵃ 6 Or *its counsel* ᵇ 8 Hebrew *aven*, a reference to Beth Aven (a derogatory name for Bethel) ᶜ 9 Or *there a stand was taken* ᵈ 2 Some Septuagint manuscripts; Hebrew *they* ᵉ 2 Septuagint; Hebrew *them*

S Eze 36:29 ◄ Hos 12:6
R Hos 9:17 ◄ Hos 10:10
R Hos 10:7 ◄ Hos 12:2

10:7–10 Hosea predicted the death of the king of Samaria and the chastening of Israel. This prophecy was fulfilled when Assyria conquered Israel in 721 B.C.

but they did not realize
  it was I who healed them.
⁴I led them with cords of human
    kindness,
  with ties of love;
I lifted the yoke from their neck
  and bent down to feed them.

⁵"Will they not return to Egypt
  and will not Assyria rule over them
  because they refuse to repent?
⁶Swords will flash in their cities,
  will destroy the bars of their gates
  and put an end to their plans.
⁷My people are determined to turn
    from me.
  Even if they call to the Most High,
  he will by no means exalt them.

⁸"How can I give you up, Ephraim?
  How can I hand you over, Israel?
  How can I treat you like Admah?
  How can I make you like Zeboiim?
  My heart is changed within me;
  all my compassion is aroused.
⁹I will not carry out my fierce anger,
  nor will I turn and devastate
    Ephraim.
  For I am God, and not man—
    the Holy One among you.
  I will not come in wrath.
¹⁰They will follow the LORD;
  he will roar like a lion.
  When he roars,
  his children will come trembling
    from the west.
¹¹They will come trembling
  like birds from Egypt,
  like doves from Assyria.
I will settle them in their homes,"
  declares the LORD.

Israel's Sin

¹²Ephraim has surrounded me with
    lies,
  the house of Israel with deceit.
  And Judah is unruly against God,
    even against the faithful Holy One.

12 ¹Ephraim feeds on the wind;
  he pursues the east wind all day
  and multiplies lies and violence.
  He makes a treaty with Assyria
  and sends olive oil to Egypt.
²The LORD has a charge to bring against
    Judah;
  he will punish Jacob according to
    his ways
  and repay him according to his
    deeds.
³In the womb he grasped his brother's
    heel;
  as a man he struggled with God.
⁴He struggled with the angel and
    overcame him;
  he wept and begged for his favor.
  He found him at Bethel
  and talked with him there—
⁵the LORD God Almighty,
  the LORD is his name of renown!
⁶But you must return to your God;
  maintain love and justice,
  and wait for your God always.

⁷The merchant uses dishonest scales;
  he loves to defraud.
⁸Ephraim boasts,
  "I am very rich; I have become
    wealthy.
  With all my wealth they will not find
    in me
  any iniquity or sin."

⁹"I am the LORD your God,
  who brought you out of Egypt;
  I will make you live in tents again,
  as in the days of your appointed
    feasts.
¹⁰I spoke to the prophets,
  gave them many visions
  and told parables through them."
¹¹Is Gilead wicked?
  Its people are worthless!
  Do they sacrifice bulls in Gilgal?

12:2 The prophet likened Judah to her father Jacob, a deceiver and schemer. Because of Judah's deceit, God would judge the nation and exile the people from the promised land.

12:9 God reminded Israel that he had delivered them from the slavery of Egypt and would "make you live in tents again." This promise will be fulfilled in the last days when the Messiah returns to establish his glorious and eternal kingdom in the land of Israel.

HOSEA 12:12　　　　　　　　　　1008

Their altars will be like piles of stones
　on a plowed field.ᵍ
¹²Jacob fled to the country of Aram;ʲ ʰ
　Israel served to get a wife,
　and to pay for her he tended sheep.ⁱ
¹³The LORD used a prophet to bring Israel up from Egypt,ʲ
　by a prophet he cared for him.ᵏ
¹⁴But Ephraim has bitterly provoked him to anger;
　his Lord will leave upon him the guilt of his bloodshed¹
　and will repay him for his contempt.ᵐ

The LORD's Anger Against Israel

13 When Ephraim spoke, men trembled;ⁿ
　he was exaltedᵒ in Israel.
　But he became guilty of Baal worshipᵖ and died.
²Now they sin more and more;
　they makeᵠ idols for themselves from their silver,ʳ
　cleverly fashioned images,
　all of them the work of craftsmen.ˢ
It is said of these people,
　"They offer human sacrifice
　and kiss¹ᵗ the calf-idols.ᵘ"

³Therefore they will be like the morning mist,
　like the early dew that disappears,ᵛ
　like chaffʷ swirling from a threshing floor,ˣ
　like smokeʸ escaping through a window.

⁴"But I am the LORD your God,
　⌊who brought you⌋ out ofᵏ Egypt.ᶻ
　You shall acknowledgeᵃ no God but me,ᵇ
　no Saviorᶜ except me.
⁵I cared for you in the desert,ᵈ
　in the land of burning heat.

R Hos 12:2 ◀▶ Hos 13:13
C Hos 10:13 ◀▶ Am 5:7
H Hos 8:7 ◀▶ Joel 1:15
O La 3:37 ◀▶ Jnh 2:9
F Hos 11:4 ◀▶ Joel 2:19

12:11 ᵍS Hos 8:11
12:12 ʰGe 28:5
　ⁱS Ge 29:18
12:13 ʲS Hos 11:1
　ᵏEx 13:3;
　14:19-22;
　Isa 63:11-14
12:14 ˡS Eze 18:13
　ᵐDa 11:18
13:1 ⁿJdg 12:1
　ᵒS Jdg 8:1
　ᵖS Hos 11:2
13:2 ᵠJer 44:8
　ʳS Isa 46:6;
　S Jer 10:4
　ˢHos 14:3
　ᵗ1Ki 19:18
　ᵘS Isa 44:17-20;
　S Hos 8:4
13:3 ᵛS Hos 6:4
　ʷS Job 13:25;
　Ps 1:4; S Isa 17:13
　ˣS Da 2:35 ʸPs 68:2
13:4 ᶻS Jer 2:6;
　S Hos 12:9
　ᵃS Hos 2:20
　ᵇS Ex 20:3
　ᶜS Dt 28:29;
　Ps 18:46; Isa 43:11;
　45:21-22
13:5 ᵈS Dt 1:19
13:6 ᵉS Ge 28:5
　ᶠS Dt 32:18;
　S Isa 17:10
　ᵍS Dt 32:12-15;
　S Pr 30:7-9;
　S Jer 5:7;
　S Hos 2:13; S 4:7
13:7 ʰS Job 10:16;
　S Jer 4:7
13:8 ⁱS 2Sa 17:8
　ʲS 1Sa 17:34;
　Ps 17:12
　ᵏPs 50:22;
　S La 3:10;
　S Hos 2:12
13:9 ˡJer 2:17-19
　ᵐS Dt 33:29
13:10 ⁿS 2Ki 17:4;
　Hos 7:7 ᵒ1Sa 8:6;
　Hos 8:4
13:11 ᵖS Nu 11:20
　ᵠS Jos 24:20;
　S 1Sa 13:14;
　S 1Ki 14:10;
　Hos 3:4; S 10:7
13:12 ʳS Dt 32:34
13:13 ˢS Isa 13:8;
　Mic 4:9-10
　ᵗ2Ki 19:3 ᵘIsa 66:9
13:14 ᵛS Ps 16:10;
　49:15;
　S Eze 37:12-13
　ʷS Isa 25:8
　ˣ1Co 15:55*
13:15 ʸS Hos 10:1
　ᶻS Job 1:19;
　S Eze 19:12;
　S Hos 4:19

⁶When I fed them, they were satisfied;
　when they were satisfied, they became proud;ᵉ
　then they forgotᶠ me.ᵍ
⁷So I will come upon them like a lion,ʰ
　like a leopard I will lurk by the path.
⁸Like a bear robbed of her cubs,ⁱ
　I will attack them and rip them open.
Like a lionʲ I will devour them;
　a wild animal will tear them apart.ᵏ

⁹"You are destroyed, O Israel,
　because you are against me,ˡ against your helper.ᵐ
¹⁰Where is your king,ⁿ that he may save you?
　Where are your rulers in all your towns,
　of whom you said,
　'Give me a king and princes'?ᵒ
¹¹So in my anger I gave you a king,ᵖ
　and in my wrath I took him away.ᵠ
¹²The guilt of Ephraim is stored up,
　his sins are kept on record.ʳ
¹³Pains as of a woman in childbirthˢ come to him,
　but he is a child without wisdom;
　when the timeᵗ arrives,
　he does not come to the opening of the womb.ᵘ
¹⁴"I will ransom them from the power of the grave¹;ᵛ
　I will redeem them from death.ʷ
　Where, O death, are your plagues?
　Where, O grave,¹ is your destruction?ˣ

"I will have no compassion,
¹⁵ even though he thrivesʸ among his brothers.
An east windᶻ from the LORD will come,

L Hos 6:3 ◀▶ Hos 14:4
R Hos 13:3 ◀▶ Hos 13:16
F Da 12:13 ◀▶ Mt 22:30–32
I Hos 12:9 ◀▶ Hos 14:4–8

ʲ 12 That is, Northwest Mesopotamia   ʲ 2 Or "Men who sacrifice / kiss
ᵏ 4 Or God / ever since you were in   ˡ 14 Hebrew Sheol

13:3–4 God likened the future existence of the rebellious nation of Israel to short-lived and vaporous clouds and dust, indicating that Ephraim (Israel) would soon vanish as a nation when they were carried into captivity. God also reminded Israel that only he was their God and Savior.

13:12–16 In this passage Hosea prophesied God's certain judgment upon Ephraim (Israel) for her wickedness. This prophecy was fulfilled in 721 B.C. when the armies of Assyria overwhelmed Israel's armies, destroying the capital city and the kingdom.

blowing in from the desert;
　his spring will fail
　　and his well dry up.ᵃ
His storehouse will be plunderedᵇ
　of all its treasures.

¹⁶The people of Samariaᶜ must bear their
　guilt,ᵈ
because they have rebelledᵉ against
　their God.
They will fall by the sword;ᶠ
　their little ones will be dashedᵍ to
　　the ground,
　their pregnant womenʰ ripped
　　open."

Repentance to Bring Blessing

14 Return,ⁱ O Israel, to the LORD
　your God.
Your sinsʲ have been your
　downfall!ᵏ
²Take words with you
　and return to the LORD.
Say to him:
"Forgiveˡ all our sins
and receive us graciously,ᵐ
that we may offer the fruit of our
　lips.ᵐⁿ
³Assyria cannot save us;ᵒ
　we will not mount war-horses.ᵖ
We will never again say 'Our gods'ᵠ
　to what our own hands have made,ʳ
for in you the fatherlessˢ find
　compassion."

R Hos 13:13 ◀▶ Hos 14:1
R Hos 13:16 ◀▶ Joel 1:4
P Hos 6:1 ◀▶ Hos 14:4
S Hos 12:6 ◀▶ Am 3:3

13:15 ᵃS Jer 51:36
ᵇJer 20:5
13:16 ᶜ2Ki 17:5
ᵈHos 10:2
ᵉS Hos 7:14
ᶠHos 11:6
ᵍS 2Ki 8:12;
S Hos 10:14
2Ki 15:16;
Isa 13:16; Am 1:13
14:1 ⁱS Isa 19:22;
S Jer 3:12
ʲS Hos 4:8
ᵏS Hos 5:5; S 9:7
14:2 ˡS Ex 34:9
ᵐPs 51:16-17;
Mic 7:18-19
ⁿHeb 13:15
14:3 ᵒS Hos 5:13
ᵖPs 33:17;
S Isa 31:1; Mic 5:10
ᵠHos 8:6 ʳver 28;
Hos 13:2 ˢPs 10:14;
68:5; Jer 49:11
14:4 ᵗS Isa 30:26;
S Hos 6:1
ᵘS Jer 2:19
ᵛS Isa 55:1;
Jer 31:20; Zep 3:17
ʷS Job 13:16
14:5 ˣS Ge 27:28;
S Isa 18:4 ʸS SS 2:1
ᶻIsa 35:2
ᵃJob 29:19
14:6 ᵇPs 52:8;
S Jer 11:16
ᶜS Ps 92:12;
S SS 4:11
14:7 ᵈPs 91:1-4
ᵉS Ge 40:10
ᶠS Hos 2:22
ᵍS Eze 17:23
14:8 ʰS ver 3
ⁱS Isa 37:24
14:9 ʲS Ps 107:43
ᵏS Pr 10:29;
S Isa 1:28;
Da 12:10
ˡPs 111:7-8;
Zep 3:5; Ac 13:10
ᵐIsa 26:7

⁴"I will healᵗ their waywardnessᵘ
　and love them freely,ᵛ
for my anger has turned awayʷ from
　them.
⁵I will be like the dewˣ to Israel;
　he will blossom like a lily.ʸ
Like a cedar of Lebanonᶻ
　he will send down his roots;ᵃ
⁶ his young shoots will grow.
His splendor will be like an
　olive tree,ᵇ
　his fragrance like a cedar of
　　Lebanon.ᶜ
⁷Men will dwell again in his shade.ᵈ
He will flourish like the grain.
He will blossomᵉ like a vine,
　and his fame will be like the wineᶠ
　　from Lebanon.ᵍ
⁸O Ephraim, what more have Iⁿ to do
　with idols?ʰ
I will answer him and care for him.
I am like a green pineⁱ tree;
　your fruitfulness comes from me."

⁹Who is wise?ʲ He will realize these
　things.
Who is discerning? He will
　understand them.ᵏ
The ways of the LORD are right;ˡ
　the righteous walkᵐ in them,
　but the rebellious stumble in
　　them.

I Hos 13:14 ◀▶ Joel 2:21
L Hos 13:9 ◀▶ Joel 2:13
P Hos 14:1–2 ◀▶ Joel 2:12–13

ᵐ 2 Or offer our lips as sacrifices of bulls ⁿ 8 Or What more has Ephraim

---

14:1 Hosea warned Israel to repent of her rebellion because of the judgment about to fall on her.
14:4–8 The prophet ended his predictions by delivering God's promise to restore Israel once again, likening the final restoration of Israel to a flourishing olive tree. Israel will ultimately be purged of its sin and experience God's full forgiveness and restoration under the coming Messiah.

Joel

Author: Joel

Theme: A locust plague foreshadows the day of the Lord

Date of Writing: c. 830 B.C.

Outline of Joel
  I. The Plague of Locusts (1:1–12)
  II. Joel's Admonition (1:13–20)
  III. Joel's Five Visions (2:1–32)
  IV. Judgment and Restoration (3:1–21)

THIS PROPHECY WAS written by Joel, a common OT name that means "Jehovah is God." Joel is mentioned only in this short book and again in Acts (see Ac 2:16); little is known about the personal life of Joel except that he was the son of Pethuel and probably lived in Judah. In addition, the political and social conditions reflected in Joel's book mirror those of the ninth century B.C. during the early years of King Joash while the high priest Jehoiada ruled in his stead (see 2Ki 11:4).

The majority of Joel's message is an apocalyptic prophecy that uses symbolic visions and language to emphasize impending judgment. A severe locust plague that devastated the land of Judah and the burning drought which followed prompted Joel's warning to the people of Judah to repent and return to God. Joel warned that these occurrences were only symbols of the great judgment that would come at the terrible "day of the Lord" (2:31). Joel also prophesied that before the fulfillment of this judgment, God would send his Holy Spirit to grant extended blessing (see 2:28–32). In the NT, on the day of Pentecost, Peter refers to a partial fulfillment of this prophecy (see Ac 2:16).

JOEL 1:17

1 The word of the LORD that came[a] to Joel[b] son of Pethuel.

An Invasion of Locusts

[2] Hear this,[c] you elders;[d]
listen, all who live in the land.[e]
Has anything like this ever happened
    in your days
or in the days of your forefathers?[f]
[3] Tell it to your children,[g]
and let your children tell it to their
    children,
and their children to the next
    generation.[h]
[4] What the locust[i] swarm has left
    the great locusts have eaten;
what the great locusts have left
    the young locusts have eaten;
what the young locusts have left[j]
    other locusts[a] have eaten.[k]
[5] Wake up, you drunkards, and weep!
Wail, all you drinkers of wine;[l]
wail because of the new wine,
for it has been snatched[m] from your
    lips.
[6] A nation has invaded my land,
    powerful and without number;[n]
it has the teeth[o] of a lion,
    the fangs of a lioness.
[7] It has laid waste[p] my vines
    and ruined my fig trees.[q]
It has stripped off their bark
    and thrown it away,
leaving their branches white.

[8] Mourn like a virgin[b] in sackcloth[r]
    grieving for the husband[c] of her
    youth.
[9] Grain offerings and drink offerings[s]
are cut off from the house of the
    LORD.
The priests are in mourning,[t]
those who minister before the LORD.
[10] The fields are ruined,
    the ground is dried up[d];[u]
the grain is destroyed,
    the new wine[v] is dried up,
    the oil fails.[w]

R Hos 14:1 ◀▶ Joel 1:7
R Joel 1:4 ◀▶ Joel 3:2

1:1 [a]S Jer 1:2
    [b]Ac 2:16
1:2 [c]Hos 5:1
    [d]Joel 2:16
    [e]S Hos 4:1 [f]Joel 2:2
1:3 [g]S Ex 10:2
    [h]S Ps 71:18
1:4 [i]S Ex 10:14
    [j]S Ex 10:5
    [k]S Ex 10:15;
    S Dt 28:39; Am 7:1;
    Na 3:15
1:5 [l]Joel 3:3
    [m]S Isa 24:7
1:6 [n]Ps 105:34;
    Joel 2:2,11,25
    [o]Rev 9:8
1:7 [p]Isa 5:6
    [q]Am 4:9
1:8 [r]ver 13;
    Isa 22:12; Am 8:10
1:9 [s]S Hos 9:4
    [t]S Isa 22:12
1:10 [u]S Isa 5:6;
    S 24:4; S Jer 3:3
    [v]S Hos 9:2
    [w]S Nu 18:12
1:11 [x]S Job 6:20;
    Am 5:16
    [y]S Ex 9:31
    [z]S Isa 17:11
1:12 [a]S Isa 15:6
    [b]S Ex 28:33
    [c]S Isa 16:8;
    Hag 2:19
1:13 [d]S Ge 37:34;
    S Jer 4:8 [e]Joel 2:17
    [f]ver 9; S Hos 9:4;
    Joel 2:14
1:14 [g]S 2Ch 20:3
    [h]S Hos 4:1 [i]Jnh 3:8
    [j]2Ch 20:4
1:15 [k]S Isa 2:12;
    Jer 30:7; S 46:10;
    S Eze 30:3; Mal 4:5
    [l]Joel 2:1,11,31;
    3:14; Am 5:18;
    Zep 1:14; Zec 14:1
    [m]S Ge 17:1
1:16 [n]Isa 3:7
    [o]S Ps 51:8
    [p]Dt 12:7
1:17
    [q]S Isa 17:10-11

[11] Despair, you farmers,[x]
    wail, you vine growers;
grieve for the wheat and the barley,[y]
    because the harvest of the field is
    destroyed.[z]
[12] The vine is dried up
    and the fig tree is withered;[a]
the pomegranate,[b] the palm and the
    apple tree—
all the trees of the field—are dried
    up.[c]
Surely the joy of mankind
is withered away.

A Call to Repentance

[13] Put on sackcloth,[d] O priests, and
    mourn;
wail, you who minister[e] before the
    altar.
Come, spend the night in sackcloth,
    you who minister before my God;
for the grain offerings and drink
    offerings[f]
are withheld from the house of your
    God.
[14] Declare a holy fast;[g]
    call a sacred assembly.
Summon the elders
    and all who live in the land[h]
to the house of the LORD your God,
    and cry out[i] to the LORD.[j]

[15] Alas for that[k] day!
For the day of the LORD[l] is near;
    it will come like destruction from
    the Almighty.[e][m]

[16] Has not the food been cut off[n]
    before our very eyes—
joy and gladness[o]
    from the house of our God?[p]
[17] The seeds are shriveled
    beneath the clods.[f][q]
The storehouses are in ruins,
    the granaries have been broken
    down,

P Da 12:1 ◀▶ Joel 2:1–11
H Hos 13:3 ◀▶ Joel 2:1–2

[a] 4 The precise meaning of the four Hebrew words used here for locusts is uncertain. [b] 8 Or young woman [c] 8 Or betrothed [d] 10 Or ground mourns [e] 15 Hebrew Shaddai [f] 17 The meaning of the Hebrew for this word is uncertain.

1:4–7 Using the occasion of a devastating plague of locusts as a prophetic type, Joel warned the people that God's judgment would certainly fall and leave the nation of Judah desolate.

1:15 Joel warned of the certainty of God's judgment when "the day of the LORD" finally comes and enemy armies invade the land.

for the grain has dried up.
¹⁸How the cattle moan!
  The herds mill about
because they have no pasture;ʳ
  even the flocks of sheep are
    suffering.ˢ

¹⁹To you, O Lᴏʀᴅ, I call,ᵗ
  for fireᵘ has devoured the open
    pasturesᵛ
  and flames have burned up all the
    trees of the field.
²⁰Even the wild animals pant for you;ʷ
  the streams of water have dried upˣ
  and fire has devoured the open
    pastures.ʸ

An Army of Locusts

2 Blow the trumpetᶻ in Zion;ᵃ
  sound the alarm on my holy hill.ᵇ
Let all who live in the land tremble,
  for the day of the Lᴏʀᴅᶜ is coming.
It is close at handᵈ—
² a day of darknessᵉ and gloom,ᶠ ᵍ
  a day of cloudsʰ and blackness.ⁱ
Like dawn spreading across the
  mountains
a large and mighty armyʲ comes,
  such as never was of oldᵏ
  nor ever will be in ages to come.

³Before them fireˡ devours,
  behind them a flame blazes.
Before them the land is like the garden
  of Eden,ᵐ
  behind them, a desert wasteⁿ—
    nothing escapes them.

⁴They have the appearance of horses;ᵒ
  they gallop along like cavalry.
⁵With a noise like that of chariotsᵖ
  they leap over the mountaintops,
  like a crackling fireᑫ consuming
    stubble,
  like a mighty army drawn up for
    battle.
⁶At the sight of them, nations are in
    anguish;ʳ
  every face turns pale.ˢ
⁷They charge like warriors;ᵗ
  they scale walls like soldiers.
They all march in line,ᵘ
  not swervingᵛ from their course.
⁸They do not jostle each other;
  each marches straight ahead.
They plunge through defenses
  without breaking ranks.
⁹They rush upon the city;
  they run along the wall.
They climb into the houses;ʷ
  like thieves they enter through the
    windows.ˣ

¹⁰Before them the earth shakes,ʸ
  the sky trembles,ᶻ
  the sun and moon are darkened,ᵃ
  and the stars no longer shine.ᵇ
¹¹The Lᴏʀᴅᶜ thundersᵈ
  at the head of his army;ᵉ
  his forces are beyond number,
  and mighty are those who obey his
    command.
The day of the Lᴏʀᴅ is great;ᶠ
  it is dreadful.
  Who can endure it?ᵍ

1:18 ʳS Ge 47:4; ˢS Jer 9:10
1:19 ᵗPs 50:15; ᵘS Ps 97:3; Am 7:4; ᵛS Jer 9:10
1:20 ʷS Ps 42:1; S 104:21; ˣ1Ki 17:7; ʸJoel 2:22
2:1 ᶻS Nu 10:2,7; ᵃver 15; ᵇS Ex 15:17; ᶜS Joel 1:15; Zep 1:14-16; ᵈS Eze 12:23; S 30:3; Ob 1:15
2:2 ᵉver 10,31; S Job 9:7; ᶠS Isa 8:22; S 13:10; Am 5:18; ᵍS Da 9:12; S Mt 24:21; ʰS Eze 34:12; ⁱS Eze 38:9; ʲZep 1:15; Rev 9:2; ᵏS Joel 1:6 ᵏJoel 1:2
2:3 ˡS Ps 97:3; S Isa 1:31; ᵐS Ge 2:8; ⁿEx 10:12-15; Ps 105:34-35; S Isa 14:17
2:4 ᵒRev 9:7
2:5 ᵖRev 9:9; ᑫIsa 5:24; 30:30
2:6 ʳS Isa 13:8; ˢS Isa 29:22
2:7 ᵗS Job 16:14; ᵘPr 30:27 ᵛIsa 5:27
2:9 ʷEx 10:6; ˣJer 9:21
2:10 ʸPs 18:7; Na 1:5; ᶻS Eze 38:19; ᵃS ver 2; S Isa 5:30; ᵇS Mt 24:29; Mk 13:24; Rev 9:2; ᵇS Job 9:7; S Ps 102:26; Isa 13:10; S Eze 32:8
2:11 ᶜS Isa 2:12; S Eze 30:3; S Joel 1:15; Ob 1:15; ᵈS Ps 29:3; ᵉS ver 2,25; ᶠZep 1:14; ᵍS Eze 22:14; Zep 2:11; Rev 6:17

P Joel 1:15 ◀▶ Joel 2:19–32
H Joel 1:15 ◀▶ Joel 2:6

H Joel 2:1–2 ◀▶ Joel 2:10–11
H Joel 2:6 ◀▶ Joel 2:31

2:1–11 The trumpet mentioned in this passage was not the silver trumpet used for feasts and festivals (see Nu 10:10). The silver trumpet's notes signified rejoicing or a call to worship. Joel instead indicated that the trumpet to be blown would be the shophar, a ram's or bull's horn used to assemble the army (see Jdg 3:27; 1Sa 13:3), to sound an attack (see Job 39:24–25) or to sound an alarm (see Jer 6:1; Hos 5:8; Am 3:6). The fearsome noise of the shophar could be heard from a great distance (see Ex 19:16) and signaled approaching danger. Joel prophesied that all who heard the sound of the shophar would tremble at that awful day.

Note also that Joel described the invaders as "cavalry" (2:4), indicating their swiftness as they crush their enemies. The sound of the invaders was "a noise like that of chariots" (2:5), possibly suggesting modern tanks or armored vehicles. However, Joel promised that God's wrath would be revealed through earthquakes and the darkening of the sun and moon. This parallels Revelation's description of God's final judgment when "the sun turned black like sackcloth made of goat hair, the whole moon turned blood red" (Rev 6:12).

Joel's prophecy indicated that God would raise up an army to fight these invaders (2:11; see also Jude 14–15). This prophecy will be fulfilled at the Battle of Armageddon when the armies of the antichrist will be defeated and Jesus Christ will set up his Messianic kingdom of peace (see Rev 9:13–19; 16:12–16; 19:11–16).

Rend Your Heart

P
R ¹²"Even now," declares the LORD,
"return[h] to me with all your heart,[i]
with fasting and weeping and
mourning."

L ¹³Rend your heart[j]
M and not your garments.[k]
Return[l] to the LORD your God,
for he is gracious and
compassionate,[m]
slow to anger and abounding in love,[n]
and he relents from sending
calamity.[o]

¹⁴Who knows? He may turn[p] and have
pity[q]
and leave behind a blessing[r]—
grain offerings and drink offerings[s]
for the LORD your God.

¹⁵Blow the trumpet[t] in Zion,[u]
declare a holy fast,[v]
call a sacred assembly.[w]
¹⁶Gather the people,
consecrate[x] the assembly;
bring together the elders,[y]
gather the children,
those nursing at the breast.
Let the bridegroom[z] leave his room
and the bride her chamber.
¹⁷Let the priests, who minister[a] before
the LORD,
weep[b] between the temple porch
and the altar.[c]
Let them say, "Spare your people,
O LORD.

P Hos 14:4 ◀ ▶ Am 5:4
R Hos 10:12 ◀ ▶ Jnh 3:5–10
L Hos 14:4 ◀ ▶ Jnh 3:10
M Hos 10:12 ◀ ▶ Ob 3–4

2:12 ʰ S Dt 4:30; S Eze 33:11; S Hos 12:6 ⁱ S 1Sa 7:3
2:13 ʲ Ps 51:17; Isa 57:15 ᵏ S Ge 37:29; S Nu 14:6; Job 1:20 ˡ S Isa 19:22 ᵐ S Dt 4:31 ⁿ Ex 34:6; S Ps 86:5,15 ᵒ S Jer 18:8; Jnh 4:2
2:14 ᵖ Jer 26:3; Jnh 3:9 ᵠ Am 5:15; Jnh 1:6 ʳ Jer 31:14; Hag 2:19; Zec 8:13; Mal 3:10 ˢ S Joel 1:13
2:15 ᵗ S Nu 10:2 ᵘ ver 1 ᵛ S 2Ch 20:3; Jer 36:9 ʷ S Ex 32:5; Nu 10:3
2:16 ˣ S Ex 19:10, 22 ʸ Joel 1:2 ᶻ Ps 19:5
2:17 ᵃ Joel 1:13 ᵇ S Isa 22:12 ᶜ Eze 8:16; Mt 23:35 ᵈ Dt 9:26-29; Ps 44:13 ᵉ S 1Ki 9:7; S Job 17:6 ᶠ S Ps 42:3
2:18 ᵍ S Isa 26:11; Zec 1:14; 8:2 ʰ S Ps 72:13
2:19 ⁱ Ps 4:7 ʲ S Jer 31:12 ᵏ S Lev 26:5 ˡ S Eze 34:29
2:20 ᵐ Jer 1:14-15 ⁿ Zec 14:8 ᵒ S Isa 34:3
2:21 ᵖ S Isa 29:22; S 54:4; Zep 3:16-17 ᵠ S Ps 9:2 ʳ S Ps 126:3; S Isa 25:1

Do not make your inheritance an
object of scorn,[d]
a byword[e] among the nations.
Why should they say among the
peoples,
'Where is their God?'""

The LORD's Answer

¹⁸Then the LORD will be jealous[g] for his
land
and take pity[h] on his people.

P
F ¹⁹The LORD will reply[g] to them:
"I am sending you grain, new wine[j]
and oil,[j]
enough to satisfy you fully;[k]
never again will I make you
an object of scorn[l] to the nations.

I ²⁰"I will drive the northern army[m] far
from you,
pushing it into a parched and barren
land,
with its front columns going into the
eastern[n] sea[h]
and those in the rear into the
western sea.[i]
And its stench[o] will go up;
its smell will rise."

Surely he has done great things.[j]
²¹   Be not afraid,[p] O land;
be glad and rejoice.[q]
Surely the LORD has done great things.[r]

P Joel 2:1–11 ◀ ▶ Joel 3:1–2
F Hos 13:5–6 ◀ ▶ Joel 2:24–26
I Hos 14:4–8 ◀ ▶ Joel 3:16–18

ᵍ 18,19 Or LORD was jealous . . . / and took pity . . . / ¹⁹The LORD replied ʰ 20 That is, the Dead Sea ⁱ 20 That is, the Mediterranean ʲ 20 Or rise. / Surely it has done great things."

2:15–16 In this passage, Joel called for the sounding of the *chatsotseroth*, the trumpets used in sacred assembly. He urged all of the people to assemble, fast and repent. No one was exempt (see Dt 24:5).

2:17 Joel gave specific instructions to the priests who were to offer prayers of intercession. The location for these prayers "between the temple porch and the altar" was the customary place in the temple for priestly intercession (see 1Ki 8:22; Eze 8:16). Though Joel's words were directed to the priests in his day, this prophecy prefigures the temple that will be rebuilt in the last days in Jerusalem (see Eze 40; 2Th. 2:4).

2:18 Joel's focus shifted from the destruction on the land to the blessings that God will give to those who repent.

2:20 Joel's vision accurately detailed an actual plague of locusts that devastated the land of Judah in his day. When the locusts died, the stench from their dead bodies was horrible. Because Israel's most powerful enemies were located geographically to the north of the promised land, this verse also foreshadows the destruction of the army from the north during the tribulation (see Eze 39:2). God will supernaturally defeat this army of the antichrist at the Battle of Armageddon. The expression "its stench will go up" suggests the magnitude of the devastation that will follow God's judgment. Compare this verse with Rev 19:17–21.

2:21–27 Joel prophesied that God would restore Israel to its place of peace and prosperity in the promised land. The land would produce an agricultural abundance and the people would eat "until

22 Be not afraid, O wild animals,
　　for the open pastures are becoming
　　　　green.ˢ
　　The trees are bearing their fruit;
　　　the fig treeᵗ and the vineᵘ yield
　　　　their riches.ᵛ
²³Be glad, O people of Zion,
　　rejoiceʷ in the LORD your God,
　　for he has given you
　　　the autumn rains in
　　　　righteousness.ᵏˣ
　　He sends you abundant showers,ʸ
　　　both autumnᶻ and spring rains,ᵃ as
　　　　before.
²⁴The threshing floors will be filled with
　　　grain;
　　the vats will overflowᵇ with new
　　　wineᶜ and oil.
²⁵"I will repay you for the years the
　　　locustsᵈ have eatenᵉ—
　　the great locust and the young
　　　locust,
　　the other locusts and the locust
　　　swarmᶠ—
　　my great armyᶠ that I sent among
　　　you.
²⁶You will have plenty to eat, until you
　　are full,ᵍ
　　and you will praiseʰ the name of the
　　　LORD your God,
　　who has worked wondersⁱ for you;
　　never again will my people be
　　　shamed.ʲ
²⁷Then you will knowᵏ that I am in
　　　Israel,
　　that I am the LORDˡ your God,
　　　and that there is no other;
　　never again will my people be
　　　shamed.ᵐ

B Hos 2:21–22 ◀▶ Joel 2:24–26
B Joel 2:22 ◀▶ Hag 2:15–19
F Joel 2:19 ◀▶ Hab 3:17–18
T Jer 1:17 ◀▶ Mal 3:16–17
L Da 9:23 ◀▶ Zec 2:8

2:22 ˢ S Ps 65:12
ᵗ S 1Ki 4:25
ᵘ S Nu 16:14
ᵛ Joel 1:18-20;
Zec 8:12
2:23 ʷ Ps 33:21;
97:12; 149:2;
Isa 12:6; 41:16;
66:14; Hab 3:18;
Zec 10:7
ˣ S Isa 45:8
ʸ S Job 36:28;
S Eze 34:26
ᶻ Ps 84:6
ᵃ S Lev 26:4;
S Ps 135:7; Jas 5:7
2:24 ᵇ Lev 26:10;
Mal 3:10
ᶜ S Pr 3:10;
Joel 3:18; Am 9:13
2:25 ᵈ S Ex 10:14;
Am 4:9 ᵉ S Dt 28:39
ᶠ S Joel 1:6
2:26 ᵍ S Lev 26:5
ʰ S Lev 23:40;
S Isa 62:9
ⁱ S Ps 126:3;
S Isa 25:1
ʲ S Isa 29:22
2:27 ᵏ S Ex 6:7
ˡ S Ex 6:2;
S Isa 44:8; Joel 3:17
ᵐ S Isa 45:17; 54:4;
Zep 3:11
2:28 ⁿ S Isa 11:2;
S 44:3
ᵒ S Nu 11:17;
S Mk 1:8; Gal 3:14
ᵖ S 1Sa 19:20
ᑫ Jer 23:25
2:29 ʳ 1Co 12:13;
Gal 3:28
ˢ S Eze 36:27
2:30 ᵗ Lk 21:11
ᵘ Mk 13:24-25
2:31 ᵛ S ver 2;
S Isa 22:5;
S Jer 4:23;
S Mt 24:29
ʷ S Joel 1:15;
Ob 1:15; Mal 3:2;
4:1,5
2:32 ˣ Ge 4:26;
S Ps 105:1
ʸ S Ps 106:8;
Ac 2:17-21*;
Ro 10:13*
ᶻ S Isa 46:13
ᵃ Ob 1:17
ᵇ S Isa 1:9; 11:11;
Mic 4:7; 7:18;
S Ro 9:27 ᶜ Ac 2:39
3:1 ᵈ S Dt 30:3;
S Jer 16:15;
S Eze 38:8;
Zep 3:20 ᵉ Jer 40:5
3:2 ᶠ Zep 3:8

The Day of the LORD

²⁸"And afterward,
　　I will pour out my Spiritⁿ on all
　　　people.ᵒ
　　Your sons and daughters will
　　　prophesy,ᵖ
　　your old men will dream dreams,ᑫ
　　your young men will see visions.
²⁹Even on my servants,ʳ both men and
　　　women,
　　I will pour out my Spirit in those
　　　days.ˢ
³⁰I will show wonders in the heavensᵗ
　　　and on the earth,ᵘ
　　blood and fire and billows of smoke.
³¹The sun will be turned to darknessᵛ
　　　and the moon to blood
　　before the coming of the great and
　　　dreadful day of the LORD.ʷ
³²And everyone who calls
　　on the name of the LORDˣ will be
　　　saved;ʸ
　　for on Mount Zionᶻ and in Jerusalem
　　　there will be deliverance,ᵃ
　　as the LORD has said,
　　　among the survivors,ᵇ
　　whom the LORD calls.ᶜ

The Nations Judged

3 "In those days and at that time,
　　when I restore the fortunesᵈ of
　　　Judahᵉ and Jerusalem,
²I will gatherᶠ all nations

B Da 6:3 ◀▶ Mic 3:8
G Da 5:14 ◀▶ Mic 3:8
M Da 6:3 ◀▶ Mic 2:7
P Eze 36:26–27 ◀▶ Zec 12:10
T Da 5:14 ◀▶ Mt 10:19–20
H Joel 2:10–11 ◀▶ Joel 3:13–14
K Eze 37:23 ◀▶ Am 5:4
P Joel 2:19–32 ◀▶ Joel 3:9–17
R Joel 1:7 ◀▶ Am 2:1–6

ᵏ 23 Or / the teacher for righteousness; ˡ 25 The precise meaning of the four Hebrew words used here for locusts is uncertain.

---

you are full, and you will praise the name of the LORD" (2:26). Joel also prophesied that God would never desert them again so that "never again will my people be shamed" (2:27).

2:28–29 God promised that in the last days he would "pour out my Spirit on all people" (2:28). The apostle Peter referred to this prophecy at the outpouring of the Holy Spirit on the day of Pentecost (see Ac 2:16–21). This was a partial fulfillment of the final outpouring of God's Spirit on Israel in the last days. This final outpouring of the Holy Spirit will transform the hearts of Israel in preparation to meet their Messiah.

2:30–32 The cosmic events noted here will accompany the day of the Lord. Joel's words are confirmed in Rev 6. As these signs occur in the heavens, the whole world will be aware of the coming judgment and wrath of God. Yet God promised mercy to a remnant of Israel who "calls on the name of the LORD" (2:32; see also Zec 12:10).

3:1–2 God declared that at the time of Israel's final redemption he would bring his people back from

and bring them down to the Valley
  of Jehoshaphat.[m]
There I will enter into judgment[h]
  against them
concerning my inheritance, my
  people Israel,
for they scattered[i] my people among
  the nations
and divided up my land.
³They cast lots[j] for my people
  and traded boys for prostitutes;
they sold girls for wine[k]
  that they might drink.

⁴"Now what have you against me,
O Tyre and Sidon[l] and all you regions of
Philistia?[m] Are you repaying me for something I have done? If you are paying me
back, I will swiftly and speedily return on
your own heads what you have done.[n]
⁵For you took my silver and my gold and
carried off my finest treasures to your
temples.[o] ⁶You sold the people of Judah
and Jerusalem to the Greeks,[p] that you
might send them far from their
homeland.
⁷"See, I am going to rouse them out of
the places to which you sold them,[q] and I
will return[r] on your own heads what you
have done. ⁸I will sell your sons[s] and
daughters to the people of Judah,[t] and
they will sell them to the Sabeans,[u] a nation far away." The LORD has spoken.[v]

⁹Proclaim this among the nations:
  Prepare for war![w]
Rouse the warriors![x]
  Let all the fighting men draw near
    and attack.
¹⁰Beat your plowshares into swords
  and your pruning hooks[y] into
    spears.[z]

Let the weakling[a] say,
  "I am strong!"[b]
¹¹Come quickly, all you nations from
    every side,
  and assemble[c] there.

Bring down your warriors,[d] O LORD!

¹²"Let the nations be roused;
  let them advance into the Valley of
    Jehoshaphat,[e]
for there I will sit
  to judge[f] all the nations on every
    side.
¹³Swing the sickle,[g]
  for the harvest[h] is ripe.
Come, trample the grapes,[i]
  for the winepress[j] is full
  and the vats overflow—
so great is their wickedness!"

¹⁴Multitudes,[k] multitudes
  in the valley[l] of decision!
For the day of the LORD[m] is near
  in the valley of decision.[n]
¹⁵The sun and moon will be darkened,
  and the stars no longer shine.[o]
¹⁶The LORD will roar[p] from Zion
  and thunder from Jerusalem;[q]
  the earth and the sky will tremble.[r]
But the LORD will be a refuge[s] for his
    people,
  a stronghold[t] for the people of
    Israel.

Blessings for God's People

¹⁷"Then you will know[u] that I, the LORD
    your God,[v]

H *Joel 2:31* ◄ ► *Am 2:14–16*
N *Hos 4:17* ◄ ► *Am 4:12*
I *Joel 2:21* ◄ ► *Joel 3:20–21*

3:2 ᵍ ver 12; S Isa 22:1
ʰ S Isa 13:9; S Jer 2:35; S Eze 36:5
ⁱ S Ge 11:4; S Lev 26:33
ʲ S Job 6:27; S Eze 24:6
ᵏ Joel 1:5; Am 2:6
3:4 ˡ S Ge 10:15; S Mt 11:21
ᵐ S Ps 87:4; Isa 14:29-31; Jer 47:1-7
ⁿ S Lev 26:28; S Isa 34:8; S Eze 25:15-17; Zec 9:5-7
3:5 ᵒ S 1Ki 15:18; S 2Ch 21:16-17
3:6 ᵖ Eze 27:13; Zec 9:13
3:7 ᵠ S Isa 43:5-6; Jer 23:8 ʳ S Isa 66:6
3:8 ˢ Isa 60:14
ᵗ Isa 14:2
ᵘ S Ge 10:7; S 2Ch 9:1
ᵛ S Isa 23:1;
S Jer 30:16
3:9 ʷ S Isa 8:9
ˣ Jer 46:4
3:10 ʸ Isa 2:4
ᶻ Nu 25:7
ᵃ Zec 12:8
ᵇ S Jos 1:6
3:11 ᶜ Eze 38:15-16; Zep 3:8 ᵈ S Isa 13:3
3:12 ᵉ S ver 2
ᶠ S Ps 82:1; S Isa 2:4
3:13 ᵍ S Mk 4:29
ʰ S Isa 17:5;
S Hos 6:11; Mt 13:39; Rev 14:15-19
ⁱ S Jer 25:30
ʲ S Jdg 6:11; S Rev 14:20
3:14 ᵏ Isa 13:4
ˡ S Isa 22:1
ᵐ Isa 34:2-8; S Joel 1:15; S Zep 1:7
ⁿ S Isa 2:4; S Eze 36:5
3:15 ᵒ S Job 9:7; S Eze 32:7
3:16 ᵖ S Isa 42:13
ᵠ Am 1:2 ʳ S Jdg 5:4; S Isa 14:16;
S Ps 46:1;
S Isa 25:4; Zec 12:8
ᵗ S 2Sa 22:3;
Jer 16:19; Zec 9:12 **3:17** ᵘ S Ex 6:7 ᵛ S Joel 2:27

ᵐ 2 *Jehoshaphat* means *the* LORD *judges*; also in verse 12.

M *Hos 3:5* ◄ ► *Joel 3:18–20*
P *Joel 3:1–2* ◄ ► *Am 1:2–15*

---

captivity and judge the nations who had gathered against Jerusalem. This judgment would take place in the Valley of Jehoshaphat. Note that this valley near Jerusalem was the site of one of the Lord's historic victories over the nations during the reign of King Jehoshaphat (see 2Ch 20:1–30).

3:9–16 Joel prophetically proclaimed God's command to the Gentiles to prepare for war, for God would bring his heavenly army against them and bring them into judgment (see Eze 38—39; Rev 19). Despite all of the talk about peace, God promised their sure destruction (see 1Th 5:3). Joel called the location of this climactic battle as "the valley of decision" (3:14). Note the parallel prophecy in Isa 34:2–8 and Am 1:2.

3:17–18 This prophecy will be fulfilled when Jesus rules from Jerusalem and establishes his Messianic kingdom. Compare with 2:27; Ps 46:4; Rev 21:3. Though strangers have ruled Jerusalem for centuries, the city will be freed from her captors and filled with God's abiding presence. Only then will Jerusalem be holy and invincible. Streams of blessing will flow from God's presence, refreshing his people. The land will no longer be barren, but well-watered and lush.

dwell in Zion,ʷ my holy hill.ˣ
Jerusalem will be holy;ʸ
    never again will foreigners invade
        her.ᶻ

¹⁸"In that day the mountains will drip
        new wine,ᵃ
    and the hills will flow with milk;ᵇ
    all the ravines of Judah will run with
        water.ᶜ
    A fountain will flow out of the LORD's
        house ᵈ
    and will water the valley of
        acacias.ⁿ ᵉ
¹⁹But Egypt ᶠ will be desolate,
    Edom ᵍ a desert waste,
        because of violence ʰ done to the
            people of Judah,
        in whose land they shed innocent
            blood.
²⁰Judah will be inhabited forever ⁱ
    and Jerusalem through all
        generations.
²¹Their bloodguilt,ʲ which I have not
        pardoned,
    I will pardon.ᵏ"

The LORD dwells in Zion! ˡ

▌Joel 3:4 ◀▶ Mic 4:3–4

3:17 ʷS Ps 74:2;
S Isa 4:3 ˣ Ps 2:6;
S Isa 2:2;
S Eze 17:22
ʸS Jer 31:40
ᶻS Isa 52:1;
S Eze 44:9; Zec 9:8
3:18 ᵃS Joel 2:24
ᵇEx 3:8; S SS 5:1
ᶜS Isa 30:25; 35:6;
S 44:3 ᵈRev 22:1-2
ᵉS Nu 25:1;
S Isa 25:6;
S Jer 31:12;
S Eze 47:1;
Am 9:13
3:19 ᶠS Isa 19:1
ᵍS Isa 11:14;
S 34:11
ʰS Jer 51:35;
Ob 1:10
3:20 ⁱS Ezr 9:12;
Am 9:15
3:21 ʲS Isa 1:15
ᵏS Eze 36:25
ˡS Ps 74:2;

▌Joel 3:16–18 ◀▶ Am 9:11–15

Isa 59:20; S Eze 48:35; Zec 8:3

ⁿ 18 Or *Valley of Shittim*

Note the parallels between this passage and Zec 13:1 as well as Ezekiel's prediction of the millennial kingdom (see Eze 47:1–8).

3:19 Joel prophesied judgment against Egypt and Edom because of their violence against God's people.

3:20–21 Joel's prophecy ends on an encouraging note: God promises that Judah and Jerusalem will dwell in peace forever under the rule of the Messiah.

Amos

Author: Amos

Theme: God will judge injustice

Date of Writing: c. 760–750 B.C.

Outline of Amos
  I. The Nations Denounced (1:1—2:5)
  II. Israel's Guilt (2:6—6:14)
  III. Five Visions of Divine Retribution (7:1—9:10)
  IV. The Promise of Restoration (9:11–15)

Amos was a shepherd or herdsman from Tekoa, a village southeast of Bethlehem, in Judah. Though he lived in the kingdom of Judah, Amos delivered God's messages to the northern kingdom of Israel, warning rulers and people alike of the danger of spiritual apathy and social injustice. Prophesying during the reigns of King Jeroboam II of Israel and King Uzziah of Judah, Amos urged the leaders to return to God and enforce justice or suffer the coming judgment of God.

Both Israel and Judah enjoyed a period of peace and prosperity during Amos's day that was marked by widespread social corruption, idolatry, injustice and rampant materialism. God was repulsed by these attitudes and actions among his people and sent Amos to warn this self-satisfied generation of impending judgment. Israel had neglected God's Word, and Amos promised that God would punish Israel if they did not "hate evil, love good; maintain justice in the courts" (5:15). Yet Amos also prophesied the future reestablishment of the kingdom of David under the rule of the Messiah.

AMOS 1:1

1 The words of Amos, one of the shepherds of Tekoa[a]—what he saw concerning Israel two years before the earthquake,[b] when Uzziah[c] was king of Judah and Jeroboam[d] son of Jehoash[a] was king of Israel.[e]

² He said:

"The LORD roars[f] from Zion
    and thunders[g] from Jerusalem;[h]
the pastures of the shepherds dry up,[b]
    and the top of Carmel[i] withers."[j]

Judgment on Israel's Neighbors

³ This is what the LORD says:

"For three sins of Damascus,[k]
    even for four, I will not turn back
    ⌊my wrath⌋.[l]
Because she threshed Gilead
    with sledges having iron teeth,
⁴ I will send fire[m] upon the house of
        Hazael[n]
    that will consume the fortresses[o] of
        Ben-Hadad.[p]
⁵ I will break down the gate[q] of
        Damascus;
    I will destroy the king who is in[c] the
        Valley of Aven[d]
and the one who holds the scepter in
        Beth Eden.[r]
The people of Aram will go into
        exile to Kir,[s]"
                            says the LORD.[t]

⁶ This is what the LORD says:

"For three sins of Gaza,[u]
    even for four, I will not turn back
    ⌊my wrath⌋.[v]
Because she took captive whole
        communities
    and sold them to Edom,[w]
⁷ I will send fire upon the walls of Gaza
    that will consume her fortresses.
⁸ I will destroy the king[e] of Ashdod[x]
    and the one who holds the scepter
        in Ashkelon.
I will turn my hand[y] against Ekron,

till the last of the Philistines[z] is
        dead,"[a]
            says the Sovereign LORD.[b]

⁹ This is what the LORD says:

"For three sins of Tyre,[c]
    even for four, I will not turn back
    ⌊my wrath⌋.[d]
Because she sold whole communities
        of captives to Edom,
    disregarding a treaty of
        brotherhood,[e]
¹⁰ I will send fire upon the walls of Tyre
    that will consume her fortresses.[f]"

¹¹ This is what the LORD says:

"For three sins of Edom,[g]
    even for four, I will not turn back
    ⌊my wrath⌋.
Because he pursued his brother with a
        sword,[h]
    stifling all compassion,[f]
because his anger raged continually
    and his fury flamed unchecked,[i]
¹² I will send fire upon Teman[j]
    that will consume the fortresses of
        Bozrah.[k]"

¹³ This is what the LORD says:

"For three sins of Ammon,[l]
    even for four, I will not turn back
    ⌊my wrath⌋.
Because he ripped open the pregnant
        women[m] of Gilead
    in order to extend his borders,
¹⁴ I will set fire to the walls of Rabbah[n]
    that will consume[o] her fortresses
    amid war cries[p] on the day of battle,
    amid violent winds[q] on a stormy
        day.
¹⁵ Her king[g] will go into exile,
    he and his officials together,[r]"
                            says the LORD.[s]

---

a 1 Hebrew *Joash*, a variant of *Jehoash*   b 2 Or *shepherds mourn*   c 5 Or *the inhabitants of*   d 5 *Aven* means *wickedness*.   e 8 Or *inhabitants*   f 11 Or *sword / and destroyed his allies*   g 15 Or / *Molech*; Hebrew *malcam*

P *Joel 3:9–17* ◀ ▶ *Ob 1–10*

1:2 Note the parallel between this verse and Joel 3:16.
1:3–5 Amos prophesied the coming judgment upon Damascus, the ancient capital of Syria, for repeated acts of rebellion. Isaiah had also prophesied the final destruction of Damascus (see Isa 17:1, 3).

1:6–7 Amos declared that the ancient Philistine city of Gaza would be consumed by fire because of God's judgment.
1:9–10 Despite Tyre's economic prosperity and virtual inaccessibility on a rocky island, Amos pronounced God's judgment on this boastful city.

2 This is what the LORD says:

"For three sins of Moab,
    even for four, I will not turn back
        my wrath.
Because he burned, as if to lime,
    the bones of Edom's king,
²I will send fire upon Moab
    that will consume the fortresses of
        Kerioth.
Moab will go down in great tumult
    amid war cries and the blast of the
        trumpet.
³I will destroy her ruler
    and kill all her officials with him,"
        says the LORD.

⁴This is what the LORD says:

"For three sins of Judah,
    even for four, I will not turn back
        my wrath.
Because they have rejected the law of
        the LORD
    and have not kept his decrees,
because they have been led astray by
        false gods,
    the gods their ancestors followed,
⁵I will send fire upon Judah
    that will consume the fortresses of
        Jerusalem."

Judgment on Israel

⁶This is what the LORD says:

"For three sins of Israel,
    even for four, I will not turn back
        my wrath.
They sell the righteous for silver,
    and the needy for a pair of sandals.
⁷They trample on the heads of the poor
    as upon the dust of the ground
    and deny justice to the oppressed.
Father and son use the same girl
    and so profane my holy name.
⁸They lie down beside every altar
    on garments taken in pledge.
In the house of their god
    they drink wine taken as fines.

⁹"I destroyed the Amorite before
        them,
    though he was tall as the cedars
    and strong as the oaks.
I destroyed his fruit above
    and his roots below.

¹⁰"I brought you up out of Egypt,
    and I led you forty years in the
        desert
    to give you the land of the
        Amorites.
¹¹I also raised up prophets from among
        your sons
    and Nazirites from among your
        young men.
    Is this not true, people of Israel?"
        declares the LORD.
¹²"But you made the Nazirites drink
        wine
    and commanded the prophets not to
        prophesy.

¹³"Now then, I will crush you
    as a cart crushes when loaded with
        grain.
¹⁴The swift will not escape,
    the strong will not muster their
        strength,
    and the warrior will not save his
        life.
¹⁵The archer will not stand his ground,
    the fleet-footed soldier will not get
        away,
    and the horseman will not save his
        life.
¹⁶Even the bravest warriors
    will flee naked on that day,"
        declares the LORD.

Witnesses Summoned Against Israel

3 Hear this word the LORD has spoken against you, O people of Israel—against the whole family I brought up out of Egypt:

²"You only have I chosen
    of all the families of the earth;
therefore I will punish you
    for all your sins."

³Do two walk together
    unless they have agreed to do so?
⁴Does a lion roar in the thicket
    when he has no prey?
Does he growl in his den
    when he has caught nothing?
⁵Does a bird fall into a trap on the
        ground
    where no snare has been set?
Does a trap spring up from the earth

h 2 Or of her cities   i 4 Or by lies   j 4 Or lies

when there is nothing to catch?
⁶When a trumpet⁽ʳ⁾ sounds in a city,
  do not the people tremble?
When disaster⁽ˢ⁾ comes to a city,
  has not the LORD caused it?⁽ᵗ⁾

⁷Surely the Sovereign LORD does nothing
  without revealing his plan⁽ᵘ⁾
  to his servants the prophets.⁽ᵛ⁾

⁸The lion⁽ʷ⁾ has roared⁽ˣ⁾—
  who will not fear?
The Sovereign LORD has spoken—
  who can but prophesy?⁽ʸ⁾

⁹Proclaim to the fortresses of Ashdod⁽ᶻ⁾
  and to the fortresses of Egypt:
"Assemble yourselves on the
    mountains of Samaria;⁽ᵃ⁾
  see the great unrest within her
  and the oppression among her
    people."

¹⁰"They do not know how to do right,⁽ᵇ⁾
    declares the LORD,
  "who hoard plunder⁽ᶜ⁾ and loot in
    their fortresses."⁽ᵈ⁾

¹¹Therefore this is what the Sovereign
LORD says:

"An enemy will overrun the land;
  he will pull down your strongholds
  and plunder your fortresses."⁽ᵉ⁾

¹²This is what the LORD says:

"As a shepherd saves from the lion's⁽ᶠ⁾
    mouth
  only two leg bones or a piece of an
    ear,
so will the Israelites be saved,
  those who sit in Samaria
  on the edge of their beds
  and in Damascus on their
    couches.⁽ᵏᵍ⁾"

¹³"Hear this and testify⁽ʰ⁾ against the
house of Jacob," declares the Lord, the
LORD God Almighty.

¹⁴"On the day I punish⁽ⁱ⁾ Israel for her
    sins,
  I will destroy the altars of Bethel;⁽ʲ⁾
  the horns⁽ᵏ⁾ of the altar will be cut off
  and fall to the ground.
¹⁵I will tear down the winter house⁽ˡ⁾

along with the summer house;⁽ᵐ⁾
the houses adorned with ivory⁽ⁿ⁾ will be
  destroyed
and the mansions⁽ᵒ⁾ will be
  demolished,⁽ᵖ⁾"
        declares the LORD.⁽ᑫ⁾

Israel Has Not Returned to God

4 Hear this word, you cows of Bashan⁽ʳ⁾
  on Mount Samaria,⁽ˢ⁾
you women who oppress the poor⁽ᵗ⁾
  and crush the needy⁽ᵘ⁾
and say to your husbands,⁽ᵛ⁾ "Bring us
  some drinks!⁽ʷ⁾"

²The Sovereign LORD has sworn by his
  holiness:
"The time⁽ˣ⁾ will surely come
  when you will be taken away⁽ʸ⁾ with
    hooks,⁽ᶻ⁾
  the last of you with fishhooks.
³You will each go straight out
  through breaks in the wall,⁽ᵃ⁾
  and you will be cast out toward
    Harmon,⁽ˡ⁾"
        declares the LORD.

⁴"Go to Bethel⁽ᵇ⁾ and sin;
  go to Gilgal⁽ᶜ⁾ and sin yet more.
Bring your sacrifices every morning,⁽ᵈ⁾
  your tithes⁽ᵉ⁾ every three years.⁽ᵐᶠ⁾
⁵Burn leavened bread⁽ᵍ⁾ as a thank
    offering
  and brag about your freewill
    offerings⁽ʰ⁾—
boast about them, you Israelites,
  for this is what you love to do,"
        declares the Sovereign LORD.

⁶"I gave you empty stomachs⁽ⁿ⁾ in every
    city
  and lack of bread in every town,
yet you have not returned to me,"
        declares the LORD.⁽ⁱ⁾

⁷"I also withheld⁽ʲ⁾ rain from you
  when the harvest was still three
    months away.
I sent rain on one town,
  but withheld it from another.⁽ᵏ⁾
One field had rain;

k 12 The meaning of the Hebrew for this line is uncertain. *l 3* Masoretic Text; with a different word division of the Hebrew (see Septuagint) *out, O mountain of oppression* *m 4* Or *tithes on the third day* *n 6* Hebrew *you cleanness of teeth*

3:7 Amos declared that God had warned the people through his prophets of his intentions, yet the people refused to listen and told the prophets to be quiet (see 2:12). Even today God desires to reveal his prophetic truth to those who seek to understand his Word.

another had none and dried up.
⁸People staggered from town to town
    for water
    but did not get enough to drink,
    yet you have not returned to me,"
        declares the LORD.

⁹"Many times I struck your gardens and
    vineyards,
    I struck them with blight and
        mildew.
    Locusts devoured your fig and olive
        trees,
    yet you have not returned to me,"
        declares the LORD.

¹⁰"I sent plagues among you
    as I did to Egypt.
    I killed your young men with the
        sword,
    along with your captured horses.
    I filled your nostrils with the stench
        of your camps,
    yet you have not returned to me,"
        declares the LORD.

¹¹"I overthrew some of you
    as I overthrew Sodom and
        Gomorrah.
    You were like a burning stick
        snatched from the fire,
    yet you have not returned to me,"
        declares the LORD.

¹²"Therefore this is what I will do to
    you, Israel,
    and because I will do this to you,
    prepare to meet your God, O Israel."

¹³He who forms the mountains,
    creates the wind,
    and reveals his thoughts to man,
    he who turns dawn to darkness,
    and treads the high places of the
        earth—
    the LORD God Almighty is his name.

A Lament and Call to Repentance

5 Hear this word, O house of Israel,
    this lament I take up concerning
    you:

²"Fallen is Virgin Israel,
    never to rise again,
    deserted in her own land,
    with no one to lift her up."

³This is what the Sovereign LORD says:

"The city that marches out a thousand
    strong for Israel
    will have only a hundred left;
    the town that marches out a hundred
        strong
    will have only ten left."

⁴This is what the LORD says to the
house of Israel:

"Seek me and live;
⁵ do not seek Bethel,
    do not go to Gilgal,
    do not journey to Beersheba.
    For Gilgal will surely go into exile,
    and Bethel will be reduced to
        nothing."

⁶Seek the LORD and live,
    or he will sweep through the house
        of Joseph like a fire;
    it will devour,
    and Bethel will have no one to
        quench it.

⁷You who turn justice into bitterness
    and cast righteousness to the
        ground

⁸(he who made the Pleiades and
    Orion,
    who turns blackness into dawn
    and darkens day into night,
    who calls for the waters of the sea
    and pours them out over the face of
        the land—
    the LORD is his name—
⁹he flashes destruction on the
    stronghold
    and brings the fortified city to
        ruin),

¹⁰you hate the one who reproves in
    court
    and despise him who tells the
        truth.

¹¹You trample on the poor
    and force him to give you grain.
    Therefore, though you have built stone
        mansions,
    you will not live in them;

K *Joel 2:32* ◄ ► *Am 5:6*
P *Joel 2:12–13* ◄ ► *Mic 7:18–19*
K *Am 5:4* ◄ ► *Ob 17*
C *Hos 13:3* ◄ ► *Am 6:12*

o 11 Hebrew *God* *p 5* Or *grief;* or *wickedness;* Hebrew *aven,* a reference to Beth Aven (a derogatory name for Bethel)

H *Am 2:14–16* ◄ ► *Am 5:16–20*
J *Da 7:9–10* ◄ ► *Mt 7:1–2*
N *Joel 3:14* ◄ ► *Zec 1:4–5*

though you have planted lush
vineyards,
you will not drink their wine.ⁱ
¹²For I know how many are your
offenses
and how great your sins.ʲ

You oppress the righteous and take
bribesᵏ
and you deprive the poorˡ of justice
in the courts.ᵐ
¹³Therefore the prudent man keeps
quietⁿ in such times,
for the times are evil.ᵒ

¹⁴Seek good, not evil,
that you may live.ᵖ
Then the LORD God Almighty will be
with you,
just as you say he is.
¹⁵Hate evil,ᑫ love good;ʳ
maintain justice in the courts.ˢ
Perhapsᵗ the LORD God Almighty will
have mercyᵘ
on the remnantᵛ of Joseph.

¹⁶Therefore this is what the Lord, the
LORD God Almighty, says:

"There will be wailingʷ in all the
streetsˣ
and cries of anguish in every public
square.
The farmersʸ will be summoned to
weep
and the mourners to wail.
¹⁷There will be wailingᶻ in all the
vineyards,
for I will pass throughᵃ your midst,"
says the LORD.ᵇ

The Day of the LORD

¹⁸Woe to you who long
for the day of the LORD!ᶜ
Why do you long for the day of the
LORD?ᵈ
That day will be darkness,ᵉ not
light.ᶠ
¹⁹It will be as though a man fled from a
lion
only to meet a bear,ᵍ
as though he entered his house
and rested his hand on the wall
only to have a snake bite him.ʰ
²⁰Will not the day of the LORD be
darkness,ⁱ not light—

pitch-dark, without a ray of
brightness?ʲ

²¹"I hate,ᵏ I despise your religious
feasts;ˡ
I cannot stand your assemblies.ᵐ
²²Even though you bring me burnt
offeringsⁿ and grain offerings,
I will not accept them.ᵒᵖ
Though you bring choice fellowship
offerings,ᑫ
I will have no regard for them.ᑫʳ
²³Away with the noise of your songs!
I will not listen to the music of your
harps.ˢ
²⁴But let justiceᵗ roll on like a river,
righteousnessᵘ like a never-failing
stream!ᵛ

²⁵"Did you bring me sacrificesʷ and
offerings
forty yearsˣ in the desert, O house
of Israel?
²⁶You have lifted up the shrine of your
king,
the pedestal of your idols,ʸ
the star of your godʳ—
which you made for yourselves.
²⁷Therefore I will send you into exileᶻ
beyond Damascus,"
says the LORD, whose name is God
Almighty.ᵃ

Woe to the Complacent

6 Woe to youᵇ who are complacentᶜ
in Zion,
and to you who feel secureᵈ on
Mount Samaria,ᵉ
you notable men of the foremost
nation,
to whom the people of Israel come!ᶠ
²Go to Calnehᵍ and look at it;
go from there to great Hamath,ʰ
and then go down to Gathⁱ in
Philistia.
Are they better off thanʲ your two
kingdoms?
Is their land larger than yours?
³You put off the evil day
and bring near a reign of terror.ᵏ
⁴You lie on beds inlaid with ivory
and lounge on your couches.ˡ
You dine on choice lambs

and fattened calves.ᵐ
⁵You strum away on your harpsⁿ like David
 and improvise on musical instruments.ᵒ
⁶You drink wineᵖ by the bowlful
 and use the finest lotions,
but you do not grieveᵠ over the ruin of Joseph.ʳ
⁷Therefore you will be among the first to go into exile;ˢ
 your feasting and lounging will end.ᵗ

The LORD Abhors the Pride of Israel

⁸The Sovereign LORD has sworn by himself ᵘ—the LORD God Almighty declares:

"I abhorᵛ the pride of Jacobʷ
 and detest his fortresses;ˣ
I will deliver upʸ the city
 and everything in it.ᶻ"

⁹If tenᵃ men are left in one house, they too will die. ¹⁰And if a relative who is to burn the bodiesᵇ comes to carry them out of the house and asks anyone still hiding there, "Is anyone with you?" and he says, "No," then he will say, "Hush!ᶜ We must not mention the name of the LORD."

¹¹For the LORD has given the command,
 and he will smashᵈ the great houseᵉ into pieces
 and the small house into bits.ᶠ

C ¹²Do horses run on the rocky crags?
S Does one plow there with oxen?
  But you have turned justice into poisonᵍ
  and the fruit of righteousnessʰ into bitternessⁱ—

¹³you who rejoice in the conquest of Lo Debarˢ
 and say, "Did we not take Karnaimᵗ by our own strength?"

¹⁴For the LORD God Almighty declares,
 "I will stir up a nationᵏ against you,
  O house of Israel,
 that will oppress you all the way
  from Leboᵘ Hamathⁱ to the valley of the Arabah.ᵐ"

C Am 5:7 ◀▶ Hab 2:4
S Am 3:3 ◀▶ Ob 17

6:4 ᵐ S Isa 1:11; S Eze 34:2-3; S Am 3:12
6:5 ⁿ S Ps 137:2; S Isa 14:11; Am 5:23
 ᵒ S 1Ch 15:16
6:6 ᵖ S Isa 28:1; S Am 2:8
 ᵠ S Eze 9:4
 ʳ S Eze 16:49
6:7 ˢ S Am 5:27
 ᵗ S Jer 16:9; S La 4:5
6:8 ᵘ S Ge 22:16; Heb 6:13
 ᵛ S Lev 26:30
 ʷ S Ps 47:4
 ˣ Am 4:2
 ʸ S Lev 26:19; Dt 32:19
6:9 ᵃ S Am 5:3
6:10 ᵇ S Isa 31:12
 ᶜ Am 8:3
6:11 ᵈ S Isa 34:5
 ᵉ S Am 3:15
 ᶠ Isa 55:11
6:12 ᵍ S Hos 10:4
 ʰ S Am 3:10
 ⁱ S Isa 1:21; S Am 5:7
6:13 ʲ S Job 8:15; Isa 28:14-15
6:14 ᵏ Jer 5:15
 ˡ S Nu 13:21
 ᵐ S Am 3:11
7:1 ⁿ ver 7; Am 8:1
 ᵒ Ps 78:46; S Jer 51:14; S Joel 1:4
7:2 ᵖ S Ex 10:15
 ᵠ S Isa 37:4
 ʳ S Eze 11:13; S Am 4:9
7:3 ˢ S Ex 32:14; Dt 32:36; S Jer 18:8; 26:19
 ᵗ S Hos 11:8
7:4 ᵘ S Isa 66:16; S Joel 1:19
 ᵛ Dt 32:22
7:5 ʷ S ver 1-2; Joel 2:17
7:6 ˣ S Ex 32:14; S Jer 18:8; Jnh 3:10
 ʸ Jer 42:10; S Ge 9:8
7:8 ᶻ Jer 1:11,13
 ᵃ Am 8:2
 ᵇ S Jer 21:13
 ᶜ S Jer 15:6; Eze 7:2-9
7:9 ᵈ S Lev 26:30
 ᵉ S Lev 26:31
 ᶠ S 1Ki 13:34; 2Ki 15:9; Isa 43:15; S Hos 10:8
7:10 ᵍ S Jos 7:2
 ʰ S 2Ki 14:23
 ⁱ Jer 38:4
 ʲ 2Ki 14:24; Jer 26:8-11

Locusts, Fire and a Plumb Line

7 This is what the Sovereign LORD showed me:ⁿ He was preparing swarms of locustsᵒ after the king's share had been harvested and just as the second crop was coming up. ²When they had stripped the land clean,ᵖ I cried out, "Sovereign LORD, forgive! How can Jacob survive?ᵠ He is so small!ʳ"

³So the LORD relented.ˢ

"This will not happen," the LORD said.ᵗ

⁴This is what the Sovereign LORD showed me: The Sovereign LORD was calling for judgment by fire;ᵘ it dried up the great deep and devouredᵛ the land. ⁵Then I cried out, "Sovereign LORD, I beg you, stop! How can Jacob survive? He is so small!ʷ"

⁶So the LORD relented.ˣ

"This will not happen either," the Sovereign LORD said.ʸ

⁷This is what he showed me: The Lord was standing by a wall that had been built true to plumb, with a plumb line in his hand. ⁸And the LORD asked me, "What do you see,ᶻ Amos?ᵃ"

"A plumb line,ᵇ" I replied.

Then the Lord said, "Look, I am setting a plumb line among my people Israel; I will spare them no longer.ᶜ

⁹"The high placesᵈ of Isaac will be destroyed
 and the sanctuariesᵉ of Israel will be ruined;
 with my sword I will rise against the house of Jeroboam.ᶠ" **R**

Amos and Amaziah

¹⁰Then Amaziah the priest of Bethelᵍ sent a message to Jeroboamʰ king of Israel: "Amos is raising a conspiracyⁱ against you in the very heart of Israel. The land cannot bear all his words.ʲ ¹¹For this is what Amos is saying:

" 'Jeroboam will die by the sword,

R Am 2:1-6 ◀▶ Am 7:16-17

ˢ 13 *Lo Debar* means nothing. ᵗ 13 *Karnaim* means *horns; horn* here symbolizes strength. ᵘ 14 Or *from the entrance to*

7:9 Amos prophesied that the centers of religious and self-righteous pride would be destroyed. Note that while Amos's words in the previous chapters were spoken to Israel's leadership as a whole, this verse is directed to one man, King Jeroboam.

and Israel will surely go into exile,ᵏ away from their native land.'"¹

¹²Then Amaziah said to Amos, "Get out, you seer!ᵐ Go back to the land of Judah. Earn your bread there and do your prophesying there.ⁿ ¹³Don't prophesy anymore at Bethel,ᵒ because this is the king's sanctuary and the templeᵖ of the kingdom.ᵠ"

¹⁴Amos answered Amaziah, "I was neither a prophetʳ nor a prophet's son, but I was a shepherd, and I also took care of sycamore-fig trees.ˢ ¹⁵But the LORD took me from tending the flockᵗ and said to me, 'Go,ᵘ prophesyᵛ to my people Israel.'ʷ ¹⁶Now then, hearˣ the word of the LORD. You say,

" 'Do not prophesy againstʸ Israel,
    and stop preaching against the
        house of Isaac.'

¹⁷"Therefore this is what the LORD says:

" 'Your wife will become a prostituteᶻ
    in the city,
and your sons and daughters will fall
    by the sword.
Your land will be measured and
    divided up,
and you yourself will die in a pagan
    country.
And Israel will certainly go into exile,ᵃ
    away from their native land.ᵇ' "

A Basket of Ripe Fruit

8 This is what the Sovereign LORD showed me:ᶜ a basket of ripe fruit. ²"What do you see,ᵈ Amos?ᵉ" he asked.
"A basketᶠ of ripe fruit," I answered.
Then the LORD said to me, "The time is ripe for my people Israel; I will spare them no longer.ᵍ

³"In that day," declares the Sovereign LORD, "the songs in the temple will turn to wailing.ʷʰ Many, many bodies—flung everywhere! Silence!¹"

⁴Hear this, you who trample the needy
    and do away with the poorʲ of the
        land,ᵏ

R *Am 7:9 ◀ ▶ Am 8:2*
R *Am 7:16–17 ◀ ▶ Am 9:5*

7:11 ᵏS Am 5:27
 ˡJer 36:16
7:12 ᵐS 1Sa 9:9
 ⁿMt 8:34
7:13 ᵒS Jos 7:2;
 S 1Ki 12:29
 ᵖJer 36:5
 ᵠS Jer 20:2;
 S Am 2:12; Ac 4:18
7:14 ʳS 1Sa 10:5;
 2Ki 2:5; 4:38;
 Zec 13:5
 ˢS 1Ki 10:27;
 S Isa 9:10
7:15 ᵗS Ge 37:2;
 S 2Sa 7:8 ᵘS Isa 6:9
 ᵛS Jer 26:12
 ʷJer 7:1-2;
 S Eze 2:3-4
7:16 ˣS Jer 22:2
 ʸS Eze 20:46;
 Mic 2:6
7:17 ᶻS Hos 4:13
 ᵃS Am 5:27
 ᵇS 2Ki 17:6;
 S Eze 4:13;
 S Hos 9:3;
 Am 2:12-13
8:1 ᶜS Am 7:1
8:2 ᵈJer 1:13; 24:3
 ᵉAm 7:8
 ᶠS Ge 40:16
 ᵍS La 4:18;
 Eze 7:2-9
8:3 ʰS Am 5:16
 ⁱAm 6:10
8:4 ʲS Pr 30:14
 ᵏS Job 20:19;
 S Ps 14:3; S Am 2:7
8:5 ˡS Nu 10:10
 ᵐIsa 58:13
 ⁿS Ne 10:31
 ᵒS Ge 31:7
 ᵖDt 25:15;
 2Ki 4:23;
 Ne 13:15-16;
 Eze 45:10-12;
 S Hos 12:7;
 Mic 6:10-11;
 Zec 5:6
8:6 ᵠAm 5:11
 ʳS Am 2:6; S 4:1
8:7 ˢS Ps 47:4
 ᵗS Hos 8:13
 ᵘS Job 35:15
8:8 ᵛS Job 9:6;
 Jer 51:29 ʷS Ps 18:7;
 S Jer 46:8; Am 9:5
8:9 ˣS Job 5:14;
 Isa 59:9-10;
 Jer 13:16; 15:9;
 S Eze 32:7;
 S Am 5:8; Mic 3:6;
 Mt 27:45;
 Mk 15:33;
 Lk 23:44-45
8:10 ʸS Lev 26:31
 ᶻS La 5:15;
 S Hos 2:11
 ᵃS Joel 1:8
 ᵇS Lev 13:40;
 S Isa 3:17
 ᶜS Ge 21:16
 ᵈS Jer 2:19;
 S Eze 7:18
8:11 ᵉJer 30:3;
 31:27 ᶠS Isa 30:20
 ᵍS 1Sa 3:1; S 28:6;
 S 2Ch 15:3

⁵saying,

"When will the New Moon¹ be over
    that we may sell grain,
and the Sabbath be ended
    that we may marketᵐ wheat?"ⁿ—
skimping the measure,
    boosting the price
    and cheatingᵒ with dishonest
        scales,ᵖ
⁶buying the poorᵠ with silver
    and the needy for a pair of sandals,
    selling even the sweepings with the
        wheat.ʳ

⁷The LORD has sworn by the Pride of Jacob:ˢ "I will never forgetᵗ anything they have done.ᵘ

⁸"Will not the land trembleᵛ for this,
    and all who live in it mourn?
The whole land will rise like the Nile;
    it will be stirred up and then sink
        like the river of Egypt.ʷ

⁹"In that day," declares the Sovereign LORD,

"I will make the sun go down at noon
    and darken the earth in broad
        daylight.ˣ
¹⁰I will turn your religious feastsʸ into
    mourning
    and all your singing into weeping.ᶻ
I will make all of you wear sackclothᵃ
    and shaveᵇ your heads.
I will make that time like mourning for
    an only sonᶜ
    and the end of it like a bitter day.ᵈ

¹¹"The days are coming,"ᵉ declares the
    Sovereign LORD,
"when I will send a famine through
    the land—
not a famine of food or a thirst for
    water,
but a famineᶠ of hearing the words
    of the LORD.ᵍ
¹²Men will stagger from sea to sea
    and wander from north to east,

E *Hos 7:2 ◀ ▶ Zec 4:10*
H *Am 5:16–20 ◀ ▶ Am 9:1–4*

ᵛ17 Hebrew *an unclean*   ʷ3 Or *"the temple singers will wail*

8:2 Ripe fruit must be eaten quickly; its shelf life is short. This metaphor indicated that Israel's judgment would come soon.

searching for the word of the LORD,
but they will not find it.ʰ

¹³"In that day

"the lovely young women and strong
young menⁱ
will faint because of thirst.ʲ
¹⁴They who swear by the shameˣ of
Samaria,ᵏ
or say, 'As surely as your god lives,
O Dan,'ˡ
or, 'As surely as the godʸ of
Beershebaᵐ lives'—
they will fall,ⁿ
never to rise again.'ᵒ

Israel to Be Destroyed

9 I saw the Lord standing by the altar,
and he said:

"Strike the tops of the pillars
so that the thresholds shake.
Bring them down on the headsᵖ of all
the people;
those who are left I will kill with the
sword.
Not one will get away,
none will escape.ᵠ
²Though they dig down to the depths of
the grave,ᶻʳ
from there my hand will take them.
Though they climb up to the heavens,ˢ
from there I will bring them down.ᵗ
³Though they hide themselves on the
top of Carmel,ᵘ
there I will hunt them down and
seize them.ᵛ
Though they hide from me at the
bottom of the sea,ʷ
there I will command the serpentˣ
to bite them.ʸᶻ
⁴Though they are driven into exile by
their enemies,
there I will command the swordᵃ to
slay them.
I will fix my eyes upon them
for evilᵇ and not for good."ᶜᵈ

H Am 8:7 ◀ ▶ Ob 15

8:12 ʰS Eze 20:3, 31
8:13 ⁱS Isa 9:17
ʲIsa 41:17; Hos 2:3
8:14 ᵏMic 1:5
ˡS 1Ki 12:29
ᵐS Am 5:5
ⁿS Ps 46:2
ᵒS Am 5:2
9:1 ᵖPs 68:21
ᵠJer 11:11
9:2 ʳS Job 7:9; S Eze 26:20
ˢJer 51:53 ᵗOb 1:4
9:3 ᵘAm 1:2
ᵛPs 139:8-10
ʷPs 68:22
ˣIsa 27:1
ʸJer 16:16-17
ᶻS Ge 49:17; S Job 11:20
9:4 ˢS Lev 26:33; S Eze 5:12
ᵇS Jer 21:10
ᶜJer 39:16; S Eze 15:7
ᵈS Jer 44:11
9:5 ᵉS Ps 46:2
ᶠS Am 8:8
9:6 ᵍJer 43:9
ʰPs 104:1-3,5-6,13; S Am 5:8
9:7 ⁱS 2Ch 12:3; Isa 20:4; 43:3
ʲS Ge 10:14
ᵏS Dt 2:23
ˡS 2Ki 16:9; S Isa 22:6; S Am 2:10
9:8 ᵐS Jer 4:27
ⁿS Jer 44:27
9:9 ᵒLk 22:31
ᵖIsa 30:28
ᵠS Jer 31:36; S Da 9:7
9:10 ʳJer 49:37
ˢJer 5:12; S 23:17; S Eze 20:38; S Am 6:3

⁵The Lord, the LORD Almighty,
he who touches the earth and it
melts,ᵉ
and all who live in it mourn—
the whole land rises like the Nile,
then sinks like the river of Egyptᶠ—
⁶he who builds his lofty palaceᵃᵍ in the
heavens
and sets its foundationᵇ on the
earth,
who calls for the waters of the sea
and pours them out over the face of
the land—
the LORD is his name.ʰ

⁷"Are not you Israelites
the same to me as the Cushitesᶜ?"ⁱ
declares the LORD.
"Did I not bring Israel up from Egypt,
the Philistinesʲ from Caphtorᵈᵏ
and the Arameans from Kir?ˡ

⁸"Surely the eyes of the Sovereign LORD
are on the sinful kingdom.
I will destroyᵐ it
from the face of the earth—
yet I will not totally destroy
the house of Jacob,"
declares the LORD.ⁿ
⁹"For I will give the command,
and I will shake the house of Israel
among all the nations
as grainᵒ is shaken in a sieve,ᵖ
and not a pebble will reach the
ground.ᵠ
¹⁰All the sinners among my people
will die by the sword,ʳ
all those who say,
'Disaster will not overtake or meet
us.'ˢ

Israel's Restoration

¹¹"In that day I will restore

R Am 8:2 ◀ ▶ Am 9:8–10
R Am 9:5 ◀ ▶ Mic 1:6
I Joel 3:20–21 ◀ ▶ Ob 17

ˣ 14 Or by Ashima; or by the idol ʸ 14 Or power ᶻ 2 Hebrew to Sheol
ᵃ 6 The meaning of the Hebrew for this phrase is uncertain.
ᵇ 6 The meaning of the Hebrew for this word is uncertain. ᶜ 7 That is, people from the upper Nile region ᵈ 7 That is, Crete

---

9:5 Note the similarity between this verse and 8:8. Because of heavy seasonal rains, the Nile River would rise as much as 20 feet over its banks, flooding the surrounding valley and depositing large amounts of topsoil on the land. Amos notes that God controls even these natural events.

9:8–10 Amos prophesied that God would judge Israel. Sinners would die for their persistent rebellion, but God would graciously spare a remnant of the faithful.

9:11 This Messianic prophecy echoes the hope that underlies Amos's words—God will bring blessing

David'sᵗ fallen tent.ᵘ
I will repair its broken places,
   restore its ruins,ᵛ
   and build it as it used to be,ʷ
¹²so that they may possess the remnant
      of Edomˣ
   and all the nations that bear my
      name,ᵉʸ"
                        declares the LORD,
               who will do these things.ᶻ

¹³"The days are coming," ᵃ declares the LORD,

"when the reaperᵇ will be overtaken
      by the plowmanᶜ
   and the planter by the one treadingᵈ
      grapes.
New wineᵉ will drip from the
      mountains
   and flow from all the hills.ᶠ
¹⁴I will bringᵍ back my exiledʰ people
      Israel;
   they will rebuild the ruined citiesⁱ
      and live in them.
   They will plant vineyardsʲ and drink
      their wine;
   they will make gardens and eat their
      fruit.ᵏ
¹⁵I will plantˡ Israel in their own land,ᵐ
   never again to be uprootedⁿ
   from the land I have given them,"ᵒ
                        says the LORD your God.ᵖ

9:11 ᵗS Isa 7:2; ᵘS Ge 26:22
ᵛPs 53:6; S Isa 49:8
ʷPs 80:12; S Eze 17:24; Mic 7:8,11; Zec 12:7; 14:10
9:12 ˣS Nu 24:18
ʸIsa 43:7; Jer 25:29
ᶻAc 15:16-17*
9:13 ᵃJer 31:38; 33:14 ᵇS Ru 2:3
ᶜLev 26:5
ᵈS Jdg 9:27
ᵉS Joel 2:24
ᶠS Joel 3:18
9:14 ᵍS Jer 29:14
ʰS Jer 33:7
ⁱS Isa 32:18; S 49:8; S 61:4
ʲS 2Ki 19:29
ᵏS Isa 62:9; S Jer 30:18; S 31:28; Eze 28:25-26; S 34:13-14; S Am 5:11
9:15 ˡS Ex 15:17; S Isa 60:21

ᵐS Jer 23:8 ⁿS Joel 3:20 ᵒS Isa 65:9; S Jer 3:18; Ob 1:17 ᵖS Jer 18:9; S 24:6; S 32:15; S Eze 28:26; S 34:25-28; S 37:12,15

ᵉ 12 Hebrew; Septuagint *so that the remnant of men / and all the nations that bear my name may seek ⸤the Lord*, ᶠ 14 Or *will restore the fortunes of my*

---

after judgment and will ultimately restore Israel. Note that the reference to the restoration of David's "tent" refers to the reinstatement of David's rule through Jesus the Messiah (see Ac 15:15–17).

9:12–15 After all of the promises of destruction and death, Amos prophesied the return of the Jewish exiles to the promised land in the last days. Note the promised prosperity and fertility of the land so that harvesting and planting will run simultaneously. The Messiah will reign over this land and even over Israel's former enemies, and Israel will never again be destroyed.

Obadiah

Author: Obadiah

Theme: God's judgment on proud Edom

Date of Writing: Disputed; possibly c. 853–841 B.C. or 605–586 B.C.

Outline of Obadiah
   I. Edom's Doom (1–9)
  II. Edom's Attitude Toward Jerusalem (10–14)
 III. Edom in the Day of the Lord (15–21)

Although the name "Obadiah" is frequently found in the OT and means "servant (or worshiper) of the Lord," nothing specific is known about this prophet beyond his identification with this short book. Even the date of this composition is obscure. Verses 11–14 contain the only datable pieces in the book and may apply to two different times in Israel's history. If these verses pertain to the invasion of Jerusalem by the Philistines during the reign of Jehoram (see 2Ki 8:20–22; 2Ch 21:8–20), the prophet Obadiah would have prophesied alongside Elisha (853–841 B.C.). However, if these verses pertain to the Babylonian destruction of Jerusalem, Obadiah would have been a contemporary of Jeremiah (605–586 B.C.). Since there are some parallels between the book of Obadiah and Jer 49:7–22 this exilic date seems more likely.

The book of Obadiah is the shortest book in the whole OT. Covering the period of judgment upon the nation of Judah, Obadiah predicts the total annihilation of the kingdom of Edom. The Edomites, who were the descendants of Esau, proudly held the mountain strongholds of Mt. Seir, the area to the south of the Dead Sea, and maliciously mocked the people of Judah when they were invaded by their enemies. The Edomites themselves participated in at least four plunderings of Jerusalem. Yet God's promised destruction of Edom was fulfilled. Following the destruction of Jerusalem in A.D. 70, the Edomites have never been heard of again.

OBADIAH 1

¹The vision^a of Obadiah.

1–4pp — Jer 49:14–16
5–6pp — Jer 49:9–10

This is what the Sovereign LORD says about Edom^b—

We have heard a message from the LORD:
> An envoy^c was sent to the nations to say,
> "Rise, and let us go against her for battle"^d—

²"See, I will make you small^e among the nations;
you will be utterly despised.
³The pride^f of your heart has deceived you,
you who live in the clefts of the rocks^{a,g}
and make your home on the heights,
you who say to yourself,
'Who can bring me down to the ground?'^h
⁴Though you soar like the eagle
and make your nestⁱ among the stars,
from there I will bring you down,"^j
declares the LORD.^k

⁵"If thieves came to you,
if robbers in the night—
Oh, what a disaster awaits you—
would they not steal only as much as they wanted?
If grape pickers came to you,
would they not leave a few grapes?^l
⁶But how Esau will be ransacked,
his hidden treasures pillaged!
⁷All your allies^m will force you to the border;
your friends will deceive and overpower you;
those who eat your breadⁿ will set a trap for you,^b
but you will not detect it.

⁸"In that day," declares the LORD,

P *Am 1:2–15* ◀ ▶ *Ob 15–16*
M *Joel 2:13* ◀ ▶ *Jnh 3:5–10*

1:1 ^aS Isa 1:1
^bS Ge 25:14;
S Isa 11:14;
S 34:11; 63:1-6;
Jer 49:7-22;
S Eze 25:12-14;
S 32:29;
S Am 1:11-12
^cIsa 18:2 ^dJer 6:4-5
1:2 ^eNu 24:18
1:3 ^fS Isa 16:6
^gfn Isa 16:1
^hS 2Ch 25:11-12
1:4 ⁱS Isa 10:14
^jS Isa 14:13
^kS Job 20:6
1:5 ^lS Dt 4:27;
24:21; S Isa 24:13
1:7 ^mJer 30:14
ⁿS Ps 41:9
1:8 ^oJob 5:12;
Isa 29:14
1:9 ^pS Ge 36:11, 34
1:10 ^qS Joel 3:19
^rPs 137:7;
Am 1:11-12
^sS Ps 137:7;
S Eze 25:12-14; 35:9
1:11 ^tS Job 6:27;
S Eze 24:6
^uS Am 1:6
1:12 ^vPr 24:17
^wS Job 31:29
^xS Eze 35:15
^yS Pr 17:5
^zPs 137:7
^aS Eze 25:6;
Mic 4:11; 7:8
1:13 ^bS Eze 35:5
1:14 ^cS 1Ki 18:4
1:15 ^dS Jer 46:10;
S Eze 30:3;
S Joel 2:31;
S Am 5:18
^eS Jer 50:29;
Hab 2:8
1:16 ^fIsa 51:17
^gS Ex 15:17

"will I not destroy^o the wise men of Edom,
men of understanding in the mountains of Esau?
⁹Your warriors, O Teman,^p will be terrified,
and everyone in Esau's mountains will be cut down in the slaughter.
¹⁰Because of the violence^q against your brother Jacob,^r
you will be covered with shame;
you will be destroyed forever.^s
¹¹On the day you stood aloof
while strangers carried off his wealth
and foreigners entered his gates
and cast lots^t for Jerusalem,
you were like one of them.^u
¹²You should not look down^v on your brother
in the day of his misfortune,^w
nor rejoice^x over the people of Judah
in the day of their destruction,^y
nor boast^z so much
in the day of their trouble.^a
¹³You should not march through the gates of my people
in the day of their disaster,
nor look down on them in their calamity^b
in the day of their disaster,
nor seize their wealth
in the day of their disaster.
¹⁴You should not wait at the crossroads
to cut down their fugitives,^c
nor hand over their survivors
in the day of their trouble.

¹⁵"The day of the LORD is near^d
for all nations.
As you have done, it will be done to you;
your deeds^e will return upon your own head.
¹⁶Just as you drank^f on my holy hill,^g

P *Ob 1–10* ◀ ▶ *Mic 1:3–7*
H *Am 9:1–4* ◀ ▶ *Mic 5:15*

^a 3 Or *of Sela* ^b 7 The meaning of the Hebrew for this clause is uncertain.

1–4 Despite the invincibility of Edom's mountain fortresses atop the cliffs, God declared that he would cut Edom down to size and destroy it. This prophecy was fulfilled when Petra was destroyed in A.D. 629–32 by the Moslems and never inhabited again. **10** Despite the natural economic and defensive advantages of the ancient nation of Edom, this prophecy has been fulfilled in totality. The powerful, rich kingdom of Edom has totally disappeared from the scene of human history, exactly as Obadiah divinely prophesied.

so all the nations will drink[h]
  continually;
they will drink and drink
  and be as if they had never been.[i]
[17]But on Mount Zion will be
  deliverance;[j]
  it will be holy,[k]
and the house of Jacob
  will possess its inheritance.[l]
[18]The house of Jacob will be a fire
  and the house of Joseph a flame;
the house of Esau will be stubble,
  and they will set it on fire[m] and
    consume[n] it.
There will be no survivors[o]
  from the house of Esau."
                The LORD has spoken.

[19]People from the Negev will occupy
  the mountains of Esau,
and people from the foothills will
  possess
  the land of the Philistines.[p]
They will occupy the fields of Ephraim
  and Samaria,[q]
  and Benjamin[r] will possess Gilead.
[20]This company of Israelite exiles who
  are in Canaan
will possess ⌊the land⌋ as far as
  Zarephath;[s]
the exiles from Jerusalem who are in
  Sepharad
will possess the towns of the
  Negev.[t]
[21]Deliverers[u] will go up on[c] Mount
  Zion
  to govern the mountains of Esau.
And the kingdom will be the
  LORD's.[v]

l Am 9:11–15 ◀▶ Mic 2:12
K Am 5:6 ◀▶ Jnh 2:9
S Am 6:12 ◀▶ Jnh 2:8

1:16 h Jer 25:15; 49:12; S La 4:21-22
i S La 4:21; S Eze 25:12-14
1:17 j S Ps 69:35; S Isa 14:1-2; Joel 2:32; S Am 9:11-15
k S Ps 74:2; S Isa 4:3 l Zec 8:12
1:18 m S Isa 1:31
n Zec 12:6
o S Jer 49:10
1:19 p Isa 11:14
q S Jer 31:5
r S Nu 1:36
1:20 s 1Ki 17:9-10; Lk 4:26
t S Jer 33:13
1:21 u S Dt 28:29; S Jdg 3:9
v S Ps 22:28; 47:9; 66:4; S Da 2:44; Zec 14:9,16; Mal 1:14; Rev 11:15

c 21 Or from

17 Obadiah prophesied God's deliverance and blessing of his chosen people and his judgment on their enemies. The Messiah's kingdom is in view when Obadiah declares that Jerusalem will no longer be occupied by her enemies; Mount Zion would once again be holy to the Lord in the last days of history (see Rev 11:15).

Jonah

Author: Jonah

Theme: God's love and forgiveness is for everyone

Date of Writing: c. 785–750 B.C.

Outline of Jonah
  I. Jonah Runs Away From God's Commission (1:1–17)
  II. Jonah's Repentance and Deliverance (2:1–10)
  III. Jonah's Mission to Nineveh (3:1–10)
  IV. Jonah's Disappointment in God's Mercy (4:1–11)

THE BOOK OF Jonah is named after its main character, a prophet and the son of Amittai. This Jonah is probably the same prophet mentioned in 2Ki 14:25, thus dating Jonah's mission to Nineveh during the latter part of King Jeroboam II's reign. Since the author is not identified in the text, others may have written this book a century or two after Jonah's trip to Nineveh. While some scholars have rejected the literal record found in Jonah, most conservative scholars acknowledge the historical truth found in its pages. Jesus also acknowledged the historical truth of Jonah's book in several direct references (see Mt 12:39–41; 16:4; Lk 11:29–32).

Jonah was given a divine commission to warn the people of Nineveh, the capital city of Assyria, of their coming judgment. Jonah did not want God to show mercy to Israel's most feared and hated enemy even if they repented, so he ran in the other direction. Through a series of supernatural events, Jonah finally relented, went to Nineveh and preached to the city. When the people of Nineveh repented, God extended his mercy to them and delayed his promised judgment against them for more than a century. As successive generations of Ninevites fell back into gross wickedness, God's judgment was finally enacted and Nineveh was destroyed.

Though only five verses of Jonah contain predictive matter, this prophetic narrative conveys a strong theme of God's forgiveness for all who repent of their sins. The prophetic sign of the three days that Jonah spent in the big fish corresponds to the three days Jesus Christ spent in the grave. Note also that while Jonah was only one witness to the Gentiles, during the seven-year tribulation Israel will win millions to Christ in the closing years leading to Armageddon.

Jonah Flees From the LORD

1 The word of the LORD came to Jonah[a] son of Amittai:[b] 2"Go to the great city of Nineveh[c] and preach against it, because its wickedness has come up before me."

3 But Jonah ran[d] away from the LORD and headed for Tarshish.[e] He went down to Joppa,[f] where he found a ship bound for that port. After paying the fare, he went aboard and sailed for Tarshish to flee from the LORD.[g]

4 Then the LORD sent a great wind on the sea, and such a violent storm arose that the ship threatened to break up.[h] 5 All the sailors were afraid and each cried out to his own god. And they threw the cargo into the sea to lighten the ship.[i]

But Jonah had gone below deck, where he lay down and fell into a deep sleep. 6 The captain went to him and said, "How can you sleep? Get up and call[j] on your god! Maybe he will take notice of us, and we will not perish."[k]

7 Then the sailors said to each other, "Come, let us cast lots to find out who is responsible for this calamity."[l] They cast lots and the lot fell on Jonah.[m]

8 So they asked him, "Tell us, who is responsible for making all this trouble for us? What do you do? Where do you come from? What is your country? From what people are you?"

9 He answered, "I am a Hebrew and I worship the LORD,[n] the God of heaven,[o] who made the sea[p] and the land.[q]"

10 This terrified them and they asked, "What have you done?" (They knew he was running away from the LORD, because he had already told them so.)

11 The sea was getting rougher and rougher. So they asked him, "What should we do to you to make the sea calm down for us?"

12 "Pick me up and throw me into the sea," he replied, "and it will become calm. I know that it is my fault that this great storm has come upon you."[r]

13 Instead, the men did their best to row back to land. But they could not, for the sea grew even wilder than before.[s] 14 Then they cried to the LORD, "O LORD, please do not let us die for taking this man's life. Do not hold us accountable for killing an innocent man,[t] for you, O LORD, have done as you pleased."[u] 15 Then they took Jonah and threw him overboard, and the raging sea grew calm.[v] 16 At this the men greatly feared[w] the LORD, and they offered a sacrifice to the LORD and made vows[x] to him.

17 But the LORD provided[y] a great fish to swallow Jonah,[z] and Jonah was inside the fish three days and three nights.

S Da 6:22–23 ◀ ▶ Jnh 2:10

1:1–3 Despite God's clear command, Jonah did not want to preach a message of repentance to the hated city of Nineveh, deciding instead to run away.
1:12 Jonah told the sailors that the storm would cease if they threw him into the sea. As soon as Jonah was thrown overboard, the sea became calm (see 1:15).
1:17 God sovereignly provided a "great fish" to swallow Jonah so that he would survive and fulfill his divine mission to preach to the Ninevites. This verse notes the duration of Jonah's ordeal as "three days and three nights." While westerners calculate a day based on a full 24-hour period, ancient middle easterners calculated a day as any portion of that day. Thus the phrase "three days and three nights" probably meant any portion of the first day, plus a full second day, plus any portion of the third day for a total time of as little as 26 hours. In a similar manner this inclusive method of reckoning time helps reconcile the 36–40 hours from Christ's burial on Friday afternoon until his supernatural resurrection on Sunday morning as "three days" (see Mt 12:40).

The Prophets in Palestine

Jonah's Prayer

2 From inside the fish Jonah prayed to the LORD his God. ²He said:

"In my distress I called[a] to the LORD,[b]
 and he answered me.
From the depths of the grave[ac] I called for help,
 and you listened to my cry.
³You hurled me into the deep,[d]
 into the very heart of the seas,
 and the currents swirled about me;
all your waves[e] and breakers swept over me.[f]
⁴I said, 'I have been banished from your sight;[g]
 yet I will look again toward your holy temple.'[h]
⁵The engulfing waters threatened me,[b]
 the deep surrounded me;
 seaweed was wrapped around my head.[i]
⁶To the roots of the mountains[j] I sank down;
 the earth beneath barred me in forever.
But you brought my life up from the pit,[k]
 O LORD my God.
⁷"When my life was ebbing away,
 I remembered[l] you, LORD,
and my prayer[m] rose to you,
 to your holy temple.[n]
⁸"Those who cling to worthless idols[o]
 forfeit the grace that could be theirs.
⁹But I, with a song of thanksgiving,[p]
 will sacrifice[q] to you.
What I have vowed[r] I will make good.
 Salvation[s] comes from the LORD."

¹⁰And the LORD commanded the fish, and it vomited Jonah onto dry land.

L Da 2:28–32 ◀▶ Mt 10:17–23
S Ob 17 ◀▶ Mic 6:7–8
K Ob 17 ◀▶ Zec 13:1
O Hos 13:4 ◀▶ Mt 7:26–27
S Jnh 1:17 ◀▶ Na 1:7

2:2 ᵃLa 3:55; ᵇPs 18:6; 120:1; ᶜPs 86:13
2:3 ᵈS Ps 88:6; ᵉS 2Sa 22:5; ᶠS Ps 42:7
2:4 ᵍPs 31:22; Jer 7:15; ʰS 1Ki 8:48
2:5 ⁱPs 69:1-2
2:6 ʲJob 28:9; ᵏS Job 17:16; S 33:18; S Ps 30:3
2:7 ˡPs 77:11-12; ᵐ2Ch 30:27; ⁿS Ps 11:4; 18:6
2:8 ᵒS Dt 32:21; S 1Sa 12:21
2:9 ᵖS Ps 42:4; ᵠPs 50:14,23; Heb 13:15; ʳS Nu 30:2; Ps 116:14; S Ecc 5:4-5; ˢS Ex 15:2; S Ps 3:8
3:1 ᵗJnh 1:1
3:4 ᵘS Jer 18:7-10
3:5 ᵛDa 9:3; Mt 11:21; 12:41; Lk 11:32
3:6 ʷEst 4:1-3; S Job 2:8,13; S Eze 27:30-31
3:7 ˣS 2Ch 20:3; S Ezr 10:6
3:8 ʸPs 130:1; Jnh 1:6 ᶻJer 25:5 ᵃJer 7:3 ᵇS Job 16:17
3:9 ᶜ2Sa 12:22 ᵈS Jer 18:8 ᵉS Joel 2:14 ᶠS Ps 85:3
3:10 ᵍS Am 7:6 ʰS Jer 18:8 ⁱS Ex 32:14

Jonah Goes to Nineveh

3 Then the word of the LORD came to Jonah[t] a second time: ²"Go to the great city of Nineveh and proclaim to it the message I give you."

³Jonah obeyed the word of the LORD and went to Nineveh. Now Nineveh was a very important city—a visit required three days. ⁴On the first day, Jonah started into the city. He proclaimed:[u] "Forty more days and Nineveh will be overturned." ⁵The Ninevites believed God. They declared a fast, and all of them, from the greatest to the least, put on sackcloth.[v]

⁶When the news reached the king of Nineveh, he rose from his throne, took off his royal robes, covered himself with sackcloth and sat down in the dust.[w] ⁷Then he issued a proclamation in Nineveh:

"By the decree of the king and his nobles:

Do not let any man or beast, herd or flock, taste anything; do not let them eat or drink.[x] ⁸But let man and beast be covered with sackcloth. Let everyone call[y] urgently on God. Let them give up[z] their evil ways[a] and their violence.[b] ⁹Who knows?[c] God may yet relent[d] and with compassion turn[e] from his fierce anger[f] so that we will not perish."

¹⁰When God saw what they did and how they turned from their evil ways, he had compassion[g] and did not bring upon them the destruction[h] he had threatened.[i]

M Ob 3–4 ◀▶ Hab 2:4
R Joel 2:12–13 ◀▶ Mt 3:2
L Joel 2:13 ◀▶ Jnh 4:2

ᵃ 2 Hebrew *Sheol* ᵇ 5 Or *waters were at my throat*

3:4–10 Jonah arrived in Nineveh and obediently proclaimed God's coming judgment. However, the people repented and God delayed his judgment in response to their unprecedented repentance. In fact, God's judgment was delayed for over a century. When the next generation of Assyrians fell back into wickedness, God's judgment was finally carried out.

3:9 The king of Assyria hoped that God would forgive. Although "the wages of sin is death" (Ro 6:23), the unchanging promise of God is that "if we confess our sins, he is faithful and just and will forgive us our sins and purify us from all unrighteousness" (1Jn 1:9).

Jonah's Anger at the LORD's Compassion

4 But Jonah was greatly displeased and became angry.[j] [2] He prayed to the LORD, "O LORD, is this not what I said when I was still at home? That is why I was so quick to flee to Tarshish. I knew[k] that you are a gracious[l] and compassionate God, slow to anger and abounding in love,[m] a God who relents[n] from sending calamity.[o] [3] Now, O LORD, take away my life,[p] for it is better for me to die[q] than to live."[r]

[4] But the LORD replied, "Have you any right to be angry?"[s]

[5] Jonah went out and sat down at a place east of the city. There he made himself a shelter, sat in its shade and waited to see what would happen to the city. [6] Then the LORD God provided[t] a vine and made it grow up over Jonah to give shade for his head to ease his discomfort, and Jonah was very happy about the vine. [7] But at dawn the next day God provided a worm, which chewed the vine so that it withered.[u] [8] When the sun rose, God provided a scorching east wind, and the sun blazed on Jonah's head so that he grew faint. He wanted to die,[v] and said, "It would be better for me to die than to live."

[9] But God said to Jonah, "Do you have a right to be angry about the vine?"[w]

"I do," he said. "I am angry enough to die."

[10] But the LORD said, "You have been concerned about this vine, though you did not tend it or make it grow. It sprang up overnight and died overnight. [11] But Nineveh[x] has more than a hundred and twenty thousand people who cannot tell their right hand from their left, and many cattle as well. Should I not be concerned[y] about that great city?"

L *Jnh 3:10* ◀▶ *Mic 6:6–8*

4:1 j ver 4; Mt 20:11; Lk 15:28
4:2 k Jer 20:7-8
 l S Dt 4:31;
 Ps 103:8
 m S Ex 22:27;
 Ps 86:5,15
 n S Nu 14:18
 o S Joel 2:13
4:3 p S Nu 11:15
 q S Job 7:15 r Jer 8:3
4:4 s Ge 4:6;
 Mt 20:11-15
4:6 t S Jnh 1:17
4:7 u Joel 1:12
4:8 v S 1Ki 19:4
4:9 w ver 4
4:11 x Jnh 1:2; 3:2
 y Jnh 3:10

4:11 Jonah's great prophecy ends with a heartfelt expression of a God who takes "no pleasure in the death of the wicked" (Eze 33:11) but rather offers grace and mercy to all.

Micah

Author: Micah

Theme: The lives of God's children should reflect God's standards

Date of Writing: c. 740–710 B.C.

Outline of Micah
  I. Samaria and Jerusalem Under Judgment (1:1–16)
  II. Guilty Leaders and Wicked Oppressors (2:1—3:12)
  III. The Promise of Divine Restoration (4:1—5:15)
  IV. God's Judgment and Mercy (6:1—7:20)

A MAN NAMED Micah from Moresheth, a small village southwest of Jerusalem, wrote this sixth book of the Minor Prophets. Though Micah was a common name in OT times that meant "Who is like the LORD?" few additional details are known about this man of God. Ministering in Judah during the reigns of King Ahaz and King Hezekiah (see Jer 26:18), Micah was a contemporary of the prophets Isaiah (1:1; see Isa 1:1), Amos and Hosea. Warning of the impending judgment of God on unrepentant Israel and Judah, Micah's words parallel the prophecies of Isaiah (see 4:1–5; Isa 2:2–4). Jesus also quoted Micah's words when instructing his disciples (see 7:6; Mt 10:35–36).

Micah's warnings are primarily directed toward the leaders of Judah and Israel in their capital cities of Jerusalem and Samaria. The prophet warns the people of Judah against their false assumption of protection from God's coming judgment simply because they possess his temple. Micah prophesied that both capitals faced certain destruction unless the people and leaders of the kingdoms repented of their sin, predicting God's use of the Assyrians as his instrument of wrath. The people, however, refused to listen to Micah's warnings, and the powerful Assyrian armies invaded the kingdom of Israel and destroyed its capital city, Samaria, in 722 B.C.

Micah concludes his prophecy by predicting the future glory of God's Messiah and his just rule. This promise of final restoration provides hope for all who put their trust in God. Jerusalem will become the center of a universal kingdom where absolute peace and justice prevail. The Messiah, whose birthplace is identified in Micah's prophecy as Bethlehem in Judah, will establish a kingdom that will last forever (see 5:2).

MICAH 1:1

1 The word of the LORD that came to Micah of Moresheth[a] during the reigns of Jotham,[b] Ahaz[c] and Hezekiah,[d] kings of Judah[e]—the vision[f] he saw concerning Samaria and Jerusalem.

² Hear,[g] O peoples, all of you,[h]
  listen, O earth[i] and all who are in it,
  that the Sovereign LORD may witness[j] against you,
  the Lord from his holy temple.[k]

Judgment Against Samaria and Jerusalem

³ Look! The LORD is coming from his dwelling[l] place;
  he comes down[m] and treads the high places of the earth.[n]
⁴ The mountains melt[o] beneath him[p]
  and the valleys split apart,[q]
  like wax before the fire,
  like water rushing down a slope.
⁵ All this is because of Jacob's transgression,
  because of the sins of the house of Israel.
  What is Jacob's transgression?
  Is it not Samaria?[r]
  What is Judah's high place?
  Is it not Jerusalem?

⁶ "Therefore I will make Samaria a heap of rubble,
  a place for planting vineyards.[s]
  I will pour her stones[t] into the valley
  and lay bare her foundations.[u]
⁷ All her idols[v] will be broken to pieces;[w]
  all her temple gifts will be burned with fire;
  I will destroy all her images.[x]
  Since she gathered her gifts from the wages of prostitutes,[y]
  as the wages of prostitutes they will again be used."

P Ob 15–16 ◄► Mic 1:9
R Am 9:8–10 ◄► Mic 2:4

Weeping and Mourning

⁸ Because of this I will weep[z] and wail;
  I will go about barefoot[a] and naked.
  I will howl like a jackal
  and moan like an owl.
⁹ For her wound[b] is incurable;[c]
  it has come to Judah.[d]
  It[a] has reached the very gate[e] of my people,
  even to Jerusalem itself.
¹⁰ Tell it not in Gath[b];
  weep not at all.[c]
  In Beth Ophrah[d]
  roll in the dust.
¹¹ Pass on in nakedness[f] and shame,
  you who live in Shaphir.[e]
  Those who live in Zaanan[f]
  will not come out.
  Beth Ezel is in mourning;
  its protection is taken from you.
¹² Those who live in Maroth[g] writhe in pain,
  waiting for relief,[g]
  because disaster[h] has come from the LORD,
  even to the gate of Jerusalem.
¹³ You who live in Lachish,[h][i]
  harness the team to the chariot.
  You were the beginning of sin
  to the Daughter of Zion,[j]
  for the transgressions of Israel
  were found in you.
¹⁴ Therefore you will give parting gifts[k]
  to Moresheth[l] Gath.
  The town of Aczib[l][m] will prove deceptive[n]
  to the kings of Israel.
¹⁵ I will bring a conqueror against you
  who live in Mareshah.[j][o]
  He who is the glory of Israel

P Mic 1:3–7 ◄► Mic 5:5

a 9 Or *He* *b* 10 *Gath* sounds like the Hebrew for *tell.* *c* 10 Hebrew; Septuagint may suggest *not in Acco.* The Hebrew for *in Acco* sounds like the Hebrew for *weep.* *d* 10 *Beth Ophrah* means *house of dust.* *e* 11 *Shaphir* means *pleasant.* *f* 11 *Zaanan* sounds like the Hebrew for *come out.* *g* 12 *Maroth* sounds like the Hebrew for *bitter.* *h* 13 *Lachish* sounds like the Hebrew for *team.* *i* 14 *Aczib* means *deception.* *j* 15 *Mareshah* sounds like the Hebrew for *conqueror.*

1:1–6 Micah declared that God had called him to prophesy to Samaria and Jerusalem because of their continued wickedness. Though directed to the two capital cities, Micah's words applied to their people as well as he prophesied their coming destruction.

1:7–16 In these verses Micah described the coming destruction of Samaria at the hands of the Assyrians (see 2Ki 17:1–18). The wealth that Israel had gained from her idolatry would be taken by Assyria and turned over for use in idol worship. Micah may have actually acted out part of this prophecy, stripped to his loincloth and wailing through the city streets. His vivid prophecy was fulfilled in 721 B.C. when the people of Israel were taken in exile to Assyria. Note that Micah also warned Jerusalem of impending doom (1:9).

will come to Adullam.ᵖ

¹⁶Shaveq your heads in mourning
  for the children in whom you
    delight;
  make yourselves as bald as the vulture,
  for they will go from you into exile.ʳ

Man's Plans and God's

2 Woe to those who plan iniquity,
  to those who plot evilˢ on their
    beds!ᵗ
  At morning's light they carry it out
  because it is in their power to do it.
²They covet fieldsᵘ and seize them,ᵛ
  and houses, and take them.
  They defraudʷ a man of his home,
  a fellowman of his inheritance.ˣ

³Therefore, the LORD says:

"I am planning disasterʸ against this
    people,
  from which you cannot save
    yourselves.
  You will no longer walk proudly,ᶻ
  for it will be a time of calamity.
⁴In that day men will ridicule you;
  they will taunt you with this
    mournful song:
'We are utterly ruined;ᵃ
  my people's possession is divided
    up.ᵇ
  He takes it from me!
  He assigns our fields to traitors.'"

⁵Therefore you will have no one in the
    assembly of the LORD
  to divide the landᶜ by lot.ᵈ

False Prophets

⁶"Do not prophesy," their prophets say.
  "Do not prophesy about these
    things;
  disgraceᵉ will not overtake us.ᶠ"

⁷Should it be said, O house of Jacob:
  "Is the Spirit of the LORD angry?
  Does he do such things?"

"Do not my words do goodᵍ
  to him whose ways are upright?ʰ

⁸Lately my people have risen up
    like an enemy.
  You strip off the rich robe
  from those who pass by without a
    care,
  like men returning from battle.
⁹You drive the women of my people
  from their pleasant homes.ⁱ
  You take away my blessing
  from their children forever.
¹⁰Get up, go away!
  For this is not your resting place,ʲ
  because it is defiled,ᵏ
  it is ruined, beyond all remedy.
¹¹If a liar and deceiverˡ comes and says,
'I will prophesy for you plenty of
  wine and beer,'ᵐ
  he would be just the prophet for this
    people!ⁿ

Deliverance Promised

¹²"I will surely gather all of you,
    O Jacob;
  I will surely bring together the
    remnantº of Israel.
  I bring them together like sheep
    in a pen,
  like a flock in its pasture;
  the place will throng with people.ᵖ
¹³One who breaks open the way will go
    up beforeq them;
  they will break through the gateʳ
    and go out.
  Their king will pass through before
    them,
  the LORD at their head."

Leaders and Prophets Rebuked

3 Then I said,

"Listen, you leadersˢ of Jacob,
  you rulers of the house of Israel.
  Should you not know justice,
² you who hate good and love evil;
  who tear the skin from my people
  and the flesh from their bones;ᵗ
³who eat my people's flesh,ᵘ
  strip off their skin

2:4 Micah predicted that the rich people would feel the brunt of God's judgment when the treacherous Assyrians conquered the land.
2:12 Despite the doom pronounced upon the wickedness of Judah and Israel, the prophet interrupted his discourse promising the ultimate restoration of "the remnant of Israel."

and break their bones in pieces;^v
who chop^w them up like meat for the
    pan,
  like flesh for the pot?^x"

⁴Then they will cry out to the LORD,
  but he will not answer them.^y
At that time he will hide his face^z from
    them
  because of the evil they have done.^a

⁵This is what the LORD says:

"As for the prophets
  who lead my people astray,^b
if one feeds them,
  they proclaim 'peace';^c
if he does not,
  they prepare to wage war against
    him.
⁶Therefore night will come over you,
    without visions,
  and darkness, without divination.^d
The sun will set for the prophets,^e
  and the day will go dark for them.^f
⁷The seers will be ashamed^g
  and the diviners disgraced.^h
They will all coverⁱ their faces^j
  because there is no answer from
    God.^k"

⁸But as for me, I am filled with power,
  with the Spirit of the LORD,
  and with justice and might,
to declare to Jacob his transgression,
  to Israel his sin.^l

⁹Hear this, you leaders of the house of
    Jacob,
  you rulers of the house of Israel,
who despise justice
  and distort all that is right;^m
¹⁰who buildⁿ Zion with bloodshed,^o
and Jerusalem with wickedness.^p
¹¹Her leaders judge for a bribe,^q
  her priests teach for a price,^r
  and her prophets tell fortunes for
    money.^s
Yet they lean^t upon the LORD and say,
  "Is not the LORD among us?
  No disaster will come upon us."^u

¹²Therefore because of you,
  Zion will be plowed like a field,
Jerusalem will become a heap of
    rubble,^v
  the temple^w hill a mound overgrown
    with thickets.^x

The Mountain of the LORD
4:1–3pp — Isa 2:1–4

4 In the last days

the mountain^y of the LORD's temple
  will be established
    as chief among the mountains;
it will be raised above the hills,^z
  and peoples will stream to it.^a

²Many nations will come and say,

"Come, let us go up to the mountain of
    the LORD,^b
  to the house of the God of Jacob.^c
He will teach us^d his ways,^e
  so that we may walk in his paths."
The law^f will go out from Zion,
  the word of the LORD from
    Jerusalem.
³He will judge between many peoples
  and will settle disputes for strong
    nations far and wide.^g
They will beat their swords into
    plowshares
  and their spears into pruning
    hooks.^h

3:12 God prophesied that Jerusalem would be utterly destroyed because of her continued wickedness. Every wall would fall and Jerusalem's enemies would plough up the foundations to signal the city's total defeat.

4:1–8 Note the similarity of this passage and Isa 2:2–4. In these verses Micah described the blessings of the millennial kingdom. Despite the certainty of God's judgment, the last days would bring a time of peace and justice. The temple would be rebuilt and the Messiah would justly "judge between many peoples" (4:3) from his throne in Jerusalem. Peace would exist between nations and they would no longer "train for war anymore" (4:3). Fear would be a thing of the past (4:4), and the kingdom of David would be reunited and restored under the glorious reign of the Messiah (4:8).

Nation will not take up sword against
  nation,
  nor will they train for war
  anymore.
⁴Every man will sit under his own vine
  and under his own fig tree,
  and no one will make them afraid,
  for the LORD Almighty has spoken.
⁵All the nations may walk
  in the name of their gods;
we will walk in the name of the LORD
  our God for ever and ever.

The LORD's Plan

⁶"In that day," declares the LORD,

"I will gather the lame;
  I will assemble the exiles
  and those I have brought to grief.
⁷I will make the lame a remnant,
  those driven away a strong nation.
The LORD will rule over them in Mount
    Zion
  from that day and forever.
⁸As for you, O watchtower of the flock,
  O stronghold of the Daughter of
    Zion,
  the former dominion will be restored
    to you;
  kingship will come to the Daughter
    of Jerusalem."

⁹Why do you now cry aloud—
  have you no king?
Has your counselor perished,
  that pain seizes you like that of a
    woman in labor?
¹⁰Writhe in agony, O Daughter of Zion,
  like a woman in labor,
for now you must leave the city
  to camp in the open field.
You will go to Babylon;
  there you will be rescued.

There the LORD will redeem you
  out of the hand of your enemies.

¹¹But now many nations
  are gathered against you.
They say, "Let her be defiled,
  let our eyes gloat over Zion!"
¹²But they do not know
  the thoughts of the LORD;
they do not understand his plan,
  he who gathers them like sheaves to
    the threshing floor.

¹³"Rise and thresh, O Daughter of Zion,
  for I will give you horns of iron;
  I will give you hoofs of bronze
  and you will break to pieces many
    nations."

You will devote their ill-gotten gains to
    the LORD,
  their wealth to the Lord of all the
    earth.

A Promised Ruler From Bethlehem

5 Marshal your troops, O city of
    troops,
  for a siege is laid against us.
They will strike Israel's ruler
  on the cheek with a rod.

²"But you, Bethlehem Ephrathah,
  though you are small among the
    clans of Judah,
  out of you will come for me
  one who will be ruler over Israel,
  whose origins are from of old,
  from ancient times."

4:11–13 These verses contain Micah's prophecy of God's judgment against the nations who laughed at Israel's devastation. Hidden within this passage is the promise of Israel's ultimate restoration in the last days when Israel will miraculously defeat her enemies. This prophecy foreshadows the supernatural deliverance of God's people at the Battle of Armageddon (see Rev 16:13–16).

5:1 To strike a ruler on the cheek was a supreme insult. Micah used this metaphor to indicate that Jerusalem's ability to resist destruction was gone. The city would be besieged and the kings seized and taken captive. This prophecy was fulfilled when Babylon carried Zedekiah into exile (see 2Ki 25:7).

5:2–3 Once again Micah makes a shift from words of doom to words of hope. This well-known prophecy clearly predicted nearly seven hundred years before its fulfillment that the town of Bethlehem in the region of Ephrathah would become the birthplace of the Messiah. This prophecy also indicated that Israel would be abandoned to the discretion of their enemies until the birth of the Messiah and the reuniting of the nation once more (see Isa 7:14).

MICAH 5:3

³Therefore Israel will be abandoned[n]
　until the time when she who is in
　　labor gives birth
and the rest of his brothers return
　to join the Israelites.

⁴He will stand and shepherd his flock[o]
　in the strength of the LORD,
　in the majesty of the name of the
　　LORD his God.
And they will live securely, for then
　his greatness[p]
will reach to the ends of the earth.
⁵ And he will be their peace.[q]

Deliverance and Destruction

When the Assyrian invades[r] our land
　and marches through our fortresses,
we will raise against him seven
　shepherds,
　even eight leaders of men.[s]
⁶They will rule[p] the land of Assyria
　with the sword,
the land of Nimrod[t] with drawn
　sword.[q][u]
He will deliver us from the Assyrian
　when he invades our land
　and marches into our borders.[v]

⁷The remnant[w] of Jacob will be
　in the midst of many peoples
like dew[x] from the LORD,
　like showers on the grass,[y]
which do not wait for man
　or linger for mankind.
⁸The remnant of Jacob will be among
　the nations,
　in the midst of many peoples,
like a lion among the beasts of the
　forest,[z]
like a young lion among flocks of
　sheep,
which mauls and mangles[a] as it goes,
　and no one can rescue.[b]

P Mic 1:9 ◀ ▶ Mic 5:15

5:3 ⁿS Jer 7:25

5:4 ᵒIsa 40:11;
49:9;
S Eze 34:11-15,23;
Mic 7:14
ᵖIsa 52:13; Lk 1:32

5:5 ᵠS Isa 9:6;
S Lk 2:14;
Col 1:19-20
ʳIsa 8:7
ˢIsa 10:24-27

5:6 ᵗGe 10:8
ᵘZep 2:13
ᵛNa 2:11-13

5:7 ʷS Am 5:15;
S Mic 2:12
ˣS Ps 133:3
ʸIsa 44:4

5:8 ᶻS Ge 49:9
ᵃMic 4:13;
Zec 10:5
ᵇS Ps 50:22;
S Isa 5:29;
S Hos 5:14

5:9 ᶜS Ps 10:12

5:10 ᵈEx 15:4,19;
S Hos 14:3;
Hag 2:22; Zec 9:10

5:11 ᵉS Dt 29:23;
Isa 6:11 ᶠS La 2:2;
S Hos 10:14;
Am 5:9

5:12 ᵍDt 18:10-12;
Isa 2:6; 8:19

5:13 ʰNa 1:14
ⁱHos 10:2
ʲS Isa 2:18;
S Eze 6:9; Zec 13:2

5:14 ᵏS Ex 34:13;
S Jdg 3:7;
S 2Ki 17:10

5:15 ˡS Isa 65:12

6:1 ᵐS Ps 50:1;
S Eze 6:2

6:2 ⁿDt 32:1
ᵒS Hos 12:2
ᵖS Isa 3:13
ᵠS Ps 50:7; S Jer 2:9

---

⁹Your hand will be lifted up[c] in triumph
　over your enemies,
　and all your foes will be destroyed.

¹⁰"In that day," declares the LORD,

"I will destroy your horses from among
　you
and demolish your chariots.[d]
¹¹I will destroy the cities[e] of your land
　and tear down all your strongholds.[f]
¹²I will destroy your witchcraft
　and you will no longer cast spells.[g]
¹³I will destroy your carved images[h]
　and your sacred stones from among
　　you;
you will no longer bow down
　to the work of your hands.[i]
¹⁴I will uproot from among you your
　Asherah poles[r][k]
and demolish your cities.
¹⁵I will take vengeance[l] in anger and
　wrath
upon the nations that have not
　obeyed me."

The LORD's Case Against Israel

6 Listen to what the LORD says:

"Stand up, plead your case before the
　mountains;[m]
let the hills hear what you have to
　say.
²Hear,[n] O mountains, the LORD's
　accusation;[o]
listen, you everlasting foundations of
　the earth.
For the LORD has a case[p] against his
　people;
he is lodging a charge[q] against
　Israel.

P Mic 5:5 ◀ ▶ Na 1:2
H Ob 15 ◀ ▶ Mic 6:13

ᵖ 6 Or *crush* ᵠ 6 Or *Nimrod in its gates* ʳ 14 That is, symbols of the goddess Asherah

---

5:4–6 Micah prophesied the future rule of the Messiah, who will rule "in the majesty of the name of the LORD" (5:4) and will defeat "the Assyrian" (5:5), a symbol of all of the enemies of God's people. Note that this title is also sometimes applied to the antichrist because of his role as the King of Babylon (see note at Isa 10:5; 14:4, 25). The antichrist will invade the promised land and will be defeated by the Messiah at the Battle of Armageddon (see Da 11:36–45; Rev 19:14–21). The reference to "seven shepherds, even eight leaders of men" (5:5) may refer to a group of great military leaders who will resist the antichrist's invasion of Israel toward the end of the seven-year tribulation period.

5:11–15 In the Messianic kingdom God's people will no longer rely on weapons of war or pagan idols. God will be the source of the people's success and strength and will bring destruction on those nations who disobey him.

³"My people, what have I done to you?
   How have I burdened⁽ʳ⁾ you?ˢ
   Answer me.
⁴I brought you up out of Egyptᵗ
   and redeemed you from the land of slavery.ᵘ
   I sent Mosesᵛ to lead you,
   also Aaronʷ and Miriam.ˣ
⁵My people, remember
   what Balakʸ king of Moab counseled
   and what Balaam son of Beor answered.
   Remember your journey from Shittimᶻ to Gilgal,ᵃ
   that you may know the righteous actsᵇ of the LORD."

⁶With what shall I come beforeᶜ the LORD
   and bow down before the exalted God?
   Shall I come before him with burnt offerings,
   with calves a year old?ᵈ
⁷Will the LORD be pleased with thousands of rams,ᵉ
   with ten thousand rivers of oil?ᶠ
   Shall I offer my firstbornᵍ for my transgression,
   the fruit of my body for the sin of my soul?ʰ
⁸He has showed you, O man, what is good.
   And what does the LORD require of you?
   To act justlyⁱ and to love mercy
   and to walk humblyʲ with your God.ᵏ

Israel's Guilt and Punishment

⁹Listen! The LORD is calling to the city—
   and to fear your name is wisdom—
   "Heed the rodˡ and the One who appointed it.ˢ
¹⁰Am I still to forget, O wicked house,
   your ill-gotten treasures
   and the short ephah,ᵗ which is accursed?ᵐ
¹¹Shall I acquit a man with dishonest scales,ⁿ
   with a bag of false weights?ᵒ
¹²Her rich men are violent;ᵖ
   her people are liarsᵠ
   and their tongues speak deceitfully.ʳ
¹³Therefore, I have begun to destroyˢ you,
   to ruin you because of your sins.
¹⁴You will eat but not be satisfied;ᵗ
   your stomach will still be empty.ᵘ
   You will store up but save nothing,ᵘ
   because what you save I will give to the sword.
¹⁵You will plant but not harvest;ᵛ
   you will press olives but not use the oil on yourselves,
   you will crush grapes but not drink the wine.ʷ
¹⁶You have observed the statutes of Omri,ˣ
   and all the practices of Ahab'sʸ house,
   and you have followed their traditions.ᶻ
   Therefore I will give you over to ruinᵃ
   and your people to derision;
   you will bear the scornᵇ of the nations."ᵛ

Israel's Misery

7 What misery is mine!
   I am like one who gathers summer fruit
   at the gleaning of the vineyard;
   there is no cluster of grapes to eat,
   none of the early figsᶜ that I crave.
²The godly have been swept from the land;ᵈ
   not oneᵉ upright man remains.
   All men lie in waitᶠ to shed blood;ᵍ
   each hunts his brotherʰ with a net.ⁱ
³Both hands are skilled in doing evil;ʲ

6:13 Micah's words indicate that God has already begun to destroy Israel with sickness and desolation as part of his judgment for their sins.
6:16 Micah indicted the leaders of Israel with following the practices of the most evil kings of Israel (see 1Ki 16:25, 30). God promised their ultimate ruin and scorn.
7:1 Micah complained that looking for the godly in Israel was like looking for fruit after the harvest over (see Jer 8:20).

the ruler demands gifts,
  the judge accepts bribes,ᵏ
  the powerful dictate what they
    desire—
  they all conspire together.
⁴The best of them is like a brier,¹
  the most upright worse than a
    thornᵐ hedge.
The day of your watchmen has come,
  the day God visits you.
  Now is the time of their confusion.ⁿ
⁵Do not trust a neighbor;
  put no confidence in a friend.ᵒ
Even with her who lies in your
    embrace
  be careful of your words.
⁶For a son dishonors his father,
  a daughter rises up against her
    mother,ᵖ
  a daughter-in-law against her
    mother-in-law—
  a man's enemies are the members of
    his own household.ᵍ

⁷But as for me, I watchʳ in hopeˢ for
    the LORD,
  I wait for God my Savior;
  my God will hearᵗ me.

Israel Will Rise

⁸Do not gloat over me,ᵘ my enemy!
  Though I have fallen, I will rise.ᵛ
  Though I sit in darkness,
    the LORD will be my light.ʷ
⁹Because I have sinned against him,
  I will bear the LORD's wrath,ˣ
  until he pleads my caseʸ
    and establishes my right.
  He will bring me out into the light;ᶻ
    I will see his righteousness.ᵃ
¹⁰Then my enemy will see it
  and will be covered with shame,ᵇ
  she who said to me,
    "Where is the LORD your God?"ᶜ
  My eyes will see her downfall;ᵈ

▎Mic 5:2 ◀▶ Mic 7:10
▎Mic 7:7–9 ◀▶ Mic 7:11–20

7:3 ᵏS Ex 23:8;
S Eze 22:12

7:4 ˡS Nu 33:55;
S Eze 2:6
ᵐS 2Sa 23:6
ⁿS Job 31:14;
Isa 22:5; S Hos 9:7

7:5 ᵒJer 9:4

7:6 ᵖS Eze 22:7
ᵍMt 10:35-36*;
S Mk 13:12

7:7 ʳS Isa 21:8
ˢPs 130:5; Isa 25:9
ᵗS Ps 4:3

7:8 ᵘS Ps 22:17;
S Pr 24:17;
S Mic 4:11
ᵛPs 20:8; 37:24;
S Am 9:11
ʷS 2Sa 22:29;
Isa 9:2

7:9 ˣLa 3:39-40
ʸS Ps 119:154
ᶻS Ps 107:10
ᵃIsa 46:13

7:10 ᵇS Ps 35:26
ᶜS Ps 42:3
ᵈS Isa 51:23
ᵉS 2Sa 22:43;
S Job 40:12;
S Isa 5:5; Zec 10:5

7:11 ᶠIsa 54:11;
S Am 9:11

7:12 ᵍS Isa 11:11
ʰIsa 19:23-25; 60:4

7:13 ⁱIsa 3:10-11;
S Eze 12:19;
S 33:28-29

7:14 ʲS Ps 28:9;
S Mic 5:4 ᵏPs 23:4
ˡPs 95:7
ᵐS Isa 33:9
ⁿS SS 4:1;
S Jer 50:19
ᵒEze 36:11

7:15 ᵖS Ex 3:20;
Ps 78:12

7:16 ᵍIsa 26:11
ʳS Jdg 18:19

7:17 ˢS Ge 3:14
ᵗ2Sa 22:46
ᵘIsa 25:3; 59:19

---

even now she will be trampledᵉ
    underfoot
  like mire in the streets.

¹¹The day for building your wallsᶠ will
    come,
  the day for extending your
    boundaries.
¹²In that day people will come to you
  from Assyriaᵍ and the cities of
    Egypt,
  even from Egypt to the Euphrates
  and from sea to sea
  and from mountain to mountain.ʰ
¹³The earth will become desolate
  because of its inhabitants,
  as the result of their deeds.ⁱ

Prayer and Praise

¹⁴Shepherdʲ your people with your
    staff,ᵏ
  the flock of your inheritance,
  which lives by itself in a forest,
    in fertile pasturelands.ʷ¹
  Let them feed in Bashanᵐ and Gileadⁿ
    as in days long ago.ᵒ

¹⁵"As in the days when you came out of
    Egypt,
  I will show them my wonders.ᵖ"

¹⁶Nations will see and be ashamed,ᵍ
  deprived of all their power.
  They will lay their hands on their
    mouthsʳ
  and their ears will become deaf.
¹⁷They will lick dustˢ like a snake,
  like creatures that crawl on the
    ground.
  They will come tremblingᵗ out of their
    dens;
  they will turn in fearᵘ to the LORD
    our God
  and will be afraid of you.

▎Mic 7:10 ◀▶ Na 1:12

w 14 Or *in the middle of Carmel*

7:7–20 Though this passage begins on a note of judgment and doom, it ends with a statement of hope. Micah clearly understood that God's judgment would come on his people for their persistent wickedness, yet he looked forward hopefully "for God my Savior" (7:7) with supreme confidence that God would hear the prayers of the godly. Micah warned his enemies not to laugh at Israel's fall into judgment, for though God would make the land desolate for a time, he would also show mercy to Israel and deliver them from their enemies. Micah ended his words with a powerful reminder to the people of God's mercy and forgiveness (7:18) that was built on the covenantal promises made to Abraham and Jacob "in days long ago" (7:20).

L ¹⁸Who is a God^v like you,
P   who pardons sin^w and forgives^x the transgression
        of the remnant^y of his inheritance?^z
You do not stay angry^a forever
    but delight to show mercy.^b
¹⁹You will again have compassion on us;
    you will tread our sins underfoot
    and hurl all our iniquities^c into the depths of the sea.^d
²⁰You will be true to Jacob,
    and show mercy to Abraham,^e
as you pledged on oath to our fathers^f
    in days long ago.^g

L *Mic 6:6–8* ◄ ► *Zec 1:3*
P *Am 5:4* ◄ ► *Zec 1:3*

7:18 ᵛS Ex 8:10; S 1Sa 2:2 ʷS Isa 43:25; S Jer 50:20; Zec 3:4 ˣS 2Ch 6:21; Ps 103:8-13 ʸS Joel 2:32; S Am 5:15; S Mic 2:12 ᶻS Ex 34:9 ᵃS Ps 103:9; S Isa 54:9 ᵇS 2Ch 30:9;

S Jer 31:20; 32:41; S Eze 18:23 **7:19** ᶜS Isa 43:25 ᵈS Jer 31:34 **7:20** ᵉGal 3:16 ᶠDt 7:8; Lk 1:72 ᵍPs 108:4

Nahum

Author: Nahum

Theme: God will judge Nineveh

Date of Writing: c. 626–585 B.C.

Outline of Nahum
   I. God's Anger Against Nineveh (1:1–15)
   II. The Fall of the Assyrian Capital (2:1–13)
   III. Woe to Nineveh (3:1–19)

The book of Nahum is like a sequel to the book of Jonah as it predicts the final fall of the powerful city of Nineveh, the great Assyrian capital. Written by Nahum the Elkoshite, a contemporary of the prophets Zephaniah, Jeremiah and Habakkuk, this book incorporates the purity of classical, poetic language with the forcefulness of prophetic imagery to convey the theme of Assyria's approaching doom. Though most of his words were directed to the Assyrians, Nahum briefly encouraged his people to observe their religious feasts, promising that the Assyrians would never again threaten Jerusalem (see 1:15).

Composed after the Assyrian conquest of Samaria in 721 B.C., Nahum's book vividly describes the ruthless subjugation of Assyria's enemies. Though the Assyrians had formerly been granted mercy because of their repentance under Jonah's ministry, Nahum stated that their return to cruelty and gross wickedness would ensure their destruction. Nahum warned that God's righteousness would not tolerate Nineveh's brutal cruelty forever. He graphically portrays the final siege and fall of the Assyrian capital. This prophecy against Assyria was ultimately fulfilled in 612 B.C. when the Babylonians invaded Assyria and destroyed Nineveh.

1 An oracle[a] concerning Nineveh.[b] The book of the vision[c] of Nahum the Elkoshite.

The LORD's Anger Against Nineveh

²The LORD is a jealous[d] and avenging God;
the LORD takes vengeance[e] and is filled with wrath.
The LORD takes vengeance on his foes
and maintains his wrath against his enemies.[f]
³The LORD is slow to anger[g] and great in power;
the LORD will not leave the guilty unpunished.[h]
His way is in the whirlwind[i] and the storm,[j]
and clouds[k] are the dust of his feet.
⁴He rebukes[l] the sea and dries it up;[m]
he makes all the rivers run dry.
Bashan and Carmel[n] wither
and the blossoms of Lebanon fade.
⁵The mountains quake[o] before him
and the hills melt away.[p]
The earth trembles[q] at his presence,
the world and all who live in it.[r]
⁶Who can withstand[s] his indignation?
Who can endure[t] his fierce anger?[u]
His wrath is poured out like fire;[v]
the rocks are shattered[w] before him.
⁷The LORD is good,[x]
a refuge in times of trouble.[y]
He cares for[z] those who trust in him,[a]
⁸ but with an overwhelming flood[b]
he will make an end of ⌞Nineveh⌟;
he will pursue his foes into darkness.
⁹Whatever they plot[c] against the LORD
he[a] will bring to an end;
trouble will not come a second time.
¹⁰They will be entangled among thorns[d]
and drunk[e] from their wine;
they will be consumed like dry stubble.[b][f]
¹¹From you, ⌞O Nineveh,⌟ has one come forth
who plots evil against the LORD
and counsels wickedness.
¹²This is what the LORD says:
"Although they have allies and are numerous,
they will be cut off[g] and pass away.
Although I have afflicted you,
⌞O Judah,⌟
I will afflict you no more.[h]
¹³Now I will break their yoke[i] from your neck
and tear your shackles away."[j]
¹⁴The LORD has given a command concerning you, ⌞Nineveh⌟:
"You will have no descendants to bear your name.[k]
I will destroy the carved images[l] and cast idols
that are in the temple of your gods.
I will prepare your grave,[m]
for you are vile."
¹⁵Look, there on the mountains,

P Mic 5:15 ◄ ► Na 1:5–12
H Mic 6:13 ◄ ► Na 1:5–6
S Mic 6:7–8 ◄ ► Zep 1:6–7
P Na 1:2 ◄ ► Na 1:15
H Na 1:2–3 ◄ ► Na 2:10
S Jnh 2:10 ◄ ► Mt 4:6

I Mic 7:11–20 ◄ ► Na 1:15
I Na 1:12 ◄ ► Zep 3:9–20
P Na 1:5–12 ◄ ► Hab 3:3–16

[a] 9 Or *What do you foes plot against the LORD? / He* [b] 10 The meaning of the Hebrew for this verse is uncertain.

1:1–3 Nahum announced that his prophecy against Nineveh was a "burden" or "oracle." In Hebrew this term relates to a word meaning "to lift up or carry" and may be understood as lifting up one's voice or carrying a burden of a message of doom. Nahum was conscious of the coming judgment of God upon Nineveh, and his words reflected the heaviness he felt in his heart as he delivered God's sentence of judgment.

In Nahum's time Nineveh was the greatest city in the world, defended by powerful armies and surrounded by reinforced walls. As the capital city of Assyria, Nineveh enjoyed an economic prosperity and military invincibility that led to arrogance and inhumanity to its enemies. Prisoners of war were cruelly tortured before they were killed. Nahum promised that God "will not leave the guilty unpunished" (1:3).

1:5–12 This prophecy of Nineveh's destruction was fulfilled in 612 B.C. when the invading armies of the Medes, the Babylonians and the Scythians overthrew this powerful city (see Eze 32:22–23).

1:15 Nahum's prophecy in this verse carried a double meaning. The direct reference here was to the good news of Judah's deliverance from the threat of the Assyrians. Yet Paul used this same imagery to announce the eternal deliverance from sin (see Ro 10:15). See also Isa 52:7.

the feet of one who brings good
    news,ⁿ
  who proclaims peace!ᵒ
Celebrate your festivals,ᵖ O Judah,
  and fulfill your vows.
No more will the wicked invade you;ᵠ
  they will be completely destroyed.

Nineveh to Fall

2 ¹An attackerʳ advances against you,
    ⌊Nineveh⌋.
  Guard the fortress,
  watch the road,
  brace yourselves,
  marshal all your strength!

²The LORD will restoreˢ the splendorᵗ of
    Jacob
  like the splendor of Israel,
though destroyers have laid them
    waste
  and have ruined their vines.

³The shields of his soldiers are red;
  the warriors are clad in scarlet.ᵘ
The metal on the chariots flashes
  on the day they are made ready;
  the spears of pine are brandished.ᶜ
⁴The chariotsᵛ storm through the
    streets,
  rushing back and forth through the
    squares.
They look like flaming torches;
  they dart about like lightning.

⁵He summons his picked troops,
  yet they stumbleʷ on their way.
They dash to the city wall;
  the protective shield is put in place.
⁶The river gatesˣ are thrown open
  and the palace collapses.
⁷It is decreedᵈ that ⌊the city⌋
  be exiled and carried away.
Its slave girls moanʸ like doves
  and beat upon their breasts.ᶻ

⁸Nineveh is like a pool,
  and its water is draining away.
"Stop! Stop!" they cry,
  but no one turns back.
⁹Plunder the silver!
  Plunder the gold!
The supply is endless,
  the wealth from all its treasures!

¹⁰She is pillaged, plundered, stripped!
  Hearts melt,ᵃ knees give way,

1:15 ⁿIsa 40:9;
Ro 10:15
ᵒS Isa 52:7;
Ac 10:36
ᵖLev 23:2-4
ᵠS Isa 52:1

2:1 ʳJer 51:20

2:2 ˢS Eze 37:23
ᵗIsa 60:15

2:3 ᵘS Eze 23:14-15

2:4 ᵛS Jer 4:13;
S Eze 23:24

2:5 ʷJer 46:12

2:6 ˣIsa 45:1;
Na 3:13

2:7 ʸS Ge 8:8;
S Isa 59:11
ᶻIsa 32:12

2:10 ᵃS Jos 2:11;
S 7:5
ᵇS Isa 29:22

2:11 ᶜIsa 5:29

2:12 ᵈS Jer 51:34
ᵉS Jer 4:7
ᶠS Isa 37:18

2:13 ᵍS Isa 10:5-13;
S Jer 21:13; Na 3:5
ʰPs 46:9
ⁱS 2Sa 2:26
ʲS Mic 5:6

3:1 ᵏS Eze 22:2;
S Mic 3:10 ˡPs 12:2

3:3 ᵐ2Ki 19:35;
Isa 34:3; Jer 47:3

3:4 ⁿS Isa 47:9
ᵒS Isa 23:17;
Eze 16:25-29

3:5 ᵖS Na 2:13;
Isa 20:4;
Jer 13:22
ᵠS Isa 47:3

3:6 ʳS Ex 29:14;
S Job 9:31

bodies tremble, every face grows
    pale.ᵇ
¹¹Where now is the lions' den,ᶜ
  the place where they fed their
    young,
  where the lion and lioness went,
  and the cubs, with nothing to fear?
¹²The lion killedᵈ enough for his cubs
  and strangled the prey for his mate,
  filling his lairsᵉ with the kill
  and his dens with the prey.ᶠ

¹³"I am againstᵍ you,"
  declares the LORD Almighty.
"I will burn up your chariots in
    smoke,ʰ
  and the swordⁱ will devour your
    young lions.
  I will leave you no prey on the
    earth.
The voices of your messengers
  will no longer be heard."ʲ

Woe to Nineveh

3 ¹Woe to the city of blood,ᵏ
    full of lies,ˡ
  full of plunder,
  never without victims!
²The crack of whips,
  the clatter of wheels,
  galloping horses
  and jolting chariots!
³Charging cavalry,
  flashing swords
  and glittering spears!
Many casualties,
  piles of dead,
  bodies without number,
  people stumbling over the
    corpsesᵐ—
⁴all because of the wanton lust of a
    harlot,
  alluring, the mistress of sorceries,ⁿ
  who enslaved nations by her
    prostitutionᵒ
  and peoples by her witchcraft.

⁵"I am againstᵖ you," declares the LORD
    Almighty.
  "I will lift your skirtsᵠ over your
    face.
  I will show the nations your
    nakednessʳ
  and the kingdoms your shame.
⁶I will pelt you with filth,ˢ

ᶜ3 Hebrew; Septuagint and Syriac / the horsemen rush to and fro
ᵈ7 The meaning of the Hebrew for this word is uncertain.

I will treat you with contempt[t]
and make you a spectacle.[u]
[7]All who see you will flee[v] from you
and say,
'Nineveh[w] is in ruins[x]—who will
mourn for her?'[y]
Where can I find anyone to comfort[z]
you?"
[8]Are you better than[a] Thebes,[e][b]
situated on the Nile,[c]
with water around her?
The river was her defense,
the waters her wall.
[9]Cush,[f][d] and Egypt were her boundless
strength;
Put[e] and Libya[f] were among her
allies.
[10]Yet she was taken captive[g]
and went into exile.
Her infants were dashed[h] to pieces
at the head of every street.
Lots[i] were cast for her nobles,
and all her great men were put in
chains.[j]
[11]You too will become drunk;[k]
you will go into hiding[l]
and seek refuge from the enemy.
[12]All your fortresses are like fig trees
with their first ripe fruit;[m]
when they are shaken,
the figs[n] fall into the mouth of the
eater.
[13]Look at your troops—
they are all women![o]
The gates[p] of your land
are wide open to your enemies;
fire has consumed their bars.[q]
[14]Draw water for the siege,[r]

strengthen your defenses![s]
Work the clay,
tread the mortar,
repair the brickwork!
[15]There the fire[t] will devour you;
the sword[u] will cut you down
and, like grasshoppers, consume
you.
Multiply like grasshoppers,
multiply like locusts![v]
[16]You have increased the number of
your merchants
till they are more than the stars of
the sky,
but like locusts[w] they strip the land
and then fly away.
[17]Your guards are like locusts,[x]
your officials like swarms of
locusts
that settle in the walls on a cold
day—
but when the sun appears they fly
away,
and no one knows where.

[18]O king of Assyria, your shepherds[g]
slumber;[y]
your nobles lie down to rest.[z]
Your people are scattered[a] on the
mountains
with no one to gather them.
[19]Nothing can heal your wound;[b]
your injury is fatal.
Everyone who hears the news about
you
claps his hands[c] at your fall,
for who has not felt
your endless cruelty?[d]

3:6 [t]S 1Sa 2:30;
S Jer 51:37
[u]Isa 14:16

3:7 [v]S Isa 13:14;
S 31:9 [w]S Na 1:1
[x]S Job 3:14
[y]S Jer 15:5
[z]S Isa 51:19

3:8 [a]Am 6:2
[b]S Jer 46:25
[c]Isa 19:6-9

3:9 [d]S Ge 10:6;
S 2Ch 12:3
[e]S Eze 27:10
[f]Eze 30:5

3:10 [g]S Isa 20:4
[h]S 2Ki 8:12;
S Isa 13:16;
Hos 13:16
[i]S Job 6:27;
S Eze 24:6
[j]S Jer 40:1

3:11 [k]S Isa 49:26
[l]S Isa 2:10

3:12 [m]S SS 2:13
[n]S Isa 28:4

3:13 [o]S Isa 19:16
[p]S Na 2:6
[q]S Isa 45:2

3:14 [r]S 2Ch 32:4
[s]Na 2:1

3:15 [t]S Isa 27:1
[u]S 2Sa 2:26
[v]S Jer 51:14;
S Joel 1:4

3:16 [w]S Ex 10:13

3:17 [x]S Jer 51:27

3:18 [y]S Ps 76:5-6;
S Jer 25:27
[z]Isa 56:10
[a]S 1Ki 22:17

3:19 [b]S Jer 30:13;
S Mic 1:9
[c]S Job 27:23;
S La 2:15; Zep 2:15
[d]Isa 37:18

[e]8 Hebrew *No Amon* [f]9 That is, the upper Nile region [g]18 Or *rulers*

3:7 Nahum declared that no one would feel sympathy when God's ultimate judgment fell upon the wicked city of Nineveh.

3:9–10 In this passage, Nahum compared Nineveh's arrogance to the arrogance of Thebes, one of the cities captured by the Assyrians. Both cities were located on rivers. Both cities thought they were invincible. Both cities had strong allies. But what the Assyrians did to Thebes would soon happen to Nineveh. Nineveh had reached the time of her final judgment by the hand of God. There was no escape.

3:11–15 Nahum's prophecy was fulfilled with chilling accuracy. Archeologists have confirmed that Nineveh was sacked and burned when the Medes, Babylonians and Scythians overran it in 612 B.C.

3:19 Nahum's prophecy revealed that God's judgment on Nineveh was irreversible. In fulfillment of this grave pronouncement, Nineveh was so totally destroyed that it was never rebuilt and the shifting desert sand covered its ruins.

Habakkuk

Author: Habakkuk

Theme: God's role in the face of evil and injustice

Date of Writing: c. 610–605 B.C.

Outline of Habakkuk
  I. Habakkuk's First Question and God's Answer (1:1–11)
  II. Habakkuk's Second Question and God's Answer (1:12—2:20)
  III. Habakkuk's Prayer of Thanksgiving (3:1–19)

LITTLE IS KNOWN about Habakkuk beyond his calling as a prophet of God. His name is unusual and comes from a Hebrew word meaning "to clasp or embrace," an appropriate name for a prophet who held to his vigorous faith in a time of national crisis. Certain statements in Habakkuk help date this prophecy to the time of King Jehoiakim and make Habakkuk a contemporary of Jeremiah. Habakkuk probably lived to see the initial fulfillment of his words when Jerusalem fell to the Babylonians in 597 B.C.

The book of Habakkuk consists of an ongoing conversation with God. The prophet recognized that the political and religious leaders of Judah had oppressed the poor and questioned why God would allow the wicked to prosper despite their obvious sins. God's answer to Habakkuk that the Babylonians would soon punish Judah led the prophet to question God's justice in allowing the Babylonians, who were more wicked than Judah's leaders, to bring judgment upon God's chosen people. God's reply silenced further questions when he reminded Habakkuk that the godly should have confidence in God's justice and mercy. Habakkuk was then assured that the Babylonians would be judged in God's time. Habakkuk closes his book with a psalm of praise that confirmed his acceptance of God's plan and his recognition of God's justice.

1 The oracle[a] that Habakkuk the prophet received.

Habakkuk's Complaint

[2] How long,[b] O LORD, must I call for help,
  but you do not listen?[c]
Or cry out to you, "Violence!"
  but you do not save?[d]
[3] Why do you make me look at injustice?
  Why do you tolerate[e] wrong?[f]
Destruction and violence[g] are before me;
  there is strife,[h] and conflict abounds.
[4] Therefore the law[i] is paralyzed,
  and justice never prevails.
The wicked hem in the righteous,
  so that justice[j] is perverted.[k]

The LORD's Answer

R [5] "Look at the nations and watch—
  and be utterly amazed.[l]
For I am going to do something in your days
  that you would not believe,
  even if you were told.[m]
[6] I am raising up the Babylonians,[a][n]
  that ruthless and impetuous people,
who sweep across the whole earth[o]
  to seize dwelling places not their own.[p]
[7] They are a feared and dreaded people;[q]
  they are a law to themselves
  and promote their own honor.
[8] Their horses are swifter[r] than leopards,
  fiercer than wolves[s] at dusk.
Their cavalry gallops headlong;
  their horsemen come from afar.
They fly like a vulture swooping to devour;
[9] they all come bent on violence.
Their hordes[b] advance like a desert wind
  and gather prisoners[t] like sand.
[10] They deride kings
  and scoff at rulers.[u]
They laugh at all fortified cities;
  they build earthen ramps[v] and capture them.
[11] Then they sweep past like the wind[w]
  and go on—
guilty men, whose own strength is their god."[x]

R Na 2:2 ◀ ▶ Hab 2:6–13

1:1 [a]S Na 1:1
1:2 [b]S Ps 6:3
  [c]Ps 13:1-2; 22:1-2
  [d]Jer 14:9; Zec 1:12
1:3 [e]ver 13
  [f]S Job 9:23
  [g]Jer 20:8
  [h]S Ps 55:9
1:4 [i]Ps 119:126
  [j]S Isa 29:21
  [k]S Job 19:7;
  S Isa 1:23; 5:20;
  S Eze 9:9
1:5 [l]S Isa 29:9
  [m]Ac 13:41*
1:6 [n]S Dt 28:49;
  S 2Ki 24:2
  [o]Rev 20:9
  [p]S Jer 13:20; S 21:5
1:7 [q]Isa 18:7;
  Jer 39:5-9
1:8 [r]S Jer 4:13
  [s]S Ge 49:27
1:9 [t]Hab 2:5
1:10 [u]S 2Ch 36:6
  [v]S Jer 33:4
1:11 [w]Jer 4:11-12
  [x]S Da 4:30
1:12 [y]S Ge 21:33
  [z]Isa 31:1; 37:23
  [a]Ps 118:17
  [b]Isa 10:6
  [c]S Ge 49:24;
  S Ex 33:22
1:13 [d]Ps 18:26
  [e]S La 3:34-36
  [f]ver 3 [g]S Ps 25:3
  [h]S Job 21:7
1:15 [i]Jer 5:26
  [j]S Isa 19:8
  [k]S Job 18:8;
  Jer 16:16
1:16 [l]Jer 44:8
1:17 [m]S Isa 14:6;
  19:8
2:1 [n]S Isa 21:8
  [o]S Ps 48:13
  [p]Ps 85:8 [q]S Ps 5:3;
  S Eze 3:17
2:2 [r]S Isa 30:8;
  S Jer 36:2;
  S Eze 24:2;
  S Ro 4:24; Rev 1:19
2:3 [s]Da 11:27
  [t]Da 8:17
  [u]S Ps 27:14
  [v]S Eze 12:25

Habakkuk's Second Complaint

[12] O LORD, are you not from everlasting?[y]
  My God, my Holy One,[z] we will not die.[a]
O LORD, you have appointed[b] them to execute judgment;
O Rock,[c] you have ordained them to punish.
[13] Your eyes are too pure[d] to look on evil;
  you cannot tolerate wrong.[e]
Why then do you tolerate[f] the treacherous?[g]
Why are you silent while the wicked
  swallow up those more righteous than themselves?[h]
[14] You have made men like fish in the sea,
  like sea creatures that have no ruler.
[15] The wicked[i] foe pulls all of them up with hooks,[j]
he catches them in his net,[k]
he gathers them up in his dragnet;
  and so he rejoices and is glad.
[16] Therefore he sacrifices to his net
  and burns incense[l] to his dragnet,
for by his net he lives in luxury
  and enjoys the choicest food.
[17] Is he to keep on emptying his net,
  destroying nations without mercy?[m]

2 I will stand at my watch[n]
  and station myself on the ramparts;[o]
I will look to see what he will say[p] to me,
  and what answer I am to give to this complaint.[c][q]

The LORD's Answer

[2] Then the LORD replied:

"Write[r] down the revelation
  and make it plain on tablets
so that a herald[d] may run with it.
[3] For the revelation awaits an appointed time;[s]
  it speaks of the end[t]
  and will not prove false.
Though it linger, wait[u] for it;
  it[e] will certainly come and will not delay.[v]

[a] 6 Or Chaldeans [b] 9 The meaning of the Hebrew for this word is uncertain. [c] 1 Or and what to answer when I am rebuked [d] 2 Or so that whoever reads it [e] 3 Or Though he linger, wait for him; / he

HABAKKUK 2:4

⁴"See, he is puffed up;
  his desires are not upright—
  but the righteous^w will live by his faith^{/x}—
⁵indeed, wine^y betrays him;
  he is arrogant^z and never at rest.
Because he is as greedy as the grave,^g
  and like death is never satisfied,^a
he gathers to himself all the nations
  and takes captive^b all the peoples.

⁶"Will not all of them taunt^c him with ridicule and scorn, saying,

" 'Woe to him who piles up stolen goods
    and makes himself wealthy by extortion!^d
  How long must this go on?'
⁷Will not your debtors^h suddenly arise?
  Will they not wake up and make you tremble?
  Then you will become their victim.^e
⁸Because you have plundered many nations,
  the peoples who are left will plunder you.^f
For you have shed man's blood;^g
  you have destroyed lands and cities
  and everyone in them.^h

⁹"Woe to him who buildsⁱ his realm by unjust gain^j
  to set his nest^k on high,
  to escape the clutches of ruin!
¹⁰You have plotted the ruin^l of many peoples,
  shaming^m your own house and forfeiting your life.
¹¹The stonesⁿ of the wall will cry out,
  and the beams of the woodwork will echo it.

¹²"Woe to him who builds a city with bloodshed^o
  and establishes a town by crime!
¹³Has not the LORD Almighty determined that the people's labor is only fuel for the fire,^p
  that the nations exhaust themselves for nothing?^q
¹⁴For the earth will be filled with the knowledge of the glory^r of the LORD,
  as the waters cover the sea.^s

¹⁵"Woe to him who gives drink^t to his neighbors,
  pouring it from the wineskin till they are drunk,
  so that he can gaze on their naked bodies.
¹⁶You will be filled with shame^u instead of glory.^v
  Now it is your turn! Drink^w and be exposed[/]!^x
The cup^y from the LORD's right hand is coming around to you,
  and disgrace will cover your glory.
¹⁷The violence^z you have done to Lebanon will overwhelm you,
  and your destruction of animals will terrify you.^a
For you have shed man's blood;^b
  you have destroyed lands and cities and everyone in them.

¹⁸"Of what value^c is an idol,^d since a man has carved it?
Or an image^e that teaches lies?
For he who makes it trusts in his own creation;
  he makes idols that cannot speak.^f
¹⁹Woe to him who says to wood, 'Come to life!'
  Or to lifeless stone, 'Wake up!'^g
Can it give guidance?
It is covered with gold and silver;^h
  there is no breath in it.ⁱ
²⁰But the LORD is in his holy temple;^j

C *Am 6:12* ◄► *Zep 1:12*
F *Jer 17:7* ◄► *Mt 11:12*
M *Jnh 3:5–10* ◄► *Zep 2:2–3*
R *Hab 1:5–12* ◄► *Hab 2:15–19*

2:4 ^wS Eze 18:9; ^xRo 1:17*; Gal 3:11*; Heb 10:37-38*
2:5 ^yS Pr 20:1; ^zS Isa 2:11; ^aS Pr 27:20; S 30:15-16; ^bHab 1:9
2:6 ^cS Isa 14:4; ^dAm 2:8
2:7 ^eS Pr 29:1
2:8 ^fIsa 33:1; Jer 50:17-18; S Ob 1:15; Zec 2:8-9 ^gver 17; ^hS Eze 39:10
2:9 ⁱS Jer 22:13; ^jS Jer 51:13; ^kS Job 39:27; S Isa 10:14
2:10 ^lJer 26:19; ^mver 16; S Na 3:6
2:11 ⁿS Jos 24:27; Zec 5:4; Lk 19:40
2:12 ^oS Eze 22:2; S Mic 3:10
2:13 ^pIsa 50:11; ^qS Isa 47:13
2:14 ^rS Ex 16:7; S Nu 14:21; ^sS Isa 11:9
2:15 ^tS Pr 23:20
2:16 ^uS ver 10; ^vS Eze 23:32-34; Hos 4:7; ^wS Lev 10:9; ^xS La 4:21; ^yS Ps 16:5; S Isa 51:22
2:17 ^zS Jer 51:35; ^aS Jer 50:15 ^bver 8
2:18 ^cS 1Sa 12:21; ^dS Jdg 10:14; S Isa 40:19; S Jer 5:21; S 14:22; ^eS Lev 26:1; ^fPs 115:4-5; Jer 10:14; 1Co 12:2
2:19 ^g1Ki 18:27; ^hS Jer 10:4; ⁱS Da 5:4,23; S Hos 4:12
2:20 ^jS Ps 11:4

K *Da 7:13–14* ◄► *Zec 14:9*
M *Mic 5:2* ◄► *Hab 2:20*
R *Hab 2:6–13* ◄► *Zep 1:2–4*
M *Hab 2:14* ◄► *Hag 2:23*

4 Or *faithfulness* *5* Hebrew *Sheol* *7* Or *creditors* *16* Masoretic Text; Dead Sea Scrolls, Aquila, Vulgate and Syriac (see also Septuagint) *and stagger*

2:14 Habakkuk's words hold a double meaning. When Babylon was destroyed by the Medo-Persians, Babylon's glory paled in comparison to God's glory. In the millennial kingdom of the Messiah, Habakkuk's words will take on their full meaning. God's glory will outshine the glory of the nations, and all of humanity will know the truth of God.

2:20 Just as stone idols maintained their silence before their worshipers, humanity will stand in silence before the Judge of all the earth (see Isa 41:1; Zep 1:7; Zec 2:13).

Habakkuk's Prayer

3 A prayer of Habakkuk the prophet. On *shigionoth*.[/1]

[2] LORD, I have heard[m] of your fame;
  I stand in awe[n] of your deeds,
    O LORD.[o]
  Renew[p] them in our day,
    in our time make them known;
  in wrath remember mercy.[q]

[3] God came from Teman,[r]
    the Holy One[s] from Mount Paran.[t]
                                  Selah
  His glory covered the heavens[u]
    and his praise filled the earth.[v]
[4] His splendor was like the sunrise;[w]
    rays flashed from his hand,
    where his power[x] was hidden.
[5] Plague[y] went before him;
    pestilence followed his steps.
[6] He stood, and shook the earth;
    he looked, and made the nations tremble.
  The ancient mountains crumbled[z]
    and the age-old hills[a] collapsed.[b]
  His ways are eternal.[c]
[7] I saw the tents of Cushan in distress,
    the dwellings of Midian[d] in anguish.[e]

[8] Were you angry with the rivers,[f]
    O LORD?
  Was your wrath against the streams?
  Did you rage against the sea[g]
    when you rode with your horses
    and your victorious chariots?[h]
[9] You uncovered your bow,
    you called for many arrows.[i] *Selah*
  You split the earth with rivers;
[10]   the mountains saw you and writhed.[j]
  Torrents of water swept by;
    the deep roared[k]
    and lifted its waves[l] on high.

[11] Sun and moon stood still[m] in the heavens
    at the glint of your flying arrows,[n]
    at the lightning[o] of your flashing spear.
[12] In wrath you strode through the earth
    and in anger you threshed[p] the nations.
[13] You came out[q] to deliver[r] your people,
    to save your anointed[s] one.
  You crushed[t] the leader of the land of wickedness,
    you stripped him from head to foot.
                                  Selah
[14] With his own spear you pierced his head
    when his warriors stormed out to scatter us,[u]
    gloating as though about to devour
    the wretched[v] who were in hiding.
[15] You trampled the sea[w] with your horses,
    churning the great waters.[x]

[16] I heard and my heart pounded,
    my lips quivered at the sound;

P Na 1:15 ◄ ► Zep 1:14–18

2:20 k S Isa 41:1
3:1 l Ps 7 Title
3:2 m S Job 26:14; Ps 44:1
  n S Ps 119:120
  o S Ps 90:16
  p Ps 85:6 q Isa 54:8
3:3 r S Ge 36:11,15
  s Isa 31:1
  t S Nu 10:12
  u S Ps 8:1 v Ps 48:10
3:4 w S Isa 18:4
  x S Job 9:6
3:5 y S Lev 26:25
3:6 z S Ps 46:2
  a Ge 49:26
  b S Ex 19:18; Ps 18:7; 114:1-6
  c S Ge 21:33
3:7 d S Ge 25:2; S Nu 25:15; Jdg 7:24-25
  e Ex 15:14
3:8 f S Ex 7:20
  g S Ps 77:16
  h S 2Ki 2:11; S Ps 68:17
3:9 i S Dt 32:23; Ps 7:12-13
3:10 j S Ps 77:16
  k Ps 98:7 l S Ps 93:3
3:11 m Jos 10:13
  n Ps 18:14
  o S Ps 144:6; Zec 9:14
3:12 p S Isa 41:15
3:13 q S Ex 13:21
  r S Ps 20:6; S 28:8
  s S 2Sa 23:1
  t Ps 68:21; 110:6
3:14 u Jdg 7:22
  v Ps 64:2-5
3:15 w S Job 9:8
  x Ex 15:8

/1 Probably a literary or musical term   k3 A word of uncertain meaning; possibly a musical term; also in verses 9 and 13

3:2 Habakkuk remembered God's miraculous works among his ancestors and asked God to intercede again in such a way. Note that Habakkuk acknowledged that God's ways are merciful even if not completely comprehensible.

3:3–16 In this passage Habakkuk recalled the events of the deliverance from Egypt, God's miraculous provision in the Sinai and the overwhelming victories of the conquest of Canaan. Habakkuk referenced well-known miracles and historical happenings such as plagues (3:5; see Ex 7—12), earthquakes (3:6; see Ex 19:18), military victories (3:8; see Jos 2:9–10), natural phenomena (3:11; see Jos 10:12–13) and the miracle at the Red Sea (3:14–15; see Ex 14:15–31). Though Habakkuk recognized the imminent judgment of God upon the people of Israel, these past events and miraculous interventions set the precedent for God's ultimate deliverance of his people.

Though Israel experienced partial restoration after their return from Babylonian exile, the final fulfillment of Israel's deliverance and restoration will not take place until Christ returns and sets up his millennial kingdom. Just as God used supernatural happenings in the past to signal his intervention in Israel's deliverance, these supernatural occurrences will also take place in the end times (see Joel 2:10; Mt 24:7, 14–15, 29; Mk 13:24; Lk 21:25; Rev 6:8).

3:13 The latter half of this verse forms a curious prophecy that has a double meaning. When the Israelites entered Canaan and began to conquer it, God gave them victory over the heads of many ruling princes and kings, razing their family line to the foundation. This prophecy may also be applied to the victory of the Messiah over the armies of the antichrist in the end times (see Ps 110:6).

HABAKKUK 3:17

decay crept into my bones,
   and my legs trembled.ʸ
Yet I will wait patientlyᶻ for the day of calamity
   to come on the nation invading us.
¹⁷Though the fig tree does not bud
   and there are no grapes on the vines,
though the olive crop fails
   and the fields produce no food,ᵃ

F Joel 2:24–26 ◀ ▶ Mt 4:11
J Isa 51:12 ◀ ▶ Mt 5:11–12

3:16 ʸS Job 4:14
     ᶻS Ps 37:7
3:17 ᵃJoel 1:10-12, 18
     ᵇJer 5:17
3:18 ᶜPs 97:12; S Isa 61:10; Php 4:4
     ᵈS Ex 15:2; S Lk 1:47
3:19 ᵉS Dt 33:29; Ps 46:1-5
     ᶠS Dt 32:13; Ps 18:33

though there are no sheep in the pen
   and no cattle in the stalls,ᵇ
¹⁸yet I will rejoice in the LORD,ᶜ
   I will be joyful in God my Savior.ᵈ

¹⁹The Sovereign LORD is my strength;ᵉ
   he makes my feet like the feet of a deer,
   he enables me to go on the heights.ᶠ

For the director of music. On my stringed instruments.

3:19 Habakkuk concluded his prophecy with a declaration of God's blessing and help despite trouble and hard times. Note the metaphor Habakkuk used is that of a deer. These sure-footed animals can walk securely on high, rocky ledges. Similarly, Habakkuk purposed to follow in the footsteps of God, knowing that God's way was the only secure way to go. We, too, should purpose to follow Christ, confident to "go on the heights" because we will be following in his footsteps.

Zephaniah

Author: Zephaniah

Theme: The coming day of the Lord

Date of Writing: c. 635–630 B.C.

Outline of Zephaniah
  I. The Day of the Lord Is Coming (1:1–18)
  II. God's Judgment on the Nations (2:1—3:8)
  III. Redemption and the Coming Kingdom (3:9–20)

THE PROPHET ZEPHANIAH, whose name means "The Lord hides (or protects)," wrote this prophecy of God's approaching judgment on Judah. His prophetic ministry is specifically dated to the reign of King Josiah (see 1:1), making him a contemporary of Jeremiah, Nahum and possibly Habakkuk. Zephaniah's words show a familiarity with royal and political issues, lending credence to the Hebrew tradition that Zephaniah may have been a descendant of King Hezekiah.

The book of Zephaniah records the warning that the "day of the LORD" will come and bring judgment upon Judah and Jerusalem. With vivid details Zephaniah describes this coming day of judgment, using the term "day of the LORD" repeatedly. This prophecy probably referred to the invasion of the Babylonians in 605–586 B.C. Though Zephaniah urged the nation of Judah to seek righteousness so that they would "be sheltered on the day of the LORD's anger" (2:3), the people refused to listen and God's promised judgment was carried out.

After calling Judah to repent, Zephaniah also foresaw the future judgment on foreign nations (see 2:13) and the final restoration of Israel under the Messiah, the future King of Israel, who will rule forever in Zion. Though Judah's guilt was certain and her punishment was inevitable, God's promise of restoration is assured too.

ZEPHANIAH 1:1

1 The word of the LORD that came to Zephaniah son of Cushi, the son of Gedaliah, the son of Amariah, the son of Hezekiah, during the reign of Josiah son of Amon king of Judah:

Warning of Coming Destruction

² "I will sweep away everything
    from the face of the earth,"
        declares the LORD.
³ "I will sweep away both men and
        animals;
    I will sweep away the birds of the
        air
    and the fish of the sea.
    The wicked will have only heaps of
        rubble
    when I cut off man from the face of
        the earth,"
        declares the LORD.

Against Judah

⁴ "I will stretch out my hand against
        Judah
    and against all who live in
        Jerusalem.
    I will cut off from this place every
        remnant of Baal,
    the names of the pagan and the
        idolatrous priests—
⁵ those who bow down on the roofs
        to worship the starry host,
    those who bow down and swear by the
        LORD
    and who also swear by Molech,
⁶ those who turn back from following
        the LORD
    and neither seek the LORD nor
        inquire of him.
⁷ Be silent before the Sovereign LORD,
    for the day of the LORD is near.
    The LORD has prepared a sacrifice;
    he has consecrated those he has
        invited.
⁸ On the day of the LORD's sacrifice
    I will punish the princes

and the king's sons
    and all those clad
        in foreign clothes.
⁹ On that day I will punish
    all who avoid stepping on the
        threshold,
    who fill the temple of their gods
        with violence and deceit.

¹⁰ "On that day," declares the LORD,
    "a cry will go up from the Fish
        Gate,
    wailing from the New Quarter,
    and a loud crash from the hills.
¹¹ Wail, you who live in the market
        district;
    all your merchants will be wiped
        out,
    all who trade with silver will be
        ruined.
¹² At that time I will search Jerusalem
        with lamps
    and punish those who are
        complacent,
    who are like wine left on its dregs,
    who think, 'The LORD will do nothing,
        either good or bad.'
¹³ Their wealth will be plundered,
    their houses demolished.
    They will build houses
        but not live in them;
    they will plant vineyards
        but not drink the wine.

The Great Day of the LORD

¹⁴ "The great day of the LORD is near—
    near and coming quickly.
    Listen! The cry on the day of the LORD
        will be bitter,
    the shouting of the warrior there.
¹⁵ That day will be a day of wrath,
    a day of distress and anguish,

R Hab 2:15–19 ◀ ▶ Zec 1:12–15
H Na 2:10 ◀ ▶ Zep 1:12
S Na 1:3 ◀ ▶ Zep 2:3

C Hab 2:4 ◀ ▶ Mal 3:13–14
H Zep 1:6–8 ◀ ▶ Zep 1:14–15
P Hab 3:3–16 ◀ ▶ Zep 3:8
H Zep 1:12 ◀ ▶ Zep 1:17–18

ᵃ 3 The meaning of the Hebrew for this line is uncertain. ᵇ 5 Hebrew *Malcam*, that is, Milcom. ᶜ 9 See 1 Samuel 5:5. ᵈ 11 Or the Mortar ᵉ 11 Or in

---

1:2–4 Zephaniah described the terrible judgment of God during the tribulation when all living things would experience God's unprecedented wrath. This sweeping destruction mirrors the destruction of the flood (see Ge 6:7), but this judgment will be carried out with fire (see 1:18; 3:8).

1:14–18 Zephaniah warned about the imminent "great day of the LORD" (1:14). With dramatic imagery Zephaniah described the worldwide destruction that would accompany this "day of wrath" (1:15). Neither wealth nor position would protect the wicked from this time of desolation and trouble.

a day of trouble and ruin,
 a day of darkness and gloom,
 a day of clouds and blackness,
¹⁶a day of trumpet and battle cry
 against the fortified cities
 and against the corner towers.

¹⁷I will bring distress on the people
 and they will walk like blind men,
 because they have sinned against
  the LORD.
 Their blood will be poured out like
  dust
 and their entrails like filth.
¹⁸Neither their silver nor their gold
 will be able to save them
 on the day of the LORD's wrath.
In the fire of his jealousy
 the whole world will be consumed,
for he will make a sudden end
 of all who live in the earth.

2 Gather together, gather together,
 O shameful nation,
²before the appointed time arrives
 and that day sweeps on like chaff,
before the fierce anger of the LORD
 comes upon you,
before the day of the LORD's wrath
 comes upon you.
³Seek the LORD, all you humble of the
 land,
 you who do what he commands.
 Seek righteousness, seek humility;
 perhaps you will be sheltered
 on the day of the LORD's anger.

Against Philistia

⁴Gaza will be abandoned
 and Ashkelon left in ruins.
 At midday Ashdod will be emptied
 and Ekron uprooted.
⁵Woe to you who live by the sea,
 O Kerethite people;
the word of the LORD is against you,
 O Canaan, land of the Philistines.
"I will destroy you,
 and none will be left."
⁶The land by the sea, where the
  Kerethites dwell,
 will be a place for shepherds and
  sheep pens.
⁷It will belong to the remnant of the
  house of Judah;
 there they will find pasture.
 In the evening they will lie down
  in the houses of Ashkelon.
 The LORD their God will care for them;
 he will restore their fortunes.

Against Moab and Ammon

⁸"I have heard the insults of Moab
  and the taunts of the Ammonites,
 who insulted my people
  and made threats against their land.
⁹Therefore, as surely as I live,"
 declares the LORD Almighty, the God
  of Israel,
 "surely Moab will become like
  Sodom,
 the Ammonites like Gomorrah—
 a place of weeds and salt pits,
  a wasteland forever.
 The remnant of my people will
  plunder them;
 the survivors of my nation will
  inherit their land."
¹⁰This is what they will get in return for
  their pride,
 for insulting and mocking the
  people of the LORD Almighty.
¹¹The LORD will be awesome to them
 when he destroys all the gods of
  the land.
 The nations on every shore will
  worship him,
 every one in its own land.

f 6 The meaning of the Hebrew for this word is uncertain. g 7 Or will bring back their captives

2:1–3 Zephaniah warned his people to repent of their wickedness in order that his people would "be sheltered on the day of the Lord's anger" (2:3).
2:4 This prophecy of judgment declared doom on four of the five great Philistine cities, indicating the extent of the destruction of this nation. Throughout the centuries following this prophecy, these ancient cities of Philistia have been conquered, rebuilt and conquered again. History records that the conquest of Gaza by Alexander the Great in 332 B.C. took over two months because of Gaza's strong defenses. When Alexander finally took the city, he killed all the male survivors and sold the women and children into slavery.

Against Cush

¹²"You too, O Cushites,ʰᵉ
    will be slain by my sword.'"

Against Assyria

¹³He will stretch out his hand against
    the north
and destroy Assyria,ᵍ
    leaving Ninevehʰ utterly desolate
    and dry as the desert.ⁱ
¹⁴Flocks and herdsʲ will lie down there,
    creatures of every kind.
The desert owlᵏ and the screech owlˡᵐ
    will roost on her columns.
Their calls will echo through the
    windows,
    rubble will be in the doorways,
    the beams of cedar will be exposed.
¹⁵This is the carefreeⁿ city
    that lived in safety.ᵒ
She said to herself,
    "I am, and there is none besides
    me."ᵖ
What a ruin she has become,
    a lair for wild beasts!ᵠ
All who pass by her scoffʳ
    and shake their fists.ˢ

The Future of Jerusalem

3 Woe to the city of oppressors,ᵗ
    rebelliousᵘ and defiled!ᵛ
²She obeysʷ no one,
    she accepts no correction.ˣ
She does not trustʸ in the LORD,
    she does not draw nearᶻ to her God.
³Her officials are roaring lions,ᵃ
    her rulers are evening wolves,ᵇ
    who leave nothing for the morning.ᶜ
⁴Her prophets are arrogant;
    they are treacherousᵈ men.
Her priests profane the sanctuary
    and do violence to the law.ᵉ
⁵The LORD within her is righteous;ᶠ
    he does no wrong.ᵍ

2:12 ᵉS Ge 10:6;
S Isa 20:4
ᶠS Jer 46:10
2:13 ᵍS Isa 10:5
ʰS Ge 10:11;
S Na 1:1 ⁱS Mic 5:6;
Zec 10:11
2:14 ʲS Isa 5:17
ᵏS Isa 14:23
ˡRev 18:2
ᵐS Ps 102:6
2:15 ⁿS Isa 32:9
ᵒIsa 47:8 ᵖEze 28:2
ᵠJer 49:33
ʳS Isa 28:22;
S Na 3:19
ˢS Eze 27:36
3:1 ᵗS Jer 6:6
ᵘS Dt 21:18
ᵛS Eze 23:30
3:2 ʷS Jer 22:21
ˣS Lev 26:23;
S Jer 7:28
ʸS Dt 1:32
ᶻS Ps 73:28
3:3 ᵃS Ps 22:13
ᵇS Ge 49:27
ᶜS Mic 3:3
3:4 ᵈS Ps 25:3;
S Isa 48:8; Jer 3:20;
9:4; Mal 2:10
ᵉS Jer 23:11;
S Eze 22:26
3:5 ᶠS Ezr 9:15
ᵍDt 32:4
ʰS Ps 5:3
ⁱS La 3:23
ʲS Jer 3:3;
S Eze 18:25
3:6 ᵏS Lev 26:31
3:7 ˡS Jer 7:28
ᵐS Hos 9:9
3:8 ⁿS Ps 27:14
ᵒS Joel 3:11
ᵖS Isa 2:3 ᵠS Ps 79:6;
Rev 16:1
ʳS Jer 10:25;
S La 4:11
ˢS Zep 1:18
3:9 ᵗS Zep 2:11
ᵘS Ge 4:26
ᵛS Isa 19:18
3:10 ʷS Ge 10:6;
S Ps 68:31

Morning by morningʰ he dispenses his
    justice,
and every new day he does not fail,ⁱ
    yet the unrighteous know no
    shame.ʲ
⁶"I have cut off nations;
    their strongholds are demolished.
I have left their streets deserted,
    with no one passing through.
Their cities are destroyed;ᵏ
    no one will be left—no one at all.
⁷I said to the city,
    'Surely you will fear me
    and accept correction!'ˡ
Then her dwelling would not be cut
    off,
nor all my punishments come upon
    her.
But they were still eager
    to act corruptlyᵐ in all they did.

⁸Therefore waitⁿ for me," declares the
    LORD,
    "for the day I will stand up to
    testify.ᵒ
I have decided to assembleᵒ the
    nations,ᵖ
    to gather the kingdoms
and to pour out my wrathᵠ on them—
    all my fierce anger.ʳ
The whole world will be consumedˢ
    by the fire of my jealous anger.

⁹"Then will I purify the lips of the
    peoples,
that all of them may callᵗ on the
    name of the LORDᵘ
and serveᵛ him shoulder to
    shoulder.
¹⁰From beyond the rivers of Cushʲʷ

P *Zep 1:14–18* ◀ ▶ *Hag 2:22*
H *Zep 2:2–3* ◀ ▶ *Zec 3:2*
I *Na 1:15* ◀ ▶ *Hag 2:7*

ʰ 12 That is, people from the upper Nile region ⁱ 8 Septuagint and Syriac; Hebrew *will rise up to plunder* ʲ 10 That is, the upper Nile region

---

3:8 This prophecy looks forward to the tribulation and the final Battle of Armageddon when Jesus Christ will destroy the armies of the antichrist and his allies. God will then judge the nations and "pour out my wrath on them." Compare this verse with Joel 3:2; Mt 25:31–32; Rev 16:14.

3:9 Though some view this verse as a prophecy regarding the reestablishment of ancient Hebrew as the language of millennial Jerusalem, others understand this verse as a prophecy of the purification of the nations. God's judgment in the last days will impact the nations so much that they will turn from their idols and worship him in both word and deed. They will call on his name and honor him and honor his chosen people. Compare this verse with Isa 6:5 and Hos 2:17.

3:10 Cush is believed to be the area of southern Egypt, Sudan and northern Ethiopia. Exiled Jews have made this part of the world their home for centuries, with some Ethiopians claiming King Solomon as their ancestor. Though some of these Jews are slowly returning to the promised land, Zephaniah's

my worshipers, my scattered people,
will bring me offerings.ˣ
¹¹On that day you will not be put to
    shameʸ
for all the wrongs you have done to
    me,ᶻ
because I will remove from this city
    those who rejoice in their pride.ᵃ
Never again will you be haughty
    on my holy hill.ᵇ
¹²But I will leave within you
    the meekᶜ and humble,
who trustᵈ in the name of the LORD.
¹³The remnantᵉ of Israel will do no
    wrong;ᶠ
they will speak no lies,ᵍ
nor will deceit be found in their
    mouths.ʰ
They will eat and lie downⁱ
and no one will make them afraid.ʲ"

¹⁴Sing, O Daughter of Zion;ᵏ
    shout aloud,¹ O Israel!
Be glad and rejoiceᵐ with all your
    heart,
    O Daughter of Jerusalem!
¹⁵The LORD has taken away your
    punishment,
he has turned back your enemy.
The LORD, the King of Israel, is with
    you;ⁿ
never again will you fearᵒ any
    harm.ᵖ

¹⁶On that day they will say to Jerusalem,
"Do not fear, O Zion;
do not let your hands hang limp.ᵠ
¹⁷The LORD your God is with you,
he is mighty to save.ʳ
He will take great delightˢ in you,
he will quiet you with his love,ᵗ
he will rejoice over you with
    singing."ᵘ
¹⁸"The sorrows for the appointed feasts
I will remove from you;
they are a burden and a reproach to
    you.ᵏ
¹⁹At that time I will deal
    with all who oppressedᵛ you;
I will rescue the lame
    and gather those who have been
        scattered.ʷ
I will give them praiseˣ and honor
    in every land where they were put
        to shame.
²⁰At that time I will gather you;
    at that time I will bringʸ you home.
I will give you honorᶻ and praiseᵃ
    among all the peoples of the earth
when I restore your fortunesˡᵇ
    before your very eyes,"
        says the LORD.

3:10 ˣ S 2Ch 32:23; S Isa 60:7
3:11 ʸ S Isa 29:22; S Joel 2:26-27 ᶻ S Ge 50:15 ᵃ S Ps 59:12 ᵇ S Ex 15:17; S Lev 26:19
3:12 ᶜ Isa 14:32 ᵈ S Jer 29:12; Na 1:7
3:13 ᵉ S Isa 10:21 ᶠ Ps 119:3; S Isa 4:3 ᵍ S Jer 33:16; Rev 14:5 ʰ S Job 16:17 ⁱ Eze 34:15; Zep 2:7 ʲ S Lev 26:6; S Eze 34:25-28
3:14 ᵏ S Ps 9:14; Zec 2:10 ˡ S Ps 95:1; Isa 12:6; Zec 2:10 ᵐ S Ps 9:2; S Isa 51:11
3:15 ⁿ Eze 37:26-28 ᵒ S Isa 54:14 ᵖ Zec 9:9
3:16 ᵠ S 2Ki 19:26; S Job 4:3; Isa 35:3-4; Heb 12:12
3:17 ʳ S Isa 63:1; S Joel 2:21 ˢ S Dt 28:63; S Isa 62:4 ᵗ S Hos 14:4 ᵘ S Isa 40:1
3:19 ᵛ S Isa 14:2 ʷ S Eze 34:16; S Mic 4:6 ˣ Isa 60:18
3:20 ʸ S Jer 29:14; S Eze 37:12 ᶻ Isa 56:5; 66:22 ᵃ S Dt 26:19; S Isa 60:18
ᵇ S Joel 3:1

k 18 Or "I will gather you who mourn for the appointed feasts; / your reproach is a burden to you" l 20 Or I bring back your captives

---

words promised that all of the Jews who were widely scattered to the far ends of the world would be restored to their homeland when the Messiah returns.
3:11—20 God promised that his people would be fully restored to Jerusalem and the promised land in the last days. There would be joy in the city, no more lying, no unrighteousness, an abundance of peace and security because the Messiah would be in their midst. Zephaniah encouraged the people to take heart because of God's assurance of restoration. In contrast to the messages of doom and judgment on Israel, this prophecy promised blessing and God's intent to give Israel "praise among all the peoples of the earth" (3:20).

Haggai

Author: Haggai

Theme: The blessing in rebuilding

Date of Writing: c. 520 B.C.

Outline of Haggai
  I. The People Stirred to Action (1:1–15)
  II. Hopes for the New Temple (2:1–9)
  III. Promised Blessings (2:10–19)
  IV. God's Final Triumph (2:20–23)

THIS VERY SHORT book takes its name from the prophet Haggai, who ministered during the reign of King Darius to the returned exiles in Jerusalem. A contemporary of Zechariah, Haggai noticed that the exiles who had returned from Babylon had not rebuilt the temple because they were too busy rebuilding their own homes. In four distinct messages Haggai vehemently reproved his people and demanded that they obey God's command to rebuild his temple in Jerusalem. Haggai is one of the few prophets who saw a positive response to his urgings.

The Babylonian exiles had been granted permission to return to the promised land to rebuild God's temple. Though the people started the project with enthusiasm, they soon turned their attention to their own needs, and God withdrew his blessing from them. Haggai assured the people that if they would give priority to God's work they would prosper. His words roused the people to action under the leadership of Zerubbabel, governor of Judea, and Joshua the high priest. As the rebuilding project resumed, many of the older exiles were saddened that the rebuilt temple was not as magnificent as Solomon's temple had been before its destruction in 586 B.C. Haggai reassured them that even though the building might be less impressive, the glory of this rebuilt temple would be greater than that of the former.

A Call to Build the House of the LORD

1 In the second year of King Darius, on the first day of the sixth month, the word of the LORD came through the prophet Haggai to Zerubbabel son of Shealtiel, governor of Judah, and to Joshua son of Jehozadak, the high priest:

²This is what the LORD Almighty says: "These people say, 'The time has not yet come for the LORD's house to be built.'"

³Then the word of the LORD came through the prophet Haggai: ⁴"Is it a time for you yourselves to be living in your paneled houses, while this house remains a ruin?"

⁵Now this is what the LORD Almighty says: "Give careful thought to your ways. ⁶You have planted much, but have harvested little. You eat, but never have enough. You drink, but never have your fill. You put on clothes, but are not warm. You earn wages, only to put them in a purse with holes in it."

⁷This is what the LORD Almighty says: "Give careful thought to your ways. ⁸Go up into the mountains and bring down timber and build the house, so that I may take pleasure in it and be honored," says the LORD. ⁹"You expected much, but see, it turned out to be little. What you brought home, I blew away. Why?" declares the LORD Almighty. "Because of my house, which remains a ruin, while each of you is busy with his own house. ¹⁰Therefore, because of you the heavens have withheld their dew and the earth its crops. ¹¹I called for a drought on the fields and the mountains, on the grain, the new wine, the oil and whatever the ground produces, on men and cattle, and on the labor of your hands."

¹²Then Zerubbabel son of Shealtiel, Joshua son of Jehozadak, the high priest, and the whole remnant of the people obeyed the voice of the LORD their God and the message of the prophet Haggai, because the LORD their God had sent him. And the people feared the LORD.

¹³Then Haggai, the LORD's messenger, gave this message of the LORD to the people: "I am with you," declares the LORD. ¹⁴So the LORD stirred up the spirit of Zerubbabel son of Shealtiel, governor of Judah, and the spirit of Joshua son of Jehozadak, the high priest, and the spirit of the whole remnant of the people. They came and began to work on the house of the LORD Almighty, their God, ¹⁵on the twenty-fourth day of the sixth month in the second year of King Darius.

The Promised Glory of the New House

2 On the twenty-first day of the seventh month, the word of the LORD came through the prophet Haggai: ²"Speak to Zerubbabel son of Shealtiel, governor of Judah, to Joshua son of Jehozadak, the high priest, and to the remnant of the people. Ask them, ³'Who of you is left who saw this house in its former glory? How does it look to you now? Does it not seem to you like nothing? ⁴But now be strong, O Zerubbabel,' declares the LORD. 'Be strong, O Joshua son of Jehozadak, the high priest. Be strong, all you people of the land,' declares the LORD, 'and work. For I am with you,' declares the LORD Almighty. ⁵'This is what I covenanted with you when you came out of Egypt. And my Spirit remains among you. Do not fear.'

⁶"This is what the LORD Almighty says: 'In a little while I will once more shake the heavens and the earth, the sea and the dry land. ⁷I will shake all nations, and

E Mic 3:8 ◄► Zec 4:6
C Da 7:13 ◄► Mt 16:27–28
I Zep 3:9–20 ◄► Zec 1:12

T Da 12:10 ◄► Hag 2:15–19

a 1 A variant of *Jeshua*; here and elsewhere in Haggai

2:6 God's promise to "shake the heavens and the earth" was initially fulfilled when Persia fell to Alexander the Great (333–330 B.C.). That tumultuous overthrow foreshadowed the judgment of the nations at the second coming of Christ. Compare this verse with Heb 12:26–27.

2:7 The Hebrew phrasing in this verse allows for a variety of translations. Some feel this verse refers to the coming of the Messiah (see Mal 3:1). Others feel this verse refers to articles of wealth and value such

the desired^k of all nations will come, and I will fill this house^l with glory,^m says the LORD Almighty. ⁸'The silver is mine and the gold^n is mine,' declares the LORD Almighty. ⁹'The glory° of this present house^p will be greater than the glory of the former house,' says the LORD Almighty. 'And in this place I will grant peace,^q' declares the LORD Almighty."

B Mic 5:1–4 ◀ ▶ Zec 9:9

2:7 ᵏS 1Sa 9:20 ˡS Isa 60:7 ᵐS Ex 16:7; S 29:43; Lk 2:32 **2:8** ⁿS 1Ch 29:2 **2:9** °S Ps 85:9; S Isa 11:10 ᵖS Ezr 3:12; S Isa 60:7 ۹S Lev 26:6; S Isa 60:17 **2:10** ʳS ver 1; S Hag 1:15 **2:11** ˢS Lev 10:10-11; Dt 17:8-11; 33:8;

Blessings for a Defiled People

¹⁰On the twenty-fourth day of the ninth month,^r in the second year of Darius, the word of the LORD came to the prophet Haggai: ¹¹"This is what the LORD Almighty says: 'Ask the priests^s what the law says: ¹²If a person carries consecrated meat^t in the fold of his garment, and that

S Jer 18:18 **2:12** ᵗJer 11:15

as King Darius's contribution to the temple (see Ezr 6:8) and thus foreshadows the offerings that the nations will bring to the millennial temple. The word "glory" in this verse could refer either to material splendor (see Isa 60:7, 13) or to God's presence (see 1Ki 8:10–11; Lk 2:27, 32).

2:9 This verse may have different interpretations. The reference to the two different temples may be a comparison between Zerubbabel's temple and Herod's temple, or it may reflect a comparison between the current temple and the one to be built during the millennium. The peace that God would grant might refer to the peace brought by Christ in his first coming and death on the cross or it may refer to the world peace of Christ's millennial reign. Either interpretation is prophetic and wonderful in its scope.

Zerubbabel's Temple

536–516 B.C.

Temple source materials are subject to academic interpretation, and subsequent art reconstructions vary.

©1981 Hugh Claycombe

Construction of the second temple was started in 536 B.C. on the Solomonic foundations leveled a half-century earlier by the Babylonians. People who remembered the earlier temple wept at the comparison (Ezr 3:12). Not until 516 B.C., the 6th year of the Persian emperor Darius I (522-486), was the temple finally completed at the urging of Haggai and Zechariah (Ezr 6:13-15).

Archaeological evidence confirms that the Persian period in Palestine was a comparatively impoverished one in terms of material culture. Later Aramaic documents from Elephantine in Upper Egypt illustrate the official process of gaining permission to construct a Jewish place of worship, and the opposition engendered by the presence of various foes during this period.

Of the temple and its construction, little is known. Among the few contemporary buildings, the Persian palace at Lachish and the Tobiad monument at Iraq el-Amir may be compared in terms of technique.

Unlike the more famous structures razed in 586 B.C. and A.D. 70, the temple begun by Zerubbabel suffered no major hostile destruction, but was gradually repaired and reconstructed over a long period. Eventually it was replaced entirely by Herod's magnificent edifice.

fold touches some bread or stew, some wine, oil or other food, does it become consecrated?^{u} '"

The priests answered, "No."

^{13}Then Haggai said, "If a person defiled by contact with a dead body touches one of these things, does it become defiled?"

"Yes," the priests replied, "it becomes defiled.^{v}"

^{14}Then Haggai said, " 'So it is with this people^w and this nation in my sight,' declares the LORD. 'Whatever they do and whatever they offer^x there is defiled.

B **T** **U** ^{15}" 'Now give careful thought^y to this from this day on^b—consider how things were before one stone was laid^z on another in the LORD's temple.^{a} ^{16}When anyone came to a heap^b of twenty measures, there were only ten. When anyone went to a wine vat^c to draw fifty measures, there were only twenty.^{d} ^{17}I struck all the work of your hands^e with blight,^{f} mildew and hail,^{g} yet you did not turn^h to me,' declares the LORD.^{i} ^{18}'From this day on, from this twenty-fourth day of the ninth month, give careful thought^j to the day when the foundation^k of the LORD's tem-

B *Joel 2:24–26* ◀▶ *Zec 8:12*
T *Hag 1:5–11* ◀▶ *1Co 11:32*
U *Da 12:3* ◀▶ *Mal 2:5*

2:12 ^{u}S Ge 7:2; S Lev 6:27; Mt 23:19
2:13 ^{v}Lev 22:4-6; Nu 19:13
2:14 ^{w}S Isa 29:13 ^{x}S Ps 51:17; S Isa 1:13
2:15 ^{y}S Hag 1:5 ^{z}S Ezr 3:10 ^{a}Ezr 4:24
2:16 ^{b}S Ru 3:7 ^{c}S Job 24:11; S Isa 5:2
2:17 ^{d}S Dt 28:38; S Hag 1:6 ^{e}Hag 1:11 ^{f}S Dt 28:22 ^{g}S Ex 9:18; Ps 78:48 ^{h}S Isa 9:13; S Jer 3:10 ^{i}S Am 4:6
2:18 ^{j}S Hag 1:5 ^{k}S Ezr 3:11
2:19 ^{l}S Ex 28:33 ^{m}S Joel 1:12 ^{n}S Ge 12:2; S Lev 25:21; Ps 128:1-6; S Joel 2:14
2:20 ^{o}S Ezr 5:1 ^{p}S ver 1; S Hag 1:15
2:21 ^{q}S Ezr 5:2 ^{r}S Isa 14:16; Eze 38:19-20
2:22 ^{s}S Ge 19:25; S Job 2:13 ^{t}S Da 2:44 ^{u}S Mic 5:10 ^{v}S Ex 15:21 ^{w}S Jdg 7:22; S Eze 38:21
2:23 ^{x}Isa 2:11;

ple was laid. Give careful thought: ^{19}Is there yet any seed left in the barn? Until now, the vine and the fig tree, the pomegranate^l and the olive tree have not borne fruit.^{m}

" 'From this day on I will bless^n you.' "

Zerubbabel the LORD's Signet Ring

^{20}The word of the LORD came to Haggai^o a second time on the twenty-fourth day of the month:^{p} ^{21}"Tell Zerubbabel^q governor of Judah that I will shake^r the heavens and the earth. ^{22}I will overturn^s **P** royal thrones and shatter the power of the foreign kingdoms.^{t} I will overthrow chariots^u and their drivers; horses and their riders^v will fall, each by the sword of his brother.^{w}

^{23}" 'On that day,^{x} declares the LORD Al- **M** mighty, 'I will take you, my servant^y Zerubbabel^z son of Shealtiel,' declares the LORD, 'and I will make you like my signet ring,^{a} for I have chosen you,' declares the LORD Almighty."

P *Zep 3:8* ◀▶ *Zec 9:2*
M *Hab 2:20* ◀▶ *Zec 2:5*

10:20; Zec 4:10 ^{y}S Isa 20:3; S Da 9:24-26 ^{z}Mt 1:12 ^{a}S Ge 38:18; S Ex 28:9; 2Co 1:22

^{b} 15 Or *to the days past*

2:18 The prophet reminded his readers that the potential for blessing that existed when the temple foundation was laid in 536 B.C. was still available to the people provided they did not fail to follow God. Note that the date given for the setting of the foundations of the second temple is the day prior to the Jewish celebration of Hanukkah.

2:21–23 Haggai declared in this prophecy that God would send miraculous, cosmic signs in the last days that will herald the fall of the heathen enemies of Israel. The millennial temple would be constructed in all its glory and the Messiah would come and rule over all the nations. Note the similarity of Haggai's words with destruction of Gog and Magog recorded in Eze 38:19–21. Haggai also stated that Zerubbabel was God's representative and guarantee that someday the Messiah would come from David's descendants (see Mt 1:1, 12; Ac 4:27). In this way Zerubbabel foreshadows the servant mentioned in Isa 42:10.

Zechariah

Author: Zechariah

Theme: Rebuilding the temple and the nation of Judah

Date of Writing: C. 520 B.C.

Outline of Zechariah
  I. The Call to Obedience (1:1–6)
  II. Eight Visions (1:7—6:8)
  III. Crowning the High Priest (6:9–15)
  IV. Obedience Versus Legalism (7:1—8:23)
  V. The King Rejected (9:1—11:17)
  VI. The King Enthroned (12:1—14:21)

THIS BOOK WAS written by the prophet Zechariah, whose name means, "The LORD remembers." Zechariah belonged to a priestly family (see 1:1, 7) and was a young man when he accompanied those who returned from Babylon in 538 B.C. Zechariah began his ministry during the reign of King Darius of Persia, about the same time as the prophet Haggai delivered his first message to the returned exiles. The duration of Zechariah's ministry is uncertain, but it is possible that he witnessed the rise of Greece as a major power (see 9:13), suggesting that he ministered to the returned exiles for almost forty years.

In his opening message, Zechariah admonished the people to learn from their ancestors' mistakes. Zechariah maintained that the Jews needed to listen to God's message through his prophets and renew their covenant relationship with God lest they fall again under his judgment. Zechariah then recorded a series of night visions meant to encourage the rebuilders of the temple. Though the exiles faced opposition to their rebuilding program (see Ezr 5—6), Zechariah's visions reminded the Jews that God was ultimately in control of everything and had a long-range plan for Israel.

The book of Zechariah, as one of the closing prophetic books of the OT, parallels the book of Revelation, the NT's last revelation of God. Both books contain apocalyptic prophecies that summarize and expand the prophecies found in the other books. Note the similarity between Zechariah's visions and those recorded in Revelation of the four horsemen (see 1:1–17; Rev 6:4), the measuring of Jerusalem (see 2:1–13; Rev 21:15–17), and the flying roll (see 5:1–4; Rev 5:1–14).

A Call to Return to the LORD

1 In the eighth month of the second year of Darius,ᵃ the word of the LORD came to the prophet Zechariahᵇ son of Berekiah,ᶜ the son of Iddo:ᵈ

²"The LORD was very angryᵉ with your forefathers. ³Therefore tell the people: This is what the LORD Almighty says: 'Return' to me,' declares the LORD Almighty, 'and I will return to you,'ᵍ says the LORD Almighty. ⁴Do not be like your forefathers,ʰ to whom the earlier prophetsⁱ proclaimed: This is what the LORD Almighty says: 'Turn from your evil ways and your evil practices.' But they would not listen or pay attention to me,ᵏ declares the LORD.ˡ ⁵Where are your forefathers now? And the prophets, do they live forever? ⁶But did not my wordsᵐ and my decrees, which I commanded my servants the prophets, overtake your forefathers?ⁿ

"Then they repented and said, 'The LORD Almighty has done to us what our ways and practices deserve,ᵒ just as he determined to do.'"ᵖ

The Man Among the Myrtle Trees

⁷On the twenty-fourth day of the eleventh month, the month of Shebat, in the second year of Darius, the word of the LORD came to the prophet Zechariah son of Berekiah, the son of Iddo.ᵠ

⁸During the night I had a vision—and there before me was a man riding a red horse! He was standing among the myrtle trees in a ravine. Behind him were red, brown and white horses.ˢ

⁹I asked, "What are these, my lord?"

The angelᵗ who was talking with me answered, "I will show you what they are."ᵘ

¹⁰Then the man standing among the myrtle trees explained, "They are the ones the LORD has sent to go throughout the earth."ᵛ

¹¹And they reported to the angel of the LORD,ʷ who was standing among the myrtle trees, "We have gone throughout the earth and found the whole world at rest and in peace."ˣ

¹²Then the angel of the LORD said, "LORD Almighty, how longʸ will you withhold mercyᶻ from Jerusalem and from the towns of Judah,ᵃ which you have been angry with these seventyᵇ years?" ¹³So the LORD spokeᶜ kind and comforting wordsᵈ to the angel who talked with me.ᵉ

¹⁴Then the angel who was speaking to me said, "Proclaim this word: This is what the LORD Almighty says: 'I am very jealousᶠ for Jerusalem and Zion, ¹⁵but I am very angry with the nations that feel secure.ᵍ I was only a little angry,ʰ but they added to the calamity.'ⁱ

¹⁶"Therefore, this is what the LORD says: 'I will returnʲ to Jerusalem with mercy, and there my house will be rebuilt. And the measuring lineᵏ will be stretched out over Jerusalem,' declares the LORD Almighty.

¹⁷"Proclaim further: This is what the

1:8–17 Zechariah saw eight visions in one night. His first vision involved a man among the myrtle trees and four horses. The imagery of this vision indicated that though Israel suffered and their oppressors were successful, God is concerned about his people and will restore them and their temple. God called Zechariah to look beyond his circumstances to God's eternal promises. The significance of the different colored horses is uncertain.

LORD Almighty says: 'My towns will again overflow with prosperity, and the LORD will again comfort Zion and choose Jerusalem.' "

Four Horns and Four Craftsmen

[18] Then I looked up—and there before me were four horns! [19] I asked the angel who was speaking to me, "What are these?"

He answered me, "These are the horns that scattered Judah, Israel and Jerusalem."

[20] Then the LORD showed me four craftsmen. [21] I asked, "What are these coming to do?"

He answered, "These are the horns that scattered Judah so that no one could raise his head, but the craftsmen have come to terrify them and throw down these horns of the nations who lifted up their horns against the land of Judah to scatter its people."

A Man With a Measuring Line

2 Then I looked up—and there before me was a man with a measuring line in his hand! [2] I asked, "Where are you going?"

He answered me, "To measure Jerusalem, to find out how wide and how long it is."

[3] Then the angel who was speaking to me left, and another angel came to meet him [4] and said to him: "Run, tell that young man, 'Jerusalem will be a city without walls because of the great number of men and livestock in it. [5] And I myself will be a wall of fire around it,'

declares the LORD, 'and I will be its glory within.'

[6] "Come! Come! Flee from the land of the north," declares the LORD, "for I have scattered you to the four winds of heaven," declares the LORD.

[7] "Come, O Zion! Escape, you who live in the Daughter of Babylon!" [8] For this is what the LORD Almighty says: "After he has honored me and has sent me against the nations that have plundered you—for whoever touches you touches the apple of his eye— [9] I will surely raise my hand against them so that their slaves will plunder them. Then you will know that the LORD Almighty has sent me.

[10] "Shout and be glad, O Daughter of Zion. For I am coming, and I will live among you," declares the LORD. [11] "Many nations will be joined with the LORD in that day and will become my people. I will live among you and you will know that the LORD Almighty has sent me to you. [12] The LORD will inherit Judah as his portion in the holy land and will again choose Jerusalem. [13] Be still before the LORD, all mankind, because he has roused himself from his holy dwelling."

Clean Garments for the High Priest

3 Then he showed me Joshua the high priest standing before the angel of the LORD, and Satan standing at his right side to accuse him. [2] The LORD said

---

1:18–21 Zechariah saw four horns in his second vision. These horns prophetically represented four empires, probably referring to Assyria, Egypt, Babylonia and Medo-Persia. These powerful nations had devastated Israel, and God promised that they in turn would be destroyed. The four craftsmen, probably Egypt, Babylonia, Medo-Persia and Greece, would come against the four horns and destroy them. This vision clearly stated that all of Judah's enemies would ultimately be defeated.

2:1–13 This third vision promised a full restoration of Jerusalem, the temple and the people during the last days when the Messiah will rule from the throne of David in the millennial kingdom. Though Jerusalem will expand beyond its walls, it will experience peace and security because of God's protection.

3:1–10 Zechariah envisioned Joshua the high priest, standing in opposition to Satan before God's angel. Just as the angel of the Lord required the cleansing of Joshua, so God required the cleansing of Israel and the removal of their sin so that they might be restored to a priestly position before God. This vi-to Satan, "The Lord rebuke you,[x] Satan! The Lord, who has chosen[y] Jerusalem, rebuke you! Is not this man a burning stick[z] snatched from the fire?"[a] ³Now Joshua was dressed in filthy clothes as he stood before the angel. ⁴The angel said to those who were standing before him, "Take off his filthy clothes." Then he said to Joshua, "See, I have taken away your sin,[b] and I will put rich garments[c] on you."

⁵Then I said, "Put a clean turban on his head." So they put a clean turban on his head and clothed him, while the angel of the Lord stood by.

⁶The angel of the Lord gave this charge to Joshua: ⁷"This is what the Lord Almighty says: 'If you will walk in my ways and keep my requirements,[e] then you will govern my house[f] and have charge[g] of my courts, and I will give you a place among these standing here.[h]

⁸" 'Listen, O high priest[i] Joshua and your associates seated before you, who are men symbolic[j] of things to come: I am going to bring my servant, the Branch.[k] ⁹See, the stone I have set in front of Joshua![l] There are seven eyes[dm] on that one stone,[n] and I will engrave an inscription on it,' says the Lord Almighty, 'and I will remove the sin[o] of this land in a single day.

¹⁰" 'In that day each of you will invite his neighbor to sit[p] under his vine and fig tree,[q]' declares the Lord Almighty."

R *Zec 1:18–21* ◀▶ *Zec 7:14*
I *Zec 3:2–5* ◀▶ *Zec 8:1–3*

3:2 ˣJude 1:9
 ʸS Isa 14:1
 ᶻS Isa 7:4
 ᵃJude 1:23
3:4 ᵇS 2Sa 12:13;
 S Eze 36:25;
 S Mic 7:18
 ᶜS Ge 41:42;
 S Ps 132:9;
 S Isa 52:1; Rev 19:8
3:5 ᵈS Ex 29:6
3:7 ᵉS Lev 8:35
 ᶠDt 17:8-11;
 S Eze 44:15-16
 ᵍ2Ch 23:6
 ʰJer 15:19;
 Zec 6:15
3:8 ⁱHag 1:1
 ʲS Dt 28:46;
 S Eze 12:11
 ᵏS Isa 4:2; S 49:3;
 S Eze 17:22
3:9 ˡS Ezr 2:2
 ᵐS 2Ch 16:9
 ⁿIsa 28:16
 ᵒS 2Sa 12:13;
 S Jer 50:20
3:10 ᵖS Job 11:18
 qS Nu 16:14;
 S 1Ki 4:25; Mic 4:4
4:1 ʳS Da 8:18
 ˢJer 31:26
4:2 ᵗS Jer 1:13
 ᵘS Ex 25:31;
 Rev 1:12 ᵛRev 4:5
4:3 ʷver 11;
 S Ps 1:3; S Jer 11:4
4:5 ˣS Zec 1:9
4:6 ʸS 1Ch 3:19;
 S Ezr 5:2
 ᶻS Isa 13:22;
 S 1Ki 19:12
 ᵃS 1Sa 2:9
 ᵇS Ne 9:20;
 Isa 11:2-4;
 S Da 2:34; Hos 1:7
4:7 ᶜS Ps 26:12;
 Jer 51:25
 ᵈS Ps 118:22
 ᵉS 1Ch 15:28
4:9 ᶠS Ezr 3:11
 ᵍEzr 3:8; S 6:15;
 Zec 6:12 ʰS Zec 2:9

The Gold Lampstand and the Two Olive Trees

4 Then the angel who talked with me returned and wakened[r] me, as a man is wakened from his sleep.[s] ²He asked me, "What do you see?"[t]

I answered, "I see a solid gold lampstand[u] with a bowl at the top and seven lights[v] on it, with seven channels to the lights. ³Also there are two olive trees[w] by it, one on the right of the bowl and the other on its left."

⁴I asked the angel who talked with me, "What are these, my lord?"

⁵He answered, "Do you not know what these are?"

"No, my lord," I replied.[x]

⁶So he said to me, "This is the word of the Lord to Zerubbabel:[y] 'Not[z] by might nor by power,[a] but by my Spirit,'[b] says the Lord Almighty.

⁷"What[c] are you, O mighty mountain? Before Zerubbabel you will become level ground.[c] Then he will bring out the capstone[d] to shouts[e] of 'God bless it! God bless it!' "

⁸Then the word of the Lord came to me: ⁹"The hands of Zerubbabel have laid the foundation[f] of this temple; his hands will also complete it.[g] Then you will know that the Lord Almighty has sent me[h] to you.

E *Hag 2:5* ◀▶ *Zec 6:8*
M *Mic 3:8* ◀▶ *Zec 6:8*
W *Mic 2:7* ◀▶ *Lk 24:49*
V *Da 11:32* ◀▶ *Zec 12:8*

d 9 Or facets e 7 Or Who

---

sion also symbolized the future cleansing of the nation of Israel at the second coming of Christ and foreshadowed the Messiah with several different symbols and titles: "servant" (3:8; see Isa 41:8–9), "Branch" (3:8; see Isa 4:2; 11:1), and "stone" (3:9; see Isa 8:13–15; 28:16).

3:9 The prophet described this "stone" as a prophetic representation of the Messiah (see Ps 118:22–23; 1Pe 2:6–8). The "seven eyes" (see 4:10) may represent infinite intelligence or may refer to the seven spirits or characteristics of God (see Isa 11:2; 1Co 12:4–11; Rev 3:1; 4:5; 5:6).

3:10 Zechariah described a vision of the messianic era of world peace and security (see 1Ki 4:25; Isa 36:16; Mic 4:4). This was a traditional Jewish image of the future messianic kingdom.

4:1–14 Zechariah's vision of the candlestick with its seven lamps depicted the divine resources available to God's people. The light from the lamps represents God's glory among his people and is made possible only by the oil that is the power of God's Spirit. Note the parallel between this vision and Christ among the seven golden candles in Rev 1:12.

4:3–14 The symbolism of the two olive trees contains a double meaning. Its initial fulfillment depicted the priestly and royal offices occupied by Joshua and Zerubbabel. The continuous supply of oil indicated God's empowering for these two men to stand as God's witnesses to oversee the reconstruction of the temple. In the last days these verses will be completely fulfilled when two mighty witnesses arise during the tribulation just prior to the Battle of Armageddon. These witnesses will be empowered by the Holy Spirit for an astonishing ministry in the last days (see Rev 11:3–12).

ZECHARIAH 4:10

¹⁰"Who despises the day of small things? Men will rejoice when they see the plumb line in the hand of Zerubbabel.

"(These seven are the eyes of the LORD, which range throughout the earth.)"

¹¹Then I asked the angel, "What are these two olive trees on the right and the left of the lampstand?"

¹²Again I asked him, "What are these two olive branches beside the two gold pipes that pour out golden oil?"

¹³He replied, "Do you not know what these are?"

"No, my lord," I said.

¹⁴So he said, "These are the two who are anointed to serve the Lord of all the earth."

The Flying Scroll

5 I looked again—and there before me was a flying scroll!

²He asked me, "What do you see?"

I answered, "I see a flying scroll, thirty feet long and fifteen feet wide."

³And he said to me, "This is the curse that is going out over the whole land; for according to what it says on one side, every thief will be banished, and according to what it says on the other, everyone who swears falsely will be banished. ⁴The LORD Almighty declares, 'I will send it out, and it will enter the house of the thief and the house of him who swears falsely by my name. It will remain in his house and destroy it, both its timbers and its stones.'"

The Woman in a Basket

⁵Then the angel who was speaking to me came forward and said to me, "Look up and see what this is that is appearing."

⁶I asked, "What is it?"

He replied, "It is a measuring basket." And he added, "This is the iniquity of the people throughout the land."

⁷Then the cover of lead was raised, and there in the basket sat a woman! ⁸He said, "This is wickedness," and he pushed her back into the basket and pushed the lead cover down over its mouth.

⁹Then I looked up—and there before me were two women, with the wind in their wings! They had wings like those of a stork, and they lifted up the basket between heaven and earth.

¹⁰"Where are they taking the basket?" I asked the angel who was speaking to me.

¹¹He replied, "To the country of Babylonia to build a house for it. When it is ready, the basket will be set there in its place."

Four Chariots

6 I looked up again—and there before me were four chariots coming out from between two mountains—mountains of bronze! ²The first chariot had red horses, the second black, ³the third white, and the fourth dappled—all of them powerful. ⁴I asked the angel who was speaking to me, "What are these, my lord?"

⁵The angel answered me, "These are the four spirits of heaven, going out from standing in the presence of the Lord of the whole world. ⁶The one with the black horses is going toward the north country, the one with the white horses toward the west, and the one with the dappled horses toward the south."

⁷When the powerful horses went out, they were straining to go throughout the earth. And he said, "Go throughout the

f 14 Or two who bring oil and g 2 Hebrew twenty cubits long and ten cubits wide (about 9 meters long and 4.5 meters wide) h 6 Hebrew an ephah; also in verses 7-11 i 6 Or appearance j 11 Hebrew Shinar k 5 Or winds l 6 Or horses after them

E Am 8:7 ◄► Mt 9:4

5:1–4 This passage marks Zechariah's sixth night vision by describing an enormous scroll that lists the curses that God has pronounced upon his people because of their sins of dishonesty, stealing and swearing.

5:5–11 Zechariah's seventh vision illustrated that the persistent wickedness of Israel would be removed from the land and deposited in Babylon. The overall message of the vision was that the whole system of evil present in Israel would be divinely removed.

6:1–8 This final night vision described four horses and chariots that represented the watchful spirit of God that overlooks the affairs of those who follow him.

earth!" So they went throughout the earth.

⁸Then he called to me, "Look, those going toward the north country have given my Spirit^m rest^h in the land of the north."^i

A Crown for Joshua

⁹The word of the LORD came to me: ¹⁰"Take ˻silver and gold˼ from the exiles Heldai, Tobijah and Jedaiah, who have arrived from Babylon.^j Go the same day to the house of Josiah son of Zephaniah. ¹¹Take the silver and gold and make a crown,^k and set it on the head of the high priest, Joshua^l son of Jehozadak.^m ¹²Tell him this is what the LORD Almighty says: 'Here is the man whose name is the Branch,^n and he will branch out from his place and build the temple of the LORD.^o ¹³It is he who will build the temple of the LORD, and he will be clothed with majesty and will sit and rule on his throne. And he will be a priest^p on his throne. And there will be harmony between the two.' ¹⁴The crown will be given to Heldai,^n Tobijah, Jedaiah and Hen^o son of Zephaniah as a memorial^q in the temple of the LORD. ¹⁵Those who are far away will come and help to build the temple of the LORD,^r and you will know that the LORD Almighty has sent me to you.^s This will happen if you diligently obey^t the LORD your God."

Justice and Mercy, Not Fasting

7 In the fourth year of King Darius, the word of the LORD came to Zechariah^u on the fourth day of the ninth month, the month of Kislev.^v ²The people of Bethel had sent Sharezer and Regem-Melech, together with their men, to entreat^w the LORD^x ³by asking the priests of the house of the LORD Almighty and the prophets, "Should I mourn^y and fast in the fifth^z

E *Zec 4:6* ◀ ▶ *Zec 7:12*
M *Zec 4:6* ◀ ▶ *Mt 3:11*
N *Da 6:3* ◀ ▶ *Zec 12:10*
Q *Mic 3:6* ◀ ▶ *Mt 12:31–32*
M *Zec 2:10–13* ◀ ▶ *Zec 8:3–8*

6:8 ^hS Eze 5:13; S 24:13 ^iS Zec 1:10
6:10 ^jEzr 7:14-16; Jer 28:6
6:11 ^kPs 21:3 ^lS Ezr 2:2; S Zec 3:1 ^mS 1Ch 6:15; S Ezr 3:2
6:12 ^nS Isa 4:2; S Eze 17:22 ^oEzr 3:8-10; Zec 4:6-9
6:13 ^pS Ps 110:4
6:14 ^qS Ex 28:12
6:15 ^rIsa 60:10 ^sZec 2:9-11 ^tIsa 58:12; Jer 7:23; S Zec 3:7
7:1 ^uS Ezr 5:1 ^vNe 1:1
7:2 ^wJer 26:19; Zec 8:21
^xHag 2:10-14
7:3 ^yZec 12:12-14 ^zKi 25:9; Jer 52:12-14
7:5 ^aIsa 58:5 ^b2Ki 25:25 ^cS Da 9:2
7:6 ^dS Isa 43:23
7:7 ^eIsa 1:11-20; Zec 1:4 ^fJer 22:21 ^gS Jer 17:26 ^hJer 44:4-5
7:9 ^iS Jer 22:3; 42:5; Zec 8:16
7:10 ^kJer 49:11 ^lS Ex 22:21 ^mS Lev 25:17; Isa 1:23 ^nS Ex 22:22; S Job 35:8; S Isa 1:17; S Eze 45:9; S Mic 6:8
7:11 ^oS Isa 9:9 ^pS Jer 32:33 ^qS Jer 5:3; 8:5; 11:10; S 17:23; S Eze 5:6
7:12 ^rS Jer 5:3; 17:1; S Eze 11:19 ^sS Ne 9:29 ^tS Jer 42:21; S Da 9:12
7:13 ^uS Jer 7:27 ^vIsa 1:15; S Jer 11:11; 14:12; S Mic 3:4 ^wS Pr 1:28; S La 3:44; S Eze 20:31
7:14 ^xS Lev 26:33; Dt 4:27; 28:64-67; S Ps 44:11 ^yJer 23:19 ^zS Isa 33:8 ^aS Jer 7:34; S 44:6; S Eze 12:19

month, as I have done for so many years?"

⁴Then the word of the LORD Almighty came to me: ⁵"Ask all the people of the land and the priests, 'When you fasted^a and mourned in the fifth and seventh^b months for the past seventy years,^c was it really for me that you fasted? ⁶And when you were eating and drinking, were you not just feasting for yourselves?^d ⁷Are these not the words the LORD proclaimed through the earlier prophets^e when Jerusalem and its surrounding towns were at rest^f and prosperous, and the Negev and the western foothills^g were settled?' "^h

⁸And the word of the LORD came again to Zechariah: ⁹"This is what the LORD Almighty says: 'Administer true justice;^i show mercy and compassion to one another.^j ¹⁰Do not oppress the widow^k or the fatherless, the alien^l or the poor.^m In your hearts do not think evil of each other.'^n

¹¹"But they refused to pay attention; stubbornly^o they turned their backs^p and stopped up their ears.^q ¹²They made their hearts as hard as flint^r and would not listen to the law or to the words that the LORD Almighty had sent by his Spirit through the earlier prophets.^s So the LORD Almighty was very angry.^t

¹³" 'When I called, they did not listen;^u so when they called, I would not listen,'^v says the LORD Almighty.^w ¹⁴'I scattered^x them with a whirlwind^y among all the nations, where they were strangers. The land was left so desolate behind them that no one could come or go.^z This is how they made the pleasant land desolate.^a' "

S *Zep 2:3* ◀ ▶ *Zec 8:16–17*
N *Zec 1:4–5* ◀ ▶ *Mal 2:2*
E *Zec 6:8* ◀ ▶ *Mt 1:18*
R *Zec 3:3–4* ◀ ▶ *Zec 8:1–2*

^m 8 Or *spirit* ^n 14 Syriac; Hebrew *Helem* ^o 14 Or *and the gracious one, the*

6:11–15 The crowning of Joshua symbolized the crowning of the Messiah who will unite the priestly and kingly roles into one divine office. Zechariah prophesied that the Messiah would rebuild God's temple during the Millennium with the help of the Gentile nations (see Eze 40—48).

7:14 The prophet revealed that God had scattered his people throughout the world in judgment for their sins.

The Lord Promises to Bless Jerusalem

8 Again the word of the LORD Almighty came to me. ²This is what the LORD Almighty says: "I am very jealous for Zion; I am burning with jealousy for her."

³This is what the LORD says: "I will return to Zion and dwell in Jerusalem. Then Jerusalem will be called the City of Truth, and the mountain of the LORD Almighty will be called the Holy Mountain."

⁴This is what the LORD Almighty says: "Once again men and women of ripe old age will sit in the streets of Jerusalem, each with cane in hand because of his age. ⁵The city streets will be filled with boys and girls playing there."

⁶This is what the LORD Almighty says: "It may seem marvelous to the remnant of this people at that time, but will it seem marvelous to me?" declares the LORD Almighty.

⁷This is what the LORD Almighty says: "I will save my people from the countries of the east and the west. ⁸I will bring them back to live in Jerusalem; they will be my people, and I will be faithful and righteous to them as their God."

⁹This is what the LORD Almighty says: "You who now hear these words spoken by the prophets who were there when the foundation was laid for the house of the LORD Almighty, let your hands be strong so that the temple may be built. ¹⁰Before that time there were no wages for man or beast. No one could go about his business safely because of his enemy, for I had turned every man against his neighbor. ¹¹But now I will not deal with the remnant of this people as I did in the past," declares the LORD Almighty.

¹²"The seed will grow well, the vine will yield its fruit, the ground will produce its crops, and the heavens will drop their dew. I will give all these things as an inheritance to the remnant of this people. ¹³As you have been an object of cursing among the nations, O Judah and Israel, so will I save you, and you will be a blessing. Do not be afraid, but let your hands be strong."

¹⁴This is what the LORD Almighty says: "Just as I had determined to bring disaster upon you and showed no pity when your fathers angered me," says the LORD Almighty, ¹⁵"so now I have determined to do good again to Jerusalem and Judah. Do not be afraid. ¹⁶These are the things you are to do: Speak the truth to each other, and render true and sound judgment in your courts; ¹⁷do not plot evil against your neighbor, and do not love to swear falsely. I hate all this," declares the LORD.

¹⁸Again the word of the LORD Almighty came to me. ¹⁹This is what the LORD Almighty says: "The fasts of the fourth, fifth, seventh and tenth months will become joyful and glad occasions and happy festivals for Judah. Therefore love truth and peace."

²⁰This is what the LORD Almighty says: "Many peoples and the inhabitants of many cities will yet come, ²¹and the inhabitants of one city will go to another and say, 'Let us go at once to entreat the LORD and seek the LORD Almighty. I myself am going.' ²²And many peoples and powerful nations will come to Jerusalem to seek the LORD Almighty and to entreat him."

²³This is what the LORD Almighty says: "In those days ten men from all languages and nations will take firm hold of one Jew by the hem of his robe and say, 'Let us go

---

8:1–5 Although God purposed to judge his people for their sins, he also promised to redeem them and restore Jerusalem and the temple. Such peace and security will pervade the city that the streets will be filled with old men and women and children at play.

8:7–8 God promised to restore his people and return them to their land in the last days.

8:20–23 Zechariah's vision of the millennial kingdom foretold a time when the Gentiles would seek the Lord (see Isa 2:2–4; Mic 4:1–5). Zechariah prophesied that the Jews would be recognized as God's chosen people and that the Gentiles would choose to come and worship their Messiah.

with you, because we have heard that
God is with you.' "ʸ

Judgment on Israel's Enemies

An Oracle ᶻ

9 The word of the LORD is against the
land of Hadrach
and will rest upon Damascus ᵃ—
for the eyes of men and all the tribes of
Israel
are on the LORD—ᵖ
²and upon Hamath ᵇ too, which borders
on it,
and upon Tyre ᶜ and Sidon, ᵈ though
they are very skillful.
³Tyre has built herself a stronghold;
she has heaped up silver like dust,
and gold like the dirt of the streets. ᵉ
⁴But the Lord will take away her
possessions
and destroy ᶠ her power on the sea,
and she will be consumed by fire. ᵍ
⁵Ashkelon ʰ will see it and fear;
Gaza will writhe in agony,
and Ekron too, for her hope will
wither.
Gaza will lose her king
and Ashkelon will be deserted.
⁶Foreigners will occupy Ashdod,
and I will cut off ⁱ the pride of the
Philistines.
⁷I will take the blood from their
mouths,
the forbidden food from between
their teeth.
Those who are left will belong to our
God ʲ
and become leaders in Judah,
and Ekron will be like the
Jebusites. ᵏ
⁸But I will defend ˡ my house
against marauding forces. ᵐ
Never again will an oppressor overrun
my people,
for now I am keeping watch. ⁿ

P *Hag 2:22* ◀ ▶ *Zec 9:5–8*
P *Zec 9:2* ◀ ▶ *Zec 9:12–16*

8:23 ʸS Ps 102:22;
S Isa 14:1; S 45:14;
S 56:3; 1Co 14:25

9:1 ᶻS Isa 13:1;
Jer 23:33 ᵃIsa 17:1;
S Am 1:5

9:2 ᵇS Jer 49:23
ᶜEze 28:1-19
ᵈS Ge 10:15

9:3 ᵉJob 27:16;
S Eze 28:4

9:4 ᶠS Isa 23:11
ᵍS Isa 23:1;
Jer 25:22;
Eze 26:3-5;
27:32-36; 28:18

9:5 ʰJer 47:5

9:6 ⁱS Isa 14:30

9:7 ʲS Job 25:2
ᵏS Jer 47:1;
S Joel 3:4; S Zep 2:4

9:8 ˡS Isa 26:1
ᵐZec 14:21
ⁿS Isa 52:1;
S 54:14; S Isa 3:17

9:9 ᵒS Isa 62:11
ᵖS 1Ki 1:39
ᵠS Ps 24:7;
S 149:2; Mic 4:8
ʳIsa 9:6-7; 43:3-11;
Jer 23:5-6;
Zep 3:14-15;
Zec 2:10
ˢS Ge 49:11;
S 1Ki 1:33
ᵗMt 21:5*;
Jn 12:15*

9:10 ᵘHos 1:7;
2:18; Mic 4:3; 5:10;
Zec 10:4 ᵛS Isa 2:4
ʷPs 72:8

9:11 ˣS Ex 24:8;
S Mt 26:28;
S Lk 22:20
ʸS Isa 10:4; S 42:7
ᶻJer 38:6

9:12 ᵃS Joel 3:16
ᵇS Dt 21:17;
S Isa 40:2

9:13 ᶜS 2Sa 22:35
ᵈS Isa 49:2
ᵉS Joel 3:6
ᶠS Jer 51:20

9:14 ᵍS Isa 31:5
ʰPs 18:14;
S Hab 3:11
ⁱS Lev 25:9;
S Mt 24:31
ʲIsa 21:1; 66:15

The Coming of Zion's King

⁹Rejoice greatly, O Daughter of Zion! ᵒ
Shout, ᵖ Daughter of Jerusalem!
See, your king ᵠ comes to you, ᵠ
righteous and having salvation, ʳ
gentle and riding on a donkey, ˢ
on a colt, the foal of a donkey. ᵗ
¹⁰I will take away the chariots from
Ephraim
and the war-horses from Jerusalem,
and the battle bow will be broken. ᵘ
He will proclaim peace ᵛ to the nations.
His rule will extend from sea to sea
and from the River ʳ to the ends of
the earth. ˢʷ
¹¹As for you, because of the blood of my
covenant ˣ with you,
I will free your prisoners ʸ from the
waterless pit. ᶻ
¹²Return to your fortress, ᵃ O prisoners of
hope;
even now I announce that I will
restore twice ᵇ as much to you.
¹³I will bend Judah as I bend my bow ᶜ
and fill it with Ephraim. ᵈ
I will rouse your sons, O Zion,
against your sons, O Greece, ᵉ
and make you like a warrior's
sword. ᶠ

The LORD Will Appear

¹⁴Then the LORD will appear over them; ᵍ
his arrow will flash like lightning. ʰ
The Sovereign LORD will sound the
trumpet; ⁱ
he will march in the storms ʲ of the
south,

B *Hag 2:9* ◀ ▶ *Zec 11:12–13*
I *Zec 8:20–23* ◀ ▶ *Zec 10:6–8*
M *Zec 8:20–23* ◀ ▶ *Zec 14:9*
U *Mic 4:3–4* ◀ ▶ *Mt 5:9*
V *Da 7:14* ◀ ▶ *Mt 22:44*
P *Zec 9:5–8* ◀ ▶ *Zec 11:8*

ᵖ *1* Or *Damascus. / For the eye of the LORD is on all mankind, / as well as on the tribes of Israel,* ᵠ *9* Or *King* ʳ *10* That is, the Euphrates ˢ *10* Or *the end of the land*

9:9–10 Over five hundred years before the birth of Jesus, Zechariah saw this vision of the Messiah riding royally into Jerusalem on a donkey just as David and his sons had ridden centuries before (see 2Sa 18:9; 1Ki 1:33). This prophecy was completely fulfilled when Christ entered Jerusalem on Palm Sunday, proving he was Israel's Messiah (see Mt 21:4–5; Jn 12:15). This triumphal entry concluded the period of the 69 weeks of years prophesied by Daniel (see Da 9:24–26). For a detailed examination of this prophecy, see the chart on "Daniel's Vision of the Seventy Weeks," p. 984. Because Israel rejected Christ at his first advent, God's mercy and the time of world peace will not be realized until the second coming of Christ in the last days.

¹⁵ and the LORD Almighty will shield^k
    them.
They will destroy
    and overcome with slingstones.^l
They will drink and roar as with
    wine;^m
they will be full like a bowl^n
    used for sprinkling^r the corners^o of
    the altar.
¹⁶ The LORD their God will save them on
    that day^p
as the flock of his people.
They will sparkle in his land
    like jewels in a crown.^q
¹⁷ How attractive and beautiful they will
    be!
Grain will make the young men
    thrive,
and new wine the young women.

The LORD Will Care for Judah

10 Ask the LORD for rain in the
    springtime;
it is the LORD who makes the storm
    clouds.
He gives showers of rain^r to men,
    and plants of the field^s to everyone.
² The idols^t speak deceit,
    diviners^u see visions that lie;
they tell dreams^v that are false,
    they give comfort in vain.^w
Therefore the people wander like
    sheep
oppressed for lack of a shepherd.^x

³ "My anger burns against the
    shepherds,
and I will punish the leaders;^y
for the LORD Almighty will care
    for his flock, the house of Judah,
and make them like a proud horse in
    battle.^z
⁴ From Judah will come the
    cornerstone,^a
from him the tent peg,^b
from him the battle bow,^c
from him every ruler.
⁵ Together they^u will be like mighty
    men
trampling the muddy streets in
    battle.^d
Because the LORD is with them,
    they will fight and overthrow the
    horsemen.^e

9:15 ^k Isa 31:5;
37:35; Zec 12:8
^l Zec 14:3
^m Zec 10:7
^n Zec 14:20
^o Ex 27:2

9:16 ^p S Isa 10:20
^q S Jer 31:11

10:1 ^r S Lev 26:4;
S 1Ki 8:36;
S Ps 104:13;
S 135:7 ^s S Job 14:9

10:2 ^t Eze 21:21
^u S Isa 44:25
^v Jer 23:16
^w S Isa 40:19
^x S Nu 27:17;
S Jer 23:1;
S Hos 3:4;
S Mt 9:36

10:3 ^y Isa 14:9;
S Jer 25:34
^z S Eze 34:8-10

10:4 ^a S Ps 118:22;
S Ac 4:11
^b S Isa 22:23
^c S Zec 9:10

10:5 ^d S 2Sa 22:43;
S Mic 7:10
^e S Am 2:15;
S Mic 5:8;
Hag 2:22; Zec 12:4

10:6 ^f S Eze 30:24
^g S Ps 102:13;
S Isa 14:1
^h S Eze 36:37;
37:19; S Zec 8:7-8
^i Ps 34:17; Isa 58:9;
65:24; Zec 13:9

10:7 ^j Zec 9:15
^k S Isa 2:1;
S Isa 60:5;
S Joel 2:23

10:8 ^l Isa 5:26
^m S Jer 33:22;
S Eze 36:11

10:9 ^n S Isa 44:21;
S Eze 6:9

10:10
^o S Isa 11:11;
S Zec 8:8
^p S Jer 50:19
^q S Isa 49:19

10:11 ^r Isa 19:5-7;
S 51:10 ^s Zep 2:13
^t Eze 30:13
^u Eze 29:15

10:12
^v S Eze 30:24
^w S Mic 4:5

11:1 ^x S Eze 31:3
^y S 2Ch 36:19;
Zec 12:6

11:2 ^z S Isa 2:13

⁶ "I will strengthen^f the house of Judah
    and save the house of Joseph.
I will restore them
    because I have compassion^g on
    them.^h
They will be as though
    I had not rejected them,
for I am the LORD their God
    and I will answer^i them.
⁷ The Ephraimites will become like
    mighty men,
and their hearts will be glad as with
    wine.^j
Their children will see it and be joyful;
    their hearts will rejoice^k in the LORD.
⁸ I will signal^l for them
    and gather them in.
Surely I will redeem them;
    they will be as numerous^m as before.
⁹ Though I scatter them among the
    peoples,
yet in distant lands they will
    remember me.^n
They and their children will survive,
    and they will return.
¹⁰ I will bring them back from Egypt
    and gather them from Assyria.^o
I will bring them to Gilead^p and
    Lebanon,
and there will not be room^q enough
    for them.
¹¹ They will pass through the sea of
    trouble;
the surging sea will be subdued
and all the depths of the Nile will
    dry up.^r
Assyria's pride^s will be brought down
    and Egypt's scepter^t will pass
    away.^u
¹² I will strengthen^v them in the LORD
    and in his name they will walk,^w"
        declares the LORD.

11 Open your doors, O Lebanon,^x
    so that fire^y may devour your
    cedars!
² Wail, O pine tree, for the cedar has
    fallen;
the stately trees are ruined!
Wail, oaks^z of Bashan;

| Zec 9:9–10 ◀ ▶ Zec 12:8

^r 15 Or bowl, / like   ^u 4,5 Or ruler, all of them together.   / ⁵ They

---

10:6–8 This prophecy declared that God would "strengthen" both Judah and Israel by reuniting them as one nation. God's mercy would bring them back together.

Christian Higher Education

Obey His Call!

www.midwest.edu

Midwest Theological Seminary
851 parr Rd.
Wentzville, MO 63385
(636)327-4645
Fax(636)327-4715

Go therefore and make disciples of all the nations, baptizing them in the name of the Father and the Son and the Holy Spirit, teaching them to observe all that I commanded you; and lo, I am with you always, even to the end of the age. Matthew 28;19-20

Degree Programs

Master of Divinity
Emphasis in:
- Christian Counseling
- Christian Education
- Christian Leadership
- Christian Mission
- Church Music
- Theology

Doctor of Ministry
Emphasis in:
- Pastoral Theology
- Christian Counseling
- Christian Education
- Christian Leadership
- Christian Mission
- Church Music

Certification and Diploma Program

ELS Program

the dense forest[a] has been cut down![b]

³Listen to the wail of the shepherds;
  their rich pastures are destroyed!
Listen to the roar of the lions;[c]
  the lush thicket of the Jordan is ruined![d]

Two Shepherds

⁴This is what the LORD my God says: "Pasture the flock marked for slaughter.[e] ⁵Their buyers slaughter them and go unpunished. Those who sell them say, 'Praise the LORD, I am rich!' Their own shepherds do not spare them.[f] ⁶For I will no longer have pity on the people of the land," declares the LORD. "I will hand everyone over to his neighbor[g] and his king. They will oppress the land, and I will not rescue them from their hands."[h]

⁷So I pastured the flock marked for slaughter,[i] particularly the oppressed of the flock. Then I took two staffs and called one Favor and the other Union, and I pastured the flock. ⁸In one month I got rid of the three shepherds.

The flock detested[j] me, and I grew weary of them ⁹and said, "I will not be your shepherd. Let the dying die, and the perishing perish.[k] Let those who are left eat[l] one another's flesh."

¹⁰Then I took my staff called Favor[m] and broke it, revoking[n] the covenant I had made with all the nations. ¹¹It was revoked on that day, and so the afflicted of the flock who were watching me knew it was the word of the LORD.

¹²I told them, "If you think it best, give me my pay; but if not, keep it." So they paid me thirty pieces of silver.[o]

¹³And the LORD said to me, "Throw it to the potter"—the handsome price at which they priced me! So I took the thirty pieces of silver[p] and threw them into the house of the LORD to the potter.[q]

¹⁴Then I broke my second staff called Union, breaking the brotherhood between Judah and Israel.

¹⁵Then the LORD said to me, "Take again the equipment of a foolish shepherd. ¹⁶For I am going to raise up a shepherd over the land who will not care for the lost, or seek the young, or heal the injured, or feed the healthy, but will eat the meat of the choice sheep, tearing off their hoofs.

¹⁷"Woe to the worthless shepherd,[r]
  who deserts the flock!
May the sword strike his arm[s] and his right eye!
May his arm be completely withered,
  his right eye totally blinded!"[t]

Jerusalem's Enemies to Be Destroyed

An Oracle[u]

12 This is the word of the LORD concerning Israel. The LORD, who

11:2 [a] Isa 32:19 [b] Isa 10:34
11:3 [c] S Isa 5:29 [d] Jer 2:15; 50:44; Eze 19:9
11:4 [e] S Jer 25:34
11:5 [f] Jer 50:7; S Eze 34:2-3
11:6 [g] Zec 14:13 [h] Isa 9:19-21; S Jer 13:14; S La 2:21; 5:8; S Mic 5:8; 7:2-6
11:7 [i] S Jer 25:34
11:8 [j] S Eze 14:5
11:9 [k] S Jer 43:11 [l] S Isa 9:20
11:10 [m] ver 7 [n] S Ps 89:39; Jer 14:21
11:12 [o] S Ge 23:16; Mt 26:15
11:13 [p] S Ex 21:32 [q] Mt 27:9-10*; Ac 1:18-19
11:17 [r] Jer 23:1 [s] S Eze 30:21-22 [t] S Jer 23:1
12:1 [u] S Isa 13:1

P Zec 9:12–16 ◀▶ Zec 12:2–6
R Zec 8:1–2 ◀▶ Zec 11:14
B Zec 9:9 ◀▶ Mt 1:21–23
R Zec 11:9–10 ◀▶ Mt 10:6

11:9–10 Zechariah declared that God would terminate his care for the people because of their rejection of the Messiah. His words "let those who are left eat one another's flesh" (11:9) foreshadowed the horror of the cannibalism that occurred during the Roman siege of Jerusalem in A.D. 70. Though God had held back the nations from oppressing Israel, because of Israel's rejection of the Messiah God would let enemies to conquer his people. This prophecy found its fulfillment in the brutal conquest of Israel by Rome.

11:12–13 Thirty pieces of silver was the price of an Israelite slave (see Ex 21:32) and was an insult to the shepherd to be of so little value. Yet this was the exact amount paid to Judas Iscariot for Christ's betrayal (see Mt 26:14–16). Note that Zechariah predicted that this money would be thrown into the potter's house. In the NT, Matthew records that the betrayal money that Judas returned to the chief priests was used to buy "the potter's field" (Mt 27:7).

11:15–17 Because Israel refused its good shepherd, the Messiah, a foolish, greedy, corrupt shepherd would replace him. This worthless shepherd is a picture of the antichrist who will neither heal nor feed God's people. The antichrist is the exact opposite of Jesus Christ, the good shepherd, who gave his life for his sheep (see Jn 10:11).

The last verse in this passage notes the wounds that will be inflicted on the antichrist. His arm will lose its strength and his eye will lose its sight symbolizing the removal of his power and insight into world affairs. This loss of eyesight may be the mysterious wound that John refers to in Rev 13:3. Some suggest that the wounds may be the result of an assassination attempt, while others state that these will be the first death blows inflicted on the antichrist.

stretches out the heavens,ᵛ who lays the foundation of the earth,ʷ and who forms the spirit of manˣ within him, declares: ᴾ ²"I am going to make Jerusalem a cupʸ that sends all the surrounding peoples reeling.ᶻ Judahᵃ will be besieged as well as Jerusalem. ³On that day, when all the nationsᵇ of the earth are gathered against her, I will make Jerusalem an immovable rockᶜ for all the nations. All who try to move it will injureᵈ themselves. ⁴On that day I will strike every horse with panic and its rider with madness," declares the LORD. "I will keep a watchful eye over the house of Judah, but I will blind all the horses of the nations.ᵉ ⁵Then the leaders of Judah will say in their hearts, 'The people of Jerusalem are strong,ᶠ because the LORD Almighty is their God.'

⁶"On that day I will make the leaders of Judah like a firepotᵍ in a woodpile, like a flaming torch among sheaves. They will consumeʰ right and left all the surrounding peoples, but Jerusalem will remain intactⁱ in her place.

⁷"The LORD will save the dwellings of Judah first, so that the honor of the house of David and of Jerusalem's inhabitants may not be greater than that of Judah.ʲ
I ⁸On that day the LORD will shieldᵏ those
V who live in Jerusalem, so that the feeblestˡ among them will be like David, and the house of David will be like God,ᵐ like the Angel of the LORD going beforeⁿ
ᴾ them. ⁹On that day I will set out to destroy all the nationsᵒ that attack Jerusalem.ᴾ

ᴾ Zec 11:8 ◄► Zec 12:9–14
I Zec 10:6–8 ◄► Zec 13:9
V Zec 4:6 ◄► Lk 21:18
ᴾ Zec 12:2–6 ◄► Zec 13:7–9

12:1 ᵛS Ge 1:8; S Ps 104:2; S Jer 51:15 ʷPs 102:25; Heb 1:10 ˣS Isa 57:16
12:2 ʸS Ps 75:8 ᶻS Ps 60:3; S Isa 51:23 ᵃZec 14:14
12:3 ᵇS Isa 66:18; Zec 14:2 ᶜS Isa 28:16; Da 2:34-35 ᵈS Isa 29:8
12:4 ᵉPs 76:6; S Zec 10:5
12:5 ᶠS Eze 30:24
12:6 ᵍIsa 10:17-18; S Zec 11:1 ʰOb 1:18 ⁱZec 14:10
12:7 ʲJer 30:18; S Am 9:11
12:8 ᵏS Ps 91:4; S Joel 3:16; S Zec 9:15 ˡJoel 3:10 ᵐPs 82:6 ⁿMic 7:8
12:9 ᵒS Isa 29:7 ᵖS Zec 1:21; 14:2-3
12:10 ᵠS Eze 37:9 ʳIsa 44:3; S Eze 39:29; Joel 2:28-29 ˢS Ps 22:16; Jn 19:34,37* ᵗJdg 11:34 ᵘS Ge 21:16; Jer 31:19
12:11 ᵛJer 50:4 ʷ2Ki 23:29
12:12 ˣMt 24:30; Rev 1:7
12:14 ʸZec 7:3
13:1 ᶻJer 17:13 ᵃS Lev 16:30; S Ps 51:2; Heb 9:14
13:2 ᵇS Jer 43:12; S Eze 6:6; S 36:25; S Hos 2:17 ᶜS Mic 5:13 ᵈ1Ki 22:22; Jer 23:14-15
13:3 ᵉS Jer 28:16

Mourning for the One They Pierced

¹⁰"And I will pour out on the house of ᶜ David and the inhabitants of Jerusalem a ᴺ spiritᵛᵠ of grace and supplication.ʳ They ᴾ will look onʷ me, the one they have ᴰ pierced,ˢ and they will mourn for him as one mourns for an only child,ᵗ and grieve bitterly for him as one grieves for a firstborn son.ᵘ ¹¹On that day the weepingᵛ in Jerusalem will be great, like the weeping of Hadad Rimmon in the plain of Megiddo.ʷ ¹²The land will mourn,ˣ each clan by itself, with their wives by themselves: the clan of the house of David and their wives, the clan of the house of Nathan and their wives, ¹³the clan of the house of Levi and their wives, the clan of Shimei and their wives, ¹⁴and all the rest of the clans and their wives.ʸ

Cleansing From Sin

13 "On that day a fountainᶻ will be ᴰ opened to the house of David and ᴷ the inhabitants of Jerusalem, to cleanseᵃ ᴸ them from sin and impurity.

²"On that day, I will banish the names of the idolsᵇ from the land, and they will be remembered no more,"ᶜ declares the LORD Almighty. "I will remove both the prophetsᵈ and the spirit of impurity from the land. ³And if anyone still prophesies, his father and mother, to whom he was born, will say to him, 'You must die, because you have told liesᵉ in the LORD's

C Mic 3:8 ◄► Lk 1:15–17
N Zec 6:8 ◄► Mt 3:11
P Joel 2:28–29 ◄► Mt 3:11
D Da 9:24–26 ◄► Zec 13:1
D Zec 12:10 ◄► Mal 1:8
K Jnh 2:9 ◄► Mt 1:21
L Zec 3:1–5 ◄► Mal 3:7

ᵛ10 Or *the Spirit* ʷ10 Or *to*

12:2–9 Zechariah prophesied that God's wrath would fall on those who lay siege to Jerusalem during the last days. At the Battle of Armageddon God will cut all of Israel's enemies in pieces even though "all the nations of the earth are gathered against her" (12:3). God will defend his people and bring supernatural forces to bear against Israel's enemies. Even the weakest inhabitants of Jerusalem will be empowered with strength so that they "will be like David" (12:8).

12:10–14 In this passage Zechariah prophesied that Israel's eyes would be opened when Christ returns. The Jews would recognize Jesus of Nazareth as their true Messiah and would realize that their ancestors had crucified him. Contrition and mourning would be felt from the highest leader to the most ordinary person and be so heartfelt that it would resemble the mourning of the ancient Israelites over the death of King Josiah in the plain of Megiddo.

13:1 Zechariah proclaimed that in the days following the victory over the antichrist's armies at the Battle of Armageddon, God would cleanse his people from their sins (see Ro 11:26–27).

name.' When he prophesies, his own parents will stab him.'

⁴"On that day every prophet will be ashamed of his prophetic vision. He will not put on a prophet's garment of hair in order to deceive. ⁵He will say, 'I am not a prophet. I am a farmer; the land has been my livelihood since my youth.ˣ'ᵏ ⁶If someone asks him, 'What are these wounds on your body?' he will answer, 'The wounds I was given at the house of my friends.'

The Shepherd Struck, the Sheep Scattered

P ⁷"Awake, O sword, against my
    shepherd,
    against the man who is close to
      me!"
    declares the LORD Almighty.
"Strike the shepherd,
    and the sheep will be scattered,
    and I will turn my hand against the
      little ones.
⁸In the whole land," declares the LORD,
    "two-thirds will be struck down and
      perish;
    yet one-third will be left in it.
I ⁹This third I will bring into the fire;
    I will refine them like silver
    and test them like gold.
They will call on my name
    and I will answer them;

P Zec 12:9–14 ◄ ► Mal 3:2–5
I Zec 12:8 ◄ ► Zec 14:8–11

I will say, 'They are my people,'
    and they will say, 'The LORD is our
      God.'"

The LORD Comes and Reigns

14 A day of the LORD is coming when your plunder will be divided among you. ²I will gather all the nations to Jerusalem to fight against it; the city will be captured, the houses ransacked, and the women raped. Half of the city will go into exile, but the rest of the people will not be taken from the city.

³Then the LORD will go out and fight against those nations, as he fights in the day of battle. ⁴On that day his feet will D stand on the Mount of Olives, east of Jerusalem, and the Mount of Olives will be split in two from east to west, forming a great valley, with half of the mountain moving north and half moving south. ⁵You will flee by my mountain valley, for it will extend to Azel. You will flee as you fled from the earthquake in the days of Uzziah king of Judah. Then the LORD my God will come, and all the holy ones with him.

⁶On that day there will be no light, no cold or frost. ⁷It will be a unique day,

D Zec 2:10 ◄ ► Zec 14:14–20

Mt 16:27; 25:31; Jude 14 14:6 ᵏS Isa 13:10; S Jer 4:23 14:7 ˡJer 30:7
ˣ5 Or *farmer; a man sold me in my youth* ʸ6 Or *wounds between your hands* ᶻ5 Or *My mountain valley will be blocked and will extend to Azel. It will be blocked as it was blocked because of the earthquake*

13:8–9 This passage indicates that God's judgment at Christ's second coming will destroy two-thirds of the Jewish people (see Isa 48:10). Only a small remnant will be left from this refining to be saved (see Ro 11:26).

14:1–5 The "day of the LORD" (14:1) is the focus of Zechariah's remaining prophecies. In this concluding vision, the prophet described the Battle of Armageddon and the final battle for Jerusalem when the armies of the antichrist would lay siege to Jerusalem in the days following their defeat at Armageddon (see Rev 19:11–21). Though many captives will be taken, Jesus and his army will descend from heaven to rescue Israel from certain destruction, and the evil nations will be supernaturally destroyed. In light of Zechariah's earlier prophecy regarding Israel's repentance after the Battle of Armageddon (see 12:10–14) it is possible that these events will be spread over a period of several days, rather than a one-day battle as some commentators have suggested.

Note that Zechariah intimated that the return of Christ would cause the Mount of Olives to split in two, revealing a valley from the Dead Sea to the Mediterranean. This valley would offer a way of escape for those survivors fleeing Jerusalem. Yet God's victory over his enemies is assured. This vision parallels the prophetic visions of Joel 3:11; Jude 14; and Rev 11–14.

14:7–11 Zechariah declared that only God knows the actual day of Christ's second coming. Note that supernatural changes will occur in the topography and political arenas when Christ returns. Zechariah indicated that the flow of water would be affected (see Eze 47:1–12), all of the land surrounding Jerusalem would be leveled, and Jerusalem would be raised to new prominence (see Isa 2:2–4). On that day Christ will be crowned "king over the whole earth" (14:9) as the peaceful, worldwide millennial kingdom of the Messiah is established. Security will be the hallmark of his reign, and the city of Jerusalem will know true peace for the first time.

without daytime or nighttime—a day known to the LORD. When evening comes, there will be light.

⁸On that day living water will flow out from Jerusalem, half to the eastern sea and half to the western sea, in summer and in winter.

⁹The LORD will be king over the whole earth. On that day there will be one LORD, and his name the only name.

¹⁰The whole land, from Geba to Rimmon, south of Jerusalem, will become like the Arabah. But Jerusalem will be raised up and remain in its place, from the Benjamin Gate to the site of the First Gate, to the Corner Gate, and from the Tower of Hananel to the royal winepresses. ¹¹It will be inhabited; never again will it be destroyed. Jerusalem will be secure.

¹²This is the plague with which the LORD will strike all the nations that fought against Jerusalem: Their flesh will rot while they are still standing on their feet, their eyes will rot in their sockets, and their tongues will rot in their mouths. ¹³On that day men will be stricken by the LORD with great panic. Each man will seize the hand of another, and they will attack each other. ¹⁴Judah too will fight at Jerusalem. The wealth of all the surrounding nations will be collected—great quantities of gold and silver and clothing. ¹⁵A similar plague will strike the horses and mules, the camels and donkeys, and all the animals in those camps.

¹⁶Then the survivors from all the nations that have attacked Jerusalem will go up year after year to worship the King, the LORD Almighty, and to celebrate the Feast of Tabernacles. ¹⁷If any of the peoples of the earth do not go up to Jerusalem to worship the King, the LORD Almighty, they will have no rain. ¹⁸If the Egyptian people do not go up and take part, they will have no rain. The LORD will bring on them the plague he inflicts on the nations that do not go up to celebrate the Feast of Tabernacles. ¹⁹This will be the punishment of Egypt and the punishment of all the nations that do not go up to celebrate the Feast of Tabernacles.

²⁰On that day HOLY TO THE LORD will be inscribed on the bells of the horses, and the cooking pots in the LORD's house will be like the sacred bowls in front of the altar. ²¹Every pot in Jerusalem and Judah will be holy to the LORD Almighty, and all who come to sacrifice will take some of the pots and cook in them. And on that day there will no longer be a Canaanite in the house of the LORD Almighty.

a 8 That is, the Dead Sea b 8 That is, the Mediterranean c 18 Or part, then the LORD d 21 Or merchant

---

14:12–15 Zechariah described terrible plagues and pestilence that will affect Israel's enemies during the final battle against Jerusalem. The prophet's graphic description of the death of the soldiers of the antichrist accurately depicts the devastation of an overexposure to radiation or biological weapons. Massive amounts of gamma rays literally melt the flesh off of living beings while leaving buildings and machinery unharmed.

14:16–21 The prophet revealed that the representatives of the nations of the world would celebrate the feast of tabernacles. Those nations that refused to celebrate this joyous feast would experience drought. Because the timing of this celebration in Zechariah's prophecy falls so close to the prophecies of the establishment of the Messiah's kingdom, some believe that the antichrist's defeat might coincide with the earlier feast of trumpets. Only God knows for sure; and only time will tell.

Malachi

Author: Malachi

Theme: Only repentance can remove skepticism and indifference

Date of Writing: c. 433–430 B.C.

Outline of Malachi
 I. God Proclaims His Love for Israel (1:1–5)
 II. Israel Offends God (1:6—2:17)
 III. God's Requirements (3:1–15)
 IV. The Righteous and the Wicked (3:16—4:6)

THIS BOOK IS attributed to Malachi, a contemporary of Ezra and Nehemiah. Since the Hebrew word *malachi* translates as "my messenger," some scholars suggest that this is a title rather than a name for an individual. Though this matter is uncertain, it is still possible that the title bears the author's name. The content of this book—religious apathy, intermarriage with foreign women, neglect of paying the tithe—are similar to the conditions in Nehemiah's time and places Malachi's active ministry during the time of the rebuilding of the temple (see Ne 13:6).

Malachi's chief concern was his people's relationship with God. In his short book, Malachi recorded several significant prophecies concerning the Messiah as he urged the exiles to repent and prepare their hearts for his coming kingdom. The people had begun to doubt God's love. They neglected God by robbing him of his tithe and failing to obey the commands of his covenant with them. Consequently, God's judgment awaited them. Yet Malachi assured the people that those who feared God and followed his ways would enjoy God's salvation forever.

1 An oracle:[a] The word[b] of the LORD to Israel through Malachi.[a]

Jacob Loved, Esau Hated

[2] "I have loved[c] you," says the LORD.

"But you ask,[d] 'How have you loved us?'

"Was not Esau Jacob's brother?" the LORD says. "Yet I have loved Jacob,[e] [3] but Esau I have hated,[f] and I have turned his mountains into a wasteland[g] and left his inheritance to the desert jackals.[h]

[4] Edom[i] may say, "Though we have been crushed, we will rebuild[j] the ruins."

But this is what the LORD Almighty says: "They may build, but I will demolish.[k] They will be called the Wicked Land, a people always under the wrath of the LORD.[l] [5] You will see it with your own eyes and say, 'Great[m] is the LORD—even beyond the borders of Israel!'[n]

Blemished Sacrifices

[6] "A son honors his father,[o] and a servant his master.[p] If I am a father, where is the honor due me? If I am a master, where is the respect[q] due me?" says the LORD Almighty.[r] "It is you, O priests, who show contempt for my name.

"But you ask,[s] 'How have we shown contempt for your name?'

[7] "You place defiled food[t] on my altar.

"But you ask,[u] 'How have we defiled you?'

"By saying that the LORD's table[v] is contemptible. [8] When you bring blind animals for sacrifice, is that not wrong? When you sacrifice crippled or diseased animals,[w] is that not wrong? Try offering them to your governor! Would he be pleased[x] with you? Would he accept you?" says the LORD Almighty.[y]

[9] "Now implore God to be gracious to us. With such offerings[z] from your hands, will he accept[a] you?"—says the LORD Almighty.

[10] "Oh, that one of you would shut the temple doors,[b] so that you would not light useless fires on my altar! I am not pleased[c] with you," says the LORD Almighty, "and I will accept[d] no offering[e] from your hands. [11] My name will be great[f] among the nations,[g] from the rising to the setting of the sun.[h] In every place incense[i] and pure offerings[j] will be brought to my name, because my name will be great among the nations," says the LORD Almighty.

[12] "But you profane it by saying of the Lord's table,[k] 'It is defiled,' and of its food,[l] 'It is contemptible.' [13] And you say, 'What a burden!'[m] and you sniff at it contemptuously,"[n] says the LORD Almighty.

"When you bring injured, crippled or diseased animals and offer them as sacrifices,[o] should I accept them from your hands?"[p] says the LORD. [14] "Cursed is the cheat who has an acceptable male in his flock and vows to give it, but then sacrifices a blemished animal[q] to the Lord. For I am a great king,"[r] says the LORD Almighty,[s] "and my name is to be feared[t] among the nations.[u]

Admonition for the Priests

2 "And now this admonition is for you, O priests.[v] [2] If you do not listen,[w] and if you do not set your heart to honor[x] my name," says the LORD Almighty, "I will send a curse[y] upon you, and I will curse your blessings.[z] Yes, I have already cursed them, because you have not set your heart to honor me.

[3] "Because of you I will rebuke[b] your descendants[c]; I will spread on your faces the offal[a] from your festival sacrifices, and you will be carried off with it.[b] [4] And you will know that I have sent you this admonition so that my covenant with Levi[c] may continue," says the LORD Almighty. [5] "My covenant was with him, a U

1:1 ªS Na 1:1
 ᵇ Ac 7:38; Ro 3:1-2;
 1Pe 4:11
1:2 ᶜS Dt 4:37
 ᵈver 6,7; Mal 2:14,
 17; 3:7,13
 ᵉS Jer 46:27;
 Ro 9:13*
1:3 ᶠLk 14:26
 ᵍS Isa 34:10
 ʰS Isa 13:22
1:4 ⁱS Isa 11:14;
 S 34:11 ʲIsa 9:10
 ᵏS Isa 34:5
 ˡS La 4:22;
 S Eze 25:12-14;
 S 26:14
1:5 ᵐ Ps 35:27;
 48:1; Mic 5:4
 ⁿ Isa 45:22; 52:10;
 S Am 1:11-12
1:6 ᵒS Lev 20:9;
 Mt 15:4; 23:9
 ᵖ Lk 6:46
 ᵠS Dt 31:12;
 ʳS Isa 1:2 ʳJob 5:17
 ˢS ver 2
1:7 ᵗver 12;
 Lev 21:6 ᵘS ver 2
 ᵛS Eze 23:41
1:8 ʷS Lev 1:3;
 S Dt 15:21
 ˣS Ge 32:20
 ʸS Isa 43:23
1:9 ᶻLev 23:33-44;
 Ps 51:17;
 Mic 6:6-8; Ro 12:1;
 Heb 13:16
 ᵃS Jer 6:20
1:10 ᵇ 2Ch 28:24
 ᶜS Hos 5:6
 ᵈ Lev 22:20
 ᵉ ver 13;
 Isa 1:11-14;
 Jer 14:12; Mal 2:12
1:11 ᶠS Isa 24:15;
 56:6 ᵍS Isa 6:3;
 S 12:4 ʰS Ps 113:3;
 S Mt 8:11
 ⁱ Isa 60:6-7;
 Rev 5:8; 8:3
 ʲS Isa 19:21;
 Heb 13:15
1:12 ᵏS Eze 41:22
 ˡS ver 7
1:13 ᵐ Isa 43:22-24
 ⁿS Nu 14:11
 ᵒS ver 10
 ᵖS Dt 15:21
1:14 ᵠ Ex 12:5;
 S Lev 22:18-21
 ʳ Ps 95:3;
 S Ob 1:21; 1Ti 6:15
 ˢ Jer 46:18
 ᵗS Dt 28:58
 ᵘ Ps 72:8-11
2:1 ᵛ ver 7
2:2 ʷ Jer 13:17
 ˣ Mt 15:7-9;
 Jn 5:23; 1Ti 6:16;
 Rev 5:12-13
 ʸS Dt 11:26;
 S 28:20
 ᶻ Nu 6:23-27
2:3 ᵃS Ex 29:14;
 S Lev 4:11;
 S Job 9:31
 ᵇ 1Ki 14:10

G Zec 1:18–21 ◀ ▶ Mt 21:41
D Mal 1:8 ◀ ▶ Mt 1:21
H Mal 1:4 ◀ ▶ Mal 3:2
N Zec 7:11–12 ◀ ▶ Mt 10:14–15
U Hag 2:15–19 ◀ ▶ Mal 3:10

2:4 ᶜS Nu 3:12

ᵃ 1 *Malachi* means *my messenger*.   ᵇ 3 Or *cut off* (see Septuagint)
ᶜ 3 Or *will blight your grain*

M Zec 14:9 ◀ ▶ Mal 3:1
H Zec 3:2 ◀ ▶ Mal 2:2
S Zec 8:16–17 ◀ ▶ Mal 2:17
D Zec 13:1 ◀ ▶ Mal 1:13–14

1:11 Despite the universal paganism of his day, Malachi prophesied that a day would come in the kingdom of the Messiah when everyone on earth would worship God.

covenant[d] of life and peace,[e] and I gave them to him; this called for reverence[f] and he revered me and stood in awe of my name. [6]True instruction[g] was in his mouth and nothing false was found on his lips. He walked[h] with me in peace[i] and uprightness,[j] and turned many from sin.[k]

[7]"For the lips of a priest[l] ought to preserve knowledge, and from his mouth men should seek instruction[m]—because he is the messenger[n] of the LORD Almighty. [8]But you have turned from the way[o] and by your teaching have caused many to stumble;[p] you have violated the covenant[q] with Levi,"[r] says the LORD Almighty. [9]"So I have caused you to be despised[s] and humiliated[t] before all the people, because you have not followed my ways but have shown partiality[u] in matters of the law."[v]

Judah Unfaithful

[10]Have we not all one Father[d]?[w] Did not one God create us?[x] Why do we profane the covenant[y] of our fathers by breaking faith[z] with one another?

[11]Judah has broken faith. A detestable[a] thing has been committed in Israel and in Jerusalem: Judah has desecrated the sanctuary the LORD loves,[b] by marrying[c] the daughter of a foreign god.[d] [12]As for the man who does this, whoever he may be, may the LORD cut him off[e] from the tents of Jacob[e][f]—even though he brings offerings[g] to the LORD Almighty.

[13]Another thing you do: You flood the LORD's altar with tears.[h] You weep and wail[i] because he no longer pays attention[j] to your offerings or accepts them with pleasure from your hands.[k] [14]You ask,[l] "Why?" It is because the LORD is acting as the witness[m] between you and the wife of your youth,[n] because you have broken faith with her, though she is your partner, the wife of your marriage covenant.[o]

[15]Has not ˻the LORD˼ made them one?[p]

In flesh and spirit they are his. And why one? Because he was seeking godly offspring.[q] So guard yourself[r] in your spirit, and do not break faith[s] with the wife of your youth.

[16]"I hate divorce,[t]" says the LORD God of Israel, "and I hate a man's covering himself[g] with violence[u] as well as with his garment," says the LORD Almighty.

So guard yourself in your spirit,[v] and do not break faith.

The Day of Judgment

[17]You have wearied[w] the LORD with your words.

"How have we wearied him?" you ask.[x]

By saying, "All who do evil are good in the eyes of the LORD, and he is pleased[y] with them" or "Where is the God of justice?"[z]

3 "See, I will send my messenger,[a] who will prepare the way before me.[b] Then suddenly the Lord[c] you are seeking will come to his temple; the messenger of the covenant,[d] whom you desire,[e] will come," says the LORD Almighty.

[2]But who can endure[f] the day of his coming?[g] Who can stand[h] when he appears? For he will be like a refiner's fire[i] or a launderer's soap.[j] [3]He will sit as a

S Mal 1:6 ◀ ▶ Mal 3:18
M Mal 1:4–5 ◀ ▶ Mal 3:17–18
I Zec 16:16–21 ◀ ▶ Mt 2:2
P Zec 13:7–9 ◀ ▶ Mal 4:1
H Mal 2:2 ◀ ▶ Mal 3:5

2:5 [d] Dt 33:9; Ps 25:10; 103:18; [e] S Mt 26:28; S Lk 22:20; [f] Heb 7:22 **2:6** [g] S Nu 25:12 [h] S Dt 14:23; S 28:58; [i] Ps 119:161; [j] Heb 12:28 **2:6** [k] S Dt 33:10 **2:7** [l] S Ge 5:22 [m] Lk 2:14; S Jn 14:27; Gal 5:22 [n] S Ps 25:21 [o] S Ro 11:16; Jas 5:19-20 **2:7** [l] S Jer 18:18 [m] S Lev 10:11; S 2Ch 17:7 [n] S Nu 27:21; S 2Ch 36:15; Mt 11:10; Mk 1:2 **2:8** [o] S Ex 32:8; Jer 2:8 [p] S Jer 18:15 [q] Jer 33:21; S Eze 22:26 [r] S Hos 4:6 **2:9** [s] S Isa 2:30; S Ps 22:6; S Jer 51:37 [t] S Ps 35:4; Jer 3:25; Ac 8:32-33 [u] S Ex 18:16; S Lev 19:15; Ac 10:34; Ro 2:11 [v] S Isa 2:17 **2:10** [w] S Ex 4:22; Mt 5:16; 6:4,18; [x] Lk 11:2; 1Co 8:6 [y] S Job 4:17; Isa 43:1 [z] Ex 19:5; S 2Ki 17:15; Jer 31:32 **2:11** [a] S Isa 1:13; S 48:8 [b] S Dt 4:37 [c] S Ne 13:23 [d] S Ex 34:16; Jer 3:7-9 **2:12** [e] S Isa 2:30-33; S Eze 24:21 [f] S Nu 24:5; 2Sa 20:1 [g] S Mal 1:10 **2:13** [h] S Jer 11:11 [i] Ps 39:12 [j] Ps 66:18; Jer 14:12 [k] Isa 58:2 **2:14** [l] S Mal 1:2 [m] S Ge 21:30; S Jos 24:22 [n] S Pr 5:18 [o] S Eze 16:8; Heb 13:4 **2:15** [p] S Ge 2:24; Mt 19:4-6 [q] S Dt 14:2; 1Co 7:14

[r] S Dt 4:15 [s] S Isa 54:6; 1Co 7:10; Heb 13:4 **2:16** [t] S Dt 24:1; Mt 5:31-32; 19:4-9; Mk 10:4-5 [u] S Ge 6:11; 34:25; S Pr 4:17; S Isa 58:4 [v] Ps 51:10 **2:17** [w] S Isa 1:14 [x] S Mal 1:2 [y] Ps 5:4 [z] S Ge 18:25; S Job 8:3; S Eze 18:25 **3:1** [a] S Nu 27:21; S 2Ch 36:15 [b] S Isa 40:3; S Mt 3:3; 11:10*; Mk 1:2*; Lk 7:27* [c] Mic 5:2 [d] S Isa 42:6 [e] S Isa 9:20 **3:2** [f] S Eze 22:14; Rev 6:17 [g] S Eze 7:7; S Da 7:13; S Joel 2:31; S Mt 16:27; Jas 5:8; 2Pe 3:4; S Rev 1:7 [h] S Isa 6:20 [i] S Isa 1:31; S 30:30; S Zec 13:9; Mt 3:10-12 [j] S Job 9:30

[d] 10 Or father   [e] 12 Or 12May the LORD cut off from the tents of Jacob anyone who gives testimony in behalf of the man who does this
[f] 15 Or 15But the one who is our father, did not do this, not as long as life remained in him. And what was he seeking? An offspring from God
[g] 16 Or his wife

3:1–5 Note that the first verse of this prophecy carries a double meaning. Initially fulfilled in the earthly ministry of John the Baptist (see Isa 40:3; Mt 11:10), this prophecy will be completely fulfilled in the last days. The Lord will mercifully send witnesses before him to prepare his people (see Rev 11:3–12) prior to his appearance at the Battle of Armageddon.

Malachi also revealed that the "day of his coming" (3:2) would be a time of affliction for God to refine and purify his people. This cleansing would begin with the tribe of Levi since the priests were supposed to be God's messengers but had instead become messengers of pagan idols and unfaithfulness. When the Lord returns he will purify the Levites and judge the people of their sins of sorcery, oppression, adultery and perjury.

refiner and purifier of silver;[k] he will purify[l] the Levites and refine them like gold and silver.[m] Then the LORD will have men who will bring offerings in righteousness,[n] [4]and the offerings[o] of Judah and Jerusalem will be acceptable to the LORD, as in days gone by, as in former years.[p]

[5]"So I will come near to you for judgment. I will be quick to testify against sorcerers,[q] adulterers[r] and perjurers,[s] against those who defraud laborers of their wages,[t] who oppress the widows[u] and the fatherless, and deprive aliens[v] of justice, but do not fear[w] me," says the LORD Almighty.

Robbing God

[6]"I the LORD do not change.[x] So you, O descendants of Jacob, are not destroyed.[y] [7]Ever since the time of your forefathers you have turned away[z] from my decrees and have not kept them. Return[a] to me, and I will return to you," says the LORD Almighty.

"But you ask,[c] 'How are we to return?'

[8]"Will a man rob[d] God? Yet you rob me.

"But you ask, 'How do we rob you?'

"In tithes[e] and offerings. [9]You are under a curse[f]—the whole nation of you—because you are robbing me. [10]Bring the whole tithe[g] into the storehouse,[h] that there may be food in my house. Test me in this," says the LORD Almighty, "and see if I will not throw open the floodgates[i] of heaven and pour out[j] so much blessing[k] that you will not have room enough for it.[l] [11]I will prevent pests from devouring[m] your crops, and the vines in your fields will not cast their fruit,[n] " says the LORD Almighty. [12]"Then all the nations will call you blessed,[o] for yours will be a delightful land,"[p] says the LORD Almighty.[q]

[13]"You have said harsh things[r] against me," says the LORD.

"Yet you ask,[s] 'What have we said against you?'

[14]"You have said, 'It is futile[t] to serve[u] God. What did we gain by carrying out his requirements[v] and going about like mourners[w] before the LORD Almighty? [15]But now we call the arrogant[x] blessed. Certainly the evildoers[y] prosper,[z] and even those who challenge God escape.'"

[16]Then those who feared the LORD talked with each other, and the LORD listened and heard.[a] A scroll[b] of remembrance was written in his presence concerning those who feared[c] the LORD and honored his name.

[17]"They will be mine,[d] " says the LORD Almighty, "in the day when I make up my treasured possession.[h,e] I will spare[f] them, just as in compassion a man spares his son[g] who serves him. [18]And you will again see the distinction between the righteous[h] and the wicked, between those who serve God and those who do not.[i]

The Day of the LORD

4 "Surely the day is coming;[j] it will burn like a furnace.[k] All the arrogant[l] and every evildoer will be stubble,[m] and that day that is coming will set them

---

3:3 [k]S Da 12:10; [l]S 1Co 3:13 [m]S 1Ch 23:28; S Isa 1:25 [n]S Job 28:1; [o]S Ps 12:6; 1Pe 1:7; Rev 3:18 [p]S Ps 132:9
3:4 [q]S 2Ch 7:12; Ps 51:19; Mal 1:11 [p]S 2Ch 7:3; S Eze 20:40
3:5 [q]S Ex 7:11; S Isa 47:9 [r]Ex 20:14; Jas 2:11; 2Pe 2:12-14 [s]Lev 19:11-12; S Jer 7:9 [t]S Lev 19:13; Jas 5:4 [u]S Ex 22:22 [v]S Ex 22:21; S Dt 24:19; S Eze 22:7 [w]S Dt 31:12; S Isa 1:2
3:6 [x]S Nu 23:19; S Heb 7:21; Jas 1:17 [y]S Job 34:15; S Hos 11:9
3:7 [z]S Ex 32:8; S Jer 7:26; Ac 7:51 [a]S Isa 44:22; S Eze 18:32 [b]S Zec 1:3; Jas 4:8 [c]S Mal 1:2
3:8 [d]S Zec 5:3 [e]S Lev 27:30; Nu 18:21; S Ne 13:10-12; Lk 18:12
3:9 [f]S Dt 11:26; 28:15-68; S Zec 5:3
3:10 [g]S Ex 22:29 [h]S Ne 13:12 [i]S 2Ki 7:2; Isa 44:3 [j]S Lev 25:21; S Joel 2:14; 2Co 9:8-11 [k]S Joel 2:24
3:11 [m]S Ex 10:15; S Dt 28:39 [n]S Ex 23:26
3:12 [o]S Dt 28:3-12; Isa 61:9 [p]S Isa 62:4; S Eze 20:6 [q]S 2Ch 31:10
3:13 [r]Mal 2:17 [s]S Mal 1:2
3:14 [t]Ps 73:13; S Isa 57:10 [u]Ps 100:2; Jn 12:26; Ro 12:11 [v]S Jos 22:5; S Isa 1:14 [w]Isa 58:3
3:15 [x]S Ps 119:21; [y]S 2Ch 31:10 [z]S Ps 73:12; Jer 7:10 [a]S Job 21:7
3:16 [b]S Ps 34:15 [c]S Ex 32:32;

C Zep 1:12 ◀ ▶ Mt 3:7
M Zep 2:2–3 ◀ ▶ Mal 4:1
T Joel 2:26 ◀ ▶ Mt 10:32–33
L Zec 2:8 ◀ ▶ Mt 6:8
M Mal 3:1 ◀ ▶ Mal 4:2–3
S Mal 2:17 ◀ ▶ Mt 1:21
P Mal 3:2–5 ◀ ▶ Mal 4:3
H Mal 3:5 ◀ ▶ Mal 4:3
M Mal 3:13 ◀ ▶ Mt 5:3–5

S Ps 56:8; S 87:6; S Lk 10:20 [c]S Dt 28:58; S 31:12; Ps 33:18; S Pr 1:7; Rev 11:18 3:17 [d]Isa 43:21 [e]S Ex 8:22; S Dt 7:6; S Ro 8:14; S Tit 2:14 [f]Ne 13:22; Ps 103:13; Isa 26:20; Lk 15:1-32 [g]S Ro 8:32 3:18 [h]S Ge 18:25 [i]Dt 32:4; Mt 25:32-33,41 4:1 [j]S Da 7:13; S Joel 2:31; Mt 11:14; Ac 2:20 [k]S Isa 31:9 [l]S Isa 2:12 [m]S Isa 5:24; S Na 1:10

H Mal 3:2 ◀ ▶ Mal 4:1
L Zec 13:1 ◀ ▶ Mt 1:21
P Zec 1:3 ◀ ▶ Mt 10:6
B Mic 3:8 ◀ ▶ Mt 3:11
P Hos 2:8 ◀ ▶ Mt 6:31–33
U Mal 2:5 ◀ ▶ Mt 5:5–12
B Zec 8:12 ◀ ▶ 2Co 9:10

[h] 17 Or *Almighty, "my treasured possession, in the day when I act*

3:16–18 Malachi declared that God kept a record of the ones who remained faithful to him despite the widespread complaining against the Lord. This book of remembrance is similar to the records that earthly kings kept of the deeds of valor performed by their faithful subjects (see Est 6:1–3; Isa 4:3; Da 7:10; 12:1). God feels a tender love for those who love and fear him, referring to them as his "treasured possession" (3:17). Yet Malachi warned the people that God would return and judge "between the righteous and the wicked" (3:18) because God knows what is in every heart.

4:1–3 Malachi warned that God's purifying fire will utterly destroy the proud and the wicked. Yet

on fire,ⁿ" says the LORD Almighty. "Not a root or a branch° will be left to them. ²But for you who revere my name,ᵖ the sun of righteousnessᑫ will rise with healingʳ in its wings. And you will go out and leapˢ like calves released from the stall. ³Then you will trampleᵗ down the wicked; they will be ashesᵘ under the soles of your feet on the day when I do these things," says the LORD Almighty.

⁴"Remember the lawᵛ of my servant Moses, the decrees and laws I gave him at Horebʷ for all Israel.ˣ

⁵"See, I will send you the prophet Elijahʸ before that great and dreadful day of the LORD comes.ᶻ ⁶He will turn the hearts of the fathers to their children,ᵃ and the hearts of the children to their fathers; or else I will come and strikeᵇ the land with a curse."ᶜ

M *Mal 3:17–18* ◀ ▶ *Mt 2:2*
P *Mal 4:1* ◀ ▶ *Mal 4:5*
H *Mal 4:1* ◀ ▶ *Mt 3:7*

4:1 ⁿS Isa 1:31 °S 2Ki 10:11; S Eze 17:8; S Mt 3:10
4:2 ᵖS Dt 28:58; Ps 61:5; 111:9; Rev 14:1 ᑫS Ps 118:27; S Isa 9:2; S 45:8; Lk 1:78; Eph 5:14 ʳS 2Ch 7:14; S Isa 30:26; S Mt 4:23; Rev 22:2 ˢS Isa 35:6
4:3 ᵗS Job 40:12; Ps 18:40-42 ᵘEze 28:18
4:4 ᵛS Dt 28:61; S Ps 147:19; Mt 5:17; 7:12; Ro 2:13; 4:15; Gal 3:24

P *Mal 4:3* ◀ ▶ *Mt 3:12*

ʷS Ex 3:1 ˣS Ex 20:1 **4:5** ʸS 1Ki 17:1; S Mt 11:14; 16:14 ᶻS Joel 2:31 **4:6** ᵃLk 1:17 ᵇS Isa 11:4; Rev 19:15 ᶜS Dt 11:26; S 13:15; S Jos 6:17; S 23:15; S Zec 5:3

God promised his people hope, healing and true peace under the coming Messiah's rule. This prophecy parallels the message in Revelation that foretells Christ's victory over the forces of the antichrist at the Battle of Armageddon (see Rev 19:11–21).

4:4–6 Malachi ended his OT prophecy with a warning to repent because of the certainty of God's judgment. Yet Malachi also delivered a promise of salvation and hope to all who love God and obey his commands. He said that God would send Elijah to prepare the people for the Lord's coming. Note too that Malachi said that a return to God would result in a restoration of familial love. This prophecy was initially fulfilled in John the Baptist who ministered "in the spirit and power of Elijah" (Lk 1:17). This prophecy will be ultimately fulfilled by the return of Elijah as one of the two witnesses during the tribulation (see Rev 11:3). For further information, see the article "The Two Witnesses," p. 1468.

New Testament

Matthew

Author: Matthew

Theme: The long-awaited Messiah has come

Date of Writing: c. A.D. 70–80

Outline of Matthew
  I. Background and Early Years (1:1—2:23)
 II. Preparation for Ministry (3:1—4:11)
III. The Galilean Ministry (4:12—18:35)
    A. The calling of the first disciples (4:12–25)
    B. The Sermon on the Mount (5:1—7:29)
    C. The ministry through miracles (8:1—11:1)
    D. Teaching through parables (11:2—13:53)
    E. Opposition and withdrawal (13:54—16:12)
    F. Jesus as the Son of God (16:13—18:35)
IV. The Final Period (19:1—28:20)
    A. Toward Jerusalem (19:1—20:34)
    B. The triumphal entry (21:1–16)
    C. Jesus as teacher (21:17—25:46)
    D. Trial, death and burial (26:1—27:66)
    E. Resurrection (28:1–20)

THOUGH THIS BOOK is anonymous, Matthew, one of the twelve disciples, is credited with the authorship of the book that bears his name. Because of the Jewish nature of the material included in this book, it seems likely that Matthew originally wrote it in Hebrew; a later Greek edition was widely known and circulated. Most scholars suggest that Matthew wrote his Gospel shortly before the destruction of Jerusalem in A.D. 70 and that he penned it from Antioch in Syria, a leading center of Christianity in the first century. It was in Antioch that the followers of Jesus were first called "Christians" (see Ac 11:26).

Although Matthew's Gospel has much in common with the books written by Mark and

Luke, there are certain characteristics that are peculiar to Matthew's own account. His approach in sharing the good news of Jesus demonstrated that Jesus is the true Messiah of Israel. Often describing Jesus as the "Son of David," Matthew repeatedly referred to the OT prophecies and illustrated how Jesus' birth, life and resurrection fulfilled them (see 1:23; 2:6, 15, 18, 23; 3:3; 4:15–16; 8:17; 12:18–21; 13:35; 21:5; 26:56). Matthew also used the phrase "kingdom of heaven" with frequency throughout his book, emphasizing the ethical and spiritual principles of the coming Messianic kingdom by acknowledging the kingdom's present existence as well as its future manifestation in the last days.

Matthew also demonstrated a strong concern for the Gentiles and their salvation (see 13:38; 28:18–20). In fact, his is the only Gospel to record the visit of non-Jewish Magi to worship the infant Jesus (see 2:1–12). Note also Matthew's mention of the teaching ministry of Jesus, particularly apparent in five sections (see 5:3—7:27; 10:5-42; 13:3–52; 18:3–35; 24:4—25:46).

The Genealogy of Jesus

1:1–17pp — Lk 3:23–38
1:3–6pp — Ru 4:18–22
1:7–11pp — 1Ch 3:10–17

1 A record of the genealogy of Jesus Christ the son of David,ᵃ the son of Abraham:ᵇ

²Abraham was the father of Isaac,ᶜ
Isaac the father of Jacob,ᵈ
Jacob the father of Judah and his brothers,ᵉ
³Judah the father of Perez and Zerah, whose mother was Tamar,ᶠ
Perez the father of Hezron,
Hezron the father of Ram,
⁴Ram the father of Amminadab,
Amminadab the father of Nahshon,
Nahshon the father of Salmon,
⁵Salmon the father of Boaz, whose mother was Rahab,ᵍ
Boaz the father of Obed, whose mother was Ruth,
Obed the father of Jesse,
⁶and Jesse the father of King David.ʰ

David was the father of Solomon, whose mother had been Uriah's wife,ⁱ
⁷Solomon the father of Rehoboam,
Rehoboam the father of Abijah,
Abijah the father of Asa,
⁸Asa the father of Jehoshaphat,
Jehoshaphat the father of Jehoram,
Jehoram the father of Uzziah,
⁹Uzziah the father of Jotham,
Jotham the father of Ahaz,
Ahaz the father of Hezekiah,
¹⁰Hezekiah the father of Manasseh,ʲ
Manasseh the father of Amon,
Amon the father of Josiah,
¹¹and Josiah the father of Jeconiahᵃ and his brothers at the time of the exile to Babylon.ᵏ

¹²After the exile to Babylon:
Jeconiah was the father of Shealtiel,ˡ
Shealtiel the father of Zerubbabel,ᵐ
¹³Zerubbabel the father of Abiud,
Abiud the father of Eliakim,
Eliakim the father of Azor,
¹⁴Azor the father of Zadok,
Zadok the father of Akim,
Akim the father of Eliud,
¹⁵Eliud the father of Eleazar,
Eleazar the father of Matthan,
Matthan the father of Jacob,
¹⁶and Jacob the father of Joseph, the husband of Mary,ⁿ of whom was born Jesus, who is called Christ.ᵒ

¹⁷Thus there were fourteen genera-

---

a 11 That is, Jehoiachin; also in verse 12

tions in all from Abraham to David, fourteen from David to the exile to Babylon, and fourteen from the exile to the Christ.*b*

The Birth of Jesus Christ

E ¹⁸This is how the birth of Jesus Christ came about: His mother Mary was pledged to be married to Joseph, but before they came together, she was found to be with child through the Holy Spirit.*p* ¹⁹Because Joseph her husband was a righteous man and did not want to expose her to public disgrace, he had in mind to divorce*q* her quietly.

E ²⁰But after he had considered this, an angel*r* of the Lord appeared to him in a dream*s* and said, "Joseph son of David, do not be afraid to take Mary home as your wife, because what is conceived in **B** her is from the Holy Spirit. ²¹She will give **D** birth to a son, and you are to give him the **K** name Jesus,*ct* because he will save his **L** people from their sins."*u*

S ²²All this took place to fulfill*v* what the Lord had said through the prophet: ²³"The virgin will be with child and will give birth to a son, and they will call him Immanuel"*dw*—which means, "God with us."

²⁴When Joseph woke up, he did what the angel*x* of the Lord had commanded him and took Mary home as his wife. ²⁵But he had no union with her until she gave birth to a son. And he gave him the name Jesus.*y*

The Visit of the Magi

2 After Jesus was born in Bethlehem in Judea,*z* during the time of King Herod,*a* Magi*e* from the east came to Jerusalem ²and asked, "Where is the one **I** who has been born king of the Jews?*b* We **M** saw his star*c* in the east*f* and have come to worship him."

³When King Herod heard this he was disturbed, and all Jerusalem with him. ⁴When he had called together all the people's chief priests and teachers of the law, he asked them where the Christ*g* was to be born. ⁵"In Bethlehem*d* in Judea," they replied, "for this is what the prophet has written:

E Zec 7:12 ◄ ► Mt 1:20
E Mt 1:18 ◄ ► Mt 3:16
B Zec 11:12–13 ◄ ► Mt 2:14–15
D Mal 1:13–14 ◄ ► Mt 20:28
K Zec 13:1 ◄ ► Mt 6:13
L Mal 3:7 ◄ ► Mt 4:16
S Mal 3:18 ◄ ► Mt 3:10

I Mal 3:2–4 ◄ ► Mt 2:6
M Mal 4:2–3 ◄ ► Mt 2:6

1:18 *p* Lk 1:35
1:19 *q* Dt 24:1
1:20 *r* S Ac 5:19; *s* S Mt 27:19
1:21 *t* S Lk 1:31; *u* Ps 130:8; S Lk 2:11; S Jn 3:17; Ac 5:31; S Ro 11:14; Tit 2:14
1:22 *v* Mt 2:15,17, 23; 4:14; 8:17; 12:17; 21:4; 26:54, 56; 27:9; Lk 4:21; 21:22; 24:44; Jn 13:18; 19:24,28, 36
1:23 *w* Isa 7:14; 8:8,10
1:24 *x* S Ac 5:19
1:25 *y* ver 21; S Lk 1:31

2:1 *z* Lk 2:4-7; *a* Lk 1:5
2:2 *b* Jer 23:5; Mt 27:11; Mk 15:2; Lk 23:38; Jn 1:49; 18:33-37; *c* Nu 24:17
2:5 *d* Jn 7:42

b 17 Or *Messiah*. "The Christ" (Greek) and "the Messiah" (Hebrew) both mean "the Anointed One." *c* 21 *Jesus* is the Greek form of *Joshua*, which means *the* LORD *saves*. *d* 23 Isaiah 7:14 *e* 1 Traditionally *Wise Men* *f* 2 Or *star when it rose* *g* 4 Or *Messiah*

1:21 The first prophecy in the NT refers to the greatest promise God ever gave to humanity. The angel of the Lord came to Joseph and instructed him to marry Mary since the child in her womb had been conceived supernaturally by the power of God. Furthermore, the angel told Joseph to name the child "Jesus, because he will save his people from their sins." The name *Jesus* means "Jehovah is salvation." What an appropriate name for one whose purpose was "to give his life as a ransom for many" (Mt 20:28).

1:22–23 Matthew reveals that this supernatural birth of Jesus to the virgin Mary would fulfill the prophecy made by Isaiah over seven hundred years earlier: "The virgin will be with child and will give birth to a son, and will call him Immanuel" (Isa 7:14).

Isaiah used the Hebrew word *almah* in this verse to refer to the child's mother. Because *almah* refers to an unmarried, young woman and does not definitely translate as "virgin," some scholars deny the possibility of the virgin birth. However, the Hebrew word *almah* carries with it an implication of morality, so that a young, unmarried woman would be expected to still be a virgin. Consider also that this prophecy was to be a supernatural sign. If *almah* did not mean a virgin, how would the birth of a son to a sexually active young woman be a prophetic sign from God since such births happen every day? Obviously, the meaning of Isaiah's prophecy signaled a virgin birth. Jesus came to humanity, revealed as God, descended from his heavenly throne, taking human flesh through the miracle of the incarnation.

2:2 The wise men were guided to Jerusalem and Bethlehem by a supernatural celestial object. Some suggest that this may have been a super nova or an unusual alignment of the constellations. Though the Bible does not give the exact details of this phenomenon, it was spectacular enough to cause these scholars to seek out the birthplace of the promised Messiah. Note that the words of the Magi, or wise men, were prophetic of Christ's final victory over Satan when Jesus will be universally acknowledged as the "king of the Jews" and rule in Jerusalem during the Millennium.

⁶"'But you, Bethlehem, in the land of Judah,
 are by no means least among the rulers of Judah;
for out of you will come a ruler
 who will be the shepherd of my people Israel.'"ᵉ

⁷Then Herod called the Magi secretly and found out from them the exact time the star had appeared. ⁸He sent them to Bethlehem and said, "Go and make a careful search for the child. As soon as you find him, report to me, so that I too may go and worship him."

⁹After they had heard the king, they went on their way, and the star they had seen in the eastⁱ went ahead of them until it stopped over the place where the child was. ¹⁰When they saw the star, they were overjoyed. ¹¹On coming to the house, they saw the child with his mother Mary, and they bowed down and worshiped him.ᶠ Then they opened their treasures and presented him with giftsᵍ of gold and of incense and of myrrh. ¹²And having been warnedʰ in a dreamⁱ not to go back to Herod, they returned to their country by another route.

The Escape to Egypt

¹³When they had gone, an angelʲ of the Lord appeared to Joseph in a dream.ᵏ "Get up," he said, "take the child and his mother and escape to Egypt. Stay there until I tell you, for Herod is going to search for the child to kill him."ˡ

¹⁴So he got up, took the child and his mother during the night and left for Egypt, ¹⁵where he stayed until the death of Herod. And so was fulfilledᵐ what the Lord had said through the prophet: "Out of Egypt I called my son."ⁿ

¹⁶When Herod realized that he had been outwitted by the Magi, he was furious, and he gave orders to kill all the boys in Bethlehem and its vicinity who were two years old and under, in accordance with the time he had learned from the Magi. ¹⁷Then what was said through the prophet Jeremiah was fulfilled:ᵒ

¹⁸"A voice is heard in Ramah,
 weeping and great mourning,
Rachelᵖ weeping for her children
 and refusing to be comforted,
 because they are no more."ᵏᑫ

The Return to Nazareth

¹⁹After Herod died, an angelʳ of the Lord appeared in a dreamˢ to Joseph in Egypt ²⁰and said, "Get up, take the child and his mother and go to the land of Israel, for those who were trying to take the child's life are dead."ᵗ

²¹So he got up, took the child and his mother and went to the land of Israel. ²²But when he heard that Archelaus was reigning in Judea in place of his father Herod, he was afraid to go there. Having been warned in a dream,ᵘ he withdrew to the district of Galilee,ᵛ ²³and he went and lived in a town called Nazareth.ʷ So was fulfilledˣ what was said through the prophets: "He will be called a Nazarene."ʸ

2:6 The chief priests and scribes told the wise men where to look for the Messiah because of Micah's words that "you, Bethlehem Ephrathah, though you are small among the clans of Judah, out of you will come for me one who will be ruler over Israel" (Mic 5:2).

2:14–15 Though this quotation from Hosea originally applied to the Israelites' exodus from Egypt under Moses, Matthew applies it also to Jesus. History does not record exactly how long Jesus and his family stayed in Egypt.

2:23 Though the exact words of this prophecy do not exist in the OT, note that Matthew indicated that the prophetical words were spoken by more than one prophet. When several of the OT prophecies are viewed together (especially Ps 22:6; Isa 11:1; and 53:3), the Messiah is pictured as someone who was despised or referred to as a branch. The Hebrew word for branch is *neser*, the root word for the name "Nazareth." In Jesus' day Nazareth was an obscure town with a bad reputation. Inhabitants of this town were despised by most of the other Jews. For both of these reasons, Jesus was "called a Nazarene."

John the Baptist Prepares the Way

3:1–12pp — Mk 1:3–8; Lk 3:2–17

3 In those days John the Baptist[z] came, preaching in the Desert of Judea [2]and saying, "Repent, for the kingdom of heaven[a] is near." [3]This is he who was spoken of through the prophet Isaiah:

"A voice of one calling in the desert,
'Prepare the way for the Lord,
  make straight paths for him.'"[/b]

[4]John's[c] clothes were made of camel's hair, and he had a leather belt around his waist.[d] His food was locusts[e] and wild honey. [5]People went out to him from Jerusalem and all Judea and the whole region of the Jordan. [6]Confessing their sins, they were baptized[f] by him in the Jordan River.

[7]But when he saw many of the Pharisees and Sadducees coming to where he was baptizing, he said to them: "You brood of vipers![g] Who warned you to flee from the coming wrath?[h] [8]Produce fruit in keeping with repentance.[i] [9]And do not think you can say to yourselves, 'We have Abraham as our father.'[j] I tell you that out of these stones God can raise up children for Abraham. [10]The ax is already at the root of the trees, and every tree that does not produce good fruit will be cut down and thrown into the fire.[k]

[11]"I baptize you with[m] water for repentance.[l] But after me will come one who is more powerful than I, whose sandals I am not fit to carry. He will baptize you with the Holy Spirit[m] and with fire.[n] [12]His winnowing fork is in his hand, and he will clear his threshing floor, gathering his wheat into the barn and burning up the chaff with unquenchable fire."[o]

The Baptism of Jesus

3:13–17pp — Mk 1:9–11; Lk 3:21,22; Jn 1:31–34

[13]Then Jesus came from Galilee to the Jordan to be baptized by John.[p] [14]But John tried to deter him, saying, "I need to be baptized by you, and do you come to me?"

[15]Jesus replied, "Let it be so now; it is proper for us to do this to fulfill all righteousness." Then John consented.

[16]As soon as Jesus was baptized, he went up out of the water. At that moment heaven was opened,[q] and he saw the Spirit of God[r] descending like a dove and lighting on him. [17]And a voice from heaven[s] said, "This is my Son,[t] whom I love; with him I am well pleased."[u]

The Temptation of Jesus

4:1–11pp — Mk 1:12,13; Lk 4:1–13

4 Then Jesus was led by the Spirit into the desert to be tempted[v] by the devil.[w] [2]After fasting forty days and forty nights,[x] he was hungry. [3]The tempter[y] came to him and said, "If you are the Son of God,[z] tell these stones to become bread."

[4]Jesus answered, "It is written: 'Man does not live on bread alone, but on ev-

---

l 3 Isaiah 40:3   m 11 Or in

3:3 John the Baptist preached about the need for the Jews to repent of their sins in preparation for the coming of the Messiah. John called upon the people to "Prepare the way for the Lord" echoing the words of Isa 40:3.

3:11–12 Matthew records John's prophecy that Jesus would "baptize you with the Holy Spirit and with fire" (3:11). This prophecy was fulfilled after Christ's resurrection on the day of Pentecost when the Holy Spirit empowered the early disciples and strengthened them to accomplish Christ's great commission (see Ac 2:1–4). However, this prophecy also looks forward to the last days when Christ will finally judge the nations and "[burn] up the chaff with unquenchable fire" (3:12).

ery word that comes from the mouth of God.'"ᵃ

⁵Then the devil took him to the holy cityᵇ and had him stand on the highest point of the temple. ⁶"If you are the Son of God,"ᶜ he said, "throw yourself down. For it is written:

" 'He will command his angels
  concerning you,
and they will lift you up in their
  hands,
so that you will not strike your foot
  against a stone.'"ᵈ

⁷Jesus answered him, "It is also written: 'Do not put the Lord your God to the test.'"ᵉ

⁸Again, the devil took him to a very high mountain and showed him all the kingdoms of the world and their splendor. ⁹"All this I will give you," he said, "if you will bow down and worship me."

¹⁰Jesus said to him, "Away from me, Satan! For it is written: 'Worship the Lord your God, and serve him only.'"ᵍ

¹¹Then the devil left him,ʰ and angels came and attended him.ⁱ

Jesus Begins to Preach

¹²When Jesus heard that John had been put in prison,ʲ he returned to Galilee.ᵏ ¹³Leaving Nazareth, he went and lived in Capernaum,ˡ which was by the lake in the area of Zebulun and Naphtali— ¹⁴to fulfillᵐ what was said through the prophet Isaiah:

¹⁵"Land of Zebulun and land of Naphtali,
  the way to the sea, along the Jordan,
  Galilee of the Gentiles—

¹⁶the people living in darkness
  have seen a great light;

S Na 1:7 ◀ ▶ Mk 4:40
F Hab 3:17–18 ◀ ▶ Mt 6:11
B Mt 3:3 ◀ ▶ Mt 12:40–41
C Mt 3:12 ◀ ▶ Mt 6:23
L Mt 1:21 ◀ ▶ Mt 5:5

4:4 ᵃDt 8:3; Jn 4:34
4:5 ᵇNe 11:1; Da 9:24; Mt 27:53
4:6 ᶜS ver 3
ᵈPs 91:11,12
4:7 ᵉDt 6:16
4:10 ᶠ1Ch 21:1; Job 1:6-9; Mt 16:23; Mk 4:15; Lk 10:18; 13:16; 22:3,31; Ro 16:20; 2Co 2:11; 11:14; 2Th 2:9; Rev 12:9
ᵍDt 6:13
4:11 ʰJas 4:7
ⁱMt 26:53; Lk 22:43; Heb 1:14
4:12 ʲMt 14:3
ᵏMk 1:14
4:13 ˡMk 1:21; 9:33; Lk 4:23,31; Jn 2:12; 4:46,47
4:14 ᵐS Mt 1:22
4:16 ⁿIsa 9:1,2; Lk 2:32; Jn 1:4,5,9
4:17 ᵒS Mt 3:2
4:18 ᵖMt 15:29; Mk 7:31; Jn 6:1
ᵍMt 16:17,18
4:19 ʳver 20,22; Mt 8:22; Mk 10:21, 28,52; Lk 5:28; Jn 1:43; 21:19,22
4:20 ˢS ver 19
4:21 ᵗMt 17:1; 20:20; 26:37; Mk 3:17; 13:3; Lk 8:51; Jn 21:2
4:22 ᵘS ver 19
4:23 ᵛMk 1:39; Lk 4:15,44
ʷMt 9:35; 13:54; Mk 1:21; 4:15; Jn 6:59; 18:20
ˣMk 1:14
ʸS Mt 3:2; Ac 20:25; 28:23,31
ᶻMt 8:16; 14:14; 15:30; Mk 3:10; Lk 7:22; Ac 10:38
4:24 ᵃS Lk 2:2
ᵇMt 8:16,28; 9:32; 12:22; 15:22; Mk 1:32; 5:15,16, 18 ᶜMt 17:15
ᵈMt 8:6; 9:2; Mk 2:3
4:25 ᵉMk 3:7,8; Lk 6:17

---

on those living in the land of the
  shadow of death
a light has dawned.'"ⁿ

¹⁷From that time on Jesus began to preach, "Repent, for the kingdom of heavenᵒ is near."

The Calling of the First Disciples

4:18–22pp — Mk 1:16–20; Lk 5:2–11; Jn 1:35–42

¹⁸As Jesus was walking beside the Sea of Galilee,ᵖ he saw two brothers, Simon called Peterᵍ and his brother Andrew. They were casting a net into the lake, for they were fishermen. ¹⁹"Come, follow me,"ʳ Jesus said, "and I will make you fishers of men." ²⁰At once they left their nets and followed him.ˢ

²¹Going on from there, he saw two other brothers, James son of Zebedee and his brother John.ᵗ They were in a boat with their father Zebedee, preparing their nets. Jesus called them, ²²and immediately they left the boat and their father and followed him.ᵘ

Jesus Heals the Sick

²³Jesus went throughout Galilee,ᵛ teaching in their synagogues,ʷ preaching the good newsˣ of the kingdom,ʸ and healing every disease and sickness among the people.ᶻ ²⁴News about him spread all over Syria,ᵃ and people brought to him all who were ill with various diseases, those suffering severe pain, the demon-possessed,ᵇ those having seizures,ᶜ and the paralyzed,ᵈ and he healed them. ²⁵Large crowds from Galilee, the Decapolis,ˢ Jerusalem, Judea and the region across the Jordan followed him.ᵉ

R Mt 3:8 ◀ ▶ Mt 6:12
E Hos 11:3 ◀ ▶ Mt 7:22

ⁿ 4 Deut. 8:3 ᵒ 6 Psalm 91:11,12 ᵖ 7 Deut. 6:16 ᵍ 10 Deut. 6:13
ʳ 16 Isaiah 9:1,2 ˢ 25 That is, the Ten Cities

4:13–16 Matthew refers to Christ's ministry in Capernaum, near Zebulun and Naphtali, as the fulfillment of Isaiah's words that "the people walking in darkness have seen a great light" (Isa 9:2). Capernaum was the home of Peter and became Jesus' base of operations during his ministry in the largely Gentile area of Galilee (see Mk 2:1; 9:33). The Jews showed disdain for anyone who came from this region, claiming that "a prophet does not come out of Galilee" (Jn 7:52). Yet their contempt was misdirected because one of Israel's greatest prophets (Jonah) had come from a town in Galilee (see 2Ki 14:25).

The Beatitudes

5:3–12pp — Lk 6:20–23

5 Now when he saw the crowds, he went up on a mountainside and sat down. His disciples came to him, ²and he began to teach them, saying:

³"Blessed are the poor in spirit,
　for theirs is the kingdom of heaven.[f]
⁴Blessed are those who mourn,
　for they will be comforted.[g]
⁵Blessed are the meek,
　for they will inherit the earth.[h]
⁶Blessed are those who hunger and
　　thirst for righteousness,
　for they will be filled.[i]
⁷Blessed are the merciful,
　for they will be shown mercy.[j]
⁸Blessed are the pure in heart,[k]
　for they will see God.[l]
⁹Blessed are the peacemakers,[m]
　for they will be called sons of God.[n]
¹⁰Blessed are those who are persecuted
　　because of righteousness,[o]
　for theirs is the kingdom of heaven.[p]

¹¹"Blessed are you when people insult you,[q] persecute you and falsely say all kinds of evil against you because of me.[r] ¹²Rejoice and be glad,[s] because great is your reward in heaven, for in the same way they persecuted the prophets who were before you.[t]

Salt and Light

¹³"You are the salt of the earth. But if the salt loses its saltiness, how can it be made salty again? It is no longer good for anything, except to be thrown out and trampled by men.[u]

¹⁴"You are the light of the world.[v] A city on a hill cannot be hidden. ¹⁵Neither do people light a lamp and put it under a bowl. Instead they put it on its stand, and it gives light to everyone in the house.[w] ¹⁶In the same way, let your light shine before men,[x] that they may see your good deeds[y] and praise[z] your Father in heaven.

The Fulfillment of the Law

¹⁷"Do not think that I have come to abolish the Law or the Prophets; I have not come to abolish them but to fulfill them.[a] ¹⁸I tell you the truth, until heaven and earth disappear, not the smallest letter, not the least stroke of a pen, will by any means disappear from the Law until everything is accomplished.[b] ¹⁹Anyone who breaks one of the least of these commandments[c] and teaches others to do the same will be called least in the kingdom of heaven, but whoever practices and teaches these commands will be called great in the kingdom of heaven. ²⁰For I tell you that unless your righteousness surpasses that of the Pharisees and the teachers of the law, you will certainly not enter the kingdom of heaven.[d]

Murder

5:25,26pp — Lk 12:58,59

²¹"You have heard that it was said to the people long ago, 'Do not murder,'[e] and anyone who murders will be subject to judgment.' ²²But I tell you that anyone who is angry[f] with his brother[*] will be subject to judgment.[g] Again, anyone who says to his brother, 'Raca,'[v] is answerable to the Sanhedrin.[h] But anyone who says, 'You fool!' will be in danger of the fire of hell.[i]

²³"Therefore, if you are offering your gift at the altar and there remember that your brother has something against you, ²⁴leave your gift there in front of the altar.

M Mal 4:1 ◄► Mt 18:1–4
N Isa 65:16–18 ◄► Heb 1:10–12
L Mt 4:16 ◄► Mt 6:14
U Mal 3:10 ◄► Mt 6:4
S Mt 3:10 ◄► Mt 5:13
U Zec 9:10 ◄► Lk 2:14
J Hab 3:17 ◄► Lk 6:22–23
S Mt 5:8 ◄► Mt 5:29–30

G Zep 1:18 ◄► Mt 7:26–27
H Mt 3:12 ◄► Mt 5:29–30

[t]21 Exodus 20:13 [u]22 Some manuscripts *brother without cause*
[v]22 An Aramaic term of contempt

5:5 Jesus' words echo the psalmist in this passage as he spoke this prophecy which will be fulfilled in the last days. In the millennial kingdom "the meek will inherit the land" (Ps 37:11) when Christ eliminates all violence (see Isa 11:4–6) and people live humbly before God in the new earth (see Rev 21:1).

5:9 Jesus blessed the peacemakers, those who strive to promote peace (see Ro 12:18), for those are the ones who truly reflect the character of God. Perfect peace will one day exist throughout the earth when Christ will reign forever as the "Prince of Peace" (Isa 9:6).

First go and be reconciled to your brother; then come and offer your gift.

²⁵"Settle matters quickly with your adversary who is taking you to court. Do it while you are still with him on the way, or he may hand you over to the judge, and the judge may hand you over to the officer, and you may be thrown into prison. ²⁶I tell you the truth, you will not get out until you have paid the last penny.ʷ

Adultery

²⁷"You have heard that it was said, 'Do not commit adultery.'ˣʲ ²⁸But I tell you that anyone who looks at a woman lustfully has already committed adultery with her in his heart.ᵏ ²⁹If your right eye causes you to sin,ˡ gouge it out and throw it away. It is better for you to lose one part of your body than for your whole body to be thrown into hell. ³⁰And if your right hand causes you to sin,ᵐ cut it off and throw it away. It is better for you to lose one part of your body than for your whole body to go into hell.

Divorce

³¹"It has been said, 'Anyone who divorces his wife must give her a certificate of divorce.'ʸⁿ ³²But I tell you that anyone who divorces his wife, except for marital unfaithfulness, causes her to become an adulteress, and anyone who marries the divorced woman commits adultery.ᵒ

Oaths

³³"Again, you have heard that it was said to the people long ago, 'Do not break your oath,ᵖ but keep the oaths you have made to the Lord.'ᑫ ³⁴But I tell you, Do not swear at all:ʳ either by heaven, for it is God's throne;ˢ ³⁵or by the earth, for it is his footstool; or by Jerusalem, for it is the city of the Great King.ᵗ ³⁶And do not swear by your head, for you cannot make even one hair white or black. ³⁷Simply let your 'Yes' be 'Yes,' and your 'No,' 'No';ᵘ anything beyond this comes from the evil one.ᵛ

An Eye for an Eye

³⁸"You have heard that it was said, 'Eye for eye, and tooth for tooth.'ᶻʷ ³⁹But I tell you, Do not resist an evil person. If someone strikes you on the right cheek, turn to him the other also.ˣ ⁴⁰And if someone wants to sue you and take your tunic, let him have your cloak as well. ⁴¹If someone forces you to go one mile, go with him two miles. ⁴²Give to the one who asks you, and do not turn away from the one who wants to borrow from you.ʸ

Love for Enemies

⁴³"You have heard that it was said, 'Love your neighborᵃᶻ and hate your enemy.'ᵃ ⁴⁴But I tell you: Love your enemiesᵇ and pray for those who persecute you,ᵇ ⁴⁵that you may be sonsᶜ of your Father in heaven. He causes his sun to rise on the evil and the good, and sends rain on the righteous and the unrighteous.ᵈ ⁴⁶If you love those who love you, what reward will you get?ᵉ Are not even the tax collectors doing that? ⁴⁷And if you greet only your brothers, what are you doing more than others? Do not even pagans do that? ⁴⁸Be perfect, therefore, as your heavenly Father is perfect.ᶠ

Giving to the Needy

6 "Be careful not to do your 'acts of righteousness' before men, to be seen by them.ᵍ If you do, you will have no reward from your Father in heaven.

²"So when you give to the needy, do not announce it with trumpets, as the hypocrites do in the synagogues and on the streets, to be honored by men. I tell you the truth, they have received their reward in full. ³But when you give to the needy, do not let your left hand know what your right hand is doing, ⁴so that your giving may be in secret. Then your Father, who sees what is done in secret, will reward you.ʰ

Prayer

6:9–13pp — Lk 11:2–4

⁵"And when you pray, do not be like the hypocrites, for they love to pray standingⁱ in the synagogues and on the street corners to be seen by men. I tell you the truth, they have received their

---

S *Mt 5:29–30* ◀ ▶ *Mt 6:21–24*
U *Mt 5:5–12* ◀ ▶ *Mt 6:6*

ʷ 26 Greek *kodrantes* ˣ 27 Exodus 20:14 ʸ 31 Deut. 24:1
ᶻ 38 Exodus 21:24; Lev. 24:20; Deut. 19:21 ᵃ 43 Lev. 19:18 ᵇ 44 Some late manuscripts *enemies, bless those who curse you, do good to those who hate you*

H *Mt 5:22* ◀ ▶ *Mt 7:13*
S *Mt 5:13* ◀ ▶ *Mt 5:48*

reward in full. ⁶But when you pray, go into your room, close the door and pray to your Father,ʲ who is unseen. Then your Father, who sees what is done in secret, will reward you. ⁷And when you pray, do not keep on babblingᵏ like pagans, for they think they will be heard because of their many words.¹ ⁸Do not be like them, for your Father knows what you needᵐ before you ask him.

⁹"This, then, is how you should pray:

" 'Our Fatherⁿ in heaven,
hallowed be your name,
¹⁰your kingdomᵒ come,
your will be doneᵖ
on earth as it is in heaven.
¹¹Give us today our daily bread.ᑫ
¹²Forgive us our debts,
as we also have forgiven our
debtors.ʳ
¹³And lead us not into temptation,ˢ
but deliver us from the evil one.ᶜʼᵗ

¹⁴For if you forgive men when they sin against you, your heavenly Father will also forgive you.ᵘ ¹⁵But if you do not forgive men their sins, your Father will not forgive your sins.ᵛ

Fasting

¹⁶"When you fast,ʷ do not look somberˣ as the hypocrites do, for they disfigure their faces to show men they are fasting. I tell you the truth, they have received their reward in full. ¹⁷But when you fast, put oil on your head and wash your face, ¹⁸so that it will not be obvious to men that you are fasting, but only to your Father, who is unseen; and your Father, who sees what is done in secret, will reward you.ʸ

U Mt 6:4 ◄ ► Mt 6:18
L Mal 3:16–17 ◄ ► Mt 6:25–34
K Zec 14:9 ◄ ► Mt 13:33
M Mt 2:6 ◄ ► Mt 6:13
F Mt 4:11 ◄ ► Mt 6:25–34
R Mt 4:17 ◄ ► Mt 6:14–15
M Mt 6:10 ◄ ► Mt 13:31–33
K Mt 1:21 ◄ ► Mt 7:24–25
L Mt 5:5 ◄ ► Mt 7:7–8
R Mt 6:12 ◄ ► Mt 18:35
U Mt 6:6 ◄ ► Mt 6:33

6:6 ʲ 2Ki 4:33
6:7 ᵏ Ecc 5:2
  ¹ 1Ki 18:26-29
6:8 ᵐ ver 32
6:9 ⁿ Jer 3:19;
Mal 2:10; 1Pe 1:17
6:10 ᵒ S Mt 3:2
  ᵖ Mt 26:39
6:11 ᑫ Pr 30:8
6:12 ʳ Mt 18:21-35
6:13 ˢ Jas 1:13
  ᵗ S Mt 5:37
6:14
ᵘ Mt 18:21-35;
Mk 11:25,26;
Eph 4:32; Col 3:13
6:15 ᵛ Mt 18:35
6:16 ʷ Lev 16:29,
31; 23:27-32;
Nu 29:7 Isa 58:5;
Zec 7:5; 8:19
6:18 ʸ ver 4,6
6:19 ᶻ Pr 23:4;
Lk 12:16-21;
Heb 13:5
  ᵃ S Jas 5:2,3
6:20 ᵇ Mt 19:21;
Lk 12:33; 16:9;
18:22; 1Ti 6:19
  ᶜ Lk 12:33
6:21 ᵈ Lk 12:34
6:24 ᵉ Lk 16:13
6:25 ᶠ ver 27,28,
31,34; Lk 10:41;
12:11,22
6:26 ᵍ Job 38:41;
Ps 104:21; 136:25;
145:15; 147:9
  ʰ Mt 10:29-31
6:27 ⁱ Ps 39:5
6:29 ʲ 1Ki 10:4-7

Treasures in Heaven
6:22,23pp — Lk 11:34–36

¹⁹"Do not store up for yourselves treasures on earth,ᶻ where moth and rust destroy,ᵃ and where thieves break in and steal. ²⁰But store up for yourselves treasures in heaven,ᵇ where moth and rust do not destroy, and where thieves do not break in and steal.ᶜ ²¹For where your treasure is, there your heart will be also.ᵈ

²²"The eye is the lamp of the body. If your eyes are good, your whole body will be full of light. ²³But if your eyes are bad, your whole body will be full of darkness. If then the light within you is darkness, how great is that darkness!

²⁴"No one can serve two masters. Either he will hate the one and love the other, or he will be devoted to the one and despise the other. You cannot serve both God and Money.ᵉ

Do Not Worry
6:25–33pp — Lk 12:22–31

²⁵"Therefore I tell you, do not worryᶠ about your life, what you will eat or drink; or about your body, what you will wear. Is not life more important than food, and the body more important than clothes? ²⁶Look at the birds of the air; they do not sow or reap or store away in barns, and yet your heavenly Father feeds them.ᵍ Are you not much more valuable than they?ʰ ²⁷Who of you by worrying can add a single hour to his lifeᵈ?ⁱ

²⁸"And why do you worry about clothes? See how the lilies of the field grow. They do not labor or spin. ²⁹Yet I tell you that not even Solomon in all his splendorʲ was dressed like one of these. ³⁰If that is how God clothes the grass of the field, which is here today and tomor-

S Mt 5:48 ◄ ► Mt 7:13–14
C Mt 4:16 ◄ ► Mt 7:16–20
C Eze 16:10 ◄ ► Lk 12:22–31
F Mt 6:11 ◄ ► Mt 14:15–21
L Mt 6:8 ◄ ► Mt 7:7–11
W Jer 10:2 ◄ ► Mt 8:26

ᶜ 13 Or *from evil;* some late manuscripts *one, / for yours is the kingdom and the power and the glory forever. Amen.* ᵈ 27 Or *single cubit to his height*

6:10, 13 In this prayer, Jesus highlights a present reality as well as a future prophecy. God's kingdom is present with us now (see Lk 17:21; Ro 14:17) yet we can still look ahead to a time when God's kingdom will be fully established on earth (see Lk 21:31). Jesus will rule from the throne of David in Jerusalem, and the peace and justice of heaven will exist on earth forever.

row is thrown into the fire, will he not much more clothe you, O you of little faith?[k] [31]So do not worry, saying, 'What shall we eat?' or 'What shall we drink?' or 'What shall we wear?' [32]For the pagans run after all these things, and your heavenly Father knows that you need them.[l] [33]But seek first his kingdom[m] and his righteousness, and all these things will be given to you as well.[n] [34]Therefore do not worry about tomorrow, for tomorrow will worry about itself. Each day has enough trouble of its own.

Judging Others

7:3–5pp — Lk 6:41,42

[7] "Do not judge, or you too will be judged.[o] [2]For in the same way you judge others, you will be judged, and with the measure you use, it will be measured to you.[p]

[3]"Why do you look at the speck of sawdust in your brother's eye and pay no attention to the plank in your own eye? [4]How can you say to your brother, 'Let me take the speck out of your eye,' when all the time there is a plank in your own eye? [5]You hypocrite, first take the plank out of your own eye, and then you will see clearly to remove the speck from your brother's eye.

[6]"Do not give dogs what is sacred; do not throw your pearls to pigs. If you do, they may trample them under their feet, and then turn and tear you to pieces.

Ask, Seek, Knock

7:7–11pp — Lk 11:9–13

[7]"Ask and it will be given to you;[q] seek and you will find; knock and the door will be opened to you. [8]For everyone who asks receives; he who seeks finds;[r] and to him who knocks, the door will be opened.

[9]"Which of you, if his son asks for bread, will give him a stone? [10]Or if he asks for a fish, will give him a snake? [11]If you, then, though you are evil, know how to give good gifts to your children, how much more will your Father in heaven give good gifts[s] to those who ask him!

6:30 [k] Mt 8:26; 14:31; 16:8; Lk 12:28
6:32 [l] ver 8
6:33 [m] S Mt 3:2 [n] Ps 37:4; Mt 19:29
7:1 [o] Lk 6:37; Ro 14:4,10,13; 1Co 4:5; 5:12; Jas 4:11,12
7:2 [p] Eze 35:11; Mk 4:24; Lk 6:38; Ro 2:1
7:7 [q] 1Ki 3:5; Mt 18:19; 21:22; Jn 14:13,14; 15:7, 16; 16:23,24; Jas 1:5-8; 4:2,3; 5:16; 1Jn 3:22; 5:14,15
7:8 [r] Pr 8:17; Jer 29:12,13
7:11 [s] Jas 1:17
7:12 [t] Lk 6:31 [u] Ro 13:8-10; Gal 5:14
7:13 [v] Lk 13:24; Jn 10:7,9
7:15 [w] Jer 23:16; Mt 24:24; Lk 6:26; 2Pe 2:1; 1Jn 4:1; Rev 19:20 [x] Eze 22:27; Ac 20:29
7:16 [y] Mt 12:33; Lk 6:44 [z] Jas 3:12
7:18 [a] Lk 6:43
7:19 [b] S Mt 3:10
7:21 [c] Hos 8:2; Mt 25:11; 1Co 12:3 [d] S Mt 3:2 [e] Mt 12:50; Ro 2:13; Jas 1:22; 1Jn 3:18
7:22 [f] S Mt 10:15 [g] Lk 10:20; Ac 19:13; 1Co 13:1-3
7:23 [h] Ps 6:8; Mt 25:12,41; Lk 13:25-27
7:24 [i] ver 21; Jas 1:22-25

[12]So in everything, do to others what you would have them do to you,[t] for this sums up the Law and the Prophets.[u]

The Narrow and Wide Gates

[13]"Enter through the narrow gate.[v] For wide is the gate and broad is the road that leads to destruction, and many enter through it. [14]But small is the gate and narrow the road that leads to life, and only a few find it.

A Tree and Its Fruit

[15]"Watch out for false prophets.[w] They come to you in sheep's clothing, but inwardly they are ferocious wolves.[x] [16]By their fruit you will recognize them.[y] Do people pick grapes from thornbushes, or figs from thistles?[z] [17]Likewise every good tree bears good fruit, but a bad tree bears bad fruit. [18]A good tree cannot bear bad fruit, and a bad tree cannot bear good fruit.[a] [19]Every tree that does not bear good fruit is cut down and thrown into the fire.[b] [20]Thus, by their fruit you will recognize them.

[21]"Not everyone who says to me, 'Lord, Lord,'[c] will enter the kingdom of heaven,[d] but only he who does the will of my Father who is in heaven.[e] [22]Many will say to me on that day,[f] 'Lord, Lord, did we not prophesy in your name, and in your name drive out demons and perform many miracles?'[g] [23]Then I will tell them plainly, 'I never knew you. Away from me, you evildoers!'[h]

The Wise and Foolish Builders

7:24–27pp — Lk 6:47–49

[24]"Therefore everyone who hears these words of mine and puts them into practice[i] is like a wise man who built his house on the rock. [25]The rain came down, the streams rose, and the winds blew and beat against that house; yet it did not fall, because it had its foundation

H Mt 5:29–30 ◀ ▶ Mt 7:19
S Mt 6:21–24 ◀ ▶ Mt 7:16–24
C Mt 6:23 ◀ ▶ Mt 7:26–27
S Mt 7:13–14 ◀ ▶ Mt 10:22
H Mt 7:13 ◀ ▶ Mt 7:26–27
E Mt 4:23–25 ◀ ▶ Mt 8:2–3
K Mt 6:13 ◀ ▶ Mt 9:6
W Mt 7:7–8 ◀ ▶ Mt 10:32

P Mal 3:10–11 ◀ ▶ Mt 17:27
U Mt 6:18 ◀ ▶ Mt 19:29
J Am 4:12 ◀ ▶ Mt 10:15
L Mt 6:14 ◀ ▶ Mt 9:12–13
W Eze 33:11 ◀ ▶ Mt 7:24
L Mt 6:25–34 ◀ ▶ Mt 8:26

on the rock. ²⁶But everyone who hears these words of mine and does not put them into practice is like a foolish man who built his house on sand. ²⁷The rain came down, the streams rose, and the winds blew and beat against that house, and it fell with a great crash."

²⁸When Jesus had finished saying these things,ʲ the crowds were amazed at his teaching,ᵏ ²⁹because he taught as one who had authority, and not as their teachers of the law.

The Man With Leprosy
8:2–4pp — Mk 1:40–44; Lk 5:12–14

8 When he came down from the mountainside, large crowds followed him. ²A man with leprosy[e1] came and knelt before himᵐ and said, "Lord, if you are willing, you can make me clean." ³Jesus reached out his hand and touched the man. "I am willing," he said. "Be clean!" Immediately he was cured[f] of his leprosy. ⁴Then Jesus said to him, "See that you don't tell anyone.ⁿ But go, show yourself to the priestᵒ and offer the gift Moses commanded,ᵖ as a testimony to them."

The Faith of the Centurion
8:5–13pp — Lk 7:1–10

⁵When Jesus had entered Capernaum, a centurion came to him, asking for help. ⁶"Lord," he said, "my servant lies at home paralyzedᵠ and in terrible suffering."

⁷Jesus said to him, "I will go and heal him."

⁸The centurion replied, "Lord, I do not deserve to have you come under my roof. But just say the word, and my servant will be healed.ʳ ⁹For I myself am a man under authority, with soldiers under me.

C Mt 7:16–20 ◀▶ Mt 8:22
G Mt 5:20 ◀▶ Mt 15:8–9
H Mt 7:19 ◀▶ Mt 8:12
O Jnh 2:9 ◀▶ Mt 10:32–33
E Mt 7:22 ◀▶ Mt 8:5–17
E Mt 8:2–3 ◀▶ Mt 8:28–32

7:28 ʲ Mt 11:1; 13:53; 19:1; 26:1
ᵏ Mt 13:54; 22:33; Mk 1:22; 6:2; 11:18; Lk 4:32;
Jn 7:46

8:2 ˡ Lev 13:45; Mt 10:8; 11:5; 26:6; Lk 5:12; 17:12 ᵐ Mt 9:18; 15:25; 18:26; 20:20

8:4 ⁿ Mt 9:30; 12:16; Mk 5:43; 7:36; S 8:30; Lk 4:41 ᵒ Lk 17:14
ᵖ Lev 14:2-32

8:6 ᵠ S Mt 4:24

8:8 ʳ Ps 107:20

8:10 ˢ Mt 15:28

8:11 ᵗ Ps 107:3; Isa 49:12; 59:19; Mal 1:11 ᵘ Lk 13:29

8:12 ᵛ Mt 13:38 ʷ Mt 13:42,50; 22:13; 24:51; 25:30; Lk 13:28

8:13 ˣ S Mt 9:22

8:16 ʸ S Mt 4:23, 24

8:17 ᶻ S Mt 1:22
ᵃ Isa 53:4

8:18 ᵇ Mk 4:35

I tell this one, 'Go,' and he goes; and that one, 'Come,' and he comes. I say to my servant, 'Do this,' and he does it."

¹⁰When Jesus heard this, he was astonished and said to those following him, "I tell you the truth, I have not found anyone in Israel with such great faith.ˢ ¹¹I say to you that many will come from the east and the west,ᵗ and will take their places at the feast with Abraham, Isaac and Jacob in the kingdom of heaven.ᵘ ¹²But the subjects of the kingdomᵛ will be thrown outside, into the darkness, where there will be weeping and gnashing of teeth."ʷ

¹³Then Jesus said to the centurion, "Go! It will be done just as you believed it would."ˣ And his servant was healed at that very hour.

Jesus Heals Many
8:14–16pp — Mk 1:29–34; Lk 4:38–41

¹⁴When Jesus came into Peter's house, he saw Peter's mother-in-law lying in bed with a fever. ¹⁵He touched her hand and the fever left her, and she got up and began to wait on him.

¹⁶When evening came, many who were demon-possessed were brought to him, and he drove out the spirits with a word and healed all the sick.ʸ ¹⁷This was to fulfillᶻ what was spoken through the prophet Isaiah:

> "He took up our infirmities
>   and carried our diseases."ᵃ ᵍ

The Cost of Following Jesus
8:19–22pp — Lk 9:57–60

¹⁸When Jesus saw the crowd around him, he gave orders to cross to the other side of the lake.ᵇ ¹⁹Then a teacher of the law came to him and said, "Teacher, I will follow you wherever you go."

²⁰Jesus replied, "Foxes have holes and

H Mt 7:26–27 ◀▶ Mt 10:14–15
H Eze 47:12 ◀▶ Mt 10:7–8

e 2 The Greek word was used for various diseases affecting the skin—not necessarily leprosy. *f* 3 Greek *made clean* *g* 17 Isaiah 53:4

8:11–12 Matthew's words are directed to all people as he records Jesus' prophecy of the great Messianic feast that will follow Christ's victory over the antichrist at Armageddon (see Isa 25:6–9). The Gentile nations "from the east and the west" (8:11) will be invited to join the Jews and celebrate the establishment of the rule of the Messiah. Jesus warns that those Jews who thought their heritage was enough to get them into the kingdom (see 3:9–10) will find themselves "thrown outside, into the darkness" (8:12).

birds of the air have nests, but the Son of Man[c] has no place to lay his head."

²¹Another disciple said to him, "Lord, first let me go and bury my father."

²²But Jesus told him, "Follow me,[d] and let the dead bury their own dead."

Jesus Calms the Storm
8:23–27pp — Mk 4:36–41; Lk 8:22–25
8:23–27Ref — Mt 14:22–33

²³Then he got into the boat and his disciples followed him. ²⁴Without warning, a furious storm came up on the lake, so that the waves swept over the boat. But Jesus was sleeping. ²⁵The disciples went and woke him, saying, "Lord, save us! We're going to drown!"

²⁶He replied, "You of little faith,[e] why are you so afraid?" Then he got up and rebuked the winds and the waves, and it was completely calm.[f]

²⁷The men were amazed and asked, "What kind of man is this? Even the winds and the waves obey him!"

The Healing of Two Demon-possessed Men
8:28–34pp — Mk 5:1–17; Lk 8:26–37

²⁸When he arrived at the other side in the region of the Gadarenes,[h] two demon-possessed[g] men coming from the tombs met him. They were so violent that no one could pass that way. ²⁹"What do you want with us,[h] Son of God?" they shouted. "Have you come here to torture us before the appointed time?"[i]

³⁰Some distance from them a large herd of pigs was feeding. ³¹The demons begged Jesus, "If you drive us out, send us into the herd of pigs."

³²He said to them, "Go!" So they came out and went into the pigs, and the whole herd rushed down the steep bank into the lake and died in the water. ³³Those tending the pigs ran off, went into the town and reported all this, including what had happened to the demon-possessed men. ³⁴Then the whole town went out to meet Jesus. And when they saw him, they pleaded with him to leave their region.[j]

C Mt 7:26–27 ◄► Mt 9:12
L Mt 7:7–11 ◄► Mt 10:29–31
W Mt 6:25–34 ◄► Mk 4:40
E Mt 8:5–17 ◄► Mt 9:2–8

8:20 ᶜDa 7:13; Mt 12:8,32,40; 16:13,27,28; 17:9; 19:28; Mk 2:10; 8:31
8:22 ᵈS Mt 4:19
8:26 ᵉS Mt 6:30 ᶠPs 65:7; 89:9; 107:29
8:28 ᵍS Mt 4:24
8:29 ʰJdg 11:12; 2Sa 16:10; 1Ki 17:18; Mk 1:24; Lk 4:34; Jn 2:4 ⁱ2Pe 2:4
8:34 ʲLk 5:8; Ac 16:39
9:1 ᵏMt 4:13
9:2 ˡS Mt 4:24 ᵐS ver 22 ⁿJn 16:33 ᵒLk 7:48
9:3 ᵖMt 26:65; Jn 10:33
9:4 ᵠPs 94:11; Mt 12:25; Lk 6:8; 9:47; 11:17; Jn 2:25
9:6 ʳS Mt 8:20
9:8 ˢMt 5:16; 15:31; Lk 7:16; 13:13; 17:15; 23:47; Jn 15:8; Ac 4:21; 11:18; 21:20
9:9 ᵗS Mt 4:19
9:11 ᵘMt 11:19; Lk 5:30; 15:2; 19:7; Gal 2:15
9:13 ᵛHos 6:6; Mic 6:6-8; Mt 12:7 ʷLk 19:10; 1Ti 1:15
9:14 ˣS Mt 3:1

Jesus Heals a Paralytic
9:2–8pp — Mk 2:3–12; Lk 5:18–26

⁹Jesus stepped into a boat, crossed over and came to his own town.[k] ²Some men brought to him a paralytic,[l] lying on a mat. When Jesus saw their faith,[m] he said to the paralytic, "Take heart,[n] son; your sins are forgiven."[o]

³At this, some of the teachers of the law said to themselves, "This fellow is blaspheming!"[p]

⁴Knowing their thoughts,[q] Jesus said, "Why do you entertain evil thoughts in your hearts? ⁵Which is easier: to say, 'Your sins are forgiven,' or to say, 'Get up and walk'? ⁶But so that you may know that the Son of Man[r] has authority on earth to forgive sins . . ." Then he said to the paralytic, "Get up, take your mat and go home." ⁷And the man got up and went home. ⁸When the crowd saw this, they were filled with awe; and they praised God,[s] who had given such authority to men.

The Calling of Matthew
9:9–13pp — Mk 2:14–17; Lk 5:27–32

⁹As Jesus went on from there, he saw a man named Matthew sitting at the tax collector's booth. "Follow me,"[t] he told him, and Matthew got up and followed him.

¹⁰While Jesus was having dinner at Matthew's house, many tax collectors and "sinners" came and ate with him and his disciples. ¹¹When the Pharisees saw this, they asked his disciples, "Why does your teacher eat with tax collectors and 'sinners'?"[u]

¹²On hearing this, Jesus said, "It is not the healthy who need a doctor, but the sick. ¹³But go and learn what means: 'I desire mercy, not sacrifice.'[v] For I have not come to call the righteous, but sinners."[w]

Jesus Questioned About Fasting
9:14–17pp — Mk 2:18–22; Lk 5:33–39

¹⁴Then John's[x] disciples came and asked him, "How is it that we and the

E Mt 8:28–32 ◄► Mt 9:18–35
E Zec 4:10 ◄► Mt 12:25
K Mt 7:24–25 ◄► Mt 11:28–29
C Mt 8:22 ◄► Mt 10:6
L Mt 7:7–8 ◄► Mt 11:28–29

ʰ 28 Some manuscripts *Gergesenes*; others *Gerasenes* ⁱ 13 Hosea 6:6

Pharisees fast,[y] but your disciples do not fast?"

[15]Jesus answered, "How can the guests of the bridegroom mourn while he is with them?[z] The time will come when the bridegroom will be taken from them; then they will fast.[a]

[16]"No one sews a patch of unshrunk cloth on an old garment, for the patch will pull away from the garment, making the tear worse. [17]Neither do men pour new wine into old wineskins. If they do, the skins will burst, the wine will run out and the wineskins will be ruined. No, they pour new wine into new wineskins, and both are preserved."

A Dead Girl and a Sick Woman
9:18–26pp — Mk 5:22–43; Lk 8:41–56

[18]While he was saying this, a ruler came and knelt before him[b] and said, "My daughter has just died. But come and put your hand on her,[c] and she will live." [19]Jesus got up and went with him, and so did his disciples.

[20]Just then a woman who had been subject to bleeding for twelve years came up behind him and touched the edge of his cloak.[d] [21]She said to herself, "If I only touch his cloak, I will be healed."

[22]Jesus turned and saw her. "Take heart,[e] daughter," he said, "your faith has healed you."[f] And the woman was healed from that moment.[g]

[23]When Jesus entered the ruler's house and saw the flute players and the noisy crowd,[h] [24]he said, "Go away. The girl is not dead[i] but asleep."[j] But they laughed at him. [25]After the crowd had been put outside, he went in and took the girl by the hand, and she got up.[k] [26]News of this spread through all that region.[l]

Jesus Heals the Blind and Mute

[27]As Jesus went on from there, two blind men followed him, calling out, "Have mercy on us, Son of David!"[m]

[28]When he had gone indoors, the blind men came to him, and he asked them, "Do you believe that I am able to do this?"

"Yes, Lord," they replied.[n]

[29]Then he touched their eyes and said, "According to your faith will it be done to you";[o] [30]and their sight was restored. Jesus warned them sternly, "See that no one knows about this."[p] [31]But they went out and spread the news about him all over that region.[q]

[32]While they were going out, a man who was demon-possessed[r] and could not talk[s] was brought to Jesus. [33]And when the demon was driven out, the man who had been mute spoke. The crowd was amazed and said, "Nothing like this has ever been seen in Israel."[t]

[34]But the Pharisees said, "It is by the prince of demons that he drives out demons."[u]

The Workers Are Few

[35]Jesus went through all the towns and villages, teaching in their synagogues, preaching the good news of the kingdom and healing every disease and sickness.[v] [36]When he saw the crowds, he had compassion on them,[w] because they were harassed and helpless, like sheep without a shepherd.[x] [37]Then he said to his disciples, "The harvest[y] is plentiful but the workers are few.[z] [38]Ask the Lord of the harvest, therefore, to send out workers into his harvest field."

Jesus Sends Out the Twelve
10:2–4pp — Mk 3:16–19; Lk 6:14–16; Ac 1:13
10:9–15pp — Mk 6:8–11; Lk 9:3–5; 10:4–12
10:19–22pp — Mk 13:11–13; Lk 21:12–17
10:26–33pp — Lk 12:2–9
10:34,35pp — Lk 12:51–53

10 He called his twelve disciples to him and gave them authority to drive out evil[j] spirits[a] and to heal every disease and sickness.[b]

[2]These are the names of the twelve

---

j 1 Greek unclean

9:15 When John's disciples complained that Jesus' disciples did not fast as often as they did, Jesus replied by predicting a future time when he would be taken away from his followers, causing them to fast.
9:37–38 The metaphor of the harvest is often used in the NT to refer to the end times. In this passage, Jesus instructs his disciples to pray to God to send workers to bring in the spiritual harvest of souls. How great that opportunity still is as we see the prophetic signs of Christ's second coming fulfilled in this generation.

apostles: first, Simon (who is called Peter) and his brother Andrew; James son of Zebedee, and his brother John; ³Philip and Bartholomew; Thomas and Matthew the tax collector; James son of Alphaeus, and Thaddaeus; ⁴Simon the Zealot and Judas Iscariot, who betrayed him.ᶜ

⁵These twelve Jesus sent out with the following instructions: "Do not go among the Gentiles or enter any town of the Samaritans.ᵈ ⁶Go rather to the lost sheep of Israel.ᵉ ⁷As you go, preach this message: 'The kingdom of heavenᶠ is near.' ⁸Heal the sick, raise the dead, cleanse those who have leprosy,ᵏ drive out demons. Freely you have received, freely give. ⁹Do not take along any gold or silver or copper in your belts;ᵍ ¹⁰take no bag for the journey, or extra tunic, or sandals or a staff; for the worker is worth his keep.ʰ

¹¹"Whatever town or village you enter, search for some worthy person there and stay at his house until you leave. ¹²As you enter the home, give it your greeting.ⁱ ¹³If the home is deserving, let your peace rest on it; if it is not, let your peace return to you. ¹⁴If anyone will not welcome you or listen to your words, shake the dust off your feetʲ when you leave that home or town. ¹⁵I tell you the truth, it will be more bearable for Sodom and Gomorrahᵏ on the day of judgmentˡ than for that town.ᵐ ¹⁶I am sending you out like sheep among wolves.ⁿ Therefore be as shrewd as snakes and as innocent as doves.ᵒ

R Zec 11:14 ◀ ▶ Mt 15:23–27
C Mt 9:12 ◀ ▶ Mt 12:30
P Mal 3:7 ◀ ▶ Mt 18:12–14
E Mt 10:1 ◀ ▶ Mt 11:4–5
H Mt 8:17 ◀ ▶ Mk 9:23
H Mt 8:12 ◀ ▶ Mt 10:28
N Mal 2:2 ◀ ▶ Mt 11:20–24
J Zep 2:4–15 ◀ ▶ Mt 11:22
J Mt 7:1–2 ◀ ▶ Mt 11:22

10:4 ᶜMt 26:14-16,25, 47; 27:3; Mk 14:10; Jn 6:71; 12:4; 13:2,26,27; Ac 1:16
10:5 ᵈ1Ki 16:24; 2Ki 17:24; Lk 9:52; 10:33; 17:16; Jn 4:4-26,39,40; 8:48; Ac 8:5,25
10:6 ᵉJer 50:6; Mt 15:24
10:7 ᶠS Mt 3:2
10:9 ᵍLk 22:35
10:10 ʰ1Ti 5:18
10:12 ⁱ1Sa 25:6
10:14 ʲNe 5:13; Mk 6:11; Lk 9:5; 10:11; Ac 13:51; 18:6
10:15 ᵏGe 18:20; 19:24; 2Pe 2:6; Jude 7 ˡMt 12:36; Ac 17:31; 2Pe 2:9; 3:7; 1Jn 4:17; Jude 6 ᵐMt 11:22, 24
10:16 ⁿLk 10:3; Ac 20:29 ᵒS 1Co 14:20
10:17 ᵖS Mt 5:22 qMt 23:34; Mk 13:9; Ac 5:40; 22:19; 26:11
10:18 ʳAc 25:24-26
10:19 ˢEx 4:12
10:20 ᵗLk 12:11, 12; Ac 4:8
10:21 ᵘver 35,36; Mic 7:6 ᵛMk 13:12
10:22 ʷS Jn 15:21 ˣMt 24:13; Mk 13:13; Lk 21:19; Rev 2:10
10:23 ʸS Lk 17:30
10:24 ᶻS Jn 13:16
10:25 ᵃS Mk 3:22
10:26 ᵇMk 4:22; Lk 8:17

¹⁷"Be on your guard against men; they will hand you over to the local councilsᵖ and flog you in their synagogues.q ¹⁸On my account you will be brought before governors and kingsʳ as witnesses to them and to the Gentiles. ¹⁹But when they arrest you, do not worry about what to say or how to say it.ˢ At that time you will be given what to say, ²⁰for it will not be you speaking, but the Spirit of your Fatherᵗ speaking through you.

²¹"Brother will betray brother to death, and a father his child; children will rebel against their parentsᵘ and have them put to death.ᵛ ²²All men will hate you because of me,ʷ but he who stands firm to the end will be saved.ˣ ²³When you are persecuted in one place, flee to another. I tell you the truth, you will not finish going through the cities of Israel before the Son of Man comes.ʸ

²⁴"A student is not above his teacher, nor a servant above his master.ᶻ ²⁵It is enough for the student to be like his teacher, and the servant like his master. If the head of the house has been called Beelzebub,ˡᵃ how much more the members of his household!

²⁶"So do not be afraid of them. There is nothing concealed that will not be disclosed, or hidden that will not be made known.ᵇ ²⁷What I tell you in the dark, speak in the daylight; what is whispered in your ear, proclaim from the roofs. ²⁸Do not be afraid of those who kill the body but cannot kill the soul. Rather, be afraid

L Jnh 2:4 ◀ ▶ Mt 26:13
G Mic 3:8 ◀ ▶ Mk 13:11
L Mt 4:1 ◀ ▶ Mk 1:12
T Joel 2:28–29 ◀ ▶ Mt 22:43–44
S Mt 7:16–24 ◀ ▶ Mt 10:37–38
H Mt 10:14–15 ◀ ▶ Mt 11:20–24

ᵏ 8 The Greek word was used for various diseases affecting the skin—not necessarily leprosy. ˡ 25 Greek *Beezeboul* or *Beelzeboul*

10:14–15 When the NT Pharisees left a Gentile area they shook the dust off their sandals to symbolize ridding themselves of any contamination from anything "unclean." This command to the disciples to "shake the dust off your feet" (10:14) is a solemn warning to those who utterly reject the message of Christ (see Lk 9:5; Ac 13:51; 18:6). Those who reject Christ will receive a worse punishment than Sodom and Gomorrah received. Scripture promises that all unrepentant sinners will be individually judged and endure hell forever (see Rev 20:12).

10:22 Matthew records Jesus' prophecy of the persecution of believers. This persecution began immediately following Christ's resurrection and has continued unabated for centuries. Worldwide persecution will increase in the last days during the tribulation. Those who stand firm against the antichrist during the years before the Battle of Armageddon and Christ's return will experience a terrible time of trial. But Jesus promised that those who stand firm "to the end will be saved."

of the One[c] who can destroy both soul and body in hell. [29]Are not two sparrows sold for a penny[m]? Yet not one of them will fall to the ground apart from the will of your Father. [30]And even the very hairs of your head are all numbered.[d] [31]So don't be afraid; you are worth more than many sparrows.[e]

[32]"Whoever acknowledges me before men,[f] I will also acknowledge him before my Father in heaven. [33]But whoever disowns me before men, I will disown him before my Father in heaven.[g]

[34]"Do not suppose that I have come to bring peace to the earth. I did not come to bring peace, but a sword. [35]For I have come to turn

" 'a man against his father,
 a daughter against her mother,
 a daughter-in-law against her
   mother-in-law[h]—
[36] a man's enemies will be the
   members of his own
   household.' "[i]

[37]"Anyone who loves his father or mother more than me is not worthy of me; anyone who loves his son or daughter more than me is not worthy of me;[j] [38]and anyone who does not take his cross and follow me is not worthy of me.[k] [39]Whoever finds his life will lose it, and whoever loses his life for my sake will find it.[l]

[40]"He who receives you receives me,[m] and he who receives me receives the one who sent me.[n] [41]Anyone who receives a prophet because he is a prophet will re-

L Mt 8:26 ◀▶ Mt 18:5–6
O Mt 7:26–27 ◀▶ Mt 15:13
T Mal 3:16–17 ◀▶ Mk 5:19
W Mt 7:24 ◀▶ Mt 11:28–29
S Mt 10:22 ◀▶ Mt 12:33–37

10:28 [c]Isa 8:12, 13; Heb 10:31
10:30 [d]1Sa 14:45; 2Sa 14:11; 1Ki 1:52; Lk 21:18; Ac 27:34
10:31 [e]Mt 6:26; 12:12
10:32 [f]Ro 10:9
10:33 [g]Mt 8:38; 2Ti 2:12
10:35 [h]ver 21
10:36 [i]Mic 7:6
10:37 [j]Lk 14:26
10:38 [k]Mt 16:24; Lk 14:27
10:39 [l]S Jn 12:25
10:40 [m]Ex 16:8; Mt 18:5; Gal 4:14
[n]Lk 9:48; 10:16; Jn 12:44; 13:20
10:42 [o]Pr 14:31; 19:17; Mt 25:40; Mk 9:41; Ac 10:4; Heb 6:10
11:1 [p]S Mt 7:28
11:2 [q]S Mt 3:1
[r]Mt 14:3
11:3 [s]Ps 118:26; Jn 11:27; Heb 10:37
11:5 [t]Isa 35:4-6; 61:1; Mt 15:31; Lk 4:18,19
11:6 [u]Mt 13:21; 26:31
11:7 [v]S Mt 3:1
[w]Mt 3:1
11:9 [x]Mt 14:5; 21:26; Lk 1:76; 7:26

ceive a prophet's reward, and anyone who receives a righteous man because he is a righteous man will receive a righteous man's reward. [42]And if anyone gives even a cup of cold water to one of these little ones because he is my disciple, I tell you the truth, he will certainly not lose his reward."[o]

Jesus and John the Baptist
11:2–19pp — Lk 7:18–35

11 After Jesus had finished instructing his twelve disciples,[p] he went on from there to teach and preach in the towns of Galilee.[o]

[2]When John[q] heard in prison[r] what Christ was doing, he sent his disciples [3]to ask him, "Are you the one who was to come,[s] or should we expect someone else?"

[4]Jesus replied, "Go back and report to John what you hear and see: [5]The blind receive sight, the lame walk, those who have leprosy[p] are cured, the deaf hear, the dead are raised, and the good news is preached to the poor.[t] [6]Blessed is the man who does not fall away on account of me."[u]

[7]As John's[v] disciples were leaving, Jesus began to speak to the crowd about John: "What did you go out into the desert[w] to see? A reed swayed by the wind? [8]If not, what did you go out to see? A man dressed in fine clothes? No, those who wear fine clothes are in kings' palaces. [9]Then what did you go out to see? A prophet?[x] Yes, I tell you, and more than a

E Mt 10:7–8 ◀▶ Mt 12:9–13

[m]29 Greek *an assarion* [n]36 Micah 7:6 [o]1 Greek *in their towns* [p]5 The Greek word was used for various diseases affecting the skin—not necessarily leprosy.

11:2–5 John's words here do not question Jesus' role as the Messiah, a fact that John clearly acknowledged (see 3:13–17; Mk 1:9–11; Lk 3:21; Jn 1:29). John was more concerned about Jesus' methods. The OT prophecies about the Messiah described a compassionate servant, a just judge, a powerful king and a mighty warrior (see Isa 9:6–8; 53:1–12; 61:1–2; Mic 5:2; Zec 9:9). The reports John heard while he languished in prison indicated that while Jesus was compassionate, he was not behaving like a warrior or a judge or a king. Jesus' response to John linked his mission to the prophetic words of Isaiah given seven centuries earlier: The Messiah would open blind eyes, deaf ears and preach good tidings to the poor (see Isa 35:5; 61:1). In this way Jesus told John to trust his mission even if his methods were not completely comprehensible.

Of the signs that Jesus used to prove his claim as Messiah, the healing of the blind is one of the most significant. When Jesus healed a blind boy (see Jn 9:1–38) it was the first time in the Jews' recorded history that anyone born blind was healed. With this miracle Jesus uniquely fulfilled a qualification of the Messiah outlined in several OT prophecies (see Ps 146:8; Isa 29:18; 42:7); he opened blind eyes for the first time in history.

Hell

ALL OF THOSE who reject God's offer of salvation will be confronted with his judgment—an eternity in hell experiencing "the lake of burning sulfur" (Rev 20:10; see Mt 25:41, 46; Rev 21:8). The Bible declares that hell is absolutely real, that it will be unpleasant and that it will last forever (see Mt 13:42; Rev 14:10). Some theologians have attempted to escape Scripture's clear teaching about the terrors of hell by assuming that it will involve the annihilation of the sinner's soul and consciousness. Jesus' words contradict this teaching and indicate that those who spend an eternity in hell will do so fully conscious with much "weeping and gnashing of teeth" (Mt 8:12).

The Bible's Description of Hell
The Bible describes hell as a "lake of burning sulfur" (Rev 20:10; see Mk 9:47) that cannot be destroyed. Several terms are used throughout Scripture when referring to hell: *Sheol, hades, gehenna* and *tartarus*. In the OT the most common word for "hell" is *Sheol*. Though the exact translation of *Sheol* is unknown, the OT often equates it with the grave (see Ge 37:35; 1Sa 2:6; Job 7:9; 14:13; Ps 6:5; 49:14; Isa 14:11) and also translates *Sheol* as "hell" (see Dt 32:22; Ps 9:17; 18:5; Isa 14:9; Am 9:2). Believed to be a shadowy underground region inhabited by disembodied souls (see Ge 37:35; Nu 16:30, 33; Job 11:8; Ps 9:17; Is 38:10; Am 9:2), Sheol became a synonym for the abode of the wretched dead. Even though God is present in Sheol (see Ps 139:8), the believer's hope for the future is ultimate deliverance from Sheol and restoration to a life in God's presence in heaven (see Job 14:13–15; 19:25–27; Ps 16:10–11; 17:15; 49:15; 73:24–26; Ac 2:27).

The NT uses the word *hades* as the Greek equivalent of *Sheol*, though *hades* rarely refers to the "grave" (see Ac 2:31). Its most common usage refers to the world of future punishment (see Mt 11:23; 16:18; Ac 2:31; Rev 1:18; 6:8; 20:13–14), describing a place where wicked spirits await the day of judgment at the end of the Millennium. Yet Scripture indicates that before Christ's death, resurrection and ascension *hades* was divided into two portions and separated by a great gulf (see Lk 16:22–26). One side of *hades* was a pleasant place known as "Abraham's side" (Lk 16:22), the repository of those righteous souls who died during the OT. Those souls who had rejected God's truth were confined to the other part of *hades* known as "the place of torment" (Lk 16:28).

Another word associated with hell is the word *tartarus*, which is found in only one place in Scripture (see 2Pe 2:4). This verse indicates that there is a special place in hell where God will imprison fallen angels "with everlasting chains for judgment on the great Day" (Jude 6).

The final word translated "hell" in the Bible is the word *gehenna*. This word occurs repeatedly in the NT (see Mt 5:22–30; Mk 9:43–47). In the Valley of Hinnom outside the walls of Jerusalem was a horrible, burning garbage pit whose fire never ceased. The bodies of criminals were thrown into this garbage pit to rot and burn. Significantly, the Scriptures liken this pit to *gehenna* and paint a graphic visual image of pain, torment and punishment in every passage in the NT where the word *gehenna* appears.

The Punished and Their Punishment

Scripture assures us of God's perfect justice (see Ge 18:25). God's holiness demands a just judgment of all sinners. Every sinner from Cain to the last rebel at the end of the Millennium will appear before the great white throne in heaven to be judged individually by God (see Rev 20:11–14). Since everyone who appears at this judgment before God's throne is an unrepentant sinner, there would be no need for this special judgment unless individual sentences were to be handed out. Though all those who enter hell will endure its flames forever, when the "books" (Rev 20:12) are opened there will be different degrees of punishment meted out in hell to reflect the evil deeds of those who reject Jesus Christ (see Ecc 12:14; Jer 17:10; 32:19; Ro 2:6; Rev 20:13). (For further information on this final judgment, see the article on "The Great White Throne Judgment" on p. 1490.)

Hell will be filled with untold billions of sinners. Their resurrected bodies will never die in hell but will feel every pain and torment of their eternal punishment. These sinners in hell will curse God and rage against his justice, desiring to avenge themselves against God, but they will not succeed (see Rev 14:11; 16:10–11).

In their frustration they may vent their anger on their weaker companions in hell. Hell has no guards or bars to protect a weaker prisoner from the cruelty of a stronger, wicked prisoner. The most a sinner could hope for in this life would be a swift death. However, in hell there will be no death. Those who reject salvation will spend eternity in hell as companions to every murderer, rapist, abuser and vile person who ever lived.

Though some liberal theologians accept the reality of hell, many seek to minimize hell's horror by suggesting that those who enter damnation will finally emerge at some point in the future to take their part among the blessed of the Lord. Others suggest that a loving God would rather annihilate the souls of those who reject Christ's salvation instead of condemning them to eternal torment. Both of these viewpoints are repudiated in Scripture. The judgment and punishment of hell will last forever (see Mt 25:41, 46; Rev 14:10), and the souls of those who reject Christ's mercy will not be annihilated but will be conscious in their eternity of torment (see Lk 16:22–28).

Final Justice

In the book of Ecclesiastes, King Solomon, the wisest man who ever lived, described the lack of justice in human life. He questioned the fact that evil deeds appear to go unpunished in this life while the righteous often have trouble all their days (see Ecc 8:11–12). God, in his mercy, often delays the punishment for sin, allowing a time for repentance and salvation (see 2Pe 3:9). And sometimes, Satan, in his cunning attempt to destroy humanity, delays the consequences of sin, leading people deeper and deeper into the whirlpool of depravity. If sin immediately resulted in painful and embarrassing consequences, many people would turn from their sinful path. However, when someone seems to "get away with it," this apparent lack of consequences leads step by step to a life lived against God's plan. Solomon's inspired conclusion was that God's justice, though delayed, would finally be revealed, and God would "bring every deed into judgment, including every hidden thing, whether it is good or evil"(Ecc 12:14). That final judgment will bring about the just punishment of hell.

prophet. ¹⁰This is the one about whom it is written:

" 'I will send my messenger ahead of you,ʸ
who will prepare your way before you.'ᵠᶻ

¹¹I tell you the truth: Among those born of women there has not risen anyone greater than John the Baptist; yet he who is least in the kingdom of heaven is **F** greater than he. ¹²From the days of John the Baptist until now, the kingdom of heaven has been forcefully advancing, and forceful men lay hold of it. ¹³For all the Prophets and the Law prophesied until John.ᵃ ¹⁴And if you are willing to accept it, he is the Elijah who was to come.ᵇ ¹⁵He who has ears, let him hear.ᶜ

¹⁶"To what can I compare this generation? They are like children sitting in the marketplaces and calling out to others:

¹⁷" 'We played the flute for you,
and you did not dance;
we sang a dirge,
and you did not mourn.'

¹⁸For John came neither eatingᵈ nor drinking,ᵉ and they say, 'He has a demon.' ¹⁹The Son of Man came eating and drinking, and they say, 'Here is a glutton and a drunkard, a friend of tax collectors and "sinners." 'ᶠ But wisdom is proved right by her actions."

Woe on Unrepentant Cities
11:21–23pp — Lk 10:13–15

H ²⁰Then Jesus began to denounce the
N cities in which most of his miracles had been performed, because they did not re-

pent. ²¹"Woe to you, Korazin! Woe to you, Bethsaida!ᵍ If the miracles that were performed in you had been performed in Tyre and Sidon,ʰ they would have repented long ago in sackcloth and ashes.ⁱ ²²But I tell you, it will be more bearable **J** for Tyre and Sidon on the day of judgment than for you.ʲ ²³And you, Capernaum,ᵏ will you be lifted up to the skies? No, you will go down to the depths.ˡ If the miracles that were performed in you had been performed in Sodom, it would have remained to this day. ²⁴But I tell you **J** that it will be more bearable for Sodom **J** on the day of judgment than for you."ᵐ

Rest for the Weary
11:25–27pp — Lk 10:21,22

²⁵At that time Jesus said, "I praise you, Father,ⁿ Lord of heaven and earth, because you have hidden these things from the wise and learned, and revealed them to little children.ᵒ ²⁶Yes, Father, for this was your good pleasure.

²⁷"All things have been committed to meᵖ by my Father.ᵠ No one knows the Son except the Father, and no one knows the Father except the Son and those to whom the Son chooses to reveal him.ʳ

²⁸"Come to me,ˢ all you who are weary **K** and burdened, and I will give you rest.ᵗ **L** ²⁹Take my yoke upon you and learn from **W** me,ᵘ for I am gentle and humble in heart, and you will find rest for your souls.ᵛ

11:10 ʸ Jn 3:28; ᶻ Mal 3:1; Mk 1:2; Lk 7:27
11:13 ᵃ Lk 16:16
11:14 ᵇ Mal 4:5; Mt 17:10-13; Mk 9:11-13; Lk 1:17; Jn 1:21
11:15 ᶜ Mt 13:9, 43; Mk 4:23; Lk 14:35; S Rev 2:7
11:18 ᵈ Mt 3:4; ᵉ S Lk 1:15
11:19 ᶠ S Mt 9:11
11:21 ᵍ Mk 6:45; 8:22; Lk 9:10; Jn 1:44; 12:21; ʰ Joel 3:4; Am 1:9; Mt 15:21; Mk 3:8; Lk 6:17; Ac 12:20; ⁱ Jnh 3:5-9
11:22 ʲ ver 24; Mt 10:15
11:23 ᵏ S Mt 4:13; ˡ Isa 14:13-15
11:24 ᵐ S Mt 10:15
11:25 ⁿ Mt 16:17; Lk 22:42; 23:34; Jn 11:41; 12:27,28; ᵒ S Mt 13:11; 1Co 1:26-29
11:27 ᵖ S Mt 28:18; ᵠ S Jn 3:35; ʳ Jn 10:15; 17:25,26
11:28 ˢ Jn 7:37; ᵗ Ex 33:14
11:29 ᵘ Jn 13:15; Php 2:5; 1Pe 2:21; 1Jn 2:6; ᵛ Ps 116:7; Jer 6:16

F Hab 2:4 ◀▶ Mt 21:31–32
H Mt 10:28 ◀▶ Mt 13:30
N Mt 10:14–15 ◀▶ Mt 12:41–42
J Mt 10:15 ◀▶ Mt 11:24
J Mt 10:15 ◀▶ Mt 11:24
J Mt 11:22 ◀▶ Mt 12:36
J Mt 11:22 ◀▶ Mt 12:36
K Mt 9:6 ◀▶ Mt 19:26
L Mt 9:12–13 ◀▶ Mt 12:20
W Mt 10:32 ◀▶ Mt 12:20

ᵠ 10 Mal. 3:1 ʳ 23 Greek *Hades*

11:21–24 Jesus chastens the unrepentant people of the cities of Korazin and Bethsaida, declaring that because of their refusal to repent they would be judged by God more harshly than the wicked Phoenician cities of Tyre and Sidon. Capernaum's indictment is more severe since it was Jesus' base of operations while he ministered in Galilee. Capernaum had its own synagogue where Jesus often taught (see Mk 1:21; Lk 4:31; Jn 6:59). Jesus also performed many miracles of healing in Capernaum: the centurion's servant (see 8:5; Lk 7:1–2), Peter's mother-in-law (see 8:14; Mk 1:30; Lk 4:38), the paralytic (see 9:1–2; Mk 2:1–3) and the demon-possessed man (see Mk 1:32; Lk 4:33). Yet the citizens of Capernaum still rejected Jesus' call to follow him.

The prophecy of judgment spoken against these three cities has been completely fulfilled. Though Korazin was a place of some importance during the ministry of Jesus, by the end of the first century it was already deserted and desolate with only a few carved stones to mark its existence. Because the destruction of the other two cities was so complete, archeologists are not even sure of the exact location of these cities that figured so prominently in Jesus' ministry.

³⁰For my yoke is easy and my burden is light."ʷ

Lord of the Sabbath
12:1–8pp — Mk 2:23–28; Lk 6:1–5
12:9–14pp — Mk 3:1–6; Lk 6:6–11

12 At that time Jesus went through the grainfields on the Sabbath. His disciples were hungry and began to pick some heads of grainˣ and eat them. ²When the Pharisees saw this, they said to him, "Look! Your disciples are doing what is unlawful on the Sabbath."ʸ

³He answered, "Haven't you read what David did when he and his companions were hungry?ᶻ ⁴He entered the house of God, and he and his companions ate the consecrated bread—which was not lawful for them to do, but only for the priests.ᵃ ⁵Or haven't you read in the Law that on the Sabbath the priests in the temple desecrate the dayᵇ and yet are innocent? ⁶I tell you that oneˢ greater than the temple is here.ᶜ ⁷If you had known what these words mean, 'I desire mercy, not sacrifice,'ᵈ you would not have condemned the innocent. ⁸For the Son of Manᵉ is Lord of the Sabbath."

⁹Going on from that place, he went into their synagogue, ¹⁰and a man with a shriveled hand was there. Looking for a reason to accuse Jesus,ᶠ they asked him, "Is it lawful to heal on the Sabbath?"ᵍ

¹¹He said to them, "If any of you has a sheep and it falls into a pit on the Sabbath, will you not take hold of it and lift it out?ʰ ¹²How much more valuable is a man than a sheep!ⁱ Therefore it is lawful to do good on the Sabbath."

¹³Then he said to the man, "Stretch out your hand." So he stretched it out and it was completely restored, just as sound as the other. ¹⁴But the Pharisees went out and plotted how they might kill Jesus.ʲ

God's Chosen Servant

¹⁵Aware of this, Jesus withdrew from that place. Many followed him, and he healed all their sick,ᵏ ¹⁶warning them not to tell who he was.ˡ ¹⁷This was to fulfillᵐ what was spoken through the prophet Isaiah:

E *Mt 11:4–5* ◀ ▶ *Mt 12:15*
E *Mt 12:9–13* ◀ ▶ *Mt 12:22–29*

11:30 ʷ 1Jn 5:3
12:1 ˣ Dt 23:25
12:2 ʸ ver 10; Ex 20:10; 23:12; Dt 5:14; Lk 13:14; 14:3; Jn 5:10; 7:23; 9:16
12:3 ᶻ 1Sa 21:6
12:4 ᵃ Lev 24:5,9
12:5 ᵇ Nu 28:9,10; Jn 7:22,23
12:6 ᶜ ver 41,42
12:7 ᵈ Hos 6:6; Mic 6:6-8; Mt 9:13
12:8 ᵉ S Mt 8:20
12:10 ᶠ Mk 3:2; 12:13; Lk 11:54; 14:1; 20:20
ᵍ S ver 2
12:11 ʰ Lk 14:5
12:12 ⁱ Mt 6:26; 10:31
12:14 ʲ Ge 37:18; Ps 71:10; Mt 26:4; 27:1; Mk 3:6; Lk 6:11; Jn 5:18; 7:1,19; 11:53
12:15 ᵏ S Mt 4:23
12:16 ˡ S Mt 8:4
12:17 ᵐ S Mt 1:22
12:18 ⁿ S Mt 3:17
ᵒ S Jn 3:34
12:21 ᵖ Isa 42:1-4
12:22 ᵠ S Mt 4:24
12:23 ʳ S Mt 9:27
12:24 ˢ S Mk 3:22
ᵗ Mt 9:34
12:25 ᵘ S Mk 9:4
12:26 ᵛ S Mt 4:10
12:27 ʷ ver 24
ˣ Ac 19:13
12:28 ʸ S Mt 3:2

¹⁸"Here is my servant whom I have chosen,
 the one I love, in whom I delight;ⁿ
I will put my Spirit on him,ᵒ
 and he will proclaim justice to the nations.
¹⁹He will not quarrel or cry out;
 no one will hear his voice in the streets.
²⁰A bruised reed he will not break,
 and a smoldering wick he will not snuff out,
till he leads justice to victory.
²¹ In his name the nations will put their hope."ᵘᵖ

Jesus and Beelzebub
12:25–29pp — Mk 3:23–27; Lk 11:17–22

²²Then they brought him a demon-possessed man who was blind and mute, and Jesus healed him, so that he could both talk and see.ᵠ ²³All the people were astonished and said, "Could this be the Son of David?"ʳ

²⁴But when the Pharisees heard this, they said, "It is only by Beelzebub,ᵛˢ the prince of demons, that this fellow drives out demons."ᵗ

²⁵Jesus knew their thoughtsᵘ and said to them, "Every kingdom divided against itself will be ruined, and every city or household divided against itself will not stand. ²⁶If Satanᵛ drives out Satan, he is divided against himself. How then can his kingdom stand? ²⁷And if I drive out demons by Beelzebub,ʷ by whom do your peopleˣ drive them out? So then, they will be your judges. ²⁸But if I drive out demons by the Spirit of God, then the kingdom of Godʸ has come upon you. ²⁹"Or again, how can anyone enter a strong man's house and carry off his possessions unless he first ties up the strong man? Then he can rob his house.

³⁰"He who is not with me is against

B *Mt 3:16* ◀ ▶ *Mk 1:8*
L *Mt 11:28–29* ◀ ▶ *Mt 12:31–32*
W *Mt 11:28–29* ◀ ▶ *Mt 20:1–16*
E *Mt 12:15* ◀ ▶ *Mt 14:14*
E *Mt 9:4* ◀ ▶ *Lk 6:8*
E *Mt 4:1* ◀ ▶ *Mt 22:43*
H *Eze 37:13–14* ◀ ▶ *Jn 3:3–8*
M *Mt 3:11* ◀ ▶ *Mk 13:11*
A *Isa 53:6* ◀ ▶ *Mt 22:11–14*
C *Mt 10:6* ◀ ▶ *Mt 13:14–15*

ˢ 6 Or *something*; also in verses 41 and 42   ᵗ 7 Hosea 6:6
ᵘ 21 Isaiah 42:1-4   ᵛ 24 Greek *Beezeboul* or *Beelzeboul*; also in verse 27

me, and he who does not gather with me scatters.[z] [31]And so I tell you, every sin and blasphemy will be forgiven men, but the blasphemy against the Spirit will not be forgiven.[a] [32]Anyone who speaks a word against the Son of Man will be forgiven, but anyone who speaks against the Holy Spirit will not be forgiven, either in this age[b] or in the age to come.[c]

[33]"Make a tree good and its fruit will be good, or make a tree bad and its fruit will be bad, for a tree is recognized by its fruit.[d] [34]You brood of vipers,[e] how can you who are evil say anything good? For out of the overflow of the heart the mouth speaks.[f] [35]The good man brings good things out of the good stored up in him, and the evil man brings evil things out of the evil stored up in him. [36]But I tell you that men will have to give account on the day of judgment for every careless word they have spoken. [37]For by your words you will be acquitted, and by your words you will be condemned."[g]

The Sign of Jonah

12:39–42pp — Lk 11:29–32
12:43–45pp — Lk 11:24–26

[38]Then some of the Pharisees and teachers of the law said to him, "Teacher, we want to see a miraculous sign[h] from you."[i]

[39]He answered, "A wicked and adulterous generation asks for a miraculous sign! But none will be given it except the sign of the prophet Jonah.[j] [40]For as Jonah was three days and three nights in the belly of a huge fish,[k] so the Son of Man[l] will be three days and three nights in the heart of the earth.[m] [41]The men of Nineveh[n] will stand up at the judgment with this generation and condemn it; for they repented at the preaching of Jonah,[o] and now one[w] greater than Jonah is here. [42]The Queen of the South will rise at the judgment with this generation and condemn it; for she came[p] from the ends of the earth to listen to Solomon's wisdom, and now one greater than Solomon is here.

[43]"When an evil[x] spirit comes out of a man, it goes through arid places seeking rest and does not find it. [44]Then it says, 'I will return to the house I left.' When it arrives, it finds the house unoccupied, swept clean and put in order. [45]Then it goes and takes with it seven other spirits more wicked than itself, and they go in and live there. And the final condition of that man is worse than the first.[q] That is how it will be with this wicked generation."

Jesus' Mother and Brothers

12:46–50pp — Mk 3:31–35; Lk 8:19–21

[46]While Jesus was still talking to the crowd, his mother[r] and brothers[s] stood

---

12:30 [z]Mk 9:40; Lk 11:23
12:31 [a]Mk 3:28, 29; Lk 12:10
12:32 [b]Tit 2:12 [c]Mk 10:30; Lk 20:34,35; Eph 1:21; Heb 6:5
12:33 [d]Mt 7:16, 17; Lk 6:43,44
12:34 [e]Mt 3:7; 23:33 [f]Mt 15:18; Lk 6:45
12:37 [g]Job 15:6; Pr 10:14; 18:21; Jas 3:2
12:38 [h]S Jn 2:11; S 4:48 [i]Mt 16:1; Mk 8:11,12; Lk 11:16; Jn 2:18; 6:30; 1Co 1:22
12:39 [j]Mt 16:4; Lk 11:29
12:40 [k]Jnh 1:17 [l]S Mt 8:20 [m]S Mt 16:21
12:41 [n]Jnh 1:2 [o]Jnh 3:5
12:42 [p]1Ki 10:1; 2Ch 9:1
12:45 [q]2Pe 2:20
12:46 [r]Mt 1:18; 2:11,13,14,20; Lk 1:43; 2:33,34, 48,51; Jn 2:1,5; 19:25,26 [s]Mt 13:55; Jn 2:12; 7:3,5; Ac 1:14; 1Co 9:5; Gal 1:19

D Isa 40:13 ◄ ► Mt 28:19
Q Zec 6:8 ◄ ► Mk 3:29
L Mt 12:20 ◄ ► Mt 18:12–14
S Mt 10:37–38 ◄ ► Mt 12:50
J Mt 11:24 ◄ ► Mt 12:42
J Mt 11:24 ◄ ► Mt 12:41–42

B Mt 4:13–15 ◄ ► Mt 27:9–10
J Mt 12:36 ◄ ► Mt 25:31–46
N Mt 11:20–24 ◄ ► Mt 13:13–15
J Mt 12:36 ◄ ► Mt 25:19

[w] 41 Or *something*; also in verse 42 [x] 43 Greek *unclean*

12:36–37 Jesus warns that all of us will be judged by our words in the final judgment. All of our words, even those carelessly spoken, are important (see 5:22; 2Co 12:20; 1Ti 1:10; Jas 3:6; Rev 21:8). Scripture clearly states that our words impact our eternal lives because "it is with your mouth that you confess and are saved" (Ro 10:10). For further information, see the article on "The Great White Throne Judgment" on p. 1490.

12:39–40 Jesus' words confirm the historical reality of Jonah's experience in the belly of the great fish. The "three days and three nights" (12:40) that Jonah spent in the great fish signify the same length of time that Jesus would be "in the heart of the earth" (12:40). Since the ancient Jews measured time inclusively, this time period is probably much shorter than three, full 24-hour periods. Though we calculate a day as 24 full hours, ancient Jews calculated any portion of one day as a full day. Thus this phrase "three days and three nights" meant any portion of the first day, plus all of the second day, plus any portion of the third day. In a similar manner, Christ's burial late Friday afternoon until his resurrection on Sunday morning occupied the same amount of time that the prophet Jonah was in the great fish.

12:42 Matthew's "Queen of the South" is probably the "queen of Sheba" from 1Ki 10:1. Just as this pagan queen stood in Solomon's presence and recognized God's touch on his life, so Matthew rebukes the scribes and Pharisees for their refusal to repent despite the overwhelming evidence of the life and ministry of Jesus Christ.

outside, wanting to speak to him. ⁴⁷Someone told him, "Your mother and brothers are standing outside, wanting to speak to you."ʸ

⁴⁸He replied to him, "Who is my mother, and who are my brothers?" ⁴⁹Pointing to his disciples, he said, "Here are my mother and my brothers. ⁵⁰For whoever does the will of my Father in heavenᵗ is my brother and sister and mother."

The Parable of the Sower

13:1–15pp — Mk 4:1–12; Lk 8:4–10
13:16,17pp — Lk 10:23,24
13:18–23pp — Mk 4:13–20; Lk 8:11–15

13 That same day Jesus went out of the houseᵘ and sat by the lake. ²Such large crowds gathered around him that he got into a boatᵛ and sat in it, while all the people stood on the shore. ³Then he told them many things in parables, saying: "A farmer went out to sow his seed. ⁴As he was scattering the seed, some fell along the path, and the birds came and ate it up. ⁵Some fell on rocky places, where it did not have much soil. It sprang up quickly, because the soil was shallow. ⁶But when the sun came up, the plants were scorched, and they withered because they had no root. ⁷Other seed fell among thorns, which grew up and choked the plants. ⁸Still other seed fell on good soil, where it produced a crop—a hundred,ʷ sixty or thirty times what was sown. ⁹He who has ears, let him hear."ˣ

¹⁰The disciples came to him and asked, "Why do you speak to the people in parables?"

¹¹He replied, "The knowledge of the secrets of the kingdom of heavenʸ has been given to you,ᶻ but not to them. ¹²Whoever has will be given more, and he will have an abundance. Whoever does not have, even what he has will be taken from him.ᵃ ¹³This is why I speak to them in parables:

"Though seeing, they do not see;
though hearing, they do not hear or understand.ᵇ

¹⁴In them is fulfilledᶜ the prophecy of Isaiah:

" 'You will be ever hearing but never understanding;
you will be ever seeing but never perceiving.
¹⁵For this people's heart has become calloused;
they hardly hear with their ears,
and they have closed their eyes.
Otherwise they might see with their eyes,
hear with their ears,
understand with their hearts
and turn, and I would heal them.'ᶻᵈ

¹⁶But blessed are your eyes because they see, and your ears because they hear.ᵉ ¹⁷For I tell you the truth, many prophets and righteous men longed to see what you seeᶠ but did not see it, and to hear what you hear but did not hear it.

¹⁸"Listen then to what the parable of the sower means: ¹⁹When anyone hears the message about the kingdomᵍ and does not understand it, the evil oneʰ comes and snatches away what was sown in his heart. This is the seed sown along the path. ²⁰The one who received the seed that fell on rocky places is the man who hears the word and at once receives it with joy. ²¹But since he has no root, he lasts only a short time. When trouble or persecution comes because of the word, he quickly falls away.ⁱ ²²The one who received the seed that fell among the thorns is the man who hears the word, but the worries of this life and the deceitfulness of wealthʲ choke it, making it unfruitful. ²³But the one who received the seed that fell on good soil is the man who hears the word and understands it. He produces a crop, yielding a hundred, sixty or thirty times what was sown."ᵏ

The Parable of the Weeds

²⁴Jesus told them another parable: "The kingdom of heaven is likeˡ a man who sowed good seed in his field. ²⁵But while everyone was sleeping, his enemy came and sowed weeds among the wheat, and went away. ²⁶When the wheat sprouted and formed heads, then the weeds also appeared.

Cross references (center column):

12:50 ᵗ Mt 6:10; Jn 15:14
13:1 ᵘ ver 36; Mt 9:28
13:2 ᵛ Lk 5:3
13:8 ʷ Ge 26:12
13:9 ˣ S Mt 11:15
13:11 ʸ S Mt 3:2; Mt 11:25; 16:17; 19:11; Jn 6:65; 1Co 2:10,14; Col 1:27; 1Jn 2:20, 27
13:12 ᵃ S Mt 25:29
13:13 ᵇ Dt 29:4; Jer 5:21; Eze 12:2
13:14 ᶜ ver 35; S Mt 1:22
13:15 ᵈ Isa 6:9,10; Jn 12:40; Ac 28:26, 27; Ro 11:8
13:16 ᵉ Mt 16:17
13:17 ᶠ Jn 8:56; Heb 11:13; 1Pe 1:10-12
13:19 ᵍ Mt 4:23
ʰ S Mt 5:37
13:21 ⁱ Mt 11:6; 26:31
13:22 ʲ Mt 19:23; 1Ti 6:9,10,17
13:23 ᵏ ver 8
13:24 ˡ ver 31,33, 45,47; Mt 18:23; 20:1; 22:2; 25:1; Mk 4:26,30

S Mt 12:33–37 ◄► Mt 13:5–8
S Mt 12:50 ◄► Mt 13:20–22
N Mt 12:41–42 ◄► Mt 21:44
C Mt 12:30 ◄► Mt 13:38

S Mt 13:5–8 ◄► Mt 16:24

ʸ 47 Some manuscripts do not have verse 47. ᶻ 15 Isaiah 6:9,10

²⁷"The owner's servants came to him and said, 'Sir, didn't you sow good seed in your field? Where then did the weeds come from?'

²⁸"'An enemy did this,' he replied.

"The servants asked him, 'Do you want us to go and pull them up?'

²⁹"'No,' he answered, 'because while you are pulling the weeds, you may root up the wheat with them. ³⁰Let both grow together until the harvest. At that time I will tell the harvesters: First collect the weeds and tie them in bundles to be burned; then gather the wheat and bring it into my barn.'"ᵐ

The Parables of the Mustard Seed and the Yeast

13:31,32pp — Mk 4:30–32
13:31–33pp — Lk 13:18–21

³¹He told them another parable: "The kingdom of heaven is likeⁿ a mustard seed,ᵒ which a man took and planted in his field. ³²Though it is the smallest of all your seeds, yet when it grows, it is the largest of garden plants and becomes a tree, so that the birds of the air come and perch in its branches."ᵖ

³³He told them still another parable: "The kingdom of heaven is likeᑫ yeast that a woman took and mixed into a large amountᵃ of flourʳ until it worked all through the dough."ˢ

P Mt 3:12 ◄► Mt 13:39–42
T Mt 3:12 ◄► Mt 24:31
H Mt 11:20–24 ◄► Mt 13:38–42
M Mt 6:13 ◄► Mt 13:43
K Mt 6:10 ◄► Mt 16:18–20

13:30 ᵐ Mt 3:12
13:31 ⁿ S ver 24
ᵒ Mt 17:20; Lk 17:6
13:32 ᵖ Ps 104:12; Eze 17:23; 31:6; Da 4:12
13:33 ᑫ S ver 24
ʳ Ge 18:6 ˢ Gal 5:9
13:34 ᵗ S Jn 16:25
13:35 ᵘ ver 14; S Mt 1:22 ᵛ Ps 78:2; Ro 16:25,26; 1Co 2:7; Eph 3:9; Col 1:26
13:36 ʷ Mt 15:15
13:37 ˣ S Mt 8:20
13:38 ʸ Jn 8:44,45; 1Jn 3:10
13:39 ᶻ Joel 3:13
ᵃ Mt 24:3; 28:20
ᵇ Rev 14:15
13:41 ᶜ S Mt 8:20
ᵈ Mt 24:31
13:42 ᵉ S Mt 8:12

³⁴Jesus spoke all these things to the crowd in parables; he did not say anything to them without using a parable.ᵗ ³⁵So was fulfilledᵘ what was spoken through the prophet:

"I will open my mouth in parables,
I will utter things hidden since the creation of the world."ᵇᵛ

The Parable of the Weeds Explained

³⁶Then he left the crowd and went into the house. His disciples came to him and said, "Explain to us the parableʷ of the weeds in the field."

³⁷He answered, "The one who sowed the good seed is the Son of Man.ˣ ³⁸The field is the world, and the good seed stands for the sons of the kingdom. The weeds are the sons of the evil one,ʸ ³⁹and the enemy who sows them is the devil. The harvestᶻ is the end of the age,ᵃ and the harvesters are angels.ᵇ

⁴⁰"As the weeds are pulled up and burned in the fire, so it will be at the end of the age. ⁴¹The Son of Manᶜ will send out his angels,ᵈ and they will weed out of his kingdom everything that causes sin and all who do evil. ⁴²They will throw them into the fiery furnace, where there will be weeping and gnashing of teeth.ᵉ

C Mt 13:14–15 ◄► Mt 15:14
H Mt 13:30 ◄► Mt 13:46–50
P Mt 13:27–30 ◄► Mt 13:47–50

ᵃ 33 Greek *three satas* (probably about 1/2 bushel or 22 liters)
ᵇ 35 Psalm 78:2

13:27–30 Some weeds resemble wheat when both plants are young. This made it very difficult to eradicate the weeds before the grain was ripe. Farmers would allow the wheat and weeds to grow together until the final harvest when the two plants would be easily distinguishable.

Jesus explains that this parable prophetically points to the final judgment when the angels of God will "weed out of his kingdom everything that causes sin and all who do evil" (13:41). After the seven-year tribulation and the Battle of Armageddon, Christ will judge the nations and usher in his millennial kingdom. The weeds (sinners) will be gathered to judgment (see 13:41–42; 25:31–33) but God will command that the reapers place the wheat (believers) in his barn (13:30). The raptured saints will return with Christ (see Rev 19:11–14) where they will be "priests of God and of Christ and will reign with him for a thousand years" (Rev 20:6).

13:31–32 The parable of the mustard seed foreshadows the amazing growth of the kingdom throughout the centuries, from the first disciples to the world dominion of the last days (see Da 2:35, 44–45; 4:21; 7:27; Rev 11:15).

13:33 It was a common practice for a baker to retain a small lump of leavened bread dough to place within a new batch of dough to raise it thoroughly. Since the Bible usually speaks of leaven as a symbol of sin and iniquity, some scholars view this parable as an indication of the growth of sin and corruption within the kingdom of heaven (see 1Co 5:6–9; Gal 5:9; 1Ti 4:1; 2Ti 4:3–4; Jude 12). Others view the meaning of leaven in this passage in a positive sense, symbolizing the growth of the kingdom of heaven because of the powerful message of the gospel.

M ⁴³Then the righteous will shine like the sun[f] in the kingdom of their Father. He who has ears, let him hear.[g]

The Parables of the Hidden Treasure and the Pearl

⁴⁴"The kingdom of heaven is like[h] treasure hidden in a field. When a man found it, he hid it again, and then in his joy went away and sold all he had and bought that field.[i]

⁴⁵"Again, the kingdom of heaven is like[j] a merchant looking for fine pearls. **H** ⁴⁶When he found one of great value, he went away and sold everything he had and bought it.

The Parable of the Net

P ⁴⁷"Once again, the kingdom of heaven is like[k] a net that was let down into the lake and caught all kinds[l] of fish. ⁴⁸When it was full, the fishermen pulled it up on the shore. Then they sat down and collected the good fish in baskets, but threw the bad away. ⁴⁹This is how it will be at the end of the age. The angels will come and separate the wicked from the righteous[m] ⁵⁰and throw them into the fiery furnace, where there will be weeping and gnashing of teeth.[n]

⁵¹"Have you understood all these things?" Jesus asked.

"Yes," they replied.

⁵²He said to them, "Therefore every teacher of the law who has been instructed about the kingdom of heaven is like the owner of a house who brings out of his storeroom new treasures as well as old."

A Prophet Without Honor

13:54–58pp — Mk 6:1–6

⁵³When Jesus had finished these parables,[o] he moved on from there. ⁵⁴Coming to his hometown, he began teaching the people in their synagogue,[p] and they were amazed.[q] "Where did this man get this wisdom and these miraculous powers?" they asked. ⁵⁵"Isn't this the carpenter's son?[r] Isn't his mother's[s] name Mary, and aren't his brothers[t] James, Joseph, Simon and Judas? ⁵⁶Aren't all his sisters with us? Where then did this man get all these things?" ⁵⁷And they took offense[u] at him.

But Jesus said to them, "Only in his hometown and in his own house is a prophet without honor."[v]

⁵⁸And he did not do many miracles **D** there because of their lack of faith.

John the Baptist Beheaded

14:1–12pp — Mk 6:14–29

14 At that time Herod[w] the tetrarch heard the reports about Jesus,[x] ²and he said to his attendants, "This is John the Baptist;[y] he has risen from the dead! That is why miraculous powers are at work in him."

³Now Herod had arrested John and bound him and put him in prison[z] because of Herodias, his brother Philip's wife,[a] ⁴for John had been saying to him: "It is not lawful for you to have her."[b] ⁵Herod wanted to kill John, but he was afraid of the people, because they considered him a prophet.[c]

⁶On Herod's birthday the daughter of Herodias danced for them and pleased Herod so much ⁷that he promised with an oath to give her whatever she asked. ⁸Prompted by her mother, she said, "Give me here on a platter the head of John the Baptist." ⁹The king was distressed, but because of his oaths and his dinner guests, he ordered that her request be granted ¹⁰and had John beheaded[d] in the prison. ¹¹His head was brought in on a platter and given to the girl, who carried it to her mother. ¹²John's disciples came and took his body

M *Mt 13:31-33* ◀ ▶ *Mt 19:28*
H *Mt 13:38-42* ◀ ▶ *Mt 15:13-14*
P *Mt 13:39-42* ◀ ▶ *Mt 24:50-51*

D *Eze 38:22* ◀ ▶ *Mk 6:5-6*

13:47–50 The parable of the net prophetically confirms the same general lesson as the parable of the weeds and wheat: The Lord will eventually judge between the righteous and the wicked. Those who have not genuinely repented of their sins will associate with the church for various reasons, but they will finally be identified and judged in the last days.

13:55–57 In this passage Jesus recognizes the truth of the adage "familiarity breeds contempt." Because Jesus' neighbors had known him since he was a child, they believed they knew him well. Yet when Jesus displayed wisdom and understanding that went beyond their preconceived notions about him, the people of Nazareth rejected his words, his works and ultimately Jesus himself.

and buried it.ᵉ Then they went and told Jesus.

Jesus Feeds the Five Thousand

14:13–21pp — Mk 6:32–44; Lk 9:10–17; Jn 6:1–13
14:13–21Ref — Mt 15:32–38

E ¹³When Jesus heard what had happened, he withdrew by boat privately to a solitary place. Hearing of this, the crowds followed him on foot from the towns. ¹⁴When Jesus landed and saw a large crowd, he had compassion on themᶠ and healed their sick.ᵍ

F ¹⁵As evening approached, the disciples came to him and said, "This is a remote place, and it's already getting late. Send the crowds away, so they can go to the villages and buy themselves some food."

¹⁶Jesus replied, "They do not need to go away. You give them something to eat."

¹⁷"We have here only five loavesʰ of bread and two fish," they answered.

¹⁸"Bring them here to me," he said. ¹⁹And he directed the people to sit down on the grass. Taking the five loaves and the two fish and looking up to heaven, he gave thanks and broke the loaves.ⁱ Then he gave them to the disciples, and the disciples gave them to the people. ²⁰They all ate and were satisfied, and the disciples picked up twelve basketfuls of broken pieces that were left over. ²¹The number of those who ate was about five thousand men, besides women and children.

Jesus Walks on the Water

14:22–33pp — Mk 6:45–51; Jn 6:16–21
14:34–36pp — Mk 6:53–56

²²Immediately Jesus made the disciples get into the boat and go on ahead of him to the other side, while he dismissed the crowd. ²³After he had dismissed them, he went up on a mountainside by himself to pray.ʲ When evening came, he was there alone, ²⁴but the boat was already a considerable distanceᶜ from land, buffeted by the waves because the wind was against it.

²⁵During the fourth watch of the night Jesus went out to them, walking on the lake. ²⁶When the disciples saw him walking on the lake, they were terrified. "It's

E Mt 12:22–29 ◀ ▶ Mt 14:34–36
F Mt 6:25–34 ◀ ▶ Mt 15:32–38

14:12 ᵉAc 8:2

14:14 ᶠS Mt 9:36
ᵍS Mt 4:23

14:17 ʰS Mt 16:9

14:19 ⁱ1Sa 9:13;
Mt 26:26; Mk 8:6;
Lk 9:16; 24:30;
Ac 2:42; 20:7,11;
27:35; 1Co 10:16;
1Ti 4:4

14:23 ʲS Lk 3:21

14:26 ᵏLk 24:37

14:27 ˡMt 9:2;
Ac 23:11
ᵐDa 10:12;
Mt 17:7; 28:10;
Lk 1:13,30; 2:10;
Ac 18:9; 23:11;
Rev 1:17

14:31 ⁿS Mt 6:30

14:33 ᵒPs 2:7;
S Mt 4:3

14:36 ᵖS Mt 9:20

15:2 ᑫLk 11:38

15:4 ʳEx 20:12;
Dt 5:16; Eph 6:2
ˢEx 21:17;
Lev 20:9

a ghost,"ᵏ they said, and cried out in fear.

²⁷But Jesus immediately said to them: "Take courage!¹ It is I. Don't be afraid."ᵐ

²⁸"Lord, if it's you," Peter replied, "tell me to come to you on the water."

²⁹"Come," he said.

Then Peter got down out of the boat, walked on the water and came toward Jesus. ³⁰But when he saw the wind, he was afraid and, beginning to sink, cried out, "Lord, save me!"

³¹Immediately Jesus reached out his hand and caught him. "You of little faith,"ⁿ he said, "why did you doubt?"

³²And when they climbed into the boat, the wind died down. ³³Then those who were in the boat worshiped him, saying, "Truly you are the Son of God."ᵒ

³⁴When they had crossed over, they **E** landed at Gennesaret. ³⁵And when the men of that place recognized Jesus, they sent word to all the surrounding country. People brought all their sick to him ³⁶and begged him to let the sick just touch the edge of his cloak,ᵖ and all who touched him were healed.

Clean and Unclean

15:1–20pp — Mk 7:1–23

15 Then some Pharisees and teachers of the law came to Jesus from Jerusalem and asked, ²"Why do your disciples break the tradition of the elders? They don't wash their hands before they eat!"ᑫ

³Jesus replied, "And why do you break the command of God for the sake of your tradition? ⁴For God said, 'Honor your father and mother'ᵈʳ and 'Anyone who curses his father or mother must be put to death.'ᵉˢ ⁵But you say that if a man says to his father or mother, 'Whatever help you might otherwise have received from me is a gift devoted to God,' ⁶he is not to 'honor his father'ᶠ with it. Thus you nullify the word of God for the sake of your tradition. ⁷You hypocrites! Isaiah was right when he prophesied about you:

⁸" 'These people honor me with their **G**
  lips,
  but their hearts are far from me.

E Mt 14:14 ◀ ▶ Mt 15:21–28
G Mt 7:26–27 ◀ ▶ Mt 22:11–14

ᶜ24 Greek many stadia ᵈ4 Exodus 20:12; Deut. 5:16
ᵉ4 Exodus 21:17; Lev. 20:9 ᶠ6 Some manuscripts father or his mother

⁹"They worship me in vain;
   their teachings are but rules taught
      by men.'"ᵍᵘ

¹⁰Jesus called the crowd to him and said, "Listen and understand. ¹¹What goes into a man's mouth does not make him 'unclean,'ᵛ but what comes out of his mouth, that is what makes him 'unclean.'"ʷ

¹²Then the disciples came to him and asked, "Do you know that the Pharisees were offended when they heard this?"

¹³He replied, "Every plant that my heavenly Father has not plantedˣ will be pulled up by the roots. ¹⁴Leave them; they are blind guides.ʰʸ If a blind man leads a blind man, both will fall into a pit."ᶻ

¹⁵Peter said, "Explain the parable to us."ᵃ

¹⁶"Are you still so dull?"ᵇ Jesus asked them. ¹⁷"Don't you see that whatever enters the mouth goes into the stomach and then out of the body? ¹⁸But the things that come out of the mouth come from the heart,ᶜ and these make a man 'unclean.' ¹⁹For out of the heart come evil thoughts, murder, adultery, sexual immorality, theft, false testimony, slander.ᵈ ²⁰These are what make a man 'unclean';ᵉ but eating with unwashed hands does not make him 'unclean.'"

The Faith of the Canaanite Woman
15:21–28pp — Mk 7:24–30

²¹Leaving that place, Jesus withdrew to the region of Tyre and Sidon.ᶠ ²²A Canaanite woman from that vicinity came to him, crying out, "Lord, Son of David,ᵍ have mercy on me! My daughter is suffering terribly from demon-possession."ʰ ²³Jesus did not answer a word. So his disciples came to him and urged him, "Send her away, for she keeps crying out after us."

²⁴He answered, "I was sent only to the lost sheep of Israel."ⁱ

²⁵The woman came and knelt before him.ʲ "Lord, help me!" she said.

²⁶He replied, "It is not right to take the children's bread and toss it to their dogs."

²⁷"Yes, Lord," she said, "but even the dogs eat the crumbs that fall from their masters' table."

²⁸Then Jesus answered, "Woman, you have great faith!ᵏ Your request is granted." And her daughter was healed from that very hour.

Jesus Feeds the Four Thousand
15:29–31pp — Mk 7:31–37
15:32–39pp — Mk 8:1–10
15:32–39Ref — Mt 14:13–21

²⁹Jesus left there and went along the Sea of Galilee. Then he went up on a mountainside and sat down. ³⁰Great crowds came to him, bringing the lame, the blind, the crippled, the mute and many others, and laid them at his feet; and he healed them.ˡ ³¹The people were amazed when they saw the mute speaking, the crippled made well, the lame walking and the blind seeing. And they praised the God of Israel.ᵐ

³²Jesus called his disciples to him and said, "I have compassion for these people;ⁿ they have already been with me three days and have nothing to eat. I do not want to send them away hungry, or they may collapse on the way."

³³His disciples answered, "Where could we get enough bread in this remote place to feed such a crowd?"

³⁴"How many loaves do you have?" Jesus asked.

"Seven," they replied, "and a few small fish."

³⁵He told the crowd to sit down on the

15:22–27 This passage reveals that Jesus' original mission was directed to "the lost sheep of Israel" (15:24). Yet this foreigner was willing to settle for "crumbs," so Jesus rewarded her persistence and great faith. It was only after the Jews had rejected Christ's claims as their Messiah that Jesus gave his disciples the command to go "and make disciples of all nations, baptizing them in the name of the Father and of the Son and of the Holy Spirit" (28:19).

ground. ³⁶Then he took the seven loaves and the fish, and when he had given thanks, he broke them° and gave them to the disciples, and they in turn to the people. ³⁷They all ate and were satisfied. Afterward the disciples picked up seven basketfuls of broken pieces that were left over.ᵖ ³⁸The number of those who ate was four thousand, besides women and children. ³⁹After Jesus had sent the crowd away, he got into the boat and went to the vicinity of Magadan.

The Demand for a Sign
16:1–12pp — Mk 8:11–21

16 The Pharisees and Sadduceesᑫ came to Jesus and tested him by asking him to show them a sign from heaven.ʳ

²He replied,ⁱ "When evening comes, you say, 'It will be fair weather, for the sky is red,' ³and in the morning, 'Today it will be stormy, for the sky is red and overcast.' You know how to interpret the appearance of the sky, but you cannot interpret the signs of the times.ˢ ⁴A wicked and adulterous generation looks for a miraculous sign, but none will be given it except the sign of Jonah."ᵗ Jesus then left them and went away.

The Yeast of the Pharisees and Sadducees

⁵When they went across the lake, the disciples forgot to take bread. ⁶"Be careful," Jesus said to them. "Be on your guard against the yeast of the Pharisees and Sadducees."ᵘ

⁷They discussed this among themselves and said, "It is because we didn't bring any bread."

E Da 12:9–10 ◄ ► Mt 24:3–6
F Mt 15:32–38 ◄ ► Mk 1:13

15:36 °S Mt 14:19
15:37 ᵖMt 16:10
16:1 ᑫS Ac 4:1; ʳS Mt 12:38
16:3 ˢLk 12:54-56
16:4 ᵗMt 12:39
16:6 ᵘLk 12:1
16:8 ᵛS Mt 6:30
16:9 ʷMt 14:17-21
16:10 ˣMt 15:34-38
16:12 ʸS Ac 4:1
16:14 ᶻS Mt 3:1; ᵃMk 6:15; Jn 1:21
16:16 ᵇS Mt 4:3; Ps 42:2; Jer 10:10; Ac 14:15; 2Co 6:16; 1Th 1:9; 1Ti 3:15; Heb 10:31; 12:22
16:17 ᶜ1Co 15:50; Eph 6:12; Heb 2:14 ᵈS Mt 13:11
16:18 ᵉJn 1:42 ᶠS Eph 2:20
16:19 ᵍIsa 22:22; Rev 3:7

⁸Aware of their discussion, Jesus asked, "You of little faith,ᵛ why are you talking among yourselves about having no bread? ⁹Do you still not understand? Don't you remember the five loaves for the five thousand, and how many basketfuls you gathered?ʷ ¹⁰Or the seven loaves for the four thousand, and how many basketfuls you gathered?ˣ ¹¹How is it you don't understand that I was not talking to you about bread? But be on your guard against the yeast of the Pharisees and Sadducees." ¹²Then they understood that he was not telling them to guard against the yeast used in bread, but against the teaching of the Pharisees and Sadducees.ʸ

Peter's Confession of Christ
16:13–16pp — Mk 8:27–29; Lk 9:18–20

¹³When Jesus came to the region of Caesarea Philippi, he asked his disciples, "Who do people say the Son of Man is?"

¹⁴They replied, "Some say John the Baptist;ᶻ others say Elijah; and still others, Jeremiah or one of the prophets."ᵃ

¹⁵"But what about you?" he asked. "Who do you say I am?"

¹⁶Simon Peter answered, "You are the Christ,ʲ the Son of the living God."ᵇ

¹⁷Jesus replied, "Blessed are you, Simon son of Jonah, for this was not revealed to you by man,ᶜ but by my Father in heaven.ᵈ ¹⁸And I tell you that you are Peter,ᵏᵉ and on this rock I will build my church,ᶠ and the gates of Hadesˡ will not overcome it.ᵐ ¹⁹I will give you the keysᵍ

K Mt 13:33 ◄ ► Mk 4:26–28
O Mt 15:13 ◄ ► Mt 18:3

ʲ2 Some early manuscripts do not have the rest of verse 2 and all of verse 3. ʲ16 Or *Messiah*; also in verse 20 ᵏ18 *Peter* means *rock*. ˡ18 Or *hell* ᵐ18 Or *not prove stronger than it*

16:3–4 Jesus criticized the religious leaders of Israel for their ability to read weather signs but their inability to read and understand the spiritual signs from the Scriptures concerning the promised Messiah. Though the leaders wanted a supernatural manifestation to prove Jesus' claim as the Messiah, Jesus warned that the only sign they would receive was the sign of Jonah's three days and three nights, words that foreshadowed his crucifixion and resurrection from the dead.
16:18 Though Jesus renamed his disciple *Peter*, which means "stone," and said that he would build his church on a "rock," the teaching of the NT is clear that the church is built solely on Jesus Christ himself. While some scholars have theorized that the church was built on Peter and his direct successors, Peter himself describes Jesus Christ as the cornerstone and foundation of the church (see 1Pe 2:4–8).
16:19 This verse does not suggest that Peter and his apostolic successors in some manner control the gates of heaven. The "keys" referred to here probably signify the authority conferred on the apostles to share the gospel message. In this way the apostles would open the kingdom to those who would believe the gospel and close the kingdom to those who would not receive Christ (see Isa 22:22; Rev 3:7).

of the kingdom of heaven; whatever you bind on earth will be[n] bound in heaven, and whatever you loose on earth will be[h] loosed in heaven." [20]Then he warned his disciples not to tell anyone[i] that he was the Christ.

Jesus Predicts His Death
16:21–28pp — Mk 8:31–9:1; Lk 9:22–27

[21]From that time on Jesus began to explain to his disciples that he must go to Jerusalem[j] and suffer many things[k] at the hands of the elders, chief priests and teachers of the law,[l] and that he must be killed[m] and on the third day[n] be raised to life.[o]

[22]Peter took him aside and began to rebuke him. "Never, Lord!" he said. "This shall never happen to you!"

[23]Jesus turned and said to Peter, "Get behind me, Satan![p] You are a stumbling block to me; you do not have in mind the things of God, but the things of men."

[24]Then Jesus said to his disciples, "If anyone would come after me, he must deny himself and take up his cross and follow me.[q] [25]For whoever wants to save his life[o] will lose it, but whoever loses his life for me will find it.[r] [26]What good will it be for a man if he gains the whole world, yet forfeits his soul? Or what can a man give in exchange for his soul? [27]For the Son of Man[s] is going to come[t] in his Father's glory with his angels, and then he will reward each person according to what he has done.[u] [28]I tell you the truth, some who are standing here will not taste death before they see the Son of Man coming in his kingdom."

S Mt 13:20–22 ◀ ▶ Mt 16:27
H Mt 15:13–14 ◀ ▶ Mt 18:6–9
C Hag 2:6–7 ◀ ▶ Mt 24:3
S Mt 16:24 ◀ ▶ Mt 18:8–9

16:19 h Mt 18:18; Jn 20:23
16:20 i S Mk 8:30
16:21 j S Lk 9:51
k Ps 22:6; Isa 53:3;
Mt 26:67,68;
Mk 10:34;
Lk 17:25; Jn 18:22,23; 19:3
l Mt 27:1,2
m Ac 2:23; 3:13
n Hos 6:2;
Mt 12:40;
Lk 24:21,46;
Jn 2:19; 1Co 15:3,4
o Mt 17:22,23; 27:63; Mk 9:31;
Lk 9:22; 18:31-33; 24:6,7
16:23 p S Mt 4:10
16:24 q Mt 10:38; Lk 14:27
16:25 r S Jn 12:25
16:27 s S Mt 8:20
t S Lk 17:30;
Jn 14:3; Ac 1:11;
S 1Co 1:7;
S 1Th 2:19; 4:16;
S Rev 1:7; 22:7,12,20
u 2Ch 6:23;
Job 34:11;
Ps 62:12; Jer 17:10;
Eze 18:20;
1Co 3:12-15;
2Co 5:10;
Rev 22:12
17:1 v S Mt 4:21
17:5 w S Mt 3:17
x Ac 3:22,23
17:7 y S Mt 14:27
17:9 z S Mk 8:30
a S Mt 8:20
b S Mt 16:21
17:11 c Mal 4:6;
Lk 1:16,17
17:12 d S Mt 11:14
e S Mt 14:3,10

The Transfiguration
17:1–8pp — Lk 9:28–36
17:1–13pp — Mk 9:2–13

17 After six days Jesus took with him Peter, James and John[v] the brother of James, and led them up a high mountain by themselves. [2]There he was transfigured before them. His face shone like the sun, and his clothes became as white as the light. [3]Just then there appeared before them Moses and Elijah, talking with Jesus.

[4]Peter said to Jesus, "Lord, it is good for us to be here. If you wish, I will put up three shelters—one for you, one for Moses and one for Elijah."

[5]While he was still speaking, a bright cloud enveloped them, and a voice from the cloud said, "This is my Son, whom I love; with him I am well pleased.[w] Listen to him!"[x]

[6]When the disciples heard this, they fell facedown to the ground, terrified. [7]But Jesus came and touched them. "Get up," he said. "Don't be afraid."[y] [8]When they looked up, they saw no one except Jesus.

[9]As they were coming down the mountain, Jesus instructed them, "Don't tell anyone[z] what you have seen, until the Son of Man[a] has been raised from the dead."[b]

[10]The disciples asked him, "Why then do the teachers of the law say that Elijah must come first?"

[11]Jesus replied, "To be sure, Elijah comes and will restore all things.[c] [12]But I tell you, Elijah has already come,[d] and they did not recognize him, but have done to him everything they wished.[e] In the same way the Son of Man is going to

[n] 19 Or *have been* [o] 25 The Greek word means either *life* or *soul*; also in verse 26.

The history of the church described in Acts defines this authority of the "keys." Peter declared the need for repentance of the Jews on the day of Pentecost (see Ac 2:38–39). Peter also was the first to accept Christ's command to preach the gospel to the Gentiles after the vision he received directed him to the house of Cornelius (see Ac 10:34–35, 45; 15:7–11). In the church council it was James, the brother of Jesus, who exercised final authority and issued the decision as to what would be required of Gentile converts to Christianity.

16:21 Jesus told his disciples the details of the remainder of his mission: his journey to Jerusalem, his trial, death and resurrection on "the third day" (see Mt 27:63; 28:1).

16:27 Jesus will return from heaven with his angelic army to defeat the antichrist and the kings of the east at the Battle of Armageddon. After his victory he will establish his Messianic millennial kingdom on earth and "reward each person according to what he has done." Compare this promised judgment with 25:31–46 and Eze 20:36–38.

suffer^f at their hands." ^13Then the disciples understood that he was talking to them about John the Baptist.^g

The Healing of a Boy With a Demon
17:14–19pp — Mk 9:14–28; Lk 9:37–42

^14When they came to the crowd, a man approached Jesus and knelt before him. ^15"Lord, have mercy on my son," he said. "He has seizures^h and is suffering greatly. He often falls into the fire or into the water. ^16I brought him to your disciples, but they could not heal him."

^17"O unbelieving and perverse generation," Jesus replied, "how long shall I stay with you? How long shall I put up with you? Bring the boy here to me." ^18Jesus rebuked the demon, and it came out of the boy, and he was healed from that moment.

^19Then the disciples came to Jesus in private and asked, "Why couldn't we drive it out?"

^20He replied, "Because you have so little faith. I tell you the truth, if you have faith^i as small as a mustard seed,^j you can say to this mountain, 'Move from here to there' and it will move.^k Nothing will be impossible for you.^p"

^22When they came together in Galilee, he said to them, "The Son of Man^l is going to be betrayed into the hands of men. ^23They will kill him,^m and on the third day^n he will be raised to life."^o And the disciples were filled with grief.

The Temple Tax

^24After Jesus and his disciples arrived in Capernaum, the collectors of the two-drachma tax^p came to Peter and asked, "Doesn't your teacher pay the temple tax^q?"

^25"Yes, he does," he replied.

When Peter came into the house, Jesus was the first to speak. "What do you think, Simon?" he asked. "From whom do the kings of the earth collect duty and taxes^q—from their own sons or from others?"

^26"From others," Peter answered.

"Then the sons are exempt," Jesus said to him. ^27"But so that we may not offend^r them, go to the lake and throw out your line. Take the first fish you catch; open its mouth and you will find a four-drachma coin. Take it and give it to them for my tax and yours."

The Greatest in the Kingdom of Heaven
18:1–5pp — Mk 9:33–37; Lk 9:46–48

18 At that time the disciples came to Jesus and asked, "Who is the greatest in the kingdom of heaven?" ^2He called a little child and had him stand among them. ^3And he said: "I tell you the truth, unless you change and become like little children,^s you will never enter the kingdom of heaven.^t ^4Therefore, whoever humbles himself like this child is the greatest in the kingdom of heaven.^u

^5"And whoever welcomes a little child like this in my name welcomes me.^v ^6But if anyone causes one of these little ones who believe in me to sin,^w it would be better for him to have a large millstone hung around his neck and to be drowned in the depths of the sea.^x

^7"Woe to the world because of the things that cause people to sin! Such things must come, but woe to the man through whom they come!^y ^8If your hand or your foot causes you to sin,^z cut it off and throw it away. It is better for you to enter life maimed or crippled than to have two hands or two feet and be thrown into eternal fire. ^9And if your eye causes you to sin,^a gouge it out and throw it away. It is better for you to enter life with one eye than to have two eyes and be thrown into the fire of hell.^b

The Parable of the Lost Sheep
18:12–14pp — Lk 15:4–7

^10"See that you do not look down on one of these little ones. For I tell you that their angels^c in heaven always see the face of my Father in heaven.^r ^12"What do you think? If a man owns a

17:12 ^f S Mt 16:21
17:13 ^g S Mt 3:1
17:15 ^h Mt 4:24
17:20 ^i S Mt 21:21; ^j Mt 13:31; Lk 17:6; ^k 1Co 13:2
17:22 ^l S Mt 8:20
17:23 ^m Ac 2:23; 3:13 ^n S Mt 16:21 ^o S Mt 16:21
17:24 ^p Ex 30:13
17:25 ^q Mt 22:17-21; Ro 13:7
17:27 ^r Jn 6:61
18:3 ^s Mt 19:14; 1Pe 2:2 ^t S Mt 3:2
18:4 ^u S Mk 9:35
18:5 ^v Mt 10:40
18:6 ^w S Mt 5:29 ^x Mk 9:42; Lk 17:2
18:7 ^y Lk 17:1
18:8 ^z S Mt 5:29
18:9 ^a S Mt 5:29 ^b S Mt 5:22
18:10 ^c Ge 48:16; Ps 34:7; Ac 12:11, 15; Heb 1:14

E *Mt 15:30–31* ◀▶ *Mt 19:1–2*
P *Mt 6:31–33* ◀▶ *Lk 22:35*

M *Mt 5:3–5* ◀▶ *Mt 18:26–27*
O *Mt 16:19* ◀▶ *Mt 18:18*
L *Mt 10:29–31* ◀▶ *Mt 18:10*
H *Mt 16:26–27* ◀▶ *Mt 21:44*
S *Mt 16:27* ◀▶ *Mt 18:17*
L *Mt 18:5–6* ◀▶ *Mt 18:19–20*
C *Mt 15:18–19* ◀▶ *Mt 22:11–14*
L *Mt 12:31–32* ◀▶ *Mt 18:26–27*
P *Mt 10:6* ◀▶ *Lk 15:3–32*

p 20 Some manuscripts you. 21But this kind does not go out except by prayer and fasting. q 24 Greek the two drachmas r 10 Some manuscripts heaven. 11The Son of Man came to save what was lost.

hundred sheep, and one of them wanders away, will he not leave the ninety-nine on the hills and go to look for the one that wandered off? ¹³And if he finds it, I tell you the truth, he is happier about that one sheep than about the ninety-nine that did not wander off. ¹⁴In the same way your Father in heaven is not willing that any of these little ones should be lost.

A Brother Who Sins Against You

¹⁵"If your brother sins against you,ˢ go and show him his fault,ᵈ just between the two of you. If he listens to you, you have won your brother over. ¹⁶But if he will not listen, take one or two others along, so that 'every matter may be established by the testimony of two or three witnesses.'ᵗᵉ ¹⁷If he refuses to listen to them, tell it to the church;ᶠ and if he refuses to listen even to the church, treat him as you would a pagan or a tax collector.ᵍ

¹⁸"I tell you the truth, whatever you bind on earth will beᵘ bound in heaven, and whatever you loose on earth will beᵘ loosed in heaven.ʰ

¹⁹"Again, I tell you that if two of you on earth agree about anything you ask for, it will be done for youⁱ by my Father in heaven. ²⁰For where two or three come together in my name, there am I with them."ʲ

The Parable of the Unmerciful Servant

²¹Then Peter came to Jesus and asked, "Lord, how many times shall I forgive my brother when he sins against me?ᵏ Up to seven times?"ˡ

²²Jesus answered, "I tell you, not seven times, but seventy-seven times.ᵛᵐ

²³"Therefore, the kingdom of heaven is likeⁿ a king who wanted to settle accountsᵒ with his servants. ²⁴As he began the settlement, a man who owed him ten thousand talentsʷ was brought to him. ²⁵Since he was not able to pay,ᵖ the master ordered that he and his wife and his children and all that he had be soldᵠ to repay the debt.

S *Mt 18:8-9* ◄ ► *Mt 18:23-35*
O *Mt 18:3* ◄ ► *Mt 22:11-14*
L *Mt 18:10* ◄ ► *Mt 21:22*
S *Mt 18:17* ◄ ► *Mt 19:16-21*

18:15 ᵈLev 19:17; Lk 17:3; Gal 6:1; Jas 5:19,20
18:16 ᵉNu 35:30; Dt 17:6; 19:15; Jn 8:17; 2Co 13:1; 1Ti 5:19; Heb 10:28
18:17 ᶠ1Co 6:1-6 ᵍS Ro 16:17
18:18 ʰMt 16:19; Jn 20:23
18:19 ⁱS Mt 7:7
18:20 ʲS Mt 28:20
18:21 ᵏS Mt 6:14 ˡLk 17:4
18:22 ᵐGe 4:24
18:23 ⁿS Mt 13:24 ᵒMt 25:19
18:25 ᵖLk 7:42 ᵠLev 25:39; 2Ki 4:1; Ne 5:5,8
18:26 ʳS Mt 8:2
18:35 ˢS Mt 6:14; S Jas 2:13
19:1 ᵗS Mt 7:28
19:2 ᵘS Mt 4:23
19:3 ᵛMt 5:31
19:4 ʷGe 1:27; 5:2

²⁶"The servant fell on his knees before him.ʳ 'Be patient with me,' he begged, 'and I will pay back everything.' ²⁷The servant's master took pity on him, canceled the debt and let him go.

²⁸"But when that servant went out, he found one of his fellow servants who owed him a hundred denarii.ˣ He grabbed him and began to choke him. 'Pay back what you owe me!' he demanded.

²⁹"His fellow servant fell to his knees and begged him, 'Be patient with me, and I will pay you back.'

³⁰"But he refused. Instead, he went off and had the man thrown into prison until he could pay the debt. ³¹When the other servants saw what had happened, they were greatly distressed and went and told their master everything that had happened.

³²"Then the master called the servant in. 'You wicked servant,' he said, 'I canceled all that debt of yours because you begged me to. ³³Shouldn't you have had mercy on your fellow servant just as I had on you?' ³⁴In anger his master turned him over to the jailers to be tortured, until he should pay back all he owed.

³⁵"This is how my heavenly Father will treat each of you unless you forgive your brother from your heart."ˢ

Divorce

19:1-9pp — Mk 10:1-12

19 When Jesus had finished saying these things,ᵗ he left Galilee and went into the region of Judea to the other side of the Jordan. ²Large crowds followed him, and he healed themᵘ there.

³Some Pharisees came to him to test him. They asked, "Is it lawful for a man to divorce his wifeᵛ for any and every reason?"

⁴"Haven't you read," he replied, "that at the beginning the Creator 'made them male and female,'ʸʷ ⁵and said, 'For this reason a man will leave his father and mother and be united to his wife, and the

L *Mt 18:12-14* ◄ ► *Mt 20:1-14*
M *Mt 18:1-4* ◄ ► *Mt 19:14*
R *Mt 6:14-15* ◄ ► *Mt 21:28-32*
E *Mt 17:14-20* ◄ ► *Mt 20:30-34*

ˢ 15 Some manuscripts do not have *against you.* ᵗ 16 Deut. 19:15 ᵘ 18 Or *have been* ᵛ 22 Or *seventy times seven* ʷ 24 That is, millions of dollars ˣ 28 That is, a few dollars ʸ 4 Gen. 1:27

two will become one flesh'.ᶻˣ ⁶So they are no longer two, but one. Therefore what God has joined together, let man not separate."

⁷"Why then," they asked, "did Moses command that a man give his wife a certificate of divorce and send her away?"ʸ

⁸Jesus replied, "Moses permitted you to divorce your wives because your hearts were hard. But it was not this way from the beginning. ⁹I tell you that anyone who divorces his wife, except for marital unfaithfulness, and marries another woman commits adultery."ᶻ

¹⁰The disciples said to him, "If this is the situation between a husband and wife, it is better not to marry."

¹¹Jesus replied, "Not everyone can accept this word, but only those to whom it has been given.ᵃ ¹²For some are eunuchs because they were born that way; others were made that way by men; and others have renounced marriageᵃ because of the kingdom of heaven. The one who can accept this should accept it."

The Little Children and Jesus
19:13–15pp — Mk 10:13–16; Lk 18:15–17

¹³Then little children were brought to Jesus for him to place his hands on themᵇ and pray for them. But the disciples rebuked those who brought them.

M ¹⁴Jesus said, "Let the little children come to me, and do not hinder them, for the kingdom of heaven belongsᶜ to such as these."ᵈ ¹⁵When he had placed his hands on them, he went on from there.

The Rich Young Man
19:16–29pp — Mk 10:17–30; Lk 18:18–30

S ¹⁶Now a man came up to Jesus and asked, "Teacher, what good thing must I do to get eternal life?"ᶠ

¹⁷"Why do you ask me about what is good?" Jesus replied. "There is only One

M Mt 18:26–27 ◀ ▶ Mt 19:23–24
S Mt 18:23–35 ◀ ▶ Mt 21:28–31

19:5 ˣGe 2:24; 1Co 6:16; Eph 5:31
19:7 ʸDt 24:1–4; Mt 5:31
19:9 ᶻS Lk 16:18
19:11 ᵃS Mt 13:11; 1Co 7:7-9,17
19:13 ᵇS Mk 5:23
19:14 ᶜS Mt 25:34 ᵈMt 18:3; 1Pe 2:2
19:16 ᵉS Mt 25:46 ᶠLk 10:25
19:17 ᵍLev 18:5
19:18 ʰJas 2:11
19:19 ⁱEx 20:12-16; Dt 5:16-20 ʲLev 19:18; S Mt 5:43
19:21 ᵏMt 5:48 ˡS Ac 2:45 ᵐS Mt 6:20
19:23 ⁿMt 13:22; 1Ti 6:9,10
19:26 ᵒGe 18:14; Job 42:2; Jer 32:17; L 1:37; 18:27; Ro 4:21
19:27 ᵖS Mt 4:19
19:28 ᵠMt 20:21; 25:31 ʳLk 22:28-30; Rev 3:21; 4:4; 20:4

who is good. If you want to enter life, obey the commandments."ᵍ

¹⁸"Which ones?" the man inquired.

Jesus replied, " 'Do not murder, do not commit adultery,ʰ do not steal, do not give false testimony, ¹⁹honor your father and mother,'ⁱ and 'love your neighbor as yourself.'ᶜ "ʲ

²⁰"All these I have kept," the young man said. "What do I still lack?"

²¹Jesus answered, "If you want to be perfect,ᵏ go, sell your possessions and give to the poor,ˡ and you will have treasure in heaven.ᵐ Then come, follow me."

²²When the young man heard this, he went away sad, because he had great wealth.

²³Then Jesus said to his disciples, "I tell M you the truth, it is hard for a rich manⁿ to enter the kingdom of heaven. ²⁴Again I tell you, it is easier for a camel to go through the eye of a needle than for a rich man to enter the kingdom of God."

²⁵When the disciples heard this, they were greatly astonished and asked, "Who then can be saved?"

²⁶Jesus looked at them and said, "With K man this is impossible, but with God all things are possible."ᵒ

²⁷Peter answered him, "We have left everything to follow you!ᵖ What then will there be for us?"

²⁸Jesus said to them, "I tell you the I truth, at the renewal of all things, when M the Son of Man sits on his glorious throne,ᵠ you who have followed me will also sit on twelve thrones, judging the twelve tribes of Israel.ʳ ²⁹And everyone U who has left houses or brothers or sisters or father or motherᵈ or children or fields

M Mt 19:14 ◀ ▶ Mt 23:12
K Mt 11:28–29 ◀ ▶ Mt 24:35
I Mt 2:6 ◀ ▶ Mt 21:5
M Mt 13:43 ◀ ▶ Mt 20:20–21
U Mt 6:33 ◀ ▶ Mk 10:28–30

ᶻ5 Gen. 2:24 ᵃ12 Or have made themselves eunuchs ᵇ19 Exodus 20:12-16; Deut. 5:16-20 ᶜ19 Lev. 19:18 ᵈ29 Some manuscripts *mother or wife*

19:28 This fascinating prophecy confirms the restoration of the kingdom of Israel during the Millennium (see Eze 37:12–22) and foresees the day when the twelve disciples of Jesus will govern the twelve tribes of Israel. Ezekiel adds that the twelve tribes will receive land allotments in the promised land during the Millennium (see Eze 47—48). Both these prophecies will necessitate the restoration of the individualities of the twelve tribes. While some Jews are able to trace their tribal identity through their family name, many Jews today are uncertain of their ancestry. These prophecies indicate that God will reveal the tribal identity of all the Jews in the last days.

for my sake will receive a hundred times as much and will inherit eternal life. ³⁰But many who are first will be last, and many who are last will be first.

The Parable of the Workers in the Vineyard

20 "For the kingdom of heaven is like a landowner who went out early in the morning to hire men to work in his vineyard. ²He agreed to pay them a denarius for the day and sent them into his vineyard.

³"About the third hour he went out and saw others standing in the marketplace doing nothing. ⁴He told them, 'You also go and work in my vineyard, and I will pay you whatever is right.' ⁵So they went.

"He went out again about the sixth hour and the ninth hour and did the same thing. ⁶About the eleventh hour he went out and found still others standing around. He asked them, 'Why have you been standing here all day long doing nothing?'

⁷"'Because no one has hired us,' they answered.

"He said to them, 'You also go and work in my vineyard.'

⁸"When evening came, the owner of the vineyard said to his foreman, 'Call the workers and pay them their wages, beginning with the last ones hired and going on to the first.'

⁹"The workers who were hired about the eleventh hour came and each received a denarius. ¹⁰So when those came who were hired first, they expected to receive more. But each one of them also received a denarius. ¹¹When they received it, they began to grumble against the landowner. ¹²'These men who were hired last worked only one hour,' they said, 'and you have made them equal to us who have borne the burden of the work and the heat of the day.'

¹³"But he answered one of them, 'Friend, I am not being unfair to you. Didn't you agree to work for a denarius? ¹⁴Take your pay and go. I want to give the man who was hired last the same as I gave you. ¹⁵Don't I have the right to do what I want with my own money? Or are you envious because I am generous?'

¹⁶"So the last will be first, and the first will be last."

Jesus Again Predicts His Death
20:17-19pp — Mk 10:32-34; Lk 18:31-33

¹⁷Now as Jesus was going up to Jerusalem, he took the twelve disciples aside and said to them, ¹⁸"We are going up to Jerusalem, and the Son of Man will be betrayed to the chief priests and the teachers of the law. They will condemn him to death ¹⁹and will turn him over to the Gentiles to be mocked and flogged and crucified. On the third day he will be raised to life!"

A Mother's Request
20:20-28pp — Mk 10:35-45

²⁰Then the mother of Zebedee's sons came to Jesus with her sons and, kneeling down, asked a favor of him.

²¹"What is it you want?" he asked.

She said, "Grant that one of these two sons of mine may sit at your right and the other at your left in your kingdom."

²²"You don't know what you are asking," Jesus said to them. "Can you drink the cup I am going to drink?"

"We can," they answered.

²³Jesus said to them, "You will indeed drink from my cup, but to sit at my right or left is not for me to grant. These places belong to those for whom they have been prepared by my Father."

²⁴When the ten heard about this, they were indignant with the two brothers. ²⁵Jesus called them together and said, "You know that the rulers of the Gentiles lord it over them, and their high officials exercise authority over them. ²⁶Not so with you. Instead, whoever wants to become great among you must be your servant, ²⁷and whoever wants to be first must be your slave— ²⁸just as the Son of Man did not come to be served, but to serve, and to give his life as a ransom for many."

20:20-21 The mother of two of Christ's disciples, James and John, requested cabinet positions in the future millennial kingdom, believing that Jesus would establish his kingdom immediately.

Two Blind Men Receive Sight

20:29-34pp — Mk 10:46-52; Lk 18:35-43

²⁹As Jesus and his disciples were leaving Jericho, a large crowd followed him. ³⁰Two blind men were sitting by the roadside, and when they heard that Jesus was going by, they shouted, "Lord, Son of David,ᵗ have mercy on us!"

³¹The crowd rebuked them and told them to be quiet, but they shouted all the louder, "Lord, Son of David, have mercy on us!"

³²Jesus stopped and called them. "What do you want me to do for you?" he asked.

³³"Lord," they answered, "we want our sight."

³⁴Jesus had compassion on them and touched their eyes. Immediately they received their sight and followed him.

The Triumphal Entry

21:1-9pp — Mk 11:1-10; Lk 19:29-38
21:4-9pp — Jn 12:12-15

21 As they approached Jerusalem and came to Bethphage on the Mount of Olives,ᵘ Jesus sent two disciples, ²saying to them, "Go to the village ahead of you, and at once you will find a donkey tied there, with her colt by her. Untie them and bring them to me. ³If anyone says anything to you, tell him that the Lord needs them, and he will send them right away."

⁴This took place to fulfillᵛ what was spoken through the prophet:

⁵"Say to the Daughter of Zion,
  'See, your king comes to you,
    gentle and riding on a donkey,
    on a colt, the foal of a donkey.' "ᵉʷ

⁶The disciples went and did as Jesus had instructed them. ⁷They brought the donkey and the colt, placed their cloaks on them, and Jesus sat on them. ⁸A very large crowd spread their cloaksˣ on the road, while others cut branches from the trees and spread them on the road. ⁹The crowds that went ahead of him and those that followed shouted,

"Hosannaᶠ to the Son of David!"ʸ

"Blessed is he who comes in the name of the Lord!"ᵍᶻ

"Hosannaᶠ in the highest!"ᵃ

¹⁰When Jesus entered Jerusalem, the whole city was stirred and asked, "Who is this?"

¹¹The crowds answered, "This is Jesus, the prophetᵇ from Nazareth in Galilee."

Jesus at the Temple

21:12-16pp — Mk 11:15-18; Lk 19:45-47

¹²Jesus entered the temple area and drove out all who were buyingᶜ and selling there. He overturned the tables of the money changersᵈ and the benches of those selling doves.ᵉ ¹³"It is written," he said to them, " 'My house will be called a house of prayer,'ʰᶠ but you are making it a 'den of robbers.' "ⁱᵍ

¹⁴The blind and the lame came to him at the temple, and he healed them.ʰ ¹⁵But when the chief priests and the teachers

---

Cross references:

20:30 ᵗS Mt 9:27
21:1 ᵘMt 24:3; 26:30; Mk 14:26; Lk 19:37; 21:37; 22:39; Jn 8:1; Ac 1:12
21:4 ᵛS Mt 1:22
21:5 ʷZec 9:9; Isa 62:11
21:8 ˣ2Ki 9:13
21:9 ʸver 15; S Mt 9:27; ᶻPs 118:26; ᵃMt 23:39 a Lk 2:14
21:11 ᵇDt 18:15; Lk 7:16,39; 24:19; Jn 1:21,25; 6:14; 7:40
21:12 ᶜDt 14:26; ᵈEx 30:13; ᵉLev 1:14
21:13 ᶠIsa 56:7; ᵍJer 7:11
21:14 ʰS Mt 4:23

E Mt 19:1-2 ◀ ▶ Mt 21:14
I Mt 19:28 ◀ ▶ Mt 27:11
M Mt 20:20-21 ◀ ▶ Mt 21:38

E Mt 20:30-34 ◀ ▶ Mk 1:23-34

ᵉ5 Zech. 9:9 ᶠ9 A Hebrew expression meaning "Save!" which became an exclamation of praise; also in verse 15 ᵍ9 Psalm 118:26 ʰ13 Isaiah 56:7 ⁱ13 Jer. 7:11

21:5 Jesus quotes the prophecy of Zec 9:9 that foretold his Messianic entrance into Jerusalem through the eastern gate in fulfillment of Da 9:24-26. See the article on "The Vision of the Seventy Weeks" on p. 986.

The Four Temples in Israel's History

Solomon's Temple	Zerubbabel's Temple		Tribulation Temple	Millennial Temple
1	2	✝	3	4
1000 B.C. (1000-587 B.C.)	536 B.C. (516 B.C.- A.D. 70)	A.D. 32 Crucifixion	The 7 year Tribulation Period	Following Battle of Armageddon

of the law saw the wonderful things he did and the children shouting in the temple area, "Hosanna to the Son of David," they were indignant.ʲ

¹⁶"Do you hear what these children are saying?" they asked him.

"Yes," replied Jesus, "have you never read,

" 'From the lips of children and infants
you have ordained praise'ʲ?"ᵏ

¹⁷And he left them and went out of the city to Bethany,ˡ where he spent the night.

The Fig Tree Withers
21:18–22pp — Mk 11:12–14,20–24

¹⁸Early in the morning, as he was on his way back to the city, he was hungry. ¹⁹Seeing a fig tree by the road, he went up to it but found nothing on it except leaves. Then he said to it, "May you never bear fruit again!" Immediately the tree withered.ᵐ

²⁰When the disciples saw this, they were amazed. "How did the fig tree wither so quickly?" they asked.

²¹Jesus replied, "I tell you the truth, if you have faith and do not doubt,ⁿ not only can you do what was done to the fig tree, but also you can say to this mountain, 'Go, throw yourself into the sea,' and it will be done. ²²If you believe, you will receive whatever you ask forᵒ in prayer."

The Authority of Jesus Questioned
21:23–27pp — Mk 11:27–33; Lk 20:1–8

²³Jesus entered the temple courts, and, while he was teaching, the chief priests and the elders of the people came to him. "By what authorityᵖ are you doing these things?" they asked. "And who gave you this authority?"

²⁴Jesus replied, "I will also ask you one question. If you answer me, I will tell you by what authority I am doing these things. ²⁵John's baptism—where did it come from? Was it from heaven, or from men?"

They discussed it among themselves and said, "If we say, 'From heaven,' he will ask, 'Then why didn't you believe him?' ²⁶But if we say, 'From men'—we are afraid of the people, for they all hold that John was a prophet."ᑫ

²⁷So they answered Jesus, "We don't know."

Then he said, "Neither will I tell you by what authority I am doing these things.

The Parable of the Two Sons

²⁸"What do you think? There was a man who had two sons. He went to the first and said, 'Son, go and work today in the vineyard.'ʳ

²⁹" 'I will not,' he answered, but later he changed his mind and went.

³⁰"Then the father went to the other son and said the same thing. He answered, 'I will, sir,' but he did not go.

³¹"Which of the two did what his father wanted?"

"The first," they answered.

Jesus said to them, "I tell you the truth, the tax collectorsˢ and the prostitutesᵗ are entering the kingdom of God ahead of you. ³²For John came to you to show you the way of righteousness,ᵘ and you did not believe him, but the tax collectorsᵛ and the prostitutesʷ did. And even after you saw this, you did not repentˣ and believe him.

The Parable of the Tenants
21:33–46pp — Mk 12:1–12; Lk 20:9–19

³³"Listen to another parable: There was a landowner who plantedʸ a vineyard. He put a wall around it, dug a winepress in it and built a watchtower.ᶻ Then he rented the vineyard to some farmers and went away on a journey.ᵃ ³⁴When the harvest time approached, he sent his servantsᵇ to the tenants to collect his fruit.

³⁵"The tenants seized his servants; they beat one, killed another, and stoned a third.ᶜ ³⁶Then he sent other servantsᵈ to them, more than the first time, and

---

21:15 ⁱ ver 9; S Mt 9:27 ʲ Lk 19:39
21:16 ᵏ Ps 8:2
21:17 ˡ Mt 26:6; Mk 11:1; Lk 24:50; Jn 11:1,18; 12:1
21:19 ᵐ Isa 34:4; Jer 8:13
21:21 ⁿ Mt 17:20; Lk 17:6; 1Co 13:2; Jas 1:6
21:22 ᵒ S Mt 7:7
21:23 ᵖ Ac 4:7; 7:27
21:26 ᑫ S Mt 11:9
21:28 ʳ ver 33; Mt 20:1
21:31 ˢ Lk 7:29 ᵗ Lk 7:50
21:32 ᵘ Mt 3:1-12 ᵛ Lk 3:12,13; 7:29 ʷ Lk 7:36-50 ˣ Lk 7:30
21:33 ʸ Ps 80:8 ᶻ Isa 5:1-7 ᵃ Mt 25:14,15
21:34 ᵇ Mt 22:3
21:35 ᶜ 2Ch 24:21; Mt 23:34,37; Heb 11:36,37
21:36 ᵈ Mt 22:4

R Mt 18:35 ◀ ▶ Mt 26:75
S Mt 19:16–21 ◀ ▶ Mt 21:34
F Mt 11:12 ◀ ▶ Mk 1:15
L Mt 20:1–14 ◀ ▶ Mt 22:9–10
S Mt 21:28–31 ◀ ▶ Mt 21:41

L Mt 18:19–20 ◀ ▶ Mt 28:20

/16 Psalm 8:2

the tenants treated them the same way. ³⁷Last of all, he sent his son to them. 'They will respect my son,' he said.

³⁸"But when the tenants saw the son, they said to each other, 'This is the heir.ᵉ Come, let's kill himᶠ and take his inheritance.'ᵍ ³⁹So they took him and threw him out of the vineyard and killed him.

⁴⁰"Therefore, when the owner of the vineyard comes, what will he do to those tenants?"

⁴¹"He will bring those wretches to a wretched end,"ʰ they replied, "and he will rent the vineyard to other tenants,ⁱ who will give him his share of the crop at harvest time."

⁴²Jesus said to them, "Have you never read in the Scriptures:

" 'The stone the builders rejected
  has become the capstoneᵏ;
the Lord has done this,
  and it is marvelous in our eyes'ʲ?ʲ

⁴³"Therefore I tell you that the kingdom of God will be taken away from youᵏ and given to a people who will produce its fruit. ⁴⁴He who falls on this stone will be broken to pieces, but he on whom it falls will be crushed."ᵐˡ

⁴⁵When the chief priests and the Pharisees heard Jesus' parables, they knew he was talking about them. ⁴⁶They looked for a way to arrest him, but they were afraid of the crowd because the people held that he was a prophet.ᵐ

21:38 ᵉ Heb 1:2
ᶠ S Mt 12:14 ᵍ Ps 2:8
21:41 ʰ Mt 8:11,
12 ⁱ S Ac 13:46
21:42 ʲ Ps 118:22,
23; S Ac 4:11
21:43 ᵏ Mt 8:12
21:44 ⁱ S Lk 2:34
21:46 ᵐ S ver 11, 26
22:2 ⁿ S Mt 13:24
22:3 ᵒ Mt 21:34
22:4 ᵖ Mt 21:36
22:7 ᵠ Lk 19:27
22:9 ʳ Eze 21:21
22:10 ˢ Mt 13:47, 48

M Mt 21:5 ◀ ▶ Mt 22:44
G Mal 1:11 ◀ ▶ Mt 21:43
R Mt 15:23–27 ◀ ▶ Mt 21:43
S Mt 21:34 ◀ ▶ Mt 22:36–40
G Mt 21:41 ◀ ▶ Mt 22:9–10
R Mt 21:41 ◀ ▶ Mt 22:7–8
H Mt 18:6–9 ◀ ▶ Mt 22:7
N Mt 13:13–15 ◀ ▶ Mt 22:1–7

The Parable of the Wedding Banquet
22:2–14Ref — Lk 14:16–24

22 Jesus spoke to them again in parables, saying: ²"The kingdom of heaven is likeⁿ a king who prepared a wedding banquet for his son. ³He sent his servantsᵒ to those who had been invited to the banquet to tell them to come, but they refused to come.

⁴"Then he sent some more servantsᵖ and said, 'Tell those who have been invited that I have prepared my dinner: My oxen and fattened cattle have been butchered, and everything is ready. Come to the wedding banquet.'

⁵"But they paid no attention and went off—one to his field, another to his business. ⁶The rest seized his servants, mistreated them and killed them. ⁷The king was enraged. He sent his army and destroyed those murderersᵠ and burned their city.

⁸"Then he said to his servants, 'The wedding banquet is ready, but those I invited did not deserve to come. ⁹Go to the street cornersʳ and invite to the banquet anyone you find.' ¹⁰So the servants went out into the streets and gathered all the people they could find, both good and bad,ˢ and the wedding hall was filled with guests.

N Mt 21:44 ◀ ▶ Mt 23:37–38
W Mt 20:1–16 ◀ ▶ Mk 3:28
H Isa 26:20–21 ◀ ▶ Mt 22:8–10
R Mt 21:43 ◀ ▶ Mt 23:37–39
H Mt 21:44 ◀ ▶ Mt 22:11–13
H Mt 22:2–3 ◀ ▶ Mt 22:14
G Mt 21:43 ◀ ▶ Mk 12:9
L Mt 21:31–32 ◀ ▶ Mt 23:37

ᵏ 42 Or *cornerstone* ˡ 42 Psalm 118:22,23 ᵐ 44 Some manuscripts do not have verse 44.

21:37–43 This prophetic parable foretells the rejection and crucifixion of the Messiah by the people of Israel. Jesus said that God would respond to Israel's rejection of his Son by rejecting Israel for a time and turning his kingdom over to "other tenants" (21:41)—a reference to the church, which is composed mainly of Gentiles.

22:2–14 Jesus continues his prophetic parables about the kingdom of heaven by comparing it to a marriage supper given for the son of a great king. Those who received the king's invitation "paid no attention and went off" (22:5). The king destroyed those who held his invitation in such contempt and sent his servants to invite "anyone you find" (22:9) to attend the marriage supper. Clearly this parable illustrates that God turned from Israel when they rejected his Son and instead offered the "wedding supper of the Lamb" (Rev 19:9) to all who would repent of their sins and trust in Christ for their salvation.

¹¹"But when the king came in to see the guests, he noticed a man there who was not wearing wedding clothes. ¹²'Friend,' he asked, 'how did you get in here without wedding clothes?' The man was speechless.

¹³"Then the king told the attendants, 'Tie him hand and foot, and throw him outside, into the darkness, where there will be weeping and gnashing of teeth.'

¹⁴"For many are invited, but few are chosen."

Paying Taxes to Caesar
22:15–22pp — Mk 12:13–17; Lk 20:20–26

¹⁵Then the Pharisees went out and laid plans to trap him in his words. ¹⁶They sent their disciples to him along with the Herodians. "Teacher," they said, "we know you are a man of integrity and that you teach the way of God in accordance with the truth. You aren't swayed by men, because you pay no attention to who they are. ¹⁷Tell us then, what is your opinion? Is it right to pay taxes to Caesar or not?"

¹⁸But Jesus, knowing their evil intent, said, "You hypocrites, why are you trying to trap me? ¹⁹Show me the coin used for paying the tax." They brought him a denarius, ²⁰and he asked them, "Whose portrait is this? And whose inscription?"

²¹"Caesar's," they replied.

Then he said to them, "Give to Caesar what is Caesar's, and to God what is God's."

²²When they heard this, they were amazed. So they left him and went away.

22:12 Mt 20:13; 26:50
22:13 S Mt 8:12
22:14 Rev 17:14
22:16 Mk 3:6
22:17 Mt 17:25
22:21 Ro 13:7
22:22 Mk 12:12
22:23 a S Ac 4:1; b Ac 23:8; 1Co 15:12
22:24 Dt 25:5,6
22:29 Jn 20:9
22:30 Mt 24:38
22:32 Ex 3:6; Ac 7:32
22:33 S Mt 7:28
22:34 S Ac 4:1
22:35 Lk 7:30; 10:25; 11:45; 14:3

A Mt 12:30 ◀▶ Lk 11:23
C Mt 18:12–14 ◀▶ Mt 23:17
G Mt 15:8–9 ◀▶ Mt 25:3
H Mt 22:7 ◀▶ Mt 22:44
O Mt 18:18 ◀▶ Mt 25:1–12
H Mt 22:8–10 ◀▶ Mt 25:1–13

Marriage at the Resurrection
22:23–33pp — Mk 12:18–27; Lk 20:27–40

²³That same day the Sadducees, who say there is no resurrection, came to him with a question. ²⁴"Teacher," they said, "Moses told us that if a man dies without having children, his brother must marry the widow and have children for him. ²⁵Now there were seven brothers among us. The first one married and died, and since he had no children, he left his wife to his brother. ²⁶The same thing happened to the second and third brother, right on down to the seventh. ²⁷Finally, the woman died. ²⁸Now then, at the resurrection, whose wife will she be of the seven, since all of them were married to her?"

²⁹Jesus replied, "You are in error because you do not know the Scriptures or the power of God. ³⁰At the resurrection people will neither marry nor be given in marriage; they will be like the angels in heaven. ³¹But about the resurrection of the dead—have you not read what God said to you, ³²'I am the God of Abraham, the God of Isaac, and the God of Jacob'? He is not the God of the dead but of the living."

³³When the crowds heard this, they were astonished at his teaching.

The Greatest Commandment
22:34–40pp — Mk 12:28–31

³⁴Hearing that Jesus had silenced the Sadducees, the Pharisees got together. ³⁵One of them, an expert in the law, tested him with this question: ³⁶"Teacher, which is the greatest commandment in the Law?"

³⁷Jesus replied: " 'Love the Lord your God with all your heart and with all your

F Hos 13:14 ◀▶ Mk 12:24–25
S Mt 21:41 ◀▶ Mt 24:13

n 32 Exodus 3:6

22:29–32 The Sadducees denied the possibility of bodily resurrection, taught the annihilation of the soul at death and rejected any portion of Scripture except the five books of Moses. Jesus answered their question about the resurrection by quoting Moses' words from Ex 3:6 that affirmed the spiritual existence of Abraham, Isaac and Jacob centuries after their physical deaths.

The Sadducees then asked a hypothetical question about a woman who died after marrying and being widowed by a series of seven brothers (see Dt 25:5). Their question concerned the law of levirate marriage that assured the preservation of both inherited land and the lineage of a departed brother. Jesus answered their specific question by declaring that marriage will not exist in the resurrection, either for angels or for believers.

soul and with all your mind.'ᵒʲ ³⁸This is the first and greatest commandment. ³⁹And the second is like it: 'Love your neighbor as yourself.'ᵖᵏ ⁴⁰All the Law and the Prophets hang on these two commandments."ˡ

Whose Son Is the Christ?
22:41–46pp — Mk 12:35–37; Lk 20:41–44

⁴¹While the Pharisees were gathered together, Jesus asked them, ⁴²"What do you think about the Christᑫ? Whose son is he?"

"The son of David,"ᵐ they replied.

⁴³He said to them, "How is it then that David, speaking by the Spirit, calls him 'Lord'? For he says,

⁴⁴ " 'The Lord said to my Lord:
"Sit at my right hand
until I put your enemies
under your feet." 'ʳⁿ

⁴⁵If then David calls him 'Lord,' how can he be his son? ⁴⁶No one could say a word in reply, and from that day on no one dared to ask him any more questions.ᵒ

Seven Woes
23:1–7pp — Mk 12:38,39; Lk 20:45,46
23:37–39pp — Lk 13:34,35

23 Then Jesus said to the crowds and to his disciples, ²"The teachers of the lawᵖ and the Pharisees sit in Moses' seat. ³So you must obey them and do everything they tell you. But do not do what they do, for they do not practice what they preach. ⁴They tie up heavy loads and put them on men's shoulders, but they themselves are not willing to lift a finger to move them.ᑫ

⁵"Everything they do is done for men to see:ʳ They make their phylacteriesˢˢ wide and the tassels on their garmentsᵗ long; ⁶they love the place of honor at banquets and the most important seats in the synagogues;ᵘ ⁷they love to be greeted in the marketplaces and to have men call them 'Rabbi.'ᵛ

⁸"But you are not to be called 'Rabbi,' for you have only one Master and you are all brothers. ⁹And do not call anyone on earth 'father,' for you have one Father,ʷ and he is in heaven. ¹⁰Nor are you to be called 'teacher,' for you have one Teacher, the Christ.ᑫ ¹¹The greatest among you will be your servant.ˣ ¹²For whoever exalts himself will be humbled, and whoever humbles himself will be exalted.ʸ

¹³"Woe to you, teachers of the law and Pharisees, you hypocrites!ᶻ You shut the kingdom of heaven in men's faces. You yourselves do not enter, nor will you let those enter who are trying to.ᵗᵃ

¹⁵"Woe to you, teachers of the law and Pharisees, you hypocrites! You travel over land and sea to win a single convert,ᵇ and when he becomes one, you make him twice as much a son of hellᶜ as you are.

¹⁶"Woe to you, blind guides!ᵈ You say, 'If anyone swears by the temple, it means nothing; but if anyone swears by the gold of the temple, he is bound by his oath.'ᵉ ¹⁷You blind fools! Which is greater: the gold, or the temple that makes the gold sacred?ᶠ ¹⁸You also say, 'If anyone swears by the altar, it means nothing; but if anyone swears by the gift on it, he is bound by his oath.' ¹⁹You blind men! Which is greater: the gift, or the altar that makes the gift sacred?ᵍ ²⁰Therefore, he who swears by the altar swears by it and by everything on it. ²¹And he who swears by

---

22:37 Dt 6:5
22:39 ᵏ Lev 19:18; S Mt 5:43
22:40 ˡ Mt 7:12; Lk 10:25-28
22:42 ᵐ S Mt 9:27
22:44 ⁿ Ps 110:1; 1Ki 5:3; Ac 2:34, 35; 1Co 15:25; Heb 1:13; 10:13
22:46 ᵒ Mk 12:34; Lk 20:40
23:2 ᵖ Ezr 7:6,25
23:4 ᑫ Lk 11:46; Ac 15:10; Gal 6:13
23:5 ʳ Mt 6:1,2,5, 16; Ex 13:9; Dt 6:8
ᵗ Nu 15:38; Dt 22:12
23:6 ᵘ Lk 11:43; 14:7; 20:46
23:7 ᵛ ver 12; Mt 26:25,49; Mk 9:5; 10:51; Jn 1:38,49; 3:2,26; 20:16
23:9 ʷ Mal 1:6; Mt 6:9; 7:11
23:11 ˣ S Mk 9:35
23:12 ʸ Isa 2:8; Ps 18:27; Pr 3:34; Isa 57:15; Eze 21:26; Lk 1:52; 14:11
23:13 ᶻ ver 15,23, 25,27,29 a Lk 11:52
23:15 ᵇ Ac 2:11; 6:5; 13:43
ᶜ S Mt 5:22
23:16 ᵈ ver 24; Isa 9:16; Mt 15:14
ᵉ Mt 5:33-35
23:17 ᶠ Ex 30:29
23:19 ᵍ Ex 29:37

M Mt 19:23–24 ◄ ► Mk 10:14–15
H Mt 22:44 ◄ ► Mt 23:33
C Mt 22:11–14 ◄ ► Mt 23:19
C Mt 23:17 ◄ ► Mt 23:25–28

ᵒ 37 Deut. 6:5 ᵖ 39 Lev. 19:18 ᑫ 42,10 Or *Messiah* ʳ 44 Psalm 110:1
ˢ 5 That is, boxes containing Scripture verses, worn on forehead and arm
ᵗ 13 Some manuscripts to. ¹⁴*Woe to you, teachers of the law and Pharisees, you hypocrites! You devour widows' houses and for a show make lengthy prayers. Therefore you will be punished more severely.*

E Mt 12:28 ◄ ► Mk 1:10
T Mt 10:19–20 ◄ ► Mk 12:36
M Mt 21:38 ◄ ► Mt 25:21
V Zec 9:10 ◄ ► Mk 12:36
H Mt 22:11–13 ◄ ► Mt 23:15

22:44 Jesus asked the Pharisees a question about the Messiah that they were unable to answer. He did so to demonstrate that the Messiah is both the Son of David and the Son of God at the same time, thus revealing the divine nature of the Messiah. King David acknowledged that God the Father told the Messiah (Jesus Christ) to "sit at my right hand until I make your enemies a footstool for your feet" (Ps 110:1). This prophecy also foreshadows the final triumph of the Messiah over all his enemies in the millennial kingdom following the Battle of Armageddon.

the temple swears by it and by the one who dwells[h] in it. ²²And he who swears by heaven swears by God's throne and by the one who sits on it.[i]

²³"Woe to you, teachers of the law and Pharisees, you hypocrites! You give a tenth[j] of your spices—mint, dill and cummin. But you have neglected the more important matters of the law—justice, mercy and faithfulness.[k] You should have practiced the latter, without neglecting the former. ²⁴You blind guides![l] You strain out a gnat but swallow a camel.

²⁵"Woe to you, teachers of the law and Pharisees, you hypocrites! You clean the outside of the cup and dish,[m] but inside they are full of greed and self-indulgence.[n] ²⁶Blind Pharisee! First clean the inside of the cup and dish, and then the outside also will be clean.

²⁷"Woe to you, teachers of the law and Pharisees, you hypocrites! You are like whitewashed tombs,[o] which look beautiful on the outside but on the inside are full of dead men's bones and everything unclean. ²⁸In the same way, on the outside you appear to people as righteous but on the inside you are full of hypocrisy and wickedness.

²⁹"Woe to you, teachers of the law and Pharisees, you hypocrites! You build tombs for the prophets[p] and decorate the graves of the righteous. ³⁰And you say, 'If we had lived in the days of our forefathers, we would not have taken part with them in shedding the blood of the prophets.' ³¹So you testify against yourselves that you are the descendants of those who murdered the prophets.[q] ³²Fill up,

C *Mt 23:19* ◀ ▶ *Mt 23:33*

23:21 h 1Ki 8:13; Ps 26:8
23:22 i Ps 11:4; Mt 5:34
23:23 j Lev 27:30 k Mic 6:8; Lk 11:42
23:24 l ver 16
23:25 m Mk 7:4 n Lk 11:39
23:27 o Lk 11:44; Ac 23:3
23:29 p Lk 11:47, 48
23:31 q S Mt 5:12
23:32 r 1Th 2:16 s Eze 20:4
23:33 t Mt 3:7; 12:34 u S Mt 5:22
23:34 v 2Ch 36:15, 16; Lk 11:49 w S Mt 10:17 x Mt 10:23
23:35 y Ge 4:8; Heb 11:4 z Zec 1:1 a 2Ch 24:21
23:36 b Mt 10:23; 24:34; Lk 11:50,51
23:37 c 2Ch 24:21; S Mt 5:12 d Ps 57:1; 61:4; Isa 31:5
23:38 e 1Ki 9:7,8; Jer 22:5
23:39 f Ps 118:26; Mt 21:9

then, the measure[r] of the sin of your forefathers![s]

³³"You snakes! You brood of vipers! **C** How will you escape being condemned **H** to hell?[t] ³⁴Therefore I am sending you prophets and wise men and teachers. Some of them you will kill and crucify;[v] others you will flog in your synagogues[w] and pursue from town to town.[x] ³⁵And so upon you will come all the righteous blood that has been shed on earth, from the blood of righteous Abel[y] to the blood of Zechariah son of Berekiah,[z] whom you murdered between the temple and the altar.[a] ³⁶I tell you the truth, all this will come upon this generation.[b]

³⁷"O Jerusalem, Jerusalem, you who **R** kill the prophets and stone those sent to **L** you,[c] how often I have longed to gather **N** your children together, as a hen gathers her chicks under her wings,[d] but you were not willing. ³⁸Look, your house is left to you desolate.[e] ³⁹For I tell you, you will not see me again until you say, 'Blessed is he who comes in the name of the Lord.'[u] [f]

Signs of the End of the Age
24:1–51pp — Mk 13:1–37; Lk 21:5–36

24 Jesus left the temple and was **R** walking away when his disciples came up to him to call his attention to its buildings. ²"Do you see all these things?" he asked. "I tell you the truth, not one

C *Mt 23:25–28* ◀ ▶ *Mt 25:2–3*
H *Mt 23:15* ◀ ▶ *Mt 24:21*
R *Mt 22:7–8* ◀ ▶ *Mt 24:1–3*
L *Mt 22:9–10* ◀ ▶ *Mk 2:17*
N *Mt 22:1–7* ◀ ▶ *Mt 24:43–44*
R *Mt 23:37–39* ◀ ▶ *Mt 24:15–22*

a 39 Psalm 118:26

23:37–39 As Jesus came to the close of his earthly ministry, he pronounced a terrible prophecy on Jerusalem that was tragically fulfilled when the Roman legions burned the temple and city to the ground in A.D. 70. Jesus also announced that the Jews would not see him again until they repented of their sins and acknowledged the return of their Messiah. This prophecy will be fulfilled when Christ triumphantly returns to save Israel from the antichrist at the Battle of Armageddon. Zechariah confirmed this prophetic picture of the repentance of Israel and says their eyes will finally be opened to see Jesus as their true Messiah (see Zec 12:9–11).

24:1–3 Jesus left the temple, knowing that it was destined to certain destruction within that generation because the Jews had rejected Jesus as their Messiah. The disciples wondered aloud when this terrible judgment would fall on the temple. Jesus gave a clear answer that was recorded in Lk 21:20–24. Then the disciples asked Jesus two additional questions regarding the signs of his second coming and the signs of the end of the world. The balance of Mt 24 reveals Jesus' detailed answer to these questions.

In order to understand the meaning of Jesus' prophetic signs in this chapter we must remember that this discourse occurred before the crucifixion. The Gentile church of believers did not exist yet.

stone here will be left on another;^g every one will be thrown down."

C
E ³As Jesus was sitting on the Mount of Olives,^h the disciples came to him privately. "Tell us," they said, "when will this happen, and what will be the sign of your comingⁱ and of the end of the age?"^j

⁴Jesus answered: "Watch out that no one deceives you.^k ⁵For many will come in my name, claiming, 'I am the Christ,'^v and will deceive many.^l ⁶You will hear of wars and rumors of wars, but see to it that you are not alarmed. Such things must happen, but the end is still to come."

24:2 ^g Lk 19:44
24:3 ^h S Mt 21:1
ⁱ S Lk 17:30
^j Mt 13:39; 28:20
24:4 ^k S Mk 13:5
24:5 ^l ver 11,23,24; 1Jn 2:18
24:7 ^m Isa 19:2
ⁿ Ac 11:28
24:9 ^o Mt 10:17
^p Jn 16:2
^q S Jn 15:21

⁷Nation will rise against nation, and kingdom against kingdom.^m There will be faminesⁿ and earthquakes in various places. ⁸All these are the beginning of birth pains.

⁹"Then you will be handed over to be persecuted^o and put to death,^p and you will be hated by all nations because of me.^q ¹⁰At that time many will turn away from the faith and will betray and hate each other, ¹¹and many false prophets^r will appear and deceive many people.^s ¹²Because of the increase of wickedness, the love of most will grow cold, ¹³but he **S**

C *Mt 16:27–28* ◀▶ *Mt 24:26–27*
E *Mt 16:3* ◀▶ *Mt 24:32–33*

24:11 ^r S Mt 7:15
^s S Mk 13:5

S *Mt 22:36–40* ◀▶ *Mt 24:48–51*

^v 5 Or *Messiah*; also in verse 23

Jesus was speaking primarily to his Jewish followers and warning of the prophetic signs that would occur just prior to his second coming.

24:4–5 Significantly, the first sign of Christ's return is the rise of false Christs who "will deceive many" (24:5). Throughout history impostors and delusional fanatics have arisen and claimed to be the Messiah. In our generation alone we have seen an explosion of those claiming to be Jesus Christ, including David Koresh, Sun Myung Moon and the Lord Maitreya.

24:6 Jesus also warned about the increase of wars before his second coming (see Joel 3:9–10). Statistics show that over the centuries our planet has endured 13 years of war for every year of peace. Despite the numerous peace and disarmament treaties enacted since 1945, we have not known a single day of worldwide peace but rather have experienced more wars than any other generation in history. Despite the growing dangers of war, Jesus told his followers not to be troubled because "the end is still to come."

24:7–8 Jesus also warned that a series of cataclysmic natural phenomena would characterize his imminent return. Famine, pestilence and earthquakes would not only increase in frequency in the last days; they would also occur in different or unusual places. Note the following statistics that herald the fulfillment of this prophecy.

Famine: Millions are at risk of famine in this decade in central Africa, India, North Korea and China. Many other nations are unable to properly feed their people due to the decreasing amounts of agricultural lands, increasing amounts of deserts and the soaring growth of their populations. Diminished food resources will be overwhelmed during the tribulation when worldwide famine destroys millions of lives (see Rev 6:5–6).

Earthquakes: Killer earthquakes (6.5 or higher on the Richter scale) occurred only once every decade during the 1800s. According to current statistics, the number of these major earthquakes has increased to over 100 in this decade alone.

Pestilence: Worldwide pestilence would also signal Jesus' return. In the past twenty years, according to the World Health Organization (WHO), health professionals have diagnosed more than 25 infectious diseases with no known treatment or cure. These have come about as a result of the ease of travel between nations, poor sanitation, growing urbanization and overpopulation. Sexually transmitted diseases are increasing, causing sterility and death. Recent studies predict that AIDS may wipe out as much as one quarter of the global population (see Rev 6:8).

Jesus warns that these terrible judgments will only set the stage for the terrible judgments of the tribulation.

24:9–12 Jesus warned that his followers would be subject to extreme persecution and martyrdom because of a profound hatred of Jesus by the religious authorities. This prophecy was initially fulfilled during the first wave of persecution by the Jewish authorities during the first century but will find its final fulfillment in the terrible persecution of the tribulation.

Because of this persecution in the last days, many will turn from their faith and betray other believers. Jesus also warned of the proliferation of false prophets and the tragic alienation of affection between people. In our generation we have seen an astonishing rise of false prophets, telepaths and cults. The growing litany of child abuse, spousal battery and abuse of the elderly reflects the widespread iniquity of our time.

24:13–14 Despite the coming trials and persecutions, Jesus promised that those who remained faithful would be saved. The generation of the last days would witness the gospel being preached in an unprecedented way throughout the world. Only then would the end come. The spectacular growth of the church in our generation is one of the great signs of

who stands firm to the end will be saved. ⁱ ¹⁴And this gospel of the kingdom ᵘ will be preached in the whole world ᵛ as a testimony to all nations, and then the end will come.

R ¹⁵"So when you see standing in the holy place ʷ 'the abomination that causes desolation,'ʷˣ spoken of through the prophet Daniel—let the reader understand— ¹⁶then let those who are in Judea flee to the mountains. ¹⁷Let no one on the roof of his house ʸ go down to take anything out of the house. ¹⁸Let no one in the field go back to get his cloak. ¹⁹How dreadful it will be in those days for pregnant women and nursing mothers! ²⁰Pray that your flight will not take place **H** in winter or on the Sabbath. ²¹For then there will be great distress, unequaled from the beginning of the world until now—and never to be equaled again.ᵃ ²²If those days had not been cut short, no one would survive, but for the sake of the elect ᵇ those days will be shortened. ²³At that time if anyone says to you, 'Look, here is the Christ!' or, 'There he is!' do not believe it.ᶜ ²⁴For false Christs and false prophets will appear and perform great signs and miracles ᵈ to deceive even the elect—if that were possible. ²⁵See, I have told you ahead of time.

C ²⁶"So if anyone tells you, 'There he is, out in the desert,' do not go out; or, 'Here he is, in the inner rooms,' do not believe it. ²⁷For as lightning ᵉ that comes from the east is visible even in the west, so will be the coming ᶠ of the Son of Man. ᵍ ²⁸Wherever there is a carcass, there the vultures will gather.ʰ

C ²⁹"Immediately after the distress of those days

" 'the sun will be darkened,
    and the moon will not give its light;
the stars will fall from the sky,
    and the heavenly bodies will be
        shaken.'ˣⁱ

³⁰"At that time the sign of the Son of Man will appear in the sky, and all the nations of the earth will mourn.ʲ They will see the Son of Man coming on the clouds of the sky,ᵏ with power and great glory. ³¹And he will send his angels ˡ with **T**

24:13 ᵗS Mt 10:22
24:14 ᵘS Mt 4:23
ᵛS Ro 10:18;
Lk 2:1; 4:5;
Ac 11:28; 17:6;
Rev 3:10; 16:14
24:15 ʷS Ac 6:13
ˣDa 9:27; 11:31;
12:11
24:17 ʸ1Sa 9:25;
Mt 10:27; Lk 12:3;
Ac 10:9
24:19 ᶻLk 23:29
24:21 ᵃEze 5:9;
Da 12:1; Joel 2:2
24:22 ᵇver 24,31
24:23 ᶜLk 17:23;
21:8
24:24 ᵈEx 7:11,
22; 2Th 2:9-11;
Rev 13:13; 16:14;
19:20
24:27 ᵉLk 17:24
ᶠS Lk 17:30
ᵍS Mt 8:20
24:28 ʰLk 17:37
24:29 ⁱIsa 13:10;
34:4; Eze 32:7;
Joel 2:10,31;
Zep 1:15; Rev 6:12,
13; 8:12
24:30 ʲRev 1:7
ᵏS Rev 1:7
24:31 ˡMt 13:41

C Mt 24:3 ◄► Mt 24:29-33
C Mt 24:26-27 ◄► Mt 24:36-51
T Mt 13:30 ◄► Lk 17:34-35

R Mt 24:1-3 ◄► Mk 12:9
H Mt 23:33 ◄► Mt 24:50-51

ʷ15 Daniel 9:27; 11:31; 12:11   ˣ29 Isaiah 13:10; 34:4

---

the nearness of Christ's return. Some studies indicate that one person in ten of the world's population today is a Christian. "Come, Lord Jesus" (Rev 22:20).

24:15—19 At the beginning of the great tribulation, when the antichrist breaks his seven-year treaty with Israel, defiles the rebuilt temple and establishes the mark of the beast, Jesus will give his followers a warning sign, the sign of the prophet Daniel (see Da 9:27; 12:11). When believers become aware of the antichrist's abomination, Jesus warns them to quickly run into the hills of Judea because the terrible wrath of God will soon be poured out on unrepentant sinners.

24:20 If this abomination occurred during the winter or on the Sabbath, escape would be much more difficult. The ancient Jews observed an orthodox ritual that prohibited travel on the Sabbath to no more than 1000 yards beyond the walls of Jerusalem lest they violate the injunction against working on the Sabbath (see Ex 16:29). This distance was considered a "Sabbath day's walk" (Ac 1:12). This verse carries added weight today as orthodox Jews become more powerful in the Israeli government and urge the reinstitution of stringent Sabbath laws to restrict Sabbath-day activities of the people.

24:21—22 Jesus warned that the tribulation to come would be unprecedented in its terror and destructiveness. All of humanity would be destroyed unless those days were shortened for the sake of the people of God. These are the tribulation saints saved during the period that follows the rapture of the church. The OT usage of the word for these "elect" or "chosen" ones clearly applies to the Jews in Isa 45:4; 65:9; 65:22.

24:23—27 Jesus warned against anyone believing another's claim that they had seen Christ. This prophetic warning should alert anyone to the claims of false messiahs. Jesus warned that these false Christs would produce deceptive signs that would be so amazing that they could even deceive, "if that were possible" (24:24), the people of God. When Jesus truly returns, his coming will be as spectacular and unmistakable as lightning. He will appear in the sky exactly as he ascended almost 2000 years ago (see Ac 1:11).

24:28 This prophecy may refer to the terrible aftermath of Armageddon when God will gather the birds of prey to eat the bodies of the dead (see Rev 19:17-18 and Job 39:30).

24:31 When Christ comes, he will send his angels to gather the "elect" from all over the world. These "elect" ones are the saints who come to faith in Christ during the terrible persecution of the tribulation. This gathering of the "elect" is a different event

a loud trumpet call,ᵐ and they will gather his elect from the four winds, from one end of the heavens to the other.

E ³²"Now learn this lesson from the fig tree: As soon as its twigs get tender and its leaves come out, you know that summer is near. ³³Even so, when you see all these things, you know that it⁷ is near, right at the door.ⁿ ³⁴I tell you the truth, this generation² will certainly not pass away until all these things have hap-
K pened.° ³⁵Heaven and earth will pass away, but my words will never pass away.ᵖ

The Day and Hour Unknown
24:37–39pp — Lk 17:26,27
24:45–51pp — Lk 12:42–46

C ³⁶"No one knows about that day or hour, not even the angels in heaven, nor the Son,ᵃ but only the Father.ᑫ ³⁷As it was in the days of Noah,ʳ so it will be at the coming of the Son of Man. ³⁸For in the days before the flood, people were eating and drinking, marrying and giving in marriage,ˢ up to the day Noah entered the ark; ³⁹and they knew nothing about what would happen until the flood came and took them all away. That is how it will be at the coming of the Son of Man.ᵗ ⁴⁰Two men will be in the field; one will be taken and the other left.ᵘ ⁴¹Two women will be grinding with a hand mill; one will be taken and the other left.ᵛ

⁴²"Therefore keep watch, because you do not know on what day your Lord will come.ʷ ⁴³But understand this: If the N owner of the house had known at what time of night the thief was coming,ˣ he would have kept watch and would not have let his house be broken into. ⁴⁴So you also must be ready,ʸ because the Son of Man will come at an hour when you do not expect him.

⁴⁵"Who then is the faithful and wise servant,ᶻ whom the master has put in charge of the servants in his household to

---

24:31 ᵐ Isa 27:13; Zec 9:14; 1Co 15:52; 1Th 4:16; Rev 8:2; 10:7; 11:15
24:33 ⁿ Jas 5:9
24:34 ° Mt 16:28; S 23:36
24:35 ᵖ S Mt 5:18
24:36 ᑫ Ac 1:7
24:37 ʳ Ge 6:5; 7:6-23
24:38 ˢ Mt 22:30
24:39 ᵗ S Lk 17:30
24:40 ᵘ Lk 17:34
24:41 ᵛ Lk 17:35
24:42 ʷ Mt 25:13; Lk 12:40
24:43 ˣ S Lk 12:39
24:44 ʸ 1Th 5:6
24:45 ᶻ Mt 25:21, 23

E Mt 24:3–6 ◄ ► Mk 13:5–13
K Mt 19:26 ◄ ► Mt 28:18
C Mt 24:29–33 ◄ ► Mt 25:1–13

N Mt 23:37–38 ◄ ► Mt 24:50–51

ʸ 33 Or he ᶻ 34 Or race ᵃ 36 Some manuscripts do not have *nor the Son.*

---

from the translation of the saints described by Paul in 1Co 15:51. Note that the angels gather these "elect," while the rapture that Paul describes indicates that the saints will rise in their resurrection bodies to meet Christ in the air (see 1Th 4:16–17). Also note that this gathering in Mt 24:31 does not mention any change in anyone's physical bodies, but the transformation to a resurrection body occurs at the rapture of the church saints prior to the tribulation.

The purposes of these two gatherings are different too. Christ will gather the "elect" to protect the tribulation saints from the wrath of God that is about to be poured out from heaven upon unrepentant sinners. The purpose of the rapture is to clothe the Christian saints, living and departed, with a glorious resurrection body like the body Jesus had when he rose from the dead (see Ro 8:22–23; Php 3:20–21; 1Jn 3:2).

24:32–35 The example of the fig tree reminded Jesus' followers to stay alert and observant. Just as the fig tree indicated the seasons by its foliage, so God's people could recognize the imminence of Christ's return by the fulfillment of these signs.

Jesus' use of the phrase "this generation will certainly not pass away" (24:34) has caused some discussion among scholars about the length of time in a "generation." In the OT, Scripture uses this term to indicate time periods of about 40 years (illustrated by the reigns of Saul, David and Solomon), 100 years (see Ge 15:13–14) and 70–80 years (a natural lifetime; Ps 90:10). The NT most often uses this term to refer to a group of people living at one particular time. The understanding in this passage is that the generation alive to witness the rebirth of Israel will still be alive when Jesus returns to establish his kingdom. Jesus also affirms that his words are more certain than the existence of the universe.

24:36 Jesus declared that only the Father knew when Christ would return. Jesus voluntarily limited his supernatural knowledge while incarnated in his human body during his earthly ministry. Yet Jesus, the Holy Spirit and the Father are three persons of the one God. Therefore, after Jesus' ascent to heaven, he possesses the knowledge of the time of his return.

24:37–51 The balance of this prophetic discourse describes the conditions in the last days and Jesus' instructions to his followers. Jesus warns that, just as in Noah's day, widespread violence, corruption and evil will characterize life on earth. As humanity rejected God's prophetic warnings from Noah, our generation has dismissed the warnings associated with Christ's return. Jesus warned that his judgment would separate the wicked from the repentant, without warning, like the unexpected appearance of a thief. Jesus challenged his followers to stay alert and faithful to the Master. Those who forget the Lord's coming will be cast into hell.

give them their food at the proper time? ⁴⁶It will be good for that servant whose master finds him doing so when he returns.ᵃ ⁴⁷I tell you the truth, he will put him in charge of all his possessions.ᵇ ⁴⁸But suppose that servant is wicked and says to himself, 'My master is staying away a long time,' ⁴⁹and he then begins to beat his fellow servants and to eat and drink with drunkards.ᶜ ⁵⁰The master of that servant will come on a day when he does not expect him and at an hour he is not aware of. ⁵¹He will cut him to pieces and assign him a place with the hypocrites, where there will be weeping and gnashing of teeth.ᵈ

The Parable of the Ten Virgins

25 "At that time the kingdom of heaven will be likeᵉ ten virgins who took their lampsᶠ and went out to meet the bridegroom.ᵍ ²Five of them were foolish and five were wise.ʰ ³The foolish ones took their lamps but did not take any oil with them. ⁴The wise, however, took oil in jars along with their lamps. ⁵The bridegroom was a long time in coming, and they all became drowsy and fell asleep.ⁱ

⁶"At midnight the cry rang out: 'Here's the bridegroom! Come out to meet him!'

⁷"Then all the virgins woke up and trimmed their lamps. ⁸The foolish ones said to the wise, 'Give us some of your oil; our lamps are going out.'ʲ

⁹"'No,' they replied, 'there may not be enough for both us and you. Instead, go to those who sell oil and buy some for yourselves.'

¹⁰"But while they were on their way to buy the oil, the bridegroom arrived. The virgins who were ready went in with him to the wedding banquet.ᵏ And the door was shut.

¹¹"Later the others also came. 'Sir! Sir!' they said. 'Open the door for us!'

¹²"But he replied, 'I tell you the truth, I don't know you.'ˡ

¹³"Therefore keep watch, because you do not know the day or the hour.ᵐ

The Parable of the Talents
25:14–30Ref – Lk 19:12–27

¹⁴"Again, it will be like a man going on a journey,ⁿ who called his servants and entrusted his property to them. ¹⁵To one he gave five talentsᵇ of money, to another two talents, and to another one talent, each according to his ability.ᵒ Then he went on his journey. ¹⁶The man who had

---

Cross references:
- S Mt 24:13 ◀▶ Mt 25:24–30
- P Mt 13:47–50 ◀▶ Lk 12:45–47
- H Mt 24:21 ◀▶ Mt 25:30–46
- N Mt 24:43–44 ◀▶ Mt 25:10–11
- C Mt 24:36–51 ◀▶ Mt 25:19
- H Mt 22:14 ◀▶ Lk 14:16
- O Mt 22:11–14 ◀▶ Mk 8:38
- C Mt 23:33 ◀▶ Mk 2:17
- G Mt 22:11–14 ◀▶ Mk 7:6–7

24:46 ᵃ Rev 16:15
24:47 ᵇ Mt 25:21, 23
24:49 ᶜ Lk 21:34
24:51 ᵈ S Mt 8:12
25:1 ᵉ S Mt 13:24; ᶠ Lk 12:35-38; Ac 20:8; Rev 4:5; ᵍ Rev 19:7; 21:2
25:2 ʰ Mt 24:45
25:5 ⁱ 1Th 5:6
25:8 ʲ Lk 12:35
25:10 ᵏ Rev 19:9
25:12 ˡ ver 41; S Mt 7:23
25:13 ᵐ Mt 24:42, 44; Mk 13:35; Lk 12:40
25:14 ⁿ Mt 21:33; Lk 19:12
25:15 ᵒ Mt 18:24, 25

N Mt 24:50–51 ◀▶ Mk 6:11

ᵇ 15 *A talent was worth more than a thousand dollars.*

25:1–13 This parable prophetically urges Israel and the tribulation saints to remain vigilant and watchful for Christ's return during the coming tribulation. Jesus details an ancient Jewish wedding to portray the varied spiritual condition of the Jewish tribulation saints prior to Christ's return at Armageddon.

Scholars differ on the interpretation of various pieces in this parable. Note that all ten virgins initially had oil. The mistake of the five foolish virgins was neglecting to take an extra supply of oil. While some contend that the "oil" in this story is symbolic of the Holy Spirit, this is highly unlikely because the Holy Spirit's presence can neither be bought, sold nor shared. Other scholars have suggested that the ten virgins represent the church. This interpretation seems inconsistent with the parable because the virgins mentioned in the text were friends of the bride who were supposed to join the procession heading for the wedding supper. Also, just as the bridegroom had only one bride, so Christ has only one bride—his church. Note that the ten virgins are waiting for the call to go to the home of the bridegroom (heaven) to attend the wedding supper (see Rev 19:7–9). The message in this parable clearly is to be watchful and in constant readiness because no one knows when Christ will return.

25:14–30 This parable stresses the need for good stewardship of the resources that God places in our hands during our earthly life. Just as the master held each servant responsible for what he had done with the talents entrusted to him, in the final judgment our Lord will also reward his servants for their faithfulness or lack of service. Our spiritual rewards and responsibilities in the millennial kingdom will reflect our use of the talents Christ entrusted to us on this earth. Those who are faithful will be given cities to govern under the leadership of Jesus the Messiah during his millennial kingdom.

received the five talents went at once and put his money to work and gained five more. ¹⁷So also, the one with the two talents gained two more. ¹⁸But the man who had received the one talent went off, dug a hole in the ground and hid his master's money.

¹⁹"After a long time the master of those servants returned and settled accounts with them.ᵖ ²⁰The man who had received the five talents brought the other five. 'Master,' he said, 'you entrusted me with five talents. See, I have gained five more.'

²¹"His master replied, 'Well done, good and faithful servant! You have been faithful with a few things; I will put you in charge of many things.ᵍ Come and share your master's happiness!'

²²"The man with the two talents also came. 'Master,' he said, 'you entrusted me with two talents; see, I have gained two more.'

²³"His master replied, 'Well done, good and faithful servant! You have been faithful with a few things; I will put you in charge of many things.ʳ Come and share your master's happiness!'

²⁴"Then the man who had received the one talent came. 'Master,' he said, 'I knew that you are a hard man, harvesting where you have not sown and gathering where you have not scattered seed. ²⁵So I was afraid and went out and hid your talent in the ground. See, here is what belongs to you.'

²⁶"His master replied, 'You wicked, lazy servant! So you knew that I harvest where I have not sown and gather where I have not scattered seed? ²⁷Well then, you should have put my money on deposit with the bankers, so that when I returned I would have received it back with interest.

²⁸"'Take the talent from him and give it to the one who has the ten talents. ²⁹For everyone who has will be given more, and he will have an abundance. Whoever does not have, even what he has will be taken from him.ˢ ³⁰And throw that worthless servant outside, into the darkness, where there will be weeping and gnashing of teeth.'ᵗ

The Sheep and the Goats

³¹"When the Son of Man comesᵘ in his glory, and all the angels with him, he will sit on his throneᵛ in heavenly glory. ³²All the nations will be gathered before him, and he will separateʷ the people one from another as a shepherd separates the sheep from the goats.ˣ ³³He will put the sheep on his right and the goats on his left.

³⁴"Then the King will say to those on his right, 'Come, you who are blessed by my Father; take your inheritance, the kingdomʸ prepared for you since the creation of the world.ᶻ ³⁵For I was hungry and you gave me something to eat, I was thirsty and you gave me something to drink, I was a stranger and you invited me in,ᵃ ³⁶I needed clothes and you clothed me,ᵇ I was sick and you looked after me,ᶜ I was in prison and you came to visit me.'ᵈ

³⁷"Then the righteous will answer him, 'Lord, when did we see you hungry and

---

25:19 ᵖ Mt 18:23
25:21 ᵍ ver 23; Mt 24:45,47; Lk 16:10
25:23 ʳ ver 21
25:29 ˢ Mt 13:12; Mk 4:25; Lk 8:18; 19:26
25:30 ᵗ S Mt 8:12
25:31 ᵘ S Lk 17:30 ᵛ Mt 19:28
25:32 ʷ Mal 3:18 ˣ Eze 34:17,20
25:34 ʸ S Mt 3:2; 5:3,10,19; 19:14; S Ac 20:32; 1Co 15:50; Gal 5:21; Jas 2:5 ᶻ Heb 4:3; 9:26; Rev 13:8; 17:8
25:35 ᵃ Job 31:32; Heb 13:2
25:36 ᵇ Isa 58:7; Eze 18:7; Jas 2:15, 16 ᶜ Jas 1:27
ᵈ 2Ti 1:16

C Mt 25:1–13 ◀▶ Mt 26:64
J Mt 12:42 ◀▶ Mt 25:31–46
M Mt 22:44 ◀▶ Mt 25:23
M Mt 25:21 ◀▶ Mt 27:11
S Mt 24:48–51 ◀▶ Mt 25:34–36
H Mt 24:50–51 ◀▶ Mt 26:24
D Zec 14:14–20 ◀▶ Mk 13:26
J Mt 25:19 ◀▶ Mk 6:11
J Mt 12:41–42 ◀▶ Mk 6:11
S Mt 25:24–30 ◀▶ Mt 25:41–43

25:31–46 Jesus Christ will judge the Gentile nations following the Battle of Armageddon and his return to earth in all his glory (see Rev 19:19–21). (Note that there is no resurrection of bodies connected with this judgment, so this reckoning is not the great white throne judgment.) The nations will be judged and separated into two categories: the sheep and the goats.

The sheep represent those saved Gentiles who cared for God's chosen people during the tribulation. These Gentiles will be invited to enter the kingdom of the Messiah, and with the saved Jews of Israel, will make up the core population of the millennial kingdom.

The goats symbolize the unsaved Gentiles who provided no aid to God's people but rather participated in their persecution. Jesus will separate these "goats" from his faithful "sheep" and condemn the unsaved Gentiles to hell. Note that this prophetic passage reveals that hell was originally "prepared for the devil and his angels" (25:41). Because unrepentant people chose to rebel against God as Satan did, unrepentant people will also suffer the same punishment as Satan.

Signs of the Second Coming

DURING THE EARLY centuries following the ascension of Jesus into heaven, Christians often greeted one another by saying, "Maranatha." This Aramaic expression means "Come, O Lord" and echoed the believers' cry for the imminent return of Christ (see 1Co 16:22). Warning signs will herald his return (see Lk 21:28). The fulfillment of several of these signs in our generation points to the imminent return of Jesus Christ.

False Christs and Rumors of War
The first prophetic sign that will signal Christ's second coming involves the rise of false Christs and false prophets in the last days (see Mt 24:4–5). Though there are no historical references to any false messiahs prior to the resurrection of Jesus, many false messiahs have appeared throughout the centuries following his ascension. In our generation alone these imposters have included Charles Manson, Rev. Sun Myung Moon, Jim Jones and David Koresh. This rising number of false messiahs will pave the way for the worship of the antichrist during the last days.

The Lord also warned that prior to his second coming we would "hear of wars and rumors of wars" (24:6). Since the end of World War II the number of wars in our world has increased dramatically. New nations have demanded independence as old empires disintegrate. Though there have been numerous peace treaties, the world has not known a single day without some nation at war with another somewhere on earth. Today's standing armies of the world comprise millions of soldiers. The continuing arms buildup among superpowers and lesser third world nations is even now setting the stage for the final Battle of Armageddon, a war that will drench the world in blood.

Famine and Pestilence
Another prophetic warning sign of Christ's imminent return is the increase of devastating, widespread famine (see 24:7). In our generation we are faced with severe drought and famine conditions throughout portions of Africa, India and Southeast Asia. Many nations in these areas are already unable to properly feed their populations. Because of severe drought, millions of acres of fertile, agricultural land have been transformed into arid wasteland. Large quantities of precious topsoil are lost each year. Tropical rain forests, which contribute significant amounts of our planet's oxygen and water supply, are shrinking every year. Compounding these problems are the staggering statistics concerning the growth rate of the world's population. Every day more than 225,000 people are added to

the earth's population with the largest percentage born in third world nations where food supplies are already compromised.

Plagues and epidemics typically follow famine and war, compounding their terrors. Jesus warned that worldwide pestilence would signify his imminent return (see 24:7). During the coming holocaust of the tribulation, these epidemics will decimate one-fourth of the world's population (see Rev 6:8).

In our generation, health officials have discovered more than 25 new infectious diseases for which there are no known cures or treatments. Growing urbanization, poor sanitation and the increase in air travel have all helped to spread these deadly diseases throughout our world. Though we try to protect ourselves with antibiotic drugs, health officials now find that we may have compounded the problem. Increasing numbers of diseases are showing resistance to traditional antibiotics. Many diseases of the past—bubonic plague, smallpox, diphtheria, yellow fever, malaria—are reemerging as strains that are resistant to standard treatments and are becoming deadly threats to human populations. Sexually transmitted diseases are also on the rise. Of these, the AIDS virus is the most dangerous plague in history.

Toxic substances are also proliferating in our environment. Untested chemicals created in laboratories every year are casually introduced into the earth's biosphere without adequate tests of their effects on humans, animals or plant life. Scientists readily recognize that a large percentage of cancers and cancerous tumors are caused by exposure to hazardous substances in our environment. In addition, the pestilence of pesticides has created an emergence of a new strain of germs highly resistant to chemical eradication.

Earthquakes
Both Jesus Christ and the OT prophets prophesied that the last days would see an increase in the number and severity of earthquakes (see Isa 29:6; Mt 24:7; Rev 11:13). Jesus also indicated that earthquakes would occur in strange places (see Mt 24:7). In our century, we have experienced an unparalleled increase in the frequency and intensity of "killer" earthquakes that register 6.5 or higher on the Richter scale. The reported number of severe earthquakes between 1900–1970 totaled only 37. The decade immediately following reported 56 occurrences, and the 1980s witnessed 74 major earthquakes. Yet the first half of the 1990s has posted a record of 125 killer earthquakes worldwide, a significant jump in the geological annals. While better reporting has influenced the total count of earthquakes per year, earthquakes of 6.5 or more on the Richter scale have always been so destructive that historical records note these killer quakes.

Increased Hatred and Alienation
While nations have always found reasons to hate one another, Jesus warned of a worldwide hatred of the Jews that would signal his impending return (see 24:9). The genocide of the Jews during Hitler's reign, the vile anti-Semitic propaganda and persecution throughout Russia and modern Arab nations, and the terrorist attacks against Jewish synagogues and cemeteries worldwide points to the fulfillment of this sign.

Note that Jesus also indicated that this hatred would extend from between nations to between families and individuals. Jesus warned that a denial of natural love would be a condition of the end times prior to his return (see 24:10–12). Familial alienation and breakdown are a common tragedy in our society. Economic and social forces bear down on families, wreaking havoc on the "normal" nuclear family unit of two parents and their own children. Such a nuclear family is now a minority in North America. Transitory relationships are the norm for many. Divorces exceed marriages in numerous communities. Many western hospitals even register more abortions than live births, exceeding one million abortions every year in North America alone.

Worldwide Evangelism

We have never seen such an astonishing move of God as we are witnessing today. Millions in Indonesia, Africa and Southeast Asia have become followers of Jesus Christ. This growth of evangelism throughout the globe during our generation is another sign of the near return of Christ (see 24:14). Statisticians in Lausanne, Switzerland, are recording an explosive growth in the number of Christians worldwide, noting that while only 1 person in 32 claimed an affiliation with Christianity in the 1940s, statistics indicate that 1 person in 10 in 1997 claimed to be a Christian.

Church membership throughout the world is on the rise, too, growing at twice the rate of the overall population growth. The evangelical church worldwide has grown from only 41 million in 1934 to 540 million today, with the greatest increase seen in the underground church in communist China. Christian radio broadcasts now reach almost half of the world's major languages. Every year more than 300 million Bibles, New Testaments and Scripture portions are distributed throughout the world. The gospel is definitely being preached to all nations. As expectant believers we must be aware of these signs, for when these signs are fulfilled "then the end will come" (24:14).

Stay Alert

Other prophecies in the Bible herald Christ's return and the beginning of the last days. Israel's rebirth as a nation in 1948 fulfilled Isaiah's words of a nation being born in one day (see Isa 66:8). Joel refers to signs and "wonders in the heavens" (Joel 2:30; see Rev 6:12–17). Even Jesus reminded his disciples to be watchful and alert, to see the signs and recognize their fulfillment, just as they knew that when a fig tree's "twigs get tender and its leaves come out" (Mt 24:32) summer was at hand. As believers we should also be alert, knowing his coming could be at any time. In light of the fulfillment of prophecies in our generation we need to heed Jesus' words to "stand up and lift up your heads, because your redemption is drawing near" (Lk 21:28). Although we may not know "the day or the hour" (Mt 25:13), the fulfillment of these specific prophecies in our lifetime indicates that Jesus Christ's second coming may occur at any time. "Come, Lord Jesus" (Rev 22:20). Maranatha!

feed you, or thirsty and give you something to drink? ³⁸When did we see you a stranger and invite you in, or needing clothes and clothe you? ³⁹When did we see you sick or in prison and go to visit you?'

⁴⁰"The King will reply, 'I tell you the truth, whatever you did for one of the least of these brothers of mine, you did for me.'ᵉ

⁴¹"Then he will say to those on his left, 'Depart from me,ᶠ you who are cursed, into the eternal fireᵍ prepared for the devil and his angels.ʰ ⁴²For I was hungry and you gave me nothing to eat, I was thirsty and you gave me nothing to drink, ⁴³I was a stranger and you did not invite me in, I needed clothes and you did not clothe me, I was sick and in prison and you did not look after me.'

⁴⁴"They also will answer, 'Lord, when did we see you hungry or thirsty or a stranger or needing clothes or sick or in prison, and did not help you?'

⁴⁵"He will reply, 'I tell you the truth, whatever you did not do for one of the least of these, you did not do for me.'ⁱ

⁴⁶"Then they will go away to eternal punishment, but the righteous to eternal life.'ʲ"ᵏ

The Plot Against Jesus
26:2–5pp — Mk 14:1,2; Lk 22:1,2

26 When Jesus had finished saying all these things,ˡ he said to his disciples, ²"As you know, the Passoverᵐ is two days away—and the Son of Man will be handed over to be crucified."

³Then the chief priests and the elders of the people assembledⁿ in the palace of the high priest, whose name was Caiaphas,ᵒ ⁴and they plotted to arrest Jesus in some sly way and kill him.ᵖ ⁵"But not during the Feast," they said, "or there may be a riotᵠ among the people."

Jesus Anointed at Bethany
26:6–13pp — Mk 14:3–9
26:6–13Ref — Lk 7:37,38; Jn 12:1–8

⁶While Jesus was in Bethanyʳ in the home of a man known as Simon the Leper, ⁷a woman came to him with an alabaster jar of very expensive perfume, which she poured on his head as he was reclining at the table.

S Mt 25:34–36 ◀ ▶ Mt 28:20

25:40 ᵉ S Mt 10:40,42; Heb 13:2

25:41 ʳ S Mt 7:23 ᵍ Isa 66:24; Mt 3:12; S 5:22; Mk 9:43,48; Lk 3:17; Jude 7 ʰ 2Pe 2:4

25:45 ⁱ Pr 14:31; 17:5

25:46 ʲ Mt 19:29; Jn 3:15,16,36; 17:2,3; Ro 2:7; Gal 6:8; 1Jn 1:2; 5:11,13,20 ᵏ Da 12:2; Jn 5:29; Ac 24:15; Ro 2:7,8; Gal 6:8

26:1 ˡ S Mt 7:28

26:2 ᵐ S Jn 11:55

26:3 ⁿ Ps 2:2 ᵒ ver 57; Lk 3:2; Jn 11:47-53; 18:13, 14,24,28; Ac 4:6

26:4 ᵖ S Mt 12:14

26:5 ᵠ Mt 27:24

26:6 ʳ S Mt 21:17

26:11 ˢ Dt 15:11

26:12 ᵗ Jn 19:40

26:14 ᵘ ver 25,47; S Mt 10:4

26:15 ᵛ Ex 21:32; Zec 11:12

26:17 ʷ Ex 12:18-20 ˣ Dt 16:5-8

26:18 ʸ Mk 14:35, 41; Jn 7:6,8,30; 8:20; 12:23; 13:1; 17:1

26:21 ᶻ Lk 22:21-23; Jn 13:21

26:23 ᵃ Ps 41:9; Jn 13:18

⁸When the disciples saw this, they were indignant. "Why this waste?" they asked. ⁹"This perfume could have been sold at a high price and the money given to the poor."

¹⁰Aware of this, Jesus said to them, "Why are you bothering this woman? She has done a beautiful thing to me. ¹¹The poor you will always have with you,ˢ but you will not always have me. ¹²When she poured this perfume on my body, she did it to prepare me for burial.ᵗ ¹³I tell you the truth, wherever this gospel is preached throughout the world, what she has done will also be told, in memory of her."

Judas Agrees to Betray Jesus
26:14–16pp — Mk 14:10,11; Lk 22:3–6

¹⁴Then one of the Twelve—the one called Judas Iscariotᵘ—went to the chief priests ¹⁵and asked, "What are you willing to give me if I hand him over to you?" So they counted out for him thirty silver coins.ᵛ ¹⁶From then on Judas watched for an opportunity to hand him over.

The Lord's Supper
26:17–19pp — Mk 14:12–16; Lk 22:7–13
26:20–24pp — Mk 14:17–21
26:26–29pp — Mk 14:22–25; Lk 22:17–20; 1Co 11:23–25

¹⁷On the first day of the Feast of Unleavened Bread,ʷ the disciples came to Jesus and asked, "Where do you want us to make preparations for you to eat the Passover?"ˣ

¹⁸He replied, "Go into the city to a certain man and tell him, 'The Teacher says: My appointed timeʸ is near. I am going to celebrate the Passover with my disciples at your house.' " ¹⁹So the disciples did as Jesus had directed them and prepared the Passover.

²⁰When evening came, Jesus was reclining at the table with the Twelve. ²¹And while they were eating, he said, "I tell you the truth, one of you will betray me."ᶻ

²²They were very sad and began to say to him one after the other, "Surely not I, Lord?"

²³Jesus replied, "The one who has dipped his hand into the bowl with me will betray me.ᵃ ²⁴The Son of Man will go

L Mt 10:17–23 ◀
H Mt 25:30–46 ◀ ▶ Mk 6:11

just as it is written about him.^b But woe to that man who betrays the Son of Man! It would be better for him if he had not been born."

²⁵Then Judas, the one who would betray him,^c said, "Surely not I, Rabbi?"^d Jesus answered, "Yes, it is you."^c

²⁶While they were eating, Jesus took bread, gave thanks and broke it,^e and gave it to his disciples, saying, "Take and eat; this is my body."

²⁷Then he took the cup,^f gave thanks and offered it to them, saying, "Drink from it, all of you. ²⁸This is my blood of the^d covenant,^g which is poured out for many for the forgiveness of sins.^h ²⁹I tell you, I will not drink of this fruit of the vine from now on until that day when I drink it anew with youⁱ in my Father's kingdom."

³⁰When they had sung a hymn, they went out to the Mount of Olives.^j

Jesus Predicts Peter's Denial
26:31–35pp — Mk 14:27–31; Lk 22:31–34

³¹Then Jesus told them, "This very night you will all fall away on account of me,^k for it is written:

" 'I will strike the shepherd,
    and the sheep of the flock will be scattered.'^e^l

³²But after I have risen, I will go ahead of you into Galilee."^m

³³Peter replied, "Even if all fall away on account of you, I never will."

³⁴"I tell you the truth," Jesus answered, "this very night, before the rooster crows, you will disown me three times."ⁿ

³⁵But Peter declared, "Even if I have to die with you,^o I will never disown you." And all the other disciples said the same.

Gethsemane
26:36–46pp — Mk 14:32–42; Lk 22:40–46

³⁶Then Jesus went with his disciples to a place called Gethsemane, and he said to them, "Sit here while I go over there and pray." ³⁷He took Peter and the two sons of Zebedee^p along with him, and he began to be sorrowful and troubled. ³⁸Then he said to them, "My soul is overwhelmed with sorrow^q to the point of death. Stay here and keep watch with me."^r

³⁹Going a little farther, he fell with his face to the ground and prayed, "My Father, if it is possible, may this cup^s be taken from me. Yet not as I will, but as you will."^t

⁴⁰Then he returned to his disciples and found them sleeping. "Could you men not keep watch with me^u for one hour?" he asked Peter. ⁴¹"Watch and pray so that you will not fall into temptation.^v The spirit is willing, but the body is weak."

⁴²He went away a second time and prayed, "My Father, if it is not possible for this cup to be taken away unless I drink it, may your will be done."^w

⁴³When he came back, he again found them sleeping, because their eyes were heavy. ⁴⁴So he left them and went away once more and prayed the third time, saying the same thing.

⁴⁵Then he returned to the disciples and said to them, "Are you still sleeping and resting? Look, the hour^x is near, and the Son of Man is betrayed into the hands of sinners. ⁴⁶Rise, let us go! Here comes my betrayer!"

Jesus Arrested
26:47–56pp — Mk 14:43–50; Lk 22:47–53

⁴⁷While he was still speaking, Judas,^y one of the Twelve, arrived. With him was a large crowd armed with swords and clubs, sent from the chief priests and the elders of the people. ⁴⁸Now the betrayer had arranged a signal with them: "The one I kiss is the man; arrest him." ⁴⁹Going at once to Jesus, Judas said, "Greetings, Rabbi!"^z and kissed him.

⁵⁰Jesus replied, "Friend,^a do what you came for."^f

Then the men stepped forward, seized

---

c 25 Or *"You yourself have said it"*   *d* 28 Some manuscripts *the new*   *e* 31 Zech. 13:7   *f* 50 Or *"Friend, why have you come?"*

D Mt 20:28 ◀ ▶ Mk 10:45

26:29 Jesus prophesied to his disciples that he would not drink wine again until they were all reunited in heaven (see Rev 19:7–9). This proves that our resurrected bodies will be able to eat and drink with our Lord to celebrate our union with him forever.

26:32 Jesus prophesied that he would meet his disciples in Galilee after his resurrection from the grave. This prophecy was fulfilled in Mt 28:16–20.

Jesus and arrested him. ⁵¹With that, one of Jesus' companions reached for his sword,ᵇ drew it out and struck the servant of the high priest, cutting off his ear.ᶜ

⁵²"Put your sword back in its place," Jesus said to him, "for all who draw the sword will die by the sword.ᵈ ⁵³Do you think I cannot call on my Father, and he will at once put at my disposal more than twelve legions of angels?ᵉ ⁵⁴But how then would the Scriptures be fulfilledᶠ that say it must happen in this way?"

⁵⁵At that time Jesus said to the crowd, "Am I leading a rebellion, that you have come out with swords and clubs to capture me? Every day I sat in the temple courts teaching,ᵍ and you did not arrest me. ⁵⁶But this has all taken place that the writings of the prophets might be fulfilled."ʰ Then all the disciples deserted him and fled.

Before the Sanhedrin

26:57–68pp — Mk 14:53–65; Jn 18:12,13,19–24

⁵⁷Those who had arrested Jesus took him to Caiaphas,ⁱ the high priest, where the teachers of the law and the elders had assembled. ⁵⁸But Peter followed him at a distance, right up to the courtyard of the high priest.ʲ He entered and sat down with the guardsᵏ to see the outcome.

⁵⁹The chief priests and the whole Sanhedrinˡ were looking for false evidence against Jesus so that they could put him to death. ⁶⁰But they did not find any, though many false witnessesᵐ came forward.

Finally twoⁿ came forward ⁶¹and declared, "This fellow said, 'I am able to destroy the temple of God and rebuild it in three days.' "ᵒ

⁶²Then the high priest stood up and said to Jesus, "Are you not going to answer? What is this testimony that these men are bringing against you?" ⁶³But Jesus remained silent.ᵖ

The high priest said to him, "I charge you under oathᑫ by the living God:ʳ Tell us if you are the Christ,ᵍˢ the Son of God."ᵗ

⁶⁴"Yes, it is as you say,"ᵘ Jesus replied. "But I say to all of you: In the future you will see the Son of Man sitting at the right hand of the Mighty One ᵛ and coming on the clouds of heaven."ʷ

⁶⁵Then the high priest tore his clothesˣ and said, "He has spoken blasphemy! Why do we need any more witnesses? Look, now you have heard the blasphemy. ⁶⁶What do you think?"

"He is worthy of death,"ʸ they answered.

⁶⁷Then they spit in his face and struck him with their fists.ᶻ Others slapped him ⁶⁸and said, "Prophesy to us, Christ. Who hit you?"ᵃ

Peter Disowns Jesus

26:69–75pp — Mk 14:66–72; Lk 22:55–62; Jn 18:16–18,25–27

⁶⁹Now Peter was sitting out in the courtyard, and a servant girl came to him. "You also were with Jesus of Galilee," she said.

⁷⁰But he denied it before them all. "I don't know what you're talking about," he said.

⁷¹Then he went out to the gateway, where another girl saw him and said to the people there, "This fellow was with Jesus of Nazareth."

⁷²He denied it again, with an oath: "I don't know the man!"

⁷³After a little while, those standing there went up to Peter and said, "Surely you are one of them, for your accent gives you away."

⁷⁴Then he began to call down curses on himself and he swore to them, "I don't know the man!"

Immediately a rooster crowed. ⁷⁵Then Peter remembered the word Jesus had spoken: "Before the rooster crows, you will disown me three times."ᵇ And he went outside and wept bitterly.

C Mt 25:19 ◄ ► Mk 4:29
R Mt 21:28–32 ◄ ► Mk 1:15

ᵍ 63 Or *Messiah*; also in verse 68

26:64 Jesus' answer to the high priest was a prophecy about his ultimate glorious return as "the Son of Man sitting at the right hand of the Mighty One." This prophecy will be fulfilled when Jesus returns at the Battle of Armageddon to save his people.

Judas Hangs Himself

27 Early in the morning, all the chief priests and the elders of the people came to the decision to put Jesus to death.^c ²They bound him, led him away and handed him over^d to Pilate, the governor.^e

³When Judas, who had betrayed him,^f saw that Jesus was condemned, he was seized with remorse and returned the thirty silver coins^g to the chief priests and the elders. ⁴"I have sinned," he said, "for I have betrayed innocent blood."

"What is that to us?" they replied. "That's your responsibility."^h

⁵So Judas threw the money into the templeⁱ and left. Then he went away and hanged himself.^j

⁶The chief priests picked up the coins and said, "It is against the law to put this into the treasury, since it is blood money." ⁷So they decided to use the money to buy the potter's field as a burial place for foreigners. ⁸That is why it has been called the Field of Blood^k to this day. ⁹Then what was spoken by Jeremiah the prophet was fulfilled:^l "They took the thirty silver coins, the price set on him by the people of Israel, ¹⁰and they used them to buy the potter's field, as the Lord commanded me."^{h,m}

Jesus Before Pilate

27:11–26pp — Mk 15:2–15; Lk 23:2,3,18–25; Jn 18:29–19:16

¹¹Meanwhile Jesus stood before the governor, and the governor asked him, "Are you the king of the Jews?"ⁿ

"Yes, it is as you say," Jesus replied.

¹²When he was accused by the chief priests and the elders, he gave no answer.^o ¹³Then Pilate asked him, "Don't you hear the testimony they are bringing against you?"^p ¹⁴But Jesus made no reply,^q not even to a single charge—to the great amazement of the governor.

B *Mt 12:40–41 ◀ ▶ Mt 27:51*
I *Mt 21:5 ◀ ▶ Mt 27:29*
M *Mt 25:23 ◀ ▶ Mt 27:29*

27:1 ^cS Mt 12:14; Mk 15:1; Lk 22:66
27:2 ^dMt 20:19 ^eMk 15:1; Lk 13:1; Ac 3:13; 1Ti 6:13
27:3 ^fS Mt 10:4 ^gMt 26:14,15
27:4 ^hver 24
27:5 ⁱLk 1:9,21 ^jAc 1:18
27:8 ^kAc 1:19
27:9 ^lS Mt 1:22
27:10 ^mZec 11:12,13; Jer 32:6-9
27:11 ⁿS Mt 2:2
27:12 ^oS Mk 14:61
27:13 ^pMt 26:62
27:14 ^qS Mk 14:61
27:15 ^rJn 18:39
27:17 ^sver 22; Mt 1:16
27:19 ^tJn 19:13 ^uver 24 ^vGe 20:6; Nu 12:6; 1Ki 3:5; Job 33:14-16; Mt 1:20; 2:12,13, 19,22
27:20 ^wAc 3:14
27:22 ^xMt 1:16
27:24 ^yMt 26:5 ^zPs 26:6 ^aDt 21:6-8 ^bver 4
27:25 ^cJos 2:19; S Ac 5:28
27:26 ^dIsa 53:5; Jn 19:1
27:27 ^eJn 18:28, 33; 19:9

¹⁵Now it was the governor's custom at the Feast to release a prisoner^r chosen by the crowd. ¹⁶At that time they had a notorious prisoner, called Barabbas. ¹⁷So when the crowd had gathered, Pilate asked them, "Which one do you want me to release to you: Barabbas, or Jesus who is called Christ?"^s ¹⁸For he knew it was out of envy that they had handed Jesus over to him.

¹⁹While Pilate was sitting on the judge's seat,^t his wife sent him this message: "Don't have anything to do with that innocent^u man, for I have suffered a great deal today in a dream^v because of him."

²⁰But the chief priests and the elders persuaded the crowd to ask for Barabbas and to have Jesus executed.^w

²¹"Which of the two do you want me to release to you?" asked the governor.

"Barabbas," they answered.

²²"What shall I do, then, with Jesus who is called Christ?"^x Pilate asked.

They all answered, "Crucify him!"

²³"Why? What crime has he committed?" asked Pilate.

But they shouted all the louder, "Crucify him!"

²⁴When Pilate saw that he was getting nowhere, but that instead an uproar^y was starting, he took water and washed his hands^z in front of the crowd. "I am innocent of this man's blood,"^a he said. "It is your responsibility!"^b

²⁵All the people answered, "Let his blood be on us and on our children!"^c

²⁶Then he released Barabbas to them. But he had Jesus flogged,^d and handed him over to be crucified.

The Soldiers Mock Jesus

27:27–31pp — Mk 15:16–20

²⁷Then the governor's soldiers took Jesus into the Praetorium^e and gathered the whole company of soldiers around him. ²⁸They stripped him and put a scar-

^h *10 See Zech. 11:12,13; Jer. 19:1-13; 32:6-9.*

27:11, 29, 37, 42 When Jesus was taken before the Roman governor Pontius Pilate, Pilate asked Jesus about his identity as "the king of the Jews" (27:11). Jesus not only affirmed his claim to that title, but also by his affirmation foreshadowed his return to rule from the throne of David in Jerusalem following the Battle of Armageddon. Though the Roman soldiers, the unrepentant thief and the people standing near the cross mocked his royal position, Jesus will one day be acclaimed the true King of the Jews.

let robe on him,[f] [29]and then twisted together a crown of thorns and set it on his head. They put a staff in his right hand and knelt in front of him and mocked him. "Hail, king of the Jews!" they said.[g] [30]They spit on him, and took the staff and struck him on the head again and again.[h] [31]After they had mocked him, they took off the robe and put his own clothes on him. Then they led him away to crucify him.[i]

The Crucifixion
27:33–44pp — Mk 15:22–32; Lk 23:33–43; Jn 19:17–24

[32]As they were going out,[j] they met a man from Cyrene,[k] named Simon, and they forced him to carry the cross.[l] [33]They came to a place called Golgotha (which means The Place of the Skull).[m] [34]There they offered Jesus wine to drink, mixed with gall;[n] but after tasting it, he refused to drink it. [35]When they had crucified him, they divided up his clothes by casting lots.[o] [36]And sitting down, they kept watch[p] over him there. [37]Above his head they placed the written charge against him: THIS IS JESUS, THE KING OF THE JEWS. [38]Two robbers were crucified with him,[q] one on his right and one on his left. [39]Those who passed by hurled insults at him, shaking their heads[r] [40]and saying, "You who are going to destroy the temple and build it in three days,[s] save yourself![t] Come down from the cross, if you are the Son of God!"[u]

[41]In the same way the chief priests, the teachers of the law and the elders mocked him. [42]"He saved others," they said, "but he can't save himself! He's the King of Israel![v] Let him come down now from the cross, and we will believe[w] in him. [43]He trusts in God. Let God rescue him[x] now if he wants him, for he said, 'I am the Son of God.' " [44]In the same way the robbers who were crucified with him also heaped insults on him.

The Death of Jesus
27:45–56pp — Mk 15:33–41; Lk 23:44–49; Jn 19:29–30

[45]From the sixth hour until the ninth hour darkness[y] came over all the land. [46]About the ninth hour Jesus cried out in a loud voice, *"Eloi, Eloi,[j] lama sabachthani?"*—which means, "My God, my God, why have you forsaken me?"[kz] [47]When some of those standing there heard this, they said, "He's calling Elijah." [48]Immediately one of them ran and got a sponge. He filled it with wine vinegar,[a] put it on a stick, and offered it to Jesus to drink. [49]The rest said, "Now leave him alone. Let's see if Elijah comes to save him."

[50]And when Jesus had cried out again in a loud voice, he gave up his spirit.[b] [51]At that moment the curtain of the temple[c] was torn in two from top to bottom. The earth shook and the rocks split.[d] [52]The tombs broke open and the bodies of many holy people who had died were raised to life. [53]They came out of the tombs, and after Jesus' resurrection they went into the holy city[e] and appeared to many people.

[54]When the centurion and those with him who were guarding[f] Jesus saw the earthquake and all that had happened, they were terrified, and exclaimed, "Surely he was the Son[l] of God!"[g]

[55]Many women were there, watching from a distance. They had followed Jesus from Galilee to care for his needs.[h] [56]Among them were Mary Magdalene,

---

B Mt 27:9–10 ◄► Mk 1:7

j 35 A few late manuscripts *lots that the word spoken by the prophet might be fulfilled: "They divided my garments among themselves and cast lots for my clothing"* (Psalm 22:18)   *j 46* Some manuscripts *Eli, Eli*   *k 46* Psalm 22:1   *l 54* Or *a son*

27:52–53 Though Matthew is the only author to record this unusual resurrection, this passage indicates that these resurrected saints went into Jerusalem and appeared to many people. The exact reason for this supernatural event is uncertain, but these resurrections proved Christ's power to defeat death and raise from the dead all those who trust in him. It is even possible that this supernatural event helped spread the truth of Christ's resurrection throughout the Roman empire. See the article on "The Resurrection of the Body" on p. 1218.

Mary the mother of James and Joses, and the mother of Zebedee's sons.ⁱ

The Burial of Jesus

27:57–61pp — Mk 15:42–47; Lk 23:50–56; Jn 19:38–42

⁵⁷As evening approached, there came a rich man from Arimathea, named Joseph, who had himself become a disciple of Jesus. ⁵⁸Going to Pilate, he asked for Jesus' body, and Pilate ordered that it be given to him. ⁵⁹Joseph took the body, wrapped it in a clean linen cloth, ⁶⁰and placed it in his own new tombʲ that he had cut out of the rock. He rolled a big stone in front of the entrance to the tomb and went away. ⁶¹Mary Magdalene and the other Mary were sitting there opposite the tomb.

The Guard at the Tomb

⁶²The next day, the one after Preparation Day, the chief priests and the Pharisees went to Pilate. ⁶³"Sir," they said, "we remember that while he was still alive that deceiver said, 'After three days I will rise again.'ᵏ ⁶⁴So give the order for the tomb to be made secure until the third day. Otherwise, his disciples may come and steal the bodyˡ and tell the people that he has been raised from the dead. This last deception will be worse than the first."

⁶⁵"Take a guard,"ᵐ Pilate answered. "Go, make the tomb as secure as you know how." ⁶⁶So they went and made the tomb secure by putting a sealⁿ on the stoneᵒ and posting the guard.ᵖ

The Resurrection

28:1–8pp — Mk 16:1–8; Lk 24:1–10; Jn 20:1–8

28 After the Sabbath, at dawn on the first day of the week, Mary Magdaleneᑫ and the other Maryʳ went to look at the tomb.

²There was a violent earthquake,ˢ for an angelᵗ of the Lord came down from heaven and, going to the tomb, rolled back the stoneᵘ and sat on it. ³His appearance was like lightning, and his clothes were white as snow.ᵛ ⁴The guards were so afraid of him that they shook and became like dead men.

⁵The angel said to the women, "Do not be afraid,ʷ for I know that you are looking for Jesus, who was crucified. ⁶He is not here; he has risen, just as he said.ˣ Come and see the place where he lay. ⁷Then go quickly and tell his disciples: 'He has risen from the dead and is going ahead of you into Galilee.ʸ There you will see him.' Now I have told you."

⁸So the women hurried away from the tomb, afraid yet filled with joy, and ran to tell his disciples. ⁹Suddenly Jesus met them.ᶻ "Greetings," he said. They came to him, clasped his feet and worshiped him. ¹⁰Then Jesus said to them, "Do not be afraid. Go and tell my brothersᵃ to go to Galilee; there they will see me."

The Guards' Report

¹¹While the women were on their way, some of the guardsᵇ went into the city and reported to the chief priests everything that had happened. ¹²When the chief priests had met with the elders and devised a plan, they gave the soldiers a large sum of money, ¹³telling them, "You are to say, 'His disciples came during the night and stole him awayᶜ while we were asleep.' ¹⁴If this report gets to the governor,ᵈ we will satisfy him and keep you out of trouble." ¹⁵So the soldiers took the money and did as they were instructed. And this story has been widely circulated among the Jews to this very day.

The Great Commission

¹⁶Then the eleven disciples went to Galilee, to the mountain where Jesus had told them to go.ᵉ ¹⁷When they saw him, they worshiped him; but some doubted. ¹⁸Then Jesus came to them and said, "All authority in heaven and on earth has been given to me.ᶠ ¹⁹Therefore go and make disciples of all nations,ᵍ baptizing them inᵐ the name of the Father and of the Son and of the Holy Spirit,ʰ ²⁰and teachingⁱ them to obey everything I have commanded you. And surely I am with youʲ always, to the very end of the age."ᵏ

K *Mt 24:35* ◄ ► *Mk 2:10*
D *Mt 12:31–32* ◄ ► *Mk 3:29*
S *Mt 25:41–43* ◄ ► *Mk 3:35*
L *Mt 21:22* ◄ ► *Mk 9:42*

ᵐ 19 Or *into*; see Acts 8:16; 19:5; Romans 6:3; 1 Cor. 1:13; 10:2 and Gal. 3:27.

Mark

Author: Mark

Theme: Jesus is God's Son, the Messiah

Date of Writing: c. A.D. 50–70

Outline of Mark
  I. Background and Preparation (1:1–13)
  II. Public Ministry of Healing and Teaching (1:14—8:26)
  III. Jesus and His Disciples (8:27—10:45)
  IV. Jericho and Jerusalem (10:46—13:37)
  V. The Passion and Death of Jesus (14:1—15:47)
  VI. The Resurrection of Jesus (16:1–20)

MOST SCHOLARS AGREE that the author of this book is Mary's son John Mark (see Ac 12:12), the cousin of Barnabas (see Col 4:10). Mary's home in Jerusalem was a center for the early church. Mark's close association with Jesus, Peter and other disciples in this house church setting would have facilitated his recording the life of Jesus according to his own and Peter's eyewitness accounts. In fact, Peter's sermon in Acts 10:34–43 is remarkably similar to an outline of Mark's Gospel. Mark likely wrote this Gospel record toward the end of Peter's lifetime or just after Peter's death.

Though surrounded by strong witnesses for Christ, Mark let fear govern his missionary zeal when he was a young man. Though he traveled with Barnabas to Antioch (see Ac 4:36–37; 12:25) and started out with Paul on his first missionary journey, Mark deserted them both in the middle of the trip and returned to Jerusalem (see Ac 13:13). Mark's immaturity led Paul to reject him as a traveling companion on his next journey to Asia, but Barnabas traveled with Mark to Cyprus. Apparently this second chance was what Mark needed to solidify his Christian witness, because ten years later Mark joined Paul in Rome (see 2Ti 4:11; Col 4:10). Peter also referred to Mark as "my son" (1Pe 5:13), suggesting that in later years Mark may have served as Peter's close associate.

Mark's terse writing style is directed toward a Roman audience. Latin words and phrases occur with frequency, sometimes being used to help explain the Greek terms. On the other hand, Jewish laws and customs are rarely emphasized in Mark's account. Dealing with precise facts, Mark records the most vivid gospel account we possess of the life of Christ. Mark presents Jesus as a man of action and frequently records the reactions of the crowds to Jesus' ministry (see 1:27; 2:7; 4:41; 7:37).

John the Baptist Prepares the Way
1:2–8pp — Mt 3:1–11; Lk 3:2–16

1 The beginning of the gospel about Jesus Christ, the Son of God.ᵃᵃ

²It is written in Isaiah the prophet:

"I will send my messenger ahead of you,
who will prepare your way"ᵇᵇ—
³"a voice of one calling in the desert,
'Prepare the way for the Lord,
make straight paths for him.'"ᶜᶜ

⁴And so Johnᵈ came, baptizing in the desert region and preaching a baptism of repentanceᵉ for the forgiveness of sins.ᶠ ⁵The whole Judean countryside and all the people of Jerusalem went out to him. Confessing their sins, they were baptized by him in the Jordan River. ⁶John wore clothing made of camel's hair, with a leather belt around his waist,ᵍ and he ate locustsʰ and wild honey. ⁷And this was his message: "After me will come one more powerful than I, the thongs of whose sandals I am not worthy to stoop down and untie.ⁱ ⁸I baptize you withᵈ water, but he will baptize you with the Holy Spirit."ʲ

The Baptism and Temptation of Jesus
1:9–11pp — Mt 3:13–17; Lk 3:21,22
1:12,13pp — Mt 4:1–11; Lk 4:1–13

⁹At that time Jesus came from Nazarethᵏ in Galilee and was baptized by Johnˡ in the Jordan. ¹⁰As Jesus was coming up out of the water, he saw heaven being torn open and the Spirit descending on him like a dove.ᵐ ¹¹And a voice came from heaven: "You are my Son,ⁿ whom I love; with you I am well pleased."ᵒ

¹²At once the Spirit sent him out into the desert, ¹³and he was in the desert forty days,ᵖ being tempted by Satan.ᵠ He was with the wild animals, and angels attended him.

The Calling of the First Disciples
1:16–20pp — Mt 4:18–22; Lk 5:2–11; Jn 1:35–42

¹⁴After Johnʳ was put in prison, Jesus went into Galilee,ˢ proclaiming the good news of God.ᵗ ¹⁵"The time has come,"ᵘ he said. "The kingdom of God is near. Repent and believeᵛ the good news!"ʷ

¹⁶As Jesus walked beside the Sea of Galilee, he saw Simon and his brother Andrew casting a net into the lake, for they were fishermen. ¹⁷"Come, follow me," Jesus said, "and I will make you fishers of men." ¹⁸At once they left their nets and followed him.ˣ

¹⁹When he had gone a little farther, he saw James son of Zebedee and his brother John in a boat, preparing their nets. ²⁰Without delay he called them, and they left their father Zebedee in the boat with the hired men and followed him.

Jesus Drives Out an Evil Spirit
1:21–28pp — Lk 4:31–37

²¹They went to Capernaum, and when

Cross references (left column):
1:1 ᵃS Mt 4:3
1:2 ᵇMal 3:1; Mt 11:10; Lk 7:27
1:3 ᶜIsa 40:3; Jn 1:23
1:4 ᵈS Mt 3:1 ᵉver 8; Jn 1:26,33; Ac 1:5,22; 11:36; 13:24; 18:25; 19:3, 4 ᶠLk 1:77
1:6 ᵍ2Ki 1:8 ʰLev 11:22
1:7 ⁱAc 13:25
1:8 ʲIsa 44:3; Joel 2:28; Jn 1:33; Ac 1:5; 2:4; 11:16; 19:4-6
1:9 ᵏS Mt 2:23 ˡS Mt 3:1
1:10 ᵐJn 1:32
1:11 ⁿS Mt 3:17 ᵒS Mt 3:17
1:13 ᵖEx 24:18; 1Ki 19:8 ᵠS Mt 4:10; Heb 4:15
1:14 ʳS Mt 3:1 ˢS Mt 4:12 ᵗS Mt 4:23
1:15 ᵘRo 5:6; Gal 4:4; Eph 1:10 ᵛS Jn 3:15 ʷAc 20:21
1:18 ˣS Mt 4:19

Reference index (bottom):

B Mt 27:51 ◀ ▶ Mk 8:31
B Mt 12:18 ◀ ▶ Mk 1:10
P Mt 3:11 ◀ ▶ Lk 3:16
B Mk 1:8 ◀ ▶ Lk 1:15
E Mt 22:43 ◀ ▶ Mk 1:12
J Mt 3:16 ◀ ▶ Lk 3:22
N Mt 3:16 ◀ ▶ Lk 3:16

E Mk 1:10 ◀ ▶ Mk 12:36
L Mt 10:19–20 ◀ ▶ Mk 12:36
F Mt 16:5–10 ◀ ▶ Mk 6:33–44
F Mt 21:31–32 ◀ ▶ Mk 16:16
R Mt 26:75 ◀ ▶ Mk 6:12

ᵃ 1 Some manuscripts do not have *the Son of God.* ᵇ 2 Mal. 3:1 ᶜ 3 Isaiah 40:3 ᵈ 8 Or *in*

the Sabbath came, Jesus went into the synagogue and began to teach.ʸ ²²The people were amazed at his teaching, because he taught them as one who had authority, not as the teachers of the law.ᶻ

E ²³Just then a man in their synagogue who was possessed by an evilᵉ spirit cried out, ²⁴"What do you want with us,ᵃ Jesus of Nazareth?ᵇ Have you come to destroy us? I know who you are—the Holy One of God!"ᶜ

²⁵"Be quiet!" said Jesus sternly. "Come out of him!"ᵈ ²⁶The evil spirit shook the man violently and came out of him with a shriek.ᵉ

²⁷The people were all so amazedᶠ that they asked each other, "What is this? A new teaching—and with authority! He even gives orders to evil spirits and they obey him." ²⁸News about him spread quickly over the whole regionᵍ of Galilee.

Jesus Heals Many
1:29–31pp — Mt 8:14,15; Lk 4:38,39
1:32–34pp — Mt 8:16,17; Lk 4:40,41

²⁹As soon as they left the synagogue,ʰ they went with James and John to the home of Simon and Andrew. ³⁰Simon's mother-in-law was in bed with a fever, and they told Jesus about her. ³¹So he went to her, took her hand and helped her up.ⁱ The fever left her and she began to wait on them.

³²That evening after sunset the people brought to Jesus all the sick and demon-possessed.ʲ ³³The whole town gathered at the door, ³⁴and Jesus healed many who had various diseases.ᵏ He also drove out many demons, but he would not let the demons speak because they knew who he was.ˡ

Jesus Prays in a Solitary Place
1:35–38pp — Lk 4:42,43

³⁵Very early in the morning, while it was still dark, Jesus got up, left the house and went off to a solitary place, where he prayed.ᵐ ³⁶Simon and his companions went to look for him, ³⁷and when they found him, they exclaimed: "Everyone is looking for you!"

³⁸Jesus replied, "Let us go somewhere else—to the nearby villages—so I can preach there also. That is why I have E come."ⁿ ³⁹So he traveled throughout Gali-

E Mt 21:14 ◀▶ Mk 1:39–45
E Mk 1:23–34 ◀▶ Mk 2:3–12

1:21 ʸ ver 39; S Mt 4:23; S Mk 10:1
1:22 ᶻ S Mt 7:28, 29
1:24 ᵃ S Mt 8:29
ᵇ Mt 2:23; Lk 24:19; Jn 1:45, 46; Ac 4:10; 24:5
ᶜ Ps 16:10; Isa 41:14,16,20; Lk 1:35; Jn 6:69; Ac 3:14; 1Jn 2:20
1:25 ᵈ ver 34
1:26 ᵉ Mk 9:20
1:27 ᶠ Mk 10:24,32
1:28 ᵍ S Mk 9:26
1:29 ʰ ver 21,23
1:31 ⁱ S Lk 7:14
1:32 ʲ S Mt 4:24
1:34 ᵏ S Mt 4:23
ˡ Mk 3:12; Ac 16:17,18
1:35 ᵐ S Lk 3:21
1:38 ⁿ Isa 61:1
1:39 ᵒ S Mt 4:23
ᵖ S Mt 4:24
1:40 ᵠ Mk 10:17
1:44 ʳ S Mt 8:4
ˢ Lev 13:49
ᵗ Lev 14:1-32
1:45 ᵘ Lk 5:15,16
ᵛ Mt 2:13; Lk 5:17; Jn 6:2
2:2 ʷ ver 13; Mk 1:45
2:3 ˣ S Mt 4:24
2:5 ʸ Lk 7:48
2:7 ᶻ Isa 43:25

lee, preaching in their synagoguesᵒ and driving out demons.ᵖ

A Man With Leprosy
1:40–44pp — Mt 8:2–4; Lk 5:12–14

⁴⁰A man with leprosyᶠ came to him and begged him on his knees,ᵠ "If you are willing, you can make me clean."

⁴¹Filled with compassion, Jesus reached out his hand and touched the man. "I am willing," he said. "Be clean!" ⁴²Immediately the leprosy left him and he was cured.

⁴³Jesus sent him away at once with a strong warning: ⁴⁴"See that you don't tell this to anyone.ʳ But go, show yourself to the priestˢ and offer the sacrifices that Moses commanded for your cleansing,ᵗ as a testimony to them." ⁴⁵Instead he went out and began to talk freely, spreading the news. As a result, Jesus could no longer enter a town openly but stayed outside in lonely places.ᵘ Yet the people still came to him from everywhere.ᵛ

Jesus Heals a Paralytic
2:3–12pp — Mt 9:2–8; Lk 5:18–26

2 A few days later, when Jesus again entered Capernaum, the people heard that he had come home. ²So manyʷ gathered that there was no room left, not even outside the door, and he preached the word to them. ³Some men came, E bringing to him a paralytic,ˣ carried by four of them. ⁴Since they could not get him to Jesus because of the crowd, they made an opening in the roof above Jesus and, after digging through it, lowered the mat the paralyzed man was lying on. ⁵When Jesus saw their faith, he said to the paralytic, "Son, your sins are forgiven."ʸ

⁶Now some teachers of the law were sitting there, thinking to themselves, ⁷"Why does this fellow talk like that? He's blaspheming! Who can forgive sins but God alone?"ᶻ

⁸Immediately Jesus knew in his spirit that this was what they were thinking in their hearts, and he said to them, "Why are you thinking these things? ⁹Which is easier: to say to the paralytic, 'Your sins are forgiven,' or to say, 'Get up, take your

E Mk 1:39–45 ◀▶ Mk 3:1–5

ᵉ 23 Greek *unclean*; also in verses 26 and 27   ᶠ 40 The Greek word was used for various diseases affecting the skin—not necessarily leprosy.

mat and walk'? ¹⁰But that you may know that the Son of Man* has authority on earth to forgive sins . . ." He said to the paralytic, ¹¹"I tell you, get up, take your mat and go home." ¹²He got up, took his mat and walked out in full view of them all. This amazed everyone and they praised God,ᵇ saying, "We have never seen anything like this!"ᶜ

The Calling of Levi
2:14–17pp — Mt 9:9–13; Lk 5:27–32

¹³Once again Jesus went out beside the lake. A large crowd came to him,ᵈ and he began to teach them. ¹⁴As he walked along, he saw Levi son of Alphaeus sitting at the tax collector's booth. "Follow me,"ᵉ Jesus told him, and Levi got up and followed him.

¹⁵While Jesus was having dinner at Levi's house, many tax collectors and "sinners" were eating with him and his disciples, for there were many who followed him. ¹⁶When the teachers of the law who were Phariseesᶠ saw him eating with the "sinners" and tax collectors, they asked his disciples: "Why does he eat with tax collectors and 'sinners'?"ᵍ

¹⁷On hearing this, Jesus said to them, "It is not the healthy who need a doctor, but the sick. I have not come to call the righteous, but sinners."ʰ

Jesus Questioned About Fasting
2:18–22pp — Mt 9:14–17; Lk 5:33–38

¹⁸Now John's disciples and the Pharisees were fasting.ⁱ Some people came and asked Jesus, "How is it that John's disciples and the disciples of the Pharisees are fasting, but yours are not?"

¹⁹Jesus answered, "How can the guests of the bridegroom fast while he is with them? They cannot, so long as they have him with them. ²⁰But the time will come when the bridegroom will be taken from them,ʲ and on that day they will fast.

²¹"No one sews a patch of unshrunk cloth on an old garment. If he does, the new piece will pull away from the old, making the tear worse. ²²And no one pours new wine into old wineskins. If he does, the wine will burst the skins, and both the wine and the wineskins will be ruined. No, he pours new wine into new wineskins."

Lord of the Sabbath
2:23–28pp — Mt 12:1–8; Lk 6:1–5
3:1–6pp — Mt 12:9–14; Lk 6:6–11

²³One Sabbath Jesus was going through the grainfields, and as his disciples walked along, they began to pick some heads of grain.ᵏ ²⁴The Pharisees said to him, "Look, why are they doing what is unlawful on the Sabbath?"ˡ

²⁵He answered, "Have you never read what David did when he and his companions were hungry and in need? ²⁶In the days of Abiathar the high priest,ᵐ he entered the house of God and ate the consecrated bread, which is lawful only for priests to eat.ⁿ And he also gave some to his companions."ᵒ

²⁷Then he said to them, "The Sabbath was made for man,ᵖ not man for the Sabbath.ᵍ ²⁸So the Son of Manʳ is Lord even of the Sabbath."

3 Another time he went into the synagogue,ˢ and a man with a shriveled hand was there. ²Some of them were looking for a reason to accuse Jesus, so they watched him closelyᵗ to see if he would heal him on the Sabbath.ᵘ ³Jesus said to the man with the shriveled hand, "Stand up in front of everyone."

⁴Then Jesus asked them, "Which is lawful on the Sabbath: to do good or to do evil, to save life or to kill?" But they remained silent.

⁵He looked around at them in anger and, deeply distressed at their stubborn hearts, said to the man, "Stretch out your hand." He stretched it out, and his hand was completely restored. ⁶Then the Pharisees went out and began to plot with the Herodiansᵛ how they might kill Jesus.ʷ

Crowds Follow Jesus
3:7–12pp — Mt 12:15,16; Lk 6:17–19

⁷Jesus withdrew with his disciples to the lake, and a large crowd from Galilee followed.ˣ ⁸When they heard all he was doing, many people came to him from Judea, Jerusalem, Idumea, and the regions across the Jordan and around Tyre and Sidon.ʸ ⁹Because of the crowd he told his disciples to have a small boat ready for him, to keep the people from crowding

---

K Mt 28:18 ◀ ▶ Mk 10:27
C Mt 25:2–3 ◀ ▶ Mk 4:12
L Mt 23:37 ◀ ▶ Mk 3:28

E Mk 2:3–12 ◀ ▶ Mk 3:10–12

him. ¹⁰For he had healed many,ᶻ so that those with diseases were pushing forward to touch him.ᵃ ¹¹Whenever the evilᵍ spirits saw him, they fell down before him and cried out, "You are the Son of God."ᵇ ¹²But he gave them strict orders not to tell who he was.ᶜ

The Appointing of the Twelve Apostles
3:16–19pp — Mt 10:2–4; Lk 6:14–16; Ac 1:13

¹³Jesus went up on a mountainside and called to him those he wanted, and they came to him.ᵈ ¹⁴He appointed twelve—designating them apostlesʰᵉ—that they might be with him and that he might send them out to preach ¹⁵and to have authority to drive out demons.ᶠ ¹⁶These are the twelve he appointed: Simon (to whom he gave the name Peter);ᵍ ¹⁷James son of Zebedee and his brother John (to them he gave the name Boanerges, which means Sons of Thunder); ¹⁸Andrew, Philip, Bartholomew, Matthew, Thomas, James son of Alphaeus, Thaddaeus, Simon the Zealot ¹⁹and Judas Iscariot, who betrayed him.

Jesus and Beelzebub
3:23–27pp — Mt 12:25–29; Lk 11:17–22

²⁰Then Jesus entered a house, and again a crowd gathered,ʰ so that he and his disciples were not even able to eat.ⁱ ²¹When his family heard about this, they went to take charge of him, for they said, "He is out of his mind."ʲ

²²And the teachers of the law who came down from Jerusalemᵏ said, "He is possessed by Beelzebub!ˡ By the prince of demons he is driving out demons."ᵐ ²³So Jesus called them and spoke to them in parables:ⁿ "How can Satan drive out Satan? ²⁴If a kingdom is divided against itself, that kingdom cannot stand. ²⁵If a house is divided against itself, that house cannot stand. ²⁶And if Satan opposes himself and is divided, he cannot stand; his end has come. ²⁷In fact, no one can enter a strong man's house and carry off his possessions unless he first ties up the strong man. Then he can rob his house.ᵖ ²⁸I tell you the truth, all the sins and blasphemies of men will be forgiven them. ²⁹But whoever blasphemes against the Holy Spirit will never be forgiven; he is guilty of an eternal sin."ᑫ

³⁰He said this because they were saying, "He has an evil spirit."

Jesus' Mother and Brothers
3:31–35pp — Mt 12:46–50; Lk 8:19–21

³¹Then Jesus' mother and brothers arrived.ʳ Standing outside, they sent someone in to call him. ³²A crowd was sitting around him, and they told him, "Your mother and brothers are outside looking for you."

³³"Who are my mother and my brothers?" he asked.

³⁴Then he looked at those seated in a circle around him and said, "Here are my mother and my brothers! ³⁵Whoever does God's will is my brother and sister and mother."

The Parable of the Sower
4:1–12pp — Mt 13:1–15; Lk 8:4–10
4:13–20pp — Mt 13:18–23; Lk 8:11–15

4 Again Jesus began to teach by the lake.ˢ The crowd that gathered around him was so large that he got into a boat and sat in it out on the lake, while all the people were along the shore at the water's edge. ²He taught them many things by parables,ᵗ and in his teaching said: ³"Listen! A farmer went out to sow his seed.ᵘ ⁴As he was scattering the seed, some fell along the path, and the birds came and ate it up. ⁵Some fell on rocky places, where it did not have much soil. It sprang up quickly, because the soil was shallow. ⁶But when the sun came up, the plants were scorched, and they withered because they had no root. ⁷Other seed fell among thorns, which grew up and choked the plants, so that they did not bear grain. ⁸Still other seed fell on good soil. It came up, grew and produced a crop, multiplying thirty, sixty, or even a hundred times."ᵛ

⁹Then Jesus said, "He who has ears to hear, let him hear."ʷ

¹⁰When he was alone, the Twelve and

3:10 ᶻ S Mt 4:23; ᵃ S Mt 9:20
3:11 ᵇ S Mt 4:3; Mk 1:23,24
3:12 ᶜ S Mt 8:4; Mk 1:24,25,34; Ac 16:17,18
3:13 ᵈ Mt 5:1
3:14 ᵉ S Mk 6:30
3:15 ᶠ S Mt 10:1
3:16 ᵍ Jn 1:42
3:20 ʰ ver 7; ⁱ Mk 6:31
3:21 ʲ Jn 10:20; Ac 26:24
3:22 ᵏ Mt 15:1; ˡ Mt 10:25; 11:18; 12:24; Jn 7:20; 8:48,52; 10:20; ᵐ Mt 9:34
3:23 ⁿ Mk 4:2; ᵒ S Mt 4:10
3:27 ᵖ Isa 49:24,25
3:29 ᑫ Mt 12:31,32; Lk 12:10
3:31 ʳ ver 21
4:1 ˢ Mk 2:13; 3:7
4:2 ᵗ ver 11; Mk 3:23
4:3 ᵘ ver 26
4:8 ᵛ Jn 15:5; Col 1:6
4:9 ʷ ver 23; S Mt 11:15

E Mk 3:1–5 ◀ ▶ Mk 3:14–15
E Mk 3:10–12 ◀ ▶ Mk 3:22–27
E Mk 3:14–15 ◀ ▶ Mk 5:1–20
L Mk 2:17 ◀ ▶ Lk 1:77–79
W Mt 22:1–10 ◀ ▶ Mk 16:15–16

D Mt 28:19 ◀ ▶ Ac 5:4
Q Mt 12:31–32 ◀ ▶ Lk 12:10
S Mt 28:20 ◀ ▶ Mk 4:5–8
S Mk 3:35 ◀ ▶ Mk 4:16–20

ᵍ 11 Greek *unclean*; also in verse 30   ʰ 14 Some manuscripts do not have *designating them apostles.*   ⁱ 22 Greek *Beezeboul* or *Beelzeboul*

the others around him asked him about the parables. ¹¹He told them, "The secret of the kingdom of God has been given to you. But to those on the outside everything is said in parables ¹²so that,

> " 'they may be ever seeing but never perceiving,
> and ever hearing but never understanding;
> otherwise they might turn and be forgiven!'"

¹³Then Jesus said to them, "Don't you understand this parable? How then will you understand any parable? ¹⁴The farmer sows the word. ¹⁵Some people are like seed along the path, where the word is sown. As soon as they hear it, Satan comes and takes away the word that was sown in them. ¹⁶Others, like seed sown on rocky places, hear the word and at once receive it with joy. ¹⁷But since they have no root, they last only a short time. When trouble or persecution comes because of the word, they quickly fall away. ¹⁸Still others, like seed sown among thorns, hear the word; ¹⁹but the worries of this life, the deceitfulness of wealth and the desires for other things come in and choke the word, making it unfruitful. ²⁰Others, like seed sown on good soil, hear the word, accept it, and produce a crop—thirty, sixty or even a hundred times what was sown."

A Lamp on a Stand

²¹He said to them, "Do you bring in a lamp to put it under a bowl or a bed? Instead, don't you put it on its stand? ²²For whatever is hidden is meant to be disclosed, and whatever is concealed is meant to be brought out into the open. ²³If anyone has ears to hear, let him hear."

²⁴"Consider carefully what you hear," he continued. "With the measure you use, it will be measured to you—and even more. ²⁵Whoever has will be given more; whoever does not have, even what he has will be taken from him."

C Mk 2:17 ◄ ► Lk 1:79
S Mk 4:5–8 ◄ ► Mk 8:34

The Parable of the Growing Seed

²⁶He also said, "This is what the kingdom of God is like. A man scatters seed on the ground. ²⁷Night and day, whether he sleeps or gets up, the seed sprouts and grows, though he does not know how. ²⁸All by itself the soil produces grain—first the stalk, then the head, then the full kernel in the head. ²⁹As soon as the grain is ripe, he puts the sickle to it, because the harvest has come."

The Parable of the Mustard Seed

4:30–32pp — Mt 13:31,32; Lk 13:18,19

³⁰Again he said, "What shall we say the kingdom of God is like, or what parable shall we use to describe it? ³¹It is like a mustard seed, which is the smallest seed you plant in the ground. ³²Yet when planted, it grows and becomes the largest of all garden plants, with such big branches that the birds of the air can perch in its shade."

³³With many similar parables Jesus spoke the word to them, as much as they could understand. ³⁴He did not say anything to them without using a parable. But when he was alone with his own disciples, he explained everything.

Jesus Calms the Storm

4:35–41pp — Mt 8:18,23–27; Lk 8:22–25

³⁵That day when evening came, he said to his disciples, "Let us go over to the other side." ³⁶Leaving the crowd behind, they took him along, just as he was, in the boat. There were also other boats with him. ³⁷A furious squall came up, and the waves broke over the boat, so that it was nearly swamped. ³⁸Jesus was in the stern, sleeping on a cushion. The disciples woke him and said to him, "Teacher, don't you care if we drown?"

³⁹He got up, rebuked the wind and said to the waves, "Quiet! Be still!" Then the wind died down and it was completely calm.

K Mt 16:18–20 ◄ ► Mk 9:1
C Mt 26:64 ◄ ► Mk 8:38
M Mt 27:42 ◄ ► Mk 10:37

*l*12 Isaiah 6:9,10

4:30–32 The parable of the mustard seed reveals the prophetic nature of the kingdom of God. This kingdom began with only twelve disciples and has grown throughout the last two thousand years to include more than 600 million Christians around the world today.

⁴⁰He said to his disciples, "Why are you so afraid? Do you still have no faith?"ᵒ

⁴¹They were terrified and asked each other, "Who is this? Even the wind and the waves obey him!"

The Healing of a Demon-possessed Man
5:1–17pp — Mt 8:28–34; Lk 8:26–37
5:18–20pp — Lk 8:38,39

5 They went across the lake to the region of the Gerasenes.ᵏ ²When Jesus got out of the boat,ᵖ a man with an evil spiritᵠ came from the tombs to meet him. ³This man lived in the tombs, and no one could bind him any more, not even with a chain. ⁴For he had often been chained hand and foot, but he tore the chains apart and broke the irons on his feet. No one was strong enough to subdue him. ⁵Night and day among the tombs and in the hills he would cry out and cut himself with stones.

⁶When he saw Jesus from a distance, he ran and fell on his knees in front of him. ⁷He shouted at the top of his voice, "What do you want with me,ʳ Jesus, Son of the Most High God?ˢ Swear to God that you won't torture me!" ⁸For Jesus had said to him, "Come out of this man, you evil spirit!"

⁹Then Jesus asked him, "What is your name?"

"My name is Legion,"ᵗ he replied, "for we are many." ¹⁰And he begged Jesus again and again not to send them out of the area.

¹¹A large herd of pigs was feeding on the nearby hillside. ¹²The demons begged Jesus, "Send us among the pigs; allow us to go into them." ¹³He gave them permission, and the evil spirits came out and went into the pigs. The herd, about two thousand in number, rushed down the steep bank into the lake and were drowned.

¹⁴Those tending the pigs ran off and reported this in the town and countryside, and the people went out to see what had happened. ¹⁵When they came to Jesus, they saw the man who had been possessed by the legionᵘ of demons,ᵛ sitting there, dressed and in his right mind; and they were afraid. ¹⁶Those who had seen it told the people what had happened to the demon-possessed man—and told about the pigs as well. ¹⁷Then the people began to plead with Jesus to leave their region.

¹⁸As Jesus was getting into the boat, the man who had been demon-possessed begged to go with him. ¹⁹Jesus did not let him, but said, "Go home to your family and tell themʷ how much the Lord has done for you, and how he has had mercy on you." ²⁰So the man went away and began to tell in the Decapolisᵐˣ how much Jesus had done for him. And all the people were amazed.

A Dead Girl and a Sick Woman
5:22–43pp — Mt 9:18–26; Lk 8:41–56

²¹When Jesus had again crossed over by boat to the other side of the lake,ʸ a large crowd gathered around him while he was by the lake.ᶻ ²²Then one of the synagogue rulers,ᵃ named Jairus, came there. Seeing Jesus, he fell at his feet ²³and pleaded earnestly with him, "My little daughter is dying. Please come and put your hands onᵇ her so that she will be healed and live." ²⁴So Jesus went with him.

A large crowd followed and pressed around him. ²⁵And a woman was there who had been subject to bleedingᶜ for twelve years. ²⁶She had suffered a great deal under the care of many doctors and had spent all she had, yet instead of getting better she grew worse. ²⁷When she heard about Jesus, she came up behind him in the crowd and touched his cloak, ²⁸because she thought, "If I just touch his clothes,ᵈ I will be healed." ²⁹Immediately her bleeding stopped and she felt in her body that she was freed from her suffering.ᵉ

³⁰At once Jesus realized that powerᶠ had gone out from him. He turned around in the crowd and asked, "Who touched my clothes?"

³¹"You see the people crowding against you," his disciples answered, "and yet you can ask, 'Who touched me?'"

³²But Jesus kept looking around to see who had done it. ³³Then the woman, knowing what had happened to her, came and fell at his feet and, trembling

---

S ⁴⁰He said...
W so afraid...
4:40 ᵒ Mt 14:31; Mk 16:14

5:2 ᵖ Mk 4:1
ᵠ Mk 1:23

5:7 ʳ S Mt 8:29
ˢ S Mt 4:3; Lk 1:32; 6:35; Ac 16:17; Heb 7:1

5:9 ᵗ ver 15

5:15 ᵘ ver 9
ᵛ ver 16,18;
S Mt 4:24

5:19 ʷ S Mt 8:4

5:20 ˣ Mt 4:25; Mk 7:31

5:21 ʸ Mt 9:1
ᶻ Mk 4:1

5:22 ᵃ ver 35,36, 38; Lk 13:14; Ac 13:15; 18:8,17

5:23 ᵇ Mt 19:13; Mk 6:5; 7:32; 8:23; 16:18; Lk 4:40; 13:13; S Ac 6:6

5:25 ᶜ Lev 15:25-30

5:28 ᵈ S Mt 9:20

5:29 ᵉ ver 34

5:30 ᶠ Lk 5:17; 6:19

T Mt 10:32–33 ◄ ► Mk 8:38
E Mk 5:1–20 ◄ ► Mk 6:5

S Mt 4:6 ◄ ► Lk 21:18
W Mt 8:26 ◄ ► Lk 8:24–25
E Mk 3:22–27 ◄ ► Mk 5:22–43

ᵏ *1* Some manuscripts *Gadarenes*; other manuscripts *Gergesenes*
ˡ *2* Greek *unclean*; also in verses 8 and 13   ᵐ *20* That is, the Ten Cities

with fear, told him the whole truth. ³⁴He said to her, "Daughter, your faith has healed you.ᵍ Go in peaceʰ and be freed from your suffering."

³⁵While Jesus was still speaking, some men came from the house of Jairus, the synagogue ruler.ⁱ "Your daughter is dead," they said. "Why bother the teacher any more?"

³⁶Ignoring what they said, Jesus told the synagogue ruler, "Don't be afraid; just believe."

³⁷He did not let anyone follow him except Peter, James and John the brother of James.ʲ ³⁸When they came to the home of the synagogue ruler,ᵏ Jesus saw a commotion, with people crying and wailing loudly. ³⁹He went in and said to them, "Why all this commotion and wailing? The child is not dead but asleep."ˡ ⁴⁰But they laughed at him.

After he put them all out, he took the child's father and mother and the disciples who were with him, and went in where the child was. ⁴¹He took her by the handᵐ and said to her, *"Talitha koum!"* (which means, "Little girl, I say to you, get up!").ⁿ ⁴²Immediately the girl stood up and walked around (she was twelve years old). At this they were completely astonished. ⁴³He gave strict orders not to let anyone know about this,ᵒ and told them to give her something to eat.

A Prophet Without Honor

6:1–6pp — Mt 13:54–58

6 Jesus left there and went to his hometown,ᵖ accompanied by his disciples. ²When the Sabbath came,ᑫ he began to teach in the synagogue,ʳ and many who heard him were amazed.ˢ

"Where did this man get these things?" they asked. "What's this wisdom that has been given him, that he even does miracles! ³Isn't this the carpenter? Isn't this Mary's son and the brother of James, Joseph,ⁿ Judas and Simon?ᵗ Aren't his sisters here with us?" And they took offense at him.ᵘ

⁴Jesus said to them, "Only in his hometown, among his relatives and in his own house is a prophet without honor."ᵛ ⁵He could not do any miracles there, except lay his hands onʷ a few sick people and heal them. ⁶And he was amazed at their lack of faith.

Jesus Sends Out the Twelve

6:7–11pp — Mt 10:1,9–14; Lk 9:1,3–5

Then Jesus went around teaching from village to village.ˣ ⁷Calling the Twelve to him,ʸ he sent them out two by twoᶻ and gave them authority over evilᵃ spirits.ᵃ

⁸These were his instructions: "Take nothing for the journey except a staff— no bread, no bag, no money in your belts. ⁹Wear sandals but not an extra tunic. ¹⁰Whenever you enter a house, stay there until you leave that town. ¹¹And if any place will not welcome you or listen to you, shake the dust off your feetᵇ when you leave, as a testimony against them."

¹²They went out and preached that people should repent.ᶜ ¹³They drove out many demons and anointed many sick people with oilᵈ and healed them.

John the Baptist Beheaded

6:14–29pp — Mt 14:1–12
6:14–16pp — Lk 9:7–9

¹⁴King Herod heard about this, for Jesus' name had become well known. Some were saying,ᵖ "John the Baptistᵉ has been raised from the dead, and that is why miraculous powers are at work in him."

¹⁵Others said, "He is Elijah."ᶠ

And still others claimed, "He is a prophet,ᵍ like one of the prophets of long ago."ʰ

¹⁶But when Herod heard this, he said,

5:34 ᵍ S Mt 9:22; ʰ S Ac 15:33
5:35 ⁱ S ver 22
5:37 ʲ S Mt 4:21
5:38 ᵏ S ver 22
5:39 ˡ S Mt 9:24
5:41 ᵐ Mk 1:31; ⁿ S Lk 7:14
5:43 ᵒ S Mt 8:4
6:1 ᵖ S Mt 2:23
6:2 ᑫ Mk 1:21; ʳ S Mt 4:23; ˢ S Mt 7:28
6:3 ᵗ S Mt 12:46; ᵘ S Mt 11:6; Jn 6:61
6:4 ᵛ Lk 4:24; Jn 4:44
6:5 ʷ S Mk 5:23
6:6 ˣ Mt 9:35; Mk 1:39; Lk 13:22
6:7 ʸ Mk 3:13; ᶻ Dt 17:6; Lk 10:1; ᵃ S Mt 10:1
6:11 ᵇ S Mt 10:14
6:12 ᶜ Lk 9:6
6:13 ᵈ S Jas 5:14
6:14 ᵉ S Mt 3:1
6:15 ᶠ Mal 4:5; ᵍ S Mt 21:11; ʰ S Mt 16:14; Mk 8:28

D Mt 13:58 ◀ ▶ Lk 1:20
E Mk 5:22–43 ◀ ▶ Mk 6:7
E Mk 6:5 ◀ ▶ Mk 6:13
J Mt 25:31–46 ◀ ▶ Lk 10:12
H Mt 26:24 ◀ ▶ Mk 8:36–38
J Mt 25:31–46 ◀ ▶ Lk 10:12–14
N Mt 25:10–11 ◀ ▶ Mk 16:15–16
R Mk 1:15 ◀ ▶ Mk 11:25
E Mk 6:7 ◀ ▶ Mk 6:54–58

ⁿ 3 Greek *Joses*, a variant of *Joseph* ᵒ 7 Greek *unclean* ᵖ 14 Some early manuscripts *He was saying*

6:11 Jesus prophesied that those who reject the offer of salvation preached by his disciples will be judged accordingly. Though these unrepentant sinners received a much greater chance to respond than the ancient cities of Sodom and Gomorrah, they still rejected salvation.

"John, the man I beheaded, has been raised from the dead!"

¹⁷For Herod himself had given orders to have John arrested, and he had him bound and put in prison.ⁱ He did this because of Herodias, his brother Philip's wife, whom he had married. ¹⁸For John had been saying to Herod, "It is not lawful for you to have your brother's wife."ʲ ¹⁹So Herodias nursed a grudge against John and wanted to kill him. But she was not able to, ²⁰because Herod feared John and protected him, knowing him to be a righteous and holy man.ᵏ When Herod heard John, he was greatly puzzled⁹; yet he liked to listen to him.

²¹Finally the opportune time came. On his birthday Herod gave a banquet¹ for his high officials and military commanders and the leading men of Galilee.ᵐ ²²When the daughter of Herodias came in and danced, she pleased Herod and his dinner guests.

The king said to the girl, "Ask me for anything you want, and I'll give it to you." ²³And he promised her with an oath, "Whatever you ask I will give you, up to half my kingdom."ⁿ

²⁴She went out and said to her mother, "What shall I ask for?"

"The head of John the Baptist," she answered.

²⁵At once the girl hurried in to the king with the request: "I want you to give me right now the head of John the Baptist on a platter."

²⁶The king was greatly distressed, but because of his oaths and his dinner guests, he did not want to refuse her. ²⁷So he immediately sent an executioner with orders to bring John's head. The man went, beheaded John in the prison, ²⁸and brought back his head on a platter. He presented it to the girl, and she gave it to her mother. ²⁹On hearing of this, John's disciples came and took his body and laid it in a tomb.

Jesus Feeds the Five Thousand

6:32–44pp — Mt 14:13–21; Lk 9:10–17; Jn 6:5–13
6:32–44Ref — Mk 8:2–9

³⁰The apostlesᵒ gathered around Jesus and reported to him all they had done and taught.ᵖ ³¹Then, because so many people were coming and going that they did not even have a chance to eat,⁹ he said to them, "Come with me by yourselves to a quiet place and get some rest."

³²So they went away by themselves in a boatʳ to a solitary place. ³³But many who saw them leaving recognized them and ran on foot from all the towns and got there ahead of them. ³⁴When Jesus landed and saw a large crowd, he had compassion on them, because they were like sheep without a shepherd.ˢ So he began teaching them many things.

³⁵By this time it was late in the day, so his disciples came to him. "This is a remote place," they said, "and it's already very late. ³⁶Send the people away so they can go to the surrounding countryside and villages and buy themselves something to eat."

³⁷But he answered, "You give them something to eat."ᵗ

They said to him, "That would take eight months of a man's wagesʳ! Are we to go and spend that much on bread and give it to them to eat?"

³⁸"How many loaves do you have?" he asked. "Go and see."

When they found out, they said, "Five—and two fish."ᵘ

³⁹Then Jesus directed them to have all the people sit down in groups on the green grass. ⁴⁰So they sat down in groups of hundreds and fifties. ⁴¹Taking the five loaves and the two fish and looking up to heaven, he gave thanks and broke the loaves.ᵛ Then he gave them to his disciples to set before the people. He also divided the two fish among them all. ⁴²They all ate and were satisfied, ⁴³and the disciples picked up twelve basketfuls of broken pieces of bread and fish. ⁴⁴The number of the men who had eaten was five thousand.

Jesus Walks on the Water

6:45–51pp — Mt 14:22–32; Jn 6:15–21
6:53–56pp — Mt 14:34–36

⁴⁵Immediately Jesus made his disciples get into the boatʷ and go on ahead of him to Bethsaida,ˣ while he dismissed the crowd. ⁴⁶After leaving them, he went up on a mountainside to pray.ʸ

⁴⁷When evening came, the boat was in the middle of the lake, and he was alone

---

F Mk 1:13 ◄ ► Mk 8:1–9

⁹ 20 Some early manuscripts *he did many things* ʳ 37 Greek *take two hundred denarii*

on land. ⁴⁸He saw the disciples straining at the oars, because the wind was against them. About the fourth watch of the night he went out to them, walking on the lake. He was about to pass by them, ⁴⁹but when they saw him walking on the lake, they thought he was a ghost. They cried out, ⁵⁰because they all saw him and were terrified.

Immediately he spoke to them and said, "Take courage! It is I. Don't be afraid." ⁵¹Then he climbed into the boat with them, and the wind died down. They were completely amazed, ⁵²for they had not understood about the loaves; their hearts were hardened.

⁵³When they had crossed over, they landed at Gennesaret and anchored there. ⁵⁴As soon as they got out of the boat, people recognized Jesus. ⁵⁵They ran throughout that whole region and carried the sick on mats to wherever they heard he was. ⁵⁶And wherever he went—into villages, towns or countryside—they placed the sick in the marketplaces. They begged him to let them touch even the edge of his cloak, and all who touched him were healed.

Clean and Unclean
7:1–23pp — Mt 15:1–20

7 The Pharisees and some of the teachers of the law who had come from Jerusalem gathered around Jesus and ²saw some of his disciples eating food with hands that were "unclean," that is, unwashed. ³(The Pharisees and all the Jews do not eat unless they give their hands a ceremonial washing, holding to the tradition of the elders. ⁴When they come from the marketplace they do not eat unless they wash. And they observe many other traditions, such as the washing of cups, pitchers and kettles.)

⁵So the Pharisees and teachers of the law asked Jesus, "Why don't your disciples live according to the tradition of the elders instead of eating their food with 'unclean' hands?"

⁶He replied, "Isaiah was right when he prophesied about you hypocrites; as it is written:

" 'These people honor me with their lips,
but their hearts are far from me.
⁷They worship me in vain;
their teachings are but rules taught by men.'

⁸You have let go of the commands of God and are holding on to the traditions of men."

⁹And he said to them: "You have a fine way of setting aside the commands of God in order to observe your own traditions! ¹⁰For Moses said, 'Honor your father and your mother,' and, 'Anyone who curses his father or mother must be put to death.' ¹¹But you say that if a man says to his father or mother: 'Whatever help you might otherwise have received from me is Corban' (that is, a gift devoted to God), ¹²then you no longer let him do anything for his father or mother. ¹³Thus you nullify the word of God by your tradition that you have handed down. And you do many things like that."

¹⁴Again Jesus called the crowd to him and said, "Listen to me, everyone, and understand this. ¹⁵Nothing outside a man can make him 'unclean' by going into him. Rather, it is what comes out of a man that makes him 'unclean.'"

¹⁷After he had left the crowd and entered the house, his disciples asked him about this parable. ¹⁸"Are you so dull?" he asked. "Don't you see that nothing that enters a man from the outside can make him 'unclean'? ¹⁹For it doesn't go into his heart but into his stomach, and then out of his body." (In saying this, Jesus declared all foods "clean.")

²⁰He went on: "What comes out of a man is what makes him 'unclean.' ²¹For from within, out of men's hearts, come evil thoughts, sexual immorality, theft, murder, adultery, ²²greed, malice, deceit, lewdness, envy, slander, arrogance and folly. ²³All these evils come from inside and make a man 'unclean.' "

The Faith of a Syrophoenician Woman
7:24–30pp — Mt 15:21–28

²⁴Jesus left that place and went to the vicinity of Tyre. He entered a house and did not want anyone to know it; yet he could not keep his presence secret.

---

s 4 Some early manuscripts *pitchers, kettles and dining couches*   *t* 6,7 Isaiah 29:13   *u* 9 Some manuscripts *set up*   *v* 10 Exodus 20:12; Deut. 5:16   *w* 10 Exodus 21:17; Lev. 20:9   *x* 15 Some early manuscripts *'unclean.' 16If anyone has ears to hear, let him hear.*   *y* 24 Many early manuscripts *Tyre and Sidon*

²⁵In fact, as soon as she heard about him, a woman whose little daughter was possessed by an evil* spirit* came and fell at his feet. ²⁶The woman was a Greek, born in Syrian Phoenicia. She begged Jesus to drive the demon out of her daughter.

²⁷"First let the children eat all they want," he told her, "for it is not right to take the children's bread and toss it to their dogs."

²⁸"Yes, Lord," she replied, "but even the dogs under the table eat the children's crumbs."

²⁹Then he told her, "For such a reply, you may go; the demon has left your daughter."

³⁰She went home and found her child lying on the bed, and the demon gone.

The Healing of a Deaf and Mute Man
7:31–37pp — Mt 15:29–31

³¹Then Jesus left the vicinity of Tyre and went through Sidon, down to the Sea of Galilee and into the region of the Decapolis. ³²There some people brought to him a man who was deaf and could hardly talk, and they begged him to place his hand on the man.

³³After he took him aside, away from the crowd, Jesus put his fingers into the man's ears. Then he spit and touched the man's tongue. ³⁴He looked up to heaven and with a deep sigh said to him, *"Ephphatha!"* (which means, "Be opened!"). ³⁵At this, the man's ears were opened, his tongue was loosened and he began to speak plainly.

³⁶Jesus commanded them not to tell anyone. But the more he did so, the more they kept talking about it. ³⁷People were overwhelmed with amazement. "He has done everything well," they said. "He even makes the deaf hear and the mute speak."

Jesus Feeds the Four Thousand
8:1–9pp — Mt 15:32–39
8:1–9Ref — Mk 6:32–44
8:11–21pp — Mt 16:1–12

8 During those days another large crowd gathered. Since they had nothing to eat, Jesus called his disciples to him and said, ²"I have compassion for these people; they have already been with me three days and have nothing to eat. ³If I send them home hungry, they will collapse on the way, because some of them have come a long distance."

⁴His disciples answered, "But where in this remote place can anyone get enough bread to feed them?"

⁵"How many loaves do you have?" Jesus asked.

"Seven," they replied.

⁶He told the crowd to sit down on the ground. When he had taken the seven loaves and given thanks, he broke them and gave them to his disciples to set before the people, and they did so. ⁷They had a few small fish as well; he gave thanks for them also and told the disciples to distribute them. ⁸The people ate and were satisfied. Afterward the disciples picked up seven basketfuls of broken pieces that were left over. ⁹About four thousand men were present. And having sent them away, ¹⁰he got into the boat with his disciples and went to the region of Dalmanutha.

¹¹The Pharisees came and began to question Jesus. To test him, they asked him for a sign from heaven. ¹²He sighed deeply and said, "Why does this generation ask for a miraculous sign? I tell you the truth, no sign will be given to it." ¹³Then he left them, got back into the boat and crossed to the other side.

The Yeast of the Pharisees and Herod

¹⁴The disciples had forgotten to bring bread, except for one loaf they had with them in the boat. ¹⁵"Be careful," Jesus warned them. "Watch out for the yeast of the Pharisees and that of Herod."

¹⁶They discussed this with one another and said, "It is because we have no bread."

¹⁷Aware of their discussion, Jesus asked them: "Why are you talking about having no bread? Do you still not see or understand? Are your hearts hardened? ¹⁸Do you have eyes but fail to see, and ears but fail to hear? And don't you remember? ¹⁹When I broke the five loaves for the five thousand, how many basketfuls of pieces did you pick up?"

"Twelve," they replied.

²⁰"And when I broke the seven loaves

for the four thousand, how many basketfuls of pieces did you pick up?"

They answered, "Seven."ˢ

²¹He said to them, "Do you still not understand?"ᵗ

The Healing of a Blind Man at Bethsaida

²²They came to Bethsaida,ᵘ and some people brought a blind manᵛ and begged Jesus to touch him. ²³He took the blind man by the hand and led him outside the village. When he had spitʷ on the man's eyes and put his hands onˣ him, Jesus asked, "Do you see anything?"

²⁴He looked up and said, "I see people; they look like trees walking around."

²⁵Once more Jesus put his hands on the man's eyes. Then his eyes were opened, his sight was restored, and he saw everything clearly. ²⁶Jesus sent him home, saying, "Don't go into the village.ᵇ"

Peter's Confession of Christ

8:27–29pp — Mt 16:13–16; Lk 9:18–20

²⁷Jesus and his disciples went on to the villages around Caesarea Philippi. On the way he asked them, "Who do people say I am?"

²⁸They replied, "Some say John the Baptist;ʸ others say Elijah;ᶻ and still others, one of the prophets."

²⁹"But what about you?" he asked. "Who do you say I am?"

Peter answered, "You are the Christ."ᶜ ᵃ

³⁰Jesus warned them not to tell anyone about him.ᵇ

Jesus Predicts His Death

8:31 — 9:1pp — Mt 16:21–28; Lk 9:22–27

³¹He then began to teach them that the Son of Manᶜ must suffer many thingsᵈ and be rejected by the elders, chief priests and teachers of the law,ᵉ and that he must be killedᶠ and after three daysᵍ rise again.ʰ ³²He spoke plainlyⁱ about this, and Peter took him aside and began to rebuke him.

³³But when Jesus turned and looked at his disciples, he rebuked Peter. "Get behind me, Satan!"ʲ he said. "You do not have in mind the things of God, but the things of men."

³⁴Then he called the crowd to him along with his disciples and said: "If anyone would come after me, he must deny himself and take up his cross and follow me.ᵏ ³⁵For whoever wants to save his lifeᵈ will lose it, but whoever loses his life for me and for the gospel will save it.ˡ ³⁶What good is it for a man to gain the whole world, yet forfeit his soul? ³⁷Or what can a man give in exchange for his soul? ³⁸If anyone is ashamed of me and my words in this adulterous and sinful generation, the Son of Manᵐ will be ashamed of himⁿ when he comesᵒ in his Father's glory with the holy angels."

9 And he said to them, "I tell you the truth, some who are standing here will not taste death before they see the kingdom of God comeᵖ with power."ᑫ

The Transfiguration

9:2–8pp — Lk 9:28–36
9:2–13pp — Mt 17:1–13

²After six days Jesus took Peter, James and Johnʳ with him and led them up a high mountain, where they were all alone. There he was transfigured before them. ³His clothes became dazzling white,ˢ whiter than anyone in the world could bleach them. ⁴And there appeared before them Elijah and Moses, who were talking with Jesus.

⁵Peter said to Jesus, "Rabbi,ᵗ it is good for us to be here. Let us put up three shelters—one for you, one for Moses and one for Elijah." ⁶(He did not know what to say, they were so frightened.)

⁷Then a cloud appeared and enveloped

8:20 ˢ ver 6-9; Mt 15:37
8:21 ᵗ Mk 6:52
8:22 ᵘ Mt 11:21 ᵛ Mk 10:46; Jn 9:1
8:23 ʷ Mk 7:33 ˣ S Mk 5:23
8:28 ʸ S Mt 3:1 ᶻ Mal 4:5
8:29 ᵃ Jn 6:69; 11:27
8:30 ᵇ S Mt 8:4; 16:20; 17:9; Mk 9:9; Lk 9:21
8:31 ᶜ S Mt 8:20 ᵈ S Mt 16:21 ᵉ Mt 27:1,2 ᶠ Ac 2:23; 3:13 ᵍ S Mt 16:21 ʰ S Mt 16:21
8:32 ⁱ Jn 18:20
8:33 ʲ S Mt 4:10
8:34 ᵏ Mt 10:38; Lk 14:27
8:35 ˡ S Jn 12:25
8:38 ᵐ S Mt 8:20 ⁿ Mt 10:33; Lk 12:9 ᵒ S 1Th 2:19
9:1 ᵖ Mk 13:30; Lk 22:18 ᑫ Mt 24:30; 25:31
9:2 ʳ S Mt 4:21
9:3 ˢ S Mt 28:3
9:5 ᵗ S Mt 23:7

S Mk 4:16–20 ◀▶ Mk 9:43–50
H Mk 6:11 ◀▶ Mk 9:42–49
C Mk 4:29 ◀▶ Mk 13:26
O Mt 25:1–12 ◀▶ Mk 10:15
T Mk 5:19 ◀▶ Lk 6:45
K Mk 4:26–28 ◀▶ Lk 11:2

ᵇ 26 Some manuscripts *Don't go and tell anyone in the village*
ᶜ 29 Or *Messiah.* "The Christ" (Greek) and "the Messiah" (Hebrew) both mean "the Anointed One." ᵈ 35 The Greek word means either *life* or *soul;* also in verse 36.

E Mk 7:25–37 ◀▶ Mk 9:14–29
B Mk 1:7 ◀▶ Mk 14:18–21

8:38 Jesus warned that those who deny their faith in him and his words will be rejected when he returns. When we face persecution for our Christian faith, we need to remember this warning and ask ourselves, "What good is it for a man to gain the whole world, yet forfeit his soul?" (Mk 8:36).

them, and a voice came from the cloud: "This is my Son, whom I love. Listen to him!"

⁸Suddenly, when they looked around, they no longer saw anyone with them except Jesus.

⁹As they were coming down the mountain, Jesus gave them orders not to tell anyone what they had seen until the Son of Man had risen from the dead. ¹⁰They kept the matter to themselves, discussing what "rising from the dead" meant.

¹¹And they asked him, "Why do the teachers of the law say that Elijah must come first?"

¹²Jesus replied, "To be sure, Elijah does come first, and restores all things. Why then is it written that the Son of Man must suffer much and be rejected? ¹³But I tell you, Elijah has come, and they have done to him everything they wished, just as it is written about him."

The Healing of a Boy With an Evil Spirit
9:14–28; 30–32pp — Mt 17:14–19; 22,23; Lk 9:37–45

¹⁴When they came to the other disciples, they saw a large crowd around them and the teachers of the law arguing with them. ¹⁵As soon as all the people saw Jesus, they were overwhelmed with wonder and ran to greet him.

¹⁶"What are you arguing with them about?" he asked.

¹⁷A man in the crowd answered, "Teacher, I brought you my son, who is possessed by a spirit that has robbed him of speech. ¹⁸Whenever it seizes him, it throws him to the ground. He foams at the mouth, gnashes his teeth and becomes rigid. I asked your disciples to drive out the spirit, but they could not."

¹⁹"O unbelieving generation," Jesus replied, "how long shall I stay with you? How long shall I put up with you? Bring the boy to me."

²⁰So they brought him. When the spirit saw Jesus, it immediately threw the boy into a convulsion. He fell to the ground and rolled around, foaming at the mouth.

²¹Jesus asked the boy's father, "How long has he been like this?"

"From childhood," he answered. ²²"It has often thrown him into fire or water to kill him. But if you can do anything, take pity on us and help us."

²³"'If you can'?" said Jesus. "Everything is possible for him who believes."

²⁴Immediately the boy's father exclaimed, "I do believe; help me overcome my unbelief!"

²⁵When Jesus saw that a crowd was running to the scene, he rebuked the evil spirit. "You deaf and mute spirit," he said, "I command you, come out of him and never enter him again."

²⁶The spirit shrieked, convulsed him violently and came out. The boy looked so much like a corpse that many said, "He's dead." ²⁷But Jesus took him by the hand and lifted him to his feet, and he stood up.

²⁸After Jesus had gone indoors, his disciples asked him privately, "Why couldn't we drive it out?"

²⁹He replied, "This kind can come out only by prayer."

³⁰They left that place and passed through Galilee. Jesus did not want anyone to know where they were, ³¹because he was teaching his disciples. He said to them, "The Son of Man is going to be betrayed into the hands of men. They will kill him, and after three days he will rise." ³²But they did not understand what he meant and were afraid to ask him about it.

Who Is the Greatest?
9:33–37pp — Mt 18:1–5; Lk 9:46–48

³³They came to Capernaum. When he was in the house, he asked them, "What were you arguing about on the road?" ³⁴But they kept quiet because on the way they had argued about who was the greatest.

³⁵Sitting down, Jesus called the Twelve and said, "If anyone wants to be first, he must be the very last, and the servant of all."

³⁶He took a little child and had him stand among them. Taking him in his arms, he said to them, ³⁷"Whoever welcomes one of these little children in my name welcomes me; and whoever welcomes me does not welcome me but the one who sent me."

Whoever Is Not Against Us Is for Us

9:38–40pp — Lk 9:49,50

[E] 38"Teacher," said John, "we saw a man driving out demons in your name and we told him to stop, because he was not one of us."[r]

39"Do not stop him," Jesus said. "No one who does a miracle in my name can in the next moment say anything bad about me, 40for whoever is not against us is for us.[s] 41I tell you the truth, anyone who gives you a cup of water in my name because you belong to Christ will certainly not lose his reward.[t]

Causing to Sin

[H]
[L] 42"And if anyone causes one of these little ones who believe in me to sin,[u] it would be better for him to be thrown into the sea with a large millstone tied
[S] around his neck.[v] 43If your hand causes you to sin,[w] cut it off. It is better for you to enter life maimed than with two hands to go into hell,[x] where the fire never goes out.[g][y] 45And if your foot causes you to sin,[z] cut it off. It is better for you to enter life crippled than to have two feet and be thrown into hell,[h][a] 47And if your eye causes you to sin,[b] pluck it out. It is better for you to enter the kingdom of God with one eye than to have two eyes and be thrown into hell,[c] 48where

" 'their worm does not die,
and the fire is not quenched.'[i][d]

49Everyone will be salted[e] with fire. 50"Salt is good, but if it loses its saltiness, how can you make it salty again?[f] Have salt in yourselves,[g] and be at peace with each other."[h]

Divorce

10:1–12pp — Mt 19:1–9

10 Jesus then left that place and went into the region of Judea and across the Jordan.[i] Again crowds of people came to him, and as was his custom, he taught them.[j]

2Some Pharisees[k] came and tested him by asking, "Is it lawful for a man to divorce his wife?"

3"What did Moses command you?" he replied.

4They said, "Moses permitted a man to write a certificate of divorce and send her away."[l]

5"It was because your hearts were hard[m] that Moses wrote you this law," Jesus replied. 6"But at the beginning of creation God 'made them male and female.'[n] 7"For this reason a man will leave his father and mother and be united to his wife,[k] 8and the two will become one flesh.'[o] So they are no longer two, but one. 9Therefore what God has joined together, let man not separate."

10When they were in the house again, the disciples asked Jesus about this. 11He answered, "Anyone who divorces his wife and marries another woman commits adultery against her.[p] 12And if she divorces her husband and marries another man, she commits adultery."[q]

The Little Children and Jesus

10:13–16pp — Mt 19:13–15; Lk 18:15–17

13People were bringing little children to Jesus to have him touch them, but the disciples rebuked them. 14When Jesus [M] saw this, he was indignant. He said to them, "Let the little children come to me, and do not hinder them, for the kingdom of God belongs to such as these.[r] 15I tell [O] you the truth, anyone who will not receive the kingdom of God like a little child will never enter it."[s] 16And he took the children in his arms,[t] put his hands on them and blessed them.

The Rich Young Man

10:17–31pp — Mt 19:16–30; Lk 18:18–30

17As Jesus started on his way, a man [G] ran up to him and fell on his knees[u] before him. "Good teacher," he asked, "what must I do to inherit eternal life?"[v]

18"Why do you call me good?" Jesus answered. "No one is good—except God alone. 19You know the commandments: 'Do not murder, do not commit adultery, do not steal, do not give false testimony,

---

9:38 r Nu 11:27–29
9:40 s Mt 12:30; Lk 11:23
9:41 t S Mt 10:42
9:42 u S Mt 5:29
v Mt 18:6; Lk 17:2
9:43 w S Mt 5:29
x Mt 5:30; 18:8
y S Mt 25:41
9:45 z S Mt 5:29
a Mt 18:8
9:47 b S Mt 5:29
c Mt 5:29; 18:9
9:48 d Isa 66:24; S Mt 25:41
9:49 e Lev 2:13
9:50 f Mt 5:13; Lk 14:34,35
g Col 4:6
h Ro 12:18; 2Co 13:11; 1Th 5:13
10:1 i Mk 1:5; Jn 10:40; 11:7
j S Mt 4:23; Mk 2:13; 4:2; 6:6, 34
10:2 k Mk 2:16
10:4 l Dt 24:1–4; Mt 5:31
10:5 m Ps 95:8; Heb 3:15
10:6 n Ge 1:27; 5:2
10:8 o Ge 2:24; 1Co 6:16
10:11 p S Lk 16:18
10:12 q Ro 7:3; 1Co 7:10,11
10:14 r S Mt 25:34
10:15 s Mt 18:3
10:16 t Mk 9:36
10:17 u Mk 1:40
v Lk 10:25;
S Ac 20:32

M Mt 23:12 ◄► Mk 10:23–25
O Mk 8:38 ◄► Mk 12:28–34
G Mk 7:6–7 ◄► Lk 18:9–14

g 43 Some manuscripts out, 44where / " 'their worm does not die, / and the fire is not quenched.' h 45 Some manuscripts hell, 46where / " 'their worm does not die, / and the fire is not quenched.' i 48 Isaiah 66:24 j 6 Gen. 1:27 k 7 Some early manuscripts do not have and be united to his wife. l 8 Gen. 2:24

E Mk 9:14–29 ◄► Mk 10:46–52
H Mk 8:36–38 ◄► Mk 12:36–40
L Mt 28:20 ◄► Mk 11:24
S Mk 8:34 ◄► Mk 12:2

do not defraud, honor your father and mother.'ᵐ ʷ

²⁰"Teacher," he declared, "all these I have kept since I was a boy."

²¹Jesus looked at him and loved him. "One thing you lack," he said. "Go, sell everything you have and give to the poor,ˣ and you will have treasure in heaven.ʸ Then come, follow me."ᶻ

²²At this the man's face fell. He went away sad, because he had great wealth.

²³Jesus looked around and said to his disciples, "How hard it is for the richᵃ to enter the kingdom of God!"

²⁴The disciples were amazed at his words. But Jesus said again, "Children, how hard it isⁿ to enter the kingdom of God!ᵇ ²⁵It is easier for a camel to go through the eye of a needle than for a rich man to enter the kingdom of God."ᶜ

²⁶The disciples were even more amazed, and said to each other, "Who then can be saved?"

²⁷Jesus looked at them and said, "With man this is impossible, but not with God; all things are possible with God."ᵈ

²⁸Peter said to him, "We have left everything to follow you!"ᵉ

²⁹"I tell you the truth," Jesus replied, "no one who has left home or brothers or sisters or mother or father or children or fields for me and the gospel ³⁰will fail to receive a hundred times as muchᶠ in this present age (homes, brothers, sisters, mothers, children and fields—and with them, persecutions) and in the age to come,ᵍ eternal life.ʰ ³¹But many who are first will be last, and the last first."ⁱ

Jesus Again Predicts His Death
10:32-34pp — Mt 20:17-19; Lk 18:31-33

³²They were on their way up to Jerusalem, with Jesus leading the way, and the disciples were astonished, while those who followed were afraid. Again he took the Twelveʲ aside and told them what was going to happen to him. ³³"We are going up to Jerusalem,"ᵏ he said, "and the Son of Manˡ will be betrayed to the chief priests and teachers of the law.ᵐ They will condemn him to death and will hand him over to the Gentiles, ³⁴who will mock him and spit on him, flog himⁿ and kill him.ᵒ Three days laterᵖ he will rise."ᑫ

The Request of James and John
10:35-45pp — Mt 20:20-28

³⁵Then James and John, the sons of Zebedee, came to him. "Teacher," they said, "we want you to do for us whatever we ask."

³⁶"What do you want me to do for you?" he asked.

³⁷They replied, "Let one of us sit at your right and the other at your left in your glory."ʳ

³⁸"You don't know what you are asking,"ˢ Jesus said. "Can you drink the cupᵗ I drink or be baptized with the baptism I am baptized with?"ᵘ

³⁹"We can," they answered.

Jesus said to them, "You will drink the cup I drink and be baptized with the baptism I am baptized with,ᵛ ⁴⁰but to sit at my right or left is not for me to grant. These places belong to those for whom they have been prepared."

⁴¹When the ten heard about this, they became indignant with James and John. ⁴²Jesus called them together and said, "You know that those who are regarded as rulers of the Gentiles lord it over them, and their high officials exercise authority over them. ⁴³Not so with you. Instead, whoever wants to become great among you must be your servant,ʷ ⁴⁴and whoever wants to be first must be slave of all. ⁴⁵For even the Son of Man did not come to be served, but to serve,ˣ and to give his life as a ransom for many."ʸ

M *Mk 4:30-32* ◀ ▶ *Mk 10:39-40*
M *Mk 10:37* ◀ ▶ *Mk 11:10*
D *Mt 26:26-28* ◀ ▶ *Mk 14:22-24*

M *Mk 10:14-15* ◀ ▶ *Lk 6:20-21*
K *Mk 2:10* ◀ ▶ *Mk 13:31*
U *Mt 19:29* ◀ ▶ *Lk 12:31*

Cross references:
10:19 ʷ Ex 20:12-16; Dt 5:16-20
10:21 ˣS Ac 2:45; ʸMt 6:20; Lk 12:33; ᶻS Mt 4:19
10:23 ᵃ Ps 52:7; 62:10; Mk 4:19; 1Ti 6:9,10,17
10:24 ᵇ Mt 7:13, 14; Jn 3:5
10:25 ᶜ Lk 12:16-20; 16:19-31
10:27 ᵈ S Mt 19:26
10:28 ᵉ S Mt 4:19
10:30 ᶠ Mt 6:33; ᵍ S Mt 12:32; ʰ S Mt 25:46
10:31 ⁱ S Mt 19:30
10:32 ʲ Mk 3:16-19
10:33 ᵏ S Lk 9:51; ˡ S Mt 8:20; ᵐ Mt 27:1,2
10:34 ⁿ S Mt 16:21; ᵒ Ac 2:23; 3:13; ᵖ S Mt 16:21; ᑫ S Mt 16:21
10:37 ʳ Mt 19:28
10:38 ˢ Job 38:2; ᵗ S Mt 20:22; ᵘ Lk 12:50
10:39 ᵛ Ac 12:2; Rev 1:9
10:43 ʷ S Mk 9:35
10:45 ˣ S Mt 20:28; ʸ S Mt 20:28

ᵐ 19 Exodus 20:12-16; Deut. 5:16-20   ⁿ 24 Some manuscripts *is for those who trust in riches*

10:37 The desire of James and John to attain cabinet positions in the coming kingdom of Jesus Christ reveals the physical reality of Christ's millennial kingdom. While many scholars have dismissed these ambitious disciples, we need to remember that even though these men did not understand that Jesus would die before returning to establish his millennial kingdom, they did understand that they had been promised the right to rule over the twelve tribes of Israel (see Mt 19:28).

Blind Bartimaeus Receives His Sight

10:46–52pp — Mt 20:29–34; Lk 18:35–43

⁴⁶Then they came to Jericho. As Jesus and his disciples, together with a large crowd, were leaving the city, a blind man, Bartimaeus (that is, the Son of Timaeus), was sitting by the roadside begging. ⁴⁷When he heard that it was Jesus of Nazareth,ᶻ he began to shout, "Jesus, Son of David,ᵃ have mercy on me!"

⁴⁸Many rebuked him and told him to be quiet, but he shouted all the more, "Son of David, have mercy on me!"

⁴⁹Jesus stopped and said, "Call him."

So they called to the blind man, "Cheer up! On your feet! He's calling you." ⁵⁰Throwing his cloak aside, he jumped to his feet and came to Jesus.

⁵¹"What do you want me to do for you?" Jesus asked him.

The blind man said, "Rabbi,ᵇ I want to see."

⁵²"Go," said Jesus, "your faith has healed you."ᶜ Immediately he received his sight and followedᵈ Jesus along the road.

The Triumphal Entry

11:1–10pp — Mt 21:1–9; Lk 19:29–38
11:7–10pp — Jn 12:12–15

11 As they approached Jerusalem and came to Bethphage and Bethany ᵉ at the Mount of Olives,ᶠ Jesus sent two of his disciples, ²saying to them, "Go to the village ahead of you, and just as you enter it, you will find a colt tied there, which no one has ever ridden.ᵍ Untie it and bring it here. ³If anyone asks you, 'Why are you doing this?' tell him, 'The Lord needs it and will send it back here shortly.'"

⁴They went and found a colt outside in the street, tied at a doorway.ʰ As they untied it, ⁵some people standing there asked, "What are you doing, untying that colt?" ⁶They answered as Jesus had told them to, and the people let them go. ⁷When they brought the colt to Jesus and threw their cloaks over it, he sat on it. ⁸Many people spread their cloaks on the road, while others spread branches they had cut in the fields. ⁹Those who went ahead and those who followed shouted,

"Hosanna!ᵒ"

"Blessed is he who comes in the name of the Lord!"ᵖⁱ

¹⁰"Blessed is the coming kingdom of our father David!"

"Hosanna in the highest!"ʲ

¹¹Jesus entered Jerusalem and went to the temple. He looked around at everything, but since it was already late, he went out to Bethany with the Twelve.ᵏ

Jesus Clears the Temple

11:12–14pp — Mt 21:18–22
11:15–18pp — Mt 21:12–16; Lk 19:45–47; Jn 2:13–16

¹²The next day as they were leaving Bethany, Jesus was hungry. ¹³Seeing in the distance a fig tree in leaf, he went to find out if it had any fruit. When he reached it, he found nothing but leaves, because it was not the season for figs.ˡ ¹⁴Then he said to the tree, "May no one ever eat fruit from you again." And his disciples heard him say it.

¹⁵On reaching Jerusalem, Jesus entered the temple area and began driving out those who were buying and selling there. He overturned the tables of the money changers and the benches of those selling doves, ¹⁶and would not allow anyone to carry merchandise through the temple courts. ¹⁷And as he taught them, he said, "Is it not written:

l Mt 27:42 ◄ ► Mk 15:2
M Mk 10:39–40 ◄ ► Mk 12:36

o 9 A Hebrew expression meaning "Save!" which became an exclamation of praise; also in verse 10 *p* 9 Psalm 118:25,26

11:10 The disciples and the people that joined this procession acknowledged Jesus' legal right to be acclaimed Israel's Messiah and loudly announced his coming kingdom.

11:13–14, 20–21 The symbol of the fig tree appears numerous times in the OT in reference to Israel (see Jdg 9:10–11; 1Ki 4:25; Isa 36:16; Mic 4:5; Zec 3:10). Jesus withered this barren fig tree because it did not bear fruit for its Creator, symbolizing that Israel had not borne spiritual fruit. God promised that Israel would produce great spiritual fruit in the last days (see Ro 11:25–29). Jesus foretold that when we see the fig tree flourishing again—Israel reborn as a nation—we will know that the end times are "near, right at the door" (Mt 24:33).

" 'My house will be called
  a house of prayer for all nations'?"
But you have made it 'a den of robbers.'"
¹⁸The chief priests and the teachers of the law heard this and began looking for a way to kill him, for they feared him, because the whole crowd was amazed at his teaching.
¹⁹When evening came, they went out of the city.

The Withered Fig Tree
11:20–24pp — Mt 21:19–22

²⁰In the morning, as they went along, they saw the fig tree withered from the roots. ²¹Peter remembered and said to Jesus, "Rabbi, look! The fig tree you cursed has withered!"
²²"Have faith in God," Jesus answered. ²³"I tell you the truth, if anyone says to this mountain, 'Go, throw yourself into the sea,' and does not doubt in his heart but believes that what he says will happen, it will be done for him. ²⁴Therefore I tell you, whatever you ask for in prayer, believe that you have received it, and it will be yours. ²⁵And when you stand praying, if you hold anything against anyone, forgive him, so that your Father in heaven may forgive you your sins."

The Authority of Jesus Questioned
11:27–33pp — Mt 21:23–27; Lk 20:1–8

²⁷They arrived again in Jerusalem, and while Jesus was walking in the temple courts, the chief priests, the teachers of the law and the elders came to him. ²⁸"By what authority are you doing these things?" they asked. "And who gave you authority to do this?"
²⁹Jesus replied, "I will ask you one question. Answer me, and I will tell you by what authority I am doing these things. ³⁰John's baptism—was it from heaven, or from men? Tell me!"
³¹They discussed it among themselves

L *Mk 9:42* ◀ ▶ *Lk 4:10–11*
R *Mk 6:12* ◀ ▶ *Lk 3:2*

11:17 m Isa 56:7
n Jer 7:11

11:18 o Mt 21:46;
Mk 12:12; Lk 20:19
p S Mt 7:28

11:19 q Lk 21:37

11:21 r S Mt 23:7

11:23 s S Mt 21:21

11:24 t S Mt 7:7

11:25 u S Mt 6:14

11:32 v S Mt 11:9

12:1 w Isa 5:1-7

12:6 x Heb 1:1-3

12:10 y S Ac 4:11

and said, "If we say, 'From heaven,' he will ask, 'Then why didn't you believe him?' ³²But if we say, 'From men' . . ." (They feared the people, for everyone held that John really was a prophet.)
³³So they answered Jesus, "We don't know."
Jesus said, "Neither will I tell you by what authority I am doing these things."

The Parable of the Tenants
12:1–12pp — Mt 21:33–46; Lk 20:9–19

12 He then began to speak to them in parables: "A man planted a vineyard. He put a wall around it, dug a pit for the winepress and built a watchtower. Then he rented the vineyard to some farmers and went away on a journey. ²At harvest time he sent a servant to the tenants to collect from them some of the fruit of the vineyard. ³But they seized him, beat him and sent him away empty-handed. ⁴Then he sent another servant to them; they struck this man on the head and treated him shamefully. ⁵He sent still another, and that one they killed. He sent many others; some of them they beat, others they killed.
⁶"He had one left to send, a son, whom he loved. He sent him last of all, saying, 'They will respect my son.'
⁷"But the tenants said to one another, 'This is the heir. Come, let's kill him, and the inheritance will be ours.' ⁸So they took him and killed him, and threw him out of the vineyard.
⁹"What then will the owner of the vineyard do? He will come and kill those tenants and give the vineyard to others. ¹⁰Haven't you read this scripture:

" 'The stone the builders rejected
  has become the capstone;

S *Mk 9:43–50* ◀ ▶ *Mk 13:13*
G *Mt 22:9–10* ◀ ▶ *Lk 14:21*
R *Mt 24:15–22* ◀ ▶ *Mk 13:1–2*

q 17 Isaiah 56:7   r 17 Jer. 7:11   s 19 Some early manuscripts he
t 22 Some early manuscripts If you have   u 25 Some manuscripts sins.
26 But if you do not forgive, neither will your Father who is in heaven forgive your sins.   v 10 Or cornerstone

---

12:9 In this prophetic parable, Jesus taught that God as "the owner of the vineyard" would destroy the generation of unrepentant Jews who rejected Jesus' claims as their Messiah. Jesus' words foreshadowed the creation of the church, composed of both Gentiles and Jews, who would accept his claims as Messiah and inherit the spiritual kingdom of heaven because of their faith in him.

¹¹the Lord has done this,
    and it is marvelous in our eyes'ʷ"?ᶻ

¹²Then they looked for a way to arrest him because they knew he had spoken the parable against them. But they were afraid of the crowd;ᵃ so they left him and went away.ᵇ

Paying Taxes to Caesar
12:13–17pp — Mt 22:15–22; Lk 20:20–26

¹³Later they sent some of the Phariseesᶜ and Herodiansᶜ to Jesus to catch himᵈ in his words. ¹⁴They came to him and said, "Teacher, we know you are a man of integrity. You aren't swayed by men, because you pay no attention to who they are; but you teach the way of God in accordance with the truth. Is it right to pay taxes to Caesar or not? ¹⁵Should we pay or shouldn't we?"

But Jesus knew their hypocrisy. "Why are you trying to trap me?" he asked. "Bring me a denarius and let me look at it." ¹⁶They brought the coin, and he asked them, "Whose portrait is this? And whose inscription?"

"Caesar's," they replied.

¹⁷Then Jesus said to them, "Give to Caesar what is Caesar's and to God what is God's."ᵉ

And they were amazed at him.

Marriage at the Resurrection
12:18–27pp — Mt 22:23–33; Lk 20:27–38

¹⁸Then the Sadducees,ᶠ who say there is no resurrection,ᵍ came to him with a question. ¹⁹"Teacher," they said, "Moses wrote for us that if a man's brother dies and leaves a wife but no children, the man must marry the widow and have children for his brother.ʰ ²⁰Now there were seven brothers. The first one married and died without leaving any children. ²¹The second one married the widow, but he also died, leaving no child. It was the same with the third. ²²In fact, none of the seven left any children. Last of all, the woman died too. ²³At the resurrectionˣ whose wife will she be, since the seven were married to her?"

²⁴Jesus replied, "Are you not in error because you do not know the Scripturesⁱ or the power of God? ²⁵When the dead rise, they will neither marry nor be given in marriage; they will be like the angels in heaven.ʲ ²⁶Now about the dead rising—have you not read in the book of Moses, in the account of the bush, how God said to him, 'I am the God of Abraham, the God of Isaac, and the God of Jacob'ʸ?ᵏ ²⁷He is not the God of the dead, but of the living. You are badly mistaken!"

The Greatest Commandment
12:28–34pp — Mt 22:34–40

²⁸One of the teachers of the lawˡ came and heard them debating. Noticing that Jesus had given them a good answer, he asked him, "Of all the commandments, which is the most important?"

²⁹"The most important one," answered Jesus, "is this: 'Hear, O Israel, the Lord our God, the Lord is one.ᶻ ³⁰Love the Lord your God with all your heart and with all your soul and with all your mind and with all your strength.'ᵃᵐ ³¹The second is this: 'Love your neighbor as yourself.'ᵇⁿ There is no commandment greater than these."

³²"Well said, teacher," the man replied. "You are right in saying that God is one and there is no other but him.ᵒ ³³To love him with all your heart, with all your understanding and with all your strength, and to love your neighbor as yourself is more important than all burnt offerings and sacrifices."ᵖ

³⁴When Jesus saw that he had answered wisely, he said to him, "You are not far from the kingdom of God."ᵠ And from then on no one dared ask him any more questions.ʳ

Whose Son Is the Christ?
12:35–37pp — Mt 22:41–46; Lk 20:41–44
12:38–40pp — Mt 23:1–7; Lk 20:45–47

³⁵While Jesus was teaching in the temple courts,ˢ he asked, "How is it that the teachers of the law say that the Christᶜ is

ʷ 11 Psalm 118:22,23 ˣ 23 Some manuscripts *resurrection, when men rise from the dead,* ʸ 26 Exodus 3:6 ᶻ 29 *Or the Lord our God is one Lord* ᵃ 30 Deut. 6:4,5 ᵇ 31 Lev. 19:18 ᶜ 35 *Or Messiah*

12:24–25 See study note at Mt 22:29–32.   **12:35–36** See study note at Mt 22:44.

the son of David?ᵗ ³⁶David himself, speaking by the Holy Spirit,ᵘ declared:

" 'The Lord said to my Lord:
"Sit at my right hand
until I put your enemies
under your feet." 'ᵈᵛ

³⁷David himself calls him 'Lord.' How then can he be his son?"

The large crowdʷ listened to him with delight.

³⁸As he taught, Jesus said, "Watch out for the teachers of the law. They like to walk around in flowing robes and be greeted in the marketplaces, ³⁹and have the most important seats in the synagogues and the places of honor at banquets.ˣ ⁴⁰They devour widows' houses and for a show make lengthy prayers. Such men will be punished most severely."

The Widow's Offering
12:41–44pp — Lk 21:1–4

⁴¹Jesus sat down opposite the place where the offerings were putʸ and watched the crowd putting their money into the temple treasury. Many rich people threw in large amounts. ⁴²But a poor widow came and put in two very small copper coins,ᵉ worth only a fraction of a penny.ᶠ

M *Mk 11:10* ◀▶ *Mk 15:2*
V *Mt 22:44* ◀▶ *Lk 1:33*
E *Mk 1:12* ◀▶ *Lk 1:15–17*
L *Mk 1:12* ◀▶ *Mk 13:11*
T *Mt 22:43–44* ◀▶ *Mk 13:11*
H *Mk 9:42–49* ◀▶ *Mk 13:19*

12:35 ᵗS Mt 9:27

12:36 ᵘ2Sa 23:2
ᵛPs 110:1;
S Mt 22:44

12:37 ʷJn 12:9

12:39 ˣLk 11:43

12:41 ʸ2Ki 12:9;
Jn 8:20

12:44 ᶻ2Co 8:12

13:2 ᵃLk 19:44

13:3 ᵇS Mt 21:1
ᶜS Mt 4:21

13:5 ᵈver 22;
Jer 29:8; Eph 5:6;
2Th 2:3,10-12;
1Ti 4:1; 2Ti 3:13;
1Jn 4:6

---

⁴³Calling his disciples to him, Jesus said, "I tell you the truth, this poor widow has put more into the treasury than all the others. ⁴⁴They all gave out of their wealth; but she, out of her poverty, put in everything—all she had to live on."ᶻ

Signs of the End of the Age
13:1–37pp — Mt 24:1–51; Lk 21:5–36

13 As he was leaving the temple, one of his disciples said to him, "Look, Teacher! What massive stones! What magnificent buildings!"

²"Do you see all these great buildings?" replied Jesus. "Not one stone here will be left on another; every one will be thrown down."ᵃ

³As Jesus was sitting on the Mount of Olivesᵇ opposite the temple, Peter, James, Johnᶜ and Andrew asked him privately, ⁴"Tell us, when will these things happen? And what will be the sign that they are all about to be fulfilled?"

⁵Jesus said to them: "Watch out that no one deceives you.ᵈ ⁶Many will come in my name, claiming, 'I am he,' and will deceive many. ⁷When you hear of wars and rumors of wars, do not be alarmed. Such things must happen, but the end is still to come. ⁸Nation will rise against nation, and kingdom against kingdom. There will be earthquakes in various

R *Mk 12:9* ◀▶ *Mk 13:14–20*
E *Mt 24:32–33* ◀▶ *Mk 13:22*

ᵈ36 Psalm 110:1   ᵉ42 Greek *two lepta*   ᶠ42 Greek *kodrantes*

13:1–2 This chapter records Christ's prophetic discourse to his disciples on the mount of Olives several days before his crucifixion (see Mt 24). Note that this discourse occurred before the crucifixion and before the establishment of the NT church.

As Jesus sat on the mount of Olives he prophesied that the temple would be totally destroyed so that "not one stone here will be left on another; every one will be thrown down" (13:2). This detailed prophecy was precisely fulfilled when the Romans burned the temple to the ground in A.D. 70. The fire melted the gold that was inlaid on the walls of the sanctuary so that it flowed down into the cracks between the huge stones. When the fire subsided, Roman soldiers and scavengers pried the stones apart to recover the valuable gold. In complete fulfillment of this prophecy, not one stone was left on top of another.

13:4 This verse records the questions of Christ's disciples regarding the coming destruction of the temple and the final signs that will indicate the return of Jesus Christ in the last days. See the study notes for Mt 24:1–3 for additional information.

13:6–7 The first prophetic sign of Christ's return will be the rise of false Christs. Though there have always been those who claimed to be the Messiah, the incidence of such claims is increasingly on the rise. Jesus also warned that "wars and rumors of wars" (13:7) would be another prophetic sign of his imminent return. Since 1945, we have endured more wars than any other generation in history (see Joel 3:9–10). See the study notes for Mt 24:4–8.

13:8 Jesus also warned that several cataclysmic signs in nature would signal his return. See the study notes for Mt 24:4–8.

places, and famines. These are the beginning of birth pains.

⁹"You must be on your guard. You will be handed over to the local councils and flogged in the synagogues.ᵉ On account of me you will stand before governors and kings as witnesses to them. ¹⁰And the gospel must first be preached to all nations. ¹¹Whenever you are arrested and brought to trial, do not worry beforehand about what to say. Just say whatever is given you at the time, for it is not you speaking, but the Holy Spirit.ᶠ

¹²"Brother will betray brother to death, and a father his child. Children will rebel against their parents and have them put to death.ᵍ ¹³All men will hate you because of me,ʰ but he who stands firm to the end will be saved.ⁱ

¹⁴"When you see 'the abomination that causes desolation'ᵍⁱ standing where itʰ does not belong—let the reader understand—then let those who are in Judea flee to the mountains. ¹⁵Let no one on the roof of his house go down or enter the house to take anything out. ¹⁶Let no one in the field go back to get his cloak. ¹⁷How dreadful it will be in those days for pregnant women and nursing mothers!ᵏ ¹⁸Pray that this will not take place in winter, ¹⁹because those will be days of distress unequaled from the beginning, when God created the world,ˡ until now—and never to be equaled again.ᵐ

²⁰If the Lord had not cut short those days, no one would survive. But for the sake of the elect, whom he has chosen, he has shortened them. ²¹At that time if anyone says to you, 'Look, here is the Christⁱ!' or, 'Look, there he is!' do not believe it.ⁿ ²²For false Christs and false prophetsᵒ will appear and perform signs and miraclesᵖ to deceive the elect—if that were possible. ²³So be on your guard;ᑫ I have told you everything ahead of time.

²⁴"But in those days, following that distress,

" 'the sun will be darkened,
    and the moon will not give its light;
²⁵the stars will fall from the sky,
    and the heavenly bodies will be shaken.'ʲʳ

²⁶"At that time men will see the Son of Man coming in cloudsˢ with great power and glory. ²⁷And he will send his angels and gather his elect from the four winds, from the ends of the earth to the ends of the heavens.ᵗ

²⁸"Now learn this lesson from the fig tree: As soon as its twigs get tender and its leaves come out, you know that summer is near. ²⁹Even so, when you see these things happening, you know that it is near, right at the door. ³⁰I tell you the truth, this generationᵏᵘ will certainly not pass away until all these things have hap-

---

13:9 ᵉ S Mt 10:17
13:11 ᶠ Mt 10:19, 20; Lk 12:11,12
13:12 ᵍ Mic 7:6; Mt 10:21; Lk 12:51-53
13:13 ʰ S Jn 15:21 ⁱ S Mt 10:22
13:14 ʲ Da 9:27; 11:31; 12:11
13:17 ᵏ Lk 23:29
13:19 ˡ Mk 10:6 ᵐ Da 9:26; 12:1; Joel 2:2
13:21 ⁿ Lk 17:23; 21:8
13:22 ᵒ S Mt 7:15 ᵖ S Jn 4:48; 2Th 2:9,10
13:23 ᑫ 2Pe 3:17
13:25 ʳ Isa 13:10; 34:4; S Mt 24:29
13:26 ˢ Rev 1:7
13:27 ᵗ Zec 2:6
13:30 ᵘ Lk 17:25

G Mt 10:19-20 ◄ ► Mk 16:17-18
L Mk 12:36 ◄ ► Lk 2:27
M Mt 12:28 ◄ ► Lk 1:15-17
T Mk 12:36 ◄ ► Mk 16:17
S Mk 12:2 ◄ ► Lk 3:9
R Mk 13:1-2 ◄ ► Lk 13:3
H Mk 12:36-40 ◄ ► Mk 14:21

E Mk 13:5-13 ◄ ► Mk 13:24
E Mk 13:22 ◄ ► Mk 13:27
C Mk 8:38 ◄ ► Mk 13:32-37
D Mt 25:31 ◄ ► 1Th 3:13
E Mk 13:24 ◄ ► Mk 13:31-32

ᵍ 14 Daniel 9:27; 11:31; 12:11 ʰ 14 Or he; also in verse 29
ⁱ 21 Or Messiah ʲ 25 Isaiah 13:10; 34:4 ᵏ 30 Or race

13:9-10 Jesus prophesied that his followers would be subject to extreme persecution by the religious authorities. Initially fulfilled during the first century, this prophecy will find its final fulfillment during the tribulation. See the study notes for Mt 24:9-14.

13:14-20 Compare this passage with Mt 24:20-22 and refer to the study notes for more information.

13:21-25 This prophetic warning should alert anyone to the claims of false Christs who produce deceptive signs. Note the expression "if that were possible" (13:22) reveals the impossibility of deceiving the elect about the true identity of the Messiah. See the study notes for Mt 24:23-27.

13:24-27 Many cataclysmic events will occur in both nature and politics just after the tribulation. Then Christ will return "in clouds with great power and glory" (13:26). His angels will gather the "elect" from all over the world. These "elect" are the saints who come to faith in Christ during the terrible persecution of the tribulation. This gathering is not the rapture described by the apostle Paul in 1Co 15:51 and 1Th 4:16-17. See the study note at Mt 24:31 for further information.

13:28-37 The parable of the fig tree predicts the generation when the Son of man will return. This prophetic passage commands the saints to "keep watch" (13:34) for his return. See the study note for Mt 24:32-35.

pened.ᵛ ³¹Heaven and earth will pass away, but my words will never pass away.ʷ

The Day and Hour Unknown

³²"No one knows about that day or hour, not even the angels in heaven, nor the Son, but only the Father.ˣ ³³Be on guard! Be alert!*¹*ʸ You do not know when that time will come. ³⁴It's like a man going away: He leaves his house and puts his servantsᶻ in charge, each with his assigned task, and tells the one at the door to keep watch.

³⁵"Therefore keep watch because you do not know when the owner of the house will come back—whether in the evening, or at midnight, or when the rooster crows, or at dawn. ³⁶If he comes suddenly, do not let him find you sleeping. ³⁷What I say to you, I say to everyone: 'Watch!' "ᵃ

Jesus Anointed at Bethany

14:1–11pp — Mt 26:2–16
14:1,2,10,11pp — Lk 22:1–6
14:3–8Ref — Jn 12:1–8

14 Now the Passoverᵇ and the Feast of Unleavened Bread were only two days away, and the chief priests and the teachers of the law were looking for some sly way to arrest Jesus and kill him.ᶜ ²"But not during the Feast," they said, "or the people may riot."

³While he was in Bethany,ᵈ reclining at the table in the home of a man known as Simon the Leper, a woman came with an alabaster jar of very expensive perfume, made of pure nard. She broke the jar and poured the perfume on his head.ᵉ

⁴Some of those present were saying indignantly to one another, "Why this waste of perfume? ⁵It could have been sold for more than a year's wagesᵐ and the money given to the poor." And they rebuked her harshly.

⁶"Leave her alone," said Jesus. "Why are you bothering her? She has done a beautiful thing to me. ⁷The poor you will always have with you, and you can help them any time you want.ᶠ But you will not always have me. ⁸She did what she could. She poured perfume on my body beforehand to prepare for my burial.ᵍ ⁹I tell you the truth, wherever the gospel is preached throughout the world,ʰ what she has done will also be told, in memory of her."

¹⁰Then Judas Iscariot, one of the Twelve,ⁱ went to the chief priests to betray Jesus to them.ʲ ¹¹They were delighted to hear this and promised to give him money. So he watched for an opportunity to hand him over.

The Lord's Supper

14:12–26pp — Mt 26:17–30; Lk 22:7–23
14:22–25pp — 1Co 11:23–25

¹²On the first day of the Feast of Unleavened Bread, when it was customary to sacrifice the Passover lamb,ᵏ Jesus' disciples asked him, "Where do you want us to go and make preparations for you to eat the Passover?"

¹³So he sent two of his disciples, telling them, "Go into the city, and a man carrying a jar of water will meet you. Follow him. ¹⁴Say to the owner of the house he enters, 'The Teacher asks: Where is my guest room, where I may eat the Passover with my disciples?' ¹⁵He will show you a large upper room,ˡ furnished and ready. Make preparations for us there."

¹⁶The disciples left, went into the city and found things just as Jesus had told them. So they prepared the Passover.

¹⁷When evening came, Jesus arrived with the Twelve. ¹⁸While they were reclining at the table eating, he said, "I tell you the truth, one of you will betray me—one who is eating with me."

¹⁹They were saddened, and one by one they said to him, "Surely not I?"

²⁰"It is one of the Twelve," he replied, "one who dips bread into the bowl with me.ᵐ ²¹The Son of Manⁿ will go just as it is written about him. But woe to that man who betrays the Son of Man! It would be better for him if he had not been born."

²²While they were eating, Jesus took bread, gave thanks and broke it,ᵒ and gave it to his disciples, saying, "Take it; this is my body."

²³Then he took the cup, gave thanks

---

¹ 33 Some manuscripts *alert and pray* *ᵐ 5* Greek *than three hundred denarii*

and offered it to them, and they all drank from it.ᵖ

²⁴"This is my blood of theⁿ covenant,ᵠ which is poured out for many," he said to them. ²⁵"I tell you the truth, I will not drink again of the fruit of the vine until that day when I drink it anew in the kingdom of God."ʳ

²⁶When they had sung a hymn, they went out to the Mount of Olives.ˢ

Jesus Predicts Peter's Denial
14:27–31pp — Mt 26:31–35

²⁷"You will all fall away," Jesus told them, "for it is written:

" 'I will strike the shepherd,
and the sheep will be scattered.'ᵒᵗ

²⁸But after I have risen, I will go ahead of you into Galilee."ᵘ

²⁹Peter declared, "Even if all fall away, I will not."

³⁰"I tell you the truth," Jesus answered, "today—yes, tonight—before the rooster crows twiceᵖ you yourself will disown me three times."ᵛ

³¹But Peter insisted emphatically, "Even if I have to die with you,ʷ I will never disown you." And all the others said the same.

Gethsemane
14:32–42pp — Mt 26:36–46; Lk 22:40–46

³²They went to a place called Gethsemane, and Jesus said to his disciples, "Sit here while I pray." ³³He took Peter, James and Johnˣ along with him, and he began to be deeply distressed and troubled. ³⁴"My soul is overwhelmed with sorrow to the point of death,"ʸ he said to them. "Stay here and keep watch."

³⁵Going a little farther, he fell to the ground and prayed that if possible the hourᶻ might pass from him. ³⁶"Abba,ᵠ Father,"ᵃ he said, "everything is possible for you. Take this cupᵇ from me. Yet not what I will, but what you will."ᶜ

³⁷Then he returned to his disciples and found them sleeping. "Simon," he said to Peter, "are you asleep? Could you not keep watch for one hour? ³⁸Watch and pray so that you will not fall into tempta-

tion.ᵈ The spirit is willing, but the body is weak."ᵉ

³⁹Once more he went away and prayed the same thing. ⁴⁰When he came back, he again found them sleeping, because their eyes were heavy. They did not know what to say to him.

⁴¹Returning the third time, he said to them, "Are you still sleeping and resting? Enough! The hourᶠ has come. Look, the Son of Man is betrayed into the hands of sinners. ⁴²Rise! Let us go! Here comes my betrayer!"

Jesus Arrested
14:43–50pp — Mt 26:47–56; Lk 22:47–50; Jn 18:3–11

⁴³Just as he was speaking, Judas,ᵍ one of the Twelve, appeared. With him was a crowd armed with swords and clubs, sent from the chief priests, the teachers of the law, and the elders.

⁴⁴Now the betrayer had arranged a signal with them: "The one I kiss is the man; arrest him and lead him away under guard." ⁴⁵Going at once to Jesus, Judas said, "Rabbi!"ʰ and kissed him. ⁴⁶The men seized Jesus and arrested him. ⁴⁷Then one of those standing near drew his sword and struck the servant of the high priest, cutting off his ear.

⁴⁸"Am I leading a rebellion," said Jesus, "that you have come out with swords and clubs to capture me? ⁴⁹Every day I was with you, teaching in the temple courts,ⁱ and you did not arrest me. But the Scriptures must be fulfilled."ʲ ⁵⁰Then everyone deserted him and fled.ᵏ

⁵¹A young man, wearing nothing but a linen garment, was following Jesus. When they seized him, ⁵²he fled naked, leaving his garment behind.

Before the Sanhedrin
14:53–65pp — Mt 26:57–68; Jn 18:12,13,19–24
14:61–63pp — Lk 22:67–71

⁵³They took Jesus to the high priest, and all the chief priests, elders and teachers of the law came together. ⁵⁴Peter followed him at a distance, right into the courtyard of the high priest.ˡ There he sat with the guards and warmed himself at the fire.ᵐ

ⁿ 24 Some manuscripts *the new*   ᵒ 27 Zech. 13:7   ᵖ 30 Some early manuscripts do not have *twice.*   ᵠ 36 Aramaic for *Father*

⁵⁵The chief priests and the whole Sanhedrin were looking for evidence against Jesus so that they could put him to death, but they did not find any. ⁵⁶Many testified falsely against him, but their statements did not agree.

⁵⁷Then some stood up and gave this false testimony against him: ⁵⁸"We heard him say, 'I will destroy this man-made temple and in three days will build another,' not made by man.' " ⁵⁹Yet even then their testimony did not agree.

⁶⁰Then the high priest stood up before them and asked Jesus, "Are you not going to answer? What is this testimony that these men are bringing against you?" ⁶¹But Jesus remained silent and gave no answer.

Again the high priest asked him, "Are you the Christ, the Son of the Blessed One?"

⁶²"I am," said Jesus. "And you will see the Son of Man sitting at the right hand of the Mighty One and coming on the clouds of heaven."

⁶³The high priest tore his clothes. "Why do we need any more witnesses?" he asked. ⁶⁴"You have heard the blasphemy. What do you think?"

They all condemned him as worthy of death. ⁶⁵Then some began to spit at him; they blindfolded him, struck him with their fists, and said, "Prophesy!" And the guards took him and beat him.

Peter Disowns Jesus

14:66–72pp — Mt 26:69–75; Lk 22:56–62; Jn 18:16–18,25–27

⁶⁶While Peter was below in the courtyard, one of the servant girls of the high priest came by. ⁶⁷When she saw Peter warming himself, she looked closely at him.

"You also were with that Nazarene, Jesus," she said.

⁶⁸But he denied it. "I don't know or understand what you're talking about," he said, and went out into the entryway.

⁶⁹When the servant girl saw him there, she said again to those standing around, "This fellow is one of them." ⁷⁰Again he denied it.

After a little while, those standing near said to Peter, "Surely you are one of them, for you are a Galilean."

⁷¹He began to call down curses on himself, and he swore to them, "I don't know this man you're talking about."

⁷²Immediately the rooster crowed the second time. Then Peter remembered the word Jesus had spoken to him: "Before the rooster crows twice you will disown me three times." And he broke down and wept.

Jesus Before Pilate

15:2–15pp — Mt 27:11–26; Lk 23:2,3,18–25; Jn 18:29–19:16

15 Very early in the morning, the chief priests, with the elders, the teachers of the law and the whole Sanhedrin, reached a decision. They bound Jesus, led him away and handed him over to Pilate.

²"Are you the king of the Jews?" asked Pilate.

"Yes, it is as you say," Jesus replied.

³The chief priests accused him of many things. ⁴So again Pilate asked him, "Aren't you going to answer? See how many things they are accusing you of."

⁵But Jesus still made no reply, and Pilate was amazed.

⁶Now it was the custom at the Feast to release a prisoner whom the people requested. ⁷A man called Barabbas was in prison with the insurrectionists who had committed murder in the uprising. ⁸The

---

14:62 These prophetic words addressed to the high priest will be fulfilled when Christ returns at Armageddon to save his people.

15:2–18, 26 Pontius Pilate asked Jesus, "Are you the king of the Jews?" (15:2). Jesus' positive response not only affirmed his claim to be Israel's Messiah and king, but foreshadowed that future day following Armageddon when he will take his position on the throne of David in Jerusalem as the King of the whole world. The Roman soldiers that mocked his royalty, the accusation affixed to the cross and the personal accusation of the unrepentant thief all unwittingly acknowledged the prophetic truth that Jesus will one day be acclaimed "KING OF THE JEWS" (15:26).

crowd came up and asked Pilate to do for them what he usually did.

⁹"Do you want me to release to you the king of the Jews?"ⁱ asked Pilate, ¹⁰knowing it was out of envy that the chief priests had handed Jesus over to him. ¹¹But the chief priests stirred up the crowd to have Pilate release Barabbasʲ instead.

¹²"What shall I do, then, with the one you call the king of the Jews?" Pilate asked them.

¹³"Crucify him!" they shouted.

¹⁴"Why? What crime has he committed?" asked Pilate.

But they shouted all the louder, "Crucify him!"

¹⁵Wanting to satisfy the crowd, Pilate released Barabbas to them. He had Jesus flogged,ᵏ and handed him over to be crucified.

The Soldiers Mock Jesus
15:16–20pp — Mt 27:27–31

¹⁶The soldiers led Jesus away into the palaceˡ (that is, the Praetorium) and called together the whole company of soldiers. ¹⁷They put a purple robe on him, then twisted together a crown of thorns and set it on him. ¹⁸And they began to call out to him, "Hail, king of the Jews!"ᵐ ¹⁹Again and again they struck him on the head with a staff and spit on him. Falling on their knees, they paid homage to him. ²⁰And when they had mocked him, they took off the purple robe and put his own clothes on him. Then they led him outⁿ to crucify him.

The Crucifixion
15:22–32pp — Mt 27:33–44; Lk 23:33–43; Jn 19:17–24

²¹A certain man from Cyrene,º Simon, the father of Alexander and Rufus,ᵖ was passing by on his way in from the country, and they forced him to carry the cross.ᑫ ²²They brought Jesus to the place called Golgotha (which means The Place of the Skull). ²³Then they offered him wine mixed with myrrh,ʳ but he did not take it. ²⁴And they crucified him. Divid-

ing up his clothes, they cast lotsˢ to see what each would get.

²⁵It was the third hour when they crucified him. ²⁶The written notice of the charge against him read: THE KING OF THE JEWS.ᵗ ²⁷They crucified two robbers with him, one on his right and one on his left.ᵛ ²⁹Those who passed by hurled insults at him, shaking their headsᵘ and saying, "So! You who are going to destroy the temple and build it in three days,ᵛ ³⁰come down from the cross and save yourself!"

³¹In the same way the chief priests and the teachers of the law mocked himʷ among themselves. "He saved others," they said, "but he can't save himself! ³²Let this Christ,ʷˣ this King of Israel,ʸ come down now from the cross, that we may see and believe." Those crucified with him also heaped insults on him.

The Death of Jesus
15:33–41pp — Mt 27:45–56; Lk 23:44–49; Jn 19:29–30

³³At the sixth hour darkness came over the whole land until the ninth hour.ᶻ ³⁴And at the ninth hour Jesus cried out in a loud voice, *"Eloi, Eloi, lama sabachthani?"*—which means, "My God, my God, why have you forsaken me?"ˣᵃ ³⁵When some of those standing near heard this, they said, "Listen, he's calling Elijah."

³⁶One man ran, filled a sponge with wine vinegar,ᵇ put it on a stick, and offered it to Jesus to drink. "Now leave him alone. Let's see if Elijah comes to take him down," he said.

³⁷With a loud cry, Jesus breathed his last.ᶜ

³⁸The curtain of the temple was torn in two from top to bottom.ᵈ ³⁹And when the centurion,ᵉ who stood there in front of Jesus, heard his cry andʸ saw how he died, he said, "Surely this man was the Sonᶻ of God!"ᶠ

⁴⁰Some women were watching from a distance.ᵍ Among them were Mary Magdalene, Mary the mother of James the

---

15:9 ⁱS ver 2
15:11 ʲAc 3:14
15:15 ᵏIsa 53:6
15:16 ˡJn 18:28, 33; 19:9
15:18 ᵐS ver 2
15:20 ⁿHeb 13:12
15:21 ºS Mt 27:32 ᵖRo 16:13 ᑫMt 27:32; Lk 23:26
15:23 ʳver 36; Ps 69:21; Pr 31:6
15:24 ˢPs 22:18
15:26 ᵗS ver 2
15:29 ᵘPs 22:7; 109:25 ᵛS Jn 2:19
15:31 ʷPs 22:7
15:32 ˣS Mk 14:61 ʸS ver 2
15:33 ᶻAm 8:9
15:34 ᵃPs 22:1
15:36 ᵇver 23; Ps 69:21
15:37 ᶜJn 19:30
15:38 ᵈHeb 10:19, 20
15:39 ᵉver 45 ᶠMk 1:1,11; 9:7; S Mt 4:3
15:40 ᵍPs 38:11

I Mk 15:2 ◀▶ Mk 15:12
M Mk 15:2 ◀▶ Mk 15:12
I Mk 15:9 ◀▶ Mk 15:17–18
M Mk 15:9 ◀▶ Mk 15:17–18
I Mk 15:12 ◀▶ Mk 15:26
M Mk 15:12 ◀▶ Mk 15:26
I Mk 15:17–18 ◀▶ Mk 15:32
M Mk 15:17–18 ◀▶ Mk 15:32
I Mk 15:26 ◀▶ Lk 1:32–33
M Mk 15:26 ◀▶ Mk 15:43

ᵛ27 Some manuscripts *left, ²⁸and the scripture was fulfilled which says, "He was counted with the lawless ones"* (Isaiah 53:12)   ʷ32 Or *Messiah*   ˣ34 Psalm 22:1   ʸ39 Some manuscripts do not have *heard his cry and*   ᶻ39 Or *a son*

younger and of Joses, and Salome.ʰ ⁴¹In Galilee these women had followed him and cared for his needs. Many other women who had come up with him to Jerusalem were also there.ⁱ

The Burial of Jesus

15:42–47pp — Mt 27:57–61; Lk 23:50–56; Jn 19:38–42

⁴²It was Preparation Day (that is, the day before the Sabbath).ʲ So as evening approached, ⁴³Joseph of Arimathea, a prominent member of the Council,ᵏ who was himself waiting for the kingdom of God,ˡ went boldly to Pilate and asked for Jesus' body. ⁴⁴Pilate was surprised to hear that he was already dead. Summoning the centurion, he asked him if Jesus had already died. ⁴⁵When he learned from the centurionᵐ that it was so, he gave the body to Joseph. ⁴⁶So Joseph bought some linen cloth, took down the body, wrapped it in the linen, and placed it in a tomb cut out of rock. Then he rolled a stone against the entrance of the tomb.ⁿ ⁴⁷Mary Magdalene and Mary the mother of Josesᵒ saw where he was laid.

The Resurrection

16:1–8pp — Mt 28:1–8; Lk 24:1–10

16 When the Sabbath was over, Mary Magdalene, Mary the mother of James, and Salome bought spicesᵖ so that they might go to anoint Jesus' body. ²Very early on the first day of the week, just after sunrise, they were on their way to the tomb ³and they asked each other, "Who will roll the stone away from the entrance of the tomb?"ᵠ

⁴But when they looked up, they saw that the stone, which was very large, had been rolled away. ⁵As they entered the tomb, they saw a young man dressed in a white robeʳ sitting on the right side, and they were alarmed.

⁶"Don't be alarmed," he said. "You are looking for Jesus the Nazarene,ˢ who was crucified. He has risen! He is not here. See the place where they laid him. ⁷But go, tell his disciples and Peter, 'He is go-

M *Mk 15:32* ◀ ▶ *Lk 1:32–33*

15:40 ʰ Mk 16:1; Lk 24:10; Jn 19:25
15:41 ⁱ Mt 27:55,56; Lk 8:2,3
15:42 ʲ Mt 27:62; Jn 19:31
15:43 ᵏ S 5:22 ˡ S Mt 3:2; Lk 2:25,38
15:45 ᵐ ver 39
15:46 ⁿ Mk 16:3
15:47 ᵒ ver 40
16:1 ᵖ Lk 23:56; Jn 19:39,40
16:3 ᵠ Mk 15:46
16:5 ʳ S Jn 20:12
16:6 ˢ S Mk 1:24
16:7 ᵗ Jn 21:1-23 ᵘ Mk 14:28
16:9 ᵛ Mk 15:47; Jn 20:11-18
16:11 ʷ ver 13,14; Lk 24:11
16:12 ˣ Lk 24:13-32
16:14 ʸ Lk 24:36-43
16:15 ᶻ Mt 28:18-20; Lk 24:47,48; Ac 1:8
16:16 ᵃ Jn 3:16,18,36; Ac 16:31
16:17 ᵇ S Jn 4:48 ᶜ Mk 9:38; Lk 10:17; Ac 5:16; 8:7; 16:18; 19:13-16 ᵈ Ac 2:4; 10:46; 19:6; 1Co 12:10,28,30; 13:1; 14:2-39
16:18 ᵉ Lk 10:19; Ac 28:3-5 ᶠ S Ac 6:6

---

ing ahead of you into Galilee. There you will see him,ᵗ just as he told you.' "ᵘ

⁸Trembling and bewildered, the women went out and fled from the tomb. They said nothing to anyone, because they were afraid.

[The earliest manuscripts and some other ancient witnesses do not have Mark 16:9–20.]

⁹When Jesus rose early on the first day of the week, he appeared first to Mary Magdalene,ᵛ out of whom he had driven seven demons. ¹⁰She went and told those who had been with him and who were mourning and weeping. ¹¹When they heard that Jesus was alive and that she had seen him, they did not believe it.ʷ

¹²Afterward Jesus appeared in a different form to two of them while they were walking in the country.ˣ ¹³These returned and reported it to the rest; but they did not believe them either.

¹⁴Later Jesus appeared to the Eleven as they were eating; he rebuked them for their lack of faith and their stubborn refusal to believe those who had seen him after he had risen.ʸ

¹⁵He said to them, "Go into all the world and preach the good news to all creation.ᶻ ¹⁶Whoever believes and is baptized will be saved, but whoever does not believe will be condemned.ᵃ ¹⁷And these signsᵇ will accompany those who believe: In my name they will drive out demons;ᶜ they will speak in new tongues;ᵈ ¹⁸they will pick up snakesᵉ with their hands; and when they drink deadly poison, it will not hurt them at all; they will place their hands onᶠ sick people, and they will get well."

E *Mk 10:46–52* ◀ ▶ *Lk 1:18*
N *Mk 6:11* ◀ ▶ *Lk 10:10–16*
O *Mk 12:28–34* ◀ ▶ *Lk 6:47–49*
W *Mk 3:28* ◀ ▶ *Lk 2:10–11*
F *Mk 1:15* ◀ ▶ *Lk 7:50*
H *Mk 14:21* ◀ ▶ *Lk 3:7*
G *Mk 13:11* ◀ ▶ *Lk 1:17*
T *Mk 13:11* ◀ ▶ *Lk 1:41–42*
H *Mk 9:23* ◀ ▶ *Lk 4:18*

15:43 Joseph of Arimathea acknowledged Jesus' claim as the Son of man who would rule in the millennial "kingdom of God" (15:43).

¹⁹After the Lord Jesus had spoken to them, he was taken up into heaven[g] and he sat at the right hand of God.[h] ²⁰Then the disciples went out and preached everywhere, and the Lord worked with them and confirmed his word by the signs[i] that accompanied it.

Luke

Author: Luke

Theme: The Savior of the world is Jesus

Date of Writing: c. A.D. 59–63

Outline of Luke
  I. Prologue (1:1–4)
  II. Jesus' Birth (1:5—2:52)
  III. Ministry of John the Baptist (3:1–20)
  IV. Jesus Is Publicly Introduced (3:21—4:44)
  V. Jesus' Ministry in Galilee (5:1—6:16)
  VI. Jesus Teaches and Heals (6:17—9:50)
  VII. Jesus Ministers in Judea and Perea (9:51—18:30)
  VIII. Suffering and Crucifixion (18:31—23:56)
  IX. The Triumphal Resurrection (24:1–53)

THIS GOSPEL IS a companion volume to the book of Acts and was written by "our dear friend Luke, the doctor" (Col 4:14). A traveling companion and fellow worker with Paul (see 2Ti 4:11; Phm 24), Luke accompanied Paul on his last trip to Rome (see Ac 21:1–17; 27:28) and probably wrote this account shortly after Paul's death.

The book of Luke is the longest and most literary of the Gospels and was written primarily for Greek believers. Emphasizing the perfect humanity of Jesus while acknowledging him as God incarnate in human flesh, Luke traces Jesus' ancestry back to Adam. Along with its presentation of Jesus as the Son of Man, this book reveals Jesus' concern for a lost humanity and the gift of salvation for all as recorded in the parables of the lost sheep, the lost coin and the lost son (see 15:3–32). Luke's association with Paul is evident in the theological perspective of the work of the Holy Spirit in Jesus' life (see 1:15; 3:22; 4:1, 14; 10:21). Note also that Luke tells about Jesus' boyhood and reveals more of his prayer life than do the other Gospel narratives.

Luke's record of Jesus' life and ministry also contains the medical terms and trained observations of a physician as well as a doctor's compassion and concern for all types of people. With the narrative of the birth and infancy of Jesus presented from the point of view of Jesus' mother, Luke shows a concern for women, children and the poor that is unparalleled in any other NT account. This Gospel also identifies by name many of the women who ministered to Jesus and stresses Jesus' sympathy for the brokenhearted, the sick and the bereaved.

Introduction

1:1–4 Ref — Ac 1:1

1 Many have undertaken to draw up an account of the things that have been fulfilled[a] among us, ²just as they were handed down to us by those who from the first[a] were eyewitnesses[b] and servants of the word.[c] ³Therefore, since I myself have carefully investigated everything from the beginning, it seemed good also to me to write an orderly account[d] for you, most excellent[e] Theophilus,[f] ⁴so that you may know the certainty of the things you have been taught.[g]

The Birth of John the Baptist Foretold

⁵In the time of Herod king of Judea[h] there was a priest named Zechariah, who belonged to the priestly division of Abijah;[i] his wife Elizabeth was also a descendant of Aaron. ⁶Both of them were upright in the sight of God, observing all the Lord's commandments and regulations blamelessly.[j] ⁷But they had no children, because Elizabeth was barren; and they were both well along in years.

⁸Once when Zechariah's division was on duty and he was serving as priest before God,[k] ⁹he was chosen by lot,[l] according to the custom of the priesthood, to go into the temple of the Lord and burn incense.[m] ¹⁰And when the time for the burning of incense came, all the assembled worshipers were praying outside.[n]

¹¹Then an angel[o] of the Lord appeared to him, standing at the right side of the altar of incense.[p] ¹²When Zechariah saw him, he was startled and was gripped with fear.[q] ¹³But the angel said to him: "Do not be afraid,[r] Zechariah; your prayer has been heard. Your wife Elizabeth will bear you a son, and you are to give him the name John.[s] ¹⁴He will be a joy and delight to you, and many will rejoice because of his birth,[t] ¹⁵for he will be great in the sight of the Lord. He is never to take wine or other fermented drink,[u] and he will be filled with the Holy Spirit[v] even from birth.[b,w] ¹⁶Many of the people of Israel will he bring back to the Lord their God. ¹⁷And he will go on be-

---

1:2 ᵃ Mk 1:1; Jn 15:27; Ac 1:21, 22 ᵇ Heb 2:3; 1Pe 5:1; 2Pe 1:16; 1Jn 1:1 ᶜ S Mk 4:14
1:3 ᵈ Ac 11:4
1:1 ᵉ Ac 24:3; 26:25 ᶠ Ac 1:1
1:4 ᵍ Jn 20:31; Ac 2:42
1:5 ʰ Mt 2:1 ⁱ 1Ch 24:10
1:6 ʲ Ge 6:9; Dt 5:33; 1Ki 9:4; Lk 2:25
1:8 ᵏ 1Ch 24:19; 2Ch 8:14
1:9 ˡ Ac 1:26 ᵐ Ex 30:7,8; 1Ch 23:13; 2Ch 29:11; Ps 141:2
1:10 ⁿ Lev 16:17
1:11 ᵒ S Ac 5:19 ᵖ Ex 30:1-10
1:12 ᵠ Jdg 6:22,23; 13:22
1:13 ʳ ver 30; S Mt 14:27 ˢ ver 60, 63; S Mt 3:1
1:14 ᵗ ver 58
1:15 ᵘ Nu 6:3; Lev 10:9; Jdg 13:4; Lk 7:33 ᵛ ver 41,67; Ac 2:4; 4:8,31; 6:3, 5; 9:17; 11:24; Eph 5:18; S Ac 10:44 ʷ Jer 1:5; Gal 1:15

R Ps 144:12 ◀ | **B** Mk 1:10 ◀ ▶ Lk 1:41
C Zec 12:10 ◀ ▶ Jn 16:7–11
E Mk 12:36 ◀ ▶ Lk 1:41
M Mk 13:11 ◀ ▶ Lk 1:80
G Mk 16:17–18 ◀ ▶ Lk 1:67
R Eze 36:25–27 ◀ ▶ Jn 3:3–8
S Mic 2:7 ◀ ▶ Ac 15:8–9

a 1 Or been surely believed *b 15 Or* from his mother's womb

1:13–17 The first prophecy in the book of Luke concerns the prediction given to the priest Zechariah that his wife Elizabeth would bear a son. This son was to be named John, and he would give joy to many. The angel predicted that John would become a Nazirite (see Jdg 13:5–7; 16:17; Nu 6; Am 2:11–12) and be filled with the Holy Spirit in his mother's womb. He would also fulfill Malachi's prophecies about Elijah as he prepared Israel for the Lord's appearance (see Mal 3:1; 4:5–6).

Note that the angel foretold that John would accomplish only one part of Malachi's prophecy to "turn the hearts of the fathers to their children" (1:17). By omitting Malachi's words about the "great and dreadful day of the Lord" (Mal 4:5) the angel revealed that John would not fulfill the totality of Malachi's prophecy. This final fulfillment will occur in the last days with the rise of the two witnesses and Elijah the prophet (see Rev 11:3–12).

fore the Lord,ˣ in the spirit and power of Elijah,ʸ to turn the hearts of the fathers to their childrenᶻ and the disobedient to the wisdom of the righteous—to make ready a people prepared for the Lord."ᵃ ¹⁸Zechariah asked the angel, "How can I be sure of this?ᵇ I am an old man and my wife is well along in years."ᶜ

¹⁹The angel answered, "I am Gabriel.ᵈ I stand in the presence of God, and I have been sent to speak to you and to tell you this good news. ²⁰And now you will be silent and not able to speakᵉ until the day this happens, because you did not believe my words, which will come true at their proper time."

²¹Meanwhile, the people were waiting for Zechariah and wondering why he stayed so long in the temple. ²²When he came out, he could not speak to them. They realized he had seen a vision in the temple, for he kept making signsᶠ to them but remained unable to speak.

²³When his time of service was completed, he returned home. ²⁴After this his wife Elizabeth became pregnant and for five months remained in seclusion. ²⁵"The Lord has done this for me," she said. "In these days he has shown his favor and taken away my disgraceᵍ among the people."

The Birth of Jesus Foretold

²⁶In the sixth month, God sent the angel Gabrielʰ to Nazareth,ⁱ a town in Galilee, ²⁷to a virgin pledged to be married to a man named Joseph,ʲ a descendant of David. The virgin's name was Mary. ²⁸The angel went to her and said, "Greetings, you who are highly favored! The Lord is with you."

²⁹Mary was greatly troubled at his words and wondered what kind of greeting this might be. ³⁰But the angel said to her, "Do not be afraid,ᵏ Mary, you have found favor with God. ³¹You will be with child and give birth to a son, and you are to give him the name Jesus.ᵐ ³²He will be great and will be called the Son of the Most High.ⁿ The Lord God will give him the throne of his father David,ᵒ ³³and he will reign over the house of Jacob forever; his kingdomᵖ will never end."ᑫ

³⁴"How will this be," Mary asked the angel, "since I am a virgin?"

³⁵The angel answered, "The Holy Spirit will come upon you,ʳ and the power of the Most Highˢ will overshadow you. So the holy oneᵗ to be born will be calledᶜ the Son of God.ᵘ ³⁶Even Elizabeth your relative is going to have a childᵛ in her old age, and she who was said to be barren is in her sixth month. ³⁷For nothing is impossible with God."ʷ

³⁸"I am the Lord's servant," Mary answered. "May it be to me as you have said." Then the angel left her.

Mary Visits Elizabeth

³⁹At that time Mary got ready and hurried to a town in the hill country of Judea,ˣ ⁴⁰where she entered Zechariah's home and greeted Elizabeth. ⁴¹When Elizabeth heard Mary's greeting, the baby leaped in her womb, and Elizabeth was filled with the Holy Spirit.ʸ ⁴²In a loud voice she exclaimed: "Blessed are you among women,ᶻ and blessed is the child you will bear! ⁴³But why am I so favored, that the mother of my Lordᵃ should come to me? ⁴⁴As soon as the sound of your greeting reached my ears, the baby in my womb leaped for joy. ⁴⁵Blessed is she who has believed that what the Lord has said to her will be accomplished!"

1:30–35 The angel prophesied that Mary would supernaturally conceive the Christ-child who would be named Jesus. The prediction included the words that Jesus would be "called the Son of the Most High" (1:32) and that, as the true Messiah, he would receive the "throne of his father David" (1:32). Finally, the angel prophesied that his kingdom would never end and that this child would be divine and be called "the Son of God" (1:35).

Mary's Song

1:46–53pp — 1Sa 2:1–10

⁴⁶And Mary said:

"My soul glorifies the Lord,
⁴⁷ and my spirit rejoices in God my Savior,
⁴⁸for he has been mindful
 of the humble state of his servant.
From now on all generations will call me blessed,
⁴⁹ for the Mighty One has done great things for me—
holy is his name.
⁵⁰His mercy extends to those who fear him,
 from generation to generation.
⁵¹He has performed mighty deeds with his arm;
 he has scattered those who are proud in their inmost thoughts.
⁵²He has brought down rulers from their thrones
 but has lifted up the humble.
⁵³He has filled the hungry with good things
 but has sent the rich away empty.
⁵⁴He has helped his servant Israel,
 remembering to be merciful
⁵⁵to Abraham and his descendants forever,
 even as he said to our fathers."

⁵⁶Mary stayed with Elizabeth for about three months and then returned home.

The Birth of John the Baptist

⁵⁷When it was time for Elizabeth to have her baby, she gave birth to a son. ⁵⁸Her neighbors and relatives heard that the Lord had shown her great mercy, and they shared her joy.

⁵⁹On the eighth day they came to circumcise the child, and they were going to name him after his father Zechariah, ⁶⁰but his mother spoke up and said, "No! He is to be called John." ⁶¹They said to her, "There is no one among your relatives who has that name."

⁶²Then they made signs to his father, to find out what he would like to name the child. ⁶³He asked for a writing tablet, and to everyone's astonishment he wrote, "His name is John." ⁶⁴Immediately his mouth was opened and his tongue was loosed, and he began to speak, praising God. ⁶⁵The neighbors were all filled with awe, and throughout the hill country of Judea people were talking about all these things. ⁶⁶Everyone who heard this wondered about it, asking, "What then is this child going to be?" For the Lord's hand was with him.

Zechariah's Song

⁶⁷His father Zechariah was filled with the Holy Spirit and prophesied:

⁶⁸"Praise be to the Lord, the God of Israel,
 because he has come and has redeemed his people.
⁶⁹He has raised up a horn of salvation for us
 in the house of his servant David
⁷⁰(as he said through his holy prophets of long ago),
⁷¹salvation from our enemies
 and from the hand of all who hate us—
⁷²to show mercy to our fathers
 and to remember his holy covenant,
⁷³ the oath he swore to our father Abraham:
⁷⁴to rescue us from the hand of our enemies,
 and to enable us to serve him without fear
⁷⁵ in holiness and righteousness before him all our days.

⁷⁶And you, my child, will be called a prophet of the Most High;
 for you will go before the Lord to prepare the way for him,

B Lk 1:41 ◀▶ Lk 3:16
E Lk 1:41 ◀▶ Lk 1:80
G Lk 1:17 ◀▶ Lk 2:40
T Lk 1:41–42 ◀▶ Lk 2:40
I Lk 1:32–33 ◀▶ Lk 2:25–26

ᵈ 69 Horn here symbolizes strength.

1:67–79 Zechariah, filled with the Holy Spirit, gave this prophecy about the role his son John the Baptist would play as "a prophet of the Most High" (1:76), who would prepare the people for the coming of the Messiah and "give his people the knowledge of salvation" (1:77).

⁷⁷to give his people the knowledge of
    salvation
  through the forgiveness of their
    sins,
⁷⁸because of the tender mercy of our
    God,
  by which the rising sun will come
    to us from heaven
⁷⁹to shine on those living in
    darkness
  and in the shadow of death,
  to guide our feet into the path of
    peace."

⁸⁰And the child grew and became strong in spirit; and he lived in the desert until he appeared publicly to Israel.

The Birth of Jesus

2 In those days Caesar Augustus issued a decree that a census should be taken of the entire Roman world. ²(This was the first census that took place while Quirinius was governor of Syria.) ³And everyone went to his own town to register.

⁴So Joseph also went up from the town of Nazareth in Galilee to Judea, to Bethlehem the town of David, because he belonged to the house and line of David. ⁵He went there to register with Mary, who was pledged to be married to him and was expecting a child. ⁶While they were there, the time came for the baby to be born, ⁷and she gave birth to her firstborn, a son. She wrapped him in cloths and placed him in a manger, because there was no room for them in the inn.

The Shepherds and the Angels

⁸And there were shepherds living out in the fields nearby, keeping watch over their flocks at night. ⁹An angel of the Lord appeared to them, and the glory of the Lord shone around them, and they were terrified. ¹⁰But the angel said to them, "Do not be afraid. I bring you good news of great joy that will be for all the people. ¹¹Today in the town of David a Savior has been born to you; he is Christ the Lord. ¹²This will be a sign to you: You will find a baby wrapped in cloths and lying in a manger."

¹³Suddenly a great company of the heavenly host appeared with the angel, praising God and saying,

¹⁴"Glory to God in the highest,
  and on earth peace to men on
    whom his favor rests."

¹⁵When the angels had left them and gone into heaven, the shepherds said to one another, "Let's go to Bethlehem and see this thing that has happened, which the Lord has told us about."

¹⁶So they hurried off and found Mary and Joseph, and the baby, who was lying in the manger. ¹⁷When they had seen him, they spread the word concerning what had been told them about this child, ¹⁸and all who heard it were amazed at what the shepherds said to them. ¹⁹But Mary treasured up all these things and pondered them in her heart. ²⁰The shepherds returned, glorifying and praising God for all the things they had heard and seen, which were just as they had been told.

Jesus Presented in the Temple

²¹On the eighth day, when it was time to circumcise him, he was named Jesus, the name the angel had given him before he had been conceived.

²²When the time of their purification according to the Law of Moses had been completed, Joseph and Mary took him to Jerusalem to present him to the Lord ²³(as it is written in the Law of the Lord, "Every firstborn male is to be consecrated to the Lord"), ²⁴and to offer a sacrifice in keeping with what is said in the Law of the Lord: "a pair of doves or two young pigeons."

---

e 11 Or *Messiah*. "The Christ" (Greek) and "the Messiah" (Hebrew) both mean "the Anointed One"; also in verse 26. *f 23* Exodus 13:2,12 *g 24* Lev. 12:8

2:14 The angelic host prophesied the assurance of peace to those who please God.

²⁵Now there was a man in Jerusalem called Simeon, who was righteous and devout.ᵏ He was waiting for the consolation of Israel,ˡ and the Holy Spirit was upon him. ²⁶It had been revealed to him by the Holy Spirit that he would not die before he had seen the Lord's Christ. ²⁷Moved by the Spirit, he went into the temple courts. When the parents brought in the child Jesus to do for him what the custom of the Law required,ᵐ ²⁸Simeon took him in his arms and praised God, saying:

²⁹"Sovereign Lord, as you have promised,ⁿ
 you now dismissʰ your servant in peace.ᵒ
³⁰For my eyes have seen your salvation,ᵖ
³¹ which you have prepared in the sight of all people,
³²a light for revelation to the Gentiles
 and for glory to your people Israel."ᑫ

³³The child's father and mother marveled at what was said about him. ³⁴Then Simeon blessed them and said to Mary, his mother:ʳ "This child is destined to cause the fallingˢ and rising of many in Israel, and to be a sign that will be spoken against, ³⁵so that the thoughts of many hearts will be revealed. And a sword will pierce your own soul too."

³⁶There was also a prophetess,ᵗ Anna, the daughter of Phanuel, of the tribe of Asher. She was very old; she had lived with her husband seven years after her marriage, ³⁷and then was a widow until she was eighty-four.ⁱᵘ She never left the temple but worshiped night and day, fasting and praying.ᵛ ³⁸Coming up to them at that very moment, she gave thanks to God and spoke about the child to all who were looking forward to the redemption of Jerusalem.ʷ

³⁹When Joseph and Mary had done everything required by the Law of the Lord, they returned to Galilee to their own town of Nazareth.ˣ ⁴⁰And the child grew and became strong; he was filled with wisdom, and the grace of God was upon him.ʸ

The Boy Jesus at the Temple

⁴¹Every year his parents went to Jerusalem for the Feast of the Passover.ᶻ ⁴²When he was twelve years old, they went up to the Feast, according to the custom. ⁴³After the Feast was over, while his parents were returning home, the boy Jesus stayed behind in Jerusalem, but they were unaware of it. ⁴⁴Thinking he was in their company, they traveled on for a day. Then they began looking for him among their relatives and friends. ⁴⁵When they did not find him, they went back to Jerusalem to look for him. ⁴⁶After three days they found him in the temple courts, sitting among the teachers, listening to them and asking them questions. ⁴⁷Everyone who heard him was amazedᵃ at his understanding and his answers. ⁴⁸When his parents saw him, they were astonished. His motherᵇ said to him, "Son, why have you treated us like this? Your fatherᶜ and I have been anxiously searching for you."

⁴⁹"Why were you searching for me?" he asked. "Didn't you know I had to be in my Father's house?"ᵈ ⁵⁰But they did not

---

2:25 ᵏ Lk 1:6
ⁱ ver 38; Isa 52:9; Lk 23:51
2:27 ᵐ ver 22
2:29 ⁿ ver 26
ᵒ Ac 2:24
2:30 ᵖ Isa 40:5; 52:10; Lk 3:6
2:32 ᑫ Isa 42:6; 49:6; Ac 13:47; 26:23
2:34 ʳ S Mt 12:46
ˢ Isa 8:14; Mt 21:44; 1Co 1:23; 2Co 2:16; Gal 5:11; 1Pe 2:7,8
2:36 ᵗ S Ac 21:9
2:37 ᵘ 1Ti 5:9
ᵛ Ac 13:3; 14:23; 1Ti 5:5
2:38 ʷ ver 25; Isa 40:2; 52:9; Lk 1:68; 24:21
2:39 ˣ ver 51; S Mt 2:23
2:40 ʸ ver 52; Lk 1:80
2:41 ᶻ Ex 23:15; Dt 16:1-8; Lk 22:8
2:47 ᵃ S Mt 7:28
2:48 ᵇ S Mt 12:46
ᶜ Lk 3:23; 4:22
2:49 ᵈ Jn 2:16

E Lk 2:25–27 ◀▶ Lk 3:22
G Lk 1:67 ◀▶ Lk 12:11–12
M Lk 1:80 ◀▶ Lk 3:16
T Lk 1:67 ◀▶ Lk 4:18

M Lk 1:32–33 ◀▶ Lk 3:5–6
L Mk 13:11 ◀▶ Lk 4:1
B Lk 1:30–35 ◀▶ Lk 2:34–35
B Lk 2:30–32 ◀▶ Lk 3:16
I Lk 2:25–26 ◀▶ Lk 23:2–3

ʰ 29 Or promised, / now dismiss ⁱ 37 Or widow for eighty-four years

---

2:25–32 Luke describes a just and devoted man named Simeon who was "waiting for the consolation of Israel" (2:25; see Isa 25:9; 40:1–2). The Holy Spirit had confirmed to Simeon that he would see the Christ before his death. When the child was brought to the temple, Simeon was there, directed to come "by the Spirit" (2:27). Simeon immediately recognized Jesus as the fulfillment of Isaiah's prophecies of the Messiah (see Isa 9:2; 42:6–7; 49:6; 60:1–3) and blessed God for his faithfulness in fulfilling his word.

2:38 There were a number of righteous Jews who anticipated the imminent arrival of the Messiah. The righteous widow Anna was one of these who knew that the Messiah was about to appear on earth. As she entered the temple, she instantly recognized Jesus as the Messiah and shared her finding with those Jews who "were looking forward to the redemption of Jerusalem" at that time.

understand what he was saying to them. ⁵¹Then he went down to Nazareth with them and was obedient to them. But his mother treasured all these things in her heart. ⁵²And Jesus grew in wisdom and stature, and in favor with God and men.

John the Baptist Prepares the Way

3:2–10pp — Mt 3:1–10; Mk 1:3–5
3:16,17pp — Mt 3:11,12; Mk 1:7,8

3 In the fifteenth year of the reign of Tiberius Caesar—when Pontius Pilate was governor of Judea, Herod tetrarch of Galilee, his brother Philip tetrarch of Iturea and Traconitis, and Lysanias tetrarch of Abilene— ²during the high priesthood of Annas and Caiaphas, the word of God came to John son of Zechariah in the desert. ³He went into all the country around the Jordan, preaching a baptism of repentance for the forgiveness of sins. ⁴As is written in the book of the words of Isaiah the prophet:

"A voice of one calling in the desert,
'Prepare the way for the Lord,
make straight paths for him.
⁵Every valley shall be filled in,
every mountain and hill made low.
The crooked roads shall become straight,
the rough ways smooth.
⁶And all mankind will see God's salvation.'"

⁷John said to the crowds coming out to be baptized by him, "You brood of vipers! Who warned you to flee from the coming wrath? ⁸Produce fruit in keeping with repentance. And do not begin to say to yourselves, 'We have Abraham as our father.' For I tell you that out of these stones God can raise up children for Abraham. ⁹The ax is already at the root of the trees, and every tree that does not produce good fruit will be cut down and thrown into the fire."

¹⁰"What should we do then?" the crowd asked.

¹¹John answered, "The man with two tunics should share with him who has none, and the one who has food should do the same."

¹²Tax collectors also came to be baptized. "Teacher," they asked, "what should we do?"

¹³"Don't collect any more than you are required to," he told them.

¹⁴Then some soldiers asked him, "And what should we do?"

He replied, "Don't extort money and don't accuse people falsely—be content with your pay."

¹⁵The people were waiting expectantly and were all wondering in their hearts if John might possibly be the Christ. ¹⁶John answered them all, "I baptize you with water. But one more powerful than I will come, the thongs of whose sandals I am not worthy to untie. He will baptize you with the Holy Spirit and with fire. ¹⁷His winnowing fork is in his hand to clear his threshing floor and to gather the wheat into his barn, but he will burn up the chaff with unquenchable fire." ¹⁸And with many other words John exhorted the people and preached the good news to them.

¹⁹But when John rebuked Herod the tetrarch because of Herodias, his brother's wife, and all the other evil things he had done, ²⁰Herod added this to them all: He locked John up in prison.

The Baptism and Genealogy of Jesus

3:21,22pp — Mt 3:13–17; Mk 1:9–11
3:23–38pp — Mt 1:1–17

²¹When all the people were being baptized, Jesus was baptized too. And as he

M Lk 2:26 ◄ ► Lk 11:2
C Lk 1:79 ◄ ► Lk 5:31
H Mk 16:16 ◄ ► Lk 3:9
R Mk 11:25 ◄ ► Lk 6:37
H Lk 3:7 ◄ ► Lk 6:25
S Mk 13:13 ◄ ► Lk 6:43–49

B Lk 2:34–35 ◄ ► Lk 9:22
B Lk 1:67 ◄ ► Lk 3:21–22
M Lk 2:40 ◄ ► Lk 4:14
N Mk 1:10 ◄ ► Lk 3:22
P Mk 1:8 ◄ ► Lk 11:9–13
B Lk 3:16 ◄ ► Lk 4:18

j 6 Isaiah 40:3-5; *k 15* Or *Messiah*; *l 16* Or *in*

3:4–6 John the Baptist was the forerunner of the Messiah, preparing people to accept the appearance of Jesus of Nazareth as the promised Messiah (see Isa 40:3). The final fulfillment of this prophecy will occur at the second coming when literally "all mankind will see God's salvation" (3:6; see Zec 12:10; Mt 24:30).

was praying,^g heaven was opened ²²and the Holy Spirit descended on him^h in bodily form like a dove. And a voice came from heaven: "You are my Son,ⁱ whom I love; with you I am well pleased."^j

²³Now Jesus himself was about thirty years old when he began his ministry.^k He was the son, so it was thought, of Joseph,^l

the son of Heli, ²⁴the son of Matthat,
the son of Levi, the son of Melki,
the son of Jannai, the son of Joseph,
²⁵the son of Mattathias, the son of Amos,
the son of Nahum, the son of Esli,
the son of Naggai, ²⁶the son of Maath,
the son of Mattathias, the son of Semein,
the son of Josech, the son of Joda,
²⁷the son of Joanan, the son of Rhesa,
the son of Zerubbabel,^m the son of Shealtiel,
the son of Neri, ²⁸the son of Melki,
the son of Addi, the son of Cosam,
the son of Elmadam, the son of Er,
²⁹the son of Joshua, the son of Eliezer,
the son of Jorim, the son of Matthat,
the son of Levi, ³⁰the son of Simeon,
the son of Judah, the son of Joseph,
the son of Jonam, the son of Eliakim,
³¹the son of Melea, the son of Menna,
the son of Mattatha, the son of Nathan,ⁿ
the son of David, ³²the son of Jesse,
the son of Obed, the son of Boaz,
the son of Salmon,^m the son of Nahshon,
³³the son of Amminadab, the son of Ram,ⁿ
the son of Hezron, the son of Perez,^o
the son of Judah, ³⁴the son of Jacob,
the son of Isaac, the son of Abraham,
the son of Terah, the son of Nahor,^p
³⁵the son of Serug, the son of Reu,
the son of Peleg, the son of Eber,
the son of Shelah, ³⁶the son of Cainan,

the son of Arphaxad,^q the son of Shem,
the son of Noah, the son of Lamech,^r
³⁷the son of Methuselah, the son of Enoch,
the son of Jared, the son of Mahalalel,
the son of Kenan,^s ³⁸the son of Enosh,
the son of Seth, the son of Adam,
the son of God.^t

The Temptation of Jesus

4:1–13pp — Mt 4:1–11; Mk 1:12,13

4 Jesus, full of the Holy Spirit,^u returned from the Jordan^v and was led by the Spirit^w in the desert, ²where for forty days^x he was tempted by the devil.^y He ate nothing during those days, and at the end of them he was hungry.

³The devil said to him, "If you are the Son of God,^z tell this stone to become bread."

⁴Jesus answered, "It is written: 'Man does not live on bread alone.'^o"^a

⁵The devil led him up to a high place and showed him in an instant all the kingdoms of the world.^b ⁶And he said to him, "I will give you all their authority and splendor, for it has been given to me,^c and I can give it to anyone I want to. ⁷So if you worship me, it will all be yours."

⁸Jesus answered, "It is written: 'Worship the Lord your God and serve him only.'^p"^d

⁹The devil led him to Jerusalem and had him stand on the highest point of the temple. "If you are the Son of God," he said, "throw yourself down from here. ¹⁰For it is written:

" 'He will command his angels concerning you
    to guard you carefully;
¹¹they will lift you up in their hands,
    so that you will not strike your foot
        against a stone.'^q"^e

E *Lk 3:22* ◀▶ *Lk 4:14*
L *Lk 2:27* ◀▶ *Lk 4:14*
L *Lk 2:10–11* ◀▶ *Lk 4:18–19*
L *Mk 11:24* ◀▶ *Lk 12:6–7*

m 32 Some early manuscripts Sala n 33 Some manuscripts Amminadab, the son of Admin, the son of Arni; other manuscripts vary widely. o 4 Deut. 8:3 p 8 Deut. 6:13 q 11 Psalm 91:11,12

E *Lk 2:40* ◀▶ *Lk 4:1*
J *Mk 1:10* ◀▶ *Jn 1:32*
N *Lk 3:16* ◀▶ *Jn 1:32*

¹²Jesus answered, "It says: 'Do not put the Lord your God to the test.'"

¹³When the devil had finished all this tempting, he left him until an opportune time.

Jesus Rejected at Nazareth

¹⁴Jesus returned to Galilee in the power of the Spirit, and news about him spread through the whole countryside. ¹⁵He taught in their synagogues, and everyone praised him.

¹⁶He went to Nazareth, where he had been brought up, and on the Sabbath day he went into the synagogue, as was his custom. And he stood up to read. ¹⁷The scroll of the prophet Isaiah was handed to him. Unrolling it, he found the place where it is written:

¹⁸"The Spirit of the Lord is on me,
 because he has anointed me
 to preach good news to the poor.
He has sent me to proclaim freedom
 for the prisoners
and recovery of sight for the blind,
to release the oppressed,
¹⁹ to proclaim the year of the Lord's favor."

²⁰Then he rolled up the scroll, gave it back to the attendant and sat down. The eyes of everyone in the synagogue were fastened on him, ²¹and he began by saying to them, "Today this scripture is fulfilled in your hearing."

²²All spoke well of him and were amazed at the gracious words that came from his lips. "Isn't this Joseph's son?" they asked.

²³Jesus said to them, "Surely you will quote this proverb to me: 'Physician, heal yourself! Do here in your hometown what we have heard that you did in Capernaum.'"

²⁴"I tell you the truth," he continued, "no prophet is accepted in his hometown. ²⁵I assure you that there were many widows in Israel in Elijah's time, when the sky was shut for three and a half years and there was a severe famine throughout the land. ²⁶Yet Elijah was not sent to any of them, but to a widow in Zarephath in the region of Sidon. ²⁷And there were many in Israel with leprosy in the time of Elisha the prophet, yet not one of them was cleansed—only Naaman the Syrian."

²⁸All the people in the synagogue were furious when they heard this. ²⁹They got up, drove him out of the town, and took him to the brow of the hill on which the town was built, in order to throw him down the cliff. ³⁰But he walked right through the crowd and went on his way.

Jesus Drives Out an Evil Spirit

4:31–37pp — Mk 1:21–28

³¹Then he went down to Capernaum, a town in Galilee, and on the Sabbath began to teach the people. ³²They were amazed at his teaching, because his message had authority.

³³In the synagogue there was a man possessed by a demon, an evil spirit. He cried out at the top of his voice, ³⁴"Ha! What do you want with us, Jesus of Nazareth? Have you come to destroy us? I know who you are—the Holy One of God!"

³⁵"Be quiet!" Jesus said sternly. "Come out of him!" Then the demon threw the man down before them all and came out without injuring him.

³⁶All the people were amazed and said to each other, "What is this teaching? With authority and power he gives orders to evil spirits and they come out!" ³⁷And the news about him spread throughout the surrounding area.

Jesus Heals Many

4:38–41pp — Mt 8:14–17
4:38–43pp — Mk 1:29–38

³⁸Jesus left the synagogue and went to the home of Simon. Now Simon's mother-in-law was suffering from a high fever, and they asked Jesus to help her. ³⁹So he bent over her and rebuked the

fever, and it left her. She got up at once and began to wait on them.

⁴⁰When the sun was setting, the people brought to Jesus all who had various kinds of sickness, and laying his hands on each one,° he healed them.ᵖ ⁴¹Moreover, demons came out of many people, shouting, "You are the Son of God!"ᵠ But he rebukedʳ them and would not allow them to speak,ˢ because they knew he was the Christ.ᵛ

⁴²At daybreak Jesus went out to a solitary place. The people were looking for him and when they came to where he was, they tried to keep him from leaving them. ⁴³But he said, "I must preach the good news of the kingdom of Godᵗ to the other towns also, because that is why I was sent." ⁴⁴And he kept on preaching in the synagogues of Judea.ʷᵘ

The Calling of the First Disciples
5:1–11pp — Mt 4:18–22; Mk 1:16–20; Jn 1:40–42

5 One day as Jesus was standing by the Lake of Gennesaret,ˣ with the people crowding around him and listening to the word of God,ᵛ ²he saw at the water's edge two boats, left there by the fishermen, who were washing their nets. ³He got into one of the boats, the one belonging to Simon, and asked him to put out a little from shore. Then he sat down and taught the people from the boat.ʷ

⁴When he had finished speaking, he said to Simon, "Put out into deep water, and let downʸ the nets for a catch."ˣ

⁵Simon answered, "Master,ʸ we've worked hard all night and haven't caught anything.ᶻ But because you say so, I will let down the nets."

⁶When they had done so, they caught such a large number of fish that their nets began to break.ᵃ ⁷So they signaled their partners in the other boat to come and help them, and they came and filled both boats so full that they began to sink.

⁸When Simon Peter saw this, he fell at Jesus' knees and said, "Go away from me, Lord; I am a sinful man!"ᵇ ⁹For he and all his companions were astonished at the catch of fish they had taken, ¹⁰and so were James and John, the sons of Zebedee, Simon's partners.

Then Jesus said to Simon, "Don't be afraid;ᶜ from now on you will catch men." ¹¹So they pulled their boats up on shore, left everything and followed him.ᵈ

The Man With Leprosy
5:12–14pp — Mt 8:2–4; Mk 1:40–44

¹²While Jesus was in one of the towns, a man came along who was covered with leprosy.ᶻᵉ When he saw Jesus, he fell with his face to the ground and begged him, "Lord, if you are willing, you can make me clean."

¹³Jesus reached out his hand and touched the man. "I am willing," he said. "Be clean!" And immediately the leprosy left him.

¹⁴Then Jesus ordered him, "Don't tell anyone,ᶠ but go, show yourself to the priest and offer the sacrifices that Moses commandedᵍ for your cleansing, as a testimony to them."

¹⁵Yet the news about him spread all the more,ʰ so that crowds of people came to hear him and to be healed of their sicknesses. ¹⁶But Jesus often withdrew to lonely places and prayed.ⁱ

Jesus Heals a Paralytic
5:18–26pp — Mt 9:2–8; Mk 2:3–12

¹⁷One day as he was teaching, Pharisees and teachers of the law,ʲ who had come from every village of Galilee and from Judea and Jerusalem, were sitting there. And the power of the Lord was present for him to heal the sick.ᵏ ¹⁸Some men came carrying a paralytic on a mat and tried to take him into the house to lay him before Jesus. ¹⁹When they could not find a way to do this because of the crowd, they went up on the roof and lowered him on his mat through the tiles into the middle of the crowd, right in front of Jesus.

²⁰When Jesus saw their faith, he said, "Friend, your sins are forgiven."ˡ

²¹The Pharisees and the teachers of the law began thinking to themselves, "Who is this fellow who speaks blasphemy? Who can forgive sins but God alone?"ᵐ

²²Jesus knew what they were thinking and asked, "Why are you thinking these

---

ᵛ 41 Or Messiah   ʷ 44 Or the land of the Jews; some manuscripts Galilee
ˣ 1 That is, Sea of Galilee   ʸ 4 The Greek verb is plural.   ᶻ 12 The Greek word was used for various diseases affecting the skin—not necessarily leprosy.

things in your hearts? ²³Which is easier: to say, 'Your sins are forgiven,' or to say, 'Get up and walk'? ²⁴But that you may know that the Son of Man[n] has authority on earth to forgive sins . . ." He said to the paralyzed man, "I tell you, get up, take your mat and go home." ²⁵Immediately he stood up in front of them, took what he had been lying on and went home praising God. ²⁶Everyone was amazed and gave praise to God.[o] They were filled with awe and said, "We have seen remarkable things today."

The Calling of Levi
5:27–32pp — Mt 9:9–13; Mk 2:14–17

²⁷After this, Jesus went out and saw a tax collector by the name of Levi sitting at his tax booth. "Follow me,"[p] Jesus said to him, ²⁸and Levi got up, left everything and followed him.[q]

²⁹Then Levi held a great banquet for Jesus at his house, and a large crowd of tax collectors[r] and others were eating with them. ³⁰But the Pharisees and the teachers of the law who belonged to their sect[s] complained to his disciples, "Why do you eat and drink with tax collectors and 'sinners'?"[t]

³¹Jesus answered them, "It is not the healthy who need a doctor, but the sick. ³²I have not come to call the righteous, but sinners to repentance."[u]

Jesus Questioned About Fasting
5:33–39pp — Mt 9:14–17; Mk 2:18–22

³³They said to him, "John's disciples[v] often fast and pray, and so do the disciples of the Pharisees, but yours go on eating and drinking."

³⁴Jesus answered, "Can you make the guests of the bridegroom[w] fast while he is with them? ³⁵But the time will come when the bridegroom will be taken from them;[x] in those days they will fast."

³⁶He told them this parable: "No one tears a patch from a new garment and sews it on an old one. If he does, he will have torn the new garment, and the patch from the new will not match the old. ³⁷And no one pours new wine into old wineskins. If he does, the new wine will burst the skins, the wine will run out

K Lk 2:10–11 ◀ ▶ Lk 6:47–48
C Lk 3:7 ◀ ▶ Lk 6:39
L Lk 4:18–19 ◀ ▶ Lk 6:37

5:24 ⁿ S Mt 8:20
5:26 ᵒ S Mt 9:8
5:27 ᵖ S Mt 4:19
5:28 ᵠ ver 11; S Mt 4:19
5:29 ʳ Lk 15:1
5:30 ˢ Ac 23:9; ᵗ S Mt 9:11
5:32 ᵘ S Jn 3:17
5:33 ᵛ Lk 7:18; Jn 1:35; 3:25,26
5:34 ʷ Jn 3:29
5:35 ˣ Lk 9:22; 17:22; Jn 16:5-7
6:1 ʸ Dt 23:25
6:2 ᶻ S Mt 12:2
6:3 ᵃ 1Sa 21:6
6:4 ᵇ Lev 24:5,9
6:5 ᶜ S Mt 8:20
6:6 ᵈ ver 1
6:7 ᵉ S Mt 12:10; ᶠ S Mt 12:2
6:8 ᵍ S Mt 9:4
6:11 ʰ Jn 5:18
6:12 ⁱ S Lk 3:21
6:13 ʲ S Mk 6:30

and the wineskins will be ruined. ³⁸No, new wine must be poured into new wineskins. ³⁹And no one after drinking old wine wants the new, for he says, 'The old is better.' "

Lord of the Sabbath
6:1–11pp — Mt 12:1–14; Mk 2:23–3:6

6 One Sabbath Jesus was going through the grainfields, and his disciples began to pick some heads of grain, rub them in their hands and eat the kernels.[y] ²Some of the Pharisees asked, "Why are you doing what is unlawful on the Sabbath?"[z]

³Jesus answered them, "Have you never read what David did when he and his companions were hungry?[a] ⁴He entered the house of God, and taking the consecrated bread, he ate what is lawful only for priests to eat.[b] And he also gave some to his companions." ⁵Then Jesus said to them, "The Son of Man[c] is Lord of the Sabbath."

⁶On another Sabbath[d] he went into the synagogue and was teaching, and a man was there whose right hand was shriveled. ⁷The Pharisees and the teachers of the law were looking for a reason to accuse Jesus, so they watched him closely[e] to see if he would heal on the Sabbath.[f] ⁸But Jesus knew what they were thinking[g] and said to the man with the shriveled hand, "Get up and stand in front of everyone." So he got up and stood there.

⁹Then Jesus said to them, "I ask you, which is lawful on the Sabbath: to do good or to do evil, to save life or to destroy it?"

¹⁰He looked around at them all, and then said to the man, "Stretch out your hand." He did so, and his hand was completely restored. ¹¹But they were furious[h] and began to discuss with one another what they might do to Jesus.

The Twelve Apostles
6:13–16pp — Mt 10:2–4; Mk 3:16–19; Ac 1:13

¹²One of those days Jesus went out to a mountainside to pray, and spent the night praying to God.[i] ¹³When morning came, he called his disciples to him and chose twelve of them, whom he also designated apostles:[j] ¹⁴Simon (whom he

E Lk 5:12–26 ◀ ▶ Lk 6:17–19
E Mt 12:25 ◀ ▶ Lk 12:2–3

named Peter), his brother Andrew, James, John, Philip, Bartholomew, ¹⁵Matthew,ᵏ Thomas, James son of Alphaeus, Simon who was called the Zealot, ¹⁶Judas son of James, and Judas Iscariot, who became a traitor.

Blessings and Woes
6:20-23pp — Mt 5:3-12

¹⁷He went down with them and stood on a level place. A large crowd of his disciples was there and a great number of people from all over Judea, from Jerusalem, and from the coast of Tyre and Sidon,ˡ ¹⁸who had come to hear him and to be healed of their diseases. Those troubled by evilᵃ spirits were cured, ¹⁹and the people all tried to touch him,ᵐ because power was coming from him and healing them all.ⁿ

²⁰Looking at his disciples, he said:

"Blessed are you who are poor,
    for yours is the kingdom of God.°
²¹Blessed are you who hunger now,
    for you will be satisfied.ᵖ
Blessed are you who weep now,
    for you will laugh.ᑫ

²²Blessed are you when men hate you,
    when they exclude youʳ and insult
        youˢ
    and reject your name as evil,
        because of the Son of Man.ᵗ

²³"Rejoice in that day and leap for joy,ᵘ because great is your reward in heaven. For that is how their fathers treated the prophets.ᵛ

²⁴"But woe to you who are rich,ʷ
    for you have already received your
        comfort.ˣ
²⁵Woe to you who are well fed now,
    for you will go hungry.ʸ
Woe to you who laugh now,
    for you will mourn and weep.ᶻ

²⁶Woe to you when all men speak well
    of you,
    for that is how their fathers treated
        the false prophets.ᵃ

Love for Enemies
6:29,30pp — Mt 5:39-42

²⁷"But I tell you who hear me: Love your enemies, do good to those who hate you,ᵇ ²⁸bless those who curse you, pray for those who mistreat you.ᶜ ²⁹If someone strikes you on one cheek, turn to him the other also. If someone takes your cloak, do not stop him from taking your tunic. ³⁰Give to everyone who asks you, and if anyone takes what belongs to you, do not demand it back.ᵈ ³¹Do to others as you would have them do to you.ᵉ

³²"If you love those who love you, what credit is that to you?ᶠ Even 'sinners' love those who love them. ³³And if you do good to those who are good to you, what credit is that to you? Even 'sinners' do that. ³⁴And if you lend to those from whom you expect repayment, what credit is that to you?ᵍ Even 'sinners' lend to 'sinners,' expecting to be repaid in full. ³⁵But love your enemies, do good to them,ʰ and lend to them without expecting to get anything back. Then your reward will be great, and you will be sonsⁱ of the Most High,ʲ because he is kind to the ungrateful and wicked. ³⁶Be merciful,ᵏ just as your Fatherˡ is merciful.

Judging Others
6:37-42pp — Mt 7:1-5

³⁷"Do not judge, and you will not be judged.ᵐ Do not condemn, and you will not be condemned. Forgive, and you will be forgiven.ⁿ ³⁸Give, and it will be given to you. A good measure, pressed down, shaken together and running over, will be poured into your lap.° For with the measure you use, it will be measured to you."ᵖ

³⁹He also told them this parable: "Can a blind man lead a blind man? Will they not both fall into a pit?ᑫ ⁴⁰A student is not above his teacher, but everyone who is fully trained will be like his teacher.ʳ

⁴¹"Why do you look at the speck of sawdust in your brother's eye and pay no attention to the plank in your own eye? ⁴²How can you say to your brother, 'Brother, let me take the speck out of your eye,' when you yourself fail to see the plank in your own eye? You hypocrite, first take the plank out of your eye,

L *Lk 5:31-32* ◀▶ *Lk 7:41-42*
R *Lk 3:8* ◀▶ *Lk 11:4*
C *Lk 5:31* ◀▶ *Lk 6:43-45*
H *Lk 6:25* ◀▶ *Lk 6:49*

ᵃ 18 Greek *unclean*

E *Lk 6:6-11* ◀▶ *Lk 7:1-22*
M *Mk 10:23-25* ◀▶ *Lk 10:13-15*
J *Mt 5:11-12* ◀▶ *Jn 16:33*
H *Lk 3:9* ◀▶ *Lk 6:39*

and then you will see clearly to remove the speck from your brother's eye.

A Tree and Its Fruit
6:43,44pp — Mt 7:16,18,20

⁴³"No good tree bears bad fruit, nor does a bad tree bear good fruit. ⁴⁴Each tree is recognized by its own fruit.ˢ People do not pick figs from thornbushes, or grapes from briers. ⁴⁵The good man brings good things out of the good stored up in his heart, and the evil man brings evil things out of the evil stored up in his heart. For out of the overflow of his heart his mouth speaks.ᵗ

The Wise and Foolish Builders
6:47–49pp — Mt 7:24–27

⁴⁶"Why do you call me, 'Lord, Lord,'ᵘ and do not do what I say?ᵛ ⁴⁷I will show you what he is like who comes to me and hears my words and puts them into practice.ʷ ⁴⁸He is like a man building a house, who dug down deep and laid the foundation on rock. When a flood came, the torrent struck that house but could not shake it, because it was well built. ⁴⁹But the one who hears my words and does not put them into practice is like a man who built a house on the ground without a foundation. The moment the torrent struck that house, it collapsed and its destruction was complete."

The Faith of the Centurion
7:1–10pp — Mt 8:5–13

7 When Jesus had finished saying all thisˣ in the hearing of the people, he entered Capernaum. ²There a centurion's servant, whom his master valued highly, was sick and about to die. ³The centurion heard of Jesus and sent some elders of the Jews to him, asking him to come and heal his servant. ⁴When they came to Jesus, they pleaded earnestly with him, "This man deserves to have you do this, ⁵because he loves our nation and has built our synagogue." ⁶So Jesus went with them.

C *Lk 6:39* ◀ ▶ *Lk 6:49*
S *Lk 3:9* ◀ ▶ *Lk 8:6–8*
T *Mk 8:38* ◀ ▶ *Lk 9:25–26*
K *Lk 5:24* ◀ ▶ *Jn 1:4*
O *Mk 16:15–16* ◀ ▶ *Lk 10:25–28*
C *Lk 6:43–45* ◀ ▶ *Lk 11:23*
H *Lk 6:39* ◀ ▶ *Lk 9:25–26*
E *Lk 6:17–19* ◀ ▶ *Lk 8:26–56*

6:44 ˢ Mt 12:33
6:45 ᵗ Pr 4:23; Mt 12:34,35; Mk 7:20
6:46 ᵘ S Jn 13:13 ᵛ Mal 1:6; Mt 7:21
6:47 ʷ Lk 8:21; 11:28; Jas 1:22-25
7:1 ˣ Mt 7:28
7:7 ʸ Ps 107:20
7:13 ᶻ ver 19; Lk 10:1; 13:15; 17:5; 22:61; 24:34; Jn 11:2
7:14 ᵃ Mt 9:25; Mk 1:31; Lk 8:54; Jn 11:43; Ac 9:40
7:16 ᵇ Lk 1:65 ᶜ S Mt 9:8 ᵈ ver 39; S Mt 21:11 ᵉ Lk 1:68
7:17 ᶠ S Mt 9:26
7:18 ᵍ S Mt 3:1 ʰ S Lk 5:33

He was not far from the house when the centurion sent friends to say to him: "Lord, don't trouble yourself, for I do not deserve to have you come under my roof. ⁷That is why I did not even consider myself worthy to come to you. But say the word, and my servant will be healed.ʸ ⁸For I myself am a man under authority, with soldiers under me. I tell this one, 'Go,' and he goes; and that one, 'Come,' and he comes. I say to my servant, 'Do this,' and he does it."

⁹When Jesus heard this, he was amazed at him, and turning to the crowd following him, he said, "I tell you, I have not found such great faith even in Israel." ¹⁰Then the men who had been sent returned to the house and found the servant well.

Jesus Raises a Widow's Son
7:11–16Ref — 1Ki 17:17–24; 2Ki 4:32–37; Mk 5:21–24,35–43; Jn 11:1–44

¹¹Soon afterward, Jesus went to a town called Nain, and his disciples and a large crowd went along with him. ¹²As he approached the town gate, a dead person was being carried out—the only son of his mother, and she was a widow. And a large crowd from the town was with her. ¹³When the Lordᶻ saw her, his heart went out to her and he said, "Don't cry." ¹⁴Then he went up and touched the coffin, and those carrying it stood still. He said, "Young man, I say to you, get up!"ᵃ ¹⁵The dead man sat up and began to talk, and Jesus gave him back to his mother.

¹⁶They were all filled with aweᵇ and praised God.ᶜ "A great prophetᵈ has appeared among us," they said. "God has come to help his people."ᵉ ¹⁷This news about Jesus spread throughout Judeaᵇ and the surrounding country.ᶠ

Jesus and John the Baptist
7:18–35pp — Mt 11:2–19

¹⁸John'sᵍ disciplesʰ told him about all these things. Calling two of them, ¹⁹he sent them to the Lord to ask, "Are you the one who was to come, or should we expect someone else?"

²⁰When the men came to Jesus, they said, "John the Baptist sent us to you to ask, 'Are you the one who was to come, or should we expect someone else?'"

ᵇ 17 Or *the land of the Jews*

²¹At that very time Jesus cured many who had diseases, sicknesses and evil spirits, and gave sight to many who were blind. ²²So he replied to the messengers, "Go back and report to John what you have seen and heard: The blind receive sight, the lame walk, those who have leprosy are cured, the deaf hear, the dead are raised, and the good news is preached to the poor. ²³Blessed is the man who does not fall away on account of me."

²⁴After John's messengers left, Jesus began to speak to the crowd about John: "What did you go out into the desert to see? A reed swayed by the wind? ²⁵If not, what did you go out to see? A man dressed in fine clothes? No, those who wear expensive clothes and indulge in luxury are in palaces. ²⁶But what did you go out to see? A prophet? Yes, I tell you, and more than a prophet. ²⁷This is the one about whom it is written:

" 'I will send my messenger ahead of you,
    who will prepare your way before you.'

²⁸I tell you, among those born of women there is no one greater than John; yet the one who is least in the kingdom of God is greater than he."

²⁹(All the people, even the tax collectors, when they heard Jesus' words, acknowledged that God's way was right, because they had been baptized by John. ³⁰But the Pharisees and experts in the law rejected God's purpose for themselves, because they had not been baptized by John.)

³¹"To what, then, can I compare the people of this generation? What are they like? ³²They are like children sitting in the marketplace and calling out to each other:

" 'We played the flute for you,
    and you did not dance;
we sang a dirge,
    and you did not cry.'

³³For John the Baptist came neither eating bread nor drinking wine, and you say, 'He has a demon.' ³⁴The Son of Man came eating and drinking, and you say, 'Here is a glutton and a drunkard, a friend of tax collectors and "sinners." ' ³⁵But wisdom is proved right by all her children."

Jesus Anointed by a Sinful Woman
7:37–39Ref — Mt 26:6–13; Mk 14:3–9; Jn 12:1–8
7:41,42Ref — Mt 18:23–34

³⁶Now one of the Pharisees invited Jesus to have dinner with him, so he went to the Pharisee's house and reclined at the table. ³⁷When a woman who had lived a sinful life in that town learned that Jesus was eating at the Pharisee's house, she brought an alabaster jar of perfume, ³⁸and as she stood behind him at his feet weeping, she began to wet his feet with her tears. Then she wiped them with her hair, kissed them and poured perfume on them.

³⁹When the Pharisee who had invited him saw this, he said to himself, "If this man were a prophet, he would know who is touching him and what kind of woman she is—that she is a sinner."

⁴⁰Jesus answered him, "Simon, I have something to tell you."

"Tell me, teacher," he said.

⁴¹"Two men owed money to a certain moneylender. One owed him five hundred denarii, and the other fifty. ⁴²Neither of them had the money to pay him back, so he canceled the debts of both. Now which of them will love him more?"

⁴³Simon replied, "I suppose the one who had the bigger debt canceled."

"You have judged correctly," Jesus said.

⁴⁴Then he turned toward the woman and said to Simon, "Do you see this woman? I came into your house. You did not give me any water for my feet, but she wet my feet with her tears and wiped them with her hair. ⁴⁵You did not give me a kiss, but this woman, from the time I entered, has not stopped kissing my feet. ⁴⁶You did not put oil on my head, but she has poured perfume on my feet. ⁴⁷Therefore, I tell you, her many sins have been forgiven—for she loved much. But he who has been forgiven little loves little."

⁴⁸Then Jesus said to her, "Your sins are forgiven."

⁴⁹The other guests began to say among

L Lk 6:37 ◄ ► Lk 7:47
L Lk 7:41–42 ◄ ► Lk 9:56

c 22 The Greek word was used for various diseases affecting the skin—not necessarily leprosy. d 27 Mal. 3:1 e 41 A denarius was a coin worth about a day's wages.

themselves, "Who is this who even forgives sins?"

⁵⁰Jesus said to the woman, "Your faith has saved you; go in peace."

The Parable of the Sower

8:4–15pp — Mt 13:2–23; Mk 4:1–20

8 After this, Jesus traveled about from one town and village to another, proclaiming the good news of the kingdom of God. The Twelve were with him, ²and also some women who had been cured of evil spirits and diseases: Mary (called Magdalene) from whom seven demons had come out; ³Joanna the wife of Cuza, the manager of Herod's household; Susanna; and many others. These women were helping to support them out of their own means.

⁴While a large crowd was gathering and people were coming to Jesus from town after town, he told this parable: ⁵"A farmer went out to sow his seed. As he was scattering the seed, some fell along the path; it was trampled on, and the birds of the air ate it up. ⁶Some fell on rock, and when it came up, the plants withered because they had no moisture. ⁷Other seed fell among thorns, which grew up with it and choked the plants. ⁸Still other seed fell on good soil. It came up and yielded a crop, a hundred times more than was sown."

When he said this, he called out, "He who has ears to hear, let him hear."

⁹His disciples asked him what this parable meant. ¹⁰He said, "The knowledge of the secrets of the kingdom of God has been given to you, but to others I speak in parables, so that,

"'though seeing, they may not see; though hearing, they may not understand.'

¹¹"This is the meaning of the parable: The seed is the word of God. ¹²Those along the path are the ones who hear, and then the devil comes and takes away the word from their hearts, so that they may not believe and be saved. ¹³Those on the rock are the ones who receive the word with joy when they hear it, but they have no root. They believe for a while, but in the time of testing they fall away. ¹⁴The seed that fell among thorns stands for those who hear, but as they go on their way they are choked by life's worries, riches and pleasures, and they do not mature. ¹⁵But the seed on good soil stands for those with a noble and good heart, who hear the word, retain it, and by persevering produce a crop.

A Lamp on a Stand

¹⁶"No one lights a lamp and hides it in a jar or puts it under a bed. Instead, he puts it on a stand, so that those who come in can see the light. ¹⁷For there is nothing hidden that will not be disclosed, and nothing concealed that will not be known or brought out into the open. ¹⁸Therefore consider carefully how you listen. Whoever has will be given more; whoever does not have, even what he thinks he has will be taken from him."

Jesus' Mother and Brothers

8:19–21pp — Mt 12:46–50; Mk 3:31–35

¹⁹Now Jesus' mother and brothers came to see him, but they were not able to get near him because of the crowd. ²⁰Someone told him, "Your mother and brothers are standing outside, wanting to see you."

²¹He replied, "My mother and brothers are those who hear God's word and put it into practice."

Jesus Calms the Storm

8:22–25pp — Mt 8:23–27; Mk 4:36–41
8:22–25Ref — Mk 6:47–52; Jn 6:16–21

²²One day Jesus said to his disciples, "Let's go over to the other side of the lake." So they got into a boat and set out. ²³As they sailed, he fell asleep. A squall came down on the lake, so that the boat was being swamped, and they were in great danger.

²⁴The disciples went and woke him, saying, "Master, Master, we're going to drown!"

He got up and rebuked the wind and the raging waters; the storm subsided, and all was calm. ²⁵"Where is your faith?" he asked his disciples.

In fear and amazement they asked one another, "Who is this? He commands even the winds and the water, and they obey him."

The Healing of a Demon-possessed Man
8:26–37pp — Mt 8:28–34
8:26–39pp — Mk 5:1–20

⁶ ²⁶They sailed to the region of the Gerasenes,ᵍ which is across the lake from Galilee. ²⁷When Jesus stepped ashore, he was met by a demon-possessed man from the town. For a long time this man had not worn clothes or lived in a house, but had lived in the tombs. ²⁸When he saw Jesus, he cried out and fell at his feet, shouting at the top of his voice, "What do you want with me,ᵖ Jesus, Son of the Most High God?ᵠ I beg you, don't torture me!" ²⁹For Jesus had commanded the evilʰ spirit to come out of the man. Many times it had seized him, and though he was chained hand and foot and kept under guard, he had broken his chains and had been driven by the demon into solitary places.

³⁰Jesus asked him, "What is your name?"

"Legion," he replied, because many demons had gone into him. ³¹And they begged him repeatedly not to order them to go into the Abyss.ʳ

³²A large herd of pigs was feeding there on the hillside. The demons begged Jesus to let them go into them, and he gave them permission. ³³When the demons came out of the man, they went into the pigs, and the herd rushed down the steep bank into the lakeˢ and was drowned.

³⁴When those tending the pigs saw what had happened, they ran off and reported this in the town and countryside, ³⁵and the people went out to see what had happened. When they came to Jesus, they found the man from whom the demons had gone out, sitting at Jesus' feet,ᵗ dressed and in his right mind; and they were afraid. ³⁶Those who had seen it told the people how the demon-possessedᵘ man had been cured. ³⁷Then all the people of the region of the Gerasenes asked Jesus to leave them,ᵛ because they were overcome with fear. So he got into the boat and left.

³⁸The man from whom the demons had gone out begged to go with him, but Jesus sent him away, saying, ³⁹"Return home and tell how much God has done for you." So the man went away and told all over town how much Jesus had done for him.

A Dead Girl and a Sick Woman
8:40–56pp — Mt 9:18–26; Mk 5:22–43

⁴⁰Now when Jesus returned, a crowd welcomed him, for they were all expecting him. ⁴¹Then a man named Jairus, a ruler of the synagogue,ʷ came and fell at Jesus' feet, pleading with him to come to his house ⁴²because his only daughter, a girl of about twelve, was dying.

As Jesus was on his way, the crowds almost crushed him. ⁴³And a woman was there who had been subject to bleedingˣ for twelve years,ⁱ but no one could heal her. ⁴⁴She came up behind him and touched the edge of his cloak,ʸ and immediately her bleeding stopped.

⁴⁵"Who touched me?" Jesus asked.

When they all denied it, Peter said, "Master,ᶻ the people are crowding and pressing against you."

⁴⁶But Jesus said, "Someone touched me;ᵃ I know that power has gone out from me."ᵇ

⁴⁷Then the woman, seeing that she could not go unnoticed, came trembling and fell at his feet. In the presence of all the people, she told why she had touched him and how she had been instantly healed. ⁴⁸Then he said to her, "Daughter, your faith has healed you.ᶜ Go in peace."ᵈ

⁴⁹While Jesus was still speaking, someone came from the house of Jairus, the synagogue ruler.ᵉ "Your daughter is dead," he said. "Don't bother the teacher any more."

⁵⁰Hearing this, Jesus said to Jairus, "Don't be afraid; just believe, and she will be healed."

⁵¹When he arrived at the house of Jairus, he did not let anyone go in with him except Peter, John and James,ᶠ and the child's father and mother. ⁵²Meanwhile, all the people were wailing and mourningᵍ for her. "Stop wailing," Jesus said. "She is not dead but asleep."ʰ

⁵³They laughed at him, knowing that

ᵍ 26 Some manuscripts *Gadarenes*; other manuscripts *Gergesenes*; also in verse 37   ʰ 29 Greek *unclean*   ⁱ 43 Many manuscripts *years, and she had spent all she had on doctors*

she was dead. ⁵⁴But he took her by the hand and said, "My child, get up!" ⁵⁵Her spirit returned, and at once she stood up. Then Jesus told them to give her something to eat. ⁵⁶Her parents were astonished, but he ordered them not to tell anyone what had happened.

Jesus Sends Out the Twelve

9:3–5pp — Mt 10:9–15; Mk 6:8–11
9:7–9pp — Mt 14:1,2; Mk 6:14–16

9 When Jesus had called the Twelve together, he gave them power and authority to drive out all demons and to cure diseases,¹ ²and he sent them out to preach the kingdom of God and to heal the sick. ³He told them: "Take nothing for the journey—no staff, no bag, no bread, no money, no extra tunic. ⁴Whatever house you enter, stay there until you leave that town. ⁵If people do not welcome you, shake the dust off your feet when you leave their town, as a testimony against them." ⁶So they set out and went from village to village, preaching the gospel and healing people everywhere.

⁷Now Herod the tetrarch heard about all that was going on. And he was perplexed, because some were saying that John had been raised from the dead, ⁸others that Elijah had appeared, and still others that one of the prophets of long ago had come back to life. ⁹But Herod said, "I beheaded John. Who, then, is this I hear such things about?" And he tried to see him.

Jesus Feeds the Five Thousand

9:10–17pp — Mt 14:13–21; Mk 6:32–44; Jn 6:5–13
9:13–17Ref — 2Ki 4:42–44

¹⁰When the apostles returned, they reported to Jesus what they had done. Then he took them with him and they withdrew by themselves to a town called Bethsaida, ¹¹but the crowds learned about it and followed him. He welcomed them and spoke to them about the kingdom of God, and healed those who needed healing.

¹²Late in the afternoon the Twelve came to him and said, "Send the crowd away so they can go to the surrounding villages and countryside and find food and lodging, because we are in a remote place here."

¹³He replied, "You give them something to eat."

They answered, "We have only five loaves of bread and two fish—unless we go and buy food for all this crowd." ¹⁴(About five thousand men were there.)

But he said to his disciples, "Have them sit down in groups of about fifty each." ¹⁵The disciples did so, and everybody sat down. ¹⁶Taking the five loaves and the two fish and looking up to heaven, he gave thanks and broke them. Then he gave them to the disciples to set before the people. ¹⁷They all ate and were satisfied, and the disciples picked up twelve basketfuls of broken pieces that were left over.

Peter's Confession of Christ

9:18–20pp — Mt 16:13–16; Mk 8:27–29
9:22–27pp — Mt 16:21–28; Mk 8:31–9:1

¹⁸Once when Jesus was praying in private and his disciples were with him, he asked them, "Who do the crowds say I am?"

¹⁹They replied, "Some say John the Baptist; others say Elijah; and still others, that one of the prophets of long ago has come back to life."

²⁰"But what about you?" he asked. "Who do you say I am?"

Peter answered, "The Christ[j] of God."

²¹Jesus strictly warned them not to tell this to anyone. ²²And he said, "The Son of Man must suffer many things and be rejected by the elders, chief priests and teachers of the law, and he must be killed and on the third day be raised to life."

²³Then he said to them all: "If anyone would come after me, he must deny himself and take up his cross daily and follow me. ²⁴For whoever wants to save his life will lose it, but whoever loses his life for me will save it. ²⁵What good is it for a man to gain the whole world, and yet

---

j 20 Or Messiah

lose or forfeit his very self? ²⁶If anyone is ashamed of me and my words, the Son of Man will be ashamed of him[m] when he comes in his glory and in the glory of the Father and of the holy angels.[n] ²⁷I tell you the truth, some who are standing here will not taste death before they see the kingdom of God."

The Transfiguration
9:28–36pp — Mt 17:1–8; Mk 9:2–8

²⁸About eight days after Jesus said this, he took Peter, John and James[o] with him and went up onto a mountain to pray.[p] ²⁹As he was praying, the appearance of his face changed, and his clothes became as bright as a flash of lightning. ³⁰Two men, Moses and Elijah, ³¹appeared in glorious splendor, talking with Jesus. They spoke about his departure,[q] which he was about to bring to fulfillment at Jerusalem. ³²Peter and his companions were very sleepy,[r] but when they became fully awake, they saw his glory and the two men standing with him. ³³As the men were leaving Jesus, Peter said to him, "Master,[s] it is good for us to be here. Let us put up three shelters—one for you, one for Moses and one for Elijah." (He did not know what he was saying.)

³⁴While he was speaking, a cloud appeared and enveloped them, and they were afraid as they entered the cloud. ³⁵A voice came from the cloud, saying, "This is my Son, whom I have chosen;[t] listen to him."[u] ³⁶When the voice had spoken, they found that Jesus was alone. The disciples kept this to themselves, and told no one at that time what they had seen.[v]

The Healing of a Boy With an Evil Spirit
9:37–42,43–45pp — Mt 17:14–18,22,23; Mk 9:14–27,30–32

³⁷The next day, when they came down from the mountain, a large crowd met him. ³⁸A man in the crowd called out, "Teacher, I beg you to look at my son, for he is my only child. ³⁹A spirit seizes him and he suddenly screams; it throws him into convulsions so that he foams at the mouth. It scarcely ever leaves him and is destroying him. ⁴⁰I begged your disciples to drive it out, but they could not."

⁴¹"O unbelieving and perverse generation,"[w] Jesus replied, "how long shall I stay with you and put up with you? Bring your son here."

⁴²Even while the boy was coming, the demon threw him to the ground in a convulsion. But Jesus rebuked the evil[k] spirit, healed the boy and gave him back to his father. ⁴³And they were all amazed at the greatness of God.

While everyone was marveling at all that Jesus did, he said to his disciples, ⁴⁴"Listen carefully to what I am about to tell you: The Son of Man is going to be betrayed into the hands of men."[x] ⁴⁵But they did not understand what this meant. It was hidden from them, so that they did not grasp it,[y] and they were afraid to ask him about it.

E Lk 9:11 ◀▶ Lk 9:49–50

9:26 m Mt 10:33; Lk 12:9; 2Ti 2:12
n S Mt 16:27
9:28 o S Mt 4:21
p S Lk 3:21
9:31 q 2Pe 1:15
9:32 r Mt 26:43
9:33 s S Lk 5:5
9:35 t Isa 42:1
u S Mt 3:17
9:36 v Mt 17:9
9:41 w Dt 32:5
9:44 x S ver 22
9:45 y S Mk 9:32

k 42 Greek *unclean*

C Mk 14:62 ◀▶ Lk 12:35–47
Q Jdg 2:10 ◀▶ Lk 16:23–25

9:26 Jesus warned that anyone who was ashamed of him and his words in this life would receive a similar response from Christ when he returns in glory at his second coming.

9:27 This prophetic statement has puzzled many, but there are two commonly accepted explanations. Some believe that this verse refers to Christ's authority and kingly reign over the kingdom of his post-resurrection church. The book of Acts confirms the disciples' participation in this growth of the early church.

Yet the context surrounding this verse seems to favor the view that this was a prediction of the transfiguration. Scholars who subscribe to this view state that the disciples experienced the kingdom of God when they were privileged to witness Jesus' supernatural appearance with Elijah and Moses on the Mount of Transfiguration only a few days later (see Mt 17:1; Mk 9:2).

9:28–33 This transfiguration visibly displayed Jesus' glory as the Son of God and prefigured his revelation in glory at his second coming at Armageddon. The fact that Elijah and Moses appeared in recognizable forms confirms that we will be recognized in heaven as ourselves and will be able to recognize other saints as well (see 2Sa 12:23). Though there appears to be a contradiction in the three gospel accounts regarding the timing of this event, Matthew and Mark counted the duration between the events exclusively while Luke counted both the initial day in which Jesus predicted the event, as well as the final day of its fulfillment as part of his eight days (see Mt 17:1–8; Mk 9:2–8).

Who Will Be the Greatest?

9:46–48pp — Mt 18:1–5
9:46–50pp — Mk 9:33–40

⁴⁶An argument started among the disciples as to which of them would be the greatest.ᶻ ⁴⁷Jesus, knowing their thoughts,ᵃ took a little child and had him stand beside him. ⁴⁸Then he said to them, "Whoever welcomes this little child in my name welcomes me; and whoever welcomes me welcomes the one who sent me.ᵇ For he who is least among you all—he is the greatest."ᶜ

⁴⁹"Master,"ᵈ said John, "we saw a man driving out demons in your name and we tried to stop him, because he is not one of us."

⁵⁰"Do not stop him," Jesus said, "for whoever is not against you is for you."ᵉ

Samaritan Opposition

⁵¹As the time approached for him to be taken up to heaven,ᶠ Jesus resolutely set out for Jerusalem.ᵍ ⁵²And he sent messengers on ahead, who went into a Samaritanʰ village to get things ready for him; ⁵³but the people there did not welcome him, because he was heading for Jerusalem. ⁵⁴When the disciples James and Johnⁱ saw this, they asked, "Lord, do you want us to call fire down from heaven to destroy themˡ?"ʲ ⁵⁵But Jesus turned and rebuked them, ⁵⁶andᵐ they went to another village.

The Cost of Following Jesus

9:57–60pp — Mt 8:19–22

⁵⁷As they were walking along the road,ᵏ a man said to him, "I will follow you wherever you go." ⁵⁸Jesus replied, "Foxes have holes and birds of the air have nests, but the Son of Manˡ has no place to lay his head." ⁵⁹He said to another man, "Follow me."ᵐ

But the man replied, "Lord, first let me go and bury my father."

⁶⁰Jesus said to him, "Let the dead bury their own dead, but you go and proclaim the kingdom of God."ⁿ

⁶¹Still another said, "I will follow you, Lord; but first let me go back and say good-by to my family."ᵒ

⁶²Jesus replied, "No one who puts his hand to the plow and looks back is fit for service in the kingdom of God."

Jesus Sends Out the Seventy-two

10:4–12pp — Lk 9:3–5
10:13–15,21,22pp — Mt 11:21–23,25–27
10:23,24pp — Mt 13:16,17

10 After this the Lordᵖ appointed seventy-twoⁿ othersᵠ and sent them two by twoʳ ahead of him to every town and place where he was about to go.ˢ ²He told them, "The harvest is plentiful, but the workers are few. Ask the Lord of the harvest, therefore, to send out workers into his harvest field.ᵗ ³Go! I am sending you out like lambs among wolves.ᵘ ⁴Do not take a purse or bag or sandals; and do not greet anyone on the road.

⁵"When you enter a house, first say, 'Peace to this house.' ⁶If a man of peace is there, your peace will rest on him; if not, it will return to you. ⁷Stay in that house, eating and drinking whatever they give you, for the worker deserves his wages.ᵛ Do not move around from house to house.

⁸"When you enter a town and are welcomed, eat what is set before you.ʷ ⁹Heal the sick who are there and tell them, 'The kingdom of Godˣ is near you.' ¹⁰But when you enter a town and are not welcomed, go into its streets and say, ¹¹'Even

S Lk 9:23 ◄ ► Lk 10:25–28
E Lk 9:49–50 ◄ ► Lk 10:17–20
N Mk 16:15–16 ◄ ► Lk 11:23

ᵗ54 Some manuscripts *them, even as Elijah did* ᵐ 55,56 Some manuscripts *them. And he said, "You do not know what kind of spirit you are of, for the Son of Man did not come to destroy men's lives, but to save them."* ⁵⁶And ⁿ1 Some manuscripts *seventy*; also in verse 17

9:46 ᶻ Lk 22:24
9:47 ᵃ S Mt 9:4
9:48 ᵇ S Mt 10:40
 ᶜ S Mk 9:35
9:49 ᵈ S Lk 5:5
9:50 ᵉ Mt 12:30; Lk 11:23
9:51 ᶠ S Mk 16:19
 ᵍ Lk 13:22; 17:11; 18:31; 19:28
9:52 ʰ S Mt 10:5
9:54 ⁱ S Mt 4:21
 ʲ 2Ki 1:10,12
9:57 ᵏ ver 51
9:58 ˡ S Mt 8:20
9:59 ᵐ S Mt 4:19
9:60 ⁿ S Mt 3:2
9:61 ᵒ 1Ki 19:20
10:1 ᵖ S Lk 7:13
 ᵠ Lk 9:1,2,51,52
 ʳ Mk 6:7 ˢ Mt 10:1
10:2 ᵗ Mt 9:37,38; Jn 4:35
10:3 ᵘ Mt 10:16
10:7 ᵛ 1Ti 5:18
10:8 ʷ 1Co 10:27
10:9 ˣ S Mt 3:2

E Lk 9:37–43 ◄ ► Lk 10:9
L Lk 7:47 ◄ ► Lk 11:9–10

10:10–15 Jesus prophesied that those cities that willfully rejected his salvation would face ultimate judgment before the throne of God. The Galilean cities of Capernaum, Korazin and Bethsaida where Jesus ministered will be judged more harshly than the wicked cities of Sodom, Sidon and Tyre because of the opportunity these people had to respond positively to the message of Jesus Christ. This prophecy confirms that individuals will be punished according to their sins, and whether they reject or receive the truth of Christ.

the dust of your town that sticks to our feet we wipe off against you.ʸ Yet be sure of this: The kingdom of God is near.' ¹²I tell you, it will be more bearable on that day for Sodomᵃ than for that town.ᵇ

¹³"Woe to you,ᶜ Korazin! Woe to you, Bethsaida! For if the miracles that were performed in you had been performed in Tyre and Sidon, they would have repented long ago, sitting in sackclothᵈ and ashes. ¹⁴But it will be more bearable for Tyre and Sidon at the judgment than for you. ¹⁵And you, Capernaum,ᵉ will you be lifted up to the skies? No, you will go down to the depths.ᵒ

¹⁶"He who listens to you listens to me; he who rejects you rejects me; but he who rejects me rejects him who sent me."ᶠ

¹⁷The seventy-twoᵍ returned with joy and said, "Lord, even the demons submit to us in your name."ʰ

¹⁸He replied, "I saw Satanⁱ fall like lightning from heaven.ʲ ¹⁹I have given you authority to trample on snakesᵏ and scorpions and to overcome all the power of the enemy; nothing will harm you. ²⁰However, do not rejoice that the spirits submit to you, but rejoice that your names are written in heaven."ˡ

²¹At that time Jesus, full of joy through the Holy Spirit, said, "I praise you, Father, Lord of heaven and earth, because you have hidden these things from the wise and learned, and revealed them to little children.ᵐ Yes, Father, for this was your good pleasure.

²²"All things have been committed to me by my Father.ⁿ No one knows who the Son is except the Father, and no one knows who the Father is except the Son and those to whom the Son chooses to reveal him."ᵒ

²³Then he turned to his disciples and said privately, "Blessed are the eyes that see what you see. ²⁴For I tell you that many prophets and kings wanted to see what you see but did not see it, and to hear what you hear but did not hear it."ᵖ

J Mk 6:11 ◀▶ Lk 10:14
H Lk 9:25–26 ◀▶ Lk 12:4–5
J Mk 6:11 ◀▶ Lk 11:31–32
M Lk 6:20–21 ◀▶ Lk 14:11
J Lk 10:12 ◀▶ Lk 11:31–32
E Lk 10:9 ◀▶ Lk 11:14–26

10:11 ʸS Mt 10:14
ᶻver 9

10:12 ᵃS Mt 10:15
ᵇMt 11:24

10:13 ᶜLk 6:24-26
ᵈS Rev 11:3

10:15 ᵉS Mt 4:13

10:16 ᶠS Mt 10:40

10:17 ᵍver 1
ʰS Mk 16:17

10:18 ⁱS Mt 4:10
ʲIsa 14:12; Rev 9:1; 12:8,9

10:19 ᵏMk 16:18; Ac 28:3-5

10:20 ˡS Rev 20:12

10:21 ᵐ1Co 1:26-29

10:22 ⁿS Mt 28:18
ᵒJn 1:18

10:24 ᵖ1Pe 1:10-12

10:25 ᵠMt 19:16; Lk 18:18

10:27 ʳDt 6:5
ˢLev 19:18; S Mt 5:43

10:28 ᵗS Ro 7:10

10:29 ᵘLk 16:15

10:31 ᵛLev 21:1-3

10:33 ʷS Mt 10:5

10:38 ˣJn 11:1; 12:2

The Parable of the Good Samaritan
10:25–28pp — Mt 22:34–40; Mk 12:28–31

²⁵On one occasion an expert in the law stood up to test Jesus. "Teacher," he asked, "what must I do to inherit eternal life?"ᵠ

²⁶"What is written in the Law?" he replied. "How do you read it?"

²⁷He answered: " 'Love the Lord your God with all your heart and with all your soul and with all your strength and with all your mind'ᵖ;ʳ and, 'Love your neighbor as yourself.'ᵠ"ˢ

²⁸"You have answered correctly," Jesus replied. "Do this and you will live."ᵗ

²⁹But he wanted to justify himself,ᵘ so he asked Jesus, "And who is my neighbor?"

³⁰In reply Jesus said: "A man was going down from Jerusalem to Jericho, when he fell into the hands of robbers. They stripped him of his clothes, beat him and went away, leaving him half dead. ³¹A priest happened to be going down the same road, and when he saw the man, he passed by on the other side.ᵛ ³²So too, a Levite, when he came to the place and saw him, passed by on the other side. ³³But a Samaritan,ʷ as he traveled, came where the man was; and when he saw him, he took pity on him. ³⁴He went to him and bandaged his wounds, pouring on oil and wine. Then he put the man on his own donkey, took him to an inn and took care of him. ³⁵The next day he took out two silver coinsʳ and gave them to the innkeeper. 'Look after him,' he said, 'and when I return, I will reimburse you for any extra expense you may have.'

³⁶"Which of these three do you think was a neighbor to the man who fell into the hands of robbers?"

³⁷The expert in the law replied, "The one who had mercy on him."

Jesus told him, "Go and do likewise."

At the Home of Martha and Mary

³⁸As Jesus and his disciples were on their way, he came to a village where a woman named Marthaˣ opened her home to him. ³⁹She had a sister called

O Lk 6:47–49 ◀▶ Lk 12:8–9
S Lk 9:62 ◀▶ Lk 11:28

ᵒ 15 Greek *Hades* ᵖ 27 Deut. 6:5 ᵠ 27 Lev. 19:18 ʳ 35 Greek *two denarii*

Mary,[y] who sat at the Lord's feet[z] listening to what he said. ⁴⁰But Martha was distracted by all the preparations that had to be made. She came to him and asked, "Lord, don't you care[a] that my sister has left me to do the work by myself? Tell her to help me!"

⁴¹"Martha, Martha," the Lord answered, "you are worried[b] and upset about many things, ⁴²but only one thing is needed.[s][c] Mary has chosen what is better, and it will not be taken away from her."

Jesus' Teaching on Prayer

11:2–4pp — Mt 6:9–13
11:9–13pp — Mt 7:7–11

11 One day Jesus was praying[d] in a certain place. When he finished, one of his disciples said to him, "Lord,[e] teach us to pray, just as John taught his disciples."

²He said to them, "When you pray, say:

" 'Father,[t]
hallowed be your name,
your kingdom[f] come.[u]
³Give us each day our daily bread.
⁴Forgive us our sins,
for we also forgive everyone who
sins against us.[v][g]
And lead us not into temptation.[w] ' "[h]

⁵Then he said to them, "Suppose one of you has a friend, and he goes to him at midnight and says, 'Friend, lend me three loaves of bread, ⁶because a friend of mine on a journey has come to me, and I have nothing to set before him.'

⁷"Then the one inside answers, 'Don't bother me. The door is already locked, and my children are with me in bed. I can't get up and give you anything.' ⁸I tell you, though he will not get up and give him the bread because he is his friend, yet because of the man's boldness[x] he will get up and give him as much as he needs.[i]

K Mk 9:1 ◀ ▶ Ac 3:21
M Lk 3:5–6 ◀ ▶ Lk 12:32
F Lk 9:12–17 ◀ ▶ Lk 12:22–31
R Lk 6:37 ◀ ▶ Lk 13:1

10:39 y Jn 11:1; 12:3 z Lk 8:35
10:40 a Mk 4:38
10:41 b Mt 6:25-34; Lk 12:11,22
10:42 c Ps 27:1
11:1 d S Lk 3:21 e S Jn 13:13
11:2 f S Mt 3:2
11:4 g Mt 18:35; Mk 11:25 h Mt 26:41; Jas 1:13
11:8 i Lk 18:1-6
11:9 j S Mt 7:7
11:14 k Mt 9:32, 33
11:15 l S Mk 3:22 m Mt 9:34
11:16 n S Mt 12:38
11:17 o S Mt 9:4
11:18 p S Mt 4:10
11:20 q Ex 8:19 r S Mt 3:2

⁹"So I say to you: Ask and it will be given to you;[j] seek and you will find; knock and the door will be opened to you. ¹⁰For everyone who asks receives; he who seeks finds; and to him who knocks, the door will be opened.

¹¹"Which of you fathers, if your son asks for[y] a fish, will give him a snake instead? ¹²Or if he asks for an egg, will give him a scorpion? ¹³If you then, though you are evil, know how to give good gifts to your children, how much more will your Father in heaven give the Holy Spirit to those who ask him!"

Jesus and Beelzebub

11:14,15,17–22,24–26pp — Mt 12:22,24–29,43–45
11:17–22pp — Mk 3:23–27

¹⁴Jesus was driving out a demon that was mute. When the demon left, the man who had been mute spoke, and the crowd was amazed.[k] ¹⁵But some of them said, "By Beelzebub,[z¹] the prince of demons, he is driving out demons."[m] ¹⁶Others tested him by asking for a sign from heaven.[n]

¹⁷Jesus knew their thoughts[o] and said to them: "Any kingdom divided against itself will be ruined, and a house divided against itself will fall. ¹⁸If Satan[p] is divided against himself, how can his kingdom stand? I say this because you claim that I drive out demons by Beelzebub. ¹⁹Now if I drive out demons by Beelzebub, by whom do your followers drive them out? So then, they will be your judges. ²⁰But if I drive out demons by the finger of God,[q] then the kingdom of God[r] has come to you.

²¹"When a strong man, fully armed, guards his own house, his possessions are

A Ps 51:10–13 ◀ ▶ Jn 4:10
P Lk 3:16 ◀ ▶ Lk 24:29
L Lk 9:56 ◀ ▶ Lk 13:34
W Lk 2:10–11 ◀ ▶ Lk 12:8
E Lk 10:17–20 ◀ ▶ Lk 13:11–17

[s] 42 Some manuscripts *but few things are needed—or only one* [t] 2 Some manuscripts *Our Father in heaven* [u] 2 Some manuscripts *come. May your will be done on earth as it is in heaven.* [v] 4 Greek *everyone who is indebted to us* [w] 4 Some manuscripts *temptation but deliver us from the evil one* [x] 8 Or *persistence* [y] 11 Some manuscripts *for bread, will give him a stone; or if he asks for* [z] 15 Greek *Beezeboul* or *Beelzeboul*; also in verses 18 and 19

11:2 When Jesus taught his disciples to pray, his words included the prophecy of the coming Millen- nium when God's kingdom will truly come on earth.

safe. ²²But when someone stronger attacks and overpowers him, he takes away the armor in which the man trusted and divides up the spoils.

²³"He who is not with me is against me, and he who does not gather with me, scatters.

²⁴"When an evil[a] spirit comes out of a man, it goes through arid places seeking rest and does not find it. Then it says, 'I will return to the house I left.' ²⁵When it arrives, it finds the house swept clean and put in order. ²⁶Then it goes and takes seven other spirits more wicked than itself, and they go and live there. And the final condition of that man is worse than the first."

²⁷As Jesus was saying these things, a woman in the crowd called out, "Blessed is the mother who gave you birth and nursed you."

²⁸He replied, "Blessed rather are those who hear the word of God and obey it."

The Sign of Jonah
11:29-32pp — Mt 12:39-42

²⁹As the crowds increased, Jesus said, "This is a wicked generation. It asks for a miraculous sign, but none will be given it except the sign of Jonah. ³⁰For as Jonah was a sign to the Ninevites, so also will the Son of Man be to this generation. ³¹The Queen of the South will rise at the judgment with the men of this generation and condemn them; for she came from the ends of the earth to listen to Solomon's wisdom, and now one[b] greater than Solomon is here. ³²The men of Nineveh will stand up at the judgment with this generation and condemn it; for they repented at the preaching of Jonah, and now one greater than Jonah is here.

A Mt 22:11-14 ◀▶ Jn 3:18
C Lk 6:49 ◀▶ Lk 11:34-35
N Lk 10:10-16 ◀▶ Lk 11:31-32
S Lk 10:25-28 ◀▶ Lk 11:34
J Lk 10:14 ◀▶ Jn 12:48
J Lk 10:12-14 ◀▶ Jn 12:48
N Lk 11:23 ◀▶ Lk 12:16-21

11:23 ˢMt 12:30; Mk 9:40; Lk 9:50
11:26 ᵗ2Pe 2:20
11:27 ᵘLk 23:29
11:28 ᵛS Heb 4:12 ʷPr 8:32; Lk 6:47; 8:21; Jn 14:21
11:29 ˣver 16; S Mt 12:38 ʸJnh 1:17; Mt 16:4
11:31 ᶻ1Ki 10:1; 2Ch 9:1
11:32 ᵃJnh 3:5
11:33 ᵇS Mt 5:15
11:37 ᶜLk 7:36; 14:1
11:38 ᵈMk 7:3,4
11:39 ᵉS Lk 7:13 ᶠMt 23:25,26; Mk 7:20-23
11:40 ᵍLk 12:20; 1Co 15:36
11:41 ʰLk 12:33 ⁱS Ac 10:15
11:42 ⁱLk 18:12 ᵏDt 6:5; Mic 6:8 ˡMt 23:23
11:43 ᵐMt 23:6,7; Lk 14:7; 20:46

The Lamp of the Body
11:34,35pp — Mt 6:22,23

³³"No one lights a lamp and puts it in a place where it will be hidden, or under a bowl. Instead he puts it on its stand, so that those who come in may see the light. ³⁴Your eye is the lamp of your body. When your eyes are good, your whole body also is full of light. But when they are bad, your body also is full of darkness. ³⁵See to it, then, that the light within you is not darkness. ³⁶Therefore, if your whole body is full of light, and no part of it dark, it will be completely lighted, as when the light of a lamp shines on you."

Six Woes

³⁷When Jesus had finished speaking, a Pharisee invited him to eat with him; so he went in and reclined at the table. ³⁸But the Pharisee, noticing that Jesus did not first wash before the meal, was surprised.

³⁹Then the Lord said to him, "Now then, you Pharisees clean the outside of the cup and dish, but inside you are full of greed and wickedness. ⁴⁰You foolish people! Did not the one who made the outside make the inside also? ⁴¹But give what is inside ₍the dish₎[c] to the poor, and everything will be clean for you.

⁴²"Woe to you Pharisees, because you give God a tenth of your mint, rue and all other kinds of garden herbs, but you neglect justice and the love of God. You should have practiced the latter without leaving the former undone.

⁴³"Woe to you Pharisees, because you love the most important seats in the synagogues and greetings in the marketplaces.

⁴⁴"Woe to you, because you are like un-

C Lk 11:23 ◀▶ Lk 12:16-21
S Lk 11:28 ◀▶ Lk 13:9

ᵃ 24 Greek *unclean* ᵇ 31 Or *something;* also in verse 32 ᶜ 41 Or *what you have*

11:31-32 The opportunities to repent are so overwhelming and numerous that the kingdom of the queen of Sheba and the ancient Ninevites will condemn the Israelites for their unrepentant hearts. Both the queen of Sheba and the city of Nineveh repented with far less spiritual revelation than those of first-century Judea who experienced and rejected the ministry of Jesus. This prophecy confirms that those condemned to eternity in hell will be judged by their own evil deeds.

marked graves,ⁿ which men walk over without knowing it."

⁴⁵One of the experts in the law° answered him, "Teacher, when you say these things, you insult us also."

⁴⁶Jesus replied, "And you experts in the law, woe to you, because you load people down with burdens they can hardly carry, and you yourselves will not lift one finger to help them.ᵖ

⁴⁷"Woe to you, because you build tombs for the prophets, and it was your forefathers who killed them. ⁴⁸So you testify that you approve of what your forefathers did; they killed the prophets, and you build their tombs.ᵠ ⁴⁹Because of this, God in his wisdomʳ said, 'I will send them prophets and apostles, some of whom they will kill and others they will persecute.'ˢ ⁵⁰Therefore this generation will be held responsible for the blood of all the prophets that has been shed since the beginning of the world, ⁵¹from the blood of Abelᵗ to the blood of Zechariah,ᵘ who was killed between the altar and the sanctuary. Yes, I tell you, this generation will be held responsible for it all.ᵛ

⁵²"Woe to you experts in the law, because you have taken away the key to knowledge. You yourselves have not entered, and you have hindered those who were entering."ʷ

⁵³When Jesus left there, the Pharisees and the teachers of the law began to oppose him fiercely and to besiege him with questions, ⁵⁴waiting to catch him in something he might say.ˣ

Warnings and Encouragements
12:2–9pp — Mt 10:26-33

12 Meanwhile, when a crowd of many thousands had gathered, so that they were trampling on one another, Jesus began to speak first to his disciples, saying: "Be on your guard against the yeast of the Pharisees, which is hypocrisy.ʸ ²There is nothing concealed that will not be disclosed, or hidden that will not be made known.ᶻ ³What you have said in the dark will be heard in the daylight, and what you have whispered in the ear in the inner rooms will be proclaimed from the roofs.

⁴"I tell you, my friends,ᵃ do not be afraid of those who kill the body and after that can do no more. ⁵But I will show you whom you should fear: Fear him who, after the killing of the body, has power to throw you into hell. Yes, I tell you, fear him.ᵇ ⁶Are not five sparrows sold for two pennies*d*? Yet not one of them is forgotten by God. ⁷Indeed, the very hairs of your head are all numbered.ᶜ Don't be afraid; you are worth more than many sparrows.ᵈ

⁸"I tell you, whoever acknowledges me before men, the Son of Man will also acknowledge him before the angels of God.ᵉ ⁹But he who disowns me before men will be disownedᶠ before the angels of God. ¹⁰And everyone who speaks a word against the Son of Manᵍ will be forgiven, but anyone who blasphemes against the Holy Spirit will not be forgiven.ʰ

¹¹"When you are brought before synagogues, rulers and authorities, do not worry about how you will defend yourselves or what you will say,ⁱ ¹²for the Holy Spirit will teach you at that time what you should say."ʲ

The Parable of the Rich Fool

¹³Someone in the crowd said to him, "Teacher, tell my brother to divide the inheritance with me."

¹⁴Jesus replied, "Man, who appointed me a judge or an arbiter between you?" ¹⁵Then he said to them, "Watch out! Be on your guard against all kinds of greed; a man's life does not consist in the abundance of his possessions."ᵏ

¹⁶And he told them this parable: "The ground of a certain rich man produced a good crop. ¹⁷He thought to himself, 'What shall I do? I have no place to store my crops.'

¹⁸"Then he said, 'This is what I'll do. I will tear down my barns and build bigger

---

11:44 ⁿ Mt 23:27
11:45 ° S Mt 22:35
11:46 ᵖ S Mt 23:4
11:48 ᵠ Mt 23:29-32; Ac 7:51-53
11:49 ʳ 1Co 1:24, 30; Col 2:3
ˢ Mt 23:34
11:51 ᵗ Ge 4:8
ᵘ 2Ch 24:20,21
ᵛ Mt 23:35,36
11:52 ʷ Mt 23:13
11:54 ˣ S Mt 12:10
12:1 ʸ Mt 16:6,11,12
12:2 ᶻ S Mk 4:22
12:4 ᵃ Jn 15:14,15
12:5 ᵇ Heb 10:31
12:7 ᶜ S Mt 10:30
ᵈ Mt 12:12
12:8 ᵉ Lk 15:10
12:9 ᶠ Mk 8:38; 2Ti 2:12
12:10 ᵍ S Mt 8:20
ʰ Mt 12:31,32; S 1Jn 5:16
12:11 ⁱ Mt 10:17,19; Lk 21:12,14
12:12 ʲ Ex 4:12; Mt 10:20; Mk 13:11; Lk 21:15
12:15 ᵏ Job 20:20; 31:24; Ps 62:10

E *Lk 6:8* ◀▶ *Lk 16:15*
H *Lk 10:12–15* ◀▶ *Lk 12:20–21*
L *Lk 4:10–11* ◀▶ *Lk 12:22–32*
O *Lk 10:25–28* ◀▶ *Lk 18:16–17*
T *Lk 9:25–26* ◀▶ *Jn 12:42–43*
W *Lk 11:9–10* ◀▶ *Lk 14:16–23*
Q *Mk 3:29* ◀▶ *Ac 5:3–4*
G *Lk 2:40* ◀▶ *Lk 21:14–15*
L *Lk 4:14* ◀▶ *Lk 21:14–15*
T *Lk 4:18* ◀▶ *Lk 21:14–15*
C *Lk 11:34–35* ◀▶ *Lk 15:24*
N *Lk 11:31–32* ◀▶ *Lk 12:39–40*

d 6 Greek *two assaria*

ones, and there I will store all my grain and my goods. ¹⁹And I'll say to myself, "You have plenty of good things laid up for many years. Take life easy; eat, drink and be merry." '

²⁰"But God said to him, 'You fool!¹ This very night your life will be demanded from you.ᵐ Then who will get what you have prepared for yourself?'ⁿ

²¹"This is how it will be with anyone who stores up things for himself but is not rich toward God."ᵒ

Do Not Worry
12:22–31pp — Mt 6:25–33

²²Then Jesus said to his disciples: "Therefore I tell you, do not worry about your life, what you will eat; or about your body, what you will wear. ²³Life is more than food, and the body more than clothes. ²⁴Consider the ravens: They do not sow or reap, they have no storeroom or barn; yet God feeds them.ᵖ And how much more valuable you are than birds! ²⁵Who of you by worrying can add a single hour to his lifeᵉ? ²⁶Since you cannot do this very little thing, why do you worry about the rest?

²⁷"Consider how the lilies grow. They do not labor or spin. Yet I tell you, not even Solomon in all his splendorᑫ was dressed like one of these. ²⁸If that is how God clothes the grass of the field, which is here today, and tomorrow is thrown into the fire, how much more will he clothe you, O you of little faith!ʳ ²⁹And do not set your heart on what you will eat or drink; do not worry about it. ³⁰For the pagan world runs after all such things, and your Fatherˢ knows that you need them.ᵗ ³¹But seek his kingdom,ᵘ and these things will be given to you as well.ᵛ

H Lk 12:4–5 ◀ ▶ Lk 12:46–48
C Mt 6:25–34 ◀ ▶ Lk 22:35
F Lk 11:3 ◀ ▶ Lk 22:35
L Lk 12:6–7 ◀ ▶ Lk 17:2
W Lk 8:24–25 ◀ ▶ Lk 18:1
U Mk 10:28–30 ◀ ▶ Lk 29:30

12:20 ˡJer 17:11; Lk 11:40 ᵐJob 27:8 ⁿPs 39:6; 49:10

12:21 ᵒver 33

12:24 ᵖJob 38:41; Ps 147:9

12:27 ᑫ1Ki 10:4-7

12:28 ʳS Mt 6:30

12:30 ˢS Lk 6:36 ᵗMt 6:8

12:31 ᵘS Mt 3:2 ᵛMt 19:29

12:32 ʷS Mt 14:27 ˣS Mt 25:34

12:33 ʸS Ac 2:45 ᶻS Mt 6:20 ᵃS Jas 5:2

12:34 ᵇMt 6:21

12:37 ᶜMt 24:42, 46; 25:13 ᵈS Mt 20:28

12:39 ᵉMt 6:19; 1Th 5:2; 2Pe 3:10; Rev 3:3; 16:15

12:40 ᶠMk 13:33; Lk 21:36

12:42 ᵍS Lk 7:13

³²"Do not be afraid,ʷ little flock, for your Father has been pleased to give you the kingdom.ˣ ³³Sell your possessions and give to the poor.ʸ Provide purses for yourselves that will not wear out, a treasure in heavenᶻ that will not be exhausted, where no thief comes near and no moth destroys.ᵃ ³⁴For where your treasure is, there your heart will be also.ᵇ

Watchfulness
12:35,36pp — Mt 25:1–13; Mk 13:33–37
12:39,40; 42–46pp — Mt 24:43–51

³⁵"Be dressed ready for service and keep your lamps burning, ³⁶like men waiting for their master to return from a wedding banquet, so that when he comes and knocks they can immediately open the door for him. ³⁷It will be good for those servants whose master finds them watching when he comes.ᶜ I tell you the truth, he will dress himself to serve, will have them recline at the table and will come and wait on them.ᵈ ³⁸It will be good for those servants whose master finds them ready, even if he comes in the second or third watch of the night. ³⁹But understand this: If the owner of the house had known at what hour the thiefᵉ was coming, he would not have let his house be broken into. ⁴⁰You also must be ready,ᶠ because the Son of Man will come at an hour when you do not expect him."

⁴¹Peter asked, "Lord, are you telling this parable to us, or to everyone?"

⁴²The Lordᵍ answered, "Who then is the faithful and wise manager, whom the master puts in charge of his servants to give them their food allowance at the proper time? ⁴³It will be good for that servant whom the master finds doing so when he returns. ⁴⁴I tell you the truth, he will put him in charge of all his posses-

M Lk 11:2 ◀ ▶ Lk 13:19
C Lk 9:26 ◀ ▶ Lk 17:23–24
N Lk 12:16–21 ◀ ▶ Lk 12:46–47

ᵉ25 Or single cubit to his height

12:32 Jesus prophesied that God has promised to deliver the millennial kingdom to the saints in the future as well as "righteousness, peace and joy in the Holy Spirit" (Ro 14:17) each day.

12:35–47 Jesus warned his followers and servants to be watchful for his return. The Lord will come in an hour when the wicked servants are not watchful, and catch them unawares as a thief who breaks into a house. Jesus' followers must be ready at any time for his return "because the Son of Man will come at an hour when you do not expect him" (12:40). Those servants who obediently watch for his return, even if it is delayed, will be rewarded; those who are not prepared will be judged.

sions. ⁴⁵But suppose the servant says to himself, 'My master is taking a long time in coming,' and he then begins to beat the menservants and maidservants and to eat and drink and get drunk. ⁴⁶The master of that servant will come on a day when he does not expect him and at an hour he is not aware of.ʰ He will cut him to pieces and assign him a place with the unbelievers.

⁴⁷"That servant who knows his master's will and does not get ready or does not do what his master wants will be beaten with many blows.ⁱ ⁴⁸But the one who does not know and does things deserving punishment will be beaten with few blows.ʲ From everyone who has been given much, much will be demanded; and from the one who has been entrusted with much, much more will be asked.

Not Peace but Division
12:51–53pp — Mt 10:34–36

⁴⁹"I have come to bring fire on the earth, and how I wish it were already kindled! ⁵⁰But I have a baptismᵏ to undergo, and how distressed I am until it is completed!ˡ ⁵¹Do you think I came to bring peace on earth? No, I tell you, but division. ⁵²From now on there will be five in one family divided against each other, three against two and two against three. ⁵³They will be divided, father against son and son against father, mother against daughter and daughter against mother, mother-in-law against daughter-in-law and daughter-in-law against mother-in-law."ᵐ

Interpreting the Times

⁵⁴He said to the crowd: "When you see a cloud rising in the west, immediately you say, 'It's going to rain,' and it does.ⁿ ⁵⁵And when the south wind blows, you say, 'It's going to be hot,' and it is. ⁵⁶Hypocrites! You know how to interpret the appearance of the earth and the sky. How is it that you don't know how to interpret this present time?ᵒ

⁵⁷"Why don't you judge for yourselves

P *Mt 24:50–51* ◀ ▶ *Lk 17:26–30*
H *Lk 12:20–21* ◀ ▶ *Lk 13:5*
N *Lk 12:39–40* ◀ ▶ *Lk 13:24–25*

12:46 ʰ ver 40
12:47 ⁱ Dt 25:2
12:48 ʲ Lev 5:17; Nu 15:27-30
12:50 ᵏ Mk 10:38 ˡ S Jn 19:30
12:53 ᵐ Mic 7:6; Mt 10:21
12:54 ⁿ Mt 16:2
12:56 ᵒ Mt 16:3
12:58 ᵖ Mt 5:25
12:59 ᵠ Mt 5:26; Mk 12:42
13:1 ʳ S Mt 27:2
13:2 ˢ Jn 9:2,3
13:4 ᵗ Jn 9:7,11
13:5 ᵘ Mt 3:2; Ac 2:38
13:6 ᵛ Isa 5:2; Jer 8:13; Mt 21:19
13:7 ʷ S Mt 3:10
13:10 ˣ S Mt 4:23
13:11 ʸ ver 16

what is right? ⁵⁸As you are going with your adversary to the magistrate, try hard to be reconciled to him on the way, or he may drag you off to the judge, and the judge turn you over to the officer, and the officer throw you into prison.ᵖ ⁵⁹I tell you, you will not get out until you have paid the last penny.ᶠ"ᵠ

Repent or Perish

13 Now there were some present at that time who told Jesus about the Galileans whose blood Pilateʳ had mixed with their sacrifices. ²Jesus answered, "Do you think that these Galileans were worse sinners than all the other Galileans because they suffered this way?ˢ ³I tell you, no! But unless you repent, you too will all perish. ⁴Or those eighteen who died when the tower in Siloamᵗ fell on them—do you think they were more guilty than all the others living in Jerusalem? ⁵I tell you, no! But unless you repent,ᵘ you too will all perish."

⁶Then he told this parable: "A man had a fig tree, planted in his vineyard, and he went to look for fruit on it, but did not find any.ᵛ ⁷So he said to the man who took care of the vineyard, 'For three years now I've been coming to look for fruit on this fig tree and haven't found any. Cut it down!ʷ Why should it use up the soil?'

⁸"'Sir,' the man replied, 'leave it alone for one more year, and I'll dig around it and fertilize it. ⁹If it bears fruit next year, fine! If not, then cut it down.'"

A Crippled Woman Healed on the Sabbath

¹⁰On a Sabbath Jesus was teaching in one of the synagogues,ˣ ¹¹and a woman was there who had been crippled by a spirit for eighteen years.ʸ She was bent over and could not straighten up at all. ¹²When Jesus saw her, he called her for-

R *Mk 13:14–20* ◀ ▶ *Lk 13:5*
R *Lk 11:4* ◀ ▶ *Lk 13:5*
R *Lk 13:3* ◀ ▶ *Lk 13:34–35*
H *Lk 12:46–48* ◀ ▶ *Lk 13:9*
R *Lk 13:3* ◀ ▶ *Lk 15:7*
H *Lk 13:5* ◀ ▶ *Lk 13:24–28*
S *Lk 11:34* ◀ ▶ *Lk 13:23–28*
E *Lk 11:14–26* ◀ ▶ *Lk 13:32–33*

ᶠ 59 Greek *lepton*

13:3–5 Jesus points out that all sinners who refuse to repent will perish.

ward and said to her, "Woman, you are set free from your infirmity." ¹³Then he put his hands on her,ᶻ and immediately she straightened up and praised God.

¹⁴Indignant because Jesus had healed on the Sabbath,ᵃ the synagogue rulerᵇ said to the people, "There are six days for work.ᶜ So come and be healed on those days, not on the Sabbath."

¹⁵The Lord answered him, "You hypocrites! Doesn't each of you on the Sabbath untie his ox or donkey from the stall and lead it out to give it water?ᵈ ¹⁶Then should not this woman, a daughter of Abraham,ᵉ whom Satanᶠ has kept bound for eighteen long years, be set free on the Sabbath day from what bound her?"

¹⁷When he said this, all his opponents were humiliated,ᵍ but the people were delighted with all the wonderful things he was doing.

The Parables of the Mustard Seed and the Yeast

13:18,19pp — Mk 4:30–32
13:18–21pp — Mt 13:31–33

¹⁸Then Jesus asked, "What is the kingdom of Godʰ like?ⁱ What shall I compare it to? ¹⁹It is like a mustard seed, which a man took and planted in his garden. It grew and became a tree,ʲ and the birds of the air perched in its branches."ᵏ

²⁰Again he asked, "What shall I compare the kingdom of God to? ²¹It is like yeast that a woman took and mixed into a large amountᵍ of flour until it worked all through the dough."ˡ

The Narrow Door

²²Then Jesus went through the towns and villages, teaching as he made his way to Jerusalem.ᵐ ²³Someone asked him, "Lord, are only a few people going to be saved?"

He said to them, ²⁴"Make every effort to enter through the narrow door,ⁿ because many, I tell you, will try to enter and will not be able to. ²⁵Once the owner of the house gets up and closes the door, you will stand outside knocking and pleading, 'Sir, open the door for us.'

"But he will answer, 'I don't know you or where you come from.'ᵒ

²⁶"Then you will say, 'We ate and drank with you, and you taught in our streets.'

²⁷"But he will reply, 'I don't know you or where you come from. Away from me, all you evildoers!'ᵖ

²⁸"There will be weeping there, and gnashing of teeth,ᵠ when you see Abraham, Isaac and Jacob and all the prophets in the kingdom of God, but you yourselves thrown out. ²⁹People will come from east and westʳ and north and south, and will take their places at the feast in the kingdom of God. ³⁰Indeed there are those who are last who will be first, and first who will be last."ˢ

Jesus' Sorrow for Jerusalem

13:34,35pp — Mt 23:37–39
13:34,35Ref — Lk 19:41

³¹At that time some Pharisees came to Jesus and said to him, "Leave this place and go somewhere else. Herodᵗ wants to kill you."

³²He replied, "Go tell that fox, 'I will drive out demons and heal people today and tomorrow, and on the third day I will reach my goal.'ᵘ ³³In any case, I must keep going today and tomorrow and the next day—for surely no prophetᵛ can die outside Jerusalem!

³⁴"O Jerusalem, Jerusalem, you who

13:13 ᶻS Mk 5:23
13:14 ᵃS Mt 12:2 ᵇS Mk 5:22 ᶜEx 20:9
13:15 ᵈLk 14:5
13:16 ᵉS Lk 3:8 ᶠS Mt 4:10
13:17 ᵍS Isa 66:5
13:18 ʰS Mt 3:2 ⁱS Mt 13:24
13:19 ʲLk 17:6 ᵏS Mt 13:32
13:21 ˡ1Co 5:6
13:22 ᵐS Lk 9:51
13:24 ⁿMt 7:13
13:25 ᵒMt 7:23; 25:10-12
13:27 ᵖS Mt 7:23
13:28 ᵠS Mt 8:12
13:29 ʳS Mt 8:11
13:30 ˢS Mt 19:30
13:31 ᵗS Mt 14:1
13:32 ᵘS Heb 2:10
13:33 ᵛS Mt 21:11

D Lk 4:23–27 ◄► Jn 5:14
M Lk 12:32 ◄► Lk 13:21
M Lk 13:19 ◄► Lk 19:11–26
S Lk 13:9 ◄► Lk 14:26–27

H Lk 13:9 ◄► Lk 14:24
N Lk 12:46–47 ◄► Lk 13:34–35
E Lk 13:11–17 ◄► Lk 14:1–6
R Lk 13:5 ◄► Lk 14:24
L Lk 11:9–10 ◄► Lk 14:21–23
N Lk 13:24–25 ◄► Lk 14:16–24

ᵍ 21 Greek *three satas* (probably about 1/2 bushel or 22 liters)

13:19 Jesus likens the kingdom of God to a "mustard seed" which is almost invisible, yet grows into "a tree." The church has grown from twelve disciples into a global church of over 600 million believers.

13:21 Jesus also compared the kingdom of God to the "yeast" that causes the whole amount of bread to rise. This comparison indicated the prophetic destiny of the church to influence the entire world with the teachings of Christ.

13:34–35 Jesus warned of God's approaching judgment on the city of Jerusalem and the temple because of the Jews refusal to repent and their rejection of Jesus as their Messiah. Jesus also warned that he would not see them again until their repentance

kill the prophets and stone those sent to you, how often I have longed to gather your children together, as a hen gathers her chicks under her wings,[w] but you were not willing! [35]Look, your house is left to you desolate.[x] I tell you, you will not see me again until you say, 'Blessed is he who comes in the name of the Lord.'[h]"[y]

Jesus at a Pharisee's House
14:8-10Ref — Pr 25:6,7

14 One Sabbath, when Jesus went to eat in the house of a prominent Pharisee,[z] he was being carefully watched.[a] [2]There in front of him was a man suffering from dropsy. [3]Jesus asked the Pharisees and experts in the law,[b] "Is it lawful to heal on the Sabbath or not?"[c] [4]But they remained silent. So taking hold of the man, he healed him and sent him away.

[5]Then he asked them, "If one of you has a son[i] or an ox that falls into a well on the Sabbath day, will you not immediately pull him out?"[d] [6]And they had nothing to say.

[7]When he noticed how the guests picked the places of honor at the table,[e] he told them this parable: [8]"When someone invites you to a wedding feast, do not take the place of honor, for a person more distinguished than you may have been invited. [9]If so, the host who invited both of you will come and say to you, 'Give this man your seat.' Then, humiliated, you will have to take the least important place. [10]But when you are invited, take the lowest place, so that when your host comes, he will say to you, 'Friend, move up to a better place.' Then you will be honored in the presence of all your fellow guests. [11]For everyone who exalts himself will be humbled, and he who humbles himself will be exalted."[f]

[12]Then Jesus said to his host, "When you give a luncheon or dinner, do not invite your friends, your brothers or relatives, or your rich neighbors; if you do, they may invite you back and so you will be repaid. [13]But when you give a banquet, invite the poor, the crippled, the lame, the blind,[g] [14]and you will be blessed. Although they cannot repay you, you will be repaid at the resurrection of the righteous."[h]

The Parable of the Great Banquet
14:16-24Ref — Mt 22:2-14

[15]When one of those at the table with him heard this, he said to Jesus, "Blessed is the man who will eat at the feast[i] in the kingdom of God."[j]

[16]Jesus replied: "A certain man was preparing a great banquet and invited many guests. [17]At the time of the banquet he sent his servant to tell those who had been invited, 'Come, for everything is now ready.'

[18]"But they all alike began to make excuses. The first said, 'I have just bought a field, and I must go and see it. Please excuse me.'

[19]"Another said, 'I have just bought five yoke of oxen, and I'm on my way to try them out. Please excuse me.'

[20]"Still another said, 'I just got married, so I can't come.'

[21]"The servant came back and reported

13:34 w S Mt 23:37
13:35 x Jer 12:17; 22:5 y Ps 118:26; Lk 19:38
14:1 z Lk 7:36; 11:37 a S Mt 12:10
14:3 b S Mt 22:35 c S Mt 12:2
14:5 d Lk 13:15
14:7 e S Lk 11:43
14:11 f S Mt 23:12
14:13 g ver 21
14:14 h Ac 24:15
14:15 i Isa 25:6; Mt 26:29; Lk 13:29; Rev 19:9 j S Mt 3:2

E Lk 13:32-33 ◄ ► Lk 17:11-19
M Lk 10:13-15 ◄ ► Lk 18:9-14
F Mk 12:24-25 ◄ ► Lk 20:34-38
H Mt 25:1-13 ◄ ► Lk 22:16
N Lk 13:34-35 ◄ ► Lk 16:30-31
W Lk 12:8 ◄ ► Lk 15:7
G Mk 12:9 ◄ ► Lk 20:16
L Lk 13:34 ◄ ► Lk 15:3-24

[h] 35 Psalm 118:26 [i] 5 Some manuscripts *donkey*

---

at his second coming at Armageddon. At the conclusion of the savage persecution under the antichrist, the Jews will finally accept their Messiah who "comes in the name of the Lord" (13:35; see Zec 12:1-14).

14:14 Jesus promised that everyone would receive just recompense for their actions at the first "resurrection of the righteous."

14:16-24 This prophetic parable illustrates the spiritual truth that God offered salvation and his kingdom to the people of Israel two thousand years ago. They rejected his offer and crucified his Son. In this parable when the first guests rejected the invitation, the master told his servants to go into the streets and invite strangers and the poor to join the feast. Likewise, Jesus turned from unrepentant Israel and offered salvation and God's kingdom to anyone, Jew or Gentile, who would repent of their sins and trust in his salvation.

this to his master. Then the owner of the house became angry and ordered his servant, 'Go out quickly into the streets and alleys of the town and bring in the poor, the crippled, the blind and the lame.'ᵏ

²²" 'Sir,' the servant said, 'what you ordered has been done, but there is still room.'

²³"Then the master told his servant, 'Go out to the roads and country lanes and make them come in, so that my house will be full. ²⁴I tell you, not one of those men who were invited will get a taste of my banquet.' "ˡ

The Cost of Being a Disciple

²⁵Large crowds were traveling with Jesus, and turning to them he said: ²⁶"If anyone comes to me and does not hate his father and mother, his wife and children, his brothers and sisters—yes, even his own life—he cannot be my disciple.ᵐ ²⁷And anyone who does not carry his cross and follow me cannot be my disciple.ⁿ

²⁸"Suppose one of you wants to build a tower. Will he not first sit down and estimate the cost to see if he has enough money to complete it? ²⁹For if he lays the foundation and is not able to finish it, everyone who sees it will ridicule him, ³⁰saying, 'This fellow began to build and was not able to finish.'

³¹"Or suppose a king is about to go to war against another king. Will he not first sit down and consider whether he is able with ten thousand men to oppose the one coming against him with twenty thousand? ³²If he is not able, he will send a delegation while the other is still a long way off and will ask for terms of peace. ³³In the same way, any of you who does not give up everything he has cannot be my disciple.ᵒ

³⁴"Salt is good, but if it loses its saltiness, how can it be made salty again?ᵖ ³⁵It is fit neither for the soil nor for the manure pile; it is thrown out.ᵠ

"He who has ears to hear, let him hear."ʳ

R Lk 13:34–35 ◀▶ Lk 19:41–44
H Lk 13:24–28 ◀▶ Lk 16:19–31
S Lk 13:23–28 ◀▶ Lk 14:33–35
S Lk 14:26–27 ◀▶ Lk 16:13

14:21 ᵏ ver 13
14:24 ˡ Mt 21:43; Ac 13:46
14:26 ᵐ Mt 10:37; S Jn 12:25
14:27 ⁿ Mt 10:38; Lk 9:23
14:33 ᵒ Php 3:7,8
14:34 ᵖ Mk 9:50
14:35 ᵠ Mt 5:13 ʳ S Mt 11:15
15:1 ˢ Lk 5:29
15:2 ᵗ S Mt 9:11
15:3 ᵘ Mt 13:3
15:4 ᵛ Ps 23; 119:176; Jer 31:10; Eze 34:11-16; Lk 5:32; 19:10
15:6 ʷ ver 9
15:7 ˣ ver 10
15:9 ʸ ver 6
15:10 ᶻ ver 7
15:11 ᵃ Mt 21:28
15:12 ᵇ Dt 21:17 ᶜ ver 30
15:13 ᵈ ver 30; Lk 16:1
15:15 ᵉ Lev 11:7

The Parable of the Lost Sheep
15:4–7pp — Mt 18:12–14

15 Now the tax collectorsˢ and "sinners" were all gathering around to hear him. ²But the Pharisees and the teachers of the law muttered, "This man welcomes sinners and eats with them."ᵗ

³Then Jesus told them this parable:ᵘ ⁴"Suppose one of you has a hundred sheep and loses one of them. Does he not leave the ninety-nine in the open country and go after the lost sheep until he finds it?ᵛ ⁵And when he finds it, he joyfully puts it on his shoulders ⁶and goes home. Then he calls his friends and neighbors together and says, 'Rejoice with me; I have found my lost sheep.'ʷ ⁷I tell you that in the same way there will be more rejoicing in heaven over one sinner who repents than over ninety-nine righteous persons who do not need to repent.ˣ

The Parable of the Lost Coin

⁸"Or suppose a woman has ten silver coinsʲ and loses one. Does she not light a lamp, sweep the house and search carefully until she finds it? ⁹And when she finds it, she calls her friends and neighbors together and says, 'Rejoice with me; I have found my lost coin.'ʸ ¹⁰In the same way, I tell you, there is rejoicing in the presence of the angels of God over one sinner who repents."ᶻ

The Parable of the Lost Son

¹¹Jesus continued: "There was a man who had two sons.ᵃ ¹²The younger one said to his father, 'Father, give me my share of the estate.'ᵇ So he divided his propertyᶜ between them.

¹³"Not long after that, the younger son got together all he had, set off for a distant country and there squandered his wealthᵈ in wild living. ¹⁴After he had spent everything, there was a severe famine in that whole country, and he began to be in need. ¹⁵So he went and hired himself out to a citizen of that country, who sent him to his fields to feed pigs.ᵉ ¹⁶He longed to fill his stomach with the

L Lk 14:21–23 ◀▶ Lk 15:32
P Mt 18:12–14 ◀▶ Ro 10:21
R Lk 13:5 ◀▶ Lk 15:10
W Lk 14:16–23 ◀▶ Lk 19:10
R Lk 15:7 ◀▶ Lk 15:18–22

ʲ 8 Greek *ten drachmas*, each worth about a day's wages

pods that the pigs were eating, but no one gave him anything.

¹⁷"When he came to his senses, he said, 'How many of my father's hired men have food to spare, and here I am starving to death! ¹⁸I will set out and go back to my father and say to him: Father, I have sinned against heaven and against you. ¹⁹I am no longer worthy to be called your son; make me like one of your hired men.' ²⁰So he got up and went to his father.

"But while he was still a long way off, his father saw him and was filled with compassion for him; he ran to his son, threw his arms around him and kissed him.

²¹"The son said to him, 'Father, I have sinned against heaven and against you. I am no longer worthy to be called your son.'

²²"But the father said to his servants, 'Quick! Bring the best robe and put it on him. Put a ring on his finger and sandals on his feet. ²³Bring the fattened calf and kill it. Let's have a feast and celebrate. ²⁴For this son of mine was dead and is alive again; he was lost and is found.' So they began to celebrate.

²⁵"Meanwhile, the older son was in the field. When he came near the house, he heard music and dancing. ²⁶So he called one of the servants and asked him what was going on. ²⁷'Your brother has come,' he replied, 'and your father has killed the fattened calf because he has him back safe and sound.'

²⁸"The older brother became angry and refused to go in. So his father went out and pleaded with him. ²⁹But he answered his father, 'Look! All these years I've been slaving for you and never disobeyed your orders. Yet you never gave me even a young goat so I could celebrate with my friends. ³⁰But when this son of yours who has squandered your property with prostitutes comes home, you kill the fattened calf for him!'

³¹"'My son,' the father said, 'you are always with me, and everything I have is yours. ³²But we had to celebrate and be glad, because this brother of yours was dead and is alive again; he was lost and is found.'"

The Parable of the Shrewd Manager

16 Jesus told his disciples: "There was a rich man whose manager was accused of wasting his possessions. ²So he called him in and asked him, 'What is this I hear about you? Give an account of your management, because you cannot be manager any longer.'

³"The manager said to himself, 'What shall I do now? My master is taking away my job. I'm not strong enough to dig, and I'm ashamed to beg— ⁴I know what I'll do so that, when I lose my job here, people will welcome me into their houses.'

⁵"So he called in each one of his master's debtors. He asked the first, 'How much do you owe my master?'

⁶"'Eight hundred gallons of olive oil,' he replied.

"The manager told him, 'Take your bill, sit down quickly, and make it four hundred.'

⁷"Then he asked the second, 'And how much do you owe?'

"'A thousand bushels of wheat,' he replied.

"He told him, 'Take your bill and make it eight hundred.'

⁸"The master commended the dishonest manager because he had acted shrewdly. For the people of this world are more shrewd in dealing with their own kind than are the people of the light. ⁹I tell you, use worldly wealth to gain friends for yourselves, so that when it is gone, you will be welcomed into eternal dwellings.

¹⁰"Whoever can be trusted with very little can also be trusted with much, and whoever is dishonest with very little will also be dishonest with much. ¹¹So if you have not been trustworthy in handling worldly wealth, who will trust you with true riches? ¹²And if you have not been trustworthy with someone else's property, who will give you property of your own?

¹³"No servant can serve two masters. Either he will hate the one and love the

---

R Lk 15:10 ◀ ▶ Lk 18:13–14
C Lk 12:16–21 ◀ ▶ Lk 15:32
C Lk 15:24 ◀ ▶ Lk 19:10
L Lk 15:3–24 ◀ ▶ Lk 16:19–22

S Lk 14:33–35 ◀ ▶ Lk 17:32

k 21 Some early manuscripts son. Make me like one of your hired men.
l 6 Greek one hundred batous (probably about 3 kiloliters)   m 7 Greek one hundred korous (probably about 35 kiloliters)

other, or he will be devoted to the one and despise the other. You cannot serve both God and Money."[y]

[14]The Pharisees, who loved money,[z] heard all this and were sneering at Jesus.[a] [15]He said to them, "You are the ones who justify yourselves[b] in the eyes of men, but God knows your hearts.[c] What is highly valued among men is detestable in God's sight.

Additional Teachings

[16]"The Law and the Prophets were proclaimed until John.[d] Since that time, the good news of the kingdom of God is being preached,[e] and everyone is forcing his way into it. [17]It is easier for heaven and earth to disappear than for the least stroke of a pen to drop out of the Law.[f]

[18]"Anyone who divorces his wife and marries another woman commits adultery, and the man who marries a divorced woman commits adultery.[g]

The Rich Man and Lazarus

[19]"There was a rich man who was dressed in purple and fine linen and lived in luxury every day.[h] [20]At his gate was laid a beggar[i] named Lazarus, covered with sores [21]and longing to eat what fell from the rich man's table.[j] Even the dogs came and licked his sores.

[22]"The time came when the beggar died and the angels carried him to Abraham's side. The rich man also died and was buried. [23]In hell,[n] where he was in torment, he looked up and saw Abraham far away, with Lazarus by his side. [24]So he called to him, 'Father Abraham,[k] have pity on me and send Lazarus to dip the tip of his finger in water and cool my tongue, because I am in agony in this fire.'[l]

[25]"But Abraham replied, 'Son, remember that in your lifetime you received

E Lk 12:2–3 ◀▶ Jn 2:24–25
H Lk 14:24 ◀▶ Lk 17:1–2
L Lk 15:32 ◀▶ Lk 18:9–14
Q Lk 9:28–33 ◀▶ 1Co 13:12

16:13 [y] ver 9,11; Mt 6:24
16:14 [z] S 1Ti 3:3 [a] Lk 23:35
16:15 [b] Lk 10:29 [c] S Rev 2:23
16:16 [d] Mt 5:17; 11:12,13 [e] Mt 4:23
16:17 [f] S Mt 5:18
16:18 [g] Mt 5:31, 32; 19:9; Mk 10:11; Ro 7:2,3; 1Co 7:10,11
16:19 [h] Eze 16:49
16:20 [i] Ac 3:2
16:21 [j] Mt 15:27; Lk 15:16
16:24 [k] ver 30; S Lk 3:8 [l] S Mt 5:22
16:25 [m] Ps 17:14 [n] Lk 6:21,24,25
16:28 [o] Ac 2:40; 20:23; 1Th 2:16
16:29 [p] S Lk 24:27,44; Jn 1:45; 5:45-47; Ac 15:21 [q] Lk 4:17; 24:27,44; Jn 1:45
16:30 [r] ver 24; S Lk 3:8
17:1 [s] S Mt 5:29 [t] Mt 18:7
17:2 [u] Mk 10:24; Lk 10:21 [v] S Mt 5:29
17:3 [w] S Mt 18:15 [x] Eph 4:32; Col 3:13
17:4 [y] Mt 18:21,22
17:5 [z] S Mk 6:30 [a] S Lk 7:13
17:6 [b] Mt 13:31; 17:20; Lk 13:19 [c] S Mt 21:21; Mk 9:23

your good things, while Lazarus received bad things,[m] but now he is comforted here and you are in agony.[n] [26]And besides all this, between us and you a great chasm has been fixed, so that those who want to go from here to you cannot, nor can anyone cross over from there to us.'

[27]"He answered, 'Then I beg you, father, send Lazarus to my father's house, [28]for I have five brothers. Let him warn them,[o] so that they will not also come to this place of torment.'

[29]"Abraham replied, 'They have Moses[p] and the Prophets;[q] let them listen to them.'

[30]" 'No, father Abraham,'[r] he said, 'but if someone from the dead goes to them, they will repent.'

[31]"He said to him, 'If they do not listen to Moses and the Prophets, they will not be convinced even if someone rises from the dead.' "

Sin, Faith, Duty

17 Jesus said to his disciples: "Things that cause people to sin[s] are bound to come, but woe to that person through whom they come.[t] [2]It would be better for him to be thrown into the sea with a millstone tied around his neck than for him to cause one of these little ones[u] to sin.[v] [3]So watch yourselves.

"If your brother sins, rebuke him,[w] and if he repents, forgive him.[x] [4]If he sins against you seven times in a day, and seven times comes back to you and says, 'I repent,' forgive him."[y]

[5]The apostles[z] said to the Lord,[a] "Increase our faith!"

[6]He replied, "If you have faith as small as a mustard seed,[b] you can say to this mulberry tree, 'Be uprooted and planted in the sea,' and it will obey you.[c]

[7]"Suppose one of you had a servant

N Lk 14:16–24 ◀▶ Lk 17:26–30
H Lk 16:19–31 ◀▶ Lk 17:26–30
L Lk 12:22–32 ◀▶ Lk 18:7–8

[n] 23 Greek Hades

16:23–25 Jesus' prophetic parable of the rich man illustrates that God judges the spiritual heart of people, not their outward condition. This parable also indicates that the conscious memory of loved ones and concern for family members continues for all the dead who are in hell awaiting the final judgment. These are aware of those who need to repent, conscious of their need for salvation and desirous that someone should warn them that there will be no second chances, but are tormented by their inability to communicate their discoveries with the living.

plowing or looking after the sheep. Would he say to the servant when he comes in from the field, 'Come along now and sit down to eat'? ⁸Would he not rather say, 'Prepare my supper, get yourself ready and wait on me[d] while I eat and drink; after that you may eat and drink'? ⁹Would he thank the servant because he did what he was told to do? ¹⁰So you also, when you have done everything you were told to do, should say, 'We are unworthy servants; we have only done our duty.' "[e]

Ten Healed of Leprosy

¹¹Now on his way to Jerusalem,[f] Jesus traveled along the border between Samaria and Galilee.[g] ¹²As he was going into a village, ten men who had leprosy[o][h] met him. They stood at a distance[i] ¹³and called out in a loud voice, "Jesus, Master,[j] have pity on us!"

¹⁴When he saw them, he said, "Go, show yourselves to the priests."[k] And as they went, they were cleansed.

¹⁵One of them, when he saw he was healed, came back, praising God[l] in a loud voice. ¹⁶He threw himself at Jesus' feet and thanked him—and he was a Samaritan.[m]

¹⁷Jesus asked, "Were not all ten cleansed? Where are the other nine? ¹⁸Was no one found to return and give praise to God except this foreigner?" ¹⁹Then he said to him, "Rise and go; your faith has made you well."[n]

The Coming of the Kingdom of God

17:26,27pp — Mt 24:37–39

²⁰Once, having been asked by the Pharisees when the kingdom of God would come,[o] Jesus replied, "The kingdom of God does not come with your careful observation, ²¹nor will people say, 'Here it is,' or 'There it is,'[p] because the kingdom of God is within[p] you."

²²Then he said to his disciples, "The time is coming when you will long to see

E Lk 14:1-6 ◄► Lk 18:35-43

17:8 d Lk 12:37
17:10 e 1Co 9:16
17:11 f S Lk 9:51
     g Lk 9:51,52; Jn 4:3,4
17:12 h S Mt 8:2
     i Lev 13:45,46
17:13 j S Lk 5:5
17:14 k Lev 14:2; Mt 8:4
17:15 l S Mt 9:8
17:16 m S Mt 10:5
17:19 n S Mt 9:22
17:20 o S Mt 3:2
17:21 p ver 23
17:22 q S Mt 8:20
     r S Lk 5:35
17:23 s Mt 24:23; Lk 21:8
17:24 t Mt 24:27
17:25 u S Mt 16:21
     v Lk 9:22; 18:32
     w Mk 13:30; Lk 21:32
17:26 x Ge 6:5-8; 7:6-24
17:28 y Ge 19:1-28
17:30 z Mt 10:23; S 16:27; 24:3,27, 37,39; 25:31; S 1Co 1:7; S 1Th 2:19; 2Th 1:7; 2:8; 2Pe 3:4; S Rev 1:7
17:31 a Mt 24:17,18
17:32 b Ge 19:26
17:33 c S Jn 12:25
17:35 d Mt 24:41

one of the days of the Son of Man,[q] but you will not see it.[r] ²³Men will tell you, 'There he is!' or 'Here he is!' Do not go running off after them.[s] ²⁴For the Son of Man in his day[q] will be like the lightning,[t] which flashes and lights up the sky from one end to the other. ²⁵But first he must suffer many things[u] and be rejected[v] by this generation.[w]

²⁶"Just as it was in the days of Noah,[x] so also will it be in the days of the Son of Man. ²⁷People were eating, drinking, marrying and being given in marriage up to the day Noah entered the ark. Then the flood came and destroyed them all.

²⁸"It was the same in the days of Lot.[y] People were eating and drinking, buying and selling, planting and building. ²⁹But the day Lot left Sodom, fire and sulfur rained down from heaven and destroyed them all.

³⁰"It will be just like this on the day the Son of Man is revealed.[z] ³¹On that day no one who is on the roof of his house, with his goods inside, should go down to get them. Likewise, no one in the field should go back for anything.[a] ³²Remember Lot's wife![b] ³³Whoever tries to keep his life will lose it, and whoever loses his life will preserve it.[c] ³⁴I tell you, on that night two people will be in one bed; one will be taken and the other left. ³⁵Two women will be grinding grain together; one will be taken and the other left."[d]

³⁷"Where, Lord?" they asked.

C Lk 12:35-47 ◄► Lk 17:26-30
C Lk 17:23-24 ◄► Lk 17:34-37
E Mk 13:31-32 ◄► Lk 21:25-31
P Lk 12:45-47 ◄► Lk 18:7-8
H Lk 17:1-2 ◄► Lk 19:27
N Lk 16:30-31 ◄► Lk 20:18
S Lk 16:13 ◄► Lk 20:10
C Lk 17:26-30 ◄► Lk 18:8
T Mt 24:31 ◄► Jn 3:8

o 12 The Greek word was used for various diseases affecting the skin—not necessarily leprosy. *p 21* Or *among* *q 24* Some manuscripts do not have *in his day*. *r 35* Some manuscripts *left.* ³⁶*Two men will be in the field; one will be taken and the other left.*

17:24–30 Jesus prophesied about the signs leading up to his return. His second coming will be as spectacular as the lightning in the sky. Spiritual conditions will mirror the violence, corruption, hatred of God and rejection of God's warnings as in the days of Noah. Even the warning of Lot and Sodom will be rejected prior to Christ's return. The tribulation judgment will fall almost immediately following the supernatural removal of all living believers to heaven.

17:34–37 Jesus reveals that, at the end of the seven-year tribulation at Armageddon, God will send

The Intermediate State

SOME SCHOLARS INTIMATE that the truth of the resurrection of the body was unknown to the OT Hebrews. Scripture indicates otherwise. Passages throughout the OT teach the reality of a bodily resurrection and a final judgment before God (see Job 19:25–26; Da 12:2). At issue, rather, is the temporary location of the souls of both believers and nonbelievers from the moment of death until their final arrival in heaven or hell. Genesis records Abraham's death and indicates that he "was gathered to his people" (Ge 25:8), intimating an intermediate state or place to await the final judgment. Yet the teachings regarding this intermediate state in the NT are not always clear. Different theories and conclusions have been suggested and are noted below. Of interest is the common agreement among scholars that although the OT speaks of *hades* and the grave as the destination of all departed souls, the Bible indicates that the experience of sinners and saints is quite different even before God's final judgment.

Hades

The word *Sheol* is the Hebrew equivalent of the Greek word *hades*. This term appears sixty-five times in the OT and is translated half of the time as "hell" and half of the time as "the grave." In the NT, the Greek usage of *hades* clearly refers to the abode of the dead. Many people speak as though unrepentant sinners immediately go to hell once they die. However, the Bible declares that these unrepentant souls descend into *hades* and are separated from the saved by a great chasm (see Lk 16:19–31). In their unjudged condition, these sinners suffer torment in this intermediate state of *hades*, awaiting the final great white throne judgment at the end of the Millennium when *hades* will surrender the wicked to God's judgment and the lake of fire (see Rev 20:13–14). Thus during the present age, the wicked who die await resurrection from *hades*, but this resurrection will only bring judgment and condemnation. For further information, see the article on "Hell" on p. 1098.

Abraham's Bosom

Scripture reveals a different end for the souls of those who died as believers in God before Christ's death and resurrection. All of the OT believers went to a place of waiting and comfort known as "Abraham's side" (Lk 16:22). Scripture indicates that though people in *hades* were aware of those in "Abraham's side," it was impossible for anyone to cross from one place to the other (see 16:26). From Abraham's bosom these righteous souls would be resurrected to heaven.

Some of these righteous souls, however, were resurrected early, immediately following Christ's resurrection (see Mt 27:52–53). This tremendous miracle of resurrecting these OT saints helped spread the truth of the resurrection of Christ and proved Christ's power over sin and death forever. Just as he resurrected those saints, someday soon he will resurrect the bodies of all living and departed believers when the church is raptured.

Paradise

A great transformation occurred in the spiritual world when Christ defeated Satan and "led captives in his train" (Eph 4:8). From the time of Christ's death on the cross, the souls of believers who die go immediately to a place called *paradise* to enjoy the presence of Jesus Christ forever (see Lk 23:43). Though the word *paradise* occurs only three times in the NT and never in Christ's public teaching, scholars have suggested various ideas about its location and characteristics.

Since the word *paradise* is of Persian origin and suggests an orchard, park or garden, some Jewish and Christian scholars believe that it is a place much like the Garden of Eden before the fall. Others suggest that paradise is merely a state of bliss that awaits the righteous after death and is an indication of the destiny of the redeemed (see Rev 22:2, 14). Still others equate paradise with the new Jerusalem, the city of God in heaven, and base their assumption on Paul's vision when he "was caught up to paradise. He heard inexpressible things, things that man is not permitted to tell" (2Co 12:4). That this viewpoint has merit is strengthened by Christ's own declaration that the tree of life exists "in the paradise of God" (Rev 2:7).

Believers who have died are with Jesus now in paradise, enjoying his presence and the presence of other saints as they all await the rapture. During this time the apostle Paul intimates that the souls of believers are conscious but merely resting in Christ (see 2Co 5:1–8; 1Th 4:14), clearly declaring that though believers are "away from the body" they will be "at home with the Lord" (2Co 5:8). When the rapture occurs, the departed souls of these righteous ones will receive their immortal, incorruptible resurrection bodies so that they can participate in all the experiences of heaven and join with Christ to rule the nations.

Different Lives, Different Conditions

The Bible teaches that the soul is neither annihilated at death nor does it sleep. In his story about the rich man and the beggar, Jesus Christ taught that the man who died in sin was alive, fully conscious and able to use his mental faculties. The sinful rich man was also tormented and unable to affect the destiny of his brothers, who faced similar punishments. There could be no change in his abode or the state of his soul. He was condemned to *hades*, and his soul would wait there until his ultimate judgment before God's great white throne. At that time all the unrepentant souls from *hades* will be resurrected to be judged for their unconfessed sins and evil works (see Rev 20:11–14). For further information, see the article on "The Great White Throne Judgment" on p. 1490.

Though some scholars subscribe to the teaching of soul sleep, Scripture clearly indicates that believers who die are alive and aware, but their souls are at rest until God resurrects them to a new immortal form for eternity. Scripture states that believers immediately join Christ's presence at the moment of death (see 2Co 5:8). In fact, Jesus promised that the thief on the cross would be with him that very day in paradise (see 23:42–43). Though a believer's body may reside in the grave where "there is neither working nor planning nor knowledge nor wisdom" (Ecc 9:10), at the rapture the believer's "spirit returns to God who gave it" (Ecc 12:7).

He replied, "Where there is a dead body, there the vultures will gather."ᵉ

The Parable of the Persistent Widow

18 Then Jesus told his disciples a parable to show them that they should always pray and not give up.ᶠ ²He said: "In a certain town there was a judge who neither feared God nor cared about men. ³And there was a widow in that town who kept coming to him with the plea, 'Grant me justiceᵍ against my adversary.'

⁴"For some time he refused. But finally he said to himself, 'Even though I don't fear God or care about men, ⁵yet because this widow keeps bothering me, I will see that she gets justice, so that she won't eventually wear me out with her coming!' "ʰ

⁶And the Lordⁱ said, "Listen to what the unjust judge says. ⁷And will not God bring about justice for his chosen ones, who cry outʲ to him day and night? Will he keep putting them off? ⁸I tell you, he will see that they get justice, and quickly. However, when the Son of Manᵏ comes,ˡ will he find faith on the earth?"

The Parable of the Pharisee and the Tax Collector

⁹To some who were confident of their own righteousnessᵐ and looked down on everybody else,ⁿ Jesus told this parable: ¹⁰"Two men went up to the temple to pray,ᵒ one a Pharisee and the other a tax collector. ¹¹The Pharisee stood upᵖ and prayed aboutˢ himself: 'God, I thank you that I am not like other men—robbers, evildoers, adulterers—or even like this tax collector. ¹²I fastᵠ twice a week and give a tenthʳ of all I get.'

¹³"But the tax collector stood at a distance. He would not even look up to heaven, but beat his breastˢ and said, 'God, have mercy on me, a sinner.'ᵗ

¹⁴"I tell you that this man, rather than the other, went home justified before God. For everyone who exalts himself will be humbled, and he who humbles himself will be exalted."ᵘ

The Little Children and Jesus

18:15–17pp — Mt 19:13–15; Mk 10:13–16

¹⁵People were also bringing babies to Jesus to have him touch them. When the disciples saw this, they rebuked them. ¹⁶But Jesus called the children to him and said, "Let the little children come to me, and do not hinder them, for the kingdom of God belongs to such as these. ¹⁷I tell you the truth, anyone who will not receive the kingdom of God like a little childᵛ will never enter it."

The Rich Ruler

18:18–30pp — Mt 19:16–29; Mk 10:17–30

¹⁸A certain ruler asked him, "Good teacher, what must I do to inherit eternal life?"ʷ

¹⁹"Why do you call me good?" Jesus answered. "No one is good—except God alone. ²⁰You know the commandments: 'Do not commit adultery, do not murder, do not steal, do not give false testimony, honor your father and mother.'ᵗ"ˣ

²¹"All these I have kept since I was a boy," he said.

²²When Jesus heard this, he said to him, "You still lack one thing. Sell everything you have and give to the poor,ʸ and you will have treasure in heaven.ᶻ Then come, follow me."

²³When he heard this, he became very sad, because he was a man of great wealth. ²⁴Jesus looked at him and said, "How hard it is for the rich to enter the kingdom of God!ᵃ ²⁵Indeed, it is easier for a camel to go through the eye of a needle than for a rich man to enter the kingdom of God."

W *Lk 12:22-32* ◀▶ *Jn 14:1*
P *Lk 17:26-30* ◀▶ *Lk 19:27*
L *Lk 17:2* ◀▶ *Lk 21:18*
C *Lk 17:34-37* ◀▶ *Lk 19:15*
G *Mk 10:17-22* ◀▶ *Lk 18:16-22*
L *Lk 16:19-22* ◀▶ *Lk 19:10*
M *Lk 14:11* ◀▶ *Lk 18:24-25*
R *Lk 15:18-22* ◀▶ *Lk 19:8-9*

17:37 ᵉ Mt 24:28
18:1 ᶠ Isa 40:31; Lk 11:5-8; S Ac 1:14; S Ro 1:10; 12:12; Eph 6:18; Col 4:2; 1Th 5:17
18:3 ᵍ Isa 1:17
18:5 ʰ Lk 11:8
18:6 ⁱ S Lk 7:13
18:7 ʲ Ex 22:23; Ps 88:1; Rev 6:10
18:8 ᵏ S Mt 8:20 ˡ S Mt 16:27
18:9 ᵐ Lk 16:15 ⁿ Isa 65:5
18:10 ᵒ Ac 3:1
18:11 ᵖ Mt 6:5; Mk 11:25
18:12 ᵠ Isa 58:3; Mt 9:14 ʳ Mal 3:8; Lk 11:42
18:13 ˢ Isa 66:2; Jer 31:19; Lk 23:48 ᵗ Lk 5:32; 1Ti 1:15
18:14 ᵘ S Mt 23:12
18:17 ᵛ Mt 11:25; 18:3
18:18 ʷ Lk 10:25
18:20 ˣ Ex 20:12-16; Dt 5:16-20; Ro 13:9
18:22 ʸ S Ac 2:45 ᶻ S Mt 6:20
18:24 ᵃ Pr 11:28

G *Lk 18:9-14* ◀▶ *Jn 1:12-13*
O *Lk 12:8-9* ◀▶ *Jn 3:3*
M *Lk 18:9-14* ◀▶ *Jn 9:39*

ˢ *11* Or *to* ᵗ *20* Exodus 20:12-16; Deut. 5:16-20

---

his angels to separate the believers and the unbelievers (see Mt 13:24–30; 24:40–42). The curious expression "there the vultures will gather" (17:37) may refer to the terrible aftermath of Armageddon when God will gather the birds of prey to eat the bodies of the dead (see Rev 19:17–18; see also Job 39:30).

18:7–8 Jesus warned that God would finally

²⁶Those who heard this asked, "Who then can be saved?"

²⁷Jesus replied, "What is impossible with men is possible with God." ᵇ

²⁸Peter said to him, "We have left all we had to follow you!" ᶜ

U ²⁹"I tell you the truth," Jesus said to them, "no one who has left home or wife or brothers or parents or children for the sake of the kingdom of God ³⁰will fail to receive many times as much in this age and, in the age to come,ᵈ eternal life." ᵉ

Jesus Again Predicts His Death
18:31–33pp — Mt 20:17–19; Mk 10:32–34

³¹Jesus took the Twelve aside and told them, "We are going up to Jerusalem,ᶠ and everything that is written by the prophetsᵍ about the Son of Manʰ will be fulfilled. ³²He will be handed over to the Gentiles.ⁱ They will mock him, insult him, spit on him, flog himʲ and kill him.ᵏ ³³On the third dayˡ he will rise again." ᵐ

³⁴The disciples did not understand any of this. Its meaning was hidden from them, and they did not know what he was talking about.ⁿ

A Blind Beggar Receives His Sight
18:35–43pp — Mt 20:29–34; Mk 10:46–52

E ³⁵As Jesus approached Jericho,ᵒ a blind man was sitting by the roadside begging. ³⁶When he heard the crowd going by, he asked what was happening. ³⁷They told him, "Jesus of Nazareth is passing by." ᵖ

³⁸He called out, "Jesus, Son of David,ᑫ have mercyʳ on me!"

³⁹Those who led the way rebuked him and told him to be quiet, but he shouted all the more, "Son of David, have mercy on me!" ˢ

U Lk 12:31 ◀▶ Jn 12:25–26
E Lk 17:11–19 ◀▶ Lk 22:50–51

18:27 ᵇS Mt 19:26
18:28 ᶜS Mt 4:19
18:30 ᵈS Mt 12:32
ᵉS Mt 25:46
18:31 ᶠS Lk 9:51
ᵍPs 22; Isa 53
ʰS Mt 8:20
18:32 ⁱLk 23:1
ʲS Mt 16:21
ᵏS Ac 2:23
18:33 ˡS Mt 16:21
ᵐS Mt 16:21
18:34 ⁿS Mk 9:32
18:35 ᵒLk 19:1
18:37 ᵖLk 19:4
18:38 ᑫver 39; S Mt 9:27
ʳMt 17:15; Lk 18:13
18:39 ˢver 38
18:42 ᵗS Mt 9:22
18:43 ᵘS Mt 9:8; Lk 13:17
19:1 ᵛLk 18:35
19:4 ʷ1Ki 10:27; 1Ch 27:28; Isa 9:10
ˣLk 18:37
19:7 ʸS Mt 9:11
19:8 ᶻS Lk 7:13
ᵃLk 3:12,13
ᵇEx 22:1; Lev 6:4,5; Nu 5:7; 2Sa 12:6; Eze 33:14,15
19:9 ᶜS Lk 3:8
19:10 ᵈEze 34:12,16; S Jn 3:17

⁴⁰Jesus stopped and ordered the man to be brought to him. When he came near, Jesus asked him, ⁴¹"What do you want me to do for you?"

"Lord, I want to see," he replied.

⁴²Jesus said to him, "Receive your sight; your faith has healed you." ᵗ ⁴³Immediately he received his sight and followed Jesus, praising God. When all the people saw it, they also praised God. ᵘ

Zacchaeus the Tax Collector

19 Jesus entered Jerichoᵛ and was passing through. ²A man was there by the name of Zacchaeus; he was a chief tax collector and was wealthy. ³He wanted to see who Jesus was, but being a short man he could not, because of the crowd. ⁴So he ran ahead and climbed a sycamore-figʷ tree to see him, since Jesus was coming that way.ˣ

⁵When Jesus reached the spot, he looked up and said to him, "Zacchaeus, come down immediately. I must stay at your house today." ⁶So he came down at once and welcomed him gladly.

⁷All the people saw this and began to mutter, "He has gone to be the guest of a 'sinner.' " ʸ

⁸But Zacchaeus stood up and said to the Lord,ᶻ "Look, Lord! Here and now I give half of my possessions to the poor, and if I have cheated anybody out of anything,ᵃ I will pay back four times the amount." ᵇ

⁹Jesus said to him, "Today salvation has come to this house, because this man, too, is a son of Abraham.ᶜ ¹⁰For the Son of Man came to seek and to save what was lost." ᵈ

R Lk 18:13–14 ◀▶ Lk 22:62
C Lk 15:32 ◀▶ Jn 3:19–20
L Lk 18:9–14 ◀▶ Lk 19:41–42
W Lk 15:7 ◀▶ Jn 1:7

R

C
L
W

---

avenge himself against the enemies of the "chosen ones"—the tribulation saints who resist the antichrist. Jesus prophesied that the antichrist would wage a devastating war against the followers of Christ during the tribulation (see Da 7:21; Rev 13:5–8), leaving very few believers alive during the final days leading up to the Battle of Armageddon. Millions of tribulation saints who become believers after the rapture will suffer martyrdom during the first half of the tribulation. Millions more will die following the persecution related to the antichrist's mark of the beast during the latter half of the tribulation (see Rev 17:5–6).

Though some contend that the church will win the world's population to Christ as a preparation for his return as Messiah, this prophecy suggests the opposite. When Jesus returns, spiritual decline and persecution will be so prevalent that those who model a faith that perseveres will be difficult to find. When all seems hopeless, Jesus will return, defeat the antichrist and cast Satan into the bottomless pit for a thousand years (see Rev 19:11–21).

The Parable of the Ten Minas

19:12–27Ref — Mt 25:14–30

¹¹While they were listening to this, he went on to tell them a parable, because he was near Jerusalem and the people thought that the kingdom of God[e] was going to appear at once.[f] ¹²He said: "A man of noble birth went to a distant country to have himself appointed king and then to return. ¹³So he called ten of his servants[g] and gave them ten minas.[u] 'Put this money to work,' he said, 'until I come back.'

¹⁴"But his subjects hated him and sent a delegation after him to say, 'We don't want this man to be our king.'

¹⁵"He was made king, however, and returned home. Then he sent for the servants to whom he had given the money, in order to find out what they had gained with it.

¹⁶"The first one came and said, 'Sir, your mina has earned ten more.'

¹⁷" 'Well done, my good servant!'[h] his master replied. 'Because you have been trustworthy in a very small matter, take charge of ten cities.'[i]

¹⁸"The second came and said, 'Sir, your mina has earned five more.'

¹⁹"His master answered, 'You take charge of five cities.'

²⁰"Then another servant came and said, 'Sir, here is your mina; I have kept it laid away in a piece of cloth. ²¹I was afraid of you, because you are a hard man. You take out what you did not put in and reap what you did not sow.'[j]

²²"His master replied, 'I will judge you by your own words,[k] you wicked servant! You knew, did you, that I am a hard man, taking out what I did not put in, and reaping what I did not sow?[l] ²³Why then didn't you put my money on deposit, so that when I came back, I could have collected it with interest?'

²⁴"Then he said to those standing by, 'Take his mina away from him and give it to the one who has ten minas.'

²⁵" 'Sir,' they said, 'he already has ten!'

²⁶"He replied, 'I tell you that to everyone who has, more will be given, but as for the one who has nothing, even what he has will be taken away.[m] ²⁷But those enemies of mine who did not want me to be king over them—bring them here and kill them in front of me.' "

The Triumphal Entry

19:29–38pp — Mt 21:1–9; Mk 11:1–10
19:35–38pp — Jn 12:12–15

²⁸After Jesus had said this, he went on ahead, going up to Jerusalem.[n] ²⁹As he approached Bethphage and Bethany[o] at the hill called the Mount of Olives,[p] he sent two of his disciples, saying to them, ³⁰"Go to the village ahead of you, and as you enter it, you will find a colt tied there, which no one has ever ridden. Untie it and bring it here. ³¹If anyone asks you, 'Why are you untying it?' tell him, 'The Lord needs it.' "

³²Those who were sent ahead went and found it just as he had told them.[q] ³³As they were untying the colt, its owners asked them, "Why are you untying the colt?"

³⁴They replied, "The Lord needs it."

³⁵They brought it to Jesus, threw their cloaks on the colt and put Jesus on it. ³⁶As

19:11 e S Mt 3:2 f Lk 17:20; Ac 1:6
19:13 g Mk 13:34
19:17 h Pr 27:18 i Lk 16:10
19:21 j Mt 25:24
19:22 k 2Sa 1:16; Job 15:6 l Mt 25:26
19:26 m S Mt 25:29
19:28 n Mk 10:32; S Lk 9:51
19:29 o S Mt 21:17 p S Mt 21:1
19:32 q Lk 22:13

M Lk 13:21 ◀▶ Lk 19:27
C Lk 18:8 ◀▶ Lk 19:23

C Lk 19:15 ◀▶ Lk 21:27–31
M Lk 19:11–26 ◀▶ Lk 20:14
P Lk 18:7–8 ◀▶ Lk 21:5–7
H Lk 17:26–30 ◀▶ Lk 20:18

[u] 13 A mina was about three months' wages.

19:11–19, 23 With this parable, Jesus wanted to correct the disciples' mistaken notion that God's kingdom would appear immediately. His story illustrated that he would be away from them in heaven for a long time. This parable confirms other statements that Jesus made about the long passage of time before the establishment of his Messianic kingdom. This parable contradicts the Preterist view of prophecy that states that all of the prophecies of Jesus' second coming were fulfilled in the destruction of Jerusalem in A.D. 70. See the information on the theories of prophetic interpretation in the article "Introduction to Prophecy" on p. vi.

19:30–38 This remarkable passage records the public presentation of Jesus as Israel's Messiah on Palm Sunday, A.D. 32, when Christ approached the eastern gate to the temple. Despite the widespread rejoicing and acclamation by "the whole crowd of disciples" (19:37), the Jewish and Roman leaders rejected Jesus' claim to be Israel's Messiah and had him crucified less than one week later, fulfilling Daniel's prophecy about the cutting off of the Messiah (see Da 9:24–27).

LUKE 19:37

he went along, people spread their cloaks[r] on the road.

[37] When he came near the place where the road goes down the Mount of Olives,[s] the whole crowd of disciples began joyfully to praise God in loud voices for all the miracles they had seen:

[38] "Blessed is the king who comes in the name of the Lord!"[v][t]

"Peace in heaven and glory in the highest!"[u]

[39] Some of the Pharisees in the crowd said to Jesus, "Teacher, rebuke your disciples!"[v]

[40] "I tell you," he replied, "if they keep quiet, the stones will cry out."[w]

[41] As he approached Jerusalem and saw the city, he wept over it[x] [42] and said, "If you, even you, had only known on this day what would bring you peace—but now it is hidden from your eyes. [43] The days will come upon you when your enemies will build an embankment against you and encircle you and hem you in on every side.[y] [44] They will dash you to the ground, you and the children within your walls.[z] They will not leave one stone on another,[a] because you did not recognize the time of God's coming[b] to you."

Jesus at the Temple

19:45,46pp — Mt 21:12–16; Mk 11:15–18; Jn 2:13–16

[45] Then he entered the temple area and began driving out those who were selling. [46] "It is written," he said to them, "'My house will be a house of prayer'[w];[c] but you have made it 'a den of robbers.'"[x][d]

[47] Every day he was teaching at the temple.[e] But the chief priests, the teachers of the law and the leaders among the people were trying to kill him.[f] [48] Yet they could

R Lk 14:24 ◀ ▶ Lk 20:9–16
L Lk 19:10 ◀ ▶ Lk 23:42–43

19:36 [r] 2Ki 9:13

19:37 [s] Mt 21:1

19:38 [t] Ps 118:26; Lk 13:35
[u] S Lk 2:14

19:39 [v] Mt 21:15, 16

19:40 [w] Hab 2:11

19:41 [x] Isa 22:4; Lk 13:34,35

19:43 [y] Isa 29:3; Jer 6:6; Eze 4:2; 26:8; Lk 21:20

19:44 [z] Ps 137:9
[a] Lk 21:6 [b] 1Pe 2:12

19:46 [c] Isa 56:7
[d] Jer 7:11

19:47 [e] S Mt 26:55
[f] S Mt 12:14; Mk 11:18

20:1 [g] S Mt 26:55
[h] Lk 8:1

20:2 [i] Jn 2:18; Ac 4:7; 7:27

20:4 [j] S Mk 1:4

20:6 [k] Lk 7:29
[l] S Mt 11:9

20:9 [m] Isa 5:1–7
[n] Mt 25:14

not find any way to do it, because all the people hung on his words.

The Authority of Jesus Questioned

20:1–8pp — Mt 21:23–27; Mk 11:27–33

20 One day as he was teaching the people in the temple courts[g] and preaching the gospel,[h] the chief priests and the teachers of the law, together with the elders, came up to him. [2] "Tell us by what authority you are doing these things," they said. "Who gave you this authority?"[i]

[3] He replied, "I will also ask you a question. Tell me, [4] John's baptism[j]—was it from heaven, or from men?"

[5] They discussed it among themselves and said, "If we say, 'From heaven,' he will ask, 'Why didn't you believe him?' [6] But if we say, 'From men,' all the people[k] will stone us, because they are persuaded that John was a prophet."[l]

[7] So they answered, "We don't know where it was from."

[8] Jesus said, "Neither will I tell you by what authority I am doing these things."

The Parable of the Tenants

20:9–19pp — Mt 21:33–46; Mk 12:1–12

[9] He went on to tell the people this parable: "A man planted a vineyard,[m] rented it to some farmers and went away for a long time.[n] [10] At harvest time he sent a servant to the tenants so they would give him some of the fruit of the vineyard. But the tenants beat him and sent him away empty-handed. [11] He sent another servant, but that one also they beat and treated shamefully and sent away empty-handed. [12] He sent still a third, and they wounded him and threw him out.

[13] "Then the owner of the vineyard said, 'What shall I do? I will send my son,

R Lk 19:41–44 ◀ ▶ Lk 21:20–24
S Lk 17:32 ◀ ▶ Jn 4:23–24

[v] 38 Psalm 118:26 [w] 46 Isaiah 56:7 [x] 46 Jer. 7:11

19:40–44 Jesus confirmed that this special day was the fulfillment of Daniel's prophecy (see Da 9:24–27) and mourned that Jerusalem did not recognize "the time of God's coming to you" (19:44). The day when Jesus presented himself as Messiah to Jerusalem was Israel's last chance to accept his claim and avoid the coming judgment of God. See the article on "The Vision of the Seventy Weeks" on p. 986. Compare also the totality of the destruction of the city mentioned in this passage with Mt 24 and the study notes at Mk 13:1–2.

20:9–16 This prophetic parable teaches about God's dealings with Israel over the centuries and their rejection of God's prophets and the crucifixion of his Son. This story of the vineyard parallels Isa 5:1–7.

whom I love;° perhaps they will respect him.'

¹⁴"But when the tenants saw him, they talked the matter over. 'This is the heir,' they said. 'Let's kill him, and the inheritance will be ours.' ¹⁵So they threw him out of the vineyard and killed him.

"What then will the owner of the vineyard do to them? ¹⁶He will come and kill those tenants ᵖ and give the vineyard to others."

When the people heard this, they said, "May this never be!"

¹⁷Jesus looked directly at them and asked, "Then what is the meaning of that which is written:

" 'The stone the builders rejected
has become the capstone ʸ'ᶻ?ᵠ

¹⁸Everyone who falls on that stone will be broken to pieces, but he on whom it falls will be crushed." ʳ

¹⁹The teachers of the law and the chief priests looked for a way to arrest him ˢ immediately, because they knew he had spoken this parable against them. But they were afraid of the people.ᵗ

Paying Taxes to Caesar
20:20-26pp — Mt 22:15-22; Mk 12:13-17

²⁰Keeping a close watch on him, they sent spies, who pretended to be honest. They hoped to catch Jesus in something he said ᵘ so that they might hand him over to the power and authority of the governor.ᵛ ²¹So the spies questioned him: "Teacher, we know that you speak and teach what is right, and that you do not show partiality but teach the way of God in accordance with the truth.ʷ ²²Is it right for us to pay taxes to Caesar or not?"

²³He saw through their duplicity and said to them, ²⁴"Show me a denarius. Whose portrait and inscription are on it?"

²⁵"Caesar's," they replied.

He said to them, "Then give to Caesar what is Caesar's,ˣ and to God what is God's."

²⁶They were unable to trap him in what he had said there in public. And astonished by his answer, they became silent.

The Resurrection and Marriage
20:27-40pp — Mt 22:23-33; Mk 12:18-27

²⁷Some of the Sadducees,ʸ who say there is no resurrection,ᶻ came to Jesus with a question. ²⁸"Teacher," they said, "Moses wrote for us that if a man's brother dies and leaves a wife but no children, the man must marry the widow and have children for his brother.ᵃ ²⁹Now there were seven brothers. The first one married a woman and died childless. ³⁰The second ³¹and then the third married her, and in the same way the seven died, leaving no children. ³²Finally, the woman died too. ³³Now then, at the resurrection whose wife will she be, since the seven were married to her?"

³⁴Jesus replied, "The people of this age marry and are given in marriage. ³⁵But those who are considered worthy of taking part in that age ᵇ and in the resurrection from the dead will neither marry nor be given in marriage, ³⁶and they can no longer die; for they are like the angels. They are God's children,ᶜ since they are children of the resurrection. ³⁷But in the account of the bush, even Moses showed that the dead rise, for he calls the Lord 'the God of Abraham, and the God of Isaac, and the God of Jacob.'ᵃᵈ ³⁸He is not the God of the dead, but of the living, for to him all are alive."

³⁹Some of the teachers of the law responded, "Well said, teacher!" ⁴⁰And no one dared to ask him any more questions.ᵉ

Whose Son Is the Christ?
20:41-47pp — Mt 22:41-23:7; Mk 12:35-40

⁴¹Then Jesus said to them, "How is it

20:13 ° S Mt 3:17
20:16 ᵖ Lk 19:27
20:17 ᵠ Ps 118:22; S Ac 4:11
20:18 ʳ Isa 8:14,15
20:19 ˢ Lk 19:47 ᵗ S Mk 11:18
20:20 ᵘ S Mt 12:10 ᵛ Mt 27:2
20:21 ʷ Jn 3:2
20:25 ˣ Lk 23:2; Ro 13:7
20:27 ʸ S Ac 4:1 ᶻ Ac 23:8; 1Co 15:12
20:28 ᵃ Dt 25:5
20:35 ᵇ S Mt 12:32
20:36 ᶜ S Jn 1:12
20:37 ᵈ Ex 3:6
20:40 ᵉ Mt 22:46; Mk 12:34

M Lk 19:27 ◀▶ Lk 20:42-43
G Lk 14:21 ◀▶ Lk 21:24
H Lk 19:27 ◀▶ Lk 20:42-43
N Lk 17:26-30 ◀▶ Jn 3:18-20

F Lk 14:13-14 ◀▶ Jn 5:25-29

ʸ 17 Or cornerstone   ᶻ 17 Psalm 118:22   ᵃ 37 Exodus 3:6

20:34-38 The Sadducees were a group of wealthy religious teachers who denied the Scriptural teaching of bodily resurrection and taught the annihilation of the soul at death. They only accepted the authority of the five books of Moses. Jesus answered their question by affirming the spiritual existence of the patriarchs. See the study notes at Mt 22:29-32 for further information.

20:41-43 Jesus took the opportunity to ask the Pharisees a question about the Messiah to demon-

that they say the Christ[b] is the Son of David?[f] ⁴²David himself declares in the Book of Psalms:

> " 'The Lord said to my Lord:
> "Sit at my right hand
> ⁴³until I make your enemies
> a footstool for your feet." '[cg]

⁴⁴David calls him 'Lord.' How then can he be his son?"

⁴⁵While all the people were listening, Jesus said to his disciples, ⁴⁶"Beware of the teachers of the law. They like to walk around in flowing robes and love to be greeted in the marketplaces and have the most important seats in the synagogues and the places of honor at banquets.[h] ⁴⁷They devour widows' houses and for a show make lengthy prayers. Such men will be punished most severely."

The Widow's Offering
21:1–4pp — Mk 12:41–44

21 As he looked up, Jesus saw the rich putting their gifts into the temple treasury.[i] ²He also saw a poor widow put in two very small copper coins.[d] ³"I tell you the truth," he said, "this poor widow has put in more than all the others. ⁴All these people gave their gifts out of their wealth; but she out of her poverty put in all she had to live on."[j]

Signs of the End of the Age
21:5–36pp — Mt 24; Mk 13
21:12–17pp — Mt 10:17–22

⁵Some of his disciples were remarking about how the temple was adorned with beautiful stones and with gifts dedicated to God. But Jesus said, ⁶"As for what you see here, the time will come when not one stone will be left on another;[k] every one of them will be thrown down."

⁷"Teacher," they asked, "when will these things happen? And what will be the sign that they are about to take place?"

⁸He replied: "Watch out that you are not deceived. For many will come in my name, claiming, 'I am he,' and, 'The time is near.' Do not follow them.[l] ⁹When you hear of wars and revolutions, do not be frightened. These things must happen first, but the end will not come right away."

¹⁰Then he said to them: "Nation will rise against nation, and kingdom against kingdom.[m] ¹¹There will be great earthquakes, famines and pestilences in vari-

20:41 ᶠ S Mt 1:1
20:43 ᵍ Ps 110:1; S Mt 22:44
20:46 ʰ S Lk 11:43
21:1 ⁱ Mt 27:6; Jn 8:20
21:4 ʲ 2Co 8:12
21:6 ᵏ Lk 19:44
21:8 ˡ Lk 17:23
21:10 ᵐ 2Ch 15:6; Isa 19:2

ᵇ 41 Or *Messiah*   ᶜ 43 Psalm 110:1   ᵈ 2 Greek *two lepta*

M Lk 20:14 ◀▶ Lk 22:29–30
V Lk 1:33 ◀▶ Ac 2:34–35
H Lk 20:18 ◀▶ Lk 20:47
H Lk 20:42–43 ◀▶ Lk 21:25–26

P Lk 19:27 ◀▶ Lk 21:9–11
P Lk 21:5–7 ◀▶ Lk 21:25–26

---

strate the truth that the Messiah is both the Son of David and the Son of God at the same time. In this statement, King David acknowledged that God the Father told the Messiah (Jesus Christ) to "sit at my right hand until I make your enemies a footstool for your feet" (Ps 110:1), revealing the final triumph of the Messiah over his enemies in the millennial kingdom following the Battle of Armageddon.

21:6–7 Jesus prophesied to his disciples that the temple would be destroyed in that generation because of Israel's rejection of Jesus as their Messiah. His disciples wondered aloud when this terrible judgment would occur and how would they know "when will these things happen?" (21:7). The first portion of this chapter provides Jesus' detailed answer about the prophetic signs pointing to his second coming. Compare this passage with Mt 24 and Mk 13.

21:7 To understand the prophetic signs of Lk 21, we must remember that this discourse was given before the crucifixion and prior to the existence of the church. Jesus' words were directed to Jewish Christians of the first century and warned of the signs that would occur when he returns.

21:8 The first prophetic sign of Jesus' return is the widespread deception surrounding the proliferation of false Christs. Many charlatans and false Christs have arisen in almost every century including Simeon Bar Kochba (A.D.135), Moses of Crete (5th century), Abraham Abulafia (A.D.1296) and Shabbethai Zebi (17th century). Yet the number of impostors claiming to be Jesus Christ are on the rise, including David Koresh, Sun Myung Moon and the Lord Maitreya in the last two decades alone.

21:9–10 Jesus also warned that the increase in wars would signal his imminent return (see Joel 3:9–10). Despite thousands of peace treaties, our generation has endured more wars than any other generation in history. Many nations are actively acquiring nuclear, biological and chemical weapons of mass destruction. The prediction of devastating ethnic strife, civil wars and conflicts are being fulfilled in our century.

21:11 Jesus also warned that a cataclysmic upheaval in the natural world would foreshadow his return. Earthquakes, famine, pestilence and unusual signs in the heavens would alert Jesus' followers to

ous places, and fearful events and great signs from heaven.ⁿ

¹²"But before all this, they will lay hands on you and persecute you. They will deliver you to synagogues and prisons, and you will be brought before kings and governors, and all on account of my name. ¹³This will result in your being witnesses to them.º ¹⁴But make up your mind not to worry beforehand how you will defend yourselves.ᵖ ¹⁵For I will give you۹ words and wisdom that none of your adversaries will be able to resist or contradict. ¹⁶You will be betrayed even by parents, brothers, relatives and friends,ʳ and they will put some of you to death. ¹⁷All men will hate you because of me.ˢ ¹⁸But not a hair of your head will perish.ᵗ ¹⁹By standing firm you will gain life.ᵘ

²⁰"When you see Jerusalem being surrounded by armies,ᵛ you will know that its desolation is near. ²¹Then let those who are in Judea flee to the mountains, let those in the city get out, and let those in the country not enter the city.ʷ ²²For this is the time of punishmentˣ in fulfillmentʸ of all that has been written. ²³How dreadful it will be in those days for pregnant women and nursing mothers! There will be great distress in the land and wrath against this people. ²⁴They will fall by the sword and will be taken as prisoners to all the nations. Jerusalem will be trampledᶻ on by the Gentiles until the times of the Gentiles are fulfilled.

²⁵"There will be signs in the sun, moon and stars. On the earth, nations will be in anguish and perplexity at the roaring and tossing of the sea.ᵃ ²⁶Men will faint from terror, apprehensive of what is coming on the world, for the heavenly bodies will be shaken.ᵇ ²⁷At that time they will see the Son of Manᶜ coming in a cloudᵈ with power and great glory. ²⁸When these things begin to take place, stand up and lift up your heads, because your redemption is drawing near."ᵉ

²⁹He told them this parable: "Look at the fig tree and all the trees. ³⁰When they sprout leaves, you can see for yourselves and know that summer is near. ³¹Even so, when you see these things happening, you know that the kingdom of Godᶠ is near.

³²"I tell you the truth, this genera-

G Lk 12:11–12 ◄► Lk 24:49
L Lk 12:11–12 ◄► Jn 4:23–24
M Lk 4:14 ◄► Lk 24:49
T Lk 12:11–12 ◄► Jn 3:34
L Lk 18:7–8 ◄► Lk 22:31–32
S Mk 4:40 ◄► Ac 18:10
V Zec 12:8 ◄► Ac 5:19
R Lk 20:9–16 ◄► Lk 23:28

21:11 ⁿ Isa 29:6; Joel 2:30
21:13 º Php 1:12
21:14 ᵖ Lk 12:11
21:15 ۹ S Lk 12:12
21:16 ʳ Lk 12:52, 53
21:17 ˢ Jn 15:21
21:18 ᵗ S Mt 10:30
21:19 ᵘ S Mt 10:22
21:20 ᵛ S Lk 19:43
21:21 ʷ Lk 17:31
21:22 ˣ Isa 63:4; Da 9:24-27; Hos 9:7 ʸ S Mt 1:22
21:24 ᶻ Isa 5:5; 63:18; Da 8:13; Rev 11:2
21:25 ᵃ 2Pe 3:10, 12
21:26 ᵇ S Mt 24:29
21:27 ᶜ S Mt 8:20 ᵈ S Rev 1:7
21:28 ᵉ Lk 18:7
21:31 ᶠ S Mt 3:2

G Lk 20:16 ◄► Jn 10:16
E Lk 17:26–30 ◄► Ac 2:17
P Lk 21:9–11 ◄► Lk 21:36
H Lk 20:47 ◄► Lk 23:30
C Lk 19:23 ◄► Lk 21:34–36

---

his imminent return (see Joel 2:10; Mt 24:29–30). See the study notes at Mt 24:7–8 for further details.
21:12–17 The Jewish believers would experience persecution and martyrdom at the hands of the religious authorities who hated Jesus. This prophecy will also be fulfilled during the seven-year tribulation when, as Jesus told his followers, "all men will hate you because of me" (21:17).
21:20–26 This passage focuses on Jesus' prophetic words concerning the destruction of the temple and Jerusalem in A.D. 70. The Roman armies burned the city and took Jewish survivors into captivity in chains. Jesus also warned about the pervading sense of fear because of the shaking of the heavens. This may refer to use of powerful nuclear weapons in the last days.
21:27–28 This passage confirms the way in which Christ will return: "in a cloud with power and great glory" (21:27; see Ac 1:9–11; Rev 1:7). Rather than being frightened or feeling despair when these signs appear, Jesus said that the fulfillment of these signs should point believers toward a positive anticipation of the glorious day when Jesus will take his place as God's Messiah and the true King of the coming millennial kingdom.
21:29–36 This parable of the fig tree points to the time when the Son of man will return. The fig tree appears in many places throughout Scripture, appearing repeatedly in the OT as a symbol of Israel's security and blessing (see 1Ki 4:25; Isa 36:16; Mic 4:4; Zec 3:10). In the NT, Jesus withered away a barren fig tree to symbolize Israel's barren spiritual life. However, Jesus promised that Israel would produce great spiritual fruit in the last days (see Ro 11:25–29). Jesus said that when the fig tree flourishes again—when Israel is reborn as a nation—God's kingdom would be close at hand. In light of the certainty of Christ's return, Jesus said his followers should wait with watchfulness for the fulfillment of these signs. Careful Bible students who observe the changes in political, social and military structures in this generation have witnessed the fulfillment of more prophecies than any other generation since the life of Jesus.

tionᵍ will certainly not pass away until all these things have happened. ³³Heaven and earth will pass away, but my words will never pass away.ʰ

³⁴"Be careful, or your hearts will be weighed down with dissipation, drunkenness and the anxieties of life,ⁱ and that day will close on you unexpectedlyʲ like a trap. ³⁵For it will come upon all those who live on the face of the whole earth. ³⁶Be always on the watch, and prayᵏ that you may be able to escape all that is about to happen, and that you may be able to stand before the Son of Man."

³⁷Each day Jesus was teaching at the temple,ˡ and each evening he went outᵐ to spend the night on the hill called the Mount of Olives,ⁿ ³⁸and all the people came early in the morning to hear him at the temple.ᵒ

Judas Agrees to Betray Jesus
22:1,2pp — Mt 26:2–5; Mk 14:1,2,10,11

22 Now the Feast of Unleavened Bread, called the Passover, was approaching,ᵖ ²and the chief priests and the teachers of the law were looking for some way to get rid of Jesus,ᑫ for they were afraid of the people. ³Then Satanʳ entered Judas, called Iscariot,ˢ one of the Twelve. ⁴And Judas went to the chief priests and the officers of the temple guardᵗ and discussed with them how he might betray Jesus. ⁵They were delighted and agreed to give him money.ᵘ ⁶He consented, and watched for an opportunity to hand Jesus over to them when no crowd was present.

The Last Supper
22:7–13pp — Mt 26:17–19; Mk 14:12–16
22:17–20pp — Mt 26:26–29; Mk 14:22–25; 1Co 11:23–25
22:21–23pp — Mt 26:21–24; Mk 14:18–21; Jn 13:21–30
22:25–27pp — Mt 20:25–28; Mk 10:42–45
22:33,34pp — Mt 26:33–35; Mk 14:29–31; Jn 13:37,38

⁷Then came the day of Unleavened Bread on which the Passover lamb had to be sacrificed.ᵛ ⁸Jesus sent Peter and John,ʷ saying, "Go and make preparations for us to eat the Passover."

⁹"Where do you want us to prepare for it?" they asked.

¹⁰He replied, "As you enter the city, a man carrying a jar of water will meet you. Follow him to the house that he enters, ¹¹and say to the owner of the house, 'The Teacher asks: Where is the guest room, where I may eat the Passover with my disciples?' ¹²He will show you a large upper room, all furnished. Make preparations there."

¹³They left and found things just as Jesus had told them.ˣ So they prepared the Passover.

¹⁴When the hour came, Jesus and his apostlesʸ reclined at the table.ᶻ ¹⁵And he said to them, "I have eagerly desired to eat this Passover with you before I suffer.ᵃ ¹⁶For I tell you, I will not eat it again until it finds fulfillment in the kingdom of God."ᵇ

¹⁷After taking the cup, he gave thanks and said, "Take this and divide it among you. ¹⁸For I tell you, I will not drink again of the fruit of the vine until the kingdom of God comes."

¹⁹And he took bread, gave thanks and broke it,ᶜ and gave it to them, saying, "This is my body given for you; do this in remembrance of me."

²⁰In the same way, after the supper he took the cup, saying, "This cup is the new covenantᵈ in my blood, which is poured out for you. ²¹But the hand of him who is going to betray me is with mine on the table.ᵉ ²²The Son of Manᶠ will go as it has been decreed,ᵍ but woe to that man who betrays him." ²³They began to question among themselves which of them it might be who would do this.

²⁴Also a dispute arose among them as to which of them was considered to be greatest.ʰ ²⁵Jesus said to them, "The kings of the Gentiles lord it over them; and those who exercise authority over them call themselves Benefactors. ²⁶But you are not to be like that. Instead, the greatest among you should be like the youngest,ⁱ and the one who rules like the one who serves.ʲ ²⁷For who is greater, the one who is at the table or the one who serves? Is it not the one who is at the table? But I am among you as one who serves.ᵏ ²⁸You are those who have

---

H *Lk 14:16* ◄► *Eph 1:10*
D *Mk 14:22–24* ◄► *Jn 1:29*

C *Lk 21:27–31* ◄► *Jn 21:22–23*
P *Lk 21:25–26* ◄► *Ac 2:19–20*

e 32 Or race

stood by me in my trials. ²⁹And I confer on you a kingdom,¹ just as my Father conferred one on me, ³⁰so that you may eat and drink at my table in my kingdom^m and sit on thrones, judging the twelve tribes of Israel.^n

³¹"Simon, Simon, Satan has asked^o to sift you^f as wheat.^p ³²But I have prayed for you,^q Simon, that your faith may not fail. And when you have turned back, strengthen your brothers."^r

³³But he replied, "Lord, I am ready to go with you to prison and to death."^s

³⁴Jesus answered, "I tell you, Peter, before the rooster crows today, you will deny three times that you know me."

³⁵Then Jesus asked them, "When I sent you without purse, bag or sandals,^t did you lack anything?"

"Nothing," they answered.

³⁶He said to them, "But now if you have a purse, take it, and also a bag; and if you don't have a sword, sell your cloak and buy one. ³⁷It is written: 'And he was numbered with the transgressors'^g;^u and I tell you that this must be fulfilled in me. Yes, what is written about me is reaching its fulfillment."

³⁸The disciples said, "See, Lord, here are two swords."

"That is enough," he replied.

Jesus Prays on the Mount of Olives
22:40–46pp — Mt 26:36–46; Mk 14:32–42

³⁹Jesus went out as usual^v to the Mount of Olives,^w and his disciples followed him. ⁴⁰On reaching the place, he said to them, "Pray that you will not fall into temptation."^x ⁴¹He withdrew about a stone's throw beyond them, knelt down^y and prayed, ⁴²"Father, if you are willing, take this cup^z from me; yet not my will, but yours be done."^a ⁴³An angel from heaven appeared to him and strength-

M Lk 20:42–43 ◀ ▶ Lk 23:2–3
L Lk 21:18 ◀ ▶ Lk 22:35
C Lk 12:22–31 ◀
F Lk 12:22–31 ◀ ▶ Jn 6:5–14
L Lk 22:31–32 ◀ ▶ Jn 10:3–4
P Mt 17:27 ◀ ▶ 2Co 9:6–11

22:29 ¹S Mt 25:34; 2Ti 2:12
22:30 ^m S Lk 14:15 ^n S Mt 19:28
22:31 ^o Job 1:6-12 ^p Am 9:9
22:32 ^q Jn 17:9,15; S Ro 8:34 ^r Jn 21:15-17
22:33 ^s Jn 11:16
22:35 ^t Mt 10:9, 10; Lk 9:3; 10:4
22:37 ^u Isa 53:12
22:39 ^v Lk 21:37 ^w S Mt 21:1
22:40 ^x Mt 6:13
22:41 ^y Lk 18:11
22:42 ^z S Mt 20:22 ^a S Mt 26:39
22:43 ^b Mt 4:11; Mk 1:13
22:46 ^c ver 40
22:49 ^d ver 38
22:52 ^e ver 4
22:53 ^f S Mt 26:55 ^g Jn 12:27 ^h Mt 8:12; Jn 1:5; 3:20
22:54 ^i Mt 26:57; Mk 14:53 ^j Mt 26:58; Mk 14:54; Jn 18:15

ened him.^b ⁴⁴And being in anguish, he prayed more earnestly, and his sweat was like drops of blood falling to the ground.^h

⁴⁵When he rose from prayer and went back to the disciples, he found them asleep, exhausted from sorrow. ⁴⁶"Why are you sleeping?" he asked them. "Get up and pray so that you will not fall into temptation."^c

Jesus Arrested
22:47–53pp — Mt 26:47–56; Mk 14:43–50; Jn 18:3–11

⁴⁷While he was still speaking a crowd came up, and the man who was called Judas, one of the Twelve, was leading them. He approached Jesus to kiss him, ⁴⁸but Jesus asked him, "Judas, are you betraying the Son of Man with a kiss?" ⁴⁹When Jesus' followers saw what was going to happen, they said, "Lord, should we strike with our swords?"^d ⁵⁰And one of them struck the servant of the high priest, cutting off his right ear.

⁵¹But Jesus answered, "No more of this!" And he touched the man's ear and healed him.

⁵²Then Jesus said to the chief priests, the officers of the temple guard,^e and the elders, who had come for him, "Am I leading a rebellion, that you have come with swords and clubs? ⁵³Every day I was with you in the temple courts,^f and you did not lay a hand on me. But this is your hour^g—when darkness reigns."^h

Peter Disowns Jesus
22:55–62pp — Mt 26:69–75; Mk 14:66–72; Jn 18:16–18,25–27

⁵⁴Then seizing him, they led him away and took him into the house of the high priest.^i Peter followed at a distance.^j ⁵⁵But when they had kindled a fire in the middle of the courtyard and had sat down together, Peter sat down with them. ⁵⁶A servant girl saw him seated there in the

E Lk 18:35–43 ◀ ▶ Jn 4:46–54

^f 31 The Greek is plural. ^g 37 Isaiah 53:12 ^h 44 Some early manuscripts do not have verses 43 and 44.

22:29–30 Jesus prophesies about the coming millennial kingdom that will be established following the Battle of Armageddon. His followers will enter into the blessings of his kingdom and rule and reign with him for a thousand years. Jesus specifically promised his disciples the privilege of ruling over the twelve tribes of Israel. This prophecy confirms that God will restore the lost tribes to their land and place of honor in God's millennial kingdom (see Eze 47—48).

firelight. She looked closely at him and said, "This man was with him."

⁵⁷But he denied it. "Woman, I don't know him," he said.

⁵⁸A little later someone else saw him and said, "You also are one of them."

"Man, I am not!" Peter replied.

⁵⁹About an hour later another asserted, "Certainly this fellow was with him, for he is a Galilean."ᵏ

⁶⁰Peter replied, "Man, I don't know what you're talking about!" Just as he was speaking, the rooster crowed. ⁶¹The Lordˡ turned and looked straight at Peter. Then Peter remembered the word the Lord had spoken to him: "Before the rooster crows today, you will disown me three times."ᵐ ⁶²And he went outside and wept bitterly.

The Guards Mock Jesus
22:63–65pp — Mt 26:67,68; Mk 14:65; Jn 18:22,23

⁶³The men who were guarding Jesus began mocking and beating him. ⁶⁴They blindfolded him and demanded, "Prophesy! Who hit you?" ⁶⁵And they said many other insulting things to him.ⁿ

Jesus Before Pilate and Herod
22:67–71pp — Mt 26:63–66; Mk 14:61–63; Jn 18:19–21
23:2,3pp — Mt 27:11–14; Mk 15:2–5; Jn 18:29–37
23:18–25pp — Mt 27:15–26; Mk 15:6–15; Jn 18:39–19:16

⁶⁶At daybreak the councilᵒ of the elders of the people, both the chief priests and teachers of the law, met together,ᵖ and Jesus was led before them. ⁶⁷"If you are the Christ,ⁱ" they said, "tell us."

Jesus answered, "If I tell you, you will not believe me, ⁶⁸and if I asked you, you would not answer.ᵠ ⁶⁹But from now on, the Son of Man will be seated at the right hand of the mighty God."ʳ

⁷⁰They all asked, "Are you then the Son of God?"ˢ

He replied, "You are right in saying I am."ᵗ

⁷¹Then they said, "Why do we need any more testimony? We have heard it from his own lips."

23
Then the whole assembly rose and led him off to Pilate.ᵘ ²And they began to accuse him, saying, "We have found this man subverting our nation.ᵛ He opposes payment of taxes to Caesarʷ and claims to be Christ,ʲ a king."ˣ

³So Pilate asked Jesus, "Are you the king of the Jews?"

"Yes, it is as you say," Jesus replied.

⁴Then Pilate announced to the chief priests and the crowd, "I find no basis for a charge against this man."ʸ

⁵But they insisted, "He stirs up the people all over Judeaᵏ by his teaching. He started in Galileeᶻ and has come all the way here."

⁶On hearing this, Pilate asked if the man was a Galilean.ᵃ ⁷When he learned that Jesus was under Herod's jurisdiction, he sent him to Herod,ᵇ who was also in Jerusalem at that time.

⁸When Herod saw Jesus, he was greatly pleased, because for a long time he had been wanting to see him.ᶜ From what he had heard about him, he hoped to see him perform some miracle. ⁹He plied him with many questions, but Jesus gave him no answer.ᵈ ¹⁰The chief priests and the teachers of the law were standing there, vehemently accusing him. ¹¹Then Herod and his soldiers ridiculed and mocked him. Dressing him in an elegant robe,ᵉ they sent him back to Pilate. ¹²That day Herod and Pilate became friendsᶠ—before this they had been enemies.

¹³Pilate called together the chief priests, the rulers and the people, ¹⁴and said to them, "You brought me this man as one who was inciting the people to rebellion. I have examined him in your presence and have found no basis for your charges against him.ᵍ ¹⁵Neither has Herod, for he sent him back to us; as you

---

23:3 When Jesus was taken before Pontius Pilate, the Roman governor asked Jesus to affirm his position as "the king of the Jews." Jesus' positive declaration affirmed his divine claim to be both Israel's Messiah and King. Jesus will one day rule from the throne of David in Jerusalem as the King of the Jews and King of the whole world after his victory at Armageddon.

can see, he has done nothing to deserve death. ¹⁶Therefore, I will punish him and then release him.'"

¹⁸With one voice they cried out, "Away with this man! Release Barabbas to us!"ⁱ ¹⁹(Barabbas had been thrown into prison for an insurrection in the city, and for murder.)

²⁰Wanting to release Jesus, Pilate appealed to them again. ²¹But they kept shouting, "Crucify him! Crucify him!"

²²For the third time he spoke to them: "Why? What crime has this man committed? I have found in him no grounds for the death penalty. Therefore I will have him punished and then release him."ʲ

²³But with loud shouts they insistently demanded that he be crucified, and their shouts prevailed. ²⁴So Pilate decided to grant their demand. ²⁵He released the man who had been thrown into prison for insurrection and murder, the one they asked for, and surrendered Jesus to their will.

The Crucifixion

23:33–43pp — Mt 27:33–44; Mk 15:22–32; Jn 19:17–24

²⁶As they led him away, they seized Simon from Cyrene,ᵏ who was on his way in from the country, and put the cross on him and made him carry it behind Jesus.¹ ²⁷A large number of people followed him, including women who mourned and wailedᵐ for him. ²⁸Jesus turned and said to them, "Daughters of Jerusalem, do not weep for me; weep for yourselves and for your children.ⁿ ²⁹For the time will come when you will say, 'Blessed are the barren women, the wombs that never bore and the breasts that never nursed!'ᵒ ³⁰Then

R *Lk 21:20–24* ◀▶ *Ro 9:25–29*
H *Lk 21:25–26* ◀▶ *Jn 3:16–19*

23:16 ʰver 22; Mt 27:26; Jn 19:1; Ac 16:37; 2Co 11:23,24
23:18 ⁱAc 3:13,14
23:22 ʲver 16
23:26 ᵏS Mt 27:32
ˡMk 15:21; Jn 19:17
23:27 ᵐLk 8:52
23:28 ⁿLk 19:41-44; 21:23,24
23:29 ᵒMt 24:19
23:30 ᵖHos 10:8; Isa 2:19; Rev 6:16
23:31 ᵠEze 20:47
23:32 ʳIsa 53:12; Mt 27:38; Mk 15:27; Jn 19:18
23:34 ˢS Mt 11:25
ᵗS Mt 5:44
ᵘPs 22:18
23:35 ᵛPs 22:17
ʷIsa 42:1
23:36 ˣPs 22:7
ʸPs 69:21; Mt 27:48
23:37 ᶻLk 4:3,9
23:38 ᵃS Mt 2:2
23:39 ᵇver 35,37
23:41 ᶜS ver 4

" 'they will say to the mountains, "Fall on us!"
and to the hills, "Cover us!" ' ᵐᵖ

³¹For if men do these things when the tree is green, what will happen when it is dry?"ᵠ

³²Two other men, both criminals, were also led out with him to be executed.ʳ ³³When they came to the place called the Skull, there they crucified him, along with the criminals—one on his right, the other on his left. ³⁴Jesus said, "Father,ˢ forgive them, for they do not know what they are doing."ⁿᵗ And they divided up his clothes by casting lots.ᵘ

³⁵The people stood watching, and the rulers even sneered at him.ᵛ They said, "He saved others; let him save himself if he is the Christ of God, the Chosen One."ʷ

³⁶The soldiers also came up and mocked him.ˣ They offered him wine vinegarʸ ³⁷and said, "If you are the king of the Jews,ᶻ save yourself."
³⁸There was a written notice above him, which read: THIS IS THE KING OF THE JEWS.ᵃ

³⁹One of the criminals who hung there hurled insults at him: "Aren't you the Christ? Save yourself and us!"ᵇ

⁴⁰But the other criminal rebuked him. "Don't you fear God," he said, "since you are under the same sentence? ⁴¹We are punished justly, for we are getting what our deeds deserve. But this man has done nothing wrong."ᶜ

⁴²Then he said, "Jesus, remember me

I *Lk 23:2–3* ◀▶ *Lk 24:21*
M *Lk 23:2–3* ◀▶ *Lk 23:42*
M *Lk 23:37–38* ◀▶ *Lk 23:51*
L *Lk 19:41–42* ◀▶ *Lk 24:46–47*

l 16 Some manuscripts him. ¹⁷Now he was obliged to release one man to them at the Feast. m 30 Hosea 10:8 n 34 Some early manuscripts do not have this sentence.

23:28 Jesus warned those who rejected his earthly ministry to "weep for yourselves and for your children." Tragically, this prophecy was fulfilled thirty-eight years later during the Roman siege of Jerusalem. Starvation and famine were so intense that parents literally ate their children in a vain attempt to stay alive while the Roman legions tightened their death grip on the city of Jerusalem.
23:37–38 The Roman soldiers hung a sign above the cross as a mockery of Jesus' royalty. Yet their derision was actually an acknowledgment of the prophetic truth that Jesus will be ultimately be acclaimed "king of the Jews" (23:3).
23:42–43 The thief on the cross acknowledged Jesus' authority and was rewarded with the immediate promise of paradise. Jesus' declaration confirms that the moment a believer dies, they will be with Jesus consciously and joyfully in heaven (see 2Co 5:8). The departed saints will then await the glorious day of the rapture when they will receive a new resurrection body like the body Jesus had when he arose from the dead (see 1Co 15:52; 1Th 4:16).

when you come into your kingdom.°"ᵈ ⁴³Jesus answered him, "I tell you the truth, today you will be with me in paradise."ᵉ

Jesus' Death

23:44–49pp — Mt 27:45–56; Mk 15:33–41; Jn 19:29–30

⁴⁴It was now about the sixth hour, and darkness came over the whole land until the ninth hour,ᶠ ⁴⁵for the sun stopped shining. And the curtain of the templeᵍ was torn in two.ʰ ⁴⁶Jesus called out with a loud voice,ⁱ "Father, into your hands I commit my spirit."ʲ When he had said this, he breathed his last.ᵏ

⁴⁷The centurion, seeing what had happened, praised Godˡ and said, "Surely this was a righteous man." ⁴⁸When all the people who had gathered to witness this sight saw what took place, they beat their breastsᵐ and went away. ⁴⁹But all those who knew him, including the women who had followed him from Galilee,ⁿ stood at a distance,° watching these things.

Jesus' Burial

23:50–56pp — Mt 27:57–61; Mk 15:42–47; Jn 19:38–42

⁵⁰Now there was a man named Joseph, a member of the Council, a good and upright man, ⁵¹who had not consented to their decision and action. He came from the Judean town of Arimathea and he was waiting for the kingdom of God.ᵖ ⁵²Going to Pilate, he asked for Jesus' body. ⁵³Then he took it down, wrapped it in linen cloth and placed it in a tomb cut in the rock, one in which no one had yet been laid. ⁵⁴It was Preparation Day,ᵠ and the Sabbath was about to begin.

⁵⁵The women who had come with Jesus from Galileeʳ followed Joseph and saw the tomb and how his body was laid in it. ⁵⁶Then they went home and prepared spices and perfumes.ˢ But they rested on the Sabbath in obedience to the commandment.ᵗ

The Resurrection

24:1–10pp — Mt 28:1–8; Mk 16:1–8; Jn 20:1–8

24 On the first day of the week, very early in the morning, the women took the spices they had preparedᵘ and went to the tomb. ²They found the stone rolled away from the tomb, ³but when they entered, they did not find the body of the Lord Jesus.ᵛ ⁴While they were wondering about this, suddenly two men in clothes that gleamed like lightningʷ stood beside them. ⁵In their fright the women bowed down with their faces to the ground, but the men said to them, "Why do you look for the living among the dead? ⁶He is not here; he has risen! Remember how he told you, while he was still with you in Galilee:ˣ ⁷'The Son of Manʸ must be delivered into the hands of sinful men, be crucified and on the third day be raised again.' "ᶻ ⁸Then they remembered his words.ᵃ

⁹When they came back from the tomb, they told all these things to the Eleven and to all the others. ¹⁰It was Mary Magdalene, Joanna, Mary the mother of James, and the others with themᵇ who told this to the apostles.ᶜ ¹¹But they did not believeᵈ the women, because their words seemed to them like nonsense. ¹²Peter, however, got up and ran to the tomb. Bending over, he saw the strips of linen lying by themselves,ᵉ and he went away,ᶠ wondering to himself what had happened.

M Lk 23:42 ◀▶ Jn 10:16

23:42 ᵈ S Mt 16:27
23:43 ᵉ 2Co 12:3, 4; Rev 2:7
23:44 ᶠ Am 8:9
23:45 ᵍ Ex 26:31-33; Heb 9:3,8
ʰ Heb 10:19,20
23:46 ⁱ Mt 27:50
ʲ Ps 31:5; 1Pe 2:23
ᵏ Jn 19:30
23:47 ˡ S Mt 9:8
23:48 ᵐ Lk 18:13
23:49 ⁿ Lk 8:2
° Ps 38:11
23:51 ᵖ Lk 2:25,38
23:54 ᵠ Mt 27:62
23:55 ʳ ver 49
23:56 ˢ Mk 16:1; Lk 24:1 ᵗ Ex 12:16; 20:10
24:1 ᵘ Lk 23:56
24:3 ᵛ ver 23,24
24:4 ʷ S Jn 20:12
24:6 ˣ Mt 17:22, 23; Lk 9:22; 24:44
24:7 ʸ S Mt 8:20
ᶻ S Mt 16:21
24:8 ᵃ Jn 2:22
24:10 ᵇ Lk 8:1-3
ᶜ S Mk 6:30
24:11 ᵈ Mk 16:11
24:12 ᵉ Jn 20:3-7
ᶠ Jn 20:10

° 42 Some manuscripts *come with your kingly power*

23:44–45 Luke records an extraordinary miracle of worldwide darkness on the day of Jesus Christ's crucifixion. For three hours God supernaturally darkened the sky because of the terrible sacrifice of his only begotten Son on the cross. Ancient secular historians record that there was an unexplained darkness on the Feast of Passover in the spring of A.D. 32. Since the Feast of the Passover was always celebrated during a full moon, the position of the earth, sun and moon made an eclipse physically impossible. Therefore, we can conclude that this "darkness" was a true miracle and a marvelous confirmation of the truthfulness of the Gospel account of the crucifixion of Jesus Christ.

23:51 Joseph of Arimathea was a member of the Sanhedrin who followed Christ and who provided the tomb for Jesus' body. Joseph believed the prophecies of the OT and "was waiting for the kingdom of God." As one of the ruling religious leaders, Joseph was undoubtedly familiar with the prophecy of Daniel's seventy weeks see Da 9:24–27) and would have anticipated the appearance of the Messiah during his lifetime.

On the Road to Emmaus

[13] Now that same day two of them were going to a village called Emmaus, about seven miles[p] from Jerusalem.[g] [14] They were talking with each other about everything that had happened. [15] As they talked and discussed these things with each other, Jesus himself came up and walked along with them;[h] [16] but they were kept from recognizing him.[i]

[17] He asked them, "What are you discussing together as you walk along?"

They stood still, their faces downcast. [18] One of them, named Cleopas,[j] asked him, "Are you only a visitor to Jerusalem and do not know the things that have happened there in these days?"

[19] "What things?" he asked.

"About Jesus of Nazareth,"[k] they replied. "He was a prophet,[l] powerful in word and deed before God and all the people. [20] The chief priests and our rulers[m] handed him over to be sentenced to death, and they crucified him; [21] but we had hoped that he was the one who was going to redeem Israel.[n] And what is more, it is the third day[o] since all this took place. [22] In addition, some of our women amazed us.[p] They went to the tomb early this morning [23] but didn't find his body. They came and told us that they had seen a vision of angels, who said he was alive. [24] Then some of our companions went to the tomb and found it just as the women had said, but him they did not see."[q]

[25] He said to them, "How foolish you are, and how slow of heart to believe all that the prophets have spoken! [26] Did not the Christ[q] have to suffer these things and then enter his glory?"[r] [27] And beginning with Moses[s] and all the Prophets,[t] he explained to them what was said in all the Scriptures concerning himself.[u]

[28] As they approached the village to which they were going, Jesus acted as if [P] he were going farther. [29] But they urged him strongly, "Stay with us, for it is nearly evening; the day is almost over." So he went in to stay with them.

[30] When he was at the table with them, he took bread, gave thanks, broke it[v] and began to give it to them. [31] Then their eyes were opened and they recognized him,[w] and he disappeared from their sight. [32] They asked each other, "Were not our hearts burning within us[x] while he talked with us on the road and opened the Scriptures[y] to us?"

[33] They got up and returned at once to Jerusalem. There they found the Eleven and those with them, assembled together [34] and saying, "It is true! The Lord[z] has risen and has appeared to Simon."[a] [35] Then the two told what had happened on the way, and how Jesus was recognized by them when he broke the bread.[b]

Jesus Appears to the Disciples

[36] While they were still talking about this, Jesus himself stood among them and said to them, "Peace be with you."[c]

[37] They were startled and frightened, thinking they saw a ghost.[d] [38] He said to them, "Why are you troubled, and why do doubts rise in your minds? [39] Look at my hands and my feet. It is I myself! Touch me and see;[e] a ghost does not have flesh and bones, as you see I have."

[40] When he had said this, he showed them his hands and feet. [41] And while they still did not believe it because of joy and amazement, he asked them, "Do you have anything here to eat?" [42] They gave him a piece of broiled fish, [43] and he took it and ate it in their presence.[f]

[44] He said to them, "This is what I told you while I was still with you:[g] Everything must be fulfilled[h] that is written about me in the Law of Moses,[i] the Prophets[j] and the Psalms."[k]

[45] Then he opened their minds so they could understand the Scriptures. [46] He [L] told them, "This is what is written: The Christ will suffer[l] and rise from the dead

---

I Lk 23:37–38 ◄ ► Jn 1:49
P Lk 11:9–13 ◄ ► Jn 1:33
L Lk 23:42–43 ◄ ► Jn 1:7

p 13 Greek *sixty stadia* (about 11 kilometers) *q 26* Or *Messiah*; also in verse 46

24:13 g Mk 16:12
24:15 h ver 36
24:16 i Jn 20:14; 21:4
24:18 j Jn 19:25
24:19 k S Mk 1:24; l S Mt 21:11
24:20 m Lk 23:13
24:21 n Lk 1:68; 2:38; 21:28; o S Mt 16:21
24:22 p ver 1-10
24:24 q ver 12
24:26 r Heb 2:10; 1Pe 1:11
24:27 s Ge 3:15; Nu 21:9; Dt 18:15; t Isa 7:14; 9:6; 40:10,11; 53; Eze 34:23; Da 9:24; Mic 7:20; Mal 3:1; u Jn 1:45
24:30 v S Mt 14:19
24:31 w ver 16
24:32 x Ps 39:3; y ver 27,45
24:34 z S Lk 7:13; a 1Co 15:5
24:35 b ver 30,31
24:36 c Jn 20:19, 21,26; S Lk 14:27
24:37 d Mk 6:49
24:39 e Jn 20:27; 1Jn 1:1
24:43 f Ac 10:41
24:44 g Lk 9:45; 18:34 h S Mt 1:22; 16:21; Lk 9:22,44; 18:31-33; 22:37 i S ver 27 j S ver 27 k Ps 2; 16; 22; 69; 72; 110; 118
24:46 l S Mt 16:21

24:13–21 This remarkable passage records the event of the two disciples who unknowingly met Jesus on the road to Emmaus. Their words revealed that they had believed that Jesus was Israel's long awaited Messiah who would redeem Israel from sin and the oppression of Rome.

on the third day,ᵐ ⁴⁷and repentance and forgiveness of sins will be preached in his nameⁿ to all nations,ᵒ beginning at Jerusalem.ᵖ ⁴⁸You are witnessesᑫ of these things. ⁴⁹I am going to send you what my Father has promised;ʳ but stay in the city until you have been clothed with power from on high."

The Ascension

⁵⁰When he had led them out to the vicinity of Bethany,ˢ he lifted up his hands and blessed them. ⁵¹While he was blessing them, he left them and was taken up into heaven.ᵗ ⁵²Then they worshiped him and returned to Jerusalem with great joy. ⁵³And they stayed continually at the temple,ᵘ praising God.

R Lk 22:62 ◄ ► Ac 2:37–38
B Lk 4:18 ◄ ► Jn 1:32–33
G Lk 21:14–15 ◄ ► Jn 3:34
M Lk 21:14–15 ◄ ► Jn 7:38–39
W Zec 4:6 ◄ ► Jn 4:23–24

24:46 ᵐ S Mt 16:21
24:47 ⁿ Ac 5:31; 10:43; 13:38
ᵒ Mt 28:19; Mk 13:10 ᵖ Isa 2:3
24:48 ᑫ S Jn 15:27; Ac 1:8; 2:32; 4:20; 5:32; 13:31; 1Pe 5:1
24:49 ʳ S Jn 14:16; Ac 1:4
24:50 ˢ S Mt 21:17
24:51 ᵗ 2Ki 2:11
24:53 ᵘ S Ac 2:46

John

Author: John

Theme: Jesus gives abundant life

Date of Writing: C. A.D. 80–95

Outline of John
  I. Prologue and Theme (1:1–18)
  II. Introduction of Jesus (1:19—4:54)
  III. Jesus' Ministry as God's Son (5:1—10:42)
  IV. In Jerusalem (11:1—12:50)
  V. Jesus With His disciples (13:1—17:26)
  VI. Trial, Death and Burial (18:1—19:42)
  VII. Resurrection and Conclusion (20:1—21:25)

JOHN, THE SON of Zebedee, composed this book before the destruction of Jerusalem in A.D. 70. John and his brother James were Galilean fishermen when Jesus called them to join him as disciples (see Mk 1:19–20). Because of their impetuosity and quick tempers, both men were given the nickname "Sons of Thunder" (Mk 3:17), yet John became one of Jesus' closest disciples and was one of the three witnesses to Jesus' transfiguration experience. Known as "the disciple whom Jesus loved" (13:23), John participated in many of the events he records, explaining Jewish feasts and customs for Greek readers who were unfamiliar with the Jewish ways of religious life.

The book of John is very different in structure and style from the other three gospel accounts. Written in simple Greek language with precise details and profound observations, John records several miracles that are not mentioned elsewhere and stresses Jesus' ministry in Judea and Jerusalem while only touching on his Galilean ministry. John also highlights many personal interviews, such as the late-night visit with Nicodemus (see 3:1–18), to stress the importance of individual relationships with Jesus.

Throughout his book John presents Jesus as God's Son (see 1:34, 49), reporting the supernatural signs that accompanied Jesus' ministry so that John's readers might believe and receive eternal life (see 20:30–31). The word "believe" occurs repeatedly in John's Gospel. Introducing Jesus as the essence of God's revelation to humanity, John portrays Jesus as the "Lamb of God" (1:29) who offers salvation to all who will repent of their sins and trust in him.

John's Gospel is the only account that records Jesus' "I am" messages. Jesus identifies himself as "the bread of life" (6:35), "the light of the world" (8:12; 9:5)," the gate" (10:7), "the good shepherd" (10:11, 14), "the resurrection and the life" (11:25), "the way and the truth and the life" (14:6) and "the true vine" (15:1).

The Word Became Flesh

1 In the beginning was the Word,[a] and the Word was with God,[b] and the Word was God.[c] ²He was with God in the beginning.[d]

³Through him all things were made; without him nothing was made that has been made.[e] ⁴In him was life,[f] and that life was the light[g] of men. ⁵The light shines in the darkness,[h] but the darkness has not understood[a] it.[i]

⁶There came a man who was sent from God; his name was John.[j] ⁷He came as a witness to testify[k] concerning that light, so that through him all men might believe.[l] ⁸He himself was not the light; he came only as a witness to the light. ⁹The true light[m] that gives light to every man[n] was coming into the world.[b]

¹⁰He was in the world, and though the world was made through him,[o] the world did not recognize him. ¹¹He came to that which was his own, but his own did not receive him.[p] ¹²Yet to all who received him, to those who believed[q] in his name,[r] he gave the right to become children of God[s]— ¹³children born not of natural descent,[c] nor of human decision or a husband's will, but born of God.[t]

¹⁴The Word became flesh[u] and made his dwelling among us. We have seen his glory,[v] the glory of the One and Only,[d] who came from the Father, full of grace[w] and truth.[x]

¹⁵John testifies[y] concerning him. He cries out, saying, "This was he of whom I said, 'He who comes after me has surpassed me because he was before me.'"[z] ¹⁶From the fullness[a] of his grace[b] we have all received one blessing after another. ¹⁷For the law was given through Moses;[c] grace and truth came through Jesus Christ.[d] ¹⁸No one has ever seen God,[e] but God the One and Only,[d,e,f] who is at the Father's side, has made him known.

John the Baptist Denies Being the Christ

¹⁹Now this was John's[g] testimony when the Jews[h] of Jerusalem sent priests and Levites to ask him who he was. ²⁰He did not fail to confess, but confessed freely, "I am not the Christ.[f]"[i]

²¹They asked him, "Then who are you? Are you Elijah?"[j]

1:1 ᵃIsa 55:11; Rev 19:13 ᵇJn 17:5; 1Jn 1:2 ᶜPhp 2:6
1:2 ᵈGe 1:1;
Jn 8:58; 17:5,24;
1Jn 1:1; Rev 1:8
1:3 ᵉver 10;
1Co 8:6; Col 1:16; Heb 1:2
1:4 ᶠS Jn 5:26;
Ac 3:15; Heb 7:16; 6:57; 11:25; 14:6;
1Jn 1:1,2; 5:20;
Rev 1:18 ᵍPs 36:9; Jn 3:19; 8:12; 9:5; 12:46
1:5 ʰPs 18:28
ⁱJn 3:19
1:6 ʲS Mt 3:1
1:7 ᵏver 15,19,32; Jn 3:26; 5:33
ˡver 12; S Jn 3:15
1:9 ᵐIsa 49:6
1:10 ᵒS ver 3
1:11 ᵖIsa 53:3
1:12 ᵠver 7;
S Jn 3:15
ʳS 1Jn 3:23
ˢDt 14:1;
S Ro 8:14; 8:16,21; Eph 5:1; 1Jn 3:1,2
1:13 ᵗJn 3:6;
Tit 3:5; Jas 1:18;
1Pe 1:23; 1Jn 3:9; 4:7; S Gal 4:4;
1:14 ᵘS Gal 4:4;
Php 2:7,8; 1Ti 3:16; Heb 2:14; 1Jn 1:1, 2; 4:2 ᵛEx 33:18; 40:34 ʷS Ro 3:24
ˣJn 14:6
1:15 ʸver 7
ᶻver 30; Mt 3:11
1:16 ʰEph 1:23;
Col 1:19; 2:9
ᵇS Ro 3:24
1:17 ᶜDt 32:46;
Jn 7:19 ᵈver 14
1:18 ᵉEx 33:20;
Jn 6:46; Col 1:15;
1Ti 6:16; 1Jn 4:12
ᶠJn 3:16,18; 1Jn 4:9

1:19 ᵍS Mt 3:1 ʰJn 2:18; 5:10,16; 6:41,52; 7:1; 10:24 **1:20** ⁱJn 3:28; Lk 3:15,16 **1:21** ʲS Mt 11:14

ᵃ5 Or *darkness, and the darkness has not overcome* ᵇ9 Or *This was the true light that gives light to every man who comes into the world* ᶜ13 Greek *of bloods* ᵈ14,18 Or *the Only Begotten* ᵉ18 Some manuscripts *but the only* (or *only begotten*) *Son* ᶠ20 Or *Messiah*. "The Christ" (Greek) and "the Messiah" (Hebrew) both mean "the Anointed One"; also in verse 25.

K Lk 6:47-48 ◀ ▶ Jn 1:12
L Lk 24:46-47 ◀ ▶ Jn 1:12
W Lk 19:10 ◀ ▶ Jn 1:9
W Jn 1:7 ◀ ▶ Jn 1:12
F Lk 8:12 ◀ ▶ Jn 3:14-18
G Lk 18:16-22 ◀ ▶ Jn 3:3
K Jn 1:4 ◀ ▶ Jn 1:29   **L** Jn 1:7 ◀ ▶ Jn 1:29
W Jn 1:9 ◀ ▶ Jn 1:29

1:15 John's declaration foreshadows the day when Jesus will be acknowledged by everyone as the true Messiah, the King of Israel (see Zep 3:15; Rev 1:7). Also note that John the Baptist's ministry would precede the earthly ministry of Jesus of Nazareth.

1:21 The people believed that Elijah would return

He said, "I am not."
"Are you the Prophet?"[k]
He answered, "No."

²²Finally they said, "Who are you? Give us an answer to take back to those who sent us. What do you say about yourself?"

²³John replied in the words of Isaiah the prophet, "I am the voice of one calling in the desert,[1] 'Make straight the way for the Lord.'"[g]

²⁴Now some Pharisees who had been sent ²⁵questioned him, "Why then do you baptize if you are not the Christ, nor Elijah, nor the Prophet?"

²⁶"I baptize with[h] water," [n] John replied, "but among you stands one you do not know. ²⁷He is the one who comes after me,[o] the thongs of whose sandals I am not worthy to untie."[p]

²⁸This all happened at Bethany on the other side of the Jordan,[q] where John was baptizing.

Jesus the Lamb of God

²⁹The next day John saw Jesus coming toward him and said, "Look, the Lamb of God,[r] who takes away the sin of the world! ³⁰This is the one I meant when I said, 'A man who comes after me has surpassed me because he was before me.'[t] ³¹I myself did not know him, but the reason I came baptizing with water was that he might be revealed to Israel."

³²Then John gave this testimony: "I saw the Spirit come down from heaven as a dove and remain on him.[u] ³³I would not have known him, except that the one who sent me to baptize with water[v] told me, 'The man on whom you see the Spirit come down and remain is he who will baptize with the Holy Spirit.'[w] ³⁴I have seen and I testify that this is the Son of God."[x]

Jesus' First Disciples

1:40–42pp — Mt 4:18–22; Mk 1:16–20; Lk 5:2–11

³⁵The next day John[y] was there again with two of his disciples. ³⁶When he saw Jesus passing by, he said, "Look, the Lamb of God!"[z]

³⁷When the two disciples heard him say this, they followed Jesus. ³⁸Turning around, Jesus saw them following and asked, "What do you want?"

They said, "Rabbi"[a] (which means Teacher), "where are you staying?"

³⁹"Come," he replied, "and you will see."

So they went and saw where he was staying, and spent that day with him. It was about the tenth hour.

⁴⁰Andrew, Simon Peter's brother, was one of the two who heard what John had said and who had followed Jesus. ⁴¹The first thing Andrew did was to find his brother Simon and tell him, "We have found the Messiah" (that is, the Christ).[b] ⁴²And he brought him to Jesus.

Jesus looked at him and said, "You are Simon son of John. You will be called[c] Cephas" (which, when translated, is Peter).[d]

Jesus Calls Philip and Nathanael

⁴³The next day Jesus decided to leave for Galilee. Finding Philip,[e] he said to him, "Follow me."[f]

⁴⁴Philip, like Andrew and Peter, was from the town of Bethsaida.[g] ⁴⁵Philip found Nathanael[h] and told him, "We have found the one Moses wrote about in the Law,[i] and about whom the prophets also wrote[j]—Jesus of Nazareth,[k] the son of Joseph."[l]

⁴⁶"Nazareth! Can anything good come from there?"[m] Nathanael asked.

---

[g] 23 Isaiah 40:3 [h] 26 Or in; also in verses 31 and 33 [i] 42 Both Cephas (Aramaic) and Peter (Greek) mean rock.

1:29 John's bold declaration foreshadowed the to announce the end times. John emphatically denied that he was Elijah and instead pointed people back to Jesus Christ as the place for their focus and attention.

glorious salvation won by Christ's sacrifice on the cross. As "the Lamb of God" (1:29), Jesus defeated sin and death forever and grants salvation to all who repent.

"Come and see," said Philip.

⁴⁷When Jesus saw Nathanael approaching, he said of him, "Here is a true Israelite,ⁿ in whom there is nothing false."ᵒ

⁴⁸"How do you know me?" Nathanael asked.

Jesus answered, "I saw you while you were still under the fig tree before Philip called you."

⁴⁹Then Nathanael declared, "Rabbi,ᵖ you are the Son of God;ᑫ you are the King of Israel."ʳ

⁵⁰Jesus said, "You believeʲ because I told you I saw you under the fig tree. You shall see greater things than that." ⁵¹He then added, "I tell youᵏ the truth, youᵏ shall see heaven open,ˢ and the angels of God ascending and descendingᵗ on the Son of Man."ᵘ

Jesus Changes Water to Wine

2 On the third day a wedding took place at Cana in Galilee.ᵛ Jesus' motherʷ was there, ²and Jesus and his disciples had also been invited to the wedding. ³When the wine was gone, Jesus' mother said to him, "They have no more wine."

⁴"Dear woman,ˣ why do you involve me?"ʸ Jesus replied. "My timeᶻ has not yet come."

⁵His mother said to the servants, "Do whatever he tells you."ᵃ

⁶Nearby stood six stone water jars, the kind used by the Jews for ceremonial washing,ᵇ each holding from twenty to thirty gallons.ˡ

⁷Jesus said to the servants, "Fill the jars with water"; so they filled them to the brim.

⁸Then he told them, "Now draw some out and take it to the master of the banquet."

They did so, ⁹and the master of the banquet tasted the water that had been turned into wine.ᶜ He did not realize where it had come from, though the servants who had drawn the water knew. Then he called the bridegroom aside ¹⁰and said, "Everyone brings out the choice wine first and then the cheaper wine after the guests have had too much to drink; but you have saved the best till now."

¹¹This, the first of his miraculous signs,ᵈ Jesus performed at Cana in Galilee. He thus revealed his glory,ᵉ and his disciples put their faith in him.ᶠ

Jesus Clears the Temple

2:14–16pp — Mt 21:12,13; Mk 11:15–17; Lk 19:45,46

¹²After this he went down to Capernaumᵍ with his motherʰ and brothersⁱ and his disciples. There they stayed for a few days.

¹³When it was almost time for the Jewish Passover,ʲ Jesus went up to Jerusalem.ᵏ ¹⁴In the temple courts he found men selling cattle, sheep and doves,ˡ and others sitting at tables exchanging money.ᵐ ¹⁵So he made a whip out of cords, and drove all from the temple area, both sheep and cattle; he scattered the coins of the money changers and overturned their tables. ¹⁶To those who sold doves he said, "Get these out of here! How dare you turn my Father's houseⁿ into a market!"

¹⁷His disciples remembered that it is written: "Zeal for your house will consume me."ᵐᵒ

¹⁸Then the Jewsᵖ demanded of him, "What miraculous signᑫ can you show us to prove your authority to do all this?"ʳ

¹⁹Jesus answered them, "Destroy this temple, and I will raise it again in three days."ˢ

²⁰The Jews replied, "It has taken forty-six years to build this temple, and you are going to raise it in three days?" ²¹But the temple he had spoken of was his body.ᵗ ²²After he was raised from the dead, his disciples recalled what he had said.ᵘ Then they believed the Scriptureᵛ and the words that Jesus had spoken.

²³Now while he was in Jerusalem at the Passover Feast,ʷ many people saw the miraculous signsˣ he was doing and be-

B Jn 1:33 ◀ ▶ Jn 3:14

ʲ 50 Or Do you believe . . . ? ᵏ 51 The Greek is plural. ˡ 6 Greek two to three metretes (probably about 75 to 115 liters) ᵐ 17 Psalm 69:9

1:49 When Jesus called Nathanael (also known as Bartholomew) to be his disciple, Nathanael acknowledged Christ's right to rule from the throne of David.

lieved in his name. ²⁴But Jesus would not entrust himself to them, for he knew all men. ²⁵He did not need man's testimony about man, for he knew what was in a man.

Jesus Teaches Nicodemus

3 Now there was a man of the Pharisees named Nicodemus, a member of the Jewish ruling council. ²He came to Jesus at night and said, "Rabbi, we know you are a teacher who has come from God. For no one could perform the miraculous signs you are doing if God were not with him."

³In reply Jesus declared, "I tell you the truth, no one can see the kingdom of God unless he is born again."

⁴"How can a man be born when he is old?" Nicodemus asked. "Surely he cannot enter a second time into his mother's womb to be born!"

⁵Jesus answered, "I tell you the truth, no one can enter the kingdom of God unless he is born of water and the Spirit. ⁶Flesh gives birth to flesh, but the Spirit gives birth to spirit. ⁷You should not be surprised at my saying, 'You must be born again.' ⁸The wind blows wherever it pleases. You hear its sound, but you cannot tell where it comes from or where it is going. So it is with everyone born of the Spirit."

⁹"How can this be?" Nicodemus asked.

¹⁰"You are Israel's teacher," said Jesus, "and do you not understand these things? ¹¹I tell you the truth, we speak of what we know, and we testify to what we have seen, but still you people do not accept our testimony. ¹²I have spoken to you of earthly things and you do not believe; how then will you believe if I speak of heavenly things? ¹³No one has ever gone into heaven except the one who came from heaven—the Son of Man. ¹⁴Just as Moses lifted up the snake in the desert, so the Son of Man must be lifted up, ¹⁵that everyone who believes in him may have eternal life.

¹⁶"For God so loved the world that he gave his one and only Son, that whoever believes in him shall not perish but have eternal life. ¹⁷For God did not send his Son into the world to condemn the world, but to save the world through him. ¹⁸Whoever believes in him is not condemned, but whoever does not believe stands condemned already because he has not believed in the name of God's one and only Son. ¹⁹This is the verdict: Light has come into the world, but men loved darkness instead of light because their deeds were evil. ²⁰Everyone who does evil hates the light, and will not come into the light for fear that his deeds will be exposed. ²¹But whoever lives by the truth comes into the light, so that it may be seen plainly that what he has done has been done through God."

John the Baptist's Testimony About Jesus

²²After this, Jesus and his disciples went out into the Judean countryside, where he spent some time with them, and baptized. ²³Now John also was baptizing at Aenon near Salim, because there was plenty of water, and people were constantly coming to be baptized. ²⁴(This

---

3:8 This verse indicates the sovereignty of the Holy Spirit. He works as he pleases when he renews human hearts.

was before John was put in prison.) ²⁵An argument developed between some of John's disciples and a certain Jew^w over the matter of ceremonial washing.^n ²⁶They came to John and said to him, "Rabbi,^o that man who was with you on the other side of the Jordan—the one you testified^p about—well, he is baptizing, and everyone is going to him."

²⁷To this John replied, "A man can receive only what is given him from heaven. ²⁸You yourselves can testify that I said, 'I am not the Christ^x but am sent ahead of him.'^q ²⁹The bride belongs to the bridegroom.^r The friend who attends the bridegroom waits and listens for him, and is full of joy when he hears the bridegroom's voice. That joy is mine, and it is now complete.^s ³⁰He must become greater; I must become less.

³¹"The one who comes from above^t is above all; the one who is from the earth belongs to the earth, and speaks as one from the earth.^u The one who comes from heaven is above all. ³²He testifies to what he has seen and heard,^v but no one accepts his testimony.^w ³³The man who has accepted it has certified that God is truthful. ³⁴For the one whom God has sent^x speaks the words of God, for God^y gives the Spirit^y without limit. ³⁵The Father loves the Son and has placed everything in his hands.^z ³⁶Whoever believes in the Son has eternal life,^a but whoever rejects the Son will not see life, for God's wrath remains on him."^z

Jesus Talks With a Samaritan Woman

4 The Pharisees heard that Jesus was gaining and baptizing more disciples than John,^b ²although in fact it was not Jesus who baptized, but his disciples. ³When the Lord^c learned of this, he left Judea^d and went back once more to Galilee. ⁴Now he had to go through Samaria.^e

⁵So he came to a town in Samaria called Sychar, near the plot of ground Jacob had given to his son Joseph.^f ⁶Jacob's well was there, and Jesus, tired as he was from the journey, sat down by the well. It was about the sixth hour.

⁷When a Samaritan woman came to draw water, Jesus said to her, "Will you give me a drink?"^g ⁸(His disciples had gone into the town^h to buy food.) ⁹The Samaritan woman said to him, "You are a Jew and I am a Samaritan^i woman. How can you ask me for a drink?" (For Jews do not associate with Samaritans.^a)

¹⁰Jesus answered her, "If you knew the gift of God and who it is that asks you for a drink, you would have asked him and he would have given you living water."^j

¹¹"Sir," the woman said, "you have nothing to draw with and the well is deep. Where can you get this living water? ¹²Are you greater than our father Jacob, who gave us the well^k and drank from it himself, as did also his sons and his flocks and herds?"

¹³Jesus answered, "Everyone who drinks this water will be thirsty again, ¹⁴but whoever drinks the water I give him will never thirst.^l Indeed, the water I give him will become in him a spring of water^m welling up to eternal life."^n

¹⁵The woman said to him, "Sir, give me this water so that I won't get thirsty^o and have to keep coming here to draw water."

¹⁶He told her, "Go, call your husband and come back."

¹⁷"I have no husband," she replied.

Jesus said to her, "You are right when you say you have no husband. ¹⁸The fact is, you have had five husbands, and the man you now have is not your husband. What you have just said is quite true."

¹⁹"Sir," the woman said, "I can see that you are a prophet.^p ²⁰Our fathers worshiped on this mountain,^q but you Jews claim that the place where we must worship is in Jerusalem."^r

---

B *Jn 1:32–33* ◀ ▶ *Jn 7:37–39*
E *Jn 1:32–33* ◀ ▶ *Jn 20:22*
G *Lk 24:49* ◀ ▶ *Jn 14:26*
N *Jn 3:8* ◀ ▶ *Jn 7:37–39*
T *Lk 21:14–15* ◀ ▶ *Jn 14:26*
F *Jn 3:14–18* ◀ ▶ *Jn 5:24*
H *Jn 3:16–19* ◀ ▶ *Jn 5:29*
L *Jn 3:14–17* ◀ ▶ *Jn 4:10*
N *Jn 3:18–20* ◀ ▶ *Jn 8:24*
O *Jn 3:18–19* ◀ ▶ *Jn 6:53*
W *Jn 3:14–18* ◀ ▶ *Jn 4:42*

A *Lk 11:9–13* ◀ ▶ *Ac 4:29–31*
K *Jn 3:14–18* ◀ ▶ *Jn 4:13–14*
L *Jn 3:36* ◀ ▶ *Jn 4:42*
K *Jn 4:10* ◀ ▶ *Jn 4:42*

^w 25 Some manuscripts *and certain Jews* ^x 28 Or *Messiah* ^y 34 Greek *he* ^z 36 Some interpreters end the quotation after verse 30. ^a 9 Or *do not use dishes Samaritans have used*

²¹Jesus declared, "Believe me, woman, a time is coming ˢ when you will worship the Father neither on this mountain nor in Jerusalem.ᵗ ²²You Samaritans worship what you do not know;ᵘ we worship what we do know, for salvation is from the Jews.ᵛ ²³Yet a time is coming and has now come ʷ when the true worshipers will worship the Father in spiritˣ and truth, for they are the kind of worshipers the Father seeks. ²⁴God is spirit,ʸ and his worshipers must worship in spirit and in truth."

²⁵The woman said, "I know that Messiah" (called Christ)ᶻ "is coming. When he comes, he will explain everything to us."

²⁶Then Jesus declared, "I who speak to you am he."ᵃ

The Disciples Rejoin Jesus

²⁷Just then his disciples returned ᵇ and were surprised to find him talking with a woman. But no one asked, "What do you want?" or "Why are you talking with her?"

²⁸Then, leaving her water jar, the woman went back to the town and said to the people, ²⁹"Come, see a man who told me everything I ever did.ᶜ Could this be the Christᵇ?"ᵈ ³⁰They came out of the town and made their way toward him.

³¹Meanwhile his disciples urged him, "Rabbi,ᵉ eat something."

³²But he said to them, "I have food to eatᶠ that you know nothing about."

³³Then his disciples said to each other, "Could someone have brought him food?"

³⁴"My food," said Jesus, "is to do the willᵍ of him who sent me and to finish his work.ʰ ³⁵Do you not say, 'Four months more and then the harvest'? I tell you, open your eyes and look at the fields! They are ripe for harvest.ⁱ ³⁶Even now the reaper draws his wages, even now he harvestsʲ the crop for eternal life,ᵏ so that the sower and the reaper may be glad together. ³⁷Thus the saying 'One sows and another reaps'ˡ is true. ³⁸I sent you to reap what you have not worked for. Others have done the hard

L Lk 21:14–15 ◀▶ Jn 16:13
W Lk 24:49 ◀▶ Jn 6:63
S Lk 20:10 ◀▶ Jn 5:14
E Jn 2:24–25 ◀▶ Jn 6:64

4:21 ˢ Jn 5:28; 16:2 ᵗ Mal 1:11; 1Ti 2:8
4:22 ᵘ 2Ki 17:28-41 ᵛ Isa 2:3; Ro 3:1,2; 9:4,5; 15:8,9
4:23 ʷ Jn 5:25; 16:32 ˣ Php 3:3
4:24 ʸ Php 3:3
4:25 ᶻ Mt 1:16; Jn 1:41
4:26 ᵃ Jn 8:24; 9:35-37
4:27 ᵇ ver 8
4:29 ᶜ ver 17,18 ᵈ Mt 12:23; Jn 7:26, 31
4:31 ᵉ S Mt 23:7
4:32 ᶠ Job 23:12; Mt 4:4; Jn 6:27
4:34 ᵍ S Mt 26:39 ʰ S Jn 19:30
4:35 ⁱ Mt 9:37; Lk 10:2
4:36 ʲ Ro 1:13 ᵏ S Mt 25:46
4:37 ˡ Job 31:8; Mic 6:15
4:39 ᵐ ver 5 ⁿ ver 29
4:42 ᵒ S Lk 2:11
4:43 ᵖ ver 40
4:44 ᵠ Mt 13:57; Lk 4:24
4:45 ʳ Jn 2:23
4:46 ˢ Jn 2:1-11
4:47 ᵗ ver 3,54
4:48 ᵘ Da 4:2,3; S Jn 2:11; Ac 2:43; 14:3; Ro 15:19; 2Co 12:12; Heb 2:4

work, and you have reaped the benefits of their labor."

Many Samaritans Believe

³⁹Many of the Samaritans from that townᵐ believed in him because of the woman's testimony, "He told me everything I ever did."ⁿ ⁴⁰So when the Samaritans came to him, they urged him to stay with them, and he stayed two days. ⁴¹And because of his words many more became believers.

⁴²They said to the woman, "We no longer believe just because of what you said; now we have heard for ourselves, and we know that this man really is the Savior of the world."ᵒ

Jesus Heals the Official's Son

⁴³After the two daysᵖ he left for Galilee. ⁴⁴(Now Jesus himself had pointed out that a prophet has no honor in his own country.)ᵠ ⁴⁵When he arrived in Galilee, the Galileans welcomed him. They had seen all that he had done in Jerusalem at the Passover Feast,ʳ for they also had been there.

⁴⁶Once more he visited Cana in Galilee, where he had turned the water into wine.ˢ And there was a certain royal official whose son lay sick at Capernaum. ⁴⁷When this man heard that Jesus had arrived in Galilee from Judea,ᵗ he went to him and begged him to come and heal his son, who was close to death.

⁴⁸"Unless you people see miraculous signs and wonders,"ᵘ Jesus told him, "you will never believe."

⁴⁹The royal official said, "Sir, come down before my child dies."

⁵⁰Jesus replied, "You may go. Your son will live."

The man took Jesus at his word and departed. ⁵¹While he was still on the way, his servants met him with the news that his boy was living. ⁵²When he inquired as to the time when his son got better, they said to him, "The fever left him yesterday at the seventh hour."

⁵³Then the father realized that this was the exact time at which Jesus had said to

K Jn 4:13–14 ◀▶ Jn 5:24
L Jn 4:10 ◀▶ Jn 5:24
W Jn 3:36 ◀▶ Jn 5:24
E Lk 22:50–51 ◀▶ Jn 5:1–16

ᵇ 29 Or *Messiah*

him, "Your son will live." So he and all his household[v] believed.

⁵⁴This was the second miraculous sign[w] that Jesus performed, having come from Judea to Galilee.

The Healing at the Pool

5 Some time later, Jesus went up to Jerusalem for a feast of the Jews. ²Now there is in Jerusalem near the Sheep Gate[x] a pool, which in Aramaic[y] is called Bethesda[c] and which is surrounded by five covered colonnades. ³Here a great number of disabled people used to lie— the blind, the lame, the paralyzed.[d] ⁵One who was there had been an invalid for thirty-eight years. ⁶When Jesus saw him lying there and learned that he had been in this condition for a long time, he asked him, "Do you want to get well?"

⁷"Sir," the invalid replied, "I have no one to help me into the pool when the water is stirred. While I am trying to get in, someone else goes down ahead of me."

⁸Then Jesus said to him, "Get up! Pick up your mat and walk."[z] ⁹At once the man was cured; he picked up his mat and walked.

The day on which this took place was a Sabbath,[a] ¹⁰and so the Jews[b] said to the man who had been healed, "It is the Sabbath; the law forbids you to carry your mat."[c]

¹¹But he replied, "The man who made me well said to me, 'Pick up your mat and walk.'"

¹²So they asked him, "Who is this fellow who told you to pick it up and walk?"

¹³The man who was healed had no idea who it was, for Jesus had slipped away into the crowd that was there.

¹⁴Later Jesus found him at the temple and said to him, "See, you are well again. Stop sinning[d] or something worse may happen to you." ¹⁵The man went away

4:53 ᵛS Ac 11:14
4:54 ʷS ver 48; S Jn 2:11
5:2 ˣNe 3:1; 12:39 ʸJn 19:13,17,20; 20:16; Ac 21:40; 22:2; 26:14
5:8 ᶻMt 9:5,6
5:9 ᵃMt 12:1-14; Jn 9:14
5:10 ᵇver 16 ᶜNe 13:15-22; Jer 17:21; S Mt 12:2
5:14 ᵈMk 2:5; Jn 8:11
5:15 ᵉS Jn 1:19
5:17 ᶠLk 2:49 ᵍJn 9:4; 14:10
5:18 ʰS Mt 12:14 ⁱJn 10:30,33; 19:7
5:19 ʲver 30; S Jn 14:24
5:20 ᵏJn 3:35 ˡJn 14:12
5:21 ᵐRo 4:17; 8:11; 2Co 1:9; Heb 11:19 ⁿJn 11:25
5:22 ᵒver 27; Ge 18:25; Jdg 11:27; Jn 9:39; S Ac 10:42
5:23 ᵖLk 10:16; S 1Jn 2:23
5:24 ᑫS Mt 10:40; S Jn 3:15; S 3:17 ʳS Mt 25:46 ˢJn 3:18 ¹ 1Jn 3:14
5:25 ᵘJn 4:23; 16:32 ᵛJn 8:43,47

and told the Jews[e] that it was Jesus who had made him well.

Life Through the Son

¹⁶So, because Jesus was doing these things on the Sabbath, the Jews persecuted him. ¹⁷Jesus said to them, "My Father[f] is always at his work[g] to this very day, and I, too, am working." ¹⁸For this reason the Jews tried all the harder to kill him;[h] not only was he breaking the Sabbath, but he was even calling God his own Father, making himself equal with God.[i]

¹⁹Jesus gave them this answer: "I tell you the truth, the Son can do nothing by himself;[j] he can do only what he sees his Father doing, because whatever the Father does the Son also does. ²⁰For the Father loves the Son[k] and shows him all he does. Yes, to your amazement he will show him even greater things than these.[l] ²¹For just as the Father raises the dead and gives them life,[m] even so the Son gives life[n] to whom he is pleased to give it. ²²Moreover, the Father judges no one, but has entrusted all judgment to the Son,[o] ²³that all may honor the Son just as they honor the Father. He who does not honor the Son does not honor the Father, who sent him.[p]

²⁴"I tell you the truth, whoever hears my word and believes him who sent me[q] has eternal life[r] and will not be condemned;[s] he has crossed over from death to life.[t] ²⁵I tell you the truth, a time is coming and has now come[u] when the dead will hear[v] the voice of the Son of God and those who hear will live. ²⁶For

F Jn 3:36 ◄ ► Jn 6:28–29
K Jn 4:42 ◄ ► Jn 6:27
L Jn 4:42 ◄ ► Jn 6:35
W Jn 4:42 ◄ ► Jn 6:35
F Lk 20:34–38 ◄ ► Jn 6:39–40
W Da 12:2 ◄ ► Ac 24:15

ᶜ2 Some manuscripts *Bethzatha*; other manuscripts *Bethsaida* ᵈ3 Some less important manuscripts *paralyzed—and they waited for the moving of the waters.* ⁴*From time to time an angel of the Lord would come down and stir up the waters. The first one into the pool after each such disturbance would be cured of whatever disease he had.*

E Jn 4:46–54 ◄ ► Jn 6:2
S Jn 4:23–24 ◄ ► Jn 5:29
D Lk 13:16 ◄ ► Jn 9:1–3

5:25–29 This passage has been interpreted in different ways. Some feel that it refers to the future resurrection of the dead to judgment. Others believe Jesus' words refer to the spiritually dead who hear him, repent and receive life from him. Still others believe that this passage is a prediction of Jesus' descent into hell following his death on the cross. Those who subscribe to this belief suggest that this prophecy of resurrection also foreshadowed the day of Jesus' resurrection when many of the OT saints rose from the dead (see Mt 27:52–53) proving the truth of Christ's power over sin and the grave.

as the Father has life in himself, so he has granted the Son to have life[w] in himself. [27]And he has given him authority to judge[x] because he is the Son of Man.

[28]"Do not be amazed at this, for a time is coming[y] when all who are in their graves will hear his voice [29]and come out—those who have done good will rise to live, and those who have done evil will rise to be condemned.[z] [30]By myself I can do nothing;[a] I judge only as I hear, and my judgment is just,[b] for I seek not to please myself but him who sent me.[c]

Testimonies About Jesus

[31]"If I testify about myself, my testimony is not valid.[d] [32]There is another who testifies in my favor,[e] and I know that his testimony about me is valid.

[33]"You have sent to John and he has testified[f] to the truth. [34]Not that I accept human testimony;[g] but I mention it that you may be saved.[h] [35]John was a lamp that burned and gave light,[i] and you chose for a time to enjoy his light.

[36]"I have testimony weightier than that of John.[j] For the very work that the Father has given me to finish, and which I am doing,[k] testifies that the Father has sent me.[l] [37]And the Father who sent me has himself testified concerning me.[m] You have never heard his voice nor seen his form,[n] [38]nor does his word dwell in you,[o] for you do not believe[p] the one he sent.[q] [39]You diligently study[e] the Scriptures[r] because you think that by them you possess eternal life.[s] These are the Scriptures that testify about me,[t] [40]yet you refuse to come to me[u] to have life.

[41]"I do not accept praise from men,[v] [42]but I know you. I know that you do not have the love of God in your hearts. [43]I have come in my Father's name, and you do not accept me; but if someone else comes in his own name, you will accept him. [44]How can you believe if you accept praise from one another, yet make no effort to obtain the praise that comes from the only God[f]?[w]

H *Jn 3:36* ◄ ► *Jn 12:48*
S *Jn 5:14* ◄ ► *Jn 8:11–12*

5:26 w Dt 30:20; Job 10:12; 33:4; Ps 36:9; S Jn 1:4
5:27 x S ver 22
5:28 y Jn 4:21; 16:2
5:29 z S Mt 25:46
5:30 a ver 19; b Isa 28:6; Jn 8:16; c S Mt 26:39
5:31 d Jn 8:14
5:32 e ver 37; Jn 8:18
5:33 f S Jn 1:7
5:34 g 1Jn 5:9; h Ac 16:30,31; Eph 2:8; Tit 3:5
5:35 i Da 12:3; 2Pe 1:19
5:36 j 1Jn 5:9; k Jn 14:11; 15:24; l S Jn 3:17
5:37 m Jn 8:18; n Dt 4:12; 1Ti 1:17; S Jn 1:18
5:38 o 1Jn 1:10; 2:14 p Isa 26:10 q S Jn 3:17
5:39 r Ro 2:17,18; s Mt 25:46; t S Lk 24:27,44; Ac 13:27
5:40 u Jn 6:44
5:41 v ver 44
5:44 w S Ro 2:29
5:45 x Jn 9:28; y Ro 2:17
5:46 z Ge 3:15; S Lk 24:27,44; Ac 26:22
5:47 a Lk 16:29,31
6:2 b S Jn 2:11
6:3 c ver 15
6:4 d S Jn 11:55
6:5 e S Jn 1:43
6:8 f Jn 1:40
6:9 g 2Ki 4:43
6:11 h ver 23; S Mt 14:19

[45]"But do not think I will accuse you before the Father. Your accuser is Moses,[x] on whom your hopes are set.[y] [46]If you believed Moses, you would believe me, for he wrote about me.[z] [47]But since you do not believe what he wrote, how are you going to believe what I say?"[a]

Jesus Feeds the Five Thousand
6:1–13pp — Mt 14:13–21; Mk 6:32–44; Lk 9:10–17

6 Some time after this, Jesus crossed to the far shore of the Sea of Galilee (that is, the Sea of Tiberias), [2]and a great crowd of people followed him because they saw the miraculous signs[b] he had performed on the sick. [3]Then Jesus went up on a mountainside[c] and sat down with his disciples. [4]The Jewish Passover Feast[d] was near.

[5]When Jesus looked up and saw a great crowd coming toward him, he said to Philip,[e] "Where shall we buy bread for these people to eat?" [6]He asked this only to test him, for he already had in mind what he was going to do.

[7]Philip answered him, "Eight months' wages[g] would not buy enough bread for each one to have a bite!"

[8]Another of his disciples, Andrew, Simon Peter's brother,[f] spoke up, [9]"Here is a boy with five small barley loaves and two small fish, but how far will they go among so many?"[g]

[10]Jesus said, "Have the people sit down." There was plenty of grass in that place, and the men sat down, about five thousand of them. [11]Jesus then took the loaves, gave thanks,[h] and distributed to those who were seated as much as they wanted. He did the same with the fish.

[12]When they had all had enough to eat, he said to his disciples, "Gather the pieces that are left over. Let nothing be wasted." [13]So they gathered them and filled twelve baskets with the pieces of

E *Jn 5:1–16* ◄ ► *Jn 7:23*
F *Lk 22:35* ◄ ► *Jn 6:31–32*

e 39 Or *Study diligently* (the imperative)   f 44 Some early manuscripts *the Only One*   g 7 Greek *two hundred denarii*

5:43 Jesus declared that, although he came in his "Father's name," many rejected him while "someone else comes in his own name" (the antichrist) and will be willingly received. This prophecy will find its tragic fulfillment during the tribulation when many will be deceived and accept the claim of the antichrist as their Messiah (see Rev 13:3–8).

The Resurrection of the Body

THE HISTORICAL TRUTH about the resurrection of Jesus Christ is the essential bedrock upon which the Christian faith stands (see 1Co 15:14, 20–23). The Gospel accounts of the life, death and resurrection of Jesus were written and distributed within thirty-five years of the occurrence of these events. Those who witnessed Jesus' appearances after his resurrection were alive to verify the facts in these widely distributed documents. Secular historians also record events that prove the historicity of Jesus' death and resurrection.

Despite Christ's victory over the grave, some people refuse to believe in a final resurrection for all human beings. Those who have rejected God seek a false comfort in believing that they will never have to face God as their judge. They believe that all life ceases after death. Yet the German philosopher and poet Goethe said, "I am fully convinced that our spirit is a being of a nature quite indestructible, and its activity continues from eternity to eternity."

The Bible clearly teaches that there is life after death. Our bodies will undergo a transformation and a transition to prepare us for eternity. The body will die, but the soul and spirit will live on.

The Two Resurrections

All people, saved and unsaved, will rise again after death. However, since the Bible describes two different resurrections, there is a great difference between the destiny of these two groups. The first resurrection leads to life whereas the second brings about spiritual death (see Jn 5:28–29; Rev 20:6).

The first resurrection involves all those who repent of their sin and accept the pardon of God. The Bible uses the word "firstfruits" to describe this first resurrection. In Israel, the Feast of Firstfruits happened in the spring of the year to celebrate the first gathering of the harvest (see Ex 23:16–19). As the Jews brought tokens of the coming harvest to God, they acknowledged that he was the provider of the harvest. In the NT, this word "firstfruits" was initially applied to Jesus Christ, who became "the firstfruits of those who have fallen asleep" (1Co 15:20). This term was thereafter applied to the resurrected saints as a token of the great harvest when Jesus, the Lord of the harvest, will come to gather the saints to meet him in the air (see 1Co 15:23; 1Th 4:14–17; Rev 14:4). These raptured believers are the firstfruits of the first resurrection (Jn 5:29). All who participate in this first resurrection to life are saved and will enjoy life in heaven forever.

This first resurrection has several different stages. Some of the OT saints participated in the first stage of this first resurrection two thousand years ago when they were called up from the grave at Christ's resurrection and appeared to many in Jerusalem (see Mt 27:52–53). With their resurrection, the Lord proved forever his claim to be the Messiah and affirmed his power over death, providing a resurrection to eternal life for all who would receive his offer of salvation.

Also included in this first resurrection is the future rapture of believers (see 1Th 4:14–17). (For further information on this, see the article on "The Rapture" on p. 1376). After this rapture a group of Jewish and Gentile tribulation saints will also be resurrected when Christ returns at Armageddon (see study note at Rev 6:9–11). Whether an OT saint, a church-age believer or a tribulation convert, those who participate in this first resurrection will be blessed and "will be priests of God and of Christ and will reign with him for a thousand years" (Rev 20:6).

The second resurrection involves those who reject God's pardon and die in their sin. There will be an interval of one thousand years between the believers' resurrection to spiritual life in heaven and the final resurrection of the wicked dead to spiritual death in hell (see 20:4–11). The wicked will rise in that last day to stand in their resurrected bodies before God's great white throne (see 20:11). All those who participate in this tragic second resurrection will experience spiritual death for eternity, for "this is the second death" (20:14).

Whether the wicked have died on land or sea, the Bible declares that the wicked dead will be resurrected to stand before God and face judgment (see 20:13). All wicked sinners who have waited in torment in *hades* will finally be judged after the Millennium. Even *hades* itself will be "thrown into the lake of fire" (20:14). Those who reject God's mercy will possess both their soul and body in "eternal punishment" (Mt 25:46) in hell forever (see Mt 10:28). For further information, see the article on "The Great White Throne Judgment" on p. 1490.

Some believe these judgments of the saved and the sinners will occur at the same moment. Because of Daniel's prophecy that "multitudes who sleep in the dust of the earth will awake: some to everlasting life, others to shame and everlasting contempt" (Da 12:2), these scholars contend that there will only be one final judgment of both the evil and the righteous. However, a careful reading of this passage reveals that Daniel is not declaring that the two resurrections will take place simultaneously. Daniel's words simply confirm the fact that two different groups will be resurrected and judged, and each will receive eternal consequences.

Our Resurrection Bodies

The clearest indication we have of our resurrection body was shown in the resurrection body of Jesus Christ. Because Jesus understood the human tendency to view bodies from the afterlife as some eerie, ghostly existence (see Lk 24:36–43), Jesus proved the reality of our future body by appearing to his disciples and his followers on many occasions after he rose from the grave. Scripture promises that our resurrection bodies will be like his body (see Php 3:21).

When Jesus rose from the dead and appeared to his disciples, his resurrected body was similar to, yet different from, his mortal body before his death on the cross. He still had flesh and bones, and his hands and feet carried the scars from the cross (see Lk 24:39). Jesus invited Thomas to put his finger on the scars in Jesus' hands and his hand on the scar on Jesus' side (see Jn 20:27). Jesus even ate and drank with his disciples after his resurrection (see Jn 21:12–14). Yet there was an indefinable quality about Christ's resurrected appearance that was different. His body was changed enough for Mary and his disciples to fail to recognize him at first glance (see 21:4). However, after being with him for a little while or hearing his voice or observing his actions, those who had known him recognized him.

As Jesus' body was changed, so shall ours be. Since our bodies will be like his, we shall have bodies of flesh and bone that are incorruptible, will never wear out, decay or die. Our resurrected bodies will never again experience pain. And our real, spiritual bodies will be able to transcend space and time. Jesus was able to enter locked rooms and disappear quickly from one place only to reappear in another (see Mt 28:10; Mk 16:11–12; Lk 24:31). In our resurrected bodies we too will have this supernatural control over matter.

Our Resurrection Mind

In the same way that our resurrected bodies will resemble Christ's, our minds and emotions and personalities will be affected by this new reality too. The Bible clearly shows that after his resurrection Jesus retained his love for his disciples, his concern for the welfare of his followers and an interest in their feelings. In our resurrection bodies we, too, will still feel the same love for our friends and families. We will experience a rich emotional life full of joy, peace, love and thanksgiving. Though Jesus said that marriage would not exist in heaven (see Mt 22:30), the spiritual essence of a pure, holy love will find its highest expression in an eternal cherishing of our loved ones.

Many assume that once we obtain our resurrection bodies and enter heaven we will automatically become bland, neutral saints without distinctive features of personality. Not so! In eternity we shall manifest the perfected form of the character we are building today. Christ will remove the sin in our lives, but we will still have those characteristics that make us unique as individuals. This diversity of personalities will provide one of the great joys of our future life and will make us recognizable to one another (see Mt 17:2–4).

Other believers have expressed the fear that once they have acquired their resurrection bodies and are residents of heaven they will not be able to enjoy the activities that they enjoy on earth. They are afraid that they will lose all knowledge and awareness of earthly relationships and interests. Why should we? Heaven is a place we will enjoy. Our creative talents will most probably flourish, and we will know and understand the vast secrets of our universe. We will be able to satisfy our curiosity about creation, history or science, and we will finally understand why certain things happened as they did. We will have greater vision and awareness because our current barriers of time and space will no longer limit us. In heaven we shall use all the faculties and gifts which our Creator has given us. And we shall do so to give him glory (see Rev 7:12).

the five barley loaves left over by those who had eaten.

¹⁴After the people saw the miraculous sign[i] that Jesus did, they began to say, "Surely this is the Prophet who is to come into the world."[j] ¹⁵Jesus, knowing that they intended to come and make him king[k] by force, withdrew again to a mountain by himself.¹

Jesus Walks on the Water
6:16–21pp — Mt 14:22–33; Mk 6:47–51

¹⁶When evening came, his disciples went down to the lake, ¹⁷where they got into a boat and set off across the lake for Capernaum. By now it was dark, and Jesus had not yet joined them. ¹⁸A strong wind was blowing and the waters grew rough. ¹⁹When they had rowed three or three and a half miles,[h] they saw Jesus approaching the boat, walking on the water;[m] and they were terrified. ²⁰But he said to them, "It is I; don't be afraid."[n] ²¹Then they were willing to take him into the boat, and immediately the boat reached the shore where they were heading.

²²The next day the crowd that had stayed on the opposite shore of the lake[o] realized that only one boat had been there, and that Jesus had not entered it with his disciples, but that they had gone away alone.[p] ²³Then some boats from Tiberias[q] landed near the place where the people had eaten the bread after the Lord had given thanks.[r] ²⁴Once the crowd realized that neither Jesus nor his disciples were there, they got into the boats and went to Capernaum in search of Jesus.

Jesus the Bread of Life

²⁵When they found him on the other side of the lake, they asked him, "Rabbi,[s] when did you get here?"

²⁶Jesus answered, "I tell you the truth, you are looking for me,[t] not because you saw miraculous signs[u] but because you ate the loaves and had your fill. ²⁷Do not work for food that spoils, but for food that endures[v] to eternal life,[w] which the Son of Man[x] will give you. On him God the Father has placed his seal[y] of approval."

²⁸Then they asked him, "What must we do to do the works God requires?"

²⁹Jesus answered, "The work of God is this: to believe[z] in the one he has sent."[a]

³⁰So they asked him, "What miraculous sign[b] then will you give that we may see it and believe you?[c] What will you do? ³¹Our forefathers ate the manna[d] in the desert; as it is written: 'He gave them bread from heaven to eat.'[e]"

³²Jesus said to them, "I tell you the truth, it is not Moses who has given you the bread from heaven, but it is my Father who gives you the true bread from heaven. ³³For the bread of God is he who comes down from heaven[f] and gives life to the world."

³⁴"Sir," they said, "from now on give us this bread."[g]

³⁵Then Jesus declared, "I am[h] the bread of life.[i] He who comes to me will never go hungry, and he who believes[j] in me will never be thirsty.[k] ³⁶But as I told you, you have seen me and still you do not believe. ³⁷All that the Father gives me[l] will come to me, and whoever comes to me I will never drive away. ³⁸For I have come down from heaven[m] not to do my will but to do the will[n] of him who sent me.[o] ³⁹And this is the will of him who sent me, that I shall lose none of all that he has given me,[p] but raise them up at the last day.[q] ⁴⁰For my Father's will is that everyone who looks to the Son[r] and believes in him shall

---

F Jn 5:24 ◄ ► Jn 6:35   **G** Jn 3:5 ◄ ► Jn 9:39
F Jn 6:5–14 ◄ ► Jn 21:8–13
K Jn 6:27 ◄ ► Jn 6:39–40
F Jn 6:28–29 ◄ ► Jn 6:40
L Jn 5:24 ◄ ► Jn 6:37
W Jn 5:24 ◄ ► Jn 6:37
L Jn 6:35 ◄ ► Jn 6:40
W Jn 6:35 ◄ ► Jn 6:40
F Jn 5:25–29 ◄ ► Jn 6:44
K Jn 6:33–35 ◄ ► Jn 6:50–51
F Jn 6:35 ◄ ► Jn 6:47
L Jn 6:37 ◄ ► Jn 6:47
W Jn 6:37 ◄ ► Jn 6:47

h 19 Greek *rowed twenty-five or thirty stadia* (about 5 or 6 kilometers)
i 31 Exodus 16:4; Neh. 9:15; Psalm 78:24,25

6:39–40 Jesus' words reveal that those who trust in him can trust in their salvation when they die. Anyone who "believes in him" (6:40) can have confidence that they will "have eternal life" (6:40) and participate in the resurrection in the last day.

have eternal life,ˢ and I will raise him up at the last day."

⁴¹At this the Jews began to grumble about him because he said, "I am the bread that came down from heaven." ⁴²They said, "Is this not Jesus, the son of Joseph,ᵗ whose father and mother we know?ᵘ How can he now say, 'I came down from heaven'?"ᵛ

⁴³"Stop grumbling among yourselves," Jesus answered. ⁴⁴"No one can come to me unless the Father who sent me draws him,ʷ and I will raise him up at the last day. ⁴⁵It is written in the Prophets: 'They will all be taught by God.'/ˣ Everyone who listens to the Father and learns from him comes to me. ⁴⁶No one has seen the Father except the one who is from God;ʸ only he has seen the Father. ⁴⁷I tell you the truth, he who believes has everlasting life.ᶻ ⁴⁸I am the bread of life.ᵃ ⁴⁹Your forefathers ate the manna in the desert, yet they died.ᵇ ⁵⁰But here is the bread that comes down from heaven,ᶜ which a man may eat and not die. ⁵¹I am the living breadᵈ that came down from heaven.ᵉ If anyone eats of this bread, he will live forever. This bread is my flesh, which I will give for the life of the world."ᶠ

⁵²Then the Jewsᵍ began to argue sharply among themselves,ʰ "How can this man give us his flesh to eat?"

⁵³Jesus said to them, "I tell you the truth, unless you eat the fleshⁱ of the Son of Manʲ and drink his blood,ᵏ you have no life in you. ⁵⁴Whoever eats my flesh and drinks my blood has eternal life, and I will raise him up at the last day.ˡ ⁵⁵For my flesh is real food and my blood is real drink. ⁵⁶Whoever eats my flesh and drinks my blood remains in me, and I in him.ᵐ ⁵⁷Just as the living Father sent meⁿ and I live because of the Father, so the one who feeds on me will live because of me. ⁵⁸This is the bread that came down from heaven. Your forefathers ate manna and died, but he who feeds on this bread will live forever."ᵒ ⁵⁹He said this while teaching in the synagogue in Capernaum.

Many Disciples Desert Jesus

⁶⁰On hearing it, many of his disciplesᵖ said, "This is a hard teaching. Who can accept it?"ᑫ

⁶¹Aware that his disciples were grumbling about this, Jesus said to them, "Does this offend you?ʳ ⁶²What if you see the Son of Manˢ ascend to where he was before!ᵗ ⁶³The Spirit gives life;ᵘ the flesh counts for nothing. The words I have spoken to you are spiritᵏ and they are life. ⁶⁴Yet there are some of you who do not believe." For Jesus had knownᵛ from the beginning which of them did not believe and who would betray him.ʷ ⁶⁵He went on to say, "This is why I told you that no one can come to me unless the Father has enabled him."ˣ

⁶⁶From this time many of his disciplesʸ turned back and no longer followed him.

⁶⁷"You do not want to leave too, do you?" Jesus asked the Twelve.ᶻ

⁶⁸Simon Peter answered him,ᵃ "Lord, to whom shall we go? You have the words of eternal life.ᵇ ⁶⁹We believe and know that you are the Holy One of God."ᶜ

⁷⁰Then Jesus replied, "Have I not chosen you,ᵈ the Twelve? Yet one of you is a devil!"ᵉ ⁷¹(He meant Judas, the son of Simon Iscariot,ᶠ who, though one of the Twelve, was later to betray him.)ᵍ

6:40 ˢ S Mt 25:46
6:42 ᵗ Lk 4:22
ᵘ Jn 7:27,28
ᵛ ver 38,62
6:44 ʷ ver 65; Jer 31:3; Jn 12:32
6:45 ˣ Isa 54:13; Jer 31:33,34; 1Co 2:13; 1Th 4:9; Heb 8:10,11; 10:16; 1Jn 2:27
6:46 ʸ S Jn 1:18; 5:37; 7:29
6:47 ᶻ S Mt 25:46
6:48 ᵃ ver 35,51
6:49 ᵇ ver 31,58
6:50 ᶜ ver 33
6:51 ᵈ ver 35,48
ᵉ ver 41,58
ᶠ Heb 10:10
6:52 ᵍ S Jn 1:19
ʰ Jn 7:43; 9:16; 10:19
6:53 ⁱ Mt 26:26
ʲ S Mt 8:20
ᵏ Mt 26:28
6:54 ˡ ver 39
6:56 ᵐ Jn 15:4-7; 1Jn 2:24; 3:24; 4:15
6:57 ⁿ S Jn 3:17
6:58 ᵒ ver 49-51; Jn 3:36; 5:24
6:60 ᵖ ver 66
ᑫ ver 52
6:61 ʳ Mt 13:57
6:62 ˢ S Mt 8:20
ᵗ S Mk 16:19; S Jn 3:13; 17:5
6:63 ᵘ 2Co 3:6
6:64 ᵛ S Jn 2:25
ʷ S Mt 10:4
6:65 ˣ ver 37,44; S Mt 13:11
6:66 ʸ ver 60
6:67 ᶻ Mt 10:2
6:68 ᵃ Mt 16:16
ᵇ ver 63; S Mt 25:46
6:69 ᶜ S Mk 1:24; 8:29; Lk 9:20
6:70 ᵈ Jn 15:16,19
ᵉ Jn 13:27; 17:12
6:71 ᶠ S Mt 26:14
ᵍ S Mt 10:4

F Jn 6:39-40 ◄ ► Jn 6:54
F Jn 6:40 ◄ ► Jn 7:38
L Jn 6:40 ◄ ► Jn 7:37
W Jn 6:40 ◄ ► Jn 7:37
K Jn 6:39-40 ◄ ► Jn 6:54-58
D Jn 3:14-17 ◄ ► Jn 10:11
O Jn 3:36 ◄ ► Jn 8:24
F Jn 6:44 ◄ ► Jn 11:23-25
K Jn 6:50-51 ◄ ► Jn 6:63

H Jn 3:3-8 ◄ ► Ro 1:4
R Jn 3:3-8 ◄ ► Ro 8:1-16
W Jn 4:23-24 ◄ ► Jn 14:16-17
K Jn 6:54-58 ◄ ► Jn 6:68
E Jn 4:29 ◄ ► Jn 16:30
K Jn 6:63 ◄ ► Jn 7:17

j 45 Isaiah 54:13 ᵏ 63 Or *Spirit*

6:44 This prophecy confirms humanity's response to God's sovereign grace. Those who respond positively to God are promised resurrection with him "at the last day."

6:54 Jesus is not teaching that the sacrament of communion is necessary for salvation, but rather indicates that without a personal appropriation of Christ one cannot have eternal life or be raised up with him in the last days.

Jesus Goes to the Feast of Tabernacles

7 After this, Jesus went around in Galilee, purposely staying away from Judea because the Jews[h] there were waiting to take his life.[i] ²But when the Jewish Feast of Tabernacles[j] was near, ³Jesus' brothers[k] said to him, "You ought to leave here and go to Judea, so that your disciples may see the miracles you do. ⁴No one who wants to become a public figure acts in secret. Since you are doing these things, show yourself to the world." ⁵For even his own brothers did not believe in him.[l]

⁶Therefore Jesus told them, "The right time[m] for me has not yet come; for you any time is right. ⁷The world cannot hate you, but it hates me[n] because I testify that what it does is evil.[o] ⁸You go to the Feast. I am not yet[1] going up to this Feast, because for me the right time[p] has not yet come." ⁹Having said this, he stayed in Galilee.

¹⁰However, after his brothers had left for the Feast, he went also, not publicly, but in secret. ¹¹Now at the Feast the Jews were watching for him[q] and asking, "Where is that man?"

¹²Among the crowds there was widespread whispering about him. Some said, "He is a good man."

Others replied, "No, he deceives the people."[r] ¹³But no one would say anything publicly about him for fear of the Jews.[s]

Jesus Teaches at the Feast

¹⁴Not until halfway through the Feast did Jesus go up to the temple courts and begin to teach.[t] ¹⁵The Jews[u] were amazed and asked, "How did this man get such learning[v] without having studied?"[w]

¹⁶Jesus answered, "My teaching is not my own. It comes from him who sent me.[x] ¹⁷If anyone chooses to do God's will, he will find out[y] whether my teaching comes from God or whether I speak on my own. ¹⁸He who speaks on his own does so to gain honor for himself,[z] but he who works for the honor of the one who sent him is a man of truth; there is nothing false about him. ¹⁹Has not Moses given you the law?[a] Yet not one of you keeps the law. Why are you trying to kill me?"[b]

²⁰"You are demon-possessed,"[c] the crowd answered. "Who is trying to kill you?"

²¹Jesus said to them, "I did one miracle,[d] and you are all astonished. ²²Yet, because Moses gave you circumcision[e] (though actually it did not come from Moses, but from the patriarchs),[f] you circumcise a child on the Sabbath. ²³Now if a child can be circumcised on the Sabbath so that the law of Moses may not be broken, why are you angry with me for healing the whole man on the Sabbath? ²⁴Stop judging by mere appearances, and make a right judgment."[g]

Is Jesus the Christ?

²⁵At that point some of the people of Jerusalem began to ask, "Isn't this the man they are trying to kill?[h] ²⁶Here he is, speaking publicly, and they are not saying a word to him. Have the authorities really concluded that he is the Christ[m]?[j] ²⁷But we know where this man is from;[k] when the Christ comes, no one will know where he is from."

²⁸Then Jesus, still teaching in the temple courts,[l] cried out, "Yes, you know me, and you know where I am from.[m] I am not here on my own, but he who sent me is true.[n] You do not know him, ²⁹but I know him[o] because I am from him and he sent me."[p]

³⁰At this they tried to seize him, but no one laid a hand on him,[q] because his time had not yet come.[r] ³¹Still, many in the crowd put their faith in him.[s] They said, "When the Christ comes, will he do more miraculous signs[t] than this man?"

³²The Pharisees heard the crowd whispering such things about him. Then the chief priests and the Pharisees sent temple guards to arrest him.

³³Jesus said, "I am with you for only a short time,[u] and then I go to the one who sent me.[v] ³⁴You will look for me, but you will not find me; and where I am, you cannot come."[w]

³⁵The Jews said to one another, "Where does this man intend to go that we cannot find him? Will he go where

E Jn 6:2 ◀ ▶ Jn 9:1–7

[1] ⁸ Some early manuscripts do not have yet. ᵐ 26 Or Messiah; also in verses 27, 31, 41 and 42

K Jn 6:68 ◀ ▶ Jn 8:12

our people live scattered* among the Greeks,* and teach the Greeks? ³⁶What did he mean when he said, 'You will look for me, but you will not find me,' and 'Where I am, you cannot come'?"²

³⁷On the last and greatest day of the Feast,ᵃ Jesus stood and said in a loud voice, "If anyone is thirsty, let him come to me and drink.ᵇ ³⁸Whoever believesᶜ in me, asⁿ the Scripture has said,ᵈ streams of living waterᵉ will flow from within him."ᶠ ³⁹By this he meant the Spirit,ᵍ whom those who believed in him were later to receive.ʰ Up to that time the Spirit had not been given, since Jesus had not yet been glorified.ⁱ

⁴⁰On hearing his words, some of the people said, "Surely this man is the Prophet."ʲ

⁴¹Others said, "He is the Christ."

Still others asked, "How can the Christ come from Galilee?ᵏ ⁴²Does not the Scripture say that the Christ will come from David's familyᵒ¹ and from Bethlehem,ᵐ the town where David lived?" ⁴³Thus the people were dividedⁿ because of Jesus. ⁴⁴Some wanted to seize him, but no one laid a hand on him.ᵒ

Unbelief of the Jewish Leaders

⁴⁵Finally the temple guards went back to the chief priests and Pharisees, who asked them, "Why didn't you bring him in?"

⁴⁶"No one ever spoke the way this man does,"ᵖ the guards declared.

⁴⁷"You mean he has deceived you also?"ᑫ the Pharisees retorted. ⁴⁸"Has any of the rulers or of the Pharisees believed in him?ʳ ⁴⁹No! But this mob that knows nothing of the law—there is a curse on them."

⁵⁰Nicodemus,ˢ who had gone to Jesus

B Jn 3:34 ◄ ► Jn 14:16–17
N Jn 3:34 ◄ ► Jn 14:16–17
P Jn 1:33 ◄ ► Jn 14:16–17
L Jn 6:47 ◄ ► Jn 8:11–12
W Jn 6:47 ◄ ► Jn 11:26
M Lk 24:49 ◄ ► Jn 14:26
F Jn 6:47 ◄ ► Jn 11:25–26
B Jn 3:14 ◄ ► Jn 19:24

7:35 ˣ S Jas 1:1
ʸ Jn 12:20; Ac 17:4; 18:4

7:36 ᶻ ver 34

7:37 ᵃ Lev 23:36
ᵇ Isa 55:1;
Rev 22:17

7:38 ᶜ S Jn 3:15
ᵈ Isa 58:11
ᵉ S Jn 4:10
ᶠ S Jn 4:14

7:39 ᵍ Joel 2:28; Jn 1:33; Ac 2:17,33
ʰ S Jn 20:22
ⁱ Jn 12:23; 13:31,32

7:40 ʲ S Mt 21:11

7:41 ᵏ ver 52; Jn 1:46

7:42 ˡ S Mt 1:1
ᵐ Mic 5:2; Mt 2:5,6; Lk 2:4

7:43 ⁿ Jn 6:52; 9:16; 10:19

7:44 ᵒ ver 30

7:46 ᵖ S Mt 7:28

7:47 ᑫ ver 12

7:48 ʳ Jn 12:42

7:50 ˢ Jn 3:1; 19:39

7:52 ᵗ ver 41

8:1 ᵘ S Mt 21:1

8:2 ᵛ ver 20; S Mt 26:55

8:5 ʷ Lev 20:10; Dt 22:22; Job 31:11

8:6 ˣ Mt 22:15,18
ʸ S Mt 12:10

8:7 ᶻ Dt 17:7; Eze 16:40 * Ro 2:1,22

8:11 ᵇ Jn 3:17

earlier and who was one of their own number, asked, ⁵¹"Does our law condemn anyone without first hearing him to find out what he is doing?"

⁵²They replied, "Are you from Galilee, too? Look into it, and you will find that a prophetᵖ does not come out of Galilee."ᵗ

[The earliest manuscripts and many other ancient witnesses do not have John 7:53–8:11.]

⁵³Then each went to his own home.

8 But Jesus went to the Mount of Olives.ᵘ ²At dawn he appeared again in the temple courts, where all the people gathered around him, and he sat down to teach them.ᵛ ³The teachers of the law and the Pharisees brought in a woman caught in adultery. They made her stand before the group ⁴and said to Jesus, "Teacher, this woman was caught in the act of adultery. ⁵In the Law Moses commanded us to stone such women.ʷ Now what do you say?" ⁶They were using this question as a trap,ˣ in order to have a basis for accusing him.ʸ

But Jesus bent down and started to write on the ground with his finger. ⁷When they kept on questioning him, he straightened up and said to them, "If any one of you is without sin, let him be the first to throw a stoneᶻ at her."ᵃ ⁸Again he stooped down and wrote on the ground.

⁹At this, those who heard began to go away one at a time, the older ones first, until only Jesus was left, with the woman still standing there. ¹⁰Jesus straightened up and asked her, "Woman, where are they? Has no one condemned you?"

¹¹"No one, sir," she said.

"Then neither do I condemn you,"ᵇ

L Jn 7:37 ◄ ► Jn 9:39
S Jn 5:29 ◄ ► Jn 8:31

ⁿ 37,38 Or / If anyone is thirsty, let him come to me. / And let him drink, ³⁸who believes in me. / As ᵒ 42 Greek seed ᵖ 52 Two early manuscripts the Prophet

---

7:52 The Pharisees and religious leaders challenged Jesus' claims by declaring that prophets did not come from Galilee. In this statement the religious leaders erred. The OT clearly records that the prophet Jonah arose from the region of Galilee before his dramatically successful missionary journey to Nineveh, the capital city of Assyria (see 2Ki 14:25).

Jesus declared. "Go now and leave your life of sin."ᶜ

───────────────

The Validity of Jesus' Testimony

K ¹²When Jesus spoke again to the people, he said, "I amᵈ the light of the world.ᵉ Whoever follows me will never walk in darkness, but will have the light of life."ᶠ

¹³The Pharisees challenged him, "Here you are, appearing as your own witness; your testimony is not valid."ᵍ

¹⁴Jesus answered, "Even if I testify on my own behalf, my testimony is valid, for I know where I came from and where I am going.ʰ But you have no idea where I come fromⁱ or where I am going. ¹⁵You judge by human standards;ʲ I pass judgment on no one.ᵏ ¹⁶But if I do judge, my decisions are right, because I am not alone. I stand with the Father, who sent me.ˡ ¹⁷In your own Law it is written that the testimony of two men is valid.ᵐ ¹⁸I am one who testifies for myself; my other witness is the Father, who sent me."ⁿ

¹⁹Then they asked him, "Where is your father?"

"You do not know me or my Father,"ᵒ Jesus replied. "If you knew me, you would know my Father also."ᵖ ²⁰He spoke these words while teachingᵠ in the temple area near the place where the offerings were put.ʳ Yet no one seized him, because his time had not yet come.ˢ

²¹Once more Jesus said to them, "I am going away, and you will look for me, and you will dieᵗ in your sin. Where I go, you cannot come."ᵘ

²²This made the Jews ask, "Will he kill himself? Is that why he says, 'Where I go, you cannot come'?"

²³But he continued, "You are from below; I am from above. You are of this
N world; I am not of this world.ᵛ ²⁴I told
O you that you would die in your sins; if you do not believe that I am ⌊the one I claim to be⌋,ᵠʷ you will indeed die in your sins."

²⁵"Who are you?" they asked.

"Just what I have been claiming all along," Jesus replied. ²⁶"I have much to

K Jn 7:17 ◀ ▶ Jn 8:36
N Jn 3:16 ◀ ▶ Jn 8:47
O Jn 6:53 ◀ ▶ Jn 10:1

8:11 ᶜ Jn 5:14
8:12 ᵈ S Jn 6:35
ᵉ S Jn 1:4 ᶠ Pr 4:18; Mt 5:14
8:13 ᵍ Jn 5:31
8:14 ʰ Jn 13:3; 16:28 ⁱ Jn 7:28; 9:29
8:15 ʲ S Jn 7:24
ᵏ Jn 3:17
8:16 ˡ Jn 5:30
8:17 ᵐ S Mt 18:16
8:18 ⁿ Jn 5:37
8:19 ᵒ Jn 16:3
ᵖ S 1Jn 2:23
8:20 ᵠ S Mt 26:55
ʳ Mk 12:41
ˢ S Mt 26:18
8:21 ᵗ Eze 3:18
ᵘ Jn 7:34; 13:33
8:23 ᵛ Jn 3:31; 17:14
8:24 ʷ Jn 4:26; 13:19
8:26 ˣ Jn 7:28
ʸ Jn 3:32; 15:15
8:28 ᶻ Jn 12:32
ᵃ Jn 14:24
8:29 ᵇ ver 16; Jn 16:32 ᶜ Isa 50:5; Jn 4:34; 5:30; 6:38
8:30 ᵈ S Jn 7:31
8:31 ᵉ Jn 15:7; 2Jn 9
8:32 ᶠ ver 36; Ro 8:2; 2Co 3:17; Gal 5:1,13
8:33 ᵍ ver 37,39; S Lk 3:8
8:34 ʰ S Ro 6:16
8:35 ⁱ Gal 4:30
8:36 ʲ ver 32
8:37 ᵏ ver 39,40
8:38 ˡ Jn 5:19,30; 14:10,24 ᵐ ver 41, 44
8:39 ⁿ ver 37; S Lk 3:8
8:40 ᵒ S Mt 12:14
ᵖ ver 26
8:41 ᵠ ver 38,44
ʳ Isa 63:16; 64:8

say in judgment of you. But he who sent me is reliable,ˣ and what I have heard from him I tell the world."ʸ

²⁷They did not understand that he was telling them about his Father. ²⁸So Jesus said, "When you have lifted up the Son of Man,ᶻ then you will know that I am ⌊the one I claim to be⌋, and that I do nothing on my own but speak just what the Father has taught me.ᵃ ²⁹The one who sent me is with me; he has not left me alone,ᵇ for I always do what pleases him."ᶜ ³⁰Even as he spoke, many put their faith in him.ᵈ

The Children of Abraham

³¹To the Jews who had believed him, S Jesus said, "If you hold to my teaching,ᵉ you are really my disciples. ³²Then you will know the truth, and the truth will set you free."ᶠ

³³They answered him, "We are Abraham's descendants,ᵍ and have never been slaves of anyone. How can you say that we shall be set free?"

³⁴Jesus replied, "I tell you the truth, ev- C
eryone who sins is a slave to sin.ʰ ³⁵Now S
a slave has no permanent place in the family, but a son belongs to it forever.ⁱ
³⁶So if the Son sets you free,ʲ you will be K
free indeed. ³⁷I know you are Abraham's descendants. Yet you are ready to kill me,ᵏ because you have no room for my word. ³⁸I am telling you what I have seen in the Father's presence,ˡ and you do what you have heard from your father."ˢ ᵐ

³⁹"Abraham is our father," they answered.

"If you were Abraham's children,"ⁿ said Jesus, "then you wouldᵗ do the things Abraham did. ⁴⁰As it is, you are determined to kill me,ᵒ a man who has told you the truth that I heard from God.ᵖ Abraham did not do such things. ⁴¹You are doing the things your own father does."ᵠ

"We are not illegitimate children," they protested. "The only Father we have is God himself."ʳ

S Jn 8:11–12 ◀ ▶ Jn 8:34–35
C Jn 3:19–20 ◀ ▶ Jn 8:44
S Jn 8:31 ◀ ▶ Jn 14:15
K Jn 8:12 ◀ ▶ Jn 8:51

ᵠ24 Or I am he; also in verse 28 ʳ33 Greek seed; also in verse 37
ˢ38 Or presence. Therefore do what you have heard from the Father.
ᵗ39 Some early manuscripts "If you are Abraham's children," said Jesus, "then"

The Children of the Devil

⁴²Jesus said to them, "If God were your Father, you would love me,ˢ for I came from God ͭ and now am here. I have not come on my own;ᵘ but he sent me.ᵛ ⁴³Why is my language not clear to you? Because you are unable to hear what I say. **C** ⁴⁴You belong to your father, the devil,ʷ and you want to carry out your father's desire.ˣ He was a murderer from the beginning, not holding to the truth, for there is no truth in him. When he lies, he speaks his native language, for he is a liar and the father of lies.ʸ ⁴⁵Yet because I tell the truth,ᶻ you do not believe me! ⁴⁶Can any of you prove me guilty of sin? If I am telling the truth, why don't you believe me? **N** ⁴⁷He who belongs to God hears what God says.ᵃ The reason you do not hear is that you do not belong to God."

The Claims of Jesus About Himself

⁴⁸The Jews answered him, "Aren't we right in saying that you are a Samaritanᵇ and demon-possessed?"ᶜ

⁴⁹"I am not possessed by a demon," said Jesus, "but I honor my Father and you dishonor me. ⁵⁰I am not seeking glory for myself;ᵈ but there is one who seeks it, and he is the judge. **K** ⁵¹I tell you the truth, if anyone keeps my word, he will never see death."ᵉ

⁵²At this the Jews exclaimed, "Now we know that you are demon-possessed! Abraham died and so did the prophets, yet you say that if anyone keeps your word, he will never taste death. ⁵³Are you greater than our father Abraham?ᵍ He died, and so did the prophets. Who do you think you are?"

⁵⁴Jesus replied, "If I glorify myself,ʰ my glory means nothing. My Father, whom you claim as your God, is the one who glorifies me.ⁱ ⁵⁵Though you do not know him,ʲ I know him.ᵏ If I said I did not, I would be a liar like you, but I do know him and keep his word.ˡ ⁵⁶Your father Abrahamᵐ rejoiced at the thought of seeing my day; he saw it ⁿ and was glad."

⁵⁷"You are not yet fifty years old," the Jews said to him, "and you have seen Abraham!"

C *Jn 8:34* ◀ ▶ *Ac 7:51*
N *Jn 8:24* ◀ ▶ *Jn 9:39–41*
K *Jn 8:36* ◀ ▶ *Jn 9:5*

8:42 ˢ 1Jn 5:1
ᵗ S Jn 13:3 ᵘ Jn 7:28
ᵛ S Jn 3:17

8:44 ʷ 1Jn 3:8
ˣ ver 38,41
ʸ Ge 3:4; 4:9;
2Ch 18:21; Ps 5:6;
12:2

8:45 ᶻ Jn 18:37

8:47 ᵃ Jn 18:37;
1Jn 4:6

8:48 ᵇ S Mt 10:5
ᶜ ver 52; S Mk 3:22

8:50 ᵈ ver 54;
Jn 5:41

8:51 ᵉ Jn 11:26

8:52 ᶠ ver 48;
S Mk 3:22

8:53 ᵍ ver 39;
Jn 4:12

8:54 ʰ ver 50
ⁱ Jn 16:14; 17:1,5

8:55 ʲ ver 19
ᵏ Jn 7:28,29
ˡ Jn 15:10

8:56 ᵐ ver 37,39;
Ge 18:18
ⁿ S Mt 13:17

8:58 ᵒ S Jn 1:2
ᵖ Ex 3:14; 6:3

8:59 ᵠ Ex 17:4;
Lev 24:16;
1Sa 30:6; Jn 10:31;
11:8 ʳ Jn 12:36

9:2 ˢ S Mt 23:7
ᵗ ver 34; Lk 13:2;
Ac 28:4 ᵘ Eze 18:20
ᵛ Ex 20:5; Job 21:19

9:3 ʷ Jn 11:4

9:4 ˣ Jn 11:9;
12:35

9:5 ʸ S Jn 1:4

9:6 ᶻ Mk 7:33; 8:23

9:7 ᵃ ver 11;
2Ki 5:10; Lk 13:4
ᵇ Isa 35:5; Jn 11:37

9:8 ᶜ Ac 3:2,10

9:11 ᵈ ver 7

9:14 ᵉ Mt 12:1–14;
Jn 5:9

9:15 ᶠ ver 10

---

⁵⁸"I tell you the truth," Jesus answered, "before Abraham was born,ᵒ I am!"ᵖ ⁵⁹At this, they picked up stones to stone him,ᵠ but Jesus hid himself,ʳ slipping away from the temple grounds.

Jesus Heals a Man Born Blind

9 As he went along, he saw a man **D** blind from birth. ²His disciples asked **E** him, "Rabbi,ˢ who sinned,ᵗ this manᵘ or his parents,ᵛ that he was born blind?"

³"Neither this man nor his parents sinned," said Jesus, "but this happened so that the work of God might be displayed in his life.ʷ ⁴As long as it is day,ˣ we must do the work of him who sent me. Night is coming, when no one can work. ⁵While I am in the world, I am the **K** light of the world."ʸ

⁶Having said this, he spitᶻ on the ground, made some mud with the saliva, and put it on the man's eyes. ⁷"Go," he told him, "wash in the Pool of Siloam"ᵃ (this word means Sent). So the man went and washed, and came home seeing.ᵇ

⁸His neighbors and those who had formerly seen him begging asked, "Isn't this the same man who used to sit and beg?"ᶜ ⁹Some claimed that he was.

Others said, "No, he only looks like him."

But he himself insisted, "I am the man."

¹⁰"How then were your eyes opened?" they demanded.

¹¹He replied, "The man they call Jesus made some mud and put it on my eyes. He told me to go to Siloam and wash. So I went and washed, and then I could see."ᵈ

¹²"Where is this man?" they asked him.

"I don't know," he said.

The Pharisees Investigate the Healing

¹³They brought to the Pharisees the man who had been blind. ¹⁴Now the day on which Jesus had made the mud and opened the man's eyes was a Sabbath.ᵉ ¹⁵Therefore the Pharisees also asked him how he had received his sight.ᶠ "He put mud on my eyes," the man replied, "and I washed, and now I see."

¹⁶Some of the Pharisees said, "This

D *Jn 5:14* ◀ ▶ *Jn 11:4*
E *Jn 7:23* ◀ ▶ *Jn 11:39–46*
K *Jn 8:51* ◀ ▶ *Jn 10:7*

man is not from God, for he does not keep the Sabbath."ᵍ

But others asked, "How can a sinner do such miraculous signs?"ʰ So they were divided.ⁱ

¹⁷Finally they turned again to the blind man, "What have you to say about him? It was your eyes he opened."

The man replied, "He is a prophet."ʲ

¹⁸The Jewsᵏ still did not believe that he had been blind and had received his sight until they sent for the man's parents. ¹⁹"Is this your son?" they asked. "Is this the one you say was born blind? How is it that now he can see?"

²⁰"We know he is our son," the parents answered, "and we know he was born blind. ²¹But how he can see now, or who opened his eyes, we don't know. Ask him. He is of age; he will speak for himself." ²²His parents said this because they were afraid of the Jews,¹ for already the Jews had decided that anyone who acknowledged that Jesus was the Christ would be put outᵐ of the synagogue.ⁿ ²³That was why his parents said, "He is of age; ask him."ᵒ

²⁴A second time they summoned the man who had been blind. "Give glory to God,"ᵛ"ᵖ they said. "We know this man is a sinner."ᑫ

²⁵He replied, "Whether he is a sinner or not, I don't know. One thing I do know. I was blind but now I see!"

²⁶Then they asked him, "What did he do to you? How did he open your eyes?"

²⁷He answered, "I have told you alreadyʳ and you did not listen. Why do you want to hear it again? Do you want to become his disciples, too?"

²⁸Then they hurled insults at him and said, "You are this fellow's disciple! We are disciples of Moses!ˢ ²⁹We know that God spoke to Moses, but as for this fellow, we don't even know where he comes from."ᵗ

³⁰The man answered, "Now that is remarkable! You don't know where he comes from, yet he opened my eyes. ³¹We know that God does not listen to sinners. He listens to the godly man who does his will.ᵘ ³²Nobody has ever heard of opening the eyes of a man born blind. ³³If this man were not from God,ᵛ he could do nothing."

³⁴To this they replied, "You were steeped in sin at birth;ʷ how dare you lecture us!" And they threw him out.ˣ

Spiritual Blindness

³⁵Jesus heard that they had thrown him out, and when he found him, he said, "Do you believeʸ in the Son of Man?"ᶻ

³⁶"Who is he, sir?" the man asked. "Tell me so that I may believe in him."ᵃ

³⁷Jesus said, "You have now seen him; in fact, he is the one speaking with you."ᵇ

³⁸Then the man said, "Lord, I believe," and he worshiped him.ᶜ

³⁹Jesus said, "For judgmentᵈ I have come into this world,ᵉ so that the blind will seeᶠ and those who see will become blind."ᵍ

⁴⁰Some Pharisees who were with him heard him say this and asked, "What? Are we blind too?"ʰ

⁴¹Jesus said, "If you were blind, you would not be guilty of sin; but now that you claim you can see, your guilt remains."ⁱ

The Shepherd and His Flock

10 "I tell you the truth, the man who does not enter the sheep pen by the gate, but climbs in by some other way, is a thief and a robber.ʲ ²The

---

9:16 ᵍ S Mt 12:2; ʰ S Jn 2:11; ⁱ S Jn 6:52
9:17 ʲ S Mt 21:11
9:18 ᵏ S Jn 1:19
9:22 ˡ S Jn 7:13; ᵐ ver 34; Lk 6:22; ⁿ Jn 12:42; 16:2
9:23 ᵒ ver 21
9:24 ᵖ Jos 7:19; ᑫ ver 16
9:27 ʳ ver 15
9:28 ˢ Jn 5:45
9:29 ᵗ Jn 8:14
9:31 ᵘ Ge 18:23-32; Ps 34:15,16; 66:18; 145:19,20; Pr 15:29; Isa 1:15; 59:1,2; Jn 15:7; Jas 5:16-18; 1Jn 5:14,15
9:33 ᵛ ver 16; Jn 3:2
9:34 ʷ ver 2; ˣ ver 22,35; Isa 66:5
9:35 ʸ S Jn 3:15; ᶻ S Mt 8:20
9:36 ᵃ Ro 10:14
9:37 ᵇ Jn 4:26
9:38 ᶜ Mt 28:9
9:39 ᵈ S Jn 5:22; ᵉ Jn 3:19; 12:47; ᶠ Lk 4:18 ᵍ Mt 13:13
9:40 ʰ Ro 2:19
9:41 ⁱ Jn 15:22,24
10:1 ʲ ver 8,10

G Jn 6:28–29 ◄ ► Jn 10:1
L Jn 8:11–12 ◄ ► Jn 11:25–26
M Lk 18:24–25 ◄ ► Ac 7:51
N Jn 8:47 ◄ ► Jn 10:26–27
G Jn 9:39 ◄ ► Ro 3:20
O Jn 8:24 ◄ ► Jn 14:6

ᵘ 22 Or *Messiah* ᵛ 24 A solemn charge to tell the truth (see Joshua 7:19)

9:32–33 The man who made this statement had been blind from birth, and his words were literally true. From the creation of Adam to that point in time, not one person born blind had ever been healed enough to allow them to see. Then Jesus came and healed this man. Isaiah had predicted that one of the miraculous signs of the Messiah was his ability to "open eyes that are blind" (Isa 42:7). This explains why the priests so vehemently rejected the possibility that the man had been truly blind (see 9:18–19). These leaders knew the prophecies about the Messiah, that only the Messiah could open the eyes of one born blind. This extraordinary miracle of healing provided supernatural proof that Jesus was the Messiah—proof that the religious leaders did not want to accept.

man who enters by the gate is the shepherd of his sheep. ³The watchman opens the gate for him, and the sheep listen to his voice. He calls his own sheep by name and leads them out. ⁴When he has brought out all his own, he goes on ahead of them, and his sheep follow him because they know his voice. ⁵But they will never follow a stranger; in fact, they will run away from him because they do not recognize a stranger's voice." ⁶Jesus used this figure of speech, but they did not understand what he was telling them.

⁷Therefore Jesus said again, "I tell you the truth, I am the gate for the sheep. ⁸All who ever came before me were thieves and robbers, but the sheep did not listen to them. ⁹I am the gate; whoever enters through me will be saved. He will come in and go out, and find pasture. ¹⁰The thief comes only to steal and kill and destroy; I have come that they may have life, and have it to the full."

¹¹"I am the good shepherd. The good shepherd lays down his life for the sheep. ¹²The hired hand is not the shepherd who owns the sheep. So when he sees the wolf coming, he abandons the sheep and runs away. Then the wolf attacks the flock and scatters it. ¹³The man runs away because he is a hired hand and cares nothing for the sheep.

¹⁴"I am the good shepherd; I know my sheep and my sheep know me— ¹⁵just as the Father knows me and I know the Father—and I lay down my life for the sheep. ¹⁶I have other sheep that are not of this sheep pen. I must bring them also. They too will listen to my voice, and there shall be one flock and one shepherd. ¹⁷The reason my Father loves me is that I lay down my life—only to take it up again. ¹⁸No one takes it from me,

but I lay it down of my own accord. I have authority to lay it down and authority to take it up again. This command I received from my Father."

¹⁹At these words the Jews were again divided. ²⁰Many of them said, "He is demon-possessed and raving mad. Why listen to him?"

²¹But others said, "These are not the sayings of a man possessed by a demon. Can a demon open the eyes of the blind?"

The Unbelief of the Jews

²²Then came the Feast of Dedication at Jerusalem. It was winter, ²³and Jesus was in the temple area walking in Solomon's Colonnade. ²⁴The Jews gathered around him, saying, "How long will you keep us in suspense? If you are the Christ, tell us plainly."

²⁵Jesus answered, "I did tell you, but you do not believe. The miracles I do in my Father's name speak for me, ²⁶but you do not believe because you are not my sheep. ²⁷My sheep listen to my voice; I know them, and they follow me. ²⁸I give them eternal life, and they shall never perish; no one can snatch them out of my hand. ²⁹My Father, who has given them to me, is greater than all; no one can snatch them out of my Father's hand. ³⁰I and the Father are one."

³¹Again the Jews picked up stones to stone him, ³²but Jesus said to them, "I have shown you many great miracles from the Father. For which of these do you stone me?"

³³"We are not stoning you for any of these," replied the Jews, "but for blasphemy, because you, a mere man, claim to be God."

³⁴Jesus answered them, "Is it not written in your Law, 'I have said you are gods'? ³⁵If he called them 'gods,' to

---

10:16 This prophecy predicts that Jesus' offer of salvation would extend from his original offer to the Jews to include all of the Gentiles who would repent of their sins and accept God's offer of salvation.

whom the word of God came—and the Scripture cannot be broken— ³⁶what about the one whom the Father set apart as his very own and sent into the world? Why then do you accuse me of blasphemy because I said, 'I am God's Son'? ³⁷Do not believe me unless I do what my Father does. ³⁸But if I do it, even though you do not believe me, believe the miracles, that you may know and understand that the Father is in me, and I in the Father." ³⁹Again they tried to seize him, but he escaped their grasp.

⁴⁰Then Jesus went back across the Jordan to the place where John had been baptizing in the early days. Here he stayed ⁴¹and many people came to him. They said, "Though John never performed a miraculous sign, all that John said about this man was true." ⁴²And in that place many believed in Jesus.

The Death of Lazarus

11 Now a man named Lazarus was sick. He was from Bethany, the village of Mary and her sister Martha. ²This Mary, whose brother Lazarus now lay sick, was the same one who poured perfume on the Lord and wiped his feet with her hair. ³So the sisters sent word to Jesus, "Lord, the one you love is sick."

⁴When he heard this, Jesus said, "This sickness will not end in death. No, it is for God's glory so that God's Son may be glorified through it." ⁵Jesus loved Martha and her sister and Lazarus. ⁶Yet when he heard that Lazarus was sick, he stayed where he was two more days.

⁷Then he said to his disciples, "Let us go back to Judea."

⁸"But Rabbi," they said, "a short while ago the Jews tried to stone you, and yet you are going back there?"

⁹Jesus answered, "Are there not twelve hours of daylight? A man who walks by day will not stumble, for he sees by this world's light. ¹⁰It is when he walks by night that he stumbles, for he has no light."

¹¹After he had said this, he went on to tell them, "Our friend Lazarus has fallen asleep; but I am going there to wake him up."

¹²His disciples replied, "Lord, if he sleeps, he will get better." ¹³Jesus had been speaking of his death, but his disciples thought he meant natural sleep.

¹⁴So then he told them plainly, "Lazarus is dead, ¹⁵and for your sake I am glad I was not there, so that you may believe. But let us go to him."

¹⁶Then Thomas (called Didymus) said to the rest of the disciples, "Let us also go, that we may die with him."

Jesus Comforts the Sisters

¹⁷On his arrival, Jesus found that Lazarus had already been in the tomb for four days. ¹⁸Bethany was less than two miles[b] from Jerusalem, ¹⁹and many Jews had come to Martha and Mary to comfort them in the loss of their brother. ²⁰When Martha heard that Jesus was coming, she went out to meet him, but Mary stayed at home.

²¹"Lord," Martha said to Jesus, "if you had been here, my brother would not have died. ²²But I know that even now God will give you whatever you ask."

²³Jesus said to her, "Your brother will rise again."

²⁴Martha answered, "I know he will

F Jn 6:54 ◀ ▶ Ac 17:18

b 18 Greek fifteen stadia (about 3 kilometers)

D Jn 9:1–3 ◀ ▶ Ac 9:8–9

11:23–26 Jesus predicted the imminent resurrection from the dead of his friend Lazarus. When Martha affirmed the known OT teaching of the resurrection of the righteous dead, Jesus responded by affirming, "I am the resurrection and the life. He who believes in me will live, even though he dies" (11:25). Jesus then added an astonishing new revelation that no one had ever heard before: "whoever lives and believes in me will never die" (11:26). Some feel that this statement means that those saints who are alive at Jesus' second coming will never die because they will be raptured in the air with him at his return (see 1Th 4:16–17). Others believe that this verse refers to the never-ending spiritual fellowship that exists between believers and God. Jesus conveys life to believers so that they will always triumph over death. The fact that this statement of Jesus was something totally new is affirmed by his question: "Do you believe this?" (11:26).

rise again in the resurrection° at the last day."ᵖ

F ²⁵Jesus said to her, "I amᑫ the resurrec-
K tion and the life.ʳ He who believesˢ in
L me will live, even though he dies; ²⁶and
W whoever lives and believesᵗ in me will
never die.ᵘ Do you believe this?"

²⁷"Yes, Lord," she told him, "I believe that you are the Christ,ᶜᵛ the Son of God,ʷ who was to come into the world."ˣ ²⁸And after she had said this, she went back and called her sister Mary aside. "The Teacherʸ is here," she said, "and is asking for you." ²⁹When Mary heard this, she got up quickly and went to him. ³⁰Now Jesus had not yet entered the village, but was still at the place where Martha had met him.ᶻ ³¹When the Jews who had been with Mary in the house, comforting her,ᵃ noticed how quickly she got up and went out, they followed her, supposing she was going to the tomb to mourn there.

³²When Mary reached the place where Jesus was and saw him, she fell at his feet and said, "Lord, if you had been here, my brother would not have died."ᵇ

³³When Jesus saw her weeping, and the Jews who had come along with her also weeping, he was deeply movedᶜ in spirit and troubled.ᵈ ³⁴"Where have you laid him?" he asked.

"Come and see, Lord," they replied.

³⁵Jesus wept.ᵉ

³⁶Then the Jews said, "See how he loved him!"ᶠ

³⁷But some of them said, "Could not he who opened the eyes of the blind manᵍ have kept this man from dying?"ʰ

Jesus Raises Lazarus From the Dead

E ³⁸Jesus, once more deeply moved,ⁱ came to the tomb. It was a cave with a stone laid across the entrance.ʲ ³⁹"Take away the stone," he said.

"But, Lord," said Martha, the sister of the dead man, "by this time there is a bad odor, for he has been there four days."ᵏ

⁴⁰Then Jesus said, "Did I not tell you that if you believed,ˡ you would see the glory of God?"ᵐ

⁴¹So they took away the stone. Then Jesus looked upⁿ and said, "Father,° I thank you that you have heard me. ⁴²I knew that you always hear me, but I said this for the benefit of the people standing here,ᵖ that they may believe that you sent me."ᑫ

⁴³When he had said this, Jesus called in a loud voice, "Lazarus, come out!"ʳ ⁴⁴The dead man came out, his hands and feet wrapped with strips of linen,ˢ and a cloth around his face.ᵗ

Jesus said to them, "Take off the grave clothes and let him go."

The Plot to Kill Jesus

⁴⁵Therefore many of the Jews who had come to visit Mary,ᵘ and had seen what Jesus did,ᵛ put their faith in him.ʷ ⁴⁶But some of them went to the Pharisees and told them what Jesus had done. ⁴⁷Then the chief priests and the Phariseesˣ called a meetingʸ of the Sanhedrin.ᶻ

"What are we accomplishing?" they asked. "Here is this man performing many miraculous signs.ᵃ ⁴⁸If we let him go on like this, everyone will believe in him, and then the Romans will come and take away both our placeᵈ and our nation."

D ⁴⁹Then one of them, named Caiaphas,ᵇ who was high priest that year,ᶜ spoke up, "You know nothing at all! ⁵⁰You do not realize that it is better for you that one man die for the people than that the whole nation perish."ᵈ

⁵¹He did not say this on his own, but as high priest that year he prophesied that Jesus would die for the Jewish nation, ⁵²and not only for that nation but also for the scattered children of God, to bring them together and make them one.ᵉ ⁵³So from that day on they plotted to take his life.ᶠ

⁵⁴Therefore Jesus no longer moved about publicly among the Jews.ᵍ Instead he withdrew to a region near the desert, to a village called Ephraim, where he stayed with his disciples.

⁵⁵When it was almost time for the Jewish Passover,ʰ many went up from the country to Jerusalem for their ceremonial cleansingⁱ before the Passover. ⁵⁶They kept looking for Jesus,ʲ and as they stood

---

F Jn 7:38 ◄ ► Jn 12:46
K Jn 10:28–29 ◄ ► Jn 12:46
L Jn 9:39 ◄ ► Jn 12:32
W Jn 7:37 ◄ ► Jn 12:32
E Jn 9:1–7 ◄ ► Jn 12:9–11

D Jn 10:15 ◄ ► Ac 8:32–35

ᶜ27 Or Messiah   ᵈ48 Or temple

in the temple area they asked one another, "What do you think? Isn't he coming to the Feast at all?" ⁵⁷But the chief priests and Pharisees had given orders that if anyone found out where Jesus was, he should report it so that they might arrest him.

Jesus Anointed at Bethany
12:1–8Ref — Mt 26:6–13; Mk 14:3–9; Lk 7:37–39

12 Six days before the Passover,ᵏ Jesus arrived at Bethany,¹ where Lazarus lived, whom Jesus had raised from the dead. ²Here a dinner was given in Jesus' honor. Martha served,ᵐ while Lazarus was among those reclining at the table with him. ³Then Mary took about a pintᵉ of pure nard, an expensive perfume;ⁿ she poured it on Jesus' feet and wiped his feet with her hair.ᵒ And the house was filled with the fragrance of the perfume.

⁴But one of his disciples, Judas Iscariot, who was later to betray him,ᵖ objected, ⁵"Why wasn't this perfume sold and the money given to the poor? It was worth a year's wages.ᶠ" ⁶He did not say this because he cared about the poor but because he was a thief; as keeper of the money bag,ᵠ he used to help himself to what was put into it.

⁷"Leave her alone," Jesus replied. "It was intended that she should save this perfume for the day of my burial.ʳ ⁸You will always have the poor among you,ˢ but you will not always have me."

⁹Meanwhile a large crowd of Jews found out that Jesus was there and came, not only because of him but also to see Lazarus, whom he had raised from the dead.ᵗ ¹⁰So the chief priests made plans to kill Lazarus as well, ¹¹for on account of himᵘ many of the Jews were going over to Jesus and putting their faith in him.ᵛ

The Triumphal Entry
12:12–15pp — Mt 21:4–9; Mk 11:7–10; Lk 19:35–38

¹²The next day the great crowd that had come for the Feast heard that Jesus was on his way to Jerusalem. ¹³They took palm branchesʷ and went out to meet him, shouting,

"Hosanna!ᵍ"

"Blessed is he who comes in the name of the Lord!"ʰˣ

"Blessed is the King of Israel!"ʸ

¹⁴Jesus found a young donkey and sat upon it, as it is written,

¹⁵"Do not be afraid, O Daughter of Zion;
see, your king is coming,
seated on a donkey's colt."ⁱᶻ

¹⁶At first his disciples did not understand all this.ᵃ Only after Jesus was glorifiedᵇ did they realize that these things had been written about him and that they had done these things to him.

¹⁷Now the crowd that was with himᶜ when he called Lazarus from the tomb and raised him from the dead continued to spread the word. ¹⁸Many people, because they had heard that he had given this miraculous sign,ᵈ went out to meet him. ¹⁹So the Pharisees said to one another, "See, this is getting us nowhere. Look how the whole world has gone after him!"ᵉ

Jesus Predicts His Death

²⁰Now there were some Greeksᶠ among those who went up to worship at the Feast. ²¹They came to Philip, who was from Bethsaidaᵍ in Galilee, with a request. "Sir," they said, "we would like to see Jesus." ²²Philip went to tell Andrew; Andrew and Philip in turn told Jesus.

²³Jesus replied, "The hourʰ has come for the Son of Man to be glorified.ⁱ ²⁴I tell you the truth, unless a kernel of wheat falls to the ground and dies,ʲ it remains only a single seed. But if it dies, it pro-

---

12:13–15 John records that many of Jesus' disciples "took palm branches and went out to meet him, shouting, 'Hosanna! . . . Blessed is the King of Israel!' " (12:13), when Jesus rode into Jerusalem on Palm Sunday. This fulfilled Zechariah's prophecy made more than five centuries earlier (see Zec 9:9).

duces many seeds. ²⁵The man who loves his life will lose it, while the man who hates his life in this world will keep it^k for eternal life.^l ²⁶Whoever serves me must follow me; and where I am, my servant also will be.^m My Father will honor the one who serves me.

²⁷"Now my heart is troubled,^n and what shall I say? 'Father,^o save me from this hour'?^p No, it was for this very reason I came to this hour. ²⁸Father, glorify your name!"

Then a voice came from heaven,^q "I have glorified it, and will glorify it again." ²⁹The crowd that was there and heard it said it had thundered; others said an angel had spoken to him. ³⁰Jesus said, "This voice was for your benefit,^r not mine. ³¹Now is the time for judgment on this world;^s now the prince of this world^t will be driven out. ³²But I, when I am lifted up from the earth,^u will draw all men to myself."^v ³³He said this to show the kind of death he was going to die.^w

³⁴The crowd spoke up, "We have heard from the Law^x that the Christ^j will remain forever,^y so how can you say, 'The Son of Man^z must be lifted up'?^a Who is this 'Son of Man'?"

³⁵Then Jesus told them, "You are going to have the light^b just a little while longer. Walk while you have the light,^c before darkness overtakes you.^d The man who walks in the dark does not know where he is going. ³⁶Put your trust in the light while you have it, so that you may become sons of light."^e When he had finished speaking, Jesus left and hid himself from them.^f

The Jews Continue in Their Unbelief

³⁷Even after Jesus had done all these miraculous signs^g in their presence, they still would not believe in him. ³⁸This was to fulfill the word of Isaiah the prophet:

"Lord, who has believed our message

and to whom has the arm of the Lord been revealed?"^k^h

³⁹For this reason they could not believe, because, as Isaiah says elsewhere:

⁴⁰"He has blinded their eyes
 and deadened their hearts,
so they can neither see with their eyes,
 nor understand with their hearts,
 nor turn—and I would heal them."^l^i

⁴¹Isaiah said this because he saw Jesus' glory^j and spoke about him.^k ⁴²Yet at the same time many even among the leaders believed in him.^l But because of the Pharisees^m they would not confess their faith for fear they would be put out of the synagogue;^n ⁴³for they loved praise from men^o more than praise from God.^p

⁴⁴Then Jesus cried out, "When a man believes in me, he does not believe in me only, but in the one who sent me.^q ⁴⁵When he looks at me, he sees the one who sent me.^r ⁴⁶I have come into the world as a light,^s so that no one who believes in me should stay in darkness.

⁴⁷"As for the person who hears my words but does not keep them, I do not judge him. For I did not come to judge the world, but to save it.^t ⁴⁸There is a judge for the one who rejects me and does not accept my words; that very word which I spoke will condemn him^u at the last day. ⁴⁹For I did not speak of my own accord, but the Father who sent me commanded me^v what to say and how to say it. ⁵⁰I know that his command leads to eternal life.^w So whatever I say is just what the Father has told me to say."^x

---

12:48 Jesus prophesied that those who rejected him and his words of salvation would be judged in the last days on the basis of Christ's own words.

Jesus Washes His Disciples' Feet

13 It was just before the Passover Feast. Jesus knew that the time had come for him to leave this world and go to the Father. Having loved his own who were in the world, he now showed them the full extent of his love.

²The evening meal was being served, and the devil had already prompted Judas Iscariot, son of Simon, to betray Jesus. ³Jesus knew that the Father had put all things under his power, and that he had come from God and was returning to God; ⁴so he got up from the meal, took off his outer clothing, and wrapped a towel around his waist. ⁵After that, he poured water into a basin and began to wash his disciples' feet, drying them with the towel that was wrapped around him.

⁶He came to Simon Peter, who said to him, "Lord, are you going to wash my feet?"

⁷Jesus replied, "You do not realize now what I am doing, but later you will understand."

⁸"No," said Peter, "you shall never wash my feet."

Jesus answered, "Unless I wash you, you have no part with me."

⁹"Then, Lord," Simon Peter replied, "not just my feet but my hands and my head as well!"

¹⁰Jesus answered, "A person who has had a bath needs only to wash his feet; his whole body is clean. And you are clean, though not every one of you." ¹¹For he knew who was going to betray him, and that was why he said not every one was clean.

¹²When he had finished washing their feet, he put on his clothes and returned to his place. "Do you understand what I have done for you?" he asked them. ¹³"You call me 'Teacher' and 'Lord,' and rightly so, for that is what I am. ¹⁴Now that I, your Lord and Teacher, have washed your feet, you also should wash one another's feet. ¹⁵I have set you an example that you should do as I have done for you. ¹⁶I tell you the truth, no servant is greater than his master, nor is a messenger greater than the one who sent him. ¹⁷Now that you know these things, you will be blessed if you do them.

Jesus Predicts His Betrayal

¹⁸"I am not referring to all of you; I know those I have chosen. But this is to fulfill the scripture: 'He who shares my bread has lifted up his heel against me.'

¹⁹"I am telling you now before it happens, so that when it does happen you will believe that I am He. ²⁰I tell you the truth, whoever accepts anyone I send accepts me; and whoever accepts me accepts the one who sent me."

²¹After he had said this, Jesus was troubled in spirit and testified, "I tell you the truth, one of you is going to betray me."

²²His disciples stared at one another, at a loss to know which of them he meant. ²³One of them, the disciple whom Jesus loved, was reclining next to him. ²⁴Simon Peter motioned to this disciple and said, "Ask him which one he means."

²⁵Leaning back against Jesus, he asked him, "Lord, who is it?"

²⁶Jesus answered, "It is the one to whom I will give this piece of bread when I have dipped it in the dish." Then, dipping the piece of bread, he gave it to Judas Iscariot, son of Simon. ²⁷As soon as Judas took the bread, Satan entered into him.

"What you are about to do, do quickly," Jesus told him, ²⁸but no one at the meal understood why Jesus said this to him. ²⁹Since Judas had charge of the money, some thought Jesus was telling him to buy what was needed for the Feast, or to give something to the poor. ³⁰As soon as Judas had taken the bread, he went out. And it was night.

Jesus Predicts Peter's Denial

13:37,38pp — Mt 26:33–35; Mk 14:29–31; Lk 22:33,34

³¹When he was gone, Jesus said, "Now is the Son of Man glorified and God is glorified in him. ³²If God is glorified in him, God will glorify the Son in himself, and will glorify him at once.

³³"My children, I will be with you only a little longer. You will look for me, and just as I told the Jews, so I tell you now: Where I am going, you cannot come.

³⁴"A new command I give you: Love one another. As I have loved you, so you

---

m 1 Or *he loved them to the last* *n 18* Psalm 41:9 *o 32* Many early manuscripts do not have *If God is glorified in him.*

The Judgments of God

THE VAST CHASM between God's holiness and humanity's sinfulness is highlighted by God's judgments. The Bible describes eight separate judgments of God.

The Judgment of a Believer's Sin
The Bible confirms that "the wages of sin is death" (Ro 6:23). God's holy law judges every sin and requires the mandatory sentence. Therefore it was necessary for Jesus Christ to die on the cross and bear the eternal punishment for sin. Thus the basis of this judgment of the believer's sin is the completed, perfect atoning work of Christ on the cross.

The Judgment of a Believer's Walk
There is a continuing judgment in a believer's daily walk of faith (see 1Co 11:31–32). The Holy Spirit awakens our conscience to an active obedience to God's will. God's chastening signals his love for us and directs us to a closer walk with him. While we sometimes resent this chastening, God corrects us because of his profound love for us and a desire for our best interests. Though not enjoyable, chastening will yield righteousness if we will learn from it (see Heb 12:1).

The Judgment of Israel
Israel's destiny as God's chosen people has truly been a two-edged sword. Blessed with God's Word, Israel bore a greater responsibility for obedience and a higher standard of spirituality than the pagan nations that surrounded her. In addition, God promised that Israel would face persecution and tribulation because of her rebellion against God's prophets and her rejection of God's commands and the Messiah. Tragically, Israel has reaped the fulfillment of this promised judgment over the centuries. Yet Israel's judgment has not come to an end.

The prophets foretold that just before the return of Jesus Christ the world would go through a time of terrible persecution under the antichrist. While this great tribulation will involve the whole world, its horrors will be focused upon Israel during the last three and one-half years before the Battle of Armageddon. God will still provide a witness for Israel and souls will be saved, beginning in Israel, during this tribulation period. Those who repent and survive through this prophesied period of trouble will be saved and blessed for eternity. Twenty-five centuries ago, the prophet Zechariah prophesied that despite the massive slaughter the Messiah would come and save Israel from her enemies (see Zec 13:1–9). At that time Israel will finally enjoy the great blessings and prosperity that have been the hope of the chosen people for centuries. For further information, see the article on "The Tribulation" on p. 990.

The Judgment of the Gentile Nations
In the last days, all the nations of the world will take part in a titanic struggle for world supremacy. Following the Battle of Armageddon, these nations will be judged by Jesus Christ based on their treatment of both Jewish and Gentile believers (see Mt 25:31–46). Those nations that have protected God's people will be preserved to enjoy the blessings of the millennial kingdom. Those nations who have despised and persecuted the people of God will be cast onto the dust heap of history.

Some have assumed that national distinctions will cease to exist once Jesus sets up his eternal kingdom on earth. However, God specifically described the future of humanity in terms of the continuation of both Israel and those nations that have blessed God's people during the tribulation. The Bible clearly states that the nations will be ruled by the saints during and after the Millennium (see Rev 5:10). After the earth is renewed, John describes a wonderful future in which the new Jerusalem will descend from heaven and Israel, the nations and Christ's kingdom will enjoy peace forever. For further information, see the article on "The New Jerusalem" on p. 1498.

The Judgment at the Great White Throne
John revealed that at the end of the Battle of Armageddon Satan would be chained in the bottomless pit for a period of one thousand years. People would enjoy peace and prosperity in God's kingdom during this Millennium. However, after the Millennium, Satan will be released to lead a final rebellion against God. The judgment at God's great white throne will occur after this rebellion. All unrepentant people who have ever lived will stand before God's throne, be judged for their wickedness and thrown into the lake of fire (see Rev 20:11–15). Note that Mt 25:41 says that the lake of fire was originally prepared for the devil and his angels. If people had never rebelled against God or stayed in their unrepentant state, they would never have been consigned to hell. For further information about this judgment, see the article on p. 1490.

The Judgment of Fallen Angels
Satan and all his rebellious angels will finally stand before Christ at the great white throne. Some say these wicked angels may have cohabited with women during the time of the flood, producing a race of wicked giants (see study note at Ge 6:1–4). Others contend that these evil angels rebelled with Satan against God before Adam and Eve sinned in the garden. In either case, these angels were chained by God in a special prison until the day of this judgment (see 2Pe 2:4; Jude 6). On this final judgment day these wicked angels will be imprisoned forever with Satan in the lake of everlasting fire (see Mt 25:41). For further information, see the article on "Satan and the Fallen Angels" on p. 926.

The Judgment of the Wicked Dead

The great white throne judgment will provide every person with a fair trial before the God of the universe. The souls of all people who have refused to repent will receive their resurrected bodies and appear before God on that ultimate judgment day. The grave and the sea will give up their dead, and even hell will surrender its souls to stand before God. All wicked persons who appear there will be judged by the works of their lives (see Rev 20:12). Many will claim to be Christians. They will point to their public religious life, but God will point to their heart and declare that their names were never entered in the book of life because they had never accepted the pardon of Jesus Christ. The only cure and deliverance from our sin and guilt is the miraculous transformation wrought by the blood of Jesus Christ.

The Bema Judgment

The apostle Paul uses the Greek word *bema* in 2Co 5:10 in reference to a judgment that will take place before Jesus Christ in heaven involving all Christians who have ever lived. A *bema* was "a raised space or bench, the official seat of a judge." Paul indicates that all believers will appear before this judgment seat of Christ to have their lives judged by Jesus on the basis of their righteous works. This *bema* judgment will occur after the resurrection of the saints and will involve the gain or loss of rewards for our service to God. Those who lived godly lives of work and service will withstand God's scrutiny and be blessed with eternal rewards in heaven; those whose works do not meet God's standards will not be rewarded (see 1Co 3:12–15). The blood of Christ will still save those who repent. For further information, see the article on "Crowns and Rewards" on p. 1326.

To reign and rule with Christ is part of the reward that will belong to faithful believers in the Millennium. Jesus Christ will rule as King of kings in Jerusalem (see Rev 19:16), and King David will be resurrected to serve as Christ's regent (see Isa 55:3–4; Jer 30:9; 33:15; Eze 34:23–24; Hos 3:5; Am 9:11). The twelve disciples will rule the twelve tribes of Israel (see Mt 19:28), and many believers will rule various cities throughout the earth (see Isa 40:10; Zec 3:7; Lk 19:12–28).

must love one another.^q ^35 By this all men will know that you are my disciples, if you love one another."^r

^36 Simon Peter asked him, "Lord, where are you going?"^s

Jesus replied, "Where I am going, you cannot follow now,^t but you will follow later."^u

^37 Peter asked, "Lord, why can't I follow you now? I will lay down my life for you."

^38 Then Jesus answered, "Will you really lay down your life for me? I tell you the truth, before the rooster crows, you will disown me three times!^v

Jesus Comforts His Disciples

14 "Do not let your hearts be troubled.^w Trust^x in God;^p,^y trust also in me. ^2 In my Father's house are many rooms; if it were not so, I would have told you. I am going there^z to prepare a place for you. ^3 And if I go and prepare a place for you, I will come back^a and take you to be with me that you also may be where I am.^b ^4 You know the way to the place where I am going."

Jesus the Way to the Father

^5 Thomas^c said to him, "Lord, we don't know where you are going, so how can we know the way?"

^6 Jesus answered, "I am^d the way^e and the truth^f and the life.^g No one comes to the Father except through me.^h ^7 If you really knew me, you would know^q my Father as well.^i From now on, you do know him and have seen him."

^8 Philip^j said, "Lord, show us the Father and that will be enough for us."

^9 Jesus answered: "Don't you know me, Philip, even after I have been among you such a long time? Anyone who has seen me has seen the Father.^k How can you say, 'Show us the Father'? ^10 Don't you believe that I am in the Father, and that the Father is in me?^l The words I say to you are not just my own.^m Rather, it is the

W *Lk 18:1* ◀ ▶ *Jn 14:27*
K *Jn 12:50* ◀ ▶ *Jn 17:3*
O *Jn 10:1* ◀ ▶ *Jn 20:23*

13:34 ^q Jn 15:12; Eph 5:2; 1Jn 4:10, 11
13:35 ^r 1Jn 3:14; 4:20
13:36 ^s Jn 16:5 ^t ver 33; Jn 14:2 ^u Jn 21:18,19; 2Pe 1:14
13:38 ^v Jn 18:27
14:1 ^w ver 27 ^x S Jn 3:15 ^y Ps 4:5
14:2 ^z Jn 13:33,36; 16:5
14:3 ^a ver 18,28; S Mt 16:27 ^b S Jn 12:26
14:5 ^c S Jn 11:16
14:6 ^d S Jn 6:35 ^e Jn 10:9; Eph 2:18; Heb 10:20 ^f Jn 1:14 ^g S Jn 1:4 ^h Ac 4:12
14:7 ^i Jn 1:18; S 1Jn 2:23
14:8 ^j S Jn 1:43
14:9 ^k Isa 9:6; Jn 1:14; 12:45; 2Co 4:4; Php 2:6; Col 1:15; Heb 1:3
14:10 ^l ver 11,20; Jn 10:38; 17:21 ^m S ver 24
14:11 ^n Jn 5:36; 10:38
14:12 ^o Mt 21:21 ^p Lk 10:17
14:13 ^q S Mt 7:7
14:15 ^r ver 21,23; Ps 103:18; Jn 15:10; 1Jn 2:3-5; 3:22,24; 5:3; 2Jn 6; Rev 12:17; 14:12
14:16 ^s ver 26; Jn 15:26; 16:7
14:17 ^t Jn 15:26; 16:13; 1Jn 4:6; 5:6 ^u 1Co 2:14
14:18 ^v 1Ki 6:13 ^w ver 3,28; S Mt 16:27
14:19 ^x Jn 7:33,34; 16:16 ^y Jn 6:57
14:20 ^z Jn 16:23, 26 ^a ver 10,11; Jn 10:38; 17:21 ^b S Ro 8:10
14:21 ^c S ver 15 ^d Dt 7:13; Jn 16:27; 1Jn 2:5
14:22 ^e Lk 6:16; Ac 1:13 ^f Ac 10:41
14:23 ^g S ver 15

Father, living in me, who is doing his work. ^11 Believe me when I say that I am in the Father and the Father is in me; or at least believe on the evidence of the miracles themselves.^n ^12 I tell you the truth, anyone who has faith^o in me will do what I have been doing.^p He will do even greater things than these, because I am going to the Father. ^13 And I will do whatever you ask^q in my name, so that the Son may bring glory to the Father. ^14 You may ask me for anything in my name, and I will do it.

Jesus Promises the Holy Spirit

^15 "If you love me, you will obey what I command.^r ^16 And I will ask the Father, and he will give you another Counselor^s to be with you forever— ^17 the Spirit of truth.^t The world cannot accept him,^u because it neither sees him nor knows him. But you know him, for he lives with you and will be^r in you. ^18 I will not leave you as orphans;^v I will come to you.^w ^19 Before long, the world will not see me anymore, but you will see me.^x Because I live, you also will live.^y ^20 On that day^z you will realize that I am in my Father,^a and you are in me, and I am in you.^b ^21 Whoever has my commands and obeys them, he is the one who loves me.^c He who loves me will be loved by my Father,^d and I too will love him and show myself to him."

^22 Then Judas^e (not Judas Iscariot) said, "But, Lord, why do you intend to show yourself to us and not to the world?"^f

^23 Jesus replied, "If anyone loves me, he will obey my teaching.^g My Father will

L *Jn 10:27–29* ◀ ▶ *Jn 16:24*
S *Jn 8:34–35* ◀ ▶ *Jn 14:21*
B *Jn 7:37–39* ◀ ▶ *Jn 14:26*
J *Jn 1:32* ◀ ▶ *Jn 14:26*
N *Jn 7:37–39* ◀ ▶ *Jn 15:26*
P *Jn 7:37–39* ◀ ▶ *Jn 14:26*
W *Jn 6:63* ◀ ▶ *Jn 16:7*
S *Jn 14:15* ◀ ▶ *Jn 15:2*
U *Jn 12:25–26* ◀ ▶ *Jn 15:7*

^p 1 Or *You trust in God* ^q 7 Some early manuscripts *If you really have known me, you will know* ^r 17 Some early manuscripts *and is*

14:16–18 This prophecy that God would send the Holy Spirit to empower believers was fulfilled on the day of Pentecost (see Ac 2:1–20). Note that Jesus promised that he would "not leave you as orphans" (14:18). This ongoing relationship of the Holy Spirit and the church will continue until the saints are resurrected to heaven when the Holy Spirit is removed in his role on earth as the restrainer of the antichrist (see 2Th 2:5–9). Satan will then be allowed to bring forth the first beast of Rev 13.

Heaven

THOUGH THE BIBLE does not reveal the exact location of heaven, Scripture tells us that heaven is the home of God and his angelic host.

Heaven in the Old Testament

The OT makes reference to heaven in several ways. The opening chapters of Genesis describe the physical, astronomical heavens. According to the OT prophets, God's coming judgment will be announced in the astronomical heavens (see Isa 13:10; Joel 2:30–31).

However, the spiritual reality of heaven is described in other OT passages as God's abode (see Ps 11:4). This view of heaven is presented throughout the OT as the hope of the saints. Few details are given other than the fact that the saints will be "gathered to their fathers" (Jdg 2:10) and that in this place they will dwell in the presence of God.

Heaven in the New Testament

Because of the advent of Christ and his teaching about God's kingdom, the NT contains many references to heaven that shed light on this glorious place. Note that occasionally a NT author may use the word *heaven* as a synonym for God to avoid the casual use of God's holy name (see Mt 23:22; Lk 15:21). Yet the majority of the NT Scriptures that deal with heaven refer to a specific place for believers. The apostle Paul suggests that heaven is full of unspeakable wonders for those who trust God (see 1Co 2:9). Fortunately, a number of NT passages describe enough details of heaven to awaken a sense of wonder and anticipation for those who long to see our Lord face to face. Many of these passages deal with references to a new heaven and a new earth that will exist after the Millennium. Cleansed by fire and housing the new Jerusalem, this eternal new heaven and new earth will no longer be subject to sin and its effects (see Rev 12:10). For further information, see the article on "A New Heaven and a New Earth" on p. 1494.

The Heavenly City

The largest percentage of teaching about heaven in the NT consists of information about the heavenly city, the new Jerusalem. This capital city of heaven is filled with God's glory and glows with an internal light, "like a jasper, clear as crystal" (Rev 21:11). New Jerusalem is an enormous city—1,500 miles long along each side. Its foundation wall is over 216 feet high, and it is full of gates, mansions, streets and inhabitants (see 21:16–18). New Jerusalem's enormous size would easily accommodate more than a billion mansions larger and grander than any palace on earth today.

The dimensions of the new Jerusalem indicate that it will also be of an unusual shape, quite possibly pyramidal. The Bible indicates that 12 layers of stone support the foundation, and each layer contains "the names of the twelve apostles of the Lamb" (21:14). The walls have three pearl gates on each side and the 12 layers of the foundations of the walls are made of precious stones like jasper, sapphire, emerald, topaz, amethyst and others (see 21:19–20). The streets in the new Jerusalem are made of pure gold, transparent like glass (see 21:21).

There will be no need of the sun or moon to provide light in the new Jerusalem because God's presence will light the whole city (see 21:23–24). His glory shines so brightly that "there will be no night there" (21:25) and no danger of an enemy or a need to shut the gates. There will be no rust or decay because sin and its effects on the universe will have ceased.

Only the redeemed, those whose names "are written in the Lamb's book of life" (21:27), will inhabit the new Jerusalem. The faithful, ever since Abel, have been longing for this city (see Heb 11). The ultimate goal of every believer is to join the Savior in the new Jerusalem, the heavenly city of God. For further information, see the article on "The New Jerusalem" on p. 1498.

Although the new Jerusalem will be the final home of all believers, we will not be restricted to it. As God's children we will be able to explore the new earth and the new heaven, able to come and go, ruling and reigning with Christ. We will have access to the "river of the water of life, as clear as crystal, flowing from the throne of God and of the Lamb" (Rev 22:1) and be able to partake freely of the tree of life (see 22:2). We have Jesus' promise that he is preparing heaven for us right now and will one day "come back and take you to be with me that you also may be where I am" (Jn 14:3). What a wonder heaven will be!

love him, and we will come to him and make our home with him.ʰ ²⁴He who does not love me will not obey my teaching. These words you hear are not my own; they belong to the Father who sent me.ⁱ

²⁵"All this I have spoken while still with you. ²⁶But the Counselor,ʲ the Holy Spirit, whom the Father will send in my name,ᵏ will teach you all things¹ and will remind you of everything I have said to you.ᵐ ²⁷Peace I leave with you; my peace I give you.ⁿ I do not give to you as the world gives. Do not let your hearts be troubledᵒ and do not be afraid.

²⁸"You heard me say, 'I am going away and I am coming back to you.'ᵖ If you loved me, you would be glad that I am going to the Father,ᵠ for the Father is greater than I.ʳ ²⁹I have told you now before it happens, so that when it does happen you will believe.ˢ ³⁰I will not speak with you much longer, for the prince of this worldᵗ is coming. He has no hold on me, ³¹but the world must learn that I love the Father and that I do exactly what my Father has commanded me.ᵘ

"Come now; let us leave.

The Vine and the Branches

15 "I amᵛ the true vine,ʷ and my Father is the gardener. ²He cuts off every branch in me that bears no fruit,ˣ while every branch that does bear fruitʸ he prunesˢ so that it will be even more fruitful. ³You are already clean because of the word I have spoken to you.ᶻ ⁴Remain in me, and I will remain in you.ᵃ No branch can bear fruit by itself; it must remain in the vine. Neither can you bear fruit unless you remain in me.

⁵"I am the vine; you are the branches. If a man remains in me and I in him, he will bear much fruit;ᵇ apart from me you can do nothing. ⁶If anyone does not remain in me, he is like a branch that is thrown away and withers; such branches are picked up, thrown into the fire and burned.ᶜ ⁷If you remain in meᵈ and my words remain in you, ask whatever you wish, and it will be given you.ᵉ ⁸This is to my Father's glory,ᶠ that you bear much fruit, showing yourselves to be my disciples.ᵍ

⁹"As the Father has loved me,ʰ so have I loved you. Now remain in my love. ¹⁰If you obey my commands,ⁱ you will remain in my love, just as I have obeyed my Father's commands and remain in his love. ¹¹I have told you this so that my joy may be in you and that your joy may be complete.ʲ ¹²My command is this: Love each other as I have loved you.ᵏ ¹³Greater love has no one than this, that he lay down his life for his friends.ˡ ¹⁴You are my friendsᵐ if you do what I command.ⁿ ¹⁵I no longer call you servants, because a servant does not know his master's business. Instead, I have called you friends, for everything that I learned from my Father I have made known to you.ᵒ ¹⁶You did not choose me, but I chose you and appointed youᵖ to go and bear fruitᵠ— fruit that will last. Then the Father will give you whatever you ask in my name.ʳ ¹⁷This is my command: Love each other.ˢ

B Jn 14:16–17 ◄ ► Jn 15:26
G Jn 3:34 ◄ ► Jn 16:13–15
J Jn 14:16–17 ◄ ► Jn 15:26
M Jn 7:38–39 ◄ ► Jn 16:7–15
P Jn 14:16–17 ◄ ► Jn 15:26
T Jn 3:34 ◄ ► Jn 15:26
W Jn 14:1 ◄ ► Php 3:1
H Jn 12:48 ◄ ► Jn 15:6
S Jn 14:21 ◄ ► Jn 15:6

14:23 ʰ Ro 8:10
14:24 ⁱ ver 10; Dt 18:18; Jn 5:19; 7:16; 8:28; 12:49, 50
14:26 ʲ ver 16; Jn 15:26; 16:7 ᵏ Ac 2:33 ˡ Jn 16:13; 1Jn 2:20,27 ᵐ Jn 2:22
14:27 ⁿ Nu 6:26; Ps 85:8; Mal 2:6; S Lk 2:14; 24:36; Jn 16:33; Php 4:7; Col 3:15 ᵒ ver 1
14:28 ᵖ ver 2-4,18; S Mt 16:27 ᵠ Jn 5:18 ʳ Jn 10:29
14:29 ˢ Jn 13:19; 16:4
14:30 ᵗ S Jn 12:31
14:31 ᵘ Jn 10:18; 12:49
15:1 ᵛ S Jn 6:35 ʷ Ps 80:8-11; Isa 5:1-7
15:2 ˣ ver 6; S Mt 3:10 ʸ Ps 92:14; Mt 3:8; 7:20; Gal 5:22; Eph 5:9; Php 1:11
15:3 ᶻ Jn 13:10; 17:17; Eph 5:26
15:4 ᵃ S Jn 6:56
15:5 ᵇ ver 16
15:6 ᶜ ver 2; Eze 15:4; S Mt 3:10
15:7 ᵈ ver 4; S Jn 6:56 ᵉ S Mt 7:7
15:8 ᶠ S Mt 9:8 ᵍ Jn 8:31
15:9 ʰ Jn 17:23,24,26
15:10 ⁱ S Jn 14:15
15:11 ʲ S Jn 3:29
15:12 ᵏ ver 17; S Jn 13:34
15:13 ˡ Ge 44:33; Jn 10:11; Ro 5:7,8
15:14 ᵐ Job 16:20; Pr 18:24; Lk 12:4 ⁿ Mt 12:50
15:15 ᵒ Jn 8:26
15:16 ᵖ ver 19; Jn 13:18 ᵠ ver 5 ʳ S Mt 7:7
15:17 ˢ ver 12

H Jn 15:2 ◄ ► Ac 1:25
S Jn 15:2 ◄ ► Jn 15:10
U Jn 14:21 ◄ ► Jn 15:11
S Jn 15:6 ◄ ► Jn 15:14
U Jn 15:7 ◄ ► Ro 8:28
L Jn 12:46–47 ◄ ► Ac 3:19
S Jn 15:10 ◄ ► Jn 17:15–20

ˢ 2 The Greek for *prunes* also means *cleans*.

14:26 Jesus promised that the Holy Spirit "will teach you all things and will remind you of everything I have said to you" (14:26). This prophecy was fulfilled on Pentecost when the disciples received the Holy Spirit.

This prophecy also guarantees the accuracy of the NT accounts of Christ's teaching because the Holy Spirit enabled the disciples to correctly recall the words of Jesus and allowed them to accurately record his messages to his believers through the NT Scriptures. Though there are minute differences in phrasing between the Gospel authors on a few occasions, the divine inspiration of the accounts is indisputable. John also indicates that "Jesus did many other things as well. If every one of them were written down, I suppose that even the whole world would not have room for the books that would be written" (21:25).

The World Hates the Disciples

[18] "If the world hates you,[t] keep in mind that it hated me first. [19] If you belonged to the world, it would love you as its own. As it is, you do not belong to the world, but I have chosen you[u] out of the world. That is why the world hates you.[v] [20] Remember the words I spoke to you: 'No servant is greater than his master.'[t][w] If they persecuted me, they will persecute you also.[x] If they obeyed my teaching, they will obey yours also. [21] They will treat you this way because of my name,[y] for they do not know the One who sent me.[z] [22] If I had not come and spoken to them,[a] they would not be guilty of sin. Now, however, they have no excuse for their sin.[b] [23] He who hates me hates my Father as well. [24] If I had not done among them what no one else did,[c] they would not be guilty of sin.[d] But now they have seen these miracles, and yet they have hated both me and my Father. [25] But this is to fulfill what is written in their Law:[e] 'They hated me without reason.'[u][f]

[26] "When the Counselor[g] comes, whom I will send to you from the Father,[h] the Spirit of truth[i] who goes out from the Father, he will testify about me.[j] [27] And you also must testify,[k] for you have been with me from the beginning.[l]

16

"All this[m] I have told you so that you will not go astray.[n] [2] They will put you out of the synagogue;[o] in fact, a time is coming when anyone who kills you will think he is offering a service to God.[p] [3] They will do such things because they have not known the Father or me.[q] [4] I have told you this, so that when the time comes you will remember[r] that I warned you. I did not tell you this at first because I was with you.[s]

The Work of the Holy Spirit

[5] "Now I am going to him who sent me,[t] yet none of you asks me, 'Where are you going?'[u] [6] Because I have said these things, you are filled with grief.[v] [7] But I tell you the truth: It is for your good that I am going away. Unless I go away, the Counselor[w] will not come to you; but if I go, I will send him to you.[x] [8] When he comes, he will convict the world of guilt[v] in regard to sin and righteousness and judgment: [9] in regard to sin,[y] because men do not believe in me; [10] in regard to righteousness,[z] because I am going to the Father,[a] where you can see me no longer; [11] and in regard to judgment, because the prince of this world[b] now stands condemned.

[12] "I have much more to say to you, more than you can now bear.[c] [13] But when he, the Spirit of truth,[d] comes, he will guide you into all truth.[e] He will not speak on his own; he will speak only what he hears, and he will tell you what is yet to come. [14] He will bring glory to me by taking from what is mine and making it known to you. [15] All that belongs to the Father is mine.[f] That is why I said the Spirit will take from what is mine and make it known to you.

[16] "In a little while[g] you will see me no more, and then after a little while you will see me."[h]

The Disciples' Grief Will Turn to Joy

[17] Some of his disciples said to one another, "What does he mean by saying, 'In

---

15:18 t Isa 66:5; Jn 7:7; 1Jn 3:13
15:19 u ver 16 v Jn 17:14
15:20 w S Jn 13:16 x 2Ti 3:12
15:21 y Isa 66:5; Mt 5:10,11; 10:22; Lk 6:22; Ac 5:41; 1Pe 4:14; Rev 2:3 z Jn 16:3
15:22 a Eze 2:5; 3:7 b Jn 9:41; Ro 1:20; 2:1
15:24 c Jn 5:36 d Jn 9:41
15:25 e S Jn 10:34 f Ps 35:19; 69:4; 109:3
15:26 g Jn 14:16 h Jn 14:26; 16:7 i S Jn 14:17 j 1Jn 5:7
15:27 k S Lk 24:48; Jn 21:24; 1Jn 1:2; 4:14 l S Lk 1:2
16:1 m Jn 15:18-27 n Mt 11:6
16:2 o Jn 9:22; 12:42 p Isa 66:5; Ac 26:9,10; Rev 6:9
16:3 q Jn 15:21; 17:25; 1Jn 3:1
16:4 r Jn 13:19; 14:29 s Jn 15:27
16:5 t ver 10,17, 28; Jn 7:33 u Jn 13:36; 14:5
16:6 v ver 22
16:7 w Jn 14:16, 26; 15:26 x Jn 7:39; 14:26
16:9 y Jn 15:22
16:10 z Ac 3:14; 7:52; Ro 1:17; 3:21, 22; 1Pe 3:18 a S ver 5
16:11 b S Jn 12:31
16:12 c Mk 4:33; 1Co 3:2
16:13 d S Jn 14:17 e Ps 25:5; Jn 15:26
16:15 f Jn 17:10
16:16 g S Jn 7:33 h ver 22; Jn 14:18-24

B Jn 14:26 ◀ ▶ Jn 16:7
J Jn 14:26 ◀ ▶ Jn 16:7
N Jn 14:16-17 ◀ ▶ Ac 2:2-4
P Jn 14:26 ◀ ▶ Jn 16:7-15
T Jn 14:26 ◀ ▶ Jn 16:7-15

B Jn 15:26 ◀ ▶ Jn 16:13
C Lk 1:15-17 ◀ ▶ Ac 11:24
J Jn 15:26 ◀ ▶ Jn 20:21-22
M Jn 14:26 ◀ ▶ Ac 1:8
P Jn 15:26 ◀ ▶ Ac 1:4-5
T Jn 15:26 ◀ ▶ Ac 1:2
W Jn 14:16-17 ◀ ▶ Ac 1:4-5

B Jn 16:7 ◀ ▶ Ac 1:4-5
G Jn 14:26 ◀ ▶ Ac 1:8
L Jn 4:23-24 ◀ ▶ Ac 1:2

t 20 John 13:16 *u* 25 Psalms 35:19; 69:4 *v* 8 Or *will expose the guilt of the world*

16:7–11 Jesus predicted that after his ascension to heaven he would send the Holy Spirit to "convict the world of guilt in regard to sin and righteousness and judgment" (16:8). The Holy Spirit also restrains "the prince of this world" (16:11) during this age of grace until the tribulation when he will be released to fulfill his prophesied role (see 2Th 2:6–9).

16:16 Jesus prophesied that he would leave his disciples soon, but he also foretold that he would physically return from heaven so that they would see him.

a little while you will see me no more, and then after a little while you will see me,'ⁱ and 'Because I am going to the Father'?'ʲ ¹⁸They kept asking, "What does he mean by 'a little while'? We don't understand what he is saying."

¹⁹Jesus saw that they wanted to ask him about this, so he said to them, "Are you asking one another what I meant when I said, 'In a little while you will see me no more, and then after a little while you will see me'? ²⁰I tell you the truth, you will weep and mournᵏ while the world rejoices. You will grieve, but your grief will turn to joy.ˡ ²¹A woman giving birth to a child has painᵐ because her time has come; but when her baby is born she forgets the anguish because of her joy that a child is born into the world. ²²So with you: Now is your time of grief,ⁿ but I will see you againᵒ and you will rejoice, and no one will take away your joy.ᵖ ²³In that dayᑫ you will no longer ask me anything. I tell you the truth, my Father will give you whatever you ask in my name. ²⁴Until now you have not asked for anything in my name. Ask and you will receive,ˢ and your joy will be complete.ᵗ

²⁵"Though I have been speaking figuratively,ᵘ a time is comingᵛ when I will no longer use this kind of language but will tell you plainly about my Father. ²⁶In that day you will ask in my name.ʷ I am not saying that I will ask the Father on your behalf. ²⁷No, the Father himself loves you because you have loved meˣ and have believed that I came from God.ʸ ²⁸I came from the Father and entered the world; now I am leaving the world and going back to the Father."ᶻ

²⁹Then Jesus' disciples said, "Now you are speaking clearly and without figures of speech.ᵃ ³⁰Now we can see that you know all things and that you do not even need to have anyone ask you questions. This makes us believeᵇ that you came from God."ᶜ

16:17 ⁱver 16
ʲver 5
16:20 ᵏMk 16:10;
Lk 23:27 ˡJn 20:20
16:21 ᵐIsa 13:8;
21:3; 26:17;
Mic 4:9; 1Th 5:3
16:22 ⁿver 6
ᵒver 16 ᵖver 20;
Jer 31:12
16:23 ᑫver 26;
Jn 14:20 ʳS Mt 7:7
16:24 ˢS Mt 7:7
ᵗS Jn 3:29
16:25 ᵘver 29;
Ps 78:2; Eze 20:49;
Mt 13:34; Mk 4:33,
34; Jn 10:6 ᵛver 2
16:26 ʷver 23,24
16:27 ˣJn 14:21,
23 ʸver 30;
S Jn 13:3
16:28 ᶻver 5,10,
17; Jn 13:3
16:29 ᵃS ver 25
16:30 ᵇ1Ki 17:24
ᶜver 27; S Jn 13:3
16:32 ᵈver 2,25
ᵉMt 26:31
ᶠMt 26:56 ᵍJn 8:16,
29
16:33 ʰS Jn 14:27
ⁱJn 15:18-21
ʲJn 8:37; 1Jn 4:4;
5:4; Rev 2:7,11,17,
26; 3:5,12,21; 21:7

17:1 ᵏJn 11:41
ˡS Mt 26:18
ᵐJn 12:23; 13:31,
32
17:2 ⁿS Mt 28:18
ᵒS Mt 25:46
ᵖver 6,9,24;
Da 7:14; Jn 6:37,39
17:3 ᑫS Php 3:8
ʳver 8,18,21,23,25;
S Jn 3:17
17:4 ˢJn 13:31
ᵗS Jn 19:30
17:5 ᵘver 1
ᵛPhp 2:6 ʷS Jn 1:2
17:6 ˣver 26;
Jn 1:18 ʸS ver 2
17:8 ᶻver 14,26;
S Jn 14:24
ᵃS Jn 13:3 ᵇver 3,
18,21,23,25;
S Jn 3:17
17:9 ᶜLk 22:32
ᵈS ver 2
17:10 ᵉJn 16:15

³¹"You believe at last!"ʷ Jesus answered. ³²"But a time is coming,ᵈ and has come, when you will be scattered,ᵉ each to his own home. You will leave me all alone.ᶠ Yet I am not alone, for my Father is with me.ᵍ

³³"I have told you these things, so that in me you may have peace.ʰ In this world you will have trouble.ⁱ But take heart! I have overcomeʲ the world."

Jesus Prays for Himself

17 After Jesus said this, he looked toward heavenᵏ and prayed:

"Father, the time has come.ˡ Glorify your Son, that your Son may glorify you.ᵐ ²For you granted him authority over all peopleⁿ that he might give eternal lifeᵒ to all those you have given him.ᵖ ³Now this is eternal life: that they may know you,ᑫ the only true God, and Jesus Christ, whom you have sent.ʳ ⁴I have brought you glory ˢ on earth by completing the work you gave me to do.ᵗ ⁵And now, Father, glorify meᵘ in your presence with the glory I had with youᵛ before the world began.ʷ

Jesus Prays for His Disciples

⁶"I have revealed youˣˣ to those whom you gave meʸ out of the world. They were yours; you gave them to me and they have obeyed your word. ⁷Now they know that everything you have given me comes from you. ⁸For I gave them the words you gave meᶻ and they accepted them. They knew with certainty that I came from you,ᵃ and they believed that you sent me.ᵇ ⁹I pray for them.ᶜ I am not praying for the world, but for those you have given me,ᵈ for they are yours. ¹⁰All I have is yours, and all you have is mine.ᵉ And glory has come to me

L Jn 14:13-14 ◀▶ Ro 8:31-39
E Jn 6:64 ◀▶ Jn 21:17

J Lk 6:22-23 ◀▶ Ac 5:41
K Jn 14:6 ◀▶ Jn 17:11-12

ʷ31 Or *"Do you now believe?"* ˣ6 Greek *your name*; also in verse 26

16:33 While Jesus warned his followers of the persecution that would afflict them, he also told them to take heart because he is the one who overcomes the world. Though the church will undergo persecution because of its faith, Christians can rejoice in the certainty that Jesus has won total victory over sin, death and Satan (see Mt 24:9-10).

through them. ¹¹"I will remain in the world no longer, but they are still in the world,ᶠ and I am coming to you.ᵍ Holy Father, protect them by the power of your name—the name you gave me—so that they may be oneʰ as we are one.ⁱ ¹²While I was with them, I protected them and kept them safe by that name you gave me. None has been lostʲ except the one doomed to destructionᵏ so that Scripture would be fulfilled.ˡ

¹³"I am coming to you now,ᵐ but I say these things while I am still in the world, so that they may have the full measure of my joyⁿ within them. ¹⁴I have given them your word and the world has hated them,ᵒ for they are not of the world any more than I am of the world.ᵖ ¹⁵My prayer is not that you take them out of the world but that you protect them from the evil one.ᑫ ¹⁶They are not of the world, even as I am not of it.ʳ ¹⁷Sanctifyʸ them by the truth; your word is truth.ˢ ¹⁸As you sent me into the world,ᵗ I have sent them into the world.ᵘ ¹⁹For them I sanctify myself, that they too may be truly sanctified.ᵛ

Jesus Prays for All Believers

²⁰"My prayer is not for them alone. I pray also for those who will believe in me through their message, ²¹that all of them may be one,ʷ Father, just as you are in me and I am in you.ˣ May they also be in us so that the world may believe that you have sent me.ʸ ²²I have given them the glory that you gave me,ᶻ that they may be one as we are one:ᵃ ²³I in them and you in me. May they be brought to complete unity to let the world know that you sent meᵇ and have loved themᶜ even as you have loved me.

²⁴"Father, I want those you have given meᵈ to be with me where I am,ᵉ and to see my glory,ᶠ the glory you have given me because you loved me before the creation of the world.ᵍ

²⁵"Righteous Father, though the world does not know you,ʰ I know you, and they know that you have sent me.ⁱ ²⁶I have made you known to them,ʲ and will continue to make you known in order that the love you have for me may be in themᵏ and that I myself may be in them."

Jesus Arrested

18:3–11pp — Mt 26:47–56; Mk 14:43–50; Lk 22:47–53

18 When he had finished praying, Jesus left with his disciples and crossed the Kidron Valley.ˡ On the other side there was an olive grove,ᵐ and he and his disciples went into it.ⁿ

²Now Judas, who betrayed him, knew the place, because Jesus had often met there with his disciples.ᵒ ³So Judas came to the grove, guidingᵖ a detachment of soldiers and some officials from the chief priests and Pharisees.ᑫ They were carrying torches, lanterns and weapons.

⁴Jesus, knowing all that was going to happen to him,ʳ went out and asked them, "Who is it you want?"ˢ

⁵"Jesus of Nazareth,"ᵗ they replied.

"I am he," Jesus said. (And Judas the traitor was standing there with them.) ⁶When Jesus said, "I am he," they drew back and fell to the ground.

⁷Again he asked them, "Who is it you want?"ᵘ

And they said, "Jesus of Nazareth."

⁸"I told you that I am he," Jesus answered. "If you are looking for me, then let these men go." ⁹This happened so that the words he had spoken would be fulfilled: "I have not lost one of those you gave me."ᶻᵛ

¹⁰Then Simon Peter, who had a sword, drew it and struck the high priest's servant, cutting off his right ear. (The servant's name was Malchus.)

¹¹Jesus commanded Peter, "Put your sword away! Shall I not drink the cupʷ the Father has given me?"

Jesus Taken to Annas

18:12,13pp — Mt 26:57

¹²Then the detachment of soldiers with its commander and the Jewish officialsˣ arrested Jesus. They bound him ¹³and brought him first to Annas, who was the father-in-law of Caiaphas,ʸ the high

---

y 17 Greek *hagiazo* (set apart for sacred use or make holy); also in verse 19 z 9 John 6:39

priest that year. ¹⁴Caiaphas was the one who had advised the Jews that it would be good if one man died for the people.ᶻ

Peter's First Denial
18:16–18pp — Mt 26:69,70; Mk 14:66–68; Lk 22:55–57

¹⁵Simon Peter and another disciple were following Jesus. Because this disciple was known to the high priest,ᵃ he went with Jesus into the high priest's courtyard,ᵇ ¹⁶but Peter had to wait outside at the door. The other disciple, who was known to the high priest, came back, spoke to the girl on duty there and brought Peter in.

¹⁷"You are not one of his disciples, are you?" the girl at the door asked Peter.

He replied, "I am not."ᶜ

¹⁸It was cold, and the servants and officials stood around a fireᵈ they had made to keep warm. Peter also was standing with them, warming himself.ᵉ

The High Priest Questions Jesus
18:19–24pp — Mt 26:59–68; Mk 14:55–65; Lk 22:63–71

¹⁹Meanwhile, the high priest questioned Jesus about his disciples and his teaching.

²⁰"I have spoken openly to the world," Jesus replied. "I always taught in synagoguesᶠ or at the temple,ᵍ where all the Jews come together. I said nothing in secret.ʰ ²¹Why question me? Ask those who heard me. Surely they know what I said."

²²When Jesus said this, one of the officialsⁱ nearby struck him in the face.ʲ "Is this the way you answer the high priest?" he demanded.

²³"If I said something wrong," Jesus replied, "testify as to what is wrong. But if I spoke the truth, why did you strike me?"ᵏ ²⁴Then Annas sent him, still bound, to Caiaphasˡ the high priest.ᵃ

Peter's Second and Third Denials
18:25–27pp — Mt 26:71–75; Mk 14:69–72; Lk 22:58–62

²⁵As Simon Peter stood warming himself,ᵐ he was asked, "You are not one of his disciples, are you?"

He denied it, saying, "I am not."ⁿ

²⁶One of the high priest's servants, a relative of the man whose ear Peter had cut off,ᵒ challenged him, "Didn't I see you with him in the olive grove?"ᵖ ²⁷Again Peter denied it, and at that moment a rooster began to crow.ᵠ

Jesus Before Pilate
18:29–40pp — Mt 27:11–18,20–23; Mk 15:2–15; Lk 23:2,3,18–25

²⁸Then the Jews led Jesus from Caiaphas to the palace of the Roman governor.ʳ By now it was early morning, and to avoid ceremonial uncleanness the Jews did not enter the palace;ˢ they wanted to be able to eat the Passover.ᵗ ²⁹So Pilate came out to them and asked, "What charges are you bringing against this man?"

³⁰"If he were not a criminal," they replied, "we would not have handed him over to you."

³¹Pilate said, "Take him yourselves and judge him by your own law."

"But we have no right to execute anyone," the Jews objected. ³²This happened so that the words Jesus had spoken indicating the kind of death he was going to dieᵘ would be fulfilled.

³³Pilate then went back inside the palace,ᵛ summoned Jesus and asked him, "Are you the king of the Jews?"ʷ

³⁴"Is that your own idea," Jesus asked, "or did others talk to you about me?"

³⁵"Am I a Jew?" Pilate replied. "It was your people and your chief priests who handed you over to me. What is it you have done?"

³⁶Jesus said, "My kingdomˣ is not of this world. If it were, my servants would fight to prevent my arrest by the Jews.ʸ But now my kingdom is from another place."ᶻ

³⁷"You are a king, then!" said Pilate.

Jesus answered, "You are right in saying I am a king. In fact, for this reason I was born, and for this I came into the world, to testify to the truth.ᵃ Everyone on the side of truth listens to me."ᵇ

l Jn 12:13–15 ◀ ▶ Jn 18:39
M Jn 12:13–15 ◀ ▶ Jn 18:39

ᵃ 24 Or (Now Annas had sent him, still bound, to Caiaphas the high priest.)

18:33–37, 39 Pilate unknowingly acknowledged Jesus as the "king of the Jews" (18:33). Jesus acknowledged, "For this reason I was born" (18:37).

³⁸"What is truth?" Pilate asked. With this he went out again to the Jews and said, "I find no basis for a charge against him.ᶜ ³⁹But it is your custom for me to release to you one prisoner at the time of the Passover. Do you want me to release 'the king of the Jews'?"

⁴⁰They shouted back, "No, not him! Give us Barabbas!" Now Barabbas had taken part in a rebellion.ᵈ

Jesus Sentenced to Be Crucified

19:1–16pp — Mt 27:27–31; Mk 15:16–20

19 Then Pilate took Jesus and had him flogged.ᵉ ²The soldiers twisted together a crown of thorns and put it on his head. They clothed him in a purple robe ³and went up to him again and again, saying, "Hail, king of the Jews!"ᶠ And they struck him in the face.ᵍ

⁴Once more Pilate came out and said to the Jews, "Look, I am bringing him outʰ to you to let you know that I find no basis for a charge against him."ⁱ ⁵When Jesus came out wearing the crown of thorns and the purple robe,ʲ Pilate said to them, "Here is the man!"

⁶As soon as the chief priests and their officials saw him, they shouted, "Crucify! Crucify!"

But Pilate answered, "You take him and crucify him.ᵏ As for me, I find no basis for a charge against him."ˡ

⁷The Jews insisted, "We have a law, and according to that law he must die,ᵐ because he claimed to be the Son of God."ⁿ

⁸When Pilate heard this, he was even more afraid, ⁹and he went back inside the palace.ᵒ "Where do you come from?" he asked Jesus, but Jesus gave him no answer.ᵖ ¹⁰"Do you refuse to speak to me?" Pilate said. "Don't you realize I have power either to free you or to crucify you?"

¹¹Jesus answered, "You would have no power over me if it were not given to you from above.ᵠ Therefore the one who handed me over to youʳ is guilty of a greater sin."

¹²From then on, Pilate tried to set Jesus free, but the Jews kept shouting, "If you let this man go, you are no friend of Caesar. Anyone who claims to be a kingˢ opposes Caesar."

¹³When Pilate heard this, he brought Jesus out and sat down on the judge's seatᵗ at a place known as the Stone Pavement (which in Aramaicᵘ is Gabbatha). ¹⁴It was the day of Preparationᵛ of Passover Week, about the sixth hour.ʷ

"Here is your king,"ˣ Pilate said to the Jews.

¹⁵But they shouted, "Take him away! Take him away! Crucify him!"

"Shall I crucify your king?" Pilate asked.

"We have no king but Caesar," the chief priests answered.

¹⁶Finally Pilate handed him over to them to be crucified.ʸ

The Crucifixion

19:17–24pp — Mt 27:33–44; Mk 15:22–32; Lk 23:33–43

So the soldiers took charge of Jesus. ¹⁷Carrying his own cross,ᶻ he went out to the place of the Skullᵃ (which in Aramaicᵇ is called Golgotha). ¹⁸Here they crucified him, and with him two othersᶜ—one on each side and Jesus in the middle.

¹⁹Pilate had a notice prepared and fastened to the cross. It read: JESUS OF NAZARETH,ᵈ THE KING OF THE JEWS.ᵉ ²⁰Many of the Jews read this sign, for the place where Jesus was crucified was near the city,ᶠ and the sign was written in Aramaic, Latin and Greek. ²¹The chief priests of the Jews protested to Pilate, "Do not write 'The King of the Jews,' but that this man claimed to be king of the Jews."ᵍ

19:2–3 The soldiers contemptuously hailed Jesus as "king of the Jews" (19:3) without knowing the truth of their statement.
19:12–15, 19–22 This account of Pilate's interaction with Jesus revealed his unknowing acknowledgment of Jesus' true position as Israel's king. Though the religious leaders challenged the title "The King of the Jews" (19:21), Pilate refused to back down and responded, "What I have written, I have written" (19:22).

²²Pilate answered, "What I have written, I have written."

²³When the soldiers crucified Jesus, they took his clothes, dividing them into four shares, one for each of them, with the undergarment remaining. This garment was seamless, woven in one piece from top to bottom. ²⁴"Let's not tear it," they said to one another. "Let's decide by lot who will get it."

This happened that the scripture might be fulfilled[h] which said,

"They divided my garments among them
and cast lots for my clothing."[b]

So this is what the soldiers did.

²⁵Near the cross[j] of Jesus stood his mother,[k] his mother's sister, Mary the wife of Clopas, and Mary Magdalene.[l] ²⁶When Jesus saw his mother[m] there, and the disciple whom he loved[n] standing nearby, he said to his mother, "Dear woman, here is your son," ²⁷and to the disciple, "Here is your mother." From that time on, this disciple took her into his home.

The Death of Jesus

19:29,30pp — Mt 27:48,50; Mk 15:36,37; Lk 23:36

²⁸Later, knowing that all was now completed,[o] and so that the Scripture would be fulfilled,[p] Jesus said, "I am thirsty." ²⁹A jar of wine vinegar[q] was there, so they soaked a sponge in it, put the sponge on a stalk of the hyssop plant, and lifted it to Jesus' lips. ³⁰When he had received the drink, Jesus said, "It is finished."[r] With that, he bowed his head and gave up his spirit.

³¹Now it was the day of Preparation,[s] and the next day was to be a special Sabbath. Because the Jews did not want the bodies left on the crosses[t] during the Sabbath, they asked Pilate to have the legs broken and the bodies taken down. ³²The soldiers therefore came and broke the legs of the first man who had been crucified with Jesus, and then those of the other.[u] ³³But when they came to Jesus and found that he was already dead, they did not break his legs. ³⁴Instead, one of the soldiers pierced[v] Jesus' side with a spear, bringing a sudden flow of blood and water.[w] ³⁵The man who saw it[x] has given testimony, and his testimony is true.[y] He knows that he tells the truth, and he testifies so that you also may believe. ³⁶These things happened so that the scripture would be fulfilled:[z] "Not one of his bones will be broken,"[ca] ³⁷and, as another scripture says, "They will look on the one they have pierced."[db]

The Burial of Jesus

19:38–42pp — Mt 27:57–61; Mk 15:42–47; Lk 23:50–56

³⁸Later, Joseph of Arimathea asked Pilate for the body of Jesus. Now Joseph was a disciple of Jesus, but secretly because he feared the Jews.[c] With Pilate's permission, he came and took the body away. ³⁹He was accompanied by Nicodemus,[d] the man who earlier had visited Jesus at night. Nicodemus brought a mixture of myrrh and aloes, about seventy-five pounds.[e] ⁴⁰Taking Jesus' body, the two of them wrapped it, with the spices, in strips of linen.[e] This was in accordance with Jewish burial customs.[f] ⁴¹At the place where Jesus was crucified, there was a garden, and in the garden a new tomb, in which no one had ever been laid. ⁴²Because it was the Jewish day of Preparation[g] and since the tomb was nearby,[h] they laid Jesus there.

The Empty Tomb

20:1–8pp — Mt 28:1–8; Mk 16:1–8; Lk 24:1–10

20 Early on the first day of the week, while it was still dark, Mary Magdalene[i] went to the tomb and saw that the stone had been removed from the entrance.[j] ²So she came running to Simon Peter and the other disciple, the one Jesus loved,[k] and said, "They have taken the Lord out of the tomb, and we don't know where they have put him!"[l]

³So Peter and the other disciple started for the tomb.[m] ⁴Both were running, but the other disciple outran Peter and reached the tomb first. ⁵He bent over and looked in[n] at the strips of linen[o] lying there but did not go in. ⁶Then Simon Peter, who was behind him, arrived and went into the tomb. He saw the strips of

B Jn 19:24 ◀ ▶ Ac 7:37–38

b 24 Psalm 22:18 c 36 Exodus 12:46; Num. 9:12; Psalm 34:20
d 37 Zech. 12:10 e 39 Greek *a hundred litrai* (about 34 kilograms)

linen lying there, ⁷as well as the burial cloth that had been around Jesus' head.ᵖ The cloth was folded up by itself, separate from the linen. ⁸Finally the other disciple, who had reached the tomb first,ᑫ also went inside. He saw and believed. ⁹(They still did not understand from Scriptureʳ that Jesus had to rise from the dead.)ˢ

Jesus Appears to Mary Magdalene

¹⁰Then the disciples went back to their homes, ¹¹but Mary stood outside the tomb crying. As she wept, she bent over to look into the tombᵗ ¹²and saw two angels in white,ᵘ seated where Jesus' body had been, one at the head and the other at the foot.

¹³They asked her, "Woman, why are you crying?"ᵛ

"They have taken my Lord away," she said, "and I don't know where they have put him."ʷ ¹⁴At this, she turned around and saw Jesus standing there,ˣ but she did not realize that it was Jesus.ʸ

¹⁵"Woman," he said, "why are you crying?ᶻ Who is it you are looking for?"

Thinking he was the gardener, she said, "Sir, if you have carried him away, tell me where you have put him, and I will get him."

¹⁶Jesus said to her, "Mary."

She turned toward him and cried out in Aramaic,ᵃ "Rabboni!"ᵇ (which means Teacher).

¹⁷Jesus said, "Do not hold on to me, for I have not yet returned to the Father. Go instead to my brothersᶜ and tell them, 'I am returning to my Fatherᵈ and your Father, to my God and your God.' "

¹⁸Mary Magdaleneᵉ went to the disciplesᶠ with the news: "I have seen the Lord!" And she told them that he had said these things to her.

Jesus Appears to His Disciples

¹⁹On the evening of that first day of the week, when the disciples were together, with the doors locked for fear of the Jews,ᵍ Jesus came and stood among them and said, "Peaceʰ be with you!" ²⁰After he said this, he showed them his hands and side.ʲ The disciples were overjoyedᵏ when they saw the Lord.

ᴶ ²¹Again Jesus said, "Peace be with you!ˡ As the Father has sent me,ᵐ I am sending you."ⁿ ²²And with that he breathed on them and said, "Receive the Holy Spirit.º ²³If you forgive anyone his sins, they are forgiven; if you do not forgive them, they are not forgiven."ᵖ ᴱ ᴷ ᴼ

Jesus Appears to Thomas

²⁴Now Thomasᑫ (called Didymus), one of the Twelve, was not with the disciples when Jesus came. ²⁵So the other disciples told him, "We have seen the Lord!"

But he said to them, "Unless I see the nail marks in his hands and put my finger where the nails were, and put my hand into his side,ʳ I will not believe it."ˢ

²⁶A week later his disciples were in the house again, and Thomas was with them. Though the doors were locked, Jesus came and stood among them and said, "Peaceᵗ be with you!"ᵘ ²⁷Then he said to Thomas, "Put your finger here; see my hands. Reach out your hand and put it into my side. Stop doubting and believe."ᵛ

²⁸Thomas said to him, "My Lord and my God!"

²⁹Then Jesus told him, "Because you have seen me, you have believed;ʷ blessed are those who have not seen and yet have believed."ˣ ᶠ

³⁰Jesus did many other miraculous signsʸ in the presence of his disciples, which are not recorded in this book.ᶻ ³¹But these are written that youᵐᵃʸ believeᵃ that Jesus is the Christ, the Son of God,ᵇ and that by believing you may have life in his name.ᶜ ᶠ

Jesus and the Miraculous Catch of Fish

21 Afterward Jesus appeared again to his disciples,ᵈ by the Sea of Tiberias.ᵍᵉ It happened this way: ²Simon Peter, Thomasᶠ (called Didymus), Nathanaelᵍ from Cana in Galilee,ʰ the sons of Zebedee,ⁱ and two other disciples were together. ³"I'm going out to fish," Simon Peter told them, and they said, "We'll go with you." So they went out and got into the boat, but that night they caught nothing.ʲ

E Jn 3:34 ◀▶ Ac 1:2
K Jn 17:11–12 ◀▶ Ac 3:26
O Jn 14:6 ◀▶ Ac 3:22–23
F Jn 12:46 ◀▶ Jn 20:31
F Jn 20:29 ◀▶ Jn 20:31

J Jn 16:7 ◀▶ Ac 9:31

⁴Early in the morning, Jesus stood on the shore, but the disciples did not realize that it was Jesus.ᵏ

⁵He called out to them, "Friends, haven't you any fish?"

"No," they answered.

⁶He said, "Throw your net on the right side of the boat and you will find some." When they did, they were unable to haul the net in because of the large number of fish.¹

⁷Then the disciple whom Jesus lovedᵐ said to Peter, "It is the Lord!" As soon as Simon Peter heard him say, "It is the Lord," he wrapped his outer garment around him (for he had taken it off) and jumped into the water. ⁸The other disciples followed in the boat, towing the net full of fish, for they were not far from shore, about a hundred yards.ʰ ⁹When they landed, they saw a fireⁿ of burning coals there with fish on it,ᵒ and some bread.

¹⁰Jesus said to them, "Bring some of the fish you have just caught."

¹¹Simon Peter climbed aboard and dragged the net ashore. It was full of large fish, 153, but even with so many the net was not torn. ¹²Jesus said to them, "Come and have breakfast." None of the disciples dared ask him, "Who are you?" They knew it was the Lord. ¹³Jesus came, took the bread and gave it to them, and did the same with the fish.ᵖ ¹⁴This was now the third time Jesus appeared to his disciplesᑫ after he was raised from the dead.

Jesus Reinstates Peter

¹⁵When they had finished eating, Jesus said to Simon Peter, "Simon son of John, do you truly love me more than these?"

"Yes, Lord," he said, "you know that I love you."ʳ

Jesus said, "Feed my lambs."ˢ

¹⁶Again Jesus said, "Simon son of John, do you truly love me?"

F Jn 6:31-32 ◀▶ 2Co 9:10

21:4 ᵏLk 24:16; Jn 20:14
21:6 ˡLk 5:4-7
21:7 ᵐS Jn 13:23
21:9 ⁿJn 18:18 ᵒver 10,13
21:13 ᵖver 9
21:14 ᑫJn 20:19, 26
21:15 ʳMt 26:33, 35; Jn 13:37 ˢLk 12:32
21:16 ᵗ2Sa 5:2; Eze 34:2; Mt 2:6; S Jn 10:11; Ac 20:28; 1Pe 5:2,3
21:17 ᵘJn 13:38 ᵛJn 16:30 ʷS ver 16
21:19 ˣJn 12:33; 18:32 ʸJn 13:36; 2Pe 1:14 ᶻS Mt 4:19
21:20 ᵃver 7; S Jn 13:23 ᵇJn 13:25
21:22 ᶜS Mt 16:27 ᵈver 19; S Mt 4:19
21:23 ᵉS Ac 1:16
21:24 ᶠS Jn 15:27 ᵍJn 19:35
21:25 ʰJn 20:30

He answered, "Yes, Lord, you know that I love you."

Jesus said, "Take care of my sheep."ᵗ

¹⁷The third time he said to him, "Simon son of John, do you love me?"

Peter was hurt because Jesus asked him the third time, "Do you love me?"ᵘ He said, "Lord, you know all things;ᵛ you know that I love you."

Jesus said, "Feed my sheep."ʷ ¹⁸I tell you the truth, when you were younger you dressed yourself and went where you wanted; but when you are old you will stretch out your hands, and someone else will dress you and lead you where you do not want to go." ¹⁹Jesus said this to indicate the kind of deathˣ by which Peter would glorify God.ʸ Then he said to him, "Follow me!"ᶻ

²⁰Peter turned and saw that the disciple whom Jesus lovedᵃ was following them. (This was the one who had leaned back against Jesus at the supper and had said, "Lord, who is going to betray you?")ᵇ ²¹When Peter saw him, he asked, "Lord, what about him?"

²²Jesus answered, "If I want him to remain alive until I return,ᶜ what is that to you? You must follow me."ᵈ ²³Because of this, the rumor spread among the brothersᵉ that this disciple would not die. But Jesus did not say that he would not die; he only said, "If I want him to remain alive until I return, what is that to you?"

²⁴This is the disciple who testifies to these thingsᶠ and who wrote them down. We know that his testimony is true.ᵍ

²⁵Jesus did many other things as well.ʰ If every one of them were written down, I suppose that even the whole world would not have room for the books that would be written.

E Jn 16:30 ◀▶ Ac 1:24
C Lk 21:34-36 ◀▶ Ac 1:11

ʰ 8 Greek about two hundred cubits (about 90 meters)

21:22-23 In this curious passage Jesus affirms the certainty of his second coming. It could occur at any time, and could theoretically, but not necessarily, occur before John's death. Jesus was simply affirming to his disciples that they should be watchfully waiting until he returns. After almost two thousand years the church still waits expectantly for Christ to come. The fulfillments of the prophecies that signal his coming point directly to the soon return of Jesus for his church.

NIV Harmony of the Gospels

	MATTHEW	MARK	LUKE	JOHN
A PREVIEW OF WHO JESUS IS				
Luke's purpose in writing a gospel			1:1–4	
John's prologue: Jesus Christ, the preexistent Word incarnate				1:1–18
Jesus' legal lineage through Joseph and natural lineage through Mary	1:1–17		3:23b–38	
THE EARLY YEARS OF JOHN THE BAPTIST				
John's birth foretold to Zechariah			1:5–25	
Jesus' birth foretold to Mary			1:26–38	
Mary's visit to Elizabeth and Elizabeth's song			1:39–45	
Mary's song of joy			1:46–56	
John's birth			1:57–66	
Zechariah's prophetic song			1:67–79	
John's growth and early life			1:80	
THE EARLY YEARS OF JESUS CHRIST				
Circumstances of Jesus' birth explained to Joseph	1:18–25			
Birth of Jesus			2:1–7	
Praise of the angels and witness of the shepherds			2:8–20	
Circumcision of Jesus			2:21	
Jesus presented in the temple with the homage of Simeon and Anna			2:22–38	
Visit of the Magi	2:1–12			
Escape into Egypt and murder of boys in Bethlehem	2:13–18			
Return to Nazareth	2:19–23		2:39	
Growth and early life of Jesus			2:40	
Jesus' first Passover in Jerusalem			2:41–50	
Jesus' growth to adulthood			2:51–52	
THE PUBLIC MINISTRY OF JOHN THE BAPTIST				
His ministry launched		1:1	3:1–2	
His person, proclamation, and baptism	3:1–6	1:2–6	3:3–6	
His messages to the Pharisees, Sadducees, crowds, tax collectors, and soldiers	3:7–10		3:7–14	
His description of Christ	3:11–12	1:7–8	3:15–18	
THE END OF JOHN'S MINISTRY AND THE BEGINNING OF CHRIST'S PUBLIC MINISTRY				
Jesus' baptism by John	3:13–17	1:9–11	3:21–23a	
Jesus' temptation in the desert	4:1–11	1:12–13	4:1–13	
John's testimony about himself to the priests and Levites				1:19–28
John's testimony to Jesus as the Son of God				1:29–34
Jesus' first followers				1:35–51
Jesus' first miracle: water becomes wine				2:1–11
Jesus' first stay in Capernaum with his relatives and early disciples				2:12
First cleansing of the temple at the Passover				2:13–22
Early response to Jesus' miracles				2:23–25
Nicodemus's interview with Jesus				3:1–21
John superseded by Jesus				3:22–36
Jesus' departure from Judea	4:12	1:14a	3:19–20; 4:14a	4:1–4
Discussion with a Samaritan woman				4:5–26
Challenge of a spiritual harvest				4:27–38
Evangelization of Sychar				4:39–42
Arrival in Galilee				4:43–45

NIV Harmony of the Gospels

	MATTHEW	MARK	LUKE	JOHN
THE MINISTRY OF CHRIST IN GALILEE				
Opposition at Home and a New Headquarters				
Nature of the Galilean ministry	4:17	1:14b–15	4:14b–15	
Child at Capernaum healed by Jesus while at Cana				4:46–54
Ministry and rejection at Nazareth			4:16–31a	
Move to Capernaum	4:13–16			
Disciples Called and Ministry Throughout Galilee				
Call of the four	4:18–22	1:16–20	5:1–11	
Teaching in the synagogue of Capernaum authenticated by healing a demoniac		1:21–28	4:31b–37	
Peter's mother-in-law and others healed	8:14–17	1:29–34	4:38–41	
Tour of Galilee with Simon and others	4:23–25	1:35–39	4:42–44	
Cleansing of a man with leprosy, followed by much publicity	8:2–4	1:40–45	5:12–16	
Forgiving and healing of a paralytic	9:1–8	2:1–12	5:17–26	
Call of Matthew	9:9	2:13–14	5:27–28	
Banquet at Matthew's house	9:10–13	2:15–17	5:29–32	
Jesus defends his disciples for feasting instead of fasting with three parables	9:14–17	2:18–22	5:33–39	
Sabbath Controversies and Withdrawals				
Jesus heals an invalid on the Sabbath				5:1–9
Effort to kill Jesus for breaking the Sabbath and saying he was equal with God				5:10–18
Discourse demonstrating the Son's equality with the Father				5:19–47
Controversy over disciples' picking grain on the Sabbath	12:1–8	2:23–28	6:1–5	
Healing of a man's shriveled hand on the Sabbath	12:9–14	3:1–6	6:6–11	
Withdrawal to the Sea of Galilee with large crowds from many places	12:15–21	3:7–12		
Appointment of the Twelve and Sermon on the Mount				
Twelve apostles chosen		3:13–19	6:12–16	
Setting of the Sermon	5:1–2		6:17–19	
Blessings of those who inherit the kingdom and woes to those who do not	5:3–12		6:20–26	
Responsibility while awaiting the kingdom	5:13–16			
Law, righteousness, and the kingdom	5:17–20			
Six contrasts in interpreting the law	5:21–48		6:27–30, 32–36	
Three hypocritical "acts of righteousness" to be avoided	6:1–18			
Three prohibitions against avarice, harsh judgment, and unwise exposure of sacred things	6:19–7:6		6:37–42	
Application and conclusion	7:7–27		6:31, 43–49	
Reaction of the crowds	7:28–8:1			
Growing Fame and Emphasis on Repentance				
A centurion's faith and the healing of his servant	8:5–13		7:1–10	
A widow's son raised at Nain			7:11–17	
John the Baptist's relationship to the kingdom	11:2–19		7:18–35	
Woes upon Korazin and Bethsaida for failure to repent	11:20–30			
Christ's feet anointed by a sinful but contrite woman			7:36–50	
First Public Rejection by Jewish Leaders				
A tour with the Twelve and other followers			8:1–3	

NIV Harmony of the Gospels

	MATTHEW	MARK	LUKE	JOHN
Blasphemous accusation by the teachers of the law and Pharisees	12:22–37	3:20–30		
Request for a sign refused	12:38–45			
Announcement of new spiritual kinship	12:46–50	3:31–35	8:19–21	
Secrets About the Kingdom Given in Parables				
To the Crowds by the Sea				
The setting of the parables	13:1–3a	4:1–2	8:4	
The parable of the soils	13:3b–23	4:3–25	8:5–18	
The parable of the seed's spontaneous growth		4:26–29		
The parable of the weeds	13:24–30			
The parable of the mustard tree	13:31–32	4:30–32		
The parable of the leavened loaf	13:33–35	4:33–34		
To the Disciples in the House				
The parable of the weeds explained	13:36–43			
The parable of the hidden treasure	13:44			
The parable of the valuable pearl	13:45–46			
The parable of the net	13:47–50			
The parable of the house owner	13:51–53			
Continuing Opposition				
Crossing the lake and calming the storm	8:18, 23–27	4:35–41	8:22–25	
Healing the Gerasene demoniacs and resultant opposition	8:28–34	5:1–20	8:26–39	
Return to Galilee, healing of a woman who touched Jesus' garment, and raising of Jairus's daughter	9:18–26	5:21–43	8:40–56	
Three miracles of healing and another blasphemous accusation	9:27–34			
Final visit to unbelieving Nazareth	13:54–58	6:1–6a		
Final Galilean Campaign				
Shortage of workers	9:35–38	6:6b		
Commissioning of the Twelve	10:1–42	6:7–11	9:1–5	
Workers sent out	11:1	6:12–13	9:6	
Antipas's mistaken identification of Jesus	14:1–2	6:14–16	9:7–9	
Earlier imprisonment and beheading of John the Baptist	14:3–12	6:17–29		
THE MINISTRY OF CHRIST AROUND GALILEE				
Lesson on the Bread of Life				
Return of the workers		6:30	9:10a	
Withdrawal from Galilee	14:13–14	6:31–34	9:10b–11	6:1–3
Feeding the five thousand	14:15–21	6:35–44	9:12–17	6:4–13
A premature attempt to make Jesus king blocked	14:22–23	6:45–46		6:14–15
Walking on the water during a storm on the lake	14:24–33	6:47–52		6:16–21
Healings at Gennesaret	14:34–36	6:53–56		
Discourse on the true bread of life				6:22–59
Defection among the disciples				6:60–71
Lesson on the Leaven of the Pharisees, Sadducees, and Herodians				
Conflict over the tradition of ceremonial uncleanness	15:1–3a, 7–9b, 3b–6, 10–20	7:1–23		7:1
Ministry to a believing Greek woman in Tyre and Sidon	15:21–28	7:24–30		
Healings in Decapolis	15:29–31	7:31–37		
Feeding the four thousand in Decapolis	15:32–38	8:1–9a		
Return to Galilee and encounter with the Pharisees and Sadducees	15:39–16:4	8:9b–12		

NIV Harmony of the Gospels

	MATTHEW	MARK	LUKE	JOHN
Warning about the error of the Pharisees, Sadducees, and Herodians	16:5–12	8:13–21		
Healing a blind man at Bethsaida		8:22–26		
Lesson of Messiahship Learned and Confirmed				
Peter's identification of Jesus as the Christ and first prophecy of the church	16:13–20	8:27–30	9:18–21	
First direct prediction of the rejection, crucifixion, and resurrection	16:21–26	8:31–37	9:22–25	
Coming of the Son of Man and judgment	16:27–28	8:38—9:1	9:26–27	
Transfiguration of Jesus	17:1–8	9:2–8	9:28–36a	
Discussion of resurrection, Elijah, and John the Baptist	17:9–13	9:9–13	9:36b	
Lessons on Responsibility to Others				
Healing of demoniac boy and unbelief rebuked	17:14–20	9:14–29	9:37–43a	
Second prediction of Jesus' death and resurrection	17:22–23	9:30–32	9:43b–45	
Payment of temple tax	17:24–27			
Rivalry over greatness in the kingdom	18:1–5	9:33–37	9:46–48	
Warning against causing believers to sin	18:6–14	9:38–50	9:49–50	
Treatment and forgiveness of a sinning brother	18:15–35			
Journey to Jerusalem for the Feast of Tabernacles				
Complete commitment required of followers	8:19–22		9:57–62	
Ridicule by Jesus' half-brothers				7:2–9
Journey through Samaria			9:51–56	7:10
THE LATER JUDEAN MINISTRY OF CHRIST				
Ministry Beginning at the Feast of Tabernacles				
Mixed reaction to Jesus' teaching and miracles				7:11–31
Frustrated attempt to arrest Jesus				7:32–52
Jesus' forgiveness of a woman caught in adultery				[7:53—8:11]
Conflict over Jesus' claim to be the light of the world				8:12–20
Jesus' relationship to God the Father				8:21–30
Jesus' relationship to Abraham, and attempted stoning				8:31–59
Healing of a man born blind				9:1–7
Response of the blind man's neighbors				9:8–12
Examination and excommunication of the blind man by the Pharisees				9:13–34
Jesus' identification of himself to the blind man				9:35–38
Spiritual blindness of the Pharisees				9:39–41
Allegory of the good shepherd and the thief				10:1–18
Further division among the Jews				10:19–21
Private Lessons on Loving Service and Prayer				
Commissioning of the seventy			10:1–16	
Return of the seventy			10:17–24	
Story of the good Samaritan			10:25–37	
Jesus' visit with Mary and Martha			10:38–42	
Lesson on how to pray and parable of the bold friend			11:1–13	
Second Debate with the Teachers of the Law and the Pharisees				
A third blasphemous accusation and a second debate			11:14–36	
Woes to the Pharisees and the teachers of the law while eating with a Pharisee			11:37–54	
Warning the disciples about hypocrisy			12:1–12	
Warning about greed and trust in wealth			12:13–34	

NIV Harmony of the Gospels

	MATTHEW	MARK	LUKE	JOHN
Warning against being unprepared for the Son of Man's coming				12:35–48
Warning about the coming division			12:49–53	
Warning against failing to discern the present time			12:54–59	
Two alternatives: repent or perish			13:1–9	
Opposition from a synagogue ruler for healing a woman on the Sabbath			13:10–21	
Another attempt to stone or arrest Jesus for blasphemy at the Feast of Dedication				10:22–39

THE MINISTRY OF CHRIST IN AND AROUND PEREA

Principles of Discipleship

	MATTHEW	MARK	LUKE	JOHN
From Jerusalem to Perea				10:40–42
Question about salvation and entering the kingdom			13:22–30	
Anticipation of Jesus' coming death and his sorrow over Jerusalem			13:31–35	
Healing of a man with dropsy while eating with a prominent Pharisee on the Sabbath, and three parables suggested by the occasion			14:1–24	
Cost of discipleship			14:25–35	
Parables in defense of association with sinners			15:1–32	
Parable to teach the proper use of money			16:1–13	
Story to teach the danger of wealth			16:14–31	
Four lessons on discipleship			17:1–10	
Sickness and death of Lazarus				11:1–16
Lazarus raised from the dead				11:17–44
Decision of the Sanhedrin to put Jesus to death				11:45–54

Teaching While on Final Journey to Jerusalem

	MATTHEW	MARK	LUKE	JOHN
Healing of ten lepers while passing through Samaria and Galilee			17:11–21	
Instructions regarding the Son of Man's coming			17:22–37	
Two parables on prayer: the persistent widow, and the Pharisee and the tax collector			18:1–14	
Conflict with Pharisaic teaching on divorce	19:1–12	10:1–12		
Example of little children in relation to the kingdom	19:13–15	10:13–16	18:15–17	
Riches and the kingdom	19:16–30	10:17–31	18:18–30	
Parable of the landowner's sovereignty	20:1–16			
Third prediction of Jesus' death and resurrection	20:17–19	10:32–34	18:31–34	
Warning against ambitious pride	20:20–28	10:35–45		
Healing of blind Bartimaeus and his companion	20:29–34	10:46–52	18:35–43	
Salvation of Zacchaeus			19:1–10	
Parable to teach responsibility while the kingdom is delayed			19:11–28	

THE FORMAL PRESENTATION OF CHRIST TO ISRAEL AND THE RESULTING CONFLICT

Triumphal Entry and the Fig Tree

	MATTHEW	MARK	LUKE	JOHN
Arrival at Bethany				11:55—12:1, 9–11
Triumphal entry into Jerusalem	21:1–3, 6–7, 4–5, 8–11, 14–17	11:1–11	19:29–44	12:12–19
Cursing of the fig tree having leaves but no figs	21:18–19a	11:12–14		
Second cleansing of the temple	21:12–13	11:15–18	19:45–48	
Request of some Greeks to see Jesus and necessity of the Son of Man's being lifted up				12:20–36a

NIV Harmony of the Gospels

	MATTHEW	MARK	LUKE	JOHN
Different responses to Jesus and Jesus' response to the crowds				12:36b–50
Withered fig tree and the lesson on faith	21:19b–22	11:19–25	21:37–38	
Official Challenge to Christ's Authority				
Questioning of Jesus' authority by the chief priests, teachers of the law, and elders	21:23–27	11:27–33	20:1–8	
Jesus' response with his own question and three parables	21:28—22:14	12:1–12	20:9–19	
Attempts by Pharisees and Herodians to trap Jesus with a question about paying taxes to Caesar	22:15–22	12:13–17	20:20–26	
Sadducees' puzzling question about the resurrection	22:23–33	12:18–27	20:27–40	
A Pharisee's legal question	22:34–40	12:28–34		
Christ's Response to His Enemies' Challenges				
Christ's relationship to David as son and Lord	22:41–46	12:35–37	20:41–44	
Seven woes against the teachers of the law and Pharisees	23:1–36	12:38–40	20:45–47	
Jesus' sorrow over Jerusalem	23:37–39			
A poor widow's gift of all she had		12:41–44	21:1–4	
PROPHECIES IN PREPARATION FOR THE DEATH OF CHRIST				
The Olivet Discourse: Jesus Speaks Prophetically About the Temple and His Own Second Coming				
Setting of the discourse	24:1–3	13:1–4	21:5–7	
Beginning of birth pains	24:4–14	13:5–13	21:8–19	
Abomination of desolation and subsequent distress	24:15–28	13:14–23	21:20–24	
Coming of the Son of Man	24:29–31	13:24–27	21:25–27	
Signs of nearness but unknown time	24:32–41	13:28–32	21:28–33	
Five parables to teach watchfulness and faithfulness	24:42—25:30	13:33–37	21:34–36	
Judgment at the Son of Man's coming	25:31–46			
Arrangements for Betrayal				
Plot by the Sanhedrin to arrest and kill Jesus	26:1–5	14:1–2	22:1–2	
Mary's anointing of Jesus for burial	26:6–13	14:3–9		12:2–8
Judas' agreement to betray Jesus	26:14–16	14:10–11	22:3–6	
The Last Supper				
Preparation for the Passover meal	26:17–19	14:12–16	22:7–13	
Beginning of the Passover meal and dissension among the disciples over greatness	26:20	14:17	22:14–16, 24–30	
Washing the disciples' feet				13:1–20
Identification of the betrayer	26:21–25	14:18–21	22:21–23	13:21–30
Prediction of Peter's denial	26:31–35	14:27–31	22:31–38	13:31–38
Conclusion of the meal and the Lord's Supper instituted (1 Cor. 11:23–26)	26:26–29	14:22–25	22:17–20	
Discourse and Prayers from the Upper Room to Gethsemane				
Questions about his destination, the Father, and the Holy Spirit answered				14:1–31
The vine and the branches				15:1–17
Opposition from the world				15:18—16:4
Coming and ministry of the Spirit				16:5–15
Prediction of joy over his resurrection				16:16–22
Promise of answered prayer and peace				16:23–33
Jesus' prayer for his disciples and all who believe				17:1–26
Jesus' three agonizing prayers in Gethsemane	26:30, 36–46	14:26, 32–42	22:39–46	18:1

NIV Harmony of the Gospels

	MATTHEW	MARK	LUKE	JOHN
THE DEATH OF CHRIST				
Betrayal and Arrest				
Jesus betrayed, arrested, and forsaken	26:47–56	14:43–52	22:47–53	18:2–12
Trial				
First Jewish phase, before Annas				18:13–14, 19–23
Second Jewish phase, before Caiaphas and the Sanhedrin	26:57, 59–68	14:53, 55–65	22:54a, 63–65	18:24
Peter's denials	26:58, 69–75	14:54, 66–72	22:54b–62	18:15–18, 25–27
Third Jewish phase, before the Sanhedrin	27:1	15:1a	22:66–71	
Remorse and suicide of Judas Iscariot (Acts 1:18–19)	27:3–10			
First Roman phase, before Pilate	27:2, 11–14	15:1b–5	23:1–5	18:28–38
Second Roman phase, before Herod Antipas			23:6–12	
Third Roman phase, before Pilate	27:15–26	15:6–15	23:13–25	18:39—19:16a
Crucifixion				
Mockery by the Roman soldiers	27:27–30	15:16–19		
Journey to Golgotha	27:31–34	15:20–23	23:26–33a	19:16b–17
First three hours of crucifixion	27:35–44	15:24–32	23:33b–43	19:18, 23–24, 19–22, 25–27
Last three hours of crucifixion	27:45–50	15:33–37	23:44–45a, 46	19:28–30
Witness of Jesus' death	27:51–56	15:38–41	23:45b, 47–49	
Burial				
Certification of Jesus' death and procurement of his body	27:57–58	15:42–45	23:50–52	19:31–38
Jesus' body placed in a tomb	27:59–60	15:46	23:53–54	19:39–42
The tomb watched by the women and guarded by the soldiers	27:61–66	15:47	23:55–56	
THE RESURRECTION AND ASCENSION OF CHRIST				
The Empty Tomb				
The tomb visited by the women	28:1	16:1		
The stone rolled away	28:2–4			
The tomb found to be empty by the women	28:5–8	16:2–8	24:1–8	20:1
The tomb found to be empty by Peter and John			24:9–12	20:2–10
The Post Resurrection Appearances				
Appearance to Mary Magdalene		[16:9–11]		20:11–18
Appearance to the other women	28:9–10			
Report of the soldiers to the Jewish authorities	28:11–15			
Appearance to the two disciples traveling to Emmaus		[16:12–13]	24:13–32	
Report of the two disciples to the rest (1 Cor. 15:5a)			24:33–35	
Appearance to the ten assembled disciples		[16:14]	24:36–43	20:19–25
Appearance to the eleven assembled disciples (1 Cor. 15:5b)				20:26–31
Appearance to the seven disciples while fishing				21:1–25
Appearance to the Eleven in Galilee (1 Cor. 15:6)	28:16–20	[16:15–18]		
Appearance to James, Jesus' brother (1 Cor. 15:7)				
Appearance to the disciples in Jerusalem (Acts 1:3–8)			24:44–49	
The Ascension				
Christ's parting blessing and departure (Acts 1:9–12)		[16:19–20]	24:50–53	

Major Archaelogical Finds Relating to the NT

SITE OR ARTIFACT	LOCATION	RELATING SCRIPTURE
ISRAEL		
Herod's temple	Jerusalem	Lk 1:9
Herod's winter palace	Jericho	Mt 2:4
The Herodium (possible site of Herod's tomb)	Near Bethlehem	Mt 2:19
Masada	Southwest of Dead Sea	Cf. Lk 21:20
Early synagogue	Capernaum	Mk 1:21
Pool of Siloam	Jerusalem	Jn 9:7
Pool of Bethesda	Jerusalem	Jn 5:2
Pilate inscription	Caesarea	Lk 3:1
Inscription: Gentile entrance of temple sanctuary	Jerusalem	Ac 21:27–29
Skeletal remains of crucified man	Jerusalem	Lk 23:33
Peter's house	Capernaum	Mt 8:14
Jacob's well	Nablus	Jn 4:5–6
ASIA MINOR		
Derbe inscription	Kerti Hüyük	Ac 14:20
Sergius Paulus inscription	Antioch in Pisidia	Ac 13:6–7
Zeus altar (Satan's throne?)	Pergamum	Rev 2:13
Fourth-century B.C. walls	Assos	Ac 20:13–14
Artemis temple and altar	Ephesus	Ac 19:27–28
Ephesian theater	Ephesus	Ac 19:29
Silversmith shops	Ephesus	Ac 19:24
Artemis statues	Ephesus	Ac 19:35
GREECE		
Erastus inscription	Corinth	Ro 16:23
Synagogue inscription	Corinth	Ac 18:4
Meat market inscription	Corinth	1Co 10:25
Cult dining rooms (in Asklepius and Demeter temples)	Corinth	1Co 8:10
Court (*bema*)	Corinth	Ac 18:12
Marketplace (*bema*)	Philippi	Ac 16:19
Starting gate for races	Isthmia	1Co 9:24,26
Gallio inscription	Delphi	Ac 18:12
Egnatian Way	Kavalla (Neapolis), Philippi, Apollonia, Thessalonica	Cf. Ac 16:11–12; 17:1
Politarch inscription	Thessalonica	Ac 17:6
ITALY		
Tomb of Augustus	Rome	Lk 2:1
Mamertime Prison	Rome	2Ti 1:16–17; 2:9; 4:6–8
Appian Way	Puteoli to Rome	Ac 28:13–16
Golden House of Nero	Rome	Cf. Ac 25:10; 1Pe 2:13
Arch of Titus	Rome	Cf. Lk 19:43–44; 21:6,20

Acts

Author: Luke

Theme: The church is established worldwide as the gospel spreads

Date of Writing: c. A.D. 63–70

Outline of Acts
  I. Jesus' Final Instructions (1:1–11)
  II. The Church in Palestine (1:12—12:25)
   A. From Judea to Galilee and Samaria (1:12—9:31)
   B. From Phoenicia to Cyprus and Antioch (9:32—12:25)
  III. The Church Expands to Rome (13:1—28:31)
   A. From Phrygia to Galatia (13:1—15:35)
    1. Paul's first missionary journey (13:1—14:28)
    2. The meeting at Jerusalem (15:1-35)
   B. Paul goes to Macedonia (15:36—21:16)
    1. Paul's second missionary journey (15:36—18:22)
    2. Paul's third missionary journey (18:23—20:2)
    3. Paul's work in Caesarea (20:3—21:16)
  IV. Paul's Mission in Rome (21:17—28:31)

ALTHOUGH THE AUTHOR of the book of Acts is anonymous, inferences from the book and from outside Scripture point to Luke as the author of this companion volume to the Gospel of Luke. Luke personally participated in many of the events recorded in this book and would have learned about other events through firsthand reports from Paul, Peter and the other disciples. With his extensive knowledge of the laws and customs of the first-century Romans, Luke's account of the spread of Christianity in the book of Acts rings with historical accuracy. Luke probably completed this account while Paul was still a prisoner in Rome.

Addressed to Theophilus, the book of Acts provides the only chronological account in the NT that shows the spread of Christianity after the crucifixion of Christ. This pivotal book traces the growth of the church throughout the Roman empire and records early stories of evangelism, ways to defend our faith, the work of the Holy Spirit and the foundational doctrines of Christianity. Although the disciples are referred to in the first chapter, the focus of Acts quickly turns to the apostle Peter's role in the Jerusalem church and Paul's emergence as the leader of the missionary effort to bring the gospel to the Gentiles.

Though the book of Acts is concerned with the expansion of the church, doctrinal messages permeate the book too. While recording specific fulfillment of prophecies about the early church, Luke places tremendous emphasis on the work of the Holy Spirit to empower the church to reach a lost world. Peter's sermon on the day of Pentecost (see 2:14–40) and Paul's sermon at Antioch (see 13:16–42) stress the resurrection of Jesus as well as his standing as the Messiah who fulfilled the words of the OT prophets (see 17:1–3). The doctrinal background of Acts forms the basis for the teaching found in the remainder of the NT epistles.

Jesus Taken Up Into Heaven

1 In my former book,[a] Theophilus, I wrote about all that Jesus began to do and to teach[b] ²until the day he was taken up to heaven,[c] after giving instructions[d] through the Holy Spirit to the apostles[e] he had chosen.[f] ³After his suffering, he showed himself to these men and gave many convincing proofs that he was alive. He appeared to them[g] over a period of forty days and spoke about the kingdom of God.[h] ⁴On one occasion, while he was eating with them, he gave them this command: "Do not leave Jerusalem, but wait[i] for the gift my Father promised, which you have heard me speak about.[j] ⁵For John baptized with[a] water,[k] but in a few days you will be baptized with the Holy Spirit."[l]

⁶So when they met together, they asked him, "Lord, are you at this time going to restore[m] the kingdom to Israel?"

⁷He said to them: "It is not for you to know the times or dates the Father has

1:1 [a] Lk 1:1-4
[b] Lk 3:23

1:2 [c] ver 9,11;
S Mk 16:19
[d] Mt 28:19,20
[e] S Mk 6:30
[f] Jn 13:18; 15:16,19

1:3 [g] Mt 28:17;
Lk 24:34,36;
Jn 20:19,26; 21:1,14; 1Co 15:5-7
[h] S Mt 3:2

1:4 [i] Ps 27:14
[j] Lk 24:49;
Jn 14:16; Ac 2:33

1:5 [k] S Mk 1:4
[l] S Mk 1:8

1:6 [m] Mt 17:11;
Ac 3:21

[a] 5 Or in

E Jn 20:22 ◀▶ Ac 1:16
L Jn 16:13 ◀▶ Ac 2:4
T Jn 16:7–15 ◀▶ Ac 1:16
B Jn 16:13 ◀▶ Ac 1:8
P Jn 16:7–15 ◀▶ Ac 1:8
W Jn 16:7 ◀▶ Ac 6:3

I Jn 19:19–22 ◀▶ Ac 2:29–31

1:4–8 The first prophecy in Acts is Christ's prophecy to his disciples concerning the baptism with the Holy Spirit. His followers seemed more interested in when he would defeat the brutal persecution of Rome and establish his Messianic kingdom. They knew the OT prophets had clearly predicted the Messiah's victory over Rome (see Da 2:44–45). Following his supernatural victory over death, the disciples wondered aloud if Jesus would now restore the kingdom. Though Jesus did not berate them for their anticipation of a restored kingdom, they mistakenly assumed that he would establish his kingdom immediately. Jesus' words to them are a warning to all believers to avoid useless speculation about the precise time of his return.

Instead, Jesus directed their thoughts to a spiritual kingdom. He promised that they would be supernaturally empowered to evangelize the entire world and prophesied that they would "be my witnesses in Jerusalem, and in all Judea and Samaria, and to the ends of the earth" (1:8). By these words Jesus predicted the unprecedented growth and penetration of the gospel message to every nation and tribe on earth. Two thousand years later we are witnesses to the nearly complete fulfillment of these words as every major language group in the world has the gospel message in its native tongue.

set by his own authority. ⁸But you will receive power when the Holy Spirit comes on you; and you will be my witnesses in Jerusalem, and in all Judea and Samaria, and to the ends of the earth."

⁹After he said this, he was taken up before their very eyes, and a cloud hid him from their sight.

¹⁰They were looking intently up into the sky as he was going, when suddenly two men dressed in white stood beside them. ¹¹"Men of Galilee," they said, "why do you stand here looking into the sky? This same Jesus, who has been taken from you into heaven, will come back in the same way you have seen him go into heaven."

Matthias Chosen to Replace Judas

¹²Then they returned to Jerusalem from the hill called the Mount of Olives, a Sabbath day's walk from the city. ¹³When they arrived, they went upstairs to the room where they were staying. Those present were Peter, John, James and Andrew; Philip and Thomas, Bartholomew and Matthew; James son of Alphaeus and Simon the Zealot, and Judas son of James. ¹⁴They all joined together constantly in prayer, along with the women and Mary the mother of Jesus, and with his brothers.

¹⁵In those days Peter stood up among the believers (a group numbering about a hundred and twenty) ¹⁶and said, "Brothers, the Scripture had to be fulfilled which the Holy Spirit spoke long ago through the mouth of David concerning Judas, who served as guide for those who arrested Jesus— ¹⁷he was one of our number and shared in this ministry."

¹⁸(With the reward he got for his wickedness, Judas bought a field; there he fell headlong, his body burst open and all his intestines spilled out. ¹⁹Everyone in Jerusalem heard about this, so they called that field in their language Akeldama, that is, Field of Blood.)

²⁰"For," said Peter, "it is written in the book of Psalms,

" 'May his place be deserted;
  let there be no one to dwell in it,'

and,

" 'May another take his place of
  leadership.'

²¹Therefore it is necessary to choose one of the men who have been with us the whole time the Lord Jesus went in and out among us, ²²beginning from John's baptism to the time when Jesus was taken up from us. For one of these must become a witness with us of his resurrection."

²³So they proposed two men: Joseph called Barsabbas (also known as Justus) and Matthias. ²⁴Then they prayed, "Lord, you know everyone's heart. Show us which of these two you have chosen ²⁵to take over this apostolic ministry, which Judas left to go where he belongs." ²⁶Then they cast lots, and the lot fell to Matthias; so he was added to the eleven apostles.

The Holy Spirit Comes at Pentecost

2 When the day of Pentecost came, they were all together in one place. ²Suddenly a sound like the blowing of a violent wind came from heaven and filled the whole house where they were sit-

---

B Ac 1:4–5 ◀ ▶ Ac 2:1–18
G Jn 16:13–15 ◀ ▶ Ac 2:3–18
M Jn 16:7–15 ◀ ▶ Ac 2:1–18
P Ac 1:4–5 ◀ ▶ Ac 2:15–18
C Jn 21:22–23 ◀ ▶ 1Co 1:7–8
E Ac 1:2 ◀ ▶ Ac 2:1–18
T Ac 1:2 ◀ ▶ Ac 2:1–18

E Jn 21:17 ◀ ▶ Ac 15:8
H Jn 15:6 ◀ ▶ Ac 2:34–35
B Ac 1:8 ◀ ▶ Ac 2:33
E Ac 1:16 ◀ ▶ Ac 2:33
M Ac 1:8 ◀ ▶ Ac 4:29–31
T Ac 1:16 ◀ ▶ Ac 6:3
N Jn 15:26 ◀ ▶ Ac 2:33

ᵇ 12 That is, about 3/4 mile (about 1,100 meters)   ᶜ 15 Greek *brothers*
ᵈ 20 Psalm 69:25   ᵉ 20 Psalm 109:8

1:10–11 These two men in white clothing were angels sent by God to instruct the disciples. These angels indicated that Jesus was taken away from them up into heaven, but declared that he "will come back in the same way you have seen him go into heaven" (1:11). Jesus will return from heaven to earth following the Battle of Armageddon just as he ascended—in full sight of his followers.

2:1 *Dispensation of the Church.* This dispensation corresponds to the church age, beginning at the cross and continuing until the resurrection of the saints (see 1Th 4:13–17). During this time period,

ting.ᵛ ³They saw what seemed to be tongues of fire that separated and came to rest on each of them. ⁴All of them were filled with the Holy Spiritʷ and began to speak in other tongues⁄ˣ as the Spirit enabled them.

⁵Now there were staying in Jerusalem God-fearingʸ Jews from every nation under heaven. ⁶When they heard this sound, a crowd came together in bewilderment, because each one heard them speaking in his own language. ⁷Utterly amazed,ᶻ they asked: "Are not all these men who are speaking Galileans?ᵃ ⁸Then how is it that each of us hears them in his own native language? ⁹Parthians, Medes and Elamites; residents of Mesopotamia, Judea and Cappadocia,ᵇ Pontusᶜ and Asia,ᵈ ¹⁰Phrygiaᵉ and Pamphylia,ᶠ Egypt and the parts of Libya near Cyrene;ᵍ visitors from Rome ¹¹(both Jews and converts to Judaism); Cretans and Arabs—we hear them declaring the wonders of God in our own tongues!" ¹²Amazed and perplexed, they asked one another, "What does this mean?"

¹³Some, however, made fun of them and said, "They have had too much wine.ᵍ"ʰ

Peter Addresses the Crowd

¹⁴Then Peter stood up with the Eleven, raised his voice and addressed the crowd: "Fellow Jews and all of you who live in Jerusalem, let me explain this to you; listen carefully to what I say. ¹⁵These men are not drunk, as you suppose. It's only nine in the morning!ⁱ ¹⁶No, this is what was spoken by the prophet Joel:

¹⁷" 'In the last days, God says,
   I will pour out my Spirit on all
      people.ʲ
   Your sons and daughters will
      prophesy,ᵏ
   your young men will see visions,
   your old men will dream dreams.
¹⁸Even on my servants, both men and
      women,
   I will pour out my Spirit in those
      days,
   and they will prophesy.ˡ
¹⁹I will show wonders in the heaven
      above
   and signs on the earth below,ᵐ

P Ac 1:8 ◀▶ Ac 2:38–39
E Lk 21:25–31 ◀▶ Ac 2:19–20
E Ac 2:17 ◀▶ 1Th 5:1–4
P Lk 21:36 ◀▶ 1Co 16:22

G Ac 1:8 ◀▶ Ac 6:3   **L** Ac 1:2 ◀▶ Ac 4:8

ᶠ4 Or languages; also in verse 11   ᵍ13 Or sweet wine

---

the continuing revelation of the previous dispensations combines with the gospel message to emphasize humanity's utter sinfulness. Only through the completed work of Christ can humanity be saved by grace though faith (see Jn 14:6; Ro 3:21–26; Eph 2:8–9; 1Ti 4:10; Heb 11:6). Those who do trust and believe in Christ are to fulfill the Lord's command to preach the Gospel to the entire world (see Mk 16:15; Lk 24:46–48). During this time many will reject Christ or pretend to believe in him and introduce false doctrines into the church, thereby hindering its growth (see 1Ti 4:1–3). This dispensation of the church concludes with the translation of the true believers from the earth to heaven as they meet the Lord in the air when he returns (see 1Th 4:17) prior to the judgments of Daniel's seventieth week (see Da 9:24–27; Rev 7:14).

The seven dispensations revealed in Scripture are the dispensations of innocence (Ge 1:28), conscience (Ge 3:7), human government (Ge 8:15), promise (Ge 12:1), law (Ex 19:1), the church (Ac 2:1) and the kingdom (Rev 20:4).

For further information on dispensations, see the article on "The Seven Dispensations" on p. 4.

2:2–6 Christ's earlier prophecy that God would send "another Counselor" (Jn 14:16) was fulfilled on the day of Pentecost. The Holy Spirit supernaturally filled the disciples with power from heaven, allowing them to miraculously "speak in other tongues as the Spirit enabled them" (2:4). These other languages were the languages spoken by foreigners of that day. Remarkably, on the day of Pentecost, thousands of Jews from every nation in the known world had made the long journey to the temple in Jerusalem to celebrate a required annual feast. Jerusalem was filled with thousands of people representing every language in the known world. These visiting Jews heard the disciples "speaking in his own language" (2:6). This miracle would have been avidly discussed everywhere as these Jewish pilgrims eventually returned to their distant homelands.

2:16–20 When some doubters suggested that the commotion could be explained by drunkenness, the apostle Peter declared that this supernatural event was a partial fulfillment of the great prophecy of Joel (see Joel 2:28–32). This prophecy will be completed in the last days when God will again pour his Spirit out on the righteous people of Israel and "they will prophesy" (2:18). Peter's words confirmed that this supernatural evidence of the Holy Spirit would be identical to what will occur in the last days.

blood and fire and billows of
   smoke.
²⁰The sun will be turned to darkness
   and the moon to blood
   before the coming of the great and
   glorious day of the Lord.
²¹And everyone who calls
   on the name of the Lord will be
   saved.'

²²"Men of Israel, listen to this: Jesus of Nazareth was a man accredited by God to you by miracles, wonders and signs, which God did among you through him, as you yourselves know. ²³This man was handed over to you by God's set purpose and foreknowledge; and you, with the help of wicked men, put him to death by nailing him to the cross. ²⁴But God raised him from the dead, freeing him from the agony of death, because it was impossible for death to keep its hold on him. ²⁵David said about him:

" 'I saw the Lord always before
   me.
Because he is at my right hand,
   I will not be shaken.
²⁶Therefore my heart is glad and my
   tongue rejoices;
my body also will live in hope,
²⁷because you will not abandon me to
   the grave,
nor will you let your Holy One see
   decay.
²⁸You have made known to me the paths
   of life;
you will fill me with joy in your
   presence.'

²⁹"Brothers, I can tell you confidently that the patriarch David died and was buried, and his tomb is here to this day. ³⁰But he was a prophet and knew that God had promised him on oath that he would place one of his descendants on his throne. ³¹Seeing what was ahead, he spoke of the resurrection of the Christ, that he was not abandoned to the grave, nor did his body see decay. ³²God has raised this Jesus to life, and we are all witnesses of the fact. ³³Exalted to the right hand of God, he has received from the Father the promised Holy Spirit and has poured out what you now see and hear. ³⁴For David did not ascend to heaven, and yet he said,

" 'The Lord said to my Lord:
   "Sit at my right hand
³⁵until I make your enemies
   a footstool for your feet." '

³⁶"Therefore let all Israel be assured of this: God has made this Jesus, whom you crucified, both Lord and Christ."

³⁷When the people heard this, they were cut to the heart and said to Peter

2:20 n S Mt 24:29
2:21 o Ge 4:26; 26:25; Ps 105:1; Ac 9:14; 1Co 1:2; 2Ti 2:22
p Joel 2:28-32; Ro 10:13
2:22 q S Mk 1:24
r S Jn 4:48 s S Jn 3:2
2:23 t Isa 53:10; Ac 3:18; 4:28
u Mt 16:21; Lk 24:20; Ac 3:13
2:24 v ver 32; Ac 13:30,33,34,37; 17:31; Ro 6:4; 8:11; 10:9; 1Co 6:14; 15:15; Eph 1:20; Col 2:12; Heb 13:20; 1Pe 1:21 w Jn 20:9
2:27 x ver 31; Ac 13:35
2:28 y Ps 16:8-11
2:29 z S Ac 22:5
a Ac 7:8,9
b Ac 13:36; 1Ki 2:10 c Ne 3:16
2:30 d S Mt 1:1
2:31 e Ps 16:10
2:32 f S ver 24
g S Lk 24:48
2:33 h S Php 2:9
i S Mk 16:19
j Ac 1:4 k Jn 7:39; 14:26; 15:26
l Ac 10:45
2:35 m Ps 110:1; S Mt 22:44
2:36 n S Mt 28:18
o S Lk 2:11

I Ac 1:6–7 ◄ ► Ro 9:4
M Jn 19:19–22 ◄ ► Ac 2:34–35
B Ac 2:1–18 ◄ ► Ac 2:38–39
E Ac 2:1–18 ◄ ► Ac 4:8
N Ac 2:2–4 ◄ ► Ac 4:31
M Ac 2:29–31 ◄ ► Ac 3:19–21
V Lk 20:42–43 ◄ ► 1Co 15:24–26
H Ac 1:25 ◄ ► Ac 3:23
R Lk 24:47 ◄ ► Ac 3:19

h 21 Joel 2:28-32 i 23 Or of those not having the law (that is, Gentiles) j 28 Psalm 16:8-11 k 31 Or Messiah. "The Christ" (Greek) and "the Messiah" (Hebrew) both mean "the Anointed One"; also in verse 36. l 35 Psalm 110:1

W Jn 12:46 ◄ ► Ac 10:34–35

2:22–35 Peter addressed his remarks to the "men of Israel" (2:22) as he recounted the well-known history of Christ's ministry, death and resurrection. Peter reminded them that they were all witnesses of his resurrection (see 2:32) and argued that the resurrection of Jesus proved his claim to be the Messiah because Jesus fulfilled the OT prophecies about rising from the dead. This argument would have been futile unless Peter knew that his audience in Jerusalem was well aware of Christ's resurrection; only ten days earlier Jesus had ascended to heaven in the sight of his disciples.

Peter reminded his listeners that David had predicted that God would "place one of his descendants on his throne" (2:30). Before the temple was burned in A.D. 70, genealogical records in the temple could be examined by anyone to trace their lineage. These genealogical records proved that Jesus was legally "the son of David" (Mt 1:1) and thus had the right to sit on his throne. However, since the destruction of the temple, it has been impossible for anyone else to ever prove that they were legally descended from King David and thus able to meet these Messianic qualifications. Jesus is the first, last and only person to prove his legal right to the throne of David as the Messiah.

2:27 Peter taught that Jesus is the true Messiah by referring to King David's prophecy of Christ's resurrection (see Ps 16:10). Peter affirmed the prediction and fulfillment when Jesus supernaturally rose from the grave on the third day without his body suffering physical decay.

and the other apostles, "Brothers, what shall we do?"ᵖ

B
P ³⁸Peter replied, "Repent and be baptized,ᵠ every one of you, in the name of Jesus Christ for the forgiveness of your sins.ʳ And you will receive the gift of the Holy Spirit.ˢ ³⁹The promise is for you and your childrenᵗ and for all who are far offᵘ—for all whom the Lord our God will call."

⁴⁰With many other words he warned them; and he pleaded with them, "Save yourselves from this corrupt generation."ᵛ ⁴¹Those who accepted his message were baptized, and about three thousand were added to their numberʷ that day.

The Fellowship of the Believers

⁴²They devoted themselves to the apostles' teachingˣ and to the fellowship, to the breaking of breadʸ and to prayer.ᶻ ⁴³Everyone was filled with awe, and many wonders and miraculous signs were done by the apostles.ᵃ ⁴⁴All the believers were together and had everything in common.ᵇ ⁴⁵Selling their possessions and goods, they gave to anyone as he had need.ᶜ ⁴⁶Every day they continued to meet together in the temple courts.ᵈ They broke breadᵉ in their homes and ate together with glad and sincere hearts, ⁴⁷praising God and enjoying the favor of all the people.ᶠ And the Lord added to their numberᵍ daily those who were being saved.

Peter Heals the Crippled Beggar

E **3** One day Peter and Johnʰ were going up to the templeⁱ at the time of prayer—at three in the afternoon.ʲ ²Now a man crippled from birthᵏ was being carried to the temple gateˡ called Beautiful, where he was put every day to begᵐ from those going into the temple courts. ³When he saw Peter and John about to enter, he asked them for money. ⁴Peter looked straight at him, as did John. Then Peter said, "Look at us!" ⁵So the man gave them his attention, expecting to get something from them.

⁶Then Peter said, "Silver or gold I do not have, but what I have I give you. In the name of Jesus Christ of Nazareth,ⁿ walk." ⁷Taking him by the right hand, he helped him up, and instantly the man's feet and ankles became strong. ⁸He jumped to his feet and began to walk. Then he went with them into the temple courts, walking and jumping,ᵒ and praising God. ⁹When all the peopleᵖ saw him walking and praising God, ¹⁰they recognized him as the same man who used to sit begging at the temple gate called Beautiful,ᵠ and they were filled with wonder and amazement at what had happened to him.

Peter Speaks to the Onlookers

¹¹While the beggar held on to Peter and John,ʳ all the people were astonished and came running to them in the place called Solomon's Colonnade.ˢ ¹²When Peter saw this, he said to them: "Men of Israel, why does this surprise you? Why do you stare at us as if by our own power or godliness we had made this man walk? ¹³The God of Abraham, Isaac and Jacob,ᵗ the God of our fathers,ᵘ has glorified his servant Jesus. You handed him overᵛ to be killed, and you disowned him before Pilate,ʷ though he had decided to let him go.ˣ ¹⁴You disowned the Holyʸ and Righteous Oneᶻ and asked that a murderer be released to you.ᵃ ¹⁵You killed the author of life, but God raised him from the dead.ᵇ We are witnessesᶜ of this. ¹⁶By faith in the name of Jesus,ᵈ this man whom you see and know was made strong. It is Jesus' name and the faith that comes through him that has given this complete healing to him, as you can all see.

¹⁷"Now, brothers,ᵉ I know that you acted in ignorance,ᶠ as did your leaders.ᵍ ¹⁸But this is how God fulfilledʰ what he had foretoldⁱ through all the prophets,ʲ

B Ac 2:33 ◄ ► Ac 4:31
P Ac 2:15–18 ◄ ► Ac 11:16
E Jn 12:17–19 ◄ ► Ac 4:8–10

3:18—21 Peter referred to the prophecies of the suffering of the Messiah (see Ps 22:1–18; Isa 52:13—53:12). These prophecies were perfectly fulfilled in the trial and cruel death of Jesus on the cross. Peter urged his listeners to repent in light of the promise of the "times of refreshing" (3:19) at the return of Christ in the last days. Peter also made reference to the prophecy that the righteous remnant of the Jews will repent just prior to the Millennium after Christ's return in glory (see Zec 12:10–14).

saying that his Christ[m] would suffer.[k] ¹⁹Repent, then, and turn to God, so that your sins may be wiped out,[l] that times of refreshing may come from the Lord, ²⁰and that he may send the Christ,[m] who has been appointed for you—even Jesus. ²¹He must remain in heaven[n] until the time comes for God to restore everything,[o] as he promised long ago through his holy prophets.[p] ²²For Moses said, 'The Lord your God will raise up for you a prophet like me from among your own people; you must listen to everything he tells you.'[q] ²³Anyone who does not listen to him will be completely cut off from among his people.'[n][r]

²⁴"Indeed, all the prophets[s] from Samuel on, as many as have spoken, have foretold these days. ²⁵And you are heirs[t] of the prophets and of the covenant[u] God made with your fathers. He said to Abraham, 'Through your offspring all peoples on earth will be blessed.'[o][v] ²⁶When God raised up[w] his servant, he sent him first[x] to you to bless you by turning each of you from your wicked ways."

Peter and John Before the Sanhedrin

4 The priests and the captain of the temple guard[y] and the Sadducees[z] came up to Peter and John while they were speaking to the people. ²They were greatly disturbed because the apostles were teaching the people and proclaiming in Jesus the resurrection of the dead.[a] ³They seized Peter and John, and because it was evening, they put them in jail[b] until the next day. ⁴But many who heard the message believed, and the number of men grew[c] to about five thousand.

⁵The next day the rulers,[d] elders and teachers of the law met in Jerusalem. ⁶Annas the high priest was there, and so were Caiaphas,[e] John, Alexander and the other men of the high priest's family. ⁷They had Peter and John brought before them and began to question them: "By what power or what name did you do this?"

⁸Then Peter, filled with the Holy Spirit,[f] said to them: "Rulers and elders of the people![g] ⁹If we are being called to account today for an act of kindness shown to a cripple[h] and are asked how he was healed, ¹⁰then know this, you and all the people of Israel: It is by the name of Jesus Christ of Nazareth,[i] whom you crucified but whom God raised from the dead,[j] that this man stands before you healed. ¹¹He is

" 'the stone you builders rejected,
which has become the capstone.'[p][q][k]

¹²Salvation is found in no one else, for there is no other name under heaven given to men by which we must be saved."[l]

¹³When they saw the courage of Peter and John[m] and realized that they were unschooled, ordinary men,[n] they were astonished and they took note that these men had been with Jesus.[o] ¹⁴But since they could see the man who had been healed standing there with them, there was nothing they could say. ¹⁵So they or-

---

3:18 k Ac 17:2,3; 26:22,23
3:19 l Ps 51:1; Isa 43:25; 44:22; S Ac 2:38
3:20 m S Lk 2:11
3:21 n Ac 1:11 o Mt 17:11; Ac 1:6 p Lk 1:70
3:22 q Dt 18:15, 18; Ac 7:37
3:23 r Dt 18:19
3:24 s S Lk 24:27
3:25 t Ac 2:39 u Ro 9:4,5 v Ge 12:3; 22:18; 26:4; 28:14
3:26 w ver 22; S Ac 2:24 x Ac 13:46; Ro 1:16
4:1 y Lk 22:4 z Mt 3:7; 16:1,6; 22:23,34; Ac 5:17; 23:6-8
4:2 a Ac 17:18
4:3 b Ac 5:18
4:4 c S Ac 2:41
4:5 d Lk 23:13
4:6 e S Mt 26:3
4:8 f S Lk 1:15 g ver 5; Lk 23:13
4:9 h Ac 3:6
4:10 i S Mk 1:24 j S Ac 2:24
4:11 k Ps 118:22; Isa 28:16; Zec 10:4; Mt 21:42; Eph 2:20; 1Pe 2:7
4:12 l S Mt 1:21; Jn 14:6; Ac 10:43; S Ro 11:14; 1Ti 2:5
4:13 m S Lk 22:8 n Mt 11:25 o Mk 3:14

M *Ac 2:34–35* ◀▶ *Ac 17:7*
L *Jn 15:13* ◀▶ *Ac 3:26*
R *Ac 2:37–38* ◀▶ *Ac 8:22*
K *Lk 11:2* ◀▶ *Ac 3:25*
N *Jn 12:48* ◀▶ *Ac 4:11–12*
O *Jn 20:23* ◀▶ *Ac 4:11–12*
H *Ac 2:34–35* ◀▶ *Ac 13:41*
K *Ac 3:21* ◀▶ *1Co 15:24–28*
K *Jn 20:23* ◀▶ *Ac 5:31*
L *Ac 3:19* ◀▶ *Ac 5:31*
S *Jn 17:15–20* ◀▶ *Ac 14:22*

E *Ac 2:33* ◀▶ *Ac 4:31*
L *Ac 2:4* ◀▶ *Ac 6:10*
E *Ac 3:1–16* ◀▶ *Ac 4:14–22*
N *Ac 3:22–23* ◀▶ *Ac 7:51–53*
O *Ac 3:22–23* ◀▶ *Ro 8:9*
E *Ac 4:8–10* ◀▶ *Ac 5:14–16*

m 18 Or *Messiah*; also in verse 20 n 23 Deut. 18:15,18,19 o 25 Gen. 22:18; 26:4 p 11 Or *cornerstone* q 11 Psalm 118:22

While some individuals followed Christ, the majority of Israel generally rejected Peter's invitation to accept Jesus as their Messiah. Because of the lack of national repentance, the prophesied judgments against Jerusalem and the temple were fulfilled a few decades later when Rome destroyed the temple and the city of Jerusalem in A.D. 70.

3:22–23 Moses prophesied that God would raise up a prophet "like me" (Dt 18:15). This prophecy was precisely fulfilled; Jesus was more like Moses in his ministry and life than any other man in history. Peter also reminded his listeners of Moses' stern warning that "anyone who does not listen to him will be completely cut off from among his people" (3:23). For further information, see the article "A Prophet Like Unto Moses" on p. 224.

dered them to withdraw from the Sanhedrin[p] and then conferred together. [16]"What are we going to do with these men?"[q] they asked. "Everybody living in Jerusalem knows they have done an outstanding miracle,[r] and we cannot deny it. [17]But to stop this thing from spreading any further among the people, we must warn these men to speak no longer to anyone in this name."

[18]Then they called them in again and commanded them not to speak or teach at all in the name of Jesus.[s] [19]But Peter and John replied, "Judge for yourselves whether it is right in God's sight to obey you rather than God.[t] [20]For we cannot help speaking[u] about what we have seen and heard."[v]

[21]After further threats they let them go. They could not decide how to punish them, because all the people[w] were praising God[x] for what had happened. [22]For the man who was miraculously healed was over forty years old.

The Believers' Prayer

[23]On their release, Peter and John went back to their own people and reported all that the chief priests and elders had said to them. [24]When they heard this, they raised their voices together in prayer to God.[y] "Sovereign Lord," they said, "you made the heaven and the earth and the sea, and everything in them.[z] [25]You spoke by the Holy Spirit through the mouth of your servant, our father David:[a]

" 'Why do the nations rage
and the peoples plot in vain?
[26]The kings of the earth take their stand
and the rulers gather together
against the Lord
and against his Anointed One.'[r]'s[b]

[27]Indeed Herod[c] and Pontius Pilate[d] met together with the Gentiles and the people[t] of Israel in this city to conspire against your holy servant Jesus,[e] whom you anointed. [28]They did what your power and will had decided beforehand should happen.[f] [29]Now, Lord, consider their threats and enable your servants to speak your word with great boldness.[g] [30]Stretch out your hand to heal and per-

form miraculous signs and wonders[h] through the name of your holy servant Jesus."[i]

[31]After they prayed, the place where they were meeting was shaken.[j] And they were all filled with the Holy Spirit[k] and spoke the word of God[l] boldly.[m]

The Believers Share Their Possessions

[32]All the believers were one in heart and mind. No one claimed that any of his possessions was his own, but they shared everything they had.[n] [33]With great power the apostles continued to testify[o] to the resurrection[p] of the Lord Jesus, and much grace[q] was upon them all. [34]There were no needy persons among them. For from time to time those who owned lands or houses sold them,[r] brought the money from the sales [35]and put it at the apostles' feet,[s] and it was distributed to anyone as he had need.[t]

[36]Joseph, a Levite from Cyprus, whom the apostles called Barnabas[u] (which means Son of Encouragement), [37]sold a field he owned and brought the money and put it at the apostles' feet.[v]

Ananias and Sapphira

5 Now a man named Ananias, together with his wife Sapphira, also sold a piece of property. [2]With his wife's full knowledge he kept back part of the money for himself,[w] but brought the rest and put it at the apostles' feet.[x]

[3]Then Peter said, "Ananias, how is it that Satan[y] has so filled your heart[z] that you have lied to the Holy Spirit[a] and have kept for yourself some of the money you received for the land?[b] [4]Didn't it belong to you before it was sold? And after it was sold, wasn't the money at your disposal?[c] What made you think of doing such a thing? You have not lied to men but to God."[d]

[5]When Ananias heard this, he fell down and died.[e] And great fear[f] seized all who heard what had happened. [6]Then

B Ac 2:38–39 ◀ ▶ Ac 5:32
E Ac 4:8 ◀ ▶ Ac 5:3
N Ac 2:33 ◀ ▶ Ac 8:39
E Ac 4:31 ◀ ▶ Ac 5:9
Q Lk 12:10 ◀ ▶ Ac 5:9
D Mk 3:29 ◀ ▶ 1Co 3:16–17

A Jn 4:10 ◀ ▶ Ac 8:14–17
M Ac 2:1–18 ◀ ▶ Ac 6:8–10

r 26 That is, Christ or Messiah   s 26 Psalm 2:1,2   t 27 The Greek is plural.

the young men came forward, wrapped up his body, and carried him out and buried him.

⁷About three hours later his wife came in, not knowing what had happened. ⁸Peter asked her, "Tell me, is this the price you and Ananias got for the land?"

"Yes," she said, "that is the price."

⁹Peter said to her, "How could you agree to test the Spirit of the Lord? Look! The feet of the men who buried your husband are at the door, and they will carry you out also."

¹⁰At that moment she fell down at his feet and died. Then the young men came in and, finding her dead, carried her out and buried her beside her husband. ¹¹Great fear seized the whole church and all who heard about these events.

The Apostles Heal Many

¹²The apostles performed many miraculous signs and wonders among the people. And all the believers used to meet together in Solomon's Colonnade. ¹³No one else dared join them, even though they were highly regarded by the people. ¹⁴Nevertheless, more and more men and women believed in the Lord and were added to their number. ¹⁵As a result, people brought the sick into the streets and laid them on beds and mats so that at least Peter's shadow might fall on some of them as he passed by. ¹⁶Crowds gathered also from the towns around Jerusalem, bringing their sick and those tormented by evil spirits, and all of them were healed.

The Apostles Persecuted

¹⁷Then the high priest and all his associates, who were members of the party of the Sadducees, were filled with jealousy. ¹⁸They arrested the apostles and put them in the public jail. ¹⁹But during the night an angel of the Lord opened the doors of the jail and brought them out. ²⁰"Go, stand in the temple courts," he said, "and tell the people the full message of this new life."

²¹At daybreak they entered the temple courts, as they had been told, and began to teach the people.

When the high priest and his associates arrived, they called together the Sanhedrin—the full assembly of the elders of Israel—and sent to the jail for the apostles. ²²But on arriving at the jail, the officers did not find them there. So they went back and reported, ²³"We found the jail securely locked, with the guards standing at the doors; but when we opened them, we found no one inside." ²⁴On hearing this report, the captain of the temple guard and the chief priests were puzzled, wondering what would come of this.

²⁵Then someone came and said, "Look! The men you put in jail are standing in the temple courts teaching the people." ²⁶At that, the captain went with his officers and brought the apostles. They did not use force, because they feared that the people would stone them.

²⁷Having brought the apostles, they made them appear before the Sanhedrin to be questioned by the high priest. ²⁸"We gave you strict orders not to teach in this name," he said. "Yet you have filled Jerusalem with your teaching and are determined to make us guilty of this man's blood."

²⁹Peter and the other apostles replied: "We must obey God rather than men! ³⁰The God of our fathers raised Jesus from the dead—whom you had killed by hanging him on a tree. ³¹God exalted him to his own right hand as Prince and Savior that he might give repentance and forgiveness of sins to Israel. ³²We are witnesses of these things, and so is the Holy Spirit, whom God has given to those who obey him."

³³When they heard this, they were furious and wanted to put them to death. ³⁴But a Pharisee named Gamaliel, a teacher of the law, who was honored by all the people, stood up in the Sanhedrin and ordered that the men be put outside for a little while. ³⁵Then he addressed them: "Men of Israel, consider carefully what you intend to do to these men.

ACTS 5:36

³⁶Some time ago Theudas appeared, claiming to be somebody, and about four hundred men rallied to him. He was killed, all his followers were dispersed, and it all came to nothing. ³⁷After him, Judas the Galilean appeared in the days of the census⁽ᵘ⁾ and led a band of people in revolt. He too was killed, and all his followers were scattered. ³⁸Therefore, in the present case I advise you: Leave these men alone! Let them go! For if their purpose or activity is of human origin, it will fail.ᵛ ³⁹But if it is from God, you will not be able to stop these men; you will only find yourselves fighting against God."ʷ

⁴⁰His speech persuaded them. They called the apostles in and had them flogged.ˣ Then they ordered them not to speak in the name of Jesus, and let them go.

⁴¹The apostles left the Sanhedrin, rejoicingʸ because they had been counted worthy of suffering disgrace for the Name.ᶻ ⁴²Day after day, in the temple courtsᵃ and from house to house, they never stopped teaching and proclaiming the good newsᵇ that Jesus is the Christ.ᵛᶜ

The Choosing of the Seven

6 In those days when the number of disciples was increasing,ᵈ the Grecian Jewsᵉ among them complained against the Hebraic Jews because their widowsᶠ were being overlooked in the daily distribution of food.ᵍ ²So the Twelve gathered all the disciplesʰ together and said, "It would not be right for us to neglect the ministry of the word of Godⁱ in order to wait on tables. ³Brothers,ʲ choose seven men from among you who are known to be full of the Spiritᵏ and wisdom. We will turn this responsibility over to themˡ ⁴and will give our attention to prayerᵐ and the ministry of the word."

⁵This proposal pleased the whole group. They chose Stephen,ⁿ a man full of faith and of the Holy Spirit;ᵒ also Philip,ᵖ Procorus, Nicanor, Timon, Parmenas,

5:37 ᵘ Lk 2:1,2
5:38 ᵛ Mt 15:13
5:39 ʷ 2Ch 13:12; Pr 21:30; Isa 46:10; Ac 7:51; 11:17
5:40 ˣ S Mt 10:17
5:41 ʸ S Mt 5:12 ᶻ S Jn 15:21
5:42 ᵃ S Ac 2:46 ᵇ S Ac 13:32 ᶜ S Ac 9:22
6:1 ᵈ S Ac 2:41 ᵉ Ac 9:29 ᶠ Ac 9:39, 41; 1Ti 5:3 ᵍ Ac 4:35
6:2 ʰ S Ac 11:26 ⁱ S Heb 4:12
6:3 ʲ S Ac 1:16 ᵏ S Lk 1:15 ˡ Ex 18:21; Ne 13:13
6:4 ᵐ S Ac 1:14
6:5 ⁿ ver 8; Ac 7:55-60; 11:19; 22:20 ᵒ S Lk 1:15 ᵖ Ac 8:5-40; 21:8
6:6 ᵠ S Ac 1:24 ʳ Nu 8:10; 27:18; Ac 9:17; 19:6; 28:8; 1Ti 4:14; S Mk 5:23
6:7 ˢ Ac 12:24; 19:20 ᵗ S Ac 2:41
6:8 ᵘ S Jn 4:48
6:9 ᵛ S Mt 27:32 ʷ Ac 15:23,41; 22:3; 23:34 ˣ S Ac 2:9
6:10 ʸ Lk 21:15
6:11 ᶻ 1Ki 21:10 ᵃ Mt 26:59-61
6:12 ᵇ S Mt 5:22
6:13 ᶜ Ex 23:1; Ps 27:12 ᵈ Mt 24:15; Ac 7:48; 21:28
6:14 ᵉ S Jn 2:19 ᶠ Ac 15:1; 21:21; 26:3; 28:17
6:15 ᵍ S Mt 5:22
7:2 ʰ Ac 22:1 ⁱ Ps 29:3 ʲ Ge 11:31; 15:7

and Nicolas from Antioch, a convert to Judaism. ⁶They presented these men to the apostles, who prayedᵠ and laid their hands on them.ʳ

⁷So the word of God spread.ˢ The number of disciples in Jerusalem increased rapidly,ᵗ and a large number of priests became obedient to the faith.

Stephen Seized

⁸Now Stephen, a man full of God's grace and power, did great wonders and miraculous signsᵘ among the people. ⁹Opposition arose, however, from members of the Synagogue of the Freedmen (as it was called)—Jews of Cyreneᵛ and Alexandria as well as the provinces of Ciliciaʷ and Asia.ˣ These men began to argue with Stephen, ¹⁰but they could not stand up against his wisdom or the Spirit by whom he spoke.ʸ

¹¹Then they secretlyᶻ persuaded some men to say, "We have heard Stephen speak words of blasphemy against Moses and against God."ᵃ

¹²So they stirred up the people and the elders and the teachers of the law. They seized Stephen and brought him before the Sanhedrin.ᵇ ¹³They produced false witnesses,ᶜ who testified, "This fellow never stops speaking against this holy placeᵈ and against the law. ¹⁴For we have heard him say that this Jesus of Nazareth will destroy this placeᵉ and change the customs Moses handed down to us."ᶠ

¹⁵All who were sitting in the Sanhedrinᵍ looked intently at Stephen, and they saw that his face was like the face of an angel.

Stephen's Speech to the Sanhedrin

7 Then the high priest asked him, "Are these charges true?"

²To this he replied: "Brothers and fathers,ʰ listen to me! The God of gloryⁱ appeared to our father Abraham while he was still in Mesopotamia, before he lived in Haran.ʲ ³'Leave your country and your

V Ac 5:19 ◀ ▶ Ac 12:7–11
J Jn 16:33 ◀ ▶ Ac 6:15
B Ac 5:32 ◀ ▶ Ac 6:5
E Ac 5:32 ◀ ▶ Ac 6:5
G Ac 2:3–18 ◀ ▶ Ac 6:8–10
T Ac 2:1–18 ◀ ▶ Ac 6:9–10
W Ac 1:4–5 ◀ ▶ Ac 7:51
B Ac 6:3 ◀ ▶ Ac 8:14–21
E Ac 6:3 ◀ ▶ Ac 6:8–10

E Ac 6:5 ◀ ▶ Ac 7:51
G Ac 6:3 ◀ ▶ Ac 10:38
M Ac 4:29–31 ◀ ▶ Ac 6:15
T Ac 6:3 ◀ ▶ Ac 7:55
L Ac 4:8 ◀ ▶ Ac 8:29
M Ac 6:8–10 ◀ ▶ Ac 10:38
J Ac 5:41 ◀ ▶ Ro 5:3

ᵛ 42 Or *Messiah*

people,' God said, 'and go to the land I will show you.'[w][k]

[4]"So he left the land of the Chaldeans and settled in Haran. After the death of his father, God sent him to this land where you are now living.[l] [5]He gave him no inheritance here,[m] not even a foot of ground. But God promised him that he and his descendants after him would possess the land,[n] even though at that time Abraham had no child. [6]God spoke to him in this way: 'Your descendants will be strangers in a country not their own, and they will be enslaved and mistreated four hundred years.[o] [7]But I will punish the nation they serve as slaves,' God said, 'and afterward they will come out of that country and worship me in this place.'[x][p] [8]Then he gave Abraham the covenant of circumcision.[q] And Abraham became the father of Isaac and circumcised him eight days after his birth.[r] Later Isaac became the father of Jacob,[s] and Jacob became the father of the twelve patriarchs.[t]

[9]"Because the patriarchs were jealous of Joseph,[u] they sold him as a slave into Egypt.[v] But God was with him[w] [10]and rescued him from all his troubles. He gave Joseph wisdom and enabled him to gain the goodwill of Pharaoh king of Egypt; so he made him ruler over Egypt and all his palace.[x]

[11]"Then a famine struck all Egypt and Canaan, bringing great suffering, and our fathers could not find food.[y] [12]When Jacob heard that there was grain in Egypt, he sent our fathers on their first visit.[z] [13]On their second visit, Joseph told his brothers who he was,[a] and Pharaoh learned about Joseph's family.[b] [14]After this, Joseph sent for his father Jacob and his whole family,[c] seventy-five in all.[d] [15]Then Jacob went down to Egypt, where he and our fathers died.[e] [16]Their bodies were brought back to Shechem and placed in the tomb that Abraham had bought from the sons of Hamor at Shechem for a certain sum of money.[f]

[17]"As the time drew near for God to fulfill his promise to Abraham, the number of our people in Egypt greatly increased.[g] [18]Then another king, who knew nothing about Joseph, became ruler of Egypt.[h] [19]He dealt treacherously with our people and oppressed our forefathers by forcing them to throw out their newborn babies so that they would die.[i]

[20]"At that time Moses was born, and he was no ordinary child.[y] For three months he was cared for in his father's house.[j] [21]When he was placed outside, Pharaoh's daughter took him and brought him up as her own son.[k] [22]Moses was educated in all the wisdom of the Egyptians[1] and was powerful in speech and action.

[23]"When Moses was forty years old, he decided to visit his fellow Israelites. [24]He saw one of them being mistreated by an Egyptian, so he went to his defense and avenged him by killing the Egyptian. [25]Moses thought that his own people would realize that God was using him to rescue them, but they did not. [26]The next day Moses came upon two Israelites who were fighting. He tried to reconcile them by saying, 'Men, you are brothers; why do you want to hurt each other?'

[27]"But the man who was mistreating the other pushed Moses aside and said, 'Who made you ruler and judge over us?[m] [28]Do you want to kill me as you killed the Egyptian yesterday?'[z] [29]When Moses heard this, he fled to Midian, where he settled as a foreigner and had two sons.[n]

[30]"After forty years had passed, an angel appeared to Moses in the flames of a burning bush in the desert near Mount Sinai. [31]When he saw this, he was amazed at the sight. As he went over to look more closely, he heard the Lord's voice:[o] [32]'I am the God of your fathers,[p] the God of Abraham, Isaac and Jacob.'[a] Moses trembled with fear and did not dare to look.[q]

[33]"Then the Lord said to him, 'Take off your sandals; the place where you are standing is holy ground.[r] [34]I have indeed seen the oppression of my people in Egypt. I have heard their groaning and have come down to set them free. Now come, I will send you back to Egypt.'[b][s]

[35]"This is the same Moses whom they had rejected with the words, 'Who made you ruler and judge?'[t] He was sent to be their ruler and deliverer by God himself, through the angel who appeared to him in the bush. [36]He led them out of Egypt[u] and did wonders and miraculous signs[v] in Egypt, at the Red Sea[c][w] and for forty years in the desert.[x]

---

[w] 3 Gen. 12:1   [x] 7 Gen. 15:13,14   [y] 20 Or *was fair in the sight of God*   [z] 28 Exodus 2:14   [a] 32 Exodus 3:6   [b] 34 Exodus 3:5,7,8,10   [c] 36 That is, Sea of Reeds

37 "This is that Moses who told the Israelites, 'God will send you a prophet like me from your own people.'ᵈʸ ³⁸He was in the assembly in the desert, with the angelᶻ who spoke to him on Mount Sinai, and with our fathers;ᵃ and he received living wordsᵇ to pass on to us.ᶜ

39 "But our fathers refused to obey him. Instead, they rejected him and in their hearts turned back to Egypt.ᵈ ⁴⁰They told Aaron, 'Make us gods who will go before us. As for this fellow Moses who led us out of Egypt—we don't know what has happened to him!'ᵉᵉ ⁴¹That was the time they made an idol in the form of a calf. They brought sacrifices to it and held a celebration in honor of what their hands had made.ᶠ ⁴²But God turned awayᵍ and gave them over to the worship of the heavenly bodies.ʰ This agrees with what is written in the book of the prophets:

" 'Did you bring me sacrifices and offerings
forty years in the desert, O house of Israel?
⁴³You have lifted up the shrine of Molech
and the star of your god Rephan, the idols you made to worship.
Therefore I will send you into exile'ⁱ beyond Babylon.

44 "Our forefathers had the tabernacle of the Testimonyʲ with them in the desert. It had been made as God directed Moses, according to the pattern he had seen.ᵏ ⁴⁵Having received the tabernacle, our fathers under Joshua brought it with them when they took the land from the nations God drove out before them.ˡ It remained in the land until the time of David,ᵐ ⁴⁶who enjoyed God's favor and asked that he might provide a dwelling place for the God of Jacob.ᵍⁿ ⁴⁷But it was Solomon who built the house for him.ᵒ

48 "However, the Most Highᵖ does not live in houses made by men.ᵠ As the prophet says:

⁴⁹ 'Heaven is my throne,
and the earth is my footstool.ʳ
What kind of house will you build for me?
says the Lord.
Or where will my resting place be?
⁵⁰Has not my hand made all these things?'ʰˢ

51 "You stiff-necked people,ᵗ with uncircumcised heartsᵘ and ears! You are just like your fathers: You always resist the Holy Spirit! ⁵²Was there ever a prophet your fathers did not persecute?ᵛ They even killed those who predicted the coming of the Righteous One. And now you have betrayed and murdered himʷ— ⁵³you who have received the law that was put into effect through angelsˣ but have not obeyed it."

The Stoning of Stephen

54 When they heard this, they were furiousʸ and gnashed their teeth at him. ⁵⁵But Stephen, full of the Holy Spirit,ᶻ looked up to heaven and saw the glory of God, and Jesus standing at the right hand of God.ᵃ ⁵⁶"Look," he said, "I see heaven openᵇ and the Son of Manᶜ standing at the right hand of God."

57 At this they covered their ears and, yelling at the top of their voices, they all rushed at him, ⁵⁸dragged him out of the cityᵈ and began to stone him.ᵉ Meanwhile, the witnessesᶠ laid their clothesᵍ at the feet of a young man named Saul.ʰ

59 While they were stoning him, Stephen prayed, "Lord Jesus, receive my spirit."ⁱ ⁶⁰Then he fell on his kneesʲ and cried out, "Lord, do not hold this sin against them."ᵏ When he had said this, he fell asleep.ˡ

E Ac 6:8-10 ◀ ▶ Ac 7:55
Q Ac 5:9 ◀ ▶ Eph 4:30
W Ac 6:3 ◀ ▶ Ac 8:14-15
C Jn 8:44 ◀ ▶ Ac 8:23
M Jn 9:39 ◀ ▶ Ac 8:22
N Ac 4:11-12 ◀ ▶ Ac 24:25
E Ac 7:51 ◀ ▶ Ac 8:14-21
T Ac 6:9-10 ◀ ▶ Ac 10:46

ᵈ 37 Deut. 18:15 ᵉ 40 Exodus 32:1 ᶠ 43 Amos 5:25-27 ᵍ 46 Some early manuscripts *the house of Jacob* ʰ 50 Isaiah 66:1,2

7:37-38 In Stephen's last message he reminds the people that Moses had specifically prophesied that God would raise up a prophet "like me" (Dt 18:15). For further information, see the article "A Prophet Like Moses" on p. 224.

8 And Saul was there, giving approval to his death.

The Church Persecuted and Scattered

On that day a great persecution broke out against the church at Jerusalem, and all except the apostles were scattered throughout Judea and Samaria. ² Godly men buried Stephen and mourned deeply for him. ³ But Saul began to destroy the church. Going from house to house, he dragged off men and women and put them in prison.

Philip in Samaria

⁴ Those who had been scattered preached the word wherever they went. ⁵ Philip went down to a city in Samaria and proclaimed the Christ there. ⁶ When the crowds heard Philip and saw the miraculous signs he did, they all paid close attention to what he said. ⁷ With shrieks, evil spirits came out of many, and many paralytics and cripples were healed. ⁸ So there was great joy in that city.

Simon the Sorcerer

⁹ Now for some time a man named Simon had practiced sorcery in the city and amazed all the people of Samaria. He boasted that he was someone great, ¹⁰ and all the people, both high and low, gave him their attention and exclaimed, "This man is the divine power known as the Great Power." ¹¹ They followed him because he had amazed them for a long time with his magic. ¹² But when they believed Philip as he preached the good news of the kingdom of God and the name of Jesus Christ, they were baptized, both men and women. ¹³ Simon himself believed and was baptized. And he followed Philip everywhere, astonished by the great signs and miracles he saw.

¹⁴ When the apostles in Jerusalem heard that Samaria had accepted the word of God, they sent Peter and John to them. ¹⁵ When they arrived, they prayed for them that they might receive the Holy Spirit, ¹⁶ because the Holy Spirit had not yet come upon any of them; they had simply been baptized into the name of the Lord Jesus. ¹⁷ Then Peter and John placed their hands on them, and they received the Holy Spirit.

¹⁸ When Simon saw that the Spirit was given at the laying on of the apostles' hands, he offered them money ¹⁹ and said, "Give me also this ability so that everyone on whom I lay my hands may receive the Holy Spirit."

²⁰ Peter answered: "May your money perish with you, because you thought you could buy the gift of God with money! ²¹ You have no part or share in this ministry, because your heart is not right before God. ²² Repent of this wickedness and pray to the Lord. Perhaps he will forgive you for having such a thought in your heart. ²³ For I see that you are full of bitterness and captive to sin."

²⁴ Then Simon answered, "Pray to the Lord for me so that nothing you have said may happen to me."

²⁵ When they had testified and proclaimed the word of the Lord, Peter and John returned to Jerusalem, preaching the gospel in many Samaritan villages.

Philip and the Ethiopian

²⁶ Now an angel of the Lord said to Philip, "Go south to the road—the desert road—that goes down from Jerusalem to Gaza." ²⁷ So he started out, and on his way he met an Ethiopian eunuch, an important official in charge of all the treasury of Candace, queen of the Ethiopians. This man had gone to Jerusalem to worship, ²⁸ and on his way home was sitting in his chariot reading the book of Isaiah the prophet. ²⁹ The Spirit told Philip, "Go to that chariot and stay near it."

³⁰ Then Philip ran up to the chariot and heard the man reading Isaiah the prophet. "Do you understand what you are reading?" Philip asked.

³¹ "How can I," he said, "unless some-

E Ac 5:14–16 ◀ ▶ Ac 9:12
A Ac 4:29–31 ◀ ▶ Eph 1:16–17
B Ac 6:5 ◀ ▶ Ac 9:17
E Ac 7:55 ◀ ▶ Ac 8:29
W Ac 7:51 ◀ ▶ Ac 9:17

M Ac 7:51 ◀ ▶ Ro 12:16
R Ac 3:19 ◀ ▶ Ac 11:18
C Ac 7:51 ◀ ▶ Ac 26:18
E Ac 8:14–21 ◀ ▶ Ac 8:39
L Ac 6:10 ◀ ▶ Ac 8:39

i 5 Or Messiah j 7 Greek unclean k 16 Or in l 27 That is, from the upper Nile region

one explains it to me?" So he invited Philip to come up and sit with him.

³²The eunuch was reading this passage of Scripture:

"He was led like a sheep to the slaughter,
and as a lamb before the shearer is silent,
so he did not open his mouth.
³³In his humiliation he was deprived of justice.
Who can speak of his descendants?
For his life was taken from the earth." ᵐˣ

³⁴The eunuch asked Philip, "Tell me, please, who is the prophet talking about, himself or someone else?" ³⁵Then Philip began ʸ with that very passage of Scripture ᶻ and told him the good news ᵃ about Jesus.

³⁶As they traveled along the road, they came to some water and the eunuch said, "Look, here is water. Why shouldn't I be baptized?" ⁿᵇ ³⁸And he gave orders to stop the chariot. Then both Philip and the eunuch went down into the water and Philip baptized him. ³⁹When they came up out of the water, the Spirit of the Lord suddenly took Philip away, ᶜ and the eunuch did not see him again, but went on his way rejoicing. ⁴⁰Philip, however, appeared at Azotus and traveled about, preaching the gospel in all the towns ᵈ until he reached Caesarea. ᵉ

Saul's Conversion

9:1–19pp — Ac 22:3–16; 26:9–18

9 Meanwhile, Saul was still breathing out murderous threats against the Lord's disciples. ᶠ He went to the high priest ²and asked him for letters to the synagogues in Damascus, ᵍ so that if he found any there who belonged to the Way, ʰ whether men or women, he might take them as prisoners to Jerusalem. ³As he neared Damascus on his journey, suddenly a light from heaven flashed around him. ⁱ ⁴He fell to the ground and heard a voice ʲ say to him, "Saul, Saul, why do you persecute me?"

⁵"Who are you, Lord?" Saul asked.

D Jn 11:49–52 ◀ ▶ Ac 20:28
E Ac 8:29 ◀ ▶ Ac 9:17
L Ac 8:29 ◀ ▶ Ac 9:31
N Ac 4:31 ◀ ▶ Ac 10:45

8:33 ˣ Isa 53:7,8
8:35 ʸ Mt 5:2
ᶻ Lk 24:27; Ac 17:2; 18:28; 28:23
ᵃ S Ac 13:32
8:36 ᵇ S Ac 2:38; 10:47
8:39 ᶜ 1Ki 18:12; 2Ki 2:16; Eze 3:12, 14; 8:3; 11:1,24; 43:5; 2Co 12:2; 1Th 4:17; Rev 12:5
8:40 ᵈ ver 25
ᵉ Ac 10:1,24; 12:19; 21:8,16; 23:23,33; 25:1,4,6, 13
9:1 ᶠ S Ac 8:3
9:2 ᵍ Isa 17:1; Jer 49:23 ʰ Ac 19:9, 23; 22:4; 24:14,22
9:3 ⁱ 1Co 15:8
9:4 ʲ Isa 6:8
9:6 ᵏ ver 16; Eze 3:22
9:7 ˡ Jn 12:29
ᵐ Da 10:7
9:8 ⁿ ver 18
9:10 ᵒ Ac 10:3,17, 19; 12:9; 16:9,10; 18:9
9:11 ᵖ ver 30; Ac 11:25; 21:39; 22:3
9:12 ᵠ S Mk 5:23
9:13 ʳ ver 32; Ac 26:10; Ro 1:7; 15:25,26,31; 16:2, 15; Eph 1:1; Php 1:1 ˢ Ac 8:3
9:14 ᵗ ver 2,21
ᵘ S Ac 2:21
9:15 ᵛ Ac 13:2; Ro 1:1; Gal 1:15; 1Ti 1:12
ʷ Ro 11:13; 15:15, 16; Gal 1:16; 2:7,8
ˣ Ac 25:22,23; 26:1
9:16 ʸ Ac 20:23; 21:11; 2Co 6:4-10; 11:23-27; 2Ti 1:8; 2:3,9
9:17 ᶻ S Ac 6:6
ᵃ S Lk 1:15
9:18 ᵇ S Ac 2:38

"I am Jesus, whom you are persecuting," he replied. ⁶"Now get up and go into the city, and you will be told what you must do." ᵏ

⁷The men traveling with Saul stood there speechless; they heard the sound ˡ but did not see anyone. ᵐ ⁸Saul got up from the ground, but when he opened his eyes he could see nothing. ⁿ So they led him by the hand into Damascus. ⁹For three days he was blind, and did not eat or drink anything.

¹⁰In Damascus there was a disciple named Ananias. The Lord called to him in a vision, ᵒ "Ananias!"

"Yes, Lord," he answered.

¹¹The Lord told him, "Go to the house of Judas on Straight Street and ask for a man from Tarsus ᵖ named Saul, for he is praying. ¹²In a vision he has seen a man named Ananias come and place his hands on ᵠ him to restore his sight."

¹³"Lord," Ananias answered, "I have heard many reports about this man and all the harm he has done to your saints ʳ in Jerusalem. ˢ ¹⁴And he has come here with authority from the chief priests ᵗ to arrest all who call on your name." ᵘ

¹⁵But the Lord said to Ananias, "Go! This man is my chosen instrument ᵛ to carry my name before the Gentiles ʷ and their kings ˣ and before the people of Israel. ¹⁶I will show him how much he must suffer for my name." ʸ

¹⁷Then Ananias went to the house and entered it. Placing his hands on ᶻ Saul, he said, "Brother Saul, the Lord—Jesus, who appeared to you on the road as you were coming here—has sent me so that you may see again and be filled with the Holy Spirit." ᵃ ¹⁸Immediately, something like scales fell from Saul's eyes, and he could see again. He got up and was baptized, ᵇ ¹⁹and after taking some food, he regained his strength.

Saul in Damascus and Jerusalem

Saul spent several days with the disci-

D Jn 11:4 ◀ ▶ Ac 10:38
E Ac 8:6–7 ◀ ▶ Ac 9:17
B Ac 8:14–21 ◀ ▶ Ac 10:44–47
E Ac 8:39 ◀ ▶ Ac 10:19
W Ac 8:14–15 ◀ ▶ Ac 19:2
E Ac 9:12 ◀ ▶ Ac 9:32–35

ᵐ 33 Isaiah 53:7,8   ⁿ 36 Some late manuscripts baptized?" ³⁷Philip said, "If you believe with all your heart, you may." The eunuch answered, "I believe that Jesus Christ is the Son of God."

ples[c] in Damascus.[d] [20]At once he began to preach in the synagogues[e] that Jesus is the Son of God.[f] [21]All those who heard him were astonished and asked, "Isn't he the man who raised havoc in Jerusalem among those who call on this name?[g] And hasn't he come here to take them as prisoners to the chief priests?"[h] [22]Yet Saul grew more and more powerful and baffled the Jews living in Damascus by proving that Jesus is the Christ.[o][i]

[23]After many days had gone by, the Jews conspired to kill him,[j] [24]but Saul learned of their plan.[k] Day and night they kept close watch on the city gates in order to kill him. [25]But his followers took him by night and lowered him in a basket through an opening in the wall.[l]

[26]When he came to Jerusalem,[m] he tried to join the disciples, but they were all afraid of him, not believing that he really was a disciple. [27]But Barnabas[n] took him and brought him to the apostles. He told them how Saul on his journey had seen the Lord and that the Lord had spoken to him,[o] and how in Damascus he had preached fearlessly in the name of Jesus.[p] [28]So Saul stayed with them and moved about freely in Jerusalem, speaking boldly in the name of the Lord. [29]He talked and debated with the Grecian Jews,[q] but they tried to kill him.[r] [30]When the brothers[s] learned of this, they took him down to Caesarea[t] and sent him off to Tarsus.[u]

[F,J,L] [31]Then the church throughout Judea, Galilee and Samaria[v] enjoyed a time of peace. It was strengthened; and encouraged by the Holy Spirit, it grew in numbers,[w] living in the fear of the Lord.

Aeneas and Dorcas

[E] [32]As Peter traveled about the country, he went to visit the saints[x] in Lydda. [33]There he found a man named Aeneas, a paralytic who had been bedridden for eight years. [34]"Aeneas," Peter said to him, "Jesus Christ heals you.[y] Get up and take care of your mat." Immediately Aeneas got up. [35]All those who lived in Lydda and Sharon[z] saw him and turned to the Lord.[a]

F *Isa 63:14* ◀ ▶ *Ac 13:52*
J *Jn 20:21–22* ◀ ▶ *Ac 13:52*
L *Ac 8:39* ◀ ▶ *Ac 10:19–20*
E *Ac 9:17* ◀ ▶ *Ac 10:38*

9:19 c S Ac 11:26
d Ac 26:20
9:20 e Ac 13:5,14; 14:1; 17:2,10,17; 18:4,19; 19:8
f S Mt 4:3
9:21 g S Ac 8:3
h ver 14
9:22 i S Lk 2:11; Ac 5:42; 17:3; 18:5, 28
9:23 j S Ac 20:3
9:24 k Ac 20:3,19; 23:16,30
9:25 l 1Sa 19:12; 2Co 11:32,33
9:26 m Ac 22:17; 26:20; Gal 1:17,18
9:27 n S Ac 4:36
o ver 3-6 p ver 20, 22
9:29 q Ac 6:1
r 2Co 11:26
9:30 s S Ac 1:16
t S Ac 8:40
u S ver 11
9:31 v S Ac 8:1
w S Ac 2:41
9:32 x S ver 13
9:34 y Ac 3:6,16; 4:10
9:35 z 1Ch 5:16; 27:29; SS 2:1; Isa 33:9; 35:2
a S Ac 2:41
9:36 b Jos 19:46; 2Ch 2:16; Ezr 3:7; Jnh 1:3; Ac 10:5
c 1Ti 2:10; Ti 3:8
9:37 d Ac 1:13; 20:8
9:38 e S Ac 11:26
9:39 f Ac 6:1; 1Ti 5:5
9:40 g Mt 6:25
h Lk 22:41; Ac 7:60
i S Lk 7:14
9:42 j S Ac 2:41
9:43 k Ac 10:6
10:1 l S Ac 8:40
10:2 m ver 22,35; Ac 13:16,26
10:3 n Ps 55:17; Ac 3:1 o S Ac 9:10
p S Ac 5:19
10:4 q Ps 20:3; S Mt 10:42; 26:13
r Rev 8:4
10:5 s S Ac 9:36
10:6 t Ac 9:43
10:8 u S Ac 9:36

[36]In Joppa[b] there was a disciple named Tabitha (which, when translated, is Dorcas[p]), who was always doing good[c] and helping the poor. [37]About that time she became sick and died, and her body was washed and placed in an upstairs room.[d] [38]Lydda was near Joppa; so when the disciples[e] heard that Peter was in Lydda, they sent two men to him and urged him, "Please come at once!"

[39]Peter went with them, and when he arrived he was taken upstairs to the room. All the widows[f] stood around him, crying and showing him the robes and other clothing that Dorcas had made while she was still with them.

[40]Peter sent them all out of the room;[g] then he got down on his knees[h] and prayed. Turning toward the dead woman, he said, "Tabitha, get up."[i] She opened her eyes, and seeing Peter she sat up. [41]He took her by the hand and helped her to her feet. Then he called the believers and the widows and presented her to them alive. [42]This became known all over Joppa, and many people believed in the Lord.[j] [43]Peter stayed in Joppa for some time with a tanner named Simon.[k]

Cornelius Calls for Peter

10 At Caesarea[l] there was a man named Cornelius, a centurion in what was known as the Italian Regiment. [2]He and all his family were devout and God-fearing;[m] he gave generously to those in need and prayed to God regularly. [3]One day at about three in the afternoon[n] he had a vision.[o] He distinctly saw an angel[p] of God, who came to him and said, "Cornelius!"

[4]Cornelius stared at him in fear. "What is it, Lord?" he asked.

The angel answered, "Your prayers and gifts to the poor have come up as a memorial offering[q] before God.[r] [5]Now send men to Joppa[s] to bring back a man named Simon who is called Peter. [6]He is staying with Simon the tanner,[t] whose house is by the sea."

[7]When the angel who spoke to him had gone, Cornelius called two of his servants and a devout soldier who was one of his attendants. [8]He told them everything that had happened and sent them to Joppa.[u]

o 22 Or *Messiah* *p 36* Both *Tabitha* (Aramaic) and *Dorcas* (Greek) mean *gazelle.*

Peter's Vision

10:9–32Ref — Ac 11:5–14

⁹About noon the following day as they were on their journey and approaching the city, Peter went up on the roof to pray. ¹⁰He became hungry and wanted something to eat, and while the meal was being prepared, he fell into a trance. ¹¹He saw heaven opened and something like a large sheet being let down to earth by its four corners. ¹²It contained all kinds of four-footed animals, as well as reptiles of the earth and birds of the air. ¹³Then a voice told him, "Get up, Peter. Kill and eat."

¹⁴"Surely not, Lord!" Peter replied. "I have never eaten anything impure or unclean."

¹⁵The voice spoke to him a second time, "Do not call anything impure that God has made clean."

¹⁶This happened three times, and immediately the sheet was taken back to heaven.

¹⁷While Peter was wondering about the meaning of the vision, the men sent by Cornelius found out where Simon's house was and stopped at the gate. ¹⁸They called out, asking if Simon who was known as Peter was staying there.

¹⁹While Peter was still thinking about the vision, the Spirit said to him, "Simon, three*q* men are looking for you. ²⁰So get up and go downstairs. Do not hesitate to go with them, for I have sent them."

²¹Peter went down and said to the men, "I'm the one you're looking for. Why have you come?"

²²The men replied, "We have come from Cornelius the centurion. He is a righteous and God-fearing man, who is respected by all the Jewish people. A holy angel told him to have you come to his house so that he could hear what you have to say." ²³Then Peter invited the men into the house to be his guests.

G Jn 10:16 ◀ ▶ Ac 10:45
E Ac 9:17 ◀ ▶ Ac 10:44–47
L Ac 9:31 ◀ ▶ Ac 11:12

10:9 ᵛ S Mt 24:17
10:10 ʷ Ac 22:17
10:11 ˣ S Mt 3:16
10:14 ʸ Ac 9:5
  ᶻ Lev 11:4-8,13-20; 20:25; Dt 14:3-20; Eze 4:14
10:15 ᵃ ver 28; Ge 9:3; Mt 15:11; Lk 11:41; Ac 11:9; Ro 14:14,17,20; 1Co 10:25; 1Ti 4:3,4; Tit 1:15
10:17 ᵇ S Ac 9:10
  ᶜ ver 7,8
10:19 ᵈ S Ac 9:10
  ᵉ S Ac 8:29
10:20 ᶠ Ac 15:7-9
10:22 ᵍ ver 2
  ʰ Ac 11:14
10:23 ⁱ S Ac 1:16
  ʲ ver 45; Ac 11:12
10:24 ᵏ S Ac 8:40
10:26 ˡ Ac 14:15; Rev 19:10; 22:8,9
10:27 ᵐ ver 24
10:28 ⁿ Jn 4:9; 18:28; Ac 11:3
  ᵒ S ver 14,15; Ac 15:8,9
10:30 ᵖ S Jn 20:12
10:34 ᵠ Dt 10:17; 2Ch 19:7; Job 34:19; Mk 12:14; Ro 2:11; Gal 2:6; Eph 6:9; Col 3:25; Jas 2:1; 1Pe 1:17
10:35 ʳ Ac 15:9
10:36 ˢ 1Jn 1:5
  ᵗ S Ac 13:32
  ᵘ S Lk 2:14
  ᵛ S Mt 28:18

Peter at Cornelius's House

The next day Peter started out with them, and some of the brothers from Joppa went along. ²⁴The following day he arrived in Caesarea. Cornelius was expecting them and had called together his relatives and close friends. ²⁵As Peter entered the house, Cornelius met him and fell at his feet in reverence. ²⁶But Peter made him get up. "Stand up," he said, "I am only a man myself."

²⁷Talking with him, Peter went inside and found a large gathering of people. ²⁸He said to them: "You are well aware that it is against our law for a Jew to associate with a Gentile or visit him. But God has shown me that I should not call any man impure or unclean. ²⁹So when I was sent for, I came without raising any objection. May I ask why you sent for me?"

³⁰Cornelius answered: "Four days ago I was in my house praying at this hour, at three in the afternoon. Suddenly a man in shining clothes stood before me ³¹and said, 'Cornelius, God has heard your prayer and remembered your gifts to the poor. ³²Send to Joppa for Simon who is called Peter. He is a guest in the home of Simon the tanner, who lives by the sea.' ³³So I sent for you immediately, and it was good of you to come. Now we are all here in the presence of God to listen to everything the Lord has commanded you to tell us."

³⁴Then Peter began to speak: "I now realize how true it is that God does not show favoritism ³⁵but accepts men from every nation who fear him and do what is right. ³⁶You know the message God sent to the people of Israel, telling the good news of peace through Jesus Christ, who is Lord of all. ³⁷You know what has happened throughout Judea, beginning in Galilee after the baptism that

W Ac 2:21 ◀ ▶ Ac 10:43

q 19 One early manuscript *two*; other manuscripts do not have the number.

10:15 The Holy Spirit came to Peter to instruct him that he was to preach the gospel to the Gentiles as well as the Jews. Using a vivid illustration, God showed Peter that the ancient laws demanding a separation from the Gentiles to insure ritual cleanliness were no longer required. The doors of salvation were now open to anyone who would sincerely repent and follow Jesus (see Mk 7:14–19).

John preached— ³⁸how God anointed Jesus of Nazareth with the Holy Spirit and power, and how he went around doing good and healing all who were under the power of the devil, because God was with him.

³⁹"We are witnesses of everything he did in the country of the Jews and in Jerusalem. They killed him by hanging him on a tree, ⁴⁰but God raised him from the dead on the third day and caused him to be seen. ⁴¹He was not seen by all the people, but by witnesses whom God had already chosen—by us who ate and drank with him after he rose from the dead. ⁴²He commanded us to preach to the people and to testify that he is the one whom God appointed as judge of the living and the dead. ⁴³All the prophets testify about him that everyone who believes in him receives forgiveness of sins through his name."

⁴⁴While Peter was still speaking these words, the Holy Spirit came on all who heard the message. ⁴⁵The circumcised believers who had come with Peter were astonished that the gift of the Holy Spirit had been poured out even on the Gentiles. ⁴⁶For they heard them speaking in tongues and praising God.

Then Peter said, ⁴⁷"Can anyone keep these people from being baptized with water? They have received the Holy Spirit just as we have." ⁴⁸So he ordered that they be baptized in the name of Jesus Christ." Then they asked Peter to stay with them for a few days.

Peter Explains His Actions

11 The apostles and the brothers throughout Judea heard that the Gentiles also had received the word of God. ²So when Peter went up to Jerusalem, the circumcised believers criticized him ³and said, "You went into the house of uncircumcised men and ate with them."

⁴Peter began and explained everything to them precisely as it had happened: ⁵"I was in the city of Joppa praying, and in a trance I saw a vision. I saw something like a large sheet being let down from heaven by its four corners, and it came down to where I was. ⁶I looked into it and saw four-footed animals of the earth, wild beasts, reptiles, and birds of the air. ⁷Then I heard a voice telling me, 'Get up, Peter. Kill and eat.'

⁸"I replied, 'Surely not, Lord! Nothing impure or unclean has ever entered my mouth.'

⁹"The voice spoke from heaven a second time, 'Do not call anything impure that God has made clean.' ¹⁰This happened three times, and then it was all pulled up to heaven again.

¹¹"Right then three men who had been sent to me from Caesarea stopped at the house where I was staying. ¹²The Spirit told me to have no hesitation about going with them. These six brothers also went with me, and we entered the man's house. ¹³He told us how he had seen an angel appear in his house and say, 'Send to Joppa for Simon who is called Peter. ¹⁴He will bring you a message through which you and all your household will be saved.'

¹⁵"As I began to speak, the Holy Spirit came on them as he had come on us at

---

10:44—11:1 The Jews found it hard to believe that God had opened the door of salvation to the Gentiles. Their lifelong training had confirmed that they alone were God's chosen people. Yet, when they saw the gift of the Holy Spirit poured out on the Gentiles, they realized that the church would be composed of people from every race.

the beginning.[g] [16]Then I remembered what the Lord had said: 'John baptized with[s] water,[h] but you will be baptized with the Holy Spirit.'[i] [17]So if God gave them the same gift[j] as he gave us,[k] who believed in the Lord Jesus Christ, who was I to think that I could oppose God?"

[18]When they heard this, they had no further objections and praised God, saying, "So then, God has granted even the Gentiles repentance unto life."[l]

The Church in Antioch

[19]Now those who had been scattered by the persecution in connection with Stephen[m] traveled as far as Phoenicia, Cyprus and Antioch,[n] telling the message only to Jews. [20]Some of them, however, men from Cyprus[o] and Cyrene,[p] went to Antioch[q] and began to speak to Greeks also, telling them the good news[r] about the Lord Jesus. [21]The Lord's hand was with them,[s] and a great number of people believed and turned to the Lord.[t]

[22]News of this reached the ears of the church at Jerusalem, and they sent Barnabas[u] to Antioch. [23]When he arrived and saw the evidence of the grace of God,[v] he was glad and encouraged them all to remain true to the Lord with all their hearts.[w] [24]He was a good man, full of the Holy Spirit[x] and faith, and a great number of people were brought to the Lord.[y]

[25]Then Barnabas went to Tarsus[z] to look for Saul, [26]and when he found him, he brought him to Antioch. So for a whole year Barnabas and Saul met with the church and taught great numbers of people. The disciples[a] were called Christians first[b] at Antioch.

[27]During this time some prophets[c] came down from Jerusalem to Antioch. [28]One of them, named Agabus,[d] stood up and through the Spirit predicted that a severe famine would spread over the entire Roman world.[e] (This happened during the reign of Claudius.)[f] [29]The disciples,[g] each according to his ability, decided to provide help[h] for the brothers[i] living in Judea. [30]This they did, sending their gift to the elders[j] by Barnabas[k] and Saul.[l]

Peter's Miraculous Escape From Prison

12 It was about this time that King Herod[m] arrested some who belonged to the church, intending to persecute them. [2]He had James, the brother of John,[n] put to death with the sword.[o] [3]When he saw that this pleased the Jews,[p] he proceeded to seize Peter also. This happened during the Feast of Unleavened Bread.[q] [4]After arresting him, he put him in prison, handing him over to be guarded by four squads of four soldiers each. Herod intended to bring him out for public trial after the Passover.[r]

[5]So Peter was kept in prison, but the church was earnestly praying to God for him.[s]

[6]The night before Herod was to bring him to trial, Peter was sleeping between two soldiers, bound with two chains,[t] and sentries stood guard at the entrance. [7]Suddenly an angel[u] of the Lord appeared and a light shone in the cell. He struck Peter on the side and woke him up. "Quick, get up!" he said, and the chains fell off Peter's wrists.[v]

[8]Then the angel said to him, "Put on your clothes and sandals." And Peter did so. "Wrap your cloak around you and follow me," the angel told him. [9]Peter followed him out of the prison, but he had no idea that what the angel was doing was really happening; he thought he was seeing a vision.[w] [10]They passed the first and second guards and came to the iron gate leading to the city. It opened for them by itself,[x] and they went through it. When they had walked the length of one street, suddenly the angel left him.

[11]Then Peter came to himself[y] and said, "Now I know without a doubt that the Lord sent his angel and rescued me[z] from Herod's clutches and from everything the Jewish people were anticipating."

[12]When this had dawned on him, he went to the house of Mary the mother of

John, also called Mark,[a] where many people had gathered and were praying.[b] [13]Peter knocked at the outer entrance, and a servant girl named Rhoda came to answer the door.[c] [14]When she recognized Peter's voice, she was so overjoyed[d] she ran back without opening it and exclaimed, "Peter is at the door!"

[15]"You're out of your mind," they told her. When she kept insisting that it was so, they said, "It must be his angel."[e]

[16]But Peter kept on knocking, and when they opened the door and saw him, they were astonished. [17]Peter motioned with his hand[f] for them to be quiet and described how the Lord had brought him out of prison. "Tell James[g] and the brothers[h] about this," he said, and then he left for another place.

[18]In the morning, there was no small commotion among the soldiers as to what had become of Peter. [19]After Herod had a thorough search made for him and did not find him, he cross-examined the guards and ordered that they be executed.[i]

Herod's Death

Then Herod went from Judea to Caesarea[j] and stayed there a while. [20]He had been quarrelling with the people of Tyre and Sidon;[k] they now joined together and sought an audience with him. Having secured the support of Blastus, a trusted personal servant of the king, they asked for peace, because they depended on the king's country for their food supply.[l]

[21]On the appointed day Herod, wearing his royal robes, sat on his throne and delivered a public address to the people. [22]They shouted, "This is the voice of a god, not of a man." [23]Immediately, because Herod did not give praise to God, an angel[m] of the Lord struck him down,[n] and he was eaten by worms and died.

[24]But the word of God[o] continued to increase and spread.[p]

[25]When Barnabas[q] and Saul had finished their mission,[r] they returned from[t] Jerusalem, taking with them John, also called Mark.[s]

Barnabas and Saul Sent Off

13 In the church at Antioch[t] there were prophets[u] and teachers:[v] Barnabas,[w] Simeon called Niger, Lucius of Cyrene,[x] Manaen (who had been brought

12:12 [a]ver 25; Ac 13:5,13; 15:37,39; Col 4:10; 2Ti 4:11; Phm 24; 1Pe 5:13 [b]ver 5
12:13 [c]Jn 18:16,17
12:14 [d]Lk 24:41
12:15 [e]S Mt 18:10
12:17 [f]Ac 13:16; 19:33; 21:40 [g]S Ac 15:13 [h]S Ac 1:16
12:19 [i]Ac 16:27 [j]S Ac 8:40
12:20 [k]S Mt 11:21 [l]1Ki 5:9,11; Eze 27:17
12:23 [m]S Ac 5:19 [n]1Sa 25:38; 2Sa 24:16,17; 2Ki 19:35
12:24 [o]S Heb 4:12 [p]Ac 6:7; 19:20
12:25 [q]S Ac 4:36 [r]Ac 11:30 [s]S ver 12
13:1 [t]S Ac 11:19 [u]S Ac 11:27 [v]S Eph 4:11 [w]S Ac 4:36 [x]S Mt 27:32 [y]S Mt 14:1
13:2 [z]S Ac 8:29 [a]Ac 14:26 [b]Ac 9:15; 22:21
13:3 [c]S Ac 6:6 [d]Ac 14:26
13:4 [e]ver 2,3 [f]Ac 4:36
13:5 [g]S Heb 4:12 [h]S Ac 9:20 [i]S Ac 12:12
13:6 [j]Ac 8:9 [k]S Mt 7:15
13:7 [l]ver 8,12; Ac 18:12; 19:38
13:8 [m]Ac 8:9 [n]S ver 7 [o]Isa 30:11; Ac 6:7
13:9 [p]S Lk 1:15
13:10 [q]Mt 13:38; Jn 8:44 [r]Hos 14:9
13:11 [s]Ex 9:3; 1Sa 5:6,7; Ps 32:4 [t]Ge 19:10,11; 2Ki 6:18
13:12 [u]S ver 7
13:13 [v]ver 6 [w]S Ac 2:10
[x]S Ac 12:12

up with Herod[y] the tetrarch) and Saul. [2]While they were worshiping the Lord and fasting, the Holy Spirit said,[z] "Set apart for me Barnabas and Saul for the work[a] to which I have called them."[b] [3]So after they had fasted and prayed, they placed their hands on them[c] and sent them off.[d]

On Cyprus

[4]The two of them, sent on their way by the Holy Spirit,[e] went down to Seleucia and sailed from there to Cyprus.[f] [5]When they arrived at Salamis, they proclaimed the word of God[g] in the Jewish synagogues.[h] John[i] was with them as their helper.

[6]They traveled through the whole island until they came to Paphos. There they met a Jewish sorcerer[j] and false prophet[k] named Bar-Jesus, [7]who was an attendant of the proconsul,[l] Sergius Paulus. The proconsul, an intelligent man, sent for Barnabas and Saul because he wanted to hear the word of God. [8]But Elymas the sorcerer[m] (for that is what his name means) opposed them and tried to turn the proconsul[n] from the faith.[o] [9]Then Saul, who was also called Paul, filled with the Holy Spirit,[p] looked straight at Elymas and said, [10]"You are a child of the devil[q] and an enemy of everything that is right! You are full of all kinds of deceit and trickery. Will you never stop perverting the right ways of the Lord?[r] [11]Now the hand of the Lord is against you.[s] You are going to be blind, and for a time you will be unable to see the light of the sun."[t] Immediately mist and darkness came over him, and he groped about, seeking someone to lead him by the hand. [12]When the proconsul[u] saw what had happened, he believed, for he was amazed at the teaching about the Lord.

In Pisidian Antioch

[13]From Paphos,[v] Paul and his companions sailed to Perga in Pamphylia,[w] where John[x] left them to return to Jerusalem.

E *Ac 11:28* ◀ ▶ *Ac 13:9*
L *Ac 11:12* ◀ ▶ *Ac 13:9*
E *Ac 13:2* ◀ ▶ *Ac 13:52*
L *Ac 13:2* ◀ ▶ *Ac 15:28*
D *Ac 10:38* ◀ ▶ *1Co 10:8*

[t] 25 Some manuscripts *to*

¹⁴From Perga they went on to Pisidian Antioch.ʸ On the Sabbathᶻ they entered the synagogueᵃ and sat down. ¹⁵After the reading from the Lawᵇ and the Prophets, the synagogue rulers sent word to them, saying, "Brothers, if you have a message of encouragement for the people, please speak."

¹⁶Standing up, Paul motioned with his handᶜ and said: "Men of Israel and you Gentiles who worship God, listen to me! ¹⁷The God of the people of Israel chose our fathers; he made the people prosper during their stay in Egypt, with mighty power he led them out of that country,ᵈ ¹⁸he endured their conductᵘᵉ for about forty years in the desert,ᶠ ¹⁹he overthrew seven nations in Canaanᵍ and gave their land to his peopleʰ as their inheritance.ⁱ ²⁰All this took about 450 years.

"After this, God gave them judgesʲ until the time of Samuel the prophet.ᵏ ²¹Then the people asked for a king,ˡ and he gave them Saulᵐ son of Kish, of the tribe of Benjamin,ⁿ who ruled forty years. ²²After removing Saul,ᵒ he made David their king.ᵖ He testified concerning him: 'I have found David son of Jesse a man after my own heart;ᑫ he will do everything I want him to do.'ʳ

²³"From this man's descendantsˢ God has brought to Israel the Saviorᵗ Jesus," as he promised.ᵛ ²⁴Before the coming of Jesus, John preached repentance and baptism to all the people of Israel.ʷ ²⁵As John was completing his work,ˣ he said: 'Who do you think I am? I am not that one.ʸ No, but he is coming after me, whose sandals I am not worthy to untie.'ᶻ

²⁶"Brothers,ᵃ children of Abraham,ᵇ and you God-fearing Gentiles, it is to us that this message of salvationᶜ has been sent. ²⁷The people of Jerusalem and their rulers did not recognize Jesus,ᵈ yet in condemning him they fulfilled the words of the prophetsᵉ that are read every Sabbath. ²⁸Though they found no proper ground for a death sentence, they asked Pilate to have him executed.ᶠ ²⁹When they had carried out all that was written about him,ᵍ they took him down from the treeʰ and laid him in a tomb.ⁱ ³⁰But God raised him from the dead,ʲ ³¹and for many days he was seen by those who had traveled with him from Galilee to Jerusalem.ᵏ They are now his witnessesˡ to our people.

³²"We tell you the good news:ᵐ What God promised our fathersⁿ ³³he has fulfilled for us, their children, by raising up Jesus.ᵒ As it is written in the second Psalm:

" 'You are my Son;
    today I have become your
        Father.'ᵛʷᵖ

³⁴The fact that God raised him from the dead, never to decay, is stated in these words:

" 'I will give you the holy and sure
    blessings promised to David.'ˣᑫ

³⁵So it is stated elsewhere:

" 'You will not let your Holy One see
    decay.'ʸʳ

³⁶"For when David had served God's purpose in his own generation, he fell asleep;ˢ he was buried with his fathersᵗ and his body decayed. ³⁷But the one whom God raised from the deadᵘ did not see decay.

³⁸"Therefore, my brothers, I want you to know that through Jesus the forgiveness of sins is proclaimed to you.ᵛ ³⁹Through him everyone who believesʷ is justified from everything you could not be justified from by the law of Moses.ˣ ⁴⁰Take care that what the prophets have said does not happen to you:

⁴¹" 'Look, you scoffers,
    wonder and perish,
for I am going to do something in your
        days
that you would never believe,
    even if someone told you.'ᶻʸ

⁴²As Paul and Barnabas were leaving the synagogue,ᶻ the people invited them to speak further about these things on the next Sabbath. ⁴³When the congregation was dismissed, many of the Jews and devout converts to Judaism followed Paul

---

13:14 ʸ Ac 14:19, 21 ᶻ ver 27,42,44; Ac 16:13; 18:4 ᵃ S Ac 9:20
13:15 ᵇ Ac 15:21
13:16 ᶜ S Ac 12:17
13:17 ᵈ Ex 6:6,7; Dt 7:6-8
13:18 ᵉ Dt 1:31 ᶠ Nu 14:33; Ps 95:10; Ac 7:36
13:19 ᵍ Dt 7:1 ʰ Jos 19:51; Ac 7:45 ⁱ Ps 78:55
13:20 ʲ Jdg 2:16 ᵏ 1Sa 3:19,20; Ac 3:24
13:21 ˡ 1Sa 8:5,19 ᵐ 1Sa 10:1 ⁿ 1Sa 9:1,2
13:22 ᵒ 1Sa 15:23, 26 ᵖ 1Sa 16:13; Ps 89:20 ᑫ 1Sa 13:14; Jer 3:15 ʳ Isa 44:28
13:23 ˢ Mt 1:1 ᵗ S Lk 2:11 ᵘ Mt 1:21 ᵛ ver 32; 2Sa 7:11; 22:51; Jer 30:9
13:24 ʷ S Mk 1:4
13:25 ˣ Ac 20:24 ʸ Jn 1:20 ᶻ Mt 3:11; Jn 1:27
13:26 ᵃ S Ac 22:5 ᵇ S Lk 3:8 ᶜ Ac 4:12; 28:28
13:27 ᵈ Ac 3:17 ᵉ S Lk 24:27; S Mt 1:22
13:28 ᶠ Mt 27:20-25; Ac 3:14
13:29 ᵍ S Mt 1:22; Lk 18:31 ʰ S Ac 5:30 ⁱ Lk 23:53
13:30 ʲ S Mt 16:21; 28:6; S Ac 2:24
13:31 ᵏ Mt 28:16 ˡ S Lk 24:48
13:32 ᵐ Isa 40:9; 52:7; Ac 5:42; 8:35; 10:36; 14:7,15,21; 17:18 ⁿ Ac 26:6; Ro 1:2; 4:13; 9:4
13:33 ᵒ S Ac 2:24 ᵖ Ps 2:7; S Mt 3:17
13:34 ᑫ Isa 55:3
13:35 ʳ Ps 16:10; Ac 2:27
13:36 ˢ Mt 9:24 ᵗ 2Sa 7:12; 1Ki 2:10; 2Ch 29:28; Ac 2:29
13:37 ᵘ S Ac 2:24
13:38 ᵛ S Lk 24:47; Ac 2:38
13:39 ʷ S Jn 3:15 ˣ S Ro 3:28
13:41 ʸ Hab 1:5
13:42 ᶻ ver 14

F Ac 10:43 ◀ ▶ Ac 16:30–31
K Ac 13:23 ◀ ▶ Ac 13:47
L Ac 11:18 ◀ ▶ Ac 13:47
W Ac 13:26 ◀ ▶ Ac 17:27
H Ac 3:23 ◀ ▶ Ro 1:18

ᵘ 18 Some manuscripts *and cared for them* ᵛ 33 Or *have begotten you* ʷ 33 Psalm 2:7 ˣ 34 Isaiah 55:3 ʸ 35 Psalm 16:10 ᶻ 41 Hab. 1:5

K Ac 10:43 ◀ ▶ Ac 13:38–39
W Ac 10:43 ◀ ▶ Ac 13:38–39

and Barnabas, who talked with them and urged them to continue in the grace of God.ᵃ ⁴⁴On the next Sabbath almost the whole city gathered to hear the word of the Lord. ⁴⁵When the Jews saw the crowds, they were filled with jealousy and talked abusivelyᵇ against what Paul was saying.ᶜ

G ⁴⁶Then Paul and Barnabas answered them boldly: "We had to speak the word of God to you first.ᵈ Since you reject it and do not consider yourselves worthy of eternal life, we now turn to the Gen-
K tiles.ᵉ ⁴⁷For this is what the Lord has
L commanded us:

" 'I have made youᵃ a light for the
  Gentiles,ᶠ
that youᵃ may bring salvation to the
  ends of the earth.'ᵇ"ᵍ

⁴⁸When the Gentiles heard this, they were glad and honored the word of the Lord;ʰ and all who were appointed for eternal life believed.

⁴⁹The word of the Lordⁱ spread through the whole region. ⁵⁰But the Jews incited the God-fearing women of high standing and the leading men of the city. They stirred up persecution against Paul and Barnabas, and expelled them from their region.ʲ ⁵¹So they shook the dust from their feetᵏ in protest against them
B and went to Iconium.ˡ ⁵²And the disci-
E plesᵐ were filled with joy and with the
F Holy Spirit.ⁿ
J

In Iconium

14 At Iconiumᵒ Paul and Barnabas went as usual into the Jewish synagogue.ᵖ There they spoke so effectively that a great numberᵍ of Jews and Gentiles believed. ²But the Jews who refused to believe stirred up the Gentiles and poisoned their minds against the brothers.ʳ ³So Paul and Barnabas spent considerable time there, speaking boldlyˢ for the Lord, who confirmed the message of his grace by enabling them to do miraculous signs and wonders.ᵗ ⁴The people of the city were divided; some sided with the Jews, others with the apostles.ᵘ ⁵There was a plot afoot among the Gentiles and Jews,ᵛ together with their leaders, to mistreat them and stone them.ʷ ⁶But they found out about it and fledˣ to the Lycaonian cities of Lystra and Derbe and to the surrounding country, ⁷where they continued to preachʸ the good news.ᶻ

In Lystra and Derbe

⁸In Lystra there sat a man crippled in his feet, who was lame from birthᵃ and had never walked. ⁹He listened to Paul as he was speaking. Paul looked directly at him, saw that he had faith to be healedᵇ ¹⁰and called out, "Stand up on your feet!"ᶜ At that, the man jumped up and began to walk.ᵈ

¹¹When the crowd saw what Paul had done, they shouted in the Lycaonian language, "The gods have come down to us in human form!"ᵉ ¹²Barnabas they called Zeus, and Paul they called Hermes because he was the chief speaker.ᶠ ¹³The priest of Zeus, whose temple was just outside the city, brought bulls and wreaths to the city gates because he and the crowd wanted to offer sacrifices to them.

¹⁴But when the apostles Barnabas and Paul heard of this, they tore their clothesᵍ and rushed out into the crowd, shouting: ¹⁵"Men, why are you doing this? We too are only men,ʰ human like you. We are bringing you good news,ⁱ

13:43 ᵃS Ac 11:23; 14:22; S Ro 3:24
13:45 ᵇAc 18:6; 1Pe 4:4; Jude 10 ᶜS 1Th 2:16
13:46 ᵈver 26; Ac 3:26 ᵉMt 21:41; Ac 18:6; 22:21; 26:20; 28:28; Ro 11:11
13:47 ᶠS Lk 2:32 ᵍIsa 49:6
13:48 ʰver 49; Ac 8:25; 15:35,36; 19:10,20
13:49 ⁱS ver 48
13:50 ʲS 1Th 2:16
13:51 ᵏS Mt 10:14 ˡAc 14:1,19,21; 16:2; 2Ti 3:11
13:52 ᵐS Ac 11:26 ⁿS Lk 1:15
14:1 ᵒS Ac 13:51 ᵖS Ac 9:20 ᵍS Ac 2:41
14:2 ʳS Ac 1:16
14:3 ˢS Ac 4:29 ᵗS Jn 4:48
14:4 ᵘAc 17:4,5; 28:24
14:5 ᵛS Ac 20:3 ʷver 19
14:6 ˣS Mt 10:23
14:7 ʸAc 16:10 ᶻver 15,21; S Ac 13:32
14:8 ᵃS Ac 3:2
14:9 ᵇS Mk 9:28,29; 13:58
14:10 ᶜEze 2:1 ᵈAc 3:8
14:11 ᵉS Ac 8:10; 28:6
14:12 ᶠEx 7:1
14:14 ᵍS Mk 14:63
14:15 ʰS Ac 10:26 ⁱver 7,21; S Ac 13:32

G Ac 11:18 ◀▶ Ac 14:27
K Ac 13:38–39 ◀▶ Ac 16:31
L Ac 13:38–39 ◀▶ Ac 15:11
B Ac 11:24 ◀▶ Ac 15:8
E Ac 13:9 ◀▶ Ac 15:8
F Ac 9:31 ◀▶ Ro 5:5   J Ac 9:31 ◀▶ Ro 5:5

E Ac 10:38 ◀▶ Ac 14:8–10
E Ac 14:3 ◀▶ Ac 14:19–20

ᵃ 47 The Greek is singular.   ᵇ 47 Isaiah 49:6

13:46–48 Paul and Barnabas declared that since the Jews who persecuted them wanted nothing to do with their message about Christ and "do not consider yourselves worthy of eternal life" (13:46), Paul and Barnabas would take their message to the Gentiles. Paul said they were going to the Gentiles in fulfillment of Isaiah's prophecy to be "a light for the Gentiles, that you may bring my salvation to the ends of the earth" (Isa 49:6). Israel had failed to fulfill this command by ignoring the Gentile nations. Paul's outreach to the Gentiles proved that God's mercy extended to include "all who were appointed for eternal life" (13:48).

telling you to turn from these worthless things to the living God, who made heaven and earth and sea and everything in them. ¹⁶In the past, he let all nations go their own way. ¹⁷Yet he has not left himself without testimony: He has shown kindness by giving you rain from heaven and crops in their seasons; he provides you with plenty of food and fills your hearts with joy." ¹⁸Even with these words, they had difficulty keeping the crowd from sacrificing to them.

¹⁹Then some Jews came from Antioch and Iconium and won the crowd over. They stoned Paul and dragged him outside the city, thinking he was dead. ²⁰But after the disciples had gathered around him, he got up and went back into the city. The next day he and Barnabas left for Derbe.

The Return to Antioch in Syria

²¹They preached the good news in that city and won a large number of disciples. Then they returned to Lystra, Iconium and Antioch, ²²strengthening the disciples and encouraging them to remain true to the faith. "We must go through many hardships to enter the kingdom of God," they said. ²³Paul and Barnabas appointed elders^c for them in each church and, with prayer and fasting, committed them to the Lord, in whom they had put their trust. ²⁴After going through Pisidia, they came into Pamphylia, ²⁵and when they had preached the word in Perga, they went down to Attalia.

²⁶From Attalia they sailed back to Antioch, where they had been committed to the grace of God for the work they had now completed. ²⁷On arriving there, they gathered the church together and reported all that God had done through them and how he had opened the door of faith to the Gentiles. ²⁸And they stayed there a long time with the disciples.

The Council at Jerusalem

15 Some men came down from Judea to Antioch and were teaching the brothers: "Unless you are circumcised, according to the custom taught by Moses, you cannot be saved." ²This brought Paul and Barnabas into sharp dispute and debate with them. So Paul and Barnabas were appointed, along with some other believers, to go up to Jerusalem to see the apostles and elders about this question. ³The church sent them on their way, and as they traveled through Phoenicia and Samaria, they told how the Gentiles had been converted. This news made all the brothers very glad. ⁴When they came to Jerusalem, they were welcomed by the church and the apostles and elders, to whom they reported everything God had done through them.

⁵Then some of the believers who belonged to the party of the Pharisees stood up and said, "The Gentiles must be circumcised and required to obey the law of Moses."

⁶The apostles and elders met to consider this question. ⁷After much discussion, Peter got up and addressed them: "Brothers, you know that some time ago God made a choice among you that the

E *Ac 14:8–10* ◀ ▶ *Ac 16:16–18*
V *Ac 12:7–11* ◀ ▶ *Ac 16:26*
S *Ac 3:26* ◀ ▶ *Ro 1:18*

G *Ac 13:46–48* ◀ ▶ *Ac 15:3*
G *Ac 14:27* ◀ ▶ *Ac 15:7–9*
G *Ac 15:3* ◀ ▶ *Ac 15:12*

^c 23 Or *Barnabas ordained elders*; or *Barnabas had elders elected*

14:27 When the church was gathered together, they discussed Isaiah's prophecies and God's offer of salvation extended to the Gentiles. This was a radical change for the Jewish believers because the Gentiles were now entering the fellowship of God on the same basis as the Jews—their repentance from sin.
15:3 The believers rejoiced when they heard that the church would include converted Gentiles.
15:7–12 The first council of the church at Jerusalem established guidelines for the proper response toward Gentile believers who accepted faith in Jesus and wished to join the church. Some Jewish believers, called Judaizers, wanted to force the Gentile converts to be circumcised and to follow the ancient Jewish law before they could be accepted as legitimate followers of Jesus. This fundamental dispute could have destroyed the early church unless it was resolved properly. Peter affirmed that God had offered salvation to the Gentiles and confirmed his gift by freely giving the Gentiles the gift of the Holy Spirit as well. "Putting on the necks of the disciples a yoke" (15:10) was not what God intended. Salvation was free, therefore acceptance and fellowship should be also.

Gentiles might hear from my lips the message of the gospel and believe.[x] [8]God, who knows the heart,[y] showed that he accepted them by giving the Holy Spirit to them,[z] just as he did to us. [9]He made no distinction between us and them,[a] for he purified their hearts by faith.[b] [10]Now then, why do you try to test God[c] by putting on the necks of the disciples a yoke[d] that neither we nor our fathers have been able to bear? [11]No! We believe it is through the grace[e] of our Lord Jesus that we are saved, just as they are."

[12]The whole assembly became silent as they listened to Barnabas and Paul telling about the miraculous signs and wonders[f] God had done among the Gentiles through them.[g] [13]When they finished, James[h] spoke up: "Brothers, listen to me. [14]Simon[d] has described to us how God at first showed his concern by taking from the Gentiles a people for himself.[i] [15]The words of the prophets are in agreement with this, as it is written:

[16]" 'After this I will return
  and rebuild David's fallen tent.
Its ruins I will rebuild,
  and I will restore it,
[17]that the remnant of men may seek the Lord,
  and all the Gentiles who bear my name,

B Ac 13:52 ◄ ► Ac 19:1–7
E Ac 13:52 ◄ ► Ac 15:28
S Lk 1:17 ◄ ► Ro 1:4
E Ac 1:24 ◄ ► Ac 15:18
L Ac 13:47 ◄ ► Ac 17:27
G Ac 15:7–9 ◄ ► Ac 18:6

15:7 [x] Ac 10:1-48
15:8 [y] S Rev 2:23
      [z] S Ac 10:44,47
15:9 [a] Ac 10:28, 34; 11:12
     [b] Ac 10:43
15:10 [c] Ac 5:9
      [d] S Mt 23:4; Gal 5:1
15:11 [e] S Ro 3:24; Gal 2:16; Eph 2:5-8
15:12 [f] S Jn 4:48
      [g] ver 4; Ac 14:27; 21:19
15:13 [h] Ac 12:17; 21:18; 1Co 15:7; Gal 1:19; 2:9,12
15:14 [i] 2Pe 1:1
15:17 [j] Am 9:11,12
15:18 [k] Isa 45:21
15:20 [l] 1Co 8:7-13; 10:14-28; Rev 2:14,20 [m] 1Co 10:7,8; Rev 2:14,20 [n] ver 29; Ge 9:4; Lev 3:17; 7:26; 17:10-13; 19:26; Dt 12:16,23
15:21 [o] Ac 13:15; 2Co 3:14,15
15:22 [p] S Ac 11:30 [q] S Ac 11:19 [r] ver 27,32,40; Ac 16:19,25,29; 2Co 1:19; 1Th 1:1; 2Th 1:1; 1Pe 5:12
15:23 [s] ver 1; S Ac 11:19 [t] S Lk 2:2 [u] ver 41; S Ac 6:9 [v] Ac 23:25, 26; Jas 1:1

says the Lord, who does these
    things'[ej]
[18]that have been known for ages.[fk] **E**

[19]"It is my judgment, therefore, that we should not make it difficult for the Gentiles who are turning to God. [20]Instead we should write to them, telling them to abstain from food polluted by idols,[l] from sexual immorality,[m] from the meat of strangled animals and from blood.[n] [21]For Moses has been preached in every city from the earliest times and is read in the synagogues on every Sabbath."[o]

The Council's Letter to Gentile Believers

[22]Then the apostles and elders,[p] with the whole church, decided to choose some of their own men and send them to Antioch[q] with Paul and Barnabas. They chose Judas (called Barsabbas) and Silas,[r] two men who were leaders among the brothers. [23]With them they sent the following letter:

The apostles and elders, your brothers,

To the Gentile believers in Antioch,[s] Syria[t] and Cilicia:[u]

Greetings.[v]

[24]We have heard that some went

E Ac 15:8 ◄ ► Ro 8:27

[d] 14 Greek *Simeon*, a variant of *Simon*; that is, Peter [e] 17 Amos 9:11,12 [f] 17,18 Some manuscripts *things*'—/ [18]*known to the Lord for ages is his work*

15:15–20 The first bishop of the church in Jerusalem was James, the brother of Jesus. He replied to Peter and Paul's messages by reminding his audience that the prophet Amos had predicted that God would reach out to the Gentiles in the last days (see Am 9:11–12) and would reinstate David's rule through Jesus the Messiah.

James' authoritative conclusion to this debate was that the Gentile converts should be given only four specific requirements: (1) they must abstain from food that had been polluted by, or offered to, idols (see 1Co 8:7–13; 10:18–22); (2) they should abstain from fornication and sexual immorality such as adultery, incest, prostitution and homosexuality; (3) Gentile converts must not eat anything strangled; and (4) these new converts were not permitted to eat blood. These last two restrictions were prudent commands for the Gentile believers because of Moses' restriction for God's people to abstain from association with any people who ate blood (see Lev 17:12). This declaration of the church settled forever that Gentiles believers did not need to become Jews or become circumcised or follow any other special Jewish legal regulation. Salvation is dependent entirely upon the atonement for sins based on the blood of Jesus Christ, not on any person's righteous works.

Note that the apostles did not demand that Gentile believers must worship on the Sabbath day (Saturday). The Gentile believers joined the Jewish believers and worshiped on the Lord's day (Sunday) in celebration of Christ's resurrection from the dead. While Jewish and Gentile believers worshiped Jesus on Sunday, many of the Jewish believers continued to celebrate the Sabbath day too and visit the temple in Jerusalem (see Ac 21:20–26).

out from us without our authorization and disturbed you, troubling your minds by what they said.[w] [25]So we all agreed to choose some men and send them to you with our dear friends Barnabas and Paul— [26]men who have risked their lives[x] for the name of our Lord Jesus Christ. [27]Therefore we are sending Judas and Silas[y] to confirm by word of mouth what we are writing. [28]It seemed good to the Holy Spirit[z] and to us not to burden you with anything beyond the following requirements: [29]You are to abstain from food sacrificed to idols, from blood, from the meat of strangled animals and from sexual immorality.[a] You will do well to avoid these things.

Farewell.

[30]The men were sent off and went down to Antioch, where they gathered the church together and delivered the letter. [31]The people read it and were glad for its encouraging message. [32]Judas and Silas,[b] who themselves were prophets,[c] said much to encourage and strengthen the brothers. [33]After spending some time there, they were sent off by the brothers with the blessing of peace[d] to return to those who had sent them.[g] [35]But Paul and Barnabas remained in Antioch, where they and many others taught and preached[e] the word of the Lord.[f]

Disagreement Between Paul and Barnabas

[36]Some time later Paul said to Barnabas, "Let us go back and visit the brothers in all the towns[g] where we preached the word of the Lord[h] and see how they are doing." [37]Barnabas wanted to take John, also called Mark,[i] with them, [38]but Paul did not think it wise to take him, because he had deserted them[j] in Pamphylia and had not continued with them in the work. [39]They had such a sharp disagreement that they parted company. Barnabas took Mark and sailed for Cyprus, [40]but Paul chose Silas[k] and left, commended by the brothers to the grace of the Lord.[l] [41]He went through Syria[m] and Cilicia,[n] strengthening the churches.[o]

E *Ac 15:8* ◀ ▶ *Ac 16:6–7*
L *Ac 13:9* ◀ ▶ *Ac 16:6–7*

15:24 w ver 1; Gal 1:7; 5:10
15:26 x Ac 9:23-25; 14:19; 1Co 15:30
15:27 y S ver 22
15:28 z Ac 4:32
15:29 a ver 20; Ac 21:25
15:32 b S ver 22 c S Ac 11:27
15:33 d 1Sa 1:17; Mk 5:34; Lk 7:50; Ac 16:36; 1Co 16:11
15:35 e Ac 8:4 f S Ac 13:48
15:36 g Ac 13:4, 13,14,51; 14:1,6, 24,25 h S Ac 13:48
15:37 i S Ac 12:12
15:38 j Ac 13:13
15:40 k S ver 22 l S Ac 11:23
15:41 m ver 23; S Lk 2:2 n S Ac 6:9 o Ac 16:5
16:1 p Ac 14:6 q Ac 17:14; 18:5; 19:22; 20:4; Ro 16:21; 1Co 4:17; 16:10; 2Co 1:1,19; Php 1:1; 2:19; Col 1:1; 1Th 1:1; 3:2,6; 2Th 1:1; 1Ti 1:2,18; 2Ti 1:2, 5,6; Phm 1 r 2Ti 1:5
16:2 s ver 40; S Ac 1:16 t S Ac 13:51
16:3 u Gal 2:3
16:4 v S Ac 11:30 w Ac 15:2 x Ac 15:28,29
16:5 y Ac 9:31; 15:41 z S Ac 2:41
16:6 a Ac 2:10; 18:23 b Ac 18:23; Gal 1:2; 3:1 c S Ac 2:9
16:7 d Ro 8:9; Gal 4:6; Php 1:19; 1Pe 1:11
16:8 e ver 11; Ac 20:5; 2Co 2:12; 2Ti 4:13
16:9 f S Ac 9:10 g Ac 19:21,29; 20:1,3; Ro 15:26; 1Co 16:5; 1Th 1:7, 8
16:10 h ver 10-17; Ac 20:5-15; 21:1-18; 27:1-28:16 i Ac 14:7
16:11 j S ver 8
16:12 k Ac 20:6; Php 1:1; 1Th 2:2 l S ver 9
16:13 m S Ac 13:14
16:14 n Rev 1:11; 2:18,24 o Lk 24:45

Timothy Joins Paul and Silas

16 He came to Derbe and then to Lystra,[p] where a disciple named Timothy[q] lived, whose mother was a Jewess and a believer,[r] but whose father was a Greek. [2]The brothers[s] at Lystra and Iconium[t] spoke well of him. [3]Paul wanted to take him along on the journey, so he circumcised him because of the Jews who lived in that area, for they all knew that his father was a Greek.[u] [4]As they traveled from town to town, they delivered the decisions reached by the apostles and elders[v] in Jerusalem[w] for the people to obey.[x] [5]So the churches were strengthened[y] in the faith and grew daily in numbers.[z]

Paul's Vision of the Man of Macedonia

[6]Paul and his companions traveled throughout the region of Phrygia[a] and Galatia,[b] having been kept by the Holy Spirit from preaching the word in the province of Asia.[c] [7]When they came to the border of Mysia, they tried to enter Bithynia, but the Spirit of Jesus[d] would not allow them to. [8]So they passed by Mysia and went down to Troas.[e] [9]During the night Paul had a vision[f] of a man of Macedonia[g] standing and begging him, "Come over to Macedonia and help us." [10]After Paul had seen the vision, we[h] got ready at once to leave for Macedonia, concluding that God had called us to preach the gospel[i] to them.

Lydia's Conversion in Philippi

[11]From Troas[j] we put out to sea and sailed straight for Samothrace, and the next day on to Neapolis. [12]From there we traveled to Philippi,[k] a Roman colony and the leading city of that district of Macedonia.[l] And we stayed there several days.

[13]On the Sabbath[m] we went outside the city gate to the river, where we expected to find a place of prayer. We sat down and began to speak to the women who had gathered there. [14]One of those listening was a woman named Lydia, a dealer in purple cloth from the city of Thyatira,[n] who was a worshiper of God. The Lord opened her heart[o] to respond to Paul's

E *Ac 15:28* ◀ ▶ *Ac 18:5*
L *Ac 15:28* ◀ ▶ *Ac 18:5*

g 33 Some manuscripts *them,* 34 *but Silas decided to remain there*

message. ¹⁵When she and the members of her household ᵖ were baptized, ᵠ she invited us to her home. "If you consider me a believer in the Lord," she said, "come and stay at my house." And she persuaded us.

Paul and Silas in Prison

E ¹⁶Once when we were going to the place of prayer, ʳ we were met by a slave girl who had a spirit ˢ by which she predicted the future. She earned a great deal of money for her owners by fortune-telling. ¹⁷This girl followed Paul and the rest of us, shouting, "These men are servants of the Most High God, ᵗ who are telling you the way to be saved." ¹⁸She kept this up for many days. Finally Paul became so troubled that he turned around and said to the spirit, "In the name of Jesus Christ I command you to come out of her!" At that moment the spirit left her. ᵘ

¹⁹When the owners of the slave girl realized that their hope of making money ᵛ was gone, they seized Paul and Silas ʷ and dragged ˣ them into the marketplace to face the authorities. ²⁰They brought them before the magistrates and said, "These men are Jews, and are throwing our city into an uproar ʸ ²¹by advocating customs unlawful for us Romans ᶻ to accept or practice." ᵃ

²²The crowd joined in the attack against Paul and Silas, and the magistrates ordered them to be stripped and beaten. ᵇ ²³After they had been severely flogged, they were thrown into prison, and the jailer ᶜ was commanded to guard them carefully. ²⁴Upon receiving such orders, he put them in the inner cell and fastened their feet in the stocks. ᵈ

²⁵About midnight ᵉ Paul and Silas ᶠ were praying and singing hymns ᵍ to God, and the other prisoners were listening to

V them. ²⁶Suddenly there was such a violent earthquake that the foundations of the prison were shaken. ʰ At once all the prison doors flew open, ⁱ and everybody's chains came loose. ʲ ²⁷The jailer woke up, and when he saw the prison doors open, he drew his sword and was about to kill himself because he thought the prisoners had escaped. ᵏ ²⁸But Paul shouted, "Don't harm yourself! We are all here!"

E *Ac 14:19–20* ◀ ▶ *Ac 19:11–12*
V *Ac 14:19–20* ◀ ▶ *Ac 18:10*

16:15 ᵖ S Ac 11:14
 ᵠ S Ac 2:38
16:16 ʳ ver 13
 ˢ Dt 18:11;
 1Sa 28:3,7
16:17 ᵗ S Mk 5:7
16:18
 ᵘ S Mk 16:17
16:19 ᵛ ver 16;
 Ac 19:25,26
 ʷ S Ac 15:22
 ˣ Ac 8:3; 17:6;
 21:30; Jas 2:6
16:20 ʸ Ac 17:6
16:21 ᶻ ver 12
 ᵃ Est 3:8
16:22 ᵇ 2Co 11:25;
 1Th 2:2
16:23 ᶜ ver 27,36
16:24 ᵈ Job 13:27;
 33:11; Jer 20:2,3;
 29:26
16:25 ᵉ Ps 119:55,
 62 ᶠ S Ac 15:22
 ᵍ S Eph 5:19
16:26 ʰ Ac 4:31
 ⁱ Ac 5:19; 12:10
 ʲ Ac 12:7
16:27 ᵏ Ac 12:19
16:29 ˡ S Ac 15:22
16:30 ᵐ Ac 2:37
16:31 ⁿ S Jn 3:15
 ᵒ S Ro 11:14
 ᵖ S Ac 11:14
16:33 ᵠ ver 25
 ʳ S Ac 2:38
16:34 ˢ S Ac 11:14
16:36 ᵗ ver 23,27
 ᵘ S Ac 15:33
16:37
 ᵛ Ac 22:25-29
16:38 ʷ Ac 22:29
16:39 ˣ Mt 8:34;
 Lk 8:37
16:40 ʸ ver 14
 ᶻ ver 2; S Ac 1:16
17:1 ᵃ ver 11,13;
 Php 4:16; 1Th 1:1;
 2Th 1:1; 2Ti 4:10
17:2 ᵇ S Ac 9:20
 ᶜ S Ac 13:14
 ᵈ Ac 8:35; 18:28
17:3 ᵉ Lk 24:26;
 Ac 3:18 ᶠ Lk 24:46;
 S Ac 2:24
 ᵍ S Ac 9:22
17:4 ʰ S Ac 15:22

²⁹The jailer called for lights, rushed in and fell trembling before Paul and Silas. ˡ ³⁰He then brought them out and asked, F "Sirs, what must I do to be saved?" ᵐ ³¹They replied, "Believe ⁿ in the Lord K Jesus, and you will be saved ᵒ—you and your household." ᵖ ³²Then they spoke the word of the Lord to him and to all the others in his house. ³³At that hour of the night ᵠ the jailer took them and washed their wounds; then immediately he and all his family were baptized. ʳ ³⁴The jailer brought them into his house and set a meal before them; he ˢ was filled with joy because he had come to believe in God—he and his whole family.

³⁵When it was daylight, the magistrates sent their officers to the jailer with the order: "Release those men." ³⁶The jailer ᵗ told Paul, "The magistrates have ordered that you and Silas be released. Now you can leave. Go in peace." ᵘ ³⁷But Paul said to the officers: "They beat us publicly without a trial, even though we are Roman citizens, ᵛ and threw us into prison. And now do they want to get rid of us quietly? No! Let them come themselves and escort us out."

³⁸The officers reported this to the magistrates, and when they heard that Paul and Silas were Roman citizens, they were alarmed. ʷ ³⁹They came to appease them and escorted them from the prison, requesting them to leave the city. ˣ ⁴⁰After Paul and Silas came out of the prison, they went to Lydia's house, ʸ where they met with the brothers ᶻ and encouraged them. Then they left.

In Thessalonica

17 When they had passed through Amphipolis and Apollonia, they came to Thessalonica, ᵃ where there was a Jewish synagogue. ²As his custom was, Paul went into the synagogue, ᵇ and on three Sabbath ᶜ days he reasoned with them from the Scriptures, ᵈ ³explaining and proving that the Christ ʰ had to suffer ᵉ and rise from the dead. ᶠ "This Jesus I am proclaiming to you is the Christ, ʰ" ᵍ he said. ⁴Some of the Jews were persuaded and joined Paul and Silas, ʰ as did

F *Ac 13:38–39* ◀ ▶ *Ac 20:21*
K *Ac 13:47* ◀ ▶ *Ac 20:32*

ʰ 3 Or *Messiah*

a large number of God-fearing Greeks and not a few prominent women.

⁵But the Jews were jealous; so they rounded up some bad characters from the marketplace, formed a mob and started a riot in the city.ⁱ They rushed to Jason'sʲ house in search of Paul and Silas in order to bring them out to the crowd.ʲ ⁶But when they did not find them, they dragged ᵏ Jason and some other brothersˡ before the city officials, shouting: "These men who have caused trouble all over the world ᵐ have now come here,ⁿ ⁷and Jason has welcomed them into his house. They are all defying Caesar's decrees, saying that there is another king, one called Jesus."ᵒ ⁸When they heard this, the crowd and the city officials were thrown into turmoil. ⁹Then they made Jason ᵖ and the others post bond and let them go.

In Berea

¹⁰As soon as it was night, the brothers sent Paul and Silasᵍ away to Berea.ʳ On arriving there, they went to the Jewish synagogue.ˢ ¹¹Now the Bereans were of more noble character than the Thessalonians,ᵗ for they received the message with great eagerness and examined the Scripturesᵘ every day to see if what Paul said was true.ᵛ ¹²Many of the Jews believed, as did also a number of prominent Greek women and many Greek men.ʷ

¹³When the Jews in Thessalonica learned that Paul was preaching the word of God at Berea,ˣ they went there too, agitating the crowds and stirring them up. ¹⁴The brothersʸ immediately sent Paul to the coast, but Silasᶻ and Timothyᵃ stayed at Berea. ¹⁵The men who escorted Paul brought him to Athensᵇ and then left with instructions for Silas and Timothy to join him as soon as possible.ᶜ

In Athens

¹⁶While Paul was waiting for them in Athens, he was greatly distressed to see that the city was full of idols. ¹⁷So he reasoned in the synagogueᵈ with the Jews and the God-fearing Greeks, as well as in the marketplace day by day with those

M Ac 3:19–21 ◀ ▶ Ro 4:13

17:5 ⁱ ver 13; S 1Th 2:16 ʲ Ro 16:21
17:6 ᵏ S Ac 16:19 ˡ S Ac 1:16 ᵐ S Mt 24:14 ⁿ Ac 16:20
17:7 ᵒ Lk 23:2; Jn 19:12
17:9 ᵖ ver 5
17:10 ᵍ S Ac 15:22 ʳ ver 13; Ac 20:4 ˢ S Ac 9:20
17:11 ᵗ S ver 1 ᵘ Lk 16:29; Jn 5:39 ᵛ Dt 29:29
17:12 ʷ S Ac 2:41
17:13 ˣ S Heb 4:12
17:14 ʸ S Ac 9:30 ᶻ S Ac 15:22 ᵃ S Ac 16:1
17:15 ᵇ ver 16,21, 22; Ac 18:1; 1Th 3:1 ᶜ Ac 18:5
17:17 ᵈ S Ac 9:20
17:18 ᵉ S Ac 13:32 ᶠ ver 31,32; Ac 4:2
17:19 ᵍ ver 22 ʰ Mk 1:27
17:21 ⁱ S ver 15
17:22 ʲ ver 19 ᵏ ver 16
17:23 ˡ Jn 4:22
17:24 ᵐ Isa 42:5; Ac 14:15 ⁿ Dt 10:14; Isa 66:1,2; Mt 11:25 ᵒ 1Ki 8:27; Ac 7:48
17:25 ᵖ Ps 50:10-12; Isa 42:5
17:26 ᵍ Dt 32:8; Job 12:23
17:27 ʳ Dt 4:7; Isa 55:6; Jer 23:23, 24
17:28 ˢ Dt 30:20; Job 12:10; Da 5:23

---

who happened to be there. ¹⁸A group of Epicurean and Stoic philosophers began to dispute with him. Some of them asked, "What is this babbler trying to say?" Others remarked, "He seems to be advocating foreign gods." They said this because Paul was preaching the good newsᵉ about Jesus and the resurrection.ᶠ ¹⁹Then they took him and brought him to a meeting of the Areopagus,ᵍ where they said to him, "May we know what this new teachingʰ is that you are presenting? ²⁰You are bringing some strange ideas to our ears, and we want to know what they mean." ²¹(All the Atheniansⁱ and the foreigners who lived there spent their time doing nothing but talking about and listening to the latest ideas.)

²²Paul then stood up in the meeting of the Areopagusʲ and said: "Men of Athens! I see that in every way you are very religious.ᵏ ²³For as I walked around and looked carefully at your objects of worship, I even found an altar with this inscription: TO AN UNKNOWN GOD. Now what you worship as somethingᵘⁿknownˡ I am going to proclaim to you.

²⁴"The God who made the world and everything in itᵐ is the Lord of heaven and earthⁿ and does not live in temples built by hands.ᵒ ²⁵And he is not served by human hands, as if he needed anything, because he himself gives all men life and breath and everything else.ᵖ ²⁶From one man he made every nation of men, that they should inhabit the whole earth; and he determined the times set for them and the exact places where they should live.ᵍ ²⁷God did this so that men would seek him and perhaps reach out for him and find him, though he is not far from each one of us.ʳ ²⁸For in him we live and move and have our being.'ˢ As some of your own poets have said, 'We are his offspring.'

²⁹"Therefore since we are God's off-

F Jn 11:23–25 ◀ ▶ Ac 23:6
L Ac 15:11 ◀ ▶ Ac 26:17–18
W Ac 13:38–39 ◀ ▶ Ro 1:16

ⁱ 5 Or the assembly of the people

17:6–7 The envious Jews who did not believe Paul's message accused the believers of preaching insurrection against Rome. Distorting the spiritual teachings that Jesus would ultimately be the Messiah, these enemies of the gospel intimated that Paul and Silas were encouraging resistance to Rome.

spring, we should not think that the divine being is like gold or silver or stone—an image made by man's design and skill.ᵗ ³⁰In the past God overlooked ᵘ such ignorance,ᵛ but now he commands all people everywhere to repent.ʷ ³¹For he has set a day when he will judgeˣ the world with justiceʸ by the man he has appointed.ᶻ He has given proof of this to all men by raising him from the dead."ᵃ

³²When they heard about the resurrection of the dead,ᵇ some of them sneered, but others said, "We want to hear you again on this subject." ³³At that, Paul left the Council. ³⁴A few men became followers of Paul and believed. Among them was Dionysius, a member of the Areopagus,ᶜ also a woman named Damaris, and a number of others.

In Corinth

18 After this, Paul left Athensᵈ and went to Corinth.ᵉ ²There he met a Jew named Aquila, a native of Pontus, who had recently come from Italy with his wife Priscilla,ᶠ because Claudiusᵍ had ordered all the Jews to leave Rome. Paul went to see them, ³and because he was a tentmaker as they were, he stayed and worked with them.ʰ ⁴Every Sabbathⁱ he reasoned in the synagogue,ʲ trying to persuade Jews and Greeks.

⁵When Silasᵏ and Timothyˡ came from Macedonia,ᵐ Paul devoted himself exclusively to preaching, testifying to the Jews that Jesus was the Christ.ʲⁿ ⁶But when the Jews opposed Paul and became abusive,ᵒ he shook out his clothes in protestᵖ and said to them, "Your blood be on your own heads!ᑫ I am clear of my responsibility.ʳ From now on I will go to the Gentiles."ˢ

⁷Then Paul left the synagogue and went next door to the house of Titius Justus, a worshiper of God.ᵗ ⁸Crispus,ᵘ the synagogue ruler,ᵛ and his entire householdʷ believed in the Lord; and many of the Corinthians who heard him believed and were baptized.

⁹One night the Lord spoke to Paul in a vision:ˣ "Do not be afraid;ʸ keep on speaking, do not be silent. ¹⁰For I am with you,ᶻ and no one is going to attack and harm you, because I have many people in this city." ¹¹So Paul stayed for a year and a half, teaching them the word of God.ᵃ

¹²While Gallio was proconsulᵇ of Achaia,ᶜ the Jews made a united attack on Paul and brought him into court. ¹³"This man," they charged, "is persuading the people to worship God in ways contrary to the law."

¹⁴Just as Paul was about to speak, Gallio said to the Jews, "If you Jews were making a complaint about some misdemeanor or serious crime, it would be reasonable for me to listen to you. ¹⁵But since it involves questions about words and names and your own lawᵈ—settle the matter yourselves. I will not be a judge of such things." ¹⁶So he had them ejected from the court. ¹⁷Then they all turned on Sosthenesᵉ the synagogue rulerᶠ and beat him in front of the court. But Gallio showed no concern whatever.

Priscilla, Aquila and Apollos

¹⁸Paul stayed on in Corinth for some time. Then he left the brothersᵍ and sailed for Syria,ʰ accompanied by Priscilla and Aquila.ⁱ Before he sailed, he had his hair cut off at Cenchreaʲ because of a vow he had taken.ᵏ ¹⁹They arrived at Ephesus,ˡ where Paul left Priscilla and Aquila. He himself went into the synagogue and reasoned with the Jews. ²⁰When they asked him to spend more time with them, he declined. ²¹But as he left, he promised, "I will come back if it is God's will."ᵐ Then he set sail from Ephe-

R Ac 11:18 ◀▶ Ac 19:18–20
J Jn 12:48 ◀▶ Ro 2:5
J Ac 10:42 ◀▶ Ac 24:25
E Ac 16:6–7 ◀▶ Ac 19:1–7
L Ac 16:6–7 ◀▶ Ac 20:22–23
G Ac 15:12 ◀▶ Ac 28:28

S Lk 21:18 ◀▶ Ac 23:11
V Ac 16:26 ◀▶ Ro 8:31

j 5 Or Messiah; also in verse 28

17:30–31 Paul reminded his listeners that God's judgment is certain and will occur on an appointed day. He emphasized that God commands repentance because of sin and because of this approaching judgment.

18:6 After preaching Christ to these Jews that so vigorously rejected his teaching, Paul gave up on them and turned to preach to the Gentiles.

sus. ²²When he landed at Caesarea,ⁿ he went up and greeted the church and then went down to Antioch.ᵒ

²³After spending some time in Antioch, Paul set out from there and traveled from place to place throughout the region of Galatiaᵖ and Phrygia,ᑫ strengthening all the disciples.ʳ

²⁴Meanwhile a Jew named Apollos,ˢ a native of Alexandria, came to Ephesus.ᵗ He was a learned man, with a thorough knowledge of the Scriptures. ²⁵He had been instructed in the way of the Lord, and he spoke with great fervorᵏᵘ and taught about Jesus accurately, though he knew only the baptism of John.ᵛ ²⁶He began to speak boldly in the synagogue. When Priscilla and Aquilaʷ heard him, they invited him to their home and explained to him the way of God more adequately.

²⁷When Apollos wanted to go to Achaia,ˣ the brothersʸ encouraged him and wrote to the disciples there to welcome him. On arriving, he was a great help to those who by grace had believed. ²⁸For he vigorously refuted the Jews in public debate, proving from the Scripturesᶻ that Jesus was the Christ.ᵃ

Paul in Ephesus

B
E **19** While Apollosᵇ was at Corinth,ᶜ Paul took the road through the
W interior and arrived at Ephesus.ᵈ There he found some disciples ²and asked them, "Did you receive the Holy Spiritᵉ when you believed?"

They answered, "No, we have not even heard that there is a Holy Spirit."

³So Paul asked, "Then what baptism did you receive?"

"John's baptism," they replied.

⁴Paul said, "John's baptismᶠ was a baptism of repentance. He told the people to believe in the one coming after him, that is, in Jesus." ᵍ ⁵On hearing this, they were baptized intoᵐ the name of the Lord
G Jesus.ʰ ⁶When Paul placed his hands on
M them,ⁱ the Holy Spirit came on them,ʲ
T and they spoke in tonguesⁿᵏ and prophe-

B Ac 15:8 ◀ ▶ Ro 8:23
E Ac 18:5 ◀ ▶ Ac 20:22–23
W Ac 9:17 ◀ ▶ Ro 1:11
G Ac 11:27–28 ◀ ▶ Ac 20:28
M Ac 11:24 ◀ ▶ Ro 1:4
T Ac 11:28 ◀ ▶ Ac 20:23

18:22 ⁿS Ac 8:40
ᵒS Ac 11:19

18:23 ᵖS Ac 16:6
ᑫAc 2:10; 16:6
ʳAc 14:22; 15:32, 41

18:24 ˢAc 19:1; 1Co 1:12; 3:5,6,22; 4:6; 16:12; Tit 3:13
ᵗS ver 19

18:25 ᵘS Ro 12:11
ᵛS Mk 1:4

18:26 ʷS ver 2

18:27 ˣS ver 12
ʸver 18; S Ac 1:16

18:28 ᶻAc 8:35; 17:2 ᵃver 5; S Ac 9:22

19:1 ᵇS Ac 18:24
ᶜS Ac 18:1
ᵈS Ac 18:19

19:2 ᵉS Jn 20:22

19:4 ᶠS Mk 1:4
ᵍJn 1:7

19:5 ʰS Ac 2:38

19:6 ⁱS Ac 6:6
ʲS Ac 10:44
ᵏS Mk 16:17

19:8 ˡS Ac 9:20
ᵐS Mt 3:2; Ac 28:23

19:9 ⁿAc 14:4
ᵒver 23; S Ac 9:2
ᵖver 30; S Ac 11:26

19:10 ᑫAc 20:31
ʳver 22,26,27; S Ac 2:9
ˢS Ac 13:48

19:11 ᵗAc 8:13

19:12 ᵘAc 5:15

19:13 ᵛMt 12:27
ʷMk 9:38

19:17 ˣS Ac 18:19
ʸAc 5:5,11

19:20 ᶻS Ac 13:48
ᵃAc 6:7; 12:24

19:21 ᵇAc 20:16, 22; 21:4,12,15; Ro 15:25
ᶜS Ac 16:9
ᵈAc 18:12
ᵉRo 15:24,28

19:22 ᶠAc 13:5
ᵍS Ac 16:1
ʰRo 16:23; 2Ti 4:20

---

sied. ⁷There were about twelve men in all.

⁸Paul entered the synagogueˡ and spoke boldly there for three months, arguing persuasively about the kingdom of God.ᵐ ⁹But some of themⁿ became obstinate; they refused to believe and publicly maligned the Way.ᵒ So Paul left them. He took the disciplesᵖ with him and had discussions daily in the lecture hall of Tyrannus. ¹⁰This went on for two years,ᑫ so that all the Jews and Greeks who lived in the province of Asiaʳ heard the word of the Lord.ˢ

¹¹God did extraordinary miraclesᵗ **E** through Paul, ¹²so that even handkerchiefs and aprons that had touched him were taken to the sick, and their illnesses were curedᵘ and the evil spirits left them.

¹³Some Jews who went around driving out evil spiritsᵛ tried to invoke the name of the Lord Jesus over those who were demon-possessed. They would say, "In the name of Jesus,ʷ whom Paul preaches, I command you to come out." ¹⁴Seven sons of Sceva, a Jewish chief priest, were doing this. ¹⁵One day the evil spirit answered them, "Jesus I know, and I know about Paul, but who are you?" ¹⁶Then the man who had the evil spirit jumped on them and overpowered them all. He gave them such a beating that they ran out of the house naked and bleeding.

¹⁷When this became known to the Jews and Greeks living in Ephesus,ˣ they were all seized with fear,ʸ and the name of the Lord Jesus was held in high honor.

¹⁸Many of those who believed now came **R** and openly confessed their evil deeds. ¹⁹A number who had practiced sorcery brought their scrolls together and burned them publicly. When they calculated the value of the scrolls, the total came to fifty thousand drachmas.ᵒ ²⁰In this way the word of the Lordᶻ spread widely and grew in power.ᵃ

²¹After all this had happened, Paul decided to go to Jerusalem,ᵇ passing through Macedoniaᶜ and Achaia.ᵈ "After I have been there," he said, "I must visit Rome also."ᵉ ²²He sent two of his helpers,ᶠ Timothyᵍ and Erastus,ʰ to Macedo-

E Ac 16:16–18 ◀ ▶ Ac 20:9–12
R Ac 17:30 ◀ ▶ Ac 20:21

ᵏ 25 Or *with fervor in the Spirit* ˡ 2 Or *after* ᵐ 5 Or *in* ⁿ 6 Or *other languages* ᵒ 19 A drachma was a silver coin worth about a day's wages.

nia, while he stayed in the province of Asia a little longer.

The Riot in Ephesus

23 About that time there arose a great disturbance about the Way. 24 A silversmith named Demetrius, who made silver shrines of Artemis, brought in no little business for the craftsmen. 25 He called them together, along with the workmen in related trades, and said: "Men, you know we receive a good income from this business. 26 And you see and hear how this fellow Paul has convinced and led astray large numbers of people here in Ephesus and in practically the whole province of Asia. He says that man-made gods are no gods at all. 27 There is danger not only that our trade will lose its good name, but also that the temple of the great goddess Artemis will be discredited, and the goddess herself, who is worshiped throughout the province of Asia and the world, will be robbed of her divine majesty."

28 When they heard this, they were furious and began shouting: "Great is Artemis of the Ephesians!" 29 Soon the whole city was in an uproar. The people seized Gaius and Aristarchus, Paul's traveling companions from Macedonia, and rushed as one man into the theater. 30 Paul wanted to appear before the crowd, but the disciples would not let him. 31 Even some of the officials of the province, friends of Paul, sent him a message begging him not to venture into the theater.

32 The assembly was in confusion: Some were shouting one thing, some another. Most of the people did not even know why they were there. 33 The Jews pushed Alexander to the front, and some of the crowd shouted instructions to him. He motioned for silence in order to make a defense before the people. 34 But when they realized he was a Jew, they all shouted in unison for about two hours: "Great is Artemis of the Ephesians!"

35 The city clerk quieted the crowd and said: "Men of Ephesus, doesn't all the world know that the city of Ephesus is the guardian of the temple of the great Artemis and of her image, which fell from heaven? 36 Therefore, since these facts are undeniable, you ought to be quiet and not do anything rash. 37 You have brought these men here, though they have neither robbed temples nor blasphemed our goddess. 38 If, then, Demetrius and his fellow craftsmen have a grievance against anybody, the courts are open and there are proconsuls. They can press charges. 39 If there is anything further you want to bring up, it must be settled in a legal assembly. 40 As it is, we are in danger of being charged with rioting because of today's events. In that case we would not be able to account for this commotion, since there is no reason for it." 41 After he had said this, he dismissed the assembly.

Through Macedonia and Greece

20 When the uproar had ended, Paul sent for the disciples and, after encouraging them, said good-by and set out for Macedonia. 2 He traveled through that area, speaking many words of encouragement to the people, and finally arrived in Greece, 3 where he stayed three months. Because the Jews made a plot against him just as he was about to sail for Syria, he decided to go back through Macedonia. 4 He was accompanied by Sopater son of Pyrrhus from Berea, Aristarchus and Secundus from Thessalonica, Gaius from Derbe, Timothy also, and Tychicus and Trophimus from the province of Asia. 5 These men went on ahead and waited for us at Troas. 6 But we sailed from Philippi after the Feast of Unleavened Bread, and five days later joined the others at Troas, where we stayed seven days.

Eutychus Raised From the Dead at Troas

7 On the first day of the week we came together to break bread. Paul spoke to the people and, because he intended to leave the next day, kept on talking until midnight. 8 There were many lamps in the upstairs room where we were meeting. 9 Seated in a window was a young man named Eutychus, who was sinking into a deep sleep as Paul talked on and on. When he was sound asleep, he fell to the ground from the third story and was picked up dead. 10 Paul went down, threw himself on the young man and put his arms around him. "Don't be alarmed," he

E *Ac 19:11–12* ◄ ► *Ac 22:11–13*

said. "He's alive!"ᵘ ¹¹Then he went upstairs again and broke bread ᵛ and ate. After talking until daylight, he left. ¹²The people took the young man home alive and were greatly comforted.

Paul's Farewell to the Ephesian Elders

¹³We went on ahead to the ship and sailed for Assos, where we were going to take Paul aboard. He had made this arrangement because he was going there on foot. ¹⁴When he met us at Assos, we took him aboard and went on to Mitylene. ¹⁵The next day we set sail from there and arrived off Kios. The day after that we crossed over to Samos, and on the following day arrived at Miletus.ʷ ¹⁶Paul had decided to sail past Ephesusˣ to avoid spending time in the province of Asia,ʸ for he was in a hurry to reach Jerusalem,ᶻ if possible, by the day of Pentecost.ᵃ

¹⁷From Miletus,ᵇ Paul sent to Ephesus for the eldersᶜ of the church. ¹⁸When they arrived, he said to them: "You know how I lived the whole time I was with you,ᵈ from the first day I came into the province of Asia.ᵉ ¹⁹I served the Lord with great humility and with tears,ᶠ although I was severely tested by the plots of the Jews.ᵍ ²⁰You know that I have not hesitated to preach anythingʰ that would be helpful to you but have taught you publicly and from house to house. ²¹I have declared to both Jewsⁱ and Greeks that they must turn to God in repentanceʲ and have faith in our Lord Jesus.ᵏ

²²"And now, compelled by the Spirit, I am going to Jerusalem,ˡ not knowing what will happen to me there. ²³I only know that in every city the Holy Spirit warns meᵐ that prison and hardships are facing me.ⁿ ²⁴However, I consider my life worth nothing to me,ᵒ if only I may finish the raceᵖ and complete the taskᑫ the Lord Jesus has given meʳ—the task of testifying to the gospel of God's grace.ˢ

²⁵"Now I know that none of you among whom I have gone about preaching the kingdomᵗ will ever see me again.ᵘ ²⁶Therefore, I declare to you today that I am innocent of the blood of all men.ᵛ

²⁷For I have not hesitated to proclaim to you the whole will of God.ʷ ²⁸Keep watch over yourselves and all the flockˣ of which the Holy Spirit has made you overseers.ᵖʸ Be shepherds of the church of God,ᑫᶻ which he boughtᵃ with his own blood.ᵇ ²⁹I know that after I leave, savage wolvesᶜ will come in among you and will not spare the flock.ᵈ ³⁰Even from your own number men will arise and distort the truth in order to draw away disciplesᵉ after them. ³¹So be on your guard! Remember that for three yearsᶠ I never stopped warning each of you night and day with tears.ᵍ

³²"Now I commit you to Godʰ and to the word of his grace, which can build you up and give you an inheritanceⁱ among all those who are sanctified.ʲ ³³I have not coveted anyone's silver or gold or clothing.ᵏ ³⁴You yourselves know that these hands of mine have supplied my own needs and the needs of my companions.ˡ ³⁵In everything I did, I showed you that by this kind of hard work we must help the weak, remembering the words the Lord Jesus himself said: 'It is more blessed to give than to receive.'"

³⁶When he had said this, he knelt down with all of them and prayed.ᵐ ³⁷They all wept as they embraced him and kissed him.ⁿ ³⁸What grieved them most was his statement that they would never see his face again.ᵒ Then they accompanied him to the ship.ᵖ

On to Jerusalem

21 After weᑫ had torn ourselves away from them, we put out to sea and sailed straight to Cos. The next day we went to Rhodes and from there to Patara. ²We found a ship crossing over to Phoenicia,ʳ went on board and set sail. ³After sighting Cyprus and passing to the south of it, we sailed on to Syria.ˢ We landed at Tyre, where our ship was to unload its cargo. ⁴Finding the disciplesᵗ

F *Ac 16:30–31* ◀▶ *Ro 1:16*
R *Ac 19:18–20* ◀▶ *Ac 26:20*
E *Ac 19:1–7* ◀▶ *Ac 20:28*
L *Ac 18:5* ◀▶ *Ac 20:28*
T *Ac 19:6* ◀▶ *Ac 21:4*

20:10 ʷ Mt 9:23, 24
20:11 ᵛ ver 7; S Mt 14:19
20:15 ʷ ver 17; 2Ti 4:20
20:16 ˣ S Ac 18:19 ʸ S Ac 2:9 ᶻ S Ac 19:21 ᵃ S Ac 2:1
20:17 ᵇ ver 15 ᶜ S Ac 11:30
20:18 ᵈ Ac 18:19-21; 19:1-41 ᵉ S Ac 2:9
20:19 ᶠ Ps 6:6 ᵍ S ver 3
20:20 ʰ ver 27; Ps 40:10; Jer 26:2; 42:4
20:21 ⁱ Ac 18:5 ʲ S Ac 2:38 ᵏ Ac 24:24; 26:18; Eph 1:15; Col 2:5; Phm 5
20:22 ˡ ver 16
20:23 ᵐ S Ac 8:29; 21:4 ⁿ S Ac 9:16
20:24 ᵒ Ac 21:13 ᵖ 2Ti 4:7 ᑫ 2Co 4:1 ʳ Gal 1:1; Tit 1:3 ˢ S Ac 11:23
20:25 ᵗ S Mt 4:23 ᵘ ver 38
20:26 ᵛ Eze 3:17-19; Ac 18:6
20:27 ʷ S ver 20
20:28 ˣ ver 29; S Jn 21:16 ʸ 1Ti 3:1 ᶻ S 1Co 10:32 ᵃ S 1Co 6:20 ᵇ S Ro 3:25
20:29 ᶜ Eze 34:5; Mt 7:15 ᵈ ver 28
20:30 ᵉ S Ac 11:26
20:31 ᶠ Ac 19:10 ᵍ ver 19
20:32 ʰ Ac 14:23 ⁱ S Eph 1:14; S Mt 25:34; Col 1:12; 3:24; Heb 9:15; 1Pe 1:4 ʲ Ac 26:18
20:33 ᵏ 1Sa 12:3; 1Co 9:12; 2Co 2:17; 7:2; 11:9; 12:14-17; 1Th 2:5
20:34 ˡ S Ac 18:3
20:36 ᵐ Lk 22:41; Ac 9:40; 21:5
20:37 ⁿ S Lk 15:20
20:38 ᵒ ver 25 ᵖ Ac 21:5
21:1 ᑫ S Ac 16:10
21:2 ʳ Ac 11:19
21:3 ˢ S Lk 2:2
21:4 ᵗ S Ac 11:26

E *Ac 20:22–23* ◀▶ *Ac 21:4*
G *Ac 19:6* ◀▶ *Ro 1:11*
L *Ac 20:22–23* ◀▶ *Ac 21:4*
D *Ac 8:32–35* ◀▶ *Ro 3:24–25*
K *Ac 16:31* ◀▶ *Ro 1:16*
E *Ac 20:28* ◀▶ *Ac 21:11*
L *Ac 20:28* ◀▶ *Ro 7:6*
T *Ac 20:23* ◀▶ *Ac 21:11*

ᵖ 28 Traditionally *bishops*   ᑫ 28 Many manuscripts *of the Lord*

there, we stayed with them seven days. Through the Spirit[u] they urged Paul not to go on to Jerusalem. [5]But when our time was up, we left and continued on our way. All the disciples and their wives and children accompanied us out of the city, and there on the beach we knelt to pray.[v] [6]After saying good-by to each other, we went aboard the ship, and they returned home.

[7]We continued our voyage from Tyre[w] and landed at Ptolemais, where we greeted the brothers[x] and stayed with them for a day. [8]Leaving the next day, we reached Caesarea[y] and stayed at the house of Philip[z] the evangelist,[a] one of the Seven. [9]He had four unmarried daughters who prophesied.[b]

[10]After we had been there a number of days, a prophet named Agabus[c] came down from Judea. [11]Coming over to us, he took Paul's belt, tied his own hands and feet with it and said, "The Holy Spirit says,[d] 'In this way the Jews of Jerusalem will bind[e] the owner of this belt and will hand him over to the Gentiles.'"[f]

[12]When we heard this, we and the people there pleaded with Paul not to go up to Jerusalem. [13]Then Paul answered, "Why are you weeping and breaking my heart? I am ready not only to be bound, but also to die[g] in Jerusalem for the name of the Lord Jesus."[h] [14]When he would not be dissuaded, we gave up[i] and said, "The Lord's will be done."[j]

[15]After this, we got ready and went up to Jerusalem.[k] [16]Some of the disciples from Caesarea[l] accompanied us and brought us to the home of Mnason, where we were to stay. He was a man from Cyprus[m] and one of the early disciples.

Paul's Arrival at Jerusalem

[17]When we arrived at Jerusalem, the brothers[n] received us warmly.[o] [18]The next day Paul and the rest of us went to see James,[p] and all the elders[q] were present. [19]Paul greeted them and reported in detail what God had done among the Gentiles[r] through his ministry.[s]

[20]When they heard this, they praised God. Then they said to Paul: "You see,

E *Ac 21:4* ◀ ▶ *Ac 28:25*
T *Ac 21:4* ◀ ▶ *Ac 28:25*

21:4 u ver 11; Ac 20:23
21:5 v Lk 22:41; Ac 9:40; 20:36
21:7 w Ac 12:20 x S Ac 1:16
21:8 y S Ac 8:40 z Ac 6:5; 8:5-40 a Eph 4:11; 2Ti 4:5
21:9 b Ex 15:20; Jdg 4:4; Ne 6:14; Lk 2:36; Ac 2:17; 1Co 11:5
21:10 c Ac 11:28
21:11 d S Ac 8:29 e ver 33 f 1Ki 22:11; Isa 20:2-4; Jer 13:1-11; Mt 20:19
21:13 g Ac 20:24 h S Jn 15:21; S Ac 9:16
21:14 i Ru 1:18 j S Mt 26:39
21:15 k S Ac 19:21
21:16 l S Ac 8:40 m ver 3,4
21:17 n S Ac 9:30 o Ac 15:4
21:18 p S Ac 15:13 q S Ac 11:30
21:19 r Ac 14:27; 15:4,12 s Ac 1:17
21:20 t Ac 22:3; Ro 10:2; Gal 1:14; Php 3:6 u Ac 15:1,5
21:21 v ver 28 w Ac 15:19-21; 1Co 7:18,19 x S Ac 6:14
21:23 y Nu 6:2,5, 18; Ac 18:18
21:24 z ver 26; Ac 24:18 a Ac 18:18
21:25 b Ac 15:20, 29
21:26 c Nu 6:13-20; Ac 24:18
21:27 d Jer 26:8; Ac 24:18; 26:21; S 1Th 2:16
21:28 e Mt 24:15; Ac 6:13; 24:5,6
21:29 f Ac 20:4; 2Ti 4:20 g S Ac 18:19
21:30 h Ac 26:21 i S Ac 16:19
21:32 j Ac 23:27

brother, how many thousands of Jews have believed, and all of them are zealous[t] for the law.[u] [21]They have been informed that you teach all the Jews who live among the Gentiles to turn away from Moses,[v] telling them not to circumcise their children[w] or live according to our customs.[x] [22]What shall we do? They will certainly hear that you have come, [23]so do what we tell you. There are four men with us who have made a vow.[y] [24]Take these men, join in their purification rites[z] and pay their expenses, so that they can have their heads shaved.[a] Then everybody will know there is no truth in these reports about you, but that you yourself are living in obedience to the law. [25]As for the Gentile believers, we have written to them our decision that they should abstain from food sacrificed to idols, from blood, from the meat of strangled animals and from sexual immorality."[b]

[26]The next day Paul took the men and purified himself along with them. Then he went to the temple to give notice of the date when the days of purification would end and the offering would be made for each of them.[c]

Paul Arrested

[27]When the seven days were nearly over, some Jews from the province of Asia saw Paul at the temple. They stirred up the whole crowd and seized him,[d] [28]shouting, "Men of Israel, help us! This is the man who teaches all men everywhere against our people and our law and this place. And besides, he has brought Greeks into the temple area and defiled this holy place."[e] [29](They had previously seen Trophimus[f] the Ephesian[g] in the city with Paul and assumed that Paul had brought him into the temple area.)

[30]The whole city was aroused, and the people came running from all directions. Seizing Paul,[h] they dragged him[i] from the temple, and immediately the gates were shut. [31]While they were trying to kill him, news reached the commander of the Roman troops that the whole city of Jerusalem was in an uproar. [32]He at once took some officers and soldiers and ran down to the crowd. When the rioters saw the commander and his soldiers, they stopped beating Paul.[j]

³³The commander came up and arrested him and ordered him to be bound with two chains. Then he asked who he was and what he had done. ³⁴Some in the crowd shouted one thing and some another, and since the commander could not get at the truth because of the uproar, he ordered that Paul be taken into the barracks. ³⁵When Paul reached the steps, the violence of the mob was so great he had to be carried by the soldiers. ³⁶The crowd that followed kept shouting, "Away with him!"

Paul Speaks to the Crowd
22:3–16pp — Ac 9:1–22; 26:9–18

³⁷As the soldiers were about to take Paul into the barracks, he asked the commander, "May I say something to you?"

"Do you speak Greek?" he replied. ³⁸"Aren't you the Egyptian who started a revolt and led four thousand terrorists out into the desert some time ago?" ³⁹Paul answered, "I am a Jew, from Tarsus in Cilicia, a citizen of no ordinary city. Please let me speak to the people."

⁴⁰Having received the commander's permission, Paul stood on the steps and motioned to the crowd. When they were all silent, he said to them in Aramaic:

22 ¹"Brothers and fathers, listen now to my defense."

²When they heard him speak to them in Aramaic, they became very quiet.

Then Paul said: ³"I am a Jew, born in Tarsus of Cilicia, but brought up in this city. Under Gamaliel I was thoroughly trained in the law of our fathers and was just as zealous for God as any of you are today. ⁴I persecuted the followers of this Way to their death, arresting both men and women and throwing them into prison, ⁵as also the high priest and all the Council can testify. I even obtained letters from them to their brothers in Damascus, and went there to bring these people as prisoners to Jerusalem to be punished.

⁶"About noon as I came near Damascus, suddenly a bright light from heaven flashed around me. ⁷I fell to the ground and heard a voice say to me, 'Saul! Saul! Why do you persecute me?'

⁸"'Who are you, Lord?' I asked.

"'I am Jesus of Nazareth,' whom you are persecuting,' he replied. ⁹My companions saw the light, but they did not understand the voice of him who was speaking to me.

¹⁰"'What shall I do, Lord?' I asked.

"'Get up,' the Lord said, 'and go into Damascus. There you will be told all that you have been assigned to do.' ¹¹My companions led me by the hand into Damascus, because the brilliance of the light had blinded me.

¹²"A man named Ananias came to see me. He was a devout observer of the law and highly respected by all the Jews living there. ¹³He stood beside me and said, 'Brother Saul, receive your sight!' And at that very moment I was able to see him.

¹⁴"Then he said: 'The God of our fathers has chosen you to know his will and to see the Righteous One and to hear words from his mouth. ¹⁵You will be his witness to all men of what you have seen and heard. ¹⁶And now what are you waiting for? Get up, be baptized and wash your sins away, calling on his name.'

¹⁷"When I returned to Jerusalem and was praying at the temple, I fell into a trance ¹⁸and saw the Lord speaking. 'Quick!' he said to me. 'Leave Jerusalem immediately, because they will not accept your testimony about me.'

¹⁹"'Lord,' I replied, 'these men know that I went from one synagogue to another to imprison and beat those who believe in you. ²⁰And when the blood of your martyr Stephen was shed, I stood there giving my approval and guarding the clothes of those who were killing him.'

²¹"Then the Lord said to me, 'Go; I will send you far away to the Gentiles.' "

Paul the Roman Citizen

²²The crowd listened to Paul until he said this. Then they raised their voices and shouted, "Rid the earth of him! He's not fit to live!"

²³As they were shouting and throwing off their cloaks and flinging dust into the air, ²⁴the commander ordered Paul to be taken into the barracks. He directed

E Ac 20:9–12 ◀▶ Ac 28:3–9

r 40 Or possibly *Hebrew*; also in 22:2 s 20 Or *witness*

that he be flogged and questioned in order to find out why the people were shouting at him like this. ²⁵As they stretched him out to flog him, Paul said to the centurion standing there, "Is it legal for you to flog a Roman citizen who hasn't even been found guilty?"ᵖ

²⁶When the centurion heard this, he went to the commander and reported it. "What are you going to do?" he asked. "This man is a Roman citizen."

²⁷The commander went to Paul and asked, "Tell me, are you a Roman citizen?"

"Yes, I am," he answered.

²⁸Then the commander said, "I had to pay a big price for my citizenship."

"But I was born a citizen," Paul replied.

²⁹Those who were about to question himᑫ withdrew immediately. The commander himself was alarmed when he realized that he had put Paul, a Roman citizen,ʳ in chains.ˢ

Before the Sanhedrin

³⁰The next day, since the commander wanted to find out exactly why Paul was being accused by the Jews,ᵗ he released himᵘ and ordered the chief priests and all the Sanhedrinᵛ to assemble. Then he brought Paul and had him stand before them.

23 Paul looked straight at the Sanhedrinʷ and said, "My brothers,ˣ I have fulfilled my duty to God in all good conscienceʸ to this day." ²At this the high priest Ananiasᶻ ordered those standing near Paul to strike him on the mouth.ᵃ ³Then Paul said to him, "God will strike you, you whitewashed wall!ᵇ You sit there to judge me according to the law, yet you yourself violate the law by commanding that I be struck!"ᶜ

⁴Those who were standing near Paul said, "You dare to insult God's high priest?"

⁵Paul replied, "Brothers, I did not realize that he was the high priest; for it is written: 'Do not speak evil about the ruler of your people.'ᵗ"ᵈ

⁶Then Paul, knowing that some of them were Sadduceesᵉ and the others Pharisees, called out in the Sanhedrin, "My brothers,ᶠ I am a Pharisee,ᵍ the son of a Pharisee. I stand on trial because of my hope in the resurrection of the dead."ʰ ⁷When he said this, a dispute broke out between the Pharisees and the Sadducees, and the assembly was divided. ⁸(The Sadducees say that there is no resurrection,ⁱ and that there are neither angels nor spirits, but the Pharisees acknowledge them all.)

⁹There was a great uproar, and some of the teachers of the law who were Phariseesʲ stood up and argued vigorously. "We find nothing wrong with this man,"ᵏ they said. "What if a spirit or an angel has spoken to him?"ˡ ¹⁰The dispute became so violent that the commander was afraid Paul would be torn to pieces by them. He ordered the troops to go down and take him away from them by force and bring him into the barracks.ᵐ

¹¹The following night the Lord stood near Paul and said, "Take courage!ⁿ As you have testified about me in Jerusalem, so you must also testify in Rome."ᵒ

The Plot to Kill Paul

¹²The next morning the Jews formed a conspiracyᵖ and bound themselves with an oath not to eat or drink until they had killed Paul.ᑫ ¹³More than forty men were involved in this plot. ¹⁴They went to the chief priests and elders and said, "We have taken a solemn oath not to eat anything until we have killed Paul.ʳ ¹⁵Now then, you and the Sanhedrinˢ petition the commander to bring him before you on the pretext of wanting more accurate information about his case. We are ready to kill him before he gets here."

¹⁶But when the son of Paul's sister heard of this plot, he went into the barracksᵗ and told Paul.

¹⁷Then Paul called one of the centurions and said, "Take this young man to

F Ac 17:18 ◀▶ Ac 23:8
F Ac 23:6 ◀▶ Ac 24:15
S Ac 18:10 ◀▶ Ac 27:23–24

t 5 Exodus 22:28

23:6–8 Paul affirmed the Biblical truth of the resurrection from the dead. The Pharisees believed this doctrine, but the Sadducees, who rejected all but the first five books of the OT, rejected this teaching too.

the commander; he has something to tell him." ¹⁸So he took him to the commander.

The centurion said, "Paul, the prisoner,ᵘ sent for me and asked me to bring this young man to you because he has something to tell you."

¹⁹The commander took the young man by the hand, drew him aside and asked, "What is it you want to tell me?"

²⁰He said: "The Jews have agreed to ask you to bring Paul before the Sanhedrinᵛ tomorrow on the pretext of wanting more accurate information about him.ʷ ²¹Don't give in to them, because more than fortyˣ of them are waiting in ambush for him. They have taken an oath not to eat or drink until they have killed him.ʸ They are ready now, waiting for your consent to their request."

²²The commander dismissed the young man and cautioned him, "Don't tell anyone that you have reported this to me."

Paul Transferred to Caesarea

²³Then he called two of his centurions and ordered them, "Get ready a detachment of two hundred soldiers, seventy horsemen and two hundred spearmenᵘ to go to Caesareaᶻ at nine tonight.ᵃ ²⁴Provide mounts for Paul so that he may be taken safely to Governor Felix."ᵇ

²⁵He wrote a letter as follows:

²⁶Claudius Lysias,

To His Excellency,ᶜ Governor Felix:

Greetings.ᵈ

²⁷This man was seized by the Jews and they were about to kill him,ᵉ but I came with my troops and rescued him,ᶠ for I had learned that he is a Roman citizen.ᵍ ²⁸I wanted to know why they were accusing him, so I brought him to their Sanhedrin.ʰ ²⁹I found that the accusation had to do with questions about their law,ⁱ but there was no charge against himʲ that deserved death or imprisonment. ³⁰When I was informedᵏ of a plotˡ to be carried out against the man, I sent him to you at once. I also ordered his accusersᵐ to present to you their case against him.

³¹So the soldiers, carrying out their or-

23:18 ᵘS Eph 3:1
23:20 ᵛver 1
ʷver 14,15
23:21 ˣver 13
ʸver 12,14
23:23 ᶻS Ac 8:40
ᵃver 33
23:24 ᵇver 26,33; Ac 24:1-3,10; 25:14
23:26 ᶜLk 1:3; Ac 24:3; 26:25
ᵈAc 15:23
23:27 ᵉAc 21:32
ᶠAc 21:33
ᵍAc 22:25-29
23:28 ʰAc 22:30
23:29 ⁱAc 18:15; 25:19 ʲS ver 9
23:30 ᵏver 20,21
ˡS Ac 20:3
ᵐver 35; Ac 24:19; 25:16
23:32 ⁿver 23
ᵒS Ac 21:34
23:33 ᵖver 23,24
ᵠS Ac 8:40 ʳver 26
23:34 ˢS Ac 6:9; 21:39
23:35 ᵗver 30; Ac 24:19; 25:16
ᵘAc 24:27
24:1 ᵛAc 23:2
ʷAc 23:30,35
ˣS Ac 23:24
24:3 ʸLk 1:3; Ac 23:26; 26:25
24:5 ᶻAc 16:20; 17:6 ᵃAc 21:28
ᵇS Mk 1:24
ᶜver 14; Ac 26:5; 28:22
24:6 ᵈAc 21:28
24:9 ᵉS 1Th 2:16
24:10 ᶠS Ac 23:24
24:11 ᵍAc 21:27; ver 1
24:12 ʰAc 25:8; 28:17 ⁱver 18

ders, took Paul with them during the night and brought him as far as Antipatris. ³²The next day they let the cavalryⁿ go on with him, while they returned to the barracks.ᵒ ³³When the cavalryᵖ arrived in Caesarea,ᵠ they delivered the letter to the governorʳ and handed Paul over to him. ³⁴The governor read the letter and asked what province he was from. Learning that he was from Cilicia,ˢ ³⁵he said, "I will hear your case when your accusersᵗ get here." Then he ordered that Paul be kept under guardᵘ in Herod's palace.

The Trial Before Felix

24 Five days later the high priest Ananiasᵛ went down to Caesarea with some of the elders and a lawyer named Tertullus, and they brought their chargesʷ against Paul before the governor.ˣ ²When Paul was called in, Tertullus presented his case before Felix: "We have enjoyed a long period of peace under you, and your foresight has brought about reforms in this nation. ³Everywhere and in every way, most excellentʸ Felix, we acknowledge this with profound gratitude. ⁴But in order not to weary you further, I would request that you be kind enough to hear us briefly.

⁵"We have found this man to be a troublemaker, stirring up riotsᶻ among the Jewsᵃ all over the world. He is a ringleader of the Nazareneᵇ sectᶜ ⁶and even tried to desecrate the temple;ᵈ so we seized him. ⁸Byᵛ examining him yourself you will be able to learn the truth about all these charges we are bringing against him."

⁹The Jews joined in the accusation,ᵉ asserting that these things were true.

¹⁰When the governorᶠ motioned for him to speak, Paul replied: "I know that for a number of years you have been a judge over this nation; so I gladly make my defense. ¹¹You can easily verify that no more than twelve daysᵍ ago I went up to Jerusalem to worship. ¹²My accusers did not find me arguing with anyone at the temple,ʰ or stirring up a crowdⁱ in the synagogues or anywhere else in the city. ¹³And they cannot prove to you the

ᵘ 23 The meaning of the Greek for this word is uncertain. ᵛ 6-8 Some manuscripts *him and wanted to judge him according to our law. ⁷But the commander, Lysias, came and with the use of much force snatched him from our hands ⁸and ordered his accusers to come before you. By*

charges they are now making against me.ʲ ¹⁴However, I admit that I worship the God of our fathersᵏ as a follower of the Way,ˡ which they call a sect.ᵐ I believe everything that agrees with the Law and that is written in the Prophets,ⁿ ¹⁵and I have the same hope in God as these men, that there will be a resurrection° of both the righteous and the wicked.ᵖ ¹⁶So I strive always to keep my conscience clearᑫ before God and man.

¹⁷"After an absence of several years, I came to Jerusalem to bring my people gifts for the poorʳ and to present offerings. ¹⁸I was ceremonially cleanˢ when they found me in the temple courts doing this. There was no crowd with me, nor was I involved in any disturbance.ᵗ ¹⁹But there are some Jews from the province of Asia,ᵘ who ought to be here before you and bring charges if they have anything against me.ᵛ ²⁰Or these who are here should state what crime they found in me when I stood before the Sanhedrin— ²¹unless it was this one thing I shouted as I stood in their presence: 'It is concerning the resurrection of the dead that I am on trial before you today.'"

²²Then Felix, who was well acquainted with the Way,ˣ adjourned the proceedings. "When Lysias the commander comes," he said, "I will decide your case." ²³He ordered the centurion to keep Paul under guardʸ but to give him some freedomᶻ and permit his friends to take care of his needs.ᵃ

²⁴Several days later Felix came with his wife Drusilla, who was a Jewess. He sent for Paul and listened to him as he spoke about faith in Christ Jesus.ᵇ ²⁵As Paul discoursed on righteousness, self-controlᶜ and the judgmentᵈ to come, Felix was afraidᵉ and said, "That's enough for now! You may leave. When I find it convenient, I will send for you." ²⁶At the same time he was hoping that Paul would offer him a bribe, so he sent for him frequently and talked with him.

F Ac 23:8 ◀ ▶ Ac 24:21
W Jn 5:25–29 ◀ ▶ 1Co 15:21–26
F Ac 24:15 ◀ ▶ Ac 26:6–8
J Ac 17:31 ◀ ▶ Ro 2:2–13
N Ac 7:51–53 ◀ ▶ Ac 26:28–29

24:13 ʲ Ac 25:7
24:14 ᵏ S Ac 3:13
ˡ S Ac 9:2 ᵐ S ver 5
ⁿ Ac 26:6,22; 28:23
24:15 ° Ac 23:6;
28:20 ᵖ S Mt 25:46
24:16 ᑫ S Ac 23:1
24:17 ʳ Ac 11:29,30; Ro 15:25-28,31; 1Co 16:1-4,15; 2Co 8:1-4; Gal 2:10
24:18 ˢ S Ac 21:26
ᵗ ver 12
24:19 ᵘ S Ac 2:9
ᵛ Ac 23:30
24:21 ʷ Ac 23:6
24:22 ˣ S Ac 9:2
24:23 ʸ Ac 23:35
ᶻ Ac 28:16
ᵃ Ac 23:16; 27:3
24:24 ᵇ S Ac 20:21
24:25 ᶜ Gal 5:23; 1Th 5:6; 1Pe 4:7; 5:8; 2Pe 1:6
ᵈ Ac 10:42
ᵉ Jer 36:16
24:27 ᶠ Ac 25:1,4,9,14 ᵍ Ac 12:3; 25:9 ʰ Ac 23:35; 25:14
25:1 ⁱ S Ac 24:27
ʲ S Ac 8:40
25:2 ᵏ ver 15; Ac 24:1
25:3 ˡ S Ac 20:3
25:4 ᵐ Ac 24:23
ⁿ S Ac 8:40
25:6 ° ver 17
ᵖ ver 10
25:7 ᑫ Mk 15:3; Lk 23:2,10; ʳ Ac 24:13
25:8 ˢ Ac 6:13; 24:12; 28:17
25:9 ᵗ Ac 24:27; 12:3 ᵘ ver 20
25:10 ᵛ ver 8
25:11 ʷ ver 21,25; Ac 26:32; 28:19

²⁷When two years had passed, Felix was succeeded by Porcius Festus,ᶠ but because Felix wanted to grant a favor to the Jews,ᵍ he left Paul in prison.ʰ

The Trial Before Festus

25 Three days after arriving in the province, Festusⁱ went up from Caesareaʲ to Jerusalem, ²where the chief priests and Jewish leaders appeared before him and presented the charges against Paul.ᵏ ³They urgently requested Festus, as a favor to them, to have Paul transferred to Jerusalem, for they were preparing an ambush to kill him along the way.ˡ ⁴Festus answered, "Paul is being heldᵐ at Caesarea,ⁿ and I myself am going there soon. ⁵Let some of your leaders come with me and press charges against the man there, if he has done anything wrong."

⁶After spending eight or ten days with them, he went down to Caesarea, and the next day he convened the court° and ordered that Paul be brought before him.ᵖ ⁷When Paul appeared, the Jews who had come down from Jerusalem stood around him, bringing many serious charges against him,ᑫ which they could not prove.ʳ

⁸Then Paul made his defense: "I have done nothing wrong against the law of the Jews or against the templeˢ or against Caesar."

⁹Festus, wishing to do the Jews a favor,ᵗ said to Paul, "Are you willing to go up to Jerusalem and stand trial before me there on these charges?"ᵘ

¹⁰Paul answered: "I am now standing before Caesar's court, where I ought to be tried. I have not done any wrong to the Jews,ᵛ as you yourself know very well. ¹¹If, however, I am guilty of doing anything deserving death, I do not refuse to die. But if the charges brought against me by these Jews are not true, no one has the right to hand me over to them. I appeal to Caesar!"ʷ

¹²After Festus had conferred with his council, he declared: "You have appealed to Caesar. To Caesar you will go!"

24:15, 21 Paul again confirmed the doctrine of the physical resurrection from the dead for the just and the unjust and affirmed the Pharisees' belief in this doctrine too.

Festus Consults King Agrippa

[13] A few days later King Agrippa and Bernice arrived at Caesarea to pay their respects to Festus. [14] Since they were spending many days there, Festus discussed Paul's case with the king. He said: "There is a man here whom Felix left as a prisoner. [15] When I went to Jerusalem, the chief priests and elders of the Jews brought charges against him and asked that he be condemned.

[16] "I told them that it is not the Roman custom to hand over any man before he has faced his accusers and has had an opportunity to defend himself against their charges. [17] When they came here with me, I did not delay the case, but convened the court the next day and ordered the man to be brought in. [18] When his accusers got up to speak, they did not charge him with any of the crimes I had expected. [19] Instead, they had some points of dispute with him about their own religion and about a dead man named Jesus who Paul claimed was alive. [20] I was at a loss how to investigate such matters; so I asked if he would be willing to go to Jerusalem and stand trial there on these charges. [21] When Paul made his appeal to be held over for the Emperor's decision, I ordered him held until I could send him to Caesar."

[22] Then Agrippa said to Festus, "I would like to hear this man myself."

He replied, "Tomorrow you will hear him."

Paul Before Agrippa

26:12–18pp — Ac 9:3–8; 22:6–11

[23] The next day Agrippa and Bernice came with great pomp and entered the audience room with the high ranking officers and the leading men of the city. At the command of Festus, Paul was brought in. [24] Festus said: "King Agrippa, and all who are present with us, you see this man! The whole Jewish community has petitioned me about him in Jerusalem and here in Caesarea, shouting that he ought not to live any longer. [25] I found he had done nothing deserving of death, but because he made his appeal to the Emperor I decided to send him to Rome. [26] But I have nothing definite to write to His Majesty about him. Therefore I have brought him before all of you, and especially before you, King Agrippa, so that as a result of this investigation I may have something to write. [27] For I think it is unreasonable to send on a prisoner without specifying the charges against him."

26 Then Agrippa said to Paul, "You have permission to speak for yourself."

So Paul motioned with his hand and began his defense: [2] "King Agrippa, I consider myself fortunate to stand before you today as I make my defense against all the accusations of the Jews, [3] and especially so because you are well acquainted with all the Jewish customs and controversies. Therefore, I beg you to listen to me patiently.

[4] "The Jews all know the way I have lived ever since I was a child, from the beginning of my life in my own country, and also in Jerusalem. [5] They have known me for a long time and can testify, if they are willing, that according to the strictest sect of our religion, I lived as a Pharisee. [6] And now it is because of my hope in what God has promised our fathers that I am on trial today. [7] This is the promise our twelve tribes are hoping to see fulfilled as they earnestly serve God day and night. O king, it is because of this hope that the Jews are accusing me. [8] Why should any of you consider it incredible that God raises the dead?

[9] "I too was convinced that I ought to do all that was possible to oppose the name of Jesus of Nazareth. [10] And that is just what I did in Jerusalem. On the authority of the chief priests I put many of the saints in prison, and when they were put to death, I cast my vote against them. [11] Many a time I went from one synagogue to another to have them punished, and I tried to force them to blaspheme. In my obsession against them, I even went to foreign cities to persecute them.

F Ac 24:21 ◀ ▶ Ac 28:20

26:6–8 When called to defend his case before King Agrippa, Paul said that the crux of the controversy between the Jewish leaders and Paul revolved around the truth of the resurrection. Paul also reminded the king that the twelve tribes of Israel had always believed this doctrine.

¹²"On one of these journeys I was going to Damascus with the authority and commission of the chief priests. ¹³About noon, O king, as I was on the road, I saw a light from heaven, brighter than the sun, blazing around me and my companions. ¹⁴We all fell to the ground, and I heard a voice saying to me in Aramaic, 'Saul, Saul, why do you persecute me? It is hard for you to kick against the goads.'

¹⁵"Then I asked, 'Who are you, Lord?'

"'I am Jesus, whom you are persecuting,' the Lord replied. ¹⁶'Now get up and stand on your feet. I have appeared to you to appoint you as a servant and as a witness of what you have seen of me and what I will show you. ¹⁷I will rescue you from your own people and from the Gentiles. I am sending you to them ¹⁸to open their eyes and turn them from darkness to light, and from the power of Satan to God, so that they may receive forgiveness of sins and a place among those who are sanctified by faith in me.'

¹⁹"So then, King Agrippa, I was not disobedient to the vision from heaven. ²⁰First to those in Damascus, then to those in Jerusalem and in all Judea, and to the Gentiles also, I preached that they should repent and turn to God and prove their repentance by their deeds. ²¹That is why the Jews seized me in the temple courts and tried to kill me. ²²But I have had God's help to this very day, and so I stand here and testify to small and great alike. I am saying nothing beyond what the prophets and Moses said would happen— ²³that the Christ would suffer and, as the first to rise from the dead, would proclaim light to his own people and to the Gentiles."

²⁴At this point Festus interrupted Paul's defense. "You are out of your mind, Paul!" he shouted. "Your great learning is driving you insane."

²⁵"I am not insane, most excellent Festus," Paul replied. "What I am saying is true and reasonable. ²⁶The king is familiar with these things, and I can speak freely to him. I am convinced that none of this has escaped his notice, because it was not done in a corner. ²⁷King Agrippa, do you believe the prophets? I know you do."

²⁸Then Agrippa said to Paul, "Do you think that in such a short time you can persuade me to be a Christian?"

²⁹Paul replied, "Short time or long—I pray God that not only you but all who are listening to me today may become what I am, except for these chains."

³⁰The king rose, and with him the governor and Bernice and those sitting with them. ³¹They left the room, and while talking with one another, they said, "This man is not doing anything that deserves death or imprisonment."

³²Agrippa said to Festus, "This man could have been set free if he had not appealed to Caesar."

Paul Sails for Rome

27 When it was decided that we would sail for Italy, Paul and some other prisoners were handed over to a centurion named Julius, who belonged to the Imperial Regiment. ²We boarded a ship from Adramyttium about to sail for ports along the coast of the province of Asia, and we put out to sea. Aristarchus, a Macedonian from Thessalonica, was with us.

³The next day we landed at Sidon; and Julius, in kindness to Paul, allowed him to go to his friends so they might provide for his needs. ⁴From there we put out to sea again and passed to the lee of Cyprus because the winds were against us. ⁵When we had sailed across the open sea off the coast of Cilicia and Pamphylia, we landed at Myra in Lycia. ⁶There the centurion found an Alexandrian ship sailing for Italy and put us on board. ⁷We made slow headway for many days and had difficulty arriving off Cnidus. When the wind did not allow us to hold our course, we sailed to the lee of Crete, opposite Salmone. ⁸We moved along the coast with difficulty and came to a place called Fair Havens, near the town of Lasea.

⁹Much time had been lost, and sailing had already become dangerous because by now it was after the Fast. So Paul warned them, ¹⁰"Men, I can see that our

---

w 14 Or Hebrew x 23 Or Messiah y 9 That is, the Day of Atonement (Yom Kippur)

voyage is going to be disastrous and bring great loss to ship and cargo, and to our own lives also."ʰ ¹¹But the centurion, instead of listening to what Paul said, followed the advice of the pilot and of the owner of the ship. ¹²Since the harbor was unsuitable to winter in, the majority decided that we should sail on, hoping to reach Phoenix and winter there. This was a harbor in Crete,ⁱ facing both southwest and northwest.

The Storm

¹³When a gentle south wind began to blow, they thought they had obtained what they wanted; so they weighed anchor and sailed along the shore of Crete. ¹⁴Before very long, a wind of hurricane force,ʲ called the "northeaster," swept down from the island. ¹⁵The ship was caught by the storm and could not head into the wind; so we gave way to it and were driven along. ¹⁶As we passed to the lee of a small island called Cauda, we were hardly able to make the lifeboatᵏ secure. ¹⁷When the men had hoisted it aboard, they passed ropes under the ship itself to hold it together. Fearing that they would run aground¹ on the sandbars of Syrtis, they lowered the sea anchor and let the ship be driven along. ¹⁸We took such a violent battering from the storm that the next day they began to throw the cargo overboard.ᵐ ¹⁹On the third day, they threw the ship's tackle overboard with their own hands. ²⁰When neither sun nor stars appeared for many days and the storm continued raging, we finally gave up all hope of being saved.

²¹After the men had gone a long time without food, Paul stood up before them and said: "Men, you should have taken my adviceⁿ not to sail from Crete;ᵒ then you would have spared yourselves this damage and loss. ²²But now I urge you to keep up your courage,ᵖ because not one of you will be lost; only the ship will be destroyed. ²³Last night an angelᑫ of the God whose I am and whom I serveʳ stood beside meˢ ²⁴and said, 'Do not be afraid, Paul. You must stand trial before Caesar;ᵗ and God has graciously given you the lives of all who sail with you.' ᵘ ²⁵So keep up your courage,ᵛ men, for I have faith in God that it will happen just as he told

me.ʷ ²⁶Nevertheless, we must run agroundˣ on some island."ʸ

The Shipwreck

²⁷On the fourteenth night we were still being driven across the Adriaticᶻ Sea, when about midnight the sailors sensed they were approaching land. ²⁸They took soundings and found that the water was a hundred and twenty feetᵃ deep. A short time later they took soundings again and found it was ninety feetᵇ deep. ²⁹Fearing that we would be dashed against the rocks, they dropped four anchors from the stern and prayed for daylight. ³⁰In an attempt to escape from the ship, the sailors let the lifeboatᶻ down into the sea, pretending they were going to lower some anchors from the bow. ³¹Then Paul said to the centurion and the soldiers, "Unless these men stay with the ship, you cannot be saved."ᵃ ³²So the soldiers cut the ropes that held the lifeboat and let it fall away.

³³Just before dawn Paul urged them all to eat. "For the last fourteen days," he said, "you have been in constant suspense and gone without food—you haven't eaten anything. ³⁴Now I urge you to take some food. You need it to survive. Not one of you will lose a single hair from his head."ᵇ ³⁵After he said this, he took some bread and gave thanks to God in front of them all. Then he broke itᶜ and began to eat. ³⁶They were all encouragedᵈ and ate some food themselves. ³⁷Altogether there were 276 of us on board. ³⁸When they had eaten as much as they wanted, they lightened the ship by throwing the grain into the sea.ᵉ

³⁹When daylight came, they did not recognize the land, but they saw a bay with a sandy beach,ᶠ where they decided to run the ship aground if they could. ⁴⁰Cutting loose the anchors,ᵍ they left them in the sea and at the same time untied the ropes that held the rudders. Then they hoisted the foresail to the wind and made for the beach. ⁴¹But the ship struck a sandbar and ran aground. The bow stuck fast and would not move, and the stern was broken to pieces by the pounding of the surf.ʰ

⁴²The soldiers planned to kill the pris-

27:10 ʰ ver 21
27:12 ⁱ S ver 7
27:14 ʲ Mk 4:37
27:16 ᵏ ver 30
27:17 ˡ ver 26,39
27:18 ᵐ ver 19,38; Jnh 1:5
27:21 ⁿ ver 10 ᵒ S ver 7
27:22 ᵖ ver 25,36
27:23 ᑫ S Ac 5:19 ʳ Ro 1:9 ˢ Ac 18:9; 23:11; 2Ti 4:17
27:24 ᵗ Ac 23:11 ᵘ ver 44
27:25 ᵛ ver 22,36 ʷ Ro 4:20,21
27:26 ˣ ver 17,39 ʸ Ac 28:1
27:30 ᶻ ver 16
27:31 ᵃ ver 24
27:34 ᵇ S Mt 10:30
27:35 ᶜ S Mt 14:19
27:36 ᵈ ver 22,25
27:38 ᵉ ver 18; Jnh 1:5
27:39 ᶠ Ac 28:1
27:40 ᵍ ver 29
27:41 ʰ 2Co 11:25

S Ac 23:11 ◀ ▶ Ro 8:31

ᶻ 27 In ancient times the name referred to an area extending well south of Italy. ᵃ 28 Greek *twenty orguias* (about 37 meters) ᵇ 28 Greek *fifteen orguias* (about 27 meters)

oners to prevent any of them from swimming away and escaping. ⁴³But the centurion wanted to spare Paul's life[i] and kept them from carrying out their plan. He ordered those who could swim to jump overboard first and get to land. ⁴⁴The rest were to get there on planks or on pieces of the ship. In this way everyone reached land in safety.[j]

Ashore on Malta

28 Once safely on shore, we[k] found out that the island[l] was called Malta. ²The islanders showed us unusual kindness. They built a fire and welcomed us all because it was raining and cold. ³Paul gathered a pile of brushwood and, as he put it on the fire, a viper, driven out by the heat, fastened itself on his hand. ⁴When the islanders saw the snake hanging from his hand,[m] they said to each other, "This man must be a murderer; for though he escaped from the sea, Justice has not allowed him to live."[n] ⁵But Paul shook the snake off into the fire and suffered no ill effects.[o] ⁶The people expected him to swell up or suddenly fall dead, but after waiting a long time and seeing nothing unusual happen to him, they changed their minds and said he was a god.[p]

⁷There was an estate nearby that belonged to Publius, the chief official of the island. He welcomed us to his home and for three days entertained us hospitably. ⁸His father was sick in bed, suffering from fever and dysentery. Paul went in to see him and, after prayer,[q] placed his hands on him[r] and healed him.[s] ⁹When this had happened, the rest of the sick on the island came and were cured. ¹⁰They honored us[t] in many ways and when we were ready to sail, they furnished us with the supplies we needed.

Arrival at Rome

¹¹After three months we put out to sea in a ship that had wintered in the island. It was an Alexandrian ship[u] with the figurehead of the twin gods Castor and Pollux. ¹²We put in at Syracuse and stayed there three days. ¹³From there we set sail

E Ac 22:11-13 ◀▶ Ro 15:18-19

and arrived at Rhegium. The next day the south wind came up, and on the following day we reached Puteoli. ¹⁴There we found some brothers[v] who invited us to spend a week with them. And so we came to Rome. ¹⁵The brothers[w] there had heard that we were coming, and they traveled as far as the Forum of Appius and the Three Taverns to meet us. At the sight of these men Paul thanked God and was encouraged. ¹⁶When we got to Rome, Paul was allowed to live by himself, with a soldier to guard him.[x]

Paul Preaches at Rome Under Guard

¹⁷Three days later he called together the leaders of the Jews.[y] When they had assembled, Paul said to them: "My brothers,[z] although I have done nothing against our people[a] or against the customs of our ancestors,[b] I was arrested in Jerusalem and handed over to the Romans. ¹⁸They examined me[c] and wanted to release me,[d] because I was not guilty of any crime deserving death.[e] ¹⁹But when the Jews objected, I was compelled to appeal to Caesar[f]—not that I had any charge to bring against my own people. ²⁰For this reason I have asked to see you and talk with you. It is because of the hope of Israel[g] that I am bound with this chain."[h]

²¹They replied, "We have not received any letters from Judea concerning you, and none of the brothers[i] who have come from there has reported or said anything bad about you. ²²But we want to hear what your views are, for we know that people everywhere are talking against this sect."[j]

²³They arranged to meet Paul on a certain day, and came in even larger numbers to the place where he was staying. From morning till evening he explained and declared to them the kingdom of God[k] and tried to convince them about Jesus[l] from the Law of Moses and from the Prophets.[m] ²⁴Some were convinced by what he said, but others would not be-

F Ac 26:6-8 ◀▶ Ro 8:11

28:17–20 Paul wanted the "leaders of the Jews" (28:17) in Rome to understand the truth about the accusations that were made against himself and other believers regarding "the hope of Israel" (28:20), that is, the hope of the resurrection from the dead.

lieve.ⁿ ²⁵They disagreed among themselves and began to leave after Paul had made this final statement: "The Holy Spirit spoke the truth to your forefathers when he said° through Isaiah the prophet:

²⁶" 'Go to this people and say,
"You will be ever hearing but never understanding;
you will be ever seeing but never perceiving."
²⁷For this people's heart has become calloused;ᵖ
they hardly hear with their ears,
and they have closed their eyes.

E *Ac 21:11* ◀▶ *Ro 1:4*
T *Ac 21:11* ◀▶ *Ro 12:6–8*
C *Ac 26:18* ◀▶ *Ro 1:20–21*

28:24 ⁿ Ac 14:4; 17:4,5
28:25 ° S Heb 3:7
28:27 ᵖ Ps 119:70
ᵠ Isa 6:9,10;
ˢ Mt 13:15
28:28 ʳ Lk 2:30
ˢ S Ac 13:46
28:31 ᵗ S Ac 4:29
ᵘ ver 23; S Mt 4:23

Otherwise they might see with their eyes,
hear with their ears,
understand with their hearts
and turn, and I would heal them.' ᶜᵠ

²⁸"Therefore I want you to know that God's salvationʳ has been sent to the Gentiles,ˢ and they will listen!"ᵈ

³⁰For two whole years Paul stayed there in his own rented house and welcomed all who came to see him. ³¹Boldlyᵗ and without hindrance he preached the kingdom of Godᵘ and taught about the Lord Jesus Christ.

G *Ac 18:6* ◀▶ *Ro 9:30*
L *Ac 26:17–18* ◀▶ *Ro 3:21–30*

ᶜ 27 *Isaiah 6:9,10* ᵈ 28 *Some manuscripts* listen!" ²⁹*After he said this, the Jews left, arguing vigorously among themselves.*

28:28 The final prophecy in the book of Acts confirms that God would send the gospel to the Gentiles because the majority of Jews had rejected the claim of Jesus of Nazareth as their promised Messiah.

Romans

Author: Paul

Theme: Justification with God through faith in Christ

Date of Writing: A.D. 57

Outline of Romans
    I. Introduction and Theme (1:1–17)
    II. All People Are Unrighteous (1:18—3:20)
    III. Righteousness Through Christ (3:21—5:21)
    IV. Sanctification (6:1—8:39)
    V. Israel's Rejection (9:1—11:36)
    VI. Righteous Living (12:1—15:13)
    VII. Conclusion, Commendation and Greetings (15:14—16:27)

PAUL ADDRESSED THIS letter to the believers in the Roman church. This church was made up primarily of Gentiles and may have been started by visitors from Rome who were present in Jerusalem on the day of Pentecost (see Ac 2:1, 10). Anticipating a visit to Rome (see Ro 15:24, 28, 32), Paul probably wrote this letter while in Corinth at the end of his third missionary journey and sent it to Rome with Phoebe (see 16:1), a helper in the church of Cenchrea, a city near Corinth.

Although the introduction and the conclusion identify Romans as a Pauline letter, this book does not display the personal character of Paul that is seen in his other epistles. Instead, Paul's words to the Roman church are instructional, revealing an orderly, doctrinal presentation of the good news of Jesus Christ. This letter to the Romans forms one of the most complete NT expositions of the key doctrines of Christianity by following a systematic presentation of God's revelation of his righteousness to humanity through Christ. Since all humanity, Jews and Gentiles, are guilty before God (see 3:19, 23), Paul is determined to make all of his readers aware of God's offer of salvation through the substitutionary death and resurrection of Jesus Christ. Paul's extensive knowledge of, and quotations from, the OT support his words that our justification from sin is received solely through our faith in Christ (see 3:28) and that our ability to live in righteousness comes only through the supernatural power of the Holy Spirit.

Throughout this letter to the Romans, Paul clearly demonstrates his gratitude, purpose and mission in life. Recognizing humanity's lost condition without Christ, Paul gratefully acknowledges God's crediting of Christ's righteousness to Paul's life as the foundation for Paul's boldness in proclaiming the gospel. In the final portion of this letter, Paul develops the practical application of these key doctrines as a way to encourage the believers' daily walk of faith.

1 Paul, a servant of Christ Jesus, called to be an apostle[a] and set apart[b] for the gospel of God[c]— ²the gospel he promised beforehand[d] through his prophets[e] in the Holy Scriptures[f] ³regarding his Son, who as to his human nature[g] was a descendant of David,[h] ⁴and who through the Spirit[a] of holiness was declared with power to be the Son of God[b][i] by his resurrection from the dead:[j] Jesus Christ our Lord.[k] ⁵Through him and for his name's sake, we received grace[l] and apostleship to call people from among all the Gentiles[m] to the obedience that comes from faith.[n] ⁶And you also are among those who are called to belong to Jesus Christ.[o]

⁷To all in Rome who are loved by God[p] and called to be saints:[q]

Grace and peace to you from God our Father and from the Lord Jesus Christ.[r]

Paul's Longing to Visit Rome

⁸First, I thank my God through Jesus Christ for all of you,[s] because your faith is being reported all over the world.[t] ⁹God, whom I serve[u] with my whole heart in preaching the gospel of his Son, is my witness[v] how constantly I remember you ¹⁰in my prayers at all times;[w] and I pray that now at last by God's will[x] the way may be opened for me to come to you.[y]

E Ac 28:25 ◀ ▶ Ro 1:11
H Jn 6:63 ◀ ▶ Ro 8:2
M Ac 19:6 ◀ ▶ Ro 1:11
N Ac 10:45 ◀ ▶ 1Co 2:11
S Ac 15:8–9 ◀ ▶ Ro 8:1–16

1:1 ªS 1Co 1:1
ᵇS Ac 9:15
ᶜRo 15:16;
S 2Co 2:12; 11:7;
1Th 2:8,9; 1Pe 4:17
1:2 ᵈS Ac 13:32;
Tit 1:2 ᵉLk 1:70;
Ro 3:21 ᶠGal 3:8
1:3 ᵍS Jn 1:14;
Ro 9:5 ʰS Mt 1:1
1:4 ⁱS Mt 4:3
ʲS Ac 2:24
ᵏ1Co 1:2
1:5 ˡ1Ti 1:14
ᵐS Ac 9:15
ⁿAc 6:7; Ro 16:26
1:6 ᵒJude 1;
Rev 17:14
1:7 ᵖRo 8:39;
1Th 1:4 ᵠS Ac 9:13
ʳ1Co 1:3; Eph 1:2;
1Ti 1:2; Tit 1:4;
1Pe 1:2
1:8 ˢ1Co 1:4;
Eph 1:16; 1Pe 1:4;
2Th 1:3; 2Ti 1:3
ᵗS Ro 10:18; 16:19
1:9 ᵘ2Ti 1:3
ᵛJob 16:19;
Jer 42:5; 2Co 1:23;
Gal 1:20; Php 1:8;
1Th 2:5,10
1:10 ʷ1Sa 12:23;
S Lk 18:1;
S Ac 1:14;
Eph 1:16; Php 1:4;
Col 1:9; 2Ti 1:11;
2Ti 1:3; Phm 4
ˣS Ac 18:21
ʸver 13; Ro 15:32
1:11 ᶻRo 15:23
ª1Co 1:7; 12:1-31
1:13 ᵇS Ro 11:25
ᶜS Ro 7:1
ᵈRo 15:22,23
1:14 ᵉ1Co 9:16
1:15 ᶠRo 15:20
1:16 ᵍ2Ti 1:8
ʰ1Co 1:18
ⁱS Jn 3:15 ʲAc 3:26;
13:46 ᵏS Ac 13:46;
Ro 2:9,10
1:17 ˡRo 3:21;
Php 3:9 ᵐS Ro 9:30
ⁿHab 2:4; Gal 3:11;
Heb 10:38
1:18 ᵒJn 3:36;
Ro 5:9; Eph 5:6;
Col 3:6; 1Th 1:10;
Rev 19:15

¹¹I long to see you[z] so that I may impart to you some spiritual gift[a] to make you strong— ¹²that is, that you and I may be mutually encouraged by each other's faith. ¹³I do not want you to be unaware,[b] brothers,[c] that I planned many times to come to you (but have been prevented from doing so until now)[d] in order that I might have a harvest among you, just as I have had among the other Gentiles. ¹⁴I am obligated[e] both to Greeks and non-Greeks, both to the wise and the foolish. ¹⁵That is why I am so eager to preach the gospel also to you who are at Rome.[f]

¹⁶I am not ashamed of the gospel,[g] because it is the power of God[h] for the salvation of everyone who believes:[i] first for the Jew,[j] then for the Gentile.[k] ¹⁷For in the gospel a righteousness from God is revealed,[l] a righteousness that is by faith[m] from first to last,[c] just as it is written: "The righteous will live by faith."[d][n]

God's Wrath Against Mankind

¹⁸The wrath of God[o] is being revealed from heaven against all the godlessness and wickedness of men who suppress the

E Ro 1:4 ◀ ▶ Ro 5:5
G Ac 20:28 ◀ ▶ Ro 12:6–8
M Ro 1:4 ◀ ▶ Ro 8:2
W Ac 19:2 ◀ ▶ Ro 7:6
F Ac 20:21 ◀ ▶ Ro 3:21–30
K Ac 20:32 ◀ ▶ Ro 3:3–4
T Jn 12:42–43 ◀ ▶ Ro 10:8–10
W Ac 17:27 ◀ ▶ Ro 3:21–24
H Ac 13:41 ◀ ▶ Ro 2:2–13
S Ac 14:22 ◀ ▶ Ro 2:6–13

ª4 Or who as to his spirit ᵇ4 Or was appointed to be the Son of God with power ᶜ17 Or is from faith to faith ᵈ17 Hab. 2:4

truth by their wickedness, ¹⁹since what may be known about God is plain to them, because God has made it plain to them.ᵖ ²⁰For since the creation of the world God's invisible qualities—his eternal power and divine nature—have been clearly seen, being understood from what has been made,ᵠ so that men are without excuse.ʳ

²¹For although they knew God, they neither glorified him as God nor gave thanks to him, but their thinking became futile and their foolish hearts were darkened.ˢ ²²Although they claimed to be wise, they became foolsᵗ ²³and exchanged the glory of the immortal God for imagesᵘ made to look like mortal man and birds and animals and reptiles.

²⁴Therefore God gave them overᵛ in the sinful desires of their hearts to sexual impurity for the degrading of their bodies with one another.ʷ ²⁵They exchanged the truth of God for a lie,ˣ and worshiped and served created thingsʸ rather than the Creator—who is forever praised.ᶻ Amen.ᵃ

²⁶Because of this, God gave them overᵇ to shameful lusts.ᶜ Even their women exchanged natural relations for unnatural ones.ᵈ ²⁷In the same way the men also abandoned natural relations with women and were inflamed with lust for one another. Men committed indecent acts with other men, and received in themselves the due penalty for their perversion.ᵉ

²⁸Furthermore, since they did not think it worthwhile to retain the knowledge of God, he gave them overᶠ to a depraved mind, to do what ought not to be done. ²⁹They have become filled with every kind of wickedness, evil, greed and depravity. They are full of envy, murder, strife, deceit and malice. They are gossips,ᵍ ³⁰slanderers, God-haters, insolent, arrogant and boastful; they invent ways of doing evil; they disobey their parents;ʰ ³¹they are senseless, faithless, heartless,ⁱ ruthless. ³²Although they know God's

C Ac 28:26–27 ◀▶ Ro 1:24
N Ac 26:28–29 ◀▶ Ro 2:5
C Ro 1:20–21 ◀▶ Ro 1:26
C Ro 1:24 ◀▶ Ro 1:28–32
C Ro 1:26 ◀▶ Ro 3:9–12

1:19 ᵖ Ac 14:17
1:20 ᵠ Ps 19:1-6
ʳ Ro 2:1
1:21 ˢ Ge 8:21; Jer 2:5; 17:9; Eph 4:17,18
1:22 ᵗ 1Co 1:20,27; 3:18,19
1:23 ᵘ Dt 4:16,17; Ps 106:20; Jer 2:11; Ac 17:29
1:24 ᵛ ver 26,28; Ps 81:12; Eph 4:19
ʷ 1Pe 4:3
1:25 ˣ Isa 44:20
ʸ Jer 10:14; 13:25; 16:19,20 ᶻ Ro 9:5; 2Co 11:31
ᵃ S Ro 11:36
1:26 ᵇ ver 24,28
ᶜ Eph 4:19; 1Th 4:5
ᵈ Lev 18:22,23
1:27 ᵉ Lev 18:22; 20:13; 1Co 6:18
1:28 ᶠ ver 24,28
1:29 ᵍ 2Co 12:20; 1Ti 5:13; Jas 3:2; 3Jn 10
1:30 ʰ 2Ti 3:2
1:31 ⁱ 2Ti 3:3
1:32 ʲ S Ro 6:23
ᵏ Ps 50:18; Lk 11:48; Ac 8:1; 22:20
2:1 ˡ Ro 1:20
ᵐ 2Sa 12:5-7; S Mt 7:1,2
2:4 ⁿ Ro 9:23; 11:33; Eph 1:7,18; 2:7; 3:8,16; Col 2:2
ᵒ Ro 11:22
ᵖ Ro 3:25 ᵠ Ex 34:6; Ro 9:22; 1Ti 1:16; 1Pe 3:20; 2Pe 3:15
ʳ 2Pe 3:9
2:5 ˢ Ps 110:5; Rev 6:17 ᵗ Jude 6
2:6 ᵘ Ps 62:12; S Mt 16:27
2:7 ᵛ ver 10
ʷ 1Co 15:53,54; 2Ti 1:10
ˣ S Mt 25:46
2:8 ʸ 2Th 2:12
ᶻ Eze 22:31
2:9 ᵃ Ps 32:10
ᵇ ver 10; Ro 1:16
2:10 ᶜ ver 9; Ro 1:16
2:11 ᵈ S Ac 10:34
2:12 ᵉ Ro 3:19; 6:14; 1Co 9:20,21; Gal 4:21; 5:18; S Ro 7:4
2:13 ᶠ Jas 1:22,23, 25

righteous decree that those who do such things deserve death,ʲ they not only continue to do these very things but also approveᵏ of those who practice them.

God's Righteous Judgment

2 You, therefore, have no excuse,ˡ you who pass judgment on someone else, for at whatever point you judge the other, you are condemning yourself, because you who pass judgment do the same things.ᵐ ²Now we know that God's judgment against those who do such things is based on truth. ³So when you, a mere man, pass judgment on them and yet do the same things, do you think you will escape God's judgment? ⁴Or do you show contempt for the richesⁿ of his kindness,ᵒ toleranceᵖ and patience,ᵠ not realizing that God's kindness leads you toward repentance?ʳ

⁵But because of your stubbornness and your unrepentant heart, you are storing up wrath against yourself for the day of God's wrath,ˢ when his righteous judgmentᵗ will be revealed. ⁶God "will give to each person according to what he has done."ᵉᵘ ⁷To those who by persistence in doing good seek glory, honorᵛ and immortality,ʷ he will give eternal life.ˣ ⁸But for those who are self-seeking and who reject the truth and follow evil,ʸ there will be wrath and anger.ᶻ ⁹There will be trouble and distress for every human being who does evil:ᵃ first for the Jew, then for the Gentile;ᵇ ¹⁰but glory, honor and peace for everyone who does good: first for the Jew, then for the Gentile.ᶜ ¹¹For God does not show favoritism.ᵈ

¹²All who sin apart from the law will also perish apart from the law, and all who sin under the lawᵉ will be judged by the law. ¹³For it is not those who hear the law who are righteous in God's sight, but it is those who obeyᶠ the law who will be declared righteous. ¹⁴(Indeed, when Gen-

H Ro 1:18 ◀▶ Ro 3:8
J Ac 24:25 ◀▶ Ro 2:16
J Ac 17:31 ◀▶ Ro 2:16
N Ro 1:20–22 ◀▶ 1Co 1:18
S Ro 1:18 ◀▶ Ro 6:1–2

ᵉ 6 Psalm 62:12; Prov. 24:12

2:5 Paul warns his readers that their hardness of heart has prepared them for God's wrath, revealed in the last day in "his righteous judgment" (2:5).

ROMANS 2:15

tiles, who do not have the law, do by nature things required by the law,[g] they are a law for themselves, even though they do not have the law, [15]since they show that the requirements of the law are written on their hearts, their consciences also bearing witness, and their thoughts now accusing, now even defending them.) [16]This will take place on the day when God will judge men's secrets[h] through Jesus Christ,[i] as my gospel[j] declares.

The Jews and the Law

[17]Now you, if you call yourself a Jew; if you rely on the law and brag about your relationship to God;[k] [18]if you know his will and approve of what is superior because you are instructed by the law; [19]if you are convinced that you are a guide for the blind, a light for those who are in the dark, [20]an instructor of the foolish, a teacher of infants, because you have in the law the embodiment of knowledge and truth— [21]you, then, who teach others, do you not teach yourself? You who preach against stealing, do you steal?[l] [22]You who say that people should not commit adultery, do you commit adultery? You who abhor idols, do you rob temples?[m] [23]You who brag about the law,[n] do you dishonor God by breaking the law? [24]As it is written: "God's name is blasphemed among the Gentiles because of you."[f][o]

[25]Circumcision has value if you observe the law,[p] but if you break the law, you have become as though you had not been circumcised.[q] [26]If those who are not circumcised keep the law's requirements,[r] will they not be regarded as though they were circumcised?[s] [27]The one who is not circumcised physically and yet obeys the law will condemn you[t] who, even though you have the[g] written code and circumcision, are a lawbreaker.

[28]A man is not a Jew if he is only one outwardly,[u] nor is circumcision merely outward and physical.[v] [29]No, a man is a Jew if he is one inwardly; and circumcision is circumcision of the heart,[w] by the Spirit,[x] not by the written code.[y] Such a man's praise is not from men, but from God.[z]

God's Faithfulness

3 What advantage, then, is there in being a Jew, or what value is there in circumcision? [2]Much in every way![a] First of all, they have been entrusted with the very words of God.[b]

[3]What if some did not have faith?[c] Will their lack of faith nullify God's faithfulness?[d] [4]Not at all! Let God be true,[e] and every man a liar.[f] As it is written:

"So that you may be proved right
 when you speak
and prevail when you judge."[h][g]

[5]But if our unrighteousness brings out God's righteousness more clearly,[h] what shall we say? That God is unjust in bringing his wrath on us? (I am using a human argument.)[i] [6]Certainly not! If that were so, how could God judge the world?[j] [7]Someone might argue, "If my falsehood enhances God's truthfulness and so increases his glory,[k] why am I still condemned as a sinner?"[l] [8]Why not say—as we are being slanderously reported as saying and as some claim that we say—"Let us do evil that good may result"?[m] Their condemnation is deserved.

No One Is Righteous

[9]What shall we conclude then? Are we any better[i]?[n] Not at all! We have already made the charge that Jews and Gentiles alike are all under sin.[o] [10]As it is written:

"There is no one righteous, not even
 one;
[11] there is no one who understands,
 no one who seeks God.
[12]All have turned away,
 they have together become
 worthless;

2:14 g Ac 10:35
2:16 h Ecc 12:14; 1Co 4:5 i Ac 10:42 j Ro 16:25; 2Ti 2:8
2:17 k ver 23; Jer 8:8; Mic 3:11; Jn 5:45; Ro 9:4
2:21 l Mt 23:3,4
2:22 m Ac 19:37
2:23 n S ver 17
2:24 o Isa 52:5; Eze 36:22; 2Pe 2:2
2:25 p ver 13,27; Gal 5:3 q Jer 4:4; 9:25,26
2:26 r Ro 8:4 s S 1Co 7:19
2:27 t Mt 12:41,42
2:28 u Mt 3:9; Jn 8:39; Ro 9:6,7 v Gal 6:15
2:29 w Dt 30:6 x Php 3:3; Col 2:11 y Ro 7:6; 2Co 3:6 z Jn 5:44; 12:43; 1Co 4:5; 2Co 10:18; Gal 1:10; 1Th 2:4; 1Pe 3:4
3:2 a Ro 9:4,5 b Dt 4:8; Ps 147:19; Ac 7:38
3:3 c Ro 10:16; Heb 4:2 d 2Ti 2:13
3:4 e Jn 3:33 f Ps 116:11 g Ps 51:4
3:5 h Ro 5:8 i Ro 6:19; Gal 3:15
3:6 j Ge 18:25; Ro 2:16
3:7 k ver 4 l Ro 9:19
3:8 m Ro 6:1
3:9 n ver 1 o ver 19, 23; 1Ki 8:46; 2Ch 6:36; Ps 106:6; Ro 5:12; 11:32; Gal 3:22

K Ro 1:16 ◀ ▶ Ro 3:24–25
J Ro 2:16 ◀ ▶ Ro 14:10–12
H Ro 2:2–13 ◀ ▶ Ro 6:23
A Jn 3:18 ◀ ▶ Ro 3:19
C Ro 1:28–32 ◀ ▶ Ro 3:17–20

f 24 Isaiah 52:5; Ezek. 36:22 g 27 Or who, by means of a h 4 Psalm 51:4 i 9 Or worse

J Ro 2:5 ◀ ▶ 1Co 4:5
J Ro 2:2–13 ◀ ▶ Ro 3:6

2:16 God will judge humanity in the final judgment day at the end of the Millennium (see Rev 20:11–15).

there is no one who does good,
     not even one."/p
¹³"Their throats are open graves;
     their tongues practice deceit."ᵏᑫ
"The poison of vipers is on their
     lips."/ʳ
¹⁴ "Their mouths are full of cursing
     and bitterness."ᵐˢ
¹⁵"Their feet are swift to shed blood;
¹⁶ ruin and misery mark their ways,
¹⁷and the way of peace they do not
     know."ⁿᵗ
¹⁸ "There is no fear of God before their
     eyes."ᵒᵘ

¹⁹Now we know that whatever the law says,ᵛ it says to those who are under the law,ʷ so that every mouth may be silencedˣ and the whole world held accountable to God.ʸ ²⁰Therefore no one will be declared righteous in his sight by observing the law;ᶻ rather, through the law we become conscious of sin.ᵃ

Righteousness Through Faith

²¹But now a righteousness from God,ᵇ apart from law, has been made known, to which the Law and the Prophets testify.ᶜ ²²This righteousness from Godᵈ comes through faithᵉ in Jesus Christᶠ to all who believe.ᵍ There is no difference,ʰ ²³for all have sinnedⁱ and fall short of the glory of God, ²⁴and are justifiedʲ freely by his graceᵏ through the redemptionˡ that came by Christ Jesus. ²⁵God presented him as a sacrifice of atonement,ᵖᵐ through faith in his blood.ⁿ He did this to demonstrate his justice, because in his forbearance he had left the sins committed beforehand unpunishedᵒ— ²⁶he did it to demonstrate his justice at the present time, so as to be just and the one who justifies those who have faith in Jesus.

²⁷Where, then, is boasting?ᵖ It is excluded. On what principle? On that of observing the law? No, but on that of faith.

3:12 ᵖ Ps 14:1-3; 53:1-3; Ecc 7:20
3:13 ᑫ Ps 5:9 ʳ Ps 140:3
3:14 ˢ Ro 10:7
3:17 ᵗ Isa 59:7,8
3:18 ᵘ Ps 36:1
3:19 ᵛ S Jn 10:34 ʷ S Ro 2:12 ˣ Ps 63:11; 107:42; Eze 16:63 ʸ ver 9
3:20 ᶻ Ac 13:39; Gal 2:16 ᵃ S Ro 4:15
3:21 ᵇ Isa 46:13; Jer 23:6; Ro 1:17; 9:30 ᶜ Ac 10:43; Ro 1:2
3:22 ᵈ Ro 1:17 ᵉ S Ro 9:30 ᶠ Gal 2:16; 3:22 ᵍ S Jn 3:15; Ro 4:11; 10:4 ʰ Ro 10:12; Gal 3:28; Col 3:11
3:23 ⁱ S ver 9
3:24 ʲ S Ro 4:25 ᵏ Jn 1:14,16,17; Ro 4:16; 5:21; 6:14; 11:5; 2Co 12:9; Eph 2:8; 4:7; Tit 2:11; Heb 4:16 ˡ Ps 130:7; 1Co 1:30; Gal 4:5; Eph 1:7,14; Col 1:14; Heb 9:12
3:25 ᵐ Ex 25:17; Lev 16:10; Ps 65:3; Heb 2:17; 9:28; 1Jn 4:10 ⁿ Ac 20:28; Ro 5:9; Eph 1:7; Heb 9:12, 14; 13:12; 1Pe 1:19; Rev 1:5 ᵒ Ac 14:16; 17:30
3:27 ᵖ Ro 2:17,23; 4:2; 1Co 1:29-31; Eph 2:9
3:28 ᑫ ver 20,21; Ac 13:39; Gal 2:16; 3:11; Eph 2:9; Jas 2:20,24,26
3:29 ʳ Ac 10:34,35; Ro 9:24; 10:12; 15:9; Gal 3:28
3:30 ˢ Ro 4:11,12; Gal 3:8
4:1 ᵗ S Ro 8:31 ᵘ S Lk 3:8
4:2 ᵛ 1Co 1:31
4:3 ʷ ver 5,9,22; Ge 15:6; Gal 3:6; Jas 2:23
4:4 ˣ Ro 11:6
4:5 ʸ ver 3,9,22; S Ro 9:30
4:8 ᶻ Ps 32:1,2; 103:12; 2Co 5:19
4:9 ᵃ Ro 3:30 ᵇ S ver 3
4:11 ᶜ Ge 17:10,11 ᵈ ver 16,17; S Lk 3:8 ᵉ S Ro 3:22

²⁸For we maintain that a man is justified by faith apart from observing the law.ᑫ ²⁹Is God the God of Jews only? Is he not the God of Gentiles too? Yes, of Gentiles too,ʳ ³⁰since there is only one God, who will justify the circumcised by faith and the uncircumcised through that same faith.ˢ ³¹Do we, then, nullify the law by this faith? Not at all! Rather, we uphold the law.

Abraham Justified by Faith

4 What then shall we sayᵗ that Abraham, our forefather,ᵘ discovered in this matter? ²If, in fact, Abraham was justified by works, he had something to boast about—but not before God.ᵛ ³What does the Scripture say? "Abraham believed God, and it was credited to him as righteousness."ᑫʷ

⁴Now when a man works, his wages are not credited to him as a gift,ˣ but as an obligation. ⁵However, to the man who does not work but trusts God who justifies the wicked, his faith is credited as righteousness.ʸ ⁶David says the same thing when he speaks of the blessedness of the man to whom God credits righteousness apart from works:

⁷"Blessed are they
     whose transgressions are forgiven,
     whose sins are covered.
⁸Blessed is the man
     whose sin the Lord will never count
          against him."ʳᶻ

⁹Is this blessedness only for the circumcised, or also for the uncircumcised?ᵃ We have been saying that Abraham's faith was credited to him as righteousness.ᵇ ¹⁰Under what circumstances was it credited? Was it after he was circumcised, or before? It was not after, but before! ¹¹And he received the sign of circumcision, a seal of the righteousness that he had by faith while he was still uncircumcised.ᶜ So then, he is the fatherᵈ of all who believeᵉ but have not been circumcised, in order that righteousness might be cred-

---

C Ro 3:9-12 ◀ ▶ Ro 6:16-17
A Ro 3:9-12 ◀ ▶ Ro 3:22
G Jn 10:1 ◀ ▶ Ro 3:27
F Ro 1:16 ◀ ▶ Ro 4:3
L Ac 28:28 ◀ ▶ Ro 4:6
W Ro 1:16 ◀ ▶ Ro 3:28-30
A Ro 3:19 ◀ ▶ Ro 3:23
A Ro 3:22 ◀ ▶ Ro 5:12
D Ac 20:28 ◀ ▶ Ro 8:32
K Ro 3:3-4 ◀ ▶ Ro 5:1-2
G Ro 3:20 ◀ ▶ Ro 4:1-4

W Ro 3:21-24 ◀ ▶ Ro 5:18
G Ro 3:27 ◀ ▶ Ro 4:14
F Ro 3:21-30 ◀ ▶ Ro 4:16
L Ro 3:21-30 ◀ ▶ Ro 4:12

ʲ 12 Psalms 14:1-3; 53:1-3; Eccles. 7:20 ᵏ 13 Psalm 5:9
ˡ 13 Psalm 140:3 ᵐ 14 Psalm 10:7 ⁿ 17 Isaiah 59:7,8 ᵒ 18 Psalm 36:1
ᵖ 25 Or *as the one who would turn aside his wrath, taking away sin*
ᑫ 3 Gen. 15:6; also in verse 22 ʳ 8 Psalm 32:1,2

ited to them. [12]And he is also the father of the circumcised who not only are circumcised but who also walk in the footsteps of the faith that our father Abraham had before he was circumcised.

[13]It was not through law that Abraham and his offspring received the promise that he would be heir of the world, but through the righteousness that comes by faith. [14]For if those who live by law are heirs, faith has no value and the promise is worthless, [15]because law brings wrath. And where there is no law there is no transgression.

[16]Therefore, the promise comes by faith, so that it may be by grace and may be guaranteed to all Abraham's offspring—not only to those who are of the law but also to those who are of the faith of Abraham. He is the father of us all. [17]As it is written: "I have made you a father of many nations." So he is our father in the sight of God, in whom he believed—the God who gives life to the dead and calls things that are not as though they were.

[18]Against all hope, Abraham in hope believed and so became the father of many nations, just as it had been said to him, "So shall your offspring be." [19]Without weakening in his faith, he faced the fact that his body was as good as dead—since he was about a hundred years old—and that Sarah's womb was also dead. [20]Yet he did not waver through unbelief regarding the promise of God, but was strengthened in his faith and gave glory to God, [21]being fully persuaded that God had power to do what he had promised. [22]This is why "it was credited to him as righteousness." [23]The words "it was credited to him" were written not for him alone, [24]but also for us, to whom God will credit righteous-

ness—for us who believe in him who raised Jesus our Lord from the dead. [25]He was delivered over to death for our sins and was raised to life for our justification.

Peace and Joy

5 Therefore, since we have been justified through faith, we have peace with God through our Lord Jesus Christ, [2]through whom we have gained access by faith into this grace in which we now stand. And we rejoice in the hope of the glory of God. [3]Not only so, but we also rejoice in our sufferings, because we know that suffering produces perseverance; [4]perseverance, character; and character, hope. [5]And hope does not disappoint us, because God has poured out his love into our hearts by the Holy Spirit, whom he has given us.

[6]You see, at just the right time, when we were still powerless, Christ died for the ungodly. [7]Very rarely will anyone die for a righteous man, though for a good man someone might possibly dare to die. [8]But God demonstrates his own love for us in this: While we were still sinners, Christ died for us.

[9]Since we have now been justified by his blood, how much more shall we be saved from God's wrath through him! [10]For if, when we were God's enemies, we were reconciled to him through the death of his Son, how much more, having been reconciled, shall we be saved through his life! [11]Not only is this so, but we also rejoice in God through our Lord Jesus Christ, through whom we have now received reconciliation.

4:13 Abraham was promised abundant offspring and given the land as his inheritance, not because of the law, but because of his faith in God (see Ge 15:4). This verse acknowledges God's promise made to Abraham and foresees the deliverance of the whole world into the hands of Jesus Christ as Messiah and "heir of the world" (4:13).

Death Through Adam, Life Through Christ

¹²Therefore, just as sin entered the world through one man,ᵈ and death through sin,ᵉ and in this way death came to all men, because all sinnedᶠ— ¹³for before the law was given, sin was in the world. But sin is not taken into account when there is no law.ᵍ ¹⁴Nevertheless, death reigned from the time of Adam to the time of Moses, even over those who did not sin by breaking a command, as did Adam,ʰ who was a pattern of the one to come.ⁱ

¹⁵But the gift is not like the trespass. For if the many died by the trespass of the one man,ʲ how much more did God's grace and the gift that came by the grace of the one man, Jesus Christ,ᵏ overflow to the many! ¹⁶Again, the gift of God is not like the result of the one man's sin: The judgment followed one sin and brought condemnation, but the gift followed many trespasses and brought justification. ¹⁷For if, by the trespass of the one man, deathˡ reigned through that one man, how much more will those who receive God's abundant provision of grace and of the gift of righteousness reign in lifeᵐ through the one man, Jesus Christ.

¹⁸Consequently, just as the result of one trespass was condemnation for all men,ⁿ so also the result of one act of righteousness was justificationᵒ that brings lifeᵖ for all men. ¹⁹For just as through the disobedience of the one manᵠ the many were made sinners,ʳ so also through the obedienceˢ of the one man the many will be made righteous.

²⁰The law was added so that the trespass might increase.ᵗ But where sin increased, grace increased all the more,ᵘ ²¹so that, just as sin reigned in death,ᵛ so also graceʷ might reign through righteousness to bring eternal lifeˣ through Jesus Christ our Lord.

Dead to Sin, Alive in Christ

6 What shall we say, then?ʸ Shall we go on sinning so that grace may increase?ᶻ ²By no means! We died to sin;ᵃ how can we live in it any longer? ³Or don't you know that all of us who were baptizedᵇ into Christ Jesus were baptized into his death? ⁴We were therefore buried with him through baptism into deathᶜ in order that, just as Christ was raised from the deadᵈ through the glory of the Father, we too may live a new life.ᵉ

⁵If we have been united with him like this in his death, we will certainly also be united with him in his resurrection.ᶠ ⁶For we know that our old selfᵍ was crucified with himʰ so that the body of sinⁱ might be done away with,ᵛ that we should no longer be slaves to sinʲ— ⁷because anyone who has died has been freed from sin.ᵏ

⁸Now if we died with Christ, we believe that we will also live with him.ˡ ⁹For we know that since Christ was raised from the dead,ᵐ he cannot die again; death no longer has mastery over him.ⁿ ¹⁰The death he died, he died to sinᵒ once for all;ᵖ but the life he lives, he lives to God.

¹¹In the same way, count yourselves dead to sinᵠ but alive to God in Christ Jesus. ¹²Therefore do not let sin reignʳ in your mortal body so that you obey its evil desires. ¹³Do not offer the parts of your body to sin, as instruments of wickedness,ˢ but rather offer yourselves to God, as those who have been brought from death to life; and offer the parts of your body to him as instruments of righteousness.ᵗ ¹⁴For sin shall not be your master,ᵘ because you are not under law,ᵛ but under grace.ʷ

Slaves to Righteousness

¹⁵What then? Shall we sin because we are not under law but under grace?ˣ By no means! ¹⁶Don't you know that when you offer yourselves to someone to obey him as slaves, you are slaves to the one whom you obeyʸ—whether you are slaves to sin,ᶻ which leads to death,ᵃ or to obedience, which leads to righteousness? ¹⁷But thanks be to Godᵇ that, though you used to be slaves to sin,ᶜ you wholeheartedly obeyed the form of teachingᵈ to which you were entrusted. ¹⁸You

---

A Ro 3:23 ◀▶ Ro 8:5–9
K Ro 5:9–11 ◀▶ Ro 7:24–25
W Ro 3:28–30 ◀▶ Ro 9:33
S Ro 2:6–13 ◀▶ Ro 6:6
S Ro 6:1–2 ◀▶ Ro 6:11–23
S Ro 6:6 ◀▶ Ro 7:4
C Ro 3:17–20 ◀▶ Ro 6:20

v 6 Or *be rendered powerless*

have been set free from sin and have become slaves to righteousness.

¹⁹I put this in human terms because you are weak in your natural selves. Just as you used to offer the parts of your body in slavery to impurity and to ever-increasing wickedness, so now offer them in slavery to righteousness leading to holiness. ²⁰When you were slaves to sin, you were free from the control of righteousness. ²¹What benefit did you reap at that time from the things you are now ashamed of? Those things result in death! ²²But now that you have been set free from sin and have become slaves to God, the benefit you reap leads to holiness, and the result is eternal life. ²³For the wages of sin is death, but the gift of God is eternal life in Christ Jesus our Lord.

An Illustration From Marriage

7 Do you not know, brothers—for I am speaking to men who know the law—that the law has authority over a man only as long as he lives? ²For example, by law a married woman is bound to her husband as long as he is alive, but if her husband dies, she is released from the law of marriage. ³So then, if she marries another man while her husband is still alive, she is called an adulteress. But if her husband dies, she is released from that law and is not an adulteress, even though she marries another man.

⁴So, my brothers, you also died to the law through the body of Christ, that you might belong to another, to him who was raised from the dead, in order that we might bear fruit to God. ⁵For when we were controlled by the sinful nature, the sinful passions aroused by the law were at work in our bodies, so that we bore fruit for death. ⁶But now, by dying to what once bound us, we have been released from the law so that we serve in the new way of the Spirit, and not in the old way of the written code.

Struggling With Sin

⁷What shall we say, then? Is the law sin? Certainly not! Indeed I would not have known what sin was except through the law. For I would not have known what coveting really was if the law had not said, "Do not covet." ⁸But sin, seizing the opportunity afforded by the commandment, produced in me every kind of covetous desire. For apart from law, sin is dead. ⁹Once I was alive apart from law; but when the commandment came, sin sprang to life and I died. ¹⁰I found that the very commandment that was intended to bring life actually brought death. ¹¹For sin, seizing the opportunity afforded by the commandment, deceived me, and through the commandment put me to death. ¹²So then, the law is holy, and the commandment is holy, righteous and good.

¹³Did that which is good, then, become death to me? By no means! But in order that sin might be recognized as sin, it produced death in me through what was good, so that through the commandment sin might become utterly sinful.

¹⁴We know that the law is spiritual; but I am unspiritual, sold as a slave to sin. ¹⁵I do not understand what I do. For what I want to do I do not do, but what I hate I do. ¹⁶And if I do what I do not want to do, I agree that the law is good. ¹⁷As it is, it is no longer I myself who do it, but it is sin living in me. ¹⁸I know that nothing good lives in me, that is, in my sinful nature. For I have the desire to do what is good, but I cannot carry it out. ¹⁹For what I do is not the good I want to do; no, the evil I do not want to do—this I keep on doing. ²⁰Now if I do what I do not want to do, it is no longer I who do it, but it is sin living in me that does it.

²¹So I find this law at work: When I want to do good, evil is right there with me. ²²For in my inner being I delight in God's law; ²³but I see another law at work in the members of my body, waging war against the law of my mind and making me a prisoner of the law of sin at work within my members. ²⁴What a wretched man I am! Who will rescue me

from this body of death?[c] [25]Thanks be to God—through Jesus Christ our Lord![d]

So then, I myself in my mind am a slave to God's law,[e] but in the sinful nature a slave to the law of sin.[f]

Life Through the Spirit

8 Therefore, there is now no condemnation[g] for those who are in Christ Jesus,[a][h] [2]because through Christ Jesus[i] the law of the Spirit of life[j] set me free[k] from the law of sin[l] and death. [3]For what the law was powerless[m] to do in that it was weakened by the sinful nature,[b][n] God did by sending his own Son in the likeness of sinful man[o] to be a sin offering.[c][p] And so he condemned sin in sinful man,[d] [4]in order that the righteous requirements[q] of the law might be fully met in us, who do not live according to the sinful nature but according to the Spirit.[r]

[5]Those who live according to the sinful nature have their minds set on what that nature desires;[s] but those who live in accordance with the Spirit have their minds set on what the Spirit desires.[t] [6]The mind of sinful man[e] is death,[u] but the mind controlled by the Spirit is life[v] and peace; [7]the sinful mind[f] is hostile to God.[w] It does not submit to God's law, nor can it do so. [8]Those controlled by the sinful nature[x] cannot please God.

[9]You, however, are controlled not by the sinful nature[y] but by the Spirit, if the Spirit of God lives in you.[z] And if anyone does not have the Spirit of Christ,[a] he does not belong to Christ. [10]But if Christ is in you,[b] your body is dead because of sin, yet your spirit is alive because of righteousness. [11]And if the Spirit of him who raised Jesus from the dead[c] is living in you, he who raised Christ from the dead will also give life to your mortal bodies[d] through his Spirit, who lives in you.

[12]Therefore, brothers, we have an obligation—but it is not to the sinful nature, to live according to it.[e] [13]For if you live according to the sinful nature, you will die;[f] but if by the Spirit you put to death the misdeeds of the body,[g] you will live,[h] [14]because those who are led by the Spirit of God[i] are sons of God.[j] [15]For you did not receive a spirit[k] that makes you a slave again to fear,[l] but you received the Spirit of sonship.[g] And by him we cry, "Abba,[h] Father."[m] [16]The Spirit himself testifies with our spirit[n] that we are God's children.[o] [17]Now if we are children, then we are heirs[p]—heirs of God and co-heirs with Christ, if indeed we share in his sufferings[q] in order that we may also share in his glory.[r]

Future Glory

[18]I consider that our present sufferings

8:11 This prophetic statement affirms the resurrection of our bodies because of the indwelling of the Holy Spirit.

8:16–25 Paul affirms that "we are God's children" (8:16) because of our identification with Jesus Christ. Whatever sufferings we may face cannot compare with "the glory that will be revealed in us" (8:18). Paul then tells us that the whole of creation awaits the day of renewal and deliverance from sin's effects. This renewal for believers will come with "the redemption of our bodies" (8:23) when Jesus raptures the saints to heaven and changes the bodies of the living and the departed saints into their glorious resurrection bodies—bodies like Jesus had after his resurrection from the grave (see 1Co 15:52).

are not worth comparing with the glory that will be revealed in us.ˢ ¹⁹The creation waits in eager expectation for the sons of God ᵗ to be revealed. ²⁰For the creation was subjected to frustration, not by its own choice, but by the will of the one who subjected it,ᵘ in hope ²¹that the creation itself will be liberated from its bondage to decay ᵛ and brought into the glorious freedom of the children of God.ʷ

²²We know that the whole creation has been groaning ˣ as in the pains of childbirth right up to the present time. ²³Not only so, but we ourselves, who have the firstfruits of the Spirit,ʸ groan ᶻ inwardly as we wait eagerly ᵃ for our adoption as sons, the redemption of our bodies.ᵇ ²⁴For in this hope we were saved.ᶜ But hope that is seen is no hope at all.ᵈ Who hopes for what he already has? ²⁵But if we hope for what we do not yet have, we wait for it patiently.ᵉ

²⁶In the same way, the Spirit helps us in our weakness. We do not know what we ought to pray for, but the Spirit ᶠ himself intercedes for us ᵍ with groans that words cannot express. ²⁷And he who searches our hearts ʰ knows the mind of the Spirit, because the Spirit intercedes ⁱ for the saints in accordance with God's will.

More Than Conquerors

²⁸And we know that in all things God works for the good ʲ of those who love him,ʲ who ᵏ have been called ᵏ according to his purpose.ˡ ²⁹For those God foreknew ᵐ he also predestined ⁿ to be conformed to the likeness of his Son,ᵒ that he might be the firstborn ᵖ among many brothers. ³⁰And those he predestined,ᵠ he also called;ʳ those he called, he also justified;ˢ those he justified, he also glorified.ᵗ

³¹What, then, shall we say in response to this?ᵘ If God is for us,ᵛ who can be against us?ʷ ³²He who did not spare his own Son,ˣ but gave him up for us all—how will he not also, along with him, graciously give us all things? ³³Who will bring any charge ʸ against those whom God has chosen? It is God who justifies. ³⁴Who is he that condemns?ᶻ Christ Jesus, who died ᵃ—more than that, who was raised to life ᵇ—is at the right hand of God ᶜ and is also interceding for us.ᵈ ³⁵Who shall separate us from the love of Christ?ᵉ Shall trouble or hardship or persecution or famine or nakedness or danger or sword?ᶠ ³⁶As it is written:

"For your sake we face death all day long;
we are considered as sheep to be slaughtered."/ᵍ

³⁷No, in all these things we are more than conquerors ʰ through him who loved us.ⁱ ³⁸For I am convinced that neither death nor life, neither angels nor demons,ᵐ neither the present nor the future,ʲ nor any powers,ᵏ ³⁹neither height nor depth, nor anything else in all creation, will be able to separate us from the love of God ˡ that is in Christ Jesus our Lord.ᵐ

God's Sovereign Choice

9 I speak the truth in Christ—I am not lying,ⁿ my conscience confirms ᵒ it in the Holy Spirit— ²I have great sorrow and unceasing anguish in my heart. ³For I could wish that I myself ᵖ were cursed ᵠ and cut off from Christ for the sake of my brothers,ʳ those of my own race,ˢ ⁴the people of Israel.ᵗ Theirs is the adoption as sons;ᵘ theirs the divine glory,ᵛ the covenants,ʷ the receiving of the law,ˣ the temple worship[y] and the promises.[z] ⁵Theirs are the patriarchs,[a] and from them is traced the human ancestry of Christ,[b] who is God over all,[c] forever praised![n][d] Amen.

⁶It is not as though God's word[e] had failed. For not all who are descended from Israel are Israel.[f] ⁷Nor because they are his descendants are they all Abraham's children. On the contrary, "It is through Isaac that your offspring will be reckoned."[o][g] ⁸In other words, it is not the natural children who are God's children,[h] but it is the children of the promise who are regarded as Abraham's offspring.[i] ⁹For this was how the promise was stated: "At the appointed time I will return, and Sarah will have a son."[p][j]

¹⁰Not only that, but Rebekah's children had one and the same father, our father Isaac.[k] ¹¹Yet, before the twins were born or had done anything good or bad[1]—in order that God's purpose[m] in election might stand: ¹²not by works but by him who calls—she was told, "The older will serve the younger."[q][n] ¹³Just as it is written: "Jacob I loved, but Esau I hated."[r][o]

¹⁴What then shall we say?[p] Is God unjust? Not at all![q] ¹⁵For he says to Moses,

"I will have mercy on whom I have mercy,
and I will have compassion on whom I have compassion."[s][r]

¹⁶It does not, therefore, depend on man's desire or effort, but on God's mercy.[s] ¹⁷For the Scripture says to Pharaoh: "I raised you up for this very purpose, that I might display my power in you and that my name might be proclaimed in all the earth."[t][t] ¹⁸Therefore God has mercy on whom he wants to have mercy, and he hardens whom he wants to harden.[u]

¹⁹One of you will say to me:[v] "Then why does God still blame us?[w] For who resists his will?"[x] ²⁰But who are you, O man, to talk back to God?[y] "Shall what

G Ro 8:9 ◀ ▶ Ro 9:31–32
K Ro 8:33–39 ◀ ▶ Ro 9:18
O Ro 8:14 ◀ ▶ Ro 10:3–4
K Ro 9:15 ◀ ▶ Ro 9:21

9:4 ʸHeb 9:1; ᶻS Ac 13:32; ˢGal 3:16
9:5 ᵃRo 11:28; ᵇMt 1:1-16; Ro 1:3; ᶜJn 1:1; Col 2:9; ᵈRo 1:25; 2Co 11:31
9:6 ᵉS Heb 4:12; ᶠRo 2:28,29; Gal 6:16
9:7 ᵍGe 21:12; Heb 11:18
9:8 ʰS Ro 8:14; ⁱS Gal 3:16
9:9 ʲGe 18:10,14
9:10 ᵏGe 25:21
9:11 ˡver 16; ᵐRo 8:28
9:12 ⁿGe 25:23
9:13 ᵒMal 1:2,3
9:14 ᵖS Ro 8:31; ᑫ2Ch 19:7
9:15 ʳEx 33:19
9:16 ˢEph 2:8; Tit 3:5
9:17 ᵗEx 9:16; 14:4; Ps 76:10
9:18 ᵘEx 4:21; 7:3; 14:4,17; Dt 2:30; Jos 11:20; Ro 11:25
9:19 ᵛRo 11:19; 1Co 15:35; Jas 2:18; ʷRo 3:7; ˣ2Sa 16:10; 2Ch 20:6; Da 4:35
9:20 ʸJob 1:22; 9:12; 40:2; ᶻIsa 64:8; Jer 18:6; ᵃIsa 29:16; 45:9; 10:15
9:21 ᵇ2Ti 2:20
9:22 ᶜS Ro 2:4; ᵈPr 16:4
9:23 ᵉS Ro 2:4; ᶠRo 8:30
9:24 ᵍS Ro 8:28; ʰS Ro 3:29
9:25 ⁱHos 2:23; 1Pe 2:10
9:26 ʲHos 1:10; ˢMt 16:16; S Ro 8:14
9:27 ᵏGe 22:17; Hos 1:10; 2Ki 19:4; Jer 44:14; 50:20; Joel 2:32; Ro 11:5
9:28 ᵐIsa 10:22, 23
9:29 ⁿJas 5:4

is formed say to him who formed it,[z] 'Why did you make me like this?'"[u][a] ²¹Does not the potter have the right to make out of the same lump of clay some pottery for noble purposes and some for common use?[b]

²²What if God, choosing to show his wrath and make his power known, bore with great patience[c] the objects of his wrath—prepared for destruction?[d] ²³What if he did this to make the riches of his glory[e] known to the objects of his mercy, whom he prepared in advance for glory[f]— ²⁴even us, whom he also called,[g] not only from the Jews but also from the Gentiles?[h] ²⁵As he says in Hosea:

"I will call them 'my people' who are not my people;
and I will call her 'my loved one' who is not my loved one,"[v][i]

²⁶and,

"It will happen that in the very place where it was said to them,
'You are not my people,'
they will be called 'sons of the living God.'"[w][j]

²⁷Isaiah cries out concerning Israel:

"Though the number of the Israelites be like the sand by the sea,[k]
only the remnant will be saved.[l]
²⁸For the Lord will carry out his sentence on earth with speed and finality."[x][m]

²⁹It is just as Isaiah said previously:

"Unless the Lord Almighty[n]
had left us descendants,
we would have become like Sodom,

K Ro 9:18 ◀ ▶ Ro 9:23
H Ro 6:23 ◀ ▶ Ro 11:20–22
K Ro 9:21 ◀ ▶ Ro 10:4
I Ro 9:4 ◀ ▶ Ro 10:21
R Lk 23:28 ◀ ▶ Ro 11:1–5

ⁿ5 Or Christ, who is over all. God be forever praised! Or Christ. God who is over all be forever praised! ᵒ7 Gen. 21:12 ᵖ9 Gen. 18:10,14 ᑫ12 Gen. 25:23 ʳ13 Mal. 1:2,3 ˢ15 Exodus 33:19 ᵗ17 Exodus 9:16 ᵘ20 Isaiah 29:16; 45:9 ᵛ25 Hosea 2:23 ʷ26 Hosea 1:10 ˣ28 Isaiah 10:22,23

9:25–30 Paul reaffirms Hosea's prophecies of Israel's rebirth as a nation in the last days (see Hos 2:23), declaring that, after repentance, Israel shall be "called 'sons of the living God'" (9:26). He also refers to the prophecies of Isaiah who declared that only a small remnant of Israel would be saved and return (see Isa 10:22).

we would have been like Gomorrah."ʸᵒ

Israel's Unbelief

³⁰What then shall we say?ᵖ That the Gentiles, who did not pursue righteousness, have obtained it, a righteousness that is by faith;ᵠ ³¹but Israel, who pursued a law of righteousness,ʳ has not attained it.ˢ ³²Why not? Because they pursued it not by faith but as if it were by works. They stumbled over the "stumbling stone."ᵗ ³³As it is written:

"See, I lay in Zion a stone that causes men to stumble
and a rock that makes them fall,
and the one who trusts in him will never be put to shame."ᶻᵘ

10 Brothers, my heart's desireᵛ and prayer to God for the Israelites is that they may be saved. ²For I can testify about them that they are zealousʷ for God, but their zeal is not based on knowledge. ³Since they did not know the righteousness that comes from God and sought to establish their own, they did not submit to God's righteousness.ˣ ⁴Christ is the end of the lawʸ so that there may be righteousness for everyone who believes.ᶻ

⁵Moses describes in this way the righteousness that is by the law: "The man who does these things will live by them."ᵃᵃ ⁶But the righteousness that is by faithᵇ says: "Do not say in your heart, 'Who will ascend into heaven?'ᵇ ᶜ (that is, to bring Christ down)⁷or 'Who will descend into the deep?'ᶜ ᵈ (that is, to bring Christ up from the dead).ᵉ ⁸But what does it say? "The word is near you;

G Ac 28:28 ◀ ▶ Ro 10:19–20
F Ro 8:24 ◀ ▶ Ro 10:4
G Ro 9:15–16 ◀ ▶ Ro 10:1–3
W Ro 5:18 ◀ ▶ Ro 10:4
G Ro 9:31–32 ◀ ▶ Ro 11:5–6
O Ro 9:15–16 ◀ ▶ 1Co 3:11
F Ro 9:30–33 ◀ ▶ Ro 10:6–11
K Ro 9:23 ◀ ▶ Ro 10:11
L Ro 8:32 ◀ ▶ Ro 10:21
W Ro 9:33 ◀ ▶ Ro 10:6–13
F Ro 10:4 ◀ ▶ Ro 11:23
W Ro 10:4 ◀ ▶ 2Co 5:14–15
T Ro 1:16 ◀ ▶ 1Co 14:24–25

9:29 ᵒ Isa 1:9; Ge 19:24-29; Dt 29:23; Isa 13:19; Jer 50:40
9:30 ᵖ S Ro 8:31 ᵠ Ro 1:17; 3:22; 4:5,13; 10:6; Gal 2:16; Php 3:9; Heb 11:7
9:31 ʳ Dt 6:25; Isa 51:1; Ro 10:2,3; 11:7 ˢ Gal 5:4
9:32 ᵗ 1Pe 2:8
9:33 ᵘ Isa 8:14; 28:16; Ro 10:11; 1Pe 2:6,8
10:1 ᵛ Ps 20:4
10:2 ʷ S Ac 21:20
10:3 ˣ Ro 1:17; S 9:31
10:4 ʸ Gal 3:24; Ro 7:1-4 ᶻ Ro 3:22
10:5 ᵃ Lev 18:5; Dt 4:1; 6:24; Ne 9:29; Pr 19:16; Isa 55:3; Eze 20:11, 13,21; S Ro 7:10
10:6 ᵇ S Ro 9:30 ᶜ Dt 30:12
10:7 ᵈ Dt 30:13 ᵉ S Ac 2:24
10:8 ᶠ Dt 30:14
10:9 ᵍ Mt 10:32 ʰ Jn 13:13 ⁱ Jn 3:15 ʲ S Ac 2:24 ᵏ S Ro 11:14
10:11 ˡ Isa 28:16; Ro 9:33
10:12 ᵐ S Ro 3:22, 29 ⁿ S Mt 28:18
10:13 ᵒ S Ac 2:21 ᵖ Joel 2:32
10:15 ᵠ Isa 52:7; Na 1:15
10:16 ʳ Heb 4:2 ˢ Isa 53:1; Jn 12:38
10:17 ᵗ Gal 3:2,5 ᵘ Col 3:16
10:18 ᵛ Ps 19:4; S Mt 24:14; Ro 1:8; Col 1:6,23; 1Th 1:8
10:19 ʷ Ro 11:11, 14 ˣ Dt 32:21

it is in your mouth and in your heart,"ᵈᶠ that is, the word of faith we are proclaiming: ⁹That if you confessᵍ with your mouth, "Jesus is Lord,"ʰ and believeⁱ in your heart that God raised him from the dead,ʲ you will be saved.ᵏ ¹⁰For it is with your heart that you believe and are justified, and it is with your mouth that you confess and are saved. ¹¹As the Scripture says, "Anyone who trusts in him will never be put to shame."ᵉˡ ¹²For there is no difference between Jew and Gentile ᵐ—the same Lord is Lord of allⁿ and richly blesses all who call on him, ¹³for, "Everyone who calls on the name of the Lordᵒ will be saved."ᶠᵖ

¹⁴How, then, can they call on the one they have not believed in? And how can they believe in the one of whom they have not heard? And how can they hear without someone preaching to them? ¹⁵And how can they preach unless they are sent? As it is written, "How beautiful are the feet of those who bring good news!"ᵍᵠ

¹⁶But not all the Israelites accepted the good news.ʳ For Isaiah says, "Lord, who has believed our message?"ʰˢ ¹⁷Consequently, faith comes from hearing the message,ᵗ and the message is heard through the word of Christ.ᵘ ¹⁸But I ask: Did they not hear? Of course they did:

"Their voice has gone out into all the earth,
their words to the ends of the world."ⁱᵛ

¹⁹Again I ask: Did Israel not understand? First, Moses says,

"I will make you enviousʷ by those who are not a nation;
I will make you angry by a nation that has no understanding."ʲˣ

²⁰And Isaiah boldly says,

"I was found by those who did not seek me;

K Ro 10:4 ◀ ▶ Ro 16:25
G Ro 9:30 ◀ ▶ Ro 11:11–12

ʸ 29 Isaiah 1:9; ᶻ 33 Isaiah 8:14; 28:16 ᵃ 5 Lev. 18:5 ᵇ 6 Deut. 30:12 ᶜ 7 Deut. 30:13 ᵈ 8 Deut. 30:14 ᵉ 11 Isaiah 28:16 ᶠ 13 Joel 2:32 ᵍ 15 Isaiah 52:7 ʰ 16 Isaiah 53:1 ⁱ 18 Psalm 19:4 ʲ 19 Deut. 32:21

10:19–21 Paul says that because God provoked Israel to jealousy, many Gentiles had accepted the Messiah that the Jews had rejected, exactly as Isaiah had prophesied centuries earlier (see Isa 65:1).

I revealed myself to those who did not ask for me."ᵏʸ

²¹But concerning Israel he says,

"All day long I have held out my hands
to a disobedient and obstinate people."ˡᶻ

The Remnant of Israel

11 I ask then: Did God reject his people? By no means!ᵃ I am an Israelite myself, a descendant of Abraham,ᵇ from the tribe of Benjamin.ᶜ ²God did not reject his people,ᵈ whom he foreknew.ᵉ Don't you know what the Scripture says in the passage about Elijah—how he appealed to God against Israel: ³"Lord, they have killed your prophets and torn down your altars; I am the only one left, and they are trying to kill me"ᵐ?ᶠ ⁴And what was God's answer to him? "I have reserved for myself seven thousand who have not bowed the knee to Baal."ⁿᵍ ⁵So too, at the present time there is a remnantʰ chosen by grace.ⁱ ⁶And if by grace, then it is no longer by works;ʲ if it were, grace would no longer be grace.ᵒ

⁷What then? What Israel sought so earnestly it did not obtain,ᵏ but the elect did. The others were hardened,ˡ ⁸as it is written:

"God gave them a spirit of stupor,
eyes so that they could not see

and ears so that they could not hear,ᵐ
to this very day."ᵖⁿ

⁹And David says:

"May their table become a snare and a trap,
a stumbling block and a retribution for them.

¹⁰May their eyes be darkened so they cannot see,ᵒ
and their backs be bent forever."ᵠᵖ

Ingrafted Branches

¹¹Again I ask: Did they stumble so as to fall beyond recovery? Not at all!ᵠ Rather, because of their transgression, salvation has come to the Gentilesʳ to make Israel envious.ˢ ¹²But if their transgression means riches for the world, and their loss means riches for the Gentiles,ᵗ how much greater riches will their fullness bring!

¹³I am talking to you Gentiles. Inasmuch as I am the apostle to the Gentiles,ᵘ I make much of my ministry ¹⁴in the hope that I may somehow arouse my own people to envyᵛ and saveʷ some of them. ¹⁵For if their rejection is the reconciliationˣ of the world, what will their acceptance be but life from the dead?ʸ ¹⁶If the part of the dough offered as firstfruitsᶻ is holy, then the whole batch is holy; if the root is holy, so are the branches.

11:1–5 Paul deals with a profound question regarding Israel's salvation. Despite the widespread rejection of Christ by the Jews, Paul says that some of the Jews secretly accepted faith in him as "a remnant chosen by grace" (11:5). These were like the faithful Israelites in the days of wicked King Ahab, who refused to worship Baal and secretly worshiped God (see 1Ki 19:18).

11:7–12 Paul discusses the mystery of Israel's rejection of the Gospel. They were spiritually "hardened" (11:7) so that in God's ultimate plan, Christ's rejection by Israel would lead to the salvation of the Gentiles.

11:15–29, 32 Paul affirms that Israel's rejection of Christ as Messiah led ultimately to the reconciling of the Gentiles because of their acceptance of salvation through the atonement of Christ on the cross. Yet Paul warns the Gentiles against pride because even though God gave them Israel's chance for salvation, Israel is still "loved on account of the patriarchs" (11:28). Paul confirms God's eternal covenant with Israel. Although individual Jews will be judged for their rejection of Christ's salvation, the nation of Israel is still a part of God's eternal plan to bring light to the Gentiles (see Isa 42:6; Ac 13:47).

[17] If some of the branches have been broken off,[a] and you, though a wild olive shoot, have been grafted in among the others[b] and now share in the nourishing sap from the olive root, [18] do not boast over those branches. If you do, consider this: You do not support the root, but the root supports you.[c] [19] You will say then, "Branches were broken off so that I could be grafted in." [20] Granted. But they were broken off because of unbelief, and you stand by faith.[d] Do not be arrogant,[e] but be afraid.[f] [21] For if God did not spare the natural branches, he will not spare you either. [22] Consider therefore the kindness[g] and sternness of God: sternness to those who fell, but kindness to you, provided that you continue[h] in his kindness. Otherwise, you also will be cut off.[i] [23] And if they do not persist in unbelief, they will be grafted in, for God is able to graft them in again.[j] [24] After all, if you were cut out of an olive tree that is wild by nature, and contrary to nature were grafted into a cultivated olive tree,[k] how much more readily will these, the natural branches, be grafted into their own olive tree!

All Israel Will Be Saved

[25] I do not want you to be ignorant[l] of this mystery,[m] brothers, so that you may not be conceited:[n] Israel has experienced a hardening[o] in part until the full number of the Gentiles has come in.[p] [26] And so all Israel will be saved,[q] as it is written:

"The deliverer will come from Zion;
    he will turn godlessness away from Jacob.
[27] And this is[r] my covenant with them
    when I take away their sins."[s][t]

[28] As far as the gospel is concerned, they are enemies[s] on your account; but as far as election is concerned, they are loved on account of the patriarchs,[t] [29] for God's gifts and his call[u] are irrevocable.[v] [30] Just as you who were at one time disobedient[w] to God have now received mercy as a result of their disobedience, [31] so they too have now become disobedient in order that they too may now[t] re-

ceive mercy as a result of God's mercy to you. [32] For God has bound all men over to disobedience[x] so that he may have mercy on them all.

Doxology

[33] Oh, the depth of the riches[y] of the
        wisdom and[u] knowledge of
        God![z]
    How unsearchable his judgments,
        and his paths beyond tracing out![a]
[34] "Who has known the mind of the
        Lord?
    Or who has been his counselor?"[v][b]
[35] "Who has ever given to God,
        that God should repay him?"[w][c]
[36] For from him and through him and to
        him are all things.[d]
    To him be the glory forever! Amen.[e]

Living Sacrifices

12 Therefore, I urge you,[f] brothers, in view of God's mercy, to offer your bodies as living sacrifices,[g] holy and pleasing to God—this is your spiritual[x] act of worship. [2] Do not conform[h] any longer to the pattern of this world,[i] but be transformed by the renewing of your mind.[j] Then you will be able to test and approve what God's will is[k]—his good, pleasing[l] and perfect will.

[3] For by the grace given me[m] I say to every one of you: Do not think of yourself more highly than you ought, but rather think of yourself with sober judgment, in accordance with the measure of faith God has given you. [4] Just as each of us has one body with many members, and these members do not all have the same function,[n] [5] so in Christ we who are many form one body,[o] and each member belongs to all the others. [6] We have different gifts,[p] according to the grace given us. If a man's gift is prophesying,[q] let him use it in proportion to his[y] faith.[r] [7] If it is serving, let him serve; if it is teaching, let him

---

t 27 Or *will be* *s 27* Isaiah 59:20,21; 27:9; Jer. 31:33,34 *t 31* Some manuscripts do not have *now*. *u 33* Or *riches and the wisdom and the* *v 34* Isaiah 40:13 *w 35* Job 41:11 *x 1* Or *reasonable* *y 6* Or *in agreement with the*

teach;ˢ ⁸if it is encouraging, let him encourage;ᵗ if it is contributing to the needs of others, let him give generously;ᵘ if it is leadership, let him govern diligently; if it is showing mercy, let him do it cheerfully.

Love

⁹Love must be sincere.ᵛ Hate what is evil; cling to what is good.ʷ ¹⁰Be devoted to one another in brotherly love.ˣ Honor one another above yourselves.ʸ ¹¹Never be lacking in zeal, but keep your spiritual fervor,ᶻ serving the Lord. ¹²Be joyful in hope,ᵃ patient in affliction,ᵇ faithful in prayer.ᶜ ¹³Share with God's people who are in need.ᵈ Practice hospitality.ᵉ

¹⁴Bless those who persecute you;ᶠ bless and do not curse. ¹⁵Rejoice with those who rejoice; mourn with those who mourn.ᵍ ¹⁶Live in harmony with one another.ʰ Do not be proud, but be willing to associate with people of low position. Do not be conceited.ⁱ

¹⁷Do not repay anyone evil for evil.ʲ Be careful to do what is right in the eyes of everybody.ᵏ ¹⁸If it is possible, as far as it depends on you, live at peace with everyone.ˡ ¹⁹Do not take revenge,ᵐ my friends, but leave room for God's wrath, for it is written: "It is mine to avenge; I will repay,"ᵃⁿ says the Lord. ²⁰On the contrary:

"If your enemy is hungry, feed him;
   if he is thirsty, give him something
      to drink.
In doing this, you will heap burning
      coals on his head."ᵇᵒ

²¹Do not be overcome by evil, but overcome evil with good.

Submission to the Authorities

13 Everyone must submit himself to the governing authorities,ᵖ for there is no authority except that which God has established.ᵠ The authorities that exist have been established by God. ²Consequently, he who rebels against the authority is rebelling against what God has instituted,ʳ and those who do so will bring judgment on themselves. ³For rulers hold no terror for those who do right, but for those who do wrong. Do you want to be free from fear of the one in authority? Then do what is right and he will commend you.ˢ ⁴For he is God's servant to do you good. But if you do wrong, be afraid, for he does not bear the sword for nothing. He is God's servant, an agent of wrath to bring punishment on the wrongdoer.ᵗ ⁵Therefore, it is necessary to submit to the authorities, not only because of possible punishment but also because of conscience.ᵘ

⁶This is also why you pay taxes,ᵛ for the authorities are God's servants, who give their full time to governing. ⁷Give everyone what you owe him: If you owe taxes, pay taxes;ʷ if revenue, then revenue; if respect, then respect; if honor, then honor.

Love, for the Day Is Near

⁸Let no debt remain outstanding, except the continuing debt to love one another, for he who loves his fellowman has fulfilled the law.ˣ ⁹The commandments, "Do not commit adultery," "Do not murder," "Do not steal," "Do not covet,"ᶜʸ and whatever other commandment there may be, are summed upᶻ in this one rule: "Love your neighbor as yourself."ᵈᵃ ¹⁰Love does no harm to its neighbor. Therefore love is the fulfillment of the law.ᵇ

¹¹And do this, understanding the present time. The hour has comeᶜ for you to wake up from your slumber,ᵈ because our salvation is nearer now than when we first believed. ¹²The night is nearly over; the day is almost here.ᵉ So let us put aside the deeds of darknessᶠ and put on the armorᵍ of light. ¹³Let us behave decently, as in the daytime, not in orgies and drunkenness,ʰ not in sexual immorality and debauchery, not in dissension and jealousy.ⁱ ¹⁴Rather, clothe yourselves

---

13:11–12 Paul declares that because "the day is almost here" (13:12), believers must awaken to their true situation and prepare for spiritual warfare.

with the Lord Jesus Christ,[j] and do not think about how to gratify the desires of the sinful nature.[e][k]

The Weak and the Strong

14 Accept him whose faith is weak,[1] without passing judgment on disputable matters. [2]One man's faith allows him to eat everything, but another man, whose faith is weak, eats only vegetables.[m] [3]The man who eats everything must not look down on[n] him who does not, and the man who does not eat everything must not condemn[o] the man who does, for God has accepted him. [4]Who are you to judge someone else's servant?[p] To his own master he stands or falls. And he will stand, for the Lord is able to make him stand.

[5]One man considers one day more sacred than another;[q] another man considers every day alike. Each one should be fully convinced in his own mind. [6]He who regards one day as special, does so to the Lord. He who eats meat, eats to the Lord, for he gives thanks to God;[r] and he who abstains, does so to the Lord and gives thanks to God. [7]For none of us lives to himself alone[s] and none of us dies to himself alone. [8]If we live, we live to the Lord; and if we die, we die to the Lord. So, whether we live or die, we belong to the Lord.[t]

[9]For this very reason, Christ died and returned to life[u] so that he might be the Lord of both the dead and the living.[v] [10]You, then, why do you judge your brother? Or why do you look down on[w] your brother? For we will all stand before God's judgment seat.[x] [11]It is written:

" 'As surely as I live,'[y] says the Lord,
'every knee will bow before me;
    every tongue will confess to God.' "[f][z]

[12]So then, each of us will give an account of himself to God.[a]

[13]Therefore let us stop passing judgment[b] on one another. Instead, make up your mind not to put any stumbling block or obstacle in your brother's way.[c] [14]As one who is in the Lord Jesus, I am fully convinced that no food[g] is unclean in itself.[d] But if anyone regards something as unclean, then for him it is unclean.[e] [15]If your brother is distressed because of what you eat, you are no longer acting in love.[f] Do not by your eating destroy your brother for whom Christ died.[g] [16]Do not allow what you consider good to be spoken of as evil.[h] [17]For the kingdom of God is not a matter of eating and drinking,[i] but of righteousness, peace[j] and joy in the Holy Spirit,[k] [18]because anyone who serves Christ in this way is pleasing to God and approved by men.[l]

[19]Let us therefore make every effort to do what leads to peace[m] and to mutual edification.[n] [20]Do not destroy the work of God for the sake of food.[o] All food is clean,[p] but it is wrong for a man to eat anything that causes someone else to stumble.[q] [21]It is better not to eat meat or drink wine or to do anything else that will cause your brother to fall.[r]

[22]So whatever you believe about these things keep between yourself and God. Blessed is the man who does not condemn[s] himself by what he approves. [23]But the man who has doubts[t] is condemned if he eats, because his eating is not from faith; and everything that does not come from faith is sin.

15 We who are strong ought to bear with the failings of the weak[u] and not to please ourselves. [2]Each of us should please his neighbor for his good,[v] to build him up.[w] [3]For even Christ did not please himself[x] but, as it is written: "The insults of those who insult you have fallen on me."[h][y] [4]For everything that was written in the past was written to teach us,[z] so that through endurance and the encouragement of the Scriptures we might have hope.

[5]May the God who gives endurance and encouragement give you a spirit of unity[a] among yourselves as you follow Christ Jesus, [6]so that with one heart and mouth you may glorify[b] the God and Father[c] of our Lord Jesus Christ.

[7]Accept one another,[d] then, just as

J Ro 3:6 ◀ ▶ 1Co 4:4–5
S Ro 13:14 ◀ ▶ Ro 14:15–18
M Ro 8:17–18 ◀ ▶ Ro 15:10
M Ro 12:16 ◀ ▶ 1Co 10:12

S Ro 14:10–12 ◀ ▶ 1Co 3:17
F Ro 8:23 ◀ ▶ Ro 15:13
J Ro 8:15 ◀ ▶ Ro 15:13
W Ro 12:6–8 ◀ ▶ 1Co 2:14

e 14 Or *the flesh* *f* 11 Isaiah 45:23 *g* 14 Or *that nothing* *h* 3 Psalm 69:9

Christ accepted you, in order to bring praise to God. ⁸For I tell you that Christ has become a servant of the Jews[fe] on behalf of God's truth, to confirm the promises[f] made to the patriarchs ⁹so that the Gentiles[g] may glorify God[h] for his mercy, as it is written:

"Therefore I will praise you among the Gentiles;
I will sing hymns to your name."[/i]

¹⁰Again, it says,

"Rejoice, O Gentiles, with his people."[kj]

¹¹And again,

"Praise the Lord, all you Gentiles,
and sing praises to him, all you peoples."[lk]

¹²And again, Isaiah says,

"The Root of Jesse[l] will spring up,
one who will arise to rule over the nations;
the Gentiles will hope in him."[mm]

¹³May the God of hope fill you with all joy and peace[n] as you trust in him, so that you may overflow with hope by the power of the Holy Spirit.[o]

Paul the Minister to the Gentiles

¹⁴I myself am convinced, my brothers, that you yourselves are full of goodness,[p] complete in knowledge[q] and competent to instruct one another. ¹⁵I have written you quite boldly on some points, as if to remind you of them again, because of the grace God gave me[r] ¹⁶to be a minister of Christ Jesus to the Gentiles[s] with the priestly duty of proclaiming the gospel of God,[t] so that the Gentiles might become an offering[u] acceptable to God, sanctified by the Holy Spirit.

¹⁷Therefore I glory in Christ Jesus[v] in my service to God.[w] ¹⁸I will not venture to speak of anything except what Christ has accomplished through me in leading the Gentiles[x] to obey God[y] by what I have said and done— ¹⁹by the power of signs and miracles,[z] through the power of the Spirit.[a] So from Jerusalem[b] all the way around to Illyricum, I have fully proclaimed the gospel of Christ.[c] ²⁰It has always been my ambition to preach the gospel[d] where Christ was not known, so that I would not be building on someone else's foundation.[e] ²¹Rather, as it is written:

"Those who were not told about him will see,
and those who have not heard will understand."[nf]

²²This is why I have often been hindered from coming to you.[g]

Paul's Plan to Visit Rome

²³But now that there is no more place for me to work in these regions, and since I have been longing for many years to see you,[h] ²⁴I plan to do so when I go to Spain.[i] I hope to visit you while passing through and to have you assist[j] me on my journey there, after I have enjoyed your company for a while. ²⁵Now, however, I am on my way to Jerusalem[k] in the service[l] of the saints[m] there. ²⁶For Macedonia[n] and Achaia[o] were pleased to make a contribution for the poor among the saints in Jerusalem.[p] ²⁷They were pleased

---

15:12 Paul quotes the ancient prophecy of Isaiah 11:10. The genealogies of Matthew and Luke confirm Jesus' claim to be the Messiah, the legitimate "son of David" (Mt 1:1) prophesied by the OT prophets (see Rev 5:5; 22:16).

15:16 The apostle affirms his role among the Gentiles and cites the Holy Spirit's sanctification as his source of power for his life and ministry.

15:27 Paul affirms that because the Jews' spiritual blessings, especially Christ and the gospel mesto do it, and indeed they owe it to them. For if the Gentiles have shared in the Jews' spiritual blessings, they owe it to the Jews to share with them their material blessings.q 28So after I have completed this task and have made sure that they have received this fruit, I will go to Spainr and visit you on the way. 29I know that when I come to you,s I will come in the full measure of the blessing of Christ.

E 30I urge you, brothers, by our Lord
F Jesus Christ and by the love of the Spirit,t to join me in my struggle by praying to God for me.u 31Pray that I may be rescuedv from the unbelievers in Judea and that my servicew in Jerusalem may be acceptable to the saintsx there, 32so that by God's willy I may come to youz with joy and together with you be refreshed.a 33The God of peaceb be with you all. Amen.

Personal Greetings

16 I commendc to you our sister Phoebe, a servanto of the church in Cenchrea.d 2I ask you to receive her in the Lorde in a way worthy of the saintsf and to give her any help she may need from you, for she has been a great help to many people, including me.

3Greet Priscillap and Aquila,g my fellow workersh in Christ Jesus.i 4They risked their lives for me. Not only I but all the churches of the Gentiles are grateful to them. 5Greet also the church that meets at their house.j

Greet my dear friend Epenetus, who was the first convertk to Christ in the province of Asia.l 6Greet Mary, who worked very hard for you. 7Greet Andronicus and Junias, my relativesm who have been in prison with me.n They are outstanding among the apostles, and they were in Christo before I was.

E Ro 15:18–19 ◀▶ 1Co 2:4–16
F Ro 15:13 ◀▶ 2Co 13:14

8Greet Ampliatus, whom I love in the Lord. 9Greet Urbanus, our fellow worker in Christ,p and my dear friend Stachys. 10Greet Apelles, tested and approved in Christ.q Greet those who belong to the householdr of Aristobulus. 11Greet Herodion, my relative.s Greet those in the householdt of Narcissus who are in the Lord. 12Greet Tryphena and Tryphosa, those women who work hard in the Lord. Greet my dear friend Persis, another woman who has worked very hard in the Lord. 13Greet Rufus,u chosenv in the Lord, and his mother, who has been a mother to me, too. 14Greet Asyncritus, Phlegon, Hermes, Patrobas, Hermas and the brothers with them. 15Greet Philologus, Julia, Nereus and his sister, and Olympas and all the saintsw with them.x 16Greet one another with a holy kiss.y

All the churches of Christ send greetings.

17I urge you, brothers, to watch out for those who cause divisions and put obstacles in your way that are contrary to the teaching you have learned.z Keep away from them.a 18For such people are not serving our Lord Christ,b but their own appetites.c By smooth talk and flattery they deceived the minds of naive people. 19Everyone has hearde about your obedience, so I am full of joy over you; but I want you to be wise about what is good, and innocent about what is evil.f

20The God of peaceg will soon crushh M Satani under your feet.

The grace of our Lord Jesus be with you.j

21Timothy,k my fellow worker, sends

M Ro 15:12 ◀▶ 1Co 6:2–3

o 1 Or deaconess p 3 Greek Prisca, a variant of Priscilla

---

sage, have been shared with the Gentiles, the Gentiles have a duty to share their material blessings with their Jewish brethren (see 1Co 16:1–4; 2Co 8—9).

16:20 The apostle Paul confirms the prophetic truth that God will ultimately defeat the antichrist and Satan (see Ge 3:15). After the Battle of Armageddon, the antichrist and false prophet will be thrown into hell, and Satan will be cast into the bottomless pit (see Rev 19:20; 20:2–3).

his greetings to you, as do Lucius,¹ Jason ᵐ and Sosipater, my relatives.ⁿ

²²I, Tertius, who wrote down this letter, greet you in the Lord.

²³Gaius,ᵒ whose hospitality I and the whole church here enjoy, sends you his greetings.

Erastus,ᵖ who is the city's director of public works, and our brother Quartus send you their greetings.q

ᴋ ²⁵Now to him who is able q to establish you by my gospel ʳ and the proclamation of Jesus Christ, according to the revelation of the mystery ˢ hidden for long ages past, ²⁶but now revealed and made known through the prophetic writings ᵗ by the command of the eternal God, so that all nations might believe and obey ᵘ him— ²⁷to the only wise God be glory forever through Jesus Christ! Amen.ᵛ

ᴋ *Ro 10:11* ◄► *1Co 1:25*

16:21 ¹ Ac 13:1; ᵐ Ac 17:5 ⁿ ver 7, 11
16:23 ᵒ Ac 19:29 ᵖ Ac 19:22; 2Ti 4:20
16:25 q 2Co 9:8; Eph 3:20; Jude 24 ʳ Ro 2:16; 2Ti 2:8 ˢ Isa 48:6; Eph 1:9; 3:3-6,9; Col 1:26, 27; 2:2; 1Ti 3:16
16:26 ᵗ Ro 13:2 ᵘ Ro 1:5
16:27 ᵛ S Ro 11:36

q 23 Some manuscripts *their greetings.* ²⁴*May the grace of our Lord Jesus Christ be with all of you. Amen.*

1 Corinthians

Author: Paul

Theme: Living the Christian life in a sinful world

Date of Writing: C. A.D. 54–55

Outline of 1 Corinthians
  I. Greetings and Introduction (1:1–9)
  II. Strife Within the Church (1:10—4:21)
  III. Moral and Ethical Behavior (5:1—6:20)
  IV. Marriage and Celibacy (7:1–40)
  V. Rights and Responsibility (8:1—11:1)
  VI. Proper Public Worship (11:2—14:40)
      A. Worshipful behavior (11:2–16)
      B. The Lord's Supper (11:17–34)
      C. Spiritual gifts (12:1—14:40)
  VII. Teaching About the Resurrection (15:1–58)
  VIII. Conclusion (16:1–24)

PAUL WROTE THIS letter to the Corinthian church during his third missionary journey and toward the end of his ministry at Ephesus. Paul had visited Corinth previously on his second missionary journey. This wealthy trading city on the Mediterranean coast contained a diverse population of Greeks, Jews and Romans. Though Paul's ministry was rejected by the Jews in Corinth, a successful house church was established among the Gentiles (see Ac 18:6–8). Paul remained with the Corinthian believers for a year and a half (see Ac 18:11), supporting himself by making tents. From Corinth, Paul continued on in his missionary journeys, accompanied by Priscilla and Aquila. During his absence, other teachers came to Corinth preaching a message that differed from Paul's words. These teachings caused confusion among the Corinthian believers. When some of the Corinthians brought a contribution to Paul, they also shared their questions and problems. The letter of 1 Corinthians contains Paul's reply to these questions.

Because of the varied makeup of the population of Corinth, the Corinthian believers were subjected to worldly influences that had affected their Christian walk. This epistle to the Corinthians addresses societal problems such as lawsuits, immorality and marriage as well as the pagan influences of idolatry and the mishandling of the sacraments. Paul also instructed the leaders on theological issues such as church finances, doctrinal divisions, disorder during worship, the gifts of the Holy Spirit, Paul's apostleship and the resurrection. Conversational in style, Paul's letter logically persuades, critiques and scolds the believers as Paul instructs them on how to apply the gospel to the challenges of everyday life in a pagan society.

1

Paul, called to be an apostle[a] of Christ Jesus by the will of God,[b] and our brother Sosthenes,[c]

[2] To the church of God[d] in Corinth,[e] to those sanctified in Christ Jesus and called[f] to be holy, together with all those everywhere who call on the name[g] of our Lord Jesus Christ—their Lord and ours:

[3] Grace and peace to you from God our Father and the Lord Jesus Christ.[h]

Thanksgiving

[4] I always thank God for you[i] because of his grace given you in Christ Jesus. [5] For in him you have been enriched[j] in every way—in all your speaking and in all your knowledge[k]— [6] because our testimony[l] about Christ was confirmed in you. [7] Therefore you do not lack any spiritual gift[m] as you eagerly wait for our Lord Jesus Christ to be revealed.[n] [8] He will keep you strong to the end, so that you will be blameless[o] on the day of our Lord Jesus Christ.[p] [9] God, who has called you[q] into fellowship with his Son Jesus Christ our Lord,[r] is faithful.[s]

Divisions in the Church

[10] I appeal to you, brothers,[t] in the name of our Lord Jesus Christ, that all of you agree with one another so that there

G Ro 15:19 ◀ ▶ 1Co 2:4–15
C Ac 1:11 ◀ ▶ 1Co 10:11

1:1 a Ro 1:1; Eph 1:1; 2Ti 1:1
b S 2Co 1:1
c Ac 18:17
1:2 d S 1Co 10:32
e S Ac 18:1 f Ro 1:7
g S Ac 2:21
1:3 h S Ro 1:7
1:4 i S Ro 1:8
1:5 j 2Co 9:11
k S 2Co 8:7
1:6 l 2Th 1:10; 1Ti 2:6; Rev 1:2
1:7 m Ro 1:11; 1Co 12:1-31
n S Mt 16:27; S Lk 17:30; 1Th 1:10; S 2:19; Tit 2:13; Jas 5:7,8; 1Pe 1:13; 2Pe 3:12;
1:8 o S 1Th 3:13
p Am 5:18; 1Co 5:5; Php 1:6,10; 2:16; 1Th 5:2
1:9 q S Ro 8:28
r 1Jn 1:3 s Dt 7:9; Isa 49:7; 1Co 10:13; 1Th 5:24; 2Th 3:3; 2Ti 2:13; Heb 10:23; 11:11
1:10 t S Ro 7:1
u 1Co 11:18
v S Ro 15:5
1:11 w S Ac 11:14
1:12 x 1Co 3:4,22
y S Ac 18:24
z Jn 1:42; 1Co 3:22; 9:5
1:13 a S Mt 28:19
1:14 b Ac 18:8
c S Ac 19:29
1:16 d S Ac 11:14
e 1Co 16:15
1:17 f Jn 4:2; S Ac 2:38 g Col 2:1, 4,13
1:18 h ver 21,23, 25; 1Co 2:14

may be no divisions among you[u] and that you may be perfectly united[v] in mind and thought. [11] My brothers, some from Chloe's household[w] have informed me that there are quarrels among you. [12] What I mean is this: One of you says, "I follow Paul";[x] another, "I follow Apollos";[y] another, "I follow Cephas[a]";[z] still another, "I follow Christ."

[13] Is Christ divided? Was Paul crucified for you? Were you baptized into[b] the name of Paul?[a] [14] I am thankful that I did not baptize any of you except Crispus[b] and Gaius,[c] [15] so no one can say that you were baptized into my name. [16] (Yes, I also baptized the household[d] of Stephanas;[e] beyond that, I don't remember if I baptized anyone else.) [17] For Christ did not send me to baptize,[f] but to preach the gospel—not with words of human wisdom,[g] lest the cross of Christ be emptied of its power.

Christ the Wisdom and Power of God

[18] For the message of the cross is foolishness[h] to those who are perishing,[i] but

G Ro 11:5–6 ◀ ▶ 1Co 1:26–31
H Ro 12:19 ◀ ▶ 1Co 3:17
N Ro 2:5 ◀ ▶ 2Co 2:15–16

i 2Co 2:15; 4:3; 2Th 2:10

a 12 That is, Peter   b 13 Or in; also in verse 15

1:7–8 Paul affirms the importance of anticipating the return of Jesus Christ. The Greek word that Paul uses in this passage for Christ's return is *apokalupsis* meaning "revelation." In this passage, it is clearly used in the context of Christ coming in the air for his church (see 1Th 4:16–17).

to us who are being saved[j] it is the power of God.[k] [19]For it is written:

> "I will destroy the wisdom of the wise;
> the intelligence of the intelligent I will frustrate."[c]

[20]Where is the wise man?[m] Where is the scholar? Where is the philosopher of this age?[n] Has not God made foolish[o] the wisdom of the world? [21]For since in the wisdom of God the world[p] through its wisdom did not know him, God was pleased through the foolishness of what was preached to save[q] those who believe.[r] [22]Jews demand miraculous signs[s] and Greeks look for wisdom, [23]but we preach Christ crucified:[t] a stumbling block[u] to Jews and foolishness[v] to Gentiles, [24]but to those whom God has called,[w] both Jews and Greeks, Christ the power of God[x] and the wisdom of God.[y] [25]For the foolishness[z] of God is wiser than man's wisdom, and the weakness[a] of God is stronger than man's strength.

[26]Brothers, think of what you were when you were called.[b] Not many of you were wise[c] by human standards; not many were influential; not many were of noble birth. [27]But God chose[d] the foolish[e] things of the world to shame the wise; God chose the weak things of the world to shame the strong. [28]He chose the lowly things of this world and the despised things—and the things that are not[f]—to nullify the things that are, [29]so that no one may boast before him.[g] [30]It is because of him that you are in Christ Jesus,[h] who has become for us wisdom from God—that is, our righteousness,[i] holiness[j] and redemption.[k] [31]Therefore, as it is written: "Let him who boasts boast in the Lord."[d]

When I came to you, brothers, I did not come with eloquence or superior wisdom[m] as I proclaimed to you the testimony about God.[e] [2]For I resolved to know nothing while I was with you except Jesus Christ and him crucified.[n] [3]I came to you[o] in weakness[p] and fear, and with much trembling.[q] [4]My message and my preaching were not with wise and persuasive words,[r] but with a demonstration of the Spirit's power,[s] [5]so that your faith might not rest on men's wisdom, but on God's power.[t]

Wisdom From the Spirit

[6]We do, however, speak a message of wisdom among the mature,[u] but not the wisdom of this age[v] or of the rulers of this age, who are coming to nothing.[w] [7]No, we speak of God's secret wisdom, a wisdom[x] that has been hidden[y] and that God destined for our glory before time began. [8]None of the rulers of this age[z] understood it, for if they had, they would not have crucified the Lord of glory.[a] [9]However, as it is written:

> "No eye has seen,
> no ear has heard,
> no mind has conceived
> what God has prepared for those who love him"[b]—

[10]but God has revealed[c] it to us by his Spirit.[d]

The Spirit searches all things, even the deep things of God. [11]For who among men knows the thoughts of a man[e] except the man's spirit[f] within him? In the same way no one knows the thoughts of God except the Spirit of God. [12]We have not received the spirit[g] of the world[h] but the Spirit who is from God, that we may understand what God has freely given us. [13]This is what we speak, not in words taught us by human wisdom[i] but in words taught by the Spirit, expressing spiritual truths in spiritual words.[g] [14]The man without the Spirit does not accept the things that come from the Spirit of God,[j] for they are foolishness[k] to him, and he cannot understand them, because they are spiritually discerned. [15]The spiritual[l] man makes judgments about all

---

1:18 [j] Ac 2:47
[k] ver 24; Ro 1:16
1:19 [l] Isa 29:14
1:20 [m] Isa 19:11,12 [n] 1Co 2:6,8; 3:18; 2Co 4:4; Gal 1:4 [o] ver 27; Job 12:17; Isa 44:25; Jer 8:9; Ro 1:22; 1Co 3:18,19
1:21 [p] ver 27,28; 1Co 6:2; 11:32 [q] S Ro 11:14 [r] S Ro 3:22
1:22 [s] S Mt 12:38; S Jn 2:11; S 4:48
1:23 [t] 1Co 2:2; Gal 3:1 [u] S Lk 2:34 [v] ver 18
1:24 [w] S Ro 8:28 [x] ver 18; Ro 1:16 [y] ver 30; S Col 2:3
1:25 [z] S ver 18 [a] 2Co 13:4
1:26 [b] S Ro 8:28 [c] ver 20
1:27 [d] Jas 2:5 [e] ver 20; Ro 1:22; 1Co 3:18,19
1:28 [f] Ro 4:17
1:29 [g] Eph 2:9
1:30 [h] S Ro 16:3 [i] Jer 23:5,6; 33:16; 2Co 5:21; Php 3:9 [j] 1Co 1:2 [k] S Ro 3:24
1:31 [l] Jer 9:23,24; Ps 34:2; 44:8; 2Co 10:17
2:1 [m] ver 4,13; 1Co 1:17
2:2 [n] Gal 6:14; 1Co 1:23
2:3 [o] Ac 18:1-18 [p] 1Co 4:10; 9:22; 2Co 11:29,30; 12:5,9,10; 13:9 [q] S 2Co 7:15
2:4 [r] ver 1 [s] S Ro 15:13
2:5 [t] 2Co 4:7; 6:7
2:6 [u] Eph 4:13; Php 3:15; Col 4:12; Heb 5:14; 6:1; Jas 1:4 [v] ver 8; S 1Co 1:20
[w] Ps 146:4
2:7 [x] ver 1 [y] Ro 16:25
2:8 [z] ver 6; S 1Co 1:20 [a] Ps 24:7; Ac 7:2; Jas 2:1
2:9 [b] Isa 64:4; 65:17
2:10 [c] S Mt 13:11; 2Co 12:1,7; Gal 1:12; 2:2; Eph 3:3,5 [d] Jn 14:26
2:11 [e] Jer 17:9 [f] Pr 20:27
2:12 [g] Ro 8:15 [h] 1Co 1:20,27; Jas 2:5
2:13 [i] ver 1,4; 1Co 1:17
2:14 [j] Jn 14:17 [k] S 1Co 1:18
2:15 [l] 1Co 3:1; Gal 6:1

E Ro 15:30 ◀▶ 1Co 3:1
G 1Co 1:4-7 ◀▶ 1Co 3:1-2
M Ro 15:19 ◀▶ 1Co 3:1
T Ro 12:6-8 ◀▶ 1Co 7:40
U Ro 8:28 ◀▶ 2Co 5:1
N Ro 1:4 ◀▶ 1Co 12:1-13
W Ro 14:17 ◀▶ 1Co 3:1-2
C Ro 8:5-8 ◀▶ 2Co 4:3-4

[c] 19 Isaiah 29:14   [d] 31 Jer. 9:24   [e] 1 Some manuscripts as I proclaimed to you God's mystery   [f] 9 Isaiah 64:4   [g] 13 Or Spirit, interpreting spiritual truths to spiritual men

---

F Ro 15:13 ◀▶ Gal 2:16
K Ro 16:25 ◀▶ 1Co 1:30
G 1Co 1:18-21 ◀▶ 1Co 3:11
K 1Co 1:25 ◀▶ 1Co 6:9-11

things, but he himself is not subject to any man's judgment:

¹⁶"For who has known the mind of the Lord
that he may instruct him?"^{*h,m*}

But we have the mind of Christ.^{*n*}

On Divisions in the Church

3 Brothers, I could not address you as spiritual^{*o*} but as worldly^{*p*}—mere infants^{*q*} in Christ. ²I gave you milk, not solid food,^{*r*} for you were not yet ready for it.^{*s*} Indeed, you are still not ready. ³You are still worldly. For since there is jealousy and quarreling^{*t*} among you, are you not worldly? Are you not acting like mere men? ⁴For when one says, "I follow Paul," and another, "I follow Apollos,"^{*u*} are you not mere men?

⁵What, after all, is Apollos?^{*v*} And what is Paul? Only servants,^{*w*} through whom you came to believe—as the Lord has assigned to each his task. ⁶I planted the seed,^{*x*} Apollos watered it, but God made it grow. ⁷So neither he who plants nor he who waters is anything, but only God, who makes things grow. ⁸The man who plants and the man who waters have one purpose, and each will be rewarded according to his own labor.^{*y*} ⁹For we are God's fellow workers;^{*z*} you are God's field,^{*a*} God's building.^{*b*}

¹⁰By the grace God has given me,^{*c*} I laid a foundation^{*d*} as an expert builder, and someone else is building on it. But each one should be careful how he builds. ¹¹For no one can lay any foundation other than the one already laid, which is Jesus Christ.^{*e*} ¹²If any man builds on this foundation using gold, silver, costly stones, wood, hay or straw, ¹³his work will be shown for what it is,^{*f*} because the Day^{*g*} will bring it to light. It will be revealed with fire, and the fire will test the quality of each man's work.^{*h*} ¹⁴If what he has built survives, he will receive his reward.^{*i*} ¹⁵If it is burned up, he will suffer loss; he himself will be saved, but only as one escaping through the flames.^{*j*}

¹⁶Don't you know that you yourselves are God's temple^{*k*} and that God's Spirit lives in you? ¹⁷If anyone destroys God's temple, God will destroy him; for God's temple is sacred, and you are that temple.

¹⁸Do not deceive yourselves. If any one of you thinks he is wise^{*m*} by the standards of this age,^{*n*} he should become a "fool" so that he may become wise. ¹⁹For the wisdom of this world is foolishness^{*o*} in God's sight. As it is written: "He catches the wise in their craftiness";^{*i;p*} ²⁰and again, "The Lord knows that the thoughts of the wise are futile."^{*j;q*} ²¹So then, no more boasting about men!^{*r*} All things are yours,^{*s*} ²²whether Paul or Apollos^{*t*} or Cephas^{*k;u*} or the world or life or death or the present or the future^{*v*}—all are yours, ²³and you are of Christ,^{*w*} and Christ is of God.

Apostles of Christ

4 So then, men ought to regard us as servants^{*x*} of Christ and as those entrusted^{*y*} with the secret things^{*z*} of God. ²Now it is required that those who have been given a trust must prove faithful. ³I care very little if I am judged by you or by any human court; indeed, I do not even judge myself. ⁴My conscience^{*a*} is clear, but that does not make me innocent.^{*b*} It is the Lord who judges me.^{*c*} ⁵Therefore

---

E 1Co 2:4–16 ◀▶ 1Co 3:16
G 1Co 2:4–15 ◀▶ 1Co 7:7
M 1Co 2:4–10 ◀▶ 2Co 3:5–18
S Ro 15:16 ◀▶ 1Co 3:16–17
W 1Co 2:14 ◀▶ 1Co 12:1–11
G 1Co 1:26–31 ◀▶ 1Co 3:19–20
O Ro 10:3–4 ◀▶ 2Co 10:17–18

D Ac 5:4 ◀▶ 2Co 3:17
E 1Co 3:1 ◀▶ 1Co 6:11
S 1Co 3:1 ◀▶ 1Co 6:11
H 1Co 1:18 ◀▶ 1Co 6:9–10
S Ro 14:15–18 ◀▶ 1Co 6:9–11
G 1Co 3:11 ◀▶ 2Co 10:18
J Ro 14:10–12 ◀▶ 2Co 5:10
J Ro 2:16 ◀▶ 2Co 5:9–11
E Ro 8:27 ◀▶ 1Th 2:4

h 16 Isaiah 40:13 *i* 19 Job 5:13 *j* 20 Psalm 94:11 *k* 22 That is, Peter

---

4:5 Paul warns Christians not to pass judgment on fellow believers' behavior or motives because Christ himself is our true judge. The final judgment of believers will occur in heaven after the rapture at "God's judgment seat" (Ro 14:10). This judgment is concerned with the giving of crowns and rewards, not with punishment for sin (see 2Co 5:10; 2Ti 4:8; Rev 22:12). Those who truly repent and follow Jesus as their Lord and Savior have already had their sins judged forever at the cross.

judge nothing[d] before the appointed time; wait till the Lord comes.[e] He will bring to light[f] what is hidden in darkness and will expose the motives of men's hearts. At that time each will receive his praise from God.[g]

[6] Now, brothers, I have applied these things to myself and Apollos for your benefit, so that you may learn from us the meaning of the saying, "Do not go beyond what is written."[h] Then you will not take pride in one man over against another.[i] [7] For who makes you different from anyone else? What do you have that you did not receive?[j] And if you did receive it, why do you boast as though you did not?

[8] Already you have all you want! Already you have become rich![k] You have become kings—and that without us! How I wish that you really had become kings so that we might be kings with you! [9] For it seems to me that God has put us apostles on display at the end of the procession, like men condemned to die[l] in the arena. We have been made a spectacle[m] to the whole universe, to angels as well as to men. [10] We are fools for Christ,[n] but you are so wise in Christ![o] We are weak, but you are strong![p] You are honored, we are dishonored! [11] To this very hour we go hungry and thirsty, we are in rags, we are brutally treated, we are homeless.[q] [12] We work hard with our own hands.[r] When we are cursed, we bless; when we are persecuted,[t] we endure it; [13] when we are slandered, we answer kindly. Up to this moment we have become the scum of the earth, the refuse[u] of the world.

[14] I am not writing this to shame you,[v] but to warn you, as my dear children.[w] [15] Even though you have ten thousand guardians in Christ, you do not have many fathers, for in Christ Jesus I became your father[x] through the gospel.[y] [16] Therefore I urge you to imitate me.[z] [17] For this reason I am sending to you Timothy,[b] my son[c] whom I love, who is faithful in the Lord. He will remind you of my way of life in Christ Jesus, which agrees with what I teach everywhere in every church.[d]

[18] Some of you have become arrogant,[e] as if I were not coming to you.[f] [19] But I will come to you very soon,[g] if the Lord is willing,[h] and then I will find out not only how these arrogant people are talking, but what power they have. [20] For the kingdom of God is not a matter of[i] talk but of power.[j] [21] What do you prefer? Shall I come to you with a whip,[k] or in love and with a gentle spirit?

Expel the Immoral Brother!

5 It is actually reported that there is sexual immorality among you, and of a kind that does not occur even among pagans: A man has his father's wife.[l] [2] And you are proud! Shouldn't you rather have been filled with grief[m] and have put out of your fellowship[n] the man who did this? [3] Even though I am not physically present, I am with you in spirit.[o] And I have already passed judgment on the one who did this, just as if I were present. [4] When you are assembled in the name of our Lord Jesus[p] and I am with you in spirit, and the power of our Lord Jesus is present, [5] hand this man over[q] to Satan,[r] so that the sinful nature[l] may be destroyed and his spirit saved on the day of the Lord.[s]

[6] Your boasting is not good.[t] Don't you know that a little yeast[u] works through the whole batch of dough?[v] [7] Get rid of the old yeast that you may be a new batch without yeast—as you really are. For Christ, our Passover lamb, has been sacrificed.[w] [8] Therefore let us keep the Festival, not with the old yeast, the yeast of malice and wickedness, but with bread without yeast,[x] the bread of sincerity and truth.

[9] I have written you in my letter not to associate[y] with sexually immoral people— [10] not at all meaning the people of this world[z] who are immoral, or the greedy and swindlers, or idolaters. In that case you would have to leave this world. [11] But now I am writing you that you must not associate with anyone who calls himself a brother[a] but is sexually immoral or greedy, an idolater[b] or a slanderer, a drunkard or a swindler. With such a man do not even eat.[c]

D *Ro 8:32* ◀ ▶ *1Co 6:20*

[5] Or that his body; *or* that the flesh

¹²What business is it of mine to judge those outside[d] the church? Are you not to judge those inside?[e] ¹³God will judge those outside. "Expel the wicked man from among you."[m][f]

Lawsuits Among Believers

6 If any of you has a dispute with another, dare he take it before the ungodly for judgment instead of before the saints?[g] ²Do you not know that the saints will judge the world?[h] And if you are to judge the world, are you not competent to judge trivial cases? ³Do you not know that we will judge angels? How much more the things of this life! ⁴Therefore, if you have disputes about such matters, appoint as judges even men of little account in the church![n] ⁵I say this to shame you.[i] Is it possible that there is nobody among you wise enough to judge a dispute between believers?[j] ⁶But instead, one brother[k] goes to law against another—and this in front of unbelievers![l]

⁷The very fact that you have lawsuits among you means you have been completely defeated already. Why not rather be wronged? Why not rather be cheated?[m] ⁸Instead, you yourselves cheat and do wrong, and you do this to your brothers.[n]

⁹Do you not know that the wicked will not inherit the kingdom of God?[o] Do not be deceived:[p] Neither the sexually immoral nor idolaters nor adulterers[q] nor male prostitutes nor homosexual offenders[r] ¹⁰nor thieves nor the greedy nor drunkards nor slanderers nor swindlers[s] will inherit the kingdom of God. ¹¹And that is what some of you were.[t] But you were washed,[u] you were sanctified,[v] you were justified[w] in the name of the Lord Jesus Christ and by the Spirit of our God.

Sexual Immorality

¹²"Everything is permissible for me"—but not everything is beneficial.[x] "Everything is permissible for me"—but I will not be mastered by anything. ¹³"Food for the stomach and the stomach for food"—but God will destroy them both.[y] The body is not meant for sexual immorality, but for the Lord,[z] and the Lord for the body. ¹⁴By his power God raised the Lord from the dead,[a] and he will raise us also.[b] ¹⁵Do you not know that your bodies are members of Christ himself?[c] Shall I then take the members of Christ and unite them with a prostitute? Never! ¹⁶Do you not know that he who unites himself with a prostitute is one with her in body? For it is said, "The two will become one flesh."[o][d] ¹⁷But he who unites himself with the Lord is one with him in spirit.[e]

¹⁸Flee from sexual immorality.[f] All other sins a man commits are outside his body, but he who sins sexually sins against his own body.[g] ¹⁹Do you not know that your body is a temple[h] of the Holy Spirit, who is in you, whom you have received from God? You are not

---

M Ro 16:20 ◄► 1Co 15:24–28
H 1Co 3:17 ◄► 1Co 10:5–12
K 1Co 1:30 ◄► 1Co 15:56–57
L Ro 10:21 ◄► 1Co 7:23
S 1Co 3:17 ◄► 1Co 6:20

B Ro 15:16 ◄► 1Co 12:1–11
E 1Co 3:16 ◄► 1Co 6:19
R Ro 8:1–16 ◄► 1Co 12:13
S 1Co 3:16–17 ◄► 2Co 3:18
F Ro 8:17–25 ◄► 1Co 15:20–26
E 1Co 6:11 ◄► 1Co 7:40

5:12 d S Mk 4:11 e ver 3-5; 1Co 6:1-4
5:13 f Dt 13:5; 17:7; 19:19; 22:21, 24; 24:7; Jdg 20:13
6:1 g Mt 18:17
6:2 h Mt 19:28; Lk 22:30; 1Co 5:12
6:5 i S 1Co 4:14 j Ac 1:15
6:6 k S Ro 7:1 l 2Co 6:14,15; 1Ti 5:8
6:7 m Mt 5:39,40
6:8 n 1Th 4:6
6:9 o S Mt 25:34 p Job 13:9; 1Co 15:33; Gal 6:7; Jas 1:16 q Lev 18:20; Dt 22:22 r Lev 18:22
6:10 s 1Ti 1:10; Rev 21:8; 22:15
6:11 t S Eph 2:2 u S Ac 22:16 v 1Co 1:2 w S Ro 4:25
6:12 x 1Co 10:23
6:13 y Col 2:22 z ver 15,19; Ro 12:1
6:14 a S Ac 2:24 b Ro 6:5; Eph 1:19,20; 1Th 4:16
6:15 c S Ro 12:5
6:16 d Ge 2:24; Mt 19:5; Eph 5:31
6:17 e Jn 17:21-23; Ro 8:9-11; Gal 2:20
6:18 f ver 9; 1Co 5:1; 2Co 12:21; Gal 5:19; Eph 5:3; 1Th 4:3,4; Heb 13:4 g Ro 6:12
6:19 h Jn 2:21

m 13 Deut. 17:7; 19:19; 21:21; 22:21,24; 24:7 n 4 Or matters, do you appoint as judges men of little account in the church? o 16 Gen. 2:24

6:1–3 Paul warns believers against taking their disputes into the law courts of the unbelievers. Believers view things from a godly point of view; the law courts of unbelievers do not have that same vantage point. Paul reminds Christians that because we will judge the world with Christ in the Millennium, we ought to be competent enough to judge cases between Christians on this earth. Paul specifically notes that the church will participate in Christ's final judgment of the nations (see Da 7:22; Mt 19:28) as well as the judgment of the wicked angels that fell during Satan's rebellion (see 2Pe 2:4; Jude 6). In light of God's promise of our future ruling status we should deal with claims against each other internally, according to Biblical principles.

6:14 In this verse, the apostle prophesies about the first resurrection from the dead for believers and affirms that God has the power to raise all of his followers from the grave. The historical reality of the resurrection of Christ was powerfully confirmed through eyewitness evidence (see 15:4–6; Mk 16:14; Lk 24:23–40). His resurrection provides proof that God has the power to resurrect all believers.

your own;[i] ²⁰you were bought at a price.[j] Therefore honor God with your body.[k]

Marriage

7 Now for the matters you wrote about: It is good for a man not to marry.[p1] ²But since there is so much immorality, each man should have his own wife, and each woman her own husband. ³The husband should fulfill his marital duty to his wife,[m] and likewise the wife to her husband. ⁴The wife's body does not belong to her alone but also to her husband. In the same way, the husband's body does not belong to him alone but also to his wife. ⁵Do not deprive each other except by mutual consent and for a time,[n] so that you may devote yourselves to prayer. Then come together again so that Satan[o] will not tempt you[p] because of your lack of self-control. ⁶I say this as a concession, not as a command.[q] ⁷I wish that all men were as I am.[r] But each man has his own gift from God; one has this gift, another has that.[s]

⁸Now to the unmarried and the widows I say: It is good for them to stay unmarried, as I am.[t] ⁹But if they cannot control themselves, they should marry, for it is better to marry than to burn with passion.

¹⁰To the married I give this command (not I, but the Lord): A wife must not separate from her husband.[v] ¹¹But if she does, she must remain unmarried or else be reconciled to her husband.[w] And a husband must not divorce his wife.

¹²To the rest I say this (I, not the Lord):[x] If any brother has a wife who is not a believer and she is willing to live with him, he must not divorce her. ¹³And if a woman has a husband who is not a believer and he is willing to live with her, she must not divorce him. ¹⁴For the unbelieving husband has been sanctified through his wife, and the unbelieving wife has been sanctified through her believing husband. Otherwise your children would be unclean, but as it is, they are holy.[y]

¹⁵But if the unbeliever leaves, let him do so. A believing man or woman is not bound in such circumstances; God has called us to live in peace.[z] ¹⁶How do you know, wife, whether you will save[a] your husband?[b] Or, how do you know, husband, whether you will save your wife?

¹⁷Nevertheless, each one should retain the place in life that the Lord assigned to him and to which God has called him.[c] This is the rule I lay down in all the churches.[d] ¹⁸Was a man already circumcised when he was called? He should not become uncircumcised. Was a man uncircumcised when he was called? He should not be circumcised.[e] ¹⁹Circumcision is nothing and uncircumcision is nothing.[f] Keeping God's commands is what counts. ²⁰Each one should remain in the situation which he was in when God called him.[g] ²¹Were you a slave when you were called? Don't let it trouble you—although if you can gain your freedom, do so. ²²For he who was a slave when he was called by the Lord is the Lord's freedman;[h] similarly, he who was a free man when he was called is Christ's slave.[i] ²³You were bought at a price;[j] do not become slaves of men. ²⁴Brothers, each man, as responsible to God, should remain in the situation God called him to.[k]

²⁵Now about virgins: I have no command from the Lord,[l] but I give a judgment as one who by the Lord's mercy[m] is trustworthy. ²⁶Because of the present crisis, I think that it is good for you to remain as you are.[n] ²⁷Are you married? Do not seek a divorce. Are you unmarried? Do not look for a wife.[o] ²⁸But if you do marry, you have not sinned;[p] and if a virgin marries, she has not sinned. But those who marry will face many troubles in this life, and I want to spare you this.

²⁹What I mean, brothers, is that the time is short.[q] From now on those who have wives should live as if they had none; ³⁰those who mourn, as if they did not; those who are happy, as if they were not; those who buy something, as if it were not theirs to keep; ³¹those who use the things of the world, as if not engrossed in them. For this world in its present form is passing away.[r]

³²I would like you to be free from concern. An unmarried man is concerned

---

D 1Co 5:7 ◀ ▶ 1Co 7:23
S 1Co 6:9–11 ◀ ▶ 1Co 9:24–27
G 1Co 3:1–2 ◀ ▶ 1Co 12:1–31

D 1Co 6:20 ◀ ▶ 1Co 11:23–25
L 1Co 6:9–11 ◀ ▶ 1Co 15:3

p1 Or "It is good for a man not to have sexual relations with a woman."

about the Lord's affairs[s]—how he can please the Lord. [33]But a married man is concerned about the affairs of this world—how he can please his wife— [34]and his interests are divided. An unmarried woman or virgin is concerned about the Lord's affairs: Her aim is to be devoted to the Lord in both body and spirit.[t] But a married woman is concerned about the affairs of this world—how she can please her husband. [35]I am saying this for your own good, not to restrict you, but that you may live in a right way in undivided[u] devotion to the Lord.

[36]If anyone thinks he is acting improperly toward the virgin he is engaged to, and if she is getting along in years and he feels he ought to marry, he should do as he wants. He is not sinning.[v] They should get married. [37]But the man who has settled the matter in his own mind, who is under no compulsion but has control over his own will, and who has made up his mind not to marry the virgin—this man also does the right thing. [38]So then, he who marries the virgin does right,[w] but he who does not marry her does even better.[q] [39]A woman is bound to her husband as long as he lives.[x] But if her husband dies, she is free to marry anyone she wishes, but he must belong to the Lord.[y] [40]In my judgment,[z] she is happier if she stays as she is—and I think that I too have the Spirit of God.

Food Sacrificed to Idols

8 Now about food sacrificed to idols:[a] We know that we all possess knowledge.[rb] Knowledge puffs up, but love builds up. [2]The man who thinks he knows something[c] does not yet know as he ought to know.[d] [3]But the man who loves God is known by God.[e]

[4]So then, about eating food sacrificed to idols:[f] We know that an idol is nothing at all in the world[g] and that there is no God but one.[h] [5]For even if there are so-called gods,[i] whether in heaven or on earth (as indeed there are many "gods" and many "lords"), [6]yet for us there is but one God,[j] the Father,[k] from whom all things came[l] and for whom we live; and

E 1Co 6:19 ◄ ► 1Co 12:1–13
L Ro 12:6–8 ◄ ► 1Co 12:3
T 1Co 2:4–16 ◄ ► 1Co 12:3

7:32 s 1Ti 5:5
7:34 t Lk 2:37
7:35 u Ps 86:11
7:36 v ver 28
7:38 w Heb 13:4
7:39 x Ro 7:2,3; y 2Co 6:14
7:40 z ver 25
8:1 a ver 4,7,10; Ac 15:20; b Ro 15:14
8:2 c 1Co 3:18; d 1Co 13:8,9,12; 1Ti 6:4
8:3 e Jer 1:5; Ro 8:29; Gal 4:9
8:4 f ver 1,7,10; Ex 34:15; g Ac 14:15; 1Co 10:19; Gal 4:8; h ver 6; Dt 6:4; Ps 86:10; Eph 4:6; 1Ti 2:5
8:5 i 2Th 2:4
8:6 j S ver 4; k Mal 2:10; l S Ro 11:36; m Eph 4:5 n S Jn 1:3
8:7 o ver 1; p Ro 14:14; 1Co 10:28
8:8 q Ro 14:17
8:9 r S 2Co 6:3; Gal 5:13 s Ro 14:1
8:10 t ver 1,4,7
8:11 u Ro 14:15,20
8:12 v Mt 18:6; w Mt 25:40,45
8:13 x S Mt 5:29
9:1 y ver 19 z S 1Co 1:1; 2Co 12:12
a S 1Co 15:8
b 1Co 3:6; 4:15
9:2 c 2Co 3:2,3
9:4 d ver 14; S Ac 18:3
9:5 e 1Co 7:7,8 f S Mt 12:46 g S 1Co 1:12
9:6 h S Ac 4:36
9:7 i 2Ti 2:3,4 j Dt 20:6; Pr 27:18; 1Co 3:6,8

there is but one Lord,[m] Jesus Christ, through whom all things came[n] and through whom we live.

[7]But not everyone knows this.[o] Some people are still so accustomed to idols that when they eat such food they think of it as having been sacrificed to an idol, and since their conscience is weak,[p] it is defiled. [8]But food does not bring us near to God;[q] we are no worse if we do not eat, and no better if we do.

[9]Be careful, however, that the exercise of your freedom does not become a stumbling block[r] to the weak.[s] [10]For if anyone with a weak conscience sees you who have this knowledge eating in an idol's temple, won't he be emboldened to eat what has been sacrificed to idols?[t] [11]So this weak brother, for whom Christ died, is destroyed[u] by your knowledge. [12]When you sin against your brothers[v] in this way and wound their weak conscience, you sin against Christ.[w] [13]Therefore, if what I eat causes my brother to fall into sin, I will never eat meat again, so that I will not cause him to fall.[x]

The Rights of an Apostle

9 Am I not free?[y] Am I not an apostle?[z] Have I not seen Jesus our Lord?[a] Are you not the result of my work in the Lord?[b] [2]Even though I may not be an apostle to others, surely I am to you! For you are the seal[c] of my apostleship in the Lord.

[3]This is my defense to those who sit in judgment on me. [4]Don't we have the right to food and drink?[d] [5]Don't we have the right to take a believing wife[e] along with us, as do the other apostles and the Lord's brothers[f] and Cephas[s]?[g] [6]Or is it only I and Barnabas[h] who must work for a living?

[7]Who serves as a soldier[i] at his own expense? Who plants a vineyard[j] and does not eat of its grapes? Who tends a flock and does not drink of the milk? [8]Do I say this merely from a human point of view? Doesn't the Law say the same thing? [9]For it is written in the Law of

q 36-38 Or [36]If anyone thinks he is not treating his daughter properly, and if she is getting along in years, and he feels she ought to marry, he should let her get married. [37]But the man who has settled the matter in his own mind, who is under no compulsion but has control over his own will, and who has made up his mind to keep the virgin unmarried—this man also does the right thing. [38]So then, he who gives his virgin in marriage does right, but he who does not give her in marriage does even better. r 1 Or "We all possess knowledge," as you say s 5 That is, Peter

Moses: "Do not muzzle an ox while it is treading out the grain."ᵗᵏ Is it about oxen that God is concerned?ˡ ¹⁰Surely he says this for us, doesn't he? Yes, this was written for us,ᵐ because when the plowman plows and the thresher threshes, they ought to do so in the hope of sharing in the harvest.ⁿ ¹¹If we have sown spiritual seed among you, is it too much if we reap a material harvest from you?ᵒ ¹²If others have this right of support from you, shouldn't we have it all the more?

But we did not use this right.ᵖ On the contrary, we put up with anything rather than hinderᵠ the gospel of Christ. ¹³Don't you know that those who work in the temple get their food from the temple, and those who serve at the altar share in what is offered on the altar?ʳ ¹⁴In the same way, the Lord has commanded that those who preach the gospel should receive their living from the gospel.ˢ

¹⁵But I have not used any of these rights.ᵗ And I am not writing this in the hope that you will do such things for me. I would rather die than have anyone deprive me of this boast.ᵘ ¹⁶Yet when I preach the gospel, I cannot boast, for I am compelled to preach.ᵛ Woe to me if I do not preach the gospel! ¹⁷If I preach voluntarily, I have a reward;ʷ if not voluntarily, I am simply discharging the trust committed to me.ˣ ¹⁸What then is my reward? Just this: that in preaching the gospel I may offer it free of charge,ʸ and so not make use of my rightsᶻ in preaching it.

¹⁹Though I am freeᵃ and belong to no man, I make myself a slave to everyone,ᵇ to win as many as possible.ᶜ ²⁰To the Jews I became like a Jew, to win the Jews.ᵈ To those under the law I became like one under the law (though I myself am not under the law),ᵉ so as to win those under the law. ²¹To those not having the law I became like one not having the lawʳ (though I am not free from God's law but am under Christ's law),ᵍ so as to win those not having the law. ²²To the weak I became weak, to win the weak.ʰ I have become all things to all menⁱ so that by all possible means I might save some.ʲ ²³I do all this for the sake of the gospel, that I may share in its blessings.

S ²⁴Do you not know that in a race all

the runners run, but only one gets the prize?ᵏ Run¹ in such a way as to get the prize. ²⁵Everyone who competes in the games goes into strict training. They do it to get a crownᵐ that will not last; but we do it to get a crown that will last forever.ⁿ ²⁶Therefore I do not run like a man running aimlessly;ᵒ I do not fight like a man beating the air.ᵖ ²⁷No, I beat my bodyᵠ and make it my slave so that after I have preached to others, I myself will not be disqualified for the prize.ʳ

Warnings From Israel's History

10 For I do not want you to be ignorantˢ of the fact, brothers, that our forefathers were all under the cloudᵗ and that they all passed through the sea.ᵘ ²They were all baptized intoᵛ Moses in the cloud and in the sea. ³They all ate the same spiritual foodʷ ⁴and drank the same spiritual drink; for they drank from the spiritual rockˣ that accompanied them, and that rock was Christ. ⁵Nevertheless, H God was not pleased with most of them; their bodies were scattered over the desert.ʸ

⁶Now these things occurred as examplesᵘᶻ to keep us from setting our hearts on evil things as they did. ⁷Do not be idolaters,ᵃ as some of them were; as it is written: "The people sat down to eat and drink and got up to indulge in pagan revelry."ᵛᵇ ⁸We should not commit sexual D immorality, as some of them did—and in one day twenty-three thousand of them died.ᶜ ⁹We should not test the Lord,ᵈ as some of them did—and were killed by snakes.ᵉ ¹⁰And do not grumble, as some of them didʳ—and were killedᵍ by the destroying angel.ʰ

¹¹These things happened to them as ex- C amplesⁱ and were written down as warn- S ings for us,ʲ on whom the fulfillment of the ages has come.ᵏ ¹²So, if you think you M are standing firm,ˡ be careful that you don't fall! ¹³No temptation has seized L you except what is common to man. And God is faithful;ᵐ he will not let you be

H 1Co 6:9–10 ◀▶ 1Co 11:32
D Ac 13:11 ◀▶ 1Co 11:29–32
C 1Co 1:7–8 ◀▶ 1Co 11:26
S 1Co 9:24–27 ◀▶ 1Co 10:31
M Ro 14:11 ◀▶ 1Co 14:24–25
L Ro 8:31–39 ◀▶ Php 4:19

S 1Co 6:20 ◀▶ 1Co 10:11–12

tempted beyond what you can bear.ⁿ But when you are tempted, he will also provide a way out so that you can stand up under it.

Idol Feasts and the Lord's Supper

¹⁴Therefore, my dear friends,ᵒ flee from idolatry.ᵖ ¹⁵I speak to sensible people; judge for yourselves what I say. ¹⁶Is not the cup of thanksgiving for which we give thanks a participation in the blood of Christ? And is not the bread that we break*q* a participation in the body of Christ?ʳ ¹⁷Because there is one loaf, we, who are many, are one body,ˢ for we all partake of the one loaf.

¹⁸Consider the people of Israel: Do not those who eat the sacrificesᵗ participate in the altar? ¹⁹Do I mean then that a sacrifice offered to an idol is anything, or that an idol is anything?ᵘ ²⁰No, but the sacrifices of pagans are offered to demons,ᵛ not to God, and I do not want you to be participants with demons. ²¹You cannot drink the cup of the Lord and the cup of demons too; you cannot have a part in both the Lord's table and the table of demons.ʷ ²²Are we trying to arouse the Lord's jealousy?ˣ Are we stronger than he?ʸ

The Believer's Freedom

²³"Everything is permissible"—but not everything is beneficial.ᶻ "Everything is permissible"—but not everything is constructive. ²⁴Nobody should seek his own good, but the good of others.ᵃ

²⁵Eat anything sold in the meat market without raising questions of conscience,ᵇ ²⁶for, "The earth is the Lord's, and everything in it."ʷᶜ ²⁷If some unbeliever invites you to a meal and you want to go, eat whatever is put before youᵈ without raising questions of conscience. ²⁸But if anyone says to you, "This has been offered in sacrifice," then do not eat it, both for the sake of the man who told you and for conscience' sakeˣᵉ— ²⁹the other man's conscience, I mean, not yours. For why should my freedomᶠ be judged by another's conscience? ³⁰If I take part in the meal with thankfulness, why am I denounced because of something I thank God for?ᵍ ³¹So whether you eat or drink or whatever you do, do it all for the glory of God.ʰ ³²Do not cause anyone to stumble,ⁱ whether Jews, Greeks or the church of Godʲ— ³³even as I try to please everybody in every way.ᵏ For I am not seeking my own good but the good of many,ˡ so that they may be saved.ᵐ ¹Follow my example,ⁿ as I follow the example of Christ.ᵒ

Propriety in Worship

²I praise youᵖ for remembering me in everythingᵠ and for holding to the teachings,ʸ just as I passed them on to you.ʳ ³Now I want you to realize that the head of every man is Christ,ˢ and the head of the woman is man,ᵗ and the head of Christ is God.ᵘ ⁴Every man who prays or prophesiesᵛ with his head covered dishonors his head. ⁵And every woman who prays or prophesiesʷ with her head uncovered dishonors her head—it is just as though her head were shaved.ˣ ⁶If a woman does not cover her head, she should have her hair cut off; and if it is a disgrace for a woman to have her hair cut or shaved off, she should cover her head. ⁷A man ought not to cover his head,ᶻ since he is the imageʸ and glory of God; but the woman is the glory of man. ⁸For man did not come from woman, but woman from man;ᶻ ⁹neither was man created for woman, but woman for man.ᵃ ¹⁰For this reason, and because of the angels, the woman ought to have a sign of authority on her head.

¹¹In the Lord, however, woman is not independent of man, nor is man independent of woman. ¹²For as woman came from man, so also man is born of woman. But everything comes from God.ᵇ ¹³Judge for yourselves: Is it proper for a woman to pray to God with her head uncovered? ¹⁴Does not the very nature of things teach you that if a man has long hair, it is a disgrace to him, ¹⁵but that if a woman has long hair, it is her glory? For long hair is given to her as a covering. ¹⁶If anyone wants to be contentious about this, we

---

w 26 Psalm 24:1 x 28 Some manuscripts conscience' sake, for "the earth is the Lord's and everything in it" y 2 Or traditions z 4-7 Or ⁴Every man who prays or prophesies with long hair dishonors his head. ⁵And every woman who prays or prophesies with no covering ⌊of hair⌋ on her head dishonors her head—she is just like one of the "shorn women." ⁶If a woman has no covering, let her be for now with short hair, but since it is a disgrace for a woman to have her hair shorn or shaved, she should grow it again. ⁷A man ought not to have long hair

Crowns and Rewards

THE LORD ADVISES believers to walk in righteousness and earn "treasures in heaven, where moth and rust do not destroy, and where thieves do not break in and steal" (Mt 6:20). These "treasures" are also referred to in other passages of the NT as "crowns." Jesus promises that when he returns, he will reward us with the crowns that we have earned and urges us to "hold on to what you have, so that no one will take your crown" (Rev 3:11). The NT highlights five special crowns for believers.

Crown of Glory: For Faithful Servants

"And when the Chief Shepherd appears, you will receive the crown of glory that will never fade away" (1 Pe 5:4).

Those who have served Jesus Christ as elders and pastors in the church will receive their reward from God. Though they have often given thanklessly of their time and resources here, in heaven they shall receive a crown of glory.

Crown of Rejoicing: For Soul Winners

"For what is our hope, our joy, or the crown in which we will glory in the presence of our Lord Jesus when he comes? Is it not you?" (1 Th 2:19).

Those who have won others to faith in Jesus Christ as their Savior will experience joy because these new believers are their spiritual children. Because others have been converted under their ministry they are promised this special reward in heaven.

Crown of Righteousness: For Those Who Love His Return

"Now there is in store for me the crown of righteousness, which the Lord, the righteous Judge, will award to me on that day—and not only to me, but also to all who have longed for his appearing" (2 Ti 4:8).

This crown will be given to all believers who long for the return of Christ. Throughout the NT, Christians are reminded to be watchful for the imminent return of their Lord. We must live active, vital lives as though we have a hundred years until he returns, while at the same time live in anticipation and holiness as though he will return today.

Incorruptible Crown: For Victorious Lives of Purity

"Everyone who competes in the games goes into strict training. They do it to get a crown that will not last; but we do it to get a crown that will last forever" (1 Co 9:25).

Borrowing imagery from athletic contests, Paul tells us that we must exercise discipline—spiritual discipline—if we are to experience victory in Christ. To be prepared for such spiritual discipline, Paul encourages us to daily "put on the full armor of God" (Eph 6:11). Accordingly, those Christians who are victorious in their daily spiritual struggle will receive an incorruptible crown.

Crown of Life: For Christian Martyrs

"Do not be afraid of what you are about to suffer. I tell you, the devil will put some of you in prison to test you, and you will suffer persecution for ten days. Be faithful, even to the point of death, and I will give you the crown of life" (Rev 2:10).

Christ promises a crown of life for all of those saints through the ages that have suffered martyrdom for their faith in him. His followers have experienced persecution in every century. Even today hundreds of thousands of Christians die throughout the world as martyrs for their faith.

have no other practice—nor do the churches of God.

The Lord's Supper
11:23–25pp — Mt 26:26–28; Mk 14:22–24; Lk 22:17–20

[17] In the following directives I have no praise for you, for your meetings do more harm than good. [18] In the first place, I hear that when you come together as a church, there are divisions among you, and to some extent I believe it. [19] No doubt there have to be differences among you to show which of you have God's approval. [20] When you come together, it is not the Lord's Supper you eat, [21] for as you eat, each of you goes ahead without waiting for anybody else. One remains hungry, another gets drunk. [22] Don't you have homes to eat and drink in? Or do you despise the church of God and humiliate those who have nothing? What shall I say to you? Shall I praise you for this? Certainly not!

[23] For I received from the Lord what I also passed on to you: The Lord Jesus, on the night he was betrayed, took bread, [24] and when he had given thanks, he broke it and said, "This is my body, which is for you; do this in remembrance of me." [25] In the same way, after supper he took the cup, saying, "This cup is the new covenant in my blood; do this, whenever you drink it, in remembrance of me." [26] For whenever you eat this bread and drink this cup, you proclaim the Lord's death until he comes.

[27] Therefore, whoever eats the bread or drinks the cup of the Lord in an unworthy manner will be guilty of sinning against the body and blood of the Lord. [28] A man ought to examine himself before he eats of the bread and drinks of the cup. [29] For anyone who eats and drinks without recognizing the body of the Lord eats and drinks judgment on himself. [30] That is why many among you are weak and sick, and a number of you have fallen asleep. [31] But if we judged ourselves, we would not come under judgment. [32] When we are judged by the Lord, we are being disciplined so that we will not be condemned with the world.

[33] So then, my brothers, when you come together to eat, wait for each other. [34] If anyone is hungry, he should eat at home, so that when you meet together it may not result in judgment.

And when I come I will give further directions.

Spiritual Gifts

12 Now about spiritual gifts, brothers, I do not want you to be ignorant. [2] You know that when you were pagans, somehow or other you were influenced and led astray to mute idols. [3] Therefore I tell you that no one who is speaking by the Spirit of God says, "Jesus be cursed," and no one can say, "Jesus is Lord," except by the Holy Spirit.

[4] There are different kinds of gifts, but the same Spirit. [5] There are different kinds of service, but the same Lord. [6] There are different kinds of working, but the same God works all of them in all men.

[7] Now to each one the manifestation of the Spirit is given for the common good. [8] To one there is given through the Spirit the message of wisdom, to another the message of knowledge by means of the same Spirit, [9] to another faith by the same Spirit, to another gifts of healing by that one Spirit, [10] to another miraculous powers, to another prophecy,

---

11:16 ᶜS 1Co 7:17; S 10:32
11:17 ᵈver 2,22
11:18 ᵉ1Co 1:10-12; 3:3
11:19 ᶠ1Jn 2:19
11:21 ᵍ2Pe 2:13; Jude 12
11:22 ʰS 1Co 10:32 ⁱJas 2:6 ⁱver 2,17
11:23 ᵏGal 1:12 ˡS ver 2
11:24 ᵐ1Co 10:16
11:25 ⁿS Lk 22:20 ᵒ1Co 10:16
11:26 ᵖS 1Co 1:7
11:27 ᵠHeb 10:29
11:28 ʳ2Co 13:5
11:30 ˢS Mt 9:24
11:31 ᵗPs 32:5; 1Jn 1:9
11:32 ᵘPs 94:12; 118:18; Pr 3:11,12; Heb 12:7-10; Rev 3:19 ᵛJn 15:18, 19
11:34 ʷver 21 ˣver 22 ʸS 1Co 4:19
12:1 ᶻRo 1:11; 1Co 1:7; 14,1,37 ᵃS Ro 11:25
12:2 ᵇS Eph 2:2 ᶜPs 115:5; Jer 10:5; Hab 2:18,19
12:3 ᵈRo 9:3; 1Co 16:22 ᵉS Jn 13:13 ᶠ1Jn 4:2,3
12:4 ᵍver 8-11; Ro 12:4-8; Eph 4:11; Heb 2:4
12:6 ʰEph 4:6 ⁱS Php 2:13
12:7 ʲ1Co 14:12; Eph 4:12
12:8 ᵏ1Co 2:6 ˡS 2Co 8:7
12:9 ᵐMt 17:19, 20; 1Co 13:2 ⁿver 28,30; Mt 10:1
12:10 ᵒver 28-30; Gal 3:5 ᵖS Eph 4:11

H 1Co 10:5–12 ◀▶ 1Co 15:25
T Hag 2:15–19 ◀▶ 2Co 1:6–9
B 1Co 6:11 ◀▶ 2Co 1:21–22
E 1Co 7:40 ◀▶ 1Co 12:28–31
G 1Co 7:7 ◀▶ 1Co 13:1–2
N 1Co 2:11 ◀▶ 2Co 3:17
W 1Co 3:1–2 ◀▶ 1Co 12:31
L 1Co 7:40 ◀▶ 1Co 14:15
T 1Co 7:40 ◀▶ 1Co 12:8
T 1Co 12:3 ◀▶ 1Co 12:10
H 1Co 15:19 ◀▶ 1Co 15:44–54
E Ro 15:18–19 ◀▶ 1Co 12:28
T 1Co 12:8 ◀▶ 1Co 14:30

D 1Co 7:23 ◀▶ 1Co 15:3
C 1Co 10:11 ◀▶ 2Co 1:14
S 1Co 10:31 ◀▶ 1Co 13:1–7
D 1Co 10:8 ◀▶ 2Co 12:7–10

11:26 Our participation in the Lord's communion supper not only affirms our belief in his death and resurrection from the grave, but also confirms our belief in his second coming. Paul reminds us to commemorate his death and resurrection "until he comes." Then we will participate in the glorious "wedding supper of the Lamb" (Rev 19:9) in heaven, celebrating our spiritual marriage to Christ forever.

to another distinguishing between spirits,[q] to another speaking in different kinds of tongues,[a][r] and to still another the interpretation of tongues.[a] [11]All these are the work of one and the same Spirit,[s] and he gives them to each one, just as he determines.

One Body, Many Parts

[12]The body is a unit, though it is made up of many parts; and though all its parts are many, they form one body.[t] So it is with Christ.[u] [13]For we were all baptized by[b] one Spirit[w] into one body—whether Jews or Greeks, slave or free[x]—and we were all given the one Spirit to drink.[y]

[14]Now the body is not made up of one part but of many.[z] [15]If the foot should say, "Because I am not a hand, I do not belong to the body," it would not for that reason cease to be part of the body. [16]And if the ear should say, "Because I am not an eye, I do not belong to the body," it would not for that reason cease to be part of the body. [17]If the whole body were an eye, where would the sense of hearing be? If the whole body were an ear, where would the sense of smell be? [18]But in fact God has arranged[a] the parts in the body, every one of them, just as he wanted them to be.[b] [19]If they were all one part, where would the body be? [20]As it is, there are many parts, but one body.[c]

[21]The eye cannot say to the hand, "I don't need you!" And the head cannot say to the feet, "I don't need you!" [22]On the contrary, those parts of the body that seem to be weaker are indispensable, [23]and the parts that we think are less honorable we treat with special honor. And the parts that are unpresentable are treated with special modesty, [24]while our presentable parts need no special treatment. But God has combined the members of the body and has given greater honor to the parts that lacked it, [25]so that there should be no division in the body, but that its parts should have equal concern for each other. [26]If one part suffers, every part suffers with it; if one part is honored, every part rejoices with it.

[27]Now you are the body of Christ,[d] and each one of you is a part of it.[e] [28]And in the church[f] God has appointed first of all apostles,[g] second prophets,[h] third teachers, then workers of miracles, also those having gifts of healing,[i] those able to help others, those with gifts of administration,[j] and those speaking in different kinds of tongues.[k] [29]Are all apostles? Are all prophets? Are all teachers? Do all work miracles? [30]Do all have gifts of healing? Do all speak in tongues[c]?[l] Do all interpret? [31]But eagerly desire[d][m] the greater gifts.

Love

And now I will show you the most excellent way.

13 If I speak in the tongues[e][n] of men and of angels, but have not love, I am only a resounding gong or a clanging cymbal. [2]If I have the gift of prophecy[o] and can fathom all mysteries[p] and all knowledge,[q] and if I have a faith[r] that can move mountains,[s] but have not love, I am nothing. [3]If I give all I possess to the poor[t] and surrender my body to the flames,[f][u] but have not love, I gain nothing.

[4]Love is patient,[v] love is kind. It does not envy, it does not boast, it is not proud.[w] [5]It is not rude, it is not self-seeking,[x] it is not easily angered,[y] it keeps no record of wrongs.[z] [6]Love does not delight in evil[a] but rejoices with the truth.[b] [7]It always protects, always trusts, always hopes, always perseveres.[c]

[8]Love never fails. But where there are prophecies,[d] they will cease; where there

---

R 1Co 6:11 ◀ ▶ 2Co 3:3

12:10 q 1Jn 4:1; r S Mk 16:17
12:11 s ver 4
12:12 t S Ro 12:5; u ver 27
12:13 v S Mk 1:8; w Eph 2:18; x Gal 3:28; Col 3:11; y Jn 7:37-39
12:14 z ver 12,20
12:18 a ver 28; b ver 11
12:20 c ver 12,14; S Ro 12:5
12:27 d Eph 1:23; 4:12; Col 1:18,24; e S Ro 12:5
12:28 f S 1Co 10:32; g Eph 4:11; h S Eph 4:11; i ver 9; j Ro 12:6-8 k ver 10; S Mk 16:17
12:30 l ver 10
12:31 m 1Co 14:1, 39
13:1 n ver 8; S Mk 16:17
13:2 o ver 8; S Eph 4:11; S Ac 11:27; p 1Co 14:2; q S Ac 8:7; r 1Co 12:9; s Mt 17:20; 21:21
13:3 t Lk 19:8; S Ac 2:45 u Da 3:28
13:4 v 1Th 5:14; w 1Co 5:2
13:5 x S 1Co 10:24; y S Mt 5:22; z Job 14:16,17; Pr 10:12; 17:9; 1Pe 4:8
13:6 a 2Th 2:12; b 2Jn 4; 3Jn 3,4
13:7 c ver 8,13
13:8 d ver 2

E 1Co 12:1–13 ◀ ▶ 2Co 1:21–22
E 1Co 12:9 ◀ ▶ Php 2:27
W 1Co 12:1–11 ◀ ▶ 1Co 14:1
G 1Co 12:1–31 ◀ ▶ 1Co 13:8
S 1Co 11:27–32 ◀ ▶ 1Co 15:2
G 1Co 13:1–2 ◀ ▶ 1Co 14:1–40

[a] 10 Or *languages*; also in verse 28 [b] 13 Or *with*; or in [c] 30 Or *other languages* [d] 31 Or *But you are eagerly desiring* [e] 1 Or *languages* [f] 3 Some early manuscripts *body that I may boast*

13:8–13 Paul reminds us that because of our earthly limitations we can only know and understand part of God's purposes. When Jesus Christ comes again, our limited knowledge and understanding will be removed, and our spiritual eyes will be opened. When we receive our glorious resurrection bodies, we will no longer need "prophecies" (13:8) because we will finally see Jesus Christ "face to face" (13:12) and know everything there is to know about him just as he already knows everything about us.

are tongues,ᵉ they will be stilled; where there is knowledge, it will pass away. ⁹For we know in partᶠ and we prophesy in part, ¹⁰but when perfection comes,ᵍ the imperfect disappears. ¹¹When I was a child, I talked like a child, I thought like a child, I reasoned like a child. When I became a man, I put childish waysʰ behind me. ¹²Now we see but a poor reflection as in a mirror;ⁱ then we shall see face to face.ʲ Now I know in part; then I shall know fully, even as I am fully known.ᵏ

¹³And now these three remain: faith, hope and love.ˡ But the greatest of these is love.ᵐ

Gifts of Prophecy and Tongues

14 Follow the way of loveⁿ and eagerly desireᵒ spiritual gifts,ᵖ especially the gift of prophecy.ᑫ ²For anyone who speaks in a tongueᵍʳ does not speak to men but to God. Indeed, no one understands him;ˢ he utters mysteriesᵗ with his spirit.ʰ ³But everyone who prophesies speaks to men for their strengthening,ᵘ encouragementᵛ and comfort. ⁴He who speaks in a tongueʷ edifiesˣ himself, but he who prophesiesʸ edifies the church. ⁵I would like every one of you to speak in tongues,ⁱ but I would rather have you prophesy.ᶻ He who prophesies is greater than one who speaks in tongues,ⁱ unless he interprets, so that the church may be edified.ᵃ

⁶Now, brothers, if I come to you and speak in tongues, what good will I be to you, unless I bring you some revelationᵇ or knowledgeᶜ or prophecy or word of instruction?ᵈ ⁷Even in the case of lifeless things that make sounds, such as the flute or harp, how will anyone know what tune is being played unless there is a distinction in the notes? ⁸Again, if the trumpet does not sound a clear call, who will get ready for battle?ᵉ ⁹So it is with you. Unless you speak intelligible words with your tongue, how will anyone know what you are saying? You will just be speaking into the air. ¹⁰Undoubtedly there are all sorts of languages in the world, yet none of them is without meaning. ¹¹If then I do not grasp the meaning of what someone is saying, I am a foreigner to the speaker, and he is a foreigner to me.ᶠ ¹²So it is with you. Since you are eager to have spiritual gifts,ᵍ try to excel in gifts that build upʰ the church.

¹³For this reason anyone who speaks in a tongue should pray that he may interpret what he says.ⁱ ¹⁴For if I pray in a tongue, my spirit prays,ʲ but my mind is unfruitful. ¹⁵So what shall I do? I will pray with my spirit,ᵏ but I will also pray with my mind; I will singˡ with my spirit, but I will also sing with my mind. ¹⁶If you are praising God with your spirit, how can one who finds himself among those who do not understandʲ say "Amen"ᵐ to your thanksgiving,ⁿ since he does not know what you are saying? ¹⁷You may be giving thanks well enough, but the other man is not edified.ᵒ

¹⁸I thank God that I speak in tongues more than all of you. ¹⁹But in the church I would rather speak five intelligible words to instruct others than ten thousand words in a tongue.ᵖ

²⁰Brothers, stop thinking like children.ᑫ In regard to evil be infants,ʳ but in your thinking be adults. ²¹In the Lawˢ it is written:

"Through men of strange tongues
    and through the lips of foreigners
I will speak to this people,
    but even then they will not listen to me,"ᵏᵗ

says the Lord.

²²Tongues, then, are a sign, not for believers but for unbelievers; prophecy,ᵘ however, is for believers, not for unbelievers. ²³So if the whole church comes together and everyone speaks in tongues, and some who do not understandˡ or some unbelievers come in, will they not say that you are out of your mind?ᵛ ²⁴But if an unbeliever or someone who does not understandᵐ comes in while everybody is prophesying, he will be convinced by all that he is a sinner and will

be judged by all, ²⁵and the secrets^w of his heart will be laid bare. So he will fall down and worship God, exclaiming, "God is really among you!"^x

Orderly Worship

²⁶What then shall we say, brothers?^y When you come together, everyone^z has a hymn,^a or a word of instruction,^b a revelation, a tongue^c or an interpretation.^d All of these must be done for the strengthening^e of the church. ²⁷If anyone speaks in a tongue, two—or at the most three—should speak, one at a time, and someone must interpret. ²⁸If there is no interpreter, the speaker should keep quiet in the church and speak to himself and God.

²⁹Two or three prophets^f should speak, and the others should weigh carefully what is said.^g ³⁰And if a revelation comes to someone who is sitting down, the first speaker should stop. ³¹For you can all prophesy in turn so that everyone may be instructed and encouraged. ³²The spirits of prophets are subject to the control of prophets.^h ³³For God is not a God of disorder^i but of peace.^j

As in all the congregations^k of the saints,^l ³⁴women should remain silent in the churches. They are not allowed to speak,^m but must be in submission,^n as the Law^o says. ³⁵If they want to inquire about something, they should ask their own husbands at home; for it is disgraceful for a woman to speak in the church.

³⁶Did the word of God^p originate with you? Or are you the only people it has reached? ³⁷If anybody thinks he is a prophet^q or spiritually gifted,^r let him acknowledge that what I am writing to you is the Lord's command.^s ³⁸If he ignores this, he himself will be ignored.^n

³⁹Therefore, my brothers, be eager^t to prophesy,^u and do not forbid speaking in tongues. ⁴⁰But everything should be done in a fitting and orderly^v way.

L 1Co 14:15 ◄ ► 2Co 12:18
T 1Co 12:10 ◄ ► Eph 1:17–19

14:25 ʷRo 2:16; ˣIsa 45:14; Zec 8:23
14:26 ʸS Ro 7:1; ᶻ1Co 12:7-10
ᵃS Eph 5:19 ᵇver 6
ᶜver 2 ᵈ1Co 12:10
ᵉS Ro 14:19
14:29 ᶠver 32,37; S 1Co 13:2
ᵍ1Co 12:10
14:32 ʰ1Jn 4:1
14:33 ⁱver 40
ʲS Ro 15:33
ᵏS 1Co 7:17; S 10:32 ˡS Ac 9:13
14:34 ᵐ1Co 11:5, 13 ⁿS Eph 5:22; 1Ti 2:11,12
ᵒver 21; Ge 3:16
14:36 ᵖS Heb 4:12
14:37
ᵠS Ac 11:27; 1Co 13:2; 2Co 10:7
ʳ1Co 2:15; S 12:1
ˢ1Jn 4:6
14:39 ᵗver 1; 1Co 12:31 ᵘver 1; S Eph 4:11
14:40 ᵛver 33; Col 2:5
15:1 ʷIsa 40:9; Ro 2:16
ˣS 1Co 3:6; ʸS Gal 1:8
15:2 ʸRo 1:16
ᶻS Ro 11:22
15:3 ᵃGal 1:12
ᵇS 1Co 11:2
ᶜIsa 53:5; Jn 1:29; ᵈS Gal 1:4; 1Pe 2:24
ᵈMt 26:24; ᵉS Lk 24:27; S 24:44; Ac 17:2; 26:22,23
15:4 ᵉMt 27:59,60
ᶠS Ac 2:24
ᵍS Mt 16:21
ʰJn 2:21,22;
15:5 ⁱLk 24:34
ʲMk 16:14; Lk 24:36-43
15:6 ᵏver 18,20; S Mt 9:24
15:7 ˡS Ac 15:13
ᵐLk 24:33,36,37; Ac 1:3,4
15:8 ⁿAc 9:3-6,17; 1Co 9:1; Gal 1:16
15:9 ᵒ2Co 12:11; Eph 3:8; 1Ti 1:15
ᵖAc 8:3
ᵠS 1Co 10:32
15:10 ʳS Ro 3:24
ˢS Ro 12:3
ᵗ2Co 11:23; Col 1:29
ᵘS Php 2:13
15:11 ᵛGal 2:6
15:12 ʷver 4
ˣS Jn 11:24
ʸAc 17:32; 23:8; 2Ti 2:18
15:14 ᶻ1Th 4:14

The Resurrection of Christ

15 Now, brothers, I want to remind you of the gospel^w I preached to you,^x which you received and on which you have taken your stand. ²By this gospel you are saved,^y if you hold firmly^z to the word I preached to you. Otherwise, you have believed in vain.

³For what I received^a I passed on to you^b as of first importance^o: that Christ died for our sins^c according to the Scriptures,^d ⁴that he was buried,^e that he was raised^f on the third day^g according to the Scriptures,^h ⁵and that he appeared to Peter,^p^i and then to the Twelve.^j ⁶After that, he appeared to more than five hundred of the brothers at the same time, most of whom are still living, though some have fallen asleep.^k ⁷Then he appeared to James,^l then to all the apostles,^m ⁸and last of all he appeared to me also,^n as to one abnormally born.

⁹For I am the least of the apostles^o and do not even deserve to be called an apostle, because I persecuted^p the church of God.^q ¹⁰But by the grace^r of God I am what I am, and his grace to me^s was not without effect. No, I worked harder than all of them^t—yet not I, but the grace of God that was with me.^u ¹¹Whether, then, it was I or they,^v this is what we preach, and this is what you believed.

The Resurrection of the Dead

¹²But if it is preached that Christ has been raised from the dead,^w how can some of you say that there is no resurrection^x of the dead?^y ¹³If there is no resurrection of the dead, then not even Christ has been raised. ¹⁴And if Christ has not been raised,^z our preaching is useless and so is your faith. ¹⁵More than that, we are then found to be false witnesses about God, for we have testified about

S 1Co 13:1–7 ◄ ► 1Co 15:33–34
D 1Co 11:23–25 ◄ ► 2Co 5:14–15
L 1Co 7:23 ◄ ► 2Co 5:18–21

ⁿ 38 Some manuscripts *If he is ignorant of this, let him be ignorant* ᵒ 3 Or *you at the first* ᵖ 5 Greek *Cephas*

15:4–6 Paul confirms the fulfillment of the prophecies that Christ would rise from the dead on the third day (see Mt 12:40; Jn 2:19–22) and confirms Christ's appearance to many of the disciples after the resurrection. These appearances to different persons at different times over a period of forty days proves that Jesus truly rose from the grave in his glorious resurrection body (see Mt 28:9, 16; Mk 16:9; Lk 24:13–31, 34; Jn 20:19, 26; 21:1–22; 1Co 15:5–7).

1 CORINTHIANS 15:16

God that he raised Christ from the dead.[a] But he did not raise him if in fact the dead are not raised. [16]For if the dead are not raised, then Christ has not been raised either. [17]And if Christ has not been raised, your faith is futile; you are still in your sins.[b] [18]Then those also who have fallen asleep[c] in Christ are lost. [19]If only for this life we have hope in Christ, we are to be pitied more than all men.[d]

F [20]But Christ has indeed been raised from the dead,[e] the firstfruits[f] of those **W** who have fallen asleep.[g] [21]For since death came through a man,[h] the resurrection of the dead[i] comes also through a man. [22]For as in Adam all die, so in Christ all will be made alive.[j] [23]But each in his own turn: Christ, the firstfruits;[k] then, when he comes,[l] those who belong to **K** him.[m] [24]Then the end will come, when he **M** hands over the kingdom[n] to God the Fa-
V ther after he has destroyed all dominion, **H** authority and power.[o] [25]For he must reign[p] until he has put all his enemies under his feet.[q] [26]The last enemy to be destroyed is death.[r] [27]For he "has put everything under his feet."[q][s] Now when it

15:15	[a] S Ac 2:24
15:17	[b] S Ro 4:25
15:18	[c] ver 6,20; S Mt 9:24
15:19	[d] S 1Co 4:9
15:20	[e] 1Pe 1:3 [f] ver 23; S Ac 26:23 [g] ver 6,18; S Mt 9:24
15:21	[h] S Ro 5:12 [i] ver 12
15:22	[j] Ro 5:14-18; S 1Co 6:14
15:23	[k] ver 20 [l] ver 52; S 1Th 2:19 [m] S 1Co 3:23
15:24	[n] Da 2:44; 7:14,27; 2Pe 1:11 [o] Ro 8:38
15:25	[p] Isa 9:7; 52:7 [q] ver 27; S Mt 22:44
15:26	[r] 2Ti 1:10; Rev 20:14; 21:4
15:27	[s] ver 25; Ps 8:6; S Mt 22:44 [t] S Mt 28:18
15:28	[u] Php 3:21 [v] 1Co 3:23
15:30	[w] 2Co 11:26
15:31	[x] S Ro 8:36
15:32	[y] 2Co 1:8 [z] S Ac 18:19 [a] Isa 22:13; Lk 12:19
15:33	[b] S 1Co 6:9 [c] Pr 22:24,25
15:34	[d] S Gal 4:8 [e] S 1Co 4:14
15:35	[f] Ro 9:19

says that "everything" has been put under him, it is clear that this does not include God himself, who put everything under Christ.[t] [28]When he has done this, then the Son himself will be made subject to him who put everything under him,[u] so that God may be all in all.[v]

[29]Now if there is no resurrection, what will those do who are baptized for the dead? If the dead are not raised at all, why are people baptized for them? [30]And as for us, why do we endanger ourselves every hour?[w] [31]I die every day[x]—I mean that, brothers—just as surely as I glory over you in Christ Jesus our Lord. [32]If I fought wild beasts[y] in Ephesus[z] for merely human reasons, what have I gained? If the dead are not raised,

"Let us eat and drink,
 for tomorrow we die."[ra]

[33]Do not be misled:[b] "Bad company cor- **S** rupts good character."[c] [34]Come back to your senses as you ought, and stop sinning; for there are some who are ignorant of God[d]—I say this to your shame.[e]

The Resurrection Body

[35]But someone may ask,[f] "How are the **F**

F 1Co 6:14 ◄ ► 1Co 15:35–55
W Ac 24:15 ◄ ► Rev 20:5–6
K Ac 3:25 ◄ ► Rev 11:15
M 1Co 6:2–3 ◄ ► Php 2:9–11
V Ac 2:34–35 ◄ ► Eph 1:21–22
H 1Co 11:32 ◄ ► 1Co 16:22

S 1Co 15:2 ◄ ► 2Co 5:10
F 1Co 15:20–26 ◄ ► 2Co 1:9

[q] 27 Psalm 8:6 [r] 32 Isaiah 22:13

15:17–19 Paul admits that if Jesus' body still lay in the grave, our faith would be in vain. The physical resurrection of Jesus' body from death to life is the most fundamental fact upon which the faith of Christianity rests. Ancient Gnostics and modern-day liberals who denied the physical resurrection of Jesus have denied the most basic and fundamental truth of Christianity. This is why the NT writers described the events of Christ's trial, crucifixion, resurrection and appearances after the resurrection with such detail. They knew that Christianity would be nothing if Jesus had not been resurrected as prophesied.

15:20–28 Paul declares God's promise of the coming harvest of believers when all those who follow Christ will participate in the bodily resurrection to eternal life in heaven. At the Feast of Firstfruits, a sheaf of grain from the first cutting of the harvest was waved by a priest in the temple before the Lord as a grateful acknowledgment of the full harvest that would follow (see Lev 23:10–11). Jesus Christ's resurrection from death is the "firstfruits" (15:20) of the final resurrection of all believers.

Paul also explains that the resurrection of believers will involve several phases. The first step occurred when Jesus Christ rose from the grave, quite possibly on the day of the Feast of Firstfruits. The apostle then refers to the resurrection or rapture of the living and departed believers, both OT and NT, raised to eternal life in Christ. The final stage is the end of all things when Christ "hands over the kingdom to God the Father" (15:24) by defeating the antichrist and the rulers of the nations at Armageddon. Then Christ will reign on earth from the throne of David in Jerusalem for the Millennium and through eternity.

There will also be a physical resurrection of all of the wicked dead at the end of the Millennium just before the great white throne judgment of God (see Rev 21:11–15). As Adam's sin brought death to all people, the resurrection power of Jesus Christ will raise all humanity from the dead—the righteous to eternal life in heaven and the unrighteous to eternal judgment in hell (see Mt 25:34–46). For further information, see the article on "The Resurrection of the Body" on p. 1218.

15:35–50 Paul deals in this passage with questions about the resurrection body that believers will receive at Christ's coming in the air

dead raised? With what kind of body will they come?"ᵍ ³⁶How foolish!ʰ What you sow does not come to life unless it dies.ⁱ ³⁷When you sow, you do not plant the body that will be, but just a seed, perhaps of wheat or of something else. ³⁸But God gives it a body as he has determined, and to each kind of seed he gives its own body.ʲ ³⁹All flesh is not the same: Men have one kind of flesh, animals have another, birds another and fish another. ⁴⁰There are also heavenly bodies and there are earthly bodies; but the splendor of the heavenly bodies is one kind, and the splendor of the earthly bodies is another. ⁴¹The sun has one kind of splendor,ᵏ the moon another and the stars another;ˡ and star differs from star in splendor.

⁴²So will it beᵐ with the resurrection of the dead.ⁿ The body that is sown is perishable, it is raised imperishable;ᵒ ⁴³it is sown in dishonor, it is raised in glory;ᵖ it is sown in weakness, it is raised in power; ⁴⁴it is sown a natural body, it is raised a spiritual body.ᵠ

If there is a natural body, there is also a spiritual body. ⁴⁵So it is written: "The first man Adam became a living being"ʳ; the last Adam,ˢ a life-giving spirit.ᵗ ⁴⁶The spiritual did not come first, but the natural, and after that the spiritual.ᵘ ⁴⁷The first man was of the dust of the earth,ᵛ the second man from heaven.ʷ ⁴⁸As was the earthly man, so are those who are of the earth; and as is the man from heaven, so also are those who are of heaven.ˣ ⁴⁹And just as we have borne the likeness of the earthly man,ʸ so shall weᶠ bear the likeness of the man from heaven.ᶻ

⁵⁰I declare to you, brothers, that flesh and bloodᵃ cannot inherit the kingdom of God,ᵇ nor does the perishable inherit the imperishable.ᶜ ⁵¹Listen, I tell you a mystery:ᵈ We will not all sleep,ᵉ but we will all be changedᶠ— ⁵²in a flash, in the twinkling of an eye, at the last trumpet. For the trumpet will sound,ᵍ the deadʰ will be raised imperishable, and we will be changed. ⁵³For the perishableⁱ must

H 1Co 12:9 ◀ ▶ 2Co 3:6

T Ro 8:17–18 ◀ ▶ Php 3:21

15:35 ᵍ Eze 37:3
15:36 ʰ Lk 11:40; 12:20 ⁱ Jn 12:24
15:38 ʲ Ge 1:11
15:41 ᵏ Ps 19:4-6 ˡ Ps 8:1,3
15:42 ᵐ Da 12:3; Mt 13:43 ⁿ ver 12 ᵒ ver 50,53,54
15:43 ᵖ Php 3:21; Col 3:4
15:44 ᵠ ver 50
15:45 ʳ Ge 2:7 ˢ Ro 5:14 ᵗ Jn 5:21; 6:57,58; Ro 8:2
15:46 ᵘ ver 44
15:47 ᵛ Ge 2:7; 3:19; Ps 90:3 ʷ Jn 3:13,31
15:48 ˣ Php 3:20, 21
15:49 ʸ Ge 5:3 ᶻ S Ro 8:29
15:50 ᵃ Eph 6:12; Heb 2:14 ᵇ S Mt 25:34 ᶜ ver 42,53,54
15:51 ᵈ 1Co 13:2; 14:2 ᵉ S Mt 9:24 ᶠ 2Co 5:4; Php 3:21
15:52 ᵍ S Mt 24:31 ʰ Jn 5:25
15:53 ⁱ ver 42,50,54

ˢ 45 Gen. 2:7 ᵗ 49 Some early manuscripts *so let us*

(see 1Th 4:16–17). A common error assumed that the resurrection body was identical to the dead body, only resuscitated like Lazarus was when he rose from the grave. The second error supposed that the resurrection body was a new creation, unrelated to the dead body. Paul indicates that the resurrection body is definitely related to the old body (15:36, 38), but that it will be transformed into a spiritual, celestial body with new capabilities (15:39–44) like the body that Jesus had when he rose from the grave (see Php 3:21; 1Jn 3:2). Our earthly bodies are prone to sin, corruption and disease and unfit for heaven's glory (15:50). But our resurrection bodies will be perfect, without sin, pain, disease or death so that we might enjoy the totality of heaven's glory and reign on the earth with Christ in the Millennium (see Rev 5:10). For further information, see the article on "The Resurrection of the Body" on p. 1218.

15:51–54 Paul reveals the "mystery" (15:51) of the rapture in this passage, that moment when all believers in Christ will be caught up into the air to receive the "redemption of our bodies" (Ro 8:23). Paul acknowledges that not every Christian will suffer death prior to this event. When Jesus returns in the air, there will be a group of living believers on earth at that moment. That generation of believers will pass from life to life eternal without ever experiencing the pangs of death. Their natural corruptible bodies will be instantaneously transformed into glorious, supernatural resurrection bodies, and they will be caught up to meet with the Lord in the air (see 1Th 4:17). At that point the rapture will signal the fulfillment of Isaiah's Messianic prophecy because "death has been swallowed up in victory" (15:54; see Isa 25:8).

Note Paul's use of the phrase "at the last trumpet" (15:52). Some scholars have suggested that this means that the resurrection of the saints will take place when the last of the seven trumpet judgments of Revelation is sounded (see Rev 11:15). However, Scripture clearly shows that this trumpet in 15:52 sounds *before* God's wrath descends, whereas the seventh trumpet blown in Revelation is sounded at the *end* of God's wrath. Note also that the trumpet that summons the church is called "the trumpet call of God" (1Th 4:16), while the seventh trumpet in Revelation is an angel's trumpet (see Rev 18:13).

It is more likely that in this verse Paul was referring to the last trumpet blasts that were given when the Israelites were traveling through the Sinai desert (see Nu 10:2–10). When the first trumpet blast sounded, the leaders gathered to Moses, and the people prepared to set out. Additional blasts were given to signal the movement for each tribe. When the last trumpet blast was sounded, this

1 CORINTHIANS 15:54

clothe itself with the imperishable,[j] and the mortal with immortality. [54]When the perishable has been clothed with the imperishable, and the mortal with immortality, then the saying that is written will come true: "Death has been swallowed up in victory."[u][k]

[55]"Where, O death, is your victory?
Where, O death, is your sting?"[v][l]

[K]
[V] [56]The sting of death is sin,[m] and the power of sin is the law.[n] [57]But thanks be to God![o] He gives us the victory through our Lord Jesus Christ.[p]

[58]Therefore, my dear brothers, stand firm. Let nothing move you. Always give yourselves fully to the work of the Lord,[q] because you know that your labor in the Lord is not in vain.[r]

The Collection for God's People

16 Now about the collection[s] for God's people:[t] Do what I told the Galatian[u] churches to do. [2]On the first day of every week,[v] each one of you should set aside a sum of money in keeping with his income, saving it up, so that when I come no collections will have to be made.[w] [3]Then, when I arrive, I will give letters of introduction to the men you approve[x] and send them with your gift to Jerusalem. [4]If it seems advisable for me to go also, they will accompany me.

Personal Requests

[5]After I go through Macedonia, I will come to you[y]—for I will be going through Macedonia.[z] [6]Perhaps I will stay with you awhile, or even spend the winter, so that you can help me on my journey,[a] wherever I go. [7]I do not want to see you now and make only a passing visit; I hope to spend some time with you, if the Lord permits.[b] [8]But I will stay on at Ephesus[c] until Pentecost,[d] [9]because a great door for effective work has opened to me,[e] and there are many who oppose me.

[10]If Timothy[f] comes, see to it that he has nothing to fear while he is with you, for he is carrying on the work of the Lord,[g] just as I am. [11]No one, then, should refuse to accept him.[h] Send him on his way[i] in peace[j] so that he may return to me. I am expecting him along with the brothers.

[12]Now about our brother Apollos:[k] I strongly urged him to go to you with the brothers. He was quite unwilling to go now, but he will go when he has the opportunity.

[13]Be on your guard; stand firm[l] in the faith; be men of courage; be strong.[m] [14]Do everything in love.[n]

[15]You know that the household of Stephanas[o] were the first converts[p] in Achaia,[q] and they have devoted themselves to the service[r] of the saints.[s] I urge you, brothers, [16]to submit[t] to such as these and to everyone who joins in the work, and labors at it. [17]I was glad when Stephanas, Fortunatus and Achaicus arrived, because they have supplied what was lacking from you.[u] [18]For they refreshed[v] my spirit and yours also. Such men deserve recognition.[w]

Final Greetings

[19]The churches in the province of Asia[x] send you greetings. Aquila and Priscilla[w][y] greet you warmly in the Lord, and so does the church that meets at their house.[z] [20]All the brothers here send you greetings. Greet one another with a holy kiss.[a]

[21]I, Paul, write this greeting in my own hand.[b]

15:53 [2]2Co 5:2,4
15:54 [k] Isa 25:8; Heb 2:14; Rev 20:14
15:55 [l] Hos 13:14
15:56 [m] S Ro 5:12; [n] S Ro 4:15
15:57 [o] S 2Co 2:14; [p] Ro 8:37; Heb 2:14,15
15:58 [q] 1Co 16:10; [r] Isa 65:23
16:1 [s] S Ac 24:17; [t] S Ac 9:13; [u] S Ac 16:6
16:2 [v] Ac 20:7; [w] 2Co 9:4,5
16:3 [x] 2Co 3:1; 8:18,19
16:5 [y] S 1Co 4:19; [z] S Ac 16:9
16:6 [a] Ro 15:24; Tit 3:13
16:7 [b] S Ac 18:21
16:8 [c] S Ac 18:19; [d] S Ac 2:1
16:9 [e] S Ac 14:27
16:10 [f] S Ac 16:1; [g] 1Co 15:58
16:11 [h] 1Ti 4:12; [i] 2Co 1:16; 3Jn 6; [j] S Ac 15:33
16:12 [k] S Ac 18:24
16:13 [l] 1Co 1:8; 2Co 1:21; Gal 5:1; Php 1:27; 1Th 3:8; S Tit 1:9; [m] S Eph 6:10
16:14 [n] 1Co 14:1
16:15 [o] 1Co 1:16; [p] Ro 16:5; [q] S Ac 18:12; [r] S Ac 24:17; [s] S Ac 9:13
16:16 [t] 1Th 5:12; Heb 13:17
16:17 [u] 2Co 11:9; Php 2:30
16:18 [v] Ro 15:32; Phm 7 v Php 2:29
16:19 [x] S Ac 2:9; [y] S Ac 18:2; [z] S Ro 16:5
16:20 [a] S Ro 16:16
16:21 [b] Gal 6:11; Col 4:18; 2Th 3:17; Phm 19

[K] 1Co 6:9–11 ◄ ► 2Co 1:20
[V] Ro 8:35–39 ◄ ► 2Co 2:14

[u] 54 Isaiah 25:8 [v] 55 Hosea 13:14 [w] 19 Greek *Prisca*, a variant of *Priscilla*

---

signified that the whole camp was on the move. Paul probably used this metaphor to symbolize God's signal to his people to be prepared to move out at the rapture.

16:2 The early Christians (including Jewish and Gentile believers) worshiped on Sunday, "the first day of every week" (16:2), in commemoration of Christ's resurrection on that day.

P ²²If anyone does not love the Lord^c—a
H cursed^d be on him. Come, O Lord^x!^e

²³The grace of the Lord Jesus be with you.^f

P *Ac 2:19–20* ◄ ► *1Th 5:3*
H *1Co 15:25* ◄ ► *2Co 2:15–16*

16:22 ^cEph 6:24
^dRo 9:3 ^eRev 22:20

16:23 ^fS Ro 16:20

²⁴My love to all of you in Christ Jesus. Amen.^y

^x22 In Aramaic the expression *Come, O Lord* is *Marana tha*.
^y24 Some manuscripts do not have *Amen*.

16:22 Paul calls attention to the fact that he wrote these closing remarks with his own hand (16:21). The end of 16:22 is actually three words, not two, as in the King James version of the Bible. The first word is the Greek word *anathema*, which means, "cursed with a great curse." The next two words, *Maran* and *Atha*, are Aramaic, the language of familiarity in the NT world. *Maran* simply means "Lord." And *Atha* translates "come." The intent, then, of Paul's last words to the Corinthians is a warning that those who reject Christ's offer of salvation are accursed because they remain dead in their sins (see Jn 3:18–20). Yet Paul's words ring with the affirmation of the imminent return of Christ to take his church home to heaven as Paul cries "Lord, come!"

2 Corinthians

Author: Paul

Theme: God's strength in our weakness

Date of Writing: C. A.D. 55

Outline of 2 Corinthians
  I. Introduction (1:1–11)
  II. Paul as God's Messenger (1:13—7:16)
  III. Stewardship in Giving (8:1—9:15)
  IV. Paul as an Apostle (10:1—13:10)
  V. Conclusion (13:11–14)

THE APOSTLE PAUL probably wrote the epistle known as 2 Corinthians a few months after his first letter to the Corinthian church. The problems that had occasioned Paul's first letter to this church were still present at the time this second letter was composed. Some of the members of the Corinthian church were unrepentant, and Paul was anxious about the welfare of the church. Reaching Macedonia, Paul was greatly relieved when Titus brought him the good news that a revival had broken out in the Corinthian church. Paul then wrote his second letter to the Corinthians, commending them for their repentance, encouraging their faithful giving to the poor and reestablishing his apostolic authority in his messages to them.

While the book of 2 Corinthians contains very few prophecies, the letter is filled with a variety of personal matters regarding Paul's feelings, obligations, ambitions and responsibilities. Containing more personal glimpses into Paul's life than any other letter, this epistle shares Paul's personal career with the Corinthian believers and deals with the attacks against his leadership (see 3:1, 8:20–23; 10:2, 8–10, 15; 11:5; 12:11–12, 16). Paul also shares some of the most significant teaching on giving, ministry and our Christian hope in this autobiographical letter.

1

¹Paul, an apostle[a] of Christ Jesus by the will of God,[b] and Timothy[c] our brother,

To the church of God[d] in Corinth,[e] together with all the saints throughout Achaia:[f]

²Grace and peace to you from God our Father and the Lord Jesus Christ.[g]

The God of All Comfort

³Praise be to the God and Father of our Lord Jesus Christ,[h] the Father of compassion and the God of all comfort, ⁴who comforts us[i] in all our troubles, so that we can comfort those in any trouble with the comfort we ourselves have received from God. ⁵For just as the sufferings of Christ flow over into our lives,[j] so also through Christ our comfort overflows. ⁶If we are distressed, it is for your comfort and salvation;[k] if we are comforted, it is for your comfort, which produces in you patient endurance of the same sufferings we suffer. ⁷And our hope for you is firm, because we know that just as you share in our sufferings,[l] so also you share in our comfort.

⁸We do not want you to be uninformed,[m] brothers, about the hardships we suffered[n] in the province of Asia.[o] We were under great pressure, far beyond our ability to endure, so that we despaired even of life. ⁹Indeed, in our hearts we felt the sentence of death. But this happened that we might not rely on ourselves but on God,[p] who raises the dead.[q] ¹⁰He has delivered us from such a deadly peril,[r] and he will deliver us. On him we have set our hope[s] that he will continue to deliver us, ¹¹as you help us by your prayers.[t] Then many will give thanks[u] on our[a] behalf for the gracious favor granted us in answer to the prayers of many.

J Ro 12:12 ◀▶ 2Co 2:14
T 1Co 11:32 ◀▶ 2Co 4:10–11
F 1Co 15:35–55 ◀▶ 2Co 4:14

1:1 a S 1Co 1:1; b 1Co 1:1; Eph 1:1; Col 1:1; 2Ti 1:1; c S Ac 16:1; d S 1Co 10:32; e S Ac 18:1; f S Ac 18:12
1:2 g S Ro 1:7
1:3 h Eph 1:3; 1Pe 1:3
1:4 i Isa 49:13; 51:12; 66:13; 2Co 7:6,7,13
1:5 j Ro 8:17; 2Co 4:10; Gal 6:17; Php 3:10; Col 1:24; 1Pe 4:13
1:6 k 2Co 4:15
1:7 l S ver 5
1:8 m S Ro 11:25; n 1Co 15:32; o S Ac 2:9
1:9 p Jer 17:5,7; q S Jn 5:21
1:10 r S Ro 15:31; s 1Ti 4:10
1:11 t Ro 15:30; Php 1:19; u 2Co 4:15; 9:11
1:12 v S Ac 23:1; w 1Th 2:10; x 2Co 2:17; y 1Co 1:17; 2:1,4, 13
1:14 z S 1Co 1:8
1:15 a S 1Co 4:19; b Ro 1:11,13; 15:29
1:16 c 1Co 16:5-7; d S Ac 16:9; e 1Co 16:11; 3Jn 6; f Ac 19:21
1:17 g 2Co 10:2,3; 11:18
1:18 h S 1Co 1:9
1:19 i S Mt 4:3; j S Ac 15:22; k S Ac 16:1; l Heb 13:8
1:20 m Ro 15:8; n S 1Co 14:16; o Ro 15:9
1:21 p S 1Co 16:13; q 1Co 2:20,27
1:22 r Ge 38:18; Eze 9:4; Hag 2:23; s 2Co 5:5
1:23 t S 1Co 1:9; u 1Co 4:21; 2Co 2:1,3; 13:2,10
1:24 v 1Pe 5:3

Paul's Change of Plans

¹²Now this is our boast: Our conscience[v] testifies that we have conducted ourselves in the world, and especially in our relations with you, in the holiness[w] and sincerity[x] that are from God. We have done so not according to worldly wisdom[y] but according to God's grace. ¹³For we do not write you anything you cannot read or understand. And I hope that, ¹⁴as you have understood us in part, you will come to understand fully that you can boast of us just as we will boast of you in the day of the Lord Jesus.[z]

¹⁵Because I was confident of this, I planned to visit you[a] first so that you might benefit twice.[b] ¹⁶I planned to visit you on my way[c] to Macedonia[d] and to come back to you from Macedonia, and then to have you send me on my way[e] to Judea.[f] ¹⁷When I planned this, did I do it lightly? Or do I make my plans in a worldly manner[g] so that in the same breath I say, "Yes, yes" and "No, no"?

¹⁸But as surely as God is faithful,[h] our message to you is not "Yes" and "No." ¹⁹For the Son of God,[i] Jesus Christ, who was preached among you by me and Silas[b][j] and Timothy,[k] was not "Yes" and "No," but in him it has always[l] been "Yes." ²⁰For no matter how many promises[m] God has made, they are "Yes" in Christ. And so through him the "Amen"[n] is spoken by us to the glory of God.[o] ²¹Now it is God who makes both us and you stand firm[p] in Christ. He anointed[q] us, ²²set his seal[r] of ownership on us, and put his Spirit in our hearts as a deposit, guaranteeing what is to come.[s]

²³I call God as my witness[t] that it was in order to spare you[u] that I did not return to Corinth. ²⁴Not that we lord it over[v] your faith, but we work with you

C 1Co 11:26 ◀▶ Php 1:6
K 1Co 15:56–57 ◀▶ 2Co 2:14
B 1Co 12:1–11 ◀▶ 2Co 5:5
E 1Co 12:28–31 ◀▶ 2Co 3:3

[a] 11 Many manuscripts *your* [b] 19 Greek *Silvanus*, a variant of *Silas*

1:9 All of us carry the sentence of death in our bodies because we are descendants of Adam and because of our individual rebellion against our Creator. Yet Paul reminds us that our hope is not based in ourselves, but resides in Christ's victory on the cross over death and sin.

1:14 Paul rejoices in their mutual salvation in Jesus Christ and confidently awaits "the day of the Lord Jesus" when all believers will leave their mortal, corrupt bodies behind and receive glorious, resurrection bodies like Jesus had when he rose from the grave (see 1Co 15:42–44).

for your joy, because it is by faith you stand firm.ʷ ¹So I made up my mind that I would not make another painful visit to you.ˣ ²For if I grieve you,ʸ who is left to make me glad but you whom I have grieved? ³I wrote as I didᶻ so that when I came I should not be distressedᵃ by those who ought to make me rejoice. I had confidenceᵇ in all of you, that you would all share my joy. ⁴For I wrote youᶜ out of great distress and anguish of heart and with many tears, not to grieve you but to let you know the depth of my love for you.

Forgiveness for the Sinner

⁵If anyone has caused grief,ᵈ he has not so much grieved me as he has grieved all of you, to some extent—not to put it too severely. ⁶The punishmentᵉ inflicted on him by the majority is sufficient for him. ⁷Now instead, you ought to forgive and comfort him,ᶠ so that he will not be overwhelmed by excessive sorrow. ⁸I urge you, therefore, to reaffirm your love for him. ⁹The reason I wrote youᵍ was to see if you would stand the test and be obedient in everything.ʰ ¹⁰If you forgive anyone, I also forgive him. And what I have forgiven—if there was anything to forgive—I have forgiven in the sight of Christ for your sake, ¹¹in order that Satanⁱ might not outwit us. For we are not unaware of his schemes.ʲ

Ministers of the New Covenant

¹²Now when I went to Troasᵏ to preach the gospel of Christˡ and found that the Lord had opened a doorᵐ for me, ¹³I still had no peace of mind,ⁿ because I did not find my brother Titusᵒ there. So I said good-by to them and went on to Macedonia.ᵖ

¹⁴But thanks be to God,ᑫ who always leads us in triumphal procession in Christ and through us spreads everywhere the fragranceʳ of the knowledgeˢ of him. ¹⁵For we are to God the aromaᵗ of Christ among those who are being saved and those who are perishing.ᵘ ¹⁶To the one we are the smell of death;ᵛ to the other, the fragrance of life. And who is equal to

such a task?ʷ ¹⁷Unlike so many, we do not peddle the word of God for profit.ˣ On the contrary, in Christ we speak before God with sincerity,ʸ like men sent from God.ᶻ

Are we beginning to commend ourselvesᵃ again? Or do we need, like some people, letters of recommendationᵇ to you or from you? ²You yourselves are our letter, written on our hearts, known and read by everybody.ᶜ ³You show that you are a letter from Christ, the result of our ministry, written not with ink but with the Spirit of the living God,ᵈ not on tablets of stoneᵉ but on tablets of human hearts.ᶠ

⁴Such confidenceᵍ as this is ours through Christ before God. ⁵Not that we are competent in ourselvesʰ to claim anything for ourselves, but our competence comes from God.ⁱ ⁶He has made us competent as ministers of a new covenantʲ—not of the letterᵏ but of the Spirit; for the letter kills, but the Spirit gives life.ˡ

The Glory of the New Covenant

⁷Now if the ministry that brought death,ᵐ which was engraved in letters on stone, came with glory, so that the Israelites could not look steadily at the face of Moses because of its glory,ⁿ fading though it was, ⁸will not the ministry of the Spirit be even more glorious? ⁹If the ministry that condemns menᵒ is glorious, how much more glorious is the ministry that brings righteousness!ᵖ ¹⁰For what was glorious has no glory now in comparison with the surpassing glory. ¹¹And if what was fading away came with glory, how much greater is the glory of that which lasts!

¹²Therefore, since we have such a hope,ᑫ we are very bold.ʳ ¹³We are not like Moses, who would put a veil over his faceˢ to keep the Israelites from gazing at it while the radiance was fading away. ¹⁴But their minds were made dull,ᵗ for to this day the same veil remains when the old covenantᵘ is read.ᵛ It has not been removed, because only in Christ is it taken away. ¹⁵Even to this day when Mo-

ses is read, a veil covers their hearts. ¹⁶But whenever anyone turns to the Lord,ʷ the veil is taken away.ˣ ¹⁷Now the Lord is the Spirit,ʸ and where the Spirit of the Lord is, there is freedom.ᶻ ¹⁸And we, who with unveiled faces all reflectᶜᵃ the Lord's glory,ᵇ are being transformed into his likenessᶜ with ever-increasing glory, which comes from the Lord, who is the Spirit.

Treasures in Jars of Clay

4 Therefore, since through God's mercyᵈ we have this ministry, we do not lose heart.ᵉ ²Rather, we have renounced secret and shameful ways;ᶠ we do not use deception, nor do we distort the word of God.ᵍ On the contrary, by setting forth the truth plainly we commend ourselves to every man's conscienceʰ in the sight of God. ³And even if our gospelⁱ is veiled,ʲ it is veiled to those who are perishing.ᵏ ⁴The godˡ of this ageᵐ has blindedⁿ the minds of unbelievers, so that they cannot see the light of the gospel of the glory of Christ,ᵒ who is the image of God.ᵖ ⁵For we do not preach ourselves,ᑫ but Jesus Christ as Lord,ʳ and ourselves as your servantsˢ for Jesus' sake. ⁶For God, who said, "Let light shine out of darkness,"ᵈᵗ made his light shine in our heartsᵘ to give us the light of the knowledge of the glory of God in the face of Christ.ᵛ

⁷But we have this treasure in jars of clayʷ to show that this all-surpassing power is from Godˣ and not from us. ⁸We are hard pressed on every side,ʸ but not crushed; perplexed,ᶻ but not in despair; ⁹persecuted,ᵃ but not abandoned;ᵇ struck

D 1Co 3:16–17 ◄ ► 2Co 6:16
J Ro 15:13 ◄ ► Gal 5:22
N 1Co 12:1–13 ◄ ► 2Co 11:4
W 2Co 3:6–11 ◄ ► 2Co 6:6
S 1Co 6:11 ◄ ► Gal 1:6
C 1Co 2:14 ◄ ► 2Co 5:14
H 2Co 2:15–16 ◄ ► 2Co 5:10–11
N 2Co 2:15–16 ◄ ► 2Co 6:2
J 2Co 2:14 ◄ ► 2Co 4:16–18

3:16 ʷ Ro 11:23; ˣ Ex 34:34; Isa 25:7
3:17 ʸ Isa 61:1,2; Gal 4:6,7 ᶻ S Jn 8:32
3:18 ᵃ 1Co 13:12 ᵇ Jn 17:22,24; 2Co 4:4,6 ᶜ S Ro 8:29
4:1 ᵈ 1Co 7:25; 1Ti 1:13,16 ᵉ ver 16; Ps 18:45; Isa 40:31
4:2 ᶠ Ro 6:21; S 1Co 4:5 ᵍ 2Co 2:17; S Heb 4:12 ʰ 2Co 5:11
4:3 ⁱ S 2Co 2:12 ʲ 2Co 3:14 ᵏ S 1Co 1:18
4:4 ˡ S Jn 12:31 ᵐ S 1Co 1:20 ⁿ 2Co 3:14 ᵒ ver 6 ᵖ S Jn 14:9
4:5 ᑫ 1Co 1:13 ʳ 1Co 1:23 ˢ 1Co 9:19
4:6 ᵗ Ge 1:3; Ps 18:28 ᵘ 2Pe 1:19 ᵛ ver 4
4:7 ʷ Job 4:19; Isa 64:8; 2Ti 2:20 ˣ Jdg 7:2; 1Co 2:5; 2Co 6:7
4:8 ʸ 2Co 7:5 ᶻ Gal 4:20
4:9 ᵃ Jn 15:20; Ro 8:35 ᵇ Heb 13:5 ᶜ Ps 37:24; Pr 24:16
4:10 ᵈ S Ro 6:6; S 2Co 1:5 ᵉ S Ro 6:5
4:11 ᶠ Ro 8:36
4:12 ᵍ 2Co 13:9
4:13 ʰ Ps 116:10 ⁱ 1Co 12:9
4:14 ʲ S Ac 2:24 ᵏ 1Th 4:14 ˡ Eph 5:27; Col 1:22; Jude 24
4:15 ᵐ 2Co 1:11; 9:11
4:16 ⁿ ver 1; Ps 18:45 ᵒ Ro 7:22 ᵖ Ps 103:5; Isa 40:31; Col 3:10
4:17 ᑫ Ps 30:5; Ro 8:18; 1Pe 1:6,7
4:18 ʳ 2Co 5:7; Ro 8:24; Heb 11:1
5:1 ˢ 1Co 15:47 ᵗ Isa 38:12; 2Pe 1:13,14
5:2 ᵘ ver 4; Ro 8:23 ᵛ ver 4; 1Co 15:53, 54
5:4 ʷ ver 2; Ro 8:23

down, but not destroyed.ᶜ ¹⁰We always carry around in our body the death of Jesus,ᵈ so that the life of Jesus may also be revealed in our body.ᵉ ¹¹For we who are alive are always being given over to death for Jesus' sake,ᶠ so that his life may be revealed in our mortal body. ¹²So then, death is at work in us, but life is at work in you.ᵍ

¹³It is written: "I believed; therefore I have spoken."ᵉʰ With that same spirit of faithⁱ we also believe and therefore speak, ¹⁴because we know that the one who raised the Lord Jesus from the deadʲ will also raise us with Jesusᵏ and present us with you in his presence.ˡ ¹⁵All this is for your benefit, so that the grace that is reaching more and more people may cause thanksgivingᵐ to overflow to the glory of God.

¹⁶Therefore we do not lose heart.ⁿ Though outwardly we are wasting away, yet inwardlyᵒ we are being renewedᵖ day by day. ¹⁷For our light and momentary troubles are achieving for us an eternal glory that far outweighs them all.ᑫ ¹⁸So we fix our eyes not on what is seen, but on what is unseen.ʳ For what is seen is temporary, but what is unseen is eternal.

Our Heavenly Dwelling

5 Now we know that if the earthlyˢ tentᵗ we live in is destroyed, we have a building from God, an eternal house in heaven, not built by human hands. ²Meanwhile we groan,ᵘ longing to be clothed with our heavenly dwelling,ᵛ ³because when we are clothed, we will not be found naked. ⁴For while we are in this tent, we groanʷ and are burdened, because we do not wish to be unclothed but to be clothed with our heavenly

T 2Co 1:6–9 ◄ ► 2Co 4:17
F 2Co 1:9 ◄ ► Php 3:11–15
J 2Co 4:8–10 ◄ ► 2Co 7:4
T 2Co 4:10–11 ◄ ► 2Co 12:7–10
U 1Co 2:9 ◄ ► 2Co 6:17

ᶜ 18 Or contemplate ᵈ 6 Gen. 1:3 ᵉ 13 Psalm 116:10

4:14 Paul reminds us that God raised Jesus from the dead and will also resurrect us. Paul also indicates that there will be a presentation of some kind, possibly after the rapture at the glorious marriage supper of the Lamb in heaven (see Rev 19:7–9).

5:1–2 This passage teaches that our heavenly home and resurrection body will replace the "earthly tent we live in" (5:1) because "the perishable must clothe itself with the imperishable, and the mortal with immortality" (1Co 15:53). Paul also says that our spirits inwardly long for this change.

dwelling,ˣ so that what is mortal may be swallowed up by life. ⁵Now it is God who has made us for this very purpose and has given us the Spirit as a deposit, guaranteeing what is to come.ʸ

⁶Therefore we are always confident and know that as long as we are at home in the body we are away from the Lord. ⁷We live by faith, not by sight.ᶻ ⁸We are confident, I say, and would prefer to be away from the body and at home with the Lord.ᵃ ⁹So we make it our goal to please him,ᵇ whether we are at home in the body or away from it. ¹⁰For we must all appear before the judgment seat of Christ, that each one may receive what is due himᶜ for the things done while in the body, whether good or bad.

The Ministry of Reconciliation

¹¹Since, then, we know what it is to fear the Lord,ᵈ we try to persuade men. What we are is plain to God, and I hope it is also plain to your conscience.ᵉ ¹²We are not trying to commend ourselves to you again,ᶠ but are giving you an opportunity to take pride in us,ᵍ so that you can answer those who take pride in what is seen rather than in what is in the heart. ¹³If we are out of our mind,ʰ it is for the sake of God; if we are in our right mind, it is for you. ¹⁴For Christ's love compels us, because we are convinced that one died for all, and therefore all died.ⁱ ¹⁵And he died for all, that those who live should no longer live for themselvesʲ but for him who died for themᵏ and was raised again.

¹⁶So from now on we regard no one from a worldlyˡ point of view. Though we once regarded Christ in this way, we do so no longer. ¹⁷Therefore, if anyone is in Christ,ᵐ he is a new creation;ⁿ the old has gone, the new has come!ᵒ ¹⁸All this is from God,ᵖ who reconciled us to himself through Christᑫ and gave us the ministry of reconciliation: ¹⁹that God was reconciling the world to himself in Christ, not counting men's sins against them.ʳ And he has committed to us the message of reconciliation. ²⁰We are therefore Christ's ambassadors,ˢ as though God were making his appeal through us.ᵗ We implore you on Christ's behalf: Be reconciled to God.ᵘ ²¹God made him who had no sinᵛ to be sinᶠ for us, so that in him we might become the righteousness of God.ʷ

6 As God's fellow workersˣ we urge you not to receive God's grace in vain.ʸ ²For he says,

"In the time of my favor I heard you,
and in the day of salvation I helped you."ᵍᶻ

I tell you, now is the time of God's favor, now is the day of salvation.

Paul's Hardships

³We put no stumbling block in anyone's path,ᵃ so that our ministry will not be discredited. ⁴Rather, as servants of God we commend ourselves in every way: in great endurance; in troubles, hardships and distresses; ⁵in beatings, im-

---

Cross references:

5:4 ˣver 2; 1Co 15:53,54
5:5 ʸRo 8:23; 2Co 1:22; Eph 1:13,14
5:7 ᶻ1Co 13:12; ᵃ2Co 4:18
5:8 ᵃS Jn 12:26
5:9 ᵇRo 14:18; Eph 5:10; Col 1:10; 1Th 5:1
5:10 ᶜS Mt 16:27; Ac 10:42; Ro 2:16; 14:10; Eph 6:8
5:11 ᵈJob 23:15; Heb 10:31; 12:29; Jude 23 ᵉ2Co 4:2
5:12 ᶠS 2Co 3:1 ᵍ2Co 1:14
5:13 ʰ2Co 11:1, 16,17; 12:11
5:14 ⁱRo 6:6,7; Gal 2:20; Col 3:3
5:15 ʲRo 14:7-9 ᵏRo 4:25
5:16 ˡ2Co 10:4; 11:18
5:17 ᵐS Ro 16:3 ⁿS Jn 1:13; S Ro 6:4; Gal 6:15 ᵒIsa 65:17; Rev 21:4,5
5:18 ᵖS Ro 11:36 ᑫS Ro 5:10
5:19 ʳS Ro 4:8
5:20 ˢ2Co 6:1; Eph 6:20 ᵗver 18 ᵘIsa 27:5
5:21 ᵛHeb 4:15; 7:26; 1Pe 2:22,24; 1Jn 3:5 ʷS Ro 1:17; S 1Co 1:30

6:1 ˣS 1Co 3:9; 2Co 5:20 ʸ1Co 15:2
6:2 ᶻIsa 49:8; Ps 69:13; Isa 55:6
6:3 ᵃS Mt 5:29; Ro 14:13,20; 1Co 8:9,13; 9:12; 10:32

B 2Co 1:21–22 ◄► Gal 3:5
J 1Co 4:5 ◄► Heb 9:27
H 2Co 4:3 ◄► 2Co 11:15
J 1Co 4:4–5 ◄► 2Ti 4:1
S 1Co 15:33–34 ◄► 2Co 5:15
A Ro 8:5–9 ◄► 2Co 13:5
C 2Co 4:3–4 ◄► Gal 5:19–21
D 1Co 15:3 ◄► 2Co 5:18–21
W Ro 10:6–13 ◄► Gal 3:6–9
S 2Co 5:10 ◄► 2Co 6:14

D 2Co 5:14–15 ◄► 2Co 9:15
L 1Co 15:3 ◄► 2Co 6:2
L 2Co 5:18–21 ◄► 2Co 9:15
N 2Co 4:3–4 ◄► 1Th 5:2–3

ᶠ21 Or *be a sin offering* ᵍ2 Isaiah 49:8

5:8 Paul affirms the clear teaching of Scripture that the moment a believer dies their spirit is taken joyfully into the presence of Jesus Christ in heaven (Paradise). Though our bodies "sleep" in the grave, our spirits do not sleep but are consciously joined with Christ in heaven (see Lk 23:43).

5:9–11 All believers should strive to live righteously because of our love for Christ. In addition, God promises rewards to faithful believers after they are raptured and stand at the judgment seat of Christ (5:10). This accounting has nothing to do with sin and justification. The payment for the penalty for sin is credited to a believer fully and forever through faith in Christ. This judgment refers to the things we have done with our lives while we are Christians (see 1Co 3:11–15). As believers we are given certain responsibilities, and this judgment will address our faithfulness to Christ's commands. God knows our hearts and motives, and this should motivate us to persuade others to faith in Christ while there is still time to repent. See the article on "The Judgments of God" on p. 1234.

prisonments[b] and riots; in hard work, sleepless nights and hunger;[c] [6]in purity, understanding, patience and kindness; in the Holy Spirit[d] and in sincere love;[e] [7]in truthful speech[f] and in the power of God;[g] with weapons of righteousness[h] in the right hand and in the left; [8]through glory and dishonor,[i] bad report[j] and good report; genuine, yet regarded as impostors;[k] [9]known, yet regarded as unknown; dying,[l] and yet we live on;[m] beaten, and yet not killed; [10]sorrowful, yet always rejoicing;[n] poor, yet making many rich;[o] having nothing,[p] and yet possessing everything.[q]

[11]We have spoken freely to you, Corinthians, and opened wide our hearts to you.[r] [12]We are not withholding our affection from you, but you are withholding yours from us. [13]As a fair exchange—I speak as to my children[s]—open wide your hearts[t] also.

Do Not Be Yoked With Unbelievers

[14]Do not be yoked together[u] with unbelievers.[v] For what do righteousness and wickedness have in common? Or what fellowship can light have with darkness?[w] [15]What harmony is there between Christ and Belial[h]?[x] What does a believer[y] have in common with an unbeliever?[z] [16]What agreement is there between the temple of God and idols?[a] For we are the temple[b] of the living God.[c] As God has said: "I will live with them and walk among them, and I will be their God, and they will be my people."[i][d]

[17]"Therefore come out from them[e]
 and be separate,
  says the Lord.
Touch no unclean thing,
 and I will receive you."[j][f]
[18]"I will be a Father to you,
 and you will be my sons and
  daughters,[g]
  says the Lord Almighty."[k][h]

7 Since we have these promises,[i] dear friends,[j] let us purify ourselves from everything that contaminates body and spirit, perfecting holiness[k] out of reverence for God.

W 2Co 3:17–18 ◀ ▶ 2Co 13:14
S 2Co 5:15 ◀ ▶ 2Co 7:1
D 2Co 3:17 ◀ ▶ 2Co 13:14
U 2Co 5:1 ◀ ▶ Gal 6:16
S 2Co 6:14 ◀ ▶ 2Co 13:11

6:5 [b] Ac 16:23; 2Co 11:23-25
[i] 1Co 4:11
6:6 [d] 1Co 2:4; 1Th 1:5 [e] Ro 12:9; 1Ti 1:5
6:7 [f] 2Co 4:2 [g] 2Co 4:7 [h] Ro 13:12; 2Co 10:4; Eph 6:10-18
6:8 [i] 1Co 4:10 [j] 1Co 4:13 [k] Mt 27:63
6:9 [l] S Ro 8:36 [m] 2Co 1:8-10; 4:10, 11
6:10 [n] S Mt 5:12; 2Co 7:4; Php 2:17; 4:4; Col 1:24; 1Th 1:6 [o] 2Co 8:9 [p] Ac 3:6 [q] Ro 8:32; 1Co 3:21
6:11 [r] 2Co 7:3
6:13 [s] S 1Th 2:11 [t] 2Co 7:2
6:14 [u] Ge 24:3; Dt 22:10; 1Co 5:9, 10 [v] 1Co 6:6 [w] Eph 5:7,11; 1Jn 1:6
6:15 [x] 1Co 10:21 [y] Ac 5:14 [z] 1Co 6:6
6:16 [a] 1Co 10:21 [b] S 1Co 3:16 [c] S Mt 16:16 [d] Lev 26:12; Jer 32:38; Eze 37:27; Rev 21:3
6:17 [e] Rev 18:4 [f] Isa 52:11; Eze 20:34,41
6:18 [g] Ex 4:22; 2Sa 7:14; 1Ch 17:13; Isa 43:6; S Ro 8:14 [h] 2Sa 7:8
7:1 [i] 2Co 6:17,18 [j] S 1Co 10:14 [k] 1Th 4:7; 1Pe 1:15,16
7:2 [l] 2Co 6:12,13
7:3 [m] 2Co 6:11,12; Php 1:7
7:4 [n] ver 14; 2Co 8:24 [o] ver 13 [p] S 2Co 6:10
7:5 [q] 2Co 2:13; S Ac 16:9 [r] 2Co 4:8 [s] Dt 32:25
7:6 [t] 2Co 1:3,4 [u] ver 13; S 2Co 2:13
7:8 [v] 2Co 2:2,4
7:10 [w] Ac 11:18
7:11 [x] ver 7
7:12 [y] ver 8; 2Co 2:3,9 [z] 1Co 5:1,2
7:13 [a] ver 6; S 2Co 2:13
7:14 [b] ver 4

Paul's Joy

[2]Make room for us in your hearts.[l] We have wronged no one, we have corrupted no one, we have exploited no one. [3]I do not say this to condemn you; I have said before that you have such a place in our hearts[m] that we would live or die with you. [4]I have great confidence in you; I take great pride in you.[n] I am greatly encouraged;[o] in all our troubles my joy knows no bounds.[p]

[5]For when we came into Macedonia,[q] this body of ours had no rest, but we were harassed at every turn[r]—conflicts on the outside, fears within.[s] [6]But God, who comforts the downcast,[t] comforted us by the coming of Titus,[u] [7]and not only by his coming but also by the comfort you had given him. He told us about your longing for me, your deep sorrow, your ardent concern for me, so that my joy was greater than ever.

[8]Even if I caused you sorrow by my letter,[v] I do not regret it. Though I did regret it—I see that my letter hurt you, but only for a little while— [9]yet now I am happy, not because you were made sorry, but because your sorrow led you to repentance. For you became sorrowful as God intended and so were not harmed in any way by us. [10]Godly sorrow brings repentance that leads to salvation[w] and leaves no regret, but worldly sorrow brings death. [11]See what this godly sorrow has produced in you: what earnestness, what eagerness to clear yourselves, what indignation, what alarm, what longing, what concern,[x] what readiness to see justice done. At every point you have proved yourselves to be innocent in this matter. [12]So even though I wrote to you,[y] it was not on account of the one who did the wrong[z] or of the injured party, but rather that before God you could see for yourselves how devoted to us you are. [13]By all this we are encouraged.

In addition to our own encouragement, we were especially delighted to see how happy Titus[a] was, because his spirit has been refreshed by all of you. [14]I had boasted to him about you,[b] and you have

---

J 2Co 4:16–18 ◀ ▶ 2Co 8:1–2
R Ac 26:20 ◀ ▶ Jas 4:8

---

[h] 15 Greek *Beliar*, a variant of *Belial*   [i] 16 Lev. 26:12; Jer. 32:38; Ezek. 37:27   [j] 17 Isaiah 52:11; Ezek. 20:34,41   [k] 18 2 Samuel 7:14; 7:8

not embarrassed me. But just as everything we said to you was true, so our boasting about you to Titusᶜ has proved to be true as well. ¹⁵And his affection for you is all the greater when he remembers that you were all obedient,ᵈ receiving him with fear and trembling.ᵉ ¹⁶I am glad I can have complete confidence in you.ᶠ

Generosity Encouraged

8 And now, brothers, we want you to know about the grace that God has given the Macedonianᵍ churches. ²Out of the most severe trial, their overflowing joy and their extreme poverty welled up in rich generosity.ʰ ³For I testify that they gave as much as they were able,ⁱ and even beyond their ability. Entirely on their own, ⁴they urgently pleaded with us for the privilege of sharingʲ in this serviceᵏ to the saints.ˡ ⁵And they did not do as we expected, but they gave themselves first to the Lord and then to us in keeping with God's will. ⁶So we urgedᵐ Titus,ⁿ since he had earlier made a beginning, to bring also to completionᵒ this act of grace on your part. ⁷But just as you excel in everythingᵖ—in faith, in speech, in knowledge,۹ in complete earnestness and in your love for usʳ—see that you also excel in this grace of giving.

⁸I am not commanding you,ʳ but I want to test the sincerity of your love by comparing it with the earnestness of others. ⁹For you know the graceˢ of our Lord Jesus Christ,ᵗ that though he was rich, yet for your sakes he became poor,ᵘ so that you through his poverty might become rich.ᵛ

¹⁰And here is my adviceʷ about what is best for you in this matter: Last year you were the first not only to give but also to have the desire to do so.ˣ ¹¹Now finish the work, so that your eager willingnessʸ to do it may be matched by your completion of it, according to your means. ¹²For if the willingness is there, the gift is acceptable according to what one has,ᶻ not according to what he does not have.

¹³Our desire is not that others might be relieved while you are hard pressed, but that there might be equality. ¹⁴At the present time your plenty will supply what they need,ᵃ so that in turn their plenty will supply what you need. Then there will be equality, ¹⁵as it is written: "He who gathered much did not have too much, and he who gathered little did not have too little."ᵐᵇ

Titus Sent to Corinth

¹⁶I thank God,ᶜ who put into the heartᵈ of Titusᵉ the same concern I have for you. ¹⁷For Titus not only welcomed our appeal, but he is coming to you with much enthusiasm and on his own initiative.ᶠ ¹⁸And we are sending along with him the brotherᵍ who is praised by all the churchesʰ for his service to the gospel.ⁱ ¹⁹What is more, he was chosen by the churches to accompany usʲ as we carry the offering, which we administer in order to honor the Lord himself and to show our eagerness to help.ᵏ ²⁰We want to avoid any criticism of the way we administer this liberal gift. ²¹For we are taking pains to do what is right, not only in the eyes of the Lord but also in the eyes of men.ˡ

²²In addition, we are sending with them our brother who has often proved to us in many ways that he is zealous, and now even more so because of his great confidence in you. ²³As for Titus,ᵐ he is my partnerⁿ and fellow workerᵒ among you; as for our brothers,ᵖ they are representatives of the churches and an honor to Christ. ²⁴Therefore show these men the proof of your love and the reason for our pride in you,۹ so that the churches can see it.

9 There is no needʳ for me to write to you about this serviceˢ to the saints.ᵗ ²For I know your eagerness to help,ᵘ and I have been boastingᵛ about it to the Macedonians, telling them that since last yearʷ you in Achaiaˣ were ready to give; and your enthusiasm has stirred most of them to action. ³But I am sending the brothersʸ in order that our boasting about you in this matter should not prove hollow, but that you may be ready, as I said you would be.ᶻ ⁴For if any Macedoniansᵃ come with me and find you unprepared, we—not to say anything about you—would be ashamed of having been so confident. ⁵So I thought it necessary to urge the brothersᵇ to visit you in advance and finish the arrangements for the generous gift you had promised. Then

---

¹⁷ Some manuscripts in our love for you   *ᵐ 15* Exodus 16:18

it will be ready as a generous gift, not as one grudgingly given.

Sowing Generously

⁶Remember this: Whoever sows sparingly will also reap sparingly, and whoever sows generously will also reap generously. ⁷Each man should give what he has decided in his heart to give, not reluctantly or under compulsion, for God loves a cheerful giver. ⁸And God is able to make all grace abound to you, so that in all things at all times, having all that you need, you will abound in every good work. ⁹As it is written:

> "He has scattered abroad his gifts to the poor;
> his righteousness endures forever."

¹⁰Now he who supplies seed to the sower and bread for food will also supply and increase your store of seed and will enlarge the harvest of your righteousness. ¹¹You will be made rich in every way so that you can be generous on every occasion, and through us your generosity will result in thanksgiving to God.

¹²This service that you perform is not only supplying the needs of God's people but is also overflowing in many expressions of thanks to God. ¹³Because of the service by which you have proved yourselves, men will praise God for the obedience that accompanies your confession of the gospel of Christ, and for your generosity in sharing with them and with everyone else. ¹⁴And in their prayers for you their hearts will go out to you, because of the surpassing grace God has given you. ¹⁵Thanks be to God for his indescribable gift!

Paul's Defense of His Ministry

10 By the meekness and gentleness of Christ, I appeal to you—I, Paul, who am "timid" when face to face with you, but "bold" when away! ²I beg you that when I come I may not have to be as bold as I expect to be toward some people who think that we live by the standards of this world. ³For though we live in the world, we do not wage war as the world does. ⁴The weapons we fight with are not the weapons of the world. On the contrary, they have divine power to demolish strongholds. ⁵We demolish arguments and every pretension that sets itself up against the knowledge of God, and we take captive every thought to make it obedient to Christ. ⁶And we will be ready to punish every act of disobedience, once your obedience is complete.

⁷You are looking only on the surface of things. If anyone is confident that he belongs to Christ, he should consider again that we belong to Christ just as much as he. ⁸For even if I boast somewhat freely about the authority the Lord gave us for building you up rather than pulling you down, I will not be ashamed of it. ⁹I do not want to seem to be trying to frighten you with my letters. ¹⁰For some say, "His letters are weighty and forceful, but in person he is unimpressive and his speaking amounts to nothing." ¹¹Such people should realize that what we are in our letters when we are absent, we will be in our actions when we are present.

¹²We do not dare to classify or compare ourselves with some who commend themselves. When they measure themselves by themselves and compare themselves with themselves, they are not wise. ¹³We, however, will not boast beyond proper limits, but will confine our boasting to the field God has assigned to us, a field that reaches even to you. ¹⁴We are not going too far in our boasting, as would be the case if we had not come to you, for we did get as far as you with the gospel of Christ. ¹⁵Neither do we go beyond our limits by boasting of work done by others. Our hope is that, as your faith continues to grow, our area of activity among you will greatly expand, ¹⁶so that we can preach the gospel in the regions beyond you. For we do not want to boast about work already done in another man's territory. ¹⁷But, "Let him

n 9 *Psalm 112:9* *o* 7 *Or Look at the obvious facts* *p* 13-15 *Or* ¹³*We, however, will not boast about things that cannot be measured, but we will boast according to the standard of measurement that the God of measure has assigned us—a measurement that relates even to you.* ¹⁴ . . . ¹⁵*Neither do we boast about things that cannot be measured in regard to the work done by others.*

who boasts boast in the Lord."^{q b} ¹⁸For it is not the one who commends himself^c who is approved, but the one whom the Lord commends.^d

Paul and the False Apostles

11 I hope you will put up with^e a little of my foolishness;^f but you are already doing that. ²I am jealous for you with a godly jealousy. I promised you to one husband,^g to Christ, so that I might present you^h as a pure virgin to him. ³But I am afraid that just as Eve was deceived by the serpent's cunning,ⁱ your minds may somehow be led astray from your sincere and pure devotion to Christ.

⁴For if someone comes to you and preaches a Jesus other than the Jesus we preached,^j or if you receive a different spirit^k from the one you received, or a different gospel^l from the one you accepted, you put up with it^m easily enough. ⁵But I do not think I am in the least inferior to those "super-apostles."ⁿ ⁶I may not be a trained speaker,^o but I do have knowledge.^p We have made this perfectly clear to you in every way.

⁷Was it a sin^q for me to lower myself in order to elevate you by preaching the gospel of God^r to you free of charge?^s ⁸I robbed other churches by receiving support from them^t so as to serve you. ⁹And when I was with you and needed something, I was not a burden to anyone, for the brothers who came from Macedonia supplied what I needed.^u I have kept myself from being a burden to you^v in any way, and will continue to do so. ¹⁰As surely as the truth of Christ is in me,^w nobody in the regions of Achaia^x will stop this boasting^y of mine. ¹¹Why? Because I do not love you? God knows^z I do!^a ¹²And I will keep on doing what I am doing in order to cut the ground from under those who want an opportunity to be considered equal with us in the things they boast about.

¹³For such men are false apostles,^b deceitful^c workmen, masquerading as apostles of Christ.^d ¹⁴And no wonder, for Satan^e himself masquerades as an angel of light. ¹⁵It is not surprising, then, if his servants masquerade as servants of righteousness. Their end will be what their actions deserve.^f

Paul Boasts About His Sufferings

¹⁶I repeat: Let no one take me for a fool.^g But if you do, then receive me just as you would a fool, so that I may do a little boasting. ¹⁷In this self-confident boasting I am not talking as the Lord would,^h but as a fool.ⁱ ¹⁸Since many are boasting in the way the world does,^j I too will boast.^k ¹⁹You gladly put up with^l fools since you are so wise!^m ²⁰In fact, you even put up withⁿ anyone who enslaves you^o or exploits you or takes advantage of you or pushes himself forward or slaps you in the face. ²¹To my shame I admit that we were too weak^p for that!

What anyone else dares to boast about—I am speaking as a fool—I also dare to boast about.^q ²²Are they Hebrews? So am I.^r Are they Israelites? So am I.^s Are they Abraham's descendants? So am I.^t ²³Are they servants of Christ?^u (I am out of my mind to talk like this.) I am more. I have worked much harder,^v been in prison more frequently,^w been flogged more severely,^x and been exposed to death again and again.^y ²⁴Five times I received from the Jews the forty lashes^z minus one. ²⁵Three times I was beaten with rods,^a once I was stoned,^b three times I was shipwrecked,^c I spent a night and a day in the open sea, ²⁶I have been constantly on the move. I have been in danger from rivers, in danger from bandits, in danger from my own countrymen,^d in danger from Gentiles; in danger in the city,^e in danger in the country, in danger at sea; and in danger from false brothers.^f ²⁷I have labored and toiled^g and have often gone without sleep; I have known hunger and thirst and have often gone without food;^h I have been cold and naked. ²⁸Besides everything else, I face daily the pressure of my concern for all the churches.ⁱ ²⁹Who is weak, and I do not feel weak?^j Who is led into sin,^k and I do not inwardly burn?

³⁰If I must boast, I will boast^l of the things that show my weakness.^m ³¹The God and Father of the Lord Jesus, who is to be praised forever,ⁿ knows^o that I am not lying. ³²In Damascus the governor under King Aretas had the city of the Dama-

---

G 1Co 3:19–20 ◀ ▶ Gal 2:16
N 2Co 3:17 ◀ ▶ Gal 5:18
H 2Co 5:10–11 ◀ ▶ Gal 5:19–21

scenes guarded in order to arrest me.ᵖ ³³But I was lowered in a basket from a window in the wall and slipped through his hands.ᵈ

Paul's Vision and His Thorn

12 I must go on boasting.ʳ Although there is nothing to be gained, I will go on to visions and revelationsˢ from the Lord. ²I know a man in Christᵗ who fourteen years ago was caught upᵘ to the third heaven.ᵛ Whether it was in the body or out of the body I do not know—God knows.ʷ ³And I know that this man—whether in the body or apart from the body I do not know, but God knows— ⁴was caught upˣ to paradise.ʸ He heard inexpressible things, things that man is not permitted to tell. ⁵I will boast about a man like that, but I will not boast about myself, except about my weaknesses.ᶻ ⁶Even if I should choose to boast,ᵃ I would not be a fool,ᵇ because I would be speaking the truth. But I refrain, so no one will think more of me than is warranted by what I do or say.

⁷To keep me from becoming conceited because of these surpassingly great revelations,ᶜ there was given me a thorn in my flesh,ᵈ a messenger of Satan,ᵉ to torment me. ⁸Three times I pleaded with the Lord to take it away from me.ᶠ ⁹But he said to me, "My graceᵍ is sufficient for you, for my powerʰ is made perfect in weakness."ⁱ Therefore I will boast all the more gladly about my weaknesses, so that Christ's power may rest on me. ¹⁰That is why, for Christ's sake, I delightᵏ in weaknesses, in insults, in hardships,ˡ in persecutions,ᵐ in difficulties. For when I am weak, then I am strong.ⁿ

D *1Co 11:29–32* ◀ ▶ *Php 2:30*
T *2Co 4:17* ◀ ▶ *Heb 5:8*
J *2Co 8:1–2* ◀ ▶ *Eph 5:20*

11:32 ᵖ Ac 9:24
11:33 ᵈ Ac 9:25
12:1 ʳ ver 5,9; 2Co 11:16,30
ˢ ver 7; S 1Co 2:10
12:2 ᵗ S Ro 16:3
ᵘ ver 4; S Ac 8:39
ᵛ Eph 4:10
ʷ 2Co 11:11
12:4 ˣ ver 2
ʸ Lk 23:43; Rev 2:7
12:5 ᶻ ver 9,10; S 1Co 2:3
12:6 ᵃ 2Co 10:8
ᵇ ver 11; 2Co 11:16
12:7 ᶜ ver 1; S 1Co 2:10
ᵈ Nu 33:55
ᵉ S Mt 4:10
12:8 ᶠ Mt 26:39,44
12:9 ᵍ S Ro 3:24
ʰ Php 4:13
ⁱ S 1Co 2:3
ʲ 1Ki 19:12
12:10 ᵏ S Mt 5:12
ˡ 2Co 6:4 m 2Th 1:4
ⁿ 2Co 13:4
12:11 ᵒ 2Co 11:1
ᵖ 2Co 11:5
ᵈ 1Co 15:9,10
12:12 ʳ S Jn 4:48
12:13 ˢ ver 14; 1Co 9:12,18
ᵗ 2Co 11:7
12:14 ᵘ 2Co 13:1
ᵛ 1Co 4:14,15
ʷ Pr 19:14
12:15 ˣ Php 2:17; 1Th 2:8
ʸ 2Co 11:11
12:16 ᶻ 2Co 11:9
12:18 ᵃ 2Co 8:6,16
ᵇ S 2Co 2:13
ᶜ 2Co 8:18
12:19 ᵈ Ro 9:1
ᵉ S 1Co 10:14
ᶠ S Ro 14:19; 2Co 10:8
12:20 ᵍ 2Co 2:1–4
ʰ 1Co 4:21
ⁱ 1Co 1:11; 3:3
ʲ Gal 5:20 ᵏ Ro 1:30
ˡ S Ro 1:29
ᵐ Gal 4:18
ⁿ 1Co 14:33
12:21 ᵒ 2Co 2:1,4
ᵖ 2Co 13:2

Paul's Concern for the Corinthians

¹¹I have made a fool of myself,ᵒ but you drove me to it. I ought to have been commended by you, for I am not in the least inferior to the "super-apostles,"ᵖ even though I am nothing.ᵈ ¹²The things that mark an apostle—signs, wonders and miraclesʳ—were done among you with great perseverance. ¹³How were you inferior to the other churches, except that I was never a burden to you?ˢ Forgive me this wrong!ᵗ

¹⁴Now I am ready to visit you for the third time,ᵘ and I will not be a burden to you, because what I want is not your possessions but you. After all, children should not have to save up for their parents,ᵛ but parents for their children.ʷ ¹⁵So I will very gladly spend for you everything I have and expend myself as well.ˣ If I love you more,ʸ will you love me less? ¹⁶Be that as it may, I have not been a burden to you.ᶻ Yet, crafty fellow that I am, I caught you by trickery! ¹⁷Did I exploit you through any of the men I sent you? ¹⁸I urgedᵃ Titusᵇ to go to you and I sent our brotherᶜ with him. Titus did not exploit you, did he? Did we not act in the same spirit and follow the same course?

¹⁹Have you been thinking all along that we have been defending ourselves to you? We have been speaking in the sight of Godᵈ as those in Christ; and everything we do, dear friends,ᵉ is for your strengthening.ᶠ ²⁰For I am afraid that when I comeᵍ I may not find you as I want you to be, and you may not find me as you want me to be.ʰ I fear that there may be quarreling,ⁱ jealousy, outbursts of anger, factions,ʲ slander,ᵏ gossip,ˡ arroganceᵐ and disorder.ⁿ ²¹I am afraid that when I come again my God will humble me before you, and I will be grievedᵒ over many who have sinned earlierᵖ and have not repented of the impurity, sexual

L *1Co 14:30* ◀ ▶ *Gal 5:5*

12:2–4 Fourteen years previous to this point Paul was given a profound vision in which he was taken up to "the third heaven" (12:2), "paradise" (12:4), the abode of God. Unsure whether he was physically taken to the third heaven to see these remarkable things or whether only his spirit was taken in vision to that place, Paul heard things in his vision that he was forbidden to reveal to the church.

The Bible reveals that there are three heavens. The atmospheric heavens include the high clouds and the sky of our atmosphere (see Ge 1:8; Ps 77:17–18). The second heaven involves outer space beyond our atmosphere that is the abode of the galaxies visible to great telescopes (see Ge 15:5). The third heaven is the heaven where the throne of God exists (see Isa 14:12–14; Eph 4:10; Rev 4:1–11).

Final Warnings

13 This will be my third visit to you.ʳ "Every matter must be established by the testimony of two or three witnesses."ʳˢ ²I already gave you a warning when I was with you the second time. I now repeat it while absent:ᵗ On my return I will not spareᵘ those who sinned earlierᵛ or any of the others, ³since you are demanding proof that Christ is speaking through me.ʷ He is not weak in dealing with you, but is powerful among you. ⁴For to be sure, he was crucified in weakness,ˣ yet he lives by God's power.ʸ Likewise, we are weakᶻ in him, yet by God's power we will live with himᵃ to serve you.

⁵Examine yourselvesᵇ to see whether you are in the faith; test yourselves.ᶜ Do you not realize that Christ Jesus is in youᵈ—unless, of course, you fail the test? ⁶And I trust that you will discover that we have not failed the test. ⁷Now we pray to God that you will not do anything wrong. Not that people will see that we have stood the test but that you will do what is right even though we may seem to have failed. ⁸For we cannot do anything against the truth, but only for the truth. ⁹We are glad whenever we are weakᵉ but you are strong;ᶠ and our prayer is for your perfection.ᵍ ¹⁰This is why I write these things when I am absent, that when I come I may not have to be harshʰ in my use of authority—the authority the Lord gave me for building you up, not for tearing you down.ⁱ

Final Greetings

¹¹Finally, brothers,ʲ good-by. Aim for perfection, listen to my appeal, be of one mind, live in peace.ᵏ And the God of loveˡ and peaceᵐ will be with you.

¹²Greet one another with a holy kiss.ⁿ ¹³All the saints send their greetings.ᵒ

¹⁴May the grace of the Lord Jesus Christ,ᵖ and the love of God,ᵍ and the fellowship of the Holy Spiritʳ be with you all.

A 2Co 5:14 ◀▶ Gal 3:22
O 2Co 10:17–18 ◀▶ Gal 1:8–9

S 2Co 7:1 ◀▶ Gal 2:17–18
D 2Co 6:16 ◀▶ Eph 2:22
F Ro 15:30 ◀▶ Gal 5:22–23
W 2Co 6:6 ◀▶ Gal 3:3

12:21 ᵠS 1Co 6:18
13:1 ʳ2Co 12:14; ˢDt 19:15; S Mt 18:16
13:2 ᵗver 10; ᵘ2Co 1:23; ᵛ2Co 12:21
13:3 ʷMt 10:20; 1Co 5:4
13:4 ˣ1Co 1:25; Php 2:7,8; 1Pe 3:18; ʸRo 1:4; 6:4; 1Co 6:14 ᶻver 9; S 1Co 2:3 ᵃS Ro 6:5
13:5 ᵇ1Co 11:28; ᶜLa 3:40; Jn 6:6; ᵈS Ro 8:10
13:9 ᵉS 1Co 2:3; ᶠ2Co 4:12 ᵍver 11; Eph 4:13
13:10 ʰS 2Co 1:23; ⁱ2Co 10:8
13:11 ʲ1Th 4:1; 2Th 3:1; ᵏS Mk 9:50; ˡ1Jn 4:16; ᵐS Ro 15:33; Eph 6:23
13:12 ⁿS Ro 16:16
13:13 ᵒPhp 4:22
13:14 ᵖS Ro 16:20; 2Co 8:9 ᵍRo 5:5; Jude 21 ʳPhp 2:1
ʳ¹ Deut. 19:15

Galatians

Author: Paul

Theme: Justification comes by faith alone

Date of Writing: C. A.D. 48–53

Outline of Galatians
  I. Introduction (1:1–9)
  II. The Gospel Paul Preached (1:10—2:21)
  III. Legalism and God's Grace (3:1—4:31)
  IV. The Gospel in Practice (5:1—6:10)
  V. Conclusion (6:11–18)

MOST SCHOLARS AGREE that Paul wrote this epistle to the Galatians, but the date and particular destination of this letter have been the subject of much discussion. Some scholars contend that Paul addressed this letter to the churches in north central Asia Minor while he was on his journey to Troas in A.D. 53. These scholars believe that these churches were established during Paul's third missionary journey (see Ac 18:23).

Others contend that this letter is the earliest of Paul's epistles, written about A.D. 48–49, before the Jerusalem council, and addressed to the churches in the southern area of Galatia—Antioch in Pisidia, Iconium, Lystra and Derbe. These were the churches Paul had established on his first missionary journey (see Ac 13—14). Accepting this view would explain the lack of reference to the Jerusalem council's discussion about keeping the Jewish law and having faith in Christ—the very problem that Paul dealt with in this letter. Still others date this book between A.D. 51–53 and suggest that it was written in Corinth or Syrian Antioch.

When Paul wrote this letter, some Jewish Christians were teaching that a number of the Jewish laws and ceremonial practices were still binding on Gentile believers. In response to this argument, Paul pointedly declares that a person is saved by faith in Jesus Christ alone. Carefully summarizing the gospel message in this letter to the Galatians, Paul stresses that salvation comes by the grace of God alone through faith in Christ's completed work on the cross and not through the Law. To support his contention, Paul notes that Abraham was saved by his faith in God alone centuries before the law was revealed through Moses. Paul tells his readers that "it is for freedom that Christ has set us free" (5:1) and encourages them to "stand firm, then" (5:1) and rather "serve one another in love" (5:13).

1

Paul, an apostle[a]—sent not from men nor by man,[b] but by Jesus Christ[c] and God the Father,[d] who raised him from the dead[e]— ²and all the brothers with me,[f]

To the churches in Galatia:[g]

³Grace and peace to you from God our Father and the Lord Jesus Christ,[h] ⁴who gave himself for our sins[i] to rescue us from the present evil age,[j] according to the will of our God and Father,[k] ⁵to whom be glory for ever and ever. Amen.[l]

No Other Gospel

⁶I am astonished that you are so quickly deserting the one who called[m] you by the grace of Christ and are turning to a different gospel[n]— ⁷which is really no gospel at all. Evidently some people are throwing you into confusion[o] and are trying to pervert[p] the gospel of Christ. ⁸But even if we or an angel from heaven should preach a gospel other than the one we preached to you,[q] let him be eternally condemned![r] ⁹As we have already said, so now I say again: If anybody is preaching to you a gospel other than what you accepted,[s] let him be eternally condemned!

¹⁰Am I now trying to win the approval of men, or of God? Or am I trying to please men?[t] If I were still trying to

D 2Co 9:15 ◀ ▶ Gal 2:20
L 2Co 9:15 ◀ ▶ Gal 2:21
O 2Co 13:5 ◀ ▶ Gal 2:16

1:1 ªS 1Co 1:1
 ᵇver 11,12 ᶜver 15,16; S Ac 9:15;
 ᵈver 15,16; S Ac 9:15; 20:24
 ᵉS Ac 2:24
1:2 ᶠPhp 4:21
 ᵍS Ac 16:6
1:3 ʰS Ro 1:7
1:4 ⁱS Mt 20:28; S Ro 4:25; S 1Co 15:3; Gal 2:20
 ʲS 1Co 1:20
 ᵏS Php 4:20
1:5 ˡS Ro 11:36
1:6 ᵐver 15; S Ro 8:28
 ⁿ2Co 11:4
1:7 ᵒAc 15:24; Gal 5:10
 ᵖJer 23:16,36
1:8 ᵠver 11,16; 1Co 15:1; 2Co 11:4; Gal 2:2
 ʳRo 9:3
1:9 ˢRo 16:17
1:10 ᵗS Ro 2:29
1:11 ᵘ1Co 15:1
 ᵛver 8
1:12 ʷver 1
 ˣver 15; S 1Co 2:10
 ʸ1Co 11:23; 15:3
1:13 ᶻAc 26:4,5
 ªS 1Co 10:32
 ᵇS Ac 8:3
1:14 ᶜS Ac 21:20
 ᵈMt 15:2
1:15 ᵉIsa 49:1,5; Jer 1:5 ᶠS Ac 9:15; S Ro 8:28
1:16 ᵍS Ac 9:15; Gal 2:9 ʰMt 16:17
1:17 ⁱAc 9:2,19-22
1:18 ʲAc 9:22,23
 ᵏAc 9:26,27
1:19 ˡMt 13:55; S Ac 15:13
1:20 ᵐS Ro 1:9
 ⁿS Ro 9:1
1:21 ᵒS Lk 2:2
 ᵖS Ac 6:9
1:22 ᵠ1Th 2:14
 ʳS Ro 16:3

please men, I would not be a servant of Christ.

Paul Called by God

¹¹I want you to know, brothers,[u] that the gospel I preached[v] is not something that man made up. ¹²I did not receive it from any man,[w] nor was I taught it; rather, I received it by revelation[x] from Jesus Christ.[y]

¹³For you have heard of my previous way of life in Judaism,[z] how intensely I persecuted the church of God[a] and tried to destroy it.[b] ¹⁴I was advancing in Judaism beyond many Jews of my own age and was extremely zealous[c] for the traditions of my fathers.[d] ¹⁵But when God, who set me apart from birth[a][e] and called me[f] by his grace, was pleased ¹⁶to reveal his Son in me so that I might preach him among the Gentiles,[g] I did not consult any man,[h] ¹⁷nor did I go up to Jerusalem to see those who were apostles before I was, but I went immediately into Arabia and later returned to Damascus.[i]

¹⁸Then after three years,[j] I went up to Jerusalem[k] to get acquainted with Peter[b] and stayed with him fifteen days. ¹⁹I saw none of the other apostles—only James,[l] the Lord's brother. ²⁰I assure you before God[m] that what I am writing you is no lie.[n] ²¹Later I went to Syria[o] and Cilicia.[p] ²²I was personally unknown to the churches of Judea[q] that are in Christ.[r] ²³They only heard the report: "The man who formerly persecuted us is now

ᵃ 15 Or from my mother's womb ᵇ 18 Greek Cephas

1:8—9 Paul's warning prophetically foreshadows the rise of false cults and religions that would attack the church, claiming that God had given them an additional revelation to supplement the teachings of the Bible. These cults, as diverse as the first-century Gnostics to the modern-day Mormons, have claimed that these new messages came from angels. Note that Paul specifically warned against those who would claim an angel visitant provided a new "gospel." Paul's condemnation of such a claimant was clear: "let him be eternally condemned" (1:9).

preaching the faith[s] he once tried to destroy."[t] 24And they praised God[u] because of me.

Paul Accepted by the Apostles

2 Fourteen years later I went up again to Jerusalem,[v] this time with Barnabas.[w] I took Titus[x] along also. 2I went in response to a revelation[y] and set before them the gospel that I preach among the Gentiles.[z] But I did this privately to those who seemed to be leaders, for fear that I was running or had run my race[a] in vain. 3Yet not even Titus,[b] who was with me, was compelled to be circumcised, even though he was a Greek.[c] 4This matter arose because some false brothers[d] had infiltrated our ranks to spy on[e] the freedom[f] we have in Christ Jesus and to make us slaves. 5We did not give in to them for a moment, so that the truth of the gospel[g] might remain with you.

6As for those who seemed to be important[h]—whatever they were makes no difference to me; God does not judge by external appearance[i]—those men added nothing to my message.[j] 7On the contrary, they saw that I had been entrusted with the task[k] of preaching the gospel to the Gentiles,[c][l] just as Peter[m] had been to the Jews.[d] 8For God, who was at work in the ministry of Peter as an apostle[n] to the Jews, was also at work in my ministry as an apostle[o] to the Gentiles. 9James,[p] Peter[e][q] and John, those reputed to be pillars,[r] gave me and Barnabas[s] the right hand of fellowship when they recognized the grace given to me.[t] They agreed that we should go to the Gentiles,[u] and they to the Jews. 10All they asked was that we should continue to remember the poor,[v] the very thing I was eager to do.

Paul Opposes Peter

11When Peter[w] came to Antioch,[x] I opposed him to his face, because he was clearly in the wrong. 12Before certain men came from James,[y] he used to eat with the Gentiles.[z] But when they arrived, he began to draw back and separate himself from the Gentiles because he was afraid of those who belonged to the circumcision group.[a] 13The other Jews joined him in his hypocrisy, so that by their hypocrisy even Barnabas[b] was led astray.

14When I saw that they were not acting in line with the truth of the gospel,[c] I said to Peter[d] in front of them all, "You are a Jew, yet you live like a Gentile and not like a Jew.[e] How is it, then, that you force Gentiles to follow Jewish customs?[f]

15"We who are Jews by birth[g] and not 'Gentile sinners'[h] 16know that a man is not justified by observing the law,[i] but by faith in Jesus Christ.[j] So we, too, have put our faith in Christ Jesus that we may be justified by faith in Christ and not by observing the law, because by observing the law no one will be justified.[k]

17"If, while we seek to be justified in Christ, it becomes evident that we ourselves are sinners,[l] does that mean that Christ promotes sin? Absolutely not![m] 18If I rebuild what I destroyed, I prove that I am a lawbreaker. 19For through the law I died to the law[n] so that I might live for God.[o] 20I have been crucified with Christ[p] and I no longer live, but Christ lives in me.[q] The life I live in the body, I live by faith in the Son of God,[r] who loved me[s] and gave himself for me.[t] 21I do not set aside the grace of God, for if righteousness could be gained through the law,[u] Christ died for nothing!"[j]

Faith or Observance of the Law

3 You foolish[v] Galatians![w] Who has bewitched you?[x] Before your very eyes Jesus Christ was clearly portrayed as crucified.[y] 2I would like to learn just one thing from you: Did you receive the Spirit[z] by observing the law,[a] or by believing what you heard?[b] 3Are you so foolish? After beginning with the Spirit, are you now trying to attain your goal by human effort? 4Have you suffered so much for nothing—if it really was for

---

F 1Co 1:21 ◄ ► Gal 3:6–9
G 2Co 10:18 ◄ ► Gal 2:21
O Gal 1:8–9 ◄ ► 1Ti 2:5
S 2Co 13:11 ◄ ► Gal 2:20
D Gal 1:4 ◄ ► Gal 3:13
S Gal 2:17–18 ◄ ► Gal 5:6
G Gal 2:16 ◄ ► Gal 3:10–12
L Gal 1:4 ◄ ► Gal 3:8
E 2Co 3:6–18 ◄ ► Gal 3:5
R 2Co 3:3 ◄ ► Gal 4:6
W 2Co 13:14 ◄ ► Gal 3:14

c 7 Greek *uncircumcised*   d 7 Greek *circumcised*; also in verses 8 and 9
e 9 Greek *Cephas*; also in verses 11 and 14   f 21 Some interpreters end the quotation after verse 14.

GALATIANS 3:5

B nothing? ⁵Does God give you his Spirit
E and work miracles[c] among you because
M you observe the law, or because you believe what you heard?[d]
F ⁶Consider Abraham: "He believed God,
W and it was credited to him as righteousness."[g][e] ⁷Understand, then, that those who believe[f] are children of Abraham.[g]
L ⁸The Scripture foresaw that God would justify the Gentiles by faith, and announced the gospel in advance to Abraham: "All nations will be blessed through you."[hh] ⁹So those who have faith[i] are blessed along with Abraham, the man of faith.[j]
G ¹⁰All who rely on observing the law[k] are under a curse,[l] for it is written: "Cursed is everyone who does not continue to do everything written in the
F Book of the Law."[m] ¹¹Clearly no one is justified before God by the law,[n] because, "The righteous will live by faith."[j][o] ¹²The law is not based on faith; on the contrary, "The man who does these things will live
D by them."[k][p] ¹³Christ redeemed us from the curse of the law[q] by becoming a curse for us, for it is written: "Cursed is everyone who is hung on a tree."[r] ¹⁴He re-
P deemed us in order that the blessing
W given to Abraham might come to the Gentiles through Christ Jesus,[s] so that by faith we might receive the promise of the Spirit.[t]

The Law and the Promise

¹⁵Brothers,[u] let me take an example from everyday life. Just as no one can set aside or add to a human covenant that has been duly established, so it is in this case. ¹⁶The promises were spoken to Abraham and to his seed.[v] The Scripture does not say "and to seeds," meaning many people, but "and to your seed,"[m][w] meaning one person, who is Christ. ¹⁷What I mean is this: The law, introduced 430 years[x] later, does not set aside the covenant previously established by

3:5 [c] 1Co 12:10
[d] ver 2,10; Gal 2:16
3:6 [e] Ge 15:6;
S Ro 4:3
3:7 [f] ver 9
[g] S Lk 3:8
3:8 [h] Ge 12:3;
18:18; 22:18; 26:4;
Ac 3:25
3:9 [i] ver 7; Ro 4:16
[j] Ro 4:18-22
3:10 [k] ver 4:5,
Gal 2:16 [l] ver 13;
S Ro 4:15
[m] Dt 27:26;
Jer 11:3
3:11 [n] S Ro 3:28
[o] Hab 2:4;
S Ro 9:30;
Heb 10:38
3:12 [p] Lev 18:5;
S Ro 10:5
3:13 [q] Gal 4:5
[r] Dt 21:23;
S Ac 5:30
3:14 [s] Ro 4:9,16
[t] ver 2; Joel 2:28;
S Jn 20:22;
S Ac 2:33
3:15 [u] S Ro 7:1
3:16 [v] Ge 17:19;
Ps 132:11;
Mic 7:20; Lk 1:55;
Ro 4:13,16; 9:4,8;
Gal 3:29; 4:28
[w] Ge 12:7; 13:15;
17:7,8,10; 24:7
3:17 [x] Ge 15:13,
14; Ex 12:40;
Ac 7:6
3:18 [y] Ro 4:14
3:19 [z] Ro 5:20
[a] ver 16 [b] Dt 33:2;
Ac 7:53 [c] Ex 20:19;
Dt 5:5
3:20 [d] 1Ti 2:5;
Heb 8:6; 9:15;
12:24
3:21 [e] Gal 2:17;
S Ro 7:12 [f] Gal 2:21
3:22 [g] Ro 3:9-19;
11:32
3:23 [h] Ro 11:32
[i] ver 25
3:24 [j] ver 19;
Ro 10:4; S 4:15
[k] Gal 2:16
3:25 [l] S Ro 7:4
3:26 [m] S Ro 8:14
3:27 [n] S Mt 28:19
[o] S Ro 13:14
3:28 [p] 1Co 12:13;
Col 3:11 [q] Ge 1:27;
5:2; Joel 2:29
[r] Jn 10:16; 17:11;
Eph 2:14,15
3:29 [s] 1Co 3:23
[t] ver 16; S Lk 3:8
[u] Ro 8:17 [v] ver 16
4:3 [w] ver 8,9,24,
25; Gal 2:4

God and thus do away with the promise.
¹⁸For if the inheritance depends on the law, then it no longer depends on a promise;[y] but God in his grace gave it to Abraham through a promise.

¹⁹What, then, was the purpose of the law? It was added because of transgressions[z] until the Seed[a] to whom the promise referred had come. The law was put into effect through angels[b] by a mediator.[c] ²⁰A mediator,[d] however, does not represent just one party; but God is one.

²¹Is the law, therefore, opposed to the G
promises of God? Absolutely not![e] For if a law had been given that could impart life, then righteousness would certainly have come by the law.[f] ²²But the Scripture de- A
clares that the whole world is a prisoner F
of sin,[g] so that what was promised, being L
given through faith in Jesus Christ, might W
be given to those who believe.

²³Before this faith came, we were held prisoners[h] by the law, locked up until faith should be revealed.[i] ²⁴So the law F
was put in charge to lead us to Christ[n][j] that we might be justified by faith.[k] ²⁵Now that faith has come, we are no longer under the supervision of the law.[l]

Sons of God

²⁶You are all sons of God[m] through faith L
in Christ Jesus, ²⁷for all of you who were baptized into Christ[n] have clothed yourselves with Christ.[o] ²⁸There is neither Jew nor Greek, slave nor free,[p] male nor female,[q] for you are all one in Christ Jesus.[r] ²⁹If you belong to Christ,[s] then you are Abraham's seed,[t] and heirs[u] according to the promise.[v]

4 What I am saying is that as long as the heir is a child, he is no different from a slave, although he owns the whole estate. ²He is subject to guardians and trustees until the time set by his father. ³So also, when we were children, we were in slavery[w] under the basic princi-

B 2Co 5:5 ◄ ► Eph 1:13–14
E Gal 3:2–3 ◄ ► Gal 4:6
M 2Co 3:5–18 ◄ ► Eph 1:17–19
F Gal 2:16 ◄ ► Gal 3:11
W 2Co 5:14–15 ◄ ► Gal 3:22
L Gal 2:21 ◄ ► Gal 3:22
G Gal 2:21 ◄ ► Gal 3:21
F Gal 3:6–9 ◄ ► Gal 3:22
D Gal 2:20 ◄ ► Gal 4:4–5
P Ac 11:16 ◄   W Gal 3:3 ◄ ► Gal 5:16

G Gal 3:10–12 ◄ ► Gal 5:4
A 2Co 13:5 ◄ ► Eph 2:1–3
F Gal 3:11 ◄ ► Gal 3:24–26
L Gal 3:8 ◄ ► Gal 3:26
W Gal 3:6–9 ◄ ► Eph 2:17–18
F Gal 3:22 ◄ ► Eph 2:8
L Gal 3:22 ◄ ► Eph 1:6–7

[g] 6 Gen. 15:6 [h] 8 Gen. 12:3; 18:18; 22:18 [i] 10 Deut. 27:26 [j] 11 Hab. 2:4 [k] 12 Lev. 18:5 [l] 13 Deut. 21:23 [m] 16 Gen. 12:7; 13:15; 24:7
[n] 24 Or *charge until Christ came*

ples of the world.ˣ ⁴But when the time had fully come,ʸ God sent his Son,ᶻ born of a woman,ᵃ born under law,ᵇ ⁵to redeemᶜ those under law, that we might receive the full rightsᵈ of sons.ᵉ ⁶Because you are sons, God sent the Spirit of his Sonᶠ into our hearts,ᵍ the Spirit who calls out, "Abba,ᵒ Father."ʰ ⁷So you are no longer a slave, but a son; and since you are a son, God has made you also an heir.ⁱ

Paul's Concern for the Galatians

⁸Formerly, when you did not know God,ʲ you were slavesᵏ to those who by nature are not gods.ˡ ⁹But now that you know God—or rather are known by Godᵐ—how is it that you are turning back to those weak and miserable principles? Do you wish to be enslavedⁿ by them all over again?ᵒ ¹⁰You are observing special days and months and seasons and years!ᵖ ¹¹I fear for you, that somehow I have wasted my efforts on you.ᵠ

¹²I plead with you, brothers,ʳ become like me, for I became like you. You have done me no wrong. ¹³As you know, it was because of an illnessˢ that I first preached the gospel to you. ¹⁴Even though my illness was a trial to you, you did not treat me with contempt or scorn. Instead, you welcomed me as if I were an angel of God, as if I were Christ Jesus himself.ᵗ ¹⁵What has happened to all your joy? I can testify that, if you could have done so, you would have torn out your eyes and given them to me. ¹⁶Have I now become your enemy by telling you the truth?ᵘ

¹⁷Those people are zealous to win you over, but for no good. What they want is to alienate you ⌊from us⌋, so that you may be zealous for them.ᵛ ¹⁸It is fine to be zealous, provided the purpose is good, and to be so always and not just when I am with you.ʷ ¹⁹My dear children,ˣ for whom I am again in the pains of childbirth until Christ is formed in you,ʸ ²⁰how I wish I could be with you now and change my tone, because I am perplexed about you!

Hagar and Sarah

²¹Tell me, you who want to be under the law,ᶻ are you not aware of what the law says? ²²For it is written that Abraham had two sons, one by the slave womanᵃ and the other by the free woman.ᵇ ²³His son by the slave woman was born in the ordinary way;ᶜ but his son by the free woman was born as the result of a promise.ᵈ

²⁴These things may be taken figuratively, for the women represent two covenants. One covenant is from Mount Sinai and bears children who are to be slaves: This is Hagar. ²⁵Now Hagar stands for Mount Sinai in Arabia and corresponds to the present city of Jerusalem, because she is in slavery with her children. ²⁶But the Jerusalem that is aboveᵉ is free, and she is our mother. ²⁷For it is written:

> "Be glad, O barren woman,
>   who bears no children;
> break forth and cry aloud,
>   you who have no labor pains;
> because more are the children of the
>   desolate woman
> than of her who has a husband."ᵖᶠ

²⁸Now you, brothers, like Isaac, are children of promise.ᵍ ²⁹At that time the son born in the ordinary wayʰ persecuted the son born by the power of the Spirit.ⁱ It is the same now. ³⁰But what does the Scripture say? "Get rid of the slave woman and her son, for the slave woman's son will never share in the inheritance with the free woman's son."ᵠʲ ³¹Therefore, brothers, we are not children of the slave woman,ᵏ but of the free woman.ˡ

Freedom in Christ

5 It is for freedom that Christ has set us free.ᵐ Stand firm,ⁿ then, and do not let yourselves be burdened again by a yoke of slavery.ᵒ

²Mark my words! I, Paul, tell you that if you let yourselves be circumcised,ᵖ Christ will be of no value to you at all. ³Again I declare to every man who lets himself be circumcised that he is obligated to obey the whole law.ᵠ ⁴You who are trying to be justified by lawʳ have been alienated from Christ; you have

---

D *Gal 3:13* ◀ ▶ *Eph 1:6–7*
E *Gal 3:5* ◀ ▶ *Gal 5:5*
R *Gal 3:2–3* ◀ ▶ *Gal 4:29*

R *Gal 4:6* ◀ ▶ *Eph 1:13–14*
G *Gal 3:21* ◀ ▶ *Eph 2:5*

o 6 Aramaic for *Father* *p* 27 Isaiah 54:1 *q* 30 Gen. 21:10

fallen away from grace. ⁵But by faith we eagerly await through the Spirit the righteousness for which we hope. ⁶For in Christ Jesus neither circumcision nor uncircumcision has any value. The only thing that counts is faith expressing itself through love.

⁷You were running a good race. Who cut in on you and kept you from obeying the truth? ⁸That kind of persuasion does not come from the one who calls you. ⁹"A little yeast works through the whole batch of dough." ¹⁰I am confident in the Lord that you will take no other view. The one who is throwing you into confusion will pay the penalty, whoever he may be. ¹¹Brothers, if I am still preaching circumcision, why am I still being persecuted? In that case the offense of the cross has been abolished. ¹²As for those agitators, I wish they would go the whole way and emasculate themselves!

¹³You, my brothers, were called to be free. But do not use your freedom to indulge the sinful nature; rather, serve one another in love. ¹⁴The entire law is summed up in a single command: "Love your neighbor as yourself." ¹⁵If you keep on biting and devouring each other, watch out or you will be destroyed by each other.

Life by the Spirit

¹⁶So I say, live by the Spirit, and you will not gratify the desires of the sinful nature. ¹⁷For the sinful nature desires what is contrary to the Spirit, and the Spirit what is contrary to the sinful nature. They are in conflict with each other, so that you do not do what you want. ¹⁸But if you are led by the Spirit, you are not under law.

E Gal 4:6 ◀ ▶ Gal 6:1
L 2Co 12:18 ◀ ▶ Gal 5:16-18
S Gal 2:20 ◀ ▶ Gal 5:19-25
L Gal 5:5 ◀ ▶ Gal 5:22-25
S 2Co 3:18 ◀ ▶ 1Th 4:7-8
W Gal 3:14 ◀ ▶ Gal 5:25
N 2Co 11:4 ◀ ▶ Eph 2:18

5:4 ˢHeb 12:15; 2Pe 3:17
5:5 ᵗRo 8:23,24
5:6 ᵘS Ro 16:3 ᵛS 1Co 7:19 ʷ1Th 1:3; Jas 2:22
5:7 ˣS 1Co 9:24 ʸGal 3:1
5:8 ᶻS Ro 8:28
5:9 ᵃ1Co 5:6
5:10 ᵇS 2Co 2:3 ᶜPhp 3:15 ᵈver 12; Gal 1:7
5:11 ᵉGal 4:29; 6:12 ᶠS Lk 2:34
5:12 ᵍver 10
5:13 ʰS ver 1 ⁱS ver 24; 1Co 8:9; 1Pe 2:16 ʲ1Co 9:19; 2Co 4:5; Eph 5:21
5:14 ᵏLev 19:18; S Mt 5:43; Gal 6:2
5:16 ˡver 18,25; Ro 8:2,4-6,9,14; S 2Co 5:17 ᵐS ver 24
5:17 ⁿRo 8:5-8 ᵒRo 7:15-23
5:18 ᵖS ver 16 ᵠS Ro 2:12; 1Ti 1:9
5:19 ʳS 1Co 6:18
5:21 ˢMt 15:19; Ro 13:13 ᵗS Mt 25:34
5:22 ᵘMt 7:16-20; Eph 5:9 ᵛCol 3:12-15 ʷMal 2:6
5:23 ˣS Ac 24:25 ʸver 18
5:24 ᶻver 13,16-21; S Ro 6:6; 7:5,18; 8:3-5,8,9, 12,13; 13:14; Gal 6:8; Col 2:11 ᵃver 16,17
5:25 ᵇS ver 16
5:26 ᶜPhp 2:3
6:1 ᵈ1Co 2:15; 3:1 ᵉS Mt 18:15; S 2Co 2:7
6:2 ᶠ1Co 9:21; Jas 2:8
6:3 ᵍRo 12:3; 1Co 8:2 ʰ1Co 3:18
6:4 ⁱ2Co 13:5 ʲ2Co 10:12
6:5 ᵏver 2; Jer 31:30
6:6 ˡ1Co 9:11,14; 1Ti 5:17,18
6:7 ᵐS 1Co 6:9 ⁿPr 22:8; Jer 34:17; Hos 10:12,13; 2Co 9:6

¹⁹The acts of the sinful nature are obvious: sexual immorality, impurity and debauchery; ²⁰idolatry and witchcraft; hatred, discord, jealousy, fits of rage, selfish ambition, dissensions, factions ²¹and envy; drunkenness, orgies, and the like. I warn you, as I did before, that those who live like this will not inherit the kingdom of God.

²²But the fruit of the Spirit is love, joy, peace, patience, kindness, goodness, faithfulness, ²³gentleness and self-control. Against such things there is no law. ²⁴Those who belong to Christ Jesus have crucified the sinful nature with its passions and desires. ²⁵Since we live by the Spirit, let us keep in step with the Spirit. ²⁶Let us not become conceited, provoking and envying each other.

Doing Good to All

6 Brothers, if someone is caught in a sin, you who are spiritual should restore him gently. But watch yourself, or you also may be tempted. ²Carry each other's burdens, and in this way you will fulfill the law of Christ. ³If anyone thinks he is something when he is nothing, he deceives himself. ⁴Each one should test his own actions. Then he can take pride in himself, without comparing himself to somebody else, ⁵for each one should carry his own load.

⁶Anyone who receives instruction in the word must share all good things with his instructor.

⁷Do not be deceived: God cannot be mocked. A man reaps what he sows. ⁸The one who sows to please his sinful

C 2Co 5:14 ◀ ▶ Eph 2:1-3
H 2Co 11:15 ◀ ▶ Gal 6:7-8
S Gal 5:6 ◀ ▶ Gal 6:7-9
F 2Co 13:14 ◀ ▶ Eph 1:3
J 2Co 3:17 ◀ ▶ 1Th 1:6
L Gal 5:16-18 ◀ ▶ Gal 6:8
W Gal 5:16 ◀ ▶ Eph 1:16-17
E Gal 5:5 ◀ ▶ Eph 1:3
H Gal 5:19-21 ◀ ▶ Eph 5:5-6
S Gal 5:19-25 ◀ ▶ Gal 6:14-16
L Gal 5:22-25 ◀ ▶ Eph 4:3-4

ʳ 13 Or *the flesh*; also in verses 16, 17, 19 and 24   ˢ 14 Lev. 19:18

5:5 Paul says that "by faith we eagerly await through the Spirit the righteousness for which we hope." This verse refers to our faith and hope of the coming resurrection when Jesus will return in the air to translate the bodies of his saints to glorious resurrection bodies fit for eternity that we might enjoy the new Jerusalem and "reign on the earth" (Rev 5:10).

nature,° from that nature' will reap destruction;ᵖ the one who sows to please the Spirit, from the Spirit will reap eternal life.ᵠ ⁹Let us not become weary in doing good,ʳ for at the proper time we will reap a harvest if we do not give up.ˢ ¹⁰Therefore, as we have opportunity, let us do goodᵗ to all people, especially to those who belong to the familyᵘ of believers.

Not Circumcision but a New Creation

¹¹See what large letters I use as I write to you with my own hand!ᵛ ¹²Those who want to make a good impression outwardlyʷ are trying to compel you to be circumcised.ˣ The only reason they do this is to avoid being persecutedʸ for the cross of Christ. ¹³Not even those who are circumcised obey the law,ᶻ yet they want you to be circumcised that they may boast about your flesh.ᵃ ¹⁴May I never boast except in the cross of our Lord Jesus Christ,ᵇ through whichᵘ the world has been crucified to me, and I to the world.ᶜ ¹⁵Neither circumcision nor uncircumcision means anything;ᵈ what counts is a new creation.ᵉ ¹⁶Peace and mercy to all who follow this rule, even to the Israel of God.

¹⁷Finally, let no one cause me trouble, for I bear on my body the marksᶠ of Jesus.

¹⁸The grace of our Lord Jesus Christᵍ be with your spirit,ʰ brothers. Amen.

6:8 ᵒS Gal 5:24 ᵖJob 4:8; Hos 8:7; S Ro 6:23 ᵠJas 3:18
6:9 ʳ1Co 15:58; 2Co 4:1 ˢJob 42:12; Ps 126:5; Heb 12:3; Rev 2:10
6:10 ᵗPr 3:27; S Tit 2:14 ᵘEph 2:19; 1Pe 4:17
6:11 ᵛS 1Co 16:21
6:12 ʷMt 23:25, 26 ˣAc 15:1 ʸGal 5:11
6:13 ᶻRo 2:25 ᵃPhp 3:3
6:14 ᵇ1Co 2:2 ᶜS Ro 6:2,6
6:15 ᵈS 1Co 7:19 ᵉS 2Co 5:17
6:17 ᶠIsa 44:5; S 2Co 1:5; 11:23
6:18 ᵍS Ro 16:20 ʰPhp 4:23; 2Ti 4:22; Phm 25

S *Gal 6:7–9* ◄► *Eph 2:10*
U *2Co 6:17* ◄► *1Ti 4:8*

ᵗ 8 Or *his flesh, from the flesh* ᵘ 14 Or *whom*

Ephesians

Author: Paul

Theme: Life in Christ

Date of Writing: C. A.D. 60–62

Outline of Ephesians
   I. Salutation (1:1–2)
   II. Christ Is the Head of the Church (1:3–23)
   III. The Church Is the Body of Christ (2:1—3:21)
   IV. The Conduct of Believers (4:1—6:9)
   V. Spiritual Warfare (6:10–20)
   VI. Conclusion (6:21–24)

IN ALL LIKELIHOOD Paul wrote this epistle during his two-year imprisonment in Rome, about A.D. 60. During this time Paul was at liberty to preach the gospel freely (see Ac 28). It is probable that Ephesians, Colossians and Philemon were all written at this same time and place too. Paul also had many companions with him at this time—Aristarchus, Epaphras, Luke, Demas, Mark, Onesimus and Tychicus (see Ac 20:4; Phm 23). Tychicus served as Paul's messenger to deliver this letter to the Ephesians (see 6:21).

Because this letter lacks personal greetings or references to specific problems or situations some scholars believe that this epistle may have been intended for a number of churches in the general area surrounding Ephesus. Embracing a broad perspective in this letter, Paul repeatedly uses the word "church" to refer to the whole body of believers. His teaching underscores the role of the church as the body of Christ as Paul reveals that God's plan and eternal purpose through redemption in Christ involved the establishment of the church.

The first portion of Paul's letter addresses the situation of the believer in Christ, contrasting the believer's conduct as a member of the body of Christ with the believer's former life of sin. The power of the Holy Spirit sets believers apart from the world and enables believers to live "in Christ." The second portion of the letter addresses a believer's conduct toward the church—not a building, but members of the body of Christ.

1

Paul, an apostle of Christ Jesus by the will of God,

To the saints in Ephesus, the faithful in Christ Jesus:

² Grace and peace to you from God our Father and the Lord Jesus Christ.

Spiritual Blessings in Christ

³ Praise be to the God and Father of our Lord Jesus Christ, who has blessed us in the heavenly realms with every spiritual blessing in Christ. ⁴ For he chose us in him before the creation of the world to be holy and blameless in his sight. In love ⁵ he predestined us to be adopted as his sons through Jesus Christ, in accordance with his pleasure and will— ⁶ to the praise of his glorious grace, which he has freely given us in the One he loves. ⁷ In him we have redemption through his blood, the forgiveness of sins, in accordance with the riches of God's grace ⁸ that he lavished on us with all wisdom and understanding. ⁹ And he made known to us the mystery of his will according to his good pleasure, which he purposed in Christ, ¹⁰ to be put into effect when the times will have reached their fulfillment—to bring all things in heaven and on earth together under one head, even Christ.

¹¹ In him we were also chosen, having been predestined according to the plan of him who works out everything in conformity with the purpose of his will, ¹² in order that we, who were the first to hope in Christ, might be for the praise of his glory. ¹³ And you also were included in Christ when you heard the word of truth, the gospel of your salvation. Having believed, you were marked in him with a seal, the promised Holy Spirit, ¹⁴ who is a deposit guaranteeing our inheritance until the redemption of those who are God's possession—to the praise of his glory.

Thanksgiving and Prayer

¹⁵ For this reason, ever since I heard about your faith in the Lord Jesus and your love for all the saints, ¹⁶ I have not stopped giving thanks for you, remembering you in my prayers. ¹⁷ I keep asking that the God of our Lord Jesus Christ, the glorious Father, may give you the Spirit of wisdom and revelation, so that you may know him better. ¹⁸ I pray also that the eyes of your heart may be enlightened in order that you may know the hope to which he has called you, the riches of his glorious inheritance in the saints, ¹⁹ and his incomparably great power for us who believe. That power is like the working of his mighty strength, ²⁰ which he exerted in Christ when he raised him from the dead and seated him at his right hand in the heavenly realms, ²¹ far above all rule and authority, power and dominion, and every title that can be given, not only in the present age but also in the one to come. ²² And God placed all things under his feet and appointed him to be head over everything for the church, ²³ which is his body, the fullness of him who fills everything in every way.

1:10 The word "dispensation" refers to a period of time in which someone is spiritually required to obey a certain revelation of truth. In this verse Paul mentions the "times" reaching "their fulfillment," referring to the first advent of Christ. This dispensation of the gospel was instituted to draw people to Christ. Compare this verse with Gal 4:4.

1:21–22 God has established his Son, Jesus Christ, far above any power or name in the universe, placing everything in subjection to him (see Ps 8:5–6; Heb 2:6–9). This prophecy will be ultimately fulfilled following the defeat of Satan at Armageddon (see Rev 11:15).

Made Alive in Christ

2 As for you, you were dead in your transgressions and sins,[g] [2]in which you used to live[h] when you followed the ways of this world[i] and of the ruler of the kingdom of the air,[j] the spirit who is now at work in those who are disobedient.[k] [3]All of us also lived among them at one time,[l] gratifying the cravings of our sinful nature[g][m] and following its desires and thoughts. Like the rest, we were by nature objects of wrath. [4]But because of his great love for us,[n] God, who is rich in mercy, [5]made us alive with Christ even when we were dead in transgressions[o]— it is by grace you have been saved.[p] [6]And God raised us up with Christ[q] and seated us with him[r] in the heavenly realms[s] in Christ Jesus, [7]in order that in the coming ages he might show the incomparable riches of his grace,[t] expressed in his kindness[u] to us in Christ Jesus. [8]For it is by grace[v] you have been saved,[w] through faith[x]—and this not from yourselves, it is the gift of God— [9]not by works,[y] so that no one can boast.[z] [10]For we are God's workmanship,[a] created[b] in Christ Jesus to do good works,[c] which God prepared in advance for us to do.

One in Christ

[11]Therefore, remember that formerly[d] you who are Gentiles by birth and called "uncircumcised" by those who call themselves "the circumcision" (that done in the body by the hands of men)[e]— [12]remember that at that time you were separate from Christ, excluded from citizenship in Israel and foreigners[f] to the covenants of the promise,[g] without hope[h] and without God in the world. [13]But now in Christ Jesus you who once[i] were far away have been brought near[j] through the blood of Christ.[k]

[14]For he himself is our peace,[l] who has made the two one[m] and has destroyed the barrier, the dividing wall of hostility, [15]by abolishing in his flesh[n] the law with its commandments and regulations.[o] His purpose was to create in himself one[p] new man out of the two, thus making peace, [16]and in this one body to reconcile both of them to God through the cross,[q] by which he put to death their hostility. [17]He came and preached peace[r] to you who were far away and peace to those who were near.[s] [18]For through him we both have access[t] to the Father[u] by one Spirit.[v]

[19]Consequently, you are no longer foreigners and aliens,[w] but fellow citizens[x] with God's people and members of God's household,[y] [20]built[z] on the foundation[a] of the apostles and prophets,[b] with Christ Jesus himself[c] as the chief cornerstone.[d] [21]In him the whole building is joined together and rises to become a holy temple[e] in the Lord. [22]And in him you too are being built together to become a dwelling in which God lives by his Spirit.[f]

Paul the Preacher to the Gentiles

3 For this reason I, Paul, the prisoner[g] of Christ Jesus for the sake of you Gentiles—

[2]Surely you have heard about the administration of God's grace that was given to me[h] for you, [3]that is, the mystery[i] made known to me by revelation,[j] as I have already written briefly. [4]In reading this, then, you will be able to understand my insight[k] into the mystery of

---

3:2–6 To the Jewish mind it was remarkable that God should freely offer salvation to the Gentiles who would repent and believe in Christ. God's offer to the Gentiles to become part "of one body, and sharers together in the promise in Christ Jesus" (3:6) revealed God's great mercy and love for all people.

Christ, ⁵which was not made known to men in other generations as it has now been revealed by the Spirit to God's holy apostles and prophets.¹ ⁶This mystery is that through the gospel the Gentiles are heirsᵐ together with Israel, members together of one body,ⁿ and sharers together in the promise in Christ Jesus.º

⁷I became a servant of this gospelᵖ by the gift of God's grace given meᵠ through the working of his power.ʳ ⁸Although I am less than the least of all God's people,ˢ this grace was given me: to preach to the Gentilesᵗ the unsearchable riches of Christ,ᵘ ⁹and to make plain to everyone the administration of this mystery,ᵛ which for ages past was kept hidden in God, who created all things. ¹⁰His intent was that now, through the church, the manifold wisdom of Godʷ should be made knownˣ to the rulers and authoritiesʸ in the heavenly realms,ᶻ ¹¹according to his eternal purposeᵃ which he accomplished in Christ Jesus our Lord. ¹²In him and through faith in him we may approach Godᵇ with freedom and confidence.ᶜ ¹³I ask you, therefore, not to be discouraged because of my sufferings for you, which are your glory.

A Prayer for the Ephesians

¹⁴For this reason I kneelᵈ before the Father, ¹⁵from whom his whole familyʰ in heaven and on earth derives its name. ¹⁶I pray that out of his glorious richesᵉ he may strengthen you with powerᶠ through his Spirit in your inner being,ᵍ ¹⁷so that Christ may dwell in your heartsʰ through faith. And I pray that you, being rootedⁱ and established in love, ¹⁸may have power, together with all the saints,ʲ to grasp how wide and long and high and deepᵏ is the love of Christ, ¹⁹and to know this love that surpasses knowledge¹— that you may be filledᵐ to the measure of all the fullness of God.ⁿ

²⁰Now to him who is ableº to do immeasurably more than all we askᵖ or imagine, according to his powerᵠ that is at work within us, ²¹to him be glory in the church and in Christ Jesus throughout all generations, for ever and ever! Amen.ʳ

Unity in the Body of Christ

4 As a prisonerˢ for the Lord, then, I urge you to live a life worthyᵗ of the callingᵘ you have received. ²Be completely humble and gentle; be patient, bearing with one anotherᵛ in love.ʷ ³Make every effort to keep the unityˣ of the Spirit through the bond of peace.ʸ ⁴There is one bodyᶻ and one Spiritᵃ—just as you were called to one hope when you were calledᵇ— ⁵one Lord,ᶜ one faith, one baptism; ⁶one God and Father of all,ᵈ who is over all and through all and in all.ᵉ

⁷But to each one of usᶠ graceᵍ has been givenʰ as Christ apportioned it. ⁸This is why itⁱ says:

"When he ascended on high,
he led captivesⁱ in his train
and gave gifts to men."ʲ

⁹(What does "he ascended" mean except that he also descended to the lower, earthly regionsᵏ? ¹⁰He who descended is the very one who ascendedᵏ higher than all the heavens, in order to fill the whole universe.)ˡ ¹¹It was he who gaveᵐ some to be apostles,ⁿ some to be prophets,º some to be evangelists,ᵖ and some to be pastors and teachers,ᵠ ¹²to prepare God's people for works of service, so that the body of Christʳ may be built upˢ ¹³until we all reach unityᵗ in the faith and in the knowledge of the Son of Godᵘ and become mature,ᵛ attaining to the whole measure of the fullness of Christ.ʷ

¹⁴Then we will no longer be infants,ˣ

tossed back and forth by the waves,ʸ and blown here and there by every wind of teaching and by the cunning and craftiness of men in their deceitful scheming.ᶻ ¹⁵Instead, speaking the truth in love,ᵃ we will in all things grow up into him who is the Head,ᵇ that is, Christ. ¹⁶From him the whole body, joined and held together by every supporting ligament, growsᶜ and builds itself upᵈ in love,ᵉ as each part does its work.

Living as Children of Light

¹⁷So I tell you this, and insist on it in the Lord, that you must no longerᶠ live as the Gentiles do, in the futility of their thinking.ᵍ ¹⁸They are darkened in their understandingʰ and separated from the life of Godⁱ because of the ignorance that is in them due to the hardening of their hearts.ʲ ¹⁹Having lost all sensitivity,ᵏ they have given themselves overˡ to sensualityᵐ so as to indulge in every kind of impurity, with a continual lust for more.

²⁰You, however, did not come to know Christ that way. ²¹Surely you heard of him and were taught in him in accordance with the truth that is in Jesus. ²²You were taught, with regard to your former way of life, to put offⁿ your old self,ᵒ which is being corrupted by its deceitful desires;ᵖ ²³to be made new in the attitude of your minds;ᵠ ²⁴and to put onʳ the new self,ˢ created to be like God in true righteousness and holiness.ᵗ

²⁵Therefore each of you must put off falsehood and speak truthfullyᵘ to his neighbor, for we are all members of one body.ᵛ ²⁶"In your anger do not sin"/:ʷ Do not let the sun go down while you are still angry, ²⁷and do not give the devil a foothold.ˣ ²⁸He who has been stealing must steal no longer, but must work,ʸ doing something useful with his own hands,ᶻ that he may have something to share with those in need.ᵃ

²⁹Do not let any unwholesome talk come out of your mouths,ᵇ but only what is helpful for building others upᶜ according to their needs, that it may benefit those who listen. ³⁰And do not grieve the Holy Spirit of God,ᵈ with whom you were sealedᵉ for the day of redemption.ᶠ ³¹Get rid ofᵍ all bitterness, rage and anger, brawling and slander, along with every form of malice.ʰ ³²Be kind and compassionate to one another,ⁱ forgiving each other, just as in Christ God forgave you.ʲ

5 Be imitators of God,ᵏ therefore, as dearly loved children¹ ²and live a life of love, just as Christ loved usᵐ and gave himself up for usⁿ as a fragrant offering and sacrifice to God.ᵒ

³But among you there must not be even a hint of sexual immorality,ᵖ or of any kind of impurity, or of greed,ᵠ because these are improper for God's holy people. ⁴Nor should there be obscenity, foolish talkʳ or coarse joking, which are out of place, but rather thanksgiving.ˢ ⁵For of this you can be sure: No immoral, impure or greedy person—such a man is an idolaterᵗ—has any inheritanceᵘ in the kingdom of Christ and of God.ᵐᵛ ⁶Let no one deceive youʷ with empty words, for because of such things God's wrathˣ comes on those who are disobedient.ʸ ⁷Therefore do not be partners with them.

⁸For you were onceᶻ darkness, but now you are light in the Lord. Live as children of lightᵃ ⁹(for the fruitᵇ of the light consists in all goodness,ᶜ righteousness and truth) ¹⁰and find out what pleases the Lord.ᵈ ¹¹Have nothing to do with the fruitless deeds of darkness,ᵉ but rather expose them. ¹²For it is shameful even to mention what the disobedient do in secret. ¹³But everything exposed by the lightᶠ becomes visible, ¹⁴for it is light that makes everything visible. This is why it is said:

"Wake up, O sleeper,ᵍ
rise from the dead,ʰ
and Christ will shine on you."ⁱ

¹⁵Be very careful, then, how you liveʲ—not as unwise but as wise, ¹⁶making the most of every opportunity,ᵏ be-

---

4:14 ʸ Isa 57:20; Jas 1:6 ᶻ Eph 6:11
4:15 ᵃ ver 2,16; Eph 1:4 ᵇ S Eph 1:22
4:16 ᶜ Col 2:19 ᵈ 1Co 12:7 ᵉ ver 2, 15; Eph 1:4
4:17 ᶠ Eph 2:1 ᵍ Ro 1:21
4:18 ʰ Dt 29:4; Ro 1:21 ⁱ Eph 2:12 ʲ 2Co 3:14
4:19 ᵏ 1Ti 4:2 ˡ Ro 1:24 ᵐ Col 3:5; 1Pe 4:3
4:22 ⁿ ver 25,31; Col 3:5,8,9; Jas 1:21; 1Pe 2:1 ᵒ S Ro 6:6 ᵖ Jer 17:9; Heb 3:13
4:23 ᵠ Ro 12:2; Col 3:10
4:24 ʳ S Ro 13:14 ˢ Ro 6:4 ᵗ Eph 2:10
4:25 ᵘ Ps 15:2; Lev 19:11; Zec 8:16; Col 3:9 ᵛ S Ro 12:5
4:26 ʷ Ps 4:4; S Mt 5:22
4:27 ˣ 2Co 2:10,11
4:28 ʸ Ac 20:35 ᶻ 1Th 4:11 ᵃ Gal 6:10
4:29 ᵇ Mt 12:36; Eph 5:4; Col 3:8 ᶜ S Ro 14:19
4:30 ᵈ Isa 63:10; 1Th 5:19 ᵉ 2Co 1:22; 5:5; Eph 1:13 ᶠ Ro 8:23
4:31 ᵍ S ver 22 ʰ Col 3:8; 1Pe 2:1
4:32 ⁱ 1Pe 3:8 ʲ Mt 6:14,15; Col 3:12,13
5:1 ᵏ Mt 5:48; Lk 6:36 ˡ S Jn 1:12
5:2 ᵐ S Jn 13:34 ⁿ ver 25; S Gal 1:4; 2:20 ᵒ Heb 7:27
5:3 ᵖ S 1Co 6:18 ᵠ Col 3:5
5:4 ʳ Eph 4:29 ˢ S ver 20
5:5 ᵗ Col 3:5 ᵘ S Ac 20:32 ᵛ S Mt 25:34
5:6 ʷ S Mk 13:5 ˣ S Ro 1:18 ʸ Eph 2:2
5:8 ᶻ S Eph 2:2 ᵃ Jn 8:12; S Lk 16:8; S Ac 26:18
5:9 ᵇ Mt 7:16-20; Gal 5:22 ᶜ Ro 15:14
5:10 ᵈ S 1Ti 5:4
5:11 ᵉ Ro 13:12; 2Co 6:14
5:13 ᶠ Jn 3:20,21
5:14 ᵍ Ro 13:11 ʰ Isa 26:19; Jn 5:25 ⁱ Isa 60:1; Mal 4:2
5:15 ʲ ver 2
5:16 ᵏ Col 4:5

L Eph 2:11–18 ◀ ▶ Eph 5:14
D Eph 2:13–18 ◀ ▶ Eph 5:25
H Gal 6:7–8 ◀ ▶ Php 1:28
S Eph 4:20–24 ◀ ▶ Eph 5:25–27
F Eph 4:3 ◀ ▶ Php 2:1
W Eph 4:3–4 ◀ ▶ Eph 5:18
C Eph 4:18 ◀ ▶ Php 2:21
K Eph 3:20 ◀ ▶ Php 4:13
L Eph 4:32 ◀ ▶ Col 1:13–14

C Eph 2:12 ◀ ▶ Eph 5:14
S Eph 4:1 ◀ ▶ Eph 5:5–6
E Eph 4:7–8 ◀ ▶ Php 3:3
Q Ac 7:51 ◀ ▶ 1Th 5:19

¹²⁶ Psalm 4:4   ᵐ 5 Or kingdom of the Christ and God

cause the days are evil.¹ ¹⁷Therefore do not be foolish, but understand what the Lord's will is.ᵐ ¹⁸Do not get drunk on wine,ⁿ which leads to debauchery. Instead, be filled with the Spirit.ᵒ ¹⁹Speak to one another with psalms, hymns and spiritual songs.ᵖ Sing and make music in your heart to the Lord, ²⁰always giving thanksᑫ to God the Father for everything, in the name of our Lord Jesus Christ.

²¹Submit to one anotherʳ out of reverence for Christ.

Wives and Husbands
5:22—6:9pp — Col 3:18—4:1

²²Wives, submit to your husbandsˢ as to the Lord.ᵗ ²³For the husband is the head of the wife as Christ is the head of the church,ᵘ his body, of which he is the Savior. ²⁴Now as the church submits to Christ, so also wives should submit to their husbandsᵛ in everything.

²⁵Husbands, love your wives,ʷ just as Christ loved the church and gave himself up for herˣ ²⁶to make her holy,ʸ cleansingⁿ her by the washingᶻ with water through the word, ²⁷and to present her to himselfᵃ as a radiant church, without stain or wrinkle or any other blemish, but holy and blameless.ᵇ ²⁸In this same way, husbands ought to love their wivesᶜ as their own bodies. He who loves his wife loves himself. ²⁹After all, no one ever hated his own body, but he feeds and cares for it, just as Christ does the church— ³⁰for we are members of his body.ᵈ ³¹"For this reason a man will leave his father and mother and be united to his wife, and the two will become one flesh."ᵒᵉ ³²This is a profound mystery— but I am talking about Christ and the church. ³³However, each one of you also must love his wifeᶠ as he loves himself, and the wife must respect her husband.

Children and Parents

6 Children, obey your parents in the Lord, for this is right.ᵍ ²"Honor your father and mother"—which is the first commandment with a promise— ³"that it may go well with you and that you may enjoy long life on the earth."ᵖʰ

⁴Fathers, do not exasperate your children;ⁱ instead, bring them up in the training and instruction of the Lord.ʲ

Slaves and Masters

⁵Slaves, obey your earthly masters with respectᵏ and fear, and with sincerity of heart,ˡ just as you would obey Christ.ᵐ ⁶Obey them not only to win their favor when their eye is on you, but like slaves of Christ,ⁿ doing the will of God from your heart. ⁷Serve wholeheartedly, as if you were serving the Lord, not men,ᵒ ⁸because you know that the Lord will reward everyone for whatever good he does,ᵖ whether he is slave or free.

⁹And masters, treat your slaves in the same way. Do not threaten them, since you know that he who is both their Master and yoursᑫ is in heaven, and there is no favoritismʳ with him.

The Armor of God

¹⁰Finally, be strong in the Lordˢ and in his mighty power.ᵗ ¹¹Put on the full armor of Godᵘ so that you can take your stand against the devil's schemes. ¹²For our struggle is not against flesh and blood,ᵛ but against the rulers, against the authorities,ʷ against the powersˣ of this dark world and against the spiritual forces of evil in the heavenly realms.ʸ ¹³Therefore put on the full armor of God,ᶻ so that when the day of evil comes, you may be able to stand your ground, and

B Eph 4:8 ◄ ► Tit 3:5–6
L Eph 4:3–4 ◄ ► Eph 6:18
N Eph 4:4 ◄ ► Heb 9:14
W Eph 5:9 ◄ ► Php 3:3
J 2Co 12:10 ◄ ► Php 1:28–29
D Eph 5:2 ◄ ► Col 1:14
S Eph 5:5–6 ◄ ► Php 2:12
H Eph 1:10 ◄ ► Rev 7:9–17

H Lk 4:18 ◄ ► Jas 5:13–18

ⁿ 26 Or *having cleansed* ᵒ 31 Gen. 2:24 ᵖ 3 Deut. 5:16

5:26–27 Paul's words foreshadow the marriage supper of the Lamb which will occur in heaven following the rapture of the church (see Rev 19:7–9). Jesus expresses his profound love for the church by perfecting and sanctifying it through the application of his atoning blood to the souls of those who repent of their sins. Though some believe that the church must endure the persecution of the tribulation as a means of purification, this passage clearly states that only the blood of Christ cleanses the church.

after you have done everything, to stand. ¹⁴Stand firm then, with the belt of truth buckled around your waist,ᵃ with the breastplate of righteousness in place,ᵇ ¹⁵and with your feet fitted with the readiness that comes from the gospel of peace.ᶜ ¹⁶In addition to all this, take up the shield of faith,ᵈ with which you can extinguish all the flaming arrows of the evil one.ᵉ ¹⁷Take the helmet of salvationᶠ and the sword of the Spirit,ᵍ which is the word of God.ʰ ¹⁸And pray in the Spiritⁱ on all occasionsʲ with all kinds of prayers and requests.ᵏ With this in mind, be alert and always keep on prayingˡ for all the saints.

C *Ac 11:24* ◀ ▶ *Rev 28:17*
T *Eph 3:16–19* ◀ ▶ *1Th 1:5*
L *Eph 5:18–19* ◀ ▶ *Php 3:3*

6:14 ᵃ Isa 11:5
ᵇ Ps 132:9; Isa 59:17; 1Th 5:8
6:15 ᶜ Isa 52:7; Ro 10:15
6:16 ᵈ 1Jn 5:4
ᵉ S Mt 5:37
6:17 ᶠ Isa 59:17
ᵍ Isa 49:2
ʰ S Heb 4:12
6:18 ⁱ Ro 8:26,27
ʲ S Lk 18:1
ᵏ Mt 26:41; Php 1:4; 4:6
ˡ S Ac 1:14; Col 1:3
6:19 ᵐ S 1Th 5:25
ⁿ S Ac 4:29
ᵒ S Ro 16:25
6:20 ᵖ 2Co 5:20
ᵠ S Ac 21:33
6:21 ʳ S Ac 20:4
6:22 ˢ Col 4:7-9
ᵗ Col 2:2; 4:8
6:23 ᵘ Gal 6:16; 2Th 3:16; 1Pe 5:14

¹⁹Pray also for me,ᵐ that whenever I open my mouth, words may be given me so that I will fearlesslyⁿ make known the mysteryᵒ of the gospel, ²⁰for which I am an ambassadorᵖ in chains.ᵠ Pray that I may declare it fearlessly, as I should.

Final Greetings

²¹Tychicus,ʳ the dear brother and faithful servant in the Lord, will tell you everything, so that you also may know how I am and what I am doing. ²²I am sending him to you for this very purpose, that you may know how we are,ˢ and that he may encourage you.ᵗ

²³Peaceᵘ to the brothers, and love with faith from God the Father and the Lord Jesus Christ. ²⁴Grace to all who love our Lord Jesus Christ with an undying love.

Philippians

Author: Paul

Theme: There is joy in a relationship with Jesus

Date of Writing: C. A.D. 60–62

Outline of Philippians
    I. Introduction (1:1–11)
    II. Paul's Circumstances and Concern (1:12–30)
    III. Serving as Christ Served (2:1–18)
    IV. Paul's Messenger (2:19–30)
    V. Warnings and Exhortations (3:1—4:20)
    VI. Conclusion (4:21–23)

THE APOSTLE PAUL wrote this letter to the Philippians during his first imprisonment in Rome (A.D. 59–61). References to Caesar's household (see 4:22) and to the praetorian guard (see 1:13) confirm this letter's origin and classify it as a "Prison Epistle," along with Ephesians, Colossians and Philemon. The believers at Philippi had sent a gift to Paul while he was in prison. The messenger who delivered the gift, Epaphroditus (see 4:18), became ill and was forced to stay with Paul while he recovered. Paul then sent this letter back to Philippi with Epaphroditus in gratitude for the Philippians' love and help.

Paul founded the church at Philippi on his second missionary journey to Macedonia. This thriving city became Paul's base of operations for several days, and many Gentiles were converted. Yet after delivering a slave girl from demons Paul found himself in the Philippian jail. A miraculous earthquake released Paul from his chains and his Philippian jailer was converted (see Ac 16:14–34). Composed primarily of Gentiles (see Ac 16:12–15), the church at Philippi grew and became a special delight to Paul because of its generous response to his pleas to aid the church in Jerusalem. Though Paul never showed favoritism to a particular church, Paul and the believers at Philippi developed a bond of love that is evoked in this personal letter as Paul shares his gratitude and Christian experience with his dear friends.

INTRODUCTION: PHILIPPIANS

Throughout this letter Paul talks about the importance of the gospel in his ministry (see 1:5, 7, 12, 16, 27; 2:22; 4:3). Although Paul was writing from prison, various forms of the words "joy" or "rejoice" occur repeatedly in this letter, reminding the Philippians that God's peace brings joy despite adverse circumstances (see 4:4–7). This letter also includes a warning against pride and a self-seeking attitude, reminding the believers to follow Christ's example through one of the most profound statements of the incarnation found in the NT (2:5–11).

1

Paul and Timothy,[a] servants of Christ Jesus,

To all the saints[b] in Christ Jesus at Philippi,[c] together with the overseers[a][d] and deacons:[e]

[2]Grace and peace to you from God our Father and the Lord Jesus Christ.[f]

Thanksgiving and Prayer

[3]I thank my God every time I remember you.[g] [4]In all my prayers for all of you, I always pray[h] with joy [5]because of your partnership[i] in the gospel from the first day[j] until now, [6]being confident of this, that he who began a good work in you will carry it on to completion[k] until the day of Christ Jesus.[l]

[7]It is right[m] for me to feel this way about all of you, since I have you in my heart;[n] for whether I am in chains[o] or defending[p] and confirming the gospel, all of you share in God's grace with me. [8]God can testify[q] how I long for all of you with the affection of Christ Jesus.

[9]And this is my prayer: that your love may abound more and more in knowledge and depth of insight,[s] [10]so that you may be able to discern what is best and may be pure and blameless until the day of Christ,[t] [11]filled with the fruit of righteousness[u] that comes through Jesus Christ—to the glory and praise of God.

C *2Co 1:14* ◀ ▶ *Php 1:10*
C *Php 1:6* ◀ ▶ *Php 2:16*

1:1 [a] S Ac 16:1; 2Co 1:1 [b] S Ac 9:13 [c] S Ac 16:12 [d] S 1Ti 3:1 [e] 1Ti 3:8
1:2 [f] S Ro 1:7
1:3 [g] S Ro 1:8
1:4 [h] S Ro 1:10
1:5 [i] Ac 2:42; Php 4:15 [j] Ac 16:12-40
1:6 [k] Ps 138:8 [l] ver 10; S 1Co 1:8
1:7 [m] 2Pe 1:13 [n] 2Co 7:3 [o] ver 13, 14,17; S Ac 21:33 [p] ver 16
1:8 [q] S Ro 1:9
1:9 [r] 1Th 3:12 [s] Eph 1:17
1:10 [t] ver 6; S 1Co 1:8
1:11 [u] S Jas 3:18
1:13 [v] ver 7,14,17; S Ac 21:33
1:14 [w] ver 7,13,17; S Ac 21:33 [x] S Ac 4:29
1:16 [y] ver 7,12
1:17 [z] Php 2:3 [a] ver 7,13,14; S Ac 21:33
1:19 [b] 2Co 1:11 [c] S Ac 16:7 [d] Phm 22
1:20 [e] Ro 8:19

Paul's Chains Advance the Gospel

[12]Now I want you to know, brothers, that what has happened to me has really served to advance the gospel. [13]As a result, it has become clear throughout the whole palace guard[b] and to everyone else that I am in chains[v] for Christ. [14]Because of my chains,[w] most of the brothers in the Lord have been encouraged to speak the word of God more courageously and fearlessly.[x]

[15]It is true that some preach Christ out of envy and rivalry, but others out of goodwill. [16]The latter do so in love, knowing that I am put here for the defense of the gospel.[y] [17]The former preach Christ out of selfish ambition,[z] not sincerely, supposing that they can stir up trouble for me while I am in chains.[ca] [18]But what does it matter? The important thing is that in every way, whether from false motives or true, Christ is preached. And because of this I rejoice.

Yes, and I will continue to rejoice, [19]for I know that through your prayers[b] and the help given by the Spirit of Jesus Christ,[c] what has happened to me will turn out for my deliverance.[dd] [20]I eagerly expect[e] and hope that I will in no way be ashamed, but will have sufficient cour-

M *Eph 3:14–19* ◀ ▶ *Col 1:9–11*

a 1 Traditionally *bishops* *b* 13 Or *whole palace* *c* 16,17 Some late manuscripts have verses 16 and 17 in reverse order. *d* 19 Or *salvation*

1:6 Paul's reference to "the day of Christ Jesus" foreshadows the day of Christ's second coming in glory.

1:10 Paul again references "the day of Christ" as Christ's second coming when believers will give an account of their life lived toward the goal of excellency, sincerity and blamelessness (see 2Co 5:10).

age^f so that now as always Christ will be exalted in my body,^g whether by life or by death.^h ^21For to me, to live is Christ^i and to die is gain. ^22If I am to go on living in the body, this will mean fruitful labor for me. Yet what shall I choose? I do not know! ^23I am torn between the two: I desire to depart^j and be with Christ,^k which is better by far; ^24but it is more necessary for you that I remain in the body. ^25Convinced of this, I know that I will remain, and I will continue with all of you for your progress and joy in the faith, ^26so that through my being with you again your joy in Christ Jesus will overflow on account of me.

^27Whatever happens, conduct yourselves in a manner worthy^l of the gospel of Christ. Then, whether I come and see you or only hear about you in my absence, I will know that you stand firm^m in one spirit, contending^n as one man for the faith of the gospel ^28without being frightened in any way by those who oppose you. This is a sign to them that they will be destroyed, but that you will be saved—and that by God. ^29For it has been granted to you^o on behalf of Christ not only to believe on him, but also to suffer^p for him, ^30since you are going through the same struggle^q you saw^r I had, and now hear^s that I still have.

Imitating Christ's Humility

2 If you have any encouragement from being united with Christ, if any comfort from his love, if any fellowship with the Spirit,^t if any tenderness and compassion,^u ^2then make my joy complete^v by being like-minded,^w having the same love, being one^x in spirit and purpose. ^3Do nothing out of selfish ambition or vain conceit,^y but in humility consider others better than yourselves.^z ^4Each of you should look not only to your own interests, but also to the interests of others.^a

^5Your attitude should be the same as that of Christ Jesus:^b

^6Who, being in very nature^e God,^c
did not consider equality with God^d
something to be grasped,
^7but made himself nothing,^e
taking the very nature^f of a
servant,^f
being made in human likeness.^g
^8And being found in appearance as a
man,
he humbled himself
and became obedient to death^h—
even death on a cross!^i
^9Therefore God exalted him^j to the
highest place
and gave him the name that is above
every name,^k
^10that at the name of Jesus every knee
should bow,^l
in heaven and on earth and under
the earth,^m
^11and every tongue confess that Jesus
Christ is Lord,^n
to the glory of God the Father.

Shining as Stars

^12Therefore, my dear friends, as you have always obeyed—not only in my presence, but now much more in my absence—continue to work out your salvation with fear and trembling,^o ^13for it is God who works in you^p to will and to act according to his good purpose.^q

^14Do everything without complaining^r or arguing, ^15so that you may become blameless^s and pure, children of God^t without fault in a crooked and depraved generation,^u in which you shine like stars in the universe ^16as you hold out^g the

---

1:20 ^f ver 14; ^g 1Co 6:20; ^h Ro 14:8
1:21 ^i Gal 2:20
1:23 ^j 2Ti 4:6; ^k S Jn 12:26
1:27 ^l S Eph 4:1; ^m S 1Co 16:13; ^n Jude 3
1:29 ^o Mt 5:11,12; Ac 5:41; ^p S Ac 14:22
1:30 ^q 1Th 2:2; Heb 10:32; ^r Ac 16:19-40; ^s ver 13
2:1 ^t 2Co 13:14; ^u Col 3:12
2:2 ^v S Jn 3:29; ^w Php 4:2; ^x S Ro 15:5
2:3 ^y Gal 5:26; ^z Ro 12:10; 1Pe 5:5
2:4 ^a S 1Co 10:24
2:5 ^b S Mt 11:29
2:6 ^c Jn 1:1; S 14:9; ^d Jn 5:18
2:7 ^e 2Co 8:9; ^f S Mt 20:28; ^g S Jn 1:14; Ro 8:3; Heb 2:17
2:8 ^h S Mt 26:39; Jn 10:18; Ro 5:19; Heb 5:8; ^i S 1Co 1:23
2:9 ^j Isa 52:13; 53:12; Da 7:14; Ac 2:33; Heb 2:9; ^k Eph 1:20,21
2:10 ^l Ps 95:6; Isa 45:23; Ro 14:11; ^m Mt 28:18; Eph 1:10; Col 1:20
2:11 ^n S Jn 13:13
2:12 ^o S 2Co 7:15
2:13 ^p Ezr 1:5; 1Co 12:6; 15:10; Gal 2:8; Heb 13:21; ^q Eph 1:5
2:14 ^r 1Co 10:10; 1Pe 4:9
2:15 ^s S 1Th 3:13; ^t Mt 5:45,48; Eph 5:1; Ac 2:40

M 1Co 15:24-28 ◄ ► 1Ti 6:15
V Eph 1:21-22 ◄ ► 2Th 2:8
S Eph 5:25-27 ◄ ► Php 2:15
S Php 2:12 ◄ ► Php 3:18
C Php 1:10 ◄ ► Php 3:20-21

^e Or in the form of ^f Or the form ^g 16 Or hold on to

H Eph 5:5-6 ◄ ► Php 3:19
J Eph 5:20 ◄ ► Php 2:17
F Eph 5:9 ◄ ► Col 1:8

2:9–11 Paul prophesied of a day after the second coming of Christ when the universe will acknowledge Christ's supremacy. Every spiritual being in heaven, earth or hell will recognize Jesus Christ as their divine King. Paul's prophetic revelation reminds us that while the return of Jesus will be the most joyful event in history for those who love him, Christ's return will produce fear among all those who have refused to repent of their sins (see Mal 3:2; Mt 24:30).

word of life—in order that I may boast on the day of Christ[v] that I did not run[w] or labor for nothing.[x] ¹⁷But even if I am being poured out like a drink offering[y] on the sacrifice[z] and service coming from your faith, I am glad and rejoice with all of you.[a] ¹⁸So you too should be glad and rejoice with me.

Timothy and Epaphroditus

¹⁹I hope in the Lord Jesus to send Timothy[b] to you soon,[c] that I also may be cheered when I receive news about you. ²⁰I have no one else like him,[d] who takes a genuine interest in your welfare. ²¹For everyone looks out for his own interests,[e] not those of Jesus Christ. ²²But you know that Timothy has proved himself, because as a son with his father[f] he has served with me in the work of the gospel. ²³I hope, therefore, to send him as soon as I see how things go with me.[g] ²⁴And I am confident[h] in the Lord that I myself will come soon.

²⁵But I think it is necessary to send back to you Epaphroditus, my brother, fellow worker[i] and fellow soldier,[j] who is also your messenger, whom you sent to take care of my needs.[k] ²⁶For he longs for all of you[l] and is distressed because you heard he was ill. ²⁷Indeed he was ill, and almost died. But God had mercy on him, and not on him only but also on me, to spare me sorrow upon sorrow. ²⁸Therefore I am all the more eager to send him,[m] so that when you see him again you may be glad and I may have less anxiety. ²⁹Welcome him in the Lord with great joy, and honor men like him,[n] ³⁰because he almost died for the work of Christ, risking his life to make up for the help you could not give me.[o]

J Php 1:28–29 ◀▶ Php 3:8
C Eph 5:14 ◀▶ Php 3:18–19
E 1Co 12:28 ◀▶ Heb 11:11–12
D 2Co 12:7–10 ◀▶ Heb 12:5–13

2:16 v S 1Co 1:8
w S 1Co 9:24
x 1Th 2:19
2:17 y 2Co 12:15;
2Ti 4:6 z Ro 15:16
a S 2Co 6:10
2:19 b S Ac 16:1
c ver 23
2:20 d 1Co 16:10
2:21 e S 1Co 10:24
2:22 f 1Co 4:17;
1Ti 1:2
2:23 g ver 19
2:24 h Php 1:25
2:25 i Ro 16:3,9, 21; 2Co 8:23;
Php 4:3; Col 4:11;
Phm 1 j Phm 2
k Php 4:18
2:26 l Php 1:8
2:28 m ver 25
2:29 n 1Co 16:18;
1Ti 5:17
2:30 o 1Co 16:17
3:1 p Php 2:18
3:2 q Ps 22:16,20;
Rev 22:15
3:3 r Ro 2:28,29;
Gal 6:15; Col 2:11
s Ro 15:17; Gal 6:14
3:4 t 2Co 11:21
3:5 u S Lk 1:59
v 2Co 11:22
w Ro 11:1 x Ac 23:6
3:6 y S Ac 21:20
z S Ac 8:3 a ver 9;
Ro 10:5
3:7 b Mt 13:44;
Lk 14:33
3:8 c ver 10;
Jer 9:23,24;
Jn 17:3; Eph 4:13;
S 2Pe 1:2
d Ps 73:25
3:9 e ver 6; Ro 10:5
f Jer 33:16
g S Ro 9:30
3:10 h S ver 8
i S 2Co 1:5
j S Ro 6:3-5
3:11 k S Jn 11:24;
S Ro 6:5; Rev 20:5,6

No Confidence in the Flesh

3 Finally, my brothers, rejoice in the Lord! It is no trouble for me to write the same things to you again,[p] and it is a safeguard for you.

²Watch out for those dogs,[q] those men who do evil, those mutilators of the flesh. ³For it is we who are the circumcision,[r] we who worship by the Spirit of God, who glory in Christ Jesus,[s] and who put no confidence in the flesh— ⁴though I myself have reasons for such confidence.[t]

If anyone else thinks he has reasons to put confidence in the flesh, I have more: ⁵circumcised[u] on the eighth day, of the people of Israel,[v] of the tribe of Benjamin,[w] a Hebrew of Hebrews; in regard to the law, a Pharisee;[x] ⁶as for zeal,[y] persecuting the church;[z] as for legalistic righteousness,[a] faultless.

⁷But whatever was to my profit I now consider loss[b] for the sake of Christ. ⁸What is more, I consider everything a loss compared to the surpassing greatness of knowing[c] Christ Jesus my Lord, for whose sake I have lost all things. I consider them rubbish, that I may gain Christ[d] ⁹and be found in him, not having a righteousness of my own that comes from the law,[e] but that which is through faith in Christ—the righteousness[f] that comes from God and is by faith.[g] ¹⁰I want to know[h] Christ and the power of his resurrection and the fellowship of sharing in his sufferings,[i] becoming like him in his death,[j] ¹¹and so, somehow, to attain to the resurrection[k] from the dead.

Pressing on Toward the Goal

¹²Not that I have already obtained all

W Jn 14:27 ◀▶ Php 4:4
E Eph 4:30 ◀▶ Col 1:8
L Eph 6:18 ◀▶ 1Th 5:19
W Eph 5:18 ◀▶ Col 1:9
G Eph 2:8–9 ◀▶ 1Ti 6:17
J Php 2:17 ◀▶ Heb 13:6
F Eph 2:8 ◀▶ Heb 3:18–19
F 2Co 4:14 ◀▶ Php 3:21

3:11–15 Paul anxiously anticipates the coming "resurrection from the dead" (3:11), admitting that he is not "perfect" (3:12). Although Paul was a mature believer, he still recognized that Christ was continuing the process of daily sanctification in his life. Paul explains that he has not yet achieved the final goal of perfection, but he will keep on toward that goal to win the prize that will be his in heaven with Christ (see 2Co 5:10). Paul then admonishes his readers to share his desire to "press on toward the goal" (3:14).

this, or have already been made perfect, but I press on to take hold^m of that for which Christ Jesus took hold of me.^n ^13Brothers, I do not consider myself yet to have taken hold of it. But one thing I do: Forgetting what is behind^o and straining toward what is ahead, ^14I press on^p toward the goal to win the prize^q for which God has called^r me heavenward in Christ Jesus.

^15All of us who are mature^s should take such a view of things.^t And if on some point you think differently, that too God will make clear to you.^u ^16Only let us live up to what we have already attained.

^17Join with others in following my example,^v brothers, and take note of those who live according to the pattern we gave you.^w ^18For, as I have often told you before and now say again even with tears,^x many live as enemies of the cross of Christ.^y ^19Their destiny^z is destruction, their god is their stomach,^a and their glory is in their shame.^b Their mind is on earthly things.^c ^20But our citizenship^d is in heaven.^e And we eagerly await a Savior from there, the Lord Jesus Christ,^f ^21who, by the power^g that enables him to bring everything under his control, will transform our lowly bodies^h so that they will be like his glorious body.^i

4 Therefore, my brothers, you whom I love and long for,^j my joy and crown, that is how you should stand firm^k in the Lord, dear friends!

Exhortations

^2I plead with Euodia and I plead with Syntyche to agree with each other^l in the Lord. ^3Yes, and I ask you, loyal yokefellow,^h help these women who have contended at my side in the cause of the gospel, along with Clement and the rest of my fellow workers,^m whose names are in the book of life.^n

^4Rejoice in the Lord always. I will say it again: Rejoice!^o ^5Let your gentleness be evident to all. The Lord is near.^p ^6Do not be anxious about anything,^q but in everything, by prayer and petition, with thanksgiving, present your requests to God.^r ^7And the peace of God,^s which transcends all understanding,^t will guard your hearts and your minds in Christ Jesus.

^8Finally, brothers, whatever is true, whatever is noble, whatever is right, whatever is pure, whatever is lovely, whatever is admirable—if anything is excellent or praiseworthy—think about such things. ^9Whatever you have learned or received or heard from me, or seen in me—put it into practice.^u And the God of peace^v will be with you.

Thanks for Their Gifts

^10I rejoice greatly in the Lord that at last you have renewed your concern for me.^w Indeed, you have been concerned, but you had no opportunity to show it. ^11I am not saying this because I am in need, for I have learned to be content^x whatever the circumstances. ^12I know what it is to be in need, and I know what it is to have plenty. I have learned the secret of being content in any and every situation, whether well fed or hungry,^y whether living in plenty or in want.^z ^13I can do

W Php 3:1 ◀▶ Php 4:6–7
C Php 3:20–21 ◀▶ Col 3:4
W Php 4:4 ◀▶ Php 4:11–13
W Php 4:6–7 ◀▶ Col 3:15
K Eph 5:14 ◀▶ Php 4:19

^h 3 Or loyal Syzygus

3:20–21 Paul encourages believers to focus on their future in heaven and reminds us that, at the resurrection, we will receive a body like the body Jesus had after he rose from the dead. Christ's resurrection body was immortal and incorruptible, able to travel instantaneously over great distances and able to appear and disappear at will (see Mt 28:10; Mk 16:11–12; Lk 24:31). Yet this body was identical in appearance to his natural body—solidly material, capable of touch and able to take sustenance (see Lk 24:38–43).

4:5 Our daily walk before the Lord should be lived in constant expectation that he could return at any moment. He has delayed his coming so that sinners could be saved and "come to a knowledge of the truth" (1Ti 2:4; see 2Pe 3:9). Therefore, as believers we must witness and live in holiness, knowing that he may return at any time, but working to fulfill his great commission even if it means another century until he returns.

everything through him who gives me strength.ᵃ

¹⁴Yet it was good of you to shareᵇ in my troubles. ¹⁵Moreover, as you Philippians know, in the early daysᶜ of your acquaintance with the gospel, when I set out from Macedonia,ᵈ not one church shared with me in the matter of giving and receiving, except you only;ᵉ ¹⁶for even when I was in Thessalonica,ᶠ you sent me aid again and again when I was in need.ᵍ ¹⁷Not that I am looking for a gift, but I am looking for what may be credited to your account.ʰ ¹⁸I have received full payment and even more; I am amply supplied, now that I have received from Epaphroditusⁱ the gifts you sent. They are a fragrantʲ offering, an acceptable sacrifice, pleasing to God. ¹⁹And my God will meet all your needsᵏ according to his glorious richesˡ in Christ Jesus.

²⁰To our God and Fatherᵐ be glory for ever and ever. Amen.ⁿ

Final Greetings

²¹Greet all the saints in Christ Jesus. The brothers who are with meᵒ send greetings. ²²All the saintsᵖ send you greetings, especially those who belong to Caesar's household.

²³The grace of the Lord Jesus Christᵍ be with your spirit.ʳ Amen.ʲ

4:13 ᵃ2Co 12:9; Eph 3:16; Col 1:1; 1Ti 1:12; 2Ti 4:17
4:14 ᵇPhp 1:7
4:15 ᶜPhp 1:5
ᵈS Ac 16:9
ᵉ2Co 11:8,9
4:16 ᶠS Ac 17:1
ᵍ1Th 2:9
4:17 ʰ1Co 9:11,12
4:18 ⁱPhp 2:25
ʲS 2Co 2:14
4:19 ᵏPs 23:1; 2Co 9:8 ˡS Ro 2:4
4:20 ᵐGal 1:4; 1Th 1:3; 3:11,13
ⁿS Ro 11:36
4:21 ᵒGal 1:2
4:22 ᵖS Ac 9:13
4:23 ᵍS Ro 16:20
ʳS Gal 6:18

K Php 4:13 ◀▶ Col 1:14

L 1Co 10:13 ◀▶ 1Ti 6:17
P 2Co 9:6–11 ◀▶ 1Ti 4:8

ʲ23 Some manuscripts do not have *Amen*.

Colossians

Author: Paul

Theme: The preeminence and glory of Christ as God's eternal Son

Date of Writing: c. A.D. 60–62

Outline of Colossians
   I. Greetings and Appreciation (1:1–8)
  II. Jesus Christ and the Believer (1:9—2:7)
 III. Dangerous Doctrines (2:8—3:4)
 IV. Practical Living (3:5—4:6)
  V. Greetings and Conclusion (4:7–18)

PAUL WROTE THIS epistle to the Colossians at about the same time as his epistle to the Ephesians. The content of the two letters, in fact, is very similar, earning Colossians the nickname as the twin epistle of Ephesians. Because Paul was imprisoned in Rome, Tychicus delivered this letter to the struggling Colossian church (see 4:7).

Colosse was located about one hundred miles east of Ephesus near modern-day Turkey. During Paul's ministry in Ephesus, Epaphras was converted and had subsequently carried the gospel message to Colosse. The small church that resulted from Epaphras's witness was under attack by false teachers. Epaphras brought news of this attack to Paul, who ultimately penned this letter in response.

Philosophers and false teachers who fused religion and Greek philosophy had attempted to modify the gospel message in the Colossian church by challenging the preeminence of Christ, relying on human wisdom and tradition, worshiping angels and encouraging severe asceticism and ceremonialism in addition to faith in Christ. Paul defends the gospel by setting forth the clear doctrine of the nature of Christ and his preeminence in the church. Paul also warns against the danger of legalism, requiring instead that ethical demands and intellectual standards be properly integrated into the pattern of Christian living.

COLOSSIANS 1:1

1 Paul, an apostle[a] of Christ Jesus by the will of God,[b] and Timothy[c] our brother,

[2] To the holy and faithful[a] brothers in Christ at Colosse:

Grace[d] and peace to you from God our Father.[b,e]

Thanksgiving and Prayer

[3] We always thank God,[f] the Father of our Lord Jesus Christ, when we pray for you, [4] because we have heard of your faith in Christ Jesus and of the love[g] you have for all the saints[h]— [5] the faith and love that spring from the hope[i] that is stored up for you in heaven[j] and that you have already heard about in the word of truth,[k] the gospel [6] that has come to you. All over the world[l] this gospel is bearing fruit[m] and growing, just as it has been doing among you since the day you heard it and understood God's grace in all its truth. [7] You learned it from Epaphras,[n] our dear fellow servant, who is a faithful minister[o] of Christ on our[c] behalf, [8] and who also told us of your love in the Spirit.[p]

[9] For this reason, since the day we heard about you,[q] we have not stopped praying for you[r] and asking God to fill you with the knowledge of his will[s] through all spiritual wisdom and understanding.[t] [10] And we pray this in order that you may live a life worthy[u] of the Lord and may please him[v] in every way: bearing fruit in every good work, growing in the knowledge of God,[w] [11] being strengthened with all power[x] according to his glorious might so that you may have great endurance and patience,[y] and joyfully [12] giving thanks to the Father,[z] who has qualified you[d] to share in the inheritance[a] of the saints in the kingdom of light.[b] [13] For he has rescued us from the dominion of darkness[c] and brought us into the kingdom[d] of the Son he loves,[e]

[14] in whom we have redemption,[e,f] the forgiveness of sins.[g]

The Supremacy of Christ

[15] He is the image[h] of the invisible God,[i] the firstborn[j] over all creation. [16] For by him all things were created:[k] things in heaven and on earth, visible and invisible, whether thrones or powers or rulers or authorities;[l] all things were created by him and for him.[m] [17] He is before all things,[n] and in him all things hold together. [18] And he is the head[o] of the body, the church;[p] he is the beginning and the firstborn[q] from among the dead,[r] so that in everything he might have the supremacy. [19] For God was pleased[s] to have all his fullness[t] dwell in him, [20] and through him to reconcile[u] to himself all things, whether things on earth or things in heaven,[v] by making peace[w] through his blood,[x] shed on the cross.

[21] Once you were alienated from God and were enemies[y] in your minds[z] because of[f] your evil behavior. [22] But now he has reconciled[a] you by Christ's physical body[b] through death to present you[c] holy in his sight, without blemish and free from accusation[d]— [23] if you continue[e] in your faith, established[f] and firm, not moved from the hope[g] held out in the gospel. This is the gospel that you heard and that has been proclaimed to every creature under heaven,[h] and of which I, Paul, have become a servant.[i]

Paul's Labor for the Church

[24] Now I rejoice[j] in what was suffered for you, and I fill up in my flesh what is still lacking in regard to Christ's afflictions,[k] for the sake of his body, which is the church.[l] [25] I have become its servant[m] by the commission God gave me[n] to present to you the word of God[o] in its fullness— [26] the mystery[p] that has been kept hidden for ages and generations, but is now disclosed to the saints. [27] To them God has chosen to make known[q] among

---

E Php 3:3 ◀▶ Col 2:5
F Php 2:1 ◀▶ 1Th 1:6
A Eph 3:14–19 ◀
G Eph 4:11–14 ◀▶ 1Th 5:20
M Php 1:19 ◀▶ 1Th 1:5
W Php 3:3 ◀▶ 1Th 4:7–8
S Php 3:18 ◀▶ Col 1:21–23
C Php 3:18–19 ◀▶ Col 1:21
L Eph 5:14 ◀▶ Col 1:19–22

1:1 a S 1Co 1:1; b S 2Co 1:1; c S Ac 16:1
1:2 d Col 4:18; e Ro 1:7
1:3 f S Ro 1:8
1:4 g Gal 5:6; h S Ac 9:13; Eph 1:15; Phm 5
1:5 i ver 23; 1Th 5:8; Tit 1:2; j 1Pe 1:4; k S 2Ti 2:15
1:6 l ver 23; S Ro 10:18 m Jn 15:16
1:7 n Col 4:12; Phm 23 o Col 4:7
1:8 p Ro 15:30
1:9 q ver 4; Eph 1:15 r S Ro 1:10 s S Eph 5:17 t S Eph 1:17
1:10 u S Eph 4:1 v S 2Co 5:9 w ver 6
1:11 x S Php 4:13 y Eph 4:2
1:12 z Eph 5:20 a S Ac 20:32 b S Ac 26:18
1:13 c S Ac 26:18 d 2Pe 1:11 e Mt 3:17
1:14 f S Ro 3:24 g Eph 1:7
1:15 h S Jn 14:9 i S Jn 1:18; 1Ti 1:17; Heb 11:27 j S ver 18
1:16 k S Jn 1:3 l Eph 1:20,21; m S Ro 11:36
1:17 n S Jn 1:2
1:18 o S Eph 1:22 p ver 24; S 1Co 12:27 q ver 15; Ps 89:27; Ro 8:29; Heb 1:6 r Ac 26:23; Rev 1:5
1:19 s S Eph 1:5 t S Jn 1:16
1:20 u S Ro 5:10 v Eph 1:10 w S Lk 2:14 x Eph 2:13
1:21 y Ro 5:10 z Eph 2:3
1:22 a ver 20; S Ro 5:10 b Ro 7:4 c S 2Co 4:14 d Eph 1:4; 5:27
1:23 e S Ro 11:22 f Eph 3:17 g ver 5; h ver 6; S Ro 10:18 i ver 25; S 1Co 3:5
1:24 j S 2Co 6:10 k S 2Co 1:5 l S 1Co 12:27
1:25 m ver 23; S 1Co 3:5 n Eph 3:2 o S Heb 4:12
1:26 p S Ro 16:25
1:27 q S Mt 13:11

D Eph 5:25 ◀▶ Col 1:20–22
K Php 4:19 ◀▶ 1Th 5:9–10
L Col 1:13–14 ◀▶ Col 2:13
D Col 1:14 ◀▶ 1Th 5:9–10
C Col 1:13 ◀▶ Col 2:13
S Col 1:10 ◀▶ Col 2:6

a 2 Or *believing* b 2 Some manuscripts *Father and the Lord Jesus Christ* c 7 Some manuscripts *your* d 12 Some manuscripts *us* e 14 A few late manuscripts *redemption through his blood* f 21 Or *minds, as shown by*

the Gentiles the glorious riches[r] of this mystery, which is Christ in you,[s] the hope of glory. [28]We proclaim him, admonishing[t] and teaching everyone with all wisdom,[u] so that we may present everyone perfect[v] in Christ. [29]To this end I labor,[w] struggling[x] with all his energy, which so powerfully works in me.[y]

2 I want you to know how much I am struggling[z] for you and for those at Laodicea,[a] and for all who have not met me personally. [2]My purpose is that they may be encouraged in heart[b] and united in love, so that they may have the full riches of complete understanding, in order that they may know the mystery[c] of God, namely, Christ, [3]in whom are hidden all the treasures of wisdom and knowledge.[d] [4]I tell you this so that no one may deceive you by fine-sounding arguments.[e] [5]For though I am absent from you in body, I am present with you in spirit[f] and delight to see how orderly[g] you are and how firm[h] your faith in Christ[i] is.

Freedom From Human Regulations Through Life With Christ

[6]So then, just as you received Christ Jesus as Lord,[j] continue to live in him, [7]rooted[k] and built up in him, strengthened in the faith as you were taught,[l] and overflowing with thankfulness.

[8]See to it that no one takes you captive through hollow and deceptive philosophy,[m] which depends on human tradition and the basic principles of this world[n] rather than on Christ.

[9]For in Christ all the fullness[o] of the Deity lives in bodily form, [10]and you have been given fullness in Christ, who is the head[p] over every power and authority.[q]

[11]In him you were also circumcised,[r] in the putting off of the sinful nature,[g][s] not with a circumcision done by the hands of men but with the circumcision done by Christ, [12]having been buried with him in baptism[t] and raised with him[u] through your faith in the power of God, who raised him from the dead.[v]

[13]When you were dead in your sins[w] and in the uncircumcision of your sinful nature,[h] God made you[i] alive[x] with Christ. He forgave us all our sins,[y] [14]having canceled the written code, with its regulations,[z] that was against us and that stood opposed to us; he took it away, nailing it to the cross.[a] [15]And having disarmed the powers and authorities,[b] he made a public spectacle of them, triumphing over them[c] by the cross.[j]

[16]Therefore do not let anyone judge you[d] by what you eat or drink,[e] or with regard to a religious festival,[f] a New Moon celebration[g] or a Sabbath day.[h] [17]These are a shadow of the things that were to come;[i] the reality, however, is found in Christ. [18]Do not let anyone who delights in false humility[j] and the worship of angels disqualify you for the prize.[k] Such a person goes into great detail about what he has seen, and his unspiritual mind puffs him up with idle notions. [19]He has lost connection with the Head,[l] from whom the whole body,[m] supported and held together by its ligaments and sinews, grows as God causes it to grow.[n]

[20]Since you died with Christ[o] to the basic principles of this world,[p] why, as though you still belonged to it, do you submit to its rules:[q] [21]"Do not handle! Do not taste! Do not touch!"? [22]These are all destined to perish[r] with use, because they are based on human commands and teachings.[s] [23]Such regulations indeed have an appearance of wisdom, with their self-imposed worship, their false humility[t] and their harsh treatment of the body, but they lack any value in restraining sensual indulgence.

Rules for Holy Living

3 Since, then, you have been raised with Christ,[u] set your hearts on things above, where Christ is seated at the right hand of God.[v] [2]Set your minds on things above, not on earthly things.[w] [3]For you died,[x] and your life is now hid-

E *Col 1:8* ◀▶ *1 Th 1:5–6*
S *Col 1:21–23* ◀▶ *Col 2:11*
S *Col 2:6* ◀▶ *Col 3:17*
C *Col 1:21* ◀▶ *Col 3:5–7*
L *Col 1:19–22* ◀▶ *1 Th 5:9–10*

M *1 Co 14:24–25* ◀▶ *1 Ti 6:3–4*

[g] 11 Or *the flesh* [h] 13 Or *your flesh* [i] 13 Some manuscripts *us* [j] 15 Or *them in him*

den with Christ in God. ⁴When Christ, who is your*ᵏ* life,*ʸ* appears,*ᶻ* then you also will appear with him in glory.*ᵃ*

⁵Put to death,*ᵇ* therefore, whatever belongs to your earthly nature:*ᶜ* sexual immorality,*ᵈ* impurity, lust, evil desires and greed,*ᵉ* which is idolatry.*ᶠ* ⁶Because of these, the wrath of God*ᵍ* is coming. ⁷You used to walk in these ways, in the life you once lived.*ʰ* ⁸But now you must rid yourselves*ⁱ* of all such things as these: anger, rage, malice, slander,*ʲ* and filthy language from your lips.*ᵏ* ⁹Do not lie to each other,*ˡ* since you have taken off your old self*ᵐ* with its practices ¹⁰and have put on the new self,*ⁿ* which is being renewed*ᵒ* in knowledge in the image of its Creator.*ᵖ* ¹¹Here there is no Greek or Jew,*ᵠ* circumcised or uncircumcised,*ʳ* barbarian, Scythian, slave or free,*ˢ* but Christ is all,*ᵗ* and is in all.

¹²Therefore, as God's chosen people, holy and dearly loved, clothe yourselves*ᵘ* with compassion, kindness, humility,*ᵛ* gentleness and patience.*ʷ* ¹³Bear with each other*ˣ* and forgive whatever grievances you may have against one another. Forgive as the Lord forgave you.*ʸ* ¹⁴And over all these virtues put on love,*ᶻ* which binds them all together in perfect unity.*ᵃ*

¹⁵Let the peace of Christ*ᵇ* rule in your hearts, since as members of one body*ᶜ* you were called to peace.*ᵈ* And be thankful. ¹⁶Let the word of Christ*ᵉ* dwell in you richly as you teach and admonish one another with all wisdom,*ᶠ* and as you sing psalms,*ᵍ* hymns and spiritual songs with gratitude in your hearts to God.*ʰ* ¹⁷And whatever you do,*ⁱ* whether in word or deed, do it all in the name of the Lord Jesus, giving thanks*ʲ* to God the Father through him.

Rules for Christian Households
3:18–4:1pp — Eph 5:22–6:9

¹⁸Wives, submit to your husbands,*ᵏ* as is fitting in the Lord.

¹⁹Husbands, love your wives and do not be harsh with them.

²⁰Children, obey your parents in everything, for this pleases the Lord.

²¹Fathers, do not embitter your children, or they will become discouraged.

²²Slaves, obey your earthly masters in everything; and do it, not only when their eye is on you and to win their favor, but with sincerity of heart and reverence for the Lord. ²³Whatever you do, work at it with all your heart, as working for the Lord, not for men, ²⁴since you know that you will receive an inheritance*ˡ* from the Lord as a reward.*ᵐ* It is the Lord Christ you are serving. ²⁵Anyone who does wrong will be repaid for his wrong, and there is no favoritism.*ⁿ*

4 Masters, provide your slaves with what is right and fair,*ᵒ* because you know that you also have a Master in heaven.

Further Instructions

²Devote yourselves to prayer,*ᵖ* being watchful and thankful. ³And pray for us, too, that God may open a door*ᵠ* for our message, so that we may proclaim the mystery*ʳ* of Christ, for which I am in chains.*ˢ* ⁴Pray that I may proclaim it clearly, as I should. ⁵Be wise*ᵗ* in the way you act toward outsiders;*ᵘ* make the most of every opportunity.*ᵛ* ⁶Let your conversation be always full of grace,*ʷ* seasoned with salt,*ˣ* so that you may know how to answer everyone.*ʸ*

Final Greetings

⁷Tychicus*ᶻ* will tell you all the news about me. He is a dear brother, a faithful minister and fellow servant*ᵃ* in the Lord. ⁸I am sending him to you for the express purpose that you may know about our*ᵐ* circumstances and that he may encourage your hearts.*ᵇ* ⁹He is coming with Onesimus,*ᶜ* our faithful and dear brother,

C Php 4:5 ◄ ► 1Th 1:10
C Col 2:13 ◄ ► 1Th 4:13
H Php 3:19 ◄ ► Col 3:25
W Php 4:11–13 ◄ ► 1Th 5:16
S Col 2:11 ◄ ► Col 3:23–25

S Col 3:17 ◄ ► 1Th 4:3
H Col 3:5–6 ◄ ► 1Th 1:10

ᵏ 4 Some manuscripts *our* *ˡ 6* Some early manuscripts *coming on those who are disobedient* *ᵐ 8* Some manuscripts *that he may know about your*

3:4 Paul foreshadows the second coming in this verse as he pictures Christ's glorious appearance. This passage also suggests that the raptured saints will also share in that visible, manifested glory. This prophecy echoes Paul's words in Romans regarding this glorious manifestation (see Ro 8:18–19).

who is one of you.ᵈ They will tell you everything that is happening here.

¹⁰My fellow prisoner Aristarchusᵉ sends you his greetings, as does Mark,ᶠ the cousin of Barnabas.ᵍ (You have received instructions about him; if he comes to you, welcome him.) ¹¹Jesus, who is called Justus, also sends greetings. These are the only Jews among my fellow workersʰ for the kingdom of God, and they have proved a comfort to me. ¹²Epaphras,ⁱ who is one of youʲ and a servant of Christ Jesus, sends greetings. He is always wrestling in prayer for you,ᵏ that you may stand firm in all the will of God, matureˡ and fully assured. ¹³I vouch for him that he is working hard for you and for those at Laodiceaᵐ and Hierapolis. ¹⁴Our dear friend Luke,ⁿ the doctor, and Demasᵒ send greetings. ¹⁵Give my greetings to the brothers at Laodicea,ᵖ and to Nympha and the church in her house.ᑫ

¹⁶After this letter has been read to you, see that it is also readʳ in the church of the Laodiceans and that you in turn read the letter from Laodicea.

¹⁷Tell Archippus:ˢ "See to it that you complete the work you have received in the Lord."ᵗ

¹⁸I, Paul, write this greeting in my own hand.ᵘ Rememberᵛ my chains.ʷ Grace be with you.ˣ

4:9 ᵈver 12
4:10 ᵉS Ac 19:29
ᶠS Ac 12:12
ᵍS Ac 4:36
4:11 ʰS Php 2:25
4:12 ⁱCol 1:7; Phm 23 ʲver 9
ᵏS Ro 15:30
ˡS 1Co 2:6
4:13 ᵐS Col 2:1
4:14 ⁿ2Ti 4:11; Phm 24 ᵒ2Ti 4:10; Phm 24
4:15 ᵖS Col 2:1
ᑫS Ro 16:5
4:16 ʳ2Th 3:14; S 1Ti 4:13
4:17 ˢPhm 2
ᵗ2Ti 4:5
4:18 ᵘS 1Co 16:21
ᵛHeb 13:3
ʷS Ac 21:33
ˣ1Ti 6:21; 2Ti 4:22; Tit 3:15; Heb 13:25

1 Thessalonians

Author: Paul

Theme: The doctrine of the return of Christ

Date of Writing: C. A.D. 50–51

Outline of 1 Thessalonians
  I. Introduction and Thanksgiving (1:1–10)
  II. Paul Defends His Actions (2:1—3:13)
  III. Practical Problems About Church Life (4:1—5:22)
  IV. Conclusion (5:23–28)

THIS LETTER IS among the earliest of Paul's writings, written while Paul ministered in the city of Corinth during his second missionary journey. While on this missionary journey, Paul had taught in the seaport of Thessalonica for three weeks. Many Greeks believed in Christ, but Paul was forced to leave suddenly for Berea because of opposition from the Jews (see Ac 17). Paul's recent converts in Thessalonica were left with little support amid much persecution. Subsequently, Timothy brought Paul a report concerning the spiritual conditions in the church at Thessalonica. Paul's letter to this young church commends the Thessalonians for their courageous behavior in the face of persecution.

There are varied themes in this letter, but the subject of the second coming is referred to in all five chapters of this epistle. The believers had raised some questions about the return of the Lord, so Paul answers these questions by focusing their hope in Christ's return, offering comfort and encouragement for those facing the death of loved ones. Paul's discussion of eschatology is concentrated in 4:13–18, but there are many predictions about the rapture and the end times unveiled throughout this brief letter. Paul also supplements his former teaching concerning the problems that these new believers faced in living the Christian life.

1 Paul, Silas[a][a] and Timothy,[b]

To the church of the Thessalonians[c] in God the Father and the Lord Jesus Christ:

Grace and peace to you.[b][d]

Thanksgiving for the Thessalonians' Faith

[2] We always thank God for all of you,[e] mentioning you in our prayers.[f] [3] We continually remember before our God and Father[g] your work produced by faith,[h] your labor prompted by love,[i] and your endurance inspired by hope[j] in our Lord Jesus Christ.

[4] For we know, brothers loved by God,[k] that he has chosen you, [5] because our gospel[l] came to you not simply with words, but also with power,[m] with the Holy Spirit and with deep conviction. You know[n] how we lived among you for your sake. [6] You became imitators of us[o] and of the Lord; in spite of severe suffering,[p] you welcomed the message with the joy given by the Holy Spirit.[q] [7] And so you became a model[s] to all the believers in Macedonia[t] and Achaia.[u] [8] The Lord's message[v] rang out from you not only in Macedonia and Achaia—your faith in God has become known everywhere.[w] Therefore we do not need to say anything about it, [9] for they themselves report what kind of reception you gave us. They tell how you turned[x] to God from idols[y] to serve the living and true God,[z] [10] and to wait for his Son from heaven,[a] whom he raised from the dead[b]—Jesus, who rescues us from the coming wrath.[c]

Paul's Ministry in Thessalonica

2 You know, brothers, that our visit to you[d] was not a failure.[e] [2] We had previously suffered[f] and been insulted in Philippi,[g] as you know, but with the help of our God we dared to tell you his gospel in spite of strong opposition.[h] [3] For the appeal we make does not spring from error or impure motives,[i] nor are we trying to trick you.[j] [4] On the contrary, we speak as men approved by God to be entrusted with the gospel.[k] We are not trying to please men[l] but God, who tests our hearts.[m] [5] You know we never used flattery, nor did we put on a mask to cover up greed[n]—God is our witness.[o] [6] We were not looking for praise from men,[p] not from you or anyone else.

As apostles[q] of Christ we could have been a burden to you,[r] [7] but we were gentle among you, like a mother caring for her little children.[s] [8] We loved you so much that we were delighted to share with you not only the gospel of God[t] but our lives as well,[u] because you had become so dear to us. [9] Surely you remember, brothers, our toil and hardship; we worked[v] night and day in order not to be a burden to anyone[w] while we preached the gospel of God to you.

[10] You are witnesses,[x] and so is God,[y] of how holy,[z] righteously and blamelessly we were among you who believed. [11] For you know that we dealt with each of you as a father deals with his own children,[a] [12] en-

E *Col 2:5* ◀ ▶ *1Th 4:8*
M *Col 1:9–11* ◀ ▶ *2Ti 1:7*
T *Eph 6:17* ◀ ▶ *1Ti 4:1*
F *Col 1:8* ◀ ▶ *2Ti 1:7*
J *Gal 5:22* ◀ ▶ *Heb 1:9*
C *Col 3:4* ◀ ▶ *1Th 2:19*
H *Col 3:25* ◀ ▶ *1Th 5:3*

E *1Co 4:5* ◀ ▶ *Heb 4:12–13*

[a] 1 Greek *Silvanus*, a variant of *Silas* [b] 1 Some early manuscripts *you from God our Father and the Lord Jesus Christ*

1:10 Paul instructs believers to confidently and expectantly wait for the second coming of Christ because Jesus has been raised from the dead. Our hope and expectation are shaped by the Bible's promise that Jesus will deliver us "from the coming wrath." While some interpret this reference of "wrath" as the punishment of hell, this interpretation seems untenable in this case because believers have already been delivered from the wrath of hell by their repentance and belief in Christ. Other scholars suggest that the "wrath" referred to here is the great white throne judgment of God. However, Revelation clearly states that that final judgment is reserved for the wicked dead (see Rev 20:11–15) and Paul appears to be addressing believers in this verse in 1 Thessalonians.

Still other scholars believe that this verse refers to a future period of tribulation, called "wrath" in Rev 6:16. Since the language of this verse indicates that Christ's return is imminent, these scholars contend that the "coming wrath" must refer to the coming wrath of God during the tribulation. Christ will deliver the Christian saints before the wrath of God is poured out on an unrepentant humanity. For further discussion of this topic, see the article on "Reasons for a Pretribulation Rapture" on p. 1384.

couraging, comforting and urging you to live lives worthy[b] of God, who calls[c] you into his kingdom and glory.

[13]And we also thank God continually[d] because, when you received the word of God,[e] which you heard from us, you accepted it not as the word of men, but as it actually is, the word of God, which is at work in you who believe. [14]For you, brothers, became imitators[f] of God's churches in Judea,[g] which are in Christ Jesus: You suffered from your own countrymen[h] the same things those churches suffered from the Jews, [15]who killed the Lord Jesus[i] and the prophets[j] and also drove us out. They displease God and are R hostile to all men [16]in their effort to keep us from speaking to the Gentiles[k] so that they may be saved. In this way they always heap up their sins to the limit.[l] The wrath of God has come upon them at last.[c]

Paul's Longing to See the Thessalonians

[17]But, brothers, when we were torn away from you for a short time (in person, not in thought),[m] out of our intense longing we made every effort to see you.[n] [18]For we wanted to come to you—certainly I, Paul, did, again and again—but C Satan[o] stopped us.[p] [19]For what is our hope, our joy, or the crown[q] in which we will glory[r] in the presence of our Lord Jesus when he comes?[s] Is it not you? [20]Indeed, you are our glory[t] and joy.

3 So when we could stand it no longer,[u] we thought it best to be left by ourselves in Athens.[v] [2]We sent Timothy,[w] who is our brother and God's fellow worker[dx] in spreading the gospel of

R Ro 11:17-28 ◀▶ Rev 12:1-6
C 1Th 1:10 ◀▶ 1Th 3:13

2:12 [b]S Eph 4:1
[c]S Ro 8:28
2:13 [d]1Th 1:2;
S Ro 1:8
[e]S Heb 4:12
2:14 [f]1Th 1:6
[g]Gal 1:22
[h]Ac 17:5; 2Th 1:4
2:15 [i]Lk 24:20;
Ac 2:23 [j]S Mt 5:12
2:16 [k]Ac 13:45, 50; 17:5; S 20:3; 21:27; 24:9
[l]Mt 23:32
2:17 [m]1Co 5:3;
Col 2:5 [n]1Th 3:10
2:18 [o]S Mt 4:10
[p]Ro 1:13; 15:22
2:19 [q]Isa 62:3;
Php 4:1 [r]2Co 1:14
[s]Mt 16:27;
S Lk 17:30;
S 1Co 1:7; 4:5;
1Th 3:13;
2Th 1:8-10;
1Pe 1:7; 1Jn 2:28;
S Rev 1:7
2:20 [t]2Co 1:14
3:1 [u]ver 5
[v]S Ac 17:15
3:2 [w]S Ac 16:1
[x]S 1Co 3:9
[y]S 2Co 2:12
3:3 [z]Mk 4:17;
Jn 16:33; Ro 5:3;
2Co 1:4; 4:17;
2Ti 3:12
[a]S Ac 9:16; 14:22
3:4 [b]1Th 2:14
3:5 [c]ver 1 [d]ver 2
[e]Mt 4:3 [f]Gal 2:2;
Php 2:16
3:6 [g]S Ac 16:1
[h]Ac 18:5 [i]1Th 1:3
[j]1Th 2:17,18
3:8 [k]S 1Co 16:13
3:9 [l]1Th 1:2
[m]1Th 2:19,20
3:10 [n]2Ti 1:3
[o]1Th 2:17
3:11 [p]ver 13;
S Php 4:20
3:12 [q]Php 1:9;
1Th 4:9,10;
2Th 1:3

Christ,[y] to strengthen and encourage you in your faith, [3]so that no one would be unsettled by these trials.[z] You know quite well that we were destined for them.[a] [4]In fact, when we were with you, we kept telling you that we would be persecuted. And it turned out that way, as you well know.[b] [5]For this reason, when I could stand it no longer,[c] I sent to find out about your faith.[d] I was afraid that in some way the tempter[e] might have tempted you and our efforts might have been useless.[f]

Timothy's Encouraging Report

[6]But Timothy[g] has just now come to us from you[h] and has brought good news about your faith and love.[i] He has told us that you always have pleasant memories of us and that you long to see us, just as we also long to see you.[j] [7]Therefore, brothers, in all our distress and persecution we were encouraged about you because of your faith. [8]For now we really live, since you are standing firm[k] in the Lord. [9]How can we thank God enough for you[l] in return for all the joy we have in the presence of our God because of you?[m] [10]Night and day we pray[n] most earnestly that we may see you again[o] and supply what is lacking in your faith.

[11]Now may our God and Father[p] himself and our Lord Jesus clear the way for us to come to you. [12]May the Lord make your love increase and overflow for each other[q] and for everyone else, just as ours does for you. [13]May he strengthen your C
D

C 1Th 2:19 ◀▶ 1Th 4:14
D Mk 13:26 ◀▶ Rev 3:12

[c]16 Or *them fully* [d]2 Some manuscripts *brother and fellow worker*; other manuscripts *brother and God's servant*

2:16 Paul predicts that the wrath of God will fall upon those Jews who persecuted the early church. The fulfillment of this prophecy occurred only twenty years later when the Roman legions invaded Israel, destroyed Jerusalem and burned the temple in A.D. 70.

2:19 Paul's joy and "crown in which we will glory" were those believers that he had won to the Lord, those who would be in Christ's presence at his second coming. Since Christ's coming will be the time when the outcome of our works for the Lord will be made manifest (see 1Co 3:14; 2Co 5:10), Paul's joy will be his spiritual children (see 2Co 1:14; Php 2:16).

Note that Paul declares the certainty that his spiritual children will be in Christ's presence at the second coming. Such a positive expression might suggest that Paul saw the coming of Jesus as our deliverance from the coming wrath of God during the "time of trouble for Jacob" (Jer 30:7) and believed that Christians would be delivered from the tribulation and the untimely martyrdom of the wicked rule of the antichrist.

3:3-4 Paul reminds the church that though it will face opposition and persecution, these afflictions will help advance God's purposes (see Ac 11:19; Ro 5:3; 2Co 4:17).

3:13 Christ will complete the process of sanctifica-

hearts so that you will be blameless and holy in the presence of our God and Father when our Lord Jesus comes with all his holy ones.

Living to Please God

4 Finally, brothers, we instructed you how to live in order to please God, as in fact you are living. Now we ask you and urge you in the Lord Jesus to do this more and more. ²For you know what instructions we gave you by the authority of the Lord Jesus.

³It is God's will that you should be sanctified: that you should avoid sexual immorality; ⁴that each of you should learn to control his own body in a way that is holy and honorable, ⁵not in passionate lust like the heathen, who do not know God; ⁶and that in this matter no one should wrong his brother or take advantage of him. The Lord will punish men for all such sins, as we have already told you and warned you. ⁷For God did not call us to be impure, but to live a holy life. ⁸Therefore, he who rejects this instruction does not reject man but God, who gives you his Holy Spirit.

⁹Now about brotherly love we do not need to write to you, for you yourselves have been taught by God to love each other. ¹⁰And in fact, you do love all the brothers throughout Macedonia. Yet we urge you, brothers, to do so more and more.

¹¹Make it your ambition to lead a quiet life, to mind your own business and to work with your hands, just as we told you, ¹²so that your daily life may win the respect of outsiders and so that you will not be dependent on anybody.

The Coming of the Lord

¹³Brothers, we do not want you to be ignorant about those who fall asleep, or to grieve like the rest of men, who have no hope. ¹⁴We believe that Jesus died and rose again and so we believe that God will bring with Jesus those who have fallen asleep in him. ¹⁵According to the Lord's own word, we tell you that we who are still alive, who are left till the coming of the Lord, will certainly not precede those who have fallen asleep. ¹⁶For the Lord himself will come down from heaven, with a loud command, with the voice of the archangel and with the trumpet call of God, and the dead in Christ will rise first. ¹⁷After that, we who are still alive and are left will be

S Col 3:23–25 ◄► 1Th 4:6–7
S 1Th 4:3 ◄► 1Th 5:22–23
S Gal 5:16 ◄► 2Th 2:13
W Col 1:9 ◄► 2Th 2:13
E 1Th 1:5–6 ◄► 2Th 2:13

F Php 3:21 ◄► 1Ti 6:13
C Col 3:5–7 ◄► 1Th 5:6
C 1Th 3:13 ◄► 1Th 5:23   T Php 3:21 ◄

e 4 Or learn to live with his own wife; or learn to acquire a wife

---

tion in the life of the believers so that they will be holy before God when Christ returns (see 1Co 1:8; Php 1:6). This verse frames a clear reference to the first resurrection of the saints when Jesus comes in the air (see 4:16–17). While some scholars have suggested that the phrase "holy ones" may mean angels, this verse seems to use this phrase to mean the departed saints who will return with Jesus.

4:13–14 In these verses, Paul begins a major teaching about the resurrection of the saints. The believers in Thessalonica were concerned that those saints who had died might miss out on Christ's second coming. Paul assures them that they should not be concerned about the departed saints because they will participate in the rapture together with the believers that are still alive when Christ returns. Paul's words affirm Jesus' meaning to the thief on the cross when he promised, "Today you will be with me in paradise" (Lk 23:43). Though the body of a believer "sleeps" until the resurrection, their soul is instantly transformed to "paradise." Paul says that the souls of departed believers will come with Jesus at the rapture to receive their eternal, resurrection bodies from God.

4:15–18 Paul reveals that Christians living at the moment Christ returns would not hinder the resurrection of the departed saints. The "dead in Christ will rise first" (4:16) to receive their resurrection bodies a moment before the living believers are transformed into their new spiritual bodies. All believers shall then be gathered together in the clouds to meet Christ and remain with him forever.

The expression "caught up" (4:17) is the only place in the NT where a "rapture" is clearly referred to. This sudden raising up of a person or object describes the supernatural action of Christ to physically lift the resurrected bodies of the saints into the air to return to heaven with him as prophesied. This rapture of reunited believers will occur as Christ returns in the air (see Ac 1:11) just prior to the tribulation (see Rev 3:10). In light of this glorious resurrection, the believers should take comfort and comfort one another.

The Rapture

THE ENGLISH WORD *rapture* comes from the Latin *rapere*, which means "to snatch away; to be caught up." The OT notes two instances of this snatching or catching away of individuals. Genesis records that a righteous man named Enoch never died, for "God took him away" (Ge 5:24). Later, the Bible tells us that the prophet Elijah also escaped death when "Elijah went up to heaven in a whirlwind" (2Ki 2:11).

However, when Bible scholars today talk about the rapture they are usually referring to the resurrection of the church, a concept that is clearly taught in several different passages of Scripture. Although the word *rapture* does not appear in English translations of the Bible, it is an excellent word that describes what the Bible declares will happen to all believers who are alive at the moment when Christ calls his church home to heaven (see 1Th 4:16–17).

Jesus and Paul Teach About the Rapture

Some scholars suggest that the first mention of the rapture and resurrection of the church in the NT occurred when Jesus comforted Martha after the death of her brother, Lazarus. Jesus promised that Lazarus would rise again. These scholars contend that Jesus was talking about more than the resurrection of those who are physically dead. They believe instead that Jesus' words in this passage indicate the first clear teaching in the NT about the translation of the church when Christ returns.

Note that Jesus appears to repeat himself when he claims that whosoever "believes in me will live, even though he dies; and whoever lives and believes in me will never die" (Jn 11:25–26). Some scholars suggest that Jesus is not being redundant but rather talking about two distinct groups of Christians. These scholars believe that the first group is composed of those Christians who have died and are buried before Christ's second coming, hence the words "he . . . will live, even though he dies" (11:25). These scholars further contend that the second group in this passage is composed of believers who are alive when Christ returns. These believers are the ones to whom Jesus refers in Jn 11:26 as those who live and believe in him and never die. This second group represents a whole generation of believers who will not have to pass through death to reach eternal life but will instead be "caught up together . . . to meet the Lord in the air" (1Th 4:17).

The apostle Paul sheds additional light on the rapture in his first letters to the Thessalonians and the Corinthians (see 1Th 4:15–18; 1Co 15:51–54). In these letters, Paul lists several components of the rapture: (1) Not all Christians will die (see 1Th 4:17; 1Co 15:51). Many will be alive in the final generation when Christ returns. They will pass from this earthly life to life eternal without passing through the portals of death. (2) Before those who are alive are translated to heaven, Christ will resurrect the bodies of those believers who have died (see 1Th 4:16; 1Co 15:52). (3) This rapture will be instantaneous (see 1Co 15:52). (4) The rapture will be accompanied by the blowing of the last trumpet (see 1Th 4:16; 1Co 15:52). (5) All believers, dead or alive, will be changed (see 1Co 15:51). Their mortal, corruptible, earthly bodies will be transformed into incorruptible, immortal, heavenly bodies fit for eternity.

The Purpose of the Rapture

Since God is a God of order there must be some reason for this rapture of the believers. Scripture clearly provides the reason for the rapture of the church. The apostle Paul reminds us that we cannot enter an incorruptible heaven in a corruptible body that is subject to decay and death, so "the perishable must clothe itself with the imperishable, and the mortal with immortality" (1Co 15:53). The rapture provides that transformation and changes our earthly bodies into new resurrection bodies that will be like Christ's resurrected body—incorruptible and immortal. The apostle John reminds us that when Christ returns "we shall be like him, for we shall see him as he is" (1Jn 3:2). For further information on our resurrection bodies, see the article "The Resurrection of the Body" on p 1218.

If believers were not raptured and transformed, we would have to spend eternity in heaven without a body. Yet we must receive a new spiritual body to enjoy all that Christ has prepared for us in heaven. Therefore, the promise to the church is that we will all be transformed, the living and the dead, at the moment of his coming. Those Christians who have died in the faith will receive their new transformed bodies as they rise to meet Christ in the air, and those who are living will simultaneously be changed as they are raptured from the earth. Those who take part in the rapture will then appear before Christ's judgment seat so "that each one may receive what is due him for the things done while in the body, whether good or bad" (2Co 5:10). Then, as God's transformed children, we shall see Jesus face to face and "so we will be with the Lord forever" (1Th 4:17).

The Timing of the Rapture

If the Bible had included one simple statement about the exact sequence of events of the rapture and the return of Christ, all confusion about the timing of these events would have been removed forever. Since there is no such clear statement in Scripture, there is a certain degree of ambiguity about the timing of the rapture. As a result, many excellent and sincere Bible teachers have formed differing conclusions regarding the timing of the rapture. Many believe that the rapture will precede the great tribulation. Others favor a midtribulation rapture. Still other scholars suggest that a posttribulation rapture will occur at the glorious return of Christ at the Battle of Armageddon. Other scholars contend that the timing of the rapture is unimportant. Whether or not the church will have to experience the mass martyrdom of the tribulation is a matter of serious study and some concern. However, the Bible urges believers to place their primary focus on Christ's return, not on their possible martyrdom or suffering.

Part of the confusion surrounding the timing of the rapture is caused by the lack of specific prophecies that reveal when it will occur. Jesus clearly said that the time of the future resurrection of the saints had been specifically hidden from everyone but God the Father (see Mt 24:36). It is therefore our responsibility as believers to wait in watchful expectation "for his Son from heaven, whom he raised from the dead—Jesus, who rescues us from the coming wrath" (1 Th 1:10).

As we await Christ's return and our translation to heaven we are forced to live in a paradox. We are to be watchful and waiting, yet busy and witnessing since we do not know when Christ will return. This sense of spiritual tension has helped keep the church alive and focused. If Christ had clearly stated that his return would not occur for centuries, the church might have lost its sense of urgency and mission to go and "make disciples of all nations, baptizing them in the name of the Father and of the Son and of the Holy Spirit" (Mt 28:19).

During the last two hundred years, this belief in the imminent return of Christ has been a strong motivator behind much of today's missionary outreach. A strong belief in the literal return of Christ will continue to spur us on to win more souls to Christ so that we all will be ready for his shout, the archangel's voice and God's trumpet calling us to meet him "in the clouds" (1 Th 4:17).

caught up together with them in the clouds[d] to meet the Lord in the air. And so we will be with the Lord[e] forever. [18]Therefore encourage each other[f] with these words.

5 Now, brothers, about times and dates[g] we do not need to write to you,[h] [2]for you know very well that the day of the Lord[i] will come like a thief in the night.[j] [3]While people are saying, "Peace and safety,"[k] destruction will come on them suddenly,[l] as labor pains on a pregnant woman, and they will not escape.[m]

[4]But you, brothers, are not in darkness[n] so that this day should surprise you like a thief.[o] [5]You are all sons of the light[p] and sons of the day. We do not belong to the night or to the darkness. [6]So then, let us not be like others, who are asleep,[q] but let us be alert[r] and self-controlled.[s] [7]For those who sleep, sleep at night, and those who get drunk, get drunk at night.[t] [8]But since we belong to the day,[u] let us be self-controlled, putting on faith and love as a breastplate,[v] and the hope of salvation[w] as a helmet.[x] [9]For God did not appoint us to suffer wrath[y] but to receive salvation through our Lord Jesus Christ.[z] [10]He died for us so that, whether we are awake or asleep, we may live together with him.[a] [11]Therefore encourage one another[b] and build each other up,[c] just as in fact you are doing.

Final Instructions

[12]Now we ask you, brothers, to respect those who work hard[d] among you, who are over you in the Lord[e] and who admonish you. [13]Hold them in the highest regard in love because of their work. Live in peace with each other.[f] [14]And we urge you, brothers, warn those who are idle,[g] encourage the timid, help the weak,[h] be patient with everyone. [15]Make sure that nobody pays back wrong for wrong,[i] but always try to be kind to each other[j] and to everyone else.

[16]Be joyful always;[k] [17]pray continually;[l] [18]give thanks in all circumstances,[m] for this is God's will for you in Christ Jesus. [19]Do not put out the Spirit's fire;[n] [20]do not treat prophecies° with contempt. [21]Test everything.[p] Hold on to the good.[q] [22]Avoid every kind of evil.

[23]May God himself, the God of peace,[r] sanctify you through and through. May your whole spirit, soul[s] and body be kept blameless[t] at the coming of our Lord

---

4:17 [d] Ac 1:9; S Ac 8:39; S Rev 1:7; 11:12 [e] S Jn 12:26
4:18 [f] 1Th 5:11
5:1 [g] Ac 1:7
[h] 1Th 4:9
5:2 [i] S 1Co 1:8 [j] S Lk 12:39
5:3 [k] Jer 4:10; 6:14; Eze 13:10 [l] Job 15:21; Ps 35:8; 55:15; Isa 29:5; 47:9,11 [m] 2Th 1:9
5:4 [n] S Ac 26:18; 1Jn 2:8 [o] ver 2
5:5 [p] S Lk 16:8
5:6 [q] Ro 13:11 [r] S Mt 25:13 [s] S Ac 24:25
5:7 [t] Ac 2:15; Ro 13:13; 2Pe 2:13
5:8 [u] ver 5 [v] S Eph 6:14 [w] Ro 8:24 [x] Isa 59:17; Eph 6:17
5:9 [y] 1Th 1:10 [z] 2Th 2:13,14
5:10 [a] Ro 14:9; 2Co 5:15
5:11 [b] 1Th 4:18 [c] Eph 4:29
5:12 [d] Ro 16:6,12; 1Co 15:10 [e] 1Ti 5:17; Heb 13:17
5:13 [f] S Mk 9:50
5:14 [g] 2Th 3:6,7, 11 [h] Ro 14:1; 1Co 8:7-12
5:15 [i] Ro 12:17; 1Pe 3:9 [j] Eph 4:32
5:16 [k] Php 4:4
5:17 [l] S Lk 18:1
5:18 [m] S Eph 5:20
5:19 [n] Eph 4:30
5:20 ° 1Co 14:1-40
5:21 [p] 1Co 14:29; 1Jn 4:1 [q] Ro 12:9
5:23 [r] S Ro 15:33 [s] Heb 4:12 [t] S 1Th 3:13

E Ac 2:19–20 ◀▶ 2Th 2:1–9
N 2Co 6:2 ◀▶ 2Th 1:7–8
P 1Co 16:22 ◀▶ 1Th 5:4
H 1Th 1:10 ◀▶ 2Th 1:5–9
P 1Th 5:3 ◀▶ 1Th 5:9
C 1Th 4:13 ◀▶ 2Th 1:8
P 1Th 5:4 ◀▶ 2Th 1:5–9
D Col 1:20–22 ◀▶ 1Ti 2:5–6
K Col 1:14 ◀▶ 2Th 3:3
L Col 2:13 ◀▶ 1Ti 1:15

W Col 3:15 ◀▶ 1Th 5:18   A Ro 8:28 ◀
W 1Th 5:16 ◀▶ 1Ti 6:6
L Php 3:3 ◀▶ Heb 9:14
Q Eph 4:30 ◀▶ Heb 10:29
G Col 1:9 ◀▶ 1Ti 4:14
S 1Th 4:6–7 ◀▶ 2Th 3:6
C 1Th 4:14 ◀▶ 2Th 1:7

5:1–8 Paul encourages the believers to be watchful for the Lord's return. His return will be unexpected and sudden for unbelievers, appearing like "a thief in the night" (5:2). Unbelievers will not pay attention to the prophetic signs of his coming or the fulfillment of the prophecies in their day. The apostle warns that these unbelievers will perceive that all is "peace and safety" (5:3) and when destruction suddenly comes, they will not be able to escape.

While Paul did not want the Thessalonians trying to fix a specific date for Christ's return (see Ac 1:17), he did want them to be aware of the fulfillment of the prophetic signs so that Christ's return will be a joy. Watchful believers will understand the fulfillment of the prophetic signs that point to the imminent return of Christ because such believers are "sons of the light and sons of the day" (5:5). Paul says that the fulfillment of the prophecies of the second coming should motivate the saints to watch for the Lord's return and be prepared for the last days.

5:9–11 Despite persecution, Paul promises the saints that God has not chosen his children for wrath, but rather "to receive salvation through our Lord Jesus Christ" (5:9). These are two opposing spiritual destinies—wrath and salvation. If the church is granted salvation, we can conclude that the church will not experience the "wrath" of God during the coming tribulation and wicked rule of the antichrist (see Rev 6:17). Paul further says that because of Christ's death and resurrection we can be comforted with the promise that whether we live or die, we will "live together with him" (5:10).

5:23 Paul concludes his prophetic passage with a benediction for the total sanctification and purification of the church "at the coming of our Lord Jesus Christ," indicating that the promise of his second coming was a major focus for this young church.

The Rapture and the Tribulation Period

THE PRETRIBULATION RAPTURE

The Church Age	The 7 Year Tribulation Period	The Millennium
Rapture-Resurrection		*Christ Descends to Defeat Antichrist*
	3.5 YRS (1260 DAYS) — 3.5 YRS (1260 DAYS)	1000 YRS
	Antichrist Signs 7 Year Treaty with Israel	Antichrist Defiles Temple — Battle of Armageddon

THE MIDTRIBULATION RAPTURE

The Church Age	The 7 Year Tribulation Period	The Millennium
	Rapture-Resurrection	*Christ Descends to Defeat Antichrist*
	3.5 YRS (1260 DAYS) — 3.5 YRS (1260 DAYS)	1000 YRS
	Antichrist Signs 7 Year Treaty with Israel	Antichrist Defiles Temple — Battle of Armageddon

THE PREWRATH RAPTURE THEORY

The Church Age	The 7 Year Tribulation Period	The Millennium
	Rapture-Resurrection	*Christ Descends to Defeat Antichrist*
	3.5 YRS (1260 DAYS) — 3.5 YRS (1260 DAYS)	1000 YRS
	Antichrist Signs 7 Year Treaty with Israel	Antichrist Defiles Temple — Battle of Armageddon

THE POSTTRIBULATION THEORY

The Church Age	The 7 Year Tribulation Period	The Millennium
	Christ Descends to Defeat Antichrist *Rapture-Resurrection*	
	3.5 YRS (1260 DAYS) — 3.5 YRS (1260 DAYS)	1000 YRS
	Antichrist Signs 7 Year Treaty with Israel	Antichrist Defiles Temple — Battle of Armageddon

Jesus Christ.ᵘ ²⁴The one who callsᵛ you is faithfulʷ and he will do it.ˣ

²⁵Brothers, pray for us.ʸ ²⁶Greet all the brothers with a holy kiss.ᶻ ²⁷I charge you before the Lord to have this letter read to all the brothers.ᵃ

²⁸The grace of our Lord Jesus Christ be with you.ᵇ

5:23 ᵘ S 1Th 2:19
5:24 ᵛ S Ro 8:28
ʷ S 1Co 1:9
ˣ Nu 23:19; Php 1:6
5:25 ʸ Eph 6:19; Col 4:3; 2Th 3:1; Heb 13:18
5:26 ᶻ S Ro 16:16
5:27 ᵃ 2Th 3:14; S 1Ti 4:13
5:28 ᵇ S Ro 16:20

2 Thessalonians

Author: Paul

Theme: The revelation of Jesus Christ at his second coming

Date of Writing: C. A.D. 51–52

Outline of 2 Thessalonians
 I. Paul's Greetings and Prayer (1:1–12)
 II. Teaching About the Day of the Lord (2:1–17)
 III. Exhortation and Instruction for the Believers (3:1–15)
 IV. Final Greetings and Benediction (3:16–18)

PAUL WROTE THIS second epistle to the church at Thessalonica shortly after his first letter to these believers. Paul was ministering in Corinth during his second missionary journey when news reached him that some of the believers in the church at Thessalonica had misunderstood the message about the second coming that he had shared in his first letter. These believers mistakenly concluded that the second coming of Christ was so imminent that they failed to live with a balanced perspective. Paul attempted to correct their unbalanced view by reminding the believers to obey Christ's command to reach the world while still maintaining an attitude of expectation for his imminent return.

In this brief letter Paul reminds the believers in Thessalonica of what he had taught in his first letter to them and severely reprimands those who remain indifferent to Christ's second coming. Filled with references to the end times, this letter reiterates the prophetic signs that will prevail just before the return of the Lord. Paul urges the believers at Thessalonica to redeem the time they are given, working with their hands and keeping busy, while understanding that Christ may delay his return or may return at any moment.

Paul, Silas[a] and Timothy,[b]

To the church of the Thessalonians[c] in God our Father and the Lord Jesus Christ: ²Grace and peace to you from God the Father and the Lord Jesus Christ.[d]

Thanksgiving and Prayer

³We ought always to thank God for you,[e] brothers, and rightly so, because your faith is growing more and more, and the love every one of you has for each other is increasing.[f] ⁴Therefore, among God's churches we boast[g] about your perseverance and faith[h] in all the persecutions and trials you are enduring.[i]

⁵All this is evidence[j] that God's judgment is right, and as a result you will be counted worthy[k] of the kingdom of God, for which you are suffering. ⁶God is just:[l] He will pay back trouble to those who trouble you[m] ⁷and give relief to you who are troubled, and to us as well. This will happen when the Lord Jesus is revealed from heaven[n] in blazing fire[o] with his powerful angels.[p] ⁸He will punish[q] those who do not know God[r] and do not obey the gospel of our Lord Jesus.[s] ⁹They will be punished with everlasting destruction[t] and shut out from the presence of the Lord[u] and from the majesty of his power,[v] ¹⁰on the day[w] he comes to be glorified[x] in his holy people and to be marveled at among all those who have believed. This includes you, because you believed our testimony to you.[y]

¹¹With this in mind, we constantly pray for you,[z] that our God may count you worthy[a] of his calling,[b] and that by his power he may fulfill every good purpose[c] of yours and every act prompted by your faith.[d] ¹²We pray this so that the name of our Lord Jesus may be glorified in you,[e] and you in him, according to the grace of our God and the Lord Jesus Christ.[b]

The Man of Lawlessness

Concerning the coming of our Lord Jesus Christ[f] and our being gathered to him,[g] we ask you, brothers, ²not to become easily unsettled or alarmed by some prophecy, report or letter[h] supposed to have come from us, saying that the day of the Lord[i] has already come.[j] ³Don't let anyone deceive you[k] in any way, for ˻that day will not come˼ until the rebellion[l] occurs and the man of lawlessness[c] is revealed,[m] the man doomed to destruction. ⁴He will oppose and will exalt himself over everything that is called

P 1Th 5:9 ◀▶ 2Th 2:8–9
H 1Th 5:3 ◀▶ 2Th 2:8
C 1Th 5:23 ◀▶ 2Th 1:10
N 1Th 5:2–3 ◀▶ 2Th 2:10–12
C 1Th 5:6 ◀▶ 2Th 2:10–12

C 2Th 1:7 ◀▶ 2Th 2:1–3
C 2Th 1:10 ◀▶ 2Th 3:5
E 1Th 5:1–4 ◀▶ 1Ti 4:1–3

[a] 1 Greek *Silvanus*, a variant of *Silas*   [b] 12 Or *God and Lord, Jesus Christ*
[c] 3 Some manuscripts *sin*

1:7–10 Paul advises the believers who were facing persecution to take heart because Paul understood the pressures they were facing (see 1Th 1:6; 2:14–18). They will all be granted relief when Christ returns in judgment against those "who do not know God and do not obey the gospel of our Lord Jesus" (1:8).

2:1–3 In these verses Paul corrects a misunderstanding held by some of the Thessalonians that they had somehow missed the resurrection because the day of the Lord had already begun. Paul's words clarify his earlier teaching and give a clear order of events concerning the rise of antichrist to power during the tribulation:
1. The forces of lawlessness were already at work in Paul's day (2:7).
2. Paul reveals that there will first be a "rebellion" (2:3). Note that though the majority of scholars believe this is an aggressive rebellion against the things of God (see Mt 24:10–12; 1Ti 4:1), a small group contend that the Greek word *apostasia* used here refers to the rapture. In Greek, the word *apostasia* means "the departure away from something or someone." While traditionally this has been applied to a departure *from* the beliefs of the church, some Bible students say that this word may refer to the departure *of* the church or its rapture from the earth. Since this interpretation is not well supported by the context of the surrounding verses, the majority of scholars believe that the concept of religious apostasy and rebellion against God is the intent of this Greek word and its English translation.
3. The "man of lawlessness" (2:3) will not be revealed until the Holy Spirit, who is restraining the antichrist's appearance, is taken out of the way (2:7).

2:4–9 Paul warns that this "man doomed to destruction" (2:3) will set himself up above every god and everything associated with the worship of the true God. He will make his blasphemous pronounce-

Reasons for a Pretribulation Rapture

DIFFERENT METHODS IN the interpretation of prophecy affect the conclusions that are drawn from prophetic passages. Those who view prophetic Scripture as a figurative compilation of apocalyptic literature will draw different conclusions from those who view Scripture from a literal point of view. If one interprets Scripture literally and consistently one arrives at the conclusion that the church, the body of Christ, will be removed from the earth before any part of the tribulation begins. Several passages of Scripture support this interpretation of the pretribulation rapture of the church.

In Christ's messages to the seven churches in the opening chapters of Revelation the church is mentioned nineteen times as being on earth. However, the central chapters of Revelation (chs. 4—19), which describe the tribulation period in great detail, make no mention of the church's presence on earth during that time of wrath. Instead, throughout this section of Revelation the church is described as participating in the marriage supper of the Lamb (see Rev 19:7–9) and standing before the judgment seat of Christ in heaven (see 2Co 5:10).

Note also that Rev 6:17 and 7:1–8 prophesy that before the great day of God's wrath, the angels will hold back their judgment until they have "put a seal on the foreheads of the servants of our God" (Rev 7:3). John's account then describes the angels sealing "144,000 from all the tribes of Israel" (7:4), describing each of the tribes of Israel by name and noting the number of each tribe that is sealed for divine protection. Because of God's great love for believers, the omission of a reference to any protection extended to the church strongly indicates that the church is already safely in heaven at this time.

John's vision in Rev 4 provides another supporting reason for a pretribulation rapture. When John was taken up to heaven to stand before the throne, he saw 24 elders with crowns on their heads. Scripture indicates that believers will be given crowns in heaven for specific behaviors and actions performed on earth. (For additional information, see the article on "Crowns and Rewards" on p. 1326.) Paul indicates that these crowns will be awarded by "the Lord, the righteous Judge" (2Ti 4:8) after Christ's return. He also indicates that all believers must "appear before the judgment seat of Christ, that each one may receive what is due him for the things done while in the body, whether good or bad" (2Co 5:10). This judgment will take place following the resurrection of all believers. Therefore John's vision of the 24 crowned elders lends great credence to the belief that these elders represent the church and that the rapture of the church must have already occurred. It is only after John sees these 24 elders that he is granted the vision of the sequential series of judgments of the tribulation.

The book of Matthew also records the events of the tribulation and focuses on Israel's participation in this time of wrath while omitting any reference to the church (see Mt 24). Specifically, those in Judea are told to flee to the hills (see 24:26); there is no mention of any other country or persons told to flee. Jesus' words also indicate that the Jews should pray that this devastation does not occur on the Sabbath (see 24:20). Jewish rabbis had interpreted God's prohibition of work on the Sabbath in Ex 16:29 to include a restriction prohibiting a Jew from walking (or fleeing) more than two thousand cubits (one thousand yards) on the Sabbath. Only the Jews would be bound by the rabbinical restriction of this "Sabbath day's walk" (Ac 1:12), so Jesus' concern would have no meaning for Christians. Obviously, Jesus was referring to the Jews enduring the tribulation, not the church.

Paul also supports the pretribulation rapture when he tells the Thessalonians that "God did not appoint us to suffer wrath but to receive salvation through our Lord Jesus Christ" (1Th 5:9). Notice that Paul contrasts two separate destinies in this verse. He reminds the church that their destiny is salvation, not God's wrath. When compared with his words earlier in this letter, Paul clearly says that Christians are to "wait for his Son from heaven, whom he raised from the dead—Jesus, who rescues us from the coming wrath" (1Th 1:10). Though some contend that this coming wrath refers to the punishment of hell, Scripture clearly states that we are delivered from hell by Christ's first coming and death on the cross, not by his second coming in the clouds. This "wrath to come" of 1Th 1:10 must refer to the tribulation, and this verse, therefore, is a clear declaration that Christ's return for his church (see 1Th 4:16–17) is the event that will deliver us from the tribulations' wrath.

The strongest proof that the rapture will precede the tribulation is found in the book of 2 Thessalonians. The church at Thessalonica was apprehensive that the great day of the Lord could occur at any moment. Paul reminded the believers of his teaching about "the coming of our Lord Jesus Christ and our being gathered to him" (2Th 2:1). He told them not to be confused about the incorrect teaching that Armageddon awaits the church and very specifically points out that Armageddon would not come "until the rebellion occurs and the man of lawlessness is revealed, the man doomed to destruction" (2:3). This man of sin is the antichrist.

Daniel clearly prophesied that the antichrist will not be revealed until he seizes power over the ten nations of revived Rome and makes a seven-year treaty with Israel (see Da 9:27). Paul declares that the antichrist will be revealed only at his appointed time (see 2Th 2:6), but until then he is restrained by supernatural powers until God releases him (see 2:7). Only then will this wicked antichrist be revealed: "The coming of the lawless one will be in accordance with the work of Satan displayed in all kinds of counterfeit miracles, signs and wonders" (2:9). For further information, see the study notes on Da 7—9 and the article on "The Vision of the Seventy Weeks" on p. 986.

Scholars have tried to identify the restrainer of the antichrist. Some believe that this restrainer is the system of human government, but that suggestion is disproved by the fact that governments and kingdoms will continue after antichrist is revealed (see Rev 13:7); they will not be taken away. Others have suggested that the church is the antichrist's restrainer; however, nowhere else in Scripture is the church referred to with the masculine pronoun "he," nor does the church ever exhibit any supernatural power except that which God manifests through it.

Most probably, therefore, the restrainer of the antichrist is God's Holy Spirit. This determination further supports the pretribulation rapture of the church because of the Holy Spirit's ministry among believers. Prior to Christ's ascension to heaven, Jesus promised his disciples that the Holy Spirit would come to empower the church (see Ac 1:8). Jesus had promised earlier that the Holy Spirit would abide in the church forever in his role as the comforter (see Jn 14:16), but that the Holy Spirit could not come until Jesus had ascended (see Jn 16:7). Unless the Holy Spirit is removed from his role as the restrainer, the antichrist will not be revealed. Therefore, because of Jesus' promise to believers of the abiding presence of the Holy Spirit, when the Holy Spirit is removed as the restrainer of the antichrist, it is because the church has already been raptured and is now in heaven at the marriage supper of the Lamb. Note that though the Holy Spirit will be removed from his role as the restrainer and comforter of the raptured church, the third person of the Trinity was, is now and always will be omnipresent. He will continue to convict sinners and thereby save a great multitude out of the tribulation (see Rev 7:9–14).

The day is coming when God will call every believer, living or dead, to meet him in the air and return home to heaven to the great marriage supper of the Lamb. Since we know not the exact time, this rapture of the church could happen without warning at any moment. It has not occurred yet, and Scripture indicates that it will occur before the tribulation begins. Until that time, "dear friends, since you are looking forward to this, make every effort to be found spotless, blameless and at peace with him" (2Pe 3:14).

God or is worshiped, so that he sets himself up in God's temple, proclaiming himself to be God.

⁵Don't you remember that when I was with you I used to tell you these things? ⁶And now you know what is holding him back, so that he may be revealed at the proper time. ⁷For the secret power of lawlessness is already at work; but the one who now holds it back will continue to do so till he is taken out of the way. ⁸And then the lawless one will be revealed, whom the Lord Jesus will overthrow with the breath of his mouth and destroy by the splendor of his coming. ⁹The coming of the lawless one will be in accordance with the work of Satan displayed in all kinds of counterfeit miracles, signs and wonders, ¹⁰and in every sort of evil that deceives those who are perishing. They perish because they refused to love the truth and so be saved. ¹¹For this reason God sends them a powerful delusion so that they will believe the lie ¹²and so that all will be condemned who have not believed the truth but have delighted in wickedness.

Stand Firm

¹³But we ought always to thank God for you, brothers loved by the Lord, because from the beginning God chose you to be saved through the sanctifying work of the Spirit and through belief in the truth. ¹⁴He called you to this through our gospel, that you might share in the glory of our Lord Jesus Christ. ¹⁵So then, brothers, stand firm and hold to the teachings we passed on to you, whether by word of mouth or by letter.

¹⁶May our Lord Jesus Christ himself and God our Father, who loved us and by his grace gave us eternal encouragement and good hope, ¹⁷encourage your hearts and strengthen you in every good deed and word.

Request for Prayer

3 Finally, brothers, pray for us that the message of the Lord may spread rapidly and be honored, just as it was with you. ²And pray that we may be delivered from wicked and evil men, for not everyone has faith. ³But the Lord is faithful, and he will strengthen and protect you from the evil one. ⁴We have confidence in the Lord that you are doing and will continue to do the things we command. ⁵May the Lord direct your hearts into God's love and Christ's perseverance.

Warning Against Idleness

⁶In the name of the Lord Jesus Christ, we command you, brothers, to keep away from every brother who is idle and does not live according to the teaching you received from us. ⁷For you your-

P 2Th 1:5–9 ◄► 2Pe 3:10–12
V Php 2:9–10 ◄► 1Ti 6:15
H 2Th 1:5–9 ◄► 2Th 2:11–12
C 2Th 1:8 ◄► 1Ti 4:2
N 2Th 1:7–8 ◄► 1Ti 4:2
H 2Th 2:8 ◄► 1Ti 6:9
E 1Th 4:8 ◄► 1Ti 3:16
S 1Th 4:7–8 ◄► Heb 10:14–15
W 1Th 4:7–8 ◄► 1Ti 4:12

K 1Th 5:9–10 ◄► 1Ti 4:8
C 2Th 2:1–3 ◄► 1Ti 6:14
S 1Th 5:22–23 ◄► 1Ti 1:19

ᵈ 13 Some manuscripts *because God chose you as his firstfruits*
ᵉ 15 Or *traditions* ᶠ 6 Or *tradition*

---

ments from the temple in Jerusalem (see Da 9:27; 11:36–45; 12:11; Mt 24:15; Rev 13:1–15), defiling the Holy of Holies.

Yet this antichrist will not be revealed until the Holy Spirit, who is restraining the antichrist's appearance, is taken out of the way (2:7). As long as the church is on earth, the indwelling Holy Spirit will continue to restrain the antichrist. However, when the saints are raptured, the Holy Spirit will be "taken out of the way" (2:7) to allow Satan to bring forth the antichrist. It is important to note that the Holy Spirit will not be removed from the earth but will still convict the world of sin (see Jn 16:7–8). Even during the tribulation millions will become believers and face martyrdom for their faith.

The apostle calls the antichrist the "lawless one" (2:8) but promises that he will be destroyed when Jesus Christ returns. Paul warns that the antichrist will deceive many because of his signs and wonders, but that the antichrist's power is all "in accordance with the work of Satan" (2:9).

3:5 Paul concludes this prophetic exhortation by urging the believers to focus on God's love and wait patiently for Christ's return (see Mk 13:33). In our waiting we are to walk in holiness as though Christ might return at any moment yet continue to work for his kingdom even if he tarries for another century.

selves know how you ought to follow our example.ᶜ We were not idle when we were with you, ⁸nor did we eat anyone's food without paying for it. On the contrary, we workedᵈ night and day, laboring and toiling so that we would not be a burden to any of you. ⁹We did this, not because we do not have the right to such help,ᵉ but in order to make ourselves a model for you to follow.ᶠ ¹⁰For even when we were with you,ᵍ we gave you this rule: "If a man will not work,ʰ he shall not eat."

¹¹We hear that some among you are idle. They are not busy; they are busybodies.ⁱ ¹²Such people we command and urge in the Lord Jesus Christʲ to settle down and earn the bread they eat.ᵏ ¹³And as for you, brothers, never tire of doing what is right.ˡ

¹⁴If anyone does not obey our instruction in this letter, take special note of him. Do not associate with him,ᵐ in order that he may feel ashamed.ⁿ ¹⁵Yet do not regard him as an enemy, but warn him as a brother.ᵒ

Final Greetings

¹⁶Now may the Lord of peaceᵖ himself give you peace at all times and in every way. The Lord be with all of you.ᑫ

¹⁷I, Paul, write this greeting in my own hand,ʳ which is the distinguishing mark in all my letters. This is how I write.

¹⁸The grace of our Lord Jesus Christ be with you all.ˢ

3:7 ᶜver 9; S 1Co 4:16
3:8 ᵈS Ac 18:3; Eph 4:28
3:9 ᵉ1Co 9:4-14 ᶠver 7; S 1Co 4:16
3:10 ᵍ1Th 3:4 ʰ1Th 4:11
3:11 ⁱver 6,7; 1Ti 5:13
3:12 ʲ1Th 4:1 ᵏ1Th 4:11; Eph 4:28
3:13 ˡGal 6:9
3:14 ᵐver 6; S Ro 16:17 ⁿS 1Co 4:14
3:15 ᵒGal 6:1; 1Th 5:14; Phm 16
3:16 ᵖS Ro 15:33 ᑫRu 2:4
3:17 ʳS 1Co 16:21
3:18 ˢS Ro 16:20

1 Timothy

Author: Paul

Theme: Instructions for a faithful ministry

Date of Writing: C. A.D. 63–65

Outline of 1 Timothy
- I. Warning Against False Teachers (1:1–17)
- II. Instructions for the Church (1:18—3:16)
- III. Instructions for Leaders (4:1—6:2)
- IV. Salutations (6:3–21)

THOUGH THE BOOKS of the NT do not always offer a clear chronology of the growth of Christianity, references in the book of Acts and the epistles help us to trace some of Paul's journeys. After Paul's first imprisonment in Rome, Paul revisited the churches in the province of Asia. On his journey to Macedonia, Paul left Timothy behind to minister at Ephesus (see 1:3) while Paul traveled on to Crete to minister there for a time. When Paul realized that he might not be able to return to Ephesus in the near future, he wrote the book of 1 Timothy to help his young protégé lead this growing congregation.

Timothy was born in Lystra, a city near Ephesus, and was converted under Paul's ministry. Timothy's mother and grandmother were apparently converted at or about that same time (see 2Ti 1:5). These women made sure that Timothy had a strong foundation in God's Word (see 2Ti 3:15)—a background that Timothy would rely on heavily in his ministry at Ephesus. When Paul came to Lystra on his second missionary journey (see Ac 16:1–3) he asked Timothy to join his mission. Timothy remained a loyal disciple of Paul throughout his ministry and even suffered imprisonment for his faith (see Heb 13:23).

This letter to Timothy is both personal and conversational as Paul instructs Timothy in the duties and qualifications of church leaders. False teachers were prevalent in Ephesus, so Paul offers guidance to Timothy as a pastor, reminding him of his duties as well as his obligations to "fight the good fight of the faith" (6:12).

1 Paul, an apostle of Christ Jesus by the command of God[a] our Savior[b] and of Christ Jesus our hope,[c]

²To Timothy[d] my true son[e] in the faith:

Grace, mercy and peace from God the Father and Christ Jesus our Lord.[f]

Warning Against False Teachers of the Law

³As I urged you when I went into Macedonia,[g] stay there in Ephesus[h] so that you may command certain men not to teach false doctrines[i] any longer ⁴nor to devote themselves to myths[j] and endless genealogies.[k] These promote controversies[l] rather than God's work—which is by faith. ⁵The goal of this command is love, which comes from a pure heart[m] and a good conscience[n] and a sincere faith.[o] ⁶Some have wandered away from these and turned to meaningless talk. ⁷They want to be teachers[p] of the law, but they do not know what they are talking about or what they so confidently affirm.[q]

⁸We know that the law is good[r] if one uses it properly. ⁹We also know that law[a] is made not for the righteous[s] but for lawbreakers and rebels,[t] the ungodly and sinful, the unholy and irreligious; for those who kill their fathers or mothers, for murderers, ¹⁰for adulterers and perverts, for slave traders and liars and perjurers—and for whatever else is contrary to the sound doctrine[u] ¹¹that conforms to the glorious gospel of the blessed God, which he entrusted to me.[v]

The Lord's Grace to Paul

¹²I thank Christ Jesus our Lord, who has given me strength,[w] that he considered me faithful, appointing me to his service.[x] ¹³Even though I was once a blasphemer and a persecutor[y] and a violent man, I was shown mercy[z] because I acted in ignorance and unbelief.[a] ¹⁴The grace of our Lord was poured out on me abundantly,[b] along with the faith and love that are in Christ Jesus.[c]

¹⁵Here is a trustworthy saying[d] that deserves full acceptance: Christ Jesus came into the world to save sinners[e]—of whom I am the worst. ¹⁶But for that very reason I was shown mercy[f] so that in me, the worst of sinners, Christ Jesus might display his unlimited patience[g] as an example for those who would believe[h] on him and receive eternal life.[i] ¹⁷Now to the King[j] eternal, immortal,[k] invisible,[l] the only God,[m] be honor and glory for ever and ever. Amen.[n]

¹⁸Timothy, my son,[o] I give you this instruction in keeping with the prophecies once made about you,[p] so that by following them you may fight the good fight, ¹⁹holding on to faith and a good conscience.[r] Some have rejected these and so have shipwrecked their faith.[s] ²⁰Among them are Hymenaeus[t] and Alexander,[u] whom I have handed over to Satan[v] to be taught not to blaspheme.

Instructions on Worship

2 I urge, then, first of all, that requests, prayers,[w] intercession and thanksgiving be made for everyone— ²for kings and all those in authority,[x] that we may live peaceful and quiet lives in all godliness[y] and holiness. ³This is good, and pleases[z] God our Savior,[a] ⁴who wants[b] all men[c] to be saved[d] and to come to a knowledge of the truth.[e] ⁵For there is one God[f] and one mediator[g] between God and men, the man Christ Jesus,[h] ⁶who gave himself as a ransom[i] for all men—the testimony[j] given in its proper time.[k] ⁷And for this purpose I was appointed a herald and an apostle—I am telling the truth, I am not lying[l]—and a teacher[m] of the true faith to the Gentiles.[n]

⁸I want men everywhere to lift up holy hands[o] in prayer, without anger or disputing.

⁹I also want women to dress modestly, with decency and propriety, not with braided hair or gold or pearls or expensive clothes,[p] ¹⁰but with good deeds,[q] appropriate for women who profess to worship God.

¹¹A woman should learn in quietness and full submission.[r] ¹²I do not permit a woman to teach or to have authority over a man; she must be silent.[s] ¹³For Adam

---

L 1Th 5:9–10 ◀▶ 1Ti 2:3–4
W Eph 2:17–18 ◀▶ 1Ti 2:3–6

S 2Th 3:6 ◀▶ 1Ti 4:16
L 1Ti 1:15 ◀▶ 1Ti 4:10
W 1Ti 1:15 ◀▶ 1Ti 4:10
D 1Ti 5:9–10 ◀▶ Tit 2:14
O Gal 2:16 ◀▶ 2Ti 2:11–12

a 9 Or *that the law*

was formed first, then Eve. 14And Adam was not the one deceived; it was the woman who was deceived and became a sinner. 15But women will be saved through childbearing—if they continue in faith, love and holiness with propriety.

Overseers and Deacons

3 Here is a trustworthy saying: If anyone sets his heart on being an overseer, he desires a noble task. 2Now the overseer must be above reproach, the husband of but one wife, temperate, self-controlled, respectable, hospitable, able to teach, 3not given to drunkenness, not violent but gentle, not quarrelsome, not a lover of money. 4He must manage his own family well and see that his children obey him with proper respect. 5(If anyone does not know how to manage his own family, how can he take care of God's church?) 6He must not be a recent convert, or he may become conceited and fall under the same judgment as the devil. 7He must also have a good reputation with outsiders, so that he will not fall into disgrace and into the devil's trap.

8Deacons, likewise, are to be men worthy of respect, sincere, not indulging in much wine, and not pursuing dishonest gain. 9They must keep hold of the deep truths of the faith with a clear conscience. 10They must first be tested; and then if there is nothing against them, let them serve as deacons.

11In the same way, their wives are to be women worthy of respect, not malicious talkers but temperate and trustworthy in everything.

12A deacon must be the husband of but one wife and must manage his children and his household well. 13Those who have served well gain an excellent standing and great assurance in their faith in Christ Jesus.

14Although I hope to come to you soon, I am writing you these instructions so that, 15if I am delayed, you will know how people ought to conduct themselves in God's household, which is the church of the living God, the pillar and foundation of the truth. 16Beyond all question, the mystery of godliness is great:

> He appeared in a body,
> was vindicated by the Spirit,
> was seen by angels,
> was preached among the nations,
> was believed on in the world,
> was taken up in glory.

Instructions to Timothy

4 The Spirit clearly says that in later times some will abandon the faith and follow deceiving spirits and things taught by demons. 2Such teachings come through hypocritical liars, whose consciences have been seared as with a hot iron. 3They forbid people to marry and order them to abstain from certain foods, which God created to be received with thanksgiving by those who believe and who know the truth. 4For everything God created is good, and nothing is to be rejected if it is received with thanksgiving, 5because it is consecrated by the word of God and prayer.

6If you point these things out to the brothers, you will be a good minister of Christ Jesus, brought up in the truths of the faith and of the good teaching that you have followed. 7Have nothing to do with godless myths and old wives' tales; rather, train yourself to be godly. 8For

E *2Th 2:13* ◀ ▶ *1Ti 4:1*
E *2Th 2:1–9* ◀ ▶ *2Ti 3:1–9*
E *1Ti 3:16* ◀ ▶ *1Ti 4:14*
T *1Th 1:5* ◀ ▶ *2Ti 3:16*
C *2Th 2:10–12* ◀ ▶ *1Ti 5:6*
N *2Th 2:10–12* ◀ ▶ *2Ti 4:3–4*
K *2Th 3:3* ◀ ▶ *2Ti 1:12*
P *Php 4:19* ◀ ▶ *Heb 6:10*
U *Gal 6:16* ◀ ▶ *1Pe 3:12*

b 15 Greek *she* *c 15* Or *restored* *d 1* Traditionally *bishop*; also in verse 2 *e 11* Or *way, deaconesses* *f 16* Some manuscripts *God* *g 16* Or *in the flesh*

4:1–3 Paul clearly says that there will be those in the last days that will openly deny the fundamental doctrines of the divinity of Jesus and the reality of his resurrection. Paul warned that these heresies would be inspired by demons and hypocritical liars. Paul's prophecy foreshadowed the cultic practices of our generation that include the acceptance of immorality and the widespread requirement to abstain from certain types of foods. In addition, liberal theologians have openly denied the fundamental doctrines of the Bible and continue to propagate these heresies both in the pulpit and in seminary classrooms.

physical training is of some value, but godliness has value for all things,^q holding promise for both the present life^r and the life to come.^s

^9This is a trustworthy saying^t that deserves full acceptance ^10(and for this we labor and strive), that we have put our hope in the living God,^u who is the Savior of all men,^v and especially of those who believe.

^11Command and teach these things.^w ^12Don't let anyone look down on you^x because you are young, but set an example^y for the believers in speech, in life, in love, in faith^z and in purity. ^13Until I come,^a devote yourself to the public reading of Scripture,^b to preaching and to teaching. ^14Do not neglect your gift, which was given you through a prophetic message^c when the body of elders^d laid their hands on you.^e

^15Be diligent in these matters; give yourself wholly to them, so that everyone may see your progress. ^16Watch your life and doctrine closely. Persevere in them, because if you do, you will save^f both yourself and your hearers.

Advice About Widows, Elders and Slaves

5 Do not rebuke an older man^g harshly,^h but exhort him as if he were your father. Treat younger men^i as brothers, ^2older women as mothers, and younger women as sisters, with absolute purity.

^3Give proper recognition to those widows who are really in need.^j ^4But if a widow has children or grandchildren, these should learn first of all to put their religion into practice by caring for their own family and so repaying their parents and grandparents,^k for this is pleasing to God.^l ^5The widow who is really in need^m and left all alone puts her hope in God^n and continues night and day to pray^o and to ask God for help. ^6But the widow who lives for pleasure is dead even while she lives.^p ^7Give the people these instructions,^q too, so that no one may be open to

L 1Ti 2:3–4 ◀▶ 2Ti 1:9
W 1Ti 2:3–6 ◀▶ Tit 2:11
W 2Th 2:13 ◀▶ 1Pe 1:2
E 1Ti 4:1 ◀▶ 2Ti 1:6–7
G 1Th 5:20 ◀▶ 2Ti 1:6–7
S 1Ti 1:19 ◀▶ 1Ti 6:12
C 1Ti 4:2 ◀▶ 2Ti 2:26

4:8 ^q 1Ti 6:6
^r Ps 37:9,11;
Pr 22:4; Mt 6:33;
Mk 10:29,30
^s Mk 10:29,30
4:9 ^t S 1Ti 1:15
4:10 ^u S Mt 16:16
^v S Lk 1:47; S 2:11
4:11 ^w 1Ti 5:7; 6:2
4:12 ^x S 2Ti 1:7;
Tit 2:15 ^y Php 3:17;
1Th 1:7; 2Th 3:9;
Tit 2:7; 1Pe 5:3
^z 1Ti 1:14
4:13 ^a 1Ti 3:14
^b Lk 4:16;
Ac 13:14-16;
Col 4:16; 1Th 5:27
4:14 ^c 1Ti 1:18
^d S Ac 11:30
^e S Ac 6:6; 2Ti 1:6
4:16 ^f S Ro 11:14
5:1 ^g Tit 2:2
^h Lev 19:32 ^i Tit 2:6
5:3 ^j ver 5,16
5:4 ^k ver 8;
Eph 6:1,2 ^l Ro 12:2;
Eph 5:10; 1Ti 2:3
5:5 ^m ver 3,16
^n 1Co 7:34; 1Pe 3:5
^o Lk 2:37; S Ro 1:10
5:6 ^p S Lk 15:24
5:7 ^q 1Ti 4:11; 6:2
5:8 ^r 2Pe 2:1;
Jude 4
5:10 ^s Ac 9:36;
1Ti 6:18; 1Pe 2:12
^t S Ro 12:13
^u S Lk 7:44 ^v ver 10
5:13 ^w S Ro 1:29
^x 2Th 3:11
5:14 ^y 1Co 7:9
^z 1Ti 6:1
5:15 ^a S Mt 4:10
5:16 ^b ver 3-5
5:17 ^c S Ac 11:30
^d Php 2:29;
1Th 5:12
5:18 ^e Dt 25:4;
1Co 9:7-9 ^f Lk 10:7;
Lev 19:13;
Dt 24:14,15;
Mt 10:10; 1Co 9:14
5:19 ^g S Ac 11:30
^h S Mt 18:16
5:20 ^i 2Ti 4:2;
Tit 1:13; 2:15
^j Dt 13:11
5:21 ^k 1Co 6:13;
2Ti 4:1
5:22 ^l S Ac 6:6
^m Eph 5:11
^n Ps 18:26
5:23 ^o 1Ti 3:8

blame. ^8If anyone does not provide for his relatives, and especially for his immediate family, he has denied^r the faith and is worse than an unbeliever.

^9No widow may be put on the list of widows unless she is over sixty, has been faithful to her husband,^h ^10and is well known for her good deeds,^s such as bringing up children, showing hospitality,^t washing the feet^u of the saints, helping those in trouble^v and devoting herself to all kinds of good deeds.

^11As for younger widows, do not put them on such a list. For when their sensual desires overcome their dedication to Christ, they want to marry. ^12Thus they bring judgment on themselves, because they have broken their first pledge. ^13Besides, they get into the habit of being idle and going about from house to house. And not only do they become idlers, but also gossips^w and busybodies,^x saying things they ought not to. ^14So I counsel younger widows to marry,^y to have children, to manage their homes and to give the enemy no opportunity for slander.^z ^15Some have in fact already turned away to follow Satan.^a

^16If any woman who is a believer has widows in her family, she should help them and not let the church be burdened with them, so that the church can help those widows who are really in need.^b

^17The elders^c who direct the affairs of the church well are worthy of double honor,^d especially those whose work is preaching and teaching. ^18For the Scripture says, "Do not muzzle the ox while it is treading out the grain,"^e and "The worker deserves his wages."^f ^19Do not entertain an accusation against an elder^g unless it is brought by two or three witnesses.^h ^20Those who sin are to be rebuked^i publicly, so that the others may take warning.

^21I charge you, in the sight of God and Christ Jesus^k and the elect angels, to keep these instructions without partiality, and to do nothing out of favoritism. ^22Do not be hasty in the laying on of hands,^l and do not share in the sins of others.^m Keep yourself pure.^n

^23Stop drinking only water, and use a little wine^o because of your stomach and your frequent illnesses.

^h 9 Or has had but one husband   ^i 18 Deut. 25:4   ^j 18 Luke 10:7

²⁴The sins of some men are obvious, reaching the place of judgment ahead of them; the sins of others trail behind them. ²⁵In the same way, good deeds are obvious, and even those that are not cannot be hidden.

6

All who are under the yoke of slavery should consider their masters worthy of full respect,ᵖ so that God's name and our teaching may not be slandered.ᑫ ²Those who have believing masters are not to show less respect for them because they are brothers.ʳ Instead, they are to serve them even better, because those who benefit from their service are believers, and dear to them. These are the things you are to teach and urge on them.ˢ

Love of Money

³If anyone teaches false doctrinesᵗ and does not agree to the sound instructionᵘ of our Lord Jesus Christ and to godly teaching, ⁴he is conceitedᵛ and understands nothing. He has an unhealthy interest in controversies and quarrels about wordsʷ that result in envy, strife, malicious talk, evil suspicions ⁵and constant friction between men of corrupt mind, who have been robbed of the truthˣ and who think that godliness is a means to financial gain.

⁶But godliness with contentmentʸ is great gain.ᶻ ⁷For we brought nothing into the world, and we can take nothing out of it.ᵃ ⁸But if we have food and clothing, we will be content with that.ᵇ ⁹People who want to get richᶜ fall into temptation and a trap,ᵈ and into many foolish and harmful desires that plunge men into ruin and destruction. ¹⁰For the love of moneyᵉ is a root of all kinds of evil. Some people, eager for money, have wandered from the faithᶠ and pierced themselves with many griefs.ᵍ

Paul's Charge to Timothy

¹¹But you, man of God,ʰ flee from all this, and pursue righteousness, godliness,ⁱ faith, love,ʲ endurance and gentleness. ¹²Fight the good fightᵏ of the faith. Take hold ofˡ the eternal lifeᵐ to which you were called when you made your good confessionⁿ in the presence of many witnesses. ¹³In the sight of God, who gives life to everything, and of Christ Jesus, who while testifying before Pontius Pilate° made the good confession,ᵖ I charge youᑫ ¹⁴to keep this command without spot or blameʳ until the appearing of our Lord Jesus Christ,ˢ ¹⁵which God will bring about in his own timeᵗ— God, the blessedᵘ and only Ruler,ᵛ the King of kings and Lord of lords,ʷ ¹⁶who alone is immortalˣ and who lives in unapproachable light,ʸ whom no one has seen or can see.ᶻ To him be honor and might forever. Amen.ᵃ

¹⁷Command those who are richᵇ in this present world not to be arrogant nor to put their hope in wealth,ᶜ which is so uncertain, but to put their hope in God,ᵈ who richly provides us with everything for our enjoyment.ᵉ ¹⁸Command them to do good, to be rich in good deeds,ᶠ and to be generous and willing to share.ᵍ ¹⁹In this way they will lay up treasure for

---

6:1 ᵖ Eph 6:5; ᑫ 1Ti 5:14; Tit 2:5,8
6:2 ʳ Phm 16; ˢ 1Ti 4:11
6:3 ᵗ 1Ti 1:3; ᵘ S 1Ti 1:10
6:4 ᵛ 1Ti 3:6; 2Ti 3:4 ʷ S 2Ti 2:14
6:5 ˣ 2Ti 3:8; Tit 1:15
6:6 ʸ Php 4:11; Heb 13:5 ᶻ 1Ti 4:8
6:7 ᵃ Job 1:21; Ps 49:17; Ecc 5:15
6:8 ᵇ Pr 30:8; Heb 13:5
6:9 ᶜ Pr 15:27; 28:20 ᵈ 1Ti 3:7
6:10 ᵉ S 1Ti 3:3 ᶠ ver 21; Jas 5:19 ᵍ Jos 7:21
6:11 ʰ 2Ti 3:17 ⁱ ver 3,5,6; S 1Ti 2:2 ʲ 1Ti 1:14; 2Ti 2:22; 3:10
6:12 ᵏ 1Co 9:25,26; S 1Ti 1:18 ˡ ver 19; Php 3:12 ᵐ S Mt 25:46 ⁿ S Heb 3:1
6:13 ° Jn 18:33-37 ᵖ ver 12 ᑫ 1Ti 5:21; 2Ti 4:1
6:14 ʳ S 1Ti 3:13 ˢ 1Ti 1:10; 4:1,8
6:15 ᵗ 1Ti 2:6; Tit 1:3 ᵘ 1Ti 1:11 ᵛ 1Ti 1:17 ʷ Dt 10:17; Ps 136:3; Da 2:47; Rev 1:5; 17:14; 19:16
6:16 ˣ 1Ti 1:17 ʸ Ps 104:2; 1Jn 1:7 ᶻ S Jn 1:18 ᵃ S Ro 11:36
6:17 ᵇ ver 9 ᶜ Ps 62:10; Jer 49:4; Lk 12:20,21 ᵈ 1Ti 4:10 ᵉ Ac 14:17
6:18 ᶠ S 1Ti 5:10 ᵍ Ro 12:8,13; Eph 4:28

M Col 2:18 ◄ ► Jas 4:6–10
W 1Th 5:18 ◄ ► 1Ti 6:8
W 1Ti 6:6 ◄ ► Heb 13:5–6
H 2Ti 2:11–12 ◄ ► Heb 2:2–3

S 1Ti 4:16 ◄ ► 2Ti 2:19
F 1Th 4:13–18 ◄ ► 2Ti 2:17–21
C 2Th 3:5 ◄ ► 2Ti 4:8
M Php 2:9–11 ◄ ► 2Ti 2:12
V 2Ti 2:8 ◄ ► Heb 1:2
G Php 3:3–10 ◄ ► 2Ti 1:9
L Php 4:19 ◄ ► Heb 1:14

6:13 The expression "who gives life to everything," refers to Jesus Christ's power to resurrect the dead.
6:14–15 Paul commands Timothy to follow Christ's commandments until the Lord returns, revealing his earnest expectation of the imminence of Christ's return for the saints. This concept of imminence accepts that Jesus could return without warning at any moment for his saints (see 1Th 4:13–17), yet recognizes that it is also possible that the signs of Ezekiel (see Eze 39) and Jesus (see Mt 24) will occur before the resurrection of the saints.

The apostle reminds us that just as Jesus' first advent occurred when God wanted (see Gal 4:4), so also Christ's return will come at the precise moment God chooses. In his first advent Jesus came in humility as the Christ-child, the wonderful teacher, the healer, the Lamb sacrificed for our sins and risen from the dead. When he returns at his second coming, however, Jesus Christ will be revealed in all of his glory and power as "the King of kings and Lord of lords" (6:15; see Rev 19:16).

themselves[h] as a firm foundation for the coming age, so that they may take hold of[i] the life that is truly life.

²⁰Timothy, guard what has been entrusted[j] to your care. Turn away from godless chatter[k] and the opposing ideas of what is falsely called knowledge, ²¹which some have professed and in so doing have wandered from the faith.[l]

Grace be with you.[m]

2 Timothy

Author: Paul

Theme: Timothy encouraged to stand firm in the faith

Date of Writing: C. A.D. 66–67

Outline of 2 Timothy
   I. Salutation (1:1–2)
   II. Faithfulness Is Essential in Service (1:3—2:13)
   III. True and False Teachings (2:14—3:17)
   IV. Paul's Charge to Timothy (4:1–8)
   V. Conclusion (4:9–22)

After Paul's fourth missionary journey, Emperor Nero imprisoned Paul in Rome. Chained in a cold dungeon like a common criminal, Paul sensed that his opportunities for preaching the gospel were coming to an end. He wrote this second letter to Timothy while in prison in an attempt to ease his own loneliness while encouraging Timothy to stand firm in his faith.

In this letter Paul senses the great task facing Timothy. Paul also realizes that his own death is imminent and seeks to strengthen his young assistant with his last words. Paul longs to see Timothy again and asks him to bring the books and parchments Paul had left behind in Troas. Paul also calls Timothy's attention to those who have deserted Paul in his time of need. Charging Timothy to maintain sound doctrine, Paul expresses his personal confidence and faith in Christ as he urges Timothy to stand firm in his faith despite persecution. Paul ultimately died in prison in Rome as a martyr to his faith in Christ.

2 TIMOTHY 1

1 Paul, an apostle of Christ Jesus by the will of God, according to the promise of life that is in Christ Jesus,

²To Timothy, my dear son:

Grace, mercy and peace from God the Father and Christ Jesus our Lord.

Encouragement to Be Faithful

³I thank God, whom I serve, as my forefathers did, with a clear conscience, as night and day I constantly remember you in my prayers. ⁴Recalling your tears, I long to see you, so that I may be filled with joy. ⁵I have been reminded of your sincere faith, which first lived in your grandmother Lois and in your mother Eunice and, I am persuaded, now lives in you also. ⁶For this reason I remind you to fan into flame the gift of God, which is in you through the laying on of my hands. ⁷For God did not give us a spirit of timidity, but a spirit of power, of love and of self-discipline.

⁸So do not be ashamed to testify about our Lord, or ashamed of me his prisoner. But join with me in suffering for the gospel, by the power of God, ⁹who has saved us and called us to a holy life—not because of anything we have done but because of his own purpose and grace. This grace was given us in Christ Jesus before the beginning of time, ¹⁰but it has now been revealed through the appearing of our Savior, Christ Jesus, who has destroyed death and has brought life and immortality to light through the gospel. ¹¹And of this gospel I was appointed a herald and an apostle and a teacher. ¹²That is why I am suffering as I am. Yet I am not ashamed, because I know whom I have believed, and am convinced that he is able to guard what I have entrusted to him for that day.

¹³What you heard from me, keep as the pattern of sound teaching, with faith and love in Christ Jesus. ¹⁴Guard the good deposit that was entrusted to you—guard it with the help of the Holy Spirit who lives in us.

¹⁵You know that everyone in the province of Asia has deserted me, including Phygelus and Hermogenes.

¹⁶May the Lord show mercy to the household of Onesiphorus, because he often refreshed me and was not ashamed of my chains. ¹⁷On the contrary, when he was in Rome, he searched hard for me until he found me. ¹⁸May the Lord grant that he will find mercy from the Lord on that day! You know very well in how many ways he helped me in Ephesus.

2 You then, my son, be strong in the grace that is in Christ Jesus. ²And the things you have heard me say in the presence of many witnesses entrust to reliable men who will also be qualified to teach others. ³Endure hardship with us like a good soldier of Christ Jesus. ⁴No one serving as a soldier gets involved in civilian affairs—he wants to please his commanding officer. ⁵Similarly, if anyone competes as an athlete, he does not receive the victor's crown unless he competes according to the rules. ⁶The hardworking farmer should be the first to receive a share of the crops. ⁷Reflect on what I am saying, for the Lord will give you insight into all this.

⁸Remember Jesus Christ, raised from the dead, descended from David. This is my gospel, ⁹for which I am suffering even to the point of being chained like a criminal. But God's word is not chained. ¹⁰Therefore I endure everything for the sake of the elect, that they too may obtain the salvation that is in Christ Jesus, with eternal glory.

¹¹Here is a trustworthy saying:

2:11–12 Paul's words here indicate that we died with Christ in the past when he died for us on the cross. Therefore we are promised that we will have eternal life in heaven with him. Paul also says that faithfully suffering in this life for our faith will result in our reigning with Christ in the coming kingdom of God on earth (see Rev 20:4). Yet Paul also warns that those who deny Jesus Christ in this life will be

If we died with him,
  we will also live with him;ⁿ
M ¹²if we endure,
T   we will also reign with him.º
If we disown him,
  he will also disown us;ᵖ
¹³if we are faithless,
  he will remain faithful,ᑫ
  for he cannot disown himself.

A Workman Approved by God

¹⁴Keep reminding them of these things. Warn them before God against quarreling about words;ʳ it is of no value, and only ruins those who listen. ¹⁵Do your best to present yourself to God as one approved, a workman who does not need to be ashamed and who correctly handles the word of truth.ᵗ ¹⁶Avoid godless chatter,ᵘ because those who indulge in it will become more and more ungodly. **F** ¹⁷Their teaching will spread like gangrene. Among them are Hymenaeusᵘ and Philetus, ¹⁸who have wandered away from the truth. They say that the resurrection has already taken place,ᵛ and they destroy **S** the faith of some.ʷ ¹⁹Nevertheless, God's solid foundation stands firm,ˣ sealed with this inscription: "The Lord knows those who are his,"ᵃʸ and, "Everyone who confesses the name of the Lordᶻ must turn away from wickedness."

M 1Ti 6:15 ◄ ► 2Ti 4:1
T 2Ti 1:8 ◄ ► Phm 6
F 1Ti 6:13 ◄ ► Heb 6:2
S 1Ti 6:12 ◄ ► Tit 1:16

2:11 ⁿ Ro 6:2-11
2:12 º Ro 8:17; 1Pe 4:13 ᵖ Mt 10:33
2:13 ᑫ Ro 3:3; S 1Co 1:9
2:14 ʳ ver 23; 1Ti 1:4; 6:4; Tit 3:9
2:15 ˢ Eph 1:13; Col 1:5; Jas 1:18
2:16 ᵗ Tit 3:9; 1Ti 6:20
2:17 ᵘ 1Ti 1:20
2:18 ᵛ 2Th 2:2 ʷ 1Ti 1:19; 6:21
2:19 ˣ Isa 28:16 ʸ Ex 33:12; Nu 16:5; Jn 10:14; 1Co 8:3; Gal 4:9 ᶻ 1Co 1:2
2:20 ᵃ Ro 9:21
2:21 ᵇ 2Co 9:8; Eph 2:10; 2Ti 3:17
2:22 ᶜ 1Ti 1:14; 6:11 ᵈ Ac 2:21 ᵉ 1Ti 1:5
2:23 ᶠ ver 14
2:24 ᵍ 1Ti 3:2,3
2:25 ʰ 1Ti 2:4
2:26 ⁱ 1Ti 3:7
3:1 ʲ 1Ti 4:1; 2Pe 3:3
3:2 ᵏ S 1Ti 3:3 ˡ Ro 1:30 ᵐ 2Pe 2:10-12 ⁿ Ro 1:30

²⁰In a large house there are articles not only of gold and silver, but also of wood and clay; some are for noble purposes and some for ignoble.ᵃ ²¹If a man cleanses himself from the latter, he will be an instrument for noble purposes, made holy, useful to the Master and prepared to do any good work.ᵇ

²²Flee the evil desires of youth, and pursue righteousness, faith, loveᶜ and peace, along with those who call on the Lordᵈ out of a pure heart.ᵉ ²³Don't have anything to do with foolish and stupid arguments, because you know they produce quarrels.ᶠ ²⁴And the Lord's servant must not quarrel; instead, he must be kind to everyone, able to teach, not resentful.ᵍ ²⁵Those who oppose him he must gently instruct, in the hope that God will grant them repentance leading them to a knowledge of the truth,ʰ ²⁶and **C** that they will come to their senses and escape from the trap of the devil,ⁱ who has taken them captive to do his will.

Godlessness in the Last Days

3 But mark this: There will be terrible **E** times in the last days.ʲ ²People will **C** be lovers of themselves, lovers of money,ᵏ boastful, proud,ˡ abusive,ᵐ disobedient to their parents,ⁿ ungrateful, unholy, ³without love, unforgiving, slan-

C 1Ti 5:6 ◄ ► 2Ti 3:1-5
E 1Ti 4:1-3 ◄ ► 2Ti 4:3-4
C 2Ti 2:26 ◄ ► 2Ti 3:8

ᵃ 19 Num. 16:5 (see Septuagint)

---

denied by him when they stand in judgment in the last days.

2:17–18 Two teachers were causing great confusion in the early church by denying the future bodily resurrection and teaching that the only resurrection was a symbolic resurrection that occurred at conversion (see 1Co 15:12–14). This teaching was devastating to the faith of those early believers who succumbed to this Gnostic heresy.

3:1–7 This prophecy describes the sinful attitudes and behaviors that will be manifest in the world from the time of Paul until the last days of this age.

1. *Self-centered.* This self-centered generation openly boasts of their dedication to personal pleasure, rather than to God or family.
2. *Lovers of money.* A value system that honors money and possessions elevates greed to a virtue in a corrupt and sinful society.
3. *Boastful and proud.* Self-promotion is emulated, boasting is widespread, and pride is no longer despised.
4. *Abusive.* Those who habitually use coarse, crude and blasphemous language are tolerated and even admired (see Eze 39:7).
5. *Disobedient.* Widespread disobedience to parents is an accepted practice despite its ban in the Ten Commandments (see Ex 20:12).
6. *Ungrateful and unholy.* An unprecedented lack of gratitude and widespread contempt for righteousness pervades society.
7. *Sexually perverted.* Public displays of immorality, sexual perversion and indecency are common and readily overlooked by society.
8. *Dishonest behavior.* The breakdown in personal righteousness and the loss of respect for honesty results in false accusers and contract breakers. The growing toleration for cheating on taxes, excessive litigation and white-collar crime shows the open contempt expressed for honest behavior.

derous, without self-control, brutal, not lovers of the good, ⁴treacherous,ᵒ rash, conceited,ᵖ lovers of pleasure rather than lovers of God— ⁵having a form of godliness૧ but denying its power. Have nothing to do with them.ʳ

⁶They are the kind who worm their wayˢ into homes and gain control over weak-willed women, who are loaded down with sins and are swayed by all kinds of evil desires, ⁷always learning but never able to acknowledge the truth.ᵗ ⁸Just as Jannes and Jambres opposed Moses,ᵘ so also these men opposeᵛ the truth—men of depraved minds,ʷ who, as far as the faith is concerned, are rejected. ⁹But they will not get very far because, as in the case of those men,ˣ their folly will be clear to everyone.

Paul's Charge to Timothy

¹⁰You, however, know all about my teaching,ʸ my way of life, my purpose, faith, patience, love, endurance, ¹¹persecutions, sufferings—what kinds of things happened to me in Antioch,ᶻ Iconiumᵃ and Lystra,ᵇ the persecutions I endured.ᶜ Yet the Lord rescuedᵈ me from all of them.ᵉ ¹²In fact, everyone who wants to live a godly life in Christ Jesus will be persecuted,ᶠ ¹³while evil men and impostors will go from bad to worse,ᵍ deceiving and being deceived.ʰ ¹⁴But as for you, continue in what you have learned and have become convinced of, because you know those from whom you learned it,ⁱ ¹⁵and how from infancyʲ you have known the holy Scriptures,ᵏ which are able to make you wiseˡ for salvation through faith in Christ Jesus. ¹⁶All Scripture is God-breathedᵐ and is useful for teaching,ⁿ rebuking, correcting and training in righteousness,ᵒ ¹⁷so that the man of Godᵖ may be thoroughly equipped for every good work.૧

4 In the presence of God and of Christ Jesus, who will judge the living and the dead,ʳ and in view of his appearingˢ and his kingdom, I give you this charge:ᵗ ²Preachᵘ the Word;ᵛ be prepared in season and out of season; correct, rebukeʷ and encourageˣ—with great patience and careful instruction. ³For the time will come when men will not put up with sound doctrine.ʸ Instead, to suit their own desires, they will gather around them a great number of teachers to say what their itching ears want to hear.ᶻ ⁴They will turn their ears away from the truth and turn aside to myths.ᵃ ⁵But you, keep your head in all situations, endure hardship,ᵇ do the work of an evangelist,ᶜ discharge all the duties of your ministry.

⁶For I am already being poured out like a drink offering,ᵈ and the time has come for my departure.ᵉ ⁷I have fought the good fight,ᶠ I have finished the race,ᵍ I have kept the faith. ⁸Now there is in store for meʰ the crown of righteousness,ⁱ

Cross references:

3:4 ᵒ Ps 25:3; ᵖ 1Ti 3:6; 6:4
3:5 ૧ S 1Ti 2:2; ʳ S Ro 16:17
3:6 ˢ Jude 4
3:7 ᵗ S 1Ti 2:4
3:8 ᵘ Ex 7:11; ᵛ Ac 13:8 ʷ 1Ti 6:5
3:9 ˣ Ex 7:12; 8:18; 9:11
3:10 ʸ 1Ti 4:6
3:11 ᶻ Ac 13:14,50; ᵃ Ac 13:51; ᵇ Ac 14:6; ᶜ 2Co 11:23-27; ᵈ S Ro 15:31; ᵉ Ps 34:19
3:12 ᶠ Jn 15:20; S Ac 14:22
3:13 ᵍ 2Ti 2:16; ʰ S Mk 13:5
3:14 ⁱ 2Ti 1:13
3:15 ʲ 2Ti 1:5; ᵏ Jn 5:39; ˡ Dt 4:6; Ps 119:98, 99
3:16 ᵐ 2Pe 1:20,21; ⁿ S Ro 4:23,24; ᵒ Dt 29:29
3:17 ᵖ 1Ti 6:11; ૧ 2Ti 2:21

4:1 ʳ S Ac 10:42; ˢ ver 8; S 1Ti 6:14; ᵗ 1Ti 5:21; 6:13
4:2 ᵘ 1Ti 4:13; ᵛ Gal 6:6; ʷ 1Ti 5:20; Tit 1:13; 2:15; ˣ Tit 2:15
4:3 ʸ S 1Ti 1:10; ᶻ Isa 30:10
4:4 ᵃ S 1Ti 1:4
4:5 ᵇ 2Ti 1:8; 2:3,9; ᶜ Ac 21:8; Eph 4:11
4:6 ᵈ Nu 15:1-12; 28:7,24; Php 2:17; ᵉ Php 1:23
4:7 ᶠ S 1Ti 1:18; ᵍ 1Co 9:24; Ac 20:24
4:8 ʰ Col 1:5; 1Pe 1:4; ⁱ S 1Co 9:25

G 2Ti 1:14 ◄ ► Heb 2:4
T 1Ti 4:1 ◄ ► Heb 3:7
M 2Ti 2:12 ◄ ► 2Ti 4:8
J 2Co 5:10 ◄ ► Heb 9:27
E 2Ti 3:1–9 ◄ ► Jas 5:1
N 1Ti 4:2 ◄ ► Heb 2:2–3
C 2Ti 3:13 ◄ ► Tit 1:16
C 1Ti 6:14 ◄ ► Tit 2:13
M 2Ti 4:1 ◄ ► 2Ti 4:18

C 2Ti 3:1–5 ◄ ► 2Ti 3:13
C 2Ti 3:8 ◄ ► 2Ti 4:4

---

9. Bankrupt values. Loving pleasure more than loving God. A value system that appears to embrace godly ideas, but has no spiritual center. A society willing to betray itself and its beliefs for worthless pleasure or goods.

Paul warned Timothy to turn away from people in his day that exemplified this sinful lifestyle. Today, we also must turn away from those who profess Christianity but deny the virgin birth, the miracles, prophecies and the resurrection of Jesus while openly endorsing sexual perversion. These are the ones that Paul says are "always learning but never able to acknowledge the truth" (3:7).

4:1–4 Paul charges Timothy to preach the word until Jesus returns. We should heed Paul's words to Timothy and reach our world with the gospel message while we still have the chance. Many in the western world have had access to the Scriptures for generations and have rejected its message due to spiritual pride and arrogance. These have turned their ears from Biblical truth in favor of modern cults and religions, fulfilling this prophecy in a tragic way.

4:8 As Paul contemplates his approaching martyrdom in Rome, he considers what lies ahead for the early church. Paul refers to that future day at the coming judgment seat of Christ (see Ro 14:10) when every believer who longs for Christ's return will win "the crown of righteousness." Paul's prophecy confirms the importance of the doctrine of the second coming and reveals that God will reward all who

which the Lord, the righteous Judge, will award to me on that day[j] —and not only to me, but also to all who have longed for his appearing.[k]

Personal Remarks

[9] Do your best to come to me quickly,[l] [10] for Demas,[m] because he loved this world,[n] has deserted me and has gone to Thessalonica.[o] Crescens has gone to Galatia,[p] and Titus[q] to Dalmatia. [11] Only Luke[r] is with me.[s] Get Mark[t] and bring him with you, because he is helpful to me in my ministry. [12] I sent Tychicus[u] to Ephesus.[v] [13] When you come, bring the cloak that I left with Carpus at Troas,[w] and my scrolls, especially the parchments.

[14] Alexander[x] the metalworker did me a great deal of harm. The Lord will repay him for what he has done.[y] [15] You too should be on your guard against him, because he strongly opposed our message.

[16] At my first defense, no one came to my support, but everyone deserted me. May it not be held against them.[z] [17] But the Lord stood at my side[a] and gave me strength,[b] so that through me the message might be fully proclaimed and all the Gentiles might hear it.[c] And I was delivered from the lion's mouth.[d] [18] The Lord will rescue me from every evil attack[e] and will bring me safely to his heavenly kingdom.[f] To him be glory for ever and ever. Amen.[g]

Final Greetings

[19] Greet Priscilla[b] and Aquila[h] and the household of Onesiphorus.[i] [20] Erastus[j] stayed in Corinth, and I left Trophimus[k] sick in Miletus.[l] [21] Do your best to get here before winter.[m] Eubulus greets you, and so do Pudens, Linus, Claudia and all the brothers.

[22] The Lord be with your spirit.[n] Grace be with you.[o]

M *2Ti 4:8* ◀ ▶ *Heb 1:8*
V *2Co 2:14* ◀ ▶ *Heb 11:32–35*

b 19 Greek *Prisca,* a variant of *Priscilla*

---

both believe and long for Christ's return with a glorious crown, an honor that will be theirs forever in the new Jerusalem.

Titus

Author: Paul

Theme: The need for order in the church

Date of Writing: C. A.D. 63–65

Outline of Titus
  I. Introduction (1:1–4)
  II. Duties of Elders and Deacons (1:5–16)
  III. Pastoral Responsibilities (2:1—3:11)
  IV. Conclusion (3:12–15)

Paul wrote this pastoral letter to his associate Titus shortly after Paul had left him in charge of the believers on the island of Crete. Titus had been Paul's trusted fellow worker for many years (see 2Co 7—8), sharing Paul's love for the believers in Corinth and assisting in his ministry throughout Asia. Though Titus was a Greek convert, he accompanied Paul and Barnabas to the Jerusalem council (see Gal 2:1–3). After Paul's first imprisonment in Rome, Titus accompanied the apostle on his missionary journeys, working with him closely on the island of Crete. Paul determined to continue his journey, but appointed Titus to stay behind and finish establishing the church. Paul may have been in Corinth when he wrote this instructional letter to Titus about church order and government.

Because the young church in Crete was disorganized and uninformed, the emphasis of this letter is similar to Paul's words in 1 Timothy. Many of the believers on Crete needed additional instruction and admonition concerning the necessity of order in the church. Paul carefully describes the qualifications for elders in the church, stresses the need for ethical behavior, strongly warns against false teachers and emphasizes the need for sound, doctrinal teaching. Paul repeatedly urges the believers to be obedient and strive to do good works. Outlining the essential elements of Christianity, this letter to Titus forms the clearest declaration in all of his writings of Paul's statement of faith.

1 Paul, a servant of God[a] and an apostle[b] of Jesus Christ for the faith of God's elect and the knowledge of the truth[c] that leads to godliness[d] — ²a faith and knowledge resting on the hope of eternal life,[e] which God, who does not lie,[f] promised before the beginning of time,[g] ³and at his appointed season[h] he brought his word to light[i] through the preaching entrusted to me[j] by the command of God[k] our Savior,[l]

⁴To Titus,[m] my true son[n] in our common faith:

Grace and peace from God the Father and Christ Jesus our Savior.[o]

Titus's Task on Crete
1:6–8Ref — 1Ti 3:2–4

⁵The reason I left you in Crete[p] was that you might straighten out what was left unfinished and appoint[a] elders[q] in every town, as I directed you. ⁶An elder must be blameless,[r] the husband of but one wife, a man whose children believe and are not open to the charge of being wild and disobedient. ⁷Since an overseer[b][s] is entrusted with God's work,[t] he must be blameless—not overbearing, not quick-tempered, not given to drunkenness, not violent, not pursuing dishonest gain.[u] ⁸Rather he must be hospitable,[v] one who loves what is good,[w] who is self-controlled,[x] upright, holy and disciplined. ⁹He must hold firmly[y] to the trustworthy message as it has been taught, so that he can encourage others by sound doctrine[z] and refute those who oppose it.

¹⁰For there are many rebellious people, mere talkers[a] and deceivers, especially those of the circumcision group.[b] ¹¹They must be silenced, because they are ruining whole households[c] by teaching things they ought not to teach—and that for the sake of dishonest gain. ¹²Even one of their own prophets[d] has said, "Cretans[e] are always liars, evil brutes, lazy gluttons." ¹³This testimony is true. Therefore, rebuke[f] them sharply, so that they will be sound in the faith[g] ¹⁴and will pay no attention to Jewish myths[h] or to the commands[i] of those who reject the truth.[j] ¹⁵To the pure, all things are pure,[k] but to those who are corrupted and do not believe, nothing is pure.[l] In fact, both their minds and consciences are corrupted.[m] ¹⁶They claim to know God, but by their actions they deny him.[n] They are detestable, disobedient and unfit for doing anything good.[o]

What Must Be Taught to Various Groups

2 You must teach what is in accord with sound doctrine.[p] ²Teach the older men[q] to be temperate,[r] worthy of respect, self-controlled,[s] and sound in faith,[t] in love and in endurance.

³Likewise, teach the older women to be reverent in the way they live, not to be slanderers[u] or addicted to much wine,[v] but to teach what is good. ⁴Then they can train the younger women[w] to love their husbands and children, ⁵to be self-controlled[x] and pure, to be busy at home,[y] to be kind, and to be subject to their husbands,[z] so that no one will malign the word of God.[a]

⁶Similarly, encourage the young men[b] to be self-controlled.[c] ⁷In everything set them an example[d] by doing what is good.[e] In your teaching show integrity, seriousness ⁸and soundness of speech that cannot be condemned, so that those who oppose you may be ashamed because they have nothing bad to say about us.[f]

⁹Teach slaves to be subject to their masters in everything,[g] to try to please them, not to talk back to them, ¹⁰and not to steal from them, but to show that they can be fully trusted, so that in every way they will make the teaching about God our Savior[h] attractive.[i]

¹¹For the grace[j] of God that brings salvation has appeared[k] to all men.[l] ¹²It teaches us to say "No" to ungodliness and worldly passions,[m] and to live self-controlled,[n] upright and godly lives[o] in this

---

C 2Ti 4:4 ◀ ▶ Tit 3:3
S 2Ti 2:19 ◀ ▶ Tit 2:11–14
K 2Ti 1:12 ◀ ▶ Heb 2:18
L 2Ti 1:9 ◀ ▶ Tit 3:3–5
S Tit 1:16 ◀ ▶ Tit 3:8
W 1Ti 4:10 ◀ ▶ Heb 2:9

a 5 Or *ordain* *b* 7 Traditionally *bishop*

present age, ¹³while we wait for the blessed hope—the glorious appearing of our great God and Savior, Jesus Christ, ¹⁴who gave himself for us to redeem us from all wickedness and to purify for himself a people that are his very own, eager to do what is good.

¹⁵These, then, are the things you should teach. Encourage and rebuke with all authority. Do not let anyone despise you.

Doing What Is Good

3 Remind the people to be subject to rulers and authorities, to be obedient, to be ready to do whatever is good, ²to slander no one, to be peaceable and considerate, and to show true humility toward all men.

³At one time we too were foolish, disobedient, deceived and enslaved by all kinds of passions and pleasures. We lived in malice and envy, being hated and hating one another. ⁴But when the kindness and love of God our Savior appeared, ⁵he saved us, not because of righteous things we had done, but because of his mercy. He saved us through the washing of rebirth and renewal by the Holy Spirit, ⁶whom he poured out on us generously through Jesus Christ our Savior, ⁷so that, having been justified by his grace, we might become heirs having the hope of eternal life. ⁸This is a trustworthy saying. And I want you to stress these things, so that those who have trusted in God may be careful to devote themselves to doing what is good. These things are excellent and profitable for everyone.

⁹But avoid foolish controversies and genealogies and arguments and quarrels about the law, because these are unprofitable and useless. ¹⁰Warn a divisive person once, and then warn him a second time. After that, have nothing to do with him. ¹¹You may be sure that such a man is warped and sinful; he is self-condemned.

Final Remarks

¹²As soon as I send Artemas or Tychicus to you, do your best to come to me at Nicopolis, because I have decided to winter there. ¹³Do everything you can to help Zenas the lawyer and Apollos on their way and see that they have everything they need. ¹⁴Our people must learn to devote themselves to doing what is good, in order that they may provide for daily necessities and not live unproductive lives.

¹⁵Everyone with me sends you greetings. Greet those who love us in the faith.

Grace be with you all.

2:13–14 Paul urges believers to be looking for the hope of the rapture and Christ's glorious second coming (see 1Th 4:16–17). Note also the mention of Jesus Christ as "our great God" (2:13), a clear affirmation of Christ's divinity.

Philemon

Author: Paul

Theme: Showing Christian love and forgiveness

Date of Writing: C. A.D. 60–62

Outline of Philemon
  I. Greetings (1–3)
  II. Paul's Concern and Love (4–7)
  III. Paul's Intercession for Onesimus (8–21)
  IV. Farewell (22–25)

During Paul's first imprisonment in Rome, Paul became associated with a runaway slave from Colosse named Onesimus. Under Paul's instruction Onesimus became a believer. Yet as a slave, Onesimus was the legal property of his owner, Philemon. Paul wrote this short letter from his prison cell, addressing it to Philemon, Apphia (who may have been Philemon's wife), Archippus (who may have been their son) and to the church which held meetings in Philemon's household, encouraging them to show Christian love and charity to Onesimus.

Slavery was a common practice in the Roman empire. Up to 50 percent of the population of some cities lived as slaves. Many slaves were respected stewards of their households. Yet this epistle does not endorse slavery as some critics have charged. With clear words and strong feelings Paul simply deals with the spiritual and moral issues involved in this incident between two believers. Onesimus had been a trusted slave who stole some of Philemon's goods when he ran away. Paul sent Onesimus back to his master with this letter, emphasizing that Christian conduct should permeate their relationship. Pleading with Philemon for forgiveness for Onesimus's sins, Paul calls upon Onesimus and Philemon to reconcile as brothers in the Lord.

PHILEMON 1

¹Paul, a prisoner[a] of Christ Jesus, and Timothy[b] our brother,[c]

To Philemon our dear friend and fellow worker,[d] ²to Apphia our sister, to Archippus[e] our fellow soldier[f] and to the church that meets in your home:[g]

³Grace to you and peace from God our Father and the Lord Jesus Christ.[h]

Thanksgiving and Prayer

⁴I always thank my God[i] as I remember you in my prayers,[j] ⁵because I hear about your faith in the Lord Jesus[k] and your love for all the saints.[l] ⁶I pray that you may be active in sharing your faith, so that you will have a full understanding of every good thing we have in Christ. ⁷Your love has given me great joy and encouragement,[m] because you, brother, have refreshed[n] the hearts of the saints.

Paul's Plea for Onesimus

⁸Therefore, although in Christ I could be bold and order you to do what you ought to do, ⁹yet I appeal to you[o] on the basis of love. I then, as Paul—an old man and now also a prisoner[p] of Christ Jesus— ¹⁰I appeal to you for my son[q] Onesimus,[a,r] who became my son while I was in chains.[s] ¹¹Formerly he was useless to you, but now he has become useful both to you and to me.

¹²I am sending him—who is my very heart—back to you. ¹³I would have liked to keep him with me so that he could take your place in helping me while I am in chains[t] for the gospel. ¹⁴But I did not want to do anything without your consent, so that any favor you do will be spontaneous and not forced.[u] ¹⁵Perhaps the reason he was separated from you for a little while was that you might have him back for good— ¹⁶no longer as a slave,[v] but better than a slave, as a dear brother.[w] He is very dear to me but even dearer to you, both as a man and as a brother in the Lord.

¹⁷So if you consider me a partner,[x] welcome him as you would welcome me. ¹⁸If he has done you any wrong or owes you anything, charge it to me.[y] ¹⁹I, Paul, am writing this with my own hand.[z] I will pay it back—not to mention that you owe me your very self. ²⁰I do wish, brother, that I may have some benefit from you in the Lord; refresh[a] my heart in Christ. ²¹Confident[b] of your obedience, I write to you, knowing that you will do even more than I ask.

²²And one thing more: Prepare a guest room for me, because I hope to be[c] restored to you in answer to your prayers.[d]

²³Epaphras,[e] my fellow prisoner[f] in Christ Jesus, sends you greetings. ²⁴And so do Mark,[g] Aristarchus,[h] Demas[i] and Luke, my fellow workers.[j]

²⁵The grace of the Lord Jesus Christ be with your spirit.[k]

1:1 [a] ver 9,23; [S] Eph 3:1; [b] S Ac 16:1; [c] 2Co 1:1; [d] S Php 2:25
1:2 [e] Col 4:17; [f] Php 2:25; [g] S Ro 16:5
1:3 [h] S Ro 1:7
1:4 [i] S Ro 1:8; [j] S Ro 1:10
1:5 [k] S Ac 20:21; [l] S Col 1:4; 1Th 3:6
1:7 [m] 2Co 7:4,13; [n] ver 20; Ro 15:32; 1Co 16:18
1:9 [o] 1Co 1:10; [p] ver 1,23; S Eph 3:1
1:10 [q] S 1Th 2:11; [r] Col 4:9; [s] S Ac 21:33
1:13 [t] ver 10; S Ac 21:33
1:14 [u] 2Co 9:7; 1Pe 5:2
1:16 [v] 1Co 7:22; [w] Mt 23:8; S Ac 1:16; 1Ti 6:2
1:17 [x] 2Co 8:23
1:18 [y] Ge 43:9
1:19 [z] S 1Co 16:21
1:20 [a] ver 7; 1Co 16:18
1:21 [b] S 2Co 2:3
1:22 [c] Php 1:25; 2:24; Heb 13:19; [d] 2Co 1:11; Php 1:19
1:23 [e] Col 1:7; [f] ver 1; Ro 16:7; Col 4:10
1:24 [g] S Ac 12:12; [h] S Ac 19:29; [i] Col 4:14; 2Ti 4:10; [j] ver 1
1:25 [k] S Gal 6:18

[a] 10 *Onesimus* means *useful.*

T 2Ti 2:12 ◄ ► Heb 3:13

Hebrews

Author: Uncertain; possibly Paul, Barnabas, Luke or Apollos

Theme: The priesthood of Jesus is superior to all others

Date of Writing: c. A.D. 60–70

Outline of Hebrews
  I. A Superior Spokesman for God (1:1—4:13)
  II. A Superior Intercessor and Priest (4:14—7:28)
  III. A Superior Covenant and Offering (8:1—10:39)
  IV. A Practical Appeal (11:1—13:25)

THOUGH THE BOOK of Hebrews does not name its author, early church scholars attributed this book to Paul. Later scholars suggested that Barnabas or Apollos wrote Hebrews. Still other scholars have suggested that this book came from the pen of Luke. Though its authorship is uncertain, the language in the book of Hebrews identifies the author as a mature, Jewish Christian who was well versed in the OT, a friend of Timothy and well known to the original recipients of this letter. The author possessed keen literary abilities and followed a style of writing that is closer to classical Greek than to the common Greek of the other NT books. The external and internal textual evidence suggests that this book was composed just prior to the destruction of Jerusalem in A.D. 70.

During the years surrounding the writing of the book of Hebrews, fear of persecution was a grim reality for the church in Rome. Directing his words to the Jewish Christians in both Palestine and throughout the Roman empire, the author of Hebrews encourages his readers to "hold on" (3:6) despite the opposition and to press on "to maturity" (6:1). In addition, Hebrews warns new believers against reverting to the legalism of the Law and stresses the utter preeminence of Jesus Christ as the only hope of salvation. Frequent warnings are given to believers against rejecting the great offer of salvation provided by Christ's completed work of atonement on the cross.

Jewish believers were also reminded that their OT religious system of sacrifices and regulations was no longer necessary. Hebrews presents Jesus as the culmination of God's revelation through the OT prophets, stating that Jesus Christ is superior in every respect to the Law. Forgiveness and salvation has been granted through the sacrificial death and resurrection of Jesus the Messiah. Hebrews also stresses the priesthood of Jesus Christ. In fact, more than twenty names and titles appear in reference to Christ in the book of Hebrews, with the office of Christ as our Priest-king receiving special consideration.

The Son Superior to Angels

1 In the past God spoke[a] to our forefathers through the prophets[b] at many times and in various ways,[c] ²but in these last days[d] he has spoken to us by his Son,[e] whom he appointed heir[f] of all things, and through whom[g] he made the universe.[h] ³The Son is the radiance of God's glory[i] and the exact representation of his being,[j] sustaining all things[k] by his powerful word. After he had provided purification for sins,[l] he sat down at the right hand of the Majesty in heaven.[m] ⁴So he became as much superior to the angels as the name he has inherited is superior to theirs.[n]

⁵For to which of the angels did God ever say,

"You are my Son;
   today I have become your
      Father"[a][b][o]?

Or again,

"I will be his Father,
   and he will be my Son"[c][p]?

⁶And again, when God brings his firstborn[q] into the world,[r] he says,

"Let all God's angels worship him."[d][s]

⁷In speaking of the angels he says,

V 1Ti 6:15 ◄ ▶ Heb 1:13
D Tit 2:14 ◄ ▶ Heb 2:9
L Tit 3:3–5 ◄ ▶ Heb 5:2

1:1 a Jn 9:29; Heb 2:2,3; 4:8; 12:25 b Lk 1:70; Ac 2:30 c Nu 12:6,8
1:2 d Dt 4:30; Heb 9:26; 1Pe 1:20 e ver 5; S Mt 3:17; Heb 3:6; 5:8; 7:28 f Ps 2:8; Mt 11:27; S 28:18 g S Jn 1:3 h Heb 11:3
1:3 i Jn 1:14 j S Jn 14:9 k Col 1:17 l Tit 2:14; Heb 7:27; 9:11-14 m S Mk 16:19
1:4 n Eph 1:21; Php 2:9,10; Heb 8:6
1:5 o Ps 2:7; S Mt 3:17 p 2Sa 7:14
1:6 q Jn 3:16; S Col 1:18 r Heb 10:5 s Dt 32:43 (LXX and DSS); Ps 97:7
1:7 t Ps 104:4
1:8 u S Lk 1:33
1:9 v Php 2:9; w Isa 61:1,3 x Ps 45:6,7
1:10 y Ps 8:6; Zec 12:1
1:11 z Isa 34:6; 51:6; S Heb 12:27
1:12 a Heb 13:8 b Ps 102:25-27

"He makes his angels winds,
   his servants flames of fire."[e][t]

⁸But about the Son he says,

"Your throne, O God, will last for ever and ever,[u]
   and righteousness will be the scepter of your kingdom.
⁹You have loved righteousness and hated wickedness;
   therefore God, your God, has set you above your companions[v]
      by anointing you with the oil[w] of joy."[f][x]

¹⁰He also says,

"In the beginning, O Lord, you laid the foundations of the earth,
   and the heavens are the work of your hands.[y]
¹¹They will perish, but you remain;
   they will all wear out like a garment.[z]
¹²You will roll them up like a robe;
   like a garment they will be changed.
But you remain the same,[a]
   and your years will never end."[g][b]

M 2Ti 4:18 ◄ ▶ Heb 1:13
B Tit 3:5–6 ◄ ▶ Heb 2:4
F 2Ti 1:7 ◄ ▶ 1Pe 1:22   J 1Th 1:6 ◄
N Mt 5:5 ◄ ▶ Heb 12:26–28

[a] 5 Or *have begotten you* [b] 5 Psalm 2:7 [c] 5 2 Samuel 7:14; 1 Chron. 17:13 [d] 6 Deut. 32:43 (see Dead Sea Scrolls and Septuagint) [e] 7 Psalm 104:4 [f] 9 Psalm 45:6,7 [g] 12 Psalm 102:25-27

1:2 This verse affirms that Jesus Christ made the world (see Jn 1:3; Col 1:16), and that, having performed the work of redemption, he was exalted to the position of the firstborn heir of God.

1:8 This reference to the ancient prophecy of Jacob (see Ge 49:10) confirms that Jesus of Nazareth is the Messiah, the King from the tribe of Judah. This prophetic fulfillment is verified in the genealogical records of both Matthew and Luke.

1:10–13 This passage is a restatement of Ps 102:25–27 and confirms Christ's hand as God in creation. Yet while the earth and heavens will ultimately change and perish, God remains unchangeable.

¹³To which of the angels did God ever say,

> "Sit at my right hand[c]
> until I make your enemies
> a footstool[d] for your feet"[h]?[e]

¹⁴Are not all angels ministering spirits[f] sent to serve those who will inherit[g] salvation?[h]

Warning to Pay Attention

2 We must pay more careful attention, therefore, to what we have heard, so that we do not drift away.[i] ²For if the message spoken[j] by angels[k] was binding, and every violation and disobedience received its just punishment,¹ ³how shall we escape if we ignore such a great salvation?[m] This salvation, which was first announced by the Lord,[n] was confirmed to us by those who heard him.[o] ⁴God also testified to it by signs, wonders and various miracles,[p] and gifts of the Holy Spirit[q] distributed according to his will.[r]

Jesus Made Like His Brothers

⁵It is not to angels that he has subjected the world to come, about which we are speaking. ⁶But there is a place where someone[s] has testified:

> "What is man that you are mindful of him,
> the son of man that you care for him?[t]
> ⁷You made him a little[i] lower than the angels;
> you crowned him with glory and honor
> ⁸ and put everything under his feet."[u]

In putting everything under him, God left nothing that is not subject to him. Yet at present we do not see everything subject to him. ⁹But we see Jesus, who was made a little lower than the angels, now crowned with glory and honor[v] because he suffered death,[w] so that by the grace of God he might taste death for everyone.[x]

¹⁰In bringing many sons to glory, it was fitting that God, for whom and through whom everything exists,[y] should make the author of their salvation perfect through suffering.[z] ¹¹Both the one who makes men holy[a] and those who are made holy[b] are of the same family. So Jesus is not ashamed to call them brothers.[c] ¹²He says,

> "I will declare your name to my brothers;
> in the presence of the congregation I will sing your praises."[k][d]

¹³And again,

> "I will put my trust in him."[l][e]

And again he says,

> "Here am I, and the children God has given me."[m][f]

¹⁴Since the children have flesh and blood,[g] he too shared in their humanity[h] so that by his death he might destroy[i] him who holds the power of death—that is, the devil[j]— ¹⁵and free those who all their lives were held in slavery by their fear[k] of death. ¹⁶For surely it is not angels he helps, but Abraham's descendants.[l] ¹⁷For this reason he had to be made like his brothers[m] in every way, in order that he might become a merciful[n] and faithful high priest[o] in service to God,[p] and that he might make atonement for[n] the sins of the people.[q] ¹⁸Because he himself suffered when he was tempted, he is able to help those who are being tempted.[r]

M Heb 1:8 ◀ ▶ Heb 2:5–8
V Heb 1:2 ◀ ▶ Rev 11:15
L 1Ti 6:17 ◀ ▶ Heb 13:5–6
S Tit 3:8 ◀ ▶ Heb 3:6
H 1Ti 6:9 ◀ ▶ Heb 6:2
N 2Ti 4:3–4 ◀ ▶ Heb 3:7–9
B Heb 1:9 ◀ ▶ Heb 10:14–15
E Tit 3:5–6 ◀ ▶ Heb 3:7
G 2Ti 3:16 ◀ ▶ 1Pe 4:10–11
H 2Co 3:6 ◀ ▶ 1Pe 3:18
M 2Ti 1:7 ◀ ▶ 2Pe 1:21
M Heb 1:13 ◀ ▶ Heb 7:2

D Heb 1:3 ◀ ▶ Heb 2:14–17
W Tit 2:11 ◀ ▶ Heb 5:9
D Heb 2:9 ◀ ▶ Heb 7:27
C Tit 3:3 ◀ ▶ Heb 3:10
K Tit 2:11 ◀ ▶ Heb 5:9

1:13 c ver 3; S Mk 16:19
d Jos 10:24; Heb 10:13
e Ps 110:1; S Mt 22:44
1:14 f Ps 91:11; 103:20; Da 7:10
g Mt 25:34; Mk 10:17; S Ac 20:32
h S Ro 11:14; Heb 2:3; 5:9; 9:28
2:1 i S Ro 11:22
2:2 j S Heb 1:1
k Dt 33:2; Ac 7:53; Gal 3:19
l Heb 10:28
2:3 m Heb 10:29; 12:25 n Heb 1:2
o S Lk 1:2
2:4 p Mk 16:20; S Jn 4:48
q S 1Co 12:4
r S Eph 1:5
2:6 s Heb 4:4
t Job 7:17; Ps 144:3
2:8 u Ps 8:4-6; S Mt 22:44
2:9 v ver 7; Ac 3:13; S Php 2:9
w Php 2:7-9
x 2Co 5:15
2:10 y S Ro 11:36
z Lk 24:26; Heb 5:8, 9; 7:28
2:11 a Heb 13:12
b S Eph 5:26
c S Mt 28:10
2:12 d Ps 22:22; 68:26
2:13 e Isa 8:17
f Isa 8:18; Jn 10:29
2:14 g 1Co 15:50; Eph 6:12
h S Jn 1:14
i Ge 3:15; 1Co 15:54-57; 2Ti 1:10 j 1Jn 3:8
2:15 k S 2Ti 1:7
2:16 l S Lk 3:8
2:17 m ver 14; S Php 2:7 n Heb 5:2
o Heb 3:1; 4:14,15; 5:5,10; 7:26,28; 8:1,3; 9:11
p Heb 5:1
q S Ro 3:25
2:18 r Heb 4:15

h 13 Psalm 110:1   i 7 Or him for a little while; also in verse 9
j 8 Psalm 8:4-6   k 12 Psalm 22:22   l 13 Isaiah 8:17   m 13 Isaiah 8:18
n 17 Or and that he might turn aside God's wrath, taking away

---

2:5–8 This passage clearly declares that Jesus Christ is the Son of God and that he is the fulfillment of King David's prophecy in Ps 8:4–6 (see 1Co 15:27; Eph 1:22).

Jesus Greater Than Moses

3 Therefore, holy brothers,[s] who share in the heavenly calling,[t] fix your thoughts on Jesus, the apostle and high priest[u] whom we confess.[v] ²He was faithful to the one who appointed him, just as Moses was faithful in all God's house.[w] ³Jesus has been found worthy of greater honor than Moses,[x] just as the builder of a house has greater honor than the house itself. ⁴For every house is built by someone, but God is the builder of everything.[y] ⁵Moses was faithful as a servant[z] in all God's house,[a] testifying to what would be said in the future. ⁶But Christ is faithful as a son[b] over God's house. And we are his house,[c] if we hold on[d] to our courage and the hope[e] of which we boast.

Warning Against Unbelief

⁷So, as the Holy Spirit says:[f]

"Today, if you hear his voice,
⁸ do not harden your hearts[g]
as you did in the rebellion,
   during the time of testing in the desert,
⁹where your fathers tested and tried me
   and for forty years saw what I did.[h]
¹⁰That is why I was angry with that generation,
   and I said, 'Their hearts are always going astray,
   and they have not known my ways.'
¹¹So I declared on oath in my anger,[i]
   'They shall never enter my rest.'"[j][o][k]

¹²See to it, brothers, that none of you has a sinful, unbelieving heart that turns away from the living God.[l] ¹³But encourage one another daily,[m] as long as it is called Today, so that none of you may be hardened by sin's deceitfulness.[n] ¹⁴We have come to share in Christ if we hold firmly[o] till the end the confidence[p] we had at first. ¹⁵As has just been said:

"Today, if you hear his voice,
do not harden your hearts
as you did in the rebellion."[p][q]

¹⁶Who were they who heard and rebelled? Were they not all those Moses led out of Egypt?[r] ¹⁷And with whom was he angry for forty years? Was it not with those who sinned, whose bodies fell in the desert?[s] ¹⁸And to whom did God swear that they would never enter his rest[t] if not to those who disobeyed[q]?[u] ¹⁹So we see that they were not able to enter, because of their unbelief.[v]

A Sabbath-Rest for the People of God

4 Therefore, since the promise of entering his rest still stands, let us be careful that none of you be found to have fallen short of it.[w] ²For we also have had the gospel preached to us, just as they did; but the message they heard was of no value to them, because those who heard did not combine it with faith.[r][x] ³Now we who have believed enter that rest, just as God has said,

"So I declared on oath in my anger,
  'They shall never enter my rest.'"[s][y]

And yet his work has been finished since the creation of the world. ⁴For somewhere he has spoken about the seventh day in these words: "And on the seventh day God rested from all his work."[t][z] ⁵And again in the passage above he says, "They shall never enter my rest."[a]

⁶It still remains that some will enter that rest, and those who formerly had the gospel preached to them did not go in, because of their disobedience.[b] ⁷Therefore God again set a certain day, calling it Today, when a long time later he spoke through David, as was said before:

"Today, if you hear his voice,
  do not harden your hearts."[p][c]

⁸For if Joshua had given them rest,[d] God would not have spoken[e] later about another day. ⁹There remains, then, a Sabbath-rest for the people of God; ¹⁰for anyone who enters God's rest also rests from his own work,[f] just as God did from his.[g]

3:1 ˢHeb 2:11
ᵗS Ro 8:28
ᵘS Heb 2:17
ᵛ1Ti 6:12;
Heb 4:14; 10:23;
2Co 9:13
3:2 ʷver 5;
Nu 12:7
3:3 ˣDt 34:12
3:4 ʸGe 1:1
3:5 ᶻEx 14:31
ᵃver 2; Nu 12:7
3:6 ᵇS Heb 1:2
ᶜS 1Co 3:16;
1Ti 3:15 ᵈver 14;
S Ro 11:22;
Heb 4:14 ᵉRo 5:2;
Heb 6:11,18,19;
7:19; 11:1
3:7 ᶠAc 28:25;
Heb 9:8; 10:15
3:8 ᵍver 15;
Heb 4:7
3:9 ʰNu 14:33;
Dt 1:3; Ac 7:36
3:11 ⁱDt 1:34,35
ʲHeb 4:3,5
ᵏPs 95:7-11
3:12 ˡS Mt 16:16
3:13 ᵐHeb 10:24,25 ⁿJer 17:9;
Eph 4:22
3:14 ᵒver 6
ᵖS Eph 3:12
3:15 ᵠver 7,8;
Ps 95:7,8; Heb 4:7
3:16 ʳNu 14:2
3:17 ˢNu 14:29;
Ps 106:26;
1Co 10:5
3:18
ᵗNu 14:20-23;
Dt 1:34,35
ᵘHeb 4:6
3:19 ᵛPs 78:22;
106:24; Jn 3:36
4:1 ʷHeb 12:15
4:2 ˣ1Th 2:13
4:3 ʸPs 95:11;
Dt 1:34,35;
Heb 3:11
4:4 ᶻGe 2:2,3;
Ex 20:11
4:5 ᵃPs 95:11;
S ver 3
4:6 ᵇver 11;
Heb 3:18
4:7 ᶜPs 95:7,8;
Heb 3:7,8,15
4:8 ᵈJos 22:4
ᵉS Heb 1:1
4:10 ᶠLev 23:3;
Rev 14:13 ᵍver 4

S Heb 2:1–3 ◀ ▶ Heb 3:12–14
E Heb 2:4 ◀ ▶ Heb 9:8
T 2Ti 3:16 ◀ ▶ Heb 6:4
N Heb 2:2–3 ◀ ▶ Heb 3:15
C Heb 2:15 ◀ ▶ Jas 1:14–15
S Heb 3:6 ◀ ▶ Heb 4:11
T Phm 6 ◀ ▶ Heb 13:15–16
N Heb 3:7–9 ◀ ▶ Heb 3:18

F Php 3:9 ◀ ▶ Heb 10:38–39
N Heb 3:15 ◀ ▶ Heb 12:25

ᵒ 11 Psalm 95:7-11 ᵖ 15,7 Psalm 95:7,8 ᵠ 18 Or *disbelieved* ʳ 2 Many manuscripts *because they did not share in the faith of those who obeyed* ˢ 3 Psalm 95:11; also in verse 5 ᵗ 4 Gen. 2:2

¹¹Let us, therefore, make every effort to enter that rest, so that no one will fall by following their example of disobedience. ¹²For the word of God is living and active. Sharper than any double-edged sword, it penetrates even to dividing soul and spirit, joints and marrow; it judges the thoughts and attitudes of the heart. ¹³Nothing in all creation is hidden from God's sight. Everything is uncovered and laid bare before the eyes of him to whom we must give account.

Jesus the Great High Priest

¹⁴Therefore, since we have a great high priest who has gone through the heavens, Jesus the Son of God, let us hold firmly to the faith we profess. ¹⁵For we do not have a high priest who is unable to sympathize with our weaknesses, but we have one who has been tempted in every way, just as we are—yet was without sin. ¹⁶Let us then approach the throne of grace with confidence, so that we may receive mercy and find grace to help us in our time of need.

5 Every high priest is selected from among men and is appointed to represent them in matters related to God, to offer gifts and sacrifices for sins. ²He is able to deal gently with those who are ignorant and are going astray, since he himself is subject to weakness. ³This is why he has to offer sacrifices for his own sins, as well as for the sins of the people. ⁴No one takes this honor upon himself; he must be called by God, just as Aaron was. ⁵So Christ also did not take upon himself the glory of becoming a high priest. But God said to him,

"You are my Son;
 today I have become your
  Father."

⁶And he says in another place,

"You are a priest forever,
 in the order of Melchizedek."

⁷During the days of Jesus' life on earth, he offered up prayers and petitions with loud cries and tears to the one who could save him from death, and he was heard because of his reverent submission. ⁸Although he was a son, he learned obedience from what he suffered ⁹and, once made perfect, he became the source of eternal salvation for all who obey him ¹⁰and was designated by God to be high priest in the order of Melchizedek.

Warning Against Falling Away
6:4–6 Ref — Heb 10:26–31

¹¹We have much to say about this, but it is hard to explain because you are slow to learn. ¹²In fact, though by this time you ought to be teachers, you need someone to teach you the elementary truths of God's word all over again. You need milk, not solid food! ¹³Anyone who lives on milk, being still an infant, is not acquainted with the teaching about righteousness. ¹⁴But solid food is for the mature, who by constant use have trained themselves to distinguish good from evil.

6 Therefore let us leave the elementary teachings about Christ and go on to maturity, not laying again the foundation of repentance from acts that lead to death, and of faith in God, ²instruction about baptisms, the laying on of hands, the resurrection of the dead, and eternal judgment. ³And God permitting, we will do so. ⁴It is impossible for those who have once been enlightened, who have tasted the heavenly gift, who have shared in the Holy Spirit, ⁵who have tasted the goodness of the word of God and the powers of the coming age, ⁶if they fall away, to be brought back to repentance, because to their loss they are crucifying

---

6:2 This verse indicates that one of the basic doctrines of the church is the "resurrection of the dead" (see 1Co 15:16–17).

the Son of God¹ all over again and subjecting him to public disgrace.

⁷Land that drinks in the rain often falling on it and that produces a crop useful to those for whom it is farmed receives the blessing of God. ⁸But land that produces thorns and thistles is worthless and is in danger of being cursed.ᵐ In the end it will be burned.

⁹Even though we speak like this, dear friends,ⁿ we are confident of better things in your case—things that accompany salvation. ¹⁰God is not unjust; he will not forget your work and the love you have shown him as you have helped his people and continue to help them.º

¹¹We want each of you to show this same diligence to the very end, in order to make your hopeᵖ sure. ¹²We do not want you to become lazy, but to imitateᵠ those who through faith and patienceʳ inherit what has been promised.ˢ

The Certainty of God's Promise

¹³When God made his promise to Abraham, since there was no one greater for him to swear by, he swore by himself,ᵗ ¹⁴saying, "I will surely bless you and give you many descendants."ᵃᵘ ¹⁵And so after waiting patiently, Abraham received what was promised.ᵛ

¹⁶Men swear by someone greater than themselves, and the oath confirms what is said and puts an end to all argument.ʷ ¹⁷Because God wanted to make the unchanging ˣ nature of his purpose very clear to the heirs of what was promised,ʸ he confirmed it with an oath. ¹⁸God did this so that, by two unchangeable things in which it is impossible for God to lie,ᶻ we who have fled to take hold of the hopeᵃ offered to us may be greatly encouraged. ¹⁹We have this hope as an anchor for the soul, firm and secure. It en-

H Heb 6:2 ◀ ▶ Heb 10:12–13
S Heb 6:1 ◀ ▶ Heb 6:11–12
P 1Ti 4:8 ◀   S Heb 6:8 ◀ ▶ Heb 9:14
K Heb 5:9 ◀ ▶ Heb 7:25

6:6 ˢ Mt 4:3
6:8 ᵐ Ge 3:17,18; Isa 5:6; 27:4
6:9 ⁿ S 1Co 10:14
6:10 º S Mt 10:40,42; 1Th 1:3
6:11 ᵖ S Heb 3:6
6:12 ᵠ Heb 13:7
   ʳ 2Ti 1:4; Jas 1:3; Rev 13:10; 14:12
   ˢ Heb 10:36
6:13 ᵗ Ge 22:16; Lk 1:73
6:14 ᵘ Ge 22:17
6:15 ᵛ Ge 21:5
6:16 ʷ Ex 22:11
6:17 ˣ ver 18; Ps 110:4 ʸ Ro 4:16; Heb 11:9
6:18 ᶻ Nu 23:19; Tit 1:2 ᵃ S Heb 3:6
6:19 ᵇ Lev 16:2; Heb 9:2,3,7
6:20 ᶜ S Heb 4:14 ᵈ S Heb 2:17 ᵉ S Heb 5:6
7:1 ᶠ Ps 76:2
   ᵍ S Mk 5:7 ʰ ver 6; Ge 14:18-20
7:3 ⁱ ver 6
   ʲ S Mt 4:3
7:4 ᵏ Ac 2:29
   ˡ Ge 14:20
7:5 ᵐ Nu 18:21,26
7:6 ⁿ Ge 14:19,20
   º Ro 4:13
7:8 ᵖ S Heb 5:6; 6:20
7:11 ᵠ ver 18,19; Heb 8:7

---

ters the inner sanctuary behind the curtain,ᵇ ²⁰where Jesus, who went before us, has entered on our behalf.ᶜ He has become a high priestᵈ forever, in the order of Melchizedek.ᵉ

Melchizedek the Priest

7 This Melchizedek was king of Salemᶠ and priest of God Most High.ᵍ He met Abraham returning from the defeat of the kings and blessed him,ʰ ²and Abraham gave him a tenth of everything. First, his name means "king of righteousness"; then also, "king of Salem" means "king of peace." ³Without father or mother, without genealogy,ⁱ without beginning of days or end of life, like the Son of Godʲ he remains a priest forever.

⁴Just think how great he was: Even the patriarchᵏ Abraham gave him a tenth of the plunder!ˡ ⁵Now the law requires the descendants of Levi who become priests to collect a tenth from the peopleᵐ—that is, their brothers—even though their brothers are descended from Abraham. ⁶This man, however, did not trace his descent from Levi, yet he collected a tenth from Abraham and blessedⁿ him who had the promises.º ⁷And without doubt the lesser person is blessed by the greater. ⁸In the one case, the tenth is collected by men who die; but in the other case, by him who is declared to be living.ᵖ ⁹One might even say that Levi, who collects the tenth, paid the tenth through Abraham, ¹⁰because when Melchizedek met Abraham, Levi was still in the body of his ancestor.

Jesus Like Melchizedek

¹¹If perfection could have been attained through the Levitical priesthood (for on the basis of it the law was given to the people),ᵠ why was there still need for an-

M Heb 2:5–8 ◀ ▶ Heb 7:11
M Heb 7:2 ◀ ▶ Heb 7:15–17

ᵃ14 Gen. 22:17

7:2 This prophetic reference describes Abram's honoring of Melchizedek (see Ge 14:17–20). Melchizedek was a "king of Salem" (Ge 14:18) and stands prophetically as a type of Christ is his role in the last days as the "king of righteousness," the "king of peace" and "a priest forever, in the order of Melchizedek" (Ps 110:4).

7:11 The OT law, subject to the rule of the Levitical priesthood under Aaron, would be replaced with a better priesthood when "another priest [would] come—one in the order of Melchizedek." This priest is clearly Jesus Christ the Messiah, who would bring salvation to all those who would follow him.

other priest to come—one in the order of Melchizedek, not in the order of Aaron? ¹²For when there is a change of the priesthood, there must also be a change of the law. ¹³He of whom these things are said belonged to a different tribe, and no one from that tribe has ever served at the altar. ¹⁴For it is clear that our Lord descended from Judah, and in regard to that tribe Moses said nothing about priests. ¹⁵And what we have said is even more clear if another priest like Melchizedek appears, ¹⁶one who has become a priest not on the basis of a regulation as to his ancestry but on the basis of the power of an indestructible life. ¹⁷For it is declared:

"You are a priest forever,
in the order of Melchizedek."

¹⁸The former regulation is set aside because it was weak and useless ¹⁹(for the law made nothing perfect), and a better hope is introduced, by which we draw near to God.

²⁰And it was not without an oath! Others became priests without any oath, ²¹but he became a priest with an oath when God said to him:

"The Lord has sworn
and will not change his mind:
'You are a priest forever.'"

²²Because of this oath, Jesus has become the guarantee of a better covenant.

²³Now there have been many of those priests, since death prevented them from continuing in office; ²⁴but because Jesus lives forever, he has a permanent priesthood. ²⁵Therefore he is able to save completely those who come to God through him, because he always lives to intercede for them.

²⁶Such a high priest meets our need—one who is holy, blameless, pure, set apart from sinners, exalted above the heavens. ²⁷Unlike the other high priests, he does not need to offer sacrifices day after day, first for his own sins, and then for the sins of the people. He sacrificed for their sins once for all when he offered himself. ²⁸For the law appoints as high priests men who are weak; but the oath, which came after the law, appointed the Son, who has been made perfect forever.

The High Priest of a New Covenant

8 The point of what we are saying is this: We do have such a high priest, who sat down at the right hand of the throne of the Majesty in heaven, ²and who serves in the sanctuary, the true tabernacle set up by the Lord, not by man.

³Every high priest is appointed to offer both gifts and sacrifices, and so it was necessary for this one also to have something to offer. ⁴If he were on earth, he would not be a priest, for there are already men who offer the gifts prescribed by the law. ⁵They serve at a sanctuary that is a copy and shadow of what is in heaven. This is why Moses was warned when he was about to build the tabernacle: "See to it that you make everything according to the pattern shown you on the mountain." ⁶But the ministry Jesus has received is as superior to theirs as the covenant of which he is mediator is superior to the old one, and it is founded on better promises.

⁷For if there had been nothing wrong with that first covenant, no place would have been sought for another. ⁸But God found fault with the people and said:

7:14–17 This passage clearly indicates that Jesus Christ, "our Lord" (7:14) fulfills the prophecy of King David that indicated the Messiah would be "a priest forever, in the order of Melchizedek" (Ps 110:4).
7:20–21 This passage is a reaffirmation that Jesus Christ is truly the fulfillment of King David's prophecy (see Ps 110:4).
8:8 *New Covenant.* The new covenant is the last of the eight, major Biblical covenants. Established on God's unconditional promises to transform the hearts of his people, the new covenant grants the personal divine manifestation of the Lord to every believer and asserts that all sin has been effectively forgiven forever through Christ's atoning work on the cross. This final covenant will also be ratified with Israel, assuring their status as God's chosen people, their

"The time is coming, declares the Lord,
when I will make a new covenant[g]
with the house of Israel
and with the house of Judah.
[9]It will not be like the covenant
I made with their forefathers[h]
when I took them by the hand
to lead them out of Egypt,
because they did not remain faithful to my covenant,
and I turned away from them,
declares the Lord.
[10]This is the covenant[i] I will make with the house of Israel
after that time, declares the Lord.
I will put my laws in their minds
and write them on their hearts.[j]
I will be their God,
and they will be my people.[k]
[11]No longer will a man teach his neighbor,
or a man his brother, saying, 'Know the Lord,'
because they will all know me,[l]
from the least of them to the greatest.
[12]For I will forgive their wickedness
and will remember their sins no more."[m]/[n]

[13]By calling this covenant "new,"[o] he has made the first one obsolete;[p] and what is obsolete and aging will soon disappear.

Worship in the Earthly Tabernacle

9 Now the first covenant had regulations for worship and also an earthly sanctuary.[q] [2]A tabernacle[r] was set up. In its first room were the lampstand,[s] the table[t] and the consecrated bread;[u] this was called the Holy Place.[v] [3]Behind the second curtain was a room called the Most Holy Place,[w] [4]which had the golden altar of incense[x] and the gold-covered ark of the covenant.[y] This ark contained the gold jar of manna,[z] Aaron's staff that had budded,[a] and the stone tablets of the covenant.[b] [5]Above the ark were the cherubim of the Glory,[c] overshadowing the atonement cover.[g][d] But we cannot discuss these things in detail now.

[6]When everything had been arranged like this, the priests entered regularly[e] into the outer room to carry on their ministry. [7]But only the high priest entered[f] the inner room,[g] and that only once a year,[h] and never without blood,[i] which he offered for himself[j] and for the sins the people had committed in ignorance.[k] [8]The Holy Spirit was showing[l] by this that the way[m] into the Most Holy Place had not yet been disclosed as long as the first tabernacle was still standing. [9]This is an illustration[n] for the present time, indicating that the gifts and sacrifices being offered[o] were not able to clear the conscience[p] of the worshiper. [10]They are only a matter of food[q] and drink[r] and various ceremonial washings[s]—external regulations[t] applying until the time of the new order.

The Blood of Christ

[11]When Christ came as high priest[u] of the good things that are already here,[h][v] he went through the greater and more perfect tabernacle[w] that is not manmade,[x] that is to say, not a part of this creation. [12]He did not enter by means of the blood of goats and calves;[y] but he entered the Most Holy Place[z] once for all[a] by his own blood,[b] having obtained eternal redemption. [13]The blood of goats and bulls[c] and the ashes of a heifer[d] sprinkled on those who are ceremonially unclean sanctify them so that they are outwardly

---

D Heb 7:27 ◀ ▶ Heb 9:11–28
E Heb 3:7 ◀ ▶ Heb 9:14
D Heb 9:7 ◀ ▶ Heb 10:12
K Heb 8:10–12 ◀ ▶ Heb 10:16–17
L Heb 8:12 ◀ ▶ Heb 9:28

K Heb 7:25 ◀ ▶ Heb 9:13–14
L Heb 7:25 ◀ ▶ Heb 9:13–14

*f*12 Jer. 31:31-34 *g*5 Traditionally *the mercy seat* *h*11 Some early manuscripts *are to come*

---

complete and ultimate redemption and conversion so that they will love and obey God forever and Israel's eternal relationship with God in the promised land.

NOTE: The seven additional covenants include the Edenic (Ge 2:15–17), Adamic (Ge 3:15–19), Noahic (Ge 9:8ff), Abrahamic (Ge 15:4ff; 17:1–22), Mosaic (Ex 19:5), Palestinian (Dt 30:1–10) and Davidic (2Sa 7:16). For further information, see the article on "The Biblical Covenants" on p. 8.

clean. ¹⁴How much more, then, will the blood of Christ, who through the eternal Spirit offered himself unblemished to God, cleanse our consciences from acts that lead to death, so that we may serve the living God!

¹⁵For this reason Christ is the mediator of a new covenant, that those who are called may receive the promised eternal inheritance—now that he has died as a ransom to set them free from the sins committed under the first covenant.

¹⁶In the case of a will, it is necessary to prove the death of the one who made it, ¹⁷because a will is in force only when somebody has died; it never takes effect while the one who made it is living. ¹⁸This is why even the first covenant was not put into effect without blood. ¹⁹When Moses had proclaimed every commandment of the law to all the people, he took the blood of calves, together with water, scarlet wool and branches of hyssop, and sprinkled the scroll and all the people. ²⁰He said, "This is the blood of the covenant, which God has commanded you to keep." ²¹In the same way, he sprinkled with the blood both the tabernacle and everything used in its ceremonies. ²²In fact, the law requires that nearly everything be cleansed with blood, and without the shedding of blood there is no forgiveness.

²³It was necessary, then, for the copies of the heavenly things to be purified with these sacrifices, but the heavenly things themselves with better sacrifices than these. ²⁴For Christ did not enter a man-made sanctuary that was only a copy of the true one; he entered heaven itself, now to appear for us in God's presence. ²⁵Nor did he enter heaven to offer himself again and again, the way the high priest enters the Most Holy Place every year with blood that is not his own. ²⁶Then Christ would have had to suffer many times since the creation of the world. But now he has appeared once for all at the end of the ages to do away with sin by the sacrifice of himself. ²⁷Just as man is destined to die once, and after that to face judgment, ²⁸so Christ was sacrificed once to take away the sins of many people; and he will appear a second time, not to bear sin, but to bring salvation to those who are waiting for him.

Christ's Sacrifice Once for All

10 The law is only a shadow of the good things that are coming—not the realities themselves. For this reason it can never, by the same sacrifices repeated endlessly year after year, make perfect those who draw near to worship. ²If it could, would they not have stopped being offered? For the worshipers would have been cleansed once for all, and would no longer have felt guilty for their sins. ³But those sacrifices are an annual reminder of sins, ⁴because it is impossible for the blood of bulls and goats to take away sins.

⁵Therefore, when Christ came into the world, he said:

"Sacrifice and offering you did not
    desire,
but a body you prepared for me;
⁶with burnt offerings and sin offerings
    you were not pleased.

D Eph 4:4 ◀▶ 1Jn 5:7
E Heb 9:8 ◀▶ Heb 10:15
L 1Th 5:19 ◀▶ 1Pe 1:12
N Eph 5:18 ◀▶ Heb 10:29
S Heb 6:11–12 ◀▶ Heb 10:26–31
O 2Ti 2:11–12 ◀▶ Jas 4:12

C Tit 2:13 ◀▶ Heb 9:28
J 2Co 5:9–11 ◀▶ Heb 10:30
J 2Ti 4:1 ◀▶ Heb 12:23
C Heb 9:26 ◀▶ Heb 10:25
L Heb 9:13–14 ◀▶ Heb 10:17

i 14 Or *from useless rituals* *j* 16 Same Greek word as *covenant*; also in verse 17 *k* 20 Exodus 24:8

9:26–28 The ancient Israelites would put away the sin of the camp by sending a scapegoat loose into the wilderness (see Lev 16:21–22). Jesus Christ becomes the fulfillment of that symbolic scapegoat as he takes away the sins of the world through his own sacrifice on the cross. Every person who rejects Christ's sacrifice and offer of salvation will ultimately appear before God at life's end to account for their refusal to believe. Yet God's offer of salvation is still available for those who will repent and believe.

10:25 Hebrews urges us to gather together as believers, encouraging each other as we await the return of Jesus Christ in glory.

[7] Then I said, 'Here I am—it is written about me in the scroll—
I have come to do your will, O God.'"

[8] First he said, "Sacrifices and offerings, burnt offerings and sin offerings you did not desire, nor were you pleased with them" (although the law required them to be made). [9] Then he said, "Here I am, I have come to do your will." He sets aside the first to establish the second. [10] And by that will, we have been made holy through the sacrifice of the body of Jesus Christ once for all.

[11] Day after day every priest stands and performs his religious duties; again and again he offers the same sacrifices, which can never take away sins. [12] But when this priest had offered for all time one sacrifice for sins, he sat down at the right hand of God. [13] Since that time he waits for his enemies to be made his footstool, [14] because by one sacrifice he has made perfect forever those who are being made holy.

[15] The Holy Spirit also testifies to us about this. First he says:

[16] "This is the covenant I will make with them
after that time, says the Lord.
I will put my laws in their hearts,
and I will write them on their minds."

[17] Then he adds:

"Their sins and lawless acts
I will remember no more."

[18] And where these have been forgiven, there is no longer any sacrifice for sin.

A Call to Persevere

[19] Therefore, brothers, since we have confidence to enter the Most Holy Place by the blood of Jesus, [20] by a new and living way opened for us through the curtain, that is, his body, [21] and since we have a great priest over the house of God, [22] let us draw near to God with a sincere heart in full assurance of faith, having our hearts sprinkled to cleanse us from a guilty conscience and having our bodies washed with pure water. [23] Let us hold unswervingly to the hope we profess, for he who promised is faithful. [24] And let us consider how we may spur one another on toward love and good deeds. [25] Let us not give up meeting together, as some are in the habit of doing, but let us encourage one another—and all the more as you see the Day approaching.

[26] If we deliberately keep on sinning after we have received the knowledge of the truth, no sacrifice for sins is left, [27] but only a fearful expectation of judgment and of raging fire that will consume the enemies of God. [28] Anyone who rejected the law of Moses died without mercy on the testimony of two or three witnesses. [29] How much more severely do you think a man deserves to be punished who has trampled the Son of God under foot, who has treated as an unholy thing the blood of the covenant that sanctified him, and who has insulted the Spirit of grace? [30] For we know him who said, "It is mine to avenge; I will repay," and again, "The Lord will judge his people." [31] It is a dreadful thing to fall into the hands of the living God.

[32] Remember those earlier days after you had received the light, when you stood your ground in a great contest in the face of suffering. [33] Sometimes you were publicly exposed to insult and persecution; at other times you stood side by side with those who were so treated. [34] You sympathized with those in prison

---

10:30 Despite the universal violence and evil during the last days, God will be the one to bring recompense, judgment and vengeance.

and joyfully accepted the confiscation of your property, because you knew that you yourselves had better and lasting possessions.ᵃ

³⁵So do not throw away your confidence;ᵇ it will be richly rewarded. ³⁶You need to persevereᶜ so that when you have done the will of God, you will receive what he has promised.ᵈ ³⁷For in just a very little while,

"He who is comingᵉ will come and
    will not delay.ᶠ
³⁸ But my righteous oneᵍ will live by
    faith.ᵍ
And if he shrinks back,
    I will not be pleased with him."ʳʰ

³⁹But we are not of those who shrink back and are destroyed, but of those who believe and are saved.

By Faith

11 Now faith is being sure of what we hope forⁱ and certain of what we do not see.ʲ ²This is what the ancients were commended for.ᵏ

³By faith we understand that the universe was formed at God's command,ˡ so that what is seen was not made out of what is visible.

⁴By faith Abel offered God a better sacrifice than Cain did. By faith he was commendedᵐ as a righteous man, when God spoke well of his offerings.ⁿ And by faith he still speaks, even though he is dead.ᵒ

⁵By faith Enoch was taken from this life, so that he did not experience death; he could not be found, because God had taken him away.ᵖ For before he was taken, he was commended as one who pleased God. ⁶And without faith it is impossible to please God, because anyone who comes to himᵠ must believe that he exists and that he rewards those who earnestly seek him.

⁷By faith Noah, when warned about things not yet seen,ʳ in holy fear built an arkˢ to save his family.ᵗ By his faith he condemned the world and became heir of the righteousness that comes by faith.ᵘ

⁸By faith Abraham, when called to go to a place he would later receive as his inheritance,ᵛ obeyed and went,ʷ even though he did not know where he was going. ⁹By faith he made his home in the promised landˣ like a stranger in a foreign country; he lived in tents,ʸ as did Isaac and Jacob, who were heirs with him of the same promise.ᶻ ¹⁰For he was looking forward to the cityᵃ with foundations,ᵇ whose architect and builder is God.ᶜ

¹¹By faith Abraham, even though he was past age—and Sarah herself was barrenᵈ—was enabled to become a fatherᵉ because heˢ considered him faithfulᶠ who had made the promise. ¹²And so from this one man, and he as good as dead,ᵍ came descendants as numerous as the stars in the sky and as countless as the sand on the seashore.ʰ

¹³All these people were still living by faith when they died. They did not receive the things promised;ⁱ they only saw them and welcomed them from a distance.ʲ And they admitted that they were aliens and strangers on earth.ᵏ ¹⁴People who say such things show that they are looking for a country of their own. ¹⁵If they had been thinking of the country they had left, they would have had opportunity to return.ˡ ¹⁶Instead, they were longing for a better country—a heavenly one.ᵐ Therefore God is not ashamedⁿ to be called their God,ᵒ for he has prepared a cityᵖ for them.

¹⁷By faith Abraham, when God tested him, offered Isaac as a sacrifice.ᵠ He who had received the promises was about to sacrifice his one and only son, ¹⁸even though God had said to him, "It is through Isaac that your offspringʳ will be reckoned."ᵘʳ ¹⁹Abraham reasoned that

---

S Heb 10:26–31 ◄ ► Heb 10:38–39
C Heb 10:25 ◄ ► Jas 5:7–9
F Heb 3:18–19 ◄ ► Heb 11:6
S Heb 10:35–36 ◄ ► Heb 12:1
H Heb 10:26–31 ◄ ► Heb 11:28
F Heb 10:38–39 ◄ ► Jas 2:23
G Tit 3:5 ◄ ► 1Pe 1:18–19

10:34 ᵃHeb 11:16; 1Pe 1:4,5
10:35 ᵇS Eph 3:12
10:36 ᶜRo 5:3; Heb 12:1; Jas 1:3,4, 12; 5:11; 2Pe 1:6
ᵈHeb 6:15; 9:15
10:37 ᵉMt 11:3
ᶠRev 22:20
10:38 ᵍRo 1:17; Gal 3:11 ʰHab 2:3, 4
11:1 ⁱS Heb 3:6
ʲS 2Co 4:18
11:2 ᵏver 4,39
11:3 ˡGe 1; Jn 1:3; Heb 1:2; 2Pe 3:5
11:4 ᵐver 2,39
ⁿGe 4:4; 1Jn 3:12
ᵒHeb 12:24
11:5 ᵖGe 5:21-24
11:6 ᵠHeb 7:19
11:7 ʳS ver 1
ˢGe 6:13-22
ᵗ1Pe 3:20 ᵘGe 6:9; Eze 14:14,20; S Ro 9:30
11:8 ᵛGe 12:7
ʷGe 12:1-4; Ac 7:2-4
11:9 ˣAc 7:5
ʸGe 12:8; 18:1,9
ᶻHeb 6:17
11:10 ᵃHeb 12:22; 13:14 ᵇRev 21:2,14
ᶜver 16
11:11
ᵈGe 17:17-19; 18:11-14 ᵉGe 21:2
ᶠS 1Co 1:9
11:12 ᵍRo 4:19
ʰGe 22:17
11:13 ⁱver 39
ʲS Mt 13:17
ᵏGe 23:4; Lev 25:23;
Php 3:20; 1Pe 1:17; 2:11
11:15 ˡGe 24:6-8
11:16 ᵐ2Ti 4:18
ⁿMk 8:38
ᵒGe 24:27; 28:13; Ex 3:6,15 ᵖver 10; Heb 13:14
11:17
ᵠGe 22:1-10; Jas 2:21
11:18 ʳGe 21:12; Ro 9:7

E Heb 10:15 ◄ ► 1Pe 1:2
E Php 2:27 ◄ ► Heb 11:34–35

ᵠ38 One early manuscript *But the righteous* ʳ38 Hab. 2:3,4 ˢ11 Or *By faith even Sarah, who was past age, was enabled to bear children because she* ᵗ18 Greek *seed* ᵘ18 Gen. 21:12

10:37 While the second coming of Christ seems delayed indefinitely, it will occur (see 2Pe 3:9). Once the conditions are right, the Lord will return in glory to defeat the antichrist and Satan.

God could raise the dead,ˢ and figuratively speaking, he did receive Isaac back from death.

²⁰By faith Isaac blessed Jacob and Esau in regard to their future.ᵗ

²¹By faith Jacob, when he was dying, blessed each of Joseph's sons,ᵘ and worshiped as he leaned on the top of his staff.

²²By faith Joseph, when his end was near, spoke about the exodus of the Israelites from Egypt and gave instructions about his bones.ᵛ

²³By faith Moses' parents hid him for three months after he was born,ʷ because they saw he was no ordinary child, and they were not afraid of the king's edict.ˣ

²⁴By faith Moses, when he had grown up, refused to be known as the son of Pharaoh's daughter.ʸ ²⁵He chose to be mistreatedᶻ along with the people of God rather than to enjoy the pleasures of sin for a short time. ²⁶He regarded disgraceᵃ for the sake of Christᵇ as of greater value than the treasures of Egypt, because he was looking ahead to his reward.ᶜ ²⁷By faith he left Egypt,ᵈ not fearing the king's anger; he persevered because he saw him who is invisible. ²⁸By faith he kept the Passover and the sprinkling of blood, so that the destroyerᵉ of the firstborn would not touch the firstborn of Israel.ᶠ

²⁹By faith the people passed through the Red Seaᵛ as on dry land; but when the Egyptians tried to do so, they were drowned.ᵍ

³⁰By faith the walls of Jericho fell, after the people had marched around them for seven days.ʰ

³¹By faith the prostitute Rahab, because she welcomed the spies, was not killed with those who were disobedient.ʷⁱ

³²And what more shall I say? I do not have time to tell about Gideon,ʲ Barak,ᵏ Samson,ˡ Jephthah,ᵐ David,ⁿ Samuel and the prophets, ³³who through faith conquered kingdoms,ᵖ administered justice, and gained what was promised; who shut the mouths of lions,ᵠ ³⁴quenched the fury of the flames,ʳ and escaped the edge of the sword;ˢ whose weakness was turned to strength;ᵗ and who became powerful in battle and routed foreign armies.ᵘ ³⁵Women received back their dead, raised to life again.ᵛ Others were tortured and refused to be released, so that they might gain a better resurrection. ³⁶Some faced jeers and flogging,ʷ while still others were chained and put in prison.ˣ ³⁷They were stonedˣ;ʸ they were sawed in two; they were put to death by the sword.ᶻ They went about in sheepskins and goatskins,ᵃ destitute, persecuted and mistreated— ³⁸the world was not worthy of them. They wandered in deserts and mountains, and in cavesᵇ and holes in the ground.

³⁹These were all commendedᶜ for their faith, yet none of them received what had been promised.ᵈ ⁴⁰God had planned something better for us so that only together with usᵉ would they be made perfect.ᶠ

God Disciplines His Sons

12 Therefore, since we are surrounded by such a great cloud of witnesses, let us throw off everything that hinders and the sin that so easily entangles, and let us runᵍ with perseveranceʰ the race marked out for us. ²Let us fix our eyes on Jesus,ⁱ the authorʲ and perfecter of our faith, who for the joy set before him endured the cross,ᵏ scorning its shame,ˡ and sat down at the right hand of the throne of God.ᵐ ³Consider him who endured such opposition from sinful men, so that you will not grow wearyⁿ and lose heart.

⁴In your struggle against sin, you have not yet resisted to the point of shedding your blood.ᵒ ⁵And you have forgotten that word of encouragement that addresses you as sons:

F Heb 6:2 ◀▶ Rev 20:5–6
S Heb 10:38–39 ◀▶ Heb 12:14
D Php 2:30 ◀ **T** Heb 5:8 ◀▶ Jas 1:2–4

ᵛ29 That is, Sea of Reeds ʷ31 Or *unbelieving* ˣ37 Some early manuscripts *stoned; they were put to the test;*

11:35 The martyrs of the church gave their lives for their faith in Jesus Christ so that "they might gain a better resurrection." This refers to the first resurrection to life (see Jn 5:29) that includes all those who participate in salvation and receive a complete transformation as they are raised to eternal life.

"My son, do not make light of the
  Lord's discipline,
and do not lose heart[p] when he
  rebukes you,
6because the Lord disciplines those he
  loves,[q]
and he punishes everyone he
  accepts as a son."[y][r]

7Endure hardship as discipline; God is treating you as sons.[s] For what son is not disciplined by his father? 8If you are not disciplined (and everyone undergoes discipline),[t] then you are illegitimate children and not true sons. 9Moreover, we have all had human fathers who disciplined us and we respected them for it. How much more should we submit to the Father of our spirits[u] and live![v] 10Our fathers disciplined us for a little while as they thought best; but God disciplines us for our good, that we may share in his holiness.[w] 11No discipline seems pleasant at the time, but painful. Later on, however, it produces a harvest of righteousness and peace[x] for those who have been trained by it.

12Therefore, strengthen your feeble arms and weak knees.[y] 13"Make level paths for your feet,"[zz] so that the lame may not be disabled, but rather healed.[a]

Warning Against Refusing God

14Make every effort to live in peace with all men[b] and to be holy;[c] without holiness no one will see the Lord.[d] 15See to it that no one misses the grace of God[e] and that no bitter root[f] grows up to cause trouble and defile many. 16See that no one is sexually immoral,[g] or is godless like Esau, who for a single meal sold his inheritance rights as the oldest son.[h] 17Afterward, as you know, when he wanted to inherit this blessing, he was rejected. He could bring about no change of mind, though he sought the blessing with tears.[i]

18You have not come to a mountain that can be touched and that is burning with fire; to darkness, gloom and storm;[j] 19to a trumpet blast[k] or to such a voice speaking words[l] that those who heard it begged that no further word be spoken to them,[m] 20because they could not bear what was commanded: "If even an animal touches the mountain, it must be stoned."[a][n] 21The sight was so terrifying that Moses said, "I am trembling with fear."[b][o]

22But you have come to Mount Zion,[p] to the heavenly Jerusalem,[q] the city[r] of the living God.[s] You have come to thousands upon thousands of angels in joyful assembly, 23to the church of the firstborn,[t] whose names are written in heaven.[u] You have come to God, the judge of all men,[v] to the spirits of righteous men made perfect,[w] 24to Jesus the mediator[x] of a new covenant, and to the sprinkled blood[y] that speaks a better word than the blood of Abel.[z]

25See to it that you do not refuse[a] him who speaks.[b] If they did not escape when they refused him who warned[c] them on earth, how much less will we, if we turn away from him who warns us from heaven?[d] 26At that time his voice shook the earth,[e] but now he has promised, "Once more I will shake not only the earth but also the heavens."[c][f] 27The words "once more" indicate the removing of what can be shaken[g]—that is, created things—so that what cannot be shaken may remain.

28Therefore, since we are receiving a kingdom that cannot be shaken,[h] let us be thankful, and so worship God acceptably with reverence and awe,[i] 29for our "God is a consuming fire."[d][j]

12:5 p ver 3
12:6 q Ps 94:12; 119:75; Rev 3:19
r Pr 3:11,12
12:7 s Dt 8:5; 2Sa 7:14; Pr 13:24
12:8 t 1Pe 5:9
12:9 u Nu 16:22; 27:16; Rev 22:6
v Isa 38:16
12:10 w S 2Pe 1:4
12:11 x Isa 32:17; Jas 3:17,18
12:12 y Isa 35:3
12:13 z Pr 4:26
a Gal 6:1
12:14 b S Ro 14:19
c Ro 6:22 d S Mt 5:8
12:15 e Gal 5:4; Heb 3:12; 4:1
f Dt 29:18
12:16 g S 1Co 6:18
h Ge 25:29-34
12:17 i Ge 27:30-40
12:18 j Ex 19:12-22; 20:18; Dt 4:11
12:19 k Ex 20:18
l Dt 4:12
m Ex 20:19; Dt 5:5, 25; 18:16
12:20 n Ex 19:12, 13
12:21 o Dt 9:19
12:22 p Isa 24:23; 60:14; Rev 14:1
q S Gal 4:26
r Heb 11:10; 13:14
s S Mt 16:16
12:23 t Ex 4:22
u S Rev 20:12
v Ge 18:25; Ps 94:2
w Php 3:12
12:24 x S Gal 3:20
y Heb 9:19; 10:22; 1Pe 1:2 z Ge 4:10; Heb 11:4
12:25 a Heb 3:12
b S Heb 1:1
c Heb 8:5; 11:7
d Dt 18:19;
Heb 2:2,3; 10:29
12:26 e Ex 19:18
f Hag 2:6
12:27 g Isa 34:4; 54:10; 1Co 7:31; Heb 1:11,12; 2Pe 3:10; 1Jn 2:17
12:28 h Ps 15:5; Da 2:44 i Mal 2:5; 4:2; Heb 13:15
12:29 j Ex 24:17; Dt 4:24; 9:3; Ps 97:3; Isa 33:14; S 2Th 1:7

J Heb 9:27 ◄▶ Jas 2:12-13
D Heb 10:12 ◄▶ Heb 13:11-12
K Heb 10:16-17 ◄▶ Heb 13:8
H Heb 11:28 ◄▶ Heb 12:29
N Heb 3:18 ◄▶ Jas 4:13-14
S Heb 12:14 ◄▶ Heb 13:20-21
N Heb 1:10-12 ◄▶ 2Pe 3:13-14
H Heb 12:25 ◄▶ 1Pe 3:12

y 6 Prov. 3:11,12 z 13 Prov. 4:26 a 20 Exodus 19:12,13
b 21 Deut. 9:19 c 26 Haggai 2:6 d 29 Deut. 4:24

S Heb 12:1 ◄▶ Heb 12:25

12:26–28 This passage corresponds to several of the OT prophecies concerning the last days (see Isa 2:9; 13:13; Joel 3:16; Hag 2:6–7). At the coming judgment of Christ, he shall destroy the works of Satan and his antichrist at the Battle of Armageddon and establish his righteous rule in his millennial kingdom forever. Though the antichrist's kingdom will be shaken, Christ's kingdom is unshakable and will remain forever (12:28).

Concluding Exhortations

13 Keep on loving each other as brothers.ᵏ ²Do not forget to entertain strangers,¹ for by so doing some people have entertained angels without knowing it.ᵐ ³Remember those in prisonⁿ as if you were their fellow prisoners, and those who are mistreated as if you yourselves were suffering.

⁴Marriage should be honored by all,ᵒ and the marriage bed kept pure, for God will judge the adulterer and all the sexually immoral.ᵖ ⁵Keep your lives free from the love of moneyᑫ and be content with what you have,ʳ because God has said,

"Never will I leave you;
  never will I forsake you."ᵉˢ

⁶So we say with confidence,

"The Lord is my helper; I will not be afraid.
What can man do to me?"ᶠᵗ

⁷Remember your leaders,ᵘ who spoke the word of Godᵛ to you. Consider the outcome of their way of life and imitateʷ their faith. ⁸Jesus Christ is the same yesterday and today and forever.ˣ ⁹Do not be carried away by all kinds of strange teachings.ʸ It is good for our hearts to be strengthenedᶻ by grace, not by ceremonial foods,ᵃ which are of no value to those who eat them.ᵇ ¹⁰We have an altar from which those who minister at the tabernacleᶜ have no right to eat.ᵈ ¹¹The high priest carries the blood of animals into the Most Holy Place as a sin offering,ᵉ but the bodies are burned outside the camp.ᶠ ¹²And so Jesus also suffered outside the city gateᵍ to make the people holyʰ through his own blood.ⁱ

¹³Let us, then, go to himʲ outside the camp, bearing the disgrace he bore.ᵏ ¹⁴For here we do not have an enduring city,¹ but we are looking for the city that is to come.ᵐ

¹⁵Through Jesus, therefore, let us continually offer to God a sacrificeⁿ of praise—the fruit of lipsᵒ that confess his name. ¹⁶And do not forget to do good and to share with others,ᵖ for with such sacrificesᑫ God is pleased.

¹⁷Obey your leadersʳ and submit to their authority. They keep watch over youˢ as men who must give an account. Obey them so that their work will be a joy, not a burden, for that would be of no advantage to you.

¹⁸Pray for us.ᵗ We are sure that we have a clear conscienceᵘ and desire to live honorably in every way. ¹⁹I particularly urge you to pray so that I may be restored to you soon.ᵛ

²⁰May the God of peace,ʷ who through the blood of the eternal covenantˣ brought back from the deadʸ our Lord Jesus, that great Shepherd of the sheep,ᶻ ²¹equip you with everything good for doing his will,ᵃ and may he work in usᵇ what is pleasing to him,ᶜ through Jesus Christ, to whom be glory for ever and ever. Amen.ᵈ

²²Brothers, I urge you to bear with my word of exhortation, for I have written you only a short letter.ᵉ

²³I want you to know that our brother Timothyᶠ has been released. If he arrives soon, I will come with him to see you.

²⁴Greet all your leadersᵍ and all God's people. Those from Italyʰ send you their greetings.

²⁵Grace be with you all.ⁱ

James

Author: Uncertain; possibly the half-brother of Jesus

Theme: The need for a practical Christian faith

Date of Writing: C. A.D. 40–50

Outline of James
  I. The Essence of True Religion (1:1–27)
  II. True Faith in Practice (2:1—3:12)
  III. True Wisdom in Practice (3:13—5:20)

THIS EPISTLE WAS written by James, who was probably the half-brother of Jesus (see Mk 6:3). James also was among the group gathered on Pentecost (see Ac 1:14) and became a leader in the Jerusalem church (see Ac 12:17), serving on the Jerusalem council where church leaders reached an agreement for the basis of Christian fellowship. The book of James may be the earliest of the NT epistles, probably written about the same time as Paul's letter to the Galatians.

Since the book of James is not directed to one particular church, it is referred to as a general epistle. Though its message reflects Jewish-Christian interests, this book is directed to all believers. James recognizes the need for a practical Christian faith that shows itself through belief and lifestyle. Using illustrations drawn from the OT, James relies on his Jewish background as he urges his readers to follow an ethical life of righteousness. Briefly mentioning the return of Christ, James emphasizes that genuine faith must produce results in good works and righteous deeds. James contends that genuine faith will be reflected in a changed life-style.

JAMES 1:1

1 James,[a] a servant of God[b] and of the Lord Jesus Christ,

To the twelve tribes[c] scattered[d] among the nations:

Greetings.[e]

Trials and Temptations

[J] [T] ²Consider it pure joy, my brothers, whenever you face trials of many kinds,[f] ³because you know that the testing of your faith[g] develops perseverance.[h] ⁴Perseverance must finish its work so that you may be mature[i] and complete, not lacking anything. ⁵If any of you lacks wisdom, he should ask God,[j] who gives generously to all without finding fault, and it will be given to him.[k] ⁶But when he asks, he must believe and not doubt,[l] because he who doubts is like a wave of the sea, blown and tossed by the wind. ⁷That man should not think he will receive anything from the Lord; ⁸he is a double-minded man,[m] unstable[n] in all he does.

⁹The brother in humble circumstances ought to take pride in his high position.[o] ¹⁰But the one who is rich should take pride in his low position, because he will pass away like a wild flower.[p] ¹¹For the sun rises with scorching heat[q] and withers[r] the plant; its blossom falls and its beauty is destroyed.[s] In the same way, the rich man will fade away even while he goes about his business.

[T] ¹²Blessed is the man who perseveres under trial,[t] because when he has stood the test, he will receive the crown of life[u] that God has promised to those who love him.[v]

[C] ¹³When tempted, no one should say, "God is tempting me." For God cannot be tempted by evil, nor does he tempt anyone; ¹⁴but each one is tempted when, by his own[w] evil desire, he is dragged away and enticed. ¹⁵Then, after desire has conceived, it gives birth to sin;[x] and sin, when it is full-grown, gives birth to death.[y]

¹⁶Don't be deceived,[z] my dear brothers.[a] ¹⁷Every good and perfect gift is from above,[b] coming down from the Father of the heavenly lights,[c] who does not change[d] like shifting shadows. ¹⁸He chose to give us birth[e] through the word of truth,[f] that we might be a kind of firstfruits[g] of all he created.

Listening and Doing

¹⁹My dear brothers,[h] take note of this: Everyone should be quick to listen, slow to speak[i] and slow to become angry, ²⁰for man's anger[j] does not bring about the righteous life that God desires. ²¹Therefore, get rid of[k] all moral filth and the evil that is so prevalent, and humbly accept the word planted in you,[l] which can save you. [K] [S]

²²Do not merely listen to the word, and so deceive yourselves. Do what it says.[m] ²³Anyone who listens to the word but does not do what it says is like a man who looks at his face in a mirror ²⁴and, after looking at himself, goes away and immediately forgets what he looks like. ²⁵But the man who looks intently into the perfect law that gives freedom,[n] and continues to do this, not forgetting what he has heard, but doing it—he will be blessed in what he does.[o]

²⁶If anyone considers himself religious and yet does not keep a tight rein on his tongue,[p] he deceives himself and his religion is worthless. ²⁷Religion that God our Father accepts as pure and faultless is this: to look after[q] orphans and widows[r] in their distress and to keep oneself from being polluted by the world.[s]

Favoritism Forbidden

2 My brothers, as believers in our glorious[t] Lord Jesus Christ, don't show favoritism.[u] ²Suppose a man comes into your meeting wearing a gold ring and fine clothes, and a poor man in shabby clothes also comes in. ³If you show special attention to the man wearing fine clothes and say, "Here's a good seat for you," but say to the poor man, "You stand there" or "Sit on the floor by my feet," ⁴have you not discriminated among yourselves and become judges[v] with evil thoughts?

⁵Listen, my dear brothers:[w] Has not God chosen those who are poor in the eyes of the world[x] to be rich in faith[y] and to inherit the kingdom[z] he promised those who love him?[a] ⁶But you have in-

---

1:1 ᵃS Ac 15:23
ᵇRo 1:1; Tit 1:1
ᶜAc 26:7
ᵈDt 32:26; Jn 7:35; 1Pe 1:1 ᵉAc 15:23
1:2 ᶠver 12;
S Mt 5:12;
Heb 10:34; 12:11
1:3 ᵍS 1Pe 1:7
ʰS Heb 10:36
1:4 ⁱS 1Co 2:6
1:5 ʲ1Ki 3:9,10;
Pr 2:3-6 ᵏPs 51:6;
Da 1:17; 2:21;
S Mt 7:7
1:6 ˡS Mt 21:21;
Mk 11:24
1:8 ᵐPs 119:113;
Jas 4:8 ⁿ2Pe 2:14;
3:16
1:9 ᵒS Mt 23:12
1:10 ᵖJob 14:2;
Ps 103:15,16;
Isa 40:6,7;
1Co 7:31; 1Pe 1:24
1:11 ᵠMt 20:12
ʳPs 102:4,11
ˢIsa 40:6-8
1:12 ᵗver 12;
1Pe 3:14
ᵘS 1Co 9:25
ᵛEx 20:6; 1Co 2:9;
8:3; Jas 2:5
1:14 ʷPr 19:3
1:15 ˣS Ge 3:6;
Job 15:35; Ps 7:14;
Isa 59:4 ʸS Ro 6:23
1:16 ᶻS 1Co 6:9
ᵃver 19; Jas 2:5
1:17 ᵇPs 85:12;
Jn 3:27; Jas 3:15,17
ᶜGe 1:16; Ps 136:7;
Da 2:22; 1Jn 1:5
ᵈNu 23:19;
Ps 102:27; Mal 3:6
1:18 ᵉS Jn 1:13
ᶠS 2Ti 2:15
ᵍJer 2:3; Rev 14:4
1:19 ʰver 16;
Jas 2:5 ⁱPr 10:19;
Jas 3:3-12
1:20 ʲS Mt 5:22
1:21 ᵏS Eph 4:22
ˡEph 1:13
1:22 ᵐS Mt 7:21;
Jas 2:14-20
1:25 ⁿPs 19:7;
Jn 8:32; Gal 2:4;
Jas 2:12
ᵒS Jn 13:17
1:26 ᵖPs 34:13;
39:1; 141:3;
Jas 3:2-12; 1Pe 3:10
1:27 ᵠMt 25:36
ʳDt 14:29;
Job 31:16,17,21;
Ps 146:9; Isa 1:17;
23 ˢRo 12:2;
Jas 4:4; 2Pe 1:4;
2:20
2:1 ᵗAc 7:2;
1Co 2:8 ᵘver 9;
Dt 1:17; Lev 19:15;
Pr 24:23;
S Ac 10:34
2:4 ᵛS Jn 7:24
2:5 ʷJas 1:16,19
ˣJob 34:19;
1Co 1:26-28
ʸLk 12:21; Rev 2:9
ᶻS Mt 25:34
ᵃS Jas 1:12

J Heb 13:6 ◀▶ Jas 5:10
T Heb 12:5–13 ◀▶ Jas 1:12
T Jas 1:2–4 ◀▶ 1Pe 1:6–7
C Heb 3:10 ◀▶ Jas 2:14–15

K Heb 13:8 ◀▶ Jas 4:12
S Heb 13:20–21 ◀▶ Jas 2:8–26

sulted the poor.[b] Is it not the rich who are exploiting you? Are they not the ones who are dragging you into court?[c] [7]Are they not the ones who are slandering the noble name of him to whom you belong?

[8]If you really keep the royal law found in Scripture, "Love your neighbor as yourself,"[ad] you are doing right. [9]But if you show favoritism,[e] you sin and are convicted by the law as lawbreakers.[f] [10]For whoever keeps the whole law and yet stumbles[g] at just one point is guilty of breaking all of it.[h] [11]For he who said, "Do not commit adultery,"[bi] also said, "Do not murder."[cj] If you do not commit adultery but do commit murder, you have become a lawbreaker.

[12]Speak and act as those who are going to be judged[k] by the law that gives freedom,[l] [13]because judgment without mercy will be shown to anyone who has not been merciful.[m] Mercy triumphs over judgment!

Faith and Deeds

[14]What good is it, my brothers, if a man claims to have faith but has no deeds?[n] Can such faith save him? [15]Suppose a brother or sister is without clothes and daily food.[o] [16]If one of you says to him, "Go, I wish you well; keep warm and well fed," but does nothing about his physical needs, what good is it?[p] [17]In the same way, faith by itself, if it is not accompanied by action, is dead.[q]

[18]But someone will say, "You have faith; I have deeds."

Show me your faith without deeds,[r] and I will show you my faith[s] by what I do.[t] [19]You believe that there is one God.[u] Good! Even the demons believe that[v]— and shudder.

[20]You foolish man, do you want evidence that faith without deeds is useless[d]?[w] [21]Was not our ancestor Abraham considered righteous for what he did when he offered his son Isaac on the altar?[x] [22]You see that his faith and his actions were working together,[y] and his faith was made complete by what he did.[z] [23]And the scripture was fulfilled that says, "Abraham believed God, and it was credited to him as righteousness,"[ea] and he was called God's friend.[b] [24]You see that a person is justified by what he does and not by faith alone.

[25]In the same way, was not even Rahab the prostitute considered righteous for what she did when she gave lodging to the spies and sent them off in a different direction?[c] [26]As the body without the spirit is dead, so faith without deeds is dead.[d]

Taming the Tongue

3 Not many of you should presume to be teachers,[e] my brothers, because you know that we who teach will be judged[f] more strictly.[g] [2]We all stumble[h] in many ways. If anyone is never at fault in what he says,[i] he is a perfect man,[j] able to keep his whole body in check.[k]

[3]When we put bits into the mouths of horses to make them obey us, we can turn the whole animal.[l] [4]Or take ships as an example. Although they are so large and are driven by strong winds, they are steered by a very small rudder wherever the pilot wants to go. [5]Likewise the tongue is a small part of the body, but it makes great boasts.[m] Consider what a great forest is set on fire by a small spark. [6]The tongue also is a fire,[n] a world of evil among the parts of the body. It corrupts the whole person,[o] sets the whole course of his life on fire, and is itself set on fire by hell.[p]

[7]All kinds of animals, birds, reptiles and creatures of the sea are being tamed and have been tamed by man, [8]but no man can tame the tongue. It is a restless evil, full of deadly poison.[q]

[9]With the tongue we praise our Lord and Father, and with it we curse men, who have been made in God's likeness.[r] [10]Out of the same mouth come praise and cursing. My brothers, this should not be. [11]Can both fresh water and salt[f] water flow from the same spring? [12]My brothers, can a fig tree bear olives, or a grapevine bear figs?[s] Neither can a salt spring produce fresh water.

S *Jas 1:21–27* ◀ ▶ *Jas 3:11–13*
A *Eph 2:1–3* ◀ ▶ *1Jn 8*
J *Heb 12:23* ◀ ▶ *1Pe 4:5*
C *Jas 1:14–15* ◀ ▶ *Jas 4:5*
F *Heb 11:6* ◀ ▶ *1Pe 1:8–9*

S *Jas 2:8–26* ◀ ▶ *Jas 4:8*

[a] 8 Lev. 19:18 [b] 11 Exodus 20:14; Deut. 5:18 [c] 11 Exodus 20:13; Deut. 5:17 [d] 20 Some early manuscripts *dead* [e] 23 Gen. 15:6 [f] 11 Greek *bitter* (see also verse 14)

Two Kinds of Wisdom

¹³Who is wise and understanding among you? Let him show it¹ by his good life, by deeds done in the humility that comes from wisdom. ¹⁴But if you harbor bitter envy and selfish ambition in your hearts, do not boast about it or deny the truth. ¹⁵Such "wisdom" does not come down from heaven but is earthly, unspiritual, of the devil. ¹⁶For where you have envy and selfish ambition, there you find disorder and every evil practice.

¹⁷But the wisdom that comes from heaven is first of all pure; then peace-loving, considerate, submissive, full of mercy and good fruit, impartial and sincere. ¹⁸Peacemakers who sow in peace raise a harvest of righteousness.

Submit Yourselves to God

4 What causes fights and quarrels among you? Don't they come from your desires that battle within you? ²You want something but don't get it. You kill and covet, but you cannot have what you want. You quarrel and fight. You do not have, because you do not ask God. ³When you ask, you do not receive, because you ask with wrong motives, that you may spend what you get on your pleasures.

⁴You adulterous people, don't you know that friendship with the world is hatred toward God? Anyone who chooses to be a friend of the world becomes an enemy of God. ⁵Or do you think Scripture says without reason that the spirit he caused to live in us envies intensely? ⁶But he gives us more grace. That is why Scripture says:

> "God opposes the proud
> but gives grace to the humble."

⁷Submit yourselves, then, to God. Resist the devil, and he will flee from you. ⁸Come near to God and he will come near to you. Wash your hands, you sinners, and purify your hearts, you double-minded. ⁹Grieve, mourn and wail. Change your laughter to mourning and your joy to gloom. ¹⁰Humble yourselves before the Lord, and he will lift you up.

¹¹Brothers, do not slander one another. Anyone who speaks against his brother or judges him speaks against the law and judges it. When you judge the law, you are not keeping it, but sitting in judgment on it. ¹²There is only one Lawgiver and Judge, the one who is able to save and destroy. But you—who are you to judge your neighbor?

Boasting About Tomorrow

¹³Now listen, you who say, "Today or tomorrow we will go to this or that city, spend a year there, carry on business and make money." ¹⁴Why, you do not even know what will happen tomorrow. What is your life? You are a mist that appears for a little while and then vanishes. ¹⁵Instead, you ought to say, "If it is the Lord's will, we will live and do this or that." ¹⁶As it is, you boast and brag. All such boasting is evil. ¹⁷Anyone, then, who knows the good he ought to do and doesn't do it, sins.

Warning to Rich Oppressors

5 Now listen, you rich people, weep and wail because of the misery that is coming upon you. ²Your wealth has rotted, and moths have eaten your clothes. ³Your gold and silver are corroded. Their corrosion will testify against you and eat your flesh like fire. You have hoarded wealth in the last days. ⁴Look! The wages you failed to pay the workmen

---

5:1–3 James warns that in the last days the rich will weep because their wealth will be worthless to help them during the famine and economic devastation that will unfold during the tribulation (see Rev 6:5–6). The rich will be left with nothing, for even gold and silver, the historic standard of value in troubled times, will be of no value. Though they have amassed great wealth for the last days, their gold and silver will tarnish because no one will want to buy.

who mowed your fields are crying out against you. The cries[r] of the harvesters have reached the ears of the Lord Almighty.[s] [5]You have lived on earth in luxury and self-indulgence. You have fattened yourselves[t] in the day of slaughter.[iu] [6]You have condemned and murdered[v] innocent men,[w] who were not opposing you.

Patience in Suffering

[7]Be patient, then, brothers, until the Lord's coming.[x] See how the farmer waits for the land to yield its valuable crop and how patient he is[y] for the autumn and spring rains.[z] [8]You too, be patient and stand firm, because the Lord's coming[a] is near.[b] [9]Don't grumble against each other, brothers,[c] or you will be judged. The Judge[d] is standing at the door![e]

[10]Brothers, as an example of patience in the face of suffering, take the prophets[f] who spoke in the name of the Lord. [11]As you know, we consider blessed[g] those who have persevered. You have heard of Job's perseverance[h] and have seen what the Lord finally brought about.[i] The Lord is full of compassion and mercy.[j]

[12]Above all, my brothers, do not swear—not by heaven or by earth or by anything else. Let your "Yes" be yes, and your "No," no, or you will be condemned.[k]

The Prayer of Faith

[13]Is any one of you in trouble? He should pray.[l] Is anyone happy? Let him sing songs of praise.[m] [14]Is any one of you sick? He should call the elders[n] of the church to pray over him and anoint him with oil[o] in the name of the Lord. [15]And the prayer offered in faith[p] will make the sick person well; the Lord will raise him up. If he has sinned, he will be forgiven. [16]Therefore confess your sins[q] to each other and pray for each other so that you may be healed.[r] The prayer of a righteous man is powerful and effective.[s]

[17]Elijah was a man just like us.[t] He prayed earnestly that it would not rain, and it did not rain on the land for three and a half years.[u] [18]Again he prayed, and the heavens gave rain, and the earth produced its crops.[v]

[19]My brothers, if one of you should wander from the truth[w] and someone should bring him back,[x] [20]remember this: Whoever turns a sinner from the error of his way will save[y] him from death and cover over a multitude of sins.[z]

5:4 r Dt 24:15; s Ro 9:29
5:5 t Eze 16:49; Am 6:1; Lk 16:19; u Jer 12:3; 25:34
5:6 v Jas 4:2; w Heb 10:38
5:7 x S 1Co 1:7; y Gal 6:9 z Dt 11:14; Jer 5:24; Joel 2:23
5:8 a S 1Co 1:7; b S Ro 13:11
5:9 c Jas 4:11; d Ps 94:2; 1Co 4:5; Jas 4:12; 1Pe 4:5; e Mt 24:33
5:10 f S Mt 5:12
5:11 g Mt 5:10; h Job 1:21,22; 2:10; S Heb 10:36; i Job 42:10,12-17; j Ex 34:6; Nu 14:18; Ps 103:8
5:12 k Mt 5:34-37
5:13 l Ps 50:15; m Col 3:16
5:14 n S Ac 11:30; o Ps 23:5; Isa 1:6; Mk 6:13; 16:18; Lk 10:34
5:15 p Jas 1:6
5:16 q Mt 3:6; Ac 19:18; r Heb 12:13; 1Pe 2:24 s S Mt 7:7; S Jn 9:31
5:17 t Ac 14:15; u 1Ki 17:1; Lk 4:25
5:18 v 1Ki 18:41-45
5:19 w Jas 3:14; x S Mt 18:15
5:20 y S Ro 11:14; z 1Pe 4:8

C Heb 10:37 ◄► 1Pe 1:5
E Jas 5:3 ◄► 2Pe 3:3–10
S Jas 4:17 ◄► Jas 5:19–20
J Jas 1:2–4 ◄► 1Pe 2:19–20
L Heb 13:5–6 ◄► 1Pe 3:12
L Jas 4:10 ◄► 1Pe 1:18–19

H Eph 6:2–3 ◄► 1Pe 3:10
P Ro 11:23–24 ◄► 1Jn 2:1–2
S Jas 5:9 ◄► 1Pe 1:2

i 5 Or yourselves as in a day of feasting

5:7–9 James commands Christians to wait patiently for the Lord's coming and likens our waiting to a farmer who waits for the harvest. The farmer can tell by the rain when the final harvest is approaching. So also believers can tell by the fulfillment of the prophecies in our generation that Christ's return is near.

Yet James advises believers to be patient in light of the imminent reality of the second coming. Expectantly hoping that Christ might return at any moment, we must always remember that God looks at time very differently then we do (see 2Pe 3:8). Therefore we must not murmur and complain against each other for "the Judge is standing at the door" (5:9). Such grudges violate Paul's command to "do everything without complaining or arguing, so that you may become blameless and pure, children of God without fault in a crooked and depraved generation" (Php 2:14–15).

1 Peter

Author: Peter

Theme: Hope in the midst of suffering

Date of Writing: C. A.D. 60–64

Outline of 1 Peter
  I. Salutation (1:1–2)
  II. A Great Salvation (1:3—2:10)
  III. Conduct of the Believer (2:11—4:11)
  IV. Ministry Through Suffering (4:12—5:11)
  V. Conclusion (5:12–14)

THIS LETTER WAS written by the apostle Peter shortly before his martyrdom under Emperor Nero of Rome. Peter wrote this letter from Babylon (see 5:13) and directed his words to the churches in the northern portion of the Roman province of Asia. Scholars disagree on the location of this "Babylon," suggesting that it could be a figurative reference to Rome or Jerusalem. There is little evidence to support these contentions since the context of 5:13 is not figurative in style, nor is there historical evidence from the first two centuries to indicate that Peter was ever in Rome or ever served as the leader of the Roman church. Other scholars suggest that Peter wrote this letter from a small, Egyptian military outpost called Babylon, though evidence to support this claim is also limited. Still other scholars contend that Peter penned these words from the small, first-century town of Babylon that was located on the Euphrates River in what is modern-day Iraq. Wherever the exact location of its composition, 1 Peter can be satisfactorily dated in the early A.D. 60s.

The recurring theme of this letter is the suffering of Christ and his saints and the glory of God that will ultimately be revealed through believers' lives. First-century Christians faced desperate times. During the rule of Emperor Nero, government policy shifted from tolerance to open persecution of Christians in Rome. Under the later rule of Emperor Domitian this persecution would spread throughout the empire. Yet sporadic waves of oppression had already begun in certain provinces and cities when Peter wrote this letter to struggling believers. Peter's message of hope, pilgrimage, courage and glory exhorts the believers to stand firm in their faith. Setting the readers' sights on their heavenly rewards, Peter's encouraging words testify to the true grace of God and fulfill Christ's command to Peter to "strengthen your brothers" (Lk 22:32).

1

¹Peter, an apostle of Jesus Christ,ᵃ

To God's elect,ᵇ strangers in the world,ᶜ scatteredᵈ throughout Pontus,ᵉ Galatia,ᶠ Cappadocia, Asia and Bithynia,ᵍ ²who have been chosen according to the foreknowledgeʰ of God the Father, through the sanctifying work of the Spirit,ⁱ for obedienceʲ to Jesus Christ and sprinkling by his blood:ᵏ

Grace and peace be yours in abundance.ˡ

Praise to God for a Living Hope

³Praise be to the God and Father of our Lord Jesus Christ!ᵐ In his great mercyⁿ he has given us new birthᵒ into a living hopeᵖ through the resurrection of Jesus Christ from the dead,ᵠ ⁴and into an inheritanceʳ that can never perish, spoil or fadeˢ—kept in heaven for you,ᵗ ⁵who through faith are shielded by God's powerᵘ until the coming of the salvationᵛ that is ready to be revealedʷ in the last time. ⁶In this you greatly rejoice,ˣ though now for a little whileʸ you may have had to suffer grief in all kinds of trials.ᶻ ⁷These have come so that your faith—of greater worth than gold, which perishes even though refined by fireᵃ—may be proved genuineᵇ and may result in praise, glory and honorᶜ when Jesus Christ is revealed.ᵈ ⁸Though you have not seen him, you love him; and even though you do not see him now, you believe in himᵉ and are filled with an inexpressible and glorious joy, ⁹for you are receiving the goal of your faith, the salvation of your souls.ᶠ

¹⁰Concerning this salvation, the prophets, who spokeᵍ of the grace that was to come to you,ʰ searched intently and with the greatest care,ⁱ ¹¹trying to find out the time and circumstances to which the Spirit of Christʲ in them was pointing when he predictedᵏ the sufferings of Christ and the glories that would follow. ¹²It was revealed to them that they were not serving themselves but you,ˡ when they spoke of the things that have now been told you by those who have preached the gospel to youᵐ by the Holy Spirit sent from heaven.ⁿ Even angels long to look into these things.

Be Holy

¹³Therefore, prepare your minds for action; be self-controlled;ᵒ set your hopeᵖ

1:1 ᵃ2Pe 1:1 ᵇMt 24:22 ᶜS Heb 11:13 ᵈS Jas 1:1 ᵃAc 2:9; 18:2 ᶠS Ac 16:6 ᵍAc 16:7
1:2 ʰRo 8:29 ⁱ2Th 2:13 ʲver 14, 22 ᵏHeb 10:22; 12:24 ˡS Ro 1:7
1:3 ᵐ2Co 1:3; Eph 1:3 ⁿTit 3:5 ᵒver 23; S Jn 1:13 ᵖver 13, 21; S Heb 3:6 ᵠ1Co 15:20; 1Pe 3:21
1:4 ʳS Ac 20:32; S Ro 8:17 ˢ1Pe 5:4 ᵗCol 1:5; 2Ti 4:8
1:5 ᵘIsa 2:9; Jn 10:28 ᵛS Ro 11:14 ʷS Ro 8:18
1:6 ˣRo 5:2 ʸ1Pe 5:10 ᶻJas 1:2; 1Pe 4:12
1:7 ᵃJob 23:10; Ps 66:10; Pr 17:3; Isa 48:10 ᵇJas 1:3 ᶜ2Co 4:17 ᵈver 13; S 1Th 2:19; 1Pe 4:13
1:8 ᵉJn 20:29
1:9 ᶠRo 6:22
1:10 ᵍS Mt 26:24 ʰver 13 ⁱS Mt 13:17
1:11 ʲS Ac 16:7; 2Pe 1:21 ᵏS Mt 26:24
1:12 ˡS Ro 4:24 ᵐver 25 ⁿS Lk 24:49
1:13 ᵒS Ac 24:25 ᵖver 3,21; S Heb 3:6

E Heb 11:11 ◄► 1Pe 1:11–12
S Heb 10:14–15 ◄► 1Pe 1:22
W 1Ti 4:12 ◄► 1Pe 2:5
S Jas 5:19–20 ◄► 1Pe 1:15–17
K Jas 4:12 ◄► 1Pe 1:9
C Jas 5:7–9 ◄► 1Pe 1:7
T Jas 1:12 ◄► 1Pe 5:10
C 1Pe 1:5 ◄► 1Pe 1:13

F Jas 2:23 ◄► 1Pe 2:6
K 1Pe 1:4–5 ◄► 1Pe 2:6
B Heb 10:14–15 ◄► 1Pe 4:10–11
E 1Pe 1:2 ◄► 1Pe 1:22
T Heb 6:4 ◄► 1Pe 4:10–11
L Heb 9:14 ◄► 1Pe 1:22
C 1Pe 1:7 ◄► 1Pe 1:20

1:5 Peter tells us that our spiritual preservation depends on "God's power" which is appropriated "through faith." The apostle also indicates that Jesus Christ will appear in the last days to establish his eternal kingdom of God on earth forever. No one can know how long Christ will delay until he returns, but the fulfillment of many specific prophecies in our generation strongly suggest that some of us may still be alive to witness the final coming of Jesus Christ to set up his kingdom on earth.

1:7 Faith will be rewarded amply when all Christians witness the glorious time "when Jesus Christ is revealed" (1:7).

1:13 Peter encourages Christians to be prepared

fully on the grace to be given you^q when Jesus Christ is revealed.^r ^14 As obedient^s children, do not conform^t to the evil desires you had when you lived in ignorance.^u ^15 But just as he who called you is holy, so be holy in all you do;^v ^16 for it is written: "Be holy, because I am holy."^a^w

^17 Since you call on a Father^x who judges each man's work^y impartially,^z live your lives as strangers^a here in reverent fear.^b ^18 For you know that it was not with perishable things such as silver or gold that you were redeemed^c from the empty way of life^d handed down to you from your forefathers, ^19 but with the precious blood^e of Christ, a lamb^f without blemish or defect.^g ^20 He was chosen before the creation of the world,^h but was revealed in these last times^i for your sake. ^21 Through him you believe in God,^j who raised him from the dead^k and glorified him,^l and so your faith and hope^m are in God.

^22 Now that you have purified^n yourselves by obeying^o the truth so that you have sincere love for your brothers, love one another deeply,^p from the heart.^b ^23 For you have been born again,^q not of perishable seed, but of imperishable,^r through the living and enduring word of God.^s ^24 For,

"All men are like grass,
  and all their glory is like the flowers of the field;
the grass withers and the flowers fall,
^25 but the word of the Lord stands forever."^c^t

And this is the word that was preached to you.

S 1Pe 1:2 ◀▶ 1Pe 2:21–22
D Heb 13:11–12 ◀▶ 1Pe 2:24
G Heb 11:6 ◀▶ Rev 3:17–18
L Jas 5:1 ◀▶ 1Pe 2:6
C 1Pe 1:13 ◀▶ 1Pe 4:7
E 1Pe 1:11–12 ◀▶ 1Pe 2:5
F Heb 1:9 ◀ L 1Pe 1:12 ◀▶ 1Pe 2:5
S 1Pe 1:2 ◀▶ Jude 19–20

1:13 ^q ver 10
^r ver 7; S 1Co 1:7
1:14 ^s ver 2,22
^t Ro 12:2 ^u Eph 4:18
1:15 ^v Isa 35:8;
1Th 4:7; 1Jn 3:3
1:16 ^w Lev 11:44,
45; 19:2; 20:7
1:17 ^x Mt 6:9
^y S Mt 16:27
^z S Ac 10:34
^a S Heb 11:13
^b Heb 12:28
1:18 ^c S Mt 20:28;
S 1Co 6:20
^d Gal 4:3
1:19 ^e S Ro 3:25
^f S Jn 1:29 ^s Ex 12:5
1:20 ^h Eph 1:4;
S Mt 25:34
^i Heb 9:26
1:21 ^j Ro 4:24;
10:9 ^k S Ac 2:24
^l Php 2:7-9; Heb 2:9
^m ver 3,13;
S Heb 3:6
1:22 ^n Jas 4:8
^o ver 2,14
^p S Jn 13:34;
S Ro 12:10
1:23 ^q ver 3;
S Jn 1:13 ^r Jn 1:13
^s S Heb 4:12
1:25 ^t Isa 40:6-8;
S Jas 1:10,11
2:1 ^u S Eph 4:22
^v S Jas 4:11
2:2 ^w 1Co 3:2;
Heb 5:12,13
^x Eph 4:15,16
2:3 ^y Ps 34:8;
Heb 6:5
2:4 ^z ver 7
^a Isa 42:1
2:5 ^b Pr 9:1;
1Co 3:9;
Eph 2:20-22
^c 1Ti 3:15 ^d ver 9;
Ex 19:6; Isa 61:6;
Rev 1:6; 5:10; 20:6
^e Php 4:18;
Heb 13:15
2:6 ^f Eph 2:20
^g Isa 28:16;
Ro 9:32,33; 10:11
2:7 ^h 2Co 2:16
^i ver 4 ^j Ps 118:22;
S Ac 4:11
2:8 ^k Isa 8:14;
S Lk 2:34 ^l Ro 9:22
2:9 ^m Dt 10:15;
1Sa 12:22 ^n ver 5
^o Ex 19:6; Dt 7:6;
Isa 62:12
^p S Tit 2:14

^2 Therefore, rid yourselves^u of all malice and all deceit, hypocrisy, envy, and slander^v of every kind. ^2 Like newborn babies, crave pure spiritual milk,^w so that by it you may grow up^x in your salvation, ^3 now that you have tasted that the Lord is good.^y

The Living Stone and a Chosen People

^4 As you come to him, the living Stone^z—rejected by men but chosen by God^a and precious to him— ^5 you also, like living stones, are being built^b into a spiritual house^c to be a holy priesthood,^d offering spiritual sacrifices acceptable to God through Jesus Christ.^e ^6 For in Scripture it says:

"See, I lay a stone in Zion,
  a chosen and precious cornerstone,^f
and the one who trusts in him
  will never be put to shame."^d^g

^7 Now to you who believe, this stone is precious. But to those who do not believe,^h

"The stone the builders rejected^i
  has become the capstone,"^e^j

^8 and,

"A stone that causes men to stumble
  and a rock that makes them fall."^g^k

They stumble because they disobey the message—which is also what they were destined for.^l

^9 But you are a chosen people,^m a royal priesthood,^n a holy nation,^o a people belonging to God,^p that you may declare the praises of him who called you out of dark-

E 1Pe 1:22 ◀▶ 1Pe 3:18–19
L 1Pe 1:22 ◀▶ 1Pe 3:18–19
W 1Pe 1:2 ◀▶ 1Pe 4:10–11
F 1Pe 1:8–9 ◀▶ 1Jn 3:23
K 1Pe 1:9 ◀▶ 1Pe 2:24
L 1Pe 1:18–19 ◀▶ 1Pe 2:24–25
T Heb 13:15–16 ◀▶ Rev 12:11

^a 16 Lev. 11:44,45; 19:2; 20:7   ^b 22 Some early manuscripts from a pure heart   ^c 25 Isaiah 40:6-8   ^d 6 Isaiah 28:16   ^e 7 Or cornerstone   ^f 7 Psalm 118:22   ^g 8 Isaiah 8:14

---

and disciplined in light of Christ's unshakable prophecies that he will return in glory. When he comes he will bring the blessedness and deliverance from sin that is the hope of every believer and the mark of the grace of God.

1:20 This verse affirms Christ's preeminence (see Jn 17:24) and reveals that none of the events of Christ's earthly ministry, trial, death or resurrection was unexpected by God. God unfolded these things in his time and his plan to win salvation for humanity and deliver us from the curse of sin.

ness into his wonderful light.ᑫ ¹⁰Once you were not a people, but now you are the people of God;ʳ once you had not received mercy, but now you have received mercy.

¹¹Dear friends,ˢ I urge you, as aliens and strangers in the world,ᵗ to abstain from sinful desires,ᵘ which war against your soul.ᵛ ¹²Live such good lives among the pagans that, though they accuse you of doing wrong, they may see your good deedsʷ and glorify Godˣ on the day he visits us.

Submission to Rulers and Masters

¹³Submit yourselves for the Lord's sake to every authorityʸ instituted among men: whether to the king, as the supreme authority, ¹⁴or to governors, who are sent by him to punish those who do wrongᶻ and to commend those who do right.ᵃ ¹⁵For it is God's willᵇ that by doing good you should silence the ignorant talk of foolish men.ᶜ ¹⁶Live as free men,ᵈ but do not use your freedom as a cover-up for evil;ᵉ live as servants of God.ᶠ ¹⁷Show proper respect to everyone: Love the brotherhood of believers,ᵍ fear God, honor the king.ʰ

¹⁸Slaves, submit yourselves to your masters with all respect,ⁱ not only to those who are good and considerate,ʲ but also to those who are harsh. ¹⁹For it is commendable if a man bears up under the pain of unjust suffering because he is conscious of God.ᵏ ²⁰But how is it to your credit if you receive a beating for doing wrong and endure it? But if you suffer for doing good and you endure it, this is commendable before God.ˡ ²¹To thisᵐ you were called,ⁿ because Christ suffered for you,ᵒ leaving you an example,ᵖ that you should follow in his steps.

²²"He committed no sin,ᑫ
  and no deceit was found in his mouth."ʳ

²³When they hurled their insults at him,ˢ he did not retaliate; when he suffered, he made no threats.ᵗ Instead, he entrusted himselfᵘ to him who judges justly.ᵛ ²⁴He himself bore our sinsʷ in his body on the tree,ˣ so that we might die to sinsʸ and live for righteousness; by his wounds you have been healed.ᶻ ²⁵For you were like sheep going astray,ᵃ but now you have returned to the Shepherdᵇ and Overseer of your souls.ᶜ

Wives and Husbands

3 Wives, in the same way be submissiveᵈ to your husbandsᵉ so that, if any of them do not believe the word, they may be won overᶠ without words by the behavior of their wives, ²when they see the purity and reverence of your lives. ³Your beauty should not come from outward adornment, such as braided hair and the wearing of gold jewelry and fine clothes.ᵍ ⁴Instead, it should be that of your inner self,ʰ the unfading beauty of a gentle and quiet spirit, which is of great worth in God's sight.ⁱ ⁵For this is the way the holy women of the past who put their hope in Godʲ used to make themselves beautiful.ᵏ They were submissive to their own husbands, ⁶like Sarah, who obeyed Abraham and called him her master.ˡ You are her daughters if you do what is right and do not give way to fear.

⁷Husbands,ᵐ in the same way be considerate as you live with your wives, and treat them with respect as the weaker partner and as heirs with you of the gracious gift of life, so that nothing will hinder your prayers.

Suffering for Doing Good

⁸Finally, all of you, live in harmony with one another;ⁿ be sympathetic, love as brothers,ᵒ be compassionate and humble.ᵖ ⁹Do not repay evil with evilᑫ or insult with insult,ʳ but with blessing,ˢ because to thisᵗ you were calledᵘ so that you may inherit a blessing.ᵛ ¹⁰For,

"Whoever would love life
  and see good days
must keep his tongue from evil
  and his lips from deceitful speech.
¹¹He must turn from evil and do good;
  he must seek peace and pursue it.

¹²For the eyes of the Lord are on the righteous
and his ears are attentive to their prayer,
but the face of the Lord is against those who do evil."ⁱʷ

¹³Who is going to harm you if you are eager to do good?ˣ ¹⁴But even if you should suffer for what is right, you are blessed.ʸ "Do not fear what they fear'; do not be frightened."ᵏᶻ ¹⁵But in your hearts set apart Christ as Lord. Always be prepared to give an answerᵃ to everyone who asks you to give the reason for the hopeᵇ that you have. But do this with gentleness and respect, ¹⁶keeping a clear conscience,ᶜ so that those who speak maliciously against your good behavior in Christ may be ashamed of their slander.ᵈ ¹⁷It is better, if it is God's will,ᵉ to suffer for doing goodᶠ than for doing evil. ¹⁸For Christ died for sinsᵍ once for all,ʰ the righteous for the unrighteous, to bring you to God.ⁱ He was put to death in the bodyʲ but made alive by the Spirit,ᵏ ¹⁹through whomˡ also he went and preached to the spirits in prison¹ ²⁰who disobeyed long ago when God waited patientlyᵐ in the days of Noah while the ark was being built.ⁿ In it only a few people, eight in all,ᵒ were savedᵖ through water, ²¹and this water symbolizes baptism that now saves youᑫ also—not the removal of dirt from the body but the pledgeᵐ of a good conscienceʳ toward God. It saves you by the resurrection of Jesus Christ,ˢ ²²who has gone into heavenᵗ and is at God's right handᵘ—with angels, authorities and powers in submission to him.ᵛ

Living for God

4 Therefore, since Christ suffered in his body,ʷ arm yourselves also with the same attitude, because he who has suffered in his body is done with sin.ˣ ²As a result, he does not live the rest of his earthly life for evil human desires,ʸ but rather for the will of God. ³For you have spent enough time in the pastᶻ doing what pagans choose to do—living in debauchery, lust, drunkenness, orgies, carousing and detestable idolatry.ᵃ ⁴They think it strange that you do not plunge with them into the same flood of dissipation, and they heap abuse on you.ᵇ ⁵But they will have to give account to him who is ready to judge the living and the dead.ᶜ ⁶For this is the reason the gospel was preached even to those who are now dead,ᵈ so that they might be judged according to men in regard to the body, but live according to God in regard to the spirit.

⁷The end of all things is near.ᵉ Therefore be clear minded and self-controlledᶠ so that you can pray. ⁸Above all, love each other deeply,ᵍ because love covers over a multitude of sins.ʰ ⁹Offer hospitalityⁱ to one another without grumbling.ʲ ¹⁰Each one should use whatever gift he has received to serve others,ᵏ faithfullyˡ administering God's grace in its various forms. ¹¹If anyone speaks, he should do it

---

3:12 ʷ Ps 34:12-16
3:13 ˣ S Tit 2:14
3:14 ʸ ver 17; 1Pe 2:19,20; 4:15, 16 ᶻ Isa 8:12,13
3:15 ᵃ Col 4:6 ᵇ S Heb 3:6
3:16 ᶜ ver 21; S Ac 23:1 ᵈ 1Pe 2:12,15
3:17 ᵉ 1Pe 2:15; 4:19 ᶠ 1Pe 2:20; 4:15,16
3:18 ᵍ 1Pe 2:21; 4:1,13 ʰ S Heb 7:27 ⁱ S Ro 5:2 ʲ Col 1:22; 1Pe 4:1 ᵏ 1Pe 4:6
3:19 ˡ 1Pe 4:6
3:20 ᵐ S Ro 2:4 ⁿ Ge 6:3,5,13,14 ᵒ Ge 8:18 ᵖ Heb 11:7
3:21 ᑫ S Ac 22:16 ʳ ver 16; S Ac 23:1 ˢ 1Pe 1:3
3:22 ᵗ S Heb 4:14 ᵘ S Mk 16:19 ᵛ S Mt 28:18; S Ro 8:38
4:1 ʷ S 1Pe 2:21 ˣ S Ro 6:18
4:2 ʸ Ro 6:2; 1Pe 1:14
4:3 ᶻ S Eph 2:2 ᵃ S Ro 13:13
4:4 ᵇ 1Pe 3:16
4:5 ᶜ S Ac 10:42
4:6 ᵈ 1Pe 3:19
4:7 ᵉ S Ro 13:11 ᶠ Ac 24:25
4:8 ᵍ S 1Pe 1:22 ʰ Pr 10:12; Jas 5:20
4:9 ⁱ S Ro 12:13 ʲ Php 2:14
4:10 ᵏ Ro 12:6,7 ˡ 1Co 4:2

H *Heb 12:29* ◀▶ *1Pe 4:17–18*
L *Jas 5:10–11* ◀▶ *1Pe 5:7*
U *1Ti 4:8* ◀▶ *1Jn 4*
J *1Pe 2:19–20* ◀▶ *1Pe 4:12–14*
W *Heb 13:5–6* ◀▶ *1Pe 5:7*
E *1Pe 2:5* ◀▶ *1Pe 4:10–11*
H *Heb 2:4* ◀▶ *Rev 11:11*
L *1Pe 2:5* ◀▶ *1Pe 4:10–11*
D *1Pe 2:24* ◀▶ *1Jn 7*
L *1Pe 2:24–25* ◀▶ *2Pe 3:9*

J *Heb 10:30* ◀▶ *2Pe 2:9*
J *Jas 2:12–13* ◀▶ *2Pe 2:4*
C *1Pe 1:20* ◀▶ *1Pe 4:13*
B *1Pe 1:11* ◀▶ *1Jn 2:20*
E *1Pe 3:18–19* ◀▶ *2Pe 1:21*
G *Heb 2:4* ◀▶ *2Pe 1:21*
L *1Pe 3:18–19* ◀▶ *Jude 19–20*
T *1Pe 1:11* ◀▶ *2Pe 1:21*
W *1Pe 2:5* ◀▶ *Jude 19–20*

ⁱ 12 Psalm 34:12-16 ʲ 14 Or *not fear their threats* ᵏ 14 Isaiah 8:12 ˡ 18,19 Or *alive in the spirit,* ¹⁹*through which* ᵐ 21 Or *response*

4:5 Everyone, both the Christian saints and the wicked dead, will be judged by Jesus Christ. Whether they are living at the time of judgment or dead and buried, every human being that has ever lived will face Jesus Christ (see Ps 1:6; Mt 25:31–46; Jn 5:22–23, 28–29; Ro 14:10; 2Ti 4:1). For those who have truly repented of their sins, the completed atonement of Christ's death on the cross will grant them justification and eternal life in heaven. But those who have continued to be unrepentant will face his wrath and eternal punishment.

4:7 Peter did not mean that Jesus' return to resurrect the saints would occur immediately. Yet the NT repeatedly promises that Christ may return without warning at any moment. Timing is not the issue; readiness is.

as one speaking the very words of God.ᵐ If anyone serves, he should do it with the strength God provides,ⁿ so that in all things God may be praisedᵒ through Jesus Christ. To him be the glory and the power for ever and ever. Amen.ᵖ

Suffering for Being a Christian

¹²Dear friends, do not be surprised at the painful trial you are suffering,ᑫ as though something strange were happening to you. ¹³But rejoiceʳ that you participate in the sufferings of Christ,ˢ so that you may be overjoyed when his glory is revealed.ᵗ ¹⁴If you are insulted because of the name of Christ,ᵘ you are blessed,ᵛ for the Spirit of glory and of God rests on you. ¹⁵If you suffer, it should not be as a murderer or thief or any other kind of criminal, or even as a meddler. ¹⁶However, if you suffer as a Christian, do not be ashamed, but praise God that you bear that name.ʷ ¹⁷For it is time for judgment to begin with the family of God;ˣ and if it begins with us, what will the outcome be for those who do not obey the gospel of God?ʸ ¹⁸And,

> "If it is hard for the righteous to be saved,
> what will become of the ungodly and the sinner?"ⁿᶻ

¹⁹So then, those who suffer according to God's willᵃ should commit themselves to their faithful Creator and continue to do good.

To Elders and Young Men

5 To the elders among you, I appeal as a fellow elder,ᵇ a witnessᶜ of Christ's sufferings and one who also will share in the glory to be revealed:ᵈ ²Be shepherds of God's flockᵉ that is under your care, serving as overseers—not because you must, but because you are willing, as God wants you to be;ᶠ not greedy for money,ᵍ but eager to serve; ³not lording it overʰ those entrusted to you, but being examplesⁱ to the flock. ⁴And when the Chief Shepherdʲ appears, you will receive the crown of gloryᵏ that will never fade away.ˡ

⁵Young men, in the same way be submissiveᵐ to those who are older. All of you, clothe yourselves with humilityⁿ toward one another, because,

> "God opposes the proud
> but gives grace to the humble."ᵒᵒ

⁶Humble yourselves, therefore, under God's mighty hand, that he may lift you up in due time.ᵖ ⁷Cast all your anxiety on himᑫ because he cares for you.ʳ

⁸Be self-controlledˢ and alert. Your enemy the devil prowls aroundᵗ like a roaring lionᵘ looking for someone to devour. ⁹Resist him,ᵛ standing firm in the faith,ʷ because you know that your brothers throughout the world are undergoing the same kind of sufferings.ˣ

¹⁰And the God of all grace, who called youʸ to his eternal gloryᶻ in Christ, after you have suffered a little while,ᵃ will himself restore you and make you strong,ᵇ firm and steadfast. ¹¹To him be the power for ever and ever. Amen.ᶜ

Final Greetings

¹²With the help of Silas,ᵖᵈ whom I regard as a faithful brother, I have written to you briefly,ᵉ encouraging you and testifying that this is the true grace of God. Stand fast in it.ᶠ

¹³She who is in Babylon, chosen together with you, sends you her greetings, and so does my son Mark.ᵍ ¹⁴Greet one another with a kiss of love.ʰ

Peaceⁱ to all of you who are in Christ.

4:13 Peter promises that those who endure suffering for Christ's sake will be rewarded for their faithful service to him "when his glory is revealed" (4:13).
5:1 Peter concludes this epistle with a promise that those faithful believers in the church who experience persecution and stand firm will be glorified and blessed at the rapture when Christ shall "be revealed" (5:1) in glory at the second coming.

2 Peter

Author: Peter

Theme: Be on your guard against false teaching

Date of Writing: c. A.D. 64–68

Outline of 2 Peter
  I. True Knowledge for the Believer (1:1–21)
  II. False Teachers and Their Doom (2:1–22)
  III. Warnings, Judgment and Exhortation (3:1–18)

THE AUTHOR IDENTIFIES himself in the first verse of this letter as "Simon Peter, a servant and apostle of Jesus Christ" (1:1). This letter was written a short time after 1 Peter and was directed to the same readers in the northern portion of the Roman province of Asia to whom Peter had addressed his first letter. The style of writing, personal illustrations, vocabulary and thoughts in this letter are also similar to Peter's first epistle, though this second letter focuses on the pressing danger of false teachers.

Traveling philosophers and teachers were perverting the message of the gospel with false doctrines and erroneous teaching about Christ's second coming. Peter's second letter urges his readers to combine Christian faith and practice while awaiting the Lord's return. Peter calls attention to the importance of knowledge in discerning between false and true teaching. He also warns that those who pervert the Word of God will face God's judgment. The Lord is certain to return, so Peter urges the believers to be ready.

1 Simon Peter, a servant[a] and apostle of Jesus Christ,[b]

To those who through the righteousness[c] of our God and Savior Jesus Christ[d] have received a faith as precious as ours:

²Grace and peace be yours in abundance[e] through the knowledge of God and of Jesus our Lord.[f]

Making One's Calling and Election Sure

³His divine power[g] has given us everything we need for life and godliness through our knowledge of him[h] who called us[i] by his own glory and goodness. ⁴Through these he has given us his very great and precious promises,[j] so that through them you may participate in the divine nature[k] and escape the corruption in the world caused by evil desires.[l]

⁵For this very reason, make every effort to add to your faith goodness; and to goodness, knowledge;[m] ⁶and to knowledge, self-control;[n] and to self-control, perseverance;[o] and to perseverance, godliness;[p] ⁷and to godliness, brotherly kindness; and to brotherly kindness, love.[q] ⁸For if you possess these qualities in increasing measure, they will keep you from being ineffective and unproductive[r] in your knowledge of our Lord Jesus Christ.[s] ⁹But if anyone does not have them, he is nearsighted and blind,[t] and has forgotten that he has been cleansed from his past sins.[u]

¹⁰Therefore, my brothers, be all the more eager to make your calling[v] and election sure. For if you do these things, you will never fall,[w] ¹¹and you will receive a rich welcome into the eternal kingdom[x] of our Lord and Savior Jesus Christ.[y]

Prophecy of Scripture

¹²So I will always remind you of these things,[z] even though you know them and are firmly established in the truth[a] you now have. ¹³I think it is right to refresh your memory[b] as long as I live in the tent of this body,[c] ¹⁴because I know that I will soon put it aside,[d] as our Lord Jesus Christ has made clear to me.[e] ¹⁵And I will make every effort to see that after my departure[f] you will always be able to remember these things.

¹⁶We did not follow cleverly invented stories when we told you about the power and coming of our Lord Jesus Christ,[g] but we were eyewitnesses of his majesty.[h] ¹⁷For he received honor and glory from God the Father when the voice came to him from the Majestic Glory, saying, "This is my Son, whom I love; with him I am well pleased."[a][i] ¹⁸We ourselves heard this voice that came from heaven when we were with him on the sacred mountain.[j]

¹⁹And we have the word of the prophets made more certain,[k] and you will do well to pay attention to it, as to a light[l] shining in a dark place, until the day dawns[m] and the morning star[n] rises in your hearts.[o] ²⁰Above all, you must understand[p] that no prophecy of Scripture came about by the prophet's own interpretation. ²¹For prophecy never had its origin in the will of man, but men spoke from God[q] as they were carried along by the Holy Spirit.[r]

1:1 a Ro 1:1; b 1Pe 1:1; c Ro 3:21-26; d Tit 2:13
1:2 e S Ro 1:7; f ver 3,8; 2Pe 2:20; 3:18; S Php 3:8
1:3 g 1Pe 1:5; h S ver 2; i S Ro 8:28
1:4 j 2Co 7:1; k Eph 4:24; Heb 12:10; 1Jn 3:2; l Jas 1:27; 2Pe 2:18-20
1:5 m S ver 2; Col 2:3
1:6 n S Ac 24:25; o S Heb 10:36; p ver 3
1:7 q S Ro 12:10; 1Th 3:12
1:8 r Jn 15:2; Col 1:10; Tit 3:14; s S ver 2
1:9 t 1Jn 2:11; u Eph 5:26; S Mt 1:21
1:10 v S Ro 8:28; w Ps 15:5; 2Pe 3:17; Jude 24
1:11 x Ps 145:13; 2Ti 4:18 y 2Pe 2:20; 3:18
1:12 z Php 3:1; 1Jn 2:21; Jude 5
a 2Jn 2
1:13 b 2Pe 3:1; c Isa 38:12; 2Co 5:1,4
1:14 d 2Ti 4:6; e Jn 13:36; 21:18, 19
1:15 f Lk 9:31
1:16 g Mk 13:26; 14:62 h Mt 17:1-8
1:17 i S Mt 3:17
1:18 j Mt 17:6
1:19 k 1Pe 1:10,11; l Ps 119:105; m Lk 1:78; n Rev 22:16; o 2Co 4:6
1:20 p 2Pe 3:3
1:21 q 2Ti 3:16; r 2Sa 23:2; Ac 1:16; 3:18; 1Pe 1:11

C 1Pe 4:13 ◀▶ 2Pe 3:3–14
E 1Pe 4:10–11 ◀▶ 1Jn 2:20
G 1Pe 4:10–11 ◀▶ 1Jn 2:20
M Heb 2:4 ◀▶ 1Jn 2:20
T 1Pe 4:10–11 ◀▶ 1Jn 2:20

S 1Pe 4:17–18 ◀▶ 2Pe 2:19–21

a 17 Matt. 17:5; Mark 9:7; Luke 9:35

1:16–18 Peter confirms that he and the other NT writers were eyewitnesses of the life and resurrection of Christ, a life that fulfilled the OT prophecies of the Messiah. Peter declares personally hearing God the Father confirm Jesus' divinity (1:17; see Mt 3:17; 17:5).

1:19–21 Peter shares some very important principles by which we should evaluate the prophecies of the Bible. First, he validates the message of prophecy (1:19), explaining that prophecy is intended to be a spiritual light to enlighten the dark times in which believers live. Peter also urges vigilance and paying close attention to prophecy because it motivates us to holy living. He also notes that prophecy is an inspired message from the Holy Spirit, not from mere humans, given so that the church will live expectantly "until the day dawns and the morning star rises in your hearts" (1:19; see Rev 22:16).

False Teachers and Their Destruction

2 But there were also false prophets among the people, just as there will be false teachers among you. They will secretly introduce destructive heresies, even denying the sovereign Lord who bought them—bringing swift destruction on themselves. ²Many will follow their shameful ways and will bring the way of truth into disrepute. ³In their greed these teachers will exploit you with stories they have made up. Their condemnation has long been hanging over them, and their destruction has not been sleeping.

⁴For if God did not spare angels when they sinned, but sent them to hell, putting them into gloomy dungeons to be held for judgment; ⁵if he did not spare the ancient world when he brought the flood on its ungodly people, but protected Noah, a preacher of righteousness, and seven others; ⁶if he condemned the cities of Sodom and Gomorrah by burning them to ashes, and made them an example of what is going to happen to the ungodly; ⁷and if he rescued Lot, a righteous man, who was distressed by the filthy lives of lawless men ⁸(for that righteous man, living among them day after day, was tormented in his righteous soul by the lawless deeds he saw and heard)— ⁹if this is so, then the Lord knows how to rescue godly men from trials and to hold the unrighteous for the day of judgment, while continuing their punishment. ¹⁰This is especially true of those who follow the corrupt desire of the sinful nature and despise authority.

Bold and arrogant, these men are not afraid to slander celestial beings; ¹¹yet even angels, although they are stronger and more powerful, do not bring slanderous accusations against such beings in the presence of the Lord. ¹²But these men blaspheme in matters they do not understand. They are like brute beasts, creatures of instinct, born only to be caught and destroyed, and like beasts they too will perish.

¹³They will be paid back with harm for the harm they have done. Their idea of pleasure is to carouse in broad daylight. They are blots and blemishes, reveling in their pleasures while they feast with you. ¹⁴With eyes full of adultery, they never stop sinning; they seduce the unstable; they are experts in greed—an accursed brood! ¹⁵They have left the straight way and wandered off to follow the way of Balaam son of Beor, who loved the wages of wickedness. ¹⁶But he was rebuked for his wrongdoing by a donkey—a beast without speech—who spoke with a man's voice and restrained the prophet's madness.

¹⁷These men are springs without water and mists driven by a storm. Blackest darkness is reserved for them. ¹⁸For they mouth empty, boastful words and, by appealing to the lustful desires of sinful human nature, they entice people who are just escaping from those who live in error. ¹⁹They promise them freedom, while they themselves are slaves of depravity—for a man is a slave to whatever has mastered him. ²⁰If they have escaped the corruption of the world by knowing our Lord and Savior Jesus Christ and are again entangled in it and overcome, they are worse off at the end than they were at

---

2:9 God can easily deliver believers from temptation if we follow his commands and resist the devil (see Ps 34:17; 1Co 10:13; 2Ti 2:22; Jas 4:7). Yet the Lord has promised to punish the wicked. Unrepentant souls who die will wait in Hades (hell) until they are resurrected to appear in heaven before God at the great white throne judgment (see Rev 20:11–15). All who appear at this judgment have chosen the punishment of hell since they have rejected the salvation of Jesus Christ. The issue to be settled at this judgment is exactly what form their punishment in hell will take (see Jer 17:10; Ro 2:5–6; Rev 2:23; 20:13).

the beginning.[f] [21]It would have been better for them not to have known the way of righteousness, than to have known it and then to turn their backs on the sacred command that was passed on to them.[g] [22]Of them the proverbs are true: "A dog returns to its vomit,"[g,h] and, "A sow that is washed goes back to her wallowing in the mud."

The Day of the Lord

3 Dear friends,[i] this is now my second letter to you. I have written both of them as reminders[j] to stimulate you to wholesome thinking. [2]I want you to recall the words spoken in the past by the holy prophets[k] and the command given by our Lord and Savior through your apostles.[l]

[3]First of all, you must understand that in the last days[m] scoffers will come, scoffing and following their own evil desires.[n] [4]They will say, "Where is this 'coming' he promised?[o] Ever since our fathers died, everything goes on as it has since the beginning of creation."[p] [5]But they deliberately forget that long ago by God's word[q] the heavens existed and the earth was formed out of water and by water.[r] [6]By these waters also the world of that time[s] was deluged and destroyed.[t] [7]By the same word the present heavens and earth are reserved for fire,[u] being kept for the day of judgment[v] and destruction of ungodly men.

[8]But do not forget this one thing, dear friends: With the Lord a day is like a thousand years, and a thousand years are like a day.[w] [9]The Lord is not slow in keeping his promise,[x] as some understand slowness. He is patient[y] with you, not wanting anyone to perish, but everyone to come to repentance.[z]

[10]But the day of the Lord will come like

C 2Pe 2:17 ◀▶ 2Pe 3:3
C 2Pe 1:16–19 ◀▶ 1Jn 2:28
E Jas 5:7 ◀▶ 1Jn 2:18
C 2Pe 2:22 ◀▶ 1Jn 2:11

2:20 [f] Mt 12:45
2:21 [g] Eze 18:24; Heb 6:4-6; 10:26, 27
2:22 [h] Pr 26:11
3:1 [i] 1Co 10:14 [j] 2Pe 1:13
3:2 [k] Lk 1:70; Ac 3:21 [l] Eph 4:11
3:3 [m] 1Ti 4:1; 2Ti 3:1 [n] 2Pe 2:10; Jude 18
3:4 [o] Isa 5:19; Eze 12:22; Mt 24:48; [S] Lk 17:30 [p] Mk 10:6
3:5 [q] Ge 1:6,9; Heb 11:3 [r] Ps 24:2
3:6 [s] 2Pe 2:5 [t] Ge 7:21,22
3:7 [u] ver 10,12; [S] 2Th 1:7 [v] [S] Mt 10:15
3:8 [w] Ps 90:4
3:9 [x] Hab 2:3; Heb 10:37 [y] [S] Ro 2:4 [z] [S] 1Ti 2:4; Rev 2:21

H 2Pe 2:17 ◀▶ Jude 5–7
J 2Pe 2:9 ◀▶ 1Jn 4:17
J 2Pe 2:9 ◀▶ 1Jn 4:17
L 1Pe 3:18 ◀▶ 1Jn 7   **R** Jas 4:8 ◀▶ 1Jn 9
W Heb 7:25 ◀▶ 1Jn 7–9
P 2Th 2:8–9 ◀▶ 2Jn 7

[g] 22 Prov. 26:11

3:3–7 The apostasy of the last days will be characterized by widespread scoffing and contempt for the doctrine of the second coming because of its long delay. Peter suggests that the scoffers will also deny the supernatural authority and truthfulness of the Scriptures, the creation by the Creator, the story of the flood and ignore the Bible's prophecies of a coming judgment. Many of these heretical tenets are taught in our modern-day seminaries. Can the "destruction of ungodly men" (3:7) be too far in the future?

3:8–9 Peter reminds us that God's view of time is different from ours (3:8; see Ps 90:4). Some suggest that these passages indicate that the six days of creation recorded in Ge 1—2 are a microcosm of six thousand years of God's dealings with humanity. These scholars suggest that just as creation took six days, with God resting on the seventh day, there would be six thousand years before the return of Christ and then the great Sabbath rest of one thousand years (the Millennium) as described in Heb 4:4, 7–9; Rev 20.

Others scholars contend that Peter's words are more direct, viewing time in its relation to eternity. Compared to eternity, an age seems no longer than a day, and a day seems no longer than a moment. These scholars suggest that Peter's words merely indicate God's patience and long-suffering versus humanity's impatience and haste. God's patience and mercy has even delayed the return of the Lord so that "everyone [should] come to repentance" (3:9).

3:10–14 Peter then warns that when the Lord appears, he will appear unexpectedly "like a thief" (3:10) to the unbelievers who have not heeded the prophecies of Scripture. (The believer is to be alert and watching for the fulfillment of these signs, so Christ's coming in the air should not be a surprise to Christians.) Peter says that Christ's coming in these days will be marked with God's wrath poured out on the earth through the judgments of the tribulation. His description of the elements melting "by fire" (3:10) may indicate multiple nuclear bombardments during the terrible judgments of the last days.

Because of such devastation, Peter urges people to consider the manner of their life (3:11). He calls upon believers to reflect their faith in Jesus in their words and actions, allowing the hope of the second coming to become a powerful motivator as they witness with urgency and walk in holiness. Note that Peter indicates that believers can speed up or hasten Christ's return by their faithful Christian walk. Since God is waiting for all who will come to salvation, the sooner we bring others to the Savior, the sooner he can return.

Finally, Peter reminds us that the final goal of our human journey is the "new heaven and a new earth" (3:13) where we will live under the righteous and just rule of Jesus Christ, the Messiah. When Jesus Christ establishes his kingdom on earth, humanity

a thief.ᵃ The heavens will disappear with a roar;ᵇ the elements will be destroyed by fire,ᶜ and the earth and everything in it will be laid bare.ʰᵈ

¹¹Since everything will be destroyed in this way, what kind of people ought you to be? You ought to live holy and godly lives ¹²as you look forwardᵉ to the day of God and speed its coming.ⁱᶠ That day will bring about the destruction of the heavens by fire, and the elements will melt in the heat.ᵍ ¹³But in keeping with his promise we are looking forward to a new heaven and a new earth,ʰ the home of righteousness.

¹⁴So then, dear friends, since you are looking forward to this, make every effort to be found spotless, blamelessⁱ and at peace with him. ¹⁵Bear in mind that our Lord's patienceʲ means salvation,ᵏ just as our dear brother Paul also wrote you with the wisdom that God gave him.ˡ ¹⁶He writes the same way in all his letters, speaking in them of these matters. His letters contain some things that are hard to understand, which ignorant and unstableᵐ people distort,ⁿ as they do the other Scriptures,ᵒ to their own destruction.

¹⁷Therefore, dear friends, since you already know this, be on your guardᵖ so that you may not be carried away by the errorᑫ of lawless menʳ and fall from your secure position.ˢ ¹⁸But grow in the graceᵗ and knowledgeᵘ of our Lord and Savior Jesus Christ.ᵛ To him be glory both now and forever! Amen.ʷ

3:10 ᵃS Lk 12:39 ᵇIsa 34:4 ᶜver 7, 12; S 2Th 1:7 ᵈMt 24:35; S Heb 12:27; Rev 21:1
3:12 ᵉS 1Co 1:7 ᶠPs 50:3 ᵍver 10
3:13 ʰIsa 65:17; 66:22; Rev 21:1
3:14 ⁱS 1Th 3:13
3:15 ʲS Ro 2:4 ᵏver 9 ˡEph 3:3
3:16 ᵐJas 1:8; 2Pe 2:14 ⁿPs 56:5; Jer 23:36 ᵒver 2
3:17 ᵖ1Co 10:12 ᑫ2Pe 2:18 ʳ2Pe 2:7 ˢRev 2:5
3:18 ᵗS Ro 3:24 ᵘS 2Pe 1:2 ᵛ2Pe 1:11; 2:20 ʷS Ro 11:36

S 2Pe 2:19–21 ◄ ► 2Pe 3:13–14
N Heb 12:26–28 ◄ ► 1Jn 2:17
S 2Pe 3:11 ◄ ► 1Jn 5–7

ʰ10 Some manuscripts *be burned up* ⁱ12 Or *as you wait eagerly for the day of God to come*

---

will finally experience the righteousness and justice it has desired for nineteen hundred years (see Isa 9:6–7). As we look for the fulfillment of these things, Paul urges us to live peaceful, blameless lives (3:14) just like Christ (see 1Pe 1:19).

1 John

Author: John

Theme: Walking in the light of Christian fellowship

Date of Writing: c. A.D. 85–95

Outline of 1 John
 I. Introduction (1:1–4)
 II. Light Is Essential for Fellowship (1:5—2:28)
 III. Love Must Permeate Life (2:29—4:21)
 IV. Faith and Certainty (5:1–21)

THIS SHORT LETTER is attributed to the apostle John, the son of Zebedee and one of Jesus' closest disciples. John also authored the Gospel of John, the book of Revelation and the other short epistles that bear his name. Though this letter does not denote its intended audience, content, style and vocabulary indicate that this epistle was probably directed to the same readers as the Gospel of John—most probably, the church in Asia for which John had some responsibilities. Though precise dating of this letter is difficult, internal and external evidence suggests that John composed this epistle shortly before his death.

False teachers had attempted to mislead first-century believers to follow their Gnostic ideas that matter is entirely evil and that the spirit is entirely good. The Gnostic solution to the tension between good and evil was to increase knowledge and thereby allow humanity to rise from the mundane to the spiritual. Gnostic teachings also perverted the gospel message by denying the true humanity of Christ, suggesting that Jesus was nothing more than a mere ghost who could manifest a dual personality, appearing at times human and at times divine. John's letter to the believers confronts this serious heresy by assuring the believers of the true message of the gospel and confirming his eyewitness testimony to the incarnation of Christ. With intimacy and warmth John also conveys the theme of Christian fellowship as he offers these first-century believers certainty for their faith in Christ.

The Word of Life

1 That which was from the beginning,[a] which we have heard, which we have seen with our eyes,[b] which we have looked at and our hands have touched[c]—this we proclaim concerning the Word of life. ² The life appeared;[d] we have seen it and testify to it,[e] and we proclaim to you the eternal life,[f] which was with the Father and has appeared to us. ³ We proclaim to you what we have seen and heard,[g] so that you also may have fellowship with us. And our fellowship is with the Father and with his Son, Jesus Christ.[h] ⁴ We write this[i] to make our[a] joy complete.[j]

Walking in the Light

⁵ This is the message we have heard[k] from him and declare to you: God is light;[l] in him there is no darkness at all. ⁶ If we claim to have fellowship with him yet walk in the darkness,[m] we lie and do not live by the truth.[n] ⁷ But if we walk in the light,[o] as he is in the light, we have fellowship with one another, and the blood of Jesus, his Son, purifies us from all[b] sin.[p]

⁸ If we claim to be without sin,[q] we deceive ourselves and the truth is not in us.[r] ⁹ If we confess our sins, he is faithful and just and will forgive us our sins[s] and purify us from all unrighteousness.[t] ¹⁰ If we claim we have not sinned,[u] we make him out to be a liar[v] and his word has no place in our lives.[w]

2 My dear children,[x] I write this to you so that you will not sin. But if anybody does sin, we have one who speaks to the Father in our defense[y]—Jesus Christ, the Righteous One. ² He is the atoning sacrifice for our sins,[z] and not only for ours but also for[c] the sins of the whole world.[a]

U 1Pe 3:12 ◀▶ 1Jn 3:22
S 2Pe 3:13–14 ◀▶ 1Jn 2:1
D 1Pe 3:18 ◀▶ 1Jn 2:2
K 2Pe 2:9 ◀▶ 1Jn 2:2   **L** 2Pe 3:9 ◀▶ 1Jn 9
W 2Pe 3:9 ◀▶ 1Jn 2:1–2
A Jas 2:10 ◀▶ 1Jn 10
L 1Jn 7 ◀▶ 1Jn 2:1–2
R 2Pe 3:9 ◀▶ Rev 2:5   **A** 1Jn 8 ◀
L 1Jn 9 ◀▶ 1Jn 2:12
P Jas 5:19–20 ◀▶ 1Jn 5:16
S 1Jn 5–7 ◀▶ 1Jn 2:3–6
W 1Jn 7–9 ◀▶ 1Jn 4:14–15
D 1Jn 7 ◀▶ 1Jn 3:5   **K** 1Jn 7 ◀▶ 1Jn 3:5

1:1 ᵃ S Jn 1:2; ᵇ S Lk 24:48; Jn 1:14; 19:35; Ac 4:20; 2Pe 1:16; ᶜ 1Jn 4:14 ᶜ Jn 20:27
1:2 ᵈ Jn 1:1-4; 11:25; 14:6; ᵉ 1Ti 3:16; 1Pe 1:20; 1Jn 3:5,8
1:3 ᵍ S ver 1; ʰ 1Co 1:9
1:4 ⁱ 1Jn 2:1; ʲ S Jn 3:29
1:5 ᵏ 1Jn 3:11 ˡ 1Ti 6:16
1:6 ᵐ Jn 3:19-21; 8:12; 2Co 6:14; Eph 5:8; 1Jn 2:11 ⁿ Jn 3:19-21; 1Jn 2:4; 4:20
1:7 ᵒ Isa 2:5 ᵖ Heb 9:14; Rev 1:5; 7:14
1:8 ᵠ Pr 20:9; Jer 2:35; Ro 3:9-19; Jas 3:2 ʳ Jn 8:44; 1Jn 2:4
1:9 ˢ Ps 32:5; 51:2; Pr 28:13 ᵗ ver 7; Mic 7:18-20; Heb 10:22
1:10 ᵘ ver 8 ᵛ 1Jn 5:10 ʷ Jn 5:38; 1Jn 2:14
2:1 ˣ ver 12,13,28; 1Jn 3:7,18; 4:4; 5:21; S 1Th 2:11 ʸ S Ro 8:34; 1Ti 2:5
2:2 ᶻ Ro 3:25; 1Jn 4:10 ᵃ S Mt 1:21; S Jn 3:17
2:3 ᵇ ver 5; 1Jn 3:24; 4:13; 5:2 ᶜ S ver 4
2:4 ᵈ S Jn 14:15 ᵉ ver 3; Tit 1:16; 1Jn 3:6; 4:7,8 ᶠ 1Jn 1:6,8
2:5 ᵍ S Jn 14:15
2:6 ʰ 1Jn 4:12 ⁱ S ver 3
2:6 ⁱ S Mt 11:29
2:7 ᵏ S 1Co 10:14 ˡ ver 24; 1Jn 3:11, 23; 4:21; 2Jn 5,6
2:8 ᵐ S Jn 13:34 ⁿ Ro 13:12; Heb 10:25 ᵒ Jn 1:9 ᵖ Eph 5:8; 1Th 5:5
2:9 ᵠ ver 11; Lev 19:17; 1Jn 3:10,15,16; 4:20,21 ʳ 1Jn 1:5
2:10 ˢ 1Jn 3:14 ᵗ ver 11; Ps 119:165
2:11 ᵘ S ver 9 ᵛ S 1Jn 1:6 ʷ Jn 11:9; 12:35
2:12 ˣ S ver 1 ʸ S 1Jn 3:23
2:13 ᶻ S Jn 1:1 ᵃ S Jn 16:33 ᵇ ver 14; S Mt 5:37 ᶜ S ver 1
2:14 ᵈ S Jn 1:1 ᵉ Eph 6:10 ᶠ S Heb 4:12 ᵍ S Jn 5:38; 1Jn 1:10 ʰ S ver 13

---

³ We know[b] that we have come to know him[c] if we obey his commands.[d] ⁴ The man who says, "I know him,"[e] but does not do what he commands is a liar, and the truth is not in him.[f] ⁵ But if anyone obeys his word,[g] God's love[d] is truly made complete in him.[h] This is how we know[i] we are in him: ⁶ Whoever claims to live in him must walk as Jesus did.[j]

⁷ Dear friends,[k] I am not writing you a new command but an old one, which you have had since the beginning.[l] This old command is the message you have heard. ⁸ Yet I am writing you a new command;[m] its truth is seen in him and you, because the darkness is passing[n] and the true light[o] is already shining.[p]

⁹ Anyone who claims to be in the light but hates his brother[q] is still in the darkness.[r] ¹⁰ Whoever loves his brother lives in the light,[s] and there is nothing in him[e] to make him stumble.[t] ¹¹ But whoever hates his brother[u] is in the darkness and walks around in the darkness;[v] he does not know where he is going, because the darkness has blinded him.[w]

¹² I write to you, dear children,[x]
   because your sins have been
   forgiven on account of his
   name.[y]
¹³ I write to you, fathers,
   because you have known him who is
   from the beginning.[z]
I write to you, young men,
   because you have overcome[a] the
   evil one.[b]
I write to you, dear children,[c]
   because you have known the
   Father.
¹⁴ I write to you, fathers,
   because you have known him who is
   from the beginning.[d]
I write to you, young men,
   because you are strong,[e]
   and the word of God[f] lives
    in you,[g]
   and you have overcome the evil
    one.[h]

S 1Jn 2:1 ◀▶ 1Jn 2:15
C 2Pe 3:3 ◀▶ 1Jn 2:15–17
L 1Jn 2:1–2 ◀▶ 1Jn 3:5

ᵃ 4 Some manuscripts *your*   ᵇ 7 Or *every*   ᶜ 2 Or *He is the one who turns aside God's wrath, taking away our sins, and not only ours but also*   ᵈ 5 Or *word, love for God*   ᵉ 10 Or *it*

Do Not Love the World

¹⁵Do not love the world or anything in the world. If anyone loves the world, the love of the Father is not in him. ¹⁶For everything in the world—the cravings of sinful man, the lust of his eyes¹ and the boasting of what he has and does—comes not from the Father but from the world. ¹⁷The world and its desires pass away, but the man who does the will of God lives forever.

Warning Against Antichrists

¹⁸Dear children, this is the last hour; and as you have heard that the antichrist is coming, even now many antichrists have come. This is how we know it is the last hour. ¹⁹They went out from us, but they did not really belong to us. For if they had belonged to us, they would have remained with us; but their going showed that none of them belonged to us.

²⁰But you have an anointing from the Holy One, and all of you know the truth.ᶠᵛ ²¹I do not write to you because you do not know the truth, but because you do know it and because no lie comes from the truth. ²²Who is the liar? It is the man who denies that Jesus is the Christ. Such a man is the antichrist—he denies the Father and the Son. ²³No one who denies the Son has the Father; whoever acknowledges the Son has the Father also.

²⁴See that what you have heard from the beginning remains in you. If it does, you also will remain in the Son and in the Father. ²⁵And this is what he promised us—even eternal life.

²⁶I am writing these things to you about those who are trying to lead you astray. ²⁷As for you, the anointing you received from him remains in you, and you do not need anyone to teach you. But as his anointing teaches you about all things and as that anointing is real, not counterfeit—just as it has taught you, remain in him.

Children of God

²⁸And now, dear children, continue in him, so that when he appears we may be confident and unashamed before him at his coming.

²⁹If you know that he is righteous, you know that everyone who does what is right has been born of him.

3 How great is the love the Father has lavished on us, that we should be called children of God! And that is what we are! The reason the world does not know us is that it did not know him. ²Dear friends, now we are children of God, and what we will be has not yet

f20 Some manuscripts and you know all things

2:17 John prophesied that this age, which has been dominated by Satan and corruption, will pass away. However, the apostle promises that eternal life is the reward of those who are obedient to God's will, which "lives forever."

2:18 The apostle prophetically warned that the clock has started to tick in a countdown to the appearance of the antichrist and the return of Christ in victory (see Rev 13:1–10). John reminded his readers that there would be a proliferation of false Christs in the last days. This increase would signal the approach of the final antichrist who will take over the ten nations of the revived Roman empire in Europe in his bid to dominate the nations of the whole earth (see Da 2:40–45; 7:7–8; Rev 13:1–10).

2:22–23 The nature of the antichrist spirit is the denial of Jesus' incarnate divinity. John confirms that this antichrist spirit produces a person who has neither the spirit nor the presence of the Son or the Father.

2:28 John commands his readers to stand firm in their faith because of the promise of the second coming of Jesus Christ. When he returns, he will appear in the air to take his saints home to heaven.

3:2 This declaration of adoption refers to the supernatural relationship of the believers to God based on their faith in Christ's atonement on the cross. The passage affirms a wonderful revelation

been made known. But we know that when he appears,^(g r) we shall be like him,^s for we shall see him as he is.^t ^3Everyone who has this hope in him purifies himself,^u just as he is pure.^v

^4Everyone who sins breaks the law; in fact, sin is lawlessness.^w ^5But you know that he appeared so that he might take away our sins.^x And in him is no sin.^y ^6No one who lives in him keeps on sinning.^z No one who continues to sin has either seen him^a or known him.^b

^7Dear children,^c do not let anyone lead you astray.^d He who does what is right is righteous, just as he is righteous.^e ^8He who does what is sinful is of the devil,^f because the devil has been sinning from the beginning. The reason the Son of God^g appeared was to destroy the devil's work.^h ^9No one who is born of God^i will continue to sin,^j because God's seed^k remains in him; he cannot go on sinning, because he has been born of God. ^10This is how we know who the children of God^l are and who the children of the devil^m are: Anyone who does not do what is right is not a child of God; nor is anyone who does not love^n his brother.^o

Love One Another

^11This is the message you heard^p from the beginning:^q We should love one another.^r ^12Do not be like Cain, who belonged to the evil one^s and murdered his brother.^t And why did he murder him? Because his own actions were evil and his brother's were righteous.^u ^13Do not be surprised, my brothers, if the world hates you.^v ^14We know that we have passed from death to life,^w because we love our brothers. Anyone who does not love remains in death.^x ^15Anyone who hates his brother^y is a murderer,^z and you know that no murderer has eternal life in him.^a

^16This is how we know what love is: Jesus Christ laid down his life for us.^b And we ought to lay down our lives for our brothers.^c ^17If anyone has material possessions and sees his brother in need but has no pity on him,^d how can the love of God be in him?^e ^18Dear children,^f let us not love with words or tongue but with actions and in truth.^g ^19This then is how we know that we belong to the truth, and how we set our hearts at rest in his presence ^20whenever our hearts condemn us. For God is greater than our hearts, and he knows everything.

^21Dear friends,^h if our hearts do not condemn us, we have confidence before God^i ^22and receive from him anything we ask,^j because we obey his commands^k and do what pleases him.^l ^23And this is his command: to believe^m in the name of his Son, Jesus Christ,^n and to love one another as he commanded us.^o ^24Those who obey his commands^p live in him,^q and he in them. And this is how we know that he lives in us: We know it by the Spirit he gave us.^r

Test the Spirits

4 Dear friends,^s do not believe every spirit,^t but test the spirits to see whether they are from God, because many false prophets have gone out into the world.^u ^2This is how you can recognize the Spirit of God: Every spirit that acknowledges that Jesus Christ has come in the flesh^v is from God,^w ^3but every spirit that does not acknowledge Jesus is not from God. This is the spirit of the

---

S 1Jn 2:15 ◄► 1Jn 3:15
D 1Jn 2:2 ◄► 1Jn 3:16
K 1Jn 2:2 ◄► 1Jn 3:8
L 1Jn 2:12 ◄► 1Jn 3:16
C 1Jn 2:15–17 ◄► 1Jn 5:12
K 1Jn 3:5 ◄► 1Jn 4:4
S 1Jn 3:3–10 ◄► 1Jn 3:24

D 1Jn 3:5 ◄► 1Jn 4:9
L 1Jn 3:5 ◄► 1Jn 4:8–10
E Heb 4:12–13 ◄► Rev 2:23
F 1Pe 2:6 ◄► 1Jn 5:1
E 1Jn 2:27 ◄► 1Jn 4:13
S 1Jn 3:15 ◄► 1Jn 4:8
N 1Jn 2:27 ◄► 1Jn 4:6

U 1Jn 4 ◄

g 2 Or when it is made known

---

that our resurrection at the rapture will transform our natural bodies to become like Jesus' resurrection body (see Php 3:21). For further information, see the article on "The Resurrection of the Body" on p. 1218.

3:3 John's prediction reminds believers of Paul's prophecy of the judgment of Christians (see Ro 14:10; 2Co 5:10), and motivates them to live in the constant expectation of the appearance of Jesus at the second coming.

4:3 The belief that Jesus, the Son of God, was incarnated in human flesh is essential to salvation.

antichrist, which you have heard is coming and even now is already in the world.

⁴You, dear children, are from God and have overcome them, because the one who is in you is greater than the one who is in the world. ⁵They are from the world and therefore speak from the viewpoint of the world, and the world listens to them. ⁶We are from God, and whoever knows God listens to us; but whoever is not from God does not listen to us. This is how we recognize the Spirit of truth and the spirit of falsehood.

God's Love and Ours

⁷Dear friends, let us love one another, for love comes from God. Everyone who loves has been born of God and knows God. ⁸Whoever does not love does not know God, because God is love. ⁹This is how God showed his love among us: He sent his one and only Son into the world that we might live through him. ¹⁰This is love: not that we loved God, but that he loved us and sent his Son as an atoning sacrifice for our sins. ¹¹Dear friends, since God so loved us, we also ought to love one another. ¹²No one has ever seen God; but if we love one another, God lives in us and his love is made complete in us.

¹³We know that we live in him and he in us, because he has given us of his Spirit. ¹⁴And we have seen and testify that the Father has sent his Son to be the Savior of the world. ¹⁵If anyone acknowledges that Jesus is the Son of God, God lives in him and he in God. ¹⁶And so we know and rely on the love God has for us.

God is love. Whoever lives in love lives in God, and God in him. ¹⁷In this way, love is made complete among us so that we will have confidence on the day of judgment, because in this world we are like him. ¹⁸There is no fear in love. But perfect love drives out fear, because fear has to do with punishment. The one who fears is not made perfect in love.

¹⁹We love because he first loved us. ²⁰If anyone says, "I love God," yet hates his brother, he is a liar. For anyone who does not love his brother, whom he has seen, cannot love God, whom he has not seen. ²¹And he has given us this command: Whoever loves God must also love his brother.

Faith in the Son of God

5 Everyone who believes that Jesus is the Christ is born of God, and everyone who loves the father loves his child as well. ²This is how we know that we love the children of God: by loving God and carrying out his commands. ³This is love for God: to obey his commands. And his commands are not burdensome, ⁴for everyone born of God overcomes the world. This is the victory that has overcome the world, even our faith. ⁵Who is it that overcomes the world? Only he who believes that Jesus is the Son of God.

⁶This is the one who came by water and blood—Jesus Christ. He did not

h 6 Or *spirit* *i* 9 Or *his only begotten Son* *j* 10 Or *the one who would turn aside his wrath, taking away*

The spirit of antichrist denies this incarnation of Christ. In addition, the denial that Jesus of Nazareth is truly the Son of God is an essential component of almost every major cult and false religion that opposes Christianity.

4:17 Since we as believers have accepted Christ's atonement on the cross for our sins, we can "have confidence on the day of judgment." We will not be subject to God's wrath at the end of the Millennium when all of the wicked souls from Cain to the last rebel soul will be judged at the great white throne judgment.

come by water only, but by water and blood. And it is the Spirit who testifies, because the Spirit is the truth.ᶻ ⁷For there are threeᵃ that testify: ⁸theᵏ Spirit, the water and the blood; and the three are in agreement. ⁹We accept man's testimony,ᵇ but God's testimony is greater because it is the testimony of God,ᶜ which he has given about his Son. ¹⁰Anyone who believes in the Son of God has this testimony in his heart.ᵈ Anyone who does not believe God has made him out to be a liar,ᵉ because he has not believed the testimony God has given about his Son. ¹¹And this is the testimony: God has given us eternal life,ᶠ and this life is in his Son.ᵍ ¹²He who has the Son has life; he who does not have the Son of God does not have life.ʰ

Concluding Remarks

¹³I write these things to you who believe in the name of the Son of Godⁱ so that you may know that you have eternal life.ʲ ¹⁴This is the confidenceᵏ we have in approaching God: that if we ask anything according to his will, he hears us.ˡ ¹⁵And if we know that he hears us—whatever we ask—we knowᵐ that we have what we asked of him.ⁿ

¹⁶If anyone sees his brother commit a sin that does not lead to death, he should pray and God will give him life.ᵒ I refer to those whose sin does not lead to death. There is a sin that leads to death.ᵖ I am not saying that he should pray about that.ᵠ ¹⁷All wrongdoing is sin,ʳ and there is sin that does not lead to death.ˢ

¹⁸We know that anyone born of Godᵗ does not continue to sin; the one who was born of God keeps him safe, and the evil oneᵘ cannot harm him.ᵛ ¹⁹We know that we are children of God,ʷ and that the whole world is under the control of the evil one.ˣ ²⁰We know also that the Son of God has comeʸ and has given us understanding,ᶻ so that we may know him who is true.ᵃ And we are in him who is true— even in his Son Jesus Christ. He is the true God and eternal life.ᵇ

²¹Dear children,ᶜ keep yourselves from idols.ᵈ

5:6 ᶻS Jn 14:17
5:7 ᵃS Mt 18:16
5:9 ᵇJn 5:34; ᶜMt 3:16,17; Jn 5:32,37; 8:17,18
5:10 ᵈRo 8:16; Gal 4:6 ᵉJn 3:33; 1Jn 1:10
5:11 ᶠS Mt 25:46 ᵍS Jn 1:4
5:12 ʰJn 3:15,16, 36
5:13 ⁱS 1Jn 3:23 ʲver 11; S Mt 25:46
5:14 ᵏS Eph 3:12; 1Jn 3:21 ˡS Mt 7:7
5:15 ᵐver 18,19, 20 ⁿ1Ki 3:12
5:16 ᵒJas 5:15 ᵖEx 23:21; Heb 6:4-6; 10:26 ᵠJer 7:16; 14:11
5:17 ʳ1Jn 3:4 ˢver 16; 1Jn 2:1
5:18 ᵗS Jn 1:13 ᵘS Mt 5:37 ᵛJn 14:30
5:19 ʷ1Jn 4:6 ˣJn 12:31; 14:30; 17:15
5:20 ʸver 5 ᶻLk 24:45 ᵃJn 17:3 ᵇver 11; S Mt 25:46
5:21 ᶜ1Jn 2:1 ᵈ1Co 10:14; 1Th 1:9

D Heb 9:14 ◄
F 1Jn 5:4–5 ◄ ► 1Jn 5:13
L 1Jn 5:1 ◄ ► 1Jn 5:16
W 1Jn 5:1 ◄ ► Rev 3:20
N Jas 4:13–14 ◄ ► 1Jn 5:12
C 1Jn 3:8 ◄ ► 1Jn 5:19
N 1Jn 5:10 ◄ ► Jude 15
O Jas 4:12 ◄ ► Rev 7:9–12
F 1Jn 5:9–10 ◄   L 1Jn 3:1 ◄

Q Heb 10:29 ◄
L 1Jn 5:9–10 ◄ ► Rev 1:5
P 1Jn 2:1–2 ◄ ► Rev 2:5
S 1Jn 5:2–3 ◄ ► 2Jn 8–9
C 1Jn 5:12 ◄ ► Jude 12

ᵏ 7,8 Late manuscripts of the Vulgate *testify in heaven: the Father, the Word and the Holy Spirit, and these three are one.* ⁸*And there are three that testify on earth: the* (not found in any Greek manuscript before the sixteenth century)

2 John

Author: John

Theme: The search for Biblical truth in light of hospitality to strangers

Date of Writing: c. A.D. 85–95

Outline of 2 John
  I. Introduction (1–3)
 II. The Path of Love and Truth (4–6)
III. Warnings About the Deceiver (7–11)
IV. Conclusion (12–13)

THE APOSTLE JOHN wrote this short epistle as well as the other short letters that bear his name (see introduction to 1 John). This second letter of John was addressed to "the chosen lady and her children" (v. 1). While some scholars feel that this greeting is used metaphorically to mean a church and its members, others feel John refers here to a specific individual and her family who allowed a church to be formed in their home. Because John's emphasis in this letter is similar to that of 1 John, scholars believe that these letters were composed at about the same time.

During the early development of the church, the gospel was taken from place to place by traveling evangelists. Believers opened their homes to these teachers and gave them provisions for their journey when they left. False teachers and philosophers also relied on this practice of hospitality, so John's letter to this "lady" urges discernment in offering hospitality to itinerant preachers. John emphasizes the importance of the knowledge of Biblical truth expressed through the life, teaching and person of Christ. With warm, personal words, John reminds this lady and her children that Jesus was truly God's Son and urges them to continue in God's love and reject false doctrine.

2 JOHN 1

¹The elder,ᵃ

To the chosenᵇ lady and her children, whom I love in the truthᶜ—and not I only, but also all who know the truthᵈ—²because of the truth,ᵉ which lives in usᶠ and will be with us forever:

³Grace, mercy and peace from God the Father and from Jesus Christ,ᵍ the Father's Son, will be with us in truth and love.

⁴It has given me great joy to find some of your children walking in the truth,ʰ just as the Father commanded us. ⁵And now, dear lady, I am not writing you a new command but one we have had from the beginning.ⁱ I ask that we love one another. ⁶And this is love:ʲ that we walk in obedience to his commands.ᵏ As you have heard from the beginning,ˡ his command is that you walk in love.

⁷Many deceivers, who do not acknowledge Jesus Christᵐ as coming in the flesh,ⁿ have gone out into the world.ᵒ Any such person is the deceiver and the antichrist.ᵖ ⁸Watch out that you do not lose what you have worked for, but that you may be rewarded fully.ᵠ ⁹Anyone who runs ahead and does not continue in the teaching of Christʳ does not have God; whoever continues in the teaching has both the Father and the Son.ˢ ¹⁰If anyone comes to you and does not bring this teaching, do not take him into your house or welcome him.ᵗ ¹¹Anyone who welcomes him sharesᵘ in his wicked work.

¹²I have much to write to you, but I do not want to use paper and ink. Instead, I hope to visit you and talk with you face to face,ᵛ so that our joy may be complete.ʷ

¹³The children of your chosenˣ sister send their greetings.

1:1 ᵃS Ac 11:30; 3Jn 1 ᵇver 13; Ro 16:13; 1Pe 5:13 ᶜver 3 ᵈJn 8:32; 1Ti 2:4
1:2 ᵉ2Pe 1:12 ᶠJn 14:17; 1Jn 1:8
1:3 ᵍS Ro 1:7
1:4 ʰ3Jn 3,4
1:5 ⁱS 1Jn 2:7
1:6 ʲ1Jn 2:5 ᵏS Jn 14:15 ˡS 1Jn 2:7
1:7 ᵐ1Jn 2:22; 4:2,3 ⁿS Jn 1:14 ᵒ1Jn 4:1 ᵖS 1Jn 2:18
1:8 ᵠS Mt 10:42; Mk 10:29,30; 1Co 3:8; Heb 10:35,36; 11:26
1:9 ʳJn 8:31 ˢS 1Jn 2:23
1:10 ᵗS Ro 16:17
1:11 ᵘ1Ti 5:22
1:12 ᵛ3Jn 13,14 ʷS Jn 3:29
1:13 ˣver 1

P 2Pe 3:10–12 ◀ ▶ Jude 14–15

S 1Jn 5:18 ◀ ▶ 3Jn 11

---

7 John said that there were many atheists even in his time who denied that Jesus was God incarnate. These "deceivers" possess the spirit of the antichrist and are fundamentally opposed to Jesus Christ. An antichrist spirit denies, at every opportunity, the gospel record that Jesus is real and that he came "in the flesh." Today, centuries later, the antichrist spirit of atheism still expresses itself in its total opposition to the historical reality that Jesus was born to the virgin Mary, lived among men, died on the cross and rose from the dead as the glorified Son of God.

3 John

Author: John

Theme: Daily life lived in the light of Biblical truth

Date of Writing: C. A.D. 85–95

Outline of 3 John
 I. Introduction (1–4)
 II. Gaius Is Commended (5–8)
 III. Diotrephes Is Condemned (9–11)
 IV. The Good Example of Demetrius (12)
 V. Conclusion (13–14)

THIS LETTER WAS written by the apostle John, the son of Zebedee and beloved disciple of Jesus (see introduction to 1 John). Composed at about the same time as his other epistles, this letter is addressed by John to his friend Gaius, who may have been a first-century church leader.

This epistle reflects the difficult experience of the church during the closing decade of the first century. A domineering leader named Diotrephes had rejected itinerant preachers that had been sent out by John to one of the churches in the province of Asia. Diotrephes also had slandered John and repudiated John's authority to teach true doctrine by removing those believers from the church who disagreed with his teaching against John. In this brief letter, John rebukes Diotrephes for his actions and instructs Gaius to support and entertain those who come as God's true messengers. John reminds Gaius that the church should be walking daily in light of Biblical truth and commends Demetrius as a strong Christian leader for basing his life upon the fundamental truths of Christianity.

3 JOHN 1

¹The elder,ᵃ

To my dear friend Gaius, whom I love in the truth.

²Dear friend, I pray that you may enjoy good health and that all may go well with you, even as your soul is getting along well. ³It gave me great joy to have some brothersᵇ come and tell about your faithfulness to the truth and how you continue to walk in the truth.ᶜ ⁴I have no greater joy than to hear that my childrenᵈ are walking in the truth.ᵉ

⁵Dear friend, you are faithful in what you are doing for the brothers,ᶠ even though they are strangers to you.ᵍ ⁶They have told the church about your love. You will do well to send them on their wayʰ in a manner worthyⁱ of God. ⁷It was for the sake of the Nameʲ that they went out, receiving no help from the pagans.ᵏ ⁸We ought therefore to show hospitality to such men so that we may work together for the truth.

⁹I wrote to the church, but Diotrephes, who loves to be first, will have nothing to do with us. ¹⁰So if I come,¹ I will call attention to what he is doing, gossiping maliciously about us. Not satisfied with that, he refuses to welcome the brothers.ᵐ He also stops those who want to do so and puts them out of the church.ⁿ

¹¹Dear friend, do not imitate what is evil but what is good.ᵒ Anyone who does what is good is from God.ᵖ Anyone who does what is evil has not seen God.ᑫ ¹²Demetrius is well spoken of by everyoneʳ—and even by the truth itself. We also speak well of him, and you know that our testimony is true.ˢ

¹³I have much to write you, but I do not want to do so with pen and ink. ¹⁴I hope to see you soon, and we will talk face to face.ᵗ

Peace to you.ᵘ The friends here send their greetings. Greet the friends there by name.ᵛ

1:1 ᵃS Ac 11:30; 2Jn 1
1:3 ᵇver 5,10; S Ac 1:16 ᶜ2Jn 4
1:4 ᵈS 1Jn 2:1 ᵉver 3
1:5 ᶠS ver 3 ᵍRo 12:13; Heb 13:2
1:6 ʰ1Co 16:11; 2Co 1:16 ⁱS Eph 4:1
1:7 ʲS Jn 15:21 ᵏAc 20:33,35
1:10 ˡver 14; 2Jn 12 ᵐver 5 ⁿJn 9:22,34
1:11 ᵒPs 34:14; 37:27 ᵖ1Jn 2:29 ᑫ1Jn 3:6,9,10
1:12 ʳ1Ti 3:7 ˢJn 19:35; 21:24
1:14 ᵗ2Jn 12 ᵘS Ro 1:7; S Eph 6:23 ᵛJn 10:3

H *1Pe 3:10* ◀ ▶ *Rev 22:2*   S *2Jn 8–9* ◀ ▶ *Jude 5–6*

Jude

Author: Jude

Theme: Believers must contend for the faith

Date of Writing: C. A.D. 65

Outline of Jude
  I. Introduction (1–2)
  II. The Reason for the Epistle (3–4)
  III. Examples of Unbelief and Rebellion (5–16)
  IV. Exhortations to Faithful Believers (17–23)
  V. Conclusion (24–25)

THE AUTHOR OF this letter was Jude, the half-brother of Jesus and brother of the apostle James (see Mk 6:3). Directed to one or more of the churches dispersed throughout the Roman empire, this letter was probably composed during the mid to late A.D. 60s.

Though the first-century Christians faced open opposition, this letter addresses the problem of heresy and false teaching. Jude had intended to write about salvation (v. 3), but he changes his appeal to a defense of faith in Christ. The similarity of the content of Jude's letter to Peter's second letter may indicate the extent to which false teachers had led believers away from the true gospel. Jude contends that the errors raised by false teachers and critics must be refuted and urges his readers to contend for their faith in Jesus Christ. Citing three examples of judgment from the OT, Jude warns that God's judgment will fall upon those who turn away from the faith even as it fell upon Cain, Korah and Balaam.

JUDE 1

¹Jude,ᵃ a servant of Jesus Christᵇ and a brother of James,

To those who have been called,ᶜ who are loved by God the Father and kept by Jesus Christ:ᵈ

²Mercy, peaceᵉ and love be yours in abundance.ᶠ

The Sin and Doom of Godless Men

³Dear friends,ᵍ although I was very eager to write to you about the salvation we share,ʰ I felt I had to write and urge you to contendⁱ for the faithʲ that was once for all entrusted to the saints.ᵏ ⁴For certain men whose condemnation was written aboutᵇ long ago have secretly slipped in among you.ˡ They are godless men, who change the grace of our God into a license for immorality and deny Jesus Christ our only Sovereign and Lord.ᵐ

⁵Though you already know all this,ⁿ I want to remind youᵒ that the Lordᶜ delivered his people out of Egypt, but later destroyed those who did not believe.ᵖ ⁶And the angels who did not keep their positions of authority but abandoned their own home—these he has kept in darkness, bound with everlasting chains for judgment on the great Day.ᵠ ⁷In a similar way, Sodom and Gomorrahʳ and the surrounding townsˢ gave themselves up to sexual immorality and perversion. They serve as an example of those who suffer the punishment of eternal fire.ᵗ

⁸In the very same way, these dreamers pollute their own bodies, reject authority and slander celestial beings.ᵘ ⁹But even the archangelᵛ Michael,ʷ when he was disputing with the devil about the body of Moses,ˣ did not dare to bring a slanderous accusation against him, but said, "The Lord rebuke you!"ʸ ¹⁰Yet these men speak abusively against whatever they do not understand; and what things they do understand by instinct, like unreasoning animals—these are the very things that destroy them.ᶻ

¹¹Woe to them! They have taken the way of Cain;ᵃ they have rushed for profit into Balaam's error;ᵇ they have been destroyed in Korah's rebellion.ᶜ

¹²These men are blemishes at your love feasts,ᵈ eating with you without the slightest qualm—shepherds who feed only themselves.ᵉ They are clouds without rain,ᶠ blown along by the wind;ᵍ autumn trees, without fruit and uprootedʰ—twice dead. ¹³They are wild waves of the sea,ⁱ foaming up their shame;ʲ wandering stars, for whom blackest darkness has been reserved forever.ᵏ

¹⁴Enoch,ˡ the seventh from Adam, prophesied about these men: "See, the Lord is comingᵐ with thousands upon thousands of his holy onesⁿ ¹⁵to judgeᵒ everyone, and to convict all the ungodly of all the ungodly acts they have done in the ungodly way, and of all the harsh words ungodly sinners have spoken against him."ᵖ ¹⁶These men are grumblersᵠ and faultfinders; they follow their own evil desires;ʳ they boastˢ about themselves and flatter others for their own advantage.

1:1 ᵃ Mt 13:55; Jn 14:22; Ac 1:13 ᵇ Ro 1:1 ᶜ Ro 1:6,7 ᵈ Jn 17:12
1:2 ᵉ Gal 6:16; 1Ti 1:2 ᶠ S Ro 1:7
1:3 ᵍ S 1Co 10:14 ʰ Tit 1:4 ⁱ 1Ti 6:12 ʲ ver 20; Ac 6:7 ᵏ S Ac 9:13
1:4 ˡ Gal 2:4 ᵐ Tit 1:16; 2Pe 2:1; 1Jn 2:22
1:5 ⁿ S 1Jn 2:20 ᵒ 2Pe 1:12,13; 3:1,2 ᵖ Nu 14:29; Dt 1:32; 2:15; Ps 106:26; 1Co 10:1-5; Heb 3:16,17
1:6 ᵠ S 2Pe 2:4,9
1:7 ʳ S Mt 10:15 ˢ Dt 29:23 ᵗ S Mt 25:41; 2Pe 3:7
1:8 ᵘ 2Pe 2:10
1:9 ᵛ 1Th 4:16 ʷ Da 10:13,21; 12:1; Rev 12:7 ˣ Dt 34:6 ʸ Zec 3:2
1:10 ᶻ 2Pe 2:12
1:11 ᵃ Ge 4:3-8; Heb 11:4; 1Jn 3:12 ᵇ S 2Pe 2:15 ᶜ Nu 16:1-3,31-35
1:12 ᵈ 2Pe 2:13; 1Co 11:20-22 ᵉ Eze 34:2,8,10 ᶠ Pr 25:14; 2Pe 2:17 ᵍ Eph 4:14 ʰ Mt 15:13
1:13 ⁱ Isa 57:20 ʲ Php 3:19 ᵏ 2Pe 2:17
1:14 ˡ Ge 5:18, 21-24 ᵐ S Mt 16:27 ⁿ Dt 33:2; Da 7:10; Zec 14:5; Heb 12:22
1:15 ᵒ 2Pe 2:6-9 ᵖ 1Ti 1:9
1:16 ᵠ 1Co 10:10 ʳ ver 18; 2Pe 2:10 ˢ 2Pe 2:18

C *1Jn 5:19* ◀ ▶ *Jude 16*
H *Jude 5–7* ◀ ▶ *Rev 1:7*
P *2Jn 7* ◀ ▶ *Rev 1:7*
J *Jude 6* ◀ ▶ *Rev 11:18*
N *1Jn 5:12* ◀ ▶ *Rev 3:17–18*
C *Jude 7* ◀ ▶ *Rev 3:17*

H *2Pe 3:6–7* ◀ ▶ *Jude 13–15*
S *3Jn 11* ◀ ▶ *Rev 2:4–5*
J *1Jn 4:17* ◀ ▶ *Rev 20:11–15*
J *1Jn 4:17* ◀ ▶ *Jude 14–15*

ᵃ 1 Or *for;* or *in* ᵇ 4 Or *men who were marked out for condemnation* ᶜ 5 Some early manuscripts *Jesus*

6–7 This prophecy refers to the evil angels who joined Satan in his wicked rebellion against God in the dateless past. Jude's prophecy reveals that these angels will be dealt with at the last judgment because of their rebellion and attempts to destroy humanity. Some scholars believe that these angels will also be judged for sexual sins because of Jude's comparison between their sin and the sin of Sodom and Gomorrah (see Ge 19). For further information, see the article on "Satan and the Fallen Angels" on p. 926.

14–15 Jude refers to an ancient prophecy of Enoch that has not survived the centuries. Yet Enoch's words echo Moses and Daniel as he prophesied that Jesus Christ will return from heaven with an enormous number of his resurrected saints (see Dt 33:2; Dan 7:9–10). Millions of resurrected saints will participate in Christ's glorious return to the earth, following his victory over the antichrist in the coming Battle of Armageddon. At that time Jesus Christ will judge everyone, convicting the ungodly of their wicked deeds.

A Call to Persevere

[E] [17] But, dear friends, remember what the apostles[t] of our Lord Jesus Christ foretold.[u] [18] They said to you, "In the last times[v] there will be scoffers who will follow their own ungodly desires."[w] [19] These are the men who divide you, who follow mere natural instincts and do not have the Spirit.[x]

[20] But you, dear friends, build yourselves up[y] in your most holy faith[z] and pray in the Holy Spirit.[a] [21] Keep yourselves in God's love as you wait[b] for the mercy of our Lord Jesus Christ to bring you to eternal life.[c]

[22] Be merciful to those who doubt; [23] snatch others from the fire and save them;[d] to others show mercy, mixed with fear—hating even the clothing stained by corrupted flesh.[e]

Doxology

[24] To him who is able[f] to keep you from falling and to present you before his glorious presence[g] without fault[h] and with great joy— [25] to the only God[i] our Savior be glory, majesty, power and authority, through Jesus Christ our Lord, before all ages, now and forevermore![j] Amen.[k]

E 1Jn 2:18 ◀ ▶ Rev 1:19
E 1Jn 5:6–8 ◀ ▶ Rev 1:4
L 1Pe 4:10–11 ◀ ▶ Rev 1:10
S 1Pe 1:22 ◀   W 1Pe 4:10–11 ◀

1:17 [t] S Eph 4:11; [u] Heb 2:3; 2Pe 3:2
1:18 [v] 1Ti 4:1; 2Ti 3:1; 2Pe 3:3
[w] ver 16; 2Pe 2:1; 3:3
1:19 [x] 1Co 2:14,15
1:20 [y] Col 2:7; 1Th 5:11 [z] ver 3
[a] Eph 6:18
1:21 [b] Tit 2:13; Heb 9:28; 2Pe 3:12
[c] S Mt 25:46
1:23 [d] Am 4:11; Zec 3:2-5; 1Co 3:15
[e] Rev 3:4
1:24 [f] S Ro 16:25
[g] S 2Co 4:14
[h] Col 1:22
1:25 [i] Jn 5:44; 1Ti 1:17 [j] Heb 13:8
[k] S Ro 11:36

K 1Jn 5:4–5 ◀ ▶ Rev 1:18

17–18 Jude's words sound a lot like Peter's words as he reminds his readers that in the last days mockers of the gospel would follow their own lusts and ignore the signs of Christ's return (see 2Pe 3:3). Despite the growing evidence that the prophetic signs are being fulfilled in our lifetime, there are still many "scoffers" who reject the prophecies and Christ's promises that he would return.

Revelation

Author: John

Theme: Christ will overcome evil when he returns

Date of Writing: c. A.D. 90–96

Outline of Revelation
- I. Jesus and the Seven Churches (1:1–20)
- II. Letters to the Seven Churches (2:1—3:22)
- III. The Throne, the Elders and the Lamb (4:1—5:14)
- IV. The Seven Seals of Judgment (6:1—8:1)
- V. The Seven Trumpets and Two Witnesses (8:2—11:19)
- VI. Different Personifications and Events (12:1—14:20)
- VII. The Seven Bowls and Armageddon (15:1—16:21)
- VIII. The Great Prostitute: Babylon (17:1—19:5)
- IX. The Marriage Supper and Return of Christ (19:6–21)
- X. The Millennium (20:1–6)
- XI. Satan's Doom (20:7–10)
- XII. The Great White Throne Judgment (20:11–15)
- XIII. A New Heaven, New Earth and New Jerusalem (21:1—22:21)

THE AUTHOR OF this book clearly identifies himself as John (see 1:1, 4, 9; 22:8) and uses the word "I" repeatedly to verify this book's authenticity. During Emperor Domitian's tyranny (A.D. 81–96), opposition to Christianity increased throughout the Roman empire. Domitian commanded that everyone worship him as a god. Anyone who refused this order was severely punished; many were imprisoned, like John. During his imprisonment on the small island of Patmos in the Aegean Sea, John received this vision and wrote the book of Revelation. Though the book is directed primarily to the seven churches of Asia, John offers a divine perspective of human history for all believers as he proclaims the hope of God's judgment on apostasy and the vindication of his children.

Often referred to as the "Apocalypse," the book of Revelation reveals the hidden happenings of the future using metaphors, symbolic language, dreams, visions and displays of supernatural power. The interpretation of the symbols and figurative language in this divine prophecy has resulted in differing viewpoints among NT scholars. Some scholars suggest that the prophecies in Revelation deal only with the struggle between the Roman empire and the first-century church. Those who adopt this preterist view believe that the prophecies of Revelation and Mt 24 were totally fulfilled in A.D. 70 when Rome destroyed Jerusalem. This view also suggests an earlier date for the writing of Revelation.

Other scholars interpret Revelation from the historical view, suggesting that John's visions reveal the major, historical developments from the day of Pentecost up until Christ's second coming. Still other scholars hold to the allegorical view, interpreting John's prophecies as a reflection of the struggle between God and the forces of evil with no particular reference to actual future events. For further information on the historical and allegorical theories of prophetic interpretation, see the article "Introduction to Prophecy" on p. vi.

The majority of scholars in this century favor a futurist interpretation for this book, suggesting that John's prophecies will be fulfilled through actual events that will occur during a future world crisis. This crisis will culminate in Christ's second coming to earth to defeat evil and establish the Messianic kingdom. For further information about the futurist theory of prophetic interpretation, see the article "Introduction to Prophecy" on p. vi.

Despite the difficulties in interpretation, the book of Revelation has drawn the interest of Christians for centuries because of its focus on Jesus Christ as our glorified Lord and coming King. Throughout his vision, John presents Jesus Christ as the divine Judge who will destroy all satanic opposition and establish his everlasting kingdom of peace and justice. John also proclaims, "Blessed is the one who reads the words of this prophecy, and blessed are those who hear it and take to heart what is written in it, because the time is near" (1:3).

Prologue

1 The revelation of Jesus Christ, which God gave^a him to show his servants what must soon take place.^b He made it known by sending his angel^c to his servant John,^d ²who testifies to everything he saw—that is, the word of God^e and the testimony of Jesus Christ.^f ³Blessed is the one who reads the words of this prophecy, and blessed are those who hear it and take to heart what is written in it,^g because the time is near.^h

Greetings and Doxology

⁴John,

1:1 a Jn 12:49; 17:8 b ver 19; Da 2:28, 29; Rev 22:6 c Rev 22:16 d ver 4, 9; Rev 22:8
1:2 e ver 9; S Heb 4:12 f ver 9; 1Co 1:6; Rev 6:9; 12:17; 19:10
1:3 g Lk 11:28; Rev 22:7 h S Ro 13:11

E *Jude 19–20* ◄ ► *Rev 1:10*
G *1Jn 2:27* ◄ ► *Rev 3:1*

1:1–3 John declares that this vision was sent to him by God through his angel. Note that John issues a unique blessing of God on anyone who reads or listens to "the words of this prophecy" (1:3).

1:4–6 John begins the first portion of his book with messages to the Asiatic churches. Though John had been a leader in many churches in the Roman province of Asia (Turkey), these particular churches were singled out because each one represented a particular situation or problem. Each letter contained Jesus Christ's divine commands for correcting that particular problem in the church; and his words are still applicable to believers two thousand years later.

Note that the number seven, which relates to divine perfection, appears repeatedly throughout this prophecy. John's declaration that Jesus is "the firstborn from the dead" (1:5) reveals Christ's majesty

To the seven churches[i] in the province of Asia:

Grace and peace to you[j] from him who is, and who was, and who is to come,[k] and from the seven spirits[a][l] before his **D** throne, [5]and from Jesus Christ, who **L** is the faithful witness,[m] the firstborn from the dead,[n] and the ruler of the kings of the earth.[o]

To him who loves us[p] and has freed us from our sins by his blood,[q] [6]and has made us to be a kingdom and priests[r] to serve his God and Father[s]—to him be glory and power for ever and ever! Amen.[t]

C [7]Look, he is coming with the clouds,[u]
P   and every eye will see him,
H   even those who pierced him;[v]
    and all the peoples of the earth will
        mourn[w] because of him.
            So shall it be! Amen.

[8]"I am the Alpha and the Omega,"[x] says the Lord God, "who is, and who

D 1Jn 4:9 ◀▶ Rev 5:9
L 1Jn 5:16 ◀▶ Rev 3:20
C 1Jn 3:2–3 ◀▶ Rev 3:11
P Jude 14–15 ◀▶ Rev 2:27
H Jude 13–15 ◀▶ Rev 3:16

1:4 [i]ver 11,20
[j]S Ro 1:7 [k]ver 8;
Rev 4:8; 11:17;
16:5 [l]Isa 11:2;
Rev 3:1; 4:5; 5:6
1:5 [m]Isa 55:4;
Jn 18:37; Rev 3:14
[n]Ps 89:27; Col 1:18
[o]1Ti 6:15
[p]S Ro 8:37
[q]S Ro 3:25
1:6 [r]S 1Pe 2:5;
Rev 5:10; 20:6
[s]Ro 15:6
[t]S Ro 11:36
1:7 [u]Da 7:13;
S Mt 16:27; 24:30;
26:64; S Lk 17:30;
[v]S 1Co 1:7;
S 1Th 2:19; 4:16,17
[v]Jn 19:34,37
[w]Zec 12:10;
Mt 24:30
1:8 [x]S ver 17;
Rev 21:6; 22:13
[y]S ver 4 [z]Rev 4:8;
15:3; 19:6
1:9 [a]ver 1
[b]S Ac 14:22;
2Co 1:7; Php 4:14
[c]ver 6 [d]2Ti 2:12
[e]ver 2; S Heb 4:12
[f]S ver 2
1:10 [g]S Ac 20:7
[h]Rev 4:2; 17:3;
21:10 [i]Ex 20:18;
Rev 4:1
1:11 [j]ver 19
[k]ver 4,20
[l]S Ac 18:19
[m]Rev 2:8
[n]Rev 2:12
[o]Ac 16:14;
Rev 2:18,24
[p]Rev 3:1 [q]Rev 3:7
[r]S Col 2:1;
Rev 3:14
1:12 [s]ver 20;

was, and who is to come,[y] the Almighty."[z]

One Like a Son of Man

[9]I, John,[a] your brother and companion in the suffering[b] and kingdom[c] and patient endurance[d] that are ours in Jesus, was on the island of Patmos because of the word of God[e] and the testimony of Jesus.[f] [10]On the Lord's Day[g] I was in the **E** Spirit,[h] and I heard behind me a loud **L** voice like a trumpet,[i] [11]which said: **T** "Write on a scroll what you see[j] and send it to the seven churches:[k] to Ephesus,[l] Smyrna,[m] Pergamum,[n] Thyatira,[o] Sardis,[p] Philadelphia[q] and Laodicea."[r]

[12]I turned around to see the voice that was speaking to me. And when I turned I saw seven golden lampstands,[s] [13]and among the lampstands[t] was someone "like a son of man,"[b][u] dressed in a robe reaching down to his feet[v] and with a golden sash around his chest.[w] [14]His head and hair were white like wool, as white as snow, and his eyes were like blazing

E Rev 1:4 ◀▶ Rev 2:7
L Jude 19–20 ◀▶ Rev 4:2
T 1Jn 2:27 ◀▶ Rev 2:7

Ex 25:31-40; Zec 4:2; Rev 2:1 1:13 [t]Rev 2:1 [u]Eze 1:26; Da 7:13; 10:16; Rev 14:14 [v]Isa 6:1 [w]Da 10:5; Rev 15:6

[a]4 Or *the sevenfold Spirit* [b]13 Daniel 7:13

---

in anticipation of his future rule as the King of kings. God's promise to make his faithful disciples "a kingdom and priests" (1:6) to serve him reveals that believers will rule and reign with him over the Jews and Gentiles that survive the tribulation and Armageddon and populate the earth during the Millennium (see 5:10).

1:7–9 Though imprisoned on Patmos, John declared these words were written for "the testimony of Jesus" (1:9) and to tell of Christ's glorious second coming in majesty and power, returning in judgment as the conquering King of kings. When he returns, there will be mourning as God's people recognize the Messiah they have rejected (see Mt 24:30).

Note that the Lord refers to himself with the first and last letters of the Greek alphabet (1:8) and declares that he alone is eternal, before everything and after everything (see Ex 3:14). This is an important declaration because some people think that Jesus only came into existence two thousand years ago when he was born in the flesh as a baby. The Scriptures clearly reveal that Jesus, the second person of the triune God, has always existed. The apostle Paul declared that Jesus created the universe (see Col 1:15–16).

1:10 This is the only place in Scripture that we find the expression "the Lord's Day." This quite possibly refers to Sunday, the first day of the week when the Lord rose from the grave. Though Sunday was designated "the first day of the week" (Mt 28:1) throughout the NT (see Lk 24:1; 1Co 16:2), the phrase "the Lord's Day" became a synonym for Sunday in the second century.

However, in this passage, "the Lord's Day" may also be a simple rearrangement of the common expression, "the day of the Lord." Because the focus of John's vision of the last days is the future "day of the Lord" some scholars believe the burden of evidence suggests this interpretation. Whether or not John received his tremendous vision on Sunday, the focus of his prophetic vision manifests the glory of Jesus Christ in the last days.

1:12–18 In his vision John saw Jesus Christ standing "among the lampstands" (1:13). The number seven appears repeatedly throughout Revelation. Seven candlesticks or lampstands represent the seven letters to the seven churches. The seven stars represent seven angelic messengers and point to the seven spirits or characteristics of God (see Zec 4:10). See study notes at Rev 4:5.

fire.ˣ ¹⁵His feet were like bronze glowing in a furnace,ʸ and his voice was like the sound of rushing waters.ᶻ ¹⁶In his right hand he held seven stars,ᵃ and out of his mouth came a sharp double-edged sword.ᵇ His face was like the sunᶜ shining in all its brilliance.

¹⁷When I saw him, I fell at his feetᵈ as though dead. Then he placed his right hand on meᵉ and said: "Do not be afraid.ᶠ I am the First and the Last.ᵍ ¹⁸I am the Living One; I was dead,ʰ and behold I am alive for ever and ever!ⁱ And I hold the keys of death and Hades.ʲ

¹⁹"Write, therefore, what you have seen,ᵏ what is now and what will take place later. ²⁰The mystery of the seven stars that you saw in my right handˡ and of the seven golden lampstandsᵐ is this: The seven stars are the angelsᶜ of the seven churches,ⁿ and the seven lampstands are the seven churches.ᵒ

To the Church in Ephesus

2 "To the angelᵈ of the church in Ephesusᵖ write:

These are the words of him who holds the seven stars in his right handᵠ and walks among the seven golden lampstands:ʳ ²I know your deeds,ˢ your hard work and your perseverance. I know that you cannot tolerate wicked men, that you have testedᵗ those who claim to be apostles but are not, and have found them false.ᵘ ³You have persevered

K *Jude 24* ◄ ► *Rev 7:14*
E *Jude 17–18* ◄ ► *Rev 4:1*

1:14 ˣDa 7:9; 10:6; Rev 2:18; 19:12
1:15 ʸEze 1:7; Da 10:6; Rev 2:18 ᶻEze 43:2; Rev 14:2; 19:6
1:16 ᵃver 20; Rev 2:1; 3:1 ᵇIsa 1:20; 49:2; Heb 4:12; Rev 2:12, 16; 19:15,21 ᶜJdg 5:31; Mt 17:2
1:17 ᵈEze 1:28; Da 8:17,18 ᵉDa 8:18 ᶠMt 14:27 ᵍIsa 41:4; 44:6; 48:12; Rev 2:8; 22:13
1:18 ʰRo 6:9; Rev 2:8 ⁱDt 32:40; Da 4:34; 12:7; Rev 4:9,10; 10:6; 15:7 ʲRev 9:1; 20:1
1:19 ᵏver 11; Hab 2:2
1:20 ˡS ver 1 ᵐS ver 12 ⁿver 4, 11 ᵒMt 5:14,15
2:1 ᵖS Ac 18:19 ᵠRev 1:16 ʳRev 1:12,13
2:2 ˢver 19; Rev 3:1,8,15 ᵗ1Jn 4:1 ᵘ2Co 11:13
2:3 ᵛS Jn 15:21
2:4 ʷJer 2:2; Mt 24:12
2:5 ˣver 16,22; Rev 3:3,19 ʸRev 1:20
2:6 ᶻver 15
2:7 ᵃS Mt 11:15; ver 11,17,29; Rev 3:6,13,22; 13:9 ᵇS Jn 16:33 ᶜGe 2:9; 3:22-24; Rev 22:2,14,19 ᵈLk 23:43
2:8 ᵉRev 1:11 ᶠS Rev 1:17 ᵍRev 1:18
2:9 ʰ2Co 6:10; Jas 2:5 ⁱRev 3:9 ʲver 13,24;
ˢMt 4:10

and have endured hardships for my name,ᵛ and have not grown weary.

⁴Yet I hold this against you: You have forsaken your first love.ʷ ⁵Remember the height from which you have fallen! Repentˣ and do the things you did at first. If you do not repent, I will come to you and remove your lampstandʸ from its place. ⁶But you have this in your favor: You hate the practices of the Nicolaitans,ᶻ which I also hate.

⁷He who has an ear, let him hearᵃ what the Spirit says to the churches. To him who overcomes,ᵇ I will give the right to eat from the tree of life,ᶜ which is in the paradiseᵈ of God.

To the Church in Smyrna

⁸"To the angel of the church in Smyrnaᵉ write:

These are the words of him who is the First and the Last,ᶠ who died and came to life again.ᵍ ⁹I know your afflictions and your poverty—yet you are rich!ʰ I know the slander of those who say they are Jews and are not,ⁱ but are a synagogue of Satan.ʲ ¹⁰Do not be afraid of what you are about to suffer. I tell you, the devil will put some of you in prison to test

S *Jude 5–6* ◄ ► *Rev 2:10*   P *1Jn 5:16* ◄
R *1Jn 9* ◄ ► *Rev 2:16*
E *Rev 1:10* ◄ ► *Rev 2:11*
T *Rev 1:10* ◄ ► *Rev 2:11*
S *Rev 2:4–5* ◄ ► *Rev 3:1–5*

ᶜ20 Or *messengers* ᵈ1 Or *messenger*; also in verses 8, 12 and 18

1:19 John was told to divide his prophecy into three parts: the past, the present and the future. The past events were contained in the introductory vision of ch. 1. The present things were the seven messages to the seven churches. The bulk of this book concerns events that will occur in the end times. Understanding this structural analysis of the book will help us better interpret the prophetic vision of Revelation.

1:20 Christ emphasized his control over the spiritual and angelic realm by holding the seven stars in his hand. So that there would be no question about the meaning of John's vision, Christ interpreted the meaning of these symbols for him. Note that these candlesticks or lampstands might either refer to tall candelabra or to golden stands that held oil lamps at an appropriate height.

2:1 The letters to the seven churches are the last direct words we have from Jesus Christ. These seven messages are similar to the parables because they are composed of Christ's own words and use symbols to paint the spiritual conditions of the churches.

Located in the region of modern-day Turkey, these seven churches flourished during the first century, but were singled out because their specific problems were characteristic of the spiritual situations faced by believers throughout all generations. Addressed to the angels, or messengers, of these seven churches, these messages form the second portion of the threefold division of Revelation referred to in 1:19. For further information on Christ's messages to these seven churches, see the article "The Seven Letters to the Churches" on p. 1456.

you,ᵏ and you will suffer persecution for ten days.ˡ Be faithful,ᵐ even to the point of death, and I will give you the crown of life.ⁿ

¹¹He who has an ear, let him hearᵒ what the Spirit says to the churches. He who overcomes will not be hurt at all by the second death.ᵖ

To the Church in Pergamum

¹²"To the angel of the church in Pergamumᵠ write:

These are the words of him who has the sharp, double-edged sword.ʳ ¹³I know where you live—where Satan has his throne. Yet you remain true to my name. You did not renounce your faith in me,ˢ even in the days of Antipas, my faithful witness,ᵗ who was put to death in your city—where Satan lives.ᵘ

¹⁴Nevertheless, I have a few things against you:ᵛ You have people there who hold to the teaching of Balaam,ʷ who taught Balak to entice the Israelites to sin by eating food sacrificed to idolsˣ and by committing sexual immorality.ʸ ¹⁵Likewise you also have those who hold to the teaching of the Nicolaitans.ᶻ ¹⁶Repentᵃ therefore! Otherwise, I will soon come to you and will fight against them with the sword of my mouth.ᵇ

¹⁷He who has an ear, let him hearᶜ what the Spirit says to the churches. To him who overcomes,ᵈ I will give some of the hidden manna.ᵉ I will also give him a white stone with a new nameᶠ written on it, known only to him who receives it.ᵍ

To the Church in Thyatira

¹⁸"To the angel of the church in Thyatiraʰ write:

These are the words of the Son of God,ⁱ whose eyes are like blazing fire and whose feet are like burnished bronze.ʲ ¹⁹I know your deeds,ᵏ your love and faith, your service and perseverance, and that you are now doing more than you did at first.

²⁰Nevertheless, I have this against you: You tolerate that woman Jezebel,ˡ who calls herself a prophetess. By her teaching she misleads my servants into sexual immorality and the eating of food sacrificed to idols.ᵐ ²¹I have given her timeⁿ to repent of her immorality, but she is unwilling.ᵒ ²²So I will cast her on a bed of suffering, and I will make those who commit adulteryᵖ with her suffer intensely, unless they repent of her ways. ²³I will strike her children dead. Then all the churches will know that I am he who searches hearts and minds,ᵠ and I will repay each of you according to your deeds.ʳ ²⁴Now I say to the rest of you in Thyatira, to you who do not hold to her teaching and have not learned Satan's so-called deep secrets (I will not impose any other burden on you):ˢ ²⁵Only hold on to what you haveᵗ until I come.ᵘ

²⁶To him who overcomesᵛ and does my will to the end,ʷ I will give authority over the nationsˣ—

²⁷'He will rule them with an iron scepter;ʸ
he will dash them to pieces like pottery'ᵉᶻ—

just as I have received authority from my Father. ²⁸I will also give him the morning star.ᵃ ²⁹He who has an ear, let him hearᵇ what the Spirit says to the churches.

To the Church in Sardis

3 "To the angelᶠ of the church in Sardisᶜ write:

These are the words of him who holds the seven spiritsᵍᵈ of God and the seven stars.ᵉ I know your

---

2:10 ᵏ Rev 3:10
ˡ Da 1:12,14
ᵐ ver 13; Rev 17:14
ⁿ S Mt 10:22;
S 1Co 9:25

2:11 ᵒ S ver 7
ᵖ Rev 20:6,14; 21:8

2:12 ᵠ Rev 1:11
ʳ ver 16; S Rev 1:16

2:13 ˢ Rev 14:12
ᵗ Rev 1:5; 11:3
ᵘ ver 9,24;
S Mt 4:10

2:14 ᵛ ver 20
ʷ S 2Pe 2:15
ˣ S Ac 15:20
ʸ 1Co 6:13

2:15 ᶻ ver 6

2:16 ᵃ S ver 5
ᵇ 2Ti 2:8;
S Rev 1:16

2:17 ᶜ S ver 7
ᵈ S Jn 16:33
ᵉ Jn 6:49,50
ᶠ Isa 56:5; 62:2; 65:15 ᵍ Rev 19:12

2:18 ʰ ver 24;
Ac 16:14; Rev 1:11
ⁱ S Mt 4:3
ʲ S Rev 1:14,15

2:19 ᵏ S ver 2

2:20 ˡ 1Ki 16:31; 21:25; 2Ki 9:7
ᵐ ver 14;
S Ac 15:20

2:21 ⁿ Ro 2:4;
2Pe 3:9 ᵒ Ro 2:5;
Rev 9:20; 16:9,11

2:22 ᵖ Rev 17:2; 18:9

2:23 ᵠ 1Sa 16:7; 1Ki 8:39; Ps 139:1, 2,23; Pr 21:2;
Jer 17:10; Lk 16:15;
Ro 8:27; 1Th 2:4
ʳ S Mt 16:27

2:24 ˢ Ac 15:28

2:25 ᵗ Rev 3:11
ᵘ S Mt 16:27

2:26 ᵛ S Jn 16:33
ʷ Mt 10:22 ˣ Ps 2:8;
Rev 3:21

2:27 ʸ Rev 12:5; 19:15 ᶻ Ps 2:9;
Isa 30:14; Jer 19:11

2:28 ᵃ Rev 22:16

2:29 ᵇ S ver 7

3:1 ᶜ Rev 1:11
ᵈ S Rev 1:4
ᵉ S Rev 1:16

E 1Jn 3:20 ◀▶ Rev 3:1
M 1Pe 5:4 ◀▶ Rev 3:7
P Rev 1:7 ◀▶ Rev 6:12
E Rev 2:17 ◀▶ Rev 3:1
T Rev 2:17 ◀▶ Rev 3:6
E Rev 2:29 ◀▶ Rev 3:6
G Rev 1:4 ◀▶ Rev 4:5   E Rev 2:23 ◀
S Rev 2:10 ◀▶ Rev 3:14–16

E Rev 2:7 ◀▶ Rev 2:17
T Rev 2:7 ◀▶ Rev 2:17   R Rev 2:5 ◀
E Rev 2:11 ◀▶ Rev 2:29
T Rev 2:11 ◀▶ Rev 2:29

ᵉ 27 Psalm 2:9 ᶠ 1 Or *messenger*; also in verses 7 and 14 ᵍ 1 Or *the sevenfold Spirit*

deeds;f you have a reputation of being alive, but you are dead.g ²Wake up! Strengthen what remains and is about to die, for I have not found your deeds complete in the sight of my God. ³Remember, therefore, what you have received and heard; obey it, and repent.h But if you do not wake up, I will come like a thief,i and you will not know at what time j I will come to you.

⁴Yet you have a few people in Sardis who have not soiled their clothes.k They will walk with me, dressed in white,l for they are worthy. ⁵He who overcomesm will, like them, be dressed in white.n I will never blot out his name from the book of life,o but will acknowledge his name before my Fatherp and his angels. ⁶He who has an ear, let him hearq what the Spirit says to the churches.

To the Church in Philadelphia

⁷"To the angel of the church in Philadelphiar write:

These are the words of him who is holys and true,t who holds the key of David.u What he opens no one can shut, and what he shuts no one can open. ⁸I know your deeds.v See, I have placed before you an open doorw that no one can shut. I know that you have little strength, yet you have kept my word and have not denied my name.x ⁹I will make those who are of the synagogue of Satan,y who claim to be Jews though they are not,z but are liars—I will make them come and fall down at your feeta and acknowledge that I have loved you.b ¹⁰Since you have kept my command to endure patiently, I will also keep youc from the hour of trial that is going to come upon the whole worldd to teste those who live on the earth.f

¹¹I am coming soon.g Hold on to what you have,h so that no one will take your crown.i ¹²Him who overcomesj I will make a pillark in the temple of my God. Never again will he leave it. I will write on him the name of my God¹ and the name of the city of my God,m the new Jerusalem,n which is coming down out of heaven from my God; and I will also write on him my new name. ¹³He who has an ear, let him hearo what the Spirit says to the churches.

To the Church in Laodicea

¹⁴"To the angel of the church in Laodiceap write:

These are the words of the Amen, the faithful and true witness,q the ruler of God's creation.r ¹⁵I know your deeds,s that you are neither cold nor hot.t I wish you were either one or the other! ¹⁶So, because you are lukewarm—neither hot nor cold—I am about to spit you out of my mouth. ¹⁷You say, 'I am rich; I have acquired wealth and do not need a thing.'u But you do not realize that you are wretched, pitiful, poor, blind and naked.v ¹⁸I counsel you to buy from me gold refined in the fire,w so you can become rich; and white clothesx to wear, so you can cover your shameful nakedness;y and salve to put on your eyes, so you can see.

¹⁹Those whom I love I rebuke and discipline.z So be earnest, and repent.a ²⁰Here I am! I stand at the doorb and knock. If anyone hears my voice and opens the door,c I will come ind and eat with him, and he with me.

²¹To him who overcomes,e I will give the right to sit with me on my throne,f just as I overcameg and sat down with my Father on his throne. ²²He who has an ear, let him hearh

what the Spirit says to the churches."

The Throne in Heaven

4 After this I looked, and there before me was a door standing open in heaven. And the voice I had first heard speaking to me like a trumpet said, "Come up here, and I will show you what must take place after this."[1] ²At once I was in the Spirit, and there before me was a throne in heaven with someone sitting on it. ³And the one who sat there had the appearance of jasper and carnelian. A rainbow, resembling an emerald, encircled the throne. ⁴Surrounding the throne were twenty-four other thrones, and seated on them were twenty-four elders. They were dressed in white and had crowns of gold on their heads. ⁵From the throne came flashes of lightning, rumblings and peals of thunder. Before the throne, seven lamps were blazing. These are the seven spirits[h] of God. ⁶Also before the throne there was what looked like a sea of glass, clear as crystal.

In the center, around the throne, were four living creatures, and they were covered with eyes, in front and in back. ⁷The first living creature was like a lion, the second was like an ox, the third had a face like a man, the fourth was like a flying eagle. ⁸Each of the four living creatures had six wings and was covered with eyes all around, even under his wings. Day and night they never stop saying:

h 5 Or the sevenfold Spirit

4:1 This chapter begins the third portion of John's revelation concerning "what will take place later" (1:19). These events will be fulfilled during the seven-year tribulation and the Millennium.

4:1–3 John begins this section on the end time events by saying "After this . . ." (4:1), indicating that something important had transpired. Some scholars feel that this phrase refers to the rapture. Others believe that this phrase is merely a transition phrase between the two visions, indicating that John had acted on the instructions of the first vision and was thereby prepared for another word from God.

In this vision, John described a voice from heaven that called him to look at the things that would happen in the future. John saw a throne in heaven and Jesus Christ sitting on it in all his glory and majesty, surrounded by a rainbow. Note the similarity between this vision of Christ and Ezekiel's vision in Eze 1:26–28. Whenever God allows humans to see him, they see Christ, "for in Christ all the fullness of the Deity lives in bodily form" (Col 2:9; see Jn 1:18; Col 1:15).

4:4 John saw twenty-four elders seated on twenty-four seats. These elders were "dressed in white." While some scholars believe these elders to be exalted angels, others believe that this court of heaven represents the resurrected saints of both the OT and NT. The fact that they are seated, wearing white raiment, and golden crowns repudiates the view that these are angelic beings but rather provides powerful evidence that these beings are raptured believers. Since we do not receive our resurrection bodies when we die (see 1Th 4:13–17), this event must take place after the rapture of the church.

Note that the word translated "elder" almost always refers to the leading representative of a family, tribe or nation and is never applied to angels since they cannot grow old or mature. Since Jesus Christ, the twenty four elders, and the saints are the only ones seen in heaven with crowns, these twenty-four elders may represent the NT and OT saints who rose with Christ at his resurrection (Mt 27:52–53). Others contend that these twenty-four are the twelve OT patriarchs and the twelve NT disciples. Since the number twelve often relates to human government, the number twenty-four possibly suggests the perfection of the government of God's kingdom.

4:5 John's reference to "seven lamps" as the "seven spirits of God," relates to seven aspects or characteristics of God. Compare this verse to Zec 4:10 and the prophet's vision of the seven eyes of the Lord, referring to seven distinct characteristics of the one triune God. Isaiah also describes the coming Messiah, the Son of God, as possessing seven spirits or divine characteristics of God (see Isa 11:2).

4:6–9 John saw the crystal sea that stretches before the throne of God. In symbolic language, John described the "four living creatures" which surround the throne of God. Some suggest that these beings are manifestations of the characteristics of God since Scripture records that they are "in the center, around the throne" (4:6). Other scholars believe that these "living creatures" are angelic beings described as seraphim (see Isa 6:1–8) and cherubim (see Eze 1:4–28), seen in this vision surrounding God's throne, worshiping him, giving him glory and praising the Lamb with harps. Later they call forth the four horsemen (see 6:1–8) and provide the seven judgment bowls to the angels (see 15:7).

"Holy, holy, holy
is the Lord God Almighty,[f]
who was, and is, and is to come."[g]

[9] Whenever the living creatures give glory, honor and thanks to him who sits on the throne[h] and who lives for ever and ever,[i] [10] the twenty-four elders[j] fall down before him[k] who sits on the throne,[l] and worship him who lives for ever and ever. They lay their crowns before the throne and say:

[11] "You are worthy, our Lord
and God,
to receive glory and honor and
power,[m]
for you created all things,
and by your will they were
created
and have their being."[n]

The Scroll and the Lamb

5 Then I saw in the right hand of him who sat on the throne[o] a scroll with writing on both sides[p] and sealed[q] with seven seals. [2] And I saw a mighty angel[r] proclaiming in a loud voice, "Who is worthy to break the seals and open the scroll?" [3] But no one in heaven or on earth or under the earth could open the scroll or even look inside it. [4] I wept and wept because no one was found who was worthy to open the scroll or look inside. [5] Then one of the elders said to me, "Do not weep! See, the Lion[s] of the tribe of Judah,[t] the Root of David,[u] has triumphed. He is able to open the scroll and its seven seals."

E Rev 4:1 ◀ ▶ Rev 22:6–7

[6] Then I saw a Lamb,[v] looking as if it had been slain, standing in the center of the throne, encircled by the four living creatures[w] and the elders.[x] He had seven horns and seven eyes,[y] which are the seven spirits[i,z] of God sent out into all the earth. [7] He came and took the scroll from the right hand of him who sat on the throne.[a] [8] And when he had taken it, the four living creatures[b] and the twenty-four elders[c] fell down before the Lamb. Each one had a harp[d] and they were holding golden bowls full of incense, which are the prayers[e] of the saints. [9] And they sang a new song:[f]

"You are worthy[g] to take the scroll
and to open its seals,
because you were slain,
and with your blood[h] you
purchased[i] men for God
from every tribe and language and
people and nation.[j]
[10] You have made them to be a kingdom
and priests[k] to serve our God,
and they will reign on the
earth."[l]

[11] Then I looked and heard the voice of many angels, numbering thousands upon thousands, and ten thousand times ten thousand.[m] They encircled the throne

E Rev 4:2 ◀ ▶ Rev 11:11
G Rev 4:5 ◀ ▶ Rev 19:10
D Rev 1:5 ◀ ▶ Rev 7:14
M Rev 3:21 ◀ ▶ Rev 11:15–19

[i] 6 Or *the sevenfold Spirit*

4:8 [f] Isa 6:3; S Rev 1:8; [g] S Rev 1:4
4:9 [h] ver 2; Ps 47:8; S Rev 5:1; [i] S Rev 1:18
4:10 [j] S ver 4; [k] Dt 33:3; Rev 5:8, 14; 7:11; 11:16; [l] S ver 2
4:11 [m] Rev 1:6; 5:12 [n] Ac 14:15; Rev 10:6
5:1 [o] ver 7,13; Rev 4:2,9; 6:16; [p] Eze 2:9,10; [q] Isa 29:11; Da 12:4
5:2 [r] Rev 10:1
5:5 [s] Ge 49:9; [t] S Heb 7:14; [u] Isa 11:1,10; Ro 15:12; Rev 22:16
5:6 [v] ver 8,9,12,13; S Jn 1:29; [w] S Rev 4:6; [x] S Rev 4:4; [y] Zec 4:10; [z] S Rev 1:4
5:7 [a] S ver 1
5:8 [b] S Rev 4:6; [c] S Rev 4:4; [d] Rev 14:2; 15:2; [e] Ps 141:2; Rev 8:3, 4
5:9 [f] Ps 40:3; 98:1; 149:1; Isa 42:10; Rev 14:3,4; [g] Rev 4:11; [h] Heb 9:12; [i] S 1Co 6:20; [j] S Rev 13:7
5:10 [k] S 1Pe 2:5; [l] Rev 3:21; 20:4
5:11 [m] Da 7:10; Heb 12:22; Jude 14

4:10–11 The twenty-four elders cast their crowns at the feet of Christ to give him glory. They announce that the purpose of all of his creation is to exist for his pleasure. Humanity's purpose is to love Christ and glorify him by their life, words and actions.

5:1–4 John saw God, seated on his throne, holding a scroll that was "sealed with seven seals" (5:1). In ancient times a scroll addressed to a king often had a secret message written on the bottom of the page. When the scroll was rolled up and sealed, this message was effectively hidden from the courier who could only read the outer portion of the scroll.

5:5–7 Only Jesus, "the Lion of the tribe of Judah" (5:5), was able to break the seals and open the scroll.

5:8–10 John described the twenty-four elders worshiping Jesus with harps and a new song. These elders held golden bowls that were full of incense and described as "the prayers of the saints" (5:8). That this incense represented the faithful prayers of believers reminds us of the incense offered in the Holy of Holies of the temple. Note also the use of harps in the worship of God. The twenty-four elders prophesied with their harps as they declared that God would make believers "a kingdom and priests to serve our God, and they will reign on the earth" (5:10).

5:11–14 The prophet described a glorious scene when the millions of inhabitants of heaven join to offer praise to Jesus Christ and worship "him who sits on the throne" (5:13).

The Seven Letters to the Churches

THE LETTERS TO the seven churches in Revelation are the last direct words we have from Jesus Christ. These seven short epistles are similar to Jesus' parables and his prophecy on the Mt. of Olives.

Ephesus (2:1–7)—The Need for Revival
Ephesus was the wealthy capital of the Roman province of Asia and an important commercial and political center. Though Ephesus was famous for its temple to Diana, one of the seven wonders of the ancient world, many of Ephesus' citizens came to faith in Christ under Paul's ministry. Paul founded the church at Ephesus and later asked Timothy to be its pastor (see Ac 19—20). The Ephesian church was also John's home church.

In the first of these brief letters the Lord commends the church at Ephesus for its genuine good works and its patient endurance. Yet Christ also criticized this church for abandoning their "first love" (Rev 2:4). Though their doctrine was uncompromised, their passion for Christ was growing dim. Jesus urged this church to "Remember the height from which you have fallen! Repent and do the things you did at first" (2:5), or else he would remove the light of God's truth from them. Tragically the church at Ephesus did not seek revival, and its spiritual light faded away, transferred to the growing, vibrant churches of the western Roman empire.

Smyrna (2:8–11)—Stand Firm in Persecution
Smyrna was a wealthy port city known for its devotion to Rome and its pagan gods. The apostle Paul probably founded the church at Smyrna on his missionary journey to Ephesus (see Ac 19:10). Christ's message to Smyrna is one of praise and commendation. Though the church was severely persecuted by both the Jews and the Romans and kept in a state of perpetual poverty, the church at Smyrna was rich in spiritual gifts, perseverance and steadfast faith.

Christ warned the believers in Smyrna that they would have to undergo more persecution, but he promised them a "crown of life" (2:10) if they would remain faithful. Christ also promised that whoever "overcomes will not be hurt at all by the second death" (2:11), referring to the spiritual death of the soul who rejects salvation.

Surely it is no accident that Smyrna and Philadelphia—the only two churches of these seven to escape Christ's condemnation—have both survived over the centuries. Today Smyrna boasts a population of over 300,000, a large percentage of which claim to be Christians.

Pergamos (2:12–17)—The Seduction of Idolatry

Pergamos, located north of Smyrna in modern-day Turkey, was noted for its temples and sensual worship of pagan gods. After the fall of Babylon, Pergamos became the center of the Babylonian mystery religions. It also housed three huge temples that were used to worship the Roman emperor. One of the chief gods of Pergamos was Aesculapius, the god of healing, represented by a serpent. This serpent image was struck into many of the city's coins. Public festivals and ceremonies often centered on licentious parties and temple prostitution.

Christ commended the church at Pergamos for its faithfulness to his name and for its good works in the midst of idolatry and satanic spiritual assaults. Yet the church was in danger of losing its holy walk with God by tolerating those who committed sexual immorality and ate foods sacrificed to idols. Jesus warned that anyone who followed these practices should have no part in the church. Christ said he would give the believers in Pergamos spiritual food from heaven if they turned from food offered to idols, and he promised to also give them "a new name written on it, known only to him who receives it" (2:17).

Thyatira (2:18–29)—The Lack of Self-discipline

Thyatira was a wealthy city known for its manufacture of purple cloth (see Ac 16:14). Located in modern-day Turkey, Thyatira is now called Ak-hissar. The church at Thyatira was commended for its love in practical service to the Lord and to others. However, it also tolerated sin within its community and lacked a zeal for true doctrine and Christian discipline.

Certain antinomian philosophers in the days of the early church taught the false doctrine that Christians could indulge in immorality as much as they desired because their sins were automatically forgiven. Though this was a direct contradiction to Scripture (see Ro 6:15), a false prophetess pressed this belief on the church at Thyatira and led the church into immorality just as Jezebel in the OT had led Israel away from the true worship of God. These sinners forgot that without holiness no one can stand before the Lord (see Heb 12:14). Though she had been given time to repent, this prophetess refused, and Christ declared that he would punish her and her followers. Those who had rejected her sinful suggestions were promised a reward—"authority over the nations" (Rev 2:26) and "the morning star" (2:28).

Sardis (3:1–7)—The Lure of Materialism

Sardis was the capital city of the wealthy King Croesus. The residents of this city carried sardis stones as amulets to ward off evil spirits. They also were consumed with securing material success and wealth. The church at Sardis had fallen prey to this lure of materialism and carnal concerns. Though they boasted in their accomplishments, this church had lost its spiritual vitality. Christ's only words of commendation were directed to a remnant who truly followed him. Christ's word to the church at Sardis was a command to "Wake up! Strengthen what remains and is about to die" (3:2).

The church at Sardis stands as a warning to churches today. While we tend to look at buildings, finances and the number of worshipers, God examines the heart of his church and its members as he evaluates the true spiritual health of the church. No matter how dead a church may seem, God may still have a faithful few "who have not soiled their clothes" (3:4). Unless we, too, watch carefully for our Lord's return, our eyes will turn to this world and its cares. The prayer of every believer should be that we join that faithful remnant and walk closely with God.

Philadelphia (3:7–13)—Faithful Love and Service

Thirty miles inland from Sardis was the city of Philadelphia. The church at Philadelphia was composed of a small group of poor Christians, rich only in the eyes of God. Of the seven churches, Philadelphia and Smyrna were the only ones to escape the Lord's criticism.

Christ commends the church at Philadelphia for its strength, faithfulness and evangelical witness. They believed the promise of Christ's second coming as they patiently watched for his appearance. Christ knew about their service for him and others and responded by giving them "an open door" (3:8) of witness that no one could shut.

Because of their faithfulness to him, Christ issued an incredible promise to spare the church at Philadelphia "from the hour of trial that is going to come upon the whole world to test those who live on the earth" (3:10). Though some suggest that this verse meant that Christ would deliver the believers at Philadelphia from the horrible persecutions of the first century, some scholars contend that this verse may also indicate a deliverance from the horrors of the tribulation.

Christ also admonishes the believers at Philadelphia to "hold on to what you have, so that no one will take your crown" (3:11). Those who remained steadfast would become pillars in God's temple in heaven. This unusual statement refers to the custom in Philadelphia that rewarded noble citizens with the honor of having their name inscribed on a temple pillar.

Laodicea (3:14–22)—Lukewarm and Self-satisfied

Built along the Meander River, Laodicea was a profitable trade center that manufactured a special eye ointment that was valued throughout the Roman empire. It also produced a unique, rich, black wool as part of a flourishing garment industry. Laodicea suffered a devastating earthquake during the reign of Rome but refused all outside help to rebuild the city. This self-sufficient attitude spilled over into the church and propelled it toward spiritual disaster.

Though some of the churches exhibited serious spiritual faults, the Lord commended something in every one of the churches with the exception of the church of Laodicea. Many of the believers in Laodicea followed a "prosperity gospel" that focused on their worldly wealth, spiritual pride and personal needs and desires. The Laodiceans believed that their success was evidence that they were pleasing God. Utterly blinded to their true spiritual condition, these believers felt that they were almost perfect even though they tolerated a hybrid worship of materialism and Christ.

The only good thing that can be said about this church is that there were still a few souls remaining within it who loved the Lord, but even their love was growing cold. The

Lord's rebuke is clear: "Because you are lukewarm—neither hot nor cold—I am about to spit you out of my mouth" (3:16). God hates lukewarm religiosity, and his judgment will fall on any church that compromises with evil.

Christ then urged the Laodiceans to turn back to true worship. To a city dependent on the garment industry and medicinal eye salve, the Lord advised the Laodicean believers to put on garments of righteousness and "salve to put on your eyes" (3:18) to heal their spiritual vision. Although the letter to the Laodiceans is filled with warnings, the Lord's chastening indicates that he still loves them even though they have gone astray.

and the living creatures[n] and the elders.[o]
[12]In a loud voice they sang:

"Worthy is the Lamb,[p] who was slain,[q]
to receive power and wealth and
  wisdom and strength
and honor and glory and praise!"[r]

[13]Then I heard every creature in heaven and on earth and under the earth[s] and on the sea, and all that is in them, singing:

"To him who sits on the throne[t] and
  to the Lamb[u]
be praise and honor and glory and
  power,
    for ever and ever!"[v]

[14]The four living creatures[w] said, "Amen,"[x] and the elders[y] fell down and worshiped.[z]

The Seals

6 I watched as the Lamb[a] opened the first of the seven seals.[b] Then I heard one of the four living creatures[c] say in a voice like thunder,[d] "Come!" [2]I looked, and there before me was a white horse![e] Its rider held a bow, and he was given a crown,[f] and he rode out as a conqueror bent on conquest.[g]

[3]When the Lamb opened the second seal, I heard the second living creature[h] say, "Come!" [4]Then another horse came out, a fiery red one.[i] Its rider was given power to take peace from the earth[j] and to make men slay each other. To him was given a large sword.

[5]When the Lamb opened the third seal, I heard the third living creature[k] say, "Come!" I looked, and there before me was a black horse![l] Its rider was holding

---

6:1 John watched Jesus open one of the seals on the scroll, indicating that the end-time judgment of the unrepentant sinners on earth had finally come. The opening of this first seal ushers in the tribulation, a seven-year period that also begins with the antichrist signing a seven-year covenant with Israel. This tribulation concludes with Christ's glorious return at the end of the Battle of Armageddon. From this moment until Christ destroys Satan's antichrist, "the great day of their wrath has come" (6:17).

6:2-8 *The Four Horsemen.* The first four seals of the seven seal judgments are commonly referred to as the four horsemen of the apocalypse because riders on horses carry out these judgments. These seven seal judgments begin the seven years of the tribulation and are part of "the great day of their wrath" (6:17). The apostle Paul clearly promised that the church would escape this coming wrath (see 1Th 1:10). Since the tribulation period begins with the wrath of God poured out in the seven seal judgments, the church will be in heaven at this time.

The first seal that begins the day of God's wrath is the white horseman of false peace. John saw a white horse and a rider with a bow. Though the color white usually represents peace, in this case this is a false peace because the rider rides out "as a conqueror bent on conquest" (6:2). Note the absence of any arrows or a quiver. This may symbolize a disarmament and false peace before his attack on his enemies. Some scholars believe that this white horseman refers to a spirit of conquest as one of the natural calamities of these judgments. Others contend that this horseman represents the antichrist who will falsely present himself to the world as a peacemaker before conquering the world. Daniel's prophecy foreshadowed the coming of this antichrist who "when they feel secure, . . . will destroy many" (Da 8:25).

The second seal opens to reveal the red horseman of war. This horseman was given a "large sword" (6:4) to create cataclysmic wars. During the tribulation, bloody warfare will devastate the world by killing millions of people. Some scholars suggest that as many as two-thirds of the world's population may die during the tribulation.

The third seal opens to reveal the third horseman holding a set of weights and balances in his hand and riding on the black horse of famine. The angel revealed that the famine would be so severe that a daily wage will only buy enough food for one person, leaving no food for other family members. Strangely, despite worldwide famine, the angel prohibited the horseman from harming the oil and wine. Some scholars feel that since olive trees and grapevines have deep roots, this famine would not immediately affect these crops. Other suggest that since oil and wine were associated with ancient wealth and comfort, this may suggest that some people will still possess great wealth and not feel the immediate effects of this worldwide famine (see Jas 5:1-3).

The fourth seal is opened to reveal a pale horse with a rider that symbolizes death and who is given the authority to destroy a fourth of the earth. The four-part judgment delivered by this horseman echoes the four judgments that are often found together in the OT as symbols of God's wrath. These four instruments are described in Eze 14:21 as "sword and famine and wild beasts and plague." Note that after the flood God instilled a fear of humanity in animals (see Ge 9:2). During the horrible judgments of the tribulation God will remove this fear, allowing the wild beasts to attack humans until the Messiah returns. The Messiah will then reinstitute a covenant of peace between humans and animals (see Isa 11:6-9; Hos 2:18).

a pair of scales in his hand. ⁶Then I heard what sounded like a voice among the four living creatures,ᵐ saying, "A quart*ʲ* of wheat for a day's wages,ᵏ and three quarts of barley for a day's wages,ᵏⁿ and do not damageᵒ the oil and the wine!"

⁷When the Lamb opened the fourth seal, I heard the voice of the fourth living creatureᵖ say, "Come!" ⁸I looked, and there before me was a pale horse!ᵠ Its rider was named Death, and Hadesʳ was following close behind him. They were given power over a fourth of the earth to kill by sword, famine and plague, and by the wild beasts of the earth.ˢ

⁹When he opened the fifth seal, I saw underᵗ the altarᵘ the souls of those who had been slainᵛ because of the word of Godʷ and the testimony they had maintained. ¹⁰They called out in a loud voice, "How long,ˣ Sovereign Lord,ʸ holy and true,ᶻ until you judge the inhabitants of the eartha and avenge our blood?"ᵇ ¹¹Then each of them was given a white robe,ᶜ and they were told to wait a little longer, until the number of their fellow servants and brothers who were to be killed as they had been was completed.ᵈ

¹²I watched as he opened the sixth

P *Rev 2:27* ◀ ▶ *Rev 9:12–15*

6:6 ᵐ S Rev 4:6,7
ⁿ Eze 4:16
ᵒ Rev 7:1,3; 9:4
6:7 ᵖ Rev 4:7
6:8 ᵠ Zec 6:3
ʳ Hos 13:14;
Rev 1:18; 20:13,14
ˢ Jer 15:2,3; 24:10;
Eze 5:12,17
6:9 ᵗ Ex 29:12;
Lev 4:7
ᵘ Rev 14:18; 16:7
ᵛ Rev 20:4 ʷ Ro 1:2;
S Heb 4:12
6:10 ˣ Ps 119:84;
Zec 1:12 ʸ Lk 2:29;
2Pe 2:1 ᶻ S Rev 3:7
ᵃ S Rev 3:10
ᵇ Dt 32:43; 2Ki 9:7;
Ps 79:10; Rev 16:6;
18:20; 19:2
6:11 ᶜ S Rev 3:4
ᵈ Heb 11:40
6:12 ᵉ Ps 97:4;
Isa 29:6; Eze 38:19;
Rev 8:5; 11:13;
16:18 ᶠ S Mt 24:29
ᵍ Isa 50:3
6:13 ʰ S Mt 24:29;
Rev 8:10; 9:1
ⁱ Isa 34:4
6:14 ʲ S 2Pe 3:10;
Rev 20:11; 21:1
ᵏ Ps 46:2; Isa 54:10;
Jer 4:24; Eze 38:20;
Na 1:5; Rev 16:20;
21:1
6:15 ˡ Rev 19:18
ᵐ Isa 2:10,19,21
6:16 ⁿ Hos 10:8;
Lk 23:30
ᵒ S Rev 5:1
6:17 ᵖ Joel 1:15;
2:1,2,11,31;
Zep 1:14,15;
Rev 16:14
ᵠ Ps 76:7; Na 1:6;

seal. There was a great earthquake.ᵉ The sun turned blackᶠ like sackclothᵍ made of goat hair, the whole moon turned blood red, ¹³and the stars in the sky fell to earth,ʰ as late figs drop from a fig treeⁱ when shaken by a strong wind. ¹⁴The sky receded like a scroll, rolling up,ʲ and every mountain and island was removed from its place.ᵏ

¹⁵Then the kings of the earth, the H princes, the generals, the rich, the N mighty, and every slave and every free manˡ hid in caves and among the rocks of the mountains.ᵐ ¹⁶They called to the mountains and the rocks, "Fall on usⁿ and hide us from the face of him who sits on the throneᵒ and from the wrath of the Lamb! ¹⁷For the great dayᵖ of their wrath has come, and who can stand?"ᵠ

144,000 Sealed

7 After this I saw four angels standing at the four cornersʳ of the earth, holding back the four windsˢ of the earth to preventᵗ any wind from blowing on

H *Rev 3:16* ◀ ▶ *Rev 11:18*
N *Rev 3:17–18* ◀ ▶ *Rev 13:9*

Mal 3:2 **7:1** ʳ Isa 11:12 ˢ Jer 49:36; Eze 37:9; Da 7:2; Zec 6:5; Mt 24:31 ᵗ S Rev 6:6

j 6 Greek *a choinix* (probably about a liter) *k 6* Greek *a denarius*

6:9–11 When Jesus opened the fifth seal, John saw the souls of those who had died for their faith. The twenty-four crowned elders in Rev 4:1–10 represent the raptured church, so this new group of believers is made up of those Jewish and Gentile disciples who became believers during the early days of the tribulation.

John then described the response of the martyrs to their oppressors, crying out to God for vengeance. This fifth seal provides additional confirmation that during the seven-year tribulation most believers will be martyred for their faith because these souls are told to wait until the other martyrs join them.

6:12–17 When Christ opens the sixth seal, he unleashes a devastating array of natural catastrophes. A massive earthquake will be the first in a series of major disturbances that mark God's wrath during the tribulation. Note that Jesus warned that the increase of earthquakes would signify his return (see Mt 24:7). In the last half-century, scientists have tracked the dramatic increase of killer earthquakes (6.5 or above on the Richter scale) from only 9 killer quakes during the 1950s to over 125 killer quakes in the first half of the 1990s alone. Jesus reminded his disciples to be alert for the signs of his coming for "when these things begin to take place,

stand up and lift up your heads, because your redemption is drawing near" (Lk 21:28).

The heavens will also signal the wrath of the Lamb with celestial phenomena that will terrify the inhabitants of earth (see Isa 2:19). John prophesies a devastating meteor shower (6:13) and a tumultuous shaking of the heavens (see Isa 34:4) that will announce "the great day of their wrath" (6:17). (Though there are many similarities between the events of the sixth seal judgment and those at Armageddon, there will be an interval of at least three and a half-years between the sixth seal judgment and this final battle. The events of Rev 7:1—19:10 will occur during this interval.)

7:1–8 There is a pause after the sixth seal during which John describes two groups of redeemed souls. The first group is identified as twelve thousand persons from each of the twelve tribes of Israel—144,000 Jews. (Though today many Jews are unsure of their tribal lineage, this sealing of the Jews by tribe indicates that God will miraculously reveal the tribal identity of his people in the last days.)

God will choose these Jews to be his witnesses to share the gospel message with the world. Revelation does not reveal how or when these Jews become followers of the Messiah. After the rapture of the

the land or on the sea or on any tree. ²Then I saw another angel coming up from the east, having the seal^u of the living God.^v He called out in a loud voice to the four angels who had been given power to harm the land and the sea:^w ³"Do not harm^x the land or the sea or the trees until we put a seal on the foreheads^y of the servants of our God." ⁴Then I heard the number^z of those who were sealed: 144,000^a from all the tribes of Israel.

⁵From the tribe of Judah 12,000 were sealed,
  from the tribe of Reuben 12,000,
  from the tribe of Gad 12,000,
⁶from the tribe of Asher 12,000,
  from the tribe of Naphtali 12,000,
  from the tribe of Manasseh 12,000,
⁷from the tribe of Simeon 12,000,
  from the tribe of Levi 12,000,
  from the tribe of Issachar 12,000,
⁸from the tribe of Zebulun 12,000,
  from the tribe of Joseph 12,000,
  from the tribe of Benjamin 12,000.

The Great Multitude in White Robes

⁹After this I looked and there before me was a great multitude that no one could count, from every nation, tribe, people and language,^b standing before the throne^c and in front of the Lamb. They were wearing white robes^d and were holding palm branches in their hands. ¹⁰And they cried out in a loud voice:

"Salvation belongs to our God,^e
who sits on the throne,^f
and to the Lamb."

¹¹All the angels were standing around the throne and around the elders^g and the four living creatures.^h They fell down on their faces^i before the throne and worshiped God, ¹²saying:

"Amen!
Praise and glory
and wisdom and thanks and honor
and power and strength
be to our God for ever and ever.
Amen!"^j

¹³Then one of the elders asked me, "These in white robes^k—who are they, and where did they come from?"

¹⁴I answered, "Sir, you know."

And he said, "These are they who have come out of the great tribulation; they have washed their robes^l and made them white in the blood of the Lamb.^m ¹⁵Therefore,

"they are before the throne of God^n
and serve him^o day and night in his temple;^p
and he who sits on the throne^q will spread his tent over them.^r
¹⁶Never again will they hunger;
never again will they thirst.^s
The sun will not beat upon them,
nor any scorching heat.^t
¹⁷For the Lamb at the center of the throne will be their shepherd;^u
he will lead them to springs of living water.^v
And God will wipe away every tear from their eyes."^w

The Seventh Seal and the Golden Censer

8 When he opened the seventh seal,^x there was silence in heaven for about half an hour.

²And I saw the seven angels^y who

H Eph 5:27 ◀ ▶ Rev 14:1–5
O 1Jn 5:12 ◀ ▶ Rev 19:1
D Rev 5:9 ◀ ▶ Rev 12:11
K Rev 1:18 ◀ ▶ Rev 12:11
S Isa 61:3 ◀ ▶ Rev 21:4

7:2 ^u Rev 9:4 ^v S Mt 16:16 ^w ver 1
7:3 ^x S Rev 6:6 ^y Eze 9:4; Rev 9:4; 14:1; 22:4
7:4 ^z Rev 9:16 ^a Rev 14:1,3
7:9 ^b S Rev 13:7 ^c ver 15 ^d S Rev 3:4
7:10 ^e Ps 3:8; Rev 12:10; 19:1 ^f S Rev 5:1
7:11 ^g S Rev 4:4 ^h S Rev 4:6 ^i S Rev 4:10
7:12 ^j S Ro 11:36; Rev 5:12-14
7:13 ^k S Rev 3:4
7:14 ^l Rev 22:14 ^m Heb 9:14; 1Jn 1:7; Rev 12:11
7:15 ^n ver 9 ^o Rev 22:3 ^p Rev 11:19 ^q S Rev 5:1 ^r Isa 4:5, 6; Rev 21:3
7:16 ^s Jn 6:35 ^t Isa 49:10
7:17 ^u S Jn 10:11 ^v S Jn 4:10 ^w Isa 25:8; 35:10; 51:11; 65:19; Rev 21:4
8:1 ^x Rev 6:1
8:2 ^y ver 6-13; Rev 9:1,13; 11:15

---

church, God would not leave the earth without a witness, so these 144,000 Jews will be divinely protected from the terrible persecution of the antichrist and the false prophet to share God's good news during the tribulation. After completing their special mission, the 144,000, identified as those who "were purchased from among men and offered as firstfruits to God and the Lamb" (14:4), will be transferred from earth to heaven.

7:9–17 John then describes "a great multitude" (7:9) from every nation and tribe who "come out of the great tribulation" (7:14), the greatest harvest of souls in history. Though millions will accept Christ during the tribulation, the persecution of that period will be so severe that most of these tribulation saints will be martyred for their faith. This "great multitude" (7:9) will rejoice in the blessings of heaven and receive special rewards and honors as they minister "before the throne of God and serve him day and night in his temple" (7:15).

8:1 The seventh seal judgment begins with an ominous "silence in heaven for about half an hour"

stand before God, and to them were given seven trumpets.[z]

[3] Another angel,[a] who had a golden censer, came and stood at the altar. He was given much incense to offer, with the prayers of all the saints,[b] on the golden altar[c] before the throne. [4] The smoke of the incense, together with the prayers of the saints, went up before God[d] from the angel's hand. [5] Then the angel took the censer, filled it with fire from the altar,[e] and hurled it on the earth; and there came peals of thunder,[f] rumblings, flashes of lightning and an earthquake.[g]

The Trumpets

[6] Then the seven angels who had the seven trumpets[h] prepared to sound them.

[7] The first angel[i] sounded his trumpet, and there came hail and fire[j] mixed with blood, and it was hurled down upon the earth. A third[k] of the earth was burned up, a third of the trees were burned up, and all the green grass was burned up.[l]

[8] The second angel sounded his trumpet, and something like a huge mountain,[m] all ablaze, was thrown into the sea. A third[n] of the sea turned into blood,[o] [9] a third[p] of the living creatures in the sea died, and a third of the ships were destroyed.

[10] The third angel sounded his trumpet, and a great star, blazing like a torch, fell from the sky[q] on a third of the rivers and on the springs of water[r]— [11] the name of the star is Wormwood.[1] A third[s] of the waters turned bitter, and many people died from the waters that had become bitter.[t]

[12] The fourth angel sounded his trumpet, and a third of the sun was struck, a third of the moon, and a third of the stars, so that a third[u] of them turned dark.[v] A third of the day was without light, and also a third of the night.[w]

[13] As I watched, I heard an eagle that was flying in midair[x] call out in a loud voice: "Woe! Woe! Woe[y] to the inhabitants of the earth,[z] because of the trumpet blasts about to be sounded by the other three angels!"

9 The fifth angel sounded his trumpet, and I saw a star that had fallen from the sky to the earth.[a] The star was given the key[b] to the shaft of the Abyss.[c]

8:2 [z] S Mt 24:31
8:3 [a] Rev 7:2; [b] Rev 5:8 [c] ver 5; Ex 30:1-6; Heb 9:4; Rev 9:13
8:4 [d] Ps 141:2
8:5 [e] Lev 16:12,13 [f] S Rev 4:5 [g] S Rev 6:12
8:6 [h] S ver 2
8:7 [i] S ver 2 [j] Eze 38:22 [k] ver 7-12; Rev 9:15,18; 12:4 [l] Rev 9:4
8:8 [m] Jer 51:25 [n] S ver 7 [o] Rev 16:3
8:9 [p] S ver 7
8:10 [q] Isa 14:12; Rev 6:13; 9:1 [r] Rev 14:7; 16:4
8:11 [s] S ver 7 [t] Jer 9:15; 23:15
8:12 [u] S ver 7 [v] Ex 10:21-23; Rev 6:12,13 [w] Eze 32:7
8:13 [x] Rev 14:6; 19:17 [y] Rev 9:12; 11:14; 12:12 [z] S Rev 3:10
9:1 [a] Rev 8:10 [b] Rev 1:18 [c] ver 2, 11; S Lk 8:31

1 11 That is, Bitterness

(8:1). After the horrors of the first six seal judgments, God pauses for a little while to allow men to reconsider their choices and repent of their sins. Though the seventh seal does not contain any special instrument of judgment itself, it does introduce the seven trumpet judgments.

8:2–5 John then receives a vision of seven angels with seven trumpets, symbolizing the coming wrath of God that will be poured out on the earth as never before. Another angel appeared and offered the prayers of the saints to God like incense. These prayers likely cry, "Come, Lord Jesus" (22:20).

8:7 The first trumpet triggers an outpouring of "hail and fire mixed with blood" (8:7). This cataclysmic judgment will burn one third of the trees and grass. Since humanity has abused the planet, the day of reckoning is at hand.

8:8–9 The second trumpet unleashes a huge chunk of a volcano or a large, burning meteor that impacts the ocean. Such an impact would create an astonishing tidal wave, sinking ships and devastating coastlands. John says this impact causes widespread death of one third of the marine life and the destruction of one third of the ships, affecting not only the food chain, but the economy as well.

8:10–11 The third trumpet judgment releases a huge meteor called "Wormwood" (8:11). Wormwood is a plant with a strong, bitter taste and is used in this passage to symbolize calamity. John warns that many will die because one third of the water will be poisoned.

8:12 The fourth trumpet will affect the heavens. One third of the sun, moon and stars will be darkened. Whether this means that daylight will be shortened or that the power of these light sources will be reduced by one-third is unclear.

8:13 The next three trumpet judgments are often called "the three woes," in recognition of the horrible judgments about to be unleashed upon the earth.

9:1–12 The fifth trumpet is also the first woe. When sounded, this trumpet releases demonic locusts from the bottomless pit that torment those "who did not have the seal of God on their foreheads" (9:4) for five months, the same length of time as the flood (see Ge 7:24). The only humans on earth immune to this terrible plague are the 144,000 (see 7:3). This is not a normal plague of locusts, because these creatures serve "the angel of the Abyss" (9:11). The locusts' stings are not deadly, but so painful that people will want to die. Note that John indicates only two groups of persons on the earth during this time—the reprobate ones afflicted by the demonic locusts and the 144,000 sealed Jews—intimating that the church must be in heaven when this terrible judgment falls on the earth.

² When he opened the Abyss, smoke rose from it like the smoke from a gigantic furnace.ᵈ The sun and sky were darkenedᵉ by the smoke from the Abyss.ᶠ ³ And out of the smoke locustsᵍ came down upon the earth and were given power like that of scorpionsʰ of the earth. ⁴ They were told not to harmⁱ the grass of the earth or any plant or tree,ʲ but only those people who did not have the seal of God on their foreheads.ᵏ ⁵ They were not given power to kill them, but only to torture them for five months.ˡ And the agony they suffered was like that of the sting of a scorpionᵐ when it strikes a man. ⁶ During those days men will seek death, but will not find it; they will long to die, but death will elude them.ⁿ

⁷ The locusts looked like horses prepared for battle.ᵒ On their heads they wore something like crowns of gold, and their faces resembled human faces.ᵖ ⁸ Their hair was like women's hair, and their teeth were like lions' teeth.ᵠ ⁹ They had breastplates like breastplates of iron, and the sound of their wings was like the thundering of many horses and chariots rushing into battle.ʳ ¹⁰ They had tails and stings like scorpions, and in their tails they had power to torment people for five months.ˢ ¹¹ They had as king over them the angel of the Abyss,ᵗ whose name in Hebrewᵘ is Abaddon,ᵛ and in Greek, Apollyon.ᵐ

P ¹² The first woe is past; two other woes are yet to come.ʷ

¹³ The sixth angel sounded his trumpet, and I heard a voice coming from the hornsⁿˣ of the golden altar that is before God.ʸ ¹⁴ It said to the sixth angel who had the trumpet, "Release the four angelsᶻ who are bound at the great river Euphrates."ᵃ ¹⁵ And the four angels who had been kept ready for this very hour and day and month and year were releasedᵇ to kill a thirdᶜ of mankind.ᵈ ¹⁶ The number of the mounted troops was two hundred million. I heard their number.ᵉ

¹⁷ The horses and riders I saw in my vision looked like this: Their breastplates were fiery red, dark blue, and yellow as sulfur. The heads of the horses resembled the heads of lions, and out of their mouthsᶠ came fire, smoke and sulfur.ᵍ ¹⁸ A thirdʰ of mankind was killedⁱ by the three plagues of fire, smoke and sulfurʲ that came out of their mouths. ¹⁹ The power of the horses was in their mouths and in their tails; for their tails were like snakes, having heads with which they inflict injury.

²⁰ The rest of mankind that were not killed by these plagues still did not repentᵏ of the work of their hands;ˡ they did not stop worshiping demons,ᵐ and idols of gold, silver, bronze, stone and wood—idols that cannot see or hear or walk.ⁿ ²¹ Nor did they repentᵒ of their murders, their magic arts,ᵖ their sexual immoralityᵠ or their thefts.

The Angel and the Little Scroll

10 Then I saw another mighty angelʳ coming down from heaven.ˢ He was robed in a cloud, with a rainbowᵗ above his head; his face was like the

P Rev 9:12–15 ◀▶ Rev 9:20
P Rev 9:18 ◀▶ Rev 10:5–7

m 11 *Abaddon* and *Apollyon* mean *Destroyer.*   *n* 13 That is, projections

---

9:13–21 The sixth trumpet (the second woe) will kill one third of humanity. God releases 200 million soldiers to wreak havoc throughout the earth (9:16). The enormous army of the kings of the east will cross into Israel from Asia to fight for world supremacy against the armies of the antichrist and his false prophet. This judgment will set the stage for the Battle of Armageddon, ending the seven-year tribulation (see Da 9:27).

For thousands of years the Euphrates River has served as a great military barrier to armies attacking from the East. However, in the late 1980s Turkey finished construction of the huge Ataturk Dam, designed to control these vast waters. For the first time in history, the flow of this great river can now be stopped at the push of a button. The prophecy of Rev 9:14 can be fulfilled in our lifetime.

Note that when God makes an appointment with destiny for a person or an empire, that appointment will not be postponed. Amazingly, despite every opportunity to repent, the sinners in the tribulation will refuse to turn from their wickedness (9:20).

10:1–4 John sees a mighty angel (see 5:2) come from heaven to announce the next series of judgments. A "little scroll" (10:2) is opened, containing information about the coming wrath of God, expressed by the "seven thunders" (10:3). Yet John prevented from writing down these things because God seals them until their proper time (see 22:10).

sun, and his legs were like fiery pillars. ²He was holding a little scroll, which lay open in his hand. He planted his right foot on the sea and his left foot on the land, ³and he gave a loud shout like the roar of a lion. When he shouted, the voices of the seven thunders spoke. ⁴And when the seven thunders spoke, I was about to write; but I heard a voice from heaven say, "Seal up what the seven thunders have said and do not write it down."

⁵Then the angel I had seen standing on the sea and on the land raised his right hand to heaven. ⁶And he swore by him who lives for ever and ever, who created the heavens and all that is in them, the earth and all that is in it, and the sea and all that is in it, and said, "There will be no more delay! ⁷But in the days when the seventh angel is about to sound his trumpet, the mystery of God will be accomplished, just as he announced to his servants the prophets."

⁸Then the voice that I had heard from heaven spoke to me once more: "Go, take the scroll that lies open in the hand of the angel who is standing on the sea and on the land."

⁹So I went to the angel and asked him to give me the little scroll. He said to me,

P Rev 9:20 ◄ ► Rev 11:14

"Take it and eat it. It will turn your stomach sour, but in your mouth it will be as sweet as honey." ¹⁰I took the little scroll from the angel's hand and ate it. It tasted as sweet as honey in my mouth, but when I had eaten it, my stomach turned sour. ¹¹Then I was told, "You must prophesy again about many peoples, nations, languages and kings."

The Two Witnesses

11 I was given a reed like a measuring rod and was told, "Go and measure the temple of God and the altar, and count the worshipers there. ²But exclude the outer court; do not measure it, because it has been given to the Gentiles. They will trample on the holy city for 42 months. ³And I will give power to my two witnesses, and they will prophesy for 1,260 days, clothed in sackcloth." ⁴These are the two olive trees and the two lampstands that stand before the Lord of the earth. ⁵If anyone tries to harm them, fire comes from their mouths and devours their enemies. This is how anyone who wants to harm them must die. ⁶These men have power to shut up the sky so that it will not rain during the time they are prophesying; and they have power to turn the waters into

G Ro 15:27 ◄ ► Rev 12:3-6

10:5-6 The mighty angel then declares that there would be no more delay. The next judgment was about to begin. Some have used this passage to mean that in heaven there would be no time. Yet Rev 22:2 indicates the passage of months in the new Jerusalem, intimating that eternity is not the absence of time; it is time without end.

10:7 The seventh trumpet (the third woe), though mentioned here, is not sounded until Rev 11:15.

11:1-2 The angel commands John to use a measuring rod and "measure the temple of God" (11:1). This seems to indicate the temple will be rebuilt during the tribulation and include the restoration of the great altar. Jerusalem will still be under the control of the Gentiles for another forty-two months (11:2) so the outer court cannot be measured. This 3 1/2 years corresponds to the great tribulation and will end at Armageddon (see Mt 24:21).

Some scholars believe that this outer court of the Gentiles encompasses the modern day Dome of the Rock. These scholars contend that the Moslem presence will still be strong in this area of Jerusalem and the court will not be completely rebuilt, so John did not need to measure it.

11:3-14 John then describes the supernatural ministry of God's two witnesses who will prophesy for 1260 days. Their supernatural power will authenticate their message. After 1260 days, they will finish their ministry and be killed by the antichrist. Unrepentant sinners will rejoice in their death, and the two will remain unburied on the streets of Jerusalem for three and a half days. The whole world will see their bodies. Yet, miraculously and fearfully, God will resurrect them and take them to heaven in the sight of their enemies. This prophecy clearly foreshadows modern-day, worldwide, television coverage. Only in this generation have people been able to see events as they occur from all over the world in live television broadcasts.

The resurrection of the two witnesses is closely followed by "a severe earthquake" (11:13) which destroys one-tenth of Jerusalem and seven thousand people. Only then will the remnant be so frightened that they will give "glory to the God of heaven" (11:13).

blood^g and to strike the earth with every kind of plague as often as they want.

⁷Now when they have finished their testimony, the beast^h that comes up from the Abyssⁱ will attack them,^j and overpower and kill them. ⁸Their bodies will lie in the street of the great city,^k which is figuratively called Sodom^l and Egypt, where also their Lord was crucified.^m ⁹For three and a half days men from every people, tribe, language and nationⁿ will gaze on their bodies and refuse them burial.^o ¹⁰The inhabitants of the earth^p will gloat over them and will celebrate by sending each other gifts,^q because these two prophets had tormented those who live on the earth.

E ¹¹But after the three and a half days^r a
H breath of life from God entered them,^s and they stood on their feet, and terror struck those who saw them. ¹²Then they heard a loud voice from heaven saying to them, "Come up here."^t And they went up to heaven in a cloud,^u while their enemies looked on.

¹³At that very hour there was a severe earthquake^v and a tenth of the city collapsed. Seven thousand people were killed in the earthquake, and the survivors were terrified and gave glory^w to the God of heaven.^x

P ¹⁴The second woe has passed; the third woe is coming soon.^y

The Seventh Trumpet

K ¹⁵The seventh angel sounded his trum-
M pet,^z and there were loud voices^a in
V heaven, which said:

E Rev 5:6 ◀▶ Rev 14:13   **H** 1Pe 3:18 ◀
P Rev 10:5–7 ◀▶ Rev 11:18–19
K 1Co 15:24–28 ◀
M Rev 5:10 ◀▶ Rev 12:5
V Heb 1:13 ◀▶ Rev 12:5

11:6 ^g Ex 7:17,19; Rev 8:8
11:7 ^h Rev 13:1-4
ⁱ S Lk 8:31
^j Da 7:21; Rev 13:7
11:8 ^k Rev 16:19
^l Isa 1:9; Jer 23:14; Eze 16:46
^m Heb 13:12
11:9 ⁿ S Rev 13:7
^o Ps 79:2,3
11:10 ^p S Rev 3:10
^q Ne 8:10,12; Est 9:19,22
11:11 ^r ver 9
^s Eze 37:5,9,10,14
11:12 ^t Rev 4:1
^u 2Ki 2:11; Ac 1:9
11:13 ^v S Rev 6:12
^w Rev 14:7; 16:9; 19:7 ^x Rev 16:11
11:14 ^y S Rev 8:13
11:15 ^z S Mt 24:31
^a Rev 16:17; 19:1
^b Rev 12:10
^c Ps 145:13; Da 2:44; 7:14,27; Mic 5:4; Zec 14:9; Lk 1:33
11:16 ^d S Rev 4:4
^e S Rev 4:10
11:17 ^f Ps 30:12
^g S Rev 1:8
^h S Rev 1:4
ⁱ Rev 19:6
11:18 ^j Ps 2:1
^k Rev 20:12
^l Rev 10:7
^m S Rev 19:5
11:19 ⁿ Rev 15:5,8
^o Ex 25:10-22; 2Ch 5:7; Heb 9:4
^p S Rev 4:5
^q Rev 16:21
12:1 ^r ver 3
^s Rev 11:19
^t Ge 37:9

"The kingdom of the world has
   become the kingdom of our
   Lord and of his Christ,^b
and he will reign for ever and
   ever."^c

¹⁶And the twenty-four elders,^d who were seated on their thrones before God, fell on their faces^e and worshiped God, ¹⁷saying:

"We give thanks^f to you, Lord God
   Almighty,^g
the One who is and who was,^h
because you have taken your great
   power
and have begun to reign.ⁱ
¹⁸The nations were angry;^j
   and your wrath has come.
The time has come for judging the
   dead,^k
and for rewarding your servants the
   prophets^l
and your saints and those who
   reverence your name,
   both small and great^m—
and for destroying those who destroy
   the earth."

¹⁹Then God's templeⁿ in heaven was opened, and within his temple was seen the ark of his covenant.^o And there came flashes of lightning, rumblings, peals of thunder,^p an earthquake and a great hailstorm.^q

The Woman and the Dragon

12 A great and wondrous sign^r ap-   **R**
peared in heaven:^s a woman clothed with the sun, with the moon under her feet and a crown of twelve stars^t

P Rev 11:14 ◀▶ Rev 12:9–17
H Rev 6:15–17 ◀▶ Rev 14:10–11
J Jude 14–15 ◀▶ Rev 14:7
R 1Th 2:16 ◀▶ Rev 12:10–13

11:15—18 The seventh trumpet sounds, ushering in the third woe. Though other significant events must still unfold, John records that the angels rejoice because the countdown to Christ's absolute victory over Satan has begun. The twenty-four elders fall upon their faces in worship of God, acknowledging that his glorious, majestic reign is about to be fulfilled at the second coming of Christ. Though the nations were angry as they endured God's judgments, when Christ returns the time for resurrection and final judgment approaches as well. Note also that God will hold people accountable for their stewardship of the earth, destroying those who destroy the earth.

11:19 John records his vision of God's temple in heaven and its "ark of his covenant" as well as various phenomena that reflect God's coming judgments upon the earth. John's vision of the ark was an unspeakable privilege. While in the tabernacle, the ark resided in the Holy of Holies, hidden by curtains and accessible only to the high priest. John's vision of the ark symbolizes God's presence with his people and indicates that God has revealed his glory to them through Jesus Christ.

12:1 The book of Revelation follows a pattern

on her head. ²She was pregnant and cried out in pain as she was about to give birth. ³Then another sign appeared in heaven: an enormous red dragon with seven heads and ten horns and seven crowns on his heads. ⁴His tail swept a third of the stars out of the sky and flung them to the earth. The dragon stood in front of the woman who was about to give birth, so that he might devour her child the moment it was born. ⁵She gave birth to a son, a male child, who will rule all the nations with an iron scepter. And her child was snatched up to God and to his throne. ⁶The woman fled into the desert to a place prepared for her by God, where she might be taken care of for 1,260 days.

⁷And there was war in heaven. Michael and his angels fought against the dragon, and the dragon and his angels fought back. ⁸But he was not strong enough, and they lost their place in heaven. ⁹The great dragon was hurled down—that ancient serpent called the devil, or Satan, who leads the whole world astray. He was hurled to the earth, and his angels with him.

¹⁰Then I heard a loud voice in heaven say:

"Now have come the salvation and
   the power and the kingdom of
   our God,
   and the authority of his Christ.
For the accuser of our brothers,
   who accuses them before our God
   day and night,
   has been hurled down.
¹¹They overcame him
   by the blood of the Lamb
   and by the word of their testimony;
   they did not love their lives so much
   as to shrink from death.
¹²Therefore rejoice, you heavens
   and you who dwell in them!
But woe to the earth and the sea,
   because the devil has gone down to
   you!
He is filled with fury,
   because he knows that his time is
   short."

¹³When the dragon saw that he had been hurled to the earth, he pursued the woman who had given birth to the male child. ¹⁴The woman was given the two wings of a great eagle, so that she might fly to the place prepared for her in the desert, where she would be taken care of for a time, times and half a time, out of the serpent's reach. ¹⁵Then from his mouth the serpent spewed water like a river, to overtake the woman and sweep her away with the torrent. ¹⁶But the earth

G Rev 11:2 ◀ ▶ Rev 13:1–18
M Rev 11:15–19 ◀ ▶ Rev 20:1–6
V Rev 11:15 ◀ ▶ Rev 17:14
P Rev 11:18–19 ◀ ▶ Rev 14:6–11
R Rev 12:1–6 ◀
D Rev 7:14 ◀   K Rev 7:14 ◀
T 1Pe 2:9 ◀ ▶ Rev 19:5

---

that is consistent with Jewish apocalyptic literature as it retells the future events of the tribulation recorded in chs. 6—11 from a different vantage point in chs. 12—19.

12:1–6 This remarkable vision of a woman has spurred different interpretations and is critical to understanding Revelation. Some have suggested that this woman is Mary, but this view seems untenable since Mary never "fled into the desert" (12:6) for 1260 days. Other scholars suggest that the "woman" is the church. This view also does not hold up under scrutiny because the woman gives birth to one child, not many believers or multiple churches.

The only tenable interpretation is to identify this "woman" with the nation of Israel. In other passages of Scripture Israel is referred to as a woman, especially in regard to her relationship with God (see Hos 2:2–13). That the woman is clothed with the sun may refer to those of Israel who believed in their Messiah. Note that the twelve stars correspond to the twelve tribes (see Ge 37:9).

The woman gives birth to a male child. This child is Jesus Christ, the Messiah. John's vision then describes a spiritual war extending over thousands of years as Satan tries to destroy the Messiah who will someday annihilate him. Though Christ returned to heaven, God will protect the "woman" for the length of the great tribulation until Christ returns at Armageddon to destroy the antichrist.

12:7–14 When Christ declares war against Satan, the archangel Michael will marshal the awesome military forces of heaven to defeat Satan and his army of fallen angels. This war at the midpoint of the seven-year tribulation will result in Satan's final expulsion from heaven to the earth. This expulsion will so enrage him that his anger will burn against God's people. Satan will realize that his wicked rule is about to end in a short time and he will terrorize Israel. God will supernaturally intervene and protect Israel from the persecution of Satan "a time, times and half a time" (12:14) or 3 1/2 years.

12:15–17 Satan will attempt to destroy the rem-

The Two Witnesses

GOD ESTABLISHED THE principle that two witnesses were required to settle the most important matters in judgment (see Dt 19:15). The Bible tells us that during the tribulation God will send two witnesses who will prophesy for 1,260 days, "that stand before the Lord of the earth" (Rev 11:4), giving testimony and tormenting evil men. Because the deception of the antichrist will have confused many, these two witnesses will be empowered to destroy God's enemies with fire from heaven. Many will respond to their message of repentance but will face martyrdom at the hands of the antichrist (see 7:9, 14). Ultimately God's two witnesses will be killed by the antichrist and left unburied on the streets of Jerusalem.

The Identity of the Two Witnesses
Though the Bible does not name the two witnesses, scholars have attempted to determine their identity. Some scholars have suggested that the two witnesses are only symbols, possibly of the OT and NT, the Bible and the Holy Spirit, or the martyrs of the faith from both the OT and NT. Yet the Bible describes these two witnesses as human beings, making this symbolic interpretation untenable. Others contend that Elijah and Enoch will be the two witnesses because they are the only two human beings who never died but were instead translated to heaven. Still others believe that Elijah and Moses will be God's two witnesses during the tribulation. While Scripture does not name the exact identity of the two witnesses, several facts are given that may help in their identification.

Elijah the Prophet
Malachi intimates that one of the two witnesses will be the prophet Elijah (see Mal 4:5). For centuries the Jews have longed for Elijah's return, recognizing that Elijah's mission would precede the Messiah's appearance. Every Passover, Jews set a place at their seder meal in anticipation of the prophet's return, leaving a door or window slightly ajar in hopes that this will be the year for Elijah's entrance to usher in the Messianic kingdom. This longing prompted the priests and Sadducees to question whether John the Baptist or even Jesus was Elijah (see Mk 8:27–28; Jn 1:21).

Elijah was a vital leader of Israel during a critical time in the life of the nation. During his ministry Elijah prayed that God would stop the rain for three and one-half years (see 1Ki 17:1; Lk 4:25; Jas 5:17). This power over the rain corresponds to one of the supernatural signs of the two witnesses and their "power to shut up the sky so that it will not rain during the time they are prophesying" (Rev 11:6)—a total of 1,260 days or three and one-half years (see 11:3). Because Elijah did not experience physical death (see 2Ki 2:9–11), he could possibly be one of the two witnesses who will return and be martyred during the tribulation.

Enoch
Many commentators suggest that Enoch is the second of the two witnesses because he is the only other person in the Bible besides Elijah who was raptured to heaven without dying (see Ge 5:24). These scholars suggest that since "man is destined to die once, and after that to face judgment" (Heb 9:27), both Enoch and Elijah must come back to earth and die since they escaped death the first time. To base the identification of one of God's witnesses on this interpretation of one verse of Scripture is a tenuous position at best. This interpretation overlooks the fact that those believers who are alive when Christ comes at the rapture will never experience death (see 1Th 4:17), yet these raptured believers are never suggested as being God's witnesses during the tribulation. Note too that the Bible indicates that several humans have actually died twice: Lazarus, Jairus's daughter and the widow of Nain's son. Complicating the identification of Enoch as one of the two witnesses is the fact that Enoch lived prior to the establishment of Israel as a nation and never figured prominently in its history or prophecy.

Moses
Because the prophet Malachi mentions both Elijah and Moses in his passage about the Messiah, some scholars conclude that Moses is the second of the two witnesses (see Mal 4:4–6). Moses was Israel's great leader and lawgiver who exercised God's miraculous power to authenticate his message and destroy Israel's spiritual enemies. Note that there are many similarities between the plagues and judgments against Egypt (see Ex 7—11) and the future plagues and judgments of the two witnesses during the tribulation.

Another indicator that suggests Moses' role as one of the two witnesses is his appearance with Elijah on the Mount of Transfiguration (see Mt 17:2–3). Moses, representing the Law, and Elijah, representing the prophets, appeared together to affirm Jesus' claim as God's Messiah. It is appropriate that these two great leaders should appear together again to witness to humanity at the end of this age.

helped the woman by opening its mouth and swallowing the river that the dragon had spewed out of his mouth. ¹⁷Then the dragon was enraged at the woman and went off to make war against the rest of her offspring—those who obey God's commandments and hold to the testimony of Jesus.

13

¹And the dragon stood on the shore of the sea.

The Beast out of the Sea

And I saw a beast coming out of the sea. He had ten horns and seven heads, with ten crowns on his horns, and on each head a blasphemous name. ²The beast I saw resembled a leopard, but had feet like those of a bear and a mouth like that of a lion. The dragon gave the beast his power and his throne and great authority. ³One of the heads of the beast seemed to have had a fatal wound, but the fatal wound had been healed. The whole world was astonished and followed the beast. ⁴Men worshiped the dragon because he had given authority to the beast, and they also worshiped the beast and asked, "Who is like the beast? Who can make war against him?"

⁵The beast was given a mouth to utter proud words and blasphemies and to exercise his authority for forty-two months. ⁶He opened his mouth to blaspheme God, and to slander his name and his dwelling place and those who live in heaven. ⁷He was given power to make war against the saints and to conquer them. And he was given authority over every tribe, people, language and nation. ⁸All inhabitants of the earth will worship the beast—all whose names have not been written in the book of life belonging to the Lamb that was slain from the creation of the world.

⁹He who has an ear, let him hear.

¹⁰If anyone is to go into captivity,
 into captivity he will go.
If anyone is to be killed with the sword,
 with the sword he will be killed.

This calls for patient endurance and faithfulness on the part of the saints.

The Beast out of the Earth

¹¹Then I saw another beast, coming out

---

nant of the righteous Jews with a flood. However, God will supernaturally open the earth and swallow the water. John then describes Satan's anger and war against all who keep God's commands and believe in Jesus Christ. In fulfillment of this prophecy, modern-day armies can cause tidal waves to swamp low-lying enemy territory with a strategically placed nuclear bomb. Whether this prophecy of a flood will be fulfilled in this military manner or in a more supernatural way, God promises to deliver his people.

13:1–2 John describes his terrible vision of this beast (the antichrist) that rises to political prominence in the world. This antichrist has "ten horns," which represent the revived Roman empire—the ten nations of Europe that will unite together under his rule (see Da 7:23–24). The "ten crowns" indicate that he has usurped all political power over these ten nations. In gaining his authority over these nations, three of the leaders of the ten kingdoms are completely overthrown or killed leaving only "seven heads" (13:1) to help bring about blasphemy against God. Whatever his status at birth, the antichrist will receive his power, throne and authority from Satan.

13:3–9 The antichrist miraculously survives an assassination attempt. Though he "seemed to have had a fatal wound" (13:3), the antichrist will be healed in a satanic imitation of Christ's resurrection, and receive the worship and wonderment of the world. For 3 1/2 years the antichrist will powerfully persecute the Jewish and Gentile tribulation saints. Everyone on earth who is not a follower of Christ will join the satanic worship of the antichrist.

13:11–18 Some say that because this second beast comes "out of the earth" (13:11) this beast is a symbol of the religious power that is now invested in the hands of secular authorities. Others propose that this beast is an individual, the antichrist's false prophet, his right-hand man, who enforces the worship of the antichrist with satanic miracles and oppression. Although countless writers have attempted to identify the future antichrist and this false prophet, it is probable that we will not know who these people are until the antichrist is revealed during the seven-year tribulation and after the rapture of the church.

Yet John give us a clear picture of the false prophet. This false prophet looks "like a lamb" (13:11) but behaves like a demon, attempting to bring down fire from heaven. Though he relies on Satan's limited power, this false prophet creates an automated image of the antichrist that people are forced to worship on penalty of death. He also devises a marking system that will be needed in

of the earth.ᵉ He had two horns like a lamb, but he spoke like a dragon.ᶠ ¹²He exercised all the authorityᵍ of the first beast on his behalf,ʰ and made the earth and its inhabitants worship the first beast,ⁱ whose fatal wound had been healed.ʲ ¹³And he performed great and miraculous signs,ᵏ even causing fire to come down from heavenˡ to earth in full view of men. ¹⁴Because of the signsᵐ he was given power to do on behalf of the first beast, he deceivedⁿ the inhabitants of the earth.ᵒ He ordered them to set up an image in honor of the beast who was wounded by the sword and yet lived.ᵖ ¹⁵He was given power to give breath to the image of the first beast, so that it could speak and cause all who refused to worshipᵠ the image to be killed.ʳ ¹⁶He also forced everyone, small and great,ˢ rich and poor, free and slave, to receive a mark on his right hand or on his forehead,ᵗ ¹⁷so that no one could buy or sell unless he had the mark,ᵘ which is the name of the beast or the number of his name.ᵛ

¹⁸This calls for wisdom.ʷ If anyone has insight, let him calculate the number of the beast, for it is man's number.ˣ His number is 666.

The Lamb and the 144,000

H **14** Then I looked, and there before me was the Lamb,ʸ standing on Mount Zion,ᶻ and with him 144,000ᵃ who had his name and his Father's nameᵇ written on their foreheads.ᶜ ²And I heard a sound from heaven like the roar of rushing watersᵈ and like a loud peal of thunder.ᵉ The sound I heard was like that of harpists playing their harps.ᶠ ³And

H *Rev 7:9–17* ◄ ► *Rev 15:2–4*

13:11 ᵉver 1,2
ᶠRev 16:13
13:12 ᵍver 4
ʰver 14; Rev 19:20
ⁱver 15; Rev 14:9, 11; 16:2; 19:20; 20:4 ʲver 3
13:13 ᵏMt 24:24
ˡ1Ki 18:38; 2Ki 1:10; Lk 9:54; Rev 20:9
13:14 ᵐ2Th 2:9, 10 ⁿRev 12:9
ᵒS Rev 3:10 ᵖver 3, 12
13:15 ᵠS ver 12
ʳDa 3:3-6
13:16 ˢS Rev 19:5
ᵗRev 7:3; 14:9; 20:4
13:17 ᵘRev 14:9
ᵛver 18; Rev 14:11; 15:2
13:18 ʷRev 17:9
ˣRev 15:2; 21:17
14:1 ʸS Rev 5:6
ᶻPs 2:6; Heb 12:22
ᵃver 3; Rev 7:4
ᵇRev 3:12; 22:4
ᶜS Rev 7:3
14:2 ᵈS Rev 1:15
ᵉRev 6:1 ᶠRev 5:8; 15:2
14:3 ᵍS Rev 5:9
ʰRev 4:6
ⁱS Rev 4:4 ʲver 1
14:4 ᵏ2Co 11:2; Rev 3:4 ˡRev 7:17
ᵐRev 5:9 ⁿJer 2:3; Jas 1:18
14:5 ᵒPs 32:2; Zep 3:13; Jn 1:47; 1Pe 2:22 ᵖEph 5:27
14:6 ᵠRev 8:13; 19:17 ʳS Rev 3:10
ˢS Rev 13:7
14:7 ᵗPs 34:9; Rev 15:4
ᵘS Rev 11:13
ᵛS Rev 10:6
ʷRev 8:10; 16:4
14:8 ˣIsa 21:9; Jer 51:8; Rev 16:19; 17:5; 18:2,10
ʸRev 17:2,4; 18:3,9
14:9 ᶻS Rev 13:12
ᵃver 13:14
ᵇS Rev 13:16
14:10 ᶜIsa 51:17; Jer 25:15 ᵈJer 51:7; Rev 18:6
ᵉS Rev 9:17
14:11 ᶠIsa 34:10; Rev 19:3 ᵍRev 4:8

they sang a new songᵍ before the throne and before the four living creaturesʰ and the elders.ⁱ No one could learn the song except the 144,000ʲ who had been redeemed from the earth. ⁴These are those who did not defile themselves with women, for they kept themselves pure.ᵏ They follow the Lamb wherever he goes.ˡ They were purchased from among menᵐ and offered as firstfruitsⁿ to God and the Lamb. ⁵No lie was found in their mouths;ᵒ they are blameless.ᵖ

The Three Angels

⁶Then I saw another angel flying in midair,ᵠ and he had the eternal gospel to proclaim to those who live on the earthʳ—to every nation, tribe, language and people.ˢ ⁷He said in a loud voice, "Fear Godᵗ and give him glory,ᵘ because the hour of his judgment has come. Worship him who madeᵛ the heavens, the earth, the sea and the springs of water."ʷ

⁸A second angel followed and said, "Fallen! Fallen is Babylon the Great,ˣ which made all the nations drink the maddening wine of her adulteries."ʸ

⁹A third angel followed them and said in a loud voice: "If anyone worships the beastᶻ and his imageᵃ and receives his mark on the foreheadᵇ or on the hand, ¹⁰he, too, will drink of the wine of God's fury,ᶜ which has been poured full strength into the cup of his wrath.ᵈ He will be tormented with burning sulfurᵉ in the presence of the holy angels and of the Lamb. ¹¹And the smoke of their torment rises for ever and ever.ᶠ There is no rest day or nightᵍ for those who worship the

P *Rev 12:9–17* ◄ ► *Rev 14:14*
J *Rev 11:18* ◄ ► *Rev 20:1–15*
G *Rev 13:1–18* ◄ ► *Rev 17:1*
H *Rev 11:18* ◄ ► *Rev 14:14–20*

---

order to buy or sell in society. For the first time in history this prophecy can now be easily fulfilled. Scientists have recently developed tiny computer chips that can be inserted beneath the skin to hold complete financial, health and identification records. Such implants would remove the necessity for money and would easily prepare the way for the implementation of a society as described in John's prophecy in this chapter.

14:1–5 John sees the 144,000 Jewish witnesses in heaven, after they "had been redeemed from the earth" (14:3). This is the same group seen earlier on earth in Rev 7. As faithful witnesses to Christ, this group is honored and called the "firstfruits to God and the Lamb" (14:4).

14:6–11 The first of a group of three angels appears and warns humanity of the coming final judgment of God. The first angel announces the gospel and calls for the worship of God. The second angel announces the fall of Babylon because of its unfaithfulness to God. This angelic announcement anticipates the final judgment of the apostate church (see ch. 17). The third angel warns humanity against worshiping the beast or receiving his mark. Anyone that gives in to the beast would be sent to the lake of fire for eternity.

beast and his image, or for anyone who receives the mark of his name." ¹²This calls for patient endurance on the part of the saints who obey God's commandments and remain faithful to Jesus.

¹³Then I heard a voice from heaven say, "Write: Blessed are the dead who die in the Lord from now on."

"Yes," says the Spirit, "they will rest from their labor, for their deeds will follow them."

The Harvest of the Earth

¹⁴I looked, and there before me was a white cloud, and seated on the cloud was one "like a son of man," with a crown of gold on his head and a sharp sickle in his hand. ¹⁵Then another angel came out of the temple and called in a loud voice to him who was sitting on the cloud, "Take your sickle and reap, because the time to reap has come, for the harvest of the earth is ripe." ¹⁶So he who was seated on the cloud swung his sickle over the earth, and the earth was harvested.

¹⁷Another angel came out of the temple in heaven, and he too had a sharp sickle. ¹⁸Still another angel, who had charge of the fire, came from the altar and called in a loud voice to him who had the sharp sickle, "Take your sharp sickle and gather the clusters of grapes from the earth's vine, because its grapes are ripe." ¹⁹The angel swung his sickle on the earth, gathered its grapes and threw them into the great winepress of God's wrath. ²⁰They were trampled in the winepress outside the city, and blood flowed out of the press, rising as high as the horses' bridles for a distance of 1,600 stadia.

Seven Angels With Seven Plagues

15 I saw in heaven another great and marvelous sign: seven angels with the seven last plagues—last, because with them God's wrath is completed. ²And I saw what looked like a sea of glass mixed with fire and, standing beside the sea, those who had been victorious over the beast and his image and over the number of his name. They held harps given them by God ³and sang the song of Moses the servant of God and the song of the Lamb:

"Great and marvelous are your deeds,
  Lord God Almighty.
Just and true are your ways,
  King of the ages.
⁴Who will not fear you, O Lord,
  and bring glory to your name?
For you alone are holy.
All nations will come
  and worship before you,
for your righteous acts have been revealed."

⁵After this I looked and in heaven the temple, that is, the tabernacle of the Testimony, was opened. ⁶Out of the temple came the seven angels with the seven plagues. They were dressed in clean, shining linen and wore golden sashes around their chests. ⁷Then one of the four living creatures gave to the seven angels seven golden bowls filled with the wrath of God, who lives for ever and ever. ⁸And the temple was filled

E *Rev 11:11* ◀▶ *Rev 17:3*
T *Rev 4:2* ◀▶ *Rev 17:3*
P *Rev 14:6–11* ◀▶ *Rev 15:5*
H *Rev 14:10–11* ◀▶ *Rev 15:1*

H *Rev 14:14–20* ◀▶ *Rev 19:3*
H *Rev 14:1–5* ◀▶ *Rev 19:7–9*
P *Rev 14:14* ◀▶ *Rev 18:19*

r 14 Daniel 7:13   s 20 That is, about 180 miles (about 300 kilometers)

14:14–20 Jesus Christ appears in John's vision wearing "a crown of gold," (14:14) representing his identity as King of kings. He also carries a "sharp sickle" (14:14) that he uses to harvest grain (the Gentiles) and grapes (the unbelieving Jews)—the unrepentant sinners of the tribulation. Christ pours out his final wrath upon the godless enemies who have gathered against the city of Jerusalem in their attempt to destroy his chosen people. The place of the final battle becomes a river of blood outside of the city, running for over 180 miles and as deep as the bridle of a horse.

15:1–8 This chapter describes an interval before the last seven plagues that will complete "God's wrath." (15:1). Once again John sees the "sea of glass, clear as crystal" (4:6), but now he sees the martyrs of the tribulation who have been resurrected to heaven to receive their reward. They have their harps and sing "the song of Moses . . . and the song of the Lamb" (15:3) in glorious worship of Jesus Christ, their King. Then John sees the temple of God and seven angels coming out of the temple, preparing to pour out the final judgment of God.

with smoke[e] from the glory of God and from his power, and no one could enter the temple[f] until the seven plagues of the seven angels were completed.

The Seven Bowls of God's Wrath

16 Then I heard a loud voice from the temple[g] saying to the seven angels,[h] "Go, pour out the seven bowls of God's wrath on the earth."[i]

²The first angel went and poured out his bowl on the land,[j] and ugly and painful sores[k] broke out on the people who had the mark of the beast and worshiped his image.[l]

³The second angel poured out his bowl on the sea, and it turned into blood like that of a dead man, and every living thing in the sea died.[m]

⁴The third angel poured out his bowl on the rivers and springs of water,[n] and

15:8 [e] Isa 6:4
[f] Ex 40:34,35; [1] Ki 8:10,11; 2 Ch 5:13,14
16:1 [g] Rev 11:19
[h] S Rev 15:1
[i] ver 2-21; Ps 79:6; Zep 3:8
16:2 [j] Rev 8:7
[k] ver 11; Ex 9:9-11; Dt 28:35
[l] Rev 13:15-17; 14:9
16:3 [m] Ex 7:17-21; Rev 8:8,9; Rev 11:6
16:4 [n] Rev 8:10

16:1–12 In this passage, John describes the last seven vial judgments. God commands the seven angels to carry out this final judgment against the earth and its wicked inhabitants. The first vial results in horrible boils and sores upon the skin of everyone who takes the mark of the beast and worships his image. The second vial will be poured out on the oceans, turning the waters to blood and killing every marine animal and fish.

The third vial will be poured out on all sources of fresh water, turning them to blood as God avenges the deaths of the saints and prophets who tried to warn the wicked. The fourth vial will be poured out on the sun, so that people will be burned "by the intense heat" (16:9). Yet the people will continue to blaspheme God and refuse "to repent and glorify him" (16:9).

The fifth vial produces supernatural darkness throughout the antichrist's kingdom, similar to the plague in Egypt (see Ex 10:21–23). The sixth vial affects the "great river Euphrates"(16:12) and dries up its riverbed in preparation for the invasion of Israel by the armies of the kings of the east.

Stages of the Battle of Armageddon

Da 11:35–45; Rev 16:16

1. The King of the South (Egypt with allies) attacks antichrist's forces in Israel.
2. The King of the North (Syria and its allies, possibly Russia) attack antichrist.
3. The Kings of the East mobilize a 200 million man army and march toward Israel.
4. The antichrist destroys his attackers from the South and North.
5. All the armies of the world gather at Armageddon in northern Israel to battle to determine who will rule the earth. Jesus Christ will descend from heaven with his army of saints to defeat these pagan armies, destroy antichrist and save Israel.

The Battle of Armageddon

THE LAST THREE years of the tribulation will be marked by a series of wars as many nations of the world rebel against the antichrist. God will allow "three evil spirits" (Rev 16:13) to summon the "kings of the whole world" (16:14) and their great armies to a valley in Israel. A fierce battle, the final conflict of the age, will then be enjoined at Armageddon.

The Location of Armageddon

Armageddon is the Greek term for the area of Palestine located along the southern rim of the plain of Esdraelon. Known alternately as the Valley of Jezreel, this great battlefield was the crossroads of two ancient trade routes and the site of major victories as well as disasters for the Israelites (see Jdg 4:15; 7; 1Sa 31:8; 2Ki 23:29–30; 2Ch 35:22). Thus Armageddon became synonymous to the Jews with terrible and final destruction.

The wars that will take place at the end of the tribulation will occur in various locations but will be centered in this area of Palestine. The prophet Joel foretold that God will "gather all nations and bring them down to the Valley of Jehoshaphat" (Joel 3:2). Isaiah indicates that the Lord will bring his armies up from the south, from Idumea or Edom (see Isa 34; 63). Zechariah indicates that Jerusalem itself will be the center of the conflict (see Zec 12:2–11; 14:2). The wide area encompassed by all of these prophecies includes the entire land of Israel and corresponds to the area that Revelation records in 14:20.

The Armies of Armageddon

At the time of the tribulation the antichrist will command the support of the majority of the nations of the west, including the nation of Israel (see Da 9:27; 11:45). These nations will be led by his inner circle of ten European and Mediterranean nations. A weakened, northern federation made up of Russia and her allies and the king of the south (most probably Egypt and her allies) will rebel against the antichrist but eventually be subdued and either conquered or annihilated (see Da 11:40; Zec 12:4). The antichrist will consolidate his military position by conquering and occupying Libya and Ethiopia, thereby controlling all of the Middle East and northern Africa, and will center his military forces in Israel because of its strategic military and economic location (see Da 11:41–42, 45; Rev 13:7).

The other major army during this time will be the army from the east (see 16:12). Though the antichrist will be able to marshal millions of soldiers at any time, he will hear disturbing reports that an enormous army of 200 million soldiers is mobilizing far to the east and north (see Da 11:44). China's current population shows a massive imbalance between the number of males and females. Currently, more than 100 million young Chinese men are of military age, and other countless millions are in its military reserve army. Should an alliance be forged between China and Japan, these eastern nations could effortlessly fill the ranks of Armageddon's prophesied 200 million soldiers (see Rev 9:14–16) and easily produce the armaments required for such an army. When the industrial might and engineering expertise of Japan is joined to the huge manpower and natural resources of China, the western world will face its greatest and final threat.

The final army to stand at the Battle of Armageddon will be the army of the Lord. Prophets in both the OT and NT foretold that the Lord would bring millions of his saints with him on the great day of the Lord (see Jude 14). Moses also described the army of heaven and the Lord coming in vengeance against Satan's forces (see Dt 33:2). The believers in Christ will return from heaven with their Messiah to join in the battle at Armageddon and win an incredible victory over the armies who attempt to destroy the Jews and each other (see Rev 19:14, 19).

The Battle Plan

At the midpoint of the seven-year tribulation, the antichrist and his ten nations will combine their forces to destroy the false church, the great whore of Babylon (see Rev 17:1–16). Obviously, this false church will have grown into a formidable power if the antichrist requires the military forces of ten nations to subdue her. Since the followers of the false church will not abandon her when she is attacked, she and her followers will be destroyed by the antichrist.

Though the nations of the world initially embrace the new world order of the antichrist, Israel and some Gentile nations will try to rebel during the tribulation (see 12:9–17). The king of the south (Egypt and her allies) will attack the antichrist's forces in Israel. The northern kingdoms will join the invasion by bringing in their forces in a lightning attack. The antichrist will swiftly retaliate and totally annihilate his enemies (see Da 11:9–12). Thus the forces of Satan will win the first round of the war. The antichrist will then hear disturbing reports about an approaching army from the east. While for thousands of years the Euphrates River has stood as a great barrier between the nations of the east and west, John prophesied that this great river would somehow dry up to allow the passage of the armies of the east to invade Israel (see Rev 16:12).

Only recently has a large dam been completed in Turkey that can control the waters of the Euphrates River. At the dam's completion the president of Turkey pressed a button that closed some of the spillways, effectively reducing 75 per cent of the river's flow. As a fulfillment of John's prophecy, the Euphrates River can now be dried up because of this massive dam.

The incredible army of the east will cross Asia, slaughtering one-third of humanity in its path as it moves toward the great Valley of Jezreel in northern Israel to meet the massed armies of the antichrist. After years of warfare this final battle between the forces of the east and the west will determine who will rule the world for the next millennium.

Although the final stages of the battle will center in Armageddon, skirmishes will engulf Asia, Africa, Europe and the Middle East. Untold millions will die in bloody warfare as nations pour their destructive nuclear, biological and chemical weapons on each other (see 19:17–18, 21).

Yet as the armies of the antichrist and the armies of the east join battle with each other, the Lord will return with his army to deliver the nation of Israel from annihilation. There will be nothing secret about his coming to destroy Satan's armies. Jesus promised that his return would be as brilliantly visible as lightning (see Mt 24:27). Yet to the consternation of the leaders of this titanic battle the armies of heaven will supernaturally intervene against both evil forces. Putting aside their own agenda, the armies of the antichrist and the armies of the east will join together to attack Christ and his heavenly army (see Rev 19:19). Despite their fearful array of military weapons, the armies of the world will be destroyed.

We are not told how long the Battle of Armageddon will rage. It may end quite quickly once the armies of heaven intervene, or it may continue for a period of time. Regardless of its duration, Christ will be the ultimate victor (see 2Th 2:8). His power and might will transcend the power of the antichrist's weapons of war (see Da 8:25; Mt 26:53). The enemies of Christ will be destroyed and the antichrist and the false prophet will be captured and thrown into the "fiery lake of burning sulfur" (Rev 19:20). Their final destruction will end the terrible persecution of God's people.

Though no one knows with certainty when this final conflict will occur, signs in the sky will announce to the nations that the Messiah's return is at hand. When Jesus returns he will not come as a meek Lamb or suffering servant. When the final day of reckoning arrives, Christ will call on the angels of heaven as well as the saints of the church to join in his triumphant return to establish his millennial kingdom. When Christ returns he will come in all the glory of Almighty God as "the King of kings and Lord of lords" (1Ti 6:15).

they became blood.º ⁵Then I heard the angel in charge of the waters say:

"You are just in these judgments,ᵖ
you who are and who were,ᑫ the Holy One,ʳ
because you have so judged;ˢ
⁶for they have shed the blood of your saints and prophets,ᵗ
and you have given them blood to drinkᵘ as they deserve."

⁷And I heard the altarᵛ respond:

"Yes, Lord God Almighty,ʷ
true and just are your judgments."ˣ

⁸The fourth angelʸ poured out his bowl on the sun,ᶻ and the sun was given power to scorch people with fire.ᵃ ⁹They were seared by the intense heat and they cursed the name of God,ᵇ who had control over these plagues, but they refused to repentᶜ and glorify him.ᵈ

¹⁰The fifth angel poured out his bowl on the throne of the beast,ᵉ and his kingdom was plunged into darkness.ᶠ Men gnawed their tongues in agony ¹¹and cursedᵍ the God of heavenʰ because of their pains and their sores,ⁱ but they refused to repent of what they had done.ʲ

¹²The sixth angel poured out his bowl on the great river Euphrates,ᵏ and its water was dried up to prepare the wayˡ for the kings from the East.ᵐ ¹³Then I saw three evil spiritsⁿ that looked like frogs;º they came out of the mouth of the dragon,ᵖ out of the mouth of the beastᑫ and out of the mouth of the false prophet.ʳ ¹⁴They are spirits of demonsˢ performing miraculous signs,ᵗ and they go out to the kings of the whole world,ᵘ to gather them for the battleᵛ on the great dayʷ of God Almighty.

¹⁵"Behold, I come like a thief!ˣ Blessed is he who stays awakeʸ and keeps his clothes with him, so that he may not go naked and be shamefully exposed."ᶻ

¹⁶Then they gathered the kings togetherᵃ to the place that in Hebrewᵇ is called Armageddon.ᶜ

¹⁷The seventh angel poured out his bowl into the air,ᵈ and out of the templeᵉ came a loud voiceᶠ from the throne, saying, "It is done!"ᵍ ¹⁸Then there came flashes of lightning, rumblings, peals of thunderʰ and a severe earthquake.ⁱ No earthquake like it has ever occurred since man has been on earth,ʲ so tremendous was the quake. ¹⁹The great cityᵏ split into three parts, and the cities of the nations collapsed. God rememberedˡ Babylon the Greatᵐ and gave her the cup filled with the wine of the fury of his wrath.ⁿ ²⁰Every island fled away and the mountains could not be found.º ²¹From the sky huge hailstonesᵖ of about a hundred pounds each fell upon men. And they cursed Godᑫ on account of the plague of hail,ʳ because the plague was so terrible.

The Woman on the Beast

17 One of the seven angelsˢ who had the seven bowlsᵗ came and said to me, "Come, I will show you the punishmentᵘ of the great prostitute,ᵛ who sits on many waters.ʷ ²With her the

G *Rev 14:8* ◂

16:13–21 John describes three evil spirits that are sent from Satan, the antichrist and the false prophet to gather the wicked kings of the whole world together for a major battle. God will allow this battle to take place at Armageddon, a huge valley in northern Israel and the site of many major historical battles.

The seventh vial will be poured into the air and a great earthquake will devastate the earth and divide Jerusalem into three parts as cities around the world fall in ruins. John warns that Babylon's day of judgment is approaching (see Rev 18). Islands will be swamped and mountains will collapse as a terrible hailstorm falls from the skies. Yet despite these judgments, the wicked will continue to curse God rather than repent of their sins.

In the middle of this passage, almost as a parenthetical thought, Christ's followers are urged to watch for his coming and be alert. The unusual phrases of 16:15 referred to the custom in John's day of the treatment of a temple guard that fell asleep while on guard duty. His clothes were taken from him, and he was forced to go home naked and in disgrace. What a warning for Christ's followers to stand firm and alert, to heed the signs and be watchful for his coming.

17:1–7 (Note that it is important to differentiate between the judgments of ecclesiastical Babylon, described in Rev 17 and the wrath of God poured out on the empire of Babylon, described in Rev 18.)

This passage is one of the most unusual prophecies in the Bible. One of the seven angels

kings of the earth committed adultery and the inhabitants of the earth were intoxicated with the wine of her adulteries."ˣ

³Then the angel carried me away in the Spiritʸ into a desert.ᶻ There I saw a woman sitting on a scarletᵃ beast that was covered with blasphemous namesᵇ and had seven heads and ten horns.ᶜ ⁴The woman was dressed in purple and scarlet, and was glittering with gold, precious stones and pearls.ᵈ She held a golden cupᵉ in her hand, filled with abominable things and the filth of her adulteries.ᶠ ⁵This title was written on her forehead:

MYSTERYᵍ
BABYLON THE GREATʰ
THE MOTHER OF PROSTITUTESⁱ
AND OF THE ABOMINATIONS OF THE EARTH.

⁶I saw that the woman was drunk with the blood of the saints,ʲ the blood of those who bore testimony to Jesus.

E *Rev 14:13* ◀ ▶ *Rev 21:10*
T *Rev 14:13* ◀

17:2 ˣS Rev 14:8
17:3 ʸS Rev 1:10; ᶻRev 12:6,14; ᵃRev 18:12,16; ᵇRev 13:1; ᶜS Rev 12:3
17:4 ᵈEze 28:13; Rev 18:16; ᵉJer 51:7; Rev 18:6; ᶠver 2; S Rev 14:8
17:5 ᵍver 7; ʰS Rev 14:8 ⁱver 1, 2
17:6 ʲRev 16:6; 18:24
17:7 ᵏver 5 ˡver 3; S Rev 12:3
17:8 ᵐS Lk 8:31; ⁿRev 13:10; ᵒS Rev 3:10; ᵖS Rev 20:12 ᵍRev 13:3
17:9 ʳRev 13:18 ˢver 3
17:11 ᵗver 8
17:12 ᵘS Rev 12:3 ᵛRev 18:10,17,19

When I saw her, I was greatly astonished. ⁷Then the angel said to me: "Why are you astonished? I will explain to you the mysteryᵏ of the woman and of the beast she rides, which has the seven heads and ten horns.ˡ ⁸The beast, which you saw, once was, now is not, and will come up out of the Abyssᵐ and go to his destruction.ⁿ The inhabitants of the earthᵒ whose names have not been written in the book of lifeᵖ from the creation of the world will be astonishedᵍ when they see the beast, because he once was, now is not, and yet will come.

⁹"This calls for a mind with wisdom.ʳ The seven headsˢ are seven hills on which the woman sits. ¹⁰They are also seven kings. Five have fallen, one is, the other has not yet come; but when he does come, he must remain for a little while. ¹¹The beast who once was, and now is not,ᵗ is an eighth king. He belongs to the seven and is going to his destruction.

¹²"The ten hornsᵘ you saw are ten kings who have not yet received a kingdom, but who for one hourᵛ will receive

---

shows John "the punishment of the great prostitute" (17:1), referring to the worldwide, ecumenical apostate religion of the last days. The spiritual imagery of fornication is repeatedly used by John to emphasize the corruption of the religious system of the last days. A pagan revival of the ancient mystery religions of Babylon will cloak themselves in the outward symbols of Christianity. This false church will be allied with the antichrist and his ten allies (17:3) and will be characterized by blasphemy and drunkenness (17:5). This false church will claim to be the true church while persecuting the tribulation saints who worship God (17:6).

17:8–18 The events of this fascinating vision occur prior to the rise of the antichrist at the middle of the tribulation and refer to the satanic nature of the antichrist and his wicked kingdom. Some say that the opening phrase of 17:8 refers to the beast; though the beast appeared once, he is not presently evident, but will in the future make his presence known. Others suggest that this phrase is an imitation of the description of Christ (see 1:18; 2:8) and an indication of the antichrist's counterfeit of God's sovereignty. Still others contend that this passage deals with the final form of the Gentile world government.

There is also an allusion here to the rise and fall of Rome. Once a powerful empire that has ceased to rule, Rome will rise again to rule the world at the end of this age (17:12). The city of Rome was commonly known in ancient times as the city on seven hills (17:9). The seven kings in this prophecy might refer to Rome's emperors or to seven secular empires that have oppressed Israel throughout her history. The five fallen empires could be Egypt, Assyria, Babylon, Medo-Persia and Greece. When John wrote Revelation, Rome was still in power. The other empire that "has not yet come" (17:10) may refer to the revived Roman empire that will be established under the antichrist as a ten-nation confederacy.

The final ruler, the antichrist, will ultimately take over the seventh kingdom, the revived Roman empire, during the first half of the seven-year treaty period. He is the eighth ruler and his kingdom will differ markedly in character from the other kingdoms because of Satan's power over him. Yet the ten separate kings will bring their kingdoms under his authority (17:12) and will build this eighth kingdom by mutual consent (17:13). This kingdom will be the most oppressive and demonic reign in history, ushering in the last 3 1/2 years of the great tribulation. Together, in the power of Satan, "they will make war against the Lamb" (17:14). Yet John prophesies that the Lamb of God will triumph.

John also sees in his vision that God will cause the ten nations to join with the antichrist and destroy the false church (17:16) as a fulfillment of God's will (17:17). Though he used the worldwide, ecumenical church to consolidate his evil rule, the antichrist will turn on her and utterly destroy her, and will instead accept the worship and deification of the people.

authority as kings along with the beast. ¹³They have one purpose and will give their power and authority to the beast.ʷ ¹⁴They will make warˣ against the Lamb, but the Lamb will overcomeʸ them because he is Lord of lords and King of kingsᶻ—and with him will be his called, chosenᵃ and faithful followers."

¹⁵Then the angel said to me, "The watersᵇ you saw, where the prostitute sits, are peoples, multitudes, nations and languages.ᶜ ¹⁶The beast and the ten hornsᵈ you saw will hate the prostitute.ᵉ They will bring her to ruinᶠ and leave her naked;ᵍ they will eat her fleshʰ and burn her with fire.ⁱ ¹⁷For God has put it into their heartsʲ to accomplish his purpose by agreeing to give the beast their power to rule,ᵏ until God's words are fulfilled.ˡ ¹⁸The woman you saw is the great cityᵐ that rules over the kings of the earth."

The Fall of Babylon

18 After this I saw another angelⁿ coming down from heaven.ᵒ He had great authority, and the earth was illuminated by his splendor.ᵖ ²With a mighty voice he shouted:

"Fallen! Fallen is Babylon the Great!ᑫ
She has become a home for demons
and a haunt for every evilᵘ spirit,ʳ
a haunt for every unclean and
detestable bird.ˢ
³For all the nations have drunk
the maddening wine of her
adulteries.ᵗ
The kings of the earth committed
adultery with her,ᵘ
and the merchants of the earth grew
richᵛ from her excessive
luxuries."ʷ

v Rev 12:5 ◄ ► Rev 19:15-16

⁴Then I heard another voice from heaven say:

"Come out of her, my people,ˣ
so that you will not share in her
sins,
so that you will not receive any of
her plagues;ʸ
⁵for her sins are piled up to heaven,ᶻ
and God has rememberedᵃ her
crimes.
⁶Give back to her as she has given;
pay her backᵇ doubleᶜ for what she
has done.
Mix her a double portion from her
own cup.ᵈ
⁷Give her as much torture and grief
as the glory and luxury she gave
herself.ᵉ
In her heart she boasts,
'I sit as queen; I am not a widow,
and I will never mourn.'ᶠ
⁸Therefore in one dayᵍ her plagues will
overtake her:
death, mourning and famine.
She will be consumed by fire,ʰ
for mighty is the Lord God who
judges her.

⁹"When the kings of the earth who committed adultery with herⁱ and shared her luxuryʲ see the smoke of her burning,ᵏ they will weep and mourn over her.ˡ ¹⁰Terrified at her torment, they will stand far offᵐ and cry:

" 'Woe! Woe, O great city,ⁿ
O Babylon, city of power!
In one hourᵒ your doom has come!'

¹¹"The merchantsᵖ of the earth will weep and mournᑫ over her because no one buys their cargoes any moreʳ— ¹²cargoes of gold, silver, precious stones and pearls; fine linen, purple, silk and

u 2 Greek unclean

18:1–19 This new vision describes the judgment of God upon the empire of Babylon, in all its commercial and political power. An angel announces the fall of this empire and focuses his words against the riches of this ungodly empire. The saints are urged to leave Babylon before God's judgment falls on this wicked nation (18:4). The antichrist will take the title "king of Babylon" (Isa 14:4) indicating his close connection with the wicked Babylonian empire during the tribulation.

In her wicked pride Babylon will show contempt for God, but John prophesies that her judgment will come and she will be destroyed by fire (18:8). Kings and merchants will mourn the loss of Babylon because they will lose their riches and wicked pleasures (18:11–13). As they watch her burning from afar, merchants and ship captains will cry out in dismay. Modern-day Iraq occupies the location of ancient Babylon. With great military power and large oil reserves, Iraq is ideally suited to become a vast commercial power that may figure prominently in the fulfillment of this prophecy in the future.

scarlet cloth; every sort of citron wood, and articles of every kind made of ivory, costly wood, bronze, iron and marble; ¹³cargoes of cinnamon and spice, of incense, myrrh and frankincense, of wine and olive oil, of fine flour and wheat; cattle and sheep; horses and carriages; and bodies and souls of men.

¹⁴"They will say, 'The fruit you longed for is gone from you. All your riches and splendor have vanished, never to be recovered.' ¹⁵The merchants who sold these things and gained their wealth from her will stand far off, terrified at her torment. They will weep and mourn ¹⁶and cry out:

" 'Woe! Woe, O great city,
dressed in fine linen, purple and scarlet,
and glittering with gold, precious stones and pearls!
¹⁷In one hour such great wealth has been brought to ruin!'

"Every sea captain, and all who travel by ship, the sailors, and all who earn their living from the sea, will stand far off. ¹⁸When they see the smoke of her burning, they will exclaim, 'Was there ever a city like this great city?' ¹⁹They will throw dust on their heads, and with weeping and mourning cry out:

" 'Woe! Woe, O great city,
where all who had ships on the sea became rich through her wealth!
In one hour she has been brought to ruin!'

²⁰Rejoice over her, O heaven!
Rejoice, saints and apostles and prophets!
God has judged her for the way she treated you.' "

²¹Then a mighty angel picked up a boulder the size of a large millstone and threw it into the sea, and said:

"With such violence
the great city of Babylon will be thrown down,
never to be found again.
²²The music of harpists and musicians,
flute players and trumpeters,
will never be heard in you again.
No workman of any trade
will ever be found in you again.
The sound of a millstone
will never be heard in you again.
²³The light of a lamp
will never shine in you again.
The voice of bridegroom and bride
will never be heard in you again.
Your merchants were the world's great men.
By your magic spell all the nations were led astray.
²⁴In her was found the blood of prophets and of the saints,
and of all who have been killed on the earth."

Hallelujah!

19 After this I heard what sounded like the roar of a great multitude in heaven shouting:

"Hallelujah!
Salvation and glory and power belong to our God,
² for true and just are his judgments.
He has condemned the great prostitute
who corrupted the earth by her adulteries.
He has avenged on her the blood of his servants."

³And again they shouted:

"Hallelujah!
The smoke from her goes up for ever and ever."

⁴The twenty-four elders and the four living creatures fell down and wor-

---

18:20–24 John hears a voice commanding the apostles and prophets to rejoice over the destruction of their deadly enemy. The angel announces that Babylon will be utterly destroyed because of her deceptive sorceries (18:23) and because of the role she played in killing the prophets and saints.

19:1–6 Following the judgment upon Babylon, John hears the voices of heaven rejoicing that God has forever destroyed the enemies of Christ.

shiped God, who was seated on the throne. And they cried:

"Amen, Hallelujah!"[i]

T ⁵Then a voice came from the throne, saying:

"Praise our God,
all you his servants,[j]
you who fear him,
both small and great!"[k]

⁶Then I heard what sounded like a great multitude,[l] like the roar of rushing waters[m] and like loud peals of thunder, shouting:

"Hallelujah![n]
For our Lord God Almighty[o] reigns.[p]
H ⁷Let us rejoice and be glad
and give him glory![q]
For the wedding of the Lamb[r] has come,
and his bride[s] has made herself ready.
⁸Fine linen,[t] bright and clean,
was given her to wear."
(Fine linen stands for the righteous acts[u] of the saints.)

T *Rev 12:11* ◀   H *Rev 15:2–4* ◀

19:4 [i] ver 1,3,6
19:5 [j] Ps 134:1
[k] ver 18; Ps 115:13; Rev 11:18; 13:16; 20:12
19:6 [l] ver 1; Rev 11:15
[m] S Rev 1:15
[n] ver 1,3,4
[o] S Rev 1:8
[p] Rev 11:15
19:7 [q] S Rev 11:13
[r] ver 9; Mt 22:2; 25:10; Eph 5:32
[s] Rev 21:2,9; 22:17
19:8 [t] ver 14; Rev 15:6
[u] Isa 61:10; Eze 44:17; Zec 3:4; Rev 15:4
19:9 [v] ver 10
[w] Rev 1:19
[x] Lk 14:15
[y] Rev 21:5; 22:6
19:10 [z] Rev 22:8
[a] Col 10:25,26; Rev 22:9
[b] S Rev 1:2
19:11 [c] S Mt 3:16
[d] ver 19,21; Rev 6:2
[e] Rev 3:14
[f] Ex 15:3; Ps 96:13; Isa 11:4
19:12 [g] S Rev 1:14
[h] Rev 6:2; 12:3
[i] ver 16 [i] S Rev 2:17
19:13 [k] Isa 63:2,3
[l] Jn 1:1
19:14 [m] ver 8
[n] S Rev 3:4
19:15 [o] ver 21;
S Rev 1:16
[p] Isa 11:4; 2Th 2:8

⁹Then the angel said to me,[v] "Write:[w] 'Blessed are those who are invited to the wedding supper of the Lamb!' "[x] And he added, "These are the true words of God."[y]

¹⁰At this I fell at his feet to worship G him.[z] But he said to me, "Do not do it! I am a fellow servant with you and with your brothers who hold to the testimony of Jesus. Worship God![a] For the testimony of Jesus[b] is the spirit of prophecy."

The Rider on the White Horse

¹¹I saw heaven standing open[c] and P there before me was a white horse, whose rider[d] is called Faithful and True.[e] With justice he judges and makes war.[f] ¹²His eyes are like blazing fire,[g] and on his head are many crowns.[h] He has a name written on him[i] that no one knows but he himself.[j] ¹³He is dressed in a robe dipped in blood,[k] and his name is the Word of God.[l] ¹⁴The armies of heaven were following him, riding on white horses and dressed in fine linen,[m] white[n] and clean. ¹⁵Out of his mouth comes a V sharp sword[o] with which to strike down[p] the nations. "He will rule them with an

G *Rev 5:6* ◀   P *Rev 18:19* ◀▶ *Rev 21:9*
V *Rev 17:14* ◀▶ *Rev 20:7–15*

19:7–9 John describes the glorious "wedding of the Lamb" (19:7) which will occur in heaven when the believers are spiritually united to Jesus Christ. The resurrected saints receive garments of "fine linen" (19:8) that signify their righteousness through the atonement of Christ's blood and God's sovereign grace. Note that this passage in ch. 19 contains the first reference to the church since the end of ch. 3 and the seven messages to the churches. This omission of the mention of the church during the seven-year tribulation reaffirms the rapture of the church before the tribulation. For further information, see the article "The Marriage Supper of the Lamb" on p. 1482.

19:11–13 John announces the second coming of Christ as heaven opens and Jesus appears in all of his glory, riding a white horse, ready to judge and make war with unrepentant sinners. Christ's garments are "dipped in blood" (19:13), reminding us of his terrible wrath and destruction of his enemies (see Isa 34:5–8).

Twice in this passage John makes reference to Jesus' name (19:12–13). Names carry a tremendous importance in the Bible because they are closely related to the character and destiny of the person so named. When the saints arrive in heaven they will even be given a "new name" (3:12). Though we do not know the name Jesus uses to refer to himself in 19:12, John reminds us that Jesus' name is "the Word of God" (19:13; see Jn 1:1).

19:14–18 Now John sees the armies of heaven which will follow Jesus out to battle. These resurrected saints are clothed in white linen and riding white horses, symbolic of their righteousness through the shed blood of Christ. These saints are probably the same ones seen at the wedding supper of the Lamb (19:7–8). Since this battle follows the wedding supper, the rapture and the judgment seat of Christ (see Ro 14:10; 2Co 5:10) must have taken place at an earlier time.

Jesus then treads the winepress in his judgment against those who have martyred his saints (see Isa 63:1–6). Jesus will rule the nations in righteousness and justice, destroying all evil during the Millennium. His glorious name is emblazoned on his garments: "KING OF KINGS AND LORD OF LORDS" (19:16). At the end of the battle of Armageddon, an angel calls the birds of the air to come and scavenge the bodies of the wicked, to cleanse the land. This gruesome "great supper of God" (19:17) is a grim contrast to the earlier wedding supper of the Lamb.

The Marriage Supper of the Lamb

THE USE OF marriage as a symbol of God's eternal spiritual union with people appears repeatedly in Scripture. In the OT, unrepentant Israel was likened to an adulterous wife (see Hos 2:1–8). In the NT, Jesus Christ referred to the faithful church as his virgin bride (see Jn 3:29).

In ancient Israel there were three phases to a legal marriage. The first stage was a betrothal, a legally binding agreement entered into by both parties. The second phase involved the coming of the bridegroom to meet his bride. The last part of a marriage celebration was the marriage supper hosted at the home of the groom.

Our spiritual life echoes this marriage ritual. Our spiritual betrothal as Christ's bride began when we accepted him as our Savior. Christ's appearance in the air to rapture the church is the equivalent of the bridegroom coming to meet the bride. John's vision in Revelation details the final phase of the church's marriage to Christ with his description of a glorious marriage supper in heaven between the complete bride of Christ and their Savior in the presence of the assembled angelic host.

Some posttribulation scholars suggest that the marriage supper of the Lamb will take place in the air while the church is being raptured. They contend that this will allow the church to rise in the air with Christ and immediately return to earth to participate in the Battle of Armageddon. This view presents some difficulties because of the clear words of Jesus' promise to bring believers to be with him in heaven (see Jn 14:3).

Other scholars suggest that the marriage supper of the Lamb must take place between Christ's coming for his church and his return with the saints at Armageddon. These scholars contend that after the rapture and the *bema* judgment, when all Christians have received their rewards for their righteous works, the believers will participate in the glorious marriage supper between Christ and his faithful bride. This supper will occur in heaven at the same time that the judgments of the tribulation are being felt on earth.

Specific grammar in John's prophecy affirms this sequence of events. Note that John says, "the wedding of the Lamb has come, and his bride has made herself ready" (Rev 19:7). The Greek word translated "has come" is written in the Greek aorist tense, signifying an act that was completed in the past and needs no other action or limitation. This indicates that the marriage will be consummated by this point and will precede the second coming of Christ. Only after describing the marriage supper does John then record his vision of Christ's return to earth at Armageddon.

There will also be guests at this wedding, those "who are invited to the wedding supper of the Lamb" (19:9). Guests are "called" or invited to a wedding, whereas the bride and bridegroom are the honored hosts. The guests of the marriage supper of the Lamb are the tribulation martyrs, OT saints and the hosts of heaven. While the saints of Israel will live with the Christian saints in the new Jerusalem, the OT saints are not the bride of Christ. Even John the Baptist referred to himself only as a wedding guest when he likened himself to a friend of the Bridegroom (see Jn 3:29).

John's detailed vision of the marriage supper includes a description of the bride's garments. Dressed in "fine linen, bright and clean" (Rev 19:8), the church is shown as completely cleansed through the atonement of Christ's completed work on the cross. Though some suggest that the church must suffer through the tribulation to cleanse and purify her in preparation for the marriage supper, these scholars have forgotten that we are not purified by tribulation. We are purified solely by Christ's righteousness applied to our hearts through faith in him as our Lord and Savior.

Because the bride is clothed with fine linen this also affirms that the church has already participated in the *bema* judgment where rewards are given for faithful works. Note also that John later describes the believers "dressed in fine linen, white and clean" (19:14) as they leave heaven to join in the Battle of Armageddon. This passage then confirms this order of events: the rapture, the *bema* judgment, the marriage supper and the return to earth at Armageddon.

iron scepter."ᵛ۹ He treads the winepressʳ of the fury of the wrath of God Almighty. ¹⁶On his robe and on his thigh he has this name written:ˢ

KING OF KINGS AND LORD OF LORDS.ᵗ

¹⁷And I saw an angel standing in the sun, who cried in a loud voice to all the birdsᵘ flying in midair,ᵛ "Come,ʷ gather together for the great supper of God,ˣ ¹⁸so that you may eat the flesh of kings, generals, and mighty men, of horses and their riders, and the flesh of all people,ʸ free and slave,ᶻ small and great."ᵃ

¹⁹Then I saw the beastᵇ and the kings of the earthᶜ and their armies gathered together to make war against the rider on the horseᵈ and his army. ²⁰But the beast was captured, and with him the false prophetᵉ who had performed the miraculous signsᶠ on his behalf.ᵍ With these signs he had deludedʰ those who had received the mark of the beastⁱ and worshiped his image.ʲ The two of them were thrown alive into the fiery lakeᵏ of burning sulfur.ˡ ²¹The rest of them were killed with the swordᵐ that came out of the mouth of the rider on the horse,ⁿ and all the birdsᵒ gorged themselves on their flesh.

H Rev 19:3 ◄ ► Rev 20:9–15

19:15 ۹ Ps 2:9; Rev 2:27; 12:5
ʳ S Rev 14:20
19:16 ˢ ver 12
ᵗ S 1Ti 6:15
19:17 ᵘ ver 21
ᵛ Rev 8:13; 14:6
ʷ Jer 12:9; Eze 39:17
ˣ Isa 34:6; Jer 46:10
19:18
ʸ Eze 39:18-20
ᶻ Rev 6:15 ˢ S ver 5
19:19 ᵇ S Rev 13:1
ᶜ Rev 16:14,16
ᵈ ver 11,21
19:20 ᵉ Rev 16:13
ᶠ S Mt 24:24
ᵍ Rev 13:12
ʰ Rev 13:14
ⁱ Rev 13:16
ʲ Rev 13:15
ᵏ Da 7:11; Rev 20:10,14,15; 21:8 ˡ S Rev 9:17
19:21 ᵐ ver 15; S Rev 1:16 ⁿ ver 11, 19 ᵒ ver 17
20:1 ᵖ Rev 10:1; 18:1 ۹ Rev 1:18
ʳ S Lk 8:31
20:2 ˢ S Mt 4:10
Isa 24:22; S 2Pe 2:4
20:3 ᵘ ver 1
ᵛ Da 6:17; Mt 27:66
ʷ ver 8,10; Rev 12:9

The Thousand Years

20 And I saw an angel coming downᴹ out of heaven,ᵖ having the keyᴶ to the Abyssʳ and holding in his hand a great chain. ²He seized the dragon, that ancient serpent, who is the devil, or Satan,ˢ and bound him for a thousand years.ᵗ ³He threw him into the Abyss,ᵘ and locked and sealedᵛ it over him, to keep him from deceiving the nationsʷ anymore until the thousand years were ended. After that, he must be set free for a short time.

⁴I saw thronesˣ on which were seated

M Rev 12:5 ◄   **J** Rev 14:7 ◄

20:4 ˣ Da 7:9
ᵛ 15 Psalm 2:9

19:19–21 The conclusion of Armageddon and the battle around Jerusalem (see Zec 12:2–9) will complete the total defeat of the antichrist and his allies by the supernatural power of Jesus Christ. The armies of the antichrist initially gathered to destroy Israel and oppose the 200 million soldiers of the kings of the east (see 9:13–21). When these armies see Jesus Christ and his armies descending from heaven, all of the wicked armies of the earth will join in battle against Jesus and his saints. However, Jesus Christ will be the ultimate victor and will annihilate the wicked, defeat the antichrist and his false prophet and cast them alive into the lake of fire in hell forever (19:20; see Da 7:11; 2Th 2:8). The remnant of the armies of the antichrist and the kings of the east will be slain with the sword of Christ (19:21).

20:1–3 John reveals the defeat of Satan as the angel of the Lord chains the Devil for a thousand years in "the Abyss" (20:3). This Abyss is not hell, the lake of fire, but is a real place where Satan will be imprisoned for the Millennium. However, John warns that after the thousand years are complete, "he must be set free for a short time" (20:3).

Many have questioned why God would release Satan for a time after imprisoning him for a thousand years. Since the Bible does not tell us, we cannot be certain. It is interesting to note, however, that even after a Millennium of peace, prosperity, and justice under the rule of the Messiah, many humans will still rebel against God because their hearts are wicked apart from the grace of God (see 20:8–9; Jer 17:9).

20:4 *Dispensation of the Kingdom.* This last dispensation concludes God's plan of redemption for humanity and reflects the establishment of God's eternal kingdom on earth. The first one thousand years (the Millennium) will see the fulfillment of God's unshakable promises to Israel, the Gentile nations and the church. For the first time since Adam, humanity will be free of the temptation of Satan. The Messiah, Jesus Christ, will rule the earth from the throne of David, and the resurrected saints will govern with him. Humanity will be subject to Christ and the laws of God's kingdom. Righteousness and justice will replace oppression and misrule; Israel will be restored and converted. Creation will be delivered from its bondage to the effects of sin (see 1Co 15:24–28; Rev 22:3).

Yet despite the blessings of the initial years of this kingdom, some will choose to rebel when the Devil is loosed from the bottomless pit (see 20:7–10). God will destroy these rebels with fire from heaven and bring to an end the rebellion of Satan, his fallen angels and unrepentant sinners. These wicked ones will be resurrected to face the great white throne judgment and be condemned to hell (see Mt 25:41, 46; Rev 14:9–11; 19:20; 20:10). Those who remain true to God during this last rebellion will enjoy the full benefits of redemption through Christ for eternity.

The seven dispensations revealed in Scripture are the dispensations of innocence (Ge 1:28), conscience (Ge 3:7), human government (Ge 8:15), promise

The Millennium

THE PREMILLENNIAL VIEW

- The Church Age
- The Tribulation Period
  - 2nd Coming of Christ
  - 1st Resurrection
  - Battle of Armageddon
- The Millennium — 1000 YRS
  - Great White Throne
  - Final War of Gog & Magog
- Eternity
  - A New Heaven & A New Earth

THE POSTMILLENNIAL VIEW

- The Church Age
- The Millennium — 1000 YRS
- The Tribulation Period
  - 2nd Coming of Christ
  - 1st Resurrection
  - Great White Throne
  - Battle of Armageddon
  - Final War of Gog & Magog
- Eternity
  - A New Heaven & A New Earth

THE AMILLENNIAL VIEW

- The Church Age / The Millennium
  - Christ Reigns with His Saints in Heaven During this Period
  - Satan Imprisoned in Chains
- The Tribulation Period
  - 2nd Coming of Christ
  - 1st Resurrection
  - Great White Throne
  - Battle of Armageddon
  - Final War of Gog & Magog
- Eternity
  - A New Heaven & A New Earth

The Millennium

THE SCRIPTURES PROMISE that Jesus Christ will rule over this earth for one thousand years. Yet the millennial kingdom of the coming Messiah is one of the most misunderstood subjects in the whole field of prophecy. Interpreters view this millennial period in three different ways.

Postmillennialism

This view suggests that Christ's spirit will work through established systems of preaching and teaching to root out evil and bring improvement to the world. Only when humanity has defeated evil will Christ return to initiate judgment and establish his kingdom for 1000 years. While this theory was popular in the late 1600s, most scholars today reject this viewpoint because of the progress of history and continued fulfillment of prophecy.

Amillennialism

Those who subscribe to a symbolic interpretation of prophecy usually advocate this view of the Millennium. This position maintains that the Millennium is currently in progress during this church age and that the 1000 years mentioned in Revelation is merely a symbol of God's kingdom promises throughout the OT. Amillennialists do not make a clear distinction between God's dealings with OT Israel and the church but rather spiritualize one with the other. Those who hold to this viewpoint also contend that Satan is already bound because of Christ's promise in Mt 18:18 that his followers would have the power to do so. However, this view minimizes the evil conditions of this present age and overlooks the apostle Paul's clear distinctions between Israel and the church (see Ro 11; 1Co 10:32).

Premillennialism

This interpretation of the Millennium bases its belief on a literal interpretation of Biblical prophecy and stresses that the 1000 years in Revelation are actual years, not symbols. The majority of conservative Bible scholars subscribe to this view. Premillennialists also recognize the power of Christ's present rule in heaven and the importance of an earthly fulfillment of God's promises to Israel. Some critics suggest that an earthly kingdom that elevates Israel to prominence would negate the spiritual blessings of Christianity. Premillennialists counter this criticism with a rejoinder that God must keep his promises to Israel so that Christians can enjoy their eternal blessings too (see Isa 65:17; 66:22; 2Pe 3:13; Rev 21:1).

Those who hold to the premillennial view believe that Christ will return from heaven to defeat the antichrist at Armageddon and then will establish his peaceful kingdom on earth and rule from the throne of David in Jerusalem for 1000 years. After that time God will allow Satan to be released to test mankind one final time. God will then defeat Satan forever by casting him into the lake of fire, and Christ will establish his eternal kingdom on the new earth.

The Importance of the Millennial Kingdom

From the moment God made his first covenant with Abraham, God committed himself to establish a theocratic kingdom in which humanity would ultimately enjoy the restoration of the peace and righteousness Adam and Eve lost in the garden. The church has often lost sight of God's commitment to establish such a kingdom and has often set out to change and rule the world on its own. Yet the Bible clearly promises that God's kingdom will come on earth and will be ruled by the Messiah.

Scripture describes in detail the Gentile empires that will rule the world prior to the Messiah's return (see Da 7—8). Though there would be many nations who would challenge one another for supremacy, only four Gentile empires would successfully govern the world during the centuries of human history. The fourth empire, Rome, would be revived as a ten-nation confederacy under the control of the antichrist. This evil world empire will gain its power and supremacy from Satan. Only Jesus Christ, as the conquering Messiah returning from heaven with his mighty army, will destroy this enemy of God. Christ will then establish his millennial kingdom of righteousness and peace and rule from the throne of David in Jerusalem (see Isa 9:7). (For further information, see the article on "The Four World Empires on p. 964 and the article on "The Battle of Armageddon" on p. 1474.)

When Christ comes to establish his kingdom, he will descend to earth on the Mt. of Olives (see Zec 14:4), opposite the temple mount. A great earthquake will split the earth from the Mediterranean through the Mt. of Olives to the Dead Sea. Ezekiel adds that the Messiah will enter the temple through the eastern gate (see Eze 43:2, 4–5). This gate would be sealed to preserve it for the coming Messiah, the Prince (see 44:2–3).

True to Ezekiel's prophecy, this eastern gate to the temple has been shut now for many centuries, sealed by the Muslims when they rebuilt the walls of Jerusalem four hundred years ago. Accumulated rubble and a Muslim graveyard now occupy the area that used to be the eastern gate to the temple. The Muslims believe that walking through a graveyard would defile a priest or holy man, and therefore the placement of a cemetery in such a strategic place would prevent the Messiah fulfilling Ezekiel's prophecy. What the Muslims failed to recognize by their attempt to prevent the Messiah's entry into the temple is that God's plans are beyond understanding and his power beyond human control. Scripture records that the Messiah will enter the temple via the eastern gate, and this prophecy will be fulfilled.

The Character of the Millennial Kingdom

Some people have supposed that the end of the Millennium would also signal the end of the kingdom of Christ. Yet the Bible teaches that Christ's kingdom is an eternal kingdom that will be established "with justice and righteousness from that time on and forever" (Isa 9:7).

The Millennium is simply the beginning of the eternal kingdom of Christ. John referred to this first period of Christ's thousand-year rule six times in Revelation 20. Both the OT and NT prophesy that the eternal kingdom begins with the return of the Messiah in glory. The spiritual character of the millennial kingdom will reflect the nature of Christ. Following the rebellion of Adam and Eve, Satan was given power to rule over this world. He became "the god of this age" (2Co 4:4), and a curse was placed on its inhabitants and on the ground. However, in the millennial kingdom of Christ, the righteousness and justice of God will finally be restored. Any sin will be dealt with judicially by Christ as he rules with "a rod of iron" (Rev 12:5). Yet even in this ideal condition, the Bible indicates that humanity will rebel.

When God releases Satan from his thousand-year imprisonment, Satan will roam freely again on the earth for "a short time" (20:3). He will gather the rebels of all nations for a last great battle against God and the beloved city of Jerusalem. Yet Satan will be defeated and condemned forever to the "lake of burning sulfur" (20:10). At that time God will renew the earth and the heavens with fire in the same way that he cleansed the world from the effects of sin with the flood in Noah's day. (For further information, see the article on "A New Heaven and a New Earth" on p. 1494.) Then Israel and the surviving Gentile nations will enjoy the blessings of God throughout eternity under the righteous rule of Christ.

The Blessings of the Millennial Kingdom

The covenant God made with Abraham, the kingdom promises he spoke to David and his descendants, the justice his prophets yearned for—all these will be finally realized in the millennial kingdom of Christ. The promises made to Israel of peace, justice, prosperity and eternal blessings will become a reality. In addition, the Lord will fulfill his promise of a new covenant with Israel in which he will give them a new heart, a willingness to obey, forgiveness of sin, the presence of his Spirit, and a peaceful existence in their land (see Eze 36:26–28)

One of the greatest blessings that will flow from the millennial kingdom of God will be the introduction of a true and lasting world peace. For the first time in human history, soldiers will put down their weapons. Armies will be unnecessary. Under the direction of Jesus Christ, the resurrected believers of the church will provide the leadership necessary to create a just society for all people. Governmental corruption will disappear. Mercy, justice, integrity, peace and righteousness will be the hallmarks of this kingdom.

The earth will also reap the benefits of Christ's righteous rule. The curse that was placed upon the earth following the sin of Adam and Eve will be lifted when the kingdom is established. The desert "will rejoice and blossom" (Isa 35:1), and the earth will produce abundantly. According to Isa 33:24, all sickness will be eliminated. The deaf and the blind will be cured (see Isa 29:18). Even the devastated land of "Lebanon shall be turned into a fertile field" (Isa 29:17) as the Messiah renews the land from the curse of sin.

Though we do not know when Christ will establish this kingdom, the Bible promises that this kingdom will one day be a reality. May we always be looking for that reality every time we pray "Your kingdom come, your will be done on earth as it is in heaven" (Mt 6:10).

those who had been given authority to judge.[y] And I saw the souls of those who had been beheaded[z] because of their testimony for Jesus[a] and because of the word of God.[b] They had not worshiped the beast[c] or his image and had not received his mark on their foreheads or their hands.[d] They came to life and reigned[e] with Christ a thousand years. [F][W] [5](The rest of the dead did not come to life until the thousand years were ended.) This is the first resurrection.[f] [6]Blessed[g] and holy are those who have part in the first resurrection. The second death[h] has no power over them, but they will be priests[i] of God and of Christ and will reign with him[j] for a thousand years.

Satan's Doom

[V] [7]When the thousand years are over,[k] Satan will be released from his prison [8]and will go out to deceive the nations[l] in the four corners of the earth[m]—Gog and Magog[n]—to gather them for battle.[o] In number they are like the sand on the seashore.[p] [9]They marched across the breadth of the earth and surrounded[q] the camp of God's people, the city he loves.[r] But fire came down from heaven[s] and devoured them. [10]And the devil, who deceived them,[t] was thrown into the lake of burning sulfur,[u] where the beast[v] and the false prophet[w] had been thrown. They will be tormented day and night for ever and ever.[x]

The Dead Are Judged

[11]Then I saw a great white throne[y] and [J] him who was seated on it. Earth and sky fled from his presence,[z] and there was no place for them. [12]And I saw the dead, [S] great and small,[a] standing before the

---

20:4 ᵛMt 19:28; Rev 3:21 ᶻRev 6:9
ᵃS Rev 1:2
ᵇS Heb 4:12
ᶜS Rev 13:12
ᵈS Rev 13:16
ᵉver 6; Rev 22:5
20:5 ᶠver 6; Lk 14:14; Php 3:11; 1Th 4:16
20:6 ᵍRev 14:13 ʰS Rev 2:11 ⁱS 1Pe 2:5 ʲver 4; Rev 22:5
20:7 ᵏver 2
20:8 ˡver 3,10; Rev 12:9 ᵐIsa 11:12; Eze 7:2; Rev 7:1 ⁿEze 38:2; 39:1 ᵒS Rev 16:14 ᵖEze 38:9,15; Heb 11:12
20:9 ᑫEze 38:9,16 ʳPs 87:2 ˢEze 38:22; 39:6; S Rev 13:13
20:10 ᵗver 3,8; Rev 12:9; 19:20 ᵘS Rev 9:17 ᵛRev 16:13 ʷRev 16:13 ˣRev 14:10,11
20:11 ʸS Rev 4:2 ᶻS Rev 6:14
20:12 ᵃS Rev 19:5

[F] Heb 11:35 ◀ [W] 1Co 15:21–26 ◀
[V] Rev 19:15–16 ◀

[H] Rev 19:20 ◀▶ Rev 21:8 [J] Jude 6 ◀
[S] Rev 3:14–16 ◀▶ Rev 21:7–8

(Ge 12:1), law (Ex 19:1), the church (Ac 2:1) and the kingdom (Rev 20:4). For further information, see the article "The Seven Dispensations" on p. 4.

20:4–6 John then describes the saints, including those saints who resisted the antichrist (20:4), reigning from thrones and governing the kingdom of God on earth (see 5:10). Those who died unrepentant for their sins will be resurrected to stand before the great white throne at the end of the Millennium. This resurrection of the wicked dead will be the second resurrection and will result in the punishment of the wicked in hell after their judgment before Christ (see 20:13–14).

John states that the first resurrection is resurrection unto eternal life in heaven. Those who are "blessed and holy" (20:6) will participate in this resurrection and will have no fear of hell because their sins are forgiven. All those who participate in this first resurrection will also "reign with him for a thousand years" (20:6). This includes the OT saints, those who were raised when Christ rose (see Mt 27:52–53), the raptured church, the 144,000 Jewish witnesses and the "great multitude" (7:9, 14) of believers who come out of the tribulation. For further information, see the article on "The Resurrection of the Body" on p. 1218.

20:7–10 John continues with his description of Satan's release after the thousand years. The armies of the nations of the world, made up of those who are born during the Millennium and who never accept the Messiah as their Lord, join with Satan in one final attempt to overthrow God.

Note that Gog and Magog are different peoples from those who take part in the battle described in Eze 38—39. Ezekiel described a battle that takes place prior to the Battle of Armageddon. The weapons, allies, motive, participants and the method of destruction used by God differ between these two battles that take place over a thousand years apart. God will destroy Satan's armies in this battle with fire from heaven (20:9) and will cast Satan into the lake of fire to be tormented forever (20:10).

20:11–15 John describes the final judgment that will occur after the completion of the Millennium. All of the wicked dead, from Cain to the last rebel killed at the end of the Millennium, will be resurrected to stand before God's great white throne to receive judgment for their sins. All those who refused Christ's mercy will face his holy and severe judgment. They will be condemned to hell for eternity and suffer eternal separation from God.

Since all of these people are destined for an eternity in hell, some say the purpose of God's record book (20:12) may be to show that this punishment is deserved. Others contend that Scripture teaches a principle of judgment on the basis of works and that this book of deeds will determine each individual sinner's punishment in hell (see Ps 62:12; Jer 17:10; Lk 12:47–48; 20:47; Ro 2:6; 1Pe 1:17). Note that "the book of life" (20:12) was also opened to prove to the wicked dead that though some of them claimed to be Christians, their claim was counterfeit, and their name was not recorded in God's book of life. Anyone not named in "the book of life" (20:12) will be cast into hell. For further information, see the article "The Great White Throne Judgment" on p. 1490.

The Great White Throne Judgment

JOHN RECEIVED A clear vision of the final judgment before God's great white throne. This judgment will occur after the Millennium. Satan will be loosed from his imprisonment and lead the rebels of the earth in one final rebellion against God. Following this rebellion all of the earth's unrepentant sinners who have ever lived will be judged by God and sentenced to hell (see Rev 20:11–15).

The Time of the Judgment

John prophesied that this judgment would occur in heaven at the end of the millennial reign of the Messiah. God will test the men and women born in the Millennium by unleashing Satan for a short time to prove that, apart from Christ's redemption, people will still choose to rebel rather than serve God. After the defeat of Satan's final rebellion at the end of the Millennium, the Lord will resurrect the bodies and souls of all wicked men and women. They will stand in judgment with the sinful angels who participated in Satan's rebellion against God. This great tribunal will seal the final judgment of all the wicked dead who have died from the beginning of the world until the end of Satan's final rebellion. While the Scriptures do not reveal the length of time the trial will take, the length of the sentence for each defendant will be eternity without end. The devil will be cast into the lake of fire forever, demonstrating the ultimate victory of Christ over sin and evil.

Who Will Be Judged?

Many writers have suggested that all people, both believers and nonbelievers, would appear at this final judgment before the throne of God to determine their destination of hell or heaven. They suggest that this judgment will occur simultaneously because Daniel prophesied that "multitudes who sleep in the dust of the earth will awake: some to everlasting life, others to shame and everlasting contempt" (Da 12:2). Yet John's vision indicates that only "death and Hades gave up the dead that were in them" (Rev 20:13) and that only unrepentant sinners who reject God's salvation will appear before this great white throne. Though this is an apparent contradiction, a careful reading of the passage in Daniel reveals that Daniel is not declaring that the two resurrections will take place simultaneously. Rather, Daniel simply records the fact that two different groups will be resurrected and judged.

The apostle Paul confirms a separate appearance for those who accept Jesus Christ as their Savior "before the judgment seat of Christ" (2Co 5:10). This judgment of believers occurs at the rapture 1000 years before the great white throne judgment and will determine the believers' rewards for faithful service to God. There is no punishment for believers at this judgment seat because our sins are dealt with forever at the cross.

John's words describe a resurrecting of the wicked from the sea, death and *hades*. The "sea" and "death" refers to the fact that the bodies of those unrepentant sinners who died in the seas as well as those who were buried on land in the grave will all be resurrected by God to stand in judgment. Note also the reference to a resurrection from *hades*. Those souls of the OT who had rejected God's truth and died were confined to the part of *hades* known as a "place of torment" (Lk 16:28). The statement that *hades* will give up its wicked dead confirms that the souls of sinners will be delivered from *hades* to God's final judgment. No sinner will be left out. The wicked dead will stand before God to hear their sentence, and they will be delivered to hell in their resurrected bodies that cannot be destroyed or die.

The only wicked people who will not be judged at the great white throne judgment are those who have already been judged by God at an earlier point in time. These individuals include the antichrist, the false prophet and those evil people who survive the Battle of Armageddon (see Rev 19:20). These evil ones will be judged at the judgment of the Gentile nations described in Mt 25. Christ referred to these evil people as the "goats" (Mt 25:33), the wicked Gentiles who will enthusiastically join in the persecution of the tribulation believers. Christ promised that these "goats" would be cursed and sent "into the eternal fire prepared for the devil and his angels" (25:41). Since these wicked individuals have already been judged by Christ and sentenced to hell following the Battle of Armageddon, they will not appear to be judged a second time a thousand years later at the great white throne judgment in heaven. (For further information, see the article on "The Battle of Armageddon" on p. 1474 and the article on "The Judgments of God" on p. 1234.)

A Just Punishment

All those who appear at the great white throne judgment are already destined to an eternity in hell because they have not "believed in the name of God's one and only Son" (Jn 3:18). Since they are summoned to stand before the Judge they will therefore receive individual sentences. Scripture clearly states that each person is responsible for his or her own actions and that God deals individually with sinners (see Ps 28:4; 62:12; Pr 24:12, 29; Ecc 12:14; Jer 17:10; 32:19; Mt 16:27; Ro 2:6). Though their fate is already sealed by their sin and rejection of Christ, God's holiness and justice will provide all with their own appointed judgment. The wicked will receive punishment according to their sinful works as every single deed, thought and act is reviewed at God's throne when the books that record the deeds of humanity are opened. Even careless words will bring added judgment, for "men will have to give account on the day of judgment for every careless word they have spoken" (Mt 12:36).

Note that John mentions that two books will be opened at this tribunal. One book is the record book of sinful humanity's deeds. The other book is "the book of life" (Rev 20:12). The wicked will be judged from this book too. Why? The book of life contains only the names of those who have accepted the salvation of Christ. There may be some at the great white throne judgment who will protest to the Judge that they are Christians. They will claim that some great mistake has been made or that they were members of the church for years or that they have done great things for God during their life on earth. Yet Christ warned that "Not everyone who says to me, 'Lord, Lord', will enter the kingdom of heaven" (Mt 7:21).

Only God knows the true heart of any person. Unless we truly repent, turn from our sinful rebellion and accept Christ as our Lord and Savior, we shall never experience the salvation of Christ and have our names recorded in the book of life. No amount of good works or theological knowledge will qualify us to enter heaven's gates. The only acceptable price for salvation and pardon from hell is the blood of Christ shed on the cross for each one of us.

throne, and books were opened.[b] Another book was opened, which is the book of life.[c] The dead were judged[d] according to what they had done[e] as recorded in the books. [13]The sea gave up the dead that were in it, and death and Hades[f] gave up the dead[g] that were in them, and each person was judged according to what he had done.[h] [14]Then death[i] and Hades[j] were thrown into the lake of fire.[k] The lake of fire is the second death.[l] [15]If anyone's name was not found written in the book of life,[m] he was thrown into the lake of fire.

The New Jerusalem

21 Then I saw a new heaven and a new earth,[n] for the first heaven and the first earth had passed away,[o] and there was no longer any sea. [2]I saw the Holy City,[p] the new Jerusalem, coming down out of heaven from God,[q] prepared as a bride[r] beautifully dressed for her husband. [3]And I heard a loud voice from the throne saying, "Now the dwelling of God is with men, and he will live with them.[s] They will be his people, and God himself will be with them and be their God.[t] [4]He will wipe every tear from their eyes.[u] There will be no more death[v] or mourning or crying or pain,[w] for the old order of things has passed away."[x]

[5]He who was seated on the throne[y] said, "I am making everything new!"[z] Then he said, "Write this down, for these words are trustworthy and true."[a]

[6]He said to me: "It is done.[b] I am the Alpha and the Omega,[c] the Beginning and the End. To him who is thirsty I will give to drink without cost[d] from the spring of the water of life.[e] [7]He who overcomes[f] will inherit all this, and I will be his God and he will be my son.[g] [8]But the cowardly, the unbelieving, the vile, the murderers, the sexually immoral, those who practice magic arts, the idolaters and all liars[h]—their place will be in the fiery lake of burning sulfur.[i] This is the second death."[j]

[9]One of the seven angels who had the seven bowls full of the seven last plagues[k] came and said to me, "Come, I will show you the bride,[l] the wife of the Lamb." [10]And he carried me away[m] in the Spirit[n] to a mountain great and high, and showed me the Holy City, Jerusalem, coming down out of heaven from God.[o] [11]It shone with the glory of God,[p] and its brilliance was like that of a very precious jewel, like a jasper,[q] clear as crystal.[r] [12]It had a great, high wall with twelve gates,[s] and with twelve angels at the gates. On the gates were written the names of the twelve tribes of Israel.[t] [13]There were three gates on the east, three on the north, three on the south and three on the west. [14]The wall of the city had twelve foundations,[u] and on them were the names of the twelve apostles[v] of the Lamb.

[15]The angel who talked with me had a measuring rod[w] of gold to measure the city, its gates[x] and its walls. [16]The city was laid out like a square, as long as it was wide. He measured the city with the rod and found it to be 12,000 stadia[w] in

---

21:1 John's vision of the "new heaven and a new earth" (21:1) reveals the fulfillment of Peter's prophecy that the first heaven and the first earth will be burned with fire and cleansed from the effects of sin (see 2Pe 3:7, 10, 12, 13). Note the absence of the oceans on the new earth. This may indicate climactic changes to the new earth as well as changes to its surface.

Though the earth will be burned with fire, Scripture seems to indicate that it will not be totally annihilated. The Bible indicates that the earth was created to last forever (see Ps 78:69; 104:5; Ecc 1:4). For further information, see the article "A New Heaven and a New Earth" on p. 1494.

21:2–27 The new Jerusalem is the capital city of heaven, and the description of this glorious city reveals the wonders that await those who love Jesus Christ. After sin is eliminated from the universe following the judgments after the Millennium, this new Jerusalem will descend to the cleansed earth. God will dwell with his people in holiness on this renewed earth. For more information, see the article on "The New Jerusalem" on p. 1498.

A New Heaven and a New Earth

BOTH ISAIAH AND John were given visions of the transformation of the heavens and the earth that will occur at the end of the Millennium (see Isa 65:17; Rev 21:1). The effects of humanity's sins have polluted the earth and the heavens since the days of Adam and Eve. God cleansed the earth with a worldwide flood during the time of Noah, but that cleansing was only a temporary one. God promised that he will purify the earth and the heavens again at the end of the Millennium, removing every vestige of sin and its effects and ushering in a time of purity in God's eternal kingdom (see 2Pe 3:10–13).

A Renovation by Fire

Though Isaiah and John glimpsed the new heavens and the new earth, the apostle Peter described a fiery destruction as the means for their renovation. This refining will be God's last judgment on earth at the end of the Millennium after God defeats Satan's final rebellion. Some suggest that this refining will involve a total annihilation of the earth (see Mk 13:31). Others contend that the earth will continue forever (see Ps 72:5; 78:69; Ecc 1:4). These scholars believe that God will merely destroy the surface of the earth with fire in much the same way that he destroyed the earth's surface with the flood in Noah's day. Whatever way God chooses to cleanse the earth, Peter encouraged believers to anticipate the new heavens and new earth, "the home of righteousness" (2Pe 3:13).

In past generations some people scoffed at Peter's words that "the elements will be destroyed by fire" (2Pe 3:10). Scientists believed that the elements were impervious to destruction. Yet the discovery of thermonuclear reactions changed those beliefs. These nuclear chain reactions convert elements into energy, producing power and heat. In fact, a continuous series of nuclear chain reactions produces the ball of fire—our sun—that gives us daylight. Peter's words may well have foreshadowed a worldwide nuclear holocaust as a means of God's cleansing for the earth.

The Redemption of Creation

In a sense, the creation of the new heavens and new earth will be a return to the conditions found in the Garden of Eden. In that glorious time of innocence, Adam and Eve had lived in perfect, peaceful harmony with God and his creation. Yet from the moment of Adam and Eve's rebellion against God, all of creation has lived under the curse of sin. Adam's descendants were deprived of immortality and intimate communion with God. The earth itself was cursed because of Adam's sin and forced to travail under the dominion of the wicked serpent, Satan. Peaceful coexistence was shattered; all who chose violence and murder were cursed. Even the eternal, perfect universe felt the shock of sin's calamity. Designed by God to renew itself, the universe was flawed by sin and began to decay, run down and degenerate to a more and more disorganized state.

The apostle Paul prophesied the redemption of all creation when Christ creates the new heavens and the new earth (see Ro 8:21). When Christ removes the curse of sin, decay will be replaced by sustainable growth; disease and death will be replaced with eternal health and immortality. Peaceful coexistence will be restored so that "The wolf will live with the lamb, the leopard will lie down with the goat, the calf and the lion and the yearling together; and a little child will lead them" (Isa 11:6; see 11:7; 65:25). When the Messiah reigns, the redeemed of the Lord will live once more in perfect harmony in a peaceful world under the rule of a loving God.

The People of the New Earth

The new earth will be inhabited. Some have thought that the nations will not exist in the future, but the Scriptures teach that the Gentile nations and Israel will exist forever under the rule of the Messiah (see Rev 21:24). God's kingdom on the new earth will be populated with the descendants of those who survived the great tribulation and the Battle of Armageddon. The resurrected saints of the church will reign over the nations under the rule of the Messiah forever. God's new heavens and new earth will be far greater than we can imagine (see 1Co 2:9–10) and filled with righteousness and justice forever.

length, and as wide and high as it is long. ¹⁷He measured its wall and it was 144 cubits thick, by man's measurement, which the angel was using. ¹⁸The wall was made of jasper, and the city of pure gold, as pure as glass. ¹⁹The foundations of the city walls were decorated with every kind of precious stone. The first foundation was jasper, the second sapphire, the third chalcedony, the fourth emerald, ²⁰the fifth sardonyx, the sixth carnelian, the seventh chrysolite, the eighth beryl, the ninth topaz, the tenth chrysoprase, the eleventh jacinth, and the twelfth amethyst. ²¹The twelve gates were twelve pearls, each gate made of a single pearl. The great street of the city was of pure gold, like transparent glass.

²²I did not see a temple in the city, because the Lord God Almighty and the Lamb are its temple. ²³The city does not need the sun or the moon to shine on it, for the glory of God gives it light, and the Lamb is its lamp. ²⁴The nations will walk by its light, and the kings of the earth will bring their splendor into it. ²⁵On no day will its gates ever be shut, for there will be no night there. ²⁶The glory and honor of the nations will be brought into it. ²⁷Nothing impure will ever enter it, nor will anyone who does what is shameful or deceitful, but only those whose names are written in the Lamb's book of life.

The River of Life

22 Then the angel showed me the river of the water of life, as clear as crystal, flowing from the throne of God and of the Lamb ²down the middle of the great street of the city. On each side of the river stood the tree of life, bearing twelve crops of fruit, yielding its fruit every month. And the leaves of the tree are for the healing of the nations. ³No longer will there be any curse. The throne of God and of the Lamb will be in the city, and his servants will serve him. ⁴They will see his face, and his name will be on their foreheads. ⁵There will be no more night. They will not need the light of a lamp or the light of the sun, for the Lord God will give them light. And they will reign for ever and ever.

⁶The angel said to me, "These words are trustworthy and true. The Lord, the God of the spirits of the prophets, sent his angel to show his servants the things that must soon take place."

H Rev 21:8 ◀ ▶ Rev 22:15
S Rev 21:7–8 ◀ ▶ Rev 22:12

H 3Jn 2 ◀   N Rev 21:1–5 ◀
E Rev 5:1 ◀ ▶ Rev 22:10

ˣ17 That is, about 200 feet (about 65 meters) ʸ17 Or *high* ᶻ20 The precise identification of some of these precious stones is uncertain.

22:1–7 The angel showed John "the river of the water of life" (22:1) that flowed from God's throne in the new Jerusalem. Note that 22:2 indicates that the "tree of life" bears fruit every month, suggesting that a way to mark time will exist in eternity. This passage also indicates that there will be food in heaven. Scripture records that believers will participate in a literal wedding supper of the Lamb (see 19:9; Isa 25:6; Lk 22:18) and even the angels in heaven partake of manna (see Ps 78:22–25).

Access to the tree of life was restricted when Adam and Eve sinned in the garden (see Ge 3:22). In the new Jerusalem the curse of sin has been removed and access to this tree is restored. Some believe that the leaves of the tree of life will be used to grant immortality to those who have been born during the Millennium. These adherents suggest that while resurrected believers receive an incorruptible body (1Co 15:51–55), those born during the Millennium will need to partake of the leaves of the tree to heal their bodies so that they may live eternally.

Other scholars believe that the absence of hunger, thirst, sickness and sorrow (7:9–17; 21:4) indicates that the need for healing is removed in the new Jerusalem. These scholars contend that this reference to the tree and its leaves is merely symbolic of continuous blessing and the restoration to fullness of life for eternity.

The angel also showed John that the curse of sin would be removed forever, allowing the holy throne of God to reside in the new Jerusalem. God's people will live and reign forever in the presence of God.

Note, too, that the Lord promises a blessing to anyone who "keeps the words of the prophecy in this book" (22:7). Several such blessings are granted throughout the book of Revelation (see 1:3; 14:13; 16:15; 19:9; 20:6; 22:7, 14). When John fell at the angel's feet to worship him because of this marvelous message (22:8), the angel constrained him, telling John that he was only a servant of God and reminding John that only God should be worshiped (22:9).

Jesus Is Coming

⁷"Behold, I am coming soon!¹ Blessed is he who keeps the words of the prophecy in this book."

⁸I, John, am the one who heard and saw these things. And when I had heard and seen them, I fell down to worship at the feet of the angel who had been showing them to me. ⁹But he said to me, "Do not do it! I am a fellow servant with you and with your brothers the prophets and of all who keep the words of this book. Worship God!"

¹⁰Then he told me, "Do not seal up the words of the prophecy of this book, because the time is near. ¹¹Let him who does wrong continue to do wrong; let him who is vile continue to be vile; let him who does right continue to do right; and let him who is holy continue to be holy."

¹²"Behold, I am coming soon! My reward is with me, and I will give to everyone according to what he has done. ¹³I am the Alpha and the Omega, the First and the Last, the Beginning and the End.

¹⁴"Blessed are those who wash their robes, that they may have the right to the tree of life and may go through the gates into the city. ¹⁵Outside are the dogs, those who practice magic arts, the sexually immoral, the murderers, the idolaters and everyone who loves and practices falsehood.

¹⁶"I, Jesus, have sent my angel to give you this testimony for the churches. I am the Root and the Offspring of David, and the bright Morning Star."

¹⁷The Spirit and the bride say, "Come!" And let him who hears say, "Come!" Whoever is thirsty, let him come; and whoever wishes, let him take the free gift of the water of life.

¹⁸I warn everyone who hears the words of the prophecy of this book: If

---

C Rev 3:11 ▶ Rev 22:12
E Rev 22:6–7 ▶   N Rev 13:9 ▶
C Rev 22:7 ▶ Rev 22:20
S Rev 21:27 ▶ Rev 22:14–15

S Rev 22:12 ◀   H Rev 21:27 ◀
E Rev 21:10 ◀   L Rev 21:6 ◀
W Rev 21:6 ◀   C Eph 6:17 ◀

a 16 The Greek is plural.

22:12–13 Christ's promise to all believers is that he will return soon. Since centuries have passed since John penned this book, God apparently views time differently than we do (see 2Pe 3:8). Yet God keeps his promises (see 1Ki 8:56), and Christ will return. When he comes, he will reward those who have been faithful witnesses for him (see 1Co 3:8, 14; 2Ti 4:8; Heb 6:10; Jas 1:12). Note that in this passage Christ reaffirms his supremacy as the God of the universe (22:13; see 1:8).

22:18–19 Revelation ends with a prophetic warning for all who would dare alter God's words in this book. God also warned about adding or subtracting from the OT (see Dt 4:2; 12:32; Pr 30:6).

Possible Sequence of Future Events

			The Tribulation Period		The Millennium		Eternity	
Rebirth of Israel / Revival of Hebrew	Israel Captured Temple Mount		Rapture	Christ's Victory at Battle of Armageddon	Satan Bound in Bottomless Pit		Great White Throne	A New Heaven & A New Earth
1948	1967							
		Nations Surround Israel	Invasion of Israel	Antichrist Signs 7 Year Treaty with Israel	Antichrist Defiles Temple		Final War of Gog & Magog	

The New Jerusalem

THE LAST PORTION of the book of Revelation deals with a new heaven, a new earth and a new Jerusalem. Scholars differ on the exact interpretation to give to John's vision of this major city. Some scholars view this vision of the new Jerusalem as a fuller picture of Jerusalem during the Millennium. Others view this city as a symbol of eternity encompassing all of the aspects of eternal life. Still other scholars who interpret Biblical prophecy literally contend that the new Jerusalem is a literal city, the eternal home of the resurrected saints of God. It is this latter interpretation to which we will turn our focus.

The City of God

At the end of the Millennium, after sin has been eliminated from the universe and Satan has been banished forever to the lake of fire, God will cleanse the earth with fire. As a holy God, the Lord could never establish his eternal throne on earth until sin and evil and its effects were eradicated. After this cleansing of the earth, the new Jerusalem will descend from heaven (see Rev 3:12).

The Bible describes the new Jerusalem in very real, physical terms and sometimes calls it by other names. The author of Hebrews calls it "mount Sion," "the city of the living God," and "the heavenly Jerusalem" in order to distinguish it from the earthly Jerusalem that will continue to exist forever (see Heb 12:22). The apostle Paul uses a similar phrase, "the Jerusalem that is above" (Gal 4:26), to make the same distinction for his readers.

The exact location of this marvelous city is unclear. It may exist as a real entity in another dimension, or possibly, somewhere out in distant space. The Bible does not give us enough information to locate it, though it consistently refers to heaven and the heavenly city as existing in an upward direction, north from the earth. John notes that when the city is revealed, it comes "down out of heaven from my God" (Rev 3:12). During this present age the new Jerusalem is still in the heavens. It will descend to its eternal location only after the earth is cleansed.

Some suggest that the new Jerusalem's eternal position will be over the earth so that the light of the city, which is the light of God's presence, will shine on the earth beneath. This shining from above onto the earth beneath will enable "the nations [to] walk by its light, and the kings of the earth will bring their splendor into it" (21:24).

A Description of the New Jerusalem

The apostle John describes the dimensions of the new Jerusalem. The distance along each side is 1,500 miles. Some writers suggest that this holy city must be either a pyramid or cube in shape, rising in tiers as a huge mountain 1,500 miles up into the sky. Its walls are 216 feet tall (see 21:17), and there are 12 gates in this wall that are used for entering and leaving the city. (A pyramidal city could logically rest on a base 216 feet high with 12 gates.) Even John had to go to the top of a high mountain in order to see all of the "Holy City, Jerusalem, coming down out of heaven from God" (21:10).

The materials described in the new Jerusalem are precious stones and metals. The walls will be laid in twelve foundation layers of jasper crystal. Each layer will be 18 feet high and embellished with every manner of precious stone. Each of the twelve foundation layers will bear the name of one of the twelve apostles in honor of their faithfulness (see 21:14). These layers are decorated with jasper, sapphire, chalcedony, emerald, sardonyx, sardius, chrysolyte, beryl, topaz, chrysoprasus, jacinth and amethyst (see 21:19–20). The twelve gates will be named in honor of the twelve tribes of Israel, indicating God's unbreakable covenant with his chosen people. These twelve gates will be "twelve pearls, each gate made of a single pearl. The great street of the city was of pure gold, like transparent glass" (21:21). For further information on the composition and character of the heavenly Jerusalem, see the article on "Heaven" on p. 1238.

The Inhabitants of the New Jerusalem

John declared that in addition to his vision he heard a "loud voice from the throne saying, 'Now the dwelling of God is with men, and he will live with them. They will be his people, and God himself will be with them and be their God'" (21:3). God the Father, Son and Holy Spirit will eternally make the new Jerusalem his home. He will dwell in it with his heavenly hosts and surround himself with his beloved.

New Jerusalem is also the home of the resurrected church and of the departed saints of the OT. All Christians who died will be present in this heavenly city in the glorious, eternal, resurrection bodies they received at the rapture of the church. After the judgment seat of Christ and the marriage supper of the Lamb, Christ's bride will settle into her permanent home in the new Jerusalem. Jesus promised he would prepare the new Jerusalem as a home for his church (see Jn 14:2). He has kept his promise and prepared the new Jerusalem, adorned with jewels, for the church in the same careful, expectant manner that a bride prepares for her prospective husband.

When Jesus defeated Satan at the cross he also freed the souls of the OT saints that rested in Abraham's bosom (see Lk 16:22). Unfallen angels, the tribulation saints and "the spirits of righteous men made perfect" (Heb 12:23) will be citizens of the heavenly new Jerusalem too.

The inhabitants of the new Jerusalem will retain their individual and national characteristics. Nations will continue to exist as political entities and will continue to have rulers who will administer their political affairs. These nations will "go up year after year to worship the King, the LORD Almighty, and to celebrate the Feast of Tabernacles" (Zec 14:16).

Life in the New Jerusalem

The new Jerusalem will "not need the sun or the moon to shine on it, for the glory of God gives it light, and the Lamb is its lamp" (Rev 21:23). In this bright and glowing city, life will be joyful and free of pain or tears (see 21:4). The martyrs for the faith will be "before the throne of God and serve him day and night in his temple; and he who sits on the throne will spread his tent over them" (7:15).

The river of life will flow through the new Jerusalem, and the tree of life will grow along its banks (see 22:1–2). Time will continue to be marked in eternity because the tree of life will bear "fruit every month" (22:2). John also indicates that we will enjoy food in this heavenly city (see 22:2).

What a joy this city will be for the saints of God. John's vision regarding the heavenly city, the new Jerusalem, was a confirmation of all of the promises made to believers for the last six thousand years. The OT saints kept their eyes focused on "the city with foundations, whose architect and builder is God" (Heb 11:10) and earned Christ's commendation for their faithfulness. When the resurrected and redeemed of the Lord possess this city as their eternal inheritance in an everlasting relationship with God who is living among them, they will have attained heaven at last.

anyone adds anything to them,ˢ God will add to him the plagues described in this book.ᵗ ¹⁹And if anyone takes words away ᵘ from this book of prophecy,ᵛ God will take away from him his share in the tree of life ʷ and in the holy city, which are described in this book.

22:18 ˢ Dt 4:2; 12:32; Pr 30:6
ᵗ Rev 15:6-16:21
22:19 ᵘ Dt 4:2; 12:32; Pr 30:6
ᵛ ver 7,10,18
ʷ S Rev 2:7
22:20 ˣ Rev 1:2
ʸ ver 7,12
ᶻ 1Co 16:22
22:21 ᵃ S Ro 16:20

²⁰He who testifies to these things ˣ says, "Yes, I am coming soon."ʸ Amen. Come, Lord Jesus.ᶻ

²¹The grace of the Lord Jesus be with God's people.ᵃ Amen.

C *Rev 22:12* ◄ ►

22:20–21 John ends this marvelous prophecy with Christ's awesome promise to return quickly. As prophecies are fulfilled in our generation, we need to stay alert (see Mk 13:33) and awaken each day with the realization that "our salvation is nearer now than when we first believed" (Ro 13:11). With John we can prayerfully say, "Come, Lord Jesus" (22:20).

Study Helps

Table of Weights and Measures

Index to Subjects

Index to Articles

Concordance

Index to Color Maps

Table of Weights and Measures

The figures of the table are calculated on the basis of a shekel equaling 11.5 grams, a cubit equaling 18 inches and an ephah equaling 22 liters. The quart referred to is either a dry quart (slightly larger than a liter) or a liquid quart (slightly smaller than a liter), whichever is applicable. The ton referred to in the footnotes is the American ton of 2,000 pounds.

This table is based upon the best available information, but it is not intended to be mathematically precise; like the measurement equivalents in the footnotes, it merely gives approximate amounts and distances. Weights and measures differed somewhat at various times and places in the ancient world. There is uncertainty particularly about the ephah and the bath; further discoveries may shed more light on these units of capacity.

	BIBLICAL UNIT		APPROXIMATE AMERICAN EQUIVALENT	APPROXIMATE METRIC EQUIVALENT
WEIGHTS	talent	(60 minas)	75 pounds	34 kilograms
	mina	(50 shekels)	1¼ pounds	0.6 kilogram
	shekel	(2 bekas)	⅖ ounce	11.5 grams
	pim	(⅔ shekel)	⅓ ounce	7.6 grams
	beka	(10 gerahs)	⅕ ounce	5.5 grams
	gerah		1/50 ounce	0.6 gram
LENGTH	cubit		18 inches	0.5 meter
	span		9 inches	23 centimeters
	handbreadth		3 inches	8 centimeters
CAPACITY				
Dry Measure	cor [homer]	(10 ephahs)	6 bushels	220 liters
	lethek	(5 ephahs)	3 bushels	110 liters
	ephah	(10 omers)	⅗ bushel	22 liters
	seah	(⅓ ephah)	7 quarts	7.3 liters
	omer	(1/10 ephah)	2 quarts	2 liters
	cab	(1/18 ephah)	1 quart	1 liter
Liquid Measure	bath	(1 ephah)	6 gallons	22 liters
	hin	(⅙ bath)	4 quarts	4 liters
	log	(1/72 bath)	⅓ quart	0.3 liter

Index to Subjects

The index to subjects will help you find information on a variety of subjects covered in the notes of the *Prophecy Study Bible*. References to articles are indicated by **A**. References to book introductions are indicated by **I**.

A

Abednego, p. 961
Abomination of desolation, p. 980 **A**; pp. 987-88 **A**
Abraham, p. 484
Abraham's bosom, p. 1098 **A**; p. 1192 **A**; p. 1499 **A**
Abrahamic covenant, p. 25; p. 38; p. 83; p. 236
Absalom, p. 606
Adam, p. 3; p. 12; p. 583; p. 1496
Adamic covenant, p. 11
Ahab, p. 389; p. 396
Ahasuerus, p. 989
Ahaz, King, p. 492
Ahijah, p. 382; p. 385; p. 386
Ahithopel, p. 606
Alertness, p. 1128 **A**
Alexander the Great, p. 976; p. 976; p. 981-982; p. 989; p. 1055; p. 1059
Amalek, p. 185
Amalekites, p. 185
Ammonites, p. 875
Amos, p. 1279
Ancient of Days, p. 976
Angel, p. 286; p. 985; p. 1162; p. 1163
Angels, p. 241; p. 406; p. 542; p. 630; p. 969; p. 970; p. 1122; p. 1321; p. 1367 **I**; p. 1446; p. 1499 **A**
  Fallen, p. 926 **A**; p. 1098 **A**; p. 1235 **A**; p. 1490 **A**
Anna, p. 1166
Antichrist, p. 9 **A**; p. 542; p. 741; p. 748; p. 767; p. 925; p. 943 **A**; p. 960 **I**; p. 976; p. 977; p. 977; pp. 978-80 **A**; p. 985; p. 987 **A**; p. 990 **A**; p. 991 **A**; p. 992 **A**; p. 1126 **A**; p. 1234 **A**; p. 1385 **A**; p. 1386 **A**; p. 1387; p. 1437; p. 1442; p. 1460; p. 1468 **A**; p. 1470; pp. 1474-76 **A**; p. 1486 **A**; p. 1491 **A**
Antiochus Epiphanes, p. 981; p. 982; p. 985; p. 989; p. 993; p. 994
Apocalypse, p. 991 **A**; p. 1010 **I**; p. 1062 **I**; p. 1384 **A**
Apocalypse, the, p. 1384 **A**; pp. 1448-49 **I**; p. 1474 **A**; pp. 1482-83 **A**; p. 1498 **A**
  Allegorical interpretation, p. 1448 **I**
  Futurist interpretation, p. 1448 **I**
  Historical interpretation, p. 1448 **I**
  Preterist interpretation, p. 1448 **I**
Apostasy, p. 393; p. 492; p. 818
Ark of the covenant, p. 306; p. 819
Armageddon, p. 4 **A**; p. 171 **A**; p. 574; p. 592-593; p. 926 **A**; p. 943 **A**; pp. 987-88 **A**; pp. 990-91 **A**; p. 1030 **I**; p. 1122
Asaph, p. 627; p. 632-633
Asher, p. 66; p. 956
Assyria, p. 399 **I**; p. 439; p. 729 **I**; p. 873; pp. 979 **A**; 997 **I**; p. 1005; p. 1006; p. 1030 **I**; p. 1035 **I**; p. 1044 **I**; p. 1045; p. 1064
Assyrians, p. 627; p. 1033; p. 1036; p. 1037
Astrologers, p. 533
Atonement, p. 115 **I**; p. 171 **A**; p. 562; p. 1279
Azariah, p. 961

B

Baasha, p. 388
Babylon, p. 170 **A**; p. 364 **I**; p. 399 **I**; p. 427; p. 432 **I**; p. 467 **I**; p. 504 **I**; p. 730 **I**; p. 747; pp. 814 **I**; p. 873; p. 895 **I**; p. 959 **I**; p. 960; p. 965 **A**; p. 979 **A**; p. 986 **A**; p. 1044 **I**; p. 1048 **I**; p. 1053 **I**; p. 1058 **I**; p. 1062 **I**; p. 1424 **I**; p. 1457 **A**; p. 1471; p. 1479
Babylonia, p. 1064
Babylonians, p. 233; p. 627; p. 1045; p. 1047
Balaam, p. 183
Baptism,
  With the Holy Spirit, p. 1258
Baruch, p. 862; p. 871
Battle of Armageddon, p. 542; p. 580; p. 680; p. 766; p. 977; p. 995; p. 1126 **A**; p. 1219 **A**; pp. 1234-35 **A**; p. 1385 **A**; pp. 1474-76 **A**; pp. 1482-83 **A**; p. 1486 **A**; p. 1491 **A**; p. 1495 **A**
Battle of Gog and Magog, pp. 942-43 **A**
Beast, the, p. 979 **A**; p. 987 **A**; p. 991 **A**
Belshazzar, p. 972; p. 973
Belteshazzar, p. 961; p. 972

Bema judgment, p. 1236 **A**; p. 1384 **A**; pp. 1482-83 **A**
　See also *First resurrection; Second resurrection; Millennium, the.*
Benjamin, p. 67; p. 956
Bethel, p. 384
Bethlehem, p. 1039
Bethsaida, p. 1179
Betrayal, p. 606; p. 623
　By Judas, p. 655
Birth of the Messiah, p. 1039
Blessing(s), pp. 4-5 **A**; p. 8 **A**; p. 9 **A**; p. 10 **A**; p. 70 **I**; p. 201 **I**; p. 399 **I**; p. 1010 **I**; p. 1058 **I**; p. 1486 **A**; p. 1488 **A**
Blind, p. 1097
Book of life, p. 1236 **A**; p. 1239 **A**; p. 1489; p. 1491 **A**
Bottomless pit, p. 926 **A**
Branch, p. 745
Bride, p. 1124
Bridegroom, p. 1124

C

Caleb, p. 172; p. 172
Canaanites, p. 221
Capernaum, p. 1088; p. 1179
Capital punishment, p. 17
Captivity, p. 424
Christ, p. 342
Church, p. 5 **A**; p. 722 **I**; p. 943 **A**; p. 987 **A**; p. 990 **A**; p. 1128 **A**; pp. 1258 **I**; p. 1354 **I**; p. 1359; p. 1361 **I**; p. 1376 **I**; p. 1385 **A**; p. 1389 **I**; p. 1395 **I**; p. 1400 **I**; p. 1403 **I**; p. 1419 **I**; p. 1443 **I**; p. 1481; p. 1482 **A**; p. 1486 **A**; p. 1499 **A**
Circumcision, p. 27; p. 1278
Civil government, p. 17
Cleansing, p. 70 **I**; p. 170 **A**
Commandment, p. 207; p. 233
Communion, p. 1222; p. 1328
Conscience, p. 1234 **A**
Covenant,
　Abrahamic, p. 1 **I**; p. 9 **A**; p. 70 **I**; p. 452; p. 484; p. 650; p. 1348 **I**; p. 1487 **A**; p. 1488 **A**
　Adamic, p. 1 **I**; pp. 8-9 **A**
　Davidic, p. 2 **I**; p. 10 **A**; p. 334 **I**; p. 454; p. 485; p. 638-639
　Edenic, p. 1 **I**; p. 8 **A**
　God's, p. 596
　Human government, p. 9 **A**
　Mosaic, p. 1 **I**; pp. 9-10 **A**; p. 70 **I**

　New, p. 1 **I**; p. 10 **A**; p. 171 **A**; p. 856; p. 857; p. 1488 **A**
　Noahic, p. 1 **I**; p. 9 **A**
　Palestinian, p. 1 **I**; p. 10 **A**; p. 517
Covenant(s), p. 115 **I**; p. 200 **I**; p. 201; p. 210; p. 232; p. 271 **I**; p. 301 **I**; p. 313; p. 432 **I**; p. 814 **I**; p. 855; p. 997 **I**; p. 1062 **I**; p. 1499 **A**
Creation, p. 1 **I**; p. 5 **A**; p. 1305; p. 1406; p. 1455; pp. 1494-95 **A**
Creator, p. 649
Cross, p. 583; p. 591
　Of Christ, p. 694
Crown, p. 1374
Crown of glory, p. 1326 **A**
Crown of life, p. 1327 **A**; p. 1456 **A**
Crown of rejoicing, p. 1326 **A**
Crown of righteousness, p. 1326 **A**; p. 1398
Crowns, p. 1236 **A**; p. 1319; pp. 1326-27 **A**; p. 1384 **A**
Crucifixion, p. 141; p. 536; p. 592; p. 592; p. 796; p. 1109; p. 1117; p. 1206
Curse(s), p. 5 **A**; p. 8 **A**; p. 9 **A**; p. 11; p. 201 **I**; p. 959 **I**; p. 1488 **A**; p. 1494 **A**
Cush, p. 752-753; p. 1056
Cyrus, p. 467 **I**; p. 504 **I**; p. 965 **A**

D

Damascus, p. 752; p. 877; p. 1018
Dan, p. 66; p. 956
Daniel, p. 961
Darius the Mede, p. 974
David, p. 314; p. 318; p. 320; p. 341; p. 359; p. 363; p. 367; p. 435; p. 606; p. 656
Davidic covenant, p. 341
Day of Atonement, p. 142
Day of judgment, p. 580
Day of Pentecost, p. 1260
Day of the Lord, p. 1010 **I**; p. 1053 **I**; p. 1385 **A**
Death, p. 1328
Deliverance, p. 69 **I**; p. 271 **I**; p. 541 **I**; p. 730 **I**
Desolation, p. 981; p. 984
Disobedience, p. 7; p. 169; p. 317
Dispensation,
　Of conscience, p. 4 **A**; p. 7
　Of grace, p. 5 **A**
　Of human government, p. 4 **A**; p. 16
　Of innocence, p. 3; p. 4 **A**
　Of promise, pp. 4-5 **A**; p. 21

Of the church, p. 1259
Of the kingdom, p. 5 **A**; p. 1484
Of the law, p. 5 **A**; p. 89
Divine inspiration, p. 574; p. 712
Dream, p. 962; p. 963
Drought, p. 392

E

Earthquake(s), p. 1121; p. 1127 **A**; p. 1200; p. 1461
Edenic covenant, p. 6
Edom, p. 1028
Edomites, p. 185
Egypt, p. 929; p. 1064
Ekron, p. 306
Elijah, p. 389; p. 392; p. 393; p. 396; p. 1079; p. 1162; p. 1178; p. 1210; p. 1211; p. 1376 **A**; pp. 1468-69 **A**
Elisha, p. 393; p. 402; p. 407
Empire(s),
Babylonian, p. 965 **A**
Greek, p. 965 **A**
Medo-Persian, p. 965 **A**
Roman, p. 965 **A**; p. 978 **A**; p. 987 **A**
Ten nations, p. 966 **A**
End times, p. 730 **I**; pp. 959-60 **I**; p. 1372 **I**; p. 1382 **I**
Enoch, p. 401; p. 1376 **A**; p. 1469 **A**
Ephesus,
Church of, p. 1456 **A**
Ephraim, p. 956
Esau, p. 37
Esther, p. 536
Evangelism, p. 1128 **A**; p. 1378 **A**
Eve, p. 3; p. 12; p. 1496
Evil angels, p. 1446
Exile, p. 170 **A**; p. 171 **A**; p. 201 **I**; p. 364 **I**; p. 419; p. 421; p. 425; p. 432 **I**; p. 467 **I**; p. 504 **I**; p. 516 **I**; p. 532 **I**; p. 837; p. 895 **I**; p. 918; p. 986 **A**; p. 1062 **I**; p. 1075 **I**
Exodus, p. 83; p. 141; p. 153; p. 169; p. 172; p. 201; p. 216; p. 837; p. 1086
Exodus, the, p. 69 **I**; p. 115 **I**
Ezra, p. 507

F

Failure, p. 206
Fall, the, p. 11

False christs, p. 1153; p. 1154; p. 1200; p. 1437
False messiahs, p. 1126 **A**
False prophet, p. 980 **A**; p. 991 **A**; p. 1126 **A**; p. 1476 **A**; p. 1491 **A**
False teachers, p. 1367 **I**; p. 1389 **I**; p. 1400 **I**; p. 1430 **I**; p. 1435 **I**; p. 1441 **I**; p. 1445 **I**; p. 1457 **A**
Famine, p. 392; p. 1121; pp. 1126-27 **A**; p. 1200; p. 1460
Fast, p. 1095
Feast of Booths, p. 143
Feast of Firstfruits, p. 141; p. 212; p. 1218 **A**; p. 1332
Feast of Tabernacles, p. 143
Feast of Trumpets, p. 142; p. 171 **A**
Feast of Weeks, p. 141
Feasts, festivals, p. 115 **I**; p. 144; p. 170 **A**; p. 224 **A**; p. 296 **I**; p. 532 **I**; p. 711 **I**; p. 1044 **I**; p. 1209 **I**; p. 1218 **A**; p. 1499 **A**
Fig tree, p. 1150
First coming, pp. 742 **A**
First resurrection, pp. 1218-19 **A**
Flood, p. 14
Foreshadow, p. 635; p. 747; p. 1359
Forgiveness, p. 701; p. 1030 **I**; p. 1403 **I**; p. 1406 **I**; p. 1488 **A**
Futurist view,
Of tribulation, p. 990 **A**

G

Gad, p. 956
Gaza, p. 1018; p. 1055
Gehenna, p. 1099 **A**
Gentiles, p. 1228; p. 1272; p. 1277; p. 1278; p. 1296; p. 1309
Giants, p. 203
Gnosticism, p. 1435 **I**
Gnostics, p. 1332; p. 1348; p. 1397
Goats, p. 1125
God,
Holiness of, p. 115 **I**
Sovereignty of, p. 959 **I**
Gog, p. 940; p. 941; pp. 942-43 **A**; p. 944
Goliath, p. 306; p. 320
Gomorrah, p. 585; p. 730; p. 747; p. 1096; p. 1142
Great tribulation, p. 635; p. 977
Great white throne, p. 553; p. 1099 **A**; p. 1193 **A**; p. 1219 **A**; p. 1235 **A**; pp. 1490-92 **A**
See also *Second resurrection*.
Great whore of Babylon, p. 1475 **A**

Greece, p. 1062 I
Greek empire, p. 981; p. 982; p. 989
Gubaru, p. 974

H

Hades, p. 1219 A; p. 1432; p. 1098 A; pp. 1192-93 A; p. 1491 A
Hagar, p. 32
Ham, p. 18
Hananiah, p. 961
Hannah, p. 303
Harlot, p. 731
Hatred, pp. 1126-28 A
Healing, p. 1097
Heaven, p. 1192 A; p. 1193 A; p. 1220 A; pp. 1238-39 A; p. 1377 A; p. 1384 A; p. 1482 A; p. 1490 A; pp. 1498-99 A
Heliopolis, p. 754
Hell, p. 580; pp. 1098-1100 A; p. 1125; p. 1192 A; p. 1235 A; p. 1385 A; p. 1432; p. 1490 A
Herod the Great, p. 855
Hezekiah, King, p. 493; p. 494
Hezekiah, p. 424; p. 775; p. 849
Hobab, p. 165
Holiness, p. 927 A; p. 960 I; p. 1099 A; p. 1491 A
Holy Spirit, p. 171 A; p. 225 A; p. 938; p. 1010 I; p. 1014; p. 1087; p. 1161 I; p. 1162; p. 1164; p. 1166; p. 1213; p. 1237; p. 1241; pp. 1258 I; p. 1260; p. 1298 I; p. 1305; p. 1317 I; p. 1354 I; p. 1386 A; p. 1387; p. 1431
    Baptism with, p. 1258
    Gift of the, p. 1273
Huldah, p. 427; p. 500
Human government, p. 1385 A

I

Idolatry, p. 206; p. 215; p. 238; p. 308; p. 384; p. 386; p. 396; p. 399 I; p. 416; p. 420; p. 421; p. 424; p. 425; p. 467 I; p. 500; p. 830; p. 840; p. 918; p. 997 I; p. 999; p. 1017 I; p. 1036; p. 1317 I; p. 1457 A
Immanuel, p. 738
Imminence of Christ's return, p. 1393; p. 1423
Imprisonment,
    Thousand-year, p. 926 A
Incarnation, p. 1085; p. 1161 I; p. 1362 I; p. 1435 I; p. 1439
    See also *First coming*.

Incense, p. 1455
Incorruptible crown, pp. 1326-27 A
Inheritance, p. 4 A
Intermediate state, pp. 1192-94 A
Iraq, p. 1479
Isaac, p. 49
Ishmael, p. 26; p. 32
Israel, p. 9 A; p. 10 A; p. 722 I; p. 729 I; p. 895 I; pp. 942-43 A; p. 965 A; p. 986 A; p. 987 A; p. 997 I; p. 1017 I; p. 1027 I; p. 1035 I; p. 1053 I; p. 1084 I; p. 1128 A; p. 1385 A; p. 1474 A; p. 1486 A; p. 1495 A
    Nation of, p. 70 I; p. 171 A; p. 224 A; p. 245 I; p. 271 I; p. 301 I; p. 334 I; p. 399 I; p. 432 I; p. 504 I; p. 1234 A; p. 1469 A
    Persecution of, p. 1234 A
Issachar, p. 66; p. 449; p. 956
Ittobaal, p. 925

J

Jacob, p. 37; p. 65
Japheth, p. 18
Jehoiachin, p. 844
Jehoram, p. 485
Jehoshaphat, p. 484; p. 1015
Jehozadak, p. 440
Jeroboam, p. 382; p. 384; p. 385; p. 386; p. 1023
Jerusalem, p. 224 A; p. 334 I; p. 504 I; p. 516 I; p. 729 I; pp. 814 I; p. 886 I; p. 943 A; p. 959 I; p. 965 A; p. 980 A; p. 986 A; p. 991 A; p. 1027 I; p. 1035 I; p. 1036; p. 1044 I; p. 1048 I; p. 1058 I; p. 1120; p. 1487 A
    Destruction of, p. 1083 I; p. 1209 I; p. 1405 I; p. 1449 I
    New, p. 1193 A; p. 1235 A; pp. 1238-39 A; pp. 1498-1501 A
Jesus Christ, p. 5 A; pp. 224 A; p. 296 I; p. 579 I; p. 583; p. 606; p. 722 I; p. 960 I; p. 1030 I; pp. 1083-84 I; p. 1098 A; pp. 1135-36 I; p. 1161 I; p. 1209 I; p. 1435 I; p. 1441 I
    As Creator, p. 649
    Atoning death, p. 553
    Cross of, p. 69 I
    Death of, p. 224 A; p. 363; p. 987 A; p. 1234 A; p. 1297 I; p. 1347 I; p. 1405 I; p. 1483 A; p. 1492 A
    Preeminence of, p. 1367 I; p. 1405-6 I
    Prophecies about, p. 9 A; p. 171 A; pp. 742-743 A
    Resurrection of, p. 224 A
    Sacrificial death of, p. 1 I

Index to Subjects

Second coming of, p. 926 **A**; p. 990 **A**; p. 992 **A**; pp. 1126-28 **A**; p. 1326 **A**; p. 1372 **I**; p. 1376 **A**; p. 1378 **A**; p. 1382 **I**; p. 1419 **I**; p. 1430 **I**; p. 1449 **I**; p. 1458 **A**; p. 1476 **A**
Jezebel, p. 390
Jezreel, p. 998
John the Baptist, p. 1077; p. 1079; p. 1087; p. 1164; p. 1167
Jonah, p. 410; p. 536; p. 1103
Joseph, p. 66; p. 68; p. 956
Joseph of Arimathea, p. 796
Joshua, p. 172; p. 172; p. 268; p. 956
Josiah, p. 384
Judah, p. 65; p. 399 **I**; p. 467 **I**; p. 516 **I**; p. 532 **I**; p. 729 **I**; pp. 814 **I**; p. 956; p. 1010 **I**; p. 1017 **I**; p. 1027 **I**; p. 1035 **I**; p. 1048 **I**; p. 1053 **I**
Judaizers, p. 1278
Judas, p. 623
    Betrayal of, p. 655
Judas Iscariot, p. 606
Judas Maccabeus, p. 981
Judgment, p. 5 **A**; p. 8 **A**; p. 9 **A**; p. 10 **A**; p. 200 **I**; p. 235; p. 399 **I**; p. 729 **I**; pp. 814 **I**; p. 886 **I**; p. 895 **I**; p. 908; p. 927 **A**; pp. 990-91 **A**; p. 998 **I**; p. 1010 **I**; p. 1017 **I**; p. 1027 **I**; p. 1030 **I**; p. 1035 **I**; p. 1044 **I**; p. 1048 **I**; p. 1053 **I**; p. 1062 **I**; p. 1075 **I**; pp. 1098-99 **A**; pp. 1192-93 **A**; pp. 1234-36 **A**; p. 1238 **A**; p. 1428; p. 1430 **I**; p. 1445 **I**; p. 1448 **I**; p. 1468 **A**; p. 1491 **A**; p. 1494 **A**
    Bema, p. 1236 **A**
    Final, p. 602
    Great white throne, p. 1099 **A**; p. 1193 **A**; p. 1219 **A**; p. 1235 **A**; pp. 1490-92 **A**
    Of believer's sin, p. 1234 **A**
    Of believer's walk, p. 1234 **A**
    Of fallen angels, p. 1235 **A**
    Of gentile nations, p. 1235 **A**
    Of Israel, pp. 1234-35 **A**
    Of wicked dead, p. 1236 **A**
Judgment seat of Christ, p. 1340
Justice, p. 5 **I**; p. 541 **I**; p. 927 **A**; p. 1035 **I**; p. 1048 **I**; pp. 1098-99 **A**; pp. 1098-1100 **A**; p. 1449 **I**; p. 1488 **A**; p. 1491 **A**; p. 1495 **A**
    God's, p. 360
Justification, p. 562

K

King Agrippa, p. 1292
King of Kings, p. 1481
King of the Jews, p. 1132; p. 1204; p. 1205; p. 1244; p. 1245
King Saul, p. 313
Kingdom, p. 580
Kingdom of God, p. 1091; p. 1159
Kingdom of the Messiah, p. 675
Korazin, p. 1179

L

Lake of fire, p. 976; p. 980 **A**; p. 992 **A**; p. 1098 **A**; p. 1219 **A**; p. 1235 **A**; p. 1476 **A**; p. 1487 **A**; p. 1489; p. 1490 **A**; p. 1498 **A**
Lamb,
    Marriage supper of the, p. 1384 **A**; p. 1386 **A**; pp. 1482-83 **A**
Lamb, the, p. 1239 **A**; p. 1476 **A**
Lamb of God, p. 135; p. 1210 **I**; p. 1211; p. 1478
Laodicea,
    Church of, p. 1458 **A**
Last days, p. 926 **A**; p. 1084 **I**; p. 1128 **A**; p. 1433; p. 1447
Last trumpet, p. 1377 **A**; p. 1378 **A**
Law, p. 4 **A**; pp. 9-10 **A**; p. 69 **I**; p. 171 **A**; p. 200 **I**; p. 225 **A**; p. 245 **I**; p. 364 **I**; p. 814 **I**
Law, the, p. 1347 **I**; p. 1405-61; p. 1469 **A**
Lazarus, p. 1229
Leah, p. 956
Leaven, p. 1105
Levi, p. 65; p. 956
Lo-ammi, p. 998
Locusts, p. 1463
Lord of lords, p. 1481
Lord's Day, p. 1279
Lo-ruhamah, p. 998
Lot, p. 1191
Love,
    Of God, p. 552

M

Magog, p. 940; pp. 942-43 **A**
Manasseh, p. 425; p. 898; p. 956
Manna, p. 153
Marriage supper of the lamb, p. 401; p. 609; p. 759; p. 1117; p. 1359; p. 1384 **A**; p. 1386 **A**; pp. 1482-83 **A**; p. 1499 **A**

Martyrdom, p. 1201
Martyrs, p. 1416
Massada, p. 141
Matthias, p. 655
Medes, p. 883; p. 1045; p. 1047
Medo-Persia, p. 989; p. 1064
Medo-Persian empire, p. 976; p. 989
Melchizedek, p. 24
Mercy, p. 8 **A**; p. 887 **I**; p. 1030 **I**; p. 1044 **I**; p. 1048 **I**; p. 1219 **A**
Meribah, p. 189; p. 206
Meshach, p. 961
Messenger, pp. 742 **A**; p. 1075 **I**
Messiah, the, p. 5 **A**; p. 10 **A**; p. 701; p. 171 **A**; p. 185; p. 222; pp. 224 **A**; p. 236; p. 318; p. 334 **I**; p. 342; p. 435; p. 454; p. 464; p. 541 **I**; p. 579 **I**; p. 580; p. 586; p. 592; p. 608; p. 609; p. 623; p. 624; p. 625-626; p. 628; p. 636; p. 638-639; p. 644; p. 656; p. 730 **I**; p. 738; pp. 742-743 **A**; p. 745; p. 777; p. 805; p. 844; p. 860; p. 960 **I**; pp. 979 **A**; p. 984; p. 986 **A**; p. 987 **A**; p. 1017 **I**; p. 1035 **I**; p. 1053 **I**; p. 1075 **I**; p. 1083 **I**; p. 1219 **A**; p. 1234 **A**; p. 1258 **I**; p. 1406 **I**; p. 1468 **A**; p. 1475 **A**; p. 1487 **A**; p. 1490 **A**; p. 1495 **A**
Messianic feast, p. 1093
Messianic kingdom, p. 4 **A**; p. 8 **A**; p. 10 **A**; p. 23; p. 172; p. 207; p. 464; p. 593-593; p. 602; p. 730 **I**; p. 926 **A**; p. 927 **A**; p. 964 **A**; p. 966 **A**; p. 1035 **I**; p. 1075 **I**; p. 1084 **I**; p. 1449 **I**; p. 1468 **A**
Millennial kingdom, p. 8 **A**; p. 10 **A**; p. 171 **A**; p. 609; p. 668; p. 688; p. 740; p. 746; p. 777; p. 860; p. 960 **I**; p. 980 **A**; p. 992 **A**; p. 1038; p. 1149; p. 1235 **A**; p. 1476 **A**
  Blessings of, p. 1488 **A**
  Character of, pp. 1487-88 **A**
  Importance of, p. 1487 **A**
Millennial temple, p. 102
Millennium, the, p. 592-593; p. 621; p. 623; p. 624-625; p. 632; p. 636-637; p. 640; p. 680; p. 770; p. 811; p. 943 **A**; p. 990 **A**; p. 1098 **A**; pp. 1098-99 **A**; p. 1192 **A**; p. 1219 **A**; p. 1235 **A**; p. 1238 **A**; pp. 1486-88 **A**; p. 1490 **A**; p. 1494 **A**
Miracles, p. 212; p. 255; p. 407; p. 738; p. 775; p. 1051; p. 1085; p. 1097; p. 1101; p. 1206
  Of healing, p. 1227
Mishael, p. 961
Moabites, p. 185; p. 402
Molech, p. 425; p. 492
Mordecai, p. 536
Mosaic covenant, p. 90
Moses, p. 70 **I**; p. 88; p. 179; p. 189; p. 200 **I**; pp. 224 **A**; p. 241; p. 1178; p. 1348 **I**; p. 1469 **A**; p. 1475 **A**
Mount of Transfiguration, p. 1178
Mt. Ebal, p. 231; p. 231

Mt. Gerizim, p. 231
Mt. Zion, p. 610

N

Nabonidus, p. 973
Naphtali, p. 66; p. 956
Nations, p. 9 **A**; p. 224 **A**; p. 730 **I**; p. 926 **A**; p. 959 **I**; p. 987 **A**; p. 1053 **I**; p. 1499 **A**
  Confederacy of, pp. 942-43 **A**; p. 966 **A**
  Confederacy of ten, p. 1385 **A**; p. 1474 **A**; p. 1475 **A**; p. 1487 **A**
  Gentile, p. 5 **A**; p. 895 **I**; p. 943 **A**; p. 979 **A**; p. 1235 **A**; p. 1487 **A**; p. 1488 **A**; p. 1491 **A**; p. 1495 **A**
  Ten, p. 979 **A**; p. 991 **A**
Natural disasters, p. 943 **A**
Nazareth, p. 1086
Nazarite, p. 159
Nebuchadnezzar, p. 234; p. 430; p. 929; p. 961
Nephilim, p. 14
New covenant, p. 856; p. 857; p. 1411
New earth, p. 632; p. 647; p. 810; p. 977; p. 1238 **A**; p. 1433; p. 1488 **A**; p. 1493; pp. 1494-95 **A**
New heart, p. 938
New heaven, p. 553; p. 647; p. 810; p. 1433; p. 1488 **A**; p. 1493; pp. 1494-95 **A**
New Jerusalem, p. 632; p. 1493
New song, p. 1455
Nineveh, p. 1031; p. 1033; p. 1045; p. 1047; p. 1182
Nisan,
  First day, p. 170 **A**
  Tenth day, p. 170 **A**
Noah, p. 14; p. 14; p. 16; p. 1123
Noahic covenant, p. 17
Noe, p. 1191
  See *Noah.*

O-P

Obadiah, p. 390
Obedience, p. 1 **I**; pp. 4-5 **A**; p. 69 **I**; p. 151 **I**; p. 169; p. 194; p. 200 **I**; p. 211; p. 215; p. 245 **I**; p. 271; p. 317; p. 364 **I**; p. 399 **I**; p. 541 **I**; p. 552; p. 562; p. 711 **I**; p. 1234 **A**; p. 1400 **I**; p. 1488 **A**
Offering, p. 121
Og, p. 204

Oppression, p. 271 **I**
Palestinian covenant, p. 236; p. 236
Palm Sunday, p. 904; p. 984; p. 1069; p. 1231
Parable, p. 1105
    Of the fig tree, p. 1154; p. 1201
    Of the great banquet, p. 1187
    Of the mustard seed, p. 1140; p. 1186
    Of the rich man, p. 1190
    Of the tenants, p. 1198
    Of yeast, p. 1186
Paradise, pp. 1193-94 **A**
Passover, p. 69 **I**; p. 70 **I**; p. 80; p. 141; p. 170 **A**; pp. 171 **A**; p. 224 **A**; p. 1468 **A**
Patmos, p. 1450
Peace, p. 1060; p. 1362 **I**; p. 1449 **I**; p. 1487 **A**; p. 1488 **A**; p. 1495 **A**
Pentecost, p. 171 **A**; p. 225 **A**; p. 296 **I**; p. 1010 **I**; p. 1014; p. 1087; p. 1237; p. 1258 **I**; p. 1297 **I**; p. 1419 **I**; p. 1449 **I**
Pergamos,
    Church of, p. 1457 **A**
Persecution, p. 1096; p. 1201; p. 1242; p. 1327 **A**; p. 1383; p. 1429; p. 1458 **A**; p. 1462; p. 1491 **A**
    In end times, p. 1476 **A**
    Of early church, p. 1372 **I**; p. 1395 **I**; p. 1405 **I**; p. 1424 **I**; p. 1448 **I**; p. 1456 **A**
    Of Israel, p. 1234 **A**
    Of the Jews, p. 1127 **A**
    Prophecies of, p. 1234 **A**
Persia, p. 532 **I**; p. 1059; p. 1062 **I**
Persians, p. 883
Pestilence, p. 1121; p. 1127 **A**; p. 1200
Peter, p. 623; p. 655; p. 1109
Petra, p. 1028
Pharisees, p. 1119; p. 1199; p. 1289; p. 1291
Philadelphia,
    Church of, p. 1458 **A**
Philistines, p. 306; p. 320
Pontius Pilate, p. 1204
Potter, p. 809
Praise, p. 359; p. 507
Prayer, p. 577
Preexistence, p. 1450
Preterist view,
    Of tribulation, p. 990 **A**
Pretribulation rapture, pp. 1384-86 **A**
Pride, p. 317
Promised land, p. 4 **A**; p. 10 **A**; p. 151 **I**; p. 200 **I**; p. 206; p. 245 **I**; p. 271 **I**; p. 341; p. 420; p. 421; p. 746; p. 896 **I**; p. 942 **A**; p. 1058 **I**

Promises, p. 11; p. 1486 **A**; p. 1500 **A**
    Of God, p. 9 **A**; p. 10 **A**; p. 245 **I**; pp. 742-743 **A**
Prophecy, prophecies, p. 1084 **I**; p. 1234 **A**; p. 1238 **A**; p. 1258 **I**; p. 1336 **I**; p. 1382 **I**; p. 1431; pp. 1448-49 **I**; p. 1475 **A**
    Of Daniel, p. 516 **I**; pp. 959-60 **I**; pp. 964-66 **A**; pp. 986 **A**; p. 1219 **A**; p. 1385 **A**; p. 1490 **A**
    Of Ezekiel, p. 895 **I**; p. 942 **A**; p. 943 **A**; p. 1487 **A**
    Of Isaiah, p. 730 **I**; p. 1128 **A**; p. 1474 **A**
    Of Jeremiah, pp. 815 **I**; p. 986 **A**
    Of Jesus, p. 1128 **A**
    Of Joel, p. 1128 **A**; p. 1474 **A**; p. 1475 **A**
    Of John, pp. 1448-49 **I**
    Of Malachi, pp. 1468-69 **A**; p. 1469 **A**
    Of Zechariah, p. 1234 **A**; p. 1474 **A**
Protevangelium, p. 11
Ptolemies, p. 989
Punishment, p. 8 **A**; p. 10 **A**; p. 1099 **A**; p. 1193 **A**; p. 1219 **A**; p. 1385 **A**; p. 1491 **A**
Purim, p. 532 **I**

Q-R

Queen of Sheba, p. 1103; p. 1182
Rachel, p. 956
Rainbow, p. 1454
Rapture, the, p. 5 **A**; p. 401; p. 943 **A**; p. 990 **A**; p. 995; p. 1123; pp. 1193-94 **A**; pp. 1218-19 **A**; p. 1333; p. 1372 **I**; p. 1375; pp. 1376-77 **A**; p. 1490 **A**
    Of the church, p. 1482 **A**; p. 1499 **A**
    Pretribulation, pp. 1384-86 **A**
Rebellion, p. 4 **A**; p. 5 **A**; p. 151 **I**; p. 317; p. 364 **I**; p. 431; p. 926 **A**; p. 978 **A**; p. 1234 **A**; p. 1235 **A**; p. 1488 **A**; p. 1490 **A**; p. 1494 **A**
Rechabites, p. 862
Reconciliation, p. 1151; p. 1403 **I**
Red heifer, p. 177
Redeemer, p. 11
Redemption, p. 1 **I**; p. 5 **A**; p. 8 **A**; p. 69 **I**; p. 151 **I**; p. 541 **I**; p. 557; p. 583; p. 730 **I**; p. 959 **I**; p. 1354 **I**; p. 1495 **A**
Remnant, p. 504 **I**; p. 744; p. 1037; p. 1307
Renewal, p. 1305
Repentance, p. 10 **A**; p. 308; p. 517; p. 562; pp. 814 **I**; p. 1010 **I**; p. 1030 **I**; p. 1033; p. 1044 **I**; p. 1053 **I**; p. 1075 **I**; pp. 1098-1100 **A**; p. 1336 **I**; p. 1468 **A**
Restoration, p. 5 **A**; p. 801; p. 806; p. 895 **I**; p. 998 **I**; p. 1035 **I**; p. 1053 **I**
    Of Israel, p. 622

Index to Subjects

Resurrection, p. 5 **A**; p. 9 **A**; p. 49; p. 65; p. 171 **A**; p. 192; p. 224 **A**; p. 273; p. 536; p. 553; p. 557; p. 559; p. 587; p. 625; p. 987 **A**; p. 995; p. 1084 **I**; p. 1098 **A**; p. 1109; p. 1118; p. 1130; p. 1133; p. 1187; pp. 1192-93 **A**; p. 1199; p. 1216; p. 1218 **A**; p. 1222; p. 1229; p. 1258 **I**; p. 1261; p. 1279; p. 1291; p. 1292; p. 1297 **I**; p. 1305; p. 1317 **I**; p. 1321; p. 1328; p. 1331; p. 1332; p. 1364; p. 1372 **I**; p. 1375; p. 1397; p. 1406 **I**; p. 1416
   First, pp. 1218-19 **A**; p. 1490 **A**
   Of Jesus Christ, p. 1218 **A**
   Of the body, pp. 1218-20 **A**
   Of the church, pp. 1376-77 **A**
   Of the dead, p. 1376 **A**
   Second, p. 1219 **A**; p. 1490 **A**
   See also Bema *judgment*.
Resurrection body, p. 1193 **A**; pp. 1219-20 **A**; p. 1377 **A**; p. 1499 **A**
Resurrection mind, p. 1220 **A**
Reuben, p. 65; p. 65; p. 956
Revelation, p. 1210 **I**; p. 1297 **I**; p. 1406 **I**
   Of God's plan, p. 1 **I**
Rewards, p. 1319; p. 1340
Righteousness, p. 5 **A**; p. 9 **A**; p. 1234 **A**; pp. 1297-98 **I**; p. 1419 **I**; p. 1487 **A**; p. 1495 **A**
River of life, p. 1239 **A**; p. 1500 **A**
Roman empire, p. 976; p. 1470; p. 1478
Rome, p. 1478
Rosh Hashanah, p. 142

S

Sabbath, p. 103; p. 145; p. 170 **A**; p. 503; p. 802; p. 1122; p. 1279
Sacrifice, p. 5 **A**; p. 69 **I**; p. 115 **I**; p. 122; p. 317; p. 363; p. 1405-6 **I**
   Of Jesus, p. 592
Sadducees, p. 1118; p. 1199; p. 1289
Salvation, p. 5 **A**; p. 70 **I**; p. 553; p. 987 **A**; p. 1075 **I**; p. 1084 **I**; p. 1098 **A**; pp. 1098-1100 **A**; p. 1161 **I**; p. 1210 **I**; p. 1219 **A**; p. 1279; p. 1297 **I**; p. 1347 **I**; p. 1379; p. 1385 **A**; p. 1405-6 **I**; p. 1445 **I**; p. 1456 **A**; p. 1491 **A**
Samaria, p. 1036
Samaritans, p. 738
Samuel, p. 303; p. 308; p. 317; p. 318
Sanctification, p. 170 **A**; p. 1313; p. 1374; p. 1379
Sanctuary, p. 96
Sardis,
   Church of, pp. 1457-58 **A**
Sargon, p. 750

Satan, p. 3; p. 4 **A**; p. 9 **A**; p. 11; p. 541 **I**; p. 542; p. 552; p. 592-593; p. 738; p. 748; p. 925; pp. 926-927 **A**; p. 978 **A**; p. 985; p. 991 **A**; p. 1064; p. 1125; p. 1235 **A**; p. 1314; p. 1387; p. 1449 **I**; p. 1467; p. 1470; p. 1475 **A**; p. 1484; p. 1486 **A**; p. 1487 **A**; p. 1488 **A**; p. 1489; p. 1490 **A**; p. 1494 **A**; p. 1498 **A**
Scapegoat, p. 1413
Science, p. 573
Scythians, p. 1045; p. 1047
Second coming, p. 746; p. 926 **A**; p. 990 **A**; p. 1121; pp. 1126-28 **A**; p. 1326 **A**; p. 1328; p. 1372 **I**; p. 1376 **A**; p. 1378 **A**; p. 1382 **I**; p. 1402; p. 1415; p. 1419 **I**; p. 1430 **I**; p. 1433; p. 1449 **I**; p. 1458 **A**; p. 1476 **A**
   Of Christ, p. 995
Second death, p. 1219 **A**; p. 1456 **A**
Second resurrection, p. 1219 **A**; p. 1236 **A**
Sela, p. 751
Seleucids, p. 989; p. 993
Seven, p. 1450
Seven letters, pp. 1456-59 **A**
Seventieth week, p. 985; p. 987 **A**
Seventy weeks, p. 102; p. 318; p. 516 **I**; pp. 987-88 **A**; p. 1385 **A**
Shadrach, p. 961
Shalmaneser, p. 750
Shearjashub, p. 738
Sheep, p. 1125
Shem, p. 18
Shema, p. 209
Sheol, p. 1098 **A**
Shepherd, p. 935
Shiloh, p. 849
Sidon, p. 1179
Signs, p. 1030 **I**; p. 1209 **I**; p. 1382 **I**; p. 1468 **A**; p. 1476 **A**
   Of second coming, pp. 1126-28 **A**
Simeon, p. 65; p. 956; p. 1166
Sinai, p. 153
Smyrna,
   Church of, p. 1456 **A**
Sodom, p. 585; p. 730; p. 747; p. 1096; p. 1142; p. 1179; p. 1191
Sodom and Gomorrah, p. 30
Solomon, p. ; p. 341; p. 367; p. 371; p. 376
   Apostasy of, p. 381
Son of David, p. 1119; p. 1200
Son of God, p. 1119; p. 1163; p. 1200
Son of man, p. 976
Song, p. 359
Soul sleep, p. 1194 **A**

Sovereign grace, p. 318; p. 1222
Sovereignty of God, p. 547
Spiritual adultery, p. 818
Spiritual warfare, p. 1311
Stephen, p. 1268
Stewardship, p. 1124
Stone, p. 967; p. 1065
Suffering, p. 1429
Suffering servant, p. 796
Syria, p. 1018

T

Tabernacle, p. 69 I; p. 70 I; p. 115 I
Tartarus, p. 1098 A
Temple, p. 96; p. 171 A; p. 363; p. 364 I; p. 432 I; p. 467 I; p. 504 I; p. 516 I; p. 532 I; pp. 814 I; p. 886 I; p. 943 A; p. 945; p. 965 A; p. 980 A; pp. 980 A; p. 1035 I; p. 1058 I; p. 1060; p. 1075 I; p. 1153
    Millennial, p. 170 A; p. 895 I
    Of Solomon, p. 376; p. 378
Temptations, p. 561
Tests, p. 561
Theophany, p. 22; p. 273; p. 286
Thousand years, p. 542; p. 1219 A; p. 1235 A
    See *Millennium, the.*
Throne, p. 458
Thyatira,
    Church of, p. 1457 A
Time calculations, p. 536; p. 1103
Tongues, p. 1260
Transfiguration, the, p. 1178
Tree of life, p. 6; p. 1496; p. 1500 A
Trials, p. 561; p. 578; p. 969
Tribulation, p. 389; p. 621; p. 758; p. 766; p. 926 A; p. 943 A; p. 960 I; p. 980 A; p. 985; p. 986-88 A; p. 987 A; p. 987 A; pp. 990-92 A; p. 1030 I; p. 1121; p. 1121; p. 1127 A; p. 1234 A; p. 1235 A; p. 1377 A; p. 1383; p. 1458 A; p. 1462; p. 1468 A; p. 1474 A; p. 1482 A; p. 1495 A
Trumpet, p. 1333; p. 1463; p. 1464
Trust, p. 359
    In God, p. 561

Turkey, p. 1451
Two witnesses, the, p. 1162; pp. 1468-70 A
Type(s), p. 70 I; p. 722 I
Tyre, p. 929; p. 1018; p. 1179

U-V-W

Unbelief, p. 206
Valley of Jehoshaphat, p. 1015
Vineyard, p. 735; p. 761
Virgin, p. 1085
Virgin birth, p. 9 A; p. 592; p. 738; p. 1085
Vision, p. 896; p. 950; p. 951; p. 955; p. 977; p. 1063; p. 1069; p. 1345; p. 1451; p. 1454
    Of Isaiah, p. 1494 A
    Of John, p. 1494 A
Wars, p. 1126 A
Wedding of the lamb, p. 1481
Wedding supper, p. 1124
Wedding supper of the lamb, p. 1328
Wicked, p. 585
Widow, p. 390
Wilderness wandering, p. 211
Wise men, p. 1085
Witnesses, p. 1258; p. 1461
Worship, p. 5 A; p. 70 I; p. 115 I; p. 151 I; pp. 200 I; p. 895 I; p. 926 A; p. 960 I; p. 997 I
    Of God, p. 363
Wrath, p. 1373; p. 1379; p. 1384 A; p. 1385 A
    Of God, p. 1123

X-Y-Z

Xerxes I, p. 989
Year of Jubilee, p. 145
Yom Kippur, p. 142
Zebulun, p. 66; p. 956
Zechariah, p. 1164
Zedekiah, p. 430; p. 866; p. 1039
Zerubbabel, p. 440
Zilpah, p. 956

Index to Articles

The Seven Dispensations 4	The Resurrection of the Body 1218
The Biblical Covenants 8	The Judgments of God 1234
The Biblical Anniversaries of Israel 170	Heaven 1238
A Prophet Like Unto Moses 224	Crowns and Rewards 1326
The Prophecies of Christ's First Coming 742	The Rapture 1376
Satan and the Fallen Angels 926	Reasons for a Pretribulation Rapture 1384
The Battle of Gog and Magog 942	The Seven Letters to the Churches 1456
The Four World Empires 964	The Two Witnesses 1468
The Antichrist 978	The Battle of Armageddon 1474
The Vision of the Seventy Weeks 986	The Marriage Supper of the Lamb 1482
The Tribulation 990	The Millennium 1486
Hell 1098	The Great White Throne Judgment 1490
Signs of the Second Coming 1126	A New Heaven and a New Earth 1494
The Intermediate State 1192	The New Jerusalem 1498

Introduction
to the NIV Concordance

The NIV Concordance, created by Edward W. Goodrick and John R. Kohlenberger III, has been developed specifically for use with the New International Version. Like all concordances, it is a special index which contains an alphabetical listing of words used in the Bible text. By looking up key words, readers can find verses and passages for which they remember a word or two but not their location.

This concordance contains 2,000 word entries, with some 13,000 Scripture references. Each word entry is followed by the Scripture references in which that particular word is found, as well as by a brief excerpt from the surrounding context. The first letter of the entry word is italicized to conserve space and to allow for a longer context excerpt. Variant spellings due to number and tense and compound forms follow the entry in parentheses, and direct the reader to check other forms of that word in locating a passage.

This concordance contains a number of "block entries," which highlight some of the key events and characteristics in the lives of certain Bible figures. The descriptive phrases replace the brief context surrounding each occurrence of the name. In those instances where more than one Bible character has the same name, that name is placed under one block entry, and each person is given a number (1), (2), etc. Insignificant names are not included.

Word or block entries marked with an asterisk (*) list every verse in the Bible in which the word appears.

This concordance is a valuable tool for Bible study. While one of its key purposes is to help the reader find forgotten references to verses, it can also be used to do word studies and to locate and trace biblical themes. Be sure to use this concordance as more than just a verse finder. Whenever you look up a verse, aim to discover the intended meaning of the verse in context. Give special attention to the flow of thought from the beginning of the passage to the end.

Concordance Abbreviations for the Books of the Bible

Genesis ....Ge	Isaiah ....Isa	Romans ....Ro
Exodus ....Ex	Jeremiah ....Jer	1 Corinthians 1Co
Leviticus ....Lev	Lamentations ....La	2 Corinthians 2Co
Numbers ....Nu	Ezekiel ....Eze	Galatians ....Gal
Deuteronomy ....Dt	Daniel ....Da	Ephesians ....Eph
Joshua ....Jos	Hosea ....Hos	Philippians ....Php
Judges ....Jdg	Joel ....Joel	Colossians ....Col
Ruth ....Ru	Amos ....Am	1 Thessalonians 1Th
1 Samuel 1Sa	Obadiah ....Ob	2 Thessalonians 2Th
2 Samuel 2Sa	Jonah ....Jnh	1 Timothy 1Ti
1 Kings 1Ki	Micah ....Mic	2 Timothy 2Ti
2 Kings 2Ki	Nahum ....Na	Titus ....Tit
1 Chronicles 1Ch	Habakkuk ....Hab	Philemon ....Phm
2 Chronicles 2Ch	Zephaniah ....Zep	Hebrews ....Heb
Ezra ....Ezr	Haggai ....Hag	James ....Jas
Nehemiah ....Ne	Zechariah ....Zec	1 Peter 1Pe
Esther ....Est	Malachi ....Mal	2 Peter 2Pe
Job ....Job	Matthew ....Mt	1 John 1Jn
Psalm ....Ps	Mark ....Mk	2 John 2Jn
Proverbs ....Pr	Luke ....Lk	3 John 3Jn
Ecclesiastes ....Ecc	John ....Jn	Jude ....Jude
Song of Songs ....SS	Acts ....Ac	Revelation ....Rev

NIV Concordance

AARON
Priesthood of (Ex 28:1; Nu 17; Heb 5:1-4; 7), garments (Ex 28; 39), consecration (Ex 29), ordination (Lev 8).

Spokesman for Moses (Ex 4:14-16, 27-31; 7:1-2). Supported Moses' hands in battle (Ex 17:8-13). Built golden calf (Ex 32; Dt 9:20). Talked against Moses (Nu 12). Priesthood opposed (Nu 16); staff budded (Nu 17). Forbidden to enter land (Nu 20:1-12). Death (Nu 20:22-29; 33:38-39).

ABANDON
Dt 4:31 he will not *a* or destroy you
1Ti 4:1 in later times some will *a* the faith

ABBA
Ro 8:15 And by him we cry, "*A*, Father."
Gal 4:6 the Spirit who calls out, "*A*, Father

ABEL
Second son of Adam (Ge 4:2). Offered proper sacrifice (Ge 4:4; Heb 11:4). Murdered by Cain (Ge 4:8; Mt 23:35; Lk 11:51; 1Jn 3:12).

ABHORS
Pr 11:1 The LORD *a* dishonest scales,

ABIGAIL
Wife of Nabal (1Sa 25:30); pled for his life with David (1Sa 25:14-35). Became David's wife (1Sa 25:36-42).

ABIJAH
Son of Rehoboam; king of Judah (1Ki 14:31-15:8; 2Ch 12:16-14:1).

ABILITY (ABLE)
Ezr 2:69 According to their *a* they gave
2Co 1:8 far beyond our *a* to endure,
    8:3 were able, and even beyond their *a*.

ABIMELECH
1. King of Gerar who took Abraham's wife Sarah, believing her to be his sister (Ge 20). Later made a covenant with Abraham (Ge 21:22-33).

2. King of Gerar who took Isaac's wife Rebekah, believing her to be his sister (Ge 26:1-11). Later made a covenant with Isaac (Ge 26:12-31).

ABLE (ABILITY ENABLE ENABLED ENABLES)
Eze 7:19 and gold will not be *a* to save them
Da 3:17 the God we serve is *a* to save us
Ro 8:39 will be *a* to separate us
   14:4 for the Lord is *a* to make him stand
   16:25 to him who is *a* to establish you
2Co 9:8 God is *a* to make all grace abound
Eph 3:20 him who is *a* to do immeasurably
2Ti 1:12 and am convinced that he is *a*
   3:15 which are *a* to make you wise
Heb 7:25 he is *a* to save completely
Jude 24 To him who is *a* to keep you
Rev 5:5 He is *a* to open the scroll

ABOLISH
Mt 5:17 that I have come to *a* the Law

ABOMINATION
Da 11:31 set up the *a* that causes desolation.

ABOUND (ABOUNDING)
2Co 9:8 able to make all grace *a* to you,
Php 1:9 that your love may *a* more

ABOUNDING (ABOUND)
Ex 34:6 slow to anger, *a* in love
Ps 86:5 *a* in love to all who call to you,

ABRAHAM
Covenant relation with the LORD (Ge 12:1-3; 13:14-17; 15; 17; 22:15-18; Ex 2:24; Ne 9:8; Ps 105; Mic 7:20; Lk 1:68-75; Ro 4; Heb 6:13-15).

Called from Ur, via Haran, to Canaan (Ge 12:1; Ac 7:2-4; Heb 11:8-10). Moved to Egypt, nearly lost Sarah to Pharaoh (Ge 12:10-20). Divided the land with Lot (Ge 13). Saved Lot from four kings (Ge 14:1-16); blessed by Melchizedek (Ge 14:17-20; Heb 7:1-20). Declared righteous by faith (Ge 15:6; Ro 4:3; Gal 3:6-9). Fathered Ishmael by Hagar (Ge 16).

Name changed from Abram (Ge 17:5; Ne 9:7). Circumcised (Ge 17; Ro 4:9-12). Entertained three visitors (Ge 18); promised a son by Sarah (Ge 18:9-15; 17:16). Moved to Gerar; nearly lost Sarah to Abimelech (Ge 20). Fathered Isaac by Sarah (Ge 21:1-7; Ac 7:8; Heb 11:11-12); sent away Hagar and Ishmael (Ge 21:8-21; Gal 4:22-30). Tested by offering Isaac (Ge 22; Heb 11:17-19; Jas 2:21-24). Sarah died; bought field of Ephron for burial (Ge 23). Secured wife for Isaac (Ge 24). Death (Ge 25:7-11).

ABSALOM
Son of David by Maacah (2Sa 3:3; 1Ch 3:2). Killed Amnon for rape of his sister Tamar; banished by David (2Sa 13). Returned to Jerusalem; received by David (2Sa 14). Rebelled against David; seized kingdom (2Sa 15-17). Killed (2Sa 18).

ABSTAIN (ABSTAINS)
1Pe 2:11 to *a* from sinful desires,

ABSTAINS* (ABSTAIN)
Ro 14:6 thanks to God; and he who *a*,

ABUNDANCE (ABUNDANT)
Lk 12:15 consist in the *a* of his possessions."
Jude 2 peace and love be yours in *a*.

ABUNDANT (ABUNDANCE)
Dt 28:11 will grant you *a* prosperity—
Ps 145:7 will celebrate your *a* goodness
Pr 28:19 works his land will have *a* food,
Ro 5:17 who receive God's *a* provision

ACCEPT (ACCEPTED ACCEPTS)
Ex 23:8 "Do not *a* a bribe,
Pr 10:8 The wise in heart *a* commands,
   19:20 Listen to advice and *a* instruction,
Ro 15:7 A one another, then, just
Jas 1:21 humbly *a* the word planted in you,

ACCEPTED (ACCEPT)
Lk 4:24 "no prophet is *a* in his hometown.

ACCEPTS (ACCEPT)
Ps 6:9 the LORD *a* my prayer.
Jn 13:20 whoever *a* anyone I send *a* me;

ACCOMPANY
Mk 16:17 these signs will *a* those who believe
Heb 6:9 your case—things that *a* salvation.

ACCOMPLISH
Isa 55:11 but will *a* what I desire

ACCORD
Nu 24:13 not do anything of my own *a*,
Jn 10:18 but I lay it down of my own *a*.
   12:49 For I did not speak of my own *a*,

ACCOUNT (ACCOUNTABLE)
Mt 12:36 to give *a* on the day of judgment
Ro 14:12 each of us will give an *a* of himself
Heb 4:13 of him to whom we must give *a*.

ACCOUNTABLE (ACCOUNT)
Eze 33:6 but I will hold the watchman *a*
Ro 3:19 and the whole world held *a* to God.

ACCUSATION (ACCUSE)
1Ti 5:19 Do not entertain an *a*

ACCUSATIONS (ACCUSE)
2Pe 2:11 do not bring slanderous *a*

ACCUSE (ACCUSATION ACCUSATIONS)
Pr 3:30 Do not *a* a man for no reason—
Lk 3:14 and don't *a* people falsely—

ACHAN*
Sin at Jericho caused defeat at Ai; stoned (Jos 7; 22:20; 1Ch 2:7).

ACHE*
Pr 14:13 Even in laughter the heart may *a*,

ACKNOWLEDGE
Mt 10:32 *a* him before my Father in heaven.
1Jn 4:3 spirit that does not *a* Jesus is not

ACQUIT
Ex 23:7 to death, for I will not *a* the guilty.

ACTION (ACTIONS ACTIVE ACTS)
Jas 2:17 if it is not accompanied by *a*,

1Pe 1:13 minds for *a*; be self-controlled;

ACTIONS (ACTION)
Mt 11:19 wisdom is proved right by her *a*."
Gal 6:4 Each one should test his own *a*.
Tit 1:16 but by their *a* they deny him.

ACTIVE (ACTION)
Heb 4:12 For the word of God is living and *a*

ACTS (ACTION)
Ps 145:12 all men may know of your mighty *a*
   150:2 Praise him for his *a* of power;
Isa 64:6 all our righteous *a* are like filthy
Mt 6:1 not to do your '*a* of righteousness'

ADAM
First man (Ge 1:26-2:25; Ro 5:14; 1Ti 2:13). Sin of (Ge 3; Hos 6:7; Ro 5:12-21). Children of (Ge 4:1-5:5). Death of (Ge 5:5; Ro 5:12-21; 1Co 15:22).

ADD
Dt 12:32 do not *a* to it or take away from it.
Pr 30:6 Do not *a* to his words,
Lk 12:25 by worrying can *a* a single hour
Rev 22:18 God will *a* to him the plagues

ADMIRABLE*
Php 4:8 whatever is lovely, whatever is *a*—

ADMONISH
Col 3:16 and *a* one another with all wisdom,

ADOPTED (ADOPTION)
Eph 1:5 In love he predestined us to be *a*

ADOPTION (ADOPTED)
Ro 8:23 as we wait eagerly for our *a* as sons,

ADORE*
SS 1:4 How right they are to *a* you!

ADORNMENT* (ADORNS)
1Pe 3:3 should not come from outward *a*,

ADORNS (ADORNMENT)
Ps 93:5 holiness *a* your house

ADULTERY
Ex 20:14 "You shall not commit *a*.
Mt 5:27 that it was said, 'Do not commit *a*.'
   5:28 lustfully has already committed *a*
   5:32 the divorced woman commits *a*.
   15:19 murder, *a*, sexual immorality, theft

ADULTS*
1Co 14:20 but in your thinking be *a*.

ADVANCED
Job 32:7 *a* years should teach wisdom.'

ADVANTAGE
Ex 22:22 "Do not take *a* of a widow
Dt 24:14 Do not take *a* of a hired man who is
1Th 4:6 should wrong his brother or take *a*

ADVERSITY
Pr 17:17 and a brother is born for *a*.

ADVICE
1Ki 12:8 rejected the *a* the elders
   12:14 he followed the *a* of the young men
Pr 12:5 but the *a* of the wicked is deceitful.
   12:15 but a wise man listens to *a*.
   19:20 Listen to *a* and accept instruction,
   20:18 Make plans by seeking *a*;

AFFLICTION
Ro 12:12 patient in *a*, faithful in prayer.

AFRAID (FEAR)
Ge 26:24 Do not be *a*, for I am with you;
Ex 3:6 because he was *a* to look at God.
Ps 27:1 of whom shall I be *a*?
   56:3 When I am *a*, / I will trust in you.
Pr 3:24 lie down, you will not be *a*;
Jer 1:8 Do not be *a* of them, for I am
Mt 8:26 You of little faith, why are you so *a*
   10:28 be *a* of the One who can destroy
   10:31 So don't be *a*; you are worth more
Mk 5:36 "Don't be *a*; just believe."
Jn 14:27 hearts be troubled and do not be *a*.
Heb 13:6 Lord is my helper; I will not be *a*.

AGED

AGED
Job 12:12 Is not wisdom found among the *a*?
Pr 17: 6 children are a crown to the *a*,

AGREE
Mt 18:19 on earth *a* about anything you ask
Ro 7:16 want to do, I *a* that the law is good.
Php 4: 2 with Syntyche to *a* with each other

AHAB
Son of Omri; king of Israel (1Ki 16:28-22:40), husband of Jezebel (1Ki 16:31). Promoted Baal worship (1Ki 16:31-33); opposed by Elijah (1Ki 17:1; 18; 21), a prophet (1Ki 20:35-43), Micaiah (1Ki 22:1-28). Defeated Ben-Hadad (1Ki 20). Killed for failing to kill Ben-Hadad and for murder of Naboth (1Ki 20:35-21:40).

AHAZ
Son of Jotham; king of Judah, (2Ki 16; 2Ch 28; Isa 7).

AHAZIAH
1. Son of Ahab; king of Israel (1Ki 22:51-2Ki 1:18; 2Ch 20:35-37).
2. Son of Jehoram; king of Judah (2Ki 8:25-29; 9:14-29), also called Jehoahaz (2Ch 21:17-22:9; 25:23).

AIM
1Co 7:34 Her *a* is to be devoted to the Lord
2Co 13:11 A for perfection, listen

AIR
Mt 8:20 and birds of the *a* have nests,
1Co 9:26 not fight like a man beating the *a*.
Eph 2: 2 of the ruler of the kingdom of the *a*,
1Th 4:17 clouds to meet the Lord in the *a*.

ALABASTER
Mt 26: 7 came to him with an *a* jar

ALERT
Jos 8: 4 All of you be on the *a*.
Mk 13:33 Be *a*! You do not know
Eph 6:18 be *a* and always keep on praying
1Th 5: 6 but let us be *a* and self-controlled.

ALIEN (ALIENATED)
Ex 22:21 "Do not mistreat an *a*

ALIENATED (ALIEN)
Gal 5: 4 by law have been *a* from Christ;

ALIVE (LIVE)
Ac 1: 3 convincing proofs that he was *a*.
Ro 6:11 but *a* to God in Christ Jesus.
1Co 15:22 so in Christ all will be made *a*.

ALMIGHTY (MIGHT)
Ge 17: 1 "I am God A; walk before me
Job 11: 7 Can you probe the limits of the A?
33: 4 the breath of the A gives me life.
Ps 91: 1 will rest in the shadow of the A.
Isa 6: 3 "Holy, holy, holy is the LORD A;

ALTAR
Ge 22: 9 his son Isaac and laid him on the *a*,
Ex 27: 1 "Build an *a* of acacia wood,
1Ki 18:30 and he repaired the *a* of the LORD
2Ch 4: 1 made a bronze *a* twenty cubits
4:19 the golden *a*; the tables

ALWAYS
Ps 16: 8 I have set the LORD *a* before me.
51: 3 and my sin is *a* before me.
Mt 26:11 The poor you will *a* have with you,
28:20 And surely I will be with you *a*,
1Co 13: 7 *a* protects, *a* trusts, *a* hopes, *a*
Php 4: 4 Rejoice in the Lord *a*.
1Pe 3:15 A be prepared to give an answer

AMAZIAH
Son of Joash; king of Judah (2Ki 14; 2Ch 25).

AMBASSADORS
2Co 5:20 We are therefore Christ's *a*,

AMBITION
Ro 15:20 It has always been my *a*
1Th 4:11 Make it your *a* to lead a quiet life,

AMON
Son of Manasseh; king of Judah (2Ki 21:18-26; 1Ch 3:14; 2Ch 33:21-25).

ANANIAS
1. Husband of Sapphira; died for lying to God (Ac 5:1-11).
2. Disciple who baptized Saul (Ac 9:10-19).
3. High priest at Paul's arrest (Ac 22:30-24:1).

ANCHOR
Heb 6:19 We have this hope as an *a*

ANCIENT
Da 7: 9 and the A of Days took his seat.

ANDREW*
Apostle; brother of Simon Peter (Mt 4:18; 10:2; Mk 1:16-18, 29; 3:18; 13:3; Lk 6:14; Jn 1:35-44; 6:8-9; 12:22; Ac 1:13).

ANGEL (ANGELS ARCHANGEL)
Ps 34: 7 The *a* of the LORD encamps
Ac 6:15 his face was like the face of an *a*.
2Co 11:14 Satan himself masquerades as an *a*
Gal 1: 8 or an *a* from heaven should preach

ANGELS (ANGEL)
Ps 91:11 command his *a* concerning you
Mt 18:10 For I tell you that their *a*
25:41 prepared for the devil and his *a*.
Lk 20:36 for they are like the *a*.
1Co 6: 3 you not know that we will judge *a*?
Heb 1: 4 as much superior to the *a*
1:14 Are not all *a* ministering spirits
2: 7 made him a little lower than the *a*;
13: 2 some people have entertained *a*
1Pe 1:12 Even *a* long to look
2Pe 2: 4 For if God did not spare *a*

ANGER (ANGERED ANGRY)
Ex 32:10 alone so that my *a* may burn
34: 6 slow to *a*, abounding in love
Dt 29:28 In furious *a* and in great wrath
2Ki 22:13 Great is the LORD's *a* that burns
Ps 30: 5 For his *a* lasts only a moment,
Pr 15: 1 but a harsh word stirs up *a*.
29:11 A fool gives full vent to his *a*,

ANGERED (ANGER)
Pr 22:24 do not associate with one easily *a*,
1Co 13: 5 it is not easily *a*, it keeps no record

ANGRY (ANGER)
Ps 2:12 Kiss the Son, lest he be *a*
Pr 29:22 An *a* man stirs up dissension,
Jas 1:19 slow to speak and slow to become *a*

ANGUISH
Ps 118: 5 In my *a* I cried to the LORD,

ANOINT
Ps 23: 5 You *a* my head with oil;
Jas 5:14 and *a* him with oil in the name

ANT*
Pr 6: 6 Go to the *a*, you sluggard;

ANTICHRIST
1Jn 2:18 have heard that the *a* is coming,
2Jn 7 person is the deceiver and the *a*.

ANTIOCH
Ac 11:26 were called Christians first at A.

ANXIETY (ANXIOUS)
1Pe 5: 7 Cast all your *a* on him

ANXIOUS (ANXIETY)
Pr 12:25 An *a* heart weighs a man down,
Php 4: 6 Do not be *a* about anything,

APOLLOS*
Christian from Alexandria, learned in the Scriptures; instructed by Aquila and Priscilla (Ac 18:24-28). Ministered at Corinth (Ac 19:1; 1Co 1:12; 3; Tit 3:13).

APOSTLES
See also Andrew, Bartholomew, James, John, Judas, Matthew, Nathanael, Paul, Peter, Philip, Simon, Thaddaeus, Thomas.
Mk 3:14 twelve—designating them *a*—
Ac 1:26 so he was added to the eleven *a*.
2:43 signs were done by the *a*.
1Co 12:28 God has appointed first of all *a*,
15: 9 For I am the least of the *a*
2Co 11:13 masquerading as *a* of Christ.
Eph 2:20 built on the foundation of the *a*

APPEAR (APPEARANCE APPEARING)
Mt 13:22 false prophets will *a* and perform
2Co 5:10 we must all *a* before the judgment
Col 3: 4 also will *a* with him in glory.
Heb 9:24 now to *a* for us in God's presence.
9:28 and he will *a* a second time,

APPEARANCE (APPEAR)
1Sa 16: 7 Man looks at the outward *a*,
Gal 2: 6 God does not judge by external *a*—

APPEARING (APPEAR)
2Ti 4: 8 to all who have longed for his *a*.

Tit 2:13 the glorious *a* of our great God

APPLY
Pr 22:17 *a* your heart to what I teach,
23:12 A your heart to instruction

APPROACH
Eph 3:12 in him we may *a* God with freedom
Heb 4:16 Let us then *a* the throne of grace

APPROVED
2Ti 2:15 to present yourself to God as one *a*,

AQUILA*
Husband of Priscilla; co-worker with Paul, instructor of Apollos (Ac 18; Ro 16:3; 1Co 16:19; 2Ti 4:19).

ARARAT
Ge 8: 4 came to rest on the mountains of A.

ARCHANGEL* (ANGEL)
1Th 4:16 with the voice of the *a*
Jude 9 *a* Michael, when he was disputing

ARCHITECT*
Heb 11:10 whose *a* and builder is God.

ARK
Ge 6:14 So make yourself an *a*
Dt 10: 5 put the tablets in the *a* I had made,
2Ch 35: 3 "Put the sacred *a* in the temple that
Heb 9: 4 This *a* contained the gold jar

ARM (ARMY)
Nu 11:23 "Is the LORD's *a* too short?
1Pe 4: 1 *a* yourselves also with the same

ARMAGEDDON*
Rev 16:16 that in Hebrew is called A.

ARMOR (ARMY)
1Ki 20:11 on his *a* should not boast like one
Eph 6:11 Put on the full *a* of God
6:13 Therefore put on the full *a* of God,

ARMS (ARMY)
Dt 33:27 underneath are the everlasting *a*.
Ps 18:32 It is God who *a* me with strength
Pr 31:20 She opens her *a* to the poor
Isa 40:11 He gathers the lambs in his *a*
Mk 10:16 And he took the children in his *a*,

ARMY (ARM ARMOR ARMS)
Ps 33:16 No king is saved by the size of his *a*
Rev 19:19 the rider on the horse and his *a*.

AROMA
2Co 2:15 For we are to God the *a* of Christ

ARRAYED*
Ps 110: 3 A in holy majesty,
Isa 61:10 and *a* me in a robe of righteousness

ARROGANT
Ro 11:20 Do not be *a*, but be afraid.

ARROWS
Eph 6:16 you can extinguish all the flaming *a*

ASA
King of Judah (1Ki 15:8-24; 1Ch 3:10; 2Ch 14-16).

ASCENDED
Eph 4: 8 "When he *a* on high,

ASCRIBE
1Ch 16:28 *a* to the LORD glory and strength,
Job 36: 3 I will *a* justice to my Maker.
Ps 29: 2 A to the LORD the glory due his

ASHAMED (SHAME)
Lk 9:26 If anyone is *a* of me and my words,
Ro 1:16 I am not *a* of the gospel,
2Ti 1: 8 So do not be *a* to testify about our
2:15 who does not need to be *a*

ASSIGNED
Mk 13:34 with his *a* task, and tells the one
1Co 3: 5 as the Lord has *a* to each his task.
7:17 place in life that the Lord *a* to him

ASSOCIATE
Pr 22:24 do not *a* with one easily angered,
Ro 12:16 but be willing to *a* with people
1Co 5:11 am writing you that you must not *a*
2Th 3:14 Do not *a* with him,

ASSURANCE
Heb 10:22 with a sincere heart in full *a* of faith

ASTRAY
Pr 10:17 ignores correction leads others *a*.
Isa 53: 6 We all, like sheep, have gone *a*,
Jer 50: 6 their shepherds have led them *a*
Jn 16: 1 you so that you will not go *a*.

1Pe 2:25 For you were like sheep going *a*,
1Jn 3: 7 do not let anyone lead you *a*.
ATHALIAH
Evil queen of Judah (2Ki 11; 2Ch 23).
ATHLETE*
2Ti 2: 5 if anyone competes as an *a*,
ATONEMENT
Ex 25:17 "Make an *a* cover of pure gold—
30:10 Once a year Aaron shall make *a*
Lev 17:11 it is the blood that makes *a*
23:27 this seventh month is the Day of A.
Nu 25:13 and made *a* for the Israelites."
Ro 3:25 presented him as a sacrifice of *a*,
Heb 2:17 that he might make *a* for the sins
ATTENTION
Pr 4: 1 pay *a* and gain understanding.
5: 1 My son, pay *a* to my wisdom,
22:17 Pay *a* and listen to the sayings
Tit 1:14 and will pay no *a* to Jewish myths
ATTITUDE (ATTITUDES)
Eph 4:23 new in the *a* of your minds;
Php 2: 5 Your *a* should be the same
1Pe 4: 1 yourselves also with the same *a*,
ATTITUDES (ATTITUDE)
Heb 4:12 it judges the thoughts and *a*
ATTRACTIVE
Tit 2:10 teaching about God our Savior *a*.
AUTHORITIES (AUTHORITY)
Ro 13: 1 it is necessary to submit to the *a*,
13: 6 for the *a* are God's servants,
Tit 3: 1 people to be subject to rulers and *a*,
1Pe 3:22 and powers in submission to him.
AUTHORITY (AUTHORITIES)
Mt 7:29 because he taught as one who had *a*
9: 6 the Son of Man has *a* on earth
28:18 "All *a* in heaven and on earth has
Ro 13: 1 for there is no *a* except that which
13: 2 rebels against the *a* is rebelling
1Co 11:10 to have a sign of *a* on her head.
1Ti 2: 2 for kings and all those in *a*,
2:12 to teach or to have *a* over a man;
Heb 13:17 your leaders and submit to their *a*.
AVENGE (VENGEANCE)
Dt 32:35 It is mine to *a*; I will repay.
AVOID
Pr 20: 3 It is to a man's honor to *a* strife,
20:19 so *a* a man who talks too much.
1Th 4: 3 you should *a* sexual immorality;
5:22 *A* every kind of evil.
2Ti 2:16 *A* godless chatter, because those
Tit 3: 9 But *a* foolish controversies
AWAKE
Ps 17:15 when I *a*, I will be satisfied
AWE (AWESOME)
Job 25: 2 "Dominion and *a* belong to God;
Ps 119:120 I stand in *a* of your laws.
Ecc 5: 7 Therefore stand in *a* of God.
Isa 29:23 will stand in *a* of the God of Israel.
Jer 33: 9 they will be in *a* and will tremble
Hab 3: 2 I stand in *a* of your deeds,
Mal 2: 5 and stood in *a* of my name.
Mt 9: 8 they were filled with *a*;
Lk 7:16 They were all filled with *a*
Ac 2:43 Everyone was filled with *a*,
Heb 12:28 acceptably with reverence and *a*,
AWESOME (AWE)
Ge 28:17 and said, "How *a* is this place!
Ex 15:11 *a* in glory,
Dt 7:21 is among you, is a great and *a* God.
10:17 the great God, mighty and *a*,
28:58 revere this glorious and *a* name—
Jdg 13: 6 like an angel of God, very *a*.
Ne 1: 5 of heaven, the great and *a* God,
9:32 the great, mighty and *a* God,
Job 10:16 again display your *a* power
37:22 God comes in *a* majesty.
Ps 45: 4 let your right hand display *a* deeds.
47: 2 How *a* is the LORD Most High,
66: 5 how *a* his works in man's behalf!
68:35 You are *a*, O God,
89: 7 he is more *a* than all who surround
99: 3 praise your great and *a* name—

111: 9 holy and *a* is his name.
145: 6 of the power of your *a* works,
Da 9: 4 "O Lord, the great and *a* God,
BAAL
1Ki 18:25 Elijah said to the prophets of B,
BAASHA
King of Israel (1Ki 15:16-16:7; 2Ch 16:1-6).
BABIES (BABY)
Lk 18:15 also bringing *b* to Jesus
1Pe 2: 2 Like newborn *b*, crave pure
BABY (BABIES)
Isa 49:15 "Can a mother forget the *b*
Lk 1:44 the *b* in my womb leaped for joy.
2:12 You will find a *b* wrapped in strips
Jn 16:21 but when her *b* is born she forgets
BABYLON
Ps 137: 1 By the rivers of B we sat and wept
BACKSLIDING
Jer 3:22 I will cure you of *b*."
14: 7 For our *b* is great;
Eze 37:23 them from all their sinful *b*,
BALAAM
Prophet who attempted to curse Israel (Nu 22-24; Dt 23:4-5; 2Pe 2:15; Jude 11). Killed (Nu 31:8; Jos 13:22).
BALM
Jer 8:22 Is there no *b* in Gilead?
BANISH
Jer 25:10 I will *b* from them the sounds of joy
BANQUET
SS 2: 4 He has taken me to the *b* hall,
Lk 14:13 when you give a *b*, invite the poor,
BAPTIZE (BAPTIZED)
Mt 3:11 He will *b* you with the Holy Spirit
Mk 1: 8 he will *b* you with the Holy Spirit."
1Co 1:17 For Christ did not send me to *b*,
BAPTIZED (BAPTIZE)
Mt 3: 6 they were *b* by him in the Jordan
Mk 1: 9 and was *b* by John in the Jordan.
10:38 or be *b* with the baptism I am
16:16 believes and is *b* will be saved,
Jn 4: 2 in fact it was not Jesus who *b*,
Ac 1: 5 but in a few days you will be *b*
BARABBAS
Mt 27:26 Then he released B to them.
BARBS*
Nu 33:55 allow to remain will become *b*
BARE
Heb 4:13 and laid *b* before the eyes of him
BARNABAS*
Disciple, originally Joseph (Ac 4:36), prophet (Ac 13:1), apostle (Ac 14:14). Brought Paul to apostles (Ac 9:27), Antioch (Ac 11:22-29; Gal 2:1-13), on the first missionary journey (Ac 13-14). Together at Jerusalem Council, they separated over John Mark (Ac 15). Later co-workers (1Co 9:6; Col 4:10).
BARREN
Ps 113: 9 He settles the *b* woman
BARTHOLOMEW*
Apostle (Mt 10:3; Mk 3:18; Lk 6:14; Ac 1:13). Possibly also known as Nathanael (Jn 1:45-49; 21:2).
BATH
Jn 13:10 person who has had a *b* needs only
BATHSHEBA
Wife of Uriah who committed adultery with and became wife of David (2Sa 11), mother of Solomon (2Sa 12:24; 1Ki 1-2; 1Ch 3:5).
BATTLE
2Ch 20:15 For the *b* is not yours, but God's.
Ps 24: 8 the LORD mighty in *b*.
Ecc 9:11 or the *b* to the strong,
BEAR (BEARING BIRTH BIRTHRIGHT BORN FIRSTBORN NEWBORN)
Ge 4:13 punishment is more than I can *b*.
Ps 38: 4 like a burden too heavy to *b*.
Isa 53:11 and he will *b* their iniquities.
Da 7: 5 beast, which looked like a *b*.
Mt 7:18 A good tree cannot *b* bad fruit,
Jn 15: 2 branch that does *b* fruit he prunes
15:16 and appointed you to go and *b* fruit—
Ro 15: 1 ought to *b* with the failings
1Co 10:13 tempted beyond what you can *b*.

Col 3:13 B with each other and forgive
BEARING (BEAR)
Eph 4: 2 *b* with one another in love.
Col 1:10 *b* fruit in every good work,
BEAST
Rev 13:18 him calculate the number of the *b*,
BEAT (BEATING)
Isa 2: 4 They will *b* their swords
Joel 3:10 B your plowshares into swords
1Co 9:27 I *b* my body and make it my slave
BEATING (BEAT)
1Co 9:26 I do not fight like a man *b* the air.
1Pe 2:20 if you receive a *b* for doing wrong
BEAUTIFUL (BEAUTY)
Ge 6: 2 that the daughters of men were *b*,
12:11 "I know what a *b* woman you are.
12:14 saw that she was a very *b* woman.
24:16 The girl was very *b*, a virgin;
26: 7 of Rebekah, because she is *b*.
29:17 Rachel was lovely in form, and *b*.
Job 38:31 "Can you bind the *b* Pleiades?
Pr 11:22 is a *b* woman who shows no
Ecc 3:11 He has made everything *b*
Isa 4: 2 of the LORD will be *b*
52: 7 How *b* on the mountains
Eze 20: 6 and honey, the most *b* of all lands.
Zec 9:17 How attractive and *b* they will be!
Mt 23:27 which look *b* on the outside
26:10 She has done a *b* thing to me.
Ro 10:15 "How *b* are the feet
1Pe 3: 5 in God used to make themselves *b*.
BEAUTY (BEAUTIFUL)
Ps 27: 4 to gaze upon the *b* of the LORD
45:11 The king is enthralled by your *b*;
Pr 31:30 is deceptive, and *b* is fleeting;
Isa 33:17 Your eyes will see the king in his *b*
53: 2 He had no *b* or majesty
61: 3 to bestow on them a crown of *b*
Eze 28:12 full of wisdom and perfect in *b*.
1Pe 3: 4 the unfading *b* of a gentle
BED
Heb 13: 4 and the marriage *b* kept pure,
BEELZEBUB
Lk 11:15 "By B, the prince of demons,
BEER
Pr 20: 1 Wine is a mocker and *b* a brawler;
BEERSHEBA
Jdg 20: 1 all the Israelites from Dan to B
BEGINNING
Ge 1: 1 In the *b* God created the heavens
Ps 102: 25 In the *b* you laid the foundations
111: 10 of the LORD is the *b* of wisdom;
Pr 1: 7 of the LORD is the *b* of knowledge
Jn 1: 1 In the *b* was the Word,
1Jn 1: 1 That which was from the *b*,
Rev 21: 6 and the Omega, the B and the End.
BEHAVE
Ro 13:13 Let us *b* decently, as in the daytime
BELIEVE (BELIEVED BELIEVER BELIEVERS BELIEVES BELIEVING)
Mt 18: 6 one of these little ones who *b* in me
21:22 If you *b*, you will receive whatever
Mk 1:15 Repent and *b* the good news!"
9:24 "I do *b*; help me overcome my
16:17 signs will accompany those who *b*:
Lk 8:50 just *b*, and she will be healed."
24:25 to *b* all that the prophets have
Jn 1: 7 that through him all men might *b*.
3:18 does not *b* stands condemned
6:29 to *b* in the one he has sent."
10:38 you do not *b* me, *b* the miracles,
11:27 "I *b* that you are the Christ,
14:11 B me when I say that I am
16:30 This makes us *b* that you came
16:31 "You *b* at last!" Jesus answered.
17:21 that the world may *b* that you have
20:27 Stop doubting and *b*."
20:31 written that you may *b* that Jesus is
Ac 16:31 They replied, "B in the Lord Jesus,
24:14 I *b* everything that agrees
Ro 3:22 faith in Jesus Christ to all who *b*.
4:11 he is the father of all who *b*

BELIEVED

10:   9 *b* in your heart that God raised him
10: 14 And how can they *b* in the one
16: 26 so that all nations might *b*
1Th   4: 14 We *b* that Jesus died and rose again
2Th   2: 11 delusion so that they will *b* the lie
1Ti   4: 10 and especially of those who *b*.
Tit   1:   6 a man whose children *b*
Heb 11:   6 comes to him must *b* that he exists
Jas   2: 19 Even the demons *b* that—
1Jn   4:   1 Dear friends, do not *b* every spirit,

BELIEVED (BELIEVE)
Ge   15:   6 Abram *b* the LORD, and he
Jnh   3:   5 The Ninevites *b* God.
Jn   1: 12 to those who *b* in his name,
          2: 22 Then they *b* the Scripture
          3: 18 because he has not *b* in the name
        20:   8 He saw and *b*.
        20: 29 who have not seen and yet have *b*."
Ac   13: 48 were appointed for eternal life *b*.
Ro   4:   3 Scripture say? "Abraham *b* God,
         10: 14 call on the one they have not *b* in?
1Co   15:   2 Otherwise, you have *b* in vain.
Gal   3:   6 Consider Abraham: "He *b* God,
2Ti   1: 12 because I know whom I have *b*,
Jas   2: 23 that says, "Abraham *b* God,

BELIEVER (BELIEVE)
1Co   7: 12 brother has a wife who is not a *b*
2Co   6: 15 What does a *b* have in common

BELIEVERS (BELIEVE)
Ac   4: 32 All the *b* were one in heart
         5: 12 And all the *b* used to meet together
1Co   6:   5 to judge a dispute between *b*?
1Ti   4: 12 set an example for the *b* in speech,
1Pe   2: 17 Love the brotherhood of *b*,

BELIEVES (BELIEVE)
Pr   14: 15 A simple man *b* anything,
Mk   9: 23 is possible for him who *b*."
        11: 23 *b* that what he says will happen,
        16: 16 Whoever *b* and is baptized will be
Jn   3: 16 that whoever *b* in him shall not
         3: 36 Whoever *b* in the Son has eternal
         5: 24 *b* him who sent me has eternal life
         6: 35 and he who *b* in me will never be
         6: 40 and *b* in him shall have eternal life,
         6: 47 he who *b* has everlasting life.
         7: 38 Whoever *b* in me, as the Scripture
        11: 26 and *b* in me will never die.
Ro   1: 16 for the salvation of everyone who *b*
        10:   4 righteousness for everyone who *b*.
1Jn   5:   1 Everyone who *b* that Jesus is
          5:   5 Only he who *b* that Jesus is the Son

BELIEVING (BELIEVE)
Jn   20: 31 and that by *b* you may have life

BELONG (BELONGS)
Dt   29: 29 The secret things *b*
Job 25:   2 "Dominion and awe *b* to God;
Ps   47:   9 for the kings of the earth *b* to God;
         95:   4 and the mountain peaks *b* to him.
Jn   8: 44 You *b* to your father, the devil,
        15: 19 As it is, you do not *b* to the world,
Ro   1:   6 called to *b* to Jesus Christ.
          7:   4 that you might *b* to another,
         14:   8 we live or die, we *b* to the Lord.
Gal   5: 24 Those who *b* to Christ Jesus have
1Th   5:   8 But since we *b* to the day, let us be

BELONGS (BELONG)
Job 41: 11 Everything under heaven *b* to me.
Ps   111: 10 To him *b* eternal praise.
Eze   18:   4 For every living soul *b* to me,
Jn   8: 47 He who *b* to God hears what God
Ro   12:   5 each member *b* to all the others.

BELOVED (LOVE)
Dt   33: 12 "Let the *b* of the LORD rest secure

BELT
Isa   11:   5 Righteousness will be his *b*
Eph   6: 14 with the *b* of truth buckled

BENEFIT (BENEFITS)
Ro   6: 22 the *b* you reap leads to holiness,
2Co   4: 15 All this is for your *b*,

BENEFITS (BENEFIT)
Ps 103:   2 and forget not all his *b*.
Jn   4: 38 you have reaped the *b* of their labor

1520

BENJAMIN
Twelfth son of Jacob by Rachel (Ge 35:16-24; 46:19-21; 1Ch 2:2). Jacob refused to send him to Egypt, but relented (Ge 42-45).

BEREANS*
Ac   17: 11 the *B* were of more noble character

BESTOWS
Ps   84: 11 the LORD *b* favor and honor;

BETHLEHEM
Mt   2:   1 After Jesus was born in *B* in Judea,

BETRAY
Pr   25:   9 do not *b* another man's confidence,

BIND (BINDS)
Dt   6:   8 and *b* them on your foreheads.
Pr   6: 21 *b* them upon your heart forever;
Isa   61:   1 me to *b* up the brokenhearted,
Mt 16: 19 whatever you *b* on earth will be

BINDS (BIND)
Ps 147:   3 and *b* up their wounds.
Isa 30: 26 when the LORD *b* up the bruises

BIRDS
Mt   8: 20 and *b* of the air have nests,

BIRTH (BEAR)
Ps   58:   3 Even from *b* the wicked go astray;
Mt   1: 18 This is how the *b* of Jesus Christ
1Pe   1:   3 great mercy he has given us new *b*

BIRTHRIGHT (BEAR)
Ge   25: 34 So Esau despised his *b*.

BLAMELESS
Ge   17:   1 walk before me and be *b*.
Job   1:   1 This man was *b* and upright;
Ps   84: 11 from those whose walk is *b*.
       119:   1 Blessed are they whose ways are *b*,
Pr   19:   1 Better a poor man whose walk is *b*
1Co   1:   8 so that you will be *b* on the day
Eph   5: 27 any other blemish, but holy and *b*.
Php   2: 15 so that you may become *b* and pure
1Th   3: 13 hearts so that you will be *b*
         5: 23 and body be kept *b* at the coming
Tit   1:   6 An elder must be *b*, the husband of
Heb   7: 26 *b*, pure, set apart from sinners,
2Pe   3: 14 effort to be found spotless, *b*

BLASPHEMES
Mk   3: 29 whoever *b* against the Holy Spirit

BLEMISH
1Pe   1: 19 a lamb without *b* or defect.

BLESS (BLESSED BLESSING BLESSINGS)
Ge   12:   3 I will *b* those who *b* you,
Ro   12: 14 Bless those who persecute you; *b*

BLESSED (BLESS)
Ge   1: 22 God *b* them and said, "Be fruitful
         2:   3 And God *b* the seventh day
        22: 18 nations on earth will be *b*,
Ps   1:   1 *B* is the man
         2: 12 *B* are all who take refuge in him.
        33: 12 *B* is the nation whose God is
        41:   1 *B* is he who has regard for the weak
        84:   5 *B* are those whose strength is
       106:   3 *B* are they who maintain justice,
       112:   1 *B* is the man who fears the LORD,
       118: 26 *B* is he who comes in the name
Pr   29: 18 but *b* is he who keeps the law.
        31: 28 Her children arise and call her *b*;
Mt   5:   3 saying: "*B* are the poor in spirit,
          5:   4 *B* are those who mourn,
          5:   5 *B* are the meek,
          5:   6 *B* are those who hunger
          5:   7 *B* are the merciful,
          5:   8 *B* are the pure in heart,
          5:   9 *B* are the peacemakers,
          5: 10 *B* are those who are persecuted
          5: 11 "*B* are you when people insult you,
Lk   1: 48 on all generations will call me *b*,
Jn   12: 13 "*B* is he who comes in the name
Ac   20: 35 'It is more *b* to give than to receive
Tit   2: 13 while we wait for the *b* hope—
Jas   1: 12 *B* is the man who perseveres
Rev   1:   3 *B* is the one who reads the words
        22: 14 "*B* are those who wash their robes,

BLESSING (BLESS)
Eze 34: 26 there will be showers of *b*.

BLESSINGS (BLESS)
Pr   10:   6 *B* crown the head of the righteous,

BLIND
Mt   15: 14 a *b* man leads a *b* man, both will fall
         23: 16 "Woe to you, *b* guides! You say,
Jn   9: 25 I was *b* but now I see!"

BLOOD
Ge   9:   6 "Whoever sheds the *b* of man,
Ex   12: 13 and when I see the *b*, I will pass
         24:   8 "This is the *b* of the covenant that
Lev   17:   1 For the life of a creature is in the *b*,
Ps   72: 14 for precious is their *b* in his sight.
Pr   6: 17 hands that shed innocent *b*,
Mt   26: 28 This is my *b* of the covenant,
Ro   3: 25 of atonement, through faith in his *b*
          5:   9 have now been justified by his *b*,
1Co   11: 25 cup is the new covenant in my *b*;
Eph   1:   7 we have redemption through his *b*,
          2: 13 near through the *b* of Christ.
Col   1: 20 by making peace through his *b*,
Heb   9: 12 once for all by his own *b*,
          9: 22 of *b* there is no forgiveness.
1Pe   1: 19 but with the precious *b* of Christ,
1Jn   1:   7 and the *b* of Jesus, his Son,
Rev   1:   5 has freed us from our sins by his *b*,
          5:   9 with your *b* you purchased men
          7: 14 white in the *b* of the Lamb.
        12: 11 him by the *b* of the Lamb

BLOT (BLOTS)
Ex   32: 32 then *b* me out of the book you have
Ps   51:   1 *b* out my transgressions.
Rev   3:   5 I will never *b* out his name

BLOTS (BLOT)
Isa   43: 25 "I, even I, am he who *b* out

BLOWN
Eph   4: 14 and *b* here and there by every wind
Jas   1:   6 doubts is like a wave of the sea, *b*

BOAST
1Ki   20: 11 armor should not *b* like one who
Ps   34:   2 My soul will *b* in the LORD;
        44:   8 In God we make our *b* all day long,
Pr   27:   1 Do not *b* about tomorrow,
1Co   1: 31 Let him who boasts *b* in the Lord."
Gal   6: 14 May I never *b* except in the cross
Eph   2:   9 not by works, so that no one can *b*.

BOAZ
Wealthy Bethlehemite who showed favor to Ruth (Ru 2), married her (Ru 4). Ancestor of David (Ru 4:18-22; 1Ch 2:12-15), Jesus (Mt 1:5-16; Lk 3:23-32).

BODIES (BODY)
Ro   12:   1 to offer your *b* as living sacrifices,
1Co   6: 15 not know that your *b* are members
Eph   5: 28 to love their wives as their own *b*.

BODY (BODIES)
Zec   13:   6 What are these wounds on your *b*?'
Mt   10: 28 afraid of those who kill the *b*
        26: 26 saying, "Take and eat; this is my *b*
        26: 41 spirit is willing, but the *b* is weak."
Jn   13: 10 wash his feet; his whole *b* is clean.
Ro   6: 13 Do not offer the parts of your *b*
        12:   4 us has one *b* with many members,
1Co   6: 19 not know that your *b* is a temple
        11: 24 "This is my *b*, which is for you;
        12: 12 The *b* is a unit, though it is made up
Eph   5: 30 for we are members of his *b*.

BOLD (BOLDNESS)
Ps 138:   3 you made me *b* and stouthearted.
Pr   21: 29 A wicked man puts up a *b* front,
         28:   1 but the righteous are as *b* as a lion.

BOLDNESS* (BOLD)
Ac   4: 29 to speak your word with great *b*.

BONDAGE
Ezr   9:   9 God has not deserted us in our *b*.

BOOK (BOOKS)
Jos   1:   8 Do not let this *B* of the Law depart
Ne   8:   8 They read from the *B* of the Law
Jn   20: 30 which are not recorded in this *b*.
Php   4:   3 whose names are in the *b* of life.
Rev   21: 27 written in the Lamb's *b* of life.

BOOKS (BOOK)
Ecc   12: 12 Of making many *b* there is no end,

BORN (BEAR)
Isa 9: 6 For to us a child is *b*,
Jn 3: 7 at my saying, 'You must be *b* again
1Pe 1:23 For you have been *b* again,
1Jn 4: 7 Everyone who loves has been *b*
 5: 1 believes that Jesus is the Christ is *b*
BORROWER
Pr 22: 7 and the *b* is servant to the lender.
BOUGHT
Ac 20:28 which he *b* with his own blood.
1Co 6:20 You are not your own; you were *b*
 7:23 You were *b* at a price; do not
2Pe 2: 1 the sovereign Lord who *b* them—
BOW
Ps 95: 6 Come, let us *b* down in worship,
Isa 45:23 Before me every knee will *b*;
Ro 14:11 'every knee will *b* before me;
Php 2:10 name of Jesus every knee should *b*,
BRANCH (BRANCHES)
Isa 4: 2 In that day the *B* of the LORD will
Jer 33:15 I will make a righteous *B* sprout
BRANCHES (BRANCH)
Jn 15: 5 "I am the vine; you are the *b*.
BRAVE
2Sa 2: 7 Now then, be strong and *b*,
BREAD
Dt 8: 3 that man does not live on *b* alone
Pr 30: 8 but give me only my daily *b*.
Ecc 11: 1 Cast your *b* upon the waters,
Isa 55: 2 Why spend money on what is not *b*
Mt 4: 4 'Man does not live on *b* alone,
 6:11 Give us today our daily *b*.
Jn 6:35 Jesus declared, "I am the *b* of life.
 21:13 took the *b* and gave it to them,
1Co 11:23 took *b*, and when he had given
BREAK (BREAKING BROKEN)
Nu 30: 2 he must not *b* his word
Jdg 2: 1 'I will never *b* my covenant
Isa 42: 3 A bruised reed he will not *b*,
Mt 12:20 A bruised reed he will not *b*,
BREAKING (BREAK)
Jas 2:10 at just one point is guilty of *b* all
BREASTPIECE (BREASTPLATE)
Ex 28:15 Fashion a *b* for making decisions—
BREASTPLATE* (BREASTPIECE)
Isa 59:17 He put on righteousness as his *b*,
Eph 6:14 with the *b* of righteousness in place
1Th 5: 8 putting on faith and love as a *b*,
BREATHED (GOD-BREATHED)
Ge 2: 7 *b* into his nostrils the breath of life,
Jn 20:22 And with that he *b* on them
BREEDS*
Pr 13:10 Pride only *b* quarrels,
BRIBE
Ex 23: 8 "Do not accept a *b*,
Pr 6:35 will refuse the *b*, however great it
BRIDE
Rev 19: 7 and his *b* has made herself ready,
BRIGHTER (BRIGHTNESS)
Pr 4:18 shining ever *b* till the full light
BRIGHTNESS (BRIGHTER)
2Sa 22:13 Out of the *b* of his presence
Da 12: 3 who are wise will shine like the *b*
BROAD
Mt 7:13 and *b* is the road that leads
BROKEN (BREAK)
Ps 51:17 The sacrifices of God are a *b* spirit;
Ecc 4:12 of three strands is not quickly *b*.
Jn 10:35 and the Scripture cannot be *b*—
BROKENHEARTED* (HEART)
Ps 34:18 The LORD is close to the *b*
 109: 16 and the needy and the *b*.
 147: 3 He heals the *b*
Isa 61: 1 He has sent me to bind up the *b*,
BROTHER (BROTHER'S BROTHERS)
Pr 17:17 and a *b* is born for adversity.
 18:24 a friend who sticks closer than a *b*.
 27:10 neighbor nearby than a *b* far away.
Mt 5:24 be reconciled to your *b*;
 18:15 "If your *b* sins against you,
Mk 3:35 Whoever does God's will is my *b*

Lk 17: 3 "If your *b* sins, rebuke him,
1Co 8:13 if what I eat causes my *b* to fall
1Jn 2:10 Whoever loves his *b* lives
 4:21 loves God must also love his *b*.
BROTHER'S (BROTHER)
Ge 4: 9 "Am I my *b* keeper?" The LORD
BROTHERS (BROTHER)
Ps 133: 1 is when *b* live together in unity!
Pr 6:19 who stirs up dissension among *b*.
Mt 25:40 one of the least of these *b* of mine,
Mk 10:29 or *b* or sisters or mother or father
Heb 13: 1 Keep on loving each other as *b*.
1Pe 3: 8 be sympathetic, love as *b*,
1Jn 3:14 death to life, because we love our *b*.
BUILD (BUILDING BUILDS BUILT)
Mt 16:18 and on this rock I will *b* my church,
Ac 20:32 which can *b* you up and give you
1Co 14:12 excel in gifts that *b* up the church.
1Th 5:11 one another and *b* each other up,
BUILDING (BUILD)
1Co 3: 9 you are God's field, God's *b*.
2Co 10: 8 us for *b* you up rather
Eph 4:29 helpful for *b* others up according
BUILDS (BUILD)
Ps 127: 1 Unless the LORD *b* the house,
1Co 3:10 one should be careful how he *b*.
 8: 1 Knowledge puffs up, but love *b* up.
BUILT (BUILD)
Mt 7:24 is like a wise man who *b* his house
Eph 2:20 *b* on the foundation of the apostles
 4:12 the body of Christ may be *b* up
BURDEN (BURDENED BURDENS)
Ps 38: 4 like a *b* too heavy to bear.
Mt 11:30 my yoke is easy and my *b* is light."
BURDENED (BURDEN)
Gal 5: 1 do not let yourselves be *b* again
BURDENS (BURDEN)
Ps 68:19 who daily bears our *b*.
Gal 6: 2 Carry each other's *b*,
BURIED
Ro 6: 4 *b* with him through baptism
1Co 15: 4 that he was *b*, that he was raised
BURNING
Lev 6: 9 the fire must be kept *b* on the altar.
Ro 12:20 you will heap *b* coals on his head."
BUSINESS
Da 8:27 and went about the king's *b*.
1Th 4:11 to mind your own *b* and to work
BUSY
1Ki 20:40 While your servant was *b* here
2Th 3:11 They are not *b*; they are
Tit 2: 5 to be *b* at home, to be kind,
CAESAR
Mt 22:21 "Give to *C* what is Caesar's,
CAIN
Firstborn of Adam (Ge 4:1), murdered brother Abel (Ge 4:1-16; 1Jn 3:12).
CALEB
Judahite who spied out Canaan (Nu 13:6); allowed to enter land because of faith (Nu 13:30-14:38; Dt 1:36). Possessed Hebron (Jos 14:6-15:19).
CALF
Ex 32: 4 into an idol cast in the shape of a *c*,
Lk 15:23 Bring the fattened *c* and kill it.
CALL (CALLED CALLING CALLS)
Ps 105: 1 to the LORD, *c* on his name;
 145: 18 near to all who *c* on him,
Pr 31:28 children arise and *c* her blessed;
Isa 55: 6 *c* on him while he is near.
 65:24 Before they *c* I will answer;
Jer 33: 3 'C to me and I will answer you
Mt 9:13 come to *c* the righteous,
Ro 10:12 and richly blesses all who *c* on him,
 11:29 gifts and his *c* are irrevocable.
1Th 4: 7 For God did not *c* us to be impure,
CALLED (CALL)
1Sa 3: 3 and said, "Here I am; you *c* me."
2Ch 7:14 if my people, who are *c*
Ps 34: 6 This poor man *c*, and the LORD
Mt 21:13 "'My house will be *c* a house

Ro 8:30 And those he predestined, he also *c*
1Co 7:15 God has *c* us to live in peace.
Gal 5:13 You, my brothers, were *c* to be free
1Pe 2: 9 of him who *c* you out of darkness
CALLING (CALL)
Jn 1:23 I am the voice of one *c* in the desert
Ac 22:16 wash your sins away, *c* on his name
Eph 4: 1 worthy of the *c* you have received.
2Pe 1:10 all the more eager to make your *c*
CALLS (CALL)
Joel 2:32 And everyone who *c*
Jn 10: 3 He *c* his own sheep by name
Ro 10:13 "Everyone who *c* on the name
CAMEL
Mt 19:24 it is easier for a *c* to go
 23:24 strain out a gnat but swallow a *c*.
CANAAN
1Ch 16:18 "To you I will give the land of *C*
CANCELED
Lk 7:42 so he *c* the debts of both.
Col 2:14 having *c* the written code,
CAPITAL
Dt 21:22 guilty of a *c* offense is put to death
CAPSTONE (STONE)
Ps 118: 22 has become the *c*;
1Pe 2: 7 has become the *c*,"
CARE (CAREFUL CARES CARING)
Ps 8: 4 the son of man that you *c* for him?
Pr 29: 7 The righteous *c* about justice
Lk 10:34 him to an inn and took *c* of him.
Jn 21:16 Jesus said, "Take *c* of my sheep."
Heb 2: 6 the son of man that you *c* for him?
1Pe 5: 2 of God's flock that is under your *c*,
CAREFUL (CARE)
Ex 23:13 "Be *c* to do everything I have said
Dt 6: 3 be *c* to obey so that it may go well
Jos 23: 6 be *c* to obey all that is written
 23:11 be very *c* to love the LORD your
Pr 13:24 he who loves him is *c*
Mt 6: 1 "Be *c* not to do your 'acts
Ro 12:17 Be *c* to do what is right in the eyes
1Co 3:10 each one should be *c* how he builds
 8: 9 Be *c*, however, that the exercise
Eph 5:15 Be very *c*, then, how you live—
CARELESS
Mt 12:36 for every *c* word they have spoken.
CARES (CARE)
Ps 55:22 Cast your *c* on the LORD
Na 1: 7 He *c* for those who trust in him,
Eph 5:29 but he feeds and *c* for it, just
1Pe 5: 7 on him because he *c* for you.
CARING* (CARE)
1Th 2: 7 like a mother *c* for her little
1Ti 5: 4 practice by *c* for their own family
CARRIED (CARRY)
Ex 19: 4 and how I *c* you on eagles' wings
Isa 53: 4 and *c* our sorrows,
Heb 13: 9 Do not be *c* away by all kinds
2Pe 1:21 as they were *c* along by the Holy
CARRIES (CARRY)
Dt 32:11 and *c* them on its pinions.
Isa 40:11 and *c* them close to his heart;
CARRY (CARRIED CARRIES)
Lk 14:27 anyone who does not *c* his cross
Gal 6: 2 *C* each other's burdens,
 6: 5 for each one should *c* his own load.
CAST
Ps 22:18 and *c* lots for my clothing.
 55:22 *C* your cares on the LORD
Ecc 11: 1 *C* your bread upon the waters,
Jn 19:24 and *c* lots for my clothing."
1Pe 5: 7 *C* all your anxiety on him
CATCH (CAUGHT)
Lk 5:10 from now on you will *c* men."
CATTLE
Ps 50:10 and the *c* on a thousand hills.
CAUGHT (CATCH)
1Th 4:17 and are left will be *c* up together
CAUSE (CAUSES)
Pr 24:28 against your neighbor without *c*,
Ecc 8: 3 Do not stand up for a bad *c*,

CAUSES

Mt	18: 7	of the things that c people to sin!
Ro	14:21	else that will c your brother
1Co	10:32	Do not c anyone to stumble,

CAUSES (CAUSE)
Isa	8:14	a stone that c men to stumble
Mt	18: 6	if anyone c one of these little ones

CAUTIOUS*
Pr	12:26	A righteous man is c in friendship,

CEASE
Ps	46: 9	He makes wars c to the ends

CENSER
Lev	16:12	is to take a c full of burning coals

CENTURION
Mt	8: 5	had entered Capernaum, a c came

CERTAIN (CERTAINTY)
2Pe	1:19	word of the prophets made more c,

CERTAINTY* (CERTAIN)
Lk	1: 4	so that you may know the c
Jn	17: 8	They knew with c that I came

CHAFF
Ps	1: 4	They are like c

CHAINED
2Ti	2: 9	But God's word is not c.

CHAMPION
Ps	19: 5	like a c rejoicing to run his course.

CHANGE (CHANGED)
1Sa	15:29	of Israel does not lie or c his mind;
Ps 110:	4	and will not c his mind.
Jer	7: 5	If you really c your ways
Mal	3: 6	"I the Lord do not c.
Mt	18: 3	unless you c and become like little
Heb	7:21	and will not c his mind:
Jas	1:17	who does not c like shifting

CHANGED (CHANGE)
1Co	15:51	but we will all be c— in a flash,

CHARACTER
Ru	3:11	that you are a woman of noble c.
Pr	31:10	A wife of noble c who can find?
Ro	5: 4	perseverance, c; and c, hope.
1Co	15:33	"Bad company corrupts good c."

CHARGE
Ro	8:33	Who will bring any c
2Co	11: 7	the gospel of God to you free of c?
2Ti	4: 1	I give you this c: Preach the Word;

CHARIOTS
2Ki	6:17	and c of fire all around Elisha.
Ps	20: 7	Some trust in c and some in horses,

CHARM
Pr	31:30	C is deceptive, and beauty is

CHASES
Pr	12:11	he who c fantasies lacks judgment.

CHATTER* (CHATTERING)
1Ti	6:20	Turn away from godless c
2Ti	2:16	Avoid godless c, because those

CHATTERING* (CHATTER)
Pr	10: 8	but a c fool comes to ruin.
	10:10	and a c fool comes to ruin.

CHEAT* (CHEATED)
Mal	1:14	"Cursed is the c who has
1Co	6: 8	you yourselves c and do wrong,

CHEATED (CHEAT)
Lk	19: 8	if I have c anybody out of anything,
1Co	6: 7	Why not rather be c? Instead,

CHEEK
Mt	5:39	someone strikes you on the right c,

CHEERFUL* (CHEERS)
Pr	15:13	A happy heart makes the face c,
	15:15	but the c heart has a continual feast
	15:30	A c look brings joy to the heart,
	17:22	A c heart is good medicine,
2Co	9: 7	for God loves a c giver.

CHEERS (CHEERFUL)
Pr	12:25	but a kind word c him up.

CHILD (CHILDISH CHILDREN)
Pr	20:11	Even a c is known by his actions,
	22: 6	Train a c in the way he should go,
	22:15	Folly is bound up in the heart of a c
	23:13	not withhold discipline from a c;
	29:15	c left to himself disgraces his mother.
Isa	7:14	The virgin will be with c
	9: 6	For to us a c is born,
	11: 6	and a little c will lead them.
	66:13	As a mother comforts her c,
Mt	1:23	"The virgin will be with c
	18: 2	He called a little c and had him
Lk	1:42	and blessed is the c you will bear!
	1:80	And the c grew and became strong
1Co	13:11	When I was a c, I talked like a c,
1Jn	5: 1	who loves the father loves his c

CHILDISH* (CHILD)
1Co	13:11	When I became a man, I put c ways

CHILDREN (CHILD)
Dt	4: 9	Teach them to your c
	11:19	them to your c, talking about them
Ps	8: 2	From the lips of c and infants
Pr	17: 6	Children's c are a crown
	31:28	Her c arise and call her blessed;
Mt	7:11	how to give good gifts to your c,
	11:25	and revealed them to little c.
	18: 3	you change and become like little c
	19:14	"Let the little c come to me,
	21:16	" 'From the lips of c and infants
Mk	9:37	one of these little c in my name
	10:14	"Let the little c come to me,
	10:16	And he took the c in his arms,
	13:12	C will rebel against their parents
Lk	10:21	and revealed them to little c.
	18:16	"Let the little c come to me,
Ro	8:16	with our spirit that we are God's c.
2Co	12:14	parents, but parents for their c.
Eph	6: 1	C, obey your parents in the Lord,
	6: 4	do not exasperate your c; instead,
Col	3:20	C, obey your parents in everything,
	3:21	Fathers, do not embitter your c,
1Ti	3: 4	and see that his c obey him
	3:12	and must manage his c and his
	5:10	bringing up c, showing hospitality,
1Jn	3: 1	that we should be called c of God!

CHOOSE (CHOOSES CHOSE CHOSEN)
Dt	30:19	Now c life, so that you
Jos	24:15	then c for yourselves this day
Pr	8:10	C my instruction instead of silver,
	16:16	to c understanding rather
Jn	15:16	You did not c me, but I chose you

CHOOSES (CHOOSE)
Jn	7:17	If anyone c to do God's will,

CHOSE (CHOOSE)
Ge	13:11	So Lot c for himself the whole plain
Ps	33:12	the people he c for his inheritance.
Jn	15:16	but I c you and appointed you to go
1Co	1:27	But God c the foolish things
Eph	1: 4	he c us in him before the creation
2Th	2:13	from the beginning God c you

CHOSEN (CHOOSE)
Isa	41: 8	Jacob, whom I have c,
Mt	22:14	For many are invited, but few are c
Lk	10:42	Mary has c what is better,
	23:35	the Christ of God, the C One."
Jn	15:19	but I have c you out of the world.
1Pe	1:20	He was c before the creation
	2: 9	But you are a c people, a royal

CHRIST (CHRIST'S CHRISTIAN CHRISTS)
Mt	1:16	was born Jesus, who is called C.
	16:16	Peter answered, "You are the C,
	22:42	"What do you think about the C?
Jn	1:41	found the Messiah" (that is, the C).
	20:31	you may believe that Jesus is the C,
Ac	2:36	you crucified, both Lord and C."
	5:42	the good news that Jesus is the C.
	9:22	by proving that Jesus is the C.
	17: 3	proving that the C had to suffer
	18:28	the Scriptures that Jesus was the C.
	26:23	that the C would suffer and,
Ro	3:22	comes through faith in Jesus C
	5: 6	we were still powerless, C died
	5: 8	While we were still sinners, C died
	5:17	life through the one man, Jesus C.
	6: 4	as C was raised from the dead
	8: 1	for those who are in C Jesus,
	8: 9	Spirit of C, he does not belong to C.
	8:35	us from the love of C?
	10: 4	C is the end of the law
	14: 9	C died and returned to life
	15: 3	For even C did not please himself
1Co	1:23	but we preach C crucified:
	2: 2	except Jesus C and him crucified.
	3:11	one already laid, which is Jesus C.
	5: 7	For C, our Passover lamb,
	8: 6	and there is but one Lord, Jesus C,
	10: 4	them, and that rock was C.
	11: 1	as I follow the example of C.
	11: 3	the head of every man is C,
	12:27	Now you are the body of C,
	15: 3	that C died for our sins according
	15:14	And if C has not been raised,
	15:22	so in C all will be made alive.
	15:57	victory through our Lord Jesus C.
2Co	3: 3	show that you are a letter from C,
	4: 5	not preach ourselves, but Jesus C
	5:10	before the judgment seat of C,
	5:17	Therefore, if anyone is in C,
	11: 2	you to one husband, to C,
Gal	2:20	I have been crucified with C
	3:13	C redeemed us from the curse
	6:14	in the cross of our Lord Jesus C,
Eph	1: 3	with every spiritual blessing in C.
	3: 8	the unsearchable riches of C,
	4:13	measure of the fullness of C.
	5: 2	as C loved us and gave himself up
	5:23	as C is the head of the church,
	5:25	just as C loved the church
Php	1:21	to live is C and to die is gain.
	1:27	worthy of the gospel of C.
	4:19	to his glorious riches in C Jesus.
Col	1:27	which is C in you, the hope of glory
	1:28	may present everyone perfect in C.
	2: 6	as you received C Jesus as Lord,
	2:17	the reality, however, is found in C.
	3:15	Let the peace of C rule
2Th	2: 1	the coming of our Lord Jesus C
1Ti	1:15	C Jesus came into the world
	2: 5	the man C Jesus, who gave himself
2Ti	2: 3	us like a good soldier of C Jesus.
	3:15	salvation through faith in C Jesus.
Tit	2:13	our great God and Savior, Jesus C,
Heb	3:14	to share in C if we hold firmly
	9:14	more, then, will the blood of C,
	9:15	For this reason C is the mediator
	9:28	so C was sacrificed once
	10:10	of the body of Jesus C once for all.
	13: 8	Jesus C is the same yesterday
1Pe	1:19	but with the precious blood of C,
	2:21	because C suffered for you,
	3:18	For C died for sins once for all,
	4:14	insulted because of the name of C,
1Jn	2:22	man who denies that Jesus is the C.
	3:16	Jesus C laid down his life for us.
	5: 1	believes that Jesus is the C is born
Rev	20: 4	reigned with C a thousand years.

CHRIST'S (CHRIST)
2Co	5:14	For C love compels us,
	5:20	We are therefore C ambassadors,
	12: 9	so that C power may rest on me.

CHRISTIAN (CHRIST)
1Pe	4:16	as a C, do not be ashamed,

CHRISTS (CHRIST)
Mt	24:24	For false C and false prophets will

CHURCH
Mt	16:18	and on this rock I will build my c,
	18:17	if he refuses to listen even to the c,
Ac	20:28	Be shepherds of the c of God,
1Co	5:12	of mine to judge those outside the c
	14: 4	but he who prophesies edifies the c.
	14:12	to excel in gifts that build up the c.
	14:26	done for the strengthening of the c.
Eph	5:23	as Christ is the head of the c,
Col	1:24	the sake of his body, which is the c.

CIRCUMCISED
Ge	17:10	Every male among you shall be c.

CIRCUMSTANCES
Php	4:11	to be content whatever the c.
1Th	5:18	continually; give thanks in all c,

CITIZENS (CITIZENSHIP)
Eph	2:19	but fellow c with God's people

CITIZENSHIP (CITIZENS)
Php	3:20	But our c is in heaven.

CITY
- Mt 5:14 A c on a hill cannot be hidden.
- Heb 13:14 here we do not have an enduring c,

CIVILIAN*
- 2Ti 2: 4 a soldier gets involved in c affairs—

CLAIM (CLAIMS)
- Pr 25: 6 do not c a place among great men;
- 1Jn 1: 6 If we c to have fellowship
- 1: 8 If we c to be without sin, we
- 1:10 If we c we have not sinned,

CLAIMS (CLAIM)
- Jas 2:14 if a man c to have faith
- 1Jn 2: 6 Whoever c to live in him must walk
- 2: 9 Anyone who c to be in the light

CLAP
- Ps 47: 1 C your hands, all you nations;
- Isa 55:12 will c their hands.

CLAY
- Isa 45: 9 Does the c say to the potter,
- 64: 8 We are the c, you are the potter;
- Jer 18: 6 "Like c in the hand of the potter,
- La 4: 2 are now considered as pots of c,
- Da 2:33 partly of iron and partly of baked c.
- Ro 9:21 of the same lump of c some pottery
- 2Co 4: 7 we have this treasure in jars of c
- 2Ti 2:20 and c; some are for noble purposes

CLEAN
- Lev 16:30 you will be c from all your sins.
- Ps 24: 4 He who has c hands and a pure
- Mt 12:44 the house unoccupied, swept c
- 23:25 You c the outside of the cup
- Mk 7:19 Jesus declared all foods "c."
- Jn 13:10 to wash his feet; his whole body is c
- 15: 3 are already c because of the word
- Ac 10:15 impure that God has made c."
- Ro 14:20 All food is c, but it is wrong

CLING (CLINGS)
- Ro 12: 9 Hate what is evil; c to what is good.

CLINGS (CLING)
- Ps 63: 8 My soul c to you;

CLOAK
- 2Ki 4:29 "Tuck your c into your belt,

CLOSE (CLOSER)
- Ps 34:18 LORD is c to the brokenhearted
- Isa 40:11 and carries them c to his heart;
- Jer 30:21 himself to be c to me?'

CLOSER (CLOSE)
- Ex 3: 5 "Do not come any c," God said.
- Pr 18:24 there is a friend who sticks c

CLOTHE (CLOTHED CLOTHES CLOTHING)
- Ps 45: 3 c yourself with splendor
- Isa 52: 1 c yourself with strength.
- Ro 13:14 c yourselves with the Lord Jesus
- Col 3:12 c yourselves with compassion,
- 1Pe 5: 5 c yourselves with humility

CLOTHED (CLOTHE)
- Ps 30:11 removed my sackcloth and c me
- Pr 31:25 She is c with strength and dignity;
- Lk 24:49 until you have been c with power

CLOTHES (CLOTHE)
- Mt 6:25 the body more important than c?
- 6:28 "And why do you worry about c?
- Jn 11:44 Take off the grave c and let him go

CLOTHING (CLOTHE)
- Dt 22: 5 A woman must not wear men's c,
- Mt 7:15 They come to you in sheep's c,

CLOUD (CLOUDS)
- Ex 13:21 them in a pillar of c to guide them
- Isa 19: 1 See, the LORD rides on a swift c
- Lk 21:27 of Man coming in a c with power
- Heb 12: 1 by such a great c of witnesses,

CLOUDS (CLOUD)
- Ps 104: 3 He makes the c his chariot
- Da 7:13 coming with the c of heaven.
- Mk 13:26 coming in c with great power
- 1Th 4:17 with them in the c to meet the Lord

CO-HEIRS* (INHERIT)
- Ro 8:17 heirs of God and c with Christ,

COALS
- Pr 25:22 you will heap burning c on his head
- Ro 12:20 you will heap burning c on his head

COLD
- Pr 25:25 Like c water to a weary soul
- Mt 10:42 if anyone gives even a cup of c water
- 24:12 the love of most will grow c,

COMFORT (COMFORTED COMFORTS)
- Ps 23: 4 rod and your staff, they c me.
- 119: 52 and I find c in them.
- 119: 76 May your unfailing love be my c,
- Zec 1:17 and the LORD will again c Zion
- 1Co 14: 3 encouragement and c.
- 2Co 1: 4 so that we can c those
- 2: 7 you ought to forgive and c him,

COMFORTED (COMFORT)
- Mt 5: 4 for they will be c.

COMFORTS* (COMFORT)
- Job 29:25 I was like one who c mourners.
- Isa 49:13 For the LORD c his people
- 51:12 "I, even I, am he who c you.
- 66:13 As a mother c her child,
- 2Co 1: 4 who c us in all our troubles,
- 7: 6 But God, who c the downcast,

COMMAND (COMMANDED COMMANDING COMMANDMENT COMMANDMENTS COMMANDS)
- Ex 7: 2 You are to say everything I c you,
- Nu 24:13 to go beyond the c of the LORD—
- Dt 4: 2 Do not add to what I c you
- 30:16 For I c you today to love
- 32:46 so that you may c your children
- Ps 91:11 For he will c his angels concerning
- Pr 13:13 but he who respects a c is rewarded
- Ecc 8: 2 Obey the king's c, I say,
- Joel 2:11 mighty are those who obey his c.
- Jn 14:15 love me, you will obey what I c.
- 15:12 My c is this: Love each other
- 1Co 14:37 writing to you is the Lord's c.
- Gal 5:14 law is summed up in a single c:
- 1Ti 1: 5 goal of this c is love, which comes
- Heb 11: 3 universe was formed at God's c,
- 1Jn 3:23 this is his c: to believe in the name
- 2Jn 6 his c is that you walk in love.

COMMANDED (COMMAND)
- Ps 33: 9 he c, and it stood firm.
- 148: 5 for he c and they were created.
- Mt 28:20 to obey everything I have c you.
- 1Co 9:14 Lord has c that those who preach
- 1Jn 3:23 and to love one another as he c us.

COMMANDING (COMMAND)
- 2Ti 2: 4 he wants to please his c officer.

COMMANDMENT (COMMAND)
- Jos 22: 5 But be very careful to keep the c
- Mt 22:38 This is the first and greatest c.
- Jn 13:34 "A new c I give you: Love one
- Ro 7:12 and the c is holy, righteous
- Eph 6: 2 which is the first c with a promise

COMMANDMENTS (COMMAND)
- Ex 20: 6 who love me and keep my c.
- 34:28 of the covenant—the Ten C.
- Ecc 12:13 Fear God and keep his c,
- Mt 5:19 one of the least of these c
- 22:40 the Prophets hang on these two c."

COMMANDS (COMMAND)
- Dt 7: 9 those who love him and keep his c.
- 11:27 the blessing if you obey the c
- Ps 112: 1 who finds great delight in his c.
- 119: 47 for I delight in your c
- 119: 86 All your c are trustworthy;
- 119: 98 Your c make me wiser
- 119:127 Because I love your c
- 119:143 but your c are my delight.
- 119:172 for all your c are righteous.
- Pr 3: 1 but keep my c in your heart,
- 6:23 For these c are a lamp,
- 10: 8 The wise in heart accept c,
- Da 9: 4 all who love him and obey his c,
- Mt 5:19 teaches these c will be called great
- Jn 14:21 Whoever has my c and obeys them,
- Ac 17:30 but now he c all people everywhere
- 1Co 7:19 Keeping God's c is what counts.
- 1Jn 5: 3 And his c are not burdensome,
- 5: 3 This is love for God: to obey his c.

COMMEND (COMMENDED COMMENDS)
- Ecc 8:15 So I c the enjoyment of life,

- Ro 13: 3 do what is right and he will c you.
- 1Pe 2:14 and to c those who do right.

COMMENDED (COMMEND)
- Heb 11:39 These were all c for their faith,

COMMENDS (COMMEND)
- 2Co 10:18 not the one who c himself who is

COMMIT (COMMITS COMMITTED)
- Ex 20:14 "You shall not c adultery.
- Ps 37: 5 C your way to the LORD;
- Mt 5:27 that it was said, 'Do not c adultery.'
- Lk 23:46 into your hands I c my spirit."
- Ac 20:32 I c you to God and to the word
- 1Co 10: 8 We should not c sexual immorality,
- 1Pe 4:19 to God's will should c themselves

COMMITS (COMMIT)
- Pr 6:32 man who c adultery lacks
- 29:22 a hot-tempered one c many sins.
- Mt 19: 9 marries another woman c adultery

COMMITTED (COMMIT)
- Nu 5: 7 and must confess the sin he has c.
- 1Ki 8:61 But your hearts must be fully c
- 2Ch 16: 9 those whose hearts are fully c
- Mt 5:28 lustfully has already c adultery
- 2Co 5:19 And he has c to us the message
- 1Pe 2:22 "He c no sin,

COMMON
- Pr 22: 2 Rich and poor have this in c:
- 1Co 10:13 has seized you except what is c
- 2Co 6:14 and wickedness have in c?

COMPANION (COMPANIONS)
- Pr 13:20 but a c of fools suffers harm.
- 28: 7 a c of gluttons disgraces his father.
- 29: 3 c of prostitutes squanders his

COMPANIONS (COMPANION)
- Pr 18:24 A man of many c may come to ruin

COMPANY
- Pr 24: 1 do not desire their c;
- Jer 15:17 I never sat in the c of revelers,
- 1Co 15:33 "Bad c corrupts good character."

COMPARED (COMPARING)
- Eze 31: 2 Who can be c with you in majesty?
- Php 3: 8 I consider everything a loss c

COMPARING* (COMPARED)
- Ro 8:18 present sufferings are not worth c
- 2Co 8: 8 the sincerity of your love by c it
- Gal 6: 4 without c himself to somebody else

COMPASSION (COMPASSIONATE COMPASSIONS)
- Ex 33:19 I will have c on whom I will have c.
- Ne 9:19 of your great c you did not
- 9:28 in your c you delivered them time
- Ps 51: 1 according to your great c
- 103: 4 and crowns you with love and c.
- 103: 13 As a father has c on his children,
- 145: 9 he has c on all he has made.
- Isa 49:10 and will have c on his afflicted ones
- 49:15 and have no c on the child she has
- Hos 2:19 in love and c.
- 11: 8 all my c is aroused.
- Jnh 3: 9 with c turn from his fierce anger
- Mt 9:36 When he saw the crowds, he had c
- Mk 8: 2 "I have c for these people;
- Ro 9:15 and I will have c on whom I have c
- Col 3:12 clothe yourselves with c, kindness,
- Jas 5:11 The Lord is full of c and mercy.

COMPASSIONATE (COMPASSION)
- Ne 9:17 gracious and c, slow to anger
- Ps 103: 8 The LORD is c and gracious,
- 112: 4 the gracious and c and righteous
- Eph 4:32 Be kind and c to one another,
- 1Pe 3: 8 love as brothers, be c and humble.

COMPASSIONS* (COMPASSION)
- La 3:22 for his c never fail.

COMPELLED (COMPELS)
- Ac 20:22 "And now, c by the Spirit,
- 1Co 9:16 I cannot boast, for I am c to preach.

COMPELS (COMPELLED)
- 2Co 5:14 For Christ's love c us, because we

COMPETENCE* (COMPETENT)
- 2Co 3: 5 but our c comes from God.

COMPETENT* (COMPETENCE)
- Ro 15:14 and c to instruct one another.

COMPETES

COMPETES*
1Co 9:25 Everyone who *c* in the games goes
2Ti 2: 5 Similarly, if anyone *c* as an athlete,
    2: 5 unless he *c* according to the rules.

COMPLACENT
Am 6: 1 Woe to you who are *c* in Zion,

COMPLAINING*
Php 2:14 Do everything without *c* or arguing

COMPLETE
Jn 15:11 and that your joy may be *c*.
   16:24 will receive, and your joy will be *c*.
   17:23 May they be brought to *c* unity
Ac 20:24 *c* the task the Lord Jesus has given
Php 2 then make my joy *c*
Col 4:17 to it that you *c* the work you have
Jas 1: 4 so that you may be mature and *c*,
    2:22 his faith was made *c* by what he did

CONCEAL (CONCEALED CONCEALS)
Ps 40:10 I do not *c* your love and your truth
Pr 25: 2 It is the glory of God to *c* a matter;

CONCEALED (CONCEAL)
Jer 16:17 nor is their sin *c* from my eyes.
Mt 10:26 There is nothing *c* that will not be
Mk 4:22 and whatever is *c* is meant

CONCEALS (CONCEAL)
Pr 28:13 He who *c* his sins does not prosper,

CONCEITED
Ro 12:16 Do not be *c*.
Gal 5:26 Let us not become *c*, provoking
1Ti 6: 4 he is *c* and understands nothing.

CONCEIVED
Mt 1:20 what is *c* in her is from the Holy
1Co 2: 9 no mind has *c*

CONCERN (CONCERNED)
Eze 36:21 I had *c* for my holy name, which
1Co 7:32 I would like you to be free from *c*.
    12:25 that its parts should have equal *c*
2Co 11:28 of my *c* for all the churches.

CONCERNED (CONCERN)
Jnh 4:10 "You have been *c* about this vine,
1Co 7:32 An unmarried man is *c* about

CONDEMN (CONDEMNATION CONDEMNED CONDEMNING CONDEMNS)
Job 40: 8 Would you *c* me to justify yourself?
Isa 50: 9 Who is he that will *c* me?
Lk 6:37 Do not *c*, and you will not be
Jn 3:17 Son into the world to *c* the world,
    12:48 very word which I spoke will *c* him
Ro 2:27 yet obeys the law will *c* you who,
1Jn 3:20 presence whenever our hearts *c* us.

CONDEMNATION (CONDEMN)
Ro 5:18 of one trespass was *c* for all men,
   8: 1 there is now no *c* for those who are

CONDEMNED (CONDEMN)
Ps 34:22 no one will be *c* who takes refuge
Mt 12:37 and by your words you will be *c*."
   23:33 How will you escape being *c* to hell
Jn 3:18 Whoever believes in him is not *c*,
   5:24 has eternal life and will not be *c*;
   16:11 prince of this world now stands *c*.
Ro 14:23 But the man who has doubts is *c*
1Co 11:32 disciplined so that we will not be *c*
Heb 11: 7 By his faith he *c* the world

CONDEMNING (CONDEMN)
Pr 17:15 the guilty and *c* the innocent—
Ro 2: 1 judge the other, you are *c* yourself,

CONDEMNS (CONDEMN)
Ro 8:34 Who is he that *c*? Christ Jesus,
2Co 3: 9 the ministry that *c* men is glorious,

CONDUCT
Pr 10:23 A fool finds pleasure in evil *c*,
   20:11 by whether his *c* is pure and right.
   21: 8 but the *c* of the innocent is upright.
Ecc 6: 6 how to *c* himself before others?
Jer 4:18 "Your own *c* and actions
   17:10 to reward a man according to his *c*,
Eze 7: 3 I will judge you according to your *c*
Php 1:27 *c* yourselves in a manner worthy

1524

3:15 to *c* themselves in God's household

CONFESS (CONFESSION)
Lev 16:21 and *c* over it all the wickedness
   26:40 " 'But if they will *c* their sins
Nu 5: 7 must *c* the sin he has committed.
Ps 38:18 I *c* my iniquity;
Ro 10: 9 That if you *c* with your mouth,
Php 2:11 every tongue *c* that Jesus Christ is
Jas 5:16 Therefore *c* your sins to each other
1Jn 1: 9 If we *c* our sins, he is faithful

CONFESSION (CONFESS)
Ezr 10:11 Now make *c* to the LORD,
2Co 9:13 obedience that accompanies your *c*

CONFIDENCE
Ps 71: 5 my *c* since my youth.
Pr 3:26 for the LORD will be your *c*
   11:13 A gossip betrays a *c*,
   25: 9 do not betray another man's *c*,
   31:11 Her husband has full *c* in her
Isa 32:17 will be quietness and *c* forever.
Jer 17: 7 whose *c* is in him.
Php 3: 3 and who put no *c* in the flesh—
Heb 3:14 till the end the *c* we had at first.
   4:16 the throne of grace with *c*,
   10:19 since we have *c* to enter the Most
   10:35 So do not throw away your *c*;
1Jn 5:14 This is the *c* we have

CONFORM* (CONFORMED)
Ro 12: 2 Do not *c* any longer to the pattern
1Pe 1:14 do not *c* to the evil desires you had

CONFORMED (CONFORM)
Ro 8:29 predestined to be *c* to the likeness

CONQUERORS
Ro 8:37 than *c* through him who loved us.

CONSCIENCE (CONSCIENCES)
Ro 13: 5 punishment but also because of *c*.
1Co 8: 7 since their *c* is weak, it is defiled.
   8:12 in this way and wound their weak *c*
   10:25 without raising questions of *c*,
   10:29 freedom be judged by another's *c*?
Heb 10:22 to cleanse us from a guilty *c*
1Pe 3:16 and respect, keeping a clear *c*,

CONSCIENCES* (CONSCIENCE)
Ro 2:15 their *c* also bearing witness,
1Ti 4: 2 whose *c* have been seared
Tit 1:15 their minds and *c* are corrupted.
Heb 9:14 cleanse our *c* from acts that lead

CONSCIOUS*
Ro 3:20 through the law we become *c* of sin
1Pe 2:19 of unjust suffering because he is *c*

CONSECRATE (CONSECRATED)
Ex 13: 2 "*C* to me every firstborn male.
Lev 20: 7 "*C* yourselves and be holy,

CONSECRATED (CONSECRATE)
Ex 29:43 and the place will be *c* by my glory.
1Ti 4: 5 because it is *c* by the word of God

CONSIDER (CONSIDERATE CONSIDERED CONSIDERS)
1Sa 12:24 *c* what great things he has done
Job 37:14 stop and *c* God's wonders.
Ps 8: 3 When I *c* your heavens,
   107: 43 and *c* the great love of the LORD.
   143: 5 and *c* what your hands have done.
Lk 12:24 *C* the ravens: They do not sow
   12:27 about the rest? "*C* how the lilies
Php 2: 3 but in humility *c* others better
   3: 8 I *c* everything a loss compared
Heb 10:24 And let us *c* how we may spur one
Jas 1: 2 *C* it pure joy, my brothers,

CONSIDERATE* (CONSIDER)
Tit 3: 2 to be peaceable and *c*,
Jas 3:17 then peace-loving, *c*, submissive,
1Pe 2:18 only to those who are good and *c*,
   3: 7 in the same way be *c* as you live

CONSIDERED (CONSIDER)
Job 1: 8 "Have you *c* my servant Job?"
   2: 3 "Have you *c* my servant Job?"
Ps 44:22 we are *c* as sheep to be slaughtered.
Isa 53: 4 yet we *c* him stricken by God,
Ro 8:36 we are *c* as sheep to be slaughtered

CONSIDERS (CONSIDER)
Pr 31:16 She *c* a field and buys it;
Ro 14: 5 One man *c* one day more sacred

Jas 1:26 If anyone *c* himself religious

CONSIST
Lk 12:15 a man's life does not *c*

CONSOLATION
Ps 94:19 your *c* brought joy to my soul.

CONSTRUCTIVE*
1Co 10:23 but not everything is *c*.

CONSUME (CONSUMING)
Jn 2:17 "Zeal for your house will *c* me."

CONSUMING (CONSUME)
Dt 4:24 For the LORD your God is a *c* fire,
Heb 12:29 and awe, for our "God is a *c* fire."

CONTAIN
1Ki 8:27 the highest heaven, cannot *c* you.
2Pe 3:16 His letters *c* some things that are

CONTAMINATES*
2Co 7: 1 from everything that *c* body

CONTEMPT
Pr 14:31 He who oppresses the poor shows *c*
   17: 5 He who mocks the poor shows *c*
   18: 3 When wickedness comes, so does *c*
Da 12: 2 others to shame and everlasting *c*
Ro 2: 4 Or do you show *c* for the riches
Gal 4:14 you did not treat me with *c*
1Th 5:20 do not treat prophecies with *c*.

CONTEND (CONTENDING)
Jude 3 you to *c* for the faith that was once

CONTENDING* (CONTEND)
Php 1:27 *c* as one man for the faith

CONTENT (CONTENTMENT)
Pr 13:25 The righteous eat to their hearts' *c*,
Php 4:11 to be *c* whatever the circumstances
   4:12 I have learned the secret of being *c*
1Ti 6: 8 and clothing, we will be *c* with that.
Heb 13: 5 and be *c* with what you have,

CONTENTMENT (CONTENT)
1Ti 6: 6 But godliness with *c* is great gain.

CONTINUAL (CONTINUE)
Pr 15:15 but the cheerful heart has a *c* feast.

CONTINUE (CONTINUAL)
Php 2:12 *c* to work out your salvation
2Ti 3:14 *c* in what you have learned
1Jn 5:18 born of God does not *c* to sin;
Rev 22:11 and let him who is holy *c* to be holy
   22:11 let him who does right *c* to do right;

CONTRITE*
Ps 51:17 a broken and *c* heart,
Isa 57:15 also with him who is *c* and lowly
   57:15 and to revive the heart of the *c*,
   66: 2 he who is humble and *c* in spirit,

CONTROL (CONTROLLED SELF-CONTROL SELF-CONTROLLED)
Pr 29:11 a wise man keeps himself under *c*.
1Co 7: 9 But if they cannot *c* themselves,
   7:37 but has *c* over his own will,
1Th 4: 4 you should learn to *c* his own body

CONTROLLED (CONTROL)
Ps 32: 9 but must be *c* by bit and bridle
Ro 8: 6 but the mind *c* by the Spirit is life
   8: 8 Those *c* by the sinful nature cannot

CONTROVERSIES
Tit 3: 9 But avoid foolish *c* and genealogies

CONVERSATION
Col 4: 6 Let your *c* be always full of grace,

CONVERT
1Ti 3: 6 He must not be a recent *c*,

CONVICT
Jn 16: 8 he will *c* the world of guilt in regard

CONVINCED (CONVINCING)
Ro 8:38 For I am *c* that neither death
2Ti 1:12 and am *c* that he is able
   3:14 have learned and have become *c*

CONVINCING* (CONVINCED)
Ac 1: 3 and gave many *c* proofs that he was

CORNELIUS*
Roman to whom Peter preached; first Gentile Christian (Ac 10).

CORNERSTONE (STONE)
Isa 28:16 a precious *c* for a sure foundation;
Eph 2:20 Christ Jesus himself as the chief *c*.

1Pe 2: 6 a chosen and precious c,
CORRECT (CORRECTING CORRECTION CORRECTS)
2Ti 4: 2 c, rebuke and encourage—
CORRECTING* (CORRECT)
2Ti 3:16 c and training in righteousness,
CORRECTION (CORRECT)
Pr 10:17 whoever ignores c leads others
 12: 1 but he who hates c is stupid.
 15: 5 whoever heeds c shows prudence.
 15:10 he who hates c will die.
 29:15 The rod of c imparts wisdom,
CORRECTS* (CORRECT)
Job 5:17 "Blessed is the man whom God c;
Pr 9: 7 Whoever c a mocker invites insult;
CORRUPT (CORRUPTS)
Ge 6:11 Now the earth was c in God's sight
CORRUPTS* (CORRUPT)
Ecc 7: 7 and a bribe c the heart.
1Co 15:33 "Bad company c good character."
Jas 3: 6 It c the whole person, sets
COST
Pr 4: 7 Though it c all you have, get
Isa 55: 1 milk without money and without c.
Rev 21: 6 to drink without c from the spring
COUNSEL (COUNSELOR)
1Ki 22: 5 "First seek the c of the LORD."
Pr 15:22 Plans fail for lack of c,
Rev 3:18 I c you to buy from me gold refined
COUNSELOR (COUNSEL)
Isa 9: 6 Wonderful C, Mighty God,
Jn 14:16 he will give you another C to be
 14:26 But the C, the Holy Spirit,
COUNT (COUNTING COUNTS)
Ro 4: 8 whose sin the Lord will never c
 6:11 c yourselves dead to sin
COUNTING (COUNT)
2Co 5:19 not c men's sins against them.
COUNTRY
Jn 4:44 prophet has no honor in his own c.)
COUNTS (COUNT)
Jn 6:63 The Spirit gives life; the flesh c
1Co 7:19 God's commands is what c.
Gal 5: 6 only thing that c is faith expressing
COURAGE (COURAGEOUS)
Ac 23:11 "Take c! As you have testified
1Co 16:13 stand firm in the faith; be men of c;
COURAGEOUS (COURAGE)
Dt 31: 6 Be strong and c.
Jos 1: 6 and c, because you will lead these
COURSE
Ps 19: 5 a champion rejoicing to run his c.
Pr 15:21 of understanding keeps a straight c.
COURTS
Ps 84:10 Better is one day in your c
 100: 4 and his c with praise;
COVENANT (COVENANTS)
Ge 9: 9 "I now establish my c with you
Ex 19: 5 if you obey me fully and keep my c,
1Ch 16:15 He remembers his c forever,
Job 31: 1 "I made a c with my eyes
Jer 31:31 "when I will make a new c"
1Co 11:25 "This cup is the new c in my blood;
Gal 4:24 One c is from Mount Sinai
Heb 9:15 Christ is the mediator of a new c,
COVENANTS (COVENANT)
Ro 9: 4 theirs the divine glory, the c,
Gal 4:24 for the women represent two c.
COVER (COVER-UP COVERED COVERS)
Ps 91: 4 He will c you with his feathers,
Jas 5:20 and c over a multitude of sins.
COVER-UP (COVER)
1Pe 2:16 but do not use your freedom as a c
COVERED (COVER)
Ps 32: 1 whose sins are c,
Isa 6: 2 With two wings they c their faces,
Ro 4: 7 whose sins are c.
1Co 11: 4 with his head c dishonors his head.
COVERS (COVER)
Pr 10:12 but love c over all wrongs.
1Pe 4: 8 love c over a multitude of sins.

COVET
Ex 20:17 You shall not c your neighbor's
Ro 13: 9 "Do not steal," "Do not c,"
COWARDLY*
Rev 21: 8 But the c, the unbelieving, the vile,
CRAFTINESS (CRAFTY)
1Co 3:19 "He catches the wise in their c";
CRAFTY (CRAFTINESS)
Ge 3: 1 the serpent was more c than any
2Co 12:16 c fellow that I am, I caught you
CRAVE
Pr 23: 3 Do not c his delicacies,
1Pe 2: 2 newborn babies, c pure spiritual
CREATE (CREATED CREATION CREATOR)
Ps 51:10 C in me a pure heart, O God,
Isa 45:18 he did not c it to be empty,
CREATED (CREATE)
Ge 1: 1 In the beginning God c the heavens
 1:21 God c the great creatures of the sea
 1:27 So God c man in his own image,
Ps 148: 5 for he commanded and they were c.
Isa 42: 5 he who c the heavens and stretched
Ro 1:25 and served c things rather
1Co 11: 9 neither was man c for woman,
Col 1:16 For by him all things were c:
1Ti 4: 4 For everything God c is good,
Rev 10: 6 who c the heavens and all that is
CREATION (CREATE)
Mk 16:15 and preach the good news to all c.
Jn 17:24 me before the c of the world.
Ro 8:19 The c waits in eager expectation
 8:39 depth, nor anything else in all c,
2Co 5:17 he is a new c; the old has gone,
Col 1:15 God, the firstborn over all c.
1Pe 1:20 chosen before the c of the world,
Rev 13: 8 slain from the c of the world.
CREATOR (CREATE)
Ge 14:22 God Most High, C of heaven
Ro 1:25 created things rather than the C—
CREATURE (CREATURES)
Lev 17:11 For the life of a c is in the blood,
CREATURES (CREATURE)
Ge 6:19 bring into the ark two of all living c,
Ps 104: 24 the earth is full of your c.
CREDIT (CREDITED)
Ro 4:24 to whom God will c righteousness
1Pe 2:20 it to your c if you receive a beating
CREDITED (CREDIT)
Ge 15: 6 and he c it to him as righteousness.
Ro 4: 5 his faith is c as righteousness.
Gal 3: 6 and it was c to him as righteousness
Jas 2:23 and it was c to him as righteousness
CRIED (CRY)
Ps 18: 6 I c to my God for help.
CRIMSON
Isa 1:18 though they are red as c,
CRIPPLED
Mk 9:45 better for you to enter life c
CRITICISM
2Co 8:20 We want to avoid any c
CROOKED
Pr 10: 9 he who takes c paths will be found
Php 2:15 children of God without fault in a c
CROSS
Mt 10:38 and anyone who does not take his c
Lk 9:23 take up his c daily and follow me.
Ac 2:23 to death by nailing him to the c.
1Co 1:17 lest the c of Christ be emptied
Gal 6:14 in the c of our Lord Jesus Christ,
Php 2: 8 even death on a c!
Col 1:20 through his blood, shed on the c.
 2:14 he took it away, nailing it to the c.
 2:15 triumphing over them by the c.
Heb 12: 2 set before him endured the c,
CROWD
Ex 23: 2 Do not follow the c in doing wrong.
CROWN (CROWNED CROWNS)
Pr 4: 9 present you with a c of splendor."
 10: 6 Blessings c the head
 12: 4 noble character is her husband's c,
 17: 6 Children's children are a c

Isa 61: 3 to bestow on them a c of beauty
Zec 9:16 like jewels in a c.
Mt 27:29 then twisted together a c of thorns
1Co 9:25 it to get a c that will last forever.
2Ti 4: 8 store for me the c of righteousness,
Rev 2:10 and I will give you the c of life.
CROWNED (CROWN)
Ps 8: 5 and c him with glory and honor.
Pr 14:18 the prudent are c with knowledge.
Heb 2: 7 you c him with glory and honor
CROWNS (CROWN)
Rev 4:10 They lay their c before the throne
 19:12 and on his head are many c.
CRUCIFIED (CRUCIFY)
Mt 20:19 to be mocked and flogged and c.
 27:38 Two robbers were c with him,
Lk 24: 7 be c and on the third day be raised
Jn 19:18 Here they c him, and with him two
Ac 2:36 whom you c, both Lord and Christ
Ro 6: 6 For we know that our old self was c
1Co 1:23 but we preach Christ c: a stumbling
 2: 2 except Jesus Christ and him c.
Gal 2:20 I have been c with Christ
 5:24 Christ Jesus have c the sinful
CRUCIFY (CRUCIFIED CRUCIFYING)
Mt 27:22 They all answered, "C him!" "Why
 27:31 Then they led him away to c him.
CRUCIFYING* (CRUCIFY)
Heb 6: 6 to their loss they are c the Son
CRUSH (CRUSHED)
Ge 3:15 he will c your head,
Isa 53:10 it was the LORD's will to c him
Ro 16:20 The God of peace will soon c Satan
CRUSHED (CRUSH)
Ps 34:18 and saves those who are c in spirit.
Isa 53: 5 he was c for our iniquities;
2Co 4: 8 not c; perplexed, but not in despair;
CRY (CRIED)
Ps 34:15 and his ears are attentive to their c;
 40: 1 he turned to me and heard my c.
 130: 1 Out of the depths I c to you,
CUP
Ps 23: 5 my c overflows.
Mt 10:42 if anyone gives even a c of cold water
 23:25 You clean the outside of the c
 26:39 may this c be taken from me.
1Co 11:25 after supper he took the c, saying,
CURSE (CURSED)
Dt 11:26 before you today a blessing and a c
 21:23 hung on a tree is under God's c.
Lk 6:28 bless those who c you, pray
Gal 3:13 of the law by becoming a c for us,
Rev 22: 3 No longer will there be any c.
CURSED (CURSE)
Ge 3:17 "C is the ground because of you;
Dt 27:15 "C is the man who carves an image
 27:17 "C is the man who dishonors his
 27:17 "C is the man who moves his
 27:18 "C is the man who leads the blind
 27:19 C is the man who withholds justice
 27:20 "C is the man who sleeps
 27:21 "C is the man who has sexual
 27:22 "C is the man who sleeps
 27:23 "C is the man who sleeps
 27:24 "C is the man who kills his
 27:25 "C is the man who accepts a bribe
 27:26 "C is the man who does not uphold
Ro 9: 3 I could wish that I myself were c
Gal 3:10 "C is everyone who does not
CURTAIN
Ex 26:33 The c will separate the Holy Place
Lk 23:45 the c of the temple was torn in two.
Heb 10:20 opened for us through the c,
CYMBAL*
1Co 13: 1 a resounding gong or a clanging c.
DANCE (DANCING)
Ecc 3: 4 a time to mourn and a time to d,
Mt 11:17 and you did not d;
DANCING (DANCE)
Ps 30:11 You turned my wailing into d;
 149: 3 Let them praise his name with d

DANGER
- Pr 27:12 The prudent see *d* and take refuge,
- Ro 8:35 famine or nakedness or *d* or sword?

DANIEL
Hebrew exile to Babylon, name changed to Belteshazzar (Da 1:6-7). Refused to eat unclean food (Da 1:8-21). Interpreted Nebuchadnezzar's dreams (Da 2; 4), writing on the wall (Da 5). Thrown into lion's den (Da 6). Visions of (Da 7-12).

DARK (DARKNESS)
- Job 34:22 There is no *d* place, no deep
- Pr 31:15 She gets up while it is still *d*;
- Ro 2:19 a light for those who are in the *d*,
- 2Pe 1:19 as to a light shining in a *d* place,

DARKNESS (DARK)
- Ge 1: 4 he separated the light from the *d*.
- 2Sa 22:29 The LORD turns my *d* into light.
- Jn 3:19 but men loved *d* instead of light
- 2Co 6:14 fellowship can light have with *d*?
- Eph 5: 8 For you were once *d*, but now you
- 1Pe 2: 9 out of *d* into his wonderful light.
- 1Jn 1: 5 in him there is no *d* at all.
- 2: 9 but hates his brother is still in the *d*.

DAUGHTERS
- Joel 2:28 sons and *d* will prophesy,

DAVID
Son of Jesse (Ru 4:17-22; 1Ch 2:13-15), ancestor of Jesus (Mt 1:1-17; Lk 3:31).
Anointed king by Samuel (1Sa 16:1-13). Musician to Saul (1Sa 16:14-23; 18:10). Killed Goliath (1Sa 17). Relation with Jonathan (1Sa 18:1-4; 19-20; 23:16-18; 2Sa 1). Disfavor of Saul (1Sa 18:6-23:29). Spared Saul's life (1Sa 24; 26). Among Philistines (1Sa 21:10-14; 27-30). Lament for Saul and Jonathan (2Sa 1).
Anointed king of Judah (2Sa 2:1-11); of Israel (2Sa 5:1-4; 1Ch 11:1-3). Promised eternal dynasty (2Sa 7; 1Ch 17; Ps 132). Adultery with Bathsheba (2Sa 11-12). Absalom's revolt (2Sa 14-18). Last words (2Sa 23:1-7). Death (1Ki 2:10-12; 1Ch 29:28).

DAWN
- Ps 37: 6 your righteousness shine like the *d*,
- Pr 4:18 is like the first gleam of *d*,

DAY (DAYS)
- Ge 1: 5 God called the light "*d*,"
- Ex 20: 8 "Remember the Sabbath *d*
- Lev 23:28 because it is the *D* of Atonement,
- Nu 14:14 before them in a pillar of cloud by *d*
- Jos 1: 8 meditate on it *d* and night,
- Ps 84:10 Better is one *d* in your courts
- 96: 2 proclaim his salvation *d* after *d*.
- 118: 24 This is the *d* the LORD has made;
- Pr 27: 1 not know what a *d* may bring forth.
- Joel 2:31 and dreadful *d* of the LORD.
- Ob 15 The *d* of the LORD is near
- Lk 11: 3 Give us each *d* our daily bread.
- Ac 17:11 examined the Scriptures every *d*
- 2Co 4:16 we are being renewed *d* by *d*.
- 1Th 5: 2 for you know very well that the *d*
- 2Pe 3: 8 With the Lord a *d* is like

DAYS (DAY)
- Dt 17:19 he is to read it a I the *d*, of his life
- Ps 23: 6 all the *d* of my life,
- 90:10 The length of our *d* is seventy years
- Ecc 12: 1 Creator in the *d* of your youth,
- Joel 2:29 I will pour out my Spirit in those *d*.
- Mic 4: 1 In the last *d*
- Heb 1: 2 in these last *d* he has spoken to us
- 2Pe 3: 3 that in the last *d* scoffers will come,

DEACONS
- 1Ti 3: 8 *D*, likewise, are to be men worthy

DEAD (DIE)
- Dt 18:11 or spiritist or who consults the *d*.
- Mt 28: 7 'He has risen from the *d*
- Ro 6:11 count yourselves *d* to sin
- Eph 2: 1 you were *d* in your transgressions
- 1Th 4:16 and the *d* in Christ will rise first.
- Jas 2:17 is not accompanied by action, is *d*.
- 2:26 so faith without deeds is *d*.

DEATH (DIE)
- Nu 35:16 the murderer shall be put to *d*.
- Ps 23: 4 the valley of the shadow of *d*,
- 116: 15 is the *d* of his saints.

- Pr 8:36 all who hate me love *d*."
- 14:12 but in the end it leads to *d*.
- Ecc 7: 2 for *d* is the destiny of every man;
- Isa 25: 8 he will swallow up *d* forever.
- 53:12 he poured out his life unto *d*,
- Jn 5:24 he has crossed over from *d* to life.
- Ro 5:12 and in this way *d* came to all men,
- 6:23 For the wages of sin is *d*,
- 8:13 put to *d* the misdeeds of the body,
- 1Co 15: 21 For since *d* came through a man,
- 15:55 Where, O *d*, is your sting?"
- Rev 1:18 And I hold the keys of *d* and Hades
- 20: 6 The second *d* has no power
- 20:14 The lake of fire is the second *d*.
- 21: 4 There will be no more *d*

DEBAUCHERY
- Ro 13:13 not in sexual immorality and *d*,
- Eph 5:18 drunk on wine, which leads to *d*.

DEBORAH
Prophetess who led Israel to victory over Canaanites (Jdg 4-5).

DEBT (DEBTORS DEBTS)
- Ro 13: 8 Let no *d* remain outstanding,
- 13: 8 continuing *d* to love one another,

DEBTORS (DEBT)
- Mt 6:12 as we also have forgiven our *d*.

DEBTS (DEBT)
- Dt 15: 1 seven years you must cancel *d*.
- Mt 6:12 Forgive us our *d*,

DECAY
- Ps 16:10 will you let your Holy One see *d*.
- Ac 2:27 will you let your Holy One see *d*.

DECEIT (DECEIVE)
- Mk 7:22 greed, malice, *d*, lewdness, envy,
- 1Pe 2: 1 yourselves of all malice and all *d*,
- 2:22 and no *d* was found in his mouth."

DECEITFUL (DECEIVE)
- Jer 17: 9 The heart is *d* above all things
- 2Co 11:13 men are false apostles, *d* workmen,

DECEITFULNESS (DECEIVE)
- Mk 4:19 the *d* of wealth and the desires
- Heb 3:13 of you may be hardened by sin's *d*.

DECEIVE (DECEIT DECEITFUL DECEITFULNESS DECEIVED DECEIVES DECEPTIVE)
- Lev 19:11 " 'Do not *d* one another.
- Pr 14: 5 A truthful witness does not *d*,
- Mt 24: 5 'I am the Christ,' and will *d* many.
- Ro 16:18 and flattery they *d* the minds
- 1Co 3:18 Do not *d* yourselves.
- Eph 5: 6 Let no one *d* you with empty words
- Jas 1:22 to the word, and so *d* yourselves.
- 1Jn 1: 8 we *d* ourselves and the truth is not

DECEIVED (DECEIVE)
- Ge 3:13 "The serpent *d* me, and I ate."
- Gal 6: 7 Do not be *d*: God cannot be
- 1Ti 2:14 And Adam was not the one *d*;
- 2Ti 3:13 to worse, deceiving and being *d*.
- Jas 1:16 Don't be *d*, my dear brothers.

DECEIVES (DECEIVE)
- Gal 6: 3 when he is nothing, he *d* himself.
- Jas 1:26 he *d* himself and his religion is

DECENCY*
- 1Ti 2: 9 women to dress modestly, with *d*

DECEPTIVE (DECEIVE)
- Pr 31:30 Charm is *d*, and beauty is fleeting;
- Col 2: 8 through hollow and *d* philosophy,

DECLARE (DECLARED DECLARING)
- 1Ch 16:24 *D* his glory among the nations,
- Ps 19: 1 The heavens *d* the glory of God;
- 96: 3 *D* his glory among the nations,
- Isa 42: 9 and new things I *d*;

DECLARED (DECLARE)
- Mk 7:19 Jesus *d* all foods "clean.")
- Ro 2:13 the law who will be *d* righteous.
- 3:20 no one will be *d* righteous

DECLARING (DECLARE)
- Ps 71: 8 *d* your splendor all day long.
- Ac 2:11 we have them *d* the wonders

DECREED (DECREES)
- La 3:37 happen if the Lord has not *d* it?
- Lk 22:22 Son of Man will go as it has been *d*,

DECREES (DECREED)
- Lev 10:11 Israelites all the *d* the LORD has
- Ps 119:112 My heart is set on keeping your *d*

DEDICATE (DEDICATION)
- Nu 6:12 He must *d* himself to the LORD
- Pr 20:25 for a man to *d* something rashly

DEDICATION (DEDICATE)
- 1Ti 5:11 sensual desires overcome their *d*

DEED (DEEDS)
- Col 3:17 you do, whether in word or *d*,

DEEDS (DEED)
- 1Sa 2: 3 and by him *d* are weighed.
- Ps 65: 5 with awesome *d* of righteousness,
- 66: 3 "How awesome are your *d*!
- 78: 4 the praiseworthy *d* of the LORD,
- 86:10 you are great and do marvelous *d*,
- 92: 4 For you make me glad by your *d*,
- 111: 3 Glorious and majestic are his *d*,
- Hab 3: 2 I stand in awe of your *d*, O LORD.
- Mt 5:16 that they may see your good *d*
- Ac 26:20 prove their repentance by their *d*.
- Jas 2:14 claims to have faith but has no *d*?
- 2:20 faith without *d* is useless?
- 1Pe 2:12 they may see your good *d*

DEEP (DEPTH)
- 1Co 2:10 all things, even the *d* things
- 1Ti 3: 9 hold of the *d* truths of the faith

DEER
- Ps 42: 1 As the *d* pants for streams of water,

DEFEND (DEFENSE)
- Ps 74:22 Rise up, O God, and *d* your cause;
- Pr 31: 9 *d* the rights of the poor and needy
- Jer 50:34 He will vigorously *d* their cause

DEFENSE (DEFEND)
- Ps 35:23 Awake, and rise to my *d*!
- Php 1:16 here for the *d* of the gospel.
- 1Jn 2: 1 speaks to the Father in our *d*—

DEFERRED*
- Pr 13:12 Hope *d* makes the heart sick,

DEFILE (DEFILED)
- Da 1: 8 Daniel resolved not to *d* himself

DEFILED (DEFILE)
- Isa 24: 5 The earth is *d* by its people;

DEFRAUD
- Lev 19:13 Do not *d* your neighbor or rob him.

DEITY*
- Col 2: 9 of the *D* lives in bodily form,

DELIGHT (DELIGHTS)
- 1Sa 15:22 "Does the LORD *d*
- Ps 1: 2 But his *d* is in the law of the LORD
- 16: 3 in whom is all my *d*.
- 35: 9 and *d* in his salvation.
- 37: 4 *D* yourself in the LORD
- 43: 4 to God, my joy and my *d*.
- 51:16 You do not *d* in sacrifice,
- 119: 77 for your law is my *d*.
- Pr 29:17 he will bring *d* to your soul.
- Isa 42: 1 my chosen one in whom I *d*;
- 55: 2 and your soul will *d* in the richest
- 58:14 I *d* greatly in the LORD;
- Jer 9:24 for in these I *d*,"
- 15:16 they were my joy and my heart's *d*,
- Mic 7:18 but *d* to show mercy.
- Zep 3:17 He will take great *d* in you,
- Mt 12:18 the one I love, in whom I *d*;
- 1Co 13: 6 Love does not *d* in evil
- 2Co 12:10 for Christ's sake, I *d* in weaknesses,

DELIGHTS (DELIGHT)
- Ps 22: 8 since he *d* in him."
- 35:27 who *d* in the well-being
- 36: 8 from your river of *d*.
- 37:23 if the LORD *d* in a man's way,
- Pr 3:12 as a father the son he *d* in.
- 12:22 but he *d* in men who are truthful.
- 23: 24 he who has a wise son *d* in him.

DELILAH*
Woman who betrayed Samson (Jdg 16:4-22).

DELIVER (DELIVERANCE DELIVERED DELIVERER DELIVERS)
- Ps 72:12 For he will *d* the needy who cry out
- 79: 9 *d* us and forgive our sins

Mt	6:13 but *d* us from the evil one."		78:52 led them like sheep through the *d*.		Zec	4:10 "Who *d* the day of small things?	
2Co	1:10 hope that he will continue to *d* us;	Mk	1:13 and he was in the *d* forty days,		**DESTINED** (DESTINY)		
DELIVERANCE (DELIVER)		**DESERTED** (DESERTS)		Lk	2:34 "This child is *d* to cause the falling		
Ps	3:8 From the LORD comes *d*.	Ezr	9:9 our God has not *d* us		**DESTINY** (DESTINED PREDESTINED)		
	32:7 and surround me with songs of *d*.	Mt	26:56 all the disciples *d* him and fled.		Ps	73:17 then I understood their final *d*.	
	33:17 A horse is a vain hope for *d;*	2Ti	1:15 in the province of Asia has *d* me,		Ecc	7:2 for death is the *d* of every man;	
DELIVERED (DELIVER)		**DESERTING** (DESERTS)		**DESTITUTE**			
Ps	34:4 he *d* me from all my fears.	Gal	1:6 are so quickly *d* the one who called		Pr	31:8 for the rights of all who are *d*.	
Ro	4:25 He was *d* over to death for our sins	**DESERTS** (DESERTED DESERTING)		Heb	11:37 *d*, persecuted and mistreated—		
DELIVERER (DELIVER)		Zec	11:17 who *d* the flock!		**DESTROY** (DESTROYED DESTROYS DESTRUCTION)		
Ps	18:2 is my rock, my fortress and my *d;*	**DESERVE** (DESERVES)		Pr	1:32 complacency of fools will *d* them;		
	40:17 You are my help and my *d;*	Ps	103:10 he does not treat us as our sins *d*		Mt	10:28 of the One who can *d* both soul	
	140:7 O Sovereign LORD, my strong *d,*	Jer	21:14 I will punish you as your deeds *d,*		**DESTROYED** (DESTROY)		
	144:2 my stronghold and my *d,*	Mt	22:8 those I invited did not *d* to come.		Job	19:26 And after my skin has been *d,*	
DELIVERS (DELIVER)		Ro	1:32 those who do such things *d* death,		Isa	55:13 which will not be *d."*	
Ps	34:17 he *d* them from all their troubles.	**DESERVES** (DESERVE)		1Co	8:11 for whom Christ died, is *d.*		
	34:19 but the LORD *d* him from them all	2Sa	12:5 the man who did this *d* to die!			15:26 The last enemy to be *d* is death.	
	37:40 The LORD helps them and *d* them	Lk	10:7 for the worker *d* his wages.		2Co	5:1 if the earthly tent we live in is *d,*	
	37:40 *d* them from the wicked	1Ti	5:18 and "The worker *d* his wages."		Heb	10:39 of those who shrink back and are *d,*	
DEMANDED		**DESIRABLE** (DESIRE)		2Pe	3:10 the elements will be *d* by fire,		
Lk	12:20 This very night your life will be *d*	Pr	22:1 A good name is more *d*		**DESTROYS** (DESTROY)		
	12:48 been given much, much will be *d;*	**DESIRE** (DESIRABLE DESIRES)		Pr	6:32 whoever does so *d* himself.		
DEMONS		Ge	3:16 Your *d* will be for your husband,			11:9 mouth the godless *d* his neighbor,	
Mt	12:27 And if I drive out *d* by Beelzebub,	Dt	5:21 You shall not set your *d*			18:9 is brother to one who *d.*	
Mk	5:15 possessed by the legion of *d,*	1Ch	29:18 keep this *d* in the hearts			28:24 he is partner to him who *d.*	
Ro	8:38 neither angels nor *d,* neither	Ps	40:6 Sacrifice and offering you did not *d*		Ecc	9:18 but one sinner *d* much good.	
Jas	2:19 Good! Even the *d* believe that—		40:8 I *d* to do your will, O my God;		1Co	3:17 If anyone *d* God's temple,	
DEMONSTRATE (DEMONSTRATES)			73:25 earth has nothing I *d* besides you		**DESTRUCTION** (DESTROY)		
Ro	3:26 he did it to *d* his justice	Pr	3:15 nothing you *d* can compare		Pr	16:18 Pride goes before *d,*	
DEMONSTRATES* (DEMONSTRATE)			10:24 what the righteous *d* will		Hos	13:14 Where, O grave, is your *d?*	
Ro	5:8 God *d* his own love for us in this:		11:23 The *d* of the righteous ends only		Mt	7:13 broad is the road that leads to *d,*	
DEN		Isa	26:8 are the *d* of our hearts.		Gal	6:8 from that nature will reap *d;*	
Da	6:16 and threw him into the lions' *d.*		53:2 appearance that we should *d* him.		2Th	1:9 punished with everlasting *d*		
Mt	21:13 you are making it a '*d* of robbers.' "		55:11 but will accomplish what I *d*		1Ti	6:9 that plunge men into ruin and *d.*	
DENARIUS		Hos	6:6 For I *d* mercy, not sacrifice,		2Pe	2:1 bringing swift *d* on themselves.	
Mk	12:15 Bring me a *d* and let me look at it."	Mt	9:13 learn what this means: 'I *d* mercy,			3:16 other Scriptures, to their own *d.*	
DENIED (DENY)		Ro	7:18 For I have the *d* to do what is good,		**DETERMINED** (DETERMINES)		
1Ti	5:8 he has *d* the faith and is worse	1Co	12:31 But eagerly *d* the greater gifts.		Job	14:5 Man's days are *d;*		
DENIES (DENY)			14:1 and eagerly *d* spiritual gifts,		Isa	14:26 This is the plan *d* for the whole	
1Jn	2:23 No one who *d* the Son has	Php	1:23 I *d* to depart and be with Christ,		Da	11:36 for what has been *d* must take place	
DENY (DENIED DENIES DENYING)		Heb	13:18 *d* to live honorably in every way.		Ac	17:26 and he *d* the times set for them	
Ex	23:6 "Do not *d* justice to your poor	Jas	1:15 Then, after *d* has conceived,		**DETERMINES*** (DETERMINED)		
Job	27:5 till I die, I will not *d* my integrity.	**DESIRES** (DESIRE)		Ps	147:4 He *d* the number of the stars		
La	3:35 to *d* a man his rights	Ge	4:7 at your door; it *d* to have you,		Pr	16:9 but the LORD *d* his steps.	
Lk	9:23 he must *d* himself and take up his	Ps	34:12 and *d* to see many good days,		1Co	12:11 them to each one, just as he *d.*	
Tit	1:16 but by their actions they *d* him.		37:4 he will give you the *d* of your heart.		**DETESTABLE** (DETESTS)		
DENYING* (DENY)			103:5 satisfies your *d* with good things,		Pr	21:27 The sacrifice of the wicked is *d*—	
Eze	22:29 mistreat the alien, *d* them justice.		145:19 He fulfills the *d* of those who fear			28:9 even his prayers are *d.*	
2Ti	3:5 a form of godliness but *d* its power.	Pr	11:6 the unfaithful are trapped by evil *d.*		Isa	1:13 Your incense is *d* to me.	
2Pe	2:1 *d* the sovereign Lord who bought		19:22 What a man *d* is unfailing love;		Lk	16:15 among men is *d* in God's sight.	
DEPART (DEPARTED)		Mk	4:19 and the *d* for other things come in		Tit	1:16 They are *d,* disobedient	
Ge	49:10 The scepter will not *d* from Judah,	Ro	8:5 set on what that nature *d;*		**DETESTS** (DETESTABLE)		
Job	1:21 and naked I will *d.*		13:14 to gratify the *d* of the sinful nature.		Dt	22:5 LORD your God *d* anyone who	
Mt	25:41 '*D* from me, you who are cursed,	Gal	5:16 and you will not gratify the *d*			23:18 the LORD your God *d* them both.	
Php	1:23 I desire to *d* and be with Christ,		5:17 the sinful nature *d* what is contrary			25:16 LORD your God *d* anyone who	
DEPARTED (DEPART)		1Ti	3:1 an overseer, he *d* a noble task.		Pr	12:22 The LORD *d* lying lips,	
1Sa	4:21 "The glory has *d* from Israel"—		6:9 and harmful *d* that plunge men			15:8 The LORD *d* the sacrifice	
Ps	119:102 I have not *d* from your laws,	2Ti	2:22 Flee the evil *d* of youth,			15:9 The LORD *d* the way	
DEPOSIT		Jas	1:20 about the righteous life that God *d.*			15:26 The LORD *d* the thoughts	
2Co	1:22 put his Spirit in our hearts as a *d,*		4:1 from your *d* that battle within you?			16:5 The LORD *d* all the proud of heart	
	5:5 and has given us the Spirit as a *d.*	1Pe	2:11 to abstain from sinful *d,* which war			17:15 The LORD *d* them both.	
Eph	1:14 who is a *d* guaranteeing our	1Jn	2:17 The world and its *d* pass away,			20:23 The LORD *d* differing weights,	
2Ti	1:14 Guard the good *d* that was	**DESOLATE**		**DEVIL** (DEVIL'S)			
DEPRAVED (DEPRAVITY)		Isa	54:1 are the children of the *d* woman		Mt	13:39 the enemy who sows them is the *d.*	
Ro	1:28 he gave them over to a *d* mind,	**DESPAIR**			25:41 the eternal fire prepared for the *d*		
Php	2:15 fault in a crooked and *d* generation,	Isa	61:3 instead of a spirit of *d.*		Lk	4:2 forty days he was tempted by the *d.*	
DEPRAVITY (DEPRAVED)		2Co	4:8 perplexed, but not in *d;* persecuted,			8:12 then the *d* comes and takes away	
Ro	1:29 of wickedness, evil, greed and *d.*	**DESPISE** (DESPISED DESPISES)		Eph	4:27 and do not give the *d* a foothold.		
DEPRIVE		Job	42:6 Therefore I *d* myself		2Ti	2:26 and escape from the trap of the *d,*	
Dt	24:17 Do not *d* the alien or the fatherless	Pr	1:7 but fools *d* wisdom and discipline.		Jas	4:7 Resist the *d,* and he will flee	
Pr	18:5 or to *d* the innocent of justice.		3:11 do not *d* the LORD's discipline		1Pe	5:8 Your enemy the *d* prowls	
Isa	10:2 to *d* the poor of their rights		23:22 do not *d* your mother		1Jn	3:8 who does what is sinful is of the *d,*	
	29:21 with false testimony *d* the innocent	Lk	16:13 devoted to the one and *d* the other.		Rev	12:9 that ancient serpent called the *d*	
1Co	7:5 Do not *d* each other.	Tit	2:15 Do not let anyone *d* you.		**DEVIL'S*** (DEVIL)		
DEPTH (DEEP)		**DESPISED** (DESPISE)		Eph	6:11 stand against the *d* schemes.		
Ro	8:39 any powers, neither height nor *d,*	Ge	25:34 So Esau *d* his birthright.		1Ti	3:7 into disgrace and into the *d* trap.	
	11:33 The *d* of the riches of the wisdom	Isa	53:3 He was *d* and rejected by men,		1Jn	3:8 was to destroy the *d* work.	
DESERT		1Co	1:28 of this world and the *d* things—		**DEVOTE** (DEVOTED DEVOTING DEVOTION DEVOUT)		
Nu	32:13 wander in the *d* forty years,	**DESPISES** (DESPISE)		Job	11:13 "Yet if you *d* your heart to him		
Ne	9:19 you did not abandon them in the *d.*	Pr	14:21 He who *d* his neighbor sins,		Jer	30:21 for who is he who will *d* himself	
Ps	78:19 "Can God spread a table in the *d?*		15:20 but a foolish man *d* his mother.		Col	4:2 *D* yourselves to prayer, being	
			15:32 who ignores discipline *d* himself,		1Ti	4:13 *d* yourself to the public reading	

DEVOTED

Tit 3: 8 may be careful to *d* themselves
DEVOTED (DEVOTE)
Ezr 7: 10 For Ezra had *d* himself to the study
Ac 2: 42 They *d* themselves
Ro 12: 10 Be *d* to one another
1Co 7: 34 Her aim is to be *d* to the Lord
DEVOTING (DEVOTE)
1Ti 5: 10 *d* herself to al kinds of good deeds.
DEVOTION (DEVOTE)
1Ch 28: 9 and serve him with wholehearted *d*
Eze 33: 31 With their mouths they express *d*,
1Co 7: 35 way in undivided *d* to the Lord.
2Co 11: 3 from your sincere and pure *d*
DEVOUR
2Sa 2: 26 "Must the sword *d* forever?"
Mk 12: 40 They *d* widows' houses
1Pe 5: 8 lion looking for someone to *d*.
DEVOUT (DEVOTE)
Lk 2: 25 Simeon, who was righteous and *d*.
DIE (DEAD DEATH DIED DIES)
Ge 2: 17 when you eat of it you will surely *d*
Ex 11: 5 Every firstborn son in Egypt will *d*,
Ru 1: 17 Where you *d* I will *d*, and there I
2Ki 14: 6 each is to *d* for his own sins."
Pr 5: 23 He will *d* for lack of discipline,
     10: 21 but fools *d* for lack of judgment.
     15: 10 he who hates correction will *d*,
     23: 13 with the rod, he will not *d*.
Ecc 3: 2 a time to be born and a time to *d*,
Isa 66: 24 their worm will not *d*, nor will their
Eze 3: 18 that wicked man will *d* for his sin,
     18: 4 soul who sins is the one who will *d*.
     33: 8 'O wicked man, you will surely *d*,'
Mt 26: 52 "for all who draw the sword will *d*
Jn 11: 26 and believes in me will never *d*.
Ro 5: 7 Very rarely will anyone *d*
     14: 8 and if we *d*, we *d* to the Lord.
1Co 15: 22 in Adam all *d*, so in Christ all will
     15: 31 I *d* every day—I mean that,
Php 1: 21 to live is Christ and to *d* is gain.
Heb 9: 27 Just as man is destined to *d* once,
Rev 14: 13 Blessed are the dead who *d*
DIED (DIE)
Ro 5: 6 we were still powerless, Christ *d*
     6: 2 By no means! We *d* to sin;
     6: 8 if we *d* with Christ, we believe that
     14: 15 brother for whom Christ *d*.
1Co 8: 11 for whom Christ *d*, is destroyed
     15: 3 that Christ *d* for our sins according
2Co 5: 14 *d* for all, and therefore all *d*.
Col 3: 3 For you *d*, and your life is now
1Th 5: 10 He *d* for us so that, whether we are
2Ti 2: 11 If we *d* with him,
Heb 9: 15 now that he has *d* as a ransom
1Pe 3: 18 For Christ *d* for sins once for all,
Rev 2: 8 who *d* and came to life again.
DIES (DIE)
Job 14: 14 If a man *d*, will he live again?
Pr 11: 7 a wicked man *d*, his hope perishes;
Jn 11: 25 in me will live, even though he *d*;
1Co 15: 36 does not come to life unless it *d*.
DIFFERENCE (DIFFERENT)
Ro 10: 12 For there is no *d* between Jew
DIFFERENT (DIFFERENCE)
1Co 12: 4 There are *d* kinds of gifts,
2Co 11: 4 or a *d* gospel from the one you
DIGNITY
Pr 31: 25 She is clothed with strength and *d*;
DIGS
Pr 26: 27 If a man *d* a pit, he will fall into it;
DILIGENCE (DILIGENT)
Heb 6: 11 to show this same *d* to the very end
DILIGENT (DILIGENCE)
Pr 21: 5 The plans of the *d* lead to profit
1Ti 4: 15 Be *d* in these matters; give yourself
DIRECT (DIRECTS)
Ps 119: 35 *D* me in the path of your
     119: 133 *D* my footsteps according
Jer 10: 23 it is not for man to *d* his steps.
2Th 3: 5 May the Lord *d* your hearts
DIRECTS (DIRECT)
Ps 42: 8 By day the LORD *d* his love,

Isa 48: 17 who *d* you in the way you should
DIRGE
Mt 11: 17 we sang a *d*,
DISAPPEAR
Mt 5: 18 will by any means *d* from the Law
Lk 16: 17 earth to *d* than for the least stroke
DISAPPOINT* (DISAPPOINTED)
Ro 5: 5 And hope does not *d* us,
DISAPPOINTED (DISAPPOINT)
Ps 22: 5 in you they trusted and were not *d*.
DISASTER
Ps 57: 1 wings until the *d* has passed.
Pr 3: 25 Have no fear of sudden *d*
     17: 5 over *d* will not go unpunished.
Isa 45: 7 I bring prosperity and create *d*;
Eze 7: 5 An unheard-of *d* is coming.
DISCERN (DISCERNING DISCERNMENT)
Ps 19: 12 Who can *d* his errors?
     139: 3 You *d* my going out and my lying
Php 1: 10 you may be able to *d* what is best
DISCERNING (DISCERN)
Pr 14: 6 knowledge comes easily to the *d*.
     15: 14 The *d* heart seeks knowledge,
     17: 24 A *d* man keeps wisdom in view,
     17: 28 and if he holds his tongue.
     19: 25 rebuke a *d* man, and he will gain
DISCERNMENT (DISCERN)
Pr 17: 10 A rebuke impresses a man of *d*
     28: 11 a poor man who has *d* sees
DISCIPLE (DISCIPLES)
Mt 10: 42 these little ones because he is my *d*,
Lk 14: 27 and follow me cannot be my *d*.
DISCIPLES (DISCIPLE)
Mt 28: 19 Therefore go and make *d*
Jn 8: 31 to my teaching, you are really my *d*
     13: 35 men will know that you are my *d*
Ac 11: 26 The *d* were called Christians first
DISCIPLINE (DISCIPLINED DISCIPLINES)
Ps 38: 1 or *d* me in your wrath.
     39: 11 You rebuke and *d* men for their sin;
     94: 12 Blessed is the man you *d*, O LORD
Pr 1: 7 but fools despise wisdom and *d*.
     3: 11 do not despise the LORD's *d*
     5: 12 You will say, "How I hated *d*!
     5: 23 He will die for lack of *d*,
     6: 23 and the corrections of *d*
     10: 17 He who heeds *d* shows the way
     12: 1 Whoever loves *d* loves knowledge,
     13: 18 He who ignores *d* comes to poverty
     13: 24 who loves him is careful to *d* him.
     15: 5 A fool spurns his father's *d*,
     15: 32 He who ignores *d* despises himself,
     19: 18 *D* your son, for in that there is hope
     22: 15 the rod of *d* will drive it far
     23: 13 Do not withhold *d* from a child;
     29: 17 *D* your son, and he will give you
Heb 12: 5 do not make light of the Lord's *d*,
     12: 7 as *d*; God is treating you
     12: 11 No *d* seems pleasant at the time,
Rev 3: 19 Those whom I love I rebuke and *d*.
DISCIPLINED (DISCIPLINE)
Pr 1: 3 for acquiring a *d* and prudent life,
Jer 31: 18 'You *d* me like an unruly calf,
1Co 11: 32 we are being *d* so that we will not
Tit 1: 8 upright, holy and *d*.
Heb 12: 7 For what son is not *d* by his father?
DISCIPLINES (DISCIPLINE)
Dt 8: 5 your heart that as a man *d* his son,
Pr 3: 12 the LORD *d* those he loves,
Heb 12: 6 because the Lord *d* those he loves,
     12: 10 but God *d* us for our good,
DISCLOSED
Lk 8: 17 is nothing hidden that will not be *d*,
DISCOURAGED
Jos 1: 9 Do not be terrified; do not be *d*,
     10: 25 "Do not be afraid; do not be *d*.
1Ch 28: 20 or *d*, for the LORD God,
Isa 42: 4 he will not falter or be *d*
Col 3: 21 children, or they will become *d*.
DISCREDITED
2Co 6: 3 so that our ministry will not be *d*.

DISCRETION*
1Ch 22: 12 May the LORD give you *d*
Pr 1: 4 knowledge and *d* to the young—
     2: 11 *D* will protect you,
     5: 2 that you may maintain *d*
     8: 12 I possess knowledge and *d*.
     11: 22 a beautiful woman who shows no *d*.
DISCRIMINATED*
Jas 2: 4 have you not *d* among yourselves
DISFIGURED
Isa 52: 14 his appearance was so *d*
DISGRACE (DISGRACEFUL DISGRACES)
Pr 11: 2 When pride comes, then comes *d*,
     14: 34 but sin is a *d* to any people.
     19: 26 is a son who brings shame and *d*.
Ac 5: 41 of suffering *d* for the Name.
Heb 13: 13 the camp, bearing the *d* he bore.
DISGRACEFUL (DISGRACE)
Pr 10: 5 during harvest is a *d* son.
     17: 2 wise servant will rule over a *d* son,
DISGRACES (DISGRACE)
Pr 28: 7 of gluttons *d* his father.
     29: 15 but a child left to itself *d* his mother
DISHONEST
Pr 11: 1 The LORD abhors *d* scales,
     29: 27 The righteous detest the *d*;
Lk 16: 10 whoever is *d* with very little will
1Ti 3: 8 wine, and not pursuing *d* gain.
DISHONOR (DISHONORS)
Lev 18: 7 "Do not *d* your father
Pr 30: 9 and so *d* the name of my God.
1Co 15: 43 it is sown in *d*, it is raised in glory;
DISHONORS (DISHONOR)
Dt 27: 16 Cursed is the man who *d* his father
DISMAYED
Isa 28: 16 the one who trusts will never be *d*.
     41: 10 do not be *d*, for I am your God.
DISOBEDIENCE (DISOBEY)
Ro 5: 19 as through the *d* of the one man
     11: 32 to *d* so that he may have mercy
Heb 2: 2 and *d* received its just punishment,
     4: 6 go in, because of their *d*.
     4: 11 fall by following their example of *d*.
DISOBEDIENT (DISOBEY)
2Ti 3: 2 proud, abusive, *d* to their parents,
Tit 1: 6 to the charge of being wild and *d*.
     1: 16 *d* and unfit for doing anything
DISOBEY (DISOBEDIENCE DISOBEDIENT)
Dt 11: 28 the curse if you *d* the commands
2Ch 24: 20 'Why do you *d* the LORD's'
Ro 1: 30 they *d* their parents; they are
DISORDER
1Co 14: 33 For God is not a God of *d*
2Co 12: 20 slander, gossip, arrogance and *d*.
Jas 3: 16 there you find *d* and every evil
DISOWN
Pr 30: 9 I may have too much and *d* you
Mt 10: 33 I will *d* him before my Father
     26: 35 To die with you, I will never *d* you."
2Ti 2: 12 If we *d* him,
DISPLAY (DISPLAYS)
Eze 39: 21 I will *d* my glory among the nations
1Ti 1: 16 Christ Jesus might *d* his unlimited
DISPLAYS (DISPLAY)
Isa 44: 23 he *d* his glory in Israel.
DISPUTE (DISPUTES)
Pr 17: 14 before a *d* breaks out.
1Co 6: 1 If any of you has a *d* with another,
DISPUTES (DISPUTE)
Pr 18: 18 Casting the lot settles *d*
DISQUALIFIED
1Co 9: 27 I myself will not be *d* for the prize.
DISREPUTE*
2Pe 2: 2 will bring the way of truth into *d*.
DISSENSION*
Pr 6: 14 he always stirs up *d*.
     6: 19 and a man who stirs up *d*
     10: 12 Hatred stirs up *d*,
     15: 18 A hot-tempered man stirs up *d*,
     16: 28 A perverse man stirs up *d*,
     28: 25 A greedy man stirs up *d*,

Ro	29:22 An angry man stirs up *d*,
Ro	13:13 debauchery, not in *d* and jealousy.

DISSIPATION*
Lk 21:34 will be weighed down with *d*,
1Pe 4: 4 with them into the same flood of *d*,

DISTINGUISH
1Ki 3: 9 and to *d* between right and wrong.
Heb 5:14 themselves to *d* good from evil.

DISTORT
2Co 4: 2 nor do we *d* the word of God.
2Pe 3:16 ignorant and unstable people *d*,

DISTRESS (DISTRESSED)
Ps 18: 6 In my *d* I called to the LORD;
Jnh 2: 2 "In my *d* I called to the LORD,
Jas 1:27 after orphans and widows in their *d*

DISTRESSED (DISTRESS)
Ro 14:15 If your brother is *d*

DIVIDED (DIVISION)
Mt 12:25 household *d* against itself will not
Lk 23:34 they *d* up his clothes by casting lots
1Co 1:13 Is Christ *d*? Was Paul crucified

DIVINATION
Lev 19:26 " 'Do not practice *d* or sorcery.

DIVINE
Ro 1:20 his eternal power and *d* nature—
2Co 10: 4 they have *d* power
2Pe 1: 4 you may participate in the *d* nature

DIVISION (DIVIDED DIVISIONS DIVISIVE)
Lk 12:51 on earth? No, I tell you, but *d*.
1Co 12:25 so that there should be no *d*

DIVISIONS (DIVISION)
Ro 16:17 to watch out for those who cause *d*
1Co 1:10 another so that there may be no *d*
  11:18 there are *d* among you,

DIVISIVE* (DIVISION)
Tit 3:10 Warn a *d* person once,

DIVORCE
Mal 2:16 "I hate *d*," says the LORD God
Mt 19: 3 for a man to *d* his wife for any
1Co 7:11 And a husband must not *d* his wife.
  7:27 Are you married? Do not seek a *d*.

DOCTOR
Mt 9:12 "It is not the healthy who need a *d*,

DOCTRINE
1Ti 4:16 Watch your life and *d* closely.
Tit 2: 1 is in accord with sound *d*.

DOMINION
Ps 22:28 for *d* belongs to the LORD

DOOR
Ps 141: 3 keep watch over the *d* of my lips.
Mt 6: 6 close the *d* and pray to your Father
  7: 7 and the *d* will be opened to you.
Rev 3:20 I stand at the *d* and knock.

DOORKEEPER
Ps 84:10 I would rather be a *d* in the house

DOUBLE-EDGED
Heb 4:12 Sharper than any *d* sword,
Rev 1:16 of his mouth came a sharp *d* sword.
  2:12 of him who has the sharp, *d* sword.

DOUBLE-MINDED (MIND)
Ps 119:113 I hate *d* men,
Jas 1: 8 he is a *d* man, unstable

DOUBT
Mt 14:31 he said, "why did you *d*?"
  21:21 if you have faith and do not *d*,
Mk 11:23 and does not *d* in his heart
Jas 1: 6 he must believe and not *d*,
Jude 22 Be merciful to those who *d*;

DOWNCAST
Ps 42: 5 Why are you *d*, O my soul?
2Co 7: 6 But God, who comforts the *d*,

DRAW (DRAWING DRAWS)
Mt 26:52 "for all who *d* the sword will die
Jn 12:32 up from the earth, will *d* all men
Heb 10:22 let us *d* near to God

DRAWING (DRAW)
Lk 21:28 because your redemption is *d* near

DRAWS (DRAW)
Jn 6:44 the Father who sent me *d* him,

DREADFUL
Heb 10:31 It is a *d* thing to fall into the hands

DRESS
1Ti 2: 9 I also want women to *d* modestly,

DRINK (DRUNK DRUNKARDS DRUNKENNESS)
Pr 5:15 *D* water from your own cistern,
Lk 12:19 Take life easy; eat, *d* and be merry
Jn 7:37 let him come to me and *d*.
1Co 12:13 were all given the one Spirit to *d*.
Rev 21: 6 to *d* without cost from the spring

DRIVES
1Jn 4:18 But perfect love *d* out fear,

DROP
Pr 17:14 so *d* the matter before a dispute
Isa 40:15 Surely the nations are like a *d*

DRUNK (DRINK)
Eph 5:18 Do not get *d* on wine, which leads

DRUNKARDS (DRINK)
Pr 23:21 for *d* and gluttons become poor,
1Co 6:10 nor the greedy nor *d* nor slanderers

DRUNKENNESS (DRINK)
Lk 21:34 weighed down with dissipation, *d*
Ro 13:13 and *d*, not in sexual immorality.
Gal 5:21 factions and envy; *d*, orgies,
1Pe 4: 3 living in debauchery, lust, *d*, orgies,

DRY
Isa 53: 2 and like a root out of *d* ground.
Eze 37: 4 '*D* bones, hear the word

DUST
Ge 2: 7 man from the *d* of the ground
Ps 103:14 he remembers that we are *d*,
Ecc 3:20 all come from *d*, and to *d* all return.

DUTY
Ecc 12:13 for this is the whole *d* of man.
Ac 23: 1 I have fulfilled my *d* to God
1Co 7: 3 husband should fulfill his marital *d*

DWELL (DWELLING)
1Ki 8:27 "But will God really *d* on earth?
Ps 23: 6 I will *d* in the house of the LORD
Isa 43:18 do not *d* on the past.
Eph 3:17 so that Christ may *d* in your hearts
Col 1:19 to have all his fullness *d* in him,
  3:16 the word of Christ *d* in you richly

DWELLING (DWELL)
Eph 2:22 to become a *d* in which God lives

EAGER
Pr 31:13 and works with *e* hands.
1Pe 5: 2 greedy for money, but *e* to serve;

EAGLE'S (EAGLES)
Ps 103: 5 your youth is renewed like the *e*.

EAGLES (EAGLE'S)
Isa 40:31 They will soar on wings like *e*;

EAR (EARS)
1Co 2: 9 no *e* has heard,
  12:16 if the *e* should say, "Because I am

EARNED
Pr 31:31 Give her the reward she has *e*,

EARS (EAR)
Job 42: 5 My *e* had heard of you
Ps 34:15 and his *e* are attentive to their cry;
Pr 21:13 If a man shuts his *e* to the cry
2Ti 4: 3 to say what their itching *e* want

EARTH (EARTHLY)
Ge 1: 1 God created the heavens and the *e*.
Ps 24: 1 *e* is the LORD's, and everything
  108: 5 and let your glory be over all the *e*.
Isa 6: 3 the whole *e* is full of his glory."
  51: 6 the *e* will wear out like a garment
  55: 9 the heavens are higher than the *e*,
  66: 1 and the *e* is my footstool.
Jer 23:24 "Do not I fill heaven and *e*?"
Hab 2:20 let all the *e* be silent before him."
Mt 6:10 done on *e* as it is in heaven.
  16:19 bind on *e* will be bound
  24:35 Heaven and *e* will pass away,
  28:18 and on *e* has been given to me.
Lk 2:14 on *e* peace to men
1Co 10:26 The *e* is the Lord's, and everything
Php 2:10 in heaven and on *e* and under the *e*,
2Pe 3:13 to a new heaven and a new *e*,

EARTHLY (EARTH)
Php 3:19 Their mind is on *e* things.
Col 3: 2 on things above, not on *e* things.

EAST
Ps 103: 12 as far as the *e* is from the west,

EASY
Mt 11:30 For my yoke is *e* and my burden is

EAT (EATING)
Ge 2:17 but you must not *e* from the tree
Isa 55: 1 come, buy and *e*!
  65:25 and the lion will *e* straw like the ox,
Mt 26:26 "Take and *e*; this is my body."
Ro 14: 2 faith allows him to *e* everything,
1Co 8:13 if what I *e* causes my brother to fall
  10:31 So whether you *e* or drink
2Th 3:10 man will not work, he shall not *e*."

EATING (EAT)
Ro 14:17 kingdom of God is not a matter of *e*

EDICT
Heb 11:23 they were not afraid of the king's *e*.

EDIFIES
1Co 14: 4 but he who prophesies *e* the church

EFFECT
Isa 32:17 *e* of righteousness will be quietness
Heb 9:18 put into *e* without blood.

EFFORT
Lk 13:24 "Make every *e* to enter
Ro 9:16 depend on man's desire or *e*,
  14:19 make every *e* to do what leads
Eph 4: 3 Make every *e* to keep the unity
Heb 4:11 make every *e* to enter that rest,
  12:14 Make every *e* to live in peace
2Pe 1: 5 make every *e* to add
  3:14 make every *e* to be found spotless,

ELAH
Son of Baasha; king of Israel (1Ki 16:6-14).

ELDERLY* (ELDERS)
Lev 19:32 show respect for the *e*

ELDERS (ELDERLY)
1Ti 5:17 The *e* who direct the affairs

ELECTION
Ro 9:11 God's purpose in *e* might stand:
2Pe 1:10 to make your calling and *e* sure.

ELI
High priest in youth of Samuel (1Sa 1-4). Blessed Hannah (1Sa 1:12-18); raised Samuel (1Sa 2:11-26).

ELIJAH
Prophet; predicted famine in Israel (1Ki 17:1; Jas 5:17). Fed by ravens (1Ki 17:2-6). Raised Sidonian widow's son (1Ki 17:7-24). Defeated prophets of Baal at Carmel (1Ki 18:16-46). Ran from Jezebel (1Ki 19:1-9). Prophesied death of Azariah (2Ki 1). Succeeded by Elishah (1Ki 19:19-21; 2Ki 2:1-18). Taken to heaven in whirlwind (2Ki 2:11-12).
Return prophesied (Mal 4:5-6); equated with John the Baptist (Mt 17:9-13; Mk 9:9-13; Lk 1:17). Appeared with Moses in transfiguration of Jesus (Mt 17:1-8; Mk 9:1-8).

ELISHA
Prophet; successor of Elijah (1Ki 19:16-21); inherited his cloak (2Ki 2:1-18). Miracles of (2Ki 2-6).

ELIZABETH*
Mother of John the Baptist, relative of Mary (Lk 1:5-58).

EMBITTER*
Col 3:21 Fathers, do not *e* your children,

EMPTY
Eph 5: 6 no one deceive you with *e* words,
1Pe 1:18 from the *e* way of life handed

ENABLE (ABLE)
Lk 1:74 to *e* us to serve him without fear
Ac 4:29 *e* your servants to speak your word

ENABLED (ABLE)
Lev 26:13 *e* you to walk with heads held high.
Jn 6:65 unless the Father has *e* him."

ENABLES (ABLE)
Php 3:21 by the power that *e* him

ENCAMPS*
Ps 34: 7 The angel of the LORD *e*

ENCOURAGE (ENCOURAGEMENT)
Ps 10:17 you *e* them, and you listen

ENCOURAGEMENT

Isa 1:17 *e* the oppressed.
Ac 15:32 to *e* and strengthen the brothers.
Ro 12: 8 if it is encouraging, let him *e*;
1Th 4:18 Therefore *e* each other
2Ti 4: 2 rebuke and *e*— with great patience
Tit 2: 6 *e* the young men to be
Heb 3:13 But *e* one another daily, as long
 10:25 but let us *e* one another—

ENCOURAGEMENT (ENCOURAGE)
Ac 4:36 Barnabas (which means Son of *E*),
Ro 15: 4 *e* of the Scriptures we might have
 15: 5 and *e* give you a spirit of unity
1Co 14: 3 to men for their strengthening, and
Heb 12: 5 word of *e* that addresses you

END
Ps 119: 33 then I will keep them to the *e*.
Pr 14:12 but in the *e* it leads to death.
 19:20 and in the *e* you will be wise.
 23:32 In the *e* it bites like a snake
Ecc 12:12 making many books there is no *e*,
Mt 10:22 firm to the *e* will be saved.
Lk 21: 9 but the *e* will not come right away
Ro 10: 4 Christ is the *e* of the law
1Co 15:24 the *e* will come, when he hands

ENDURANCE (ENDURE)
Ro 15: 4 through *e* and the encouragement
 15: 5 May the God who gives *e*
2Co 1: 6 which produces in you patient *e*
Col 1:11 might so that you may have great *e*
1Ti 6:11 faith, love, and gentleness.
Tit 2: 2 and sound in faith, in love and in *e*.

ENDURE (ENDURANCE ENDURES)
Ps 72:17 May his name *e* forever;
Pr 12:19 Truthful lips *e* forever,
 27:24 for riches do not *e* forever,
Ecc 3:14 everything God does will *e* forever;
Mal 3: 2 who can *e* the day of his coming?
2Ti 2: 3 *E* hardship with us like a good
 2:12 if we *e*, / we will also reign
Heb 12: 7 *E* hardship as discipline; God is
Rev 3:10 kept my command to *e* patiently,

ENDURES (ENDURE)
Ps 112: 9 his righteousness *e* forever;
 136: 1 His love *e* forever.
Da 9:15 made for yourself a name that *e*

ENEMIES (ENEMY)
Ps 23: 5 in the presence of my *e*.
Mic 6: a man's *e* are the members
Mt 5:44 Love your *e* and pray
Lk 20:43 hand until I make your *e*

ENEMY (ENEMIES ENMITY)
Pr 24:17 Do not gloat when your *e* falls;
 25:21 If your *e* is hungry, give him food
 27: 6 but an *e* multiplies kisses.
1Co 15:26 The last *e* to be destroyed is death.
1Ti 5:14 and to give the *e* no opportunity

ENJOY (JOY)
Dt 6: 2 and so that you may *e* long life.
Eph 6: 3 and that you may *e* long life
Heb 11:25 rather than to *e* the pleasures of sin

ENJOYMENT (JOY)
Ecc 4: 8 and why am I depriving myself of *e*
1Ti 6:17 us with everything for our *e*.

ENLIGHTENED* (LIGHT)
Eph 1:18 that the eyes of your heart may be *e*
Heb 6: 4 for those who have once been *e*,

ENMITY* (ENEMY)
Ge 3:15 And I will put *e*

ENOCH
Walked with God and taken by him (Ge 5:18-24; Heb 11:5). Prophet (Jude 14).

ENTANGLED (ENTANGLES)
2Pe 2:20 and are again *e* in it and overcome,

ENTANGLES* (ENTANGLED)
Heb 12: 1 and the sin that so easily *e*,

ENTER (ENTERED ENTERS ENTRANCE)
Ps 100: 4 *E* his gates with thanksgiving
Mt 5:20 will certainly not *e* the kingdom
 7:13 *E* through the narrow gate.
 18: 8 It is better for you to *e* life maimed
Mk 10:15 like a little child will never *e* it."
 10:23 is for the rich to *e* the kingdom

ENTERED (ENTER)
Ro 5:12 as sin *e* the world through one man,
Heb 9:12 but he *e* the Most Holy Place once

ENTERS (ENTER)
Mk 7:18 you see that nothing that *e* a man
Jn 10: 2 The man who *e* by the gate is

ENTERTAIN
1Ti 5:19 Do not *e* an accusation
Heb 13: 2 Do not forget to *e* strangers,

ENTHRALLED*
Ps 45:11 The king is *e* by your beauty;

ENTHRONED (THRONE)
1Sa 4: 4 who is *e* between the cherubim.
Ps 2: 4 The One *e* in heaven laughs;
 102: 12 But you, O LORD, sit *e* forever;
Isa 40:22 He sits *e* above the circle

ENTICE
Pr 1:10 My son, if sinners *e* you,
2Pe 2:18 they *e* people who are just escaping

ENTIRE
Gal 5:14 The *e* law is summed up

ENTRUSTED (TRUST)
1Ti 6:20 guard what has been *e* to your care.
2Ti 1:12 able to guard what I have *e* to him
 1:14 Guard the good deposit that was *e*
Jude 3 once for all *e* to the saints.

ENVY
Pr 3:31 Do not *e* a violent man
 14:30 but *e* rots the bones.
1Co 13: 4 It does not *e*, it does not boast,

EPHRAIM
1. Second son of Joseph (Ge 41:52; 46:20). Blessed as firstborn by Jacob (Ge 48).
2. Synonymous with Northern Kingdom (Isa 7:17; Hos 5).

EQUAL
Isa 40:25 who is my *e*?" says the Holy One.
Jn 5:18 making himself *e* with God.
1Co 12:25 that its parts should have *e* concern

EQUIP* (EQUIPPED)
Heb 13:21 *e* you with everything good

EQUIPPED (EQUIP)
2Ti 3:17 man of God may be thoroughly *e*

ERROR
Jas 5:20 Whoever turns a sinner from the *e*

ESAU
Firstborn of Isaac, twin of Jacob (Ge 25:21-26). Also called Edom (Ge 25:30). Sold Jacob his birthright (Ge 25:29-34); lost blessing (Ge 27). Reconciled to Jacob (Gen 33).

ESCAPE (ESCAPING)
Ro 2: 3 think you will *e* God's judgment?
Heb 2: 3 how shall we *e* if we ignore such

ESCAPING (ESCAPE)
1Co 3:15 only as one *e* through the flames.

ESTABLISH
Ge 6:18 But I will *e* my covenant with you,
1Ch 28: 7 I will *e* his kingdom forever
Ro 10: 3 God and sought to *e* their own,

ESTEEMED
Pr 22: 1 to be *e* is better than silver or gold.
Isa 53: 3 he was despised, and we *e* him not.

ESTHER
Jewess who lived in Persia; cousin of Mordecai (Est 2:7). Chosen queen of Xerxes (Est 2:8-18). Foiled Haman's plan to exterminate the Jews (Est 3-4; 7-9).

ETERNAL (ETERNALLY ETERNITY)
Ps 16:11 with *e* pleasures at your right hand.
 111: 10 To him belongs *e* praise.
 119: 89 Your word, O LORD, is *e*;
Isa 26: 4 LORD, the LORD, is the Rock *e*.
Mt 19:16 good thing must I do to get *e* life?"
 25:41 into the fire prepared for the devil
 25:46 they will go away to *e* punishment,
Jn 3:15 believes in him may have *e* life.
 3:16 him shall not perish but have *e* life.
 3:36 believes in the Son has *e* life,
 4:14 spring of water welling up to *e* life."
 5:24 believes him who sent me has *e* life
 6:68 You have the words of *e* life.
 10:28 I give them *e* life, and they shall

 17: 3 this is *e* life: that they may know
Ro 1:20 his *e* power and divine nature—
 6:23 but the gift of God is *e* life
2Co 4:17 for us an *e* glory that far outweighs
 4:18 temporary, but what is unseen is *e*.
1Ti 1:16 believe on him and receive *e* life.
 1:17 Now to the King *e*, immortal,
Heb 9:12 having obtained *e* redemption.
1Jn 5:11 God has given us *e* life,
 5:13 you may know that you have *e* life.

ETERNALLY (ETERNAL)
Gal 1: 8 let him be *e* condemned! As we

ETERNITY (ETERNAL)
Ps 93: 2 you are from all *e*.
Ecc 3:11 also set *e* in the hearts of men;

ETHIOPIAN
Jer 13:23 Can the *E* change his skin

EUNUCHS
Mt 19:12 For some are *e* because they were

EVANGELIST (EVANGELISTS)
2Ti 4: 5 hardship, do the work of an *e*,

EVANGELISTS* (EVANGELIST)
Eph 4:11 some to be prophets, some to be *e*,

EVE
2Co 11: 3 as *E* was deceived by the serpent's
1Ti 2:13 For Adam was formed first, then *E*

EVEN-TEMPERED*
Pr 17:27 and a man of understanding is *e*.

EVER (EVERLASTING FOREVER)
Ex 15:18 LORD will reign for *e* and *e*."
Dt 8:19 If you *e* forget the LORD your
Ps 5:11 let them *e* sing for joy.
 10:16 The LORD is King for *e* and *e*;
 25: 3 will *e* be put to shame,
 26: 3 for your love is *e* before me,
 45: 6 O God, will last for *e* and *e*;
 52: 8 God's unfailing love for *e* and *e*.
 89:33 nor will I *e* betray my faithfulness.
 145: 1 I will praise your name for *e* and *e*.
Pr 4:18 shining *e* brighter till the full light
 5:19 may you *e* be captivated
Isa 66: 8 Who has *e* heard of such a thing?
Jer 31:36 the descendants of Israel *e* cease
Da 7:18 it forever—yes, for *e* and *e*.'
 12: 3 like the stars for *e* and *e*.
Mk 4:12 *e* hearing but never understanding;
Jn 1:18 No one has *e* seen God.
Rev 1:18 and behold I am alive for *e* and *e*!
 22: 5 And they will reign for *e* and *e*.

EVER-INCREASING* (INCREASE)
Ro 6:19 to impurity and to *e* wickedness,
2Co 3:18 into his likeness with *e* glory,

EVERLASTING (EVER)
Dt 33:27 and underneath are the *e* arms.
Ne 9: 5 your God, who is from *e* to *e*."
Ps 90: 2 from *e* to *e* you are God.
 139: 24 and lead me in the way *e*.
Isa 9: 6 *E* Father, Prince of Peace.
 33:14 Who of us can dwell with *e* burning
 35:10 *e* joy will crown their heads.
 45:17 the LORD is an *e* salvation;
 54: 8 but with *e* kindness
 55: 3 I will make an *e* covenant with you,
 63:12 to gain for himself *e* renown,
Jer 31: 3 "I have loved you with an *e* love;
Da 9:24 to bring in *e* righteousness,
 12: 2 some to *e* life, others to shame
Jn 6:47 the truth, he who believes has *e* life.
2Th 1: 9 punished with *e* destruction
Jude 6 bound with *e* chains for judgment

EVER-PRESENT*
Ps 46: 1 an *e* help in trouble

EVIDENCE (EVIDENT)
Jn 14:11 on the *e* of the miracles themselves.

EVIDENT (EVIDENCE)
Php 4: 5 Let your gentleness be *e* to all.

EVIL
Ge 2: 9 of the knowledge of good and *e*.
Job 1: 1 he feared God and shunned *e*.
 1: 8 a man who fears God and shuns *e*."
 34:10 Far be it from God to do *e*,
Ps 23: 4 I will fear no *e*,

FAITH

	34:14	Turn from *e* and do good;
	51: 4	and done what is *e* in your sight,
	97:10	those who love the LORD hate *e*,
	101: 4	I will have nothing to do with *e*.
Pr	8:13	To fear the LORD is to hate *e*;
	10:23	A fool finds pleasure in *e* conduct,
	11:27	*e* comes to him who searches for it.
	24:19	Do not fret because of *e* men
	24:20	for the *e* man has no future hope,
Isa	5:20	Woe to those who call *e* good
	13:11	I will punish the world for its *e*,
	55: 7	and the *e* man his thoughts.
Hab	1:13	Your eyes are too pure to look on *e*;
Mt	5:45	He causes his sun to rise on the *e*
	6:13	but deliver us from the *e* one.'
	7:11	If you, then, though you are *e*,
	12:35	and the *e* man brings *e* things out
Jn	17:15	you protect them from the *e* one.
Ro	2: 9	for every human being who does *e*:
	12: 9	Hate what is *e*; cling
	12:17	Do not repay anyone *e* for *e*.
	16:19	and innocent about what is *e*.
1Co	13: 6	Love does not delight in *e*
	14:20	In regard to *e* be infants,
Eph	6:16	all the flaming arrows of the *e* one.
1Th	5:22	Avoid every kind of *e*.
1Ti	6:10	of money is a root of all kinds of *e*.
2Ti	2:22	Flee the *e* desires of youth,
Jas	1:13	For God cannot be tempted by *e*,
1Pe	2:16	your freedom as a cover-up for *e*;
	3: 9	Do not repay *e* with *e* or insult

EXACT
Heb 1: 3 the *e* representation of his being,

EXALT (EXALTED EXALTS)
Ps	30: 1	I will *e* you, O LORD,
	34: 3	let us *e* his name together.
	118:28	you are my God, and I will *e* you.
Isa	24:15	*e* the name of the LORD, the God

EXALTED (EXALT)
2Sa	22:47	*E* be God, the Rock, my Savior!
1Ch	29:11	you are *e* as head over all.
Ne	9: 5	and may it be above all blessing
Ps	21:13	Be *e*, O LORD, in your strength;
	46:10	I will be *e* among the nations,
	57: 5	Be *e*, O God, above the heavens;
	97: 9	you are *e* far above all gods.
	99: 2	he is *e* over all the nations.
	108: 5	Be *e*, O God, above the heavens,
	148:13	for his name alone is *e*;
Isa	6: 1	*e*, and the train of his robe filled
	12: 4	and proclaim that his name is *e*.
	33: 5	The LORD is *e*, for he dwells
Eze	21:26	The lowly will be *e* and the *e* will be
Mt	23:12	whoever humbles himself will be *e*.
Php	1:20	always Christ will be *e* in my body,
	2: 9	Therefore God *e* him

EXALTS (EXALT)
Ps	75: 7	He brings one down, he *e* another.
Pr	14:34	Righteousness *e* a nation,
Mt	23:12	For whoever *e* himself will be

EXAMINE (EXAMINED)
Ps	26: 2	*e* my heart and my mind;
Jer	17:10	and *e* the mind,
La	3:40	Let us *e* our ways and test them,
1Co	11:28	A man ought to *e* himself
2Co	13: 5	*E* yourselves to see whether you

EXAMINED (EXAMINE)
Ac 17:11 *e* the Scriptures every day to see

EXAMPLE (EXAMPLES)
Jn	13:15	have set you an *e* that you should
1Co	11: 1	Follow my *e*, as I follow
1Ti	4:12	set an *e* for the believers in speech,
Tit	2: 7	In everything set them an *e*
1Pe	2:21	leaving you an *e*, that you should

EXAMPLES* (EXAMPLE)
1Co	10: 6	Now these things occurred as *e*
	10: 11	as *e* and were written down
1Pe	5: 3	to you, but being *e* to the flock.

EXASPERATE*
Eph 6: 4 Fathers, do not *e* your children;

EXCEL (EXCELLENT)
1Co 14:12 to *e* in gifts that build up the church

| 2Co | 8: 7 | But just as you *e* in everything— |

EXCELLENT (EXCEL)
1Co	12:31	now I will show you the most *e* way
Php	4: 8	if anything is *e* or praiseworthy—
1Ti	3:13	have served well gain an *e* standing
Tit	3: 8	These things are *e* and profitable

EXCHANGED
| Ro | 1:23 | *e* the glory of the immortal God |
| | 1:25 | They *e* the truth of God for a lie, |

EXCUSE (EXCUSES)
| Jn | 15:22 | they have no *e* for their sin. |
| Ro | 1:20 | so that men are without *e*. |

EXCUSES* (EXCUSE)
Lk 14:18 "But they all alike began to make *e*.

EXISTS
| Heb | 2:10 | and through whom everything *e*, |
| | 11: 6 | to him must believe that he *e* |

EXPECT (EXPECTATION)
Mt 24:44 at an hour when you do not *e* him.

EXPECTATION (EXPECT)
| Ro | 8:19 | waits in eager *e* for the sons |
| Heb | 10:27 | but only a fearful *e* of judgment |

EXPEL*
1Co 5:13 *E* the wicked man from among you

EXPENSIVE
1Ti 2: 9 or gold or pearls or *e* clothes,

EXPLOIT
| Pr | 22:22 | Do not *e* the poor because they are |
| 2Co | 12:17 | Did I *e* you through any |

EXPOSE
| 1Co | 4: 5 | will *e* the motives of men's hearts. |
| Eph | 5:11 | of darkness, but rather *e* them. |

EXTENDS
| Pr | 31:20 | and *e* her hands to the needy. |
| Lk | 1:50 | His mercy *e* to those who fear him, |

EXTINGUISHED
2Sa 21:17 the lamp of Israel will not be *e*."

EXTOL*
Job	36:24	Remember to *e* his work,
Ps	34: 1	I will *e* the LORD at all times;
	68: 4	*e* him who rides on the clouds—
	95: 2	and *e* him with music and song.
	109:30	mouth I will greatly *e* the LORD;
	111: 1	I will *e* the LORD with all my heart
	115:18	it is we who *e* the LORD,
	117: 1	*e* him, all you peoples.
	145: 2	and *e* your name for ever and ever.
	145:10	your saints will *e* you.
	147:12	*E* the LORD, O Jerusalem;

EXTORT*
Lk 3:14 "Don't *e* money and don't accuse

EYE (EYES)
Ex	21:24	you are to take life for life, *e* for *e*,
Ps	94: 9	Does he who formed the *e* not see?
Mt	5:29	If your right *e* causes you to sin,
	5:38	'*E* for *e*, and tooth for tooth'.
	7: 3	of sawdust in your brother's *e*
1Co	2: 9	"No *e* has seen,
Col	3:22	not only when their *e* is on you
Rev	1: 7	and every *e* will see him,

EYES (EYE)
Nu	33:55	remain will become barbs in your *e*
Jos	23:13	on your backs and thorns in your *e*,
2Ch	16: 9	For the *e* of the LORD range
Job	31: 1	"I made a covenant with my *e*
	36: 7	He does not take his *e*
Ps	119: 18	Open my *e* that I may see
	121: 1	I lift up my *e* to the hills—
	141: 8	But my *e* are fixed on you,
Pr	3: 7	Do not be wise in your own *e*;
	4:25	Let your *e* look straight ahead,
	15: 3	The *e* of the LORD are everywhere
Isa	6: 5	and my *e* have seen the King,
Hab	1:13	Your *e* are too pure to look on evil;
Jn	4:35	open your *e* and look at the fields!
2Co	4:18	So we fix our *e* not on what is seen,
Heb	12: 2	Let us fix our *e* on Jesus, the author
Jas	5: 2	poor in the *e* of the world to be rich
1Pe	3:12	For the *e* of the Lord are
Rev	7:17	wipe away every tear from their *e*."
	21: 4	He will wipe every tear from their *e*

EZEKIEL
Priest called to be prophet to the exiles (Eze 1-3).

EZRA
Priest and teacher of the Law who led a return of exiles to Israel to reestablish temple and worship (Ezr 7-8). Corrected intermarriage of priests (Ezr 9-10). Read Law at celebration of Feast of Tabernacles (Neh 8).

FACE (FACES)
Ge	32:30	"It is because I saw God *f* to *f*,
Ex	34:29	was not aware that his *f* was radiant
Nu	6:25	the LORD make his *f* shine
1Ch	16:11	seek his *f* always.
2Ch	7:14	and seek my *f* and turn
Ps	4: 6	Let the light of your *f* shine upon us
	27: 8	Your *f*, LORD, I will seek.
	31:16	Let your *f* shine on your servant;
	105: 4	seek his *f* always.
	119:135	Make your *f* shine
Isa	50: 7	Therefore have I set my *f* like flint,
Mt	17: 2	His *f* shone like the sun,
1Co	13:12	mirror; then we shall see *f* to *f*.
2Co	4: 6	the glory of God in the *f* of Christ.
1Pe	3:12	but the *f* of the Lord is
Rev	1:16	His *f* was like the sun shining

FACES (FACE)
2Co 3:18 who with unveiled *f* all reflect

FACTIONS
Gal 5:20 selfish ambition, dissensions, *f*

FADE
1Pe 5: 4 of glory that will never *f* away.

FAIL (FAILING FAILINGS FAILS)
1Ch	28:20	He will not *f* you or forsake you
2Ch	34:33	they did not *f* to follow the LORD,
Ps	89:28	my covenant with him will never *f*.
Pr	15:22	Plans *f* for lack of counsel,
Isa	51: 6	my righteousness will never *f*.
La	3:22	for his compassions never *f*.
2Co	13: 5	unless, of course, you *f* the test?

FAILING (FAIL)
1Sa 12:23 sin against the LORD by *f* to pray

FAILINGS (FAIL)
Ro 15: 1 ought to bear with the *f* of the weak

FAILS (FAIL)
1Co 13: 8 Love never *f*.

FAINT
Isa 40:31 they will walk and not be *f*.

FAIR
| Pr | 1: 3 | doing what is right and just and *f*; |
| Col | 4: 1 | slaves with what is right and *f*, |

FAITH (FAITHFUL FAITHFULLY FAITHFULNESS FAITHLESS)
2Ch	20:20	Have *f* in the LORD your God
Hab	2: 4	but the righteous will live by his *f*—
Mt	9:29	According to your *f* will it be done
	17:20	if you have *f* as small as a mustard
	24:10	many will turn away from the *f*
Mk	11:22	"Have *f* in God," Jesus answered.
Lk	7: 9	I have not found such great *f*
	12:28	will he clothe you, O you of little *f*!
	17: 5	"Increase our *f*!" He replied,
	18: 8	will he find *f* on the earth?"
Ac	14: 9	saw that he had *f* to be healed
	14:27	the door of *f* to the Gentiles.
Ro	1:12	encouraged by each other's *f*.
	1:17	is by *f* from first to last,
	1:17	"The righteous will live by *f*."
	3: 3	What if some did not have *f*?
	3:22	comes through *f* in Jesus Christ
	3:25	a sacrifice of atonement, through *f*
	4: 5	his *f* is credited as righteousness.
	5: 1	we have been justified through *f*,
	10:17	*f* comes from hearing the message,
	14: 1	Accept him whose *f* is weak,
	14:23	that does not come from *f* is sin.
1Co	13: 2	and if I have a *f* that can move
	13:13	And now these three remain: *f*,
	16:13	stand firm in the *f*; be men
2Co	5: 7	We live by *f*, not by sight.
	13: 5	to see whether you are in the *f*;
Gal	2:16	Jesus that we may be justified by *f*
	2:20	I live by *f* in the Son of God,
	3:11	"The righteous will live by *f*."

FAITHFUL

	3:24 that we might be justified by f.	
Eph	2: 8 through f— and this not	
	4: 5 one Lord, one f, one baptism;	
	6:16 to all this, take up the shield of f,	
Col	1:23 continue in your f, established	
1Th	5: 8 on f and love as a breastplate,	
1Ti	2:15 if they continue in f, love	
	4: 1 later times some will abandon the f	
	5: 8 he has denied the f and is worse	
	6:12 Fight the good fight of the f.	
2Ti	3:15 wise for salvation through f	
	4: 7 finished the race, I have kept the f.	
Phm	6 may be active in sharing your f,	
Heb	10:38 But my righteous one will live by f.	
	11: 1 f is being sure of what we hope for	
	11: 3 By f we understand that	
	11: 5 By f Enoch was taken from this life	
	11: 6 And without f it is impossible	
	11: 7 By f Noah, when warned about	
	11: 8 By f Abraham, when called to go	
	11:17 By f Abraham, when God tested	
	11:20 By f Isaac blessed Jacob	
	11:21 By f Jacob, when he was dying,	
	11:22 By f Joseph, when his end was near	
	11:24 By f Moses, when he had grown up	
	11:31 By f the prostitute Rahab,	
	12: 2 the author and perfecter of our f,	
Jas	2:14 if a man claims to have f	
	2:17 In the same way, f by itself,	
	2:26 so f without deeds is dead.	
2Pe	1: 5 effort to add to your f goodness;	
1Jn	5: 4 overcome the world, even our f.	
Jude	3 to contend for the f that was once	

FAITHFUL (FAITH)
Nu	12: 7 he is f in all my house.	
Dt	7: 9 your God is God; he is the f God,	
	32: 4 A f God who does no wrong,	
2Sa	22:26 "To the f you show yourself f,	
Ps	25:10 of the LORD are loving and f	
	31:23 The LORD preserves the f,	
	33: 4 he is f in all he does.	
	37:28 and will not forsake his f ones.	
	97:10 for he guards the lives of his f ones	
	145: 13 The LORD is f to all his promises	
	146: 6 the LORD, who remains f forever.	
Pr	31:26 and f instruction is on her tongue.	
Mt	25:21 'Well done, good and f servant!	
Ro	12:12 patient in affliction, f in prayer.	
1Co	4: 2 been given a trust must prove f.	
	10:13 And God is f; he will not let you be	
1Th	5:24 The one who calls you is f	
2Ti	2:13 he will remain f,	
Heb	3: 6 But Christ is f as a son	
	10:23 for he who promised is f.	
1Pe	4:19 themselves to their f Creator	
1Jn	1: 9 he is f and just and will forgive us	
Rev	1: 5 who is the f witness, the firstborn	
	2:10 Be f, even to the point of death,	
	19:11 whose rider is called F and True.	

FAITHFULLY (FAITH)
Dt	11:13 if you f obey the commands I am	
1Sa	12:24 and serve him f with all your heart;	
1Ki	2: 4 and if they walk f before me	
1Pe	4:10 f administering God's grace	

FAITHFULNESS (FAITH)
Ps	57:10 your f reaches to the skies.	
	85:10 Love and f meet together;	
	86:15 to anger, abounding in love and f.	
	89: 1 mouth I will make your f known	
	89:14 love and f go before you.	
	91: 4 his f will be your shield	
	117: 2 the f of the LORD endures forever.	
	119: 75 and in f you have afflicted me.	
Pr	3: 3 Let love and f never leave you;	
Isa	11: 5 and f the sash around his waist.	
La	3:23 great is your f.	
Ro	3: 3 lack of faith nullify God's f?	
Gal	5:22 patience, kindness, goodness, f,	

FAITHLESS (FAITH)
Ps	119:158 I look on the f with loathing,	
Jer	3:22 "Return, f people;	
Ro	1:31 they are senseless, f, heartless,	
2Ti	2:13 if we are f,	

FALL (FALLEN FALLING FALLS)
Ps	37:24 though he stumble, he will not f,	
	55:22 he will never let the righteous f.	
	69: 9 of those who insult you f on me.	
Pr	11:28 Whoever trusts in his riches will f,	
Lk	11:17 a house divided against itself will f.	
Ro	3:23 and f short of the glory of God,	
Heb	6: 6 if they f away, to be brought back	

FALLEN (FALL)
2Sa	1:19 How the mighty have f!	
Isa	14:12 How you have f from heaven,	
1Co	15:20 of those who have f asleep.	
Gal	5: 4 you have f away from grace.	
1Th	4:15 precede those who have f asleep.	

FALLING (FALL)
Jude	24 able to keep you from f	

FALLS (FALL)
Pr	24:17 Do not gloat when your enemy f.	
Jn	12:24 a kernel of wheat f to the ground	
Ro	14: 4 To his own master he stands or f.	

FALSE (FALSEHOOD FALSELY)
Ex	20:16 "You shall not give f testimony	
	23: 1 "Do not spread f reports.	
Pr	13: 5 The righteous hate what is f,	
	19: 5 A f witness will not go unpunished,	
Mt	7:15 "Watch out for f prophets.	
	19:18 not steal, do not give f testimony,	
	24:11 and many f prophets will appear	
Php	1:18 whether from f motives or true,	
1Ti	1: 3 not to teach f doctrines any longer	
2Pe	2: 1 there will be f teachers among you.	

FALSEHOOD (FALSE)
Ps	119:163 I hate and abhor f	
Pr	30: 8 Keep f and lies far from me;	
Eph	4:25 each of you must put off f	

FALSELY (FALSE)
Lev	19:12 " 'Do not swear f by my name	
Lk	3:14 and don't accuse people f—	
1Ti	6:20 ideas of what is f called knowledge,	

FALTER*
Pr	24:10 If you f in times of trouble,	
Isa	42: 4 he will not f or be discouraged	

FAMILIES (FAMILY)
Ps	68: 6 God sets the lonely in f,	

FAMILY (FAMILIES)
Pr	15:27 greedy man brings trouble to his f,	
	31:15 she provides food for her f	
Lk	9:61 go back and say good-by to my f."	
	12:52 one f divided against each other,	
1Ti	3: 4 He must manage his own f well	
	3: 5 how to manage his own f,	
	5: 4 practice by caring for their own f	
	5: 8 and especially for his immediate f,	

FAMINE
Ge	41:30 seven years of f will follow them.	
Am	8:11 but a f of hearing the words	
Ro	8:35 or persecution or f or nakedness	

FAN*
2Ti	1: 6 you to f into flame the gift of God,	

FAST
Dt	13: 4 serve him and hold f to him.	
Jos	22: 5 to hold f to him and to serve him	
	23: 8 to hold f to the LORD your God,	
Ps	119: 31 I hold f to your statutes, O LORD;	
	139: 10 your right hand will hold me f.	
Mt	6:16 "When you f, do not look somber	
1Pe	5:12 Stand f in it.	

FATHER (FATHER'S FATHERLESS FATHERS FOREFATHERS)
Ge	2:24 this reason a man will leave his f	
	17: 4 You will be the f of many nations.	
Ex	20:12 "Honor your f and your mother,	
	21:15 "Anyone who attacks his f	
	21:17 "Anyone who curses his f	
Lev	18: 7 " 'Do not dishonor your f	
	19: 3 you must respect his mother and f,	
Dt	5:16 "Honor your f and your mother,	
	21:18 son who does not obey his f	
Ps	27:10 Though my f and mother forsake	
	68: 5 A f to the fatherless, a defender	
Pr	10: 1 A wise son brings joy to his f,	
	17:21 there is no joy for the f of a fool.	

	23:22 Listen to your f, who gave you life,	
	23:24 f of a righteous man has great joy;	
	28: 7 of gluttons disgraces his f.	
	29: 3 loves wisdom brings joy to his f,	
Isa	9: 6 Everlasting F, Prince of Peace.	
Mt	6: 9 " 'Our F in heaven,	
	10:37 "Anyone who loves his f	
	15: 4 'Honor your f and mother'	
	19: 5 this reason a man will leave his f	
Lk	12:53 f against son and son against f,	
	23:34 Jesus said, "F, forgive them,	
Jn	6:44 the F who sent me draws him,	
	6:46 No one has seen the F	
	8:44 You belong to your f, the devil,	
	10:30 I and the F are one."	
	14: 6 No one comes to the F	
	14: 9 who has seen me has seen the F.	
Ro	4:11 he is the f of all who believe	
2Co	6:18 "I will be a F to you,	
Eph	6: 2 "Honor your f and mother"—	
Heb	12: 7 what son is not disciplined by his f?	

FATHER'S (FATHER)
Pr	13: 1 A wise son heeds his f instruction,	
	15: 5 A fool spurns his f discipline,	
	19:13 A foolish son is his f ruin,	
Lk	2:49 had to be in my F house?"	
Jn	2:16 How dare you turn my F house	
	10:29 can snatch them out of my F hand.	
	14: 2 In my F house are many rooms;	

FATHERLESS (FATHER)
Dt	10:18 He defends the cause of the f	
	24:17 Do not deprive the alien or the f	
	24:19 Leave it for the alien, the f	
Ps	68: 5 A father to the f, a defender	
Pr	23:10 or encroach on the fields of the f,	

FATHERS (FATHER)
Ex	20: 5 for the sin of the f to the third	
Lk	11:11 "Which of you f, if your son asks	
Eph	6: 4 F, do not exasperate your children;	
Col	3:21 F, do not embitter your children,	

FATHOM*
Job	11: 7 "Can you f the mysteries of God?	
Ps	145: 3 his greatness no one can f.	
Ecc	3:11 yet they cannot f what God has	
Isa	40:28 and his understanding no one can f	
1Co	13: 2 and can f all mysteries and all	

FAULT (FAULTS)
Mt	18:15 and show him his f, just	
Php	2:15 of God without f in a crooked	
Jas	1: 5 generously to all without finding f,	
Jude	24 his glorious presence without f	

FAULTFINDERS*
Jude	16 These men are grumblers and f;	

FAULTS (FAULT)
Ps	19:12 Forgive my hidden f.	

FAVORITISM*
Ex	23: 3 and do not show f to a poor man	
Lev	19:15 to the poor or f to the great,	
Ac	10:34 true it is that God does not show f	
Ro	2:11 For God does not show f.	
Eph	6: 9 and there is no f with him.	
Col	3:25 for his wrong, and there is no f.	
1Ti	5:21 and to do nothing out of f.	
Jas	2: 1 Lord Jesus Christ, don't show f.	
	2: 9 But if you show f, you sin	

FEAR (AFRAID FEARS)
Dt	6:13 F the LORD your God, serve him	
	10:12 but to f the LORD your God,	
	31:12 and learn to f the LORD your God	
Ps	19: 9 The f of the LORD is pure,	
	23: 4 I will f no evil,	
	27: 1 whom shall I f?	
	91: 5 You will not f the terror of night,	
	111: 10 f of the LORD is the beginning	
Pr	8:13 To f the LORD is to hate evil;	
	9:10 f of the LORD is the beginning	
	10:27 The f of the LORD adds length	
	14:27 The f of the LORD is a fountain	
	15:33 f of the LORD teaches a man	
	16: 6 through the f of the LORD a man	
	19:23 The f of the LORD leads to life:	
	29:25 F of man will prove to be a snare,	
Isa	11: 3 delight in the f of the LORD.	

FLESH

	41:10	So do not *f*, for I am with you;
Lk	12: 5	I will show you whom you should *f*:
Php	2:12	work out your salvation with *f*
1Jn	4:18	But perfect love drives out *f*,

FEARS (FEAR)
Job	1: 8	a man who *f* God and shuns evil."
Ps	34: 4	he delivered me from all my *f*.
Pr	31:30	a woman who *f* the LORD is
1Jn	4:18	The one who *f* is not made perfect

FEED
Jn	21:15	Jesus said, "*F* my lambs."
	21:17	Jesus said, "*F* my sheep.
Ro	12:20	"If your enemy is hungry, *f* him;
Jude	12	shepherds who *f* only themselves.

FEET (FOOT)
Ps	8: 6	you put everything under his *f*:
	22:16	have pierced my hands and my *f*.
	40: 2	he set my *f* on a rock
	110: 1	a footstool for your *f*."
	119:105	Your word is a lamp to my *f*
Ro	10:15	"How beautiful are the *f*
1Co	12:21	And the head cannot say to the *f*,
	15:25	has put all his enemies under his *f*.
Heb	12:13	"Make level paths for your *f*,"

FELLOWSHIP
2Co	6:14	what *f* can light have with darkness
	13:14	and the *f* of the Holy Spirit be
Php	3:10	the *f* of sharing in his sufferings,
1Jn	1: 6	claim to have *f* with him yet walk
	1: 7	we have *f* with one another,

FEMALE
| Ge | 1:27 | male and *f* he created them. |
| Gal | 3:28 | *f*, for you are all one in Christ Jesus |

FERVOR
| Ro | 12:11 | but keep your spiritual *f*, serving |

FIELD (FIELDS)
Mt	6:28	See how the lilies of the *f* grow.
	13:38	*f* is the world, and the good seed
1Co	3: 9	you are God's *f*, God's building.

FIELDS (FIELD)
| Lk | 2: 8 | were shepherds living out in the *f* |
| Jn | 4:35 | open your eyes and look at the *f*! |

FIG (FIGS)
| Ge | 3: 7 | so they sewed *f* leaves together |

FIGHT (FOUGHT)
Ex	14:14	The LORD will *f* for you; you need
Dt	1:30	going before you, will *f* for you,
	3:22	the LORD your God himself will *f*
Ne	4:20	Our God will *f* for us!"
Ps	35: 1	*f* against those who *f* against me.
Jn	18:36	my servants would *f*
1Co	9:26	I do not *f* like a man beating the air.
2Co	10: 4	The weapons we *f*
1Ti	1:18	them you may *f* the good *f*,
	6:12	Fight the good *f* of the faith.
2Ti	4: 7	fought the good *f*, I have finished

FIGS (FIG)
| Lk | 6:44 | People do not pick *f* |

FILL (FILLED FILLS FULL FULLNESS FULLY)
Ge	1:28	and increase in number; *f* the earth
Ps	16:11	you will *f* me with joy
	81:10	wide your mouth and I will *f* it.
Pr	28:19	who chases fantasies will have his *f*
Hag	2: 7	and I will *f* this house with glory',
Jn	6:26	you ate the loaves and had your *f*.
Ac	2: 2	All of them were *f*
Ro	15:13	The God of hope *f* you with all joy

FILLED (FILL)
Ps	72:19	may the whole earth be *f*
	119: 64	The earth is *f* with your love,
Eze	43: 5	the glory of the LORD *f* the temple
Hab	2:14	For the earth will be *f*
Lk	1:15	and he will be *f* with the Holy Spirit
	1:41	and Elizabeth was *f* with the Holy
Jn	12: 3	the house was *f* with the fragrance
Ac	2: 4	All of them were *f*
	4: 8	Then Peter, *f* with the Holy Spirit,
	9:17	and be *f* with the Holy Spirit."
	13: 9	called Paul, *f* with the Holy Spirit,
Eph	5:18	Instead, be *f* with the Spirit.
Php	1:11	*f* with the fruit of righteousness

FILLS (FILL)
Nu	14:21	of the LORD *f* the whole earth,
Ps	107: 9	and *f* the hungry with good things.
Eph	1:23	fullness of him who *f* everything

FILTHY
Isa	64: 6	all our righteous acts are like *f* rags;
Col	3: 8	and *f* language from your lips.
2Pe	2: 7	by the *f* lives of lawless men

FIND (FINDS FOUND)
Nu	32:23	be sure that your sin will *f* you out.
Dt	4:29	you will *f* him if you look for him
1Sa	23:16	and helped him *f* strength in God.
Ps	36: 7	*f* refuge in the shadow
	91: 4	under his wings you will *f* refuge;
Pr	14:22	those who plan what is good *f* love
	31:10	A wife of noble character who can *f*
Jer	6:16	and you will *f* rest for your souls.
Mt	7: 7	seek and you will *f*; knock
	11:29	and you will *f* rest for your souls.
	16:25	loses his life for me will *f* it.
Lk	18: 8	will he *f* faith on the earth?"
Jn	10: 9	come in and go out, and *f* pasture.

FINDS (FIND)
Ps	62: 1	My soul *f* rest in God alone;
	112: 1	who *f* great delight
	119:162	like one who *f* great spoil.
Pr	18:22	He who *f* a wife *f* what is good
Mt	7: 8	he who seeks *f*; and to him who
	10:39	Whoever *f* his life will lose it,
Lk	12:37	whose master *f* them watching
	15: 4	go after the lost sheep until he *f* it?

FINISH (FINISHED)
Jn	4:34	him who sent me and to *f* his work.
	5:36	that the Father has given me to *f*,
Ac	20:24	if only I may *f* the race
2Co	8:11	Now *f* the work, so that your eager
Jas	1: 4	Perseverance must *f* its work

FINISHED (FINISH)
Ge	2: 2	seventh day God had *f* the work he
Jn	19:30	the drink, Jesus said, "It is *f*."
2Ti	4: 7	I have *f* the race, I have kept

FIRE
Ex	13:21	in a pillar of *f* to give them light,
Lev	6:12	*f* on the altar must be kept burning;
Isa	30:27	and his tongue is a consuming *f*.
Jer	23:29	my word like *f*," declares
Mt	3:11	you with the Holy Spirit and with *f*.
	5:22	will be in danger of the *f* of hell.
	25:41	into the eternal *f* prepared
Mk	9:43	where the *f* never goes out.
Ac	2: 3	to be tongues of *f* that separated
1Co	3:13	It will be revealed with *f*,
1Th	5:19	Do not put out the Spirit's *f*;
Heb	12:29	for our "God is a consuming *f*."
Jas	3: 5	set on *f* by a small spark.
2Pe	3:10	the elements will be destroyed by *f*,
Jude	23	snatch others from the *f*
Rev	20:14	The lake of *f* is the second death.

FIRM
Ex	14:13	Stand *f* and you will see
2Ch	20:17	stand *f* and see the deliverance
Ps	33:11	of the LORD stand *f* forever,
	37:23	he makes his steps *f*;
	40: 2	and gave me a *f* place to stand.
	89: 2	that your love stands *f* forever,
	119: 89	it stands *f* in the heavens.
Pr	4:26	and take only ways that are *f*.
Zec	8:23	nations will take *f* hold of one Jew
Mk	13:13	he who stands *f* to the end will be
1Co	16:13	on your guard; stand *f* in the faith;
2Co	1:24	because it is by faith you stand *f*.
Eph	6:14	Stand *f* then, with the belt
Col	4:12	that you may stand *f* in all the will
2Th	2:15	stand *f* and hold to the teachings
2Ti	2:19	God's solid foundation stands *f*,
Heb	6:19	an anchor for the soul, *f* and secure
1Pe	5: 9	Resist him, standing *f* in the faith,

FIRST
Isa	44: 6	I am the *f* and I am the last;
	48:12	I am the *f* and I am the last.
Mt	5:24	*F* go and be reconciled
	6:33	But seek *f* his kingdom
	7: 5	*f* take the plank out
	20:27	wants to be *f* must be your slave—
	22:38	This is the *f* and greatest
	23:26	*F* clean the inside of the cup
Mk	13:10	And the gospel must *f* be preached
Ac	11:26	disciples were called Christians *f*
Ro	1:16	*f* for the Jew, then for the Gentile.
1Co	12:28	in the church God has appointed *f*
2Co	8: 5	they gave themselves *f* to the Lord
1Ti	2:13	For Adam was formed *f*, then Eve.
Jas	3:17	comes from heaven is *f* of all pure;
1Jn	4:19	We love because he *f* loved us.
3Jn	9	but Diotrephes, who loves to be *f*,
Rev	1:17	I am the *F* and the Last.
	2: 4	You have forsaken your *f* love.

FIRSTBORN (BEAR)
| Ex | 11: 5 | Every *f* son in Egypt will die, |

FIRSTFRUITS
| Ex | 23:19 | "Bring the best of the *f* of your soil |

FISHERS
| Mk | 1:17 | "and I will make you *f* of men." |

FITTING*
Ps	33: 1	it is *f* for the upright to praise him.
	147: 1	how pleasant and *f* to praise him!
Pr	10:32	of the righteous know what is *f*,
	19:10	It is not *f* for a fool to live in luxury
	26: 1	honor is not *f* for a fool.
1Co	14:40	everything should be done in a *f*
Col	3:18	to your husbands, as is *f* in the Lord
Heb	2:10	sons to glory, it was *f* that God,

FIX
Dt	11:18	*F* these words of mine
Pr	4:25	*f* your gaze directly before you.
2Co	4:18	we *f* our eyes not on what is seen,
Heb	3: 1	heavenly calling, *f* your thoughts
	12: 2	Let us *f* our eyes on Jesus,

FLAME (FLAMES FLAMING)
| 2Ti | 1: 6 | you to fan into *f* the gift of God, |

FLAMES (FLAME)
| 1Co | 3:15 | only as one escaping through the *f*. |
| | 13: 3 | and surrender my body to the *f*, |

FLAMING (FLAME)
| Eph | 6:16 | you can extinguish all the *f* arrows |

FLASH
| 1Co | 15:52 | in a *f*, in the twinkling of an eye, |

FLATTER (FLATTERING FLATTERY)
| Job | 32:21 | nor will I *f* any man; |
| Jude | 16 | *f* others for their own advantage. |

FLATTERING (FLATTER)
Ps	12: 2	their *f* lips speak with deception.
	12: 3	May the LORD cut off all *f* lips
Pr	26:28	and a *f* mouth works ruin.

FLATTERY (FLATTER)
| Ro | 16:18 | and *f* they deceive the minds |
| 1Th | 2: 5 | You know we never used *f*, |

FLAWLESS*
2Sa	22:31	the word of the LORD is *f*.
Job	11: 4	You say to God, 'My beliefs are *f*
Ps	12: 6	And the words of the LORD are *f*,
	18:30	the word of the LORD is *f*.
Pr	30: 5	"Every word of God is *f*;
SS	5: 2	my dove, my *f* one.

FLEE
Ps	139: 7	Where can I *f* from your presence?
1Co	6:18	*F* from sexual immorality.
	10:14	my dear friends, *f* from idolatry.
1Ti	6:11	But you, man of God, *f* from all this
2Ti	2:22	*F* the evil desires of youth,
Jas	4: 7	Resist the devil, and he will *f*

FLEETING
| Ps | 89:47 | Remember how *f* is my life. |
| Pr | 31:30 | Charm is deceptive, and beauty is *f* |

FLESH
Ge	2:23	and of my *f*;
	2:24	and they will become one *f*.
Job	19:26	yet in my *f* I will see God;
Eze	11:19	of stone and give them a heart of *f*.
	36:26	of stone and give you a heart of *f*.
Mk	10: 8	and the two will become one *f*.'
Jn	1:14	The Word became *f* and made his
	6:51	This bread is my *f*, which I will give
1Co	6:16	"The two will become one *f*."
Eph	5:31	and the two will become one *f*."

FLOCK

6:12 For our struggle is not against *f*
FLOCK (FLOCKS)
Isa 40:11 He tends his *f* like a shepherd:
Eze 34:2 not shepherds take care of the *f*?
Zec 11:17 who deserts the *fl*
Mt 26:31 the sheep of the *f* will be scattered.'
Ac 20:28 all the *f* of which the Holy Spirit
1Pe 5:2 Be shepherds of God's *f* that is
FLOCKS (FLOCK)
Lk 2:8 keeping watch over their *f* at night.
FLOG
Ac 22:25 to *f* a Roman citizen who hasn't
FLOODGATES
Mal 3:10 see if I will not throw open the *f*
FLOURISHING
Ps 52:8 *f* in the house of God;
FLOW (FLOWING)
Nu 13:27 and it does *f* with milk and honey!
Jn 7:38 streams of living water will *f*
FLOWERS
Isa 40:7 The grass withers and the *f* fall,
FLOWING (FLOW)
Ex 3:8 a land *f* with milk and honey—
FOLDING
Pr 6:10 a little *f* of the hands to rest—
FOLLOW (FOLLOWING FOLLOWS)
Ex 23:2 Do not *f* the crowd in doing wrong.
Lev 18:4 and be careful to *f* my decrees.
Dt 5:1 Learn them and be sure to *f* them.
Ps 23:6 Surely goodness and love will *f* me
Mt 16:24 and take up his cross and *f* me.
Jn 10:4 his sheep *f* him because they know
1Co 14:1 *F* the way of love and eagerly
Rev 14:1 They *f* the Lamb wherever he goes.
FOLLOWING (FOLLOW)
1Ti 1:18 by *f* them you may fight the good
FOLLOWS (FOLLOW)
Jn 8:12 Whoever *f* me will never walk
FOOD (FOODS)
Pr 20:13 you will have *f* to spare.
22:9 for he shares his *f* with the poor.
25:21 If your enemy is hungry, give him *f*
31:15 she provides *f* for her family
Da 1:8 to defile himself with the royal *f*
Jn 6:27 Do not work for *f* that spoils,
Ro 14:14 fully convinced that no *f* is unclean
1Co 8:8 But *f* does not bring us near to God
1Ti 6:8 But if we have *f* and clothing,
Jas 2:15 sister is without clothes and daily *f*.
FOODS (FOOD)
Mk 7:19 Jesus declared all *f* "clean.")
FOOL (FOOLISH FOOLISHNESS FOOLS)
Ps 14:1 The *f* says in his heart,
Pr 15:5 A *f* spurns his father's discipline,
17:28 Even a *f* is thought wise
18:2 A *f* finds no pleasure
26:5 Answer a *f* according to his folly,
28:26 He who trusts in himself is a *f*,
Mt 5:22 But anyone who says, 'You *f*!'
FOOLISH (FOOL)
Pr 10:1 but a *f* son grief to his mother.
17:25 A *f* son brings grief to his father
Mt 7:26 practice is like a *f* man who built
25:2 of them were *f* and five were wise.
1Co 1:27 God chose the *f* things of the world
FOOLISHNESS (FOOL)
1Co 1:18 the cross is *f* to those who are
1:25 For the *f* of God is wiser
2:14 for they are *f* to him, and he cannot
3:19 of this world is *f* in God's sight.
FOOLS (FOOL)
Pr 14:9 *F* mock at making amends for sin,
1Co 4:10 We are *f* for Christ, but you are
FOOT (FEET FOOTHOLD)
Jos 1:3 every place where you set your *f*,
Isa 1:6 From the sole of your *f* to the top
1Co 12:15 If the *f* should say, "Because I am
FOOTHOLD (FOOT)
Eph 4:27 and do not give the devil a *f*.
FORBEARANCE*
Ro 3:25 because in his *f* he had left the sins

FORBID
1Co 14:39 and do not *f* speaking in tongues.
FOREFATHERS (FATHER)
Heb 1:1 spoke to our *f* through the prophets
FOREKNEW* (KNOW)
Ro 8:29 For those God *f* he
11:2 not reject his people, whom he *f*.
FOREVER (EVER)
1Ch 16:15 He remembers his covenant *f*,
16:34 his love endures *f*.
Ps 9:7 The LORD reigns *f*;
23:6 dwell in the house of the LORD *f*.
33:11 the plans of the LORD stand firm *f*
86:12 I will glorify your name *f*.
92:8 But you, O LORD, are exalted *f*.
110:4 "You are a priest *f*,
119:111 Your statutes are my heritage *f*;
Jn 6:51 eats of this bread, he will live *f*.
14:16 Counselor to be with you *f*—
1Co 9:25 it to get a crown that will last *f*.
1Th 4:17 And so we will be with the Lord *f*.
Heb 13:8 same yesterday and today and *f*.
1Pe 1:25 but the word of the Lord stands *f*."
1Jn 2:17 who does the will of God lives *f*.
FORFEIT
Lk 9:25 and yet lose or *f* his very self?
FORGAVE (FORGIVE)
Ps 32:5 and you *f*
Eph 4:32 just as in Christ God *f* you.
Col 2:13 He *f* us all our sins, having
3:13 Forgive as the Lord *f* you.
FORGET (FORGETS FORGETTING)
Dt 6:12 that you do not *f* the LORD,
Ps 103:2 and *f* not all his benefits.
137:5 may my right hand *f* its skill
Isa 49:15 "Can a mother *f* the baby
Heb 6:10 he will not *f* your work
FORGETS (FORGET)
Jn 16:21 her baby is born she *f* the anguish
Jas 1:24 immediately *f* what he looks like.
FORGETTING (FORGET)
Php 3:13 *f* what is behind and straining
FORGIVE (FORGAVE FORGIVENESS FORGIVING)
2Ch 7:14 will *f* their sin and will heal their
Ps 19:12 *f* my hidden faults.
Mt 6:12 *F* us our debts,
6:14 For if you *f* men when they sin
18:21 many times shall I *f* my brother
Mk 11:25 in heaven may *f* you your sins."
Lk 11:4 *F* us our sins,
23:34 Jesus said, "Father, *f* them,
Col 3:13 *F* as the Lord forgave you.
1Jn 1:9 and just and will *f* us our sins
FORGIVENESS (FORGIVE)
Ps 130:4 But with you there is *f*;
Ac 10:43 believes in him receives *f* of sins
Eph 1:7 through his blood, the *f* of sins,
Col 1:14 in whom we have redemption, the *f*
Heb 9:22 the shedding of blood there is no *f*.
FORGIVING (FORGIVE)
Ne 9:17 But you are a *f* God, gracious
Eph 4:32 to one another, *f* each other,
FORMED
Ge 2:7 And the LORD God *f* man
Ps 103:14 for he knows how we are *f*,
Isa 45:18 but *f* it to be inhabited—
Ro 9:20 "Shall what is *f* say to him who *f*,
1Ti 2:13 For Adam was *f* first, then Eve.
Heb 11:3 understand that the universe was *f*
FORSAKE (FORSAKEN)
Jos 1:5 I will never leave you nor *f* you.
24:16 "Far be it from us to *f* the LORD
2Ch 15:2 but if you *f* him, he will *f* you.
Ps 27:10 Though my father and mother *f* me
Isa 55:7 Let the wicked *f* his way
Heb 13:5 never will I *f* you."
FORSAKEN (FORSAKE)
Ps 22:1 my God, why have you *f* me?
37:25 I have never seen the righteous *f*
Mt 27:46 my God, why have you *f* me?"
Rev 2:4 You have *f* your first love.

FORTRESS
Ps 18:2 The LORD is my rock, my *f*
71:3 for you are my rock and my *f*.
FOUGHT (FIGHT)
2Ti 4:7 I have *f* the good fight, I have
FOUND (FIND)
1Ch 28:9 if you seek him, he will be *f* by you;
Isa 55:6 Seek the LORD while he may be *f*;
Da 5:27 on the scales and *f* wanting.
Lk 15:6 with me; I have *f* my lost sheep.'
15:9 with me; I have *f* my lost coin.'
Ac 4:12 Salvation is *f* in no one else,
FOUNDATION
Isa 28:16 a precious cornerstone for a sure *f*;
1Co 3:11 For no one can lay any other *f*
Eph 2:20 built on the *f* of the apostles
2Ti 2:19 God's solid *f* stands firm,
FOXES
Mt 8:20 "*F* have holes and birds
FRAGRANCE
2Co 2:16 of death; to the other, the *f* of life.
FREE (FREED FREEDOM FREELY)
Ps 146:7 The LORD sets prisoners *f*,
Jn 8:32 and the truth will set you *f*."
Ro 6:18 You have been set *f* from sin
Gal 3:28 slave nor *f*, male nor female,
1Pe 2:16 *f* men, but do not use your freedom
FREED (FREE)
Rev 1:5 has *f* us from our sins by his blood,
FREEDOM (FREE)
Ro 8:21 into the glorious *f* of the children
2Co 3:17 the Spirit of the Lord is, there is *f*.
Gal 5:13 But do not use your *f* to indulge
1Pe 2:16 but do not use your *f* as a cover-up
FREELY (FREE)
Isa 55:7 and to our God, for he will *f* pardon
Mt 10:8 Freely you have received, *f* give.
Ro 3:24 and are justified *f* by his grace
Eph 1:6 which he has *f* given us
FRIEND (FRIENDS)
Ex 33:11 as a man speaks with his *f*.
Pr 17:17 A *f* loves at all times,
18:24 there is a *f* who sticks closer
27:6 Wounds from a *f* can be trusted,
27:10 Do not forsake your *f* and the *f*
Jas 4:4 Anyone who chooses to be a *f*
FRIENDS (FRIEND)
Pr 16:28 and a gossip separates close *f*.
Zec 13:6 given at the house of my *f*.'
Jn 15:13 that he lay down his life for his *f*.
FRUIT (FRUITFUL)
Ps 1:3 which yields its *f* in season
Pr 11:30 The *f* of the righteous is a tree
Mt 7:16 By their *f* you will recognize them.
Jn 15:2 branch in me that bears no *f*,
Gal 5:22 But the *f* of the Spirit is love, joy,
Rev 22:2 of *f*, yielding its *f* every month.
FRUITFUL (FRUIT)
Ge 1:22 "Be *f* and increase in number
Ps 128:3 Your wife will be like a *f* vine
Jn 15:2 prunes so that it will be even more *f*.
FULFILL (FULFILLED FULFILLMENT)
Ps 116:14 I will *f* my vows to the LORD
Mt 5:17 come to abolish them but to *f* them.
1Co 7:3 husband should *f* his marital duty
FULFILLED (FULFILL)
Pr 13:19 A longing *f* is sweet to the soul,
Mk 14:49 But the Scriptures must be *f*."
Ro 13:8 loves his fellowman has *f* the law.
FULFILLMENT (FULFILL)
Ro 13:10 Therefore love is the *f* of the law.
FULL (FILL)
Ps 127:5 whose quiver is *f* of them.
Pr 31:11 Her husband has *f* confidence
Isa 6:3 the whole earth is *f* of his glory."
11:9 for the earth will be *f*
Jn 10:10 may have life, and have it to the *f*.
Ac 6:3 known to be *f* of the Spirit
FULLNESS (FILL)
Col 1:19 to have all his *f* dwell in him,
2:9 in Christ all the *f* of the Deity lives

GLORY

FULLY (FILL)
- 1Ki 8:61 your hearts must be *f* committed
- 2Ch 16:9 whose hearts are *f* committed
- Ps 119:4 that are to be *f* obeyed.
- 119:138 they are *f* trustworthy.
- 1Co 15:58 Always give yourselves *f*

FUTURE
- Ps 37:37 there is a *f* for the man of peace.
- Pr 23:18 There is surely a *f* hope for you,
- Ro 8:38 neither the present nor the *f*,

GABRIEL*
Angel who interpreted Daniel's visions (Da 8:16-26; 9:20-27); announced births of John (Lk 1:11-20), Jesus (Lk 1:26-38).

GAIN (GAINED)
- Ps 60:12 With God we will *g* the victory,
- Mk 8:36 it for a man to *g* the whole world,
- 1Co 13:3 but have not love, I *g* nothing.
- Php 1:21 to live is Christ and to die is *g*.
- 3:8 that I may *g* Christ and be found
- 1Ti 6:6 with contentment is great *g*.

GAINED (GAIN)
- Ro 5:2 through whom we have *g* access

GALILEE
- Isa 9:1 but in the future he will honor G

GALL
- Mt 27:34 mixed with *g*; but after tasting it,

GAP
- Eze 22:30 stand before me in the *g* on behalf

GARDENER
- Jn 15:1 true vine, and my Father is the *g*.

GARMENT (GARMENTS)
- Ps 102:26 they will all wear out like a *g*.
- Mt 9:16 of unshrunk cloth on an old *g*,
- Jn 19:23 This *g* was seamless, woven

GARMENTS (GARMENT)
- Ge 3:21 The LORD God made *g* of skin
- Isa 61:10 me with *g* of salvation
- 63:1 with his *g* stained crimson?
- Jn 19:24 "They divided my *g* among them

GATE (GATES)
- Mt 7:13 For wide is the *g* and broad is
- Jn 10:9 I am the *g*; whoever enters

GATES (GATE)
- Ps 100:4 Enter his *g* with thanksgiving
- Mt 16:18 the *g* of Hades will not overcome it

GATHER (GATHERS)
- Zec 14:2 I will *g* all the nations to Jerusalem
- Mt 12:30 he who does not *g* with me scatters
- 23:37 longed to *g* your children together,

GATHERS (GATHER)
- Isa 40:11 He *g* the lambs in his arms
- Mt 23:37 a hen *g* her chicks under her wings,

GAVE (GIVE)
- Ezr 2:69 According to their ability they *g*
- Job 1:21 LORD *g* and the LORD has taken
- Jn 3:16 so loved the world that he *g* his one
- 2Co 8:5 they *g* themselves first to the Lord
- Gal 2:20 who loved me and *g* himself for me
- 1Ti 2:6 who *g* himself as a ransom

GAZE
- Ps 27:4 to *g* upon the beauty of the LORD
- Pr 4:25 fix your *g* directly before you.

GENEALOGIES
- 1Ti 1:4 themselves to myths and endless *g*.

GENERATIONS
- Ps 22:30 future *g* will be told about the Lord
- 102:12 your renown endures through all *g*.
- 145:13 dominion endures through all *g*.
- Lk 1:48 now on all *g* will call me blessed,
- Eph 3:5 not made known to men in other *g*

GENEROUS
- Ps 112:5 Good will come to him who is *g*
- Pr 22:9 A *g* man will himself be blessed,
- 2Co 9:5 Then it will be ready as a *g* gift,
- 1Ti 6:18 and to be *g* and willing to share.

GENTILE (GENTILES)
- Ro 1:16 first for the Jew, then for the G.
- 10:12 difference between Jew and G—

GENTILES (GENTILE)
- Isa 42:6 and a light for the G,
- Ro 3:9 and G alike are all under sin.
- 11:13 as I am the apostle to the G,
- 1Co 1:23 block to Jews and foolishness to G,

GENTLE (GENTLENESS)
- Pr 15:1 A *g* answer turns away wrath,
- Zec 9:9 *g* and riding on a donkey,
- Mt 11:29 for I am *g* and humble in heart,
- 21:5 *g* and riding on a donkey,
- 1Co 4:21 or in love and with a *g* spirit?
- 1Pe 3:4 the unfading beauty of a *g*

GENTLENESS* (GENTLE)
- 2Co 10:1 By the meekness and *g* of Christ,
- Gal 5:23 faithfulness, *g* and self-control.
- Php 4:5 Let your *g* be evident to all.
- Col 3:12 kindness, humility, *g* and patience.
- 1Ti 6:11 faith, love, endurance and *g*,
- 1Pe 3:15 But do this with *g* and respect,

GETHSEMANE
- Mt 26:36 disciples to a place called G,

GIDEON*
Judge, also called Jerub-Baal; freed Israel from Midianites (Jdg 6-8; Heb 11:32). Given sign of fleece (Jdg 8:36-40).

GIFT (GIFTS)
- Pr 21:14 A *g* given in secret soothes anger,
- Mt 5:23 if you are offering your *g*
- Ac 2:38 And you will receive the *g*
- Ro 6:23 but the *g* of God is eternal life
- 1Co 7:7 each man has his own *g* from God;
- 2Co 8:12 the *g* is acceptable according
- 9:15 be to God for his indescribable *g!*
- Eph 2:8 it is the *g* of God—not by works,
- 1Ti 4:14 not neglect your *g*, which was
- 2Ti 1:6 you to fan into flame the *g* of God,
- Jas 1:17 and perfect *g* is from above,
- 1Pe 4:10 should use whatever *g* he has

GIFTS (GIFT)
- Ro 11:29 for God's *g* and his call are
- 12:6 We have different *g*, according
- 1Co 12:4 There are different kinds of *g*,
- 12:31 But eagerly desire the greater *g*.
- 14:1 and eagerly desire spiritual *g*,
- 14:12 excel in *g* that build up the church.

GILEAD
- Jer 8:22 Is there no balm in G?

GIVE (GAVE GIVEN GIVER GIVES GIVING)
- Nu 6:26 and *g* you peace." '
- 1Sa 1:11 then I will *g* him to the LORD
- 2Ch 15:7 be strong and do not *g* up,
- Pr 21:26 but the righteous *g* without sparing
- 23:26 My son, *g* me your heart
- 30:8 but *g* me only my daily bread.
- 31:31 G her the reward she has earned,
- Isa 42:8 I will not *g* my glory to another
- Eze 36:26 I will *g* you a new heart
- Mt 6:11 G us today our daily bread.
- 10:8 Freely you have received, freely *g*.
- 22:21 "G to Caesar what is Caesar's,
- Mk 8:37 Or what can a man *g* in exchange
- Lk 6:38 G, and it will be given to you.
- 11:13 Father in heaven *g* the Holy Spirit
- Jn 10:28 I *g* them eternal life, and they shall
- 13:34 "A new commandment I *g* you:
- Ac 20:35 blessed to *g* than to receive.'"
- Ro 12:8 let him *g* generously;
- 13:7 G everyone what you owe him:
- 14:12 each of us will *g* an account
- 2Co 9:7 Each man should *g* what he has
- Rev 14:7 "Fear God and *g* him glory,

GIVEN (GIVE)
- Nu 8:16 are to be *g* wholly to me.
- Ps 115:16 but the earth he has *g* to man.
- Isa 9:6 to us a son is *g*,
- Mt 6:33 and all these things will be *g* to you
- 7:7 "Ask and it will be *g* to you;
- Lk 22:19 saying, "This is my body *g* for you;
- Jn 3:27 man can receive only what is *g* him
- Ro 5:5 the Holy Spirit, whom he has *g* us.
- 1Co 4:2 those who have been *g* a trust must
- 12:13 we were all *g* the one Spirit to drink
- Eph 4:7 to each one of us grace has been *g*

GIVER* (GIVE)
- Pr 18:16 A gift opens the way for the *g*
- 2Co 9:7 for God loves a cheerful *g*.

GIVES (GIVE)
- Ps 119:130 The unfolding of your words *g* light;
- Pr 14:30 A heart at peace *g* life to the body,
- 15:30 good news *g* health to the bones.
- 28:27 He who *g* to the poor will lack
- Isa 40:29 He *g* strength to the weary
- Mt 10:42 if anyone *g* even a cup of cold water
- Jn 6:63 The Spirit *g* life; the flesh counts
- 1Co 15:57 He *g* us the victory
- 2Co 3:6 the letter kills, but the Spirit *g* life.

GIVING (GIVE)
- Ne 8:8 *g* the meaning so that the people
- Ps 19:8 *g* joy to the heart.
- Mt 6:4 so that your *g* may be in secret.
- 2Co 8:7 also excel in this grace of *g*.

GLAD (GLADNESS)
- Ps 31:7 I will be *g* and rejoice in your love,
- 46:4 whose streams make *g* the city
- 97:1 LORD reigns, let the earth be *g*;
- 118:24 Let us rejoice and be *g* in it.
- Pr 23:25 May your father and mother be *g*;
- Zec 2:10 and be *g*, O Daughter of Zion.
- Mt 5:12 be *g*, because great is your reward

GLADNESS (GLAD)
- Ps 45:15 They are led in with joy and *g*;
- 51:8 Let me hear joy and *g*;
- 100:2 Serve the LORD with *g*;
- Jer 31:13 I will turn their mourning into *g*;

GLORIFIED (GLORY)
- Jn 13:31 Son of Man *g* and God is *g* in him.
- Ro 8:30 those he justified, he also *g*.
- 2Th 1:10 comes to be *g* in his holy people

GLORIFY (GLORY)
- Ps 34:3 G the LORD with me;
- 86:12 I will *g* your name forever.
- Jn 13:32 God will *g* the Son in himself,
- 17:1 G your Son, that your Son may

GLORIOUS (GLORY)
- Ps 45:13 All *g* is the princess
- 111:3 G and majestic are his deeds,
- 145:5 of the *g* splendor of your majesty,
- Isa 4:2 the LORD will be beautiful and *g*,
- 12:5 for he has done *g* things;
- 42:21 to make his law great and *g*
- 63:15 from your lofty throne, holy and *g*.
- Mt 19:28 the Son of Man sits on his *g* throne,
- Lk 9:31 appeared in *g* splendor, talking
- Ac 2:20 of the great and *g* day of the Lord.
- 2Co 3:8 of the Spirit be even more *g*?
- Php 3:21 so that they will be like his *g* body.
- 4:19 to his *g* riches in Christ Jesus.
- Tit 2:13 the *g* appearing of our great God
- Jude 24 before his *g* presence without fault

GLORY (GLORIFIED GLORIFY GLORIOUS)
- Ex 15:11 awesome in *g*,
- 33:18 Moses said, "Now show me your *g*
- 1Sa 4:21 "The *g* has departed from Israel"—
- 1Ch 16:24 Declare his *g* among the nations,
- 16:28 ascribe to the LORD *g*
- 29:11 and the *g* and the majesty
- Ps 8:5 and crowned him with *g* and honor
- 19:1 The heavens declare the *g* of God;
- 24:7 that the King of *g* may come in.
- 29:1 ascribe to the LORD *g*
- 72:19 the whole earth be filled with his *g*.
- 96:3 Declare his *g* among the nations,
- Pr 19:11 it is to his *g* to overlook an offense.
- 25:2 It is the *g* of God to conceal
- Isa 6:3 the whole earth is full of his *g*."
- 48:11 I will not yield my *g* to another.
- Eze 43:2 and the land was radiant with his *g*.
- Mt 24:30 of the sky, with power and great *g*.
- 25:31 the Son of Man comes in his *g*,
- Mk 8:38 in his Father's *g* with the holy
- 13:26 in clouds with great power and *g*.
- Lk 2:9 and the *g* of the Lord shone
- 2:14 saying, "G to God in the highest,
- Jn 1:14 We have seen his *g*, the *g* of the One
- 17:5 presence with the *g* I had with you
- 17:24 to see my *g*, the *g* you have given

GLUTTONS

Ac	7: 2	The God of g appeared
Ro	1:23	exchanged the g of the immortal
	3:23	and fall short of the g of God,
	8:18	with the g that will be revealed
	9: 4	theirs the divine g, the covenants,
1Co	10:31	whatever you do, do it all for the g
	11: 7	but the woman is the g of man.
	15:43	it is raised in g; it is sown
2Co	3:10	comparison with the surpassing g.
	3:18	faces all reflect the Lord's g,
	4:17	us an eternal g that far outweighs
Col	1:27	Christ in you, the hope of g.
	3: 4	also will appear with him in g.
1Ti	3:16	was taken up in g.
Heb	1: 3	The Son is the radiance of God's g
	2: 7	you crowned him with g and honor
1Pe	1:24	and all their g is like the flowers
Rev	4:11	to receive g and honor and power,
	21:23	for the g of God gives it light,

GLUTTONS
Tit	1:12	always liars, evil brutes, lazy g."

GNASHING
Mt	8:12	where there will be weeping and g

GNAT*
Mt	23:24	You strain out a g but swallow

GOAL
2Co	5: 9	So we make it our g to please him,
Gal	3: 3	to attain your g by human effort?
Php	3:14	on toward the g to win the prize

GOAT (GOATS SCAPEGOAT)
Isa	11: 6	the leopard will lie down with the g

GOATS (GOAT)
Nu	7:17	five male g and five male lambs

GOD (GOD'S GODLINESS GODLY GODS)
Ge	1: 1	In the beginning G created
	1: 2	and the Spirit of G was hovering
	1:26	Then G said, "Let us make man
	1:27	So G created man in his own image
	1:31	G saw all that he had made,
	2: 3	And G blessed the seventh day
	2:22	Then the Lord G made a woman
	3:21	The Lord G made garments
	3:23	So the Lord G banished him
	5:22	Enoch walked with G 300 years
	6: 2	sons of G saw that the daughters
	9:16	everlasting covenant between G
	17: 1	"I am G Almighty; walk before me
	21:33	name of the Lord, the Eternal G.
	22: 8	"G himself will provide the lamb
	28:12	and the angels of G were ascending
	32:28	because you have struggled with G
	32:30	"It is because I saw G face to face,
	35:10	G said to him, "Your name is Jacob
	41:51	G has made me forget all my
	50:20	but G intended it for good
Ex	2:24	G heard their groaning
	3: 6	because he was afraid to look at G.
	6: 7	own people, and I will be your G.
	8:10	is no one like the Lord our G.
	13:18	So G led the people
	15: 2	He is my G, and I will praise him,
	17: 9	with the staff of G in my hands."
	19: 3	Then Moses went up to G,
	20: 2	the Lord your G, who brought
	20: 5	the Lord your G, am a jealous G,
	20:19	But do not have G speak to us
	22:28	"Do not blaspheme G
	31:18	inscribed by the finger of G.
	34: 6	the compassionate and gracious G,
	34:14	name is Jealous, is a jealous G.
Lev	18:21	not profane the name of your G.
	19: 2	the Lord your G, am holy.
	26:12	walk among you and be your G,
Nu	22:38	I must speak only what G puts
	23:19	G is not a man, that he should lie,
Dt	1:17	for judgment belongs to G.
	3:22	Lord your G himself will fight
	3:24	For what g is there in heaven
	4:24	is a consuming fire, a jealous G.
	4:31	the Lord your G is a merciful G,
	4:39	heart this day that the Lord is G
	5:11	the name of the Lord your G,
	5:14	a Sabbath to the Lord your G.
	5:26	of the living G speaking out of fire,
	6: 4	Lord our G, the Lord is one.
	6: 5	Love the Lord your G
	6:13	the Lord your G, serve him only
	6:16	Do not test the Lord your G.
	7: 9	your G is G; he is the faithful G,
	7:12	the Lord your G will keep his
	7:21	is a great and awesome G.
	8: 5	the Lord your G disciplines you.
	10:12	but to fear the Lord your G,
	10:14	the Lord your G belong
	10:17	For the Lord your G is G of gods
	11:13	to love the Lord your G
	13: 3	The Lord your G is testing you
	13: 4	the Lord your G you must
	15: 6	the Lord your G will bless you
	19: 9	to love the Lord your G
	25:16	the Lord your G detests anyone
	29:29	belong to the Lord our G,
	30: 2	return to the Lord your G
	30:16	today to love the Lord your G,
	30:20	you may love the Lord your G,
	31: 6	for the Lord your G goes
	32: 3	Oh, praise the greatness of our G!
	32: 4	A faithful G who does no wrong,
	33:27	The eternal G is your refuge,
Jos	1: 9	for the Lord your G will be
	14: 8	the Lord my G wholeheartedly.
	22: 5	to love the Lord your G,
	22:34	Between Us that the Lord is G.
	23: 11	careful to love the Lord your G.
	23:14	the Lord your G gave you has
Jdg	16:28	O G, please strengthen me just
Ru	1:16	be my people and your G my G.
1Sa	2: 2	there is no Rock like our G.
	2: 3	for the Lord is a G who knows,
	2:25	another man, G may mediate
	10:26	men whose hearts G had touched.
	12:12	the Lord your G was your king.
	17:26	defy the armies of the living G?"
	17:46	world will know that there is a G
	30: 6	strength in the Lord his G.
2Sa	14:14	But G does not take away life;
	22: 3	my G is my rock, in whom I take
	22:31	"As for G, his way is perfect;
1Ki	4:29	G gave Solomon wisdom
	8:23	there is no G like you in heaven
	8:27	"But will G really dwell on earth?
	8:61	committed to the Lord our G,
	18:21	If the Lord is G, follow him;
	18:37	are G, and that you are turning
	20:28	a g of the hills and not a g
2Ki	19:15	G of Israel, enthroned
1Ch	16:35	Cry out, "Save us, O G our Savior;
	28: 2	for the footstool of our G,
	28: 9	acknowledge the G of your father,
	29:10	G of our father Israel,
	29:17	my G, that you test the heart
2Ch	2: 4	for the Name of the Lord my G
	5:14	of the Lord filled the temple of G
	6:18	"But will G really dwell on earth
	18:13	I can tell him only what my G says
	20: 6	are you not the G who is in heaven?
	25: 8	for G has the power to help
	30: 9	for the Lord your G is gracious
	33:12	the favor of the Lord his G
Ezr	8:22	"The good hand of our G is
	9: 6	"O my G, I am too ashamed
	9:13	our G, you have punished us less
Ne	1: 5	the great and awesome G,
	8: 8	from the Book of the Law of G,
	9:17	But you are a forgiving G,
	9:32	the great, mighty and awesome G,
Job	1: 1	he feared G and shunned evil.
	2:10	Shall we accept good from G,
	4:17	a mortal be more righteous than G?
	5:17	is the man whom G corrects;
	11: 7	Can you fathom the mysteries of G
	19:26	yet in my flesh I will see G;
	22:13	Yet you say, 'What does G know?
	25: 4	can a man be righteous before G?
	33:14	For G does speak—now one way,
	34:12	is unthinkable that G would do
	36:26	is G— beyond our understanding!
Ps	37:22	G comes in awesome majesty.
	18: 2	my G is my rock, in whom I take
	18:28	my G turns my darkness into light.
	19: 1	The heavens declare the glory of G;
	22: 1	G, my G, why have you forsaken
	29: 3	the G of glory thunders,
	31:14	I say, "You are my G."
	40: 3	a hymn of praise to our G.
	40: 8	I desire to do your will, O my G;
	42: 2	thirsts for G, for the living G.
	42:11	Put your hope in G,
	45: 6	O G, will last for ever and ever;
	46: 1	G is our refuge and strength,
	46:10	"Be still, and know that I am G;
	47: 7	For G is the King of all the earth;
	50: 3	Our G comes and will not be silent;
	51: 1	Have mercy on me, O G,
	51:10	Create in me a pure heart, O G,
	51:17	O G, you will not despise.
	62: 7	my honor depend on G;
	65: 5	O G our Savior,
	66: 1	Shout with joy to G, all the earth!
	66:16	listen, all you who fear G;
	68: 6	G sets the lonely in families,
	71:17	my youth, O G, you have taught
	71:19	reaches to the skies, O G,
	71:22	harp for your faithfulness, O my G;
	73:26	but G is the strength of my heart
	77:13	What g is so great as our God?
	78:19	Can G spread a table in the desert?
	81: 1	Sing for joy to G our strength;
	84: 2	out for the living G.
	84:10	a doorkeeper in the house of my G
	86:12	O Lord my G, with all my heart;
	89: 7	of the holy ones G is greatly feared;
	90: 2	to everlasting you are G.
	91: 2	my G, in whom I trust."
	95: 7	for he is our G
	100: 3	Know that the Lord is G.
	108: 1	My heart is steadfast, O G;
	113: 5	Who is like the Lord our G,
	139:23	Search me, O G, and know my
Pr	3: 4	in the sight of G and man.
	25: 2	of G to conceal a matter;
	30: 5	"Every word of G is flawless;
Ecc	3:11	cannot fathom what G has done
	11: 5	cannot understand the work of G,
	12:13	Fear G and keep his
Isa	9: 6	Wonderful Counselor, Mighty G,
	37:16	you alone are G over all
	40: 3	a highway for our G.
	40: 8	the word of our G stands forever."
	40:28	The Lord is the everlasting G,
	41:10	not be dismayed, for I am your G.
	44: 6	apart from me there is no G.
	52: 7	"Your G reigns!"
	55: 7	to our G, for he will freely pardon;
	57:21	says my G, "for the wicked."
	59: 2	you from your G;
	61:10	my soul rejoices in my G.
	62: 5	so will your G rejoice over you.
Jer	23:23	"Am I only a G nearby,"
	31:33	I will be their G,
	32:27	"I am the Lord, the G
Eze	28:13	the garden of G;
Da	3:17	the G we serve is able to save us
	9: 4	O Lord, the great and awesome G,
Hos	12: 6	and wait for your G always.
Joel	2:13	Return to the Lord your G,
Am	4:12	prepare to meet your G, O Israel."
Mic	6: 8	and to walk humbly with your G.
Na	1: 2	Lord is a jealous and avenging G;
Zec	14: 5	Then the Lord my G will come,
Mal	3: 8	Will a man rob G? Yet you rob me.
Mt	1:23	which means, "G with us."
	5: 8	for they will see G.
	6:24	You cannot serve both G
	19: 6	Therefore what G has joined
	19:26	but with G all things are possible."
	22:21	and to G what is God's."
	22:37	" 'Love the Lord your G
	27:46	which means, "My G, my G,
Mk	12:29	the Lord our G, the Lord is one.
	16:19	and he sat at the right hand of G.

Lk	1:37	For nothing is impossible with G."
	1:47	my spirit rejoices in G my Savior,
	10:9	'The kingdom of G is near you.'
	10:27	" 'Love the Lord your G
	18:19	"No one is good—except G alone.
Jn	1:1	was with G, and the Word was G.
	1:18	seen G, but G the One and Only,
	3:16	"For G so loved the world that he
	4:24	G is spirit, and his worshipers must
	14:1	Trust in G; trust also in me.
	20:28	"My Lord and my G!"
Ac	2:24	But G raised him from the dead,
	5:4	You have not lied to men but to G
	5:29	"We must obey G rather than men!
	7:55	to heaven and saw the glory of G,
	17:23	TO AN UNKNOWN G.
	20:27	to you the whole will of G.
	20:32	"Now I commit you to G
Ro	1:17	a righteousness from G is revealed,
	2:11	For G does not show favoritism.
	3:4	Let G be true, and every man a liar.
	3:23	and fall short of the glory of G,
	4:24	to whom G will credit
	5:8	G demonstrates his own love for us
	6:23	but the gift of G is eternal life
	8:28	in all things G works for the good
	11:22	the kindness and sternness of G:
	14:12	give an account of himself to G.
1Co	1:20	Has not G made foolish
	2:9	what G has prepared
	3:6	watered it, but G made it grow.
	6:20	Therefore honor G with your body.
	7:24	each man, as responsible to G.
	8:8	food does not bring us near to G;
	10:13	G is faithful; he will not let you be
	10:31	do it all for the glory of G.
	14:33	For G is not a G of disorder
	15:28	so that G may be all in all.
2Co	1:9	rely on ourselves but on G,
	2:14	be to G, who always leads us
	3:5	but our competence comes from G.
	4:7	this all-surpassing power is from G
	5:19	that G was reconciling the world
	5:21	G made him who had no sin
	6:16	we are the temple of the living G.
	9:7	for G loves a cheerful giver.
	9:8	G is able to make all grace abound
Gal	2:6	G does not judge by external
	6:7	not be deceived: G cannot be
Eph	2:10	which G prepared in advance for us
	4:6	one baptism; one G and Father
	5:1	Be imitators of G, therefore,
Php	2:6	Who, being in very nature G,
	4:19	And my G will meet all your needs
1Th	2:4	trying to please men but G,
	4:7	For G did not call us to be impure,
	4:9	taught by G to love each other.
	5:9	For G did not appoint us
1Ti	2:5	one mediator between G and men,
	4:4	For everything G created is good,
	5:4	for this is pleasing to G.
Tit	2:13	glorious appearing of our great G
Heb	1:1	In the past G spoke
	4:12	For the word of G is living
	6:10	G is not unjust; he will not forget
	10:31	to fall into the hands of the living G
	11:6	faith it is impossible to please G,
	12:10	but G disciplines us for our good,
	12:29	for our "G is a consuming fire."
	13:15	offer to G a sacrifice of praise—
Jas	1:13	For G cannot be tempted by evil,
	2:19	You believe that there is one G.
	2:23	"Abraham believed G,
	4:4	the world becomes an enemy of G.
	4:8	Come near to G and he will come
1Pe	4:11	it with the strength G provides,
2Pe	1:21	but men spoke from G
1Jn	1:5	G is light; in him there is no
	3:20	For G is greater than our hearts,
	4:7	for love comes from G.
	4:9	This is how G showed his love
	4:11	Dear friends, since G so loved us,
	4:12	No one has ever seen G;
	4:16	G is love.
Rev	4:8	holy is the Lord G Almighty,
	7:17	G will wipe away every tear
	19:6	For our Lord G Almighty reigns.

GOD-BREATHED* (BREATHED)
2Ti	3:16	All Scripture is G and is useful

GOD'S (GOD)
2Ch	20:15	For the battle is not yours, but G.
Job	37:14	stop and consider G wonders.
Ps	52:8	I trust in G unfailing love
	69:30	I will praise G name in song
Mk	3:35	Whoever does G will is my brother
Jn	7:17	If anyone chooses to do G will,
	10:36	'I am G Son'? Do not believe me
Ro	2:3	think you will escape G judgment?
	2:4	not realizing that G kindness leads
	3:3	lack of faith nullify G faithfulness?
	7:22	in my inner being I delight in G law
	9:16	or effort, but on G mercy.
	11:29	for G gifts and his call are
	12:2	and approve what G will is—
	12:13	Share with G people who are
	13:6	for the authorities are G servants,
1Co	7:19	Keeping G commands is what
2Co	6:2	now is the time of G favor,
Eph	1:7	riches of G grace that he lavished
1Th	4:3	It is G will that you should be
	5:18	for this is G will for you
1Ti	1:4	so that G name and our teaching
2Ti	2:19	G solid foundation stands firm,
Tit	1:7	overseer is entrusted with G work,
Heb	1:3	The Son is the radiance of G glory
	9:24	now to appear for us in G presence.
	11:3	was formed at G command,
1Pe	2:15	For it is G will that
	3:4	which is of great worth in G sight.
1Jn	2:5	G love is truly made complete

GODLINESS (GOD)
1Ti	2:2	and quiet lives in all g and holiness.
	4:8	but g has value for all things,
	6:6	g with contentment is great gain.
	6:11	and pursue righteousness, g, faith,

GODLY (GOD)
Ps	4:3	that the Lord has set apart the g
2Co	7:10	G sorrow brings repentance that
	11:2	jealous for you with a g jealousy.
2Ti	3:12	everyone who wants to live a g life
2Pe	3:11	You ought to live holy and g lives

GODS (GOD)
Ex	20:3	"You shall have no other g
Ac	19:26	He says that man-made g are no g

GOLD
Job	23:10	tested me, I will come forth as g.
Ps	19:10	They are more precious than g,
	119:127	more than g, more than pure g,
Pr	22:1	esteemed is better than silver or g.

GOLGOTHA
Jn	19:17	(which in Aramaic is called G).

GOLIATH
Philistine giant killed by David (1Sa 17; 21:9).

GOOD
Ge	1:4	God saw that the light was g,
	1:31	he had made, and it was very g.
	2:18	"It is not g for the man to be alone.
	50:20	but God intended it for g
Job	2:10	Shall we accept g from God,
Ps	14:1	there is no one who does g.
	34:8	Taste and see that the Lord is g;
	37:3	Trust in the Lord and do g;
	84:11	no g thing does he withhold
	86:5	You are forgiving and g, O Lord
	103:5	satisfies your desires with g things,
	119:68	You are g, and what you do is g;
	133:1	How g and pleasant it is
	147:1	How g it is to sing praises
Pr	3:4	you will win favor and a g name
	11:27	He who seeks g finds g will,
	17:22	A cheerful heart is g medicine,
	18:22	He who finds a wife finds what is g
	22:1	A g name is more desirable
	31:12	She brings him g, not harm,
Isa	5:20	Woe to those who call evil g
	52:7	the feet of those who bring g news,
Jer	6:16	ask where the g way is,
Mic	6:8	has showed you, O man, what is g.
Mt	5:45	sun to rise on the evil and the g,
	7:17	Likewise every g tree bears g fruit,
	12:35	The g man brings g things out
	19:17	"There is only One who is g.
	25:21	'Well done, g and faithful servant!
Mk	3:4	lawful on the Sabbath: to do g
	8:36	What g is it for a man
Lk	6:27	do g to those who hate you,
Jn	10:11	"I am the g shepherd.
Ro	8:28	for the g of those who love him,
	10:15	feet of those who bring g news!"
	12:9	Hate what is evil; cling to what is g.
1Co	10:24	should seek his own g, but the g
	15:33	Bad company corrupts g character
2Co	9:8	you will abound in every g work,
Gal	6:9	us not become weary in doing g,
	6:10	as we have opportunity, let us do g
Eph	2:10	in Christ Jesus to do g works,
Php	1:6	that he who began a g work
1Th	5:21	Hold on to the g.
1Ti	3:7	have a g reputation with outsiders,
	4:4	For everything God created is g,
	6:12	Fight the g fight of the faith.
	6:18	them to do g, to be rich in g deeds,
2Ti	3:17	equipped for every g work.
	4:7	I have fought the g fight, I have
Heb	12:10	but God disciplines us for our g,
1Pe	2:3	you have tasted that the Lord is g.
	2:12	Live such g lives among the pagans

GOSPEL
Ro	1:16	I am not ashamed of the g,
	15:16	duty of proclaiming the g of God,
1Co	1:17	to preach the g— not with words
	9:16	Woe to me if I do not preach the g!
	15:1	you of the g I preached to you,
Gal	1:7	a different g— which is really no g
Php	1:27	in a manner worthy of the g

GOSSIP
Pr	11:13	A g betrays a confidence,
	16:28	and a g separates close friends.
	18:8	of a g are like choice morsels;
	26:20	without a g a quarrel dies down.
2Co	12:20	slander, g, arrogance and disorder.

GRACE (GRACIOUS)
Ps	45:2	lips have been anointed with g,
Jn	1:17	g and truth came through Jesus
Ac	20:32	to God and to the word of his g,
Ro	3:24	and are justified freely by his g
	5:15	came by the g of the one man,
	5:17	God's abundant provision of g
	5:20	where sin increased, g increased all
	6:14	you are not under law, but under g.
	11:6	if by g, then it is no longer by works
2Co	6:1	not to receive God's g in vain.
	8:9	For you know the g
	9:8	able to make all g abound to you,
	12:9	"My g is sufficient for you,
Gal	2:21	I do not set aside the g of God,
	5:4	you have fallen away from g.
Eph	1:7	riches of God's g that he lavished
	2:5	it is by g you have been saved.
	2:7	the incomparable riches of his g,
	2:8	For it is by g you have been saved,
Php	1:7	all of you share in God's g with me.
Col	4:6	conversation be always full of g,
2Th	2:16	and by his g gave us eternal
2Ti	2:1	be strong in the g that is
Tit	2:11	For the g of God that brings
	3:7	having been justified by his g,
Heb	2:9	that by the g of God he might taste
	4:16	find g to help us in our time of need
	4:16	throne of g with confidence,
Jas	4:6	but gives g to the humble."
2Pe	3:18	But grow in the g and knowledge

GRACIOUS (GRACE)
Nu	6:25	and be g to you;
Pr	22:11	a pure heart and whose speech is g
Isa	30:18	Yet the Lord longs to be g to you

GRAIN
1Co	9:9	ox while it is treading out the g."

GRANTED
Php 1:29 For it has been *g* to you on behalf

GRASS
Ps 103:15 As for man, his days are like *g*,
1Pe 1:24 "All men are like *g*,

GRAVE (GRAVES)
Pr 7:27 Her house is a highway to the *g*,
Hos 13:14 Where, O *g*, is your destruction?

GRAVES (GRAVE)
Jn 5:28 are in their *g* will hear his voice
Ro 3:13 "Their throats are open *g*;

GREAT (GREATER GREATEST GREATNESS)
Ge 12:2 "I will make you into a *g* nation
Dt 10:17 the *g* God, mighty and awesome,
2Sa 22:36 you stoop down to make me *g*.
Ps 19:11 in keeping them there is *g* reward.
    89:1 of the Lord's *g* love forever;
    103:11 so *g* is his love for those who fear
    107:43 consider the *g* love of the Lord.
    108:4 For *g* is your love, higher
    119:165 *G* peace have they who love your
    145:3 *G* is the Lord and most worthy
Pr 23:24 of a righteous man has *g* joy;
Isa 42:21 to make his law *g* and glorious.
La 3:23 *g* is your faithfulness.
Mk 10:43 whoever wants to become *g*
Lk 21:27 in a cloud with power and *g* glory.
1Ti 6:6 with contentment is *g* gain.
Tit 2:13 glorious appearing of our *g* God
Heb 2:3 if we ignore such a *g* salvation?
1Jn 3:1 How *g* is the love the Father has

GREATER (GREAT)
Mk 12:31 There is no commandment *g*
Jn 1:50 You shall see *g* things than that."
    15:13 *G* love has no one than this,
1Co 12:31 But eagerly desire the *g* gifts.
Heb 11:26 as of *g* value than the treasures
1Jn 3:20 For God is *g* than our hearts,
    4:4 is in you is *g* than the one who is

GREATEST (GREAT)
Mt 22:38 is the first and *g* commandment.
Lk 9:48 least among you all—he is the *g*."
1Co 13:13 But the *g* of these is love.

GREATNESS (GREAT)
Ps 145:3 his *g* no one can fathom.
    150:2 praise him for his surpassing *g*.
Isa 63:1 forward in the *g* of his strength?
Php 3:8 compared to the surpassing *g*

GREED (GREEDY)
Lk 12:15 on your guard against all kinds of *g*
Ro 1:29 kind of wickedness, evil, *g*
Eph 5:3 or of any kind of impurity, or of *g*,
Col 3:5 evil desires and *g*, which is idolatry
2Pe 2:14 experts in *g*—an accursed brood!

GREEDY (GREED)
Pr 15:27 A *g* man brings trouble
1Co 6:10 nor thieves nor the *g* nor drunkards
Eph 5:5 No immoral, impure *g* person—
1Pe 5:2 not *g* for money, but eager to serve;

GREEN
Ps 23:2 makes me lie down in *g* pastures,

GREW (GROW)
Lk 2:52 And Jesus *g* in wisdom and stature,
Ac 16:5 in the faith and *g* daily in numbers.

GRIEF (GRIEVE)
Ps 10:14 O God, do see trouble and *g*;
Pr 14:13 and joy may end in *g*.
La 3:32 Though he brings *g*, he will show
Jn 16:20 but your *g* will turn to joy.
1Pe 1:6 had to suffer *g* in all kinds of trials.

GRIEVE (GRIEF)
Eph 4:30 do not *g* the Holy Spirit of God,
1Th 4:13 or to *g* like the rest of men,

GROUND
Ge 3:17 "Cursed is the *g* because of you;
Ex 3:5 where you are standing is holy *g*."
Eph 6:13 you may be able to stand your *g*,

GROW (GREW)
Pr 13:11 by little makes it *g*.
1Co 3:6 watered it, but God made it *g*.
2Pe 3:18 But *g* in the grace and knowledge

GRUMBLE (GRUMBLING)
1Co 10:10 And do not *g*, as some of them did
Jas 5:9 Don't *g* against each other,

GRUMBLING (GRUMBLE)
Jn 6:43 "Stop *g* among yourselves,"
1Pe 4:9 to one another without *g*.

GUARANTEE (GUARANTEEING)
Heb 7:22 Jesus has become the *g*

GUARANTEEING (GUARANTEE)
2Co 1:22 as a deposit, *g* what is to come.
Eph 1:14 who is a deposit *g* our inheritance

GUARD (GUARDS)
Ps 141:3 Set a *g* over my mouth, O Lord;
Pr 4:23 Above all else, *g* your heart,
Isa 52:12 the God of Israel will be your rear *g*
Mk 13:33 Be on *g*! Be alert! You do not know
1Co 16:13 Be on your *g*; stand firm in the faith
Php 4:7 will *g* your hearts and your minds
1Ti 6:20 *g* what has been entrusted

GUARDS (GUARD)
Pr 13:3 He who *g* his lips *g* his life,
    19:16 who obeys instructions *g* his life,
    21:23 He who *g* his mouth and his tongue
    22:5 he who *g* his soul stays far

GUIDE
Ex 13:21 of cloud to *g* them on their way
    15:13 In your strength you will *g* them
Ne 9:19 cease to *g* them on their path,
Ps 25:5 *g* me in your truth and teach me,
    43:3 let them *g* me;
    48:14 he will be our *g* even to the end.
    67:4 and *g* the nations of the earth.
    73:24 You *g* me with your counsel,
    139:10 even there your hand will *g* me,
Pr 4:11 I *g* you in the way of wisdom
    6:22 When you walk, they will *g* you;
Isa 58:11 The Lord will *g* you always;
Jn 16:13 comes, he will *g* you into all truth.

GUILTY
Ex 34:7 does not leave the *g* unpunished;
Jn 8:46 Can any of you prove me *g* of sin?
Heb 10:22 to cleanse us from a *g* conscience
Jas 2:10 at just one point is *g* of breaking all

HADES
Mt 16:18 the gates of *H* will not overcome it.

HAGAR
Servant of Sarah, wife of Abraham, mother of Ishmael (Ge 16:1-6; 25:12). Driven away by Sarah while pregnant (Ge 16:5-16); after birth of Isaac (Ge 21:9-21; Gal 4:21-31).

HAGGAI*
Post-exilic prophet who encouraged rebuilding of the temple (Ezr 5:1; 6:14; Hag 1-2).

HAIR (HAIRS)
Lk 21:18 But not a *h* of your head will perish
1Co 11:6 for a woman to have her *h* cut

HAIRS (HAIR)
Mt 10:30 even the very *h* of your head are all

HALLELUJAH*
Rev 19:1

HALLOWED (HOLY)
Mt 6:9 *h* be your name,

HAND (HANDS)
Ps 16:8 Because he is at my right *h*,
    37:24 the Lord upholds him with his *h*.
    139:10 even there your *h* will guide me,
Ecc 9:10 Whatever your *h* finds to do,
Mt 6:3 know what your right *h* is doing,
Jn 10:28 one can snatch them out of my *h*.
1Co 12:15 I am not a *h*, I do not belong

HANDS (HAND)
Ps 22:16 they have pierced my *h*
    24:4 He who has clean *h* and a pure
    31:5 Into your *h* I commit my spirit;
    31:15 My times are in your *h*;
Pr 10:4 Lazy *h* make a man poor,
    31:20 and extends her *h* to the needy.
Isa 55:12 will clap their *h*.
    65:2 All day long I have held out my *h*
Lk 23:46 into your *h* I commit my spirit."
1Th 4:11 and to work with your *h*,
1Ti 2:8 to lift up holy *h* in prayer,

5:22 hasty in the laying on of *h*,

HANNAH*
Wife of Elkanah, mother of Samuel (1Sa 1). Prayer at dedication of Samuel (1Sa 2:1-10). Blessed (1Sa 2:18-21).

HAPPY
Ps 68:3 may they be *h* and joyful.
Pr 15:13 A *h* heart makes the face cheerful,
Ecc 3:12 better for men than to be *h*
Jas 5:13 is anyone *h*? Let him sing songs

HARD (HARDEN HARDSHIP)
Ge 18:14 Is anything too *h* for the Lord?
Mt 19:23 it is *h* for a rich man
1Co 4:12 We work *h* with our own hands.
1Th 5:12 to respect those who work *h*

HARDEN (HARD)
Ro 9:18 he hardens whom he wants to *h*.
Heb 3:8 do not *h* your hearts

HARDHEARTED* (HEART)
Dt 15:7 do not be *h* or tightfisted

HARDSHIP (HARD)
Ro 8:35 Shall trouble or *h* or persecution
2Ti 2:3 Endure *h* with us like a good
    4:5 endure *h*, do the work
Heb 12:7 Endure *h* as discipline; God is

HARM
Ps 121:6 the sun will not *h* you by day,
Pr 3:29 not plot *h* against your neighbor,
    31:12 She brings him good, not *h*,
Ro 13:10 Love does no *h* to its neighbor.
1Jn 5:18 and the evil one cannot *h* him.

HARMONY
Ro 12:16 Live in *h* with one another.
2Co 6:15 What *h* is there between Christ
1Pe 3:8 live in *h* with one another;

HARVEST
Mt 9:37 *h* is plentiful but the workers are
Jn 4:35 at the fields! They are ripe for *h*.
Gal 6:9 at the proper time we will reap a *h*
Heb 12:11 it produces a *h* of righteousness

HASTE (HASTY)
Pr 21:5 as surely as *h* leads to poverty.
    29:20 Do you see a man who speaks in *h*?

HASTY* (HASTE)
Pr 19:2 nor to be *h* and miss the way.
Ecc 5:2 be not *h* in your heart
1Ti 5:22 Do not be *h* in the laying

HATE (HATED HATES HATRED)
Lev 19:17 "'Do not *h* your brother
Ps 5:5 you *h* all who do wrong.
    45:7 righteousness and *h* wickedness;
    97:10 those who love the Lord *h* evil,
    139:21 Do I not *h* those who *h* you,
Pr 8:13 To fear the Lord is to *h* evil;
Am 5:15 *H* evil, love good;
Mal 2:16 "I *h* divorce," says the Lord God
Mt 5:43 your neighbor and *h* your enemy.'
    10:22 All men will *h* you because of me,
Lk 6:27 do good to those who *h* you,
Ro 12:9 *H* what is evil; cling to what is good

HATED (HATE)
Ro 9:13 "Jacob I loved, but Esau I *h*."
Eph 5:29 no one ever *h* his own body,
Heb 1:9 righteousness and *h* wickedness;

HATES (HATE)
Pr 6:16 There are six things the Lord *h*,
    13:24 He who spares the rod *h* his son,
Jn 3:20 Everyone who does evil *h* the light,
1Jn 2:9 *h* his brother is still in the darkness.

HATRED (HATE)
Pr 10:12 *H* stirs up dissension,
Jas 4:4 with the world is *h* toward God?

HAUGHTY
Pr 16:18 a *h* spirit before a fall.

HAY
1Co 3:12 costly stones, wood, *h* or straw,

HEAD (HEADS HOTHEADED)
Ge 3:15 he will crush your *h*,
Ps 23:5 You anoint my *h* with oil;
Pr 25:22 will heap burning coals on his *h*,
Isa 59:17 and the helmet of salvation on his *h*

HERITAGE

Mt 8:20 of Man has no place to lay his *h*."
Ro 12:20 will heap burning coals on his *h*."
1Co 11: 3 and the *h* of Christ is God.
 12:21 And the *h* cannot say to the feet,
Eph 5:23 For the husband is the *h* of the wife
2Ti 4: 5 keep your *h* in all situations,
Rev 19:12 and on his *h* are many crowns.

HEADS (HEAD)
Lev 26:13 you to walk with *h* held high.
Isa 35:10 everlasting joy will crown their *h*.

HEAL (HEALED HEALING HEALS)
2Ch 7:14 their sin and will *h* their land.
Ps 41: 4 *h* me, for I have sinned against you
Mt 10: 8 *H* the sick, raise the dead,
Lk 4:23 to me: 'Physician, *h* yourself!
 5:17 present for him to *h* the sick.

HEALED (HEAL)
Isa 53: 5 and by his wounds we are *h*.
Mt 9:22 he said, "your faith has *h* you."
 14:36 and all who touched him were *h*.
Ac 4:10 this man stands before you *h*.
 14: 9 saw that he had faith to be *h*
Jas 5:16 for each other so that you may be *h*
1Pe 2:24 by his wounds you have been *h*.

HEALING (HEAL)
Eze 47:12 for food and their leaves for *h*."
Mal 4: 2 rise with *h* in its wings.
1Co 12: 9 to another gifts of *h*
 12:30 Do all have gifts of *h*? Do all speak
Rev 22: 2 are for the *h* of the nations.

HEALS (HEAL)
Ex 15:26 for I am the LORD, who *h* you."
Ps 103: 3 and *h* all your diseases;
 147: 3 He *h* the brokenhearted

HEALTH (HEALTHY)
Pr 3: 8 This will bring *h* to your body
 15:30 and good news gives *h* to the bones

HEALTHY (HEALTH)
Mk 2:17 "It is not the *h* who need a doctor,

HEAR (HEARD HEARING HEARS)
Dt 6: 4 *H*, O Israel: The LORD our God,
 31:13 must *h* it and learn
2Ch 7:14 then will I *h* from heaven
Ps 94: 9 he who implanted the ear not *h*?
Isa 29:18 that day the deaf will *h* the words
 65:24 while they are still speaking I will *h*
Mt 11:15 He who has ears, let him *h*.
Jn 8:47 reason you do not *h* is that you do
2Ti 4: 3 what their itching ears want to *h*.

HEARD (HEAR)
Job 42: 5 My ears had *h* of you
Isa 66: 8 Who has ever *h* of such a thing?
Mt 5:21 "You have *h* that it was said
 5:27 "You have *h* that it was said,
 5:33 you have *h* that it was said
 5:38 "You have *h* that it was said
 5:43 "You have *h* that it was said,
1Co 2: 9 no ear has *h*,
1Th 2:13 word of God, which you *h* from us,
2Ti 1:13 What you *h* from me, keep
Jas 1:25 not forgetting what he has *h*,

HEARING (HEAR)
Ro 10:17 faith comes from *h* the message,

HEARS (HEAR)
Jn 5:24 whoever *h* my word and believes
1Jn 5:14 according to his will, he *h* us.
Rev 3:20 If anyone *h* my voice and opens

HEART (BROKENHEARTED HARDHEARTED HEARTS WHOLEHEARTEDLY)
Ex 25: 2 each man whose *h* prompts him
Lev 19:17 Do not hate your brother in your *h*.
Dt 4:29 if you look for him with all your *h*
 6: 5 LORD your God with all your *h*
 10:12 LORD your God with all your *h*
 15:10 and do so without a grudging *h*;
 30: 6 you may love him with all your *h*
 30:10 LORD your God with all your *h*
Jos 22: 5 and to serve him with all your *h*
1Sa 13:14 sought out a man after his own *h*
 16: 7 but the LORD looks at the *h*."
2Ki 23: 3 with all his *h* and all his soul,
1Ch 28: 9 for the LORD searches every *h*

2Ch 7:16 and my *h* will always be there.
Job 22:22 and lay up his words in your *h*.
 37: 1 "At this my *h* pounds
Ps 14: 1 The fool says in his *h*,
 19:14 and the meditation of my *h*
 37: 4 will give you the desires of your *h*.
 45: 1 My *h* is stirred by a noble theme
 51:10 Create in me a pure *h*, O God,
 51:17 a broken and contrite *h*,
 66:18 If I had cherished sin in my *h*,
 86:11 give me an undivided *h*,
 119: 11 I have hidden your word in my *h*
 119: 32 for you have set my *h* free.
 139: 23 Search me, O God, and know my *h*
Pr 3: 5 Trust in the LORD with all your *h*
 4:21 keep them within your *h*;
 4:23 Above all else, guard your *h*,
 7: 3 write them on the tablet of your *h*.
 13:12 Hope deferred makes the *h* sick,
 14:13 Even in laughter the *h* may ache,
 15:30 A cheerful look brings joy to the *h*,
 17:22 A cheerful *h* is good medicine,
 24:17 stumbles, do not let your *h* rejoice,
 27:19 so a man's *h* reflects the man.
Ecc 8: 5 wise *h* will know the proper time
SS 4: 9 You have stolen my *h*, my sister,
Isa 40:11 and carries them close to his *h*;
 57:15 and to revive the *h* of the contrite.
Jer 17: 9 The *h* is deceitful above all things
 29:13 when you seek me with all your *h*.
Eze 36:26 I will give you a new *h*
Mt 5: 8 Blessed are the pure in *h*,
 6:21 treasure is, there your *h* will be
 12:34 of the *h* the mouth speaks.
 22:37 the Lord your God with all your *h*
Lk 6:45 overflow of his *h* his mouth speaks.
Ro 2:29 is circumcision of the *h*,
 10:10 is with your *h* that you believe
1Co 14:25 the secrets of his *h* will be laid bare.
Eph 5:19 make music in your *h* to the Lord,
 6: 6 doing the will of God from your *h*.
Col 3:23 work at it with all your *h*,
1Pe 1:22 one another deeply, from the *h*.

HEARTS (HEART)
Dt 11:18 Fix these words of mine in your *h*
1Ki 8:39 for you alone know the *h* of all men
 8:61 your *h* must be fully committed
Ps 62: 8 pour out your *h* to him,
Ecc 3:11 also set eternity in the *h* of men;
Jer 31:33 and write it on their *h*.
Lk 16:15 of men, but God knows your *h*.
 24:32 "Were not our *h* burning within us
Jn 14: 1 "Do not let your *h* be troubled.
Ac 15: 9 for he purified their *h* by faith.
Ro 2:15 of the law are written on their *h*,
2Co 3: 2 written on our *h*, known
 3: 3 but on tablets of human *h*.
 4: 6 shine in our *h* to give us the light
Eph 3:17 dwell in your *h* through faith.
Col 3: 1 set your *h* on things above,
Heb 3: 8 do not harden your *h*
 10:16 I will put my laws in their *h*,
1Jn 3:20 For God is greater than our *h*,

HEAT
2Pe 3:12 and the elements will melt in the *h*.

HEAVEN (HEAVENLY HEAVENS)
Ge 14:19 Creator of *h* and earth.
1Ki 8:27 the highest *h*, cannot contain you.
2Ki 2: 1 up to *h* in a whirlwind,
2Ch 7:14 then will I hear from *h*
Isa 14:12 How you have fallen from *h*,
 66: 1 "*H* is my throne,
Da 7:13 coming with the clouds of *h*.
Mt 6: 9 " 'Our Father in *h*,
 6:20 up for yourselves treasures in *h*,
 6:19 bind on earth will be bound in *h*,
 19:23 man to enter the kingdom of *h*.
 24:35 *H* and earth will pass away,
 26:64 and coming on the clouds of *h*."
 28:18 "All authority in *h*
Mk 16:19 he was taken up into *h*
Lk 15: 7 in *h* over one sinner who repents
 18:22 and you will have treasure in *h*.

Ro 10: 6 'Who will ascend into *h*?' " (that is,
2Co 5: 1 an eternal house in *h*, not built
 12: 2 ago was caught up to the third *h*.
Php 2:10 *h* and on earth and under the earth,
 3:20 But our citizenship is in *h*.
1Th 1:10 and to wait for his Son from *h*,
Heb 8: 5 and shadow of what is in *h*.
 9:24 he entered *h* itself, now to appear
2Pe 3:13 we are looking forward to a new *h*
Rev 21: 1 Then I saw a new *h* and a new earth

HEAVENLY (HEAVEN)
Ps 8: 5 him a little lower than the *h* beings
2Co 5: 2 to be clothed with our *h* dwelling,
Eph 1: 3 in the *h* realms with every spiritual
 1:20 at his right hand in the *h* realms,
2Ti 4:18 bring me safely to his *h* kingdom.
Heb 12:22 to the *h* Jerusalem, the city

HEAVENS (HEAVEN)
Ge 1: 1 In the beginning God created the *h*
1Ki 8:27 The *h*, even the highest heaven,
2Ch 2: 6 since the *h*, even the highest
Ps 8: 3 When I consider your *h*,
 19: 1 The *h* declare the glory of God;
 102:25 the *h* are the work of your hands.
 108: 4 is your love, higher than the *h*;
 119:89 it stands firm in the *h*.
 139: 8 If I go up to the *h*, you are there;
Isa 51: 6 Lift up your eyes to the *h*,
 55: 9 "As the *h* are higher than the earth,
 65:17 new *h* and a new earth.
Joel 2:30 I will show wonders in the *h*
Eph 4:10 who ascended higher than all the *h*,
2Pe 3:10 The *h* will disappear with a roar;

HEBREW
Ge 14:13 and reported this to Abram the *H*.

HEEDS
Pr 13: 1 wise son *h* his father's instruction,
 13:18 whoever *h* correction is honored.
 15: 5 whoever *h* correction shows
 15:32 whoever *h* correction gains

HEEL
Ge 3:15 and you will strike his *h*."

HEIRS (INHERIT)
Ro 8:17 then we are *h*—*h* of God
Gal 3:29 and *h* according to the promise.
Eph 3: 6 gospel the Gentiles are *h* together
1Pe 3: 7 as *h* with you of the gracious gift

HELL
Mt 5:22 will be in danger of the fire of *h*.
Lk 16:23 In *h*, where he was in torment,
2Pe 2: 4 but sent them to *h*, putting them

HELMET
Isa 59:17 and the *h* of salvation on his head;
Eph 6:17 Take the *h* of salvation
1Th 5: 8 and the hope of salvation as a *h*.

HELP (HELPED HELPER HELPING HELPS)
Ps 18: 6 I cried to my God for *h*.
 30: 2 my God, I called to you for *h*
 46: 1 an ever-present *h* in trouble.
 79: 9 *H* us, O God our Savior,
 121: 1 where does my *h* come from?
Isa 41:10 I will strengthen you and *h* you;
Jnh 2: 2 depths of the grave I called for *h*,
Mk 9:24 *h* me overcome my unbelief!"
Ac 16: 9 Come over to Macedonia and *h* us
1Co 12:28 those able to *h* others, those

HELPED (HELP)
1Sa 7:12 "Thus far has the LORD *h* us."

HELPER (HELP)
Ge 2:18 I will make a *h* suitable for him."
Ps 10:14 you are the *h* of the fatherless.
Heb 13: 6 Lord is my *h*; I will not be afraid.

HELPING (HELP)
Ac 9:36 always doing good and *h* the poor.
1Ti 5:10 *h* those in trouble and devoting

HELPS (HELP)
Ro 8:26 the Spirit *h* us in our weakness.

HEN
Mt 23:37 as a *h* gathers her chicks

HERITAGE (INHERIT)
Ps 127: 3 Sons are a *h* from the LORD,

HEROD
1. King of Judea who tried to kill Jesus (Mt 2; Lk 1:5).
2. Son of 1. Tetrarch of Galilee who arrested and beheaded John the Baptist (Mt 14:1-12; Mk 6:14-29; Lk 3:1, 19-20; 9:7-9); tried Jesus (Lk 23:6-15).
3. Grandson of 1. King of Judea who killed James (Ac 12:2); arrested Peter (Ac 12:3-19). Death (Ac 12:19-23).

HERODIAS
Wife of Herod the Tetrarch who persuaded her daughter to ask for John the Baptist's head (Mt 14:1-12; Mk 6:14-29).

HEZEKIAH
King of Judah. Restored the temple and worship (2Ch 29-31). Sought the LORD for help against Assyria (2Ki 18-19; 2Ch 32:1-23; Isa 36-37). Illness healed (2Ki 20:1-11; 2Ch 32:24-26; Isa 38). Judged for showing Babylonians his treasures (2Ki 20:12-21; 2Ch 32:31; Isa 39).

HID (HIDE)
Ge 3: 8 and they *h* from the LORD God
Ex 2: 2 she *h* him for three months.
Jos 6:17 because she *h* the spies we sent.
Heb 11:23 By faith Moses' parents *h* him

HIDDEN (HIDE)
Ps 19:12 Forgive my *h* faults.
  119: 11 I have *h* your word in my heart
Pr 2: 4 and search for it as for *h* treasure,
Isa 59: 2 your sins have *h* his face from you,
Mt 5:14 A city on a hill cannot be *h*.
  13:44 of heaven is like treasure *h*
Col 1:26 the mystery that has been kept *h*
  2: 3 in whom are all the treasures
  3: 3 and your life is now *h* with Christ

HIDE (HID HIDDEN)
Ps 17: 8 *h* me in the shadow of your wings
  143: 9 for I *h* myself in you.

HILL (HILLS)
Mt 5:14 A city on a *h* cannot be hidden.

HILLS (HILL)
Ps 50:10 and the cattle on a thousand *h*.
  121: 1 I lift up my eyes to the *h*—

HINDER (HINDERS)
1Sa 14: 6 Nothing can *h* the LORD
Mt 19:14 come to me, and do not *h* them,
1Co 9:12 anything rather than *h* the gospel
1Pe 3: 7 so that nothing will *h* your prayers.

HINDERS (HINDER)
Heb 12: 1 let us throw off everything that *h*

HINT*
Eph 5: 3 even a *h* of sexual immorality,

HOLD
Ex 20: 7 LORD will not *h* anyone guiltless
Lev 19:13 " 'Do not *h* back the wages
Jos 22: 5 to *h* fast to him and to serve him
Ps 73:23 you *h* me by my right hand.
Pr 4: 4 "Lay *h* of my words
Isa 54: 2 do not *h* back;
Mk 11:25 if you *h* anything against anyone,
Php 2:16 as you *h* out the word of life—
  3:12 but I press on to take *h* of that
Col 1:17 and in him all things *h* together.
1Th 5:21 *H* on to the good.
1Ti 6:12 Take *h* of the eternal life
Heb 10:23 Let us *h* unswervingly

HOLINESS (HOLY)
Ex 15: 11 majestic in *h*,
Ps 29: 2 in the splendor of his *h*.
  96: 9 in the splendor of his *h*;
Ro 6:19 to righteousness leading to *h*.
2Co 7: 1 perfecting *h* out of reverence
Eph 4:24 God in true righteousness and *h*.
Heb 12: 10 that we may share in his *h*.
  12:14 without *h* no one will see the Lord.

HOLY (HALLOWED HOLINESS)
Ex 19: 6 kingdom of priests and a *h* nation.'
  20: 8 the Sabbath day by keeping it *h*.
Lev 11:44 and be *h*, because I am *h*.
  20: 7 " 'Consecrate yourselves and be *h*,
  20:26 You are to be *h* to me because I,
  21: 8 Consider them *h*, because I
  22:32 Do not profane my *h* name.
Ps 16:10 will you let your *H* One see decay.

24: 3 Who may stand in his *h* place?
77:13 Your ways, O God, are *h*.
99: 3 he is *h*.
99: 5 he is *h*.
99: 9 for the LORD our God is *h*.
111: 9 *h* and awesome is his name.
Isa 5:16 the *h* God will show himself *h*
6: 3 *H, h, h* is the LORD Almighty;
40:25 who is my equal?" says the *H* One.
57:15 who lives forever, whose name is *h*:
Eze 28:25 I will show myself *h* among them
Da 9:24 prophecy and to anoint the most *h*.
Hab 2:20 But the LORD is in his *h* temple;
Ac 2:27 will you let your *H* One see decay.
Ro 7:12 and the commandment is *h*,
12: 1 as living sacrifices, *h* and pleasing
Eph 5: 3 improper for God's *h* people.
2Th 1: 10 to be glorified in his *h* people
2Ti 1: 9 saved us and called us to a *h* life—
3:15 you have known the *h* Scriptures,
Tit 1: 8 upright, *h* and disciplined.
1Pe 1:15 But just as he who called you is *h*,
1:16 is written: "Be *h*, because I am *h*."
2: 9 a royal priesthood, a *h* nation,
2Pe 3: 11 You ought to live *h* and godly lives
Rev 4: 8 "*H, h, h* is the Lord God

HOME (HOMES)
Dt 6: 7 Talk about them when you sit at *h*
Ps 84: 3 Even the sparrow has found a *h*,
Pr 3:33 but he blesses the *h* of the righteous
Mk 10:29 "no one who has left *h* or brothers
Jn 14:23 to him and make our *h* with him.
Tit 2: 5 to be busy at *h*, to be kind,

HOMES (HOME)
Ne 4:14 daughters, your wives and your *h*."
1Ti 5:14 to manage their *h* and to give

HOMOSEXUAL*
1Co 6: 9 male prostitutes nor *h* offenders

HONEST
Lev 19:36 Use *h* scales and *h* weights,
Dt 25:15 and *h* weights and measures,
Job 31: 6 let God weigh me in *h* scales
Pr 12:17 truthful witness gives *h* testimony,

HONEY
Ex 3: 8 a land flowing with milk and *h*—
Ps 19: 10 than *h* from the comb.
119: 103 sweeter than *h* to my mouth!

HONOR (HONORABLE HONORABLY HONORED HONORS)
Ex 20: 12 "*H* your father and your mother,
Nu 25:13 he was zealous for the *h* of his God
Dt 5:16 "*H* your father and your mother,
1Sa 2:30 Those who *h* me I will *h*,
Ps 8: 5 and crowned him with glory and *h*.
Pr 3: 9 *H* the LORD with your wealth,
15:33 and humility comes before *h*.
20: 3 It is to a man's *h* to avoid strife,
Mt 15: 4 '*H* your father and mother'
Ro 12: 10 *H* one another above yourselves.
1Co 6:20 Therefore *h* God with your body.
Eph 6: 2 "*H* your father and mother"—
1Ti 5:17 well are worthy of double *h*,
Heb 2: 7 you crowned him with glory and *h*
Rev 4: 9 *h* and thanks to him who sits

HONORABLE (HONOR)
1Th 4: 4 body in a way that is holy and *h*,

HONORABLY (HONOR)
Heb 13:18 and desire to live *h* in every way.

HONORED (HONOR)
Ps 12: 8 when what is vile is *h* among men.
Pr 13:18 but whoever heeds correction is *h*.
1Co 12:26 if one part is *h*, every part rejoices
Heb 13: 4 Marriage should be *h* by all,

HONORS (HONOR)
Ps 15: 4 but *h* those who fear the LORD,
Pr 14: 31 to the needy *h* God.

HOOKS
Isa 2: 4 and their spears into pruning *h*.
Joel 3: 10 and your pruning *h* into spears.

HOPE (HOPES)
Job 13:15 Though he slay me, yet will I *h*
Ps 42: 5 Put your *h* in God,

62: 5 my *h* comes from him.
119: 74 for I have put my *h* in your word.
130: 7 O Israel, put your *h* in the LORD,
147: 11 who put their *h* in his unfailing love
Pr 13:12 *H* deferred makes the heart sick,
Isa 40: 31 but those who *h* in the LORD
Ro 5: 4 character; and character, *h*.
8:24 But *h* that is seen is no *h* at all.
12:12 Be joyful in *h*, patient in affliction,
15: 4 of the Scriptures we might have *h*.
1Co 13:13 now these three remain: faith, *h*
15:19 for this life we have *h* in Christ,
Col 1:27 Christ in you, the *h* of glory.
1Th 5: 8 and the *h* of salvation as a helmet.
1Ti 6:17 but to put their *h* in God,
Tit 2:13 while we wait for the blessed *h*—
Heb 6:19 We have this *h* as an anchor
11: 1 faith is being sure of what we *h* for
1Jn 3: 3 Everyone who has this *h*

HOPES (HOPE)
1Co 13: 7 always *h*, always perseveres.

HORSE
Ps 147: 10 not in the strength of the *h*,
Pr 26: 3 A whip for the *h*, a halter
Zec 1: 8 before me was a man riding a red *h*
Rev 6: 2 and there before me was a white *h*!
6: 4 "Come!" Then another *h* came out,
6: 5 and there before me was a black *h*!
6: 8 and there before me was a pale *h*!
19: 11 and there before me was a white *h*,

HOSANNA
Mt 21: 9 "*H* in the highest!"

HOSHEA
Last king of Israel (2Ki 15:30; 17:1-6).

HOSPITABLE* (HOSPITALITY)
1Ti 3: 2 self-controlled, respectable, *h*,
Tit 1: 8 Rather he must be *h*, one who loves

HOSPITALITY (HOSPITABLE)
Ro 12:13 Practice *h*.
1Ti 5: 10 as bringing up children, showing *h*,
1Pe 4: 9 Offer *h* to one another

HOSTILE
Ro 8: 7 the sinful mind is *h* to God.

HOT
1Ti 4: 2 have been seared as with a *h* iron.
Rev 3:15 that you are neither cold nor *h*.

HOT-TEMPERED
Pr 15:18 A *h* man stirs up dissension,
19:19 A *h* man must pay the penalty;
22:24 Do not make friends with a *h* man,
29:22 and a *h* one commits many sins.

HOTHEADED (HEAD)
Pr 14:16 but a fool is *h* and reckless.

HOUR
Ecc 9:12 knows when his *h* will come:
Mt 6:27 you by worrying can add a single *h*
Lk 12:40 the Son of Man will come at an *h*
Jn 12:23 The *h* has come for the Son of Man
12:27 for this very reason I came to this *h*

HOUSE (HOUSEHOLD STOREHOUSE)
Ex 20:17 shall not covet your neighbor's *h*.
Ps 23: 6 I will dwell in the *h* of the LORD
84: 10 a doorkeeper in the *h* of my God
122: 1 "Let us go to the *h* of the LORD."
127: 1 Unless the LORD builds the *h*,
Pr 7:27 Her *h* is a highway to the grave,
21: 9 than share a *h* with a quarrelsome
Isa 56: 7 a *h* of prayer for all nations."
Zec 13: 6 given at the *h* of my friends'.
Mt 7:24 is like a wise man who built his *h*
12:29 can anyone enter a strong man's *h*
21:13 My *h* will be called a *h* of prayer',
Mk 3:25 If a *h* is divided against itself,
Lk 11:17 a *h* divided against itself will fall.
Jn 2:16 How dare you turn my Father's *h*
12: 3 the *h* was filled with the fragrance
14: 2 In my Father's *h* are many rooms;
Heb 3: 3 the builder of a *h* has greater honor

HOUSEHOLD (HOUSE)
Jos 24:15 my *h*, we will serve the LORD."
Mic 7: 6 are the members of his own *h*.
Mt 10: 36 will be the members of his own *h*.'

	12:25 or *h* divided against itself will not
1Ti	3:12 manage his children and his *h* well.
	3:15 to conduct themselves in God's *h*,

HUMAN (HUMANITY)
Gal 3: 3 to attain your goal by *h* effort?
HUMANITY* (HUMAN)
Heb 2:14 he too shared in their *h* so that
HUMBLE (HUMBLED HUMBLES HUMILIATE HUMILITY)
2Ch 7:14 will *h* themselves and pray
Ps 25: 9 He guides the *h* in what is right
Pr 3:34 but gives grace to the *h*.
Isa 66: 2 he who is *h* and contrite in spirit,
Mt 11:29 for I am gentle and *h* in heart,
Eph 4: 2 Be completely *h* and gentle;
Jas 4:10 *H* yourselves before the Lord,
1Pe 5: 6 *H* yourselves,
HUMBLED (HUMBLE)
Mt 23:12 whoever exalts himself will be *h*,
Php 2: 8 he *h* himself
HUMBLES (HUMBLE)
Mt 18: 4 whoever *h* himself like this child is
23:12 whoever *h* himself will be exalted.
HUMILIATE* (HUMBLE)
Pr 25: 7 than for him to *h* you
1Co 11:22 *h* those who have nothing?
HUMILITY (HUMBLE)
Pr 11: 2 but with *h* comes wisdom.
15:33 and *h* comes before honor.
Php 2: 3 but in *h* consider others better
Tit 3: 2 and to show true *h* toward all men.
1Pe 5: 5 clothe yourselves with *h*
HUNGRY
Ps 107: 9 and fills the *h* with good things.
146: 7 and gives food to the *h*.
Pr 25:21 If your enemy is *h*, give him food
Eze 18: 7 but gives his food to the *h*
Mt 25:35 For I was *h* and you gave me
Lk 1:53 He has filled the *h* with good things
Jn 6:35 comes to me will never go *h*,
Ro 12:20 "If your enemy is *h*, feed him;
HURT (HURTS)
Ecc 8: 9 it over others to his own *h*.
Mk 16:18 deadly poison, it will not *h* them
Rev 2:11 He who overcomes will not be *h*
HURTS* (HURT)
Ps 15: 4 even when it *h*,
Pr 26:28 A lying tongue hates those it *h*,
HUSBAND (HUSBAND'S HUSBANDS)
1Co 7: 3 The *h* should fulfill his marital duty
7:10 wife must not separate from her *h*.
7:11 And a *h* must not divorce his wife.
7:13 And if a woman has a *h* who is not
7:39 A woman is bound to her *h* as long
2Co 11: 2 I promised you to one *h*, to Christ,
Eph 5:23 For the *h* is the head of the wife
5:33 and the wife must respect her *h*.
1Ti 3: 2 the *h* of but one wife, temperate,
HUSBAND'S (HUSBAND)
Pr 12: 4 of noble character is her *h* crown,
1Co 7: 4 the *h* body does not belong
HUSBANDS (HUSBAND)
Eph 5:22 submit to your *h* as to the Lord.
5:25 *H*, love your wives, just
Tit 2: 4 the younger women to love their *h*
1Pe 3: 1 same way be submissive to your *h*
3: 7 *H*, in the same way be considerate
HYMN
1Co 14:26 everyone has a *h*, or a word
HYPOCRISY (HYPOCRITE HYPOCRITES)
Mt 23:28 but on the inside you are full of *h*
1Pe 2: 1 *h*, envy, and slander of every kind.
HYPOCRITE (HYPOCRISY)
Mt 7: 5 You *h*, first take the plank out
HYPOCRITES (HYPOCRISY)
Ps 26: 4 nor do I consort with *h*;
Mt 6: 5 when you pray, do not be like the *h*
HYSSOP
Ps 51: 7 with *h*, and I will be clean;
IDLE (IDLENESS)
1Th 5:14 those who are *i*, encourage

2Th 3: 6 away from every brother who is *i*
1Ti 5:13 they get into the habit of being *i*.
IDLENESS* (IDLE)
Pr 31:27 and does not eat the bread of *i*.
IDOL (IDOLATRY IDOLS)
Isa 44:17 From the rest he makes a god, his *i*;
1Co 8: 4 We know that an *i* is nothing at all
IDOLATRY (IDOL)
Col 3: 5 evil desires and greed, which is *i*.
IDOLS (IDOL)
1Co 8: 1 Now about food sacrificed to *i*:
IGNORANT (IGNORE)
1Co 15:34 for there are some who are *i* of God
Heb 5: 2 to deal gently with those who are *i*
1Pe 2:15 good you should silence the *i* talk
2Pe 3:16 which *i* and unstable people distort
IGNORE (IGNORANT IGNORES)
Dt 22: 1 do not *i* it but be sure
Ps 9:12 he does not *i* the cry of the afflicted
Heb 2: 3 if we *i* such a great salvation?
IGNORES (IGNORE)
Pr 10:17 whoever *i* correction leads others
15:32 He who *i* discipline despises
ILLUMINATED*
Rev 18: 1 and the earth was *i* by his splendor.
IMAGE
Ge 1:26 "Let us make man in our *i*,
1:27 So God created man in his own *i*,
1Co 11: 7 since he is the *i* and glory of God;
Col 1:15 He is the *i* of the invisible God,
3:10 in knowledge in the *i* of its Creator.
IMAGINE
Eph 3:20 more than all we ask or *i*,
IMITATE (IMITATORS)
1Co 4:16 Therefore I urge you to *i* me.
Heb 6:12 but to *i* those who through faith
13: 7 of their way of life and *i* their faith.
3Jn 11 do not *i* what is evil but what is
IMITATORS* (IMITATE)
Eph 5: 1 Be *i* of God, therefore,
1Th 1: 6 You became *i* of us and of the Lord
2:14 became *i* of God's churches
IMMANUEL
Isa 7:14 birth to a son, and will call him *I*.
Mt 1:23 and they will call him *I*"—
IMMORAL* (IMMORALITY)
Pr 6:24 keeping you from the *i* woman,
1Co 5:10 to associate with sexually *i* people
5:10 the people of this world who are *i*,
5:11 but is sexually *i* or greedy,
6: 9 Neither the sexually *i* nor idolaters
Eph 5: 5 No *i*, impure or greedy person—
Heb 12:16 See that no one is sexually *i*,
13: 4 the adulterer and all the sexually *i*.
Rev 21: 8 the murderers, the sexually *i*,
22:15 the sexually *i*, the murderers,
IMMORALITY (IMMORAL)
1Co 6:13 The body is not meant for sexual *i*,
6:18 Flee from sexual *i*.
10: 8 We should not commit sexual *i*,
Gal 5:19 sexual *i*, impurity and debauchery;
Eph 5: 3 must not be even a hint of sexual *i*,
1Th 4: 3 that you should avoid sexual *i*;
Jude 4 grace of our God into a license for *i*.
IMMORTAL* (IMMORTALITY)
Ro 1:23 glory of the *i* God for images made
1Ti 1:17 Now to the King eternal, *i*,
6:16 who alone is *i* and who lives
IMMORTALITY (IMMORTAL)
Ro 2: 7 honor and *i*, he will give eternal life
1Co 15:53 and the mortal with *i*.
2Ti 1:10 and *i* to light through the gospel.
IMPERISHABLE
1Pe 1:23 not of perishable seed, but of *i*,
IMPORTANCE* (IMPORTANT)
1Co 15: 3 passed on to you as of first *i*:
IMPORTANT (IMPORTANCE)
Mt 6:25 Is not life more *i* than food,
23:23 have neglected the more *i* matters
Mk 12:29 "The most *i* one," answered Jesus,
12:33 as yourself is more *i* than all burnt

Php 1:18 The *i* thing is that in every way,
IMPOSSIBLE
Mt 17:20 Nothing will be *i* for you."
Lk 1:37 For nothing is *i* with God."
18:27 "What is *i* with men is possible
Heb 6:18 things in which it is *i* for God to lie,
11: 6 without faith it is *i* to please God,
IMPROPER*
Eph 5: 3 these are *i* for God's holy people.
IMPURE (IMPURITY)
Ac 10:15 not call anything *i* that God has
Eph 5: 5 No immoral, *i* or greedy person—
1Th 4: 7 For God did not call us to be *i*,
Rev 21:27 Nothing *i* will ever enter it,
IMPURITY (IMPURE)
Ro 1:24 hearts to sexual *i* for the degrading
Eph 5: 3 of any kind of *i*, or of greed,
INCENSE
Ex 40: 5 Place the gold altar of *i* in front
Ps 141: 2 my prayer be set before you like *i*;
Mt 2:11 him with gifts of gold and of *i*
INCOME
Ecc 5:10 wealth is never satisfied with his *i*.
1Co 16: 2 sum of money in keeping with his *i*,
INCOMPARABLE*
Eph 2: 7 ages he might show the *i* riches
INCREASE (EVER-INCREASING INCREASED INCREASES INCREASING)
Ge 1:22 "Be fruitful and *i* in number
Ps 62:10 though your riches *i*,
Isa 9: 7 Of the *i* of his government
Lk 17: 5 said to the Lord, "*I* our faith!"
1Th 3:12 May the Lord make your love *i*
INCREASED (INCREASE)
Ac 6: 7 of disciples in Jerusalem *i* rapidly,
Ro 5:20 But where sin *i*, grace *i* all the more
INCREASES (INCREASE)
Pr 24: 5 and a man of knowledge *i* strength;
INCREASING (INCREASE)
Ac 6: 1 when the number of disciples was *i*,
2Th 1: 3 one of you has for each other is *i*.
2Pe 1: 8 these qualities in *i* measure,
INDEPENDENT*
1Co 11:11 however, woman is not *i* of man,
11:11 of man, nor is man *i* of woman.
INDESCRIBABLE*
2Co 9:15 Thanks be to God for his *i* gift!
INDISPENSABLE*
1Co 12:22 seem to be weaker are *i*,
INEFFECTIVE*
2Pe 1: 8 they will keep you from being *i*
INEXPRESSIBLE*
2Co 12: 4 He heard *i* things, things that man
1Pe 1: 8 are filled with an *i* and glorious joy,
INFANTS
Mt 21:16 "'From the lips of children and *i*
1Co 14:20 In regard to evil be *i*,
INFIRMITIES
Isa 53: 4 Surely he took up our *i*
INHERIT (CO-HEIRS HEIRS HERITAGE INHERITANCE)
Ps 37:11 But the meek will *i* the land
37:29 the righteous will *i* the land
Mt 5: 5 for they will *i* the earth.
Mk 10:17 "what must I do to *i* eternal life?"
1Co 15:50 blood cannot *i* the kingdom of God
INHERITANCE (INHERIT)
Dt 4:20 to be the people of his *i*,
Pr 13:22 A good man leaves an *i*
Eph 1:14 who is a deposit guaranteeing our *i*
5: 5 has any *i* in the kingdom of Christ
Heb 9:15 receive the promised eternal *i*—
1Pe 1: 4 and into an *i* that can never perish,
INIQUITIES (INIQUITY)
Ps 78:38 he forgave their *i*
103:10 or repay us according to our *i*.
Isa 59: 2 But your *i* have separated
Mic 7:19 and hurl all our *i* into the depths
INIQUITY (INIQUITIES)
Ps 51: 2 Wash away all my *i*
Isa 53: 6 the *i* of us all.

INJUSTICE

INJUSTICE
2Ch 19: 7 the LORD our God there is no *i*
INNOCENT
Pr 17:26 It is not good to punish an *i* man,
Mt 10:16 shrewd as snakes and as *i* as doves.
   27: 4 "for I have betrayed *i* blood."
1Co 4: 4 but that does not make me *i*.
INSCRIPTION
Mt 22:20 And whose *i*?" "Caesar's,"
INSOLENT
Ro 1:30 God-haters, *i*, arrogant
INSTITUTED
Ro 13: 2 rebelling against what God has *i*,
1Pe 2:13 to every authority *i* among men:
INSTRUCT (INSTRUCTION)
Ps 32: 8 I will *i* you and teach you
Pr 9: 9 *i* a wise man and he will be wiser
Ro 15:14 and competent to *i* one another.
2Ti 2:25 who oppose him he must gently *i*,
INSTRUCTION (INSTRUCT)
Pr 1: 8 Listen, my son, to your father's *i*
   4: 1 Listen, my sons, to a father's *i*;
   4:13 Hold on to *i*, do not let it go;
   8:10 Choose my *i* instead of silver,
   8:33 Listen to my *i* and be wise;
   13: 1 A wise son heeds his father's *i*,
   13:13 He who scorns *i* will pay for it,
   16:20 Whoever gives heed to *i* prospers,
   16:21 and pleasant words promote *i*.
   19:20 Listen to advice and accept *i*,
   23:12 Apply your heart to *i*
1Co 14: 6 or prophecy or word of *i*?
   14:26 or a word of *i*, a revelation,
Eph 6: 4 up in the training and *i* of the Lord.
1Th 4: 8 he who rejects this *i* does not reject
2Th 3:14 If anyone does not obey our *i*
1Ti 1:18 I give you this *i* in keeping
   6: 3 to the sound *i* of our Lord Jesus
2Ti 4: 2 with great patience and careful *i*.
INSULT
Pr 9: 7 corrects a mocker invites *i*;
   12:16 but a prudent man overlooks an *i*.
Mt 5:11 Blessed are you when people *i* you,
Lk 6:22 when they exclude you and you
1Pe 3: 9 evil with evil or *i* with *i*,
INTEGRITY
1Ki 9: 4 if you walk before me in *i* of heart
Job 2: 3 And he still maintains his *i*,
   27: 5 till I die, I will not deny my *i*.
Pr 10: 9 The man of *i* walks securely,
   11: 3 The *i* of the upright guides them,
   29:10 Bloodthirsty men hate a man of *i*
Tit 2: 7 your teaching show *i*, seriousness
INTELLIGENCE
Isa 29:14 the *i* of the intelligent will vanish."
1Co 1:19 *i* of the intelligent I will frustrate."
INTELLIGIBLE
1Co 14:19 I would rather speak five *i* words
INTERCEDE (INTERCEDES INTERCESSION)
Heb 7:25 he always lives to *i* for them.
INTERCEDES (INTERCEDE)
Ro 8:26 but the Spirit himself *i* for us
INTERCESSION* (INTERCEDE)
Isa 53:12 and made *i* for the transgressors.
1Ti 2: 1 *i* and thanksgiving be made
INTERESTS
1Co 7:34 his wife—and his *i* are divided.
Php 2: 4 only to your own *i*, but also to the *i*
   2: 21 everyone looks out for his own *i*,
INTERMARRY (MARRY)
Dt 7: 3 Do not *i* with them.
INVENTED*
2Pe 1:16 We did not follow cleverly *i* stories
INVESTIGATED
Lk 1: 3 I myself have carefully *i* everything
INVISIBLE
Ro 1:20 of the world God's *i* qualities—
Col 1:15 He is the image of the *i* God,
1Ti 1:17 immortal, *i*, the only God,
INVITE (INVITED INVITES)
Lk 14:13 you give a banquet, *i* the poor,

INVITED (INVITE)
Mt 22:14 For many are *i*, but few are chosen
   25:35 I was a stranger and you *i* me in,
INVITES (INVITE)
1Co 10:27 If some unbeliever *i* you to a meal
INVOLVED
2Ti 2: 4 a soldier gets *i* in civilian affairs—
IRON
1Ti 4: 2 have been seared as with a hot *i*.
Rev 2:27 He will rule them with an *i* scepter;
IRREVOCABLE*
Ro 11:29 for God's gifts and his call are *i*.
ISAAC
Son of Abraham by Sarah (Ge 17:19; 21:1-7; 1Ch 1:28). Offered up by Abraham (Ge 22; Heb 11:17-19). Rebekah taken as wife (Ge 24). Fathered Esau and Jacob (Ge 25:19-26; 1Ch 1:34). Tricked into blessing Jacob (Ge 27). Father of Israel (Ex 3:6; Dt 29:13; Ro 9:10).
ISAIAH
Prophet to Judah (Isa 1:1). Called by the LORD (Isa 6).
ISHMAEL
Son of Abraham by Hagar (Ge 16; 1Ch 1:28). Blessed, but not son of covenant (Ge 17:18-21; Gal 4:21-31). Sent away by Sarah (Ge 21:8-21).
ISRAEL (ISRAELITES)
1. Name given to Jacob (see JACOB).
2. Corporate name of Jacob's descendants; often specifically Northern Kingdom.
Dt 6: 4 Hear, O *I*: The LORD our God,
1Sa 4:21 "The glory has departed from *I*"—
Isa 27: 6 *I* will bud and blossom
Jer 31:10 'He who scattered *I* will gather
Eze 39:23 of *I* went into exile for their sin,
Mk 12:29 'Hear, O *I*, the Lord our God,
Lk 22:30 judging the twelve tribes of *I*.
Ro 9: 8 all who are descended from *I* are *I*.
   11:26 And so all *I* will be saved,
Eph 2:12 Gentiles are heirs together with *I*,
ISRAELITES (ISRAEL)
Ex 14:22 and the *I* went through the sea
   16:35 The *I* ate manna forty years,
Hos 1:10 "Yet the *I* will be like the sand
Ro 9:27 the number of the *I* be like the sand
ITCHING*
2Ti 4: 3 to say what their *i* ears want to hear
JACOB
Second son of Isaac, twin of Esau (Ge 26:21-26; 1Ch 1:34). Bought Esau's birthright (Ge 26:29-34); tricked Isaac into blessing him (Ge 27:1-37). Abrahamic covenant perpetuated through (Ge 28:13-15; Mal 1:2). Vision at Bethel (Ge 28:10-22). Wives and children (Ge 29:1-30:24; 35:16-26; 1Ch 2-9). Wrestled with God; name changed to Israel (Ge 32:22-32). Sent sons to Egypt during famine (Ge 42-43). Settled in Egypt (Ge 46). Blessed Ephraim and Manasseh (Ge 48). Blessed sons (Ge 49:1-28; Heb 11:21). Death (Ge 49:29-33). Burial (Ge 50:1-14).
JAMES
1. Apostle; brother of John (Mt 4:21-22; 10:2; Mk 3:17; Lk 5:1-10). At transfiguration (Mt 17:1-13; Mk 9:1-13; Lk 9:28-36). Killed by Herod (Ac 12:2).
2. Apostle; son of Alphaeus (Mt 10:3; Mk 3:18; Lk 6:15).
3. Brother of Jesus (Mt 13:55; Mk 6:3; Lk 24:10; Gal 1:19) and Judas (Jude 1). With believers before Pentecost (Ac 1:13). Leader of church at Jerusalem (Ac 12:17; 15; 21:18; Gal 2:9, 12). Author of epistle (Jas 1:1).
JAPHETH
Son of Noah (Ge 5:32; 1Ch 1:4-5). Blessed (Ge 9:18-28).
JARS
2Co 4: 7 we have this treasure in *j* of clay
JEALOUS (JEALOUSY)
Ex 20: 5 the LORD your God, am a *j* God,
   34:14 whose name is Jealous, is a *j* God.
Dt 4:24 God is a consuming fire, a *j* God.
Joel 2:18 the LORD will be *j* for his land
Zec 1:14 I am very *j* for Jerusalem and Zion,
2Co 11: 2 I am *j* for you with a godly jealousy
JEALOUSY (JEALOUS)
1Co 3: 3 For since there is *j* and quarreling
2Co 11: 2 I am jealous for you with a godly *j*.

Gal 5:20 hatred, discord, *j*, fits of rage,
JEHOAHAZ
1. Son of Jehu; king of Israel (2Ki 13:1-9).
2. Son of Josiah; king of Judah (2Ki 23:31-34; 2Ch 36:1-4).
JEHOASH
Son of Jehoahaz; king of Israel (2Ki 13-14; 2Ch 25).
JEHOIACHIN
Son of Jehoiakim; king of Judah exiled by Nebuchadnezzar (2Ki 24:8-17; 2Ch 36:8-10; Jer 22:24-30; 24:1). Raised from prisoner status (2Ki 25:27-30; Jer 52:31-34).
JEHOIAKIM
Son of Josiah; king of Judah (2Ki 23:34-24:6; 2Ch 36:4-8; Jer 22:18-23; 36).
JEHORAM
Son of Jehoshaphat; king of Judah (2Ki 8:16-24).
JEHOSHAPHAT
Son of Asa; king of Judah (1Ki 22:41-50; 2Ki 3; 2Ch 17-20).
JEHU
King of Israel (1Ki 19:16-19; 2Ki 9-10).
JEPHTHAH
Judge from Gilead who delivered Israel from Ammon (Jdg 10:6-12:7). Made rash vow concerning his daughter (Jdg 11:30-40).
JEREMIAH
Prophet to Judah (Jer 1:1-3). Called by the LORD (Jer 1). Put in stocks (Jer 20:1-3). Threatened for prophesying (Jer 11:18-23; 26). Opposed by Hananiah (Jer 28). Scroll burned (Jer 36). Imprisoned (Jer 37). Thrown into cistern (Jer 38). Forced to Egypt with those fleeing Babylonians (Jer 43).
JEROBOAM
1. Official of Solomon; rebelled to become first king of Israel (1Ki 11:26-40; 12:1-20; 2Ch 10). Idolatry (1Ki 12:25-33); judgment for (1Ki 13-14; 2Ch 13).
2. Son of Jehoash; king of Israel (1Ki 14:23-29).
JERUSALEM
2Ki 23:27 and I will reject *J*, the city I chose,
2Ch 6: 6 now I have chosen *J* for my Name
Ne 2:17 Come, let us rebuild the wall of *J*,
Ps 122: 6 Pray for the peace of *J*:
   125: 2 As the mountains surround *J*,
   137: 5 If I forget you, O *J*,
Isa 40: 9 You who bring good tidings to *J*,
   65:18 for I will create *J* to be a delight
Joel 3:17 *J* will be holy;
Zep 3:16 On that day they will say to *J*,
Zec 2: 4 '*J* will be a city without walls
   8: 8 I will bring them back to live in *J*;
   14: 8 living water will flow out from *J*,
Mt 23:37 "O *J*, *J*, you who kill the prophets
Lk 13:34 die outside *J*! "O *J*, *J*,
   21:24 *J* will be trampled
Jn 4:20 where we must worship is in *J*."
Ac 1: 8 and you will be my witnesses in *J*,
Gal 4:25 corresponds to the present city of *J*
Rev 21: 2 I saw the Holy City, the new *J*,
JESUS
LIFE: Genealogy (Mt 1:1-17; Lk 3:21-37). Birth announced (Mt 1:18-25; Lk 1:26-45). Birth (Mt 2:1-12; Lk 2:1-40). Escape to Egypt (Mt 2:13-23). As a boy in the temple (Lk 2:41-52). Baptism (Mt 3:13-17; Mk 1:9-11; Lk 3:21-22; Jn 1:32-34). Temptation (Mt 4:1-11; Mk 1:12-13; Lk 4:1-13). Ministry in Galilee (Mt 4:12-18:35; Mk 1:14-9:50; Lk 4:14-13:9; Jn 1:35-2:11; 4; 6), Transfiguration (Mt 17:1-8; Mk 9:2-8; Lk 9:28-36), on the way to Jerusalem (Mt 19-20; Mk 10; Lk 13:10-19:27), in Jerusalem (Mt 21-25; Mk 11-13; Lk 19:28-21:38; Jn 2:12-3:36; 5; 7-12). Last supper (Mt 26:17-35; Mk 14:12-31; Lk 22:1-38; Jn 13-17). Arrest and trial (Mt 26:36-27:31; Mk 14:43-15:20; Lk 22:39-23:25; Jn 18:1-19:16). Crucifixion (Mt 27:32-66; Mk 15:21-47; Lk 23:26-55; Jn 19:28-42). Resurrection and appearances (Mt 28; Mk 16; Lk 24; Jn 20-21; Ac 1:1-11; 7:56; 9:3-6; 1Co 15:1-8; Rev 1:1-20).

MIRACLES. Healings: official's son (Jn 4:43-54), demoniac in Capernaum (Mk 1:23-26; Lk 4:33-35), Peter's mother-in-law (Mt 8:14-17; Mk 1:29-31; Lk 4:38-39), leper (Mt 8:2-4; Mk 1:40-45; Lk 5:12-16), paralytic (Mt 9:1-8; Mk 2:1-12; Lk 5:17-26), cripple (Jn 5:1-9), shriveled hand (Mt 12:10-13; Mk 3:1-5; Lk 6:6-11), centurion's servant (Mt 8:5-13; Lk 7:1-10), widow's son raised (Lk 7:11-17), demoniac (Mt 12:22-23; Lk 11:14), Gadarene demoniacs (Mt 8:28-34; Mk 5:1-20; Lk 8:26-39), woman's bleeding and Jairus' daughter (Mt 9:18-26; Mk 5:21-43; Lk 8:40-56), blind man (Mt 9:27-31), mute man (Mt 9:32-33), Canaanite woman's daughter (Mt 15:21-28; Mk 7:24-30), deaf man (Mk 7:31-37), blind man (Mk 8:22-26), demoniac boy (Mt 17:14-18; Mk 9:14-29; Lk 9:37-43), ten lepers (Lk 17:11-19), man born blind (Jn 9:1-7), Lazarus raised (Jn 11), crippled woman (Lk 13:11-17), man with dropsy (Lk 14:1-6), two blind men (Mt 20:29-34; Mk 10:46-52; Lk 18:35-43), Malchus' ear (Lk 22:50-51). Other Miracles: water to wine (Jn 2:1-11), catch of fish (Lk 5:1-11), storm stilled (Mt 8:23-27; Mk 4:37-41; Lk 8:22-25), 5,000 fed (Mt 14:15-21; Mk 6:35-44; Lk 9:10-17; Jn 6:1-14), walking on water (Mt 14:25-33; Mk 6:48-52; Jn 6:15-21), 4,000 fed (Mt 15:32-39; Mk 8:1-9), money from fish (Mt 17:24-27), fig tree cursed (Mt 21:18-22; Mk 11:12-14), catch of fish (Jn 21:1-14).

MAJOR TEACHING: Sermon on the Mount (Mt 5-7; Lk 6:17-49), to Nicodemus (Jn 3), to Samaritan woman (Jn 4), Bread of Life (Jn 6:22-59), at Feast of Tabernacles (Jn 7-8), woes to Pharisees (Mt 23; Lk 11:37-54), Good Shepherd (Jn 10:1-18), Olivet Discourse (Mt 24-25; Mk 13; Lk 21:5-36), Upper Room Discourse (Jn 13-16).

PARABLES: Sower (Mt 13:3-23; Mk 4:3-25; Lk 8:5-18), seed's growth (Mk 4:26-29), wheat and weeds (Mt 13:24-30, 36-43), mustard seed (Mt 13:31-32; Mk 4:30-32), yeast (Mt 13:33; Lk 13:20-21), hidden treasure (Mt 13:44), valuable pearl (Mt 13:45-46), net (Mt 13:47-51), house owner (Mt 13:52), good Samaritan (Lk 10:25-37), unmerciful servant (Mt 18:15-35), lost sheep (Mt 18:10-14; Lk 15:4-7), lost coin (Lk 15:8-10), prodigal son (Lk 15:11-32), dishonest manager (Lk 16:1-13), rich man and Lazarus (Lk 16:19-31), persistent widow (Lk 18:1-8), Pharisee and tax collector (Lk 18:9-14), payment of workers (Mt 20:1-16), tenants and the vineyard (Mt 21:28-46; Mk 12:1-12; Lk 20:9-19), wedding banquet (Mt 22:1-14), faithful servant (Mt 24:45-51), ten virgins (Mt 25:1-13), talents (Mt 25:14-30; Lk 19:12-27).

DISCIPLES see APOSTLES. Call of (Jn 1:35-51; Mt 4:18-22; 9:9; Mk 1:16-20; 2:13-14; Lk 5:1-11, 27-28). Named Apostles (Mt 10:2-4; Mk 3:13-19; Lk 6:12-16). Twelve sent out (Mt 10; Mk 6:7-11; Lk 9:1-5). Seventy sent out (Lk 10:1-24). Defection of (Jn 6:60-71; Mt 26:56; Mk 14:50-52). Final commission (Mt 28:16-20; Jn 21:15-23; Ac 1:3-8).

Ac	2:32	God has raised this *J* to life,
	9: 5	"I am *J*, whom you are persecuting
	15:11	of our Lord *J* that we are saved,
	16:31	"Believe in the Lord *J*,
Ro	3:24	redemption that came by Christ *J*.
	5:17	life through the one man, *J* Christ.
	8: 1	for those who are in Christ *J*,
1Co	2: 2	except *J* Christ and him crucified.
	8: 6	and there is but one Lord, *J* Christ,
	12: 3	and no one can say, "*J* is Lord,"
2Co	4: 5	not preach ourselves, but *J* Christ
Gal	2:16	but by faith in *J* Christ.
	3:28	for you are all one in Christ *J*.
	5: 6	in Christ *J* neither circumcision
Eph	2:10	created in Christ *J*
	2:20	with Christ *J* himself as the chief
Php	1: 6	until the day of Christ *J*.
	2: 5	be the same as that of Christ *J*:
	2:10	name of *J* every knee should bow,
Col	3:17	do it all in the name of the Lord *J*,
2Th	2: 1	the coming of our Lord *J* Christ
1Ti	1:15	Christ *J* came into the world
2Ti	3:12	life in Christ *J* will be persecuted,
Tit	2:13	our great God and Savior, *J* Christ,
Heb	2: 9	But we see *J*, who was made a little
	3: 1	fix your thoughts on *J*, the apostle
	4:14	through the heavens, *J* the Son
	7:22	*J* has become the guarantee
	7:24	but because *J* lives forever,
	12: 2	Let us fix our eyes on *J*, the author
2Pe	1:16	and coming of our Lord *J* Christ,
1Jn	1: 7	and the blood of *J*, his Son,
	2: 1	*J* Christ, the Righteous One.
	2: 6	to live in him must walk as *J* did.
	4:15	anyone acknowledges that *J* is
Rev	22:20	Come, Lord *J*.

JEW (JEWS JUDAISM)

Zec	8:23	of one *J* by the edge of his robe
Ro	1:16	first for the *J*, then for the Gentile.
	10:12	there is no difference between *J*
1Co	9:20	To the Jews I became like a *J*,
Gal	3:28	There is neither *J* nor Greek,

JEWELRY (JEWELS)

1Pe	3: 3	wearing of gold *j* and fine clothes.

JEWELS (JEWELRY)

Isa	61:10	as a bride adorns herself with her *j*.
Zec	9:16	like *j* in a crown.

JEWS (JEW)

Mt	2: 2	who has been born king of the *J*?
	27:11	"Are you the king of the *J*?" "Yes,
Jn	4:22	for salvation is from the *J*.
Ro	3:29	Is God the God of *J* only?
1Co	1:22	*J* demand miraculous signs
	9:20	To the *J* I became like a Jew,
	12:13	whether *J* or Greeks, slave or free
Gal	2: 8	of Peter as an apostle to the *J*,
Rev	3: 9	claim to be *J* though they are not,

JEZEBEL

Sidonian wife of Ahab (1Ki 16:31). Promoted Baal worship (1Ki 16:32-33). Killed prophets of the LORD (1Ki 18:4, 13). Opposed Elijah (1Ki 19:1-2). Had Naboth killed (1Ki 21). Death prophesied (1Ki 21:17-24). Killed by Jehu (2Ki 9:30-37).

JOASH

Son of Ahaziah; king of Judah. Sheltered from Athaliah by Jehoiada (2Ki 11; 2Ch 22:10-23:21). Repaired temple (2Ki 12; 2Ch 24).

JOB

Wealthy man from Uz; feared God (Job 1:1-5). Righteousness tested by disaster (Job 1:6-22), personal affliction (Job 2). Maintained innocence in debate with three friends (Job 3-31), Elihu (Job 32-37). Rebuked by the LORD (Job 38-41). Vindicated and restored to greater stature by the LORD (Job 42). Example of righteousness (Eze 14:14, 20).

JOHN

1. Son of Zechariah and Elizabeth (Lk 1). Called the Baptist (Mt 3:1-12; Mk 1:2-8). Witness to Jesus (Mt 3:11-12; Mk 1:7-8; Lk 3:15-18; Jn 1:6-35; 3:27-30; 5:33-36). Doubts about Jesus (Mt 11:2-6; Lk 7:18-23). Arrest (Mt 4:12; Mk 1:14). Execution (Mt 14:1-12; Mk 6:14-29; Lk 9:7-9). Ministry compared to Elijah (Mt 11:7-19; Mk 9:11-13; Lk 7:24-35).

2. Apostle; brother of James (Mt 4:21-22; 10:2; Mk 3:17; Lk 5:1-10). At transfiguration (Mt 17:1-13; Mk 9:1-13; Lk 9:28-36). Desire to be greatest (Mk 10:35-45). Leader of church at Jerusalem (Ac 4:1-3; Gal 2:9). Elder who wrote epistles (2Jn 1; 3Jn 1). Prophet who wrote Revelation (Rev 1:1; 22:8).

3. Cousin of Barnabas, co-worker with Paul, (Ac 12:12-13:13; 15:37), see MARK.

JOIN (JOINED)

Pr	23:20	Do not *j* those who drink too much
	24:21	and do not *j* with the rebellious,
Ro	15:30	to *j* me in my struggle by praying
2Ti	1: 8	*j* with me in suffering for the gospel

JOINED (JOIN)

Mt	19: 6	Therefore what God has *j* together,
Mk	10: 9	Therefore what God has *j* together,
Eph	2:21	him the whole building is *j* together
	4:16	*j* and held together

JOINTS

Heb	4:12	even to dividing soul and spirit, *j*

JOKING

Eph	5: 4	or coarse *j*, which are out of place,

JONAH

Prophet in days of Jeroboam II (2Ki 14:25). Called to Nineveh; fled to Tarshish (Jnh 1:1-3). Cause of storm; thrown into sea (Jnh 1:4-16). Swallowed by fish (Jnh 1:17). Prayer (Jnh 2). Preached to Nineveh (Jnh 3). Attitude reproved by the LORD (Jnh 4). Sign of (Mt 12:39-41; Lk 11:29-32).

JONATHAN

Son of Saul (1Sa 13:16; 1Ch 8:33). Valiant warrior (1Sa 13-14). Relation to David (1Sa 18:1-4; 19-20; 23:16-18). Killed at Gilboa (1Sa 31). Mourned by David (2Sa 1).

JORAM

1. Son of Ahab; king of Israel (2Ki 3; 8-9; 2Ch 22).

JORDAN

Nu	34:12	boundary will go down along the *J*
Jos	4:22	Israel crossed the *J* on dry ground."
Mt	3: 6	baptized by him in the *J* River.

JOSEPH

1. Son of Jacob by Rachel (Ge 30:24; 1Ch 2:2). Favored by Jacob, hated by brothers (Ge 37:3-4). Dreams (Ge 37:5-11). Sold by brothers (Ge 37:12-36). Served Potiphar; imprisoned by false accusation (Ge 39). Interpreted dreams of Pharaoh's servants (Ge 40), of Pharaoh (Ge 41:4-40). Made greatest in Egypt (Ge 41:41-57). Sold grain to brothers (Ge 42-45). Brought Jacob and sons to Egypt (Ge 46-47). Sons Ephraim and Manasseh blessed (Ge 48). Blessed (Ge 49:22-26; Dt 33:13-17). Death (Ge 50:22-26; Ex 13:19; Heb 11:22). 12,000 from (Rev 7:8).

2. Husband of Mary, mother of Jesus (Mt 1:16-24; 2:13-19; Lk 1:27; 2; Jn 1:45).

3. Disciple from Arimathea, who gave his tomb for Jesus' burial (Mt 27:57-61; Mk 15:43-47; Lk 24:50-52).

4. Original name of Barnabas (Ac 4:36).

JOSHUA

1. Son of Nun; name changed from Hoshea (Nu 13:8, 16; 1Ch 7:27). Fought Amalekites under Moses (Ex 17:9-14). Servant of Moses on Sinai (Ex 24:13; 32:17). Spied Canaan (Nu 13). With Caleb, allowed to enter land (Nu 14:6, 30). Succeeded Moses (Dt 1:38; 31:1-8; 34:9).

Charged Israel to conquer Canaan (Jos 1). Crossed Jordan (Jos 3-4). Circumcised sons of wilderness wanderings (Jos 5). Conquered Jericho (Jos 6), Ai (Jos 7-8), five kings at Gibeon (Jos 10:1-28), southern Canaan (Jos 10:29-43), northern Canaan (Jos 11-12). Defeated at Ai (Jos 7). Deceived by Gibeonites (Jos 9). Renewed covenant (Jos 8:30-35; 24:1-27). Divided land among tribes (Jos 13-22). Last words (Jos 23). Death (Jos 24:28-31).

2. High priest during rebuilding of temple (Hag 1-2; Zec 3:1-9; 6:11).

JOSIAH

Son of Amon; king of Judah (2Ki 22-23; 2Ch 34-35).

JOTHAM

Son of Azariah (Uzziah); king of Judah (2Ki 15:32-38; 2Ch 26:21-27:9).

JOY (ENJOY ENJOYMENT JOYFUL OVERJOYED REJOICE REJOICES REJOICING)

Dt	16:15	and your *j* will be complete.
1Ch	16:27	strength and *j* in his dwelling place.
Ne	8:10	for the *j* of the LORD is your
Est	9:22	their sorrow was turned into *j*
Job	38: 7	and all the angels shouted for *j*?
Ps	4: 7	have filled my heart with greater *j*
	21: 6	with the *j* of your presence.
	30:11	sackcloth and clothed me with *j*,
	43: 4	to God, my *j* and my delight.
	51:12	to me the *j* of your salvation
	66: 1	Shout with *j* to God, all the earth!
	96:12	the trees of the forest will sing for *j*;
	107:22	and tell of his works with songs of *j*
	119:111	they are the *j* of my heart.
Pr	10: 1	A wise son brings *j* to his father,
	10:28	The prospect of the righteous is *j*,
	12:20	but *j* for those who promote peace.
Isa	35:10	everlasting *j* will crown their heads
	51:11	Gladness and *j* will overtake them,
	55:12	You will go out in *j*
Lk	1:44	the baby in my womb leaped for *j*.
	2:10	news of great *j* that will be
Jn	15:11	and that your *j* may be complete.
	16:20	but your grief will turn to *j*.
2Co	8: 2	their overflowing *j* and their
Php	2: 2	then make my *j* complete
	4: 1	and long for, my *j* and crown,
1Th	2:19	For what is our hope, our *j*,
Phm		7 Your love has given me great *j*
Heb	12: 2	for the *j* set before him endured
Jas	1: 2	Consider it pure *j*, my brothers,
1Pe	1: 8	with an inexpressible and glorious *j*
2Jn		4 It has given me great *j* to find some
3Jn		4 I have no greater *j*

JOYFUL (JOY)

Ps	100: 2	come before him with *j* songs.

JUDAH

Hab 3:18 I will be *j* in God my Savior.
1Th 5:16 Be *j* always; pray continually;

JUDAH
1. Son of Jacob by Leah (Ge 29:35; 35:23; 1Ch 2:1). Tribe of blessed as ruling tribe (Ge 49:8-12; Dt 33:7).
2. Name used for people and land of Southern Kingdom.
Jer 13:19 All *J* will be carried into exile.
Zec 10: 4 From *J* will come the cornerstone,
Heb 7:14 that our Lord descended from *J*,

JUDAISM (JEW)
Gal 1:13 of my previous way of life in *J*,

JUDAS
1. Apostle (Lk 6:16; Jn 14:22; Ac 1:13). Probably also called Thaddaeus (Mt 10:3; Mk 3:18).
2. Brother of James and Jesus (Mt 13:55; Mk 6:3), also called Jude (Jude 1).
3. Apostle, also called Iscariot, who betrayed Jesus (Mt 10:4; 26:14-56; Mk 3:19; 14:10-50; Lk 6:16; 22:3-53; Jn 6:71; 12:4; 13:2-30; 18:2-11). Suicide of (Mt 27:3-5; Ac 1:16-25).

JUDGE (JUDGED JUDGES JUDGING JUDGMENT)
Ge 18:25 Will not the *J* of all the earth do
1Ch 16:33 for he comes to *j* the earth.
Ps 9: 8 He will *j* the world in righteousness
Joel 3:12 sit to *j* all the nations on every side.
Mt 7: 1 Do not *j*, or you too will be judged.
Jn 12:47 For I did not come to *j* the world,
Ac 17:31 a day when he will *j* the world
Ro 2:16 day when God will *j* men's secrets
1Co 4: 3 indeed, I do not even *j* myself.
6: 2 that the saints will *j* the world?
Gal 2: 6 not *j* by external appearance—
2Ti 4: 1 who will *j* the living and the dead,
4: 8 which the Lord, the righteous *J*,
Jas 4:12 There is only one Lawgiver and *J*,
4:12 who are you to *j* your neighbor?
Rev 20: 4 who had been given authority to *j*.

JUDGED (JUDGE)
Mt 7: 1 "Do not judge, or you too will be *j*.
1Co 11:31 But if we *j* ourselves, we would not
Jas 3: 1 who teach will be *j* more strictly.
Rev 20:12 The dead were *j* according

JUDGES (JUDGE)
Jdg 2:16 Then the LORD raised up *j*,
Ps 58:11 there is a God who *j* the earth."
Heb 4:12 it *j* the thoughts and attitudes
Rev 19:11 With justice he *j* and makes war.

JUDGING (JUDGE)
Mt 19:28 *j* the twelve tribes of Israel.
Jn 7:24 Stop *j* by mere appearances,

JUDGMENT (JUDGE)
Dt 1:17 of any man, for *j* belongs to God.
Ps 1: 5 the wicked will not stand in the *j*,
119: 66 Teach me knowledge and good *j*,
Pr 6:32 man who commits adultery lacks *j*;
12:11 but he who chases fantasies lacks *j*.
Ecc 12:14 God will bring every deed into *j*,
Isa 66:16 the LORD will execute *j*
Mt 5:21 who murders will be subject to *j*.'
10:15 on the day of *j* than for that town.
12:36 have to give account on the day of *j*
Jn 5:22 but has entrusted all *j* to the Son,
7:24 appearances, and make a right *j*."
16: 8 to sin and righteousness and *j*;
Ro 14:10 stand before God's *j* seat.
14:13 Therefore let us stop passing *j*
1Co 11:29 body of the Lord eats and drinks *j*
2Co 5:10 appear before the *j* seat of Christ,
Heb 9:27 to die once, and after that to face *j*,
10:27 but only a fearful expectation of *j*
1Pe 4:17 For it is time for *j* to begin
Jude 6 bound with everlasting chains for *j*

JUST (JUSTICE JUSTIFICATION JUSTIFIED JUSTIFY JUSTLY)
Dt 32: 4 and all his ways are *j*.
Ps 37:28 For the LORD loves the *j*
111: 7 of his hands are faithful and *j*;
Pr 1: 3 doing what is right and *j* and fair;
2: 8 for he guards the course of the *j*
Da 4:37 does is right and all his ways *j*.
Ro 3:26 as to be *j* and the one who justifies
Heb 2: 2 received its *j* punishment,

1Jn 1: 9 and *j* and will forgive us our sins
Rev 16: 7 true and *j* are your judgments."

JUSTICE (JUST)
Ex 23: 2 do not pervert *j* by siding
23: 6 "Do not deny *j* to your poor people
Job 37:23 in his *j* and great righteousness,
Ps 9: 8 he will govern the peoples with *j*.
9:16 The LORD is known by his *j*;
11: 7 he loves *j*.
45: 6 a scepter of *j* will be the scepter
101: 1 I will sing of your love and *j*;
106: 3 Blessed are they who maintain *j*,
Pr 21:15 When *j* is done, it brings joy
28: 5 Evil men do not understand *j*,
29: 4 By *j* a king gives a country stability
29:26 from the LORD that man gets *j*.
Isa 9: 7 it with *j* and righteousness
28:17 I will make *j* the measuring line
30:18 For the LORD is a God of *j*.
42: 1 and he will bring *j* to the nations.
42: 4 till he establishes *j* on earth.
56: 1 "Maintain *j*
61: 8 "For I, the LORD, love *j*;
Jer 30:11 I will discipline you but only with *j*;
Eze 34:16 I will shepherd the flock with *j*.
Am 5:15 maintain *j* in the courts.
5:24 But let *j* roll on like a river,
Zec 7: 9 'Administer true *j*; show mercy
Lk 11:42 you neglect *j* and the love of God.
Ro 3:25 He did this to demonstrate his *j*,

JUSTIFICATION (JUST)
Ro 4:25 and was raised to life for our *j*.
5:18 of righteousness was *j* that brings

JUSTIFIED (JUST)
Ac 13:39 him everyone who believes is *j*
Ro 3:24 and are *j* freely by his grace
3:28 For we maintain that a man is *j*
5: 1 since we have been *j* through faith,
5: 9 Since we have now been *j*
8:30 those he called, he also *j*; those he *j*.
1Co 6:11 you were *j* in the name
Gal 2:16 observing the law no one will be *j*,
3:11 Clearly no one is *j* before God
3:24 to Christ that we might be *j* by faith
Jas 2:24 You see that a person is *j*

JUSTIFY (JUST)
Gal 3: 8 that God would *j* the Gentiles

JUSTLY (JUST)
Mic 6: 8 To act *j* and to love mercy

KEEP (KEEPER KEEPING KEEPS KEPT)
Ge 31:49 "May the LORD *k* watch
Ex 20: 6 and *k* my commandments.
Nu 6:24 and *k* you;
Ps 18:28 You, O LORD, *k* my lamp burning
19:13 *K* your servant also from willful
119: 9 can a young man *k* his way pure?
121: 7 The LORD will *k* you
141: 3 *k* watch over the door of my lips.
Pr 4:24 corrupt talk far from your lips.
Isa 26: 3 You will *k* in perfect peace
Mt 10:10 for the worker is worth his *k*.
Lk 12:35 and *k* your lamps burning,
Gal 5:25 let us *k* in step with the Spirit.
Eph 4: 3 Make every effort to *k* the unity
1Ti 5:22 *K* yourself pure.
2Ti 4: 5 *k* your head in all situations,
Heb 13: 5 *K* your lives free from the love
Jas 1:26 and yet does not *k* a tight rein
2: 8 If you really *k* the royal law found
Jude 24 able to *k* you from falling

KEEPER (KEEP)
Ge 4: 9 I my brother's *k*?" The LORD

KEEPING (KEEP)
Ex 20: 8 the Sabbath day by *k* it holy.
Ps 19:11 in *k* them there is great reward.
Mt 3: 8 Produce fruit in *k* with repentance.
Lk 2: 8 *k* watch over their flocks at night.
1Co 7:19 *K* God's commands is what counts.
2Pe 3: 9 Lord is not slow in *k* his promise,

KEEPS (KEEP)
Pr 17:28 a fool is thought wise if he *k* silent,
Am 5:13 Therefore the prudent man *k* quiet
1Co 13: 5 is not easily angered, it *k* no record

Jas 2:10 For whoever *k* the whole law

KEPT (KEEP)
Ps 130: 3 If you, O LORD, *k* a record of sins,
2Ti 4: 7 finished the race, I have *k* the faith.
1Pe 1: 4 spoil or fade—*k* in heaven for you,

KEYS
Mt 16:19 I will give you the *k* of the kingdom

KILL (KILLS)
Mt 17:23 They will *k* him, and on the third

KILLS (KILL)
Lev 24:21 but whoever *k* a man must be put
2Co 3: 6 for the letter *k*, but the Spirit gives

KIND (KINDNESS KINDS)
Ge 1:24 animals, each according to its *k*."
2Ch 10: 7 "if you will be *k* to these people
Pr 11:17 A *k* man benefits himself,
12:25 but a *k* word cheers him up.
14:21 blessed is he who is *k* to the needy.
14:31 whoever is *k* to the needy honors
19:17 He who is *k* to the poor lends
Da 2:27 by being *k* to the oppressed.
Lk 6:35 because he is *k* to the ungrateful
1Co 13: 4 Love is patient, love is *k*.
15:35 With what *k* of body will they
Eph 4:32 Be *k* and compassionate
1Th 5:15 but always try to be *k* to each other
2Ti 2:24 instead, he must be *k* to everyone,
Tit 2: 5 to be busy at home, to be *k*,

KINDNESS (KIND)
Ac 14:17 He has shown *k* by giving you rain
Ro 11:22 Consider therefore the *k*
Gal 5:22 peace, patience, *k*, goodness,
Eph 2: 7 expressed in his *k* to us
2Pe 1: 7 brotherly *k*; and to brotherly *k*,

KINDS (KIND)
1Co 12: 4 There are different *k* of gifts,
1Ti 6:10 of money is a root of all *k* of evil.

KING (KINGDOM KINGS)
1. Kings of Judah and Israel: see Saul, David, Solomon.
2. Kings of Judah: see Rehoboam, Abijah, Asa, Jehoshaphat, Jehoram, Ahaziah, Athaliah (Queen), Joash, Amaziah, Uzziah, Jotham, Ahaz, Hezekiah, Manasseh, Amon, Josiah, Jehoahaz, Jehoiakim, Jehoiachin, Zedekiah.
3. Kings of Israel: see Jeroboam I, Nadab, Baasha, Elah, Zimri, Tibni, Omri, Ahab, Ahaziah, Joram, Jehu, Jehoahaz, Jehoash, Jeroboam II, Zechariah, Shallum, Menahem, Pekah, Pekahiah, Hoshea.
Jdg 17: 6 In those days Israel had no *k*;
1Sa 12:12 the LORD your God was your *k*.
Ps 24: 7 that the *K* of glory may come in.
Isa 32: 1 See, a *k* will reign in righteousness
Zec 9: 9 See, your *k* comes to you,
1Ti 6:15 the *K* of kings and Lord of lords,
1Pe 2:17 of believers, fear God, honor the *k*.
Rev 19:16 *K* OF KINGS AND LORD

KINGDOM (KING)
Ex 19: 6 you will be for me a *k* of priests
1Ch 29: 1 Yours, O LORD, is the *k*;
Ps 45: 6 justice will be the scepter of your *k*.
Da 4: 3 His *k* is an eternal *k*;
Mt 3: 2 Repent, for the *k* of heaven is near
5: 3 for theirs is the *k* of heaven.
6:10 your *k* come,
6:33 But seek first his *k* and his
7:21 Lord,' will enter the *k* of heaven,
11:11 least in the *k* of heaven is greater
13:24 "The *k* of heaven is like a man who
13:31 *k* of heaven is like a mustard seed,
13:33 "The *k* of heaven is like yeast that
13:44 *k* of heaven is like treasure hidden
13:45 the *k* of heaven is like a merchant
13:47 *k* of heaven is like a net that was let
16:19 the keys of the *k* of heaven;
18:23 the *k* of heaven is like a king who
19:24 for a rich man to enter the *k* of God
24: 7 rise against nation, and *k* against *k*.
24:14 gospel of the *k* will be preached
25:34 he prepared for you
Mk 9:47 better for you to enter the *k* of God
10:14 for the *k* of God belongs to such
10:23 for the rich to enter the *k* of God!"

Lk 10: 9 'The *k* of God is near you.'
   12: 31 seek his *k*, and these things will be
   17: 21 because the *k* of God is within you
Jn 3: 5 no one can enter the *k* of God
   18: 36 "My *k* is not of this world.
1Co 6: 9 the wicked will not inherit the *k*
   15: 24 hands over the *k* to God the Father
Rev 1: 6 has made us to be a *k* and priests
   11: 15 of the world has become the *k*

KINGS (KING)
Ps 2: 2 The *k* of the earth take their stand
   72: 11 All *k* will bow down to him
Da 7: 24 ten horns are ten *k* who will come
1Ti 2: 2 for *k* and all those in authority,
Rev 1: 5 and the ruler of the *k* of the earth.

KINSMAN-REDEEMER (REDEEM)
Ru 3: 9 over me, since you are a *k*."

KISS
Ps 2: 12 *K* the Son, lest he be angry
Pr 24: 26 is like a *k* on the lips.
Lk 22: 48 the Son of Man with a *k*?"

KNEE (KNEES)
Isa 45: 23 Before me every *k* will bow;
Ro 14: 11 'every *k* will bow before me;
Php 2: 10 name of Jesus every *k* should bow,

KNEES (KNEE)
Isa 35: 3 steady the *k* that give way;
Heb 12: 12 your feeble arms and weak *k*.

KNEW (KNOW)
Job 23: 3 If only I *k* where to find him;
Jnh 4: 2 I *k* that you are a gracious
Mt 7: 23 tell them plainly, 'I never *k* you.

KNOCK
Mt 7: 7 *k* and the door will be opened
Rev 3: 20 I am! I stand at the door and *k*.

KNOW (FOREKNEW KNEW KNOWING KNOWLEDGE KNOWN KNOWS)
Dt 18: 21 "How can we *k* when a message
Job 19: 25 I *k* that my Redeemer lives,
   42: 3 things too wonderful for me to *k*.
Ps 46: 10 "Be still, and *k* that I am God;
   139: 1 and you *k* me.
   139: 23 Search me, O God, and *k* my heart;
Pr 27: 1 for you do not *k* what a day may
Jer 24: 7 I will give them a heart to *k* me,
   31: 34 his brother, saying, '*K* the LORD',
Mt 6: 3 let your left hand *k* what your right
   24: 42 you do not *k* on what day your
Lk 1: 4 so that you may *k* the certainty
Jn 3: 11 we speak of what we *k*,
   4: 22 we worship what we do *k*,
   9: 25 One thing I do *k*.
   10: 14 I *k* my sheep and my sheep *k* me—
   17: 3 that they may *k* you, the only true
   21: 24 We *k* that his testimony is true.
Ac 1: 7 "It is not for you to *k* the times
Ro 6: 6 For we *k* that our old self was
   7: 18 I *k* that nothing good lives in me,
   8: 28 we *k* that in all things God works
1Co 2: 2 For I resolved to *k* nothing
   6: 15 Do you not *k* that your bodies are
   6: 19 Do you not *k* that your body is
   13: 12 Now I *k* in part; then I shall *k* fully,
   15: 58 because you *k* that your labor
Php 3: 10 I want to *k* Christ and the power
2Ti 1: 12 because I *k* whom I have believed,
Jas 4: 14 *k* what will happen tomorrow.
1Jn 2: 4 The man who says, "I *k* him,"
   3: 14 We *k* that we have passed
   3: 16 This is how we *k* what love is:
   5: 2 This is how we *k* that we love
   5: 13 so that you may *k* that you have

KNOWING (KNOW)
Ge 3: 5 and you will be like God, *k* good
Php 3: 8 of *k* Christ Jesus my Lord,

KNOWLEDGE (KNOW)
Ge 2: 9 the tree of the *k* of good and evil.
Job 42: 3 obscures my counsel without *k*?'
Ps 19: 2 night after night they display *k*.
   73: 11 Does the Most High have *k*?"
   139: 6 Such *k* is too wonderful for me,
Pr 1: 7 of the LORD is the beginning of *k*,

   10: 14 Wise men store up *k*,
   12: 1 Whoever loves discipline loves *k*,
   13: 16 Every prudent man acts out of *k*,
   19: 2 to have zeal without *k*,
Isa 11: 9 full of the *k* of the LORD
Hab 2: 14 filled with the *k* of the glory
Ro 11: 33 riches of the wisdom and *k* of God!
1Co 8: 1 *K* puffs up, but love builds up.
   8: 11 Christ died, is destroyed by your *k*.
   13: 2 can fathom all mysteries and all *k*,
2Co 2: 14 everywhere the fragrance of the *k*
   4: 6 light of the *k* of the glory of God
Eph 3: 19 to know this love that surpasses *k*
Col 2: 3 all the treasures of wisdom and *k*.
1Ti 6: 20 ideas of what is falsely called *k*,
2Pe 3: 18 grow in the grace and *k* of our Lord

KNOWN (KNOW)
Ps 16: 11 You have made *k* to me the path
   105: 1 make *k* among the nations what he
Isa 46: 10 *k* the end from the beginning,
Mt 10: 26 or hidden that will not be made *k*.
Ro 1: 19 since what may be *k* about God is
   11: 34 "Who has *k* the mind of the Lord?
   15: 20 the gospel where Christ was not *k*,
2Co 3: 2 written on our hearts, *k*
2Pe 2: 21 than to have *k* it and then

KNOWS (KNOW)
1Sa 2: 3 for the LORD is a God who *k*,
Job 23: 10 But he *k* the way that I take;
Ps 44: 21 since he *k* the secrets of the heart?
   94: 11 The LORD *k* the thoughts of man;
Ecc 8: 7 Since no man *k* the future,
Mt 6: 8 for your Father *k* what you need
   24: 36 "No one *k* about that day or hour,
Ro 8: 27 who searches our hearts *k* the mind
1Co 8: 2 who thinks he *k* something does
2Ti 2: 19 The Lord *k* those who are his," and

LABAN
Brother of Rebekah (Ge 24:29-51), father of Rachel and Leah (Ge 29-31).

LABOR
Ex 20: 9 Six days you shall *l* and do all your
Isa 55: 2 and your *l* on what does not satisfy
Mt 6: 28 They do not *l* or spin.
1Co 3: 8 rewarded according to his own *l*.
   15: 58 because you know that your *l*

LACK (LACKING LACKS)
Pr 15: 22 Plans fail for *l* of counsel,
Ro 3: 3 Will their *l* of faith nullify God's
Col 2: 23 any value in restraining sensual

LACKING (LACK)
Ro 12: 11 Never be *l* in zeal, but keep your
Jas 1: 4 and complete, not *l* anything.

LACKS (LACK)
Pr 6: 32 who commits adultery *l* judgment;
   12: 11 he who chases fantasies *l* judgment
Jas 1: 5 any of you *l* wisdom, he should ask

LAID (LAY)
Isa 53: 6 and the LORD has *l* on him
1Co 3: 11 other than the one already *l*,
1Jn 3: 16 Jesus Christ *l* down his life for us.

LAKE
Rev 19: 20 into the fiery *l* of burning sulfur.
   20: 14 The *l* of fire is the second death.

LAMB (LAMB'S LAMBS)
Ge 22: 8 "God himself will provide the *l*
Ex 12: 21 and slaughter the Passover *l*.
Isa 11: 6 The wolf will live with the *l*,
   53: 7 he was led like a *l* to the slaughter,
Jn 1: 29 *L* of God, who takes away the sin
1Co 5: 7 our Passover *l*, has been sacrificed.
1Pe 1: 19 a *l* without blemish or defect.
Rev 5: 6 Then I saw a *L*, looking
   5: 12 "Worthy is the *L*, who was slain,
   14: 1 They follow the *L* wherever he

LAMB'S (LAMB)
Rev 21: 27 written in the *L* book of life.

LAMBS (LAMB)
Lk 10: 3 I am sending you out like *l*—
Jn 21: 15 Jesus said, "Feed my *l*."

LAMENT
2Sa 1: 17 took up this *l* concerning Saul

LAMP (LAMPS)
2Sa 22: 29 You are my *l*, O LORD;
Ps 18: 28 You, O LORD, keep my *l* burning;
   119: 105 Your word is a *l* to my feet
Pr 21: 18 and her *l* does not go out at night.
Lk 8: 16 "No one lights a *l* and hides it
Rev 21: 23 gives it light, and the Lamb is its *l*.

LAMPS (LAMP)
Mt 25: 1 be like ten virgins who took their *l*
Lk 12: 35 for service and keep your *l* burning,

LAND
Ge 1: 10 God called the dry ground "*l*,"
   1: 11 "Let the *l* produce vegetation:
   12: 7 To your offspring I will give this *l*."
Ex 3: 8 a *l* flowing with milk and honey—
Nu 35: 33 Do not pollute the *l* where you are.
Dt 34: 1 LORD showed him the whole *l*—
Jos 13: 2 "This is the *l* that remains:
   14: 3 Levites received no share of the *l*
2Ch 7: 14 their sin and will heal their *l*.
   7: 20 then I will uproot Israel from my *l*,
Eze 36: 24 and bring you back into your own *l*.

LANGUAGE
Ge 11: 1 Now the whole world had one *l*
Ps 19: 3 There is no speech or *l*
Jn 8: 44 When he lies, he speaks his native *l*
Ac 2: 6 heard them speaking in his own *l*.
Col 3: 8 slander, and filthy *l* from your lips.
Rev 5: 9 from every tribe and *l* and people

LAST (LASTING LASTS LATTER)
2Sa 23: 1 These are the *l* words of David:
Isa 44: 6 I am the first and I am the *l*;
Mt 19: 30 But many who are first will be *l*,
Mk 10: 31 are first will be *l*, and the *l* first."
Jn 15: 16 and bear fruit—fruit that will *l*.
Ro 1: 17 by faith from first to *l*,
2Ti 3: 1 will be terrible times in the *l* days.
2Pe 3: 3 in the *l* days scoffers will come,
Rev 1: 17 I am the First and the *L*.
   22: 13 the First and the *L*, the Beginning

LASTING (LAST)
Ex 12: 14 to the LORD—a *l* ordinance.
Lev 24: 8 of the Israelites, as a *l* covenant.
Nu 25: 13 have a covenant of a *l* priesthood,
Heb 10: 34 had better and *l* possessions.

LASTS (LAST)
Ps 30: 5 For his anger *l* only a moment,
2Co 3: 11 greater is the glory of that which *l*!

LATTER (LAST)
Job 42: 12 The LORD blessed the *l* part

LAUGH (LAUGHS)
Ecc 3: 4 a time to weep and a time to *l*,

LAUGHS (LAUGH)
Ps 2: 4 The One enthroned in heaven *l*;
   37: 13 but the Lord *l* at the wicked,

LAVISHED
Eph 1: 8 of God's grace that he *l* on us
1Jn 3: 1 great is the love the Father has *l*

LAW (LAWS)
Dt 31: 11 you shall read this *l* before them
   31: 26 "Take this Book of the *L*
Jos 1: 8 of the *L* depart from your mouth;
Ne 8: 8 from the Book of the *L* of God,
Ps 1: 2 and on his *l* he meditates day
   19: 7 The *l* of the LORD is perfect,
   119: 18 wonderful things in your *l*.
   119: 72 *l* from your mouth is more precious
   119: 97 Oh, how I love your *l*!
   119: 165 peace have they who love your *l*,
Isa 8: 20 To the *l* and to the testimony!
Jer 31: 33 "I will put my *l* in their minds
Mt 5: 17 that I have come to abolish the *L*
   7: 12 sums up the *L* and the Prophets.
   22: 40 All the *L* and the Prophets hang
Lk 16: 17 stroke of a pen to drop out of the *L*.
Jn 1: 17 For the *l* was given through Moses;
Ro 2: 12 All who sin apart from the *l* will
   2: 15 of the *l* are written on their hearts,
   5: 13 for before the *l* was given,
   5: 20 *l* was added so that the trespass
   6: 14 because you are not under *l*,
   7: 6 released from the *l* so that we serve

LAWLESSNESS

	7:12	l is holy, and the commandment is
	8: 3	For what the l was powerless to do
	10: 4	Christ is the end of the l
	13:10	love is the fulfillment of the l.
Gal	3:13	curse of the l by becoming a curse
	3:24	So the l was put in charge to lead us
	5: 3	obligated to obey the whole l.
	5: 4	justified by l have been alienated
	5:14	The entire l is summed up
Heb	7:19	(for the l made nothing perfect),
	10: 1	The l is only a shadow
Jas	1:25	intently into the perfect l that gives
	2:10	For whoever keeps the whole l

LAWLESSNESS*
2Th	2: 3	and the man of l is revealed,
	2: 7	power of l is already at work;
1Jn	3: 4	sins breaks the law; in fact, sin is l.

LAWS (LAW)
Lev	25:18	and be careful to obey my l,
Ps	119: 30	I have set my heart on your l.
	119: 120	I stand in awe of your l.
Heb	8:10	I will put my l in their minds
	10:16	I will put my l in their hearts,

LAY (LAID LAYING)
Job	22:22	and l up his words in your heart.
Isa	28:16	"See, I l a stone in Zion,
Mt	8:20	of Man has no place to l his head."
Jn	10:15	and I l down my life for the sheep.
	15:13	that he l down his life
1Co	3:11	no one can l any foundation other
1Jn	3:16	And we ought to l down our lives
Rev	4:10	They l their crowns

LAYING (LAY)
| 1Ti | 5:22 | Do not be hasty in the l on of hands |
| Heb | 6: 1 | not l again the foundation |

LAZARUS
1. Poor man in Jesus' parable (Lk 16:19-31).
2. Brother of Mary and Martha whom Jesus raised from the dead (Jn 11:1-12:19).

LAZY
| Pr | 10: 4 | L hands make a man poor, |
| Heb | 6:12 | We do not want you to become l, |

LEAD (LEADERS LEADERSHIP LEADS LED)
Ex	15:13	"In your unfailing love you will l
Ps	27:11	l me in a straight path
	61: 2	l me to the rock that is higher
	139: 24	and l me in the way everlasting.
	143: 10	l me on level ground.
Ecc	5: 6	Do not let your mouth l you
Isa	11: 6	and a little child will l them.
Da	12: 3	those who l many to righteousness,
Mt	6:13	And l us not into temptation,
1Jn	3: 7	do not let anyone l you astray.

LEADERS (LEAD)
| Heb | 13: 7 | Remember your l, who spoke |
| | 13:17 | Obey your l and submit |

LEADERSHIP (LEAD)
| Ro | 12: 8 | if it is l, let him govern diligently; |

LEADS (LEAD)
Ps	23: 2	he l me beside quiet waters,
Pr	19:23	The fear of the LORD l to life:
Isa	40:11	he gently l those that have young.
Mt	7:13	and broad is the road that l
	15:14	If a blind man l a blind man,
Jn	10: 3	sheep by name and l them out.
Ro	14:19	effort to do what l to peace
2Co	2:14	always l us in triumphal procession

LEAH
Wife of Jacob (Ge 29:16-30); bore six sons and one daughter (Ge 29:31-30:21; 34:1; 35:23).

LEAN
| Pr | 3: 5 | not on your own understanding; |

LEARN (LEARNED LEARNING)
| Isa | 1:17 | l to do right! |
| Mt | 11:29 | yoke upon you and l from me, |

LEARNED (LEARN)
| Php | 4:11 | for l have l to be content whatever |
| 2Ti | 3:14 | continue in what you have l |

LEARNING (LEARN)
| Pr | 1: 5 | let the wise listen and add to their l, |
| 2Ti | 3: 7 | always l but never able |

LED (LEAD)
Ps	68:18	you l captives in your train;
Isa	53: 7	he was l like a lamb to the slaughter
Am	2:10	and I l you forty years in the desert
Ro	8:14	those who are l by the Spirit
Eph	4: 8	he l captives in his train

LEFT
Jos	1: 7	turn from it to the right or to the l,
Pr	4:27	Do not swerve to the right or the l;
Mt	6: 3	do not let your l hand know what
	25:33	on his right and the goats on his l.

LEGION
| Mk | 5: 9 | "My name is L," he replied, |

LEND (LENDS)
Dt	15: 8	freely l him whatever he needs.
Ps	37:26	are always generous and l freely;
Lk	6:34	if you l to those from whom you

LENDS (LEND)
| Pr | 19:17 | to the poor l to the LORD, |

LENGTH (LONG)
| Ps | 90:10 | The l of our days is seventy years— |
| Pr | 10:27 | The fear of the LORD adds l to life |

LEPROSY
| 2Ki | 7: 3 | men with l at the entrance |

LETTER (LETTERS)
Mt	5:18	not the smallest l, not the least
2Co	2	You yourselves are our l, written
	3	for the l kills, but the Spirit gives
2Th	3:14	not obey our instruction in this l,

LETTERS (LETTER)
2Co	3: 7	which was engraved in l on stone,
	10:10	"His l are weighty and forceful,
2Pe	3:16	His l contain some things that are

LEVEL
Ps	143: 10	lead me on l ground.
Pr	4:26	Make l paths for your feet
Isa	26: 7	The path of the righteous is l;
Heb	12:13	"Make l paths for your feet,"

LEVI (LEVITES)
1. Son of Jacob by Leah (Ge 29:34; 46:11; 1Ch 2:1). Tribe of blessed (Ge 49:5-7; Dt 33:8-11), chosen as priests (Nu 3-4), numbered (Nu 3:39; 26:62), allotted cities, but not land (Nu 18; 35; Dt 10:9; Jos 13:14; 21), land (Eze 48:8-22), 12,000 from (Rev 7:7).
2. See MATTHEW.

LEVITES (LEVI)
Nu	1:53	The L are to be responsible
	8: 6	"Take the L from among the other
	18:21	I give to the L all the tithes in Israel

LEWDNESS
| Mk | 7:22 | malice, deceit, l, envy, slander, |

LIAR (LIE)
Pr	19:22	better to be poor than a l.
Jn	8:44	for he is a l and the father of lies.
Ro	3: 4	Let God be true, and every man a l.

LIBERATED*
| Ro | 8:21 | that the creation itself will be l |

LIE (LIAR LIED LIES LYING)
Lev	19:11	" 'Do not l.
Nu	23:19	God is not a man, that he should l,
Dt	6: 7	when you l down and when you get
Ps	23: 2	me l down in green pastures,
Isa	11: 6	leopard will l down with the goat,
Eze	34:14	they will l down in good grazing
Ro	1:25	exchanged the truth of God for a l,
Col	3: 9	Do not l to each other,
Heb	6:18	which it is impossible for God to l,

LIED (LIE)
| Ac | 5: 4 | You have not l to men but to God." |

LIES (LIE)
| Ps | 34:13 | and your lips from speaking l. |
| Jn | 8:44 | for he is a liar and the father of l. |

LIFE (LIVE)
Ge	2: 7	into his nostrils the breath of l;
	2: 9	of the garden were the tree of l
	9:11	Never again will l be cut
Ex	21:23	you are to take l for l, eye for eye,
Lev	17:14	l of every creature is its blood.
	24:18	must make restitution—l for l.
Dt	30:19	Now choose l, so that you
Ps	16:11	known to me the path of l;

	23: 6	all the days of my l
	34:12	Whoever of you loves l
	39: 4	let me know how fleeting is my l.
	49: 7	No man can redeem the l
	104: 33	I will sing to the LORD all my l;
Pr	1: 3	a disciplined and prudent l,
	6:23	are the way to l,
	7:23	little knowing it will cost him his l.
	8:35	For whoever finds me finds l
	11:30	of the righteous is a tree of l,
	21:21	finds l, prosperity and honor.
Jer	10:23	that a man's l is not his own;
Eze	37: 5	enter you, and you will come to l.
Da	12: 2	some to everlasting l, others
Mt	6:25	Is not l more important than food,
	7:14	and narrow the road that leads to l,
	10:39	Whoever finds his l will lose it,
	16:25	wants to save his l will lose it,
	20:28	to give his l as a ransom for many."
Mk	10:45	to give his l as a ransom for many."
Lk	12:15	a man's l does not consist
	12:22	do not worry about your l,
	14:26	even his own l— he cannot be my
Jn	1: 4	In him was l, and that l was
	3:15	believes in him may have eternal l.
	3:36	believes in the Son has eternal l,
	4:14	of water welling up to eternal l."
	5:24	him who sent me has eternal l
	6:35	Jesus declared, "I am the bread of l
	6:47	he who believes has everlasting l.
	6:68	You have the words of eternal l.
	10:10	I have come that they may have l,
	10:15	and I lay down my l for the sheep.
	10:28	I give them eternal l, and they shall
	11:25	"I am the resurrection and the l.
	14: 6	am the way and the truth and the l.
	15:13	lay down his l for his friends.
	20:31	that by believing you may have l
Ac	13:48	appointed for eternal l believed.
Ro	4:25	was raised to l for our justification.
	6:13	have been brought from death to l;
	6:23	but the gift of God is eternal l
	8:38	convinced that neither death nor l,
1Co	15:19	If only for this l we have hope
2Co	3: 6	letter kills, but the Spirit gives l.
Gal	2:20	The l I live in the body, I live
Eph	4: 1	I urge you to live a l worthy
Php	2:16	as you hold out the word of l—
Col	1:10	order that you may live a l worthy
1Th	4:12	so that your daily l may win
1Ti	4: 8	for both the present l and the l
	4:16	Watch your l and doctrine closely.
	6:19	hold of the l that is truly l.
2Ti	3:12	to live a godly l in Christ Jesus will
Jas	1:12	crown of l that God has promised
	3:13	Let him show it by his good l,
1Pe	3:10	"Whoever would love l
2Pe	1: 3	given us everything we need for l
1Jn	3:14	we have passed from death to l,
	5:11	has given us eternal l, and this l is
Rev	13: 8	written in the book of l belonging
	20:12	was opened, which is the book of l.
	21:27	written in the Lamb's book of l.
	22: 2	side of the river stood the tree of l,

LIFT (LIFTED)
Ps	121: 1	I l up my eyes to the hills—
	134: 2	L up your hands in the sanctuary
La	3:41	Let us l up our hearts and our
1Ti	2: 8	everywhere to l up holy hands

LIFTED (LIFT)
Ps	40: 2	He l me out of the slimy pit,
Jn	3:14	Moses l up the snake in the desert,
	12:32	when I am l up from the earth,

LIGHT (ENLIGHTENED)
Ge	1: 3	"Let there be l," and there was l.
2Sa	22:29	LORD turns my darkness into l.
Job	38:19	"What is the way to the abode of l?
Ps	4: 6	Let the l of your face shine upon us
	19: 8	giving l to the eyes.
	27: 1	LORD is my l and my salvation—
	56:13	God in the l of life.
	76: 4	You are resplendent with l,
	104: 2	He wraps himself in l

LORD‡

	119: 105	and a *l* for my path.
	119: 130	The unfolding of your words gives *l*;
Isa	2: 5	let us walk in the *l* of the LORD.
	9: 2	have seen a great *l*;
	49: 6	also make you a *l* for the Gentiles,
Mt	4: 16	have seen a great *l*;
	5: 16	let your *l* shine before men,
	11: 30	yoke is easy and my burden is *l*."
Jn	3: 19	but men loved darkness instead of *l*
	8: 12	he said, "I am the *l* of the world.
2Co	4: 6	made his *l* shine in our hearts
	6: 14	Or what fellowship can *l* have
	11: 14	masquerades as an angel of *l*.
1Ti	6: 16	and who lives in unapproachable *l*,
1Pe	2: 9	of darkness into his wonderful *l*.
1Jn	1: 5	God is *l*; in him there is no
	1: 7	But if we walk in the *l*,
Rev	21: 23	for the glory of God gives it *l*,

LIGHTNING
Da	10: 6	his face like *l*, his eyes like flaming
Mt	24: 27	For as the *l* that comes from the east
	28: 3	His appearance was like *l*,

LIKENESS
Ge	1: 26	man in our image, in our *l*,
Ps	17: 15	I will be satisfied with seeing your *l*.
Isa	52: 14	his form marred beyond human *l*—
Ro	8: 3	Son in the *l* of sinful man
	8: 29	to be conformed to the *l* of his Son,
2Co	3: 18	his *l* with ever-increasing glory,
Php	2: 7	being made in human *l*.
Jas	3: 9	who have been made in God's *l*.

LILIES
Lk	12: 27	"Consider how the *l* grow.

LION
Isa	11: 7	and the *l* will eat straw like the ox.
1Pe	5: 8	around like a roaring *l* looking
Rev	5: 5	See, the *L* of the tribe of Judah,

LIPS
Ps	8: 2	From the *l* of children and infants
	34: 1	his praise will always be on my *l*.
	119: 171	May my *l* overflow with praise,
Pr	13: 3	He who guards his *l* guards his life,
	27: 2	someone else, and not your own *l*.
Isa	6: 5	For I am a man of unclean *l*,
Mt	21: 16	"'From the *l* of children
Col	3: 8	and filthy language from your *l*.

LISTEN (LISTENING LISTENS)
Dt	30: 20	to his voice, and hold fast to him.
Pr	1: 5	let the wise *l* and add
Jn	10: 27	My sheep *l* to my voice; I know
Jas	1: 19	Everyone should be quick to *l*,
	1: 22	Do not merely *l* to the word,

LISTENING (LISTEN)
1Sa	3: 9	Speak, LORD, for your servant is *l*
Pr	18: 13	He who answers before *l*—

LISTENS (LISTEN)
Pr	12: 15	but a wise man *l* to advice.

LIVE (ALIVE LIFE LIVES LIVING)
Ex	20: 12	so that you may *l* long
	33: 20	for no one may see me and *l*."
Dt	8: 3	to teach you that man does not *l*
Job	14: 14	If a man dies, will he *l* again?
Ps	119: 175	Let me *l* that I may praise you,
Isa	55: 3	hear me, that your soul may *l*.
Eze	37: 3	can these bones *l*?" I said,
Hab	2: 4	but the righteous will *l* by his faith
Mt	4: 4	'Man does not *l* on bread alone,
Ac	17: 28	'For in him we *l* and move
Ro	1: 17	"The righteous will *l* by faith."
2Co	5: 7	We *l* by faith, not by sight.
Gal	2: 20	The life I *l* in the body, I *l* by faith
	5: 25	Since we *l* by the Spirit, let us keep
Php	1: 21	to *l* is Christ and to die is gain.
1Th	5: 13	*L* in peace with each other.
2Ti	3: 12	who wants to *l* a godly life
Heb	12: 14	Make every effort to *l* in peace
1Pe	1: 17	*l* your lives as strangers here

LIVES (LIVE)
Job	19: 25	I know that my Redeemer *l*,
Isa	57: 15	he who *l* forever, whose name is
Da	3: 28	to give up their *l* rather than serve
Jn	14: 17	for he *l* with you and will be in you.
Ro	7: 18	I know that nothing good *l* in me,
	14: 7	For none of us *l* to himself alone
1Co	3: 16	and that God's Spirit *l* in you?
Gal	2: 20	I no longer live, but Christ *l* in me.
Heb	13: 5	Keep your *l* free from the love
2Pe	3: 11	You ought to live holy and godly *l*
1Jn	3: 16	to lay down our *l* for our brothers.
	4: 16	Whoever *l* in love *l* in God,

LIVING (LIVE)
Ge	2: 7	and man became a *l* being.
Jer	2: 13	the spring of *l* water,
Mt	22: 32	the God of the dead but of the *l*."
Jn	7: 38	streams of *l* water will flow
Ro	12: 1	to offer your bodies as *l* sacrifices,
Heb	4: 12	For the word of God is *l* and active.
	10: 31	to fall into the hands of the *l* God.
Rev	1: 18	I am the *L* One; I was dead,

LOAD
Gal	6: 5	for each one should carry his own *l*.

LOCUSTS
Mt	3: 4	His food was *l* and wild honey.

LOFTY
Ps	139: 6	too *l* for me to attain.
Isa	57: 15	is what the high and *l* One says—

LONELY
Ps	68: 6	God sets the *l* in families,

LONG (LENGTH LONGED LONGING LONGS)
1Ki	18: 21	"How *l* will you waver
Jn	9: 4	As *l* as it is day, we must do
Eph	3: 18	to grasp how wide and *l* and high
1Pe	1: 12	Even angels *l* to look

LONGED (LONG)
Mt	13: 17	righteous men *l* to see what you see
	23: 37	how often I have *l*
2Ti	4: 8	to all who have *l* for his appearing.

LONGING (LONG)
Pr	13: 19	A *l* fulfilled is sweet to the soul,
2Co	5: 2	*l* to be clothed with our heavenly

LONGS (LONG)
Isa	30: 18	Yet the LORD *l* to be gracious

LOOK (LOOKING LOOKS)
Dt	4: 29	you will find him if you *l* for him
Job	31: 1	not to *l* lustfully at a girl.
Ps	34: 5	Those who *l* to him are radiant;
Pr	4: 25	Let your eyes *l* straight ahead,
Isa	60: 5	Then you will *l* and be radiant,
Hab	1: 13	Your eyes are too pure to *l* on evil;
Zec	12: 10	They will *l* on me, the one they
Mk	13: 21	'*L*, here is the Christ!' or, '*L*,
Lk	24: 39	*L* at my hands and my feet.
Jn	1: 36	he said, "*L*, the Lamb of God!"
	4: 35	open your eyes and *l* at the fields!
	19: 37	"They will *l* on the one they have
Jas	1: 27	to *l* after orphans and widows
1Pe	1: 12	long to *l* into these things.

LOOKING (LOOK)
2Co	10: 7	You are *l* only on the surface
Rev	5: 6	I saw a Lamb, *l* as if it had been

LOOKS (LOOK)
1Sa	16: 7	Man *l* at the outward appearance,
Lk	9: 62	and *l* back is fit for service
Php	2: 21	For everyone *l* out

LORD† (LORD'S† LORDING)
Ne	4: 14	Remember the *L*, who is great
Job	28: 28	'The fear of the *L*— that is wisdom,
Ps	54: 4	the *L* is the one who sustains me.
	62: 12	and that you, O *L*, are loving.
	86: 5	You are forgiving and good, O *L*,
	110: 1	The LORD says to my *L*:
	147: 5	Great is our *L* and mighty in power
Isa	6: 1	I saw the *L* seated on a throne,
Da	9: 4	"O *L*, the great and awesome God,
Mt	3: 3	'Prepare the way for the *L*,
	4: 7	'Do not put the *L* your God
	7: 21	"Not everyone who says to me, '*L*,
	22: 37	" 'Love the *L* your God
	22: 44	For he says, " 'The *L* said to my *L*:
Mk	12: 11	the *L* has done this,
	12: 29	the *L* our God, the *L* is one.
Lk	2: 9	glory of the *L* shone around them,
	6: 46	"Why do you call me, '*L*, *L*,'
	10: 27	" 'Love the *L* your God
Ac	2: 21	on the name of the *L* will be saved.'
	16: 31	replied, "Believe in the *L* Jesus,
Ro	10: 9	with your mouth, "Jesus is *L*,"
	10: 13	on the name of the *L* will be saved
	12: 11	your spiritual fervor, serving the *L*.
	14: 8	we live to the *L*; and if we die,
1Co	1: 31	Let him who boasts boast in the *L*."
	3: 5	the *L* has assigned to each his task.
	7: 34	to be devoted to the *L* in both body
	10: 9	We should not test the *L*,
	11: 23	For I received from the *L* what I
	12: 3	"Jesus is *L*," except by the Holy
	15: 57	victory through our *L* Jesus Christ.
	16: 22	If anyone does not love the *L*—
2Co	3: 17	Now the *L* is the Spirit,
	8: 5	they gave themselves first to the *L*
	10: 17	Let him who boasts boast in the *L*."
Gal	6: 14	in the cross of our *L* Jesus Christ,
Eph	4: 5	one *L*, one faith, one baptism;
	5: 10	and find out what pleases the *L*.
	5: 19	make music in your heart to the *L*,
Php	2: 11	confess that Jesus Christ is *L*,
	3: 1	my brothers, rejoice in the *L*!
	4: 4	Rejoice in the *L* always.
Col	2: 6	as you received Christ Jesus as *L*,
	3: 17	do it all in the name of the *L* Jesus,
	3: 23	as working for the *L*, not for men,
	4: 17	work you have received in the *L*."
1Th	3: 12	May the *L* make your love increase
	5: 2	day of the *L* will come like a thief
	5: 23	at the coming of our *L* Jesus Christ.
2Th	2: 1	the coming of our *L* Jesus Christ
2Ti	2: 19	"The *L* knows those who are his,"
Heb	12: 14	holiness no one will see the *L*.
	13: 6	*L* is my helper; I will not be afraid.
Jas	4: 10	Humble yourselves before the *L*,
1Pe	1: 25	the word of the *L* stands forever."
	2: 3	you have tasted that the *L* is good.
	3: 15	in your hearts set apart Christ as *L*.
2Pe	1: 16	and coming of our *L* Jesus Christ,
	2: 1	the sovereign *L* who bought
	3: 9	The *L* is not slow in keeping his
Jude	14	the *L* is coming with thousands
Rev	4: 8	holy, holy is the *L* God Almighty,
	4: 11	"You are worthy, our *L* and God,
	17: 14	he is *L* of lords and King of kings—
	22: 20	Come, *L* Jesus.

LORD'S† (LORD†)
Ac	21: 14	and said, "The *L* will be done."
1Co	10: 26	"The earth is the *L*, and everything
	11: 26	you proclaim the *L* death
2Co	3: 18	faces all reflect the *L* glory,
2Ti	2: 24	And the *L* servant must not quarrel
Jas	4: 15	you ought to say, "If it is the *L* will,

LORDING* (LORD†)
1Pe	5: 3	not *l* it over those entrusted to you,

LORD‡ (LORD'S‡)
Ge	2: 4	When the *L* God made the earth
	2: 7	the *L* God formed the man
	3: 21	The *L* God made garments of skin
	7: 16	Then the *L* shut him in.
	15: 6	Abram believed the *L*,
	18: 14	Is anything too hard for the *L*?
	31: 49	"May the *L* keep watch
Ex	3: 2	the angel of the *L* appeared to him
	9: 12	he hardened Pharaoh's heart
	14: 30	That day the *L* saved Israel
	20: 2	"I am the *L* your God, who
	33: 11	The *L* would speak to Moses face
	40: 34	glory of the *L* filled the tabernacle.

‡This entry represents the translation of the Hebrew name for God. *Yahweh*, always indicated in the NIV by Lord. For LORD, see the concordance entries LORD† and LORD'S†.

LORD'S‡

Lev	19: 2	'Be holy because I, the L your God,
Nu	8: 5	L said to Moses: "Take the Levites
	14: 21	glory of the L fills the whole earth,
Dt	2: 7	forty years the L your God has
	5: 9	the L your God, am a jealous God,
	6: 4	The L our God, the L is one.
	6: 5	Love the L your God
	6: 16	Do not test the L your God
	10: 14	To the L your God belong
	10: 17	For the L your God is God of gods
	11: 1	Love the L your God and keep his
	28: 1	If you fully obey the L your God
	30: 16	today to love the L your God,
	30: 20	For the L is your life, and he will
	31: 6	for the L your God goes with you;
Jos	22: 5	to love the L your God, to walk
	24: 15	my household, we will serve the L
1Sa	1: 28	So now I give him to the L.
	2: 2	"There is no one holy like the L;
	7: 12	"Thus far has the L helped us."
	12: 22	his great name the L will not reject
	15: 22	"Does the L delight
2Sa	22: 2	"The L is my rock, my fortress
1Ki	2: 3	and observe what the L your God
	8: 11	the glory of the L filled his temple
	8: 61	fully committed to the L our God,
	18: 21	If the L is God, follow him;
2Ki	13: 23	But the L was gracious to them
1Ch	16: 8	Give thanks to the L, call
	16: 23	Sing to the L, all the earth;
	28: 9	for the L searches every heart
	29: 11	O L, is the greatness and the power
2Ch	5: 14	the glory of the L filled the temple
	16: 9	of the L range throughout the earth
	19: 6	judging for man but for the L,
	30: 9	for the L your God is gracious
Ne	1: 5	Then I said: "O L, God of heaven,
Job	1: 21	L gave and the L has taken away;
	38: 1	the L answered Job out
	42: 9	and the L accepted Job's prayer.
Ps	1: 2	But his delight is in the law of the L
	9: 9	The L is a refuge for the oppressed,
	12: 6	And the words of the L are flawless
	16: 8	I have set the L always before me.
	18: 30	the word of the L is flawless.
	19: 7	The law of the L is perfect,
	19: 14	O L, my Rock and my Redeemer.
	23: 1	The L is my shepherd, I shall not be
	23: 6	I will dwell in the house of the L
	27: 1	The L is my light and my salvation
	27: 4	to gaze upon the beauty of the L
	29: 1	Ascribe to the L, O mighty ones,
	32: 2	whose sin the L does not count
	33: 12	is the nation whose God is the L,
	33: 18	But the eyes of the L are
	34: 3	Glorify the L with me;
	34: 7	The angel of the L encamps
	34: 8	Taste and see that the L is good;
	34: 18	The L is close to the brokenhearted
	37: 4	Delight yourself in the L
	40: 1	I waited patiently for the L;
	47: 2	How awesome is the L Most High,
	48: 1	Great is the L, and most worthy
	55: 22	Cast your cares on the L
	75: 8	In the hand of the L is a cup
	84: 11	For the L God is a sun and shield;
	86: 11	Teach me your way, O L,
	89: 5	heavens praise your wonders, O L,
	91: 2	I will say of the L, "He is my refuge
	95: 1	Come, let us sing for joy to the L;
	96: 1	Sing to the L a new song;
	98: 4	Shout for joy to the L, all the earth,
	100: 1	Shout for joy to the L, all the earth.
	103: 1	Praise the L, O my soul;
	103: 8	The L is compassionate
	104: 1	O L my God, you are very great;
	107: 8	to the L for his unfailing love
	110: 1	The L says to my Lord:
	113: 4	L is exalted over all the nations,
	115: 1	Not to us, O L, not to us
	116: 15	Precious in the sight of the L
	118: 1	Give thanks to the L, for he is good
	118: 24	This is the day the L has made;
	121: 2	My help comes from the L,
	121: 5	The L watches over you—
	125: 2	so the L surrounds his people
	127: 1	Unless the L builds the house,
	127: 3	Sons are a heritage from the L,
	130: 3	If you, O L, kept a record of sins,
	135: 6	The L does whatever pleases him,
	136: 1	Give thanks to the L, for he is good
	139: 1	O L, you have searched me
	144: 3	O L, what is man that you care
	145: 3	Great is the L and most worthy
	145: 18	The L is near to all who call on him
Pr	1: 7	The fear of the L is the beginning
	3: 5	Trust in the L with all your heart
	3: 9	Honor the L with your wealth,
	3: 12	the L disciplines those he loves,
	3: 19	By wisdom the L laid the earth's
	5: 21	are in full view of the L,
	6: 16	There are six things the L hates,
	10: 27	The fear of the L adds length to life
	11: 1	The L abhors dishonest scales,
	12: 22	The L detests lying lips,
	14: 26	He who fears the L has a secure
	15: 3	The eyes of the L are everywhere,
	16: 2	but motives are weighed by the L.
	16: 4	The L works out everything
	16: 9	but the L determines his steps.
	16: 33	but its every decision is from the L.
	18: 10	The name of the L is a strong tower
	18: 22	and receives favor from the L.
	19: 14	but a prudent wife is from the L.
	19: 17	to the poor lends to the L,
	21: 3	to the L than sacrifice.
	21: 30	that can succeed against the L.
	21: 31	but victory rests with the L.
	22: 2	The L is the Maker of them all.
	24: 18	or the L will see and disapprove
	31: 30	a woman who fears the L is
Isa	6: 3	holy, holy is the L Almighty;
	11: 2	The Spirit of the L will rest on him
	11: 9	full of the knowledge of the L
	12: 2	The L, the L, is my strength
	24: 1	the L is going to lay waste the earth
	25: 8	The Sovereign L will wipe away
	29: 15	to hide their plans from the L,
	33: 6	the fear of the L is the key
	35: 10	the ransomed of the L will return.
	40: 5	the glory of the L will be revealed,
	40: 7	the breath of the L blows on them.
	40: 10	the Sovereign L comes with power,
	40: 28	The L is the everlasting God,
	40: 31	but those who hope in the L
	42: 8	"I am the L; that is my name!
	43: 11	I, even I, am the L,
	44: 24	I am the L,
	45: 5	I am the L, and there is no other;
	45: 21	Was it not I, the L?
	51: 11	The ransomed of the L will return.
	53: 6	and the L has laid on him
	53: 10	and the will of the L will prosper
	55: 6	Seek the L while he may be found;
	58: 8	of the L will be your rear guard.
	58: 11	The L will guide you always;
	59: 1	the arm of the L is not too short
	61: 3	a planting of the L
	61: 10	I delight greatly in the L;
Jer	1: 9	Then the L reached out his hand
	9: 24	I am the L, who exercises kindness,
	16: 19	O L, my strength and my fortress,
	17: 7	is the man who trusts in the L,
La	3: 40	and let us return to the L.
Eze	1: 28	of the likeness of the glory of the L.
Hos	1: 7	horsemen, but by the L their God."
	3: 5	They will come trembling to the L
	6: 1	"Come, let us return to the L.
Joel	2: 1	for the day of the L is coming.
	2: 11	The day of the L is great;
	3: 14	For the day of the L is near
Am	5: 18	long for the day of the L?
Jnh	1: 3	But Jonah ran away from the L
Mic	4: 2	up to the mountain of the L,
	6: 8	And what does the L require of you
Na	1: 2	The L takes vengeance on his foes
	1: 3	The L is slow to anger
Hab	2: 14	knowledge of the glory of the L,
Zep	2: 20	But the L is in his holy temple;
	3: 17	The L your God is with you,
Zec	1: 17	and the L will again comfort Zion
	9: 16	The L their God will save them
	14: 5	Then the L my God will come,
	14: 9	The L will be king
Mal	4: 5	and dreadful day of the L comes.

LORD'S‡ (LORD‡)

Ex	34: 34	he entered the L presence
Nu	14: 41	you disobeying the L command?
Dt	6: 18	is right and good in the L sight,
	32: 9	For the L portion is his people,
Jos	21: 45	Not one of all the L good promises
Ps	24: 1	The earth is the L, and everything
	32: 10	but the L unfailing love
	89: 1	of the L great love forever;
	103: 17	L love is with those who fear him,
Pr	3: 11	do not despise the L discipline
Isa	24: 14	west they acclaim the L majesty.
	62: 3	of splendor in the L hand,
Jer	48: 10	lax in doing the L work!
La	3: 22	of the L great love we are not
Mic	4: 1	of the L temple will be established

LOSE (LOSES LOSS LOST)

1Sa	17: 32	"Let no one / heart on account
Mt	10: 39	Whoever finds his life will / it,
Lk	9: 25	and yet / or forfeit his very self?
Jn	6: 39	that I shall / none of all that he has
Heb	12: 3	will not grow weary and / heart.
	12: 5	do not / heart when he rebukes you

LOSES (LOSE)

Mt	5: 13	But if the salt / its saltiness,
Lk	15: 4	you has a hundred sheep and / one
	15: 8	has ten silver coins and / one.

LOSS (LOSE)

Ro	11: 12	and their / means riches
1Co	3: 15	he will suffer /; he himself will be
Php	3: 8	I consider everything / compared

LOST (LOSE)

Ps	73: 2	I had nearly / my foothold.
Jer	50: 6	"My people have been / sheep;
Eze	34: 4	the strays or searched for the /.
	34: 16	for the / and bring back the strays.
Mt	18: 14	any of these little ones should be /.
Lk	15: 4	go after the / sheep until he finds it?
	15: 6	with me; I have found my / sheep.'
	15: 9	with me; I have found my / coin.'
	15: 24	is alive again; he was / and is found
	19: 10	to seek and to save what was /."
Php	3: 8	for whose sake I have / all things.

LOT (LOTS)

Nephew of Abraham (Ge 11:27; 12:5). Chose to live in Sodom (Ge 13). Rescued from Sodom (Ge 14). Rescued from Sodom (Ge 19:1-29; 2Pe 2:7). Fathered Moab and Ammon by his daughters (Ge 19:30-38).

Est	3: 7	the (/) in the presence of Haman
	9: 24	the (/) for their ruin and destruction.
Pr	16: 33	The / is cast into the lap,
	18: 18	Casting the / settles disputes
Ecc	3: 22	his work, because that is his /.
Ac	1: 26	Then they drew lots, and the / fell

LOTS (LOT)

| Ps | 22: 18 | and cast / for my clothing. |
| Mt | 27: 35 | divided up his clothes by casting /. |

LOVE (BELOVED LOVED LOVELY LOVER LOVERS LOVES LOVING)

Ge	22: 2	your only son, Isaac, whom you /,
Ex	15: 13	"In your unfailing / you will lead
	20: 6	showing / to a thousand generations
	20: 6	of those who / me
	34: 6	abounding in / and faithfulness,
Lev	19: 18	but / your neighbor as yourself.
	19: 34	L him as yourself,
Nu	14: 18	abounding in / and forgiving sin
Dt	5: 10	showing / to a thousand generations
	5: 10	of those who / me
	6: 5	L the LORD your God
	7: 13	He will / you and bless you
	10: 12	to walk in all his ways, to / him,
	11: 13	to / the LORD your God
	13: 6	wife you /, or your closest friend
	30: 6	so that you may / him
Jos	22: 5	to / the LORD your God, to walk

1Ki	3: 3	Solomon showed his *l*
	8:23	you who keep your covenant of *l*
2Ch	5:13	his *l* endures forever."
Ne	1: 5	covenant of *l* with those who / him
Ps	18: 1	I love you, O Lord, my strength.
	23: 6	Surely goodness and *l* will follow
	25: 6	O Lord, your great mercy and *l*,
	31:16	save me in your unfailing *l*.
	32:10	but the Lord's unfailing *l*
	33: 5	the earth is full of his unfailing *l*.
	33:18	whose hope is in his unfailing *l*,
	36: 5	Your *l*, O Lord, reaches
	36: 7	How priceless is your unfailing *l*!
	45: 7	You *l* righteousness and hate
	51: 1	according to your unfailing *l*;
	57:10	For great is your *l*, reaching
	63: 3	Because your *l* is better than life,
	66:20	or withheld his *l* from me!
	70: 4	may those who *l* your salvation
	77: 8	Has his unfailing *l* vanished forever
	85: 7	Show us your unfailing *l*, O Lord
	85:10	*L* and faithfulness meet together;
	86:13	For great is your *l* toward me;
	89: 1	I will sing of the Lord's *l* forever;
	89:33	but I will not take my *l* from him,
	92: 2	to proclaim your *l* in the morning
	94:18	your *l*, O Lord, supported me.
	100: 5	is good and his *l* endures forever;
	101: 1	I will sing of your *l* and justice;
	103: 4	crowns you with *l* and compassion.
	103: 8	slow to anger, abounding in *l*.
	103:11	so great is his *l* for those who fear
	107: 8	to the Lord for his unfailing *l*
	108: 4	For great is your *l*, higher
	116: 1	I *l* the Lord, for he heard my
	118: 1	his *l* endures forever.
	119: 47	because I *l* them.
	119: 64	The earth is filled with your *l*,
	119: 76	May your unfailing *l* be my
	119: 97	Oh, how I *l* your law!
	119:119	therefore I *l* your statutes.
	119:124	your servant according to your *l*
	119:132	to those who *l* your name.
	119:159	O Lord, according to your *l*.
	119:163	but I *l* your law.
	119:165	peace have they who *l* your law,
	122: 6	"May those who *l* you be secure.
	130: 7	for with the Lord is unfailing *l*
	136: 1	*l* -26 His *l* endures forever.
	143: 8	of your unfailing *l*,
	145: 8	slow to anger and rich in *l*.
	145: 20	over all who *l* him,
	147: 11	who put their hope in his unfailing *l*
Pr	3: 3	Let *l* and faithfulness never leave
	4: 6	*l* her, and she will watch over you.
	5:19	you ever be captivated by her *l*.
	8:17	I *l* those who *l* me,
	9: 8	rebuke a wise man and he will *l* you
	10:12	but *l* covers over all wrongs.
	14:22	those who plan what is good find *l*
	15:17	of vegetables where there is *l*
	17: 9	over an offense promotes *l*,
	19:22	What a man desires is unfailing *l*;
	20: 6	claims to have unfailing *l*,
	20:13	Do not *l* sleep or you will grow
	20:28	through / his throne is made secure
	21: 21	who pursues righteousness and *l*
	27: 5	rebuke than hidden *l*.
Ecc	9: 6	Their *l*, their hate
	9: 9	life with your wife, whom you *l*
SS	2: 4	and his banner over me is *l*.
	8: 6	for *l* is as strong as death,
	8: 7	Many waters cannot quench *l*;
	8: 7	all the wealth of his house for *l*,
Isa	5: 1	I will sing for the one I *l*
	16: 5	In *l* a throne will be established;
	38:17	In your *l* you kept me
	54:10	yet my unfailing *l* for you will not
	55: 3	my faithful *l* promised to David.
	61: 8	"For I, the Lord, *l* justice;
	63: 9	In his *l* and mercy he redeemed
Jer	5: 31	and my people *l* it this way.
	31: 3	you with an everlasting *l*;
	32:18	You show *l* to thousands
La	3:22	of the Lord's great *l* we are not
	3:32	so great is his unfailing *l*.
Eze	33:32	more than one who sings *l* songs
Da	9: 4	covenant of *l* with all who *l* him
Hos	2:19	in *l* and compassion.
	3: 1	Go, show your *l* to your wife again,
	11: 4	with ties of *l*;
	12: 6	maintain *l* and justice,
Joel	2:13	slow to anger and abounding in *l*,
Am	5:15	Hate evil, *l* good;
Mic	3: 2	you who hate good and *l* evil;
	6: 8	To act justly and to *l* mercy
Zep	3:17	he will quiet you with his *l*,
Zec	8:19	Therefore *l* truth and peace."
Mt	3:17	"This is my Son, whom I *l*;
	5:44	*L* your enemies and pray
	6:24	he will hate the one and *l* the other,
	17: 5	"This is my Son, whom I *l*;
	19:19	and *l* your neighbor as yourself'."
	22:37	"*L* the Lord your God
Lk	6:32	Even 'sinners' *l* those who *l* them.
	7:42	which of them will *l* him more?"
	20:13	whom I *l*; perhaps they will respect
Jn	13:34	I give you: *L* one another.
	13:35	disciples, if you *l* one another."
	14:15	"If you *l* me, you will obey what I
	15:13	Greater *l* has no one than this,
	15:17	This is my command: *L* each other.
	21:15	do you truly *l* me more than these
Ro	5: 5	because God has poured out his *l*
	5: 8	God demonstrates his own *l* for us
	8:28	for the good of those who *l* him,
	8:35	us from the *l* of Christ?
	8:39	us from the *l* of God that is
	12: 9	*L* must be sincere.
	12:10	to one another in brotherly *l*.
	13: 8	continuing debt to *l* one another,
	13: 9	"*L* your neighbor as yourself."
	13:10	Therefore *l* is the fulfillment
	13:10	*L* does no harm to its neighbor.
1Co	2: 9	prepared for those who *l* him"—
	8: 1	Knowledge puffs up, but *l* builds up
	13: 1	have not *l*, I am only a resounding
	13: 2	but have not *l*, I am nothing.
	13: 3	but have not *l*, I gain nothing.
	13: 4	Love is patient, *l* is kind.
	13: 4	*L* is patient, love is kind.
	13: 6	does not delight in evil
	13: 8	*L* never fails.
	13:13	But the greatest of these is *l*.
	13:13	three remain: faith, hope and *l*.
	14: 1	way of *l* and eagerly desire spiritual
	16:14	Do everything in *l*.
2Co	5:14	For Christ's *l* compels us,
	8: 8	sincerity of your *l* by comparing it
	8:24	show these men the proof of your *l*
Gal	5: 6	is faith expressing itself through *l*.
	5:13	rather, serve one another in *l*.
	5:22	But the fruit of the Spirit is *l*, joy,
Eph	1: 4	In *l* he predestined us
	2: 4	But because of his great *l* for us,
	3:17	being rooted and established in *l*,
	3:18	and high and deep is the *l* of Christ,
	3:19	and to know this *l* that surpasses
	4: 2	bearing with one another in *l*.
	4:15	Instead, speaking the truth in *l*,
	5: 2	loved children and live a life of *l*,
	5:25	your wives, just as Christ loved
	5:28	husbands ought to *l* their wives
	5:33	each one of you also must *l* his wife
Php	1: 9	that your *l* may abound more
	2: 2	having the same *l*, being one
Col	1: 5	*l* that spring from the hope that is
	2: 2	in heart and united in *l*,
	3:14	And over all these virtues put on *l*,
	3:19	your wives and do not be harsh
1Th	1: 3	your labor prompted by *l*,
	4: 9	taught by God to *l* each other.
	5: 8	on faith and *l* as a breastplate,
2Th	3: 5	direct your hearts into God's *l*
1Ti	1: 5	The goal of this command is *l*,
	2:15	*l* and holiness with propriety.
	4:12	in life, in *l*, in faith and in purity.
	6:10	For the *l* of money is a root
	6:11	faith, *l*, endurance and gentleness.
2Ti	1: 7	of power, of *l* and of self-discipline.
	2:22	and pursue righteousness, faith, *l*
	3:10	faith, patience, *l*, endurance,
Tit	2: 4	women to *l* their husbands
Phm	9	yet I appeal to you on the basis of *l*.
Heb	6:10	and the *l* you have shown him
	10:24	may spur one another on toward *l*
	13: 5	free from the *l* of money
Jas	1:12	promised to those who *l* him.
	2: 5	he promised those who *l* him?
	2: 8	"*L* your neighbor as yourself,"
1Pe	1:22	the truth so that you have sincere *l*
	1:22	*l* one another deeply,
	2:17	*L* the brotherhood of believers,
	3: 8	be sympathetic, *l* as brothers,
	3:10	"Whoever would *l* life
	4: 8	Above all, *l* each other deeply,
	4: 8	*l* covers over a multitude of sins.
	5:14	Greet one another with a kiss of *l*.
2Pe	1: 7	and to brotherly kindness, *l*.
	1:17	"This is my Son, whom I *l*;
1Jn	2: 5	God's *l* is truly made complete
	2:15	Do not *l* the world or anything
	3: 1	How great is the *l* the Father has
	3:10	anyone who does not *l* his brother.
	3:11	We should *l* one another.
	3:14	Anyone who does not *l* remains
	3:16	This is how we know what *l* is:
	3:18	let us not *l* with words or tongue
	3:23	to *l* one another as he commanded
	4: 7	Dear friends, let us *l* one another,
	4: 7	for *l* comes from God.
	4: 8	Whoever does not *l* does not know
	4: 9	This is how God showed his *l*
	4:10	This is *l*: not that we loved God,
	4:11	we also ought to *l* one another.
	4:12	and his *l* is made complete in us.
	4:16	God is *l*.
	4:16	Whoever lives in *l* lives in God,
	4:17	*l* is made complete among us
	4:18	But perfect *l* drives out fear,
	4:19	We *l* because he first loved us.
	4:20	If anyone says, "I *l* God,"
	4:21	loves God must also *l* his brother.
	5: 2	we know that we *l* the children
	5: 3	This is *l* for God: to obey his
2Jn	5	I ask that we *l* one another.
	6	his command is that you walk in *l*.
	6	this is *l*: that we walk in obedience
Jude	12	men are blemishes at your *l* feasts,
	21	Keep yourselves in God's *l*
Rev	2: 4	You have forsaken your first *l*.
	3:19	Those whom I *l* I rebuke
	12:11	they did not *l* their lives so much

LOVED (LOVE)
Ge	24:67	she became his wife, and he *l* her;
	29:30	and he *l* Rachel more than Leah.
	37: 3	Now Israel *l* Joseph more than any
Dt	7: 8	But it was because the Lord *l* you
1Sa	1: 5	a double portion because he *l* her,
	20:17	because he *l* him as he *l* himself.
Ps	44: 3	light of your face, for you *l* them.
Jer	2: 2	how as a bride you *l* me
	31: 3	"I have *l* you with an everlasting
Hos	2:23	to the one I called 'Not my *l* one.'
	3: 1	though she is *l* by another
	9:10	became as vile as the thing they *l*.
	11: 1	"When Israel was a child, I *l* him,
Mal	1: 2	"But you ask, 'How have you *l* us?'
Mk	12: 6	left to send, a son, whom he *l*.
Jn	3:16	so *l* the world that he gave his one
	3:19	but men *l* darkness instead of light
	11: 5	Jesus *l* Martha and her sister
	12:43	for they *l* praise from men more
	13: 1	Having *l* his own who were
	13:23	the disciple whom Jesus *l*,
	13:34	As I have *l* you, so you must love
	14:21	He who loves me will be *l*
	15: 9	the Father has *l* me, so have I *l* you.
	15:12	Love each other as I have *l* you.
	19:26	the disciple whom he *l* standing
Ro	8:37	conquerors through him who *l* us.

LOVELY

	9:13	"Jacob I *l*, but Esau I hated."
	9:25	her 'my / one' who is not my / one',
	11:28	they are / on account
Gal	2:20	who / me and gave himself for me.
Eph	5: 2	as Christ / us and gave himself up
	5:25	just as Christ / the church
2Th	2:16	who / us and by his grace gave us
2Ti	4:10	for Demas, because he / this world,
Heb	1: 9	You have / righteousness
1Jn	4:10	This is love: not that we / God,
	4:11	Dear friends, since God so / us,
	4:19	We love because he first / us.

LOVELY (LOVE)

Ps	84: 1	How / is your dwelling place,
SS	2:14	and your face is /.
	5:16	he is altogether *l*.
Php	4: 8	whatever is /, whatever is

LOVER (LOVE)

SS	2:16	*Beloved* My / is mine and I am his;
	7:10	I belong to my /,
1Ti	3: 3	not quarrelsome, not a / of money.

LOVERS (LOVE)

2Ti	3: 2	People will be / of themselves,
	3: 3	without self-control, brutal, not /
	3: 4	/ of pleasure rather than / of God—

LOVES (LOVE)

Ps	11: 7	he / justice;
	33: 5	The LORD / righteousness
	34:12	Whoever of you / life
	91:14	Because he / me," says the LORD,
	127: 2	for he grants sleep to those he /.
Pr	3:12	the LORD disciplines those he /,
	12: 1	Whoever / discipline / knowledge,
	13:24	he who / him is careful
	17:17	A friend / at all times,
	17:19	He who / a quarrel / sin;
	22:11	He who / a pure heart and whose
Ecc	5:10	whoever / wealth is never satisfied
Mt	10:37	anyone who / his son or daughter
Lk	7:47	has been forgiven little / little."
Jn	3:35	Father / the Son and has placed
	10:17	reason my Father / me is that I lay
	12:25	The man who / his life will lose it,
	14:21	obeys them, he is the one who / me.
	14:23	Jesus replied, "If anyone / me,
Ro	13: 8	for he who / his fellowman has
2Co	9: 7	for God / a cheerful giver.
Eph	5:28	He who / his wife / himself.
	5:33	must love his wife as he / himself,
Heb	12: 6	the Lord disciplines those he /,
1Jn	2:10	Whoever / his brother lives
	2:15	If anyone / the world, the love
	4: 7	Everyone who / has been born
	4:21	Whoever / God must also love his
	5: 1	who / the father / his child
3Jn	9	but Diotrephes, who / to be first,
Rev	1: 5	To him who / us and has freed us

LOVING (LOVE)

Ps	25:10	All the ways of the LORD are /
	62:12	and that you, O Lord, are /.
	145: 17	and / toward all he has made.
Heb	13: 1	Keep on / each other as brothers.
1Jn	5: 2	by / God and carrying out his

LOWLY

Job	5:11	The / he sets on high,
Pr	29:23	but a man of / spirit gains honor.
Isa	57:15	also with him who is contrite and /
Eze	21:26	/ will be exalted and the exalted
1Co	1:28	He chose the / things of this world

LUKE*

Co-worker with Paul (Col 4:14; 2Ti 4:11; Phm 24)

LUKEWARM*

Rev	3:16	So, because you are /— neither hot

LUST

Pr	6:25	Do not / in your heart
Col	3: 5	sexual immorality, impurity, /,
1Th	4: 5	not in passionate / like the heathen,
1Jn	2:16	the / of his eyes and the boasting

LYING (LIE)

Pr	6:17	a / tongue,
	26:28	A / tongue hates those it hurts,

MACEDONIA

Ac	16: 9	"Come over to *M* and help us."

MADE (MAKE)

Ge	1:16	He also *m* the stars.
	1:25	God *m* the wild animals according
	2:22	Then the LORD God *m* a woman
2Ki	19:15	You have *m* heaven and earth.
Ps	95: 5	The sea is his, for he *m* it,
	100: 3	It is he who *m* us, and we are his;
	118: 24	This is the day the LORD has *m*;
	139: 14	I am fearfully and wonderfully *m*;
Ecc	3:11	He has *m* everything beautiful
Mk	2:27	"The Sabbath was *m* for man,
Jn	1: 3	Through him all things were *m*;
Ac	17:24	"The God who *m* the world
Heb	1: 2	through whom he *m* the universe,
Rev	14: 7	Worship him who *m* the heavens,

MAGI

Mt	2: 1	*M* from the east came to Jerusalem

MAGOG

Eze	38: 2	of the land of *M*, the chief prince
	39: 6	I will send fire on *M*
Rev	20: 8	and *M*— to gather them for battle.

MAIDEN

Pr	30:19	and the way of a man with a *m*.
Isa	62: 5	As a young man marries a *m*,
Jer	2:32	Does a *m* forget her jewelry,

MAIMED

Mt	18: 8	It is better for you to enter life *m*

MAJESTIC (MAJESTY)

Ex	15: 6	was *m* in power.
	15:11	*m* in holiness,
Ps	8: 1	how *m* is your name in all the earth
	29: 4	the voice of the LORD is *m*.
	111: 3	Glorious and *m* are his deeds,
SS	6:10	*m* as the stars in procession?
2Pe	1:17	came to him from the *M* Glory,

MAJESTY (MAJESTIC)

Ex	15: 7	In the greatness of your *m*
Dt	33:26	and on the clouds in his *m*.
1Ch	16:27	Splendor and *m* are before him;
Est	1: 4	the splendor and glory of his *m*.
Job	37:22	God comes in awesome *m*.
	40:10	and clothe yourself in honor and *m*
Ps	45: 4	In your *m* ride forth victoriously
	93: 1	The LORD reigns, he is robed in *m*
	110: 3	Arrayed in holy *m*,
	145: 5	of the glorious splendor of your *m*,
Isa	53: 2	or *m* to attract us to him,
Eze	31: 2	can be compared with you in *m*?
2Pe	1:16	but we were eyewitnesses of his *m*.
Jude	25	only God our Savior be glory, *m*,

MAKE (MADE MAKER MAKES MAKING)

Ge	1:26	"Let us *m* man in our image,
	2:18	I will *m* a helper suitable for him."
	12: 2	"I will *m* you into a great nation
Ex	22: 3	thief must certainly *m* restitution,
Nu	6:25	the LORD *m* his face shine
Ps	108: 1	*m* music with all my soul.
Isa	14:14	I will *m* myself like the Most High
	29:16	"He did not *m* me"?
Jer	31:31	"when I will *m* a new covenant
Mt	3: 3	*m* straight paths for him!' "
	28:19	and *m* disciples of all nations,
Mk	1:17	and I will *m* you fishers of men."
Lk	13:24	"*M* every effort to enter
	14:23	country lanes and *m* them come in,
Ro	14:19	*m* every effort to do what leads
2Co	5: 9	So we *m* it our goal to please him,
Eph	4: 3	*M* every effort to keep the unity
Col	4: 5	*m* the most of every opportunity,
1Th	4:11	*M* it your ambition
Heb	4:11	*m* every effort to enter that rest,
	12:14	*M* every effort to live in peace
2Pe	1: 5	*m* every effort to add
	3:14	*m* every effort to be found spotless,

MAKER (MAKE)

Job	4:17	Can a man be more pure than his *M*
	36: 3	I will ascribe justice to my *M*.
Ps	95: 6	kneel before the LORD our *M*;
Pr	22: 2	The LORD is the *M* of them all.
Isa	45: 9	to him who quarrels with his *M*,
	54: 5	For your *M* is your husband—

1550

Jer	10:16	for he is the *M* of all things,

MAKES (MAKE)

1Co	3: 7	but only God, who *m* things grow.

MAKING (MAKE)

Ps	19: 7	*m* wise the simple.
Ecc	12:12	Of *m* many books there is no end,
Jn	5:18	*m* himself equal with God.
Eph	5:16	*m* the most of every opportunity,

MALE

Ge	1:27	*m* and female he created them.
Gal	3:28	slave nor free, *m* nor female,

MALICE (MALICIOUS)

Ro	1:29	murder, strife, deceit and *m*.
Col	3: 8	*m*, slander, and filthy language
1Pe	2: 1	rid yourselves of all *m*

MALICIOUS (MALICE)

Pr	26:24	A *m* man disguises himself
1Ti	3:11	not *m* talkers but temperate
	6: 4	*m* talk, evil suspicions

MAN (MEN WOMAN WOMEN)

Ge	1:26	"Let us make *m* in our image,
	2: 7	God formed the *m* from the dust
	2:18	for the *m* to be alone
	2:23	she was taken out of *m*.
	9: 6	Whoever sheds the blood of *m*,
Dt	8: 3	does not live on bread
1Sa	13:14	a *m* after his own heart
	15:29	he is not a *m* that he
Job	14: 1	*M* born of woman is of few
	14:14	If a *m* dies, will he live
Ps	1: 1	Blessed is the *m* who does
	8: 4	what is *m* that you are
	119: 9	can a young *m* keep his
	127: 5	Blessed is the *m* whose quiver
Pr	14:12	that seems right to a *m*,
	30:19	way of a *m* with a maiden.
Isa	53: 3	a *m* of sorrows,
Mt	19: 5	a *m* will leave his father
Mk	8:36	What good is it for a *m*
Lk	4: 4	'*M* does not live on bread
Ro	5:12	entered the world through one *m*
1Co	7: 2	each *m* should have his own
	11: 3	head of every *m* is Christ,
	11: 3	head of woman is *m*
	13:11	When I became a *m*,
Php	2: 8	found in appearance as a *m*,
1Ti	2: 5	the *m* Christ Jesus,
	2:11	have authority over a *m*;
Heb	9:27	as *m* is destined to die

MANAGE

Jer	12: 5	how will you *m* in the thickets
1Ti	3: 4	He must *m* his own family well
	3:12	one wife and must *m* his children
	5:14	to *m* their homes and to give

MANASSEH

1. Firstborn of Joseph (Ge 41:51; 46:20). Blessed (Ge 48).

2. Son of Hezekiah; king of Judah (2Ki 21:1-18; 2Ch 33:1-20).

MANGER

Lk	2:12	in strips of cloth and lying in a *m*."

MANNA

Ex	16:31	people of Israel called the bread *m*.
Dt	8:16	He gave you *m* to eat in the desert,
Jn	6:49	Your forefathers ate the *m*
Rev	2:17	I will give some of the hidden *m*.

MANNER

1Co	11:27	in an unworthy *m* will be guilty
Php	1:27	conduct yourselves in a *m* worthy

MARITAL* (MARRY)

Ex	21:10	of her food, clothing and *m* rights.
Mt	5:32	except for *m* unfaithfulness,
	19: 9	except for *m* unfaithfulness,
1Co	7: 3	husband should fulfill his *m* duty

MARK (MARKS)

Cousin of Barnabas (Col 4:10; 2Ti 4:11; Phm 24; 1Pe 5:13), see JOHN.

Ge	4:15	Then the LORD put a *m* on Cain
Rev	13:16	to receive a *m* on his right hand

MARKS (MARK)

Jn	20:25	Unless I see the nail *m* in his hands
Gal	6:17	bear on my body the *m* of Jesus.

MARRED
Isa 52:14 his form *m* beyond human likeness
MARRIAGE (MARRY)
Mt 22:30 neither marry nor be given in *m*;
24:38 marrying and giving in *m*,
Ro 7: 2 she is released from the law of *m*.
Heb 13: 4 by all, and the *m* bed kept pure,
MARRIED (MARRY)
Ro 7: 2 by law a *m* woman is bound
1Co 7:27 Are you *m*? Do not seek a divorce.
7:33 But a *m* man is concerned about
7:36 They should get *m*.
MARRIES (MARRY)
Mt 5:32 and anyone who *m* the divorced
19: 9 and *m* another woman commits
Lk 16:18 the man who *m* a divorced woman
MARRY (INTERMARRY MARITAL MARRIAGE MARRIED MARRIES)
Mt 22:30 resurrection people will neither *m*
1Co 7: 1 It is good for a man not to *m*.
7: 9 control themselves, they should *m*,
1Ti 5:14 So I counsel younger widows to *m*,
MARTHA*
Sister of Mary and Lazarus (Lk 10:38-42; Jn 11; 12:2).
MARVELED
Lk 2:33 mother *m* at what was said about
MARY
1. Mother of Jesus (Mt 1:16-25; Lk 1:27-56; 2:1-40). With Jesus at temple (Lk 2:41-52), at the wedding in Cana (Jn 2:1-5), questioning his sanity (Mk 3:21), at the cross (Jn 19:25-27). Among disciples after Ascension (Ac 1:14).
2. Magdalene; former demoniac (Lk 8:2). Helped support Jesus' ministry (Lk 8:1-3). At the cross (Mt 27:56; Mk 15:40; Jn 19:25), burial (Mt 27:61; Mk 15:47). Saw angel after resurrection (Mt 28:1-10; Mk 16:1-9; Lk 24:1-12); also Jesus (Jn 20:1-18).
3. Sister of Martha and Lazarus (Jn 11). Washed Jesus' feet (Jn 12:1-8).
MASQUERADES*
2Co 11:14 for Satan himself *m* as an angel
MASTER (MASTERED MASTERS)
Mt 10:24 nor a servant above his *m*.
23: 8 for you have only one *M*
24:46 that servant whose *m* finds him
25:21 "His *m* replied, 'Well done,
Ro 6:14 For sin shall not be your *m*,
14: 4 To his own *m* he stands or falls.
2Ti 2:21 useful to the *M* and prepared
MASTERED* (MASTER)
1Co 6:12 but I will not be *m* by anything.
2Pe 2:19 a slave to whatever has *m* him.
MASTERS (MASTER)
Mt 6:24 "No one can serve two *m*.
Eph 6: 5 obey your earthly *m* with respect
6: 9 And *m*, treat your slaves
Tit 2: 9 subject to their *m* in everything,
MATTHEW*
Apostle; former tax collector (Mt 9:9-13; 10:3; Mk 3:18; Lk 6:15; Ac 1:13). Also called Levi (Mk 2:14-17; Lk 5:27-32).
MATURE (MATURITY)
Eph 4:13 of the Son of God and become *m*,
Php 3:15 of us who are *m* should take such
Heb 5:14 But solid food is for the *m*,
Jas 1: 4 work so that you may be *m*
MATURITY* (MATURE)
Heb 6: 1 about Christ and go on to *m*,
MEAL
Pr 15:17 Better a *m* of vegetables where
1Co 10:27 some unbeliever invites you to a *m*
Heb 12:16 for a single *m* sold his inheritance
MEANING
Ne 8: 8 and giving the *m* so that the people
MEANS
1Co 9:22 by all possible *m* I might save some
MEAT
Ro 14: 6 He who eats *m*, eats to the Lord,
14:21 It is better not to eat *m*
MEDIATOR
1Ti 2: 5 and one *m* between God and men,

Heb 8: 6 of which he is *m* is superior
9:15 For this reason Christ is the *m*
12:24 to Jesus the *m* of a new covenant,
MEDICINE*
Pr 17:22 A cheerful heart is good *m*,
MEDITATE (MEDITATES MEDITATION)
Jos 1: 8 from your mouth; *m* on it day
Ps 119:15 I *m* on your precepts
119:78 but I will *m* on your precepts.
119: 97 I *m* on it all day long.
145: 5 I will *m* on your wonderful works.
MEDITATES* (MEDITATE)
Ps 1: 2 and on his law he *m* day and night.
MEDITATION* (MEDITATE)
Ps 19:14 of my mouth and the *m* of my heart
104: 34 May my *m* be pleasing to him,
MEDIUM
Lev 20:27 " 'A man or woman who is a *m*
MEEK (MEEKNESS)
Ps 37:11 But the *m* will inherit the land
Mt 5: 5 Blessed are the *m*,
MEEKNESS* (MEEK)
2Co 10: 1 By the *m* and gentleness of Christ,
MEET (MEETING)
Ps 85:10 Love and faithfulness *m* together;
Am 4:12 prepare to *m* your God, O Israel."
1Th 4:17 them in the clouds to *m* the Lord
MEETING* (MEET)
Heb 10:25 Let us not give up *m* together,
MELCHIZEDEK
Ge 14:18 *M* king of Salem brought out bread
Ps 110: 4 in the order of *M*."
Heb 7:11 in the order of *M*, not in the order
MELT
2Pe 3:12 and the elements will *m* in the heat.
MEMBERS
Mic 7: 6 a man's enemies are the *m*
Ro 7:23 law at work in the *m* of my body,
12: 4 we have one body with many *m*,
1Co 6:15 not know that your bodies are *m*
12:24 But God has combined the *m*
Eph 4:25 for we are all *m* of one body.
Col 3:15 as *m* of one body you were called
MEN (MAN)
Mt 4:19 will make you fishers of *m*
5:16 your light shine before *m*
12:36 *m* will have to give account
Jn 12:32 will draw all *m* to myself
Ac 5:29 obey God rather than *m*!
Ro 1:27 indecent acts with other *m*,
5:12 death came to all *m*,
1Co 9:22 all things to all *m*
2Co 5:11 we try to persuade *m*.
1Ti 2: 4 wants all *m* to be saved
2Ti 2: 2 entrust to reliable *m*
2Pe 1:21 but *m* spoke from God
MENAHEM
King of Israel (2Ki 15:17-22).
MERCIFUL (MERCY)
Dt 4:31 the LORD your God is a *m* God;
Ne 9:31 for you are a gracious and *m* God.
Mt 5: 7 Blessed are the *m*,
Lk 6:36 Be *m*, just as your Father is *m*.
Heb 2:17 in order that he might become a *m*
Jude 22 Be *m* to those who doubt; snatch
MERCY (MERCIFUL)
Ex 33:19 *m* on whom I will have *m*,
Ps 25: 6 O LORD, your great *m* and love,
Isa 63: 9 and *m* he redeemed them;
Hos 6: 6 For I desire *m*, not sacrifice,
Mic 6: 8 To act justly and to love *m*
Hab 3: 2 in wrath remember *m*.
Mt 12: 7 'I desire *m*, not sacrifice,' you
23:23 justice, *m* and faithfulness.
Ro 9:15 "I will have *m* on whom I have *m*,
Eph 2: 4 who is rich in *m*, made us alive
Jas 2:13 *M* triumphs over judgment!
1Pe 1: 3 In his great *m* he has given us new
MESSAGE
Isa 53: 1 Who has believed our *m*
Jn 12:38 "Lord, who has believed our *m*

Ro 10:17 faith comes from hearing the *m*,
1Co 1:18 For the *m* of the cross is
2Co 5:19 to us the *m* of reconciliation.
MESSIAH*
Jn 1:41 "We have found the *M*" (that is,
4:25 "I know that *M*" (called Christ) "is
METHUSELAH
Ge 5:27 Altogether, *M* lived 969 years,
MICHAEL
Archangel (Jude 9); warrior in angelic realm, protector of Israel (Da 10:13, 21; 12:1; Rev 12:7).
MIDWIVES
Ex 1:17 The *m*, however, feared God
MIGHT (ALMIGHTY MIGHTY)
Jdg 16:30 Then he pushed with all his *m*,
2Sa 6:14 before the LORD with all his *m*,
Ps 21:13 we will sing and praise your *m*.
Zec 4: 6 'Not by *m* nor by power,
1Ti 6:16 To him be honor and *m* forever.
MIGHTY (MIGHT)
Ex 6: 1 of my *m* hand he will drive them
Dt 7: 8 he brought you out with a *m* hand
2Sa 1:19 How the *m* have fallen!
23: 8 the names of David's *m* men:
Ps 24: 8 The LORD strong and *m*,
50: 1 The *M* One, God, the LORD,
89: 8 You are *m*, O LORD,
136: 12 with a *m* hand and outstretched
147: 5 Great is our Lord and *m* in power;
Isa 9: 6 Wonderful Counselor, *M* God,
Zep 3:17 he is *m* to save.
Eph 6:10 in the Lord and in his *m* power.
MILE*
Mt 5:41 If someone forces you to go one *m*,
MILK
Ex 3: 8 a land flowing with *m* and honey—
Isa 55: 1 Come, buy wine and *m*
1Co 3: 2 I gave you *m*, not solid food,
Heb 5:12 You need *m*, not solid food!
1Pe 2: 2 babies, crave pure spiritual *m*,
MILLSTONE (STONE)
Lk 17: 2 sea with a *m* tied around his neck
MIND (DOUBLE-MINDED MINDFUL MINDS)
1Sa 15:29 Israel does not lie or change his *m*;
1Ch 28: 9 devotion and with a willing *m*,
Ps 26: 2 examine my heart and my *m*;
Isa 26: 3 him whose *m* is steadfast,
Mt 22:37 all your soul and with all your *m*.'
Ac 4:32 believers were one in heart and *m*.
Ro 7:25 I myself in my *m* am a slave
8: 7 the sinful *m* is hostile to God.
12: 2 by the renewing of your *m*.
1Co 2: 9 no *m* has conceived
14:14 spirit prays, but my *m* is unfruitful.
2Co 13:11 be of one *m*, live in peace.
Php 3:19 Their *m* is on earthly things.
1Th 4:11 to *m* your own business
Heb 7:21 and will not change his *m*:
MINDFUL* (MIND)
Ps 8: 4 what is man that you are *m* of him,
Lk 1:48 God my Savior, for he has been *m*
Heb 2: 6 What is man that you are *m* of him,
MINDS (MIND)
Ps 7: 9 who searches *m* and hearts,
Jer 31:33 "I will put my law in their *m*
Eph 4:23 new in the attitude of your *m*;
Col 3: 2 Set your *m* on things above,
Heb 8:10 I will put my laws in their *m*
Rev 2:23 I am he who searches hearts and *m*,
MINISTERING (MINISTRY)
Heb 1:14 Are not all angels *m* spirits sent
MINISTRY (MINISTERING)
Ac 6: 4 to prayer and the *m* of the word."
2Co 5:18 gave us the *m* of reconciliation:
2Ti 4: 5 discharge all the duties of your *m*.
MIRACLES (MIRACULOUS)
1Ch 16:12 his *m*, and the judgments he
Ps 77:14 You are the God who performs *m*;
Mt 11:20 most of his *m* had been performed,
11:21 If the *m* that were performed
24:24 and perform great signs and *m*
Mk 6: 2 does *m*! Isn't this the carpenter?

MIRACULOUS

Jn	10:32	"I have shown you many great *m*
	14:11	the evidence of the *m* themselves.
Ac	2:22	accredited by God to you by *m*,
	19:11	God did extraordinary *m*
1Co	12:28	third teachers, then workers of *m*,
Heb	2: 4	it by signs, wonders and various *m*,

MIRACULOUS (MIRACLES)

Jn	3: 2	could perform the *m* signs you are
	9:16	"How can a sinner do such *m* signs
	20:30	Jesus did many other *m* signs
1Co	1:22	Jews demand *m* signs and Greeks

MIRE

Ps	40: 2	out of the mud and *m*;
Isa	57:20	whose waves cast up *m* and mud.

MIRIAM

Sister of Moses and Aaron (Nu 26:59). Led dancing at Red Sea (Ex 15:20-21). Struck with leprosy for criticizing Moses (Nu 12). Death (Nu 20:1).

MIRROR

Jas	1:23	a man who looks at his face in a *m*

MISERY

Ex	3: 7	"I have indeed seen the *m*
Jdg	10:16	he could bear Israel's *m* no longer.
Hos	5:15	in their *m* they will earnestly seek
Ro	3:16	ruin and *m* mark their ways,
Jas	5: 1	of the *m* that is coming upon you.

MISLED

1Co	15:33	Do not be *m*: "Bad company

MISS

Pr	19: 2	nor to be hasty and *m* the way.

MIST

Hos	6: 4	Your love is like the morning *m*,
Jas	4:14	You are a *m* that appears for a little

MISUSE*

Ex	20: 7	"You shall not *m* the name
Dt	5:11	"You shall not *m* the name
Ps	139:20	your adversaries *m* your name.

MOCK (MOCKED MOCKER MOCKERS MOCKING)

Ps	22: 7	All who see me *m* me;
Pr	14: 9	Fools *m* at making amends for sin,
Mk	10:34	who will *m* him and spit on him,

MOCKED (MOCK)

Mt	27:29	knelt in front of him and *m* him.
	27:41	of the law and the elders *m* him.
Gal	6: 7	not be deceived: God cannot be *m*.

MOCKER (MOCK)

Pr	9: 7	corrects a *m* invites insult;
	9:12	if you are a *m*, you alone will suffer
	20: 1	Wine is a *m* and beer a brawler,
	22:10	Drive out the *m*, and out goes strife

MOCKERS (MOCK)

Ps	1: 1	or sit in the seat of *m*.

MOCKING (MOCK)

Isa	50: 6	face from *m* and spitting.

MODEL*

Eze	28:12	" 'You were the *m* of perfection,
1Th	1: 7	And so you became a *m*
2Th	3: 9	to make ourselves a *m* for you

MOMENT

Job	20: 5	the joy of the godless lasts but a *m*.
Ps	30: 5	For his anger lasts only a *m*,
Isa	66: 8	or a nation be brought forth in a *m*?
Gal	2: 5	We did not give in to them for a *m*,

MONEY

Ecc	5:10	Whoever loves *m* never has *m*
Isa	55: 1	and you who have no *m*,
Mt	6:24	You cannot serve both God and M.
Lk	9: 3	no bread, no *m*, no extra tunic.
1Co	16: 2	set aside a sum of *m* in keeping
1Ti	3: 3	not quarrelsome, not a lover of *m*.
	6:10	For the love of *m* is a root
2Ti	3: 2	lovers of *m*, boastful, proud,
Heb	13: 5	free from the love of *m*
1Pe	5: 2	not greedy for *m*, but eager to serve

MOON

Ps	121: 6	nor the *m* by night.
Joel	2:31	and the *m* to blood
1Co	15:41	*m* another and the stars another;

MORNING

Ge	1: 5	and there was *m*— the first day.
Dt	28:67	In the *m* you will say, "If only it

MORTAL

Ps	5: 3	In the *m*, O Lord,
2Pe	1:19	and the *m* star rises in your hearts.
Rev	22:16	of David, and the bright *M* Star."

MORTAL

1Co	15:53	and the *m* with immortality.

MOSES

Levite; brother of Aaron (Ex 6:20; 1Ch 6:3). Put in basket into Nile; discovered and raised by Pharaoh's daughter (Ex 2:1-10). Fled to Midian after killing Egyptian (Ex 2:11-15). Married to Zipporah, fathered Gershom (Ex 2:16-22).

Called by the Lord to deliver Israel (Ex 3-4). Pharaoh's resistance (Ex 5). Ten plagues (Ex 7-11). Passover and Exodus (Ex 12-13). Led Israel through Red Sea (Ex 14). Song of deliverance (Ex 15:1-21). Brought water from rock (Ex 17:1-7). Raised hands to defeat Amalekites (Ex 17:8-16). Delegated judges (Ex 18; Dt 1:9-18).

Received Law at Sinai (Ex 19-23; 25-31; Jn 1:17). Announced Law to Israel (Ex 19:7-8; 24; 35). Broke tablets because of golden calf (Ex 32; Dt 9). Saw glory of the Lord (Ex 33-34). Supervised building of tabernacle (Ex 36-40). Set apart Aaron and priests (Lev 8-9). Numbered tribes (Nu 1-4; 26). Opposed by Aaron and Miriam (Nu 12). Sent spies into Canaan (Nu 13). Announced forty years of wandering for failure to enter land (Nu 14). Opposed by Korah (Nu 16). Forbidden to enter land for striking rock (Nu 20:1-13; Dt 1:37). Lifted bronze snake for healing (Nu 21:4-9; Jn 3:14). Final address to Israel (Dt 1-33). Succeeded by Joshua (Nu 27:12-23; Dt 34). Death (Dt 34:5-12).

"Law of Moses" (1Ki 2:3; Ezr 3:2; Mk 12:26; Lk 24:44). "Book of Moses" (2Ch 25:12; Ne 13:1). "Song of Moses" (Ex 15:1-21; Rev 15:3). "Prayer of Moses" (Ps 90).

MOTH

Mt	6:19	where *m* and rust destroy,

MOTHER (MOTHER'S)

Ge	2:24	and *m* and be united to his wife,
	3:20	because she would become the *m*
Ex	20:12	"Honor your father and your *m*,
Lev	20: 9	" 'If anyone curses his father or *m*,
Dt	5:16	"Honor your father and your *m*,
	21:18	who does not obey his father and *m*
	27:16	who dishonors his father or his *m*."
1Sa	2: 9	Each year his *m* made him a little
Ps	113: 9	as a happy *m* of children.
Pr	23:25	May your father and *m* be glad;
	29:15	child left to himself disgraces his *m*.
	31: 1	an oracle his *m* taught him:
Isa	49:15	"Can a *m* forget the baby
	66:13	As a *m* comforts her child,
Mt	10:37	or *m* more than me is not worthy
	15: 4	'Honor your father and *m*'
	19: 5	and *m* and be united to his wife,
Mk	7:10	'Honor your father and *m*,'
	10:19	honor your father and *m*.' "
Jn	19:27	to the disciple, "Here is your *m*."

MOTHER'S (MOTHER)

Job	1:21	"Naked I came from my *m* womb,
Pr	1: 8	and do not forsake your *m* teaching

MOTIVES*

Pr	16: 2	but *m* are weighed by the Lord.
1Co	4: 5	will expose the *m* of men's hearts.
Php	1:18	whether from false *m* or true,
1Th	2: 3	spring from error or impure *m*,
Jas	4: 3	because you ask with wrong *m*,

MOUNTAIN (MOUNTAINS)

Mic	4: 2	let us go up to the *m* of the Lord,
Mt	17:20	say to this *m*, 'Move from here

MOUNTAINS (MOUNTAIN)

Isa	52: 7	How beautiful on the *m*
	55:12	the *m* and hills
1Co	13: 2	if I have a faith that can move *m*,

MOURN (MOURNING)

Ecc	3: 4	a time to *m* and a time to dance,
Isa	61: 2	to comfort all who *m*,
Mt	5: 4	Blessed are those who *m*,
Ro	12:15	*m* with those who *m*.

MOURNING (MOURN)

Jer	31:13	I will turn their *m* into gladness;
Rev	21: 4	There will be no more death or *m*

MOUTH

Jos	1: 8	of the Law depart from your *m*;
Ps	19:14	May the words of my *m*
	40: 3	He put a new song in my *m*,
	119:103	sweeter than honey to my *m*!
Pr	16:23	A wise man's heart guides his *m*,
	27: 2	praise you, and not your own *m*;
Isa	51:16	I have put my words in your *m*
Mt	12:34	overflow of the heart the *m* speaks.
	15:11	into a man's *m* does not make him
Ro	10: 9	That if you confess with your *m*,

MUD

Ps	40: 2	out of the *m* and mire;
Isa	57:20	whose waves cast up mire and *m*.
2Pe	2:22	back to her wallowing in the *m*."

MULTITUDE (MULTITUDES)

Isa	31: 1	who trust in the *m* of their chariots
1Pe	4: 8	love covers over a *m* of sins.
Rev	7: 9	me was a great *m* that no one could

MULTITUDES (MULTITUDE)

Joel	3:14	*M*, *m* in the valley of decision!

MURDER (MURDERER MURDERERS)

Ex	20:13	"You shall not *m*.
Mt	15:19	*m*, adultery, sexual immorality,
Ro	13: 9	"Do not *m*," "Do not steal,"
Jas	2:11	adultery," also said, "Do not *m*."

MURDERER (MURDER)

Nu	35:16	he is a *m*; the *m* shall be put
Jn	8:44	He was a *m* from the beginning,
1Jn	3:15	who hates his brother is a *m*,

MURDERERS (MURDER)

1Ti	1: 9	for *m*, for adulterers and perverts,
Rev	21: 8	the *m*, the sexually immoral,

MUSIC

Jdg	5: 3	I will make *m* to the Lord,
Ps	27: 6	and make *m* to the Lord.
	95: 2	and extol him with *m* and song.
	98: 4	burst into jubilant song with *m*;
	108: 1	I make *m* with all my soul.
Eph	5:19	make *m* in your heart to the Lord,

MUSTARD

Mt	13:31	kingdom of heaven is like a *m* seed,
	17:20	you have faith as small as a *m* seed,

MUZZLE

Dt	25: 4	Do not *m* an ox while it is treading
Ps	39: 1	I will put a *m* on my mouth
1Co	9: 9	"Do not *m* an ox while it is

MYRRH

Mt	2:11	of gold and of incense and of *m*.
Mk	15:23	offered him wine mixed with *m*,

MYSTERY

Ro	16:25	to the revelation of the *m* hidden
1Co	15:51	I tell you a *m*: We will not all sleep,
Eph	5:32	This is a profound *m*—
Col	1:26	the *m* that has been kept hidden
1Ti	3:16	the *m* of godliness is great:

MYTHS

1Ti	4: 7	Have nothing to do with godless *m*

NADAB

Son of Jeroboam I; king of Israel (1Ki 15:25-32).

NAIL* (NAILING)

Jn	20:25	"Unless I see the *n* marks

NAILING* (NAIL)

Ac	2:23	him to death by *n* him to the cross.
Col	2:14	he took it away, *n* it to the cross.

NAKED

Ge	2:25	The man and his wife were both *n*,
Job	1:21	*N* I came from my mother's womb,
Isa	58: 7	when you see the *n*, to clothe him,
2Co	5: 3	are clothed, we will not be found *n*.

NAME

Ex	3:15	This is my *n* forever, the *n*
	20: 7	"You shall not misuse the *n*
Dt	5:11	"You shall not misuse the *n*
	28:58	this glorious and awesome *n*—'
1Ki	5: 5	will build the temple for my *N*.'
2Ch	7:14	my people, who are called by my *n*,
Ps	34: 3	let us exalt his *n* together.
	103: 1	my inmost being, praise his holy *n*.
	147: 4	and calls them each by *n*.
Pr	22: 1	A good *n* is more desirable

Isa	30: 4	What is his *n*, and the *n* of his son?
Isa	40:26	and calls them each by *n*.
	57:15	who lives forever, whose *n* is holy:
Jer	14: 7	do something for the sake of your *n*
Da	12: 1	everyone whose *n* is found written
Joel	2:32	on the *n* of the LORD will be saved
Zec	14: 9	one LORD, and his *n* the only *n*.
Mt	1:21	and you are to give him the *n* Jesus,
	6: 9	hallowed be your *n*,
	18:20	or three come together in my *n*,
Jn	10: 3	He calls his own sheep by *n*
	16:24	asked for anything in my *n*.
Ac	4:12	for there is no other *n*
Ro	10:13	"Everyone who calls on the *n*
Php	2: 9	him the *n* that is above every *n*,
Col	3:17	do it all in the *n* of the Lord Jesus,
Heb	1: 4	as the *n* he has inherited is superior
Rev	20:15	If anyone's *n* was not found written

NAOMI
Mother-in-law of Ruth (Ru 1). Advised Ruth to seek marriage with Boaz (Ru 2-4).

NARROW
Mt 7:13 "Enter through the *n* gate.

NATHANAEL
Apostle (Jn 1:45-49; 21:2). Probably also called Bartholomew (Mt 10:3).

NATION (NATIONS)
Ge	12: 2	"I will make you into a great *n*
Ps	33:12	Blessed is the *n* whose God is
Pr	14:34	Righteousness exalts a *n*,
Isa	65: 1	To a *n* that did not call on my name
1Pe	2: 9	a royal priesthood, a holy *n*,
Rev	5: 9	from every *n*, tribe, people

NATIONS (NATION)
Ge	17: 4	You will be the father of many *n*.
	18:18	and all *n* on earth will be blessed
Ex	19: 5	of all *n* you will be my treasured
Ne	1: 8	I will scatter you among the *n*,
Ps	96: 3	Declare his glory among the *n*,
Isa	40:15	Surely the *n* are like a drop
Eze	36:23	*n* will know that I am the LORD,
Hag	2: 7	and the desired of all *n* will come,
Zec	8:23	*n* will take firm hold of one Jew
	14: 2	I will gather all the *n* to Jerusalem
Mt	28:19	and make disciples of all *n*,
Rev	21:24	The *n* will walk by its light,

NATURAL (NATURE)
Ro 6:19 you are weak in your *n* selves.
1Co 15:44 If there is a *n* body, there is

NATURE (NATURAL)
Ro	8: 4	do not live according to the sinful *n*
	8: 8	by the sinful *n* cannot please God.
Gal	5:19	The acts of the sinful *n* are obvious:
	5:24	Jesus have crucified the sinful *n*
Php	2: 6	Who, being in very *n* God,

NAZARENE
Mt 2:23 prophets: "He will be called a *N*."

NAZIRITE
Jdg 13: 7 because the boy will be a *N* of God

NECESSARY
Ro 13: 5 it is *n* to submit to the authorities,

NEED (NEEDS NEEDY)
Ps	116: 6	when I was in great *n*, he saved me.
Mt	6: 8	for your Father knows what you *n*
Ro	12:13	with God's people who are in *n*.
1Co	12:21	say to the hand, "I don't *n* you!"
1Jn	3:17	sees his brother in *n* but has no pity

NEEDLE
Mt 19:24 go through the eye of a *n*

NEEDS (NEED)
Isa 58:11 he will satisfy your *n*
Php 4:19 God will meet all your *n* according

NEEDY
Pr	14:21	blessed is he who is kind to the *n*.
	14:31	to the *n* honors God.
	31:20	and extends her hands to the *n*.
Mt	6: 2	"So when you give to the *n*,

NEGLECT (NEGLECTED)
Ne	10:39	We will not *n* the house of our God
Ps	119: 16	I will not *n* your word.
Ac	6: 2	for us to *n* the ministry of the word
1Ti	4:14	Do not *n* your gift, which was

	6:16	to *o*, which leads to righteousness?
2Jn	6	that we walk in *o* to his commands.

OBEDIENT (OBEY)
Lk 2:51 with them and was *o* to them.
Php 2: 8 and became *o* to death—
1Pe 1:14 As *o* children, do not conform

OBEY (OBEDIENCE OBEDIENT OBEYED)
Ex	12:24	"*O* these instructions as a lasting
Dt	6: 3	careful to *o* so that it may go well
	13: 4	Keep his commands and *o* him;
	21:18	son who does not *o* his father
	30: 2	and *o* him with all your heart
	32:46	children to *o* carefully all the words
1Sa	15:22	To *o* is better than sacrifice,
Ps	119: 34	and *o* it with all my heart.
Mt	28:20	to *o* everything I have commanded
Jn	14:23	loves me, he will *o* my teaching.
Ac	5:29	"We must *o* God rather than men!
Ro	6:16	slaves to the one whom you *o*—
Gal	5: 3	obligated to *o* the whole law.
Eph	6: 1	*o* your parents in the Lord,
	6: 5	*o* your earthly masters with respect
Col	3:20	*o* your parents in everything,
1Ti	3: 4	and see that his children *o* him
Heb	13:17	*O* your leaders and submit
1Jn	5: 3	love for God: to *o* his commands.

OBEYED (OBEY)
Ps	119: 4	that are to be fully *o*.
Jnh	3: 3	Jonah *o* the word of the LORD
Jn	17: 6	and they have *o* your word.
Ro	6:17	you wholeheartedly *o* the form
Heb	11: 8	*o* and went, even though he did not
1Pe	3: 6	who *o* Abraham and called him her

OBLIGATED
Ro 1:14 I am *o* both to Greeks
Gal 5: 3 himself to be circumcised that he is *o*

OBSCENITY
Eph 5: 4 Nor should there be *o*, foolish talk

OBSOLETE
Heb 8:13 he has made the first one *o*;

OBTAINED
Ro 9:30 not pursue righteousness, have *o* it,
Php 3:12 Not that I have already *o* all this,
Heb 9:12 having *o* eternal redemption.

OFFENDED (OFFENSE)
Pr 18:19 An *o* brother is more unyielding

OFFENSE (OFFENDED OFFENSIVE)
Pr 17: 9 over an *o* promotes love,
19:11 it is to his glory to overlook an *o*.

OFFENSIVE (OFFENSE)
Ps 139: 24 See if there is any *o* way in me,

OFFER (OFFERED OFFERING OFFERINGS)
Ro 12: 1 to *o* your bodies as living sacrifices,
Heb 13:15 therefore, let us continually *o*

OFFERED (OFFER)
Heb 7:27 once for all when he *o* himself.
11: 4 By faith Abel *o* God a better

OFFERING (OFFER)
Ge	22: 8	provide the lamb for the burnt *o*,
Ps	40: 6	Sacrifice and *o* you did not desire,
Isa	53:10	the LORD makes his life a guilt *o*,
Mt	5:23	if you are *o* your gift at the altar
Eph	5: 2	as a fragrant *o* and sacrifice to God.
Heb	10: 5	"Sacrifice and *o* you did not desire,

OFFERINGS (OFFER)
Mal 3: 8 do we rob you?" "In tithes and *o*.
Mk 12:33 is more important than all burnt *o*

OFFICER
2Ti 2: 4 wants to please his commanding *o*.

OFFSPRING
Ge 3:15 and between your *o* and hers;
12: 7 "To your *o* I will give this land."

OIL
Ps 23: 5 You anoint my head with *o*;
Isa 61: 3 the *o* of gladness
Heb 1: 9 by anointing you with the *o* of joy."

OLIVE (OLIVES)
Zec 4: 3 Also there are two *o* trees by it,
Ro 11:17 and you, though a wild *o* shoot,
Rev 11: 4 These are the two *o* trees

NEGLECT (NEGLECTED)
Mt 23:23 But you have *n* the more important

NEHEMIAH
Cupbearer of Artaxerxes (Ne 2:1); governor of Israel (Ne 8:9). Returned to Jerusalem to rebuild walls (Ne 2-6). With Ezra, reestablished worship (Ne 8). Prayer confessing nation's sin (Ne 9). Dedicated wall (Ne 12).

NEIGHBOR (NEIGHBOR'S)
Ex	20:16	give false testimony against your *n*.
Lev	19:13	Do not defraud your *n* or rob him.
	19:18	but love your *n* as yourself.
Pr	27:10	better a *n* nearby than a brother far
Mt	19:19	and 'love your *n* as yourself.' "
Lk	10:29	who is my *n*?" In reply Jesus said:
Ro	13:10	Love does no harm to its *n*.

NEIGHBOR'S (NEIGHBOR)
Ex	20:17	You shall not covet your *n* wife,
Dt	5:21	not set your desire on your *n* house
	19:14	not move your *n* boundary stone
Pr	25:17	Seldom set foot in your *n* house—

NEW
Ps	40: 3	He put a *n* song in my mouth,
Ecc	1: 9	there is nothing *n* under the sun.
Isa	65:17	*n* heavens and a *n* earth.
Jer	31:31	"when I will make a *n* covenant
Eze	36:26	give you a *n* heart and put a *n* spirit
Mt	9:17	Neither do men pour *n* wine
Lk	22:20	"This cup is the *n* covenant
2Co	5:17	he is a *n* creation; the old has gone,
Eph	4:24	and to put on the *n* self, created
2Pe	3:13	to a *n* heaven and a *n* earth,
1Jn	2: 8	Yet I am writing you a *n* command;

NEWBORN (BEAR)
1Pe 2: 2 Like *n* babies, crave pure spiritual

NEWS
Isa	52: 7	the feet of those who bring good *n*,
Mk	1:15	Repent and believe the good *n*!"
	16:15	preach the good *n* to all creation.
Lk	2:10	I bring you good *n*
Ac	5:42	proclaiming the good *n* that Jesus
	17:18	preaching the good *n* about Jesus
Ro	10:15	feet of those who bring good *n*!"

NICODEMUS*
Pharisee who visted Jesus at night (Jn 3). Argued fair treatment of Jesus (Jn 7:50-52). With Joseph, prepared Jesus for burial (Jn 19:38-42).

NIGHT
Job	35:10	who gives songs in the *n*,
Ps	1: 2	on his law he meditates day and *n*.
	91: 5	You will not fear the terror of *n*,
Jn	3: 2	He came to Jesus at *n* and said,
1Th	5: 2	Lord will come like a thief in the *n*.
	5: 5	We do not belong to the *n*.
Rev	21:25	for there will be no *n* there.

NOAH
Righteous man (Eze 14:14, 20) called to build ark (Ge 6-8; Heb 11:7; 1Pe 3:20; 2Pe 2:5). God's covenant with (Ge 9:1-17). Drunkenness of (Ge 9:18-23). Blessed sons, cursed Canaan (Ge 9:24-27).

NOBLE
Ru	3:11	you are a woman of *n* character.
Ps	45: 1	My heart is stirred by a *n* theme
Pr	12: 4	of *n* character is her husband's
	31:10	A wife of *n* character who can find?
	31:29	"Many women do *n* things,
Isa	32: 8	But the *n* man makes *n* plans,
Lk	8:15	good soil stands for those with a *n*
Ro	9:21	of clay some pottery for *n* purposes
Php	4: 8	whatever is *n*, whatever is right,
2Ti	2:20	some are for *n* purposes

NOTHING
Ne 9:21 in the desert; they lacked *n*,
Jer 32:17 *N* is too hard for you
Jn 15: 5 apart from me you can do *n*.

NULLIFY
Ro 3:31 Do we, then, *n* the law by this faith

OATH
Dt 7: 8 and kept the *o* he swore

OBEDIENCE (OBEY)
2Ch 31:21 in *o* to the law and the commands,
Pr 30:17 that scorns *o* to a mother,
Ro 1: 5 to the *o* that comes from faith.

OLIVES

OLIVES (OLIVE)
Jas 3:12 a fig tree bear o, or a grapevine bear

OMEGA
Rev 1: 8 "I am the Alpha and the O,"

OMRI
King of Israel (1Ki 16:21-26).

OPINIONS*
1Ki 18:21 will you waver between two o?
Pr 18: 2 but delights in airing his own o.

OPPORTUNITY
Ro 7:11 seizing the o afforded
Gal 6:10 as we have o, let us do good
Eph 5:16 making the most of every o,
Col 4: 5 make the most of every o.
1Ti 5:14 to give the enemy no o for slander.

OPPOSES
Jas 4: 6 "God o the proud
1Pe 5: 5 because, "God o the proud

OPPRESS (OPPRESSED)
Ex 22:21 "Do not mistreat an alien or o him,
Zec 7:10 Do not o the widow

OPPRESSED (OPPRESS)
Ps 9: 9 The LORD is a refuge for the o,
Isa 53: 7 He was o and afflicted,
Zec 10: 2 o for lack of a shepherd.

ORDAINED
Ps 8: 2 you have o praise

ORDERLY
1Co 14:40 done in a fitting and o way.
Col 2: 5 and delight to see how o you are

ORGIES*
Ro 13:13 not in o and drunkenness,
Gal 5:21 drunkenness, o, and the like.
1Pe 4: 3 o, carousing and detestable

ORIGIN
2Pe 1:21 For prophecy never had its o

ORPHANS
Jn 14:18 will not leave you as o; I will come
Jas 1:27 to look after o and widows

OUTCOME
Heb 13: 7 Consider the o of their way of life
1Pe 4:17 what will the o be for those who do

OUTSIDERS*
Col 4: 5 wise in the way you act toward o;
1Th 4:12 daily life may win the respect of o
1Ti 3: 7 also have a good reputation with o,

OUTSTANDING
SS 5:10 o among ten thousand.
Ro 13: 8 no debt remain o,

OUTSTRETCHED
Ex 6: 6 and will redeem you with an o arm
Jer 27: 5 and o arm I made the earth
Eze 20:33 an o arm and with outpoured wrath

OUTWEIGHS
2Co 4:17 an eternal glory that far o them all.

OVERCOME (OVERCOMES)
Mt 16:18 and the gates of Hades will not o it.
Mk 9:24 I do believe; help me o my unbelief
Jn 16:33 But take heart! I have o the world."
Ro 12:21 Do not be o by evil, but o evil
1Jn 5: 4 is the victory that has o the world,
Rev 17:14 but the Lamb will o them

OVERCOMES* (OVERCOME)
1Jn 5: 4 born of God o the world.
5: 5 Who is it that o the world?
Rev 2: 7 To him who o, I will give the right
2:11 He who o will not be hurt at all
2:17 To him who o, I will give some
2:26 To him who o and does my will
3: 5 He who o will, like them, be
3:12 Him who o I will make a pillar
3:21 To him who o, I will give the right
21: 7 He who o will inherit all this,

OVERFLOW (OVERFLOWS)
Ps 119:171 May my lips o with praise,
Lk 6:45 out of the o of his heart his mouth
Ro 15:13 so that you may o with hope
2Co 4:15 to o to the glory of God.
1Th 3:12 o for each other and for everyone

OVERFLOWS* (OVERFLOW)
Ps 23: 5 my cup o.

2Co 1: 5 also through Christ our comfort o.

OVERJOYED* (JOY)
Da 6:23 The king was o and gave orders
Mt 2:10 they saw the star, they were o.
Jn 20:20 The disciples were o
Ac 12:14 she was so o she ran back
1Pe 4:13 so that you may be o

OVERSEER (OVERSEERS)
1Ti 3: 1 anyone sets his heart on being an o,
3: 2 Now the o must be above reproach,
Tit 1: 7 Since an o is entrusted

OVERSEERS* (OVERSEER)
Ac 20:28 the Holy Spirit has made you o.
Php 1: 1 together with the o and deacons:
1Pe 5: 2 as o— not because you must,

OVERWHELMED
Ps 38: 4 My guilt has o me
65: 3 When we were o by sins,
Mt 26:38 "My soul is o with sorrow
Mk 7:37 People were o with amazement.

OWE
Ro 13: 7 If you o taxes, pay taxes; if revenue
Phm 19 to mention that you o me your very

OX
Dt 25: 4 Do not muzzle an o
Isa 11: 7 and the lion will eat straw like the o
1Co 9: 9 "Do not muzzle an o

PAGANS
Mt 5:47 Do not even p do that? Be perfect,
1Pe 2:12 such good lives among the p that,

PAIN (PAINFUL)
Ge 3:16 with p you will give birth
Job 33:19 may be chastened on a bed of p
Jn 16:21 woman giving birth to a child has p

PAINFUL (PAIN)
Ge 3:17 through p toil you will eat of it
Heb 12:11 seems pleasant at the time, but p.
1Pe 4:12 at the p trial you are suffering,

PALMS
Isa 49:16 you on the p of my hands;

PANTS
Ps 42: 1 As the deer p for streams of water,

PARADISE*
Lk 23:43 today you will be with me in p."
2Co 12: 4 God knows—was caught up to p.
Rev 2: 7 of life, which is in the p of God.

PARALYTIC
Mk 2: 3 bringing to him a p, carried by four

PARDON (PARDONS)
Isa 55: 7 and to our God, for he will freely p.

PARDONS* (PARDON)
Mic 7:18 who p sin and forgives

PARENTS
Pr 17: 6 and p are the pride of their children
Lk 18:29 left home or wife or brothers or p
21:16 You will be betrayed even by p,
Ro 1:30 they disobey their p; they are
2Co 12:14 for their p, but p for their children.
Eph 6: 1 Children, obey your p in the Lord,
Col 3:20 obey your p in everything,
2Ti 3: 2 disobedient to their p, ungrateful,

PARTIALITY
Dt 10:17 who shows no p and accepts no
2Ch 19: 7 our God there is no injustice or p
Lk 20:21 and that you do not show p

PARTICIPATION
1Co 10:16 is not the bread that we break a p

PASS
Ex 12:13 and when I see the blood, I will p
La 1:12 to you, all you who p by?
Lk 21:33 Heaven and earth will p away,
1Co 13: 8 there is knowledge, it will p away.

PASSION (PASSIONS)
1Co 7: 9 better to marry than to burn with p.

PASSIONS (PASSION)
Gal 5:24 crucified the sinful nature with its p
Tit 2:12 to ungodliness and worldly p,

PASSOVER
Ex 12:11 Eat it in haste; it is the LORD's P.
Dt 16: 1 celebrate the P of the LORD your
1Co 5: 7 our P lamb, has been sacrificed.

PAST
Isa 43:18 do not dwell on the p.
Ro 15: 4 in the p was written to teach us,
Heb 1: 1 In the p God spoke

PASTORS*
Eph 4:11 and some to be p and teachers,

PASTURE (PASTURES)
Ps 37: 3 dwell in the land and enjoy safe p.
100: 3 we are his people, the sheep of his p
Jer 50: 7 against the LORD, their true p,
Eze 34:13 I will p them on the mountains
Jn 10: 9 come in and go out, and find p.

PASTURES (PASTURE)
Ps 23: 2 He makes me lie down in green p,

PATCH
Mt 9:16 No one sews a p of unshrunk cloth

PATH (PATHS)
Ps 27:11 lead me in a straight p
119:105 and a light for my p.
Pr 15:19 the p of the upright is a highway.
15:24 The p of life leads upward
Isa 26: 7 The p of the righteous is level;
Lk 1:79 to guide our feet into the p of peace
2Co 6: 3 no stumbling block in anyone's p,

PATHS (PATH)
Ps 23: 3 He guides me in p of righteousness
25: 4 teach me your p;
Pr 3: 6 and he will make your p straight.
Ro 11:33 and his p beyond tracing out!
Heb 12:13 "Make level p for your feet,"

PATIENCE (PATIENT)
Pr 19:11 A man's wisdom gives him p;
2Co 6: 6 understanding, p and kindness,
Gal 5:22 joy, peace, p, kindness, goodness,
Col 1:11 may have great endurance and p,
3:12 humility, gentleness and p.

PATIENT (PATIENCE PATIENTLY)
Pr 15:18 but a p man calms a quarrel.
Ro 12:12 Be joyful in hope, p in affliction,
1Co 13: 4 Love is p, love is kind.
Eph 4: 2 humble and gentle; be p,
1Th 5:14 help the weak, be p with everyone.

PATIENTLY (PATIENT)
Ps 40: 1 I waited p for the LORD;
Ro 8:25 we do not yet have, we wait for it p.

PATTERN
Ro 5:14 who was a p of the one to come.
12: 2 longer to the p of this world,
2Ti 1:13 keep as the p of sound teaching,

PAUL
Also called Saul (Ac 13:9). Pharisee from Tarsus (Ac 9:11; Php 3:5). Apostle (Gal 1). At stoning of Stephen (Ac 8:1). Persecuted Church (Ac 9:1-2; Gal 1:13). Vision of Jesus on road to Damascus (Ac 9:4-9; 26:12-18). In Arabia (Gal 1:17). Preached in Damascus; escaped death through the wall in a basket (Ac 9:19-25). In Jerusalem; sent back to Tarsus (Ac 9:26-30).
Brought to Antioch by Barnabas (Ac 11:22-26). First missionary journey to Cyprus and Galatia (Ac 13-14). Stoned at Lystra (Ac 14:19-20). At Jerusalem council (Ac 15). Split with Barnabas over Mark (Ac 15:36-41).
Second missionary journey with Silas (Ac 16-20). Called to Macedonia (Ac 16:6-10). Freed from prison in Philippi (Ac 16:16-40). In Thessalonica (Ac 17:1-9). Speech in Athens (Ac 17:16-33). In Corinth (Ac 18). In Ephesus (Ac 19). Return to Jerusalem (Ac 20). Farewell to Ephesian elders (Ac 20:13-38). Arrival in Jerusalem (Ac 21:1-26). Arrested (Ac 21:27-36). Addressed crowds (Ac 22), Sanhedrin (Ac 23:1-11). Transferred to Caesarea (Ac 23:12-35). Trial before Felix (Ac 24), Festus (Ac 25:1-12). Before Agrippa (Ac 25:13-26:32). Voyage to Rome; shipwreck (Ac 27). Arrival in Rome (Ac 28).

PAY (REPAID REPAY)
Lev 26:43 They will p for their sins
Pr 22:17 P attention and listen
Mt 22:17 is it right to p taxes to Caesar
Ro 13: 6 This is also why you p taxes,
2Pe 1:19 you will do well to p attention to it,

PEACE (PEACEMAKERS)
Nu 6:26 and give you p."
Ps 34:14 seek p and pursue it.
85:10 righteousness and p kiss each other

119:165 Great p have they who love your
122: 6 Pray for the p of Jerusalem:
Pr 14:30 A heart at p gives life to the body,
   17: 1 Better a dry crust with p and quiet
Isa 9: 6 Everlasting Father, Prince of P.
    26: 3 You will keep in perfect p
    48:22 "There is no p," says the LORD,
Zec 9:10 He will proclaim p to the nations.
Mt 10:34 I did not come to bring p,
Lk   2:14 on earth p to men on whom his
Jn 14:27 P I leave with you; my p
    16:33 so that in me you may have p.
Ro   5: 1 we have p with God
1Co 7:15 God has called us to live in p.
    14:33 a God of disorder but of p.
Gal 5:22 joy, p, patience, kindness,
Eph 2:14 he himself is our p, who has made
Php 4: 7 the p of God, which transcends all
Col 1:20 by making p through his blood,
     3:15 Let the p of Christ rule
1Th 5: 3 While people are saying, "P
2Th 3:16 the Lord of p himself give you p
2Ti 2:22 righteousness, faith, love and p,
1Pe 3:11 he must seek p and pursue it.
Rev 6: 4 power to take p from the earth
PEACEMAKERS* (PEACE)
Mt   5: 9 Blessed are the p,
Jas 3:18 P who sow in peace raise a harvest
PEARL* (PEARLS)
Rev 21:21 each gate made of a single p.
PEARLS (PEARL)
Mt   7: 6 do not throw your p to pigs.
    13:45 like a merchant looking for fine p.
1Ti 2: 9 or gold or p or expensive clothes,
Rev 21:21 The twelve gates were twelve p,
PEKAH
King of Israel (2Ki 15:25-31; Isa 7:1).
PEKAHIAH*
Son of Menahem; king of Israel (2Ki 15:22-26).
PEN
Mt   5:18 letter, not the least stroke of a p,
PENTECOST
Ac   2: 1 of P came, they were all together
PEOPLE (PEOPLES)
Dt 32: 9 the LORD's portion is his p,
Ru   1:16 Your p will be my p
2Ch 7:14 if my p, who are called
Jer 24: 7 They will be my p,
Zec 2:11 and will become my p.
Lk   2:10 joy that will be for all the p.
Ac 15:14 from the Gentiles a p.
2Co 6:16 and they will be my p."
Tit 2:14 a p that are his very own,
1Pe 2: 9 you are a chosen p,
Rev 21: 3 They will be his p,
PEOPLES (PEOPLE)
Da   7:14 all p, nations and men
Mic 4: 1 and p will stream to it.
PERCEIVING
Isa 6: 9 be ever seeing, but never p.'
PERFECT (PERFECTER PERFECTION)
SS   5: 2 but my dove, my p one, is unique,
Isa 26: 3 You will keep in p peace
Mt   5:48 as your heavenly Father is p.
Ro 12: 2 his good, pleasing and p will.
2Co 12: 9 for my power is made p
Col 1:28 so that we may present everyone p
     3:14 binds them all together in p unity.
Heb 9:11 and more p tabernacle that is not
    10:14 he has made p forever those who
Jas 1:17 Every good and p gift is from above
     1:25 into the p law that gives freedom,
     3: 2 he is a p man, able
1Jn 4:18 But p love drives out fear,
PERFECTER* (PERFECT)
Heb 12: 2 the author and p of our faith,
PERFECTION (PERFECT)
Ps 119: 96 To all p I see a limit;
2Co 13: 11 Aim for p, listen to my appeal,
Heb 7:11 If p could have been attained
PERFORMS
Ps 77:14 You are the God who p miracles;

PERISH (PERISHABLE)
Ps   1: 6 but the way of the wicked will p.
   102:26 They will p, but you remain;
Lk 13: 3 unless you repent, you too will all p
Jn 10:28 eternal life, and they shall never p;
Col 2:22 These are all destined to p with use,
Heb 1:11 They will p, but you remain;
2Pe 3: 9 not wanting anyone to p,
PERISHABLE (PERISH)
1Co 15:42 The body that is sown is p,
PERJURERS
1Ti 1:10 for slave traders and liars and p—
PERMISSIBLE (PERMIT)
1Co 10:23 "Everything is p"— but not
PERMIT (PERMISSIBLE)
1Ti 2:12 I do not p a woman to teach
PERSECUTE (PERSECUTED PERSECUTION)
Mt   5:11 p you and falsely say all kinds
Lk 15:20 they persecuted me, they will p you
Ac   9: 4 why do you p me?" "Who are you,
Ro 12:14 Bless those who p you; bless
PERSECUTED (PERSECUTE)
1Co 4:12 when we are p, we endure it;
2Ti 3:12 life in Christ Jesus will be p,
PERSECUTION (PERSECUTE)
Ro   8:35 or hardship or p or famine
PERSEVERANCE (PERSEVERE)
Ro   5: 3 we know that suffering produces p;
     5: 4 p, character; and character, hope.
Heb 12: 1 run with p the race marked out
Jas 1: 3 the testing of your faith develops p.
2Pe 1: 6 p; and to p, godliness;
PERSEVERE* (PERSEVERANCE PERSEVERED PERSEVERES)
1Ti 4:16 P in them, because if you do,
Heb 10:36 You need to p so that
PERSEVERED* (PERSEVERE)
Heb 11:27 he p because he saw him who is
Jas 5:11 consider blessed those who have p.
Rev 3: 3 You have p and have endured
PERSEVERES* (PERSEVERE)
1Co 13: 7 trusts, always hopes, always p.
Jas 1:12 Blessed is the man who p
PERSUADE
2Co 5:11 is to fear the Lord, we try to p men.
PERVERSION (PERVERT)
Lev 18:23 sexual relations with it; that is a p.
Jude   7 up to sexual immorality and p.
PERVERT (PERVERSION PERVERTS)
Gal 1: 7 are trying to p the gospel of Christ.
PERVERTS* (PERVERT)
1Ti 1:10 for murderers, for adulterers and p,
PESTILENCE
Ps 91: 6 nor the p that stalks in the darkness
PETER
Apostle, brother of Andrew, also called Simon (Mt 10:2; Mk 3:16; Lk 6:14; Ac 1:13), and Cephas (Jn 1:42). Confession of Christ (Mt 16:13-20; Mk 8:27-30; Lk 9:18-27). At transfiguration (Mt 17:1-8; Mk 9:2-8; Lk 9:28-36; 2Pe 1:16-18). Caught fish with coin (Mt 17:24-27). Denial of Jesus predicted (Mt 26:31-35; Mk 14:27-31; Lk 22:31-34; Jn 13:31-38). Denied Jesus (Mt 26:69-75; Mk 14:66-72; Lk 22:54-62; Jn 18:15-27). Commissioned by Jesus to shepherd his flock (Jn 21:15-23).
Speech at Pentecost (Ac 2). Healed beggar (Ac 3:1-10). Speech at temple (Ac 3:11-26), before Sanhedrin (Ac 4:1-22). In Samaria (Ac 8:14-25). Sent by vision to Cornelius (Ac 10). Announced salvation of Gentiles in Jerusalem (Ac 11; 15). Freed from prison (Ac 12). Inconsistency at Antioch (Gal 2:11-21). At Jerusalem Council (Ac 15).
PHARISEES
Mt   5:20 surpasses that of the P
PHILIP
1. Apostle (Mt 10:3; Mk 3:18; Lk 6:14; Jn 1:43-48; 14:8; Ac 1:13).
2. Deacon (Ac 6:1-7); evangelist in Samaria (Ac 8:4-25), to Ethiopian (Ac 8:26-40).
PHILOSOPHY*
Col 2: 8 through hollow and deceptive p,

PHYLACTERIES*
Mt 23: 5 They make their p wide
PHYSICAL
1Ti 4: 8 For p training is of some value,
Jas 2:16 but does nothing about his p needs,
PIECES
Ge 15:17 and passed between the p.
Jer 34:18 and then walked between its p.
PIERCED
Ps 22:16 they have p my hands and my feet.
Isa 53: 5 But he was p for our transgressions,
Zec 12:10 look on me, the one they have p,
Jn 19:37 look on the one they have p."
PIGS
Mt   7: 6 do not throw your pearls to p.
PILATE
Governor of Judea. Questioned Jesus (Mt 27:1-26; Mk 15:15; Lk 22:66-23:25; Jn 18:28-19:16); sent him to Herod (Lk 23:6-12); consented to his crucifixion when crowds chose Barabbas (Mt 27:15-26; Mk 15:6-15; Lk 23:13-25; Jn 19:1-10).
PILLAR
Ge 19:26 and she became a p of salt.
Ex 13:21 ahead of them in a p of cloud
1Ti 3:15 the p and foundation of the truth.
PIT
Ps 40: 2 He lifted me out of the slimy p,
   103: 4 who redeems your life from the p
Mt 15:14 a blind man, both will fall into a p."
PITIED
1Co 15:19 we are to be p more than all men.
PLAGUE
2Ch 6:28 "When famine or p comes
PLAIN
Ro   1:19 what may be known about God is p
PLAN (PLANNED PLANS)
Job 42: 2 no p of yours can be thwarted.
Pr 14:22 those who p what is good find love
Eph 1:11 predestined according to the p
PLANK
Mt   7: 3 attention to the p in your own eye?
Lk   6:41 attention to the p in your own eye?
PLANNED (PLAN)
Ps 40: 5 The things you p for us
Isa 46:11 what I have p, that will I do.
Heb 11:40 God had p something better for us
PLANS (PLAN)
Ps 20: 4 and make all your p succeed.
    33:11 p of the LORD stand firm forever,
Pr 20:18 Make p by seeking advice;
Isa 32: 8 But the noble man makes noble p,
PLANTED (PLANTS)
Ps   1: 3 He is like a tree p by streams
Mt 15:13 Father has not p will be pulled
1Co 3: 6 I p the seed, Apollos watered it,
PLANTS (PLANTED)
1Co 3: 7 So neither he who p nor he who
     9: 7 Who p a vineyard and does not eat
PLATTER
Mk   6:25 head of John the Baptist on a p."
PLAYED
Lk   7:32 " 'We p the flute for you,
1Co 14: 7 anyone know what tune is being p
PLEADED
2Co 12: 8 Three times I p with the Lord
PLEASANT (PLEASE)
Ps 16: 6 for me in p places;
   133: 1 How good and p it is
   147: 1 how p and fitting to praise him!
Heb 12:11 No discipline seems p at the time,
PLEASE (PLEASANT PLEASED PLEASES PLEASING PLEASURE PLEASURES)
Pr 20:23 and dishonest scales do not p him.
Jer 6:20 your sacrifices do not p me."
Jn   5:30 for I seek not to p myself
Ro   8: 8 by the sinful nature cannot p God.
    15: 2 Each of us should p his neighbor
1Co 7:32 affairs—how he can p the Lord.
    10:33 I try to p everybody in every way.
2Co 5: 9 So we make it our goal to p him,
Gal 1:10 or of God? Or am I trying to p men

1Th 4: 1 how to live in order to *p* God,
2Ti 2: 4 wants to *p* his commanding officer.
Heb 11: 6 faith it is impossible to *p* God,

PLEASED (PLEASE)
Mt 3:17 whom I love; with him I am well *p*
1Co 1:21 God was *p* through the foolishness
Col 1:19 For God was *p* to have all his
Heb 11: 5 commended as one who *p* God.
2Pe 1:17 whom I love; with him I am well *p*

PLEASES (PLEASE)
Ps 135: 6 The LORD does whatever *p* him,
Pr 15: 8 but the prayer of the upright *p* him.
Jn 3: 8 The wind blows wherever it *p*.
8:29 for I always do what *p* him."
Col 3:20 in everything, for this *p* the Lord.
1Ti 2: 3 This is good, and *p* God our Savior,
1Jn 3:22 his commands and do what *p* him.

PLEASING (PLEASE)
Ps 104: 34 May my meditation be *p* to him,
Ro 12: 1 *p* to God—which is your spiritual
Php 4:18 an acceptable sacrifice, *p* to God.
Heb 13:21 may he work in us what is *p* to him,

PLEASURE (PLEASE)
Ps 5: 4 You are not a God who takes *p*
147: 10 His *p* is not in the strength
Pr 21:17 He who loves *p* will become poor;
Eze 18:32 For I take no *p* in the death
Eph 1: 5 in accordance with his *p* and will—
1: 9 of his will according to his good *p*,
2Ti 3: 4 lovers of *p* rather than lovers

PLEASURES (PLEASE)
Ps 16: 11 with eternal *p* at your right hand.
Heb 11:25 rather than to enjoy the *p* of sin
2Pe 2:13 reveling in their *p* while they feast

PLENTIFUL
Mt 9:37 harvest is *p* but the workers are

PLOW (PLOWSHARES)
Lk 9:62 "No one who puts his hand to the *p*

PLOWSHARES (PLOW)
Isa 2: 4 They will beat their swords into *p*
Joel 3:10 Beat your *p* into swords

PLUNDER
Ex 3:22 And so you will *p* the Egyptians."

POINT
Jas 2:10 yet stumbles at just one *p* is guilty

POISON
Mk 16:18 and when they drink deadly *p*,
Jas 3: 8 It is a restless evil, full of deadly *p*.

POLLUTE* (POLLUTED)
Nu 35:33 " 'Do not *p* the land where you are.
Jude 8 these dreamers *p* their own bodies,

POLLUTED* (POLLUTE)
Ezr 9: 11 entering to possess is a land *p*
Pr 25:26 Like a muddied spring or a *p* well
Ac 15:20 to abstain from food *p* by idols,
Jas 1:27 oneself from being *p* by the world.

PONDER
Ps 64: 9 and *p* what he has done.
119: 95 but I will *p* your statutes.

POOR (POVERTY)
Dt 15: 4 there should be no *p* among you,
15: 11 There will always be *p* people
Ps 34: 6 This *p* man called, and the LORD
82: 3 maintain the rights of the *p*
112: 9 scattered abroad his gifts to the *p*,
Pr 10: 4 Lazy hands make a man *p*,
13: 7 to be *p*, yet has great wealth.
14:31 oppresses the *p* shows contempt
19: 1 Better a *p* man whose walk is
19:17 to the *p* lends to the LORD,
22: 2 Rich and *p* have this in common:
22: 9 for he shares his food with the *p*.
28: 6 Better a *p* man whose walk is
31:20 She opens her arms to the *p*
Isa 61: 1 me to preach good news to the *p*.
Mt 5: 3 saying: "Blessed are the *p* in spirit,
11: 5 the good news is preached to the *p*.
19:21 your possessions and give to the *p*,
26: 11 The *p* you will always have
Mk 12:42 But a *p* widow came and put
Ac 10: 4 and gifts to the *p* have come up
1Co 13: 3 If I give all I possess to the *p*
2Co 8: 9 yet for your sakes he became *p*,
Jas 2: 2 and a *p* man in shabby clothes

PORTION
Dt 32: 9 For the LORD's *p* is his people,
2Ki 2: 9 "Let me inherit a double *p*
La 3:24 to myself, "The LORD is my *p*;

POSSESS (POSSESSING POSSESSION POSSESSIONS)
Nu 33:53 for I have given you the land to *p*.
Jn 5:39 that by them you *p* eternal life.

POSSESSING* (POSSESS)
2Co 6:10 nothing, and yet *p* everything.

POSSESSION (POSSESS)
Ge 15: 7 to give you this land to take *p* of it
Nu 13:30 "We should go up and take *p*
Eph 1:14 of those who are God's *p*—

POSSESSIONS (POSSESS)
Lk 12:15 consist in the abundance of his *p*."
2Co 12:14 what I want is not your *p* but you.
1Jn 3:17 If anyone has material *p*

POSSIBLE
Mt 19:26 but with God all things are *p*."
Mk 9:23 "Everything is *p* for him who
10:27 all things are *p* with God."
Ro 12:18 If it is *p*, as far as it depends on you,
1Co 9:22 by all *p* means I might save some.

POT (POTSHERD POTTER POTTERY)
2Ki 4:40 there is death in the *p*!"
Jer 18: 4 But the *p* he was shaping

POTSHERD (POT)
Isa 45: 9 a *p* among the potsherds

POTTER (POT)
Isa 29:16 Can the pot say of the *p*,
45: 9 Does the clay say to the *p*,
64: 8 We are the clay, you are the *p*;
Jer 18: 6 "Like clay in the hand of the *p*,
Ro 9:21 Does not the *p* have the right

POTTERY (POT)
Ro 9:21 of clay some *p* for noble purposes

POUR (POURED)
Ps 62: 8 *p* out your hearts to him,
Joel 2:28 I will *p* out my Spirit on all people.
Mal 3:10 *p* out so much blessing that you
Ac 2:17 I will *p* out my Spirit on all people.

POURED (POUR)
Ac 10:45 of the Holy Spirit had been *p* out
Ro 5: 5 because God has *p* out his love

POVERTY (POOR)
Pr 14:23 but mere talk leads only to *p*.
21: 5 as surely as haste leads to *p*.
30: 8 give me neither *p* nor riches,
Mk 12:44 out of her *p*, put in everything—
2Co 8: 2 and their extreme *p* welled up
8: 9 through his *p* might become rich.

POWER (POWERFUL POWERS)
1Ch 29: 11 LORD, is the greatness and the *p*
2Ch 32: 7 for there is a greater *p* with us
Job 36:22 "God is exalted in his *p*.
Ps 63: 2 and beheld your *p* and your glory.
68:34 Proclaim the *p* of God,
147: 5 Great is our Lord and mighty in *p*;
Pr 24: 5 A wise man has great *p*,
Isa 40:10 the Sovereign LORD comes with *p*
Zec 4: 6 nor by *p*, but by my Spirit,'
Mt 22:29 do not know the Scriptures or the *p*
24:30 on the clouds of the sky, with *p*
Ac 1: 8 you will receive *p* when the Holy
4:33 With great *p* the apostles
10:38 with the Holy Spirit and *p*,
Ro 1:16 it is the *p* of God for the salvation
1Co 1:18 to us who are being saved it is the *p*
15:56 of death is sin, and the *p*
2Co 12: 9 for my *p* is made perfect
Eph 1:19 and his incomparably great *p*
Php 3:10 and the *p* of his resurrection
Col 1: 11 strengthened with all *p* according
2Ti 1: 7 but a spirit of *p*, of love
Heb 7:16 of the *p* of an indestructible life.
Rev 4: 11 to receive glory and honor and *p*,
19: 1 and glory and *p* belong to our God,
20: 6 The second death has no *p*

POWERFUL (POWER)
Ps 29: 4 The voice of the LORD is *p*;
Lk 24:19 *p* in word and deed before God
2Th 1: 7 in blazing fire with his *p* angels.
Heb 1: 3 sustaining all things by his *p* word.
Jas 5:16 The prayer of a righteous man is *p*

POWERLESS
Ro 5: 6 when we were still *p*, Christ died
8: 3 For what the law was *p* to do

POWERS (POWER)
Ro 8:38 nor any *p*, neither height nor depth
1Co 12:10 to another miraculous *p*,
Col 1:16 whether thrones or *p* or rulers
2:15 And having disarmed the *p*

PRACTICE
Lev 19:26 " 'Do not *p* divination or sorcery.
Mt 23: 3 for they do not *p* what they preach.
Lk 8:21 hear God's word and put it into *p*."
Ro 12:13 *P* hospitality.
1Ti 5: 4 to put their religion into *p* by caring

PRAISE (PRAISED PRAISES PRAISING)
Ex 15: 2 He is my God, and I will *p* him,
Dt 32: 3 Oh, *p* the greatness of our God!
Ru 4:14 said to Naomi: "*P* be to the LORD,
2Sa 22:47 The LORD lives! *P* be to my Rock
1Ch 16:25 is the LORD and most worthy of *p*;
2Ch 20:21 and to *p* him for the splendor
Ps 8: 2 you have ordained *p*
33: 1 it is fitting for the upright to *p* him.
34: 1 his *p* will always be on my lips.
40: 3 a hymn of *p* to our God.
48: 1 the LORD, and most worthy of *p*,
68:19 *P* be to the Lord, to God our Savior
89: 5 The heavens *p* your wonders,
100: 4 and his courts with *p*;
105: 2 Sing to him, sing *p* to him;
106: 1 *P* the LORD.
119:175 Let me live that I may *p* you,
139: 14 I *p* you because I am fearfully
145: 21 Let every creature *p* his holy name
146: 1 *P* the LORD, O my soul.
150: 2 *p* him for his surpassing greatness.
150: 6 that has breath *p* the LORD.
Pr 27: 2 Let another *p* you, and not your
27:21 man is tested by the *p* he receives.
31:31 let her works bring her *p*
Mt 5:16 and *p* your Father in heaven.
21:16 you have ordained *p*'?"
Jn 12:43 for they loved *p* from men more
Eph 1: 6 to the *p* of his glorious grace,
1:12 might be for the *p* of his glory.
1:14 to the *p* of his glory.
Heb 13:15 offer to God a sacrifice of *p*—
Jas 5:13 happy? Let him sing songs of *p*.

PRAISED (PRAISE)
1Ch 29:10 David *p* the LORD in the presence
Ne 8: 6 Ezra *p* the LORD, the great God;
Da 2:19 Then Daniel *p* the God of heaven
Ro 9: 5 who is God over all, forever *p*!
1Pe 4: 11 that in all things God may be *p*

PRAISES (PRAISE)
2Sa 22:50 I will sing *p* to your name.
Ps 47: 6 Sing *p* to God, sing *p*;
147: 1 How good it is to sing *p* to our God,
Pr 31:28 her husband also, and he *p* her:

PRAISING (PRAISE)
Ac 10:46 speaking in tongues and *p* God.
1Co 14:16 If you are *p* God with your spirit,

PRAY (PRAYED PRAYER PRAYERS PRAYING)
Dt 4: 7 is near us whenever we *p* to him?
1Sa 12:23 the LORD by failing to *p* for you.
2Ch 7:14 will humble themselves and *p*
Job 42: 8 My servant Job will *p* for you,
Ps 122: 6 *P* for the peace of Jerusalem:
Mt 5:44 and *p* for those who persecute you,
6: 5 "And when you *p*, do not be like
6: 9 "This, then, is how you should *p*:
26:36 Sit here while I go over there and *p*
Lk 6:28 *p* for those who mistreat you.
18: 1 them that they should always *p*
22:40 "*P* that you will not fall
Ro 8:26 do not know what we ought to *p*,
1Co 14:13 in a tongue should *p* that he may
1Th 5:17 Be joyful always; *p* continually;
Jas 5:13 one of you in trouble? He should *p*.

PRAYED (PRAY)
1Sa 1:27 I *p* for this child, and the Lord
Jnh 2: 1 From inside the fish Jonah *p*
Mk 14:35 *p* that if possible the hour might

PRAYER (PRAY)
2Ch 30:27 for their *p* reached heaven,
Ezr 8:23 about this, and he answered our *p*.
Ps 6: 9 the Lord accepts my *p*.
  86: 6 Hear my *p*, O Lord;
Pr 15: 8 but the *p* of the upright pleases him
Isa 56: 7 a house of *p* for all nations."
Mt 21:13 house will be called a house of *p*,'
Mk 11:24 whatever you ask for in *p*,
Jn 17:15 My *p* is not that you take them out
Ac 6: 4 and will give our attention to *p*
Php 4: 6 but in everything, by *p* and petition
Jas 5:15 *p* offered in faith will make the sick
1Pe 3:12 and his ears are attentive to their *p*,

PRAYERS (PRAY)
1Ch 5:20 He answered their *p*, because they
Mk 12:40 and for a show make lengthy *p*.
1Pe 3: 7 so that nothing will hinder your *p*.
Rev 5: 8 which are the *p* of the saints.

PRAYING (PRAY)
Mk 11:25 And when you stand *p*,
Jn 17: 9 I am not *p* for the world,
Ac 16:25 and Silas were *p* and singing hymns
Eph 6:18 always keep on *p* for all the saints.

PREACH (PREACHED PREACHING)
Mt 23: 3 they do not practice what they *p*.
Mk 16:15 and *p* the good news to all creation.
Ac 9:20 At once he began to *p*
Ro 10:15 how can they *p* unless they are sent
  15:20 to *p* the gospel where Christ was
1Co 1:17 to *p* the gospel—not with words
  1:23 wisdom, but we *p* Christ crucified;
  9:14 that those who *p* the gospel should
  9:16 Woe to me if I do not *p* the gospel!
2Co 10:16 so that we can *p* the gospel
Gal 1: 8 from heaven should *p* a gospel
2Ti 4: 2 I give you this charge: *P* the Word;

PREACHED (PREACH)
Mk 13:10 And the gospel must first be *p*
Ac 8: 4 had been scattered *p* the word
1Co 9:27 so that after I have *p* to others,
  15: 1 you of the gospel I *p* to you,
2Co 11: 4 other than the Jesus we *p*,
Gal 1: 8 other than the one we *p* to you,
Php 1:18 false motives or true, Christ is *p*.
1Ti 3:16 was *p* among the nations,

PREACHING (PREACH)
Ro 10:14 hear without someone *p* to them?
1Co 9:18 in *p* the gospel I may offer it free
1Ti 4:13 the public reading of Scripture, to *p*
  5:17 especially those whose work is *p*

PRECEPTS
Ps 19: 8 The *p* of the Lord are right,
  111: 7 All his *p* are trustworthy.
  111: 10 who follow his *p* have good
  119: 40 How I long for your *p*!
  119: 69 I keep your *p* with all my heart.
  119: 104 I gain understanding from your *p*;
  119: 159 See how I love your *p*;

PRECIOUS
Ps 19:10 They are more *p* than gold,
  116: 15 *P* in the sight of the Lord
Pr 8:11 for wisdom is more *p* than rubies,
Isa 28:16 a *p* cornerstone for a sure
1Pe 1:19 but with the *p* blood of Christ,
  2: 6 a chosen and *p* cornerstone,
2Pe 1: 4 us his very great and *p* promises,

PREDESTINED* (DESTINY)
Ro 8:29 *p* to be conformed to the likeness
  8:30 And those he *p*, he also called;
Eph 1: 5 In love he *p* us to be adopted
  1:11 having been *p* according

PREDICTION*
Jer 28: 9 only if his *p* comes true."

PREPARE (PREPARED)
Ps 23: 5 You *p* a table before me
Am 4:12 *p* to meet your God, O Israel."

Jn 14: 2 there to *p* a place for you.
Eph 4:12 to *p* God's people for works

PREPARED (PREPARE)
Mt 25:34 the kingdom *p* for you
1Co 2: 9 what God has *p* for those who love
Eph 2:10 which God *p* in advance for us
2Ti 4: 2 be *p* in season and out of season;
1Pe 3:15 Always be *p* to give an answer

PRESENCE (PRESENT)
Ex 25:30 Put the bread of the *P* on this table
Ezr 9:15 one of us can stand in your *p*."
Ps 31:20 the shelter of your *p* you hide them
  89:15 who walk in the light of your *p*,
  90: 8 our secret sins in the light of your *p*
  139: 7 Where can I flee from your *p*?
Jer 5:22 "Should you not tremble in my *p*?
Heb 9:24 now to appear for us in God's *p*.
Jude 24 before his glorious *p* without fault

PRESENT (PRESENCE)
2Co 11: 2 so that I might *p* you as a pure
Eph 5:27 and to *p* her to himself
2Ti 2:15 Do your best to *p* yourself to God

PRESERVES
Ps 1 19:50 Your promise *p* my life.

PRESS (PRESSED PRESSURE)
Php 3:14 I *p* on toward the goal

PRESSED (PRESS)
Lk 6:38 *p* down, shaken together

PRESSURE (PRESS)
2Co 1: 8 We were under great *p*, far
  11:28 I face daily the *p* of my concern

PREVAILS
1Sa 2: 9 "It is not by strength that one *p*;

PRICE
Job 28:18 the *p* of wisdom is beyond rubies.
1Co 6:20 your own; you were bought at a *p*.
  7:23 bought at a *p*; do not become slaves

PRIDE (PROUD)
Pr 8:13 I hate *p* and arrogance,
  16:18 *P* goes before destruction,
Da 4:37 And those who walk in *p* he is able
Gal 6: 4 Then he can take *p* in himself,
Jas 1: 9 ought to take *p* in his high position.

PRIEST (PRIESTHOOD PRIESTS)
Heb 4:14 have a great high *p* who has gone
  4:15 do not have a high *p* who is unable
  7:26 Such a high *p* meets our need—
  8: 1 We do have such a high *p*,

PRIESTHOOD (PRIEST)
Heb 7:24 lives forever, he has a permanent *p*.
1Pe 2: 5 into a spiritual house to be a holy *p*,
  2: 9 you are a chosen people, a royal *p*,

PRIESTS (PRIEST)
Ex 19: 6 you will be for me a kingdom of *p*
Rev 5:10 to be a kingdom and *p*

PRINCE
Isa 9: 6 Everlasting Father, *P* of Peace.
Jn 12:31 now the *p* of this world will be
Ac 5:31 as *P* and Savior that he might give

PRISON (PRISONER)
Isa 42: 7 to free captives from *p*
Mt 25:36 I was in *p* and you came to visit me
1Pe 3:19 spirits in *p* who disobeyed long ago
Rev 20: 7 Satan will be released from his *p*

PRISONER (PRISON)
Ro 7:23 and making me a *p* of the law of sin
Gal 3:22 declares that the whole world is a *p*
Eph 3: 1 the *p* of Christ Jesus for the sake

PRIVILEGE*
2Co 8: 4 pleaded with us for the *p* of sharing

PRIZE
1Co 9:24 Run in such a way as to get the *p*.
Php 3:14 on toward the goal to win the *p*

PROCLAIM (PROCLAIMED PROCLAIMING)
1Ch 16:23 *p* his salvation day after day.
Ps 1: the skies *p* the work of his hands.
  50: 6 the heavens *p* his righteousness,
  68:34 *P* the power of God,
  118: 17 will *p* what the Lord has done.
Zec 9:10 He will *p* peace to the nations.
Ac 20:27 hesitated to *p* to you the whole will

1Co 11:26 you *p* the Lord's death

PROCLAIMED (PROCLAIM)
Ro 15:19 I have fully *p* the gospel of Christ.
Col 1:23 that has been *p* to every creature

PROCLAIMING (PROCLAIM)
Ro 10: 8 the word of faith we are *p*:

PRODUCE (PRODUCES)
Mt 3: 8 *P* fruit in keeping with repentance.
  3:10 tree that does not *p* good fruit will

PRODUCES (PRODUCE)
Pr 30:33 so stirring up anger *p* strife."
Ro 5: 3 that suffering *p* perseverance;
Heb 12:11 it *p* a harvest of righteousness

PROFANE
Lev 22:32 Do not *p* my holy name.

PROFESS*
1Ti 2:10 for women who *p* to worship God.
Heb 4:14 let us hold firmly to the faith we *p*.
  10:23 unswervingly to the hope we *p*,

PROMISE (PROMISED PROMISES)
1Ki 8:20 The Lord has kept the *p* he made
Ac 2:39 The *p* is for you and your children
Gal 3:14 that by faith we might receive the *p*
1Ti 4: 8 holding *p* for both the present life
2Pe 3: 9 Lord is not slow in keeping his *p*,

PROMISED (PROMISE)
Ex 3:17 And I have *p* to bring you up out
Dt 26:18 his treasured possession as he *p*,
Ps 119: 57 I have *p* to obey your words.
Ro 4:21 power to do what he had *p*.
Heb 10:23 for he who *p* is faithful.
2Pe 3: 4 "Where is this 'coming' he *p*?

PROMISES (PROMISE)
Jos 21:45 one of all the Lord's good *p*
Ro 9: 4 the temple worship and the *p*.
2Pe 1: 4 us his very great and precious *p*,

PROMPTED
1Th 1: 3 your labor *p* by love, and your
2Th 1:11 and every act *p* by your faith.

PROPHECIES (PROPHESY)
1Co 13: 8 where there are *p*, they will cease;
1Th 5:20 do not treat *p* with contempt.

PROPHECY (PROPHESY)
1Co 14: 1 gifts, especially the gift of *p*.
2Pe 1:20 you must understand that no *p*

PROPHESY (PROPHECIES PROPHECY PROPHESYING PROPHET PROPHETS)
Joel 2:28 Your sons and daughters will *p*,
Mt 7:22 Lord, did we not *p* in your name,
1Co 14:39 my brothers, be eager to *p*,

PROPHESYING (PROPHESY)
Ro 12: 6 If a man's gift is *p*, let him use it

PROPHET (PROPHESY)
Dt 18:18 up for them a *p* like you
Am 7:14 "I was neither a *p* nor a prophet's
Mt 10:41 Anyone who receives a *p*
Lk 4:24 "no *p* is accepted in his hometown.

PROPHETS (PROPHESY)
Ps 105: 15 do my *p* no harm."
Mt 5:17 come to abolish the Law or the *P*;
  7:12 for this sums up the Law and the *P*.
  24:24 false Christs and false *p* will appear
Lk 24:25 believe all that the *p* have spoken!
Ac 10:43 All the *p* testify about him that
1Co 12:28 second *p*, third teachers, then
  14:32 The spirits of *p* are subject
Eph 2:20 foundation of the apostles and *p*,
Heb 1: 1 through the *p* at many times
1Pe 1:10 Concerning this salvation, the *p*,
2Pe 1:19 word of the *p* made more certain,

PROSPER (PROSPERITY PROSPERS)
Pr 28:25 he who trusts in the Lord will *p*.

PROSPERITY (PROSPER)
Ps 73: 3 when I saw the *p* of the wicked.
Pr 13:21 but *p* is the reward of the righteous.

PROSPERS (PROSPER)
Ps 1: 3 Whatever he does *p*.

PROSTITUTE (PROSTITUTES)
1Co 6:15 of Christ and unite them with a *p*?

PROSTITUTES (PROSTITUTE)
Lk 15:30 property with *p* comes home,

PROSTRATE

1Co 6: 9 male *p* nor homosexual offenders
PROSTRATE
Dt 9:18 again I fell *p* before the LORD
PROTECT (PROTECTS)
Ps 32: 7 you will *p* me from trouble
Pr 2:11 Discretion will *p* you,
Jn 17:11 *p* them by the power of your name
PROTECTS (PROTECT)
1Co 13: 7 It always *p*, always trusts,
PROUD (PRIDE)
Pr 16: 5 The LORD detests all the *p*
Ro 12:16 Do not be *p*, but be willing
1Co 13: 4 it does not boast, it is not *p*.
PROVE
Ac 26:20 *p* their repentance by their deeds.
1Co 4: 2 been given a trust must *p* faithful.
PROVIDE (PROVIDED PROVIDES)
Ge 22: 8 "God himself will *p* the lamb
Isa 43:20 because I *p* water in the desert
1Ti 5: 8 If anyone does not *p*
PROVIDED (PROVIDE)
Jnh 1:17 But the LORD *p* a great fish
4: 6 Then the LORD God *p* a vine
4: 7 dawn the next day God *p* a worm,
4: 8 God *p* a scorching east wind,
PROVIDES (PROVIDE)
1Ti 6:17 who richly *p* us with everything
1Pe 4:11 it with the strength God *p*,
PROVOKED
Ecc 7: 9 Do not be quickly *p* in your spirit,
PRUDENT
Pr 14:15 a *p* man gives thought to his steps.
19:14 but a *p* wife is from the LORD.
Am 5:13 Therefore the *p* man keeps quiet
PRUNING
Isa 2: 4 and their spears into *p* hooks.
Joel 3:10 and your *p* hooks into spears.
PSALMS
Eph 5:19 Speak to one another with *p*,
Col 3:16 and as you sing *p*, hymns
PUBLICLY
Ac 20:20 have taught you *p* and from house
1Ti 5:20 Those who sin are to be rebuked *p*,
PUFFS
1Co 8: 1 Knowledge *p* up, but love builds up
PULLING
2Co 10: 8 building you up rather than *p* you
PUNISH (PUNISHED PUNISHES)
Ex 32:34 I will *p* them for their sin."
Pr 23:13 if you *p* him with the rod, he will
Isa 13:11 I will *p* the world for its evil,
1Pe 2:14 by him to *p* those who do wrong
PUNISHED (PUNISH)
La 3:39 complain when *p* for his sins?
2Th 1: 9 be *p* with everlasting destruction
Heb 10:29 to be *p* who has trampled the Son
PUNISHES (PUNISH)
Heb 12: 6 everyone he accepts
PURE (PURIFIES PURIFY PURITY)
2Sa 22:27 to the *p* you show yourself *p*,
Ps 24: 4 who has clean hands and a *p* heart,
51:10 Create in me a *p* heart, O God,
119: 9 can a young man keep his way *p*?
Pr 20: 9 can say, "I have kept my heart *p*;
Isa 52:11 Come out from it and be *p*,
Hab 1:13 Your eyes are too *p* to look on evil;
Mt 5: 8 Blessed are the *p* in heart,
2Co 11: 2 I might present you as a *p* virgin
Php 4: 8 whatever is *p*, whatever is lovely,
1Ti 5:22 Keep yourself *p*.
Tit 1:15 To the *p*, all things are *p*,
2: 5 to be self-controlled and *p*,
Heb 13: 4 and the marriage bed kept *p*,
1Jn 3: 3 him purifies himself, just as he is *p*.
PURGE
Pr 20:30 and beatings *p* the inmost being.
PURIFIES* (PURE)
1Jn 1: 7 of Jesus, his Son, *p* us from all sin.
3: who has this hope in him *p* himself,
PURIFY (PURE)
Tit 2:14 to *p* for himself a people that are

1Jn 1: 9 and *p* us from all unrighteousness.
PURITY (PURE)
2Co 6: 6 in *p*, understanding, patience
1Ti 4:12 in life, in love, in faith and in *p*.
PURPOSE
Pr 19:21 but it is the LORD's *p* that prevails
Isa 55:11 and achieve the *p* for which I sent it
Ro 8:28 have been called according to his *p*.
Php 2: 2 love, being one in spirit and *p*.
PURSES
Lk 12:33 Provide *p* for yourselves that will
PURSUE
Ps 34:14 seek peace and *p* it.
2Ti 2:22 and *p* righteousness, faith,
1Pe 3:11 he must seek peace and *p* it.
QUALITIES (QUALITY)
2Pe 1: 8 For if you possess these *q*
QUALITY (QUALITIES)
1Co 3:13 and the fire will test the *q*
QUARREL (QUARRELSOME)
Pr 15:18 but a patient man calms a *q*.
17:14 Starting a *q* is like breaching a dam;
17:19 He who loves a *q* loves sin;
2Ti 2:24 And the Lord's servant must not *q*;
QUARRELSOME (QUARREL)
Pr 19:13 a *q* wife is like a constant dripping.
1Ti 3: 3 not violent but gentle, not *q*,
QUICK-TEMPERED
Tit 1: 7 not *q*, not given to drunkenness,
QUIET (QUIETNESS)
Ps 23: 2 he leads me beside *q* waters,
Zep 3:17 he will *q* you with his love,
Lk 19:40 he replied, "if they keep *q*,
1Ti 2: 2 we may live peaceful and *q* lives
1Pe 3: 4 beauty of a gentle and *q* spirit,
QUIETNESS (QUIET)
Isa 30:15 in *q* and trust is your strength,
32:17 the effect of righteousness will be *q*
1Ti 2:11 A woman should learn in *q*
QUIVER
Ps 127: 5 whose *q* is full of them.
RACE
Ecc 9:11 The *r* is not to the swift
1Co 9:24 that in a *r* all the runners run,
2Ti 4: 7 I have finished the *r*, I have kept
Heb 12: 1 perseverance the *r* marked out
RACHEL
Daughter of Laban (Ge 29:16); wife of Jacob (Ge 29:28); bore two sons (Ge 30:22-24; 35:16-24; 46:19).
RADIANCE (RADIANT)
Heb 1: 3 The Son is the *r* of God's glory
RADIANT (RADIANCE)
Ex 34:29 he was not aware that his face was *r*
Ps 34: 5 Those who look to him are *r*;
SS 5:10 Beloved My lover is *r* and ruddy,
Isa 60: 5 Then you will look and be *r*,
Eph 5:27 her to himself as a *r* church,
RAIN (RAINBOW)
Mt 5:45 and sends *r* on the righteous
RAINBOW (RAIN)
Ge 9:13 I have set my *r* in the clouds,
RAISED (RISE)
Ro 4:25 was *r* to life for our justification.
10: 9 in your heart that God *r* him
1Co 15: 4 that he was *r* on the third day
RAN (RUN)
Jnh 1: 3 But Jonah *r* away from the LORD
RANSOM
Mt 20:28 and to give his life as a *r* for many."
Heb 9:15 as a *r* to set them free
RAVENS
1Ki 17: 6 The *r* brought him bread
Lk 12:24 Consider the *r*: They do not sow
READ (READS)
Jos 8:34 Joshua *r* all the words of the law—
Ne 8: 8 They *r* from the Book of the Law
2Co 3: 2 known and *r* by everybody.
READS (READ)
Rev 1: 3 Blessed is the one who *r* the words

REAL (REALITY)
Jn 6:55 is *r* food and my blood is *r* drink.
REALITY* (REAL)
Col 2:17 the *r*, however, is found in Christ.
REAP (REAPS)
Job 4: 8 and those who sow trouble *r* it.
2Co 9: 6 generously will also *r* generously.
REAPS (REAP)
Gal 6: 7 A man *r* what he sows.
REASON
Isa 1:18 "Come now, let us *r* together,"
1Pe 3:15 to give the *r* for the hope that you
REBEKAH
Sister of Laban, secured as bride for Isaac (Ge 24). Mother of Esau and Jacob (Ge 25:19-26). Taken by Abimelech as sister of Isaac; returned (Ge 26:1-11). Encouraged Jacob to trick Isaac out of blessing (Ge 27:1-17).
REBEL
Mt 10:21 children will *r* against their parents
REBUKE (REBUKED REBUKING)
Pr 9: 8 *r* a wise man and he will love you.
27: 5 Better is open *r*
Lk 17: 3 "If your brother sins, *r* him,
2Ti 4: 2 correct, *r* and encourage—
Rev 3:19 Those whom I love I *r*
REBUKED (REBUKE)
1Ti 5:20 Those who sin are to be *r* publicly,
REBUKING (REBUKE)
2Ti 3:16 *r*, correcting and training
RECEIVE (RECEIVED RECEIVES)
Ac 1: 8 you will *r* power when the Holy
20:35 'It is more blessed to give than to *r*
2Co 6:17 and I will *r* you."
Rev 4:11 to *r* glory and honor and power,
RECEIVED (RECEIVE)
Mt 6: 2 they have *r* their reward in full.
10: 8 Freely you have *r*, freely give.
1Co 11:23 For I *r* from the Lord what I
Col 2: 6 just as you *r* Christ Jesus as Lord,
1Pe 4:10 should use whatever gift he has *r*
RECEIVES (RECEIVE)
Mt 7: 8 everyone who asks *r*; he who seeks
10:40 he who *r* me *r* the one who sent me.
Ac 10:43 believes in him *r* forgiveness of sins
RECKONING
Isa 10: 3 What will you do on the day of *r*,
RECOGNIZE (RECOGNIZED)
Mt 7:16 By their fruit you will *r* them.
RECOGNIZED (RECOGNIZE)
Mt 12:33 for a tree is *r* by its fruit.
Ro 7:13 in order that sin might be *r* as sin,
RECOMPENSE
Isa 40:10 and his *r* accompanies him.
RECONCILE (RECONCILED RECONCILIATION)
Eph 2:16 in this one body to *r* both of them
RECONCILED (RECONCILE)
Mt 5:24 First go and be *r* to your brother;
Ro 5:10 we were *r* to him through the death
2Co 5:18 who *r* us to himself through Christ
RECONCILIATION* (RECONCILE)
Ro 5:11 whom we have now received *r*.
11:15 For if their rejection is the *r*
2Co 5:18 and gave us the ministry of *r*:
5:19 committed to us the message of *r*.
RECORD
Ps 130: 3 If you, O LORD, kept a *r* of sins,
RED
Isa 1:18 though they are *r* as crimson,
REDEEM (KINSMAN-REDEEMER REDEEMED REDEEMER REDEMPTION)
2Sa 7:23 on earth that God went out to *r*
Ps 49: 7 No man can *r* the life of another
Gal 4: 5 under law, to *r* those under law,
REDEEMED (REDEEM)
Gal 3:13 Christ *r* us from the curse
1Pe 1:18 or gold that you were *r*
REDEEMER (REDEEM)
Job 19:25 I know that my *R* lives,

RICHES

REDEMPTION (REDEEM)
Ps 130: 7 and with him is full *r*.
Lk 21:28 because your *r* is drawing near."
Ro 8:23 as sons, the *r* of our bodies.
Eph 1: 7 In him we have *r* through his blood
Col 1:14 in whom we have *r*, the forgiveness
Heb 9:12 having obtained eternal *r*.

REFLECT
2Co 3:18 unveiled faces all *r* the Lord's

REFUGE
Nu 35:11 towns to be your cities of *r*,
Dt 33:27 The eternal God is your *r*,
Ru 2:12 wings you have come to take *r*."
Ps 46: 1 God is our *r* and strength,
    91: 2 "He is my *r* and my fortress,

REHOBOAM
Son of Solomon (1Ki 11:43; 1Ch 3:10). Harsh treatment of subjects caused divided kingdom (1Ki 12:1-24; 14:21-31; 2Ch 10-12).

REIGN
Ex 15:18 The LORD will *r*
Ro 6:12 Therefore do not let sin *r*
1Co 15:25 For he must *r* until he has put all
2Ti 2:12 we will also *r* with him.
Rev 20: 6 will *r* with him for a thousand years

REJECTED (REJECTS)
Ps 118: 22 The stone the builders *r*
Isa 53: 3 He was despised and *r* by men,
1Ti 4: 4 nothing is to be *r* if it is received
1Pe 2: 4 *r* by men but chosen by God
    2: 7 "The stone the builders *r*

REJECTS (REJECTED)
Lk 10:16 but he who *r* me *r* him who sent me
Jn 3:36 whoever *r* the Son will not see life,

REJOICE (JOY)
Ps 2:11 and *r* with trembling.
    66: 6 come, let us *r* in him.
    118: 24 let us *r* and be glad in it.
Pr 5:18 may you *r* in the wife of your youth
Lk 10:20 but *r* that your names are written
    15: 6 '*R* with me; I have found my lost
Ro 12:15 Rejoice with those who *r*; mourn
Php 4: 4 *R* in the Lord always.

REJOICES (JOY)
Isa 61:10 my soul *r* in my God.
Lk 1:47 and my spirit *r* in God my Savior,
1Co 12:26 if one part is honored, every part *r*
    13: 6 delight in evil but *r* with the truth.

REJOICING (JOY)
Ps 30: 5 but *r* comes in the morning.
Lk 15: 7 in the same way there will be more *r*
Ac 5:41 *r* because they had been counted

RELIABLE
2Ti 2: 2 witnesses entrust to *r* men who will

RELIGION
1Ti 5: 4 all to put their *r* into practice
Jas 1:27 *R* that God our Father accepts

REMAIN (REMAINS)
Nu 33:55 allow to *r* will become barbs
Jn 15: 7 If you *r* in me and my words
Ro 13: 8 Let no debt *r* outstanding,
1Co 13:13 And now these three *r*: faith,
2Ti 2:13 he will *r* faithful,

REMAINS (REMAIN)
Ps 146: 6 the LORD, who *r* faithful forever.
Heb 7: 3 Son of God he *r* a priest forever.

REMEMBER (REMEMBERS REMEMBRANCE)
Ex 20: 8 "*R* the Sabbath day
1Ch 16:12 *R* the wonders he has done,
Ecc 12: 1 *R* your Creator
Jer 31:34 and will *r* their sins no more."
Gal 2:10 we should continue to *r* the poor,
Php 1: 3 I thank my God every time I *r* you.
Heb 8:12 and will *r* their sins no more."

REMEMBERS (REMEMBER)
Ps 103: 14 he *r* that we are dust.
    111: 5 he *r* his covenant forever.
Isa 43:25 and *r* your sins no more.

REMEMBRANCE (REMEMBER)
1Co 11:24 which is for you; do this in *r* of me

REMIND
Jn 14:26 will *r* you of everything I have said

REMOVED
Ps 30:11 you *r* my sackcloth and clothed me
    103: 12 so far has he *r* our transgressions
Jn 20: 1 and saw that the stone had been *r*

RENEW (RENEWED RENEWING)
Ps 51:10 and *r* a steadfast spirit within me.
Isa 40:31 will *r* their strength.

RENEWED (RENEW)
Ps 103: 5 that your youth is *r* like the eagle's.
2Co 4:16 yet inwardly we are being *r* day

RENEWING (RENEW)
Ro 12: 2 transformed by the *r* of your mind.

RENOUNCE (RENOUNCES)
Da 4:27 *R* your sins by doing what is right,

RENOUNCES (RENOUNCE)
Pr 28:13 confesses and *r* them finds

RENOWN
Isa 63:12 to gain for himself everlasting *r*,
Jer 32:20 have gained the *r* that is still yours.

REPAID (PAY)
Lk 14:14 you will be *r* at the resurrection
Col 3:25 Anyone who does wrong will be *r*

REPAY (PAY)
Dt 32:35 It is mine to avenge; I will *r*.
Ru 2:12 May the LORD *r* you
Ps 116: 12 How can I *r* the LORD
Ro 12:19 "It is mine to avenge; I will *r*,"
1Pe 3: 9 Do not *r* evil with evil

REPENT (REPENTANCE REPENTS)
Job 42: 6 and *r* in dust and ashes."
Jer 15:19 "If you *r*, I will restore you
Mt 4:17 *R*, for the kingdom of heaven is
Lk 13: 3 unless you *r*, you too will all perish.
Ac 2:38 Peter replied, "*R* and be baptized,
   17:30 all people everywhere to *r*.

REPENTANCE (REPENT)
Lk 3: 8 Produce fruit in keeping with *r*.
   5:32 call the righteous, but sinners to *r*."
Ac 26:20 and prove their *r* by their deeds.
2Co 7:10 Godly sorrow brings *r* that leads

REPENTS (REPENT)
Lk 15:10 of God over one sinner who *r*."
   17: 3 rebuke him, and if he *r*, forgive him

REPROACH
1Ti 3: 2 Now the overseer must be above *r*,

REPUTATION
1Ti 3: 7 also have a good *r* with outsiders,

REQUESTS
Ps 20: 5 May the LORD grant all your *r*.
Php 4: 6 with thanksgiving, present your *r*

REQUIRE
Mic 6: 8 And what does the LORD *r* of you

RESCUE (RESCUES)
Da 6:20 been able to *r* you from the lions?"
2Pe 2: 9 how to *r* godly men from trials

RESCUES (RESCUE)
1Th 1:10 who *r* us from the coming wrath.

RESIST
Jas 4: 7 *R* the devil, and he will flee
1Pe 5: 9 *R* him, standing firm in the faith,

RESOLVED
Ps 17: 3 I have *r* that my mouth will not sin.
Da 1: 8 But Daniel *r* not to defile himself
1Co 2: 2 For I *r* to know nothing while I was

RESPECT (RESPECTABLE)
Lev 19: 3 " 'Each of you must *r* his mother
   19:32 show *r* for the elderly and revere
Pr 11:16 A kindhearted woman gains *r*,
Mal 1: 6 where is the *r* due me?" says
1Th 4:12 so that your daily life may win the *r*
   5:12 to those who work hard
1Ti 3: 4 children obey him with proper *r*.
1Pe 2:17 Show proper *r* to everyone:
    3: 7 them with *r* as the weaker partner

RESPECTABLE* (RESPECT)
1Ti 3: 2 self-controlled, *r*, hospitable,

REST
Ex 31:15 the seventh day is a Sabbath of *r*,
Ps 91: 1 will *r* in the shadow
Jer 6:16 and you will find *r* for your souls.
Mt 11:28 and burdened, and I will give you *r*.

RESTITUTION
Ex 22: 3 "A thief must certainly make *r*,
Lev 6: 5 He must make *r* in full, add a fifth

RESTORE (RESTORES)
Ps 51:12 *R* to me the joy of your salvation
Gal 6: 1 are spiritual should *r* him gently.

RESTORES (RESTORE)
Ps 23: 3 he *r* my soul.

RESURRECTION
Mt 22:30 At the *r* people will neither marry
Lk 14:14 repaid at the *r* of the righteous."
Jn 11:25 Jesus said to her, "I am the *r*
Ro 1: 4 Son of God by his *r* from the dead:
1Co 15:12 some of you say that there is no *r*
Php 3:10 power of his *r* and the fellowship
Rev 20: 5 This is the first *r*.

RETRIBUTION
Jer 51:56 For the LORD is a God of *r*;

RETURN
2Ch 30: 9 If you *r* to the LORD, then your
Ne 1: 9 but if you *r* to me and obey my
Isa 55:11 It will not *r* to me empty,
Hos 6: 1 "Come, let us *r* to the LORD.
Joel 2:12 "*r* to me with all your heart,

REVEALED (REVELATION)
Dt 29:29 but the things *r* belong to us
Isa 40: 5 the glory of the LORD will be *r*,
Mt 11:25 and *r* them to little children.
Ro 1:17 a righteousness from God is *r*,
    8:18 with the glory that will be *r* in us.

REVELATION (REVEALED)
Gal 1:12 I received it by *r* from Jesus Christ.
Rev 1: 1 *r* of Jesus Christ, which God gave

REVENGE (VENGEANCE)
Lev 19:18 " 'Do not seek *r* or bear a grudge
Ro 12:19 Do not take *r*, my friends,

REVERE (REVERENCE)
Ps 33: 8 let all the people of the world *r* him

REVERENCE (REVERE)
Lev 19:30 and have *r* for my sanctuary.
Ps 5: 7 in *r* will I bow down
Col 3:22 of heart and *r* for the Lord.
1Pe 3: 2 when they see the purity and *r*

REVIVE (REVIVING)
Ps 85: 6 Will you not *r* us again,
Isa 57:15 to *r* the spirit of the lowly

REVIVING (REVIVE)
Ps 19: 7 *r* the soul.

REWARD (REWARDED)
Ps 19:11 in keeping them there is great *r*.
   127: 3 children a *r* from him.
Pr 19:17 he will *r* him for what he has done.
   25:22 and the LORD will *r* you.
   31:31 Give her the *r* she has earned,
Jer 17:10 to *r* a man according to his conduct
Mt 5:12 because great is your *r* in heaven,
    6: 5 they have received their *r* in full.
   16:27 and then he will *r* each person
1Co 3:14 built survives, he will receive his *r*.
Rev 22:12 I am coming soon! My *r* is with me

REWARDED (REWARD)
Ru 2:12 May you be richly *r* by the LORD,
Ps 18:24 The LORD has *r* me according
Pr 14:14 and the good man *r* for his.
1Co 3: 8 and each will be *r* according

RICH (RICHES)
Pr 23: 4 Do not wear yourself out to get *r*;
Jer 9:23 or the *r* man boast of his riches,
Mt 19:23 it is hard for a *r* man
2Co 6:10 yet making many *r*; having nothing
    8: 9 he was *r*, yet for your sakes he
1Ti 6:17 Command those who are *r*

RICHES (RICH)
Ps 119: 14 as one rejoices in great *r*.
Pr 30: 8 give me neither poverty nor *r*,
Isa 10: 3 Where will you leave your *r*?
Ro 9:23 to make the *r* of his glory known
   11:33 the depth of the *r* of the wisdom
Eph 2: 7 he might show the incomparable *r*

RID

	3: 8 to the Gentiles the unsearchable *r*
Col	1:27 among the Gentiles the glorious *r*

RID
Ge	21:10 "Get *r* of that slave woman
1Co	5: 7 Get *r* of the old yeast that you may
Gal	4:30 "Get *r* of the slave woman

RIGHT (RIGHTS)
Ge	18:25 the Judge of all the earth do *r*?"
Ex	15:26 and do what is *r* in his eyes,
Dt	5:32 do not turn aside to the *r*
	6: 18 Because he is at my *r* hand,
Ps	16: 8 Because he is at my *r* hand,
	19: 8 The precepts of the LORD are *r*,
	63: 8 your *r* hand upholds me.
	110: 1 "Sit at my *r* hand
Pr	4:27 Do not swerve to the *r* or the left;
	14:12 There is a way that seems *r*
Isa	1:17 learn to do *r*
Jer	23: 5 and do what is just and *r* in the land
Hos	14: 9 The ways of the LORD are *r*;
Mt	6: 3 know what your *r* hand is doing,
Jn	1:12 he gave the *r* to become children
Ro	9:21 Does not the potter have the *r*
	12:17 careful to do what is *r* in the eyes
Eph	1:20 and seated him at his *r* hand
Php	4: 8 whatever is *r*, whatever is pure,
2Th	3:13 never tire of doing what is *r*.

RIGHTEOUS (RIGHTEOUSNESS)
Ps	34:15 The eyes of the LORD are on the *r*
	37:25 yet I have never seen the *r* forsaken
	119:137 *R* are you, O LORD,
	143: 2 for no one living is *r* before you.
Pr	3:33 but he blesses the home of the *r*.
	11:30 The fruit of the *r* is a tree of life,
	18:10 the *r* run to it and are safe.
Isa	64: 6 and all our *r* acts are like filthy rags
Hab	2: 4 but the *r* will live by his faith—
Mt	5:45 rain on the *r* and the unrighteous.
	9:13 For I have not come to call the *r*,
	13:49 and separate the wicked from the *r*
	25:46 to eternal punishment, but the *r*
Ro	1:17 as it is written: "The *r* will live
	3:10 "There is no one *r*, not even one;
1Ti	1: 9 that law is made not for the *r*
1Pe	3:18 the *r* for the unrighteous,
1Jn	3: 7 does what is right is *r*, just as he is *r*.
Rev	19: 8 stands for the *r* acts of the saints.)

RIGHTEOUSNESS (RIGHTEOUS)
Ge	15: 6 and he credited it to him as *r*.
1Sa	26:23 LORD rewards every man for his *r*
Ps	9: 8 He will judge the world in *r*;
	23: 3 He guides me in paths of *r*
	45: 7 You love *r* and hate wickedness;
	85:10 *r* and peace kiss each other.
	89:14 *R* and justice are the foundation
	111: 3 and his *r* endures forever.
Pr	14:34 *R* exalts a nation,
	21:21 He who pursues *r* and love
Isa	5:16 will show himself holy by his *r*
	59:17 He put on *r* as his breastplate,
Eze	18:20 The *r* of the righteous man will be
Da	9:24 to bring in everlasting *r*,
	12: 3 and those who lead many to *r*,
Mal	4: 2 the sun of *r* will rise with healing
Mt	5: 6 those who hunger and thirst for *r*,
	5:20 unless your *r* surpasses that
	6:33 But seek first his kingdom and his *r*
Ro	4: 3 and it was credited to him as *r*."
	4: 9 faith was credited to him as *r*.
	6:13 body to him as instruments of *r*.
2Co	5:21 that in him we might become the *r*
Gal	2:21 for if *r* could be gained
	3: 6 and it was credited to him as *r*."
Eph	6:14 with the breastplate of *r* in place,
Php	3: 9 not having a *r* of my own that
2Ti	3:16 correcting and training in *r*,
	4: 8 is in store for me the crown of *r*,
Heb	11: 7 became heir of the *r* that comes
2Pe	2:21 not to have known the way of *r*,

RIGHTS (RIGHT)
| La | 3:35 to deny a man his *r* |
| Gal | 4: 5 that we might receive the full *r* |

RISE (RAISED)
| Isa | 26:19 their bodies will *r*. |

1560

Mt	27:63 'After three days I will *r* again'.
Jn	5:29 those who have done good will *r*
1Th	4:16 and the dead in Christ will *r* first.

ROAD
| Mt | 7:13 and broad is the *r* that leads |

ROBBERS
Jer	7:11 become a den of *r* to you?
Mk	15:27 They crucified two *r* with him,
Lk	19:46 but you have made it 'a den of *r*.' "
Jn	10: 8 came before me were thieves and *r*,

ROCK
Ps	18: 2 The LORD is my *r*, my fortress
	40: 2 he set my feet on a *r*
Mt	7:24 man who built his house on the *r*.
	16:18 and on this *r* I will build my church
Ro	9:33 and a *r* that makes them fall,
1Co	10: 4 the spiritual *r* that accompanied

ROD
Ps	23: 4 your *r* and your staff,
Pr	13:24 He who spares the *r* hates his son,
	23:13 if you punish him with the *r*,

ROOM (ROOMS)
Mt	6: 6 But when you pray, go into your *r*,
Lk	2: 7 there was no *r* for them in the inn.
Jn	21:25 the whole world would not have *r*

ROOMS (ROOM)
| Jn | 14: 2 In my Father's house are many *r*; |

ROOT
| Isa | 53: 2 and like a *r* out of dry ground. |
| 1Ti | 6:10 of money is a *r* of all kinds of evil. |

ROYAL
| Jas | 2: 8 If you really keep the *r* law found |
| 1Pe | 2: 9 a *r* priesthood, a holy nation, |

RUBBISH*
| Php | 3: 8 I consider them *r*, that I may gain |

RUDE*
| 1Co | 13: 5 It is not *r*, it is not self-seeking, |

RUIN (RUINS)
| Pr | 18:24 many companions may come to *r*, |
| 1Ti | 6: 9 desires that plunge men into *r* |

RUINS (RUIN)
| Pr | 19: 3 A man's own folly *r* his life, |
| 2Ti | 2:14 and only *r* those who listen. |

RULE (RULER RULERS RULES)
1Sa	12:12 'No, we want a king to *r* over us'—
Ps	2: 9 You will *r* them with an iron
	119:133 let no sin *r* over me.
Zec	9:10 His *r* will extend from sea to sea
Col	3:15 the peace of Christ *r* in your hearts,
Rev	2:27 He will *r* them with an iron scepter;

RULER (RULE)
Ps	8: 6 You made him *r* over the works
Eph	2: 2 of the *r* of the kingdom of the air,
1Ti	6:15 God, the blessed and only *R*,

RULERS (RULE)
| Ps | 2: 2 and the *r* gather together |
| Col | 1:16 or powers or *r* or authorities; |

RULES (RULE)
Ps	103: 19 and his kingdom *r* over all.
Lk	22:26 one who *r* like the one who serves.
2Ti	2: 5 he competes according to the *r*.

RUMORS
| Mt | 24: 6 You will hear of wars and *r* of wars, |

RUN (RAN)
Isa	40:31 they will *r* and not grow weary,
1Co	9:24 *R* in such a way as to get the prize.
Heb	12: 1 let us *r* with perseverance the race

RUST
| Mt | 6:19 where moth and *r* destroy, |

RUTH*
Moabitess; widow who went to Bethlehem with mother-in-law Naomi (Ru 1). Gleaned in field of Boaz; shown favor (Ru 2). Proposed marriage to Boaz (Ru 3). Married (Ru 4:1-12); bore Obed, ancestor of David (Ru 4:13-22), Jesus (Mt 1:5).

SABBATH
Ex	20: 8 "Remember the *S* day
Dt	5:12 "Observe the *S* day
Col	2:16 a New Moon celebration or a *S* day

SACKCLOTH
| Mt | 11:21 would have repented long ago in *s* |

SACRED
| Mt | 7: 6 "Do not give dogs what is *s*; |
| 1Co | 3:17 for God's temple is *s*, and you are |

SACRIFICE (SACRIFICED SACRIFICES)
Ge	22: 2 *S* him there as a burnt offering
Ex	12:27 'It is the Passover *s* to the LORD,
1Sa	15:22 To obey is better than *s*,
Hos	6: 6 For I desire mercy, not *s*,
Mt	9:13 this means: 'I desire mercy, not *s*.'
Heb	9:26 away with sin by the *s* of himself.
	13:15 offer to God a *s* of praise—
1Jn	2: 2 He is the atoning *s* for our sins,

SACRIFICED (SACRIFICE)
1Co	5: 7 our Passover lamb, has been *s*.
	8: 1 Now about food *s* to idols:
Heb	9:28 so Christ was *s* once

SACRIFICES (SACRIFICE)
| Ps | 51:17 The *s* of God are a broken spirit; |
| Ro | 12: 1 to offer your bodies as living *s*, |

SADDUCEES
| Mk | 12:18 *S*, who say there is no resurrection, |

SAFE (SAVE)
| Ps | 37: 3 in the land and enjoy *s* pasture. |
| Pr | 18:10 the righteous run to it and are *s*. |

SAFETY (SAVE)
| Ps | 4: 8 make me dwell in *s*. |
| 1Th | 5: 3 people are saying, "Peace and *s*," |

SAINTS
Ps	116: 15 is the death of his *s*.
Ro	8:27 intercedes for the *s* in accordance
Eph	1:18 of his glorious inheritance in the *s*,
	6:18 always keep on praying for all the *s*
Rev	5: 8 which are the prayers of the *s*.
	19: 8 for the righteous acts of the *s*.)

SAKE
Ps	44:22 Yet for your *s* we face death all day
Php	3: 7 loss for the *s* of Christ.
Heb	11:26 He regarded disgrace for the *s*

SALT
| Ge | 19:26 and she became a pillar of *s*. |
| Mt | 5:13 "You are the *s* of the earth. |

SALVATION (SAVE)
Ex	15: 2 He has become my *s*.
1Ch	16:23 proclaim his *s* day after day.
Ps	27: 1 The LORD is my light and my *s*—
	51:12 Restore to me the joy of your *s*
	62: 2 He alone is my rock and my *s*;
	85: 9 Surely his *s* is near those who fear
	96: 2 proclaim his *s* day after day.
Isa	25: 9 let us rejoice and be glad in his *s*."
	45:17 with an everlasting *s*;
	51: 6 But my *s* will last forever,
	59:17 and the helmet of *s* on his head;
	61:10 me with garments of *s*
Jnh	2: 9 *S* comes from the LORD."
Zec	9: 9 righteous and having *s*,
Lk	2:30 For my eyes have seen your *s*,
Jn	4:22 for *s* is from the Jews.
Ac	4:12 *S* is found in no one else,
	13:47 that you may bring *s* to the ends
Ro	11:11 *s* has come to the Gentiles
2Co	7:10 brings repentance that leads to *s*
Eph	6:17 Take the helmet of *s* and the sword
Php	2:12 to work out your *s* with fear
1Th	5: 8 and the hope of *s* as a helmet.
2Ti	3:15 wise for *s* through faith
Heb	2: 3 escape if we ignore such a great *s*?
	6: 9 case—things that accompany *s*.
1Pe	1:10 Concerning this *s*, the prophets,
	2: 2 by it you may grow up in your *s*,

SAMARITAN
| Lk | 10:33 But a *S*, as he traveled, came where |

SAMSON
Danite judge. Birth promised (Jdg 13). Married to Philistine (Jdg 14). Vengeance on Philistines (Jdg 15). Betrayed by Delilah (Jdg 16:1-22). Death (Jdg 16:23-31). Feats of strength: killed lion (Jdg 14:6), 30 Philistines (Jdg 14:19), 1,000 Philistines with jawbone (Jdg 15:13-17), carried off gates of Gaza (Jdg 16:3), pushed down temple of Dagon (Jdg 16:25-30).

SAMUEL
Ephraimite judge and prophet (Heb 11:32). Birth

prayed for (1Sa 1:10-18). Dedicated to temple by Hannah (1Sa 1:21-28). Raised by Eli (1Sa 2:11, 18-26). Called as prophet (1Sa 3). Led Israel to victory over Philistines (1Sa 7). Asked by Israel for a king (1Sa 8). Anointed Saul as king (1Sa 9-10). Farewell speech (1Sa 12). Rebuked Saul for sacrifice (1Sa 13). Announced rejection of Saul (1Sa 15). Anointed David as king (1Sa 16). Protected David from Saul (1Sa 19:18-24). Death (1Sa 25:1). Returned from dead to condemn Saul (1Sa 28).

SANCTIFIED (SANCTIFY)
Ac 20:32 among all those who are s.
Ro 15:16 to God, s by the Holy Spirit.
1Co 6:11 But you were washed, you were s,
7:14 and the unbelieving wife has been s
Heb 10:29 blood of the covenant that s him,

SANCTIFY (SANCTIFIED SANCTIFYING)
1Th 5:23 s you through and through.

SANCTIFYING (SANCTIFY)
2Th 2:13 through the s work of the Spirit

SANCTUARY
Ex 25: 8 "Then have them make a s for me,

SAND
Ge 22:17 and as the s on the seashore.
Mt 7:26 man who built his house on s.

SANDALS
Ex 3: 5 off your s, for the place where you
Jos 5:15 off your s, for the place where you

SANG (SING)
Job 38: 7 while the morning stars s together
Rev 5: 9 And they s a new song:

SARAH
Wife of Abraham, originally named Sarai; barren (Ge 11:29-31; 1Pe 3:6). Taken by Pharaoh as Abraham's sister; returned (Ge 12:10-20). Gave Hagar to Abraham; sent her away in pregnancy (Ge 16). Name changed; Isaac promised (Ge 17:15-21; 18:10-15; Heb 11:11). Taken by Abimelech as Abraham's sister; returned (Ge 20). Isaac born; Hagar and Ishmael sent away (Ge 21:1-21; Gal 4:21-31). Death (Ge 23).

SATAN
Job 1: 6 and S also came with them.
Zec 3: 2 said to S, "The LORD rebuke you,
Mk 4:15 S comes and takes away the word
2Co 11:14 S himself masquerades
12: 7 a messenger of S, to torment me.
Rev 12: 9 serpent called the devil, or S,
20: 2 or S, and bound him for a thousand
20: 7 S will be released from his prison

SATISFIED (SATISFY)
Isa 53:11 he will see the light ⌊of life⌋ and be s

SATISFIES (SATISFY)
Ps 103: 5 who s your desires with good things,

SATISFY (SATISFIED SATISFIES)
Isa 55: 2 and your labor on what does not s?

SAUL
1. Benjamite; anointed by Samuel as first king of Israel (1Sa 9-10). Defeated Ammonites (1Sa 11). Rebuked for offering sacrifice (1Sa 13:1-15). Defeated Philistines (1Sa 14). Rejected as king for failing to annihilate Amalekites (1Sa 15). Soothed from evil spirit by David (1Sa 16:14-23). Sent David against Goliath (1Sa 17). Jealousy and attempted murder of David (1Sa 18:1-11). Gave David Michal as wife (1Sa 18:12-30). Second attempt to kill David (1Sa 19). Anger at Jonathan (1Sa 20:26-34). Pursued David; killed priests at Nob (1Sa 22), went to Keilah and Ziph (1Sa 23), life spared by David at En Gedi (1Sa 24) and in his tent (1Sa 26). Rebuked by Samuel's spirit for consulting witch at Endor (1Sa 28). Wounded by Philistines; took his own life (1Sa 31; 1Ch 10).
2. See PAUL

SAVE (SAFE SAFETY SALVATION SAVED SAVIOR)
Isa 63: 1 mighty to s."
Da 3:17 the God we serve is able to s us
Zep 3:17 he is mighty to s.
Mt 1:21 he will s his people from their sins
16:25 wants to s his life will lose it,
Lk 19:10 to seek and to s what was lost."
Jn 3:17 but to s the world through him.
1Ti 1:15 came into the world to s sinners—
Jas 5:20 of his way will s him from death

SAVED (SAVE)
Ps 34: 6 he s him out of all his troubles.
Isa 45:22 "Turn to me and be s,
Joel 2:32 on the name of the LORD will be s;
Mk 13:13 firm to the end will be s.
16:16 believes and is baptized will be s,
Jn 10: 9 enters through me will be s.
Ac 4:12 to men by which we must be s."
16:30 do to be s?" They replied,
Ro 9:27 only the remnant will be s.
10: 9 him from the dead, you will be s.
1Co 3:15 will suffer loss; he himself will be s,
15: 2 By this gospel you are s,
Eph 2: 5 it is by grace you have been s.
2: 8 For it is by grace you have been s,
1Ti 2: 4 who wants all men to be s

SAVIOR (SAVE)
Ps 89:26 my God, the Rock my S.'
Isa 43:11 and apart from me there is no s.
Hos 13: 4 no S except me.
Lk 1:47 and my spirit rejoices in God my S,
2:11 of David a S has been born to you;
Jn 4:42 know that this man really is the S
Eph 5:23 his body, of which he is the S.
1Ti 4:10 who is the S of all men,
Tit 2:10 about God our S attractive.
2:13 appearing of our great God and S,
3: 4 and love of God our S appeared,
1Jn 4:14 Son to be the S of the world.
Jude 25 to the only God our S be glory,

SCALES
Lev 19:36 Use honest s and honest weights,
Da 5:27 You have been weighed on the s

SCAPEGOAT (GOAT)
Lev 16:10 by sending it into the desert as a s.

SCARLET
Isa 1:18 "Though your sins are like s,

SCATTERED
Jer 31:10 'He who s Israel will gather them
Ac 8: 4 who had been s preached the word

SCEPTER
Rev 19:15 "He will rule them with an iron s."

SCHEMES
2Co 2:11 For we are not unaware of his s.
Eph 6:11 stand against the devil's s.

SCOFFERS
2Pe 3: 3 that in the last days s will come,

SCORPION
Rev 9: 5 sting of a s when it strikes a man.

SCRIPTURE (SCRIPTURES)
Jn 10:35 and the S cannot be broken—
1Ti 4:13 yourself to the public reading of S,
2Ti 3:16 All S is God-breathed
2Pe 1:20 that no prophecy of S came about

SCRIPTURES (SCRIPTURE)
Lk 24:27 said in all the S concerning himself.
Jn 5:39 These are the S that testify about
Ac 17:11 examined the S every day to see

SCROLL
Eze 3: 1 eat what is before you, eat this s;

SEA
Ex 14:16 go through the s on dry ground.
Isa 57:20 the wicked are like the tossing s,
Mic 7:19 iniquities into the depths of the s.
Jas 1: 6 who doubts is like a wave of the s,
Rev 13: 1 I saw a beast coming out of the s.

SEAL (SEALS)
Jn 6:27 God the Father has placed his s
2Co 1:22 set his s of ownership on us,
Eph 1:13 you were marked in him with a s,

SEALS (SEAL)
Rev 5: 2 "Who is worthy to break the s
6: 1 opened the first of the seven s.

SEARCH (SEARCHED SEARCHES SEARCHING)
Ps 4: 4 s your hearts and be silent.
139: 23 S me, O God, and know my heart;
Pr 2: 4 and s for it as for hidden treasure,
Jer 17:10 "I the LORD s the heart
Eze 34:16 I will s for the lost and bring back
Lk 15: 8 and s carefully until she finds it?

SEARCHED (SEARCH)
Ps 139: 1 O LORD, you have s me

SEARCHES (SEARCH)
Ro 8:27 And he who s our hearts knows
1Co 2:10 The Spirit s all things,

SEARCHING (SEARCH)
Am 8:12 s for the word of the LORD,

SEARED
1Ti 4: 2 whose consciences have been s

SEASON
2Ti 4: 2 be prepared in s and out of s;

SEAT (SEATED SEATS)
Ps 1: 1 or sit in the s of mockers.
Da 7: 9 and the Ancient of Days took his s.
2Co 5:10 before the judgment s of Christ,

SEATED (SEAT)
Ps 47: 8 God is s on his holy throne.
Isa 6: 1 I saw the Lord s on a throne,
Col 3: 1 where Christ is s at the right hand

SEATS (SEAT)
Lk 11:43 you love the most important s

SECRET (SECRETS)
Dt 29:29 The s things belong
Jdg 16: 6 Tell me the s of your great strength
Ps 90: 8 our s sins in the light
Pr 11:13 but a trustworthy man keeps a s.
Mt 6: 4 so that your giving may be in s.
2Co 4: 2 we have renounced s and shameful
Php 4:12 I have learned the s

SECRETS (SECRET)
Ps 44:21 since he knows the s of the heart?
1Co 14:25 the s of his heart will be laid bare.

SECURE (SECURITY)
Ps 112: 8 His heart is s, he will have no fear;
Heb 6:19 an anchor for the soul, firm and s.

SECURITY (SECURE)
Job 31:24 or said to pure gold, 'You are my s,'

SEED (SEEDS)
Lk 8:11 of the parable: The s is the word
1Co 3: 6 I planted the s, Apollos watered it,
2Co 9:10 he who supplies s to the sower
Gal 3:29 then you are Abraham's s,
1Pe 1:23 not of perishable s,

SEEDS (SEED)
Jn 12:24 But if it dies, it produces many s.
Gal 3:16 Scripture does not say "and to s,"

SEEK (SEEKS SELF-SEEKING)
Dt 4:29 if from there you s the LORD your
1Ch 28: 9 If you s him, he will be found
2Ch 7:14 themselves and pray and s my face
Ps 119: 10 I s you with all my heart;
Isa 55: 6 S the LORD while he may be
65: 1 found by those who did not s me.
Mt 6:33 But s first his kingdom
Lk 19:10 For the Son of Man came to s
Ro 10:20 found by those who did not s me;
1Co 7:27 you married? Do not s a divorce.

SEEKS (SEEK)
Jn 4:23 the kind of worshipers the Father s.

SEER
1Sa 9: 9 of today used to be called a s.)

SELF-CONTROL (CONTROL)
1Co 7: 5 you because of your lack of s.
Gal 5:23 faithfulness, gentleness and s.
2Pe 1: 6 and to knowledge, s; and to s,

SELF-CONTROLLED* (CONTROL)
1Th 5: 6 are asleep, but let us be alert and s.
5: 8 let us be s, putting on faith and love
1Ti 3: 2 s, respectable, hospitable,
Tit 1: 8 who is s, upright, holy
2: 2 worthy of respect, s, and sound
2: 5 to be s and pure, to be busy at home
2: 6 encourage the young men to be s.
2:12 to live s, upright and godly lives
1Pe 1:13 prepare your minds for action; be s;
4: 7 and s so that you can pray.
5: 8 Be s and alert.

SELF-INDULGENCE
Mt 23:25 inside they are full of greed and s.

SELF-SEEKING (SEEK)
1Co 13: 5 it is not s, it is not easily angered,

SELFISH

SELFISH*
Ps 119: 36 and not toward s gain.
Pr 18: 1 An unfriendly man pursues s ends;
Gal 5: 20 fits of rage, s ambition, dissensions,
Php 1: 17 preach Christ out of s ambition,
2: 3 Do nothing out of s ambition
Jas 3: 14 and s ambition in your hearts,
3: 16 you have envy and s ambition,
SEND (SENDING SENT)
Isa 6: 8 S me!" He said, "Go and tell this
Mt 9: 38 to s out workers into his harvest
Jn 16: 7 but if I go, I will s him to you.
SENDING (SEND)
Jn 20: 21 Father has sent me, I am s you."
SENSES*
Lk 15: 17 "When he came to his s, he said,
1Co 15: 34 Come back to your s as you ought,
2Ti 2: 26 and that they will come to their s
SENSUAL
Col 2: 23 value in restraining s indulgence.
SENT (SEND)
Isa 55: 11 achieve the purpose for which I s it.
Mt 10: 40 me receives the one who s me.
Jn 4: 34 "is to do the will of him who s me
Ro 10: 15 can they preach unless they are s?
1Jn 4: 10 but that he loved us and s his Son
SEPARATE (SEPARATED SEPARATES)
Mt 19: 6 has joined together, let man not s."
Ro 8: 35 Who shall s us from the love
1Co 7: 10 wife must not s from her husband.
2Co 6: 17 and be s, says the Lord.
SEPARATED (SEPARATE)
Isa 59: 2 But your iniquities have s
SEPARATES (SEPARATE)
Pr 16: 28 and a gossip s close friends.
SERPENT
Ge 3: 1 the s was more crafty than any
Rev 12: 9 that ancient s called the devil
SERVANT (SERVANTS)
1Sa 3: 10 "Speak, for your s is listening."
Mt 20: 26 great among you must be your s,
25: 21 'Well done, good and faithful s!
Lk 16: 13 "No s can serve two masters.
Php 2: 7 taking the very nature of a s,
2Ti 2: 24 And the Lord's s must not quarrel;
SERVANTS (SERVANT)
Lk 17: 10 should say, 'We are unworthy s;
Jn 15: 15 longer call you s, because a servant
SERVE (SERVICE SERVING)
Dt 10: 12 to s the LORD your God
Jos 22: 5 and to s him with all your heart
24: 15 this day whom you will s,
Mt 4: 10 Lord your God, and s him only."
6: 24 "No one can s two masters.
20: 28 but to s, and to give his life
Eph 6: 7 S wholeheartedly,
SERVICE (SERVE)
1Co 12: 5 There are different kinds of s,
Eph 4: 12 God's people for works of s,
SERVING (SERVE)
Ro 12: 11 your spiritual fervor, s the Lord.
Eph 6: 7 as if you were s the Lord, not men,
Col 3: 24 It is the Lord Christ you are s.
2Ti 2: 4 No one s as a soldier gets involved
SEVEN (SEVENTH)
Ge 7: 2 Take with you s of every kind
Jos 6: 4 march around the city s times,
1Ki 19: 18 Yet I reserve s thousand in Israel—
Pr 6: 16 s that are detestable to him:
24: 16 a righteous man falls s times,
Isa 4: 1 In that day s women
Da 9: 25 comes, there will be s 'sevens',
Mt 18: 21 Up to s times?" Jesus answered,
Lk 11: 26 takes s other spirits more wicked
Ro 11: 4 for myself s thousand who have not
Rev 1: 4 To the s churches in the province
6: 1 opened the first of the s seals.
8: 2 and to them were given s trumpets.
10: 4 And when the s thunders spoke,
15: 7 to the s angels s golden bowls filled
SEVENTH (SEVEN)
Ge 2: 2 By the s day God had finished

Ex 23: 12 but on the s day do not work,
SEXUAL (SEXUALLY)
1Co 6: 13 body is not meant for s immorality,
6: 18 Flee from s immorality.
10: 8 should not commit s immorality,
Eph 5: 3 even a hint of s immorality,
1Th 4: 3 that you should avoid s immorality
SEXUALLY (SEXUAL)
1Co 5: 9 to associate with s immoral people
6: 18 he who sins s sins against his own
SHADOW
Ps 23: 4 through the valley of the s of death,
36: 7 find refuge in the s of your wings.
Heb 10: 1 The law is only a s
SHALLUM
King of Israel (2Ki 15:10-16).
SHAME (ASHAMED)
Ps 34: 5 their faces are never covered with s
Pr 13: 18 discipline comes to poverty and s,
Heb 12: 2 endured the cross, scorning its s,
SHARE (SHARED)
Ge 21: 10 that slave woman's son will never s
Lk 3: 11 "The man with two tunics should s
Gal 4: 30 the slave woman's son will never s
6: 6 in the word must s all good things
Eph 4: 28 something to s with those in need.
1Ti 6: 18 and to be generous and willing to s.
Heb 12: 10 that we may s in his holiness.
13: 16 to do good and to s with others,
SHARED (SHARE)
Heb 2: 14 he too s in their humanity so that
SHARON
SS 2: 1 I am a rose of S,
SHARPER*
Heb 4: 12 S than any double-edged sword,
SHED (SHEDDING)
Ge 9: 6 by man shall his blood be s;
Col 1: 20 through his blood, s on the cross.
SHEDDING (SHED)
Heb 9: 22 without the s of blood there is no
SHEEP
Ps 100: 3 we are his people, the s
119: 176 I have strayed like a lost s.
Isa 53: 6 We all, like s, have gone astray,
Jer 50: 6 "My people have been lost s;
Eze 34: 11 I myself will search for my s
Mt 9: 36 helpless, like s without a shepherd.
Jn 10: 3 He calls his own s by name
10: 15 and I lay down my life for the s.
10: 27 My s listen to my voice; I know
21: 17 Jesus said, "Feed my s.
1Pe 2: 25 For you were like s going astray,
SHELTER
Ps 61: 4 take refuge in the s of your wings.
91: 1 in the s of the Most High
SHEM
Son of Noah (Ge 5:32; 6:10). Blessed (Ge 9:26).
Descendants (Ge 10:21-31; 11:10-32).
SHEPHERD (SHEPHERDS)
Ps 23: 1 LORD is my s, I shall not be in want.
Isa 40: 11 He tends his flock like a s:
Jer 31: 10 will watch over his flock like a s.'
Eze 34: 12 As a s looks after his scattered
Zec 11: 17 "Woe to the worthless s,
Mt 9: 36 and helpless, like sheep without a s.
Jn 10: 11 The good s lays down his life
10: 16 there shall be one flock and one s.
1Pe 5: 4 And when the Chief S appears,
SHEPHERDS (SHEPHERD)
Jer 23: 1 "Woe to the s who are destroying
Lk 2: 8 there were s living out in the fields
Ac 20: 28 Be s of the church of God,
1Pe 5: 2 Be s of God's flock that is
SHIELD
Ps 28: 7 LORD is my strength and my s;
Eph 6: 16 to all this, take up the s of faith,
SHINE (SHONE)
Ps 4: 6 Let the light of your face s upon us,
80: 1 between the cherubim, s forth
Isa 60: 1 "Arise, s, for your light has come,
Da 12: 3 are wise will s like the brightness

Mt 5: 16 let your light s before men,
13: 43 the righteous will s like the sun
2Co 4: 6 made his light s in our hearts
Eph 5: 14 and Christ will s on you."
SHIPWRECKED*
2Co 11: 25 I was stoned, three times I was s,
1Ti 1: 19 and so have s their faith.
SHONE (SHINE)
Mt 17: 2 His face s like the sun,
Lk 2: 9 glory of the Lord s around them,
Rev 21: 11 It s with the glory of God,
SHORT
Isa 59: 1 of the LORD is not too s to save,
Ro 3: 23 and fall s of the glory of God,
SHOULDERS
Isa 9: 6 and the government will be on his s
Lk 15: 5 he joyfully puts it on his s
SHOWED
1Jn 4: 9 This is how God s his love
SHREWD
Mt 10: 16 Therefore be as s as snakes and
SHUN*
Job 28: 28 and to s evil is understanding.'"
Pr 3: 7 fear the LORD and s evil.
SICK
Pr 13: 12 Hope deferred makes the heart s,
Mt 9: 12 who need a doctor, but the s.
25: 36 I was s and you looked after me,
Jas 5: 14 of you s? He should call the elders
SICKLE
Joel 3: 13 Swing the s,
SIDE
Ps 91: 7 A thousand may fall at your s,
124: 1 If the LORD had not been on our s
2Ti 4: 17 But the Lord stood at my s
SIGHT
Ps 90: 4 For a thousand years in your s
116: 15 Precious in the s of the LORD
2Co 5: 7 We live by faith, not by s.
1Pe 3: 4 which is of great worth in God's s.
SIGN (SIGNS)
Isa 7: 14 the Lord himself will give you a s:
SIGNS (SIGN)
Mk 16: 17 these s will accompany those who
Jn 20: 30 Jesus did many other miraculous s
SILENT
Pr 17: 28 a fool is thought wise if he keeps s,
Isa 53: 7 as a sheep before her shearers is s,
Hab 2: 20 let all the earth be s before him."
1Co 14: 34 women should remain s
1Ti 2: 12 over a man; she must be s.
SILVER
Pr 25: 11 is like apples of gold in settings of s.
Hag 2: 8 'The s is mine and the gold is mine,'
1Co 3: 12 s, costly stones, wood, hay or straw
SIMON
1. See PETER.
2. Apostle, called the Zealot (Mt 10:4; Mk 3:18; Lk 6:15; Ac 1:13).
3. Samaritan sorcerer (Ac 8:9-24).
SIN (SINFUL SINNED SINNER SINNERS SINNING SINS)
Nu 5: 7 and must confess the s he has
32: 23 be sure that your s will find you
Dt 24: 16 each is to die for his own s.
1Ki 8: 46 for there is no one who does not s
2Ch 7: 14 and will forgive their s and will heal
Ps 4: 4 In your anger do not s;
32: 2 whose s the LORD does not count
32: 5 Then I acknowledged my s to you
51: 2 and cleanse me from my s.
66: 18 If I had cherished s in my heart,
119: 11 that I might not s against you.
119: 133 let no s rule over me.
Isa 6: 7 is taken away and your s atoned
Mic 7: 18 who pardons s and forgives
Mt 18: 6 little ones who believe in me to s,
Jn 1: 29 who takes away the s of the world!
8: 34 everyone who sins is a slave to s.
Ro 5: 12 as s entered the world
5: 20 where s increased, grace increased
6: 11 count yourselves dead to s

SONS

	6:23	For the wages of *s* is death,
	14:23	that does not come from faith is *s*.
2Co	5:21	God made him who had no *s* to be *s*
Gal	6:1	if someone is caught in a *s*,
Heb	9:26	to do away with *s* by the sacrifice
	11:25	the pleasures of *s* for a short time.
	12:1	and the *s* that so easily entangles,
1Pe	2:22	"He committed no *s*,
1Jn	1:8	If we claim to be without *s*,
	3:4	in fact, *s* is lawlessness.
	3:5	And in him is no *s*.
	3:9	born of God will continue to *s*,
	5:18	born of God does not continue to *s*;

SINCERE
Ro	12:9	Love must be *s*.
Heb	10:22	near to God with a *s* heart

SINFUL (SIN)
Ps	51:5	Surely I was *s* at birth
	51:5	*s* from the time my mother
Ro	7:5	we were controlled by the *s* nature,
	8:4	not live according to the *s* nature
	8:9	are controlled not by the *s* nature
Gal	5:19	The acts of the *s* nature are obvious
	5:24	Jesus have crucified the *s* nature
1Pe	2:11	abstain from *s* desires, which war

SING (SANG SINGING SONG SONGS)
Ps	30:4	*S* to the LORD, you saints of his;
	47:6	*S* praises to God, *s* praises;
	59:16	But I will *s* of your strength,
	89:1	I will *s* of the LORD'S great love
	101:1	I will *s* of your love and justice;
Eph	5:19	*S* and make music in your heart

SINGING (SING)
Ps	63:5	with *s* lips my mouth will praise
Ac	16:25	Silas were praying and *s* hymns

SINNED (SIN)
2Sa	12:13	"I have *s* against the LORD."
Job	1:5	"Perhaps my children have *s*
Ps	51:4	Against you, you only, have I *s*
Da	9:5	we have *s* and done wrong.
Mic	7:9	Because I have *s* against him,
Lk	15:18	I have *s* against heaven
Ro	3:23	for all have *s* and fall short
1Jn	1:10	claim we have not *s*, we make him

SINNER (SIN)
Ecc	9:18	but one *s* destroys much good.
Lk	15:7	in heaven over one *s* who repents
	18:13	'God, have mercy on me, a *s*.'
1Co	14:24	convinced by all that he is a *s*
Jas	5:20	Whoever turns a *s* from the error
1Pe	4:18	become of the ungodly and the *s*?"

SINNERS (SIN)
Ps	1:1	or stand in the way of *s*
Pr	23:17	Do not let your heart envy *s*,
Mt	9:13	come to call the righteous, but *s*."
Ro	5:8	While we were still *s*, Christ died
1Ti	1:15	came into the world to save *s*—

SINNING (SIN)
Ex	20:20	be with you to keep you from *s*."
1Co	15:34	stop *s*; for there are some who are
Heb	10:26	If we deliberately keep on *s*
1Jn	3:6	No one who lives in him keeps on *s*
	3:9	go on *s*, because he has been born

SINS (SIN)
2Ki	14:6	each is to die for his own *s*."
Ezr	9:6	our *s* are higher than our heads
Ps	19:13	your servant also from willful *s*;
	32:1	whose *s* are covered.
	103:3	who forgives all your *s*
	130:3	O LORD, kept a record of *s*,
Pr	28:13	who conceals his *s* does not
Isa	1:18	"Though your *s* are like scarlet,
	43:25	and remembers your *s* no more.
	59:2	your *s* have hidden his face
Eze	18:4	soul who *s* is the one who will die.
Mt	1:21	he will save his people from their *s*
	18:15	"If your brother *s* against you,
Lk	11:4	Forgive us our *s*,
	17:3	"If your brother *s*, rebuke him,
Ac	22:16	be baptized and wash your *s* away,
1Co	15:3	died for our *s* according
Eph	2:1	dead in your transgressions and *s*,
Col	2:13	us all our *s*, having canceled

Heb	1:3	he had provided purification for *s*,
	7:27	He sacrificed for their *s* once for all
	8:12	and will remember their *s* no more
	10:12	for all time one sacrifice for *s*,
Jas	4:17	ought to do and doesn't do it, *s*.
	5:16	Therefore confess your *s*
	5:20	and cover over a multitude of *s*.
1Pe	2:24	He himself bore our *s* in his body
	3:18	For Christ died for *s* once for all,
1Jn	1:9	If we confess our *s*, he is faithful
Rev	1:5	has freed us from our *s* by his blood

SITS
Ps	99:1	*s* enthroned between the cherubim,
Isa	40:22	He *s* enthroned above the circle
Mt	19:28	of Man *s* on his glorious throne,
Rev	4:9	thanks to him who *s* on the throne

SKIN
Job	19:20	with only the *s* of my teeth.
	19:26	And after my *s* has been destroyed,
Jer	13:23	Can the Ethiopian change his *s*

SLAIN (SLAY)
Rev	5:12	"Worthy is the Lamb, who was *s*,

SLANDER (SLANDERED SLANDERERS)
Lev	19:16	" 'Do not go about spreading *s*
1Ti	5:14	the enemy no opportunity for *s*.
Tit	3:2	to *s* no one, to be peaceable

SLANDERED (SLANDER)
1Co	4:13	when we are *s*, we answer kindly.

SLANDERERS (SLANDER)
Ro	1:30	They are gossips, *s*, God-haters,
1Co	6:10	nor the greedy nor drunkards nor *s*
Tit	2:3	not to be *s* or addicted

SLAUGHTER
Isa	53:7	he was led like a lamb to the *s*,

SLAVE (SLAVERY SLAVES)
Ge	21:10	"Get rid of that *s* woman
Mt	20:27	wants to be first must be your *s*—
Jn	8:34	everyone who sins is a *s* to sin.
1Co	12:13	whether Jews or Greeks, *s* or free
Gal	3:28	*s* nor free, male nor female,
	4:30	Get rid of the *s* woman and her son
2Pe	2:19	a man is a *s* to whatever has

SLAVERY (SLAVE)
Ro	6:19	parts of your body in *s* to impurity
Gal	4:3	were in *s* under the basic principles

SLAVES (SLAVE)
Ro	6:6	that we should no longer be *s* to sin
	6:22	and have become *s* to God,

SLAY (SLAIN)
Job	13:15	Though he *s* me, yet will I hope

SLEEP (SLEEPING)
Ps	121:4	will neither slumber nor *s*.
1Co	15:51	We will not all *s*, but we will all be

SLEEPING (SLEEP)
Mk	13:36	suddenly, do not let him find you *s*.

SLOW
Ex	34:6	and gracious God, *s* to anger,
Jas	1:19	*s* to speak and *s* to become angry,
2Pe	3:9	The Lord is not *s* in keeping his

SLUGGARD
Pr	6:6	Go to the ant, you *s*;
	20:4	A *s* does not plow in season;

SLUMBER
Ps	121:3	he who watches over you will not *s*;
Pr	6:10	A little sleep, a little *s*,
Ro	13:11	for you to wake up from your *s*,

SNAKE (SNAKES)
Nu	21:8	"Make a *s* and put it up on a pole;
Pr	23:32	In the end it bites like a *s*
Jn	3:14	Moses lifted up the *s* in the desert,

SNAKES (SNAKE)
Mt	10:16	as shrewd as *s* and as innocent
Mk	16:18	they will pick up *s* with their hands;

SNATCH
Jn	10:28	no one can *s* them out of my hand.
Jude	23	*s* others from the fire and save

SNOW
Ps	51:7	and I will be whiter than *s*.

SOAR
Isa	40:31	They will *s* on wings like eagles;

SODOM
Ge	19:24	rained down burning sulfur on *S*
Ro	9:29	we would have become like *S*,

SOIL
Ge	4:2	kept flocks, and Cain worked the *s*.
Mt	13:23	on good *s* is the man who hears

SOLDIER
1Co	9:7	as a *s* at his own expense?
2Ti	2:3	with us like a good *s* of Christ Jesus

SOLE
Dt	28:65	place for the *s* of your foot.
Isa	1:6	From the *s* of your foot to the top

SOLID
2Ti	2:19	God's *s* foundation stands firm,
Heb	5:12	You need milk, not *s* food!

SOLOMON
Son of David by Bathsheba; king of Judah (2Sa 12:24; 1Ch 3:5, 10). Appointed king by David (1Ki 1); adversaries Adonijah, Joab, Shimei killed by Benaiah (1Ki 2). Asked for wisdom (1Ki 3; 2Ch 1). Judged between two prostitutes (1Ki 3:16-28). Built temple (1Ki 5-7; 2Ch 2-5); prayer of dedication (1Ki 8; 2Ch 6). Visited by Queen of Sheba (1Ki 10; 2Ch 9). Wives turned his heart from God (1Ki 11:1-13). Jeroboam rebelled against (1Ki 11:26-40). Death (1Ki 11:41-43; 2Ch 9:29-31).

Proverbs of (1Ki 4:32; Pr 1:1; 10:1; 25:1); psalms of (Ps 72; 127); song of (SS 1:1).

SON (SONS)
Ge	22:2	"Take your *s*, your only *s*, Isaac,
Ex	11:5	Every firstborn *s* in Egypt will die,
Dt	21:18	rebellious *s* who does not obey his
Ps	2:7	He said to me, "You are my *S*;
	2:12	Kiss the *S*, lest he be angry
Pr	10:1	A wise *s* brings joy to his father,
	13:24	He who spares the rod hates his *s*,
	29:17	Discipline your *s*, and he will give
Isa	7:14	with child and will give birth to a *s*,
Hos	11:1	and out of Egypt I called my *s*.
Mt	2:15	"Out of Egypt I called my *s*."
	3:17	"This is my *S*, whom I love;
	11:27	one knows the *S* except the Father,
	16:16	"You are the Christ, the *S*
	17:5	"This is my *S*, whom I love;
	20:18	and the *S* of Man will be betrayed
	24:30	They will see the *S* of Man coming
	24:44	the *S* of Man will come at an hour
	27:54	"Surely he was the *S* of God!"
	28:19	and of the *S* and of the Holy Spirit,
Mk	10:45	even the *S* of Man did not come
	14:62	you will see the *S* of Man sitting
Lk	9:58	but the *S* of Man has no place
	18:8	when the *S* of Man comes,
	19:10	For the *S* of Man came to seek
Jn	3:14	so the *S* of Man must be lifted up,
	3:16	that he gave his one and only *S*,
	17:1	Glorify your *S*, that your *S* may
Ro	8:29	conformed to the likeness of his *S*,
	8:32	He who did not spare his own *S*,
1Co	15:28	then the *S* himself will be made
Gal	4:30	rid of the slave woman and her *s*,
1Th	1:10	and to wait for his *S* from heaven,
Heb	1:2	days he has spoken to us by his *S*,
	10:29	punished who has trampled the *S*
1Jn	1:7	his *S*, purifies us from all sin.
	4:9	only *S* into the world that we might
	5:5	he who believes that Jesus is the *S*
	5:11	eternal life, and this life is in his *S*.

SONG (SING)
Ps	40:3	He put a new *s* in my mouth;
	96:1	Sing to the LORD a new *s*;
	149:1	Sing to the LORD a new *s*,
Isa	49:13	burst into *s*, O mountains!
	55:12	will burst into *s* before you,
Rev	5:9	And they sang a new *s*:
	15:3	and sang the *s* of Moses the servant

SONGS (SING)
Job	35:10	who gives *s* in the night,
Ps	100:2	come before him with joyful *s*.
Eph	5:19	with psalms, hymns and spiritual *s*.
Jas	5:13	Is anyone happy? Let him sing *s*

SONS (SON)
Joel	2:28	Your *s* and daughters will prophesy
Jn	12:36	so that you may become *s* of light."

SORROW

Ro 8:14 by the Spirit of God are s of God.
2Co 6:18 and you will be my s and daughters
Gal 4: 5 we might receive the full rights of s.
Heb 12: 7 discipline; God is treating you as s.

SORROW (SORROWS)
Jer 31:12 and they will s no more.
Ro 9: 2 I have great s and unceasing
2Co 7:10 Godly s brings repentance that

SORROWS (SORROW)
Isa 53: 3 a man of s, and familiar

SOUL (SOULS)
Dt 6: 5 with all your s and with all your
 10:12 all your heart and with all your s,
Jos 22: 5 with all your heart and all your s."
Ps 23: 3 he restores my s.
 42: 1 so my s pants for you, O God.
 42:11 Why are you downcast, O my s?
 103: 1 Praise the LORD, O my s;
Pr 13:19 A longing fulfilled is sweet to the s,
Isa 55: 2 your s will delight in the richest
Mt 10:28 kill the body but cannot kill the s.
 16:26 yet forfeits his s? Or what can
 22:37 with all your s and with all your
Heb 4:12 even to dividing s and spirit,

SOULS (SOUL)
Pr 11:30 and he who wins s is wise.
Jer 6:16 and you will find rest for your s.
Mt 11:29 and you will find rest for your s.

SOUND
1Co 14: 8 if the trumpet does not s a clear call
 15:52 the trumpet will s, the dead will
2Ti 4: 3 men will not put up with s doctrine.

SOVEREIGN
Da 4:25 that the Most High is s

SOW (SOWS)
Job 4: 8 and those who s trouble reap it.
Mt 6:26 they do not s or reap or store away
2Pe 2:22 and, "A s that is washed goes back

SOWS (SOW)
Pr 11:18 he who s righteousness reaps a sure
 22: 8 He who s wickedness reaps trouble
2Co 9: 6 Whoever s sparingly will
Gal 6: 7 A man reaps what he s.

SPARE (SPARES)
Ro 8:32 He who did not s his own Son,
 11:21 natural branches, he will not s you

SPARES (SPARE)
Pr 13:24 He who s the rod hates his son,

SPEARS
Isa 2: 4 and their s into pruning hooks.
Joel 3:10 and your pruning hooks into s.
Mic 4: 3 and their s into pruning hooks.

SPECTACLE
1Co 4: 9 We have been made a s
Col 2:15 he made a public s of them,

SPIN
Mt 6:28 They do not labor or s.

SPIRIT (SPIRIT'S SPIRITS SPIRITUAL SPIRITUALLY)
Ge 1: 2 and the S of God was hovering
 6: 3 "My S will not contend
2Ki 2: 9 inherit a double portion of your s,"
Job 33: 4 The S of God has made me;
Ps 31: 5 Into your hands I commit my s;
 51:10 and renew a steadfast s within me.
 51:11 or take your Holy S from me.
 51:17 sacrifices of God are a broken s;
 139: 7 Where can I go from your S?
Isa 57:15 him who is contrite and lowly in s,
 63:10 and grieved his Holy S.
Eze 11:19 an undivided heart and put a new s
 36:26 you a new heart and put a new s
Joel 2:28 I will pour out my S on all people.
Zec 4: 6 but by my S,' says the LORD
Mt 1:18 to be with child through the Holy S
 3:11 will baptize you with the Holy S
 3:16 he saw the S of God descending
 4: 1 led by the S into the desert
 5: 3 saying: "Blessed are the poor in s,
 26:41 s is willing, but the body is weak."
 28:19 and of the Son and of the Holy S,
Lk 1:80 child grew and became strong in s;
 11:13 Father in heaven give the Holy S
Jn 4:24 God is s, and his worshipers must
 7:39 Up to that time the S had not been
 14:26 But the Counselor, the Holy S,
 16:13 But when he, the S of truth, comes,
 20:22 and said, "Receive the Holy S.
Ac 1: 5 will be baptized with the Holy S."
 2: 4 of them were filled with the Holy S
 2:38 will receive the gift of the Holy S.
 6: 3 who are known to be full of the S
 19: 2 "Did you receive the Holy S
Ro 8: 9 And if anyone does not have the S
 8:26 the S helps us in our weakness.
1Co 2:10 God has revealed it to us by his S.
 2:14 man without the S does not accept
 6:19 body is a temple of the Holy S,
 12:13 baptized by one S into one body—
2Co 3: 6 the letter kills, but the S gives life.
 5: 5 and has given us the S as a deposit,
Gal 5:16 by the S, and you will not gratify
 5:22 But the fruit of the S is love, joy,
 5:25 let us keep in step with the S.
Eph 1:13 with a seal, the promised Holy S,
 4:30 do not grieve the Holy S of God,
 5:18 Instead, be filled with the S.
 6:17 of salvation and the sword of the S,
2Th 2:13 the sanctifying work of the S
Heb 4:12 even to dividing soul and s,
1Pe 3: 4 beauty of a gentle and quiet s,
2Pe 1:21 carried along by the Holy S.
1Jn 4: 1 Dear friends, do not believe every s

SPIRIT'S (SPIRIT)
1Th 5:19 not put out the S fire; do not treat

SPIRITS (SPIRIT)
1Co 12:10 to another distinguishing between s,
 14:32 The s of prophets are subject
1Jn 4: 1 test the s to see whether they are

SPIRITUAL (SPIRIT)
Ro 12: 1 this is your s act of worship.
 12:11 but keep your s fervor, serving
1Co 2:13 expressing s truths in s words.
 3: 1 I could not address you as s but
 12: 1 Now about s gifts, brothers,
 14: 1 of love and eagerly desire s gifts,
 15:44 a natural body, it is raised a s body.
Gal 6: 1 you who are s should restore him
Eph 1: 3 with every s blessing in Christ.
 5:19 with psalms, hymns and s songs,
 6:12 and against the s forces of evil
1Pe 2: 2 newborn babies, crave pure s milk,
 2: 5 are being built into a s house

SPIRITUALLY (SPIRIT)
1Co 2:14 because they are s discerned.

SPLENDOR
1Ch 16:29 the LORD in the s of his holiness.
 29:11 the glory and the majesty and the s,
Job 37:22 of the north he comes in golden s;
Ps 29: 2 in the s of his holiness.
 45: 3 clothe yourself with s and majesty.
 96: 6 S and majesty are before him;
 96: 9 in the s of his holiness;
 104: 1 you are clothed with s and majesty.
 145: 5 of the glorious s of your majesty,
Isa 61: 3 the LORD for the display of his s.
 63: 1 Who is this, robed in s,
Lk 9:31 appeared in glorious s, talking
2Th 2: 8 and destroy by the s of his coming.

SPOIL
Ps 119:162 like one who finds great s.

SPOTLESS
2Pe 3:14 make every effort to be found s,

SPREAD (SPREADING)
Ac 12:24 of God continued to increase and s.
 19:20 the word of the Lord s widely

SPREADING (SPREAD)
1Th 3: 2 God's fellow worker in s the gospel

SPRING
Jer 2:13 the s of living water,
Jn 4:14 in him a s of water welling up
Jas 3:12 can a salt s produce fresh water.

SPUR*
Heb 10:24 how we may s one another

SPURNS*
Pr 15: 5 A fool s his father's discipline,

STAFF
Ps 23: 4 your rod and your s,

STAKES
Isa 54: 2 strengthen your s.

STAND (STANDING STANDS)
Ex 14:13 S firm and you will see
2Ch 20:17 s firm and see the deliverance
Ps 1: 5 Therefore the wicked will not s
 40: 2 and gave me a firm place to s.
 119:120 I s in awe of your laws.
Eze 22:30 s before me in the gap on behalf
Zec 14: 4 On that day his feet will s
Mt 12:25 divided against itself will not s.
Ro 14:10 we will all s before God's judgment
1Co 10:13 out so that you can s up under it.
 15:58 Therefore, my dear brothers, s firm
Eph 6:14 S firm then, with the belt
2Th 2:15 s firm and hold to the teachings we
Jas 5: 8 You too, be patient and s firm,
Rev 3:20 Here I am! I s at the door

STANDING (STAND)
Ex 3: 5 where you are s is holy ground."
Jos 5:15 the place where you are s is holy."
1Pe 5: 9 Resist him, s firm in the faith,

STANDS (STAND)
Ps 89: 2 that your love s firm forever,
 119: 89 it s firm in the heavens.
Mt 10:22 but he who s firm to the end will be
2Ti 2:19 God's solid foundation s firm,
1Pe 1:25 but the word of the Lord s forever

STAR (STARS)
Nu 24:17 A s will come out of Jacob;
Rev 22:16 and the bright Morning S."

STARS (STAR)
Da 12: 3 like the s for ever and ever.
Php 2:15 in which you shine like s

STATURE
Lk 2:52 And Jesus grew in wisdom and s,

STEADFAST
Ps 51:10 and renew a s spirit within me.
Isa 26: 3 him whose mind is s,
1Pe 5:10 and make you strong, firm and s.

STEAL
Ex 20:15 "You shall not s.
Mt 19:18 do not s, do not give false
Eph 4:28 has been stealing must s no longer,

STEP (STEPS)
Gal 5:25 let us keep in s with the Spirit.

STEPS (STEP)
Pr 16: 9 but the LORD determines his s.
Jer 10:23 it is not for man to direct his s.
1Pe 2:21 that you should follow in his s.

STICKS
Pr 18:24 there is a friend who s closer

STIFF-NECKED
Ex 34: 9 Although this is a s people,

STILL
Ps 46:10 "Be s, and know that I am God;
Zec 2:13 Be s before the LORD, all mankind

STIRS
Pr 6:19 and a man who s up dissension
 10:12 Hatred s up dissension,
 15: 1 but a harsh word s up anger.
 15:18 hot-tempered man s up dissension,
 16:28 A perverse man s up dissension,
 28:25 A greedy man s up dissension,
 29:22 An angry man s up dissension,

STONE (CAPSTONE CORNERSTONE MILLSTONE)
1Sa 17:50 the Philistine with a sling and a s;
Isa 8:14 a s that causes men to stumble
Eze 11:19 remove from them their heart of s
Mk 16: 3 "Who will roll the s away
Lk 4: 3 tell this s to become bread."
Jn 8: 7 the first to throw a s at her."
2Co 3: 3 not on tablets of s but on tablets

STOOP
2Sa 22:36 you s down to make me great.

STORE
Pr 10:14 Wise men s up knowledge,

TAKEN

Mt	6:19	not *s* up for yourselves treasures

STOREHOUSE (HOUSE)
Mal 3:10 Bring the whole tithe into the *s*,

STRAIGHT
Pr 3: 6 and he will make your paths *s*.
4:25 Let your eyes look *s* ahead,
15:21 of understanding keeps a *s* course.
Jn 1:23 'Make *s* the way for the Lord.' "

STRAIN
Mt 23:24 You *s* out a gnat but swallow

STRANGER (STRANGERS)
Mt 25:35 I was a *s* and you invited me in,
Jn 10: 5 But they will never follow a *s*;

STRANGERS (STRANGER)
1Pe 2:11 as aliens and *s* in the world,

STREAMS
Ps 1: 3 He is like a tree planted by *s*
46: 4 is a river whose *s* make glad
Ecc 1: 7 All *s* flow into the sea,
Jn 7:38 *s* of living water will flow

STRENGTH (STRONG)
Ex 15: 2 The LORD is my *s* and my song;
Dt 6: 5 all your soul and with all your *s*.
2Sa 22:33 It is God who arms me with *s*
Ne 8:10 for the joy of the LORD is your *s*."
Ps 28: 7 The LORD is my *s* and my shield;
46: 1 God is our refuge and *s*,
96: 7 ascribe to the LORD glory and *s*.
118: 14 The LORD is my *s* and my song;
147: 10 not in the *s* of the horse,
Isa 40:31 will renew their *s*.
Mk 12:30 all your mind and with all your *s*.'
1Co 1:25 of God is stronger than man's *s*.
Php 4:13 through him who gives me *s*.
1Pe 4:11 it with the *s* God provides,

STRENGTHEN (STRONG)
2Ch 16: 9 to *s* those whose hearts are fully
Ps 119: 28 *s* me according to your word.
Isa 35: 3 *S* the feeble hands,
41:10 I will *s* you and help you;
Eph 3:16 of his glorious riches he may *s* you
2Th 2:17 and *s* you in every good deed
Heb 12:12 *s* your feeble arms and weak knees.

STRENGTHENING (STRONG)
1Co 14:26 done for the *s* of the church.

STRIFE
Pr 20: 3 It is to a man's honor to avoid *s*,
22:10 out the mocker, and out goes *s*;

STRIKE (STRIKES)
Ge 3:15 and you will *s* his heel."
Zec 13: 7 "*S* the shepherd,
Mt 26:31 " 'I will *s* the shepherd,

STRIKES (STRIKE)
Mt 5:39 If someone *s* you on the right

STRONG (STRENGTH STRENGTHEN STRENGTHENING)
Dt 31: 6 Be *s* and courageous.
1Ki 2: 2 "So be *s*, show yourself a man,
Pr 18:10 The name of the LORD is a *s* tower
31:17 her arms are *s* for her tasks.
SS 8: 6 for love is as *s* as death,
Lk 2:40 And the child grew and became *s*;
Ro 15: 1 We who are *s* ought to bear
1Co 1:27 things of the world to shame the *s*.
16:13 in the faith; be men of courage; be *s*
2Co 12:10 For when I am weak, then I am *s*.
Eph 6:10 be *s* in the Lord and in his mighty

STRUGGLE
Ro 15:30 me in my *s* by praying to God
Eph 6:12 For our *s* is not against flesh
Heb 12: 4 In your *s* against sin, you have not

STUDY
Ezr 7:10 Ezra had devoted himself to the *s*
Ecc 12:12 and much *s* wearies the body.
Jn 5:39 You diligently *s* the Scriptures

STUMBLE (STUMBLING)
Ps 37:24 though he *s*, he will not fall,
119:165 and nothing can make them *s*.
Isa 8:14 a stone that causes men to *s*
Jer 31: 9 a level path where they will not *s*,
Eze 7:19 for it has made them *s* into sin.
1Co 10:32 Do not cause anyone to *s*,

STUMBLING (STUMBLE)
1Pe 2: 8 and, "A stone that causes men to *s*
Ro 14:13 up your mind not to put any *s* block
1Co 8: 9 freedom does not become a *s* block
2Co 6: 3 We put no *s* block in anyone's path,

SUBDUE
Ge 1:28 in number; fill the earth and *s* it.

SUBJECT (SUBJECTED)
1Co 14:32 of prophets are *s* to the control
15:28 then the Son himself will be made *s*
Tit 2: 5 and to be *s* to their husbands,
2: 9 slaves to be *s* to their masters
3: 1 Remind the people to be *s* to rulers

SUBJECTED (SUBJECT)
Ro 8:20 For the creation was *s*

SUBMISSION
1Co 14:34 but must be in *s*, as the Law says.
1Ti 2:11 learn in quietness and full *s*.

SUBMISSIVE (SUBMIT)
Jas 3:17 then peace-loving, considerate, *s*,
1Pe 3: 1 in the same way be *s*
5: 5 in the same way be *s*

SUBMIT (SUBMISSION SUBMISSIVE SUBMITS)
Ro 13: 1 Everyone must *s* himself
13: 5 necessary to *s* to the authorities,
1Co 16:16 to *s* to such as these
Eph 5:21 *S* to one another out of reverence
Col 3:18 Wives, *s* to your husbands,
Heb 12: 9 How much more should we *s*
13:17 Obey your leaders and *s*
Jas 4: 7 *S* yourselves, then, to God.
1Pe 2:18 *s* yourselves to your masters

SUBMITS* (SUBMIT)
Eph 5:24 Now as the church *s* to Christ,

SUCCESSFUL
Jos 1: 7 that you may be *s* wherever you go.
2Ki 18: 7 he was *s* in whatever he undertook.
2Ch 20:20 in his prophets and you will be *s*."

SUFFER (SUFFERED SUFFERING SUFFERINGS SUFFERS)
Isa 53:10 to crush him and cause him to *s*,
Mk 8:31 the Son of Man must *s* many things
Lk 24:26 the Christ have to *s* these things
24:46 The Christ will *s* and rise
Php 1:29 to *s* for him, since you are going
1Pe 4:16 However, if you *s* as a Christian,

SUFFERED (SUFFER)
Heb 2: 9 and honor because he *s* death,
2:18 Because he himself *s*
1Pe 2:21 Christ *s* for you, leaving you

SUFFERING (SUFFER)
Isa 53: 3 of sorrows, and familiar with *s*.
Ac 5:41 worthy of *s* disgrace for the Name.
2Ti 1: 8 But join with me in *s* for the gospel,
Heb 2:10 of their salvation perfect through *s*.

SUFFERINGS (SUFFER)
Ro 8:17 share in his *s* in order that we may
8:18 that our present *s* are not worth
2Co 1: 5 as the *s* of Christ flow
Php 3:10 the fellowship of sharing in his *s*,

SUFFERS (SUFFER)
Pr 13:20 but a companion of fools *s* harm.
1Co 12:26 If one part *s*, every part *s* with it;

SUFFICIENT
2Co 12: 9 said to me, "My grace is *s* for you,

SUITABLE
Ge 2:18 I will make a helper *s* for him."

SUN
Ecc 1: 9 there is nothing new under the *s*.
Mal 4: 2 the *s* of righteousness will rise
Mt 5:45 He causes his *s* to rise on the evil
17: 2 His face shone like the *s*,
Rev 1:16 His face was like the *s* shining
21:23 The city does not need the *s*

SUPERIOR
Heb 1: 4 he became as much *s* to the angels
8: 6 ministry Jesus has received is as *s*

SUPERVISION
Gal 3:25 longer under the *s* of the law.

SUPREMACY* (SUPREME)
Col 1:18 in everything he might have the *s*.

SUPREME (SUPREMACY)
Pr 4: 7 Wisdom is *s*; therefore get wisdom.

SURE
Nu 32:23 you may be *s* that your sin will find
Dt 6:17 Be *s* to keep the commands
14:22 Be *s* to set aside a tenth
Isa 28:16 cornerstone for a *s* foundation;
Heb 11: 1 faith is being *s* of what we hope for
2Pe 1:10 to make your calling and election *s*.

SURPASS* (SURPASSES SURPASSING)
Pr 31:29 but you *s* them all."

SURPASSES (SURPASS)
Mt 5:20 unless your righteousness *s* that
Eph 3:19 to know this love that *s* knowledge

SURPASSING* (SURPASS)
Ps 150: 2 praise him for his *s* greatness.
2Co 3:10 in comparison with the *s* glory.
9:14 of the *s* grace God has given you.
Php 3: 8 the *s* greatness of knowing Christ

SURROUNDED
Heb 12: 1 since we are *s* by such a great cloud

SUSPENDS*
Job 26: 7 he *s* the earth over nothing.

SUSTAINING* (SUSTAINS)
Heb 1: 3 *s* all things by his powerful word.

SUSTAINS (SUSTAINING)
Ps 18:35 and your right hand *s* me;
146: 9 and *s* the fatherless and the widow,
147: 6 The LORD *s* the humble
Isa 50: 4 to know the word that *s* the weary.

SWALLOWED
1Co 15:54 "Death has been *s* up in victory."
2Co 5: 4 so that what is mortal may be *s* up

SWEAR
Mt 5:34 Do not *s* at all: either by heaven,

SWORD (SWORDS)
Ps 45: 3 Gird your *s* upon your side,
Pr 12:18 Reckless words pierce like a *s*,
Mt 10:34 come to bring peace, but a *s*.
26:52 all who draw the *s* will die by the *s*.
Lk 2:35 a *s* will pierce your own soul too."
Ro 13: 4 for he does not bear the *s*
Eph 6:17 of salvation and the *s* of the Spirit,
Heb 4:12 Sharper than any double-edged *s*,
Rev 1:16 came a sharp double-edged *s*.

SWORDS (SWORD)
Isa 2: 4 They will beat their *s*
Joel 3:10 Beat your plowshares into *s*

SYMPATHETIC*
1Pe 3: 8 in harmony with one another; be *s*,

SYNAGOGUE
Lk 4:16 the Sabbath day he went into the *s*,
Ac 17: 2 custom was, Paul went into the *s*,

TABERNACLE
Ex 40:34 the glory of the LORD filled the *t*.

TABLE (TABLES)
Ps 23: 5 You prepare a *t* before me

TABLES (TABLE)
Ac 6: 2 word of God in order to wait on *t*.

TABLET (TABLETS)
Pr 3: 3 write them on the *t* of your heart.
7: 3 write them on the *t* of your heart.

TABLETS (TABLET)
Ex 31:18 he gave him the two *t*
Dt 10: 5 and put the *t* in the ark I had made,
2Co 3: 3 not on *t* of stone but on *t*

TAKE (TAKEN TAKES TAKING TOOK)
Dt 12:32 do not add to it or *t* away from it.
31:26 "*T* this Book of the Law
Job 23:10 But he knows the way that I *t*;
Ps 49:17 for he will *t* nothing with him
51: 11 or *t* your Holy Spirit from me.
Mt 10:38 anyone who does not *t* his cross
11:29 *T* my yoke upon you and learn
16:24 deny himself and *t* up his cross

TAKEN (TAKE)
Lev 6: 4 must return what he has stolen or *t*
Isa 6: 7 your guilt is *t* away and your sin
Mt 24:40 one will be *t* and the other left.
Mk 16:19 he was *t* up into heaven
1Ti 3:16 was *t* up in glory.

TAKES

TAKES (TAKE)
- 1Ki 20:11 should not boast like one who t it
- Ps 5:4 You are not a God who t pleasure
- Jn 1:29 who t away the sin of the world!
- Rev 22:19 And if anyone t words away

TAKING (TAKE)
- Ac 15:14 by t from the Gentiles a people
- Php 2:7 t the very nature of a servant,

TALENT
- Mt 25:15 to another one t, each according

TAME*
- Jas 3:8 but no man can t the tongue.

TASK
- Mk 13:34 each with his assigned t,
- Ac 20:24 complete the t the Lord Jesus has
- 1Co 3:5 the Lord has assigned to each his t.
- 2Co 2:16 And who is equal to such a t?

TASTE (TASTED)
- Ps 34:8 T and see that the LORD is good;
- Col 2:21 Do not t! Do not touch!"?
- Heb 2:9 the grace of God he might t death

TASTED (TASTE)
- 1Pe 2:3 now that you have t that the Lord

TAUGHT (TEACH)
- Mt 7:29 he t as one who had authority,
- 1Co 2:13 but in words t by the Spirit,
- Gal 1:12 nor was I t it; rather, I received it

TAXES
- Mt 22:17 Is it right to pay t to Caesar or not
- Ro 13:7 If you owe t, pay t; if revenue,

TEACH (TAUGHT TEACHER TEACHERS TEACHES TEACHING)
- Ex 33:13 t me your ways so I may know you
- Dt 4:9 T them to your children
- 8:3 to t you that man does not live
- 11:19 T them to your children, talking
- 1Sa 12:23 I will t you the way that is good
- Ps 32:8 t you in the way you should go;
- 51:13 I will t transgressors your ways,
- 90:12 T us to number our days aright,
- 143:10 T me to do your will,
- Jer 31:34 No longer will a man t his neighbor
- Lk 11:1 said to him, "Lord, t us to pray,
- Jn 14:26 will t you all things and will remind
- 1Ti 2:12 I do not permit a woman to t
- 3:2 respectable, hospitable, able to t,
- Tit 2:1 You must t what is in accord
- Heb 8:11 No longer will a man t his neighbor
- Jas 3:1 know that we who t will be judged
- 1Jn 2:27 you do not need anyone to t you.

TEACHER (TEACH)
- Mt 10:24 "A student is not above his t,
- Jn 13:14 and T, have washed your feet,

TEACHERS (TEACH)
- 1Co 12:28 third t, then workers of miracles,
- Eph 4:11 and some to be pastors and t,
- Heb 5:12 by this time you ought to be t,

TEACHES (TEACH)
- 1Ti 6:3 If anyone t false doctrines

TEACHING (TEACH)
- Pr 1:8 and do not forsake your mother's t.
- Mt 28:20 t them to obey everything I have
- Jn 7:17 whether my t comes from God or
- 14:23 loves me, he will obey my t.
- 1Ti 4:13 of Scripture, to preaching and to t.
- 2Ti 3:16 is God-breathed and is useful for t,
- Tit 2:7 In your t show integrity,

TEAR (TEARS)
- Rev 7:17 God will wipe away every t

TEARS (TEAR)
- Ps 126:5 Those who sow in t
- Php 3:18 and now say again even with t,

TEETH (TOOTH)
- Mt 8:12 will be weeping and gnashing of t."

TEMPERATE*
- 1Ti 3:2 t, self-controlled, respectable,
- 3:11 not malicious talkers but t
- Tit 2:2 Teach the older men to be t,

TEMPEST
- Ps 55:8 far from the t and storm."

TEMPLE (TEMPLES)
- 1Ki 8:27 How much less this t I have built!
- Hab 2:20 But the LORD is in his holy t;
- 1Co 3:16 that you yourselves are God's t
- 6:19 you not know that your body is a t
- 2Co 6:16 For we are the t of the living God.

TEMPLES (TEMPLE)
- Ac 17:24 does not live in t built by hands.

TEMPT (TEMPTATION TEMPTED)
- 1Co 7:5 again so that Satan will not t you

TEMPTATION (TEMPT)
- Mt 6:13 And lead us not into t,
- 26:41 pray so that you will not fall into t.
- 1Co 10:13 No t has seized you except what is

TEMPTED (TEMPT)
- Mt 4:1 into the desert to be t by the devil.
- 1Co 10:13 he will not let you be t
- Heb 2:18 he himself suffered when he was t,
- 4:15 but we have one who has been t
- Jas 1:13 For God cannot be t by evil,

TEN (TENTH TITHE TITHES)
- Ex 34:28 covenant—the T Commandments.
- Ps 91:7 t thousand at your right hand,
- Mt 25:28 it to the one who has the t talents.
- Lk 15:8 suppose a woman has t silver coins

TENTH (TEN)
- Dt 14:22 Be sure to set aside a t

TERRIBLE (TERROR)
- 2Ti 3:1 There will be t times

TERROR (TERRIBLE)
- Ps 91:5 You will not fear the t of night,
- Lk 21:26 Men will faint from t, apprehensive
- Ro 13:3 For rulers hold no t

TEST (TESTED TESTS)
- Dt 6:16 Do not t the LORD your God
- Ps 139:23 t me and know my anxious
- Ro 12:2 Then you will be able to t
- 1Co 3:13 and the fire will t the quality
- 1Jn 4:1 t the spirits to see whether they are

TESTED (TEST)
- Ge 22:1 Some time later God t Abraham.
- Job 23:10 when he has t me, I will come forth
- Pr 27:21 man is t by the praise he receives.
- 1Ti 3:10 They must first be t; and then

TESTIFY (TESTIMONY)
- Jn 5:39 are the Scriptures that t about me,
- 2Ti 1:8 ashamed to t about our Lord,

TESTIMONY (TESTIFY)
- Isa 8:20 and to the t! If they do not speak
- Lk 18:20 not give false t, honor your father

TESTS (TEST)
- Pr 17:3 but the LORD t the heart.
- 1Th 2:4 but God, who t our hearts.

THADDAEUS
Apostle (Mt 10:3; Mk 3:18); probably also known as Judas son of James (Lk 6:16; Ac 1:13).

THANKFUL (THANKS)
- Heb 12:28 let us be t, and so worship God

THANKS (THANKFUL THANKSGIVING)
- 1Ch 16:8 Give t to the LORD, call
- Ne 12:31 assigned two large choirs to give t.
- Ps 100:4 give t to him and praise his name.
- 1Co 15:57 t be to God! He gives us the victory
- 2Co 2:14 t be to God, who always leads us
- 9:15 T be to God for his indescribable
- 1Th 5:18 give t in all circumstances,

THANKSGIVING (THANKS)
- Ps 95:2 Let us come before him with t
- 100:4 Enter his gates with t
- Php 4:6 by prayer and petition, with t,
- 1Ti 4:3 created to be received with t

THIEF (THIEVES)
- Ex 22:3 A t must certainly make restitution
- 1Th 5:2 day of the Lord will come like a t
- Rev 16:15 I come like a t! Blessed is he who

THIEVES (THIEF)
- 1Co 6:10 nor homosexual offenders nor t

THINK (THOUGHT THOUGHTS)
- Ro 12:3 Do not t of yourself more highly
- Php 4:8 praiseworthy—t about such things

THIRST (THIRSTY)
- Ps 69:21 and gave me vinegar for my t.
- Mt 5:6 Blessed are those who hunger and t
- Jn 4:14 the water I give him will never t.

THIRSTY (THIRST)
- Isa 55:1 "Come, all you who are t,
- Jn 7:37 "If anyone is t, let him come to me
- Rev 22:17 Whoever is t, let him come;

THOMAS
Apostle (Mt 10:3; Mk 3:18; Lk 6:15; Jn 11:16; 14:5; 21:2; Ac 1:13). Doubted resurrection (Jn 20:24-28).

THONGS
- Mk 1:7 t of whose sandals I am not worthy

THORN (THORNS)
- 2Co 12:7 there was given me a t in my flesh,

THORNS (THORN)
- Nu 33:55 in your eyes and t in your sides.
- Mt 27:29 then twisted together a crown of t
- Heb 6:8 But land that produces t

THOUGHT (THINK)
- Pr 14:15 a prudent man gives t to his steps.
- 1Co 13:11 I talked like a child, I t like a child,

THOUGHTS (THINK)
- Ps 94:11 The LORD knows the t of man;
- 139:23 test me and know my anxious t.
- Isa 55:8 "For my t are not your t,
- Heb 4:12 it judges the t and attitudes

THREE
- Ecc 4:12 of t strands is not quickly broken.
- Mt 12:40 t nights in the belly of a huge fish,
- 18:20 or t come together in my name,
- 27:63 'After t days I will rise again'.
- 1Co 13:13 And now these t remain: faith,
- 14:27 or at the most t—should speak,
- 2Co 13:1 testimony of two or t witnesses."

THRESHING
- 2Sa 24:18 an altar to the LORD on the t floor

THRONE (ENTHRONED)
- 2Sa 7:16 your t will be established forever
- Ps 45:6 Your t, O God, will last for ever
- 47:8 God is seated on his holy t.
- Isa 6:1 I saw the Lord seated on a t,
- 66:1 "Heaven is my t
- Heb 4:16 Let us then approach the t of grace
- 12:2 at the right hand of the t of God.
- Rev 4:10 They lay their crowns before the t
- 20:11 Then I saw a great white t
- 22:3 t of God and of the Lamb will be

THROW
- Jn 8:7 the first to t a stone at her."
- Heb 10:35 So do not t away your confidence;
- 12:1 let us t off everything that hinders

THWART*
- Isa 14:27 has purposed, and who can t him?

TIBNI
King of Israel (1Ki 16:21-22).

TIME (TIMES)
- Est 4:14 come to royal position for such a t
- Da 7:25 to him for a t, times and half a t.
- Hos 10:12 for it is t to seek the LORD,
- Ro 9:9 "At the appointed t I will return,
- Heb 9:28 and he will appear a second t,
- 10:12 for all t one sacrifice for sins,
- 1Pe 4:17 For it is t for judgment to begin

TIMES (TIME)
- Ps 9:9 a stronghold in t of trouble,
- 31:15 My t are in your hands;
- 62:8 Trust in him at all t, O people;
- Pr 17:17 A friend loves at all t,
- Am 5:13 for the t are evil.
- Mt 18:21 how many t shall I forgive my
- Ac 1:7 "It is not for you to know the t
- Rev 12:14 t and half a time, out

TIMIDITY*
- 2Ti 1:7 For God did not give us a spirit of t.

TIMOTHY
Believer from Lystra (Ac 16:1). Joined Paul on second missionary journey (Ac 16-20). Sent to settle problems at Corinth (1Co 4:17; 16:10). Led church at Ephesus (1Ti 1:3). Co-writer with Paul (1Th 1:1; 2Th 1:1; Phm 1).

TIRE (TIRED)
2Th 3:13 never *t* of doing what is right.
TIRED (TIRE)
Ex 17:12 When Moses' hands grew *t*,
Isa 40:28 He will not grow *t* or weary,
TITHE (TEN)
Lev 27:30 " 'A *t* of everything from the land,
Dt 12:17 eat in your own towns the *t*
Mal 3:10 the whole *t* into the storehouse,
TITHES (TEN)
Mal 3:8 'How do we rob you?' "In *t*
TITUS
Gentile co-worker of Paul (Gal 2:1-3; 2Ti 4:10); sent to Corinth (2Co 2:13; 7-8; 12:18), Crete (Tit 1:4-5).
TODAY
Mt 6:11 Give us *t* our daily bread.
Lk 23:43 *t* you will be with me in paradise."
Heb 3:13 daily, as long as it is called *T*,
13: 8 Christ is the same yesterday and *t*
TOIL
Ge 3:17 through painful *t* you will eat of it
TOLERATE
Hab 1:13 you cannot *t* wrong.
Rev 2: 2 that you cannot *t* wicked men,
TOMB
Mt 27:65 make the *t* as secure as you know
Lk 24: 2 the stone rolled away from the *t*,
TOMORROW
Pr 27: 1 Do not boast about *t*,
Isa 22:13 "for *t* we die!"
Mt 6:34 Therefore do not worry about *t*,
Jas 4:13 "Today or *t* we will go to this
TONGUE (TONGUES)
Ps 39: 1 and keep my *t* from sin;
Pr 12:18 but the *t* of the wise brings healing.
1Co 14: 4 He who speaks in a *t* edifies himself
14:13 in a *t* should pray that he may
14:19 than ten thousand words in a *t*
Php 2:11 every *t* confess that Jesus Christ is
Jas 1:26 does not keep a tight rein on his *t*,
3: 8 but no man can tame the *t*.
TONGUES (TONGUE)
Isa 28:11 with foreign lips and strange *t*
66:18 and gather all nations and *t*,
Mk 16:17 in new *t*; they will pick up snakes
Ac 2: 4 and began to speak in other *t*
10:46 For they heard them speaking in *t*
19: 6 and they spoke in *t* and prophesied
1Co 12:30 Do all speak in *t*? Do all interpret?
14:18 speak in *t* more than all of you.
14:39 and do not forbid speaking in *t*.
TOOK (TAKE)
1Co 11:23 the night he was betrayed, *t* bread,
Php 3:12 for which Christ Jesus *t* hold of me.
TOOTH (TEETH)
Ex 21:24 eye for eye, *t* for *t*, hand for hand,
Mt 5:38 'Eye for eye, and *t* for *t*.'
TORMENTED
Rev 20:10 They will be *t* day and night
TORN
Gal 4:15 you would have *t* out your eyes
Php 1:23 I do not know! I am *t*
TOUCH (TOUCHED)
Ps 105: 15 "Do not *t* my anointed ones;
Lk 24:39 It is I myself! *T* me and see;
2Co 6:17 *T* no unclean thing,
Col 2:21 Do not taste! Do not *t*!"?
TOUCHED (TOUCH)
1Sa 10:26 men whose hearts God had *t*.
Mt 14:36 and all who *t* him were healed.
TOWER
Ge 11: 4 with a *t* that reaches to the heavens
Pr 18:10 of the LORD is a strong *t*;
TOWNS
Nu 35: 2 to give the Levites *t* to live
35:15 These six *t* will be a place of refuge
TRACING*
Ro 11:33 and his paths beyond *t* out!
TRADITION
Mt 15: 6 word of God for the sake of your *t*.

Col 2: 8 which depends on human *t*
TRAIN (TRAINING)
Pr 22: 6 *T* a child in the way he should go,
Eph 4: 8 he led captives in his *t*
TRAINING (TRAIN)
1Co 9:25 in the games goes into strict *t*.
2Ti 3:16 correcting and *t* in righteousness,
TRAMPLED
Lk 21:24 Jerusalem will be *t*
Heb 10:29 to be punished who has *t* the Son
TRANCE
Ac 10:10 was being prepared, he fell into a *t*.
TRANSCENDS*
Php 4: 7 which *t* all understanding,
TRANSFIGURED
Mt 17: 2 There he was *t* before them.
TRANSFORM* (TRANSFORMED)
Php 3:21 will *t* our lowly bodies
TRANSFORMED (TRANSFORM)
Ro 12: 2 be *t* by the renewing of your mind.
2Co 3:18 are being *t* into his likeness
TRANSGRESSION (TRANSGRESSIONS TRANSGRESSORS)
Isa 53: 8 for the *t* of my people he was
Ro 4:15 where there is no law there is no *t*.
TRANSGRESSIONS (TRANSGRESSION)
Ps 32: 1 whose *t* are forgiven,
51: 1 blot out my *t*.
103: 12 so far has he removed our *t* from us
Isa 53: 5 But he was pierced for our *t*,
Eph 2: 1 you were dead in your *t* and sins,
TRANSGRESSORS (TRANSGRESSION)
Ps 51:13 Then I will teach *t* your ways,
Isa 53:12 and made intercession for the *t*.
53:12 and was numbered with the *t*.
TREADING
Dt 25: 4 an ox while it is *t* out the grain.
1Co 9: 9 an ox while it is *t* out the grain."
TREASURE (TREASURED TREASURES)
Isa 33: 6 of the LORD is the key to this *t*.
Mt 6:21 For where your *t* is, there your
2Co 4: 7 But we have this *t* in jars of clay
TREASURED (TREASURE)
Dt 7: 6 to be his people, his *t* possession.
Lk 2:19 But Mary *t* up all these things
TREASURES (TREASURE)
Mt 6:19 up for yourselves *t* on earth,
Col 2: 3 in whom are hidden all the *t*
Heb 11:26 of greater value than the *t* of Egypt,
TREAT
Lev 22: 2 sons to *t* with respect the sacred
1Ti 5: 1 *T* younger men as brothers,
1Pe 3: 7 and *t* them with respect
TREATY
Dt 7: 2 Make no *t* with them, and show
TREE
Ge 2: 9 and the *t* of the knowledge of good
2: 9 of the garden were the *t* of life
Dt 21:23 hung on a *t* is under God's curse.
Ps 1: 3 like a *t* planted by streams
Mt 3:10 every *t* that does not produce good
12:33 for a *t* is recognized by its fruit.
Gal 3:13 is everyone who is hung on a *t*."
Rev 22:14 they may have the right to the *t*
TREMBLE (TREMBLING)
1Ch 16:30 *T* before him, all the earth!
Ps 114: 7 *T*, O earth, at the presence
TREMBLING (TREMBLE)
Ps 2:11 and rejoice with *t*.
Php 2:12 out your salvation with fear and *t*,
TRESPASS
Ro 5:17 For if, by the *t* of the one man,
TRIALS
1Th 3: 3 one would be unsettled by these *t*.
Jas 1: 2 whenever you face *t* of many kinds,
2Pe 2: 9 how to rescue godly men from *t*
TRIBES
Ge 49:28 All these are the twelve *t* of Israel,
Mt 19:28 judging the twelve *t* of Israel.

TRIBULATION*
Rev 7:14 who have come out of the great *t*;
TRIUMPHAL* (TRIUMPHING)
Isa 60:11 their kings led in *t* procession.
2Co 2:14 us in *t* procession in Christ
TRIUMPHING* (TRIUMPHAL)
Col 2:15 of them, *t* over them by the cross.
TROUBLE (TROUBLED TROUBLES)
Job 14: 1 is of few days and full of *t*.
Ps 46: 1 an ever-present help in *t*.
107: 13 they cried to the LORD in their *t*,
Pr 11:29 He who brings *t* on his family will
24: 10 If you falter in times of *t*,
Mt 6:34 Each day has enough of its own.
Jn 16:33 In this world you will have *t*.
Ro 8:35 Shall *t* or hardship or persecution
TROUBLED (TROUBLE)
Jn 14: 1 "Do not let your hearts be *t*.
14:27 Do not let your hearts be *t*
TROUBLES (TROUBLE)
1Co 7:28 those who marry will face many *t*
2Co 1: 4 who comforts us in all our *t*,
4:17 and momentary *t* are achieving
TRUE (TRUTH)
Dt 18:22 does not take place or come *t*,
1Sa 9: 6 and everything he says comes *t*.
Ps 119:160 All your words are *t*;
Jn 17: 3 the only *t* God, and Jesus Christ,
Ro 3: 4 Let God be *t*, and every man a liar.
Php 4: 8 whatever is *t*, whatever is noble,
Rev 22: 6 These words are trustworthy and *t*.
TRUMPET
1Co 14: 8 if the *t* does not sound a clear call,
15:52 For the *t* will sound, the dead will
TRUST (ENTRUSTED TRUSTED TRUSTS TRUSTWORTHY)
Ps 20: 7 we *t* in the name of the LORD our
37: 3 *T* in the LORD and do good;
56: 4 in God I *t*; I will not be afraid.
119: 42 for I *t* in your word.
Pr 3: 5 *T* in the LORD with all your heart
Isa 30:15 in quietness and *t* is your strength,
Jn 14: 1 *T* in God; *t* also in me.
1Co 4: 2 been given a *t* must prove faithful.
TRUSTED (TRUST)
Ps 26: 1 I have *t* in the LORD
Isa 25: 9 in him, and he saved us.
Da 3:28 They *t* in him and defied the king's
Lk 16:10 *t* with very little can also be *t*
TRUSTS (TRUST)
Ps 32:10 surrounds the man who *t* in him.
Pr 11:28 Whoever *t* in his riches will fall,
28:26 He who *t* in himself is a fool,
Ro 9:33 one who *t* in him will never be put
TRUSTWORTHY (TRUST)
Ps 119:138 they are fully *t*.
Pr 11:13 but a *t* man keeps a secret.
Rev 22: 6 "These words are *t* and true.
TRUTH (TRUE TRUTHFUL TRUTHS)
Ps 51: 6 Surely you desire *t*
Isa 45:19 I, the LORD, speak the *t*;
Zec 8:16 are to do: Speak the *t* to each other,
Jn 4:23 worship the Father in spirit and *t*,
8:32 Then you will know the *t*,
8:32 and the *t* will set you free."
14: 6 I am the way and the *t* and the life.
16:13 comes, he will guide you into all *t*.
18:38 "What is *t*?" Pilate asked.
Ro 1:25 They exchanged the *t* of God
1Co 13: 6 in evil but rejoices with the *t*.
2Co 13: 8 against the *t*, but only for the *t*.
Eph 4:15 Instead, speaking the *t* in love,
6:14 with the belt of *t* buckled
2Th 2:10 because they refused to love the *t*
1Ti 2: 4 to come to a knowledge of the *t*.
3:15 the pillar and foundation of the *t*.
2Ti 2:15 correctly handles the word of *t*.
3: 7 never able to acknowledge the *t*.
Heb 10:26 received the knowledge of the *t*,
1Pe 1:22 by obeying the *t* so that you have
2Pe 2: 2 the way of *t* into disrepute.
1Jn 1: 6 we lie and do not live by the *t*.

TRUTHFUL

1: 8 deceive ourselves and the t is not
TRUTHFUL (TRUTH)
Pr 12:22 but he delights in men who are t.
Jn 3:33 it has certified that God is t.
TRUTHS (TRUTH)
1Co 2:13 expressing spiritual t
1Ti 3: 9 hold of the deep t of the faith
Heb 5:12 to teach you the elementary t
TRY (TRYING)
Ps 26: 2 Test me, O Lord, and t me,
Isa 7:13 enough to t the patience of men?
1Co 14:12 t to excel in gifts that build up
2Co 5: 11 is to fear the Lord, we t
1Th 5:15 always t to be kind to each other
TRYING (TRY)
2Co 5:12 We are not t to commend ourselves
1Th 2: 4 We are not t to please men but God
TUNIC
Lk 6:29 do not stop him from taking your t.
TURN (TURNED TURNS)
Ex 32:12 T from your fierce anger; relent
Dt 5:32 do not t aside to the right
28:14 Do not t aside from any
Jos 1: 7 do not t from it to the right
2Ch 7:14 and t from their wicked ways,
30: 9 he will not t his face from you
Ps 78: 6 they in t would tell their children.
Pr 22: 6 when he is old he will not t from it.
Isa 29:16 You t things upside down,
30:21 Whether you t to the right
45:22 "T to me and be saved,
55: 7 Let him t to the Lord,
Eze 33: 11 T! T from your evil ways!
Mal 4: 6 He will t the hearts of the fathers
Mt 5:39 you on the right cheek, t
10:35 For I have come to t
Jn 12:40 nor t— and I would heal them."
Ac 3:19 Repent, then, and t to God,
26:18 and t them from darkness to light,
1Ti 6:20 T away from godless chatter
1Pe 3: 11 He must t from evil and do good;
TURNED (TURN)
Ps 30: 11 You t my wailing into dancing;
40: 1 he t to me and heard my cry.
Isa 53: 6 each of us has t to his own way;
Hos 7: 8 Ephraim is a flat cake not t over.
Joel 2: 31 The sun will be t to darkness
Ro 3:12 All have t away,
TURNS (TURN)
2Sa 22:29 the Lord t my darkness into light
Pr 15: 1 A gentle answer t away wrath,
Isa 44:25 and t it into nonsense,
Jas 5:20 Whoever t a sinner from the error
TWELVE
Ge 49:28 All these are the t tribes of Israel,
Mt 10: 1 He called his t disciples to him
TWINKLING*
1Co 15:52 in a flash, in the t of an eye,
UNAPPROACHABLE*
1Ti 6:16 immortal and who lives in u light,
UNBELIEF (UNBELIEVER UNBELIEVERS UNBELIEVING)
Mk 9:24 help me overcome my u!"
Ro 11:20 they were broken off because of u,
Heb 3:19 able to enter, because of their u.
UNBELIEVER* (UNBELIEF)
1Co 7:15 But if the u leaves, let him do so.
10:27 If some u invites you to a meal
14:24 if an u or someone who does not
2Co 6:15 have in common with an u?
1Ti 5: 8 the faith and is worse than an u.
UNBELIEVERS (UNBELIEF)
1Co 6: 6 another—and this in front of u!
2Co 6:14 Do not be yoked together with u.
UNBELIEVING (UNBELIEF)
1Co 7:14 For the u husband has been
Rev 21: 8 But the cowardly, the u, the vile,
UNCERTAIN*
1Ti 6:17 which is so u, but to put their hope
UNCHANGEABLE*
Heb 6:18 by two u things in which it is

UNCIRCUMCISED
1Sa 17:26 Who is this u Philistine that he
Col 3: 11 circumcised or u, barbarian,
UNCIRCUMCISION
1Co 7:19 is nothing and u is nothing.
Gal 5: 6 neither circumcision nor u has any
UNCLEAN
Isa 6: 5 ruined! For I am a man of u lips,
Ro 14:14 fully convinced that no food is u
2Co 6:17 Touch no u thing,
UNCONCERNED*
Eze 16:49 were arrogant, overfed and u;
UNCOVERED
Heb 4:13 Everything is u and laid bare
UNDERSTAND (UNDERSTANDING UNDERSTANDS)
Job 42: 3 Surely I spoke of things I did not u,
Ps 73:16 When I tried to u all this,
119: 125 that I may u your statutes.
Lk 24:45 so they could u the Scriptures.
Ac 8:30 "Do you u what you are reading?"
Ro 7:15 I do not u what I do.
1Co 2:14 and he cannot u them,
Eph 5:17 but u what the Lord's will is.
2Pe 3:16 some things that are hard to u,
UNDERSTANDING (UNDERSTAND)
Ps 119: 104 I gain u from your precepts;
147: 5 his u has no limit.
Pr 3: 5 and lean not on your own u;
4: 7 Though it cost all you have, get u.
10:23 but a man of u delights in wisdom.
11:12 but a man of u holds his tongue.
15:21 a man of u keeps a straight course.
15:32 whoever heeds correction gains u.
23:23 get wisdom, discipline and u.
Isa 40:28 and his u no one can fathom.
Da 5:12 a keen mind and knowledge and u,
Mk 4:12 and ever hearing but never u;
12:33 with all your u and with all your
Php 4: 7 of God, which transcends all u,
UNDERSTANDS (UNDERSTAND)
1Ch 28: 9 and u every motive
1Ti 6: 4 he is conceited and u nothing.
UNDIVIDED*
1Ch 12:33 to help David with u loyalty—
Ps 86: 11 give me an u heart,
Eze 11:19 I will give them an u heart
1Co 7:35 way in u devotion to the Lord.
UNDOING
Pr 18: 7 A fool's mouth is his u,
UNDYING*
Eph 6:24 Lord Jesus Christ with an u love.
UNFADING*
1Pe 3: 4 the u beauty of a gentle
UNFAILING
Ps 33: 5 the earth is full of his u love.
119: 76 May your u love be my comfort,
143: 8 bring me word of your u love,
Pr 19:22 What a man desires is u love;
La 3:32 so great is his u love.
UNFAITHFUL (UNFAITHFULNESS)
Lev 6: 2 is u to the Lord by deceiving his
1Ch 10: 13 because he was u to the Lord;
Pr 13:15 but the way of the u is hard.
UNFAITHFULNESS (UNFAITHFUL)
Mt 5:32 except for marital u, causes her
19: 9 for marital u, and marries another
UNFOLDING
Ps 119: 130 the u of your words gives light;
UNGODLINESS
Tit 2:12 It teaches us to say "No" to u
UNIT
1Co 12:12 body is a u, though it is made up
UNITED (UNITY)
Ro 6: 5 If we have been u with him
Php 2: 1 from being u with Christ,
Col 2: 2 encouraged in heart and u in love,
UNITY (UNITED)
Ps 133: 1 is when brothers live together in u!
Ro 15: 5 a spirit of u among yourselves
Eph 4: 3 effort to keep the u of the Spirit
4:13 up until we all reach u in the faith

UNIVERSE
Col 3: 14 them all together in perfect u.
Php 2:15 which you shine like stars in the u
Heb 1: 2 and through whom he made the u.
UNKNOWN
Ac 17:23 TO AN U GOD.
UNLEAVENED
Ex 12:17 "Celebrate the Feast of U Bread,
UNPROFITABLE
Tit 3: 9 because these are u and useless.
UNPUNISHED
Ex 34: 7 Yet he does not leave the guilty u;
Pr 19: 5 A false witness will not go u,
UNREPENTANT*
Ro 2: 5 stubbornness and your u heart,
UNRIGHTEOUS*
Zep 3: 5 yet the u know no shame.
Mt 5:45 rain on the righteous and the u.
1Pe 3:18 the righteous for the u, to bring you
2Pe 2: 9 and to hold the u for the day
UNSEARCHABLE
Ro 11:33 How u his judgments,
Eph 3: 8 preach to the Gentiles the u riches
UNSEEN
2Co 4:18 on what is seen, but on what is u.
4:18 temporary, but what is u is eternal.
UNSTABLE*
Jas 1: 8 he is a double-minded man, u
2Pe 2:14 they seduce the u; they are experts
3:16 ignorant and u people distort,
UNTHINKABLE*
Job 34:12 It is u that God would do wrong,
UNVEILED*
2Co 3:18 with u faces all reflect the Lord's
UNWORTHY
Job 40: 4 "I am u— how can I reply to you?
Lk 17: 10 should say, 'We are u servants;
UPRIGHT
Job 1: 1 This man was blameless and u;
Pr 2: 7 He holds victory in store for the u,
15: 8 but the prayer of the u pleases him.
Tit 1: 8 who is self-controlled, u, holy
2:12 u and godly lives in this present
UPROOTED
Jude 12 without fruit and u— twice dead.
USEFUL
2Ti 2:21 u to the Master and prepared
3: 16 Scripture is God-breathed and is u
USELESS
1Co 15:14 our preaching is u
Jas 2: 20 faith without deeds is u?
USURY
Ne 5: 10 But let the exacting of u stop!
UTTER
Ps 78: 2 I will u hidden things, things from of
UZZIAH
Son of Amaziah; king of Judah also known as Azariah (2Ki 15:1-7; 1Ch 6:24; 2Ch 26).
VAIN
Ps 33:17 A horse is a v hope for deliverance;
Isa 65:23 They will not toil in v
1Co 15: 2 Otherwise, you have believed in v.
15:58 labor in the Lord is not in v.
2Co 6: 1 not to receive God's grace in v.
VALLEY
Ps 23: 4 walk through the v of the shadow
Isa 40: 4 Every v shall be raised up,
Joel 3:14 multitudes in the v of decision!
VALUABLE (VALUE)
Lk 12:24 And how much more v you are
VALUE (VALUABLE)
Mt 13:46 When he found one of great v,
1Ti 4: 8 For physical training is of some v,
Heb 11:26 as of greater v than the treasures
VEIL
Ex 34:33 to them, he put a v over his face.
2Co 3:14 for to this day the same v remains
VENGEANCE (AVENGE REVENGE)
Isa 34: 8 For the Lord has a day of v,

VICTORIES (VICTORY)
Ps 18:50 He gives his king great v;
  21: 1 great is his joy in the v you give!
VICTORIOUSLY* (VICTORY)
Ps 45: 4 In your majesty ride forth v
VICTORY (VICTORIES VICTORIOUSLY)
Ps 60:12 With God we will gain the v,
1Co 15:54 "Death has been swallowed up in v
  15:57 He gives us the v through our Lord
1Jn 5: 4 This is the v that has overcome
VINDICATED
1Ti 3:16 was v by the Spirit,
VINE
Jn 15: 1 "I am the true v, and my Father is
VINEGAR
Mk 15:36 filled a sponge with wine v,
VIOLATION
Heb 2: 2 every v and disobedience received
VIOLENCE
Isa 60:18 No longer will v be heard
Eze 45: 9 Give up your v and oppression
VIPERS
Ro 3:13 "The poison of v is on their lips."
VIRGIN
Isa 7:14 The v will be with child
Mt 1:23 "The v will be with child
2Co 11: 2 that I might present you as a pure v
VIRTUES*
Col 3:14 And over all these v put on love,
VISION
Ac 26:19 disobedient to the v from heaven.
VOICE
Ps 95: 7 Today, if you hear his v,
Isa 30:21 your ears will hear a v behind you,
Jn 5:28 are in their graves will hear his v
  10: 3 and the sheep listen to his v.
Heb 3: 7 "Today, if you hear his v,
Rev 3:20 If anyone hears my v and opens
VOMIT
Pr 26:11 As a dog returns to its v,
2Pe 2:22 "A dog returns to its v," and,
VOW
Nu 30: 2 When a man makes a v
WAGES
Lk 10: 7 for the worker deserves his w.
Ro 4:4 his w are not credited to him
  6:23 For the w of sin is death,
WAILING
Ps 30:11 You turned my w into dancing;
WAIST
2Ki 1: 8 with a leather belt around his w."
Mt 3: 4 he had a leather belt around his w.
WAIT (WAITED WAITS)
Ps 27:14 W for the LORD;
  130: 1 I w for the LORD, my soul waits,
Isa 30:18 Blessed are all who w for him!
Ac 1: 4 w for the gift my Father promised,
Ro 8:23 as we w eagerly for our adoption
1Th 1:10 and to w for his Son from heaven,
Tit 2:13 while we w for the blessed hope—
WAITED (WAIT)
Ps 40: 1 I w patiently for the LORD;
WAITS (WAIT)
Ro 8:19 creation w in eager expectation
WALK (WALKED WALKS)
Dt 11:19 and when you w along the road,
Ps 1: 1 who does not w in the counsel
  23: 4 Even though I w
  89:15 who w in the light of your presence
Isa 2: 5 let us w in the light of the LORD.
  30:21 saying, "This is the way; w in it."
  40:31 they will w and not be faint.
Jer 6:16 ask where the good way is, and w
Da 4:37 And those who w in pride he is able
Am 3: 3 Do two w together
Mic 6: 8 and to w humbly with your God.
Mk 2: 9 'Get up, take your mat and w'?
Jn 8:12 Whoever follows me will never w
1Jn 1: 7 But if we w in the light,
2Jn 6 his command is that you w in love.

WALKED (WALK)
Ge 5:24 Enoch w with God; then he was no
Jos 14: 9 which your feet have w will be your
Mt 14:29 w on the water and came toward
WALKS (WALK)
Pr 13:20 He who w with the wise grows wise
WALL
Jos 6:20 w collapsed; so every man charged
Ne 2:17 let us rebuild the w of Jerusalem,
Rev 21:12 It had a great, high w
WALLOWING
2Pe 2:22 back to her w in the mud."
WANT (WANTED WANTING WANTS)
1Sa 8:19 "We w a king over us.
Ps 23: 1 is my shepherd, I shall not be in w.
Lk 19:14 'We don't w this man to be our king
Ro 7:15 For what I w to do I do not do,
Php 3:10 I w to know Christ and the power
WANTED (WANT)
1Co 12:18 of them, just as he w them to be.
WANTING (WANT)
Da 5:27 weighed on the scales and found w.
2Pe 3: 9 with you, not w anyone to perish,
WANTS (WANT)
Mt 20:26 whoever w to become great
Mk 8:35 For whoever w to save his life will
Ro 9:18 he hardens whom he w to harden.
1Ti 2: 4 who w all men to be saved
WAR (WARS)
Isa 2: 4 nor will they train for w anymore.
Da 9:26 W will continue until the end,
2Co 10: 3 we do not wage w as the world does
Rev 19:11 With justice he judges and makes w
WARN (WARNED WARNINGS)
Eze 3:19 But if you do w the wicked man
  33: 9 if you do w the wicked man to turn
WARNED (WARN)
Ps 19:11 By them is your servant w;
WARNINGS (WARN)
1Co 10:11 and were written down as w for us,
WARS (WAR)
Ps 46: 9 He makes w cease to the ends
Mt 24: 6 You will hear of w and rumors of w,
WASH (WASHED WASHING)
Ps 51: 7 w me, and I will be whiter
Jn 13: 5 and began to w his disciples' feet,
Ac 22:16 be baptized and w your sins away,
Rev 22:14 Blessed are those who w their robes
WASHED (WASH)
1Co 6:11 you were w, you were sanctified,
Rev 7:14 they have w their robes
WASHING (WASH)
Eph 5:26 cleansing her by the w with water
Tit 3: 5 us through the w of rebirth
WATCH (WATCHES WATCHING WATCHMAN)
Ge 31:49 "May the LORD keep w
Jer 31:10 will w over his flock like a shepherd
Mt 24:42 "Therefore keep w, because you do
  26:41 W and pray so that you will not fall
Lk 2: 8 keeping w over their flocks at night
1Ti 4:16 W your life and doctrine closely.
WATCHES (WATCH)
Ps 1: 6 For the LORD w over the way
  121: 3 he who w over you will not slumber
WATCHING (WATCH)
Lk 12:37 whose master finds them w
WATCHMAN (WATCH)
Eze 3:17 I have made you a w for the house
WATER (WATERED WATERS)
Ps 1: 3 like a tree planted by streams of w,
  22:14 I am poured out like w,
Pr 25:21 if he is thirsty, give him w to drink.
Isa 49:10 and lead them beside springs of w.
Jer 2:13 broken cisterns that cannot hold w.
Zec 14: 8 On that day living w will flow out
Mk 9:41 anyone who gives you a cup of w
Jn 4:10 he would have given you living w."
  7:38 streams of living w will flow
Eph 5:26 washing with w through the word,
1Pe 3:21 this w symbolizes baptism that now
Rev 21: 6 cost from the spring of the w of life.

WATERED (WATER)
1Co 3: 6 I planted the seed, Apollos w it,
WATERS (WATER)
Ps 23: 2 he leads me beside quiet w,
Ecc 11: 1 Cast your bread upon the w,
Isa 58:11 like a spring whose w never fail.
1Co 3: 7 plants nor he who w is anything,
WAVE (WAVES)
Jas 1: 6 he who doubts is like a w of the sea,
WAVES (WAVE)
Isa 57:20 whose w cast up mire and mud.
Mt 8:27 Even the winds and the w obey him
Eph 4:14 tossed back and forth by the w,
WAY (WAYS)
Dt 1:33 to show you the w you should go.
2Sa 22:31 "As for God, his w is perfect;
Job 23:10 But he knows the w that I take;
Ps 1: 1 or stand in the w of sinners
  37: 5 Commit your w to the LORD;
  119: 9 can a young man keep his w pure?
  139: 24 See if there is any offensive w in me
Pr 14:12 There is a w that seems right
  16:17 he who guards his w guards his life.
  22: 6 Train a child in the w he should go,
Isa 30:21 saying, "This is the w; walk in it."
  53: 6 each of us has turned to his own w;
  55: 7 Let the wicked forsake his w
Mt 3: 3 'Prepare the w for the Lord,
Jn 14: 6 "I am the w and the truth
1Co 10:13 also provide a w out so that you can
  12:31 will show you the most excellent w.
Heb 4:15 who has been tempted in every w,
  9: 8 was showing by this that the w
  10:20 and living w opened for us
WAYS (WAY)
Ex 33:13 teach me your w so I may know
Ps 25:10 All the w of the LORD are loving
  51:13 I will teach transgressors your w,
Pr 3: 6 in all your w acknowledge him,
Isa 55: 8 neither are your w my w,"
Jas 3: 2 We all stumble in many w.
WEAK (WEAKER WEAKNESS)
Mt 26:41 spirit is willing, but the body is w."
Ro 14: 1 Accept him whose faith is w,
1Co 1:27 God chose the w things
  8: 9 become a stumbling block to the w.
  9:22 To the w I became w, to win the w.
2Co 12: 10 For when I am w, then I am strong.
Heb 12:12 your feeble arms and w knees.
WEAKER (WEAK)
1Co 12:22 seem to be w are indispensable,
1Pe 3: 7 them with respect as the w partner
WEAKNESS (WEAK)
Ro 8:26 the Spirit helps us in our w.
1Co 1:25 and the w of God is stronger
2Co 12: 9 for my power is made perfect in w
Heb 5: 2 since he himself is subject to w.
WEALTH
Pr 3: 9 Honor the LORD with your w,
Mk 10:22 away sad, because he had great w.
Lk 15:13 and there squandered his w
WEAPONS
2Co 10: 4 The w we fight with are not
WEARIES (WEARY)
Ecc 12:12 and much study w the body.
WEARY (WEARIES)
Isa 40:31 they will run and not grow w,
Mt 11:28 all you who are w and burdened,
Gal 6: 9 Let us not become w in doing good,
WEDDING
Mt 22:11 who was not wearing w clothes.
Rev 19: 7 For the w of the Lamb has come,
WEEP (WEEPING WEPT)
Ecc 3: 4 a time to w and a time to laugh,
Lk 6:21 Blessed are you who w now,
WEEPING (WEEP)
Ps 30: 5 w may remain for a night,
  126: 6 He who goes out w,
Mt 8:12 where there will be w and gnashing
WELCOMES
Mt 18: 5 whoever w a little child like this
2Jn 11 Anyone who w him shares

WELL
- Lk 17:19 your faith has made you *w*."
- Jas 5:15 in faith will make the sick person *w*

WEPT (WEEP)
- Ps 137:1 of Babylon we sat and *w*
- Jn 11:35 Jesus *w*.

WEST
- Ps 103:12 as far as the east is from the *w*,

WHIRLWIND (WIND)
- 2Ki 2:1 to take Elijah up to heaven in a *w*,
- Hos 8:7 and reap the *w*.
- Na 1:3 His way is in the *w* and the storm,

WHITE (WHITER)
- Isa 1:18 they shall be as *w* as snow;
- Da 7:9 His clothing was as *w* as snow;
- Rev 1:14 hair were *w* like wool, as *w* as snow,
- 3:4 dressed in *w*, for they are worthy.
- 20:11 Then I saw a great *w* throne

WHITER (WHITE)
- Ps 51:7 and I will be *w* than snow.

WHOLE
- Mt 16:26 for a man if he gains the *w* world,
- 24:14 will be preached in the *w* world
- Jn 13:10 to wash his feet; his *w* body is clean
- 21:25 the *w* world would not have room
- Ac 20:27 proclaim to you the *w* will of God.
- Ro 3:19 and the *w* world held accountable
- 8:22 know that the *w* creation has been
- Gal 3:22 declares that the *w* world is
- 5:3 obligated to obey the *w* law.
- Eph 4:13 attaining to the *w* measure
- Jas 2:10 For whoever keeps the *w* law
- 1Jn 2:2 but also for the sins of the *w* world.

WHOLEHEARTEDLY (HEART)
- Dt 1:36 because he followed the LORD *w*
- Eph 6:7 Serve *w*, as if you were serving

WICKED (WICKEDNESS)
- Ps 1:1 walk in the counsel of the *w*
- 1:5 Therefore the *w* will not stand
- 73:3 when I saw the prosperity of the *w*.
- Pr 10:20 the heart of the *w* is of little value.
- 11:21 The *w* will not go unpunished,
- Isa 53:9 He was assigned a grave with the *w*
- 55:7 Let the *w* forsake his way
- 57:20 But the *w* are like the tossing sea,
- Eze 3:18 that *w* man will die for his sin,
- 18:23 pleasure in the death of the *w*?
- 33:14 to the *w* man, 'You will surely die,'

WICKEDNESS (WICKED)
- Eze 28:15 created till *w* was found in you.

WIDE
- Isa 54:2 stretch your tent curtains *w*,
- Mt 7:13 For *w* is the gate and broad is
- Eph 3:18 to grasp how *w* and long and high

WIDOW (WIDOWS)
- Dt 10:18 cause of the fatherless and the *w*,
- Lk 21:2 saw a poor *w* put in two very small

WIDOWS (WIDOW)
- Jas 1:27 look after orphans and *w*

WIFE (WIVES)
- Ge 2:24 and mother and be united to his *w*,
- 24:67 she became his *w*, and he loved her;
- Ex 20:17 shall not covet your neighbor's *w*,
- Dt 5:21 shall not covet your neighbor's *w*.
- Pr 5:18 in the *w* of your youth.
- 12:4 *w* of noble character is her
- 18:22 He who finds a *w* finds what is
- 19:13 quarrelsome *w* is like a constant
- 31:10 *w* of noble character who can find?
- Mt 19:3 For a man to divorce his *w* for any
- 1Co 7:2 each man should have his own *w*,
- 7:33 how he can please his *w*—
- Eph 5:23 the husband is the head of the *w*
- 5:33 must love his *w* as he loves himself,
- 1Ti 3:2 husband of but one *w*, temperate,
- Rev 21:9 I will show you the bride, the *w*

WILD
- Lk 15:13 squandered his wealth in *w* living.
- Ro 11:17 and you, though a *w* olive shoot,

WILL (WILLING WILLINGNESS)
- Ps 40:8 I desire to do your *w*, O my God;
- 143:10 Teach me to do your *w*,

- Isa 53:10 Yet it was the LORD's *w*
- Mt 6:10 your *w* be done
- 26:39 Yet not as I *w*, but as you *w*."
- Jn 7:17 If anyone chooses to do God's *w*,
- Ac 20:27 to you the whole *w* of God.
- Ro 12:2 and approve what God's *w* is—
- 1Co 7:37 but has control over his own *w*,
- Eph 5:17 understand what the Lord's *w* is.
- Php 2:13 for it is God who works in you to *w*
- 1Th 4:3 God's *w* that you should be
- 5:18 for this is God's *w* for you
- Heb 9:16 In the case of a *w*, it is necessary
- 10:7 I have come to do your *w*, O God
- Jas 4:15 "If it is the Lord's *w*,
- 1Jn 5:14 we ask anything according to his *w*,
- Rev 4:11 and by your *w* they were created

WILLING (WILL)
- Ps 51:12 grant me a *w* spirit, to sustain me.
- Da 3:28 were *w* to give up their lives rather
- Mt 18:14 Father in heaven is not *w* that any
- 23:37 her wings, but you were not *w*.
- 26:41 The spirit is *w*, but the body is weak

WILLINGNESS (WILL)
- 2Co 8:12 For if the *w* is there, the gift is

WIN (WINS)
- Php 3:14 on toward the goal to *w* the prize
- 1Th 4:12 your daily life may *w* the respect

WIND (WHIRLWIND)
- Jas 1:6 blown and tossed by the *w*.

WINE
- Pr 20:1 *W* is a mocker and beer a brawler;
- Isa 55:1 Come, buy *w* and milk
- Mt 9:17 Neither do men pour new *w*
- Lk 23:36 They offered him *w* vinegar
- Ro 14:21 not to eat meat or drink *w*
- Eph 5:18 on *w*, which leads to debauchery.

WINESKINS
- Mt 9:17 do men pour new wine into old *w*.

WINGS
- Ru 2:12 under whose *w* you have come
- Ps 17:8 hide me in the shadow of your *w*
- Isa 40:31 They will soar on *w* like eagles;
- Mal 4:2 rise with healing in its *w*.
- Lk 13:34 hen gathers her chicks under her *w*,

WINS (WIN)
- Pr 11:30 and he who *w* souls is wise.

WIPE
- Rev 7:17 God will *w* away every tear

WISDOM (WISE)
- 1Ki 4:29 God gave Solomon *w* and very
- Ps 111:10 of the LORD is the beginning of *w*;
- Pr 31:26 She speaks with *w*,
- Jer 10:12 he founded the world by his *w*
- Mt 11:19 But *w* is proved right by her actions
- Lk 2:52 And Jesus grew in *w* and stature,
- Ro 11:33 the depth of the riches of the *w*
- Col 2:3 are hidden all the treasures of *w*
- Jas 1:5 of you lacks *w*, he should ask God,

WISE (WISDOM WISER)
- 1Ki 3:12 give you a *w* and discerning heart,
- Job 5:13 He catches the *w* in their craftiness
- Ps 19:7 making *w* the simple.
- Pr 3:7 Do not be *w* in your own eyes;
- 9:8 rebuke a *w* man and he will love
- 10:1 A *w* son brings joy to his father,
- 11:30 and he who wins souls is *w*.
- 13:20 He who walks with the *w* grows *w*,
- 17:28 Even a fool is thought *w*
- Da 12:3 Those who are *w* will shine like
- Mt 11:25 hidden these things from the *w*
- 1Co 1:27 things of the world to shame the *w*;
- 2Ti 3:15 able to make you *w* for salvation

WISER (WISE)
- 1Co 1:25 of God is *w* than man's wisdom,

WITHER (WITHERS)
- Ps 1:3 and whose leaf does not *w*.

WITHERS (WITHER)
- Isa 40:7 The grass *w* and the flowers fall,
- 1Pe 1:24 the grass *w* and the flowers fall,

WITHHOLD
- Ps 84:11 no good thing does he *w*
- Pr 23:13 Do not *w* discipline from a child;

WITNESS (WITNESSES)
- Jn 1:8 he came only as a *w* to the light.

WITNESSES (WITNESS)
- Dt 19:15 by the testimony of two or three *w*.
- Ac 1:8 and you will be my *w* in Jerusalem,

WIVES (WIFE)
- Eph 5:22 *W*, submit to your husbands
- 5:25 love your *w*, just as Christ loved
- 1Pe 3:1 words by the behavior of their *w*,

WOE
- Isa 6:5 "*W* to me!" I cried.

WOLF
- Isa 65:25 *w* and the lamb will feed together,

WOMAN (MAN)
- Ge 2:22 God made a *w* from
- 3:15 between you and the *w*,
- Lev 20:13 as one lies with a *w*,
- Dt 22:5 *w* must not wear men's
- Ru 3:11 a *w* of noble character
- Pr 31:30 a *w* who fears the LORD
- Mt 5:28 looks at a *w* lustfully
- Jn 8:3 a *w* caught in adultery.
- Ro 7:2 a married *w* is bound to
- 1Co 11:3 the head of the *w* is man,
- 11:13 a *w* to pray to God with
- 1Ti 2:11 A *w* should learn in

WOMEN (MAN)
- Lk 1:42 Blessed are you among *w*,
- 1Co 14:34 *w* should remain silent in
- 1Ti 2:9 want *w* to dress modestly
- Tit 2:3 teach the older *w* to be
- 1Pe 3:5 the holy *w* of the past

WOMB
- Job 1:21 Naked I came from my mother's *w*,
- Jer 1:5 you in the *w* I knew you,
- Lk 1:44 the baby in my *w* leaped for joy.

WONDER (WONDERFUL WONDERS)
- Ps 17:7 Show the *w* of your great love,

WONDERFUL (WONDER)
- Job 42:3 things too *w* for me to know.
- Ps 31:21 for he showed his *w* love to me
- 119:18 *w* things in your law.
- 119:129 Your statutes are *w*;
- 139:6 Such knowledge is too *w* for me,
- Isa 9:6 *W* Counselor, Mighty God,
- 1Pe 2:9 out of darkness into his *w* light.

WONDERS (WONDER)
- Job 37:14 stop and consider God's *w*.
- Ps 119:27 then I will meditate on your *w*.
- Joel 2:30 I will show *w* in the heavens
- Ac 2:19 I will show *w* in the heaven above

WOOD
- Isa 44:19 Shall I bow down to a block of *w*?"
- 1Co 3:12 costly stones, *w*, hay or straw,

WORD (WORDS)
- Dt 8:3 but on every *w* that comes
- 2Sa 22:31 the *w* of the LORD is flawless.
- Ps 119:9 By living according to your *w*.
- 119:11 I have hidden your *w* in my heart
- 119:105 Your *w* is a lamp to my feet
- Pr 12:25 but a kind *w* cheers him up.
- 25:11 A *w* aptly spoken
- 30:5 "Every *w* of God is flawless;
- Isa 55:11 so is my *w* that goes out
- Jn 1:1 was the *W*, and the *W* was
- 1:14 The *W* became flesh and made his
- 2Co 2:17 we do not peddle the *w* of God
- 4:2 nor do we distort the *w* of God.
- Eph 6:17 of the Spirit, which is the *w* of God.
- Php 2:16 as you hold out the *w* of life—
- Col 3:16 Let the *w* of Christ dwell
- 2Ti 2:15 and who correctly handles the *w*
- Heb 4:12 For the *w* of God is living
- Jas 1:22 Do not merely listen to the *w*,
- 2Pe 1:19 And we have the *w* of the prophets

WORDS (WORD)
- Dt 11:18 Fix these *w* of mine in your hearts
- Ps 119:103 How sweet are your *w* to my taste
- 119:130 The unfolding of your *w* gives light;
- 119:160 All your *w* are true;
- Pr 30:6 Do not add to his *w*,
- Jer 15:16 When your *w* came, I ate them;

Mt	24:35	but my *w* will never pass away.
Jn	6:68	You have the *w* of eternal life.
	15: 7	in me and my *w* remain in you,
1Co	14:19	rather speak five intelligible *w*
Rev	22:19	And if anyone takes *w* away

WORK (WORKER WORKERS WORKING WORKMAN WORKMANSHIP WORKS)

Ex	23:12	"Six days do your *w*,
Nu	8:11	ready to do the *w* of the LORD.
Dt	5:14	On it you shall not do any *w*,
Ecc	5:19	his lot and be happy in his *w*—
Jer	48:10	lax in doing the LORD's *w*!
Jn	6:27	Do not *w* for food that spoils,
	9: 4	we must do the *w* of him who sent
1Co	3:13	test the quality of each man's *w*.
Php	1: 6	that he who began a good *w*
	2:12	continue to *w* out your salvation
Col	3:23	Whatever you do, *w* at it
1Th	5:12	to respect those who *w* hard
2Th	3:10	If a man will not *w*, he shall not eat
2Ti	3:17	equipped for every good *w*.
Heb	6:10	he will not forget your *w*

WORKER (WORK)

Lk	10: 7	for the *w* deserves his wages.
1Ti	5:18	and "The *w* deserves his wages."

WORKERS (WORK)

Mt	9:37	is plentiful but the *w* are few.
1Co	3: 9	For we are God's fellow *w*;

WORKING (WORK)

Col	3:23	as *w* for the Lord, not for men,

WORKMAN (WORK)

2Ti	2:15	a *w* who does not need

WORKMANSHIP* (WORK)

Eph	2:10	For we are God's *w*, created

WORKS (WORK)

Pr	31:31	let her *w* bring her praise
Ro	8:28	in all things God *w* for the good
Eph	2: 9	not by *w*, so that no one can boast.
	4:12	to prepare God's people for *w*

WORLD (WORLDLY)

Ps	50:12	for the *w* is mine, and all that is in it
Isa	13:11	I will punish the *w* for its evil,
Mt	5:14	"You are the light of the *w*.
	16:26	for a man if he gains the whole *w*,
Mk	16:15	into all the *w* and preach the good
Jn	1:29	who takes away the sin of the *w*!
	3:16	so loved the *w* that he gave his one
	8:12	he said, "I am the light of the *w*.
	15:19	As it is, you do not belong to the *w*,
	16:33	In this *w* you will have trouble.
	18:36	"My kingdom is not of this *w*.
Ro	3:19	and the whole *w* held accountable
1Co	3:19	the wisdom of this *w* is foolishness
2Co	5:19	that God was reconciling the *w*
	10: 3	For though we live in the *w*,
1Ti	6: 7	For we brought nothing into the *w*,
1Jn	2: 2	but also for the sins of the whole *w*.
	2:15	not love the *w* or anything in the *w*.
Rev	13: 8	slain from the creation of the *w*.

WORLDLY (WORLD)

Tit	2:12	to ungodliness and *w* passions,

WORM

Mk	9:48	" 'their *w* does not die,

WORRY (WORRYING)

Mt	6:25	I tell you, do not *w* about your life,
	10:19	do not *w* about what to say

WORRYING (WORRY)

Mt	6:27	of you by *w* can add a single hour

WORSHIP

1Ch	16:29	*w* the LORD in the splendor
Ps	95: 6	Come, let us bow down in *w*,
Mt	2: 2	and have come to *w* him."
Jn	4:24	and his worshipers must *w* in spirit
Ro	12: 1	this is your spiritual act of *w*.

WORTH (WORTHY)

Job	28:13	Man does not comprehend its *w*;
Pr	31:10	She is *w* far more than rubies.
Mt	10:31	are *w* more than many sparrows.
Ro	8:18	sufferings are not *w* comparing
1Pe	1: 7	of greater *w* than gold,
	3: 4	which is of great *w* in God's sight.

WORTHLESS

Pr	11: 4	Wealth is *w* in the day of wrath,
Jas	1:26	himself and his religion is *w*.

WORTHY (WORTH)

1Ch	16:25	For great is the LORD and most *w*
Eph	4: 1	to live a life *w* of the calling you
Php	1:27	in a manner *w* of the gospel
3Jn	6	on their way in a manner *w* of God.
Rev	5: 2	"Who is *w* to break the seals

WOUNDS

Pr	27: 6	*W* from a friend can be trusted,
Isa	53: 5	and by his *w* we are healed.
Zec	13: 6	'What are these *w* on your body?'
1Pe	2:24	by his *w* you have been healed.

WRATH

2Ch	36:16	scoffed at his prophets until the *w*
Ps	2: 5	and terrifies them in his *w*, saying,
	76:10	Surely your *w* against men brings
Pr	15: 1	A gentle answer turns away *w*,
Jer	25:15	filled with the wine of my *w*
Ro	1:18	The *w* of God is being revealed
	5: 9	saved from God's *w* through him!
1Th	5: 9	God did not appoint us to suffer *w*
Rev	6:16	and from the *w* of the Lamb!

WRESTLED

Ge	32:24	and a man *w* with him till daybreak

WRITE (WRITING WRITTEN)

Dt	6: 9	*W* them on the doorframes
Pr	7: 3	*w* them on the tablet of your heart.
Heb	8:10	and *w* them on their hearts.

WRITING (WRITE)

1Co	14:37	him acknowledge that what I am *w*

WRITTEN (WRITE)

Jos	1: 8	careful to do everything *w* in it.
Da	12: 1	everyone whose name is found *w*
Lk	10:20	but rejoice that your names are *w*

Jn	20:31	these are *w* that you may believe
1Co	4: 6	"Do not go beyond what is *w*."
2Co	3: 3	*w* not with ink but with the Spirit
Col	2:14	having canceled the *w* code,
Heb	12:23	whose names are *w* in heaven.

WRONG (WRONGDOING WRONGED WRONGS)

Ex	23: 2	Do not follow the crowd in doing *w*
Nu	5: 7	must make full restitution for his *w*,
Job	34:12	unthinkable that God would do *w*,
1Th	5:15	that nobody pays back *w* for *w*,

WRONGDOING (WRONG)

Job	1:22	sin by charging God with *w*.

WRONGED (WRONG)

1Co	6: 7	not rather be *w*? Why not rather

WRONGS (WRONG)

Pr	10:12	but love covers over all *w*.
1Co	13: 5	angered, it keeps no record of *w*.

YEARS

Ps	90: 4	For a thousand *y* in your sight
	90:10	The length of our days is seventy *y*
2Pe	3: 8	The Lord a day is like a thousand *y*,
Rev	20: 2	and bound him for a thousand *y*.

YESTERDAY

Heb	13: 8	Jesus Christ is the same *y*

YOKE (YOKED)

Mt	11:29	Take my *y* upon you and learn

YOKED (YOKE)

2Co	6:14	Do not be *y* together

YOUNG (YOUTH)

Ps	119: 9	How can a *y* man keep his way
1Ti	4:12	down on you because you are *y*,

YOUTH (YOUNG)

Ps	103: 5	so that your *y* is renewed like
Ecc	12: 1	Creator in the days of your *y*,
2Ti	2:22	Flee the evil desires of *y*,

ZEAL

Pr	19: 2	to have *z* without knowledge,
Ro	12:11	Never be lacking in *z*,

ZECHARIAH

1. Son of Jeroboam II; king of Israel (2Ki 15:8-12).
2. Post-exilic prophet who encouraged rebuilding of temple (Ezr 5:1; 6:14; Zec 1:1).
3. Father of John the Baptist (Lk 1:13; 3:2).

ZEDEKIAH

Mattaniah, son of Josiah (1Ch 3:15), made king of Judah by Nebuchadnezzar (2Ki 24:17-25:7; 2Ch 36:10-14; Jer 37-39; 52:1-11).

ZERUBBABEL

Descendant of David (1Ch 3:19; Mt 1:3). Led return from exile (Ezr 2-3; Ne 7:7; Hag 1-2; Zec 4).

ZIMRI

King of Israel (1Ki 16:9-20).

ZION

Ps	137: 3	"Sing us one of the songs of *Z*!"
Jer	50: 5	They will ask the way to *Z*
Ro	9:33	I lay in *Z* a stone that causes men
	11:26	"The deliverer will come from *Z*;

Index to Color Maps

A

Abana River	6 D1
Abarim Mts.	2 E3
Abel Meholah	6 C3
Abel Shittim	3 D3
Abilene	11 H4
Acco	2 D1; 4 B2; 5 A3; 9 B2
Achaia	11 D3; 13 D3
Adriatic Sea	11 C1; 13 C2
Aegean Sea	1 A1; 11 E3; 13 D3
Afghanistan	12 F2
Africa	11 A4; 13 B3
Ai	1 C3; 3 D3
Alaska	12 A1
Albania	12 g6
Aleppo	1 C2; 5 C1; 7a B2; 7b B5; 10 C1; 11 H3
Alexandria	13 D4
Algeria	12 D2
Alps	13 B2
Altar	8 C3
Amman	2 E3
Ammon	3 D3; 4 D4; 5 B4; 6 D4
Amphipolis	11 E2
Anathoth	6 B4
Andorra	12 f6
Angola	12 E3
Anguilla	12 c5
Antigua and Barbuda	12 c5
Antinoe	13 E4
Antioch	10 C1; 11 H3; 13 E3
Antonia Fortress	8 C2
Aphek	4 B3; 6 B4
Apollonia	11 E2
Arabah	2 D5
Arabia	1 D3; 11 H5
Arabian Desert	13 F4
Arabians	7a B3
Arad	6 B5
Aram	4 D1; 5 B3; 6 D1
Aramean Desert	5 D3
Ararat	7a C1; 7b C4;
Ararat, Mt.	1 E1; 7a C1
Araxes River	1 E1; 7a D1
Arbela	7b C5
Argentina	12 C4
Armenia	12 h6; 13 F3
Arnon River	2 E3; 3 D3; 4 C5; 6 C5
Aroer	4 C5
Arrapkha	7a C2; 7b C5
Aruba	12 b5
Arubu	7a B3
Arvad	5 B2; 7a B2; 7b B5
Ashdod	4 A4; 5 A4
Asher	4 B2
Ashkelon	4 A4
Ashtaroth	4 D2; 5 B4
Asia	11 F3
Asshur	1 E2; 7a C2; 7b C5
Assos	11 F3
Athens	11 E3; 13 D3
Atlantic Ocean	13 A1
Attalia	11 G3
Australia	12 H4
Austria	12 g5
Azekah	3 C3
Azerbaijan	12 h6
Azotus	10 A6

B

Babylon	1 E3; 7a C2; 7b C5
Babylonians	1 E2
Bahamas, The	12 b5
Bangladesh	12 G2
Barbados	12 c6
Bashan	3 D2
Beautiful, Gate	8 C3
Beersheba	1 C3; 2 D4; 3 C3; 4 B5; 5 A5; 6 B5
Beersheba, Desert of	6 B5
Behistun	7b D5
Belarus	12 g5
Belgium	12 f5
Belize	12 a5
Benin	12 D3
Benjamin	4 B4
Benjamin Mts.	2 D3
Berea	11 E2
Berothai	5 B3
Besor Brook	2 C4; 3 C3; 6 A5
Beth Horon	3 C3
Beth Shan	4 C3; 5 B4
Beth Shemesh	4 B4
Bethany	9 B6
Bethany beyond Jordan	9 C4; 9 C5
Bethel	1 C3; 3 D2; 4 B4; 6 B4
Bethesda Pool	8 C2
Bethlehem	2 D3; 4 B4; 9 B6
Bethsaida	9 C3
Bethsura	10 B6
Betogabris	10 A6
Bezer	4 C4
Bhutan	12 G2
Bithynia & Pontus	11 G2; 13 E3
Black Sea	1 B1; 7a B1; 11 G1; 13 E2
Bolivia	12 C3
Bosnia and Herzegovina	12 g5
Botswana	12 E4
Brazil	12 C3
Britain	13 B1
Brunei	12 G3
Bulgaria	12 g6
Burkina	12 D2
Burma	12 G2
Burundi	12 E3
Byblos	1 C2; 5 B2; 7a B2; 7b B5; 10 B3
Byzantium	13 D2

C

Cabul	4 B2
Caesarea	9 A4; 10 A5; 11 H5
Caesarea Philippi	9 D2; 10 B4
Calah	7a C2
Cambodia	12 G3
Cameroon	12 E3
Cana	9 B3
Canaan	3 D2
Canada	12 B1
Cape Verde	12 D2
Capernaum	9 C3; 10 B5
Caphtor	1 A2
Cappadocia	11 H3; 13 E3
Carchemish	1 D2; 7a B2; 7b B5
Carmel, Mt.	2 D2; 6 B2
Carthage	13 B3
Caspian Sea	1 F1; 7a D1; 7b D4; 13 F2
Caucasus Mts.	1 E1; 13 E2
Cayman Islands	12 a5
Cenchrea	11 E3
Central African Republic	12 E3
Chad	12 E2
Chile	12 C4
China	12 G2
Cilicia	10 A1; 11 H3; 13 E3
Cnidus	11 F3
Cologna	13 B1
Colombia	12 B3
Colosse	11 F3
Commagene	11 H3
Comoros	12 E3
Congo	12 E3
Corinth	11 E3; 13 D3
Corsica	11 A2; 13 B2
Cos	11 F3
Costa Rica	12 a6
Crete	1 A2; 11 E4; 13 D3
Croatia	12 g5
Cuba	12 b5
Cyprus	1 C2; 5 A2; 10 A2; 11 G4; 12 h6; 13 E3
Cyrenaica	11 E5
Cyrene (region)	13 D4
Cyrene (town)	13 D4
Cyrus River	13 F2
Czech Republic	12 g5

Index to color Maps

D

Dacia	11 E1; 13 D2
Dalmatia	11 D1
Damascus	1 C3; 2 E1; 4 D1; 5 B3; 6 D1; 7a B2; 7b B5; 10 C4; 11 H4; 13 E3
Dan (town)	2 E1; 4 C1; 5 B3
Dan (tribe)	4 B4
Danube River	13 C2
Dead Sea	2 E4
Debir	3 C3
Decapolis	9 D4
Delphi	11 E3
Denmark	12 g5
Derbe	11 G3; 13 E3
Dibon	3 D3; 4 C5
Djibouti	12 E3
Dnieper River	13 D1
Dominica	12 c5
Dominican Republic	12 b5
Dophkah	3 B5
Dor	4 B3
Dothan	1 C3; 6 B3
Dur Sharrukin	7a C2; 7b C5
Dura-Europos	13 E3

E

Eastern Desert	2 F5; 5 C4
Ebal, Mt.	2 D2; 4 B3
Ebla	1 C2
Ecbatana	7a D2; 7b D5
Ecuador	12 B3
Edessa	13 E3
Edom	3 D4; 4 C6; 5 B5; 6 C6
Edom, Desert of	2 E5
Edrei	3 D2; 4 D3; 5 B4
Eglon	3 C3; 4 B4
Egypt	2 A3; 11 F6; 12 E2; 13 E4
Egyptians	1 C4
Egypt, Wadi of	2 C4; 3 C3; 5 A5
Ekron	4 B4
El Salvador	12 a6
Elim	3 B5
Emmaus	9 B5; 10 B6
En Gedi	2 D3; 4 C4
Ephesus	11 F3; 13 D3
Ephraim	4 B4
Epirus	11 D3
Equatorial Guinea	12 E3
Erech	1 E3; 7a C3; 7b C6
Eritrea	12 E2
Essene Gate	8 B6
Essene Quarter	8 B5
Estonia	12 g5
Ethiopia	12 E3
Euphrates River	1 D2; 5 D1; 7a C2; 7b C5; 10 D1; 11 H3; 13 E3
Ezion Geber	2 D6; 3 C4; 5 A6

F

Faeroe Islands	12 f5
Fair Havens	11 E4
Falkland Islands	12 C4
Finland	12 E1
First Wall	8 B4
Fish Gate	8 B2
Foothills	2 D3
Forum of Appius	11 C2
France	12 f5
French Guiana	12 C3

G

Gabon	12 E3
Gad	4 C4
Gadara	9 C3
Galatia	11 G2; 13 E3
Galilean Mts.	2 D1
Galilee	6 B2; 9 C3; 10 B5
Galilee, Sea of	2 E1; 9 C3; 10 B5
Gallia	11 A1
Gambia	12 D2
Garden Tomb	8 B1
Gath	4 B4; 5 A4
Gath Hepher	6 C2
Gaul	13 B2
Gaza	2 C3; 4 A5; 5 A5; 10 A6
Gebal	5 B2
Gennath Gate	8 B4
Gentiles, Court of the	8 C4
Georgia	12 h6
Gerar	1 C3; 4 A5
Gerasa	9 D4
Gergesa	9 C3
Gerizim, Mt.	2 D2; 4 B3; 9 B4; 10 B5
German Sea	13 B1
Germania	11 D1
Germany	12 g5; 13 C1
Gethsemane	8 D3
Gezer	4 B4; 5 A4
Ghana	12 D3
Gibeah	5 B4
Gibeon	3 D3; 4 B4
Gibraltar	12 f6
Gihon Spring	8 D5
Gilboa, Mt.	2 D2; 3 D2; 5 B4
Gilead	6 C3
Gilgal	3 D2; 4 C4; 6 C4
Gimirrai	7a B1
Golan	4 C2
Golden Gate	8 D3
Golgotha	8 B3
Gomer	7a B1
Goshen	3 A3
Gozan	7a C2; 7b C5
Great Bitter Lake	2 A5; 3 B4
Great Sea, The	1 B3; 2 B2; 3 B2; 4 A2; 5 A3; 6 A2; 7a A2; 7b A5; 9 A2; 10 A3; 11 E4
Greece	12 g6
Greenland	12 D1
Grenada	12 c6
Guadeloupe	12 c5
Guatemala	12 a6

Guinea	12 D3
Guinea Bissau	12 D3
Gulf of Aqaba	5 A6
Guyana	12 C3

H

Habor River	7a C2; 7b C5
Haiti	12 b5
Halak, Mt.	2 D4
Hamath (region)	5 C1
Hamath (town)	5 C2; 7a B2; 7b B5; 10 C2
Haran	1 D2; 7a B2; 7b B5
Hattusha	1 C1
Hawaii	12 A2
Hazeroth	3 C5
Hazor	1 C3; 3 D2; 4 C2; 5 B3
Hebron	1 C3; 2 D3; 3 D3; 4 B4; 5 B5
Heliopolis	1 B3; 3 A4
Hermon, Mt.	2 E1; 4 C1; 5 B3; 9 D1
Herod Antipas's Palace	8 B4
Herod's Palace	8 B4
Heshbon	3 D3; 4 C4
Hezekiah's Tunnel	8 C5
High Priest's House	8 B5
Hinnom Valley	8 B6
Hippicus, Tower of	8 A4
Hittites	1 C1
Honduras	12 a6
Horeb, Mt.	2 C7
Hormah	4 B5
Hulda Gates	8 C4
Hungary	12 g5

I

Iceland	12 D1
Iconium	11 G3
Ijon	4 C1
Illyricum	13 C2
India	12 F2
Indonesia	12 G3
Inner Court	8 C3
Ionian Sea	11 D3
Iran	12 F2
Iraq	12 h6
Ireland	12 f5
Israel	12 h6
Israel Pool	8 C2
Issachar	4 C3
Issus	11 H3
Italy	11 B1; 12 g6; 13 C2
Ivory Coast	12 D3
Iye Abarim	3 D3

J

Jabbok River	2 E2; 4 C3; 6 C3; 9 D4; 10 B5
Jabesh Gilead	4 C3
Jahaz	3 D3
Jamaica	12 b5

Index to color Maps

Japan	12 H2
Jarmuth	3 C3
Jazer	4 C4
Jericho	2 E3; 3 D3; 4 C4; 6 C4; 9 C5
Jerusalem	2 D3; 3 D3; 4 B4; 5 B4; 6 B4; 7a B2; 7b B5; 9 B6; 10 B6; 11 H5; 13 E4
Jezreel	4 B3; 6 C3
Joppa	2 D3; 4 B4; 5 A4; 6 B4; 10 A5
Jordan	12 h6
Jordan River	2 E2; 3 D2; 4 C3; 5 B4; 6 C3; 7a B2; 7b B5; 9 C4; 10 B5; 11 H5
Judah	4 B5; 6 B5
Judea	9 B6; 10 B6; 11 H5; 13 E4
Judean Mts.	2 D3

K

Kadesh	5 B2
Kadesh Barnea	1 C3; 3 C4; 5 A5
Kazakstan	12 F1
Kedesh	3 D2; 4 C2; 5 B3
Kenya	12 E3
Kerith Ravine	6 C3
Khersa	9 C3
Kidron Valley	8 D1, D5
Kinnereth, Sea of	2 E1; 3 D2; 4 C2; 5 B3; 6 C2
Kios	11 E3
Kir Haresheth	5 B5; 6 C5
Kiriath Jearim	4 B4
Kishon River	2 D2; 4 B3; 6 B2
Kittim	1 C2; 5 A2
Knossos	1 A2
Korazin	9 C2
Kuwait	12 h6
Kyrgyzstan	12 F2

L

Lachish	3 C3; 4 B4
Laodicea	11 F3
Laos	12 G2
Lasea	11 E4
Latvia	12 g5
Lebanon	12 h6
Lesotho	12 E4
Liberia	12 D3
Libnah	3 C3
Libya	12 E2
Liechtenstein	12 g5
Litani River	2 D1; 4 C1; 5 B3; 10 B4
Lithuania	12 g5
Little Bitter Lake	2 A5
Loire River	13 B2
London	13 B1
Lower City	8 C5
Luxembourg	12 f5
Lycaonia	11 G3
Lycia	11 F3
Lydda	10 A5
Lydia	11 F3
Lyons	13 B2
Lystra	11 G3

M

Macedonia, Former Yugoslav Republic of	11 D2; 12 g5; 13 D3
Machaerus	9 C6
Madagascar	12 E4
Magdala	9 C3
Mahanaim	4 C3; 5 B4
Mainz	13 B1
Makkedah	3 C3
Malawi	12 E3
Malaysia	12 G3
Maldives	12 F3
Mali	12 D2
Malta	11 C4; 12 g6
Manasseh	4 B3
Manasseh, East	4 C2
Marah	3 B4
Mari	1 D2
Mariamne, Tower of	8 A4
Martinique	12 c6
Mauretania	13 A3
Mauritania	12 D2
Mauritius	12 F3
Medeba	5 B4
Media	7a D2; 7b D5
Mediterranean Sea	2 B2; 13 C4
Megiddo	1 C3; 4 B3; 5 B4
Memphis	1 B3; 3 A4; 7a A3; 7b A6; 13 E4
Men, Court of	8 C3
Menzaleh, Lake	3 A3
Merom	3 D2; 4 C2
Mesopotamia	13 F3
Mexico	12 B2
Midian	3 C5
Miletus	11 F3
Mitylene	11 F3
Mizpah	4 B4; 6 B4; 7b B5
Moab	3 D3; 4 C5; 5 B5; 6 C5
Moesia	11 E1; 13 D2
Moldova	12 g5
Monaco	12 f5
Mongolia	12 G2
Montserrat	12 c5
Moreh, Mt.	2 D2; 4 C3
Moresheth Gath	6 B4
Morocco	12 D2
Mozambique	12 E3
Mycenae	1 A1
Myra	11 F4
Mysia	11 F3; 13 D3

N

Nabatea	13 E4
Nain	9 C3
Namibia	12 E3
Naphtali	4 C2
Nazareth	2 D2; 9 B3
Neapolis	11 E2
Nebo, Mt.	2 E3; 3 D3; 4 C4
Negev	2 D4
Nepal	12 F2
Netherlands	12 f5
Netherlands Antilles	12 b6
New Caledonia	12 H4
New Zealand	12 H4
Nicaragua	12 a6
Niger	12 E2
Nigeria	12 D3
Nile River	1 B4; 3 A5; 11 G6; 13 E4
Nineveh	1 E2; 7a C2; 7b C5
Nippur	1 E3; 7a C2; 7b C5
Noph	1 B3; 3 A4
North Korea	12 G2
Norway	12 D1
Numidia	11 A4
Nuzi	1 E2

O

Oboth	3 D3
Olives, Mt. of	2 D3; 8 D3; 9 B5
Olympus, Mt.	11 E2
Oman	12 F2
On	1 B3; 3 A4
Orontes River	5 B1; 7a B2; 7b B5; 10 C3

P

Paddan Aram	1 D2
Pakistan	12 F2
Pamphylia	11 G3
Panama	12 b6
Paphos	11 G4
Papua New Guinea	12 H3
Paraguay	12 C4
Paran, Desert of	2 C6; 3 C4
Parthia	13 F3
Patara	11 F4
Patmos	11 F3
Pella	13 E4
Perea	9 C5
Perga	11 G3
Pergamum	11 F3; 13 D3
Persian Gulf	1 F4; 7a D3; 7b D6; 13 F4
Peru	12 B3
Pharpar River	4 D1; 6 D1
Phasael, Tower of	8 A4
Philadelphia	11 F3
Philippi	11 E2; 13 D3
Philippines	12 G2
Philistia	3 C3; 5 A4; 6 A5
Phoenicia	5 B3; 6 C1; 9 C1; 11 H4
Phoenix	11 E4
Phrygia	11 F3; 13 D3
Pinnacle of the Temple	8 D4
Pisidia	11 G3
Pisidian Antioch	11 G3
Pithom	3 A4
Po River	13 B2
Poland	12 g5
Portugal	12 f6
Ptolemais	9 B2; 10 B5; 11 H5
Puerto Rico	12 c5
Punon	3 D4
Puteoli	11 C2; 13 C3

Q-R

Qatar	12 F2
Qatna	5 C2
Rabbah	2 E3; 4 C4; 5 B4
Ramah	6 B4
Rameses	3 A3
Ramoth Gilead	4 D3; 5 B4; 6 D3
Red Sea	1 C4; 2 D8; 3 C6; 7a B3; 7b B6; 11 H6; 13 E4
Rephidim	3 C5
Reuben	4 C4
Reunion	12 F4
Rezeph	7a B2; 7b B5
Rhegium	11 C3
Rhine River	13 B1
Rhodes	11 F4
Rhone River	13 B2
Riblah	7b B5
Rimmon	4 B2
Robinson's Arch	8 C4
Romania	12 g5
Rome	11 B2; 13 C2
Royal Porch	8 C4
Russia	12 F1
Rwanda	12 E3

S

St. Kitts and Nevis	12 c5
St. Lucia	12 c6
St. Vincent and the Grenadines	12 c6
Salamis	11 G4
Salim	9 C4
Salmone	11 F4
Salt Sea	2 E4; 3 D3; 4 C5; 5 B5; 6 C5; 9 C6; 10 B6; 11 H5
Samaria (region)	6 B3; 9 B4; 10 B5
Samaria (town)	4 B3; 6 B3; 7a B2; 10 B5
Samos	11 F3
Samothrace	11 E2
San Marino	12 g6
Sã o Tomè and Prìncipe	12 D3
Sardinia	11 A2; 13 B3
Sardis	11 F3
Sarmatia	13 D2
Saudi Arabia	12 E2
Sebaste	10 B5
Second Quarter	8 B3
Second Wall,	8 B2
Seir, Mt.	2 E4
Seleucia	10 B2; 11 H3
Senegal	12 D2
Serpent's Pool	8 A5
Seychelles	12 F3
Sharon, Plain of	2 D2
Shechem	1 C3; 2 D2; 3 D2; 4 B3; 5 B4
Sheep Gate	8 C2
Sheep Pool	8 C2
Shephelah	2 D3
Shiloh	3 D2; 4 B4; 6 B4
Shunem	6 C3
Shur, Desert of	2 B5; 3 B4
Sicily	11 C3; 13 C3
Sidon	5 B3; 6 C1; 10 B4; 11 H4; 13 E3
Sierra Leone	12 D3
Siloam, Pool of	8 C5
Simeon	4 A5
Sinai	1 C4; 2 C6; 3 C4; 5 A6
Sin, Desert of	2 B7; 3 B5
Sinai, Desert of	2 C8
Sinai, Mt.	2 C7; 3 C5
Singapore	12 G3
Slovakia	12 g5
Slovenia	12 g5
Smyrna	11 F3
Solomon Islands	12 H3
Solona	13 C2
Somalia	12 E3
South Africa	12 E4
South Korea	12 G2
Spain	12 f6; 13 A2
Sparta	11 E3
Sri Lanka	12 F3
Strato's Tower	9 A4
Succoth	1 C3; 3 A3; 4 C3
Sudan	12 E2
Suriname	12 C3
Susa	7a D2; 7b D5
Svalbard	12 E1
Swaziland	12 E4
Sweden	12 E1
Switzerland	12 f5
Sychar	9 B4; 10 B5
Syracuse	11 C3; 13 C3
Syria	10 C2; 11 H4; 12 h6; 13 E3

T

Taanach	4 B3; 5 B4
Tabor, Mt.	2 D2; 3 D2; 4 C2; 9 C3
Tadmor	1 D2; 5 D2; 7a B2; 7b B5
Tagus River	13 A2
Taiwan	12 G2
Tajikistan	12 F2
Tamar	5 B5
Tanis	1 B3
Tanzania	12 E3
Tarsus	10 A1; 11 H3; 13 E3
Taurus Mountains	1 C2
Tekoa	6 B4
Tel Aviv	2 D3
Temple	8 C3
Thailand	12 G2
Theater	8 B4
Thessalonica	11 E2; 13 D3
Thrace	11 E2; 13 D3
Three Taverns	11 B2
Thyatira	11 F3
Tiberias	2 E2; 9 C3
Tigris River	1 E2; 7a C2; 7b C5; 13 F3
Tiphsah	5 D1; 7a B2
Tirzah	4 B3
Tishbe	6 C3
Togo	12 D3
Towers' Pool	8 A3
Trinidad and Tobago	12 c6
Tripolitania	11 B5
Troas	11 F3
Troy	1 B1
Tunisia	12 g6
Turkey	12 h6
Turkmenistan	12 F2
Turks & Caicos Islands	12 b5
Tyre	2 D1; 4 B1; 5 B3; 6 B1; 9 B1; 10 B4; 11 H4; 13 E3
Tyropoeon Valley	8 B3, C5
Tyrrhenian Sea	11 B2; 13 C3

U

Uganda	12 E3
Ugarit	1 C2
Ukraine	12 g5
United Arab Emirates	12 F2
United Kingdom	12 f5
United States	12 B2
Upper City	8 B4
Upper Room	8 B5
Ur	1 E3; 7a D3; 7b D6
Urartu	7a C1; 7b C4
Urmia, Lake	1 E2; 7a C1; 7b C4
Uruguay	12 C4
Uruk	1 E3
Uzbekistan	12 F2

V

Valley Gate	8 C4
Van, Lake	7a C1; 7b C4
Vanuatu	12 H3
Venezuela	12 C3
Vietnam	12 G3
Virgin Islands	12 c5
Vistula River	13 C1
Volga River	13 F1

W-Y

Water Gate	8 C5
West Bank	12 h6
Western Sahara	12 D2
Wilson's Arch	8 C3
Women, Court of	8 C3
Yarkon River	2 D3
Yarmuk River	2 E2; 4 C2; 6 C3; 9 C3
Yemen	12 E2
Yugoslavia	12 g6

Z

Zaire	12 E3
Zambia	12 E3
Zarephath	6 B1
Zebulun	4 B2
Zered Brook	2 E4; 3 D3; 4 C5; 6 C6
Ziklag	4 A5; 5 A5
Zimbabwe	12 E3
Zin, Desert of	2 D4; 3 C5
Zoan	1 B3
Zoar	1 C3

NIV Prophecy
Marked Reference Study Bible

Project management and editorial by Gary Knapp

Editorial assistance by Sally M. Hupp

Production management by Mark Luce

Interior design by Sharon Wright, Belmont, MI

Art direction by Cindy Davis

Cover design by Christine Gannon

Interior proofreading by Peachtree Editorial and Proofreading Service, Peachtree City, GA

Interior typesetting by Auto-Graphics, Inc., Pomona, CA

Printing and binding by R.R. Donnelley, Crawfordsville, IN

Guarantee

Zondervan Publishing House guarantees leather Bibles unconditionally against manufacturing defects for six years and hardcover and softcover Bibles for four years. This guarantee does not apply to normal wear. Contact Zondervan Customer Service, 800-727-1309, for replacement instructions.

Care

We suggest loosening the binding of your new Bible by gently pressing on a small section of pages at a time from the center. To ensure against breakage of the spine, it is best not to bend the cover backward around the spine or to carry study notes, church bulletins, pens, etc., inside the cover. Because a felt-tipped marker will "bleed" through the pages, we recommend use of a ball-point pen or pencil to underline favorite passages. Your Bible should not be exposed to excessive heat, cold, or humidity. Protecting the gold or silver edges of the paper from moisture will avoid spotting, streaking, or fading.

Definitions

Bonded leather: no less than 90% leather fibers with latex base.
Top-Grain leather: 100% pigskin
Cowhide: 100% cowhide

Map 1: WORLD OF THE PATRIARCHS

Map 2: PALESTINE AND SINAI

Great Bitter Lake
Little Bitter Lake

DESERT OF SHUR
DESERT OF SIN
DESERT OF PARAN
SINAI
DESERT OF SINAI
▲ Mt. Sinai (Mt. Horeb)

Ezion Geber

ARABAH
DESERT OF EDOM
EASTERN

Red Sea

0 10 20 30 40 mi.
0 10 20 30 40 50 60 km.

© 1986 The Zondervan Corporation

Map 3: EXODUS AND CONQUEST OF CANAAN

Map 4: **LAND OF THE TWELVE TRIBES**

Map 5: KINGDOM OF DAVID AND SOLOMON

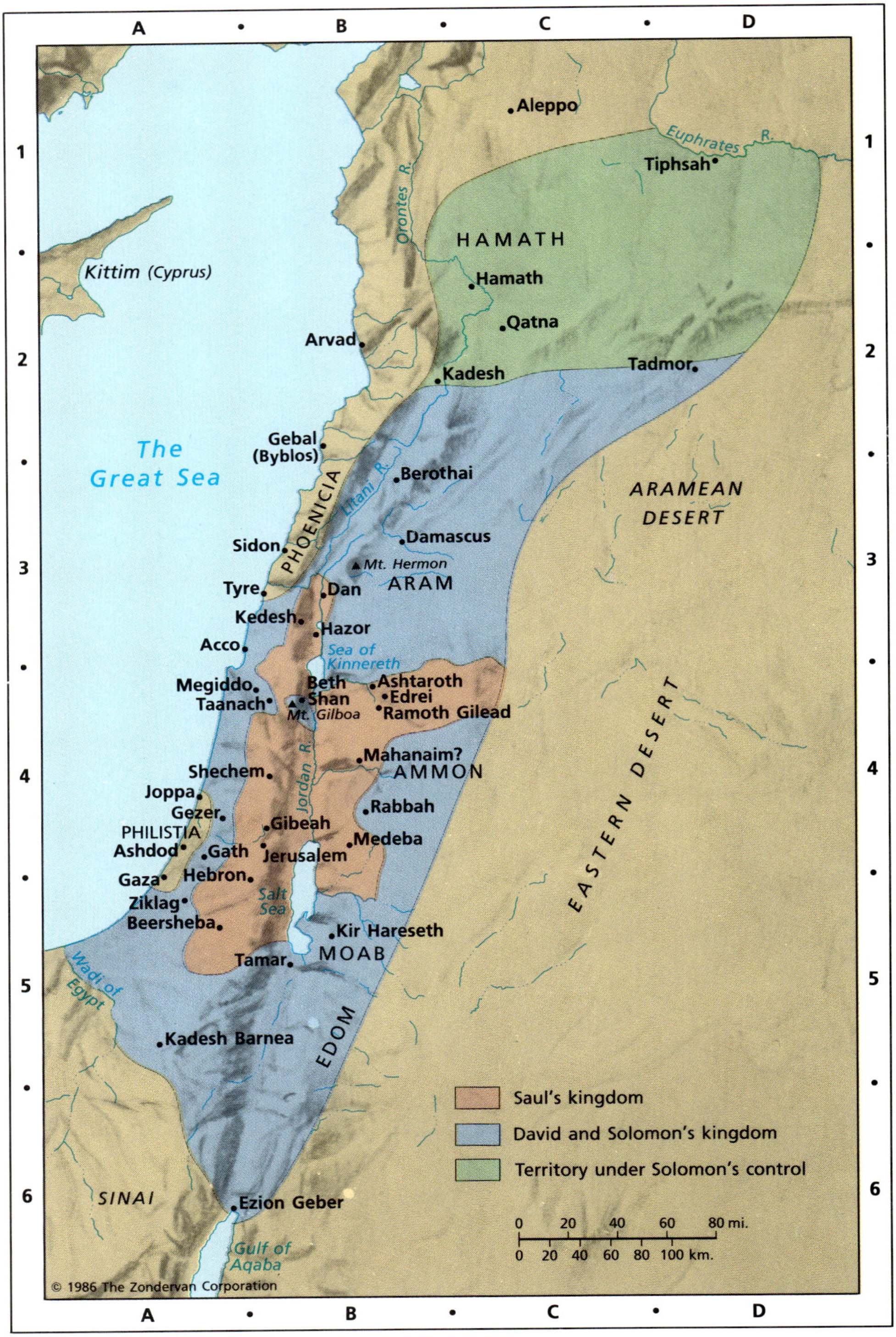

- Saul's kingdom
- David and Solomon's kingdom
- Territory under Solomon's control

© 1986 The Zondervan Corporation

Map 6: PROPHETS IN ISRAEL AND JUDAH

Map 7: ASSYRIAN AND BABYLONIAN EMPIRES

Map 7a: ASSYRIAN EMPIRE (c. 700 B.C.)

— Exiles from Israel into Assyrian captivity (722 B.C.)

© 1986 The Zondervan Corporation

Map 7b: BABYLONIAN EMPIRE (c. 600 B.C.)

— Exiles from Judah into Babylonian captivity (605, 597, 586 B.C.)
— Return of exiles under Sheshbazzar and Zerubbabel 537 B.C.
— Return of exiles under Ezra (458 B.C.) and Nehemiah (445 B.C.)

© 1986 The Zondervan Corporation

Map 8: JERUSALEM IN JESUS' TIME

Legend:
- City walls in Jesus' time
- "City of David"
- The "Old City" (surviving walls, built in 16th century)

Labels on map:

- Garden Tomb (alternate site of crucifixion)
- Second Wall
- Fish Gate
- Sheep Pool (Bethesda Pool)
- Antonia Fortress
- Sheep Gate
- Israel Pool
- Jesus arrested
- Preaching
- Gethsemane
- Crucifixion and burial
- Inner Court
- Altar
- Golden Gate
- Gate Beautiful
- Golgotha (traditional site)
- SECOND QUARTER
- TYROPOEON VALLEY
- TEMPLE
- Court of Women
- Mt. of Olives
- Court of Men
- Court of the Gentiles
- Clearing of temple
- Towers' Pool
- Gennath Gate
- First Wall
- Bridge (Wilson's Arch)
- Royal Porch
- Pinnacle of the Temple (traditional location)
- Tower of Phasael
- Tower of Hippicus
- Stairs (Robinson's Arch)
- Huldah Gates
- Tower of Mariamne
- Herod Antipas's Palace
- Herod's Palace
- UPPER CITY
- Valley Gate
- Theater
- KIDRON VALLEY
- Jesus before high priests; Peter's denial
- Gihon Spring
- Serpent's Pool
- High Priest's House
- ESSENE QUARTER
- LOWER CITY (Possibly part of Jerusalem in Jesus' time)
- Upper Room (traditional site)
- Last Supper
- Pool of Siloam
- Water Gate
- Hezekiah's Tunnel
- Essene Gate
- HINNOM VALLEY

Scale: 0 — 0.1 — 0.2 mi.
0 — 0.1 — 0.2 — 0.3 km.

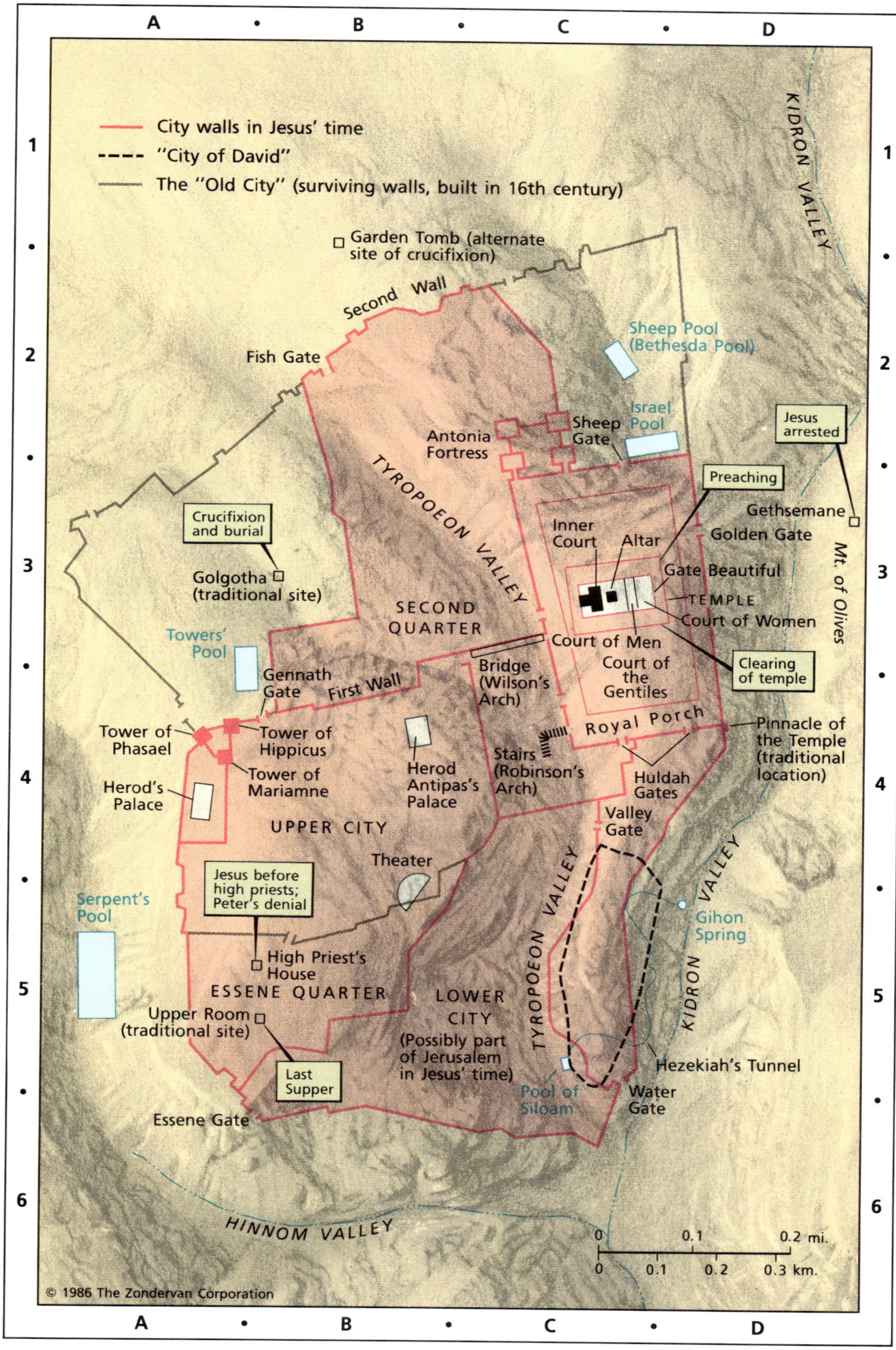

© 1986 The Zondervan Corporation

Map 9: JESUS' MINISTRY

Map 10: APOSTLES' EARLY TRAVELS

Map 11: PAUL'S MISSIONARY JOURNEYS

← First Missionary Journey (A.D. 46–48)
← Second Missionary Journey (A.D. 49–52)
← Third Missionary Journey (A.D. 53–57)
← Trip to Rome (A.D. 59–60)

© 1986 The Zondervan Corporation

Map 12: THE WORLD TODAY

Map of Asia, Oceania, Africa, and Europe

Main Map (Asia, Oceania, Eastern Africa, Australia)

Grid references: E, F, G, H (columns) / 1, 2, 3, 4 (rows)

- SVALBARD (NOR.)
- FINLAND
- DEN.
- See inset below
- RUSSIA
- KAZAKSTAN
- MONGOLIA
- TURKEY
- UZBEKISTAN
- KYRGYZSTAN
- TURKMENISTAN
- TAJIKISTAN
- NORTH KOREA
- SOUTH KOREA
- JAPAN
- IRAQ
- IRAN
- AFGHANISTAN
- CHINA
- North Pacific Ocean
- LIBYA
- EGYPT
- SAUDI ARABIA
- QATAR
- UNITED ARAB EMIRATES
- PAKISTAN
- NEPAL
- BHUTAN
- OMAN
- BANGLADESH
- INDIA
- BURMA (MYANMAR)
- LAOS
- TAIWAN
- CHAD
- SUDAN
- ERITREA
- YEMEN
- DJIBOUTI
- THAILAND
- CAMBODIA
- VIETNAM
- PHILIPPINES
- CENTRAL AFRICAN REPUBLIC
- ETHIOPIA
- SRI LANKA
- BRUNEI
- CAMEROON
- CONGO
- UGANDA
- SOMALIA
- MALDIVES
- MALAYSIA
- SINGAPORE
- PAPUA NEW GUINEA
- RWANDA
- BURUNDI
- KENYA
- SEYCHELLES
- INDONESIA
- ZAIRE
- TANZANIA
- Indian Ocean
- SOLOMON ISLANDS
- ANGOLA
- COMOROS
- VANUATU
- MALAWI
- ZAMBIA
- MOZAMBIQUE
- NAMIBIA
- ZIMBABWE
- MAURITIUS
- RÉUNION (FR.)
- NEW CALEDONIA (FR.)
- BOTSWANA
- MADAGASCAR
- AUSTRALIA
- SWAZILAND
- SOUTH AFRICA
- LESOTHO
- NEW ZEALAND

© 1996 The Zondervan Corporation

Inset Map (Europe)

Grid references: e, f, g, h (columns) / 5, 6 (rows)

- FAEROE IS. (DEN.)
- NORWAY
- FINLAND
- SWEDEN
- EST.
- LATVIA
- UNITED KINGDOM
- DENMARK
- LITH.
- RUSSIA
- IRELAND
- NETHERLANDS
- BELARUS
- BELGIUM
- GERMANY
- POLAND
- LUXEMBOURG
- CZECH REPUBLIC
- SLOVAKIA
- UKRAINE
- KAZAKSTAN
- SWITZERLAND
- AUSTRIA
- HUNGARY
- MOLDOVA
- FRANCE
- LIECH.
- SLOV.
- CROATIA
- BOS. & HERZ.
- ROMANIA
- MONACO
- SAN MARINO
- YUGO.
- BULGARIA
- ANDORRA
- ITALY
- ALBANIA
- GEORGIA
- PORTUGAL
- SPAIN
- F.Y.R. MACED.
- GREECE
- ARMENIA
- TURKEY
- AZERBAIJAN
- GIBRALTAR (U.K.)
- MALTA
- CYPRUS
- SYRIA
- MOROCCO
- TUNISIA
- LEBANON
- WEST BANK
- ISRAEL
- IRAQ
- ALGERIA
- LIBYA
- EGYPT
- JORDAN
- KUWAIT

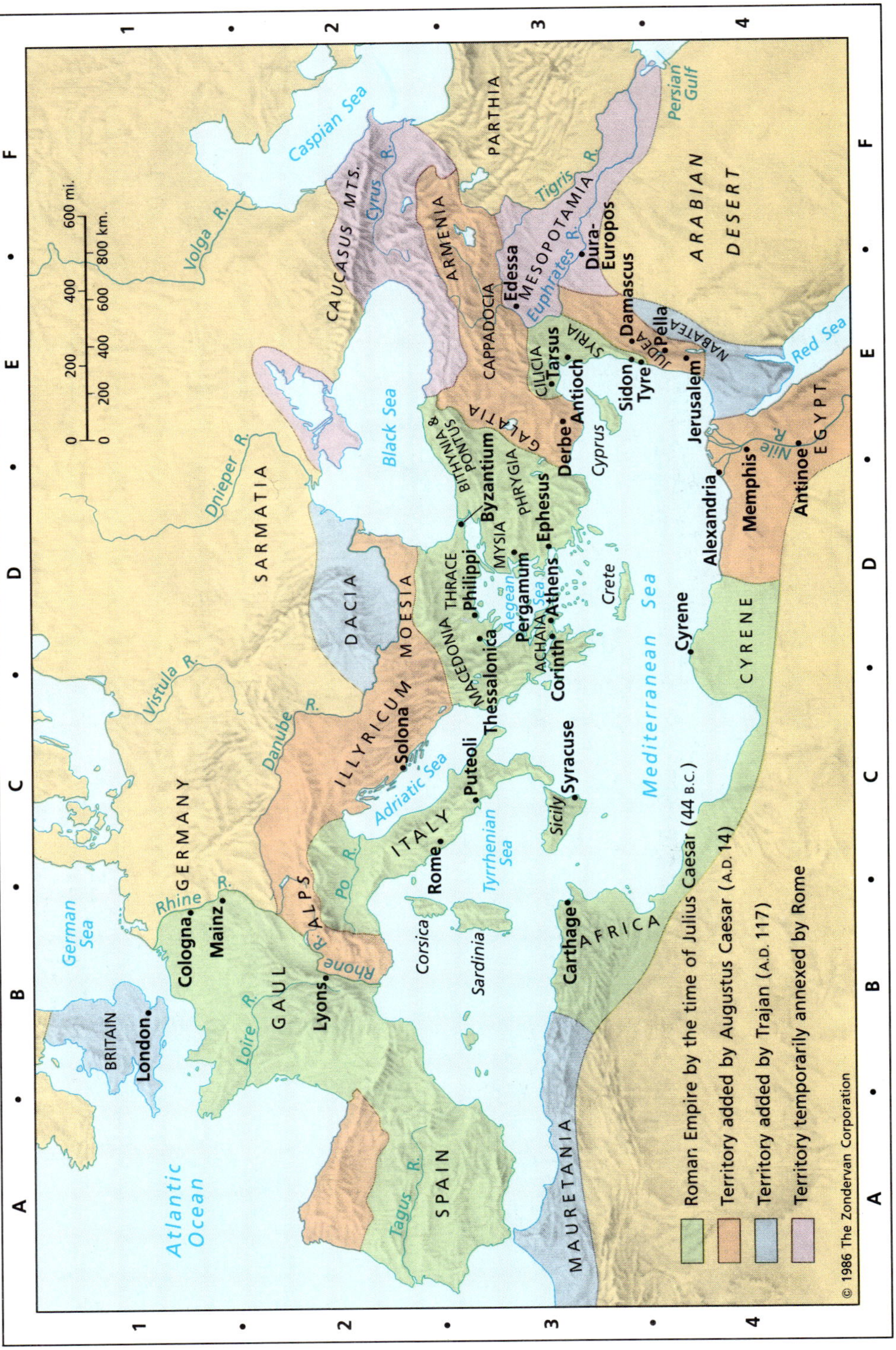

Map 13: ROMAN EMPIRE

- Roman Empire by the time of Julius Caesar (44 B.C.)
- Territory added by Augustus Caesar (A.D. 14)
- Territory added by Trajan (A.D. 117)
- Territory temporarily annexed by Rome

© 1986 The Zondervan Corporation

Mark
Mark 11:22
01:14-56
95-4/:10